EUROPEA[illegible]L TIMETABLE

Summer 2016

Rail and ferry services
throughout Europe

An expanded edition of the monthly
European Rail Timetable

Published by
European Rail Timetable Limited
28 Monson Way
Oundle
Northamptonshire
PE8 4QG
United Kingdom

ISBN 978–0–9929073–6–5

Director and Editor-in-Chief : John Potter

Editor : Chris Woodcock

Editorial team : Peter Bass, David Turpie, Peter Weller

Additional compiling : Brendan Fox

Marketing and Advertising Manager: Keri Blunston

Commercial Manager : Gemma Donaldson

Social Media Manager: Reuben Turner

Subscriptions : Peter Weller

Telephone (Editorial & Sales) +44 (0)1832 270198
e-mail (Sales): sales@europeanrailtimetable.eu
e-mail (Editorial): editorial@europeanrailtimetable.eu

Website and on-line bookshop : www.europeanrailtimetable.eu

Every care has been taken to render the timetable correct in accordance with the latest information, but changes may be made by the railway authorities and the publishers cannot hold themselves responsible for the consequences of either changes or inaccuracies.

Cover created by Andrea Collins:
www.millstonecreative.co.uk
millstonecreative@btinternet.com

Front cover photograph:
Train 8643, the 1534 from Alcamo Diramazione to Trapani, at Santa Ninfa, Sicily, between the stations of Salemi-Gibellina and Castelvetrano (Table 646) on May 8, 2015.
© Giuseppe Pastorello

Printed and bound by CPI Group (UK) Ltd, Croydon, CR0 4YY

INTRODUCTION

This **Summer 2016** edition is a specially enlarged version of the monthly European Rail Timetable, published by European Rail Timetable Limited and recognised throughout the world as the indispensable compendium of European rail schedules. Seasonal editions appear twice yearly, in Summer and Winter versions, and they now replace the June and December monthly editions. Regular monthly editions continue to be published January to May and July to November and these include the latest updates to schedules around Europe.

Previously published by Thomas Cook, the European Rail Timetable is still compiled by the same dedicated team and has been the travelling companion of the tourist and business traveller, InterRailer and Eurailer for many years.

The intention of this special seasonal edition is to make the timetable more widely available to the increasing numbers of holidaymakers who are touring Europe by train, whether using InterRail, Eurail or one of the other popular European rail passes, or simply travelling point to point. It includes additional information of use to rail travellers, especially those trying this kind of holiday for the first time.

Our feature on **Rail Passes** (pages v to xi) includes full details of the InterRail Global Pass and InterRail One Country Pass schemes (for European residents), as well as latest details of the various Eurail passes for those resident outside Europe. Many other passes are also featured, including a selection of citywide tickets and visitor cards for those visiting major European cities.

The **Country-by-Country** section (pages xii to xxiv) is packed with useful information about each country, and there is a chart of visa requirements on page xxiv. In the main body of the timetable, **Newslines** on page 3 has information about the latest changes and about the particular contents of this edition. Pages 8 and 9 help you make vital preparations for your journey, whilst a little time spent reading the notes on pages 4 to 7, explaining how to read the timetable, will be amply repaid when you get down to the task of planning your travels.

Whether you intend to travel only in one or two countries, or are attempting a spectacular grand tour of Europe, the timetables in this book will cover most of the routes you will need and will enable you to pre-plan your journey, which is often half the fun. Rail timetables are, however, always liable to change and you are recommended to consult the latest monthly edition of the European Rail Timetable or local information before travelling.

BEYOND EUROPE

Our Beyond Europe pages cover eight different areas around the world, with each section appearing twice a year in our regular monthly publication. As a special bonus we include the latest information from all eight areas in this special edition. Further details will be found on page 577.

TRAVEL TIPS

ACCOMMODATION

Hotels:

Europe offers an excellent choice, from five-star hotels to room only. Your main problem may lie in finding somethi to suit your budget. Rooms in private houses are often a good, inexpensive and friendly option (local tourist office often have lists), but you may be expected to stay for more than one night. The quality of cheaper hotels in Easte Europe may still be less than inspiring and you may do better with a private room. Local tourist offices are almo always your best starting point if you haven't pre-booked. If they don't handle bookings themselves (there's usually small charge), they will re-direct you to someone who does and/or supply you with the information to do it yourself tell them your price horizons.

Hostels:

For those on a tight budget, the best bet is to join **HI** (Hostelling International); there's no age limit. Membership of national association will entitle you to use over 5000 HI hostels in 60 different countries and, apart from camping, the often provide the cheapest accommodation. The norm is dormitory-style, but many hostels also have single and fami rooms.

Many offer excellent-value dining and many have self-catering and/or laundry facilities. Some hostels are open 2 hours, but most have lock-out times and reception's hours are usually limited; advise them if you are arriving out hours. Reservation is advisable – many hostels fill well in advance and even those with space are likely to limit yo stay to three nights if you just turn up without booking. In winter (except around Christmas) you may be able to g special price deals.

Buy the HI's directory Europe, which lists hostel addresses, contact numbers, locations and facilities; the HI website *www.hihostels.com.*

Camping:

This is obviously the cheapest accommodation if you're prepared to carry the equipment. There are campsites rig across Europe, from basic (just toilets and showers) to luxury family-oriented sites with dining-rooms, swimming poo and complexes of permanent tents. The drawback is that sites are often miles from the city centres. There's no real good pan-European guide to campsites, but most tourist offices can provide a directory for their country.

WHAT TO TAKE WITH YOU

Luggage:

Backpack (not more than 50 litres for women or 60 litres for men) plus day sack; sort your luggage into see-throug polythene bags (makes fishing out your socks from the backpack much easier), plus take plastic bags for dirty clothe etc, and elastic bands for sealing them. If flying to or from your holiday you will need to check your airlines baggag regulations.

Clothing:

Lightweight clothing, preferably of a type that doesn't need ironing; smart casual clothes for evening wear, swimsui sun hat, long-sleeved garment to cover shoulders (essential in some churches/temples; women may nee headscarves); non-slip foot-wear – and don't forget underwear! All-purpose hiking boots (useful for big walks aroun cities) or rubber sandals with chunky soles are good when it's hot; flip flops for the shower etc.

First Aid/Medical:

Insect repellent and antihistamine cream, sun-screen cream, after-sun lotion, water-sterilising tablets, something fo headaches and tummy troubles, antiseptic spray or cream, medicated wet-wipes, plasters for blisters, bandage contraceptives and tampons (especially if visiting Eastern Europe, where they can be sometimes difficult to get – or tr the luxury shop in the city's biggest hotel). Spare spectacles/contact lenses and a copy of your prescription.

Overnight Equipment:

Lightweight sleeping-bag (optional), sheet liner (for hostelling), inflatable travel pillow, earplugs, and eyemask.

Documents:

Passport, tickets, photocopies of passport/visas (helps if you lose the passport itself) and travel insurance, travellers cheques counterfoil, passport photos, student card, numbers of credit cards and where to phone if you lose them.

Other items:

A couple of lightweight towels, small bar of soap, water-bottle, pocket knife, torch (flashlight), sewing kit, padlock an chain (for anchoring your luggage), safety matches, mug and basic cutlery, toothbrush, travel wash, string (for washing-line), travel adapter, mobile (cell) phone charger, universal bath plug (often missing from wash-basins) sunglasses, alarm clock, notepad and pen, pocket calculator (to convert money), a money-belt and a good book/game (for long journeys).

EUROPEAN RAIL PASSES

›asses represent excellent value for train travellers who are touring ıd Europe (or parts of it) or making a number of journeys within a : period. They can offer substantial savings over point-to-point ts, as well as greater flexibility. Passes may cover most of Europe InterRail or Eurail), a specific group of countries, single countries, or a certain area. InterRail passes are only available to European lents, whereas Eurail passes are only for non-European residents. : passes cannot be used in your country of residence.

›es either cover a specified number of consecutive days, or are of the type where you get so many 'travel days' within a specified period e are boxes on the pass where you write each date). Free travel ires the use of a travel day, whereas discounted travel does not.

With InterRail and Eurail *flexi* passes, direct night trains or ferries leaving after 1900 hrs can count as the next travel day (as long as it's not the first day of validity). Free overnight ferries count as either the day of departure or the next day. Passes generally cover the ordinary services of the national rail companies, but supplements often have to be paid for travel on high-speed services, night trains, and 'global price' trains. 'Independent' operators may not accept passes but may give discounts to passholders. Extra charges always apply for travel in sleeping cars or couchettes.

Passes can be purchased from appointed agents and their websites, and some may be available from principal railway stations. Your passport may be required for identification, also one or two passport-size photos. In this feature USD = US dollars, € = euros, £ = pounds sterling.

InterRail

Europe-wide or single-country passes for European residents website: www.interrail.eu

:RRAIL GLOBAL PASS - valid in 30 European countries:
ria, Belgium, Bosnia-Herzegovina, Bulgaria, Croatia, Czech Repub-)enmark, Finland, France, Germany, Great Britain, Greece, Hungary, ɪnd (including Northern Ireland), Italy, Luxembourg, FYR Macedonia, tenegro, Netherlands, Norway, Poland, Portugal, Romania, Serbia, akia, Slovenia, Spain, Sweden, Switzerland and Turkey.
' VALID in the passholder's country of residence (but see below).

:ES - GLOBAL PASS

)uth is 12 - 25 years	Youth 1st / 2nd cl.	Adult 2nd class	Adult 1st class
ıys within 15 days (flexi)	€331 / 200	€264	€413
ıys within 1 month (flexi)	€393 / 246	€315	€491
lays within 1 month (flexi)	€471 / 292	€374	€588
ays within 1 month (flexi)	€579 / 361	€463	€723
lays continuous	€520 / 338	€414	€650
lays continuous	€608 / 374	€484	€760
›nth continuous	€787 / 479	€626	€983

›s correct as at 14/01/16. Accompanied children aged 4 - 11 travel with a Child Pass; two children can travel with each adult. Global ; Senior (60+) gives 10% discount (not for One Country passes).

:RRAIL ONE COUNTRY PASS (O.C.P.) - valid in one country
ers any <u>one</u> of the participating countries above (except Bosnia- zegovina and Montenegro). NOT available for the passholder's ıtry of residence. Note that Benelux (Belgium, Luxembourg and ıerlands) counts as one country. *Greece Plus* and *Italy Plus* passes ıdes Italy - Greece ferry services operated by Attica Group (Superfast ies - some routes are run jointly with Anek Lines). 1st class Youth ses are also available (except Norway). Prices correct as at 14/01/16.

:ES - ONE COUNTRY PASS *3, 4, 6 or 8 days within 1 month*

	Youth	2nd	1st		Youth	2nd	1st
ıce, Germany or Great Britain:							
ays	€154	€203	€317	6 days	€208	€283	€445
ays	€164	€223	€349	8 days	€232	€313	€492
tria, Italy Plus, Norway (2nd class only), Spain or Sweden:							
ays	€131	€173	€272	6 days	€187	€256	€401
ays	€154	€197	€308	8 days	€219	€297	€465
elux, Denmark, Finland, Greece Plus, Ireland, Italy or Switzerland:							
ays	€87	€118	€185	6 days	€141	€199	€311
ays	€108	€149	€233	8 days	€176	€239	€376
ɟaria, Croatia, Czech Republic, Greece, Hungary, Poland, Portugal, ıania, Slovakia, Slovenia or Turkey:							
ays	€57	€78	€121	6 days	€93	€125	€197
ays	€69	€95	€148	8 days	€107	€148	€231
! Macedonia or Serbia:							
ays	€42	€56	€89	6 days	€81	€106	€166
ays	€57	€78	€121	8 days	€91	€126	€199

O CAN BUY INTERRAIL PASSES
national of a European country (including Russia) with a valid sport, or anyone who has lived in Europe for at least six months. ses can be purchased up to three months before travel begins.

PPLEMENTS AND RESERVATION FEES
ɪuired for certain types of high-speed or 'global price' train.

rnational day train examples, 2nd class (subject to change): ıce - Italy *TGV* €33 - 60 (€48 - 80 in 1st class); *Berlin - Warszawa ›ress* €4; *EC Switzerland - Italy* €11; *Eurostar* passholder fare (e.g. don - Paris from €89); *TGV / ICE* France - Germany €13; *TGV Lyria* ınce - Switzerland) from €25; *Thalys* passholder fare from €15; *TGV* ssels - France €9; *SJ Snabbtåg* Stockholm - København €7. *IC bus* Klagenfurt - Venezia €9 (€13 1st class). Domestic examples: **Croatia** *IC / ICN* €1. **Czech Republic** *SC* €8. **Finland** *Pendolino* €3 - 7. **France** *TGV* €9 (peak €18), *Intercités* with compulsory reservation €6. **Germany** free on *ICE*. **Greece** *IC* €7 - 28. **Hungary** *IC* €3. **Italy** *FA*, *FB* and *FR* €10, *IC* €3. **Norway** long-distance trains €6.3. **Poland** *EIP* €10, *EIC / TLK* free. **Portugal** *AP / IC* €5. **Romania** *IC/IR* €1 - 1.2. **Slovakia** *IC* €5. **Slovenia** *ICS* €3.4 (€5.1 1st class). **Spain** *AVE* €10, most other long-distance trains €6.5, *MD* €4.5. **Sweden** *Snabbtåg* €7.

Night trains: Passes do not include sleeping accommodation, which is typically €15 to €75 for a couchette, and €35 to €155 for a berth in a sleeping car. Some trains also include reclining seats. Many night trains are globally priced and fares for passholders vary widely. *Thello* (France / Italy) gives 25% discount. Holders of a Global or Sweden One Country Pass can obtain a couchette berth on the *Berlin Night Express* (Berlin - Malmö and v.v.) for €29.

The number of seats allocated to InterRail holders may be limited (e.g. on *TGV* and *Thalys* trains). If sold out, you may have to buy an ordinary ticket. The fold-out Travel Report inside the ticket cover must be filled in. Direct night trains or ferries leaving after 1900 hrs can count as next day.

FREE TRAVEL TO THE BORDER, AIRPORT OR SEAPORT
Although it is not possible to purchase an InterRail pass for the holder's own country of residence, from 2016 a Global pass entitles the holder to two free journeys (one outbound, one inbound) between any station in their country of residence and its border, an airport or seaport. Each journey must be completed in one day (no overnight stops allowed), within the overall validity of the pass, or include a travel day if using a flexi pass. Details must be entered in the travel diary.

VALIDITY ON PRIVATE RAILWAYS
InterRail passes are valid on the national railway companies in each country, plus many privately run railways (some give discounts). For details see the InterRail Traveller's Guide or www.interrail.eu. Selected details are as follows (subject to change): **Austria**: free travel on WESTbahn and ROeEE. **Denmark**: free travel on Arriva and DSB-Øresund, 50% discount on Nordjyske Jernbaner (Hjørring - Hirtshals and Frederikshavn - Skagen). **France**: SNCF bus services included. **Germany**: free on most regional services. **Hungary**: GySEV services are included. **Italy**: not valid on NTV's *Italo* trains. **Netherlands**: privately run regional lines are included. **Norway**: Flåmsbana (Myrdal - Flåm) gives 30% discount. **Spain**: FGC gives 50% discount. **Sweden**: most private operators are included. **Switzerland**: free travel on BLS, FART/SSIF, MOB, RhB, SOB, THURBO and ZB. Many others offer 25 - 50% discount, including AB, ASM, CJ, FB, LEB, MBC, NStCM, RA, RB, RBS, SZU, TMR, TPC, TPF, TRN, WB, WSB. The MGB (Disentis - Brig - Zermatt) offers 50% to under-26s only. Discounted fare on William Tell Express (rail and boat tour). No discounts available on BRB or narrow gauge railways in Jungfrau area (BOB, JB, WAB).

VALIDITY ON FERRY AND BUS SERVICES
The pass includes free deck passage between Italy and Greece on SuperFast Ferries and Minoan Lines (you pay port taxes €7, high-season surcharge €10 June / Sept., €20 July / Aug., and possibly a fuel surcharge); free air-type seats for 1st class pass holders. Many other ferry companies offer discounts (not on cabins), for example: Balearia 20%, Finnlines 30%, Fjord Line 20% (10% high-season), Grimaldi 20%, Irish Ferries 30%, Stena Line 30%, Tallink Silja 20% (high-season), 40% (low-season), Viking Line 50%. Special fares apply on Destination Gotland.

Most Swiss lakes give 50% discount, as does Fjord1 on Norwegian Fjords. Certain bus services in Scandinavia (including Luleå - Haparanda - Tornio - Kemi) and some railway museums are free or discounted. A limited number of tourist attractions, hotels, hostels and cycle hire outlets also offer discounts.

Eurail

Eurail Global Pass *For non-European residents.* website: www.eurail.com www.eurailgroup.org

Area of validity

The *Eurail Global Pass* is valid for unlimited travel on the national railways of 28 European countries, namely Austria, Belgium, Bosnia-Herzegovina, Bulgaria, Croatia, Czech Republic, Denmark, Finland, France, Germany, Greece, Hungary, Ireland (including Northern Ireland), Italy, Luxembourg, Montenegro, the Netherlands, Norway, Poland, Portugal, Romania, Serbia, Slovakia, Slovenia, Spain, Sweden, Switzerland and Turkey.

Who can buy the pass?

The pass can be purchased by anyone resident outside Europe (but excluding residents of Russia and CIS or Turkey). Passes are sold through official Eurail Sales Agents (see www.eurailgroup.org) and can also be bought directly from Eurail through www.eurail.com.

The option exists to buy the passes after arrival in Europe but it is much cheaper to buy them beforehand, and since you can buy them up to eleven months in advance, there is no point in waiting until the last minute. Pass validity cannot be changed once in Europe, and passes must be validated before first use.

Periods of validity and prices

Adult *Eurail Global Passes* are only available as a first class pass (naturally you can also travel in second class). Prices (from eurail.com) in US dollars are as follows:

Youth is 12 - 25 years	Youth 1st class	Youth 2nd class	Adult 1st class
5 days within 1 month	424 USD	345 USD	528 USD
7 days within 1 month	516 USD	420 USD	643 USD
10 days within 2 months	636 USD	518 USD	793 USD
15 days within 2 months	833 USD	678 USD	1039 USD
15 days continuous	541 USD	441 USD	673 USD
22 days continuous	696 USD	566 USD	868 USD
1 month continuous	854 USD	695 USD	1065 USD
2 months continuous	1203 USD	979 USD	1501 USD
3 months continuous	1482 USD	1206 USD	1851 USD

Prices correct as at 14/01/16. Accompanied children aged 4 - 11 travel free with a Child Pass; two children can travel with each adult.

Supplements payable

Eurostar and *Thalys* charge a passholder rate, as do other 'global price' trains (see the InterRail page for further details). French *TGV* and certain *Intercités* require the reservation fee only. In Spain most long-distance trains have a supplement/reservation fee (sample 2nd class rates: regional trains €4.5, long-distance €6.5, *AVE* Turista class €10; where meal provided in 1st/Preferente class €23.5). Supplements are also payable on *Freccia* services in Italy (€10) and *SJ Snabbtåg* (€7). Further details are given in the InterRail section on the previous page.

As with all passes, sleeper/couchette supplements and seat reserva are extra.

Validity on other railways

Eurail passes are valid on the principal railway companies in country, but may not be valid on 'private' or locally run railways (s give discounts). Selected details are as follows (some require rese tions): **Austria**: free travel on WESTbahn and ROeEE. **Denmark**: travel on Arriva and DSB-Øresund, 50% discount on Hjørring - Hirts and Frederikshavn - Skagen. **France**: SNCF buses included. **Hung** GySEV services are included. **Italy**: not valid on NTV's *Italo* tr **Norway**: Flåmsbana (Myrdal - Flåm) gives 30% discount. **Spain**: gives 50% discount. **Sweden**: most private operators are inclu **Switzerland**: free travel on many railways including AB, ASM, BLS, CJ, FART/SSIF, FB, LEB, MBC, MOB, NStCM, RA, RhB, SOB, THURBO, TMR, TPC, TPF, TRN, WB, WSB, ZB. There is 50% disc on Arth-Goldau/Vitznau - Rigi, the Pilatus line (and cable car) offers and there is a 25% discount on railways in the Jungfrau region (B BLM, JB, WAB) and the MGB (Disentis - Brig - Zermatt). There reductions on some cable cars as well. A list of bonuses is included ir Traveler's Guide issued with your pass.

Ferry services

Free passage or fare reductions are available on various ferry servi the main ones are shown below. Ferry discounts usually exclude c accommodation, and other restrictions (such as compulsory reserva may apply: free deck passage between Italy and Greece on Super Ferries and Minoan Lines (you pay port taxes €7, high-season surch €10 June/Sept., €20 July/Aug., and possibly a fuel surcharge); airline-type seats for 1st class pass holders. Many other ferry compa offer discounts (not on cabins), for example: Balearia 20%, Blue Star (domestic routes), Finnlines 30%, Fjord Line 20% (10% high-seas Grimaldi 20%, Irish Ferries 30%, SNAV 20%, Stena Line 30%, Ta Silja 40% (20% high-season), Viking Line 50%. Special fares apply Destination Gotland. Most boat services on the Swiss lakes are inclu Bodensee ferries operated by BSB, SBS, ÖBB give 50% discount. Th are also reductions on some river cruises (e.g. certain DDSG sailin KD Line gives a 20% discount on its scheduled Rhine and Mosel bo

Other discounts

Certain bus services in Norway offer a 50% discount. Some rail museums offer free or discounted entry and a limited number of to attractions, hotels and hostels offer discounts. If in doubt, ask!

Note regarding flexi passes: free travel requires the use of a 'tr day', whereas discounted travel does not, provided it is within the ov validity of the pass. For free overnight travel by ferry you can enter ei the day of departure or day of arrival. A direct overnight train leaving a 1900 hrs requires only the following day to be used as a 'travel day'

Eurail Select Pass *For non-European residents*

Revamped for 2016 combining the Select with the former Regional pass, a *Eurail (Two / Three / Four Country) Select Pass* allows unlimited travel in 2, 3 or 4 bordering countries selected from the following (some countries are grouped together and count as one):

• Austria • Benelux (Belgium/Netherlands/Luxembourg) • Bulgaria • Croatia/Slovenia • Czech Republic • Denmark • Finland • France • Germany • Greece • Hungary • Ireland (including NIR) • Italy • Norway • Poland • Portugal • Romania • Serbia/Montenegro • Slovakia • Spain • Sweden • Switzerland • Turkey.

'Bordering' means linked by a direct train (not through another country) or shipping line included in the Eurail scheme; for example Italy's links include Spain and Greece.

The Two Country Select Pass is available for 4, 5, 6, 8 or 10 travel days within a two-month period, in both youth (12 - 25 years) and adult 1st and 2nd class versions. The Three and Four Country Select passes offer 5, 6, 8 and 10 days travel within a two-month period; there is no 2nd class adult version. Prices vary depending on countries chosen; some examples are shown below. Children aged 4 - 11 travel free with a Child Pass when accompanied by an adult; two children can travel with each adult.

International Ferries: *Select* and *One Country* passes must be valid in both the countries of departure and arrival to obtain free travel, but only need to be valid in one of the countries to obtain discounted travel.

Two Country Select Pass (examples):

Austria & Germany; France & Switzerland; Portugal & Spain.

(USD prices)	4 days	5 days	6 days	8 days	10 da
Youth 1st/2nd cl.	294/240	331/271	365/298	425/347	479/3
Adult 1st/2nd cl.	365/294	411/331	455/365	529/425	596/4

Three Country Select Pass (examples):

Czech Republic, Slovakia & Hungary; France, Spain & Portugal; Gree Italy & Slovenia/Croatia.

(USD prices)	5 days	6 days	8 days	10 da
Youth 1st/2nd cl.	310/253	343/280	398/325	450/3
Adult 1st class	385	426	496	561

Four Country Select Pass (examples):

France, Italy, Portugal & Spain; Benelux, France, Germany & Italy.

(USD prices)	5 days	6 days	8 days	10 da
Youth 1st/2nd cl.	387/316	421/344	492/401	561/4
Adult 1st class	481	525	612	699

Denmark, Sweden, Norway & Finland; Austria, Czech Republic, Slova & Hungary; Bulgaria, Greece, Italy & Romania.

(USD prices)	5 days	6 days	8 days	10 da
Youth 1st/2nd cl	339/276	373/304	435/355	490/4
Adult 1st class	421	464	541	611

Eurail One Country Passes *For non-European residents*

A *Eurail One Country Pass* allows unlimited travel in a single European country as listed below (Benelux and Scandinavia each count as one). Each pass has its own characteristics regarding class of travel, number of travel days (usually 3, 4, 5 or 8 days within 1 month), and availability of adult, youth and family versions. For prices and further information see www.eurail.com.

• Austria • Benelux (Belgium, Luxembourg, the Netherlands) • Bulgaria • Croatia • Czech Republic • Denmark • Finland • Greece • Greek Islands • Hungary • Ireland • Italy • Norwa • Poland • Portugal • Romania • Scandinavia (Denmark, Finlan Norway, Sweden) • Slovakia • Slovenia • Spain • Sweden

BritRail

Rail is a pass for overseas visitors to Great Britain, allowing unlimited el on the national rail network in England, Scotland and Wales. It is available to residents of Great Britain, Northern Ireland, the Isle of or the Channel Islands. It is best to buy the pass before arriving in ain. Youth prices apply to ages 16 to 25, senior applies to 60+. Child es (ages 5 to 15) are approx 50% of the adult fare. Prices correct as at 1/16. See www.britrail.net.

TRAIL CONSECUTIVE PASS

vel for a certain number of consecutive days, First or Standard class.

D prices)	Adult 1st cl.	Youth 1st cl.	Senior 1st cl.	Adult Std cl.	Youth Std cl.	Senior Std cl.
ays	339	271	288	224	179	224
ays	421	337	358	278	222	278
ays	600	480	510	403	323	403
days	886	709	754	600	480	600
days	1126	901	957	750	600	750
onth	1334	1067	1134	886	709	886

TRAIL FLEXIPASS

xi version gives 3, 4, 8 or 15 days travel within a one-month period.

D prices)	Adult 1st cl.	Youth 1st cl.	Senior 1st cl.	Adult Std cl.	Youth Std cl.	Senior Std cl.
ays	410	328	347	277	222	277
ays	504	403	427	347	277	347
ays	741	593	629	497	398	497
days	1106	885	939	747	598	747

TRAIL ENGLAND PASSES

Britrail England Pass excludes Wales and Scotland. A Britrail South st pass is also available. Both passes are available in Consecutive Flexi versions.

BRITRAIL LONDON PLUS PASS

This 'flexi' pass allows unlimited rail travel in London and the surrounding area for either 3, 4 or 8 days within a one-month period. You can visit such places as Canterbury, Salisbury, Bristol, Bath, Oxford, Cambridge, Stratford-Upon-Avon, Worcester, and anywhere on the coast between Harwich to Weymouth.

(USD prices)	Adult 1st cl.	Youth 1st cl.	Senior 1st cl.	Adult Std cl.	Youth Std cl.	Senior Std cl.
3 days	242	193	205	172	138	172
4 days	279	224	238	210	168	210
8 days	395	316	336	291	233	291

BRITRAIL SCOTLAND PASSES

Three different passes are available; Freedom of Scotland (available as 4 days within 8, and 8 days within 15 versions), Central Scotland (3 days within 7), and Highlands (4 days within 8; standard (2nd) class only).

DISCOUNTS

The following reductions are available on passes but only one type of discount can be used. Discounts cannot be applied to London Plus and any Scotland passes.

Saver Discount: small groups of 3 to 9 people receive a discount of up to 20%. Passes must be of the same type and duration and the party must travel together at all times.

Family Discount: if any adult or senior pass is purchased, one accompanying child (aged 5-15) may receive a free pass of the same type and duration. Any further children travelling receive a 50% discount. All children under 5 travel free.

Other International Passes

ALKAN FLEXIPASS

imited travel (see note below) in Bosnia, Bulgaria, Greece, cedonia, Montenegro, Romania, Serbia and Turkey for any 5/7/ 15 days in one month. 1st class €120/162/210/252, 2nd class 8/120/156/186. 40% discount for under 26s, 20% for over 60s, 50% children (4-12). Supplements for *IC* trains. Allows travel on Attica up (Superfast) ferries international routes and 30% discount on nestic routes. Prices correct as at 19/01/16 from Bosnian Railways RS). Only 1st class 5, 10 and 15 day passes are usually offered outside ticipating countries (with increased prices). Not available to residents he above countries.

e that if purchased from one of the above countries the pass allows a return journey from place of issue to the border of a neighbouring ticipating country before unlimited travel is possible.

JREGIO-BODENSEE TAGESKARTE

e day's unlimited travel by rail, bus and ferry in border region Austria/ rmany/Switzerland surrounding Lake Constance. In Germany valid y on DB local trains. Adult 45 CHF/€31, small groups (1 or 2 adults l up to 4 children) 84 CHF/€58. Zonal versions also available for aller areas.

JREGIO TICKET MAAS-RHEIN

e days unlimited travel in border region Belgium/Netherlands/ rmany by rail and bus (covers Liège, Hasselt, Maastricht, Roer-nd, Aachen, Düren). In Germany and Belgium covers only local trains l buses. Price €18.5. At weekends/public holidays valid as a family et (2 adults plus 3 children under 12).

JROPEAN EAST PASS

ers unlimited rail travel throughout Austria, Czech Republic, Hungary l Slovakia for any 5 to 10 days within a month. Valid also on direct vices through Germany between Kufstein and Salzburg (the ssholder cannot leave the train). Now available to European residents cept those from countries where the ticket is valid) as well as non-opean residents. Price for 5 days: 1st class €236, 2nd class €162 to 5 extra days €25/21 per day 1st/2nd class). Children aged 4-11 f price. Discounts available on river cruises, Children's Railway etc.

ÖRESUND RUNDT

Two days unlimited travel on trains and buses in the København, Malmö and Helsingborg area (includes the metro in København), 249 SEK. Children 7-15 half price. The Öresund can only be crossed by rail in one direction; the Helsingborg - Helsingør ferry (operated by Scandlines, included) must be used in the other direction. Available in Denmark from København Tourist Office and in Sweden from Skånetrafiken.

PASS ALSACE-RHEIN-NECKAR

A day ticket valid on Saturdays, Sundays and public holidays covering local trains, buses and trams in the Rhein-Neckar area (VRN) of Germany, plus local trains in the Bas Rhin area of France. Therefore covers the Mannheim, Heidelberg and Strasbourg areas. Price €17.50 for one person or €28.50 for a group of 2-5 people.

PASSBASK

Covers the area between Bayonne in France and San Sebastian in Spain on SNCF trains (includes *TGV* but not night trains) and EuskoTren services. Valid for one day in July or August, or for Saturdays and Sundays (i.e. two days) rest of the year. A barrier pass for EuskoTren should be obtained at Hendaye station. Price €11, child aged 4-12 €7.

SAAR-LOR-LUX TICKET

One day's unlimited 2nd class travel on Saturday or Sunday throughout Saarland (i.e. Saarbrücken area of Germany, local trains only), Lorraine (i.e. Metz, Nancy, Épinal area of France) and all CFL trains in Luxembourg. Price €26; for groups of 2-5 people add €10 per extra person. Not valid on *TGV* or *ICE* trains.

OTHER PASSES

A range of day tickets is available covering areas of the Czech Republic and adjoining countries, i.e. **Euro-Neisse Tageskarte** (Liberec, Jelenia Góra, Zittau/Görlitz; www.zvon.de), the **EgroNet-Ticket** (Cheb, Karlovy Vary, Plauen, Zwickau; www.egronet.de), the **Bayern-Böhmen Ticket** (Bavaria/Bohemia), the **Sachsen-Böhmen Ticket** (Saxony/Bohemia) and the **Elbe-Labe Ticket**.

Railplus

ilplus cards are valid for one year and offer a discount of 25% on ss-border rail travel (excluding supplements) between the participating untries, which are Austria, Belgium, Bulgaria, Croatia, Czech Republic, nmark, Finland, Germany, Great Britain, Greece, Hungary, Italy, via, Lithuania, Luxembourg, Macedonia, Montenegro, Netherlands, land, Romania, Serbia, Slovakia, Slovenia, Switzerland and Ukraine. France, Norway, Portugal, Spain and Sweden only grant discounts to youth (12-25) and seniors (60+). Cards are not available for sale in all participating countries, and you may be required to hold a national railcard for the country where you buy the pass, in addition to the Railplus card.

Passes for Domestic Travel

Every effort has been made to show latest prices, but some may have changed. Most cities offer day tickets valid on public transport (some include local trains), and larger cities often have Visitor Cards available from airports and tourist information offices (often also from hotels and online).

AUSTRIA

European residents: InterRail Global Pass and One Country Pass.
Non-European residents: Eurail Global Pass, Eurail Select / One Country Passes.
Also European East Pass, Euregio-Bodensee Tageskarte.

Einfach-Raus-Ticket: one day's 2nd class travel on regional and local trains for groups of 2 to 5 people, €33 - 45. On Mon to Fri not valid before 0900 hrs.

Vorteilscard annual cards giving 45-50% discount; the *Classic* version (€99) is available to all but there are cheaper cards for families, seniors and those under 26.

ÖSTERREICHcard Classic gives unlimited travel for 1 year, €1,719 (1st class €2,414). Cheaper cards for families, seniors and youths.

Wien metro / tram / bus: 24 / 48 / 72 hours €7.6 / 13.3 / 16.5; any 8 days (not necessarily consecutive) €38.4; weekly ticket (only available from Monday 0000 to the following Monday 0900) €16.2. For journeys from / to the airport buy an additional zone ticket (€2.2). **Wien-Karte**: unlimited travel on local transport in Vienna plus discounted museum entry, 48 / 72 hours €18.9 / 21.9. One child up to age 15 free.

Other visitor cards giving local travel plus museum / sights discounts for 24 / 48 / 72 hours: **Salzburg Card** €27 / 36 / 42 (reduced by €3-5 low season Nov to Apr); **Innsbruck Card** €33 / 41 / 47. Children half price.

BELARUS

Minsk: 10-day public transport passes are available from metro stations.

BELGIUM

European residents: InterRail Global Pass and One Country Pass.
Non-European residents: Eurail Global Pass, Eurail Select / One Country (Benelux) Passes. Also Euregio Ticket Maas-Rhein.

Nettreinkaart / Carte Train Réseau : unlimited travel on rail network; 1 month €292 / 450, 3 months €818 / 1260, 1 year €2923 / 4502. Add-ons for city transport also available.

Discounts on SNCB point to point tickets: **Rail Pass** (age 26 +) allows 10 single journeys between two specified stations (not frontier) for €76 2nd class, €117 1st class, valid 1 year. **Go Pass 10** is under 26 version, €51 2nd class. **Weekend Ticket**: 50% discount, from Friday 1900 hrs. **Senior Ticket** (65 +), flat fare of €6 2nd class, €13 1st class, from 0900 Mon-Fri, not Sat/Sun in peak summer.

Brussels: **Jump ticket** covers all transport in greater Brussels (De Lijn / SNCB / STIB / TEC) 1 / 2 / 3 days €7.5 / 14 / 18. Personal Mobib or Mobib Basic card required (€5).

De Lijn has 1 / 3 / 5 day system passes €6 / 12 / 17 (in advance). Day Pass may also be purchased from driver (€8). Includes coastal tram. Also West Flanders province 7 day pass valid by tram and bus €24 (€36 for 2 people).

BOSNIA-HERZEGOVINA

European residents: InterRail Global Pass. Also Balkan Flexipass.
Non-European residents: Eurail Global Pass.

BULGARIA

European residents: InterRail Global Pass and One Country Pass.
Non-European residents: Eurail Global Pass, Eurail Select / One Country Passes. Also Balkan Flexipass.

Sofia: all SKGT metro, tram and bus: 1 day 4 BGN, 10 trips 8 BGN.

CROATIA

European residents: InterRail Global Pass and One Country Pass.
Non-European residents: Eurail Global Pass, Eurail Select / One Country passes.

Zagreb: day ticket (dnevna karta) all ZET tram / bus (zone 1): 30 HRK. Also multi-day tickets (višednevne karte): 3 / 7 / 15 / 30 days, 70 / 150 / 200 / 400 HRK. **Zagreb Card** adds museums, discounts, 24 hrs 60 HRK, 72 hrs 90 HRK.

CZECH REPUBLIC

European residents: InterRail Global Pass and One Country Pass.
Non-European residents: Eurail Global Pass, Eurail Select / One Country Passes. Also European East Pass.

Day ticket (Celodenni Jizdenka): 2nd class travel on whole rail network 579 CZK (on *SC* trains 200 CZK reservation payable). 13 regional areas also available, 159 - 239 CZK. Certain regions also have day tickets including border areas of Germany or Poland, 250 - 300 CZK. Other day tickets cover specific cross-border areas: Vltava-Dunaj (486 CZK), EgroNet (200 CZK), Labe-Elbe (250 CZK), Euro-Nisa (160 CZK).

Group Weekend ticket (Skupinová víkendová jízdenka): 2nd [...] travel on whole network on Sat or Sun for 2 adults and up to 3 chil[...] 679 CZK (829 CZK including local transport in Praha). Reservatio[...] payable on *SC* trains. Valid cross-border to first station on local t[...] (except Austria). Regional areas also available, 229 - 319 CZK. Vers[...] for Czech Republic plus border areas of Germany or Poland, inclu[...] regional areas, are also available.

Praha: all public transport (including most trains): 24 hrs 110 CZ[...] days 310 CZK. Wider areas available. **Prague Card**: 2 / 3 / 4 [...] admission card, includes transport when booked online, €4[...] (student €33 - 47). Most cities have day tickets for city transport.

DENMARK

European residents: InterRail Global Pass and One Country Pass.
Non-European residents: Eurail Global Pass, Eurail Select / One Cou[...] Passes (also Scandinavia). Also Öresund Rundt.

Fares based on national zonal system; 30-day **Pendlerkort** [...] commuters (photocard required) including all-zones version. 10-jou[...] tickets also available. **Rejsekortet** is a new pre-pay travel card aime[...] Danish residents, but a **Rejsekort Anonymt** may be purchase[...] anyone (card costs 80 DKK, plus an initial 600 DKK for travel purpo[...]

København: **City Pass** zones 1 - 4 (including from / to airport) on [...] metro and train 24 / 72 hrs 80 / 200 DKK (child half price). **24-Hour Ti[...]** adds greater København, 130 DKK (child 65 DKK). **FlexCard**: 7 [...] travel in choice of zones, 250 - 675 DKK.

Copenhagen Card: greater København public transport, free entry t[...] attractions, 24 / 48 / 72 / 120 hrs €48 / 65 / 78 / 110 (2 children unde[...] free).

ESTONIA

Tallinn: tram / bus / trolley-bus **Ühiskaart** pre-pay travel card (de[...] €2) available for 1 / 3 / 5 / 30 days: €3 / 5 / 6 / 23 (supplement on exp[...] buses). One hour ticket €1.10. **Tallinn Card**: adds museums etc., 24[...] €32, 48 hrs €42, 72 hrs €52. Under 15s half price.

FINLAND

European residents: InterRail Global Pass and One Country Pass.
Non-European residents: Eurail Global Pass, Eurail Select / One Cou[...] Passes (also Scandinavia).

Helsinki: single-charge electronic cards for all public transport inclu[...] local trains: 1 / 2 / 3 days €8 / 12 / 16; 7 days €32 (1 - 7 days availa[...]
Helsinki Card: public transport plus free entry to main sights, 24 / 48[...] hrs €39 / 49 / 59, child 7-16 €22 / 27 / 32.

FRANCE

European residents: InterRail Global Pass and One Country Pass.
Non-European residents: Eurail Global Pass and Eurail Select P[...]
Also Pass Alsace - Rhein-Neckar, Passbask, Saar-Lor-Lux.

France Railpass: only available to non-European residents, valid for [...] days within one month. Adult 3 days 256 / 206 USD 1st / 2nd class [...] approx 35 / 30 USD per extra day (9-day: 468 / 374 USD). Approx [...] discount for Youth (aged 12 - 25), 12% discount for Senior (60 +). S[...] version for 2 - 5 people: 15% discount. Also, 15 days within two m[...] pass 610 / 488 USD, 1st / 2nd class. Passes also available for 2, 4, [...] and 15 days continuous travel: 1st / 2nd class, 155 / 126 - 488 / 391 U[...]

Reservations required for most trains. Special Passholder fare pay[...] on *Eurostar*. Pass is available from RailEurope and other agents.

Annual railcards are available for children, young people (ages 12 - [...] and seniors (60 +) giving 25% - 50% discount off rail fares. A **C[...] Week-End** is available for all ages giving discounts at weekends.

Regional Tickets: several regions offer day tickets on TER (local) tr[...] at weekends and holidays. Conditions vary and some only vali[...] summer. Details generally available on TER website www.sncf.co[...] trains/ter. The **Lille City Pass** 24 / 48 / 72 hrs, €25 / 35 / 45 includes l[...] transport (3-day pass includes TER trains in Nord-Pas de Calais re[...] on one day). **Alsa Plus 24h**: a zonal day pass for Alsace, €35.9 for [...] whole region; group ticket (2-5 people) available at weekends for €[...]

Paris Visite: public transport within Paris, plus discounted entry [...] attractions: zones 1 - 3: €11.15 / 18.15 / 24.80 / 35.70 for 1 / 2 / 3 / 5 da[...] Zones 1 - 5 (includes suburbs and airports): €23.50 / 35.70 / 50.[...] 61.25. Children 4 - 11 half price. **Mobilis**: Paris one-day ticket [...] available on airport services), €7 (zones 1 - 2) to €16.6 (zones 1 - 5[...] Most cities have bus / tram day tickets, e.g. **Lyon** €5.5, **Lille** €4.8.

GERMANY

European residents: InterRail Global Pass and One Country Pass.
Non-European residents: Eurail Global Pass and Eurail Select Pa[...]
Also Euregio-Bodensee, Euregio Mass-Rhein, Sar-Lor-Lux.

For non-European residents, **German Rail Pass FLEXI**: 3, 4, 5, 7 and [...] days unlimited travel within one month. 3 days €258 / 191 1st / 2nd cla[...] 4 days €277 / 205, 5 days €296 / 219, 7 days €367 / 272, 10 d[...] €471 / 348. **German Rail Pass CONSECUTIVE**: 5 / 10 / 15 consecu[...] days 1st class €288 / 417 / 585 (€213 / 309 / 434 2nd class). A **T[...]**

s offers a discount of approximately 50% for second adult. Youth ses also available. No supplements on *ICE, IC, EC*. 20% discount on nantische Strasse bus.

öնes-Wochenende-Ticket: one day's unlimited travel on Saturday Sunday (to 0300 following day) on local trains (IRE/RE/RB/S-Bahn), class. Price €40 from machines, €42 from ticket offices. Valid for up people (+€4 for each additional traveller), buy on the day. Also valid trams/buses in certain areas, and on certain rail lines across the der into Poland.

er-durchs-Land-Ticket: one day's unlimited travel (not before 0900 - Fri, but valid until 0300 following day) on local trains (IRE/RE/RB/S-n), 2nd class. Valid for up to 5 people. €44 for one person, then add for each additional person in the group (€76 for a group of five).

ional tickets (Länder-Tickets): one day's unlimited 2nd class travel up to 5 people on DB local trains (not before 0900 on Mon-Fri, valid to 0 the following day). **Baden-Württemberg** €23 for one person (add for each additional person). **Bayern** €23 for one person (add €5 for h additional person). **Brandenburg-Berlin** €29. **Hessen** (includes st buses) €33. **Mecklenburg-Vorpommern** €23 for one person (add for each additional person). **Niedersachsen** €23 for one person (add for each additional person). **Nordrhein-Westfalen** (SchönerTag ket) one person €29.5, 2-5 people €43. **Rheinland-Pfalz** plus arland €24 for one person (add €5 for each additional person). chsen including **Sachsen-Anhalt** and **Thüringen** €23 for one person d €5 for each additional person). **Schleswig-Holstein** €28 for one son (add €3 for each additional person; includes public transport in nburg). All Länder tickets may be purchased on the day from ticket chines (most cost €2 more if purchased from travel centres).

ncard 25/50: valid for 1 year, giving discounts of 25% or 50% on all onal DB trains for €62 or €255 in 2nd class (1st class €125/515). h cards entitle the holder to a 25% discount for international journeys ween Germany and 30 European countries (except where global fares charged). Half price Bahncards available for young people and iors. **Bahncard 100** (passport photo required) gives unlimited travel 1 year, €4,090 in 2nd class, €6,890 in 1st class. All available from London.

z: HSB narrow gauge railway 3/5 days €78/117, child 6-11 50%.

geskarte (day ticket): most urban areas offer 24/48/72 hour tickets d on most public transport; generally a zonal system operates.

lcome Tickets: most public transport in selected cities, also includes e or reduced entry to many museums and visitor attractions. Buy from urist Information, main stations, some airports and hotels. Examples: **rlin Welcome Card**: one adult and up to 3 children under 15; 48 hrs 1.5, 72 hrs €29.5, 4 days €34.5, 5 days €40.5, 6 days €45.5. vers zones A, B and C and includes DB trains. **Dresden City Card**: 1 €10; family card also available for 2 adults and up to 4 children under €15. Includes ferry trips within the Dresden tariff zone. **Frankfurt rd**: 1 day €10.5, 2 days €15.5; group ticket (up to 5) €20.5 (1 day)/ 0.5 (2 days). Includes travel from/to the airport. **Hamburg Card**: Day ket €9.9. Also 2-5 days €18.9 - 40.9. Group versions (up to 5) 7.9/32.9-72.9. **Hannover Card**: 1 day €9.5, 2 days €15, 3 days 8, group ticket (up to 5) €20/27/35. **Köln Welcome Card**: 24/48 hrs /18, group ticket (up to 5) €19/38. Wider areas also available. **pzig Card**: 1 day €11.5, 3 days €22.5, 3 day group (2 adults and up 3 children under 14) €39.9. **Nürnberg Card**: 2 days €25 companied children aged 6-11 €5).

REAT BRITAIN

ropean (non-UK) residents: InterRail Global Pass and One Country ss. Non-UK residents: Britrail.

ilcards: annual cards giving 34% discount on most rail fares; 16-25 ilcard, Two Together, Family & Friends, Senior: all £30; Disabled rsons £20. Network Railcard gives off-peak discount in South East gland, £30.

-Line Rail Rover: covers whole National Rail network. 1st/standard ss £731/483 (7 days), £1117/731 (14 days), children 5-15 half price. % discount for holders of Senior/Disabled/Two Together railcard, and andard class only) 16-25/Family & Friends railcard. Some restrictions fore 1000 Mon-Fri. Not valid on Eurostar, Heathrow Express, London derground. Valid on Ffestiniog Railway but not other private railways.

irit of Scotland Travelpass: all rail services in Scotland (includes rlisle and Berwick) plus Caledonian MacBrayne ferry services and me buses. Standard class only. Valid 4 out of 8 days, £134; not before 15 Mon to Fri (except on Glasgow - Oban/Mallaig/Stranraer services d north of Inverness). 34% discount with 16-25/Two Together/ nior/Disabled railcard; 50% discount for children (5-15). 20% count on Northlink Ferries to Orkney and Shetland. Smaller areas o available: **Highland Rover**, 4 days out of 8 £81.50; **Central otland Rover** 3 in 7 days, £36.30.

plore Wales: standard class rail travel on any 4 days out of 8 (not valid fore 0930 Mon-Fri), price £99, children half price. Tickets available line and at most staffed stations. Other areas available: South Wales 69), North and Mid Wales (£69).

A range of **Rover** tickets is available covering various areas, typically for 7 days, 3 in 7 days, 4 in 8 days, or 8 in 15 days. Most not valid until after the morning peak on Mon to Fri. Examples: Anglia Plus, Coast and Peaks, East Midlands, Heart of England, Kent, North Country, North Wales, Severn & Solent, Thames.

Ranger day tickets also available: e.g. Cambian coast, Cheshire, Cornwall, Cotswolds, Cumbria, Devon, East Midlands, Isle of Wight, Lakes, Lancashire, Lincolnshire, North Downs, Oxfordshire, South Pennines, Thames branches, Tyne & Tees, West Midlands, West Wales, West Yorkshire, Yorkshire Coast. Details: nationalrail.co.uk.

All-day tickets (some off-peak) covering local rail and most buses are available in Derbyshire, Glasgow, Greater Manchester, Merseyside, South Yorkshire, West Yorkshire, Tyneside and West Midlands.

London: Day Travelcards cover almost all transport (Underground, bus and rail) in the London area; peak version from £12.10 (central London, zones 1-4) to £17.20 (zones 1-6), off-peak version (not before 0930 Mon-Fri) £12.10 (zones 1-6). 7-day tickets from £32.40 (zones 1-2) to £59.10 (zones 1-6), no off-peak version. Travelcard holders may take up to four children aged 1-15 for £2 each after 1000 (otherwise half fare). For single journeys contactless debit and credit cards, or stored-value Oyster cards offer the best value as prices are capped. Visitor Oyster cards are available preloaded from £10 to £50 (plus £3 fee, non-refundable). Children under 11 travel free on buses and trams (also on Tube, DLR and some rail services when accompanied by a fare paying adult; up to four children per adult).

Isle of Man **Go Explore** cards (£2 fee): most trains (not Groudle Glen) and buses: 1/3/5/7 days, £16/32/39/47, children 5-15 half price. Family card: 2 adults and up to 3 children, £39/75/95/115.

GREECE

European residents: InterRail Global Pass and One Country Pass (also Greece Plus).

Non-European residents: Eurail Global Pass, Eurail Select/One Country Passes. Also Balkan Flexipass.

Athens: 24-hour ticket valid on metro, tram and bus €4.5, 5 days €9 (excludes airport, €9 single). 3-day tourist ticket including airport €22.

HUNGARY

European residents: InterRail Global Pass and One Country Pass.

Non-European residents: Eurail Global Pass, Eurail Select/One Country Passes. Also European East Pass. Travel by rail and local transport is free for over-65s with an EU passport or ID card.

START Klub Card: gives 50% discount on 2nd class travel. Valid for either 6 months or one year: HUF 19900/34900 (HUF 14900/24900 under 26 years). Requires passport style photograph. Cardholders may obtain 50% discount for a second person on Saturday.

Balaton Mix: rail and shipping services around Lake Balaton, valid Mar. 26 - Oct. 23, 2016. 3-day ticket gives 1 day's unlimited travel HUF 3590, child 6-14 HUF 2190, family (2 adults + 2 children) HUF 9490. 7-day ticket gives any 2 days travel for HUF 5990/3590/16190. 50% discount on rail journey to/from the area within period of validity.

Budapest: BKV tram/metro/bus/rail, 24 hrs HUF 1650, 72 hrs HUF 4150, 7 days HUF 4950. Also 24 hr group ticket (2-5 people), HUF 3300. **Budapest Card** also includes museums, walking tour and discounts: 24 hrs HUF 4900, 48 hrs HUF 7900, 72 hrs HUF 9900.

IRELAND

European residents: InterRail Global Pass and One Country Pass.

Non-European residents: Eurail Global/Select/One Country Passes. InterRail and Eurail passes valid in the Republic of Ireland are also valid in Northern Ireland.

REPUBLIC OF IRELAND ONLY:

Irish Explorer: any 5 days in 15 on IÉ rail services, €160 (child €80), standard class. **Trekker** gives 4 consecutive days on Irish Rail for €110.

Dublin area: **Short Hop Zone** tickets: Rail only 1 day €11.4, 3 days €26.5. **Leap Visitor Card**: 1 day €10, 3 days €19.5, 7days €40. Includes rail in short hop zone, Luas tram and bus (also Airlink); purchase at airport or tourist offices (not railway stations). Luas **Flexi** ticket (tram only): 1 day €6.8, 7 day €24.9 (child €2.8/8.9). **Rambler** (bus only, includes Airlink): 5 days €30.6.

NORTHERN IRELAND ONLY:

iLink integrated smartcard gives unlimited bus and rail travel on Translink services (Northern Ireland Railways, Ulsterbus and Belfast Citybus). Zone 4 covers the whole of Northern Ireland: 1 day £17.50, 7 days £61, 1 month £211. Zone 1 covers Belfast city (£6.50/23/78). Children half price. New North West zone: £14.50/52/181. Initial £1 fee for card. **Belfast Visitor Pass** includes visitor discounts: 1/2/3 days, adult £6.50/11/14.50, child £3.75/6/7.75. **Select**: 3 days travel within 7 on pre-selected dates and journeys gives 16% discount on normal fares.

ITALY

European residents: InterRail Global Pass and One Country Pass (also Italy Plus).

Passes for Domestic Travel

Non-European residents : Eurail Global Pass, Eurail Select / One Country Passes.

Mobilcard Südtirol : regional trains, buses, funiculars and cable cars in Bolzano, Malles, Brennero area: 1 / 3 / 7 days; €15 / 23 / 28 respectively.

Roma: Biglietto Integrato Giornaliero (BIG) covers rail / metro / bus in urban area for one day, €6 (excludes Fiumicino airport, restrictions on rail / metro). Biglietto Turistico Integrato (BTI) valid 3 days €16.5, weekly ticket (CIS) €24. **Roma Pass**: 2 / 3 day transport pass (€28 / 36) with museum discounts.

Milano: 24 hour ticket (abbonamento giornaliero): ATM city services plus local Trenitalia, Trenord rail services, €4.5. Also 48 hour ticket €8.25.

Napoli: 'Campania > artecard' is a transport + museum visitors card, with various options. The 3 day card (€32) allows free entry to two museums with 50% off others; the 7 day version (€34) allows 5 free then 50% off.

Venezia: Travel cards for ACTV buses and boats: 1 / 2 / 3 / 7 days €20 / 30 / 40 / 60. Each card is also available with airport transfer add-on (€8).

LATVIA

Riga Card: public transport, bus tour, plus free / discounted museum entry; €25 / 30 / 35 for 24 / 48 / 72 hours.

LITHUANIA

Vilnius : 1 / 3 / 10 day tickets available on local VVT buses / trolleybuses; €3.5 / 6 / 12. **Vilnius Card** includes public transport, museums and discounts; 24 / 72 hrs, €20 / 30.

LUXEMBOURG

European residents : InterRail Global Pass and One Country Pass (Benelux).
Non-European residents : Eurail Global Pass, Eurail Select / One Country Passes (Benelux). See also Sar-Lor-Lux Ticket.

Dagesbilljee / Billet longue durée: day ticket €4, unlimited 2nd class travel on all public transport throughout the country (until 0400 hrs following morning); not valid to border points. €5 if bought on board the train. Carnet of 5 day tickets €16. **Oeko Pass**: valid one month €50 2nd class, €75 1st class; from CFL offices.

Luxembourg Card: unlimited travel on trains and buses throughout the country, plus free entry to 70 attractions. 1 day €13, 2 days €20, 3 days €28. Family pass for 2 - 5 people (max 3 adults) for 1 / 2 / 3 days: €28 / 48 / 68.

MACEDONIA

European residents : InterRail Global Pass and One Country Pass.
Also Balkan Flexipass.

MONTENEGRO

European residents : InterRail Global Pass and One Country Pass.
Non-European residents : Eurail Global Pass, Eurail Select Pass.
Also Balkan Flexipass.

NETHERLANDS

European residents : InterRail Global Pass and One Country Pass (Benelux).
Non-European residents : Eurail Global Pass, Eurail Select / One Country Passes (Benelux). Also Euregio Maas-Rhein.

A national stored-value OV-chipkaart is used for public transport, initial cost €7.50, which can be loaded with day tickets. A single-use chipcard or e-ticket may be used by less frequent travellers. **Day ticket**: unlimited travel on NS trains; 1st / 2nd class €89.4 / 52.6. **Railrunner**: Children aged 4 - 11 travel for a flat rate of €2.50 each in 2nd class. Must be accompanied by an adult in 1st class; maximum 3 children per adult. Excludes *Thalys*.

Amsterdam Travel Ticket: GVB tram / bus / metro (also includes one return journey from / to airport on NS train): 24 hrs €15, 48 hrs €20, 72 hrs €25. **Amsterdam & Region Day Ticket**: a 1-day GVB ticket including Connexxion and EBS (not valid on trains), €13.5. **I amsterdam Card**: GVB tram / bus / metro, one free canal tour plus free / discounted entry to various attractions; 24 / 48 / 72 / 96 hrs, €55 / 65 / 75 / 85.

NORWAY

European residents : InterRail Global Pass and One Country Pass.
Non-European residents : Eurail Global Pass, Eurail Select / One Country Passes (also Scandinavia).

Oslo: 24 hour ticket for all 'Ruter' public transport in zone 1 (wider areas available): 90 NOK, 7 days 240 NOK; children half price. **Oslo Pass**: all public transport including NSB local trains (zones 1 - 2, excludes airport), free entry to attractions, discounts on sightseeing buses / boats: 24 / 48 / 72 hours 335 / 490 / 620 NOK (children pay approximately 50%).

Bergen Card: local bus travel plus free or discounted entry to various attractions; 24 / 48 / 72 hrs, 240 / 310 / 380 NOK (children aged 3 - 15, 90 / 120 / 150 NOK).

POLAND

European residents : InterRail Global Pass and One Country Pass.
Non-European residents : Eurail Global Pass, Eurail Select / One Cou
Passes.

PKP Intercity operates *EIC, EIP, IC, TLK* trains and offers the follo
passes for its trains: **Bilet Weekendowy** (weekend ticket): valid 190
to 0600 Mon (extended if Thurs or Mon is a public holiday). Basic ti
valid only in *TLK* and *IC* trains (with seats); 79 / 109 PLN 2nd / 1st c
(this version was formerly called Bilet Podróznika). **Weekendowy M**
valid in *EIC, EIP, IC* and *TLK*: 154 PLN 2nd class, 247 PLN 1st c
(supplement of 10 PLN for each *EIP* journey). Seat reservations free
not compulsory). Both the above also available from train conductor

Bilety Sieciowe (network tickets): 3 months 2900 / 4050 PLN (2nd,
class); 6 months 5400 / 7500 PLN; annual 9900 / 14600 PLN. Versi
with unnamed holder are also available.

Przewozy Regionalne (PR) operates REGIO, IR and RE trains: **Bi
Sieciowe** (network tickets): weekly / monthly 159 / 369 PLN. **REGIO
net**: valid for any 3 days out of 2 months, 75 PLN; 65 PLN for RE
trains only; validate at ticket office before travel. **Bilet Turystyc**
(tourist ticket): valid 1800 Friday to 0600 Monday, 45 PLN; 39 PLN
REGIO trains only. **Bilet Turystyczny + Czechy** adds border area
Czech Republic; 55 PLN. Passes valid on REGIO trains also valid
Arriva RP and Koleje Dolnoślaskie.

Koleje Mazowieckie (KM) trains: wide area around Warsaw, 24 hr B
dobowy imienny 35 PLN.

Warsaw ZTM tram / bus / metro / rail (includes Chopin airport): 1 day z
1 only, 15 PLN; zones 1 & 2, 26 PLN. Weekend ticket valid 1900 F
0800 Mon valid zones 1 & 2, 24 PLN.

PORTUGAL

European residents : InterRail Global Pass and One Country Pass.
Non-European residents : Eurail Global Pass, Eurail Select / One Cou
Passes.

Intra-Rail : for ages 12 - 30 with free nights at youth hostels; *Xc*
version valid 3 days €58 (€64 without youth card). *Xplore* version val
days €127 (€146 without youth card). Not valid on *AP* trains. Bu
major stations. Card and ID must be presented to obtain a (free) tra
ticket.

Lisboa: Carris tram / bus / metro - one-day ticket (bilhete 24h Rede) €
conjunction with reusable *7 Colinas* smartcard (€0.50). Includes
funiculars and lift. **Lisboa Card** includes free and discounted attractio
24 / 48 / 72 hrs, €18.5 / 31.5 / 39 (ages 4 - 15: €11.5 / 17.5 / 20.5).

Coimbra : day ticket on SMTUC local buses €3.50.

Porto: *Andante Tour Card* gives metro + STCP bus + local rail, all zon
24 hrs €7, 72 hrs €15. **Porto Card** also includes free / discounted en
to tourist attractions, 1 day €13, 2 days €20, 3 days €25.

ROMANIA

European residents : InterRail Global Pass and One Country Pass.
Non-European residents : Eurail Global Pass, Eurail Select / One Cour
Passes. Also Balkan Flexipass.

Bucuresti : RATB tram, bus and trolleybus network (not express buse
1 / 7 / 15 days, 8 / 17 / 25 RON. An 'Activ' or 'Multiplu' card may be requi
(1.6 RON). The **Bucharest City Card** is issued *free* and incluc
museum and other discounts, valid 3 days.

RUSSIA

Moskva : smart cards for unlimited number of journeys on metro; 1 c
210 RUB, 3 days 400 RUB, 7 days 800 RUB. Bus /tram tickets availa
from kiosks in strips of 10 / 20. Monthly *yediniy bilyet* covers bus / tra
metro (limited to 70 journeys) 2550 RUB. No tourist tickets.

St Peterburg : bus / tram tickets available in packs of 10; multi-jour
cards can be bought for the metro. A **Guest Petersburg Card** is availa
for 2 / 3 / 5 / 7 days.

SERBIA

European residents : InterRail Global Pass and One Country Pass.
Non-European residents : Eurail Global Pass, Eurail Select Pass.
Also Balkan Flexipass.

SLOVAKIA

European residents : InterRail Global Pass and One Country Pass.
Non-European residents : Eurail Global Pass, Eurail Select / One Coun
Passes. Also European East Pass.

Bratislava : urban tram / bus network, 24 hrs €6.9, 3 days €8, 7 da
€11.4 **Bratislava City Card** includes many discounts, 1 day €10
days €12, 3 days €15, available from tourist offices.

SLOVENIA

European residents : InterRail Global Pass and One Country Pass.
Non-European residents : Eurail Global Pass, Eurail Select / One Coun
Passes.

Ljubljana City Card : city buses, castle funicular, tourist boat a
museums, valid for 24, 48 or 72 hours, €23 / 30 / 35 (10% discou
available online).

Passes for Domestic Travel

·AIN

ropean residents: InterRail Global Pass and One Country Pass.
n-European residents: Eurail Global Pass, Eurail Select / One Country
sses. Also Passbask.

NFE Spain Pass: for people resident outside Spain giving 4, 6, 8, 10 12 individual journeys. Tickets must be obtained in advance using the s; reservations are compulsory but free. Valid 1 month from first rney. Can be purchased online (www.renfe.com).

drid: Abono Turístico (Tourist Ticket) gives all public transport in e A, 1/2/3 days €8.4/14.2/18.4, also 5/7 days €26.8/35.4, dren 50%. Available for wider area (zone T) at double the price. **drid Card** gives discounts at various attractions, 24/48/72/120 hrs 7/60/67/77 (cheaper online); combine with Tourist Ticket above for nsport.

rcelona T-Dia ticket: valid 1 day on metro / TMB bus / tram / local rail, n €8.4 (zone 1, includes airport) to €22.5 (all 6 zones, wide area und the city). **Hola BCN** zone 1 travelcards available for 2/3/4/5 ys, €14/20.5/26.5/32 (cheaper online). **Barcelona Card**: adds free discounted museums, 3 to 5 days €45/55/60 (children 4-12 years 1/27/32).

WEDEN

ropean residents: InterRail Global Pass and One Country Pass.
n-European residents: Eurail Global Pass, Eurail Select / One Country
sses (also Scandinavia). Also Öresund Rundt.

ockholm: all SL public transport in Greater Stockholm, 24/72 hours 5/230 SEK. 7 days 300 SEK, plus smartcard 20 SEK. Reduced 40% under 20s/over 65s. **Stockholm Pass** includes museums, 710/ 25/1225/1755 SEK for 24/48/72/120 hours (approximately half ce for ages 6-17). A cheaper version excluding travel is also available.

WITZERLAND

ropean residents: InterRail Global Pass and One Country Pass.
n-European residents: Eurail Global Pass, Eurail Select Pass.
o Euregio-Bodensee.

viss Travel Pass: available to all non-Swiss residents. Consecutive ys on Swiss Railways, boats and most alpine postbuses and city ses. Valid for 3, 4, 8 or 15 days; 1st class 336/402/581/704 CHF, 2nd ss 210/251/363/440 CHF. Youth Pass (16-25 years) gives approxi- tely 20% reduction. All versions give 50% reduction on most funicular d mountain railways. Also includes the Swiss Museum Pass - free trance to over 400 sites. Children aged 6-15 travel free with a Family rd if accompanied by a parent (not other relatives), otherwise half fare.

viss Travel Pass Flex: as above but for 3/4/8/15 non-consecutive ys within 1 month. Prices 1st/2nd class: 382/239 CHF (3 days), 458/ 6 CHF (4 days), 651/407 CHF (8 days), 774/484 CHF (15 days). uth discounts. Offers 50% reduction on most funicular and mountain ways on selected days only.

viss Transfer Ticket: return ticket from any airport / border station to y other Swiss station; use within 1 month. Each journey must be mpleted on day of validation and by the most direct route. 1st class 6 CHF, 2nd class 141 CHF. Family Card valid, see above. Cannot be tained in Switzerland.

viss Transfer Ticket Combi: as Swiss Transfer Ticket but also offers limited half-fare tickets for 1 month on trains, buses, boats and most untain railways and cable cars. 1st / 2nd class 286/201 CHF. Family card valid, see above under Swiss Travel Pass. No youth discount. Cannot be obtained in Switzerland.

Swiss Half Fare Card: discount card offering 50% off most public transport, valid for 1 month, 120 CHF.

Swiss Half Fare Card Combi: available to holders of the Swiss Travel Pass Flex or Swiss Transfer Ticket, 60 CHF. Offers the same benefits as the Swiss Half Fare Card.

The **9 o'clock Travelpass** is valid for travel within the GA area after 0900 hrs (not valid at weekends) to holders of Half Fare travelcards; 1st/ 2nd class 96/58 CHF. Packs of 6 can be bought for price of 5.

The above passes are available online (some may be printed at home), from Switzerland Travel Centre or from major Swiss stations. Not available to Swiss residents.

Bernese Oberland Regional Pass: valid May to October. Available for 4, 6, 8 or 10 days unlimited travel; 240/300/340/380 CHF 2nd class, 288/360/408/456 CHF 1st class.

Regional Passes: several other areas are available including Adventure Card Upper Valais - Uri - Grisons, Graubünden Pass, Lake Geneva - Alps and Tell-Pass.

Jungfrau Travel Pass: valid May to October for 3/4/5/6 days consecutive travel, 180/205/230/255 CHF. Covers most routes; 50% discount Eigergletscher - Jungfraujoch. 5 and 6 day passes also include boats on Lakes Brienz and Thun. **Summer Season Pass**: unlimited travel May to November, 550 CHF. Covers most routes; 50% discount Eigergletscher - Jungfraujoch. Discounts for holders of Half Fare Card, GA or Swiss Travel Pass on both the above. Not available in Switzerland.

Bern: day ticket for all transport in city 12.4 CHF. The **Bern Ticket** is issued to overnight guests offering free bus and tram travel within the inner city.

Genève: Day ticket (Carte 24 Heures) includes buses, trams, trains and boats: 10 CHF (valid for 2 people at weekends). **Carte 9 h** is valid from 0900 hrs, 8 CHF. Day ticket for wider regional area 18.5 CHF (13.2 CHF after 0900). The **Geneva Transport Card** is given to those staying at a hotel or youth hostel in the city and allows unrestricted travel on all public transport for the duration of the stay.

Zürich: ZVV Tageskarte gives 24 hours on all transport including SBB trains, 14.2/8.6 CHF 1st/2nd class (central zone only); all zones in Canton 55.6/33.6 CHF. Off-peak version is 9-UhrPass, all zones, not before 0900 Mon-Fri, 42.8/26 CHF. **Zürich Card** includes all museums: 24 hours 24 CHF, 72 hours 48 CHF (children 16/32 CHF), includes airport.

TURKEY

European residents: InterRail Global Pass and One Country Pass.
Non-European residents: Eurail Global Pass, Eurail Select Pass.
Also Balkan Flexipass.

Tren Tur Karti: 30 day network pass. *Ekspres* version covers day trains excluding high-speed (YTL 210), *Yatakli Karti* includes night trains (YTL 550). Various *YHT* cards cover high-speed lines. Buy from main stations.

UKRAINE

Kyïv: a unlimited use metro pass valid for 1 calendar month is available, 95 UAH (48 UAH if purchased after the 15th), but there are no tourist tickets.

Where to Buy your Pass

urces of rail passes (and point to point tickets) include the following:

THE UNITED KINGDOM

:P Rail - see www.acprail.com and www.britrail.net

eutsche Bahn UK (German Railways)
< Booking Centre, ✆ 08718 80 80 66 www.bahn.com

Rail Travel Ltd
Tileyard Studios, Tileyard Road, London, N7 9AH
0207 619 1083 www.etrains4u.com

estiniog Travel
nit 6, Snowdonia Business Park, Penrhyndeudraeth, Gwynedd LL48 6LD
01766 772030 www.ffestiniogtravel.com

ternational Rail
) Box 153, Alresford, Hampshire SO24 4AQ
0871 231 0790 www.internationalrail.com

ail Canterbury
Palace Street, Canterbury, Kent CT1 2DZ
01227 450088 www.rail-canterbury.co.uk

ailTourGuide
iite 42, 7-15 Pink Lane, Newcastle upon Tyne, NE1 5DW
0191 246 0708 www.railtourguide.com

Real Russia
Unit 5, The Ivories, Northampton Street, Islington, London, N1 2HY
✆ 0207 100 7370 www.realrussia.co.uk

Switzerland Travel Centre
30 Bedford Street, 1st Floor, London, WC2E 9ED
0207 420 49 34 www.stc.co.uk

Trainseurope
4 Station Approach, March, Cambs PE15 8SJ
Also at St Pancras International station (East Midlands Trains ticket office). ✆ 0871 700 7722 www.trainseurope.co.uk

Voyages sncf
www.voyages-sncf.com

IN THE USA AND CANADA

Rail Europe Inc.
44 South Broadway, White Plains, NY 10601, USA
✆ 1-800-622-8600 www.raileurope.com

Rail Europe, Canada
✆ 1-800-361 7245 (1-800-361-RAIL) www.raileurope.ca

See also **Rick Steve's** comprehensive website: www.ricksteves.com.
For a list of **Eurail** agents worldwide see www.eurailgroup.org.

AUSTRIA

CAPITAL

Vienna (Wien).

CURRENCY

Euro (EUR / €). 1 euro = 100 cent. For exchange rates see page 9.

EMBASSIES IN VIENNA

Australia: Mattiellistraße 2-4, ✆ 1 506 740. **Canada**: Laurenzenberg 2, ✆ 1 531 383 000. **New Zealand** Mattiellistraße 2-4/3, ✆ 1 505 3021. **UK**: Jaurèsgasse 12, ✆ 1 716 130. **USA**: Boltzmanngasse 16, ✆ 1 313 390.

EMBASSIES OVERSEAS

Australia: 12 Talbot St, Forrest, Canberra, ACT 2603, ✆ 2 629 515 33. **Canada**: 445 Wilbrod St, Ottawa ON, KIN 6M7, ✆ 613 789 1444. **UK**: 18 Belgrave Mews West, London SW1X 8HU, ✆ 020 7344 3250. **USA**: 3524 International Court NW, Washington DC 20008, ✆ 202 895 6700.

LANGUAGE

German. English is widely spoken in tourist areas.

PUBLIC TRANSPORT

Most long-distance travel is by rail (see below). Inter-urban buses operated by ÖBB-Postbus (www.postbus.at); stops usually located by rail stations or post offices. City transport is efficient with integrated ticketing; buy tickets from machines or Tabak/Trafik booths. Wien has an extensive metro and tram system; for day tickets see Passes section. Other cities with tram networks include Graz, Innsbruck and Linz. Taxis are metered; extra charges for luggage (fixed charges in smaller towns).

RAIL TRAVEL

See Tables **950 - 999**. Operated by Österreichische Bundesbahnen (ÖBB) www.oebb.at. *RJ* (*Railjet*) / *EC* / *IC*) operate every 1–2 hrs on main domestic and international routes. *ICE* trains operate certain international services to / from Germany. Other train categories: *D* (ordinary fast trains); *REX* (semi-fast local trains); *R* (local stopping trains). S-Bahn services operate in major cities. Private operator *Westbahn* also operate fast trains between Wien and Salzburg. Most overnight trains convey sleeping-cars (up to three berths), couchettes (four/six berths) and 2nd-class seats. Seat reservations available on long-distance services.

TELEPHONES

Dial in: ✆ +43 then number (omit initial 0). Outgoing: ✆ 00. Emergency: ✆ 112. Police: ✆ 133. Fire: ✆ 122. Ambulance: ✆ 144.

TOURIST INFORMATION

Austrian National Tourist Office (*Fremdenverkehrsbüro*) www.austria.info. Vienna: Albertinaplatz / Maysedergasse, ✆ 01 24 555.

TOURIST OFFICES OVERSEAS

Australia: 36 Carrington St, 1st floor, Sydney NSW 2000, ✆ 02 9299 3621, info@antosyd.org.au. **Canada**: 2 Bloor St West, Suite 400, Toronto ON, M4W 3E2, ✆ 416 967 3381, travel@austria.info. **UK**: 9-11 Richmond Buildings, off Dean St., London W1D 3HF, ✆ 0845 101 18 18, holiday@austria.info. **USA**: P.O. Box 1142, New York NY 10108-1142, ✆ 212 944 6880, travel@austria.info.

VISAS

See page xxiv for visa requirements.

BELGIUM

CAPITAL

Brussels (Bruxelles / Brussel).

CURRENCY

Euro (EUR / €). 1 euro = 100 cent. For exchange rates see page 9.

EMBASSIES IN BRUSSELS

Australia: Ave des Arts 56, ✆ 02 286 0500. **Canada**: Avenue de Tervueren 2, ✆ 02 741 0611. **New Zealand**: Avenue des Nerviens 9/31, ✆ 02 512 1040. **UK**: Avenue d'Auderghem 10, ✆ 02 287 6211. **USA**: Boulevard du Regentlaan 27, ✆ 02 811 4000.

EMBASSIES OVERSEAS

Australia: 19 Arkana St, Yarralumla, Canberra, ACT 2600, ✆ 2 627 325 01. **Canada**: 360 Albert St, Suite 820, Ottawa ON, K1R 7X7, ✆ 613 236 7267. **UK**: 17 Grosvenor Crescent, London SW1X 7EE, ✆ 020 7470 3700. **USA**: 3330 Garfield St NW, Washington DC 20008, ✆ 202 333 6900.

LANGUAGE

Dutch (north), French (south) and German (east). Many speak both French and Dutch, plus often English and/or German.

PUBLIC TRANSPORT

National bus companies: De Lijn (Flanders), TEC (Wallonia, i.e. the French-speaking areas); few long-distance buses. Brussels has extensive metro / tram / bus system operated by STIB with integrated ticketing; tickets can be purchased from tram / bus driver but it's cheaper to buy in advance from machines at metro stations or special kiosks (also offices labelled *Bootik*). For day tickets see Passes section. Some tram and bus stops are request stops – raise your hand. Taxis seldom pick up in the street, so find a rank or phone; double rates outside city limits.

RAIL TRAVEL

See Tables **400 - 448**. Operated by NMBS (in Dutch) / SNCB (in French) www.b-rail.be. Rail information offices: 'B' in an oval logo. Some platforms serve more than one train at a time; check carefully. Left luggage and cycle hire at many stations. Timetables usually in two sets: Mondays to Fridays and weekends/holidays.

TELEPHONES

Dial in: ✆ +32 then number (omit initial 0). Outgoing: ✆ 00. Emergency: ✆ 112. Police: ✆ 101. Fire, ambulance: ✆ 100.

TOURIST INFORMATION

Dutch: *Dienst voor Toerisme*. French: *Office de Tourisme*. Toerisme Vlaanderen www.toervl.be / www.visitflanders.co.uk. Office de Promotion du Tourisme de Wallonie et de Bruxelles www.belgium-tourism.net. Brussels: Hôtel de Ville, Grand Place or rue Royale 2, ✆ 025 138 940.

TOURIST OFFICES OVERSEAS

UK: Tourism Flanders - Brussels, 1a Cavendish Square, London W1G 0LD. ✆ 020 7307 7738, info@visitflanders.co.uk; Belgian Tourist Office Brussels-Wallonia, 217 Marsh Wall, London E14 9FJ. ✆ 020 7531 0390, ✆ 0800 954 5245, info@belgiumtheplaceto.be. **USA / Canada**: 220 East 42nd St, Suite 3402, New York NY 10017, ✆ 212 758 8130, info@visitbelgium.com.

VISAS

See page xxiv for visa requirements.

BULGARIA

CAPITAL

Sofia (Sofiya).

CURRENCY

Lev (BGN or Lv.); 1 lev = 100 stotinki (st). Tied to euro. For exchange rates see page 9.

EMBASSIES IN SOFIA

Australia *refer to Australian Embassy in Greece.* **Canada**: (Consulate) 7 Pozitano St, ✆ 02 969 9710. **New Zealand**: *refer to NZ Embassy in Belgium.* **UK**: ul. Moskovska 9, ✆ 02 933 9222. **USA**: ulitsa Kozyak 16, ✆ 02 937 5100.

EMBASSIES OVERSEAS

Australia: 29 Pindary Crescent str. O'Malley, Canberra, ACT 2606, ✆ 2 628 697 11. **Canada**: 325 Steward St, Ottawa ON, K1N 6K5, ✆ 613 789 3215. **UK**: 186 - 188 Queen's Gate, London SW7 5HL, ✆ 020 7584 9400. **USA**: 1621 22nd St NW, Washington DC 20008, ✆ 202 387 0174.

LANGUAGE

Bulgarian (written in the Cyrillic alphabet). English, German, Russian and French in tourist areas.

PUBLIC TRANSPORT

There is an extensive bus network but quality is variable. They are slightly more expensive than trains but both are very cheap for hard currency travellers. In Sofia buses and trams use the same ticket; punch it at the machine after boarding, get a new ticket if you change. For day tickets see Passes section.

RAIL TRAVEL

See Tables **1500 - 1560**. Bulgarian State Railways (BDZ) www.bdz.bg run express, fast and stopping trains. Reservations are recommended (obligatory for express trains). Overnight trains convey 1st- and 2nd-class sleeping cars and seats. One platform may serve two tracks, platforms and tracks are both numbered. Station signs are in Cyrillic.

TELEPHONES

Dial in: ✆ +359 then number (omit initial 0). Outgoing: ✆ 00. Emergency: ✆ 112.

TOURIST INFORMATION

Bulgarian Tourism Authority www.bulgariatravel.org. Sofia: St Klimet Ohridski Sofia University, ✆ 02 491 83 44.

TOURIST OFFICES OVERSEAS

UK and **USA**: Tourist information available at the Bulgarian Embassies listed above.

VISAS

See page xxiv for visa requirements. Passports must have 3 months validity remaining. Visitors staying with friends or family (i.e. not in paid accommodation) need to register on arrival.

CROATIA

CAPITAL

Zagreb.

CURRENCY

Kuna (HRK or kn); 1 kuna = 100 lipa. For exchange rates see page 9.

EMBASSIES IN ZAGREB

Australia: Centar Kaptol, 3rd Floor, Nova Ves 11, ✆ 1 4891 200. **Canada**: Prilaz Gjure Dezelica 4, ✆ 1 4881 200. **New Zealand** (Consulate): Vlaska ulica 50A, ✆ 1 4612 060. **UK**: Ivana Lučića 4, ✆ 1 6009 100. **USA**: Ulica Thomasa Jeffersona 2, ✆ 1 6612 200.

EMBASSIES OVERSEAS

Australia: 14 Jindalee Crescent, O'Malley, Canberra, ACT 2606, ✆ 2 6286 6988. **Canada**: 229 Chapel St, Ottawa ON, K1N 7Y6, ✆ 613 562 7820. **New Zealand** (Consulate): 131 Lincoln Rd, Henderson, PO Box 83-200, Edmonton, Auckland, ✆ 9 836 5581. **UK**: 21 Conway St, London, W1T 6BN, ✆ 020 7387 2022. **USA**: 2343 Massachusetts Ave. NW, Washington DC 20008-2803, ✆ 202 588 5899.

LANGUAGE

Croatian. English, German and Italian spoken in tourist areas.

PUBLIC TRANSPORT

Buses and trams are cheap, regular and efficient. Zagreb and Osijek have tram networks. Jadrolinija maintains most domestic ferry lines; main office in Rijeka, ✆ +385 51 666 111.

RAIL TRAVEL

See Tables **1300 - 1359**. National railway company: Hrvatske željeznice (HŽ) www.hzpp.hr. Zagreb is a major hub for international trains. Efficient services but there is a limited network and services can be infrequent on some routes. Daytime trains on the Zagreb - Split line are operated by modern tilting diesel trains. Station amenities: generally left luggage, a bar and WCs.

TELEPHONES

Dial in: ✆ +385 then number (omit initial 0). Outgoing: ✆ 00. Police: ✆ 92. Fire: ✆ 93. Ambulance: ✆ 94.

TOURIST INFORMATION

Croatian National Tourist Board www.croatia.hr. Zagreb: Iblerov trg 10/IV, ✆ 014 699 333. Zagreb Tourist Board www.infozagreb.hr, Kaptol 5, ✆ 014 898 555.

TOURIST OFFICES OVERSEAS

UK: Elsinore House, 77 Fulham Palace Rd, London, W6 8JA, ✆ 020 8563 7979, info@croatia-london.co.uk. **Germany**: Rumfordstrasse 7, 80469 Munich ✆ 089 223 344, kroatien-tourismus@online.de. **USA**: 350 Fifth Ave., Suite 4003, New York NY 10118, ✆ 212 279 8672, cntony@earthlink.net or info@htz.hr.

VISAS

See page xxiv for visa requirements.

CZECH REPUBLIC

CAPITAL

Prague (Praha).

CURRENCY

Czech crown or koruna (CZK or Kč); 1 koruna = 100 haléřu. For exchange rates see page 9.

EMBASSIES IN PRAGUE

Australia (Consulate): 6th Floor, Solitaire Building, ulica Klimentska 10, ✆ 221 729 260. **Canada**: Ve Struhach 95/2, ✆ 272 101 800. **New Zealand** (Consulate): Václavské náměstí 11, ✆ 234 784 777. **UK**: Thunovská 14, ✆ 257 402 111. **USA**: Tržiště 15, ✆ 257 022 000.

EMBASSIES OVERSEAS

Australia: 8 Culgoa Circuit, O'Malley, Canberra, ACT 2606, ✆ 2 6290 1386. **Canada**: 251 Cooper St., Ottawa ON, K2P 0G2, ✆ 613 562 3875. **New Zealand** (Consulate): 110 Customs Street West, Auckland 1010, ✆ 9 306 5883. **UK**: 26–30 Kensington Palace Gardens, London W8 4QY, ✆ 020 7243 1115. **USA**: 3900 Spring of Freedom St NW, Washington DC 20008, ✆ 202 274 9100.

LANGUAGE

Czech. Czech and Slovak are closely related Slavic tongues. English, German and Russian are widely understood, but Russian is less popular.

PUBLIC TRANSPORT

Extensive long-distance bus network competing with the railways, run by private companies (many previously part of the nationalised ČSAD). In Prague the long-distance bus station is close to Florenc metro station. If boarding at a bus station with a ticket window, buy your ticket in advance, otherwise pay the driver. Good urban networks with integrated ticketing. Prague (Praha) has metro and tram system - see Passes feature for day tickets. Other cities with trams include Brno, Ostrava, Plzeň, Olomouc, Liberec.

RAIL TRAVEL

See Tables **1100 - 1169**. National rail company is České Dráhy (ČD) www.cd.cz. An extensive network with many branch lines and cheap fares, but sometimes crowded trains. The best mainline trains are classified *IC*, *EC* or *Ex*. The fastest Praha - Ostrava trains are classified *SC* meaning *SuperCity* and are operated by Pendolino tilting trains - a compulsory reservation fee of CZK 250 or €9.00 applies on these. Other fast (*R* for rychlík) trains are shown in our tables with just the train number. Semi-fast trains are *Sp* or spešný, local trains (very slow) are *Os* or osobný. Some branch lines are now operated by private companies, and on the Praha - Ostrava route ČD compete with two private operators: RegioJet and Leo Express. Many long-distance trains have dining or buffet cars. Seats for express trains may be reserved at least one hour before departure at the counter marked R at stations.

TELEPHONES

Dial in: ✆ +420 then number. Outgoing: ✆ 00. Police: ✆ 158. Fire: ✆ 150. Ambulance: ✆ 155. Also 112.

TOURIST INFORMATION

Czech Tourism www.czechtourism.com. Prague: Vinohradská 46, 120 41 Praha 2, Vinohrady, ✆ 221 580 611. Prague Information Service, www.prague.eu, Information centre, Old Town Hall, Staroměstské náměsti 1, Praha 1.

TOURIST OFFICES OVERSEAS

Canada: See USA. **UK**: 13 Harley Street, London W1G 9QG, ✆ 020 7631 0427, info-uk@czechtourism.com. **USA**: 1109 Madison Ave., New York NY 10028, ✆ 212 288 0830, info-usa@czechtourism.com.

VISAS

See page xxiv for visa requirements.

DENMARK

CAPITAL

Copenhagen (København).

CURRENCY

Danish crown or krone, DKK or kr; 1 krone = 100 øre. For exchange rates see page 9.

EMBASSIES IN COPENHAGEN
Australia: Dampfaergevej 26, ✆ 70 26 36 76. **Canada**: Kristen Bernikowsgade 1, ✆ 33 48 32 00. **New Zealand** (Consulate): Store Strandstraede 21, ✆ 33 37 77 02. **UK**: Kastelsvej 36-40, ✆ 35 44 52 00. **USA**: Dag Hammarskjölds Allé 24, ✆ 33 41 71 00.

EMBASSIES OVERSEAS
Australia: 15 Hunter St, Yarralumla, Canberra, ACT 2600, ✆ 2 6270 5333. **Canada**: 47 Clarence St, Suite 450, Ottawa ON, K1N 9K1, ✆ 613 562 1811. **New Zealand** (Consulate): 273 Bleakhouse Rd, Howick, Auckland 2014, ✆ 9 537 3099. **UK**: 55 Sloane St, London SW1X 9SR, ✆ 020 7333 0200. **USA**: 3200 Whitehaven St NW, Washington DC 20008-3683, ✆ 202 234 4300.

LANGUAGE
Danish. English is almost universally spoken.

PUBLIC TRANSPORT
Long-distance travel is easiest by train (see below). Excellent regional and city bus services, many connecting with trains. Modern and efficient metro www.m.dk and suburban rail network in and around the capital; see Passes feature for day tickets. No trams in København; bus network can be tricky to fathom. Bridges or ferries link all the big islands. Taxis: green *Fri* sign when available; metered, and most accept major credit cards. Many cycle paths and bike hire shops; free use of City Bikes in Copenhagen central area (returnable coin required).

RAIL TRAVEL
See Tables **700 - 728**. Operator: Danske Statsbaner (DSB) www.dsb.dk. Some independent lines, and certain former DSB services are operated by private company ArrivaTog www.arriva.dk. *IC* trains reach up to 200 km/h. *Re* (regionaltog) trains are frequent, but slower. Reservations are recommended (not compulsory) on *IC* and *Lyn* trains - DKK 30 in standard class; reservation included in business class. Reservations close 15 minutes before a train leaves its originating station. Nationwide reservations ✆ 70 13 14 15. Baggage lockers at most stations, usually DKK 30 per 24 hrs. Usually free trolleys, but you may need a (returnable) coin.

TELEPHONES
Dial in: ✆ + 45 then number. Outgoing: ✆ 00.
Emergency services: ✆ 112. Police ✆ 114.

TOURIST INFORMATION
Danish Tourist Board www.visitdenmark.com.

TOURIST OFFICES OVERSEAS
UK: 55 Sloane St, London SW1X 9SY, ✆ 020 7259 5958, london@visitdenmark.com. **USA / Canada**: P.O.Box 4649, Grand Central Station, New York NY 10163-4649, ✆ 212 885 9700, info@goscandinavia.com.

VISAS
See page xxiv for visa requirements.

ESTONIA

CAPITAL
Tallinn.

CURRENCY
Euro (EUR / €). 1 euro = 100 cent. For exchange rates see page 9.

EMBASSIES IN TALLINN
Australia (Consulate): c/- Standard Ltd Marja 9, ✆ 650 9308.
Canada (Consulate): Toom Kooli 13, ✆ 627 3311.
New Zealand: See Germany.
UK: Wismari 6, ✆ 667 4700. **USA**: Kentmanni 20, ✆ 668 8100.

EMBASSIES OVERSEAS
Australia (Consulate): Suite 1, 144 Pacific Highway, Sydney, NSW 2060, ✆ 2 8014 8999. **Canada**: 260 Dalhousie St, Suite 210, Ottawa ON, K1N 7E4, ✆ 613 789 4222. **New Zealand** (Consulate): 3 Olliver Grove, Waikanae Beach, Wellington 5036, ✆ 4 293 1361. **UK**: 16 Hyde Park Gate, London SW7 5DG, ✆ 020 7838 5388. **USA**: 2131 Massachusetts Ave. NW, Washington DC 20008, ✆ 202 588 0101.

LANGUAGE
Estonian. Some English is spoken but some Finnish is also useful, plus Russian in Tallinn and the north-east.

PUBLIC TRANSPORT
Long-distance bus services are often quicker, cleaner, and more efficient than rail, but more expensive. The main domestic long-distance bus operator is Tpilet www.tpilet.ee; for international bus journeys book in advance with Luxexpress www.luxexpress.eu or ecolines www.ecolines.net. Tallinn has a tram network.

RAIL TRAVEL
See Tables **1800 - 1890**. Local rail services are operated by Elron www.elron.ee. Comfortable overnight train to Moscow via St Peterburg. Very little English spoken at stations.

TELEPHONES
Dial in: ✆ + 372 then number. Outgoing: ✆ 00.
Police: ✆ 110. Fire, ambulance: ✆ 112.

TOURIST INFORMATION
Estonian Tourist Board www.visitestonia.com, tourism@eas.ee.
Tallinn: Niguliste 2 / Kullassepa 4, ✆ 645 7777, turismiinfo@tallinnlv.ee.

TOURIST OFFICES OVERSEAS
UK: Tourism brochures available from the Estonian Embassy (see above) Mon-Fri 0900 - 1700. **Germany**: Baltikum Tourismus Zentrale, Katharinenstraße 19-20, 10711 Berlin, ✆ 030 89 00 90 91, www.baltikuminfo.de, info@baltikuminfo.de.

VISAS
See page xxiv for visa requirements.

FINLAND

CAPITAL
Helsinki (Helsingfors).

CURRENCY
Euro (EUR / €). 1 euro = 100 cent. For exchange rates see page 9.

EMBASSIES IN HELSINKI
Australia (Consulate): c/- Tradimex Oy, Museokatu 25B, ✆ 04 204 492. **Canada**: Pohjoisesplanadi 25B, ✆ 09 228 530.
New Zealand (Consulate): Erottajankatu 9, ✆ 50 342 9950.
UK: Itäinen Puistotie 17, ✆ 09 2286 5100. **USA**: Itäinen Puistotie 14B, ✆ 09 616 250.

EMBASSIES OVERSEAS
Australia: 12 Darwin Ave., Yarralumla, Canberra, ACT 2600, ✆ 2 6273 3800. **Canada**: 55 Metcalfe St, Suite 850, Ottawa ON, K1P 6L5, ✆ 613 288 2233. **New Zealand** (Consulate): 1 Kimberley Rd, Epsom, Auckland 1023, ✆ 9 368 5711. **UK**: 38 Chesham Place, London SW1X 8HW, ✆ 020 7838 6200. **USA**: 3301 Massachusetts Ave. NW, Washington DC 20008, ✆ 202 298 5800.

LANGUAGE
Finnish, and, in the north, Lapp/Sami. Swedish, the second language, often appears on signs after the Finnish. English is widely spoken. German is also reasonably widespread.

PUBLIC TRANSPORT
There are more than 300 bus services daily from Helsinki to all parts of the country. The main long-distance bus operators are Matkahuolto www.matkahuolto.fi and the Expressbus consortium www.expressbus.com. Bus stations (*Linja-autoasema*) often have restaurants and shops. It is usually cheaper to buy tickets in advance. Bus stop signs show a black bus on a yellow background (local services) or a white bus on a blue background (long distance). Helsinki has metro / tram / bus network with integrated ticketing.

RAIL TRAVEL
See Tables **790 - 799**. National rail company: VR www.vr.fi; tilting Pendolinos (up to 220 km/h) run on certain lines. Fares depend on train type - those for *S220* (Pendolino), *IC* (InterCity) and *P* (express) trains include a seat reservation. Travel classes are referred to as *Eco* (2nd class) and *Extra* (1st class). Sleeping-cars: one, two or three berth compartments (variable supplement in addition to the appropriate *Eco* class express fare). In winter sleeping accommodation generally costs less on Mondays to Thursdays. Rail station: *Rautatieasema* or *Järnvägsstation*; some larger stations have luggage lockers. Only the largest stations have open ticket offices, although most stations have automatic ticket machines.

TELEPHONES
Dial in: ✆ +358 then number (omit initial 0). Outgoing: ✆ 00. Emergency services: ✆ 112.

TOURIST INFORMATION
Finnish Tourist Board www.visitfinland.com. Helsinki: PO Box 625, Töölönkatu 11, ✆ 029 50 58000, mek@visitfinland.com.

TOURIST OFFICES OVERSEAS
USA: 297 York Street, Jersey City, NJ 07302, ✆ 917 863 5484.

VISAS
See page xxiv for visa requirements.

FRANCE

CAPITAL
Paris, divided into *arrondissements* 1 to 20 (1er, 2e etc).

CURRENCY
Euro (EUR / €). 1 euro = 100 cent. For exchange rates see page 9.

EMBASSIES IN PARIS
Australia: 4 rue Jean Rey, ✆ 01 40 59 33 00. **Canada**: 35 avenue Montaigne, ✆ 01 44 43 29 00. **New Zealand**: 7 ter, rue Léonard de Vinci, ✆ 01 45 01 43 43. **UK**: 35 rue du Faubourg St Honoré, ✆ 01 44 51 31 00. **USA**: 2 avenue Gabriel, ✆ 01 43 12 22 22.

EMBASSIES OVERSEAS
Australia: 6 Perth Ave. Yarralumla, Canberra, ACT 2600, ✆ 2 6216 0100. **Canada**: 42 Sussex Drive, Ottawa ON, K1M 2C9, ✆ 613 789 1795. **New Zealand**: 34-42 Manners St, Wellington, ✆ 4 384 2555. **UK**: 58 Knightsbridge, London SW1X 7JT, ✆ 020 7073 1000. **USA**: 4101 Reservoir Rd, NW, Washington DC 20007, ✆ 202 944 6000.

LANGUAGE
French. Many people can speak a little English, particularly in Paris.

PUBLIC TRANSPORT
In Paris, use the Métro where possible: clean, fast, cheap and easy. For urban and suburban transport, *carnets* (sets of 10 tickets) are cheaper than individual tickets; for day tickets see Passes feature. Bus and train timetable leaflets (free) are available from tourist offices, bus and rail stations. Many cities have modern tram / light rail networks; Lyon, Marseille and Toulouse also have metro systems. Bus services are infrequent after 2030 and on Sundays. Sparse public transport in rural areas, and few long-distance bus services. Licensed taxis (avoid others) are metered; white roof-lights when free; surcharges for luggage, extra passengers, and journeys beyond the centre.

RAIL TRAVEL
See Tables **250 - 399**. Société Nationale des Chemins de fer Français (SNCF) www.sncf.com, ✆ 3635 (premium rate, in French), followed by 1 for traffic status, 2 for timetables, 3 for reservations and tickets, 4 for other services. Excellent network from Paris to major cities with *TGV* trains using dedicated high-speed lines (up to 320 km/h on the *Est Européen* line to eastern France) as well as conventional track. However, some cross-country journeys can be slow and infrequent. Trains can get very full at peak times, so to avoid having to spend the journey standing, book a seat. Prior reservation is compulsory on *TGV* high-speed trains and the charge is included in the ticket price; rail pass holders will have to pay at least the reservation fee. Tickets can cost more at busy times (known as 'white' periods). Long distance trains on non-TGV routes are usually branded *Intercités* using refurbished rolling stock - some have compulsory reservation as shown in our tables. Reservation is also compulsory on all overnight trains: most convey couchettes and reclining seats only (sleeping cars are only conveyed on international trains). A certain number of couchette compartments are reserved for women only or those with small children; otherwise, couchette accommodation is mixed. There is a minimal bar/trolley service on some long-distance trains. Larger stations have 24-hour coin-operated left-luggage lockers, and sometimes pay-showers.

TELEPHONES
Dial in: ✆ +33 then number (omit initial 0). Outgoing: ✆ 00. Emergency: ✆ 112. Police: ✆ 17. Fire: ✆ 18. Ambulance: ✆ 15.

TOURIST INFORMATION
Maison de la France www.franceguide.com. Paris: 79/81 Rue de Clichy, ✆ 0 142 967 000. Local tourist offices: *Syndicat d'Initiative* or *Office de Tourisme*.

TOURIST OFFICES OVERSEAS
Australia: Level 13, 25 Bligh St, Sydney NSW 2000, ✆ 02 9231 6277, info.au@franceguide.com. **Canada**: 1800 avenue McGill College, Suite 1010, Montréal QC, H3A 3J6, ✆ 514 288 2026, canada@franceguide.com. **UK**: Lincoln House, 300 High Holborn, London WC1V 7JH, ✆ 0207 061 6600, info.uk@franceguide.com. **USA**: 825 Third Avenue, 29th floor, New York NY 10022, ✆ 212 838 7800, info.us@franceguide.com. Also in Los Angeles and Chicago.

VISAS
See page xxiv for visa requirements.

GERMANY

CAPITAL
Berlin.

CURRENCY
Euro (EUR / €). 1 euro = 100 cent. For exchange rates see page 9.

EMBASSIES IN BERLIN
Australia: Wallstraße 76-79, ✆ 030 88 00 880. **Canada**: Leipziger Platz 17, ✆ 030 203 12 470. **New Zealand**: Friedrichstraße 60, ✆ 030 206 210. **UK**: Wilhelmstraße 70/71, ✆ 030 204 570. **USA**: Clayallee 170, ✆ 030 830 50.

EMBASSIES OVERSEAS
Australia: 119 Empire Circuit, Yarralumla, Canberra, ACT 2600, ✆ 2 6270 1911. **Canada**: 1 Waverley St, Ottawa ON, K2P 0T8, ✆ 613 232 1101. **New Zealand**: 90-92 Hobson St, Thorndon, Wellington, ✆ 4 473 6063. **UK**: Embassy, 23 Belgrave Sq., London SW1X 8PZ, ✆ 020 7824 1300. **USA**: 2300 M Street, NW, Suite 300 Washington DC, 20037, ✆ 202 298 4000.

LANGUAGE
German. English and French widely spoken.

PUBLIC TRANSPORT
Most large cities have U-Bahn (U) underground railway and S-Bahn (S) urban rail service, many have trams. City travel passes cover these and other public transport, including local ferries in some cities (e.g. Hamburg). International passes usually cover S-Bahn. Single fares are expensive; a day card (*Tagesnetzkarte*) or multi-ride ticket (*Mehrfahrkarte*) pays for itself if you take more than three rides (see Passes feature for selected day tickets). Long-distance buses are not common.

RAIL TRAVEL
See Tables **800 - 949**. Deutsche Bahn (DB) www.bahn.de. ✆ 01805 99 66 33 (20ct per call) for timetable and fares information, ticket purchase and reservations. Timetable freephone (automated): ✆ 0800 1507090. UK booking centre ✆ 08718 80 80 66 (8p per minute). *Sparpreis* are good value single fares valid for travel on a fixed day / train. Long-distance day trains: *ICE* (modern high-speed trains; up to 300km/h; higher fares but no extra charge for InterRail pass holders), *IC*, *EC* and *D*. Regional trains: *IRE*, *RE*, *RB* (modern, comfortable and connect with long-distance network). Frequent local S-Bahn services operate in major cities. Many local services are now run by private operators. Overnight services (*CNL*, *EN*, *D*) convey sleeping-cars (up to three berths) and/or couchettes (six berths), also seats. Reservation on overnight trains is usually compulsory. However, the seating cars on *CNL* trains are now classified *IC*, are allocated a different train number to the main train and, in most cases, can be used without prior reservation. Most long-distance trains convey a bistro or restaurant car (an at-seat service is offered in first class). Seat reservations possible on long-distance trains. Stations are well staffed, often with left luggage and bicycle hire. Main station is *Hauptbahnhof* (Hbf).

TELEPHONES
Dial in: ✆ +49 then number (omit initial 0). Outgoing: ✆ 00. Police: ✆ 110. Fire: ✆ 112. Ambulance: ✆ 112.

TOURIST INFORMATION
German National Tourist Office www.germany-tourism.de. Main office: Beethovenstraße 69, 60325 Frankfurt am Main, ✆ 069 974 640, info@germany.travel.

TOURIST OFFICES OVERSEAS

Australia: c/o Gate 7 Pty Ltd, Level 1, 97 Rose St. Chippendale, Sydney NSW 2008, ✆ 02 9331 6202, germanytourism@smink.com.au. **Canada**: Vox International Inc, 2 Bloor St West, Suite 2601, Toronto ON, M4W 3E2, ✆ 416 935 1896, info@-gnto.ca. **UK**: PO Box 2695, London W1A 3TN, ✆ 020 7317 0908, office-britain@germany.travel. **USA**: 122 East 42nd Street, New York NY 10168-0072, ✆ 212 661 7200, office-usa@germany.travel. Also in Chicago (✆ 773 539 6303) and Los Angeles (✆ 310 545 1350).

VISAS

See page xxiv for visa requirements.

GREECE

CAPITAL

Athens (Athína).

CURRENCY

Euro (EUR/€). 1 euro = 100 cent. For exchange rates see page 9.

EMBASSIES IN ATHENS

Australia: Level 6, Thon Building, Kifisias/Alexandras, Ambelokipi, ✆ 210 870 4000. **Canada**: Ioannou Ghennadiou 4, ✆ 210 727 3400. **New Zealand** (Consulate): Kifissias Avenue 76, Ambelokipi, ✆ 210 6924 136. **UK**: Ploutarchou 1, ✆ 210 727 2600. **USA**: Vasilissis Sophias 91, ✆ 210 721 2951.

EMBASSIES OVERSEAS

Australia: 9 Turrana St, Yarralumla, Canberra, ACT 2600, ✆ 2 6273 3011. **Canada**: 76-80 MacLaren St, Ottawa ON, K2P 0K6, ✆ 613 238 6271. **New Zealand**: 38-42 Waring Taylor St, Wellington 6142, ✆ 4 473 7775. **UK**: 1A Holland Park, London W11 3TP, ✆ 020 7229 3850. **USA**: 2217 Massachusetts Ave. NW, Washington DC 20008, ✆ 202 939 1300.

LANGUAGE

Greek. English widely spoken in Athens and tourist areas (also some German, French or Italian).

PUBLIC TRANSPORT

KTEL buses: fast, punctual, fairly comfortable long-distance services; well-organised stations in most towns (tickets available from bus terminals), www.ktelbus.com. Islands connected by ferries and hydrofoils. City transport: bus or (in Athens) trolleybus and metro. Outside Athens, taxis are plentiful and good value.

RAIL TRAVEL

See Tables **1400 - 1499**. Operator: TrainOSE S.A. (OSE) www.trainose.gr. English language call centre for reservations and information (0600 - 2300): ✆ 14511. Limited rail network, especially away from the main Athens - Thessaloniki axis. Reservations are essential on most express trains. *ICity* trains are fast and fairly punctual, but supplements can be expensive. Stations: often no left luggage or English-speaking staff, but many have bars.

TELEPHONES

Dial in: ✆ +30 then number. Outgoing: ✆ 00.
Emergency: ✆ 112. Police: ✆ 100. Fire: ✆ 199. Ambulance: ✆ 166.
Tourist police (24 hrs, English-speaking): ✆ 171.

TOURIST INFORMATION

Greek National Tourist Organisation www.visitgreece.gr. Athens: Tsoha 7, ✆ 2 108 707 000. Athens information: Amalias 26, ✆ 2 103 310 392.

TOURIST OFFICES OVERSEAS

Australia: 37-49 Pitt St, Sydney NSW 2000, ✆ 02 9241 1663, hto@tpg.com.au. **UK**: 4 Great Portland St, London W1W 8QJ, ✆ 020 7495 9300, info@gnto.co.uk. **USA**: 305 East 47th Street, New York NY10017, ✆ 212 421 5777, info@greektourism.com.

VISAS

See page xxiv for visa requirements.

HUNGARY

CAPITAL

Budapest.

CURRENCY

Forint (HUF or Ft). For exchange rates see page 9.

EMBASSIES IN BUDAPEST

Australia: *refer to Australian Embassy in Austria.* **Canada**: Ganz utca 12–14, ✆ 1 392 3360. **New Zealand** (Consulate): Nagymazö utca 47, ✆ 1 302 2484. **UK**: Harmincad utca 6, ✆ 1 266 2888. **USA**: Szabadság tér 12, ✆ 1 475 4400.

EMBASSIES OVERSEAS

Australia: 17 Beale Crescent, Deakin, Canberra, ACT 2600, ✆ 2 6282 3226. **Canada**: 299 Waverley St, Ottawa ON, K2P 0V9, ✆ 613 230 2717. **New Zealand** (Consulate): 23 Fife St, Coxs Bay, Auckland 1144, ✆ 9 376 3609. **UK**: 35 Eaton Place, London SW1X 8BY, ✆ 020 7201 3440. **USA**: 3910 Shoemaker St NW, Washington DC 20008, ✆ 202 362 6730.

LANGUAGE

Hungarian. English and German are both widely understood.

PUBLIC TRANSPORT

Long-distance buses: *Volánbusz* www.volanbusz.hu, ✆ +36 1 382 0888. Extensive metro/tram/bus system in Budapest with integrated tickets; for day tickets see Passes section. Purchase tickets in advance and validate on board. Debrecen, Miskolc and Szeged also have trams. Ferry and hydrofoil services operate on the Danube.

RAIL TRAVEL

See Tables **1200 - 1299**. A comprehensive network operated by Hungarian State Railways (MÁV) www.mav.hu connects most towns and cities. Express services link Budapest to major centres and Lake Balaton: *IC* trains require compulsory reservation, also a supplement which varies according to distance (passholders pay only the reservation fee). Most *EC* trains do not require reservation for international journeys; trains to Romania have compulsory reservation. Other trains include *gyorsvonat* (fast trains) and *sebesvonat* (semi-fast). Local trains (*személyvonat*) are very slow. Book sleepers well in advance.

TELEPHONES

Dial in: ✆ +36 then number (omit initial 06, which is only used when dialing from city to city within Hungary). Outgoing: ✆ 00.
Emergency: ✆ 112. Police: ✆ 107. Fire: ✆ 105. Ambulance: ✆ 104.

TOURIST INFORMATION

Hungarian National Tourist Office (*Tourinform*) www.gotohungary.com. Call Centre 0800 - 2000 Mon - Fri, ✆ 01 438 80 80, info@itthon.hu.

TOURIST OFFICES OVERSEAS

UK: 46 Eaton Place, London SW1X 8AL, ✆ 020 7823 0132, htlondon@hungarytourism.hu. **USA**: 470 7th Avenue, Suite 2601, New York NY 10123, ✆ 212 695 1221, info@gotohungary.com.

VISAS

See page xxiv for visa requirements.

IRELAND

CAPITAL

Dublin. For Northern Ireland see under United Kingdom.

CURRENCY

Euro (EUR/€). 1 euro = 100 cent. For exchange rates see page 9.

EMBASSIES IN DUBLIN

Australia: Fitzwilton House, Wilton Terrace, ✆ 01 664 5300. **Canada**: 7–8 Wilton Terrace, ✆ 01 234 4000. **New Zealand** (Consulate): P.O. Box 9999, Dublin, ✆ 01 660 4233. **UK**: 29 Merrion Road, ✆ 01 205 3700. **USA**: 42 Elgin Road, ✆ 01 668 8777.

EMBASSIES OVERSEAS

Australia: 20 Arkana St, Yarralumla, Canberra, ACT 2600, ✆ 2 6214 0000. **Canada**: Suite 1105, 130 Albert St, Ottawa ON, K1P 5G4, ✆ 613 233 6281. **New Zealand** (Consulate): 205 Queen Street, Auckland 1140, ✆ 9 977 2252. **UK**: 17 Grosvenor Place, London SW1X 7HR, ✆ 020 7235 2171. **USA**: 2234 Massachusetts Ave. NW, Washington DC 20008, ✆ 202 462 3939.

LANGUAGE

Most people speak English. The Irish language (Gaeilge) is spoken in several areas (known as the Gaeltacht) scattered over seven counties and four provinces, mostly along the western seaboard. Official documents use both languages.

PUBLIC TRANSPORT

A modern tramway system in Dublin called *Luas* www.luas.ie has two unconnected lines; the red line is the most useful for visitors as it connects Connolly and Heuston stations. Dublin Bus operates an extensive network throughout the capital. Almost all bus services outside Dublin are operated by Bus Éireann www.buseireann.ie, ✆ 01 836 6111 (daily 0830–1900). Long distance services leave from the Dublin bus station (*Busáras*) in Store St, near Connolly rail station.

RAIL TRAVEL

See Tables **230 - 249**. Rail services are operated by Iarnród Éireann (IÉ) www.irishrail.ie. Timetable and fares enquiries: ✆ 01 850 366 222 (0900–1700 Mon-Fri). The *Enterprise* express service Dublin - Belfast is operated jointly with Northern Ireland Railways. Local IÉ north-south electric line in Dublin is called DART.

TELEPHONES

Dial in: ✆ +353 then number (omit initial 0). Outgoing: ✆ 00 (048 for Northern Ireland). Emergency services: ✆ 112 or 999.

TOURIST INFORMATION

Fáilte Ireland www.discoverireland.ie or www.ireland.com. Dublin: 14 Upper O'Connell Street, infooconnell@failteireland.ie.

TOURIST OFFICES OVERSEAS

Australia: Level 5, 36 Carrington St, Sydney NSW 2000, ✆ 02 9964 6900. **Canada**: 2 Bloor St West, Suite 3403, Toronto ON, M4W 3E2, ✆ 416 925 6368. **UK**: 103 Wigmore St, London W1U 1QS, ✆ 020 7518 0800. **USA**: 345 Park Avenue, 17th floor, New York NY 10154, ✆ 212 418 0800.

VISAS

See page xxiv for visa requirements.

ITALY

CAPITAL

Rome (Roma).

CURRENCY

Euro (EUR/€). 1 euro = 100 cent. For exchange rates see page 9.

EMBASSIES IN ROME

Australia: Via Antonio Bosio 5, ✆ 06 852 721. **Canada**: Via Zara 30, ✆ 06 85 44 42 911. **New Zealand**: Via Clitunno 44, ✆ 06 853 7501. **UK**: Via XX Settembre 80a, ✆ 06 4220 0001. **USA**: Via Vittorio Veneto 121, ✆ 06 46 741.

EMBASSIES OVERSEAS

Australia: 12 Grey St, Deakin, Canberra ACT 2600, ✆ 2 6273 3333. **Canada**: 275 Slater St, Ottawa ON, K1P 5H9, ✆ 613 232 2401. **New Zealand**: 34-38 Grant Rd, Thorndon, Wellington, ✆ 4 473 5339. **UK**: 14 Three Kings Yard, London W1K 4EH, ✆ 020 7312 2200. **USA**: 3000 Whitehaven St NW, Washington DC 20008, ✆ 202 612 4400.

LANGUAGE

Italian. Standard Italian is spoken across the country though there are marked regional pronunciation differences. Some dialects in more remote areas. Many speak English in cities and tourist areas. In the south and Sicily, French is often more useful than English.

PUBLIC TRANSPORT

Buses are often crowded, but regular, and serve many areas inaccessible by rail. Services may be reduced at weekends. Tickets are usually purchased from newsagents. Roma, Milano and Napoli have metro systems; most major cities have trams. Taxis (metered) can be expensive; steer clear of unofficial ones.

RAIL TRAVEL

See Tables **580 - 648**. The national operator is Trenitalia, a division of Ferrovie dello Stato (FS) www.trenitalia.com. 24-hr national rail information ✆ 89 20 21 (from abroad +39 06 68 47 54 75; 0700 - 2400). The trunk high-speed line from Torino to Salerno via Milano, Roma and Napoli allows fast journey times between major cities. Core services are branded *Frecciarossa*, whilst tilting *Frecciargento* trains divert off the high-speed lines to serve other cities. *Frecciabianca* services are fast premium fare services which use traditional lines. Reservation is compulsory on all types of service except *EC* (EuroCity) trains to Austria operated in Italy by LeNord. Other services are classified *Regionale Veloce* (fast regional train) and *Regionale* (stops at most stations). Services are reasonably punctual. Some long-distance trains do not carry passengers short distances. Sleepers: single or double berths in 1st class, three (sometimes doubles) in 2nd. Couchettes: four berths in 1st class, six in 2nd, although there is a number of four-berth 2nd-class couchettes. Refreshments on most long-distance trains. There are often long queues at stations; buy tickets and make reservations at travel agencies (look for FS symbol).

TELEPHONES

Dial in: ✆ +39 then number. Outgoing: ✆ 00.
Carabinieri: ✆ 112. Police: ✆ 113. Fire: ✆ 115. Ambulance: ✆ 118.

TOURIST INFORMATION

Italian State Tourist Board www.enit.it. Roma: Via Marghera 2/6, ✆ 0 649 711, sedecentrale@enit.it. Most towns and resorts have an *Azienda Autonoma di Soggiorno e Turismo* (AAST), many with their own websites, or *Pro Loco* (local tourist board).

TOURIST OFFICES OVERSEAS

Australia: Ground Floor, 140 William St, East Sydney NSW 2011, ✆ 02 9357 2561, sydney@enit.it. **Canada**: 110 Yonge Street, Suite 503, Toronto ON, M5C 1T4, ✆ 416 925 4882, toronto@enit.it. **UK**: 1 Princes St, London W1B 2AY, ✆ 020 7408 1254, info.london@enit.it. **USA**: 630 Fifth Avenue, Suite 1965, New York NY 10111, ✆ 212 245 5618, newyork@enit.it. Also Chicago (✆ 312 644 0996) chicago@enit.it. and Los Angeles (✆ 310 820 1898) losangeles@enit.it.

VISAS

See page xxiv for visa requirements.

LATVIA

CAPITAL

Riga.

CURRENCY

Euro (EUR/€). 1 euro = 100 cent. For exchange rates see page 9.

EMBASSIES IN RIGA

Australia: (Consulate) c/- Airtour, 7 Vilandes ✆ 6732 0509. **Canada**: Baznicas iela 20/22, ✆ 6781 3945. **New Zealand**: *refer to NZ Embassy in Germany*. **UK**: J Alunana iela 5, ✆ 6777 4700. **USA**: Samnera Velsa St. 1, ✆ 6710 7000.

EMBASSIES OVERSEAS

Australia: (Consulate) 2 Mackennel Street, Melbourne, VIC 3079, ✆ 3 9499 6920. **Canada**: 350 Sparks St, Suite 1200, Ottawa ON, K1R 7S8, ✆ 613 238 6014. **New Zealand** (Consulate): 166 St Asaphs St., Te Whare Ta Wahi, Christchurch 8140, ✆ 3 365 3505. **UK**: 45 Nottingham Place, London W1U 5LY, ✆ 020 7312 0041. **USA**: 2306 Massachusetts Ave. NW, Washington DC 20008, ✆ 202 328 2840.

LANGUAGE

Latvian is the majority language. Russian is the first language of around 30% and is widely understood. English and German can often be of use, especially in the larger towns.

PUBLIC TRANSPORT

Very cheap for Westerners. Taxis generally affordable (agree fare first if not metered). Long-distance bus network preferred to slow domestic train service.

RAIL TRAVEL

See Tables **1800 - 1899**. The national operator is Latvian Railways www.ldz.lv. Comfortable overnight train to Moscow and St Peterburg; best to take berth in 2nd-class coupé (4-berth compartment). Reservation is compulsory for all sleepers; Russia-bound sleepers may require proof of entry visa when booking. Very little English spoken at stations.

TELEPHONES

Dial in: ✆ +371 then number. Outgoing: ✆ 00.
Emergency: ✆ 112. Police: ✆ 02. Fire: ✆ 01. Ambulance: ✆ 03.

TOURIST INFORMATION

Latvian Tourism Development Agency www.latvia.travel/en. Riga: Brivibas iela 55, ✆ 67 229 945, info@latvia.travel. Tourist Hotline: ✆ 1188.

TOURIST OFFICES OVERSEAS

Germany: Baltikum Tourismus Zentrale, Katharinenstraße 19-20, 10711 Berlin, ✆ 030 89 00 90 91, info@baltikuminfo.de.

VISAS

See page xxiv for visa requirements. Applications may take up to 30 days; confirmed hotel reservations are required. Visas may also be valid for Estonia and Lithuania. Passports must be valid for at least 3 months following the stay. Visas issued on arrival at the airport (not train border crossings) are valid 10 days.

LITHUANIA

CAPITAL

Vilnius.

CURRENCY

Euro (EUR/€). 1 euro = 100 cent. For exchange rates see page 9.

EMBASSIES IN VILNIUS

Australia (Consulate): 23 Vilniaus St. ✆ 05 212 33 69. **Canada** (Consulate): Jogailos St. 4, ✆ 05 249 09 50. **New Zealand**: *refer to NZ Embassy in Germany*. **UK**: Antakalnio Str. 2, ✆ 05 246 29 00. **USA**: Akmenu gatve 6, ✆ 05 266 55 00.

EMBASSIES OVERSEAS

Australia (Consulate): 39 The Boulevarde. Doncaster, VIC 3108, ✆ 3 9840 0070. **Canada**: 150 Metcalfe St. Suite 1600, Ottawa ON, K2P 1P1, ✆ 613 567 5458. **UK**: 2 Bessborough Gardens, London SW1V 2JE, ✆ 020 7592 2840. **USA**: 2622 16 Street NW, Washington DC 20009, ✆ 202 234 5860.

LANGUAGE

Lithuanian. Russian is the first language of around 10% of the population. English and German can often be of use, especially in the larger towns.

PUBLIC TRANSPORT

Similar to Latvia (see above).

RAIL TRAVEL

See Tables **1800 - 1899**. The national operator is Lithuanian Railways www.litrail.lt. Comfortable overnight train to Moscow via Minsk. Very little English spoken at stations.

TELEPHONES

Dial in: ✆ +370 then number (omit initial 8). Outgoing: ✆ 00. Emergency: ✆ 112. Police: ✆ 02. Fire: ✆ 01. Ambulance: ✆ 03.

TOURIST INFORMATION

Lithuania State Department of Tourism www.tourism.lt and www.travel.lt. Vilnius: Vilniaus g. 22, ✆ 526 296 60, tic@vilnius.lt.

TOURIST OFFICES OVERSEAS

Germany: Lituanian Tourism, Jösephspitalstr 15, 80331 Muenchen, ✆ 089 55 25 33 406, info@baltikuminfo.de. **UK**: Lithuanian National Tourism Office, 11 Blades Court, London SW15 2NU, ✆ 0208 877 4546, lithuania@representationplus.co.uk.

VISAS

See page xxiv for visa requirements.

LUXEMBOURG

CAPITAL

Luxembourg City (Ville de Luxembourg).

CURRENCY

Euro (EUR/€). 1 euro = 100 cent. For exchange rates see page 9.

EMBASSIES IN LUXEMBOURG

Australia: *refer to Australian Embassy in Belgium*. **Canada** (Consulate): 15, rue Guillaume Schneider, ✆ 26 270 570. **New Zealand**: *refer to NZ Embassy in Belgium*. **UK**: 5 Boulevard Joseph II, ✆ 22 98 64. **USA**: 22 Boulevard Emmanuel Servais, ✆ 46 01 23.

EMBASSIES OVERSEAS

Australia (Consulate): 6 Damour Ave, Sydney, NSW 2070, ✆ 2 9880 8002. **UK**: 27 Wilton Crescent, London SW1X 8SD, ✆ 020 7235 6961 (visa info. between 1000 and 1145). **USA / Canada**: 2200 Massachusetts Ave. NW, Washington DC 20008 ✆ 202 265 4171.

LANGUAGE

Luxembourgish is the national tongue, but almost everyone also speaks fluent French and/or German, plus often some English.

PUBLIC TRANSPORT

Good bus network between most towns. Taxis not allowed to pick up passengers in the street; most stations have ranks.

RAIL TRAVEL

See Table **449** for local services. Operator: Société Nationale des Chemins de fer Luxembourgeois (CFL) www.cfl.lu, ✆ +352 2489 2489 Frequent rail services converge on Luxembourg City. Inexpensive multi-ride passes (good for one hour or up to 24 hours) are valid on trains and local buses. Most rail stations are small with few facilities.

TELEPHONES

Dial in: ✆ +352 then number. Outgoing: ✆ 00. Police: ✆ 113. Fire and ambulance: ✆ 112.

TOURIST INFORMATION

Office National du Tourisme www.visitluxembourg.com. Luxembourg: Gare Centrale, P.O. Box 1001, ✆ 4 282 8210, info@visitluxembourg.com. Luxembourg City Tourist Office www.lcto.lu, 30 Place Guillaume II, ✆ 222 809, touristinfo@lcto.lu.

TOURIST OFFICES OVERSEAS

Germany: Klingelofer Straße 7 D 10785 Berlin, ✆ 03 2575 773, info@visitluxembourg.de. **USA**: 17 Beekman Place, New York NY 10022, ✆ 212 935 8888, info@visitluxembourg.com.

VISAS

See page xxiv for visa requirements.

NETHERLANDS

CAPITAL

Amsterdam is the capital city. The Hague (Den Haag) is the seat of government.

CURRENCY

Euro (EUR/€). 1 euro = 100 cent. For exchange rates see page 9.

EMBASSIES IN THE HAGUE

Australia: Carnegielaan 4, ✆ 0 70 310 8200. **Canada**: Sophialaan 7, ✆ 0 70 311 1600. **New Zealand**: Eisenhowerlaan 77N, ✆ 0 70 346 9324. **UK**: Lange Voorhout 10, ✆ 0 70 427 0427. **USA**: Lange Voorhout 102, ✆ 0 70 310 2209.

EMBASSIES OVERSEAS

Australia: 120 Empire Circuit, Yarralumla, Canberra, ACT 2600, ✆ 2 6220 9400. **Canada**: Constitution Square Building, 350 Albert St, Suite 2020, Ottawa ON, K1R 1A4, ✆ 1 877 388 2443. **New Zealand**: Investment House, cnr Ballance & Featherston Streets, Wellington, ✆ 4 471 6390. **UK**: 38 Hyde Park Gate, London SW7 5DP, ✆ 020 7590 3200. **USA**: 4200 Linnean Ave. NW, Washington DC 20008, ✆ 202 244 5300.

LANGUAGE

Dutch. English is very widely spoken.

PUBLIC TRANSPORT

Premium rate number for all rail and bus enquiries (computerised, fast and accurate): ✆ 09 009 292 www.9292ov.nl. Taxis are best boarded at ranks or ordered by phone as they seldom stop in the street. In many cities (not Amsterdam) a *Zonetaxi* can be prebooked for an onward journey at a fixed price (€6 for the first two kilometres, then an extra €3 for every two kilometres thereafter; ✆ 0900 6798294 or purchase on-line). A nationwide stored value contactless Smartcard system called OV-Chipcard is used for all public transport. Personalised and anonymous cards are available, together with disposable cards for visitors. These can be purchased at ticket offices and also from machines (payment by cash or credit card). OV-Chipcard readers are located on railway platforms and on trams and buses etc. (remember to swipe your card at the beginning and end of your journey).

RAIL TRAVEL

See Tables **450 - 499**. National rail company Nederlandse Spoorwegen (NS) www.ns.nl provides most services, though private operators run local train services in some parts of the north and east. Through tickets can be purchased between all stations in the Netherlands, regardless of operator. Cycle hire and cycle and baggage storage are usually available at larger stations. Smaller stations are usually unstaffed, but all stations have ticket vending machines. Most paper tickets have been replaced by the OV-Chipcard (see previous paragraph). Travellers found to have boarded a train without a valid ticket must pay a fine of €35 plus the cost of their fare. *Intercity direct* are fast services between Amsterdam, Schiphol, Rotterdam and Breda via the high-speed line (supplement payable, except for local journeys Amsterdam - Schiphol and Rotterdam - Breda). Other fast trains, calling only at principal stations, are classified *Intercity*. Local stopping trains are branded *Sprinter*. Seat reservations are not available except for international journeys and for travel on *Intercity direct* services.

TELEPHONES

Dial in: ✆ +31 then number (omit initial 0). Outgoing: ✆ 00. Emergency services: ✆ 112.

TOURIST INFORMATION

Netherlands Board of Tourism *Vereniging voor Vreemdelingenverkeer* www.holland.com, Vlietweg 15, 2260 MG Leidschendam, ✆ 070 370 5705, info@holland.com.

TOURIST OFFICES OVERSEAS

See www.holland.com.

VISAS

See page xxiv for visa requirements.

NORWAY

CAPITAL

Oslo.

CURRENCY

Norwegian crown or krone (NOK or kr); 1 krone = 100 øre. For exchange rates see page 9.

EMBASSIES IN OSLO

Australia (Consulate): Wilh. Wilhelmsen ASA, Strandveien 20, Lysaker, ✆ 67 58 48 48. **Canada**: Wergelandsveien 7, ✆ 22 99 53 00. **New Zealand** (Consulate): c/o Halfdan Ditlev-Simonsen & Co AS, Strandveien 50, Lysaker, ✆ 67 11 00 30. **UK**: Thomas Heftyesgate 8, ✆ 23 13 27 00. **USA**: Henrik Ibsens gate 48, ✆ 21 30 85 40.

EMBASSIES OVERSEAS

Australia: 17 Hunter St, Yarralumla, Canberra, ACT 2600, ✆ 2 6270 5700. **Canada**: 150 Metcalfe St. Suite 1300, Ottawa ON, K2P 1P1, ✆ 613 238 6571. **New Zealand** (Consulate): 6b Wagener Place, Mt Albert, Auckland 1025, ✆ 21 780 726. **UK**: 25 Belgrave Sq., London SW1X 8QD, ✆ 020 7591 5500. **USA**: 2720 34th St NW, Washington D.C. 20008, ✆ 202 333 6000.

LANGUAGE

Norwegian, which has two official versions: *Nynorsk* and *Bokmål*. Norwegian has three additional vowels: æ, ø, å, which (in that order) follow z. Almost everyone speaks English; if not, try German.

PUBLIC TRANSPORT

Train, boat and bus schedules are linked to provide good connections. It is often worth using buses or boats to connect two dead-end rail lines (e.g. Bergen and Stavanger), rather than retracing your route. Rail passes sometimes offer good discounts, even free travel, on linking services. NorWay Bussekspress www.nor-way.no, Karl Johans gate 2, N-0154 Oslo, ✆ 82 021 300 (premium rate) has the largest bus network with routes going as far north as Kirkenes. Long-distance buses are comfortable, with reclining seats, ample leg room. Tickets: buy on board or reserve, ✆ 81 544 444 (premium-rate). Taxis: metered, can be picked up at ranks or by phoning; treat independent taxis with caution.

RAIL TRAVEL

See Tables **770 - 789**. Operated by: Norges Statsbaner (NSB) www.nsb.no. All trains convey 2nd-class seating. Most medium- and long-distance trains also convey *NSB Komfort* accommodation, a dedicated area with complimentary tea/coffee and newspapers (supplement payable). Sleeping cars have one- and two-berth compartments; a sleeper supplement is payable per compartment (for two people travelling together, or sole use for single travellers). Long-distance trains convey a bistro car serving hot and cold meals, drinks and snacks. Reservation possible (and recommended) on all long-distance trains, ✆ (within Norway) 81 500 888, then dial 9 for an english speaking operator. Reserved seats not marked, but your confirmation specifies carriage and seat/berth numbers. Carriage numbers shown by the doors, berth numbers outside compartments, seat numbers on seat-backs or luggage racks. Most larger stations have luggage lockers. Narvesen chain (at most stations; open long hours) sells English-language publications and a good range of snacks.

TELEPHONES

Dial in: ✆ +47 then number. Outgoing: ✆ 00. Police: ✆ 112. Fire: ✆ 110. Ambulance: ✆ 113.

TOURIST INFORMATION

Innovation Norway www.visitnorway.com. Oslo: Akersgata 13, ✆ 2200 2500. Tourist offices (*Turistkontorer*) and bureaux (*Reiselivslag / Turistinformasjon*) exist in almost all towns.

TOURIST OFFICES OVERSEAS

UK: Charles House, 5 Lower Regent St, London SW1Y 4LR, ✆ 020 7389 8800, infouk@innovationnorway.no. **USA**: 655 Third Avenue, 18th floor, New York NY 10017, ✆ 212 885 9700, newyork@innovationnorway.no.

VISAS

See page xxiv for visa requirements.

POLAND

CAPITAL

Warsaw (Warszawa).

CURRENCY

Złoty (PLN or zł); 1 złoty = 100 groszy. For exchange rates see page 9.

EMBASSIES IN WARSAW

Australia: ul. Nowogrodzka 11, ✆ 22 521 34 44. **Canada**: ul. Jana Matejki 1/5, ✆ 22 584 31 00. **New Zealand**: Aleje Ujazdowskie 51, ✆ 22 521 05 00. **UK**: ul Kawalerii 12, ✆ 22 311 00 00. **USA**: Aleje Ujazdowskie 29/31, ✆ 22 504 20 00.

EMBASSIES OVERSEAS

Australia: 7 Turrana St, Yarralumla, Canberra, ACT 2600, ✆ 2 6272 1000. **Canada**: 443 Daly Ave., Ottawa ON, K1N 6H3, ✆ 613 789 0468. **New Zealand**: 142-4 Featherston St, Wellington, ✆ 4 475 9453. **UK**: 47 Portland Place, London W1B 1JH, ✆ 020 7291 3520. **USA**: 2640 16th St NW, Washington DC 20009, ✆ 202 499 1700.

LANGUAGE

Polish. Many older Poles speak German, younger Poles are likely to understand English. Russian is widely understood, but unpopular.

PUBLIC TRANSPORT

Buses are cheap and sometimes more practical than trains. Main long-distance bus station in Warszawa is adjacent to the Zachodnia (western) station. Some services (including PolskiBus) leave from suburban metro stations. Tickets normally include seat reservations (seat number is on back), bookable from bus station. In rural areas, bus drivers will often halt between official stops if you flag them down. Extensive tram networks in Warszawa and most other cities; Warszawa also has a modern north-south metro line.

RAIL TRAVEL

See Tables **1000 - 1099**. Most long-distance trains are classified *EC*, *EIC*, *EIP* or *TLK* and are operated by PKP Intercity, www.intercity.pl. *TLK* are lower-cost daytime and overnight services. Reservation is compulsory on all trains operated by PKP Intercity. Purely local trains (*osobowy*) are classified *R* (REGIO) and are operated by a separate company, Przewozy Regionalne (www.przewozyregionalne.pl), which also operates longer distance *IR* (InterREGIO) and *RE* services, often in competition with PKP Intercity, but tickets are not interchangeable. In some areas local services are operated by different companies (e.g. Koleje Śląskie around Katowice). At stations, departures (*odjazdy*) are shown on yellow paper, arrivals (*przyjazdy*) on white. Note that long distance trains are shown in red print on timetables at stations. Fares are about 50% higher for 1st class, but still cheap by western standards and probably worth it. Overnight trains usually have 1st and 2nd-class sleepers, plus 2nd-class couchettes and seats. Left luggage and refreshments in major stations.

TELEPHONES
Dial in: ✆ +48 then number (omit initial 0). Outgoing: ✆ 0*0 *(wait for tone after first 0)*. Police: ✆ 997. Fire: ✆ 998. Ambulance: ✆ 999. Emergency (from mobile): ✆ 112.

TOURIST INFORMATION
Polish National Tourist Office www.poland.travel.

TOURIST OFFICES OVERSEAS
UK: Level 3, Westgate House, West Gate, London W5 1YY, ✆ 0300 303 1812, london@poland.travel. **USA**: 5 Marine View Plaza, Hoboken NJ 07030, ✆ 201 420 9910, info.na@poland.travel.

VISAS
See page xxiv for visa requirements.
For travellers in Germany, visas are obtainable from the Polish consulate in Berlin www.berlin.polemb.net.

PORTUGAL

CAPITAL
Lisbon (Lisboa).

CURRENCY
Euro (EUR/€). 1 euro = 100 cent. For exchange rates see page 9.

EMBASSIES IN LISBON
Australia: Avenida da Liberdade 200, ✆ 21 310 1500.
Canada: Avenida da Liberdade 198–200, ✆ 21 316 4600.
New Zealand: (Consulate) Rua da Sociedade Farmaceutica 68 ✆ 213 140 780. **UK**: Rua de São Bernardo 33, ✆ 21 392 4000.
USA: Avenida das Forças Armadas, ✆ 21 727 3300.

EMBASSIES OVERSEAS
Australia: 32 Thesiger Court, Deakin, ACT 2600, ✆ 2 6260 4970.
Canada: 645 Island Park Dr., Ottawa ON, K1Y OB8, ✆ 613 729 2922.
New Zealand: (Consulate) 21 Marion St, Wellington, ✆ 4 382 7655.
UK: 11 Belgrave Sq., London SW1X 8PP, ✆ 020 723 5533.
USA: 2012 Massachusetts Ave. NW, Washington DC 20036, ✆ 202 332 3007.

LANGUAGE
Portuguese. Older people often speak French as a second language, young people Spanish and/or English. English, French, and German in some tourist areas.

PUBLIC TRANSPORT
Usually buy long-distance bus tickets before boarding. Bus stops: *paragem;* extend your arm to stop a bus. Taxis: black with green roofs or beige; illuminated signs; cheap, metered in cities, elsewhere fares negotiable; drivers may ask you to pay for their return journey; surcharges for luggage over 30 kg and night travel; 10% tip. City transport: single tickets can be bought as you board, but day tickets or passes are cheaper.

RAIL TRAVEL
See Tables **690 - 699**. Operator: Comboios de Portugal (CP) www.cp.pt. Cheap and generally punctual; 1st/2nd class on long-distance. Fastest trains are *IC* and *AP* (Alfa Pendular), modern, fast; supplement payable; seat reservations compulsory, buffet cars. CP information line, ✆ 808 208 208. Left-luggage lockers in most stations.

TELEPHONES
Dial in: ✆ +351 then number. Outgoing: ✆ 00.
Emergency services: ✆ 112.

TOURIST INFORMATION
Portuguese National Tourist Office www.visitportugal.com. info@visitportugal.com, ✆ 211 140 200.

TOURIST OFFICES OVERSEAS
UK: 11 Belgrave Square, London SW1X 8PP, ✆ 0207 201 6666, tourism.london@portugalglobal.pt. **USA**: 590 Fifth Avenue, 4th floor, New York NY 10036, ✆ 646 723 0200, tourism@iecp.pt.

VISAS
See page xxiv for visa requirements.

ROMANIA

CAPITAL
Bucharest (Bucuresti).

CURRENCY
Leu (plural: lei). 1 leu = 100 bani. For exchange rates see page 9.

EMBASSIES IN BUCHAREST
Australia (Consulate): The Group, Praga St 3 ✆ 21 206 22 00.
Canada: 1-3 Tuberozelor St, ✆ 21 307 50 00. **New Zealand**: *refer to NZ Embassy in Belgium*. **UK**: Jules Michelet 24, ✆ 21 201 72 00.
USA: Dr Liviu Librescu Blvd. 4–6, ✆ 21 200 33 00.

EMBASSIES OVERSEAS
Australia: 4 Dalman Crescent, O'Malley, Canberra ACT 2606, ✆ 2 6286 2343. **Canada**: 655 Rideau St, Ottawa ON, K1N 6A3, ✆ 613 789 3709. **New Zealand** (Consulate): 53 Homewood Ave, Karori, Wellington 6012, ✆ 4 476 6883. **UK**: Arundel House, 4 Palace Green, London W8 4QD, ✆ 020 7937 9666. **USA**: 1607 23rd St NW, Washington DC, 20008, ✆ 202 332 4846.

LANGUAGE
Romanian. English is understood by younger people, plus some French, German, and Hungarian throughout Transylvania.

PUBLIC TRANSPORT
Buy bus/tram/metro tickets in advance from kiosks (as a rule) and cancel on entry. Taxis are plentiful and inexpensive; if the meter is not in use agree price first and always pay in lei, not foreign currency. Avoid unlicensed vehicles. Trains are best for long-distance travel, although bus routes are expanding and connect important towns and cities.

RAIL TRAVEL
See Tables **1600 - 1699**. Societatea Natională de Transport Feroviar de Călători (CFR) operates an extensive network linking all major towns www.cfrcalatori.ro. Most main lines are electrified and quite fast, but branch line services are very slow. Trains are fairly punctual and very cheap. Except for local trains, reserve and pay a speed supplement in advance (tickets issued abroad include the supplement): cheapest are *regio* (very slow), then *Interregio* and finally *IC* trains (prices approaching Western levels). Food and drink is normally available only on *IC* and some *IR* trains. Couchette (*cușetă*) or sleeper (*vagon de dormit*) accommodation is inexpensive. An increasing number of services are now operated by private operators, such as Regiotrans, Transferoviar Grup SA, and Softrans S.R.L.

TELEPHONES
Dial in: ✆ +40 then number (omit initial 0). Outgoing: ✆ 00. Emergency: ✆ 112. Police: ✆ 955. Fire: ✆ 981. Ambulance: ✆ 961.

TOURIST INFORMATION
Romanian National Tourist Office www.romaniatourism.com.
Bucharest TIC www.tourism-bucharest.com: ✆ 021 305 55 00, turism@bucuresti-primaria.ro.

TOURIST OFFICES OVERSEAS
UK: 12 Harley St, London W1G 9PG, ✆ 020 7224 3692, romaniatravel@btconnect.com. **USA**: 355 Lexington Ave., 8th floor, New York NY 10017, ✆ 212 545 8484, info@romaniatourism.com.

VISAS
See page xxiv for visa requirements. Make sure you keep your visa papers when you enter – you'll pay a large fine if you don't have them when you leave Romania.

SLOVAKIA

CAPITAL
Bratislava.

CURRENCY
Euro (EUR/€). 1 euro = 100 cent. For exchange rates see page 9.

EMBASSIES IN BRATISLAVA
Australia: *refer to Australian Embassy in Austria*. **Canada**: Carlton Court Yard & Savoy Buildings, Mostova 2, ✆ 2 5920 4031.
New Zealand: *refer to NZ Embassy in Austria*. **UK**: Panská 16, ✆ 2 5998 2000. **USA**: Hviezdoslavovo námestie 4, ✆ 2 5443 0861.

EMBASSIES OVERSEAS

Australia: 47 Culgoa Circuit, O'Malley, Canberra, ACT 2606, ✆ 2 6290 1516. **Canada**: 50 Rideau Terrace, Ottawa ON, K1M 2A1, ✆ 613 749 4442. **New Zealand** (Consulate): 188 Quayt St, Auckland 1010, ✆ 9 366 5111. **UK**: 25 Kensington Palace Gardens, London W8 4QY, ✆ 020 7313 6470. **USA**: 3523 International Court NW, Washington DC 20008, ✆ 202 237 1054.

LANGUAGE

Slovak, a Slavic tongue closely related to Czech. Some Russian (unpopular), German, Hungarian (especially in the south), plus a little English and French.

PUBLIC TRANSPORT

There is a comprehensive long-distance bus network, often more direct than rail in upland areas. Buy tickets from the driver; priority is given to those with bookings.

RAIL TRAVEL

See Tables **1170 - 1199**. The national rail operator is Železničná spoločnosť (ŽSSK) www.slovakrail.sk, running on the network of ŽSR. Trains are cheap, but often crowded. Apart from a small number of *EC* and *IC* trains (for which higher fares apply), the fastest trains are *expresný* (*Ex*) and *Rýchlik* (*R*). Cheaper are *zrýchlený* (semi-fast) and *osobný* (very slow). At stations, departures (*odjezdy*) are shown on yellow posters, arrivals (*prijezdy*) on white. Sleeping cars/couchettes (reserve at all main stations, well in advance in summer) are provided on most overnight trains. Seat reservations (at station counters marked R) are recommended for express trains. Private operators Regiojet and Leo Express also run on main route to Kosice.

TELEPHONES

Dial in: ✆ +421 then number (omit initial 0). Outgoing: ✆ 00. Emergency: ✆ 112. Police: ✆ 158. Fire: ✆ 150. Ambulance: ✆ 155.

TOURIST INFORMATION

Slovak Tourist Board www.slovakia.travel. Main office: Námestie L'. Štúra 1, P.O. Box 35, 974 05 Banská Bystrica, ✆ 0 484 136 146, sacr@sacr.sk. Bratislava Tourist Information Centre: Klobučnicka 2, www.bratislava.sk, ✆ 0 216 186, touristinfo@bratislava.sk.

TOURIST OFFICES OVERSEAS

Germany: Slowakische Zentrale für Tourismus, Zimmerstr. 27, D-10969, Berlin, ✆ +49 (0) 30 2594 2640. **USA** Phorall LLC, 18 Florence St., Edison NY08817 nyoffice@slovakia.travel

VISAS

See page xxiv for visa requirements.

SLOVENIA

CAPITAL

Ljubljana.

CURRENCY

Euro (EUR/€). 1 euro = 100 cent. For exchange rates see page 9.

EMBASSIES IN LJUBLJANA

Australia (Consulate): *refer to Australian Embassy in Austria.*
Canada (Consulate): Linhartova cesta 49a, ✆ 1 252 4444.
New Zealand: (Consulate) Lek d.d., Verovskova 57, ✆ 1 580 3055.
UK: Trg Republike 3, ✆ 1 200 3910.
USA: Prešernova 31, ✆ 1 200 5500.

EMBASSIES OVERSEAS

Australia: 26 Akame Circuit, O'Malley, Canberra, ACT 2606, ✆ 2 6290 0000. **Canada**: 150 Metcalfe St. Suite 2200, Ottawa, ON, K2P 1P1, ✆ 613 565 5781. **UK**: 10 Little College St, London SW1P 3SH, ✆ 020 7222 5700. **USA**: 2410 California St., Washington DC 20008, ✆ 202 386 6610.

LANGUAGE

Slovenian. English, German and Italian are often spoken in tourist areas.

PUBLIC TRANSPORT

Long-distance bus services are frequent and inexpensive; normally, buy your ticket on boarding. Information: Trg Osvobodilne Fronte 5, next to Ljubljana station, ✆ 012 344 606. On city buses pay by dropping the exact flat fare or a cheaper token (available from news-stands and post offices) into the farebox next to the driver. Daily and weekly passes are available in the main cities.

RAIL TRAVEL

See Tables **1300 - 1359**. Operator: Slovenske železnice (SŽ) www.slo-zeleznice.si. Information: ✆ 012 913 332 (+386 129 13 332 from abroad). Good, efficient network, but fewer services run on Saturdays. Reserve for *ICS* trains; supplements are payable on other express services.

TELEPHONES

Dial in: ✆ +386 then number (omit initial 0). Outgoing: ✆ 00. Police: ✆ 113. Fire and ambulance: ✆ 112.

TOURIST INFORMATION

Slovenian Tourist Board www.slovenia.info. Ljubljana: Krekov trg 10, ✆ 01 306 45 75, stic@visitljubljana.si.

TOURIST OFFICES OVERSEAS

UK: Slovenian Tourist Board, 10 Little College Street, London SW1P 3SH, ✆ 0870 225 53 05, london@slovenia.info.
USA: 2929 East Commercial Boulevard, Suite 201, Fort Lauderdale, FL 33308, ✆ 954 491 0112, info@slovenia.info.

VISAS

See page xxiv for visa requirements.

SPAIN

CAPITAL

Madrid.

CURRENCY

Euro (EUR/€). 1 euro = 100 cent. For exchange rates see page 9.

EMBASSIES IN MADRID

Australia: Paseo de la Castellana, 259D, ✆ 913 536 600.
Canada: Paseo de la Castellana, 259D, ✆ 913 828 400.
New Zealand: Pinar 7, ✆ 915 230 226. **UK**: Paseo de la Castellana 259D, ✆ 917 146 300. **USA**: Serrano 75, ✆ 915 872 200.

EMBASSIES OVERSEAS

Australia: 15 Arkana St, Yarralumla, Canberra, ACT 2600, ✆ 2 6273 3555. **Canada**: 74 Stanley Avenue, Ottawa ON, K1M 1P4, ✆ 613 747 2252. **New Zealand**: 50 Manners St, Wellington 6142, ✆ 4 802 5665. **UK**: 39 Chesham Place, London SW1X 8SB, ✆ 020 7235 5555. **USA**: 2375 Pennsylvania Ave. NW, Washington DC 20037, ✆ 202 452 0100.

LANGUAGE

Castilian Spanish is the most widely spoken language. There are three other official languages: Catalan in the east; Galician (*Galego*) in the north-west, and Basque (*Euskera*) in the Basque country and parts of Navarre. English is fairly widely spoken in tourist areas. Note that in Spanish listings *Ch* often comes after the *C*'s, *Ll* after the *L*'s, and *Ñ* after the *N*'s.

PUBLIC TRANSPORT

Numerous regional bus companies provide a fairly comprehensive and cheap (if sometimes confusing) service. The largest bus operating groups are ALSA www.alsa.es and Avanzabus www.avanzabus.com. City buses are efficient and there are metro systems in Madrid, Barcelona, València and Bilbao.

RAIL TRAVEL

See Tables **650 - 689**. National rail company: Red Nacional de los Ferrocarriles Españoles (RENFE) www.renfe.es. FEVE and a number of regionally-controlled railways operate lines in coastal regions. General information: RENFE ✆ 902 320 320; FEVE ✆ 902 100 818; AVE (high-speed): ✆ 915 066 329; Grandes Líneas (other long-distance): ✆ 902 105 205; international: ✆ 934 901 122. Spain's high-speed network has expanded considerably over the last few years and the Barcelona - Madrid service has some of the fastest trains in Europe. As well as *AVE* high-speed trains, other long-distance categories include *Altaria*, *Euromed*, *Talgo* (light articulated trains) and IC expresses (see page 321 for further train categories). *Trenhotel* (hotel train): night train offering sleeping compartments with their own shower and WC. Long-distance trains convey 1st and 2nd-class accommodation (known as *Preferente* and *Turista*) and require advance reservation. *Regionales*: local stopping service; *Cercanias*: suburban trains. In remoter parts of country, services may be very infrequent. Reservation is compulsory on all services for which a train category (*Talgo*, *IC* etc) is shown in the timing column of this timetable. RENFE offer money back if their AVE trains on the Sevilla line arrive more than 5 minutes late.

TELEPHONES
Dial in: ✆ +34 then number. Outgoing: ✆ 00.
Emergency (police / fire / ambulance): ✆ 112.

TOURIST INFORMATION
Spanish Tourist Office / Turespaña (*Oficinas de Turismo*) www.tourspain.es. Also in the USA: www.spain.info/en_US, and in the UK: www.spain.info/en_GB.

TOURIST OFFICES OVERSEAS
Canada: 2 Bloor Street West, Suite 3402, Toronto ON M4W 3E2, ✆ 416 961 3131, toronto@tourspain.es. **UK**: 64 North Row, 6th floor, London W1K 7DE, ✆ 0207 317 2011, londres@tourspain.es.
USA: 60 East 42nd Street, Suite 5300 (53rd floor), New York NY 10165-0039, ✆ 212 265 8822, nuevayork@tourspain.es.
Also in Chicago ✆ 312 642 1992, Los Angeles ✆ 323 658 7188, Miami ✆ 305 476 1966.

VISAS
See page xxiv for visa requirements.

SWEDEN

CAPITAL
Stockholm.

CURRENCY
Swedish crown or krona (SEK, kr, or Skr); 1 krona = 100 öre. For exchange rates see page 9.

EMBASSIES IN STOCKHOLM
Australia: Klarabergsviadukten 63, ✆ 08 613 2900.
Canada: Klarabergsgatan 23, ✆ 08 453 3000. **New Zealand**: *refer to NZ Embassy in Belgium*. **UK**: Skarpögatan 6–8, ✆ 08 671 3000.
USA: Dag Hammarskjölds Väg 31, ✆ 08 783 5300.

EMBASSIES OVERSEAS
Australia: 5 Turrana St, Yarralumla, Canberra, ACT 2600, ✆ 2 6270 2700. **Canada**: 377 Dalhousie St, Ottawa ON, K1N 9N8, ✆ 613 244 8200. **New Zealand** (Consulate): Molesworth House, 101 Molesworth Street, Wellington, ✆ 4 499 9895. **UK**: 11 Montagu Pl., London W1H 2AL, ✆ 020 7917 6400. **USA**: 2900 K Street NW, Washington DC 20007, ✆ 202 467 2600.

LANGUAGE
Swedish. English is widely spoken.

PUBLIC TRANSPORT
The transport system is highly efficient; ferries are covered (in whole or part) by rail passes and city transport cards. Swebus www.swebus.se, ✆ 0771 218 218 (+46 771 218 218 from abroad) is the biggest operator of long-distance buses. Advance booking is essential, tickets may be purchased at sales offices, by telephone or via the website. Bus terminals usually adjoin rail stations.

RAIL TRAVEL
See Tables **730 - 769**. National rail company: SJ AB, formerly part of Statens Järnvägar (SJ) www.sj.se or www.samtrafiken.se. Best services are operated by high-speed trains (*Snabbtåg*, shown as *Sn* in our tables) running at up to 200 km/h and using either SJ 2000 trains (formerly X2000) or new SJ 3000 units. Supplements are required on *Snabbtåg*. Some local lines are run by regional authorities or private companies such as Veolia Transport www.veolia.se; see page 349 for other operators. SJ information and sales line, ✆ (0) 771 75 75 75, Veolia ✆ (0) 771 260 000. Sleeping-cars: one or two berths in 2nd class; couchettes: six berths; female-only compartment available. 1st-class sleeping-cars (en-suite shower and WC) on many overnight services; 2nd-class have wash-basins, shower and WC are at the end of the carriage. Long-distance trains have a refreshment service. Many trains have a family coach with a playroom, and facilities for the disabled. Seat reservations are compulsory on *Sn* and night trains. *Sn* services also operate between Sweden and Copenhagen via the Öresund bridge and tunnel but it is better to use the frequent local trains for short journeys. 'C' (for Central) in timetables etc. means the town's main station. *Biljetter* indicates the station ticket office, often with limited opening hours, but ticket machines are widely in use. *Pressbyrån* kiosks (at stations) sell snacks and English-language publications.

TELEPHONES
Dial in: ✆ +46 then number (omit initial 0). Outgoing: ✆ 00.
Emergency services (police / fire / ambulance): ✆ 112.

TOURIST INFORMATION
Swedish Travel & Tourism Council www.visitsweden.com info@visitsweden.com. Stockholm Visitor Centre: Kulturhuset, Sergel Torg 3, ✆ 085 0828 508, touristinfo@stockholm.se.

TOURIST OFFICES OVERSEAS
UK: 5 Upper Montagu St, London W1H 2AG, ✆ 020 7108 6168 uk@visitsweden.com. **USA**: PO Box 4649, Grand Central Station, New York NY10163-4649, ✆ 212 885 9700, usa@visitsweden.com.

VISAS
See page xxiv for visa requirements.

SWITZERLAND

CAPITAL
Berne (Bern).

CURRENCY
Swiss franc (CHF or Sfr.); 1 franc = 100 centimes. For exchange rates see page 9.

EMBASSIES IN BERNE
Australia (Consulate in Geneva): Chemin des Fins 2, Geneva, ✆ 0 22 799 91 00. **Canada**: Kirchenfeldstrasse 88, ✆ 0 31 357 32 00 **New Zealand** (Consulate in Geneva): 2 Chemin des Fins, Geneva, ✆ 0 22 929 03 50. **UK**: Thunstrasse 50, ✆ 0 31 359 77 00.
USA: Sulgeneckstrasse 19, ✆ 0 31 357 70 11.

EMBASSIES OVERSEAS
Australia: 7 Melbourne Avenue, Forrest, Canberra, ACT 2603, ✆ 2 6162 8400. **Canada**: 5 Marlborough Avenue, Ottawa ON, K1N 8E6 ✆ 613 235 1837. **New Zealand**: 10 Customhouse Quay, Wellington 6040, ✆ 4 472 1593. **UK**: 16-18 Montagu Place, London W1H 2BQ, ✆ 020 7616 6000. **USA**: 2900 Cathedral Ave. NW, Washington DC 20008, ✆ 202 745 7900.

LANGUAGE
German, French, Italian, and Romansch are all official languages. Most Swiss people are at least bilingual. English is widespread.

PUBLIC TRANSPORT
Swiss buses are famously punctual. Yellow postbuses call at rail stations; free timetables from post offices. Swiss Pass valid (see Passes feature), surcharge for some scenic routes. The best way to get around centres is often on foot. Most cities have efficient tram and bus networks with integrated ticketing.

RAIL TRAVEL
See Tables **500 - 579**. The principal rail carrier is Swiss Federal Railways (SBB / CFF / FFS) www.sbb.ch. Information: ✆ 0 900 300 300 (English-speaking operator). There are also many local lines with independent operators. Services are fast and punctual, trains spotlessly clean. Reservations are required on some sightseeing trains (e.g. Glacier Express, Bernina-Express). All main stations have information offices (and usually tourist offices), shopping and eating facilities. Bicycle hire at most stations.

TELEPHONES
Dial in: ✆ +41 then number (omit initial 0). Outgoing: ✆ 00.
Emergency: ✆ 112. Police: ✆ 117. Fire: ✆ 118. Ambulance: ✆ 114.

TOURIST INFORMATION
Switzerland Tourism www.myswitzerland.com. Zürich: Tödistrasse 7, (Not open to the public). International toll-free ✆ 00800 100 200 29.

TOURIST OFFICES OVERSEAS
Canada: 480 University Ave, Suite 1500, Toronto ON, M5G 1V2, ✆ 800 794 7795 (toll-free), info.caen@myswitzerland.com. **UK**: 30 Bedford Street, London WC2E 9ED, ✆ 00800 100 200 29 (free-phone), info.uk@myswitzerland.com. **USA**: 608 Fifth Ave., New York NY 10020, ✆ 01 800 794 7795 (toll-free), info.usa@myswitzerland.com.

VISAS
See page xxiv for visa requirements.

TURKEY

CAPITAL
Ankara.

CURRENCY
New Turkish lira (TRY or YTL). 1 lira = 100 kurus. For exchange rates see page 9.

CONSULATES IN ISTANBUL
Australia: Ritz Carlton residences, Asker Ocaği Caddesi No 15, Elmadağ 34367, ✆ 393 8542. **Canada**: 209 Buyukdere Caddesi Tekfen Tower, ✆ 385 9700. **New Zealand**: Inonu Caddesi No 48/3 Taksim, Istanbul 34437, ✆ 244 0272. **UK**: Mesrutiyet Caddesi No 34, Tepebasi Beyoglu, ✆ 334 6400. **USA**: istinye Mahallesi, Kaplı calar Mekvii Sokak No 2, istinye 34460, ✆ 335 9000.

EMBASSIES OVERSEAS
Australia: 6 Moonah Place, Yarralumla, Canberra, ACT 2600, ✆ 2 6234 0000. **Canada**: 197 Wurtemburg St., Ottawa ON, K1N 8L9, ✆ 613 244 2470. **New Zealand**: 17-17 Murphy St, Thorndon, Wellington 6011, ✆ 4 472 1290. **UK**: (Consulate) Rutland Lodge Rutland Gardens, Knightsbridge, London SW7 1BW, ✆ 020 7591 6900. **USA**: 2525 Massachusetts Ave, NW, Washington, DC 20008, ✆ 202 612 6700.

LANGUAGE
Turkish, which is written using the Latin alphabet. English and German are often understood.

PUBLIC TRANSPORT
An excellent long-distance bus system, run by competing companies (amongst the best are Varan and Ulusoy), generally provides quicker journeys than rail. *Dolmus* minibuses that pick up passengers like a taxi, but at much cheaper rates and operating along set routes, can be used for shorter journeys. Istanbul has a modern metro line, as well as a light-rail and tram route. Passenger ferries link major ports.

RAIL TRAVEL
See Tables **1570 - 1590** (also **1550** for European Turkey). Operator: TCDD (Turkish State Railways) www.tcdd.gov.tr. Traditional routes are tortuous and journeys slow, but the coaching stock is generally comfortable. Ankara and Istanbul are connected by a new high-speed route via Eskişehir with another high-speed section linking these cities with Konya. Further high speed lines are under construction. The Marmaray Tunnel under the Bosphorus opened in 2013, joining the Asian and European parts of Istanbul by rail for the first time. The historic terminal stations of Sirkeci and Haydarpasa are currently closed to all rail traffic. No domestic passenger rail services currently operate in European Turkey, other than in and around Istanbul itself.

TELEPHONES
Dial in: ✆ +90 then number (omit initial 0). Outgoing: ✆ 00. Emergency: ✆ 112. Police: ✆ 155. Fire: ✆ 110. Ambulance: ✆ 112.

TOURIST INFORMATION
Turkish National Tourist Office www.gototurkey.com. Ministry of Culture and Tourism www.kultur.gov.tr: Atatürk Bulvarı 29, 06050 Opera, Ankara, ✆ 312 309 0850.

TOURIST OFFICES OVERSEAS
UK: 4th Floor, 29-30 St James's Street, London SW1A 1HB, ✆ 020 7839 7778, info@gototurkey.co.uk. **USA**: 825 3rd Avenue 5 floor, New York NY 10022, ✆ 212 687 2194, ny@tourismturkey.org. Also Los Angeles ✆ 323 937 8066, Washington ✆ 202 612 6800.

VISAS
See page xxiv for visa requirements.

UNITED KINGDOM

CAPITAL
London.

CURRENCY
Pounds Sterling (GBP or £). £1 = 100 pence (p). For exchange rates see page 09.

EMBASSIES IN LONDON
Australia (High Commission): Australia House, The Strand, ✆ 020 7379 4334. **Canada** (High Commission) Macdonald House, 1 Grosvenor Square, ✆ 020 7258 6600.
New Zealand (High Commission): New Zealand House, 80 Haymarket, ✆ 020 7930 8422. **USA**: 24 Grosvenor Square, ✆ 020 7499 9000.

EMBASSIES OVERSEAS
Australia (High Commission): Commonwealth Ave, Yarralumla, Canberra, ACT 2600, ✆ 2 6270 6666. **Canada** (High Commission): 80 Elgin St, Ottawa ON, K1P 5K7, ✆ 613 237 1530. **New Zealand** (High Commission): 44 Hill St, Wellington, ✆ 4 924 2888. **USA**: 3100 Massachusetts Ave. NW, Washington DC 20008, ✆ 202 588 6500.

LANGUAGE
English, plus Welsh in Wales and Gaelic in parts of Scotland.

PUBLIC TRANSPORT
Intercity express bus services (coaches) are generally cheaper, but slower, than trains, and mostly require prebooking. The main long-distance coach operator in England and Wales is National Express www.nationalexpress.com, or Citylink www.citylink.co.uk in Scotland. Comprehensive local bus network; most companies belong to large groups such as Stagecoach, First or Arriva. Bus stations are rarely adjacent to railway stations. Traveline www.traveline.org.uk is an on-line and telephone service for all UK timetables: ✆ 0871 200 22 23 (10p per minute). Extensive 'Underground' railway network in London operated by Transport for London www.tfl.gov.uk who also control the bus service using private companies. In Northern Ireland, Ulsterbus (part of Translink) is the principal bus operator www.translink.co.uk.

RAIL TRAVEL
See Tables **100 - 234**. Passenger services in Great Britain are provided by a number of train operating companies, working together as National Rail www.nationalrail.co.uk. Through tickets are available to all stations in the country. If asked, booking-office staff will quote the cheapest through fare regardless of operator (time period restrictions apply to the very cheapest fares). National Rail enquiries: ✆ 08457 48 49 50. Fast trains, comfortable and frequent, have first and standard class. Other long- and medium-distance regional services are often standard-class only. Refreshments are often available on board. Sleepers: cabins are two-berth or (higher charge) single. Advance reservation (essential for sleepers) is available for most long-distance services - a fee may be charged. Travel between Saturday evening and Sunday afternoon is sometimes interrupted by engineering works and buses may replace trains.
In Northern Ireland, trains are operated by Northern Ireland Railways (NIR), part of Translink. NIR enquiries: ✆ 028 90 666 630.

TELEPHONES
Dial in: ✆ +44 then number (omit initial 0). Outgoing: ✆ 00.
Emergency services: ✆ 999 or 112.

TOURIST INFORMATION
VisitBritain www.visitbritain.com. London: 20 Great Smith Street, ✆ 020 7578 1000. There are local tourist offices in most towns and cities.

TOURIST OFFICES OVERSEAS
Australia: The Gateway, 1 Macquarie Place Sidney, NSW 2000, ✆ 2 8247 2275. **Canada**: 777 Bay Street Suite, 2800 Toronto ON M5G 2G2, ✆ 664 666 77. **USA** 845 Third Avenue, 10th Floor New York NY 10022, ✆ 212 850 0349. Also in Los Angeles, ✆ 310 481 2989. Intending visitors should refer to the website www.visitbritain.com.

VISAS
See page xxiv for visa requirements.

Visa Requirements

The table below shows whether nationals from selected countries (shown in columns) need visas to visit countries in Europe (shown in rows) - the symbol ▲ indicates that a visa **is** required. This information applies to tourist trips for up to 30 days - different requirements may apply for longer trips or for visits for other purposes, also if you are resident in a country other than your own. To enter certain countries you may need up to three months remaining validity on your passport. Holders of biometric ordinary passports sometimes do not require a visa.

The first row and column, labelled **Schengen area**, apply to the 26 European countries which have signed the Schengen Agreement whereby border controls between the member countries have been abolished. It is possible to obtain a single Schengen visa to cover all these countries, which are:

Austria, Belgium, Czech Republic, Denmark, Estonia, Finland, France, Germany, Greece, Hungary, Iceland, Italy, Latvia, Liechtenstein, Lithuania, Luxembourg, Malta, Netherlands, Norway, Poland, Portugal, Slovakia, Slovenia, Spain, Sweden, Switzerland.

Note that the Schengen area and the European Union (EU) differ in the following respects: Iceland, Liechtenstein, Norway and Switzerland are not in the EU but have implemented the Schengen agreement, whereas the United Kingdom and the Republic of Ireland are in the EU but have opted out of Schengen. Andorra is not included in the Schengen area. Croatia, Cyprus, Romania and Bulgaria are in the EU and are legally obliged to join Schengen once certain requirements are met.

Visas should generally be applied for in advance from an Embassy or Consulate of the country you are visiting, although sometimes they are available on arrival. Transit visas may be available for those travelling through a country in order to reach another, but these may also need to be purchased in advance. **The information show below is given as a guide only - entry requirements may be subject to change.**

NATIONALS OF →

▲ VISA REQUIRED

TRAVELLING TO ↓	Schengen area	Albania	Belarus	Bosnia-Herzegovina	Bulgaria	Croatia	Cyprus	Macedonia	Moldova	Montenegro	Romania	Russia	Serbia	Switzerland	Turkey	UK / Ireland	Ukraine	Australia	Canada	Japan	New Zealand	USA
Schengen area	–	:	▲	:	:	:	:	:	:	:	:	▲	:	:	▲	:	▲	:	:	:	:	:
Albania ◇	:	–	▲	:	:	:	:	:	▲	:	:	▲	:	:	:	:	:	:	:	:	:	:
Belarus	▲	▲	–	▲	▲	▲	▲	▲	:	▲	▲	:	:	▲	:	▲	:	▲	▲	▲	▲	▲
Bosnia-Herzegovina	:	:	▲	–	:	:	:	:	▲	:	:	:	:	:	:	:	:	:	:	:	:	:
Bulgaria	:	▲[1]	▲	▲[1]	–	:	:	▲[1]	▲[1]	▲[1]	:	▲	▲[1]	:	▲	:	▲	:	:	:	:	:
Croatia	:	:	▲	:	:	–	:	:	:	:	:	▲	:	:	▲	:	▲	:	:	:	:	:
Cyprus	:	▲[1]	▲	▲[1]	:	:	–	▲[1]	▲[1]	▲[1]	:	▲	▲[1]	:	▲	:	▲	:	:	:	:	:
Macedonia	:	▲[1]	▲	:	:	:	:	–	▲	▲[1]	:	:	▲[1]	:	:	:	:	:	:	:	:	:
Moldova	:	:	:	:	:	:	:	:	–	:	:	:	▲[1]	:	:	:	:	:	:	:	:	:
Montenegro	:	:	▲	:	:	:	:	:	:	–	:	:	:	:	:	:	:	:	:	:	:	:
Romania	:	▲[1]	▲	▲[1]	:	:	:	▲[1]	▲[1]	▲[1]	–	▲	▲[1]	:	▲	:	▲	:	:	:	:	:
Russia	▲	▲	:	:	▲	▲	▲	▲	:	:	▲	–	:	▲	:	▲	:	▲	▲	▲	▲	▲
Serbia	:	:	:	:	:	:	:	:	▲[1]	:	:	:	–	:	:	:	:	:	:	:	:	:
Switzerland	:	▲[1]	▲	▲[1]	:	:	:	▲[1]	▲[1]	▲[1]	:	▲	▲[1]	–	▲	:	▲	:	:	:	:	:
Turkey	●[2]	:	:	:	:	●	●	:	:	:	:	:	:	:	–	●	:	●	●	:	:	●
UK / Ireland	:	▲	▲	▲	:	:	:	▲	▲	▲	:	▲	▲	:	▲	–	▲	:	:	:	:	:
Ukraine	:	▲	:	:	:	:	:	:	:	:	:	:	:	:	:	:	–	▲	:	:	▲	:

NOTES

▲ – Visa required (see also general notes above table).

▲[1] – Visa not required by holders of 'biometric' passports.

● – Electronic visa required before entering the country (prices vary according to nationality). For further information and to make a visa application see www.evisa.gov.tr.

●[2] – ● applies to nationals of Austria, Belgium, Malta, Netherlands, Norway, Poland, Portugal and Spain.

◇ – Tax of 10 euro may be payable on entry to Albania.

EUROPEAN RAIL TIMETABLE

JUNE 2016

GENERAL INFORMATION

FEATURES

TIMETABLES

CONTACT DETAILS

Director and Editor-in-chief	John Potter
Editor	Chris Woodcock
Editorial Team	Peter Bass David Turpie Peter Weller
Additional compiling	Brendan Fox
Marketing and Advertising Manager	Keri Blunston
Commercial Manager	Gemma Donaldson
Subscriptions Manager	Peter Weller
Social Media Manager	Reuben Turner
General sales enquiries	Mon-Fri 0900 - 1700 +44 (0)1832 270198
e-mail	editorial@europeanrailtimetable.eu
sales	sales@europeanrailtimetable.eu
website	www.europeanrailtimetable.eu

ISSN 1748-0817 Published monthly.

Printed and bound by CPI Group (UK) Ltd, Croydon, CR0 4YY

Cover created by Andrea Collins website: www.millstonecreative.co.uk
e-mail: millstonecreative@btinternet.com

European Rail Timetable Limited
28 Monson Way
Oundle
Northamptonshire PE8 4QG, United Kingdom

Company Number 8590554

2016

CALENDRIER CALENDARIO KALENDER CALENDARIO

JANUARY

M	T	W	T	F	S	S
①	②	③	④	⑤	⑥	⑦
–	–	–	–	1	2	3
4	5	6	7	8	9	10
11	12	13	14	15	16	17
18	19	20	21	22	23	24
25	26	27	28	29	30	31

FEBRUARY

M	T	W	T	F	S	S
①	②	③	④	⑤	⑥	⑦
1	2	3	4	5	6	7
8	9	10	11	12	13	14
15	16	17	18	19	20	21
22	23	24	25	26	27	28
29	–	–	–	–	–	–

MARCH

M	T	W	T	F	S	S
①	②	③	④	⑤	⑥	⑦
–	1	2	3	4	5	6
7	8	9	10	11	12	13
14	15	16	17	18	19	20
21	22	23	24	25	26	27
28	29	30	31	–	–	–

APRIL

M	T	W	T	F	S	S
①	②	③	④	⑤	⑥	⑦
–	–	–	–	1	2	3
4	5	6	7	8	9	10
11	12	13	14	15	16	17
18	19	20	21	22	23	24
25	26	27	28	29	30	–

MAY

M	T	W	T	F	S	S
①	②	③	④	⑤	⑥	⑦
30	31	–	–	–	–	1
2	3	4	5	6	7	8
9	10	11	12	13	14	15
16	17	18	19	20	21	22
23	24	25	26	27	28	29

JUNE

M	T	W	T	F	S
①	②	③	④	⑤	⑥
–	–	1	2	3	4
6	7	8	9	10	11
13	14	15	16	17	18
20	21	22	23	24	25
27	28	29	30	–	–

JULY

M	T	W	T	F	S	S
①	②	③	④	⑤	⑥	⑦
–	–	–	–	1	2	3
4	5	6	7	8	9	10
11	12	13	14	15	16	17
18	19	20	21	22	23	24
25	26	27	28	29	30	31

AUGUST

M	T	W	T	F	S	S
①	②	③	④	⑤	⑥	⑦
1	2	3	4	5	6	7
8	9	10	11	12	13	14
15	16	17	18	19	20	21
22	23	24	25	26	27	28
29	30	31	–	–	–	–

SEPTEMBER

M	T	W	T	F	S	S
①	②	③	④	⑤	⑥	⑦
–	–	–	1	2	3	4
5	6	7	8	9	10	11
12	13	14	15	16	17	18
19	20	21	22	23	24	25
26	27	28	29	30	–	–

OCTOBER

M	T	W	T	F	S	S
①	②	③	④	⑤	⑥	⑦
31	–	–	–	–	1	2
3	4	5	6	7	8	9
10	11	12	13	14	15	16
17	18	19	20	21	22	23
24	25	26	27	28	29	30

NOVEMBER

M	T	W	T	F	S	S
①	②	③	④	⑤	⑥	⑦
–	1	2	3	4	5	6
7	8	9	10	11	12	13
14	15	16	17	18	19	20
21	22	23	24	25	26	27
28	29	30	–	–	–	–

DECEMBER

M	T	W	T	F	S
①	②	③	④	⑤	⑥
–	–	–	1	2	3
5	6	7	8	9	10
12	13	14	15	16	17
19	20	21	22	23	24
26	27	28	29	30	31

2017

JANUARY

M	T	W	T	F	S	S
①	②	③	④	⑤	⑥	⑦
30	31	–	–	–	–	1
2	3	4	5	6	7	8
9	10	11	12	13	14	15
16	17	18	19	20	21	22
23	24	25	26	27	28	29

FEBRUARY

M	T	W	T	F	S	S
①	②	③	④	⑤	⑥	⑦
–	–	1	2	3	4	5
6	7	8	9	10	11	12
13	14	15	16	17	18	19
20	21	22	23	24	25	26
27	28	–	–	–	–	–

MARCH

M	T	W	T	F	S	S
①	②	③	④	⑤	⑥	⑦
–	–	1	2	3	4	5
6	7	8	9	10	11	12
13	14	15	16	17	18	19
20	21	22	23	24	25	26
27	28	29	30	31	–	–

APRIL

M	T	W	T	F	S	S
①	②	③	④	⑤	⑥	⑦
–	–	–	–	–	1	2
3	4	5	6	7	8	9
10	11	12	13	14	15	16
17	18	19	20	21	22	23
24	25	26	27	28	29	30

MAY

M	T	W	T	F	S	S
①	②	③	④	⑤	⑥	⑦
1	2	3	4	5	6	7
8	9	10	11	12	13	14
15	16	17	18	19	20	21
22	23	24	25	26	27	28
29	30	31	–	–	–	–

JUNE

M	T	W	T	F	S
①	②	③	④	⑤	⑥
–	–	–	1	2	3
5	6	7	8	9	10
12	13	14	15	16	17
19	20	21	22	23	24
26	27	28	29	30	–

PUBLIC HOLIDAYS 2016

JOURS FÉRIÉS GIORNI FESTIVI FEIERTAGE DÍAS FESTIVOS

The dates given below are those of national public holidays. They do not include regional, half-day or unofficial holidays. Passengers intending to trav public holidays, or on days immediately preceding or following them, are strongly recommended to reserve seats and to confirm timings locally. Fu information regarding special transport conditions applying on holiday dates may be found in the introduction to each country.

Austria: Jan. 1, 6, Mar. 28, May 1, 5, 16, 26, Aug. 15, Oct. 26, Nov. 1, Dec. 8, 25, 26.

Belarus: Jan. 1, 7, Mar. 8, May 1, 9, 10, July 3, Nov. 7, Dec. 25.

Belgium: Jan. 1, Mar. 28, May 1, 5, 16, July 21, Aug. 15, Nov. 1, 11, Dec. 25.

Bosnia-Herzegovina: Jan. 1, 2, Mar. 1, May 1, 2, Nov. 25. *Other religious holidays are observed in certain areas.*

Bulgaria: Jan. 1, Mar. 3, Apr. 29, 30, May 1, 2, 6, 24, Sept. 6, 22, Dec. 24, 25, 26.

Croatia: Jan. 1, 6, Mar. 28, May 1, 26, June 22, 25, Aug. 5, 15, Oct. 8, Nov. 1, Dec. 25, 26.

Czech Republic: Jan. 1, Mar. 28, May 1, 8, July 5, 6, Sept. 28, Oct. 28, Nov. 17, Dec. 24, 25, 26.

Denmark: Jan. 1, Mar. 24, 25, 28, Apr. 22, May 5, 16, Dec. 25, 26.

Estonia: Jan. 1, Feb. 24, Mar. 25, May 1, June 23, 24, Aug. 20, Dec. 24, 25, 26.

Finland: Jan. 1, 6, Mar. 25, 28, May 1, 5, June 25, Nov. 5, Dec. 6, 25, 26.

France: Jan. 1, Mar. 28, May 1, 5, 8, 16, July 14, Aug. 15, Nov. 1, 11, Dec. 25.

Germany: Jan. 1, 6*, Mar. 25, 28, May 1, 5, 16, 26*, Aug. 15*, Oct. 3, 31*, Nov. 1*, 16*, Dec. 25, 26. ** Observed in certain regions: see also page 367.*

Great Britain: *England & Wales*: Jan. 1, Mar. 25, 28, May 2, 30, Aug. 29, Dec. 25, 26, 27. *Scotland*: Jan. 1, 4, Mar. 25, May 2, 30, Aug. 1, Dec. 25, 26, 27.

Greece: Jan. 1, 6, Mar. 14, 25, Apr. 29, May 1, 2, June 20, Aug. 15, Oct. 28, Dec. 25, 26.

Hungary: Jan. 1, Mar. 15, 28, May 1, 16, Aug. 20, Oct. 23, Nov. 1, Dec. 25, 26.

Iceland: Jan. 1, Mar. 24, 25, 28, Apr. 21, May 1, 5, 16, June 17, Aug. 1, Dec. 24, 25, 26, 31.

Ireland (Northern): Jan. 1, Mar. 17, 25, 28, May 2, 30, July 12, Aug. 29, Dec. 25, 26, 27.

Ireland (Republic): Jan. 1, Mar. 17, 28, May 2, June 6, Aug. 1, Oct. 31, Dec. 25, 26.

Italy: Jan. 1, 6, Mar. 28, Apr. 25, May 1, June 2, Aug. 15, Nov. 1, Dec. 8, 25, 26.

Latvia: Jan. 1, Mar. 25, 28, May 1, 2, 4, June 23, 24, Nov. 18, Dec. 24, 25, 26, 31.

Lithuania: Jan. 1, Feb. 16, Mar. 11, 28, May 1, June 24, July 6, Aug. 15, Nov. 1, Dec. 24, 25, 26.

Luxembourg: Jan. 1, Mar. 28, May 1, 5, 16, June 23, Aug. 15, Nov. 1, Dec. 25, 26.

Macedonia: Jan. 1, 7, May 1, 2, 24, Aug. 2, Sept. 8, Oct. 11, 23, Dec. 8. *Other religious holidays are observed in certain areas.*

Moldova: Jan. 1, 2, 7, 8, Mar. 8, May 1, 2, 9, Aug. 27, 31, Dec. 25.

Netherlands: Jan. 1, Mar. 28, Apr. 27, May 5, 16, Dec. 25, 26.

Norway: Jan. 1, Mar. 24, 25, 28, May 1, 5, 16, 17, Dec. 25, 26.

Poland: Jan. 1, 6, Mar. 28, May 1, 3, 26, Aug. 15, Nov. 1, 11, Dec. 25, 26.

Portugal: Jan. 1, Mar. 25, Apr. 25, May 1, June 10, Aug. 15, Dec. 8, 25.

Romania: Jan. 1, 2, 24, May 1, 2, June 20, Aug. 15, Nov. 30, Dec. 1, 25, 26.

Russia: Jan. 1, 4, 5, 6, 7, 8, Feb. 23, Mar. 8, May 2, 9, June 13, Nov. 4.

Serbia: Jan. 1, 2, 7, Feb. 15, 16, Apr. 29, 30, May 1, 2, Nov. 11.

Slovakia: Jan. 1, 6, Mar. 25, 28, May 1, 8, July 5 Aug. 29, Sept. 1, 15, Nov. 1, 17, Dec. 24, 25, 2

Slovenia: Jan. 1, Feb. 8, Mar. 28, Apr. 27, May June 25, Aug. 15, Oct. 25, 31, Nov. 1, Dec. 2

Spain: Jan. 1, 6, Mar. 19*, 24*, 25, 28*, May 1, 2* July 25*, Aug. 15, Oct. 12, Dec. 6*, 8, 25, 26*. *some local holidays. * Observed in certain reg*

Sweden: Jan. 1, 6, Mar. 25, 28, May 1, 5, June 6 Nov. 5, Dec. 25, 26.

Switzerland: Jan. 1, 2 •, 6 •, Mar. 19 •, Mar. 25* May 1 •, 5, 16*, 26 •, Aug. 1, 15 •, Nov. 1 •, Dec 25, 26*. *Also some local holidays.*
** Observed in most regions; • some regions.*

Turkey: Jan. 1, Apr. 23, May 1, 19, Aug. 30, Oc (also 2016 festival periods July 5 – 7, Sept. 12 -

Ukraine: Jan. 1, 7, 8, 9, Mar. 8, May 1, 2, 3, 9, Ju 20, 28, Aug. 24.

MOVABLE HOLIDAYS

Fêtes mobiles – Feste mobile
Bewegliche Feste – Fiestas movibles

	2016	2017
Good Friday	Mar. 25 •	Apr. 1
Easter Monday	Mar. 28 •	Apr. 1
Ascension Day	May 5 •	May 2
Whit Monday (Pentecost)	May 16 •	June
Corpus Christi	May 26	June

• *Five weeks later in the Orthodox calen*

TIME COMPARISON

COMPARAISON DES HEURES COMPARAZIONE DELLE ORE ZEITVERGLEICH COMPARACIÓN DE LAS HORAS

West European Time	*WINTER: GMT* *SUMMER: GMT +1*	Ireland Portugal United Kingdom	Iceland *(GMT all year)*
Central European Time	*WINTER: GMT +1* *SUMMER: GMT +2*	Albania, Austria, Belgium, Bosnia, Croatia, Czech Rep., Denmark, France, Germany, Hungary, Italy, Luxembourg, Macedonia, Malta, Montenegro, Netherlands, Norway, Poland, Serbia, Slovakia, Slovenia, Spain, Sweden, Switzerland	
East European Time	*WINTER: GMT +2* *SUMMER: GMT +3*	Bulgaria, Estonia, Finland, Greece, Latvia, Lithuania, Moldova, Romania, Turkey, Ukraine	Belarus *(GMT+3 all year)* Kaliningrad *(GMT+2 all year)* Western Russia *(GMT+3 all year)*

Daylight Saving Time ('Summer Time') applies between 0100 GMT on March 27 and 0100 GMT on October 30, 2016 *(GMT = Greenwich Mean Time = U*

Time comparison for countries which appear only in the shipping section are shown on page 542

What's new this month

ELCOME

come to our expanded Summer 2016 edition of the European Rail etable which includes updated schedules for most countries valid December 10. As always, there are a number of exceptions and ders are advised to consult individual country headings to confirm validity of timings in each section.

he front of this edition are an extra 24 pages (numbered i–xxiv) ch include useful country by country information on subjects such mbassies, tourist offices and public transport. Our full seven page passes feature will also be found in these pages.

well as the African and Middle Eastern Beyond Europe section on es 558 to 569, this edition also has an additional 72 pages, found at back of the timetable, containing all of the other Beyond Europe tions that are published throughout the year.

aders are reminded that, in addition to our regular printed timetable, e is now a digital version available for you to download onto your artphone, tablet, eBook and to view on your computer. Please ck our website for further information regarding this new way to ain the European Rail Timetable (www.europeanrailtimetable.eu).

JROPE BY RAIL

idea what it might be like to ride over the Lika Railway as it climbs ugh formidably barren terrain on its way to Split? Or what you ht see as you take the Torre del Oro Talgo train all the way from celona to Seville? You can find out in our brand new guide book, *ope by Rail: The Definitive Guide for Independent Travellers.* tten by Nicky Gardner and Susanne Kries, authors of our regular *ute of the Month* feature, this fourteenth edition of the much loved (previously published by Thomas Cook) has been entirely orked in a completely new format. Two sample page layouts of exciting new publication will be found on page 517.

OUTE OF THE MONTH

ky Gardner and Susanne Kries, our regular roving travel writers, the eastbound EuroCity service *Transalpin* at Feldkirch for a ctacular trip over the Arlberg route to Innsbruck. The description of ir journey will be found on page 35 and the latest timings for vices along the route are shown in Table **951**.

P OF THE MONTH

all groups of two to five people wishing to explore Austria on a dget by train can do so by investing in an *Einfach-Raus-Ticket*. In *Tip of the Month*, which will be found on page 36, Nicky and sanne offer some advice on how to use this popular product and o explain the restrictions that apply to it.

TERNATIONAL

ere are a couple of additional stops to report on trains between nce and Russia. Train **24/23** Paris – Moskva makes an extra stop at ernay (Table **24**) and train **18/17** Nice – Moskva calls additionally at l am See (Table **25**).

m July 9 to 24 *ICE* services between Amsterdan and Frankfurt are erted via Venlo and Mönchengladbach and amended timings are own in a special table on page 62. The overnight service between sterdam and Zürich / München is also affected during this period.

reported in the French entry below, the TGV Est high-speed line ension to Strasbourg is due to open on July 3 affecting services ween France and Germany. This month we have produced two sions of Table **30** (Paris - Frankfurt) and Table **32** (London - Paris - ttgart - München). A summary of the service until July 2 can be nd on page 68 whilst fully updated versions of Tables **30** and **32**, id from July 3, can be found on pages 64 and 65 respectively.

V services **9241**, **9245** and **9249** from Paris to Milano will leave the ench capital up to 60 minutes earlier until August 31 (Table **44**).

ring the summer season, *EC* **85** München – Bologna is extended to nini on Fridays and Saturdays with the return train, *EC* **84**, starting m Rimini on Saturdays and Sundays (Table **70**).

Mondays to Fridays from July 4 the Marseille to Milano *EC* service, erated by *Thello*, will run approximately four hours earlier (Table **90**). is change means that, on Mondays to Fridays, train **148/147** will no ger have a connection from London, but the earlier departure from arseille of train **146/147** will mean connections can be made at Milano for onward journeys to Venezia and Roma. Please note that the service on Saturdays and Sundays remains unchanged, as does the daily service in the opposite direction.

GREAT BRITAIN

Services operated by *Southeastern* are currently valid until August 27, after which services to London Charing Cross and London Cannon Street will be revised as work continues to upgrade the area around London Bridge station. Precise details of the service from August 28 are not yet available, but readers should be aware that all *Southeastern* services are subject to change, even those that do not pass through London Bridge (Tables **101** and **102**).

South West Trains has introduced a summer Saturday service from London Waterloo to Weymouth via Yeovil (Tables **113** and **139**).

Most journeys to and from stations on the Windermere branch now require a change of trains at Oxenholme (Table **158**).

Arriva Trains Wales has extended a number of its services between Manchester and North Wales to serve Manchester Airport (Table **160**).

On Mondays to Fridays *Virgin Trains East Coast* has added four additional through services in each direction between London and Edinburgh, achieved by extending services that previously ran only between London and Newcastle (Table **180**). This means there is now almost a half-hourly service between London and Edinburgh throughout the day.

FRANCE

Timings in the French section are generally valid until December 10 although there are a number of tables which are valid for a shorter period. These are clearly indicated in the applicable tables or at the top of the page.

The high-speed line extension to Strasbourg is due to open on July 3 and timings of most *TGV* services to and from Strasbourg will be altered. In the French section we have taken the decision to show the new timings in this edition and so readers intending travel up to July 2 are advised to consult the May edition. From July 3 the fastest journey time between Paris and Strasbourg will be just 1 hour 46 minutes. However, other journey times do vary considerably as a temporary single track section is currently in use.

Engineering work will affect services using the Lyon to Chambéry route until August 31. *TGV* services between Paris and Chambéry, Annecy and Milano that are routed via Lyon St Exupéry are retimed or cancelled during this period (Table **341**). The local service is completely recast from June 23 to August 31 with services diverted and journey times extended (Table **344**).

The 2016 European football championship takes place in France from June 10 to July 10 and during this period there may be alterations to certain *TGV* services and some additional trains will also be provided. Readers intending to travel in France during this period are advised to check their reservation for confirmed *TGV* timings.

SPAIN

We have received the proposed new timetable for the Lleida to La Pobla de Segur line (Table **655**) but unfortunately a start date had yet to be announced at the time of going to press. Therefore both versions of the timetable have been included on page 323.

The Madrid to Cadiz service increases to five daily trains with an additional journey on Thursdays, Fridays and Sundays during the summer season (Tables **660** and **671**).

Journey times on services between Madrid and Alacant and València have increased by a few minutes (Table **668**).

We understand that the engineering work taking place between Antequera-Santa Ana and Granada via Antequera-Ciudad will not now be completed by the end of June as originally planned. The amended timings, including bus replacement services, will now remain in place until further notice (Table **673**).

CONTINUED ON PAGE 34

EXPLANATION OF STANDARD SYMBOLS

	EXPLANATION OF SYMBOLS	*EXPLICATION DES SIGNES*	*DELUCIDAZIONE DEI SEGNI*	*ZEICHENERKLÄRUNG*	*EXPLICACIÓN DE LOS SIGNOS*
	SERVICES	**SERVICES**	**SERVIZI**	**DIENSTE**	**SERVICIOS**
12	Through service (1st and 2nd class seats)	Relation directe (places assises 1re et 2e classe)	Relazione diretta (con posti di 1a e 2a classe)	Direkte Verbindung (Sitzplätze 1. und 2. Klasse)	Relación directa (con asientos de 1a y 2a clase
	Sleeping car	Voiture-lits	Carrozza letti	Schlafwagen	Coche-camas
	Couchette car	Voiture-couchettes	Carrozza cuccette	Liegewagen	Coche-literas
✕	Restaurant car	Voiture-restaurant	Carrozza ristorante	Speisewagen	Coche-restaurante
	Snacks and drinks available *(see page 8)*	Voiture-bar ou vente ambulante *(voir page 8)*	Carrozza bar o servizio di buffet *(vedere pagina 8)*	Imbiss und Getränke im Zug *(siehe Seite 8)*	Servicio de cafeteria o bar móvil *(véase pág. 8)*
2	Second class only	Uniquement deuxième classe	Sola seconda classe	Nur zweite Klasse	Sólo segunda clase
	Bus or coach service	Service routier	Servizio automobilistico	Buslinie	Servicio de autobuses
	Shipping service	Service maritime	Servizio marittimo	Schifffahrtslinie	Servicio marítimo
	DAYS OF RUNNING	**JOURS DE CIRCULATION**	**GIORNI DI EFFETTUAZIONE**	**VERKEHRSTAGE**	**DÍAS DE CIRCULACIÓN**
⚒	Mondays to Saturdays except holidays*	Du lundi au samedi, sauf les fêtes*	Dal lunedì al sabato, salvo i giorni festivi*	Montag bis Samstag außer Feiertage*	De lunes a sábado, excepto festivos*
Ⓐ	Mondays to Fridays except holidays*	Du lundi au vendredi, sauf les fêtes*	Dal lunedì al venerdì, salvo i giorni festivi*	Montag bis Freitag außer Feiertage*	De lunes a viernes, excepto festivos*
Ⓑ	Daily except Saturdays	Tous les jours sauf les samedis	Giornalmente, salvo il sabato	Täglich außer Samstag	Diario excepto sábados
Ⓒ	Saturdays, Sundays and holidays*	Les samedis, dimanches et fêtes*	Sabato, domenica e giorni festivi*	Samstage, Sonn- und Feiertage*	Sábados, domingos y festivos*
†	Sundays and holidays*	Les dimanches et fêtes*	Domenica e giorni festivi*	Sonn- und Feiertage*	Domingos y festivos*
①②	Mondays, Tuesdays	Les lundis, mardis	Lunedì, martedì	Montag, Dienstag	Lunes, martes
③④	Wednesdays, Thurdays	Les mercredis, jeudis	Mercoledì, giovedì	Mittwoch, Donnerstag	Miércoles, jueves
⑤⑥	Fridays, Saturdays	Les vendredis, samedis	Venerdì, sabato	Freitag, Samstag	Viernes, sábados
⑦	Sundays	Les dimanches	Domenica	Sonntag	Domingos
①–④	Mondays to Thursdays	Des lundis aux jeudis	Dal lunedì al giovedì	Montag bis Donnerstag	De lunes a jueves
	OTHER SYMBOLS	**AUTRES SIGNES**	**ALTRI SIMBOLI**	**SONSTIGE SYMBOLE**	**OTROS SÍMBOLOS**
IC **29**	Train number (**bold figures** above train times)	Numéro du train (en **caractères gras** au-dessus de l'horaire du train)	Numero del treno (in **neretto** sopra gli orari del treno)	Zugnummer (über den Fahrplanzeiten in **fetter Schrift** gesetzt)	Número del tren (figura en **negrita** encima del horario del tren)
♦	See footnotes (listed by train number)	Renvoi aux notes données en bas de page (dans l'ordre numérique des trains)	Vedi in calce alla pagina l'annotazione corrispondente al numero del treno	Siehe die nach Zugnummern geordneten Fußnoten	Véase al pie de la página la nota correspondiente al número del tren
R	Reservation compulsory	Réservation obligatoire	Prenotazione obbligatoria	Reservierung erforderlich	Reserva obligatoria
	Frontier station	Gare frontalière	Stazione di frontiera	Grenzbahnhof	Estación fronteriza
✈	Airport	Aéroport	Aeroporto	Flughafen	Aeropuerto
|	Train does not stop	Sans arrêt	Il treno non ferma qui	Zug hält nicht	El tren no para aquí
—	Separates two trains in the same column between which no connection is possible	Sépare deux trains de la même colonne qui ne sont pas en correspondance	Separa due treni della stessa colonna che non sono in coincidenza	Trennt zwei in derselben Spalte angegebene Züge, zwischen denen kein Anschluß besteht	Separa dos trenes de la misma columna entre los cuales no hay enlace
→	Continued in later column	Suite dans une colonne à droite	Continuazione più avanti a destra	Fortsetzung weiter rechts	Continuación a la derecha
←	Continued from earlier column	Suite d'une colonne à gauche	Seguito di una colonna a sinistra	Fortsetzung von links	Continuación desde la izquierda
v.v.	Vice versa	Vice versa	Viceversa	Umgekehrt	A la inversa
	** Public holiday dates for each country are given on page 2.*	** Les dates des fêtes légales nationales sont données en page 2.*	** Per le date dei giorni festivi civili nei diversi paesi vedere pagina 2.*	** Gesetzlichen Feiertage der jeweiligen Länder finden Sie auf Seite 2.*	** Las fechas de los días festivos en cada país figuran en la página 2.*
	Other, special symbols are explained in table footnotes or in the introduction to each country.	*D'autres signes particuliers sont expliqués dans les notes ou bien dans l'avant-propos relatif à chaque pays.*	*Altri segni particolari vengono spiegati nelle note in calce ai quadri o nella introduzione attinente a ogni paese.*	*Besondere Symbole sind in den Fußnoten bzw. in der Einleitung zu den einzelnen Ländern erklärt.*	*La explicación de otros signos particulares se da en las notas o en el preámbulo correspondiente a cada país.*

For explanation of train types (AP, IC, TGV etc) see the introduction to each country section

at is the European Rail Timetable?

European Rail Timetable is a concise guide to rail and ferry schedules ghout Europe, and even includes each month an area of the world de Europe. Needless to say, it cannot be comprehensive (it would run into sands of pages), but through our knowledge and experience, together with ble feedback from our readers, we can select those services which we ve will satisfy the needs of most travellers.

en do the services change?

e is a major annual timetable change in mid-December affecting almost all pean countries, with many countries having a second change in mid- . There are, of course, exceptions. For example, the British summer able starts in late May, Sweden changes again in mid-August, whilst ia and the other CIS countries have their main change at the end of May. v holiday areas also have separate timetables for the high-summer period, cularly areas of France and Italy. In fact, changes can happen at any time ar, and railways issue amendments either on set dates or as and when ssary. Engineering work also causes frequent changes, and shipping dules can change at any time.

w are the trains selected for inclusion?

ple travel for many reasons, whether for leisure, business, sightseeing, ng friends or relations, or just for the fun of it, and there are no hard and rules for selecting the services that we show. Naturally, major towns and -city services are shown as a matter of course, but the level of smaller es and local trains shown will depend on the country and even the area. urprising just how many minor lines we manage to squeeze in! Generally vill show a greater number of local trains in areas which are popular tourist nations or where other services are sparse.

not possible to show suburban trains within cities or conurbations, or most -suburban routes to places close to large cities. However, where there places of particular interest or importance in this category we do try to v brief details of frequency and journey time.

When should I use the International section?

The rail tables are divided into two sections - International (Tables **9** to **99**) and Country by Country (Tables **100** upwards). For some international services between adjacent countries (for example Stockholm - Oslo or Hamburg - Århus) it is necessary to use the relevant Country tables - the index or maps will guide you. Local trains which cross international frontiers will usually only be found in the Country sections.

Some international trains also carry passengers internally within each country and will therefore be found in the Country tables as well as the International section. Some services are primarily for international travel and will therefore only be found in the International section - this includes *Eurostar* trains (London - Paris/Brussels) and *Thalys* services (Paris - Brussels - Amsterdam/ Köln), as well as certain long-distance night trains.

What about places outside Europe?

The European Rail Timetable includes the whole of Turkey and Russia. Furthermore, our **Beyond Europe** section at the back of each edition features timetables from different areas of the world each month. Eight areas are covered, each appearing at least twice a year as follows: **India** (Jan/July), **South East Asia, Australia, New Zealand** (Feb/Aug), **China** (March/Sept), **Japan** (April/Oct), **South America** (April/Oct), **North America** (May/Nov), **South Korea** (May/Nov) and **Africa and the Middle East** (June/Dec). In our expanded June and December editions we include all eight of the latest Beyond Europe sections.

What else does it contain?

A summary of international sleeper services will be found on page 33, listing types of accommodation, operators and facilities on board.

We also include a summary of European rail passes (see the list of contents on page 1 for its current location) with a more detailed version appearing in our expanded June and December editions.

Each month a different rail journey is described in our *Route of the Month* feature, written by Nicky Gardner and Susanne Kries, editors of Hidden Europe magazine. They also offer useful information in our *Tip of the Month*.

Our timetables and other products may be purchased from our website **www.europeanrailtimetable.eu**.

HOW TO USE THE TIMETABLE

Using the index

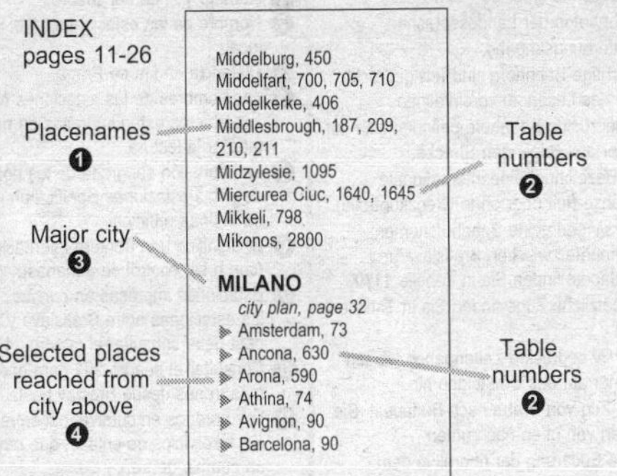

Look up the two places between which you are travelling. It can often be helpful to start your search from the *smaller* of the two locations. ❺

Using the maps

The maps can be the quickest way of finding the required table number, if you already know the geographical location of the places required. ❿

MMENT TROUVER VOTRE TRAIN

❶ ocalité.
❷ Numéros des tableaux.
❸ Grande ville.
❹ Localités sélectionnées à gagner de la grande ville en haut.
❺ Cherchez les deux bouts du parcours désiré sur la liste des villes. Commencer par la ville de moindre importance peut faciliter la recherche.
❻ Ligne principale.
❼ Ligne secondaire.
❽ Ligne à grande vitesse.
❾ Liaison en autocar.
❿ La consultation des cartes – si vous savez déjà la location géographique de vos points de départ et d'arrivée – est e moyen le plus rapide de repérer les numéros des tableaux relatifs à votre parcours.

COME TROVARE IL VOSTRO TRENO

❶ Località.
❷ Numeri dei quadri-orario.
❸ Grandi città.
❹ Principali destinazione raggiungibili dalla località in neretto sopra.
❺ Cercate le localita' tra le quali dovrete viaggiare; spesso può essere di aiuto iniziare la ricerca dalla località più piccola.
❻ Principale linea ferroviaria.
❼ Linea ferroviaria secondaria.
❽ Linea ad alta velocità.
❾ Autobus.
❿ Le mappe sono il metodo più rapido per trovare i numeri dei quadri-orario di cui avete bisogno, quando gia' siete a conoscenza della collocazione geografica delle localita' di partenza e arrivo del vostro viaggio.

WIE FINDE ICH MEINEN ZUG?

❶ Ortsname.
❷ Tabellennummer.
❸ Großstadt.
❹ Knotenpunkte erreichbar von der Großstadt oben.
❺ Suchen Sie Ihre Start- und Endbahnhof im Ortsverzeichnis. Dazu empfehlen wir, Ihre Suche aus der Richtung des *kleineren* Ortes aufzunehmen.
❻ Hauptstrecke.
❼ Nebenstrecke.
❽ Hochgeschwindigkeitsstrecke.
❾ Busverbindung.
❿ Kennen Sie die geographische Lage der Ausgangs- und Bestimmungsorte Ihrer Reise, dann empfehlen wir einen Blick in die im Kursbuch enthaltene Übersichtskarte.

COMO BUSCAR SU TREN

❶ Localidad.
❷ Números de los cuadros horarios.
❸ Gran ciudad.
❹ Principales destinos accesibles a través de esta localidad.
❺ Busque los dos lugares a través de los cuales viaja. Normalmente facilita la búsqueda empezar por la localidad más pequeña.
❻ Línea principal.
❼ Línea secundaria.
❽ Línea de alta velocidad.
❾ Línea de autobuses.
❿ Los mapas pueden ser la forma más rápida de encontrar los cuadros que debe consultar, si ya conoce el punto de inicio y conclusión de su viaje.

Numbers in circles refer to translations below

Reading the tables

Trains run daily unless otherwise shown by symbol or footnote

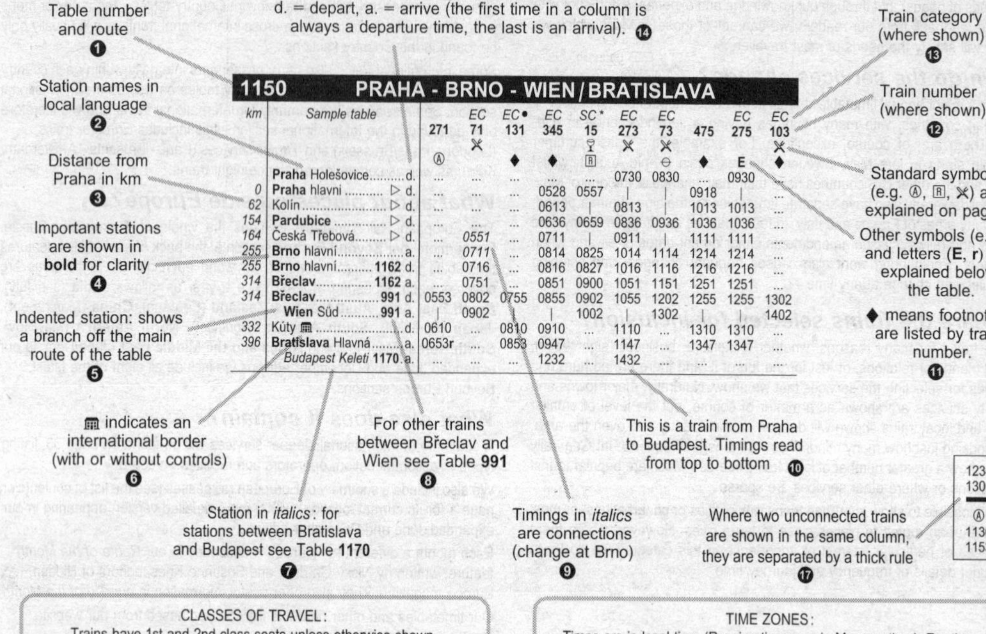

Table number and route ❶
Station names in local language ❷
Distance from Praha in km ❸
Important stations are shown in **bold** for clarity ❹
Indented station: shows a branch off the main route of the table ❺
🏢 indicates an international border (with or without controls) ❻
Station in *italics*: for stations between Bratislava and Budapest see Table **1170** ❼
For other trains between Břeclav and Wien see Table **991** ❽
Timings in *italics* are connections (change at Brno) ❾
This is a train from Praha to Budapest. Timings read from top to bottom ❿
d. = depart, a. = arrive (the first time in a column is always a departure time, the last is an arrival). ⓮
Train category (where shown) ⓭
Train number (where shown) ⓬
Standard symbols (e.g. Ⓐ, 🅁, ✕) are explained on page
Other symbols (e.g. and letters (**E**, **r**) a explained below the table.
♦ means footnote are listed by train number. ⓫
Where two unconnected trains are shown in the same column, they are separated by a thick rule ⓱
1234
1306
Ⓐ
1130
1153

1150 PRAHA - BRNO - WIEN / BRATISLAVA

km	*Sample table*		*EC*	*EC*•	*EC*	*SC**	*EC*	*EC*		*EC*	*EC*
		271	**71**	**131**	**345**	**15**	**273**	**73**	**475**	**275**	**103**
			✕			🍷	✕	✕			✕
		Ⓐ		♦	♦	🅁		⊖	♦	**E**	♦
	Praha Holešovice.......... d.	...	...	...	...	...	0730	0830	...	0930	...
0	**Praha** hlavni .... ▷ d.	...	...	...	0528	0557	|	|	0918	|	...
62	Kolín .... ▷ d.	...	...	...	0613	|	0813	|	1013	1013	...
154	**Pardubice** .... ▷ d.	...	...	...	0636	0659	0836	0936	1036	1036	...
164	Česká Třebová......... ▷ d.	...	*0551*	...	0711	|	0911	|	1111	1111	...
255	**Brno** hlavní.................. a.	...	*0711*	...	0814	0825	1014	1114	1214	1214	...
255	**Brno** hlavní.......... **1162** d.	...	0716	...	0816	0827	1016	1116	1216	1216	...
314	**Břeclav**............... **1162** a.	...	0751	...	0851	0900	1051	1151	1251	1251	...
314	**Břeclav**................. **991** d.	0553	0802	0755	0855	0902	1055	1202	1255	1255	1302
	Wien Süd .... **991** a.	|	0902	|	|	1002	|	1302	|	|	1402
332	Kúty 🏢 ....d.	0610	...	0810	0910	...	1110	...	1310	1310	...
396	**Bratislava** Hlavná.........a.	0653**r**	...	0853	0947	...	1147	...	1347	1347	...
	Budapest Keleti **1170**.a.	...	...	...	1232	...	1432	...	...	...	...

CLASSES OF TRAVEL:
Trains have 1st and 2nd class seats unless otherwise shown.
However, local trains may only have 2nd class seats. ⓯

TIME ZONES:
Times are in local time (Russian times are in Moscow time). For time zones see page 2. Timings are given in 24 hour clock (see page 9). ⓰

COMMENT LIRE LES TABLEAUX

❶ Numéro et parcours du tableau.
❷ Nom de la gare en langue locale.
❸ La distance en km de Praha.
❹ Les noms de gares importantes sont imprimés en **gras** pour faciliter la lecture.
❺ La mise en retrait des noms de gares indique une ligne d'embranchement.
❻ 🏢 indique une frontière internationale (avec ou sans le contrôle).
❼ Les noms de gares imprimés en *italique*: vous trouverez des gares sur le trajet Bratislava - Budapest en consultant le tableau **1170**.
❽ Consultez le tableau **991** pour trouver des trains supplémentaires de Břeclav à Wien.
❾ Les heures en *italique* indiquent une *correspondance* et supposent dans tous les cas un changement de train.
❿ Ici un train de Praha à Budapest. Lire de haut en bas.
⓫ Les signes conventionnels sont expliqués à la page 4. Les autres signes et lettres sont expliqués en bas du tableau. Le symbole ♦ à l'en-tête d'une colonne signifie qu'il faut consulter le note qui porte le numéro du train concerné.
⓬ Le numéro du train (en cas échéant).
⓭ Indication de catégorie (en cas échéant).
⓮ d. = départ, a. = arrivée. Pour chaque train la *première* mention est toujours une heure de *départ*, la *dernière* toujours une heure d'*arrivée*.
⓯ Sauf indication contraire, les trains circulent *tous les jours* et y compris des places assises de 1ère et 2ème classe.
⓰ Toutes les indications horaires sont données en heures locales (voir page 2). En Russie c'est à l'heure Moskva.
⓱ Deux trains de la même colonne qui ne sont pas en correspondance sont separés par une règle épaisse:

COME SI CONSULTA UN QUADRO ORARIO

❶ Numero del quadro e percorso.
❷ Nome della stazione nella lingua locale.
❸ Distanze in km da Praha.
❹ I nomi delle stazioni piu' importante sono stampati in **neretto** per renderne più facile la lettura.
❺ I nomi delle stazioni rientrati rispetto alla colonna principale indicano una diramazione dal percorso principale del quadro-orario in questione.
❻ 🏢 indica una stazione di confine (con o senza controllo).
❼ Stazioni in *corsivo*: per gli orari tra le stazione di Bratislava e Budapest bisogna consultare il quadro **1170**.
❽ Consultare il quadro **991** per ulteriori treni da Břeclav a Wien.
❾ Gli orari *in corsivo* si riferiscono a servizi *in coincidenza* che implicano un cambio di treno.
❿ Questo e' un treno da Praha a Budapest. La lettura viene fatta dall'alto verso il basso.
⓫ I simboli convenzionali sono spiegate a pagina 4. Altri simboli e lettere sono spiegati sotto il quadro-orario in questione. Il simbolo ♦ all'inizio di una colonna-orario significa che bisogna fare riferimento alla nota corrispondente al numero del treno in questione.
⓬ Numero del treno (quando indicato).
⓭ Classificazione del treno (quando indicato).
⓮ d. = partenza, a. = arrivo. Notare che l'orario che compare per *primo* nel quadro-orario è sempre un l'orario di *partenza*, mentre quello che compare per *ultimo* è sempre l'orario di *arrivo*.
⓯ Se non ci sono altre indicazioni i treni si intendono giornalieri, con prima e seconda classe di viaggio.
⓰ Gli orari sono sempre espressi in ora locale (in Russia e' utilizzati l'ora di Mosca). Per informazioni sui fusi orari vedere a pagina 2.
⓱ Quando nella colonna-orario ci sono due treni che non sono in coincidenza tra loro, questo e' indicato dalla linea in grassetto che li separa.

WIE LESE ICH DIE FAHRPLÄNE

❶ Tabellennummer und Strecke.
❷ Bahnhof in der Landessprache.
❸ Entfernungsangabe.
❹ Wichtige Bahnhöfe sind **fett** gedruckt um das Lesen zu vereinfachen.
❺ Eingerückte Bahnhöfe befinden sich auf einer abzweigenden Strecke.
❻ 🏢 Bezeichnet eine internationale Grenze (mit oder ohne Grenzkontrolle).
❼ *Kursiv* gedruckte Bahnhofsnamen: Bahnhöfe zwischen Bratislava und Budapest finden Sie in Tabelle **1170**.
❽ Zusätzliche Züge finden Sie in Tabelle **991**.
❾ *Kursiv* gedruckte Zeitangaben weisen immer auf das Umsteigen hin.
❿ Ein Zug von Praha nach Budapest. Sie lesen von oben nach unten.
⓫ Eine Erklärung der überall in dem Kursbuch verwendeten konventionellen Zeichen finden Sie auf Seite 4. Anderen Zeichen und Buchstaben finden Sie unter der Fahrplantabelle. Das Zeichen ♦ im Kopf der Zugspalte bedeutet: Sehen Sie bei der Fußnote des Zuges mit der betreffenden Zugnummer nach.
⓬ Zugnummer (wo zutreffend).
⓭ Zuggattung (wo zutreffend).
⓮ d. = Abfahrt, a. = Ankunft. Es handelt sich stets bei der ersten für einen Zug angegebenen Zeit um eine Abfahrtzeit, bei der letzten um eine Ankunftzeit.
⓯ Sofern nicht anders angemeldet, verkehren die Züge *täglich*. Im Allgemeinen führen die Züge die 1. und 2. Wagenklasse.
⓰ Fahrzeiten sind immer in der jeweiligen Landeszeit angegeben (Seite 2). Russische Fahrzeiten sind auf Moskauer Zeit.
⓱ Im Falle von zwei Züge in der gleichen Spalte ohne Anschlussmöglichkeit, liegt das Zeichen ▬ zwischen den Zügen.

COMO LEER LOS CUADROS

❶ Número y línea del cuadro.
❷ Nombre de las estaciones en el idi local.
❸ Distancia en km de Praga.
❹ Los nombres de las estaciones má importantes están impresas en neg facilitar la lectura.
❺ La impresión sangrada de los nom de estas estaciones significa un ra de la línea principal.
❻ 🏢 significa una frontera internacior (con o sin control de aduanas).
❼ Estaciones impresas en *cursiva*: pa las estaciones entre Bratislava y Bu pest debe consultar el cuadro **1170**
❽ Consultar el cuadro **991** para enco más trenes desde Břeclav hasta Vi
❾ Los horarios en cursiva, hacen refe cia a servicios de enlace, que requ un cambio de tren.
❿ Esto un tren desde Praga hasta Bu pest. Leer de arriba a abajo.
⓫ La explicación de los signos convencionales se da en la página Ostros símbolos y letras se explica pie del cuadro. El símbolo ♦ en el encabezamiento de la columna qui decir: consulte la nota que lleva el número del tren interesado.
⓬ Número de tren (si se indica).
⓭ Tipo de tren (si se indica).
⓮ d. = salida, a. = llegada. Nótese que primer horario indicado en las colur es siempre un horario de salida, y e último un horario de llegada.
⓯ Salvo indicación contraria, los trene circulan a *diario* y llevan plazas sentadas de primera y segunda cla
⓰ Todas las indicaciones horarias sor horario local (Para Rusia se utiliza hora local de Moscú). Para compro las franjas horarias mirar la página Los horarios utilizan el sistema hora de 24h (ver página 9).
⓱ Cuando dos trenes que no tienen conexión aparecen en la misma columna, estos se encuentran sepa dos por el símbolo ▬.

Reading the footnotes

These footnotes relate to the sample table on page 6 ❶

In certain tables, footnotes are listed by train number, shown by ♦ on relevant trains ❷

♦ – **NOTES** (LISTED BY TRAIN NUMBERS)

102/3 – POLONIA – [12] ✕ Warszawa - Ostrava - Břeclav - Wien and v.v.

131 – MORAVIA – [12] Bohumin - Ostrava - Břeclav - Bratislava.

345 – AVALA – [12] ✕ Praha - Bratislava - Budapest - Beograd. Conveys on ⑤ June 12 - Sept. 18 ▬ 2 cl. Praha - Beograd (**335**) - Thessaloniki.

475 – JADRAN – June 19 - Sept. 4. 🛏 1, 2 cl., ▬ 2 cl., [2] Praha - Bratislava - Zagreb - Split (Table **92**); [12] Praha - Bratislava.

E – SLOVAN, not June 19 - Sept. 4.

r – 0659 on ©.

▷ – See also Table **1160**.

⊖ – Runs 10 mins later on Aug. 15.

• – *Ex* in Slovakia.

* – Pendolino tilting train. Classified *EC* in Austria.

OTHER TRAIN NAMES:

71 – GUSTAV MAHLER

73 – FRANZ SCHUBERT

Letters and symbols may be found above the timings (e.g. **E**) or against individual times (e.g. **r**). Symbols may also appear in the station column (e.g. ▷). ❻

Train names are sometimes listed separately. ❺

Train **345** is named 'AVALA' and runs daily from Praha to Beograd with 1st and 2nd class seats and a restaurant car. On Fridays June 12 to September 18, a through couchette car runs from Praha to Thessaloniki, attached to train **335** between Beograd and Thessaloniki. ❸

Train **475** is named 'JADRAN' and runs only from June 19 to September 4. It has a sleeper, couchettes and second class seats from Praha to Split via Bratislava and Zagreb, as well as first and second class seats only going as far as Bratislava. Further details will be found in Table **92**. ❹

Always read the footnotes; they may contain important information. Standard symbols are explained on page 4. ❼

Dates shown are where a train **starts** its journey (unless otherwise noted). Some notes show both directions of the train (e.g. **102/3**) with "and v.v." ❽

FURTHER HINTS ON READING THE TIMETABLE

Refer to the introduction to each country for important information such as train types, supplements, compulsory reservation, and the dates of validity of the timings. Exceptions are noted in individual tables.

For dates of public holidays see page 2.

- Please allow adequate time for changing trains, especially at large stations. Connections are not guaranteed, especially when late running occurs (connecting trains are sometimes held for late running trains).
- A Glossary of common terms appears on page 10.

LES NOTES EN BAS DU TABLEAU

Ces notes se rapportent au example de tableau à la page 6.

Dans certains tableaux, le symbole ♦ à l'en-tête d'une colonne signifie qu'il faut consulter le note qui porte le numéro du train concerné.

Le train **345** s'appelle AVALA et circule tous les jours de Praha à Beograd avec des places assises de 1ère et 2ème classe et une voiture-restaurant. Tous les vendredis du 12 juin jusqu'au 18 sept il y a aussi une voiture-couchettes de Praha à Thessaloniki, qui se joint au train **335** entre Beograd et Thessaloniki.

Le train **475** s'appelle JADRAN et circule seulement entre le 19 juin et le 4 septembre. Il compris des voitures-lits, couchettes et places assises de 2ème classe à Split via Zagreb, et des places assises de 1ère et 2ème classe jusqu'à Bratislava. Voir le tableau **92**.

Les noms des trains sont parfois indiqués séparément.

Les lettres et signes sont situés à l'en-tête d'une colonne ou à côté d'une heure dans la colonne. Une signe peut sortir également a côté d'un nom de gare.

Les notes peuvent vous donner des informations importantes. Les signes conventionnels sont expliqués à la page 4.

Sauf indication contraire, les jours et dates de circulation mentionnés sont ceux applicables à la *gare d'origine* du train (mentionnée si elle ne figure pas sur le tableau même dans les notes). Les notes peuvent expliquer les deux sens d'un train (e.g. **102/3**) utilisant "and v.v." (et vice versa).

JS DE CONSEILS

Il vous est fortement recommandé de consulter aussi l'introduction à chaque section nationale: vous y trouverez des précisions concernant la classification des trains, les prestations offertes à bord des trains, les suppléments, la réservation des places, etc.

Jours fériés - voir page 2.

Aucune correspondance n'est garantie pourtant. N'oubliez pas non plus que dans les grandes gares les changements peuvent entraîner une longue marche et l'emprunt d'escaliers.

Lexique - voir page 10.

NOTE ALLA FINE DEL QUADRO-ORARIO

❶ Queste note si riferiscono all' esempio a pagina 6.

❷ In certi quadri-orario, il simbolo ♦ nelle note di testa significa che bisogna fare riferimento alla nota con il numero di treno corrispondente.

❸ Il treno **345** si chiama AVALA ed e' giornaliero tra Praha e Beograd con posti di 1ª e 2ª classe e carrozza ristorante. Il venerdi dal 12 giugno fino al 18 settembre e' aggiunta a Beograd una carrozza cuccette diretta a Thessaloniki, combinandosi con il treno **335** tra Beograd e Thessaloniki.

❹ Il treno **475** si chiama JADRAN ed e' operativo solo dal 19 giugno al 4 settembre. Il treno si compone di carrozze letti, carrozze cuccette, e posti di 2ª classe tra Praha e Split, via Bratislava e Zagrabria; inoltre ci sono anche posti di 1ª e 2ª classe fino a Bratislava. Consultare anche il quadro-orario **92** al riguardo

❺ I nomi dei treni sono talvolta indicati separatamente.

❻ Lettere e simboli possono essere sia alla testa di una colonna-orario, che accanto all'orario del treno stesso. Un simbolo potrebbe anche essere accanto al nome di una stazione.

❼ E' importante leggere sempre le note a le informazioni a fine quadro. I segni convenzionali sono elencati e spiegati a pagina 4.

❽ Salvo casi in cui sia diversamente indicato, le date di circolazione dei treni si riferiscono sempre alla stazione dove il treno inizia il suo viaggio (come viene riportato nelle note a fine quadro, e Inoltre nel quadro stesso).

ALTRI CONSIGLI UTILI

- Vi consigliamo vivamente di consultare anche l'introduzione dedicata ad ogni nazione. Troverete importanti informazioni riguardanti i servizi di trasporto di ciascun paese, così come le categorie dei treni, la ristorazione, il pagamento di supplementi, le necessità di prenotazione, ecc.
- I giorni festivi suddivisi per paese sono elencati a pagina 2.
- Le coincidenze indicate non sono garantite. Tenete presente che che nelle grandi stazioni il trasferimento tra due binari potrebbe significare un lungo tratto da percorrere a piedi e con l'uso di scale.
- Il glossario si trova a pagina 10.

FUSSNOTEN

❶ Fußnoten beziehen sich auf die Beispieltabelle auf Seite 6.

❷ ♦: Sehen Sie bei der Fußnote des Zuges mit der betreffenden Zugnummer nach.

❸ Zug **345** heißt AVALA und fährt täglich zwischen Praha und Beograd mit Sitzplätzen 1. und 2. Klasse. An Freitagen vom 12. Juni bis 18. September führt dieser Zug durchgehende Liegewagen von Praha nach Thessaloniki (mit Zug **335** vereinigt von Beograd nach Thessaloniki).

❹ Zug **475** heißt JADRAN und fährt nur von 19. Juni bis 4. September. Er führt Schlaf-, Liege und Sitzwagen 2. Klasse von Praha nach Split über Zagreb, auch Sitzwagen 1. und 2. Klasse, die nur bis Bratislava fahren. Auf Tabelle **92** finden Sie weitere Informationen.

❺ Zugnamen können besonders aufgeführt sein.

❻ Zeichen und Buchstaben finden sich im Kopf der Zugspalte oder neben einer bestimmten Zeitangabe. Zeichen sind auch in der Bahnhofsspalte möglich.

❼ In Fußnoten findet man wichtige Informationen. Standardzeichen sind auf Seite 4 erklärt.

❽ Die erwähnten Tage und Zeitabschnitte für Züge, die nicht täglich verkehren, gelten für den Ausgangsbahnhof des Zuges (wenn dieser nicht in der Tabelle steht, ist er in einer Fußnote erwähnt). Fußnoten dürfen beide Richtungen erklären (z.B. **102/3**), mit "and v.v." (und umgekehrt).

WEITERE HINWEISE

- Es ist zu empfehlen, die Einleitungen zu jedem einzelnen Land zu lesen. Darin werden Sie wichtige Informationen über die Besonderheiten jedes Landes finden: Zugcharakterisierung, Services an Bord der Züge, Zuschlagpflicht, Reservierungsbedingungen usw.
- Feiertage - siehe Seite 2.
- Anschlussversäumnisse durch Verspätung oder Ausfall von Zügen sind immer möglich. Bitte beachten Sie, dass auf Großstadtbahnhöfen häufig längere Fußwege zurückgelegt bzw. Treppen benutzen werden müssen.
- Glossar - siehe Seite 10.

LAS NOTAS AL PIE DEL CUADRO

❶ Estas notas hacen referencia al ejemplo de la página 6.

❷ El símbolo ♦ ciertas tablas horarias significa: que hay que consultar la nota a pie de página con el número correspondiente.

❸ El Tren **345** se llama AVALA y circula a diario entre Praga y Belgrado con plazas sentadas de 1ra y 2da clase, además de con coche-restaurante. Los Viernes del 12 de junio al 18 de septiembre el tren lleva coches litera desde Praga hasta Tesalónica que se combinan con el tren **335** entre Belgrado y Tesalónica.

❹ El Tren **475** se llama JADRAN y circula solamente del 19 de junio al 4 de septiembre. El Tren **475** se llama JADRAN y circula solamente del 19 de junio al 4 de sept. El tren dispone de lleva vagones de coches cama, litera, y plazas sentadas de 2da clase entre Praga y Split a través de Zagreb, también plazas sentadas de 1ra y 2da clase hasta Bratislava. Consulte el cuadro **92**.

❺ Los nombres de los Trenes a veces son enumerados por separado.

❻ Las letras y signos se encuentran en el encabezamiento de las distintas columnas horarias o adyacentes a horas de salida individuales. Los símbolos también pueden aparecer en la columna de la estación.

❼ Lea siempre las notas a pie de cuadro ya que pueden contener información importante. La explicación de los signos convencionales se da en la página 4.

❽ Salvo indicación contraria los días y fechas de circulación de los trenes son aquéllos mencionados en la estación de *origen* del tren. Algunas notas muestran ambas direcciones del tren mediante la nota "and v.v." (y viceversa).

INFORMACIÓN ADICIONAL

- Se recomienda vivamente que consulte también los preámbulos al comienzo de cada sección nacional: le proporcionarán datos importantes sobre las particularidades de cada pais: tipos de trenes, restauración, pago de suplementos, y necesidades de reservación anticipada.
- Días festivos - cunsulte la página 2.
- Los trasbordos no se pueden garantizar, sobretodo en el caso de retrasos. Hay que ser consciente también que el trasbordo en las estaciones de grandes ciudades puede suponer un desplazamiento bastante largo a pie y el uso de escaleras.
- Glosario - cunsulte la página 10.

The following is designed to be an outline guide to travelling around Europe by train. For further details of types of accommodation available, catering, supplements etc., see the introduction to each country.

BUYING YOUR TICKET

Train tickets must be purchased before travelling, either from travel agents or at the station ticket office (or machine). Where a station has neither a ticket office nor a ticket machine, the ticket may usually be purchased on the train.

Tickets which are not dated when purchased (for example in France and Italy) must be validated before travel in one of the machines at the entrance to the platform.

In certain Eastern European countries foreign nationals may have to buy international rail tickets at the office of the state tourist board concerned and not at the railway station. The tickets can sometimes only be purchased in western currency and buying tickets can take a long time.

Most countries in Europe offer two classes of rail accommodation, usually 1st and 2nd class. 1st class is more comfortable and therefore more expensive than 2nd class. Local trains are often 2nd class only. In Southern and Eastern Europe, 1st class travel is advisable for visitors as fares are reasonable and 2nd class can be very overcrowded.

RESERVATIONS

Many express trains in Europe are restricted to passengers holding advance seat reservations, particularly in France, Italy, Sweden and Spain. This is indicated by the symbol R in the tables, or by notes in the introduction to each country. All *TGV*, *Eurostar* and *Thalys* trains require advance reservation, as do all long-distance trains in Spain.

Reservations can usually be made up to two months in advance. A small fee is charged, but where a supplement is payable the reservation fee is often included. Reservations can often be made on other long-distance services and this is recommended at busy times.

SUPPLEMENTS

Many countries have faster or more luxurious train services for which an extra charge is made. This supplement is payable when the ticket is purchased and often includes the price of a seat reservation. The supplement can sometimes be paid on the train, but usually at extra cost. The introduction to each country gives further information. On certain high-speed services, the first class fare includes the provision of a meal.

RAIL PASSES

Passes are available which give unlimited travel on most trains in a given area. These range from InterRail and Eurail passes which cover most of Europe for up to one month, to local passes which cover limited areas for one day. Further details of InterRail and Eurail passes appear elsewhere in this edition, and a special feature on rail passes appears in the twice-yearly Independent Travellers Edition.

FINDING YOUR TRAIN

At most stations departures are listed on large paper sheets (often yellow), and/or on electronic departure indicators. These list trains by departure, giving principal stops, and indicate from which platform they leave.

On each platform of principal European stations, a display board can be found giving details of the main trains calling at that platform. This includes the location of individual coaches, together with their destinations and the type of accommodation provided.

A sign may be carried on the side of the carriage indicating the train name, principal stops and destination and a label or sign near the door will indicate the number allocated to the carriage, which is shown on reservation tickets. 1st class accommodation is usually indicated by a yellow band above the windows and doors and/or a figure '1' near the door or on the windows

A sign above the compartment door will indicate seat numbers and which seats are reserved. In non-compartment trains, reserved seats have labels on their headrests. In some countries reserved seats are not marked and occupants will be asked to move when the passenger who has reserved the seat boards the train.

LUGGAGE & BICYCLES

Luggage may be registered at many larger stations and sent separately by rail to your destination. In some countries, bicycles may also be registered in advance and certain local and some express trains will convey bicycles (there may be a charge). The relevant railways will advise exact details on request.

✕ CATERING 🍸

Many high-quality and long-distance trains in Europe have restaurant cars serving full meals, usually with waiter service. An at-seat service may also be provided to passengers in first class accommodation. Such trains are identified with the symbol ✕ in the tables. Full meals may only be available at set times, sometimes with separate sittings, and may only be available to passengers holding first class tickets. However, the restaurant car is often supplemented by a counter or trolley service offering light snacks and drinks.

Other types of catering are shown with the symbol 🍸. This varies from a self-service buffet car serving light meals (sometimes called bistro or café) to a trolley which is wheeled through the train, serving drinks and light refreshments. Where possible, the introduction to each country gives further information on the level of catering to be expected on particular types of train.

Please note that the catering shown may not be available throughout the journey and may be suspended or altered at weekends or on holidays.

SLEEPING CARS

Sleeping cars are indicated by the symobol in the tables. Stan sleeping car types have bedroom style compartments with limited was facilities and full bedding. Toilets are located at one or both ends of the cc An attendant travels with each car or pair of cars and will serve drinks, sn and breakfast at an extra charge. 1st class sleeping compartments have or two berths (in Britain and Norway, and in older Swedish sleeping cars, berth compartments require only 2nd class tickets) and 2nd class com ments have three berths. Some trains convey special T2 cabins, shown (T2) in the tables, with one berth in 1st class and two berths in 2nd c

Compartments are allocated for occupation exclusively by men or by wo except when married couples or families occupy all berths. Children trave alone, or who cannot be accommodated in the same compartment as family, are placed in women's compartments. In Russia and other countri the CIS, however, berths are allocated in strict order of booking and men women often share the same compartments.

Some trains have communicating doors between sleeping compartm which can be opened to create a larger room if both compartments occupied by the same family group. Berths can be reserved up to 2 mo (3 months on certain trains) before the date of travel and early reservatic recommended as space is limited, especially on French ski trains an Eastern Europe. Berths must be claimed within 15 minutes of boarding train or they may be resold.

HOTEL TRAINS

A new generation of overnight trains known collectively as Hotel trains now running on a selection of national and international routes. The facil are of a higher standard than those offered in conventional sleeping cars, special fares are payable. The trains fall into the following categories:

City Night Line: Many night trains radiating from Germany, as wel domestic overnight trains within Germany, come under the *City Night* banner. They operate on ten routes serving six countries, and are show *CNL* in our tables. *Deluxe* cabins can be configured with one, two or th berths and have a table, chairs and an en-suite washroom with tc washbasin and shower. *Economy* compartments have one, two or th berths and a washbasin. Breakfast is included in the sleeping car fare. A class ticket is required for *Deluxe* compartments (but not for single occupa of an *Economy* compartment). Six-berth couchettes are also avail although only a maximum of five passengers will normally be booked couchette compartment. Reservation is compulsory for travel in sleeping and couchettes. Seating cars are also conveyed but are now classified have a different train number and, in most cases, can be used without p reservation.

Trenhotel (Spain). These *Talgo*-type trains run on the international ro from Madrid to Lisboa and from Irún/Hendaye to Lisboa. They also ope on internal routes within Spain, from Barcelona to A Coruña, Granada Vigo, and from Madrid to A Coruña, Ferrol and Pontevedra. The highest c of accommodation is *Gran Clase*, which has shower and toilet facilitie each compartment and can be used for single or double occupancy.

Compartments with showers are also available on some domestic overn services in Sweden and Italy, and on certain other international routes indicated on our international overnight services summary on page 33.

COUCHETTES

Couchettes ( ) are a more basic form of overnight accommodation cons ing of simple bunk beds with a sheet, blanket and pillow. The couchettes converted from ordinary seating cars for the night, and there are usual berths per compartment in 1st class, 6 berths in 2nd class. On certain tra (e.g. in Austria and Italy), 4 berth compartments are available to 2nd cl passengers, at a higher supplement. Washing and toilet facilities are provi at the ends of each coach. Men and women are booked into the sa compartments and are expected to sleep in daytime clothes. A small num of trains in Germany, however, have women-only couchette compartmen

INTERNATIONAL OVERNIGHT SERVICES

A summary of international overnight services will be found on page 33 wh specifies the various types of accommodation and catering provided on ea individual service (including details of the operator).

CAR-SLEEPERS

Trains which convey motor cars operate throughout much of Europe and shown in Table **1** for international services and Table **2** for other servic The motor cars are conveyed in special wagons while passengers trave sleeping cars or couchettes, usually (but not always) in the same train.

WHEELCHAIR ACCESS ♿

Most main-line domestic and international trains, together with an increas number of local trains, are specially equipped to accommodate passengers wheelchairs. Access ramps are available at many stations and some tra are fitted with special lifts. These trains have at least one wheelchair spa and are equipped with accessible toilets.

Most railways publish guides to accessibility, and many countries prov dedicated staff to assist disabled travellers. Wheelchair users normally ne to reserve in advance, stating their requirements.

HEALTH REQUIREMENTS

ot mandatory for visitors to Europe to be vaccinated against infectious ses unless they are travelling from areas where these are endemic. For llers' peace of mind, however, protection against the following diseases d be considered:

HIV	Cholera
Hepatitis A	Hepatitis B
Polio	Rabies
Tetanus	Typhoid

nformation is available from the manual published by the World Health nisation, and travellers should seek advice from their Travel Agent.

DRINKING WATER

water is usually safe to drink in most parts of Europe. The water in rooms or toilets on trains is, however, not suitable for drinking. Those doubt the purity of the tap water are recommended to boil it, to use sterion tablets, or to drink bottled water.

CLIMATE

of Europe lies within the temperate zone but there can be considerable rences between North and South, East and West, as illustrated in the below. Local temperatures are also affected by altitude and the diffe-e between summer and winter temperatures tends to be less marked in tal regions than in areas far removed from the sea.

	Bucuresti	Dublin	Madrid	Moskva
UARY				
Highest	2°	8°	10°	– 6°
Lowest	– 6°	3°	3°	– 12°
Rain days	6	13	9	11
RIL				
Highest	18°	11°	18°	10°
Lowest	6°	4°	7°	2°
Rain days	7	10	11	9
Y				
Highest	29°	19°	31°	23°
Lowest	16°	11°	18°	14°
Rain days	7	9	3	12
TOBER				
Highest	18°	14°	19°	8°
Lowest	6°	8°	10°	2°
Rain days	5	11	9	10

est = Average highest daily temperature in °C
est = Average lowest daily temperature in °C
days = Average number of days with recorded precipitation
ce: World Weather Information Service

FIND US ON FACEBOOK!

www.facebook.com/EuropeanRailTimetable

and on **Twitter** @EuropeanRailTT

CURRENCY CONVERSION

The information shown below is intended to be indicative only. Rates fluctuate from day to day and commercial exchange rates normally include a commission element.

Country	unit	1 GBP =	1 USD =	1 EUR =	100 JPY =
Euro zone (‡)	**euro**	**1.29**	**0.89**	**1.00**	**0.82**
Albania	lek	178.47	123.40	138.20	112.75
Belarus	rubl	28492.14	19700.00	22062.97	17999.91
Bosnia	marka	2.52	1.75	1.96	1.59
Bulgaria	lev	2.53	1.75	1.96	1.59
Croatia	kuna	9.67	6.69	7.49	6.11
Czech Republic	koruna	34.91	24.14	27.03	22.05
Denmark	krone	9.60	6.64	7.43	6.06
Georgia	lari	3.11	2.14	2.40	1.96
Hungary	forint	410.12	283.56	317.57	259.09
Iceland	krona	180.29	124.66	139.61	113.90
Macedonia	denar	79.52	54.98	61.58	50.24
Moldova	leu	28.77	19.89	22.28	18.18
Norway	krone	12.09	8.36	9.36	7.64
Poland	złoty	5.74	3.97	4.44	3.63
Romania	leu nou	5.83	4.03	4.51	3.68
Russia	rubl	96.98	67.05	75.09	61.26
Serbia	dinar	158.58	109.64	122.80	100.18
Sweden	krona	12.09	8.36	9.36	7.63
Switzerland	franc	1.43	0.99	1.11	0.91
Turkey	yeni lira	4.33	2.99	3.35	2.73
Ukraine	hryvnya	36.34	25.12	28.14	22.96
United Kingdom	pound	1.00	0.69	0.77	0.63

‡ – Austria, Belgium, Cyprus, Estonia, Finland, France, Germany, Greece, Ireland, Italy, Latvia, Lithuania, Luxembourg, Malta, the Netherlands, Portugal, Slovakia, Slovenia and Spain.

The euro is also legal tender in Andorra, Kosovo, Monaco, Montenegro, San Marino, and the Vatican City.

PASSPORTS AND VISAS

Nationals of one country intending to travel to or pass through another country normally require a valid passport and will also require a visa unless a special visa-abolition agreement has been made between the countries concerned. The limit of stay permitted in each country is usually 3 months.

Applications for visas should be made well in advance of the date of travel to the local consulate of the country concerned. Consuls usually make a charge for issuing a visa. Before issuing a transit visa, a consul normally requires to see the visa of the country of destination.

The possession of a valid passport or visa does not necessarily grant the holder automatic access to all areas of the country to be visited. Certain countries have zones which are restricted or prohibited to foreign nationals.

All border controls have been abolished, however, between those countries which have signed the **Schengen Agreement** (see list below), and a visa allowing entry to any of these countries is valid in all of them.

LIST OF SCHENGEN AREA COUNTRIES

Austria, Belgium, Czech Republic, Denmark, Estonia, Finland, France, Germany, Greece, Hungary, Iceland, Italy, Latvia, Lithuania, Luxembourg, Malta, Netherlands, Norway, Poland, Portugal, Slovakia, Slovenia, Spain, Sweden, Switzerland.

METRIC CONVERSION TABLES

ne Celsius system of temperature measurement, the metric system of ance measurement and the twenty-four hour clock are used throughout s book. The tables below give Fahrenheit, mile and twelve-hour clock equivalents.

TEMPERATURE

°C	°F
–20	–4
–15	5
–10	14
–5	23
0	32
5	41
10	50
15	59
20	68
25	77
30	86
35	95
40	104

Conversion formulae :
C = (°F – 32) x 5 / 9
F = (°C x 9 / 5) + 32

DISTANCE

km	miles	km	miles	km	miles
1	0.62	45	27.96	300	186.41
2	1.24	50	31.07	400	248.55
3	1.86	55	34.18	500	310.69
4	2.49	60	37.28	600	372.82
5	3.11	65	40.39	700	434.96
6	3.73	70	43.50	800	497.10
7	4.35	75	46.60	900	559.23
8	4.97	80	49.71	1000	621.37
9	5.59	85	52.82	1100	683.51
10	6.21	90	55.92	1200	745.65
15	9.32	95	59.03	1300	807.78
20	12.43	100	62.14	1400	869.92
25	15.53	125	77.67	1500	932.06
30	18.64	150	93.21	2000	1242.74
35	21.75	175	108.74	3000	1864.11
40	24.85	200	124.27	4000	2485.48

TIME

24 hour clock

Midnight departure	0000
1 am	0100
5 am	0500
5.30 am	0530
11 am	1100
12 noon	1200
1 pm	1300
3.45 pm	1545
Midnight arrival	2400

GLOSSARY

🔑	*FRANCAIS*	*ITALIANO*	*DEUTSCH*	*ESPAÑOL*
additional trains	d'autres trains	ulteriori treni	weitere Züge	otros trenes
also	[circule] aussi	[si effettua] anche	[verkehrt] auch	[circula] también
alteration	modification	variazione	Änderung	modificación
approximately	environ	circa	ungefähr	aproximadamente
arrival, arrives (a.)	arrivée, arrive	arrivo, arriva	Ankunft, kommt an	llegada, llega
and at the same minutes past each hour until	puis toutes les heures aux mêmes minutes jusqu'à	poi ai stessi minuti di ogni ora fino a	und so weiter im Takt bis	luego a los mismos mir de cada hora hasta
calls at	s'arrête à	ferma a	hält in	efectúa parada en
certain	déterminé	certo	bestimmt	determinado
change at	changer à	cambiare a	umsteigen in	cambiar en
composition	composition	composizione	Zugbildung	composición
confirmation	confirmation	conferma	Bestätigung	confirmación
connection	correspondance, relation	coincidenza, relazione	Anschluss, Verbindung	correspondencia, enlac
conveys	comporte, achemine	ha in composizione	befördert, führt	lleva
daily	tous les jours	giornalmente	täglich	diariamente
delay	retard	ritardo	Verspätung	retraso
departure, departs (d.)	départ, part	partenza, parte	Abfahrt, fährt ab	salida, sale
earlier	plus tôt	più presto	früher	más temprano
engineering work	travaux de voie	lavori sul binario	Bauarbeiten	obras de vía
even / uneven dates	jours pairs / impairs	giorni pari / dispari	gerade / ungerade Daten	fechas pares / impares
every 30 minutes	toutes les 30 minutes	ogni 30 minuti	alle 30 Minuten	cada 30 minutos
except	sauf	escluso	außer	excepto
fast(er)	(plus) rapide	(più) rapido	schnell(er)	(más) rápido
for	pour	per	für	para
from Rennes	(en provenance) de Rennes	(proviene) da Rennes	von Rennes	(procede) de Rennes
from Jan. 15	à partir du 15 janvier	dal 15 di gennaio	vom 15. Januar (an)	desde el 15 de enero
hourly	toutes les heures	ogni ora	stündlich	cada hora
hours (hrs)	heures	ore	Stunden	horas
journey	voyage, trajet	viaggio, percorso	Reise	viaje, trayecto
journey time	temps de parcours	tempo di tragitto	Reisezeit	duración del recorrido
later	plus tard	più tardi	später	más tarde
may	peut, peuvent	può, possono	kann, können	puede(n)
minutes (mins)	minutes	minuti	Minuten	minutos
not	ne [circule] pas	non [si effettua]	[verkehrt] nicht	no [circula]
not available	pas disponible	non disponibile	nicht erhältlich	no disponible
on the dates shown in Table **81**	les jours indiqués dans le tableau **81**	nei giorni indicati nel quadro **81**	an den in der Tabelle **81** angegebene Daten	los días indicados en el cuadro **81**
only	seulement	esclusivamente	nur	sólo
operator	entreprise de transports	azienda di trasporto	Verkehrsunternehmen	empresa de transportes
other	autre	altro	andere	otros
runs	circule	circola, si effettua	verkehrt	circula
sailing	traversée	traversata	Überfahrt	travesía
ship	bateau, navire	nave, battello	Schiff	barco
stopping trains	trains omnibus	treni regionali	Nahverkehrszüge	trenes regionales
stops	s'arrête	ferma	hält	efectúa parada
subject to	sous réserve de	soggetto a	vorbehaltlich	sujeto a
summer	été	estate	Sommer	verano
supplement payable	avec supplément	con pagamento di supplemento	zuschlagpflichtig	con pago de suplement
then	puis	poi	dann	luego
through train	train direct	treno diretto	durchgehender Zug	tren directo
timings	horaires	orari	Zeitangaben	horarios
to York	vers, à destination de York	(diretto) a York	nach York	(continúa) a York
to / until July 23	jusqu'au 23 juillet	fino al 23 di luglio	bis zum 23. Juli	hasta el día 23 de julio
to pick up	pour laisser monter	per viaggiatori in partenza	zum Zusteigen	para recoger viajeros
to set down	pour laisser descendre	per viaggiatori in arrivo	zum Aussteigen	para dejar viajeros
unless otherwise shown	sauf indication contraire	salvo indicazione contraria	sofern nicht anders angezeigt	salvo indicación contrari
valid	valable	valido	gültig	válido
when train **44** runs	lors de la circulation du train **44**	quando circola il treno **44**	beim Verkehren des Zuges **44**	cuando circula el tren 4
winter	hiver	inverno	Winter	invierno

INDEX OF PLACES by table number

The BEYOND EUROPE section is indexed separately - see the back of each edition

Connection by train from the nearest station shown in this timetable.
Connection by boat from the nearest station shown in this timetable.
🚌 Connection by bus from the nearest station shown in this timetable.
10/355 Consult both indicated tables to find the best connecting services.

P

PARIS

PARIS ✈ CHARLES DE GAULLE

POZNAŃ

PRAHA

CRUISE TRAINS

services shown in the European Rail Timetable are the regular scheduled services of the railway companies concerned. However, a number of specialised operators also run ious cruise trains taking several days to complete their journey. Overnight accommodation is provided either on the train or in hotels. Cruise trains are bookable only through perating company or its appointed agents and normal rail tickets are not valid on these trains. A selection of operators is shown below.

Danube Express : Fully escorted holidays in central and eastern Europe by luxury private train based in Budapest. Operator: Danube Express, Offley Holes Farm, Charlton Road, Preston, Hitchin, SG4 7TD, UK; ✆ +44 (0)1462 441400. Website: www.danube-express.com

ond Royal Scotsman : Luxury tours of Scotland starting from Edinburgh. Operator: Belmond Royal Scotsman, 1st Floor, Shackleton House, 4 Battle Bridge Lane, London, SE1 2HP, UK; ✆ 0845 077 2222 (UK only) or +44 (0) 20 3117 1380. Website: www.royalscotsman.com

anscantábrico and **El Expreso de La Robla** : Rail cruises along Spain's northern coast. Operator: Trenes Turísticos de Lujo, Plaza de los Ferroviarios s/n., 33012 Oviedo, Asturias, Spain; ✆ +34 902 555 902, fax +34 985 981 711. Website: www.trenesturisticosdelujo.com

s-Siberian Express : Tours by private hotel train along the Trans-Siberian Railway. Operator: Golden Eagle Luxury Trains, Denzell House, Denzell Gardens, Dunham Road, Altrincham, WA14 4QF, UK; ✆ +44 (0)16 1 928 9410, fax +44 (0)161 941 6101. Website: www.goldeneagleluxurytrains.com.

ce Simplon-Orient-Express : This well-known luxury train runs once or twice weekly from late March to early November, mostly on its established London - Paris - Venezia route. Operator: Orient-Express Hotels Ltd., 1st Floor, Shackleton House, 4 Battle Bridge Lane, London, SE1 2HP, UK; ✆ 0845 077 2222 (UK only) or +44 (0) 20 3117 1380. Website: www.vsoe.com

LIST OF ADVERTISERS

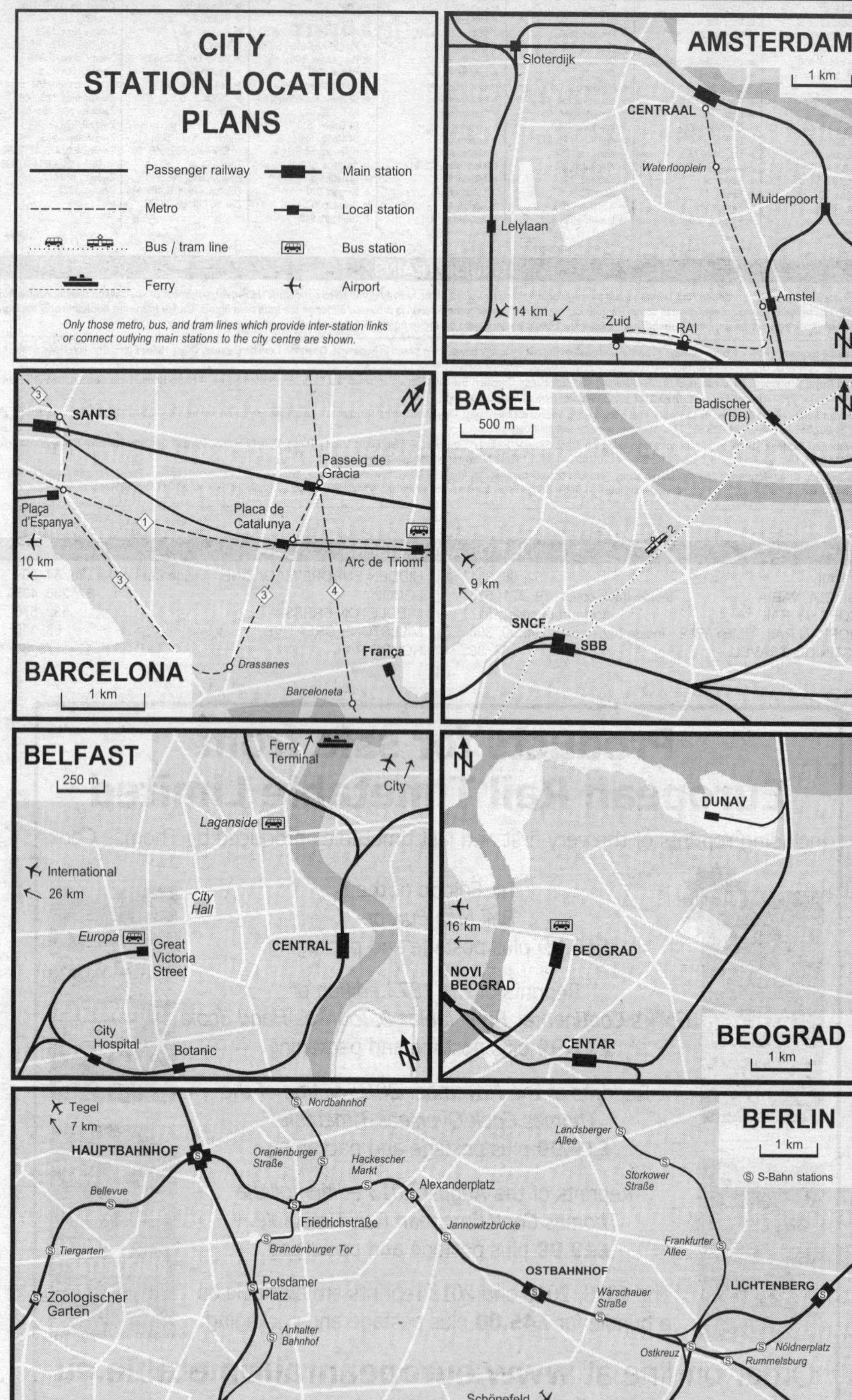

CITY STATION LOCATION PLANS
Passenger railway
Main station
Metro
Local station
Bus / tram line
Bus station
Ferry
Airport
Only those metro, bus, and tram lines which provide inter-station links or connect outlying main stations to the city centre are shown.
AMSTERDAM
1 km
Sloterdijk
CENTRAAL
Waterlooplein
Muiderpoort
Lelylaan
Amstel
14 km
Zuid
RAI
BARCELONA
1 km
SANTS
Passeig de Gràcia
Plaça d'Espanya
Placa de Catalunya
Arc de Triomf
10 km
Drassanes
França
Barceloneta
BASEL
500 m
Badischer (DB)
9 km
SNCF
SBB
BELFAST
250 m
Ferry Terminal
City
Laganside
International
26 km
City Hall
Europa
Great Victoria Street
CENTRAL
City Hospital
Botanic
DUNAV
16 km
BEOGRAD
NOVI BEOGRAD
CENTAR
BEOGRAD
1 km
BERLIN
1 km
S-Bahn stations
Tegel
7 km
Nordbahnhof
HAUPTBAHNHOF
Oranienburger Straße
Hackescher Markt
Landsberger Allee
Storkower Straße
Bellevue
Alexanderplatz
Friedrichstraße
Jannowitzbrücke
Tiergarten
Brandenburger Tor
Frankfurter Allee
OSTBAHNHOF
LICHTENBERG
Zoologischer Garten
Potsdamer Platz
Warschauer Straße
Anhalter Bahnhof
Ostkreuz
Nöldnerplatz
Rummelsburg
Schönefeld
18 km
Yorckstraße (Großgörschenstraße)
Yorckstraße
Treptower Park
Betriebsbahnhof Rummelsburg

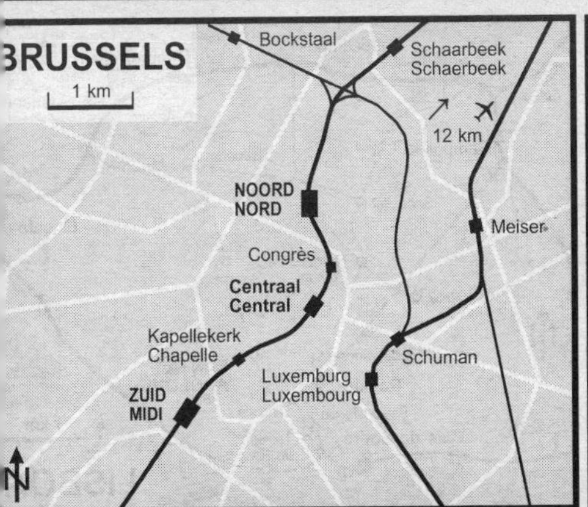
BRUSSELS
1 km
Bockstaal
Schaarbeek
Schaerbeek
12 km
NOORD
NORD
Meiser
Congrès
Centraal
Central
Kapellekerk
Chapelle
Schuman
Luxemburg
Luxembourg
ZUID
MIDI

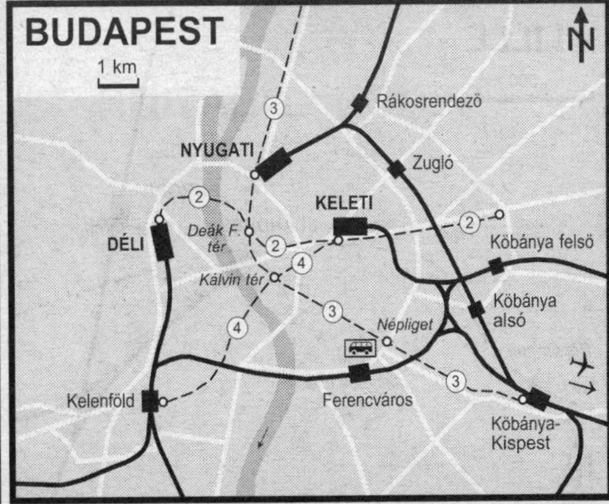
BUDAPEST
1 km
Rákosrendezö
NYUGATI
Zugló
KELETI
DÉLI
Deák F. tér
Kőbánya felsö
Kálvin tér
Kőbánya alsó
Népliget
Kelenföld
Ferencváros
Kőbánya-Kispest

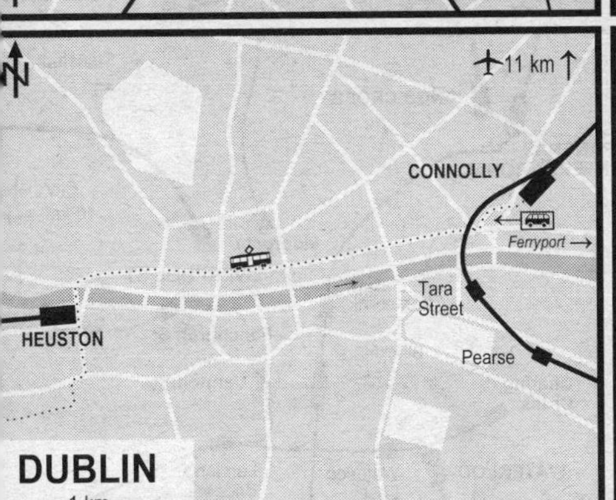
11 km
CONNOLLY
Ferryport
HEUSTON
Tara Street
Pearse
DUBLIN
1 km

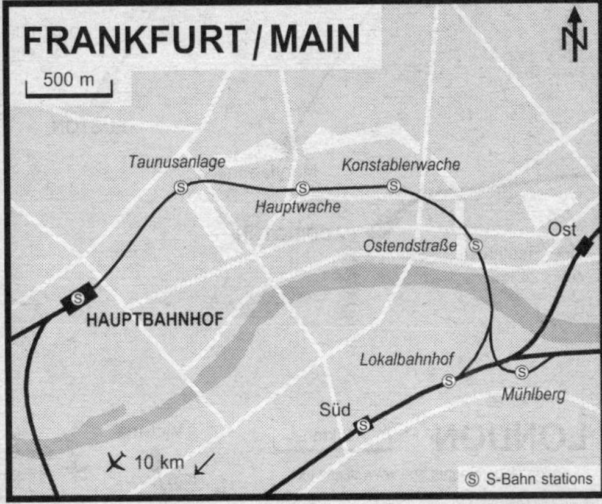
FRANKFURT / MAIN
500 m
Taunusanlage
Konstablerwache
Hauptwache
Ost
Ostendstraße
HAUPTBAHNHOF
Lokalbahnhof
Mühlberg
Süd
10 km
S-Bahn stations

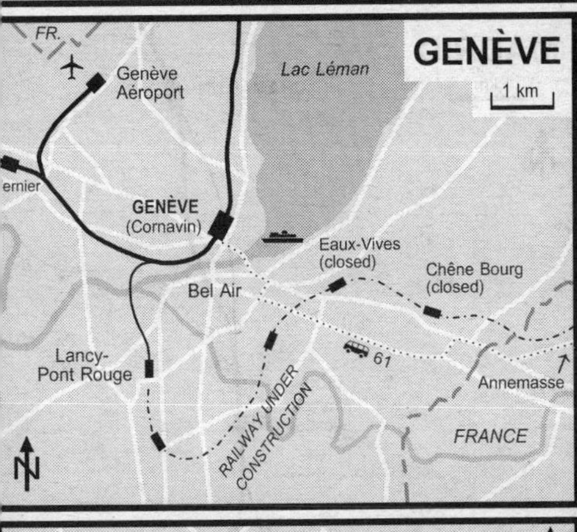
FR.
Genève Aéroport
Lac Léman
GENÈVE
1 km
GENÈVE
(Cornavin)
Eaux-Vives
(closed)
Chêne Bourg
(closed)
Bel Air
Lancy-
Pont Rouge
61
Annemasse
RAILWAY UNDER CONSTRUCTION
FRANCE

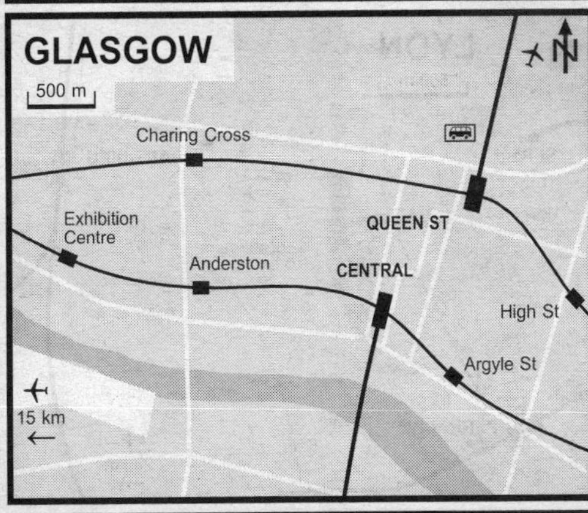
GLASGOW
500 m
Charing Cross
Exhibition
Centre
QUEEN ST
Anderston
CENTRAL
High St
Argyle St
15 km

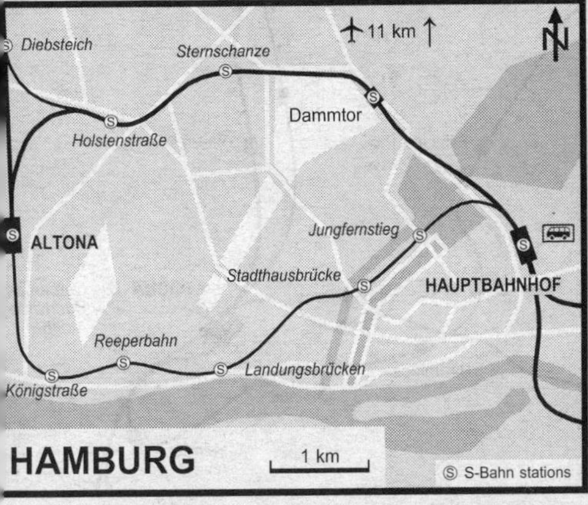
Diebsteich
Sternschanze
11 km
Dammtor
Holstenstraße
ALTONA
Jungfernstieg
Stadthausbrücke
HAUPTBAHNHOF
Reeperbahn
Landungsbrücken
Königstraße
HAMBURG
1 km
S-Bahn stations

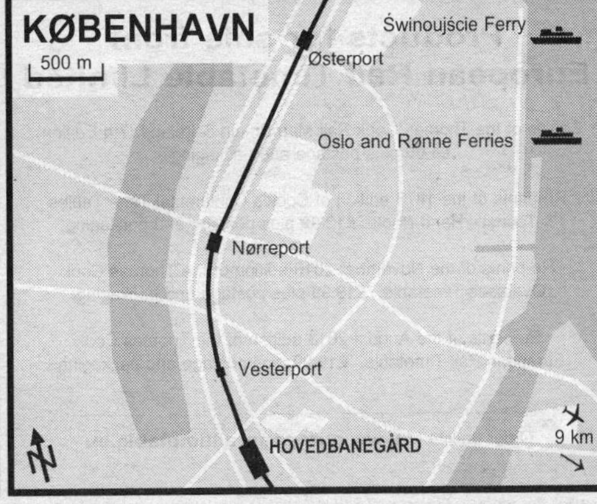
KØBENHAVN
500 m
Świnoujście Ferry
Østerport
Oslo and Rønne Ferries
Nørreport
Vesterport
HOVEDBANEGÅRD
9 km

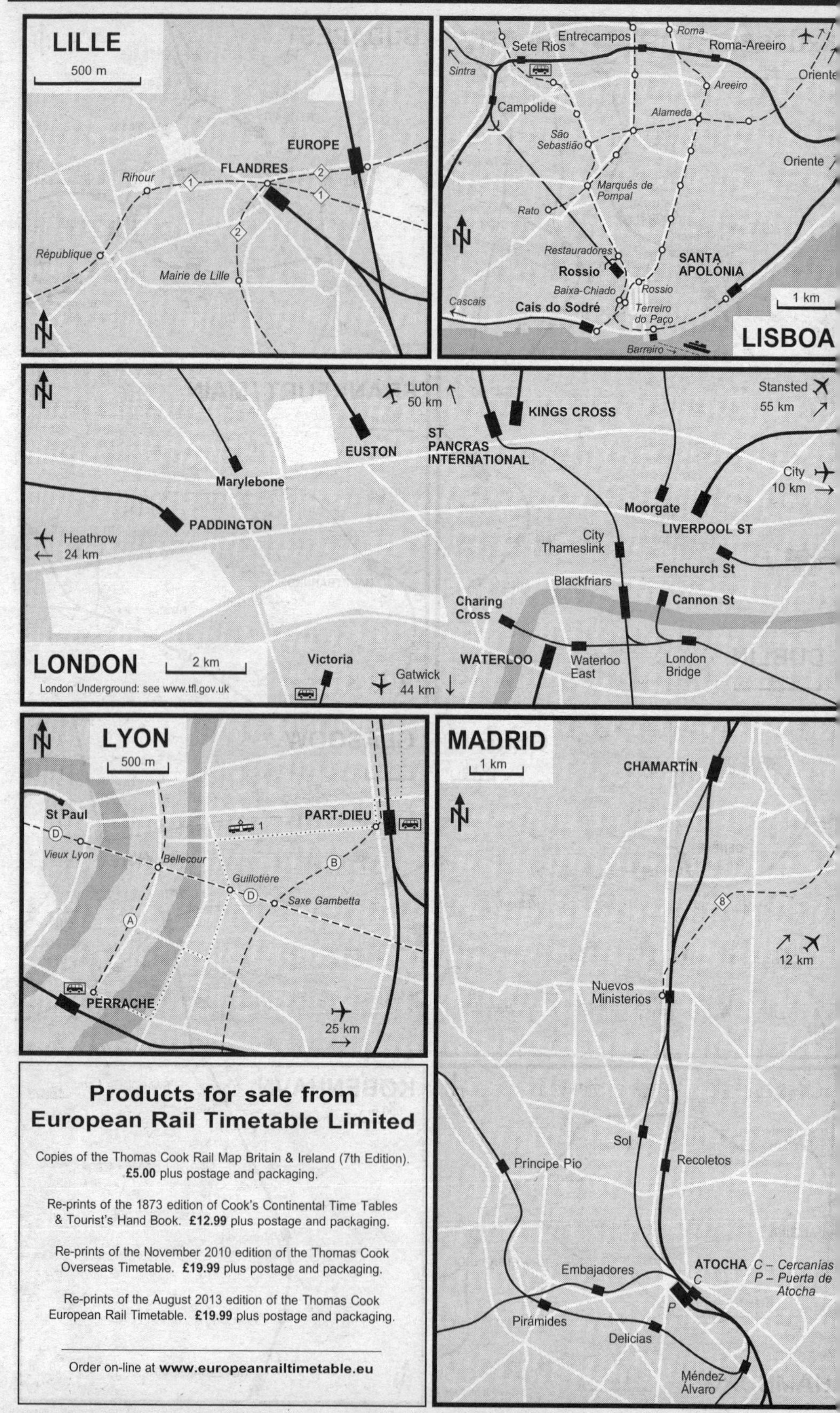
LILLE
500 m
EUROPE
FLANDRES
Rihour
République
Mairie de Lille
LISBOA
1 km
Entrecampos
Roma
Sete Rios
Roma-Areeiro
Sintra
Oriente
Areeiro
Campolide
Alameda
São Sebastião
Oriente
Marquês de Pompal
Rato
Restauradores
Rossio
SANTA APOLÓNIA
Baixa-Chiado
Rossio
Cascais
Cais do Sodré
Terreiro do Paço
Barreiro
LONDON
2 km
London Underground: see www.tfl.gov.uk
Luton 50 km
Stansted 55 km
KINGS CROSS
EUSTON
ST PANCRAS INTERNATIONAL
Marylebone
City 10 km
Moorgate
PADDINGTON
LIVERPOOL ST
Heathrow 24 km
City Thameslink
Fenchurch St
Blackfriars
Charing Cross
Cannon St
Victoria
WATERLOO
Waterloo East
London Bridge
Gatwick 44 km
LYON
500 m
St Paul
PART-DIEU
Vieux Lyon
Bellecour
Guillotière
Saxe Gambetta
PERRACHE
25 km
MADRID
1 km
CHAMARTÍN
12 km
Nuevos Ministerios
Sol
Príncipe Pío
Recoletos
Embajadores
ATOCHA
C – Cercanías
P – Puerta de Atocha
Pirámides
Delicias
Méndez Álvaro

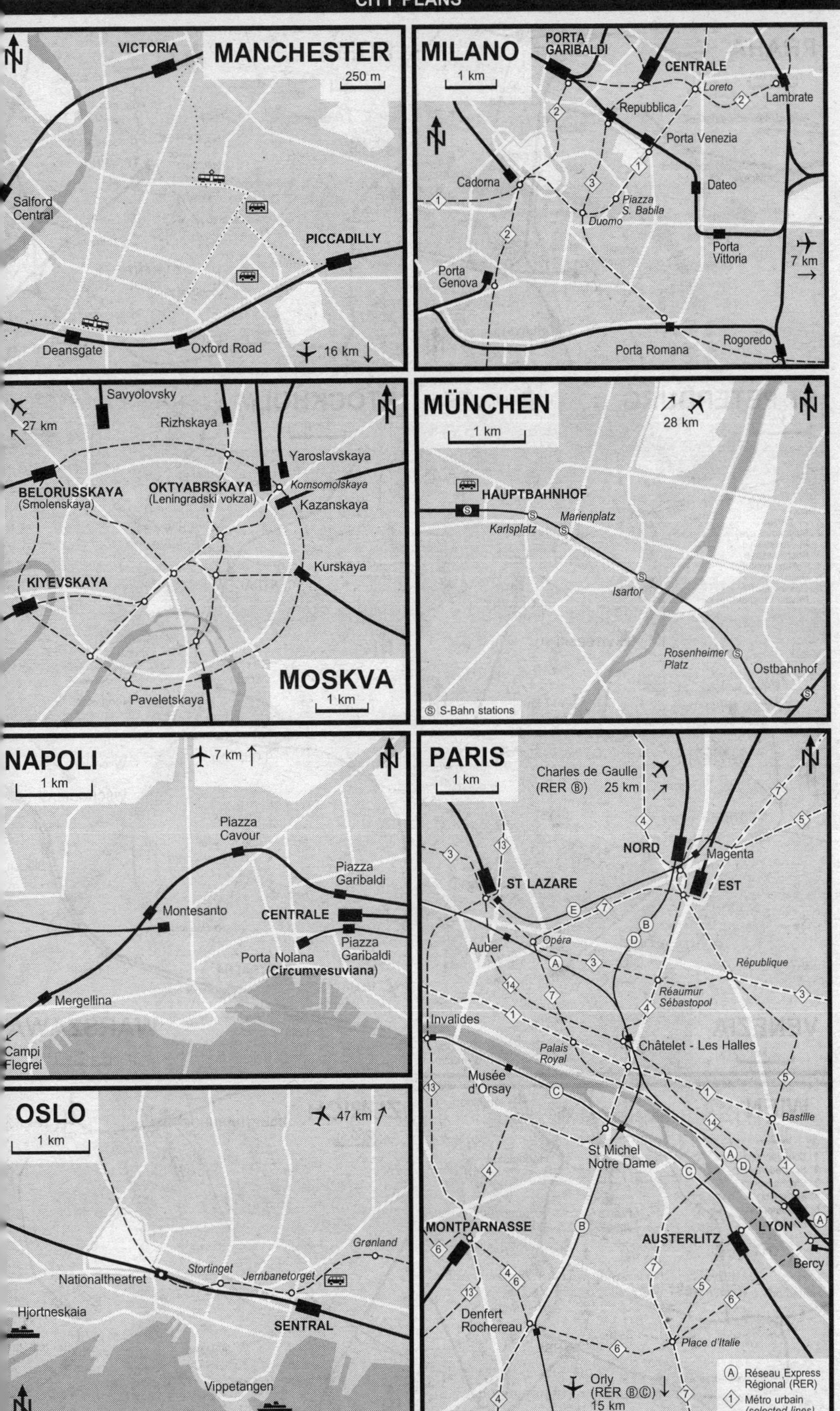
MANCHESTER
250 m
VICTORIA
Salford Central
PICCADILLY
Deansgate
Oxford Road
16 km
MILANO
1 km
PORTA GARIBALDI
CENTRALE
Loreto
Lambrate
Repubblica
Porta Venezia
Cadorna
Dateo
Piazza S. Babila
Duomo
Porta Vittoria
7 km
Porta Genova
Porta Romana
Rogoredo
Savyolovsky
Rizhskaya
27 km
Yaroslavskaya
BELORUSSKAYA
(Smolenskaya)
OKTYABRSKAYA
(Leningradski vokzal)
Komsomolskaya
Kazanskaya
KIYEVSKAYA
Kurskaya
Paveletskaya
MOSKVA
1 km
MÜNCHEN
1 km
28 km
HAUPTBAHNHOF
Marienplatz
Karlsplatz
Isartor
Rosenheimer Platz
Ostbahnhof
S-Bahn stations
NAPOLI
1 km
7 km
Piazza Cavour
Piazza Garibaldi
Montesanto
CENTRALE
Piazza Garibaldi
Porta Nolana
(Circumvesuviana)
Mergellina
Campi Flegrei
OSLO
1 km
47 km
Grønland
Stortinget
Jernbanetorget
Nationaltheatret
Hjortneskaia
SENTRAL
Vippetangen
PARIS
1 km
Charles de Gaulle
(RER B) 25 km
NORD
Magenta
ST LAZARE
EST
Opéra
Auber
République
Réaumur Sébastopol
Invalides
Châtelet - Les Halles
Palais Royal
Musée d'Orsay
Bastille
St Michel Notre Dame
MONTPARNASSE
AUSTERLITZ
LYON
Bercy
Denfert Rochereau
Place d'Italie
Orly
(RER B C)
15 km
Réseau Express Régional (RER)
Métro urbain
(selected lines)

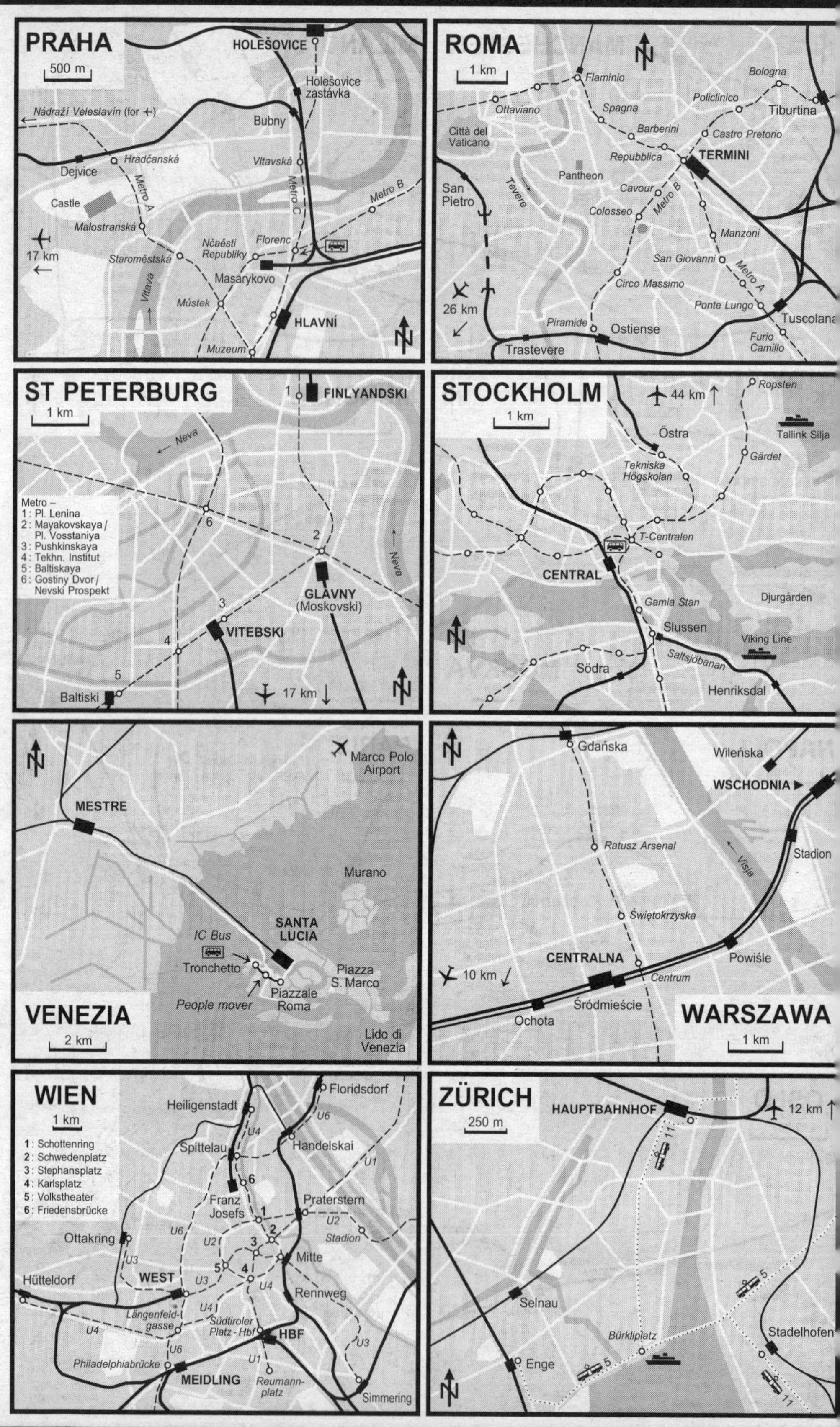
PRAHA
500 m
HOLEŠOVICE
Holešovice zastávka
Nádraží Veleslavín (for ✈)
Bubny
Dejvice
Hradčanská
Vltavská
Metro A
Metro C
Metro B
Castle
Malostranská
17 km
Staroměstská
Nčaěsti Republiky
Florenc
Masarykovo
Vltava
Můstek
HLAVNÍ
Muzeum
ROMA
1 km
Flaminio
Bologna
Ottaviano
Spagna
Policlinico
Tiburtina
Città del Vaticano
Barberini
Castro Pretorio
Repubblica
TERMINI
Pantheon
San Pietro
Tevere
Cavour
Metro B
Colosseo
Manzoni
San Giovanni
Metro A
Circo Massimo
26 km
Ponte Lungo
Tuscolana
Piramide
Ostiense
Furio Camillo
Trastevere
ST PETERBURG
1 km
FINLYANDSKI
Neva
Metro –
1: Pl. Lenina
2: Mayakovskaya / Pl. Vosstaniya
3: Pushkinskaya
4: Tekhn. Institut
5: Baltiskaya
6: Gostiny Dvor / Nevski Prospekt
GLAVNY (Moskovski)
VITEBSKI
Baltiski
17 km
STOCKHOLM
1 km
44 km
Ropsten
Östra
Tallink Silja
Tekniska Högskolan
Gärdet
T-Centralen
CENTRAL
Djurgården
Gamla Stan
Slussen
Viking Line
Saltsjöbanan
Södra
Henriksdal
Marco Polo Airport
MESTRE
Murano
SANTA LUCIA
IC Bus
Tronchetto
Piazza S. Marco
Piazzale Roma
People mover
VENEZIA
2 km
Lido di Venezia
Gdańska
Wileńska
WSCHODNIA ▶
Ratusz Arsenal
Stadion
Wisła
Świętokrzyska
CENTRALNA
Powiśle
10 km
Centrum
Śródmieście
Ochota
WARSZAWA
1 km
WIEN
1 km
Heiligenstadt
Floridsdorf
U6
U4
Handelskai
Spittelau
U1
1: Schottenring
2: Schwedenplatz
3: Stephansplatz
4: Karlsplatz
5: Volkstheater
6: Friedensbrücke
Franz Josefs
Praterstern
U2
Stadion
Ottakring
U6
U3
Mitte
Hütteldorf
WEST
U3
U4
Rennweg
Längenfeldgasse
Südtiroler Platz - Hbf
HBF
U4
U3
U6
U1
Philadelphiabrücke
MEIDLING
Reumannplatz
Simmering
ZÜRICH
250 m
HAUPTBAHNHOF
12 km
11
5
Selnau
Bürkliplatz
Stadelhofen
Enge
5
11

SELECTED DAILY INTERNATIONAL SLEEPER SERVICES

n	To	Train Number	Brand	Facilities and owner	Train Name	International table number
	Warszawa	447/446	Euro Night	🛏 1, 2 cl. 🚿(pkp), ▬ 2 cl.(db), ✗(pkp)	Jan Kiepura	54, 56
eldorf	Wien	421/420	Euro Night	🛏 1, 2 cl. 🚿(öbb), ▬ 2 cl.(öbb)		28, 66
erdam	München	419/418	City Night Line	🛏 1, 2 cl. 🚿(db), ▬ 2 cl.(sbb), 🍸	Pollux	28
	Praha	40458/40447	City Night Line	🛏 1, 2 cl. 🚿(cd), ▬ 2 cl.(db), 🍸	Kopernikus	20, 28, 54
chen	Budapest	463/462	Euro Night	🛏 1, 2 cl.(mav), ▬ 2 cl.(mav)	Kálmán Imre	32
	Bucuresti	347/346	Euro Night	🛏 1, 2 cl.(cfr), ▬ 2 cl.(cfr), ✗(cfr)	Dacia	32, 61
apest	Bucuresti	473/472	Euro Night	🛏 1, 2 cl.(cfr), ▬ 1, 2 cl.(cfr)	Ister	32, 61
	Venezia	221/220	Thello Euro Night	🛏 1, 2 cl.(ti), ▬ 2 cl.(ti), ✗(ti)		44
/ Hendaye	Lisboa	312/310	Trenhotel talgo	🛏 1, 2 cl. 🚿(renfe), ✗(renfe)	Surex / Sud Expresso	45
ba	Madrid	335/332	Trenhotel talgo	🛏 1, 2 cl. 🚿(renfe), ✗(renfe)	Lusitania	45
n	Malmö	301/300	Euro Night	▬ 2 cl.(bne)	Berlin Night Express	50
h	Praha	40470/458	City Night Line	🛏 1, 2 cl. 🚿(cd), ▬ 2 cl.(sbb), 🍸	Canopus	54
h	Hamburg	479/478	City Night Line	🛏 1, 2 cl. 🚿(sbb), ▬ 2 cl.(sbb), 🍸	Komet	54, 73
h	Berlin	471/470	City Night Line	🛏 1, 2 cl. 🚿(sbb), ▬ 2 cl.(sbb), 🍸	Sirius	54, 73
szawa	Kyïv	68/67		🛏 1, 2 cl.(uz)	Kyïv Ekspres	56
szawa	Moskva	10/9		🛏 1, 2 cl.(rzd)	Polonez	56
n	Budapest	477/476	Euro Night	🛏 1, 2 cl.(cd), ▬ 2 cl.(mav)	Metropol	60
n	Wien	477/476	Euro Night	🛏 1, 2 cl.(cd), ▬ 2 cl.(mav)	Metropol	60
a	Budapest	477/476	Euro Night	🛏 1, 2 cl. 🚿(cd), ▬ 2 cl.(cd)	Metropol	60
apest	Beograd	341/340		🛏 1, 2 cl.(zs), ▬ 2 cl.(zs)	Beograd	61
grad	Skopje	335/334		▬ 2 cl.(mz)	Hellas Express	61
uresti	istanbul	491/490 ❖		🛏 1, 2 cl.(cfr), ▬ 2 cl.(tcdd)	Bosphor	61
grad	Sofia	293/292		▬ 2 cl.(zs)	Nušić	61
ch	Beograd	315/314		🛏 1, 2 cl.(zs), ▬ 2 cl.(zs)		62
burg	Wien	491/490	Euro Night	🛏 1, 2 cl. 🚿(öbb), ▬ 2 cl.(öbb)	Hans Albers	64
chen	Budapest	463/462	Euro Night	🛏 1, 2 cl.(mav), ▬ 2 cl.(mav)	Kálmán Imre	65
chen	Roma	485/484	City Night Line	🛏 1, 2 cl. 🚿(db), ▬ 2 cl.(db), 🍸	Lupus	70
chen	Venezia	40463/40236	City Night Line	🛏 1, 2 cl. 🚿(db), ▬ 2 cl.(db), 🍸	Pictor	70
chen	Milano	40485/40481	City Night Line	🛏 1, 2 cl. 🚿(db), ▬ 2 cl.(db), 🍸	Apus	70
terdam	Zürich	40419/40478	City Night Line	🛏 1, 2 cl. 🚿(cnl), ▬ 2 cl.(cnl), 🍸	Pegasus	73
ch	Zagreb	465/414	Euro Night	🛏 1, 2 cl.(hz), ▬ 2 cl.(hz)		86
ch	Budapest	467/466	Euro Night	🛏 1, 2 cl.(mav), ▬ 2 cl.(mav)	Wiener Walzer	86
ch	Graz	465/464	Euro Night	🛏 1, 2 cl. 🚿(öbb), ▬ 2 cl.(öbb)	Zürichsee	86
n	Roma	1235/1234	Euro Night	🛏 1, 2 cl. 🚿(öbb), ▬ 2 cl.(öbb)	Tosca	88
n	Venezia	237/236	Euro Night	🛏 1, 2 cl. 🚿(öbb), ▬ 2 cl.(öbb)	Vienna - Venezia Express	88
n	Milano	1235/1234	Euro Night	🛏 1, 2 cl.(ti), ▬ 2 cl.(ti)		88
na	Moskva	22/21		🛏 1, 2 cl.(rzd)	Vltava	95
b	Moskva	22/21		🛏 1, 2 cl.(rzd)	Vltava	95
n	Moskva	22/21		🛏 1, 2 cl.(rzd)	Vltava	95
kow	Kyïv	36/35		🛏 1, 2 cl. 🚿(pkp)		1075
na	Kyïv	801/143		🛏 1, 2 cl.(uz)		96
islava	Kyïv	801/143		🛏 1, 2 cl.(uz)		96
apest	Kyïv	34/33		🛏 1, 2 cl.(uz)	Latorca	96
szawa	Lviv	35/36		🛏 1, 2 cl.(uz)		97
szawa	Budapest	407/476		🛏 1, 2 cl.(pkp), ▬ 2 cl.(pkp)		99
szawa	Wien	407/406		🛏 1, 2 cl. 🚿(pkp), ▬ 2 cl.(öbb)	Chopin	99
szawa	Praha	407/443		🛏 1, 2 cl.(pkp), ▬ 2 cl.(pkp)		99
ków	Budapest	402/476		🛏 1, 2 cl.(pkp), ▬ 2 cl.(pkp)		99
ków	Wien	402/406		🛏 1, 2 cl.(pkp), ▬ 2 cl.(pkp)		99
ków	Praha	403/402		🛏 1, 2 cl.(cd), ▬ 2 cl.(cd)	Silesia	99
kow	Kyïv	36/35		🛏 1, 2 cl. 🚿(pkp)		1075
sinki	Moskva	31/32	Firménny	🛏 1, 2 cl. 🚿(rzd), ✗	Lev Tolstoi	1910
daily sleepers (other seasonal services operate):						
s	Moskva	453/452	Euro Night	🛏 1, 2 cl. 🚿(rzd), ✗(pkp, rzd)	Trans European Express	24

Key to ownership of sleeping cars:

: - Bulgarian, bc - Belarussian, bne - Berlin Night Express, cd - Czech, cfr - Romanian, cnl - City Night Line, db - German, hz - Croatian, v - Hungarian, mz - Macedonain, öbb - Austrian, pkp - Polish, renfe - Spanish, rzd - Russian, sbb - Swiss, ti - Italian, uz - Ukrainian, - Serbian.

Reported as not running most nights.
No sleeping cars conveyed until further notice.
🚿 – Shower.

✗ – Restaurant car.
❖ – The composition of this train is subject to confirmation.

te : This list excludes trains not shown in our International section (e.g. Czech Republic to Slovakia, Ukraine to Russia etc.).

What's new this month *(continued from page 3)*

ITALY

New schedules come into effect from June 12. Information was unavailable at press date, although only minor alterations are expected. However, readers should be cautious of any exception dates if travelling on or around public holidays, or during August.

SWEDEN

Tables have been updated following receipt of further information; most schedules are now valid until August 14.

FINLAND

Our Finnish section has been updated with timings for the summer period from June 20 to August 14. This latest timetable change includes significant alterations on many long-distance routes.

The daytime service between Helsinki and Oulu now consists of five *InterCity* trains in each direction, evenly spaced to run approximately every three hours (Table **794**). An additional *Pendolino* service also runs twice a week in each direction between these cities. Only a single through service remains between Helsinki and Rovaniemi with the northbound departure from Helsinki considerably later than before, at 1527. Other journeys are still possible to the far north by changing trains at Oulu. Overnight services remain unchanged, apart from some minor timing alterations.

The number of through trains between Helsinki and Vaasa has increased from three to five in each direction. An additional connecting service is also provided (Table **794**).

All services via Jyväskylä (Table **795**) now run to/from Helsinki meaning that journeys to and from Turku require a change of train at Tampere. Through services via Jyväskylä to Kuopio and beyond have also been withdrawn (apart from one *Pendolino* train pair on Sundays).

The service between Kouvola and Oulu (Table **798**) has been recast with numerous train category changes and retimings. Please be aware that some trains are replaced by bus between Kajaani and Oulu on Mondays to Fridays from July 11 to August 12.

GERMANY

During the Summer period (until mid-September) engineering work will affect many long-distance services at a number of key locations around the country. It is not possible to show all variations in our tables so we have included a special shaded panel on page 367 with a summary of locations, dates and brief descriptions of how services are affected. Readers travelling in Germany during the summer are strongly advised to consult this panel and check timings of services that may be affected.

AUSTRIA

Journeys on the Linz to Selzthal route are disrupted from June 20 due to engineering work taking place between Spital am Pyhrn and Selzthal. All regional trains are replaced by bus over the affected section with journey times extended by a few minutes. *IC* trains between Linz and Graz are replaced by a fast bus between Kirchdorf and Selzthal with overall timings unaffected. Table **974** has been updated with the revised timings from June 20.

POLAND

Retimings are expected from June 12, but unfortunately information was not available as we went to press. We hope to show updated tables next month.

CZECH REPUBLIC

The Praha – Ostrava – Žilina line has a number of minor changes June 12 and Table **1160** is therefore valid from that date. *Leo Exp* has recently withdrawn the first journey in each direction (0611 Praha and 0355 from Bohumín), whilst the 0811 from Praha and Karvina – Praha no longer run on Tuesdays.

SLOVAKIA

The three trains each way between Bratislava and Košice operate *RegioJet* are retimed by a few minutes from June 12; the revised t are shown in Table **1180**. These trains no longer call at Pova Bystrica, and one train each way now omits Štrba. *Regio* overnight Praha – Košice train is also retimed between Žilina Košice, arriving 27 minutes earlier at 0614.

HUNGARY

Summer timings for services in the Lake Balaton area will apply June 18 to August 28, mostly affecting Tables **1220**, **1225** and **1** Unfortunately timings were not available in time for this edition bu appear in the July edition.

SERBIA, MONTENEGRO, FYRo MACEDONIA and GREECE

Normal service is reported to have resumed between Beograd and following repairs to the weather damaged infrastructure (Table **13**

Readers are reminded that international services between Beo and Skopje (trains **334**–**337**) are suspended until mid-June owir engineering work between Niš and Preševo. Work will be halted fo summer season but is expected to resume in early September (T **1380**). No replacement bus service is provided.

ROMANIA

Details of seasonal summer trains to the Black Sea coast have b received and relevant tables updated accordingly. This year s through coaches to Mangalia from Arad, Craiova, Deva, Ora Reşiţa, Satu Mare, Sibiu, Sighetu Marmaţiei, Suceava, Târgu M and Timişoara.

Journey time on CFR Călători operated Bucureşti – Constanţa n stop services is reduced to two hours (Table **1680**).

RUSSIA

Although the main timetable change in Russia is in December, th are certain minor changes from the end of May which have b incorporated into the tables. *Go Rail*'s Tallinn – St Peterburg – Mos train (Table **1870**) is retimed from May 29 to leave at 17 approximately 30 minutes later than before.

BEYOND EUROPE

In this expanded edition of the European Rail Timetable, we are abl show all eight of the latest Beyond Europe sections. A list of the a included and their locations within the timetable will be found on p 577. There have been some major alterations to services in Malay North America and Japan since these areas last appeared in previ monthly editions and we have made sure that all the relevant tab have been updated with the latest timings for this edition.

In the African section we have added a new Table **4345** which inclu timings of the recently restored passenger services in Botswana. In Algerian table **4020** we have added the reinstated service betw Mohammadia and Mostaganem.

To the Tyrol (Table 951)

Berlin-based travel writers Nicky Gardner and Susanne Kries invite readers to join them on the morning Eurocity train over the Arlberg rail route.

The very mention of the word Arlberg evokes memories of a *belle époque* of continental rail travel. The Arlberg is the rugged mountain region which separates Austria's westernmost province, Vorarlberg, from the Tyrol. The mountains achieve no spectacular heights – there are no summits in excess of 3,000 metres.

But the difficult terrain was for centuries an obstacle to travel until the Arlberg Railway was completed in 1884. It is the principal west to east route through the region, and it has long been a major artery for international trains – as well as for Austrian domestic services.

EC163 TRANSALPIN

Reckon on two hours for the 157-km run from Feldkirch to Innsbruck. Make time to look around Feldkirch before departure. The station has a memorial to James Joyce, who passed through Feldkirch in 1915 en route from Trieste to Switzerland.

Most daytime services over the Arlberg line are ÖBB Railjets, but there is one nicely timed Eurocity (EC163 *Transalpin* from Zürich to Graz). This train leaves Feldkirch at 10.16 each morning. It's the only train of the day where you can ride in a very chic Swiss panorama car from Feldkirch to Innsbruck. That carriage is first class only, but the views are superb, so this is perhaps a case where it's worth trading up to first class.

Time and technology have tamed the mountains. In the early days of the line, specially designed locomotives were needed to cope with the gradients. Today, the trains slide with seeming ease over the Arlberg line, although a second locomotive is still added to the *Transalpin* for the leg over the Arlberg to Innsbruck.

THE ARLBERG WATERSHED

The railway climbs through glorious Alpine scenery to over 1,300 metres, passing under the watershed in a ten-kilometre long tunnel. It all seems too easy, compared with the arduous rigours of travel in the region before the coming of the railway. An early John Murray guide recalls the days when travellers perished in the Arlberg snows, their corpses left to rot by the side of the path with birds pecking at their eyes.

On the west side of the Arlberg, the waters drain west towards the Rhine and thus eventually decant into the North Sea. On the east side, the clear mountain streams flow east, joining the Inn and then the Danube. Eventually those waters reach the Black Sea. Emerging from the Arlberg Tunnel, the train stops immediately at St Anton am Arlberg – an upmarket ski resort as full of glitz and gloss as the ultra-modern station building suggests.

Beyond St Anton, the railway follows the River Rosanna downstream through lovely Tyrolean landscapes to the town of Landeck, which would hardly warrant a mention were it not for its key position on the Tyrolean transport network. It's the jumping-off point for buses which run up to Nauders and Martina (ERT 954), from where there are onward bus connections to the Engadine area of eastern Switzerland and to Malles in Italy.

THE INN VALLEY

After Landeck, the railway follows the valley downstream through Imst, a town which once thrived on the twin industries of mining and breeding canaries, prosecuting the latter with such success that birds from Imst were once delivered on foot to potentates across the Middle East. East from Imst, the valley becomes more heavily industrialised on the approach to Innsbruck, the administrative capital of the Tyrol region.

Innsbruck is a good spot for an overnight stay, and a chance to plan your next move. South over the Brenner to Italy? North via Mittenwald to Upper Bavaria? Or east through the Kitzbühel Alps to Zell am See?

Susanne and Nicky are the authors of 'Europe by Rail: The Definitive Guide for Independent Travellers'. The book is published this month by European Rail Timetable Limited.

Tip of the Month

Exploring Austria

by Nicky Gardner and Susanne Kries

There are some German phrases which cannot easily be translated into English. "Einfach Raus" is one of them. A close English idiom (though not a literal translation) might be "Let's head out!" But you do not need to be a linguist to realise that Austria's *Einfach-Raus-Ticket* is a great deal for couples or small groups keen to explore Austria by train for a day.

The *Einfach-Raus-Ticket* is valid any day of the week, although on weekday mornings travel may not start until 09.00. The ticket is valid right through until 03.00 the following morning. It requires a minimum of two passengers travelling together and may be used by up to a maximum of five people. The fare for the ticket is currently €33 for two, €37 for three, €41 for four and €45 for five travellers.

This is effectively a rover ticket, allowing travellers to roam at will across the Austrian rail network. But the small print is important. The ticket can only be used on local and regional train services. So don't even think of hopping on a Railjet, Eurocity, Intercity or Euronight train. The *Einfach-Raus-Ticket* is a great deal for those who are not in a hurry, but have time to wander. It's perfect for travellers wanting to explore Austrian secondary routes or branch lines – provided of course there are always at least two people travelling together.

Although the *Einfach-Raus-Ticket* is promoted as being valid across the Austrian rail network, it's worth bearing in mind that the restriction on faster services does create some no-go zones. The most conspicuous of these is the Arlberg route, which features as the *Route of the Month* in this issue of the *European Rail Timetable*. There are no regional trains over the central section of the Arlberg line (the 36 km between Bludenz and St Anton) and hence the *Einfach-Raus-Ticket* cannot be used on that particular stretch. So before investing in one of these great-value tickets it is worth checking if your intended journey can indeed be completed without recourse to premium trains.

◆

Our *Tip of the Month* (like our *Route of the Month*) is always contributed by Susanne Kries and Nicky Gardner. They are the editors of *hidden europe* magazine (www.hiddeneurope.co.uk). The two women are also the authors of a new book published by European Rail Timetable Limited. The book is called *Europe by Rail: The Definitive Guide for Independent Travellers*. It is available through all good bookshops. The book can also be ordered at www.europeanrailtimetable.eu or www.amazon.co.uk.

AUTO-TRAIN, AUTOREISEZÜGE, MOTORAIL

ırrying trains are composed of special wagons or vans for the conveyance of cars usually with sleeping cars and couchettes enabling the driver and ngers to travel overnight in comfort in the same train. Some services ularly in France) convey vehicles separately allowing passengers a choice of for their own journey. Some shorter distance services run by day and convey g coaches.

are often loaded on the trains at separate stations from the passenger station and be loaded some time before the passenger train departs. International carng trains are shown in Table **1**, Domestic car-carrying trains in Table **2**. Some es also carry passengers without cars.

s of Channel Tunnel shuttle services may be found on page 46. Austrian and alpine tunnel car-carrying trains are shown in the relevant country section - see 458 and 260 respectively for details.

Readers should be careful to check that dates refer to current schedules, as old dates may be left in the table until such time as current information is received. Loading and train times may vary on some dates, but will be confirmed by the agent when booking.

> Some services shown in Table **1** are operated by organisations other than national railway companies. Contact details for these are:
>
> *Services from Germany (except Düsseldorf - Verona service):*
> DB AutoZug, (UK booking centre); ✆ 08718 80 80 66.
>
> *Düsseldorf - Verona service:*
> Treinreiswinkel, ANVR 2407, Oude Vest 7 - 9, 2312 XP Leiden; ✆ 071-513 70 08.
>
> *Certain Eastern European services (see table for details):*
> Optima Tours, Karlstrasse 56, 80333 D - München; ✆ +49 89 54880 - 111, fax +49 89 54880 - 155.

INTERNATIONAL CAR - CARRYING TRAINS 1

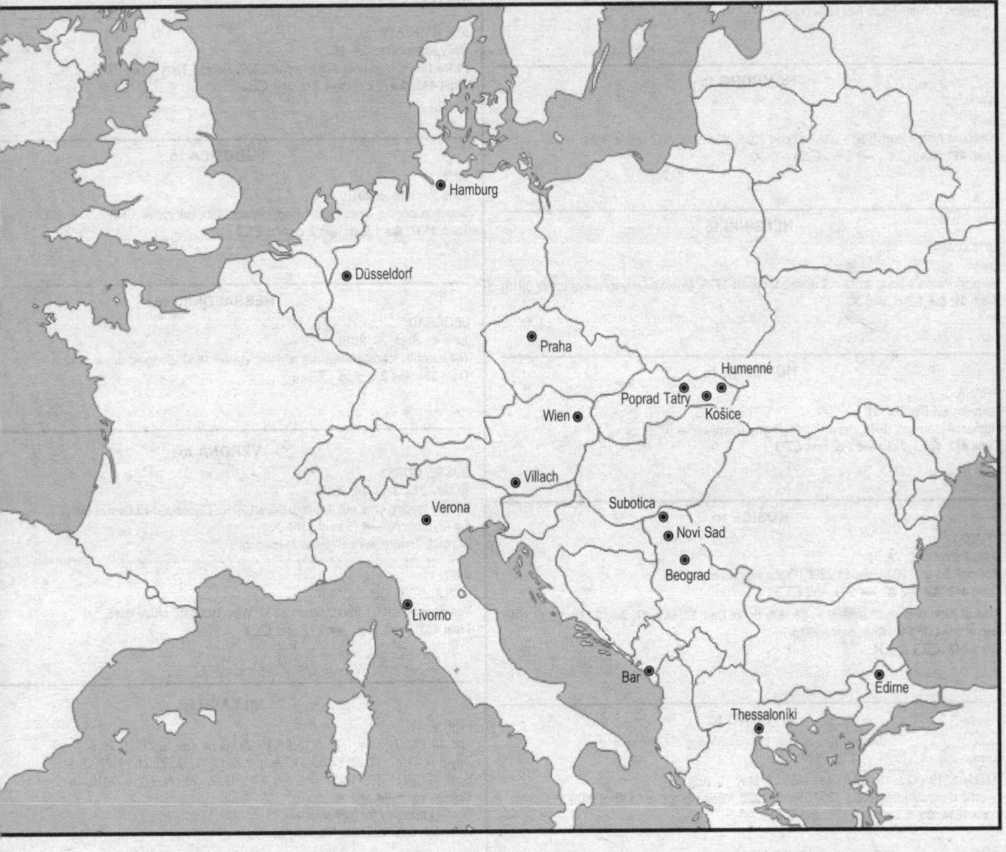

BAR to

GRAD:
·
oading times not advised, depart 1900, Beograd arrive 0602.
ional train June 4 - Sept. 5: Bar depart 2000, Beograd arrive 0824.
daily day train: Bar depart 0900, Beograd arrive 1953.
1342: 1, 2 cl. and 2 cl.

I SAD:
4 - Sept. 5, 2016.
oading times not advised, depart 1700, Novi Sad arrive 0602.
1136: 1, 2 cl., 2 cl. and 2.

OTICA:
4 - Sept. 5, 2016.
oading times not advised, depart 1700, Subotica arrive 0909.
1136: 1, 2 cl., 2 cl. and 2.

BEOGRAD to

BAR:
Daily.
Beograd loading times not advised, depart 2010, Bar arrive 0738.
Additional train June 3 - Sept. 4: Beograd depart 2110, Bar arrive 0938.
Also daily day train: Beograd depart 0910, Bar arrive 2031.
Train **1343**: 1, 2 cl. and 2 cl.

THESSALONÍKI:
June 3 - Sept. 25, 2016.
Beograd loading times not advised, depart 1850, Thessaloníki arrive 1007.
Train **335**: 2 cl. and 2.

DÜSSELDORF to

VERONA:
⑤ May 20 - Sept. 23, 2016.
Düsseldorf Hbf loading time not advised, depart 2005, Verona arrive 0902.
🛏 (2/3 berth), 🛏 (5 berth) and ✕.
Contact: Treinreiswinkel (see table heading).

WIEN:
Daily.
Düsseldorf Hbf load 2015 - 2035, depart 2054, Wien Hbf ARZ arrive 0828.
Train **421**: 🛏 1, 2 cl., 🛏 2 cl., 2 and ✕.

EDIRNE to

VILLACH:
Apr. 21, 25, 29, May 5, 9, 13, 19, 23, 27, June 2, 6, 10, 16, 21, 27, July 1, 7, 11, 15, 19, 24, 28, 29, Aug. 1, 4, 11, 12, 15, 18, 19, 22, 25, 26, 29, Sept. 1, 2, 5, 8, 9, 15, 19, 23, 29, Oct. 3, 7, 13, 17, 21, 27, 31, Nov. 4, 9, 2016.
Timings vary. 🛏 and ✕.
Contact operator for further details.
Operator: Optima Tours (see table heading).

HAMBURG to

WIEN:
Daily.
Hamburg Altona load 1950 - 2020, depart 2035, Wien Hbf ARZ arrive 0824.
Train **491**: 🛏 1, 2 cl., 🛏 2 cl., 2 and ✕.

HELSINKI to

MOSKVA:
Daily.
Helsinki Pasila loading times not advised, depart 1729, Moskva Oktyabrskaya arrive 0919.
Train **31**: 🛏 1, 2 cl. and ✕.

HUMENNÉ to

PRAHA:
Daily except Dec. 24, 31.
Humenné load until 1845, depart 1946, Praha hlavní arrive 0739.
Train **442**: 🛏 1, 2 cl., 🛏 2 cl. and 2.

KOŠICE to

PRAHA:
Daily except Dec. 24, 31.
Košice load until 2035, depart 2208, Praha hlavní arrive 0739.
Train **442**: 🛏 1, 2 cl., 🛏 2 cl. and 2.
Also daytime train on ⑦ (also Mar. 28, July 6; not Dec. 27, Mar. 27, July 3): load until 1045, depart 1144, Praha hlavní arrive 1915.
Train **242**: 12 and ✕.

LIVORNO to

German services may be bookable only in Germany.

WIEN:
④⑥ Mar. 19 - Oct. 15, 2016 (also Mar. 28, May 16, Aug. 15).
Livorno Centrale load 1630 - 1800, depart 1920, Wien Hbf arrive 0840 or 0922.
Train **1234**: 🛏 1, 2 cl., 🛏 2 cl. and 2.

MOSKVA to

HELSINKI:
Daily.
Moskva Oktyabrskaya loading times not advised, depart 2310, Helsinki Pasila arrive 1250.
Train **32**: 🛏 1, 2 cl. and ✕.

NOVI SAD to

BAR:
June 3 - Sept. 4, 2016.
Novi Sad loading times not advised, depart 2132, Bar arrive 1049.
Train **1137**: 🛏 1, 2 cl., 🛏 2 cl. and 2.

POPRAD TATRY to

PRAHA:
Daily except Dec. 24, 31.
Poprad Tatry load until 2040, depart 2153, Praha hlavni arrive 0638.
Train **444**: 🛏 1, 2 cl., 🛏 2 cl. and 2.

PRAHA to

HUMENNÉ:
Daily except Dec. 24, 31.
Praha hlavní load until 2100, depart 2200, Humenné arrive 1033.
Train **445**: 🛏 1, 2 cl., 🛏 2 cl. and 2.

KOŠICE:
Daily except Dec. 24, 31.
Praha hlavní load until 2100, depart 2200, Košice arrive 0741.
Train **445**: 🛏 1, 2 cl., 🛏 2 cl. and 2.
Also daytime train on ⑤ (also Dec. 23, Oct. 27, Nov. 16; not Dec. 25, Jan. 1, Oct. 28, Nov. 18): load until 1215, depart 1306, Košice arrive 2045.
Train **243**: 12 and ✕.

POPRAD TATRY:
Daily except Dec. 24, 31.
Praha hlavní load until 2200, depart 2309, Poprad Tatry arrive 0705.
Train **443**: 🛏 1, 2 cl., 🛏 2 cl. and 2.

SUBOTICA to

BAR:
June 3 - Sept. 4, 2016.
Subotica loading times not advised, depart 1830, Bar arrive 1049.
Train **1137**: 🛏 1, 2 cl., 🛏 2 cl. and 2.

THESSALONÍKI to

BEOGRAD:
June 4 - Sept. 26, 2016.
Thessaloníki loading times not advised, depart 1830, Beograd arrive 0742.
Train **334**: 🛏 2 cl. and 2.

VERONA to

DÜSSELDORF:
⑥ May 21 - Sept. 24, 2016.
Verona loading time not advised, depart 2010, Düsseldorf Hbf arrive 0907.
🛏 (2/3 berth), 🛏 (5 berth) and ✕.
Contact: Treinreiswinkel (see table heading).

WIEN:
⑤⑦ Apr. 29 - Oct. 16, 2016.
Verona load 2100 - 2200, depart 2330, Wien Hbf ARZ arrive 0958.
Train **481**: 🛏 1, 2 cl., 🛏 2 cl. and 2.

VILLACH to

EDIRNE:
Apr. 18, 23, 27, May 1, 7, 11, 15, 21, 25, 29, June 4, 8, 12, 18, 25, 29, July 3, 9, 13, 17, 21, 23, 27, 30, 31, Aug. 3, 6, 13, 14, 17, 20, 21, 24, 27, 28, 31, Sept. 3, 4, 7, 11, 17, 21, 25, Oct. 1, 5, 9, 15, 19, 23, 29, Nov. 2, 6, 2016.
Timings vary. 🛏 and ✕.
Contact operator for further details.
Operator: Optima Tours (see table heading).

WIEN to

DÜSSELDORF:
Daily.
Wien Hbf ARZ load 2030 - 2050, depart 2127, Düsseldorf Hbf arrive 0841.
Train **420**: 🛏 1, 2 cl., 🛏 2 cl., 2 and ✕.

HAMBURG:
Daily.
Wien Hbf ARZ load 1930 - 2000, depart 2027, Hamburg Altona arrive 0806.
Train **490**: 🛏 1, 2 cl., 🛏 2 cl., 2 and ✕.

LIVORNO:
③⑤ Mar. 18 - Oct. 14, 2016 (also Mar. 27, May 15, Aug. 14).
Wien Hbf ARZ load 1815 - 1945, depart 2010, Livorno Centrale arrive 0850.
Train **1237**: 🛏 1, 2 cl., 🛏 2 cl. and 2.

VERONA:
④⑥ Apr. 28 - Oct. 15, 2016.
Wien Hbf ARZ load 1740 - 1820, depart 1910, Verona arrive 0635.
Train **60235**: 🛏 1, 2 cl., 🛏 2 cl. and 2.

AUSTRIA

to 10/12/16

rch - Graz: daily.
rch - Villach: daily.
rch - Wien Hbf ARZ: daily.
- Feldkirch: daily.
n - Feldkirch: daily.
Hbf ARZ - Feldkirch: daily.

CROATIA

to 10/12/16

Zagreb: daily in summer (dates to be confirmed).
b - Split: daily in summer (dates to be confirmed).

FINLAND

to 10/12/16

nki - Kemijärvi: ⑤ (not June 24).
nki - Kolari: ③⑤⑥ (also June 15, 17, 18, 23; not June 24, 25).
nki - Oulu: daily (not June 24, 25, Aug. 12, Sept. 23, Oct. 14, Nov. 4, Dec. 2, 9).
nki - Rovaniemi: daily (not June 24, 25).
ärvi - Helsinki: ⑥ (not June 25).
- Helsinki: ④⑥⑦ (also June 16, 18, 19; not June 25).
- Tampere: ④⑥⑦ (also June 16, 18, 19; not June 25).
- Helsinki: daily (not June 24, 25, Aug. 13, Sept. 24, Oct. 15, Nov. 5, Dec. 3, 10).
niemi - Helsinki: daily (not June 24, 25).
niemi - Tampere: daily (not June 24, 25).
niemi - Turku: daily (not June 24, 25, Aug. 13, Sept. 24).
ere - Kolari: ③⑤⑥ (also June 15, 17, 18, 23; not June 24, 25).
ere - Rovaniemi: daily (not June 24, 25).
- Rovaniemi: daily (not June 24, 25, Aug. 12, Sept. 23).

ote: Helsinki trains load and unload at Pasila station (3km north of Helsinki station)

FRANCE

to 10/12/16

non - Paris: ⑥ Dec. 19, 2015 - Apr. 2; ④⑥ Apr. 7 - June 18; daily June 23 - Sept. 8; ④⑥ Sept. 10 - Oct. 8; ⑥ Oct. 15 - Dec. 10, 2016.

tz - Paris▲: ⑥ Apr. 16 - May 7; ④⑥ May 12 - June 11; ②④⑥ June 14 - 30; ①②③④⑤⑥ July 1 - Sept. 5; ④⑥ Sept. 8 - Oct. 1, 2016.

eaux - Paris: ⑥ Dec. 19, 2015 - Apr. 9; ⑥ Apr. 16 - May 7; ④⑥ May 12 - June 11; ②④⑥ June 14 - 30; ①②③④⑤⑥ July 1 - Sept. 5; ④⑥ Sept. 8 - Oct. 1; ⑥ Oct. 8 - Dec. 10, 2016.

çon - Paris▲: ④⑥ June 16 - 25; ②④⑥ June 28 - Sept. 10, 2016.

- Paris: ⑥ Apr. 16 - May 7; ④⑥ May 12 - June 11; ②④⑥ June 14 - 30; ①②③④⑤⑥ July 1 - Sept. 5; ④⑥ Sept. 8 - Oct. 1, 2016.

s-St. Raphaël – see St. Raphaël.

- Paris: ⑥ Dec. 19, 2015 - June 25; ②⑥ June 28 - Sept. 10; ⑥ Sept. 17 - Dec. 10, 2016.

seille - Paris: ⑥ Dec. 19, 2015 - Apr. 2; ④⑥ Apr. 7 - June 18; daily June 23 - Sept. 8; ④⑥ Sept. 10 - Oct. 8; ⑥ Oct. 15 - Dec. 10, 2016.

onne - Paris▲: ⑥ Dec. 19, 2015 - May 7; ④⑥ May 12 - June 11; ②④⑥ June 14 - 30; ①②③④⑤⑥ July 1 - Sept. 5; ④⑥ Sept. 8 - Oct. 1; ⑥ Oct. 8 - Dec. 10, 2016.

- Paris▲: ⑥ Dec. 19, 2015 - Apr. 2; ④⑥ Apr. 7 - May 14; ②④⑥ May 17 - June 21; daily June 23 - Sept. 8; ②④⑥ Sept. 10 - Oct. 8; ④⑥ Oct. 13 - 29; ⑥ Nov. 5 - Dec. 10, 2016.

s - Avignon: ⑤ Dec. 18, 2015 - Apr. 1; ③⑤ Apr. 6 - June 17; daily June 22 - Sept. 7; ③⑤ Sept. 9 - Oct. 7; ⑤ Oct. 14 - Dec. 9, 2016.

s - Biarritz▲: ⑤ Apr. 15 - May 6; ③⑤ May 11 - June 10; ①③⑤ June 13 - 29; ①②③④⑤⑥ June 30 - Sept. 3; ③⑤ Sept. 7 - 30, 2016.

s - Bordeaux: ⑤ Dec. 18, 2015 - Apr. 8; ⑤ Apr. 15 - May 6; ③⑤ May 11 - June 10; ①③⑤ June 13 - 29; ①②③④⑤⑥ June 30 - Sept. 3; ③⑤ Sept. 7 - 30; ⑤ Oct. 7 - Dec. 9, 2016.

s - Briançon▲: ③⑤ June 15 - 24; ①③⑤ June 27 - Sept. 9, 2016.

s - Brive: ⑤ Apr. 15 - May 6; ③⑤ May 11 - June 10; ①③⑤ June 13 - 29; ①②③④⑤⑥ June 30 - Sept. 3; ③⑤ Sept. 7 - 30, 2016.

s - Lyon: ⑤ Dec. 18, 2015 - June 24; ①⑤ June 27 - Sept. 9; ⑤ Sept. 16 - Dec. 9, 2016.

s - Marseille: ⑤ Dec. 18, 2015 - Apr. 1; ③⑤ Apr. 6 - June 17; daily June 22 - Sept. 7; ③⑤ Sept. 9 - Oct. 7; ⑤ Oct. 14 - Dec. 9, 2016.

s - Narbonne▲: ⑤ Dec. 18, 2015 - May 6; ③⑤ May 11 - June 10; ①③⑤ June 13 - 29; ①②③④⑤⑥ June 30 - Sept. 3; ③⑤ Sept. 7 - 30; ⑤ Oct. 7 - Dec. 9, 2016.

s - Nice▲: ⑤ Dec. 18, 2015 - Apr. 1; ③⑤ Apr. 6 - May 13; ①③⑤ May 16 - June 20; daily June 22 - Sept. 7; ①③⑤ Sept. 9 - Oct. 7; ③⑤ Oct. 12 - 28; ⑤ Nov. 4 - Dec. 9, 2016.

FRANCE (continued)

to 10/12/16

Paris - St. Raphaël▲: ⑤ Dec. 18, 2015 - Apr. 1; ③⑤ Apr. 6 - May 13; ①③⑤ May 16 - June 20; daily June 22 - Sept. 7; ①③⑤ Sept. 9 - Oct. 7; ③⑤ Oct. 12 - 28; ⑤ Nov. 4 - Dec. 9, 2016.

Paris - Toulon▲: ⑤ Dec. 18, 2015 - Apr. 1; ③⑤ Apr. 6 - May 13; ①③⑤ May 16 - June 20; daily June 22 - Sept. 7; ①③⑤ Sept. 9 - Oct. 7; ③⑤ Oct. 12 - 28; ⑤ Nov. 4 - Dec. 9, 2016.

Paris - Toulouse▲: ⑤ Dec. 18, 2015 - May 6; ③⑤ May 11 - June 10; ①③⑤ June 13 - 29; ①②③④⑤⑥ June 30 - Sept. 3; ③⑤ Sept. 7 - 30; ⑤ Oct. 7 - Dec. 9, 2016.

St. Raphaël - Paris▲: ⑥ Dec. 19, 2015 - Apr. 2; ④⑥ Apr. 7 - May 14; ②④⑥ May 17 - June 21; daily June 23 - Sept. 8; ②④⑥ Sept. 10 - Oct. 8; ④⑥ Oct. 13 - 29; ⑥ Nov. 5 - Dec. 10, 2016.

Toulon - Paris▲: ⑥ Dec. 19, 2015 - Apr. 2; ④⑥ Apr. 7 - May 14; ②④⑥ May 17 - June 21; daily June 23 - Sept. 8; ②④⑥ Sept. 10 - Oct. 8; ④⑥ Oct. 13 - 29; ⑥ Nov. 5 - Dec. 10, 2016.

Toulouse - Paris▲: ⑥ Dec. 19, 2015 - May 7; ④⑥ May 12 - June 11; ②④⑥ June 14 - 30; ①②③④⑤⑥ July 1 - Sept. 5; ④⑥ Sept. 8 - Oct. 1; ⑥ Oct. 8 - Dec. 10, 2016.

Passengers are offered a choice of departure times, mostly by day train but those noted ▲ also include night trains (Briançon night train only).

GERMANY

to 10/12/16

Basel (Lörrach) - Hamburg Altona: ①⑥⑦ Dec. 19, 2015 - Jan. 11; ⑥ Jan. 16 - Feb. 27; ①⑤⑥⑦ Mar. 5 - Apr. 30; ①④⑤⑥⑦ May 1 - June 13; daily June 16 - Sept. 5; ①⑤⑥⑦ Sept. 9 - Oct. 31; ⑥ Nov. 5 - Dec. 10, 2016 (also Dec. 23, 30, Jan. 6, 8; not Mar. 6, 27).

Hamburg Altona - Basel (Lörrach): ⑤⑥⑦ Dec. 18, 2015 - Jan. 10; ⑤ Jan. 15 - Feb. 26; ④⑤⑥⑦ Mar. 4 - Apr. 30; ③④⑤⑥⑦ May 1 - June 12; daily June 15 - Sept. 4; ④⑤⑥⑦ Sept. 8 - Oct. 30; ⑤ Nov. 4 - Dec. 9, 2016 (also Dec. 22, 29, Jan. 5, 7; not Mar. 7, 26).

Hamburg Altona - München Ost: ②⑤⑦ Dec. 18, 2015 - Jan. 5; ⑤⑦ Jan. 8 - Feb. 28; ②⑤⑦ Mar. 9 - Oct. 30; ⑤ Nov. 4 - Dec. 9, 2016.

München Ost - Hamburg Altona: ①③⑥ Dec. 19, 2015 - Jan. 6; ①⑥ Jan. 9 - Feb. 29; ①④⑥ Mar. 5 - Oct. 31; ⑥ Nov. 5 - Dec. 10, 2016.

Niebüll - Westerland: Daily shuttle service; 18 - 28 per day in summer, 12 - 14 per day in winter.

Westerland - Niebüll: Daily shuttle service; 18 - 28 per day in summer, 12 - 14 per day in winter.

***CNL** – DB City Night Line* (see page **8** for description).

GREECE

to 10/12/16

Athína - Thessaloníki: daily.
Thessaloníki - Athína: daily.

RUSSIA

to 10/12/16

Moskva - Astrakhan and v.v.
Moskva - Petrozavodsk and v.v.
Moskva - Pskov and v.v.
Moskva - St. Peterburg and v.v.
Moskva - Sochi - Adler and v.v.
St. Peterburg - Astrakhan and v.v.
St. Peterburg - Sochi - Adler and v.v.

Contact operator for days and dates of running.

SLOVAKIA

to 10/12/16

Bratislava - Humenné: daily (not Dec. 24, 31).
Humenné - Bratislava: daily (not Dec. 24, 31).

SLOVENIA

to 10/12/16

Bohinjska Bistrica - Podbrdo - Most na Soči: daily.
Most na Soči - Podbrdo - Bohinjska Bistrica: daily.

Note: service operates through the Julian Alps. Passengers remain in their vehicles. Also accepts passengers without vehicles.

Scenic Rail Routes of Europe

The following is a list of some of the most scenic rail routes of Europe, timings for most of which can be found within the timetable (the relevant table number has been specified in bold). Routes marked * are some of the editorial team's favourite journeys. Please note that this list does not include specialised mountain and tourist railways.

Types of scenery : C-Coastline, F-Forest, G-Gorge, L-Lake, M-Mountain, R-River.

ALBANIA

Route	Scenery	Table
Elbasan - Pogradec	M L G R	**1390**

AUSTRIA

Route	Scenery	Table
Bruck an der Mur - Villach	M R	**980**
Gmunden - Stainach Irdning*	M L	**961**
Innsbruck - Brennero	M	**595**
Innsbruck - Garmisch*	M	**895**
Innsbruck - Schwarzach-St Veit	M G	**960**
Krems - Emmersdorf	R	**991**
Landeck - Bludenz*	M	**951**
St Pölten - Mariazell*	M	**994**
Salzburg - Villach*	M G	**970**
Selzthal - Kleinreifling - Steyr	M G R	**976/977**
Wiener Neustadt - Graz	M	**980**

BELGIUM and LUXEMBOURG

Route	Scenery	Table
Liège - Luxembourg*	R	**444**
Liège - Marloie	R	
Namur - Dinant	R	**440**

BULGARIA

Route	Scenery	Table
Septemvri - Dobriniste	M	**1510**
Sofia - Burgas	M	**1500**
Tulovo - Gorna Oryakhovitsa	M	**1525**

CROATIA and BOSNIA

Route	Scenery	Table
Rijeka - Ogulin	M	**1310**
Ogulin - Split	M	**1330**
Sarajevo - Ploče	M G R	**1355**

CZECH REPUBLIC

Route	Scenery	Table
Karlovy Vary - Mariánské Lázně	R F	**1123**
Karlovy Vary - Chomutov	R	**1110**
Praha - Děčín	R	**1100**

DENMARK

Route	Scenery	Table
Struer - Thisted	C	**716**

FINLAND

Route	Scenery	Table
Kouvola - Joensuu	L F	**797**

FRANCE

Route	Scenery	Table
Aurillac - Neussargues	M G	**331**
Bastia - Ajaccio	M	**369**
Bourg-en-Bresse - Bellegarde	M	**341**
Chambéry - Bourg St Maurice	M	**366**
Chambéry - Modane	M L	**367**
Chamonix - Martigny*	M G	**572**
Clermont Ferrand - Béziers	M G	**332**
Clermont Ferrand - Nîmes*	M G R	**333**
Gap - Briançon	M L	**362**
Genève - Aix les Bains	M R	**364**
Grenoble - Veynes - Marseille	M	**632**
Marseille - Ventimiglia	C	**360/361**
Mouchard - Montbéliard	R	**378**
Nice - Digne	M	**359**
Nice - Cuneo*	M G	**581**
Perpignan - Latour de Carol*	M G	**354**
Portbou - Perpignan	C	**355**
Sarlat - Bergerac	R	**318**
Toulouse - Latour de Carol	M	**312**
Valence - Veynes	M	**362**

GERMANY

Route	Scenery	Table
Arnstadt - Meiningen	M	**870**
Dresden - Děčín	G R	**1100**
Freiburg - Donaueschingen	G F	**938**
Garmisch - Reutte - Kempten	M	**888**
Heidelberg - Neckarelz	R	**923/924**
Koblenz - Mainz*	G R	**911/914**
München - Lindau	M	**935**
Murnau - Oberammergau	M L	**897**
Naumburg - Saalfeld	R	**849/851**
Niebüll - Westerland	C	**821**
Nürnberg - Pegnitz	G R	**880**

GERMANY - continued

Route	Scenery	Table
Offenburg - Konstanz	M F	**916**
Pforzheim - Nagold / Wildbad	F	**941**
Plattling - Bayerisch Eisenstein	F	**929**
Rosenheim - Berchtesgaden	M L	**890/891**
Rosenheim - Wörgl	M	**951**
Siegburg/Bonn - Siegen	R	**807**
Stuttgart - Singen	F	**940**
Titisee - Seebrugg	L F	**938**
Trier - Koblenz - Giessen	R	**906/915**
Ulm - Göppingen	M	**930**
Ulm - Tuttlingen	R	**938**

GREAT BRITAIN and IRELAND

Route	Scenery	Table
Alnmouth - Dunbar	C	**180**
Barrow in Furness - Maryport	C	**159**
Coleraine - Londonderry	C	**231**
Dun Laoghaire - Wicklow	C	**237**
Edinburgh - Aberdeen	C	**224**
Exeter - Newton Abbot	C	**115/116**
Glasgow - Oban / Mallaig*	M L	**218**
Inverness - Kyle of Lochalsh*	M C	**226**
Lancaster - Carlisle - Carstairs	M G R	**151**
Liskeard - Looe	R	**118**
Llanelli - Craven Arms	M	**146**
Machynlleth - Pwllheli	M C	**148**
Perth - Inverness	M	**221**
Plymouth - Gunnislake	R	**118**
St Erth - St Ives	C	**118**
Sheffield - Chinley	M	**193/206**
Shrewsbury - Aberystwyth	M R	**147**
Skipton - Settle - Carlisle	M R	**173**

GREECE

Route	Scenery	Table
Korinthos - Patras	C	**1450**
Diakoptó - Kalávrita	M G	**1455**

HUNGARY

Route	Scenery	Table
Budapest - Szob	R	**1255**
Eger - Szilvásvárad	M	**1299**
Székesfehérvár - Balatonszentgyörgy	L	**1220**
Székesfehérvár - Tapolca	L	**1225**

ITALY

Route	Scenery	Table
Bologna - Pistoia	M	**609**
Bolzano - Merano	M	**597**
Brennero - Verona*	M	**595**
Brig - Arona	M L	**590**
Domodossola - Locarno*	M G	**551**
Firenze - Viareggio	M	**614**
Fortezza - San Candido	M	**596**
Genova - Pisa	C	**610**
Genova - Ventimiglia	C	**580**
Lecco - Tirano	M L	**593**
Messina - Palermo	C	**641**
Napoli - Sorrento	C	**639**
Roma - Pescara	M	**624**
Salerno - Reggio Calabria	C	**640**
Taranto - Reggio Calabria	C	**635**
Torino - Aosta	M	**586**
Ventimiglia - Cuneo*	M G	**581**

NORWAY

Route	Scenery	Table
Bergen - Oslo*	M L	**780/781**
Bodø - Trondheim	M L	**787**
Dombås - Åndalsnes	M	**785**
Drammen - Larvik	C	**783**
Myrdal - Flåm*	M C	**781**
Oslo - Kongsvinger	R	**750**
Oslo / Røros - Trondheim	M L	**784/785**
Stavanger - Kristiansand	M	**775**

POLAND

Route	Scenery	Table
Jelenia Góra - Walbrzych	M	**1084**
Kraków - Zakopane	M	**1066**
Olsztyn - Elk	L	**1035**
Olsztyn - Morag	L	**1035**
Tarnów - Krynica	M	**1078**

PORTUGAL

Route	Scenery	Table
Covilhã - Entroncamento	M R	
Pampilhosa - Guarda	M	
Porto - Coimbra	C R	
Porto - Pocinho*	R	
Porto - Valenca	M C	

ROMANIA

Route	Scenery	Table
Brasov - Ploiesti	M	
Caransebes - Craiova	M G R	
Fetesti - Constanta	R	
Oradea - Cluj Napoca	R	

SERBIA and MONTENEGRO

Route	Scenery	Table
Priboj - Bar	M L	

SLOVAKIA

Route	Scenery	Table
Banská Bystrica - Brezno - Košice	M	
Žilina - Poprad Tatry	M	

SLOVENIA

Route	Scenery	Table
Jesenice - Sežana	M G R	
Maribor - Zidani Most	M	
Maribor - Bleiburg	M G R	
Villa Opicina - Ljubljana - Zagreb	G R	

SPAIN

Route	Scenery	Table
Algeciras - Ronda	M R	
Barcelona - Latour de Carol	M	
Bilbao - San Sebastián	M	
Bilbao - Santander	M	
Ferrol - Gijón*	C	
Granada - Almería	M	
Huesca - Canfranc	M G R	
León - Monforte de Lemos	M	
León - Oviedo	M	
Lleida - La Pobla de Segur	M L	
Málaga - Bobadilla	G	
Santander - Oviedo	M C	
Zaragoza - València	M R	

SWEDEN

Route	Scenery	Table
Bollnäs - Ånge - Sundsvall	M L	
Borlänge - Mora	M L F	
Borlänge - Ludvika - Frövi	M L F	
Narvik - Kiruna	M F	
Östersund - Storlien	L F	

SWITZERLAND

Route	Scenery	Table
Andermatt - Göschenen	G	
Basel - Delémont - Moutier	M R	
Chur - Arosa	M G	
Chur - Brig - Zermatt*	M	**575**
Chur - St Moritz*	M G	
Davos - Filisur	M G	**5**
Davos - Landquart	M	
Interlaken Ost - Jungfraujoch*	M	
Interlaken Ost - Luzern	M L	
Interlaken West - Spiez	L	
Lausanne - Brig	M L R	
Lausanne - Neuchâtel - Biel	M L	
Montreux - Zweisimmen - Lenk	M L G	
Rorschach - Kreuzlingen	L	
St Moritz - Scuol Tarasp	M	
St Moritz - Tirano*	M	
Spiez - Zweisimmen	G	
Thun - Kandersteg - Brig*	M L	
Zürich / Luzern - Chiasso	M L	
Zürich - Chur	M L	

Plans are on pages 28 - 32

AIRPORT → CITY CENTRE LINKS

5

ort code and name	City	Distance	Journey	Transport ‡	City terminal	Table
Aarhus	Århus	37 km	40 mins	🚌 flybus, connects with flights	Banegårdspladsen, Central rail station	
Aberdeen, Dyce	Aberdeen	11 km	33 mins	🚌 **727**, ①–⑤ every 30 mins; ⑥⑦ hourly	Union Square bus station. Also ①–⑤ 🚌 **80** to Dyce rail station	
Alacant	Alacant	12 km	30 mins	🚌 **C6**, every 20 mins 0600 - 0000	Plaza Puerta del Mar	
Amsterdam, Schiphol	Amsterdam	17 km	20 mins	Train, every 10 mins (every hour 2400 - 0600)	Centraal rail station	**451, 454**
	Rotterdam	65 km	45 mins	Train, every 30 mins (every hour 2400 - 0600)	Centraal rail station	**450, 454**
	Den Haag	43 km	35 mins	Train, every 30 mins (every hour 2400 - 0600)	Centraal rail station	**450, 454**
Ancona, Falconara	Ancona	16 km	30 mins	1) 🚌 Linea **J**, 2) Train hourly at peak times: 17 mins	Main rail station	
Athína, Elefthérios Venizélos	Athína	27 km	39 mins	Metro (line **3**), every 30 mins 0635 - 2335	Syntagma	**1440**
	Pireás	41 km	90 mins	🚌 **X96**, 3 - 4 per hour	Platia Karaiskáki	
Barcelona, Aeroport del Prat	Barcelona	14 km	19 mins	Train, 0513, 0535, 0609, then every 30 mins: 0609 - 2314	Sants. Also calls at Passeig de Gràcia rail station (26 mins)	**659**
Basel - Mulhouse - Freiburg	Basel	9 km	20 mins	🚌 **50**, ①–⑤ 8 per hour; ⑥⑦ 6 per hour	SBB rail station / Kannenfeldplatz	
	Freiburg	60 km	55 mins	🚌 ①–⑤ every 1 - 2 hours; ⑥⑦ every 2 hours	Rail station	
Belfast, City, George Best	Belfast	2 km	15 mins	🚌 *Airlink* **600**, ①–⑥ every 20 mins; ⑦ every 40 mins	Europa Buscentre. Also train from Sydenham rail station	
Belfast, International	Belfast	26 km	40 mins	🚌 *Airbus* **300**, Ⓐ every 15 mins; ⑥ every 20; ⑦ every 30	Europa Buscentre (adjacent to Great Victoria St rail station)	
Beograd, Nikola Tesla	Beograd	18 km	30 mins	🚌 **72**, every 32 minutes	Rail station	
Berlin, Schönefeld	Berlin	24 km	28 mins	Train, *AirportExpress* **RE7/ RB14** 2 per hour 0631 - 2331	Hbf, also Ost, Alexanderplatz and Zoo rail stations	**847**
Berlin, Tegel	Berlin	7 km	40 mins	🚌 *JetExpressBus TXL*, Ⓐ every 10 mins, Ⓒ every 20 mins	Hauptbahnhof rail station	
Biarritz - Anglet - Bayonne	Biarritz	3 km	22 mins	🚌 *STAB* **6**, every hour approx.	Town centre	
	Bayonne	7 km	28 mins	🚌 *STAB* **6**, every hour approx.	Rail station	
Bilbao, Sondika	Bilbao	10 km	45 mins	🚌 Bizkaibus **A-3247**, every 20 mins 0620 - 0000	Plaza Moyúa (Metro station Moyúa)	
Billund	Vejle	25 km	34 mins	🚌 *Sydtrafik* **43**	Town centre	
Birmingham, International	Birmingham	12 km	11 mins	Train, ①–⑥ ± 9 per hour, ⑦ 6 per hour	New Street rail station from International	**129, 142, 143**
Bologna, Guglielmo Marconi	Bologna	8 km	25 mins	🚌 *Aerobus* BLQ, every 15 mins 0600 - 2315	Centrale rail station	
Bordeaux, Mérignac	Bordeaux	12 km	45 mins	🚌 Jet' Bus, every 45 mins 0745 - 2245	St Jean rail station	
Bournemouth, Hurn	Bournemouth	10 km	15 mins	🚌 **A 1** *Airport Shuttle*, hourly 0730 - 1830	Rail station, Bus station (Travel Interchange)	
Bratislava, Milan Rastislav Štefánika	Bratislava	10 km	25 mins	🚌 **61**, 3 - 4 per hour	Main rail station (Hlavná stanica)	
Bremen	Bremen	3 km	20 mins	Tram **6**, ①–⑥ every 10 mins, ⑦ every 20 mins	Main rail station	
Brescia, Montichiari, Verona	Verona	50 km	45 mins	🚌, connects with Ryanair flights	Main rail station	
	Brescia	18 km	20 mins	🚌, connects with Ryanair flights	Main rail station	
Bristol, International	Bristol	13 km	30 mins	🚌 *International Flyer*, ①–⑥ 3 - 6 per hour; ⑦ 2 - 6 per hour	Temple Meads rail station, also bus station	
Brno	Brno	8 km	20 mins	🚌 **76**, 2 per hour	Main rail station, also bus station	
Brussels, Nationaal / Zaventem	Brussels	12 km	25 mins	Train, 6 per hour	Midi / Zuid rail station (also calls at Central and Nord)	**401**
	Antwerpen	38 km	34 mins	Train, Ⓐ 2 per hour, Ⓒ hourly.	Centraal	**420, 432**
Bucuresti, Henri Coanda, Otopeni	Bucuresti	16 km	45 mins	🚌 **783**, ①–⑤ every 15 - 30 mins; ⑥⑦ every 30 mins	Piata Victoriei (800m from Nord station or 1 stop on subway)	
Budapest, Ferihegy	Budapest	16 km	40 mins	🚌 **200E**, every 10 - 20 mins	Köbánya-Kispest metro station (metro connection to city centre)	
	Budapest	18 km	25 mins	Train, 2 - 6 per hour	🚌 **200E**, to Ferihegy station then train to Nyugati rail station.	
Bydgoszcz	Bydgoszcz	4 km	30 mins	🚌 **80**, 2 per hour	Main rail station	
Carcassonne, Salvaza	Carcassonne	5 km	10 mins	🚌, connects with Ryanair flights	Place Davilla and Carcassonne rail station	
Cardiff	Cardiff	19 km	40 mins	🚌 *Airbus Xpress* **X91**, ①–⑥ hourly, ⑦ every 2 hours	Central rail station, city centre	
	Cardiff	19 km	50 mins	🚌 to Rhoose then Train: ①–⑥ hourly, ⑦ every 2 hours	Central rail station	
Charleroi, Brussels South	Brussels	55 km	60 mins	🚌 *Brussels City Shuttle*, every 30 mins	Brussels Midi (corner of Rue de France / Rue de l'Instruction)	
	Charleroi		18 mins	🚌 *Line* **A**, ①–⑤ 2 per hour, ⑥⑦ hourly	Main rail station	
Cork	Cork	8 km	25 mins	🚌 **226**, ①–⑥ 2 per hour, ⑦ hourly	Rail station, also Parnell Place bus station	
Derry (Londonderry)	Londonderry	11 km	30 mins	🚌 connects with flights	Foyle Street bus station	
Dinard - Pleurtuit - St-Malo	St Malo	14 km	20 mins	Taxis only. Dinard 6 km 10 mins		
Doncaster - Sheffield	Doncaster	10 km	25 mins	🚌 **91**, ①–⑥ 2 per hour; ⑦ hourly	Frenchgate Interchange (bus station)	
Donetsk	Donetsk	13 km	40 mins	Fixed-run taxi **5**	Main rail station	
Dortmund, Wickede	Dortmund	10 km	25 mins	🚌 every hour, AirportExpress	Main rail station (Hbf). Also 🚌 to Holzwickede rail station	
Dresden	Dresden	15 km	21 mins	Train (S-Bahn **S2**) every 30 mins	Main rail stations (Hbf and Neustadt)	**857a**
Dublin	Dublin	11 km	60 mins	🚌 *Airlink* **747**, every 10 mins (15 - 20 mins on ⑦)	Bus station (Busáras) 30min, O'Connell St., Heuston rail station	
	Belfast	157 km	130 mins	🚌 **001 / 200**, hourly 0520 - 2120 also 2320, 0120, 0320	Europa Buscentre. Also 2220, 0020, 0220, 0420 June 3 - Sept. 22	
Dubrovnik, Čilipi	Dubrovnik	24 km	30 mins	🚌 *Atlas Bus*, connects with flights	Bus station	
Düsseldorf, International	Düsseldorf	7 km	12 mins	Train (S-Bahn **S1**) Ⓐ every 20 mins, Ⓒ every 30 mins	Main rail station (Hauptbahnhof)	**800, 802**
East Midlands, Nottingham - - Leicester - Derby	East Midlands	10 km	10 mins	Taxi shuttle	East Midlands Parkway rail station	
	Nottingham	21 km	55 mins	🚌 *Skylink*, every 30 min. 0505 - 0105, also 0205, 0305, 0405	Broadmarsh bus station	
	Derby	19 km	40 mins	🚌 *Skylink* every 30 min. 0615 - 1855; (60 mins 1945 - 0545)	Bus station	
	Loughborough	8 km	25 mins	🚌 *Skylink* every 30 min. 0715 - 2017; (60 mins 2057 - 0657)	Swan Street	
	Leicester	23 km	55 mins	🚌 *Skylink* every 30 min. 0715 - 1948; (60 mins 2057 - 0657)	St Margaret's bus station	
Edinburgh, Turnhouse	Edinburgh	11 km	25 mins	🚌 *Airlink* **100**, every 10 mins. **N 22** 2400 - 0600 every 30mins.	Haymarket rail station; Waverley Bridge (next to Waverley station)	
Erfurt	Erfurt	6 km	22 mins	Tram, Line 4, Ⓐ 3 - 6 per hour; Ⓒ 2 per hour	Main rail station (Hauptbahnhof)	
Esbjerg	Esbjerg	12 km	21 mins	🚌 **8**, hourly	*Bybusterminal*	
Exeter	Exeter	8 km	25 mins	🚌 **56, 56A, 56B**, 1 per hour	St Davids rail station	
Faro	Faro	6 km	20 mins	🚌 *Proxima* **16**, 1 per hour	Rail station, Bus station	
Firenze, Amerigo Vespucci	Firenze	7 km	20 mins	🚌 Ataf *Vola in bus* **62**, every 30 mins	Santa Maria Novella rail station	
Frankfurt, Hahn	Frankfurt	120 km	105 mins	🚌, connects with Ryanair flights	Mannheimer Straße, adjacent to main rail station (Hauptbahnhof)	
Also 🚌 to Bingen, 60 mins; Heidelberg hbf, 140 mins; Koblenz, 70 mins; Köln hbf, 135 mins; Luxembourg, 105 mins; Mainz, 70 mins; Mannheim, 110 mins						
Frankfurt	Frankfurt	10 km	15 mins	Train (S-Bahn **S8** or **S9**), 4 - 6 times hourly	Main rail station (Hauptbahnhof)	**917a**
Friedrichshafen	Friedrichshafen	4 km	7 mins	1 - 2 trains per hour	Main rail station (Stadt) or Harbour (Hafen)	**933**
Gdańsk, Lech Walesa	Gdańsk	10 km	22 mins	Train *PKM*, Port Lotniczy, 3 - 4 per hour	Wrzeszcz rail station, then 3 stops (every 15 mins) to Główny	
Genève	Genève	6 km	6 mins	Train, 5 times hourly	Cornavin rail station	**500, 570**
Genova, Cristoforo Colombo	Genova	7 km	20 mins	🚌 *Volabus*, 1 - 2 per hour	Principe rail station	
Girona	Girona	12 km	25 mins	🚌, hourly	Rail / Bus station (Estación autobuses)	
	Barcelona	102 km	70 mins	🚌, connects with Ryanair flights	Estacio del Nord, corner of carrer Ali Bei 80 / Sicilia	

The frequencies shown apply during daytime on weekdays and are from the airport to the city centre. There may be fewer journeys in the evenings, at weekends and during the winter months. Extended 🚌 journey times could apply during peak hours.

5 AIRPORT → CITY CENTRE LINKS

City Plans are on pages 28

Airport code and name		City	Distance	Journey	Transport ‡	City terminal	
GLA	Glasgow, International	Glasgow	15 km	15 mins	🚌 *GlasgowFlyer*, ①–⑥ every 10 mins, ⑦ every 15 mins.	Central rail station	
PIK	Glasgow, Prestwick	Glasgow	61 km	50 mins	Train, ①–⑥ 4 per hour, ⑦ 2 per hour	Central rail station	
GSE	Göteborg, City	Göteborg	17 km	30 mins	🚌, connects with Ryanair, Air Berlin and Wizz Air flights	Nils Ericson Terminalen (bus station) / Central rail station	
GOT	Göteborg, Landvetter	Göteborg	25 km	30 mins	🚌, ①–⑤ 3 per hour, ⑥⑦ 2 - 3 per hour	Nils Ericson Terminalen (bus station) / Central rail station	
GRZ	Graz	Graz	9 km	9 mins	Train ①–⑥ 1 - 2 per hour, ⑦ every 2 hours	Main rail station (Hauptbahnhof)	
GNB	Grenoble, St Geoirs	Grenoble	37 km	45 mins	🚌, connects with flights	Main rail station, also bus station	
HAM	Hamburg, Fuhlsbüttel	Hamburg	11 km	24 mins	Train (S-Bahn **S1**), every 10 mins	Main rail station (Hauptbahnhof)	
HAJ	Hannover, Langenhagen	Hannover	15 km	17 mins	Train (S-Bahn **S5**), every 30 mins	Main rail station (Hauptbahnhof)	
HEL	Helsinki, Vantaa	Helsinki	19 km	35 mins	Train ①–⑥ 4 - 6 per hour, ⑦ 3 - 4 per hour	Helsinki (Ring Rail Line)	
NOC	Ireland West Airport Knock	Ballyhaunis	22 km	30 mins	🚌 **64**, 0855, 1250	Rail station	
IOM	Isle of Man, Ronaldsway	Douglas	16 km	30 mins	🚌 **1**, hourly (every 30 mins in peak periods)	Lord street	
IST	İstanbul, Atatürk	İstanbul	28 km	40 mins	🚌, *Havas Airport Shuttle* hourly 0400 - 2400	Taksim	
		İstanbul	28 km	60 mins	Metro to Zeytinburnu, then over bridge for Tram **T1**	Sirkeci rail station	
SAW	İstanbul, Sabiha Gökcen	İstanbul	32 km	60 mins	🚌, 1–2 per hour, 0540 - 2040	Bus station. Also Pendik rail station is 4km from airport	
XRY	Jerez	Jerez	10 km	9 mins	Train, 11 trains per day	Jerez de la Frontera, then to Cadiz	
FKB	Karlsruhe - Baden-Baden	Baden-Baden	8 km	15 mins	🚌 **205**, connects with Ryanair flights	Rail station; also 🚌 **140** to Karlsruhe Hbf, 25 mins	
KTW	Katowice, Pyrzowice	Katowice	34 km	50 mins	🚌 *Lotnisko, PKM*, 1 per hour approx	Katowice Dworzec (main rail station)	
KUN	Kaunas	Kaunas	13 km	40 mins	🚌 **120, 29**	City centre	
		Vilnius	102 km	90 mins	🚌 connects with Ryanair flights	Hotel Panorama, close to bus and rail stations	
KLU	Klagenfurt	Klagenfurt	5 km	25 mins	🚌 **45**, to Annabichl rail station, then train or 🚌 **40**	Main rail station and bus station	
CPH	København, Kastrup	København	12 km	15 mins	Train, every 10 mins	Main rail station (Hovedbanegård)	
		Malmö	36 km	22 mins	Train, every 20 mins	Central rail station	
CGN	Köln / Bonn, Konrad Adenauer	Bonn	25 km	32 mins	🚌 **SB60**, ①–⑤ 2 per hour; ⑥⑦ 1 - 2 per hour	Main rail station (Hauptbahnhof)	
		Köln	15 km	16 mins	Train **S13**, ①–⑤ every 20 mins, ⑥⑦ every 30 mins	Main rail station (Hbf). Also to Mönchengladbach, Koblenz	
KRK	Kraków, Balice	Kraków	12 km	18 mins	Train, 2 per hour	Kraków Główny	
KBP	Kyïv, Boryspil	Kyïv	34 km	60 mins	🚌 **322** *Polit*, 2 - 3 per hour	Main rail station	
LBA	Leeds - Bradford	Leeds	16 km	40 mins	🚌 **757**, 2 per hour	Main rail station and bus station	
		Bradford	11 km	40 mins	🚌 **737, 747**, 2 per hour	Interchange rail station	
AOC	Leipzig, Altenburg - Nobitz	Leipzig	75 km	70 mins	🚌 **250** *ThüSac*, connects with Ryanair flights	Main rail station. Also stops at Altenburg rail station after 15 r	
LEJ	Leipzig - Halle	Leipzig	20 km	14 mins	Train, 2 - 3 per hour	Main rail station (Hauptbahnhof)	
		Halle	18 km	12 mins	Train, 2 per hour	Main rail station (Hauptbahnhof)	
LNZ	Linz, Blue Danube	Linz	12 km	19 mins	🚌, connects with Ryanair flights	Main rail station. Also free 🚌 to Hörsching rail station, 3 mi	
LIS	Lisboa, Portela	Lisboa	3 km	9 mins	Train, Red (Vermelho) line. Every 5 - 9 mins	Oriente rail station. For Santa Apolónia change at São Sebastiã	
LPL	Liverpool, John Lennon	Liverpool	11 km	37 mins	🚌 **500**, every 30 mins 0545 - 1945	Lime Street rail station, Liverpool One bus station	
LJU	Ljubljana, Jože Pučnik, Brnik	Ljubljana	26 km	45 mins	🚌, Ⓐ hourly 0500 - 2000; Ⓒ 0700, every 2 hours 1000 - 2000	Bus station (Avtobusna pos	
LCJ	Łódź, Lublinek	Łódź	6 km	20 mins	🚌 **65**	Kaliska rail station	
LCY	London, City	London	12 km	25 mins	Train (Docklands Light Railway), every 8 - 10 mins	Bank underground (tube) station	
LGW	London, Gatwick	London	44 km	30 mins	Train *Gatwick Express*, every 15 minutes	Victoria rail station	**103, 105,**
LHR	London, Heathrow	London	24 km	15 mins	Train *Heathrow Express*, every 15 minutes	Paddington rail station	
		London	24 km	58 mins	Underground train (tube), every 6 - 12 mins	King's Cross St Pancras rail station	
LTN	London, Luton	London	50 km	35 mins	6 - 7 per hour (🚌 between and Parkway rail station)	St Pancras International rail station	**103, 140,**
SEN	London, Southend	London	64 km	55 mins	Train, 3 per hour	Liverpool Street rail station	
STN	London, Stansted	London	55 km	46 mins	Train *Stansted Express*, every 15 minutes	Liverpool Street rail station	
LBC	Lübeck, Blankensee	Lübeck	8 km	30 mins	🚌 **6**, every 20 mins	Bus station (bus stop 5). Also train from Flughafen 300m walk	
		Hamburg	59 km	75 mins	🚌 *VHHAG*, connects with Ryanair flights	Corner Adenaueralle / Brockesstrasse (ZOB) near main rail stat	
LUZ	Lublin	Lublin	10 km	15 mins	Train, ①–⑥ 5 per day, ⑦ 3 per day, connects with flights	Main rail station	
LUX	Luxembourg, Findel	Luxembourg	7 km	25 mins	🚌 **16**, every 15 mins ①–⑥, every 30 mins ⑦	Central rail station	
LWO	Lviv, Skniliv	Lvov	10 km		🚌, Taxi-bus *Marshrutka*	City Centre	
LYS	Lyon, St Exupéry	Lyon	23 km	30 mins	Tram *RhôneExpress*, 4 per hour	Part Dieu rail station	
		Chambéry	87 km	60 mins	🚌 Altibus, 4 - 5 times daily	Bus station (gare routière)	
		Grenoble	91 km	65 mins	🚌 Faure Vercors, 0630 Ⓐ, hourly 0730 - 2330	Bus station (gare routière); Place de la Résistance	
MAD	Madrid, Barajas T4	Madrid	12 km	11 mins	Train, Cercanías every 30 mins 0628 - 2258	Chamartín, also Atocha Cercanías 25 mins (see city plans p3	
AGP	Málaga	Málaga	8 km	12 mins	Train, every 30 mins	María Zambrano (renfe) and Centro-Alameda rail stations	
MMX	Malmö, Sturup	Malmö	30 km	45 mins	🚌 *flygbussarna*, 1 - 2 per hour	Central rail station	
MAN	Manchester	Manchester	16 km	14 mins	Train, up to 9 per hour (hourly through the night)	Piccadilly rail station	
MSE	Manston	Ramsgate	3 km	9 mins	🚌 **38**, ①–⑥ hourly 0943 - 1343	Rail station	
MRS	Marseille, Provence	Marseille	28 km	25 mins	🚌, every 20 mins. See also rail / bus on Table **351**	St Charles rail station; also 🚌 to Aix TGV rail stn. every 30 m	
FMM	Memmingen	Memmingen	5 km	10 mins	🚌 **2, 810, 811**	Bus station and rail station; also 🚌 to München, 95 mins	
LIN	Milano, Linate	Milano	9 km	20 mins	1) 🚌 **73** every 10 mins; 2) 🚌 *Starfly*, every 30 mins	1) Piazza S. Babila, Metro line 1; 2) Centrale rail static	
MXP	Milano, Malpensa	Milano	45 km	40 mins	1) *Malpensa Express* train, every 30 mins; 2) 1 - 2 per hour	1) Cadorna and Bovisa rail stations; 2) Centrale rail station	
				50 mins	🚌 *Bus Express*, 2 per hour / *Shuttle Air* 3 per hour	Centrale rail station. Also 🚌 to Gallarate (Table **590**)	
BGY	Milano, Orio al Serio, Bergamo	Milano	45 km	60 mins	🚌, 1 - 2 per hour	Centrale rail station (Air Terminal)	
		Bergamo	4 km	15 mins	🚌, 2 per hour	Rail station	
MSQ	Minsk	Minsk	42 km	90 mins	🚌, **112, 300**,	Vostochniy and Moskovskiy bus stations	
DME	Moskva, Domodedovo	Moskva	35 km	47 mins	Train, *Aeroexpress*, 1 - 2 per hour approx, 0600 - 0000	Paveletskaya rail station	**19**
SVO	Moskva, Sheremetyevo	Moskva	35 km	35 mins	Train, *Aeroexpress*, 1 - 2 per hour approx, 0500 - 0030	Belorusskaya rail station	**1**
VKO	Moskva, Vnukovo	Moskva	28 km	40 mins	Train, *Aeroexpress*, 1 per hour approx, 0600 - 0000	Kiyevskaya rail station	**1**
MUC	München, International	München	37 km	40 mins	Train **S1**, **S8** for Hbf, every 10 mins; **S8** for Ost, every 20 mins	Main rail stations (Hauptbahnhof, Ostbahnhof)	**8**
		Freising	6 km	24 mins	🚌 *MVV* **635**, every 20 mins	Rail station for connections to Regensburg, Passau	**878, 9**
NTE	Nantes, Atlantique	Nantes	9 km	30 mins	🚌 *Tan Air*, ± hourly; connects with flights	Main rail station	
NAP	Napoli, Capodichino	Napoli	7 km	20 mins	🚌 *ANM* **3S** line, 2 per hour; *Alibus*, 2 per hour	Piazza Garibaldi (Centrale rail station)	
NCL	Newcastle, International	Newcastle	9 km	25 mins	Metro train, every 12 mins	Main rail station	

‡ – The frequencies shown apply during daytime on weekdays and are from the airport to the city centre. There may be fewer journeys in the evenings, at weekends and during the winter months. Extended 🚌 journey times could apply during peak hours.

¶ – Graz Airport - Feldkirchen rail station is loca about 300 metres away from the airport.

Plans are on pages 28-32

AIRPORT → CITY CENTRE LINKS 5

ort code and name	City	Distance	Journey	Transport ‡	City terminal	Table
Nice, Côte d'Azur	Nice	7 km	20 mins	🚌 **99**, 2 per hour	SNCF rail station ¶	
		7 km	20 mins	🚌 **98**, 3 per hour	City centre, Riquier	
Nîmes - Arles - Camargue	Nîmes	12 km	20 mins	🚌, connects with Ryanair flights	Rail station	
Norwich	Norwich	8 km	24 mins	🚌 **603**, ①–⑥ 4 per hour 0700 - 1800, 1835, 1905, 1935, 2002	Bus station	
Nürnberg	Nürnberg	6 km	12 mins	Train, U-bahn **U2**, 4 - 6 per hour	Main rail station (Hauptbahnhof)	
Odesa	Odesa	9 km	30mins	🚌 **129**	Rail station	
Oslo, Gardermoen	Oslo	49 km	19 mins	Train *Flytoget*, 3 - 6 per hour	Central rail station	**771**
Oslo, Sandefjord Torp	Oslo	123 km	116 mins	🚌 to Torp rail station (4 mins) for train to Oslo	Also 🚌 to Oslo Bus terminal	**783**
Oslo, Rygge	Oslo	69 km	51 mins	🚌 connects with Ryanair flights, to Rygge rail station (4 km).	Sentral rail station (51 mins Rygge to Sentral)	**770**
) Palermo, Falcone-Borsellino	Palermo	24 km	45 mins	Train *Trinacria express*, ①–⑥ 2 per hour, ⑦ hourly	Centrale rail station	
Palma, Mallorca	Palma	11 km	30 mins	🚌 **1**, every 15 mins	Paseo de Mallorca, Placa d'Espanya (for rail stations), the Port	
Paris, Beauvais	Paris	80 km	75 mins	🚌, connects with Ryanair and WizzAir flights	Porte Maillot, Metro (Line 1) for Châtelet Les Halles, Gare de Lyon	
Paris, Charles de Gaulle	Paris	25 km	35 mins	RER train, (Line B), every 7 - 15 mins	Nord, Châtelet Les Halles, and St Michel rail stations	**398**
	Disneyland	23 km	45 mins	🚌 **VEA** Navette / Shuttle, every 20 minutes	Disneyland Resort, Disneyland hotels	
Paris, Orly	Paris	15 km	35 mins	🚌 to Pont de Rungis, then RER train, (Line C) 4 per hr.	Austerlitz, St Michel, Musée d'Orsay, and Invalides rail stns.	**398**
	Paris	15 km	33 mins	ORLYVAL shuttle to Antony then RER train, (Line B) 4 per hr.	Châlet-Les-Halles, Nord rail stations	**398**
Perpignan, Rivesaltes	Perpignan	5 km	15 mins	🚌, connects with flights	Rail station, bus station (gare routière)	
Pisa, Galileo Galilei	Pisa	2 km	8 mins	🚌 every 10 minutes	Centrale rail station	**613**
) Porto	Porto	17 km	35 mins	Metro Train, Line E, 3 per hour	Campanhã rail station	
Poznań, Ławica	Poznań	6 km	20 mins	🚌 **L** *MPK*, 2 per hour	Rail station	
Praha, Václav Havel	Praha	19 km	46 mins	🚌 **AE** *Airport Express*, every 20 - 30 mins	hlavní rail station	
	Praha	17 km	60 mins	🚌 **119**, every 10 mins	Nádraží Veleslavín metro station, then Metro line A to muzeum	
Pula	Pula	6 km	15 mins	🚌, connects with Ryanair flights	Town centre	
Reus	Reus	6 km	20 mins	🚌 **50**, *Hispano Igualadina*, hourly	Rail station	**652**
	Barcelona	90 km	90 mins	🚌 *Hispano Igualadina* connects with Ryanair flights	Sants rail station	
Reykjavík, Keflavík	Reykjavík	50 km	45 mins	🚌 *flybus*, connects with all flights	BSÍ bus terminal	
Riga	Riga	13 km	30 mins	🚌 **22**, every 10 - 30 mins	Abrenes iela (street) next to rail station	
Rijeka	Rijeka	30 km	45 mins	🚌 *Autotrans*, connects with flights	Bus station, Jelačić Square	
Roma, Ciampino	Roma	15 km	40 mins	🚌 *Terravision* 1 - 3 per hour	Termini rail station	**622**
) Roma, Fiumicino	Roma	26 km	42 mins	Train, ①–⑥ 4 per hour, ⑦ 2 per hour	Ostiense and Tiburtina rail stations	**622**
(also known as Leonardo da Vinci)		26 km	31 mins	*Leonardo Express* rail service, every 30 mins	Termini rail station	**622**
Rotterdam	Rotterdam	5 km	20 mins	*Airport Shuttle* **33**, ①–⑤ every 10 mins, ⑥⑦ every 15 mins	Groot Handelsgebouw (adjacent to Centraal rail station)	
Rzeszów, Jasionka	Rzeszów	15 km	20 mins	🚌 **L**, connects with flights	Main rail station and bus station	
St Peterburg, Pulkovo II	St Peterburg	17 km	60 mins	🚌 **13**	Moskovskaya Metro station, Line 2 for Nevski Pr. (see City Plans)	
Salzburg, W. A. Mozart	Salzburg	5 km	22 mins	🚌 **2**, ①–⑥ every 10 - 20 mins, ⑦ every 20 mins	Main rail station	
Simferopol	Simferopol	12 km	28 mins	🚌 **9** (trolleybus), every 10–15 mins	Main rail station	
Skopje, Alexander the Great	Skopje	14 km	25 mins	🚌 Vardar Ekspres, connects with flights	Bus station	
Sofia, International	Sofia	10 km	25 mins	🚌 **84**, **384**, every 10 - 20 mins	University	
Southampton	Southampton	8 km	8 mins	Train, 50 metres from terminal, 4 - 5 trains per hour	Central rail station	**108, 129**
Split, Kaštela	Split	16 km	50 mins	🚌 connects with flights	Bus station. Departs 200m from Airport terminal	
Stavanger, Sola	Stavanger	14 km	30 mins	🚌, ①–⑤ every 20 mins, ⑥ 2 per hour, ⑦ hourly	Atlantic Hotel / Fiskepiren	
Stockholm, Arlanda	Stockholm	44 km	20 mins	*Arlanda Express* train, every 15 mins	Central rail station	**747, 760**
Stockholm, Skavsta	Stockholm	103 km	80 mins	🚌, connects with Ryanair flights	Cityterminal (bus station), also 🚌 to Nyköping rail station	
Stockholm, Västerås	Stockholm	107 km	75 mins	🚌, connects with Ryanair flights	Cityterminal (bus station), also 🚌 **941** to Västerås rail station	
Strasbourg, Entzheim	Strasbourg	10 km	9 mins	Train from Entzheim Aéroport (300m walk) 1 - 4 per hour	Gare Centrale (Central rail station)	**388**
Stuttgart, Echterdingen	Stuttgart	20 km	27 mins	Train (S-Bahn **S2**, **S3**), 2 - 4 times hourly 0508 - 0008	Main rail station (Hauptbahnhof)	**932**
Szczecin, Goleniów	Szczecin	43 km	56 mins	Train, 0832, 1552 Ⓑ, 1905.	Szczecin Główny. Also 🚌 connects with Ryanair/Norwegian flights	
Tallinn, Ülemiste	Tallinn	5 km	22 mins	🚌 **90K**, every 30 mins 0800 - 1800	Balti jaam (rail station)	
Tampere, Pirkkala	Tampere	18 km	25 mins	🚌, connects with Ryanair flights	Main rail station (Rautatieasemalta)	
Tbilisi	Tbilisi	19 km	30 mins	Train, 2 per day: 0845, 1805	Rail station	
Tirana (Tiranë), Nënë Tereza	Tirana	12 km	45 mins	🚌 *Rinas Express*, every hour 0600 - 1800	National Museum in city centre	
Torino, Caselle	Torino	16 km	20 mins	*SATTI* train every 30 mins	Torino Dora rail station, Piazza Baldissera	
	Torino	16 km	40 mins	🚌, ①–⑥ 2 - 3 per hour; ⑦ 1 - 2 per hour	Torino Porta Nuova and Porta Susa rail stations	
Toulouse, Blagnac	Toulouse	8 km	38 mins	Tram, **T2** every 15 minutes for Arènes then Metro line **A**	for Marengo-SNCF, then 300m to Matabiau rail station	
	Toulouse	8 km	20 mins	🚌 *Aero*, every 20 minutes	Place Jeanne d'Arc / Matabiau rail / bus station (gare routière)	
Trieste, Ronchi dei Legionari	Trieste	33 km	50 mins	🚌 **51**, ①–⑥ 1 - 2 per hour; ⑦ hourly	Bus station, next to rail station	
	Monfalcone	4 km	17 mins	🚌 **10**, ①–⑥ 1 - 2 per hour; ⑦ hourly	Rail station	
Trondheim, Værnes	Trondheim	33 km	37 mins	Train, ①–⑤ hourly, ⑥⑦ every two hours	Rail station. Værnes rail station is 220m from Airport terminal	**787**
València	València	9 km	22 mins	Train, Lines **3**, **5**, Ⓐ every 6 - 9 mins; ⑥⑦ every 8 - 12 mins	Xátiva for Nord rail station	
Venezia, Marco Polo	Venezia	12 km	25 mins	🚌 **5**, 2 per hour	Piazzale Roma (see city plans p32)	
	Venezia		80 mins	Waterbus *Alilaguna* ± every 30 mins	Lido 53 - 63 mins / Piazza S. Marco, 72 - 80 mins	
Venezia, Treviso	Venezia	30 km	70 mins	🚌, connects with flights	Mestre rail station, Piazzale Roma (see city plans p32)	
Verona, Villafranca	Verona	12 km	20 mins	🚌, every 20 mins 0635 - 2335	Rail station	
Vilnius	Vilnius	4 km	7 mins	Train, 0637, 0728 and every ± 40 minutes until 1944	Rail station	**1812**
W Warszawa, Frederic Chopin, Okęcie,	Warszawa	13 km	23 mins	SKM / KM train, 3 - 5 per hour	Śródmieście (2 - 3 per hr) or Centralna (1 - 2 per hr) rail stations	
Warszawa, Modlin	Warszawa	44 km	47 mins	🚌, to Modlin rail stn, then train, approx 1 - 2 per hour	Centralna or Gdánska rail stations	**1030**
Weeze, Niederhein	Düsseldorf	70 km	75 mins	🚌, connects with Ryanair flights	Main rail station (Hauptbahnhof) Worringer Street	
	Düsseldorf	74 km	82 mins	🚌 **SW1**, to Weeze rail station, then train, Table **802**	Main rail station (Hauptbahnhof)	**802**
Wien, Schwechat	Wien	21 km	16 mins	*City Airport Train (CAT)*, every 30 mins; special fares	Mitte rail station	**985**
	Wien	21 km	25 mins	S-bahn, every 30 mins	Mitte rail station	**985**
	Bratislava	54 km	60 mins	🚌 *ÖBB - Postbus / Slovak Lines*, hourly	AS Mlynské nivy (bus station) / Einsteinnova/Petrzalka	**985**
RO Wrocław, Copernicus	Wrocław	10 km	30 mins	🚌 **406**, ①–⑥ 2 - 3 per hour; ⑦ every 40 mins	Rail station, bus station	
G Zagreb	Zagreb	17 km	25 mins	🚌, 1 - 2 per hour	Bus station (Autobusni kolodvor), Avenija Marina Drzica	
Z Zaragoza	Zaragoza	10 km	30 mins	🚌, ①–⑥ 1 - 2 per hour 0615 - 2315; ⑦ hourly 0645 - 2245	Paseo María Agustín, 150m from Portillo rail station	
H Zürich	Zürich	10 km	13 mins	Train, 7 - 8 per hour	Main rail station (HB)	**529**

The frequencies shown apply during daytime on weekdays and are from the airport to the city centre. There may be fewer journeys in the evenings, at weekends and during the winter months. Extended 🚌 journey times could apply during peak hours.

¶ – Also train, from Nice St Augustin, ± hourly; 800m from Terminal 1.

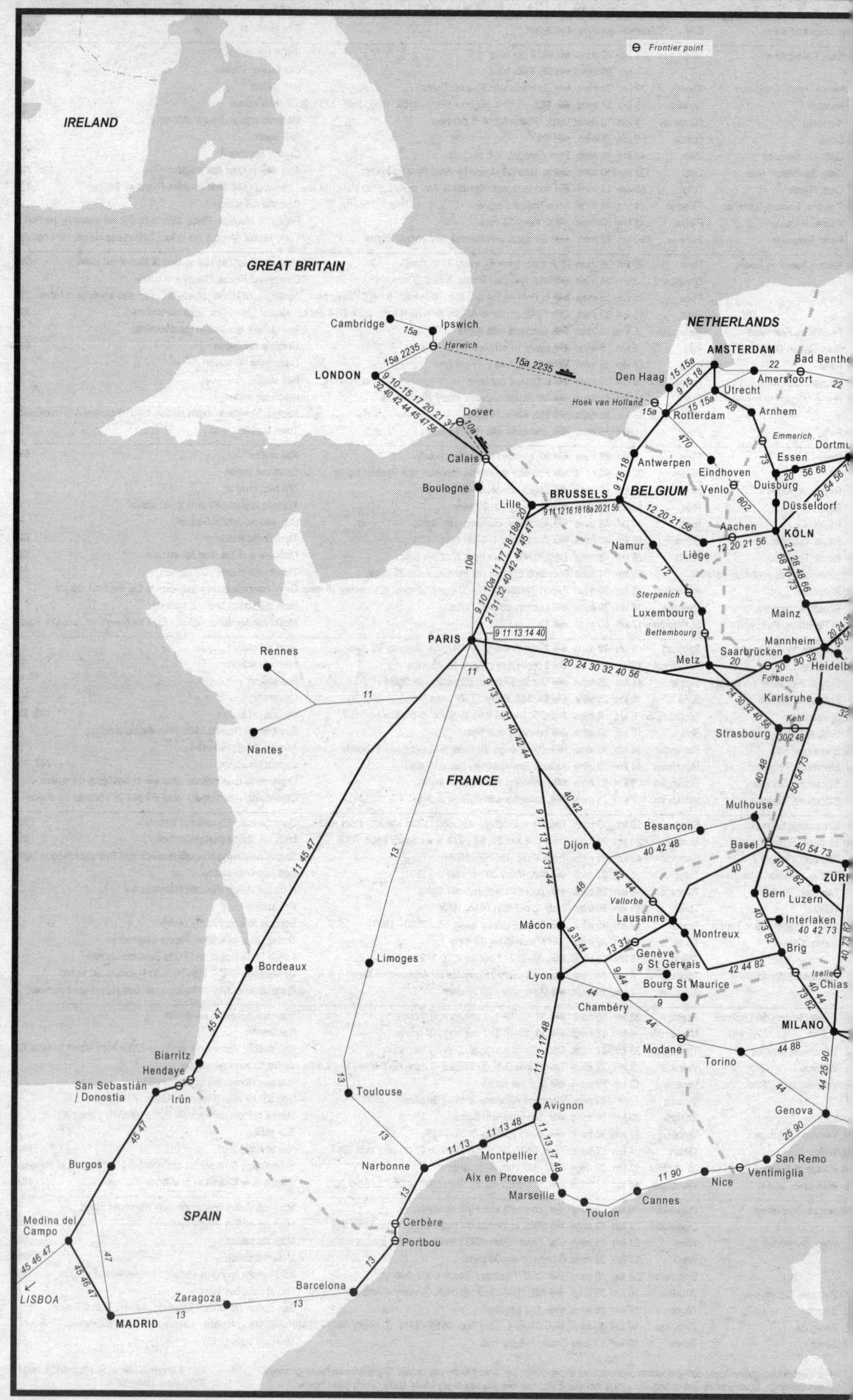

Frontier point
IRELAND
GREAT BRITAIN
NETHERLANDS
BELGIUM
FRANCE
SPAIN
Cambridge
Ipswich
Harwich
LONDON
Dover
Calais
Boulogne
Lille
BRUSSELS
AMSTERDAM
Den Haag
Hoek van Holland
Rotterdam
Utrecht
Amersfoort
Bad Benthe
Arnhem
Emmerich
Antwerpen
Eindhoven
Venlo
Essen
Duisburg
Düsseldorf
Dortmu
Aachen
KÖLN
Namur
Liège
Sterpenich
Luxembourg
Bettembourg
Mainz
Mannheim
Heidelb
Saarbrücken
Forbach
Metz
Karlsruhe
Kehl
Strasbourg
PARIS
Rennes
Nantes
Mulhouse
Besançon
Dijon
Basel
ZÜRI
Bern
Luzern
Interlaken
Vallorbe
Lausanne
Montreux
Brig
Iselle
Chias
Mâcon
Genève
St Gervais
Bourg St Maurice
Lyon
Chambéry
Modane
MILANO
Torino
Genova
Limoges
Bordeaux
Biarritz
Hendaye
San Sebastián / Donostia
Irún
Toulouse
Avignon
Montpellier
Narbonne
Aix en Provence
Marseille
Toulon
Cannes
Nice
Ventimiglia
San Remo
Cerbère
Portbou
Barcelona
Burgos
Medina del Campo
LISBOA
Zaragoza
MADRID

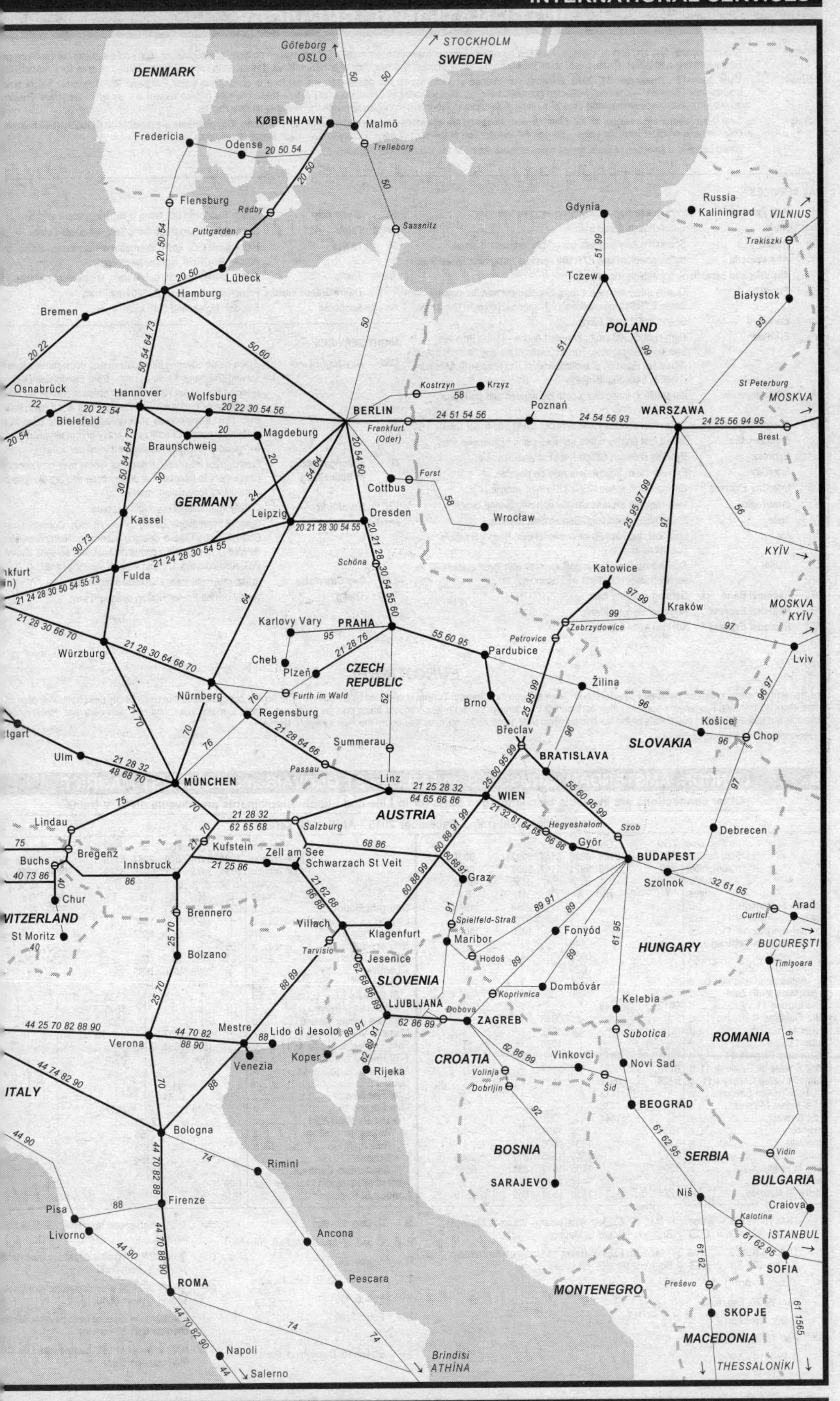
DENMARK
SWEDEN
KØBENHAVN
Malmö
Trelleborg
Göteborg
OSLO
STOCKHOLM
Fredericia
Odense
Flensburg
Rødby
Puttgarden
Lübeck
Hamburg
Bremen
Sassnitz
Gdynia
Russia
Kaliningrad
VILNIUS
Trakiszki
Tczew
Białystok
POLAND
Osnabrück
Hannover
Wolfsburg
Bielefeld
Braunschweig
Magdeburg
BERLIN
Frankfurt (Oder)
Kostrzyn
Krzyz
Poznań
WARSZAWA
St Peterburg
MOSKVA
Brest
Cottbus
Forst
Wrocław
GERMANY
Kassel
Leipzig
Dresden
Fulda
Schöna
KYÏV
Katowice
Kraków
Zebrzydowice
Petrovice
Würzburg
Karlovy Vary
PRAHA
Cheb
Plzeň
CZECH REPUBLIC
Pardubice
Brno
Žilina
Lviv
Nürnberg
Furth im Wald
Regensburg
Košice
Chop
SLOVAKIA
Břeclav
BRATISLAVA
Ulm
Summerau
MÜNCHEN
Passau
Linz
WIEN
AUSTRIA
Salzburg
Lindau
Bregenz
Kufstein
Hegyeshalom
Szob
Győr
BUDAPEST
Debrecen
Buchs
Innsbruck
Zell am See
Schwarzach St Veit
Graz
Szolnok
Arad
Curtici
Chur
SWITZERLAND
St Moritz
Brennero
Villach
Tarvisio
Klagenfurt
Spielfeld-Straß
Maribor
Hodoš
Fonyód
HUNGARY
BUCUREŞTI
Timişoara
Bolzano
Jesenice
SLOVENIA
Koprivnica
Dombóvár
Kelebia
LJUBLJANA
Dobova
ZAGREB
Subotica
ROMANIA
Verona
Mestre
Lido di Jesolo
Venezia
Koper
Rijeka
CROATIA
Vinkovci
Novi Sad
Volinja
Dobrljin
Šid
BEOGRAD
ITALY
Bologna
Rimini
BOSNIA
SARAJEVO
SERBIA
Vidin
BULGARIA
Pisa
Livorno
Firenze
Ancona
Niš
Craiova
Kalotina
İSTANBUL
SOFIA
ROMA
Pescara
MONTENEGRO
Preševo
SKOPJE
Napoli
Salerno
Brindisi
ATHÍNA
MACEDONIA
THESSALONÍKI

INTERNATIONAL SERVICES

Services All trains convey first and second classes of seating accommodation unless otherwise noted. For information on types of sleeping car (🛏) and couchette car (▬) see pa Restaurant (✕) and buffet (🍸) cars vary considerably from country to country in standard of service offered. The catering car may not be carried or open for the whole jou

Timings **Valid June 12 - December 12, 2016**. Services can change at short notice and passengers are advised to consult the latest European Rail Timetable before trav International trains are not normally affected by public holidays, but may alter at Christmas and Easter - these changes (where known) are shown in the tables. Reade advised to cross-check timings and days of running of services in the International section with the relevant country section.

Tickets **Seat reservations** are available for most international trains and are advisable as some trains can get very crowded. **Supplements** are payable on **EuroCity** (*EC*) trains in countries and on most InterCity trains – consult the introduction at the start of each country to see which supplements apply.

Listed below is a selection of the different types of trains found in the International Section.

DAY SERVICES:

AP	***Alfa Pendular***	Portuguese high-quality tilting express train.
Alvia	***Alvia***	Spanish high-speed train.
Alta	***Altaria***	Spanish quality express using light, articulated stock.
AV	***Alta Velocità***	Italian premium fare **ETR 500** services using high-speed lines.
AVE	***Alta Velocidad Española***	Spanish high-speed train.
EC	***EuroCity***	Quality international express. Supplement may be payable. Italian **ETR 610** international high-speed (200 km/h) tilting train.
Em	***Euromed***	Spanish 200 km/h train.
☆	***Eurostar***	High-speed (300 km/h) service London - Paris / Brussels. Special fares payable. Three classes of service on most trains: (Business Premier, Standard Premier and Standard). Minimum check-in time 30 minutes.
FA	***Frecciargento***	Italian tilting trains using both high-speed and traditional lines.
FB	***Frecciabianca***	Italian fast premium fare services using traditional lines.
FR	***Frecciarossa***	Italian fast premium fare services using high-speed lines.
Ex	***Express***	Express between Czech Republic and Slovakia.
IC	***InterCity***	Express train. Supplement may be payable.
ICE	***InterCity Express***	German high-speed (230 - 320 km/h) service.
IR	***InterRegio***	Inter-regional express usually with refurbished coaches.
ITA	***.italo***	Italian high-speed train. Supplement payable.
izy	***izy***	Low cost, high-speed international train Paris - Brussels Special fares apply.
RJ	***Railjet***	Austrian quality international express with three classes of service: (Business, First and Economy).
RB	***Regional Bahn***	German stopping train.
RE	***Regional Express***	Regional semi-fast train.
REX	***Regional Express***	Austrian semi-fast train.
SC	***Super City***	Czech Pendolino **680** tilting train, supplement payable.
Talgo	***Talgo***	Spanish quality express using light, articulated stock.
⇌	***Thalys***	High-speed (300 km/h) international train Paris - Brussels Amsterdam / Köln. Special fares apply.
Thello	***Thello***	Jointly owned French / Italian train, supplement payable.
TGV	**Train à Grande Vitesse**	French high-speed (270 - 320 km/h) train.
Sn	***Snabbtåg***	Swedish high-speed (210 km/h) train.

NIGHT SERVICES:

CNL	***City Night Line***	Brand name covering international and domestic services serving Germany. Facilities range from *Comfortline Deluxe* sleeping cars (1 and 2 berth) with en-suite shower and WC modernised *Comfortline Economy* sleeper and 6 berth couc cars. Most trains convey shower facilities and 🍸 (also ✕ c certain services). Special fares apply and reservation is compulsory (except in seating) on most services.
D	***Durchgangszug*** or **Schnellzug**	Overnight or international express. Some may only convey passengers to international destinations and are likely to b compulsory reservation, marked R.
EN	***EuroNight***	Quality international overnight express.
Hotel	***Trenhotel***	Spanish international quality overnight train. Conveys Gran Clase / Grande Classe sleeping accommodation comprising *de luxe* (1 and 2 berth) compartments with en-suite showe WC. Also conveys 1, 2 and 4 berth sleeping cars.
ICN	***InterCity Notte***	Italian overnight train, supplement payable.
Thello	***Thello***	Jointly owned French / Italian overnight train.

EUROTUNNEL

The frequent car-carrying service between Folkestone and Calais through the **Channel Tunnel** is operated by Eurotunnel. The service operates up to four times hourly (less frequently at night takes about 35 minutes. Passengers stay with their cars during the journey. Separate less-frequent trains operate for lorries, coaches, motorcycles, and cars with caravans. Reservation advisable but passengers can buy tickets at the toll booths when they arrive at the terminal and board the next available shuttle.

Reservations: ✆ 08443 35 35 35.

9 LONDON, AMSTERDAM, BRUSSELS and LILLE - ST GERVAIS and BOURG ST MAURICE

Other connections are available by changing in Paris (or in Lille and Lyon). Supplements are payable on TGV trains

Winter ski trains December 2015 - April 2016 service

train type	*TGV*		*TGV*	⇌	*TGV*	☆		☆	
train number	**964**		**5108**	**9920**	**5146**	**9092**		**9096**	
train number	**965**		**5109**	**9921**	**5147**	**9093**		**9097**	
notes			R 🍸	R 🍸	R 🍸	R ✕		R ✕	
notes	**Y**		**H**	**A**	**F**	**M**		**E◐**	
London St Pancras d.	...	...	...	...	...	0945	...	1945	...
Ashford International **11** a.	...	...	...	...	...	1016	...	2016	...
Ashford International **11** d.	...	...	...	...	...	1028	...	2028	...
Amsterdam Centraal d.	...	...	...	0540	...	|	...	|	...
Schiphol d.	...	...	...	0558	...	|	...	|	...
Rotterdam CS d.	...	...	...	0625	...	|	...	|	...
Antwerpen Centraal d.	...	...	...	0705	...	|	...	|	...
Brussels Midi / Zuid d.	...	...	...	0759	...	|	...	|	...
Lille Europe 11 d.	0612	...	0743	|	...	|	...	|	...
Lille Flandres ◇ d.	|	...	|	|	0943	|	...	|	...
Douai **11** d.	|	...	|	|	1012	|	...	|	...
Arras **11** d.	|	...	|	|	1030	|	...	|	...
TGV Haute Picardie **11** d.	|	...	0813	|	|	|	...	|	...
Paris Charles de Gaulle ✈ **11** d.	0713	...	0853	|	1117	|	...	|	...
Marne la Valleé Chessy § **11** d.	0728	...	0912	|	1131	|	...	|	...
Cluses (Haute Savoie) a.	|	...	1418	|	|	|	...	|	...
Salanches Megève a.	|	...	1436	|	|	|	...	|	...
St Gervais a.	|	...	1444	|	|	|	...	|	...
Chambéry a.	1030	...	...	1221	1427	|	...	|	...
Albertville a.	1109	...	...	1304	1506	|	...	|	...
Moûtiers-Salins a.	1142	...	...	1345	1545	1811	...	0533	...
Aime la Plagne a.	1204	...	...	1405	1613	1831	...	0557	...
Landry a.	1215	...	...	1417	1623	|	...	|	...
Bourg St Maurice a.	1225	...	...	1430	1634	1850	...	0616	...

train type	☆	*TGV*	*TGV*	⇌	*TGV*		☆	☆
train number	**9095**	**5174**	**970**	**9987**	**5178**		**9099**	**9099**
train number	**9094**	**5175**	**971**	**9986**	**5179**		**9098**	**9098**
notes	R ✕	R 🍸	R 🍸	R 🍸	R 🍸		R ✕	R ✕
notes	**G**	**K**	**Z**	**B**	**T**		**P◧**	**Q◧**
Bourg St Maurice d.	0934	1413	1517	1536	...	...	2212	2212
Landry d.	|	1422	1527	1546	...	...	|	|
Aime la Plagne d.	|	1433	1539	1557	...	...	|	|
Moûtiers-Salins a.	1007	|	|	|	...	...	2242	2242
Moûtiers-Salins d.	1014	1451	1608	1625	...	...	2254	2254
Albertville d.	|	1528	1646	1658	...	...	|	|
Chambéry d.	|	1614	|	1750	...	...	|	|
St Gervais d.	|	|	|	|	1530	...	|	|
Salanches Megève d.	|	|	|	|	1548	...	|	|
Cluses (Haute Savoie) d.	|	|	|	|	1606	...	|	|
Marne la Vallée Chessy § **11** a.	|	1917	2017	|	|	...	|	|
Paris Charles de Gaulle ✈ **11** a.	|	1934	2031	2045	|	...	|	|
TGV Haute Picardie **11** a.	|	2006	|	|	2048	...	|	|
Arras **11** a.	|	|	|	|	|	...	|	|
Douai **11** a.	|	|	|	|	|	...	|	|
Lille Flandres ◇ a.	|	|	2131	|	|	...	|	|
Lille Europe 11 a.	|	2038	...	|	2117	...	|	|
Brussels Midi / Zuid a.	|	...	...	2211	...	...	|	|
Antwerpen Centraal a.	|	...	...	2256	...	...	|	|
Rotterdam CS a.	|	...	...	2333	...	...	|	|
Schiphol a.	|	...	...	2354	...	...	|	|
Amsterdam Centraal a.	|	...	...	0012	...	...	|	|
Ashford International **11** a.	1537	...	...	...	...	...	0633	|
London St Pancras a.	1613	...	...	...	...	...	0716	0705

A – THALYS NEIGE – ⑥ Dec. 19 - Mar. 19: 🚃12 🍸 Amsterdam - Bourg St Maurice; ⑥ Dec. 19 - Apr. 9: 🚃12 🍸 Brussels - Bourg St Maurice.

B – THALYS NEIGE – ⑥ Dec. 26 - Mar. 26: 🚃12 🍸 Bourg St Maurice - Amsterdam; ⑥ Dec. 19 - Apr. 9: 🚃12 🍸 Bourg St Maurice - Brussels.

E – ⑤ Jan. 1 - Apr. 1.

F – Dec. 19, 26, Feb. 6, 13.

G – ⑥ Dec. 26 - Apr. 9.

H – Dec. 19, 26, Feb. 6, 13.

K – ⑥ Dec. 19 - Apr. 2.

M – ⑥ Dec. 19 - Apr. 2.

P – ⑥ Jan. 2 - Apr. 9 (not Feb. 20).

Q – ⑥ Feb. 20.

T – Dec. 26, Jan. 2, Feb. 13, 20.

Y – Feb. 6, 13

Z – Feb. 13, 20.

§ – Station for Disneyland, Paris.

⇌ – *Thalys* high-speed train R 🍸. Special far payable.

◐ – 🍸 until 2400. ✕ after departure from Ash ✕ and 🍸 from 0500.

◧ – 🍸 until 2400. ✕ after departure from Moût ✕ and 🍸 from 0500.

☆ – Eurostar train. Special fares payable. Minir check-in time 30 minutes.

◇ – 500 metres from Lille Europe (see Lille Ci Plan on page 30).

For explanation of standard symbols see page 4

LONDON - LILLE - PARIS and BRUSSELS *by Eurostar* 10

Minimum check-in time is 30 minutes, but passengers are advised to allow longer due to immigration procedures.
Not available for London - Ebbsfleet - Ashford or v.v. Special fares payable that include three classes of service: business premier, standard premier and standard. All times shown are local times (France and Belgium are one hour ahead of Great Britain).
All Eurostar services are 🅁, non-smoking and convey ✕ in Business Premier and Standard Premier, 🍸 in Standard.

Service May 29 - December 10

February 1 - July 15 Engineering work on the high speed line between Calais and Paris will affect services: Departures from Paris will be 3 - 15 minutes earlier and the last two arrivals at Paris will be up to 60 minutes later.

km	*train number*	9080	9108	9002	9110	9110	9004	9008	9008	9114	9010	9010	9116	9116	9116	9014	9014	9014	9016	9018	9126	9126	9020	9022
	notes	①–⑤	①	⑥		⑥	①–⑤	⑥	①–⑤	①–⑤	⑦	①–⑥		①	⑥⑦	①–⑤	⑦	⑥		Ⓑ		⑦	⑥	⑥
	notes	f	K	r	L		j		j	j	y	j	W	M	y	j	y		A		Y	Z	w	
0	**London** St Pancras ....d.	0540	0613	0618	0650	0657	0701	0752	0755	0804	0819	0831	0855	0855	0858	0917	0922	0924	1001	1024	1058	1104	1101	1122
35	Ebbsfleet International ....d.	0558	0630		0707			0812	0812		0838		0914	0914	0915	0934		0941		1042	1115			
90	Ashford International ....d.	0624	0652	0655	0728	0728										0955	0955							1155
166	Calais Fréthun ....a.				0859									1059	1059									
267	Lille Europe ....a.				0930	0926				1026			1126	1130	1130						1326	1326		
373	**Brussels** Midi / Zuid ....a.		0958		1007	1005				1105			1205	1208	1208						1405	1405		
	Paris Nord ....a.	0917	...	0947	...	...	1017	1117	1117	...	1147	1147	...	...	...	1247	1247	1247	1317	1347	...	...	1417	1447

train number	9022	9060	9024	9132	9028	9030	9136	9032	9140	9036	9038	9144	9040	9148	9044	9152	9046	9152	9048	9050	9156	9158	9054	9162	9056
notes		①④⑤				⑦			Ⓑ			⑥				⑦	①–⑤	①–⑤		Ⓑ	⑥⑦	①–⑤		⑦	
notes	Q	H			R	y	F				B			V		y	j	j	C		y	j			S
on St Pancras .... d.	1131	1201	1224	1258	1331	1401	1404	1422	1504	1531	1601	1604	1631	1704	1731	1755	1801	1804	1831	1901	1904	1934	2001	2003	2031
leet International .... d.			1242	1315																					
rd International .... d.								1455								1828									
s Fréthun .... a.				1459																	2059	2129			
Europe .... a.				1530			1626		1726			1826		1926		2026		2026			2130	2200		2226	
ussels Midi / Zuid.......... a.				1608			1705		1805			1905		2005		2105		2105			2208	2238		2305	
Nord........................... a.	1447	1517	1547	...	1647	1717	...	1747	...	1847	1917	...	1947	...	2047	...	2117	...	2147	2217	...	...	2317	...	2347

train number	9109	9005	9007	9113	9009	9011	9117	9013	9015	9019	9125	9021	9023	9129	9025	9027	9133	9029	9029	9031	9031	9033	9035	9037	9141
notes	①	①	①–⑥	①–⑥	①–⑤	⑥⑦								⑦	⑥		①–⑥		⑦	⑦	①–⑥	⑥	⑥⑦		⑦
notes	k	p	q	j	j	y		D		T	X	N		b		U	j	H	y	y	j	G	b	J	y
Nord........................... d.	...	0643	0713	...	0743	0813	...	0843	0913	1013	...	1043	1113	...	1133	1213	...	1233	1243	1313	1313	1333	1413	1443	...
ussels Midi / Zuid.......... d.	0656			0756			0852				1056			1156			1252								1452
Europe .... d.	0736			0836			0930				1136			1236			1330								1530
s Fréthun .... d.							1001										1401								1601
rd International .... a.								0937					1207												
fleet International .... a.									1018								1345		1348		1418				1545
on St Pancras .... a.	0759	0802	0832	0857	0900	0930	0957	1009	1039	1130	1157	1200	1239	1257	1300	1330	1405	1400	1409	1430	1439	1500	1530	1602	1605

train number	9141	9039	9145	9043	9045	9045	9149	9149	9047	9153	9153	9051	9157	9053	9055	9161	9059	9061	9063						
notes	①–⑥				⑦		①–⑥	⑦		①–⑤	⑦	Ⓑ	Ⓑ					⑦	Ⓑ						
notes	j	t	F		y	E	j	y		j	y			P				m							
Nord........................... d.	...	1513	...	1613	1643	1643	...	...	1713	...	...	1813	...	1843	1913	...	2013	2043	2113	...	...	...	...	...	...
ussels Midi / Zuid.......... d.	1456		1556				1656	1656		1756	1756		1856			1952				...	...	...	...	...	...
Europe .... d.	1536		1636				1736	1736		1836	1836		1935			2030				...	...	...	...	...	...
s Fréthun .... d.																2101				...	...	...	...	...	...
rd International .... a.					1737		1734				1835				2007					...	...	...	...	...	...
fleet International .... a.	1545			1718		1748		1745		1845		1918				2045	2118		2218	...	...	...	...	...	...
on St Pancras .... a.	1605	1630	1657	1739	1812	1812	1806	1803	1832	1903	1910	1939	1957	2002	2039	2103	2139	2200	2239	...	...	...	...	...	...

⑥⑦ May 29 - July 23. ⑦ July 24 - Sept. 3 (also Aug. 27).
④⑤⑦ May 29 - July 23 (also May 30). ⑤⑦ July 24 - Dec. 10 (also Aug. 29).
Daily May 29 - July 23. ①④⑤⑥⑦ July 24 - Sept. 3. ⑤⑥⑦ Sept. 4 - Nov. 4. ⑤⑦ Nov. 5 - Dec. 10.
①–⑤ (① July 24 - Sept. 3; not May 30, Aug. 29, Nov. 11).
⑦ Sept. 4 - Dec. 10 (also Aug. 26, Nov. 11).
Ⓑ May 29 - Sept. 3. ⑤⑦ Sept. 4 - Dec. 10 (also Oct. 24–27).
⑥ (not July 24 - Sept. 3) also Aug. 27.
①④⑤ May 29 - Sept. 3 (also May 31, June 1; not May 30, Aug. 29).
Ⓑ May 29 - July 23 (not May 30). ①④⑤⑦ July 24 - Sept. 3 (not Aug. 29).
⑤ Sept. 4 - Dec. 10 (not Nov. 11).
① July 24 - Dec. 10 (not Aug. 15).
①–⑤ May 31 - July 23. ②–⑤ July 24 - Dec. 10 (not Aug. 29, Nov. 1, 11).
① July 24 - Dec. 10 (not Oct. 24).
⑤ June 3 - Sept. 3 (also May 29, June 5).

P – ②③④⑤⑦ (also May 30, July 25, Aug. 29; not Nov. 11).
Q – Ⓑ May 29 - July 3. ①④⑤⑦ July 4 - Dec. 10 (not Aug. 29).
R – Daily May 29 - July 3. ⑤⑥⑦ July 4 - Dec. 10.
S – ⑤⑦ May 29 - Sept. 3 (also Aug. 29). ⑦ Sept. 4 - Dec. 10, (also Nov. 11).
T – Daily May 29 - Sept. 3. ①④⑤⑥ Sept. 4 - Nov. 4. ④⑤⑥ Nov. 5 - Dec. 10.
U – Ⓑ May 29 - Sept. 3 (also June 4). ①⑤⑦ Sept. 4 - Dec. 10.
V – Daily May 29 - Sept. 3. Ⓑ Sept. 4 - Dec. 10.
W – ①–⑤ May 31 - July 23. ②–⑤ July 24 - Dec. 10 (also Oct. 24; not Aug. 29, Nov. 11).
X – ①–⑥ May 29 - Sept. 3. ①–⑤ Sept. 4 - Dec. 10 (not Nov. 11).
Y – ①–⑥ May 31 - Nov. 4 (not Aug. 29). Daily Nov. 5 - Dec. 10.
Z – ⑦ May 29 - Nov. 4 (also May 30, Aug. 29).

b – Also Nov. 11.
f – Not May 30, July 14, July 24 - Sept. 3, Nov. 1, 11.
h – Not Aug. 29.
j – Not May 30, Aug. 29, Nov. 11.
k – Not May 30, Aug. 29.
m – Also June 2, July 1, Aug. 29, Nov. 11.
p – Not May 30, July 24 - Sept. 3.
q – Not May 30, July 14, Aug. 29, Nov. 1, 11, 12.
r – Not Nov. 12.
t – Not May 29, Aug. 28.
w – Also May 29, 30, June 5.
y – Also May 30, Aug. 29, Nov. 11.

LONDON – PARIS *by rail – sea – rail* 10a

r services are available by taking normal service trains between London and Dover (Tables **100**, **101**), sailings between Dover and Calais (Table **2110**) and normal service trains between Calais and Paris, by changing at Boulogne (Table **261**), passengers making their own way between stations and docks at Dover and Calais, allowing at least 1 hour for connections.

Services between London and Dover are disrupted until December, please see Newslines on page 3, and Tables 101 and 102.

French train number	⚡	⚡	⛴	TGV⚡	2	2026				⚡	⚡	⛴	2	2030	2	2030	2034		⚡	⛴	2	2036	
sea crossing (see below)	⑥	①–⑤	①–⑥	7254	①–⑥	①–⑥	⑦	⑥	①–⑤	⑥	Ⓑ		⑦	⑦	①–⑤	①–⑤	⑥	⑦	⑦	⑦	⑦	⑦	
notes		p		🅁A	f	f	q		p				h	h	f	f		q	q		h	h	
don St Pancras................d.	0637	0722	...	...	...	...	...	...	...	0934	0937	...	...	...	...	...	...	...	1137	...	...	...	...
don Charing Cross...........d.			...	...	...	...	0840c	0840	0833			...	...	...	...	...	...	1040c		...	...	...	...
er Priory ❦.........................a.	0741	0828	...	...	...	...	1031	1031	1033	1041	1041	...	...	...	...	...	...	1231	1241	...	...	...	...
over Eastern Docks ▦ ❦ ..d.	...	...	0955	...	...	...	...	...	...	...	...	1210	...	...	...	...	...	...	...	1425	...	...	...
alais Port ▦ ❖....................a.	...	...	1225	...	...	...	...	...	...	...	...	1440	...	...	...	...	...	...	...	1655	...	...	...
ais Ville ❖.........................d.	...	...	...	1325	1335	...	...	...	...	...	...	...	1548	...	1558	...	...	...	...	...	1807	...	...
logne Ville.........................d.	...	...	...		1410	1436	...	...	...	...	...	...	1623	1633	1633	1646	1733	...	...	...	1847	1933	...
ens ....a.	...	...	...		...	1609	...	...	...	...	...	...	...	1809	...	1809	1909	...	...	...	...	2108	...
s Nord.................................a.	...	...	...	1514	...	1729	...	...	...	...	...	...	...	1929	...	1929	2029	...	...	...	...	2229	...

French train number	TGV⚡	⛴	⚡		2005	2	2009	2	⛴			2011	2	⛴			2017	2	2021	2	⛴	⚡	
sea crossing (see below)	7223	①–⑥	①–⑥	①–⑥	①–⑤	①–⑤	⑥	⑥	①–⑥	⑥	⑥	⑦	⑦	⑦	⑦	⑦	Ⓑ	①–⑤	⑥	⑥⑦			①–⑥
notes	🅁A		p	p	f	f						h	h					f		h			
s Nord.................................d.	0946	...	...	...	0731	...	0831	...	...	...	...	0931	...	...	...	...	1331	...	1431	...	...	...	...
ens ....d.		...	...	...	0853	...	0951	...	...	...	...	1051	...	...	...	...	1451	...	1551	...	...	...	...
logne Ville.........................d.		...	...	...	1015	1227	1126	1227	...	...	...	1226	1248	...	...	...	1613x	1711	1713	1723	...	...	...
ais Ville ❖.........................a.	1132	...	...	...	...	1310	...	1310	...	...	...	...	1323	...	...	...	...	1750	...	1757	...	...	...
alais Port ▦ ❖....................d.	...	1305	...	...	...	...	...	...	1410	...	...	...	...	1525	...	...	...	...	...	...	2000	...	...
over Eastern Docks ▦ ❦ ..a.	...	1335	...	...	...	...	...	...	1440	...	...	...	...	1555	...	...	...	...	...	...	2030	...	...
er Priory ❦.........................d.	...	...	1449	1500	...	...	...	...	...	1549	1603	...	...	...	1725	1745	...	...	...	...	...	2145	2203
don Charing Cross...........a.	...	...		1655	...	...	...	...	...		1752	...	...	...	1922		...	...	...	...	...		2357
don St Pancras................a.	...	...	1554	...	...	...	...	...	...	1654	...	...	...	...	...	1853	...	...	...	...	...	2254	...

①–⑥ (not July 14, Aug. 15, Nov. 1, 11).
London **Cannon Street**.
f – Not July 14, Aug. 15, Nov. 1, 11.
h – Also July 14, Aug. 15, Nov. 1, 11.
p – Not Aug. 29.
q – Also Aug. 29.
x – 1625 on ⑦.
⚡ – Supplement payable.

⛴ – Ship service, operated by P & O Ferries. ✕ on ship. One class only on ship. For additional ferry services see Table **2110**. Passengers make their own way between Dover Priory and Dover Eastern Docks.

❖ – 🚌 service (not a guaranteed connection):
From Calais Port to Calais Ville station 1120, 1220, 1305, 1405, 1500, 1640, 1740, 1835.
From Calais Ville station to Calais Port 1040, 1135, 1235, 1320, 1420, 1515, 1655, 1755.

11 LONDON / BRUSSELS - LILLE - CHARLES DE GAULLE ✈ - WESTERN / SOUTHERN FRANCE

DAY TRAINS (FOR NIGHT TRAINS SEE TABLE 13). Supplements are payable on *TGV* trains. Connections at Lille are not guaranteed. Other connections available via Paris.

km	train type	TGV	TGV	TGV	TGV	TGV		TGV	TGV	TGV	TGV	TGV	TGV	TGV	TGV	⇌	☆	☆	☆	EC	☆	TGV
	train number	5102	5104	5200	5110	9810		9870	9870	5214	5211	9800	9812	5202	5202	9926	9110	9110	9084	147	9114	5164
	train number	5103	5105	5201	9811	9811	17483	9871	9871	5215		9801	9811	5450	5450	9927			9085	148		9826
	notes	R 🍸	R 🍸	R 🍸	R 🍸	R 🍸		R 🍸	R 🍸	R 🍸	R 🍸	R 🍸	R 🍸	R 🍸 Ⓐ	R 🍸 Ⓒ	R 🍸	R ✕ ①–⑤	R ✕ ⑥	R ✕	♣	R ✕ ①–⑤	R 🍸
								T	V							S	L		M	E	q	
	London St Pancras **12** d.	...	...	...	...	...	...	...	...	...	...	...	...	...	...	...	0650	0657	0719x	...	0804	...
	Ebbsfleet International **12** d.	...	...	...	...	...	...	...	...	...	...	...	...	...	...	...	0708	|	...	...	|	...
	Ashford International **12** d.	...	...	...	...	...	...	...	...	...	...	...	...	...	...	...	0728	0728	0755	...	|	...
	Brussels Midi / Zuid **12** d.	...	...	...	...	0710	...	0717	0717	...	...	0817	0817	...	...	0925	|	|	|	...	|	...
	Lille Europe **12** a.	...	...	...	...	|	...	0752	0752	...	...	0852	0852	...	...	|	0930	0926	|	...	1026	...
0	**Lille** Europe d.	0537	...	0717	0654f	|	...	0802	0802	0836	0836	0902	0902	0921	0921	|	...	...	|	...	...	1043
	Douai d.	|	...	|	0716	|	...	|	|	|	|	|	|	|	|	|	...	...	|	...	...	|
	Arras d.	0559	...	|	0732	|	...	|	|	|	|	|	|	|	|	|	...	...	|	...	...	|
99	TGV Haute Picardie d.	0618	...	0747	|	|	...	|	|	0915	0915	|	|	|	|	|	...	...	|	...	...	1115
203	Paris Charles de Gaulle ✈ a.	0648	...	0814	0821	0826	...	0854	0854	0944	0944	0952	0952	1011	1011	1041	...	...	|	...	...	1144
203	Paris Charles de Gaulle ✈ d.	0658	0658	0819	0831	0831	...	0859	0859	0949	0949	0958	0958	1016	1016	1050	...	...	|	...	...	1158
227	Marne la Vallée § d.	0711	0711	0833	0843	0843	...	|	|	1003	1003	1011	1011	1033	1033	|	...	...	|	...	...	1211
	Strasbourg a.	|	|	|	|	|	...	1123	1049	|	|	|	|	|	|	|	...	...	|	...	...	|
289	Massy TGV d.	|	|	0908	|	|	...	...	...	1038	1038	|	|	1108	1108	|	...	...	|	...	...	|
	Le Mans a.	|	|	|	|	|	...	...	...	1127	1127	|	|	|	|	|	...	...	|	...	...	|
	Rennes a.	|	|	|	|	|	...	...	...	|	1248	|	|	|	|	|	...	...	|	...	...	|
	Angers St Laud a.	|	|	|	|	|	...	...	...	1208	...	|	|	|	|	|	...	...	|	...	...	|
	Nantes a.	|	|	|	|	|	...	...	...	1246	...	|	|	|	|	|	...	...	|	...	...	|
	St Pierre des Corps a.	|	|	1001	|	|	...	...	...	...	...	|	|	1201	1201	|	...	...	|	...	...	|
	Futuroscope a.	|	|	|	|	|	...	...	...	...	...	|	|	|	1239	|	...	...	|	...	...	|
	Poitiers a.	|	|	1042	|	|	...	...	...	...	...	|	|	1242	1249	|	...	...	|	...	...	|
	Angoulême a.	|	|	1135	|	|	...	...	...	...	...	|	|	1335	1335	|	...	...	|	...	...	|
	Bordeaux a.	|	|	1237	|	|	...	...	...	...	...	|	|	1437	1437	|	...	...	|	...	...	|
521	Le Creusot TGV a.	|	|	...	|	|	...	...	...	...	...	|	|	...	...	|	...	...	|	...	...	|
645	**Lyon** Part Dieu a.	0900	0900	...	1030	1030	...	...	...	...	...	1200	1200	...	...	|	...	...	1300z	...	...	1400
	Lyon Perrache a.	|	|	...	|	|	...	...	...	...	...	|	|	...	...	|	...	...	|	...	...	|
	Lyon St Exupéry ✈ a.	|	|	...	|	|	...	...	...	...	...	|	|	...	...	|	...	...	|	...	...	|
	Valence TGV a.	|	0945	...	1111	1111	...	...	...	...	...	|	1244	...	...	1304	...	...	|	...	...	1439
	Avignon TGV a.	1008	|	...	1145	1145	...	...	...	...	...	1308	|	...	...	1338	...	...	1408	...	...	|
	Nîmes a.	|	1033	...	|	|	...	...	...	...	...	|	1332	...	...	|	...	...	|	...	...	|
	Montpellier a.	|	1103	...	|	|	...	...	...	...	...	|	1402	...	...	|	...	...	|	...	...	|
	Béziers a.	|	...	...	|	|	...	...	...	...	...	|	...	...	...	|	...	...	|	...	...	|
	Narbonne a.	|	...	...	|	|	...	...	...	...	...	|	...	...	...	|	...	...	|	...	...	|
	Toulouse Matabiau a.	|	...	...	|	|	...	...	...	...	...	|	...	...	...	|	...	...	|	...	...	|
	Perpignan a.	|	...	...	|	|	...	...	...	...	...	|	...	...	...	|	...	...	|	...	...	|
	Aix en Provence TGV a.	1031	...	...	|	|	...	...	...	...	...	1331	...	...	...	1401	...	...	|	...	...	1529
	Marseille St Charles a.	1046	...	...	1216	1216	1231	...	...	...	...	1346	...	...	...	1416	...	...	1445	1531	...	1546
	Toulon a.	...	...	...	...	...	1314	...	...	...	...	1502	...	...	...	...	...	...	...	1614	...	...
	St Raphaël - Valescure a.	...	...	...	...	...	1409	...	...	...	...	...	...	...	...	...	...	...	...	1709	...	...
	Cannes a.	...	...	...	...	...	1436	...	...	...	...	...	...	...	...	...	...	...	...	1735	...	...
	Nice a.	...	...	...	...	...	1506	...	...	...	...	...	...	...	...	...	...	...	...	1803	...	...

train type	☆	☆	TGV		☆	TGV		☆	☆	TGV	TGV	TGV	TGV		☆	TGV	TGV	TGV	TGV	TGV		
train number	9116	9116	9828		9074	5452		9126	9126	6811	5232	5209	5222		9132	5134	6183	5119	6217	9874		
train number			5028			5453				6810	5233		5223			5135				9875		
notes	R ✕ ①–⑤	R ✕ ⑥⑦	R 🍸		R ✕	R 🍸		R ✕ ①–⑥	R ✕ ⑦	R 🍸	R 🍸	R 🍸	R 🍸		R ✕	R 🍸	R 🍸 ⑤⑥⑦	R 🍸	R 🍸	R 🍸		
	q	y			A	C		Y	Z	¶		W					w			V		
London St Pancras **12** d.	0855	0858	...	...	1014	...	...	1058	1104	...	...	...	...	...	1258	...	...	...	...	...	...	...
Ebbsfleet International **12** d.	0914	0915	...	...	1034	...	...	1115	|	...	...	...	...	...	1315	...	...	...	...	...	...	...
Ashford International **12** d.	|	|	...	...	1058	...	...	|	|	...	...	...	...	...	|	...	...	...	...	...	...	...
Brussels Midi / Zuid **12** d.	|	|	1217	...	|	...	...	|	|	...	...	...	...	...	|	...	...	...	...	1517	...	...
Lille Europe **12** a.	1126	1130	1253	...	1254s	...	...	1326	1326	...	...	...	...	...	1530	...	...	...	...	1552	...	...
Lille Europe d.	...	...	1303	...	|	...	...	...	...	...	1352	1352	1445f	...	...	1554	...	1554	...	1602	...	...
Douai d.	...	...	|	...	|	...	...	...	...	...	|	|	1508	...	...	|	...	|	...	|	...	...
Arras d.	...	...	|	...	|	...	...	...	...	...	|	|	1526	...	...	|	...	|	...	|	...	...
TGV Haute Picardie d.	...	...	|	...	|	...	...	...	...	...	|	|	1551	...	...	1622	...	1622	...	|	...	...
Paris Charles de Gaulle ✈ a.	...	...	1353	...	|	...	...	...	...	...	1444	1444	1617	...	...	1651	...	1651	...	1554	...	...
Paris Charles de Gaulle ✈ d.	...	...	1358	...	|	...	...	...	...	...	1449	1449	1621	...	...	1656	...	1656	...	1659	...	...
Marne la Vallée § d.	...	...	1411	...	1402	1433	...	...	...	...	1503	1503	1633	...	...	1711	...	1711	...	|	...	...
Strasbourg a.	...	...	|	...	...	|	...	...	...	...	|	|	|	...	...	|	...	|	...	1901	...	...
Massy TGV d.	...	...	|	...	...	1508	...	...	...	...	1538	1538	1708	...	...	|	...	|	...	...	...	...
Le Mans a.	...	...	|	...	...	|	...	...	...	...	1627	1627	|	...	...	|	...	|	...	...	...	...
Rennes a.	...	...	|	...	...	|	...	...	...	...	1747	|	|	...	...	|	...	|	...	...	...	...
Angers St Laud a.	...	...	|	...	...	|	...	...	...	...	...	1708	|	...	...	|	...	|	...	...	...	...
Nantes a.	...	...	|	...	...	|	...	...	...	...	...	1750	|	...	...	|	...	|	...	...	...	...
St Pierre des Corps a.	...	...	|	...	...	1600	...	...	...	...	...	...	1759	...	...	|	...	|	...	...	...	...
Futuroscope a.	...	...	|	...	...	|	...	...	...	...	...	...	|	...	...	|	...	|	...	...	...	...
Poitiers a.	...	...	|	...	...	1642	...	...	...	...	...	...	1842	...	...	|	...	|	...	...	...	...
Angoulême a.	...	...	|	...	...	1732	...	...	...	...	...	...	1935	...	...	|	...	|	...	...	...	...
Bordeaux a.	...	...	|	...	...	1837	...	...	...	...	...	...	2037	...	...	|	...	|	...	...	...	...
Le Creusot TGV a.	...	...	|	...	...	...	...	...	...	...	...	...	...	...	...	|	...	|	...	...	...	...
Lyon Part Dieu a.	...	...	1600	...	...	...	...	...	...	1810	...	...	...	...	...	1900	...	1900	...	...	...	...
Lyon Perrache a.	...	...	|	...	...	...	...	...	...	|	...	...	...	...	...	|	...	|	...	...	...	...
Lyon St Exupéry ✈ a.	...	...	|	...	...	...	...	...	...	|	...	...	...	...	...	|	...	|	...	...	...	...
Valence TGV a.	...	...	|	...	...	...	...	...	...	1844	...	...	...	...	...	|	...	1947	...	...	...	...
Avignon TGV a.	...	...	1709	...	...	...	...	...	...	|	...	...	...	...	...	2009	...	|	...	...	...	...
Nîmes a.	...	...	|	...	...	...	...	...	...	1933	...	...	...	...	...	|	...	2034	...	...	...	...
Montpellier a.	...	...	|	...	...	...	...	...	...	2002	...	...	...	...	...	|	...	2102	2141	...	...	...
Béziers a.	...	...	|	...	...	...	...	...	...	2040	...	...	...	...	...	|	...	...	2233	...	...	...
Narbonne a.	...	...	|	...	...	...	...	...	...	2101	...	...	...	...	...	|	...	...	2248	...	...	...
Toulouse Matabiau a.	...	...	|	...	...	...	...	...	...	2217	...	...	...	...	...	|	...	...	|	...	...	...
Perpignan a.	...	...	|	...	...	...	...	...	...	...	...	...	...	...	...	|	...	...	2324	...	...	...
Aix en Provence TGV a.	...	...	1731	...	...	...	...	...	...	...	...	...	...	...	...	2031	2117	...	...	...	...	...
Marseille St Charles a.	...	...	1746	...	...	...	...	...	...	...	...	...	...	...	...	2046	|	...	...	...	...	...
Toulon a.	...	...	1844	...	...	...	...	...	...	...	...	...	...	...	...	...	2206	...	...	...	...	...
St Raphaël - Valescure a.	...	...	1938	...	...	...	...	...	...	...	...	...	...	...	...	...	2259	...	...	...	...	...
Cannes a.	...	...	2003	...	...	...	...	...	...	...	...	...	...	...	...	...	2324	...	...	...	...	...
Nice a.	...	...	2037	...	...	...	...	...	...	...	...	...	...	...	...	...	2355	...	...	...	...	...

A – ①③⑤⑦ May 28 - July 22 (also May 28, 31, June 2, 4); ①③⑤⑥⑦ July 23 - Sept. 5; ①③⑤⑦ Sept. 6 - Dec. 9 (also Oct. 22, 25, 27, 29, Nov. 1, 3, 5; not Nov. 27). On Nov 27 depart London 1024, Ebbsfleet 1044, not call at Ashford.
C – July 3 - Aug. 28.
E – Daily until July 3. ⑥⑦ from July 4.
L – ①–⑤ May 29 - July 23 (not May 30). ②–⑤ July 24 - Dec. 10, (not Aug. 29, Nov. 1, 11).
M – ①⑤⑥ May 29 - July 2; ①④⑤⑥⑦ July 3 - Sept. 3; ①⑤⑥ Sept. 4 - Oct. 29; see Tables **13**, **17**.
S – ⑥ July 2 - Sept. 3: *THALYS* SOLEIL – 12 🍸 Amsterdam (depart 0720 see Table **18**) - Brussels - Valence *TGV* - Marseille.

T – Apr. 3 - July 2.
V – July 3 - Dec. 10.
W – ①②③④⑦.
Y – ①–⑥ May 31 - Nov. 4 (also Aug. 29). Daily Nov. 5 - Dec. 10.
Z – ⑦ May 29 - Nov. 4, (also May 30, Aug. 29).
f – Lille **Flandres** (◇).
q – Not Aug. 29, Nov. 11.
s – Calls to set down only.
w – Not June 27.

x – 0715 on ⑦ (also Aug. 29).
y – Also Aug. 29, Nov. 11.
z – Lyon **St Exupéry** ✈ on Oct. 29.

§ – Marne la Vallée - Chessy (station for Disneyland).
⇌ – *Thalys* high-speed train. R 🍸. Special fares payable.
☆ – Eurostar train. Special fares payable. ✕ in Business Premier and Stan Premier, 🍸 in Standard. Business Premier not available to Marne la Val Chessy and Marseille. Minimum check-in time 30 minutes. Valid May 29 - Dec. 10.
◇ – 500 metres from Lille Europe (see Lille City Plan on page 30).

¶ – Not Oct. 29, 30, 31, Nov. 12,
♣ – *EC Thello*. To Milano, Table
⊖ – To St Malo on dates in Table

LONDON / BRUSSELS - LILLE - CHARLES DE GAULLE ✈ - WESTERN / SOUTHERN FRANCE 11

DAY TRAINS (FOR NIGHT TRAINS SEE TABLE 13). Supplements payable on all *TGV* services. Connections at Lille are not guaranteed. Other connections available via Paris.

train type	☆	*TGV*	*TGV*	☆	*TGV*	*TGV*	*TGV*	☆	*TGV*	☆	*TGV*	*TGV*	*TGV*
train number	**9136**	**9836**	**5240**	**9140**	**5237**	**5230**	**5124**	**9144**	**5130**	**9148**	**5234**	**9846**	**9846**
train number		**9837**	**5241**			**5231**	**5125**		**5131**		**5235**	**9847**	**5137**
notes	R ✕	R 🍷	R 🍷	R ✕ Ⓑ	R 🍷	R 🍷	R 🍷	R ✕ ⑥	R 🍷	R ✕	R 🍷 ⑤	R 🍷	R 🍷 ⑦
	F				△	▽			▷	V			
lon St Pancras **12** d.	1404	...	...	1504	...	...	...	1604	...	1704	...	...	...
fleet International **12** d.	│	...	...	│	...	...	...	│	...	│	...	...	...
ɔrd International **12** d.	│	...	...	│	...	...	...	│	...	│	...	...	...
ussels Midi / Zuid **12** d.	│	1617	...	│	...	...	...	│	...	│	...	1917	...
Europe **12** a.	1626	1653	...	1726	...	...	...	1826	...	1926	...	1952	...
Europe d.	...	1703	1709**f**	...	1752	1752	1826	...	1900**f**	...	1952	2002	2002
ai d.	...	│	│	...	│	│	│	...	│	...	│	│	│
s d.	...	│	│	...	│	│	│	...	│	...	│	2028	2028
Haute Picardie d.	...	│	│	...	│	│	1854	...	│	...	│	│	│
Charles de Gaulle ✈ a.	...	1753	1804	...	1842	1842	1923	...	1953	...	2045	2112	2112
Charles de Gaulle ✈ d.	...	1758	1809	...	1847	1847	1928	...	1958	...	2050	2117	2117
e la Vallée § d.	...	1811	1833	...	1901	1901	1941	...	2007	...	2103	2130	2130
Strasbourg a.	...	│	│	...	│	│	│	...	...	...	│	│	│
assy TGV d.	...	│	1908	...	1938	1938	│	...	...	...	2138	│	│
Mans a.	...	│	│	...	2028	2028	│	...	...	...	2228	│	│
Rennes a.	...	│	│	...	2158	│	│	...	...	...	│	│	│
Angers St Laud a.	...	│	│	...	...	2110	│	...	...	...	2308	│	│
Nantes a.	...	│	│	...	...	2149	│	...	...	...	2346	│	│
Pierre des Corps a.	...	│	1959	...	...	...	│	...	...	...	...	│	│
turoscope a.	...	│	│	...	...	...	│	...	...	...	...	│	│
itiers a.	...	│	2041	...	...	...	│	...	...	...	...	│	│
goulême a.	...	│	2135	...	...	...	│	...	...	...	...	│	│
rdeaux a.	...	│	2237	...	...	...	│	...	...	...	...	│	│
reusot TGV a.	...	│	...	...	...	...	│	...	...	...	...	2239	2239
Part Dieu a.	...	2000	...	...	...	...	2130	...	...	...	...	2324	2324
Perrache a.	...	│	...	...	...	...	│	...	...	...	...	2337	│
on St Exupéry ✈ a.	...	│	...	...	...	...	│	...	...	...	...	...	│
nce TGV a.	...	2044	...	...	...	...	│	...	...	...	...	...	0007
non TGV a.	...	│	...	...	...	...	2240	...	...	...	...	...	│
mes a.	...	2133	...	...	...	...	│	...	...	...	...	...	0054
ontpellier a.	...	2202	...	...	...	...	│	...	...	...	...	...	0132
ziers a.	...	2250**t**	...	...	...	...	│	...	...	...	...	...	...
arbonne a.	...	2308**t**	...	...	...	...	│	...	...	...	...	...	...
Toulouse Matabiau a.	...	│	...	...	...	...	│	...	...	...	...	...	...
erpignan a.	...	2344**t**	...	...	...	...	│	...	...	...	...	...	...
en Provence TGV a.	...	...	...	...	...	...	2303	...	...	...	...	...	...
seille St Charles a.	...	...	...	...	...	...	2318	...	...	...	...	...	...
on a.	...	...	...	...	...	...	...	...	...	...	...	...	...
aphaël - Valescure a.	...	...	...	...	...	...	...	...	...	...	...	...	...
nes a.	...	...	...	...	...	...	...	...	...	...	...	...	...
a.	...	...	...	...	...	...	...	...	...	...	...	...	...

train type	*TGV*	*TGV*	*TGV*	☆	*TGV*	*TGV*	*TGV*	*TGV*	☆	☆	*TGV*	*TGV*	*TGV*	☆	*TGV*	*TGV*	*TGV*	*TGV*	*TGV*	*TGV*	☆
train number	**9809**	**9852**	**9890**	**9117**	**5152**	**5254**	**5252**	**9854**	**9125**	**9129**	**5144**	**9862**	**5260**	**9133**	**9860**	**5166**	**5270**	**5272**	**5264**	**5264**	**9141**
train number		**9853**	**9891**		**5153**	**5255**		**9855**			**9862**	**9863**	**5261**		**9861**	**9860**	**5271**		**5265**	**5265**	
notes	R 🍷 Ⓐ	R 🍷	R 🍷	R ✕	R 🍷	R 🍷 ⚒	R 🍷 ⚒	R 🍷	R ✕	R ✕ ⑦	R 🍷	R 🍷	R 🍷	R ✕ ①–⑥	R 🍷	R 🍷	R 🍷	R 🍷	R 🍷 Ⓐ	R 🍷 Ⓒ	R ✕
			A		▷				X	y				g			▽	△			
d.	...	...	...	...	...	...	...	...	...	...	...	...	...	...	0602	...	...	...	...	...	...
nes d.	...	...	...	...	...	...	...	...	...	...	...	...	...	...	0641	...	...	...	...	...	...
Raphaël - Valescure d.	...	...	...	...	...	...	...	...	...	...	...	...	...	...	0708	...	...	...	...	...	...
on d.	...	...	...	...	...	...	...	...	...	...	...	...	...	...	0816	...	...	...	...	...	...
seille St Charles d.	...	...	...	...	...	...	...	0614	...	...	0714	...	...	...	0914	...	...	...	...	...	...
en Provence TGV d.	...	...	...	...	...	...	...	0629	...	...	0728	...	...	...	0929	...	...	...	...	...	...
erpignan d.	...	...	...	...	...	...	...	│	...	...	│	0515**z**	...	...	│	...	...	...	...	...	...
Toulouse Matabiau d.	...	...	...	...	...	...	...	│	...	...	│	│	...	...	│	...	...	...	...	...	...
arbonne d.	...	...	...	...	...	...	...	│	...	...	│	0552**z**	...	...	│	...	...	...	...	...	...
éziers d.	...	...	...	...	...	...	...	│	...	...	│	0608**z**	...	...	│	...	...	...	...	...	...
ontpellier d.	...	...	...	...	...	...	...	│	...	...	│	0658	...	...	│	0858	...	...	...	...	...
îmes d.	...	...	...	...	...	...	...	│	...	...	│	0726	...	...	│	0924	...	...	...	...	...
non TGV d.	...	...	...	...	...	...	...	│	...	...	│	│	...	...	0950	│	...	...	...	...	...
ence TGV d.	...	...	...	...	...	...	...	0720	...	...	│	0818	...	...	│	1015	...	...	...	...	...
yon St Exupéry ✈ d.	...	...	...	...	...	...	...	│	...	...	│	│	...	...	│	│	...	...	...	...	...
n Perrache d.	...	...	...	...	...	...	...	│	...	...	│	│	...	...	│	│	...	...	...	...	...
n Part Dieu d.	...	0550	...	...	...	...	...	0800	...	...	0900	0900	...	...	1100	1100	...	...	...	...	...
Creusot TGV d.	...	0632	...	...	...	...	...	│	...	...	│	│	...	...	│	│	...	...	...	...	...
ordeaux d.	...	│	...	...	...	...	...	│	...	...	│	│	0723	...	│	│	...	...	0923	0923	...
ngoulême d.	...	│	...	...	...	...	...	│	...	...	│	│	0826	...	│	│	...	...	1026	1026	...
oitiers d.	...	│	...	...	...	...	...	│	...	...	│	│	0917	...	│	│	...	...	1117	1117	...
uturoscope d.	...	│	...	...	...	...	...	│	...	...	│	│	│	...	│	│	...	...	│	│	...
t Pierre des Corps d.	...	│	...	...	...	...	...	│	...	...	│	│	1001	...	│	│	...	...	1200	1200	...
Nantes d.	...	│	...	...	...	...	0605	│	...	...	│	│	│	...	│	│	1005	...	│	│	...
Angers St Laud d.	...	│	...	...	...	...	0643	│	...	...	│	│	│	...	│	│	1044	...	│	│	...
Rennes d.	...	│	...	...	...	0610	│	│	...	...	│	│	│	...	│	│	│	1005	│	│	...
e Mans d.	...	│	...	...	...	0733	0733	│	...	...	│	│	│	...	│	│	1133	1133	│	│	...
lassy TGV d.	...	│	...	...	...	0825	0825	│	...	...	│	│	1055	...	│	│	1225	1225	1255	1255	...
Strasbourg d.	...	│	0608	...	...	│	│	│	...	...	│	│	│	...	│	│	│	│	│	│	...
ne la Vallée § d.	...	0749	│	...	0853	0901	0901	0951	...	...	1052	1052	1135	...	1252	1252	1301	1301	│	1331	...
s Charles de Gaulle ✈ a.	...	0801	0757	...	0903	0911	0911	1001	...	...	1102	1102	1145	...	1302	1302	1311	1311	1331	1341	...
s Charles de Gaulle ✈ d.	...	0807	0807	...	0908	0916	0916	1006	...	...	1107	1107	1157	...	1307	1307	1316	1316	1336	1346	...
/ Haute Picardie d.	...	│	│	...	│	0950	0950	1037	...	...	│	│	1230	...	1337	1337	│	│	│	│	...
as a.	...	│	│	...	│	│	│	│	...	...	│	│	│	...	1356**e**	1356**e**	│	│	│	│	...
ai a.	...	│	│	...	│	│	│	│	...	...	│	│	│	...	│	│	│	│	│	│	...
e Europe a.	...	0856	0856	...	0958	1017	1017	1103	...	...	1156	1156	1301**f**	...	1421**e**	1421**e**	1407	1407	1430	1437	...
e Europe **12** d.	0732	0908	0908	0930	...	...	...	1117	1136	1236	...	1208	...	1330	1435**e**	...	...	...	...	...	1536**v**
russels Midi / Zuid **12** a.	0808	0943	0943	│	...	...	...	1151	│	│	...	1252	...	│	1512**e**	...	...	...	...	...	│
ford International **12** a.	...	...	...	│	...	...	...	...	│	│	...	...	...	│	...	...	...	...	...	...	│
sfleet International **12** a.	...	...	...	│	...	...	...	...	│	│	...	...	...	1345	...	...	...	...	...	...	1545
ndon St Pancras **12** a.	...	...	...	0957	...	...	...	...	1157	1257	...	...	...	1405	...	...	...	...	...	...	1605

July 3 - Dec. 10.

Ⓑ May 29 - Sept. 3. ⑤⑦ Sept. 4 - Dec. 10 (also Oct. 24–27).

Daily May 29 - Sept. 3. Ⓑ Sept. 4 - Dec. 10.

①–⑥ May 29 - Sept. 3. ①–⑤ Sept. 4 - Dec. 10, (not Nov. 11).

On Ⓒ does not call at Arras, arrives Lille 1403, Brussels 1457.

f – Lille **Flandres** (◇).

g – Not May 30, Aug. 29, Nov. 11.

t – ⑤⑦.

v – 1530 on ⑦ (also May 30, Aug. 29, Nov. 11).

y – Also Nov. 11.

z – ①⑥.

▽ – To / from Le Croisic on dates in Table **288**.

△ – To / from Lorient or Quimper on dates in Table **285**.

▷ – To / from Dijon, Besancon and Mulhouse (Table **370**).

§ – Marne la Vallée - Chessy. Station for Disneyland Paris.

◇ – 500 metres from Lille Europe (see Lille City Plan on page 30).

☆ – Eurostar train. Special fares payable. ✕ in Business Premier and Standard Premier, 🍷 in Standard. Minimum check-in time 30 minutes. Valid May 29 - Dec. 10.

11 SOUTHERN / WESTERN FRANCE - CHARLES DE GAULLE ✈ - LILLE - BRUSSELS / LONDON

DAY TRAINS (FOR NIGHT TRAINS SEE TABLE 13). Supplements payable on all *TGV* services. Connections at Lille are not guaranteed. Other connections available via Paris.

train type	*TGV*	☆		*TGV*	*TGV*	*TGV*	☆	☆	☆	*TGV*	*TGV*	*TGV*	*TGV*	☆	☆	☆	*TGV*	*TGV*	*TGV*	☆
train number	**5256**	**9145**		**5442**	**5184**	**9866**	**9149**	**9149**	**9057**	**9894**	**9894**	**5278**	**5280**	**9153**	**9153**	**9057**	**6859**	**5192**	**9868**	**9161**
train number	**5257**			**5443**	**9866**	**9867**				**9895**	**9895**		**5281**				**6858**	**5193**	**9869**	
notes	🅁 🍷 ⑦	🅁 ✕		🅁 🍷	🅁 🍷	🅁 🍷	🅁 ✕ ①–⑥	🅁 ✕ ⑦	🅁 ✕	🅁 🍷	🅁 🍷	🅁 🍷	🅁 🍷	🅁 ✕ ①–⑤	🅁 ✕ ⑦	🅁 ✕	🅁 🍷	🅁 🍷	🅁 🍷	🅁 ✕
		F		**V**			**y**	**q**	**R**	**X**	**W**			**y**	**q**	**S**				
Nice d.	...	...	...	...	0924	...	...	...	...	...	...	...	...	...	...	...	...	...	...	...
Cannes d.	...	...	...	...	0953	...	...	...	...	...	...	...	...	...	...	...	...	...	...	...
St Raphaël - Valescure d.	...	...	...	...	1020	...	...	...	...	...	...	...	...	...	...	...	...	...	...	...
Toulon d.	...	...	...	...	1116	...	...	...	...	...	...	...	...	...	...	...	...	...	...	...
Marseille St Charles d.	...	...	...	...	1214	1214	...	...	...	...	...	...	...	...	...	...	...	1409	...	...
Aix en Provence TGV d.	...	...	...	...	1229	1229	...	...	...	...	...	...	...	...	...	...	...	1424	...	...
Perpignan d.	...	...	...	...	|	|	...	...	...	...	...	...	...	...	...	...	...	|	...	...
Toulouse Matabiau d.	...	...	...	...	|	|	...	...	...	...	...	...	...	...	...	...	1049	|	...	...
Narbonne d.	...	...	...	...	|	|	...	...	...	...	...	...	...	...	...	...	1204	|	...	...
Béziers d.	...	...	...	...	|	|	...	...	...	...	...	...	...	...	...	...	1220	|	...	...
Montpellier d.	...	...	...	...	|	|	...	...	...	...	...	...	...	...	...	...	1304	|	1458	...
Nîmes d.	...	...	...	...	|	|	...	...	...	...	...	...	...	...	...	...	1333	|	1526	...
Avignon TGV d.	...	...	...	...	1251	1251	...	...	...	...	...	...	...	...	...	...	|	1451	|	...
Valence TGV d.	...	...	...	...	|	|	...	...	...	...	...	...	...	...	...	...	|	|	1615	...
Lyon St Exupéry ✈ d.	...	...	...	...	|	|	...	...	...	...	...	...	...	...	...	...	|	|	|	...
Lyon Perrache d.	...	...	...	...	|	|	...	...	...	...	...	...	...	...	...	...	|	|	|	...
Lyon Part Dieu d.	...	...	...	...	1400	1400	...	...	...	...	...	...	...	...	...	...	1454	1600	1700	...
Le Creusot TGV d.	...	...	...	...	|	|	...	...	...	...	...	...	...	...	...	...	...	|	|	...
Bordeaux d.	...	...	...	1123	|	|	...	...	...	...	...	...	...	...	...	...	...	|	|	...
Angoulême d.	...	...	...	1226	|	|	...	...	...	...	...	...	...	...	...	...	...	|	|	...
Poitiers d.	...	...	...	1317	|	|	...	...	...	...	...	...	...	...	...	...	...	|	|	...
Futuroscope d.	...	...	...	|	|	|	...	...	...	...	...	...	...	...	...	...	...	|	|	...
St Pierre des Corps d.	...	...	...	1359	|	|	...	...	...	...	...	...	...	...	...	...	...	|	|	...
Nantes d.	...	...	...	|	|	|	...	...	...	...	...	1408	...	...	...	...	...	|	|	...
Angers St Laud d.	...	...	...	|	|	|	...	...	...	...	...	1445	...	...	...	...	...	|	|	...
Rennes d.	1110	...	...	|	|	|	...	...	...	...	...	|	1410	...	...	...	...	|	|	...
Le Mans d.	1232	...	...	|	|	|	...	...	...	...	...	1533	1533	...	...	...	...	|	|	...
Massy TGV d.	1325	...	...	1455	|	|	...	...	...	...	...	1625	1625	...	...	...	...	|	|	...
Strasbourg d.	|	...	...	|	|	|	...	...	...	1424	1510	|	|	...	...	...	...	|	|	...
Marne la Vallée § d.	1401	...	...	1527	1552	1552	...	...	1707	|	|	1701	1701	...	...	1802	...	1752	1852	...
Paris Charles de Gaulle ✈ a.	1411	...	...	...	1602	1602	...	...	|	1704	1703	1711	1711	...	...	|	...	1802	1902	...
Paris Charles de Gaulle ✈ d.	1416	...	...	...	1607	1607	...	...	|	1707	1709	1716	1716	...	...	|	...	1807	1907	...
TGV Haute Picardie d.	|	...	...	...	|	|	...	...	|	|	|	|	|	...	...	|	...	1841	|	...
Arras a.	|	...	...	...	|	|	...	...	|	|	|	|	|	...	...	|	...	1859	|	...
Douai a.	|	...	...	...	|	|	...	...	|	|	|	|	|	...	...	|	...	1917	|	...
Lille Europe a.	1507	...	...	...	1657	1657	...	...	|	1804	1758	1808	1808	...	...	|	...	1944f	1956	...
Lille Europe **12** d.	...	1636	...	...	...	1707	1736	1736	|	1822	1810	...	...	1836	1836	|	...	...	2008	2030
Brussels Midi / Zuid **12** a.	...	|	...	...	...	1743	|	|	|	1901	1845	...	...	|	|	|	...	...	2043	|
Ashford International **12** a.	...	|	...	...	...	...	1734	|	1806	...	...	...	...	|	1835	1904	...	...	...	|
Ebbsfleet International **12** a.	...	|	...	...	...	...	|	1745	1827	...	...	...	...	1845	|	1926	...	...	...	2045
London St Pancras **12** a.	...	1657	...	...	...	...	1806	1806	1847	...	...	...	...	1903	1910	1946	...	...	...	2103

train type	☆	☆		*TGV*	⇌		*TGV*	*TGV*		*TGV*	*TGV*		*TGV*	*TGV*		*TGV*				
train number	**9087**	**9087**		**5266**	**9955**		**6861**	**9882**		**5284**	**5284**		**5186**	**5180**		**5194**				
train number	**9086**	**9086**		**5267**	**9954**		**6860**	**5017**		**5285**	**5285**		**5187**	**5186**		**5195**				
notes	🅁 ✕	🅁 ✕		🅁 🍷	🅁 🍷		🅁 🍷 ⚒	🅁 🍷		🅁 🍷 Ⓐ	🅁 🍷 Ⓒ		🅁 🍷	🅁 🍷		🅁 🍷 ⑦				
	M	**M**			**T**											**D**				
Nice d.	...	...	...	...	...	...	...	...	...	...	...	...	...	...	...	...	...	...	...	...
Cannes d.	...	...	...	...	...	...	...	...	...	...	...	...	...	...	...	...	...	...	...	...
St Raphaël - Valescure d.	...	...	...	...	...	...	...	...	...	...	...	...	...	...	...	...	...	...	...	...
Toulon d.	...	...	...	...	...	...	...	...	...	...	...	...	...	...	...	...	...	...	...	...
Marseille St Charles d.	1522	...	...	...	1606	...	...	1714	...	...	...	...	...	1814	...	1910	...	...	...	...
Aix en Provence TGV d.	|	...	...	...	1621	...	...	1729	...	...	...	...	...	1829	...	1924	...	...	...	...
Perpignan d.	|	...	...	...	|	...	...	|	...	...	...	...	...	|	...	|	...	...	...	...
Toulouse Matabiau d.	|	...	...	...	|	...	1449	|	...	...	...	...	...	|	...	|	...	...	...	...
Narbonne d.	|	...	...	...	|	...	1604	|	...	...	...	...	...	|	...	|	...	...	...	...
Béziers d.	|	...	...	...	|	...	1620	|	...	...	...	...	...	|	...	|	...	...	...	...
Montpellier d.	|	...	...	...	|	...	1706	|	...	...	...	...	1757	|	...	|	...	...	...	...
Nîmes d.	|	...	...	...	|	...	1735	|	...	...	...	...	1826	|	...	|	...	...	...	...
Avignon TGV d.	1559	...	...	...	1645	...	|	1752	...	...	...	...	|	1852	...	1946	...	...	...	...
Valence TGV d.	|	...	...	...	1731	...	|	|	...	...	...	...	1915	|	...	|	...	...	...	...
Lyon St Exupéry ✈ d.	|	...	...	...	|	...	|	|	...	...	...	...	|	|	...	|	...	...	...	...
Lyon Perrache d.	|	...	...	...	|	...	|	|	...	...	...	...	|	|	...	|	...	...	...	...
Lyon Part Dieu d.	1725z	...	...	...	|	...	1850	1900	...	...	...	...	2000	2000	...	2100	...	...	...	...
Le Creusot TGV d.	|	...	...	...	|	...	...	|	...	...	...	...	|	|	...	|	...	...	...	...
Bordeaux d.	|	...	...	1523	|	...	...	|	...	1723	1723	...	|	|	...	|	...	...	...	...
Angoulême d.	|	...	...	1626	|	...	...	|	...	1825	1826	...	|	|	...	|	...	...	...	...
Poitiers d.	|	...	...	1716	|	...	...	|	...	1913	|	...	|	|	...	|	...	...	...	...
Futuroscope d.	|	...	...	1725	|	...	...	|	...	|	1921	...	|	|	...	|	...	...	...	...
St Pierre des Corps d.	|	...	...	1801	|	...	...	|	...	2002	2000	...	|	|	...	|	...	...	...	...
Nantes d.	|	...	...	|	|	...	...	|	...	|	|	...	|	|	...	|	...	...	...	...
Angers St Laud d.	|	...	...	|	|	...	...	|	...	|	|	...	|	|	...	|	...	...	...	...
Rennes d.	|	...	...	|	|	...	...	|	...	|	|	...	|	|	...	|	...	...	...	...
Le Mans d.	|	...	...	|	|	...	...	|	...	|	|	...	|	|	...	|	...	...	...	...
Massy TGV d.	|	...	...	1855	|	...	...	|	...	2055	2055	...	|	|	...	|	...	...	...	...
Strasbourg d.	|	...	...	|	|	...	...	|	...	|	|	...	|	|	...	|	...	...	...	...
Marne la Vallée § d.	|	...	...	1931	|	...	...	2052	...	2131	2131	...	2152	2152	...	2253	...	...	...	...
Paris Charles de Gaulle ✈ a.	|	...	...	1941	1953	...	...	2102	...	2141	2141	...	2202	2202	...	2303	...	...	...	...
Paris Charles de Gaulle ✈ d.	|	...	...	1950	2009	...	...	2107	...	2146	2146	...	2207	2207	...	2308	...	...	...	...
TGV Haute Picardie d.	|	...	...	|	|	...	...	|	...	2215	2215	...	2238	2238	...	2338	...	...	...	...
Arras a.	|	...	...	2033	|	...	...	|	...	|	|	...	|	|	...	|	...	...	...	...
Douai a.	|	...	...	2049	|	...	...	|	...	|	|	...	|	|	...	|	...	...	...	...
Lille Europe a.	2021	...	...	2111f	|	...	...	2159	...	2244	2244	...	2304	2304	...	0005	...	...	...	...
Lille Europe **12** d.	...	2136	...	...	|	...	...	2222	...	...	...	...	...	...	...	...	...	...	...	...
Brussels Midi / Zuid **12** a.	...	|	...	...	2123	...	...	2256	...	...	...	...	...	...	...	...	...	...	...	...
Ashford International **12** a.	...	2134	...	...	...	...	...	...	...	...	...	...	...	...	...	...	...	...	...	...
Ebbsfleet International **12** a.	...	|	...	...	...	...	...	...	...	...	...	...	...	...	...	...	...	...	...	...
London St Pancras **12** a.	...	2212	...	...	...	...	...	...	...	...	...	...	...	...	...	...	...	...	...	...

D – ⑦ until Aug. 28 (also Aug. 15).
F – ⑧ May 29 - Sept. 3. ⑤⑦ Sept. 4 - Dec. 10 (also Oct. 24–27).
M – ①⑤⑥ May 29 - July 2, ①④⑤⑥⑦ July 3 - Sept. 3, ①⑤⑥ Sept. 4 - Oct. 29, see Table **17**.
R – ⑤⑦ May 29 - July 22 (also May 28, June 4; not July 10, 15); ⑤⑥⑦ July 23 - Sept. 5; ⑤⑦ Sept. 6 - Dec. 9 (also Oct. 22, 29, Nov. 5). Depart Marne la Vallée 1649 on certain dates: see Table **17**.
S – ①③ May 29 - Dec. 9 (also May 31, June 2, Oct 25, 27, Nov. 1, 3). Depart Marne la Vallée 1756 on certain dates: see Table **17**.
T – ⑥ July 2 - Sept. 3: *THALYS* SOLEIL – 🚌12 🍷 Marseille - Valence *TGV* - Brussels - Amsterdam (arrive 2320; Table **18**).

V – July 3 - Aug. 28.
W – July 3 - Dec. 10.
X – Apr. 3 - July 2.

f – Lille **Flandres** (◇).
q – Also Aug. 29, Nov. 11.
y – Not Aug. 29, Nov. 11.
z – 1656 on Oct. 29 from Lyon **St Exupéry** ✈.

⊖ – From St Malo on dates in Table **261**.
☆ – Eurostar train. Special fares payable. ✕ in Business Premi and Standard Premier, 🍷 in Standard. Business Premier n available from Marne la Vallée - Chessy and Marseille. Minim check-in time 30 minutes. Valid May 29 - Dec. 10.
◇ – 500 metres from Lille Europe (see Lille City Plan on page 3
§ – Marne la Vallée - Chessy, station for Disneyland Paris.
⇌ – *Thalys* high-speed train. 🅁 🍷. Special fares payable.

LONDON - LILLE - BRUSSELS *by Eurostar* — 12

All times shown are local times (France and Belgium are one hour ahead of Great Britain).
For the complete service London - Lille see Table 10. For other services Lille - Brussels (by TGV) see Table 16.
All Eurostar services are 🅁 and convey ✕ in Business Premier and Standard Premier, 🍷 in Standard.

Eurostar service May 29 - Dec. 10.

train type	☆	☆	*ICE*			☆				☆					☆	☆					☆	☆	*ICE*		
train number	**9108**	**9110**	**15**			**9110**				**9114**					**9116**	**9116**					**9126**	**9126**	**17**		
notes			🍷		Ⓐ	⑥				①–⑤		Ⓐ		Ⓒ	①–⑤	⑥⑦		Ⓐ		Ⓒ	①–⑥	⑦	🍷		
notes	K	L z	F							j					j	y z					Y	Z	F		
London St Pancras ...... d.	0613	0650	...	...	...	0657	...	...	...	0804	...	...	...	...	0855	0858	...	...	...	...	1058	1104	...	...	...
Ebbsfleet International ... d.	0630	0707	...	...	...	│	...	...	...	│	...	...	...	...	0914	0915	...	...	...	...	1115	│	...	...	...
Ashford International ..... d.	0652	0728	...	...	...	0728	...	...	...	│	...	...	...	...	│	│	...	...	...	...	│	│	...	...	...
Lille Europe .... a.	│	0930	...	...	...	0926	...	...	...	1026	...	...	...	...	1126	1130	...	...	...	...	1326	│	...	...	...
Lille Europe .... d.	│	0933	...	...	...	0930	...	...	...	1030	...	...	...	...	1130	1133	...	...	...	...	1330	1326	...	...	...
Brussels Midi / Zuid ...... a.	0958	1007	1025	1026	1031	1005	1033	1058	1105	1105	1126	1131	1133	1158	1205	1208	1226	1231	1233	1258	1405	1405	1425	1431x	1433
Brugge .... a.	...	...	│	1124	│	...	│	│	1201	...	1224	│	│	│	...	...	1324	│	│	│	*1524*	...	│	│	│
Leuven .... a.	...	...	│	...	1057	...	│	1125	...	...	...	1157	│	1225	...	...	...	1257	│	1325	...	...	│	1457x	│
Liège Guillemins ..... a.	...	...	1112	...	1155	...	│	1200	...	...	...	1255	│	1300	...	...	...	1355	│	1400	...	...	1512	1555	│
Namur .... a.	...	...	...	...	...	...	1139	...	...	...	...	...	1239	...	...	...	...	...	1346	...	...	...	...	...	1539
Luxembourg .... a.	...	...	...	...	...	...	1340	...	...	...	...	...	1445	...	...	...	...	...	1552	...	...	...	...	...	1740

train type	☆						☆		⇌					☆	*ICE*						☆		⇌			
train number	**9132**						**9136**		**9461**					**9140**	**19**						**9144**		**9473**			
notes			Ⓐ		Ⓒ					Ⓐ		Ⓒ		Ⓑ	🍷		Ⓐ		Ⓒ		⑥				Ⓒ	
notes	z						A		D						F								D			
don St Pancras ....d.	1258	...	...	...	...	...	1404	...	...	...	...	...	...	1504	...	...	...	...	...	...	1604	...	...	...	...	...
sfleet International ....d.	1315	...	...	...	...	...	│	...	...	...	...	...	...	│	...	...	...	...	...	...	│	...	...	...	...	...
ord International ....d.	│	...	...	...	...	...	│	...	...	...	...	...	...	│	...	...	...	...	...	...	│	...	...	...	...	...
Europe ....a.	1530	...	...	...	...	...	1626	...	...	...	...	...	...	1726	...	...	...	...	...	...	1826	...	...	...	...	...
Europe ....d.	1533	...	...	...	...	...	1630	...	...	...	...	...	...	1730	...	...	...	...	...	...	1830	...	...	...	...	...
ssels Midi / Zuid ....a.	1608	1626	1631	1633	1658	...	1705	1726	1728	1731	1733	1758	...	1805	1825	1826	1831	1833	1858	...	1905	1926	1928	1933	1958	...
ugge ....a.	...	1724	│	│	│	...	...	1824	│	│	│	│	...	...	│	1924	│	│	│	...	...	2024	│	│	│	...
Leuven......................a.	...	...	1657	│	1725	...	...	...	│	1757	│	1825	...	...	│	...	1857	│	1925	...	...	...	│	│	2025	...
Liège Guillemins ......a.	...	...	1755	│	1800	...	...	...	1811	1855	│	1900	...	...	1912	...	1955	│	2000	...	...	...	2011	│	2100	...
Namur ....a.	...	...	...	1740	...	...	...	...	...	...	1840	...	...	...	...	...	...	1939	...	...	...	...	...	2039	...	...
Luxembourg ....a.	...	...	...	1940	...	...	...	...	...	...	2040	...	...	...	...	...	...	2140	...	...	...	...	...	2240	...	...

train type	☆						☆	☆						☆					☆						☆	
train number	**9148**						**9152**	**9152**						**9156**					**9158**						**9162**	
notes			Ⓐ		Ⓒ		⑦	①–⑤		Ⓐ		Ⓒ		⑥⑦		Ⓒ			①–⑤	Ⓐ	Ⓒ		Ⓒ		⑦	
notes	V						y	j						y z					j z							
don St Pancras ....d.	1704	...	...	...	...	...	1755	1804	...	...	...	...	...	1904	...	...	...	...	1934	...	...	...	...	...	2003	...
sfleet International ....d.	│	...	...	...	...	...	│	│	...	...	...	...	...	│	...	...	...	...	│	...	...	...	...	...	│	...
ord International ....d.	│	...	...	...	...	...	1828	│	...	...	...	...	...	│	...	...	...	...	│	...	...	...	...	...	│	...
Europe ....a.	1926	...	...	...	...	...	2026	2026	...	...	...	...	...	2130	...	...	...	...	2200	...	...	...	...	...	2225	...
Europe ....d.	1930	...	...	...	...	...	2030	2030	...	...	...	...	...	2133	...	...	...	...	2203	...	...	...	...	...	2230	...
ssels Midi / Zuid ....a.	2005	2026	2031	2033	2058	...	2105	2105	2126	2131	2133	2158	...	2208	2226	2258	2233	...	2238	2257	2258	2305	2333	...	2304	...
ugge ....a.	...	2124	│	│	│	...	...	...	2224	│	│	│	...	...	2324	│	│	...	...	│	│	0001	│	...	...	...
Leuven......................a.	...	...	2057	│	2125	...	...	...	...	2157	│	2225	...	...	...	2327	│	...	...	2323	2327	...	│	...	...	...
Liège Guillemins ......a.	...	...	2155	│	2200	...	...	...	...	2255	│	2302	...	...	...	0023	│	...	...	0023	0023	...	│	...	...	...
Namur ....a.	...	...	...	2139	...	...	...	...	...	...	2241	...	...	...	...	...	2339	...	...	...	...	...	0046	...	...	...
Luxembourg ....a.	...	...	...	2340	...	...	...	...	...	...	...	...	...	...	...	...	...	...	...	...	...	...	...	...	...	...

train type				☆						☆					☆						☆					☆
train number				**9109**						**9113**					**9117**						**9125**					**9129**
notes	Ⓐ		Ⓐ	①		Ⓐ	Ⓒ			①–⑥							Ⓐ									⑦
notes				k						j					z						X					f
Luxembourg ....d.	...	...	...	...	...	...	...	...	...	...	...	...	...	...	...	0620	0650	...	...	...	...	0720	...	...	...	...
Namur ....d.	0411	...	...	...	...	...	...	0551	...	...	...	...	0651	...	...	0820	0843	...	0851	...	...	0921	...	0951	...	...
Liège Guillemins ......d.	│	...	0443	...	...	...	...	│	0600	...	...	...	│	0700	...	│	│	...	│	0900	...	│	...	│	1000	...
Leuven......................d.	│	...	0537	...	...	...	...	│	0637	...	...	...	│	0734	...	│	│	...	│	0937	...	│	...	│	1037	...
rugge ....d.	│	0450	│	...	...	0557	0559	│	│	...	...	0658	│	│	...	│	│	0859	│	│	...	│	0959	│	│	...
ssels Midi / Zuid ....d.	0545	0555	0603	0656	...	0655	0655	0657	0703	0756	...	0755	0757	0803	0852	0927	0945	0955	0957	1003	1056	1027	1055	1057	1103	1156
Europe ....a.	...	...	...	0731	...	...	...	...	...	0830	...	...	...	...	0926	...	...	...	...	...	1130	...	...	...	...	1230
Europe ....d.	...	...	...	0736	...	...	...	...	...	0836	...	...	...	...	0930	...	...	...	...	...	1136	...	...	...	...	1236
ford International.......a.	...	...	...	│	...	...	...	...	...	│	...	...	...	...	│	...	...	...	...	...	│	...	...	...	...	│
sfleet International ....a.	...	...	...	│	...	...	...	...	...	│	...	...	...	...	│	...	...	...	...	...	│	...	...	...	...	│
don St Pancras ....a.	...	...	...	0759	...	...	...	...	...	0857	...	...	...	...	0957	...	...	...	...	...	1157	...	...	...	...	1257

train type					☆					☆	☆					☆					☆	☆				
train number					**9133**					**9141**	**9141**					**9145**					**9149**	**9149**				
notes					①–⑤					⑦	①–⑥										①–⑥	⑦				
notes					j z					y z	j					A					j	y				
Luxembourg ....d.	0820	...	...	...	...	1020	...	...	...	...	...	1120	...	...	...	...	1220	...	...	...	...	...	...	...	...	...
Namur ....d.	1021	...	1051	...	...	1221	...	1251	...	...	...	1321	...	1351	...	...	1421	...	1451	...	...	...	...	...	...	...
Liège Guillemins ......d.	│	...	│	1100	...	│	...	│	1300	...	...	│	...	│	1400	...	│	...	│	1500	...	...	...	...	...	...
Leuven......................d.	│	...	│	1137	...	│	...	│	1337	...	...	│	...	│	1437	...	│	...	│	1537	...	...	...	...	...	...
rugge ....d.	│	1059	│	│	...	│	1259	│	│	...	...	│	1359	│	│	...	│	1459	│	│	...	...	...	...	...	...
ssels Midi / Zuid ....d.	1127	1155	1157	1203	1252	1327	1355	1357	1403	1452	1456	1427	1455	1457	1503	1556	1527	1555	1557	1603	1656	1656	...	...	...	...
Europe ....a.	...	...	...	...	1326	...	...	...	...	1526	1532	...	...	...	...	1630	...	...	...	...	1732	1732	...	...	...	...
Europe ....d.	...	...	...	...	1330	...	...	...	...	1530	1536	...	...	...	...	1636	...	...	...	...	1736	1736	...	...	...	...
ford International.......a.	...	...	...	...	│	...	...	...	...	│	│	...	...	...	...	│	...	...	...	...	1734	│	...	...	...	...
sfleet International ....a.	...	...	...	...	1345	...	...	...	...	1545	1545	...	...	...	...	│	...	...	...	...	│	1745	...	...	...	...
don St Pancras ....a.	...	...	...	...	1405	...	...	...	...	1605	1605	...	...	...	...	1657	...	...	...	...	1806	1806	...	...	...	...

train type					☆	☆					☆						☆									
train number					**9153**	**9153**					**9157**						**9161**									
notes					①–⑤	⑦					Ⓑ															
notes					j	y											z									
Luxembourg ....d.	1324	...	...	...	...	...	...	1420	...	...	...	...	1520	...	...	...	...	...	...	...	...	...	...	...	...	...
Namur ....d.	1521	...	1551	...	...	...	...	1621	...	1651	...	...	1721	...	1751	...	...	...	...	...	...	...	...	...	...	...
Liège Guillemins ......d.	│	...	│	1600	...	...	...	│	...	│	1700	...	│	...	│	1800	...	...	...	...	...	...	...	...	...	...
Leuven......................d.	│	...	│	1637	...	...	...	│	...	│	1737	...	│	...	│	1837	...	...	...	...	...	...	...	...	...	...
rugge ....d.	│	1559	│	│	...	...	...	│	1659	│	│	...	│	1759	│	│	...	...	...	...	...	...	...	...	...	...
ssels Midi / Zuid ....d.	1627	1655	1657	1703	1756	1756	...	1727	1755	1757	1803	1856	...	1827	1855	1857	1903	1952	...	...	...	...	...	...	...	...
Europe ....a.	...	...	...	...	1830	1830	...	...	...	...	...	1930	...	...	...	...	...	2026	...	...	...	...	...	...	...	...
Europe ....d.	...	...	...	...	1836	1836	...	...	...	...	...	1935	...	...	...	...	...	2030	...	...	...	...	...	...	...	...
ford International.......a.	...	...	...	...	│	1835	...	...	...	...	...	│	...	...	...	...	...	│	...	...	...	...	...	...	...	...
sfleet International ....a.	...	...	...	...	1845	│	...	...	...	...	...	│	...	...	...	...	...	2045	...	...	...	...	...	...	...	...
don St Pancras ....a.	...	...	...	...	1903	1910	...	...	...	...	...	1957	...	...	...	...	...	2103	...	...	...	...	...	...	...	...

Ⓑ May 29 - Sept. 3. ⑤⑦ Sept. 4 - Dec. 10 (also Oct. 24–27).
To Dortmund (Table **20**).
To Köln and Frankfurt (Table **21**).
① July 24 - Dec. 10 (not Aug. 15).
①–⑤ May 29 - July 23 (not May 30).
②–⑤ July 24 - Dec. 10 (not Aug. 29, Nov. 1, 11).

V – Daily May 29 - Sept. 3. Ⓑ Sept. 4 - Dec. 10.
X – ①–⑥ May 29 - Sept. 3. ①–⑤ Sept. 4 - Dec. 10, (not Nov. 11).
Y – ①–⑥ May 31 - Nov. 4 (not Aug. 29). Daily Nov. 5 - Dec. 10.
Z – ⑦ May 29 - Nov. 4 (also May 30, Aug. 29).
f – Also Nov. 11.
j – Not May 30, Aug. 29, Nov. 11.

k – Not May 30, Aug. 29.
x – 27–28 minutes later on Ⓒ.
y – Also May 30, Aug. 29, Nov. 11.
z – Calls at Calais Fréthun, see Table **10**.
⇌ – *Thalys* high-speed train. 🅁 🍷. Special fares payable. Valid May 30 - Dec. 10.
☆ – Eurostar train. 🅁, ✕ in Business Premier and Standard Premier, 🍷 in Standard. Special fares payable. Minimum check-in time is 30 minutes. Not available for London - Ebbsfleet - Ashford or v.v. journeys. Valid May 29 - Dec. 10.

13 LONDON - PARIS - BARCELONA - MADRID

train type	AVE	AVE	AVE	TGV	AVE	TGV		☆		☆	TGV	AVE	TGV	☆		☆	☆	❖		AVE	A
train number	9729	3122	9730	9711	3142	9713		9084		9110	5164	9743	9756	9014		9022	9040	3731		9729	3
train number/notes			9731					9085		①–⑤	9826		9757					3733			
notes	B			C				Q		z						T		G 🅁	2	B	
London St Pancras **10** d.	...	...	...	...	...	...	...	0719r	...	0804	...	...	...	0917t	...	1131j	1631	...	...	...	
Lille Europe d.	...	...	...	...	...	...	...	|	...	1026	1043	...	...	|	...	|	|	...	...	...	
Paris Nord **10** a.	...	...	...	...	...	...	...	|	...	...	|	...	...	1247	...	1447	1947	...	...	...	
														TGV **9715**		*TGV* **9717** **A S**					
Paris Gare de Lyon d.	...	...	...	0715	...	1007	...	|	...	...	|	...	...	1407	...	1607	...	...	...	...	
Paris Austerlitz d.	...	...	...	|	...	|	...	|	...	...	|	...	...	|	...	|	...	2139	...	...	
Les Aubrais-Orléans d.	...	...	...	|	...	|	...	|	...	...	|	...	...	|	...	|	...	2240	...	...	
Genève 🏛 d.	...	...	...	|	...	|	...	|	1130	...	|	...	1242	|	1500	|	...	|	...	...	
Lyon Part Dieu d.	...	...	...	|	...	|	...	1300e	1324	...	1400	1423	1436	|	|	|	...	|	...	...	
Valence TGV d.	...	...	...	|	...	1221	...	...	...	...	...	1503	1510	1621	1804	1821	...	|	...	...	
Marseille St Charles d.	...	...	0805	|	...	|	...	...	...	...	...	|	...	|	...	|	...	|	...	...	
Aix en Provence TGV d.	...	...	0821	|	...	|	...	...	...	...	...	|	...	|	...	|	...	|	...	...	
Avignon TGV d.	...	...	0843	|	...	|	...	...	...	...	...	|	...	|	...	|	...	|	...	...	
Nimes d.	...	...	0904	1008	...	1308	...	...	...	...	...	1548	...	1708	...	1907	...	|	...	...	
Montpellier d.	...	...	0933	1037	...	1338	...	...	...	...	...	1625	...	1738	...	1941	...	|	...	...	
Béziers d.	...	...	1015	|	...	1421	...	...	...	...	...	1716	...	|	...	2029	...	|	...	...	
Toulouse Matabiau d.	0806	...	|	|	...	|	...	...	...	...	...	|	...	|	...	|	...	|	...	...	
Carcassonne d.	0857	...	|	|	...	|	...	...	...	...	...	|	...	|	...	|	...	0525	...	...	
Narbonne d.	|	...	1034	1135	...	1439	...	...	...	...	...	1735	...	1834	...	2048	...	0628	...	...	
Perpignan d.	1000	...	1117	1212	...	1517	...	...	...	...	...	1809	...	1913	...	2125	...	0716	...	1000	
Cerbère 🏛 a.	|	...	|	|	...	|	...	...	...	...	...	|	...	|	...	|	...	0800	...	|	
Portbou 🏛 a.	|	...	|	|	...	|	...	...	...	...	...	|	...	|	...	|	...	0810	0833	|	
Figueres Vilafant ◇ a.	1023	...	1140	1236	...	1536	*AVE*	...	...	...	...	1833	*AVE*	1936	*AVE*	2148	...	...	0857x	1021	
Girona a.	1040	...	1157	1253	...	1553	**3172**	...	...	...	...	1850	**3202**	1953	**3212**	2205	...	...	0935	1038	
Barcelona Sants a.	1121	...	1238	1334	...	1634	...	...	...	...	...	1931	...	2034	...	2246	...	...	1109	1121	
Barcelona Sants d.	...	1200	1250	...	1400	...	1700	...	...	...	...	...	2000	...	2100c	...	...	...	...	...	1
Zaragoza Delicias a.	...	1340	1423	...	1540	...	1828	...	...	...	...	...	2140	...	2240	...	...	...	...	...	1
Madrid Puerta de Atocha a.	...	1510	1545	...	1710	...	1950	...	...	...	...	...	2310	...	0002	...	...	...	...	...	1

train type	TGV	☆	AVE		TGV	☆	AVE	AVE	TGV	☆		AVE	TGV	TGV		AVE	TGV	AVE	AVE	❖	
train number	9700	9039	9734		9866	9149	3053	3061	9702	9055		3093	9704	5380		3123	9706	9724	9732	3730	9
train number/notes					9867		①④⑤	①–④						5381				9725		3732	
notes	R D	h													2		C		E	H 🅁	
Madrid Puerta de Atocha d.	...	...	...	...	...	...	0550	0610	...	...	...	0930	...	...	...	1230	...	1325	...	...	
Zaragoza Delicias d.	...	...	...	...	...	...	0706	|	...	...	...	1046	...	...	...	1346	...	1452	...	...	
Barcelona Sants a.	...	...	...	...	...	...	0855	0840	...	...	...	1234	...	...	...	1530	...	1624	...	...	
Barcelona Sants d.	0610	...	0720	...	...	...	...	...	0925	...	...	...	1317	...	1516	...	1620	1645	1830	...	
Girona d.	0651	...	0801	...	...	...	...	...	1006	...	...	...	1358	...	1648	...	1701	1726	1911	...	
Figueres Vilafant ◇ d.	0708	...	0818	...	...	...	...	...	1023	...	...	...	1415	...	1727x	...	1718	1743	1928	...	
Portbou 🏛 d.	|	...	|	...	...	...	...	...	|	...	...	...	|	...	1753	...	|	|	|	...	
Cerbère 🏛 d.	|	...	|	...	...	...	...	...	|	...	...	...	|	...	1757	...	|	|	|	2005	
Perpignan a.	0731	...	0843	...	...	...	...	...	1046	...	...	...	1440	...		...	1742	1806	1951	2055d	
Narbonne a.	0811	...	0922	...	...	...	...	...	1127	...	...	...	1525	...	...	...	1823	1854	|	2213d	
Carcassonne a.	|	...	|	...	...	...	...	...	|	...	...	...	|	...	...	...	|	|	2056	2249d	
Toulouse Matabiau a.	|	...	|	...	...	...	...	...	|	...	...	...	|	...	...	...	|	|	2142	0049d	
Béziers a.	0829	...	0938	...	...	...	...	...	|	...	...	...	|	...	...	...	1839	1910	...	|	
Montpellier a.	0924	...	1024	...	...	...	...	...	1221	...	...	...	1618	1627	...	...	1920	1954	...	|	
Nimes a.	0952	...	1056	...	...	...	...	...	1251	...	...	...	1652	1655	...	...	1952	2022	...	|	
Avignon TGV a.	|	...	|	...	...	...	...	...	|	...	...	...	|	|	...	...	|	2043	...	|	
Aix en Provence TGV a.	|	...	|	...	...	...	...	...	|	...	...	...	|	|	...	...	|	2105	...	|	
Marseille St Charles a.	|	...	|	...	...	...	...	...	|	...	...	...	|	|	...	...	|	2120	...	|	
Valence TGV a.	|	...	1146	...	...	...	...	...	1338	...	1357	...	1738	1746	...	...	|	...	...	|	
Lyon Part Dieu a.	|	...	1226	1238	1400	...	...	...	|	...	|	...	|	1824	1836	...	|	...	...	|	
Genève 🏛 a.	|	...	...	1427	|	...	...	...	|	...	1700	...	|	...	2027	...	|	...	...	|	
Les Aubrais-Orléans a.	|	...	...	...	|	...	...	...	|	...	...	...	|	...	...	...	|	...	...	0620	
Paris Austerlitz a.	|	...	...	...	|	...	...	...	|	...	...	...	|	...	...	...	|	...	...	0723	
Paris Gare de Lyon a.	1245	...	...	...	|	...	...	...	1553	...	...	...	1953	...	...	...	2245	...	...	...	
	☆ **9037** **J**								☆ **9051** Ⓑ												
Paris Nord **10** d.	1443	1513	...	...	|	...	...	...	1813	1913	...	...	...	...	...	...	...	...	...	...	09
Lille Europe a.	|	|	...	...	1657	1736	...	...	|	|	...	...	...	...	...	...	...	...	...	...	
London St Pancras **10** a.	1602	1639	...	...	...	1806	...	...	1939	2039	...	...	...	...	...	...	...	...	...	...	10

A – July 3 - Aug. 28.
B – June 2 - Sept. 26.
C – June 2 - Aug. 28.
D – Calls at Agde, a. 0843, Sète, a. 0858.
E – June 2 - Sept. 25.
G – *INTERCITÉS* – 🛏 1, 2 cl., (2) (reclining) Paris - Portbou. (not Oct. 22, 29, 30, 31) ❖.
H – *INTERCITÉS* – 🛏 1, 2 cl., (2) (reclining) Cerbère - Paris. (not Oct. 22, 29, 30, 31) ❖.
J – Ⓑ May 29 - July 23 (not May 30). ①④⑤⑦ July 24 - Sept. 3, (not Aug. 29). ⑤ Sept. 4 - Dec. 10 (not Nov. 11).
Q – ①⑤⑥ May 29 - July 2, ①④⑤⑥⑦ July 3 - Sept. 3, ①⑤⑥ Sept. 4 - Oct. 29, see Tables **11**, **17**.
R – July 4 - Aug. 28.

S – Calls at Sète 1958, Agde 2014.
T – Daily May 29 - July 3. ①④⑤⑥⑦ July 4 - Dec. 10 (not Aug. 29).

c – 2115 on ①②③④⑥.
d – Departure time.
e – Lyon **St Exupéry** ✈ on Oct. 29.
h – Not May 29, Aug. 28.
j – 1122 on ⑥.
r – 0715 on ⑦ (also Aug. 29).
t – 0922 on ⑦ (also May 30, Aug. 29, Nov. 11). 0924 on ⑥.
x – Figueres.

z – Not May 30, Aug. 29, Nov. 11.

❖ – Subject to confirmation from July 1.
TGV – *Train à Grande Vitesse* 🅁 🍸 ✗.
AVE – Alta Velocidad Española 🅁 🍸 ✗.
✗ – Supplement payable.
◇ – 🚌 connections available to Figueres bus station (Table **657**).
☆ – Eurostar train. 🅁, ✕ in Business Premier and Standa Premier, 🍸 in Standard. Special fares payable. Minim check-in time 30 minutes. Additional services are show on Table **10**. Valid May 29 - Dec. 10.

LONDON - ROTTERDAM - AMSTERDAM *by Eurostar* 15

train type	☆	☆	☆	*IC*		☆	*IC*	⇌		☆	☆	*IC*	⇌		☆	☆	*IC*	⇌	⇌	
train number	**9108**	**9110**	**9110**	**9231**		**9114**	**9235**	**9327**		**9116**	**9116**	**9239**	**9993**		**9126**	**9126**	**9247**	**9397**	**9351**	
notes	**K**	**L**	⑥	❖		**A**	❖			**A**	**B**	❖			**Y**	**J**	❖	**C**		
on St Pancras **12** d.	0613	0650	0657	...	...	0804	...	...	...	0855	0858	...	...	...	1058	1104	...	...	...	...
eet International **12** d.	0630	0707	|	...	...	|	...	...	...	0914	0915	...	...	...	1115	|	...	...	...	...
rd International d.	0652	0728	0728	...	...	|	...	...	...	|	|	...	...	...	|	|	...	...	...	...
urope **12** d.	|	0933	0930	...	...	1030	...	...	...	1130	1133	...	...	...	1330	1330	...	...	...	...
sels Midi/Zuid **12** a.	0958	1007	1005	...	...	1105	...	...	...	1205	1208	...	...	...	1405	1405	...	...	...	...
sels Midi/Zuid d.	...	...	...	1045	...	...	1145	1152	...	...	...	1245	1252	...	...	...	1445	1452	1552	...
erpen Centraal a.	...	...	...	1143	...	...	1243	1227	...	...	...	1343	1327	...	...	...	1543	1527	1627	...
endaal 🏨 a.	...	...	...	1211	...	...	1311	|	...	...	...	1411	|	...	...	...	1611	|	|	...
rdam Centraal a.	...	...	...	1256	...	...	1356	1302	...	...	...	1456	1402	...	...	...	1656	1602	1702	...
Haag HS a.	...	...	...	1317	...	...	1417	|	...	...	...	1517	|	...	...	...	1717	|	|	...
hol ✈ a.	...	...	...	1348	...	...	1448	1324	...	...	...	1548	1424	...	...	...	1748	1624	1724	...
erdam Centraal a.	...	...	...	1405	...	...	1505	1342	...	...	...	1605	1442	...	...	...	1805	1642	1742	...

train type		☆	*IC*	⇌		☆	*IC*	⇌		☆	*IC*	⇌		☆	*IC*	⇌				
train number		**9132**	**9255**	**9357**		**9136**	**9259**	**9363**		**9140**	**9263**	**9369**		**9144**	**9267**	**9375**				
notes			❖	Ⓑ **w**		**F**	❖	Ⓑ **g**		Ⓑ	❖			⑥	❖	**H**				
on St Pancras **12** d.	...	1258	...	...	...	1404	...	...	...	1504	...	...	...	1604	...	...	...	...	...	...
leet International **12** d.	...	1315	...	...	...	|	...	...	...	|	...	...	...	|	...	...	...	...	...	...
rd International d.	...	|	...	...	...	|	...	...	...	|	...	...	...	|	...	...	...	...	...	...
urope **12** d.	...	1533	...	...	...	1630	...	...	...	1730	...	...	...	1830	...	...	...	...	...	...
sels Midi/Zuid **12** a.	...	1608	...	...	...	1705	...	...	...	1805	...	...	...	1905	...	...	...	...	...	...
sels Midi/Zuid d.	...	...	1645	1652	...	...	1745	1752	...	...	1845	1852	...	...	1945	1952	...	...	...	...
erpen Centraal a.	...	...	1743	1727	...	...	1843	1827	...	...	1943	1927	...	...	2043	2027	...	...	...	...
endaal 🏨 a.	...	...	1811	|	...	...	1911	|	...	...	2011	|	...	...	2111	|	...	...	...	...
rdam Centraal a.	...	...	1856	1802	...	...	1956	1902	...	...	2056	2002	...	...	2156	2102	...	...	...	...
Haag HS a.	...	...	1917	|	...	...	2017	|	...	...	2117	|	...	...	2217	|	...	...	...	...
hol ✈ a.	...	...	1948	1824	...	...	2048	1924	...	...	2148	2024	...	...	2248	2124	...	...	...	...
erdam Centraal a.	...	...	2005	1842	...	...	2105	1942	...	...	2205	2042	...	...	2305	2142	...	...	...	...

train type		☆	*IC*	⇌		☆	☆	⇌												
train number		**9148**	**9271**	**9381**		**9152**	**9152**	**9995**												
notes		**V**	❖			⑦ **y**	**A**	⑤⑥⑦ **k**												
on St Pancras **12** d.	...	1704	...	...	...	1755	1804		...	...	...	...	...	...	...	...	...	...	...	...
leet International **12** d.	...	|	...	...	...	|	|	...	...	...	...	...	...	...	...	...	...	...	...	...
rd International d.	...	|	...	...	...	1828	|	...	...	...	...	...	...	...	...	...	...	...	...	...
urope **12** d.	...	1930	...	...	...	2030	2030	...	...	...	...	...	...	...	...	...	...	...	...	...
sels Midi/Zuid **12** a.	...	2005	...	...	...	2105	2105	...	...	...	...	...	...	...	...	...	...	...	...	...
sels Midi/Zuid d.	...	...	2045	2052	...	...	...	2152	...	...	...	...	...	...	...	...	...	...	...	...
erpen Centraal a.	...	...	2143	2127	...	...	...	2227	...	...	...	...	...	...	...	...	...	...	...	...
endaal 🏨 a.	...	...	2211	|	...	...	...	|	...	...	...	...	...	...	...	...	...	...	...	...
rdam Centraal a.	...	...	2256	2202	...	...	...	2302	...	...	...	...	...	...	...	...	...	...	...	...
n Haag HS a.	...	...	2317	|	...	...	...	|	...	...	...	...	...	...	...	...	...	...	...	...
hol ✈ a.	...	...	2348	2224	...	...	...	2324	...	...	...	...	...	...	...	...	...	...	...	...
erdam Centraal a.	...	...	0005	2242	...	...	...	2342	...	...	...	...	...	...	...	...	...	...	...	...

train type		⇌	☆		⇌	*IC*	☆			⇌	*IC*	☆		⇌ **h**	*IC*	☆				
train number		**9310**	**9117**		**9322**	**9216**	**9125**			**9328**	**9220**	**9129**		**9334**	**9224**	**9133**				
notes		**P**				■	**X**			**Z**	■	⑦ **t**		⑤⑥⑦	■	**E**				
erdam Centraal d.	...	0617	...	...	0817	0652	...	...	...	0917	0752	...	...	1017	0852	...	...	...	...	...
hol ✈ △ d.	...	0633	...	...	0833	0707	...	...	...	0933	0807	...	...	1033	0907	...	...	...	...	...
n Haag HS d.	...	|	...	...	|	0743	...	...	...	|	0843	...	...	|	0943	...	...	...	...	...
rdam Centraal d.	...	0658	...	...	0858	0805f	...	...	...	0958	0908	...	...	1058	1005f	...	...	...	...	...
endaal 🏨 d.	...	|	...	...	|	0847	...	...	...	|	0947	...	...	|	1047	...	...	...	...	...
verpen Centraal d.	...	0734	...	...	0933	0917	...	...	...	1033	1017	...	...	1133	1117	...	...	...	...	...
sels Midi/Zuid a.	...	0808	...	...	1008	1015	...	...	...	1108	1115	...	...	1208	1215	...	...	...	...	...
sels Midi/Zuid **12** d.	...	...	0852	...	...	...	1056	...	...	...	...	1156	...	...	...	1252	...	...	...	...
Europe **12** a.	...	...	0926	...	...	...	1130	...	...	...	...	1230	...	...	...	1330	...	...	...	...
ord International a.	...	...	|	...	...	...	|	...	...	...	...	|	...	...	...	|	...	...	...	...
fleet International **12** a.	...	...	|	...	...	...	|	...	...	...	...	|	...	...	...	1345	...	...	...	...
lon St Pancras **12** a.	...	...	0957	...	...	...	1157	...	...	...	...	1257	...	...	...	1405	...	...	...	...

train type		*IC*	⇌	☆	☆		⇌	*IC*	☆			⇌	*IC*	☆	☆					
train number		**9232**	**9340**	**9141**	**9141**		**9352**	**9236**	**9145**			**9358**	**9240**	**9149**	**9149**					
notes		■		⑦ **y**	**E**			■	**F**			Ⓑ **w**	■	**E**	⑦ **y**					
terdam Centraal d.	...	1052	1117	...	...	...	1317	1152	...	...	...	1417	1252	...	...	...	...	...	...	...
hol ✈ △ d.	...	1107	1133	...	...	...	1333	1207	...	...	...	1433	1307	...	...	...	...	...	...	...
n Haag HS d.	...	1143	|	...	...	...	|	1243	...	...	...	|	1343	...	...	...	...	...	...	...
rdam Centraal d.	...	1205f	1158	...	...	...	1358	1308	...	...	...	1458	1405f	...	...	...	...	...	...	...
sendaal 🏨 d.	...	1247	|	...	...	...	|	1347	...	...	...	|	1447	...	...	...	...	...	...	...
verpen Centraal d.	...	1317	1233	...	...	...	1433	1417	...	...	...	1533	1517	...	...	...	...	...	...	...
sels Midi/Zuid a.	...	1415	1308	...	...	...	1508	1515	...	...	...	1608	1615	...	...	...	...	...	...	...
sels Midi/Zuid **12** d.	...	...	...	1452	1456	...	...	...	1556	...	...	...	...	1656	1656	...	...	...	...	...
Europe **12** a.	...	...	...	1526	1530	...	...	...	1632	...	...	...	...	1732	1732	...	...	...	...	...
ord International a.	...	...	...	|	|	...	...	...	|	...	...	...	...	1734	|	...	...	...	...	...
sfleet International **12** a.	...	...	...	1545	1545	...	...	...	|	...	...	...	...	|	1745	...	...	...	...	...
don St Pancras **12** a.	...	...	...	1605	1605	...	...	...	1657	...	...	...	...	1806	1803	...	...	...	...	...

train type		⇌	*IC*	☆	☆		⇌ **w**	*IC*	☆		⇌	*IC*	☆							
train number		**9364**	**9244**	**9153**	**9153**		**9370**	**9248**	**9157**		**9376**	**9252**	**9161**							
notes		**9996**	■	**A**	⑦ **y**		**9998**	■	Ⓑ		Ⓑ **w**	■								
terdam Centraal d.	...	1517	1352	...	...	...	1617	1452	...	...	1717	1552	...	...	...	...	...	...	...	...
hol ✈ △ d.	...	1533	1407	...	...	...	1633	1507	...	...	1733	1607	...	...	...	...	...	...	...	...
en Haag HS d.	...	|	1443	...	...	...	|	1543	...	...	|	1643	...	...	...	...	...	...	...	...
erdam Centraal d.	...	1558	1508	...	...	...	1658	1605f	...	...	1758	1708	...	...	...	...	...	...	...	...
sendaal 🏨 a.	...	|	1547	...	...	...	|	1647	...	...	|	1747	...	...	...	...	...	...	...	...
verpen Centraal d.	...	1633	1617	...	...	...	1733	1717	...	...	1833	1817	...	...	...	...	...	...	...	...
ssels Midi/Zuid a.	...	1708	1715	...	...	...	1808	1815	...	...	1908	1915	...	...	...	...	...	...	...	...
ssels Midi/Zuid **12** d.	...	...	...	1756	1756	...	...	...	1856	...	...	...	1952	...	...	...	...	...	...	...
Europe **12** a.	...	...	...	1832	1832	...	...	...	1930	...	...	...	2026	...	...	...	...	...	...	...
ord International a.	...	...	...	|	1835	...	...	...	|	...	...	...	|	...	...	...	...	...	...	...
sfleet International **12** a.	...	...	...	1845	|	...	...	...	|	...	...	...	2045	...	...	...	...	...	...	...
don St Pancras **12** a.	...	...	...	1903	1910	...	...	...	1957	...	...	...	2103	...	...	...	...	...	...	...

①–⑤ (not May 30, Aug. 29, Nov. 11).
⑥⑦ (also May 30, Aug. 29, Nov. 11).
①–④ (not Aug. 15).
①–⑥ (not May 30, Aug. 29, Nov. 11).
Ⓑ May 29 - Sept. 3. ⑤⑦ Sept. 4 - Dec. 10 (also Oct. 24–27).
Ⓑ (not Nov. 11). Train number **9975** on ①–④.
⑦ May 29 - Nov. 4 (also May 30, Aug. 29).
① July 24 - Dec. 10 (not Aug. 15).
①–⑤ May 29 - July 23 (not May 30). ②–⑤ July 24 - Dec. 10, (not Aug. 29, Nov. 1, 11).
①–⑤ (not Aug. 15, Nov. 11).
Daily May 29 - Sept. 3. Ⓑ Sept. 4 - Dec. 10.
①–⑥ May 29 - Sept. 3. ①–⑤ Sept. 4 - Dec. 10 (not Nov. 11).

Y – ①–⑥ May 31 - Nov. 4 (not Aug. 29). Daily Nov. 5 - Dec. 10.
Z – ①–⑥ (not Aug. 15).

f – 3 minutes later on ©.
g – Not Aug. 15.
h – Also Aug. 15, Nov. 11.
k – Also Aug. 15.
t – Also Nov. 11.
w – Not Nov. 11.
y – Also May 30, Aug. 29, Nov. 11.

△ – Trains stop to pick up only.
⇌ – *Thalys* high-speed train. 🅁 🍸. Valid May 30 - Dec. 10. Special fares payable.
☆ – Eurostar train. 🅁, ✕ in Business Premier and Standard Premier, 🍸 in Standard. Special fares payable. Minimum check-in time 30 minutes. Not available for London - Ebbsfleet - Ashford or v.v. journeys. Valid May 29 - Dec. 10.
❖ – Service calls at Mechelen 37 minutes after Brussels Midi/Zuid, and at Dordrecht 28 minutes after Roosendaal; see Table **18** for full timings.
■ – Service calls at Dordrecht 14-15 minutes after Rotterdam Centraal and at Mechelen 18 minutes after Antwerpen Centraal; see Table **18** for full timings.

15a LONDON - AMSTERDAM *by rail–sea–rail via Harwich - Hoek van Holland*

notes	①–⑥	⑥	①–⑤	①–⑥	①–⑥	①–⑥	①–⑥	⑦	⑦	⑦	⑦	⑦	⑦	①–⑤	⑥	①–⑥	①–⑥	①–⑥	①–⑥	①–⑥
				⛴						⛴							⛴			
London Liverpool Street d.	...	0638	0638	...	...	...	...	...	0755	...	...	...	...	1932	1932	...	...	...	...	...
Colchester d.	...	0740	0743	...	...	...	...	...	0859	...	...	...	...	2025	2032	...	...	...	...	...
Manningtree d.	...	0748	0751	...	...	...	...	...	0907	...	...	...	...	2034	2040	...	...	...	...	...
Cambridge d.	...	|	|	...	...	...	...	...	|	...	...	...	...	|	|	1944	...	...	...	...
Ipswich d.	0659	|	|	...	...	...	...	0751	|	...	...	...	...	|	|	2101	...	...	...	...
Harwich International d.	0727	0809	0810	0900	...	...	...	0816	0925	1000	...	...	...	2054	2056	2129	2300	...	...	...
Hoek van Holland Haven a.	...	...	...	1715	1756	...	...	...	...	1800	1856	...	...	...	...	...	0800	0826	...	...
Schiedam Centrum a.	...	...	...	...	1821	1826	...	...	...	...	1921	1926	...	...	...	...	...	0851	...	0856
Rotterdam Centraal a.	...	...	...	...	1827	|	1835	...	...	...	1927	|	1935	...	...	...	...	0857	0905	|
Utrecht Centraal a.	...	...	...	...	...	|	1913	...	...	...	...	|	2013	...	...	...	...	...	0943	|
Amersfoort a.	...	...	...	...	...	|	1934	...	...	...	...	|	2034	...	...	...	...	...	1004	|
Den Haag HS a.	...	...	...	...	...	1843	...	...	...	...	...	1943	...	...	...	...	...	...	...	0913
Schiphol ✈ a.	...	...	...	...	...	1914	...	...	...	...	...	2014	...	...	...	...	...	...	...	0944
Amsterdam Centraal a.	...	...	...	...	...	1931	...	...	...	...	...	2031	...	...	...	...	...	...	...	1001

notes	⑦	⑦	⑦	⑦	⑦	⑦
			⛴			
London Liverpool Street d.	1932	...	...	...	...	...
Colchester d.	2046	...	...	...	...	...
Manningtree d.	2055	...	...	...	...	...
Cambridge d.	|	1912	...	...	...	...
Ipswich d.	|	2036	...	...	...	...
Harwich International d.	2114	2105	2300	...	...	...
Hoek van Holland Haven a.	...	...	0800	0826	...	...
Schiedam Centrum a.	...	...	...	0851	...	0856
Rotterdam Centraal a.	...	...	...	0857	0905	|
Utrecht Centraal a.	...	...	...	...	0943	|
Amersfoort a.	...	...	...	...	1004	|
Den Haag HS a.	...	...	...	...	...	0913
Schiphol ✈ a.	...	...	...	...	...	0944
Amsterdam Centraal a.	...	...	...	...	...	1001

notes	⑥⑦	⑥⑦	⑥⑦	⑥⑦	⑦	⑥	⑦	⑥
				⛴				
Amsterdam Centraal d.	1128	...	...	...	...	...	...	...
Schiphol ✈ d.	1146	...	...	...	...	...	...	...
Den Haag HS d.	1219	...	...	...	...	...	...	...
Amersfoort d.	|	1126	...	...	...	...	...	...
Utrecht d.	|	1147	...	...	...	...	...	...
Rotterdam Centraal d.	|	1225	1232	...	...	...	...	...
Schiedam Centrum d.	1233	...	1237	...	...	...	...	...
Hoek van Holland Haven d.	...	...	1302	1345	...	...	...	...
Harwich International a.	...	...	...	1945	2035	2045	2110	2138
Ipswich a.	...	...	...	...	|	|	2137	2203
Cambridge a.	...	...	...	...	|	|	...	...
Manningtree a.	...	...	...	...	2048	2058	...	...
Colchester a.	...	...	...	...	2057	2107	...	...
London Liverpool Street a.	...	...	...	...	2202	2214	...	...

notes	①–⑤	①–⑤	①–⑤	①–⑤	①–⑤	①–⑤					①–⑤	⑥	⑦	①–⑥	⑦
				⛴						⛴					
Amsterdam Centraal d.	1128	...	...	...	...	...	...	1928	...	...	...	...	...	...	...
Schiphol ✈ d.	1146	...	...	...	...	...	...	1946	...	...	...	...	...	...	...
Den Haag HS d.	1219	...	...	...	...	...	...	2019	...	...	...	...	...	...	...
Amersfoort d.	|	1126	...	...	...	...	1926	|	...	...	...	...	...	...	...
Utrecht d.	|	1147	...	...	...	...	1947	|	...	...	...	...	...	...	...
Rotterdam Centraal d.	|	1225	1232	...	...	...	2025	|	2032	...	...	...	...	...	...
Schiedam Centrum d.	1233	...	1237	...	...	...	...	2033	2037	...	...	...	...	...	...
Hoek van Holland Haven d.	...	...	1302	1415	...	...	...	...	2102	2200	...	...	...	...	...
Harwich International a.	...	...	...	1945	2045	2138	...	...	...	0630	0715	0720	0720	0750	0830
Ipswich a.	...	...	...	...	|	2204	...	...	...	...	|	|	|	0817	0856
Cambridge a.	...	...	...	...	|	...	...	...	...	...	|	|	|	0939	1025
Manningtree a.	...	...	...	...	2058	...	...	...	...	...	0731	0733	0733	...	...
Colchester a.	...	...	...	...	2107	...	...	...	...	...	0741	0742	0742	...	...
London Liverpool Street a.	...	...	...	...	2214	...	...	...	...	...	0854	0845	0859	...	...

SEA CROSSING (for rail / sea / rail journeys): ⛴ – Ship service, operated by Stena Line. [R] One class only on ship. ✕ on ship. A cabin berth is necessary on night sailings.

16 LILLE - BRUSSELS (Summary Table)

train type	TGV	TGV	☆	☆	☆	TGV	☆	☆	⇌	TGV	☆	☆	☆	TGV	☆	☆	⇌	☆	TGV	☆	⇌	☆	☆	☆
train number	**9809**	**9852**	**9110**	**9110**	**9114**	**9854**	**9116**	**9116**	**9993**	**9862**	**9126**	**9132**	**9136**	**9866**	**9140**	**9144**	**9975**	**9148**	**9868**	**9152**	**9995**	**9156**	**9158**	**9162**
notes	Ⓐ		⑥		①–⑤		①–⑤	⑥⑦							Ⓑ	⑥	①–④			Ⓑ	⑤⑥⑦	⑥⑦	①–⑤	⑦
notes				L	j		j	y	A				F				A r	V			A n	y	j	
Lille Europe d.	0732	0908	0930	0933	1030	1117	1130	1133	1159	1208	1330	1533	1630	1707	1730	1830	1907	1930	2008	2030	2104	2133	2203	2230
Brussels Midi / Zuid a.	0808	0943	1005	1007	1105	1151	1205	1208	1235	1252	1405	1608	1705	1743	1805	1905	1943	2005	2043	2105	2141	2208	2238	2305

train type	☆	☆	TGV	☆	⇌	☆	☆	TGV	☆	☆	☆	☆	TGV	☆	⇌	☆	⇌	☆	TGV	☆
train number	**9109**	**9113**	**9800**	**9117**	**9994**	**9125**	**9129**	**9828**	**9133**	**9141**	**9141**	**9145**	**9836**	**9149**	**9996**	**9153**	**9996**	**9157**	**9846**	**9161**
notes	①	①–⑥					⑦		①–⑥	⑦	①–⑥				①–④	Ⓑ	⑤⑥⑦	Ⓑ		
notes	k	j			A	X	t		j	y	j	F			Ar		A n			
Brussels Midi / Zuid d.	0656	0756	0817	0852	0917	1056	1156	1217	1252	1452	1456	1556	1617	1656	1717	1756	1817	1856	1917	1952
Lille Europe a.	0731	0830	0852	0926	0953	1130	1230	1253	1326	1526	1532	1630	1653	1732	1752	1830	1854	1930	1952	2026

A – To / from Amsterdam (Table **18**).
F – Ⓑ May 29 - Sept. 3. ⑤⑦ Sept. 4 - Dec. 10 (also Oct. 24–27).
L – ①–⑤ May 29 - July 23 (not May 30). ②–⑤ July 24 - Dec. 10, (not Aug. 29, Nov. 1, 11).
V – Daily May 29 - Sept. 3. Ⓑ Sept. 4 - Dec. 10.
X – ①–⑥ May 29 - Sept. 3. ①–⑤ Sept. 4 - Dec. 10 (not Nov. 11).

j – Not May 30, Aug. 29, Nov. 11.
k – Not May 30, Aug. 29.
n – Also Aug. 15.
r – Not Aug. 15.
t – Also Nov. 11.
y – Also May 30, Aug. 29, Nov. 11.

☆ – Eurostar train. [R], ✕ in Business Premier and Standard Premier, Standard. Special fares payable. Minimun check-in time 30 mi[n] departure from Brussels. Valid May 29 - Dec. 10.
⇌ – *Thalys* high-speed train. [R] 🍸. Special fares payable. Valid May 30 - Dec. 10.
TGV– High-speed train. [R] 🍸.

17 LONDON - MARSEILLE and MARNE LA VALLÉE

train type	☆		☆	☆		
train number	**9084**		**9074**	**9074**		
train number	**9085**					
notes	**M**		**A**	**Y**		
London St Pancras d.	0719**x**	...	1014	1024	...	...
Ebbsfleet International d.	|	...	1034	1044	...	...
Ashford International d.	0755	...	1058	|	...	...
Lille Europe a.	|	...	1254**s**	1254**s**	...	...
Marne la Vallée § a.	|	...	1402	1402	...	...
Lyon Part Dieu a.	1300**z**	...	...	...	...	...
Avignon TGV a.	1408	...	...	...	...	...
Marseille St Charles a.	1445	...	...	...	...	...

train type	☆	☆	☆	☆	☆	
train number	**9057**	**9057**	**9057**	**9057**	**9087**	**9(**
train number					**9086**	**9(**
notes	**T**	**Y**	**B**	**C**	**M**	
Marseille St Charles d.	...	...	...	...	1522	
Avignon TGV d.	...	...	...	...	1559	
Lyon Part Dieu d.	...	...	...	...	1725**z**	
Marne la Vallée § d.	1649	1707	1707**e**	1802**c**	|	
Lille Europe d.	|	|	|	|	2021	21
Ashford International a.	1806	|	1806	1904	...	21
Ebbsfleet International a.	1827	1827	1827	1926	...	
London St Pancras a.	1847	1847	1847	1946	...	22

A – ①③⑤⑦ May 28 - July 22 (also May 28, 31, June 2, 4); ①③⑤⑥⑦ July 23 - Sept. 5; ①③⑤⑦ Sept. 6 - Dec. 9 (also Oct. 22, 25, 27, 29, Nov. 1, 3, 5; not Nov. 27).
B – ⑤⑦ May 29 - July 22 (also May 28, June 4; not July 10, 15); ⑤⑥⑦ July 23 - Sept. 5; ⑤⑦ Sept. 6 - Dec. 9 (also Oct. 22, 29, Nov. 5).
C – ①③ May 29 - Dec. 9 (also May 31, June 2, Oct 25, 27, Nov. 1, 3).
M – ①⑤⑥ May 29 - July 2, ①④⑤⑥⑦ July 3 - Sept. 3, ①⑤⑥ Sept. 4 - Oct. 29, see Tables **11**, **13**.
T – July 10, 15. **Y** – Nov. 27.

c – 1756 May 29 - July 8 (also July 11, 13).
e – 1649 May 29 - July 8.
s – Calls to set down only.
x – 0715 on ⑦ (also Aug. 29).
z – Lyon **St Exupéry** ✈ on Oct. 29. Train **9087** depart St Exupéry 1656.
§ – Marne la Vallée - Chessy (station for Disneyland).
☆ – Eurostar train. [R], ✕ in Standard Premier, 🍸 in Standard. Special fares payable. Minimum check-in time 30 minutes. Not available for London - Ashford or v.v. journey[s]. Valid May 29 - Dec. 10.

18a PARIS - BRUSSELS

train type / number	izy	izy	izy	izy	izy	izy	izy	izy	izy
train number									
notes	⑥	①⑤	A	⑦	⑥	①–⑤	⑦		
Brussels Midi / Zuid d.	0829	1028	1446	1629	1821	1859	2031	...	...
Paris Nord a.	1042	1250	1700	1844	2032	2129	2243	...	...

train type / number	izy	izy	izy	izy	izy	izy	izy	izy
train number								
notes	①	B	⑦	⑥	⑤	⑦	⑦	①–⑤
Paris Nord d.	0949	1134	1344	1506	1536	1728	1946	2001
Brussels Midi / Zuid a.	1208	1344	1552	1714	1755	1953	2211	2212

A – ②③④⑤⑦. **B** – ②③④⑤⑥.

Low-cost *TGV* services branded **izy**, internet booking only through www.izy.com, special conditions ap[ply]

For the full service London - Brussels and v.v. see Table **12**. Connections at Brussels are not guaranteed.

	train type	⇌	⇌	⇌	⇌	⇌	⇌	⇌	⇌	*IC*	⇌	*IC*	⇌	⇌	⇌	*IC*	⇌	⇌	*IC*	⇌	⇌	*IC*		
	train number	**9300**	**9304**	**9308**	**9310**	**9412**	**9316**	**9994**	**9926/7**	**9212**	**9322**	**9216**	**9424**	**9328**	**9328**	**9220**	**9334**	**9334**	**9224**	**9336**	**9340**	**9228**		
	notes	①–④	①–⑤	①–⑥	①–⑤				⊕					①–⑥	⑦		⑤	⑥⑦		①–⑤				
		S	**f**	**h**	**p**		**K**		**A**					**g**	**Y**			**q**		**p**				
0	**Amsterdam** Centraal d.	...	...	...	0617	...	...	0717	0720	0552	0817	0652	...	0917	...	0752	1017	1017	0852	...	1117	0952	...	...
17	Schiphol ✈ ⊕ d.	...	...	...	0633	...	...	0733	0736	0607	0833	0707	...	0933	...	0807	1033	1033	0907	...	1133	1007	...	...
	Den Haag HS d.	...	...	...	|	...	...	|	|	0643	|	0743	...	|	...	0843	|	|	0943	...	|	1043	...	...
70	**Rotterdam** Centraal d.	...	...	...	0658	...	...	0758	0803	0705j	0858	0805j	...	0958	...	0908	1058	1058	1005j	...	1158	1108	...	...
	Dordrecht d.	...	...	...	|	...	...	|	|	0720	|	0820	...	|	...	0922	|	|	1020	...	|	1122	...	...
	Roosendaal 🏛 d.	...	...	...	|	...	...	|	|	0747	|	0847	...	|	...	0947	|	|	1047	...	|	1147	...	...
165	**Antwerpen** Centraal d.	...	...	...	0734	...	...	0833	0837	0817	0933	0917	...	1033	...	1017	1133	1133	1117	...	1233	1217	...	...
	Mechelen d.	...	...	...	|	...	...	|	|	0835	|	0935	...	|	...	1035	|	|	1135	...	|	1235	...	...
	Brussels Nationaal ✈ d.	...	...	...	|	...	...	|	|	0849	|	0949	...	|	...	1049	|	|	1149	...	|	1249	...	...
212	**Brussels** Midi / Zuid △ a.	...	...	...	0808	...	...	0908	|	0915	1008	1015	...	1108	...	1115	1208	1208	1215	...	1308	1315	...	...
212	**Brussels** Midi / Zuid d.	0613	0713	0743	0813	0843	0913	0917	0925	...	1013	...	1043	1113	1113	...	...	1213	...	1237	1313	...	...	...
	Lille Europe a.	|	|	|	|	|	|	0953	...	...	|	...	|	|	|	...	...	|	...	|	|	...	...	...
524	**Paris** Nord a.	0735	0835	0905	0935	1005	1035	...	...	...	1135	...	1205	1235	1235	...	...	1335	...	1359	1435	...	...	...

train type	⇌	*IC*	⇌	⇌	*IC*	⇌	⇌	*IC*	⇌	⇌	⇌	⇌	*IC*	⇌	⇌	⇌	⇌	*IC*	⇌	⇌	⇌	*IC*	⇌	⇌	
train number	**9346**	**9232**	**9448**	**9352**	**9236**	**9358**	**9358**	**9240**	**9360**	**9364**	**9996**	**9364**	**9244**	**9368**	**9370**	**9998**	**9370**	**9248**	**9472**	**9376**	**9376**	**9252**	**9380**	**9382**	
notes	①–④					Ⓑ	⑥			①–④	①–④	⑤⑥⑦			⑦	⑤⑥⑦	①–⑤			⑥	Ⓑ		⑤		
	g					**w**	**m**		**G**	**g**	**g**	**k**		**Q**	**k**	**k**	**p**			**F**	**w**		**F**		
erdam Centraal d.	1217	1052	...	1317	1152	1417	...	1252	...	...	1517	1517	1352	...	...	1617	1617	1452	...	...	1717	1552	...	1817	...
hol ✈ ⊕ d.	1233	1107	...	1333	1207	1433	...	1307	...	...	1533	1533	1407	...	...	1633	1633	1507	...	...	1733	1607	...	1833	...
Haag HS d.	|	1143	...	|	1243	|	...	1343	...	...	|	|	1443	...	...	|	|	1543	...	...	|	1643	...	|	...
rdam Centraal d.	1258	1205j	...	1358	1308	1458	...	1405j	...	...	1558	1558	1508	...	...	1658	1658	1608j	...	...	1758	1708	...	1858	...
echt d.	|	1220	...	|	1322	|	...	1420	...	...	|	|	1522	...	...	|	|	1620	...	...	|	1722	...	|	...
endaal 🏛 d.	|	1247	...	|	1347	|	...	1447	...	...	|	|	1547	...	...	|	|	1647	...	...	|	1747	...	|	...
erpen Centraal d.	1333	1317	...	1433	1417	1533	...	1517	...	...	1633	1633	1617	...	...	1733	1733	1717	...	...	1833	1817	...	1933	...
elen d.	|	1335	...	|	1435	|	...	1535	...	...	|	|	1635	...	...	|	|	1735	...	...	|	1835	...	|	...
sels Nationaal ✈ d.	|	1349	...	|	1449	|	...	1549	...	...	|	|	1649	...	...	|	|	1749	...	...	|	1849	...	|	...
sels Midi / Zuid △ a.	1408	1415	...	1508	1515	1608	...	1615	...	...	1708	1708	1715	...	...	1808	1808	1815	...	...	1908	1915	...	2008	...
sels Midi / Zuid d.	...	...	1443	1513	...	1613	1613	...	1637	1713	1717	1713	...	1743	1813	1817	1813	...	1843	1913	1913	...	1943	2013	...
e Europe a.	...	...	|	|	...	|	|	...	|	|	1752	|	...	|	|	1854	|	...	|	|	|	...	|	|	...
Nord a.	...	...	1605	1635	...	1735	1735	...	1759	1835	...	1835	...	1905	1935	...	1935	...	2005	2035	2035	...	2105	2135	...

train type	*IC*	⇌	⇌	*IC*	⇌	⇌	*IC*	*IC*	*IC*	
train number	**9256**	**9484**	**9388**	**9260**	**9394**	**9394**	**9264**	**9268**	**9272**	
notes			Ⓑ		①–⑤	⑦				
			w		**p**	**k**				
erdam Centraal d.	1652	...	1917	1752	2017	2017	1852	1952	2052	...
hol ✈ ⊕ d.	1707	...	1933	1807	2033	2033	1907	2007	2107	...
Haag HS d.	1743	...	|	1843	|	|	1943	2043	2143	...
rdam Centraal d.	1805j	...	1958	1908	2058	2058	2005j	2108	2205j	...
echt d.	1820	...	|	1922	|	|	2020	2122	2220	...
endaal 🏛 d.	1847	...	|	1947	|	|	2047	2147	2247	...
erpen Centraal d.	1917	...	2033	2017	2133	2133	2117	2217	2317	...
elen d.	1935	...	|	2035	|	|	2135	2235	2335	...
sels Nationaal ✈ d.	1949	...	|	2049	|	|	2149	2249	2349	...
sels Midi / Zuid △ a.	2015	...	2108	2115	2208	2208	2215	2315	0015	...
sels Midi / Zuid d.	...	2043	2113	...	...	2213	...	...	...	...
e Europe a.	...	|	|	...	...	|	...	...	...	...
Nord a.	...	2205	2235	...	...	2335	...	...	...	...

train type	*IC*	⇌	*IC*	⇌	*IC*	⇌	⇌	*IC*	⇌	
train number	**9211**	**9391**	**9215**	**9401**	**9219**	**9303**	**9305**	**9223**	**9309**	
notes		①–⑤				①–⑤	①–④		①–⑥	
		g				**p**	**N**		**g**	
Paris Nord d.	...	...	...	0601	...	0625	0655	...	0725	...
Lille Europe d.	...	...	...	|	...	|	|	...	|	...
Brussels Midi / Zuid a.	...	...	...	0723	...	0747	0817	...	0847	...
Brussels Midi / Zuid ▽ d.	0545	0652	0645	...	0745	0752	...	0845	0852	...
Brussels Nationaal ✈ d.	0611	|	0711	...	0811	|	...	0911	|	...
Mechelen d.	0625	|	0725	...	0825	|	...	0925	|	...
Antwerpen Centraal a.	0643	0727	0743	...	0843	0827	...	0943	0927	...
Roosendaal 🏛 a.	0711	|	0811	...	0911	|	...	1011	|	...
Dordrecht a.	0740	|	0840	...	0940	|	...	1040	|	...
Rotterdam Centraal a.	0756	0803	0856	...	0956	0902	...	1056	1002	...
Den Haag HS a.	0817	|	0917	...	1017	|	...	1117	|	...
Schiphol ✈ ⊗ a.	0848	0824	0948	...	1048	0924	...	1148	1024	...
Amsterdam Centraal a.	0905	0842	1005	...	1105	0942	...	1205	1042	...

train type	⇌	*IC*	⇌	⇌	*IC*	⇌	⇌	*IC*	⇌	*IC*	⇌	⇌	⇌	*IC*	⇌	⇌	⇌	*IC*	*IC*	⇌	*IC*	⇌	⇌	*IC*	
train number	**9413**	**9227**	**9315**	**9319**	**9231**	**9321**	**9325**	**9235**	**9327**	**9239**	**9993**	**9333**	**9437**	**9243**	**9339**	**9341**	**9397**	**9247**	**9251**	**9351**	**9255**	**9357**	**9461**	**9259**	
notes							①–⑤										①–④					Ⓑ			
				R		**H**	**T**					**J**				**C**	**g**					**w**			
Nord d.	0755	...	0825	0901	...	0925	1001	...	1025	...	...	1125	1155	...	1225	1246	...	...	...	1425	...	1525	1555	...	...
le Europe d.	|	...	|	|	...	|	|	...	|	...	1159	|	|	...	|	|	...	...	...	|	...	|	|	...	...
sels Midi / Zuid a.	0917	...	0947	1023	...	1047	1123	...	1147	...	1235	1247	1317	...	1347	1412	...	...	...	1547	...	1647	1717	...	...
sels Midi / Zuid ▽ d.	...	0945	0952	...	1045	...	...	1145	1152	1245	1252	...	...	1345	1352	...	1452	1445	1545	1552	1645	1652	...	1745	...
sels Nationaal ✈ d.	...	1011	|	...	1111	...	...	1211	|	1311	|	...	...	1411	|	...	|	1511	1611	|	1711	|	...	1811	...
elen d.	...	1025	|	...	1125	...	...	1225	|	1325	|	...	...	1425	|	...	|	1525	1625	|	1725	|	...	1825	...
erpen Centraal a.	...	1043	1027	...	1143	...	...	1243	1227	1343	1327	...	...	1443	1427	...	1527	1543	1643	1627	1743	1727	...	1843	...
endaal 🏛 a.	...	1111	|	...	1211	...	...	1311	|	1411	|	...	...	1511	|	...	|	1611	1711	|	1811	|	...	1911	...
recht a.	...	1140	|	...	1240	...	...	1340	|	1440	|	...	...	1540	|	...	|	1640	1740	|	1840	|	...	1940	...
erdam Centraal a.	...	1156	1102	...	1256	...	...	1356	1302	1456	1402	...	...	1556	1502	...	1602	1656	1756	1702	1856	1802	...	1956	...
n Haag HS a.	...	1217	|	...	1317	...	...	1417	|	1517	|	...	...	1617	|	...	|	1717	1817	|	1917	|	...	2017	...
hol ✈ ⊗ a.	...	1248	1124	...	1348	...	...	1448	1324	1548	1424	...	...	1648	1524	...	1624	1748	1848	1724	1948	1824	...	2048	...
terdam Centraal a.	...	1305	1142	...	1405	...	...	1505	1342	1605	1442	...	...	1705	1542	...	1642	1805	1905	1742	2005	1842	...	2105	...

train type	⇌	⇌	⇌	*IC*	⇌	⇌	*IC*	⇌	⇌	⇌	⇌	*IC*	⇌	⇌	⇌	⇌	⇌	⇌	⇌	⇌					
train number	**9363**	**9363**	**9365**	**9263**	**9369**	**9473**	**9267**	**9975**	**9375**	**9375**	**9377**	**9271**	**9381**	**9955/4**	**9995**	**9387**	**9389**	**9393**	**9395**	**9399**					
notes	⑤⑦	①–④						①–④	⑤⑦					⊗	⑤⑥⑦					⑦					
	kw	**g**	**L**					**g**	**kw**	**D**	**V**			**B**	**k**	**P**	**Z**	**M**	**E**	**z**					
Nord d.	1625	...	1655	...	1725	1755	...	...	1825	1825	1855	...	1925	...	...	2025	2055	2125	2155	2225	...	...	...	...	...
le Europe d.	|	...	|	...	|	|	...	1907	|	|	|	...	|	...	2104	|	|	|	|	|	...	...	...	...	...
sels Midi / Zuid a.	1747	...	1817	...	1847	1917	...	1943	1947	1947	2017	...	2047	2123	2141	2147	2217	2247	2317	2347	...	...	...	...	...
sels Midi / Zuid ▽ d.	1752	1752	...	1845	1852	...	1945	1952	1952	...	...	2045	2052	|	2152	...	...	...	...	...	...	...	...	...	...
sels Nationaal ✈ d.	|	|	...	1911	|	...	2011	|	|	...	...	2110	|	|	|	...	...	...	...	...	...	...	...	...	...
elen d.	|	|	...	1925	|	...	2025	|	|	...	...	2125	|	|	|	...	...	...	...	...	...	...	...	...	...
erpen Centraal a.	1827	1827	...	1943	1927	...	2043	2027	2027	...	...	2143	2127	2204	2227	...	...	...	...	...	...	...	...	...	...
endaal 🏛 a.	|	|	...	2011	|	...	2111	|	|	...	...	2211	|	|	|	...	...	...	...	...	...	...	...	...	...
recht a.	|	|	...	2040	|	...	2140	|	|	...	...	2240	|	|	|	...	...	...	...	...	...	...	...	...	...
erdam Centraal a.	1902	1902	...	2056	2002	...	2156	2102	2102	...	...	2256	2202	2238	2302	...	...	...	...	...	...	...	...	...	...
n Haag HS a.	|	|	...	2117	|	...	2217	|	|	...	...	2317	|	|	|	...	...	...	...	...	...	...	...	...	...
hol ✈ ⊗ a.	1924	1924	...	2148	2024	...	2248	2124	2124	...	...	2348	2224	2300	2324	...	...	...	...	...	...	...	...	...	...
terdam Centraal a.	1942	1942	...	2205	2042	...	2305	2142	2142	...	...	0005	2242	2320	2342	...	...	...	...	...	...	...	...	...	...

⑥ July 2 - Sept. 3: *THALYS* SOLEIL – (12) 🍷 Amsterdam - Brussels - Valence *TGV* - Marseille (Table **11**).
⑥ July 2 - Sept. 3: *THALYS* SOLEIL – (12) 🍷 Marseille - Valence *TGV* - Brussels - Amsterdam (Table **11**).
①–⑤ May 30 - July 9. ①–⑥ July 10 - Aug. 27 (not Aug. 15).
①⑤ Aug. 28 - Dec. 10 (not Nov. 11).
Daily May 30 - July 9. Ⓑ July 10 - Dec. 10 (not Nov. 11).
①⑤ May 30 - July 9. ⑤ July 10 - Dec. 10 (not Nov. 11).
Apr. 3 - July 9.
②③④⑤ Apr. 3 - July 9 and Aug. 28 - Dec. 10 (not Nov. 11).
②③④⑦ May 30 - July 9. ①–④ July 10 - Aug. 27 (not Aug. 15).
①⑦ (⑦ July 10 - Aug. 27) also Aug. 15.
①–⑤ (⑥ July 10 - Aug. 27). Not Oct. 31, Nov. 1, 11.
Daily May 30 - July 9. ①⑤ July 10 - Aug. 27 (not Aug. 15).
Ⓑ Aug. 28 - Dec. 10 (not Nov. 11).
②③④⑥ May 30 - July 9. ⑦ July 10 - Aug. 27 (also Aug. 15).
①–④ Aug. 28 - Dec. 10.
Not July 10 - Aug. 27, Oct. 31, Nov. 1.

P – Ⓑ (⑤⑦ July 10 - Aug. 27) also Aug. 15; not Nov. 11.
Q – Ⓑ May 30 - July 9. ②③④⑤⑦ Aug. 28 - Dec. 10 (not Nov. 11).
R – ①⑤⑥ May 30 - July 9. ⑤ July 10 - Aug. 27. ①–⑥ Aug. 28 - Dec. 10.
S – Not July 10 - Aug. 27, Nov. 1.
T – ①–⑥ (not July 10 - Aug. 27, Oct. 31).
V – Ⓑ (⑤ July 10 - Aug. 27) not Nov. 11.
Y – ⑦ (not July 10 - Aug. 27).
Z – ⑦ May 30 - July 9. ①②③④⑥ July 10 - Aug. 27 (not Aug. 15). ⑥⑦ Aug. 28 - Dec. 10 (also Nov. 11).

f – Not July 14, 21, Aug. 15.
g – Not Aug. 15.
h – Not Aug. 15, Oct. 31, Nov. 1.
j – 3 minutes later on ⑥⑦.
k – Also Aug. 15.

m – Also Nov. 11.
p – Not Aug. 15, Nov. 11.
q – Also Aug. 15, Nov. 11.
w – Not Nov. 11.
z – Also Aug. 15; not Aug. 14.

⊗ – Calls to set down only.
⊕ – Calls to pick up only.
⇌ – *Thalys* high-speed train. Ⓡ 🍷. Special fares payable. Valid May 30 - Dec. 10.
▽ – All services, except *Thalys*, call at Brussels Central 4 minutes, and Brussels Noord 10 minutes, after Brussels Midi / Zuid.
△ – All services, except *Thalys*, call at Brussels Noord 10 minutes, and Brussels Central 5 minutes, before Brussels Midi / Zuid.

20 LONDON, PARIS and BRUSSELS - KÖLN, HAMBURG and BERLIN

For the full service London - Brussels and v.v. see Table **12**. For Paris - Brussels and v.v. see Table **18**. Connections at Brussels are not guaranteed.

train type	ICE	ICE	IC	RE	IC	⇌	ICE	EC	IC	IC	ICE	ICE	⇌	IC	ICE	EC	IC	⇌	☆	☆	☆	ICE	RE	ICE	IC
train number	11	545	2037	10508	2310	9401	847	177	2441	2204	1028	37	9413	2202	859	179	2049	9315	9108	9110	9110	15	10516	559	2431
notes								✗				↗				✗			①		⑥				
												D	S						K	L					
London St Pancras d.	...	...	...	...	...	...	...	...	...	...	...	...	...	...	...	...	...	...	0613	0650	0657	...	...	...	...
Ebbsfleet International d.	...	...	...	...	...	...	...	...	...	...	...	...	...	...	...	...	...	...	0630	0707	|	...	...	...	...
Ashford International d.	...	...	...	...	...	...	...	...	...	...	...	...	...	...	...	...	...	...	0652	0728	0728	...	...	...	...
Lille Europe d.	...	...	...	...	...	...	...	...	...	...	...	...	...	...	...	...	...	...	|	0933	0930	...	...	...	...
Paris Nord d.	...	...	...	...	...	0601	...	...	...	...	...	...	0755	...	...	...	...	0825	|	|	|	...	...	...	...
Brussels Midi/Zuid a.	...	...	...	...	...	0723	...	...	...	...	...	...	0917	...	...	...	...	0947	0958	1007	1005	...	...	...	...
Brussels Midi/Zuid d.	0625	...	...	...	...	0728	...	...	...	...	...	...	0928	...	...	...	...	▬	▬	▬	...	1025	...	...	...
Brussels Nord d.	0633	...	...	...	...	|	...	...	...	...	...	...	|	...	...	...	...	*RE*	...	...	...	1034	...	...	...
Liège Guillemins a.	0710	...	...	...	...	0811	...	...	...	...	...	...	1011	...	...	...	...	**10121**	...	...	...	1112	...	...	...
Liège Guillemins d.	0712	...	...	...	...	0814	...	...	...	...	...	...	1014	...	...	...	...		*IC*	...	...	1114	...	...	...
Aachen 🏛 a.	0737	...	...	...	...	0836	...	...	...	...	...	...	1036	...	...	...	...	1051	**2226**	...	...	1136	...	...	...
Köln Hbf a.	0815	...	...	...	...	0915	...	...	...	...	...	...	1115	...	...	...	...	1144	...	...	...	1215	...	...	...
Köln Hbf d.	...	0828	...	0831	0910	0918	0928	...	...	0946	1010	...	1119	1146	1148	...	...	1149	1210	...	...	...	1231	1248	...
Wuppertal Hbf a.	...	|	...	|	|	|	|	...	...	|	1041	...	|	|	1214	...	...	|	1241	...	...	...	|	1314	...
Hagen Hbf a.	...	|	...	|	|	|	|	...	...	|	1100	...	|	|	1233	...	...	|	1259	...	...	...	|	1333	...
Düsseldorf Hbf a.	...	0850	...	0901	0931	0940	0950	...	...	1009	|	...	1140	1209	|	...	...	1219	|	...	...	...	1301	|	...
Duisburg Hbf a.	...	0908	...	0918	0944	0954	1008	...	...	1024	|	...	1200	1224	|	...	...	1236	|	...	...	...	1318	|	...
Oberhausen a.	...	|	...	0926	|	|	|	...	...	1031	|	...	|	1231	|	...	...	|	|	...	...	...	1326	|	...
Essen Hbf a.	...	0921	...	...	0957	1007	1021	...	...	|	|	...	1214	|	|	...	...	1250	|	...	...	...	...	|	...
Bochum Hbf a.	...	0933	...	...	1008	▬	1033	...	...	|	|	...	|	|	|	...	...	1303	|	...	...	...	...	|	...
Dortmund Hbf a.	...	0946	...	...	1021	...	1046	...	...	|	1123	...	1241	|	|	...	...	1315	1321	...	...	...	...	|	...
Hamm (Westf) a.	...	1006	...	...	|	...	1106	...	...	|	|	...	...	|	1302	...	...	1336	|	...	...	...	...	1402	...
Bielefeld Hbf a.	...	1036	...	...	|	...	1136	...	...	|	|	...	...	|	1336	...	...	...	|	...	...	...	...	1436	...
Münster a.	...	|	...	...	1054	*ICE*	|	...	...	1128	1155	...	...	1328	|	...	...	...	1354	*ICE*	...	...	...	|	...
Osnabrück Hbf a.	...	|	...	...	1121	**35**	|	...	...	...	1222	...	...	...	|	...	...	...	1421	**39**	...	...	...	|	...
Bremen Hbf a.	...	|	...	...	1215	↗	|	...	...	...	1315	...	...	...	|	...	...	...	1515	↗	...	...	...	|	...
Hannover Hbf a.	...	1128	1135	...	|	**D**	1228	...	1236	...	|	...	...	...	1428	...	1436	...	|	**D**	...	...	...	1528	1535
Hamburg Hbf a.	...	|	|	...	1313	1328	|	...	|	...	1413	1528	...	...	|	...	|	...	1613	1728	...	...	...	|	|
København H ⊙ a.	...	|	|	...	...	1822	|	...	|	...	...	2022	...	...	|	...	|	...	...	2222	...	...	...	|	|
Wolfsburg a.	...	|	|	...	...	...	1303	...	|	...	...	...	...	...	1503	...	|	...	...	...	...	...	...	|	|
Braunschweig Hbf a.	...	|	1208	...	...	...	|	...	1309	...	...	...	...	...	|	...	1509	...	...	...	...	...	...	|	1608
Magdeburg Hbf a.	...	|	1257	...	...	...	|	...	1356	...	...	...	...	...	|	...	1556	...	...	...	...	...	...	|	1657
Halle Hbf a.	...	|	1350	...	...	...	|	...	1452	...	...	...	...	...	|	...	1652	...	...	...	...	...	...	|	...
Leipzig Hbf a.	...	|	1419	...	...	...	|	...	1517	...	...	...	...	...	|	...	1717	...	...	...	...	...	...	|	...
Berlin Hbf a.	...	1306	...	...	...	...	1409	1448	|	...	...	...	...	...	1609	1648	|	...	...	...	...	...	...	1706	...
Dresden Hbf a.	...	...	...	...	...	...	...	1653	1637	...	...	...	...	...	...	1853	1837	...	...	...	...	...	...	...	...
Bad Schandau 🏛 a.	...	...	...	...	...	...	...	1736	...	...	...	...	...	...	...	1936	...	...	...	...	...	...	...	...	...
Děčín a.	...	...	...	...	...	...	...	1753	...	...	...	...	...	...	...	1953	...	...	...	...	...	...	...	...	...
Praha Holešovice a.	...	...	...	...	...	...	...	1918	...	...	...	...	...	...	...	2118	...	...	...	...	...	...	...	...	...
Praha hlavní a.	...	...	...	...	...	...	...	1928	...	...	...	...	...	...	...	2128	...	...	...	...	...	...	...	...	...

train type	☆	☆	⇌	IC	ICE	IC	RE	ICE	⇌	☆	☆	⇌	ICE	RE	ICE		RE	EC	☆	☆	⇌	RE	ICE	EC	ICE
train number	9116	9116	9437	2004	953	2045	10129	1026	9339	9126	9126	9341	17	10524	653		10131	8	9132	9136	9461	10530	947	114	957
notes	①–⑤	⑥⑦		2014	Ⓑ	Ⓑ					⑦												⚒		⑦
	p	y		Ⓑ						Y	Z	A								F					
London St Pancras d.	0855	0858	...	...	...	...	...	...	...	1058	1104	...	...	...	...	...	...	...	1258	1404	...	...	...	...	...
Ebbsfleet International d.	0914	0915	...	...	...	...	...	...	...	1115	|	...	...	...	...	...	...	...	1315	|	...	...	...	...	...
Ashford International d.	|	|	...	...	...	...	...	...	...	|	|	...	...	...	...	...	...	...	|	|	...	...	...	...	...
Lille Europe d.	1130	1133	...	...	...	...	...	...	...	1330	1330	...	...	...	...	...	...	...	1533	1630	...	...	...	...	...
Paris Nord d.	|	|	1155	...	...	...	...	...	1225	|	|	1246	...	...	...	...	...	...	|	|	1555	...	...	...	...
Brussels Midi/Zuid a.	1205	1208	1317	...	...	...	...	...	1347	1405	1405	1412	...	...	...	...	...	...	1608	1705	1717	...	...	...	...
Brussels Midi/Zuid d.	...	...	1328	...	...	...	...	...	...	...	...	...	1425	...	...	...	...	...	...	...	1728	...	...	...	...
Brussels Nord d.	...	...	|	...	...	...	...	...	...	...	...	...	1434	...	...	...	...	...	...	...	|	...	...	...	...
Liège Guillemins a.	...	...	1411	...	...	...	...	...	...	...	...	...	1512	...	...	...	...	...	...	...	1811	...	...	...	...
Liège Guillemins d.	...	...	1414	...	...	...	...	...	...	...	...	...	1514	...	...	...	...	...	...	...	1814	...	...	...	...
Aachen 🏛 a.	...	...	1436	...	...	...	...	...	...	...	...	...	1536	...	...	...	...	...	...	...	1836	...	...	...	...
Köln Hbf a.	...	...	1515	...	...	...	...	...	...	...	...	...	1615	...	...	...	...	...	...	...	1915	...	...	...	...
Köln Hbf d.	...	...	...	1546	1548	...	1549	1610	...	...	...	...	...	1631	1648	...	1649	1710	...	...	1918	1931	1927	1946	1948
Wuppertal Hbf a.	...	...	...	|	1614	...	|	1641	...	...	...	...	...	|	1714	...	|	|	...	...	|	|	|	|	2014
Hagen a.	...	...	...	|	1633	...	|	1700	...	...	...	...	...	|	1733	...	|	|	...	...	|	|	|	|	2033
Düsseldorf Hbf a.	...	...	...	1609	|	...	1619	|	...	...	...	...	...	1701	|	...	1719	1731	...	...	1940	2001	1950	2008	|
Duisburg Hbf a.	...	...	...	1624	|	...	1636	|	...	...	...	...	...	1718	|	...	1736	1744	...	...	1953	2018	2008	2022	|
Oberhausen a.	...	...	...	1631	|	...	|	|	...	...	...	...	...	1726	|	...	|	|	...	...	|	2026	|	|	|
Essen Hbf a.	...	...	...	|	|	...	1650	|	...	...	...	...	...	...	|	...	1750	1757	...	...	2006	...	2021	2037	|
Bochum Hbf a.	...	...	...	|	|	...	1703	|	...	...	...	...	...	...	|	...	1803	1809	...	...	|	...	2033	2047	|
Dortmund Hbf a.	...	...	...	|	|	...	1715	1721	...	...	...	...	...	...	|	...	1815	1821	...	...	2036	...	2046	2100	|
Hamm (Westf) a.	...	...	...	|	1702	...	1736	|	...	...	...	...	...	...	1802	...	1836	|	...	...	...	...	2106	...	2102
Bielefeld a.	...	...	...	|	1736	...	...	|	...	...	...	...	...	...	1836	...	...	|	...	...	...	...	2136	...	2136
Münster a.	...	...	...	1728	|	...	...	1755	...	...	...	...	...	...	|	*IC*	...	1854	...	...	...	...	|	...	|
Osnabrück a.	...	...	...	...	|	...	...	1821	...	...	...	...	...	...	|	**2435**	...	1921	...	...	...	...	|	...	|
Bremen Hbf a.	...	...	...	...	|	...	...	1914	...	...	...	...	...	...	|	...	...	2015	...	...	...	...	|	...	|
Hannover Hbf a.	...	...	...	...	1828	1836	...	|	...	...	...	...	...	...	1928	1935	...	|	...	...	...	...	2228	...	2228
Hamburg Hbf a.	...	...	...	...	|	|	...	2013	...	...	...	...	...	...	|	|	...	2113	...	...	...	...	|	...	|
København H ⊙ a.	...	...	...	...	|	|	...	...	...	...	...	...	...	...	|	|	...	...	...	...	...	...	|	...	|
Wolfsburg a.	...	...	...	...	1903	|	...	...	...	...	...	...	...	...	|	|	...	...	...	...	...	...	2303	...	2303
Braunschweig Hbf a.	...	...	...	...	|	1909	...	...	...	...	...	...	...	...	|	2008	...	...	...	...	...	...	|	...	|
Magdeburg Hbf a.	...	...	...	...	|	1956	...	...	...	...	...	...	...	...	|	2057	...	...	...	...	...	...	|	...	|
Halle a.	...	...	...	...	|	2052	...	...	...	...	...	...	...	...	|	2150	...	...	...	...	...	...	|	...	|
Leipzig Hbf a.	...	...	...	...	|	2117	...	...	...	...	...	...	...	...	|	2219	...	...	...	...	...	...	|	...	|
Berlin Hbf a.	...	...	...	...	2009	|	...	...	...	...	...	...	...	...	2106	|	...	...	...	...	...	...	0009	...	0009
Dresden Hbf a.	...	...	...	...	...	2237	...	...	...	...	...	...	...	...	...	2339x	...	...	...	...	...	...	...	...	...
Bad Schandau 🏛 a.	...	...	...	...	...	...	...	...	...	...	...	...	...	...	...	...	...	...	...	...	...	...	...	...	...
Děčín a.	...	...	...	...	...	...	...	...	...	...	...	...	...	...	...	...	...	...	...	...	...	...	...	...	...
Praha Holešovice a.	...	...	...	...	...	...	...	...	...	...	...	...	...	...	...	...	...	...	...	...	...	...	...	...	...
Praha hlavní a.	...	...	...	...	...	...	...	...	...	...	...	...	...	...	...	...	...	...	...	...	...	...	...	...	...

A – ①–⑤ May 30 - July 9. ①–⑥ July 10 - Aug. 27 (not Aug. 15). ①⑤ Aug. 28 - Dec. 10 (not Nov. 11).

D – [12] 🍷 ↗ Hamburg - København (Table **50**).

F – Ⓑ May 29 - Sept. 3. ⑤⑦ Sept. 4 - Dec. 10 (also Oct. 24–27).

K – ① July 24 - Dec. 10 (not Aug. 15).

L – ①–⑤ May 29 - July 23 (not May 30). ②–⑤ July 24 - Dec. 10 (not Aug. 29, Nov. 1, 11).

S – Calls at Düsseldorf Flughafen ✈, arrives 1149.

Y – ①–⑥ May 31 - Nov. 4 (not Aug. 29). Daily Nov. 5 - Dec. 10.

Z – ⑦ May 29 - Nov. 4 (also May 30, Aug. 29).

p – Not May 30, Aug. 29, Nov. 11.

x – ⑥ (also Oct. 2).

y – Also May 30, Aug. 29, Nov. 11.

↗ – Supplement payable.

⇌ – *Thalys* high-speed train. Ⓡ 🍷. Special fares payable. Valid May 30 - Dec. 10.

⊙ – 🏛 between Hamburg and København is Rødby, see Table **720**.

☆ – Eurostar train. Ⓡ, ✗ in Business Premier and Standard Premier, 🍷 in Standard. Special fares payable. Minimum check-in time 30 minutes. Not available for London - Ebbsfleet - Ashford or v.v. journeys. Valid May 29 - Dec. 10.

LONDON, PARIS and BRUSSELS - KÖLN, HAMBURG and BERLIN 20

For the full service London - Brussels and v.v. see Table **12**. For Paris - Brussels and v.v. see Table **18**. Connections at Brussels are not guaranteed.

train type		⇌	☆	⇌	*ICE*	*RE*	*ICE*	*IC*	*ICE*	*ICE*		☆	⇌	*RE*	*RE*	*ICE*	*ICE*	*CNL*	*EN*	*IC*	*ICE*	*IC*
train number		**9461**	**9140**	**9365**	**19**	**10542**	**657**	**2318**	**1102**	**102**		**9144**	**9473**	**10534**	**10141**	**1522**	**512**	**457**	**447**	**2020**	**31**	**2241**
notes			Ⓑ			**10532**	⑦	Ⓑ	⑥	Ⓑ		⑥							🅁			⚒
				L									**G**					**B**	**A**		**D K**	
on St Pancras d.	...	...	1504	...	...	...	...	...	...	...	...	1604	...	...	...	...	...	...	...	...	...	...
fleet International d.	...	...	|	...	...	...	...	...	...	...	...	|	...	...	...	...	...	...	...	...	...	...
ord International d.	...	...	|	...	...	...	...	...	...	...	...	|	...	...	...	...	...	...	...	...	...	...
Europe d.	...	...	1730	...	...	...	...	...	...	...	...	1830	...	...	...	...	...	...	...	...	...	...
ris Nord d.	...	1555	|	1655	...	...	...	...	...	...	...	|	1755	...	...	...	...	...	...	...	...	...
sels Midi/Zuid a.	...	1717	1805	1817	...	...	...	...	...	...	...	1905	1917	...	...	...	...	...	...	...	...	...
sels Midi/Zuid d.	...	...	...	...	1825	...	...	...	...	...	...	...	1928	...	...	...	...	...	...	...	...	...
sels Nord d.	...	...	...	...	1834	...	...	...	...	...	...	...	|	...	...	...	...	...	...	...	...	...
Guillemins a.	...	...	...	...	1912	...	...	...	...	...	...	...	2011	...	...	...	...	...	...	...	...	...
Guillemins d.	...	...	...	...	1914	...	...	...	...	...	...	...	2014	...	...	...	...	...	...	...	...	...
en a.	...	...	...	...	1936	...	...	...	...	...	...	...	2036	...	...	...	...	...	...	...	...	...
Hbf a.	...	...	...	...	2015	...	...	...	...	...	...	...	2115	...	...	...	...	...	...	...	...	...
Hbf d.	...	...	...	...	...	2031	2048	2110	2110	2110	...	...	2118	2131	2149	2210	2210	2313	2313	0210	...	...
uppertal Hbf a.	...	...	...	...	...	|	2114	|	|	2141	...	...	|	|	|	2241	|	|	|	|	...	...
gen Hbf a.	...	...	...	...	...	|	2133	|	|	2159	...	...	|	|	|	2300	|	|	|	|	...	...
eldorf Hbf a.	...	...	...	...	...	2101	|	2131	2131	|	...	...	2140	2201	2219	|	2231	2335	2335	0232	...	...
burg Hbf a.	...	...	...	...	...	2118	|	2144	2144	|	...	...	2159	2218	2236	|	2244	2349	2349	0250	...	...
hausen a.	...	...	...	...	...	2126	|	|	|	|	...	...	|	2226	|	|	|	|	|	|	...	...
n Hbf a.	...	...	...	...	...	...	|	2157	2157	|	...	...	2215	...	2250	|	2257	0004	0004	0305	...	...
um Hbf a.	...	...	...	...	...	...	|	2208	2208	|	...	...	|	...	2303	|	|	0015	0015	0315	...	...
mund Hbf a.	...	...	...	...	...	...	|	2221	2221	2221	...	...	2241	...	2315	2322	|	0029	0029	0328	...	...
m (Westf) a.	...	...	...	...	...	...	2202	|	2248	2248	...	...	...	...	2345	...	|	0047	0047	|	...	...
feld Hbf a.	...	...	...	...	...	...	2236	|	2318	2318	...	...	...	...	...	...	|	0122	0122	|	...	...
inster a.	...	...	...	...	...	...	|	2254**j**	|	|	...	...	...	...	...	...	2356	|	|	0414	...	0538
snabrück Hbf a.	...	...	...	...	...	...	|	...	|	|	...	...	...	...	...	...	...	|	|	0446	...	0602
emen Hbf a.	...	...	...	...	...	...	|	...	|	|	...	...	...	...	...	...	...	|	|	0552	...	|
nover Hbf a.	...	...	...	...	...	...	2328	...	0018	0018	...	...	...	...	...	...	...	0223	0223	|	...	0718
amburg Hbf a.	...	...	...	...	...	...	|	...	...	...	...	...	...	...	...	...	...	|	|	0651	0724	|
København H ⊙ a.	...	...	...	...	...	...	|	...	...	...	...	...	...	...	...	...	...	|	|	...	1222	|
olfsburg a.	...	...	...	...	...	...	0002	...	...	...	...	...	...	...	...	...	...	|	|	...	...	0753
nschweig Hbf a.	...	...	...	...	...	...	|	...	...	...	...	...	...	...	...	...	...	0314	0314	...	...	|
deburg Hbf a.	...	...	...	...	...	...	|	...	...	...	...	...	...	...	...	...	...	0402	0402	...	...	|
lle Hbf a.	...	...	...	...	...	...	|	...	...	...	...	...	...	...	...	...	...	|	|	...	...	|
ipzig Hbf a.	...	...	...	...	...	...	|	...	...	...	...	...	...	...	...	...	...	|	|	...	...	|
n Hbf a.	...	...	...	...	...	...	0110	...	...	...	...	...	...	...	...	...	...	0515**w**	0625	...	...	0922
esden Hbf a.	...	...	...	...	...	...	...	...	...	...	...	...	...	...	...	...	...	0858	...	...	...	...
d Schandau a.	...	...	...	...	...	...	...	...	...	...	...	...	...	...	...	...	...	0936	...	...	...	...
čin a.	...	...	...	...	...	...	...	...	...	...	...	...	...	...	...	...	...	0953	...	...	...	...
aha Holešovice a.	...	...	...	...	...	...	...	...	...	...	...	...	...	...	...	...	...	1118	...	...	...	...
aha hlavní a.	...	...	...	...	...	...	...	...	...	...	...	...	...	...	...	...	...	1128	...	...	...	...

train type			*ICE*	*ICE*	*IC*	*RE*	⇌		*ICE*	*IC*	*EN*	*CNL*	*RE*	*RE*	*ICE*	⇌	☆	☆				
train number			**32**	**30**	**2021**	**10503**	**9412**		**101**	**2319**	**446**	**40458**	**10106**	**10505**	**18**	**9322**	**9125**	**9129**				
notes						Ⓐ				⚒	🅁	**61458**	**10104**			**9422**		⑦				
			K	**C K**			**H**				**A**	**F**					**X**	**y**				
aha hlavní d.	...	...	...	...	...	...	...	...	...	...	...	1827	...	...	...	...	...	...	...	...	...	...
aha Holešovice d.	...	...	...	...	...	...	...	...	...	...	...	1836	...	...	...	...	...	...	...	...	...	...
čin d.	...	...	...	...	...	...	...	...	...	...	...	2000	...	...	...	...	...	...	...	...	...	...
d Schandau d.	...	...	...	...	...	...	...	...	...	...	...	2017	...	...	...	...	...	...	...	...	...	...
esden Hbf d.	...	...	...	...	...	...	...	...	...	...	...	2054	...	...	...	...	...	...	...	...	...	...
in Hbf d.	...	...	...	...	...	...	...	...	...	...	2344	2344	...	...	...	...	...	...	...	...	...	...
eipzig Hbf d.	...	...	...	...	...	...	...	...	...	...	|	|	...	...	...	...	...	...	...	...	...	...
alle Hbf d.	...	...	...	...	...	...	...	...	...	...	|	|	...	...	...	...	...	...	...	...	...	...
deburg Hbf d.	...	...	...	...	...	...	...	...	...	...	0109	0109	...	...	...	...	...	...	...	...	...	...
nschweig Hbf d.	...	...	...	...	...	...	...	...	...	...	0209	0209	...	...	...	...	...	...	...	...	...	...
olfsburg d.	...	...	...	...	...	...	...	...	...	...	|	|	...	...	...	...	...	...	...	...	...	...
København H ⊙ d.	...	...	1537	1737	...	...	...	...	...	...	|	|	...	...	...	...	...	...	...	...	...	...
amburg Hbf d.	...	...	2021	2223	2246	...	...	...	...	...	|	|	...	...	...	...	...	...	...	...	...	...
nover Hbf d.	...	...	...	...	|	...	...	...	...	...	0340	0340	...	...	...	...	...	...	...	...	...	...
emen Hbf d.	...	...	...	...	2344	...	...	...	...	...	|	|	...	...	...	...	...	...	...	...	...	...
snabrück Hbf d.	...	...	...	...	0037	...	...	...	...	...	|	|	...	...	...	...	...	...	...	...	...	...
ünster d.	...	...	...	...	0105	...	...	...	...	0503**c**	|	|	...	...	...	...	...	...	...	...	...	...
efeld Hbf d.	...	...	...	...	|	...	...	...	...	|	0439	0439	...	...	...	...	...	...	...	...	...	...
m (Westf) d.	...	...	...	...	0125	...	...	...	...	|	0512	0512	0515	...	...	...	...	...	...	...	...	...
tmund Hbf d.	...	...	...	...	0144	...	0520	...	0537	0537	0535	0535	0545	...	...	...	...	...	...	...	...	...
hum Hbf d.	...	...	...	...	0155	...	|	...	|	0549	|	|	0556	...	...	...	...	...	...	...	...	...
en Hbf d.	...	...	...	...	0206	...	0542	...	|	0600	0604	0604	0609	...	...	...	...	...	...	...	...	...
rhausen d.	...	...	...	...	|	0534	|	...	|	|	|	|	|	0634	...	...	...	...	...	...	...	...
sburg Hbf d.	...	...	...	...	0219	0542	0556	...	|	0612	0618	0618	0623	0642	...	...	...	...	...	...	...	...
seldorf Hbf d.	...	...	...	...	0239	0558	0617	...	|	0627	0633	0633	0640	0658	...	...	...	...	...	...	...	...
agen Hbf d.	...	...	...	...	|	|	|	...	0557	|	|	|	|	|	...	...	...	...	...	...	...	...
uppertal Hbf d.	...	...	...	...	|	|	|	...	0614	|	|	|	|	|	...	...	...	...	...	...	...	...
Hbf a.	...	...	...	...	0301	0629	0642	...	0646	0649	0656	0656	0712	0729	...	...	...	...	...	...	...	...
Hbf d.	...	...	...	...	...	...	0645	...	...	...	...	...	...	...	0743	...	...	...	...	...	...	...
hen d.	...	...	...	...	...	...	0724	...	...	...	...	...	...	...	0821	...	...	...	...	...	...	...
e Guillemins a.	...	...	...	...	...	...	0749	...	...	...	...	...	...	...	0844	...	...	...	...	...	...	...
e Guillemins d.	...	...	...	...	...	...	0752	...	...	...	...	...	...	...	0846	...	...	...	...	...	...	...
ssels Nord a.	...	...	...	...	...	...	|	...	...	...	...	...	...	...	0926	...	...	...	...	...	...	...
ssels Midi/Zuid a.	...	...	...	...	...	...	0832	...	...	...	...	...	...	...	0935	...	...	...	...	...	...	...
ssels Midi/Zuid d.	...	...	...	...	...	...	0843	...	...	...	...	...	...	...	...	1013	1056	1156	...	...	...	...
aris Nord a.	...	...	...	...	...	...	1005	...	...	...	...	...	...	...	...	1135	|	|	...	...	...	...
Europe a.	...	...	...	...	...	...	...	...	...	...	...	...	...	...	...	...	1130	1230	...	...	...	...
ford International a.	...	...	...	...	...	...	...	...	...	...	...	...	...	...	...	...	|	|	...	...	...	...
sfleet International. a.	...	...	...	...	...	...	...	...	...	...	...	...	...	...	...	...	|	|	...	...	...	...
don St Pancras a.	...	...	...	...	...	...	...	...	...	...	...	...	...	...	...	...	1157	1257	...	...	...	...

JAN KIEPURA – 🛏 1, 2 cl., 🛌 2 cl., (2) (reclining) 🍷 Köln - Berlin - Warszawa and v.v.

City Night Line KOPERNIKUS – 🛏 1, 2 cl., 🛌 2 cl., 🍷 (*CNL* **40458** 🅁) Praha - Köln; (2) (*IC* **61458**) Praha - Köln. Special fares apply.

Mar. 18 - June 17.

Mar. 18 - June 17.

City Night Line KOPERNIKUS – 🛏 1, 2 cl., 🛌 2 cl., 🍷 (*CNL* **40447** 🅁) Köln - Praha; (2) (*IC* **61447**) Köln - Praha. Special fares apply.

Calls at Düsseldorf Flughafen ✈ arrives 2148.

Calls at Düsseldorf Flughafen ✈ departs 0607.

(12) 🍷 ✓ Hamburg - København and v.v.

Daily May 30 - July 9. ①⑤ July 10 - Aug. 27 (not Aug. 15). Ⓑ Aug. 28 - Dec. 10 (not Nov. 11).

①–⑥ May 29 - Sept. 3. ①–⑤ Sept. 4 - Dec. 10 (not Nov. 11).

c – ① (also May 17; not May 16).

j – ⑦ (also May 16; not May 15).

s – Calls to set down only.

u – Calls to pick up only.

w – Berlin **Wannsee**.

y – Also May 30, Aug. 29, Nov. 11.

☆ – Eurostar train. 🅁, ✕ in Business Premier and Standard Premier, 🍷 in Standard. Special fares payable. Minimum check-in time 30 minutes. Not available for London - Ebbsfleet - Ashford or v.v. journeys. Valid May 29 - Dec. 10.

⇌ – *Thalys* high-speed train. 🅁 🍷. Special fares payable. Valid May 30 - Dec. 10.

⊙ – between Hamburg and København is Rødby (Table **720**).

20 BERLIN, HAMBURG and KÖLN - BRUSSELS, PARIS and LONDON

For the full service Brussels - London and v.v. see Table **12**. For Brussels - Paris and v.v. see Table **18**. Connections at Brussels are not guaranteed.

train type	*ICE*	*RE*	*EC*	⇌	☆	*EC*	*IC*	*IC*	*ICE*	*ICE*	⇌	☆	☆	*IC*	*IC*	*ICE*	*IC*	⇌	*IC*	*IC*	*ICE*	*RE*	*RE*	*ICE*	⇌
train number	**1521**	**10110**	**115**	**9424**	**9129**	**9**	**2013**	**2434**	**654**	**16**	**9448**	**9141**	**9141**	**2023**	**2044**	**954**	**2009**	**9448**	**2217**	**2430**	**650**	**10126**	**10521**	**14**	**9370**
notes		**10108**	🍷		⑦ **p**			①–⑥		🍷		⑦ **y**	①–⑤ **q**		①–⑥	①–⑥									Ⓑ **w**
Praha hlavní ... d.	...	...	...	...	...	...	...	...	...	...	...	...	...	...	...	...	...	...	...	...	...	...	...	...	...
Praha Holešovice ... d.	...	...	...	...	...	...	...	...	...	...	...	...	...	...	...	...	...	...	...	...	...	...	...	...	...
Děčín ... d.	...	...	...	...	...	...	...	...	...	...	...	...	...	...	...	...	...	...	...	...	...	...	...	...	...
Bad Schandau 🏛 ... d.	...	...	...	...	...	...	...	...	...	...	...	...	...	...	...	...	...	...	...	...	...	...	...	...	...
Dresden Hbf ... d.	...	...	...	...	...	...	...	...	...	...	...	...	...	...	0520r	...	...	...	...	...	...	...	...	...	...
Berlin Hauptbahnhof . d.	...	...	...	...	...	...	...	...	0652	...	...	...	...	...	|	0749	...	...	...	...	1052	...	...	...	...
Leipzig Hbf ... d.	...	...	...	...	...	...	0430j	0539	|	...	...	...	...	...	0643	|	...	...	...	0939	|	...	...	...	...
Halle Hbf ... d.	...	...	...	...	...	...	|	0607	|	...	...	...	...	...	0707	|	...	...	...	1007	|	...	...	...	...
Magdeburg Hbf ... d.	...	...	...	...	...	...	0601f	0700	|	...	...	...	...	...	0804	|	...	...	...	1059	|	...	...	...	...
Braunschweig Hbf ... d.	...	...	...	...	...	...	0651	0751	|	...	...	...	...	...	0851	|	...	...	...	1151	|	...	...	...	...
Wolfsburg ... d.	...	...	...	...	...	...	|	|	0757	...	...	...	...	...	|	0856	...	...	...	|	|	...	...	...	...
København H ⊙ d.	...	...	...	...	...	...	|	|	|	...	...	...	...	...	|	|	...	...	...	|	|	...	...	...	...
Hamburg Hbf ... d.	...	...	...	...	...	0646	|	|	|	...	...	...	...	0746	|	|	...	...	1046	|	|	...	...	...	...
Hannover Hbf ... d.	...	...	...	...	...	|	0740	0823	0831	...	...	...	...	|	0923	0931	...	...	|	1223	1231	...	...	...	...
Bremen Hbf ... d.	...	...	...	...	...	0744	|	▬	|	...	...	...	...	0844	▬	|	...	...	1144	▬	|	...	...	...	...
Osnabrück Hbf ... d.	...	...	...	...	...	0837	|	...	|	...	...	...	...	0937	...	|	...	...	1237	...	|	...	...	...	...
Münster ... d.	...	...	0631	...	...	0903	|	...	|	...	...	...	...	1003	*ICE*	|	1032	...	1303	...	|	...	...	...	...
Bielefeld Hbf ... d.	...	...	|	...	...	|	0842	...	0922	...	...	...	...	|	**517**	1022	|	...	|	...	1322	...	...	...	...
Hamm (Westf) ... d.	...	0615	|	...	...	|	0914	...	0954	...	...	...	...	|		1054	|	...	|	...	1354	1322	...	...	...
Dortmund Hbf ... d.	0636	0645	|	0714	...	0937	0952	...	|	...	...	...	...	1036	1037	|	|	...	1337	...	|	1345	...	...	...
Bochum Hbf ... d.	|	0656	|	|	...	0949	1003	*RE*	|	...	...	...	...	|	1049	|	|	...	1349	...	|	1356	...	...	...
Essen Hbf ... d.	|	0709	|	0750	...	1000	1014	**10513**	|	...	...	...	...	|	1100	|	|	...	1400	...	|	1409	...	...	...
Oberhausen ... d.	|	|	0727	|	...	|	|	1034	|	...	...	...	...	|	|	|	1127	...	|	...	|	|	1434	...	...
Duisburg Hbf ... d.	|	0723	0734	0803	...	1012	1030	1042	|	...	...	...	...	|	1112	|	1134	...	1412	...	|	1423	1442	...	...
Düsseldorf Hbf ... d.	|	0740	0751	0818	...	1027	1051	1058	|	...	...	...	...	|	1127	|	1149	...	1427	...	|	1440	1458	...	...
Hagen Hbf ... d.	0657	|	|	|	...	|	|	|	1024	...	...	...	...	1057	|	1124	|	...	|	...	1424	|	|	...	...
Wuppertal Hbf ... d.	0714	|	|	|	...	|	|	|	1041	...	...	...	...	1114	|	1141	|	...	|	...	1441	|	|	...	...
Köln Hbf ... a.	0746	0812	0815	0842	...	1050	1115	1129	1109	...	...	...	...	1146	1149	1209	1215	...	1450	...	1509	1512	1529	...	...
Köln Hbf ... d.	...	...	...	0845	...	▬	...	...	...	1143	...	...	...	...	...	...	...	1245	▬	...	▬	...	...	1542	...
Aachen 🏛 ... d.	...	...	...	0924	...	...	...	...	...	1221	...	...	...	...	...	...	...	1324	...	...	...	...	...	1621	...
Liège Guillemins ... a.	...	...	...	0946	...	☆	...	...	...	1244	...	...	...	...	...	...	...	1346	...	☆	...	...	...	1644	...
Liège Guillemins ... d.	...	...	...	0949	...	**9133**	...	...	...	1246	...	...	...	...	...	...	...	1349	☆	**9149**	☆	...	...	1646	...
Brussels Nord ... a.	...	...	...	|	...	①–⑥	...	...	...	1326	...	...	...	...	...	...	...	|	**9145**	①–⑥	**9149**	...	...	1726	...
Brussels Midi/Zuid ... a.	...	...	...	1032	...	**q**	...	...	...	1335	...	...	...	...	...	...	...	1432	**F**	**q**	⑦ **y**	...	...	1735	...
Brussels Midi/Zuid ... d.	...	...	...	1043	1156	1252	...	...	...	...	1443	1452	1456	...	...	...	...	1443	1556	1656	1656	...	...	...	1813
Paris Nord ... a.	...	...	...	1205	|	|	...	...	...	...	1605	|	|	...	...	...	...	1605	|	|	|	...	...	...	1935
Lille Europe ... a.	...	...	...	...	1230	1326	...	...	...	...	...	1526	1532	...	...	...	...	...	1630	1732	1732	...	...	...	...
Ashford International .. a.	...	...	...	...	|	|	...	...	...	...	...	|	|	...	...	...	...	...	|	1734	|	...	...	...	...
Ebbsfleet International . a.	...	...	...	...	|	1345	...	...	...	...	...	1545	1545	...	...	...	...	...	|	|	1745	...	...	...	...
London St Pancras ... a.	...	...	...	...	1257	1405	...	...	...	...	...	1605	1605	...	...	...	...	...	1657	1806	1803	...	...	...	...

train type	*IC*	*IC*	*EC*	*ICE*	*IC*	⇌	☆	*ICE*	*IC*	*IC*	*IC*	*EC*	*ICE*	*IC*	⇌		*ICE*	*IC*	*RE*	*IC*	*ICE*	*RE*	*ICE*	⇌	
train number	**2327**	**2048**	**178**	**950**	**2203**	**9472**	**9161**	**38**	**2311**	**2229**	**2440**	**176**	**858**	**2205**	**9484**		**36**	**2213**	**10134**	**2036**	**556**	**10529**	**10**	**9394**	
notes	**2027**		✕		**2019**			**K**				✕					**K**			Ⓑ	✕			⑦ **h**	
Praha hlavní ... d.	...	...	0627	...	...	...	...	...	...	...	...	0827	...	...	...	...	...	...	...	...	...	...	...	...	...
Praha Holešovice ... d.	...	...	0626	...	...	...	...	...	...	...	...	0836	...	...	...	...	...	...	...	...	...	...	...	...	...
Děčín ... d.	...	...	0800	...	...	...	...	...	...	...	...	1000	...	...	...	...	...	...	...	...	...	...	...	...	...
Bad Schandau 🏛 ... d.	...	...	0817	...	...	...	...	...	...	...	...	1017	...	...	...	...	...	...	...	...	...	...	...	...	...
Dresden Hbf ... d.	...	0919	0907	...	...	...	...	...	...	...	1120	1107	...	...	...	...	...	...	...	...	...	...	...	...	...
Berlin Hauptbahnhof . d.	...	|	1115	1149	...	...	...	...	...	...	|	1315	1349	...	...	...	...	...	...	...	1452	...	...	...	...
Leipzig Hbf ... d.	...	1040	...	|	...	...	...	...	...	...	1243	...	|	...	...	...	...	...	...	1339	|	...	...	...	...
Halle Hbf ... d.	...	1107	...	|	...	...	...	...	...	...	1307	...	|	...	...	...	...	...	...	1407	|	...	...	...	...
Magdeburg Hbf ... d.	...	1202	...	|	...	...	...	...	...	...	1404	...	|	...	...	...	...	...	...	1459	|	...	...	...	...
Braunschweig Hbf ... d.	...	1251	...	|	...	...	...	...	...	...	1451	...	|	...	...	...	...	...	...	1551	|	...	...	...	...
Wolfsburg ... d.	...	|	...	1256	...	...	...	...	...	...	|	...	1456	...	...	...	...	...	...	|	|	...	...	...	...
København H ⊙ d.	...	|	...	|	...	...	...	0737	...	...	|	...	|	...	...	...	0937	...	...	|	|	...	...	...	...
Hamburg Hbf ... d.	1146	|	...	|	...	...	...	1221	1246	1346	|	...	|	...	...	...	1421	1446	...	|	|	...	...	...	...
Hannover Hbf ... d.	|	1323	...	1331	...	...	...	...	|	|	1523	...	1531	...	...	...	...	|	...	1623	1631	...	...	...	...
Bremen Hbf ... d.	1244	...	...	|	...	...	...	...	1344	1444	...	...	|	...	...	...	...	1544	...	...	|	...	...	...	...
Osnabrück Hbf ... d.	1337	...	...	|	...	...	...	...	1437	1537	...	...	|	...	...	...	...	1637	...	...	|	...	...	...	...
Münster ... d.	1403	...	...	|	1432	...	...	...	1503	1603	...	...	|	1632	...	...	...	1703	...	...	|	...	...	...	...
Bielefeld Hbf ... d.	|	...	...	1422	|	...	...	...	|	|	...	...	1622	|	...	...	...	|	...	...	1722	...	...	...	...
Hamm (Westf) ... d.	|	...	...	1454	|	...	...	...	|	|	...	...	1654	|	...	...	...	|	1722	...	1754	...	...	...	...
Dortmund Hbf ... d.	1436	...	...	|	|	1514	...	...	1537	1636	...	...	|	|	...	...	...	1737	1745	...	|	...	...	...	...
Bochum Hbf ... d.	|	...	...	|	|	|	...	...	1549	|	...	...	|	|	...	...	...	1749	1756	...	|	...	...	...	...
Essen Hbf ... d.	|	...	...	|	|	1550	...	...	1600	|	...	...	|	|	1750	...	...	1800	1809	...	|	...	...	...	...
Oberhausen ... d.	|	...	...	|	1527	|	...	...	|	|	...	...	|	1727	|	...	...	|	|	...	|	1834	...	...	...
Duisburg Hbf ... d.	|	...	...	|	1534	1603	...	...	1612	|	...	...	|	1734	1803	...	...	1812	1823	...	|	1842	...	...	...
Düsseldorf Hbf ... d.	|	...	...	|	1549	1618	...	...	1627	|	...	...	|	1749	1818	...	...	1827	1840	...	|	1858	...	...	...
Hagen Hbf ... d.	1457	...	...	1524	|	|	...	...	|	1657	...	...	1724	|	|	...	...	|	|	...	1824	|	...	...	...
Wuppertal Hbf ... d.	1514	...	...	1541	|	|	...	...	|	1714	...	...	1741	|	|	...	...	|	|	...	1841	|	...	...	...
Köln Hbf ... a.	1546	...	...	1609	1613	1641	...	...	1650	1746	...	...	1809	1813	1841	...	...	1850	1912	...	1909	1929	...	...	...
Köln Hbf ... d.	...	...	...	...	...	1644	...	...	...	...	...	...	...	...	1844	...	...	...	...	...	...	...	1943	...	...
Aachen 🏛 ... d.	...	...	...	...	...	1724	...	...	...	...	...	...	...	...	1924	...	...	...	...	...	...	...	2021	...	...
Liège Guillemins ... a.	...	...	...	...	...	1746	...	...	...	...	...	...	...	...	1946	...	...	...	...	...	...	...	2044	...	...
Liège Guillemins ... d.	...	...	...	...	...	1749	...	...	...	...	...	...	...	...	1949	...	...	...	...	...	...	...	2046	...	...
Brussels Nord ... a.	...	...	...	...	...	|	...	...	...	...	...	...	...	...	|	...	...	...	...	...	...	...	2126	...	...
Brussels Midi/Zuid ... a.	...	...	...	...	...	1832	...	...	...	...	...	...	...	...	2032	...	...	...	...	...	...	...	2135	...	...
Brussels Midi/Zuid ... d.	...	...	...	...	...	1843	1952	...	...	...	...	...	...	...	2043	...	...	...	...	...	...	...	...	2213	...
Paris Nord ... a.	...	...	...	...	...	2005	|	...	...	...	...	...	...	...	2205	...	...	...	...	...	...	...	...	2335	...
Lille Europe ... a.	...	...	...	...	...	...	2026	...	...	...	...	...	...	...	...	...	...	...	...	...	...	...	...	...	...
Ashford International .. a.	...	...	...	...	...	...	|	...	...	...	...	...	...	...	...	...	...	...	...	...	...	...	...	...	...
Ebbsfleet International . a.	...	...	...	...	...	...	2045	...	...	...	...	...	...	...	...	...	...	...	...	...	...	...	...	...	...
London St Pancras ... a.	...	...	...	...	...	...	2103	...	...	...	...	...	...	...	...	...	...	...	...	...	...	...	...	...	...

F – Ⓑ May 29 - Sept. 3. ⑤⑦ Sept. 4 - Dec. 10 (also Oct. 24–27).
K – (12) 🍷 ✓ København - Hamburg.

f – ①–⑥.
h – Also Aug. 15.
j – ①.
p – Also Nov. 11.
q – Not May 30, Aug. 29, Nov. 11.

r – ①–⑤.
w – Not Nov. 11.
y – Also May 30, Aug. 29, Nov. 11.

☆ – Eurostar train. 🅁, ✕ in Business Premier and Standard Premier, 🍷 in Standard. Special fares paya[ble]. Minimum check-in time 30 minutes. Not available for London - Ebbsfleet - Ashford or v.v. journeys. Valid May 29 - Dec. 10.
⇌ – *Thalys* high-speed train. 🅁 🍷. Special fares payable. Valid May 30 - Dec. 10.
⊙ – 🏛 between Hamburg and København is Rødby (Table **720**).

LONDON and BRUSSELS - FRANKFURT, WIEN and MÜNCHEN 21

train type	ICE	ICE	ICE	EC	ICE	RJ	🚌	🚌	ALX	ICE	⇌	ICE	IC	ICE	IC	RJ	EC	IC	ICE	EN	🚌	⇌	ICE	ICE	EC	IC
train number	11	11	529	89	91	67	42010	42012	355	593 1091	9401	621	115	515	1281	69	83	119	27	347	42014	9413	625	517	189	2023 1023
notes	①–⑤	⑥⑦		✕	R		® 🍷 T	® 🍷	J				✕	🍷	G	🍷	🍷	🍷 C	🍷 S	✕ A	® 🍷				✕	🍷
on St Pancras ... d.	...	...	...	...	...	...	...	...	...	...	...	...	...	...	...	...	...	...	...	...	...	...	...	...	...	...
'leet International d.	...	...	...	...	...	...	...	...	...	...	...	...	...	...	...	...	...	...	...	...	...	...	...	...	...	...
rd International .. d.	...	...	...	...	...	...	...	...	...	...	...	...	...	...	...	...	...	...	...	...	...	...	...	...	...	...
Europe .... d.	...	...	...	...	...	...	...	...	...	...	...	...	...	...	...	...	...	...	...	...	...	...	...	...	...	...
ris Nord .... d.	...	...	...	...	...	...	...	...	...	...	0601	...	...	...	...	...	...	...	...	...	...	0755	...	...	...	...
sels Midi / Zuid ... a.	...	...	...	...	...	...	...	...	...	...	0723	...	...	...	...	...	...	...	...	...	...	0917	...	...	...	...
sels Midi / Zuid ... d.	0625	0625	...	...	...	...	...	...	...	...	0728	...	...	...	...	...	...	...	...	...	...	0928	...	...	...	...
els Nord .... d.	0633	0633	...	...	...	...	...	...	...	...	|	...	...	...	...	...	...	...	...	...	...	|	...	...	...	...
Guillemins .... a.	0710	0710	...	...	...	...	...	...	...	...	0811	...	...	...	...	...	...	...	...	...	...	1011	...	...	...	...
Guillemins .... d.	0712	0712	...	...	...	...	...	...	...	...	0814	...	...	...	...	...	...	...	...	...	...	1014	...	...	...	...
en Hbf 🏛 .... a.	0737	0737	...	...	...	...	...	...	...	...	0836	...	...	...	...	...	...	...	...	...	...	1036	...	...	...	...
Hbf .... a.	0815	0815	...	...	...	...	...	...	...	...	0915	...	...	...	...	...	...	...	...	...	...	1115	...	...	...	...
Hbf .... d.	0827	0820	...	...	...	...	...	...	...	...	...	0936x	...	0955	...	...	...	...	0953	...	...	...	1130x	1155	...	1153
Hbf .... a.	|	|	...	...	...	...	...	...	...	...	...	|	...	|	...	...	...	...	1012	...	...	...	|	|	...	1212
nz Hbf .... a.	⊖	⊖	...	...	...	...	...	...	...	...	...	⊖	...	⊖	...	...	...	...	1046	...	...	...	⊖	⊖	...	1246
z Hbf .... a.	|	|	...	...	...	...	...	...	...	...	...	|	...	|	...	...	...	...	1138	...	...	...	|	|	...	1337
nkfurt Flughafen ✈ a.	0916	0926	...	...	...	...	...	...	...	...	...	1034	...	1050	...	...	...	...	1159	...	...	...	1234	1250	...	1359
nkfurt (Main) Hbf . a.	0930	0941	0954	...	...	...	...	...	...	0950	...	1048	...	|	...	...	...	...	1213	...	...	...	1248	|	...	1412
rzburg Hbf .... a.	...	...	1102	...	...	...	...	...	...	|	...	1202	...	|	...	...	...	...	1331	...	...	...	1402	|	...	...
rnberg Hbf .... a.	...	...	1159	...	1230	...	1240	1340	...	|	...	1259	...	|	...	...	...	...	1427	...	1540	...	1459	|	...	...
gensburg Hbf ..... a.	...	...	|	...	1324	...	|	|	1419	|	...	|	...	|	...	...	...	...	1525	...	|	...	|	|	...	...
Praha hlavní ...... a.	...	...	|	...	|	...	1618	1718	1843	|	...	|	...	|	...	...	...	...	|	...	1918	...	|	|	...	...
heim Hbf .... a.	...	...	|	...	|	...	...	...	...	1027	...	|	...	1123	...	...	...	1154	|	...	...	...	|	1323	...	...
gart Hbf .... a.	...	...	|	...	|	...	...	...	...	1108	...	|	...	1208	...	...	...	1245	|	...	...	...	|	1408	...	...
Hbf .... a.	...	...	|	...	|	...	...	...	...	1207	...	|	...	1307	...	...	...	1400	|	...	...	...	|	1507	...	...
burg Hbf .... a.	...	...	|	...	|	...	...	...	...	1253	...	|	...	1353	...	...	...	|	|	...	...	...	|	1553	...	...
chen Hbf .... a.	...	...	1304	1338	|	1334	...	...	...	1327	...	1404	1417	1427	1522	1534	1538	|	|	...	...	...	1606	1627	1738	...
zburg .... a.	...	...	...	|	|	1508	...	...	...	...	...	...	1558	...	|	1702	|	|	|	...	...	...	...	...	|	...
ein 🏛 .... a.	...	...	...	1438	|	|	...	...	...	...	...	...	|	...	1619	|	1638	◧	|	...	...	...	...	...	1838	...
l .... a.	...	...	...	1449	|	|	...	...	...	...	...	...	|	...	1635	|	1649	|	|	...	...	...	...	...	1849	...
ühel .... a.	...	...	...	|	|	|	...	...	...	...	...	...	|	...	1728	|	|	|	|	...	...	...	...	...	|	...
m See .... a.	...	...	...	|	|	|	...	...	...	...	...	...	|	...	1824	|	|	|	|	...	...	...	...	...	|	...
arzach St Veit .... a.	...	...	...	|	|	|	...	...	...	...	...	...	1709	...	1854	|	|	|	|	...	...	...	...	...	|	...
sbruck Hbf .... a.	...	...	...	1522	|	|	...	...	...	...	...	...	|	...	...	|	1722	1901	|	...	...	...	...	...	1922	...
Gastein .... a.	...	...	...	...	|	|	...	...	...	...	...	...	1741	...	...	|	...	...	|	...	...	...	...	...	...	...
h .... a.	...	...	...	...	|	|	...	...	...	...	...	...	1843	...	...	|	...	...	|	...	...	...	...	...	...	...
enfurt .... a.	...	...	...	...	|	|	...	...	...	...	...	...	1915	...	...	|	...	...	|	...	...	...	...	...	...	...
ssau 🏛 .... a.	...	...	...	...	1432	|	...	...	...	...	...	...	...	...	...	|	...	...	1633	...	...	...	...	...	...	...
z .... a.	...	...	...	...	1543	1612	...	...	...	...	...	...	...	...	...	1812	...	...	1742	...	...	...	...	...	...	...
en Hbf .... a.	...	...	...	...	1708	1730	...	...	...	...	...	...	...	...	...	1930	...	...	1908	1942	...	...	...	...	...	...
dapest Keleti ▲ .. a.	...	...	...	...	...	2019	...	...	...	...	...	...	...	...	...	...	...	...	...	2220	...	...	...	...	...	...

train type / number	⇌	☆	☆	☆	ICE	ICE	ICE	EC	ICE	🚌	ALX	EC	☆	☆	⇌	ICE	ICE	⇌	⇌	☆	☆	ICE	ICE	ICE	EN	EN
train number	9315	9108	9110	9110	15	627	597	189	29	42016	357	117	9116	9116	9437	125	723	9339	9341	9126	9126	17	691	725	463	463 499
notes		① K	H	⑥				✕	🍷	® 🍷 U	J	Ⓑ	①–⑤ j	⑥⑦ k			Ⓑ		E	①–⑥ Y	⑦ Z	🍷			B	L
don St Pancras ... d.	...	0613	0650	0657	...	...	...	...	...	...	...	...	0855	0858	...	...	...	...	...	1058	1104	...	...	...	...	...
fleet International d.	...	0630	0707	|	...	...	...	...	...	...	...	...	0914	0915	...	...	...	...	...	1115	|	...	...	...	...	...
ord International .. d.	...	0652	0728	0728	...	...	...	...	...	...	...	...	|	|	...	...	...	...	...	|	|	...	...	...	...	...
Europe .... d.	...	|	0933	0930	...	...	...	...	...	...	...	...	1130	1133	...	...	...	...	...	1330	1330	...	...	...	...	...
ris Nord .... d.	0825	|	|	|	...	...	...	...	...	...	...	...	|	|	1155	...	...	1225	1246	|	|	...	...	...	...	...
sels Midi / Zuid ... a.	0947	0958	1007	1005	...	...	...	...	...	...	...	...	1205	1208	1317	...	...	1347	1412	1405	1405	...	...	...	...	...
sels Midi / Zuid ... d.	...	...	...	...	1025	...	...	...	...	...	...	...	▬	▬	1328	...	...	▬	▬	▬	...	1425	...	...	...	...
sels Nord .... d.	...	...	...	...	1034	...	...	...	...	...	...	...	...	...	|	...	...	...	...	...	...	1434	...	...	...	...
Guillemins .... a.	...	...	...	...	1112	...	...	...	...	...	...	...	...	...	1411	...	...	...	...	...	...	1512	...	...	...	...
Guillemins .... d.	...	...	...	...	1114	...	...	...	...	...	...	...	...	*IC*	1414	...	...	...	...	*IC*	...	1514	...	...	...	...
en Hbf 🏛 .... a.	...	...	...	...	1136	...	...	...	...	...	...	...	...	**2313**	1436	...	...	*ICE*	...	**2027**	...	1536	...	...	...	...
Hbf .... a.	...	...	...	...	1215	...	...	...	...	...	...	...	...	🍷	1515	...	...	**611**	...	**2327**	...	1615	...	...	...	...
Hbf .... d.	...	...	...	...	1218	...	...	...	...	...	...	...	...	1253	...	1529	...	1555	...	1553	...	1620	...	...	...	...
Hbf .... a.	...	...	...	...	|	...	...	...	...	...	...	...	...	1312	...	|	...	|	...	1612	...	|	...	...	...	...
enz Hbf .... a.	...	...	...	...	⊖	...	...	...	...	...	...	...	...	1346	...	⊖	...	⊖	...	1646	...	⊖	...	...	...	...
z Hbf .... a.	...	...	...	...	|	...	...	...	...	...	...	...	...	1437	...	|	...	|	...	1738	...	|	...	...	...	...
nkfurt Flughafen ✈ a.	...	...	...	...	1316	...	...	...	...	...	...	...	...	|	...	1616	...	1650	...	1759	...	1709z	...	...	...	...
nkfurt (Main) Hbf . a.	...	...	...	...	1330	1354	1350	...	1416	...	...	1420	...	|	...	1630	1654	|	...	1813	...	1722z	1750	1754	...	...
rzburg Hbf .... a.	...	...	...	...	...	1502	|	...	1531	...	...	|	...	|	...	...	1802	|	...	1931	...	...	|	1902	...	...
rnberg Hbf .... a.	...	...	...	...	...	1559	|	...	1626	1740	...	|	...	|	...	...	1859	|	...	2027	...	...	|	1959	...	...
gensburg Hbf ..... a.	...	...	...	...	...	|	|	...	1725	|	1835	|	*EC*	|	...	...	|	|	...	2131	...	...	|	|	...	...
Praha hlavní ...... a.	...	...	...	...	...	|	|	...	|	2118	2243	|	**1217**	|	...	...	|	|	*CNL*	|	...	...	|	|	...	...
heim Hbf .... a.	...	...	...	...	...	|	1427	...	|	...	...	|	⑥	1521	...	...	|	1723	**485**	|	...	...	1827	|	...	...
gart Hbf .... a.	...	...	...	...	...	|	1508	...	|	...	...	1553	1557	1622	...	...	|	1808	**40463**	|	...	...	1908	|	...	...
Hbf .... a.	...	...	...	...	...	|	1607	...	|	...	...	1652	1652	...	...	...	|	1907	**D**	|	...	...	2007t	|	...	...
burg Hbf .... a.	...	...	...	...	...	|	1653	...	|	...	...	1739	1739	...	...	...	|	1953	®	|	...	...	2053t	|	...	...
chen Hbf .... a.	...	...	...	...	...	1704	1727	1738	|	...	...	1811	1811	...	...	...	2004	2027	2103	|	...	...	2127t	2105	2336	2336
lzburg .... a.	...	...	...	...	...	...	...	|	|	...	...	1958	1959	...	...	...	...	...	|	|	...	...	...	...	0118	0118
ein 🏛 .... a.	...	...	...	...	...	...	...	1838	|	...	...	|	|	...	...	...	...	...	2204	|	...	...	...	...	|	|
gl .... a.	...	...	...	...	...	...	...	1849	|	...	...	|	|	...	...	...	...	...	2215	|	...	...	...	...	|	|
ühel .... a.	...	...	...	...	...	...	...	|	|	...	...	|	|	...	...	...	...	...	|	|	...	...	...	...	|	|
am See .... a.	...	...	...	...	...	...	...	|	|	...	...	|	|	...	...	...	...	...	|	|	...	...	...	...	|	|
varzach St Veit .... a.	...	...	...	...	...	...	...	|	|	...	...	2109	2109	...	...	...	...	...	|	|	...	...	...	...	|	0223
nsbruck Hbf .... a.	...	...	...	...	...	...	...	1922	|	...	...	|	|	...	...	...	...	...	2258	|	...	...	...	...	|	|
Gastein .... a.	...	...	...	...	...	...	...	...	|	...	...	2141	2141	...	...	...	...	...	...	|	...	...	...	...	|	|
ch .... a.	...	...	...	...	...	...	...	...	|	...	...	2243	2243	...	...	...	...	...	...	|	...	...	...	...	|	0351
enfurt .... a.	...	...	...	...	...	...	...	...	|	...	...	2315	2315	...	...	...	...	...	...	|	...	...	...	...	|	...
ssau 🏛 .... a.	...	...	...	...	...	...	...	...	1832	...	...	...	...	...	...	...	...	...	...	2241	...	...	...	...	|	...
nz .... a.	...	...	...	...	...	...	...	...	1942	...	...	...	...	...	...	...	...	...	...	...	...	...	...	...	0458	...
ien Hbf .... a.	...	...	...	...	...	...	...	...	2108	...	...	...	...	...	...	...	...	...	...	...	...	...	...	...	0634	...
dapest Keleti ▲ .. a.	...	...	...	...	...	...	...	...	...	...	...	...	...	...	...	...	...	...	...	...	...	...	...	...	0924	...

DACIA – 🛏 1, 2 cl., 🛌 2 cl., [2] ✕ Wien - Budapest - Bucuresti.
KÁLMÁN IMRE – 🛏 1, 2 cl., 🛌 2 cl., [2] München - Wien - Budapest.
[12] 🍷 Munster - Köln - Stuttgart - Lindau 🏛 - Innsbruck (Table **70**).
City Night Line LUPUS / PICTOR – 🛏 1, 2 cl., 🛌 2 cl., [2] 🍷 München - Innsbruck - Roma / Venezia. Special fares apply.
①–⑤ May 30 - July 9. ①–⑥ July 10 - Aug. 27 (not Aug. 15). ①⑤ Aug. 28 - Dec. 10 (not Nov. 11).
GROSSGLOCKNER – ⑥ July 2 - Sept. 3: [12] München - Kufstein 🏛 - Wörgl - Zell am See - Schwarzach St Veit.
①–⑤ May 31 - July 23. ②–⑤ July 24 - Dec. 10 (not Aug. 29, Nov. 1, 11).
[12] München - Praha. *EC* in the Czech Republic (Table **76**).
① July 24 - Dec. 10 (not Aug. 15).
LISINSKI – 🛏 1, 2 cl., 🛌 2 cl., [2] München - Salzburg - Villach - Zagreb (Table **62**).
[12] ✕ Hamburg - Nürnberg - Wien.

S – [12] ✕ Dortmund - Köln - Wien.
T – Mar. 28 - Oct. 4.
U – Ⓑ Mar. 29 - Oct. 4.
Y – ①–⑥ May 31 - Nov. 4 (not Aug. 29). Daily Nov. 5 - Dec. 10.
Z – ⑦ May 29 - Nov. 4 (also May 30, Aug. 29).

j – Not May 30, Aug. 29, Nov. 11.
k – Also May 30, Aug. 29, Nov. 11.
t – Ⓑ.
x – Köln **Messe / Deutz** (Table **910**). Connections from Köln Hbf depart every 2 - 5 minutes, journey time 2 - 3 minutes.
z – 17 - 19 minutes later on ⑥⑦.

◧ – 🏛 is at Lindau.
▲ – 🏛 is at Hegyeshalom.
⊖ – Via Köln - Frankfurt high speed line.
⇌ – *Thalys* high-speed train. ® 🍷. Special fares payable. Valid May 30 - Dec. 10.
🚌 – **DB / ČD** *ExpressBus*. ® 🍷. Rail tickets valid. 🏛 is Waidhaus (Germany). (Table **76**).
RJ – ÖBB *Railjet* service. [1] (business class), [1] (first class), [2] (economy class), ✕.
☆ – Eurostar train. ®, ✕ in Business Premier and Standard Premier, 🍷 in Standard. Special fares payable. Minimum check-in time 30 minutes. Not available for London - Ebbsfleet - Ashford or v.v. journeys. Valid May 29 - Dec. 10.

21 LONDON and BRUSSELS - FRANKFURT, WIEN and MÜNCHEN

train type	☆	☆	⇌	*ICE*	*ICE*	☆	⇌	*ICE*	*ICE*	*ICE*	*IC*	*EN*	☆	⇌	*ICE*	*IC*	*EN*	*EC*	*CNL*	*IC*	*CNL*	*RJ*	*EC*	*EC*
train number	**9132**	**9136**	**9461**	**1029**	**615**	**9140**	**9365**	**19**	**773**	**1029**	**2315**	**421**	**9144**	**9473**	**227**	**2395**	**421**	**345**	**459**	**2221**	**419**	**61**	**81**	**111**
notes		Ⓑ				Ⓑ					**2215**	🅁	⑥			⑥	🅁	🍷	🅁	**2321**	**60419**		**1289**	
		F					**G**					**B**					**B**	**R**	**A**		**L**			
London St Pancras .....d.	1258	1404	...	...	...	1504	...	...	...	...	...	...	1604	...	...	...	...	...	...	...	...	...	...	...
Ebbsfleet International ..d.	1315	│	...	...	...	│	...	...	...	...	...	...	│	...	...	...	...	...	...	...	...	...	...	...
Ashford International ....d.	│	│	...	...	...	│	...	...	...	...	...	...	│	...	...	...	...	...	...	...	...	...	...	...
Lille Europe ....d.	1533	1630	...	...	...	1730	...	...	...	...	...	...	1830	...	...	...	...	...	...	...	...	...	...	...
Paris Nord ....d.	│	│	1555	...	...	│	1655	...	...	...	...	...	│	1755	...	...	...	...	...	...	...	...	...	...
Brussels Midi / Zuid .....a.	1608	1705	1717	...	...	1805	1817	...	...	...	...	...	1905	1917	...	...	...	...	...	...	...	...	...	...
Brussels Midi / Zuid .....d.	...	...	1728	...	...	...	...	1825	...	...	...	...	...	1928	...	...	...	...	...	...	...	...	...	...
Brussels Nord ....d.	...	...	│	...	...	...	...	1834	...	...	...	...	...	│	...	...	...	...	...	...	...	...	...	...
Liège Guillemins ....a.	...	...	1811	...	...	...	...	1912	...	...	...	...	...	2011	...	...	...	...	...	...	...	...	...	...
Liège Guillemins ....d.	...	...	1814	...	...	...	...	1914	...	...	...	...	...	2014	...	...	...	...	...	...	...	...	...	...
Aachen Hbf 🛃 ....a.	...	...	1836	...	...	...	...	1936	...	...	...	...	...	2036	...	...	...	...	...	...	...	...	...	...
Köln Hbf ....a.	...	...	1915	...	...	...	...	2015	...	...	...	...	...	2115	...	...	...	...	...	...	...	...	...	...
Köln Hbf ....d.	...	...	...	1953	1957	...	...	2028	...	...	2053	2122	...	...	2128	...	...	...	...	2153	2318	...	...	...
Bonn Hbf ....a.	...	...	...	2012	│	...	...	│	...	...	2112	2143**d**	...	...	│	...	...	...	...	2212	2337	...	...	...
Koblenz Hbf ....a.	...	...	...	2046	⊖	...	...	⊖	...	...	2146	2217**d**	...	...	⊖	...	←	...	...	2246	0015	...	...	...
Mainz Hbf ....a.	...	...	...	2141	│	...	...	│	...	...	2241	2315	...	...	│	...	2317**d**	...	...	2338	0111	...	...	...
Frankfurt Flughafen ✈ .a.	...	...	...	...	2050	...	...	2116	2120	...	...	→	...	...	2216	...	2353**d**	...	...	...	0129	...	...	...
Frankfurt (Main) Hbf ...a.	...	...	...	...	│	...	...	2130	│	2218	...	...	...	...	2230	2308	0004**j**	...	0054**j**	...	0142	...	...	...
Würzburg Hbf ....a.	...	...	...	...	│	...	...	...	│	2341	...	...	...	...	...	│	│	...	│	...	│	...	...	...
Nürnberg Hbf ....a.	...	...	...	...	│	...	...	...	│	0037	...	...	...	...	...	│	│	...	│	...	│	...	...	...
Regensburg Hbf ....a.	...	...	...	...	│	...	...	...	│	...	...	...	...	...	...	│	│	...	│	...	│	...	...	...
Praha hlavní ....a.	...	...	...	...	│	...	...	...	│	...	...	...	...	...	...	│	│	...	0928	...	│	...	...	...
Mannheim Hbf ....a.	...	...	...	...	2123	...	...	...	2154	...	...	...	...	...	...	│	│	...	...	...	│	...	...	...
Stuttgart Hbf ....a.	...	...	...	...	2208	...	...	...	2250	...	...	...	...	...	...	0050	│	...	...	...	0421	...	...	...
Ulm Hbf ....a.	...	...	...	...	2307	...	...	...	...	...	...	...	...	...	...	...	│	...	...	...	0540	...	...	...
Augsburg Hbf ....a.	...	...	...	...	2352	...	...	...	...	...	...	...	...	...	...	...	│	...	...	...	0633	...	...	...
München Hbf ....a.	...	...	...	...	0027	...	...	...	...	...	...	...	...	...	...	...	│	...	...	...	0710	0733	0738	0818
Salzburg ....a.	...	...	...	...	...	...	...	...	...	...	...	...	...	...	...	...	│	...	...	...	...	0902	│	0959
Kufstein 🛃 ....a.	...	...	...	...	...	...	...	...	...	...	...	...	...	...	...	...	│	...	...	...	...	│	0838	│
Wörgl ....a.	...	...	...	...	...	...	...	...	...	...	...	...	...	...	...	...	│	...	...	...	...	│	0849	│
Kitzbühel ....a.	...	...	...	...	...	...	...	...	...	...	...	...	...	...	...	...	│	...	...	...	...	│	│	│
Zell am See ....a.	...	...	...	...	...	...	...	...	...	...	...	...	...	...	...	...	│	...	...	...	...	│	│	│
Schwarzach St Veit ......a.	...	...	...	...	...	...	...	...	...	...	...	...	...	...	...	...	│	...	...	...	...	│	│	1109
Innsbruck Hbf ....a.	...	...	...	...	...	...	...	...	...	...	...	...	...	...	...	...	│	...	...	...	...	│	0922	│
Bad Gastein ....a.	...	...	...	...	...	...	...	...	...	...	...	...	...	...	...	...	│	...	...	...	...	│	...	1141
Villach ....a.	...	...	...	...	...	...	...	...	...	...	...	...	...	...	...	...	│	...	...	...	...	│	...	1243
Klagenfurt ....a.	...	...	...	...	...	...	...	...	...	...	...	...	...	...	...	...	│	...	...	...	...	│	...	1315
Passau 🛃 ....a.	...	...	...	...	...	...	...	...	...	...	...	...	...	...	...	...	0518	...	...	...	...	│	...	...
Linz ....a.	...	...	...	...	...	...	...	...	...	...	...	...	...	...	...	...	0633	...	...	...	...	1011	...	...
Wien Hbf ....a.	...	...	...	...	...	...	...	...	...	...	...	...	...	...	...	...	0820	0842	...	...	...	1130	...	...
Budapest Keleti ▲....a.	...	...	...	...	...	...	...	...	...	...	...	...	...	...	...	...	...	1119	...	...	...	1419	...	...

train type	*EC*	*EC*	*RJ*	*CNL*	⇌	*CNL*	*IC*	*EC*	*EN*	*ICE*	⇌	*EN*	*IC*	*ICE*	*ICE*	⇌	☆	☆	*IC*	*ICE*	*ICE*	*ICE*	⇌	☆	
train number	**110**	**188**	**68**	**418**	**9412**	**458**	**2212**	**148**	**420**	**18**	**9322**	**420**	**2220**	**616**	**226**	**9424**	**9129**	**9133**	**2216**	**728**	**692**	**16**	**9448**	**9141**	**9**
notes		**1288**							🅁		**9422**	🅁	**2320**				⑦	①–⑥						⑦	①
notes				**M**		**A**			**B**			**B**					**q**	**h**						**y**	
Budapest Keleti ▲....d.	...	...	1540	...	...	...	...	1840	...	...	...	...	...	...	...	...	...	...	...	...	...	...	...	...	
Wien Hbf ....d.	...	...	1830	...	...	...	...	2118	2139	...	...	...	...	...	...	...	...	...	...	...	...	...	...	...	
Linz ....d.	...	...	1948	...	...	...	...	▬	2319	...	...	...	...	...	...	...	...	...	...	...	...	...	...	...	
Passau 🛃 ....d.	...	...	│	...	...	...	...	...	0030	...	...	...	...	...	...	...	...	...	...	...	...	...	...	...	
Klagenfurt ....d.	1642	...	│	...	...	...	...	...	│	...	...	...	...	...	...	...	...	...	...	...	...	...	...	...	
Villach ....d.	1716	...	│	...	...	...	...	...	│	...	...	...	...	...	...	...	...	...	...	...	...	...	...	...	
Bad Gastein ....d.	1817	...	│	...	...	...	...	...	│	...	...	...	...	...	...	...	...	...	...	...	...	...	...	...	
Innsbruck Hbf ....d.	│	2036	│	...	...	...	...	...	│	...	...	...	...	...	...	...	...	...	...	...	...	...	...	...	
Schwarzach St Veit ......d.	1849	│	│	...	...	...	...	...	│	...	...	...	...	...	...	...	...	...	...	...	...	...	...	...	
Zell am See ....d.	│	│	│	...	...	...	...	...	│	...	...	...	...	...	...	...	...	...	...	...	...	...	...	...	
Kitzbühel ....d.	│	│	│	...	...	...	...	*ICE*	│	...	...	...	...	...	...	...	...	...	...	...	...	...	...	...	
Wörgl ....d.	│	2109	│	...	...	...	...	**618**	│	...	...	...	...	...	...	...	...	...	...	...	...	...	...	...	
Kufstein 🛃 ....d.	│	2119	│	...	...	...	...	**1018**	│	...	...	...	...	...	...	...	...	...	...	...	...	...	...	...	
Salzburg ....d.	2000	│	2056	...	...	...	...	🍷	│	...	...	...	...	...	...	...	...	...	...	...	...	...	...	...	
München Hbf ....d.	2141	2221	2226	2250	...	...	...	0001	│	...	...	...	...	0325	...	...	...	...	...	0652	0630**c**	...	...	...	
Augsburg Hbf ....d.	...	...	...	2320	...	...	...	0031	│	...	...	...	...	0357	...	...	...	...	...	│	0706**c**	...	...	...	
Ulm Hbf ....d.	...	...	...	0010	...	...	...	0116	│	...	...	...	...	0440	...	...	...	...	...	│	0751**c**	...	...	...	
Stuttgart Hbf ....d.	...	...	...	0135	...	...	...	0230	│	...	...	...	...	0551	...	...	...	...	0737	│	0851	...	...	...	
Mannheim Hbf ....d.	...	...	...	│	...	...	...	0440	│	...	...	...	...	0636	...	...	...	...	0839	│	0932	...	...	...	
Praha hlavní ....d.	...	...	...	│	...	1827	...	│	│	...	...	...	...	│	...	...	...	...	│	│	│	...	...	...	
Regensburg Hbf ....d.	...	...	...	│	...	│	...	│	│	...	...	...	...	│	...	...	...	...	│	│	│	...	...	...	
Nürnberg Hbf ....d.	...	...	...	│	...	│	...	│	│	...	...	...	...	│	...	...	...	...	│	0800	│	...	...	...	
Würzburg Hbf ....d.	...	...	...	│	...	│	...	│	│	...	...	...	...	│	...	...	...	...	│	0855	│	...	...	...	
Frankfurt (Main) Hbf...d.	...	...	...	0345	...	0359**j**	...	0544	0527**j**	0629	...	←	...	│	0727	...	...	...	│	1004	1008	1029**e**	...	...	
Frankfurt Flughafen ✈..d.	...	...	...	0358	...	...	...	0601	0536**s**	0643	...	0538**s**	...	0709	0743	...	...	...	│	...	...	1043**e**	...	...	
Mainz Hbf ....d.	...	...	...	0420	...	...	...	│	→	│	...	0602**s**	0617**n**	│	│	...	...	...	0920	...	...	│	...	...	
Koblenz Hbf ....d.	...	...	...	0513	...	...	0605	⊖	...	⊖	...	0705**s**	0713	⊖	⊖	...	...	...	1013	...	...	⊖	...	...	
Bonn Hbf ....d.	...	...	...	0547	...	...	0644	│	...	│	...	│	0744	│	│	...	...	...	1044	...	...	│	...	...	
Köln Hbf ....a.	...	...	...	0615	...	...	0705	0705	...	0739	...	0815	0805	0805	0832	...	...	...	1105	...	...	1132	...	...	
Köln Hbf ....d.	...	...	...	...	0645	...	...	...	...	0743	...	▬	...	...	...	0845	...	...	...	...	...	1143	...	...	
Aachen Hbf 🛃 ....d.	...	...	...	...	0724	...	...	...	...	0821	...	...	...	...	...	0924	...	...	...	...	...	1221	...	...	
Liège Guillemins ....a.	...	...	...	...	0749	...	...	...	...	0844	...	...	...	...	...	0946	...	...	...	...	...	1244	...	...	
Liège Guillemins ....d.	...	...	...	...	0752	...	...	...	...	0846	...	☆	...	...	...	0949	...	...	...	...	...	1246	...	...	
Brussels Nord ....a.	...	...	...	...	│	...	...	...	...	0926	...	**9125**	...	...	...	│	...	...	...	...	...	1326	...	...	
Brussels Midi / Zuid .....a.	...	...	...	...	0832	...	...	...	...	0935	...	**X**	...	...	...	1032	...	...	...	...	...	1335	...	...	
Brussels Midi / Zuid .....d.	...	...	...	...	0843	...	...	...	...	...	1013	1056	...	...	...	1043	1156	1252	...	...	...	...	1443	1452	14
Paris Nord ....d.	...	...	...	...	1005	...	...	...	...	...	1135	│	...	...	...	1205	│	│	...	...	...	...	1605	│	
Lille Europe ....a.	...	...	...	...	...	...	...	...	...	...	...	1130	...	...	...	...	1229	1326	...	...	...	...	...	1526	15
Ashford International ....a.	...	...	...	...	...	...	...	...	...	...	...	│	...	...	...	...	│	│	...	...	...	...	...	│	
Ebbsfleet International .a.	...	...	...	...	...	...	...	...	...	...	...	│	...	...	...	...	│	1345	...	...	...	...	...	1545	15
London St Pancras .....a.	...	...	...	...	...	...	...	...	...	...	...	1157	...	...	...	...	1257	1405	...	...	...	...	...	1605	16

A – *City Night Line* CANOPUS – 🛏 1,2 cl., 🛌 2 cl., 🍷 (*CNL* **40470** 🅁) Zürich - Frankfurt (Main) **Süd** - Praha; [2] (*IC* **60470**) Zürich - Frankfurt (Main) **Süd** - Praha. Special fares apply.

B – 🛏 1, 2 cl., 🛌 2 cl. (4, 6 berth), [2] 🍷 Düsseldorf - Köln - Frankfurt - Passau 🛃 - Wien and v.v. 🅁 Special fares apply. For international journeys only.

E – ①–⑤ (not May 25).

F – Ⓑ May 29 - Sept. 3. ⑤⑦ Sept. 4 - Dec. 10 (also Oct. 24–27).

G – Daily May 30 - July 9. ①⑤ July 10 - Aug. 27 (not Aug. 15). Ⓑ Aug. 28 - Dec. 10 (not Nov. 11).

L – *City Night Line* POLLUX – 🛏 1,2 cl., 🛌 2 cl. 🍷 (*CNL* **419** 🅁) Amsterdam - Köln - München; [2] (*IC* **60419**) Amsterdam - Köln - München. Special fares apply.

M – *City Night Line* POLLUX – 🛏 1,2 cl., 🛌 2 cl. 🍷 (*CNL* **418** 🅁) München - Köln - Amsterdam; [2] (*IC* **60418**) München - Köln - Amsterdam. Special fares apply.

R – AVALA – [1,2] 🍷 Wien - Budapest - Beograd and v.v. (Table **61**).

X – ①–⑥ May 29 - Sept. 3. ①–⑤ Sept. 4 - Dec. 10 (not Nov. 11).

c – ①–⑤ (not May 16).

d – Departure time.

e – On ⑦ depart Frankfurt Hbf 1016, Frankfurt Flughafen 1031.

h – Not May 30, Aug. 29, Nov. 11.

j – Frankfurt (Main) **Süd**.

n – ①–⑥.

q – Also Nov. 11.

s – Calls to set down only.

t – ⑥ Dec. 19 - Apr. 2.

y – Also May 30, Aug. 29, Nov. 11.

▲ – 🛃 is at Hegyeshalom.

⇌ – *Thalys* high-speed train. 🅁 🍷. Special far payable. Valid May 30 - Dec. 10.

☆ – Eurostar train. 🅁, ✕ in Business Premier, Standard Premier, 🍷 in Standard. Special fares payable. Minimum check-in time 30 minutes. Valid May 29 - Dec. 10.

⊖ – Via Köln - Frankfurt high speed line.

RJ – ÖBB *Railjet* service. ✕, [ ] (business cla [1] (first class), [2] (economy class).

MÜNCHEN, WIEN and FRANKFURT - BRUSSELS and LONDON 21

train type	IC	EN	EN	CNL	ICE	ICE	⇌	☆	IC	ICE	RJ	ALX	🚌	ICE	IC	ICE	ICE	ICE	⇌	☆	ICE	🚌	EC	ICE	⇌	☆
train number	2226	462	498	484	612	726	9448	9145	2024	208	260	356	42005	228	2312	598	720	14	9370	9157	518	42007	218	628	9472	9161
notes			462	40236		①–⑥				1208			Ⓡ						Ⓑ	Ⓑ		Ⓡ				
notes		K	L	C Ⓡ				A		✕		A							w			Q	g			
apest Keleti ▲.. d.	...	2040	...	...	...	...	...	...	...	...	...	...	...	...	...	...	...	...	...	...	...	...	...	...	...	...
n Hbf d.	...	2325	...	...	...	...	...	...	...	...	0630	...	...	0652	...	...	...	...	...	...	...	...	...	...	...	...
d.	...	0101	...	...	...	...	...	...	...	...	0748	...	...	0816	...	...	...	...	...	...	...	...	...	...	...	...
sau 🏛 d.	...	│	...	...	...	...	...	...	0717	...	│	...	...	0924	...	...	...	...	...	...	...	...	...	...	...	...
nfurt d.	...	│	...	...	...	...	...	...	│	...	│	...	...	│	...	...	...	...	...	...	...	...	...	...	...	...
d.	...	│	0146	...	...	...	...	...	│	...	│	...	...	│	...	...	...	...	...	...	...	...	...	...	...	...
iastein d.	...	│	0254	...	...	...	...	...	│	...	│	...	...	│	...	...	...	...	...	...	...	...	...	...	...	...
sbruck Hbf d.	...	│	│	0436	...	...	...	...	│	0709	│	...	...	│	...	...	...	...	...	...	...	...	...	...	...	...
arzach St Veit d.	...	│	0320	│	...	...	...	...	│	│	│	...	...	│	...	...	...	...	...	...	...	...	...	...	...	...
n See d.	...	│	│	│	...	...	...	...	│	│	│	...	...	│	...	...	...	...	...	...	...	...	...	...	...	...
hel d.	...	│	│	│	...	...	...	...	│	│	│	...	...	│	...	...	...	...	...	...	...	...	...	...	...	...
d.	...	│	│	0518	...	...	...	...	│	0746	│	...	...	│	...	...	...	...	...	...	...	...	...	...	...	...
ein 🏛 d.	...	│	│	0529	...	...	...	...	│	0758	│	...	...	│	...	...	...	...	...	...	...	...	...	...	...	...
zburg d.	...	0428	0428	│	...	...	...	...	│	│	0856	...	...	│	...	...	...	...	...	...	...	...	1000	...	...	...
hen Hbf d.	...	0609	0609	0629	0727	0755	...	...	│	0859	1024	...	...	│	...	1028	1055	...	...	...	1129	...	1141	1155	...	...
burg Hbf d.	...	...	...	...	0803	│	...	...	│	...	...	...	...	│	...	1103	│	...	...	...	1203	...	...	│	...	...
lbf d.	...	...	...	...	0851	│	...	...	│	...	...	...	...	│	...	1151	│	...	...	...	1251	...	...	│	...	...
gart Hbf d.	...	...	...	...	0951	│	...	...	│	...	...	...	...	│	...	1251	│	...	...	...	1351	...	...	│	...	...
heim Hbf d.	...	...	...	...	1036	│	...	...	│	...	...	...	...	│	...	1332	│	...	...	...	1436	...	...	│	...	...
raha hlavni d.	...	...	...	...	│	│	...	...	│	...	...	0514	0700	│	...	│	│	...	...	...	│	0812	...	│	...	...
gensburg Hbf d.	...	...	...	...	│	│	...	...	0827	...	...	0929	│	1028	...	│	│	...	...	...	│	│	...	│	...	...
rnberg Hbf d.	0729c	...	...	...	│	0900	...	...	0929	...	...	...	1050	1128	...	│	1200	...	...	...	│	1150	...	1300	...	...
rzburg Hbf d.	0826c	...	...	...	│	0955	...	...	1026	...	...	...	...	1227	...	│	1257	...	...	...	│	...	...	1355	...	...
nkfurt (Main) Hbf. d.	0942	...	...	...	│	1110	...	...	1142	...	...	...	...	1340	...	1408	1404	1429	...	...	│	...	...	1510	...	...
kfurt Flughafen ✈ d.	0958	...	...	...	1109	1122	...	...	1158	...	...	...	...	...	...	...	...	1443	...	...	1509	...	...	1525	...	...
Hbf d.	1020	...	...	...	│	│	...	...	1220	...	...	...	...	...	1320	...	...	│	...	...	│	...	...	│	...	...
nz Hbf d.	1113	...	...	...	⊖	⊖	...	...	1313	...	...	...	...	...	1413	...	...	⊖	...	...	⊖	...	...	⊖	...	...
Hbf d.	1144	...	...	...	│	│	...	...	1344	...	...	...	...	...	1444	...	...	│	...	...	│	...	...	│	...	...
Hbf a.	1205	...	...	...	1205	1225x	...	...	1405	...	...	...	...	...	1505	...	...	1533	...	...	1605	...	...	1614x	...	...
Hbf d.	...	...	...	...	...	...	1245	...	...	...	...	...	...	...	...	...	...	1542	...	...	...	...	...	...	1644	...
en Hbf 🏛 d.	...	...	...	...	...	...	1324	...	...	...	...	...	...	...	...	...	...	1621	...	...	...	...	...	...	1724	...
Guillemins a.	...	...	...	...	...	...	1346	...	...	...	...	...	...	...	...	...	...	1644	...	...	...	...	...	...	1746	...
Guillemins d.	...	...	...	...	...	...	1349	...	...	...	...	...	...	...	...	...	...	1646	...	...	...	...	...	...	1749	...
els Nord a.	...	...	...	...	...	...	│	...	...	...	...	...	...	...	...	...	...	1726	...	...	...	...	...	...	│	...
sels Midi / Zuid a.	...	...	...	...	...	...	1432	...	...	...	...	...	...	...	...	...	...	1735	...	...	...	...	...	...	1832	...
sels Midi / Zuid d.	...	...	...	...	...	...	1443	1556	...	...	...	...	...	...	...	...	...	...	1813	1856	...	...	...	...	1843	1952
is Nord a.	...	...	...	...	...	...	1605	│	...	...	...	...	...	...	...	...	...	...	1935	│	...	...	...	...	2005	│
urope a.	...	...	...	...	...	...	...	1630	...	...	...	...	...	...	...	...	...	...	...	1930	...	...	...	...	...	2026
rd International a.	...	...	...	...	...	...	...	│	...	...	...	...	...	...	...	...	...	...	...	│	...	...	...	...	...	│
leet International a.	...	...	...	...	...	...	...	│	...	...	...	...	...	...	...	...	...	...	...	│	...	...	...	...	...	2045
lon St Pancras a.	...	...	...	...	...	...	...	1657	...	...	...	...	...	...	...	...	...	...	...	1957	...	...	...	...	...	2103

train type	EC	IC	ICE	ICE	EC	EN	ICE	ICE	IC	RE	ICE	ICE	⇌	RJ	🚌	ICE	EC	IC	ICE	EC	RJ	ICE	ICE	EC	ICE	⇌
train number	218	1280	596	106	82	346	28	626	118	79022	516	624	9484	60	42009	26	114	1284	1090	88	60	622	572	6	10	9394
notes								826							Ⓡ				594			1222				⑦
notes	g	G				D		Ⓑ	E							F		H								h
dapest Keleti ▲.. d.	...	...	...	...	...	0540	...	...	...	...	...	...	...	0740	...	...	...	...	...	...	0740	...	...	...	...	...
en Hbf d.	...	...	...	...	...	0818	0852	...	...	...	...	...	...	1018	...	1052	...	...	...	...	1030	...	...	...	...	...
z d.	...	...	...	...	...	...	1016	...	...	...	...	...	...	━━	...	1216	...	...	...	...	1148	...	...	...	...	...
ssau 🏛 d.	...	...	...	...	...	...	1124	...	...	...	...	...	...	...	...	1324	...	...	...	...	│	...	...	...	...	...
enfurt d.	...	...	...	...	...	...	│	...	...	...	...	...	...	...	...	│	0842	...	...	...	│	...	...	...	...	...
h d.	...	...	...	...	...	...	│	...	...	...	...	...	...	...	...	│	0916	...	...	...	│	...	...	...	...	...
Gastein d.	...	...	...	...	...	...	│	...	...	...	...	...	...	...	...	│	1017	...	...	...	│	...	...	...	...	...
sbruck Hbf d.	...	...	...	...	1036	...	│	...	0901	...	...	...	...	...	...	│	│	...	...	1236	│	...	...	...	...	...
varzach St Veit d.	...	...	...	...	│	...	│	...	│	...	...	...	...	...	...	│	1049	1005	...	│	│	...	...	...	...	...
am See d.	...	0839	...	...	│	...	│	...	│	...	...	...	...	...	...	│	│	1035	...	│	│	...	...	...	...	...
ühel d.	...	0931	...	...	│	...	│	...	│	...	...	...	...	...	...	│	│	1127	...	│	│	...	...	...	...	...
l d.	...	1024	...	...	1109	...	│	...	│	...	...	...	...	...	...	│	│	1222	...	1309	│	...	...	...	...	...
ein 🏛 d.	...	1037	...	...	1119	...	│	...	◧	...	...	...	...	...	...	│	│	1234	...	1319	│	...	...	...	...	...
lzburg d.	1000	│	...	...	│	...	│	...	│	1109	...	...	...	...	...	│	1200	│	...	│	1256	...	...	...	...	...
chen Hbf d.	1146	1133f	1228	...	1221	...	│	1255	│	1317	1328	1355	...	...	...	│	1340	1345	1428	1421	1424	1455	...	...	...	...
burg Hbf d.	1216	...	1303	...	...	...	│	│	│	...	1403	│	...	...	...	│	...	...	1503	...	...	│	...	...	...	...
Hbf d.	1304	...	1351	...	...	...	│	│	1356	...	1451	│	...	ALX	...	│	...	...	1551	...	...	│	...	...	...	...
gart Hbf d.	1405	...	1451	...	...	...	│	│	1512	...	1551	│	...	354	...	│	...	...	1651	...	...	│	1726	...	...	...
nheim Hbf d.	│	...	1529	1536	...	...	│	│	1606	...	1636	│	...	A	...	│	...	...	1732	...	...	│	1806	...	...	...
Praha hlavní d.	│	...	...	│	...	...	│	│	...	...	│	│	...	0914	1042	│	...	...	│	...	...	│	│	...	...	...
gensburg Hbf d.	│	...	...	│	...	...	1228	│	...	...	│	│	...	1330	│	1428	...	...	│	...	...	│	│	...	...	...
rnberg Hbf d.	│	...	...	│	...	...	1328	1400	...	...	│	1500	...	...	1420	1528	...	...	│	...	...	1600	│	...	...	...
ürzburg Hbf d.	│	...	...	│	...	...	1427	1455	...	...	│	1555	...	...	...	1627	...	...	│	...	...	1655	│	...	...	...
ankfurt (Main) Hbf. d.	1540	...	...	│	...	...	1536	1609	...	...	│	1710	...	...	...	1736	...	...	1808	...	...	1804	│	...	1829	...
nkfurt Flughafen ✈ d.	...	...	...	1609	...	...	...	1630	...	...	1709	1725	...	...	...	...	...	...	...	...	...	...	1838	...	1843	...
z Hbf d.	...	...	...	│	...	...	...	│	...	...	│	│	...	...	...	...	...	...	...	...	...	...	...	1720	│	...
enz Hbf d.	...	...	...	⊖	...	...	...	⊖	...	...	⊖	⊖	...	...	...	...	...	...	...	...	...	...	...	1813	⊖	...
Hbf d.	...	...	...	│	...	...	...	│	...	...	│	│	...	...	...	...	...	...	...	...	...	...	...	1844	│	...
Hbf a.	...	...	...	1705	...	...	...	1742e	...	...	1805	1813x	...	...	...	...	...	...	...	...	...	...	...	1905	1939	...
Hbf d.	...	...	...	...	...	...	...	...	...	...	...	...	1844	...	...	...	...	...	...	...	...	...	...	...	1943	...
en Hbf 🏛 d.	...	...	...	...	...	...	...	...	...	...	...	...	1924	...	...	...	...	...	...	...	...	...	...	...	2021	...
e Guillemins a.	...	...	...	...	...	...	...	...	...	...	...	...	1946	...	...	...	...	...	...	...	...	...	...	...	2044	...
e Guillemins d.	...	...	...	...	...	...	...	...	...	...	...	...	1949	...	...	...	...	...	...	...	...	...	...	...	2046	...
sels Nord a.	...	...	...	...	...	...	...	...	...	...	...	...	│	...	...	...	...	...	...	...	...	...	...	...	2126	...
ssels Midi / Zuid a.	...	...	...	...	...	...	...	...	...	...	...	...	2032	...	...	...	...	...	...	...	...	...	...	...	2135	...
ssels Midi / Zuid d.	...	...	...	...	...	...	...	...	...	...	...	...	2043	...	...	...	...	...	...	...	...	...	...	...	...	2213
ris Nord d.	...	...	...	...	...	...	...	...	...	...	...	...	2205	...	...	...	...	...	...	...	...	...	...	...	...	2335
Europe a.	...	...	...	...	...	...	...	...	...	...	...	...	...	...	...	...	...	...	...	...	...	...	...	...	...	...
ord International a.	...	...	...	...	...	...	...	...	...	...	...	...	...	...	...	...	...	...	...	...	...	...	...	...	...	...
sfleet International a.	...	...	...	...	...	...	...	...	...	...	...	...	...	...	...	...	...	...	...	...	...	...	...	...	...	...
don St Pancras a.	...	...	...	...	...	...	...	...	...	...	...	...	...	...	...	...	...	...	...	...	...	...	...	...	...	...

Ⓑ May 29 - Sept. 3. ⑤⑦ Sept. 4 - Dec. 10 (also Oct. 24–27).

City Night Line LUPUS / PICTOR – 🛏 1, 2 cl., ▬ 2 cl., (2) 🍷 Roma / Venezia - Innsbruck - München. Special fares apply (Table **70**).

DACIA – 🛏 1, 2 cl., ▬ 2 cl., (2) ✕ Bucuresti - Budapest - Wien.

(12) 🍷 Innsbruck - Lindau 🏛 - Stuttgart - Köln - Munster (Table **70**).

(12) ✕ Wien - Nürnberg - Frankfurt - Köln - Dortmund.

GROSSGLOCKNER – ⑥ July 9 - Sept. 3: (12) Zell am See - Wörgl - Kufstein 🏛 - München.

GROSSGLOCKNER – ⑦ July 3 - Sept. 4: (12) Schwarzach St Veit - Zell am See - Wörgl - Kufstein 🏛 - München.

KÁLMÁN IMRE – 🛏 1, 2 cl., ▬ 2 cl., (2) Budapest - Wien - München.

LISINSKI – 🛏 1, 2 cl., ▬ 2 cl., (2) Zagreb - Villach - Salzburg - München (Table **62**).

Q – Mar. 28 - Oct. 4.

c – ①–⑥.

e – On ⑥ arrive at Köln **Messe / Deutz** at 1714, see note **x**.

f – 1158 Aug. 6 - Sept. 3.

g – From Graz (Table **68**).

h – Also Aug. 15.

w – Not Nov. 11.

x – Köln **Messe / Deutz** (Table **910**). Connections to Köln Hbf depart every 2 - 5 minutes, journey time 2 - 3 minutes.

⊖ – Via Köln - Frankfurt high speed line.

▲ – 🏛 is at Hegyeshalom.

◧ – 🏛 is at Lindau.

⇌ – *Thalys* high-speed train. Ⓡ 🍷. Special fares payable. Valid May 30 - Dec. 10.

🚌 – DB / ČD *ExpressBus*. Ⓡ 🍷. Rail tickets valid. 1st and 2nd class. 🏛 is Waidhaus (Germany). Timings subject to alteration (Table **57**).

☆ – Eurostar train. Ⓡ, ✕ in Business Premier and Standard Premier, 🍷 in Standard. Special fares payable. Minimum check-in time 30 minutes. Not available for London - Ebbsfleet - Ashford or v.v. journeys. Valid May 29 - Dec. 10.

RJ – ÖBB *Railjet* service. (business class), (first class), (economy class) ✕.

For explanation of standard symbols see page 4

22 AMSTERDAM - BERLIN

train type	IC	IC	IC	IC	IC	IC	IC	IC	IC	ICE	RE	RE	IC
train number	**245**	**141**	**143**	**145**	**147**	**149**	**241**	**241**	**241**	**645**			**243**
notes	①–⑥						⑥	⑧	⑦	**655**			⑦
								A	**q**				
Amsterdam Centraal ... d.	0502	0701	0901	1101	1301	1501	1701	1701	1701	...	...	...	1901
Hilversum ... d.	0526	0722	0922	1122	1322	1522	1722	1722	1722	...	...	...	1922
Amersfoort ... d.	0538	0737	0937	1137	1337	1537	1737	1737	1737	...	...	...	1937
Apeldoorn ... d.	0603	0803	1003	1203	1403	1603	1803	1803	1803	...	...	...	2003
Deventer ... d.	0616	0819	1019	1219	1419	1619	1819	1819	1819	...	...	...	2019
Almelo ... d.	0641	0845	1045	1245	1445	1645	1845	1845	1845	...	...	...	2045
Hengelo ... d.	0654	0859	1059	1259	1459	1659	1859	1859	1859	...	...	...	2059
Bad Bentheim 🛃 ... a.	0711	0916	1116	1316	1516	1716	1916	1916	1916	...	1957	...	2116
Rheine ... a.	0733	0940	1140	1340	1540	1740	...	1940	1940	...	2012	...	2140
Osnabrück Hbf ... a.	0803	1006	1206	1406	1606	1806	...	2006	2006	...	2046	2116	2206
Minden ... a.	0847	1047	1247	1447	1647	1847	...	2047	2047	...	...	2207	2250
Hannover Hbf ... a.	0918	1118	1318	1518	1718	1918	...	2118	2118	2131	...	2251	2326
Wolfsburg ... a.	0953	1153	1353	1553	1753	1953	...	...	2153	|	...	...	...
Stendal ... a.	1025	1225	1425	1625	1825	2025	...	...	2225	|	...	...	...
Berlin Hauptbahnhof ... a.	1122	1322	1522	1722	1922	2122	...	...	2317	2306	...	...	...
Berlin Ostbahnhof ... a.	1134	1334	1534	1734	1934	2134	...	...	2329	...	...	...	...

train type	IC	ICE	IC	RE	RE	IC	IC	IC	IC	IC	IC	IC	IC
train number	**244**	**646**	**242**			**240**	**240**	**240**	**148**	**146**	**144**	**142**	**140**
notes	①	①–⑤	①–⑥			①–⑥	①–⑥	⑦					
		p					**B**						
Berlin Ostbahnhof ... d.	...	...	...	...	...	0623	...	...	0823	1023	1223	1423	1623
Berlin Hauptbahnhof ... d.	...	0430	...	...	...	0634	...	...	0834	1034	1234	1434	1634
Stendal ... d.	...	0516	...	...	...	0734	...	...	0934	1134	1334	1534	1734
Wolfsburg ... d.	...	0548	...	...	...	0804	...	...	1004	1204	1404	1604	1804
Hannover Hbf ... d.	...	0618	0640	0709	...	0840	0840	...	1040	1240	1440	1640	1840
Minden ... d.	...	...	0712	0752	...	0912	0912	...	1112	1312	1512	1712	1912
Osnabrück Hbf ... d.	...	...	0753	0841	0914	0953	0953	...	1153	1353	1553	1753	1953
Rheine ... d.	...	...	0821	...	0948	1021	1021	...	1221	1421	1621	1821	2021
Bad Bentheim 🛃 ... d.	0744	...	0844	...	1003	1044	1044	1044	1244	1444	1644	1844	2044
Hengelo ... a.	0801	...	0901	...	...	1101	1101	1101	1301	1501	1701	1901	2101
Almelo ... a.	0814	...	0914	...	...	1114	1114	1114	1314	1514	1714	1914	2114
Deventer ... a.	0842	...	0942	...	...	1142	1142	1142	1342	1542	1742	1942	2142
Apeldoorn ... a.	0859	...	0959	...	...	1159	1159	1159	1359	1559	1759	1959	2159
Amersfoort ... a.	0924	...	1024	...	...	1224	1224	1224	1424	1624	1824	2024	2224
Hilversum ... a.	0938	...	1038	...	...	1238	1238	1238	1438	1638	1838	2038	2238
Amsterdam Centraal ... a.	1000	...	1100	...	...	1300	1300	1300	1500	1700	1900	2100	2300

A – ⑧ (daily Mar. 13 - Nov. 4).
B – ①–⑥ (daily Mar. 14 - Nov. 5).
p – Not Oct. 3.
q – Also Oct. 3; not Oct. 2.

24 PARIS - MOSKVA

train number	24 *JI*	24 *JI*
train number	**453**	**453**
notes	**A P**	**A Q**
	③⑥⑦	③⑥⑦
Paris Est ... d.	1858	1858
Épernay ... d.	2020	2020
Strasbourg ... d.	2325	2325
Karlsruhe Hbf ... d.	0045	0045
Frankfurt (Main) Süd ... d.	0156	0156
Erfurt Hbf ... d.	0442	0442
Berlin Hbf ... a.	0708	0708
Berlin Hbf ... d.	0713	0713
Berlin Lichtenberg ... a.	0729	0729
Berlin Lichtenberg ... d.	0750	0750
Frankfurt (Oder) 🛃 ... d.	0855	0855
Rzepin ... d.	0919	0919
Poznań Gł. ... d.	1045	1045
Warszawa Centralna ... d.	1340	1340
Warszawa Wschodnia ... a.	1347	1347
Warszawa Wschodnia ... d.	1417	1417
Terespol ... a.	1617	1617
Terespol 🛃 ... d.	1704	1704
Brest Tsentralny 🛃 ... a.	1950	1950
Brest Tsentralny ... d.	2107	2200
Baranavichy ... a.	2305	0001
Minsk ... a.	0050	0139
Orsha Tsentralnaya § ... a.	0318	0406
Smolensk Tsentralny § ... a.	0446	0535
Vyazma ... a.	0634	0723
Moskva Belorusskaya ... a.	0921	1010

train number	23 *JI*	23 *JI*
train number	**452**	**452**
notes	**B P**	**B Q**
	①④⑤	①④⑤
Moskva Belorusskaya ... d.	2111	2215
Vyazma ... d.	2356	0100
Smolensk Tsentralny § ... d.	0151	0255
Orsha Tsentralnaya § ... d.	0317	0417
Minsk ... d.	0556	0657
Baranavichy ... d.	0752	0856
Brest Tsentralny ... a.	0950	1052
Brest Tsentralny 🛃 ... d.	1303	1303
Terespol 🛃 ... a.	1121	1121
Terespol ... d.	1201	1201
Warszawa Wschodnia ... a.	1353	1353
Warszawa Wschodnia ... d.	1423	1423
Warszawa Centralna ... d.	1435	1435
Poznań Gł. ... d.	1727	1727
Rzepin ... d.	1902	1902
Frankfurt (Oder) 🛃 ... a.	1924	1924
Berlin Lichtenberg ... a.	2022	2022
Berlin Lichtenberg ... d.	2046	2046
Berlin Hbf ... a.	2104	2104
Berlin Hbf ... d.	2109	2109
Erfurt ... d.	2324	2324
Frankfurt (Main) Süd ... a.	0138	0138
Karlsruhe ... a.	0304	0304
Strasbourg ... a.	0449	0449
Épernay ... a.	0828	0828
Paris Nord ... a.	0933	0933

25 NICE - MOSKVA

train number	18 *BJ*	18 *BJ*	
notes	⑥	⑥	
notes	**D P**	**D Q**	
Nice ... d.	2147	2147	⑥
Monaco-Monte Carlo ... d.	2204	2204	:
Menton ... d.	2214	2214	:
Ventimiglia 🛃 ... d.	2246	2246	:
Bordighera ... d.	2255	2255	:
San Remo ... d.	2305	2305	:
Genova Piazza Principe ... d.	0115	0115	⑦
Milano Rogoredo ... d.	0249	0249	:
Verona ... d.	0436	0436	:
Bolzano / Bozen ... d.	0627	0627	:
Brennero / Brenner 🛃 ... d.	0837	0837	:
Innsbruck Hbf ... d.	0938	0938	:
Zell am See ... d.	1156	1156	:
Salzburg Hbf ... d.	|	|	:
Linz Hbf ... d.	1506	1506	:
Wien Hbf ... d.	1641	1641	:
Břeclav 🛃 ... d.	1810	1810	:
Bohumín 🛃 ... d.	2025	2025	:
Zebrzydowice 🛃 ... d.	2102	2102	:
Katowice ... d.	2208	2208	①
Warszawa Centralna ... a.	0051	0051	:
Warszawa Wschodnia ... a.	0103	0103	:
Warszawa Wschodnia ... d.	0202	0202	:
Terespol ... a.	0410	0410	:
Terespol 🛃 ... d.	0455	0455	:
Brest Tsentralny 🛃 ... a.	0741	0741	:
Brest Tsentralny ... d.	0840	0940	:
Baranavichy ... a.	|	|	:
Minsk ... a.	1221	1315	:
Orsha Tsentralnaya § ... a.	1500	1558	:
Smolensk Tsentralny § ... a.	1632	1730	:
Vyazma ... a.	1840	1938	:
Moskva Belorusskaya ... a.	2130	2230	:

train number	17 *BJ*	17 *BJ*
notes	④	④
notes	**C P**	**C Q**
Moskva Belorusskaya ... d.	1018	1118
Vyazma ... d.	1333	1447
Smolensk Tsentralny § ... d.	1526	1638
Orsha Tsentralnaya § ... d.	1703	1803
Minsk ... d.	1933	2035
Baranavichy ... d.	|	|
Brest Tsentralny ... a.	2310	0010
Brest Tsentralny 🛃 ... d.	2315	0015
Terespol 🛃 ... a.	0033	0033
Terespol ... d.	0113	0113
Warszawa Wschodnia ... a.	0317	0317
Warszawa Wschodnia ... d.	0400	0400
Warszawa Centralna ... d.	0412	0412
Katowice ... d.	0657	0657
Zebrzydowice 🛃 ... d.	0813	0813
Bohumín 🛃 ... d.	0833	0833
Břeclav 🛃 ... d.	1118	1118
Wien Hbf ... d.	1241	1241
Linz Hbf ... d.	1426	1426
Salzburg Hbf ... d.	|	|
Zell am See ... d.	1840	1840
Innsbruck Hbf ... d.	2144	2144
Brennero / Brenner 🛃 ... d.	2243	2243
Bolzano / Bozen ... d.	2346	2346
Verona ... d.	0136	0136
Milano Rogoredo ... d.	0257	0257
Genova Piazza Principe ... d.	0454	0454
San Remo ... d.	0659	0659
Bordighera ... d.	0712	0712
Ventimiglia 🛃 ... d.	0751	0751
Menton ... a.	0803	0803
Monaco-Monte Carlo ... a.	0813	0813
Nice ... a.	0830	0830

Notes for tables 24 and 25

A – TRANSEUROPEAN EXPRESS ③⑥⑦: 🛏 1, 2 cl. Paris (**453**) - Berlin - Brest (**24** *JI*) - Moskva. ✕ (PKP) Paris - Warszawa. ✕ (RZD) Brest - Moskva.

B – TRANSEUROPEAN EXPRESS ①④⑤: 🛏 1, 2 cl. Moskva (**23** *JI*) - Brest (**452**) - Berlin - Paris. ✕ (RZD) Moskva - Brest. ✕ (PKP) Warszawa - Paris.

C – ④: 🛏 1 cl. (lux), 🛏 1, 2 cl. Moskva - Nice. ✕ (RZD) Moskva - Brest and ✕ (PKP) Warszawa - Nice (journey two nights).

D – ⑥: 🛏 1 cl. (lux), 🛏 1, 2 cl. Nice - Moskva. ✕ (PKP) Nice - Warszawa and ✕ (RZD) Brest - Moskva (journey two nights).

P – Mar. 27 - Oct. 29.

Q – Oct. 30 - Dec. 10.

✕ (PKP) – Polish railways restaurant car.

✕ (RZD) – Russian railways restaurant car.

§ – 🛃: Osinovka (BY) / Krasnoye (R

AMSTERDAM - FRANKFURT, WIEN and MÜNCHEN

train type		ICE	ICE	ICE		ICE	ICE	ICE	🚌		ICE	ICE	ICE	ICE	🚌		ICE	ICE	ICE		ICE	ICE	ICE		ICE	ICE
train number		121	621	515		105	595	27	42014		123	629	519	229	42018		125	723	611		127	727	613		129	615
notes	①–⑤	①–⑥				D			Ⓡ 🍷 2						Ⓡ 🍷 2			Ⓑ			V	Ⓑ				
erdam Centraal d.	...	0635	...	...	...	0805	...	...	...	...	1035	...	...	...	...	...	1235	...	...	...	1435	...	...	...	1635	...
terdam Centraal d.	0605	|	...	...	0735	|	...	...	...	1005	|	...	...	...	...	1205	|	...	...	1405	|	...	...	1605	|	...
ht Centraal d.	0643	0702	...	...	0813	0832	...	...	...	1043	1102	...	...	...	...	1243	1302	...	...	1443	1502	...	...	1643	1702	...
em ◐ d.	...	0737	...	...	...	0907	...	...	...	...	1137	...	...	...	...	...	1337	...	...	...	1537	...	...	...	1737	...
hausen Hbf ◐ d.	...	0826	...	...	...	0958	...	...	...	...	1224	...	...	...	...	...	1424	...	...	...	1626	...	...	...	1824	...
urg Hbf d.	...	0834	...	...	...	1006	...	...	...	...	1232	...	...	...	...	...	1432	...	...	...	1638	...	...	...	1832	...
eldorf Hbf d.	...	0848	...	...	...	1020	...	...	...	...	1246	...	...	...	...	...	1446	...	...	...	1653	...	...	...	1846	...
Hbf a.	...	0912	...	...	...	1045	...	...	...	...	1312	...	...	...	...	...	1512	...	...	...	1718	...	...	...	1912	...
Hbf d.	...	0927	...	...	...	1055	...	...	...	...	1328	...	...	...	...	...	1528	...	...	...	1728	...	...	...	1920	...
Hbf d.	...	|	...	...	...	|	...	...	...	...	|	...	...	...	...	...	|	...	...	...	|	...	...	...	|	...
nz d.	...	⊖	...	...	...	⊖	...	...	...	...	⊖	...	...	...	...	...	⊖	...	...	...	⊖	...	...	...	⊖	...
z d.	...	|	...	...	...	|	...	...	...	...	|	...	...	...	...	...	|	...	...	...	|	...	...	...	|	...
nkfurt Flughafen ✈ d.	...	1018	...	1053	...	1150	...	1202	...	...	1416	...	1453	...	...	...	1616	...	1653	...	1818	...	1853	...	2016	2053
nkfurt (Main) Hbf a.	...	1030	1054	|	...	|	...	1213	...	...	1430	1454	|	1620	...	...	1630	1654	|	...	1830	1854	|	...	2030	|
rzburg a.	...	...	1202	|	...	|	...	1331	...	...	...	1602	|	1731	...	...	...	1802	|	...	...	2002	|	...	...	|
rnberg a.	...	...	1259	|	...	|	...	1427	1540	...	...	1659	|	1827	1840	...	...	1859	|	...	...	2059	|	...	...	|
gensburg a.	...	...	|	|	...	|	...	1525	|	...	...	|	|	1925	|	...	...	|	|	...	...	|	|	...	...	|
Praha hlavní a.	...	...	|	|	...	|	...	|	1918	...	...	|	|	|	2230	...	...	|	|	...	...	|	|	...	...	|
heim a.	...	...	|	1123	...	1223	1230	|	...	...	...	|	1523	|	...	...	...	|	1723	...	...	|	1923	...	...	2123
gart a.	...	...	|	1208	...	...	1308	|	...	...	...	|	1608	|	...	...	...	|	1808	...	...	|	2008	...	...	2208
a.	...	...	|	1307	...	...	1407	|	...	...	...	|	1707	|	...	...	...	|	1907	...	...	|	2107	...	...	2307
ourg a.	...	...	|	1353	...	...	1453	|	...	...	...	|	1753	|	...	...	...	|	1953	...	...	|	2153	...	...	2353
chen Hbf a.	...	...	1404	1427	...	...	1528	|	...	...	...	1804	1827	|	...	...	...	2004	2027	...	...	2205	2226	...	...	0027
ssau 🏛 a.	...	...	...	...	...	...	...	1633	...	...	...	...	...	2033	...	...	...	...	...	...	...	...	...	...	...	...
z a.	...	...	...	...	...	...	...	1742	...	...	...	...	...	2143	...	...	...	...	...	...	...	...	...	...	...	...
en Hbf a.	...	...	...	...	...	...	...	1908	...	...	...	...	...	2308	...	...	...	...	...	...	...	...	...	...	...	...

train type		ICE	EN	CNL	CNL		CNL	RJ		
train number		221	421	40470	40447		419	61		
notes				60470	61447					
			A	P	K		B			
erdam Centraal d.	...	1835	...	...	...	...	2031	...	...	...
tterdam Centraal d.	1805	|	...	...	...	1950	|	...	...	...
ht Centraal d.	1843	1902	...	...	...	2028	2100	...	...	...
em ◐ d.	...	1937	...	...	...	...	2133	...	...	...
hausen Hbf ◐ d.	...	2026	...	...	...	...	|	...	...	...
burg Hbf d.	...	2034	...	...	2353x	...	2234	...	...	...
eldorf Hbf d.	...	2048	2054	...	2337x	...	2249	...	...	...
Hbf a.	...	2112	2118	...	|	...	2315	...	...	...
Hbf d.	...	2128	2121	...	2313x	...	2318	...	...	...
Hbf d.	...	|	2143	...	|	...	2339	...	...	...
enz d.	...	⊖	2217	...	|	...	0017	...	...	...
z d.	...	|	2317	...	|	...	0113	...	...	...
ankfurt Flughafen ✈ d.	...	2218	2353	...	|	...	0131	...	...	...
ankfurt (Main) Hbf a.	...	2230	0004k	0054k	|	...	0142	...	...	...
ürzburg a.	...	...	|	|	|	...	|	...	...	...
rnberg a.	...	...	|	|	|	...	|	...	...	...
gensburg a.	...	...	|	|	|	...	|	...	...	...
Praha hlavní a.	...	...	|	0928	1128	...	|	...	...	...
nheim a.	...	...	|	...	...	...	|	...	...	...
gart a.	...	...	|	...	...	...	0421	...	...	...
a.	...	...	|	...	...	...	0540	...	...	...
burg a.	...	...	|	...	...	...	0633	...	...	...
chen Hbf a.	...	...	|	...	...	...	0710	0733	...	...
nnsbruck Hbf a.	...	...	|	...	...	...	...	|	...	...
ssau 🏛 a.	...	...	0518	...	...	...	...	|	...	...
z a.	...	...	0633	...	...	...	...	1012	...	...
en Hbf a.	...	...	0820	...	...	...	...	1130	...	...

train type	RJ	CNL		CNL	CNL		EN	ICE	ICE		
train number	68	418		40458	458		420	616	220		
notes				61458	60458						
		C		J	Q		A				
Wien Hbf d.	1830	...	...	...	...	...	2139	...	...	...	...
Linz d.	1948	...	...	...	...	...	2319	...	...	...	...
Passau 🏛 d.	|	...	...	...	...	...	0030	...	...	...	...
Innsbruck Hbf d.	|	...	...	...	...	...	|	...	...	...	...
München Hbf d.	2226	2250	...	...	...	...	|	0325	...	...	...
Augsburg d.	...	2320	...	...	...	...	|	0357	...	...	...
Ulm d.	...	0010	...	...	...	...	|	0440	...	...	...
Stuttgart d.	...	0135	...	...	...	...	|	0551	...	...	...
Mannheim d.	...	|	...	...	...	...	|	0636	...	...	...
Praha hlavní d.	...	|	...	1827	1827	...	|	|	...	...	...
Regensburg d.	...	|	...	|	|	...	|	|	...	...	...
Nürnberg d.	...	|	...	|	|	...	|	|	...	...	...
Würzburg d.	...	|	...	|	|	...	|	|	...	...	...
Frankfurt (Main) Hbf d.	...	0345	...	|	0359k	...	0527k	|	0729	...	...
Frankfurt Flughafen ✈ d.	...	0356a	...	|	...	...	0536a	0709	0745	...	...
Mainz a.	...	0418	...	|	...	...	0602	|	|	...	...
Koblenz a.	...	0511	...	|	...	...	0705	⊖	⊖	...	...
Bonn Hbf a.	...	0548	...	|	...	...	|	|	|	...	...
Köln Hbf a.	...	0615	...	0656z	...	...	0815	0805	0834	...	...
Köln Hbf d.	...	0626	...	|	...	...	0817	...	0846	...	...
Düsseldorf Hbf a.	...	0651	...	0631z	...	...	0841	...	0913	...	...
Duisburg Hbf a.	...	0710	...	0616z	...	...	...	...	0926	...	...
Oberhausen Hbf ◐ a.	...	0719	...	...	...	...	...	...	0934	...	...
Arnhem ◐ a.	...	0827	...	...	...	...	...	...	1031	...	...
Utrecht Centraal a.	...	0903	0917	...	...	0917	...	...	1103	1117	...
Rotterdam Centraal a.	...	|	0955	...	...	0955	...	...	|	1155	...
Amsterdam Centraal a.	...	0934	...	...	...	...	...	...	1129	...	...

train type	ICE	ICE	ICE		ICE	ICE	ICE	IC	ICE	ICE	ICE	EC	ICE	ICE	ICE	ICE		🚌	ICE	ICE	ICE	ICE	🚌	ICE	ICE	
train number	614	820	128		612	726	126	2024	610	722	124	8	28	596	626	122		42009	26	1090	104	514	42011	620	120	
notes		①–⑥				①–⑥	V			1122					826			Ⓡ 🍷 2		594	D		Ⓡ 🍷 2		Ⓑ	
en Hbf d.	...	...	...	...	...	...	...	...	...	...	...	...	0852	...	...	...	...	...	1052	...	...	...	...	...	...	...
z d.	...	...	...	...	...	...	...	...	...	...	...	...	1016	...	...	...	...	...	1216	...	...	...	...	...	...	...
ssau 🏛 d.	...	...	...	...	...	...	...	0718	...	...	...	...	1124	...	...	...	...	...	1324	...	...	...	...	...	...	...
chen Hbf d.	0527	0552	...	...	0728	0755	...	|	0928	0955	...	...	|	1228	1255	...	...	...	|	1428	...	1528	...	1555	...	...
burg d.	0602	|	...	...	0803	|	...	|	1003	|	...	...	|	1303	|	...	...	...	|	1503	...	1603	...	|	...	...
d.	0651	|	...	...	0851	|	...	|	1051	|	...	...	|	1351	|	...	...	...	|	1551	...	1651	...	|	...	...
gart d.	0751	|	...	...	0951	|	...	|	1151	|	...	...	|	1451	|	...	...	...	|	1651	...	1751	...	|	...	...
nheim d.	0836	|	...	...	1036	|	...	|	1236	|	...	1439	|	1532	|	...	...	...	|	1729	1736	1836	...	|	...	...
Praha hlavní d.	|	|	...	...	|	|	...	|	|	|	...	|	|	|	|	...	...	1042	|	...	|	|	1242	|	...	...
egensburg d.	|	|	...	...	|	|	...	0827	|	|	...	|	1228	|	|	...	...	|	1428	...	|	|	|	|	...	...
rnberg d.	|	0700	...	...	|	0900	...	0928	|	1100	...	|	1328	|	1400	...	...	1420	1528	...	|	|	1620	1700	...	...
ürzburg d.	|	0755	...	...	|	0955	...	1027	|	1155	...	|	1427	|	1455	...	...	...	1627	...	|	|	...	1755	...	...
ankfurt (Main) Hbf d.	|	0904	0927	...	|	1104	1129	1142	|	1304	1329	|	1536	1608	1604	1629	...	...	1745	...	|	|	...	1904	1929	...
ankfurt Flughafen ✈ a.	0906	...	0943	...	1106	...	1140	1158	1306	...	1343	|	...	...	...	1643	...	...	1756	...	1809	1906	...	...	1940	...
z a.	...	...	|	...	...	...	|	1220	...	...	|	1518	...	...	...	|	...	...	...	...	|		...	...	|	...
enz a.	...	...	⊖	...	...	...	⊖	1313	...	...	⊖	1611	...	...	...	⊖	...	...	...	...	⊖	...	...	...	⊖	...
Hbf a.	...	...	|	...	...	...	|	1344	...	...	|	1642	...	...	...	|	...	...	...	...	|	...	...	...	|	...
Hbf a.	...	...	1032	...	...	...	1232	1405	...	...	1432	1705	...	...	...	1739	...	...	...	...	1905	...	...	...	2032	...
Hbf d.	...	...	1042	...	...	...	1241		...	...	1446		...	...	...	1746	...	...	...	...	1917	...	...	...	2042	...
seldorf Hbf a.	...	...	1114	...	...	...	1305	...	...	...	1514	...	...	...	...	1814	...	...	...	...	1940	...	...	...	2105	...
burg Hbf a.	...	...	1128	...	...	...	1322	...	...	...	1529	...	...	...	...	1826	...	...	...	...	1953	...	...	...	2122	...
hausen Hbf ◐ a.	...	...	1135	...	...	...	1332	...	...	...	1536	...	...	...	...	1834	...	...	...	...	2000	...	...	...	2132	...
em ◐ a.	...	...	1229	...	...	...	1429	...	...	...	1629	...	...	...	...	1929	...	...	...	...	2053	...	...	...	2229	...
cht Centraal a.	...	...	1300	1317	...	...	1500	1517	...	...	1701	1717	...	...	...	2000	2017	...	...	...	2128	2147	...	...	2300	...
tterdam Centraal a.	...	...	|	1355	...	...	|	1555	...	...	|	1755	...	...	...	|	2055	...	...	...	|	2225	...	...	|	...
sterdam Centraal a.	...	...	1327	...	...	...	1527	...	...	...	1727	...	...	...	...	2027	...	...	...	...	2155	...	...	...	2327	...

🛏 1, 2 cl., 🛌 2 cl. (4, 6 berth), (2) 🍷: Düsseldorf - Köln - Frankfurt - Passau 🏛 - Wien and v.v. Ⓡ Special fares apply. For international journeys only.

City Night Line POLLUX – 🛏 1, 2 cl., 🛌 2 cl. 🍷 (*CNL* **419** Ⓡ) Amsterdam - Köln - München; (2) (*IC* **60419**) Amsterdam - Köln - München. Special fares apply.

City Night Line POLLUX – 🛏 1, 2 cl., 🛌 2 cl. 🍷 (*CNL* **418** Ⓡ) München - Köln - Amsterdam; (2) (*IC* **60418**) München - Köln - Amsterdam. Special fares apply.

(12) 🍷 Amsterdam - Mannheim - Basel and v.v. (Table **73**).

City Night Line KOPERNIKUS – 🛏 1, 2 cl., 🛌 2 cl., 🍷 (*CNL* **40458** Ⓡ) Praha - Köln; (2) (*IC* **61458**) Praha - Köln. Special fares apply.

City Night Line KOPERNIKUS – 🛏 1, 2 cl., 🛌 2 cl., 🍷 (*CNL* **40447** Ⓡ) Köln - Praha; (2) (*IC* **61447**) Köln - Praha. Special fares apply.

City Night Line CANOPUS – 🛏 1, 2 cl., 🛌 2 cl. 🍷 (*CNL* **40470** Ⓡ) Zürich - Basel - Frankfurt (Main) **Süd** - Děčín 🏛 - Praha; (2) (*IC* **60470**) Zürich - Basel - Frankfurt (Main) **Süd** - Děčín 🏛 - Praha. Special fares apply.

City Night Line CANOPUS – 🛏 1, 2 cl., 🛌 2 cl. 🍷 (*CNL* **458** Ⓡ) Praha - Děčín 🏛 - Frankfurt (Main) **Süd** - Basel - Zürich; (2) (*IC* **60458**) Praha - Děčín 🏛 - Frankfurt (Main) **Süd** - Basel - Zürich. Special fares apply.

V – ⑤ (daily Mar. 18 - Oct. 30).

a – Arrival time.
k – Frankfurt (Main) **Süd**.
x – Train calls in the following order: Köln - Düsseldorf - Duisburg.
z – Train calls in the following order: Duisburg - Düsseldorf - Köln.

🚌 – **DB / ČD** *ExpressBus*. Ⓡ 🍷. Rail tickets valid. 2nd class only. (Table **76**).
RJ – ÖBB *Railjet* service. (1) (business class), (1) (firstclass), (2) (economy class) ✕.
◐ – 🏛 between Arnhem and Oberhausen is Emmerich.
⊖ – Via Köln - Frankfurt high speed line.

30 PARIS - FRANKFURT - BERLIN, LEIPZIG, DRESDEN and PRAHA

Alternative services Paris - Frankfurt are available via Brussels (Table **21**). Alternative services Paris - Berlin are available via Brussels (Table **20**).

Service from July 3. Service until July 2 is on page 68.

train type	TGV	ICE	ICE	EC	ICE	TGV	ICE	ICE	EC	ICE		ICE	ICE	ICE	ICE	ICE	ICE	ICE	ICE	ICE	ICE	ICE		ICE	CNL	CNL	
train number	9561	372	1559	177	623	9551	370	1651	179	627		9553	276	1655	725	9563	274	1657	729	9555	1659	1029		9557 9559	470	459	
notes	[R]★	🍷	🍷	🍴	🍷	[R]★	🍷	🍷	🍴	🍷		[R]★	🍷	🍷	🍷	[R]★	🍷	🍷	🍷	[R]★	🍷	🍷		[R]★			
notes	①–⑥																			Ⓑ	Ⓑ						
		J		G					D																C	B	
Paris Est d.	0720	...	...	...	...	0906	...	...	...	...	...	1301	...	...	...	1520	...	...	...	1710	...	...	...	1906	...	...	...
Strasbourg d.	0913	...	...	...	...	|	...	...	...	...	...	|	...	...	...	1713	...	...	...	|	...	...	...	|	...	...	...
Forbach 🏛 d.	◧	...	...	...	...	1047	...	...	...	...	...	|	...	...	...	◧	...	...	...	|	...	...	...	2049	...	...	...
Saarbrücken a.	|	...	...	...	...	1055	...	...	...	...	...	1457	...	...	...	|	...	...	...	1857	...	...	...	2057	...	...	...
Kaiserlautern a.	|	...	...	...	...	1133	...	...	...	...	...	1535	...	...	...	|	...	...	...	1935	...	...	...	2135	...	...	...
Karlsruhe Hbf d.	0955	...	...	...	...	|	...	...	...	...	...	|	...	...	...	1752	...	...	...	|	...	...	...	|	...	...	...
Mannheim a.	1018	...	...	...	...	1215	...	...	...	...	...	1617	...	...	...	1818	...	...	...	2017	...	...	...	2217	0005	0005	...
Frankfurt (Main) Hbf d.	1058x	1113	1119	...	1154	1258z	1313	1319	...	1354	...	1658z	1713	1720	1754	1858x	1913	1919	1954	2058z	2119	2218	...	2258z	0054f	0054f	...
Würzburg a.	...	|	|	...	1303	...	|	|	...	1502	...	...	|	|	1902	...	|	|	2102	...	|	2341	...	...	|	|	...
Nürnberg a.	...	|	|	...	1403	...	|	|	...	1559	...	...	|	|	1959	...	|	|	2159	...	|	0037	...	...	|	|	...
Fulda a.	...	1209	1212	...	...	...	1409	1412	...	...	...	...	1809	1812	...	...	2009	2012	...	...	2212	...	...	...	|	|	...
Erfurt a.	...	|	1337	...	...	...	|	1537	...	...	...	...	|	1937	...	...	|	2137	...	...	2341	...	...	...	0337	0337	...
Leipzig Hbf a.	...	|	1422	...	...	...	|	1622	...	...	...	...	|	2022	...	...	|	2222	...	...	0026r	...	...	...	0450	0450	...
Dresden Hbf a.	...	|	1539	1707	...	...	|	1737	1907	...	...	...	|	2137	...	...	|	2339t	...	...	...	...	...	...	|	0706	...
Děčín (🏛 = Schöna) a.	...	|	...	1753	...	...	|	...	1953	...	...	...	|	...	...	...	|	...	...	...	...	...	...	...	|	0753	...
Praha Holešovice a.	...	|	...	1918	...	...	|	...	2118	...	...	...	|	...	...	...	|	...	...	...	...	...	...	...	|	0918	...
Praha hlavní a.	...	|	...	1928	...	...	|	...	2128	...	...	...	|	...	...	...	|	...	...	...	...	...	...	...	|	0928	...
Kassel Wilhelmshöhe a.	...	1241	...	...	...	...	1441	...	...	...	...	...	1841	...	...	...	2041	...	...	...	...	...	...	...	|	...	...
Göttingen a.	...	1301	...	...	...	...	1501	...	...	...	...	...	1901	...	...	...	2101	...	...	...	...	...	...	...	|	...	...
Braunschweig a.	...	1357	...	...	...	...	1557	...	...	...	...	...	1957	...	...	...	2157	...	...	...	...	...	...	...	|	...	...
Wolfsburg a.	...	1415	...	...	...	...	1615	...	...	...	...	...	2015	...	...	...	2215	...	...	...	...	...	...	...	|	...	...
Berlin Hauptbahnhof a.	...	1528	...	...	...	...	1728	...	...	...	...	...	2128	...	...	...	2326	...	...	...	...	...	...	...	0723	...	...

train type	CNL	CNL	ICE	ICE	ICE	ICE	ICE	ICE	ICE	ICE	ICE	ICE	ICE	ICE	ICE	ICE	TGV	TGV	ICE	ICE	EC	ICE	TGV	ICE	EC	ICE	ICE
train number	458	1258	9558	9568	9586	822	1656	275	9566	9556	277	9554	9554	724	1652	279	9552	9552	626	373	176	1558	9560	622	174	1556	375
notes			[R]★	[R]★	[R]★	🍷	🍷	🍷	[R]★	[R]★	🍷	[R]★	[R]★	🍷	🍷	🍷	[R]★	[R]★	🍷	🍷	🍴	🍷	[R]★	🍷	🍴	🍷	🍷
notes			①–⑤	Ⓑ	⑥	①–⑥	①–⑥	①–⑤	⑥	①–⑤		⑥	⑦				Ⓑ	⑥									
	B	C						J												J	G		A		E		
Berlin Hauptbahnhof d.	...	2150	...	...	...	...	...	0432	...	...	0631	...	...	...	...	0831	...	...	...	1231	...	...	...	...	...	...	1431
Wolfsburg d.	...	|	...	...	...	...	...	0540	...	...	0740	...	...	...	...	0940	...	...	...	1340	...	...	...	...	...	...	1540
Braunschweig d.	...	|	...	...	...	...	...	0558	...	...	0758	...	...	...	...	0958	...	...	...	1358	...	...	...	...	...	...	1558
Göttingen d.	...	|	...	...	...	...	...	0655	...	...	0855	...	...	...	...	1055	...	...	...	1455	...	...	...	...	...	...	1655
Kassel Wilhelmshöhe d.	...	|	...	...	...	...	...	0716	...	...	0916	...	...	...	...	1116	...	...	...	1516	...	...	...	...	...	...	1716
Praha hlavní d.	1827	|	...	...	...	...	...	|	...	...	|	...	...	...	...	|	...	...	...	|	0827	...	...	...	1027	..	|
Praha Holešovice d.	1836	|	...	...	...	...	...	|	...	...	|	...	...	...	...	|	...	...	...	|	0836	...	...	...	1036	...	|
Děčín (🏛 = Schöna) d.	2000	|	...	...	...	...	...	|	...	...	|	...	...	...	...	|	...	...	...	|	1000	...	...	...	1200	...	|
Dresden Hbf d.	2054	|	...	...	...	...	...	|	...	...	|	...	...	...	0820	|	...	...	...	|	1045	1220	...	...	1245	1420	|
Leipzig Hbf d.	0005	0005	...	...	...	...	0533	|	...	...	|	...	...	...	0933	|	...	...	...	|	...	1333	...	...	...	1533	|
Erfurt d.	0133	0133	...	...	...	...	0618	|	...	...	|	...	...	...	1018	|	...	...	...	|	...	1418	...	...	...	1618	|
Fulda d.	|	|	...	...	...	...	0744	0748	...	...	0948	...	...	...	1144	1148	...	...	...	1548	...	1544	...	...	...	1744	1748
Nürnberg d.	|	|	...	...	...	0600	|	|	...	...	|	...	...	1000	|	|	...	...	1400	|	...	|	...	1600	...	|	|
Würzburg d.	|	|	...	...	...	0655	|	|	...	...	|	...	...	1055	|	|	...	...	1455	|	...	|	...	1655	...	|	|
Frankfurt (Main) Hbf d.	0402f	0402f	0558¶	0658§	0658¶	0804	0837	0844	0856§	0856¶	1044	1058¶	1058¶	1204	1237	1244	1258¶	1258¶	1604	1644	...	1637	1657	1804	...	1837	1844
Mannheim d.	0440	0440	0639	0739	0738	...	...	...	0940¶	0940	...	1142	1142	...	..	...	1340	1340	...	...	...	...	1740	...	...	...	...
Karlsruhe Hbf d.	...	...	|	0807	|	...	...	...	1006	|	...	|	|	...	...	...	|	|	...	...	...	...	1807	...	...	...	...
Kaiserlautern d.	...	...	0721	|	0822	...	...	...	|	1022	...	1230	1228	...	...	...	1422	1422	...	...	...	...	|	...	...	...	...
Saarbrücken d.	...	...	0800	|	0902	...	...	...	|	1101	...	1307	1307	...	...	...	1501	1501	...	...	...	...	|	...	...	...	...
Forbach 🏛 a.	...	...	0809	◧	0911	...	...	...	◧	|	...	|	1316	...	...	...	|	1510	...	...	...	...	◧	...	...	...	...
Strasbourg a.	...	...	|	0851	|	...	...	...	1051	|	...	|	|	...	...	...	|	|	...	...	...	...	1847	...	...	...	...
Paris Est a.	...	...	0951	1038	1053	...	...	...	1238	1251	...	1454	1458	...	...	...	1650	1658	...	...	...	...	2041	...	...	...	...

A – July 16 - Aug. 28 depart Frankfurt 1649, runs 17-27 minutes later, arrive Paris 2106.

B – *City Night Line* CANOPUS – 🛏 1,2 cl., ▬ 2 cl., [2] (reclining) 🍷 Zürich - Basel - Frankfurt - Děčín 🏛 - Praha and v.v. [R] Special fares apply.

C – *City Night Line* SIRIUS – 🛏 1,2 cl., 🛏 1,2 cl. (T4), ▬ 2 cl. (4,6 berth), [2] (reclining) 🍷 Zürich - Basel - Mannheim - Frankfurt - Berlin and v.v. [R] Special fares apply.

D – ALOIS NEGRELLI – [12] 🍴 Hamburg - Berlin - Dresden - Praha.

E – [12] 🍴 Praha - Dresden - Berlin - Hamburg.

G – JOHANNES BRAHMS – [12] 🍴 Praha - Dresden - Berlin - Hamburg and v.v.

J – [12] 🍷 Interlaken Ost - Basel - Mannheim - Berlin and v.v.

T – Runs as *ICE* **9566** on certain dates.

f – Frankfurt (Main) **Süd**.

r – ①⑥.

t – Not ⑥.

x – 26-35 minutes later July 16 - Aug. 28.

z – 18-21 minutes later July 16 - Aug. 28.

◧ – 🏛 is at Kehl.

★ – *Alleo* ICE / TGV service. A DB / SNCF jo[int] enterprise.

¶ – 15-21 minutes earlier July 16 - Aug. 28

§ – 29-31 minutes earlier July 16 - Aug. 28

31 LONDON - GENÈVE

For the full service Paris - Genève, see Table **341**. 90 minutes (including Eurostar check-in time of 30 minutes) has been allowed between Paris Nord and Paris Gare de Lyon. Additional Eurostar services are available, see Table **10**.

train type	☆	☆	TGV	☆	☆	☆	☆	TGV	TGV	☆	TGV	☆	TGV	☆	TGV	☆	TGV		☆	TGV	☆	T
train number	9002	9004	9773	9108	9110	9110	9114	5164	9750 9751	9018	9775	9022	9777	9028	9781	9132	5134 5119		9032	9785	9036	9
notes	⑥			①	①–⑤	⑥	①–⑤			Ⓑ			Ⓑ									
notes	r	g	♥	K	L		g	[R]	[R]		♥		♥	R	♥		[R]			♥		
London St Pancras **10** d.	0618	0701	...	0613	0650	0657	0804	...	...	1024	...	1131e	...	1331	...	1258	...	...	1422	...	1531	
Lille Europe d.	|	|	...	0958	0930	0926	1026	1043	...	|	...	|	...	|	...	1530	1554	...	|	...	|	
Paris Nord **10** a.	0947	1017	...	...	...	...	...	|	...	1347	...	1447	...	1647	...	...	|	...	1747	...	1847	
Paris Gare de Lyon d.	...	...	1211	...	...	...	...	|	...	...	1511	...	1611	...	1811	...	|	...	...	1911	...	2
Lyon Part Dieu a.	...	...	|	...	...	...	...	1400	1534	...	|	...	|	...	|	...	1900	2034	...	|	...	
Bellegarde a.	...	...	1457	...	...	...	...	...	1648	...	1747	...	1858	...	2058	...	...	2159	...	2151	...	2
Genève a.	...	...	1527	...	...	...	...	...	1716	...	1816	...	1927	...	2127	...	...	2232	...	2220	...	2

train type	TGV	☆	TGV	☆	☆	TGV	☆	TGV	☆	TGV	TGV	TGV	☆	TGV	☆		TGV	☆			
train number	9760	9023	9764	9031	9031	9768	9039	9770	9047	9756 9757	5192	9868	9161	9772	9055		9774	9059			
notes	⚒			⑦	①–⑥			①–⑤						Ⓒ			Ⓐ				
notes	♥		♥	q	g	♥	n	♥		[R]				♥			♥				
Genève d.	0614	...	0742	...	...	0942	...	1142	...	1242	...	...	...	1342	...	...	1442	...	...	...	...
Bellegarde d.	0643	...	0810	...	...	1010	...	1210	...	1311	...	...	...	1410	...	...	1510	...	...	...	...
Lyon Part Dieu d.	|	...	|	...	...	|	...	|	...	1426	1600	1700	...	|	...	...	|	...	...	...	...
Paris Gare de Lyon a.	0927	...	1049	...	...	1249	...	1452	...	...	|	|	...	1649	...	...	1749	...	...	...	...
Paris Nord **10** d.	...	1113	...	1313	1313	...	1513	...	1713	...	|	|	...	...	1913	...	...	2013	...	...	...
Lille Europe d.	...	|	...	|	|	...	|	...	|	...	1944f	1956	2030	...	|	...	...	|	...	...	...
London St Pancras **10** a.	...	1239	...	1430	1439	...	1630	...	1832	...	...	...	2103	...	2039	...	...	2139	...	...	...

e – 1122 on ⑥.

f – Lille **Flandres** (◇).

g – Not May 30, Aug. 29, Nov. 11.

n – Not May 29, Aug. 28.

q – Also May 30, Aug. 29, Nov. 11.

r – Not Nov. 12.

K – ① July 24 - Dec. 10 (not Aug. 15).

L – ①–⑤ May 29 - July 23 (not May 30). ②–⑤ July 24 - Dec. 10 (not Aug. 29, Nov. 1, 11).

R – Daily May 29 - July 3. ⑤⑥⑦ July 4 - Dec. 10.

◇ – 500 metres from Lille Europe (see Lille City Plan on page 30).

♥ – *TGV Lyria* service. [R] special fares payable. At-seat meal service in first class.

🚌 – *SNCF* service; see table **366a**.

☆ – Eurostar train. [R], 🍴 in Business Premier and Standard Premier, 🍷 in Stand[ard]. Special fares payable. Minimum check-in time 30 minutes. Additional servi[ces] are shown in Table **10**. Connections across Paris between *TGV* and Euros[tar] services are not guaranteed. Valid May 29 - Dec. 10.

LONDON - PARIS - MÜNCHEN - WIEN - BUDAPEST - BUCURESTI

Alternative services London - München and London - Wien - Budapest are available via Brussels (Table **21**)

Service from July 3. Service until July 2 is on page 68.

train type	RJ	EN	IC	RJ	ICE	EC	RJ	EN	TGV	TGV	ICE	EC	RJ	ICE	TGV	ICE	RJ	☆	ICE	☆	TGV	ICE	EC	RJ
train number	**61**	**473**	**2265**	**65**	**9571**	**113**	**165**	**347**	**9591**	**9551**	**595**	**219**	**567**	**9573**	**9593**	**517**	**261**	**9010**	**9553**	**9014**	**9575**	**599**	**391**	**361**
train number/notes	✕	¶	🍷	✕	★	🍷	✕	¶	★	★	🍷	🍷	✕	Ⓑ	⑥	🍷	✕		★		★	🍷		✕
notes		**S**						**M**	**A**			**x**												
on St Pancras **10** .... d.	...	...	...	...	...	...	...	...	...	...	...	...	...	...	...	...	...	0831t	...	0917j	...	...	...	...
Nord **10** .... a.	...	...	...	...	...	...	...	...	...	...	...	...	...	...	...	...	...	1147	...	1247	...	...	...	...
Est .... d.	...	...	...	...	0639	...	...	...	0825	0906	...	...	...	1054	1055	...	...	...	1301	...	1355	...	...	...
bourg .... d.	...	...	...	...	0831	...	...	...	1026	|	...	...	...	1246	1246	...	...	...	|	...	1546	...	...	...
🛃 .... d.	...	...	...	...	|	...	...	...	|	◧	...	...	...	|	|	...	...	...	◧	...	|	...	...	...
ruhe Hbf .... d.	...	...	0806	...	0910	...	...	...	1114	|	...	...	...	1328	1328	...	...	...	|	...	1628	...	...	...
nnheim Hbf .... d.	...	...	|	...	|	...	...	...	|	1215	1230	...	...	|	|	...	...	...	1617	...	|	1630	...	...
gart Hbf .... d.	...	...	0853	...	0948	0958	...	...	1219	...	1313	1358	...	1404	1404	1413	...	...	...	...	1704	1712	1758	...
Hbf .... d.	...	...	0956	...	...	1057	...	...	1316	...	1409	1456	...	...	...	1509	...	...	...	...	...	1809	1856	...
burg Hbf .... d.	...	...	1039	...	...	1142	...	...	1403	...	1455	1542	...	...	...	1555	...	...	...	...	...	1855	1942	...
hen Pasing .... a.	...	...	1101	...	...	|	...	...	|	...	1518	|	...	...	...	1618	...	...	...	...	...	1918	|	...
chen Hbf .... a.	...	...	1111	...	...	1210	...	...	1434	...	1528	1610	...	...	...	1627	...	...	...	...	...	1927	2011	...
chen Hbf .... d.	0733	...	...	1134	...	1218	...	...	...	...	...	1618	...	...	...	...	1734	...	...	...	...	...	2018	...
burg Hbf 🛃 .... a.	0902	...	...	1302	...	1359	1608	...	...	...	...	1759	1808	...	...	...	1902	...	...	...	...	...	2203	2208
Hbf .... a.	1012	...	...	1412	...	...	1712	...	...	...	...	...	1912	...	...	...	2012	...	...	...	...	...	2326f	2312
ölten Hbf .... a.	1100	...	...	1500	...	...	1800	...	...	...	...	...	2000	...	...	...	2100	...	...	...	...	...	...	2400
Hbf .... a.	1130	...	...	1530	...	...	1830	1942	...	...	...	...	2030	...	...	...	2130	...	...	...	...	...	...	0030
eshalom 🛃 .... a.	1225	...	...	1625	...	...	1925	2025	...	...	...	...	...	...	...	...	...	...	...	...	...	...	...	...
.... a.	1250	...	...	1651	...	...	1950	2050	...	...	...	...	...	...	...	...	...	...	...	...	...	...	...	...
apest Keleti .... a.	1418	1910	...	1819	...	...	2118	2218	...	...	...	...	...	...	...	...	...	...	...	...	...	...	...	...
resti Nord .... a.	...	1200	...	...	...	...	...	1504	...	...	...	...	...	...	...	...	...	...	...	...	...	...	...	...

train type	☆	☆	TGV	EN	☆	TGV	TGV	ICE	☆	ICE	ICE
train number	**9018**	**9020**	**9577**	**463**	**9024**	**9579**	**9579**	**693**	**9032**	**9557**	**1093**
train number/notes	Ⓑ	⑥	★	**K**		★	★	🍷		**9559**	**695**
notes		**p**	Ⓑ			⑥	Ⓑ	Ⓑ		★	
don St Pancras **10** .... d.	1024	1101	...	...	1224	...	...	...	1422	...	...
Nord **10** .... a.	1347	1417	...	...	1547	...	...	...	1747	...	...
Est .... d.	...	...	1555	...	...	1755	1755	...	...	1906	...
sbourg .... d.	...	...	1746	...	...	1946	1946	...	...	|	...
🛃 .... d.	...	...	|	...	...	|	|	...	...	◧	...
sruhe Hbf .... d.	...	...	1828	...	...	2028	2025	...	...	|	...
annheim Hbf .... d.	...	...	|	...	...	|	|	...	...	2217	2231
tgart Hbf .... d.	...	...	1922	...	...	2112	2104	2113	...	...	2310
Hbf .... d.	...	...	2020	...	...	2210	...	2209	...	...	...
sburg Hbf .... d.	...	...	2103	...	...	2258e	...	2255	...	...	...
chen Pasing .... a.	...	...	|	...	...	|	...	2320	...	...	...
chen Hbf .... a.	...	...	2136z	...	...	2329e	...	2329	...	...	...
chen Hbf .... d.	...	...	...	2336	...	...	...	...	...	...	...
burg Hbf 🛃 .... a.	...	...	...	0118	...	...	...	...	...	...	...
Hbf .... a.	...	...	...	0458	...	...	...	...	...	...	...
ölten Hbf .... a.	...	...	...	0558	...	...	...	...	...	...	...
Hbf .... a.	...	...	...	0634	...	...	...	...	...	...	...
yeshalom 🛃 .... a.	...	...	...	0725	...	...	...	...	...	...	...
.... a.	...	...	...	0751	...	...	...	...	...	...	...
apest Keleti .... a.	...	...	...	0919	...	...	...	...	...	...	...
uresti Nord .... a.	...	...	...	...	...	...	...	...	...	...	...

train type	RJ	ICE	ICE	☆	TGV	ICE	ICE	☆	☆
train number	**66**	**616**	**9558**	**9023**	**9578**	**9586**	**9568**	**9027**	**9031**
train number/notes	✕		★		★	★	★		①–⑥
notes			①–⑤		①–⑥	⑥	Ⓑ	**U**	**g**
Bucuresti Nord .... d.	...	...	...	...	...	...	...	...	...
Budapest Keleti .... d.	1340	...	...	...	...	...	...	...	...
Györ .... d.	1501	...	...	...	...	...	...	...	...
Hegyeshalom 🛃 .... d.	1532	...	...	...	...	...	...	...	...
Wien Hbf .... d.	1630	...	...	...	...	...	...	...	...
St Pölten Hbf .... d.	1700	...	...	...	...	...	...	...	...
Linz Hbf .... d.	1748	...	...	...	...	...	...	...	...
Salzburg Hbf 🛃 .... d.	1856	...	...	...	...	...	...	...	...
München Hbf .... a.	2024	...	...	...	...	...	...	...	...
München Hbf .... d.	2045n	0325	...	...	...	...	...	...	...
München Pasing .... d.	|	0333	...	...	...	...	...	...	...
Augsburg Hbf .... d.	2117n	0357	...	...	...	...	...	...	...
Ulm Hbf .... d.	2204n	0440	...	...	...	...	...	...	...
Stuttgart Hbf .... d.	2305n	0551	...	...	0654	...	...	...	...
Mannheim Hbf .... d.	2343n	0628	0639	...	|	0738	0739	...	...
Karlsruhe Hbf .... d.	...	...	|	...	0732	|	0807	...	...
Kehl 🛃 .... d.	...	...	◧	...	|	◧	◧	...	...
Strasbourg .... a.	...	...	|	...	0813	|	|	...	...
Paris Est .... a.	...	...	0951	...	1005	1053	1038	...	...
Paris Nord **10** .... d.	...	...	...	1113	...	...	...	1213	1313
London St Pancras **10** .... a.	...	...	...	1239	...	...	...	1330	1439

train type	IC	EN	TGV	TGV	☆	☆	IC	ICE	TGV	RJ	EC	ICE	ICE	TGV	ICE	EN	RJ	RJ	EC	TGV	ICE	TGV	EN	RJ	IC
train number	**72**	**462**	**9576**	**9576**	**9035**	**9039**	**1296**	**690**	**9574**	**560**	**218**	**596**	**9572**	**9592**	**1090**	**346**	**60**	**564**	**112**	**9590**	**592**	**9570**	**472**	**62**	**2264**
train number/notes	🅁		★	★	⑥⑦		🍷	🍷	★	✕	🍷	🍷	★	★	**594**	¶	✕	✕	🍷	★	🍷	★	¶	✕	
notes	**T**	**K**	①–⑤	⑥⑦	**b**		①–⑥						Ⓑ	Ⓑ	🍷	**M**				**A**			**S**		
uresti Nord .... d.	0545	...	...	...	...	...	...	...	...	...	...	...	...	...	...	1300	...	...	...	...	...	...	1735	...	...
apest Keleti .... d.	1850	2040	...	...	...	...	...	...	...	...	...	...	...	...	...	0540	0740	...	...	...	...	...	0850	0940	...
.... d.	...	2201	...	...	...	...	...	...	...	...	...	...	...	...	...	0701	0901	...	...	...	...	...	...	1101	...
yeshalom 🛃 .... d.	...	2232	...	...	...	...	...	...	...	...	...	...	...	...	...	0732	0932	...	...	...	...	...	...	1132	...
Hbf .... d.	...	2325	...	...	...	...	...	...	...	0730	...	...	...	...	...	0818	1030	1130	...	...	...	...	...	1230	...
ölten Hbf .... d.	...	0002	...	...	...	...	...	...	...	0800	...	...	...	...	...	▬	1100	1200	...	...	...	...	...	1300	...
Hbf .... d.	...	0101	...	...	...	...	...	...	...	0848	...	...	...	...	...	...	1148	1248	...	...	...	...	...	1348	...
burg Hbf 🛃 .... d.	...	0428	...	...	...	...	0545	...	...	0952	1000	...	...	...	...	...	1256	1352	1400	...	...	...	...	1456	...
chen Hbf .... a.	...	0609	...	...	...	...	0730	...	...	▬	1141	...	...	...	...	...	1424	...	1541	...	...	...	...	1624	...
chen Hbf .... d.	...	...	0625	0629	...	...	0746	0828	...	...	1146	1228	...	...	1428	...	...	...	1546	1607	1628	...	...	...	1648
chen Pasing .... d.	...	...	|	|	...	...	|	0837	...	...	|	1237	...	...	1437	...	...	...	|	|	1637	...	...	...	1656
sburg Hbf .... d.	...	...	0657	0706	...	...	0817	0903	...	...	1217	1303	...	...	1503	TGV	...	...	1617	1636	1703	...	...	...	1721
Hbf .... d.	...	...	0743	0751	...	...	0904	0951	...	...	1304	1351	...	...	1551	**9560**	...	...	1703	1724	1751	...	...	...	1804
tgart Hbf .... d.	...	...	0855	0855	...	...	1000	1046	1055	...	1400	1446	1454	1454	1651	★	...	...	1800	1831	1846	1854	...	...	1911
annheim Hbf .... d.	...	...	|	|	...	...	...	...	|	...	...	...	|	|	1729	1740	...	...	...	|	...	|	...	...	1953
sruhe Hbf .... d.	...	...	0933	0933	...	...	...	...	1133	...	...	...	1532	1532	...	1807	...	...	...	1917	...	1932	...	...	...
🛃 .... d.	...	...	|	|	...	...	...	...	|	☆	...	...	|	|	...	◧	...	...	...	|	...	|	...	...	...
sbourg .... a.	...	...	1012	1012	...	...	...	...	1213	**9051**	...	...	1612	1612	...	|	...	...	...	2019	...	2013	...	...	...
s Est .... a.	...	...	1205	1205	...	...	...	...	1405	Ⓑ	...	...	1804	1804	...	2041	...	...	...	2205	...	2205	...	...	...
s Nord **10** .... d.	...	...	...	...	1413	1513	...	...	...	1813	...	...	...	...	...	...	...	...	...	...	...	...	...	...	...
don St Pancras **10** .... a.	...	...	...	...	1530	1639	...	...	...	1939	...	...	...	...	...	...	...	...	...	...	...	...	...	...	...

Sept. 23, 25, 30, Oct. 3.

KÁLMÁN IMRE – 🛏 1, 2 cl., ▬ 2 cl., (2) München - Budapest and v.v.

DACIA – 🛏 1, 2 cl., ▬ 2 cl., (2) ✕ Wien - Budapest - Bucuresti and v.v.

EuroNight ISTER – 🛏 1, 2 cl., ▬ 1, 2 cl., (2) ✕ Budapest - Bucuresti and v.v.

TRAIANUS – (12) Bucuresti - Budapest.

Ⓑ May 29 - Sept. 3 (also June 4). ①⑤⑦ Sept. 4 - Dec. 10.

Also Nov. 11.

12 - 14 minutes later July 30 - Sept. 10.

Not ⑥ (not May 15).

Not May 30, Aug. 29, Nov. 11.

0922 on ⑦ (also May 30, Aug. 29, Nov. 11). 0924 on ⑥.

⑤⑥ (also May 15).

p – Also May 29, 30, June 5.

q – Also June 4.

t – 0819 on ⑦ (also May 30, Aug. 29, Nov. 11).

x – To Graz (arrive 2214; Table **68**).

z – 2200 July 31 - Sept. 11.

◧ – 🛃 is at Forbach.

RJ – ÖBB *Railjet* service. ✕, (1) (business class), (1) (first class), (2) (economy class).

★ – *Alleo* ICE / TGV service. A DB / SNCF joint enterprise.

TGV – 🅁, supplement payable, 🍷.

¶ – Compulsory reservation for international journeys between Hungary and Romania.

☆ – Eurostar train. 🅁, ✕ in Business Premier and Standard Premier, 🍷 in Standard. Special fares payable. Minimum check-in time 30 minutes. Additional services are shown in Table **10**. Valid May 29 - Dec. 10.

40 LONDON - PARIS - BASEL - ZÜRICH, INTERLAKEN, BRIG and MILANO

train type/number	TGV	IC	IC	IC	IC	EC	☆	TGV	IC	EC	IC	IR	IC	☆	☆	TGV	IC	EC	IC	IC	IR
train number	**9203**	**567**	**1067**	**967**	**671**	**57**	**9080**	**9211**	**573**	**21**	**1073**	**2327**	**820**	**9002**	**9004**	**9213**	**577**	**23**	**1077**	**824**	**2331**
notes	♥ k ①–⑥					🅁 🍷 ⊗	①–⑤ h	♥		🅁 🍷 ⊗				⑥	①–⑤ j	♥	🍷	🅁 🍷 ⊗			
London St Pancras d.	...	...	...	...	...	...	0540	...	...	...	...	...	...	0618	0701	...	...	...	...	...	...
Paris Nord a.	...	...	...	...	...	...	0917	...	...	...	...	...	...	0947	1017	...	...	...	...	...	...
Paris Gare de Lyon d.	0723	...	...	...	...	...	...	1023	...	...	...	...	...	...	...	1223	...	...	...	...	...
Dijon d.	│	...	...	...	...	...	...	1201	...	...	...	...	...	...	...	1402	...	...	...	...	...
Besançon TGV ⊖ d.	│	...	...	...	...	...	...	│	...	...	...	...	...	...	...	│	...	...	...	...	...
Belfort TGV ⊡ d.	0941	...	...	...	...	...	...	│	...	...	...	...	...	...	...	│	...	...	...	...	...
Mulhouse d.	1006	...	...	...	...	...	...	1306	...	...	...	...	...	...	...	1507	...	...	...	...	...
Basel SBB a.	1026	...	...	...	...	...	...	1326	...	...	...	...	...	...	...	1526	...	...	...	...	...
Basel SBB d.	1033	...	1031	1059	1104	1231	...	1333	...	...	1331	1404	...	...	...	1533	...	...	1531	...	1604
Zürich HB a.	1126	1137	│	│	│	│	...	1426	1437	1532	│	│	...	...	...	1626	1637	1732	│	...	│
Landquart a.	...	1241	│	│	│	│	...	...	1541	│	│	│	...	...	...	...	1741	│	│	...	│
Chur a.	...	1252	│	│	│	│	...	...	1552	│	│	│	...	...	...	...	1752	│	│	...	│
Chur d.	...	*1258*	│	│	│	│	...	...	*1558*	│	│	│	...	...	...	...	*1758*	│	│	...	│
St Moritz a.	...	*1455*	│	│	│	│	...	...	*1755*	│	│	│	...	...	...	...	*1955*	│	│	...	│
Luzern a.	...	...	│	│	1205	│	...	...	...	│	│	1505	...	...	...	...	...	│	│	...	1705
Arth Goldau a.	...	...	│	│	1244	│	...	...	...	1614	│	1544	...	...	...	...	...	1814	│	...	1744
Bellinzona a.	...	...	│	│	1423	│	...	...	...	1759	│	1753	...	...	...	...	...	1959	│	...	1953
Locarno a.	...	...	│	│	│	│	...	...	...	│	│	1813	...	...	...	...	...	│	│	...	2013
Lugano a.	...	...	│	│	1448	│	...	...	...	1825	│	...	...	...	...	...	...	2025	│	...	...
Chiasso 🏛 a.	...	...	│	│	...	│	...	...	...	1848	│	...	...	...	...	...	...	2048	│	...	...
Bern a.	...	...	1127	1156	...	1327	...	...	...	│	1427	...	1507	...	...	...	...	│	1627	1707	...
Thun a.	...	...	1152	1221	...	1352	...	...	...	│	1452	...	1524	...	...	...	...	│	1652	1724	...
Spiez a.	...	...	1202	1231	...	1402	...	...	...	│	1502	...	1534	...	...	...	...	│	1702	1734	...
Interlaken West a.	...	...	│	1251	...	│	...	...	...	│	1522	...	│	...	...	...	...	│	1722	│	...
Interlaken Ost a.	...	...	│	1257	...	│	...	...	...	│	1528	...	│	...	...	...	...	│	1728	│	...
Brig a.	...	...	1240	...	...	1440	...	...	...	│	...	...	1611	...	...	...	...	│	...	1811	...
Como San Giovanni a.	...	...	...	...	...	◧	...	...	...	│	...	...	...	...	...	...	...	2056	...	...	...
Milano Centrale a.	...	...	...	...	...	1637	...	...	...	1935	...	...	...	...	...	...	...	2135	...	...	...

train type/number	☆	TGV	EC		IC	IR	EC	☆	☆	TGV	IC	ICN	IC	ICE	IR	☆	☆	TGV	RE	TGV	IR
train number	**9014**	**9215**	**59**		**581**	**2335**	**25**	**9018**	**9022**	**9219**	**585**	**889**	**1085**	**373**	**2339**	**9024**	**9028**	**9223**	**5093**	**9225**	**2343**
notes		♥ Ⓑ g	🅁 🍷 ⊗		🍷		🅁 🍷 ⊗	Ⓑ		♥							R	♥		♥	
London St Pancras d.	0917t	...	...	...	...	...	...	1024	1131f	...	...	...	...	...	...	1224	1331	...	...	...	...
Paris Nord a.	1247	...	...	...	...	...	...	1347	1447	...	...	...	...	...	...	1547	1647	...	...	...	...
Paris Gare de Lyon d.	...	1423	...	...	...	...	...	...	...	1623	...	...	...	...	...	...	...	1823	...	1823	...
Dijon d.	...	│	...	...	...	...	...	...	...	│	...	...	...	...	...	...	...	2001	...	2001	...
Besançon TGV ⊖ d.	...	│	...	...	...	...	...	...	...	│	...	...	...	...	...	...	...	│	...	│	...
Belfort TGV ⊡ d.	...	1641	...	...	...	...	...	...	...	1841	...	...	...	...	...	...	...	│	...	│	...
Mulhouse d.	...	1706	...	...	...	...	...	...	...	1907	...	...	...	...	...	...	...	2106	...	2106	...
Basel SBB a.	...	1726	...	...	...	...	...	...	...	1926	...	...	...	...	...	...	...	2126	...	2126	...
Basel SBB d.	...	...	1731	...	1733	1804	...	...	...	1933	...	...	1931	1959	2004	...	...	2133	...	2136	2202
Zürich HB a.	...	...	│	...	1826	│	1932	...	...	2026	2037	2109	│	│	│	...	...	2226	2312	│	│
Landquart a.	...	...	│	...	1941	│	│	...	...	...	2141	│	│	│	│	...	...	...	0037	│	│
Chur a.	...	...	│	...	1952	│	│	...	...	...	2152	│	│	│	│	...	...	...	0047	│	│
Chur d.	...	...	│	...	*1958*	│	│	...	...	...	...	│	│	│	│	...	...	...	...	│	│
St Moritz a.	...	...	│	...	*2157*	│	│	...	...	...	...	│	│	│	│	...	...	...	...	│	│
Luzern a.	...	...	│	...	...	1905	│	...	...	...	...	│	│	│	2105	...	...	...	...	│	2305
Arth Goldau a.	...	...	│	...	...	1944	2014	...	...	...	...	2146	│	│	2144	...	...	...	...	│	...
Bellinzona a.	...	...	│	...	...	2153	2159	...	...	...	...	2323	│	│	...	...	...	...	...	│	...
Locarno a.	...	...	│	...	...	2213	│	...	...	...	...	*2356*	│	│	...	...	...	...	...	│	...
Lugano a.	...	...	│	...	...	...	2225	...	...	...	...	2348	│	│	...	...	...	...	...	│	...
Chiasso 🏛 a.	...	...	│	...	...	...	2248	...	...	...	...	0012	│	│	...	...	...	...	...	│	...
Bern a.	...	...	1827	...	...	...	│	...	...	...	...	...	2027	2056	...	...	...	...	...	2250	...
Thun a.	...	...	1852	...	...	...	│	...	...	...	...	...	2052	2124	...	...	...	...	...	│	...
Spiez a.	...	...	1902	1905	...	...	│	...	...	...	...	...	2102	2134	...	...	...	...	...	│	...
Interlaken West a.	...	...	│	1923	...	...	│	...	...	...	...	...	│	2151	...	...	...	...	...	2343	...
Interlaken Ost a.	...	...	│	1928	...	...	│	...	...	...	...	...	│	2157	...	...	...	...	...	2353	...
Brig a.	...	...	1940	...	...	...	│	...	...	...	...	...	2140	...	...	...	...	...	...	...	...
Como San Giovanni a.	...	...	◧	...	...	...	2256	...	...	...	...	...	...	...	...	...	...	...	...	...	...
Milano Centrale a.	...	...	2137	...	...	...	2335	...	...	...	...	...	...	...	...	...	...	...	...	...	...

train type	IR	IC	IC	TGV	☆	☆	IC	IR	IC	ICN	IC	TGV	TGV	☆		EC	IR	IC	IC	TGV	☆
train number	**2308**	**1058**	**558**	**9206**	**9031**	**9031**	**1060**	**2314**	**1062**	**862**	**562**	**9214**	**9210**	**9039**		**50**	**2316**	**1066**	**566**	**9218**	**9047**
notes			🍷	♥ k	y ⑦	j ①–⑥	🍷			🍷	🍷	♥	♥	t		🅁 🍷 ⊗			🍷	♥	
Milano Centrale d.	...	...	...	...	...	...	...	...	...	...	...	...	...	...	...	0723	...	...	...	...	...
Como San Giovanni d.	...	...	...	...	...	...	...	...	...	...	...	...	...	...	...	◧	...	...	...	...	...
Brig d.	...	...	...	...	...	...	0720	...	...	...	...	...	...	...	...	0920	...	...	...	...	...
Interlaken Ost d.	...	0627	...	...	...	...	│	...	0830	...	...	...	...	...	...	│	...	1030	...	...	...
Interlaken West d.	...	0632	...	...	...	...	│	...	0835	...	...	...	...	...	...	│	...	1035	...	...	...
Spiez d.	...	0654	...	...	...	...	0754	...	0854	...	...	...	...	...	...	0954	...	1054	...	...	...
Thun d.	...	0704	...	...	...	...	0804	...	0904	...	...	...	...	...	...	1004	...	1104	...	...	...
Bern d.	...	0734	...	...	...	...	0834	...	0934	...	...	0910	...	...	...	1034	...	1134	...	...	...
Chiasso 🏛 d.	...	│	...	...	...	...	│	...	│	0545	...	│	...	...	...	│	0710	│	...	...	...
Lugano d.	...	│	...	...	...	...	│	...	│	0611	...	│	...	...	...	│	0737	│	...	...	...
Locarno d.	...	│	...	...	...	...	│	...	│	│	...	│	...	...	...	│	│	│	...	...	...
Bellinzona d.	...	│	...	...	...	...	│	...	│	0634	...	│	...	...	...	│	0806	│	...	...	...
Arth Goldau d.	...	│	...	...	...	...	│	...	│	0813	...	│	...	...	...	│	1014	│	...	...	...
Luzern d.	0654	│	...	...	...	...	│	0854	│	│	...	│	...	...	...	│	1054	│	...	...	...
St Moritz d.	│	│	...	...	...	...	│	│	│	│	...	│	...	...	...	│	│	│	*0802*	...	...
Chur a.	│	│	...	...	...	...	│	│	│	│	...	│	...	...	...	│	│	│	*1003*	...	...
Chur d.	│	│	0609	...	...	...	│	│	│	│	0809	│	...	...	...	│	│	│	1009	...	...
Landquart d.	│	│	0619	...	...	...	│	│	│	│	0819	│	...	...	...	│	│	│	1019	...	...
Zürich HB d.	│	│	0723	0734	...	...	│	│	│	0851	0923	│	0934	...	...	│	│	│	1123	1134	...
Basel SBB a.	0755	0829	...	0827	...	...	0929	0955	1029	...	...	1023	1027	...	...	1129	1155	1229	...	1227	...
Basel SBB d.	...	...	...	0834	...	...	...	...	...	...	...	1034	1034	...	...	...	...	...	...	1234	...
Mulhouse a.	...	...	...	0853	...	...	...	...	...	...	...	1053	1053	...	...	...	...	...	...	1254	...
Belfort TGV ⊡ a.	...	...	...	0918	...	...	...	...	...	...	...	│	│	...	...	...	...	...	...	1320	...
Besançon TGV ⊖ a.	...	...	...	│	...	...	...	...	...	...	...	│	│	...	...	...	...	...	...	│	...
Dijon a.	...	...	...	│	...	...	...	...	...	...	...	1158	1158	...	...	...	...	...	...	│	...
Paris Gare de Lyon a.	...	...	...	1137	...	...	...	...	...	...	...	1337	1337	...	...	...	...	...	...	1537	...
Paris Nord d.	...	...	...	...	1313	1313	...	...	...	...	...	...	...	1513	...	...	...	...	...	...	1713
London St Pancras a.	...	...	...	...	1430	1439	...	...	...	...	...	...	...	1630	...	...	...	...	...	...	1832

R – Daily May 29 - July 3. ⑤⑥⑦ July 4 - Dec. 10.

f – 1122 on ⑥.

g – Not Oct. 8, 15, Nov. 5, 6.

h – Not May 30, July 14, July 24 -. Sept. 3, Nov. 1, 11.

j – Not May 30, Aug. 29, Nov. 11.

k – Not Aug. 15, Nov. 1.

t – 0922 on ⑦ (also May 30, Aug. 29, Nov. 11). 0924 on ⑥.

y – Also May 30, Aug. 29, Nov. 11.

⊖ – Full name: Besancon Franche-Comté TGV.

⊡ – Full name: Belfort Montbéliard TGV.

♥ – *TGV Lyria* service. 🅁 🍷 special fares payable. At-seat meal service in first class.

⊗ – Compulsory reservation for international journeys. Supplement payable for international journeys and internal journeys within Italy.

☆ – Eurostar train. 🅁, ✕ in Business Premier and Standard Premier, 🍷 in Standard. Special fares paya Minimum check-in time 30 minutes. Valid May 29 - Dec. 10.

◧ – 🏛 between Brig and Milano is Domodossola. Ticket point is **Iselle**.

MILANO, BRIG, INTERLAKEN and ZÜRICH - BASEL - PARIS - LONDON — 40

train type	IC	IR	IC	EC	IC	TGV	☆		EC	EC	IR	IC	IC	TGV	☆		EC	IC	IR	IC	ICE	TGV	
train number	1068	2320	1070	12	570	9222	9055		14	52	2324	1074	574	9226	9063		16	1076	2328	578	332	9230	
notes				🅁 🍷 ⊗	🍷	♥			🅁 🍷 ⊗	🅁 🍷 ⊗			🍷	♥ Ⓑ	Ⓑ		🅁 🍷 ⊗			🍷		♥	
o Centrale d.	...	...	...	0825	...	...	...	...	1025	1123	...	...	...	...	...	...	1225	...	...	...	...	...	...
San Giovanni d.	...	...	...	0903	...	...	...	...	1103	◧	...	...	...	...	...	...	|	...	...	...	...	...	...
d.	1120	...	...	|	...	...	...	...	|	1320	...	...	...	...	...	...	|	1520	...	...	...	...	...
erlaken Ost d.	|	...	1230	|	...	...	...	...	|	|	...	1430	...	...	...	...	|	|	...	...	1630	...	...
erlaken West d.	|	...	1235	|	...	...	...	...	|	|	...	1435	...	...	...	...	|	|	...	...	1635	...	...
z d.	1154	...	1254	|	...	...	...	...	|	1354	...	1454	...	...	...	...	|	1554	...	...	1654	...	...
d.	1204	...	1304	|	...	...	...	...	|	1404	...	1504	...	...	...	...	|	1604	...	...	1704	...	...
d.	1234	...	1334	|	...	...	...	...	|	1434	...	1534	...	...	...	...	|	1634	...	...	1734	...	...
iasso 🏛 d.	|	...	|	0912	...	...	...	...	1112	|	...	|	...	...	...	...	1312	|	...	...	|	...	...
gano d.	|	...	|	0933	...	...	...	...	1133	|	...	|	...	...	...	...	1333	|	...	...	|	...	...
Locarno d.	|	0947	|	|	...	...	...	...	|	|	1147	|	...	...	...	...	|	|	1347	...	|	...	...
llinzona d.	|	1006	|	0959	...	...	...	...	1159	|	1206	|	...	...	...	...	1359	|	1406	...	|	...	...
h Goldau d.	|	1214	|	1145	...	...	...	...	1345	|	1414	|	...	...	...	...	1545	|	1614	...	|	...	...
zern d.	|	1254	|	|	...	...	...	...	|	|	1454	|	...	...	...	...	|	|	1654	...	|	...	...
St Moritz d.	|	|	|	|	*1002*	...	...	...	|	|	|	|	*1202*	...	...	...	|	|	|	*1302*	|	...	...
Chur d.	|	|	|	|	*1203*	...	...	...	|	|	|	|	*1403*	...	...	...	|	|	|	*1503*	|	...	...
ur d.	|	|	|	|	1209	...	...	...	|	|	|	|	1409	...	...	...	|	|	|	1609	|	...	...
ndquart d.	|	|	|	|	1219	...	...	...	|	|	|	|	1419	...	...	...	|	|	|	1619	|	...	...
rich HB d.	|	|	|	1228	1323	1334	...	...	1428	|	|	|	1523	1534	...	...	1628	|	|	1734	|	...	...
el SBB a.	1329	1355	1429	...	...	1427	...	...	...	1529	1555	1629	...	1627	...	...	...	1729	1755	1827	1829	...	...
el SBB d.	...	...	...	...	...	1434	...	...	...	...	...	...	...	1634	...	...	...	...	...	...	...	1834	...
ouse a.	...	...	...	...	...	1453	...	...	...	...	...	...	...	1653	...	...	...	...	...	...	...	1856	...
rt TGV ⊡ a.	...	...	...	...	...	|	...	...	...	...	...	...	...	|	...	...	...	...	...	...	...	1921	...
nçon TGV ⊖ a.	...	...	...	...	...	|	...	...	...	...	...	...	...	|	...	...	...	...	...	...	...	|	...
a.	...	...	...	...	...	1558	...	...	...	...	...	...	...	1758	...	...	...	...	...	...	...	|	...
s Gare de Lyon a.	...	...	...	...	...	1737	...	...	...	...	...	...	...	1937	...	...	...	...	...	...	...	2138	...
s Nord d.	...	...	...	...	...	...	1913	...	...	...	...	...	...	...	2113	...	...	...	...	...	...	...	...
don St Pancras a.	...	...	...	...	...	...	2039	...	...	...	...	...	...	...	2239	...	...	...	...	...	...	...	...

Full name: Besancon Franche-Comté TGV.

Full name: Belfort Montbéliard TGV.

🏛 between Brig and Milano is Domodossola. Ticket point is **Iselle**.

☆ – Eurostar train. 🅁, ✕ in Business Premier and Standard Premier, 🍷 in Standard. Special fares payable. Minimum check-in time 30 minutes. Valid May 29 - Dec. 10.

♥ – *TGV Lyria* service. 🅁 🍷 special fares payable. At-seat meal service in first class.

⊗ – Compulsory reservation for international journeys. Supplement payable for international journeys and for internal journeys within Italy.

LONDON - PARIS - LAUSANNE - BRIG — 42

train type	TGV	IR		☆	☆	TGV	IR		TGV	☆	TGV	IR		☆	☆	TGV	IR			☆	TGV	IR	
train number	9261	1717		9002	9004	9269	1725		9773	9014	9271	1731		9022	9022	9273	1737			9028	9277	1741	
notes	♥ 🍷			⑥ r	①–⑤ g	♥ 🍷			♥ 🍷 ①–④	⑦ h	♥ 🍷 ⑦			⑥	Q	♥ 🍷				R	♥ 🍷		
don St Pancras **10** d.	...	...	...	0618	0701	...	...	...	...	0922	...	...	...	1122	1131	...	...	...	...	1331	...	...	...
s Nord **10** a.	...	...	...	0947	1017	...	...	...	...	1247	...	...	...	1447	1447	...	...	...	...	1647	...	...	...
s Gare de Lyon d.	0757	...	...	...	...	1157	...	...	1211	...	1357	...	...	...	...	1557	...	...	...	...	1757	...	...
n d.	0931	...	...	...	...	1336	...	...	|	...	1531	...	...	...	...	1732	...	...	...	...	1932	...	...
ne a.	1040	...	...	...	...	1441	...	...	◧	...	1639	...	...	...	...	1841	...	...	...	...	2041	...	...
rbe 🏛 a.	1057	...	...	...	...	1457	...	...	|	...	1657	...	...	...	...	1857	...	...	...	...	2057	...	...
sanne a.	1137	...	...	...	...	1537	...	...	1615	...	1737	...	...	...	...	1937	...	...	...	...	2137	...	...
sanne d.	...	1220	...	...	...	...	1620	...	...	...	...	1818	...	...	...	...	2020	...	...	...	...	2220	...
treux a.	...	1240	...	...	...	...	1640	...	...	...	...	1835	...	...	...	...	2040	...	...	...	...	2240	...
e a.	...	1251	...	...	...	...	1651	...	...	...	...	1846	...	...	...	...	2051	...	...	...	...	2251	...
igny a.	...	1311	...	...	...	...	1711	...	...	...	...	1905	...	...	...	...	2111	...	...	...	...	2311	...
a.	...	1325	...	...	...	...	1725	...	...	...	...	1920	...	...	...	...	2125	...	...	...	...	2325	...
re a.	...	1337	...	...	...	...	1737	...	...	...	...	1932	...	...	...	...	2137	①–⑥	⑦	...	...	2337	...
a.	...	1353	1408	...	...	...	1753	1808	...	...	...	1953	2008	...	...	...	2153	2241	2323	...	...	2353	...
ermatt a.	...	|	1513	...	...	...	|	1913	...	...	...	|	2113	...	...	...	|	2336	0018	...	...	|	...
a.	...	1402	...	...	...	...	1802	...	...	...	...	2002	...	...	...	...	2202	...	...	...	...	0002	...

train type	IR	TGV	☆	IR	IR	TGV	☆		IR	TGV	☆	☆		IR	EC	TGV	TGV		IR	TGV			
train number	1806	9260	9027	1712	1710	9264	9039		1720	9268	9051	9055		1728	34	9270	9778		1732	9272			
notes		♥ 🍷 ①–⑥	U	Ⓒ	Ⓐ	♥ 🍷	t			♥ 🍷	Ⓑ				🅁 🍷 ⊗	♥ 🍷 ⑤⑦	♥ 🍷 ①–④			♥ 🍷			
d.	0428	...	...	0558	0601	...	...	...	0958	...	...	...	...	1358	1418			...	1558	...	...	...	...
ermatt d.	|	...	...	|	|	...	...	0837	|	...	...	...	1237	|	|	...	...	1437	|	...	...	...	...
d.	0435	...	...	0606	0609	...	...	0945	1006	...	...	...	1345	1406	|	...	...	1545	1606	...	...	...	...
re d.	0453	...	...	0622	0628	...	...	...	1021	...	...	...	...	1421	|	...	...	...	1622	...	...	...	...
d.	0505	...	...	0634	0640	...	...	...	1033	...	...	...	...	1433	1446	...	...	...	1634	...	...	...	...
igny d.	0518	...	...	0648	0654	...	...	...	1047	...	...	...	...	1447	|	...	...	...	1648	...	...	...	...
e d.	0542	...	...	0707	0714	...	...	...	1106	...	...	...	...	1506	|	...	...	...	1707	...	...	...	...
treux d.	0553	...	...	0718	0725	...	...	...	1117	...	...	...	...	1517	1525	...	...	...	1718	...	...	...	...
sanne a.	0614	...	...	0740	0743	...	...	...	1139	...	...	...	...	1539	1542	...	...	...	1740	...	...	...	...
sanne d.	...	0623	...	...	...	0823	...	...	...	1223	...	...	...	...	...	1623	1638	...	...	1823	...	...	...
orbe 🏛 d.	...	0700	...	...	...	0900	...	...	...	1300	...	...	...	...	...	1700	|	...	...	1900	...	...	...
sne d.	...	0714	...	...	...	0915	...	...	...	1315	...	...	...	...	...	1717	◧	...	...	1915	...	...	...
n a.	...	0822	...	...	...	1024	...	...	...	1425	...	...	...	...	...	1822	|	...	...	2022	...	...	...
s Gare de Lyon a.	...	1003	...	...	...	1203	...	...	...	1603	...	...	...	...	...	2003	2049	...	...	2203	...	...	...
is Nord 10 d.	...	...	1213	...	...	...	1513	...	...	...	1813	1913	...	...	...	...	...	...	...	...	...	...	...
don St Pancras **10** a.	...	...	1330	...	...	...	1639	...	...	...	1939	2039	...	...	...	...	...	...	...	...	...	...	...

Ⓑ May 29 - July 3. ①④⑤⑦ July 4 - Dec. 10 (not Aug. 29).

Daily May 29 - July 3. ⑤⑥⑦ July 4 - Dec. 10.

Ⓑ May 29 - Sept. 3 (also June 4). ①⑤⑦ Sept. 4 - Dec. 10.

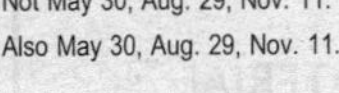

Not May 30, Aug. 29, Nov. 11.

Also May 30, Aug. 29, Nov. 11.

k – Also June 4.

r – Not Nov. 12.

t – Not May 29, Aug. 28.

◧ – Via Genève.

◇ – Stopping train. 2nd class only.

♥ – *TGV Lyria* service. 🅁. Special fares payable. At-seat meal service in first class.

⊗ – Compulsory reservation for international journeys. Supplement payable for international journeys and for internal journeys within Italy.

☆ – Eurostar train. 🅁, ✕ in Business Premier and Standard Premier, 🍷 in Standard. Special fares payable. Minimum check-in time 30 minutes. Valid May 29 - Dec. 10. Additional Eurostar services are available, see Table **10**.

30 PARIS - FRANKFURT - BERLIN, LEIPZIG, DRESDEN and PRAHA

Alternative services Paris - Frankfurt are available via Brussels (Table **21**). Alternative services Paris - Berlin are available via Brussels (Table **20**).

Service until July 2. Service from July 3 is on page 64.

train type	ICE		TGV	TGV		ICE		ICE		ICE
train number	**9551**		**9553**	**9553**		**9555**		**9557**		**9559**
notes	🄡★		🄡★	🄡★		🄡★		🄡★		🄡★
notes	①–⑥		⑦	①–⑥				Ⓑ		
notes										
Paris Est ... d.	0706	...	0906	0910	...	1309	...	1710	...	1906
Strasbourg ... d.	|	...	|	|	...	|	...	|	...	|
Forbach 🏛 ... d.	0848	...	1047	|	...	|	...	|	...	2049
Saarbrücken ... a.	0856	...	1055	1055	...	1457	...	1857	...	2057
Kaiserlautern ... a.	0935	...	1133	1133	...	1535	...	1935	...	2135
Karlsruhe Hbf ... d.	|	...	|	|	...	|	...	|	...	|
Mannheim ... a.	1017	...	1215	1215	...	1617	...	2017	...	2217
Frankfurt (Main) Hbf ... a.	1058	...	1258	1258	...	1658	...	2058	...	2258

train type	ICE	ICE		ICE	ICE		ICE		TGV
train number	**9558**	**9568**		**9556**	**9556**		**9554**		**9552**
notes	🄡★	🄡★		🄡★	🄡★		🄡★		🄡★
notes	①–⑤	⑥		①–⑥	⑦				
notes									
Frankfurt (Main) Hbf ... d.	0559	0658	...	0857	0857	...	1300	...	1658
Mannheim ... d.	0640	0739	...	0941	0941	...	1341	...	1743
Karlsruhe Hbf ... d.	|	|	...	|	|	...	|	...	|
Kaiserlautern ... d.	0722	0823	...	1023	1023	...	1423	...	1824
Saarbrücken ... d.	0800	0903	...	1102	1102	...	1502	...	1903
Forbach 🏛 ... a.	0808	0912	...	|	1110	...	|	...	1911
Strasbourg ... a.	|	|	...	|	|	...	|	...	|
Paris Est ... a.	0950	1054	...	1251	1251	...	1650	...	2054

★ – *Alleo* ICE / TGV service. A DB / SNCF joint enterprise.

32 LONDON - PARIS - MÜNCHEN - WIEN - BUDAPEST - BUCURESTI

Alternative services London - München and London - Wien - Budapest are available via Brussels (Table **21**)

Service until July 2. Service from July 3 is on page 65.

train type	IC	TGV	ICE	EC	TGV	ICE	EC	☆	☆	TGV	ICE	EC	☆	☆	ICE	ICE	☆	☆	TGV	TGV	☆	TGV	ICE	☆	ICE
train number	**2265**	**9571**	**1091**	**115**	**9553**	**595**	**219**	**9002**	**9004**	**9573**	**597**	**117**	**9008**	**9010**	**9555**	**599**	**9018**	**9020**	**9575**	**9575**	**9024**	**9577**	**693**	**9032**	**9559**
train number / notes	🍷	★	**593**	🍷	★	🍷	🍷	⑥	①–⑤	★	🍷	**1217**	①–⑥	⑦	★	🍷	Ⓑ	⑥	★	★		★	🍷		★
notes			🍷				x					🍷							⑥	Ⓑ		Ⓑ			
London St Pancras **10** ... d.	...	...	...	...	...	...	...	0618	0701	...	...	...	0755v	0819	...	...	1024	1101	...	...	1224	...	...	1422	...
Paris Nord **10** ... a.	...	...	...	...	...	...	...	0947	1017	...	...	...	1117	1147	...	...	1347	1417	...	...	1547	...	...	1747	...
Paris Est ... d.	...	0725	...	...	0910e	...	...	...	...	1125	...	...	...	...	1309	...	...	...	1525	1525	...	1725	...	...	1906
Strasbourg ... d.	...	0947	...	...	|	...	...	...	...	1347	...	...	...	...	|	...	...	...	1747	1747	...	1947	...	...	|
Kehl 🏛 ... d.	...	|	...	...	◧	...	...	...	...	|	...	...	...	...	◧	...	...	...	|	|	...	|	...	...	◧
Mannheim Hbf ... d.	...	|	...	...	1215	1230	...	...	...	|	...	...	...	...	1617	1630	...	...	|	|	...	|	...	...	2217
Karlsruhe Hbf ... d.	0806	1028	...	...	...	|	...	...	...	1428	...	...	...	...	...	|	...	...	1828	1828	...	2028	...	...	...
Stuttgart Hbf ... d.	0853	1104	1113	1157	...	1313	1358	...	...	1504	1513	1557	...	...	...	1712	...	...	1913	1922	...	2104	2113	...	...
Ulm Hbf ... d.	0956	...	1209	1255	...	1409	1456	...	...	...	1609	1656	...	...	...	1809	...	...	2010	2019	...	...	2209	...	...
Augsburg Hbf ... d.	1039	...	1255	1342	...	1455	1542	...	...	...	1655	1741	...	...	...	1855	...	...	2058	2103	...	...	2255	...	...
München Pasing ... a.	1101	...	1318	|	...	1518	|	...	...	...	1718	|	...	...	...	1918	...	...	|	|	...	...	2320	...	...
München Hbf ... a.	1111	...	1327	1410	...	1528	1610	...	...	...	1727	1811	...	...	...	1927	...	...	2129	2136	...	...	2329	...	...

train type	ICE	ICE	☆	TGV	ICE	☆	☆	TGV	☆	☆	EC	ICE	TGV	☆	EC	TGV	ICE	TGV	EC	TGV	ICE	ICE	IC		
train number	**616**	**9558**	**9023**	**9578**	**9568**	**9027**	**9031**	**9576**	**9035**	**9039**	**390**	**598**	**9574**	**9051**	**114**	**9572**	**1090**	**9552**	**112**	**9570**	**592**	**9550**	**2264**		
train number / notes		★		★	★		①–⑥	★	⑥⑦		🍷	🍷	★	Ⓑ	🍷	★	**594**	★	🍷	★	🍷	★			
notes		①–⑤		①–⑥	⑥	G				t						⑥⑦	🍷			①–⑤		Ⓑ			
München Hbf ... d.	0325	...	...	...	...	...	...	0624	...	...	0946	1028	...	...	1345	...	1428	...	1546	...	1628	...	1648	...	...
München Pasing ... d.	0333	...	...	...	...	...	...	|	...	...	|	1037	...	...	|	...	1437	...	|	...	1637	...	1656	...	...
Augsburg Hbf ... d.	0357	...	...	...	...	...	...	0656	...	...	1017	1103	...	...	1417	...	1503	...	1617	...	1703	...	1721	...	...
Ulm Hbf ... d.	0440	...	...	...	...	...	...	0743	...	...	1104	1151	...	...	1504	...	1551	...	1703	...	1751	...	1804	...	...
Stuttgart Hbf ... d.	0551	...	...	0655	...	...	...	0854	...	...	1201	1246	1250	...	1609	1650	1651j	...	1800	1850	1851j	...	1911	...	...
Karlsruhe Hbf ... d.	|	...	...	0733	...	...	...	0932	...	...	...	...	1333	...	|	1733	|	...	...	1933	|	...	1953	...	...
Mannheim Hbf ... d.	0628	0640	...	|	0739	...	...	|	...	...	...	...	|	...	1656	|	1729	1743	...	|	1929	1940	...	...	...
Kehl 🏛 ... d.	...	◧	...	|	◧	...	...	|	...	...	...	...	|	...	...	|	...	◧	...	|	...	◧	...	...	...
Strasbourg ... a.	...	|	...	0811	|	...	...	1011	...	...	...	...	1411	...	...	1810	...	|	...	2011	...	|	...	...	...
Paris Est ... a.	...	0950	...	1038	1054	...	...	1235	...	...	...	...	1635	...	...	2035	...	2054	...	2235	...	2250	...	...	...
Paris Nord **10** ... d.	...	...	1113	...	...	1213	1313	...	1413	1513	...	...	...	1813	...	...	...	...	...	...	...	...	...	...	...
London St Pancras **10** ... a.	...	...	1239	...	...	1330	1439	...	1530	1639	...	...	...	1939	...	...	...	...	...	...	...	...	...	...	...

G – Ⓑ May 29 - Sept. 3 (also June 4).

e – 0906 on ⑦.

j – Arrive 5 minutes earlier.

v – 0752 on ⑥.

x – To Graz (arrive 2214; Table **68**).

◧ – 🏛 is at Forbach.

★ – *Alleo* ICE / TGV service. A DB / SNCF joint enterprise.

TGV – 🄡, supplement payable, 🍷.

☆ – Eurostar train. 🄡, ✕ in Business Premier and Standard Premier, 🍷 in Standard. Special fares payable. Minimum check-in 30 minutes. Additional services are shown in Table **10**. Valid Dec. 13 - May 28.

LONDON - PARIS - TORINO - MILANO - VENEZIA and ROMA

train type	TGV	TGV	TGV	FR⚡	IC	FB	ITA			TGV	☆		TGV	TGV	FB	ITA		FR	FR	
train number	9241	9241	9241	9569 9571	597	9727	9925 9927			9245	9080	18503	9245	9245	9745	9977		9655	9557	
notes	[R] ✕	[R] ✕	[R] ✕	[R] ✕	⚡	[R] 🍷	[R] ✕			[R] ✕			[R] ✕	[R] ✕	[R] 🍷	[R] ✕		[R] ✕	[R] ✕	
notes	♣ A	♣ B	♣ C	⑧		⚡	⚡			♣ P	①–⑤ b		♣ Q	♣ R	⚡	⚡		⚡	⚡	
n St Pancras **10 12** d.	...	...	...	...	...	...	...	...	...	...	0540	...	...	...	...	...	...	...	...	...
Nord **10** a.	...	...	...	...	...	...	...	...	...	...	0917	...	...	...	...	...	...	...	...	...
Gare de Lyon d.	0611	0620	0629	...	...	...	...	...	...	0941	...	...	1027j	1041	...	...	...	...	...	...
n Part Dieu d.	|	|	0831	...	...	...	...	...	...	|	...	1140	|	|	...	...	...	...	...	...
n St Exupéry TGV ✈ d.	|	|	|	...	...	...	...	...	...	1138f	...	|	|	1236	...	...	...	...	...	...
béry d.	0935	0933	0942	...	...	...	...	...	...	|	...	1259	1333	1344	...	...	...	...	...	...
e 🏛 d.	1055	1055	1055	...	...	...	...	...	...	1455	...	...	1455	1455	...	...	...	...	...	...
▲ a.	1123	1123	1123	...	...	...	...	...	...	1523	...	...	1523	1523	...	...	...	...	...	...
o Porta Susa § a.	1224	1224	1224	1320	...	1319	1335	...	...	1615	...	...	1615	1615	1710	1712	...	1800	1822	...
o Porta Nuova § a.	|	|	|	|	...	|	|	1330	...	|	...	...	|	|	|	|	1730	|	|	...
a a.	|	|	|	|	...	1411	|	|	...	1711	...	...	1711	1711	1811	|	|	|	|	...
o Porta Garibaldi a.	1350	1350	1350	1418**d**	...	|	|	|	...	1750	...	...	1750	1750	|	|	|	|	|	...
o Centrale a.	...	...	...	|	...	1450	1425	|	...	...	...	...	...	...	1854	1800	|	1850	1910	...
o Centrale d.	...	...	...	|	1450	1505	1435	|	...	...	...	...	...	...	1905	1815	|	1900	1920	1920
ssandria a.	...	...	...	|	|	|	|	1429	...	...	...	...	...	...	|	|	1829	|	|	|
ova Piazza Principe a.	...	...	...	|	|	|	|	1530	...	...	...	...	...	...	|	|	1930	|	|	|
Spezia a.	...	...	...	|	|	|	|	...	...	...	...	...	...	...	|	|	...	|	|	|
eggio a.	...	...	...	|	|	|	|	...	...	...	...	...	...	...	|	|	...	|	|	|
a Centrale a.	...	...	...	|	|	|	|	...	...	...	...	...	...	...	|	|	...	|	|	|
rno a.	...	...	...	|	|	|	|	...	...	...	...	...	...	...	|	|	...	|	|	|
sseto a.	...	...	...	|	|	|	|	...	...	...	...	...	...	...	|	|	...	|	|	|
rescia a.	...	...	...	|	|	1551	|	...	...	...	...	...	...	...	1951	|	...	|	|	|
erona Porta Nuova a.	...	...	...	|	|	1628	|	...	...	...	...	...	...	...	2028	|	...	|	|	|
cenza a.	...	...	...	|	|	1654	|	...	...	...	...	...	...	...	2054	|	...	|	|	|
adova a.	...	...	...	|	|	1712	|	...	...	...	...	...	...	...	2112	|	...	|	|	|
enezia Mestre a.	...	...	...	|	|	1728	|	...	...	...	...	...	...	...	2128	|	...	|	|	|
enezia Santa Lucia a.	...	...	...	|	|	1740	|	...	...	...	...	...	...	...	2140	|	...	|	|	|
nza a.	...	...	...	|	1543	...	|	...	...	...	...	...	...	...	...	|	...	|	|	2012
a a.	...	...	...	|	1614	...	|	...	...	...	...	...	...	...	...	|	...	|	|	2054
o Emilia a.	...	...	...	1509	1631	...	1521	...	...	...	...	...	...	...	...	|	...	|	|	2112
na a.	...	...	...	|	1648	...	|	...	...	...	...	...	...	...	...	|	...	|	|	2132
na Centrale a.	...	...	...	1537	1714	...	1547	...	...	...	...	...	...	...	...	|	...	|	2022	2214
ze SMN a.	...	...	...	1615	1817**v**	...	1625	...	...	...	...	...	...	...	...	|	...	|	2059	...
Tiburtina a.	...	...	...	1743	2118	...	1753	...	...	...	...	...	...	...	...	|	...	|	2228	...
Termini a.	...	...	...	|	|	...	1805	...	...	...	...	...	...	...	...	2110	...	2155	2240	...
i Centrale a.	...	...	...	1855	2330	...	1925	...	...	...	...	...	...	...	...	2230	...	2315	...	...
no a.	...	...	...	1942	...	...	2016	...	...	...	...	...	...	...	...	...	...	...	...	...

train type	☆			TGV	TGV		ICN	ICN	☆	EN	FR⚡		ITA	IC	EC	IC	ITA	FR⚡		
train number	9014	18517	18519 17931	9249	9249		797	799	9032	221	9503 9505	2004	9901	583	141	505	9961 9963	9509		
notes				[R] ✕	[R] ✕		[R] ⚡	[R] ⚡			[R] 🍷		[R] ✕	[R] 🍷	[R] 🍷	[R] 🍷	[R] ✕	[R] 🍷		
notes			Ⓐ	♣ S	♣ T		H	E		V	⚒		⚡ Ⓐ	⚡	⚡	⚡	⚡			
on St Pancras **10 12** d.	0917**e**	...	...	...	...	...	...	...	1422	...	...	...	...	...	...	...	...	...	...	...
Nord **10** a.	1247	...	...	...	...	...	...	...	1747	...	...	...	...	...	...	...	...	...	...	...
Gare de Lyon d.	...	...	...	1427**k**	1441	...	...	...	...	1911	...	...	...	...	...	...	...	...	...	...
d.	...	...	...	|	|	...	...	...	...	2157	...	...	...	...	...	...	...	...	...	...
on Part Dieu d.	...	1450	1540	|	|	...	...	...	...	|	...	...	...	...	...	...	...	...	...	...
n St Exupéry TGV ✈ d.	...	|	|	|	1637	...	...	...	...	|	...	...	...	...	...	...	...	...	...	...
béry d.	...	1616	1658	1735	1744	...	...	...	...	|	...	...	...	...	...	...	...	...	...	...
ne 🏛 d.	...	...	...	1855	1855	...	...	...	...	⊙	...	...	...	...	...	...	...	...	...	...
▲ a.	...	...	...	1923	1923	...	...	...	...	|	...	...	...	...	...	...	...	...	...	...
o Porta Susa § a.	...	...	...	2018	2018	...	2140	...	...	|	...	...	...	...	...	...	...	...	...	...
o Porta Nuova § a.	...	...	...	|	|	2130	|	2155	...	|	...	...	...	...	...	...	...	...	...	...
a a.	...	...	...	|	|	|	2238**d**	|	...	|	...	...	...	...	...	...	...	...	...	...
o Porta Garibaldi a.	...	...	...	2150	2150	|	2317**d**	|	...	|	...	...	...	...	...	...	...	...	...	...
o Centrale a.	...	...	...	...	...	|	|	|	...	0550	...	...	...	...	...	...	...	...	...	...
o Centrale d.	...	...	...	...	...	|	|	|	...	|	0615	0618	0635	0650	0705	...	0715	0720	...	...
a a.	...	...	...	...	...	|	|	|	...	|	|	0656	|	|	|	...	|	|	...	...
o Porta Susa a.	...	...	...	...	...	|	|	|	...	|	|	0758	|	|	|	...	|	|	...	...
ssandria a.	...	...	...	...	...	2229	|	2257	...	|	|	...	|	|	|	...	|	|	...	...
nova Piazza Principe a.	...	...	...	...	...	2330	|	2350	...	|	|	...	|	|	0840	0851	|	|	...	...
Spezia a.	...	...	...	...	...	...	|	0124	...	|	|	...	|	|	...	1004	|	|	...	...
reggio a.	...	...	...	...	...	...	|	|	...	|	|	...	|	|	...	1039	|	|	...	...
a Centrale a.	...	...	...	...	...	...	|	0216	...	|	|	...	|	|	...	1056	|	|	...	...
orno a.	...	...	...	...	...	...	|	0237	...	|	|	...	|	|	...	1119	|	|	...	...
sseto a.	...	...	...	...	...	...	|	0355	...	|	|	...	|	|	...	1228	|	|	...	...
Brescia a.	...	...	...	...	...	...	|	|	...	0712	|	...	|	|	...	|	|	|	...	...
Verona Porta Nuova a.	...	...	...	...	...	...	|	|	...	0754	|	...	|	|	...	|	|	|	...	...
Vicenza a.	...	...	...	...	...	...	|	|	...	0843	|	...	|	|	...	|	|	|	...	...
Padova a.	...	...	...	...	...	...	|	|	...	0906	|	...	|	|	...	|	|	|	...	...
Venezia Mestre a.	...	...	...	...	...	...	|	|	...	0923	|	...	|	|	...	|	|	|	...	...
Venezia Santa Lucia a.	...	...	...	...	...	...	|	|	...	0935	|	...	|	|	...	|	|	|	...	...
nza a.	...	...	...	...	...	...	0008	|	...	...	|	...	|	0743	...	|	|	|	...	...
a a.	...	...	...	...	...	...	0059	|	...	...	|	...	|	0814	...	|	|	|	...	...
io Emilia a.	...	...	...	...	...	...	|	|	...	...	0701	...	0721	0831	...	|	|	|	...	...
ena a.	...	...	...	...	...	...	|	|	...	...	|	...	|	0848	...	|	|	|	...	...
gna Centrale a.	...	...	...	...	...	...	0215	|	...	...	0722	...	0747	0914	...	|	|	0822	...	...
ze SMN a.	...	...	...	...	...	...	0407**t**	|	...	...	0759	...	0825	1011**v**	...	|	|	0859	...	...
a Tiburtina a.	...	...	...	...	...	...	0717	|	...	...	0928	...	0953	1317	...	1420**o**	|	1028	...	...
a Termini a.	...	...	...	...	...	...	|	0554**o**	...	...	0940**c**	...	1005	|	...	1433	1010**c**	1040**c**	...	...
li Centrale a.	...	...	...	...	...	...	0938	0817	...	...	1100	...	...	1529	...	...	1130	1200	...	...
no a.	...	...	...	...	...	...	1032	0912	...	...	1154	...	...	...	...	...	1232	...	...	...

①–⑤ June 23 - Aug. 31 (not July 14, Aug. 15).
⑥⑦ June 25 - Aug. 28 (also July 14, Aug. 15).
June 1 - 22. Sept. 1 - Dec. 10 (not Oct. 31, 31).
🛏 1, 2 cl., 🛌 2 cl., (2) Torino - Roma - Napoli - Salerno.
🛏 1, 2 cl., 🛌 2 cl. (4 berth), (2) Torino - Milano - Salerno.
July 3 - Aug. 31.
June 1 - July 2.
Sept. 1 - Dec. 10.
June 1 - Aug. 31
Sept. 1 - Dec. 10.
Thello - 🛏 1, 2 cl. (1, 2, 3 berth), 🛌 2 cl. (4, 6 berth), ✕ Paris - Milano - Venezia.
For use by passengers making international journeys only. Special fares payable.

Not May 30, July 14, July 24 - Sept. 3, Nov. 1, 11.
Depart 10 - 19 minutes later.
Departure time.
0922 on ⑦ (also May 30, Aug. 29, Nov. 11). 0924 on ⑥.

f – 1243 ⑥⑦ July 3 - Aug. 28 (also July 14, Aug. 15).
k – 1428, 1433 on certain dates.
j – 1019 on June 25.
o – Roma **Ostiense**.
t – Firenze **Campo di Marte**.
v – Firenze **Rifredi**.

⚡ – Supplement payable.
♣ – *TGV* France-Italy service. [R] ✕ Special fares payable.
▲ – Station for the resorts of Cesana, Claviere and Sestriere.
☆ – Eurostar train. [R], ✕ in Business Premier and Standard Premier, 🍷 in Standard. Special fares payable. Minimum check-in time 30 minutes. Valid May 29 - Dec. 10. Additional Eurostar services are available, see Table **10**.
⊙ – Frontier / ticketing points 🏛 are Vallorbe and Domodossola. Ticket point for Domodossola is **Iselle**.
§ – Local train services (Tables **585**, **586**) and metro services run between Torino **Porta Susa** and Torino **Porta Nuova**.

44 ROMA and VENEZIA - MILANO - TORINO - PARIS - LONDON

train type	TGV	TGV	TGV			☆	ICN	ICN	IC	TGV	TGV		☆	☆		FB	FB		ITA	FR	TGV	TGV
train number	9240	9240	9240	18548	18550	9039	798	796	500	9244	9244	83270	9051	9055		9714	9810		9908 9910	9622	9248	9248
notes	🅁✕	🅁✕	🅁✕				🅁⚡	🅁⚡	⚡	🅁✕	🅁✕					🅁🍷	🅁🍷		🅁✕	🅁✕	🅁✕	🅁✕
notes	♣ A	♣ B	♣ C	Ⓒ	Ⓐ	f	H	E	⚒	♣ Pg	♣ Qh		Ⓑ			⚡	⚡		🅁✕ ⚡	⚡ ①–⑥	⑤⑥⑦ S ♣	⑤⑥⑦ R ♣
Salerno d.	...	...	...	...	...	...	2038	2050	...	...	...	...	...	...	...	...	...	...	0737	...	...	...
Napoli Centrale d.	...	...	...	...	...	...	2132	2142	...	...	...	...	...	...	...	...	...	...	0825	0940	...	...
Roma Termini d.	...	...	...	...	...	...	|	0003**o**	...	...	...	...	...	...	...	...	...	...	0945	1100	...	...
Roma Tiburtina d.	...	...	...	...	...	...	2343	|	...	...	...	...	...	...	...	...	...	...	0955	|	...	...
Firenze SMN d.	...	...	...	...	...	...	0257**t**	|	...	...	...	...	...	...	...	...	...	...	1125	|	...	...
Bologna Centrale d.	...	...	...	...	...	...	0418	|	...	...	...	...	...	...	...	...	1118	...	1203	|	...	...
Modena d.	...	...	...	...	...	...	|	|	...	...	...	...	...	...	...	...	1141	...	|	|	...	...
Reggio Emilia d.	...	...	...	...	...	...	|	|	...	...	...	...	...	...	...	...	1154	...	1224	|	...	...
Parma d.	...	...	...	...	...	...	0521	|	...	...	...	...	...	...	...	...	1210	...	|	|	...	...
Piacenza d.	...	...	...	...	...	...	0602	|	...	...	...	...	...	...	...	...	1241	...	|	|	...	...
Venezia Santa Lucia d.	...	...	...	...	...	...	|	|	...	...	...	...	...	...	...	1050	|	...	|	|	...	...
Venezia Mestre d.	...	...	...	...	...	...	|	|	...	...	...	...	...	...	...	1102	|	...	|	|	...	...
Padova d.	...	...	...	...	...	...	|	|	...	...	...	...	...	...	...	1118	|	...	|	|	...	...
Vicenza d.	...	...	...	...	...	...	|	|	...	...	...	...	...	...	...	1135	|	...	|	|	...	...
Verona Porta Nuova d.	...	...	...	...	...	...	|	|	...	...	...	...	...	...	...	1202	|	...	|	|	...	...
Brescia d.	...	...	...	...	...	...	|	|	...	...	...	...	...	...	...	1239	|	...	|	|	...	...
Grosseto d.	...	...	...	...	...	...	|	0153	...	...	...	...	...	...	...	|	|	...	|	|	...	...
Livorno d.	...	...	...	...	...	...	|	0309	...	...	...	...	...	...	...	|	|	...	|	|	...	...
Pisa Centrale d.	...	...	...	...	...	...	|	0326	...	...	...	...	...	...	...	|	|	...	|	|	...	...
Viareggio d.	...	...	...	...	...	...	|	|	...	...	...	...	...	...	...	|	|	...	|	|	...	...
La Spezia d.	...	...	...	...	...	...	|	0425	...	...	...	...	...	...	...	|	|	...	|	|	...	...
Genova Piazza Principe d.	...	...	...	...	...	...	|	0606	0708	...	...	...	...	...	...	|	|	1330	|	|	...	...
Alessandria d.	...	...	...	...	...	...	|	0657	0757	...	...	...	...	...	...	|	|	1431	|	|	...	...
Milano Centrale a.	...	...	...	...	...	...	|	|	|	...	...	...	...	...	...	1325	1325	|	1315	1355	...	...
Milano Centrale d.	...	...	...	...	...	...	|	|	|	...	...	...	...	...	...	...	...	|	1325	1405	...	...
Milano Porta Garibaldi d.	0600	0600	0600	...	...	...	0711**a**	|	|	0845	0845	...	...	...	...	...	...	|	|	|	1440	1440
Novara d.	0631	0631	0631	...	...	...	0805	|	|	|	|	...	...	...	...	...	...	|	|	|	|	|
Torino Porta Nuova § d.	|	|	|	...	...	...	|	0810	0855	|	|	...	...	...	...	...	...	1530	|	|	|	|
Torino Porta Susa § d.	0739	0739	0739	...	...	...	0910	...	...	1011	1011	...	...	...	...	...	...	...	1413	1452	1611	1611
Oulx ▲ d.	0836	0836	0836	...	...	...	...	...	...	1113	1113	...	...	...	...	...	...	...	...	...	1716	1716
Modane 🏛 a.	0905	0905	0905	...	...	...	...	...	...	1144	1144	...	...	...	...	...	...	...	...	...	1747	1747
Chambéry a.	1015	1013	1013	1043	1207	...	...	...	...	1257	1249	1302	...	...	...	...	...	...	...	...	1905	1852
Lyon St Exupéry TGV ✈ a.	1123	|	|	|	|	...	...	...	...	|	|	|	...	...	...	...	...	...	...	...	|	|
Lyon Part Dieu a.	|	|	|	1210	1326	...	...	...	...	|	|	1420	...	...	...	...	...	...	...	...	|	2032
Paris Gare de Lyon a.	1319**j**	1320	1319	...	...	...	...	...	...	1611	1611	...	...	...	...	...	...	...	...	...	2230**z**	2238
Paris Nord **10** d.	...	...	...	...	...	1513	...	...	...	...	...	...	1813	1913	...	...	...	...	...	...	...	...
London St Pancras **10 12** a.	...	...	...	...	...	1630	...	...	...	...	...	...	1939	2039	...	...	...	...	...	...	...	...

train type	FB		FR	IC	IC		ITA	TGV	TGV			FB	IC	FR		IC	ITA	FR	EN	☆	☆	
train number	9718	2280	9524 9526	746	670		9914 9916	9250	9250			9826	728	9552		1534	9940	9654	220	9027	9031	
notes	🅁🍷		🅁✕	🍷	🍷		🅁✕	🅁✕	🅁✕			🅁✕	🅁🍷	🅁✕		🅁	🅁✕	🅁✕				
notes	⚡		⚡	⚡	⚡		⚡	①–④ J ♣	①–④ K ♣			⚡	⚡	⚡		⚡	⚡	⚡	V	U		
Salerno d.	...	...	0914	...	...	...	0936			...	...	...	1536	...	...	...	...	...	...	...	...	...
Napoli Centrale d.	...	...	1000	...	...	...	1027	...	...	...	...	...	1615	1700	...	...	1725	...	...	...	...	...
Roma Termini d.	...	...	1120	...	...	...	1145	...	...	...	...	...	...	1820	...	...	1845	1900	...	...	...	...
Roma Tiburtina d.	...	...	1129	...	...	...	1155	...	...	...	...	...	...	1829	...	...	1855	|	...	...	...	...
Firenze SMN d.	...	...	1300	...	...	...	1325	...	...	...	...	...	...	2000	...	...	2025	|	...	...	...	...
Bologna Centrale d.	...	1152	1338	...	...	...	1403	...	...	...	...	1918	...	2038	...	...	2103	|	...	...	...	...
Modena d.	...	1225	|	...	...	...	|	...	...	...	...	1941	...	|	...	...	|	|	...	...	...	...
Reggio Emilia d.	...	1242	|	...	...	...	1424	...	...	...	...	1954	...	|	...	...	2124	2118	...	...	...	...
Parma d.	...	1305	|	...	...	...	|	...	...	...	...	2010	...	|	...	...	|	|	...	...	...	...
Piacenza d.	...	1350	|	...	...	...	|	...	...	...	...	2041	...	|	...	...	|	|	...	...	...	...
Venezia Santa Lucia d.	1150	|	|	...	...	...	|	...	...	...	...	|	...	|	...	...	|	|	1920	...	...	...
Venezia Mestre d.	1202	|	|	...	...	...	|	...	...	...	...	|	...	|	...	...	|	|	1932	...	...	...
Padova d.	1218	|	|	...	...	...	|	...	...	...	...	|	...	|	...	...	|	|	1948	...	...	...
Vicenza d.	1235	|	|	...	...	...	|	...	...	...	...	|	...	|	...	...	|	|	2012	...	...	...
Verona Porta Nuova d.	1302	|	|	...	...	...	|	...	...	...	...	|	...	|	...	...	|	|	2050	...	...	...
Brescia d.	1339	|	|	...	...	...	|	...	...	...	...	|	...	|	...	...	|	|	2133	...	...	...
Grosseto d.	|	|	|	...	...	...	|	...	...	...	...	|	...	|	...	1604	|	|	|	...	...	...
Livorno d.	|	|	|	...	1124	...	|	...	...	...	...	|	...	|	...	1718	|	|	|	...	...	...
Pisa Centrale d.	|	|	|	...	1142	...	|	...	...	...	...	|	...	|	...	1736	|	|	|	...	...	...
Viareggio d.	|	|	|	...	1200	...	|	...	...	...	...	|	...	|	...	1753	|	|	|	...	...	...
La Spezia d.	|	|	|	...	1238	...	|	...	...	...	...	|	...	|	...	1838	|	|	|	...	...	...
Genova Piazza Principe d.	|	|	|	1322	1415	1430	|	...	...	...	...	|	...	|	...	2018	|	|	|	...	...	...
Alessandria d.	|	|	|	|	...	1531	|	...	...	...	...	|	...	|	...	|	|	|	|	...	...	...
Torino Porta Susa d.	|	|	|	|	...	|	|	...	...	...	...	|	...	|	2002	|	|	|	|	...	...	...
Novara d.	|	|	|	|	...	|	|	...	...	...	...	|	...	|	2103	|	|	|	|	...	...	...
Milano Centrale a.	1425	1445	1440	1450	...	|	1515	...	...	...	...	2125	...	2140	2145	2150	2215	2202	2240	...	...	...
Milano Centrale d.	...	...	...	...	...	|	1525	...	...	...	...	...	...	...	...	...	...	...	2305	...	...	...
Milano Porta Garibaldi d.	...	...	...	...	...	|	|	1608	1608	...	...	...	...	...	...	...	...	...	|	...	...	...
Novara d.	...	...	...	...	...	|	|	|	|	...	...	...	...	...	...	...	...	...	|	...	...	...
Torino Porta Nuova § d.	...	...	...	...	...	1630	|	|	|	...	...	...	...	...	...	...	...	...	|	...	...	...
Torino Porta Susa § d.	...	...	...	...	...	...	1613	1735	1735	...	...	...	...	...	...	...	...	...	|	...	...	...
Oulx ▲ d.	...	...	...	...	...	...	...	1837	1837	...	...	...	...	...	...	...	...	...	⊙	...	...	...
Modane 🏛 a.	...	...	...	...	...	...	...	1912	1912	...	...	...	...	...	...	...	...	...	|	...	...	...
Chambéry a.	...	...	...	...	...	...	...	2027	2015	...	...	...	...	...	...	...	...	...	|	...	...	...
Lyon St Exupéry TGV ✈ a.	...	...	...	...	...	...	...	|	|	...	...	...	...	...	...	...	...	...	|	...	...	...
Lyon Part Dieu a.	...	...	...	...	...	...	...	|	2131	...	...	...	...	...	...	...	...	...	0642	...	...	...
Dijon a.	...	...	...	...	...	...	...	|	|	...	...	...	...	...	...	...	...	...	0955	...	...	...
Paris Gare de Lyon a.	...	...	...	...	...	...	...	2342**x**	2332	...	...	...	...	...	...	...	...	...	...	...	...	...
Paris Nord **10** d.	...	...	...	...	...	...	...	...	...	...	...	...	...	...	...	...	...	...	...	1213	1313	...
London St Pancras **10 12** a.	...	...	...	...	...	...	...	...	...	...	...	...	...	...	...	...	...	...	...	1330	1439	...

A – June 1 - 21, Aug. 1 - Dec. 10 (also July 1; not June 5, Aug. 30, 31).
B – ①②③④⑥⑦ June 23 - July 2 (not June 25). ⑤⑦ July 3 - 31 (also July 13).
C – ①②③④⑥ July 4 - 30 (also June 24, 25; not July 13).
E – 🛏 1, 2 cl., ▬ 2 cl., (2) Salerno - Napoli - Roma - Torino.
H – 🛏 1, 2 cl., ▬ 2 cl. (4 berth), (2) Salerno - Torino.
J – ①–④ June 1 - Aug. 31.
K – ①–④ Sept. 1 - Dec. 10.
P – June 1 - July 2.
Q – July 3 - Dec. 10.
R – ⑤⑥⑦ Sept. 2 - Dec. 10 (not Oct. 29).
S – ⑤⑥⑦ June 1 - Sept. 1.
U – Ⓑ May 29 - Sept. 3 (also June 4). ①⑤⑦ Sept. 4 - Dec. 10.
V – *Thello* – 🛏 1, 2 cl. (1, 2, 3 berth), ▬ 2 cl. (4, 6 berth), ✕ Venezia - Milano - Paris. For use by passengers making international journeys only. Special fares payable.

a – Arrival time.
f – Not May 29, Aug. 28.

g – Calls at Aix les Bains at 1310, Bourg-en-Bresse 1411, Mâcon Loché TGV 1432.
h – Calls at Aix les Bains at 1303, Bourg-en-Bresse 1410, Mâcon Loché TGV 1432.
j – 1335 on July 1.
o – Roma **Ostiense**.
t – Firenze **Campo di Marte**.
x – 2333, 2337, 2338, 2346 on certain dates.
z – 2227, 2232 on certain dates.

⚡ – Supplement payable.
♣ – *TGV* France-Italy service. 🅁 ✕ Special fares payable.
▲ – Station for the resorts of Cesana, Claviere and Sestriere.
☆ – Eurostar train. 🅁, ✕ in Business Premier and Standard Premier, 🍷 in Standard. Special fare payable. Minimum check-in time 30 minutes. Valid May 29 - July 23. Additional Eurostar service available, see Table **10**.
⊙ – Frontier / ticketing points 🏛 are Vallorbe and Domodossola. Ticket point for Domodossola is Is
§ – Local train services (Tables **585, 586**) and metro services run between Torino **Porta Susa** a Torino **Porta Nuova**.

LONDON - PARIS/MADRID - LISBOA and PORTO 45

train type/number		☆	TGV	Hotel	Hotel	IR
train number		9008	8537	312	332	823
notes		①–⑥	🅁 ↗	🅁 🍸	🅁 🍸	🅁 🍸
		g	🍸	A	L	
on St Pancras 10	d.	0755f	...	...	...	...
Nord 10	a.	1117	...	...	...	...
Montparnasse	d.	...	1228	...	...	...
aux St Jean	d.	...	1551	...	...	...
z	d.	...	1746	...	...	...
aye	d.	...	1811	...	...	...
🏛	d.	...	1820	1850	...	...
Sebastián/Donostia	a.	...	...	1908	...	...
a/Gasteiz	a.	...	...	2045	...	...
da de Ebro	a.	...	...	2109	...	...
s Rosa de Lima	a.	...	...	2204	...	...
dolid Campo Grande	a.	...	...	2320	...	...
drid Chamartín	d.	...	...	|	2150	...
la	d.	...	...	|	2311	...
na del Campo	a.	...	...	2351	2355	...
nanca	a.	...	...	0057	0057	...
d Rodrigo	a.	...	...	0206	0206	...
es d'Oñoro 🏛 ES	d.	...	...	0230	0230	...
Formoso 🏛 PT	d.	...	...	0150	0150	...
da	a.	...	...	0222	0222	...
ualde	a.	...	...	0323	0323	...
bra-B	a.	...	...	0446	0446	0520
bal	a.	...	...	0521	0521	|
oncamento	a.	...	...	0605	0605	|
oa Oriente	a.	...	...	0720	0720	|
oa Santa Apolónia	a.	...	...	0730	0730	|
Aveiro	a.	...	...	...	...	0601
Porto Campanhã	a.	...	...	...	...	0650

train type/number		IR	Hotel	Hotel	TGV	
train number		822	335	310	8544	
notes		🅁 🍸	🅁 🍸	🅁 🍸	🅁 ↗	
			L	B	⑧	
Porto Campanhã	d.	2155	...	...	...	...
Aveiro	d.	2245	...	...	...	...
Lisboa Santa Apolónia	d.	|	2125	2125	...	...
Lisboa Oriente	d.	|	2134	2134	...	...
Entroncamento	d.	|	2230	2230	...	...
Pombal	d.	|	2306	2306	...	...
Coimbra-B	d.	2325	2332	2332	...	...
Mangualde	d.	...	0046	0046	...	...
Guarda	d.	...	0145	0146	...	...
Vilar Formoso 🏛 PT	d.	...	0235	0235	...	...
Fuentes d'Oñoro 🏛 ES	d.	...	0340	0340	...	...
Ciudad Rodrigo	d.	...	0359	0359	...	...
Salamanca	d.	...	0456	0456	...	...
Medina del Campo	d.	...	0618	0600	...	...
Ávila	a.	...	0705	|	...	...
Madrid Chamartín	a.	...	0840	|	...	...
Valladolid Campo Grande	d.	...	...	0629	...	...
Burgos Rosa de Lima	d.	...	...	0748	...	...
Miranda de Ebro	d.	...	...	0848	...	...
Vitoria/Gasteiz	d.	...	...	0912	...	...
San Sebastián/Donostia	d.	...	...	1055	...	...
Irún	a.	...	...	1118	...	...
Hendaye 🏛	a.	...	...	1128	1419	...
Biarritz	a.	...	...	...	1443	...
Bordeaux St Jean	a.	...	...	...	1711	...
Paris Montparnasse	a.	...	...	...	2033	...
Paris Nord 10	d.	...	...	...	...	...
London St Pancras 10	a.	...	...	...	...	...

ES FOR TABLES 45 AND 46

SUREX/SUD EXPRESSO *Trenhotel* – 🛏 *Gran Clase/Gran Classe* (1, 2 berths), 🛏 *Preferente* (1, 2 berths), 🛏 *Turista* (4 berths), [2] 🍸 Irún (**312**) - Vilar Formoso (**313**) - Lisboa.
SUD EXPRESSO/SUREX *Trenhotel* – 🛏 *Gran Clase/Gran Classe* (1, 2 berths), 🛏 *Preferente* (1, 2 berths), 🛏 *Turista* (4 berths), [2] 🍸 Lisboa (**310**) - Vilar Formoso (**311**) - Hendaye.
🚌 operated by Avanza, additional buses operate, rail tickets not valid; www.avanzabus.com
LUSITANIA *Hotel Train* – 🛏 *Gran Clase/Gran Classe* (1, 2 berths), 🛏 *Preferente* (1, 2 berths), 🛏 *Turista* (4 berths), [2] 🍸 🅁 Madrid (**332/3**) - Medina del Campo (**312**) - Lisboa and Lisboa (**310**) - Medina del Campo (**330/5**) - Madrid. Special fares apply.

MADRID - LISBOA 46

		🚌	🚌	🚌	332
		C	C	C	L
			①–⑤		
Madrid Chamartín	d.	...	...	...	2150
Madrid Estación Sur ✥	d.	1000	1430	2100	|
Cáceres	d.	|	1915	|	|
Badajoz ❦ 🏛 ES	d.	1530	2030	0230	|
Elvas 🏛 PT	d.	|	|	|	|
Lisboa Oriente	a.	1700	2200	0400	0730

		🚌	🚌	🚌	335
		C	C	C	L
			①–⑤		
Lisboa Oriente	d.	0915	1215	2015	2125
Elvas 🏛 PT	d.	|	|	|	|
Badajoz ❦ 🏛 ES	d.	1330	1630	0015	|
Cáceres	a.	|	1800	|	|
Madrid Estación Sur ✥	a.	1840	2155	0530	|
Madrid Chamartín	a.	...	...	...	0840

NOTES FOR TABLES 45 AND 46

f – 0752 on ⑥.
g – Not May 30, Aug. 29, Nov. 11.

↗ – Supplement payable.
ES – Spain (Central European Time).
PT – Portugal (West European Time).
✥ – Madrid south bus station close to Méndez Álvaro metro (see Madrid city plan on page 30).
❦ – Badajoz railway station is 1 km north of Badajoz city centre and Badajoz bus station is 2.5 km south of Badajoz city centre.
☆ – Eurostar train. 🅁, ✕ in Business Premier and Standard Premier, 🍸 in Standard. Special fares payable. Minimum check-in time 30 minutes. Valid May 29 - Dec. 10. Additional Eurostar services are available, see Table **10**.

LONDON - PARIS - HENDAYE / IRÚN - MADRID 47

train type/number		TGV	MD	Alvia	MD	☆		MD	RE	
train number		8531	18014	4166	18310	9044	4053	18012	18318	
notes		🅁 ↗	2		2		🅁	2	2	
		①–⑥					P✥			
don St Pancras 10	d.	...	...	...	...	1731	...	...	...	...
s Nord 10	a.	...	...	...	...	2047	...	...	...	...
s Montparnasse	d.	0728	...	...	...	...	...	...	...	...
ris Austerlitz	d.	|	...	...	...	...	2152	...	...	...
s Aubrais-Orléans	d.	|	...	...	...	...	2252	...	...	...
eaux St Jean	d.	1051	...	...	...	...	|	...	...	...
itz	d.	1247	...	...	...	...	0848	...	...	...
daye	a.	1316	...	...	...	...	0914a	...	...	...
🏛	a.	1325	1350	1615	...	...	0925	1050	...	...
Sebastián/Donostia	a.	...	1407	1631	...	...	...	1107	...	...
ia/Gasteiz	a.	...	1555	1807	...	...	...	1255	...	...
nda de Ebro	a.	...	1616	1829	...	...	...	1316	...	...
os Rosa de Lima	a.	...	1713	1931	...	...	...	1413	...	...
adolid Campo Grande	a.	...	1845	2048	2135	...	...	1543	1905	...
na del Campo	a.	...	1911	|	2209	...	...	1609	1932	...
manca	a.	...	|	|	2252	...	...	|	2021	...
vila	d.	...	1958	|	...	...	...	1658	...	...
adrid Chamartín	d.	...	2144	2206	...	...	...	1840	...	...

train type/number		RE	Alvia	TGV	MD	Av	MD		☆	
train number		18302	4087	8544	18061	8109	18061	4052	9015	
notes		2	🍸	🅁 ↗	2		2	🅁		
				⑧		2		Q✥		
Madrid Chamartín	d.	...	0800	...	0905	1015	...	...	...	...
Ávila	a.	...	|	...	1038	|	...	...	...	...
Salamanca	d.	0712	|	...	|	|	...	...	...	...
Medina del Campo	d.	0802	|	...	1125	|	←	...	...	...
Valladolid Campo Grande	d.	0830	0918	...	1149	1120	1150	...	...	...
Burgos Rosa de Lima	d.	...	1028	...	→	...	1320	...	...	...
Miranda de Ebro	d.	...	1128	...	...	...	1417	...	...	...
Vitoria/Gasteiz	d.	...	1151	...	...	...	1440	...	...	...
San Sebastián/Donostia	d.	...	1326	...	...	...	1629	...	...	...
Irún	a.	...	1348	...	...	...	1651	...	...	...
Hendaye 🏛	a.	...	1355	1445	...	...	...	1924	...	...
Biarritz	a.	...	...	1511	...	...	...	1954	...	...
Bordeaux St Jean	a.	...	...	1711	...	...	...	|	...	...
Les Aubrais-Orléans	a.	...	...	|	...	...	...	0608	...	...
Paris Austerlitz	a.	...	...	|	...	...	...	0720	...	...
Paris Montparnasse	a.	...	...	2033	...	...	...	...	...	...
Paris Nord 10	d.	...	...	...	...	...	...	...	0913	...
London St Pancras 10	a.	...	...	...	...	...	...	...	1039	...

INTERCITÉS – for dates of running see Table **305**.
🛏 1, 2 cl. [2] (reclining) Paris - Irún ✥.
INTERCITÉS – for dates of running see Table **305**.
🛏 1, 2 cl. [2] (reclining) Hendaye - Paris ✥.

✥ – Subject to confirmation from July 1.
↗ – Supplement payable.
Alvia – 🅁 🍸 ↗.

☆ – Eurostar train. 🅁, ✕ in Business Premier and Standard Premier, 🍸 in Standard. Special fares payable. Minimum check-in time 30 minutes. Valid May 29 - Dec. 10. Additional Eurostar services are available, see Table **10**.

FRANKFURT - STRASBOURG - LYON - MARSEILLE 48

Service from July 3. Service December 13 - July 2 is on page 71.

train type				ICE	TGV	ICE			TGV	TGV	
train number				9568	9877	107			9580	9836	
notes			①–⑤	🅁★	9876			①–⑤	9581	9837	
				⑧	🅁★				🅁★	🅁	
öln Hbf	d.	...	...	...	...	1255	...	...	...	...	...
nkfurt (Main) Hbf	d.	...	...	0658	...	|	...	...	1359	...	...
nheim	d.	...	...	0739	...	1423	...	...	1439	...	...
sruhe	d.	...	...	0807	...	...	...	...	1512	...	...
en-Baden	d.	...	...	|	...	...	...	...	1534	...	...
ffenburg	d.	0734	0804	|	...	...	1434	1504	|	...	...
l 🏛	d.	0754	0822	|	...	...	1452	1522	|	...	...
asbourg	a.	0805	0834	0851	...	...	1504	1534	1600	...	...
asbourg	d.	...	...	...	0906	...	...	...	1615	...	...
house	a.	...	...	...	1003	...	...	...	1705	...	...
ort Montbéliard TGV	a.	...	...	...	1030	...	...	...	1732	...	...
ançon TGV ⊖	a.	...	...	...	1054	...	...	...	1756	...	...
lon sur Saône	a.	...	...	...	|	...	...	...	1853	...	...
n Part Dieu	a.	...	...	...	1256	...	...	...	1956	2010	...
non TGV	a.	...	...	...	1407	...	...	...	2108	|	...
en Provence TGV	a.	...	...	...	1431	...	...	...	2131	|	...
seille St Charles	a.	...	...	...	1446	...	...	...	2142	|	...
imes	a.	...	...	...	...	...	...	...	...	2133	...
ontpellier	a.	...	...	...	...	...	...	...	...	2204	...

train type		TGV	TGV			ICE	TGV		TGV	ICE	ICE
train number		9862	9582			106	6874		9577	100	590
notes		9863	9583	①–⑤			6875		🅁		698
		🅁	🅁★				🅁★		⑧		992
Montpellier	d.	0656	...	...	...	...	...	...	...	...	...
Nimes	d.	0726	...	...	...	...	...	...	...	...	...
Marseille St Charles	d.	|	0814	...	...	...	1244	...	...	...	...
Aix en Provence TGV	d.	|	0829	...	...	...	1259	...	...	...	...
Avignon TGV	d.	|	0851	...	...	...	1321	...	...	...	...
Lyon Part Dieu	d.	0854	1004	...	...	...	1432	...	...	...	...
Chalon sur Saône	d.	...	1108	...	...	...	|	...	...	...	...
Besançon TGV ⊖	d.	...	1205	...	...	...	1657	...	...	...	...
Belfort Montbéliard TGV	d.	...	1230	...	...	...	1730	...	...	...	...
Mulhouse	d.	...	1257	...	...	...	1804	...	...	...	...
Strasbourg	a.	...	1344	...	...	...	1857	...	...	...	...
Strasbourg	d.	...	1355	1422	1452	...	...	1922	1947	...	...
Kehl 🏛	a.	...	|	1433	1503	...	...	1933	|	...	...
Offenburg	a.	...	|	1452	1522	...	...	1952	|	2028	...
Baden-Baden	a.	...	1422	...	...	...	...	...	|	2042	...
Karlsruhe	a.	...	1446	...	...	...	...	...	2025	2059	...
Mannheim	a.	...	1518	...	...	1536	...	...	...	2124	2132
Frankfurt (Main) Hbf	a.	...	1558	...	...	|	...	...	...	|	2208
Köln Hbf	a.	...	...	...	...	1705	...	...	...	2307	...

Alleo ICE/TGV service. A DB/SNCF joint enterprise.

⊖ – Full name: Besançon Franche-Comté TGV.

50 OSLO, STOCKHOLM and KØBENHAVN - HAMBURG - BERLIN

train type / train number	EC	ICE			ICE		1/3			ICE	ICE		Sn			ICE	IC					
train number	232	209			38		[R]			36	1719		519	1039		34	2071					
notes	🍷	🍷			🍷		Ⓑ			🍷	🍷		①–⑤	①–⑥		🍷	🍷					
notes	Pc				c		J			c			Q			c						
Stockholm Central d.	...	...	...	...	...	...	2310	...	...	...	...	...	0521	...	...	...	...	...	...	...	...	...
Göteborg d.	...	...	...	...	...	...	|	...	...	...	...	...	|	0655	...	...	...	...	...	...	...	...
Malmö C ⊡ d.	...	...	...	0653	...	...	0648	0653	0833	...	...	...	0950	0953	1033	...	...	...	...	...	...	...
København H. ⊡ d.	0537	...	...	0728	0737	...	...	0728	0908	0937	...	...	1024j	1028	1108	1137	...	...	...	...	...	...
Rødby Ferry ⛴ d.	0736	...	...	...	0936	...	...	...	...	1136	...	...	...	...	...	1336	...	...	...	...	...	...
Puttgarden ⛴ a.	0836	...	...	...	1036	...	...	...	...	1236	...	...	...	...	...	1436	...	...	...	...	...	...
Lübeck Hbf a.	|	...	...	...	1137	...	...	...	...	1337	...	...	...	...	...	1537	...	...	...	...	...	...
Hamburg Hbf a.	1021	1051	...	...	1221	...	...	...	...	1421	1505	...	...	...	...	1622	1629	...	...	...	...	...
Berlin Hbf a.	...	1235	...	...	...	...	...	...	...	...	1643	...	...	...	...	...	1834	...	...	...	...	...

train type / train number	Sn	Sn			EC	IC	Sn	391			ICE	ICE	Sn	Sn			ICE	EC		EN	IC	
train number	521	523	1051		1238	2073	527	105	1063		32	905	529	531	1075		30	1130		301	70187	
notes	①–⑥	①–⑤			🍷	🍷		①–⑥			🍷									①④⑥	230	
notes					Pc						c			R			Tc	Pc		Gb	K	
Oslo Sentral d.	...	...	...	...	...	...	...	0701	...	...	...	...	...	...	...	...	...	...	...	...	...	...
Stockholm Central d.	0621	0721	...	...	...	...	0921	|	...	...	...	...	1021	1121	...	...	...	...	...	...	...	...
Göteborg d.	|	|	0855	...	...	...	|	1040	1055	...	...	...	|	|	1255	...	...	...	...	...	...	...
København H. ⊡ d.	|	|	|	...	...	...	...	...	|	...	...	...	|	|	|	...	...	...	1552	...	...	...
Malmö C ⊡ d.	1050	1147	1153	1233	...	...	1347	...	1353	1433	...	...	1450	1547	1553	1633	...	...	1626	1700	...	...
København H. ⊡ d.	1124	...	1228	1308	1337	...	...	...	1428	1508	1537	...	1524	...	1628	1708	1737	1737	...	|	2202	...
Rødby Ferry ⛴ d.	...	...	...	...	1536	...	...	...	...	...	1736	...	...	...	...	...	1936	1936	...	|	|	...
Puttgarden ⛴ a.	...	...	...	...	1636	...	...	...	...	...	1836	...	...	...	...	...	2036	2036	...	|	|	...
Lübeck Hbf a.	...	...	...	...	1737	...	...	...	...	...	1937	...	...	...	...	...	2137	2137	...	|	|	...
Hamburg Hbf a.	...	...	...	...	1822	1827	...	...	...	...	2021	2121	...	...	...	...	2223	2223	...	|	0528	...
Berlin Hbf a.	...	...	...	...	...	2035	...	...	...	...	...	2312	...	...	...	...	...	...	...	0625	...	...

train type	EN			394	Sn	ICE	EC			398	Sn	Sn	ICE	IC	ICE			Sn	ICE	IC	EC	
train number	300		1020	124	528	31	1131		1056	134	540	512	1618	2070	33		1068	544	806	2072	1233	
notes	③⑤⑦										Ⓑ	⑥			🍷						🍷	
notes	Cb				M	Tc	Pc								c						Pc	
Berlin Hbf d.	1928	...	...	...	...	...	...	...	...	...	...	...	0638	0706	...	...	...	...	0839	0906	...	...
Hamburg Hbf d.	|	...	...	...	...	0724	0724	...	...	...	...	...	0824	0910	0928	...	...	...	1021	1111	1126	...
Lübeck Hbf d.	|	...	...	...	...	0806	0806	...	...	...	...	...	...	...	1006	...	...	...	...	...	1206	...
Puttgarden ⛴ d.	|	...	...	...	...	0908	0908	...	...	...	...	...	...	...	1108	...	...	...	...	...	1308	...
Rødby Ferry ⛴ a.	|	...	...	...	...	1008	1008	...	...	...	...	...	...	...	1208	...	...	...	...	...	1408	...
København H. ⊡ d.	|	...	...	...	...	1222	1222	1232	1332	...	...	1424f	...	...	1422	1432	1532	...	...	...	1622	1632
Malmö C ⊡ a.	0725	0733	0808	...	0811	...	...	1306	1406	...	1411	1459	...	...	...	1506	1606	1611	...	...	...	1706
København H. ⊡ d.	...	0808	|	...	|	...	...	...	|	...	|	|	...	...	...	...	|	|	...	...	...	...
Göteborg a.	...	...	1105	1300	|	...	...	...	1705	1755	|	|	...	...	...	...	1905	|	...	...	...	...
Stockholm Central a.	...	...	...	|	1239	...	...	...	...	|	1839	1939	...	...	...	...	...	2039	...	...	...	...
Oslo Sentral a.	...	...	...	1652	...	...	...	...	...	2149	...	...	...	...	...	...	...	...	...	...	...	...

train type / train number	ICE	ICE			Sn		ICE	ICE		2		ICE	ICE			ICE	EC			IC		Sn
train number	1616	35		1092	550		1034	37		[R]		800	39			802	239			231		516
notes	①–⑥				Ⓑ		1714			Ⓑ						1610				1231		526
notes		c						c		J			c				Pc			K		
Berlin Hbf d.	1039	...	...	...	...	...	1238	...	...	...	...	1439	...	...	...	1639	...	...	...	...	...	...
Hamburg Hbf d.	1221	1328	...	...	...	...	1422	1528	...	...	...	1621	1728	...	...	1821	1925	...	...	2342	...	...
Lübeck Hbf d.	...	1406	...	...	...	...	...	1606	...	...	...	...	1806	...	...	...	2006	...	...	|	...	...
Puttgarden ⛴ d.	...	1508	...	...	...	...	...	1708	...	...	...	...	1908	...	...	...	2108	...	...	|	...	...
Rødby Ferry ⛴ a.	...	1608	...	...	...	...	...	1808	...	...	...	...	2008	...	...	...	2208	...	...	|	...	...
København H. ⊡ d.	...	1822	1832	1932	...	...	...	2022	2032	...	...	...	2222	2232	...	...	0029	0112	...	0540	0612	...
Malmö C ⊡ a.	...	...	1906	2006	1911	...	...	...	2106	2237	...	...	...	2306	...	...	...	0146	...	...	0646	0711
Göteborg a.	...	...	...	2305	|	...	...	...	...	|	...	...	...	...	...	...	...	...	...	...	...	|
Stockholm Central a.	...	...	...	...	2339	...	...	...	...	0616	...	...	...	...	...	...	...	...	...	...	...	1139

C – BERLIN NIGHT EXPRESS – ③⑤⑦ June 27 - Aug. 28: 2 cl., 🍷 (✕ on board ferry) Berlin - Malmö. [R] Special fares apply.

G – BERLIN NIGHT EXPRESS – ①④⑥ June 27 - Aug. 28: 2 cl., 🍷 (✕ on board ferry) Malmö - Berlin. [R] Special fares apply. *EN* **301** arrives Berlin Hbf 0625, passengers are allowed on until 0700.

J – Ⓑ: 1,2 cl., 2 cl., (2. cl.) 🍷 [R] Stockholm - Malmö and v.v.

K – June 24 - Sept. 4. Via Flensburg ⛴ and Padborg ⛴. Depart Hamburg 2357, arrive København 0556, 0608, 0612, 0623, 0656, 0756 on certain dates.

L – June 24 - Sept. 4. Via Padborg ⛴ and Flensburg ⛴. Depart København 2302, arrive Hamburg 0540, 0541 on certain dates.

M – ①–⑤ Apr. 4 - July 4. ①⑥ July 9 - Aug. 13. ①–⑤ Aug. 15 - Dec. 9.

P – June 18 - Sept. 4.

Q – Not June 24 - Aug. 28.

R – July 3 - Aug. 13.

S – Mar. 18 - June 17.

T – Mar. 18 - June 17; Sept. 5 - Oct. 30.

b – Train is conveyed by train-ferry Trelleborg ⛴ - Sassnitz Fährhafen ⛴ (Mukran) and v.v.

c – Passengers to / from Rødby or Puttgarden may be required to leave / board the train on board the f

f – Not Apr. 9 - June 25.

j – 1042 until June 23.

Sn – *Snabbtåg* high speed train. [R] ✕.

⊡ – Additional services Malmö - København and v.v. are available, see Table **703**.

51 BERLIN - TORUN / GDYNIA

train type	EC	
train number	55	88100
notes	[R]	
notes	H	A
Berlin Hbf d.	1437	...
Berlin Ost d.	1450	...
Berlin Lichtenberg d.	|	1837
Frankfurt (Oder) ⛴ d.	1545	|
Rzepin a.	1605	|
Kostrzyn ⛴ a.	|	1948
Gorzów Wlkp. a.	|	2030
Krzyż a.	|	2118
Poznań Gł. a.	1724	...
Gniezno a.	1757	...
Inowrocław a.	1827	...
Piła a.	|	...
Bydgoszcz Gł. a.	1853	...
Torun Gł. d.	|	...
Tczew a.	2001	...
Gdańsk Gł. a.	2018	...
Sopot a.	2035	...
Gdynia Gł. a.	2044	...

train type		EC
train number	88033	54
notes		[R]
notes	A	H
Gdynia Gł. d.	...	0711
Sopot d.	...	0720
Gdańsk Gł. d.	...	0737
Tczew d.	...	0754
Torun Gł. d.	...	|
Bydgoszcz Gł. d.	...	0901
Piła d.	...	|
Inowrocław d.	...	0928
Gniezno d.	...	1000
Poznań Gł. d.	...	1032
Krzyż d.	0732	|
Gorzów Wlkp. d.	0828	|
Kostrzyn ⛴ d.	0911	|
Rzepin d.	|	1152
Frankfurt (Oder) ⛴ a.	|	1212
Berlin Lichtenberg a.	1028	|
Berlin Ost a.	...	1306
Berlin Hbf a.	...	1315

A – Operated by Arriva (Table **1000**).

H – BERLIN GDANSK EXPRESS (12) ✕ [R] Berlin - Poznań - Gdynia and v.v.(Table **1020**).

52 PRAHA - ZÜRICH

train type				CNL
train number	1541	1543	1545	458
notes				B
Praha hlavní d.	0535	0935	1335	1827
Praha Holešovice d.	|	|	|	1836
Tábor d.	0701	1101	1501	|
Veselí nad Lužnicí d.	0729	1129	1529	|
České Budějovice d.	0813	1213	1613	|
Summerau ⛴ d.	0913	1314	1714	◧
Linz Hbf a.	1024	1424	1824	|
	RJ	*RJ*	*RJ*	|
	162	**166**	**760**	|
	🍷	🍷	🍷	|
Linz Hbf d.	1048	1448	1848	|
Salzburg a.	1152	1552	1952	|
Innsbruck Hbf a.	1340	1738	2138	|
Zürich HB a.	1720	2120	...	0905

train type	RJ	EC	RJ
train number	765	163	563
notes	🍷	🍷	🍷
Zürich HB d.	...	0840	...
Innsbruck Hbf d.	0820	1216	1220
Salzburg d.	1008	...	1408
Linz Hbf a.	1112	...	1512
	1540		**1542**
Linz Hbf d.	1135	...	1535
Summerau ⛴ a.	1243	...	1642
České Budějovice a.	1345	...	1745
Veselí nad Lužnicí a.	1429	...	1829
Tábor a.	1458	...	1858
Praha Holešovice a.	|	...	|
Praha hlavní a.	1623	...	2023

A – *City Night Line* CANOPUS – 1,2 cl., 2 cl. 🍷 (*CNL* **40470** [R]) Zürich - Frankfurt - Praha; (2. cl.) (*IC* **60470**) Zürich - Frankfurt - Praha. Special fares apply.

B – *City Night Line* CANOPUS – 1,2 cl., 2 cl. 🍷 (*CNL* **458** [R]) Praha - Frankfurt - Zürich; (2. cl.) (*IC* **60458**) Praha - Frankfurt - Zürich. Special fares apply.

RJ – ÖBB *Railjet* service. (premium class), (first class), (economy class), ✕.

◧ – ⛴ at Bad Schandau and Basel Bad Bf.

TRAIN NAMES: **1540 / 1541** – F A GERSTNER **1542 / 1543** – ANTON BRUCKNER **1545** – FERDINAND KINDERMANN

ZÜRICH and KÖLN - WARSZAWA, PRAHA and BERLIN 54

		CNL 470 61470	CNL 40470 60470	CNL 478 60478		EN 447 ®	CNL 40447 61447			
		S	A	P		J	H			
ı HB d.	...	1942	1942	2142	...	...	...	...	...	...
SBB d.	...	2113	2113	2313	...	...	...	...	...	...
ıhe Hbf d.	...	2304	2304	0129	...	...	...	...	...	...
furt (Main) Süd d.	...	0054	0054	0349f	...	...	...	...	...	...
Hbf a.	...	0337	0337	|	...	...	...	...	...	...
ar a.	...	0353	0353	|	...	...	...	...	...	...
g Hbf a.	...	0450	0450	|	...	...	...	...	...	...
ı Hbf d.	...	|	|	|	...	2313	2313	...	...	...
seldorf Hbf d.	...	|	|	|	...	2337	2337	...	...	...
ıburg Hbf d.	...	|	|	|	...	2353	2353	...	...	...
tmund Hbf d.	...	|	|	|	...	0032	0032	...	...	...
ım (Westf) d.	...	|	|	|	...	0049	0049	...	...	...
efeld Hbf d.	...	|	|	|	...	0124	0124	...	...	...
ı Wannsee a.	...	|	|	|	...	0515	0515	...	...	...
ı Hbf a.	...	0723	|	|	...	0625	|	...	...	...
Ostbahnhof a.	...	...	|	|	...	0647	|	...	...	...
/arszawa Centralna a.	...	...	|	|	...	1215	|	...	...	...
sden Hbf a.	...	...	0706	|	...	...	0858	...	...	...
ha hlavní a.	...	...	0928	|	...	...	1128	...	...	...
›ver a.	...	...	...	0658	...	...	...	...	...	...
urg Hbf a.	...	...	...	0836	...	...	...	...	...	...

		CNL 479 60479	CNL 458 60458	CNL 471 60471		EN 446 ®	CNL 40458 61458			
		Q	B	T		J	K			
Hamburg Hbf d.	...	2029	...	...	...	...	...	...	...	...
Hannover d.	...	2201	...	...	...	...	...	...	...	...
Praha hlavní d.	...	|	1827	...	...	...	1827	...	...	...
Dresden Hbf d.	...	|	2054	...	...	...	2107	...	...	...
Warszawa Centralna d.	...	|	|	...	...	1800	|	...	...	...
Berlin Ostbahnhof d.	...	|	|	...	...	2333	2333	...	...	...
Berlin Hbf d.	...	|	|	2150	...	2344	2344	...	...	...
Berlin Wannsee d.	...	|	|	|	...	|	|	...	...	...
Bielefeld Hbf a.	...	|	|	|	...	0437	0437	...	...	...
Hamm (Westf) a.	...	|	|	|	...	0510	0510	...	...	...
Dortmund Hbf a.	...	|	|	|	...	0531	0531	...	...	...
Duisburg Hbf a.	...	|	|	|	...	0616	0616	...	...	...
Düsseldorf Hbf a.	...	|	|	|	...	0631	0631	...	...	...
Köln Hbf a.	...	|	|	|	...	0656	0656	...	...	...
Leipzig Hbf d.	...	|	0005	0005	...	...	...	...	...	...
Weimar d.	...	|	0116	0116	...	...	...	...	...	...
Erfurt Hbf d.	...	|	0133	0133	...	...	...	...	...	...
Frankfurt (Main) Süd a.	...	0113f	0359	0359	...	...	...	...	...	...
Karlsruhe Hbf a.	...	0400	0507	0507	...	...	...	...	...	...
Basel SBB a.	...	0619	0720	0720	...	...	...	...	...	...
Zürich HB a.	...	0805	0905	0905	...	...	...	...	...	...

City Night Line CANOPUS – 1, 2 cl., 2 cl. (*CNL* **40470** ®) Zürich - Frankfurt - Bad Schandau - Praha; 2 (*IC* **60470**) Zürich - Frankfurt - Praha. Special fares apply.
City Night Line CANOPUS – 1, 2 cl., 2 cl. (*CNL* **458** ®) Praha - Frankfurt - Zürich; 2 (*IC* **60458**) Praha - Bad Schandau - Frankfurt - Zürich. Special fares apply.
City Night Line KOPERNIKUS – 1, 2 cl., 2 cl., (*CNL* **40447** ®) Köln - Berlin (**171**) - Praha; 2 (*IC* **61447**) Köln - Berlin (**171**) - Praha. Special fares apply.
JAN KIEPURA – 1, 2 cl., 2 cl., 2 (reclining) Köln - Warszawa and v.v. (Table **56**).
City Night Line KOPERNIKUS – 1, 2 cl., 2 cl., (*CNL* **40458** ®) Praha - Köln; 2 (*IC* **61458**) Praha - Köln. Special fares apply.
City Night Line KOMET – 1, 2 cl., 2 cl. (*CNL* **478**) Zürich - Hamburg; 2 (*IC* **60478**) Zürich - Hamburg. Special fares apply.

Q – *City Night Line* KOMET – 1, 2 cl., 2 cl. (*CNL* **479**) Hamburg - Zürich; 2 (*IC* **60479**) Hamburg - Zürich. Special fares apply.
S – *City Night Line* SIRIUS – 1, 2 cl., 2 cl. (*CNL* **470** ®) Zürich - Frankfurt - Berlin; 2 (*IC* **61470**) Zürich - Frankfurt - Berlin. Special fares apply.
T – *City Night Line* SIRIUS – 1, 2 cl., 2 cl. (*CNL* **471** ®) Berlin - Frankfurt - Zürich; 2 (*IC* **60471**) Berlin - Frankfurt - Zürich. Special fares apply.

f – Frankfurt (Main) **Hbf**.

FRANKFURT - LEIPZIG - DRESDEN - PRAHA 55

train type	*CNL*	*IC*		*EC*	*IC*	*IC*	*EC*	*ICE*	*IC*	*EC*	*ICE*	*IC*	*EC*	*IC*	*IC*	*EC*	*ICE*	*IC*	*EC*	*IC*	*IC*	*EN*	*EN*	
train number	**40470**	**60470**		**171**	**2153**	**2447**	**173**	**2157**	**2445**	**379**	**1597**	**2443**	**175**	**2159**	**2441**	**177**	**1651**	**2049**	**179**	**2251**	**2047**	**477**	**60477**	
notes		2		✕	Ⓐ		✕	🍸	①–⑥	✕	🍸	①–⑥	✕	🍸		✕	🍸	**2249**	✕	🍸	Ⓑ	🍸	**407**	
	A	**A**		**L**			**C**									**P**			**Q**			**M**		
furt Flughafen ✈ d.	...	...	...	...	...	...	...	...	...	...	0902	...	...	1102	...	...	1302	...	...	1502	...	...	...	...
furt (Main) Hbf d.	...	...	...	...	0452f	...	...	0718	...	...	0919	...	...	1119	...	...	1319	...	...	1520	...	...	...	...
furt (Main) Süd d.	0054	0054	...	...	|	...	...	|	...	...	|	...	...	|	...	...	|	...	...	|	...	...	...	...
d.	|	|	...	...	0551f	...	...	0814	...	...	1014	...	...	1214	...	...	1414	...	...	1614	...	...	...	...
Hbf d.	|	0339	...	...	0732	...	...	0934	...	...	1134	...	...	1334	...	...	1534	...	...	1734	...	...	...	...
ar d.	|	0355	...	...	0749	...	...	|	...	...	|	...	...	|	...	...	|	...	...	|	...	...	...	...
ig d.	0458s	0557	...	...	0846	0929	...	1046	1129	...	1246	1329	...	1446	1529	...	1646	1729	...	1846	1929	...	...	...
len Hbf d.	0706s	0708	...	0908	...	1037	1108	...	1237	1308	...	1437	1508	...	1637	1708	...	1837	1908	...	2037	2108	2108	...
Schandau 🏛 ◧ d.	0736s	0738	...	0938	...	...	1138	...	...	1338	...	...	1538	...	...	1738	...	...	1938	...	...	|	|	...
🏛 ◧ d.	0753s	0756	...	0957	...	...	1157	...	...	1357	...	...	1557	...	...	1757	...	...	1957	...	...	2157	2157	...
Holešovice a.	0918	0918	...	1118	...	...	1318	...	...	1518	...	...	1718	...	...	1918	...	...	2118	...	...	2318	2318	...
a hlavní a.	0928	0928	...	1128	...	...	1328	...	...	1528	...	...	1728	...	...	1928	...	...	2128	...	...	2328	2328	...
en Hbf **1150** a.	...	...	...	...	...	...	|	...	...	...	...	...	...	...	...	...	...	...	...	...	...	|	0706	...
tislava hlavná **1150** a.	...	...	...	...	...	...	1750	...	...	...	...	...	...	...	...	...	...	...	...	...	...	0536	...	...
dapest Keleti **1175** a.	...	...	...	...	...	...	2035	...	...	...	...	...	...	...	...	...	...	...	...	...	...	0835	...	...

train type	*EC*	*IC*	*ICE*	*EC*	*IC*	*ICE*	*EC*	*IC*	*IC*	*EC*	*IC*	*ICE*	*EC*	*IC*	*IC*	*EC*	*IC*	*IC*	*CNL*		*EN*	*EN*	*IC*	*IC*
train number	**178**	**2048**	**2250**	**176**	**2440**	**1558**	**174**	**2442**	**2154**	**378**	**2444**	**1554**	**172**	**2446**	**2152**	**170**	**2030**	**60458**	**458**		**476**	**60406**	**2046**	**2252**
notes	✕			✕			✕			✕			✕			✕	Ⓑ	2			🍸	**476**	①–⑥	
	D			**P**									**C**			**L**		**B**	**B**		**M**			
dapest Keleti **1175** d.	...	...	...	...	...	...	...	...	...	...	...	...	0725	...	...	...	...	...	...	...	2005	...	...	...
tislava hlavná **1150** d.	...	...	...	...	...	...	...	...	...	...	...	...	1010	...	...	...	...	...	...	...	2301	...	...	...
en Hbf **1150** d.	...	...	...	...	...	...	...	...	...	...	...	...	|	...	...	...	...	...	...	...	|	2250	...	...
a hlavní d.	0627	...	...	0827	...	...	1027	...	...	1227	...	...	1427	...	...	1627	...	1827	1827	...	0427	0427	...	...
a Holešovice d.	0636	...	...	0836	...	...	1036	...	...	1236	...	...	1436	...	...	1636	...	1836	1836	...	0436	0436	...	...
🏛 ◧ d.	0800	...	...	1000	...	...	1200	...	...	1400	...	...	1600	...	...	1800	...	2000	2000u	...	0600	0600	...	...
Schandau 🏛 ◧ a.	0815	...	...	1015	...	...	1215	...	...	1415	...	...	1615	...	...	1815	...	2015	2017u	...	|	|	...	...
len Hbf a.	0844	0920	...	1044	1120	...	1244	1320	...	1444	1520	...	1644	1720	...	1844	1920	2045	2054u	...	0644	0644	0720	...
ig a.	...	1028	1111	...	1228	1311	...	1428	1511	...	1628	1711	...	1828	1911	...	2028	2226	2336u	...	...	...	0828	0911
ar a.	...	...	|	...	...	|	...	...	|	...	...	|	...	...	|	...	...	|	|	...	...	...	...	|
Hbf a.	...	...	1223	...	...	1423	...	...	1623	...	...	1823	...	...	2027	...	...	0131	|	...	...	...	...	1023
a.	...	...	1342	...	...	1542	...	...	1742	...	...	1942	...	...	2152	...	...	0254	|	...	...	...	...	1142
furt (Main) Süd a.	...	...	|	...	...	|	...	...	|	...	...	|	...	...	|	...	...	0359	0359	...	...	...	...	|
kfurt (Main) Hbf a.	...	...	1437	...	...	1637	...	...	1837	...	...	2037	...	...	2254	...	...	...	...	...	...	...	...	1237
furt Flughafen ✈ a.	...	...	1455	...	...	1655	...	...	1855	...	...	2055	...	...	...	...	...	...	...	...	...	...	...	1255

City Night Line CANOPUS – 1, 2 cl., 2 cl. (*CNL* **40470** ®) Zürich - Frankfurt - Bad Schandau 🏛 - Praha; 2 (*IC* **60470**) Zürich - Frankfurt - Praha. Special fares apply.
City Night Line CANOPUS – 1, 2 cl., 2 cl. (*CNL* **458** ®) Praha - Frankfurt - Zürich; 2 (*IC* **60458**) Praha - Bad Schandau 🏛 - Frankfurt - Zürich. Special fares apply.
HUNGARIA – 12 ✕ Hamburg - Berlin - Dresden - Praha - Budapest and v.v.
ALOIS NEGRELLI – 12 ✕ Praha - Dresden - Berlin.
PORTA BOHEMICA – 12 ✕ Berlin - Dresden - Praha and v.v.
METROPOL – 1, 2 cl., 2 cl., 2 Berlin - Dresden - Praha - Budapest and v.v.

P – JOHANNES BRAHMS – 12 ✕ Hamburg - Berlin - Dresden - Praha and v.v.
Q – ALOIS NEGRELLI – 12 ✕ Hamburg - Berlin - Dresden - Praha.

f – ①.
s – Calls to set down only.
u – Calls to pick up only.

◧ – Ticketing point is Schöna.

56 LONDON - KÖLN - BERLIN - WARSZAWA - MOSKVA

Services between Berlin and Frankfurt (Oder) will be subject to alteration Aug. 2-4, Nov. 19-28.

train type	*EC*	☆		*ICE*	*EC*			*ICE*	*EC*	⇌	*ICE*	*EC*	⇌	*ICE*	*EC*	☆	*ICE*	☆	⇌	*EN*
train number	**41**	**9032**	**24*JI***	**541**	**43**	**10*ZH***	**68*KJ***	**855**	**45**	**9401**	**857**	**55**	**9413**	**859**	**47**	**9140**	**19**	**9144**	**9473**	**447**
notes	①-⑥		**453**	①-⑥				🍷			🍷			🍷	Ⓑ	Ⓑ	🍷	⑥		
	T		**M**	**b** 🍷	**T**	**P**	**C**	**A**	**T**		**A**	**N**		**A**	**T**					**J**
London St Pancras d.	...	1422	...	...	...	...	...	...	...	...	...	...	...	...	...	1504	...	1604	...	...
Ashford International d.	...	1455	...	...	...	...	...	...	...	...	...	...	...	...	...	|	...	|	...	...
Lille Europe d.	...	|	...	...	...	...	...	...	...	...	...	...	...	...	...	1730	...	1830	...	...
Paris Nord d.	...	1747	1858**e**	...	...	...	...	...	...	0601	...	...	0755	...	...	|	...	|	1755	...
Brussels Midi/Zuid d.	...	...	|	...	...	...	...	...	...	0728	...	...	0928	...	...	1805	1825	1905	1928	...
Liège Guillemins d.	...	...	|	...	...	...	...	...	...	0814	...	...	1014	...	...	...	1914	...	2014	...
Aachen 🏛 d.	...	...	|	...	...	...	...	...	...	0840	...	...	1040	...	...	...	1940	...	2040	...
Köln Hbf a.	...	...	|	...	...	...	...	...	...	0915	...	...	1115	...	...	...	2015	...	2115	...
Köln Hbf d.	...	...	|	0429	...	...	...	0748	...	...	0948	...	...	1148	...	...	...	...	...	2313
Bielefeld Hbf d.	...	...	|	0640	...	...	...	0938	...	...	1138	...	...	1338	...	...	...	...	...	0124
Hannover Hbf d.	...	...	|	0731	...	...	...	1031	...	...	1231	...	...	1431	...	...	...	...	...	0240
Berlin Hbf a.	...	...	0709	0906	...	...	...	1209	...	...	1409	...	...	1609	...	...	...	...	...	0625
Berlin Hbf d.	0637	...	0713	...	0937	...	...	...	1237	...	...	1437	...	...	1637	...	...	...	...	|
Berlin Ostbahnhof d.	0650	...	0750**k**	...	0950	...	...	...	1250	...	...	1450	...	...	1650	...	...	...	...	0647**s**
Frankfurt (Oder) 🏛 d.	0745	...	0855	...	1045	...	...	...	1345	...	...	1545	...	...	1745	...	...	...	...	0742**s**
Rzepin d.	0808	...	0919	...	1108	...	...	...	1408	...	...	1608	...	...	1808	...	...	...	...	0805**s**
Poznań Gł. d.	0938	...	1045	...	1240	...	...	...	1540	...	...	1724	...	...	1930	...	...	...	...	0924**s**
Warszawa Centralna a.	1215	...	1335	...	1515	1840	1850	...	1815	...	...	...	...	...	2205	...	...	...	...	1215**s**
Warszawa Wschodnia d.	1237	...	1417	...	1532	1927	1858	...	1832	...	...	...	...	...	2227	...	...	...	...	1237**s**
Terespol a.	...	...	1617	...	...	2159	...	...	...	...	...	...	...	...	...	...	...	...	...	...
Brest Tsentralny 🏛 a.	...	...	1950**r**	...	...	0139	|	...	...	...	...	...	...	...	...	...	...	...	...	...
Yahodyn 🏛 a.	...	...	|	...	...	|	0030	...	...	...	...	...	...	...	...	...	...	...	...	...
Kyïv a.	...	...	|	...	...	|	1320	...	...	...	...	...	...	...	...	...	...	...	...	...
Minsk a.	...	...	0050	...	...	0724	...	...	...	...	...	...	...	...	...	...	...	...	...	...
Orsha Tsentralnaya § a.	...	...	0318	...	...	1018	...	...	...	...	...	...	...	...	...	...	...	...	...	...
Smolensk Tsentralny 🏛 § a.	...	...	0446	...	...	1148	...	...	...	...	...	...	...	...	...	...	...	...	...	...
Moskva Belorusskaya ‡ a.	...	...	0921	...	...	1620	...	...	...	...	...	...	...	...	...	...	...	...	...	...

train type/number	*EC*	*ICE*	⇌	☆	*EC*	*ICE*	⇌			*EC*	*ICE*	*EC*	*ICE*	*EC*	*EN*	*ICE*	☆	☆		☆
train number	**46**	**950**	**9472**	**9161**	**54**	**858**	**9484**	**9*JA***	**67*KJ***	**44**	**856**	**42**	**842**	**40**	**446**	**18**	**9125**	**9129**	**23*JI***	**9023**
notes	①-⑥	🍷				🍷					🍷		🍷	Ⓑ		🍷		⑦	**452**	
	T	**A**			**N**			**P**	**C**	**T**		**T**		**T**	**J**		**X**		**F**	
Moskva Belorusskaya ‡ d.	...	...	...	...	...	...	...	1627	...	...	...	...	...	...	...	...	...	...	2111	...
Smolensk Tsentralny 🏛 § d.	...	...	...	...	...	...	...	2110	...	...	...	...	...	...	...	...	...	...	0151	...
Orsha Tsentralnaya § d.	...	...	...	...	...	...	...	2234	...	...	...	...	...	...	...	...	...	...	0317	...
Minsk d.	...	...	...	...	...	...	...	0116	...	...	...	...	...	...	...	...	...	...	0556	...
Kyïv d.	...	...	...	...	...	...	...	|	1615	...	...	...	...	...	...	...	...	...	|	...
Yahodyn 🏛 d.	...	...	...	...	...	...	...	|	0415	...	...	...	...	...	...	...	...	...	|	...
Brest Tsentralny 🏛 d.	...	...	...	...	...	...	...	0654	|	...	...	...	...	...	...	...	...	...	1203**f**	...
Terespol d.	...	...	...	...	...	...	...	0601	|	...	...	...	...	...	...	...	...	...	1201	...
Warszawa Wschodnia a.	0548	...	...	...	...	...	...	0831	0901	0948	...	1343	...	1743	1743	...	...	...	1353	...
Warszawa Centralna d.	0600	...	...	...	...	...	...	0855	0910	1000	...	1400	...	1800	1800**u**	...	...	...	1435	...
Poznań Gł. d.	0832	...	...	...	1032	...	...	...	...	1232	...	1632	...	2032	2032**u**	...	...	...	1727	...
Rzepin d.	0952	...	...	...	1152	...	...	...	...	1352	...	1752	...	2152	2152**u**	...	...	...	1902	...
Frankfurt (Oder) 🏛 a.	1012	...	...	...	1212	...	...	...	...	1412	...	1812	...	2207	2209**u**	...	...	...	1924	...
Berlin Ostbahnhof a.	1118	...	...	...	1306	...	...	...	...	1518	...	1918	...	2258	2306**u**	...	...	...	2022**k**	...
Berlin Hbf a.	1143	...	...	...	1315	...	...	...	...	1543	...	1943	...	2321	2340	...	...	...	2104	...
Berlin Hbf d.	...	1149	...	...	...	1349	...	...	...	...	1549	...	1949	...	2344	...	...	...	2109	...
Hannover Hbf a.	...	1328	...	...	...	1528	...	...	...	...	1728	...	2128	...	0244	...	...	...	|	...
Bielefeld Hbf a.	...	1420	...	...	...	1620	...	...	...	...	1820	...	2220	...	0437	...	...	...	|	...
Köln Hbf a.	...	1609	...	...	...	1809	...	...	...	...	2009	...	0030	...	0656	...	...	...	|	...
Köln Hbf d.	...	...	1644	...	...	...	1844	...	...	...	...	...	...	...	...	0743	...	...	|	...
Aachen 🏛 a.	...	...	1720	...	...	...	1920	...	...	...	...	...	...	...	...	0821	...	...	|	...
Liège Guillemins a.	...	...	1746	...	...	...	1946	...	...	...	...	...	...	...	...	0844	...	...	|	...
Brussels Midi/Zuid a.	...	...	1832	1952	...	...	2032	...	...	...	...	...	...	...	...	0935	1056	1156	|	...
Paris Nord a.	...	...	2005	|	...	...	2205	...	...	...	...	...	...	...	...	...	|	|	0933**e**	1113
Lille Europe a.	...	...	...	2026	...	...	...	...	...	...	...	...	...	...	...	...	1130	1230	...	|
Ashford International a.	...	...	...	|	...	...	...	...	...	...	...	...	...	...	...	...	|	|	...	1207
London St Pancras a.	...	...	...	2103	...	...	...	...	...	...	...	...	...	...	...	...	1157	1257	...	1239

A – [1,2] ✕ Köln - Wuppertal - Hamm - Berlin and Düsseldorf - Hamm - Berlin and v.v. Table **810**.

C – KYÏV EKSPRES / KIEV EXPRESS – 🛏 1, 2 cl. Warszawa - Kyïv and v.v.

F – TRANSEUROPEAN EXPRESS ①④⑤: 🛏 1, 2 cl. Moskva (**23** *JI*) - Brest (**452**) - Berlin - Paris. ✕ (RZD) Moskva - Brest. ✕ (PKP) Warszawa - Paris.

J – JAN KIEPURA – 🛏 1, 2 cl., ▬ 2 cl., [2] (reclining) 🍷 [R] Köln - Berlin - Warszawa and v.v. ✕ ①-⑥ Berlin - Warszawa. ✕ Ⓑ Warszawa - Berlin.

M – TRANSEUROPEAN EXPRESS ③⑥⑦: 🛏 1, 2 cl. Paris (**453**) - Berlin - Brest (**24** *JI*) - Moskva. ✕ (PKP) Paris - Warszawa. ✕ (RZD) Brest - Moskva.

N – BERLIN GDANSK EXPRESS [1,2] ✕ [R] Berlin - Poznań - Gdynia and v.v.

P – POLONEZ – 🛏 1, 2 cl., 🍷 Warszawa - Moskva and v.v. ✕ Brest - Moskva and v.v.

T – BERLIN WARSZAWA EXPRESS – [1,2] ✕ Berlin - Poznań - Warszawa and v.v. [R] Special fares apply. Supplement payable in Poland.

X – ①-⑥ May 29 - Sept. 3. ①-⑤ Sept. 4 - Dec. 10 (not Nov. 11).

b – Not Oct. 3.

e – Paris **Est**.

f – Arrive 0950.

k – Berlin **Lichtenberg**.

r – Depart 2107.

s – Calls to set down only.

u – Calls to pick up only.

⇌ – *Thalys* high-speed train. [R] 🍷. Special payable. Valid May 30 - Dec. 10.

§ – 🏛: Osinovka (BY) / Krasnoye (RU).

‡ – Also known as Moskva **Smolenskaya** station.

☆ – Eurostar train. Special fares payable. ✕ in Business Premier and Star Premier, 🍷 in Standard. Minimum che time 30 minutes. Valid May 29 - Dec.

58 BERLIN - COTTBUS - FORST - WROCLAW

	RE	
	5825	
	⑥⑦	
	K	
Berlin Lichtenberg d.	0831	...
Berlin Ostkreuz d.	0836	...
Cottbus d.	0953	...
Forst 🏛 a.	|	...
Forst 🏛 d.	1008	...
Tuplice d.	|	...
Żary d.	1041	...
Żagań d.	1058	...
Legnica d.	1219	...
Wrocław Gł. a.	1305	...

	RE	*RE*
	5826	**5824**
	⑦	⑥
	K	**K**
Wrocław Gł. d.	1629	1921
Legnica d.	1713	2006
Żagań d.	1846	2133
Żary d.	1858	2148
Tuplice d.	|	|
Forst 🏛 a.	1930	2220
Forst 🏛 d.	|	|
Cottbus a.	2005	2236
Berlin Ostkreuz a.	2126	2348
Berlin Lichtenberg a.	2135	2354

K – KULTURZUG - [2] Berlin - Wrocław and v.v. For Intenational journeys only. Special fares apply.

For explanation of standard symbols see page 4

HAMBURG - BERLIN - PRAHA - WIEN / BUDAPEST 60

train type	EC	EC	RJ	EC	RJ		EC	RJ	EC	EC	RJ	EC	EC	RJ	EC	EC	RJ	EC	EC	RJ	EC	EC	EN	EN	EN
train number	271	273	71	275	73	459	277	75	171	279	77	131	173	79	379	281	371	175	283	373	177	179	477	477	60477 407
notes	✕	✕	✕	✕	✕	2 E	✕ S	✕	✕ E	✕	✕	✕ V	✕ J	✕	✕ H	✕	✕	✕	✕	✕	✕	✕	C	A	B
urg Altona..........d.	...	...	...	...	...	...	...	...	...	...	...	...	0636	...	...	...	...	...	...	...	1239	1437	...	...	...
urg Hbf.............d.	...	...	...	...	...	...	...	...	...	...	...	...	0648	...	0851	...	...	...	...	...	1251	1451	...	...	...
Hbf....................d.	...	...	...	...	...	...	...	...	0658	...	...	...	0900	...	1100	...	...	1300	...	...	1500	1700	...	1814	1814
Südkreuz..........d.	...	...	...	...	...	...	...	...	0704	...	...	...	0907	...	1107	...	...	1307	...	...	1507	1707	...	1821	1821
en Hbf...............d.	...	...	...	...	...	0708	...	...	0908	...	...	...	1108	...	1308	...	...	1508	...	...	1708	1908	...	2108	2108
chandau 🏛 ⊖....d.	...	...	...	...	...	0738	...	...	0938	...	...	...	1138	...	1338	...	...	1538	...	...	1738	1938	...	|	|
..........................d.	...	...	...	...	...	0756	...	...	0956	...	...	...	1156	...	1356	...	...	1556	...	...	1756	1956	...	2157	2156
ad Labem hlavní.d.	...	...	...	...	...	0813	...	...	1013	...	...	...	1213	...	1413	...	...	1613	...	...	1813	2013	...	2213	2213
Holešovice........a.	...	...	...	...	...	0918	...	...	1118	...	...	...	1318	...	1518	...	...	1718	...	...	1918	2118	...	2316	2316
hlavní................a.	...	...	...	...	...	0928	...	...	1128	...	...	...	1328	...	1528	...	...	1728	...	...	1928	2128	...	2326	2326
hlavní................d.	...	0552	0652	0752	0852	...	0952	1052	...	1152	1252	...	1352	1452	...	1552	1652	...	1752	1852	...	...	2358	2358	2358
bice....................d.	...	0649	0749	0849	0949	...	1049	1149	...	1249	1349	...	1449	1549	...	1649	1749	...	1849	1949	...	...	0108	0108	0108
hlavní..................d.	0622	0824	0924	1024	1124	...	1224	1324	...	1424	1524	...	1624	1724	...	1824	1924	...	2024	2124	...	...	0315	0315	0315
av.........................a.	0652	0853	0953	1053	1153	...	1253	1353	...	1453	1553	...	1653	1753	...	1853	1953	...	2053	2153	...	...	0353	0353	0353
av.........................d.	0659	0859	0956	1059	1156	...	1259	1356	...	1459	1556	1559	1659	1756	...	1859	1956	...	2059	2156	...	...	0440	0440	0549
en Hbf..................a.	|	|	1051	|	1251	...	|	1451	...	|	1651	|	|	1851	...	|	2051	...	|	2251	...	...	|	|	0705
en Meidling..........a.	|	|	1102	|	1302	...	|	1502	...	|	1702	|	|	1902	...	|	2105	...	|	...	...	...	|	|	...
ner Neustadt Hbf..a.	|	|	1128	|	1328	...	|	1528	...	|	1730	|	|	1928	...	|	2128	...	|	...	...	...	|	|	...
z Hbf.....................a.	|	|	1333	|	1533	...	|	1733	...	|	1933	|	|	2133	...	|	2333	...	|	...	...	...	|	|	...
🏛..........................d.	0713	0913	...	1113	...	...	1313	...	...	1513	...	1613	1713	...	...	1913	...	...	2113	...	...	...	0455	0455	...
slava hlavná........d.	0753	0953	...	1153	...	...	1353	...	...	1553	...	1653	1753	...	...	1953	...	...	2150	...	...	...	0548	0548	...
vo 🏛 △..............a.	0910	1111	...	1311	...	...	1511	...	...	1711	...	1811	1911	...	...	2111	...	...	...	...	...	...	0710	0710	...
pest Keleti..........a.	1035	1235	...	1435	...	...	1635	...	...	1835	...	1935	2035	...	...	2235	...	...	...	...	...	...	0835	0835	...

train type/number	EC	EC	EC	EC	RJ	EC	EC	RJ	EC	EC	RJ	EC	EC	RJ	EC		RJ	EC	RJ	EC	RJ	EC	EN	EN	EN
train number	178	176	282	174	70	280	378	72	172	130	74	278	170	76	276	458	78	274	370	272	372	270	60406 476	476	476 878
notes	✕	✕	✕	✕	✕	✕	✕ G	✕	✕ K	✕ V	✕	✕	✕	✕	✕ T	2 E	✕	✕	✕	✕	✕	✕	X	A	D
pest Keleti..........d.	...	...	...	...	...	0525	...	...	0725	0800	...	0925	...	...	1125	...	...	1325	...	1525	...	1725	...	2005	2005
vo 🏛 △..............d.	...	...	...	...	...	0649	...	...	0849	0949	...	1049	...	...	1249	...	...	1449	...	1649	...	1850	...	2124	2124
slava hlavná........d.	...	...	0610	...	...	0810	...	...	1010	1110	...	1210	...	...	1410	...	...	1610	...	1810	...	2010	...	2301	2301
🏛..........................d.	...	...	0649	...	...	0849	...	...	1049	1149	...	1249	...	...	1449	...	...	1649	...	1849	...	2049	...	2343	2343
az Hbf....................d.	...	...	|	...	...	|	...	0625	|	|	0825	|	...	1025	|	...	1225	|	1425	|	1625	|	...	|	|
ener Neustadt Hbf..d.	...	...	|	...	...	|	...	0832	|	|	1032	|	...	1232	|	...	1432	|	1632	|	1832	|	...	|	|
en Meidling..........d.	...	...	|	...	...	|	...	0858	|	|	1058	|	...	1258	|	...	1458	|	1658	|	1858	|	...	|	|
en Hbf..................d.	...	...	|	...	0709	|	...	0909	|	|	1109	|	...	1309	|	...	1509	|	1709	|	1909	|	2250	|	|
av.........................a.	...	...	0701	...	0804	0901	...	1004	1101	1201	1204	1301	...	1404	1501	...	1604	1701	1804	1901	2004	2101	2350	2356	2356
av.........................d.	...	...	0707	...	0807	0907	...	1007	1107	...	1207	1307	...	1407	1507	...	1607	1707	1807	1907	2007	2107	0020	0020	0017
hlavní..................d.	...	...	0738	...	0838	0938	...	1038	1138	...	1238	1338	...	1438	1538	...	1638	1738	1838	1938	2038	2136	0127	0127	0127
ıbice....................d.	...	...	0912	...	1012	1112	...	1212	1312	...	1412	1512	...	1612	1712	...	1812	1912	2012	2112	2212	...	0309	0309	0534
hlavní................a.	...	...	1010	...	1108	1208	...	1308	1410	...	1508	1608	...	1708	1808	...	1908	2008	2108	2208	2308	...	0408	0408	0643
hlavní................d.	0627	0827	...	1027	...	...	1227	...	1427	...	...	...	1627	...	...	1827	...	...	...	...	...	...	0427	0427	...
Holešovice........d.	0636	0836	...	1036	...	...	1236	...	1436	...	...	...	1636	...	...	1836	...	...	...	...	...	...	0436	0436	...
nad Labem hlavní.d.	0743	0943	...	1143	...	...	1343	...	1543	...	...	...	1743	...	...	1943	...	...	...	...	...	...	0543	0545	...
n..........................d.	0800	1000	...	1200	...	...	1400	...	1600	...	...	...	1800	...	...	2000	...	...	...	...	...	...	0600	0600	...
Schandau 🏛 ⊖.....a.	0815	1015	...	1215	...	...	1415	...	1615	...	...	...	1815	...	...	2015	...	...	...	...	...	...	|	|	...
den Hbf................a.	0844	1044	...	1244	...	...	1444	...	1644	...	...	...	1844	...	...	2045	...	...	...	...	...	...	0644	0644	...
n Südkreuz...........a.	1050	1250	...	1450	...	...	1650	...	1850	...	...	...	2050	...	...	|	...	...	...	...	...	...	0904	0904	...
n Hbf......................a.	1058	1258	...	1458		...	1658	...	1858	...	...	...	2058	...	...	2309¶	...	...	...	...	...	...	0911	0911	...
ourg Hbf...............a.	...	1511	...	1710	...	...	1911	...	2115	...	...	...	...	...	...	...	...	...	...	...	...	...	...	...	...
ourg Altona...........a.	...	1525	...	1724	...	...	...	...	2137	...	...	...	...	...	...	...	...	...	...	...	...	...	...	...	...

METROPOL – 🛏 1, 2 cl., ▬ 2 cl., (2) Berlin - Praha - Budapest and v.v.

METROPOL – 🛏 1, 2 cl., ▬ 2 cl., (2) Berlin (**477**) - Praha - Břeclav (**407**) - Wien.

🛏 1, 2 cl., ▬ 2 cl., Praha - Pardubice - Břeclav - Budapest.

🛏 1, 2 cl., ▬ 2 cl., Budapest (**476**) - Břeclav - Pardubice (**878**) - Praha.

For additional cars see Table **54**.

CARL MARIA VON WEBER – (2) ✕ Praha - Berlin - Hamburg - Kiel (arrive 2018).

CARL MARIA VON WEBER – (2) ✕ Kiel (depart 0742) - Hamburg - Berlin - Praha.

HUNGARIA – (12) ✕ Hamburg - Berlin - Praha - Břeclav - Budapest. Conveys ②⑤ June 17 - Sept. 2: 🛏 1, 2 cl., ▬ 2 cl. Praha (**173**) - Budapest (**341**) - Bar.

HUNGARIA – (12) ✕ Budapest - Břeclav - Praha - Berlin - Hamburg. Conveys ④⑦ June 19 - Sept. 4: 🛏 1, 2 cl., ▬ 2 cl. Bar (**340**) - Budapest (**172**) - Praha.

SLOVAN – (12) ✕ Praha - Břeclav - Budapest. Conveys on ②⑤ June 17 - Aug. 26: 🛏 1, 2 cl. Praha - Budapest - Split.

SLOVAN – (12) ✕ Budapest - Břeclav - Praha. Conveys on ③⑥ June 18 - Aug. 27: 🛏 1, 2 cl. Split - Budapest - Praha.

VARSOVIA – (12) ✕ Warszawa - Katowice - Břeclav - Budapest and v.v. (Table **99**).

METROPOL – 🛏 1, 2 cl., ▬ 2 cl., (2) Wien (**406**) - Břeclav (**476**) - Praha - Berlin.

Routeing point for international tickets: Szob.

Routeing point for international tickets: Schöna.

Berlin **Ostbahnhof**.

ÖBB *Railjet* service. (B) (business class), (1) (first class), (2) (economy class), ✕.

OTHER TRAIN NAMES:

70 / 71 –	GUSTAV MAHLER
72 / 73 –	BEDŘICH SMETANA
74 / 75 –	FRANZ SCHUBERT
76 / 77 –	ANTONÍN DVOŘÁK
78 / 79 –	JOHANN STRAUSS
130 / 131 –	VARSOVIA
170 / 171 –	PORTA BOHEMICA
172 / 173 –	HUNGARIA
174 / 175 –	ROBERT SCHUMANN
176 / 177 –	JOHANNES BRAHMS
178 / 179 –	ALOIS NEGRELLI
270 / 271 –	PETROV
272 / 273 –	CSÁRDÁS
274 / 275 –	JAROSLAV HAŠEK
278 / 279 –	DANUBIUS
280 / 281 –	JÁN JESENIUS/JESZENSZKY JÁNOS
282 / 283 –	SLOVENSKÁ STRELA
370 / 371 –	JOSEPH HAYDN
372 / 373 –	W. A. MOZART

61 WIEN - BUDAPEST - BEOGRAD / BUCUREŞTI and İSTANBUL / THESSALONÍKI

Services to / from İstanbul are subject to alteration until further notice. Trains are replaced by 🚌 Çerkezköy - İstanbul and v.v.

train type	IC		IC		IC	EC			EN	461					491	EN
train number	73	481	343	335	75	345	293	361	473	491	461	341	337	491	81031	347
notes	R		🍸	❦	R	✕			R	81031	R	R	❦			R
	H	Q	B	K	P	J	N		R	R S	W	G	Y	D	C	E
Wien Hbf d.	...	...	...	...	...	0842	...	...	...	...	...	...	...	...	...	1942
Budapest Kelenföld d.	...	...	...	...	...	1104	...	...	...	...	...	...	...	...	...	2204
Budapest Keleti d.	0710	0710	0805	...	0910	1205	...	...	1910	...	...	2225	...	...	...	2250
Lökösháza a.	1010	1010	│	...	1210	│	...	...	2210	...	...	│	...	...	...	0140
Curtici 🛃 a.	1145	1145	│	...	1345	│	...	...	2350	...	...	│	...	...	...	0335
Arad a.	1227	1227	│	...	1418	│	...	...	0023	...	...	│	...	...	...	0435
Timişoara a.	1318	1318	│	...	│	│	...	...	│	...	...	│	...	...	...	│
Craiova a.	1947	1947	│	...	│	│	...	...	│	...	...	│	...	...	...	│
Braşov a.	│	│	│	...	2245	│	...	...	0917	...	...	│	...	...	...	1336
Bucureşti Nord a.	2252	│	│	...	...	│	...	...	1200	...	...	│	...	...	...	1550
Bucureşti Nord d.	...	│	│	...	...	│	...	...	...	1250	1250	│	...	...	...	...
Videle a.	...	│	│	...	...	│	...	...	...	1339	1339	│	...	...	...	...
Giurgiu Nord 🛃 a.	...	│	│	...	...	│	...	...	...	1447	1447	│	...	...	...	...
Giurgiu Nord 🛃 d.	...	│	│	...	...	│	...	...	...	1525	1525	│	...	...	...	...
Ruse 🛃 a.	...	│	│	...	...	│	...	...	...	1550	1550	│	...	...	...	...
Ruse 🛃 d.	...	│	│	...	...	│	...	...	...	1630	1630	│	...	...	...	...
Gorna Oryakhovitsa a.	...	│	│	...	...	│	...	...	...	1827	1827	│	...	...	...	...
Varna a.	...	│	│	...	...	│	...	...	...	│	│	│	...	...	...	...
Burgas a.	...	│	│	...	...	│	...	...	...	│	│	│	...	...	...	...
Subotica 🛃 a.	...	│	1155	...	...	1555	...	...	...	│	│	0154	...	...	...	...
Novi Sad a.	...	│	1455	...	...	1840	...	...	...	│	│	0448	...	...	...	...
Beograd a.	...	│	1632	1850	...	2013	2205	...	...	│	│	0621	0735	0735	...	...
Niš a.	...	│	...	2259	...	...	0214	...	...	│	│	...	1144	1144	...	...
Tabanovci 🛃 a.	...	│	...	0305	...	...	│	...	...	│	│	...	1602	│	...	...
Skopje a.	...	│	...	0420	...	...	│	...	...	│	│	...	1715	│	...	...
Idoméni 🛃 a.	...	│	..	0828	...	...	│	...	...	│	│	...	...	│	...	...
Dimitrovgrad (Serbia) 🛃 a.	...	│	...	│	...	...	0510	...	...	│	│	...	...	1455	...	...
Kalotina Zapad 🛃 a.	...	│	...	│	...	...	0640	...	...	│	│	...	...	1628	...	...
Pleven a.	...	│	...	│	...	...	│	...	...	│	1940	...	...	│	...	...
Mezdra a.	...	│	...	│	...	...	│	...	...	│	2059	...	...	│	...	...
Vidin 🛃 a.	...	2330	...	│	...	...	│	...	...	│	│	...	...	│	...	...
Sofia a.	...	0540	...	│	...	...	0830	...	...	│	2225	...	...	1815	...	...
Sofia d.	...	...	...	│	...	...	...	1520	...	│	...	...	...	...	1915	...
Dimitrovgrad (Bulgaria) a.	...	...	...	│	...	...	...	│	...	2251	...	...	...	...	2308	...
Svilengrad a.	...	...	...	│	...	...	...	│	...	0044	...	...	...	...	0044	...
Kapikule 🛃 a.	...	...	...	│	...	...	...	│	...	0150	...	...	...	...	0150	...
İstanbul Sirkeci a.	...	...	...	│	...	...	...	│	...	*0752**	...	...	...	...	*0752**	...
Kulata 🛃 a.	...	...	...	│	...	...	...	1843	...	...	...	...	...	...	...	...
Thessaloníki a.	...	...	...	1007	...	...	...	2222	...	...	...	...	...	...	...	...

train type/number	EN	81032			81032			EN			EC	IC		IC	IC	
train number	346	492	460	336	492	490	340	472	360	292	344	74	334	342	72	480
notes	R	460	R	❦			R	R			✕	R	❦	🍸	R	
	E	R S	W	Y	C	D	M	R		N	J	P	K	B	H	Q
Thessaloníki d.	...	...	...	...	...	...	...	...	0655	...	...	...	1830	...	...	...
Kulata 🛃 d.	...	...	...	...	...	...	...	...	1026	...	...	...	│	...	...	...
İstanbul Sirkeci d.	...	*2200**	...	...	*2200**	...	...	...	│	...	...	...	│	...	...	...
Kapikule 🛃 d.	...	0405	...	...	0405	...	...	...	│	...	...	...	│	...	...	...
Svilengrad d.	...	0510	...	...	0510	...	...	...	│	...	...	...	│	...	...	...
Dimitrovgrad (Bulgaria) d.	...	0655	...	...	0630	...	...	...	│	...	...	...	│	...	...	...
Sofia a.	...	│	...	...	1105	...	...	...	1345	...	...	...	│	...	...	...
Sofia d.	...	│	0800	...	...	1130	...	...	...	2025	...	...	│	...	...	2300
Vidin 🛃 d.	...	│	│	...	...	│	...	...	...	│	...	...	│	...	...	0505
Mezdra d.	...	│	0928	...	...	│	...	...	...	│	...	...	│	...	...	│
Pleven d.	...	│	1045	...	...	│	...	...	...	│	...	...	│	...	...	│
Kalotina Zapad 🛃 d.	...	│	│	...	...	1312	...	...	...	2152	...	...	│	...	...	│
Dimitrovgrad (Serbia) 🛃 d.	...	│	│	...	...	1240	...	...	...	2120	...	...	│	...	...	│
Idomeni 🛃 d.	...	│	│	...	...	│	...	...	...	│	...	...	2011	...	...	│
Skopje d.	...	│	│	0820	...	│	...	...	...	│	...	...	2219	...	...	│
Tabanovci 🛃 d.	...	│	│	0926	...	│	...	...	...	│	...	...	2329	...	...	│
Niš d.	...	│	│	1335	...	1530	...	...	...	0016	...	...	0330	...	...	│
Beograd d.	...	│	│	1808	...	1935	2150	...	...	0436	0720	...	0742	1135	...	│
Novi Sad d.	...	│	│	...	...	...	2320	...	...	...	0900	...	...	1304	...	│
Subotica 🛃 d.	...	│	│	...	...	...	0216	...	...	...	1159	...	...	1600	...	│
Burgas d.	...	│	│	...	...	...	│	...	...	...	│	...	...	│	...	│
Varna d.	...	│	│	...	...	...	│	...	...	...	│	...	...	│	...	│
Gorna Oryakhovitsa d.	...	1208	1208	...	...	...	│	...	...	...	│	...	...	│	...	│
Ruse 🛃 a.	...	1405	1405	...	...	...	│	...	...	...	│	...	...	│	...	│
Ruse 🛃 d.	...	1435	1435	...	...	...	│	...	...	...	│	...	...	│	...	│
Giurgiu Nord 🛃 a.	...	1500	1500	...	...	...	│	...	...	...	│	...	...	│	...	│
Giurgiu Nord 🛃 d.	...	1517	1517	...	...	...	│	...	...	...	│	...	...	│	...	│
Videle d.	...	1627	1627	...	...	...	│	...	...	...	│	...	...	│	...	│
Bucureşti Nord a.	...	1724	1724	...	...	...	│	...	...	...	│	...	...	│	...	│
Bucureşti Nord d.	1400	...	...	...	...	...	│	1745	...	...	│	...	...	│	0545	│
Braşov d.	1631	...	...	...	...	...	│	2022	...	...	│	0600	...	│	│	│
Craiova d.	│	...	...	...	...	...	│	│	...	...	│	│	...	│	0900	0900
Timişoara d.	│	...	...	...	...	...	│	│	...	...	│	│	...	│	1448	1448
Arad d.	0128	...	...	...	...	...	│	0522	...	...	│	1428	...	│	1539	1539
Curtici 🛃 d.	0205	...	...	...	...	...	│	0605	...	...	│	1514	...	│	1614	1614
Lököshaza d.	0150	...	...	...	...	...	│	0549	...	...	│	1449	...	│	1549	1549
Budapest Keleti a.	0455	...	...	...	...	...	0546	0850	...	...	1554	1750	...	1954	1850	1850
Budapest Kelenföld a.	0554	...	...	...	...	...	...	...	...	...	1653	...	...	...	...	...
Wien Hbf a.	0818	...	...	...	...	...	...	...	...	...	1918	...	...	...	...	...

B – IVO ANDRIC – 12 🍸 Budapest - Beograd and v.v.

C – BALKAN EXPRESS – 🛏 2 cl. Sofia - İstanbul and v.v.

D – BALKAN – 2 Beograd - Sofia and v.v.

E – DACIA – 🛏 1, 2 cl., 🛏 2 cl., 2 ✕ Wien - Bucureşti and v.v.

G – BEOGRAD – 🛏 1, 2 cl., 🛏 2 cl., 12 Budapest - Beograd. Conveys ②⑤ June 17 - Sept. 2: 🛏 1, 2 cl., 🛏 2 cl. Praha (**173**) - Budapest (**341**) - Bar.

H – TRAIANUS – 12 Budapest - Bucureşti and v.v.

J – AVALA – 12 ✕ Wien - Budapest - Beograd and v.v.

K – HELLAS EXPRESS – 🛏 2 cl., 2 Beograd - Skopje - Thessaloníki and v.v.

M – BEOGRAD – 🛏 1, 2 cl., 🛏 2 cl., 12 Beograd - Budapest. Conveys ④⑦ June 19 - Sept. 4: 🛏 1, 2 cl., 🛏 2 cl. Bar (**340**) - Budapest (**172**) - Praha.

N – NUŠIĆ – 🛏 2 cl., 2 Beograd - Sofia and v.v.

P – TRANSSYLVANIA / TRANSILVANIA – 12 Budapest - Braşov and v.v.

Q – SERDICA – 🛏 1, 2 cl., 🛏 2 cl., 2 Budapest - Vidin 🛃 - Sofia and v.v.

R – *EuroNight* ISTER – 🛏 1, 2 cl., 🛏 1, 2 cl., 2 ✕ Budapest - Bucureşti and v

S – BOSPHOR – 🛏 1, 2 cl., 🛏 2 cl. Bucureşti - İstanbul and v.v. (The compostio this train is subject to confirmation).

W – ROMANIA – 2 Bucureşti - Sofia and v.v.

Y – OLYMPUS – 2 Beograd - Skopje and v.v.

❦ – Service expected to commence from June 12.

¶ – Train number for international bookings.

⁄ – Supplement payable.

* – 🚌 Çerkezköy - İstanbul and v.v., see Table **1550**.

MÜNCHEN - LJUBLJANA - ZAGREB - BEOGRAD - THESSALONÍKI 62

train type/number		EC	EC		EC113		EC	D	D				EN	D				
train number		111	211		EC213		115	315	411	491	337		463	415	335	293		
notes		🍷			🍷 ◧		🍷				❖		499		❖			
			T		M		W		Y	A	K		L	F	E	H		
en Hbf d.	...	0818	...	...	1218	...	1417	...	...	...	...	...	2336	...	...	...	...	...
rg Hbf 🏛 d.	...	1012	...	...	1412	...	1612	...	...	...	...	...	0134	...	...	...	...	...
fshofen d.	...	1054	...	...	1454	...	1654	...	...	...	...	...	|	...	...	...	...	...
rzach St Veit d.	...	1111	...	...	1511	...	1711	...	...	...	...	...	0226	0427	...	...	...	...
astein d.	...	1142	...	...	1542	...	1742	...	...	...	...	...	|	0500	...	...	...	...
Hbf d.	...	1243	1253	...	1653	...	1843	1853	...	...	...	...	0415	0625	...	...	...	...
ce 🏛 a.	...	...	1333	...	1733	...	...	1933	...	...	...	...	0454	0705	...	...	...	...
ana a.	...	...	1431	...	1832	...	...	2040	2105	...	...	...	0559	0812	...	...	...	...
a 🏛 a.	...	...	1620	...	2005	...	...	...	2242	...	...	...	0750	0957	...	...	...	...
b a.	...	...	1712	...	2054	...	...	...	2328	...	...	...	0838	1046	...	...	...	...
b d.	...	...	1742	...	...	...	...	...	2348	...	...	...	...	1106	...	...	...	...
ci a.	...	...	2107	...	...	...	...	...	0312	...	...	...	...	1438	...	...	...	...
a.	...	...	...	...	...	...	...	...	0345	...	...	...	...	1515	...	...	...	...
rad a.	...	...	...	...	...	...	...	...	0554	0735	0735	...	...	1733	1850	2205	...	...
a.	...	...	...	...	...	...	...	...	...	1144	1144	...	...	...	2259	0214	...	...
itrovgrad 🏛 a.	...	...	...	...	...	...	...	...	...	1455	|	...	...	...	|	0510	...	...
tina Zapad 🏛 a.	...	...	...	...	...	...	...	...	...	1628	|	...	...	...	|	0640	...	...
a a.	...	...	...	...	...	...	...	...	...	1815	|	...	...	...	|	0830	...	...
ovci 🏛 a.	...	...	...	...	...	...	...	...	...	...	1602	...	...	...	0305	...	...	...
e a.	...	...	...	...	...	...	...	...	...	...	1715	...	...	...	0420	...	...	...
ni 🏛 a.	...	...	...	...	...	...	...	...	...	...	...	...	...	...	0828	...	...	...
aloníki a.	...	...	...	...	...	...	...	...	...	...	...	...	...	...	1007	...	...	...

train type				D	EN				D	D	EC		EC212		EC	EC		
train number		292	334	414	498		336	490	410	314	114		EC112		210	110		
notes			❖		462		❖				🍴		🍷 ◧			🍷		
		H	E	F	L		K	A	Y		W		M		T			
aloníki d.	...	...	1830	...	...	...	...	...	...	...	...	...	...	...	...	...	...	...
ni 🏛 d.	...	...	2011	...	...	...	...	...	...	...	...	...	...	...	...	...	...	...
e d.	...	...	2219	...	...	...	0820	...	...	...	...	...	...	...	...	...	...	...
ovci 🏛 d.	...	...	2329	...	...	...	0926	...	...	...	...	...	...	...	...	...	...	...
ia d.	...	2025	|	...	...	...	|	1130	...	...	...	...	...	...	...	...	...	...
tina Zapad 🏛 d.	...	2152	|	...	...	...	|	1312	...	...	...	...	...	...	...	...	...	...
itrovgrad 🏛 d.	...	2120	|	...	...	...	|	1240	...	...	...	...	...	...	...	...	...	...
d.	...	0016	0330	...	...	...	1335	1530	...	...	...	...	...	...	...	...	...	...
rad d.	...	0436	0742	1100	...	...	1808	1935	2130	...	...	...	...	...	...	...	...	...
d.	...	...	...	1356	...	...	...	...	0026	...	...	...	...	...	...	...	...	...
vci d.	...	...	...	1442	...	...	...	...	0105	...	...	...	...	...	0900	...	...	...
eb a.	...	...	...	1812	...	...	...	...	0428	...	...	...	...	...	1224	...	...	...
eb d.	...	...	...	1838	2122	...	...	...	0445	...	...	...	0655	...	1237	...	...	...
va 🏛 d.	...	...	...	1925	2208	...	...	...	0531x	0541	...	...	0744	...	1338	...	...	...
jana d.	...	...	...	2110	2355	...	...	...	0708	0728	...	...	0923	...	1527	...	...	...
ice 🏛 d.	...	...	...	2205	0050	...	...	...	...	0827	...	...	1016	...	1627	...	...	...
n Hbf a.	...	...	...	2243	0130	...	...	...	...	0908	0916	...	1056	...	1707	1716	...	...
Gastein a.	...	...	...	0024	0250	...	...	...	...	...	1016	...	1216	...	...	1816	...	...
arzach St Veit a.	...	...	...	0057	0318	...	...	...	...	...	1047	...	1247	...	...	1847	...	...
ofshofen a.	...	...	...	...	|	...	...	...	...	...	1103	...	1303	...	...	1903	...	...
urg Hbf 🏛 a.	...	...	...	...	0409	...	...	...	...	...	1147	...	1347	...	...	1947	...	...
hen Hbf a.	...	...	...	...	0609	...	...	...	...	...	1340	...	1541	...	...	2141	...	...

BALKAN – [2] Beograd - Sofia and v.v.

HELLAS EXPRESS – 🛏 2 cl., [2] Beograd - Skopje - Thessaloníki and v.v.

[2] Zürich (**465**) - Schwarzach St Veit (**415**) - Zagreb - Beograd and Beograd (**414**) - Zagreb - Schwarzach St Veit (**464**) - Zürich. [12] Villach - Beograd and v.v. Table **86**.

NUŠIĆ – 🛏 2 cl., [2] Beograd - Sofia and v.v.

OLYMPUS – [2] Beograd - Skopje and v.v.

LISINSKI – 🛌 1, 2 cl., 🛏 2 cl., [2] München - Salzburg - Zagreb and v.v.

[12] Frankfurt - München - Zagreb and v.v. 🍴 München - Villach and v.v.

SAVA – [2] Villach - Jesenice 🏛 - Ljubljana - Zagreb - Vinkovci and v.v.

W – WÖRTHERSEE – [12] 🍴 Münster - Klagenfurt and Klagenfurt - Dortmund.

Y – 🛏 2 cl., [12] Ljubljana - Beograd and v.v.

x – Arrive 0516.

◧ – Supplement payable: Jesenice 🏛 - Zagreb - Beograd and v.v.

⁄ – Supplement payable.

❖ – Service expected to commence from June 12.

HAMBURG and BERLIN - WIEN - BUDAPEST 64

For alternative services via Břeclav see Table **60**

train type	ICE	ICE	ICE	RJ	ICE	ICE	ICE	RJ	ICE	ICE	IC	ICE	EN	ICE	ICE	ICE	ICE	ICE	IC	ICE	ICE		EN	EC	
train number	1003	783	23	65	1585	1005	91	67	1587	787	2355	27	347	1589	1609	789	29	1209	2301	881	229		491	345	
notes	1583	①–⑥	🍷	🍴		1605	🍷	🍴	🍷	🍷	🍷	🍷	[R]	🍷	🍷	🍷	🍷	🍷	🍷	🍷	🍷		🍷	🍷	
	①–⑥			B	Q	P		B	Q		P		D	Q	P			Q	P				A	J	
burg Hbf d.	...	0555	...	...	...	...	0803	...	...	1001	...	...	...	...	...	1201	...	...	...	1401	...	...	2052	...	...
over Hbf d.	...	0726	...	...	...	...	0926	...	...	1126	...	...	...	...	...	1326	...	...	...	1526	...	...	2227	...	...
rlin Hbf d.	0432	|	...	...	0627	0730	|	...	0827	|	0930	...	...	1027	1130	|	...	1227	1330	|	...	...	|	...	...
pzig Hbf d.	0543	|	...	...	0748	0848	|	...	0948	|	1043	...	...	1143	1248	|	...	1348	1448	|	...	...	|	...	...
berg Hbf d.	0928	1024	1029	...	1128	1223	1230	...	1328	1424	1425	1430	...	1525	1623	1624	1629	1728	1823	1824	1830	...	0300	...	...
au 🏛 d.	...	...	1238	...	...	...	1438	...	...	...	...	1638	...	...	...	...	1838	...	...	...	2038	...	0512	...	...
Hbf a.	...	...	1342	1414	...	...	1543	1614	...	...	...	1742	...	...	...	...	1942	...	...	...	2143	...	0623	...	...
Hbf a.	...	...	1508	1530	...	...	1708	1730	...	...	...	1908	1942	...	...	...	2108	...	...	...	2308	...	0816	0842	...
pest Keleti § a.	...	...	...	1819	...	...	...	2019	...	...	...	...	2220	...	...	...	...	...	...	...	...	...	...	1119	...

train type	ICE	ICE	ICE	ICE	EN	ICE	ICE	IC	ICE	RJ	ICE	ICE	ICE	ICE	RJ	ICE	ICE	ICE	RJ	ICE	ICE	ICE	ICE	RJ	EN
train number	228	880	1610	1588	346	28	788	2356	1586	60	26	786	1006	1584	62	90	1604	1582	64	22	782	1000	1000	42	490
notes	🍷	🍷	🍷	🍷	[R]	🍷	🍷	🍷	🍷	🍴	🍷	🍷	704	🍷	🍴	🍷	🍷	🍷	🍴	🍷	1182	⑤⑦	⑤⑦	🍴	🍷
			P	Q	D				Q	B			P	Q	B		P	Q	B		🍷	P	Q		A
pest Keleti § d.	...	...	...	...	0540	...	...		...	0740	...	...	...	...	0940	...	...	...	1140	...	...	...	...	1740	...
Hbf d.	0652	...	...	...	0818	0852	...		...	1030	1052	...	...	...	1230	1252	...	...	1430	1452	...	...	...	2018	2039
Hbf d.	0816	...	...	...	...	1016	...		...	1146	1216	...	...	...	1346	1416	...	...	1546	1616	...	...	...	2146	2219
au 🏛 a.	0917	...	...	...	...	1117	...		...	...	1317	...	...	...	...	1518	...	...	...	1717	...	...	...	...	2326
berg Hbf a.	1125	1133	1134	1233	...	1325	1333		1433	...	1525	1534	1534	1633	...	1726	1736	1833	...	1925	1934	1935	2033	...	0132
pzig Hbf a.	...	|	1510	1610	...	...	|		1810	...	...	|	1910	2010	...	|	2110	2210	...	...	|	2308	0043	...	|
rlin Hbf a.	...	|	1630	1733	...	...	|		1933	...	...	|	2033	2133	...	|	2230	2333	...	...	|	0030	0206	...	|
over Hbf a.	...	1432	...	...	...	...	1632		...	...	...	1832	...	...	...	2032	...	...	...	...	2240	...	...	...	0613
burg Hbf a.	...	1554	...	...	...	...	1753		...	...	...	1953	...	...	...	2153	...	...	...	...	0008	...	...	...	0749

HANS ALBERS – 🛌 1, 2 cl., 🛏 2 cl., [2] 🍷 Hamburg - Passau 🏛 - Wien and v.v.

ÖBB *Railjet* service: München - Wien - Budapest and v.v.

DACIA – 🛌 1, 2 cl., 🛏 2 cl., [2] 🍴 Wien - Budapest - Bucuresti and v.v.

AVALA – [12] 🍷 Wien - Budapest - Beograd and v.v.

Sept. 4 - Dec. 10.

Q – June 1 - Sept. 3.

§ – 🏛 is at Hegyeshalom.

RJ – ÖBB *Railjet* service. 🍴, [1] (business class), [1] (first class), [2] (economy class).

65 MÜNCHEN - SALZBURG - WIEN - BUDAPEST - BUCUREŞTI

train type	RJ	EN	EC	RJ	RJ	RJ	RJ	EC	RJ	EC	EC	RJ	EN	EC	EC	RJ	EC	RJ	EN	EC	RJ	EC	IC	EC
train number	41	467	345	949	49	265	61	111	63	217	145	65	473	113	147	67	115	69	347	219	261	117	1269	391
notes	✕		🍸	✕	✕	✕	✕	✕	✕	✕	✕	✕	[R]	✕	✕	✕	✕	✕	[R]		✕	1217		
		W	K	⑦		C			F				Y		G				D			✕	⑧	
München Hbf d.	...	...	...	...	...	0624	0733	0818	0934	1018	...	1134	...	1218	...	1334	1418	1534	...	1618	1734	1818	1918	2018
Salzburg Hbf 🏛 a.	...	...	...	...	...	0802	0902	0959	1102	1159	...	1302	...	1359	...	1502	1559	1702	...	1759	1902	1959	2059	2203
						|	|	RJ 765 ✕	|	RJ 161 ✕		|		RJ 563 ✕		|	RJ 165 ✕	|		RJ 167 ✕	|	RJ 169 ✕	RJ 663 ✕	RJ 361 ✕
Salzburg Hbf 🏛 d.	...	0439	...	0708	0708r	0808	0908	1008	1108	1208	...	1308	...	1408	...	1508	1608	1708	...	1808	1908	2008	2108	2208
Linz Hbf d.	...	0610	...	0814	0814r	0914	1014	1114	1214	1314	...	1414	...	1514	...	1614	1714	1814	...	1914	2014	2114	2214	2314
St Pölten Hbf d.	...	0715	...	0902	0902r	1002	1102	1202	1302	1402	...	1502	...	1602	...	1702	1802	1902	...	2002	2102	2202	2302	0002
Wien Meidling d.	...	0746	...	0926	0926r	1026	1126	1226	1326	1426	...	1526	...	1626	...	1726	1826	1926	...	2026	2126	2226	2326	0026
Wien Hbf d.	0742	0755	0842	0930	0942	1030	1142	1230	1342	1430	1442	1542	...	1630	1642	1742	1842	1930	1942	2030	2130	2230	2330	0030
Hegyeshalom 🏛 a.	0825	...	0925	...	1025	...	1225	...	1425	...	1525	1625	...	...	1728	1825	1925	...	2025	...	...	...	...	...
Györ a.	0853	...	0953	...	1053	...	1253	...	1453	...	1553	1653	...	...	1753	1853	1953	...	2053	...	...	...	...	...
Budapest Keleti a.	1019	...	1119	...	1219	...	1419	...	1619	...	1719	1819	1910	...	1919	2019	2119	...	2220	...	...	...	...	...
Bucureşti Nord a.	...	...	...	...	...	...	...	...	...	...	...	...	1200	...	...	...	...	...	1550	...	...	...	...	...

train type	RJ	RJ	RJ	EN	RJ	RJ	RJ	EC	RJ	EN	RJ	RJ	RJ	RJ	RJ	RJ	RJ	EC	RJ	RJ	EC	EN	IC	EN
train number	362	260	160	346	262	162	60	140	564	472	62	166	64	168	66	760	68	344	762	42	148	466	72	462
notes	✕	✕	✕	[R]	✕	✕	✕	✕	✕	[R]	✕	✕	✕	✕	✕	✕	✕	🍸	✕	✕	✕		[R]	
	C			D				J		Y					F			K				W	H	A
Bucureşti Nord d.	...	...	...	1400	...	...	...	...	...	1745	...	...	...	...	...	...	...	...	...	...	...	...	0545	...
Budapest Keleti d.	...	...	...	0540	...	0640	0740	0840	...	0850	0940	...	1140	...	1340	...	1540	1640	...	1740	1840	...	1850	2040
Györ d.	...	...	...	0702	...	0802	0902	1002	...	...	1102	...	1302	...	1502	...	1702	1802	...	1902	2002	...	...	2202
Hegyeshalom 🏛 d.	...	...	...	0732	...	0832	0932	1032	...	...	1132	...	1332	...	1532	...	1732	1832	...	1932	2032	...	...	2232
Wien Hbf d.	0530	0630	0730	0818	0830	0930	1030	1118	1130	...	1230	1330	1430	1530	1630	1730	1830	1918	1930	2030	2118	2125	...	2325
Wien Meidling d.	0537	0637	0737	...	0837	0937	1037	...	1137	...	1237	1337	1437	1537	1637	1737	1837	...	1937	2037	...	2133	...	2332
St Pölten Hbf d.	0600	0700	0800	...	0900	1000	1100	...	1200	...	1300	1400	1500	1600	1700	1800	1900	...	2000	2100	...	2205	...	0002
Linz Hbf d.	0648	0748	0848	...	0948	1048	1148	...	1248	...	1348	1448	1548	1648	1748	1848	1948	...	2048	2148	...	2311	...	0101
Salzburg Hbf 🏛 a.	0752	0852	0952	...	1052	1152	1252	...	1352	...	1452	1552	1652	1752	1852	1952	2052	...	2152	2252	...	0032	...	0210
	EC 390	|	EC 218		|	EC 114	|		EC 112		|	EC 216	|	79042 2	|	EC 110	|			79050 2				|
Salzburg Hbf 🏛 d.	0800	0856	1000	...	1056	1200	1256	...	1400	...	1456	1600	1656	1813	1856	2000	2056	...	...	2300	...	...	...	0428
München Hbf a.	0941	1024	1141	...	1224	1341	1424	...	1541	...	1624	1741	1824	2006	2024	2141	2226	...	...	0055	...	...	...	0609

A – KÁLMÁN IMRE – 🛏 1, 2 cl., ▬ 2 cl. [2] 🍸 München - Wien - Budapest and v.v.
C – ①–⑥ (not Jan. 1, 2, 6, Mar. 28, May 16, Dec. 8).
D – DACIA – 🛏 1, 2 cl., ▬ 2 cl., [2] ✕ Wien - Budapest - Bucureşti and v.v.
F – From/to Frankfurt (Main) Hbf on dates shown in Table **930**.
G – [12] Wien - Budapest - Szolnok (arrive 2029) - Debrecen (2149).
H – TRAIANUS – [12] 🍸 Bucureşti - Budapest.
J – [12] Debrecen (depart 0607) - Szolnok (0727) - Budapest - Wien.
K – AVALA – [12] 🍸 Wien - Budapest - Beograd and v.v.

W – WIENER WALZER – 🛏 1, 2 cl., ▬ 2 cl., [2] Zürich - Salzburg - Wien and v.
Y – *EuroNight* ISTER – 🛏 1, 2 cl., ▬ 1, 2 cl., [2] ✕ Budapest - Bucureşti and v.

r – ①–⑥ (not Aug. 15).

RJ – ÖBB *Railjet* service, ✕, [1] (business class), [1] (first class), [2] (economy

66 DORTMUND - KÖLN - FRANKFURT - WIEN - BUDAPEST

train type	ICE	RJ	ICE	ICE	ICE	RJ	ICE	EN	ICE	ICE	EN	EC
train number	21	63	23	1521	91	67	27	347	29	229	421	345
notes	🍸	✕	🍸		🍸	✕	🍸	D [R]	🍸	🍸	A	✕
Dortmund Hbf d.	...	...	0437	0636	...	...	0838	...	...	...	...	...
Düsseldorf Hbf d.	...	...	0527	⊙	...	...	0927	...	...	...	2054	...
Köln Hbf d.	...	...	0553	0753	...	...	0953	...	...	...	2121	...
Bonn Hbf d.	...	...	0614	0814	...	...	1014	...	...	...	2143	...
Koblenz Hbf d.	...	...	0648	0848	...	...	1048	...	...	...	2217	...
Mainz Hbf d.	...	...	0740	0940	...	...	1140	...	...	...	2317	...
Frankfurt Flug. ✈ d.	...	...	0802	1002	...	...	1202	...	...	...	2353	...
Frankfurt (M) Hbf d.	0622	...	0819	1018	...	...	1220	...	1416	1620	0007f	...
Würzburg Hbf d.	0733	...	0932	1125	1135	...	1333	...	1533	1733	|	...
Nürnberg Hbf d.	0829	...	1029	▬	1230	...	1430	...	1629	1830	|	...
Regensburg Hbf d.	0927	...	1127	...	1326	...	1527	...	1727	1927	|	...
Passau Hbf 🏛 d.	1038	...	1238	RJ	1438	...	1638	...	1838	2038	0522	...
Linz a.	1142	...	1342	65	1543	...	1742	...	1942	2143	0633	...
Wien Hbf a.	1308	1342	1508	1542	1708	1742	1908	1942	2108	2308	0820	0842
Hegyeshalom 🏛 a.	...	1425	...	1625	...	1825	...	2025	...	...	...	0925
Budapest Keleti a.	...	1619	...	1819	...	2019	...	2219	...	...	...	1119

train type	ICE	EN	ICE	RJ	ICE	RJ	ICE	RJ	ICE	RJ	ICE	EC
train number	228	346	28	60	26	62	90	64	22	66	20	148
notes	🍸	D [R]	🍸	✕	🍸	✕	🍸	✕	🍸	✕	🍸	
Budapest Keleti d.	...	0540	...	0740	...	0940	...	1140	...	1340	...	1840
Hegyeshalom 🏛 d.	...	0732	...	0932	...	1132	...	1332	...	1532	...	2032
Wien Hbf d.	0652	0818	0852	1018	1052	1218	1252	1418	1452	1618	1652	2118
Linz d.	0816	...	1016	...	1216	...	1416	▬	1616	...	1816	...
Passau Hbf 🏛 a.	0917	...	1117	...	1317	...	1518	ICE	1717	...	1917	...
Regensburg Hbf a.	1026	...	1226	...	1426	...	1626	1522	1826	...	2026	...
Nürnberg Hbf a.	1125	...	1325	...	1525	...	1725	🍸	1925	...	2125	...
Würzburg Hbf a.	1223	...	1423	...	1623	...	1821	1829	2023	...	2222	...
Frankfurt (M) Hbf a.	1340	...	1536	...	1736	...	...	1936	2135	...	2339	...
Frankfurt Flug. ✈ a.	...	...	...	...	1755	...	...	1956	2157	...	...	...
Mainz Hbf a.	...	...	...	...	1818	...	...	2018	2218	...	...	...
Koblenz Hbf a.	...	...	...	...	1911	...	...	2111	2311	...	...	...
Bonn Hbf a.	...	...	...	...	1942	...	...	2143	2342	...	...	...
Köln Hbf a.	...	...	...	...	2005	...	...	2205	0005	...	...	...
Düsseldorf Hbf a.	...	...	...	...	⊙	...	...	⊙	0032	...	...	...
Dortmund Hbf a.	...	...	...	...	2122	...	...	2322	0121	...	...	...

A – 🛏 1, 2 cl., ▬ 2 cl. (4, 6 berth), [2] 🍸 Düsseldorf - Köln - Frankfurt - Passau 🏛 - Wien and v.v. [R] Special fares apply. For international journeys only.
D – DACIA – 🛏 1, 2 cl., ▬ 2 cl., [2] ✕ Wien - Budapest - Bucureşti and v.v.

f – Frankfurt (Main) **Süd**.

⊙ – Via Hagen, Wuppertal (Table **800**).
RJ – ÖBB *RailJet* service. [1] (business c [1] (first class), [2] (economy clas

68 DORTMUND - KÖLN - MÜNCHEN - GRAZ and KLAGENFURT

train type/number	EC	EC	EC	IC	EC	EC	EC	D	EC	EC	EN
train number	111	211	217	690	113	113	115	315	219	117	499
notes	🍸	H	✕	🍸	✕	213	✕		🍸	1217	L
			Y			A	W			✕	
Dortmund Hbf d.	...	...	...	...	...	...	...	...	...	...	...
Münster Hbf d.	...	...	...	...	...	...	0631	...	...	...	...
Köln Hbf d.	...	...	...	...	...	...	0818	...	...	...	...
Frankfurt (Main) Hbf d.	...	...	...	...	0822	0822	|	...	1220	1420t	...
Saarbrücken d.	...	...	0528	...	|	|	|	...	|	|	...
Mannheim d.	...	...	0711	...	|	|	1101	...	|	|	...
Heidelberg d.	...	...	|	...	0913	0913	|	...	1314	1514t	...
Stuttgart Hbf d.	...	...	0758	...	0958	0958	1157	...	1358	1557	...
Ulm d.	...	...	0856	...	1054	1054	1255	...	1456	1655	...
Augsburg d.	...	...	0942	...	1142	1142	1342	...	1542	1741	...
München Hbf d.	0818	...	1018	...	1218	1218	1417	...	1618	1818	2336
Salzburg 🏛 a.	0959	...	1158	1212	1359	1359	1558	...	1759	1958	0119
Bischofshofen a.	1052	...	1302	1252	1452	1452	1652	...	1902	2052	|
Selzthal a.	|	...	1439	|	|	|	|	...	2039	|	|
Graz a.	|	...	1614	|	|	|	|	...	2214	|	|
Schwarzach St Veit a.	1109	...	...	1309	1509	1509	1709	...	...	2109	0223
Villach Hbf a.	1243	1253	...	1443	1643	1643	1843	1853	...	2243	0351
Klagenfurt a.	1315	|	...	...	1715	|	1915	|	...	2315	|
Ljubljana a.	...	1431	...	...	...	1831	...	2040	...	...	0559

train type/number	IC	EC	D	EC	EC	EC	EC	EC	EC	EN
train number	693	218	314	114	112	212	216	210	110	498
notes	🍸	🍸		✕	🍸	112	✕	H	🍸	L
				W		A	Y			
Ljubljana d.	...	...	0726	...	...	0922	...	1525	...	2355
Klagenfurt d.	0645	...	|	0842	1027	|	...	|	1642	|
Villach Hbf d.	0716	...	0907	0916	1116	1116	...	1707	1716	0146
Schwarzach St Veit d.	0850	...	...	1049	1249	1249	...	...	1849	0320
Graz d.	|	0545	...	|	|	|	1145	...	|	|
Selzthal d.	|	0719	...	|	|	|	1319	...	|	|
Bischofshofen d.	0905	0857	...	1105	1305	1305	1457	...	1905	|
Salzburg 🏛 d.	0948	1000	...	1200	1400	1400	1600	...	2000	0428
München Hbf a.	...	1141	...	1340	1541	1541	1741	...	2141	0610
Augsburg a.	...	1214	...	1415	1615	1615	1815	...	...	...
Ulm a.	...	1302	...	1502	1701	1701	1901	...	...	...
Stuttgart Hbf a.	...	1401	...	1600	1800	1800	2000	...	...	...
Heidelberg a.	...	1444	...	|	1843	1843	|	...	...	...
Mannheim a.	...	|	...	1657	|	|	2047	...	...	...
Saarbrücken a.	...	|	...	|	|	|	2219	...	...	...
Frankfurt (Main) Hbf a.	...	1540	...	|	1940	1940	...	...	...	...
Köln Hbf a.	...	...	...	1942	...	...	...	...	...	...
Münster Hbf a.	...	...	...	|	...	...	...	...	...	...
Dortmund Hbf a.	...	...	...	2100	...	...	...	...	...	...

A – [12] 🍸 Frankfurt - Stuttgart - München - Villach - Ljubljana - Zagreb and v.v.
H – SAVA – [2] Villach - Jesenice 🏛 - Ljubljana - Zagreb - Vinkovci and v.v. ✕ Jesenice 🏛 - Zagreb and v.v.
L – LISINSKI – 🛏 1, 2 cl., ▬ 2 cl., [2] München - Ljubljana - Zagreb and v.v.
W – WÖRTHERSEE – [12] ✕ Münster - Klagenfurt and Klagenfurt - Dortmund.

Y – [12] ✕ Saarbrücken - Mannheim - Graz an

t – Not ⑥.

DORTMUND - MÜNCHEN - INNSBRUCK - VENEZIA and MILANO

train type / number	*ICE*	*CNL*	*IC*	*EC*	*EC*	*EC*	*FB*	*ICE*	*ICE*	*EC*	*FB*	*FB*	*FA*	*IC*	*ICE*	*ICE*	*IC*	*EC*	*EC*	*FA*			
train number	**823**	**419**	**61479**	**1289**	**81**	**37**	**9722**	**521**	**699**	**85**	**9725**	**9728**	**9439**	**2021**	**1125**	**525**	**2265**	**87**	**42**	**9483**			
notes	①–⑤		2	✕♥	✕♥	[R] 🍷	[R]	🍷	*RJ*	✕♥	[R] ⚡	[R]	[R] ⚡		⑦	①–⑥	🍷	✕	[R] 🍷	[R] ⚡			
		L		⑥⑦	①–⑤	⊗	🍷 ⚡		**63**	**R**	🍷	🍷 ⚡	🍷			🍷		♥	⊗	✕			
und Hbf ... d.	...	...	...	...	...	...	...	...	...	...	...	...	...	0144	0514	0524	...	...	...	...	...	...	...
m Hbf ... d.	...	...	...	...	...	...	...	...	...	...	...	...	...	0155	0526	0538	...	...	...	...	...	...	...
Hbf ... d.	...	...	...	...	...	...	...	...	...	...	...	...	...	0206	0538	0553	...	...	...	...	...	...	...
urg Hbf ... d.	...	2234	...	...	...	...	...	...	...	...	...	...	...	0219	0550	0607	...	...	...	...	...	...	...
eldorf Hbf ... d.	...	2249	...	...	...	...	...	...	...	...	...	...	...	0239	0605	0621	...	...	...	...	...	...	...
Messe/Deutz ... d.	...	|	...	...	...	...	...	...	...	...	...	...	...	|	0628	0644	...	...	...	...	...	...	...
Hbf ... d.	...	2318	...	...	...	...	...	0418	...	...	...	...	...	0353	|	|	...	...	...	...	...	...	...
Hbf ... d.	...	2339	...	...	...	...	...	|	...	...	...	...	...	0416	|	|	...	...	...	...	...	...	...
nz Hbf ... d.	...	0017	...	...	...	...	...	⊖	...	...	...	...	...	0531	⊖	⊖	...	...	...	...	...	...	...
Hbf ... d.	...	0113	...	...	...	...	...	|	...	...	...	...	...	0628	|	|	...	...	...	...	...	...	...
furt Flughafen ✈ ... d.	...	0131	...	...	...	...	...	0534	...	...	...	...	...	0648	0736	0735	...	...	...	...	...	...	...
nkfurt (Main) Hbf ... d.	...	0213	...	...	...	...	...	0551	...	...	...	...	...	0702	0754	0754	...	...	...	...	...	...	...
heim Hbf ... d.	...	|	...	...	...	...	...	|	...	...	...	...	...	...	|	|	...	...	...	...	...	...	...
lberg Hbf ... d.	...	|	...	...	...	...	...	|	...	...	...	...	...	...	|	|	...	...	...	...	...	...	...
nberg Hbf ... d.	0558	|	...	...	...	...	...	0802	...	...	...	...	...		1002	1002	...	...	...	...	...	...	...
gart Hbf ... d.	|	0435	0435	...	...	...	...	|	0656	...	...	...	...	...	|	|	0853	...	...	...	...	...	...
Hbf ... d.	|	0542	0542	...	...	...	...	|	0756	...	...	...	...	...	|	|	0956	...	...	...	...	...	...
burg Hbf ... d.	|	0636	0636	...	...	...	...	|	0842	...	...	...	...	...	|	|	1039	...	...	...	...	...	...
chen Hbf ... d.	0703	0710	0710	0738	0738	...	...	0904	0913	0938	...	...	...	...	1104	1104	1111	1138	...	...	...	...	...
hen Ost ▲ ... d.	...	...	...	0747	0747	...	...		...	0947	...	...	...	...	...	...	...	1147	...	...	...	...	...
ein 🏛 ... a.	...	...	...	0840	0840	...	...		...	1040	...	...	...	...	...	...	...	1240	...	...	...	...	...
... a.	...	...	...	0851	0851	...	...		...	1051	...	...	...	...	...	...	...	1251	...	...	...	...	...
ch ... a.	...	...	...	0903	0903	...	...		...	1103	...	...	...	...	...	...	...	1303	...	...	...	...	...
ruck Hbf ... a.	...	...	...	0922	0922	...	...		...	1122	...	...	...	...	...	...	...	1322	...	...	...	...	...
ruck Hbf ... d.	...	...	...	0926	0927	...	...		...	1127	...	...	...	...	...	...	...	1327	...	...	...	...	...
ero / Brenner 🏛 ... a.	...	...	...	1001	1002	...	...		...	1202	...	...	...	...	...	...	...	1402	...	...	...	...	...
no / Bozen ... a.	...	...	...	1117	1127	...	...		...	1327	...	...	...	...	...	...	...	1527	...	...	...	...	...
o ... a.	...	...	...	1148	1202	...	...		...	1402	...	...	...	...	...	...	...	1602	...	...	...	...	...
na ... a.	...	...	...	1242	1256	1329	1402		...	1456	1529	1532	...	...	...	...	...	1656	1732	1750	...	...	...
dova ... a.	...	...	...	1325	|	1412	|		...	|	1612	|	...	...	...	...	...	1741	|	|	...	...	...
nezia Santa Lucia ... a.	...	...	...	1356	|	1440	|		...	|	1640	|	...	...	...	...	...	1810	|	|	...	...	...
Milano Centrale ... a.	...	...	...	...	|	...	1525		...	|	...	1655	...	...	...	...	...	...	1855	|	...	...	...
na Centrale ... a.	...	...	...	...	1406	...	...		...	1606	...	...	1653	...	...	...	...	...	...	1840	...	...	...
ze SMN ... a.	...	...	...	...	...	...	...		...	...	...	...	1730	...	...	...	...	...	...	1920¶	...	...	...
a Termini ... a.	...	...	...	...	...	...	...		...	...	...	...	1910	...	...	...	...	...	...	2040	...	...	...
i Centrale ... a.	...	...	...	...	...	...	...		...	...	...	...	2035	...	...	...	...	...	...	...	...	...	...

train type / number	*ICE*	*ICE*	*EC*		*FB*	*IC*	*EC*	*ICE*	*ICE*	*IC*	*EC*	*FB*	*ICE*	*ICE*	*EC*		*ICE*	*ICE*	*CNL*	*CNL*	*CNL*		
train number	**513**	**529**	**89**	**2107**	**9746**	**119**	**115**	**515**	**623**	**2261**	**83**	**9749**	**517**	**627**	**189**		**723**	**611**	**485** **60485**	**40485**	**40463** **60463**		
notes	🍷		✕	2	[R] ⚡	🍷	✕	🍷	🍷	🍷	✕	[R]	🍷	🍷	✕		🍷	🍷					
			♥			**K**	**Q**				♥	🍷 ⚡			♥		Ⓑ		**B**	**T**	**C**		
nund Hbf ... d.	0637	0724	...	...	...	...	...	0837	...	...	...	...	1037	...	...	...	...	1437	...	...	...	...	...
um Hbf ... d.	0649	0738	...	...	...	...	...	|	...	...	...	...	1049	...	...	...	...	1449	...	...	...	...	...
n Hbf ... d.	0700	0754	...	...	...	0823	...	|	0941	...	...	...	1100	1153	...	...	1453	1500	...	...	...	...	...
urg Hbf ... d.	0712	0808	...	...	...	0838	0734	|	0955	...	...	...	1112	1207	...	...	1507	1512	...	...	...	...	...
eldorf Hbf ... d.	0727	0822	...	...	...	0852	0751	|	1012	...	...	...	1127	1221	...	...	1521	1527	...	...	...	...	...
Messe/Deutz ... d.	|	0844	...	...	...	|	|	|	1033	...	...	...	|	1244	...	...	1544	|	...	...	...	...	...
Hbf ... d.	0755	|	...	...	...	0918	0818	0955	|	...	...	...	1155	|	...	...	|	1555	...	...	...	...	...
Hbf ... d.	|	|	...	...	...	0937	0837	|	|	...	...	...	|	|	...	...	|	|	...	...	...	...	...
enz Hbf ... d.	⊖	⊖	...	...	...	1017	0917	⊖	⊖	...	...	...	⊖	⊖	...	...	⊖	⊖	...	...	...	...	...
z Hbf ... d.	|	|	...	...	...	1112	1017	|	|	...	...	...	|	|	...	...	|	|	...	...	...	...	...
kfurt Flughafen ✈ ... d.	0853	0935	...	...	...	|	|	1053	1135	...	...	...	1253	1332	...	...	1635	1653	...	...	...	...	...
ankfurt (Main) Hbf ... d.	|	0954	...	...	...	|	|	|	1154	...	...	...	|	1354	...	...	1654	|	...	...	...	...	...
heim Hbf ... d.	0931	|	...	...	...	1154	1102	1131	|	...	...	...	1331	|	...	...	|	1731	...	...	...	...	...
elberg Hbf ... d.	|	|	...	...	...	1206	|	|	|	...	...	...	|	|	...	...	|	|	...	...	...	...	...
rnberg Hbf ... d.	|	1202	...	...	...	|	|	|	1406	...	...	...	|	1602	...	...	1902	|	...	...	...	...	...
gart Hbf ... d.	1013	|	...	...	...	1257	1158	1213	|	1253	...	...	1413	|	...	...	|	1813	...	...	...	...	...
Hbf ... d.	1109	|	...	...	...	1411	1256	1309	|	1356	...	...	1509	|	...	...	|	1909	...	...	...	...	...
burg Hbf ... d.	1155	|	...	...	...	|	1342	1355	|	1440	...	...	1555	|	...	...	|	1955	...	...	...	...	...
chen Hbf ... d.	1227	1304	1338	...	...	|	1411	1427	1508	1512	1538	...	1627	1704	1738	...	2004	2027	2108	2108	2336	...	...
chen Ost ▲ ... d.	...	...	1347	...	...	|	...	...	...	...	1547	...	...	...	1747	...	...	...	|	|	|	...	...
ein 🏛 ... d.	...	...	1440	...	...	|	...	...	...	...	1640	...	...	...	1840	...	...	...	2207	2207	|	...	...
gl ... d.	...	...	1451	...	...	|	...	...	...	...	1651	...	...	...	1851	...	...	...	2217	2217	|	...	...
ach ... a.	...	...	1503	...	...	|	...	...	...	...	1703	...	...	...	1903	...	...	...	2232	2232	|	...	...
bruck Hbf ... a.	...	...	1522	...	...	1901	...	...	...	...	1722	...	...	...	1922	...	...	...	2258	2258	|	...	...
bruck Hbf ... d.	...	...	1527	...	...	...	...	...	...	...	1727	...	...	...	...	...	...	...	2305	2305	|	...	...
nero / Brenner 🏛 ... a.	...	...	1602	...	...	...	...	...	...	...	1802	...	...	...	...	...	...	...	2341	2341	◧	...	...
ano / Bozen ... a.	...	...	1727	...	...	...	...	...	...	...	1927	...	...	...	...	...	...	...	0106	0106	|	...	...
o ... a.	...	...	1802	...	...	...	...	...	...	...	2002	...	...	...	...	...	...	...	0141	0141	|	...	...
na ... a.	...	...	1856	1918	1932	...	...	...	...	...	2056	2129	...	...	...	...	...	...	0237	0237e	|	...	...
dova ... a.	...	...	...	2021	|	...	...	...	...	...	...	2212	...	...	...	...	...	...	|	|	|	...	...
nezia Santa Lucia ... a.	...	...	...	2054	|	...	...	...	...	...	...	2240	...	...	...	...	...	...	|	|	0834	...	...
Milano Centrale ... a.	...	...	...	...	2055	...	...	...	...	...	...	...	...	...	...	...	...	...	|	0912	...	...	...
gna Centrale ... a.	...	...	...	...	...	...	...	...	...	...	...	...	...	...	...	...	...	...	0420	...	...	...	...
ze SMN ... a.	...	...	...	...	...	...	...	...	...	...	...	...	...	...	...	...	...	...	0607	...	..	...	...
a Termini ... a.	...	...	...	...	...	...	...	...	...	...	...	...	...	...	...	...	...	...	0922	...	...	...	...
li Centrale ... a.	...	...	...	...	...	...	...	...	...	...	...	...	...	...	...	...	...	...	...	...	...	...	...

B – *City Night Line* LUPUS – 🛏 1, 2 cl., ▬ 2 cl., (2) 🍷 München - Innsbruck - Roma. Special fares apply. [R] for journeys to / from Italy.

C – *City Night Line* PICTOR – 🛏 1, 2 cl., ▬ 2 cl., (2) 🍷 München - Tarvisio 🏛 - Venezia. Special fares apply. [R] for journeys to / from Italy.

K – (1,2) 🍷 Munster - Köln - Stuttgart - Lindau 🏛 - Innsbruck and v.v.

L – *City Night Line* POLLUX – 🛏 1, 2 cl., ▬ 2 cl. 🍷 (*CNL* **419** [R]) Amsterdam - Köln - München; (2) (*IC* **60419**) Amsterdam - Köln - München. Special fares apply.

Q – WÖRTHERSEE – (1,2) ✕ Münster - München - Klagenfurt.

R – On ⑤⑥ June 17 - Sept. 10 to Rimini, arrive 1729.

T – *City Night Line* APUS – 🛏 1, 2 cl., ▬ 2 cl., [R] München - Innsbruck - Verona - Milano. Special fares apply.

e – Depart 0720.

◧ – 🏛 is Tarvisio (Table **88**).

⊗ – Compulsory reservation for international journeys. Supplement payable for international journeys and for internal journeys within Italy.

⊖ – Via Köln - Frankfurt high speed line.

¶ – Firenze **Campo di Marte**.

⚡ – Supplement payable.

▲ – Change here for München Airport (Table **892**).

♥ – DB-ÖBB EuroCity service.

70 MILANO and VENEZIA - INNSBRUCK - MÜNCHEN - DORTMUND

train type/number	IC	EC	ICE	ICE	FB	FB		EC	ICE	FR	FB	FB	EC	ICE	ICE	FB	FB	FB	FR	EC	ICE	ICE
train number	118	82	626	516	9704	9703		88	622	9460	9712	9713	80	528	512	9715	9791	9714	9518	84	524	510 1010 1110
notes	🍷 K	✕ ♥	🍷	🍷	🍷⚡ Ⓡ	🍷⚡ Ⓡ		✕ ♥	🍷	Ⓡ⚡ 🍷	🍷⚡ Ⓡ	🍷⚡ Ⓡ	✕ ♥	🍷	🍷	🍷⚡ Ⓡ	Ⓡ⚡ ⑥⑦	🍷⚡ Ⓡ	Ⓡ⚡ 🍷	✕♥ R	🍷	
Napoli Centrale d.	...	...	...	...	...	...	...	...	...	...	...	...	...	...	...	...	...	...	0800	...	...	...
Roma Termini d.	...	...	...	...	...	...	...	...	...	0630	...	...	...	...	...	...	...	...	0920	...	...	...
Firenze SMN d.	...	...	...	...	...	...	...	...	...	0750c	...	...	...	...	...	...	...	...	1100	...	...	...
Bologna Centrale d.	...	...	...	...	...	...	0710	...	...	0830	...	...	...	...	...	...	...	...	1135	1152	...	...
Milano Centrale d.	...	...	...	...	...	0705	|	...	...	|	...	0905	...	...	...	0935	1035	...	...	|	...	...
Venezia Santa Lucia d.	...	...	...	...	0650	|	|	...	...	|	0850	|	...	...	...	|	|	1050	...	|	...	...
Padova d.	...	...	...	...	0718	|	|	...	...	|	0918	|	...	...	...	|	|	1118	...	|	...	...
Verona d.	...	...	...	...	0800	0827	0838	0904	...	0920	1000	1027	1104	...	...	1057	1157	1200	...	1304	...	...
Trento d.	...	...	...	...	...	...	...	0959	...	—	...	...	1159	...	...	...	...	...	...	1359	...	...
Bolzano/Bozen d.	...	...	...	...	...	...	...	1033	...	...	...	...	1233	...	...	...	...	...	...	1433	...	...
Brennero/Brenner 🏛 d.	...	...	...	...	...	...	...	1200	...	...	...	...	1400	...	...	...	...	...	...	1600	...	...
Innsbruck Hbf a.	...	...	...	...	...	...	...	1231	...	...	...	...	1431	...	...	...	...	...	...	1631	...	...
Innsbruck Hbf d.	0901	1036	...	...	...	...	...	1236	...	...	...	...	1436	...	...	...	...	...	...	1636	...	...
Jenbach d.	|	1055	...	...	...	...	...	1255	...	...	...	...	1455	...	...	...	...	...	...	1655	...	...
Wörgl d.	|	1109	...	...	...	...	...	1309	...	*ICE*	...	...	1509	...	...	...	...	...	...	1709	...	...
Kufstein 🏛 a.	|	1119	...	...	...	...	...	1319	...	**514**	...	...	1517	...	...	...	...	...	...	1717	...	...
München Ost ▲ a.	|	1209	...	...	...	...	...	1409	...	🍷	...	...	1609	...	...	...	...	...	...	1809	...	...
München Hbf a.	|	1221	1255	1328	...	...	...	1421	1455	1528	...	...	1621	1652	1727	...	...	...	...	1821	1855	1928
Augsburg Hbf a.	|	...	|	1400	...	...	...	...	|	1600	...	...	...	|	1800	...	...	...	...	...	|	2000
Ulm Hbf a.	1345	...	|	1447	...	...	...	...	|	1647	...	...	...	|	1847	...	...	...	...	...	|	2047
Stuttgart Hbf a.	1458	...	|	1546	...	...	...	...	|	1746	...	...	...	|	1946	...	...	...	...	...	|	2146
Nürnberg Hbf a.	|	...	1357	|	...	...	...	...	1557	|	...	...	...	1757	|	...	...	...	...	...	1957	|
Heidelberg Hbf a.	1553	...	|	|	...	...	...	...	|	|	...	...	...	|	|	...	...	...	...	...	|	|
Mannheim Hbf a.	1606	...	|	1628	...	...	...	...	|	1828	...	...	...	|	2028	...	...	...	...	...	|	2229
Frankfurt (Main) Hbf a.	|	...	1604	|	...	...	...	...	1804	|	...	...	...	2004	|	...	...	...	...	...	2204	|
Frankfurt Flughafen ✈ a.	|	...	1622	1706	...	...	...	...	1822	1906	...	...	...	2022	2106	...	...	...	...	...	2222	2308
Mainz Hbf a.	1646	...	|	|	...	...	...	...	|	|	...	...	...	|	|	...	...	...	...	...	|	...
Koblenz Hbf a.	1741	...	⊖	⊖	...	...	...	...	⊖	⊖	...	...	...	⊖	⊖	...	...	...	...	...	⊖	...
Bonn Hbf a.	1820	...	|	|	...	...	...	...	|	|	...	...	...	|	|	...	...	...	...	...	|	...
Köln Hbf a.	1842	...	|	1805	...	...	...	...	|	2005	...	...	...	|	2205	...	...	...	...	...	|	...
Köln Messe/Deutz a.	|	...	1714	|	...	...	...	...	1914	|	...	...	...	2114	|	...	...	...	...	...	2339	...
Dusseldorf Hbf a.	1907	...	1736	1831	...	...	...	...	1944	2031	...	...	...	2136	2231	...	...	...	...	...	2400	...
Duisburg Hbf a.	1922	...	1749	1844	...	...	...	...	1957	2044	...	...	...	2149	2244	...	...	...	...	...	0013	...
Essen Hbf a.	1934	...	1802	1857	...	...	...	...	2015	2057	...	...	...	2202	2257	...	...	...	...	...	0026	...
Bochum Hbf a.	...	...	...	1908	...	...	...	...	2027	2108	...	...	...	2214	...	...	...	...	...	...	0036	...
Dortmund Hbf a.	...	...	...	1921	...	...	...	...	2042	2121	...	...	...	2230	...	...	...	...	...	...	0049	...

train type	FA	FB	EC	ICE		FB	FB	EC	EC	CNL	IC		CNL	CNL	CNL	ICE	ICE
train number	9416	9723	86	990		9727	9732	188	1288	418	60418		40236 60236	484 60484	40481	728	612
notes	Ⓡ⚡	Ⓡ⚡	✕ ♥	*RJ* 66 1590		Ⓡ⚡	Ⓡ⚡	✕♥ ①–⑤	✕♥ ⑥⑦	L			C	B	T	🍷	🍷
Napoli Centrale d.	...	...	...	...	...	...	...	...	...	...	...	...	...	...	...	...	...
Roma Termini d.	1035	...	...	...	...	...	...	...	...	...	...	...	...	1904	...	...	...
Firenze SMN d.	1215	...	...	...	...	...	...	...	...	...	...	...	...	2214	...	...	...
Bologna Centrale d.	1255	...	...	...	1410	...	...	1552	...	...	...	...	...	2345	...	...	...
Milano Centrale d.	|	1305	...	...	|	1505	...	|	...	...	...	...	...	|	2105	...	...
Padova d.	|	|	1334	...	|	|	1520	|	1541	...	...	...	...	|	|	...	...
Venezia Santa Lucia d.	1352	|	1407	...	|	|	1548	|	1614	...	...	...	2057	|	|	...	...
Verona d.	...	1427	1504	...	1538	1627	1630	1704	1704	...	...	...	|	0111	0111z	...	...
Trento d.	...	...	1559	...	...	...	...	1759	1759	...	...	...	|	|	|	...	...
Bolzano/Bozen d.	...	...	1633	...	...	...	...	1833	1833	...	...	...	|	|	|	...	...
Brennero/Brenner 🏛 d.	...	...	1800	...	...	...	...	2000	2000	...	...	...	◧	0357	0357	...	...
Innsbruck Hbf a.	...	...	1831	...	...	...	...	2032	2032	...	...	...	|	0430	0430	...	...
Innsbruck Hbf d.	...	...	1836	...	...	...	...	2036	2036	...	...	...	|	0436	0436	...	...
Jenbach d.	...	...	1855	...	...	...	...	2055	2055	...	...	...	|	0500	0500	...	...
Wörgl d.	...	...	1909	...	...	...	...	2109	2109	...	...	...	|	0518	0518	...	...
Kufstein 🏛 d.	...	...	1917	...	...	...	...	2117	2117	...	...	...	|	0527	0527	...	...
München Ost ▲ d.	...	...	2009	...	...	...	...	2209	2209	...	...	...	|	|	|	...	...
München Hbf a.	...	...	2021	2045	...	...	...	2221	2221	2250	2250	...	0610	0630	0630	0652	0727
Augsburg Hbf a.	...	...	...	2115	...	...	...	...	...	2318	2318	...	...	...	...	|	0800
Ulm Hbf a.	...	...	...	2202	...	...	...	...	...	0008	0008	...	...	...	...	|	0847
Stuttgart Hbf a.	...	...	...	2259	...	...	...	...	...	0116	0116	...	...	...	...	|	0946
Nürnberg Hbf a.	...	...	...	|	...	...	...	...	...	|	...	...	...	...	...	0757	|
Heidelberg Hbf a.	...	...	...	|	...	...	...	...	...	|	...	...	...	...	...	|	|
Mannheim Hbf a.	...	...	...	2345	...	...	...	...	...	|	...	...	...	...	...	|	1028
Frankfurt (Main) Hbf a.	...	...	...	0042r	...	...	...	...	...	0312	...	...	...	...	...	1004	|
Frankfurt Flughafen ✈ a.	...	...	...	0023r	...	...	...	...	...	0356	...	...	...	...	...	1022	1106
Mainz Hbf a.	...	...	...	...	...	...	...	...	...	0418	...	...	...	...	...	|	|
Koblenz Hbf a.	...	...	...	...	...	...	...	...	...	0511	...	...	...	...	...	⊖	⊖
Bonn Hbf a.	...	...	...	...	...	...	...	...	...	0545	...	...	...	...	...	|	|
Köln Hbf a.	...	...	...	...	...	...	...	...	...	0615	...	...	...	...	...	|	1205
Köln Messe/Deutz a.	...	...	...	...	...	...	...	...	...	|	...	...	...	...	...	1114	|
Dusseldorf Hbf a.	...	...	...	...	...	...	...	...	...	0651	...	...	...	...	...	1136	1231
Duisburg Hbf a.	...	...	...	...	...	...	...	...	...	0710	...	...	...	...	...	1149	1244
Essen Hbf a.	...	...	...	...	...	...	...	...	...	...	...	...	...	...	...	1202	1257
Bochum Hbf a.	...	...	...	...	...	...	...	...	...	...	...	...	...	...	...	1214	1308
Dortmund Hbf a.	...	...	...	...	...	...	...	...	...	...	...	...	...	...	...	1230	1321

B – *City Night Line* LUPUS – 🛏 1, 2 cl., 🛏 2 cl., (2) 🍷 Roma - Innsbruck - München. Special fares apply. Ⓡ for journeys to/from Italy.

C – *City Night Line* PICTOR – 🛏 1, 2 cl., 🛏 2 cl., (2) 🍷 Venezia - Tarvisio 🏛 - München. Special fares apply. Ⓡ for journeys to/from Italy.

K – (12) 🍷 Innsbruck - Lindau 🏛 - Stuttgart - Köln - Munster.

L – *City Night Line* POLLUX – 🛏 1, 2 cl., 🛏 2 cl., (2), 🍷 Ⓡ München - Köln - Amsterdam. Special fares apply.

R – On ⑥⑦ June 17 - Sept. 10 from Rimini, depart 1035.

T – *City Night Line* APUS – 🛏 1, 2 cl., 🛏 2 cl., Ⓡ Milano - Verona - Innsbruck - München. Special fares apply.

c – Firenze **Campo di Marte**.

r – Train stops at Frankfurt Flughafen before Frankfurt (Main).

z – Arrive 2240.

◧ – 🏛 is Tarvisio (Table **88**).

⊖ – Via Köln - Frankfurt high speed line.

⚡ – Supplement payable.

▲ – Change here for München Airport (Table **892**).

♥ – DB-ÖBB EuroCity service.

AMSTERDAM, BERLIN, DORTMUND and KÖLN - BASEL - ZÜRICH and MILANO 73

train type	ICE	EC	ICE	ICE	IR	EC	ICE	ICE	EC	ICE	EC	ICE	ICE	ICE	IR	EC	ICE	ICE	EC	ICE	EC	EC	
train number	3	15	271	5	2319	17	101	275	57	71	7	121	515	277	2327	21	105	73	9	279	9	23	
notes	🍷	[R] 🍷	M	🍷		[R] 🍷	🍷	🍷	[R] 🍷	🍷	🍴	①–⑥	🍷			[R] 🍷	505	1173	🍴	🍷	🍴	[R] 🍷	
		⊗	①–⑥			⊗			⊗		B					⊗	🍷	🍷	D		D	⊗	
urg Hbf d.	...	...	0044e	...	...	...	...	...	...	0618	0442v	...	...	...	...	...	...	0824	0646	...	...	...	...
en Hbf d.	...	...	|	...	...	...	...	...	...	|	0540v	...	...	...	...	...	...	|	0744	...	...	...	...
lin Hbf d.	...	...	|	...	...	...	...	0432p	...	|	|	...	...	0631	...	...	...	|	|	0831	...	...	...
nover Hbf d.	...	...	0210e	...	...	...	...	|	...	0741	|	...	...	|	...	...	...	0941	|	|	...	...	...
und Hbf d.	...	...	|	...	...	...	0537	|	...	|	0737	...	0837	|	...	...	...	|	0937	|	...	...	...
Hbf d.	...	...	|	...	...	...	|	|	...	|	0800	...	|	|	...	...	...	|	1000	|	...	...	...
sterdam Centraal d.	...	...	|	...	...	...	|	|	...	|	|	0635	|	|	...	...	0805	|	|	|	...	...	...
echt Centraal d.	...	...	|	...	...	...	|	|	...	|	|	0702	|	|	...	...	0832	|	|	|	...	...	...
hem ⊙ d.	...	...	|	...	...	...	|	|	...	|	|	0737	|	|	...	...	0907	|	|	|	...	...	...
urg Hbf d.	...	...	|	...	...	...	h	|	...	|	0812	0834	h	|	...	...	1008	|	1012	|	...	...	...
eldorf Hbf d.	...	...	|	...	...	...	|	|	...	|	0827	0848	|	|	...	...	1022	|	1027	|	...	...	...
Hbf d.	...	...	|	...	...	...	0654	|	...	|	0853	0927	0955	|	...	...	1055	|	1053	|	...	...	...
Hbf d.	...	...	|	...	...	...	|	|	...	|	0914	|	|	|	...	...	|	|	1114	|	...	...	...
nz Hbf d.	...	...	|	...	...	...	⊖	|	...	|	0948	⊖	⊖	|	...	...	⊖	|	1148	|	...	...	...
Hbf d.	...	...	|	...	...	...	|	|	...	|	1040	|	|	|	...	...	|	|	1240	|	...	...	...
furt Flughafen ✈ d.	...	...	|	...	...	...	0753	|	...	|	|	1018	1053	|	...	...	1153	|	|	|	...	...	...
nkfurt (Main) Hbf d.	...	...	0550	0650	...	...	|	0850	...	1005	|	1030	|	1050	...	...	|	1205	|	1250	...	...	...
heim Hbf d.	...	...	0633	0736	...	...	0836	0936	...	1045	1123	...	1123	1136	...	...	1236	1245	1323	1336	...	...	...
uhe Hbf d.	0556p	...	0658	0800	...	...	0900	1000	...	1110	1149	...	...	1200	...	...	1300	1310	1349	1400	...	...	...
urg (Brsg) Hbf d.	0702p	...	0802	0901	...	...	1007	1101	...	1212	1251	...	...	1306	...	...	1401	1412	1455	1501	...	...	...
Bad Bf 🏛 a.	0735p	...	0834	0934	...	...	1038	1134	...	1245	1322	...	...	1338	...	...	1434	1445	1527	1534	←	...	...
SBB a.	0747p	...	0847	0947	...	...	1047	1147	...	1254	1330	...	...	1347	...	...	1447	1454	1535	1547	1535	...	...
SBB ★ d.	0807	...	0907	...	1004	...	...	1159	1231	1307	1359	...	...	...	1404	...	...	1507	1607	...	1607	...	...
a.	|	...	|	...	|	...	...	1256	1324	|	1456	...	...	...	|	...	...	|	→	...	|	...	...
erlaken Ost a.	|	...	|	...	|	...	...	1357	|	|	1557	...	...	...	|	...	...	|	...	...	|	...	...
h HB a.	0900	0932	1000	...	|	1132	...	...	|	1400	...	...	...	...	|	1532	...	1600	...	...	1700	1732	...
ur a.	...	|	1122	...	|	|	...	...	|	1522	...	...	...	...	|	|	...	...	...	...	...	|	...
Goldau a.	...	1014	...	...	1144	1214	...	...	|	...	...	...	...	...	1544	1614	...	...	...	...	...	1814	...
zona a.	...	1155	...	...	...	1355	...	...	|	...	...	...	...	...	...	1755	...	...	...	...	...	1955	...
no a.	...	1223	...	...	...	1423	...	...	|	...	...	...	...	...	...	1823	...	...	...	...	...	2023	...
so 🏛 a.	...	1248	...	...	...	1448	...	...	◧	...	...	...	...	...	...	1848	...	...	...	...	...	2048	...
San Giovanni a.	...	|	...	...	...	1456	...	...	|	...	...	...	...	...	...	|	...	...	...	...	...	2056	...
o Centrale a.	...	1335	...	...	...	1535	...	...	1635	...	...	...	...	...	...	1935	...	...	...	...	...	2135	...

train type	ICE	ICE	EC	EC	ICE	ICE	ICE	ICE	ICE	ICE	ICE		IC	IC	CNL	CNL	CNL	EC	IC	IR	EC		
train number	107	75	59	25	123	371	109	77	125	373	79		2307	61419	40419	479	471	15	60458	2315	15		
notes	🍷	1175	[R] 🍷	[R] 🍷	🍷	🍷	🍷	🍷	🍷	🍷	🍷		🍷	2		60479	60471	[R] 🍷			[R] 🍷		
		🍷	⊗	⊗										A	A	K	G	⊗			⊗		
burg Hbf d.	...	1024	...	...	...	...	...	1224	...	...	1424	...	1846	...	...	2029	...	...	...	...	...	...	...
en Hbf d.	...	|	...	...	...	...	...	|	...	...	|	...	1944	...	...	|	...	...	...	...	...	...	...
rlin Hbf d.	...	|	...	...	...	1035	...	|	...	1231	|	...	|	...	...	|	2150	...	...	...	...	...	...
nnover Hbf d.	...	1141	...	...	...	|	...	1341	...	|	1541	...	|	...	...	2201	|	...	...	...	...	...	...
mund Hbf d.	...	|	...	...	...	|	1337c	|	...	|	|	...	2137	...	...	|	|	...	...	...	...	...	...
n Hbf d.	...	|	...	...	...	|	|	|	...	|	|	...	2200	...	...	|	|	...	...	...	...	...	...
sterdam Centraal d.	...	|	...	...	1035	|	|	|	1235	|	|	...	|	2031	2031	|	|	...	...	...	...	...	...
echt Centraal d.	...	|	...	...	1102	|	|	|	1302	|	|	...	|	2100	2100u	|	|	...	...	...	...	...	...
hem ⊙ d.	...	|	...	...	1137	|	|	|	1337	|	|	...	|	2133	2133u	|	|	...	...	...	...	...	...
burg Hbf d.	...	|	...	...	1234	|	h	|	1438	|	|	...	2212	2234	2234u	|	|	...	...	...	...	...	...
seldorf Hbf d.	...	|	...	...	1248	|	|	|	1454	|	|	...	2227	2249	2249u	|	|	...	...	...	...	...	...
Hbf d.	1255	|	...	...	1328	|	1455	|	1529	|	|	...	2250	2318	2318u	|	|	...	...	...	...	...	...
Hbf d.	|	|	...	...	|	|	|	|	|	|	|	...	2314	2339	2339u	|	|	...	...	...	...	...	...
enz Hbf d.	⊖	|	...	...	⊖	|	⊖	|	⊖	|	|	...	2354	0017	0017u	|	|	...	...	...	...	...	...
z Hbf d.	|	|	...	...	|	|	|	|	|	|	|	...	...	0113	0113u	|	|	...	...	...	...	...	...
kfurt Flughafen ✈ d.	1353	|	...	...	1418	|	1553	|	1618	|	|	...	...	0131	0131u	|	|	...	...	...	...	...	...
nkfurt (Main) Hbf d.	|	1405	...	...	1430	1450	|	1605	1630	1650	1805	...	...	0248	|	0248	0359z	...	0402z	...	...	...	...
heim Hbf d.	1434	1445	...	...	...	1536	1636	1645	...	1736	1845	...	...	0331	|	0331	0440s	...	0442	...	...	...	...
ruhe Hbf d.	1458	1510	...	...	...	1600	1700	1710	...	1800	1910	...	...	0402	0400s	0402	0507s	...	0509	...	...	...	...
urg (Brsg) Hbf d.	1601	1612	...	...	...	1701	1801	1812	...	1901	2012	...	...	0531	0529s	0531	0620s	...	0622	...	...	...	...
Bad Bf 🏛 a.	1634	1645	...	...	...	1734	1834	1845	...	1934	2045	...	...	0609	0609	0609	0706s	...	0706	...	...	...	...
l SBB a.	1647	1654	...	...	...	1747	1847	1854	...	1947	2054	...	...	0619	0619	0619	0720s	...	0720	...	...	...	...
l SBB ★ d.	...	1707	1731	...	...	1759	...	1907	...	1959	2107	...	...	|	|	|	|	...	...	0804	...	...	...
a.	...	|	1824	...	...	1856	...	|	...	2056	|	...	...	|	|	|	|	...	...	|	...	...	...
erlaken Ost a.	...	|	|	...	...	1957	...	|	...	2157	|	...	...	|	|	|	|	...	...	|	...	...	...
n a.	...	|	|	...	...	...	...	|	...	...	|	...	...	0741	0741	0741	0841	...	...	|	...	...	...
ch HB a.	...	1800	|	1932	...	...	...	2000	...	...	2200	...	...	0805	0805	0805	0905	0932	...	|	...	...	...
ur a.	...	1922	|	|	...	...	...	...	...	...	...	...	...	...	...	...	...	|	...	|	...	...	...
Goldau a.	...	...	|	2014	...	...	...	...	...	...	...	...	...	...	...	...	...	1014	...	0944	1017	...	...
zona a.	...	...	|	2155	...	...	...	...	...	...	...	...	...	...	...	...	...	1155	...	...	1155	...	...
no a.	...	...	|	2223	...	...	...	...	...	...	...	...	...	...	...	...	...	1223	...	...	1223	...	...
sso 🏛 a.	...	...	◧	2248	...	...	...	...	...	...	...	...	...	...	...	...	...	1248	...	...	1248	...	...
o San Giovanni a.	...	...	|	2256	...	...	...	...	...	...	...	...	...	...	...	...	...	|	...	...	|	...	...
o Centrale a.	...	...	2135	2335	...	...	...	...	...	...	...	...	...	...	...	...	...	1335	...	...	1335	...	...

City Night Line PEGASUS – 🛏 1, 2 cl., 🛏 2 cl., 🍷 (*CNL* **40419** [R]) Amsterdam - Zürich; 🚃2 (*IC* **61419**) Amsterdam - Zürich. Special fares apply.

🚃12 🍴 (Hamburg ①–⑥) - Dortmund - Köln - Basel - Interlaken Ost.

🚃12 🍴 Hamburg - Dortmund - Köln - Basel - Zürich.

City Night Line SIRIUS – 🛏 1, 2 cl., 🛏 2 cl. 🍷 (*CNL* **471** [R]) Berlin - Frankfurt - Zürich; 🚃2 (*IC* **60471**) Berlin - Frankfurt - Zürich. Special fares apply. *Conveys City Night Line* (*CNL* **458** [R], *IC* **60458**) CANOPUS Praha - Dresden - Frankfurt - Zürich (Table **54**).

City Night Line KOMET – 🛏 1, 2 cl., 🛏 2 cl. 🍷 (*CNL* **479**) Hamburg - Zürich; 🚃2 (*IC* **60479**) Hamburg - Zürich. Special fares apply.

🚃12 🍷 (Hamburg ①) - (Frankfurt ①–⑥) - Basel - Chur.

Not ⑥.

① only.

Via Hagen and Wuppertal.

p – ①–⑤.

s – Calls to set down only.

u – Calls to pick up only.

v – ①–⑥.

z – Frankfurt (Main) **Süd**.

⊙ – 🏛 is at Emmerich.

◧ – Via Brig. 🏛 is at Domodossola; ticket point is **Iselle**.

⊖ – Via Köln - Frankfurt high speed line.

★ – Connections at Basel are not guaranteed.

⊗ – Compulsory reservation for international journeys. Supplement payable for international journeys and for internal journeys within Italy.

CONNECTING SERVICES

Basel - Luzern - Chiasso : Table **550**, Basel - Bern - Interlaken and Brig : Table **560**.

Zürich - Landquart - Chur : Table **520**, Chur - St Moritz : Table **540**, Zürich - Bellinzona - Chiasso : Table **550**.

73 MILANO and ZÜRICH - KÖLN, DORTMUND, BERLIN and AMSTERDAM

train type	ICE	ICE	ICE	ICE	ICE	ICE		ICE		EC	EC	ICE	EC	ICE	ICE		ICE	EC	EC	ICE	ICE	
train number	78	372	126	76	370	124		74		8	50	278	8	72	122		276	6	12	70	104 504	
notes	🍷	🍷	🍷 T	🍷	🍷	🍷		🍷		✕	Ⓡ 🍷 ⊗	🍷	✕	🍷	🍷			✕ G	Ⓡ 🍷 ⊗	🍷	🍷	
Milano Centrale d.	...	...	...	...	...	...	...	...	...	...	0725	...	...	...	...	...	...	...	0825	...	...	...
Como San Giovanni d.	...	...	...	...	...	...	...	...	...	...	|	...	...	...	...	...	...	...	0903	...	...	...
Chiasso 🏛 d.	...	...	...	...	...	...	...	...	...	...	◧	...	...	...	...	...	...	...	0912	...	...	...
Lugano d.	...	...	...	...	...	...	...	...	...	...	|	...	...	...	...	...	...	...	0934	...	...	...
Bellinzona d.	...	...	...	...	...	...	...	...	...	...	|	...	...	...	...	...	...	...	1000	...	...	...
Arth-Goldau d.	...	...	...	...	...	...	...	...	...	...	|	...	...	...	...	...	...	...	1145	...	...	...
Chur d.	...	...	...	...	...	...	...	...	...	...	|	...	...	1039	...	...	...	...	|	1239	...	...
Zürich HB d.	0600	...	...	0800	...	...	...	1000	...	1100	|	...	...	1200	...	...	...	...	1228	1400	...	...
Interlaken Ost d.	|	0600	...	|	...	...	...	|	...	|	|	1000	...	|	...	...	...	1200	...	|	...	...
Bern d.	|	0704	...	|	...	...	...	|	...	|	1036	1104	←	|	...	...	...	1304	...	|	...	...
Basel SBB ★ a.	0652	0759	...	0852	...	...	...	1052	...	1152	1129	1159	1152	1252	...	...	...	1359	...	1452	...	...
Basel SBB d.	0706	0813	...	0906	1013	...	...	1106	...	1220	...	1213	1220	1306	...	...	1413	1427	...	1506	1513	...
Basel Bad Bf 🏛 d.	0715	0823	...	0915	1023	...	...	1115	...	→	...	1223	1230	1315	...	...	1423	1435	...	1515	1523	...
Freiburg (Brsg) Hbf d.	0749	0857	...	0949	1057	...	...	1149	...	...	...	1257	1304	1349	...	...	1455	1507	...	1549	1557	...
Karlsruhe Hbf d.	0851	1000	...	1051	1200	...	...	1251	...	...	...	1400	1412	1451	...	...	1601	1612	...	1651	1700	...
Mannheim Hbf a.	0914	1024	...	1116	1223	...	...	1314	...	...	...	1423	1437	1514	...	...	1624	1637	...	1714	1723	...
Frankfurt (Main) Hbf a.	0953	1108	1129	1153	1308	1329	...	1353	...	...	...	1508	|	1553	1629	...	1708	|	...	1753	|	...
Frankfurt Flughafen ✈ a.	|	|	1140	|	|	1340	...	|	...	...	...	|	|	|	1640	...	|	|	...	|	1806	...
Mainz Hbf a.	|	|	|	|	|	|	...	|	...	...	...	|	1518	|	|	...	|	1718	...	|	|	...
Koblenz Hbf a.	|	|	⊖	|	|	⊖	...	|	...	...	...	|	1611	|	⊖	...	|	1811	...	|	⊖	...
Bonn Hbf a.	|	|	|	|	|	|	...	|	...	...	...	|	1642	|	|	...	|	1842	...	|	|	...
Köln Hbf a.	|	|	1232	|	|	1432	...	|	...	...	...	|	1705	|	1732	...	|	1905	...	|	1905	...
Düsseldorf Hbf a.	|	|	1305	|	|	1511	...	|	...	...	...	|	1731	|	1812	...	|	1931	...	|	1936	...
Duisburg Hbf a.	|	|	1322	|	|	1525	...	|	...	...	...	|	1744	|	1824	...	|	1944	...	|	1949	...
Arnhem ⊙ a.	|	|	1429	|	|	1629	...	|	...	...	...	|	|	|	1929	...	|	|	...	|	2053	...
Utrecht Centraal a.	|	|	1500	|	|	1700	...	|	...	...	...	|	|	|	2000	...	|	|	...	|	2128	...
Amsterdam Centraal a.	|	|	1527	|	|	1726	...	|	...	...	...	|	|	|	2027	...	|	|	...	|	2156	...
Essen Hbf a.	|	|	...	|	|	...	...	|	...	...	...	|	1757	|	...	...	|	1957	...	|	...	...
Dortmund Hbf a.	|	|	...	|	|	...	...	|	...	...	...	|	1821	|	...	...	|	2021	...	|	...	...
Hannover Hbf a.	1217	|	...	1417	|	...	...	1617	...	...	...	|	|	1817	...	...	|	|	...	2017	...	...
Berlin Hbf a.	|	1528	...	|	1728	...	...	|	...	...	...	1928	|	|	...	...	2128	|	...	|	...	...
Bremen Hbf a.	|	...	...	|	...	...	...	|	...	...	...	...	2015	|	...	...	...	2216x	...	|	...	...
Hamburg Hbf a.	1335	...	...	1535	...	...	...	1735	...	...	...	...	2113	1935	...	...	...	2314x	...	2138	...	...

train type	EC	ICE	ICE		ICE	EC		EC	ICE	ICE		EC	ICE	CNL	EC	EC	CNL	CNL	IC	IC		
train number	52	274	120		376 396	102 1102		16	272 292 1172	100		18	4	470	20	56	478	40478	61478	2212		
notes	Ⓡ 🍷 ⊗	🍷	Ⓑ		🍷			Ⓡ 🍷 ⊗		🍷		Ⓡ ⊗		🍷 C	Ⓡ ⊗	Ⓡ 🍷 ⊗	K	A	2			
Milano Centrale d.	1125	...	...	...	...	...	...	1225	...	...	...	1424	...	...	1625	1825	...	...	...	...	...	...
Como San Giovanni d.	|	...	...	...	...	...	...	|	...	...	...	|	...	...	|	|	...	...	...	...	...	...
Chiasso 🏛 d.	◧	...	...	...	...	...	...	1312	...	...	...	1512	...	...	1715	◧	...	...	...	...	...	...
Lugano d.	|	...	...	...	...	...	...	1334	...	...	...	1534	...	...	1734	|	...	...	...	...	...	...
Bellinzona d.	|	...	...	...	...	...	...	1400	...	...	...	1600	...	...	1800	|	...	...	...	...	...	...
Arth-Goldau d.	|	...	...	...	...	...	...	1545	...	...	...	1745	...	...	1945	|	...	...	...	...	...	...
Chur d.	|	...	...	...	...	...	...	|	...	...	...	|	...	...	|	|	...	...	...	...	...	...
Zürich HB d.	|	...	...	...	...	...	...	1628	1700	...	...	1828	1900	1942	2028	|	2142	2142	2142	...	...	...
Baden d.	|	...	...	...	...	...	...	...	|	...	...	...	|	2000	...	|	2200	2200	2200	...	...	...
Interlaken Ost d.	|	...	...	...	1500	...	...	...	|	...	...	...	|	|	...	|	|	|	|	...	...	...
Bern d.	1436	...	...	...	1604	...	...	...	|	...	...	...	|	|	...	2136	|	|	|	...	...	...
Basel SBB ★ a.	1529	...	...	...	1659	...	...	...	1752	...	...	...	1952	|	...	2229	|	|	|	...	...	...
Basel SBB d.	...	1613	...	...	1706	1713	...	...	1813	1913	...	...	2013	2113u	...	...	2313u	2313u	2313	...	...	...
Basel Bad Bf 🏛 d.	...	1623	...	...	1715	1723	...	...	1823	1923	...	...	2023	2122u	...	...	2323u	2323u	2323	...	...	...
Freiburg (Brsg) Hbf d.	...	1655	...	...	1749	1756	...	...	1857	1956	...	...	2055	2158u	...	...	0000u	0005u	0005	...	...	...
Karlsruhe Hbf d.	...	1801	...	...	1851	1900	...	...	2000	2101	...	...	2201	2304u	...	...	0129u	0129u	0129	...	...	...
Mannheim Hbf a.	...	1824	...	...	1914	1924	...	...	2024	2124	...	...	2224	0005u	...	...	0213	|	0213	...	...	...
Frankfurt (Main) Hbf a.	...	1908	1929	...	1953	|	...	...	2108	|	...	...	2315	0054z	...	...	0259	|	|	...	...	...
Frankfurt Flughafen ✈ a.	...	|	1940	...	|	2006	...	...	...	2206	...	...	...	|	...	...	|	|	0356	...	...	...
Mainz Hbf a.	...	|	|	...	|	|	...	...	...	|	...	...	...	|	...	...	|	|	0418	...	...	...
Koblenz Hbf a.	...	|	⊖	...	|	⊖	...	...	...	⊖	...	...	...	|	...	...	|	0511	0511	0605	...	...
Bonn Hbf a.	...	|	|	...	|	|	...	...	...	|	...	...	...	|	...	...	|	0545	0545	0642	...	...
Köln Hbf a.	...	|	2032	...	|	2105	...	...	...	2307	...	...	...	|	...	...	|	0615	0615	0705	...	...
Düsseldorf Hbf a.	...	|	2105	...	|	|	...	...	...	2339	...	...	...	|	...	...	|	0651	0651	0731	...	...
Duisburg Hbf a.	...	|	2122	...	|	h	...	...	...	2357	...	...	...	|	...	...	|	0710	0710	0744	...	...
Arnhem ⊙ a.	...	|	2229	...	|	|	...	...	...	|	...	...	...	|	...	...	|	0827	0827	|	...	...
Utrecht Centraal a.	...	|	2300	...	|	|	...	...	...	|	...	...	...	|	...	...	|	0903	0903	|	...	...
Amsterdam Centraal a.	...	|	2327	...	|	|	...	...	...	|	...	...	...	|	...	...	|	0934	0934	|	...	...
Essen Hbf a.	...	|	...	...	|	|	...	...	...	0009	...	...	...	|	...	...	|	...	...	0757	...	...
Dortmund Hbf a.	...	|	...	...	|	2221	...	...	...	0033	...	...	...	|	...	...	|	...	...	0821	...	...
Hannover Hbf a.	...	|	...	...	2217j	...	...	...	...	...	...	...	...	|	...	...	0658s	...	...	|	...	...
Berlin Hbf a.	...	2326y	...	...	|	...	...	...	...	...	...	...	...	0723	...	...	|	...	...	|	...	...
Bremen Hbf a.	...	...	...	...	|	...	...	...	...	...	...	...	...	...	...	...	|	...	...	1014	...	...
Hamburg Hbf a.	...	...	...	...	2351j	...	...	...	...	...	...	...	...	...	...	...	0836e	...	...	1112	...	...

A – *City Night Line* PEGASUS – 🛏 1, 2 cl., 🛌 2 cl., 🍷 (*CNL* **40478** Ⓡ) Zürich - Amsterdam; (2) (*IC* **61478**) Zürich - Amsterdam. Special fares apply.

S – *City Night Line* SIRIUS – 🛏 1, 2 cl., 🛌 2 cl. 🍷 (*CNL* **470** Ⓡ) Zürich - Frankfurt - Berlin; (2) (*IC* **61470**) Zürich - Frankfurt - Berlin. Special fares apply. Conveys *City Night Line* (*CNL* **40470** Ⓡ, *IC* **60470**) CANOPUS Zürich - Frankfurt - Dresden - Praha (Table **54**).

G – (12) ✕ Basel - Köln - Dortmund (- Hamburg Ⓑ).

K – *City Night Line* KOMET – 🛏 1, 2 cl., 🛌 2 cl. 🍷 (*CNL* **478**) Zürich - Hamburg; (2) (*IC* **60478**) Zürich - Hamburg. Special fares apply.

T – ⑤ (daily Mar. 18 - Oct. 30).

e – Arrive Hamburg 0905 on certain dates.

h – Via Wuppertal, Hagen.

j – ⑤⑦.

s – Calls to set down only.

u – Calls to pick up only.

x – Ⓑ.

z – Frankfurt (Main) **Süd**. Calls to pick up only.

⊙ – 🏛 is at Emmerich.

◧ – Via Brig. 🏛 is at Domodossola; ticket point is Is

★ – Connections at Basel are not guaranteed.

⊖ – Via Köln - Frankfurt high speed line.

⊗ – Compulsory reservation for international journe Supplement payable for international journeys for internal journeys within Italy.

CONNECTING SERVICES

Basel - Luzern - Chiasso: Table **550**, Basel - Bern - Interlaken and Brig: Table **560**.

Zürich - Landquart - Chur: Table **520**, Chur - St Moritz: Table **540**, Zürich - Bellinzona - Chiasso: Table **550**.

 ① – Mondays ② – Tuesdays ③ – Wednesdays ④ – Thursdays ⑤ – Fridays ⑥ – Saturdays ⑦ – Sundays Ⓑ – Not Saturdays

MILANO and ROMA - PÁTRA - ATHÍNAI 74

train type		FB			IC	FB	FA	
train number	2320	9803			605	9809	9355	
notes		[R] 🍴	🚢		[R] 🍴	[R] 🍴	[R] 🍴	🚢
		⚡	SF		⚡	⚡	⚡	SF
o Centrale d.	...	0735	...	...	...	1035	...	...
na d.	...	0942	...	...	1000	1242	...	...
ma Termini d.	0545	|	...	...	|	|	1450	...
gno d.	0742	|	...	...	|	|	|	...
a d.	0950	1129	...	...	1217	1431	|	...
a Marittima d.	...	...	1330	...	|	|	|	...
ra Centrale d.	...	....	|	...	1352	1540	|	...
serta d.	...	...	|	...	|	|	1603	...
a d.	...	...	|	...	1538	1714	1750	...
entrale a.	...	...	|	...	1700	1820	1848	...
arittima d.	...	...	|	...	...	...	...	2000
a.	...	...	1430	...	...	...	...	1300
a Lárisa a.	...	...	❖	...	...	...	...	❖

train type		FB		IC			FB	IC	FA	
train number		9818	2327	541			9822	612	9354	
notes	🚢	[R] 🍴		[R] 🍴		🚢	[R] 🍴	[R] 🍴	[R] 🍴	
	SF	⚡		⚡		SF	⚡	⚡	⚡	
Athína Lárisa d.	❖	...	...	...	...	❖	...	...	...	...
Pátra d.	1430	...	...	...	...	1800	...	...	...	...
Bari Marittima a.	|	...	...	...	...	0930	...	...	...	...
Bari Centrale d.	|	...	...	...	...	...	1138	1204	1317	...
Foggia a.	|	...	...	...	...	...	1237	1319	1413	...
Caserta a.	|	...	...	...	...	...	|	|	1602	...
Pescara Centrale a.	|	...	...	...	...	...	1412	1503	|	...
Ancona Marittima a.	1030	...	...	...	...	...	|	|	|	...
Ancona a.	...	1326	1344	1530	...	...	1523	1633	|	...
Foligno a.	...	|	1543	1711	...	...	|	|	|	...
Roma Termini a.	...	|	1746	1856	...	...	|	|	1720	...
Bologna a.	...	1514	...	...	...	...	1714	1900	...	...
Milano Centrale a.	...	1725	...	...	...	...	1925	...	...	...

Supplement payable.

❖ – For 🚌/rail connections Pátra - Athína and v.v. see Table **1450**.

SF – **Superfast Ferries**, for days of running see Tables **2715**, **2755**.

MÜNCHEN - ZÜRICH 75

train type	EC	EC		EC		EC		EC	
train number	196	196		194		192		190	
notes	🍴	🍴		🍴		🍴		🍴	
	A	B							
chen Hbf d.	0717	0703	...	1233	...	1633	...	1833	...
oe d.	0758	0748	...	1317	...	1717	...	1917	...
mingen d.	|	0820	...	1346	...	1746	...	1946	...
mpten Hbf d.	0841	|	...	|	...	|	...	|	...
u 🛂 d.	0954	0954	...	1455	...	1854	...	2054	...
enz 🛂 d.	1006	1006	...	1506	...	1906	...	2106	...
argrethen 🛂 a.	1018	1018	...	1518	...	1918	...	2118	...
allen a.	1041	1041	...	1541	...	1941	...	2141	...
erthur a.	1126	1126	...	1626	...	2026	...	2226	...
n Flughafen ✈ a.	1141	1141	...	1641	...	2041	...	2241	...
ch HB a.	1152	1152	...	1652	...	2052	...	2252	...
l SBB a.	...	...	...	...	...	2212	...	...	...

train type	EC		EC		EC		EC	EC	
train number	191		193		195		197	197	
notes	🍴		🍴		🍴		🍴	🍴	
							A	B	
Basel SBB d.	0547	...	0747	...	...	...	...	...	...
Zürich HB d.	0709	...	0909	...	1309	...	1809	1809	...
Zürich Flughafen ✈ d.	0721	...	0921	...	1321	...	1821u	1821u	...
Winterthur d.	0737	...	0937	...	1337	...	1837u	1837u	...
St Gallen d.	0821	...	1021	...	1420	...	1921u	1921u	...
St Margrethen 🛂 d.	0842	...	1042	...	1442	...	1942u	1942u	...
Bregenz 🛂 d.	0855	...	1055	...	1455	...	1955	1955	...
Lindau 🛂 a.	0905	...	1105	...	1505	...	2005	2005	...
Kempten Hbf a.	|	...	|	...	|	...	2122	|	...
Memmingen a.	1013	...	1213	...	1613	...	|	2120	...
Buchloe a.	1041	...	1241	...	1641	...	2203	2203	...
München Hbf a.	1128	...	1328	...	1728	...	2245	2245	...

Oct. 21 - Dec. 10.

B – Apr. 3 - Oct. 20.

u – Calls to pick up only.

MÜNCHEN and NÜRNBERG - PRAHA 76

train type	RE	ALX	ALX	🚌	🚌	🚌	RE	ALX	🚌	🚌	🚌	🚌	RE	ALX	🚌	🚌	🚌	🚌	RE	ALX	🚌		
train number		351	351	P	Q	P		353	Q	P	P	P		355	Q	P	P	Q		357	P		
notes		①–⑥		[R]	[R]	[R]		¶	[R]	[R]	[R]	[R]		¶	[R]	[R]	[R]	[R]		¶	[R]		
notes		¶	¶								B			🍷			⑦	m		🍷			
chen Hbf d.	...	0455	...	...	0715	...	...	0901	1015	...	...	...	...	1244	1415	...	...	1700	...	1702	...	...	...
rnberg Hbf d.	0536	|	...	0740	|	0940	0943	|	|	1130	1240	1340	1343	|	|	1540	1740	|	1743	|	1840	...	...
nsburg d.	|	0623	...	|	|	|	|	1031	|	|	|	|	|	1419	|	|	|	|	|	1835	|	...	...
vandorf d.	0643	0705	0705	|	|	|	1048	1107	|	|	|	|	1448	1507	|	|	|	|	1848	1909	|	...	...
im Wald 🛂 d.	...	0750	0750	◐	|	◐	...	1150	|	◐	◐	◐	...	1550	|	◐	◐	|	...	1952	◐	...	...
ň hlavní a.	...	0857	0857	|	|	1210	...	1257	|	|	|	|	...	1657	|	|	|	|	...	2059	2110	...	...
a hlavní a.	...	1041	1041	1118	1153	1318	...	1441	1453	1508	1618	1718	...	1841	1853	1918	2118	2153	...	2241	2218	...	...

train type	ALX	RE	🚌	🚌	🚌	ALX	RE	🚌	🚌	🚌	🚌	ALX	RE	🚌	🚌	🚌	🚌	ALX	RE	🚌			
train number	356		P	Q	P	354		P	Q	P	P	352		Q	P	P	Q	350		P			
notes	¶		[R]	[R]	[R]	¶		[R]	[R]	[R]	[R]	¶		[R]	[R]	[R]	[R]	¶		[R]			
notes	🍷			r	B	🍷				⑦													
a hlavní d.	0512	...	0712	0800	0830	0912	...	1042	1115	1130	1242	1312	...	1415	1530	1612	1715	1712	...	1842	...	...	...
ň hlavní d.	0700	...	0820	|	|	1100	...	|	|	|	|	1500	...	|	|	|	|	1900	...	|	...	...	...
im Wald 🛂 a.	0810	...	◐	|	◐	1210	...	◐	|	◐	◐	1610	...	|	◐	◐	|	2012	...	◐	...	...	...
vandorf a.	0854	0906	|	|	|	1254	1306	|	|	|	|	1655	1705	|	|	|	|	2056	2106	|	...	...	...
nsburg a.	0929	|	|	|	|	1330	|	|	|	|	|	1737	|	|	|	|	|	2133	|	|	...	...	...
rnberg Hbf a.	|	1014	1050	|	1208	|	1414	1420	|	1508	1620	|	1814	|	1908	1950	|	|	2222	2220	...	...	...
chen Hbf a.	1118	...	...	1253	...	1505	...	...	1553	...	...	1915	...	1853	...	...	2153	2305	...	...	...	...	...

①④⑤⑥.

🚌 **DB / ČD** *IC Bus*. Rail tickets valid. [R] 🍷. Supplement payable. 2nd class only. At Praha hlavní railway station the bus stop is located outside the old building on the upper level (access from platform one); street name is Wilsonova. At Nürnberg Hbf the bus stop is at Bahnhofvorplatz Hauptausgang (main entrance). At Plzeň the bus stop is located at Plzeň Autobusove nadrazi (Husova).

🚌 **DB / Czech Student Agency** *IC Bus*. Rail tickets valid. [R] 🍷. Supplement payable. 2nd class only. At Praha hlavní railway station the bus stop is located outside the old building on the upper level (access from platform one); street name is Wilsonova. The bus stop for München is at Hackerbrücke (approx. 700 metres from München Hbf).

Also calls at München Flughafen Terminal 2, Halt 22 (depart 1745).

Calls at München Flughafen Terminal 2, Halt 22 (arrive 1208).

¶ – *Ex* in the Czech Republic.

◐ – 🛂 is Waidhaus (Germany).

ALX – Arriva Länderbahn Express.

CONNECTING SERVICES

Hamburg - Hannover - Nürnberg : Table **900**
Köln - Frankfurt - Nürnberg : Table **920**
Karlsruhe - Stuttgart - Nürnberg : Table **925**

ER TRAIN NAMES: **351 / 352** – JAN HUS **350 / 353** – ALBERT EINSTEIN **354 / 357** – FRANZ KAFKA **355 / 356** – KAREL ČAPEK

82 GENÈVE, BASEL and ZÜRICH - MILANO, VENEZIA and ROMA

train type	IC	EC	FR	FB	IR	EC	FB	IR	EC	IC	IC	EC	FR	EC	IR	EC	FR	IR	EC	FR	IR	EC	FB	FR
train number	802	35	9521	9791	1807	51	9719	2311	13	959	806	37	9529	153	2315	15	9537	2319	17	9545	1819	57	9737	9549
notes		R 🍷 ⊗	R ✖ ⚡	R 🍷 ⑥⑦		R 🍷 ⊗	R ✖ ⚡		R 🍷 ⊗			R 🍷 ⊗	R ✖ ⚡	🍷 ⊗		R 🍷 ⊗	R ✖ ⚡		R 🍷 ⊗	R ✖ ⚡		R 🍷 ⊗	R 🍷 ⚡	R ✖ ⚡
Genève Aéroport ✈ d.	...	...	...	...	...	...	...	...	...	...	...	...	...	...	...	...	...	...	...	...	1151	...	...	...
Genève d.	...	0539	...	...	0612	...	...	...	...	...	...	0739	...	...	...	...	...	...	...	...	1200	...	...	...
Lausanne d.	...	0618	...	...	0650	...	...	...	...	...	...	0818	...	...	...	...	...	...	...	...	1250	...	...	...
Montreux d.	...	0636	...	...	0710	...	...	...	...	...	...	0836	...	...	...	...	...	...	...	...	1310	...	...	...
Aigle d.	...	|	...	...	0721	...	...	...	...	...	...	|	...	...	...	...	...	...	...	...	1321	...	...	...
Martigny d.	...	|	...	...	0743	...	...	...	...	...	...	|	...	...	...	...	...	...	...	...	1343	...	...	...
Sion d.	...	0713	...	...	0758	...	...	...	...	...	...	0913	...	...	...	...	...	...	...	...	1358	...	...	...
Zürich HB d.	...	|	...	...	|	...	...	...	0732	...	...	|	...	...	...	0932	...	...	1132	...	|	...	...	...
Basel SBB d.	...	|	...	...	|	0631	...	0604	|	0659	...	|	...	...	0804	|	...	1004	|	...	|	1231	...	...
Olten d.	...	|	...	...	|	0657	...	0630	|	0729	...	|	...	...	0830	|	...	1030	|	...	|	1257	...	...
Bern d.	0606	|	...	...	|	0734	...	|	|	0756	0806	|	...	...	|	|	...	|	|	...	|	1334	...	...
Spiez d.	0636	|	...	...	|	0805	...	|	|	...	0836	|	...	...	|	|	...	|	|	...	|	1405	...	...
Luzern d.	|	|	...	...	|	|	...	0718	|	...	|	|	...	0847	0918	|	...	1118	|	...	|	|	...	...
Arth-Goldau d.	|	|	...	...	|	|	...	0744	0817	...	|	|	...	0916	0944	1017	...	1144	1217	...	|	|	...	...
Bellinzona d.	|	|	...	...	|	|	...	...	0956	...	|	|	...	1056	...	1156	...	...	1356	...	|	|	...	...
Lugano d.	|	|	...	...	|	|	...	...	1025	...	|	|	...	1125	...	1225	...	...	1425	...	|	|	...	...
Chiasso 🏛 d.	|	|	...	...	|	|	...	...	1052	...	|	|	...	1152	...	1252	...	...	1452	...	|	|	...	...
Como San Giovanni a.	|	|	...	...	|	|	...	...	1056	...	|	|	...	1158	...	|	...	...	1456	...	|	|	...	...
Visp d.	0703	|	...	...	0825	0832	...	...	|	...	0903	|	...	|	...	|	...	...	|	...	1425	1432	...	...
Brig d.	0711	0744	...	...	0832	0844	...	...	|	...	0911	0944	...	|	...	|	...	...	|	...	1432	1444	...	...
Domodossola 🏛 ¶ a.	...	0812	...	...	...	0912	...	...	|	...	...	1012	...	|	...	|	...	...	|	...	...	1512	...	...
Stresa a.	...	0838	...	...	...	0938	...	...	|	...	...	|	...	|	...	|	...	...	|	...	...	1538	...	...
Gallarate a.	...	|	...	...	...	|	...	...	|	...	...	1102	...	|	...	|	...	...	|	...	...	|	...	...
Milano Centrale a.	...	0937	...	...	...	1037	...	...	1135	...	...	1137	...	1250	...	1335	...	...	1535	...	...	1637	...	...
		FR 9619 ✖ ⚡ R				FR 9525 ✖ ⚡ R						|		FR 9533 ✖ ⚡ R		FB 9725 R 🍷 ⚡			FB 9733 R 🍷 ⚡					
Milano Centrale d.	...	1000	1020	1035	...	1120	1135	...	...	...	...	1205	1220	1320	...	1405	1420	...	1605	1620	...	...	1705	1720
Verona Porta Nuova a.	...	|	|	1158	...	|	1258	...	...	...	...	1328	|	|	...	1528	|	...	1728	|	...	...	1828	|
Venezia Mestre a.	...	|	|	1258	...	|	1358	...	...	...	...	1428	|	|	...	1628	|	...	1828	|	...	...	1928	|
Venezia Santa Lucia a.	...	|	|	1310	...	|	1410	...	...	...	...	1440	|	|	...	1640	|	...	1840	|	...	...	...	|
Bologna Centrale a.	...	|	1122	...	...	1222	...	...	...	...	...	...	1322	1422	...	...	1522	...	...	1722	...	...	...	1822
Firenze SMN a.	...	|	1159	...	...	1259	...	...	...	...	...	...	1359	1459	...	...	1559	...	...	1759	...	...	...	1859
Roma Termini a.	...	1255	1340	...	...	1440	...	...	...	...	...	...	1540	1640	...	...	1740	...	...	1940	...	...	...	2040
Napoli Centrale a.	...	1415	1500	...	...	1602	...	...	...	...	...	...	1700	1800	...	...	1900	...	...	2100	...	...	...	2200

train type	IC	IC	EC	IR	EC	FR ⚡	FB	FR	IR	EC	FB	FR ⚡		IR	EC	IR	EC		ICN	ICE	IC	EC	IR	EC
train number	971	818	39	2323	19	9651	9741	9553	2327	21	9745	9559		2331	23	1829	59	2117	797	371	828	41	2335	25
notes			R 🍷 ⊗		R ✖ ⊗	R ✖	R 🍷 ⚡	R ✖ ⚡		R ✖ ⊗	R 🍷	R ✖			R ✖ ⊗		R 🍷 ⊗		R ⚡ K			R 🍷 ⊗		R ✖ ⊗
Genève Aéroport ✈ d.	...	...	...	...	...	...	...	...	...	...	...	...	...	...	...	1651	...	...	...	...	...	...	...	...
Genève d.	...	...	1339	...	...	...	...	...	...	...	...	...	...	...	...	1700	...	...	...	...	...	1839	...	...
Lausanne d.	...	...	1418	...	...	...	...	...	...	...	...	...	...	...	...	1750	...	...	...	...	...	1918	...	...
Montreux d.	...	...	1436	...	...	...	...	...	...	...	...	...	...	...	...	1810	...	...	...	...	...	1936	...	...
Aigle d.	...	...	|	...	...	...	...	...	...	...	...	...	...	...	...	1821	...	...	...	...	...	|	...	...
Martigny d.	...	...	|	...	...	...	...	...	...	...	...	...	...	...	...	1843	...	...	...	...	...	|	...	...
Sion d.	...	...	1513	...	...	...	...	...	...	...	...	...	...	...	...	1858	...	...	...	...	...	2013	...	...
Zürich HB d.	...	...	|	...	1332	...	...	...	...	1532	...	...	...	...	1732	|	...	...	...	...	1802	|	...	1932
Basel SBB d.	1259	...	|	1204	|	...	...	...	1404	|	...	...	...	1604	|	|	1731	...	...	1759	|	|	1804	|
Oltern d.	1329	...	|	1230	|	...	...	...	1430	|	...	...	...	1630	|	|	1757	...	...	1829	|	|	1830	|
Bern d.	1356	1406	|	|	|	...	...	...	|	|	...	...	...	|	|	|	1834	...	...	1856	1906	|	|	|
Spiez d.	...	1436	|	|	|	...	...	...	|	|	...	...	...	|	|	|	1905	...	...	...	1936	|	|	|
Luzern d.	...	|	|	1318	|	...	...	...	1518	|	...	...	...	1718	|	|	|	...	...	...	|	|	1918	|
Arth-Goldau d.	...	|	|	1344	1417	...	...	...	1544	1617	...	...	...	1744	1817	|	|	...	...	...	|	|	1944	2017
Bellinzona d.	...	|	|	...	1556	...	...	...	...	1756	...	...	...	...	1956	|	|	...	...	...	|	|	...	2156
Lugano d.	...	|	|	...	1625	...	...	...	...	1825	...	...	...	...	2025	|	|	...	...	...	|	|	...	2225
Chiasso 🏛 d.	...	|	|	...	1652	...	...	...	...	1852	...	...	...	...	2052	|	|	...	...	...	|	|	...	2252
Como San Giovanni a.	...	|	|	...	|	...	...	...	...	|	...	...	...	...	2056	|	|	...	...	...	|	|	...	2256
Visp d.	...	1503	|	...	|	...	...	...	...	|	...	...	...	...	|	1925	1932	...	...	...	2003	|	...	|
Brig d.	...	1511	1544	...	|	...	...	...	...	|	...	...	...	...	|	1932	1944	...	...	...	2011	2044	...	|
Domodossola 🏛 ¶ a.	...	...	1612	...	|	...	...	...	...	|	...	...	...	...	|	...	2012	...	...	...	...	2112	...	|
Stresa a.	...	...	1638	...	|	...	...	...	...	|	...	...	...	...	|	...	|	...	...	...	...	2138	...	|
Gallarate a.	...	...	|	...	|	...	...	...	...	|	...	...	...	...	|	...	2103	...	...	...	...	|	...	|
Milano Centrale a.	...	...	1737	...	1735	...	...	...	...	1935	...	...	...	...	2135	...	2137	...	...	...	...	2237	...	2335
Milano Centrale d.	...	...	...	...	...	1800	1805	1820	...	...	1905	2020	...	...	...	...	...	2225	2317g	...	...	...	...	...
Verona Porta Nuova a.	...	...	...	...	...	|	1928	|	...	...	2028	|	...	...	...	...	...	0020	|	...	...	...	...	...
Venezia Mestre a.	...	...	...	...	...	|	2028	|	...	...	2128	|	...	...	...	...	...	...	|	...	...	...	...	...
Venezia Santa Lucia a.	...	...	...	...	...	|	...	|	...	...	2140	|	...	...	...	...	...	...	|	...	...	...	...	...
Bologna Centrale a.	...	...	...	...	...	|	...	1922	...	...	...	2122	...	...	...	...	...	...	0215	...	...	...	...	...
Firenze SMN a.	...	...	...	...	...	|	...	1959	...	...	...	2159	...	...	...	...	...	...	0407y	...	...	...	...	...
Roma Termini a.	...	...	...	...	...	2055	...	2140	...	...	...	2340	...	...	...	...	...	...	0717t	...	...	...	...	...
Napoli Centrale a.	...	...	...	...	...	2215	...	2300	...	...	...	...	...	...	...	...	...	...	0938	...	...	...	...	...

K – 🛏 1, 2 cl., 🛏 2 cl. (4 berth), 🚃 Milano - Napoli - Salerno.

g – Milano **Porta Garibaldi**.
t – Roma **Tiburtina**.
y – Firenze **Campo di Marte**.

⚡ – Supplement payable.
¶ – Ticket point is **Iselle**.

⊗ – Compulsory reservation for international journe[ys]. Supplement payable for international journeys a[nd] for internal journeys within Italy.

ROMA, VENEZIA and MILANO - ZÜRICH, BASEL and GENÈVE 82

train type	EC	E		EC	IC	IC	EC	IR	FR⚡	FR	FB	EC	IR	FB⚡	FR	FR⚡	EC	IR	FB	FR	FR	IC	ICE	EC	IR
train number	**50**	**796**	**2122**	**32**	**817**	**968**	**12**	**2320**	**9504**	**9606**	**9790**	**14**	**2324**	**9708**	**9508**	**9610**	**52**	**1822**	**9712**	**9514**	**9614**	**825**	**376** **396**	**16**	**2328**
notes	🅁 🍷	**A**		🅁 🍷			🅁 ✕		🅁 ✕	🅁 ✕	🅁 ✕	🅁 ✕		🅁 ✕	🅁 ✕	🅁 ✕	🅁 🍷		🅁 ✕	🅁 ✕	🅁 ✕			🅁 ✕	
	⊗			⊗			⊗		①–⑥	⚡	⚡	⊗		①–⑤	⚡		⊗		⚡	⚡	⚡			⊗	
Centrale d.	...	2132	...	...	...	...	...	...	...	...	...	...	...	...	...	0640	...	...	...	0700	0740	...	...	...	...
Termini d.	...	2343t	...	...	...	...	...	...	0620	0700	...	...	...	...	0720	0800	...	...	...	0820	0900	...	...	...	...
e SMN d.	...	|	...	...	...	...	...	...	0800	|	...	...	...	...	0900	|	...	...	...	1000	|	...	...	...	...
a Centrale d.	...	|	0528	...	...	...	...	...	0838	|	...	...	...	...	0938	|	...	...	...	1038	|	...	...	...	...
ezia Santa Lucia d.	...	|	|	...	...	...	...	...	|	|	...	...	...	0750	|	|	...	...	0850	|	|	...	...	...	...
ezia Mestre d.	...	|	|	...	...	...	...	...	|	|	0750	...	...	0802	|	|	...	...	0902	|	|	...	...	...	...
ona Porta Nuova d.	...	|	|	...	...	...	...	...	|	|	0845	...	...	0902	|	|	...	...	1002	|	|	...	...	...	...
Centrale a.	...	0711g	0800	...	...	...	...	...	0942	0959	1000	...	...	1025	1040	1055	...	...	1125	1140	1155	...	...	...	...
																					EC				
																					34				
																					🅁 🍷				
																					⊗				
Centrale d.	0723	...	...	0823	...	...	0825	...	...	...	...	1025	...	...	...	...	1123	...	...	...	1223	...	...	1225	...
ate d.	0757	*IR*	...	|	...	...	|	...	...	...	...	|	...	...	...	...	|	...	...	...	|	...	...	|	...
d.	|	**1814**	...	0921	...	...	|	...	...	...	...	|	...	...	...	...	1221	...	...	...	1321	...	...	|	...
dossola 🏛 ¶ d.	0848		...	0948	...	...	|	...	...	...	...	|	...	...	...	...	1248	...	...	...	1348	...	...	|	...
a.	0916	0927	...	1016	1049	...	|	...	...	...	...	|	...	...	...	...	1316	1327	...	...	1416	1449	...	|	...
a.	0926	0933	...	|	1055	...	|	...	...	...	...	|	...	...	...	...	1326	1333	...	...	|	1455	...	|	...
o San Giovanni d.	|	|	...	|	|	...	0903	...	...	...	...	1103	...	...	...	...	|	|	...	...	|	|	...	|	...
sso 🏛 a.	|	|	...	|	|	...	0908	...	...	...	...	1108	...	...	...	...	|	|	...	...	|	|	...	1308	...
ano a.	|	|	...	|	|	...	0932	...	...	...	...	1132	...	...	...	...	|	|	...	...	|	|	...	1332	...
inzona a.	|	|	...	|	|	...	0959	...	...	...	...	1159	...	...	...	...	|	|	...	...	|	|	...	1359	...
-Goldau a.	|	|	...	|	|	...	1143	1214	...	...	...	1343	1414	...	...	...	|	|	...	...	|	|	...	1543	1614
n a.	|	|	...	|	|	...	|	1241	...	...	...	|	1441	...	...	...	|	|	...	...	|	|	...	|	1641
a.	0953	|	...	|	1124	...	|	|	...	...	...	|	|	...	...	...	1353	|	...	...	|	1524	...	|	|
a.	1023	|	...	|	1154	1204	|	|	...	...	...	|	|	...	...	...	1423	|	...	...	|	1554	1604	|	|
a.	1102	|	...	|	...	1230	|	1327	...	...	...	|	1527	...	...	...	1502	|	...	...	|	...	1630	|	1727
SBB a.	1129	|	...	|	...	1259	|	1355	...	...	...	|	1555	...	...	...	1529	|	...	...	|	...	1659	|	1755
ich HB a.	...	|	...	|	...	...	1228	...	...	...	...	1428	...	...	...	...	...	|	...	...	|	...	...	1628	...
a.	...	0959	...	1047	...	...	...	...	...	...	...	...	...	...	...	...	...	1359	...	...	1447	...	...	...	...
gny a.	...	1013	...	|	...	...	...	...	...	...	...	...	...	...	...	...	...	1413	...	...	|	...	...	...	...
a.	...	1036	...	|	...	...	...	...	...	...	...	...	...	...	...	...	...	1436	...	...	|	...	...	...	...
eux a.	...	1047	...	1123	...	...	...	...	...	...	...	...	...	...	...	...	...	1447	...	...	1523	...	...	...	...
nne a.	...	1110	...	1142	...	...	...	...	...	...	...	...	...	...	...	...	...	1510	...	...	1542	...	...	...	...
ve a.	...	1200	...	1221	...	...	...	...	...	...	...	...	...	...	...	...	...	1600	...	...	1621	...	...	...	...
ve Aéroport ✈ a.	...	1209	...	...	...	...	...	...	...	...	...	...	...	...	...	...	...	1609	...	...	...	...	...	...	...

train type/number	FB	FR	IR	FR	EC	FR	FB	IR	FR	FB	EC	IC	FR	FB	FR	IR	EC	FR	FR⚡	EC	IC	ICE	FR	FB	EC
train number	**9714**	**9520**	**2332**	**9526**	**158**	**9528**	**9726**	**2336**	**9532**	**9728**	**36**	**1084**	**9536**	**9732**	**9638**	**1836**	**22**	**9540**	**9642**	**42**	**1088**	**338**	**9544**	**9740**	**24**
notes	🅁 ✕	🅁 ✕		🅁 ✕	🅁 🍷	🅁 ✕	🅁 ✕		🅁 ✕	🅁 ✕	🅁 🍷		🅁 ✕	🅁 ✕	🅁 ✕		🅁 ✕	🅁 ✕	🅁 ✕	🅁 🍷			🅁 ✕	🅁 ✕	🅁 ✕
	⚡	⚡		⚡	⊗	⚡	⚡		⚡	⚡	⊗		⚡	⚡	⚡		⊗	⚡	Ⓑ	⊗			⚡	⚡	⊗
i Centrale d.	...	0900	...	1000	...	1100	...	...	1200	...	...	...	1300	...	...	...	...	1400	1440	...	...	...	1500	...	...
Termini d.	...	1020	...	1120	...	1220	...	...	1320	...	...	...	1420	...	1500	...	...	1520	1600	...	...	...	1620	...	...
ze SMN d.	...	1200	...	1300	...	1400	...	...	1500	...	...	...	1600	...	|	...	...	1700	|	...	...	...	1800	...	...
na Centrale d.	...	1238	...	1338	...	1438	...	...	1538	...	...	...	1638	...	|	...	...	1738	|	...	...	...	1838	...	...
nezia Santa Lucia d.	1050	|	...	|	...	|	1320	...	|	1420	...	...	|	1520	|	...	...	|	|	1620	...	...	|	1720	...
nezia Mestre d.	1102	|	...	|	...	|	1332	...	|	1432	...	...	|	1532	|	...	...	|	|	1632	...	...	|	1732	...
ona Porta Nuova d.	1202	|	...	|	...	|	1432	...	|	1532	...	...	|	1632	|	...	...	|	|	1732	...	...	|	1832	...
o Centrale a.	1325	1340	...	1440	...	1540	1555	...	1640	1655	...	...	1740	1755	1755	...	...	1842	1855	1855	...	...	1940	1955	...
		EC					*EC*								*EC*					|					
		18					**20**								**56**					|					
		🅁 ✕					🅁 🍷								🅁 🍷					|					
		⊗					⊗								⊗					|					
o Centrale d.	...	1425	...	...	1510	...	1625	...	...	...	1723	...	...	...	1823	...	1825	...	...	1923	...	...	...	...	2025
rate d.	...	|	...	...	|	...	|	...	...	...	|	...	...	...	|	...	|	...	...	1957	...	...	...	...	|
a d.	...	|	...	...	|	...	|	...	...	...	1821	...	...	...	1921	...	|	...	...	|	...	...	...	...	|
dossola 🏛 ¶ d.	...	|	...	...	|	...	|	...	...	...	1848	...	...	...	1948	...	|	...	...	2048	...	...	...	...	|
a.	...	|	...	...	|	...	|	...	...	...	1916	1920	...	...	2016	2027	|	...	...	2116	2120	...	...	...	|
a.	...	|	...	...	|	...	|	...	...	...	|	1926	...	...	2026	2033	|	...	...	|	2126	...	...	...	|
mo San Giovanni d.	...	|	...	...	1601	...	|	...	...	...	|	|	...	...	|	|	|	...	...	|	|	...	...	...	2101
asso 🏛 a.	...	1508	...	...	1608	...	1708	...	...	...	|	|	...	...	|	|	1908	...	...	|	|	...	...	...	2108
gano a.	...	1532	...	...	1632	...	1732	...	...	...	|	|	...	...	|	|	1932	*IR*	...	|	|	...	...	...	2132
llinzona a.	...	1559	...	...	1659	...	1759	...	...	...	|	|	...	...	|	|	1959	**2340**	...	|	|	...	...	...	2159
h-Goldau a.	...	1743	1814	...	1843	...	1943	2014	...	...	|	|	...	...	|	|	2143	2214	...	|	|	...	...	...	2343
rn a.	...	|	1841	...	1913	...	|	2041	...	...	|	|	...	...	|	|	|	2241	...	|	|	...	...	...	|
a.	...	|	|	...	...	...	|	|	...	...	|	1953	...	...	2053	|	|	|	...	|	2153	...	...	...	|
a.	...	|	|	...	...	...	|	|	...	...	|	2023	...	...	2123	|	|	|	...	|	2223	2236	...	...	|
a.	...	|	1927	...	...	...	|	2127	...	...	|	2102	...	...	2202	|	|	2327	...	|	...	2303	...	...	|
l SBB a.	...	|	1955	...	...	...	|	2155	...	...	|	2129	...	...	2229	|	|	2359	...	|	...	2330	...	...	|
rich HB a.	...	1828	...	...	...	...	2028	...	...	...	|	...	...	...	...	|	2228	...	...	|	...	...	...	...	0028
a.	...	...	...	...	...	...	...	...	...	...	1947	...	...	...	...	2059	...	...	...	2147	...	...	...	...	...
gny a.	...	...	...	...	...	...	...	...	...	...	|	...	...	...	...	2113	...	...	...	|	...	...	...	...	...
a.	...	...	...	...	...	...	...	...	...	...	|	...	...	...	...	2136	...	...	...	|	...	...	...	...	...
reux a.	...	...	...	...	...	...	...	...	...	...	2023	...	...	...	...	2147	...	...	...	2223	...	...	...	...	...
anne a.	...	...	...	...	...	...	...	...	...	...	2042	...	...	...	...	2210	...	...	...	2242	...	...	...	...	...
ève a.	...	...	...	...	...	...	...	...	...	...	2121	...	...	...	...	2316	...	...	...	2321	...	...	...	...	...
ève Aéroport ✈ a.	...	...	...	...	...	...	...	...	...	...	...	...	...	...	...	...	...	...	...	...	...	...	...	...	...

A – 🛏 1, 2 cl., 🛏 2 cl. (4 berth), (12) Salerno - Napoli - Milano.

g – Milano **Porta Garibaldi**.

t – Roma **Tiburtina**.

⚡ – Supplement payable.

¶ – Ticket point is **Iselle**.

⊗ – Compulsory reservation for international journeys. Supplement payable for international journeys and for internal journeys within Italy.

86 ZÜRICH - INNSBRUCK - WIEN, GRAZ, ZAGREB and BUDAPEST

train type/number	RJ	RJ	IC	EC	IC	RJ	IC	EC	EC	RJ	EC	EC	RJ	EC	D	IC	RJ	EC	RJ	EC	RJ	RJ	EN	EN	EN
train number	49	765	515	111	211	161	690	217	163	563	113	113 213	165	115	315	611	167	219	169	117 1217	361	363	465	465 415	60467
notes	🍷 ①–⑥	🍷	🍷			🍷	🍷	🍷	🍷 B		🍴			🍴			🍷		🍷	🍴	🍷	🍷	Z	A	C
Zürich HB d.	...	...	...	...	...	0640	...	...	0840	...	...	...	1040	...	...	...	1240	...	1440	...	1640	1840	2040	2040	2140
Sargans d.	...	...	...	...	...	0737	...	...	0937	...	...	...	1137	...	...	...	1337	...	1537	...	1737	1937	2137	2137	2237
Buchs 🏛 d.	...	...	...	...	...	0753	...	...	0959	...	...	...	1154	...	...	...	1353	...	1553	...	1759	1953	2205	2205	2305
Bregenz d.	...	0547	...	...	...	|	...	...	|	...	...	...	|	...	...	...	|	...	|	...	|	|	|	|	|
Feldkirch d.	...	0614	...	...	...	0815	...	...	1016	...	...	...	1215	...	...	...	1415	...	1615	...	1816	2015	2242	2242	2324
Bludenz d.	...	0628	...	...	...	0828	...	...	1029	...	...	...	1228	...	...	...	1428	...	1628	...	1829	2028	2257	2257	2340
Langen am Arlberg d.	...	0654	...	...	...	0854	...	...	1055	...	...	...	1254	...	...	...	1454	...	|	...	|	2054	2331	2331	|
St Anton am Arlberg d.	...	0704	...	...	...	0905	...	...	1105	...	...	...	1305	...	...	...	1505	...	1701	...	1905	2105	2340	2340	|
Landeck-Zams d.	...	0729	...	...	...	0929	...	...	1129	...	...	...	1329	...	...	...	1528	...	1725	...	1929	2129	0009	0009	|
Ötztal d.	...	0753	...	...	...	0953	...	...	1153	...	...	...	1353	...	...	...	1553	...	1753	...	1953	2153	|	|	|
Innsbruck Hbf d.	0505	0820	0824	...	...	1022	...	...	1224e	1220	...	...	1420	...	...	...	1622	...	1822	...	2022	2216	0056	0056	0128
Jenbach d.	0522	|	0846	...	...	|	...	...	1245	|	...	...	|	...	...	...	|	...	|	...	|	...	0118	0118	|
Wörgl d.	0537	|	0902	...	...	|	...	...	1302	|	...	...	|	...	...	...	|	...	|	...	|	...	0138	0138	|
Kitzbühel d.	|	|	0932	...	...	|	...	...	1332	|	...	...	|	...	...	...	|	...	|	...	|	...	|	|	|
St Johann in Tirol d.	|	|	0940	...	...	|	...	...	1340	|	...	...	|	...	...	...	|	...	|	...	|	...	|	|	|
Saalfelden d.	|	|	1008	...	...	|	...	...	1408	|	...	...	|	...	...	...	|	...	|	...	|	...	|	|	|
Zell am See d.	|	|	1019	...	...	|	...	...	1419	|	...	...	|	...	...	...	|	...	|	...	|	...	|	|	|
Schwarzach St Veit d.	|	|	|	...	...	|	...	...	|	|	...	...	|	...	...	...	|	...	|	...	|	...	0323	0427	|
Salzburg Hbf d.	0708	1008	|	1012	...	1208	1212	1215	|	1408	...	...	1608	1612	...	1615	1808	1815	2008	2012	2208	...	|	|	0350
Bischofshofen a.	|	|	|	1052	...	|	1252	1302	|	|	...	...	|	1652	...	1702	|	1902	|	2052	|	...	0336	|	|
Schwarzach St Veit a.	|	|	1048	1109	...	|	1309	|	1448	|	1511	1511	|	1709	...	|	|	|	|	2109	|	...	|	|	|
Selzthal a.	|	|	1240	|	...	|	|	1439	1639	|	|	|	|	|	...	1839	|	2039	|	|	|	...	0503	|	|
Graz Hbf a.	|	|	1414	|	...	|	|	1614	1814	|	|	|	|	|	...	2014	|	2214	|	|	|	...	0700	|	|
Villach Hbf a.	|	|	▬	1243	1253	|	1443	...	...	|	1643	1643	|	1843	1853	...	|	...	|	2243	|	...	...	0604	|
Klagenfurt a.	|	|	...	1315	|	|	▬	...	...	|	1715	|	|	1915	|	...	|	...	|	2315	|	...	...	|	|
Jesenice 🏛 a.	|	|	...	...	1333	|	...	...	...	|	▬	1733	|	...	1933	...	|	...	|	...	|	...	...	0705	|
Ljubljana ⊙ a.	|	|	...	...	1431	|	...	...	...	|	...	1832	|	...	2040	...	|	...	|	...	|	...	...	0812	|
Zagreb ⊙ a.	|	|	...	...	1712	|	...	...	...	|	...	2054	|	...	...	...	|	...	|	...	|	...	...	1046	|
Vinkovci ⊕ a.	|	|	...	...	2107	|	...	...	...	|	...	...	|	...	...	...	|	...	|	...	|	...	...	1438	|
Beograd ⊕ a.	|	|	...	...	...	|	...	...	...	|	...	...	|	...	...	...	|	...	|	...	|	...	...	1733	|
Linz Hbf a.	0812	1112	...	...	...	1312	...	...	...	1512	...	...	1712	...	...	...	1912	...	2112	...	2312	...	...	...	0501
St Pölten a.	0900	1200	*RJ*	...	...	1400	*EC*	...	...	1600	*EC*	...	1800	...	...	...	2000	...	2200	...	2400	...	...	...	0558
Wien Meidling a.	0923	1223	**63**	...	...	1423	**145**	...	...	1623	**147**	...	1823	...	...	...	2023	...	2223	...	0023	...	...	...	0627
Wien Hbf a.	0930	1230	🍷	...	...	1430	🍷	...	...	1630	**D**	...	1830	...	...	...	2030	...	2230	...	0030	...	...	...	0635
Wien Hbf d.	0942	...	1342	...	...	...	1442	...	...	...	1642	...	1842	...	...	...	...	...	...	...	...	...	...	...	0642
Hegyeshalom 🏛 a.	1025	...	1425	...	...	...	1525	...	...	...	1725	...	1925	...	...	...	...	...	...	...	...	...	...	...	0725
Györ a.	1053	...	1453	...	...	...	1553	...	...	...	1753	...	1953	...	...	...	...	...	...	...	...	...	...	...	0753
Budapest Keleti a.	1219	...	1619	...	...	...	1719	...	...	...	1919	...	2119	...	...	...	...	...	...	...	...	...	...	...	0924

train type/number	RJ	RJ	EC	IC	RJ	IC	EC	RJ	EC	EC	RJ	RJ	EC	EC	RJ	RJ	RJ	RJ	IC	EC	RJ	RJ	EN	EN	EN
train number	360	362	218	693	160	512	114	162	212 112	112	60	860	164	216	62	166	64	168	610	210	66	760	466	60466	414 464
notes	🍷	🍷	🍷	🍷	🍷	🍷	🍴	🍷		🍴	🍷	🍷	🍷 B	🍷	🍷	🍷	🍷	🍷	🍷		🍷	🍷	W	C	A
Budapest Keleti d.	...	...	...	...	...	...	...	0640	...	...	0740	...	...	...	0940	...	1140	...	...	...	1340	...	...	2040	...
Györ d.	...	...	...	...	...	...	...	0802	...	...	0902	...	...	...	1102	...	1302	...	...	...	1502	...	...	2202	...
Hegyeshalom 🏛 d.	...	...	...	...	...	...	...	0832	...	...	0932	...	...	...	1132	...	1332	...	...	...	1532	...	...	2232	...
Wien Hbf a.	...	...	...	...	...	...	...	0918	...	...	1018	...	...	...	1218	...	1418	...	...	...	1618	...	...	2318	...
Wien Hbf d.	...	0530x	...	...	0730	...	...	0930	...	...	1030	1030	...	...	▬	1330	▬	1530	...	...	▬	1730	2125	2325	...
Wien Meidling d.	...	0537x	...	...	0737	...	...	0937	...	...	1037	1037	...	...	...	1337	...	1537	...	...	...	1737	2133	2333	...
St Pölten d.	...	0600x	...	...	0800	...	...	1000	...	...	1100	1100	...	...	...	1400	...	1600	...	...	...	1800	2205	0002	...
Linz Hbf d.	...	0648x	...	...	0848	...	...	1048	...	...	1148	1148	...	...	...	1448	...	1648	...	...	...	1848	2311	0102	...
Beograd ⊕ d.	...	|	...	...	|	...	...	|	...	...	|	|	...	...	...	|	...	|	...	...	...	|	|	|	1100
Vinkovci ⊕ d.	...	|	...	...	|	...	...	|	...	...	|	|	...	...	...	|	...	|	...	0900	...	|	|	|	1442
Zagreb ⊙ d.	...	|	...	...	|	...	...	|	0655	...	|	|	...	...	...	|	...	|	...	1237	*EC*	|	|	|	1838
Ljubljana ⊙ d.	...	|	...	...	|	...	...	|	0923	...	|	|	...	...	*IC*	|	...	|	...	1527	**110**	|	|	|	2110
Jesenice 🏛 d.	...	|	...	...	|	...	...	|	1016	...	|	|	...	...	**691**	|	*IC*	|	...	1627	🍷	|	|	|	2205
Klagenfurt d.	...	|	...	0645	|	...	0842	|	|	1027	|	|	...	...	1245	|	**518**	|	...	|	1642	|	|	|	|
Villach Hbf d.	...	|	...	0716	|	...	0916	|	1116	1116	|	|	...	...	1316	|	🍷	|	...	1707	1716	|	|	|	2316
Graz Hbf d.	...	|	0545	|	|	0745	|	|	|	|	|	|	0945	1145	|	|	1345	|	1545	...	|	|	|	|	|
Selzthal d.	...	|	0719	|	|	0919	|	|	|	|	|	|	1119	1319	|	|	1519	|	1719	...	|	|	|	|	|
Schwarzach St Veit d.	...	|	|	0850	|	|	1049	|	1247	1247	|	|	1312	|	1450	|	|	|	|	...	1849	|	|	|	|
Bischofshofen d.	...	|	0857	0905	|	1057	1105	|	...	...	|	|	|	1457	1505	|	1650	|	1857	...	1905	|	|	|	|
Salzburg Hbf d.	...	0756	0944	0948	0956	1144	1147	1156	...	...	1252	1300	|	1544	1548	1556	|	1756	1944	...	1947	1956	0230	0230	|
Schwarzach St Veit d.	...	|	...	...	|	...	...	|	...	...	...	|	|	...	...	|	1712	|	...	...	...	|	|	|	0232
Zell am See d.	...	|	...	...	|	...	...	|	...	...	...	|	1343	...	...	|	1743	|	...	...	...	|	|	|	|
Saalfelden d.	...	|	...	...	|	...	...	|	...	...	...	|	1352	...	...	|	1752	|	...	...	...	|	|	|	|
St Johann in Tirol d.	...	|	...	...	|	...	...	|	...	...	...	|	1420	...	...	|	1820	|	...	...	...	|	|	|	|
Kitzbühel d.	...	|	...	...	|	...	...	|	...	...	...	|	1428	...	...	|	1828	|	...	...	...	|	|	|	|
Wörgl d.	...	|	...	...	|	...	...	|	...	...	...	1424	1500	...	...	|	1859	|	...	...	...	|	|	|	|
Jenbach d.	...	|	...	...	|	...	...	|	...	...	...	1438	1516	...	...	|	1916	|	...	...	...	|	|	|	|
Innsbruck Hbf d.	0740	0944	...	...	1144	...	...	1344	...	...	...	1454	1543	...	...	1744	1936	1944	...	...	...	2144	0431	0431	0453
Ötztal d.	0804	1008	...	...	1208	...	...	1408	...	...	...	...	1607	...	...	1808	...	2008	...	...	...	2208	|	|	|
Landeck-Zams d.	0827	1034	...	...	1232	...	...	1432	...	...	...	...	1630	...	...	1832	...	2032	...	...	...	2232	|	|	0545
St Anton am Arlberg d.	0852	1057	...	...	1256	...	...	1456	...	...	...	...	1654	...	...	1856	...	2055	...	...	...	2256	|	|	0610
Langen am Arlberg d.	0902	1108	...	...	1306	...	...	1506	...	...	...	...	1704	...	...	1906	...	2106	...	...	...	2306	|	|	0622
Bludenz d.	0929	1134	...	...	1333	...	...	1533	...	...	...	...	1731	...	...	1933	...	2133	...	...	...	2333	0623	0623	0706
Feldkirch d.	0943	1148	...	...	1348	...	...	1548	...	...	...	...	1744	...	...	1948	...	2148	...	...	...	2346	0640	0640	0738
Bregenz a.	|	|	...	...	|	...	...	|	...	...	...	...	|	...	...	|	...	|	...	...	...	0010	|	|	|
Buchs 🏛 a.	0958	1205	...	...	1406	...	...	1606	...	...	...	...	1758	...	...	2006	...	2203	...	...	...	...	0656	0656	0753
Sargans a.	1022	1222	...	...	1422	...	...	1622	...	...	...	...	1822	...	...	2022	...	2222	...	...	...	...	0723	0723	0823
Zürich HB a.	1120	1320	...	...	1520	...	...	1720	...	...	...	...	1920	...	...	2120	...	2320	...	...	...	...	0820	0820	0920

A – ALPINE PEARLS – 🛏 1,2 cl., ▬ 2 cl. Zürich - Zagreb and v.v. [2] Zürich - Beograd and v.v. [12] Villach - Beograd and v.v.

B – TRANSALPIN – [1] (observation car), [12] 🍷 Zürich - Innsbruck - Graz and v.v.

C – 🛏 1,2 cl., ▬ 2 cl., [2] Zürich - Wien - Budapest and v.v. Special fares payable.

D – [12] 🍴 Wien - Budapest - Szolnok (arrive 2029) - Debrecen (2149).

W – WIENER WALZER – 🛏 1,2 cl., ▬ 2 cl., [2] Zürich - Wien and v.v. Special fares payable.

Z – ZÜRICHSEE – 🛏 1,2 cl., ▬ 2 cl., [2] Zürich - Graz and v.v.

e – Arrive 1216.

x – ①–⑥.

RJ – ÖBB *Railjet* service. 🍴, [1] (business cl [1] (first class), [2] (economy class).

⊙ – 🏛 between Ljubljana and Zagreb is Dobc

⊕ – 🏛 between Vinkovci and Beograd is Šid.

◧ – 🏛 is St Margrethen (Table 75).

WIEN - KLAGENFURT - VENEZIA, MILANO and ROMA 88

train type/number	🚌		REX	IC		RJ	🚌		RJ	🚌		RJ	REX			EN	EN	EN		EN		
train number	831		1881	31		533	835		535	837		539	1883			235	60235 480	1237		237		
notes	🅁			✕		✕	🅁		✕	🅁		✕				R	V	C		G		
			2				A			A			2			⚡	⚡	⚡		⚡		
Hbf d.	...	...	...	0625	...	0825	...	...	1025	...	...	1425	...	...	...	1923	1923	2023	...	2125	...	...
Meidling d.	...	...	...	0632	...	0832	...	...	1032	...	...	1432	...	...	...	1931	1931	2031	...	2133	...	...
an der Mur d.	...	...	...	0815	...	1015	...	...	1215	...	...	1615	...	...	...	2125	2125	2222	...	|	...	...
nfurt Hbf d.	0605	...	...	1022	...	1222	1210	...	1422	1410	...	1822	...	...	...	2335	2335	0021	...	|	...	...
: Hbf d.	|	...	...	|	...	|	|	...	|	|	...	|	...	...	...	|	|	|	...	2305	...	...
burg Hbf d.	|	...	...	|	...	|	|	...	|	|	...	|	...	...	...	|	|	|	...	0134	...	...
Hbf d.	0650	...	0945	1050	...	1246	1256	...	1446	1456	...	1846	1929	...	...	0003	0003	0045	...	0445	...	...
io 🏛 a.	|	...	1012	1112	...	...	|	...	...	|	...	...	1956	...	...	0026	0026	0108	...	0508	...	...
a.	0825	...	1130	1216	...	...	1430	...	...	1630	...	...	2115	...	...	|	|	0217	...	0632	...	...
ia Mestre a.	1000	...	...	1353	...	...	1605	...	...	1805	...	...	...	...	...	0256	0256h	|	...	0821	...	...
ezia Tronchetto ★ a.	1020	...	...	|	...	...	1625	...	...	1825	...	...	...	...	...	|	|	|	...	|	...	...
ezia Santa Lucia a.	...	...	...	1405	...	...	...	...	...	...	...	...	...	...	...	|	|	|	...	0834	...	...
va a.	...	...	...	...	...	...	...	...	...	...	...	...	...	...	...	|	0547	0415	...	...	...	...
ona Porta Nuova a.	...	...	...									...	...	...	...	|	0645	|	...	...	...	...
ano Centrale a.	...	...	...									...	...	...	...	|	0930	|	...	...	...	...
na Centrale a.	...	...	...									...	...	...	...	0448	...	0541	...	...	...	...
e SMN a.	...	...	...									...	...	...	...	0607	...	0655	...	...	...	...
entrale a.	...	...	...									...	...	...	...	|	...	0830	...	...	...	...
o Centrale a.	...	...	...	...	...	...	...	...	...	...	...	...	...	...	...	|	...	0849	...	...	...	...
Termini a.	...	...	...	...	...	...	...	...	...	...	...	...	...	...	...	0922	...	...	...	...	...	...

OTHER CONNECTING SERVICES
Venezia - Roma: Table **600**
Venezia - Milano: Table **605**

train type/number	REX	RJ		🚌	RJ		🚌	RJ		REX	IC	🚌			EN	EN	EN	EN	EN			
train number	1880	534		830	538		832	630		1882	30	838			236	1236	481	234	1234/6			
notes		✕		🅁	✕		🅁	✕			✕	🅁			H	D	234	R	1238			
	2			A						2		A			⚡	⚡	W⚡	⚡	E⚡			
Termini d.	...	...	...	...	...	...	...	...	...	...	...	...	...	...	...	...	...	1904	...	...	...	...
o Centrale d.	...	...	...	...	...	...	...	...	...	...	...	...	...	...	...	1920	...	|	1920	...	...	...
Centrale d.	...	...	...	...	...	...	...	...	...	...	...	...	...	...	...	1946	...	|	1946	...	...	...
e SMN d.	...	...	...	...	...	...	...	...	...	...	...	...	...	...	...	2105	...	2209	2105	...	...	...
na Centrale d.	...	...	...	...	...	...	...	...	...	...	...	...	...	...	...	2224	...	2330	2224	...	...	...
ano Centrale d.	...	...	...	...	...	...	...	...	...	...	...	...	...	...	...	|	2105	|	|	...	...	...
ona Porta Nuova d.	...	...	...	...	...	...	...	...	...	...	...	...	...	...	...	|	2330	|	|	...	...	...
va d.	...	...	...	...	...	...	...	...	...	...	...	...	...	...	...	2349	0024	0041	2349	...	...	...
ezia Santa Lucia d.	...	...	...	...	...	...	...	...	...	...	1555	...	...	...	2057	|	|	|	|	...	...	...
ezia Tronchetto ★ d.	...	...	...	0920	...	...	1120	...	...	...	|	1820	...	...	|	|	|	|	|	...	...	...
zia Mestre d.	...	...	...	0940	...	...	1140	...	...	...	1607	1840	...	...	2109	|	0130g	0130	|	...	...	...
d.	0707	...	...	1115	...	...	1315	...	...	1717	1742	2015	...	...	2246	0201	|	|	0201	...	...	...
sio 🏛 d.	0827	...	...	|	...	...	|	...	...	1840	1849	|	...	...	0020	0319	0420	0420	0319	...	...	...
h Hbf a.	0854	0914	...	1250	1314	...	1450	1514	...	1907	1911	2150	...	...	0042	0341	0442	0442	0341	...	...	...
zburg Hbf a.	...	|	...	|	|	...	|	|	...	...	|	|	...	...	0409	|	|	|	|	...	...	...
z Hbf a.	...	|	...	|	|	...	|	|	...	...	|	|	...	...	0601	|	|	|	|	...	...	...
nfurt Hbf a.	...	0937	...	1335	1337	...	1535	1537	...	...	1937	2235	...	...	|	0407	0532	0532	0407	...	...	...
an der Mur a.	...	1144	...	...	1544	...	...	1744	...	...	2144	...	...	...	|	0621	0731	0731	0621	...	...	...
Meidling a.	...	1328	...	...	1728	...	...	1928	...	...	2328	...	...	...	0746	0826	0940	0940	0855	...	...	...
Hbf a.	...	1335	...	...	1735	...	...	1935	...	...	2335	...	...	...	0755	0832	0948	0948	0903	...	...	...

Mar. 19 - Oct. 26.
TOSCANA MARE ③⑤ Mar. 18 - Oct. 14 (also Aug. 14): 🛏 1, 2 cl. (T2), ▬ 2 cl. (6 berth), (2) 🅁 Wien - Firenze - Pisa - Livorno.
TOSCANA MARE ⑥ Mar. 19 - Oct. 15 (also Aug. 15): 🛏 1, 2 cl. (T2), ▬ 2 cl. (6 berth), (2) 🅁 Livorno - Pisa - Firenze - Wien.
TOSCANA MARE ④ Mar. 24 - Oct. 13: 🛏 1, 2 cl. (T2), ▬ 2 cl. (6 berth), (2) 🅁 Livorno - Pisa - Firenze - Wien.
VIENNA-VENEZIA EXPRESS – 🛏 1, 2 cl., 🛏 1, 2 cl. (T2), ▬ 2 cl. (6 berth), (2) Wien (**944**) - Salzburg (**499**) - Villach (**237**) - Udine - Venezia.
VENEZIA-VIENNA EXPRESS – 🛏 1, 2 cl., 🛏 1, 2 cl. (T2), ▬ 2 cl. (6 berth), (2) Venezia (**236**) - Udine - Villach (**498**) - Salzburg (**945**) - Wien.
ALLEGRO TOSCA – 🛏 1, 2 cl., ▬ 2 cl. (6 berth), (2) Wien - Roma and v.v.
🛏 1, 2 cl., ▬ 2 cl. (4 berth), (2) Wien (**235, 60235**) - Venezia Mestre (**480**) - Milano.
🛏 1, 2 cl., ▬ 2 cl. (4 berth), (2) Milano (**481**) - Venezia Mestre (**234**) - Wien.

g – Arrive 0043.
h – Depart 0530. Train **480**.

★ – See Venezia City Plan on page 32.
🚌 – From June 1 to Sept. 15, an **ÖBB** *IC Bus* departs Venezia Mestre 0825 for Lido di Jesolo (arrives 0920). Also departs Lido di Jesolo 1945 for Venezia Mestre (arrives 2040). Rail tickets **not** valid.
⚡ – Supplement payable.
RJ – ÖBB *Railjet* service. (business class), (first class), (economy class), ✕.
🚌 – **ÖBB** *IC Bus*. Rail tickets valid. 🅁. Supplement payable. 1st and 2nd class. 🍸 in first class. Connections to/from Wien are made at Villach.

VENEZIA - LJUBLJANA - ZAGREB - BUDAPEST and BEOGRAD 89

train type	IC	D	EC	IC		🚌	EC	1604			
train number	201	415	247	205		832	213	1247	1205	1205	
notes						🅁					
notes	A		M	R				K	C	E	
zia Santa Lucia d.	...	...	...	...	...	...	...	...	...	...	...
zia Tronchetto d.	...	...	...	...	...	1120	...	...	...	...	...
zia Mestre d.	...	...	...	...	...	1140	...	...	...	...	...
h Hbf d.	...	0625	...	...	...	1450	1653	...	...	...	...
per a.	...	|	...	...	...	...	|	2017	...	...	...
ljana d.	...	0825	0845	...	...	...	1835	2250	...	...	...
va 🏛 d.	...	1015	|	...	...	...	2023	|	...	...	...
eka d.	...	|	|	...	...	...	|	|	...	2310	...
lit d.	...	|	|	...	...	...	|	|	1837	|	...
eb a.	...	1046	|	...	...	...	2054	|	0310	0310	...
eb d.	1007	1106	|	1434	...	...	...	|	0328	0328	...
nkovci a.	|	1438	|	|	...	...	...	|	|	|	...
d 🏛 a.	|	1515	|	|	...	...	...	|	|	|	...
ograd a.	|	1733	|	|	...	...	...	|	|	|	...
ivnica 🏛 d.	1121	...	◧	1615	...	...	...	◧	0434	0434	...
kényes a.	1135	...	|	1629	...	...	...	|	0459	0459	...
kanizsa a.	1244	...	|	|	...	...	...	|	0600	0600	...
posvár a.	|	...	|	1815	...	...	...	|	|	|	...
mbóvár a.	|	...	|	1847	...	...	...	|	|	|	...
ód a.	1414	...	|	|	...	...	...	|	0702	0702	...
k a.	1501	...	|	|	...	...	...	|	0752	0752	...
esfehérvár a.	1535	...	1641	|	...	...	...	0741	0829	0829	...
apest Déli a.	1624	...	1729	|	...	...	...	0829	|	|	...
apest Keleti a.	...	...	...	2114	...	...	...	1044	0936	0936	...

train type	D	EC	EC	🚌	IC	D	EC	IC			1246
train number	314	31	212	835	200	414	246	204	1204	1204	1605
notes		🅁		🅁							
notes				T	A		M	R	D	G	J
Budapest Keleti a.	...	...	...	...	...	...	...	1445	1823	1823	1815
Budapest Déli d.	...	...	...	...	0600	...	0830	|	|	|	2030
Székesfehérvár d.	...	...	...	...	0646	...	0916	|	1925	1925	2116
Siófok d.	...	...	...	...	0723	...	|	|	2000	2000	|
Fonyód d.	...	...	...	...	0815	...	|	|	2043	2043	|
Dombóvár d.	...	...	...	...	|	...	|	1700	|	|	|
Kaposvár d.	...	...	...	...	|	...	|	1736	|	|	|
Nagykanizsa d.	...	...	...	...	0929	...	|	|	2154	2154	|
Gyékényes d.	...	...	...	...	1045	...	|	1916	2251	2251	|
Koprivnica 🏛 a.	...	...	...	...	1058	...	◧	1929	2303	2303	◧
Beograd d.	...	...	...	...	|	1100	|	|	|	|	|
Šid 🏛 d.	...	...	...	...	|	1356	|	|	|	|	|
Vinkovci d.	...	...	...	...	|	1442	|	|	|	|	|
Zagreb a.	...	...	...	...	1248	1812	|	2046	0011	0011	|
Zagreb d.	...	...	0655	...	...	1838	|	...	0030	0030	|
Split a.	...	...	|	...	...	|	|	...	0824	|	|
Rijeka a.	...	...	|	...	...	|	|	...	...	0530	|
Dobova 🏛 d.	0541	...	0744	...	...	1925	|	...	...	...	|
Ljubljana d.	0728	...	0923	...	...	2110	1643	...	...	...	0610
Koper a.	|	...	|	...	...	|	...	...	...	...	0834
Villach Hbf a.	0908	1050	1058	1256	...	2243	...	...	...	...	...
Venezia Mestre a.	...	1353	...	1605	...	...	...	...	...	...	...
Venezia Tronchetto a.	...	|	...	1625	...	...	...	...	...	...	...
Venezia Santa Lucia a.	...	1405	...	...	...	...	...	...	...	...	...

AGRAM (12) Budapest - Zagreb and v.v.
ADRIA ①③⑥ June 18 - Aug. 27: 🛏 1, 2 cl., ▬ 2 cl., (2) Split - Zagreb - Budapest. ②④⑦ (2) Zagreb - Budapest. Conveys on ③⑥ June 18 - Aug. 27: 🛏 1, 2 cl. Split (**1205**) - Budapest (**276**) - Praha.
ADRIA ②⑤⑦ June 17 - Aug. 26: 🛏 1, 2 cl., ▬ 2 cl., (2) Budapest - Zagreb - Split. (2) Budapest - Zagreb. Conveys on ②⑤ June 17 - Aug. 26: 🛏 1, 2 cl. Praha (**277**) - Budapest (**1204**) - Split.
ADRIA ①③⑥ June 18 - Aug. 27: 🛏 1, 2 cl., ▬ 2 cl., (2) 🍸 Rijeka - Zagreb - Budapest.
ADRIA ②⑤⑦ June 17 - Aug. 26: 🛏 1, 2 cl., ▬ 2 cl., (2) 🍸 Budapest - Zagreb - Rijeka.
ISTRA ①④ June 30 - Aug. 29: 🛏 1, 2 cl., ▬ 2 cl., (2) Budapest (**1246**) - Hodoš - Maribor (**1605**) - Koper.
ISTRA ②⑤ July 1 - Aug. 30: 🛏 1, 2 cl., ▬ 2 cl., (2) Koper (**1604**) - Maribor (**1247**) - Hodoš - Budapest.
CITADELLA – (12) ✕ Ljubljana - Hodoš - Budapest and v.v. (Table **91**).

R – RIPPL-RÓNAI – (12) 🍸 Zagreb - Budapest and v.v.
T – Mar. 19 - Oct. 26.

k – Budapest **Kelenfold**.

◧ – 🏛 is Hodoš.
🚌 – **ÖBB** *IC Bus*. 🅁 Rail tickets valid. Supplement payable. 1st and 2nd class. 🍸 in first class.

90 MARSEILLE - NICE - MILANO, ROMA and VENEZIA

train type	EC	FB	IC	FB	FR				IC	IC	FB	FB	FR	EC	EC	EC	IC	FR	FB	EC	EC	EC	ICN
train number	139	9773	511	9723	9533		17473		745	665	9777	9727	9541	145	145	145	673	9557	9749	147	147	147	799
notes	140	[R] 🍸	[R] 🍸	[R] 🍸	[R] ✕			◇	746	[R]	[R] ✕	[R] 🍸	[R] ✕	146	146	146	[R] 🍸	[R] ✕	[R] 🍸	148	148	148	[R]
notes		✓	✓	✓	✓		Ⓐ		[R]	✓	✓	✓	✓	♣	♣Q	♣Q	✓	✓	✓	♣	♣Q	♣Q	✓
notes	♣								✓					P	①–⑤	⑥⑦				P	①–⑤	⑥⑦	A
Marseille St Charles d.	...	...	...	...	...	...	0630	...	...	...	...	...	...	...	1131	...	...	...	...	1531	...	1531	...
Toulon d.	...	...	...	...	...	...	0713	...	...	...	...	...	...	...	1218	...	...	...	...	1617	...	1617	...
Cannes d.	...	...	...	...	...	...	0839	...	...	...	...	...	...	...	1335	...	...	...	...	1738	...	1738	...
Nice d.	0808	...	...	...	...	...	0906	0950	...	...	...	...	...	1406	1406	1406	...	...	...	1807	1807	1807	...
Monaco - Monte Carlo d.	0825	...	...	...	...	...	...	1016	...	...	...	...	...	1423	1423	1423	...	...	...	1825	1825	1825	...
Ventimiglia 🏛 d.	0901	...	...	...	...	...	...	1040	1049	...	...	...	...	1502	1502	1502	...	...	...	1902	1902	1902	...
San Remoth a.	0913	...	...	...	...	...	...	...	1108	...	...	...	...	1513	1513	1513	...	...	...	1913	1913	1913	...
Genova Piazza Principe a.	1107	1212	1238	...	...	...	...	...	1306	1347	1502	...	...	1707	1707	1707	1747	...	...	2106	2106	2106	2353
Milano Centrale a.	1250	|	|	1305	1320	...	...	...	1450	|	|	1505	1520	1850	1850	1850	|	1920	2005	2250	2250	2250	|
Verona a.	...	|	|	1428	|	...	...	...	...	|	|	1628	|	...	...	...	|	|	2128	...	...	...	|
Venezia Santa Lucia a.	...	|	|	1540	|	...	...	...	...	|	|	1740	|	...	...	...	|	|	2240	...	...	...	|
La Spezia a.	...	1312	1355	...	|	...	...	...	...	1521	1618	...	|	...	...	...	1921	|	...	...	...	...	0124
Pisa Centrale a.	...	1355	1452	...	|	...	...	...	...	...	1710	...	|	...	...	...	2017	|	...	...	...	...	0216
Firenze SMN a.	...	|	|	...	1459	...	...	...	...	...	|	...	1659	...	...	...	...	2059	...	...	...	...	|
Roma Termini a.	...	1632	1803	...	1640	...	...	...	...	...	2003	...	1840	...	...	...	...	2240	...	...	...	...	0555o
Napoli Centrale a.	...	...	2029	...	1800	...	...	...	...	...	...	...	2000	...	...	...	...	...	...	...	...	...	0817

train type	ICN	IC	EC	TGV	FB	FB	FR	FR	FB	EC		IC	FB	FR	EC		FR	FB	FB	IC			
train number	796	658	141	6864	9708	9764	9508	9610	9710	143	17490	674	9718	9526	159		9532	9726	9774	675			
notes	[R]	[R] 🍸	142	[R]	[R]	[R] 🍸	[R] 🍸	[R]	[R] 🍸	144		[R] 🍸	[R] 🍸	[R] ✕	160		[R] ✕	[R] 🍸	[R] 🍸	676	◇		
notes	✓	✓		✓	✓	✓	✓	✓	✓			✓	✓	✓			✓	✓	✓	[R] ✓			
notes	A		♣		①–⑤			①–⑤		♣					♣								
Napoli Centrale d.	2142	...	...	...	...	...	...	0640	...	...	...	...	...	1000	...	...	1200	...	...	...	...	...	...
Roma Termini d.	0003o	...	...	...	...	0657	0720	0800	...	...	...	...	...	1120	...	...	1320	...	1357	...	...	...	...
Firenze SMN d.	|	...	...	...	...	|	0900	|	...	...	...	...	...	1300	...	...	1500	...	|	...	...	...	...
Pisa Centrale d.	0326	0542	...	...	...	0947	|	|	...	...	...	1342	...	|	...	...	|	...	1629	...	...	...	...
La Spezia d.	0425	0638	...	...	...	1039	|	|	...	...	...	1438	...	|	...	...	|	...	1715	...	...	...	...
Venezia Santa Lucia d.	|	|	...	...	0750	|	|	|	0832q	...	...	|	1150	|	...	...	|	1320	|	...	...	...	...
Verona d.	|	|	...	...	0902	|	|	|	0932	...	...	|	1302	|	...	...	|	1432	|	...	...	...	...
Milano Centrale d.	|	|	0705	...	1025	|	1040	1055	1055	1110	...	|	1425	1440	1510	...	1640	1555	|	1705	...	...	...
Genova Piazza Principe d.	0601	0815	0856	...	...	1156	...	...	...	1258	...	1615	...	...	1658	...	...	...	1816	1858	...	...	...
San Remo d.	...	...	1049	...	...	...	...	...	...	1447	...	...	...	...	1848	...	...	...	...	2054	...	...	...
Ventimiglia 🏛 a.	...	...	1101	...	...	...	...	...	...	1501	...	...	...	...	1901	...	...	...	...	2115	2240	...	...
Monaco - Monte Carlo a.	...	...	1148	...	...	...	...	...	...	1543	...	...	...	...	1946	...	...	...	...	...	2305	...	...
Nice a.	...	...	1204	1223	...	...	...	...	...	1600	1655	...	...	...	2005	...	...	...	...	...	2330	...	...
Cannes a.	...	...	...	1253	...	...	...	...	...	...	1719	...	...	...	2039	...	...	...	...	...	...	...	...
Toulon a.	...	...	...	1412	...	...	...	...	...	...	1844	...	...	...	2158	...	...	...	...	...	...	...	...
Marseille St Charles a.	...	...	...	1459	...	...	...	...	...	...	1929	...	...	...	2241	...	...	...	...	...	...	...	...

A – 🛏 1, 2 cl., 🛌 2 cl. (4 berth), 🚃2 Torino - Genova - Napoli - Salerno and v.v.
P – Until July 3.
Q – From July 4.
f – Not Apr. 2.
j – Firenze **Campo di Marte**.

o – Roma **Ostiense**.
q – Venezia **Mestre**.

✓ – Supplement payable.
♣ – *EC Thello.*

◇ – Stopping train. Alternative services available, see Table **361**.
★ – Service offering Executive, Business, Premium and Standard cl

91 WIEN - LJUBLJANA and ZAGREB

train type		EC			EC	EC	ICS	1246	
train number		151	483	2752	246	159	23	1605	
notes		✕		2	✕	✕ ✓	[R]		
		E			M	C		J	
Wien Hbf d.	...	0758	...	...	...	1558	...	...	...
Wien Meidling d.	...	0805	...	...	...	1605	...	...	...
Wiener Neustadt Hbf d.	...	0832	...	...	...	1632	...	...	...
Graz Hbf d.	...	1038	...	...	...	1838	...	...	...
Spielfeld-Straß 🏛 d.	...	1120	...	...	...	1920	...	...	...
Budapest Déli d.	...	|	...	...	0830	|	...	2030	...
Hodoš 🏛 d.	...	|	...	...	1303	|	...	0105	...
Maribor a.	...	1137	...	...	|	1938	1945	0240	...
Pragersko a.	...	1205	...	...	1430	2011	2001	|	...
Zidani Most a.	...	1310	...	...	1541	|	2052	0505	...
Dobova 🏛 a.	...	|	...	...	|	2156	|	|	...
Zagreb a.	...	|	...	...	|	2242	|	|	...
Ljubljana a.	...	1406	1510	1542	1643	...	2138	0606	...
Koper a.	...	...	|	1813	...	...	...	0840	...
Rijeka a.	...	...	1755	...	...	...	...	...	...

train type / number	IC	ICS	EC	EC			EC	1604
train number	508	14	158	247	2751	482	150	1247
notes		[R]	✕ ✓		2		✕	
			C	M			E	K
Rijeka d.	...	...	...	...	...	1200	...	...
Koper d.	0525	...	...	...	1003	|	...	2015
Ljubljana d.	0748	0805	...	0845	1240	1450	1600	2250
Zagreb d.	...	|	0725	|	...	...	|	|
Dobova 🏛 d.	...	|	0813	|	...	...	|	|
Zidani Most d.	...	0850	|	0941	...	...	1657	2349
Pragersko d.	...	0942	1000	1100	...	...	1800	|
Maribor d.	...	0955	1019	|	...	...	1819	0200
Hodoš 🏛 a.	...	...	|	1229	...	...	|	0331
Budapest Déli a.	...	...	|	1729	...	...	|	0829
Spielfeld-Straß 🏛 a.	...	...	1036	...	...	...	1836	...
Graz Hbf a.	...	...	1120	...	...	...	1920	...
Wiener Neustadt Hbf a.	...	...	1328	...	...	...	2128	...
Wien Meidling a.	...	...	1355	...	...	...	2155	...
Wien Hbf a.	...	...	1402	...	...	...	2202	...

C – CROATIA 🚃12 ✕ Wien - Zagreb and v.v.
E – EMONA 🚃12 ✕ Wien - Ljubljana and v.v.
M – CITADELLA 🚃12 ✕ Budapest - Hodoš - Ljubljana and v.v. (Table **89**).

J – ISTRA ①④ June 30 - Aug. 29: 🛏 1, 2 cl., 🛌 2 cl., 🚃2 Budapest (**1246**) - Hodoš - Maribor (**1605**) - Koper.
K – ISTRA ②⑤ July 1 - Aug. 30: 🛏 1, 2 cl., 🛌 2 cl., 🚃2 Koper (**1604**) - Maribor (**1247**) - Hodoš - Budapest.

✓ – Supplement paya
◇ – Stopping train.

92 ZAGREB - SARAJEVO

train number		397	
notes		A	
Zagreb d.	...	0859	...
Sunja d.	...	1015	...
Volinja 🏛 d.	...	1112	...
Dobrljin 🏛 d.	...	1145	...
Novi Grad d.	...	1204	...
Banja Luka d.	...	1342	...
Doboj d.	...	1523	...
Zenica d.	...	1657	...
Sarajevo a.	...	1817	...

train number		396	
notes		A	
Sarajevo d.	...	1043	...
Zenica d.	...	1205	...
Doboj d.	...	1348	...
Banja Luka d.	...	1531	...
Novi Grad d.	...	1704	...
Dobrljin 🏛 d.	...	1721	...
Volinja 🏛 d.	...	1759	...
Sunja d.	...	1827	...
Zagreb a.	...	1942	...

A – 🚃2 Zagreb - Sarajevo and v.v.

93 WARSZAWA - VILNIUS

train number	TLK	TLK	
notes	31010	10108	
	H	W	
		⑧	
Warszawa Centralna d.	0736	1505	...
Warszawa Wschodnia d.	0744	1517	...
Małkinia d.	0857	1634	...
Białystok d.	1015	1754	...
Suwałki d.	1207	1954	...
Mockava 🏛 ◐ a.	1430	...	...
Šeštokai a.	...	...	...
Kaunas a.	...	...	...
Vilnius a.	...	...	...

train number	TLK	TLK
notes	10118	13010
	W	H
	①–⑥	
Vilnius d.	...	...
Kaunas d.	...	...
Šeštokai d.	...	...
Mockava 🏛 ◐ d.	...	1510
Suwałki d.	0439	1528
Białystok d.	0700	1746
Małkinia a.	0800	1849
Warszawa Wschodnia a.	0911	1958
Warszawa Centralna a.	0920	2006

H – HAŃCZA – 🚃12 [R] Kraków - Warszawa - Białystok - Suwałki - Mockava and v.v.
W – WIGRY – 🚃12 [R] Warszawa - Białystok - Suwałki and v.v.

◐ – 🏛 = Trakiszki (Poland) / Mockava (Lithuania); ticketing point is Mockava.

For explanation of standard symbols see page 4

MOSKVA / St PETERBURG - WARSZAWA 94

train number	17BJ	17BJ	9JA	9JA	23JI	23JI	57MJ	57MJ	21JA	21JA
train number					452	452	404	404	404	404
notes	HW	HX	RW	RX	BW	BX	SW	SX	PW	PX
…kva Belorusskaya .... d.	1018	1118	1506	1627	2111	2215	...	...	0644	0746
…ensk Tsentralny ▦ ...§ d.	1526	1638	1949	2110	0151	0255	...	...	1116	1224
…Peterburg Vitebski ..... d.	|	|	|	|	|	|	2147	2147	|	|
…a Tsentralnaya ....§ d.	1703	1803	2113	2234	0317	0417	1242z	1349z	1242	1349
…k .... d.	1933	2035	2356	0116	0556	0657	1517	1625	1517	1625
… Tsentralny ▦ .... d.	2315	0015	0554	0654	1203t	1303t	2115	2215	2115	2215
…spol .... a.	0033	0033	0513	0513	1121	1121	2033	2033	2033	2033
…szawa Wschodnia .... a.	0319	0319	0832	0832	1353	1353	2319	2319	2319	2319
…szawa Centralna .... a.	0407	0407	0855	0855	1430	1430	2340	2340	2340	2340

train number	18BJ	18BJ	405ZH	405ZH	22AJ	22AJ	10ZH	10ZH	24JI	24JI
train number			22AJ	22AJ	20GJ	20GJ			453	453
notes	GW	GX	QW	QX	TW	TX	RW	RX	AW	AX
Warszawa Centralna ....d.	0056	0056	0310	0310	0310	0310	1840	1840	1340	1340
Warszawa Wschodnia ....d.	0202	0202	0332	0332	0332	0332	1927	1927	1417	1417
Terespol ....d.	0455	0455	0630	0630	0630	0630	2252	2252	1704	1704
Brest Tsentralny ▦ ....a.	0641	0741	0841	0941	0841	0941	0039	0139	1850f	1950f
Minsk ....a.	1221	1315	1406	1501	1406	1501	0633	0724	0050	0139
Orsha Tsentralnaya .... § a.	1500	1558	1638	1730	1638	1730	0935	1018	0318	0406
St Peterburg Vitebski ....a.	|	|	|	|	0723	0723	|	|	|	|
Smolensk Tsentralny ▦ .... § a.	1632	1730	1806	1858	...	...	1111	1148	0446	0535
Moskva Belorusskaya ....a.	2130	2230	2243	2335	...	...	1539	1620	0921	1010

TRANSEUROPEAN EXPRESS ③⑥⑦: 🛏 1, 2 cl. Paris (**453**) - Berlin - Brest (**24** *JI*) - Moskva. ✕ (RZD) Brest - Moskva.

TRANSEUROPEAN EXPRESS ①④⑤: 🛏 1, 2 cl. Moskva (**23** *JI*) - Brest (**452**) - Berlin - Paris. ✕ (RZD) Moskva - Brest.

⑥: 🛏 1 cl. (lux), 🛏 1, 2 cl. Nice - Warszawa - Moskva. ✕ (RZD) Brest - Moskva (journey two nights).

④: 🛏 1 cl. (lux), 🛏 1, 2 cl. Moskva - Warszawa - Nice. ✕ (RZD) Moskva - Brest (journey two nights).

VLTAVA ③⑤: 🛏 1, 2 cl. Moskva (**21***JA*) - Terespol (**404**) - Praha (Table **95**). Conveys on ③⑤: 🛏 1, 2 cl. Moskva - Wien. Conveys on ③ June 1 - Sept. 7 🛏 1, 2 cl. Moskva - Budapest.

VLTAVA ④⑥: 🛏 1, 2 cl. Praha (**405**) - Brest (**22***AJ*) - Moskva (Table **95**). Conveys on ④⑥: 🛏 1, 2 cl. Wien - Moskva. Conveys on ④ June 2 - Sept. 8 🛏 1, 2 cl. Budapest - Moskva.

POLONEZ – 🛏 1, 2 cl. 🍸 Moskva - Warszawa and v.v. ✕ Moskva - Brest and v.v. Conveys 🛏 1, 2 cl. Moskva - Budapest and Sofia and v.v.

④: 🛏 1, 2 cl. St Peterburg (**57***MJ*) - Orsha (**21***JA*) - Terespol (**404**) - Praha (journey 2 nights). Conveys 🛏 1, 2 cl. St Peterburg (**57***MJ*) - Orsha (**21***JA*) - Terespol (**404**) - Bohumín (**101**) - Wien (journey 2 nights).

⑥: 🛏 1, 2 cl. Praha (**405**) - Brest (**22***AJ*) - Orsha (**52***BJ*) - St Peterburg (journey 2 nights). Conveys 🛏 1, 2 cl. Wien (**100**) - Bohumín (**405**) - Brest (**22***AJ*) - Orsha (**20***GJ*) - St Peterburg (journey 2 nights).

W – Mar. 27 - Oct. 29.

X – Oct. 30 - Dec. 10.

f – Depart 2200 Mar. 27 - Oct. 29; depart 2107 from Oct. 30.

t – Arrive 0950 Mar. 27 - Oct. 29; arrive 1052 from Oct. 30.

z – Arrive 0909.

§ – ▦: Osinovka (BY) / Krasnoye (RU).

MOSKVA and St PETERBURG - PRAHA, WIEN and BUDAPEST 95

train number	57MJ	57MJ	21JA	21EJ	21EJ		17BJ	9SZ
notes	B	Q	V	J	C		S	D
…kva Belorusskaya .... d.	...	...	0746	0746	0746	...	1118	1627
…lensk Tsentralny ▦ ....§ d.	...	...	1225	1225	1225	...	1639	2110
…Peterburg Vitebski ...... d.	2147	2147	|	|	|	...	|	|
…a Tsentralnaya ....§ d.	1349x	1349x	1349	1349	1349	...	1803	2234
…sk .... d.	1625	1625	1625	1625	1625	...	2035	0116
…t Tsentralny ▦ .... a.	1952	1952	1952	1952	1952	...	0010	0440
…st Tsentralny ▦ .... d.	2215	2215	2215	2215	2215	...	0015	0654
…spol .... a.	2033	2033	2033	2033	2033	...	0033	0513
…szawa Centralna .... a.	2340	2340	2340	2340	2340	...	0407	0855
…wice .... a.	0253	0253	0253	0253	0253	...	0651	1225
…umín ▦ .... a.	0410	0410	0410	0410	0410	...	0831	1350
…ava hlavní .... a.	0419	0419r	0419	0419	0419r	...	|	1358
…eclav .... a.	|	0848	|	|	0848	...	1047	1548
Bratislava hlavná .... a.	|	|	|	|	|	...	|	1649
Budapest Keleti .... a.	|	|	|	|	|	...	|	1935
Beograd .... a.	|	|	|	|	|	...	|	0621
Sofia .... a.	|	|	|	|	|	...	|	1815
…ien Hbf .... a.	|	0951	|	|	0951	...	1232	...
…nouc .... a.	0555	...	0555	0555	...	...	...	...
…lubice .... a.	0718	...	0718	0718	...	...	...	...
…ha hlavní .... a.	0828	...	0828	0828	...	...	...	...
…arlovy Vary .... a.	...	...	...	1240	...	...	...	...
…heb .... a.	...	...	...	1329	...	...	...	...

train number	10ZJ		18BJ	22IJ	22AJ	22AJ	22IJ	22AJ
notes	E		T	H	K	W	P	A
Cheb .... d.	...	...	...	...	1427	...	...	...
Karlovy Vary .... d.	...	...	...	...	1515	...	...	...
Praha hlavní .... d.	...	...	...	...	1846	1846	...	1846
Pardubice .... d.	...	...	...	...	1941	1941	...	1941
Olomouc .... d.	...	...	...	...	2101	2101	...	2101
Wien Hbf .... d.	...	...	1641	1809	|	|	1809	|
Sofia .... d.	1130	...	|	|	|	|	|	|
Beograd .... d.	2150	...	|	|	|	|	|	|
Budapest Keleti .... d.	0800	...	|	|	|	|	|	|
Bratislava hlavná ..... d.	1110	...	|	|	|	|	|	|
Břeclav .... d.	1213	...	1810	1913	|	|	1913	|
Ostrava hlavní .... d.	1359	...	|	2237	2237	2237	2237	2237
Bohumín ▦ .... d.	1407	...	2025	2246	2246	2246	2246	2246
Katowice .... d.	1529	...	2208	2359	2359	2359	2359	2359
Warszawa Centralna .... d.	1840	...	0056	0310	0310	0310	0310	0310
Terespol .... d.	2252	...	0455	0630	0630	0630	0630	0630
Brest Tsentralny ▦ .... a.	0139	...	0741	0941	0941	0941	0941	0941
Brest Tsentralny ▦ .... d.	0348	...	0940	1120	1120	1120	1120	1120
Minsk .... a.	0724	...	1315	1501	1501	1501	1501	1501
Orsha Tsentralnaya ....§ a.	1018	...	1558	1730	1730	1730	1730t	1730t
St Peterburg Vitebski ... a.	|	...	|	|	|	|	0723	0723
Smolensk Tsentralny ▦ .§ a.	1148	...	1730	1858	1858	1858	...	...
Moskva Belorusskaya ...... a.	1620	...	2230	2335	2335	2335	...	...

A – ⑥: 🛏 1, 2 cl. Praha (**405**) - Brest (**22***AJ*) - Orsha (**52***BJ*) - St Peterburg (journey 2 nights).

B – ④: 🛏 1, 2 cl. St Peterburg (**57***MJ*) - Orsha (**21***JA*) - Terespol (**404**) - Praha (journey 2 nights).

C – ③⑤: 🛏 1, 2 cl. Moskva (**21***EJ*) - Terespol (**404**) - Bohumín (**101**) - Wien.

D – 🛏 1, 2 cl. Moskva (**9***SZ*) - Brest - Warszawa (**131**) - Budapest. Conveys 🛏 1, 2 cl. Moskva - Budapest (**341**) - Beograd (**491**) - Sofia (journey 2 nights). For additional cars see Table **1360**.

E – 🛏 1, 2 cl. Budapest (**130**) - Warszawa (**10***ZJ*) - Brest - Moskva. Conveys 🛏 1, 2 cl. Sofia (**490**) - Beograd (**340**) - Budapest - Moskva (journey 2 nights). For additional cars see Table **1360**.

H – ④⑥: 🛏 1, 2 cl. Wien (**100**) - Bohumín (**405**) - Brest (**22***IJ*) - Moskva.

J – ③⑤: 🛏 1, 2 cl. Moskva (**21***EJ*) - Terespol (**404**) - Praha (**612**) - Cheb.

K – ④⑥: 🛏 1, 2 cl. Cheb (**613**) - Praha (**405**) - Brest (**22***AJ*) - Moskva.

P – ⑥: 🛏 1, 2 cl. Wien (**100**) - Ostrava (**405**) - Brest (**22***IJ*) - Orsha (**52***BJ*) - St Peterburg, (journey 2 nights).

Q – ④: 🛏 1, 2 cl. St Peterburg (**57***MJ*) - Orsha (**21***EJ*) - Terespol (**404**) - Ostrava (**101**) - Wien, (journey 2 nights).

S – ④: 🛏 1 cl. (lux), 🛏 1, 2 cl. Moskva - Wien - Nice. ✕ (RZD) Moskva - Brest and ✕ (PKP) Warszawa - Nice (journey two nights).

T – ⑥: 🛏 1 cl. (lux), 🛏 1, 2 cl. Nice - Wien - Moskva. ✕ (PKP) Nice - Warszawa and ✕ (RZD) Brest - Moskva (journey two nights).

V – VLTAVA ③⑤: 🛏 1, 2 cl. Moskva (**21***JA*) - Terespol (**404**) - Praha.

W – VLTAVA ④⑥: 🛏 1, 2 cl. Praha (**405**) - Brest (**22***AJ*) - Moskva.

r – Depart 0700.

t – Depart 2052.

x – Arrive 0909.

§ – ▦: Osinovka (BY) / Krasnoye (RU).

BUDAPEST / PRAHA / BRATISLAVA - KYÏV 96

train number	801	443	34KJ
train number	801LJ	443KJ	
notes	A	C	L
…dapest Nyugati .... d.	...	...	0723
…lnok .... d.	...	...	0838
…recen .... d.	...	...	0951
…ony ▦ .... a.	...	...	1121
…raha hlavní .... d.	...	2309	|
Bratislava hlavná .... d.	2349	|	|
…ilina .... d.	|	0516	|
Zvolen .... d.	0316	|	|
…ice .... d.	1006	1006	|
…na nad Tisou ▦ .... a.	1151	1151	|
…p ▦ .... a.	1410	1410	1340
…v .... a.	2222	2222	2222
…nelnytsky .... a.	0230	0230	0230
…nytsya .... a.	0434	0434	0434
…v .... a.	0743	0743	0743

train number	81DJ	771	771
train number		800	442
notes	L	B	D
Kyïv ....d.	2022	2312	2312
Vinnytsya ....d.	2329	0204	0204
Khmelnytsky ....d.	0122	0537	0537
Lviv ....d.	0544	1010	1010
Chop ▦ ....d.	1420	1735	1735
Čierna nad Tisou ▦ ....d.	|	1804	1804
Košice ....a.	|	1954	1954
Zvolen ....a.	|	0155	|
Žilina ....a.	|	|	0115
Bratislava hlavná ....a.	|	0525	|
Praha hlavní ....a.	|	...	0739
Záhony ▦ ....a.	1440	...	...
Debrecen ....a.	1605	...	...
Szolnok ....a.	1720	...	...
Budapest Nyugati ....a.	1837	...	...

A – ①–⑤: 🛏 1, 2 cl. Bratislava (**801**) - Košice (**8807**) - Čierna nad Tisou (**8862**) - Chop (**801** *LJ*) - Lviv - Kyïv (journey two nights).

B – ①②③⑥⑦: 🛏 1, 2 cl. Kyïv (**771**) - Khmelnytsky - Lviv - Chop (**8863**) - Čierna nad Tisou (**8820**) - Košice (**800**) - Bratislava (journey two nights).

C – 🛏 1, 2 cl. Praha (**443**) - Košice (**8807**) - Čierna nad Tisou (**8862**) - Chop (**443** *KJ*) - Lviv - Kyïv (journey two nights).

D – 🛏 1, 2 cl. Kyïv - Khmelnytsky - Lviv - Chop (**8863**) - Čierna nad Tisou (**8820**) - Košice (**442**) - Praha (journey two nights).

L – LATORCA – 🛏 1, 2 cl. Budapest - Lviv - Kyïv and v.v.

WARSZAWA - LVIV 97

train type/number	1326	1326
notes	6300	6300
notes	35	51
	AP	AQ
Warszawa Centralna . d.	1850	1850
Kraków Gł. .... d.	2205	2205
Przemyśl .... d.	0252	0356
Medyka ▦ .... d.	|	|
Mostiska **II** ▦ .... ‡ a.	0421	0530
Lviv .... ‡ a.	0603	0715

train type/number	52	36
notes	3600	3600
notes	3124	3124
	BP	BQ
Lviv .... ‡ d.	2259	2359
Mostiska **II** ▦ ..... ‡ d.	0045	0145
Medyka ▦ .... d.	|	|
Przemyśl .... a.	0020	0117
Kraków Gł. .... a.	0555	0555
Warszawa Centralna d.	0854	0854

A – LVIV EXPRESS – 🛏 2 cl. Warszawa (**1326**) - Kraków (**6300**) - Przemyśl (**35/51**) - Lviv.

B – LVIV EXPRESS – 🛏 2 cl. Lviv (**52/36**) - Przemyśl (**3600**) - Kraków (**3124**) - Warszawa.

P – Runs on even dates in May, Aug., Nov., Dec.; uneven dates in June, July, Sept., Oct.

Q – Runs on even dates in June, July, Sept., Oct.; uneven dates in May, Aug., Nov., Dec.

‡ – Ukrainian (East European) time.

99 WARSZAWA and KRAKÓW - PRAHA, WIEN and BUDAPEST

train type/train number	*EC*	*IC*	*EC*	*SC*	*EC*	*EC*		*EC*	*SC*	*EC*	*EC*		*IC*	*EC*					402		
train number	**116**	**38102**	**103**	**508**	**277**	**131**		**105**	**502**	**281**	**112**		**37200**	**110**		**407**		**407**	**407**	**402**	**402**
notes/train number	✕	**38103**	✕	🍷	✕	✕		✕	🍷	✕	✕		**37201**	✕		**477**	**407**	**444**	**477**	**407**	**442**
notes	⊡		⊡	🅁⚡		⊡	2	⊡	⚡		⊡			🅁							
notes	**Y**		**X**	Ⓑ	**Z**	**V**		**W**		**K**	**M**			**T**		**B**	**C**	**P**	**A**	**D**	**R**
Gdynia Główny ..... d.	...	...	...	...	...	...	...	0925	...	...	...	...	...	...	...	...	...	...	...	...	...
Gdańsk Główny ..... d.	...	...	...	...	...	...	...	0950	...	...	...	...	...	...	...	...	...	...	...	...	...
Warszawa Wschodnia ..... d.	0529	...	0644	...	...	0944	...	1234	...	...	1339	...	...	1744	...	2119	2119	2119	...	...	...
Warszawa Centralna ..... d.	0540	...	0655	...	...	0955	...	1255	...	...	1355	...	...	1755	...	2130	2130	2130	...	...	...
Kraków Główny ..... d.	|	0650	|	...	...	|	1314	|	...	...	|	...	1815	|	...	|	|	|	2202	2202	2202
Katowice ..... d.	0818	0850	0925	...	...	1226	1515	1528	...	...	1631	...	2006	2032	...	0007	0007	0007	|	|	|
Zebrzydowice 🛂 ..... d.	|	...	1023	...	...	1323	...	1623	...	...	|	...	...	|	...	0103	0103	0103	0054	0054	0054
Bohumín 🛂 ..... a.	0941	...	1040	...	...	1340	...	1640	...	...	1750	...	...	|	...	0120	0120	0120	0111	0111	0111
Bohumín 🛂 ..... d.	1007	...	1052	...	...	1352	...	1652	...	...	1807	...	...	|	...	0210	0210	0210	0210	0210	0346
Ostrava hlavní ..... a.	1013	...	1059	1114	...	1359	...	1659	1714	...	1813	...	...	2156	...	0217	0217	0217	0217	0217	0354
Přerov ..... a.	|	...	1149	|	...	1449	...	1749	|	...	|	...	...	...	...	0309	0309	0309	0309	0309	|
Olomouc ..... a.	1116	...	|	1209	...	|	...	|	1809	...	1916	...	...	...	...	|	|	0358	|	|	0515
Pardubice ..... a.	1236	...	|	1320	...	|	...	|	1920	...	2036	...	...	...	...	|	|	0525	|	|	0640
Praha hlavní ..... a.	1339	...	|	1415	...	|	...	|	2015	...	2139	...	...	...	...	|	|	0638	|	|	0740
Břeclav ..... a.	...	...	1246	...	1258	1547	...	1847	...	1858	...	...	...	...	...	0405	0405	...	0405	0405	...
Wien Hbf ..... a.	...	...	1351	...	|	|	...	1951	...	|	...	...	...	...	...	|	0705	...	|	0705	...
Kúty 🛂 ..... a.	...	...	...	...	1310	1610	...	...	...	1910	...	...	...	...	...	0453	...	...	0453	...	...
Bratislava hlavná ..... a.	...	...	...	...	1349	1649	...	...	...	1949	...	...	...	...	...	0536	...	...	0536	...	...
Štúrovo 🛂 △ ..... a.	...	...	...	...	1511	1811	...	...	...	2111	...	...	...	...	...	0710	...	...	0710	...	...
Budapest Keleti ..... a.	...	...	...	...	1635	1935	...	...	...	2235	...	...	...	...	...	0835	...	...	0835	...	...

train type/train number	*EC*			*EC*	*EC*	*SC*	*EC*		*EC*		*EC*	*SC*	*EC*		*EC*						**476**
train number	**111**			**113**	**280**	**503**	**104**		**130**		**276**	**509**	**102**		**117**		**445**		**406**	**476**	**406**
notes/train number	✕			✕	✕	🍷	✕		✕		✕	🍷	✕		✕		**403**	**406**	**403**	**406**	**403**
notes	🅁	2		⊡		🅁	⊡		⊡	2		🅁	⊡	2	⊡						
notes	**T**			**M**	**K**	⚡	**W**		**V**		**Z**	⚡	**X**		**Y**		**S**	**C**	**E**	**G**	**F**
Budapest Keleti ..... d.	...	...	...	...	0525	...	...	...	0800	...	1125	...	...	...	...	...	...	...	...	2005	2005
Štúrovo 🛂 △ ..... d.	...	...	...	...	0649	...	...	...	0949	...	1249	...	...	...	...	...	...	...	...	2124	2124
Bratislava hlavná ..... d.	...	...	...	...	0811	...	...	...	1110	...	1411	...	...	...	...	...	...	...	...	2258	2258
Kúty 🛂 ..... d.	...	...	...	...	0850	...	...	...	1150	...	1450	...	...	...	...	...	...	...	...	2340	2340
Wien Hbf ..... d.	...	...	...	...	|	...	0809	...	|	...	...	...	1409	...	...	...	...	2250	2250	|	|
Břeclav ..... d.	...	...	...	...	0902	...	0913	...	1213	...	1502	...	1513	...	...	...	...	0025	0025	0025	0025
Praha hlavní ..... d.	...	...	...	0624	...	0743	|	...	|	...	...	1343	|	...	1424	...	2200	|	|	|	|
Pardubice ..... d.	...	...	...	0725	...	0837	|	...	|	...	...	1437	|	...	1525	...	2316	|	|	|	|
Olomouc ..... d.	...	...	...	0845	...	0950	|	...	|	...	...	1550	|	...	1645	...	0041	|	|	|	|
Přerov ..... d.	...	...	...	|	...	|	1008	...	1309	...	...	|	1608	...	|	...	0126	0119	0119	0119	0119
Ostrava hlavní ..... d.	0556	...	...	0948	...	1044	1059	...	1359	...	...	1644	1659	...	1748	...	0217	0156	0156	0156	0156
Bohumín 🛂 ..... a.	|	...	...	0955	...	...	1105	...	1406	...	...	...	1705	...	1755	...	0225	0203	0203	0203	0203
Bohumín 🛂 ..... d.	|	...	...	1007	...	...	1120	...	1420	...	...	...	1720	...	1809	...	0404	0300	0404	0300	0404
Zebrzydowice 🛂 ..... d.	|	...	...	|	...	...	1138	...	1438	...	...	...	1738	...	|	...	0424	0319	0424	0319	0424
Katowice ..... a.	0722	0742	...	1128	...	...	1233	...	1534	1620	...	...	1835	1907	1932	...	|	0409	|	0409	|
Kraków Główny ..... a.	|	0952	...	|	...	...	|	...	|	1824	...	...	|	2110	|	...	0709	|	0709	|	0709
Warszawa Centralna ..... a.	0950	...	...	1358	...	...	1505	...	1800	...	...	...	2103	...	2215	...	...	0646	...	0646	...
Warszawa Wschodnia ..... a.	1006	...	...	1416	...	...	1526	...	1816	...	...	...	2131	...	2226	...	...	0656	...	0656	...
Gdańsk Główny ..... a.	...	...	...	...	...	...	1808	...	...	...	...	...	...	...	...	...	...	...	...	...	...
Gdynia Główny ..... a.	...	...	...	...	...	...	1833	...	...	...	...	...	...	...	...	...	...	...	...	...	...

A – 🛏 1, 2 cl., ▬ 2 cl. Kraków (**402**) - Bohumín (**407**) - Břeclav (**477**) - Budapest.

B – 🛏 1, 2 cl., ▬ 2 cl., (2) Warszawa (**407**) - Břeclav (**477**) - Bratislava - Budapest.

C – CHOPIN – 🛏 1, 2 cl., ▬ 2 cl. (2) Warszawa - Wien and v.v.

D – 🛏 1, 2 cl. (also ▬ 2 cl. Mar. 11 - Nov. 1) Kraków (**402**) - Bohumín (**407**) - Wien.

E – 🛏 1, 2 cl. (also ▬ 2 cl. Mar. 12 - Nov. 2) Wien (**406**) - Bohumín (**403**) - Kraków.

F – 🛏 1, 2 cl., ▬ 2 cl. Budapest (**476**) - Břeclav (**406**) - Bohumín (**403**) - Kraków.

G – 🛏 1, 2 cl., ▬ 2 cl., (2) Budapest (**476**) - Břeclav (**406**) - Warszawa.

K – JÁN JESENIUS / JESZENSZKY JÁNOS – (12) ✕ Praha - Břeclav - Budapest and v.v. (Table **60**).

M – PORTA MORAVICA – (12) ✕ Warszawa - Katowice - Praha and v.v.

P – 🛏 1, 2 cl., (2) (also ▬ 2 cl. Mar. 11 - Nov. 1) Warszawa (**407**) - Bohumín (**444**) - Praha.

Q – 🛏 1, 2 cl., (2) (also ▬ 2 cl. Mar. 12 - Nov. 2) Praha (**445**) - Bohumín (**406**) - Warszawa.

R – SILESIA – 🛏 1, 2 cl., (2) (also ▬ 2 cl. Mar. 12 - Nov. 2) Kraków (**402**) - Bohumín (**442**) - Praha.

S – SILESIA – 🛏 1, 2 cl., ▬ 2 cl. (2) (also ▬ 2 cl. Mar. 11 - Nov. 1) Praha (**443**) - Bohumín (**403**) - Kraków.

T – JAGELLO – (12) ✕ Warszawa - Katowice - Ostrava and v.v.

V – VARSOVIA – (12) ✕ Warszawa - Katowice - Břeclav - Budapest and v.v.

W – SOBIESKI – (12) ✕ Gdynia - Warszawa - Katowice - Wien and v.v.

X – POLONIA – (12) ✕ Warszawa - Katowice - Wien and v.v.

Y – PRAHA – (12) ✕ Warszawa - Katowice - Praha and v.v.

Z – SLOVAN – (12) ✕ Praha - Břeclav - Budapest and v.v. (Table **60**).

△ – Routeing point for international tickets: Szob.

⊡ – Supplement payable in Poland; Reservation compulsory in Poland.

SC – *SUPERCITY PENDOLINO* train, 🍷 🅁 ⚡; operated by tilting trains.

⚡ – 🅁 with supplement payable.

GREAT BRITAIN

SEE MAP PAGES 92/93

ators: Passenger services are provided by a number of private passenger train companies operating the **National Rail** (www.nationalrail.co.uk) network on lines owned by the British national railway infrastructure company **Network Rail**. The following Network Rail codes are used in the table headings to indicate the operators of trains in each table:

AW	Arriva Trains Wales	GR	Virgin Trains East Coast	ME	Merseyrail	SW	South West Trains
CC	c2c	GW	Great Western Railway	NT	Arriva Rail North	TL	Thameslink Railway
CH	Chiltern Railways	HT	Hull Trains	NY	North Yorkshire Moors Railway	TP	TransPennine Express
CS	Caledonian Sleeper	IL	Island Line	SE	Southeastern	VT	Virgin Trains West Coast
EM	East Midlands Trains	LE	Greater Anglia	SN	Southern	XC	Arriva Cross Country
GC	Grand Central Railway	LM	London Midland	SR	Abellio ScotRail		

ngs: Except where indicated otherwise, timings are valid **May 15 – December 10, 2016.** As service patterns at weekends (especially on ⑦) usually differ greatly from those applying on Mondays to Fridays, the timings in most tables are grouped by days of operation: Ⓐ = Mondays to Fridays; ⚒ = Mondays to Saturdays; ⑥ = Saturdays; ⑦ = Sundays. Track engineering work, affecting journey times, frequently takes place at weekends, so it is advisable to confirm your journey details locally if planning to travel in the period between the late evening of ⑥ and the late afternoon of ⑦. Confirm timings, too, if you intend travelling on public holidays (see page **2**) as there may be alterations to services at these times. Suburban and commuter services are the most likely to be affected; the majority of long-distance and cross-country trains marked Ⓐ and ⚒ run as normal on these dates. No trains (except limited Gatwick and Heathrow Express services) run on **December 25**, with only a limited service on certain routes on **December 26**. In Scotland only trains between Edinburgh/Glasgow and England run on **January 1**.

ces: Unless indicated otherwise (by '2' in the train column or '2nd class' in the table heading), trains convey both **first** (1st) and **standard** (2nd) classes of seated accommodation. Light refreshments (snacks, hot and cold drinks) are available from a **buffet car** or a **mobile trolley service** on board those trains marked 🍸 and ✕: the latter also convey a **restaurant car** or serve meals to passengers at their seats (this service is in some cases available to first-class ticket holders only). Note that catering facilities may not be available for the whole of a train's journey. **Sleeping-cars** (🛏) have one berth per compartment in first class and two in standard class.

rvations: Seats on most long-distance trains and berths in sleeping-cars can be reserved in advance when purchasing travel tickets at rail stations or directly from train operating companies (quote the departure time of the train and your destination). Seat reservation is normally free of charge.

LONDON AIRPORT LINKS — 100

wick ✈

VICK EXPRESS: Daily non-stop rail service from/to **London Victoria**. Journey time: 30 minutes (35 minutes on ⑦).

London Victoria: 0002, 0030, 0500 and every 15 minutes until 2045, 2100⑥, 2115Ⓑ, 2130⑥, 2145Ⓑ, 2200, 2215, 2230, 2300, 2330, 2345.
Gatwick Airport: 0020, 0035, 0050, 0135, 0545, 0600 and every 15 minutes until 2045, then 2-3 trains per hour until 2330⑥, 2335Ⓐ, 2350⑦.

· rail services via Gatwick Airport: London Victoria - Eastbourne Table **102**; Bedford - Brighton Table **103**; London Victoria - Brighton Table **105**; Reading - Gatwick Airport Table **134**.

athrow ✈

THROW EXPRESS: Daily non-stop rail service **London** Paddington - **Heathrow** Terminal 5 and v.v. Journey times: **Heathrow** Central ♣ 15 minutes, Heathrow Terminal 5 21 minutes.

London Paddington: 0510⚒/0625⑦ and every 15 minutes until 2155, then every 30 minutes (15 minutes on ⑤⑦) until 2325.
Heathrow Terminal 5 (5 mins. later from Heathrow Central): 0507⚒/0618⑦ and every 15 minutes until 2212, then every 30 minutes (15 mins. on ⑤⑦) until 2342⚒ / 2348⑦.

THROW CONNECT: Daily rail service **London** Paddington - **Heathrow** Central ♣ and v.v. Journey time 32 minutes.

London Paddington: on ⚒ at 0442, 0513, 0533 and every 30 minutes until 2103 (additional later trains on ⑤⑥); on ⑦ at 0612, 0712, 0812, 0907 and hourly until 2312.
Heathrow Central ♣: on ⚒ at 0529, 0557 and every 30 minutes until 2127 (additional later trains on ⑤⑥); on ⑦ at 0713 and hourly until 2313.

Heathrow Central serves Terminals 1, 2 and 3. A free rail transfer service operates every 15 minutes Heathrow Central - Heathrow **Terminals 4 and 5 and v.v.**

CADILLY LINE: London Underground service between **Kings Cross St Pancras** and all Heathrow terminals via Central London. Journey time: 50-58 minutes.
ıent trains (every 4 - 10 minutes) 0530⚒/0730⑦ - 2300⚒/2330⑦.

AIR LINK 🚌 **Reading** railway station - **Heathrow Airport** (Service **X25**).

Reading: Services call at Heathrow Terminal 5 (±40 minutes), Heathrow Terminal 1 (±50 minutes) and Heathrow Terminal 3 (±56 minutes):
) at 0400, 0500, 0530, 0555, 0608, 0620, 0640, 0700, 0720, 0740, 0800, 0820, 0840, 0905 and every 20 minutes until 1805, 1835, 1905, 1935, 2005, 2035, 2105, 2205, 2305.
) at 0400, 0500, 0545, 0615, 0645 and every 30 minutes until 1915, 1945, 2025, 2055, 2205, 2305.

Heathrow Airport Bus Station: Services call at Heathrow Terminal 5 (±10 minutes) and Reading Railway Station (±50 minutes).
) at 0005, 0500, 0600, 0630, 0657, 0720 and every 20 minutes until 1000, 1015, and every 20 minutes until 1755, 1815, 1835, 1855, 1915, 1940, 2010, 2040, 2110, 2140, 2215, 2305.
) at 0005, 0500, 0600, 0700, 0730 and every 30 minutes until 1900, 1920, 1950, 2020, 2050, 2130, 2200, 2305.

AIR LINK 🚌 **Woking** rail station - **Heathrow Airport** (Service **701**).

Woking: Services call at Heathrow Terminal 5 (±25 - 45 minutes) and Heathrow Central Bus Station (±40 - 60 minutes).
, 0400, 0500, 0600, 0640, 0740, 0845, 0945, 1050, 1135 and hourly until 1735, 1845, 1945, 2045, 2130, 2220.

Heathrow Central Bus Station: Services call at Heathrow Terminal 5 (±15 minutes) and Woking (±45 - 65 minutes).
, 0745, 0845, 0950, 1040, 1140, 1230 and hourly until 1630, 1735, 1835, 1940, 2040, 2130, 2215, 2315.

ton ✈

neslink Railway services Brighton - Gatwick Airport - London St Pancras - Luton Airport Parkway ◧ - Luton ◧ - Bedford: Table **103**.
Midlands Trains services London St Pancras - Luton Airport Parkway ◧ - Luton ◧ - Leicester - Nottingham/Derby/Sheffield: Table **170**.

A frequent shuttle 🚌 service operates between each of the railway stations and the airport terminal.

service **Milton Keynes - Luton Airport** and v.v. (Stagecoach route **99**. Journey 55 minutes) for connections from/to **Birmingham**, **Liverpool** and **Manchester** (Table **150**).

Milton Keynes railway station: on Ⓐ at 0630, 0720, 0750, 0855 and hourly until 1655, 1735, 1805, 1835, 1905, 2010, 2110, 2210; on ⑥ at 0630, 0750, 0855 and hourly until 2055; on ⑦ at · and hourly until 2120.

Luton Airport: on Ⓐ at 0540, 0650, 0750, 0905 and hourly until 1705, 1735, 1805, 1835, 1905, 1935, 2005, 2110; on ⑥ at 0540, 0650, 0750, 0905 and hourly until 2005; on ⑦ at 0820 and y until 2020.

nsted ✈

NSTED EXPRESS: Daily rail service from/to **London** Liverpool St. Journey time ± 45 minutes.

London Liverpool Street: on ⚒ at 0440, 0510 and every 15 minutes until 2255, 2325; on ⑦ at 0440, 0510, 0540, 0610 and every 15 minutes until 2255, 2325.
Stansted Airport: on ⚒ at 0600 and every 15 minutes until 2345, 2359; on ⑦ at 0530, 0600, 0630, 0700 and every 15 minutes until 2345, 2359.

trains call at **Tottenham Hale** for London Underground (Victoria Line) connections to/from Kings Cross, St Pancras, Euston, and Victoria stations.
Cross Country services to/from Cambridge, Peterborough, Leicester and Birmingham see Table **208**.

y ✈

CKLANDS LIGHT RAILWAY from/to **Bank** (interchange with London Underground: Central, Circle, District, Northern, and Waterloo & City Lines).
ıs run every 7-10 minutes 0530 - 0030 on ⚒, 0700 - 2330 on ⑦. Journey time: ± 22 minutes.

er- Airport 🚌 links

Operator: National Express ✆ 08717 81 81 81. www.nationalexpress.com

wick North Terminal - **Heathrow** Central. — Journey 1½ hours
, 0155, 0320, 0440, 0540, 0640, 0700, 0740, 0825, 0840, 0925, 0955 and every 30 tes until 1555, 1655, 1735, 1755Ⓒ, 1805Ⓐ, 1825, 1955Ⓒ, 2005Ⓐ, 2055, 2200, 2255, .

Heathrow Central - **Gatwick** North Terminal.
0015, 0035, 0240, 0340, 0535, 0635, 0720Ⓐ, 0735Ⓒ, 0835, 0905, 0935, 1025, 1035, 1120, 1135, 1235, 1245, 1335, 1340, 1435, 1455, 1535, 1545, 1635, 1720, 1735, 1835, 1920, 1935, 1950, 2035, 2130, 2205, 2305.

wick North Terminal - **Stansted**. — Journey 3 hours
, 0535, 0720Ⓐ, 0735Ⓒ, 0935, 1135, 1335, 1535, 1735, 1935, 2205.

Stansted - Gatwick North Terminal.
0140, 0405, 0605, 0815, 1015, 1215, 1415, 1615Ⓒ, 1625Ⓐ, 1815Ⓒ, 1825Ⓐ, 2115.

throw Central - **Luton**. — Journey 1–1½ hours
, 0550Ⓐ, 0605Ⓒ, 0730, 0750Ⓐ, 0805Ⓒ, 0830, 0930, 1005, 1030, 1130, 1205, 1300, , 1405, 1415, 1530, 1605, 1730, 1805, 1930, 2005, 2130, 2205, 2345.

From **Luton** to **Heathrow** Central.
0215, 0355, 0405, 0450, 0520, 0605, 0625Ⓐ, 0640Ⓒ, 0740Ⓐ, 0755Ⓒ, 0805, 0820Ⓐ, 0850Ⓒ, 1005, 1050, 1130, 1205, 1250, 1400, 1450, 1605, 1650, 1725, 1805, 1850, 1955, 2005, 2205.

throw Central - **Stansted**. — Journey 1½ hours
, 0705, 0905, 1105, 1305, 1505, 1705, 1905, 2105, 2335.

Stansted - Heathrow Central.
0140, 0405, 0605, 0815, 1015, 1215, 1415, 1615Ⓒ, 1625Ⓐ, 1815Ⓒ, 1825Ⓐ, 2115.

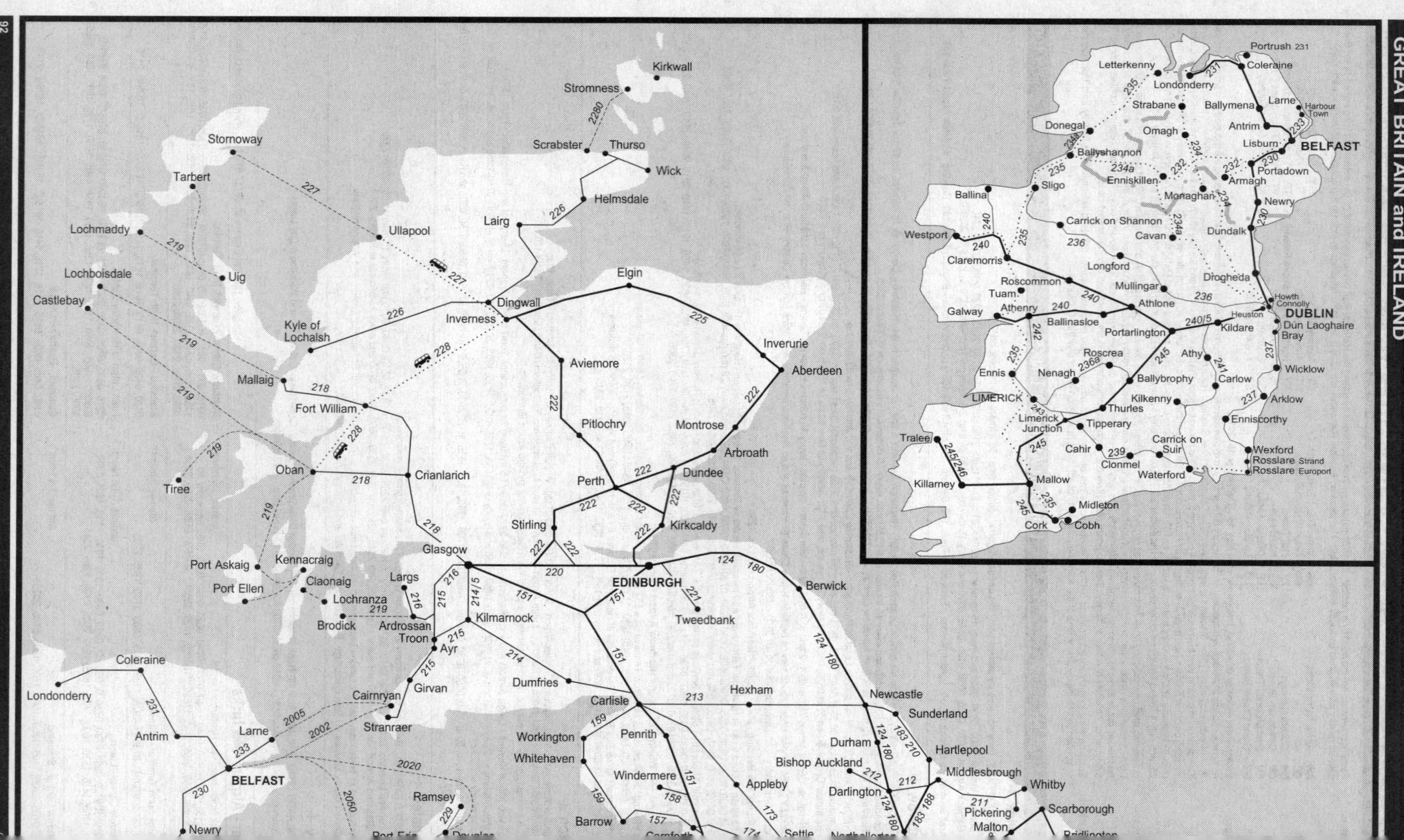
Kirkwall
Stromness
Stornoway
Scrabster
Thurso
Wick
Tarbert
Helmsdale
Lairg
Lochmaddy
Ullapool
Uig
Lochboisdale
Elgin
Castlebay
Dingwall
Inverness
Kyle of Lochalsh
Inverurie
Aberdeen
Aviemore
Mallaig
Fort William
Pitlochry
Montrose
Arbroath
Oban
Crianlarich
Dundee
Perth
Tiree
Stirling
Kirkcaldy
Glasgow
Port Askaig
Kennacraig
Claonaig
Port Ellen
Largs
Lochranza
EDINBURGH
Berwick
Tweedbank
Brodick
Ardrossan
Troon
Kilmarnock
Ayr
Coleraine
Londonderry
Girvan
Dumfries
Cairnryan
Carlisle
Hexham
Newcastle
Stranraer
Antrim
Larne
Workington
Penrith
Sunderland
Whitehaven
Durham
Hartlepool
Bishop Auckland
BELFAST
Middlesbrough
Windermere
Appleby
Darlington
Whitby
Ramsey
Pickering
Scarborough
Barrow
Malton
Newry
Settle
Portrush
Coleraine
Letterkenny
Londonderry
Strabane
Ballymena
Larne
Harbour Town
Donegal
Antrim
Omagh
Lisburn
BELFAST
Ballyshannon
Enniskillen
Portadown
Armagh
Sligo
Monaghan
Ballina
Newry
Carrick on Shannon
Cavan
Dundalk
Westport
Claremorris
Longford
Drogheda
Roscommon
Mullingar
Tuam
Howth
Connolly
Athlone
DUBLIN
Galway
Athenry
Heuston
Ballinasloe
Dún Laoghaire
Bray
Kildare
Portarlington
Roscrea
Athy
Ennis
Nenagh
Carlow
Wicklow
Ballybrophy
LIMERICK
Kilkenny
Arklow
Thurles
Limerick Junction
Tipperary
Enniscorthy
Tralee
Carrick on Suir
Cahir
Wexford
Rosslare Strand
Rosslare Europort
Clonmel
Waterford
Killarney
Mallow
Midleton
Cork
Cobh

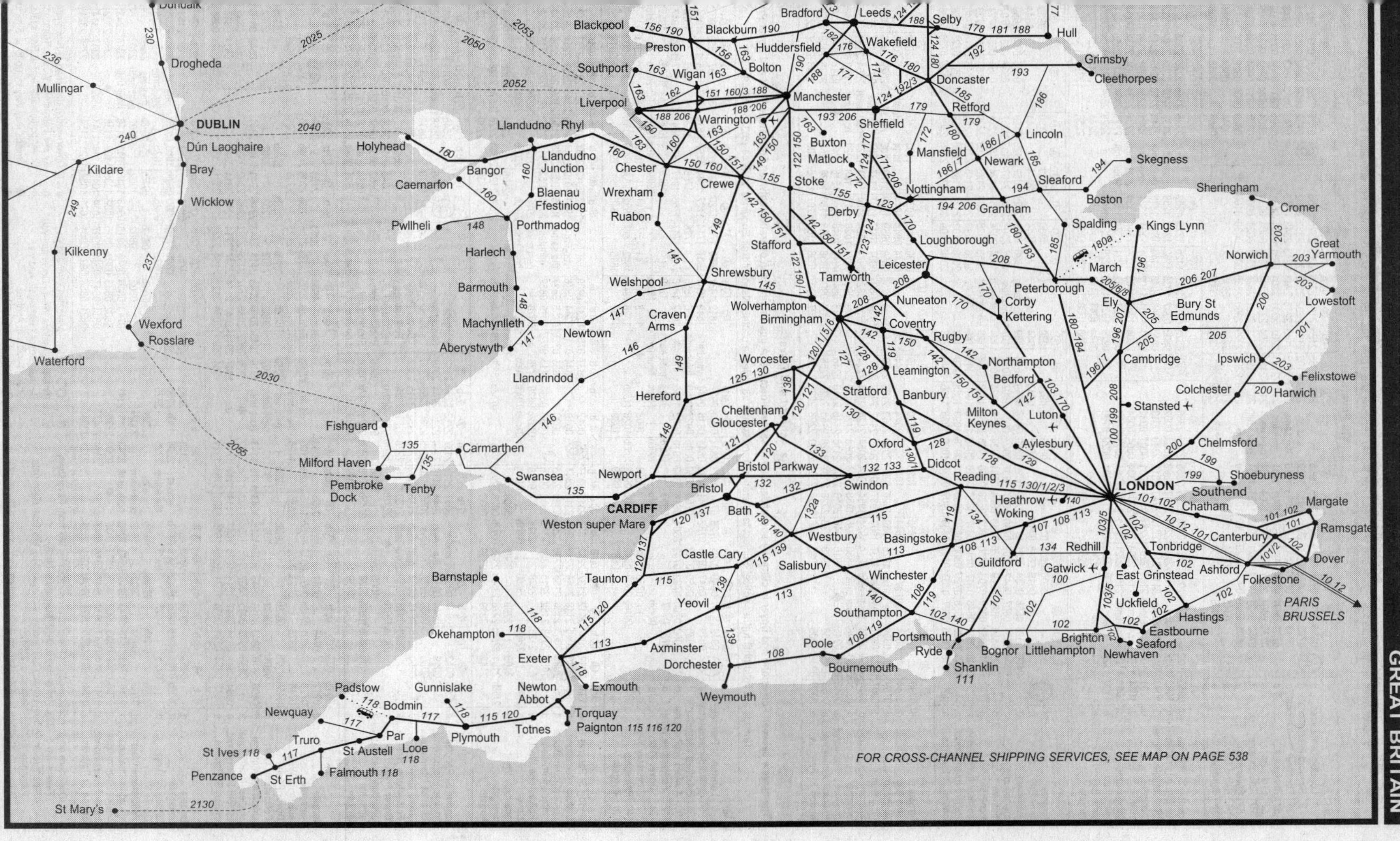
Drogheda
Mullingar
DUBLIN
Dún Laoghaire
Bray
Wicklow
Kildare
Kilkenny
Wexford
Rosslare
Waterford
Blackpool
Preston
Southport
Liverpool
Wigan
Warrington
Bolton
Blackburn
Bradford
Huddersfield
Leeds
Wakefield
Selby
Hull
Grimsby
Cleethorpes
Doncaster
Manchester
Sheffield
Retford
Lincoln
Skegness
Holyhead
Llandudno
Rhyl
Llandudno Junction
Bangor
Caernarfon
Blaenau Ffestiniog
Pwllheli
Porthmadog
Harlech
Barmouth
Machynlleth
Aberystwyth
Newtown
Welshpool
Chester
Wrexham
Ruabon
Crewe
Stoke
Buxton
Matlock
Mansfield
Newark
Nottingham
Sleaford
Boston
Grantham
Derby
Loughborough
Spalding
Kings Lynn
Sheringham
Cromer
Norwich
Great Yarmouth
Lowestoft
Stafford
Shrewsbury
Tamworth
Leicester
March
Peterborough
Ely
Wolverhampton
Birmingham
Nuneaton
Corby
Kettering
Bury St Edmunds
Craven Arms
Coventry
Rugby
Northampton
Cambridge
Ipswich
Felixstowe
Harwich
Llandrindod
Worcester
Leamington
Bedford
Colchester
Stansted
Hereford
Stratford
Banbury
Milton Keynes
Luton
Cheltenham
Gloucester
Aylesbury
Fishguard
Carmarthen
Milford Haven
Pembroke Dock
Tenby
Swansea
Newport
CARDIFF
Bristol Parkway
Bristol
Bath
Swindon
Oxford
Didcot
Reading
Chelmsford
LONDON
Shoeburyness
Southend
Heathrow
Woking
Chatham
Margate
Ramsgate
Canterbury
Dover
Weston super Mare
Westbury
Basingstoke
Redhill
Tonbridge
Castle Cary
Salisbury
Guildford
Gatwick
East Grinstead
Ashford
Folkestone
Barnstaple
Taunton
Winchester
Uckfield
Hastings
PARIS
BRUSSELS
Yeovil
Southampton
Eastbourne
Seaford
Okehampton
Axminster
Poole
Portsmouth
Bognor
Littlehampton
Brighton
Newhaven
Exeter
Dorchester
Bournemouth
Ryde
Shanklin
Exmouth
Weymouth
Padstow
Gunnislake
Newton Abbot
Newquay
Bodmin
Torquay
Paignton
Par
Totnes
Plymouth
Looe
Truro
St Austell
St Ives
Penzance
St Erth
Falmouth
St Mary's
FOR CROSS-CHANNEL SHIPPING SERVICES, SEE MAP ON PAGE 538

101 LONDON - MARGATE via HS1 HIGH SPEED LINE

2nd class

Special fares are payable for high-speed services. For slower services see Table **102**. Service may be subject to alteration from August 28.

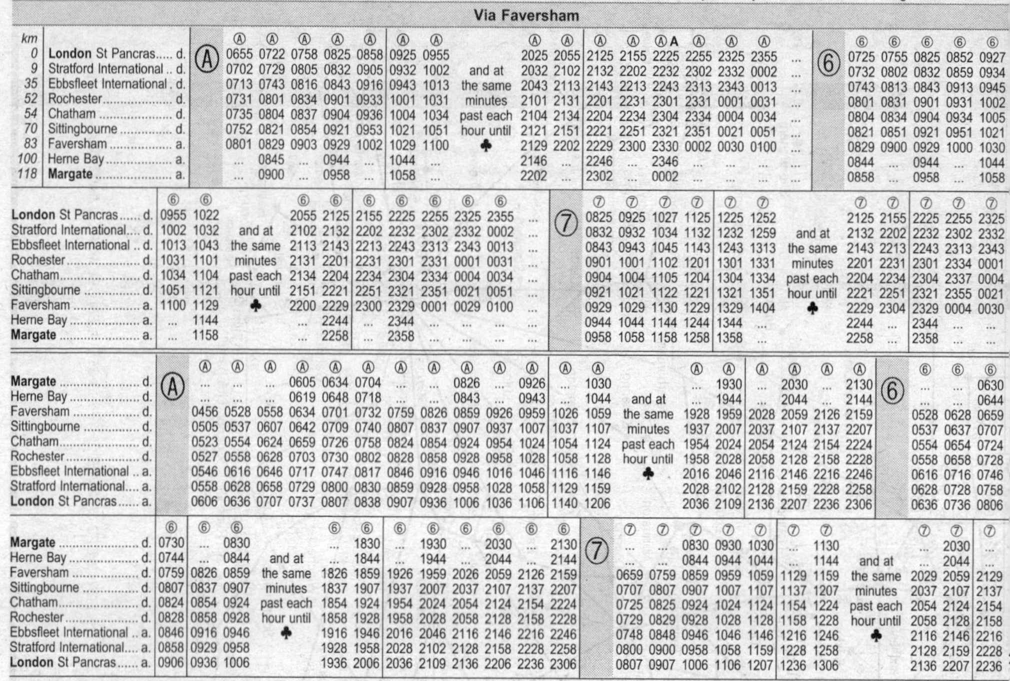

Via Faversham

km		Ⓐ	Ⓐ	Ⓐ	Ⓐ	Ⓐ	Ⓐ	Ⓐ	Ⓐ		Ⓐ	Ⓐ	Ⓐ	Ⓐ	ⒶA	Ⓐ	Ⓐ	Ⓐ		⑥	⑥	⑥	⑥	⑥	⑥
0	**London** St Pancras..... d.		0655	0722	0758	0825	0858	0925	0955		2025	2055	2125	2155	2225	2255	2325	2355	...		0725	0755	0825	0852	0927
9	Stratford International .. d.		0702	0729	0805	0832	0905	0932	1002	and at	2032	2102	2132	2202	2232	2302	2332	0002	...		0732	0802	0832	0859	0934
35	Ebbsfleet International . d.		0713	0743	0816	0843	0916	0943	1013	the same	2043	2113	2143	2213	2243	2313	2343	0013	...		0743	0813	0843	0913	0945
52	Rochester.................. d.		0731	0801	0834	0901	0933	1001	1031	minutes	2101	2131	2201	2231	2301	2331	0001	0031	...		0801	0831	0901	0931	1002
54	Chatham .... d.		0735	0804	0837	0904	0936	1004	1034	past each	2104	2134	2204	2234	2304	2334	0004	0034	...		0804	0834	0904	0934	1005
70	Sittingbourne .... d.		0752	0821	0854	0921	0953	1021	1051	hour until	2121	2151	2221	2251	2321	2351	0021	0051	...		0821	0851	0921	0951	1021
83	Faversham .... a.		0801	0829	0903	0929	1002	1029	1100	♣	2129	2202	2229	2300	2330	0002	0030	0100	...		0829	0900	0929	1000	1030
100	Herne Bay .... a.		...	0845	...	0944	...	1044	...		2146	...	2246	...	2346	...	...	...	...		0844	...	0944	...	1044
118	**Margate** .... a.		...	0900	...	0958	...	1058	...		2202	...	2302	...	0002	...	...	...	...		0858	...	0958	...	1058

	⑥	⑥		⑥	⑥	⑥	⑥	⑥	⑥	⑥		⑦	⑦	⑦	⑦	⑦	⑦	⑦		⑦	⑦	⑦	⑦	⑦
London St Pancras...... d.	0955	1022		2055	2125	2155	2225	2255	2325	2355	...		0825	0925	1027	1125	1225	1252		2125	2155	2225	2255	2325
Stratford International.... d.	1002	1032	and at	2102	2132	2202	2232	2302	2332	0002	...		0832	0932	1034	1132	1232	1259	and at	2132	2202	2232	2302	2332
Ebbsfleet International .. d.	1013	1043	the same	2113	2143	2213	2243	2313	2343	0013	...		0843	0943	1045	1143	1243	1313	the same	2143	2213	2243	2313	2343
Rochester.................. d.	1031	1101	minutes	2131	2201	2231	2301	2331	0001	0031	...		0901	1001	1102	1201	1301	1331	minutes	2201	2231	2301	2334	0001
Chatham.................... d.	1034	1104	past each	2134	2204	2234	2304	2334	0004	0034	...		0904	1004	1105	1204	1304	1334	past each	2204	2234	2304	2337	0004
Sittingbourne .... d.	1051	1121	hour until	2151	2221	2251	2321	2351	0021	0051	...		0921	1021	1122	1221	1321	1351	hour until	2221	2251	2321	2355	0021
Faversham .... a.	1100	1129	♣	2200	2229	2300	2329	0001	0029	0100	...		0929	1029	1130	1229	1329	1404	♣	2229	2304	2329	0004	0030
Herne Bay .... a.	...	1144		...	2244	...	2344	...	...	...	...		0944	1044	1144	1244	1344	...		2244	...	2344	...	...
Margate .... a.	...	1158		...	2258	...	2358	...	...	...	...		0958	1058	1158	1258	1358	...		2258	...	2358	...	...

	Ⓐ	Ⓐ	Ⓐ	Ⓐ	Ⓐ	Ⓐ	Ⓐ	Ⓐ	Ⓐ	Ⓐ	Ⓐ	Ⓐ	Ⓐ	Ⓐ		Ⓐ	Ⓐ	Ⓐ	Ⓐ	Ⓐ	Ⓐ	⑥	⑥	⑥	⑥
Margate .... d.		...	...	...	0605	0634	0704	...	...	0826	...	0926	...	1030		...	1930	...	2030	...	2130		...	...	0630
Herne Bay .... d.		...	...	...	0619	0648	0718	...	...	0843	...	0943	...	1044	and at	...	1944	...	2044	...	2144		...	...	0644
Faversham .... d.		0456	0528	0558	0634	0701	0732	0759	0826	0859	0926	0959	1026	1059	the same	1928	1959	2028	2059	2126	2159		0528	0628	0659
Sittingbourne .... d.		0505	0537	0607	0642	0709	0740	0807	0837	0907	0937	1007	1037	1107	minutes	1937	2007	2037	2107	2137	2207		0537	0637	0707
Chatham.................... d.		0523	0554	0624	0659	0726	0758	0824	0854	0924	0954	1024	1054	1124	past each	1954	2024	2054	2124	2154	2224		0554	0654	0724
Rochester.................. d.		0527	0558	0628	0703	0730	0802	0828	0858	0928	0958	1028	1058	1128	hour until	1958	2028	2058	2128	2158	2228		0558	0658	0728
Ebbsfleet International .. a.		0546	0616	0646	0717	0747	0817	0846	0916	0946	1016	1046	1116	1146	♣	2016	2046	2116	2146	2216	2246		0616	0716	0746
Stratford International.... a.		0558	0628	0658	0729	0800	0830	0859	0928	0958	1028	1058	1129	1159		2028	2102	2128	2159	2228	2258		0628	0728	0758
London St Pancras...... a.		0606	0636	0707	0737	0807	0838	0907	0936	1006	1036	1106	1140	1206		2036	2109	2136	2207	2236	2306		0636	0736	0806

	⑥	⑥	⑥		⑥	⑥	⑥	⑥	⑥	⑥	⑥	⑥	⑦	⑦	⑦	⑦	⑦	⑦	⑦	⑦		⑦	⑦	⑦
Margate .... d.	0730	...	0830		...	1830	...	1930	...	2030	...	2130		...	...	0830	0930	1030	...	1130		...	2030	...
Herne Bay .... d.	0744	...	0844	and at	...	1844	...	1944	...	2044	...	2144		...	...	0844	0944	1044	...	1144	and at	...	2044	...
Faversham .... d.	0759	0826	0859	the same	1826	1859	1926	1959	2026	2059	2126	2159		0659	0759	0859	0959	1059	1129	1159	the same	2029	2059	2129
Sittingbourne .... d.	0807	0837	0907	minutes	1837	1907	1937	2007	2037	2107	2137	2207		0707	0807	0907	1007	1107	1137	1207	minutes	2037	2107	2137
Chatham.................... d.	0824	0854	0924	past each	1854	1924	1954	2024	2054	2124	2154	2224		0725	0825	0924	1024	1124	1154	1224	past each	2054	2124	2154
Rochester.................. d.	0828	0858	0928	hour until	1858	1928	1958	2028	2058	2128	2158	2228		0729	0829	0928	1028	1128	1158	1228	hour until	2058	2128	2158
Ebbsfleet International .. a.	0846	0916	0946	♣	1916	1946	2016	2046	2116	2146	2216	2246		0748	0848	0946	1046	1146	1216	1246	♣	2116	2146	2216
Stratford International.... a.	0858	0929	0958		1928	1958	2028	2102	2128	2158	2228	2258		0800	0900	0958	1058	1159	1228	1258		2128	2159	2228
London St Pancras...... a.	0906	0936	1006		1936	2006	2036	2109	2136	2206	2236	2306		0807	0907	1006	1106	1207	1236	1306		2136	2207	2236

Via Ashford and Dover

The service between Folkestone and Dover is currently suspended due to sea-wall damage. A bus service is in operation between Folkestone West and Dover Pric

Timings are valid until further notice. Subject to alteration from August 28 - please contact National Rail Enquiries ✆ +44 (0)3457 48 49 50.

km		Ⓐ	②–⑤	Ⓐb	Ⓐ	Ⓐ	Ⓐ	Ⓐb	Ⓐ	Ⓐb	Ⓐ	Ⓐb		Ⓐ	Ⓐb	Ⓐ	Ⓐ	Ⓐ	Ⓐb	ⒶD	Ⓐb	Ⓐ	Ⓐb	Ⓐ	Ⓐb
0	**London** St Pancras..... d.		0012	...	0640	0704	0725	0737	0812	0837	0909	0937		1612	1637	1650	1707	1720	1737	1750	1807	1820	1837	1850	1907
9	Stratford International .. d.		0019	...	0647	0711	0732	0744	0819	0844	0916	0944	and at	1619	1644	1657	1714	1727	1744	1757	1814	1827	1845	1857	1914
35	Ebbsfleet International . d.		0030	...	0659	0722	|	0755	0830	0855	0927	0955	the same	1630	1655	|	1726	|	1756	|	1826	|	1856	|	1926
90	Ashford International.... d.		0050	0700	0722	0742	0801	0816	0852	0915	0952	1015	minutes	1652	1718	1726	1747	1756	1817	1826	1847	1856	1917	1926	1947
112	**Folkestone** West...... a.		*0122*	0717	|	|	...	0833	|	0928	|	1028	past each	|	1730	|	...	|	1829	|	1909c	|	1929	|	1959
124	**Dover** Priory .... a.		...	*0749*b	|	|	...	*0905*b	|	*1000*b	|	*1100*b	hour until	|	*1802*b	|	...	|	*1901*b	1946e	*1941*b	|	*2001*b	|	*2031*b
112	Canterbury West .... a.		...	|	0738	0758	...	|	0908	|	1008	|	♠	1708	|	1741	...	1811	|	1842	|	1911	|	1941	...
140	Ramsgate.................. d.		...	*0910*b	0803	0819	...	*0953*b	0928	*1053*b	1028	*1153*b		1728	*1844*b	1802	...	1832	*1953*b	1905	*2030*b	1932	*2056*b	2002	...
149	**Margate** .... a.		...	...	...	0831	...	...	0939	...	1039	...		1739	...	1815	...	1845	...	1918	...	1945	...	2015	...

	Ⓐb	Ⓐ	Ⓐb	Ⓐ	Ⓐb	ⒶB	Ⓐb	ⒶC	Ⓐg	⑥	⑥b	⑥b	⑥b	⑥	⑥b	⑥		⑥b	⑥	⑥b	⑥	⑥b	⑥	⑥b	⑥
London St Pancras...... d.	1937	2012	2037	2112	2137	2212	2237	2312	2337		0012	...	0637	0708	0737	0809		1937	2012	2037	2112	2137	2212	2237	2312
Stratford International.... d.	1944	2019	2044	2119	2144	2219	2244	2319	2344		0019	...	0644	0715	0744	0816	and at	1944	2019	2044	2119	2144	2219	2244	2319
Ebbsfleet International .. d.	1955	2030	2055	2130	2155	2230	2255	2330	2355		0030	...	0655	0726	0755	0827	the same	1955	2030	2055	2130	2155	2230	2255	2330
Ashford International..... d.	2015	2052	2115	2152	2215	2252	2315	2352	0015		0050	0615	0715	0752	0815	0852	minutes	2015	2052	2115	2152	2215	2252	2315	2352
Folkestone West .... a.	2028	|	2128	|	2228	|	2328	|	0028		0122c	0628	0728	|	0828	|	past each	2028	|	2128	|	2228	|	2328	|
Dover Priory.............. a.	*2100*b	|	*2200*b	|	*2300*b	|	*0001*b	|	*0101*g		*0154*b	*0700*b	*0800*b	|	*0900*b	|	hour until	*2100*b	|	*2200*b	|	*2300*b	|	*0001*b	|
Canterbury West........... a.	|	2108	|	2208	|	2308	|	0008	|		...	|	|	0808	|	0908	♠	|	2108	|	2208	|	2308	|	0008
Ramsgate.................... d.	*2156*b	2131	*2256*b	2228	*2356*b	2328	*0047*b	0028	*0202*g		...	*0753*b	*0853*b	0828	*0953*b	0928		*2153*b	2128	*2253*b	2228	*2353*b	2328	*0047*b	0028
Margate .... a.	...	2142	...	2239	...	2339	...	0039	...		...	...	...	0839	...	0939		...	2139	...	2239	...	2339	...	0039

	⑦	⑦	⑦b	⑦b	⑦		⑦b	⑦	⑦b	⑦	⑦b	⑦
London St Pancras...... d.		0012	...	0837	0909		2037	2112	2137	2212	2237	2312
Stratford International.... d.		0019	...	0844	0916	and at	2044	2119	2144	2219	2244	2319
Ebbsfleet International .. d.		0030	...	0855	0927	the same	2055	2130	2155	2230	2255	2330
Ashford International..... d.		0050	0816	0915	0952	minutes	2115	2152	2215	2252	2315	2352
Folkestone West .... a.		...	0828	0928	|	past each	2130	|	2228	|	2328	|
Dover Priory.............. a.		...	*0901*b	*1001*b	|	hour until	*2201*b	|	*2301*b	|	*0001*b	|
Canterbury West........... a.		...	|	|	1008	♠	|	2208	|	2308	|	0008
Ramsgate.................... d.		...	*0953*b	*1053*b	1028		*2253*b	2228	*2353*b	2328	*0047*b	0028
Margate .... a.		...	...	...	1039		...	2239	...	2339	...	0039

	Ⓐ	Ⓐ	Ⓐb	Ⓐ	Ⓐb	ⒶD	Ⓐb	Ⓐ
Margate .... d.		...	...	0546	...	0614	...	0646
Ramsgate.......................... d.		0455	...	0558	*0450*b	0629	*0520*b	0658
Canterbury West............. d.		0518	...	0618	|	0649	|	0718
Dover Priory................. d.		|	*0524*b	|	*0557*b	0542h	*0627*b	|
Folkestone West .... d.		|	0558	|	0631	|	0701	|
Ashford Intl .... d.		0543	0613	0636	0646	0707	0716	0736
Ebbsfleet Intl.................... a.		0602	0632	0655	0705	|	0735	|
Stratford Intl..................... a.		0614	0644	0707	0717	0735	0747	0804
London St Pancras....... a.		0621	0651	0714	0725	0743	0754	0813

	ⒶD	Ⓐ	Ⓐ	Ⓐb	Ⓐ	Ⓐ	Ⓐb	Ⓐ	Ⓐb	Ⓐ		Ⓐb	Ⓐ	Ⓐb	Ⓐ	Ⓐb	Ⓐ	Ⓐb	Ⓐ	Ⓐb	Ⓐ		⑥	⑥	⑥b
Margate .... d.	0712	...	0749	...	0851	...	...	0953	...	1053		...	1853	...	1953	...	2053	...	2153	...	2253	...		...	...
Ramsgate .... d.	0728	...	0801	*0742*b	0903	0932	*0805*b	1005	*0936*b	1105	and at	*1736*b	1905	*1836*b	2005	*1938*b	2105	*2038*b	2205	*2138*b	2305	...		0505	...
Canterbury West........... d.	0748	...	0825	|	0923	0952	|	1025	|	1125	the same	|	1925	|	2025	|	2125	|	2225	|	2325	...		0525	...
Dover Priory.............. d.	0645h	*0727*b	|	*0828*b	|	|	*0928*b	|	*1028*b	†	minutes	*1828*b	|	*1928*b	|	*2028*b	|	*2128*b	|	*2228*b	|	...		|	*0528*b
Folkestone West .... d.	|	0801	|	0902	|	|	1002	|	1102	|	past each	1902	|	2002	|	2102	|	2202	|	2302	|	...		|	0602
Ashford International..... d.	0806	0816	0843	0916	0943	1010	1016	1043	1116	1143	hour until	1916	1943	2016	2043	2116	2143	2216	2243	2316	2341	...		0543	0616
Ebbsfleet International .. a.	|	0835	0902	0935	1002	|	1035	1102	1135	1202	♠	1935	2002	2035	2102	2135	2202	2235	2302	2335	...	...		0602	0635
Stratford International.... a.	0834	0847	0914	0947	1014	1038	1047	1114	1147	1214	d	1947	2014	2047	2114	2147	2214	2247	2314	2347	...	...		0614	0647
London St Pancras...... a.	0842	0854	0921	0954	1021	1046	1055	1121	1154	1221		1954	2021	2054	2121	2154	2221	2254	2321	2354	...	...		0621	0654

	⑥b	⑥	⑥b	⑥	⑥b	⑥	⑥b		⑥	⑥b	⑥		⑦	⑦	⑦	⑦	⑦b	⑦	⑦b	⑦	⑦b		⑦b	⑦
Margate .... d.	...	0653	...	0753	...	0853	...		2153	...	2253	...		...	...	0753	...	0853	...	0953	...		...	2153
Ramsgate .... d.	*0536*b	0705	*0636*b	0805	*0736*b	0905	*0836*b	and at	2205	*2136*b	2305	...		...	...	0805	*0736*b	0905	*0836*b	1005	*0936*b	and at	*2036*b	2205
Canterbury West........... d.	|	0725	|	0825	|	0925	|	the same	2225	|	2325	...		...	...	0825	|	0925	|	1025	|	the same	|	2225
Dover Priory.............. d.	*0628*b	|	*0728*b	|	*0828*b	|	*0928*b	minutes	|	*2228*b	|	...		...	*0728*b	|	*0828*b	|	*0928*b	|	*1028*b	minutes	*2128*b	|
Folkestone West .... d.	0702	|	0802	|	0902	|	1002	past each	|	2302	|	...		...	0802	|	0902	|	1002	|	1102	past each	2202	|
Ashford International..... d.	0716	0743	0816	0843	0916	0943	1016	hour until	2243	2316	2341	...		0743	0816	0843	0916	0943	1016	1043	1116	hour until	2216	2243
Ebbsfleet International .. a.	0735	0802	0835	0902	0935	1002	1035	♠	2302	2335	...	...		0802	0835	0902	0935	1002	1035	1102	1135	♠	2235	2302
Stratford International.... a.	0747	0814	0847	0914	0947	1014	1047		2314	2347	...	...		0814	0847	0914	0947	1014	1047	1114	1147		2247	2314
London St Pancras...... a.	0754	0821	0855	0921	0954	1021	1055		2321	2354	...	...		0821	0854	0921	0954	1021	1054	1121	1154		2254	2321

A – Departure on ② from London St Pancras is operated by 🚌 from Faversham (Faversham d. 2336, Herne Bay d. 0012, Margate a. 0043).
B – Departure on ② from London St Pancras is operated by 🚌 from Ramsgate (Ramsgate d. 2335, Margate a. 2354).
C – Subject to alteration from Ashford on ①②. Timings vary, check with operator.
D – 2 London - Margate/Dover and v.v.
b – By 🚌 Folkestone West - Dover and v.v. By train Dover - Ramsgate and v.v.
c – Change trains at Ashford.
d – Ramsgate d. 1526 (not 1536).
e – Dover portion detached at Ramsgate.
g – By 🚌 Folkestone West to Ramsgate
h – Dover portion attached at Ramsgate.
♣ – Timings may vary by up to ± 3 minu
♠ – Timings may vary by up to ± 4 minu

Services marked ⊠ are valid until August 27. For service from August 28 please contact National Rail Enquires ✆ +44 (0)3457 48 49 50.

off-peak journey time in hours and minutes
AD DOWN ↓ READ UP ↑

Journey times may be extended during peak hours on Ⓐ (0600 - 0900 and 1600 - 1900) and also at weekends.
The longest journey time by any train is noted in the table heading.

DON VICTORIA - RAMSGATE – SEE NOTE ⊠ ABOVE

Longest journey: 2 hours 10 minutes SE

Down		Station		Up
0h00	↓	d.**London** Victoria.....a.	↑	1h57
0h17		d.Bromley South ....d.		1h40
0h47	↓	d.Rochester...............d.	↑	1h12
0h50		d.Chatham.................d.		1h10
1h09	↓	d.Sittingbourne..........d.	↑	0h50
1h21		d.Faversham..............d.		0h42
1h36	↓	d.Herne Bay ....d.	↑	0h26
1h49		d.Margate ....d.		0h10
1h59		a.**Ramsgate** ....d.		0h00

From London Victoria: on Ⓐ at 0007②–⑥ **f**, 0522, 0552, 0622 **g**, 0652 **g**, 0736, 0837 and hourly until 1537, 1637 **g**, 1636 **c**, 1657, 1727, 1730 **c**, 1752 **c m**, 1757 **m**, 1814 **c**, 1827, 1844 **c m**, 1857, 1937, 2037, 2137, 2207 **f g**, 2237 **f**, 2307 **f**; on ⑥ at 0707 **g**, 0737 and hourly until 2237, 2307; on ⑦ at 0007, 0745 and hourly until 2245, 2304 **h**, 2345 **h**.

From Ramsgate: on Ⓐ at 0432, 0506, 0539, 0608, 0629 **m c**, 0632, 0651 **m c**, 0703, 0708 **m c**, 0719 **b**, 0754 and hourly until 1354, 1450, 1545, 1648, 1748, 1848, 1954, 2050, 2154, 2310 **h**; on ⑥ at 0430, 0554 and hourly until 2154, 2310 **h**; on ⑦ at 0705, and hourly until 2105, 2120 **g**, 2235.

b – To London Blackfriars, not Victoria.
c – From/to London Bridge and London Cannon Street, not Victoria.
f – On Tuesday night/Wednesday mornings does not call at Herne Bay or Margate.
h – To Faversham.
g – Change at Faversham.
m – To/from Margate.

DON VICTORIA - DOVER – SEE NOTE ⊠ ABOVE

Longest journey: 2 hours 10 minutes SE

Down		Station		Up
0h00	↓	d.**London** Victoria.....a.	↑	2h02
0h17		d.Bromley South ......d.		1h43
0h47	↓	d.Rochester ....d.	↑	1h17
0h50		d.Chatham.................d.		1h15
1h09	↓	d.Sittingbourne..........d.	↑	0h58
1h21		d.Faversham..............d.		0h47
1h37	↓	d.Canterbury East.....d.	↑	0h27
1h58		a.**Dover** Priory ....d.		0h00

From London Victoria: on Ⓐ at 0552 **g**, 0622, 0652, 0734, 0807, 0834 and at the same minutes past each hour until 1407, 1437 **g**, 1507, 1537 **g**, 1607, 1637, 1655 **b**, 1727, 1757, 1827, 1857, 1927 **b**, 1937 **g**, 2007, 2034 **e**, 2107, 2134 **e**, 2207; on ⑥ at 0522, 0634, 0707, 0734 and at the same minutes past each hour until 1934, 2007, 2034 **e**, 2107, 2134 **e**, 2207; on ⑦ at 0745, 0804 **e**, 0845, 0904 **e** and at the same minutes past each hour until 1804 **e**,1845 then hourly until 2145.

From Dover Priory: on Ⓐ at 0430, 0500 **g**, 0545 **b**, 0605 **g**, 0628 **g**, 0702, 0735, 0820, 0852, 0920, 0952 and at the same minutes past each hour until 1520, 1551, 1620, 1651 **g**, 1720, 1751, 1820, 1851, 1920, 2005, 2105, 2205; on ⑥ at 0520, 0620, 0652 and at the same minutes past each hour until 1920, 2005, 2105, 2205; on ⑦ at 0705, 0805, 0904 **e**, 0905 and at the same minutes past each hour until 2005, 2105, 2235 **g**.

rom/to London Blackfriars, not Victoria.
e – To/from Canterbury East.
g – Change at Faversham.

DON CHARING CROSS - CANTERBURY WEST – SEE NOTE ⊠ ABOVE

Longest journey: 1 hour 55 minutes SE

Down		Station		Up
0h00	↓	d.**London** C Cross ...a.	↑	1h46
0h03		d.**London** Waterloo ‡ a.		1h42
|	↓	d.**London** Bridge ......a.	↑	|
0h32		d.Sevenoaks..............d.		1h13
0h40	↓	d.Tonbridge ....d.	↑	1h04
1h20		a.Ashford Int'l ....d.		0h27
1h38	↓	a.**Canterbury** West...d.	↑	0h00

From London Charing Cross: on Ⓐ at 0530 **d**, 0636 **c**, 0710, 0740, 0813, 0913, 1010 and hourly until 1610, 1640, 1714, 1739, 1806 **c**, 1841, 1910, 2010, 2110, 2210 **e**, 2310 **e**, 2340 **e**; on ⑥ at 0606, 0706, 0810 and hourly until 2210, 2310, 2340; on ⑦ at 0810, 0910 and hourly until 2110, 2210.

From Canterbury West: on Ⓐ at 0600, 0634 **c**, 0703, 0736, 0838, 0939, 1045 and hourly until 1545, 1641, 1741, 1806, 1838, 1941, 2041, 2141; on ⑥ at 0542, 0639, 0739, 0845 and hourly until 1845, 1941, 2041, 2141; on ⑦ at 0742, 0842, 0945 and hourly until 1845, 1942, 2042, 2142.

☛ Additional Services are available with a change at Ashford.

To/from London Cannon Street (also calls at London Bridge; see map on page 30).
Change trains at Ashford.
e – On ① change trains at Ashford for replacement 🚌 to Canterbury.
‡ – London Waterloo East.

DON CHARING CROSS - DOVER – SEE NOTE ⊠ ABOVE

Longest journey: 2 hours 06 minutes SE

Down		Station		Up
0h00	↓	d.**London** C Cross ...a.	↑	2h02
0h03		d.**London** Waterloo ‡ a.		1h58
|	↓	d.**London** Bridge ......a.	↑	|
0h32		d.Sevenoaks..............d.		1h28
0h40	↓	d.Tonbridge ....d.	↑	1h16
1h20		d.Ashford Int'l ....d.		0h39
1h40	↓	d.Folkstone West ✣ ..d.	↑	0h12
		a.**Dover** Priory ✣ ......d.		0h00

From London Charing Cross: on Ⓐ at 0530, 0710, 0740, 0833, 0940 and hourly until 1340, 1410, 1440, 1510, 1540, 1610, 1640 **d**, 1657, 1724 **c**, 1739 **d**, 1745 **c**, 1803, 1820 **d**, 1832 **c**, 1910, 1940, 2040, 2140, 2240, 2340; on ⑥ at 0740 and hourly until 2340; on ⑦ at 0840 and hourly until 2240.

From Folkestone West: on Ⓐ at 0443 **c**, 0544, 0612 **c**, 0643, 0717 **c**, 0738, 0813, 0838, 0915, 0940, 1015 and hourly until 1415, 1515, 1613, 1640, 1712, 1740, 1813, 1840, 1913, 2015, 2115, 2215; on ⑥ at 0509, 0609, 0715 and hourly until 2215; on ⑦ at 0815 and hourly until 2115.

c – From/to London Cannon Street (also calls at London Bridge; see map on page 30).
d – Change trains at Ashford.
‡ – London Waterloo East.

The service between Folkestone and Dover is currently suspended due to seawall damage. A replacement bus service is in operation between Folkestone West and Dover Priory.

DON VICTORIA - ASHFORD INTERNATIONAL – SEE NOTE ⊠ ABOVE

Longest journey: 1 hours 40 minutes SE

Down		Station		Up
0h00	↓	d.**London** Victoria.....a.	↑	1h29
0h17		d.Bromley South ....d.		1h14
0h28	↓	d.Swanley.................d.	↑	1h03
0h52		d.West Malling..........d.		0h42
1h03	↓	d.Maidstone East......d.	↑	0h30
1h09		d.Bearsted ....d.		0h25
1h31	↓	a.**Ashford** Int'l ....d.	↑	0h00

From London Victoria: on Ⓐ at 0022②–⑤, 0555, 0637, 0707, 0752, 0822, 0852 and every 30 minutes until 1622, 1652, 1712, 1742, 1747 **b**, 1818, 1842, 1904 **b**, 1922, 1952, 2022, 2052, 2122, 2152, 2222, 2252, 2322; on ⑥ at 0022, 0622, 0722, 0752 and every 30 minutes until 2322; on ⑦ at 0022, 0736 and hourly until 2336.

From Ashford International: on Ⓐ at 0514, 0532 **b**, 0547, 0601, 0617, 0624 **b**, 0640, 0656, 0711, 0748, 0830, 0910, 0930, 1010, 1038 and at the same minutes past each hour until 1538, 1602, 1638, 1702, 1738, 1802, 1838, 1900, 1938, 2002, 2038, 2102, 2132, 2232; on ⑥ at 0532, 0610, 0638 and at the same minutes past each hour until 2038, 2110, 2132, 2232; on ⑦ at 0646 and hourly until 2146.

b – From/to Blackfriars, not Victoria.

NDON CHARING CROSS - HASTINGS – SEE NOTE ⊠ ABOVE

Longest journey: 1 hour 53 minutes SE

Down		Station		Up
0h00	↓	d.**London** C Cross ...a.	↑	1h43
0h03		d.**London** Waterloo ‡ a.		1h39
|	↓	d.**London** Bridge ......a.	↑	|
0h34		d.Sevenoaks..............d.		1h09
0h43	↓	d.Tonbridge ....d.	↑	1h00
0h55		d.Tunbridge Wells.....d.		0h49
1h33	↓	d.Battle.....................d.	↑	0h16
1h45		a.**Hastings** ....d.		0h00

From London Charing Cross: on Ⓐ at 0630, 0715, 0746 **c**, 0817, 0842 **c**, 0914 **c**, 0945 and every 30 minutes until 1545, 1615, 1620*, 1643, 1702 **c**, 1717*, 1737 **c***, 1759*, 1828 **c***, 1845, 1904 **c**, 1915, 1945, 2015, 2045, 2145 ◐, 2245 ◐, 2356 ◐; on ⑥ at 0745, 0815, 0845, and every 30 minutes until 2015, 2045, 2145, 2245, 2356; on ⑦ at 0825, 0855, and every 30 minutes until 1925, 1955, 2025, 2125, 2225, 2325.

From Hastings: on Ⓐ at 0517, 0537 **c**, 0548 **c**, 0604*, 0620*, 0628*, 0643 **c***, 0703*, 0726 **c***, 0744 **c**, 0804*, 0814, 0847, 0929, 0950, 1031, 1050 and at the same minutes past each hour until 1531, 1545 **c**, 1619, 1645, 1719, 1750, 1819, 1846, 1950, 2050, 2150 ◐; on ⑥ at 0550, 0620, 0650, 0720, 0750, 0820, 0850, 0931, 0950 and at the same minutes past each hour until 1650, 1720, 1750, 1820, 1850, 1950, 2050, 2150; on ⑦ at 0720, 0750, 0831, 0850 and at the same minutes past each hour until 1831, 1850, 1950, 2050, 2150.

From/to London Cannon Street (also calls at London Bridge; see map on page 30).
Train subject to alteration on ①②. Timings vary, please check with operator.
* – Does not call at Sevenoaks and Tonbridge. Frequent trains call at these stations.
‡ – London Waterloo East.

NDON VICTORIA - EASTBOURNE

Longest journey: 1 hour 44 minutes SN

Down		Station		Up
0h00	↓	d.**London** Victoria.....a.	↑	1h26
0h16		d.East Croydon.........d.		1h09
0h33	↓	d.Gatwick Airport ......d.	↑	0h53
0h50		d.Haywards Heath ....d.		0h34
1h06	↓	d.Lewes....................d.	↑	0h19
1h27		a.**Eastbourne**...........d.		0h00

From London Victoria: on Ⓐ at 0005②–⑤, 0532, 0647, 0747, 0817, 0847, 0917 and every 30 minutes until 1647, 1722 **b**, 1727, 1757, 1823 **b**, 1846, 1917, 1947, 2017, 2047, 2117, 2147, 2247; on ⑥ at 0005, 0747 and every 30 minutes until 2147, 2247; on ⑦ at 0005, 0847 and hourly until 2247.

From Eastbourne: on Ⓐ at 0508, 0543 **b**, 0621 **b**, 0654 **g**, 0712 **g b**, 0731 **g**, 0757, 0818, 0853, 0931, 0955, 1035, 1055 and at the same minutes past each hour until 1435, 1453, 1535, 1553, 1635, 1653, 1733, 1755, 1831, 1859, 1931, 2031, 2131, 2216; on ⑥ at 0503, 0628, 0655, 0735, 0755 and at the same minutes past each hour until 1935, 2035, 2135, 2218; on ⑦ at 0658, 0755, 0859 and hourly

From/to London Bridge, not Victoria.
g – Does not call at Gatwick Airport.

HFORD - HASTINGS - EASTBOURNE - BRIGHTON

Longest journey: 2 hours 07 minutes SN

Down		Station		Up
0h00	↓	d.**Ashford** Int'l ....a.	↑	1h46
0h23		d.Rye..........................d.		1h24
0h42	↓	d.**Hastings** ....d.	↑	1h04
0h52		d.Bexhill.....................d.		0h52
1h07	↓	a.**Eastbourne**...........d.	↑	0h37
1h15		d.**Eastbourne**...........a.		0h32
1h35	↓	d.Lewes.....................d.	↑	0h12
1h48		a.**Brighton** ....d.		0h00

From Ashford International: on Ⓐ at 0614, 0715, 0833, 0853 **h**, 0933 and hourly until 1933, 1959 **h**, 2033, 2133, 2234 **h**; on ⑥ at 0615, 0733 and hourly until 2133, 2234 **h**; on ⑦ at 0811, 0916 and hourly until 2116, 2234 **h**.

From Brighton: on Ⓐ at 0521 **h**, 0546 **h**, 0619 **h**, 0615, 0732 and hourly until 1532, 1632, 1709 **h**, 1730, 1832, 1932, 2030; on ⑥ at 0520 **h**, 0618 **h**, 0632 and hourly until 2032; on ⑦ at 0722 **h**, 0814 **h**, 0812 and hourly until 2012.

h – Additional service Ashford - Hastings and v.v.

☛ Additional local services are available Brighton/Lewes - Eastbourne - Hastings v.v.

102 LONDON - THE SOUTH and SOUTH EAST

Typical off-peak journey time in hours and minutes
READ DOWN ↓ READ UP ↑

Journey times may be extended during peak hours on Ⓐ (0600 - 0900 and 1600 - 1900) and also at weekends.
The longest journey time by any train is noted in the table heading.

LONDON BRIDGE - UCKFIELD

Longest journey: 1 hour 19 minutes

km					
0	0h00	↓	d.**London** Bridge ......a.	↑	1h15
16	0h16	↓	d.East Croydon ....d.	↑	0h59
32	0h29	↓	d.Oxted.....................d.	↑	0h44
57	0h55		d.Eridge △ ....d.		0h17
70	1h01	↓	d.Crowborough ....d.	↑	0h12
74	1h15		a.**Uckfield** ....d.		0h00

From London Bridge: on Ⓐ at 0602, 0638, 0703, 0755, 0902, 1008 and hourly until 1508, 1538, 1608, 1638, 1708, 1806, 1908, 2104, 2204, 2304; on ⑥ at 0608 and hourly until 2208, 2304.

From Uckfield: on Ⓐ at 0516, 0540, 0630, 0705, 0731, 0801, 0833. 0934 and hourly until 1534, 1633, 1732, 1832, 1900, 1933, 2034, 2134, 2234; on ⑥ at 0634 and hourly until 2234.

On ⑦ services run Oxted - Uckfield and v.v. only. Connections available from / to London Victoria (see East Grinstead Table). From O 0937⑦ and hourly until 2237⑦. From Uckfield at 1034⑦ and hourly until 2234⑦.

△ – **Spa Valley Railway** (🚂 Eridge - Tunbridge Wells West: *8 km*). ✆ 01892 537715. www.spavalleyrailway.co.uk

LONDON VICTORIA - EAST GRINSTEAD

Longest journey: 60 minutes

km					
0	0h00	↓	d.**London** Victoria.....a.	↑	0h56
17	0h17		d.East Croydon ....d.		0h37
33	0h37	↓	d.Oxted.....................d.	↑	0h16
48	0h54		a.**East Grinstead** ▽.d.		0h00

From London Victoria: on Ⓐ at 0526, 0547, 0624, 0654, 0710, 0718 **b**, 0732, 0750 **b**, 0824 **b**, 0853 and every 30 minutes until 1713 **b**, 1723, 1744 **b**, 1753, 1817 **b**, 1823, 1847 **b**, 1853, and every 30 minutes until 2323; on ⑥ at 0523, 0623, 0653 and every 30 m until 2253, 2324; on ⑦ at 0747, 0853, 0923, 0953 and every 30 minutes until 2053, 2153, 2236.

From East Grinstead: on Ⓐ at 0545 **b**, 0555, 0613 **b**, 0632, 0640 **b**, 0702, 0716 **b**, 0733, 0749 **b**, 0807 and every 30 minutes until 2254; on ⑥ at 0637 and every 30 minutes until 2237, 2257; on ⑦ at 0820, 0912, and every 30 minutes until 2012, 2112, 2212, 2

b – From / to London Bridge (not Victoria). ▽ – **Bluebell Railway** (🚂 East Grinstead - Sheffield Park: *18 km*). ✆ 01825 720800. www.bluebell-railway.com

LONDON VICTORIA - LITTLEHAMPTON

Longest journey: 1 hour 47 minutes

km					
0	0h00	↓	d.**London** Victoria.....a.	↑	1h42
17	0h16	↓	d.East Croydon ....a.	↑	1h25
43	0h33	↓	d.Gatwick Airport ......a.	↑	1h09
61	0h50	↓	d.Haywards Heath ....a.	↑	0h54
82	1h06	↓	d.Hove ....a.	↑	0h35
96	1h21	↓	d.Worthing ....d.	↑	0h21
114	1h41	↓	a.**Littlehampton** ....d.	↑	0h00

From London Victoria: on Ⓐ at 0747, 0817, 0847 and every 30 minutes until 1617, 1657 **bg**, 1718, 1740 **bg**, 1746, 1810 **bg**, 18 1846, 1917, 1947, 2017, 2047, 2147; on ⑥ at 0747, 0817, 0847 and every 30 minutes until 2017, 2047, 2147; on ⑦ at 0817 and until 2117.

From Littlehampton: on Ⓐ at 0552 **b**, 0629 **b**, 0640 **g**, 0700 **g**, 0729, 0814, 0851, 0914, 0947, 1014, 1051 and at the same minut past each hour until1514, 1549, 1614, 1651, 1714, 1751, 1814, 1914, 2014, 2114; on ⑥ at 0545, 0614, 0651 and at the same mi past each hour until 1814, 1914, 2014, 2114; on ⑦ at 0715 and hourly until 2015.

b – From / to London Bridge (not Victoria). **g** – Does not call at Gatwick Airport.

LONDON VICTORIA - BOGNOR REGIS

Longest journey: 1 hour 57 minutes

km					
0	0h00	↓	d.**London** Victoria.....a.	↑	1h50
17	0h16		d.East Croydon ....d.		1h30
43	0h37	↓	d.Gatwick Airport ......d.	↑	1h08
61	1h03		d.Horsham..................d.		0h50
94	1h30	↓	d.Arundel ....d.	↑	0h16
110	1h40		d.Barnham ....d.		0h07
116	1h46	↓	a.**Bognor Regis** ....d.	↑	0h00

From London Victoria: on Ⓐ at 0602, 0803, 0832, 0902, 0932, 1006 and every 30 minutes until 1636, 1702 **g**, 1734 **g**, 1803 **g**, 1 1902, 1932, 2002, 2032, 2117 **k**, 2217 **k**; on ⑥ at 0736, 0806, 0836 and every 30 minutes until 1836, 1902, 1932, 2002, 2032, 21 2217 **k**; on ⑦ at 0702 and hourly until 2202.

From Bognor Regis: on Ⓐ at 0605, 0640 **g**, 0717 **g**, 0755, 0826, 0856, 0930, 0956 and at the same minutes past each hour unti 1456, 1527, 1556, 1630, 1656, 1730, 1756, 1833 **k**, 1940 **k**, 2040 **k**; on ⑥ at 0630, 0656 and at the same minutes past each hour 1756, 1833 **k**, 1940 **k**, 2040 **k**; on ⑦ at 0652, 0759 and hourly until 2159.

g – Does not call at Gatwick Airport. **k** – Does not call at Arundel and Horsham.

SEAFORD - BRIGHTON

Longest journey: 42 minutes

km					
0	0h00	↓	d.**Seaford** ....a.	↑	0h36
4	0h05		d.Newhaven Harbour..d.		0h30
5	0h07	↓	d.Newhaven Town ....d.	↑	0h28
15	0h19		d.Lewes......................d.		0h18
22	0h26	↓	d.Falmer.....................d.	↑	0h09
28	0h35		a.**Brighton** ....d.		0h00

From Seaford: on Ⓐ at 0509, 0544, 0627, 0717, 0733, 0759, 0855, 0925, 0954 and at the same minutes past each hour until 1654, 1757, 1824, 1841, 1859, 1917, 1937, 1957, 2028, 2057, 2128, 2157, 2220, 2257, 2325; on ⑥ at 0505, 0628, 0657, 0725, 0757 and same minutes past each hour until 2057, 2128, 2157, 2220, 2257, 2325; on ⑦ at 0757 and every 30 minutes until 2127, 2153, 2227,

From Brighton: on Ⓐ at 0545, 0639, 0652, 0717, 0740, 0810, 0845, 0910 and every 30 minutes until 1710, 1745, 1802, 1822, 1838, 1940, 2010, 2040, 2104, 2140, 2204, 2234, 2336; on ⑥ at 0552, 0610, 0640 and every 30 minutes until 2040, 2104, 2140, 2204, 2336; on ⑦ at 0715, 0749, 0817, 0849, 0917, 0947 and every 30 minutes until 2147, 2209, 2239.

BRIGHTON - PORTSMOUTH HARBOUR

Longest journey: 1 hour 49 minutes

km	⚒	⑦				⚒	⑦
0	0h00	0h00	↓	d.**Brighton**..............d.	↑	1h19	1h44
2	0h04	0h10		d.Hove ....d.		1h15	1h40
16	0h22	0h31	↓	d.Worthing ....d.	↑	0h57	1h19
35	0h39	0h54		d.Barnham ....d.		0h39	0h57
45	0h47	1h02	↓	d.Chichester...............d.	↑	0h31	0h43
59	1h02	1h23		d.Havant ....d.		0h17	0h22
71	1h14	1h37	↓	a.**Portsmouth** S ▽.d.	↑	0h04	0h04
72	1h18	1h41		a.**Portsmouth** H .....d.		0h00	0h00

From Brighton: on Ⓐ at 0553, 0635, 0715, 0737, 0803, 0904, 1003 and hourly until 1503, 1603 **p**, 1705, 1800, 1900 **p**, 2103, 2133, 2203; on ⑥ at 0601, 0703 and hourly until 1903, 1956, 2103, 2133, 2203; on ⑦ at 0715 **r**, 0719, 0820 **r**, 083 hourly until 2030, 2125, 2146 **r**.

From Portsmouth Harbour: on Ⓐ at 0528, 0604, 0701, 0720, 0829 and hourly until 1629, 1640, 1729, 1827, 1932 **p**, 2 2115 **pt**, 2215 **t**, 2240 **t**; on ⑥ at 0629, 0648, 0729 and hourly until 1929, 2028, 2111 **t**, 2215 **t**, 2244 **t**; on ⑦ at 0714 and hourly until 1914, 2011, 2114, 2144.

p – To / from Portsmouth & Southsea only. **t** – Runs in ⑦ (slower) timings.
r – Runs in ⚒ (faster) timings. ▽ – Portsmouth and Southsea.

BRIGHTON - SOUTHAMPTON CENTRAL

Longest journey: 2 hours 1 minute

km	⚒	⑦				⚒	⑦
0	0h00	0h00	↓	d.**Brighton**..............d.	↑	1h45	1h50
2	0h04	0h04		d.Hove ....d.		1h41	1h46
16	0h22	0h25	↓	d.Worthing ....d.	↑	1h23	1h25
35	0h44	0h48		d.Barnham ....d.		1h00	1h03
45	0h52	0h56	↓	d.Chichester...............d.	↑	0h52	0h54
59	1h04	1h08		d.Havant ....d.		0h38	0h42
75	1h23	1h25	↓	d.Fareham ....d.	↑	0h23	0h24
98	1h46	1h56		a.**Southampton** C ..d.		0h00	0h00

From Brighton: on Ⓐ at 0512, 0530, 0627, 0705, 0730, 0833, 0859, 0933 and hourly until 1633, 1702, 1733, 1828, 1930, on ⑥ at 0515, 0527, 0634, 0733, 0833, 0900, 0933 and hourly until 1633, 1700, 1733, 1833, 1929, 2030; on ⑦ at 0800 and hourly until 2100.

From Southampton Central: on Ⓐ at 0610, 0733, 0832 and hourly until 1332, 1426, 1434, 1532 and hourly until 2032, on ⑥ at 0632 and hourly until 1332, 1426, 1434, 1532 and hourly until 2032, 2113; on ⑦ at 0730, 0827, 0831, 0930 and hourly until 1930, 2029, 2130.

LONDON WATERLOO - READING

Longest journey: 1 hour 35 minutes

km					
0	0h00	↓	d.**London** Waterloo ..a.	↑	1h22
16	0h16		d.Richmond ....d.		1h03
18	0h20	↓	d.Twickenham.............d.	↑	0h58
30	0h33		d.Staines ....d.		0h36
46	0h53	↓	d.Ascot ....d.	↑	0h28
70	1h20		a.**Reading** ....d.		0h00

From London Waterloo: on Ⓐ at 0505, 0550 and every 30 minutes until 2350; on ⑥ at 0505, 0550 and every 30 minutes until 2 on ⑦ at 0709, 0809 and every 30 minutes until 2339.

From Reading: on Ⓐ at 0542 and every 30 minutes until 2242, 2312; on ⑥ at 0542 and every 30 minutes until 2242, 2312; on ⑦ at 0754 0824, 0854 and every 30 minutes until 2154, 2224, 2254.

LONDON WATERLOO - WINDSOR

Longest journey: 1 hour 09 minutes

km					
0	0h00	↓	d.**London** Waterloo ..a.	↑	0h56
16	0h20	↓	d.Richmond ....d.	↑	0h34
18	0h24	↓	d.Twickenham.............d.	↑	0h30
30	0h39		d.Staines ....d.		0h15
41	0h53	↓	a.**Windsor** ▷ ....d.	↑	0h00

From London Waterloo: on Ⓐ at 0558 and every 30 minutes until 2328; on ⑥ at 0558 and every 30 minutes until 2328; on ⑦ at 0744, 0825, 0844 and at the same minutes past each hour until 1944, 2025, 2044, 2144, 2244.

From Windsor and Eton Riverside: on Ⓐ at 0553, 0623 and every 30 minutes until 2223, 2253; on ⑥ at 0553, 0623 and every 30 mi until 2223, 2253; on ⑦ at 0701, 0801, 0901, 0934 and at the same minutes past each hour until 2101, 2201, 2301.

▷ – Windsor and Eton Riverside.

BEDFORD - LUTON ✈ - LONDON - GATWICK ✈ - BRIGHTON 103

Additional trains are available London Bridge - Brighton and v.v.

Other services: Bedford - Luton Airport - London St Pancras see Table **170**; London Victoria - Gatwick Airport - Brighton see Table **105**; London Victoria - Gatwick Airport *Gatwick Express* see Table **100**.

(A)	Ⓐ	Ⓐ	Ⓐ	Ⓐ	Ⓐ	Ⓐ	Ⓐ	Ⓐ	Ⓐ	Ⓐ	Ⓐ	Ⓐ	Ⓐ	Ⓐ	Ⓐ	Ⓐ	Ⓐ	Ⓐ	Ⓐ	Ⓐ	Ⓐ	Ⓐ		Ⓐ	Ⓐ	Ⓐ
Bedford d.	0040	0140	0220	0240	0320	0340	0416	0446	0518	0544	0600	0618	0654	0658	0730	0734	0748	0804	0824	0840	0854	0910	and at	1440	1454	1510
Luton d.	0104	0204	0244	0304	0344	0404	0440	0510	0542	0604	0624	0638	0714	0722	0750	0758	0812	0828	0848	0904	0918	0934	the same	1504	1518	1534
Luton Airport ✈ d.	0107	0207	0247	0307	0347	0407	0443	0513	0544	|	0627	0641	|	0725	|	0800	0815	0831	0851	0907	0921	0937	minutes	1507	1521	1537
St Albans City d.	0119	0219	0259	0319	0359	0419	0455	0525	0556	0616	0638	0652	0726	0738	0802	0812	0828	0843	0903	0918	0933	0948	past	1518	1533	1548
London St Pancras d.	0154	0254	0324	0354	0424	0454	0524	0552	0620	0634	0656	0714	0744	0756	0820	0832	0848	0904	0924	0940	0954	1010	each	1540	1554	1610
London Blackfriars d.	0205	0305	0335	0405	0435	0505	0535	0603	0633	0646	0708	0728	0756	0808	0832	0844	0900	0918	0938	0952	1008	1022	hour	1552	1608	1622
East Croydon d.	0236	0336	0406	0436	0506	0532	0602	0632	0702	0716	0736	0758	0826	0838	0858	0912	0931	0949	1004	1019	1034	1049	until	1619	1634	1651
Gatwick Airport ✈ d.	0256	0356	0426	0457	0527	0548	0618	0648	0717	0732	0754	0814	0842	0854	0914	0928	0958	1005	1034	1035	1102	1105		1635	1702	1707
Haywards Heath d.	...	...	...	0512	0542	0602	0634	0704	0731	0748	0808	0830	0858	...	0928	0945	...	1019	...	1049	...	1119	♣	1649	...	1721
Brighton a.	...	...	...	0534	0602	0622	0654	0726	0750	0808	0823	0850	0918	...	0948	1005	...	1039	...	1109	...	1139		1709	...	1743

	Ⓐ	Ⓐ	Ⓐ	Ⓐ	Ⓐ	Ⓐ	Ⓐ	Ⓐ	Ⓐ	Ⓐ	Ⓐ	Ⓐ	Ⓐ	Ⓐ	Ⓐ	Ⓐ	Ⓐ	Ⓐ	Ⓐ	Ⓐ	Ⓐ	Ⓐ	Ⓐ	Ⓐ	(6) ⑥	⑥	⑥	⑥
ord d.	1524	1550	1608	1626	1640	1708	1720	1734	1800	1810	1824	1840	1854	1908	1940	2010	2040	2110	2140	2152	2222	2240	2310	2340	0040	0140	0220	0240
d.	1548	1610	1632	1650	1704	1732	1744	1758	1819	1834	1848	1904	1918	1932	2004	2034	2104	2134	2204	2216	2246	2306	2334	0004	0104	0204	0244	0304
Airport ✈ d.	1551	1613	1635	1652	1707	1735	1747	1801	1822	1837	1851	1907	1921	1935	2007	2037	2107	2137	2207	2219	2249	2309	2337	0007	0107	0207	0247	0307
ans City d.	1603	1624	1647	1704	1718	1748	1758	1812	1834	1848	1903	1918	1933	1946	2018	2048	2118	2148	2218	2230	2300	2321	2349	0019	0119	0219	0259	0319
on St Pancras d.	1624	1646	1708	1728	1740	1808	1818	1834	1854	1910	1924	1940	1954	2010	2040	2110	2140	2210	2240	2254	2324	2354	0024	0054	0154	0254	0324	0354
on Blackfriars d.	1638	1658	1720	1740	1752	1820	1830	1846	1908	1922	1938	1952	2008	2022	2052	2122	2152	2222	2252	2308	2336	0005	0035	0105	0205	0305	0335	0405
Croydon d.	1704	1726	1748	1809	1825	1850	1901	1918	1939	1951	2010	2021	2039	2051	2121	2151	2221	2251	2321	2339	0006	0032	0106	0136	0236	0336	0406	0436
ck Airport ✈ d.	1729	1742	1814	1824	1852	1906	1927	1935	2003	2007	2026	2037	2054	2107	2137	2207	2237	2307	2340	2357	0026	0054	0127	0156	0256	0356	0426	0456
ards Heath d.	...	1758	1832	1840	...	1920	...	1949	...	2021	...	2051	2110	2121	2153	2221	2253	2321	2355	0011	0043	...	...	...	...	...	...	...
ton a.	...	1819	1852	1903	...	1942	...	2010	...	2041	...	2111	2124	2141	2213	2241	2313	2341	0015	0031	0103	...	...	...	...	...	...	...

	⑥	⑥	⑥	⑥	⑥	⑥	⑥	⑥	⑥	⑥		⑥	⑥	⑥	⑥	⑥	⑥	⑥	⑥		⑥	⑥	⑥	⑥	⑥	⑥	⑥	⑥
ord d.	0320	0340	0412	0450	0520	0540	0554	0610	0624	0640	and at	1754	1810	1824	1840	1854	1910	1940	2010	...	2040	2110	2140	2152	2222	2240	2310	2340
d.	0344	0404	0436	0514	0544	0604	0618	0634	0648	0704	the same	1818	1834	1848	1904	1918	1934	2004	2034	...	2104	2134	2204	2216	2246	2306	2334	0004
Airport ✈ d.	0347	0407	0439	0517	0547	0607	0621	0637	0651	0707	minutes	1821	1837	1851	1907	1921	1937	2007	2037	...	2107	2137	2207	2219	2249	2309	2337	0007
ans City d.	0359	0419	0451	0528	0558	0618	0633	0648	0703	0718	past	1833	1848	1903	1918	1933	1948	2018	2048	...	2118	2148	2218	2230	2300	2321	2349	0019
on St Pancras d.	0424	0454	0524	0554	0624	0640	0654	0710	0724	0740	each	1854	1910	1924	1940	1954	2010	2040	2110	...	2140	2210	2240	2254	2324	2354	0024	0054
on Blackfriars d.	0435	0505	0535	0608	0638	0652	0708	0722	0738	0752	hour	1908	1922	1938	1952	2008	2022	2052	2122	...	2152	2222	2252	2308	2336	0005	0035	0105
Croydon d.	0506	0532	0602	0634	0704	0719	0734	0749	0804	0819	until	1934	1951	2004	2021	2034	2051	2121	2151	...	2221	2251	2321	2339	0004	0032	0106	0136
ick Airport ✈ d.	0526	0548	0618	0650	0720	0735	0802	0805	0834	0835		2002	2007	2034	2037	2102	2107	2137	2207	...	2237	2307	2337	2357	0024	0054	0126	0156
ards Heath d.	0543	0603	0633	0703	0733	0751	...	0819	...	0849	♣	...	2021	...	2051	2116	2121	2153	2221	...	2253	2321	2353	0011	0041	0109	...	...
ton a.	0606	0624	0654	0724	0754	0811	...	0839	...	0909		...	2041	...	2111	2132	2141	2213	2241	...	2313	2341	0013	0031	0101	0129	...	...

(7)	⑦	⑦	⑦	⑦	⑦	⑦	⑦	⑦	⑦		⑦	⑦	⑦	⑦	⑦	⑦	⑦	⑦	⑦	⑦	⑦	⑦	⑦	⑦	⑦	⑦	⑦
ord d.	...	0558	0628	0658	0728	0750	0806	0820	0836	and at	1636	1650	1706	1720	1736	1806	1836	1906	1936	2006	2028	2058	2128	2158	2228	2300	2340
d.	...	0622	0652	0722	0752	0814	0830	0844	0900	the same	1700	1714	1730	1744	1800	1830	1900	1930	2000	2030	2052	2122	2152	2222	2252	2324	0004
Airport ✈ d.	...	0625	0655	0725	0755	0817	0833	0847	0903	minutes	1703	1717	1733	1747	1803	1833	1903	1933	2003	2033	2055	2125	2155	2225	2255	2327	0007
ans City d.	...	0637	0707	0737	0807	0829	0845	0859	0915	past	1715	1729	1745	1759	1815	1845	1915	1945	2015	2045	2107	2137	2207	2237	2307	2339	0019
on St Pancras d.	...	0710	0740	0810	0840	0854	0910	0924	0940	each	1740	1754	1810	1824	1840	1910	1940	2010	2040	2110	2140	2210	2240	2310	2340	0014	0054
on Blackfriars d.	0652	0722	0752	0822	0852	0906	0922	0936	0952	hour	1752	1806	1822	1836	1852	1922	1952	2022	2052	2122	2152	2222	2252	2322	2352	0025	0105
Croydon d.	0723	0753	0821	0856	0926	0939	0956	1009	1026	until	1826	1839	1856	1909	1926	1956	2026	2056	2126	2156	2226	2256	2326	2357	0029	0059	0136
ick Airport ✈ d.	0744	0818	0842	0912	0942	0956	1012	1026	1042		1842	1856	1912	1926	1942	2012	2042	2112	2142	2212	2242	2312	2342	0020	0049	0119	0156
ards Heath d.	0758	0834	0856	0926	0956	...	1028	...	1056	♣	1856	...	1928	...	1956	2028	2056	2128	2156	2228	2256	2328	2356	0036	...	...	...
nton a.	0818	0854	0916	0948	1016	...	1048	...	1116		1916	...	1948	...	2016	2048	2116	2148	2216	2248	2316	2348	0016	0056	...	...	...

(A)	Ⓐ	Ⓐ	Ⓐ	Ⓐ	Ⓐ	Ⓐ	Ⓐ	Ⓐ	Ⓐ	Ⓐ	Ⓐ	Ⓐ	Ⓐ	Ⓐ	Ⓐ	Ⓐ	Ⓐ	Ⓐ	Ⓐ	Ⓐ	Ⓐ	Ⓐ	Ⓐ	Ⓐ	Ⓐ	Ⓐ	
nton d.	...	...	...	...	...	...	...	0510	0530	0544	0606	0619	0657	0722	0748	0800	0818	0833	0905	0935	1005	1035	...	1105	...	1135	and at
vards Heath d.	...	...	...	...	...	...	...	0531	0551	0603	0629	0642	0720	0746	0809	0822	0839	0856	0926	0956	1026	1056	...	1126	...	1156	the same
ick Airport ✈ d.	0121	0221	0321	0351	0421	0455	0525	0548	0608	0617	0643	0700	0738	0801	0823	0839	0853	0910	0940	1010	1040	1110	1108	1140	1138	1210	minutes
Croydon a.	0139	0239	0339	0409	0439	0517	0546	0602	0622	0639	0657	0723	0753	0822	0838	0853	0907	0924	0954	1024	1054	1124	1137	1154	1207	1224	past
don Blackfriars a.	0208	0308	0408	0438	0508	0541	0611	0628	0650	0707	0725	0752	0820	0849	0909	0921	0938	0953	1021	1051	1121	1151	1207	1221	1237	1251	each
don St Pancras a.	0219	0319	0419	1449	0518	0555	0621	0640	0702	0718	0736	0804	0832	0900	0920	0932	0948	1003	1033	1103	1133	1203	1218	1233	1248	1303	hour
bans City a.	0253	0353	0453	0513	0553	0617	0643	0702	0722	0741	0756	0825	0851	0919	0940	0951	1008	1024	1054	1125	1154	1224	1238	1255	1309	1324	until
Airport ✈ a.	0305	0405	0505	0525	0605	0629	0655	0714	0734	0754	0807	0837	0902	0928	0951	1002	1020	1037	1106	1137	1206	1237	1250	1306	1320	1337	
a.	0308	0408	0508	0528	0608	0632	0658	0717	0737	0757	0810	0840	0905	0931	0954	1005	1023	1040	1109	1140	1209	1240	1253	1309	1323	1340	♣
ford a.	0335	0435	0535	0557	0637	0700	0724	0743	0803	0823	0837	0905	0925	0957	1020	1025	1053	1105	1135	1205	1235	1305	1319	1335	1349	1405	

	Ⓐ	Ⓐ	Ⓐ	Ⓐ	Ⓐ	Ⓐ	Ⓐ	Ⓐ	Ⓐ	Ⓐ	Ⓐ	Ⓐ	Ⓐ	Ⓐ	Ⓐ	Ⓐ	Ⓐ	Ⓐ	Ⓐ	Ⓐ	Ⓐ	Ⓐ	Ⓐ	Ⓐ	Ⓐ	Ⓐ	Ⓐ	Ⓐ	Ⓐ
nton d.	...	1505	...	1535	...	1602	...	1635	...	1701	...	1735	...	1805	1835	...	1905	...	1933	...	2003	...	2033	2105	2133	2205	2233	2305	2337
vards Heath d.	...	1526	...	1556	...	1623	...	1656	...	1722	...	1756	...	1826	1856	...	1926	...	1954	...	2026	...	2054	2126	2154	2226	2254	2326	2358
vick Airport ✈ d.	1508	1540	1538	1610	1608	1640	1638	1710	1710	1740	1745	1810	1815	1840	1910	1917	1940	1947	2010	2018	2040	2047	2110	2140	2210	2240	2310	2340	0015
Croydon a.	1537	1554	1607	1624	1637	1655	1703	1724	1738	1754	1802	1824	1831	1855	1924	1932	1954	2004	2025	2034	2054	2104	2125	2154	2225	2254	2325	2356	0037
don Blackfriars a.	1607	1621	1637	1650	1707	1721	1735	1751	1809	1821	1835	1850	1905	1921	1951	2007	2021	2037	2051	2107	2121	2137	2151	2221	2251	2321	2351	0022	0103
don St Pancras a.	1617	1631	1647	1701	1717	1731	1745	1801	1819	1831	1845	1901	1915	1933	2003	2018	2033	2048	2103	2118	2133	2148	2203	2231	2301	2331	0001	0033	0114
lbans City a.	1638	1649	1709	1719	1735	1749	1805	1819	1941	1849	1906	1919	1935	1955	2025	2038	2055	2109	2125	2138	2155	2209	2225	2256	2326	2356	0026	0107	0147
Airport ✈ a.	1651	|	1720	|	1747	|	1818	|	1853	|	1918	|	1948	2007	2037	2050	2107	2120	2137	2150	2207	2220	2237	2308	2338	0008	0038	0119	0159
a.	1654	1702	1723	1732	1750	1802	1821	1832	1856	1902	1921	1932	1951	2010	2040	2053	2110	2123	2140	2153	2210	2223	2240	2311	2341	0011	0041	0122	0202
ford a.	1719	1723	1749	1753	1813	1823	1846	1853	1926	1923	1948	1953	2013	2035	2105	2119	2135	2150	2205	2219	2235	2249	2305	2338	0008	0038	0108	0149	0229

(6)	⑥	⑥	⑥	⑥	⑥	⑥	⑥	⑥	⑥	⑥		⑥	⑥	⑥	⑥	⑥	⑥	⑥	⑥		⑥	⑥	⑥	⑥	⑥	⑥	⑥
hton d.	...	...	...	...	...	...	0533	0605	0602	0635	...	0632	0705	0737	0734	0805	...	0835	...	and at	2005	...	2033	...	2105	2133	2205
vards Heath d.	...	...	...	...	...	...	0554	0626	0620	0656	...	0647	0726	0756	0751	0826	...	0856	...	the same	2026	...	2054	...	2126	2154	2226
vick Airport ✈ d.	0121	0221	0321	0421	0455	0525	0610	0640	0638	0710	...	0708	0740	0810	0808	0840	0838	0910	0908	minutes	2040	2038	2110	2108	2140	2210	2240
Croydon a.	0139	0239	0339	0439	0517	0546	0625	0654	0707	0724	...	0737	0754	0824	0837	0854	0907	0924	0937	past	2054	2107	2125	2137	2154	2225	2254
don Blackfriars a.	0208	0308	0408	0508	0541	0612	0651	0721	0737	0751	...	0807	0821	0851	0907	0921	0937	0951	1007	each	2121	2137	2151	2207	2221	2251	2321
don St Pancras a.	0219	0319	0419	0518	0551	0623	0703	0733	0748	0803	...	0818	0833	0903	0918	0933	0948	1003	1018	hour	2133	2148	2203	2218	2233	2301	2331
lbans City a.	0253	0353	0453	0553	0625	0645	0725	0755	0808	0825	...	0838	0855	0925	0938	0955	1009	1025	1038	until	2155	2208	2225	2238	2258	2326	2356
n Airport ✈ a.	0305	0405	0505	0605	0637	0657	0736	0807	0820	0837	...	0850	0907	0937	0950	1007	1020	1037	1050		2207	2220	2237	2250	2310	2338	0008
n a.	0308	0408	0508	0608	0640	0700	0739	0810	0823	0840	...	0853	0910	0940	0953	1010	1023	1040	1053	♣	2210	2223	2240	2253	2313	2341	0011
ford a.	0335	0435	0535	0635	0709	0725	0805	0835	0849	0905	...	0919	0935	1005	1019	1035	1049	1105	1119		2235	2249	2305	2319	2340	0008	0038

	⑥	⑥	⑥	(7) ⑦	⑦	⑦	⑦	⑦	⑦	⑦	⑦	⑦	⑦		⑦	⑦	⑦	⑦	⑦	⑦	⑦	⑦	⑦	⑦	⑦	⑦	⑦
hton d.	2233	2305	2337	0010	0606	0636	0704	0736	0804	...	0844	...	0914	and at	...	1844	...	1914	1944	2014	2044	2114	2144	2214	2244	2312	2342
wards Heath d.	2254	2326	2358	0026	0624	0654	0724	0754	0824	...	0903	...	0933	the same	...	1903	...	1933	2003	2033	2103	2133	2203	2233	2303	2331	0002
wick Airport ✈ d.	2310	2340	0015	0039	0638	0708	0738	0808	0838	0859	0917	0929	0947	minutes	1859	1917	1929	1947	2017	2047	2117	2147	2217	2247	2317	2345	0015
Croydon a.	2325	2356	0037	0100	0656	0727	0756	0826	0855	0917	0932	0943	1003	past	1916	1932	1943	2003	2032	2103	2132	2203	2232	2303	2332	0001	0037
don Blackfriars a.	2351	0022	0103	0128	0724	0754	0824	0854	0924	0949	1007	1019	1037	each	1949	2007	2019	2037	2107	2137	2207	2237	2307	2337	0005	0031	0103
don St Pancras a.	0001	0033	0114	0139	0734	0804	0834	0904	0934	1004	1018	1032	1048	hour	2002	2018	2032	2048	2118	2148	2218	2248	2318	2348	0018	0042	0114
lbans City a.	0026	0107	0147	0213	0807	0837	0907	0937	1007	1037	1042	1056	1112	until	2026	2042	2056	2112	2142	2212	2242	2321	2351	0021	0051	0117	0147
n Airport ✈ a.	0038	0119	0159	0225	0819	0849	0919	0949	1019	1049	1054	1108	1124		2038	2054	2108	2124	2154	2224	2254	2333	0003	0033	0103	0129	0159
n a.	0041	0122	0202	0228	0822	0852	0922	0952	1022	1052	1057	1111	1127	♣	2041	2057	2111	2127	2157	2227	2257	2336	0006	0036	0106	0132	0202
ford a.	0108	0149	0229	0255	0849	0919	0949	1019	1049	1119	1124	1138	1154		2108	2124	2138	2154	2225	2254	2324	0003	0033	0103	0133	0159	0229

- Timings may vary by up to 5 minutes.

105 LONDON - GATWICK ✈ - BRIGHTON

For other services London - Gatwick Airport - Brighton and v.v. see Tables **100** and **103**.

km		Ⓐ	②–⑤	Ⓐ	Ⓐ	Ⓐ	Ⓐ	Ⓐ	Ⓐ	Ⓐ	Ⓐ	Ⓐ	Ⓐ	Ⓐ	Ⓐ	Ⓐ	Ⓐ	Ⓐ	Ⓐ	Ⓐ	Ⓐ		Ⓐ	Ⓐ	Ⓐ	Ⓐ
0	**London** Victoria.....d.		0005	0100	0400	0452	0606	0615	0617	0630	0715	0736	0800	0807	0821	0830	0838	0900	0920	0930	0950	and at the same	1550	1600	1620	1630
17	East Croydon.........d.		0027	0124	0427	0519	0623	|	0634	|	|	0752	|	0823	0841	|	0854	|	0936	|	1006	minutes past	1606	|	1636	|
43	Gatwick Airport ✈..d.		0045	0150	0452	0548	|	0646	0706	0704	0750	0808	0833	|	0857	0902	0910	0932	0952	1002	|	each hour until	|	1632	1652	1702
82	**Brighton** ....a.		0118	0225	0523	0626	0705	0716	0741	0735	0820	0838	0857	0912	0938	0926	0942	0954	1017	1024	1046	✣	1646	1654	1720	1732

	Ⓐ	Ⓐ	Ⓐ	Ⓐ	Ⓐ	Ⓐ	Ⓐ	Ⓐ	Ⓐ	Ⓐ		Ⓐ	Ⓐ	Ⓐ	Ⓐ	Ⓐ	Ⓐ		⑥	⑥	⑥	⑥	⑥		⑥	⑥
London Victoria .....d.	1730	1742	1800	1815	1830	1844	1900	1920	1930	1950	and at the same	2200	2220	2230	2250	2307	2332	...		0005	0100	0400	0502	...	0532	0600
East Croydon..........d.	|	|	|	|	1847	|	|	1936	|	2007	minutes past	|	2238	|	2306	2324	2350	...		0027	0124	0424	0524	...	0548	|
Gatwick Airport ✈...d.	1807	1815	1837	1847	|	1917	1932	1952	2002	2023	each hour until	2232	2254	2302	2322	|	0015	...		0045	0151	0449	0553	...	0622	0632
Brighton ....a.	1839	1848	1912	1921	1939	1952	2002	2019	2027	2049	✣	2257	2319	2327	2346	0003	0053	...		0118	0226	0517	0630	...	0706	0702

	⑥	⑥	⑥	⑥		⑥	⑥	⑥	⑥	⑥		⑥	⑥	⑥	⑥	⑥		⑦	⑦	⑦	⑦	⑦	⑦		⑦	⑦
London Victoria .....d.	0700	0720	0730	0750	and at the same	2100	2120	2130	2150	2200	...	2220	2230	2250	2307	2332	...		0005	0100	0400	0502	0547	...	0632	0726
East Croydon..........d.	|	0736	|	0806	minutes past	|	2136	|	2206	|	...	2236	|	2306	2324	2349	...		0027	0126	0426	0525	0610	...	0655	0748
Gatwick Airport ✈...d.	0732	0751	0802	|	each hour until	2132	2152	2202	2222	2232	...	2252	2302	2322	|	0013	...		0046	0154	0453	0550	0633	...	0723	0813
Brighton ....a.	0757	0816	0824	0846	✣	2157	2221	2227	2247	2259	...	2318	2327	2346	0003	0050	...		0117	0225	0522	0620	0709	...	0759	0851

	⑦	⑦	⑦		⑦	⑦	⑦	⑦		⑦	
London Victoria .....d.	0907	0927	0932	and at the same	2032	2106	2127	2227	...	2332	...
East Croydon..........d.	0923	0942	0949	minutes past	2049	2123	2142	2242	...	2353	...
Gatwick Airport ✈...d.	0939	1006	|	each hour until	|	2139	2207	2306	...	0015	...
Brighton ....a.	1003	1043	1024	✣	2124	2203	2243	2345	...	0052	...

		Ⓐ	Ⓐ		Ⓐ	Ⓐ	Ⓐ	Ⓐ	Ⓐ	Ⓐ
Brighton ....d.	Ⓐ	0350	0523	...	0630	0640	0646	0712	0729	0744
Gatwick Airport ✈..........d.		0505	0555	...	0704	0719	|	0749	0802	0820
East Croydon..................d.		0532	0610	...	|	|	0739	|	|	|
London Victoria..........a.		0552	0628	...	0741	0754	0758	0823	0839	0855

	Ⓐ	Ⓐ	Ⓐ	Ⓐ	Ⓐ	Ⓐ		Ⓐ	Ⓐ	Ⓐ	Ⓐ	Ⓐ		Ⓐ	Ⓐ	Ⓐ	Ⓐ	Ⓐ	Ⓐ	Ⓐ	Ⓐ	Ⓐ	Ⓐ	Ⓐ	Ⓐ	Ⓐ
Brighton ....d.	0830	0846	0918	0928	0948	0958	and at the same	1418	1428	1448	1458	1518	...	1526	1548	1618	1648	1720	1728	1750	1758	1818	1828	1848	1915	1928
Gatwick Airport ✈...d.	0906	0914	0945	0953	1015	|	minutes past	1445	1453	1515	|	1545	...	1553	1615	1645	1716	1748	1753	1817	1823	1850	1853	1921	1945	1953
East Croydon..........d.	|	0929	|	1008	|	1038	each hour until	|	1508	|	1538	|	...	1608	|	|	|	|	1808	|	1838	|	1909	|	|	2008
London Victoria .....a.	0939	0949	1016	1026	1045	1056	✣	1515	1524	1546	1554	1615	...	1626	1647	1717	1747	1822	1824	1852	1856	1926	1928	1951	2015	2026

	Ⓐ	Ⓐ	Ⓐ	Ⓐ	Ⓐ	Ⓐ	Ⓐ	Ⓐ	Ⓐ	Ⓐ	Ⓐ	Ⓐ			⑥	⑥	⑥	⑥	⑥	⑥	⑥	⑥		⑥	⑥	⑥
Brighton ....d.	1958	2020	2028	2048	2058	2120	2128	2149	2158	2226	2255	2310	...	⑥	0350	0523	0550	0556	0618	0628	0648	0658	and at the same	2118	2128	2148
Gatwick Airport ✈...d.	2023	2045	2053	2115	2123	2145	2153	2215	2223	2250	2320	2353	...		0503	0553	0626	0633	0645	0653	0715	|	minutes past	2145	2153	2215
East Croydon..........d.	2038	|	2108	|	2138	|	2208	|	2238	|	|	0019	...		0529	0608	0641	0653	|	0708	|	0738	each hour until	|	2208	|
London Victoria .....a.	2054	2117	2125	2144	2156	2214	2224	2243	2256	2321	2354	0041	...		0556	0624	0657	0710	0715	0724	0746	0754	✣	2215	2224	2245

	⑥	⑥	⑥			⑦	⑦		⑦	⑦		⑦	⑦	⑦	⑦	⑦		⑦	⑦	⑦	⑦	⑦	⑦		⑦	⑦
Brighton ....d.	2218	2255	2308	...	⑦	0350	0613	...	0706	0747	...	0825	0838	0910	0859	0935	and at the same	1910	1859	1935	2010	1959	2035	...	2104	2204
Gatwick Airport ✈...d.	2245	2321	2354	...		0502	0648	...	0743	0830	...	|	0901	|	0941	0957	minutes past	|	1941	1957	|	2041	2057	...	2141	2241
East Croydon..........d.	|	|	0020	...		0527	0706	...	0804	0858	...	0908	0916	0946	1001	1014	each hour until	1946	2001	2014	2046	2101	2114	...	2201	2301
London Victoria .....a.	2315	2355	0041	...		0555	0727	...	0825	0914	...	0924	0932	1003	1018	1030	✣	2003	2018	2031	2105	2118	2130	...	2218	2319

✣ – Timings may vary by ± 3 minutes.

107 LONDON - GUILDFORD - PORTSMOUTH

km			Ⓐ	Ⓐ		Ⓐ	Ⓐ	Ⓐ	Ⓐ	Ⓐ	Ⓐ	Ⓐ		Ⓐ	Ⓐ	Ⓐ	Ⓐ	Ⓐ	Ⓐ	Ⓐ	Ⓐ	Ⓐ	Ⓐ	Ⓐ
0	**London** Waterloo....... 113 d.	Ⓐ	0500	0520	...	0615	0645	0730	0800	0830	0900	0930	and at	1700	1730	1800	1815	1830	1900	1930	2000	2030	2100	2130
39	Woking.................... 113 d.		0553	0611	...	0643	0713	0755	0825	0855	0925	0955	the same	1725	1756	|	|	1858	1925	1955	2025	2055	2125	2155
49	Guildford.....................d.		0604	0630	...	0655	0725	0804	0840	0907	0934	1004	minutes	1737	1808	1833	1851	1908	1937	2004	2034	2104	2134	2204
69	Haslemere....................d.		0628	0655	...	0720	0753	0825	0856	0925	0949	1021	past each	1754	1826	1852	1906	1926	1953	2023	2055	2122	2155	2225
88	Petersfield...................d.		0645	0711	...	0736	0811	0836	0907	0936	1000	1034	hour until	1805	1837	1903	1923	1937	2004	2034	2106	2133	2206	2236
107	Havant.........................a.		0659	0727	...	0751	0826	0849	0919	0949	1015	1049		1819	1850	1915	1940	1951	2016	2048	2118	2145	2218	2248
118	**Portsmouth** & Southsea...a.		0716	0746	...	0807	0843	0902	0932	1003	1028	1102	♣	1832	1903	1929	1959	2004	2029	2101	2132	2158	2232	2303
120	**Portsmouth** Harbour........a.		0720	0751	...	0812	0848	0907	0937	1008	1033	1107		1839	1910	1936	...	2010	2034	2106	2137	2202	2237	2308

	Ⓐ	Ⓐ	Ⓐ	Ⓐ			⑥	⑥	⑥	⑥	⑥		⑥	⑥	⑥	⑥	⑥	⑥	⑥	⑥	⑥	⑥	⑥	⑥
London Waterloo ....113 d.	2230	2245	2315	2345	...	⑥	0520	0645	0730	0800	0830	and at	1800	1830	1900	1930	2000	2030	2100	2130	2200	2230	2245	2315
Woking........................113 d.	2256	2313	2343	0013	...		0613	0713	0755	0825	0855	the same	1825	1855	1925	1955	2025	2055	2125	2155	2225	2255	2313	2343
Guildford..............................d.	2305	2325	2352	0025	...		0625	0725	0804	0834	0904	minutes	1834	1904	1934	2004	2034	2104	2134	2204	2234	2304	2325	2352
Haslemere..............................d.	2325	2350	0012	0050	...		0645	0745	0821	0849	0921	past each	1849	1921	1949	2021	2049	2121	2155	2225	2255	2325	2350	0012
Petersfield.............................d.	2336	0006	0023	0106	...		0701	0801	0832	0900	0932	hour until	1900	1932	2000	2032	2100	2132	2206	2236	2306	2336	0006	0023
Havant...................................a.	2348	0020	0036	0121	...		0719	0816	0849	0915	0949		1915	1949	2015	2049	2115	2144	2218	2248	2318	2348	0020	0036
Portsmouth & Southsea ....a.	0002	0038	0050	0138	...		0735	0832	0902	0928	1002	♣	1928	2002	2028	2102	2128	2158	2232	2302	2331	0002	0037	0049
Portsmouth Harbour..........a.	0007	...	0055	...	...		0740	0837	0907	0933	1007		1933	2007	2033	2107	2133	2203	2236	2308	2336	0007	...	0054

		⑦	⑦	⑦	⑦	⑦	⑦	⑦	⑦	⑦	⑦	⑦		⑦	⑦	⑦	⑦	⑦	⑦	⑦	⑦	⑦	⑦	⑦
London Waterloo ....113 d.	⑦	...	0800	0830	0900	0930	1000	1030	1100	1130	1200	1230	and at	1800	1830	1900	1930	2000	2030	2100	2130	2200	2230	2300
Woking........................113 d.		0732	0835	0904	0935	1004	1032	1102	1132	1202	1232	1302	the same	1832	1902	1932	2002	2032	2102	2132	2202	2232	2302	2332
Guildford..............................d.		0741	0845	0914	0945	1014	1042	1112	1142	1212	1242	1312	minutes	1842	1912	1942	2012	2042	2112	2142	2212	2242	2312	2342
Haslemere..............................d.		0807	0912	0929	1012	1029	1107	1127	1207	1227	1307	1327	past each	1907	1927	2007	2027	2107	2127	2207	2227	2307	2327	0007
Petersfield.............................d.		0823	0928	0940	1028	1040	1123	1138	1223	1238	1323	1338	hour until	1923	1938	2023	2038	2123	2138	2223	2238	2323	2338	0023
Havant...................................a.		0838	0943	0952	1043	1052	1138	1150	1238	1250	1338	1350		1938	1950	2038	2050	2138	2150	2238	2250	2338	2350	0038
Portsmouth & Southsea ....a.		0853	0958	1006	1058	1105	1153	1204	1253	1304	1353	1404	♣	1953	2004	2053	2104	2153	2204	2253	2304	2353	0004	0053
Portsmouth Harbour..........a.		0857	1003	1011	1103	1111	1158	1211	1258	1311	1358	1411		1958	2011	2058	2109	2158	2208	2258	2309	2358	0009	0058

		ⒶA	ⒶB	ⒶA	ⒶB	Ⓐ	Ⓐ	Ⓐ	Ⓐ	Ⓐ	Ⓐ	Ⓐ	Ⓐ	Ⓐ	Ⓐ	Ⓐ		Ⓐ	Ⓐ	Ⓐ	Ⓐ	Ⓐ	Ⓐ	Ⓐ
Portsmouth Harbour..........d.	Ⓐ	0425	0430	0514	0519	0550	0615	...	0642	...	0713	0745	0815	0845	0915	0945	and at	1515	1545	1615	...	1645	1715	1745
Portsmouth & Southsea ....d.		0430	0435	0519	0524	0555	0620	...	0647	...	0718	0750	0820	0850	0920	0950	the same	1520	1550	1620	...	1650	1720	1750
Havant...................................d.		0446	0451	0535	0540	0611	0634	0650	0700	0711	0732	0804	0834	0904	0934	1004	minutes	1534	1604	1634	1656	1704	1734	1804
Petersfield.............................d.		0503	0508	0552	0557	0629	0648	0707	0714	0725	0746	0818	0848	0918	0948	1018	past each	1548	1618	1648	1710	1718	1748	1818
Haslemere..............................d.		0521	0526	0614	0616	0647	0702	0726	0735	0740	0800	0832	0902	0932	1002	1032	hour until	1602	1637	1702	1732	1737	1802	1832
Guildford.............................d.		0550	0550	0631	0631	0707	0717	0745	0754	0803	0815	0854	0917	0947	1017	1047		1617	1700	1717	1747	1800	1817	1855
Woking........................113 a.		0600	0600	0640	0640	0715	0725	0755	|	0811	0826	|	0927	0959	1025	1057	♣	1625	1711	1725	1758	1811	|	1903
London Waterloo ....113 a.		0629	0629	0712	0712	0745	0754	0824	0832	0841	0855	0931	0955	1027	1051	1124		1654	1743	1754	1827	1843	1859	1929

	Ⓐ	Ⓐ	Ⓐ	Ⓐ	Ⓐ	Ⓐ	Ⓐ	Ⓐ			⑥C	⑥D	⑥C	⑥D	⑥	⑥	⑥	⑥		⑥	⑥	⑥	⑥	⑥
Portsmouth Harbour..........d.	1845	1915	1945	2015	2045	2119	2219	2319	...	⑥	0438	0443	0514	0519	0619	0645	0715	0745	and at	1615	1645	...	1719	1745
Portsmouth & Southsea ....d.	1850	1920	1950	2020	2050	2124	2224	2324	...		0443	0448	0519	0524	0624	0650	0720	0750	the same	1620	1650	1710	1724	1750
Havant...................................d.	1904	1934	2004	2034	2104	2140	2240	2340	...		0459	0504	0535	0540	0640	0704	0734	0804	minutes	1634	1704	1726	1740	1804
Petersfield.............................d.	1918	1948	2018	2048	2118	2157	2257	2357	...		0515	0520	0552	0557	0657	0718	0748	0818	past each	1648	1718	1743	1757	1818
Haslemere..............................d.	1932	2002	2032	2102	2132	2215	2315	0015	...		0534	0539	0613	0615	0715	0732	0802	0832	hour until	1702	1732	1802	1815	1832
Guildford.............................d.	1947	2017	2047	2117	2147	2239	2339	0037	...		0602	0602	0634	0634	0734	0747	0817	0847		1717	1747	1817	1834	1847
Woking........................113 a.	1957	2025	2058	2125	2157	2249	2349	...	...		0611	0611	0644	0644	0744	0757	0826	0857	♣	1725	1757	1825	1844	1857
London Waterloo ....113 a.	2024	2050	2129	2150	2227	2319	0033	...	...		0640	0640	0713	0713	0813	0823	0851	0923		1751	1823	1851	1913	1923

	⑥	⑥	⑥	⑥	⑥	⑥	⑥	⑥			⑦E	⑦F	⑦E	⑦F	⑦	⑦E	⑦F	⑦	⑦	⑦		⑦	⑦	⑦
Portsmouth Harbour..........d.	1845	1915	1945	2015	2045	2119	2219	2319	...	⑦	0643	0648	0729	0732	0748	0829	0832	0848	0932	0948	and at	2132	2148	2232
Portsmouth & Southsea ....d.	1850	1920	1950	2020	2050	2124	2224	2324	...		0648	0653	0734	0737	0753	0834	0837	0853	0937	0953	the same	2137	2153	2237
Havant...................................d.	1904	1934	2004	2034	2104	2140	2240	2340	...		0702	0707	0747	0750	0807	0847	0850	0907	0950	1007	minutes	2150	2207	2250
Petersfield.............................d.	1918	1948	2018	2048	2118	2157	2257	2357	...		0719	0724	0801	0804	0824	0901	0904	0924	1004	1024	past each	2204	2224	2304
Haslemere..............................d.	1932	2002	2032	2102	2132	2215	2315	0015	...		0737	0742	0814	0817	0842	0914	0917	0942	1017	1042	hour until	2217	2242	2317
Guildford.............................d.	1947	2017	2047	2117	2149	2239	2339	0037	...		0805	0805	0835	0835	0905	0935	0935	1005	1035	1106		2235	2305	2335
Woking........................113 a.	1957	2025	2059	2125	2157	2249	2349	...	...		0813	0813	0842	0842	0915	0942	0942	1015	1042	1113	♣	2242	2313	2342
London Waterloo ....113 a.	2023	2050	2127	2150	2224	2318	0032	...	...		0850	0850	0916	0916	0948	1014	1014	1046	1114	1149		2314	2344	0014

A – From Oct. 10.
B – Until Oct. 7.
C – From Oct. 15.
D – Until Oct. 8.
E – From Oct. 9.
F – Until Oct. 2.
s – Calls to set down only.
♣ – Timings may vary by ± 6 minutes.

LONDON - SOUTHAMPTON - BOURNEMOUTH - WEYMOUTH 108

	Ⓐ	Ⓐ	Ⓐ	Ⓐ	Ⓐ	Ⓐ	Ⓐ	Ⓐ	Ⓐ	Ⓐ		Ⓐ	Ⓐ	Ⓐ	Ⓐ	Ⓐ	Ⓐ	Ⓐ	Ⓐ	Ⓐ	Ⓐ	Ⓐ
London Waterloo...... 113 d.	...	...	...	0530	0630	0703	0735	0805	0835	0905		1635	1705	1735	1805	1835	1905	1935	2005	2035	2105	2135
Woking...... 113 d.	...	...	...	0601	0657	0730	0800	|	0900	|	and	1700u	|	|	|	|	|	2000	|	2100	2132	2200
Basingstoke...... 119 d.	...	...	0540	0621	0718	0750	0820	0849	|	0949	at	|	|	|	|	|	1949	|	2049	|	2152	|
Winchester...... 119 d.	...	...	0559	0638	0734	0806	0837	0905	0933	1005	the	1733	1800	1830	1900	1930	2005	2033	2105	2133	2208	2233
Southampton Airport. 119 d.	...	...	0613	0653	0749	0815	0852	0914	0942	1014	same	1742	1809	1839	1909	1939	2014	2042	2115	2142	2222	2242
Southampton Central 119 d.	...	...	0625	0701	0759	0827	0901	0924	0951	1024	minutes	1753	1821	1851	1919	1951	2024	2051	2125	2151	2231	2251
Brockenhurst...... 119 d.	...	0616	0644	0718	0820	0846	0918	0938	1005	1038	past	1808	|	|	1936	|	2038	2108	2144	2205	2250	2305
Bournemouth...... 119 d.	0611	0644	0711	0746	0848	0913	0945	1004	1024	1104	each	1824	1850	1921	2007	2021	2104	2127	2212	2224	2317	2329
Poole...... d.	0624	0657	0724	0758	0900	0926	0958	1014	1037	1114	hour	1837	1903	1934	2019	2034	2115	2139	2223	2237	2329	2342
Wareham...... d.	0638	0711	0738	0812	0912	0940	1010	1028	1050	1128	until	1849	1917	1946	2033	2046	2127	2151	...	2249	...	2354
Dorchester South...... d.	0658	0731	0758	0833	0933	1000	1026	1054	1106	1149	♠	1908	1937	2003	2054	2102	2147	2212	...	2309	...	0014
Weymouth...... a.	0714	0747	0814	0844	0944	1011	1035	1106	1115	1202		1919	1950	2015	2107	2115	2200	2223	...	2320	...	0025

	Ⓐ	Ⓐ	Ⓐ		⑥	⑥	⑥	⑥	⑥	⑥	⑥	⑥		⑥	⑥	⑥	⑥	⑥	⑥	⑥	⑥	⑥	⑥	⑥
on Waterloo...... 113 d.	2205	2235	2305	⑥	...	...	...	0530	0630	0735	0805	0835		1805	1835	1905	1935	2005	2035	2105	2135	2205	2235	2305
g...... 113 d.	2232	2300	2332		...	...	...	0601	0657	0800	|	0900	and	|	1900	|	2000	|	2100	2132	2200	2232	2300	2332
gstoke...... 119 d.	2252	|	2353		...	...	...	0621	0718	0821	0849	|	at	1849	|	1949	|	2049	|	2152	|	2252	|	2352
ester...... 119 d.	2308	2333	0012		...	...	...	0641	0734	0838	0905	0933	the	1905	1933	2005	2033	2105	2133	2208	2233	2308	2333	0011
ampton Airport. 119 d.	2322	2342	0028		...	...	...	0656	0748	0851	0914	0942	same	1914	1942	2014	2042	2114	2142	2222	2242	2322	2342	0025
ampton Central 119 d.	2330	2351	0038		...	...	0621	0705	0800	0900	0924	0951	minutes	1924	1951	2024	2051	2124	2151	2230	2251	2330	2351	0035
enhurst...... 119 d.	2349	0005	0054s		...	0616	0640	0722	0817	0917	0938	1005	past	1938	2005	2038	2105	2143	2205	2249	2305	2349	0005	0051s
nemouth...... 119 d.	0016	0022	0118		0611	0644	0711	0749	0844	0944	1004	1024	each	2004	2024	2104	2124	2210	2224	2317	2329	0016	0022	0115
...... d.	0028	0035	0130		0624	0657	0724	0802	0857	0957	1014	1037	hour	2014	2037	2114	2137	2223	2237	2329	2342	0030	0035	0127
ham...... d.	...	...	...		0638	0711	0738	0814	0909	1009	1028	1049	until	2028	2049	2128	2149	...	2249	...	2354	...	...	...
ester South...... d.	...	...	...		0658	0731	0758	0834	0929	1027	1049	1105	♠	2049	2105	2149	2209	...	2309	...	0014	...	...	...
outh...... a.	...	...	...		0709	0742	0809	0845	0940	1035	1100	1113		2100	2113	2200	2220	...	2320	...	0025	...	...	...

		⑦	⑦	⑦	⑦	⑦	⑦	⑦	⑦		⑦	⑦	⑦	⑦	⑦		⑦	⑦	⑦	⑦		⑦	⑦
on Waterloo...... 113 d.	⑦	...	...	...	0754	0835	0854	0935	0954		1435	1454	1535	1605	1635		2005	2035	2105	2135	...	2205	2305
ng...... 113 d.		...	...	...	0828	0909	0928	1008	1028	and	1507	1528	1607	1637	1707	and	2037	2107	2137	2207	...	2237	2337
gstoke...... 119 d.		...	0748	...	0848	0929	0948	1028	1048	at	1528	1548	1628	1657	1728	at	2057	2128	2157	2228	...	2257	2357
nester...... 119 d.		...	0808	...	0908	0946	1008	1044	1108	the	1544	1608	1644	1714	1744	the	2114	2144	2214	2244	...	2314	0014
hampton Airport. 119 d.		...	0827	...	0927	0955	1027	1053	1127	same	1553	1627	1653	1727	1753	same	2127	2153	2227	2253	...	2327	0028
hampton Central 119 d.		...	0835	0903	0935	1003	1035	1103	1135	minutes	1603	1635	1703	1736	1803	minutes	2136	2203	2236	2303	...	2336	0042
enhurst...... 119 d.		...	0857	0917	0957	1018	1057	1117	1157	past	1617	1657	1717	1757	1817	past	2157	2217	2257	2317	...	2355	0058s
nemouth...... 119 d.		0839	0927	0939	1024	1039	1124	1139	1224	each	1639	1724	1739	1825	1839	each	2225	2239	2325	2339	...	0022	0122
...... d.		0851	0936	0951	1033	1051	1133	1151	1233	hour	1651	1733	1751	1834	1851	hour	2234	2251	2334	2351	...	0034	0134
ham...... d.		0903	...	1003	...	1103	...	1203	...	until	1703	...	1803	...	1903	until	...	2303	...	0003		...	...
ester South...... d.		0924	...	1024	...	1124	...	1224	...	♠	1724	...	1824	...	1924	♠	...	2325	...	0025		...	...
outh...... a.		0935	...	1035	...	1135	...	1235	...		1735	...	1835	...	1935		...	2336	...	0036		...	...

		Ⓐ	Ⓐ	Ⓐ	Ⓐ	Ⓐ	Ⓐ	Ⓐ	Ⓐ	Ⓐ	Ⓐ	Ⓐ	Ⓐ		Ⓐ	Ⓐ	Ⓐ	Ⓐ	Ⓐ	Ⓐ	Ⓐ	Ⓐ	Ⓐ	Ⓐ
nouth...... d.	Ⓐ	...	...	...	*0550*	*0620*	0650	...	0725	0755	0820	0903	0920		1703	1720	1803	1820	1903	1920	2010	2110	2210	2310
nester South...... d.		...	...	...	*0602*	*0632*	0702	...	0737	0807	0833	0913	0933	and	1713	1733	1813	1833	1913	1937	2022	2122	2222	2322
ham...... d.		...	...	...	*0622*	*0652*	0722	...	0757	0827	0853	0928	0953	at	1728	1753	1828	1853	1928	1957	2042	2142	2242	2342
...... d.		0457	0542	*0608*	*0639*	*0709*	0739	0755	0811	0841	0907	0940	1007	the	1740	1807	1840	1907	1940	2009	2054	2154	2254	2354
nemouth...... 119 d.		0512	0554	*0625*	*0656*	*0726*	0759	0810	0825	0859	0918	0955	1022	same	1759	1822	1859	1922	1959	2022	2112	2212	2312	0003
enhurst...... 119 d.		0538	0614	|	|	|	0815	0841	0852	0915	0941	1011	1045	minutes	1815	1845	1915	1945	2015	2045	2140	2240	2340	...
hampton Central 119 d.		0555	0630	0700	0730	0800	0830	0900	*0916*	0930	1000	1030	1100	past	1830	1900	1930	2000	2030	2100	2200	2300	2359	...
hampton Airport. 119 d.		0603	0638	0708	0738	0808	0838	0908	*0923*	0938	1008	1038	1108	each	1838	1908	1938	2008	2038	2108	2208	2308	0010	...
hester...... 119 d.		0618	0648	0718	0748	0818	0848	0918	*0932*	0948	1018	1048	1118	hour	1848	1918	1948	2018	2048	2118	2218	2324	...	...
gstoke...... 119 a.		0634	|	|	|	0834	|	0935	*0946*	|	1034	|	1134	until	|	1934	|	2034	|	2134	2234	2343	...	...
ng...... 113 a.		0653	|	|	|	0853	0922	0954	...	1020	|	1119	|	♠	1925	|	2019	|	2119	|	2254	0018	...	...
don Waterloo...... 113 a.		0724	0747	0816	0850	0925	0953	1023		1049	1120	1149	1220		1952	2020	2049	2124	2149	2222	2323	0104	...	...

		⑥	⑥	⑥	⑥	⑥	⑥	⑥	⑥	⑥	⑥	⑥		⑥	⑥	⑥	⑥	⑥	⑥	⑥		⑥	⑥	⑥
mouth...... d.	⑥	...	0537	...	0650	0720	0758	0820	0903	0920	1003	1020		1703	1720	1803	1820	1903	1920	2010	...	2110	2210	2310
nester South...... d.		...	0547	...	0702	0733	0808	0833	0913	0933	1013	1033	and	1713	1733	1813	1833	1913	1933	2022	...	2122	2222	2322
eham...... d.		...	0605	...	0722	0753	0823	0853	0928	0953	1028	1053	at	1728	1753	1828	1853	1928	1953	2042	...	2142	2242	2342
e...... d.		0528	0622	0707	0739	0807	0835	0907	0940	1007	1040	1107	the	1740	1807	1840	1907	1940	2007	2054	...	2154	2254	2354
rnemouth...... 119 d.		0542	0642	0722	0759	0822	0859	0922	0959	1022	1059	1122	same	1759	1822	1859	1922	1959	2022	2112	...	2212	2312	0003
kenhurst...... 119 d.		0610	0710	0745	0815	0845	0915	0945	1015	1045	1115	1145	minutes	1815	1845	1915	1945	2015	2045	2140	...	2240	2340	...
hampton Central 119 d.		0630	0730	0800	0830	0900	0930	1000	1030	1100	1130	1200	past	1830	1900	1930	2000	2030	2100	2200	2230	2300	2359	...
hampton Airport. 119 d.		0638	0738	0808	0838	0908	0938	1008	1038	1108	1138	1208	each	1838	1908	1938	2008	2038	2108	2208	2238	2308	0010	...
hester...... 119 d.		0652	0748	0818	0848	0918	0948	1018	1048	1118	1148	1218	hour	1848	1918	1948	2018	2048	2118	2218	2255	2324	...	...
ngstoke...... 119 a.		0708	|	0834	|	0934	|	1034	|	1134	|	1234	until	|	1934	|	2034	|	2134	2234	2311	2343	...	...
ng...... 113 a.		0727	0821	|	0919	|	1019	|	1119	|	1219	|	♠	1919	|	2019	|	2119	|	2253	2332	0018	...	...
don Waterloo...... 113 a.		0753	0849	0920	0949	1020	1049	1120	1149	1221	1251	1321		1949	2020	2049	2124	2149	2222	2322	0003	0104	...	...

		⑦	⑦	⑦	⑦	⑦	⑦	⑦		⑦	⑦	⑦	⑦	⑦		⑦	⑦	⑦	⑦	⑦	⑦	⑦	⑦
mouth...... d.	⑦	...	...	0743	...	0843	...	0948		...	1248	...	1348	...		1748	...	1848	...	1958	2058	2158	2258
hester South...... d.		...	...	0755	...	0855	...	1000	and	...	1300	...	1400	...	and	1800	...	1900	...	2010	2110	2210	2310
eham...... d.		...	...	0815	...	0915	...	1020	at	...	1320	...	1420	...	at	1820	...	1920	...	2030	2130	2230	2330
e...... d.		*0650e*	*0750e*	0830	*0855e*	0930	*0955e*	1032	the	*1255e*	1332	*1355e*	1432	1455	the	1832	1855	1932	1955	2050	2150	2250	2350
rnemouth...... 119 d.		*0706e*	*0806e*	0850	*0906e*	0950	*1006e*	1050	same	*1306e*	1350	*1406e*	1450	1506	same	1850	1906	1950	2006	2106	2206	2306	0003
kenhurst...... 119 d.		*0734e*	*0834e*	0909	*0934e*	1009	*1034e*	1109	minutes	*1334e*	1409	*1434e*	1509	1534	minutes	1909	1934	2009	2034	2134	2234	2334	...
hampton Central 119 d.		*0755e*	*0855e*	0925	*0955e*	1025	*1055e*	1125	past	*1355e*	1425	*1455e*	1525	1555	past	1925	1955	2025	2055	2155	2255	2353	...
hampton Airport. 119 d.		*0803e*	*0903e*	0933	*1003e*	1033	*1103e*	1133	each	*1403e*	1433	*1503e*	1533	1603	each	1933	2003	2033	2103	2203	2303	...	...
hester...... 119 d.		0823	0923	0942	1023	1042	1123	1142	hour	1423	1442	1523	1542	1617	hour	1942	2017	2042	2117	2218	2323	...	...
gstoke...... 119 a.		0842	0942	0958	1042	1058	1142	1158	until	1442	1458	1542	1558	1633	until	1958	2033	2058	2133	2235	2342	...	...
ing...... 113 a.		0902	1002	1019	1102	1118	1202	1218	♠	1502	1518	1602	1618	1653	♠	2018	2053	2118	2153	2254	0002	...	...
don Waterloo...... 113 a.		0941	1039	1050	1139	1150	1237	1249		1537	1549	1637	1649	1724		2049	2124	2149	2224	2325	0033	...	...

ckenhurst - Lymington Pier (for ⛴ to Isle of Wight).
ney 11 minutes. Trains call at Lymington Town 6 minutes later:
0559 and every 30 minutes until 0929, 1012 and every 30 minutes until 1812, 1848 and every 30 minutes until 2218.
0612, 0642 and every 30 minutes until 2112, 2148, 2218.
0859, 0929 and every 30 minutes until 2059, 2129, 2159.

Lymington Pier - Brockenhurst.
Journey 11 minutes. Trains call at Lymington Town 2 minutes later:
Ⓐ: 0614 and every 30 minutes until 0944, 1027 and every 30 minutes until 1827, 1903 and every 30 minutes until 2203, 2236.
⑥: 0627, 0657 and every 30 minutes until 2127, 2203, 2236.
⑦: 0914, 0944 and every 30 minutes until 2114, 2144, 2214.

Change at Eastleigh.
Calls to set down only.
u – Calls to pick up only.
♠ – Timings may vary by ± 3 minutes.
☞ For ⛴ services Weymouth / Poole – Jersey / Guernsey / St Malo and v.v., see Table **2100**.

2nd class PORTSMOUTH - RYDE - SHANKLIN 111

ough fares including ferry travel are available. Allow 10 minutes for connections between trains and ferries. Operator: Wightlink ✆ 0871 376 4342. www.wightlink.co.uk

smouth Harbour - Ryde Pierhead: ⛴
5Ⓐ, 0615⚒, 0715 and hourly until 1815, 1920, 2020, 2120, 2245.

Ryde Pierhead - Portsmouth Harbour — Journey time: ± 20 minutes
0547Ⓐ, 0647⚒, 0747 and hourly until 2147, 2310.

Service until December 18, 2016. Additional services operate on Ⓐ and on public holidays.

e Pierhead - Shanklin: *14 km*
0549, 0607, 0649, 0707, 0749, 0807, 0849, 0907, 0949, 1007, 1049*, 1107, 1149*, 1207*, 1249*, 1307*, 1349, 1407, 1449*, 1507*, 1549*, 1607*, 1649, 1707, 1749, 1807, 1849, 1907, 1949, 2007, 2049, 2149.
0649, 0749, 0849, 0907, 0949, 1007, 1049*, 1107, 1149*, 1207*, 1249*, 1307*, 1349, 1407, 1449*, 1507*, 1549*, 1607*, 1649, 1707, 1749, 1807, 1849, 1907, 1949, 2049, 2149.

Shanklin - Ryde Pierhead — Journey time: ± 24 minutes
⚒: 0618, 0638, 0718, 0738, 0818, 0838, 0918, 0938, 1018, 1038*, 1118, 1138*, 1218*, 1238*, 1318*, 1338, 1418, 1438*, 1518*, 1538*, 1618*, 1638, 1718, 1738, 1818, 1838, 1918, 1938, 2018, 2118, 2238.
⑦: 0718, 0818, 0838, 0918, 0938, 1018, 1038*, 1118, 1138*, 1218*, 1238*, 1318*, 1338, 1418, 1438*, 1518*, 1538*, 1618*, 1638, 1718, 1738, 1818, 1838, 1918, 1938, 2018, 2118, 2238.

Also calls at Smallbrook Junction (connection with **Isle of Wight Steam Railway**, see note △) 9 minutes from Ryde / 15 minutes from Shanklin, when Steam Railway is operating.

△ – **Isle of Wight Steam Railway** (🚂 Smallbrook Junction - Wootton: *9 km*). ✆ 01983 882204. www.iwsteamrailway.co.uk

113 LONDON - SALISBURY - EXETER

km	Ⓐ	Ⓐ	Ⓐ	Ⓐ	Ⓐ	Ⓐ	Ⓐ	Ⓐ	ⒶB	Ⓐ	Ⓐ	ⒶB	Ⓐ	Ⓐ	Ⓐ	Ⓐ	Ⓐ	Ⓐ	Ⓐ	Ⓐ	Ⓐ	Ⓐ	Ⓐ	Ⓐ
0	**London** W'loo.... **108** d.	...	...	...	...	*0630*	0710	0820	0920	1020	1120	1220	1250	1320	1350	1420	1520	1550	1620	1650	1720	1750	1820	1850
39	Woking .... **108** d.	...	...	...	...	*0657*	0736	0846	0946	1046	1146	1246	1316	1346	1416	1446	1546	1616	1646	1716**u**	1746**u**	|	1846	1918
77	Basingstoke .... **108** d.	...	...	...	...	0722	0757	0907	1007	1107	1207	1307	1338	1407	1438	1507	1607	1638	1707	1738	1807	1838	1907	1939
107	Andover .... d.	...	...	...	...	0744	0819	0924	1024	1124	1224	1324	1400	1424	1500	1524	1624	1700	1729	1800	1829	1900	1929	2001
134	**Salisbury** .... a.	...	...	...	...	0803	0839	0943	1042	1142	1242	1343	1419	1442	1520	1542	1642	1720	1748	1820	1850	1920	1948	2021
134	**Salisbury** .... d.	...	...	0608	0740	0808	0847	0947	1047	1147	1247	1347	1424	1447	1523	1547	1647	1723	1753	1823	1854	1923	1953	2025
169	Gillingham .... d.	...	...	0642	0811	0837	0917	1017	1117	1217	1317	1417	|	1517	1552	1617	1717	1753	1820	1851	1919	1954	2022	2052
190	Sherborne .... d.	...	...	0657	0826	...	0932	1032	1132	1232	1332	1432	◧	1532	1607	1632	1732	1808	1835	1906	1934	2009	2037	2107
197	**Yeovil** Junction .... a.	...	...	0703	0832	...	0938	1038	1138	1238	1338	1438	|	1538	1613	1638	1738	1813	1840	1912	1939	2015	2043	2113
197	**Yeovil** Junction .... d.	...	0615	0707	0839	...	0939	1039	1139	1239	1339	1439	|	1539	1620	1639	1739	...	1842	1917	1941	2020	2044	2117
200	**Yeovil** Pen Mill ...... a.	...	|	|	|	...	|	|	|	|	|	|	1537	|	1627	|	|	...	|	1925	|	2025	|	2123
211	Crewkerne .... d.	...	0624	0716	0849	...	0949	1049	1149	1249	1349	1449	...	1549	...	1649	1749	...	1851	...	1950	...	2054	...
233	Axminster .... d.	0552	0656	0737	0903	...	1003	1103	1203	1303	1403	1503	...	1603	...	1703	1803	...	1905	...	2004	...	2108	...
249	Honiton .... d.	0607	0712	0753	0916	...	1016	1116	1216	1316	1416	1516	...	1616	...	1716	1818	...	1919	...	2017	...	2120	...
277	**Exeter** St Davids ..△ a.	0635	0742	0821	0944	...	1042	1143	1243	1343	1443	1544	...	1643	...	1742	1843	...	1946	...	2043	...	2147	...

	Ⓐ	Ⓐ	Ⓐ	Ⓐ	⑥	⑥	⑥	⑥	⑥	⑥A	⑥	⑥B	⑥	⑥c	⑥	⑥A	⑥B	⑥	⑥	⑥	⑥	⑥	⑥	⑥B
London Waterloo **108** d.	2020	2120	2220	2340	...	...	...	...	0710	0750	0820	0920	1020	...	1120	...	1220	1320	1420	1520	1620	1720	1820	1920
Woking .... **108** d.	2046	2149	2249	0008	...	...	...	...	0736	0816	0846	0946	1046	...	1146	...	1246	1346	1446	1546	1646	1746	1846	1946
Basingstoke .... **108** d.	2107	2214	2311	0028	...	...	...	...	0759	0838	0907	1007	1107	...	1207	...	1307	1407	1507	1607	1707	1807	1907	2007
Andover .... d.	2129	2236	2333	0050	...	...	...	...	0821	0900	0924	1024	1124	...	1224	...	1324	1424	1524	1624	1724	1824	1924	2024
Salisbury .... a.	2148	2255	2353	0110	...	...	...	...	0842	0920	0942	1042	1142	...	1242	...	1342	1442	1542	1642	1742	1843	1943	2042
Salisbury .... d.	2206	2303	...	...	...	...	0615	0745	0847	0924	0947	1047	1147	...	1247	...	1347	1447	1547	1647	1747	1847	1947	2047
Gillingham .... d.	2235	2327**s**	...	...	...	...	0642	0811	0917	0952	1017	1117	1217	...	1317	...	1417	1517	1617	1717	1817	1919	2017	2117
Sherborne .... d.	2250	2342**s**	...	...	...	...	0657	0826	0932	1007	1032	1132	1232	...	1332	...	1432	1532	1632	1732	1832	1934	2032	2132
Yeovil Junction .... a.	2255	2348	...	...	...	...	0703	0832	0938	1012	1038	1138	1238	...	1338	...	1438	1538	1638	1738	1838	1939	2038	2138
Yeovil Junction ...... ■ d.	2257	...	...	...	...	0615	0707	0839	0939	1016	1039	1139	1239	1345	1339	1405	1439	1539	1639	1739	1839	1941	2039	2139
Yeovil Pen Mill... ■ a.	|	...	...	...	...	|	|	|	|	1021	|	|	|	1350	|	1410	|	|	|	|	|	|	|	|
Crewkerne .... d.	2306	...	...	...	...	0624	0716	0849	0949	...	1049	1149	1249	...	1349	...	1449	1549	1649	1749	1849	1950	2049	2149
Axminster .... d.	2320	...	...	...	0552	0656	0738	0903	1003	...	1103	1203	1303	...	1403	...	1503	1603	1703	1803	1903	2005	2103	2203
Honiton .... d.	2332	...	...	...	0607	0712	0754	0916	1016	...	1116	1216	1316	...	1416	...	1516	1616	1716	1817	1916	2017	2117	2217
Exeter St Davids ... △ a.	0001	...	...	...	0635	0742	0822	0944	1042	...	1142	1242	1342	...	1442	...	1542	1642	1742	1842	1942	2044	2142	2245

	⑥	⑥	⑥	⑦	⑦	⑦	⑦	⑦	⑦	⑦B	⑦	⑦	⑦	⑦	⑦	⑦	⑦B	⑦	⑦	⑦	⑦	⑦	⑦e	⑦
London Waterloo **108** d.	2120	2220	2340	...	...	0815	0915	1015	1115	1215	1315	1415	1515	1615	1715	1745	1815	1845	1915	1945	2015	2045	2115	2215
Woking .... **108** d.	2149	2249	0008	...	...	0847	0947	1046	1146	1246	1346	1446	1546	1646	1746	|	1846	|	1946	|	2046	|	2146	2246
Basingstoke .... **108** d.	2214	2311	0028	...	0805	0908	1008	1107	1207	1307	1407	1507	1607	1707	1807	|	1907	|	2007	|	2107	|	2207	2307
Andover .... d.	2236	2333	0050	...	0827	0930	1025	1129	1224	1329	1424	1529	1624	1729	1824	1849	1929	1949	2024	2049	2129	|	2226	2329
Salisbury .... a.	2255	2353	0110	...	0846	0946	1045	1145	1245	1345	1445	1545	1645	1745	1845	1905	1945	2005	2045	2105	2145	2205	2245	2348
Salisbury .... d.	2303	...	...	0706	0851	0951	1051	1151	1251	1351	1451	1551	1651	1751	1851	...	1951	...	2051	...	2151	...	2251	...
Gillingham .... d.	2327**s**	...	...	0731	0921	1021	1121	1221	1321	1421	1521	1621	1721	1821	1921	...	2021	...	2121	...	2221	...	2322	...
Sherborne .... d.	2342**s**	...	...	0746	0936	1036	1136	1236	1336	1436	1536	1636	1736	1836	1936	...	2036	...	2136	...	2236	...	2337	...
Yeovil Junction .... a.	2348	...	...	0751	0941	1041	1141	1241	1341	1441	1541	1641	1741	1841	1941	...	2041	...	2141	...	2242	...	2343	...
Yeovil Junction .... d.	...	...	...	0753	0943	1043	1143	1243	1343	1443	1543	1643	1743	1843	1943	...	2043	...	2143	...	...	...	2344	...
Yeovil Pen Mill .... a.	...	...	...	|	|	|	|	|	|	|	|	|	|	|	|	...	|	...	|	...	...	...	|	...
Crewkerne .... d.	...	...	...	0802	0952	1052	1152	1252	1352	1452	1552	1652	1752	1852	1952	...	2052	...	2152	...	...	...	2354	...
Axminster .... d.	...	...	...	0816	1006	1106	1206	1306	1406	1506	1606	1706	1806	1906	2006	...	2106	...	2206	...	...	...	0008	...
Honiton .... d.	...	...	...	0831	1018	1118	1218	1318	1418	1518	1618	1718	1818	1918	2018	...	2118	...	2220	...	...	...	0020	...
Exeter St Davids ... △ a.	...	...	...	0859	1045	1145	1245	1345	1445	1545	1645	1745	1845	1945	2045	...	2146	...	2248	...	...	...	0046	...

	Ⓐ	Ⓐ	Ⓐ	Ⓐ	Ⓐ	Ⓐ	Ⓐ	Ⓐ	Ⓐ	ⒶB	Ⓐ	Ⓐ	Ⓐ	ⒶB	Ⓐ	Ⓐ	Ⓐ	ⒶB	Ⓐ	Ⓐ	Ⓐ	Ⓐ	Ⓐ	Ⓐ
Exeter St Davids ... ▽ d.	...	...	...	...	0510	...	0641	0725	...	0823	0925	1025	1125	1225	1325	1425	...	1525	...	1624	1725	1746	1825	1925
Honiton .... d.	...	...	...	...	0541	0619	0712	0752	...	0855	0955	1055	1155	1255	1355	1455	...	1555	...	1656	1755	1819	1859	1955
Axminster .... d.	...	...	...	...	0552	0630	0723	0803	...	0906	1006	1106	1206	1306	1406	1506	...	1606	...	1707	1806	1829	1910	2006
Crewkerne .... d.	...	...	...	...	0605	0643	0736	0816	...	0919	1019	1119	1219	1319	1419	1519	...	1619	...	1720	1819	...	1923	2019
Yeovil Pen Mill .... d.	...	...	...	0541	|	|	|	|	...	|		|	|	|	|	|	1542	|	1653	|	|	...	|	|
Yeovil Junction .... a.	...	...	...	0546	0614	0652	0745	0825	...	0927	1027	1127	1227	1327	1427	1527	1547	1627	|	1728	1827	...	1931	2028
Yeovil Junction .... d.	...	...	0511	0550	0620	0653	0750	0829	...	0929	1029	1129	1229	1329	1429	1529	1553	1629	1648**b**	1730	1829	...	1933	2029
Sherborne .... d.	...	...	0517	0556	0626	0700	0756	0835	...	0935	1035	1135	1235	1335	1435	1535	1559	1635	◧	1736	1835	...	1939	2036
Gillingham .... d.	...	...	0533	0612	0642	0715	0812	0851	0918	0951	1051	1151	1251	1351	1451	1551	1617	1651	|	1752	1851	...	1955	2051
Salisbury .... a.	...	...	0601	0639	0707	0740	0837	0916	0942	1016	1116	1216	1316	1416	1516	1616	1643	1716	1817	1822	1923	...	2022	2122
Salisbury .... d.	0512	0540	0603	0645	0715	0745	0847	0921	0947	1021	1121	1221	1321	1421	1521	1621	1647	1721	1827	1827	1926	...	2026	2126
Andover .... d.	0532	0600	0623	0705	0735	0805	0906	0938	1006	1038	1138	1238	1338	1438	1538	1638	1706	1738	1844	1844	1945	...	2045	2145
Basingstoke .... **108** a.	0558	0626	0649	0728	0758	0828	0928	0955	1028	1055	1155	1255	1355	1455	1555	1655	1729	1755	1901	1901	2008	...	2108	2207
Woking .... **108** a.	0618	0646	|	|	0818	0848	0949	1015	1049	1115	1215	1315	1415	1515	1615	1715	1749	1815	1921	1921	2029	...	2129	2228
London Waterloo **108** a.	0649	0714	0739	0814	0846	0917	1019	1049	1119	1149	1249	1349	1449	1549	1649	1749	1821	1849	1950	1950	2100	...	2204	2258

	Ⓐ	Ⓐ	⑥	⑥	⑥	⑥	⑥	⑥	⑥	⑥	⑥B	⑥	⑥	⑥	⑥A	⑥B	⑥c	⑥	⑥	⑥B	⑥	⑥A	⑥	⑥
Exeter St Davids ... ▽ d.	2125	2257	...	...	...	...	0510	...	0641	0725	0824	0925	1025	1125	...	1225	...	1325	1425	1525	1625	...	1725	1825
Honiton .... d.	2159	2332	...	...	...	...	0541	0619	0713	0755	0855	0955	1055	1155	...	1255	...	1355	1455	1555	1655	...	1757	1855
Axminster .... d.	2210	2343	...	...	...	...	0552	0630	0724	0806	0906	1006	1106	1206	...	1306	...	1406	1506	1606	1706	...	1808	1906
Crewkerne .... d.	2223	2356	...	...	...	...	0605	0643	0737	0819	0919	1019	1119	1219	...	1319	...	1419	1519	1619	1719	...	1821	1919
Yeovil Pen Mill... ■ d.	|	|	...	...	...	...	|	|	|	|	|	|	|	|	1258	|	1328	|	|	|	|	1739	|	|
Yeovil Junction...... ■ a.	2231	0004	...	...	...	...	0614	0652	0745	0827	0927	1027	1127	1227	1303	1327	1333	1427	1527	1627	1727	1745	1829	1927
Yeovil Junction .... d.	2233	0006	...	...	...	...	0620	0653	0750	0829	0929	1029	1129	1229	...	1329	...	1429	1529	1629	1729	1750	1831	1929
Sherborne .... d.	2239	|	...	...	...	...	0626	0700	0756	0835	0935	1035	1135	1235	...	1335	...	1435	1535	1635	1735	1757	1837	1935
Gillingham .... d.	2255	|	...	...	...	...	0642	0715	0812	0851	0951	1051	1151	1251	...	1351	...	1451	1551	1651	1751	1816	1853	1951
Salisbury .... a.	2329	0040	...	...	...	...	0707	0740	0837	0916	1016	1116	1216	1316	...	1416	...	1516	1616	1716	1816	1841	1918	2016
Salisbury .... d.	...	...	0512	0544	0618	0647	0721	0747	0847	0921	1021	1121	1221	1321	...	1421	...	1521	1621	1721	1821	1847	1926	2026
Andover .... d.	...	...	0532	0603	0635	0706	0738	0806	0906	0938	1038	1138	1238	1338	...	1438	...	1538	1638	1738	1838	1906	1945	2045
Basingstoke .... **108** a.	...	...	0558	0628	0655	0728	0755	0828	0928	0955	1055	1155	1255	1355	...	1455	...	1555	1655	1755	1855	1928	2008	2108
Woking .... **108** a.	...	...	0618	0649	0715	0749	0817	0849	0949	1015	1115	1215	1315	1415	...	1515	...	1615	1715	1815	1915	1949	2029	2129
London Waterloo **108** a.	...	...	0649	0719	0749	0819	0849	0919	1019	1049	1149	1249	1349	1449	...	1549	...	1649	1749	1849	1949	2019	2104	2204

	⑥	⑥	⑥	⑦	⑦	⑦	⑦	⑦	⑦	⑦	⑦	⑦	⑦	⑦	⑦	⑦B	⑦	⑦	⑦	⑦	⑦	⑦	⑦	⑦
Exeter St Davids ... ▽ d.	2025	2125	2257	...	...	...	...	...	0925	1025	1125	1225	1325	1425	...	1525	...	1625	...	1725	1825	1925	2025	2125
Honiton .... d.	2056	2157	2332	...	...	...	...	0858	0957	1057	1157	1257	1357	1457	...	1557	...	1657	...	1757	1857	1957	2057	2159
Axminster .... d.	2107	2208	2343	...	...	...	...	0909	1009	1109	1209	1309	1409	1509	...	1609	...	1709	...	1809	1909	2009	2109	2210
Crewkerne .... d.	2120	2221	2356	...	...	...	...	0922	1022	1122	1222	1322	1422	1522	...	1622	...	1722	...	1822	1922	2022	2122	2223
Yeovil Pen Mill .... d.	|	|	|	...	...	...	...	|	|	|	|	|	|	|	...	|	...	|	...	|	|	|	|	|
Yeovil Junction .... a.	2129	2229	0004	...	...	...	...	0930	1030	1130	1230	1330	1430	1530	...	1630	...	1730	...	1830	1930	2030	2131	2232
Yeovil Junction .... d.	2130	2231	0006	...	...	0732	...	0932	1032	1132	1232	1332	1432	1532	...	1632	...	1732	...	1832	1932	2032	2132	2233
Sherborne .... d.	2137	2237	|	...	...	0738	...	0938	1038	1138	1238	1338	1438	1538	...	1638	...	1738	...	1838	1938	2038	2138	2240
Gillingham .... d.	2152	2253	|	...	...	0754	0854	0954	1054	1154	1254	1354	1454	1554	1621	1654	1721	1754	...	1854	1954	2054	2154	2256
Salisbury .... a.	2223	2329	0041	...	...	0820	0920	1020	1120	1220	1320	1420	1520	1620	1647	1720	1747	1820	...	1920	2020	2120	2220	2321
Salisbury .... d.	2227	...	...	0642	0724	0827	0927	1027	1129	1227	1327	1427	1527	1627	1652	1727	1752	1827	1852	1927	2027	2127	2227	...
Andover .... d.	2247	...	...	0659	0743	0846	0946	1044	1146	1244	1346	1444	1546	1644	1709	1746	1809	1844	1909	1946	2044	2146	2246	...
Basingstoke .... **108** a.	2309	...	...	0719	0808	0908	1002	1106	1204	1306	1402	1506	1602	1706	1726	1802	1826	1906	1926	2002	2106	2203	2308	...
Woking .... **108** a.	*2332*	...	...	0739	0828	0928	1028	1128	1228	1328	1428	1528	1628	1728	1748	1828	1848	1928	1948	2028	2128	2228	*2350*	...
London Waterloo **108** a.	*0003*	...	...	0820	0912	1011	1104	1204	1304	1359	1459	1559	1659	1759	1819	1859	1919	1959	2019	2059	2159	2259	*0033*	...

☛ Full service **London** Waterloo - **Salisbury** and v.v. :

From **London** Waterloo on Ⓐ at 0710, 0750, 0820, 0850 and every 30 minutes until 1920, 1950, 2020, 2120, 2220, 2340; on ⑥ at 0710, 0750, 0820, 0850 and every 30 minutes until 2020, 2120, 2220, 2340; on ⑦ at 0815 and hourly until 2215, 2335 (also 1745, 1845, 1945, 2045. Please see timings above for calling points between London and Salisbury).

From **Salisbury** on Ⓐ at 0512, 0540, 0603, 0645, 0715, 0745, 0815, 0847, 0921, 0947 and at the same minutes past each hour until 1747, 1827, 1847, 1926, 2026, 2126; on ⑥ at 0512, 0544, 0618, 0647, 0721, 0747 and at the same minutes past each hour until 1847, 1926, 2026, 2126; on ⑦ at 0642, 0724, 0827 and hourly until 2127 (also 1652, 1752, 1852).

A – May 21 - Sept. 3. To / from Weymouth (Table **139**).
B – Conveys (12) London Waterloo - Bristol and v.v. (Table **140**).
b – Calls at Yeovil Junction before Yeovil Pen Mill.
c – May 21 - Sept. 3.
e – Does not call at Exeter Central.
s – Calls to set down only.
u – Calls to pick up only.
◧ – Via Westbury (Tables **140** and **139**).
■ – Additional trains Yeovil Pen Mill to Ye Junction and v.v.: from Yeovil Junction 1307⑥ **c**; from Yeovil Pen Mill at 1355
△ – Trains to Exeter St Davids also call at **Exeter Central** 5 - 6 minutes earlier
▽ – Trains from Exeter St Davids also call **Exeter Central** 4 - 5 minutes later.

For explanation of standard symbols see page 4

LONDON - EXETER - PAIGNTON and PLYMOUTH — 115

Service on ⑦ is valid until Sept. 11. For service on ⑦ from Sept. 18 please contact National Rail Enquiries ✆ + 44 (0)3457 48 49 50.

Ⓐ	Ⓐ2 B★	Ⓐ2 D★	Ⓐ2 a★	Ⓐ 2	Ⓐ 🍷	Ⓐ 🍷★	Ⓐ 2	Ⓐ 2★	Ⓐ 🍷D	Ⓐ 🍷a	Ⓐ 2F	Ⓐ2 G★	Ⓐ 🍴	Ⓐ 🍷★	Ⓐ 🍷	Ⓐ 🍷	Ⓐ 🍴	Ⓐ 2	Ⓐ 🍴	Ⓐ 2	Ⓐ 🍷	⑤ 2	⑤ 🍷H
London Paddington .. 132 d.	...	...	...	...	0706	0730	...	...	0906	0906	...	...	1006	1000	1106	1133	1205	...	1305	...	1406	...	1434
Reading .... 132 d.	...	...	...	...	0733	0759	...	...	0935	0935u	...	...	1032	1028	1133u	1201	1233u	...	1333	...	1434u	...	1501u
Newbury .... d.	...	...	...	...	0749	|	...	...	|	|	...	...	|	|	|	1223	|	...	|	...	|	...	|
Westbury .... d.	...	...	...	...	0826	|	...	...	|	|	...	...	|	|	1217	1300	|	...	|	...	|	1520	1610
Castle Cary .... d.	...	...	...	...	|	|	...	...	1031	1031	...	...	|	|	1235	|	|	...	|	...	|	1550	1628
Bristol Temple M. .. 120 d.	...	0524	0524	0642	|	0913	...	0855	|	|	0955	0955	|	1147	|	|	|	1319	|	1357	|	|	|
Taunton .... 120 d.	...	0620	0620	0739	0903	0945	...	1001	1053	1053	1100	1100	|	1229	1259	1340	|	1400	1448	1458	1549	1621	1651
Tiverton Parkway ...... 120 d.	...	0635	0635	0755	0916	|	...	|	1106	1106	1116	1116	|	|	1312	|	|	1415	1501	1514	1602	1637	1704
Exeter St Davids .... 120 a.	...	0652	0652	0812	0930	1009	...	1031	1121	1121	1132	1132	1206	1254	1328	1404	1406	1433	1516	1532	1617	1658	1720
Exeter St Davids. 116 120 d.	0628	0655	0655	0814	0933	1010	1018	1032	1125	1125	1135	1135	1208	1257	1329	...	1410	...	1519	...	1620	...	...
Newton Abbot .... 116 120 d.	0655	0728	0728	0835	0955	1038	1041	1101	1145	1145	1157	1214	1229	1323	1349	...	1429	...	1542	...	1641	...	...
Torquay .... 116 120 d.	|	|	|	|	|	1050	|	1113	|	|	1209	1227	|	1337	|	...	|	...	|	...	|	...	...
Paignton .... 116 120 a.	|	|	|	|	|	1057	|	1120	|	|	1242	1301	|	1345	|	...	|	...	|	...	|	...	...
Totnes .... 120 d.	0709	0742	0742	0849	1007	...	1053	...	1158	1158	...	...	|	...	1403	...	|	...	1554	...	1653	...	...
Plymouth .... 120 a.	0740	0811	0811	0919	1033	...	1124	...	1227	1227	...	...	1305	...	1433	...	1505	...	1623	...	1721	...	...
Newquay 117 .... a.	...	|	1009	|	|	...	|	...	|	1419	...	...	|	...	...	...	|	...	|	...	|	...	...
Penzance 117 .... a.	...	1016	...	1126	1237	...	1325	...	*1439*	*1444*	...	...	1511	...	...	...	1712	...	1833a	...	1933	...	...

	Ⓐ 🍷	Ⓐ 🍷	①–④ 🍷	⑤ 🍷	Ⓐ 🍷	Ⓐ 🍷★	Ⓐ 🍴	Ⓐ 🍷	①–④ 🍷	⑤ 🍷	①–④ 🍴	⑤ 🍴	Ⓐ 🍷	Ⓐ 🍷	Ⓐ 2	Ⓐ 2	Ⓐ 🍷	Ⓐ A	⑥ ⑥2 c★	⑥2 d★	⑥2 d★	⑥🍷 c★	⑥ 2	⑥ 🍷c
n Paddington ... 132 d.	1506	1606	1636	1636	1703	1733	1803	1805	1835	1835	1903	1903	1945	2035	...	...	2145	2345‡	...	...	...	...	...	0736
ng .... 132 d.	1533u	1632u	1704	1704	1730u	1801	1831u	1837	1903	1903	1933	1933u	2012	2102	...	...	2212	0046u	...	...	...	...	...	0804u
ury .... d.	|	|	1719	1719	1748	1819	|	1904	1919	1919	1950	1950	2028	2119	...	...	|	|	...	...	...	...	...	|
ury .... d.	1623	|	1803	1803	|	1900	|	1955	2006	2006	|	|	2106	2156	...	...	|	|	...	...	...	...	...	|
Cary .... d.	1641	|	1822	1822	|	1919	|	...	2024	2024	|	|	2126	2215	...	...	|	|	...	...	...	...	...	|
stol Temple M ... 120 d.	|	|	|	|	|	|	|	...	|	|	|	|	|	|	2156	2306	2335	|	0524	0524	0636	0644	...	|
on .... 120 d.	1705	1750	1844	1844	1852	1942	1948	...	2046	2046	2054	2054	2148	2237	2303	0014s	0036s	0235	0618	0618	0725	0730	...	0925
on Parkway ...... 120 d.	1718	1803	1857	1857	1905	1955	|	...	2059	2059	2107	2107	2202	2250	2318	0031s	0049s	|	0633	0633	0741	0743	...	|
St Davids .... 120 a.	1733	1818	1914	1913	1920	2009	2013	...	2116	2116	2122	2122	2217	2305	2337	0050	0107	0337	0652	0652	0759	0758	...	0950
St Davids.. 116 120 d.	1737	1822	...	1916	1922	2020	2016	...	...	2117	2125	2125	2219	2308	...	...	...	0411	0653	0653	0800	0800	0928	0953
n Abbot ..... 116 120 d.	1758	1843	...	1936	1942	2058	2036	...	...	2137	2145	2145	2240	2328	...	...	...	0433	0727	0727	0831	0832	0949	1015
quay .... 116 120 d.	|	|	...	|	|	2112	|	...	...	|	|	|	|	|	...	...	...	|	|	|	|	|	|	|
gnton .... 116 120 a.	|	|	...	|	|	2122	|	...	...	|	|	|	|	|	...	...	...	|	|	|	|	|	|	|
s .... 120 d.	1811	1856	...	|	1956	...	2050	...	...	|	2158	2158	2253	2342	...	...	...	|	0740	0740	0845	0846	1001	|
outh .... 120 a.	1839	1926	...	2015	2024	...	2118	...	...	2215	2226	2226	2325	0011	...	...	...	0514	0813	0813	0916	0916	1032	1051
wquay 117 .... a.	|	|	...	...	|	...	|	...	...	...	|	|	...	...	...	...	...	|	|	|	|	|	|	1242
zance 117 .... a.	2042	2131	...	...	2230	...	2313	...	...	...	*0046*	0040	...	...	...	...	...	0753	*1028*	1018	1126	1127	1237	...

	⑥ 🍷	⑥ 🍷d	⑥🍷 c★	⑥ 🍷d	⑥ 🍷c	⑥ 🍷	⑥ 2★	⑥🍷 c★	⑥ 🍷c	⑥ 🍷d	⑥ 🍷	⑥🍷 c★	⑥ 🍷c	⑥ 🍷d	⑥ 🍷	⑥ 🍷	⑥ 2★	⑥ 🍷	⑥ 🍷	⑥ 🍷	⑥ 🍷	⑥ 🍷	⑥ 🍷★	⑥ 2	⑥ 🍷
on Paddington ... 132 d.	0730	0806	0835	0906	0906	1006	...	1035	1106	1106	1206	1235	1306	1306	1406	1506	...	1606	1706	1630	1806	1906	2006	...	2030
ng .... 132 d.	0759	0834	0903u	0932	0934u	1033v	...	1104u	1134u	1132	1233v	1305u	1332u	1332	1434u	1532	...	1634v	1732	1659	1834u	1932	2033	...	2059
ury .... d.	|	0859	0919	|	|	|	...	|	|	|	|	1322	|	|	|	|	...	|	|	|	|	1949	2047	...	|
oury .... d.	|	0942	0956	|	|	|	...	1154	|	1221	|	1358	|	1424	|	1623	...	|	1823	|	|	2027	2126	...	|
e Cary .... d.	|	1002	1015	|	|	|	...	1212	|	1239	|	1416	|	1442	|	1641	...	|	1841	|	|	2044	2144	...	|
stol Temple M ... 120 d.	0917	|	|	|	|	|	*1144*	|	|	|	|	|	|	|	|	|	...	|	|	1818	|	|	|	2159	2217
on .... 120 d.	0951	1025	1037	1048	1050	|	*1216*	1235	|	1302	|	1440	1448	1504	1549	1704	...	1749	1903	1907	1948	2107	2206	2305	2318
on Parkway ...... 120 d.	|	1038	1050	1101	1103	|	*1228*	1248	|	1315	|	|	1501	1517	1602	1717	...	1802	1916	1923	|	2120	2219	2321	2331
St Davids .... 120 a.	1015	1053	1105	1116	1118	1208	*1243*	1302	1312	1330	1409	1503	1516	1532	1617	1731	...	1817	1932	1938	2012	2135	2234	2339	2347
r St Davids.. 116 120 d.	1019	...	1108	1119	1122	1212	1250	1308	1316	1333	1413	1507	1519	1534	1619	1735	1750	1819	1934	1940	2015	2139	2239	...	...
on Abbot ..... 116 120 d.	1039	...	1142	1138	1145	1235	1319	1349	1336	1353	1434	1540	1543	1555	1640	1757	1822	1841	1954	2000	2036	2159	2303	...	...
quay .... 116 120 d.	|	...	1155	|	|	|	|	1402	|	|	|	1553	|	|	|	|	|	|	|	2015	|	|	|	...	...
gnton .... 116 120 a.	|	...	1204	|	|	|	|	1412	|	|	|	1600	|	|	|	|	|	|	|	2022	|	|	|	...	...
s .... 120 d.	1052	...	...	1152	1158	|	1332	...	1348	1405	|	...	1556	1609	1652	1810	1835	1854	2008	...	2050	2212	2316	...	...
outh .... 120 a.	1120	...	...	1224	1226	1313	1405	...	1417	1434	1510	...	1623	1636	1724	1839	1906	1924	2035	...	2118	2243	2346	...	...
wquay 117 .... a.	|	...	...	...	|	|	|	...	|	...	|	...	|	|	|	|	|	|	|	...	|	...	...	...	...
nzance 117 .... a.	1321	...	...	...	1429	1518	*1621*	...	1621	...	1710	...	1825	1854	1924	2041d	2111	2127c	2242d	...	2322	...	...	...	...

⑦	⑦ 2★	⑦ 2★	⑦ 🍷★	⑦ 🍷	⑦ 2	⑦ 🍷	⑦ 🍷	⑦ 🍷★	⑦ 🍷	⑦ 🍷	⑦ 🍷	⑦ 2★	⑦ 🍷	⑦ 🍷	⑦ 🍷	⑦ 🍷	⑦ 2	⑦ 🍷		⑦ 🍷★	⑦ 🍷	⑦ 🍷	⑦ 🍷	⑦ A
on Paddington ... 132 d.	...	...	0800	0851	...	0957	1057	1127	1157	1257	1300	...	1357	1457	1557	1657	...	1757	...	1857	1903	1957	2057	2350‡
ing .... 132 d.	...	...	0839	0932	...	1032	1133	1208	1233	1332	1338	...	1432	1532	1632	1732	...	1832	...	1932	1938	2032	2132	0038u
ury .... d.	...	...	|	0948	...	|	|	|	1248	|	|	...	1448	|	1648	|	...	1849	...	|	|	2048	|	|
oury .... d.	...	...	|	1022	...	|	|	1305	|	1419	|	...	|	|	1724	|	...	1927	...	|	|	2127	|	|
e Cary .... d.	...	...	|	|	...	1133	|	1324	|	|	|	...	1536	|	1743	|	...	|	...	2030	|	2144	|	|
stol Temple M ... 120 d.	0726	0828	1000	|	...	|	|	|	|	|	1456	...	|	|	|	|	1830	|	...	|	2100	|	|	|
ton .... 120 d.	0820	0932	1034	1058	...	1156	1247	1345	1354	1455	1529	...	1557	1651	1805	1851	1933	2002	...	2052	2151	2206	2246s	|
ton Parkway ...... 120 d.	0835	0947	1048	1112	...	|	|	1359	1407	|	|	...	|	1704	1818	1904	1949	2017	...	2106	2205	2219	2300s	|
er St Davids .... 120 a.	0853	1004	1102	1126	...	1221	1314	1413	1421	1518	1553	...	1622	1718	1834	1919	2007	2030	...	2121	2221	2235	2319	0305
er St Davids.. 116 120 d.	0905	1006	1105	1126	1215	1223	1315	1415	1424	1521	1555	1605	1624	1721	1836	1921	...	2030	...	2122	...	2236	...	0435
on Abbot ..... 116 120 d.	0928	1032	1132	1147	1236	1244	1337	1442	1447	1542	1616	1637	1643	1740	1858	1940	...	2053	...	2149	...	2257	...	0456
rquay .... 116 120 d.	|	|	|	|	|	|	|	1453	|	|	|	|	|	|	|	|	...	|	...	|	...	|	...	|
ignton .... 116 120 a.	|	|	|	|	|	|	|	1502	|	|	|	|	|	|	|	|	...	|	...	|	...	|	...	|
es .... 120 d.	0941	1044	1144	1201	1248	1257	|	...	1459	1554	|	1651	1701	1755	|	1955	...	2106	...	2203	...	2310	...	|
outh .... 120 a.	1012	1113	1214	1230	1318	1325	1413	...	1527	1622	1653	1721	1730	1821	1934	2022	...	2133	...	2231	...	2340	...	0535
wquay 117 .... a.	|	|	|	|	...	1512	|	...	|	|	...	|	...	|	|	|	...	|	...	...	...	...	...	|
nzance 117 .... a.	1224	1315	1416	1433	...	...	1612	...	1728	1824	...	1937	...	2029	*2142*	2224	...	2335	...	...	...	...	...	0859

THE NIGHT RIVIERA – Conveys 🛏 1, 2. cl and (2). To Par May 16 - July 1 / from Sept. 5 (Table **117**). May 16 - July 1 and from Sept. 5.

F – From Sept. 12.
G – May 16 - Sept. 9.
H – July 8 - Sept. 2.
a – July 4 - Sept. 2.
b – Also calls at Dawlish 0621.
c – May 21 - Sept. 10.
d – From Sept. 17.
s – Stops to set down only.

NOTES CONTINUE ON NEXT PAGE →

EXETER - PAIGNTON — 116

2nd class

Ⓐ	Ⓐ	Ⓐ	Ⓐ	Ⓐ	Ⓐ	Ⓐ	Ⓐ	Ⓐ	Ⓐ	Ⓐ	Ⓐ	Ⓐ	Ⓐ	Ⓐ	Ⓐ	Ⓐ	Ⓐ	Ⓐ	Ⓐ	Ⓐ	Ⓐ
Exeter St Davids .... 115 d.	0534	0611	0718	0750	0842	0858	0958	1032	1058	1158	1249	1303	1358	1503	1558	1628	1655	1728	1751	1836	1933
Dawlish .... 115 d.	0555	0631	0738	0810	0857	0925	1019	1048	1118	1228	|	1324	1428	1523	1619	1648	1715	1755	1812	1902	1959
Teignmouth .... 115 d.	0600	0636	0743	0815	0902	0930	1024	1053	1123	1233	|	1329	1433	1528	1624	1653	1720	1800	1817	1907	2004
Newton Abbot .... 115 d.	0609	0645	0752	0824	0911	0938	1032	1101	1132	1241	1313	1338	1442	1537	1632	1702	1729	1810	1826	1916	2013
Torquay .... 115 d.	0620	0656	0803	0836	0922	0950	1044	1113	1143	1253	1324	1349	1453	1548	1644	1713	1740	1821	1837	1927	2024
Paignton .... 🚂 115 a.	0628	0706	0812	0844	0929	0957	1053	1120	1152	1301	1333	1358	1500	1557	1654	1722	1750	1830	1846	1934	2032

	Ⓐ	Ⓐ	Ⓐ	⑥ ⑥	⑥	⑥	⑥	⑥	⑥	⑥	⑥	⑥	⑥	⑥	⑥	⑥	⑥	⑥	⑥	⑥	⑥	⑥
er St Davids .... 115 d.	2020	2129	2246	0518	0536	0611	0750	0837	0856	0956	1025	1035	1059	1157	1258	1359	1430	1458	1558	1655	1727	1827
ish .... 115 d.	2043	2149	2306	0539	0557	0631	0810	0851	0925	1016	|	1051	1119	1217	1318	1429	1446	1518	1617	1715	1753	1846
mouth .... 115 d.	2050	2154	2311	0544	0602	0636	0815	0856	0930	1021	|	1056	1124	1222	1323	1434	1451	1523	1622	1720	1758	1851
on Abbot .... 115 d.	2058	2203	2319	0552	0611	0645	0824	0906	0939	1030	1048	1104	1136	1233	1332	1444	1500	1532	1631	1729	1808	1901
uay .... 115 d.	2112	2214	2330	0603	0622	0656	0835	0916	0950	1042	1059	1114	1147	1243	1343	1456	1511	1543	1642	1740	1819	1912
nton .... 🚂 115 a.	2122	2223	2339	0611	0630	0706	0844	0925	1000	1052	1107	1123	1157	1256	1351	1504	1519	1553	1652	1750	1826	1921

	⑥	⑥	⑥	⑥		⑦ ⑦	⑦	⑦	⑦	⑦	⑦	⑦	⑦	⑦	⑦	⑦	⑦	⑦	⑦	⑦	⑦	⑦
er St Davids .... 115 d.	1856	1913	2019	2056	...	0849	0954	1053	1158	1302	1326	1359	1415	1505	1531	1600	1657	1757	1857	1957	2102	2202
ish .... 115 d.	1909	1933	2039	2116	...	0909	1014	1113	1218	1317	1339	1419	1429	1517	1543	1615	1710	1817	1917	2017	2115	2222
mouth .... 115 d.	1914	1938	2044	2121	...	0914	1019	1118	1223	1322	1344	1424	1435	1522	1548	1620	1715	1822	1922	2022	2120	2227
on Abbot .... 115 d.	1922	1947	2053	2132	...	0924	1037	1127	1232	1330	1352	1435	1442	1530	1556	1629	1723	1831	1931	2031	2128	2236
uay .... 115 d.	1932	1958	2104	2143	...	0935	1048	1138	1243	1341	1404	1446	1453	1542	1607	1640	1735	1842	1942	2042	2140	2247
nton .... 🚂 115 a.	1940	2006	2111	2150	...	0942	1054	1145	1251	1348	1411	1452	1502	1550	1615	1647	1742	1849	1949	2049	2147	2255

\- Dartmouth Steam Railway (Paignton - Kingswear: *10 km*). ✆ 01803 555 872. www.dartmouthrailriver.co.uk

115 PLYMOUTH and PAIGNTON - EXETER - LONDON

Service on ⑦ is valid until Sept. 11. For service on ⑦ from Sept. 18 please contact National Rail Enquiries ✆ +44 (0)3457 48 49 50.

km		Ⓐ 🍷w	Ⓐ 🍷	Ⓐ 2	Ⓐ 🍴	Ⓐ 🍷b	Ⓐ 🍷	Ⓐ 🍴	Ⓐ 🍷	Ⓐ 🍷☆	Ⓐ 2☆	Ⓐ 🍷	Ⓐ 🍷	Ⓐ 🍷	Ⓐ 🍷☆	Ⓐ 🍴	Ⓐ 2☆	Ⓐ 🍴	Ⓐ 🍷☆	Ⓐ 🍷	Ⓐ 🍷	Ⓐ 🍷
	Penzance **117** d.	...	...	...	...	...	...	0505	0541	...	0600	0645	0741	0844	...	1000	...	1047a	...	...	1303	*1345*
	Newquay **117** d.	...	...	...	...	...	...	|	|	...	|	|	|	|	...	|	...	|	...	...	|	|
0	**Plymouth** 120 d.	...	...	...	0553	0530	0509	0655	0748	...	0809	0853	0948	1044	...	1201	...	1256	...	...	1503	1602
38	Totnes 120 d.	...	...	...	|	0558	|	|	0816	...	0839	0923	1019	|	...	1229	...	1324	...	...	|	1629
	Paignton 116 120 d.	...	...	...	|	|	|	|	|	0740	|	|	|	|	1132	|	1248	|	1413	...	|	|
	Torquay 116 120 d.	...	...	...	|	|	|	|	|	0746	|	|	|	|	1138	|	1254	|	1419	...	|	|
52	Newton Abbot 116 120 d.	...	...	...	0631	0611	0547	0732	0829	0806	0852	0936	1032	|	1150	1242	1308	1337	1432	...	1541	1642
84	**Exeter** St Davids 116 120 a.	...	...	...	0651	0633	0610	0752	0849	0839	0918	0956	1054	1137	1215	1302	1332	1357	1458	...	1601	1702
84	**Exeter** St Davids 120 d.	...	0546	0600	0652	0635	0612	0753	0851	0841	0933	0958	1056	1139	1217	1304	1336	1359	1501	1453	1603	1708
110	Tiverton Parkway 120 d.	...	0602	0617	|	0651	0627	|	0906	|	0950	1013	1111	|	1231	1319	1353	|	1516	1508	1617	1723
133	Taunton 120 d.	...	0617	0634	0718	0706	0654	0819	0921	0905	1007	1028	1125	|	1245	1334	1410	1424	1531	1523	1631	1736
205	**Bristol** Temple M 120 a.	0518	|	0741	|	|	0757	|	|	0957	1110	|	1158	|	|	|	1513	|	|	|	|	|
	Castle Cary d.	|	0639	...	|	0727	|	|	0942	|	...	|	|	|	1306	|	...	1446	1553	|	|	|
	Westbury d.	0603	0701	...	|	0751	|	|	1002	|	...	1105	|	|	1327	|	...	1504	|	1608	|	|
	Newbury a.	0648	0745	...	|	0829	|	|	|	|	...	|	|	|	1403	|	...	|	|	1649	|	|
337	**Reading** 132 a.	0716	0806	...	0832	0850	0914	0932	1050	1108	...	1150	1308	1316	1420	1450	...	1549	1650	1716	1749	1851
395	**London** Paddington 132 a.	0749	0838	...	0900	0921	0944	1002	1124	1139	...	1224	1339	1344	1454	1521	...	1622	1724	1745	1821	1924

	⑤ 🍷H	Ⓐ 🍴	Ⓐ 2☆	①–④ 🍷	⑤ 🍷	⑤ 🍷	①–④ 🍷	Ⓐ 🍷	Ⓐ 2☆	Ⓐ 2☆	Ⓐ A	⑥ 2	⑥ 🍷	⑥ 🍷	⑥ 🍷	⑥ 2c	⑥ 🍷	⑥ 🍷	⑥ 🍷☆	⑥ 🍷c	⑥ 🍷d	⑥ 🍷
Penzance **117** d.	...	1559	...	*1644*	*1644*	1739	1739	...	...	*1913*	2145‡	...	...	...	...	0527	*0537*d	0650	...	0718	0759	0839
Newquay **117** d.	...	|	...	|	|	|	|	...	...	|	|	...	...	...	...	|	|	|	...	|	|	|
Plymouth 120 d.	...	1803	...	*1844*	*1844*	1942	1942	...	...	2125	2354	...	0540	0655	...	0735	0747	0852	...	0930	1001	1044
Totnes 120 d.	...	1831	...	*1913*	*1913*	2010	2010	...	...	2154	0022	...	0607	|	...	0803	0814	0919	...	0959	1031	|
Paignton 116 120 d.	...	|	1852	|	|	|	|	*2014*	*2035*	|	|	...	|	|	...	|	|	|	0918	|	|	|
Torquay 116 120 d.	...	|	1857	|	|	|	|	*2020*	*2040*	|	|	...	|	|	...	|	|	|	0925	|	|	|
Newton Abbot 116 120 d.	...	1844	1909	*1926*	*1926*	2023	2023	*2031*	*2053*	2206	0036	...	0620	0732	...	0815	0827	0932	0939	1012	1044	|
Exeter St Davids 116 120 a.	...	1903	1939	*1948*	*1948*	2043	2043	*2050*	*2128*	2240	0058	...	0640	0752	...	0842	0847	0952	1013	1032	1104	1138
Exeter St Davids 120 d.	1817	1906	1939	1955	*1948*	2045	2045	*2052*	2149	...	0106	0600	0641	0754	0729	...	0849	0954	1015	1035	1106	1140
Tiverton Parkway 120 d.	|	1921	|	2010	*2005*	2100	2100	*2105*	2206	...	|	0617	0656	0809	0744	...	0904	1009	1030	|	1121	|
Taunton 120 d.	1842	1936	2010	2025	2027	2115	2115	2129	2223	...	0142	0634	0711	0824	0759	...	0919	1024	1045	1100	1136	|
Bristol Temple M 120 a.	|	|	2054	|	|	2147	2147	2232	2312	...	|	0742	|	|	0857	...	|	|	1133	|	|	|
Castle Cary d.	|	|	...	2046	2046	|	|	|	...	...	|	...	0733	|	|	...	0940	|	|	1121	|	|
Westbury d.	|	|	...	2105	2105	|	|	|	...	...	|	...	0756	|	|	...	0959	1102	|	1143	|	|
Newbury a.	|	|	...	2142	2142	|	|	|	...	...	|	...	0833	|	|	...	|	|	|	|	|	|
Reading 132 a.	2018	2050	...	2159	2159	2308	2304	2354	...	...	0400s	...	0851	0942	1011	...	1050	1147	1246	1237	1251	1316
London Paddington 132 a.	2052	2124	...	2241	2230	2341	2344	0039	...	...	0523	...	0922	1010	1039	...	1121	1223	1315	1309	1321	1344

	⑥ 🍷c	⑥ 🍷d	⑥ 🍷d	⑥ 🍷c	⑥ 🍷c	⑥ 2 c☆	⑥ 🍷c	⑥ 🍷d	⑥ 🍷 c☆	⑥ 🍷c	⑥ 🍷d	⑥ 🍷	⑥ 🍷d	⑥ 🍷 c☆	⑥ 🍷	⑥ 2 d☆	⑥ 2 c☆	⑥ 🍷c	⑥ 🍷	⑥ 2☆	⑦ 2	⑦ 🍷
Penzance **117** d.	0954	1000	1058	1100	...	...	1158	*1146*	...	*1300*x	*1300*	1401	*1452*	...	1552	1641	1655	...	1740	1906	...	...
Newquay **117** d.	|	|	|	|	1130	...	|	|	...	1319	|	|	|	...	|	|	|	1726	|	|	...	...
Plymouth 120 d.	1200	1159	1254	1302	1314	1335	1359	1400	...	1506	1504	1600	1656	...	1754	1851	1904	1918	1942	2115	...	...
Totnes 120 d.	1229	1229	1321	|	1341	1407	|	|	...	|	1531	1628	1727	...	1821	1922	1934	|	2009	2144	...	...
Paignton 116 120 d.	|	|	|	|	|	|	|	|	1448	|	|	|	|	1700	|	|	|	|	|	|	...	...
Torquay 116 120 d.	|	|	|	|	|	|	|	|	1455	|	|	|	|	1707	|	|	|	|	|	|	...	...
Newton Abbot 116 120 d.	1302	1242	1335	|	1354	1421	1435	1435	1507	1542	1544	1641	1740	1719	1834	1935	1946	1955	2022	2156	...	...
Exeter St Davids 116 120 a.	1305	1302	1355	1402	1415	1453	1456	1456	1533	1604	1604	1702	1800	1751	1854	2001	...	2014	2042	2222	...	...
Exeter St Davids 120 d.	1320	1304	1357	1404	1418	...	1459	1459	1536	1607	1606	1703	1802	1802	1856	...	...	2016	2044	...	0801	0839
Tiverton Parkway 120 d.	1335	1319	|	|	|	...	1514	1514	|	1622	1621	1717	1817	1817	1911	...	...	|	2059	...	0818	0854
Taunton 120 d.	|	1334	1423	1430	|	...	1529	1529	1601	1636	1636	1732	1832	1832	1926	...	...	2042	2114	...	0835	0908
Bristol Temple M 120 a.	|	|	|	|	|	...	|	|	|	|	|	|	|	|	|	...	...	|	2147	...	0938	|
Castle Cary d.	|	|	1444	|	|	...	|	1550	1623	|	|	|	1853	1853	1947	...	...	|	|	...	...	0930
Westbury d.	|	|	1502	|	|	...	|	1616	1642	|	|	|	1913	1913	2006	...	...	|	|	...	...	0950
Newbury a.	|	|	|	|	|	...	|	1654	|	|	|	|	1946	1946	|	...	...	|	|	...	...	1027
Reading 132 a.	1450	1449	1549	1546	1554	...	1648	1711	1734	1753	1751	1849	2004	2004	2056	...	...	2157	2304	...	...	1045
London Paddington 132 a.	1521	1521	1621	1621	1632	...	1721	1741	1808	1821	1821	1921	2037	2037	2132	...	...	2232	2342	...	...	1123

	⑦ 🍷☆	⑦ 🍷	⑦ 🍷	⑦ 🍷	⑦ 🍷	⑦ 🍷	⑦ 2☆	⑦ 🍷	⑦ 🍷	⑦ 🍷	⑦ 🍷☆	⑦ 2	⑦ 🍷	⑦ 2☆		⑦	⑦ 🍷	⑦ 🍷		⑦ 🍷		⑦ 🍷	⑦ 2☆
Penzance **117** d.	...	...	0830	0947	1100	1140	1205	1256	...	...	...	1339	...	1437	...	1500	1550	...	...	1731	...	...	1900
Newquay **117** d.	...	...	|	|	|	|	|	|	...	...	...	|	...	|	...	|	|	1621	...	|	...	...	|
Plymouth 120 d.	0840	1010	1038	1145	1300	1345	1407	1455	1510	1542	...	1551	1612	1638	...	1700	1745	1810	...	1930	...	2000	2115
Totnes 120 d.	0907	1040	1105	1213	1328	1413	1436	1525	|	1608	...	1620	1639	1707	...	1728	1816	1840	...	1957	...	|	2144
Paignton 116 120 d.	|	|	|	|	|	|	|	|	|	|	1545	|	|	|	...	|	|	|	...	|	...	|	|
Torquay 116 120 d.	|	|	|	|	|	|	|	|	|	|	1550	|	|	|	...	|	|	|	...	|	...	|	|
Newton Abbot 116 120 d.	0921	1054	1119	1227	1341	1426	1449	1538	1547	1623	1605	1633	1655	1720	...	1740	1829	1852	...	2010	...	2036	2157
Exeter St Davids 116 120 a.	0947	1114	1139	1247	1401	1447	1515	1558	1607	1643	1631	1654	1715	1746	...	1801	1850	1913	...	2030	...	2057	2222
Exeter St Davids 120 d.	0949	1118	1141	1248	1403	1449	...	1601	1609	1644	1633	...	1717	1747	...	1802	1852	1915	...	2031	...	2059	...
Tiverton Parkway 120 d.	|	1133	1156	|	1417	|	...	1616	1624	1700	|	...	1732	|	...	1819	|	1930	...	2047	...	2114	...
Taunton 120 d.	1013	1148	1210	1314	1432	1514	...	1631	1639	1714	1658	...	1746	1818	...	1834	1916	1944	...	2100	...	2127	...
Bristol Temple M 120 a.	|	1224	|	|	|	|	...	|	1720	|	1757	...	1822	1917	...	|	|	|	...	|	...	2159	...
Castle Cary d.	|	|	1231	|	|	1536	...	|	|	1736	|	...	|	...	...	|	|	2006	...	2124	...	|	...
Westbury d.	1049	|	1251	1358	|	1553	...	|	|	1756	|	...	|	...	...	|	1955	2027	...	2144	...	|	...
Newbury a.	1123	|	1328	|	|	1632	...	|	|	1833	|	...	|	...	...	|	2028	|	...	2219	...	|	...
Reading 132 a.	1144	1344	1348	1444	1551	1650	...	1749	1844	1852	1914	...	1941	...	...	1952	2048	2114	...	2241	...	2326	...
London Paddington 132 a.	1222	1423	1427	1526	1628	1729	...	1827	1925	1930	1954	...	2025	...	...	2030	2127	2153	...	2328	...	0007	...

NOTES (continued from previous page)

u – Stops to pick up only.
v – Until Sept. 10 stops to pick up only.
w – Via Trowbridge (Table **140**).
x – Change at Par.
★ – Also calls at Dawlish (10 – 15 minutes after Exeter) and Teignmouth (15 – 18 minutes after Exeter).
☆ – Also calls at Teignmouth (7 – 10 minutes after Newton Abbot) and Dawlish (12 – 15 minutes after Newton Abb
‡ – Passengers may occupy cabins at London Paddington from 2230 and at Penzance from 2045⑦/2115Ⓐ.

116 PAIGNTON - EXETER

2nd class

	Ⓐ	Ⓐ	Ⓐ	Ⓐ	Ⓐ	Ⓐ	Ⓐ	Ⓐ	Ⓐ	Ⓐ	Ⓐ	Ⓐ	Ⓐ	Ⓐ	Ⓐ	Ⓐ	Ⓐ	Ⓐ	Ⓐ	Ⓐ	Ⓐ
Paignton 🚂 115 d.	0603	0634	0711	0740	0820	0912	1021	1033	1115	1213	1308	1421	1513	1612	1630	1657	1726	1752	1834	1937	2035
Torquay 115 d.	0608	0639	0716	0746	0825	0917	1026	1038	1120	1218	1313	1426	1518	1617	1635	1702	1731	1757	1839	1942	2040
Newton Abbot 115 d.	0621	0652	0737	0806	0838	0939	1039	1051	1133	1231	1326	1439	1531	1631	1648	1715	1744	1810	1852	1954	2053
Teignmouth 115 d.	0628	0659	0745	0813	0845	0945	1046	1058	1140	1238	1333	1446	1538	1638	1655	1722	1751	1817	1859	2002	2100
Dawlish 115 d.	0633	0704	0750	0819	0850	0950	1051	1103	1145	1243	1338	1451	1543	1643	1700	1727	1756	1822	1904	2007	2105
Exeter St Davids 115 a.	0703	0733	0814	0839	0912	1014	1113	1128	1208	1313	1408	1513	1612	1711	1718	1751	1819	1845	1932	2029	2128

	Ⓐ	Ⓐ	⑥	⑥	⑥	⑥	⑥	⑥	⑥	⑥	⑥	⑥	⑥a	⑥b	⑥	⑥	⑥	⑥	⑥b	⑥a	⑥
Paignton 🚂 115 d.	2230	2341	0613	0634	0806	0904	0930	1015	1058	1120	1213	1243	1300	1313	1412	1513	1543	1613	1711	1718	1751
Torquay 115 d.	2235	2346	0618	0639	0811	0909	0935	1020	1103	1125	1218	1248	1305	1318	1417	1518	1548	1618	1716	1723	1756
Newton Abbot 115 d.	2248	2359	0631	0652	0834	0935	0949	1033	1122	1138	1232	1307	1318	1338	1439	1533	1606	1631	1729	1736	1809
Teignmouth 115 d.	2255	0006	0638	0659	0841	0942	0956	1040	1130	1145	1239	1314	1325	1346	1447	1541	1613	1638	1736	1744	1817
Dawlish 115 d.	2300	0011	0643	0704	0846	0947	1002	1045	1135	1150	1244	1319	1330	1351	1452	1546	1618	1643	1741	1749	1822
Exeter St Davids 115 a.	2322	0034	0706	0733	0909	1009	1018	1117	1158	1213	1313	1336	1354	1413	1513	1614	1631	1714	1810	1812	1844

	⑥	⑥	⑥	⑥	⑥	⑦	⑦	⑦	⑦	⑦	⑦	⑦	⑦	⑦	⑦	⑦		⑦	⑦	⑦	⑦
Paignton 🚂 115 d.	1921	1951	2013	2115	2153	0949	1058	1149	1257	1352	1419	1457	1555	1619	1654	1749	...	1855	1955	2055	2152
Torquay 115 d.	1926	1956	2018	2120	2158	0954	1103	1154	1302	1357	1424	1501	1600	1624	1659	1754	...	1900	2000	2100	2157
Newton Abbot 115 d.	1940	2008	2031	2133	2211	1007	1121	1207	1315	1409	1437	1516	1613	1637	1712	1807	...	1913	2014	2113	2209
Teignmouth 115 d.	1947	2015	2038	2140	2218	1014	1128	1214	1322	1416	1444	1523	1620	1644	1719	1814	...	1920	2021	2120	2216
Dawlish 115 d.	1952	2020	2043	2145	2223	1019	1133	1219	1327	1421	1449	1528	1625	1649	1724	1819	...	1925	2026	2125	2221
Exeter St Davids 115 a.	2025	2038	2105	2207	2245	1040	1147	1242	1340	1442	1512	1541	1642	1711	1741	1840	...	1948	2049	2138	2242

a – May 21 - Sept. 10.
b – From Sept. 17.
🚂 – Dartmouth Steam Railway (Paignton - Kingswear). ✆ 01803 555 872. www.dartmouthrailriver.co.uk

XC PLYMOUTH - NEWQUAY and PENZANCE 117

Service on ⑦ is valid until Sept. 11. For service on ⑦ from Sept. 18 please contact National Rail Enquiries ✆ +44 (0)3457 48 49 50.

Ⓐ	②–⑤	①	②–⑤	①	Ⓐ	Ⓐ2	Ⓐ	Ⓐ	Ⓐ	Ⓐ	Ⓐ	Ⓐ	Ⓐ	Ⓐ	Ⓐ	Ⓐ	Ⓐ2	Ⓐ	Ⓐ	Ⓐ	Ⓐ	Ⓐ	Ⓐ	Ⓐ	Ⓐ	Ⓐ
	A			A	🍷	B a	2 b	2 a	2 a	🍷 b	2	🍷	2	2 B	🍷 b	2 a	G b	🍷	2 a	2	🍷	2 b	2 a	🍷 b	2	🍷
London Pad. **115** d.	2345p	...	...	2350p	...	...	...	...	...	...	...	0706	...	*0730*e	0906	*0906*	...	1006	...	...	1205	...	...	1305	*1305*	1406
Bristol § **115 120** d.	|	...	...	|	...	...	0524	0524	...	...	0642	|	...	*0913*e	|	*0944*	...	*1045*	...	*1144*	*1245*	*1344*	*1344*	*1344*	*1445*	*1513*e
Plymouth d.	0543	0600	0628	0628	0702	0753	0814	0814	...	0820	0921	1039	...	1125	1228	1239	...	1311	...	1349	1512	1557	1557	1628	1701	1723
Saltash d.	|	|	|	|	0715	0802	|	0824	...	0832	0931	|	...	1134	1238	1248	...	|	...	1358	|	1611	1612	|	1714	1734
Liskeard d.	0608	0623	0651	0709	0736	0820	0839	0843	...	0853	0950	1103	...	1153	1258	1307	...	1335	...	1417	1537	1633	1633	1653	1738	1754
Bodmin Parkway 🚂 d.	0622	0635	0703	0723	0749	0833	0851	0855	...	|	1002	1116	...	1205	1312	1319	...	1348	...	1429	1549	▬	1645	1706	...	1807
Lostwithiel d.	0628	0641	0708	0729	0755	0840	0856	0900	...	|	1007	|	...	1211	1318	1324	...	|	...	1434	|	Ⓐ2	1650	1712	...	1813
Par ♡ d.	0637	0648	0715	0738	0803	0854	0917	0908	0917	0914	1015	1128	1140	1218	1328	1332	1338	1400	1407	1442	1601	1610	1658	1721	...	1822
Newquay ♡ a.	|	|	|	|	|	...	1009	|	1009	|	|	|	1231	|	1419	|	|	|	1459	|	|	1702	|	|	...	|
St Austell d.	0646	0655	0721	0746	0811	...	...	0916	...	0923	1022	1136	...	1225	...	1339	1345	1407	...	1449	1608	...	1706	1728	...	1829
Truro d.	0706	0711	0738	0806	0829	...	...	0934	...	0940	1040	1154	...	1242	...	1357	1403	1425	...	1507	1626	...	1723	1746	...	1847
Redruth d.	0718	0723	0749	0820	0841	...	...	0947	...	0953	1053	1206	...	1256	...	1410	1416	1437	...	1520	1638	...	1736	1759	...	1859
Camborne d.	0726	0730	0755	0827	0848	...	...	0953	...	1000	1059	1214	...	1302	...	1416	1422	1445	...	1526	1646	...	1742	1807	...	1907
St Erth d.	0742	0743	0807	0845	0902	...	...	1008	...	1014	1110	1225	...	1314	...	1428	1433	1459	...	1538	1700	...	1754	1822	...	1921
Penzance a.	0753	0752	0816	0859	0912	...	...	1016	...	1027	1126	1237	...	1325	...	1439	1444	1511	...	1549	1712	...	1806	1833	...	1933

	Ⓐ	Ⓐ	Ⓐ	Ⓐ	Ⓐ	Ⓐ	Ⓐ	Ⓐ	Ⓐ	Ⓐ	Ⓐ	⑤	①–④	⑥	⑥	⑥	⑥	⑥	⑥	⑥	⑥	⑥	⑥	⑥	⑥	⑥	⑥
	2	2	2	🍷	C	🍷	2	D	🍷	C	🍷	🍷	2	2 c	A	2 c	c	d	2 c	d	2 c	2 d	c	🍷 d	2 c	2 B	🍷 d
don Pad. **115**. d.	...	...	...	1506	...	1606	...	...	1703	...	1803	1903	*1903*	...	2345p	...	...	...	...	...	...	...	...	...	...	...	0736
tol § **115 120**.. d.	...	*1544*	...	|	1645	|	...	1744	|	1844	|	*1945*	*1945*	...	|	...	...	...	0524	*0524*	...	...	0636	0644	...	*0812*e	*0845*
uth d.	...	1755	1817	1842	1901	1931	...	1949	2026	2050	2120	2229	2242	...	0543	...	0628	0725	0818	0818	...	...	0919	0923	0951	1033	1054
h d.	...	1804	1831	|	|	1940	...	|	2037	|	|	2239	2251	...	|	...	|	|	0828	0828	...	...	0928	0933	1001	1044	|
rd d.	...	1820	1854	1907	1924	1957	...	2012	2056	2113	2145	2259	2310	...	0608	...	0651	0749	0847	0848	...	...	0949	0950	1022	1103	1119
n Parkway 🚂 d.	...	1832	...	1919	1936	2010	...	2024	2109	2125	2159	2313	2326	...	0622	...	0703	0802	0859	0901	...	...	1002	1003	1034	1115	|
thiel d.	...	1837	...	|	|	|	...	|	|	2131	|	2319	2331	...	0628	...	0708	0808	0904	0907	...	...	|	1009	1039	1120	|
♡ d.	1829	1845	...	1931	1946	2022	2028	2034	2121	2137	2211	2328	2339	0609	0637	0652	0714	0818	0912	0916	0918	0946	1014	1016	1046	1128	1141
vquay ♡ a.	1921	|	...	|	|	|	2120	|	|	|	|	|	|	|	|	0744	|	0908	|	|	1010	1047	|	|	|	|	1242
stell d.	...	1853	...	1939	1952	2029	...	2041	2128	2144	2218	2335	2346	0616	0646	...	0721	...	0920	0923	...	...	1022	1024	1054	1137	...
d.	...	1910	...	2000	2018	2047	...	2102	2146	2203	2237	2353	0005	0635	0706	...	0737	...	0937	0942	...	...	1040	1042	1110	1155	...
th d.	...	1923	...	2010	2029	2059	...	2118	2158	2214	2248	0006	0018	0648	0718	...	0748	...	0950	0955	...	...	1055	1054	1124	1208	...
orne d.	...	1929	...	2018	2035	2107	...	2125	|	2220	|	0014	0024	0654	0726	...	0755	...	0956	1002	...	...	1102	1101	1130	1214	...
n d.	...	1942	...	2028	2046	2120	...	2135	2216	2232	|	0028	0035	0704	0742	...	0807	...	1008	1018	...	...	1117	1116	1142	1225	...
ance a.	...	1954	...	2042	2054	2131	...	2143	2230	2241	2313	0040	0046	0716	0753	...	0815	...	1018	1028	...	...	1126	1127	1155	1237	...

	⑥	⑥	⑥	⑥	⑥	⑥	⑥	⑥🍷	⑥	⑥	⑥	⑥	⑥	⑥	⑥	⑥	⑥🍷	⑥	⑥	⑥	⑥	⑥	⑥	⑥	⑥	⑥	⑥	⑥
	🍷	2 c	🍷 d	🍷 d	2 c	🍷	2 c	H d	🍷 d	2 c	🍷 d	🍷	2 c	2	🍷 d	🍷 c	J d	🍷	2 c	🍷 d	2 c	2 d	🍷 c	C	2 d	2 B	2 c	🍷 d
don Pad. **115**. d.	0730	...	0906	...	*0906*	1006	...	...	1106	...	1135	1206	...	...	1306	1306	...	1406	...	...	...	...	1506	...	...	...	...	1606
tol § **115 120**.. d.	0917	...	|	1020	*1044*	|	...	1144	|	*1144*	*1244*	*1244*	...	*1344*	|	|	1444	*1444*	...	1544	*1544*	...	|	1644	...	...	...	|
outh d.	1123	...	1228	1239	1245	1315	...	1348	1424	1415	1456	1511	...	1603	1626	1649	1650	1726	...	1742	1752	1752	1842	1855	...	1908	...	1930
sh d.	|	...	1238	|	1254	|	...	|	|	1424	|	|	...	1612	|	|	|	|	...	|	1806	1805	|	|	...	1917	...	|
ard d.	1147	...	1255	1305	1313	1340	...	1411	1449	1445	|	1536	...	1633	1650	1713	1713	1751	...	1805	1826	1829	1907	1921	...	1936	...	1955
in Parkway 🚂 d.	1200	...	1308	1321	1325	1354	...	1424	1502	1458	|	1549	...	1645	1703	1728	1729	1803	...	1817	1838	1842	1920	1933	...	1948	...	2008
ithiel d.	|	...	|	|	1330	|	...	|	|	1504	1535	|	...	1650	|	|	|	|	...	|	1844	1848	|	|	...	1953c	...	|
♡ d.	1211	1215	|	1333	1337	1406	1410	1434	|	1512	1546	1601	1615	1657	|	|	1741	1816	1821	1828	1852	1857	1931	1944	1948	2001	2015	2020
wquay ♡ a.	|	1307	|	1431	|	|	1457	|	|	|	1647	|	1707	|	|	|	1839	|	1913	|	|	|	|	|	2040	|	2107	|
stell d.	1219	...	1323	...	1345	1413	...	1442	1517	1521	...	1608	...	1704	1720	1745	...	1823	...	1834	1859	1904	1940	1952	...	2008	...	2027
d.	1237	...	1341	...	1402	1430	...	1500	1535	1539	...	1626	...	1723	1737	1802	...	1841	...	1852	1917	1923	2000	2015	...	2026	...	2046
th d.	1249	...	1355	...	1415	1443	...	1512	1548	1553	...	1638	...	1736c	1750	1815	...	1853	...	1908	1930	1935	2010	2027	...	2042	...	2059
orne d.	1256	...	1402	...	1421	1450	...	1519	1555	1600	...	1646	...	1742c	1757	1822	...	1901	...	1915	1936	1943	2018	2035	...	2049	...	2107
h d.	1308	...	1419	...	1433	1505	...	1532	1610	1612	...	1658	...	1754c	1813	1842	...	1912	...	1925	1948	1957	2029	2046	...	2058	...	2117
ance a.	1321	...	1429	...	1442	1518	...	1541	1621	1621	...	1710	...	1803c	1825	1854	...	1924	...	1934	1957	2007	2041	2056	...	2111	...	2127

	⑥	⑥	⑥	⑥	⑥	⑦	⑦	⑦	⑦	⑦	⑦	⑦	⑦	⑦	⑦	⑦	⑦	⑦	⑦	⑦	⑦	⑦	⑦	⑦	⑦	⑦	⑦
	D	🍷 c	2 d	C c	🍷	2	2	2	2	2	2	🍷	🍷	F	🍷	🍷	2	🍷	2	🍷	2 B	🍷	E	2	🍷	C	🍷
don Pad. **115**.. d.	...	1706	*1706*	...	1806	...	...	...	...	...	...	0800	0851	...	0957	1057	...	1157	...	1257	*1300*	1457	...	*1557*	1657	...	1757
stol § **115 120**.. d.	1744	|	|	1844	|	...	...	...	0726	...	0828	1000	|	1057	|	*1154*	...	*1254*	...	*1344*	*1455*	|	1644	|	|	1844	|
outh d.	1948	2040	2040	2058	2120	...	0901	0909	1020	...	1115	1215	1235	1255	1328	1415	1450	1530	...	1625	1735	1825	1853	1943	2025	2050	2135
sh d.	|	2051	2054	|	|	...	|	0921	1030	...	1126	|	|	|	|	|	1459	|	...	|	1745	|	|	1952	|	|	|
ard d.	2011	2110	2113	2125	2146	...	0925	0943	1051	...	1145	1243	1301	1318	1352	1440	1518	1553	...	1650	1806	1852	1916	2011	2050	2113	2200
in Parkw'y 🚂 d.	2023	2123	2125	2137	2159	...	0938	0955	1103	...	1157	1256	1314	1330	1405	1454	1530	1608	...	1703	1818	1906	1928	2023	2103	2125	2213
ithiel d.	2028	|	2130	|	|	...	|	1001	1108	...	1202	|	|	|	1411	|	1536	|	...	|	1823	|	|	2028	|	|	|
♡ d.	2035	2135	2138	2147	2211	0900	0955	1009	1116	1149	1210	1308	1325	1340	1422	|	1544	1620	1630	1714	1831	1918	1938	2036	2115	2135	2227
wquay ♡ a.	|	|	|	|	|	0950	1100	|	|	1245	|	|	|	|	1512	|	|	|	1734	|	|	|	|	|	|	|	|
stell d.	2041	2143	2145	2201	2218	...	...	1016	1125	...	1218	1315	1333	1351	...	1510	1551	1629	...	1722	1838	1925	1945	2043	2121	2143	2234
d.	2102	2203	2203	2218	2236	...	...	1035	1144	...	1235	1334	1351	1409	...	1528	1610	1646	...	1740	1856	1942	2001	2100	2139	2200	2250
uth d.	2113	2213	2217	2229	2248	...	...	1048	1157	...	1248	1346	1404	1420	...	1539	1623	1659	...	1753	1909	1954	2012	2114	2152	2211	2304
orne d.	2119	|	2223	2235	2256	...	...	1054	1203	...	1254	1354	1411	1427	...	1547	1629	1706	...	1801	1915	2004	2021	2120	2158	2220	2311
th d.	2131	2230	2234	2245	2309	...	...	1106	1214	...	1305	1406	1423	1437	...	1559	1641	1719	...	1813	1925	2017	2031	2132	2212	2230	2324
ance a.	2140	2242	2244	2254	2322	...	...	1115	1224	...	1315	1416	1433	1447	...	1612	1651	1728	...	1824	1937	2029	2039	2142	2224	2242	2335

THE NIGHT RIVIERA – Conveys 🛏 1, 2. cl and [2]. See also note ‡ on page 102.
From Exeter St Davids (Table **115**).
From Glasgow Central (Table **120**).
From Aberdeen (Table **120**).
From Edinburgh (Table **120**).
From Birmingham New Street (Table **120**).
From Newquay.

H – From York (Table **120**).
J – From Dundee (Table **120**).

a – May 16 - July 1 and from Sept. 5.
b – July 4 - Sept. 2.
c – From Sept. 17.
d – May 21 - Sept. 10.
e – Change at Exeter St Davids.

p – Previous night.
s – Stops to set down only.
u – Stops to pick up only.

§ – Bristol Temple Meads.
♡ – Par - Newquay: *'The Atlantic Coast Line'*.
🚂 – Bodmin & Wenford Railway (Bodmin Parkway - Bodmin General - Boscarne Junction *10 km*). ✆ 01208 73555. www.bodminrailway.co.uk

2nd class BRANCH LINES and BUS CONNECTIONS IN DEVON and CORNWALL 118

ETER - EXMOUTH *'The Avocet Line'* *18 km*

n Exeter St Davids: on ⚒ at 0544, 0606Ⓐ, 0629, 0707, 0736, 0815, 0845, 0915, 0948 at the same minutes past each hour until 1616, 1646, 1716, 1745⑥, 1753Ⓐ, 1816⑥, Ⓐ, 1847, 1931, 2031, 2131Ⓐ, 2141⑥, 2231Ⓐ, 2241⑥, 2309⑥, 2328Ⓐ; at 0830, 0940, 1044, 1151, 1247, 1348, 1446, 1518, 1546, 1646, 1746, 1846, 1951, , 2148, 2248, 2325.

n Exmouth: on ⚒ at 0001, 0614, 0643Ⓐ, 0712, 0751, 0821, 0852, 0921, 0953 and at ame minutes past each hour until 1653, 1723, 1753⑥, 1801Ⓐ, 1825⑥, 1832Ⓐ, 1854⑥, Ⓐ, 1939, 2007⑥, 2015Ⓐ, 2111Ⓐ, 2116⑥, 2207Ⓐ, 2219⑥, 2307Ⓐ, 2317⑥, 2345⑥;) at 0910, 1019, 1124, 1228, 1255, 1324, 1358, 1427, 1523, 1623, 1655, 1723, 1755, , 1923, 2028, 2128, 2227, 2329.

ney: 37 – 40 minutes. Trains call at Exeter Central 3 – 4 minutes from Exeter St Davids.

ETER - BARNSTAPLE *'The Tarka Line'* *63 km*

n Exeter St Davids: on ⚒ at 0550Ⓐ, 0554⑥, 0648Ⓐ, 0655⑥, 0831, 0927, 1027, 1127, , 1327, 1427, 1527, 1657⑥, 1702Ⓐ, 1757, 1859, 2100, 2253⑤; on ⑦ at 0843, 0954, , 1408, 1604, 1807, 2001.

n Barnstaple: on ⚒ at 0700Ⓐ, 0705⑥, 0843, 0943, 1043, 1143, 1243, 1343, 1443, 1543, ⑥, 1713Ⓐ, 1813, 1916, 2024, 2216Ⓐ, 2230⑥; on ⑦ at 1000, 1129, 1323, 1529, 1721, , 2130.

ney: 65 minutes. Trains call at ***Crediton*** *(11 minutes from Exeter / 54 minutes from staple) and* ***Eggesford*** *(40 minutes from Exeter / 25 minutes from Barnstaple).*

PLYMOUTH - GUNNISLAKE *'The Tamar Valley Line'* *24 km*

From Plymouth: on Ⓐ at 0506, 0641, 0840, 1054, 1254, 1454, 1638, 1823, 2131; on ⑥ at 0627, 0854, 1054, 1254, 1448, 1638, 1823, 2131; on ⑦ at 0920, 1106, 1306, 1511, 1741.

From Gunnislake: on Ⓐ at 0551, 0731, 0929, 1145, 1345, 1545, 1729, 1913, 2221; on ⑥ at 0717, 0945, 1145, 1345, 1545, 1729, 1913, 2221; on ⑦ at 1018, 1207, 1358, 1604, 1835.

Journey: 45 – 60 minutes.

LISKEARD - LOOE *'The Looe Valley Line'* *14 km*

From Liskeard: on Ⓐ at 0605, 0714, 0833, 0959, 1111, 1216, 1321, 1425, 1541, 1641, 1806, 1918; on ⑥ at 0550**a**, 0601**b**, 0713, 0835, 0958, 1108**b**, 1112**a**, 1212, 1324, 1428, 1543, 1656, 1801, 1928, 2040**a**; on ⑦ until Oct. 23 at 1012, 1126, 1250, 1400, 1503**c**, 1523**d**, 1610**c**, 1635**d**, 1735**c**, 1740**d**, 2015.

From Looe: on Ⓐ at 0637, 0746, 0909, 1030, 1143, 1248, 1353, 1459, 1613, 1715, 1840, 1952; on ⑥ at 0622**a**, 0633**b**, 0747, 0909, 1032, 1137, 1244, 1356, 1456, 1615, 1728, 1833, 2000, 2112**a**; on ⑦ until Oct. 23 at 1044, 1158, 1322, 1432, 1535**c**, 1555**d**, 1642**c**, 1717**d**, 1815, 2050.

Journey: 28 – 33 minutes.

a – To Sept. 10. **b** – From Sept. 17. **c** – To Sept. 11. **d** – From Sept. 18.

EXETER - OKEHAMPTON *Service runs only on ⑦ until Sept. 11* *40 km*

From Exeter St. Davids: on ⑦ until Sept. 11 at 0908, 1109, 1435, 1637.
From Okehampton: on ⑦ until Sept. 11 at 0955, 1158, 1523, 1759.

Journey: 40 – 42 minutes. Trains call at ***Crediton*** *(approx. 10 minutes from Exeter).*

117 PENZANCE and NEWQUAY - PLYMOUTH

GW

Service on ⑦ is valid until Sept. 11. For service on ⑦ from Sept. 18 please contact National Rail Enquiries ✆ +44 (0)3457 48 49 50.

Ⓐ		Ⓐ 🍷	Ⓐ 2	Ⓐ 🍷	Ⓐ 2	Ⓐ D	Ⓐ 🍷	Ⓐ 🍷	Ⓐ D	Ⓐ 🍷	Ⓐ E	Ⓐ 2	Ⓐ 🍷	Ⓐ 2a	Ⓐ ✕b	Ⓐ 2	Ⓐ2 Jb	Ⓐ 2a	Ⓐ 🍷	Ⓐ 2	Ⓐ 2a	Ⓐ 2a	Ⓐ 2b	Ⓐ 🍷b	Ⓐ 🍷	①–④ 2B
Penzance	d.	0505	0520	0541	0600	0628	0645	0741	0828	0844	0935	...	1000	1046	1047	1141	...	...	1303	1345	...	1449	1452	...	1559	1644
St Erth	d.	|	|	|	0609	0636	0655	0751	0836	0854	0943	...	1010	1055	1057	1150	...	...	1313	1354	...	1458	1501	...	1610	1653
Camborne	d.	|	0539	0559	0622	0646	0707	0806	0846	0907	0956	...	1023	1108	1112	1203	...	...	1325	1407	...	1511	1514	...	1621	1706
Redruth	d.	0526	|	0606	0628	0652	0714	0813	0852	0914	1003	...	1030	1114	1119	1209	...	...	1332	1413	...	1517	1520	...	1629	1712
Truro	d.	0538	0554	0619	0640	0704	0727	0826	0904	0927	1015	...	1043	1126	1132	1220	...	...	1345	1424	...	1528	1531	...	1642	1725
St Austell	d.	0556	...	0636	0657	0720	0745	0844	0920	0944	1031	...	1100	1143	1150	1237	...	...	1402	1441	...	1545	1548	...	1659	1742
Newquay ♡	d.	|	...	|	|	|	|	|	|	|	|	1013	|	|	|	|	1240	1303	|	|	1501	|	|	1506	|	|
Par ♡	d.	|	...	0643	0703	0727	0752	0851	0927	0951	1038	1102	1108	1150	1157	1244	1335	1352	1410	1448	1547	1552	1554	1600	1707	1748
Lostwithiel	d.	|	...	0651	0710	|	0800	|	|	|	1045	...	|	1156	|	1250	...	...	|	1455	...	1558	...	1609	1714	1755
Bodmin Parkway 🚂	d.	0614	...	0657	0716	0737	0806	0903	0937	1003	1051	...	1119	1202	1208	1256	...	...	1421	1501	...	1604	...	1616	1721	1801
Liskeard	d.	0627	...	0711	0729	0753	0820	0916	0950	1016	1104	...	1133	1217	1241	1309	...	...	1434	1514	...	1617	...	1629	1734	1814
Saltash	d.	|	...	0730	0747	|	0839	0934	|	|	|	...	|	1234	|	1328	...	...	|	1532	...	1637	...	|	|	1832
Plymouth	a.	0651	...	0741	0804	0820	0849	0946	1018	1040	1127	...	1157	1244	1252	1337	...	...	1459	1543	...	1651	...	1654	1758	1842
Bristol § **115 120**	a.	0926	...	|	1110	1025	|	1158	1224	1324	1355	...	|	1523	1523	1623	...	...	1724	1823	...	1925	...	1925	2025	|
London Pad. **115**	a.	1003	...	1124	...	...	1224	1339	...	1344	...	...	1521	1622	1622	...	...	...	1821	1924	...	2039	...	2039	2124	2241e

		Ⓐ 2	⑤ 🍷	①–④ 🍷	Ⓐ 2	Ⓐ 2b	Ⓐ 2a	Ⓐ 2b	Ⓐ 2	Ⓐ 2	Ⓐ A	Ⓐ	⑥	⑥ 2d	⑥ 2c	⑥2 Bd	⑥ 2c	⑥ D	⑥ 🍷	⑥ 🍷d	⑥ 2c	⑥ 2c	⑥ 🍷c	⑥ D	⑥ 🍷	⑥🍷 Hd	⑥ Ec
Penzance	d.	...	1739	1739	...	1913	1916	...	2018	...	2145	2208		0510	0520	0527	0537	0630	0650	0718	...	0735	0759	0828	0839	...	0943
St Erth	d.	...	1749	1749	...	1923	1925	...	2027	...	2155	2216		|	|	0535	0545	0638	0700	0729	...	0748	0809	0836	0850	...	0951
Camborne	d.	...	1804	1804	...	1939	1938	...	2042	...	2208	2230		0528	0537	0549	0559	0651	0712	0745	...	0803	0924	0846	0906	...	1001
Redruth	d.	...	1812	1812	...	1946	1944	...	2050	...	2216	2236		0534	0543	0555	0605	0657	0719	0752	...	0810	0831	0852	0913	...	1007
Truro	d.	...	1824	1824	...	1959	1956	...	2103	...	2229	2248		0546	0555	0606	0616	0709	0732	0806	...	0821	0844	0904	0926	...	1019
St Austell	d.	...	1841	1841	...	2016	2013	...	2120	...	2247	2304		...	...	0623	0633	0725	0749	0823	...	0837	0902	0920	0944	...	1035
Newquay ♡	d.	1722	|	|	1924	|	|	...	|	2126	|	|		...	...	|	|	|	|	|	0748	|	|	|	|	0935	|
Par ♡	d.	1813	1849	1849	2013	2024	2019	...	2127	2216	2257	2311		...	...	0629	0639	0732	0756	0830	0839	0844	0909	0927	0951	1031	1041
Lostwithiel	d.	...	|	|	...	2031	2026	...	2134	...	|	2318		...	...	0636	0646	0739	0804	0838	...	0851	|	|	|	|	1048
Bodmin Parkway 🚂	d.	...	1901	1901	...	2038	2032	...	2140	...	2309	2325		...	...	0642	0652	0746	0810	0844	...	0857	0920	0937	1002	1045	1055
Liskeard	d.	...	1914	1914	...	2051	2045	2103	2153	...	2325	2337		...	...	0656	0707	0758	0823	0857	...	0910	0933	0950	1015	1058	1107
Saltash	d.	...	|	|	...	|	2104	2130	2211	...	|	|		...	...	0715	0726	|	|	0917	...	0929	|	|	|	|	|
Plymouth	a.	...	1938	1938	...	2116	2119	2146	2224	...	2348	0001		...	...	0731	0742	0821	0848	0930	...	0940	0958	1017	1040	1121	1130
Bristol § **115 120**	a.	...	2145	2145	...	...	...	...	...	...	|	...		...	...	|	|	1025	1126	|	...	...	|	1225	|	1325	1355
London Pad. **115**	a.	...	2341	2344	...	...	...	...	...	...	0523	...		...	...	1121	1124	...	1223	1309	...	...	1321	...	1344	...	...

		⑥ 🍷d	⑥ 🍷c	⑥ 2d	⑥ 2c	⑥ 🍷c	⑥ 🍷d	⑥ 🍷d	⑥ 2c	⑥ 2c	⑥ 🍷d	⑥ 2c	⑥ 2d	⑥ 🍷d	⑥ 🍷	⑥ 2c	⑥ 2c	⑥ 🍷d	⑥🍷 Ed	⑥ 🍷	⑥2 Bc	⑥2 Kd	⑥ 2c	⑥ 🍷d	⑥ 🍷	⑥ 2d	⑥ d
Penzance	d.	0954	1000	...	1037	1058	1100	...	1146	...	1158	1300	1300	...	1401	...	1452	1500	...	1552	1641	1655	...	...	1740	...	...
St Erth	d.	1005	1010	...	1045	1108	1111	...	1155	...	1209	1309	1309	...	1411	...	1501	1510	...	1602	1651	1705	...	...	1750	...	...
Camborne	d.	1021	1022	...	1059	1120	1127	...	1209	...	1225	1322	1322	...	1423	...	1515	1526	...	1614	1706	1721	...	...	1805	...	...
Redruth	d.	1028	1029	...	1105	1127	1134	...	1215	...	1232	1328	1328	...	1430	...	1521	1533	...	1621	1713	1728	...	...	1812	...	...
Truro	d.	1041	1042	...	1116	1140	1147	...	1227	...	1245	1339	1339	...	1443	...	1532	1546	...	1634	1726	1741	...	...	1825	...	...
St Austell	d.	1059	1059	...	1133	1157	1205	...	1244	...	1303	1356	1356	...	1500	...	1549	1604	...	1652	1744	1758	...	...	1842	...	...
Newquay ♡	d.	|	|	...	|	|	|	1130	|	1309	|	|	|	1319	|	1459	|	|	1530	|	|	|	1721	1726	|	...	1900
Par ♡	d.	1106	1107	1125	1139	|	|	1226	1253	1358	|	1403	1424g	1414	1507	1548	1155	1611	1627	1659	1751	1805	1810	1822	1849	1901	1954
Lostwithiel	d.	|	|	1133	1146	|	|	|	1300	...	|	1409	1429	|	|	...	1602	1619	|	1706	1758	1813	...	|	|	1908	|
Bodmin Parkway 🚂	d.	1118	1118	1139	1152	1213	1221	|	1306	...	1319	1415	1435	|	1519	...	1608	1625	1638	1713	1805	1819	...	1835	1901	1914	2006
Liskeard	d.	1131	1131	1154	1207	1226	1234	|	1319	...	1332	1428	1448	1436	1533	...	1621	1638	1651	1726	1819	1832	...	1848	1914	1927	2020
Saltash	d.	|	|	1218	1226	|	|	|	1339	...	|	1447	1509	|	|	...	1640	1659	|	|	1838	1851	...	|	|	1945	|
Plymouth	a.	1156	1156	1229	1237	1251	1258	1311	1350	...	1356	1458	1520	1501	1559	...	1650	1710	1714	1750	1849	1901	...	1914	1938	1956	2044
Bristol § **115 120**	a.	1425	1425	...	...	1525	1525	1525	1625	...	1625	1725	1725	|	1825c	...	1924	...	1923	2024	...	...	...	|	2147	...	...
London Pad. **115**	a.	1521	1521	...	...	1621	1621	1632	1741	...	1721	1821	...	1821	1921	...	2037	...	...	2132	...	...	...	2232	2342	...	...

		⑥ 2B	⑥ 2d	⑥ 2c	⑥	⑦	⑦ 🍷	⑦ F	⑦ 🍷	⑦ 🍷	⑦🍷 Fd	⑦ 🍷	⑦ 2B	⑦ E	⑦ 🍷	⑦ 2B	⑦ 2	⑦ 🍷	⑦ G	⑦ 🍷	⑦ 🍷	⑦ 2	⑦ 🍷	⑦ 2	⑦ 2B	⑦ 2	⑦ 2
Penzance	d.	1906	...	...	2129		0830	0930	0947	1100	...	1140	1205	1230	1256	1339	1437	1500	1530	1550	...	...	1731	1750	1900	...	2005
St Erth	d.	1915	...	...	2138		0839	0938	0956	1110	...	1149	1214	1238	1306	1349	1447	1510	1538	1559	...	...	1740	1800	1909	...	2014
Camborne	d.	1928	...	...	2149		0856	0948	1008	1124	...	1201	1226	1251	1320	1402	1500	1523	1549	1612	...	...	1753	1813	1921	...	2027
Redruth	d.	1934	...	...	2156		0902	0954	1014	1130	...	1207	1232	1258	1326	1408	1506	1530	1555	1618	...	...	1800	1819	1927	...	2033
Truro	d.	1945	...	...	2209		0916	1006	1027	1143	...	1221	1244	1309	1339	1419	1517	1542	1607	1633	...	...	1812	1831	1939	...	2045
St Austell	d.	2002	...	...	2226		0932	1022	1044	1200	...	1237	1300	1326	1357	1436	1534	1600	1623	1649	...	...	1831	1848	1956	...	2102
Newquay ♡	d.	|	2045	2118	|		|	|	|	|	1132	|	|	|	|	|	|	|	|	|	1621	1738	|	|	|	2015	|
Par ♡	d.	2009	2140	2209	2233		0940	1029	1052	1207	1226	1245	1306	1332	1403	1443	1540	1607	1630	1656	1715	1827	1838	1855	2003	2102	2109
Lostwithiel	d.	2015	2148	2218	|		|	|	|	|	|	|	1313	1339	|	1449	1547	|	|	|	|	...	|	1901	2009	...	2115
Bodmin Parkway 🚂	d.	2021	2154	2224	2244		0952	1039	1105	1219	1237	1258	1319	1346	1416	1455	1553	1618	1640	1709	1727	...	1849	1908	2015	...	2122
Liskeard	d.	2035	2207	2237	2258		1005	1052	1118	1233	1251	1311	1333	1358	1429	1508	1609	1631	1652	1722	1741	...	1902	1922	2028	...	2136
Saltash	d.	2054	2225	2255	|		1021	|	|	|	|	|	1354	|	|	1526	1626	|	|	|	1758	...	|	1940	2047	...	2154
Plymouth	a.	2110	2242	2312	2322		1029	1115	1142	1257	1315	1336	1403	1423	1454	1534	1636	1657	1715	1745	1810	...	1926	1951	2100	...	2204
Bristol § **115 120**	a.	...	...	...	...		|	1326	|	|	1526	|	1626	1647	1720	1822	1917	|	1922	1957	|	...	2159	...	...	...	...
London Pad. **115**	a.	...	...	...	...		1427	...	1526	1628	...	1729	...	...	1827	2025	...	2030	...	2127	2153	...	2328	...	...	...	...

A – THE NIGHT RIVIERA – Conveys 🛏 1, 2. cl and (2). See also note ‡ on page 102.
B – To Exeter St Davids (Table **115**).
C – To Taunton (Table **115**).
D – To Glasgow Central (Table **120**).
E – To Manchester Piccadilly (Table **120**).
F – To Edinburgh (Table **120**).
G – To Leeds (Table **120**).
H – To Dundee (Table **120**).
J – To Penzance.
K – To Newton Abbot (Table **115**).
a – May 16 - July 1 and from Sept. 5.
b – July 4 - Sept. 2.
c – From Sept. 17.
d – May 21 - Sept. 10.
e – Change at Exeter St Davids.
g – Arrives 1402.
n – Change at Taunton.
♡ – Par - Newquay: *'The Atlantic Coast Line'*.
🚂 – Bodmin & Wenford Railway (Bodmin Parkwa[y] - Bodmin General - Boscarne Junction *10 km*). ✆ 01208 73555. www.bodminrailway.co.uk

118 BRANCH LINES and BUS CONNECTIONS IN DEVON and CORNWALL

2nd class

Rail tickets are generally not valid on 🚌 services shown in this table.

BODMIN PARKWAY - PADSTOW — *Plymouth City Bus 🚌 service 11A*

From Bodmin Parkway station: on ⚒ at 0627, 0727, 0827, 0922, 1022, 1122, 1222, 1322, 1422, 1522, 1622, 1727, 1822; on ⑦ at 0751, 1001, 1201, 1401, 1601, 1756.

From Padstow Bus Terminus: on ⚒ at 0620, 0735, 0835, 0935, 1035, 1135, 1235, 1335, 1435, 1535, 1635, 1730, 1835, 1930; on ⑦ at 0855, 1105, 1305, 1505, 1705, 1905.

Journey: 60 minutes. Buses also make calls in Bodmin town centre and at Bodmin General station, and call at ***Wadebridge*** *(35 minutes after Bodmin/25 minutes after Padstow).*

TRURO - FALMOUTH DOCKS — *'The Maritime Line'* — *20 km*

From Truro: on ⚒ at 0604, 0631, 0714, 0747, 0820, 0851 and at the same minutes past each hour until 1620, 1651, 1727, 1759, 1831, 1902, 2004, 2105, 2208Ⓐ, 2212⑥; on ⑦ at 0901, 1039, 1209, 1308, 1412, 1535, 1700, 1813, 1946, 2103, 2204.

From Falmouth Docks: on ⚒ at 0631, 0715, 0747, 0820, 0850 and at the same minutes past each hour until 1620, 1650, 1727, 1759, 1831, 1902, 1929, 2031, 2132, 2235Ⓐ, 2239⑥; on ⑦ at 0935, 1106, 1236, 1335, 1439, 1602**e**, 1614**k**, 1735, 1840, 2013, 2130, 2233.

Trains call at ***Falmouth Town*** *22 minutes after Truro and 3 minutes after Falmouth Docks.*

Journey: 25 minutes.

a – From Sept. 12.
b – Until Sept. 9.
c – Until Sept. 10.
d – From Sept. 17.
e – Until Sept. 11.
f – Sept. 18 - Oct. 23.
g – From Oct. 30.
h – Until Oct. 23.
k – From Sept. 18.

ST AUSTELL - EDEN PROJECT — *First Kernow 🚌 service*

From St Austell bus station: on Ⓐ at 0846, 0930, 1040, 1146, 1241, 1412, 1454, 1550, 1[…] on ⑥ at 0846, 0930, 1040, 1143, 1247, 1417, 1503, 1552, 1636, 1735; on ⑦ at 0846. […] 1130, 1225, 1330, 1440, 1527, 1612, 1735.

From Eden Project: on Ⓐ at 0906, 1110, 1210, 1330, 1432, 1515, 1615, 1715, 1800; on ⑥ at 0906, 1105, 1205, 1330, 1437, 1524, 1614, 1656, 1759; on ⑦ at 0950, 1055, 1[…] 1250, 1400, 1505, 1550, 1635, 1800.

Journey 20 minutes.

ST ERTH - ST IVES — *'The St Ives Bay Line'* — *7*

From St Erth: on Ⓐ at 0706, 0759, 0905, 0938, 1018, 1048. 1118, 1148**a**, 1152**b**, 1218**a**, 1[…] 1318, 1348, 1418**a**, 1448, 1518, 1548, 1618**a**, 1648, 1717, 1748 and every 30 minutes […] 2048, 2123, 2158; on ⑥ at 0650, 0800, 0903, 0935, 1013, 1048, 1119, 1148, 1218, 1248, 1[…] 1348**d**, 1418, 1448, 1518, 1548, 1618, 1648, 1717, 1759, 1859**c** 1904**d**, 1953**d**, 2001**c** 2[…] 2106, 2147; on ⑦ at 0853**e**, 0927**e**, 1000**e**, 1030**h**, 1113**e**, 1118**f**, 1142**e**, 1148**f**, 1156**g**, 12[…] 1230**g**, 1248**f**, 1318, 1348, 1418, 1448, 1518**k**, 1548, 1618, 1648, 1726, 1755**k**, 1803**e**, 18[…] 1835**e**, 1931.

From St Ives: on Ⓐ at 0725, 0815, 0922, 0953, 1033, 1103, 1133, 1203**a**, 1233, 1303, 1[…] 1403**a**, 1433, 1503, 1533, 1603**a**, 1633, 1703, 1731, 1803, 1833, 1905, 1932, 2003, 2[…] 2103, 2137, 2231; on ⑥ at 0712, 0815, 0920, 0950, 1027, 1103, 1133, 1203, 1233, 1[…] 1333**d**, 1403 and every 30 minutes until 1703, 1732, 1817, 1926, 2010**d**, 2017**c**, 2049, 2[…] 2205; on ⑦ at 0910**e**, 0941**e**, 1015**e**, 1050, 1127**e**, 1133**f**, 1157**e**, 1203**f**, 1213**g**, 1233**f**, 12[…] 1303**h**, 1333, 1403, 1432, 1503**k**, 1533, 1603, 1633, 1703, 1740, 1810**k**, 1819**e**, 1850, 1[…]

Journey: 15 minutes.

BIRMINGHAM - READING - SOUTHAMPTON - BOURNEMOUTH 119

Most services convey 🍸

		Ⓐ	Ⓐ	Ⓐ	Ⓐ	Ⓐ	Ⓐ	Ⓐ	Ⓐ	Ⓐ	Ⓐ	Ⓐ	Ⓐ	Ⓐ	Ⓐ	Ⓐ	Ⓐ	Ⓐ	Ⓐ	Ⓐ	Ⓐ	Ⓐ	Ⓐ
						A							E										G
Manchester Piccadilly **122** .. d.	Ⓐ	...	...	0511	...	...	...	0727	...	0827	...	0927	...	1027	...	1127	...	1227	...	1327	...	1427	...
Newcastle **124** .... d.		...	...	|	...	...	...	|	0625	|	0725	|	0835	|	0935	|	1035	|	1135	|	1235	|	1335
York **124** .... d.		...	...	|	...	...	...	|	0727	|	0826	|	0935	|	1035	|	1135	|	1235	|	1335	|	1435
Leeds **124** .... d.		...	...	|	...	...	0616	|	|	|	|	|	|	|	|	|	|	|	|	|	|	|	|
Sheffield **124** .... d.		...	...	|	0601	...	0718	|	0821	|	0924	|	1024	|	1124	|	1224	|	1324	|	1424	|	1524
Derby **124** .... d.		...	...	|	0648	0706	0750	|	0853	|	0953	|	1053	|	1153	|	1253	|	1353	|	1453	|	1553
Birmingham New Street **150** d.		0604	0633	0704	0733	0804	0833	0904	0933	1004	1033	1104	1133	1204	1233	1304	1333	1404	1433	1504	1533	1604	1633
Birmingham Intl ✈ .... **150** d.		0614	|	0714	|	0814	|	0914	|	1014	|	1114	|	1214	|	1314	|	1414	|	1514	|	1614	|
Coventry .... **150** d.		0625	|	0725	|	0825	|	0925	|	1025	|	1125	|	1225	|	1325	|	1425	|	1525	|	1625	|
Leamington Spa .... **128** d.		0637	0700	0738	0759	0838	0900	0938	1000	1038	1100	1138	1201	1238	1300	1338	1400	1438	1500	1538	1601	1638	1700
Banbury .... **128** a.		0653	0718	0755	0815	0854	0918	0954	1017	1054	1117	1156	1217	1254	1318	1354	1417	1454	1517	1554	1617	1654	1717
Oxford .... **131** a.		0714	0741	0814	0839	0914	0941	1013	1040	1113	1141	1214	1240	1314	1341	1413	1440	1514	1540	1614	1640	1713	1741
Reading .... **131** a.		0740	0809	0840	0908	0941	1010	1041	1109	1140	1209	1241	1307	1340	1409	1440	1508	1541	1611	1640	1708	1740	1808
Basingstoke .... **108** a.		0808	0841	0908	...	1008	1039	1108	...	1208	1239	1308	...	1408	1439	1508	...	1608	1639	1708	...	1808	...
Winchester .... **108** a.		0824	0856	0925	...	1024	1054	1124	...	1224	1254	1324	...	1424	1454	1524	...	1624	1659	1724	...	1824	...
Southampton Airport ✈. **108** a.		0833	0908	0933	...	1032	1107	1133	...	1232	1308	1332	...	1434	1509	1532	...	1632	1709	1732	...	1833	...
Southampton Central .... **108** a.		0844	0917	0943	...	1043	1117	1143	...	1241	1317	1341	...	1441	1517	1541	...	1641	1717	1741	...	1843	...
Brockenhurst .... **108** a.		0859	...	0958	...	1058	...	1158	...	1256	...	1356	...	1456	...	1556	...	1656	...	1756	...	1857	...
Bournemouth .... **108** a.		0914	...	1013	...	1113	...	1213	...	1311	...	1411	...	1511	...	1611	...	1711	...	1815	...	1912	...

	Ⓐ	Ⓐ	Ⓐ	Ⓐ	Ⓐ		Ⓐ	Ⓐ			Ⓐ		Ⓐ		Ⓐ		⑥	⑥	⑥	⑥	⑥	⑥	⑥	⑥
																					A			
anchester Piccadilly **122** .. d.	1527	...	1627	...	1727	...	...	1827	...	...	...	...	1927	...	...	⑥	...	...	0511	...	...	...	0727	...
Newcastle **124** .... d.	|	1435	|	1505	|	...	1635	|	...	...	1732	...	|	...	...		...	...	|	...	...	...	|	0623
York **124** .... d.	|	1535	|	1605	|	...	1735	|	...	...	1835	...	|	...	...		...	...	|	...	...	...	|	0727
Leeds **124** .... d.	|	|	|	1640	|	...	|	|	...	...	|	...	|	...	...		...	...	|	...	...	0616	|	|
Sheffield **124** .... d.	|	1624	|	1724	|	...	1824	|	...	...	1924	...	|	...	...		...	...	|	0545a	...	0718	|	0820
Derby **124** .... d.	|	1653	|	1753	|	...	1853	|	...	...	1954	...	|	...	...		...	...	|	0648	0706	0751	|	0853
ingham New Street **150** d.	1704	1733	1804	1833	1904	...	1933	2004	...	...	2033	...	2104	...	2204		0604	0633	0704	0733	0804	0833	0904	0933
ingham Intl ✈ .... **150** d.	1714	|	1814	|	1914	...	|	2014	...	...	|	...	2114	...	2214		0614	|	0714	|	0814	|	0914	|
entry .... **150** d.	1725	|	1825	|	1925	...	|	2025	...	...	|	...	2125	...	2225		0625	|	0725	|	0825	|	0925	|
nington Spa .... **128** d.	1738	1801	1837	1901	1938	...	2004	2037	...	...	2100	...	2138	...	2239		0638	0700	0738	0800	0838	0900	0938	1000
oury .... **128** a.	1754	1818	1855	1917	1954	...	2021	2054	...	...	2117	...	2154	...	2255		0654	0717	0754	0817	0854	0917	0955	1017
rd .... **131** a.	1814	1840	1913	1940	2013	...	2040	2114	...	...	2140	...	2214	...	2314		0714	0741	0814	0841	0914	0940	1015	1041
ding .... **131** a.	1842	1910	1940	2009	2041	...	2107	2142	...	...	2216	...	2242	...	2347		0741	0809	0841	0909	0940	1008	1041	1111
ngstoke .... **108** a.	1908	...	2009	...	2109	...	...	2209	...	...	2239	...	2305	...	...		0808	0839	0908	...	1008	1039	1108	...
chester .... **108** a.	1924	...	2024	...	2124	...	...	2224	...	...	2256	...	2324	...	...		0824	0854	0924	...	1024	1054	1124	...
thampton Airport ✈. **108** a.	1932	...	2033	...	2133	...	...	2233	...	...	2312	...	2336	...	...		0832	0908	0932	...	1032	1108	1132	...
thampton Central .... **108** a.	1940	...	2041	...	2140	...	...	2242	...	...	2320	...	2343	...	...		0841	0917	0940	...	1041	1117	1141	...
kenhurst .... **108** a.	1956	...	2058	...	2155	...	...	2256	...	...	...	...	...	...	...		0856	...	0957	...	1057	...	1157	...
rnemouth .... **108** a.	2011	...	2115	...	2215	...	...	2319	...	...	...	...	...	...	...		0914	...	1011	...	1113	...	1212	...

	⑥	⑥	⑥	⑥	⑥	⑥	⑥	⑥	⑥	⑥	⑥	⑥	⑥	⑥	⑥	⑥	⑥	⑥	⑥	⑥	⑥	⑥	⑥	
				E										G										
anchester Piccadilly **122** .. d.	0827	...	0927	...	1027	...	1127	...	1227	...	1327	...	1427	...	1527	...	1627	...	1727	...	1827	...	1927	...
Newcastle **124** .... d.	|	0735	|	0835	|	0935	|	1035	|	1135	|	1235	|	1335	|	1435	|	1505	|	1635	|	1732	|	...
York **124** .... d.	|	0835	|	0935	|	1035	|	1135	|	1235	|	1335	|	1435	|	1535	|	1606	|	1735	|	1835	|	...
Leeds **124** .... d.	|	|	|	|	|	|	|	|	|	|	|	|	|	|	|	|	|	1640	|	|	|	|	|	...
Sheffield **124** .... d.	|	0924	|	1024	|	1124	|	1224	|	1324	|	1424	|	1524	|	1624	|	1724	|	1824	|	1924	|	...
Derby **124** .... d.	|	0953	|	1053	|	1153	|	1253	|	1353	|	1453	|	1553	|	1653	|	1753	|	1853	|	1954	|	...
ingham New Street **150** d.	1004	1033	1104	1133	1204	1233	1304	1333	1404	1433	1504	1533	1604	1633	1704	1733	1804	1833	1904	1933	2004	2033	2104	...
ingham Intl ✈ .... **150** d.	1014	|	1114	|	1214	|	1314	|	1414	|	1514	|	1614	|	1714	|	1814	|	1914	|	2014	|	2114	...
entry .... **150** d.	1025	|	1125	|	1225	|	1325	|	1425	|	1525	|	1625	|	1725	|	1825	|	1925	|	2025	|	2125	...
nington Spa .... **128** d.	1038	1100	1138	1200	1238	1300	1338	1400	1438	1500	1538	1602	1638	1700	1738	1802	1838	1900	1938	2003	2038	2100	2138	...
oury .... **128** a.	1054	1117	1154	1217	1254	1317	1354	1417	1454	1518	1554	1618	1654	1717	1754	1818	1854	1917	1954	2019	2054	2119	2154	...
rd .... **131** a.	1114	1141	1214	1241	1314	1339	1414	1440	1514	1539	1614	1640	1714	1740	1814	1841	1914	1939	2014	2040	2114	2141	2214	...
ding .... **131** a.	1138	1206	1241	1309	1340	1408	1441	1508	1540	1609	1641	1710	1739	1810	1841	1910	1941	2009	2041	2108	2142	2214	2245	...
ngstoke .... **108** a.	1208	1240	1308	...	1408	1440	1508	...	1608	1640	1708	...	1808	...	1908	...	2008	...	2107	...	2209	2239	2307	...
chester .... **108** a.	1224	1255	1324	...	1424	1455	1524	...	1624	1655	1724	...	1824	...	1924	...	2024	...	2124	...	2226	2256	2324	...
thampton Airport ✈. **108** a.	1232	1308	1332	...	1432	1508	1532	...	1632	1708	1732	...	1832	...	1932	...	2032	...	2131	...	2234	2312	2332	...
thampton Central .... **108** a.	1241	1317	1341	...	1441	1517	1541	...	1641	1717	1741	...	1841	...	1941	...	2041	...	2140	...	2242	2320	2341	...
kenhurst .... **108** a.	1257	...	1357	...	1457	...	1557	...	1657	...	1757	...	1857	...	1957	...	2057	...	2156	...	2258	...	...	...
rnemouth .... **108** a.	1312	...	1412	...	1512	...	1612	...	1712	...	1812	...	1912	...	2012	...	2112	...	2215	...	2318	...	...	...

		⑦	⑦	⑦	⑦	⑦	⑦	⑦	⑦	⑦	⑦	⑦	⑦	⑦	⑦	⑦	⑦	⑦	⑦	⑦		⑦	⑦	⑦
																		E					G	
anchester Piccadilly **122** .. d.	⑦	...	0827	0927	1027	...	1127	...	1226	...	1326	...	1427	...	1527	...	1627	...	1727	...	...	1827	...	1927
Newcastle **124** .... d.		...	|	|	|	...	|	...	|	...	|	...	|	1335	|	1435	|	1523	|	1635	...	|	1735	|
York **124** .... d.		...	|	|	|	...	|	...	|	...	|	...	|	1435	|	1535	|	1624	|	1735	...	|	1835	|
Leeds **124** .... d.		...	|	|	|	...	|	...	|	...	|	...	|	|	|	|	|	|	|	|	...	|	|	|
Sheffield **124** .... d.		...	|	|	|	...	|	...	|	...	|	1422	|	1524	|	1624	|	1724	|	1824	...	|	1924	|
Derby **124** .... d.		...	|	|	|	...	|	...	|	1355	|	1453	|	1553	|	1654	|	1754	|	1854	...	|	1956	|
ningham New Street **150** d.		0904	1004	1104	1204	1233	1304	1333	1404	1433	1504	1533	1604	1633	1704	1733	1804	1833	1904	1933	...	2004	2033	2104
ingham Intl ✈ .... **150** d.		0914	1014	1114	1214	1245	1314	|	1414	1445	1514	|	1614	1645	1714	|	1814	1845	1914	1945	...	2014	|	2114
entry .... **150** d.		0925	1025	1125	1225	1255	1325	|	1425	1455	1525	|	1625	1655	1725	|	1825	1855	1925	1955	...	2025	|	2124
mington Spa .... **128** d.		0938	1038	1138	1238	1308	1338	1359	1438	1508	1538	1559	1638	1708	1738	1759	1838	1908	1938	2008	...	2038	2100	2136
bury .... **128** a.		0954	1054	1154	1254	1324	1354	1415	1454	1525	1554	1615	1654	1724	1754	1816	1854	1924	1954	2024	...	2054	2117	2152
rd .... **131** a.		1014	1114	1214	1314	1343	1414	1435	1514	1544	1614	1635	1714	1743	1814	1835	1914	1944	2014	2043	...	2114	2138	2211
ding .... **131** a.		1042	1140	1240	1341	1412	1440	1504	1540	1612	1640	1704	1739	1809	1840	1904	1939	2009	2040	2114	...	2140	2206	2238
ngstoke .... **108** a.		1109	1208	1308	1408	...	1508	...	1608	...	1708	...	1808	...	1909	...	2009	...	2108	...	...	2209	...	...
chester .... **108** a.		1124	1224	1324	1424	...	1524	...	1624	...	1724	...	1824	...	1924	...	2024	...	2124	...	...	2223	...	...
thampton Airport ✈. **108** a.		1133	1233	1333	1433	...	1533	...	1633	...	1733	...	1833	...	1933	...	2033	...	2133	...	...	2233	...	...
thampton Central .... **108** a.		1142	1242	1342	1442	...	1542	...	1642	...	1740	...	1842	...	1940	...	2041	...	2142	...	...	2242	...	...
kenhurst .... **108** a.		1206	1306	1406	1506	...	1603	...	1706	...	1806	...	1903	...	2006	...	2106	...	2206	...	...	...	...	...
rnemouth .... **108** a.		1226	1326	1426	1526	...	1626	...	1726	...	1826	...	1926	...	2026	...	2126	...	2226	...	...	...	...	...

From Nottingham (Table **121**).
From Edinburgh Waverley (Table **124**).

G – To Guildford (Table **134**).

a – May 21 - Sept. 10.

119 BOURNEMOUTH - SOUTHAMPTON - READING - BIRMINGHAM

Most services convey 🍸

Ⓐ

	Ⓐ	Ⓐ G	Ⓐ	Ⓐ	Ⓐ	Ⓐ	Ⓐ	Ⓐ	Ⓐ	Ⓐ	Ⓐ	Ⓐ	Ⓐ	Ⓐ	Ⓐ	Ⓐ	Ⓐ	Ⓐ E	Ⓐ	Ⓐ	Ⓐ b	Ⓐ
Bournemouth 108 d.	...	...	...	...	0630	...	0730	...	0845	...	0945	...	1045	...	1145	...	1245	...	1345	...	1445	...
Brockenhurst 108 d.	...	...	...	...	0645	...	0750	...	0900	...	1000	...	1100	...	1200	...	1300	...	1400	...	1500	...
Southampton Central 108 d.	0515	...	0615	...	0715	...	0815	...	0916	0946	1017	...	1117	1146	1217	...	1316	1346	1417	...	1516	1546
Southampton Airport ✈ 108 d.	0522	...	0622	...	0722	...	0822	...	0923	0955	1024	...	1124	1153	1224	...	1323	1354	1424	...	1523	1553
Winchester 108 d.	0531	...	0631	...	0731	0812	0831	...	0932	1003	1033	...	1133	1202	1233	...	1332	1403	1433	...	1532	1602
Basingstoke 108 d.	0547	...	0647	...	0747	0828	0847	...	0949	1019	1049	...	1149	1218	1249	...	1349	1419	1449	...	1548	1618
Reading 131 d.	0615	0645	0715	0746	0815	0850	0915	0945	1015	1045	1115	1145	1215	1245	1315	1345	1415	1445	1515	1545	1615	1645
Oxford 131 d.	0638	0709	0739	0812	0839	0915	0939	1015	1039	1113	1139	1213	1239	1313	1339	1413	1439	1513	1539	1613	1639	1713
Banbury 128 d.	0657	0726	0757	0830	0857	0933	0957	1032	1057	1130	1157	1232	1257	1331	1357	1431	1457	1532	1557	1631	1657	1732
Leamington Spa 128 d.	0714	0744	0814	0847	0914	0950	1014	1050	1114	1148	1214	1250	1314	1348	1414	1450	1514	1550	1614	1648	1714	1750
Coventry 150 d.	0727	|	0827	|	0927	|	1027	|	1127	|	1227	|	1327	|	1427	|	1527	|	1627	|	1727	|
Birmingham Intl ✈ 150 d.	0738	|	0838	|	0938	|	1038	|	1138	|	1238	|	1338	|	1438	|	1538	|	1638	|	1738	|
Birmingham New Street 150 a.	0748	0810	0848	0918	0948	1018	1048	1118	1148	1218	1248	1318	1348	1418	1448	1518	1548	1618	1648	1718	1748	1818
Derby 124 a.	|	0905	|	1005	|	1105	|	1205	|	1305	|	1405	|	1505	|	1605	|	1705	|	1805	|	1905
Sheffield 124 a.	|	0944	|	1044	|	1144	|	1244	|	1344	|	1444	|	1544	|	1644	|	1742	|	1844	|	1940
Leeds 124 a.	|	|	|	|	|	|	|	|	|	|	|	|	|	|	|	|	|	1834	|	|	|	|
York 124 a.	|	1039	|	1139	|	1240	|	1340	|	1439	|	1539	|	1639	|	1739	|	1901	|	1939	|	2038
Newcastle 124 a.	|	1145	|	1244	|	1345	|	1443	|	1545	|	1645	|	1745	|	1847	|	2001	|	2042	|	2144
Manchester Piccadilly 122 a.	0938	...	1035	...	1135	...	1235	...	1334	...	1435	...	1535	...	1635	...	1735	...	1835	...	1935	...

	Ⓐ	Ⓐ	Ⓐ	Ⓐ	Ⓐ	Ⓐ	Ⓐ	Ⓐ	Ⓐ	
Bournemouth 108 d.	...	1645	...	1745	...	1845	...	1945	...	...
Brockenhurst 108 d.	...	1700	...	1800	...	1900	...	2000	...	...
Southampton Central 108 d.	...	1717	1746	1815	...	1917	...	2017	...	...
Southampton Airport ✈ 108 d.	...	1724	1753	1822	...	1924	...	2024	...	...
Winchester 108 d.	...	1733	1802	1831	...	1933	...	2033	...	...
Basingstoke 108 d.	...	1749	1818	1847	...	1949	...	2049	...	...
Reading 131 d.	1745	1815	1845	1915	1945	2015	2045	2111	2145	...
Oxford 131 d.	1810	1838	1913	1939	2013	2039	2114	2136	2230	...
Banbury 128 d.	1827	1857	1930	1957	2032	2057	2133	2154	2248	...
Leamington Spa 128 d.	1845	1914	1948	2014	2050	2114	2152	2211	2305	...
Coventry 150 d.	|	1927	|	2027	|	2127	|	2225	2317	...
Birmingham Intl ✈ 150 d.	|	1938	|	2038	|	2138	|	2235	2327	...
Birmingham New Street 150 a.	1918	1948	2018	2048	2123	2148	2218	2245	2356	...
Derby 124 a.	2005	|	2109	|	...	|	...	...	...	...
Sheffield 124 a.	2040	|	2150	|	...	|	...	...	...	...
Leeds 124 a.	|	|	|	|	...	|	...	...	...	...
York 124 a.	2140	|	2252	|	...	|	...	...	...	...
Newcastle 124 a.	2247	|	...	|	...	|	...	...	...	...
Manchester Piccadilly 122 a.	...	2140	...	2234	...	2337	...	...	...	...

⑥

	⑥	⑥ G	⑥	⑥	⑥	⑥	⑥	⑥	⑥	⑥	⑥	⑥
Bournemouth 108 d.	...	...	...	0625	0637	...	0747	...	0847	...	0947	...
Brockenhurst 108 d.	...	...	...	0639	0655	...	0802	...	0902	...	1002	...
Southampton Central 108 d.	0509	...	0620	0653	0720	0747	0820	...	0918	0947	1017	...
Southampton Airport ✈ 108 d.	0516	...	0627	0701	0727	0754	0827	...	0925	0954	1024	...
Winchester 108 d.	0525	...	0636	0709	0736	0803	0836	...	0934	1003	1033	...
Basingstoke 108 d.	0541	...	0652	0725	0752	0819	0852	...	0952	1019	1052	...
Reading 131 d.	0615	0645	0715	0747	0815	0845	0912	0945	1015	1045	1115	1145
Oxford 131 d.	0639	0712	0740	0812	0840	0912	0936	1012	1040	1112	1140	1212
Banbury 128 d.	0657	0729	0757	0829	0857	0929	0953	1029	1057	1129	1157	1229
Leamington Spa 128 d.	0714	0747	0814	0847	0914	0947	1011	1047	1114	1147	1214	1247
Coventry 150 d.	0727	|	0827	|	0927	|	1027	|	1127	|	1227	|
Birmingham Intl ✈ 150 d.	0738	|	0838	|	0938	|	1038	|	1138	|	1238	|
Birmingham New Street 150 a.	0748	0818	0848	0918	0948	1018	1048	1118	1148	1218	1248	1318
Derby 124 a.	|	0905	|	1005	|	1105	|	1205	|	1305	|	1405
Sheffield 124 a.	|	0944	|	1044	|	1144	|	1244	|	1344	|	1444
Leeds 124 a.	|	|	|	|	|	|	|	|	|	|	|	|
York 124 a.	|	1039	|	1139	|	1239	|	1339	|	1439	|	1539
Newcastle 124 a.	|	1146	|	1245	|	1345	|	1443	|	1545	|	1645
Manchester Piccadilly 122 a.	0935	...	1035	...	1135	...	1235	...	1335	...	1435	...

	⑥	⑥	⑥	⑥	⑥	⑥	⑥	⑥	⑥	⑥	⑥	⑥	⑥	⑥ a	⑥ c	⑥	⑥	⑥	⑥	⑥
Bournemouth 108 d.	...	1147	...	1247	...	1347	...	1447	...	1547	...	1647	...	1747	1747	...	1847	...	1947	...
Brockenhurst 108 d.	...	1202	...	1302	...	1402	...	1502	...	1602	...	1702	...	1802	1802	...	1902	...	2002	...
Southampton Central 108 d.	1147	1220	...	1318	1347	1420	...	1518	1547	1620	...	1720	1747	1820	1820	...	1920	...	2020	...
Southampton Airport ✈ 108 d.	1154	1227	...	1325	1354	1427	...	1525	1554	1627	...	1727	1754	1827	1827	...	1927	...	2027	...
Winchester 108 d.	1203	1236	...	1334	1403	1436	...	1534	1603	1636	...	1736	1803	1836	1836	...	1936	...	2036	...
Basingstoke 108 d.	1219	1252	...	1352	1419	1452	...	1552	1618	1652	...	1752	1818	1852	1852	...	1952	...	2052	...
Reading 131 d.	1245	1315	1345	1415	1445	1515	1545	1615	1645	1715	1745	1815	1845	1915	1915	1945	2015	2045	2115	2145
Oxford 131 d.	1312	1340	1412	1440	1512	1540	1612	1640	1712	1740	1812	1840	1912	1940	1940	2012	2040	2112	2139	2212
Banbury 128 d.	1329	1357	1429	1457	1529	1557	1629	1657	1729	1757	1829	1857	1929	1957	1957	2029	2057	2129	2157	2229
Leamington Spa 128 d.	1347	1414	1447	1514	1547	1614	1647	1714	1747	1814	1847	1914	1947	2015	2015	2047	2115	2147	2214	2247
Coventry 150 d.	|	1427	|	1527	|	1627	|	1727	|	1827	|	1927	|	2027	2027	|	2127	2159	2226	|
Birmingham Intl ✈ 150 d.	|	1438	|	1538	|	1638	|	1738	|	1838	|	1938	|	2039	2039	|	2138	2211	2237	|
Birmingham New Street 150 a.	1418	1448	1518	1548	1618	1648	1718	1748	1818	1848	1918	1948	2018	2049	2049	2116	2148	2221	2247	2317
Derby 124 a.	1505	|	1605	|	1705	|	1805	|	1905	|	2005	|	2124	|	2141	...	|	...	...	...
Sheffield 124 a.	1544	|	1644	|	1744	|	1844	|	1947	|	2049	|	2159	|	2223	...	|	...	...	...
Leeds 124 a.	|	|	|	|	1829	|	|	|	|	|	|	|	|	|	2325	...	|	...	...	...
York 124 a.	1639	|	1739	|	1901	|	1939	|	2039	|	2144	|	2246	|	...	...	|	...	...	...
Newcastle 124 a.	1745	|	1843	|	2001	|	2042	|	2144	|	2247	|	...	|	...	...	|	...	...	...
Manchester Piccadilly 122 a.	...	1635	...	1735	...	1835	...	1935	...	2035	...	2136	...	2235	...	...	2330	...	...	...

⑦

	⑦	⑦
Bournemouth 108 d.	...	...
Brockenhurst 108 d.	...	...
Southampton Central 108 d.	...	0915
Southampton Airport ✈ 108 d.	...	0922
Winchester 108 d.	...	0931
Basingstoke 108 d.	...	0947
Reading 131 d.	0912	1011
Oxford 131 d.	0937	1037
Banbury 128 d.	0955	1055
Leamington Spa 128 d.	1012	1112
Coventry 150 d.	1029	1129
Birmingham Intl ✈ 150 d.	1040	1141
Birmingham New Street 150 a.	1050	1151
Derby 124 a.	|	|
Sheffield 124 a.	|	|
Leeds 124 a.	|	|
York 124 a.	|	|
Newcastle 124 a.	|	|
Manchester Piccadilly 122 a.	1241	1340

	⑦	⑦ G	⑦	⑦		⑦	⑦	⑦	⑦ E		⑦	⑦	⑦	⑦		⑦	⑦	⑦	⑦		⑦	⑦	⑦
Bournemouth 108 d.	1040	...	1140	...	...	1240	...	1340	...	...	1440	...	1540	...	...	1640	...	1740	...	...	1840	...	1940
Brockenhurst 108 d.	1057	...	1157	...	...	1257	...	1357	...	...	1457	...	1557	...	...	1657	...	1757	...	...	1857	...	1957
Southampton Central 108 d.	1115	...	1215	...	...	1315	...	1415	...	...	1515	...	1615	...	...	1715	...	1815	...	...	1915	...	2015
Southampton Airport ✈ 108 d.	1122	...	1222	...	...	1322	...	1422	...	...	1522	...	1622	...	...	1722	...	1822	...	...	1922	...	2022
Winchester 108 d.	1131	...	1231	...	...	1331	...	1431	...	...	1531	...	1631	...	...	1731	...	1831	...	...	1931	...	2031
Basingstoke 108 d.	1147	...	1247	...	...	1347	...	1447	...	...	1547	...	1647	...	...	1747	...	1847	...	...	1947	...	2047
Reading 131 d.	1211	1254	1310	1341	...	1411	1441	1511	1541	...	1611	1641	1711	1741	...	1811	1841	1911	1941	...	2011	2041	2111
Oxford 131 d.	1237	1317	1337	1406	...	1437	1506	1537	1606	...	1637	1706	1737	1806	...	1837	1906	1937	2006	...	2037	2106	2137
Banbury 128 d.	1255	1335	1355	1424	...	1455	1524	1555	1624	...	1655	1724	1754	1824	...	1855	1924	1955	2024	...	2055	2124	2154
Leamington Spa 128 d.	1312	1352	1412	1442	...	1512	1540	1612	1640	...	1712	1740	1812	1842	...	1912	1941	2012	2041	...	2112	2141	2212
Coventry 150 d.	1327	|	1427	1454	...	1527	1554	1627	1654	...	1727	1754	1827	1855	...	1927	1954	2027	2054	...	2127	2153	2224
Birmingham Intl ✈ 150 d.	1338	|	1438	1504	...	1538	1604	1638	1704	...	1738	1804	1838	1905	...	1938	2004	2038	2104	...	2138	2203	2234
Birmingham New Street 150 a.	1348	1419	1448	1514	...	1548	1614	1648	1714	...	1748	1814	1848	1915	...	1948	2014	2048	2115	...	2148	2214	2243
Derby 124 a.	|	1501	|	1601	...	|	1702	|	1802	...	|	1903	|	2001	...	|	...	|	...	...	|	...	...
Sheffield 124 a.	|	1547	|	1648	...	|	1749	|	1845	...	|	1940	|	2041	...	|	...	|	...	...	|	...	...
Leeds 124 a.	|	|	|	|	...	|	1851	|	|	...	|	|	|	|	...	|	...	|	...	...	|	...	...
York 124 a.	|	1638	|	1740	...	|	1921	|	1939	...	|	2039	|	2143	...	|	...	|	...	...	|	...	...
Newcastle 124 a.	|	1744	|	1841	...	|	2019	|	2041	...	|	2144	|	2312	...	|	...	|	...	...	|	...	...
Manchester Piccadilly 122 a.	1539	...	1640	...	...	1740	...	1840	...	...	1940	...	2040	...	...	2140	...	2239	...	...	2340	...	...

E – To Edinburgh Waverley (Table **124**).
G – From Guildford (Table **134**).

a – From Sept. 17.
b – Not Dec. 9.
c – May 21 - Sept. 10.

Most services convey 🍸

BIRMINGHAM - BRISTOL - PAIGNTON and PLYMOUTH 120

		Ⓐ	Ⓐ	Ⓐ	Ⓐ	Ⓐ	Ⓐ	Ⓐ	Ⓐ	Ⓐ	Ⓐ	Ⓐ	Ⓐ	Ⓐ	Ⓐ	Ⓐ	Ⓐ	Ⓐ	Ⓐ	Ⓐ	Ⓐ	Ⓐ	Ⓐ	Ⓐ
									★d							A					★	B		
Glasgow Central **124** d.	Ⓐ	...	...	...	...	...	...	...	...	...	...	...	...	0601	...	...	...	0750	...	0900	...	...	...	1100
Edinburgh Waverley **124** d.		...	...	...	...	...	...	...	...	...	...	0606	...	0707	...	0810	...	0908	...	1010	...	1106	...	1208
Newcastle **124** d.		...	...	...	...	...	...	...	...	0645	...	0740	...	0843	...	0942	...	1042	...	1144	...	1241	...	1343
York **124** d.		...	...	...	...	...	...	0640	...	0743	...	0845	...	0945	...	1045	...	1145	...	1245	...	1345	...	1445
Leeds **124** d.		...	...	...	...	0600	...	0705	...	0811	...	0911	...	1011	...	1111	...	1211	...	1311	...	1411	...	1511
Sheffield **124** d.		...	...	...	...	0652	...	0753	...	0854	...	0954	...	1055	...	1154	...	1255	...	1355	...	1455	...	1555
Derby **124** d.		...	...	0610	...	0727	...	0828	...	0928	...	1030	...	1128	...	1230	...	1328	...	1428	...	1528	...	1628
Manchester P'dilly **122** d.		...	...	|	0600	|	0707	|	0807	|	0907	|	1007	|	1107	|	1207	|	1307	|	1407	|	1507	|
Birmingham New St **121** d.		...	0642	0712	0742	0812	0842	0917	0942	1017	1042	1117	1142	1217	1242	1317	1342	1417	1442	1517	1542	1612	1642	1712
Cheltenham Spa **121** a.		...	0721	0751	0824	0850	0924	0958	1024	1059	1124	1157	1224	1259	1324	1357	1424	1458	1524	1558	1624	1649	1724	1751
Bristol Parkway a.		...	0754	0826	0854	0925	0954	1030	1054	1131	1154	1229	1254	1330	1354	1429	1454	1529	1554	1630	1654	1724	1754	1828
Bristol Temple Meads a.		...	0805	0839	0910	0939	1008	1042	1110	1141	1205	1242	1309	1341	1408	1442	1510	1541	1611	1643	1710	1739	1807	1841
Bristol Temple Meads **115** d.		0634	0810	0844	...	0944	...	1045	1115	1144	...	1245	...	1344	...	1445	1513	1544	...	1645	1713	1744	...	1844
Taunton **115** a.		0707	0842	0914	...	1015	...	1116	1158	1214	...	1316	...	1414	...	1516	1544	1614	...	1716	1744	1815	...	1915
Tiverton Parkway **115** a.		0719	0854	0926	...	1028	...	1129	1210	1226	...	1328	...	1426	...	1528	1556	1626	...	1728	1756	1827	...	1927
Exeter St Davids **115** a.		0732	0907	0940	...	1042	...	1143	1224	1240	...	1343	...	1440	...	1543	1612	1640	...	1742	1811	1841	...	1942
Newton Abbot **115** a.		0754	0927	0959	...	1104	...	1204	1248	1259	...	1403	...	1459	...	1603	...	1704	...	1811	1835	1905	...	2002
Torquay **115** a.		|	0939	|	...	|	...	|	1300	|	...	|	...	|	...	|	...	|	...	|	1847	|	...	|
Paignton **115** a.		|	0947	|	...	|	...	|	1308	|	...	|	...	|	...	|	...	|	...	|	1855	|	...	|
Totnes **115** a.		0807	...	1014	...	1117	...	1218	...	1311	...	1416	...	1511	...	1619	...	1716	...	1823	...	1917	...	2014
Plymouth **115** a.		0833	...	1042	...	1144	...	1247	...	1338	...	1443	...	1540	...	1648	...	1742	...	1849	...	1943	...	2040
Newquay **117** a.		...	...	...	...	...	...	...	...	...	...	...	...	...	...	...	...	...	...	|	...	|	...	|
Penzance **117** a.		...	...	...	...	...	...	...	...	...	...	...	...	...	...	...	...	...	...	2054	...	2143	...	2241

	Ⓐ	Ⓐ	Ⓐ	Ⓐ	Ⓐ	Ⓐ	Ⓐ	Ⓐ	Ⓐ		⑥	⑥	⑥	⑥	⑥	⑥	⑥	⑥	⑥	⑥	⑥	⑥	⑥	⑥	⑥
		b	D					c							e	★f	e	f		★d	e	f			
Glasgow Central **124** d.	...	...	...	1300	...	...	...	1500	...	⑥	...	...	...	...	...	...	...	...	...	...	...	...	...	...	...
Edinburgh Waverley **124** d.	...	1307	...	1408	...	1508	...	1606	1708		...	...	...	...	...	...	...	...	...	...	...	...	...	0608	...
Newcastle **124** d.	...	1442	...	1541	...	1641	...	1741	1843		...	...	...	...	...	...	...	...	...	...	0645	...	...	0741	...
York **124** d.	...	1545	...	1645	...	1745	...	1845	1945		...	...	...	...	...	...	...	...	0620g	...	0745	0745	...	0845	...
Leeds **124** d.	...	1611	...	1711	...	1811	...	1911	2011		...	...	...	...	0600	0600	...	...	0711	...	0811	0811	...	0911	...
Sheffield **124** d.	...	1655	...	1758	...	1858	...	1958	2058		...	...	...	...	0650	0650	...	...	0756	...	0855	0854	...	0955	...
Derby **124** d.	...	1729	...	1829	...	1930	...	2029	2129		...	...	0610	...	0726	0726	...	...	0828	...	0930	0930	...	1028	...
Manchester P'dilly **122** d.	1607	|	1705	|	1805	|	1907	|	|		...	...	|	0600	|	|	0707	0707	|	0807	|	|	0907	|	1007
Birmingham New St **121** d.	1742	1812	1842	1912	1942	2012	2042	2112	2212		...	0642	0712	0742	0812	0812	0842	0842	0912	0942	1012	1012	1042	1112	1142
Cheltenham Spa **121** a.	1824	1850	1924	1950	2024	2052	2126	2151	2251		...	0724	0750	0824	0851	0851	0924	0924	0951	1024	1051	1051	1124	1153	1224
Bristol Parkway a.	1854	1933	1954	2030	2054	2125	2201	2233	2322		...	0753	0824	0853	0924	0924	0953	0953	1029	1054	1125	1125	1153	1229	1253
Bristol Temple Meads a.	1906	1943	2009	2041	2108	2136	2214	2243	2340		...	0805	0838	0906	0939	0939	1004	1004	1042	1109	1138	1138	1204	1242	1307
Bristol Temple Meads **115** d.	...	1945	...	2044	2113	2144	...	...	...		0608	0812	0845	...	0944	0944	...	1020	1044	1112	1144	1144	...	1244	...
Taunton **115** a.	...	2016	...	2115	2143	2215	...	...	...		0715	0842	0915	...	1017	1017	...	1100	1115	1159	1215	1216	...	1315	...
Tiverton Parkway **115** a.	...	2029	...	2127	2155	2227	...	...	...		0727	0854	0927	...	1030	1030	...	1112	1127	1211	1227	1229	...	1327	...
Exeter St Davids **115** a.	...	2043	...	2144	2209	2241	...	...	...		0740	0907	0940	...	1044	1044	...	1126	1141	1225	1241	1243	...	1341	...
Newton Abbot **115** a.	...	2103	...	2205	2228	2301	...	...	...		0759	0928	1000	...	1109	1111	...	1151	1201	1250	1300	1304	...	1401	...
Torquay **115** a.	...	|	...	|	|	|	...	...	...		|	0939	|	...	|	1125	...	|	|	1302	|	|	...	|	...
Paignton **115** a.	...	|	...	|	|	|	...	...	...		|	0947	|	...	|	1135	...	|	|	1310	|	|	...	|	...
Totnes **115** a.	...	2116	...	2217	2241	2313	...	...	...		0812	...	1012	...	1122	...	...	1204	1213	...	1312	1317	...	1416	...
Plymouth **115** a.	...	2146	...	2243	2313	2339	...	...	...		0838	...	1039	...	1151	...	...	1233	1240	...	1339	1345	...	1444	...
Newquay **117** a.	...	...	...	...	...	...	...	...	...		...	...	...	...	...	...	...	1431	...	...	...	|	...	...	...
Penzance **117** a.	...	...	...	...	...	...	...	...	...		...	...	...	...	...	...	...	...	...	...	...	1541	...	...	...

	⑥	⑥	⑥	⑥	⑥	⑥	⑥	⑥	⑥	⑥	⑥	⑥	⑥	⑥	⑥	⑥	⑥	⑥	⑥	⑥	⑥	⑥	⑥		⑦
	e	★f		A	★f	e				f	★e	B					D		f	e			c		
Glasgow Central **124** d.	0601	0601	...	...	...	...	0750	...	0900	...	...	...	...	1100	...	...	...	1300	...	...	...	...	1500	⑦	...
Edinburgh Waverley **124** d.	0707	0707	...	0805	...	...	0908	...	1005	...	...	1108	...	1204	...	1309	...	1405	...	...	1508	...	1605		...
Newcastle **124** d.	0843	0842	...	0942	...	...	1044	...	1142	...	...	1244	...	1344	...	1444	...	1544	...	...	1644	...	1744		...
York **124** d.	0945	0945	...	1045	...	...	1145	...	1245	...	...	1345	...	1445	...	1545	...	1645	...	...	1745	...	1845		...
Leeds **124** d.	1011	1011	...	1111	...	...	1211	...	1311	...	...	1411	...	1511	...	1611	...	1711	...	...	1811	...	1911		...
Sheffield **124** d.	1055	1054	...	1155	...	...	1255	...	1355	...	...	1455	...	1555	...	1655	...	1755	...	...	1858	...	1955		...
Derby **124** d.	1130	1130	...	1230	...	...	1328	...	1430	...	...	1528	...	1628	...	1728	...	1829	...	...	1929	...	2028		...
Manchester P'dilly **122** d.	|	|	1107	|	1207	1207	|	1307	|	1407	1407	|	1507	|	1607	|	1706	|	1805	1805	|	1907	|		...
Birmingham New St **121** d.	1212	1212	1242	1312	1342	1342	1412	1442	1512	1542	1542	1612	1642	1712	1742	1812	1842	1912	1942	1942	2012	2042	2112		...
Cheltenham Spa **121** a.	1251	1251	1325	1350	1424	1424	1451	1524	1550	1624	1624	1650	1724	1750	1824	1850	1924	1950	2024	2024	2051	2124	2150		...
Bristol Parkway a.	1324	1324	1355	1426	1456	1456	1524	1554	1629	1653	1653	1725	1753	1829	1853	1925	1955	2029	2053	2053	2122	2158	2231		...
Bristol Temple Meads a.	1338	1339	1405	1440	1509	1509	1538	1607	1642	1707	1707	1738	1807	1842	1904	1938	2005	2042	2104	2104	2135	2212	2241		...
Bristol Temple Meads **115** d.	1344	1344	...	1444	1512	1512	1544	...	1644	...	1710	1744	...	1844	...	1944	...	2044	...	2111	2144	...	...		0844
Taunton **115** a.	1415	1416	...	1516	1542	1542	1614	...	1716	...	1740	1815	...	1915	...	2015	...	2115	...	2141	2215	...	...		0915
Tiverton Parkway **115** a.	1427	1429	...	1528	1554	1554	1626	...	1729	...	1752	1827	...	1927	...	2027	...	2127	...	2153	2229	...	...		0927
Exeter St Davids **115** a.	1441	1443	...	1543	1607	1609	1640	...	1743	...	1805	1841	...	1944	...	2040	...	2143	...	2207	2244	...	...		0939
Newton Abbot **115** a.	1502	1516	...	1603	1647	...	1700	...	1810	...	1830	1904	...	2005	...	2100	...	2204	...	2226	2311	...	...		0959
Torquay **115** a.	|	1528	...	|	1659	...	|	...	|	...	1841	|	...	|	...	|	...	|	...	|	|	...	...		|
Paignton **115** a.	|	1538	...	|	1710	...	|	...	|	...	1849	|	...	|	...	|	...	|	...	|	|	...	...		|
Totnes **115** a.	1514	...	...	1616	...	...	1712	...	1823	...	...	1916	...	2017	...	2112	...	2220	...	2238	2327	...	...		1012
Plymouth **115** a.	1541	...	...	1643	...	...	1739	...	1851	...	...	1942	...	2043	...	2138	...	2250	...	2305	2356	...	...		1037
Newquay **117** a.	...	...	...	1839f	...	...	|	...	|	...	...	|	...	|	...	...	...	...	...	...	...	...	...		...
Penzance **117** a.	...	...	...	...	...	...	1934f	...	2056	...	...	2140	...	2254e	...	...	...	...	...	...	...	...	...		...

	⑦	⑦	⑦	⑦	⑦	⑦	⑦	⑦	⑦	⑦	⑦		⑦	⑦	⑦	⑦	⑦h	⑦k	⑦	⑦	⑦	⑦	⑦	⑦	⑦
								★									★a	★a	B						
Glasgow Central **124** d.	...	...	...	...	...	...	...	...	...	...	...	...	...	1055	...	1200	...	...	...	...	1348	...	1455	...	...
Edinburgh Waverley **124** d.	...	...	...	...	...	...	0908	...	1008	...	1105	...	...	1208	...	1308	...	...	1408	...	1508	...	1608	...	1708
Newcastle **124** d.	...	...	...	...	0935	...	1039	...	1140	...	1240	...	...	1340	...	1440	...	...	1540	...	1640	...	1740	...	1840
York **124** d.	...	...	...	0933	1033	...	1141	...	1241	...	1341	...	...	1441	...	1541	...	...	1641	...	1741	...	1841	...	1941
Leeds **124** d.	...	0810	0900	1000	1100	...	1211	...	1311	...	1411	...	...	1511	...	1611	...	...	1711	...	1811	...	1911	...	2011
Sheffield **124** d.	...	0854	0957	1057	1157	...	1257	...	1357	...	1455	...	...	1555	...	1654	...	...	1754	...	1855	...	1955	...	2054
Derby **124** d.	...	0928	1033	1129	1229	...	1332	...	1429	...	1526	...	...	1627	...	1727	...	...	1826	...	1927	...	2027	...	2126
Manchester P'dilly **122** d.	...	|	|	|	|	...	|	1307	|	1407	|	...	1507	|	1607	|	1707	1707	|	1807	|	1907	|	2007	|
Birmingham New St **121** d.	0930	1030	1130	1212	1312	1342	1412	1442	1512	1542	1612	...	1642	1712	1742	1812	1842	1842	1912	1942	2012	2042	2112	2142	2212
Cheltenham Spa **121** a.	1008	1109	1208	1251	1351	1423	1450	1524	1550	1624	1650	...	1724	1751	1824	1851	1924	1924	1951	2024	2051	2124	2151	2223	2252
Bristol Parkway a.	1037	1139	1238	1320	1420	1453	1523	1559	1620	1654	1720	...	1803	1820	1854	1921	2003	2003	2020	2056	2120	2159	2233	2252	2322
Bristol Temple Meads a.	1048	1151	1249	1331	1431	1508	1534	1611	1631	1708	1733	...	1814	1835	1908	1932	2014	2014	2031	2106	2130	2210	2244	2306	2333
Bristol Temple Meads **115** d.	1057	1154	1254	1344	1444	...	1544	1614	1644	...	1744	...	...	1844	...	1944	2019	2019	2044	...	2144	...	...	...	...
Taunton **115** a.	1129	1225	1325	1414	1514	...	1614	1644	1714	...	1817	...	...	1916	...	2017	2058	2057	2114	...	2214	...	...	...	...
Tiverton Parkway **115** a.	1141	1235	1336	1426	1526	...	1626	1656	1726	...	1829	...	...	1928	...	2029	2111	2111	2126	...	2227	...	...	...	...
Exeter St Davids **115** a.	1154	1252	1352	1439	1539	...	1640	1709	1739	...	1845	...	...	1945	...	2043	2127	2127	2139	...	2245	...	...	...	...
Newton Abbot **115** a.	1214	1312	1412	1459	1600	...	1701	1736	1800	...	1905	...	...	2007	...	2101	2153	2154	2159	...	2304	...	...	...	...
Torquay **115** a.	|	|	|	|	|	...	|	1748	|	...	|	...	...	|	...	|	|	2205	|	...	|	...	...	...	...
Paignton **115** a.	|	|	|	|	|	...	|	1756	|	...	|	...	...	|	...	|	|	2214	|	...	|	...	...	...	...
Totnes **115** a.	1226	1325	1425	1511	1612	...	1714	...	1812	...	1917	...	...	2019	...	2113	|	...	2217	...	2317	...	...	...	...
Plymouth **115** a.	1252	1352	1452	1537	1638	...	1742	...	1838	...	1943	...	...	2045	...	2141	2237	...	2245	...	2346	...	...	...	...
Newquay **117** a.	|	...	...	...	...	...	...	...	|	...	...	...	...	|	...	...	...	...	...	...	...	...	...	...	...
Penzance **117** a.	1447	...	...	...	...	...	...	...	2039	...	...	...	...	2242	...	...	...	...	...	...	...	...	...	...	...

– From Dundee (Table **222**).
– From Aberdeen (Table **222**).
– To Cardiff Central May 16 - Sept. 10 and from Oct. 24 (Table **121**).

– Also calls at Weston-super-Mare (d. 2036).
– Also calls at Gloucester (a. 1901).

c – Also calls at Gloucester (a. 2202 on Ⓐ and ⑦, 2200 on ⑥).
d – Also calls at Weston-super-Mare (d. 1132 on Ⓐ, 1129 on ⑥).
e – From Sept. 17.
f – May 21 - Sept. 10.
g – 0645 May 21 - Sept. 10.
h – From Sept. 18.
k – May 15 - Sept. 11.

★ – Also calls at Dawlish (10 – 15 minutes after Exeter) and Teignmouth (15 – 18 minutes after Exeter).

120 PLYMOUTH and PAIGNTON - BRISTOL - BIRMINGHAM

Ⓐ	Ⓐ E	Ⓐ	Ⓐ	Ⓐ D	Ⓐ	Ⓐ ☆e	Ⓐ	Ⓐ	Ⓐ	Ⓐ	Ⓐ B	Ⓐ ☆	Ⓐ	Ⓐ	Ⓐ A	Ⓐ	Ⓐ	Ⓐ	Ⓐ	Ⓐ ☆a	Ⓐ	Ⓐ
Penzance **117** d.	...	...	...	...	...	...	...	...	0628	...	...	...	0828	...	...	0935	...	...	...	...	...	...
Newquay **117** d.	...	...	...	...	...	...	...	...	|	...	...	...	|	...	...	|	...	...	...	...	...	...
Plymouth **115** d.	...	...	0520	...	0625	...	0725	...	0825	...	0925	...	1025	...	1125	1150	1225	...	1325	...	1425	...
Totnes **115** d.	...	...	0545	...	0650	...	0750	...	0850	...	0950	...	1050	...	1150	1215	1251	...	1351	...	1450	...
Paignton **115** d.	...	...	|	...	|	0702	|	...	|	...	|	1007	|	...	|	|	|	...	|	1404	|	...
Torquay **115** d.	...	...	|	...	|	0708	|	...	|	...	|	1013	|	...	|	|	|	...	|	1410	|	...
Newton Abbot **115** d.	...	...	0602	...	0703	0719	0803	...	0903	...	1003	1024	1103	...	1203	1228	1304	...	1404	1421	1503	...
Exeter St Davids **115** d.	...	...	0624	...	0724	0745	0824	...	0924	...	1024	1050	1124	...	1224	1250	1324	...	1424	1448	1524	...
Tiveton Parkway **115** d.	...	...	0637	...	0737	0758	0837	...	0938	...	1037	1103	1137	...	1238	1306	1338	...	1438	1502	1537	...
Taunton **115** d.	...	...	0651	...	0751	0812	0851	...	0951	...	1051	1117	1151	...	1251	1322	1351	...	1451	1515	1551	...
Bristol Temple Meads **115** a.	0620	...	0726	...	0827	0854	0926	...	1025	...	1124	1152	1224	...	1324	1355	1426	...	1523	1556	1623	...
Bristol Temple Meads d.	0627	0700	0730	0800	0830	0900	0930	1000	1030	1100	1130	1200	1230	1300	1330	1400	1430	1500	1530	1600	1630	1700
Bristol Parkway d.	0638	0709	0739	0809	0839	0909	0939	1009	1039	1109	1139	1209	1239	1309	1339	1409	1440	1509	1540	1609	1639	1709
Cheltenham Spa **121** d.	0710	0740	0811	0840	0912	0942	1010	1041	1111	1142	1211	1240	1311	1342	1410	1441	1511	1542	1611	1641	1711	1742
Birmingham New St **121** a.	0756	0826	0856	0926	0958	1023	1056	1126	1158	1226	1256	1326	1356	1423	1456	1523	1556	1623	1656	1723	1756	1823
Manchester P'dilly **122** a.	|	0959	|	1059	|	1159	|	1259	|	1359	|	1459	|	1559	|	1657	|	1759	|	1859	|	1959
Derby **124** a.	0841	...	0939	...	1038	...	1138	...	1241	...	1339	...	1440	...	1540	...	1641	...	1739	...	1839	...
Sheffield **124** a.	0917	...	1017	...	1118	...	1217	...	1317	...	1418	...	1517	...	1618	...	1718	...	1818	...	1918	...
Leeds **124** a.	1001	...	1101	...	1201	...	1301	...	1401	...	1501	...	1601	...	1704	...	1802	...	1903	...	2005	...
York **124** a.	1030	...	1130	...	1230	...	1330	...	1430	...	1530	...	1630	...	1730	...	1831	...	1930	...	2030	...
Newcastle **124** a.	1129	...	1229	...	1329	...	1430	...	1529	...	1629	...	1730	...	1833	...	1932	...	2033	...	2128	...
Edinburgh Waverley **124** a.	1306	...	1410	...	1507	...	1606	...	1706	...	1807	...	1906	...	2009	...	2108	...	2214	...	2303	...
Glasgow Central **124** a.	1412	...	...	...	1612	...	...	...	1811	...	...	...	2015	...	...	...	2224	...	...	...	...	...

	Ⓐ	Ⓐ	Ⓐ	Ⓐ	Ⓐ b	Ⓐ	Ⓐ	⑥ c	⑥	⑥	⑥ D	⑥	⑥ ☆	⑥	⑥	⑥	⑥ df	⑥ g	⑥f ☆B	⑥g B	⑥ ☆	⑥
Penzance **117** d.	...	...	...	...	...	...	...	...	...	...	...	...	...	...	...	0630	...	...	...	...	...	0828
Newquay **117** d.	...	...	...	...	...	...	...	...	...	...	...	...	...	...	...	|	...	...	...	...	...	|
Plymouth **115** d.	...	1625	...	1725	...	1825	...	...	...	0525	...	0625	...	0725	...	0825	0839	...	0918	0925	...	1025
Totnes **115** d.	...	1650	...	1751	...	1850	...	...	...	0550	...	0650	...	0750	...	0850	0904	...	0943	0950	...	1050
Paignton **115** d.	...	|	...	|	...	|	2014	...	...	|	...	|	0702	|	...	|	|	...	|	|	1006	|
Torquay **115** d.	...	|	...	|	...	|	2020	...	...	|	...	|	0708	|	...	|	|	...	|	|	1012	|
Newton Abbot **115** d.	...	1703	...	1804	...	1903	2031	...	...	0603	...	0703	0719	0803	...	0903	0917	...	0956	1003	1023	1103
Exeter St Davids **115** d.	1654	1724	...	1825	...	1924	2052	...	...	0623	...	0723	0745	0823	...	0923	0945	...	1025	1023	1049	1123
Tiveton Parkway **115** d.	1708	1737	...	1839	...	1937	2105	...	...	0637	...	0737	0758	0837	...	0937	0958	...	1038	1037	1102	1137
Taunton **115** d.	1722	1751	...	1851	...	1951	2119	...	...	0650	...	0750	0811	0850	...	0950	1011	...	1051	1050	1117	1150
Bristol Temple Meads **115** a.	1754	1823	...	1925	...	2025	2152	...	...	0722	...	0824	0849	0925	...	1025	1051	...	1126	1123	1154	1225
Bristol Temple Meads d.	1800	1830	1900	1930	2000	2030	2200	0615	0700	0730	0800	0830	0900	0930	1000	1030	1100	1100	1130	1130	1200	1230
Bristol Parkway d.	1809	1839	1909	1940	2009	2040	2210	0624	0709	0739	0809	0839	0909	0939	1009	1039	1109	1109	1139	1139	1209	1239
Cheltenham Spa **121** d.	1841	1911	1940	2011	2056	2117	2242	0711	0741	0811	0841	0911	0941	1011	1041	1111	1141	1141	1211	1211	1241	1311
Birmingham New St **121** a.	1923	1956	2022	2051	2137	2202	2343	0756	0825	0856	0926	0956	1025	1056	1126	1156	1226	1226	1256	1256	1326	1356
Manchester P'dilly **122** a.	2058	|	2200	|	...	...	...	|	0959	|	1059	|	1159	|	1259	|	1359	1359	|	|	1459	|
Derby **124** a.	...	2038	...	2143	...	...	...	0841	...	0939	...	1038	...	1138	...	1238	...	...	1341	1341	...	1440
Sheffield **124** a.	...	2115	...	2224	...	...	...	0917	...	1017	...	1117	...	1217	...	1317	...	...	1418	1418	...	1517
Leeds **124** a.	...	2204	...	2315	...	...	...	1001	...	1101	...	1200	...	1302	...	1401	...	...	1501	1501	...	1601
York **124** a.	...	...	...	...	...	...	...	1030	...	1130	...	1230	...	1330	...	1430	...	...	1530	1530	...	1630
Newcastle **124** a.	...	...	...	...	...	...	...	1129	...	1229	...	1329	...	1429	...	1529	...	...	1629	1629	...	1729
Edinburgh Waverley **124** a.	...	...	...	...	...	...	...	1302	...	1406	...	1504	...	1604	...	1707	...	...	1803	1803	...	1906
Glasgow Central **124** a.	...	...	...	...	...	...	...	1412	...	...	...	1612	...	...	...	1811	...	...	...	...	...	2012

	⑥ A	⑥ g	⑥ f	⑥ ☆f	⑥ g	⑥	⑥	⑥ ☆a		⑥	⑥	⑥	⑥ g	⑥ f	⑥ ☆f	⑥ g	⑥	⑥ f		⑥ g	⑥ f	⑥ g	⑥ f
Penzance **117** d.	...	0943	...	...	...	...	...	...	...	...	...	...	...	...	...	...	...	...	...	...	...	...	1625
Newquay **117** d.	0935f	|	...	...	...	...	...	...	...	...	...	...	...	...	...	...	...	1530	...	...	...	...	|
Plymouth **115** d.	1125	1148	...	...	1225	...	1325	...	...	1425	...	1525	...	...	...	1625	...	1725	...	1725	...	...	1825
Totnes **115** d.	1150	1213	...	...	1251	...	1350	...	...	1450	...	1550	...	...	...	1650	...	1750	...	1751	...	...	1851
Paignton **115** d.	|	|	...	1235	|	...	|	1355	...	|	...	|	...	...	1637	|	...	|	...	|	1811	...	|
Torquay **115** d.	|	|	...	1242	|	...	|	1401	...	|	...	|	...	...	1644	|	...	|	...	|	1818	...	|
Newton Abbot **115** d.	1203	1225	...	1254	1304	...	1403	1412	...	1503	...	1603	...	...	1656	1703	...	1803	...	1804	1830	...	1904
Exeter St Davids **115** d.	1223	1248	...	1323	1323	...	1425	1437	...	1523	...	1623	1653	...	1723	1723	...	1823	...	1824	1850	...	1924
Tiveton Parkway **115** d.	1237	1302	...	1337	1337	...	1438	1450	...	1537	...	1637	1707	...	1737	1737	...	1837	...	1838	1904	...	1938
Taunton **115** d.	1250	1315	...	1350	1350	...	1451	1503	...	1550	...	1650	1721	...	1750	1750	...	1850	...	1851	1917	...	1951
Bristol Temple Meads **115** a.	1325	1355	...	1425	1425	...	1525	1549	...	1625	...	1725	1755	...	1825	1825	...	1923	...	1924	1953	...	2024
Bristol Temple Meads d.	1330	1400	1400	1430	1430	1500	1530	1600	...	1630	1700	1730	1800	1800	1830	1830	1900	1930	...	1930	2000	2000	2030
Bristol Parkway d.	1339	1409	1409	1440	1440	1509	1539	1609	...	1639	1709	1739	1809	1809	1839	1839	1909	1940	...	1940	2009	2009	2040
Cheltenham Spa **121** d.	1411	1441	1441	1511	1511	1541	1611	1641	...	1711	1741	1813	1841	1841	1911	1911	1941	2013	...	2011	2041	2041	2111
Birmingham New St **121** a.	1456	1526	1526	1556	1556	1626	1656	1726	...	1756	1826	1856	1926	1926	1958	1958	2026	2050	...	2052	2138	2138	2151
Manchester P'dilly **122** a.	|	1659	1659	|	|	1759	|	1859	...	|	1959	|	2059	2059	|	|	2202	2235	...	|	...	...	2229
Derby **124** a.	1540	...	...	1640	1640	...	1739	...	...	1839	...	1939	...	...	2039	2039	...	...	...	2143	...	...	2309
Sheffield **124** a.	1618	...	...	1717	1717	...	1817	...	...	1917	...	2022	...	...	2119	2119	...	...	...	2223	...	...	2351
Leeds **124** a.	1701	...	...	1802	1802	...	1901	...	...	2004	...	2104	...	...	2202	2202	...	...	...	2325	...	...	...
York **124** a.	1729	...	...	1830	1830	...	1930	...	...	2030	...	2155	...	...	...	...	...	...	...	...	...	...	...
Newcastle **124** a.	1831	...	...	1932	1932	...	2028	...	...	2128	...	...	...	...	...	...	...	...	...	...	...	...	...
Edinburgh Waverley **124** a.	2006	...	...	2108	2108	...	2208	...	...	2257	...	...	...	...	...	...	...	...	...	...	...	...	...
Glasgow Central **124** a.	...	...	...	2220	2220	...	...	...	...	...	...	...	...	...	...	...	...	...	...	...	...	...	...

⑦	⑦ c	⑦	⑦ B	⑦	⑦ ☆a	⑦	⑦	⑦		⑦	⑦	⑦	⑦	⑦ d	⑦	⑦	⑦	⑦	⑦	⑦	⑦	
Penzance **117** d.	...	...	...	...	...	0930	...	...	...	...	...	...	...	1230	...	...	...	...	1530	...	...	...
Newquay **117** d.	...	...	...	...	...	|	...	...	...	...	1132h	...	...	|	...	...	...	...	|	...	...	...
Plymouth **115** d.	...	...	0925	1025	...	1125	1200	1225	...	1252	1325	...	1425	1435	1524	...	1625	...	1725	...	1825	...
Totnes **115** d.	...	...	0950	1050	...	1150	|	1250	...	|	1351	...	1451	1501	1550	...	1650	...	1750	...	1852	...
Paignton **115** d.	...	...	|	|	1050	|	|	|	...	|	|	...	|	|	|	...	|	...	|	1820	|	...
Torquay **115** d.	...	...	|	|	1056	|	|	|	...	|	|	...	|	|	|	...	|	...	|	1826	|	...
Newton Abbot **115** d.	...	...	1003	1103	1108	1203	1236	1303	...	1327	1404	...	1504	1513	1603	...	1703	...	1803	1837	1905	...
Exeter St Davids **115** d.	...	...	1023	1123	1133	1223	1256	1323	...	1347	1424	...	1524	1532	1624	...	1726	...	1823	1858	1925	...
Tiveton Parkway **115** d.	...	...	1037	1137	1147	1237	1310	1337	...	|	1438	...	1537	1546	1637	...	1739	...	1837	1911	1938	...
Taunton **115** d.	...	...	1050	1152	1200	1250	1323	1350	...	|	1451	...	1551	1559	1651	...	1753	...	1850	1924	1952	...
Bristol Temple Meads **115** a.	...	...	1124	1227	1244	1326	1354	1421	...	1442	1526	...	1626	1647	1726	...	1827	...	1922	1957	2025	...
Bristol Temple Meads d.	0915	1030	1130	1230	1300	1330	1400	1430	...	1500	1530	1600	1630	1700	1730	1800	1830	1900	1930	2000	2030	...
Bristol Parkway d.	0924	1039	1139	1239	1309	1339	1409	1439	...	1509	1540	1609	1640	1709	1740	1809	1839	1909	1939	2009	2040	...
Cheltenham Spa **121** d.	1012	1110	1210	1310	1341	1410	1441	1510	...	1541	1611	1640	1712	1741	1811	1840	1910	1941	2010	2040	2111	...
Birmingham New St **121** a.	1049	1148	1249	1348	1427	1448	1527	1548	...	1627	1649	1726	1749	1827	1848	1926	1948	2027	2049	2118	2148	...
Manchester P'dilly **122** a.	|	|	|	|	1559	|	1700	|	...	1759	|	1859	|	1959	|	2100	|	2157	|	...	|	...
Derby **124** a.	1137	1238	1337	1439	...	1537	...	1638	...	...	1740	...	1839	...	1940	...	2038	...	2141	...	2240	...
Sheffield **124** a.	1218	1318	1417	1517	...	1618	...	1717	...	...	1819	...	1920	...	2018	...	2116	...	2218	...	2318	...
Leeds **124** a.	1301	1401	1501	1602	...	1701	...	1801	...	...	1904	...	2005	...	2107	...	2204	...	2302	...	0008	...
York **124** a.	1327	1427	1527	1627	...	1727	...	1827	...	...	1929	...	2030	...	2132	...	...	...	...	...	...	...
Newcastle **124** a.	1426	1526	1625	1725	...	1825	...	1925	...	...	2031	...	2131	...	...	...	...	...	...	...	...	...
Edinburgh Waverley **124** a.	1602	1656	1757	1856	...	1957	...	2056	...	...	2212	...	2304	...	...	...	...	...	...	...	...	...
Glasgow Central **124** a.	...	1812	...	2021	...	...	...	2213	...	...	...	...	...	...	...	...	...	...	...	...	...	...

A – To Dundee (Table **222**).
B – To Aberdeen (Table **222**).
D – From Cardiff Central May 16 - Sept. 10 and from Oct. 24 (Table **121**).
E – From Bath Spa (d. 0609).

a – Also calls at Weston-super-Mare (d. 1538 on Ⓐ, 1529 on ⑥, 1221 on ⑦).
b – Also calls at Gloucester (d. 2046).
c – Also calls at Gloucester (d. 0700 on ⑥, 1000 on ⑦).
d – Also calls at Weston-super-Mare (d. 1033 on ⑥, 1628 on ⑦).
e – Also calls at Weston-super-Mare (d. 0833).
f – May 21 - Sept. 10.

g – From Sept. 17.
h – May 15 - Sept. 11.

☆ – Also calls at Teignmouth (7 – 10 minutes af Newton Abbot) and Dawlish (12 – 15 minute after Newton Abbot).

BIRMINGHAM - CARDIFF 121

On ⑥ May 21 - June 18 and from Sept. 17 Newport and Cardiff arrivals may be up to 8 minutes earlier, departures up to 10 minutes later.

		Ⓐ 2	Ⓐ	Ⓐ	Ⓐ 2	Ⓐ	Ⓐ 2	Ⓐ	Ⓐ	Ⓐ 2	Ⓐ	Ⓐ 2	Ⓐ	Ⓐ	Ⓐ 2a	Ⓐ 2b	Ⓐ	Ⓐ 2 Bb	Ⓐ 2 Ba	Ⓐ	Ⓐ	Ⓐ 2
Nottingham 123 d.	Ⓐ	...	...	...	...	0600	...	0704	0812	...	0910	...	1010	1110	...	...	1210	...	...	1310	1410	...
Derby 123 d.		...	...	...	...	0636	...	0736	0837	...	0936	...	1037	1137	...	...	1237	...	...	1337	1436	...
Birmingham New Street 120 d.		...	0500	0537	...	0730	...	0830	0930	...	1030	...	1130	1230	...	...	1330	...	...	1430	1530	...
Cheltenham 120 d.		0537	0602	0643	0746	0811	0846	0910	1010	1045	1110	1146	1210	1310	1345	1352	1410	...	...	1510	1610	1645
Gloucester d.		0550	0614	0701d	0758	0825c	0858	0925c	1025c	1058	1125c	1159	1225c	1325c	1358	1403	1425	1442	1448	1525c	1625c	1658
Lydney 🚂 d.		0609	0633	0720	0817	|	0917	|	1044	1117	|	1218	|	1344	1417	1422	|	1501	1507	|	1644	1717
Chepstow d.		0619	0642	0729	0827	0851	0927	0951	|	1127	1151	1228	1251	|	1427	1432	1451	1511	1517	1551	1653	1727
Caldicot d.		0626	0651	0738	0835	|	0935	|	|	1135	|	1236	|	|	1435	1440	|	1519	1525	|	|	1735
Newport 132 136 149 a.		0641	0705	0752	0850	0912	0953	1011	1111	1152	1210	1253	1311	1411	1450	1455	1511	1538	1540	1612	1713	1750
Cardiff Central 132 136 149 a.		0700	0721	0808	0909	0930	1012	1028	1127	1212	1226	1310	1330	1427	1515	1515	1530	1600	1558	1629	1730	1810

	Ⓐ	Ⓐ 2	Ⓐ	Ⓐ 2b	Ⓐ 2a	Ⓐ	Ⓐ Aa	Ⓐ 2	Ⓐ	Ⓐ	Ⓐ 2	⑤ 2		⑥	⑥	⑥	⑥ 2	⑥	⑥ 2	⑥	⑥	⑥ 2
ngham 123 d.	1510	...	1610	...	...	1710	...	...	1810	1910	...	...	⑥	...	...	...	...	0558	...	0658	0812	...
y 123 d.	1537	...	1637	...	...	1737	...	...	1837	1937	*2129*	...		...	...	...	...	0636	...	0736	0837	...
gham New Street 120 d.	1630	...	1730	...	...	1830	1842	...	1930	2030	*2212*	2300		...	0500	0542	...	0730	...	0830	0930	...
nham 120 d.	1714	1745	1817	...	1845	1913	1925	1945	2011	2110	2300	0008		...	0603	0642	0745	0810	0845	0910	1010	1045
ster d.	1725	1758	1831	1845	1900	1925	|	1958	2025c	2121	2313	0019		0550	0614	0657	0758	0822	0858	0922	1022	1058
🚂 d.	1744	1817	|	1904	1920	|	|	2017	|	2140	2333	...		0609	0633	0716	0817	|	0917	|	1041	1117
ow d.	|	1827	|	1914	1929	|	|	2027	|	2149	2342	...		0619	0642	0726	0827	0848	0927	0948	|	1127
ot d.	|	1835	|	1921	1937	|	|	2035	|	2158	2351	...		0627	0651	0734	0835	|	0935	|	|	1135
rt 132 136 149 a.	1812	1850	1914	1945	1953	2011	2047	2050	2110	2212	0006	...		0647	0711	0754	0856	0912	0956	1012	1112	1156
Central 132 136 149 a.	1829	1910	1932	2009	2012	2027	2102	2110	2128	2230	0036	...		0705	0727	0810	0916	0930	1010	1028	1129	1211

	⑥	⑥ 2	⑥	⑥	⑥ 2	⑥		⑥ 2 Bg	⑥ 2 Bh	⑥	⑥	⑥ 2	⑥	⑥ 2	⑥	⑥ 2	⑥	⑥ A	⑥ 2	⑥	⑥	⑥	⑥ 2
ingham 123 d.	0910	...	1010	1110	...	1210	...	...	...	1310	1410	...	1510	...	1610	...	1710	...	...	1810	1910	...	...
y 123 d.	0936	...	1037	1137	...	1237	...	...	...	1337	1437	...	1537	...	1637	...	1737	...	...	1837	1937	2028	...
gham New Street 120 d.	1030	...	1130	1230	...	1330	...	...	...	1430	1530	...	1630	...	1730	...	1830	1842	...	1930	2030	2112	...
nham 120 d.	1110	1146	1210	1310	1345	1410	...	...	...	1510	1610	1645	1710	1745	1816	1845	1910	1925	1945	2010	2110	2151	...
ester d.	1122	1158	1222	1322	1358	1422	...	1435	1443	1522	1621	1658	1722	1758	1827	1858	1922	|	1958	2022	2122	2200	2309
🚂 d.	|	1217	|	1341	1417	|	...	1454	1502	|	1640	1717	1741	1817	|	1917	|	|	2017	|	2141	...	2328
tow d.	1148	1227	1248	|	1427	1448	...	1504	1512	1548	1650	1727	|	1827	|	1927	|	|	2027	|	2150	...	2338
ot d.	|	1235	|	|	1435	|	...	1512	1520	|	|	1735	|	1835	|	1934	|	|	2035	|	2159	...	2346
rt 132 136 149 a.	1212	1255	1312	1412	1456	1513	...	1536	1541	1612	1714	1756	1812	1856	1915	1955	2010	2049	2055	2110	2219	...	0012
f Central 132 136 149 a.	1228	1315	1328	1429	1517	1529	...	1555	1558	1628	1730	1816	1832	1915	1932	2014	2026	2105	2114	2126	2242	...	0039

		⑦ 2	⑦		⑦	⑦ 2	⑦	⑦		⑦	⑦	⑦		⑦ 2	⑦	⑦		⑦ 2	⑦	⑦	⑦ 2	⑦	⑦ 2
ingham 123 d.	⑦	...	...	...	0954	...	1111	1210	...	...	1310	1410	...	...	1510	1610	...	...	1710	1810	...	...	...
by 123 d.		...	...	...	1018	...	1136	1236	...	...	1336	1435	...	...	1535	1635	...	...	1736	1836	...	2027	...
gham New Street 120 d.		...	1012	...	1112	...	1230	1330	...	...	1430	1530	...	...	1630	1730	...	...	1830	1930	...	2112	...
nham 120 d.		...	1052	...	1152	1219	1310	1410	...	1419	1510	1610	...	1619	1711	1810	...	1835	1912	2010	2019	2152	...
ester d.		1048	1105	...	1205	1232	1323	1424	...	1433	1523	1623	...	1636d	1723	1823	...	1848	1928	2022	2033	2202	2233
🚂 d.		1107	|	...	|	1251	|	|	...	1452	|	|	...	1655	|	|	...	1907	|	|	2052	...	2252
tow d.		1117	|	...	|	1301	|	|	...	1502	|	|	...	1706	|	|	...	1917	|	|	2102	...	2302
ot d.		1125	|	...	|	1309	|	|	...	1510	|	|	...	1712	|	|	...	1925	|	|	2110	...	2309
rt 132 136 149 a.		1145	1153	...	1252	1334	1411	1514	...	1531	1609	1706	...	1737	1814	1912	...	1954	2016	2110	2135	...	2331
f Central 132 136 149 a.		1205	1209	...	1316	1353	1429	1534	...	1554	1634	1728	...	1756	1830	1929	...	2012	2032	2130	2153	...	2350

		Ⓐ	Ⓐ 2b	Ⓐ 2a	Ⓐ	Ⓐ 2	Ⓐ A	Ⓐ	Ⓐ	Ⓐ 2	Ⓐ	Ⓐ 2	Ⓐ	Ⓐ	Ⓐ 2b	Ⓐ 2a	Ⓐ	Ⓐ 2b	Ⓐ 2a	Ⓐ	Ⓐ	Ⓐ 2b	Ⓐ 2a
f Central 132 136 149 d.	Ⓐ	...	0609	0611	0640	0705	0700	0745	0845	0910	0945	1009	1045	1145	1210	1212	1245	1310	1312	1345	1445	1508	1512
ort 132 136 149 d.		...	0625	0628	0655	0723	0715	0802	0900	0925	1000	1025	1100	1200	1225	1228	1301	1324	1328	1400	1500	1525	1528
ot d.		...	0637	0640	0708	0736	|	|	|	0937	|	1038	|	|	1238	1242	|	1338	1342	|	|	1537	1541
stow d.		...	0646	0649	0716	0745	|	|	0918	0946	1018	1047	|	1218	1247	1251	1318	1347	1351	|	1518	1546	1550
y 🚂 d.		...	0655	0658	0725	0754	|	0825	|	0955	|	1056	1125	|	1256	1300	|	1356	1400	1425	|	1555	1559
ester d.		0710	0721	0721	0746	0821c	|	0849	0950c	1017	1050c	1117	1150c	1248	1318	1322	1350c	1417	1421	1450c	1550c	1618	1622
nham 120 d.		0721	0734	0735	0757	0837	0840	0900	1001	1031	1101	1132	1201	1258	1328	1333	1401	...	...	1501	1601	1631	1631
gham New Street 120 a.		0816	*0826*	*0826*	0845	...	0926	0945	1045	...	1145	...	1245	1345	...	...	1445	...	...	1545	1645	...	...
by 123 a.		...	...	...	0934	...	...	1034	1134	...	1234	...	1334	1434	...	...	1534	...	...	1634	1734	...	...
ingham 123 a.		...	...	...	1003	...	...	1103	1203	...	1303	...	1403	1503	...	...	1603	...	...	1703	1803	...	...

	Ⓐ	Ⓐ 2	Ⓐ	Ⓐ 2b	Ⓐ 2a	Ⓐ	Ⓐ 2	Ⓐ	Ⓐ	Ⓐ	Ⓐ 2	Ⓐ	Ⓐ 2		⑥	⑥ 2	⑥	⑥ 2h	⑥ 2g	⑥ A	⑥	⑥	⑥ 2h
ff Central 132 136 149 d.	1545	1611	1645	1710	1712	1745	1809	1845	1950	2105	2110	2150	2320	⑥	...	0604	0630	0706	0708	0654	0740	0842	0907
ort 132 136 149 d.	1600	1626	1700	1725	1728	1800	1824	1900	2005	2119	2125	2205	2335		...	0619	0646	0721	0723	0708	0754	0856	0921
ot d.	|	1639	|	1738	1741	|	1837	|	2018	|	2138	|	2356		...	0639	0706	0741	0736	|	|	|	0940
stow d.	1618	1648	|	1747	1750	1818	1846	1917	2026	|	2147	|	0005		...	0648	0714	0750	0745	|	|	0918	0950
y 🚂 d.	|	1657	1725	1756	1759	|	1855	|	2035	|	2156	|	0014		...	0657	0723	0759	0754	|	0825	|	0958
ester d.	1650c	1719	1750c	1818	1821	1846	1919	1945	2059c	2204	2219	2247	0039		0707	0721	0746	0822	0822	|	0850c	0950c	1021
nham 120 d.	1701	1732	1801	...	1830	1857	1931	1957	2111	2215	2234	2258	...		0718	0734	0757	0835	0835	0841	0901	1001	1032
ngham New Street 120 a.	1745	...	1845	...	...	1945	...	2040	2151	2305	...	2359	...		0808	...	0845	...	...	0926	0945	1045	...
by 123 a.	1834	...	1934	...	...	2034	...	2132	...	...	...	...	...		...	...	0934	...	...	...	1034	1134	...
tingham 123 a.	1903	...	2003	...	...	2103	...	2208	...	...	...	...	...		...	...	1003	...	...	...	1103	1203	...

	⑥ 2g	⑥	⑥ 2k	⑥ 2g	⑥	⑥	⑥ 2	⑥	⑥ 2k	⑥ 2g	⑥	⑥	⑥ 2	⑥	⑥ 2h	⑥ 2g	⑥	⑥ 2	⑥	⑥ 2	⑥	⑥	⑥
ff Central 132 136 149 d.	0909	0942	1007	1010	1042	1142	1207	1242	1308	1312	1342	1442	1507	1542	1608	1609	1642	1707	1742	1807	1841	1955	2045
ort 132 136 149 d.	0923	0956	1028	1025	1056	1156	1222	1256	1323	1327	1356	1456	1522	1556	1622	1623	1656	1722	1756	1822	1855	2010	2100
cot d.	0935	|	1042	1038	|	|	1240	|	1343	1340	|	|	1538	|	1643	1637	|	1738	|	1840	|	2028	|
stow d.	0945	1018	1051	1047	|	1218	1249	1318	1352	1349	|	1517	1547	1618	1652	1646	|	1747	1818	1849	1918	2036	|
ey 🚂 d.	0953	|	1100	1056	1125	|	1258	|	1401	1358	1425	|	1556	|	1701	1655	1725	1756	|	1858	|	2045	|
cester d.	1021	1050c	1122	1122	1150c	1248	1322	1350c	1423	1420	1450c	1550c	1621	1650c	1723	1720	1750c	1824c	1848	1921	1946	2107	2148
enham 120 d.	1032	1101	1133	1132	1201	1259	1332	1401	...	...	1501	1601	1632	1701	1733	1730	1801	1833	1859	1931	1957	2118	2200
ngham New Street 120 a.	...	1145	...	...	1245	1345	...	1445	...	...	1545	1645	...	1745	...	...	1845	...	1945	...	2042	2207	2242
by 123 a.	...	1234	...	...	1334	1434	...	1535	...	...	1634	1734	...	1835	...	...	1934	...	2034	...	2133	2253	...
tingham 123 a.	...	1303	...	...	1403	1503	...	1603	...	...	1703	1803	...	1903	...	...	2003	...	2103	...	2208	2327	...

	⑥ 2	⑥ 2		⑦ 2	⑦	⑦		⑦ 2	⑦	⑦	⑦ 2	⑦	⑦	⑦ 2	⑦	⑦	⑦	⑦	⑦	⑦ 2m	⑦ 2n	⑦	⑦ 2
ff Central 132 136 149 d.	2107	2320	⑦	1023	1045	1145	...	1225	1245	1345	1423	1445	1545	1623	1645	1745	1824	1845	1945	2024	2024	2045	2226
ort 132 136 149 d.	2122	2336		1038	1059	1159	...	1240	1259	1359	1438	1459	1558	1638	1659	1759	1839	1859	2000	2039	2039	2059	2249
cot d.	2140	2354		1058	|	|	...	1257	|	|	1458	|	|	1658	|	|	1859	|	|	2059	2104	|	2309
stow d.	2149	0003		1107	|	|	...	1306	|	|	1507	|	|	1707	|	|	1908	|	|	2108	2113	|	2318
ey 🚂 d.	2158	0012		1116	|	|	...	1315	|	|	1516	|	|	1716	|	|	1917	|	|	2117	2122	|	2327
cester d.	2221	0035		1142c	1150	1248	...	1339	1348	1448	1538	1548	1648	1740	1748	1848	1942c	1950	2049	2142	2146	2148	2350
enham 120 d.	...	...		1158	1201	1258	...	1352	1358	1458	1550	1558	1658	1750	1758	1858	1955	2000	2100	...	...	2159	...
ngham New Street 120 a.	...	...		...	1243	1341	...	...	1441	1541	...	1641	1741	...	1841	1941	...	2043	2144	...	...	2242	...
by 123 a.	...	...		...	1333	1434	...	...	1533	1634	...	1733	1833	...	1933	2034	...	2133	...	...	...	...	...
tingham 123 a.	...	...		...	1400	1500	...	...	1600	1700	...	1800	1900	...	2000	2100	...	2200	...	...	...	...	...

Not ①–⑥ Sept. 12 – Oct. 22. [12] Manchester Piccadilly - Bristol Temple Meads - Cardiff Central and v.v. (Table **122**).
To Fishguard Harbour (Table **135**).

May 16 - Sept. 9 and from Oct. 24.
Sept. 12 - Oct. 21.
Arrives up to 2 - 6 minutes earlier.

d – Arrives 7–8 minutes earlier.
g – May 21 - June 18 and Sept.17 - Dec.10.
h – June 25 - Sept. 10.
k – June 25 - Sept. 10 and Oct. 29 - Dec. 10.
m – May 15 - June 19 and Sept. 18 - Oct. 23.
n – June 26 - Sept. 11 and Oct. 30 - Dec. 4.

🚂 – DEAN FOREST RAILWAY (Lydney Junction - Parkend. *7 km*). ✆ 01594 845840. www.deanforestrailway.co.uk. Lydney Junction station is 10 minutes walk from the National Rail station.

122 BIRMINGHAM - MANCHESTER

Most services convey 🍸

km		Ⓐ	Ⓐ	Ⓐ	Ⓐ	Ⓐ	Ⓐ	Ⓐ	Ⓐ	Ⓐ	Ⓐ	Ⓐ	Ⓐ	Ⓐ	Ⓐ	Ⓐ	Ⓐ	Ⓐ	Ⓐ	Ⓐ	Ⓐ	Ⓐ
									A												H	
	Bournemouth **119** d.	...	...	...	...	...	...	...	...	0630	...	0730	...	0845	...	0945	...	1045	...	1145	...	1245
	Southampton Central **119** d.	...	...	...	...	0515	...	0615	...	0715	...	0815	...	0916	...	1017	...	1117	...	1217	...	1316
	Reading **119** d.	...	...	...	...	0615	...	0715	...	0815	...	0915	...	1015	...	1115	...	1215	...	1315	...	1415
	Paignton **120** d.	...	...	...	...		...		...		0702		...		...		1007		...		...	
	Exeter St Davids **120** d.	...	...	...	...		...		...		0745		...		...		1050		...		1250	
	Bristol T Meads **120** d.	...	...	...	...		0700		0800		0900		1000		1100		1200		1300		1400	
0	**Birmingham** New Street **150** d.	0557	0622	0657	0731	0757	0831	0857	0931	0957	1031	1057	1131	1157	1231	1257	1331	1357	1431	1457	1531	1557
20	Wolverhampton **150** d.	0616	0641	0715	0750	0815	0849	0915	0949	1015	1049	1115	1149	1216	1249	1315	1349	1415	1449	1515	1548	1615
46	Stafford **150** d.	0632	0655	0731	0802	0832	0902	0932	1002	1032	1102	1132	1202	1232	1302	1332	1402	1432	1502	1532	1602	1632
72	Stoke on Trent **150** d.	0651	0714		0821	0854	0920	0954	1020	1054	1120	1154	1220	1254	1320	1354	1420	1454	1520	1554	1619	1654
104	Macclesfield **150** d.	0712	0731		0838	0911		1011		1111		1211		1311		1411		1511		1611		1711
123	Stockport **150** d.	0726	0750	0824	0851	0927	0950	1025	1050	1125	1150	1225	1250	1324	1350	1425	1450	1525	1550	1625	1648	1725
132	**Manchester** Piccadilly **150** a.	0734	0800	0834	0900	0938	0959	1035	1059	1135	1159	1235	1259	1334	1359	1435	1459	1535	1559	1635	1657	1735

	Ⓐ	Ⓐ	Ⓐ	Ⓐ	Ⓐ	Ⓐ	Ⓐ	Ⓐ	Ⓐ	Ⓐ	Ⓐ	
			a									
Bournemouth **119** d.	1345	...	1445	...	1545	...	1645	...	1745	1845	...	...
Southampton Central **119** d.	1417	...	1516	...	1617	...	1717	...	1815	1917	...	...
Reading **119** d.	1515	...	1615	...	1715	...	1815	...	1915	2015	...	...
Paignton **120** d.		1404		...		...		...			...	...
Exeter St Davids **120** d.		1448		...		1654		...			...	...
Bristol T Meads **120** d.		1600		1700		1800		1900			...	...
Birmingham New Street **150** d.	1657	1731	1757	1831	1857	1931	1957	2031	2057	2157	2230	...
Wolverhampton **150** d.	1715	1750	1815	1849	1915	1949	2016	2049	2116	2216	2248	...
Stafford **150** d.	1732	1802	1832	1902	1932	2002	2032	2102	2132	2235	2301	...
Stoke on Trent **150** d.	1754	1821	1854	1920	1954	2020	2055	2119	2154	2256	2320	...
Macclesfield **150** d.	1811		1911		2011		2112		2211	2314		...
Stockport **150** d.	1825	1850	1925	1951	2025	2049	2129	2149	2225	2328		...
Manchester Piccadilly **150** a.	1835	1859	1935	1959	2035	2058	2140	2200	2234	2337	0011	...

	⑥	⑥	⑥	⑥	⑥	⑥	⑥	⑥	⑥	⑥
								A		
Bournemouth **119** d.	...	...	...	...	...	...	...	...	0637	...
Southampton Central **119** d.	...	...	...	...	0509	...	0620	...	0720	...
Reading **119** d.	...	...	...	...	0615	...	0715	...	0815	...
Paignton **120** d.	...	...	...	...		...		...		0702
Exeter St Davids **120** d.	...	...	...	...		...		...		0745
Bristol T Meads **120** d.	...	...	...	...		0700		0800		0900
Birmingham New Street **150** d.	0557	0631	0657	0731	0757	0831	0857	0931	0957	1031
Wolverhampton **150** d.	0616	0649	0715	0749	0815	0849	0915	0949	1015	1049
Stafford **150** d.	0632	0702	0731	0802	0832	0902	0932	1002	1032	1102
Stoke on Trent **150** d.	0651	0719		0820	0854	0920	0954	1020	1054	1120
Macclesfield **150** d.	0712	0737		0837	0911		1011		1111	
Stockport **150** d.	0726	0750	0818	0850	0925	0950	1025	1050	1125	1150
Manchester Piccadilly **150** a.	0734	0759	0835	0859	0935	0959	1035	1059	1135	1159

	⑥	⑥	⑥	⑥	⑥	⑥	⑥		⑥	⑥	⑥	⑥	⑥	⑥	⑥	⑥	⑥	⑥	⑥	⑥	⑥	⑥	⑥
			G							P											bN	c	
Bournemouth **119** d.	...	0847	...	0947	...	1047	...	...	1147	...	1247	...	1347	...	1447	...	1547	...	1647	...	...	1747	1847
Southampton Central **119** d.	...	0918	...	1017	...	1120	...	...	1220	...	1318	...	1420	...	1518	...	1620	...	1720	...	...	1820	1920
Reading **119** d.	...	1015	...	1115	...	1215	...	...	1315	...	1415	...	1515	...	1615	...	1715	...	1815	...	...	1915	2015
Paignton **120** d.	...		...		1006		...	...		...		...		1355		...		...		...	...		
Exeter St Davids **120** d.	...		0945b		1049		...	...		1248c		...		1437		...		1653c		...	1823		
Bristol T Meads **120** d.	1000		1100		1200		1300	...		1400		1500		1600		1700		1800		1900	1930		
Birmingham New Street **150** d.	1131	1157	1231	1257	1331	1357	1431	...	1457	1531	1557	1631	1657	1731	1757	1831	1857	1931	1957	2031	2057	2057	2157
Wolverhampton **150** d.	1149	1215	1249	1315	1349	1415	1449	...	1515	1549	1615	1649	1715	1749	1815	1849	1915	1949	2015	2049	2117	2117	2215
Stafford **150** d.	1202	1232	1302	1332	1402	1432	1502	...	1532	1602	1632	1702	1732	1802	1832	1902	1932	2002	2032	2102	2132	2132	2232
Stoke on Trent **150** d.	1220	1254	1320	1354	1420	1454	1520	...	1554	1620	1655	1720	1754	1820	1854	1920	1955	2020	2055	2120	2153	2153	2251
Macclesfield **150** d.		1311		1411		1511		...	1611		1712		1811		1911		2012	2037	2112	2138	2212	2212	2308
Stockport **150** d.	1250	1325	1350	1425	1450	1525	1550	...	1625	1650	1725	1750	1825	1849	1925	1950	2025	2050	2125	2153	2226	2226	2321
Manchester Piccadilly **150** a.	1259	1335	1359	1435	1459	1535	1559	...	1635	1659	1735	1759	1835	1859	1935	1959	2035	2059	2136	2202	2235	2235	2330

	⑦	⑦	⑦	⑦	⑦	⑦	⑦	⑦	⑦	⑦		⑦	⑦	⑦	⑦	⑦	⑦	⑦	⑦	⑦	⑦	⑦
										F			F				H					
Bournemouth **119** d.	...	...	...	...	0940	...	1040	...	1140	...	...	1240	...	1340	...	1440	...	1540	...	1640	...	1740
Southampton Central **119** d.	...	...	...	0915	1015	...	1115	...	1215	...	...	1315	...	1415	...	1515	...	1615	...	1715	...	1815
Reading **119** d.	...	...	0912	1011	1111	...	1211	...	1310	...	...	1411	...	1511	...	1611	...	1711	...	1811	...	1911
Paignton **120** d.	...	...				...		1050		...	...		...		...		...		...		...	
Exeter St Davids **120** d.	...	...				...		1133		1256	...		1347		...		1532		...		...	
Bristol T Meads **120** d.	...	...				...		1300		1400	...		1500		1600		1700		1800		1900	
Birmingham New Street **150** d.	0901	1001	1101	1201	1301	1331	1401	1431	1501	1531	...	1601	1631	1701	1731	1801	1831	1901	1931	2001	2031	2101
Wolverhampton **150** d.	0919	1019	1119	1219	1319	1349	1419	1449	1519	1549	...	1619	1649	1719	1749	1819	1849	1919	1949	2019	2053	2119
Stafford **150** d.	0933	1033	1132	1232	1333		1433		1533		...	1630		1737		1837		1936		2037		2137
Stoke on Trent **150** d.		1052	1152	1253	1357	1421	1457	1521	1558	1621	...	1658	1720	1758	1821	1857	1921	1958	2019	2057	2122	2157
Macclesfield **150** d.		1109	1210	1311	1415		1515		1615		...	1716		1815		1915		2015		2115		2215
Stockport **150** d.	1022	1123	1227	1330	1429		1529		1629		...	1729		1829		1929		2030		2129		2228
Manchester Piccadilly **150** a.	1037	1133	1241	1340	1440	1459	1539	1559	1640	1700	...	1740	1759	1840	1859	1940	1959	2040	2100	2140	2157	2239

	Ⓐ	Ⓐ	Ⓐ	Ⓐ	Ⓐ	Ⓐ	Ⓐ	Ⓐ	Ⓐ	Ⓐ	Ⓐ	Ⓐ	Ⓐ	Ⓐ	Ⓐ	Ⓐ	Ⓐ	Ⓐ	Ⓐ	Ⓐ	Ⓐ	Ⓐ
Manchester Piccadilly **150** d.	0511	0600	0627	0707	0727	0807	0827	0907	0927	1007	1027	1107	1127	1207	1227	1307	1327	1407	1427	1507	1527	1607
Stockport **150** d.		0608	0635	0716	0735	0816	0835	0916	0935	1016	1035	1116	1135	1216	1235	1316	1335	1416	1435	1516	1535	1616
Macclesfield **150** d.			0648		0749		0849		0949		1049		1149		1249		1349		1449		1549	
Stoke on Trent **150** d.	0607		0706	0744	0807	0844	0907	0944	1007	1044	1107	1144	1207	1244	1307	1344	1407	1444	1508	1544	1607	1644
Stafford **150** d.	0625	0700	0724	0801	0825	0902	0925	1000	1026	1101	1125	1201	1225	1301	1326	1401	1426	1501	1526	1603	1625	1702
Wolverhampton **150** d.	0641	0716	0745	0816	0841	0916	0942	1017	1041	1116	1141	1216	1241	1317	1341	1417	1441	1517	1541	1617	1641	1717
Birmingham New Street **150** a.	0657	0733	0807	0833	0858	0933	0958	1033	1058	1133	1158	1233	1258	1333	1358	1433	1458	1533	1558	1633	1658	1733
Bristol T Meads **120** a.		0910	...	1008		1110		1205		1309		1408		1510		1611		1710		1807		1906
Exeter St Davids **120** a.		...	...	...		1224		...		...		...		1612		...		1811		...		...
Paignton **120** a.		...	...	...		1308		...		...		...		...		...		1855		...		...
Reading **119** a.	0840	...	...	...	1041	...	1140	...	1241	...	1340	...	1440	...	1541	...	1640	...	1740	...	1842	...
Southampton Central **119** a.	0943	...	...	...	1143	...	1241	...	1341	...	1441	...	1541	...	1641	...	1741	...	1843	...	1940	...
Bournemouth **119** a.	1013	...	...	...	1213	...	1311	...	1411	...	1511	...	1611	...	1711	...	1815	...	1912	...	2011	...

	Ⓐ	Ⓐ	Ⓐ	Ⓐ	Ⓐ	Ⓐ	Ⓐ	Ⓐ	Ⓐ	Ⓐ	
	A		F								
Manchester Piccadilly **150** d.	1705	1727	1805	1827	1907	1927	2007	2027	2127	2207	...
Stockport **150** d.	1714	1735	1813	1835	1916	1936	2017	2035	2135	2216	...
Macclesfield **150** d.	1728		1826			1949		2049	2149	2229	...
Stoke on Trent **150** d.	1745		1844	1906	1944	2007	2045	2107	2208	2247	...
Stafford **150** d.	1802	1828	1901	1925	2001	2026	2102	2125	2226	2304	...
Wolverhampton **150** d.	1816	1841	1917	1941	2017	2044	2116	2141	2242	2318	...
Birmingham New Street **150** a.	1833	1858	1933	1958	2033	2100	2132	2200	2259	2336	...
Bristol T Meads **120** a.	2009		2108		2214		...	...	...	...	...
Exeter St Davids **120** a.	...		2209		...		...	...	...	...	...
Paignton **120** a.	...				...		...	...	...	...	...
Reading **119** a.	...	2041	...	2142	...	2242	...	...	...	...	...
Southampton Central **119** a.	...	2140	...	2242	...	2343	...	...	...	...	...
Bournemouth **119** a.	...	2215	...	2319	...	...	...	...	...	...	...

	⑥	⑥	⑥	⑥	⑥	⑥	⑥	⑥	⑥	⑥	⑥
			M								
Manchester Piccadilly **150** d.	0511	0600	0707	0727	0807	0827	0907	0927	1007	1027	1107
Stockport **150** d.		0608	0716	0735	0816	0835	0916	0935	1016	1035	1116
Macclesfield **150** d.		0621		0749		0849		0949		1049	
Stoke on Trent **150** d.	0608	0640	0744	0807	0844	0907	0944	1007	1044	1107	1144
Stafford **150** d.	0626	0700	0803	0825	0900	0925	1001	1025	1101	1125	1201
Wolverhampton **150** d.	0641	0716	0818	0841	0917	0941	1017	1041	1117	1141	1217
Birmingham New Street **150** a.	0657	0733	0834	0858	0933	0958	1033	1058	1133	1159	1233
Bristol T Meads **120** a.		0906	1004		1109		1204		1307		1405
Exeter St Davids **120** a.		...	1126b		1225		...		...		...
Paignton **120** a.		...			1310		...		...		...
Reading **119** a.	0841	...	...	1041	...	1138	...	1241	...	1340	...
Southampton Central **119** a.	0940	...	...	1141	...	1241	...	1341	...	1441	...
Bournemouth **119** a.	1011	...	...	1212	...	1312	...	1412	...	1512	...

A – From/to Cardiff May 16 - Sept. 10 and from Oct. 24 (Table **121**).
F – To/from Plymouth (Table **120**).
G – From Plymouth May 21 - Sept. 10 (Table **120**).
H – From Penzance (Tables **117** and **120**).
M – To Newquay May 21 - Sept. 10 (Tables **117** and **120**).
N – From Newquay (Tables **117** and **120**).
P – From Penzance from Sept. 17 (Tables **117** and **120**).

a – Not Dec. 9.
b – May 21 - Sept. 10.
c – From Sept. 17.

For explanation of standard symbols see page 4

MANCHESTER - BIRMINGHAM 122

Most services convey 🍷

	⑥	⑥	⑥	⑥	⑥	⑥	⑥	⑥	⑥	⑥	⑥ A	⑥	⑥ F	⑥	⑥	⑥	⑥	⑥	⑥	⑥			⑦	⑦
hester Piccadilly .... 150 d.	1207	1227	1307	1327	1407	1427	1507	1527	1607	1627	1706	1727	1805	1827	1907	1927	2007	2027	2107	2127	...	⑦	0827	0927
port .... 150 d.	1216	1235	1316	1335	1416	1435	1516	1535	1616	1635	1715	1736	1813	1835	1916	1935	2016	2035	|	2135	...		0836	0936
esfield .... 150 d.	|	1249	|	1349	|	1449	|	1549	|	1649	1727	|	1826	|	|	1949	|	2049	|	2149	...		|	0949
on Trent .... 150 d.	1244	1307	1344	1407	1444	1507	1544	1607	1644	1707	1745	1807	1844	1907	1944	2007	2044	2107	2144	2207	...		|	1007
rd .... 150 d.	1301	1325	1401	1425	1500	1525	1601	1625	1701	1725	1802	1825	1901	1925	2001	2025	2101	2125	2202	2230	...		0926	1026
erhampton .... 150 d.	1317	1341	1417	1441	1517	1541	1617	1641	1717	1741	1817	1840	1917	1941	2017	2041	2115	2142	2217	2245	...		0941	1043
ngham New Street 150 a.	1333	1358	1433	1458	1533	1558	1633	1658	1733	1758	1833	1858	1933	1959	2033	2058	2131	2159	2233	2301	...		0958	1059
ristol T Meads 120 .... a.	1509	|	1607	|	1707	|	1807	|	1904	|	2005	|	2104	|	2212	|	...	...	...	...	...		|	|
xeter St Davids 120 .... a.	1609a	|	...	|	1805b	|	...	|	...	|	...	|	2207b	|	...	|	...	...	...	...	...		|	|
aignton 120 .... a.	1710a	|	...	|	1849b	|	...	|	...	|	...	|	...	|	...	|	...	...	...	...	...		|	|
ading 119 .... a.	...	1540	...	1641	...	1739	...	1841	...	1941	...	2041	...	2142	...	2245	...	...	...	...	...		1140	1240
thampton Central 119 .... a.	...	1641	...	1741	...	1841	...	1941	...	2041	...	2140	...	2242	...	2341	...	...	...	...	...		1242	1342
rnemouth 119 .... a.	...	1712	...	1812	...	1912	...	2012	...	2112	...	2215	...	2318	...	...	...	...	...	...	...		1326	1426

	⑦	⑦	⑦	⑦		⑦	⑦	⑦	⑦		⑦	⑦	⑦	⑦ d	⑦ cG	⑦	⑦	⑦	⑦		⑦	⑦	⑦	⑦
hester Piccadilly .... 150 d.	1027	1127	1226	1307	...	1326	1407	1427	1507	...	1527	1607	1627	1707	1707	1727	1807	1827	1907	...	1927	2007	2107	2207
port .... 150 d.	1036	1136	1235	|	...	1336	|	1436	|	...	1536	|	1636	|	|	1736	|	1836	|	...	1936	2016	2116	2216
esfield .... 150 d.	1049	1149	1249	|	...	1349	|	1449	|	...	1549	|	1649	|	|	1749	|	1849	|	...	1949	2029	2129	2229
on Trent .... 150 d.	1107	1207	1307	1343	...	1407	1443	1507	1543	...	1607	1643	1708	1743	1743	1808	1843	1907	1943	...	2007	2047	2147	2247
rd .... 150 d.	1127	1224	1325	|	...	1425	|	1524	|	...	1624	|	1725	|	|	1825	|	1925	|	...	2024	2104	2204	2304
erhampton .... 150 d.	1143	1241	1341	1416	...	1441	1515	1541	1615	...	1641	1715	1741	1815	1815	1841	1915	1941	2015	...	2041	2122	2222	2319
ngham New Street 150 a.	1158	1258	1358	1432	...	1458	1531	1558	1631	...	1658	1731	1758	1831	1831	1858	1931	1958	2031	...	2057	2139	2240	2336
ristol T Meads 120 .... a.	|	|	|	1611	...	|	1708	|	1814	...	|	1908	|	2014	2014	|	2106	|	2210	...	|	2306	...	...
xeter St Davids 120 .... a.	|	|	|	1709	...	|	...	|	...	...	|	...	|	2127	2127	|	...	|	...	...	|	...	...	...
aignton 120 .... a.	|	|	|	1756	...	|	...	|	...	...	|	...	|	2214	...	|	...	|	...	...	|	...	...	...
ading 119 .... a.	1341	1440	1540	...	...	1640	...	1739	...	...	1840	...	1939	...	...	2040	...	2140	...	...	2238	...	...	...
thampton Central 119 .... a.	1442	1542	1642	...	...	1740	...	1842	...	...	1940	...	2041	...	...	2142	...	2242	...	...	...	...	...	...
rnemouth 119 .... a.	1526	1626	1726	...	...	1826	...	1926	...	...	2026	...	2126	...	...	2226	...	...	...	...	...	...	...	...

To Cardiff May 21 - Sept. 10 and from Oct. 29 (Table **121**).
To Plymouth from Sept. 17 (Table **120**).
To Plymouth (Table **120**).

a – May 21 - Sept. 10.
b – From Sept. 17.
c – From Sept. 18.

d – May 15 - Sept. 11.

BIRMINGHAM - NOTTINGHAM 123

		Ⓐ	Ⓐ	Ⓐ	Ⓐ	Ⓐ	Ⓐ	Ⓐ	Ⓐ		Ⓐ	Ⓐ	Ⓐ	Ⓐ	Ⓐ			⑥	⑥	⑥	⑥	⑥
Cardiff Central 121 .... d.	Ⓐ	...	...	...	...	...	0640	...	0745	and at	...	1745	1845	*1950*	...	...	⑥	...	...	...	...	...
Birmingham New Street .... d.		0619	0649	0719	0749	0819	0849	0919	0949	the same	1919	1949	2049	2203	2309	...		0619	0649	0719	0749	0819
Tamworth .... d.		0639	0707	0739	0807	0836	0909	0936	1007	minutes	1936	2009	2109	2227	2328	...		0639	0707	0739	0807	0836
Burton-on-Trent .... d.		0651	0720	0750	0819	0848	0921	0948	1019	past each	1948	2021	2121	2239	2340	...		0651	0719	0750	0819	0848
Derby .... a.		0704	0735	0805	0836	0900	0934	1000	1034	hour until	2000	2034	2132	2251	2353	...		0703	0734	0805	0835	0900
Derby .... d.		0708	0743	0810	0840	0908	0940	1008	1040		2008	2040	2138	2259	2357	...		0709	0740	0809	0840	0908
Nottingham .... a.		0738	0809	0834	0906	0928	1003	1028	1103		2028	2103	2208	2327	0016	...		0738	0806	0832	0906	0928

	⑥	⑥	⑥	⑥		⑥	⑥	⑥	⑥	⑥	⑥		⑦	⑦	⑦	⑦	⑦	⑦	⑦	⑦	⑦	⑦	⑦
rdiff Central 121 .... d.	0630	...	0740	...	and at	1642	...	1742	1841	1955	...	⑦	...	1045	1145	1245	1345	1445	1545	1645	1745	1845	*1945*
ingham New Street .... d.	0849	0919	0949	1019	the same	1849	1919	1949	2049	2210	2249		1149	1249	1349	1449	1549	1649	1749	1849	1949	2049	2203
worth .... d.	0909	0936	1007	1036	minutes	1909	1936	2009	2109	2227	2308		1207	1307	1407	1509	1607	1707	1807	1909	2007	2106	2219
n-on-Trent .... d.	0921	0948	1019	1048	past each	1921	1948	2021	2121	2239	2320		1219	1319	1419	1521	1619	1719	1819	1921	2019	2119	|
y .... a.	0934	1000	1034	1100	hour until	1934	2000	2034	2133	2253	2333		1234	1333	1434	1533	1634	1733	1833	1933	2034	2133	2240
y .... d.	0940	1008	1040	1108		1940	2008	2040	2140	2259	...		1240	1340	1440	1540	1640	1740	1840	1940	2040	2140	...
ngham .... a.	1003	1028	1103	1131		2003	2028	2103	2208	2327	...		1300	1400	1500	1600	1700	1800	1900	2000	2100	2200	...

		Ⓐ	Ⓐ A	Ⓐ	Ⓐ	Ⓐ	Ⓐ	Ⓐ		Ⓐ	Ⓐ	Ⓐ	Ⓐ	Ⓐ	Ⓐ		⑥	⑥ A	⑥	⑥	⑥	⑥	⑥
ngham .... d.	Ⓐ	0600	0637	0704	0737	0812	0841	0910	and at	1841	1910	1940	2040	2139	...	⑥	0558	0637	0658	0737	0812	0841	0910
y .... a.		0632	0659	0731	0802	0833	0907	0931	the same	1906	1931	2006	2104	2208	...		0628	0659	0729	0802	0831	0909	0931
y .... d.		0636	0706	0736	0806	0837	0911	0936	minutes	1910	1937	2010	2110	2212	2245		0636	0706	0736	0806	0837	0912	0936
n-on-Trent .... d.		0648	0717	0750	0818	0849	0922	0950	past each	1921	1949	2021	2124	2223	2256		0648	0717	0750	0818	0849	0924	0949
worth .... d.		0701	0730	0803	0830	0902	0934	1002	hour until	1933	2003	2033	2134	2235	2307		0701	0730	0802	0830	0902	0935	1002
ingham New Street .... a.		0725	0753	0825	0855	0924	0955	1024		1955	2025	2055	2157	2301	2325		0724	0752	0824	0855	0924	0956	1024
rdiff Central 121 .... a.		0930	...	1028	...	1127	...	1232		...	2234	...	...	...	...		0930	...	1028	...	1129	...	1232

		⑥	⑥	⑥	⑥	⑥	⑥		⑦	⑦	⑦		⑦	⑦	⑦		⑦	⑦	⑦	⑦	⑦	⑦	⑦
ngham .... d.	and at	1841	1910	1941	2037	2139	...	⑦	0954	1111	1210	...	1310	1410	1510	...	1610	1710	1810	1910	2010	2110	...
y .... a.	the same	1906	1932	2007	2102	2208	...		1012	1131	1230	...	1330	1429	1530	...	1630	1729	1830	1930	2030	2130	...
y .... d.	minutes	1910	1937	2011	2110	2212	2226		1018	1136	1236	...	1336	1435	1535	...	1635	1736	1836	1936	2036	2136	2226
n-on-Trent .... d.	past each	1921	1949	2022	2124	2222	2237		1029	1147	1247	...	1347	1447	1547	...	1647	1747	1847	1948	2048	2148	2237
worth .... d.	hour until	1933	2002	2034	2135	2235	2247		1042	1200	1300	...	1400	1500	1600	...	1700	1800	1900	2000	2100	2200	2247
ingham New Street .... a.		1955	2024	2055	2156	2302	2306		1102	1221	1320	...	1422	1520	1621	...	1719	1819	1921	2021	2119	2223	2305
rdiff Central 121 .... a.		...	2242	...	...	...	...		1316	1429	1534	...	1634	1728	1830	...	1929	2032	2130	...	...	...	...

To Bournemouth (Table **119**).

124 BIRMINGHAM - SHEFFIELD - LEEDS - YORK - NEWCASTLE - EDINBURGH - GLASGOW

km		Ⓐ	Ⓐ	Ⓐ	Ⓐ	Ⓐ	Ⓐ	Ⓐ	Ⓐ	Ⓐ	Ⓐ	Ⓐ	Ⓐ	Ⓐ	Ⓐ	Ⓐ	Ⓐ	Ⓐ	Ⓐ	Ⓐ	Ⓐ	Ⓐ	Ⓐ
								H	G				A			B		C		B		D	
	Plymouth 120 d.	...	...	...	...	...	...	...	...	0520	...	0625	...	0725	...	0825	...	0925	...	1025	...	1125	...
	Bristol T Meads 120 d.	...	...	...	...	...	...	0627	...	0730	...	0830	...	0930	...	1030	...	1130	...	1230	...	1330	...
	Southampton Central 119 d.	...	...	...	...	...	...	|	...	|	...	|	...	|	...	|	0946	|	...	|	1146	|	...
	Reading 119 d.	...	...	...	...	...	...	|	0645	|	0746	|	0850	|	0945	|	1045	|	1145	|	1245	|	1345
0	**Birmingham** New Street 123 d.	...	...	0600	0630	0703	0730	0803	0830	0903	0930	1003	1030	1103	1130	1203	1230	1303	1330	1403	1430	1503	1530
28	Tamworth 123 d.	...	...	|	|	0719	|	0819	|	|	|	1019	|	|	|	1219	|	|	|	1419	|	|	|
48	Burton on Trent 123 d.	...	...	|	|	0731	|	0829	|	0927	|	|	|	1126	|	|	|	1328	|	|	|	1526	|
67	**Derby** 123 170 d.	...	0556	0635	0713	0744	0813	0844	0916a	0944b	1016a	1044b	1116a	1144b	1216a	1244	1316a	1344b	1416a	1444	1516a	1544	1616a
105	Chesterfield 170 d.	...	0617	0654	0732	0803	0832	0903	|	1003	|	1103	|	1203	|	1303	|	1403	|	1503	|	1603	|
125	**Sheffield** 170 d.	...	0633	0709	0754d	0822b	0847	0921	0947	1021	1047	1121	1147	1221	1247	1321	1347	1421	1447	1521	1547	1621	1647
154	Doncaster 180 d.	...	0603b	|	0825	|	0919	|	1019	|	1119	|	1219	|	1319	|	1419	|	1519	|	1619	|	1719
171	Wakefield Westgate 180 d.	...	|	0737	|	0848	|	0947	|	1047	|	1147	|	1247	|	1347	|	1447	|	1547	|	1650	|
187	**Leeds** 180 d.	...	|	0757d	|	0908d	|	1008d	|	1108d	|	1208d	|	1308d	|	1408d	|	1508d	|	1608d	|	1708	|
199	**York** 180 a.	...	0723	0822	0847	0932	0940	1030	1039	1130	1139	1230	1240	1330	1340	1430	1439	1530	1539	1630	1639	1730	1739
	York 180 d.	...	0732	0829	0850	0934	0948	1032	1048	1132	1148	1232	1248	1332	1348	1432	1448	1532	1548	1632	1648	1732	1748
270	Darlington 180 d.	...	0800	0858	0917	1000	1015	1100	1115	1200	1215	1300	1315	1401	1414	1500	1515	1600	1615	1700	1715	1800	1815
305	Durham 180 d.	...	0818	0915	0934	1018	1032	1117	1132	1217	1232	1317	1332	1418	1431	1517	1532	1617	1632	1718	1732	1817	1833
328	**Newcastle** 180 a.	...	0838	0935	0947	1030	1045	1129	1145	1229	1244	1329	1345	1430	1443	1529	1545	1629	1645	1730	1745	1833	1847
	Newcastle 180 d.	0735	...	0927	...	1035	...	1140	...	1239	...	1338	...	1436	...	1537	...	1637	...	1737	...	1840	...
384	Alnmouth 180 d.	|	...	1000	...	|	...	|	...	|	...	1402	...	|	...	1602	...	1702	...	1802	...	|	...
436	Berwick upon Tweed 180 d.	0819	...	1021	...	|	...	1222	...	|	...	1423	...	|	...	1622	...	|	...	1822	...	1922	...
528	**Edinburgh** Waverley 180 220 a.	0918	...	1106	...	1204	...	1306	..	1410	...	1507	...	1606	...	1706	...	1807	...	1906	...	2009	...
599	Motherwell 220 a.	1002	...	1152	...	...	...	1353	...	...	...	1552	...	...	...	1752	...	...	...	1953	...	...	...
620	**Glasgow** Central 220 a.	1025	...	1212	...	...	...	1412	...	...	...	1612	...	...	...	1811	...	...	...	2015	...	...	...

	Ⓐ	Ⓐ	Ⓐ	Ⓐ	Ⓐ	Ⓐ	Ⓐ	Ⓐ	Ⓐ	Ⓐ
Plymouth 120 d.	...	1325	...	1425	...	1525	...	1625	...	1725
Bristol T Meads 120 d.	...	1530	...	1630	...	1730	...	1830	...	1930
Southampton Central 119 d.	1346	|	...	|	1546	|	...	|	1746	|
Reading 119 d.	1445	|	1545	|	1645	|	1745	|	1845	|
Birmingham New Street 123 d.	1630	1703	1730	1803	1830	1903	1930	2003	2030	2103
Tamworth 123 d.	|	|	|	1819	|	|	|	2019	|	2119
Burton on Trent 123 d.	|	1726	|	|	|	1929	|	|	|	2130
Derby 123 170 d.	1711b	1742	1816a	1844b	1909	1943	2009	2044b	2119a	2144
Chesterfield 170 d.	|	1803	|	1903	1928	2004	|	2103	2138	2207
Sheffield 170 d.	1747b	1821	1847	1926d	1956g	2021	2053a	2121b	2154	2230b
Doncaster 180 d.	|	|	1918	|	2018	|	2120	|	2231	|
Wakefield Westgate 180 d.	1819	1848	|	1951	|	2048	|	2148	|	2301
Leeds 180 d.	1838	1908b	|	2008	|	2106	|	2204	|	2315
York 180 a.	1901	1930	1939	2030	2038	...	2140	...	2252	...
York 180 d.	1904	1933	1945	2032	2048	...	2147	...	...	...
Darlington 180 d.	1932	2002	2012	2059	2115	...	2213	...	...	...
Durham 180 d.	1949	2020	2029	2116	2132	...	2230	...	...	...
Newcastle 180 a.	2001	2033	2042	2128	2144	...	2247	...	...	...
Newcastle 180 d.	2003	2036	...	2135	...	...	...	...	...	...
Alnmouth 180 d.	2027	|	...	2201	...	...	...	...	...	...
Berwick upon Tweed 180 d.	|	2125	...	|	...	...	...	...	...	...
Edinburgh Waverley 180 220 a.	2128	2214	...	2303	...	...	...	...	...	...
Motherwell 220 a.	...	...	...	...	...	...	...	...	...	...
Glasgow Central 220 a.	...	...	...	...	...	...	...	...	...	...

	⑥	⑥	⑥	⑥	⑥	⑥	⑥	⑥	⑥	⑥	⑥	⑥	⑥
								G		E			
Plymouth 120 d.	...	...	...	...	...	...	...	...	0525	...	0625	...	0725
Bristol T Meads 120 d.	...	...	...	...	...	...	0615	...	0730	...	0830	...	0930
Southampton Central 119 d.	...	...	...	...	...	...	|	...	|	0653	|	0747	|
Reading 119 d.	...	...	...	...	...	...	|	0645	|	0747	|	0845	|
Birmingham New Street 123 d.	...	...	0557	0630	0703	0730	0803	0830	0903	0930	1003	1030	1103
Tamworth 123 d.	...	...	0613	0646	0719	0746	0819	|	|	|	1019	|	|
Burton on Trent 123 d.	...	...	0624	0656	0731	0756	0829	|	0928	|	|	|	1128
Derby 123 170 d.	...	0556	0638	0713	0744	0813	0844	0916a	0944b	1016a	1044b	1116a	1144b
Chesterfield 170 d.	...	0631	0657	0732	0803	0832	0903	|	1003	|	1103	|	1203
Sheffield 170 d.	...	0649b	0712	0754d	0822b	0847	0921	0947	1021	1047	1121	1147	1221
Doncaster 180 d.	...	0719	|	0825	|	0919	|	1019	|	1119	|	1217	|
Wakefield Westgate 180 d.	...	|	0740	|	0848	|	0947	|	1047	|	1147	|	1247
Leeds 180 d.	...	|	0757	|	0908d	|	1008d	|	1108d	|	1208d	|	1308b
York 180 a.	...	0743	0819	0847	0930	0940	1030	1039	1130	1139	1230	1239	1330
York 180 d.	...	0748	0829	0850	0932	0948	1032	1048	1132	1148	1232	1248	1332
Darlington 180 d.	...	0815	0858	0917	1000	1015	1100	1115	1200	1215	1300	1315	1400
Durham 180 d.	...	0832	0915	0934	1017	1032	1117	1132	1217	1232	1317	1332	1417
Newcastle 180 a.	...	0845	0927	0947	1030	1044	1129	1146	1229	1245	1329	1345	1429
Newcastle 180 d.	0738	...	0935	...	1035	...	1136	...	1236	...	1335	...	1434
Alnmouth 180 d.	|	...	0959	...	|	...	|	...	|	...	1400	...	|
Berwick upon Tweed 180 d.	0824	...	1020	...	|	...	1220	...	|	...	1420	...	|
Edinburgh Waverley 180 220 a.	0907	...	1103	...	1205	...	1302	...	1406	...	1504	...	1604
Motherwell 220 a.	0954	...	1152	...	...	...	1353	...	...	...	1552	...	...
Glasgow Central 220 a.	1015	...	1212	...	...	...	1412	...	...	...	1612	...	...

	⑥	⑥	⑥	⑥	⑥	⑥	⑥	⑥	⑥	⑥	⑥	⑥	⑥	⑥	⑥	⑥	⑥	⑥	⑥	⑥	⑥	⑥	⑥
	B		C		B		DF		Jc	e								Jc	e		Ec	e	Bc
Plymouth 120 d.	0825	...	0918f	...	1025	...	1125	...	...	1225	...	1325	...	1425	...	1525	...	...	1625	...	...	1725	1825
Bristol T Meads 120 d.	1030	...	1130	...	1230	...	1330	...	1430	1430	...	1530	...	1630	...	1730	...	1830	1830	...	...	1930	2030
Southampton Central 119 d.	|	0947	|	...	|	1147	|	...	|	|	1347	|	...	|	1547	|	...	|	|	1747	1820	|	|
Reading 119 d.	|	1045	|	1145	|	1245	|	1345	|	|	1445	|	1545	|	1645	|	1745	|	|	1845	1915	|	|
Birmingham New Street 123 d.	1203	1230	1303	1330	1403	1430	1503	1530	1603	1603	1630	1703	1730	1803	1830	1903	1930	2003	2003	2030	2103	2103	2156
Tamworth 123 d.	1219	|	|	|	1419	|	|	|	1619	1619	|	|	|	1819	|	|	|	2019	2019	|	2119	2119	|
Burton on Trent 123 d.	|	|	1327	|	|	|	1527	|	|	|	1654	1726	|	|	|	1927	|	|	|	|	2130	2130	|
Derby 123 170 d.	1244b	1316a	1344	1416a	1444	1516a	1544	1616a	1643	1643	1716a	1744b	1816a	1844b	1916a	1944b	2016a	2044b	2044b	2127	2147	2147	2233
Chesterfield 170 d.	1303	|	1403	|	1503	|	1603	|	1704	1704	|	1803	|	1903	1935	2005	2035	2105	2105	2147	2208	2208	2255
Sheffield 170 d.	1321	1347	1421	1447	1521	1547	1621	1647	1721	1721	1747	1821	1847	1921	1956d	2024	2053	2121	2121	2203	2230d	2230d	2312
Doncaster 180 d.	|	1419	|	1519	|	1619	|	1719	|	|	|	|	1919	|	2019	|	2124	|	|	2226	|	2253	|
Wakefield Westgate 180 d.	1347	|	1447	|	1547	|	1647	|	1748	1748	1815	1848	|	1951	|	2049	|	2148	2148	|	2311	2311	|
Leeds 180 d.	1408d	|	1508d	|	1608d	|	1708d	|	1808b	1808b	1838d	1908d	|	2008	|	2119g	|	2202	2202	|	2325	2325	2351
York 180 a.	1430	1439	1530	1539	1630	1639	1729	1739	1830	1830	1901	1930	1939	2030	2039	2155	2144	...	...	2246	...	...	...
York 180 d.	1432	1448	1532	1548	1632	1648	1731	1748	1832	1832	1904	1932	1945	2032	2048	...	2148	...	...	...	...	...	...
Darlington 180 d.	1500	1515	1600	1615	1700	1715	1758	1814	1901	1901	1932	1959	2012	2059	2115	...	2215	...	...	...	...	...	...
Durham 180 d.	1517	1532	1617	1632	1717	1732	1814	1831	1919	1919	1949	2016	2029	2116	2132	...	2232	...	...	...	...	...	...
Newcastle 180 a.	1529	1545	1629	1645	1729	1745	1827	1843	1932	1932	2001	2028	2042	2128	2144	...	2247	...	...	...	...	...	...
Newcastle 180 d.	1535	...	1634	...	1735	...	1837	...	1935	1935	...	2035	...	2132	...	...	...	...	...	...	...	...	...
Alnmouth 180 d.	1600	...	1658	...	1800	...	|	...	2003	2003	...	|	...	2156	...	...	...	...	...	...	...	...	...
Berwick upon Tweed 180 d.	1620	...	|	...	1820	...	1919	...	2024	2024	...	2120	...	|	...	...	...	...	...	...	...	...	...
Edinburgh Waverley 180 220 a.	1707	...	1803	...	1906	...	2006	...	2108	2108	...	2208	...	2257	...	...	...	...	...	...	...	...	...
Motherwell 220 a.	1752	...	...	...	1953	...	...	...	2159	2159	...	...	...	...	...	...	...	...	...	...	...	...	...
Glasgow Central 220 a.	1811	...	...	...	2012	...	...	...	2220	2220	...	...	...	...	...	...	...	...	...	...	...	...	...

	⑦	⑦	⑦	⑦	⑦	⑦	⑦	⑦	⑦	⑦	⑦	⑦	⑦		⑦	⑦	⑦	⑦	⑦	⑦	⑦	⑦	⑦	⑦
								C			G	B					F							B
Plymouth 120 d.	...	...	...	...	...	...	...	0925	...	1025	...	1125	...	...	1225	...	1325	...	1425	...	1524	...	1625	1725
Bristol T Meads 120 d.	...	...	...	...	0915	1030	...	1130	...	1230	...	1330	...	...	1430	...	1530	...	1630	...	1730	...	1830	1930
Southampton Central 119 d.	...	...	...	...	|	|	...	|	...	|	...	|	...	...	|	...	|	...	|	...	|	...	|	|
Reading 119 d.	...	...	...	...	|	|	...	|	...	|	1254	|	1341	...	|	1441	|	1541	|	1641	|	1741	|	|
Birmingham New Street 123 d.	...	...	0903	1003	1103	1203	1230	1303	1330	1403	1430	1503	1530	...	1603	1630	1703	1730	1803	1830	1903	1930	2003	2103
Tamworth 123 d.	...	...	0919	1018	|	1219	|	|	|	1419	|	|	|	...	1619	|	|	|	1819	|	|	|	2019	2119
Burton on Trent 123 d.	...	...	0928	1029	1125	|	|	1326	|	|	|	1525	|	...	|	|	1728	|	|	|	1926	|	|	2129
Derby 123 170 d.	...	...	0944	1044	1144d	1244b	1311a	1344d	1411a	1444b	1511a	1544d	1611a	...	1644b	1712a	1743	1812a	1843	1906	1942	2009d	2044b	2144
Chesterfield 170 d.	...	...	1003	1103	1203	1303	1330	1403	1430	1503	|	1603	|	...	1703	|	1804	|	1905	|	2003	|	2103	2203
Sheffield 170 d.	...	0921	1021b	1121	1221	1321	1351d	1421	1451b	1521	1551	1621	1651	...	1721	1752	1821	1852d	1921	1952a	2021	2052a	2121b	2221
Doncaster 180 d.	...	|	|	|	|	|	1417	|	1522d	|	1618	|	1719b	...	|	1817	|	1919	|	2018	|	2123	|	|
Wakefield Westgate 180 d.	...	0946	1046	1146	1246	1346	|	1446	|	1546	|	1646	|	...	1745	1835	1849	|	1950	|	2053	|	2148	2244
Leeds 180 d.	0920	1008b	1105b	1205	1305	1405	|	1505	|	1605	|	1705	|	...	1805	1859d	1908	|	2008	|	2108	|	2204	2302
York 180 a.	0942	1029	1127	1227	1327	1427	1437	1527	1543	1627	1638	1727	1740	...	1827	1921	1929	1939	2030	2039	2132	2143	...	...
York 180 d.	0944	1032	1129	1229	1329	1429	1448	1529	1545	1629	1647	1729	1745	...	1829	1923	1932	1945	2032	2048	...	2149	...	...
Darlington 180 d.	1011	1059	1156	1256	1357	1457	1515	1556	1612	1656	1714	1756	1811	...	1856	1950	2000	2012	2100	2115	...	2226	...	...
Durham 180 d.	1028	1116	1213	1313	1414	1514	1532	1613	1629	1713	1731	1813	1828	...	1913	2007	2018	2029	2118	2132	...	2243	...	...
Newcastle 180 a.	1040	1128	1225	1325	1426	1526	1544	1625	1642	1725	1744	1825	1841	...	1925	2019	2031	2041	2131	2144	...	2312	...	...
Newcastle 180 d.	1042	1134	1230	1328	1432	1528	...	1628	...	1728	...	1828	...	...	1928	...	2034	2056	2134	...	...	...	...	...
Alnmouth 180 d.	|	|	|	1352	|	1553	...	1652	...	1753	...	|	...	...	1953	...	|	|	2202	...	...	...	...	...
Berwick upon Tweed 180 d.	1124	1218	|	1413	|	1613	...	|	...	1813	...	1910	...	...	2013	...	2122	|	|	...	...	...	...	...
Edinburgh Waverley 180 220 a.	1207	1259	1400	1456	1602	1656	...	1757	...	1856	...	1957	...	...	2056	...	2212	2221	2304	...	...	...	...	...
Motherwell 220 a.	1258	1353	...	1554	...	1755	...	...	...	1959	...	...	...	...	2156	...	...	...	...	...	...	...	...	...
Glasgow Central 220 a.	1317	1412	...	1613	...	1812	...	...	...	2021	...	...	...	...	2213	...	...	...	...	...	...	...	...	...

A – From Winchester (Table **119**).
B – From Penzance (Tables **117**/**120**).
C – To Aberdeen (Table **222**).
D – To Dundee (Table **222**)
E – From Bournemouth (Table **119**).
F – From Newquay May 15 - Sept. 11 (Tables **117**/**120**).
G – From Guildford (Table **134**).
H – From Bath Spa (Table **120**).
J – From Paignton (Table **120**).
a – Arrives 10–12 minutes earlier.
b – Arrives 5–6 minutes earlier.
c – May 21 - Sept. 10.
d – Arrives 7–9 minutes earl
e – From Sept. 17.
f – 0925 from Sept. 17.
g – Arrives 15–16 minutes ea

GLASGOW - EDINBURGH - NEWCASTLE - YORK - LEEDS - SHEFFIELD - BIRMINGHAM 124

Ⓐ

	Ⓐ	Ⓐ	Ⓐ	Ⓐ	Ⓐ	Ⓐ	Ⓐ	Ⓐ	Ⓐ	Ⓐ	Ⓐ	Ⓐ	Ⓐ	Ⓐ	Ⓐ	Ⓐ	Ⓐ	Ⓐ	Ⓐ	Ⓐ	Ⓐ	Ⓐ	Ⓐ	Ⓐ
													D				B		C B	G	B			
gow **Central** 220 d.	...	...	...	...	...	...	...	...	...	...	0601	...	...	...	0750	...	0900	...	...	...	1100	...	...	...
erwell 220 d.	...	...	...	...	...	...	...	...	...	...	0617	...	...	...	0805	...	0915	...	...	...	1116	...	...	...
burgh Waverley 180 220 d.	...	...	...	...	...	...	...	...	0606	0700	0707	...	0810	...	0908	...	1010	...	1106	...	1208	...	1307	...
ick upon Tweed 180 d.	...	...	...	...	...	...	...	...	0647	0739	|	...	0851	...	0951	...	1049	...	1149	...	1248	...	|	...
outh 180 d.	...	...	...	...	...	...	...	...	0708	0759	|	...	|	...	|	...	|	...	1209	...	|	...	1411	...
castle 180 a.	...	...	...	...	...	...	...	...	0738	0830	0834	...	0940	...	1038	...	1137	...	1238	...	1334	...	1440	...
castle 180 d.	...	...	...	...	...	0625	0645	0725	0740	0835	0843	0935	0942	1035	1042	1135	1144	1235	1241	1335	1343	1435	1442	1505
am 180 d.	...	...	...	...	...	0638	0658	0738	0755	0848	0856	0949	0956	1048	1055	1149	1157	1248	1254	1349	1356	1448	1456	1518
ngton 180 d.	...	...	...	...	...	0655	0715	0755	0812	0905	0913	1007	1013	1105	1113	1206	1214	1305	1313	1407	1413	1505	1513	1535
180 a.	...	...	...	...	...	0722	0741	0821	0840	0932	0941	1033	1041	1131	1140	1232	1240	1331	1340	1433	1440	1531	1541	1601
180 d.	...	...	...	...	0640	0727	0743	0826	0845	0935	0945	1035	1045	1135	1145	1235	1245	1335	1345	1435	1445	1535	1545	1605
eds 180 d.	...	...	0600	0616	0705	|	0811	|	0911	|	1011	|	1111	|	1211	|	1311	|	1411	|	1511	|	1611	1640**c**
akefield Westgate 180 d.	...	...	0612	0628	0719	|	0823	|	0923	|	1023	|	1124	|	1223	|	1323	|	1423	|	1523	|	1623	1652
caster 180 d.	...	...	|	0646	|	0756**b**	|	0851	|	0959	|	1059	|	1159	|	1259	|	1359	|	1459	|	1559	|	|
field 170 d.	...	0601	0652**e**	0718**d**	0753	0821	0854	0924**d**	0954	1024	1055	1124	1154	1224	1255	1324	1355	1424	1455	1524	1555	1624	1655	1724
terfield 170 d.	...	0626	0706	0730	0806	0833	0907	|	1008	|	1107	|	1208	|	1307	|	1407	|	1507	|	1607	|	1708	|
y 123 170 d.	0610	0648**b**	0727	0750	0828	0853	0928	0953	1030	1053	1128	1153	1230	1253	1328	1353	1428	1453	1528	1553	1628	1653	1729	1753
on on Trent 123 d.	0620	0658	0738	0800	0838	|	0938	|	|	|	|	|	|	|	1338	|	|	|	1538	|	|	|	1740	|
worth 123 d.	0631	0709	0750	0811	0850	|	|	|	1050	|	|	|	1249	|	|	|	1447	|	|	|	1647	|	|	|
ingham New Street 123 a.	0652	0727	0808	0827	0910	0927	1008	1027	1109	1127	1207	1227	1308	1327	1408	1427	1508	1527	1602	1628	1708	1728	1806	1827
eading 119 a.	|	0908	|	1010	|	1109	|	1209	|	1307	|	1409	|	1508	|	1611	|	1708	|	1808	|	1910	|	2009
uthampton Central 119 a.	|	...	|	1117	|	...	|	1317	|	...	|	1517	|	...	|	1717	|	...	|	...	|	...	|	...
Bristol T Meads 120 a.	0839	...	0939	...	1042	...	1141	...	1242	...	1341	...	1442	...	1541	...	1643	...	1739	...	1841	...	1943	...
Plymouth 120 a.	1042	...	1144	...	1247	...	1338	...	1443	...	1540	...	1648	...	1742	...	1849	...	1943	...	2040	...	2146	...

	Ⓐ	Ⓐ	Ⓐ	Ⓐ	Ⓐ	Ⓐ	Ⓐ	Ⓐ	Ⓐ	Ⓐ
sgow **Central** 220 d.	1300	...	...	...	1500	...	...	...	1700	1900
herwell 220 d.	1316	...	...	...	1516	...	...	...	1716	1916
burgh Waverley 180 220 d.	1408	...	1508	...	1606	...	1708	...	1805	2002
wick upon Tweed 180 d.	1450	...	|	...	|	...	1751	...	1849	2045
nouth 180 d.	|	...	|	...	1702	...	|	...	1910	2105
castle 180 a.	1534	...	1634	...	1734	...	1837	...	1939	2134
castle 180 d.	1541	1635	1641	1732	1741	1835	1843	1935	1942	...
am 180 d.	1554	1648	1653	1748	1754	1848	1856	1950	1955	...
ngton 180 d.	1613	1706	1712	1805	1813	1907	1913	2007	2013	...
k 180 a.	1640	1731	1740	1831	1839	1933	1940	2032	2040	
k 180 d.	1645	1735	1745	1835	1845	1936	1945	2035	2045	...
eds 180 d.	1711	|	1811	|	1911	|	2011	|	2111	...
akefield Westgate 180 d.	1723	|	1823	|	1923	|	2024	|	2123	...
caster 180 d.	|	1759	|	1859	|	2000	|	2102	|	...
field 170 d.	1758**d**	1824	1858**d**	1924	1958**d**	2024	2058**b**	2129	2200**d**	...
sterfield 170 d.	1810	|	1911	|	2010	|	2110	2141	2225	...
by 123 170 d.	1829	1853	1930	1954	2029	2054	2129	2202	2245	...
on on Trent 123 d.	|	|	1941	|	|	|	2140	|	2256	...
worth 123 d.	1848	|	|	|	2047	|	2150	|	2307	...
ingham New Street 123 a.	1908	1927	2007	2027	2107	2129	2209	2251	2325	...
eading 119 a.	|	2107	|	2216	|	...	|	...	...	...
outhampton Central 119 a.	|	...	|	2320	|	...	|	...	...	...
Bristol T Meads 120 a.	2041	...	2136	...	2243	...	2340	...	...	...
Plymouth 120 a.	2243	...	2339	...	...	...	...	...	...	...

⑥

	⑥	⑥	⑥	⑥	⑥	⑥	⑥	⑥	⑥	⑥	⑥	⑥	⑥	⑥
			g	H a				g	B a				H a	g
sgow **Central** 220 d.	...	...	...	...	...	...	...	...	...	...	...	...	0601	0601
herwell 220 d.	...	...	...	...	...	...	...	...	...	...	...	...	0617	0617
burgh Waverley 180 220 d.	...	...	...	...	...	...	...	...	...	...	0608	0700	0707	0707
wick upon Tweed 180 d.	...	...	...	...	...	...	...	...	...	...	0647	0740	|	|
nouth 180 d.	...	...	...	...	...	...	...	...	...	...	0707	0800	|	|
castle 180 a.	...	...	...	...	...	...	...	...	...	...	0736	0831	0836	0836
castle 180 d.	...	...	...	...	...	...	0623	0645	...	0735	0741	0835	0842	0843
am 180 d.	...	...	...	...	...	...	0638	0658	...	0748	0754	0848	0856	0856
ngton 180 d.	...	...	...	...	...	...	0655	0715	...	0805	0813	0905	0913	0913
k 180 a.	...	...	...	...	...	...	0721	0741	...	0831	0840	0932	0941	0941
k 180 d.	...	...	...	...	...	0620**f**	0727	0745	0745	0835	0845	0935	0945	0945
eds 180 d.	...	...	0600	0600	0616	0711**e**	|	0811	0811	|	0911	|	1011	1011
akefield Westgate 180 d.	...	...	0612	0612	0629	0723	|	0823	0824	|	0924	|	1024	1024
caster 180 d.	...	...	|	|	0647	|	0756**d**	|	|	0859	|	0959	|	|
field 170 d.	...	0545**a**	0650**c**	0650**c**	0718**d**	0756**b**	0820	0855	0854	0924	0955	1024	1054	1055
sterfield 170 d.	...	0557**a**	0704	0704	0730	0808	0832	0907	0908	|	1007	|	1108	1107
by 123 170 d.	0610	0648	0726	0726	0751	0828	0853	0930**b**	0930**b**	0953	1028	1053	1130**b**	1130**b**
on on Trent 123 d.	0620	0658	0737	0737	0800	0838	|	0941	0941	|	|	|	1141	1140
worth 123 d.	0631	0709	0748	0748	0811	0849	|	|	|	|	1048	|	|	|
ingham New Street 123 a.	0650	0728	0808	0808	0827	0908	0927	1006	1006	1027	1107	1127	1208	1208
eading 119 a.	|	0909	|	|	1008	|	1111	|	|	1206	|	1309	|	|
outhampton Central 119 a.	|	...	|	|	1117	|	...	|	|	1317	|	...	|	|
Bristol T Meads 120 a.	0838	...	0939	0939	...	1042	...	1138	1138	...	1242	...	1339	1338
Plymouth 120 a.	1039	...	1151	...	...	1240	...	1339	1345	...	1444	...	...	1541

	⑥	⑥	⑥	⑥	⑥	⑥	⑥	⑥	⑥	⑥	⑥	⑥	⑥	⑥	⑥	⑥	⑥	⑥	⑥		⑥	⑥	⑥	⑥	⑥
		D F		B a	g		B		C B	G	B g	a													
sgow **Central** 220 d.	...	...	...	0750	0750	...	0900	...	...	...	1100	1100	...	...	...	1300	...	...	...	...	1500	...	...	...	1700
herwell 220 d.	...	...	...	0805	0805	...	0915	...	...	...	1116	1116	...	...	...	1316	...	...	...	...	1516	...	...	...	1716
burgh Waverley 180 220 d.	...	0805	...	0908	0908	...	1005	...	1108	...	1204	1204	...	1309	...	1405	...	1508	...	...	1605	...	1708	...	1808
wick upon Tweed 180 d.	...	0847	...	0951	0951	...	1045	...	1151	...	1246	1246	...	|	...	1447	...	|	...	...	|	...	1752	...	1851
nouth 180 d.	...	0909	...	|	|	...	|	...	1211	...	|	|	...	1409	...	|	...	|	...	...	1703	...	|	...	1911
castle 180 a.	...	0939	...	1038	1038	...	1138	...	1240	...	1332	1332	...	1348	...	1532	...	1634	...	...	1734	...	1838	...	1940
castle 180 d.	0935	0942	1035	1044	1044	1135	1142	1235	1244	1335	1344	1344	1435	1444	1505	1544	1635	1644	1732	...	1744	1835	1844	1935	1945
ham 180 d.	0949	0956	1048	1056	1056	1149	1155	1248	1256	1349	1356	1356	1448	1456	1518	1556	1648	1656	1749	...	1756	1849	1857	1950	1957
ington 180 d.	1006	1013	1105	1113	1113	1206	1212	1305	1313	1406	1413	1413	1505	1513	1535	1613	1705	1713	1806	...	1813	1906	1914	2007	2014
k 180 a.	1032	1041	1131	1140	1140	1232	1240	1331	1340	1432	1440	1440	1531	1540	1601	1640	1731	1740	1831	...	1841	1932	1941	2033	2041
k 180 d.	1035	1045	1135	1145	1145	1235	1245	1335	1345	1435	1445	1445	1535	1545	1606	1645	1735	1745	1835	...	1845	1936	1945	2035	2045
eeds 180 d.	|	1111	|	1211	1211	|	1311	|	1411	|	1511	1511	|	1611	1640**c**	1711	|	1811	|	...	1911	|	2011	|	2111
akefield Westgate 180 d.	|	1123	|	1223	1223	|	1323	|	1423	|	1523	1523	|	1623	1652	1723	|	1823	|	...	1924	|	2023	|	2123
caster 180 d.	1059	|	1159	|	|	1259	|	1359	|	1459	|	|	1559	|	|	|	1759	|	1859	...	|	2000	|	2059	|
ffield 170 d.	1124	1155	1224	1255	1255	1324	1355	1424	1455	1524	1555	1555	1624	1655	1724	1755	1824	1858**d**	1924	...	1955	2024	2055	2125	2155
sterfield 170 d.	|	1209	|	1307	1307	|	1408	|	1507	|	1607	1607	|	1707	|	1807	|	1910	|	...	2007	|	2107	2137	2207
by 123 170 d.	1153	1230	1253	1328	1328	1353	1430	1453	1528	1553	1628	1628	1653	1728	1753	1829**b**	1853	1929	1954	...	2028	2053	2128	2156	2226
on on Trent 123 d.	|	|	|	1338	1338	|	|	|	1538	|	|	|	|	1738	|	|	|	1939	|	...	|	|	2138	|	2237
worth 123 d.	|	1249	|	|	|	|	1449	|	|	|	1648	1648	|	|	|	1847	|	|	|	...	2046	|	2149	|	2247
ningham New Street 123 a.	1227	1308	1327	1402	1402	1426	1508	1527	1602	1627	1707	1707	1727	1807	1827	1907	1927	2006	2027	...	2104	2125	2206	2244	2306
eading 119 a.	1408	|	1508	|	|	1609	|	1710	|	1810	|	|	1910	|	2009	|	2108	|	2214	...	|	...	...	...	...
outhampton Central 119 a.	1517	|	...	|	|	1717	|	...	|	...	|	|	...	|	...	|	...	|	2320	...	|	...	...	...	...
Bristol T Meads 120 a.	...	1440	...	1538	1538	...	1642	...	1738	...	1842	1842	...	1938	...	2042	...	2135	...	...	2241	...	...	...	...
Plymouth 120 a.	...	1643	...	1739	1739	...	1851	...	1942	...	2043	2043	...	2138	...	2250	...	2356	...		...	...	...	...	...

⑦

	⑦	⑦	⑦	⑦	⑦	⑦	⑦	⑦	⑦	⑦	⑦		⑦	⑦	⑦	⑦	⑦	⑦	⑦	⑦	⑦	⑦	⑦	⑦
						B				B					C			G						
sgow **Central** 220 d.	...	...	...	...	...	...	...	...	...	1055	...	...	1200	...	...	...	1348	...	1455	...	...	...	1655	1900
herwell 220 d.	...	...	...	...	...	...	...	...	...	1113	...	...	1217	...	...	...	1404	...	1512	...	...	...	1712	1915
nburgh Waverley 180 220 d.	...	...	...	...	0908	1008	...	1105	...	1208	...	...	1308	1355	1408	...	1508	...	1608	...	1708	...	1808	2018
wick upon Tweed 180 d.	...	...	...	...	0949	|	...	1148	...	1248	...	...	|	1434	1447	...	|	...	|	...	1751	...	1851	2039
mouth 180 d.	...	...	...	...	|	1105	...	1208	...	|	...	...	1408	|	|	...	|	...	1705	...	|	...	|	2103
wcastle 180 a.	...	...	...	...	1036	1136	...	1237	...	1335	...	...	1437	1520	1535	...	1634	...	1736	...	1837	...	1937	2149
wcastle 180 d.	...	...	...	0935	1039	1140	...	1240	1335	1340	1435	...	1440	1523	1540	1635	1640	1735	1740	1825	1840	1926	1940	...
ham 180 d.	...	...	...	0948	1053	1153	...	1253	1348	1353	1449	...	1454	1536	1553	1648	1653	1748	1754	1837	1853	1939	1953	...
lington 180 d.	...	...	...	1005	1110	1210	...	1310	1406	1410	1506	...	1511	1553	1610	1705	1710	1806	1811	1854	1910	1956	2010	...
k 180 a.	...	...	...	1031	1138	1237	...	1337	1432	1437	1532	...	1537	1620	1636	1731	1737	1832	1838	1920	1937	2022	2037	...
k 180 d.	...	...	0933	1033	1141	1241	...	1341	1435	1441	1535	...	1541	1624	1641	1735	1741	1835	1841	1924	1941	2024	2041	...
eeds 180 d.	0810	0900	1000	1100	1211**b**	1311**d**	...	1411**d**	|	1511**d**	|	...	1611**d**	|	1711**b**	|	1811**b**	|	1911**d**	|	2011**b**	|	2111**d**	...
Wakefield Westgate 180 d.	0823	0911	1012	1112	1224	1324	...	1423	|	1523	|	...	1623	|	1723	|	1823	|	1923	|	2023	|	2123	...
caster 180 d.	|	0932	1030	1130	|	|	...	|	1459	|	1559	...	|	1651	|	1759	|	1859	|	1954**b**	|	2051	|	...
effield 170 d.	0854	0957	1057	1157	1257	1357	1422	1455	1524	1555	1624	...	1654	1724	1754	1824	1855	1924	1955	2021	2054	2120	2154	...
esterfield 170 d.	0907	1009	1109	1209	1309	1409	1432	1507	|	1607	|	...	1707	|	1807	|	1907	|	2007	|	2106	2132	2206	...
rby 123 170 d.	0928	1033	1129	1229	1332	1429	1453	1526	1553	1627	1654	...	1727	1754	1826	1854	1927	1956	2027	2054**b**	2126	2153	2226	...
ton on Trent 123 d.	|	|	1140	|	1343	|	|	1537	|	|	|	...	1737	|	|	|	1938	|	|	|	2137	2203	2237	...
nworth 123 d.	|	1053	|	1248	|	1448	|	|	|	1648	|	...	|	|	1845	|	|	|	2046	|	2147	2214	2247	...
mingham New Street 123 a.	1018	1121	1205	1306	1409	1505	1526	1602	1626	1705	1726	...	1802	1826	1904	1928	2005	2027	2103	2126	2205	2231	2305	...
Reading 119 a.	|	|	|	|	|	|	1704	|	1809	|	1904	...	|	2009	|	2114	|	2206	|	...	|	...	...	...
Southampton Central 119 a.	|	|	|	|	|	|	...	|	...	|	...	...	|	...	|	...	|	...	|	...	|	...	...	...
Bristol T Meads 120 a.	1151	1249	1331	1431	1534	1631	...	1733	...	1835	...	...	1932	...	2031	...	2130	...	2244	...	2333	...	...	...
Plymouth 120 a.	1352	1452	1537	1638	1742	1838	...	1943	...	2045	...	...	2141	...	2245	...	2346	...	...	...	...	...	...	...

To Winchester (Table **119**).
To Penzance (Tables **117**/**120**).
From Aberdeen (Table **222**).
From Dundee (Table **222**).

E – To Bournemouth (Table **119**).
F – To Newquay May 21 - Sept. 10 (Tables **117**/**120**).
G – To Guildford (Table **134**).
H – To Paignton (table **120**).

a – May 21 - Sept. 10.
b – Arrives 5–6 minutes earlier.
c – Arrives 9–10 minutes earlier.
d – Arrives 7–8 minutes earlier.

e – Arrives 12 minutes earlier.
f – 0645 May 21 - Sept. 10.
g – From Sept 17.

125 BIRMINGHAM - WORCESTER - HEREFORD

2nd class

km			Ⓐ	Ⓐ	Ⓐ	Ⓐ		Ⓐ	Ⓐ	Ⓐ	Ⓐ	Ⓐ	Ⓐ	Ⓐ	Ⓐ	Ⓐ	Ⓐ		⑥	⑥		⑥	⑥	⑥	⑥
0	**Birmingham** New Str d.	Ⓐ	0659	0719	0759	0849		1549	1649	1719	1749	1759	1819	1919	1959	2059	2300	⑥	0649	0749		1749	1849	1919	2059
21	Bromsgrove d.		0721	0744	0821	0910		1610	1710	1740	1809	1820	1842	1942	2019	2120	2320		0710	0810		1810	1910	1940	2120
32	Droitwich Spa d.		0730	0754	0830	0920	and	1620	1720	1752	1819	1835	1857	1952	2029	2130	2330		0720	0820	and	1820	1920	1951	2130
41	**Worcester** Foregate St d.		0742	0811	0840	0932	hourly	1630	1735	1807	1835	1857	1910**h**	2015	2036**h**	2141	2339**h**		0732	0832	hourly	1835	1938	2000	2150
54	Great Malvern d.		0800	0822	0853	0945	until	1643	1747	1819	1849	1910	*1954*	2027	*2100*	2154	...		0745	0845	until	1848	1950	2025	2202
65	Ledbury d.		0813	...	0907	0958		1659	1800	1831	1904	...	*2010*	2041	*2116*	2209	...		0759	0859		1901	...	2039	2215
87	**Hereford** a.		0833	...	0927	1019		1719	1821	1851	1923	...	*2031*	2101	*2136*	2228	...		0819	0919		1919	...	2102	2235

		⑦	⑦	⑦	⑦	⑦	⑦	⑦	⑦	⑦
Birmingham New Str d.	⑦	1000	1200	1400	1558	1758	1900	2000	2100	2205
Bromsgrove d.		1020	1220	1420	1618	1818	1920	2020	2120	2225
Droitwich Spa d.		1030	1232	1430	1628	1828	1930	2030	2130	2236
Worcester Foregate St d.		1054	1250	1454	1642	1842	1944	2100	2144	2254
Great Malvern d.		1106	1302	1506	1703	1859	*2033*	*2139*	2156	2307
Ledbury d.		1118	1315	1518	1716	1912	*2048*	...	2209	...
Hereford a.		1134	1332	1534	1734	1930	*2104*	...	2227	...

		Ⓐ	Ⓐ	Ⓐ	Ⓐ	Ⓐ	Ⓐ	Ⓐ	Ⓐ	Ⓐ	
Hereford d.	Ⓐ	*0450*	*0528*	...	...	0709	0734	...	0846	0940	
Ledbury d.		|	*0545*	...	...	0725	0750	...	0906	0958	
Great Malvern d.		0549	*0559*	0647	0702	0737	0807	0837	0917	1010	and
Worcester F'gate St. d.		0602	0626**h**	0658	0716	0749	0824	0852	0930	1024	hourly
Droitwich Spa d.		0611	0633	0713	0733	0805	0833	0901	0943	1033	until
Bromsgrove d.		0621	0643	0723	|	|	0843	0911	0953	1043	
Birmingham N Str a.		0650	0710	0748	0810	0840	0909	0940	1020	1110	

	Ⓐ	Ⓐ	Ⓐ	Ⓐ	Ⓐ		⑥	⑥	⑥	⑥		⑥	⑥	⑥	⑥	⑥	⑥		⑦	⑦	⑦	⑦	⑦	⑦	⑦
Hereford d.	1848	1950	2056	2129	2259	⑥	...	*0617*	0740	0840		1740	1912	2000	*2020*	*2135*	2250	⑦	1006	1200	1406	1609	*1634*	1809	*1830*
Ledbury d.	1904	2009	2114	2145	2315		...	*0634*	0758	0858		1758	1928	2016	*2040*	*2151*	2306		1022	1216	1422	1625	*1652*	1825	*1848*
Great Malvern d.	1915	2020	2125	2156	2327		0622	0707	0810	0910	and	1810	1939	2027	2130	*2203*	2317		1034	1230	1434	1637	*1705*	1837	*1911*
Worcester Foregate St d.	1928	2031	2136	2210	2339		0634	0728	0824	0924	hourly	1825	1951	2040	2142	2247**h**	2327		1046	1242	1446	1649	1757**h**	1849	1949
Droitwich Spa d.	1937	2045	...	2219	...		0643	0743	0833	0933	until	1833	2000	2049	2202	2255	...		1103	1303	1503	1703	1805	1903	2003
Bromsgrove d.	1947	2055	...	2229	...		0653	0753	0843	0943		1844	|	2059	|	|	...		1113	1313	1513	1713	1815	1913	2013
Birmingham New Str a.	2018	2120	...	2254	...		0718	0818	0909	1009		1909	2055**n**	2120	2255**n**	2336**n**	...		1137	1337	1537	1737	1837	1937	2037

h – Worcester Shrub Hill.

n – Birmingham Snow Hill.

126 BIRMINGHAM - KIDDERMINSTER - WORCESTER

2nd class

km			Ⓐ	Ⓐ	Ⓐ	Ⓐ	Ⓐ	Ⓐ	Ⓐ	Ⓐ	Ⓐ	Ⓐ	Ⓐ	Ⓐ	Ⓐ	Ⓐ	Ⓐ	Ⓐ	Ⓐ	Ⓐ		Ⓐ	Ⓐ	Ⓐ	Ⓐ	Ⓐ
0	**Birmingham** Moor St d.	Ⓐ	0604	0649	0718	0748	0834	0909	0939	1009	1039	1109	1139	1209	1239	1309	1339	1409	1439	1509	...	1539	1609	1639	1709	1732
1	**Birmingham** Sn'w Hill d.		0607	0653	0723	0753	0843	0913	0943	1013	1043	1113	1143	1213	1243	1313	1343	1413	1443	1513	...	1543	1613	1643	1713	1736
31	Kidderminster △ d.		0648	0734	0804	0834	0920	0947	1018	1047	1118	1147	1218	1247	1318	1347	1418	1447	1518	1552	...	1620	1647	1722	1752	1814
45	Droitwich Spa d.		0658	0747	0817	0847	0930	1000	1030	1100	1130	1200	1230	1300	1330	1400	1430	1500	1530	1606	...	1631	1700	1737	1804	1828
54	**Worcester** Shr Hill a.		|	|	0824	|	0940	|	|	|	1138	|	1238	|	|	1408	1440	1510	|	1614	...	|	|	|	1812	|
54	**Worcester** F'gate St. a.		0709	0757	0833	0858	...	1009	1039	1109	...	1209	...	1309	1340	...	1446	...	1539	1625	...	1640	1709	1746	...	1839

	Ⓐ	Ⓐ	Ⓐ	Ⓐ	Ⓐ	Ⓐ		⑥	⑥	⑥	⑥	⑥	⑥	⑥	⑥		⑥	⑥	⑥	⑥	⑥	⑥	⑥	⑥	⑥	⑥
Birmingham Moor St d.	1839	1924	1954	2052	2155	2256	⑥	0633	0701	0749	0845	0909	0939	1009	1039	...	1109	1139	1209	1239	1309	1339	1409	1439	1509	1539
Birmingham Sn'w Hill d.	1843	1928	1958	2055	2158	2300		0637	0705	0753	0853	0913	0943	1013	1043	...	1113	1143	1213	1243	1313	1343	1413	1443	1513	1543
Kidderminster △ d.	1920	2009	2039	2139	2238	2341		0717	0745	0831	0933	0947	1018	1047	1118	...	1147	1218	1247	1318	1347	1418	1447	1518	1547	1618
Droitwich Spa d.	1932	2022	2050	2152	2252	2352		0731	0756	0842	0944	1000	1030	1100	1130	...	1200	1230	1300	1330	1400	1430	1500	1530	1600	1630
Worcester Shr'b Hill a.	|	|	2059	2159	2259	0001		0740	0805	|	0952	|	1038	|	1138	...	|	|	|	1338	|	1439	|	1538	|	|
Worcester F'gate St a.	1943	2031	...	2210	2310	...		...	0813	0851	...	1009	...	1109	...	...	1209	1239	1309	...	1409	1446	1509	...	1609	1639

	⑥	⑥	⑥	⑥	⑥	⑥	⑥	⑥	⑥	⑥		⑦	⑦	⑦	⑦	⑦	⑦	⑦	⑦	⑦		⑦	⑦	⑦	⑦	⑦
Birmingham Moor St d.	1639	1709	1739	1818	1849	1924	1953	2052	2152	2257	⑦	0924	1015	1115	1215	1315	1415	1515	1615	1702	...	1715	1815	1915	2015	2143
Birmingham Sn'w Hill d.	1643	1713	1743	1823	1853	1928	1956	2056	2156	2301		0928	1022	1122	1222	1322	1422	1522	1622	1706	...	1722	1822	1922	2022	2146
Kidderminster △ d.	1718	1749	1820	1900	1934	2009	2036	2136	2236	2341		1003	1059	1159	1259	1357	1459	1557	1657	1733	...	1757	1859	1957	2057	2220
Droitwich Spa d.	1730	1802	1834	1914	1946	2022	2048	2148	2250	2353		1015	1111	1211	1311	1408	1511	1608	1708	1745	...	1809	1911	2009	2109	2231
Worcester Shr'b Hill a.	|	1812	|	|	1954	2031	2056	2156	2257	0001		1022	1119	1219	|	|	|	|	|	1752	...	|	1919	2017	2118	2239
Worcester F'gate St a.	1739	...	1843	1923	...	...	2101	...	2302	...		1030	1135	...	1320	1417	1520	1617	1717	...	...	1819	...	...	2124	...

		Ⓐ	Ⓐ	Ⓐ	Ⓐ	Ⓐ	Ⓐ	Ⓐ	Ⓐ	Ⓐ	Ⓐ	Ⓐ	Ⓐ	Ⓐ	Ⓐ	Ⓐ	Ⓐ	Ⓐ	Ⓐ	Ⓐ	Ⓐ	Ⓐ	Ⓐ	Ⓐ	Ⓐ	Ⓐ
Worcester F'gate St d.	Ⓐ	...	...	...	...	0714	...	0802	0839	0903	...	1016	...	1116	1151	1216	...	...	1351	1416	...	...	1533	1613	1634	1647
Worcester Shr'b Hill d.		0530	0612	0635	0650	|	0735	|	0845	|	0952	|	1052	|	|	|	1252	1317	|	|	1452	1517	1547	|	1640	|
Droitwich Spa d.		0538	0620	0643	0703	0723	0743	0811	0853	0912	1000	1025	1100	1125	1200	1225	1300	1325	1400	1425	1500	1525	1555	1622	1648	1655
Kidderminster △ d.		0548	0633	0656	0716	0736	0754	0824	0906	0925	1010	1038	1110	1138	1210	1238	1310	1338	1410	1438	1510	1538	1608	1635	1701	1706
Birmingham Sn'w Hill a.		0627	0722	0738	0759	0815	0835	0905	0945	1004	1045	1115	1145	1215	1245	1315	1345	1415	1445	1515	1545	1616	1645	1718	1739	1745
Birmingham Moor St a.		0638	0728	0743	0806	0820	0840	0910	0950	1010	1050	1120	1150	1220	1250	1320	1350	1420	1450	1520	1550	1620	1650	1725	1745	1750

	Ⓐ	Ⓐ	Ⓐ	Ⓐ	Ⓐ	Ⓐ	Ⓐ		⑥	⑥	⑥	⑥	⑥	⑥	⑥	⑥	⑥	⑥	⑥	⑥	⑥	⑥	⑥	⑥	⑥	⑥
Worcester F'gate St d.	1756	...	1846	1946	2051	...	2217	⑥	...	...	...	0747	...	0856	0916	...	1016	...	...	1151	1216	1251	...	1351	1416	...
Worcester Shr'b Hill d.	|	1837	|	|	|	2154	2227		0544	0625	0701	|	0815	|	|	0948	|	1052	1117	|	|	|	1317	|	|	1452
Droitwich Spa d.	1805	1845	1855	1955	2100	2202	2235		0552	0633	0709	0756	0823	0905	0925	0956	1025	1100	1125	1200	1225	1300	1325	1400	1425	1500
Kidderminster △ d.	1815	1855	1910	2010	2113	2213	2248		0602	0646	0722	0806	0836	0916	0938	1006	1038	1110	1138	1210	1238	1310	1338	1410	1438	1510
Birmingham Sn'w Hill a.	1855	1934	1955	2055	2155	2255	2328		0645	0732	0805	0845	0915	0956	1015	1041	1115	1145	1215	1245	1315	1345	1415	1445	1515	1545
Birmingham Moor St a.	1900	...	2000	2100	2200	2300	2337		0653	0740	0810	0850	0920	1001	1020	1050	1120	1150	1220	1250	1320	1350	1420	1450	1520	1550

	⑥	⑥	⑥	⑥	⑥	⑥	⑥	⑥	⑥	⑥	⑥		⑦	⑦	⑦	⑦	⑦	⑦	⑦	⑦	⑦	⑦	⑦	⑦	⑦	⑦
Worcester F'gate St d.	1547	1614	1647	...	1747	1812	1851	1951	...	2142	...	⑦	0920	1025	1112	1220	1326	1426	1528	1545	1626	1727	1826	...	...	2118
Worcester Shr'b Hill d.	|	|	|	1715	|	1818	|	|	2052	2154	2247		0926	|	1126	1226	|	|	|	|	|	|	|	1938	2037	2125
Droitwich Spa d.	1556	1623	1656	1723	1756	1826	1900	2000	2100	2202	2255		0935	1035	1135	1235	1335	1435	1537	1554	1635	1736	1835	1946	2046	2133
Kidderminster △ d.	1610	1636	1706	1736	1806	1836	1913	2013	2113	2213	2305		0945	1045	1145	1245	1345	1445	1547	1604	1645	1746	1845	1956	2056	2143
Birmingham Sn'w Hill a.	1645	1715	1745	1815	1845	1916	1955	2055	2154	2255	2336		1022	1122	1222	1322	1422	1522	1623	1636	1722	1824	1921	2033	2133	2219
Birmingham Moor St a.	1650	1720	1750	1820	1858	1920	2000	2100	2200	2300	2340		1029	1130	1230	1330	1430	1530	1630	1645	1730	1830	1925	2037	2137	2223

△ – **Severn Valley Railway** (🚂 Kidderminster - Bridgnorth : *26 km*). ✆ 01299 403816. www.svr.co.uk.

127 STRATFORD UPON AVON - BIRMINGHAM

2nd class

km			Ⓐ	Ⓐ	Ⓐ	Ⓐ	Ⓐ	Ⓐ	Ⓐ		Ⓐ	Ⓐ	Ⓐ	Ⓐ	Ⓐ	Ⓐ	Ⓐ	Ⓐ	Ⓐ	Ⓐ	Ⓐ	Ⓐ		⑥
0	**Stratford upon Avon** d.	Ⓐ	0626	0652	0719	0743	0826	0926	1003	and at the same	1603	1626	1727	1755	1827	1851	1903	1926	2026	2126	2233	2330	⑥	0700
13	Henley in Arden d.		0641	0707	0735	0758	0841	0941	|	minutes	|	1641	1743	1807	1843	1907	|	1941	2041	2139	2246	|		0715
40	**Birmingham** Moor Str d.		0724	0748	0808	0839	0918	1018	1049	past each	1649	1719	1818	1839	1919	1935	1954	2018	2118	2218	2319	0006		0755
41	**Birmingham** Snow Hill a.		0726	0750	0810	0842	0920	1020	1052	hour until	1652	1721	1821	1841	1922	1937	1956	2020	2120	2220	2321	0008		0757

	⑥	⑥		⑥	⑥	⑥	⑥	⑥	⑥	⑥	⑥	⑥	⑥		⑦	⑦	⑦	⑦	⑦	⑦	⑦	⑦	⑦	⑦
Stratford upon Avon d.	0826	0903	and at the same	1703	1726	1754	1813	1848	1926	2026	2126	2233	2330	⑦	0929	1029	1129	1229	1329	1429	1529	1629	1729	1829
Henley in Arden d.	0841	|	minutes	|	1741	1808	1828	1903	1941	2041	2140	2247	|		0943	1043	1143	1243	1343	1443	1543	1643	1743	1843
Birmingham Moor Str d.	0918	0949	past each	1749	1818	1839	1909	1944	2018	2118	2218	2319	0008		1015	1115	1215	1315	1415	1515	1615	1715	1815	1915
Birmingham Snow Hill a.	0920	0952	hour until	1752	1820	1843	1911	1946	2020	2120	2220	2322	0010		1017	1117	1217	1317	1417	1517	1617	1717	1817	1917

		Ⓐ	Ⓐ	Ⓐ	Ⓐ	Ⓐ	Ⓐ	Ⓐ		Ⓐ	Ⓐ	Ⓐ	Ⓐ	Ⓐ	Ⓐ	Ⓐ	Ⓐ	Ⓐ	Ⓐ	Ⓐ	Ⓐ		⑥	⑥
Birmingham Snow Hill d.	Ⓐ	0553	0630	0640	0725	0828	0858	0928	and at the same	1458	1528	1628	1703	1728	1747	1758	1828	1928	2028	2128	2228	⑥	0725	0828
Birmingham Moor Str d.		0556	0633	0643	0728	0831	0901	0931	minutes	1501	1531	1631	1706	1731	1750	1801	1831	1931	2031	2131	2231		0728	0831
Henley in Arden d.		|	0705	0720	0806	0906	|	1006	past each	|	1606	1707	1736	1807	1828	|	1907	2007	2107	2207	2307		0806	0906
Stratford upon Avon a.		0648	0720	0736	0823	0923	0949	1023	hour until	1541	1623	1724	1749	1824	1843	1859	1923	2023	2123	2223	2323		0821	0923

	⑥	⑥	⑥		⑥	⑥	⑥	⑥	⑥	⑥	⑥	⑥	⑥			⑦	⑦	⑦	⑦	⑦	⑦	⑦	⑦	⑦
Birmingham Snow Hill d.	0928	0958	1028	and at the same	1628	1658	1707	1747	1828	1928	2028	2128	2228	...	⑦	0927	1026	1127	1227	1327	1427	1527	1627	1727
Birmingham Moor Str d.	0931	1001	1031	minutes	1631	1701	1710	1750	1831	1931	2031	2131	2231	...		0930	1029	1130	1230	1330	1430	1530	1630	1730
Henley in Arden d.	1006	|	1106	past each	1706	|	1748	1828	1906	2007	2107	2207	2307	...		1001	1101	1201	1301	1401	1501	1601	1701	1801
Stratford upon Avon a.	1023	1041	1123	hour until	1723	1741	1803	1843	1923	2023	2123	2223	2323	...		1015	1115	1215	1315	1415	1515	1615	1715	1815

🚂 – THE SHAKESPEARE EXPRESS – 🚃12, ✕ (1st class only) and 🍸 Birmingham Snow Hill - Stratford upon Avon and v.v. Runs ⑦ July 17 - Sept. 4, 2016. National Rail tickets NOT valid. From Birmingham Snow Hill 1023 and 1356 (Birmingham Moor Street 5 minutes later). From Stratford upon Avon at 1023 and 1356. Journey time: 59–74 minutes. To book contact Vintage Trains Ltd. ✆ 0121 708 4960. www.shakespeareexpress.com.

2nd class

LONDON - OXFORD, STRATFORD UPON AVON and BIRMINGHAM 128

LONDON - BIRMINGHAM

		Ⓐ	Ⓐ	Ⓐ	Ⓐ	Ⓐ	Ⓐ	Ⓐ	Ⓐ	Ⓐ	Ⓐ	Ⓐ	Ⓐ	Ⓐ	Ⓐ	Ⓐ	Ⓐ	Ⓐ	Ⓐ	Ⓐ	Ⓐ	Ⓐ
London Marylebone ◇ d.	Ⓐ	...	0605	0711	0748	0814	0841	0911	0940	1010	1040	1110	1140	1210	1240	1310	1340	1410	1440	1510	1540	1615
High Wycombe ◇ d.			|	|	0814	|	|	0936	|	1036	|	1134	|	1234	|	1334	|	1433	|	1534	|	|
Bicester North ◇ d.		0546	0647	0754	0836	|	0932	|	1028	|	1131	|	1227	|	1327	|	1427	|	1527	|	1627	|
Banbury ◇ d.		0604	0703	0807	0850	0908	0946	1008	1042	1107	1145	1210	1240	1307	1340	1410	1440	1507	1540	1609	1640	1708
Leamington Spa d.		0624	0721	0825	0907	0926	1004	1025	1100	1125	1204	1227	1258	1325	1358	1427	1458	1525	1558	1626	1658	1726
Warwick d.		0629	0726	0829	0912	0930	1009	|	1105	|	1209	|	1302	|	1402	|	1502	|	1602	|	1702	|
Warwick Parkway d.		0632	0729	0833	0915	0934	1013	1032	1109	1132	1213	1233	1306	1332	1406	1433	1506	1530	1606	1632	1706	1732
Solihull a.		0648	0750	0844	0930	0945	1030	1044	1124	1144	1230	1244	1321	1344	1421	1444	1521	1544	1621	1643	1721	1744
Birmingham Moor Street a.		0658	0802	0853	0942	0954	1044	1053	1133	1159	1241	1259	1333	1359	1433	1459	1533	1559	1633	1653	1736	1754
Birmingham Snow Hill a.		0706	0810	0901	...	1002	...	1101	1142	...	1248	...	1341	...	1441	...	1541	...	1641	1701	1744	1757

	Ⓐ	Ⓐ	Ⓐ	Ⓐ	Ⓐ	Ⓐ	Ⓐ	Ⓐ	Ⓐ	Ⓐ	Ⓐ	Ⓐ	Ⓐ	Ⓐ	Ⓐ		⑥	⑥	⑥	⑥	⑥	⑥	⑥
London Marylebone ◇ d.	1621	1647	1715	1747	1815	1847	1915	1947	2010	2040	2110	2140	2210	2237	2307	⑥	...	0700	0810	0840	0910	0940	1010
High Wycombe ◇ d.	1646	|	|	|	|	|	|	|	2034	2105	2134	2204	2235	2302	|		0612	0724	0834	|	0934	|	1034
Bicester North ◇ d.	1710	1734	|	1835	|	1936	2003	2032	2058	2126	2157	2228	2259	2327	2350		0645	0751	0857	0926	|	1024	|
Banbury ◇ d.	1723	1747	1807	1848	1910	1951	2016	2045	2112	2139	2214	2241	2313	2341	0003		0703	0804	0910	0940	1007	1037	1107
Leamington Spa d.	1740	1804	1826	1905	1928	2009	2035	2103	2130	2157	2231	2259	2331	2359	0021		0721	0823	0928	0958	1025	1055	1125
Warwick d.	1744	1808	|	1909	|	2013	|	2107	|	2201	|	2303	|	0003	0025		0725	|	0932	1002	|	1059	|
Warwick Parkway d.	1748	1812	1832	1913	1934	2017	2043	2110	2136	2205	2238	2307	2337	0007	0029		0729	0829	0935	1006	1031	1103	1132
Solihull a.	1803	1826	1845	1928	1950	2032	2058	2132	2148	2220	2250	2330	2348	0023	0040		0747	0846	0950	1021	1043	1120	1144
Birmingham Moor Street a.	1812	1841	1855	1938	2000	2041	2113	2142	2158	2230	2259	2339	0004	0039	0055		0803	0859	1001	1033	1058	1133	1159
Birmingham Snow Hill a.	1822	...	1858	1946	2004	2049	...	2150	2206	2238	2302	2347	...	...	...		...	0907	1009	1041	...	1141	...

	⑥	⑥	⑥	⑥	⑥	⑥	⑥	⑥	⑥	⑥	⑥	⑥	⑥	⑥	⑥	⑥	⑥	⑥	⑥	⑥	⑥	⑥	⑥
London Marylebone ◇ d.	1040	1110	1140	1210	1240	1310	1340	1410	1440	1510	1540	1610	1640	1710	1740	1810	1840	1910	1940	2010	2040	2110	2210
High Wycombe ◇ d.	|	1134	|	1234	|	1334	|	1434	|	1534	|	1634	|	1734	|	1834	|	1934	|	2034	|	2134	2234
Bicester North ◇ d.	1127	|	1224	|	1324	|	1424	|	1524	|	1624	|	1724	|	1824	|	1924	|	2024	|	2124	2157	2257
Banbury ◇ d.	1143	1210	1237	1307	1337	1409	1437	1507	1537	1609	1637	1707	1737	1809	1837	1907	1937	2009	2037	2107	2137	2210	2310
Leamington Spa d.	1201	1227	1255	1325	1355	1426	1455	1525	1555	1626	1655	1725	1755	1826	1855	1926	1955	2027	2055	2125	2155	2228	2328
Warwick d.	1205	|	1259	|	1359	|	1459	|	1559	|	1659	|	1759	|	1859	|	1959	|	2059	|	2159	2232	2332
Warwick Parkway d.	1209	1234	1303	1332	1403	1433	1503	1532	1603	1633	1703	1732	1803	1833	1903	1933	2003	2033	2103	2132	2203	2236	2337
Solihull a.	1224	1245	1320	1344	1420	1444	1520	1544	1620	1644	1720	1744	1820	1847	1918	1946	2018	2045	2118	2144	2218	2256	2354
Birmingham Moor Street a.	1233	1259	1333	1359	1433	1459	1533	1559	1633	1659	1733	1759	1833	1858	1927	1958	2027	2100	2127	2200	2227	2306	0009
Birmingham Snow Hill a.	1241	...	1341	...	1441	...	1541	...	1641	...	1741	...	1841	1907	1935	2007	2035	...	2135	...	2235	2314	...

		⑦	⑦	⑦	⑦	⑦	⑦	⑦	⑦	⑦		⑦	⑦	⑦	⑦	⑦		⑦	⑦	⑦	⑦	⑦
London Marylebone ◇ d.	⑦	0815	0910	0940	1010	1040	1110	1140	1210	1240		1710	1740	1810	1840	1910	...	1940	2010	2040	2110	2208
High Wycombe ◇ d.		0845	0934	|	1034	|	1134	|	1234	|	and at	1734	|	1834	|	1934	...	|	2034	|	2134	2234
Bicester North ◇ d.		0910	|	1024	|	1124	|	1224	|	1326	the	|	1826	|	1926	|	...	2026	|	2126	|	2256
Banbury ◇ d.		0929	1007	1037	1107	1137	1207	1237	1307	1339	same	1807	1839	1907	1939	2007	...	2039	2107	2139	2207	2309
Leamington Spa d.		0947	1025	1055	1125	1155	1225	1255	1325	1357	minutes	1825	1857	1925	1957	2025	...	2057	2125	2157	2225	2327
Warwick d.		0951	|	1059	|	1159	|	1259	|	1401	past	|	1901	|	2001	|	...	2101	|	2201	2229	2331
Warwick Parkway d.		0955	1032	1103	1132	1203	1232	1303	1332	1405	each	1832	1905	1932	2005	2032	...	2105	2132	2205	2234	2334
Solihull a.		1016	1044	1118	1144	1218	1244	1320	1344	1420	hour	1844	1920	1943	2020	2044	...	2128	2144	2220	2257	2349
Birmingham Moor Street a.		1024	1053	1127	1159	1227	1259	1329	1359	1429	until	1859	1929	1959	2029	2059	...	2137	2159	2229	2306	2358
Birmingham Snow Hill a.		1032	1101	1135	...	1235	...	1337	...	1437		...	1937	...	2037	...	...	2145	...	2237	2314	0007

		Ⓐ	Ⓐ	Ⓐ	Ⓐ	Ⓐ	Ⓐ	Ⓐ	Ⓐ	Ⓐ	Ⓐ	Ⓐ	Ⓐ	Ⓐ	Ⓐ	Ⓐ		Ⓐ	Ⓐ	Ⓐ	Ⓐ	Ⓐ	Ⓐ
Birmingham Snow Hill d.	Ⓐ	...	...	...	...	0650	0707	0750	0807	0822	0852	0912	...	1012	...	1112	...	...	1212	...	1312	...	1412
Birmingham Moor Street d.		0515	0542	0610	0628	0655	0711	0755	0810	0825	0855	0915	0955	1015	1055	1115	...	1155	1215	1255	1315	1355	1415
Solihull d.		0524	0551	0619	0638	0704	0720	0804	0819	0837	0907	0924	1004	1024	1104	1124	...	1204	1224	1304	1324	1404	1424
Warwick Parkway d.		0536	0605	0634	0659	0718	0737	0816	0834	0902	0919	0939	1016	1039	1116	1139	...	1216	1239	1316	1339	1416	1439
Warwick d.		|	0608	|	0702	|	|	|	0837	0906	|	0942	|	1042	|	1142	...	|	1242	|	1342	|	1442
Leamington Spa d.		0541	0613	0641	0706	0724	0744	0822	0842	0912	0925	0946	1022	1046	1123	1146	...	1222	1246	1322	1346	1422	1446
Banbury ◇ d.		0559	0631	0659	0724	|	0803	0840	0900	0930	0944	1005	1040	1104	1140	1204	...	1240	1304	1340	1404	1440	1504
Bicester North ◇ d.		0612	0646	0711	0739	|	0816	|	0913	0942	|	1018	|	1116	|	1216	...	|	1316	|	1416	|	1516
High Wycombe ◇ d.		|	|	|	|	|	0836	|	|	1007	|	|	1110	|	1210	|	...	1310	|	1410	|	1510	|
London Marylebone ◇ a.		0703	0735	0802	0833	0834	0906	0938	0959	1036	1040	1108	1140	1208	1239	1308	...	1341	1408	1441	1508	1538	1608

	Ⓐ	Ⓐ	Ⓐ	Ⓐ	Ⓐ	Ⓐ	Ⓐ	Ⓐ	Ⓐ	Ⓐ	Ⓐ	Ⓐ			⑥	⑥	⑥	⑥	⑥	⑥	⑥	⑥	⑥
Birmingham Snow Hill d.	...	1512	...	1612	1652	1707	1752	1812	1840	1914	2015	2115	...	⑥	0612	0646	0712	0751	...	0853	0912	0951	1012
Birmingham Moor Street d.	1455	1515	1555	1615	1655	1710	1755	1815	1843	1917	2018	2118	...		0615	0649	0715	0755	0815	0856	0915	0955	1015
Solihull d.	1504	1524	1604	1624	1704	1719	1806	1824	1852	1926	2027	2127	...		0624	0702	0724	0805	0824	0905	0924	1004	1024
Warwick Parkway d.	1516	1539	1616	1639	1716	1736	1822	1845	1907	1946	2042	2147	...		0644	0714	0739	0818	0839	0916	0939	1018	1039
Warwick d.	|	1542	|	1642	1719	1739	|	1848	|	1949	2045	2150	...		0647	|	0742	|	0842	|	0942	|	1042
Leamington Spa d.	1522	1546	1622	1646	1723	1743	1828	1853	1912	1954	2050	2155	...		0652	0720	0746	0824	0846	0922	0946	1024	1046
Banbury ◇ d.	1540	1604	1640	1704	1741	1801	1845	1912	1930	2012	2113	2213	...		0710	0739	0804	0844	0904	0940	1004	1043	1104
Bicester North ◇ d.	|	1616	|	1716	|	1814	1857	1928	1946	2025	2125	2225	...		0722	0751	0816	|	0916	|	1016	|	1116
High Wycombe ◇ d.	1610	|	1710	|	1811	1838	|	|	2013	|	2145	2245	...		0746	0811	|	0914	|	1014	|	1118	|
London Marylebone ◇ a.	1642	1711	1742	1813	1840	1911	1944	2023	2043	2112	2212	2312	...		0813	0840	0910	0941	1010	1041	1110	1146	1211

	⑥	⑥	⑥	⑥	⑥	⑥	⑥	⑥	⑥	⑥	⑥	⑥	⑥	⑥	⑥	⑥	⑥	⑥	⑥	⑥	⑥	⑥	⑥
Birmingham Snow Hill d.	...	1112	...	1212	...	...	1312	...	1412	...	1512	...	1612	...	1712	...	1812	...	1912	...	2012	...	2115
Birmingham Moor Street d.	1055	1115	1155	1215	1255	...	1315	1355	1415	1455	1515	1555	1615	1655	1715	1755	1815	1855	1915	1955	2015	2045	2118
Solihull d.	1104	1124	1204	1224	1304	...	1324	1404	1424	1504	1524	1604	1624	1704	1724	1804	1824	1904	1924	2004	2024	2055	2127
Warwick Parkway d.	1116	1139	1220	1239	1316	...	1339	1416	1439	1516	1539	1616	1639	1716	1739	1816	1839	1916	1939	2016	2039	2113	2149
Warwick d.	|	1142	|	1242	|	...	1342	|	1442	|	1542	|	1642	|	1742	|	1842	|	1942	|	2042	2117	2152
Leamington Spa d.	1121	1146	1226	1246	1322	...	1346	1422	1446	1522	1546	1622	1646	1722	1746	1822	1846	1922	1946	2022	2046	2122	2157
Banbury ◇ d.	1139	1204	1244	1304	1340	...	1407	1440	1504	1540	1604	1640	1704	1740	1804	1840	1904	1940	2004	2040	2104	2140	2215
Bicester North ◇ d.	|	1216	|	1316	|	...	1420	|	1516	|	1616	|	1716	|	1816	|	1916	|	2016	|	2116	2152	2230
High Wycombe ◇ d.	1214	|	1314	|	1414	...	|	1514	|	1614	|	1714	|	1814	|	1914	|	2014	|	2114	|	2214	2259
London Marylebone ◇ a.	1241	1310	1341	1411	1441	...	1510	1541	1610	1646	1710	1741	1810	1841	1910	1941	2010	2041	2110	2141	2210	2241	2330

		⑦	⑦		⑦	⑦	⑦	⑦	⑦	⑦	⑦	⑦		⑦	⑦	⑦		⑦	⑦	⑦	⑦	⑦
Birmingham Snow Hill d.	⑦	...	...	...	0912	...	1012	...	1112	...	1212	...		1712	...	1812	...	...	1912	...	2012	2115
Birmingham Moor Street d.		0825	0855	...	0915	0955	1015	1055	1115	1155	1215	1255	and at	1715	1755	1815	...	1855	1915	1939	2015	2118
Solihull d.		0834	0904	...	0924	1004	1024	1104	1124	1204	1224	1304	the	1724	1804	1824	...	1904	1924	1948	2024	2127
Warwick Parkway d.		0849	0916	...	0939	1016	1039	1116	1139	1216	1239	1316	same	1739	1816	1839	...	1916	1939	|	2039	2144
Warwick d.		0852	|	...	0942	|	1042	|	1142	|	1242	|	minutes	1742	|	1842	...	|	1942	2011	2042	2147
Leamington Spa d.		0858	0922	...	0946	1022	1046	1122	1146	1222	1246	1322	past	1746	1822	1846	...	1922	1946	2017	2046	2152
Banbury ◇ d.		0916	0940	...	1004	1040	1104	1140	1204	1240	1304	1340	each	1804	1840	1904	...	1941	2004	2036	2104	2215
Bicester North ◇ d.		0929	|	...	1016	|	1116	|	1216	|	1316	|	hour	1816	|	1916	...	1953	2016	2052	2116	2230
High Wycombe ◇ d.		|	1012	...	|	1114	|	1212	|	1313	|	1412	until	|	1912	|	...	2016	|	2116	|	2302
London Marylebone ◇ a.		1018	1041	...	1108	1142	1210	1240	1308	1340	1410	1440		1910	1940	2010	...	2042	2108	2153	2209	2347

Frequent additional services are available between these stations.

128 LONDON - OXFORD, STRATFORD UPON AVON and BIRMINGHAM 2nd class

LONDON - STRATFORD UPON AVON

km		Ⓐ	Ⓐ	Ⓐ	Ⓐ	Ⓐ	Ⓐ		Ⓐ	Ⓐ	Ⓐ	Ⓐ	⑥	⑥	⑥	⑥	⑥	⑥	⑥	⑥	⑦	⑦	⑦	⑦		⑦	
0	London Marylebone .. d.		...	0618	*0814*	*1010*	*1210*	...	*1410*	*1621*	1824	2043		*0700*	*1010*	*1210*	*1410*	*1610*	*1810*	*2010*		0943	*1210*	*1410*	...	*1610*	1
45	High Wycombe .... d.		...	0701	|	*1036*	*1234*	...	*1433*	*1646*	1900	2114		*0724*	*1034*	*1234*	*1434*	*1634*	*1834*	*2034*		1018	*1234*	*1434*	...	*1634*	1
88	Bicester North .... d.		0546	0733	|	|	|	...	|	*1710*	1941	2143		*0751*	|	|	|	|	|	|		1047	|	|	...	|	
111	Banbury .... d.		*0604*	0749	*0908*	*1107*	*1307*	...	*1507*	*1723*	2006	2201		*0804*	*1107*	*1307*	*1507*	*1707*	*1907*	*2107*		1111	*1307*	*1507*	...	*1707*	1
143	Leamington Spa .... a.		*0623*	0808	*0925*	*1124*	*1324*	...	*1524*	*1740*	2025	2219		*0822*	*1124*	*1324*	*1524*	*1724*	*1924*	*2124*		1130	*1324*	*1524*	...	*1724*	1
	Leamington Spa .... d.		0653	0808	0940	1132	1332	...	1532	1811	2026	2220		0830	1132	1332	1532	1732	1932	2132		1132	1332	1532	...	1732	1
146	Warwick .... d.		0658	0813	0945	1137	1337	...	1537	1816	|	2224		0834	1138	1337	1537	1737	1937	2137		1138	1337	1537	...	1737	1
167	**Stratford upon Avon** . a.		0728	0846	1014	1203	1407	...	1607	1851	2054	2255		0912	1205	1409	1608	1815	2010	2210		1207	1406	1606	...	1806	2

	Ⓐ	Ⓐ	Ⓐ	Ⓐ	Ⓐ	Ⓐ	Ⓐ	Ⓐ	Ⓐ	Ⓐ	Ⓐ	⑥	⑥	⑥	⑥	⑥	⑥	⑥	⑥	⑥	⑦	⑦	⑦	⑦	⑦	⑦	
Stratford upon Avon...d.		0606	0733	0900	1037	1240	1437	1736	*1912*h	2139	2315		0756	1040	1242	1442	1641	1841	2042	2215		0938	1246	1446	1646	1846	2
Warwick.......................d.		0640	0803	0927	1104	1304	1505	1803	1949	2206	2334		0824	1108	1309	1509	1709	1909	2109	2235		1001	1311	1511	1711	1911	2
Leamington Spa..........a.		0645	0807	0934	1111	1311	1515	1807	1953	2210	2338		0828	1115	1316	1516	1716	1916	2115	2240		1005	1317	1517	1717	1917	2
Leamington Spa..........d.		*0706*	0808	*0946*	*1123*	*1322*	*1546*	1808	1954	2210	2339		0829	*1146*	*1346*	*1546*	*1746*	*1946*	*2157*	2241		1006	*1346*	*1546*	*1746*	*1946*	2
Banbury........................d.		*0724*	0826	*1005*	*1140*	*1340*	*1604*	1827	2012	2230	2357		0848	*1204*	*1407*	*1604*	*1804*	*2004*	*2215*	2302		1024	*1404*	*1604*	*1804*	*2004*	2
Bicester North.............d.		*0739*	0841	*1018*	|	|	*1616*	1843	2025	2246	...		0903	*1216*	*1420*	*1616*	*1816*	*2016*	*2230*	...		1036	*1416*	*1616*	*1816*	*2016*	2
High Wycombe ....d.		|	0905	|	*1210*	*1410*	|	|	|	2317	...		0930	|	|	|	|	|	*2259*	...		1103	|	|	|	|	2
London Marylebone ...a.		*0833*	0935	*1108*	*1239*	*1441*	*1711*	1941	2112	2358	...		1005	*1310*	*1510*	*1710*	*1910*	*2110*	*2330*	...		1139	*1510*	*1710*	*1910*	*2108*	2

LONDON - OXFORD

km		Ⓐ	Ⓐ	Ⓐ	Ⓐ	Ⓐ	Ⓐ	Ⓐ	Ⓐ	Ⓐ	Ⓐ	Ⓐ	Ⓐ	Ⓐ		Ⓐ	Ⓐ	Ⓐ	Ⓐ	Ⓐ	Ⓐ	Ⓐ	Ⓐ	
0	London Marylebone . d.		0609	0648	0715	0740	0808	0837	0907	0935	1005	1035	1105	1135	and at	1435	1505	1535	1618	1650	1718	1750	1818	1
45	High Wycombe.......... d.		0640	0713	0738	0804	0833	0903	|	1002	|	1100	|	1200	the same	|	1530	1559	|	1715	|	1816	|	1
90	Bicester Village .... d.		0708	0745	0802	0832	0856	0924	0956	1032	1053	1132	1154	1223	minutes past	1526	1556	1621	1706	1740	1805	1841	1908	1
103	**Oxford** Parkway .... a.		0720	0755	0812	0840	0905	0933	1003	1040	1101	1140	1203	1232	each hour until ♠	1535	1605	1631	1715	1749	1812	1852	1917	1

	Ⓐ	Ⓐ	Ⓐ	Ⓐ	Ⓐ		Ⓐ	Ⓐ	Ⓐ	Ⓐ	⑥	⑥	⑥	⑥	⑥	⑥	⑥	⑥	⑥	⑥	⑥		⑥	
London Marylebone .. d.	1950	1950	2007	2037	2107	...	2135	2207	2240	2310		0557	0625	0705	0735	0805	0835	0905	0935	1005	1035	and at	1905	1
High Wycombe .... d.	2014	2014	|	|	|	...	2159	|	2309	2337		0627	0652	0729	0759	|	0859	|	0959	|	1059	the same	|	1
Bicester Village......... d.	2039	2039	2055	2124	2154	...	2222	2256	2335	0006		0656	0724	0757	0827	0854	0922	0954	1022	1054	1125	minutes past	1954	2
Oxford Parkway .... a.	2049	2049	2106	2135	2205	...	2235	2306	2343	0017		0707	0737	0808	0840	0906	0935	1005	1033	1105	1136	each hour until ♠	2005	2

		⑥	⑥	⑥		⑥	⑥	⑥	⑥		⑦	⑦		⑦	⑦	⑦		⑦	⑦	⑦	⑦		⑦	
London Marylebone .. d.	...	2005	2035	2105	...	2135	2205	2235	2310	...		0735	...	0835	0905	0935	and at	2005	2035	2105	2135	...	2215	2
High Wycombe .... d.	...	|	2059	|	...	2159	|	2306	2336	...		0806	...	0859	|	0959	the same	|	2059	|	2159	...	|	2
Bicester Village......... d.	...	2054	2122	2154	...	2222	2254	2331	2359	...		0837	...	0922	0953	1022	minutes past	2053	2122	2153	2222	...	2309	0
Oxford Parkway .... a.	...	2105	2135	2205	...	2233	2305	2342	0013	...		0849	...	0933	1004	1035	each hour until ♠	2104	2133	2204	2235	...	2320	0

	Ⓐ	Ⓐ	Ⓐ	Ⓐ	Ⓐ	Ⓐ	Ⓐ		Ⓐ	Ⓐ	Ⓐ	Ⓐ	Ⓐ	Ⓐ	Ⓐ	Ⓐ	Ⓐ	Ⓐ	Ⓐ	Ⓐ		Ⓐ	Ⓐ	
Oxford Parkway .... d.		0542	0612	0631	0647	0724	0753	...	0808	0827	0850	0922	0947	0953	1017	1047	1117	1147	1217	1247	and at	1617	1645	17
Bicester Village......... d.		0552	0621	0640	0656	0734	0802	...	0820	0836	0859	0931	0957	1002	1026	1056	1126	1156	1226	1256	the same	1626	1656	1
High Wycombe .... d.		0625	0644	|	0726	|	0830	...	0850	|	0927	0956	|	1030	1051	|	1151	|	1251	|	minutes past	1651	|	1
London Marylebone .. a.		0700	0723	0730	0757	0820	0856	...	0927	0930	0956	1027	1043	1105	1118	1146	1218	1246	1318	1346	each hour until ♠	1721	1744	1

	Ⓐ	Ⓐ	Ⓐ	Ⓐ	Ⓐ	Ⓐ	Ⓐ	Ⓐ	Ⓐ	Ⓐ	Ⓐ	Ⓐ	⑥	⑥	⑥	⑥	⑥	⑥	⑥	⑥	⑥		⑥	
Oxford Parkway .... d.	1809	1829	1909	1929	2008	2031	2101	2121	2143	2221	2245	2321		0618	0644	0715	0745	0817	0848	0915	0948	and at	1917	1
Bicester Village......... d.	1822	1838	1918	1939	2019	2040	2110	2130	2155	2230	2256	2330		0628	0653	0726	0755	0826	0857	0926	0957	the same	1926	1
High Wycombe .... d.	|	1906	|	2007	|	2110	2139	|	2221	2300	2324	0004		0656	|	0754	|	0851	|	0951	|	minutes past	1951	
London Marylebone .. a.	1912	1933	2015	2037	2107	2138	2206	2218	2253	2336	0011	...		0727	0740	0828	0854	0918	0946	1018	1047	each hour until ♠	2018	2

	⑥	⑥	⑥		⑥	⑥	⑦	⑦	⑦		⑦	⑦	⑦	⑦	⑦		⑦	⑦	⑦	⑦	⑦		⑦	
Oxford Parkway .... d.	2017	2048	2115	...	2148	2215		0749	0813	...	0844	0904	0948	1017	1048	and at	1817	1847	1915	1947	2017	...	2115	2
Bicester Village......... d.	2026	2057	2126	...	2157	2226		0758	0822	...	0853	0915	0957	1026	1057	the same	1826	1856	1926	1956	2026	...	2126	2
High Wycombe .... d.	2051	|	2151	...	2222	2251		0823	0850	...	|	0944	|	1051	|	minutes past	1851	|	1951	|	2051	...	2151	2
London Marylebone .. a.	2118	2147	2218	...	2249	2327		0851	0925	...	0942	1011	1045	1118	1145	each hour until ♠	1918	1943	2017	2047	2117	...	2217	2

h – Change at **Hatton** (a. 1936 / d. 1941).

♠ – Timings may vary by up to 5 minutes.

129 LONDON - AYLESBURY 2nd class

km		Ⓐ	Ⓐ	Ⓐ	Ⓐ	Ⓐ	Ⓐ	Ⓐ	Ⓐ	Ⓐ	Ⓐ	Ⓐ	Ⓐ	Ⓐ	Ⓐ	Ⓐ	Ⓐ	Ⓐ	Ⓐ	Ⓐ	Ⓐ	Ⓐ	Ⓐ	Ⓐ	
0	**London** Marylebone .... △ d.		0633	0652	0757	0857	0957	1057	1157	1257	1357	1457	1527	1612	1642	1730	1759	1832	1859	1932	1956	2057	2157	2257	2
38	Amersham .... △ d.		0708	0727	0832	0932	1032	1132	1232	1332	1432	1532	1602	1647	1717	|	1829	|	1934	2008	2031	2132	2232	2332	0
60	**Aylesbury** .... △ d.		0730	0754	0854	0954	1054	1154	1254	1354	1454	1554	1626	1709	1739	1824	1855	1924	2003	2030	2053	2154	2254	2354	0
65	**Aylesbury** Vale Parkway .....a.		0739	0802	0903	1003	1103	1203	1303	1403	1503	1603	1634	1718	1748	1832	1904	1936	2011	2039	2102	2203	2303	0003	0

	⑥	⑥	⑥	⑥	⑥		⑥	⑥	⑥	⑥	⑦	⑦	⑦	⑦	⑦	⑦		⑦	⑦	⑦	⑦
London Marylebone........△ d.		...	0727	0757	0857	0957	and at	2057	2157	2227	2257		0757	0857	0957	1057	1157	and at	1957	2057	2157	2227
Amersham.......................△ d.		0702	0802	0832	0932	1032	the same	2132	2232	2302	2332		0832	0932	1032	1132	1232	the same	2032	2132	2232	2302
Aylesbury........................△ d.		0726	0824	0854	0954	1054	minutes	2154	2254	2324	2354		0854	0954	1054	1154	1254	minutes	2054	2154	2254	2324
Aylesbury Vale Parkway ..... a.		...	0833	0903	1003	1103	past each hour until	2203	2303	2333	0003		0903	1003	1103	1203	1303	past each hour until	2103	2203	2303	2333

	Ⓐ	Ⓐ	Ⓐ	Ⓐ	Ⓐ	Ⓐ	Ⓐ	Ⓐ	Ⓐ	Ⓐ	Ⓐ	Ⓐ	Ⓐ	Ⓐ	Ⓐ	Ⓐ	Ⓐ	Ⓐ	Ⓐ	Ⓐ	Ⓐ	Ⓐ	Ⓐ	Ⓐ	
Aylesbury Vale Parkway..... d.		0513	0541	0616	0650	0722	0749	0809	0836	0915	1010	1110	1210	1310	1410	1510	1610	1640	1734	1813	1839	1910	1940	2045	2
Aylesbury........................▽ d.		0518	0546	0621	0655	0727	0759	0814	0841	0920	1015	1115	1215	1315	1415	1515	1615	1645	1747	1818	1844	1915	1945	2050	2
Amersham.......................▽ d.		0540	0608	0644	0718	0750	0822	0836	0902	0941	1036	1136	1236	1336	1436	1536	1636	1706	1808	1839	1905	1936	2006	2111	2
London Marylebone........▽ a.		0616	0649	0722	0753	0826	0900	0916	0944	1023	1120	1220	1320	1420	1520	1620	1720	1748	1850	1918	1948	2020	2049	2152	2

	⑥	⑥	⑥	⑥	⑥		⑥	⑥	⑥	⑥	⑥	⑦	⑦	⑦	⑦	⑦	⑦		⑦	⑦	⑦	⑦	
Aylesbury Vale Parkway..... d.		0610	0710	0810	0910	and at	1910	2010	2110	2210			0710	0810	0910	1010	1110	and at	1810	1910	2010	2110	2
Aylesbury........................▽ d.		0615	0715	0815	0915	the same	1915	2015	2115	2215	2315		0715	0815	0915	1015	1115	the same	1815	1915	2015	2115	2
Amersham.......................▽ d.		0636	0736	0836	0936	minutes	1936	2036	2136	2236	2342		0736	0836	0936	1036	1136	minutes	1836	1936	2036	2136	2
London Marylebone........▽ a.		0720	0820	0920	1020	past each hour until	2020	2120	2220	2320			0820	0920	1020	1120	1220	past each hour until	1920	2020	2120	2220	

△ – Additional trains London Marylebone - Aylesbury on Ⓐ at 0727 and hourly until 1427, 1557, 1627, 1711, 1742, 1812, 1843, 1918, 2023, 2127, 2227, 2327; on ⑥ at 0827 and hourly until 2127, 2327, 2357; on ⑦ at 1527 and hourly until 2127, 2327.

▽ – Additional trains Aylesbury - London Marylebone on Ⓐ at 0604, 0635, 0709, 0738, 0859, 0945 and hourly until 1545, 1712, 2018, 2145, 2245; on ⑥ at 0645 and hourly until 2145; on ⑦ at 0845, 0945, 1445 and hourly until 2245.

LONDON - WORCESTER - HEREFORD — 130

Most trains convey 🍸

Other services: London Paddington - Oxford see Table **131**; Worcester - Hereford see Table **125**.

		Ⓐ	Ⓐ	Ⓐ	Ⓐ	Ⓐ	Ⓐ	Ⓐ	Ⓐ	Ⓐ	Ⓐ	Ⓐ	Ⓐ	Ⓐ	Ⓐ	Ⓐ	Ⓐ	Ⓐ	Ⓐ	Ⓐ	Ⓐ	Ⓐ	⑤		⑥	⑥
London Paddington .. d.	Ⓐ	...	0512	0545	0652	...	0821	0921	1022	1120	1220	1322	1421	1522	1552	1622	1722	1749	1822	1922	2022	2148	2318	⑥	0517	0621
Reading .... d.		...	0550	0619	0722	...	0853	0953	1052	1153	1251	1352	1453	1552	|	1652u	1750	1822	1851	1952	2053	2225	0005		0554	0654
Oxford .... d.		0514	0621	0649	0801	0858	0924	1019	1119	1220	1321	1418	1520	1621	1646	1725	1817	1850	1923	2021	2121	2253	0036		0623	0723
Moreton in Marsh ...... d.		0542	0648	0726	0839	0936	0959	1055	1156	1256	1358	1456	1555	1656	1725	1812	1855	1929	2002	2059	2157	2334	0115		0700	0757
Evesham .... a.		0559	...	0743	0856	...	1018	1109	1216	1313	1416	1511	1612	1715	...	1831	1915	1945	2021	2118	2217	2353	...		0720	0816
Evesham .... d.		0559	...	0751	0857	...	1025	1110	1224	1317	1428	1511	1621	1717	...	1838	1915	1946	2022	2122	2218	2354	...		0724	0821
Worcester Shrub Hill a.		0619	...	0810	0915	...	1044	1128	1243	1336	1447	1525	1640	1736	...	1857	1935	2005	2041	2147	2240	0013	...		0743	0840
Worcester F'gate St.. a.		0625	...	0816	0919	...	1050	1134	1248	1340	...	1540	1644	1744	...	1911	1939	...	2044	2151	2244	...	...		0748	0844
Great Malvern .... a.		...	...	...	0932	...	1107	...	1302	1356	...	...	...	1758	...	1926	1953	...	2059	2207	2301	...	...		0802	0901
Ledbury .... a.		...	...	...	...	...	1120	...	1323	...	...	...	...	...	...	...	2008	...	2114	2235	...	...	...		...	...
Hereford .... a.		...	...	...	...	...	1141	...	1347	...	...	...	...	...	...	...	2031	...	2136	2257	...	...	...		...	...

	⑥	⑥	⑥	⑥	⑥	⑥	⑥	⑥	⑥	⑥	⑥	⑥	⑥		⑦	⑦	⑦	⑦	⑦	⑦	⑦	⑦	⑦	⑦	⑦	⑦	⑦
n Paddington ... d.	0721	0821	0921	1021	1121	1321	1421	1521	1621	1721	1821	1950	2148	⑦	0803	0842	0935	1042	1242	1342	1442	1542	1642	1742	1842	1942	2142
g .... d.	0754	0853	0954	1054	1154	1354	1454	1554	1654	1754	1854	2022	2221		0845	0924	1016	1122	1322	1422	1521	1622	1725	1825	1925	2022	2222
d .... d.	0823	0924	1025	1123	1223	1425	1523	1623	1723	1823	1923	2049	2251		0917	0952	1052	1154	1352	1452	1556	1656	1756	1856	1956	2054	2254
n in Marsh .... d.	0857	1000	1059	1159	1300	1502	1557	1657	1803	1859	1959	2125	2328		0952	1025	1125	1230	1430	1526	1628	1728	1833	1933	2033	2131	2331
am .... a.	0916	1020	1118	1219	1318	1521	1616	1716	1823	1919	2019	2144	2345		1010	1041	1142	1248	1451	1544	1649	1744	1850	1954	2050	2150	2350
am .... d.	0921	1024	1131	1227	1323	1522	1621	1721	1824	1920	2023	2144	2346		1014	1045	1148	1250	1452	1545	1649	1744	1851	1955	2051	2151	2351
ster Shrub Hill .. a.	0940	1043	1150	1246	1342	1541	1640	1740	1844	1939	2043	2204	0008		1033	1059	1207	1310	1510	1604	1708	1803	1910	2014	2111	2210	0013
ster F'gate St ... a.	0944	1048	1156	1250	1344	1545	1644	1744	1856	1944	2049	2207	...		1036	1103	1210	1314	1514	1607	1711	1806	1913	2018	...	2214	...
Malvern .... a.	1000	1101	...	1305	1400	1600	1700	1801	1910	...	2102	2222	...		1054	1117	1222	1327	1528	...	1723	...	1925	2032	...	2227	...
y .... a.	...	1119	...	1321	...	...	...	...	1924	...	2116	...	...		...	1132	...	1342	1542	...	1736	...	...	2046	...	...	...
rd .... a.	...	1138	...	1339	...	...	...	...	1945	...	2135	...	...		...	1151	...	1407	1601	...	1753	...	...	2104	...	...	...

		Ⓐ	Ⓐ	Ⓐ	Ⓐ	Ⓐ	Ⓐ	Ⓐ	Ⓐ	Ⓐ	Ⓐ	Ⓐ	Ⓐ	Ⓐ	Ⓐ	Ⓐ	Ⓐ	Ⓐ	Ⓐ	Ⓐ	Ⓐ	Ⓐ	Ⓐ		⑥	⑥	⑥
ord .... d.	Ⓐ	...	0450	0528	...	...	0642	...	...	...	...	...	1209	...	...	...	1514	...	...	...	...	...	2151	⑥	...	0617	0710
ry .... d.		...	|	0545	...	...	0659	...	...	...	...	...	1224	...	...	...	1531	...	...	...	...	...	2209		...	0634	0730
Malvern .... d.		...	0517	0559	...	...	0712	...	...	0954	...	...	1236	1425	...	...	1545	...	...	1835	1944	...	2222		0556	0649	0744
ster F'gate St ... d.		...	0531	0614	...	0653	0728	0826	...	1007	...	1206	1256	1438	...	1550	1601	...	1728	1848	1956	2059	2234		0609	0704	0759
ster Shrub Hill .. d.		0511	0536	0619	...	0655	0732	0839	...	1010	1122	1208	1258	1442	1521	1554	1605	...	1731	1852	2004	2103	2243		0612	0708	0804
am .... a.		0525	0553	0635	...	0712	0749	0854	...	1026	1136	1224	1316	1458	1535	1607	1622	...	1746	1908	2019	2120	2300		0629	0725	0821
am .... d.		0527	0558	0637	...	0712	0750	0905	...	1030	1136	1232	1330	1502	1535	1608	1625	...	1747	1908	2019	2121	2301		0629	0726	0825
n in Marsh .... d.		0547	0614	0656	0710	0727	0811	0923	0950	1048	1152	1250	1349	1520	1552	1624	1645	1732	1805	1926	2047	2141	2326		0648	0745	0845
d .... a.		0626	0652	0731	0751	0812	0849	0959	1028	1127	1227	1325	1423	1555	1628	1653	1728	1801	1900	2000	2124	2227	2358		0725	0826	0925
g .... a.		0653	0725	0756	0822	...	0916	1024	1054	1154	1255	1354	1454	1624	1654	1726	1754	1825	1930	2024	2155	2253	0042		0754	0852	0952
n Paddington ... a.		0729	0801	0829	0851	...	0947	1057	1129	1227	1330	1428	1530	1659	1729	1759	1829	1859	2006	2059	2243a	2340	0122		0828	0927	1025

	⑥	⑥	⑥	⑥	⑥	⑥	⑥	⑥	⑥	⑥	⑥	⑥	⑥		⑦	⑦	⑦	⑦	⑦	⑦	⑦	⑦	⑦	⑦	⑦	⑦	⑦
ord .... d.	...	...	...	...	1213	...	1513	...	...	...	...	2020	...	⑦	...	...	...	...	1332	...	1432	...	1634	...	1830	...	...
ry .... d.	...	...	...	...	1231	...	1531	...	...	...	...	2040	...		...	...	...	...	1351	...	1452	...	1652	...	1848	...	...
Malvern .... d.	0843	0951	1058	...	1246	1434	1544	1634	1749	1835	...	2053	2241		0920	...	1115	1315	1407	...	1509	...	1705	...	1911	2015	...
ster F'gate St ... d.	0858	1004	1111	1206	1301	1457	1559	1655	1802	1849	2002	2111	2253		0932	1023	1128	1327	1422	...	1524	1628	1724	1826	1929	2028	...
ster Shrub Hill .. d.	0902	1008	1115	1210	1306	1501	1604	1702	1806	1902	2006	2115	2256		0935	1029	1131	1331	1429	...	1528	1632	1728	1830	1933	2031	2128
am .... a.	0919	1024	1131	1228	1323	1518	1620	1718	1823	1918	2023	2132	2314		0951	1045	1147	1347	1446	...	1546	1646	1747	1848	1948	2048	2145
am .... d.	0929	1030	1132	1230	1326	1526	1621	1726	1827	1927	2024	2133	...		0952	1049	1149	1349	1449	...	1549	1649	1749	1849	1949	2049	2149
n in Marsh .... d.	0948	1049	1150	1249	1345	1545	1641	1744	1845	1945	2043	2152	...		1011	1108	1208	1408	1508	...	1608	1708	1813	1908	2012	2108	2208
d .... a.	1028	1124	1226	1324	1426	1623	1723	1823	1924	2023	2126	2235	...		1049	1149	1249	1449	1549	...	1649	1752	1849	1953	2049	2148	2243
g .... a.	1054	1152	1255	1352	1452	1654	1754	1854	1953	2052	2156	2310	...		1125	1225	1325	1525	1620	...	1725	1823	1922	2026	2123	2220	2314
n Paddington ... a.	1128	1229	1330	1427	1527	1728	1829	1929	2027	2126	2229	2352	...		1206	1306	1406	1608	1708	...	1808	1908	2007	2109	2205	2301	0007

2236 on ⑤.

u – Calls to pick up only.

LONDON - OXFORD — 131

		②–⑤	Ⓐ	Ⓐ	Ⓐ	Ⓐ	Ⓐ	Ⓐ	Ⓐ	Ⓐ	Ⓐ	Ⓐ	Ⓐ	Ⓐ	Ⓐ	Ⓐ	Ⓐ	Ⓐ	Ⓐ	Ⓐ	Ⓐ	Ⓐ	Ⓐ	Ⓐ	Ⓐ
London P ◇ **130 132** d.	Ⓐ	0022	0512	0545	0620	0652	0721	0750	0821	0851	0921	0950	1022	1050	1120	1150	1220	1250	1322	1350	1421	1450	1522	1552	1622
Reading .... **130 132** d.		0101	0550	0619	0651	0722	0753	0822	0853	0922	0953	1020	1052	1119	1153	1220	1251	1320	1352	1420	1453	1522	1552	|	1652u
Didcot .... **130 132** d.		0119	0606	|	0708	0744	|	|	|	0938	|	|	|	1134	|	|	|	1338	|	|	|	1538	|	|	|
Oxford .... **130** a.		0134	0619	0648	0720	0758	0818	0848	0918	0952	1017	1047	1117	1149	1218	1248	1316	1350	1416	1447	1517	1550	1616	1644	1723

	Ⓐ	Ⓐ	Ⓐ	Ⓐ	Ⓐ		Ⓐ	Ⓐ	Ⓐ	Ⓐ	Ⓐ	Ⓐ	⑤	①–④	⑤	①–④	Ⓐ	⑤	Ⓐ		⑥	⑥	⑥	⑥	⑥	⑥
on P ◇ **130 132** d.	1649	1722	1749	1822	1850	...	1922	1950	2022	2048	2118	2148	2218	2218	2248	2248	2318	2342	2333	⑥	0022	0517	0550	0621	0650	0721
ng .... **130 132** d.	1721	1750	1822	1851	1922	...	1952	2022	2053	2122	2151	2225	2250	2300	2329	2334	0005	0027	0027		0104	0554	0622	0654	0722	0754
.... **130 132** d.	1738	|	|	|	|	...	|	|	|	|	|	|	|	|	|	|	|	0046	0056		0122	0608	0638	|	|	|
d .... **130** a.	1753	1814	1848	1920	1950	...	2020	2052	2117	2151	2218	2247	2325	2330	2357	0001	0034	0102	0120		0137	0621	0652	0719	0748	0818

	⑥	⑥	⑥	⑥	⑥	⑥	⑥	⑥	⑥	⑥	⑥	⑥	⑥	⑥	⑥	⑥	⑥	⑥	⑥	⑥	⑥	⑥	⑥	⑥	⑥	⑥
on P ◇ **130 132** d.	0750	0821	0850	0921	0950	1021	1050	1121	1150	1221	1250	1321	1350	1421	1450	1521	1550	1621	1650	1721	1750	1821	1850	1921	1950	2018
ng .... **130 132** d.	0822	0853	0922	0954	1022	1054	1122	1154	1222	1254	1322	1354	1422	1454	1522	1554	1622	1654	1722	1754	1822	1854	1922	1954	2022	2051
.... **130 132** d.	|	|	|	|	|	|	|	|	|	|	|	|	|	|	|	|	|	|	|	|	|	|	|	|	|	|
d .... **130** a.	0847	0917	0949	1017	1050	1118	1149	1219	1250	1318	1350	1418	1450	1518	1549	1618	1649	1717	1750	1817	1849	1917	1950	2018	2049	2116

	⑥	⑥	⑥	⑥	⑥	⑥			⑦	⑦	⑦	⑦		⑦	⑦	⑦	⑦	⑦	⑦	⑦	⑦	⑦	⑦	⑦	⑦	⑦
on P ◇ **130 132** d.	2050	2118	2148	2218	2248	2333	...	⑦	0803	0842	0935	1042	...	1142	1242	1342	1442	1542	1642	1742	1842	1942	2042	2142	2203	2242
ng .... **130 132** d.	2122	2154	2221	2255	2326	0017	...		0845	0924	1016	1122	...	1221	1322	1422	1521	1622	1725	1825	1925	2022	2120	2222	2246	2321
t .... **130 132** d.	2139	2210	2237	2312	2344	0033	...		0901	0940	1032	1138	...	1237	1338	1438	1537	1638	1742	1842	1942	2038	2137	2238	2302a	2339a
d .... **130** a.	2151	2223	2248	2326	2358	0054	...		0912	0949	1045	1150	...	1250	1349	1449	1549	1649	1754	1854	1954	2052	2150	2252	*2355**	*0015**

		②–⑤	②–⑤	Ⓐ	Ⓐ	Ⓐ	Ⓐ	Ⓐ	Ⓐ	Ⓐ	Ⓐ	Ⓐ	Ⓐ	Ⓐ	Ⓐ	Ⓐ	Ⓐ	Ⓐ	Ⓐ	Ⓐ	Ⓐ	Ⓐ	Ⓐ	Ⓐ	Ⓐ	Ⓐ
rd .... **130** d.	Ⓐ	0007	0027	0400b	0501	0542	0559	0630	0655	0734	0753	0808	0851	0901	0931	1001	1031	1101	1131	1201	1231	1301	1329	1401	1431	1501
t .... **130 132** d.		0021	0046	0412	0516	0600	0613	|	0710	|	|	0821	|	0915	|	|	|	|	|	|	|	|	|	|	|	|
ng .... **130 132** a.		0037	0113	0440	0541	0616	0627	0653	0725	0756	0822	0834	0916	0933	0954	1024	1054	1124	1154	1224	1255	1324	1354	1425	1454	1523
on P ◇ **130 132** a.		0122	0207	0546	0644	0654	0708	0729	0801	0829	0851	0907	0947	1009	1029	1057	1129	1159	1227	1306	1330	1356	1428	1459	1530	1557

	Ⓐ	Ⓐ	Ⓐ	Ⓐ	Ⓐ	Ⓐ	Ⓐ	Ⓐ	Ⓐ	Ⓐ	Ⓐ	Ⓐ	⑤	①–④	Ⓐ	Ⓐ	Ⓐ		⑥	⑥	⑥	⑥	⑥	⑥	⑥	⑥
rd .... **130** d.	1531	1601	1631	1701	1730	1801	1831	1905	1931	2001	2031	2101	2132	2132	2211	2230	2309	⑥	0007	0027	0359	0514	0549	0631	0659	0730
t .... **130 132** d.	|	|	|	|	|	|	|	|	|	|	|	|	|	|	2226	|	2323		0021	0046	0410	0531	0601	|	|	|
ng .... **130 132** a.	1555	1624	1654	1726	1754	1825	1855	1930	1953	2024	2055	2126	2155	2155	2243	2253	2341		0042	0113	0430	0558	0627	0657	0723	0754
on P ◇ **130 132** a.	1629	1659	1729	1759	1829	1859	1929	2006	2027	2059	2130	2201	2236	2243	2324	2340	0027		0122	0207	0532	0703	0732	0737	0758	0828

	⑥	⑥	⑥	⑥	⑥	⑥	⑥	⑥	⑥	⑥	⑥	⑥	⑥	⑥	⑥	⑥	⑥	⑥	⑥	⑥	⑥	⑥	⑥	⑥	⑥	⑥
rd .... **130** d.	0801	0829	0901	0929	1001	1031	1101	1129	1201	1231	1301	1329	1401	1429	1501	1530	1601	1629	1701	1731	1801	1829	1901	1929	2001	2027
t .... **130 132** d.	|	|	|	|	|	|	|	|	|	|	|	|	|	|	|	|	|	|	|	|	|	|	|	|	|	|
ing .... **130 132** a.	0825	0852	0924	0952	1025	1054	1124	1152	1225	1255	1326	1352	1425	1452	1522	1554	1625	1654	1725	1754	1825	1854	1925	1953	2025	2052
on P ◇ **130 132** a.	0859	0927	0959	1025	1059	1128	1159	1229	1259	1330	1359	1427	1459	1527	1559	1628	1659	1728	1759	1829	1859	1929	1959	2027	2059	2126

	⑥	⑥	⑥	⑥	⑥	⑥		⑦	⑦	⑦**A**	⑦**B**	⑦	⑦	⑦	⑦	⑦	⑦	⑦**C**	⑦	⑦	⑦	⑦	⑦	⑦	⑦	⑦
rd .... **130** d.	2101	2128	2201	2235	2301	2310	⑦	*0715**	0850	0950	0955	1055	1155	1255	1355	1455	1550	1631	1650	1750	1850	1955	2050	2150	2244	*2300**
t .... **130 132** d.	|	2142	2213	2251	2315	2334		0759	0903	1002	1010	1108	1208	1308	1408	1508	1605	|	1705	1805	1905	2008	2104	2204	2257	2350
ng .... **130 132** a.	2125	2156	2228	2310	2332	2359		0818	0919	1018	1026	1125	1225	1325	1425	1525	1620	1700	1725	1823	1922	2026	2123	2220	2314	0016
on P ◇ **130 132** a.	2159	2229	2302	2352	0017	0105		0903	0958	1057	1104	1206	1306	1406	1506	1608	1708	1744	1808	1908	2007	2109	2205	2301	0007	0115

May 15 - Sept. 11.
Sept. 18 - Dec. 4.

C – July 3 - Sept. 11.

a – Arrival time.
b – ①–⑤ May 16 - June 24; ②–⑤ June 28 - Dec. 9.

* – Connection by 🚌.
◇ – London Paddington.

132 LONDON - BRISTOL - CARDIFF - SWANSEA

🍸 available on most services

LONDON - BRISTOL TEMPLE MEADS - TAUNTON

km			Ⓐ	Ⓐ	Ⓐ	Ⓐ	Ⓐ	Ⓐ	Ⓐ	Ⓐ	Ⓐ	Ⓐ	Ⓐ	Ⓐ	Ⓐ		Ⓐ	Ⓐ	Ⓐ	Ⓐ	Ⓐ	Ⓐ	Ⓐ	Ⓐ
			F			A					A													
0	**London** Paddington 130 131 d.	Ⓐ	0518	0630	0700	0730	0800	0830	0900	0930	1000	1030	1100	1130	1200	...	1230	1300	1330	1400	1430	1500	1530	1600
58	Reading 130 131 d.		0554	0657	0730	0759	0828	0859	0928	0959	1028	1059	1127	1159	1228	...	1259	1328	1359	1428	1459	1527	1558	1628
85	Didcot Parkway 131 d.		0609	0712	0744	|	0841	|	0942	|	1042	|	1142	|	1242	...	|	1342	1413	|	1513	|	1612	|
124	Swindon d.		0627	0730	0801	0827	0900	0933	1000	1025	1059	1126	1200	1230	1300	...	1328	1400	1430	1456	1530	1556	1629	1657
151	Chippenham d.		0641	0744	0817	0842	0915	0945	1014	1039	1113	1140	1213	1244	1313	...	1343	1414	1444	1510	1544	1609	1644	1711
172	Bath a.		0655	0757	0829	0855	0927	0959	1028	1054	1128	1156	1227	1259	1327	...	1356	1428	1459	1524	1600	1623	1658	1724
190	**Bristol** Temple Meads 137 a.		0710	0817	0845	0910	0943	1015	1043	1111	1144	1213	1242	1315	1344	...	1412	1443	1515	1540	1615	1638	1714	1739
221	Weston-super-Mare 137 a.		...	...	...	|	...	...	...	...	1206	...	...	...	...	...	...	...	...	...	1652	...	1752	...
262	**Taunton** 137 a.		...	...	...	0944	...	...	...	...	1229	...	...	...	...	...	...	...	...	...	...	...	...	...

	Ⓐ	Ⓐ	Ⓐ	Ⓐ	Ⓐ	Ⓐ	Ⓐ	Ⓐ	Ⓐ	⑤	①–④	Ⓐ		⑥	⑥	⑥	⑥	⑥	⑥	⑥	⑥	⑥	⑥	⑥
									B			C				D								
London Paddington. 130 131 d.	1700	1730	1800	1830	1900	1930	2000	2045	2145	2215	2215	2330	⑥	0630	0700	0730	0800	0830	0900	0930	1000	1030	1100	1130
Reading 130 131 d.	1727	1757	1828	1858	1928	1959	2029	2112	2212	2243	2255	0010		0659	0729	0759	0828	0858	0928	0959	1028	1059	1128	1159
Didcot Parkway 131 d.	1742	1811	1842	1913	1942	2012	2042	2127	2231	2303	2314	0028		0713	|	0812	|	0912	|	1012	|	1112	|	1212
Swindon d.	1800	1830	1900	1930	2001	2030	2100	2144	2249	2322	2333	0048		0731	0756	0830	0856	0930	0955	1030	1055	1130	1156	1230
Chippenham d.	1814	1845	1914	1946	2016	2044	2116	2158	2303	2336	2346	0103		0745	0811	0845	0909	0944	1009	1044	1109	1144	1209	1244
Bath a.	1827	1858	1928	1959	2029	2059	2129	2212	2317	2349	2358	0115		0800	0824	0900	0924	1000	1026	1100	1126	1200	1226	1259
Bristol Temple Meads 137 a.	1844	1913	1943	2014	2044	2114	2144	2228	2331	0004	0014	0130		0815	0839	0915	0939	1015	1040	1115	1141	1215	1241	1314
Weston-super-Mare 137 a.	...	1948	...	2053	...	2149	...	...	0005**s**	...	...	...		...	...	|	...	...	1106**b**	...	...	1235**b**	...	...
Taunton 137 a.	...	2023	...	...	...	...	...	...	0036	...	...	...		...	...	0950	...	...	...	...	...	...	...	...

	⑥	⑥	⑥	⑥	⑥	⑥	⑥	⑥	⑥	⑥	⑥	⑥	⑥	⑥	⑥	⑥	⑥	⑥	⑥	⑥		⑦	⑦	⑦
									A								B					D	c	d
London Paddington. 130 131 d.	1230	1300	1330	1400	1430	1500	1530	1600	1630	1700	1730	1800	1830	1900	1930	2000	2030	2130	2235	2330	⑦	0800	0900	0900
Reading 130 131 d.	1259	1328	1359	1428	1459	1528	1559	1628	1659	1728	1759	1828	1859	1928	1959	2028	2059	2159	2303	0006		0839	0938	0940
Didcot Parkway 131 d.	1312	|	1412	|	1512	|	1612	|	1712	|	1811	|	1912	|	2012	2042	2112	2213	2322	0021		0855	0952	0958
Swindon d.	1330	1356	1431	1456	1530	1556	1631	1656	1730	1755	1829	1855	1930	1955	2030	2100	2130	2231	2340	0041		0914	1011	1015
Chippenham d.	1344	1409	1444	1509	1544	1609	1645	1709	1744	1809	1843	1909	1944	2009	2044	2114	2145	2246	2354	0056		0929	1026	1029
Bath a.	1400	1425	1500	1526	1600	1626	1700	1726	1800	1826	1858	1926	2000	2026	2059	2131	2200	2300	0009	0110		0944	1039	1044
Bristol Temple Meads 137 a.	1415	1440	1515	1541	1615	1641	1715	1741	1815	1842	1913	1940	2015	2043	2114	2145	2214	2315	0023	0124		0958	1056	1059
Weston-super-Mare 137 a.	1435**b**	...	...	...	1635**b**	...	1735**b**	...	1836	...	1950	...	2036	2126	...	...	2247**s**	...	...	...		|	1119	...
Taunton 137 a.	...	...	...	...	...	...	...	...	1907	...	...	...	2102	2159	...	...	2317	...	...	...		1034	...	...

	⑦	⑦	⑦	⑦	⑦	⑦	⑦	⑦	⑦	⑦	⑦	⑦	⑦	⑦	⑦	⑦	⑦	⑦	⑦	⑦	⑦	⑦	⑦	⑦
	H		De	E				Ee					De			e	B		Ee				d	
London Paddington. 130 131 d.	1100	1200	1233	1300	1400	1500	1527	1533	1600	1622	1700	1727	1757	1800	1827	1900	1903	1927	1957	2003	2103	2203	2237	2303
Reading 130 131 d.	1140	1240	1309	1338	1438	1538	1603	1609	1638	1700	1738	1806	1832	1838	1903	1936	1938	2006	2032	2038	2143	2246	2317	2346
Didcot Parkway 131 d.	1153	1253	|	1353	1453	1553	|	|	1653	|	1753	|	|	1853	|	|	1953	|	|	2053	2200	2303	2332**s**	0002**s**
Swindon d.	1210	1310	1344	1410	1510	1610	1630	1637	1710	1728	1810	1833	1904	1910	1929	2002	2010	2031	2100	2110	2218	2322	2348**s**	0021**s**
Chippenham d.	1225	1325	|	1425	1525	1624	1645	|	1724	1741	1825	1848	|	1925	1944	|	2025	2045	|	2125	2232	2337	|	0035**s**
Bath a.	1239	1339	|	1439	1539	1639	1659	|	1739	1802	1839	1902	|	1939	2003	|	2041	2102	|	2141	2246	2351	|	0051**s**
Bristol Temple Meads 137 a.	1255	1355	|	1455	1555	1653	1717	|	1756	1816	1855	1920	1950**u**	1955	2017	2043	2055	2116	|	2155	2302	0006	0030	0105
Weston-super-Mare 137 a.	1317**e**	1429	|	|	...	1724	...	|	...	...	...	1957	|	...	...	...	2127	...	|	2229	...	...	...	...
Taunton 137 a.	1340**e**	...	1448	1528	...	1759	...	1743	...	...	...	...	2021	...	...	...	2150	...	2216	...	...	...	...	...

LONDON - BRISTOL PARKWAY - CARDIFF - SWANSEA

Valid May 21 - September 11. For service from September 12 please contact National Rail Enquiries ✆ +44 (0)3457 48 49 50.

km			Ⓐ	Ⓐ	Ⓐ	Ⓐ	Ⓐ	Ⓐ	Ⓐ	Ⓐ	Ⓐ	Ⓐ	Ⓐ	Ⓐ	Ⓐ	Ⓐ	Ⓐ	Ⓐ	Ⓐ	Ⓐ	Ⓐ	Ⓐ	Ⓐ
												✕											
0	**London** Paddington. 130 131 d.	Ⓐ	0518	0645	0715	0745	0815	0845	0915	0945	1015	1045	1115	1145	1215	1245	1315	1345	1415	1445	1515	1545	1615
58	Reading 130 131 d.		0554	0711	0742	0811	0841	0911	0941	1011	1042	1111	1142	1211	1241	1310	1341	1411	1441	1511	1541	1611	1642
85	Didcot Parkway 131 d.		0609	|	0757	|	0854	|	0956	|	1056	|	1156	|	1256	|	1356	|	1455	|	1556	|	1658
124	Swindon d.		0627	0739	0815	0841	0916	0940	1014	1042	1113	1140	1213	1242	1313	1338	1415	1442	1516	1539	1614	1641	1716
180	**Bristol** Parkway d.		0709**t**	0808	0841	0908	0943	1008	1041	1108	1143	1208	1242	1309	1341	1408	1442	1508	1544	1608	1640	1708	1745
215	Newport 136 149 a.		0748	0832	0907	0929	1005	1031	1106	1131	1204	1231	1304	1331	1402	1430	1505	1531	1607	1630	1706	1732	1807
234	**Cardiff** Central . 135 136 149 a.		0803	0847	0923	0946	1022	1046	1123	1146	1221	1246	1322	1346	1422	1446	1522	1547	1623	1646	1722	1748	1822
266	Bridgend 135 a.		0826	0910	...	1009	...	1109	...	1209	...	1309	...	1409	...	1509	...	1610	...	1709	...	1811	1848
286	Port Talbot 135 a.		0839	0926	...	1022	...	1122	...	1222	...	1322	...	1424	...	1522	...	1623	...	1722	...	1824	1901
295	Neath 135 a.		0847	0932	...	1030	...	1130	...	1230	...	1330	...	1433	...	1530	...	1630	...	1730	...	1830	1909
307	**Swansea** 135 a.		0900	0947	...	1044	...	1143	...	1243	...	1344	...	1447	...	1543	...	1644	...	1743	...	1845	1922

	Ⓐ	Ⓐ	Ⓐ	Ⓐ	①–④	⑤	Ⓐ	Ⓐ	⑤	①–④	⑤	①–④		⑥	⑥	⑥	⑥	⑥	⑥	⑥	⑥	⑥
	G													n	n	Kn	n	n	n	n	n	n
London Paddington 130 131 d.	1715	1745	1815	1845	1915	1915	2015	2115	2245	2245	2330	2330	⑥	...	0745	0845	0945	1045	1145	1245	1345	1445
Reading 130 131 d.	1742	1811	1840	1911	1942	1948**u**	2040	2142	2311	2323	0010	0010		...	0811	0911	1011	1111	1211	1311	1411	1511
Didcot Parkway 131 d.	1758	|	1856	|	1957	|	2056	2201	2332	2343	0029	0028		...	|	|	|	|	|	|	|	|
Swindon d.	1815	1845	1916	1941	2016	2017	2115	2219	2350	0001	0048	0048		...	0839	0938	1037	1138	1239	1338	1440	1538
Bristol Parkway d.	1842	1910	1942	2008	2042	2043	2141	2247	0016	0027	0130**t**	0130**t**		0711	0908	1008	1108	1208	1308	1408	1508	1608
Newport 136 149 a.	1910	1933	2005	2031	2104	2105	2204	2321	0038	0057	0203**s**	0215**s**		0740	0936	1038	1138	1238	1337	1438	1536	1636
Cardiff Central 135 136 149 a.	1925	1949	2022	2048	2119	2119	2221	2340	0054	0112	0220	0232		0756	0952	1053	1154	1253	1355	1453	1552	1653
Bridgend 135 a.	1949	2011	2045	2115	2145	2145	2246	0003	0119	0140	...	...		0817	1014	1115	1217	1315	1417	1515	1615	1715
Port Talbot 135 a.	2002	2026	2058	2128	2158	2158	2300	0017	0133	0154	...	...		0830	1027	1128	1230	1328	1430	1528	1628	1728
Neath 135 a.	2009	2034	2105	2136	2206	2206	2308	0025	0141	0202	...	...		0839	1035	1136	1238	1336	1438	1536	1635	1735
Swansea 135 a.	2021	2047	2119	2150	2220	2220	2322	0039	0155	0216	...	...		0852	1049	1149	1251	1349	1451	1549	1649	1749

	⑥	⑥	⑥	⑥	⑥	⑥			⑦	⑦	⑦	⑦	⑦	⑦	⑦	⑦	⑦	⑦	⑦	⑦	⑦	⑦
	n	Gn	n	n						G		G		G								
London Paddington 130 131 d.	1645	1745	1845	1945	2045	2200	...	⑦	0837	0930	1037	1137	1237	1337	1437	1537	1637	1737	1837	1900	1937	2037
Reading 130 131 d.	1711	1811	1911	2011	2111	2229	...		0915	1007	1117	1213	1314	1414	1514	1614	1714	1814	1914	1939	2014	2114
Didcot Parkway 131 d.	|	|	|	|	|	2248	...		0932	|	1132	1229	1329	1429	1529	1629	1729	1829	1929	|	2029	2129
Swindon d.	1739	1838	1938	2038	2139	2305	...		0950	1041	1148	1248	1348	1448	1548	1648	1748	1848	1948	2005	2048	2148
Bristol Parkway d.	1808	1908	2008	2108	2211**a**	2333	...		1016	1106	1215	1314	1414	1514	1614	1714	1814	1914	2014	2033	2114	2214
Newport 136 149 a.	1837	1937	2037	2137	2243	0003	...		1042	1131	1240	1340	1440	1540	1640	1740	1840	1940	2040	2056	2140	2239
Cardiff Central 135 136 149 a.	1853	1952	2051	2153	2303	0023	...		1100	1150	1303	1400	1502	1603	1700	1802	1901	2001	2102	2118	2158	2300
Bridgend 135 a.	1916	2016	2115	2216	2325	...	...		1122	1214	1325	1421	1525	1623	1724	1822	1923	2024	2122	2139	2221	2322
Port Talbot 135 a.	1929	2029	2128	2229	2338	...	...		1135	1227	1337	1435	1537	1635	1735	1836	1936	2037	2135	2152	2234	2336
Neath 135 a.	1937	2036	2136	2237	2346	...	...		1144	1235	1344	1443	1545	1643	1743	1843	1945	2045	2143	2200	2241	2344
Swansea 135 a.	1950	2050	2149	2251	0001	...	...		1157	1249	1400	1458	1600	1656	1758	1857	1959	2059	2156	2214	2255	0001

A – To Paignton (Table **115**).
B – To Exeter St Davids (Table **115**).
C – Continues to Cardiff Central (see London to Swansea panel).
D – To Penzance (Tables **115**/**117**).
E – To Plymouth (Table **115**).
F – Continues to Swansea (see London to Swansea panel).
G – To Carmarthen (Table **135**).
H – To Paignton Sept. 18 - Oct. 23.
K – To Pembroke Dock (Table **135**).

a – Arrives 8 minutes earlier.
b – May 21 - Sept. 10.
c – May 15 - Sept. 11.
d – From Sept. 18.
e – Sept. 18 - Oct. 23.
k – May 16 - Sept. 9 and from Oct. 24.
n – Arrival times Newport - Swansea are 5–9 minutes earlier May 21 - June 18.
s – Calls to set down only.
t – Bristol Temple Meads.
u – Calls to pick up only.

TAUNTON - BRISTOL TEMPLE MEADS - LONDON

		Ⓐ	Ⓐ	Ⓐ	Ⓐ	Ⓐ	Ⓐ	Ⓐ	Ⓐ	Ⓐ	Ⓐ	Ⓐ	Ⓐ	Ⓐ	Ⓐ	Ⓐ	Ⓐ	Ⓐ	Ⓐ	Ⓐ	Ⓐ	Ⓐ	Ⓐ	Ⓐ	Ⓐ
								E				A				D									
on 137 d.	Ⓐ	...	...	...	...	...	...	0654	0712	...	...	0905	...	...	...	1125	...	...	...	...	...	...	...	...	...
on-super-Mare 137 d.		...	...	...	...	0620	0648	0725	0749	...	...	0929	...	...	...	|	...	...	...	...	...	...	...	...	...
ol Temple Meads 137 d.		0447	0529	0600	0633	0700	0730	0800	0830	0900	0930	1000	1030	1100	1130	1200	1230	1300	1330	1400	1430	1500	1530	1600	1630
d.		|	0541	0613	0646	0713	0743	0813	0843	0913	0943	1013	1043	1113	1143	1212	1243	1313	1343	1413	1443	1513	1543	1613	1643
enham d.		|	0554	0625	0658	0725	0755	0825	0855	0925	0955	1025	1055	1125	1155	1225	1255	1325	1355	1425	1455	1525	1555	1625	1655
on d.		0523	0610	0641	0715	0741	0811	0841	0911	0941	1011	1041	1110	1141	1211	1241	1311	1341	1411	1441	1511	1541	1611	1641	1711
t Parkway 131 a.		0541	0627	0658	|	0801	0828	0858	0928	|	1031	|	1128	|	1229	|	1328	|	1428	|	1528	|	1628	|	1728
ng 130 131 a.		0556	0641	0713	0743	0816	0843	0914	0944	1008	1046	1108	1143	1208	1243	1308	1343	1408	1443	1509	1543	1608	1643	1708	1743
on Paddington 130 131 a.		0626	0717	0746	0814	0845	0914	0944	1015	1037	1114	1139	1214	1238	1314	1339	1414	1438	1514	1544	1614	1644	1714	1738	1815

	Ⓐ	Ⓐ	Ⓐ	Ⓐ	Ⓐ	Ⓐ	①-④	⑤	Ⓐ		⑥	⑥	⑥	⑥	⑥	⑥	⑥	⑥	⑥	⑥	⑥	⑥	⑥	⑥	⑥
							D	D				F						B					Ac	Ab	
on 137 d.	...	...	...	...	...	...	2115	2115	2129	⑥	...	...	...	...	...	0654	...	0759	...	...	...	...	1045	1045	...
on-super-Mare 137 d.	...	1710	...	1808	...	...	|	|	2201		...	...	...	0624	...	0724	...	0830	...	...	...	...	1107	|	1131b
ol Temple Meads 137 d.	1700	1730	1800	1830	1930	2030	2150	2150	2235		0530	0600	0630	0700	0730	0800	0830	0900	0930	1000	1030	1100	1130	1130	1200
d.	1713	1743	1813	1843	1943	2043	2202	2202	2247		0543	0613	0643	0713	0743	0813	0843	0913	0943	1013	1043	1113	1143	1143	1213
enham d.	1725	1755	1825	1855	1955	2055	2215	2215	2300		0555	0625	0655	0725	0755	0825	0855	0925	0955	1025	1055	1125	1155	1155	1225
on d.	1741	1811	1841	1911	2011	2111	2232	2232	2316		0611	0641	0711	0741	0811	0841	0911	0941	1011	1041	1111	1141	1211	1211	1241
t Parkway 131 a.	1759	1828	|	1928	2028	2129	2248	2250	2333		0628	0658	0728	0759	0829	0859	0932a	|	1032a	|	1132a	|	1232a	1228	|
ng 130 131 a.	1813	1844	1909	1943	2043	2144	2304	2308	2354		0642	0714	0743	0813	0843	0914	0946a	1011	1046a	1108	1147a	1209	1246	1245	1309
on Paddington 130 131 a.	1844	1916	1939	2014	2114	2216	2344	2341	0039		0714	0744	0814	0844	0914	0944	1015	1039	1115	1138	1215	1239	1314	1314	1338

	⑥	⑥	⑥	⑥	⑥	⑥	⑥	⑥	⑥	⑥	⑥	⑥	⑥	⑥	⑥	⑥	⑥		⑦	⑦	⑦	⑦	⑦	⑦	⑦
																D					d		Bd		
on 137 d.	...	...	...	...	...	...	...	...	...	...	...	...	...	...	...	2114	2130	⑦	...	...	...	...	0904	...	...
on-super-Mare 137 d.	...	...	1301b	...	...	...	1501b	...	...	...	1701b	...	1801b	...	2010	|	2153		...	...	...	0811	|	...	0956
ol Temple Meads 137 d.	1230	1300	1330	1400	1430	1500	1530	1600	1630	1700	1730	1800	1830	1930	2033	2147	2230		0745	0815	0820	0845	|	0948	1030
d.	1243	1313	1343	1413	1443	1513	1543	1613	1643	1713	1743	1813	1843	1943	2046	2202	2243		0758	0828	|	0858	|	1001	1043
enham d.	1255	1325	1355	1425	1455	1525	1555	1625	1655	1725	1755	1825	1855	1955	2058	2215	2255		0810	0840	|	0910	|	1013	1055
don d.	1311	1341	1411	1441	1511	1541	1611	1641	1711	1741	1811	1841	1911	2011	2114	2231	2311		0826	0856	0856	0926	1021	1029	1111
t Parkway 131 a.	1332a	|	1432a	|	1532a	|	1628a	|	1728a	|	1828a	|	1928a	2027a	2131	2248	2329		0844	|	|	0943	|	1045	1127
ng 130 131 a.	1346a	1411	1446a	1509	1546a	1610	1645a	1708	1743a	1808	1845a	1908	1944a	2044a	2146	2304	2345		0900	0926	0927	1000	1048	1102	1146
on Paddington 130 131 a.	1415	1440	1515	1538	1615	1640	1715	1738	1815	1838	1915	1938	2015	2115	2214	2342	0033		0940	1008	1004	1041	1127	1143	1227e

	⑦	⑦	⑦	⑦	⑦	⑦	⑦	⑦	⑦	⑦	⑦	⑦	⑦	⑦	⑦	⑦	⑦	⑦	⑦	⑦	⑦	⑦	⑦	⑦	⑦
				E	Dd		k	h					h	k	E	A	Ed	E	m	n				Dd	E
ton 137 d.	...	...	...	1148	1210	...	...	...	...	...	...	...	...	...	1639	1658	1708	1746	...	...	...	1856	...	2100	2127
on-super-Mare 137 d.	...	...	1139h	|	|	...	1320	1320	...	1451	...	...	...	...	1701	1729	|	|	...	...	...	1925	2026	|	|
ol Temple Meads 137 d.	1100	1130	1200	1230	|	1330	1400	1400	1500	1530	1600	1630	1700	1705	1730	1800	|	1830	1900	1905	1930	2000	2100	|	2210
d.	1113	1143	1213	1243	|	1343	1413	1413	1513	1543	1613	1643	1713	1718	1743	1813	|	1843	1913	1918	1943	2013	2113	|	2223
enham d.	1125	1155	1225	1255	|	1355	1425	1425	1525	1555	1625	1655	1725	1730	1755	1825	|	1855	1925	1930	1955	2025	2125	|	2235
don d.	1141	1211	1241	1311	1329	1411	1440	1442	1541	1611	1641	1711	1740	1745	1811	1841	1824	1911	1941	1948	2011	2041	2141	2221	2252
t Parkway 131 a.	|	1227	|	1327	|	1427	|	1458	1557	|	1658	|	1756	1801	|	1858	|	|	1958	2005	|	2058	2158	|	2310
ng 130 131 a.	1214	1245	1314	1344	1357	1444	1509	1515	1615	1642	1714	1743	1815	1819	1844	1914	1852	1943	2014	2020	2044	2114	2216	2252	2326
on Paddington 130 131 a.	1257g	1323	1359g	1423	1442	1523	1557	1554	1657	1725	1757	1824	1853	1857	1925	1957	1927	2025	2059	2059	2123	2201	2258	2330	0012

SWANSEA - CARDIFF - BRISTOL PARKWAY - LONDON

Valid May 21 - September 11. For service from September 12 please contact National Rail Enquiries ✆ +44 (0)3457 48 49 50.

		Ⓐ	Ⓐ	Ⓐ	Ⓐ	Ⓐ	Ⓐ	Ⓐ	Ⓐ	Ⓐ	Ⓐ	Ⓐ	Ⓐ	Ⓐ	Ⓐ	Ⓐ	Ⓐ	Ⓐ	Ⓐ	Ⓐ	Ⓐ	Ⓐ	Ⓐ
					✂					G													
sea 135 d.	Ⓐ	0352	0458	0527	0558	0628	0658	0728	0758	0828	...	0928	...	1028	...	1128	...	1228	...	1328	...	1428	...
135 d.		0404	0510	0539	0610	0640	0710	0740	0810	0840	...	0940	...	1040	...	1140	...	1240	...	1340	...	1440	...
Talbot 135 d.		0412	0518	0547	0618	0648	0718	0748	0818	0848	...	0948	...	1048	...	1148	...	1248	...	1348	...	1448	...
end 135 d.		0425	0531	0600	0631	0701	0731	0801	0831	0902	...	1001	...	1101	...	1201	...	1301	...	1401	...	1501	...
ff Central 135 136 149 d.		0512	0555	0624	0655	0725	0755	0825	0855	0925	0955	1025	1055	1125	1155	1225	1255	1325	1355	1425	1455	1525	1555
ort 136 149 d.		0529	0609	0638	0709	0739	0809	0839	0909	0939	1009	1039	1109	1139	1209	1239	1309	1339	1409	1439	1509	1539	1609
l Parkway d.		0601	0632	0702	0732	0802	0832	0902	0932	1002	1032	1103	1132	1202	1232	1302	1332	1402	1432	1502	1532	1602	1632
don d.		0627	0658	0728	0758	0828	0859	0929	0959	1029	1059	1129	1159	1229	1259	1329	1359	1429	1459	1529	1559	1629	1659
t Parkway 131 a.		0645	|	0745	|	|	|	|	1015	1045	1116	|	1215	1245	1315	|	1415	1445	1516	|	1616	1645	1716
ing 130 131 a.		0659	0728	0800	|	0855	0925	0958	1030	1100	1130	1158	1230	1300	1331	1356	1430	1500	1530	1557	1630	1700	1731
on Paddington 130 131 a.		0730	0802	0833	0854	0924	0959	1032	1059	1132	1202	1229	1300	1333	1406	1432	1502	1533	1600	1633	1708	1732	1809

	Ⓐ	Ⓐ	Ⓐ	Ⓐ	Ⓐ	Ⓐ	Ⓐ	①-④	⑤			⑥	⑥	⑥	⑥	⑥	⑥	⑥	⑥	⑥	⑥	⑥	⑥
													p	p	p	p	p	p	p	p	Gp	p	Hp
sea 135 d.	1528	...	1628	...	1728	1828	1929	2028	2028	...	⑥	0358	0450	0520	0550	0620	0650	0720	0822	0922	1022	1122	1222
135 d.	1540	...	1640	...	1740	1840	1940	2040	2040	...		0410	0502	0532	0602	0632	0703	0732	0834	0934	1034	1134	1234
Talbot 135 d.	1548	...	1648	...	1748	1848	1948	2048	2048	...		0418	0510	0540	0610	0640	0711	0740	0842	0942	1042	1142	1242
end 135 d.	1601	...	1701	...	1801	1901	2001	2101	2101	...		0430	0523	0553	0623	0653	0724	0753	0855	0955	1055	1155	1255
ff Central 135 136 149 d.	1625	1655	1725	1755	1825	1925	2025	2125	2125	...		0455	0547	0617	0646	0717	0748	0817	0919	1019	1119	1218	1319
ort 136 149 d.	1639	1709	1739	1809	1839	1939	2039	2139	2139	...		0509	0601	0631	0700	0731	0801	0831	0933	1033	1133	1232	1333
l Parkway d.	1702	1733	1802	1832	1902	2002	2104	2202	2202	...		0600t	0634	0704	0732	0804	0832	0904	1004	1104	1204	1304	1402
don d.	1729	1800	1829	1859	1929	2029	2133	2225	2228	...		0641	0701	0731	0759	0831	0859	0931	1031	1131	1231	1331	1431
t Parkway 131 a.	|	1817	1846	|	1946	2046	2152	*2248*	...	...		0658	|	|	0815	|	0916	|	|	|	|	|	|
ing 130 131 a.	1758	1831	1900	1925	2000	2100	2211	*2304*	2302	...		0714	0727	0757	0831	0857	0931	0957	1058	1157	1259	1357	1457
on Paddington 130 131 a.	1832	1902	1932	1954	2037	2132	2249	*2344*	2338	...		0744	0800	0830	0902	0930	1002	1028	1132	1230	1333	1430	1530

	⑥	⑥	⑥	⑥	⑥	⑥	⑥			⑦	⑦	⑦	⑦	⑦	⑦	⑦	⑦	⑦	⑦	⑦	⑦	⑦	⑦
	p	p	p	p	Hp	p	p												G		G		G
sea 135 d.	1322	1422	1522	1622	1722	1822	1922	...	⑦	...	0810	0921	1021	1121	1221	1321	1421	1521	1551	1651	1751	1851	1955
135 d.	1334	1434	1534	1634	1734	1834	1934	...		...	0822	0933	1033	1133	1233	1333	1433	1533	1603	1703	1803	1903	2007
Talbot 135 d.	1342	1442	1542	1642	1742	1842	1942	...		...	0829	0940	1040	1140	1240	1340	1440	1540	1610	1710	1810	1910	2014
end 135 d.	1355	1455	1557	1655	1755	1855	1955	...		...	0843	0953	1053	1153	1253	1353	1453	1553	1623	1723	1823	1923	2028
ff Central 135 136 149 d.	1419	1519	1619	1719	1819	1919	2018	...		0800	0905	1015	1115	1215	1314	1415	1515	1614	1649	1750	1849	1949	2054
ort 136 149 d.	1433	1533	1634	1733	1833	1933	2032	...		0818	0920	1032	1131	1231	1332	1432	1532	1632	1704	1804	1904	2004	2108
l Parkway d.	1504	1604	1704	1804	1903	2004	2102	...		0847	0949	1102	1201	1302	1401	1501	1601	1701	1732	1832	1933	2034	2138
don d.	1531	1631	1731	1831	1929	2031	2129	...		0915	1017	1129	1228	1328	1429	1529	1629	1729	1801	1859	1959	2059	2205
t Parkway 131 a.	|	|	|	|	|	|	2146	...		|	|	1146	1245	1345	1446	1546	|	1746	1818	1918	2018	|	|
ing 130 131 a.	1557	1658	1758	1858	1957	2057	2202	...		0949	1049	1201	1302	1401	1502	1602	1656	1801	1833	1934	2034	2129	2240
on Paddington 130 131 a.	1638	1731	1832	1931	2030	2129	2238	...		1030	1127	1240	1340	1440	1544	1641	1736	1839	1911	2012	2114	2222	2322

From Paignton (Table **115**).
From Exeter St Davids (Table **115**).
From Penzance (Tables **115**/**117**).
From Plymouth (Table **115**).
From Swansea (see Swansea to London panel).
From Carmarthen (Table **135**).
From Pembroke Dock (Table **135**).

a – Arrives 3–4 minutes earlier May 21 - Sept. 10 and from Oct. 29.
b – May 21 - Sept. 10.
c – From Sept. 17.
d – Sept. 18 - Oct. 23.
e – Arrives 4–5 Minutes earlier Sept. 18 - Oct. 23.
g – Arrives 5–7 minutes earlier May 15 - Oct. 23.

h – May 15 - Sept. 11.
k – From Sept. 18.
m – May 15 - Sept. 11 and from Oct. 30.
n – Sept. 18 - Oct. 23.
p – Departure times Swansea to Newport are 6–9 minutes later May 21 - June 18.
t – Bristol Temple Meads.

132a SWINDON - WESTBURY

2nd class

km		Ⓐ	Ⓐ	Ⓐ	Ⓐ	Ⓐ	Ⓐ	Ⓐ	Ⓐ	Ⓐ	⑥	⑥	⑥	⑥	⑥	⑥	⑥	⑥	⑦ b	⑦ c	⑦	⑦ d	⑦ e	⑦
	Gloucester 133 ... d.	0517	...	...	...	...	...	...	1754	...	...	...	...	...	...	...	...	2013	...	...	...	...	...	...
0	**Swindon** 132 d.	0612	0849	1047	1247	1319	1512	1736	1848	2006	0836	1036	1236	1436	1522	1736	1936	2108a	0926	1128	1326	1528	1718	1953
27	Chippenham 132 d.	0629	0906	1104	1304	1336	1529	1753	1905	2023	0853	1053	1253	1453	1539	1753	1953	2125a	0943	1145	1343	1545	1735	2010
37	Melksham d.	0638	0915	1113	1313	1347	1539	1803	1915	2032	0902	1102	1302	1503	1548	1802	2002	2134a	0952	1154	1352	1554	1744	2019
46	Trowbridge 139 d.	0648	0933	1124	1323	1359	1549	1813	1924	2042	0912	1112	1312	1512	1558	1812	2012	2144a	1001	1203	1401	1603	1754	2029
52	**Westbury** 139 a.	0655	0942	1133	1332	1407	1557	1821	1931	2049	0920	1120	1320	1520	1607	1818	2020	2152a	1008	1210	1410	1610	1801	2038

	Ⓐ	Ⓐ	Ⓐ	Ⓐ	Ⓐ	Ⓐ	Ⓐ	Ⓐ	Ⓐ	⑥	⑥		⑥	⑥	⑥	⑥	⑥	⑥	⑦ b	⑦ c	⑦ k	⑦ m	⑦ d	⑦ m
Westbury 139 d.	0704	0733	0948	1147	1220	1414	1621	1832	1932	0732	0822	...	0930	1132	1332	1506	1633	1832	0830	1030	1230	1435	1620	1839
Trowbridge 139 d.	0710	0739	0954	1153	1226	1420	1627	1838	1938	0738	0828	...	0936	1138	1338	1512	1639	1838	0835	1035	1235	1440	1625	1845
Melksham d.	0720	0749	1004	1203	1237	1430	1637	1848	1947	0748	0837	...	0946	1148	1348	1521	1649	1848	0846	1046	1246	1450	1635	1854
Chippenham 132 d.	0730	0800	1014	1212	1246	1441	1646	1900	2000	0800	0847	...	1000	1200	1400	1531	1700	1900	0855	1100h	1300	1500	1645	1904
Swindon 132 a.	0748	0823	1034	1236	1305	1503	1706	1923	2021	0820	0906	...	1024	1223	1425	1550	1725	1922	0919	1120	1320	1519	1705	1922
Gloucester 133 a.	0852	...	...	...	...	...	...	...	2123	...	...	...	...	...	...	...	...	...	...	...	...	...	...	...

a – Runs 5 minutes later Sept. 17 - Oct. 22.
b – May 15 - Sept. 11.
c – Runs 25 minutes earlier Sept. 18 - Oct. 23.
d – Runs 11 minutes earlier Sept. 18 - Oct. 23.
e – Runs 13 minutes earlier Sept. 18 - Oct. 23.
g – Sept. 18 - Oct. 23.
h – Departs 30 minutes earlier Sept. 18 - Oct 23.
k – Runs 16 minutes earlier Sept. 18 - Oct. 23.
m – Runs 20 minutes earlier Sept. 18 - Oct. 23.

133 LONDON - CHELTENHAM

Most London trains convey 🍸

Service on ⑦ is valid May 15 - Sept. 11. For service on ⑦ from Sept. 18 please contact National Rail Enquiries ✆ +44 (0)3457 48 49 50.

km		Ⓐ	Ⓐ 2A	Ⓐ	Ⓐ 2	Ⓐ	Ⓐ 2	Ⓐ	Ⓐ 2		Ⓐ	Ⓐ 2	Ⓐ	Ⓐ 2	Ⓐ	Ⓐ	Ⓐ 2A	Ⓐ	Ⓐ 2	Ⓐ 2	⑥ 2	⑥		⑥ 2
0	**London** Paddington 132 d.	...	...	0736	...	0936	...	1136	...	...	1336	...	1536	...	1742	1847	...	1948	...	...	...	0815a	...	...
58	Reading 132 d.	...	...	0802	...	1003	...	1203	...	...	1404	...	1602	...	|	1919	...	2018	...	...	...	0841a	...	...
85	Didcot Parkway 132 d.	...	...	0817	...	1018	...	1218	...	...	1419	...	1617	...	1821	1934	...	2034	...	...	...	0855a	...	...
124	**Swindon** 132 d.	0640	0750	0840	0936	1039	1136	1239	1336	...	1439	1536	1638	1754	1841	1955	2025	2055	2154	2336	0716	0914	...	1014
164	Stroud d.	0709	0820	0910	1005	1107	1205	1307	1405	...	1507	1605	1707	1822	1911	2025	2053	2124	2223	0005	0745	0945	...	1043
183	Gloucester a.	0731	0848	0929	1028	1130	1228	1330	1428	...	1530	1628	1730	1849	1931	2046	2115	2146	2246	0028	0806	1006	...	1105
194	**Cheltenham** Spa 138 a.	0749	0905	0952	1048	1152	1245	1352	1447	...	1552	1647	1752	1905	1947	2102	2133	2202	2304	0045	0824	1022	...	1122
	Worcester Shrub Hill 138 a.	...	...	...	...	...	...	...	...	...	...	...	...	...	...	...	...	2224	...	...	...	...	...	...

	⑥ 2	⑥	⑥ 2	⑥		⑥ 2	⑥	⑥ 2	⑥	⑥ 2	⑥	⑥ 2		⑦	⑦ 2	⑦	⑦	⑦ 2		⑦	⑦	⑦ 2	⑦	⑦ 2A	⑦
London Paddington 132 d.	...	1215a	...	1415a	...	...	1614a	...	1815a	...	2015a	...	...	0827	...	1027	1227	...	...	1427	1627	...	1822	...	2022
Reading 132 d.	...	1241a	...	1441a	...	...	1641a	...	1841a	...	2041a	...	...	0903	...	1105	1303	...	...	1503	1703	...	1901	...	2059
Didcot Parkway 132 d.	...	1255a	...	1455a	...	...	1655a	...	1855a	...	2055a	...	...	|	...	|	|	...	...	|	|	...	|	...	|
Swindon 132 d.	1214	1314	1414	1514	...	1614	1714	1814	1914	2000	2117	2241	...	0937	1047	1137	1337	1429	...	1537	1733	1843	1930	2029	2129
Stroud d.	1243	1345	1443	1545	...	1643	1745	1843	1945	2029	2145	2310	...	1004	1116	1204	1404	1459	...	1604	1801	1911	1957	2058	2158
Gloucester a.	1303	1406	1503	1605	...	1703	1806	1903	2006	2049	2206	2331	...	1026	1136	1226	1426	1519	...	1626	1822	1934	2024	2118	2219
Cheltenham Spa 138 a.	1324	1422	1525	1621	...	1725	1822	1925	2022	2102	2221	...	...	1042	1149	1244	1446	1533	...	1646	1845	...	2046	2130	2236
Worcester Shrub Hill 138 a.	...	...	...	...	...	...	...	...	...	...	...	...	...	...	...	...	...	...	...	...	...	...	...	...	...

	Ⓐ 2A	Ⓐ b	Ⓐ c	Ⓐ	Ⓐ	Ⓐ	Ⓐ 2	Ⓐ	Ⓐ 2	Ⓐ	Ⓐ 2	Ⓐ	Ⓐ 2	Ⓐ	Ⓐ 2A	Ⓐ	Ⓐ 2b	Ⓐ 2c	Ⓐ 2b	Ⓐ 2c	Ⓐ 2	⑥ 2	⑥ d	⑥ e
Worcester Shrub Hill 138 d.	...	0521	0521	...	0706	...	...	...	...	...	...	...	...	...	...	...	...	...	...	...	...	...	...	...
Cheltenham Spa 138 d.	...	0551	0553	0630	0729	0831	0918	1036	1120	1236	1320	1436	1520	1620	1740	1834	2001	2001	2100	2100	2201	0530	0720	0731
Gloucester d.	0517	0606	0608	0645	0745	0848	0932	1051	1133	1252	1333	1452	1533	1643	1754	1850	2013	2025	2121	2126	2213	0542	0735	0746
Stroud d.	0535	0627	0629	0705	0805	0908	0952	1113	1152	1314	1352	1514	1552	1704	1812	1911	2031	2045	2138	2145	2232	0601	0754	0805
Swindon 132 a.	0605	0656	0658	0735	0834	0941	1023	1142	1224	1343	1424	1543	1624	1733	1843	1939	2105	2117	2209	2216	2305	0632	0824	0835
Didcot Parkway 132 a.	...	|	0718	0753	0853	1002	...	1202	...	1402	...	1602	...	|	...	1958	...	...	...	...	...	...	...	0853a
Reading 132 a.	...	0728	0733	0811	0908	1016	...	1217	...	1417	...	1617	...	1803	...	2014	...	...	...	...	...	...	...	0908a
London Paddington 132 a.	...	0802	0809	0842	0940	1047	...	1247	...	1445	...	1653	...	1839	...	2046	...	...	...	...	...	...	...	0940a

	⑥ h	⑥ 2	⑥		⑥ 2	⑥	⑥ 2	⑥	⑥ 2	⑥	⑥ 2	⑥	⑥ 2A	⑥ 2	⑦ 2	⑦		⑦ 2	⑦	⑦	⑦ 2	⑦		⑦ 2	⑦
Worcester Shrub Hill 138 d.	0836	...	...	...	...	...	...	...	...	...	...	...	...	...	...	...	...	...	...	...	...	...	...	...	...
Cheltenham Spa 138 d.	0859	1001	1100	...	1201	1300	1401	1500	1601	1700	1801	1900	2001	2120	0924	1118	...	1230	1333	1533	1632	1733	...	...	2001
Gloucester d.	0914	1013	1114	...	1213	1315	1413	1514	1613	1714	1813	1916	2013	2134	0937	1134	...	1245	1349	1546	1645	1749	...	1934	2016
Stroud d.	0935	1032	1135	...	1232	1336	1432	1535	1632	1735	1832	1936	2032	2153	0955	1154	...	1303	1409	1606	1702	1809	...	1952	2036
Swindon 132 a.	1016	1104	1204	...	1304	1404	1504	1604	1704	1804	1904	2005	2103	2225	1024	1222	...	1332	1437	1634	1733	1838	...	2021	2104
Didcot Parkway 132 a.	...	...	1222a	...	...	1423a	...	1622a	...	1822a	...	2023a	...	...	...	|	...	...	|	|	...	|	...	...	2125
Reading 132 a.	...	...	1236a	...	...	1437a	...	1636a	...	1836a	...	2037a	...	...	...	1252	...	...	1505	1706	...	1909	...	...	2144
London Paddington 132 a.	...	...	1306a	...	...	1506a	...	1707a	...	1906a	...	2107a	...	...	...	1330	...	...	1551	1751	...	1951	...	...	2229

A – To/from Westbury (Table **132a**).
a – May 21 - Sept. 10.
b – Sept. 12 - Oct. 21.
c – May 16 - Sept. 9 and from Oct. 24.
d – Sep. 17 - Oct. 22.
e – May 21 - Sept. 10 and from Oct. 29.
g – May 21 - Oct. 22.
h – From Oct. 29.

134 GATWICK AIRPORT ✈ - READING

km		Ⓐ A	Ⓐ	Ⓐ	Ⓐ	Ⓐ	Ⓐ	Ⓐ		Ⓐ	Ⓐ	Ⓐ	Ⓐ	Ⓐ	Ⓐ	Ⓐ	Ⓐ	Ⓐ	⑥ A	⑥	⑥	⑥	
0	**Gatwick** Airport ✈ d.	...	0531	0556	0658	0758	0910	1003	and	1503	1603	1703	1803	1913	2003	2103	2222	2318	...	0531	0603	0703	and
10	Redhill △ d.	...	0543	0613	0710	0808	0923	1014	hourly	1514	1614	1713	1813	1926	2014	2114	2233	2334	...	0542	0613	0713	hourly
43	Guildford △ d.	0602	0613	0643	0743	0838	0954	1044	until	1544	1644	1744	1847	1955	2044	2144	2314	0002	0609	0612	0644	0744	until
84	**Reading** △ a.	0632	0700	0731	0830	0919	1025	1121		1626	1721	1826	1927	2034	2121	2221	0003	0041	0643	0701	0719	0819	

	⑥	⑥		⑥	⑥	⑦	⑦		⑦	⑦	⑦	⑦	⑦ A	⑦	⑦	⑦		⑦	⑦	⑦	⑦	⑦	⑦		⑦	⑦
Gatwick Airport ✈ d.	2003	2103	...	2219	2318	0611	0711	...	0811	0909	1009	1109	...	1209	1309	1409	...	1509	1609	1709	1809	1909	2009	...	2109	2209
Redhill △ d.	2014	2114	...	2233	2329	0620	0720	...	0820	0920	1020	1120	...	1220	1320	1420	...	1520	1620	1720	1820	1920	2020	...	2120	2220
Guildford △ d.	2044	2144	...	2314	0002	0651	0752	...	0900	0952	1100	1152	1214	1300	1352	1500	...	1552	1700	1752	1900	1952	2100	...	2152	2300
Reading △ a.	2119	2219	...	0001	0037	0726	0835	...	0938	1035	1135	1235	1248	1335	1435	1535	...	1635	1735	1835	1935	2035	2136	...	2236	2336

	Ⓐ	Ⓐ	Ⓐ	Ⓐ	Ⓐ	Ⓐ		Ⓐ	Ⓐ	Ⓐ	Ⓐ	Ⓐ A	Ⓐ	Ⓐ		Ⓐ	Ⓐ	Ⓐ	Ⓐ	⑥	⑥		⑥
Reading ▽ d.	0432	0522	0632	0732	0832	0932	and	1432	1526	1632	1732	1821	1832	1932	...	2032	2132	2232	2332	0434	0534	and	1734
Guildford ▽ d.	0510	0600	0710	0818	0913	1010	hourly	1510	1610	1710	1818	1859	1910	2010	...	2110	2218	2318	0021	0510	0610	hourly	1810
Redhill ▽ a.	0539	0629	0738	0846	0942	1038	until	1538	1640	1738	1847	...	1940	2038	...	2146	2248	2358	0049	0539	0639	until	1838
Gatwick Airport ✈ a.	0555	0642	0750	0859	0957	1050		1551	1659	1754	1900	...	1956	2050	...	2204	2304	0011	0103	0558	0650		1850

	⑥	⑥	⑥	⑥	⑥	⑥	⑦	⑦	⑦	⑦	⑦		⑦	⑦	⑦	⑦	⑦	⑦	⑦	⑦	⑦		⑦	⑦	⑦ A	⑦
Reading ▽ d.	1834	1934	2034	2134	2234	2334	0603	0703	0818	0918	1018	...	1118	1218	1318	1418	1518	1618	1718	1818	1918	...	2018	2118	2214	2218
Guildford ▽ d.	1910	2010	2110	2218	2318	0021	0639	0747	0856	1001	1056	...	1201	1256	1401	1456	1601	1656	1801	1856	2001	...	2056	2201	2242	2256
Redhill ▽ a.	1938	2038	2146	2253	2358	0049	0708	0816	0936	1035	1136	...	1235	1336	1435	1536	1635	1736	1835	1936	2035	...	2136	2235	...	2336
Gatwick Airport ✈ a.	1950	2050	2159	2305	0008	0100	0727	0828	0947	1047	1147	...	1247	1347	1447	1547	1647	1747	1847	1947	2047	...	2147	2247	...	2347

A – To/from Newcastle (Table **124**).

△ – Additional trains Redhill - Reading on Ⓐ at 0624, 0728, 0833, 0934 and hourly ur 1434, 1529, 1632, 1743, 1843, 2034, 2135; on ⑥ at 0634 and hourly until 2034, 2 Journey time 80 – 92 minutes.

▽ – Additional trains Reading - Redhill on Ⓐ at 0552, 0702 and hourly until 1802, 200 on ⑥ at 0604 and hourly until 2004. Journey time 85 – 90 minutes.

Service on ⑦ is valid May 15 - Sept. 11. For service on ⑦ from Sept. 18 please contact National Rail Enquires ✆ +44 (0)3457 48 49 50.

Ⓐ	Ⓐ	Ⓐ	Ⓐ	Ⓐ	Ⓐ	Ⓐ	Ⓐ	Ⓐ	Ⓐ	Ⓐ	Ⓐ	Ⓐ	Ⓐ	Ⓐ	Ⓐ	Ⓐ	Ⓐ	Ⓐ	Ⓐ	Ⓐ	Ⓐ	Ⓐ	Ⓐ	Ⓐ	Ⓐ
																								B	
Manchester Picc. **149** d.	...	...	...	...	...	...	...	...	...	...	...	...	0630	0730	...	...	0830	0930	...	1030	1130	...	1230	...	1330
Cardiff Central **149 132** d.	...	...	...	...	...	...	0535	0642	...	0750	0904	0912	1004**a**	1042	1058	...	1138	1239	...	1341	1443	...	1539	1604	1704
Bridgend **132** d.	...	...	...	...	...	...	0607	0705	...	0809	0923	0934	1023**a**	1101	1119	...	1159	1258	...	1404	1502	...	1601	1625	1727
Port Talbot **132** d.	...	...	...	...	...	...	0623	0722	...	0825	0936	0952	1036**a**	1114	|	...	1211	1311	...	1418	1515	...	1614	1641	1742
Neath **132** d.	...	...	...	...	...	...	0634	0733	...	0835	0943	1003	1043**a**	1121	|	...	1218	1318	...	1425	1522	...	1621	1649	1752
Swansea **132** a.	...	...	...	...	...	...	0651	0749	...	0854	0955	1021	1055**a**	1134	|	...	1234	1333	...	1434	1534	...	1633	1702	1807
Swansea d.	...	...	...	...	...	0545	0653	0752	0814	0900	1002	▬	1100	1138	|	1200	1240	1337	1400	1437	1537	1600	1640	1705	1814
Llanelli d.	...	...	...	...	...	0604	0711	0810	0831	0919	1021	Ⓐ	1118	1154	1203	1219	1259	1356	1416	1456	1556	1618	1659	1724	1833
Carmarthen a.	...	...	...	...	...	0638	0743	0841	|	0955	1053		1144	1226	|	1248	1322	1430	1445	1522	1630	1647	1728	1755	1902
Carmarthen d.	0450	0530	0550	0558	...	0639	0746	0843	|	0959	...	1058	1148	...	|	1251	1330	...	1451	1528	...	1651	1731	1757	1905
Whitland d.	0503	0547	0605	0613	...	0656	0800	0902	0910	1014	...	1113	1201	...	1245	1306	1345	...	1506	1543	...	1706	1746	1813	1921
Tenby a.	|	0624	|	|	...	0724	|	0930	|	|	...	1141	|	...	|	1334	|	...	1534	|	...	1734	|	|	1957
Pembroke Dock a.	|	0654	|	|	...	0807	|	1018	|	|	...	1223	|	...	|	1419	|	...	1619	|	...	1819	|	|	*2035*
Clarbeston Road d.	0518**x**	...	0620**x**	0627**x**	0720	...	0814**x**	...	0925**x**	1028**x**	...	...	1215**x**	...	|	...	1359**x**	...	...	1557**x**	...	...	1800**x**	1827**x**	...
Haverfordwest d.	0529	...	|	0635	|	...	0823	...	|	1036	...	...	1223	...	|	...	1408	...	...	1606	...	...	1808	|	...
Milford Haven a.	0552	...	|	0658	|	...	0843	...	|	1057	...	...	1248	...	|	...	1431	...	...	1629	...	...	1831	|	...
Fishguard Harbour a.	...	...	0644	...	0744	...	...	...	0950	...	...	...	...	...	1327	...	...	...	...	...	...	...	...	1856	...

	Ⓐ	Ⓐ	Ⓐ	Ⓐ	Ⓐ	Ⓐ	Ⓐ	Ⓐ	①–④	⑤	Ⓐ	Ⓐ
				Ab	Ac	c	b					
nchester Picc. **149** d.	1430	...	1530	...	...	1630	1630	...	1830	1830	...	1930
ff Central **149 132** d.	1740	1806	1904	1929	1956	1946	1946	2104	2209	2209	...	2315
end **132** d.	1800	1831	1923	1950	2015	2005	2005	2127	2235	2235	...	2345
Talbot **132** d.	1818	1848	1938	2003	2028	2021	2021	2145	2247	2247	...	0001
132 d.	1826	1859	1948	2010	2036	2028	2028	2152	|	2254	...	0013
sea **132** a.	1838	1914	2004	2021	2051	2042	2042	2205	|	2307	...	0028
sea d.	1841	*1934*	2011	2033	2104	2048	2048	2227	|	2311	2345	0045
lli d.	1900	*1954*	2030	2050	2121	2107	2111	2246	2321	2331	0002	0102**s**
arthen a.	1927	*2029*	2055	2122	2153	2135	2139	2315	2357	0007	0033	0140
arthen d.	1930	▬	*2110*	...	...	2154	2141	2320	...	...	0035	...
and d.	1946		*2125*	...	...	2209	2156	2335	...	...	0051	...
nby a.	|	Ⓐ	*2152*	...	...	|	|	|	...	...	|	...
mbroke Dock a.	|	...	*2226*	...	...	|	|	|	...	...	|	...
eston Road d.	2000**x**	2005	...	...	...	2223**x**	2210**x**	2350**x**	...	...	0104**x**	...
rfordwest d.	2009	|	...	...	...	2232	2223	2358	...	...	|	...
rd Haven a.	2032	|	...	...	...	2255	2246	0021	...	...	|	...
shguard Harbour a.	...	2029	...	...	...	...	...	...	...	...	0133	...

⑥	⑥	⑥	⑥	⑥	⑥	⑥	⑥	⑥	⑥	⑥	⑥	⑥	⑥	⑥
							r	p	g	g	h			
Manchester Picc. **149** d.	...	...	...	...	...	...	...	...	...	...	...	...	...	...
Cardiff Central **149 132** d.	...	...	...	...	...	...	0533	0533	0642	...	0642	0754	0904	0914
Bridgend **132** d.	...	...	...	...	...	...	0601	0604	0702	...	0702	0814	0923	0934
Port Talbot **132** d.	...	...	...	...	...	...	0617	0620	0718	...	0718	0826	0936	0952
Neath **132** d.	...	...	...	...	...	...	0628	0631	0729	...	0729	0833	0943	1003
Swansea **132** a.	...	...	...	...	...	...	0648	0648	0745	...	0745	0855	1000	1021
Swansea d.	...	...	...	...	...	0545	0653	0659	0750	...	0750	0858	1004	▬
Llanelli d.	...	...	...	...	...	0604	0711	0717	0808	...	0808	0919	1022	⑥
Carmarthen a.	...	...	...	...	...	0637	0744	0749	0840	...	0840	0948	1051	
Carmarthen d.	0450	0530	0550	0558	...	0638	0746	0751	0843	...	0845	0957	...	1056
Whitland d.	0503	0546	0606	0613	...	0656	0800	0805	0902	0907	0901	1014	...	1111
Tenby a.	|	0624	|	|	...	0724	|	|	0930	|	|	|	...	1139
Pembroke Dock a.	|	0659	|	|	...	0807	|	|	1017	|	|	|	...	1220
Clarbeston Road d.	0518**x**	...	0621**x**	0627**x**	0720	...	0815**x**	0820**x**	...	0922**x**	0915**x**	1028**x**	...	...
Haverfordwest d.	0530	...	|	0635	|	...	0823	0828	...	|	|	1036	...	...
Milford Haven a.	0553	...	|	0658	|	...	0848	0853	...	|	|	1058	...	...
Fishguard Harbour a.	...	...	0646	...	0744	...	...	...	...	0947	0943	...	...	...

	⑥	⑥	⑥	⑥	⑥	⑥	⑥	⑥	⑥	⑥	⑥	⑥	⑥	⑥	⑥	⑥	⑥	⑥	⑥	⑥	⑥	⑥	⑥	⑥	⑥	⑥	⑥
			Am	Ak	g									g	h			Bg	Bh						Ae	Ad	
nchester Picc. **149** d.	0630	...	...	...	...	0730	...	0830	0930	...	...	1030	1130	...	...	...	1230	...	...	...	1330	1430	...	1530	...	...	1630
iff Central **132** d.	1000	1059	1048	1054	...	1105	1114	1204	1304	...	1310	1404	1504	...	...	1513	1540	1600	1604	...	1704	1804	...	1904	1948	1954	2001
end **132** d.	1022	1119	1109	1115	...	1124	1134	1223	1323	...	1332	1423	1523	...	...	1533	1600	1620	1624	...	1725	1825	...	1924	2009	2016	2020
Talbot **132** d.	1033	|	1122	1128	...	1138	1150	1236	1336	...	1348	1436	1536	...	...	1549	1617	1636	1640	...	1740	1841	...	1939	2022	2029	2033
h **132** d.	1042	|	1130	1136	...	1146	1201	1243	1343	...	1359	1443	1543	...	...	1600	1624	1644	1648	...	1750	1849	...	1949	2030	2036	|
nsea **132** a.	1055	|	1143	1149	...	1203	1220	1255	1357	...	1418	1455	1555	...	...	1617	1638	1657	1701	...	1805	1902	...	2005	2043	2050	|
nsea d.	1100	|	1150	1157	1150	1205	...	1302	1405	1350	...	1500	1600	1605	1605	1620	1640	1701	1706	1750	1809	1904	1934	2013	2100	2100	|
elli d.	1118	1202	1208	1214	1211	1224	...	1322	1424	1406	...	1520	1619	1628	1632	1647	1659	1719	1724	1809	1828	1924	1954	2032	2116	2116	2106
arthen a.	1145	|	1239	1242	1240	1257	...	1347	1453	1440	...	1545	1653	1657	1709	...	1730	1750	1755	1854	1905	1951	2029	2057	2148	2148	2134
arthen d.	1148	|	1246	1249	1258	...	...	1351	...	1458	...	1549	...	1659	1714	...	1731	1752	1757	...	1905	1955	▬	2100	...	...	2205
and d.	1203	1238	1305	1308	1312	...	...	1406	...	1512	...	1604	...	1714	1732	...	1746	1808	1813	...	1921	2010		2115	...	...	2220
nby a.	|	|	1333	1336	1340	...	...	|	...	1540	...	|	...	1741	1800	...	|	|	|	...	1957	|	⑥	2142	...	...	|
mbroke Dock a.	|	|	1414	1414	1419	...	...	|	...	1619	...	|	...	1821	1840	...	|	|	|	...	2029	|		2218	...	...	|
eston Road d.	1217**x**	|	...	...	...	...	...	1420**x**	...	...	...	1618**x**	...	...	...	...	1800**x**	1822**x**	1851**x**	...	...	2025**x**	2030	...	...	...	2234**x**
rfordwest d.	1225	|	...	...	...	...	...	1429	...	...	...	1626	...	...	...	...	1808	|	|	...	...	2033	|	...	...	...	2242
rd Haven a.	1248	|	...	...	...	...	...	1500	...	...	...	1649	...	...	...	...	1833	|	|	...	...	2056	|	...	...	...	2305
shguard Harbour a.	...	1327	...	...	...	...	...	...	...	...	...	...	...	...	...	...	...	1846	1851	...	...	...	2054	...	...	...	...

	⑥	⑥	⑥	⑥
nchester Picc. **149** d.	...	1830	...	...
iff Central **132** d.	2104	2207	...	2235
end **132** d.	2123	2233	...	2302
Talbot **132** d.	2139	2245	...	2319
h **132** d.	2146	2252	...	2331
nsea **132** a.	2157	2308	...	2347
nsea d.	2225	2310	2347	0008
elli d.	2244	2329	0004	0027**s**
arthen a.	2318	0006	0035	0104
arthen d.	...	...	0037	...
and d.	...	...	0053	...
nby a.	...	...	|	...
mbroke Dock a.	...	...	|	...
eston Road d.	...	...	0106**x**	...
rfordwest d.	...	...	|	...
rd Haven a.	...	...	|	...
shguard Harbour a.	...	...	0135	...

⑦	⑦	⑦	⑦	⑦	⑦	⑦	⑦	⑦	⑦	⑦	⑦	⑦	⑦	⑦	⑦	⑦	⑦	⑦	⑦	⑦	⑦	⑦
							A		t	v	A			A			v	t				
Manchester Picc. **149** d.	...	...	...	...	...	...	...	...	...	...	...	1031	...	...	1233	...	1430	1430	...	...	...	...
Cardiff Central **132** d.	...	0710	...	...	0954	1112	1152	1205	*1303*	*1304*	1402	1412	*1504*	1604	1614	*1704*	1752	1807	...	*1902*	2014	2230
Bridgend **132** d.	...	0732	...	...	1024	1132	1215	1235	*1322*	*1325*	1422	1442	*1525*	1624	1644	*1725*	1841	1838	...	*1922*	2035	2251
Port Talbot **132** d.	...	0746	...	...	1040	1146	1228	1254	*1335*	*1338*	1435	1458	*1538*	1635	1701	*1736*	1857	1854	...	*1935*	2052	2305
Neath **132** d.	...	0754	...	...	1048	1154	1236	|	*1343*	*1345*	1443	1506	*1545*	1643	1709	*1744*	1905	1902	...	*1943*	2100	2313
Swansea **132** a.	...	0807	...	...	1100	1213	1249	|	*1357*	*1400*	1458	1519	*1600*	1656	1723	*1758*	1918	1915	...	*1959*	2112	2325
Swansea d.	...	0815	...	...	1104	1216	1255	|	1402	1407	1507	1536	1638	1708	1725	1837	1922	1920	...	2050	2118	2338
Llanelli d.	...	0835	...	...	1124	1234	1313	1326	1422	1427	1524	1555	1658	1726	1744	1857	1941	1939	...	2110	2137	2358
Carmarthen a.	...	0907	...	...	1156	1306	1342	1359	1455	1500	1552	1625	1730	1755	1814	1929	2009	2007	...	2142	2206	0030
Carmarthen d.	0820	0910	0955	1019	1206	1308	...	1405	1457	1502	...	1627	1732	...	1820	1932	2010	2008	...	...	2210	0034
Whitland d.	0836	0926	1011	1034	1222	1323	...	1421	1512	1513	...	1645	1748	...	1837	1948	2030	2030	2037	...	2226	0050
Tenby a.	|	0954	|	1101	|	|	...	|	1540	1545	...	|	1820	...	|	|	|	|	2102	...	|	|
Pembroke Dock a.	|	1027	|	1141	|	|	...	|	1617	1622	...	|	1859	...	|	|	|	|	2136	...	|	|
Clarbeston Road d.	0852**x**	...	1027**x**	...	1238**x**	|	...	1437**x**	...	...	...	1700**x**	...	...	1853**x**	2004**x**	2046**x**	2046**x**	...	...	2242**x**	0103**x**
Haverfordwest d.	0900	...	1035	...	1246	|	...	1445	...	...	...	1709	...	...	1901	2012	2054	2054	...	...	2250	|
Milford Haven a.	0920	...	1055	...	1306	|	...	1509	...	...	...	1729	...	...	1925	...	2120	2120	...	...	2310	|
Fishguard Harbour a.	...	...	...	...	...	1400	...	...	...	...	...	...	...	...	...	...	...	...	...	...	...	0132

From London (operated by GW, see Table **132**). Conveys 🍷.
From Gloucester (Table **121**).

Runs 10 minutes earlier Sept. 12 - Oct. 21.
May 16 - Sept. 9 and from Oct. 24.

c – Sept. 12 - Oct. 21.
d – June 25 - Sept.10 and from Oct. 29.
e – May 21 - June 18 and Sept. 17 - Oct. 22.
g – From Sept. 17.
h – May 21 - Sept. 10.
k – June 25 - Sept. 10.
m – May 21 - June 18.
p – From Oct. 29.
r – May 21 - Oct. 22.
s – Calls to set down only.
t – June 26 - Sept. 11.
v – May 15 - June 19.
x – Calls on request.

135 SOUTH WEST WALES - SWANSEA - CARDIFF

2nd class

Service on ⑦ is valid May 15 - Sept. 11. For service on ⑦ from Sept. 18 please contact National Rail Enquires ✆ +44 (0)3457 48 49 50.

		②–⑤	Ⓐ	Ⓐ	Ⓐ	Ⓐ	Ⓐ	Ⓐ	Ⓐ	Ⓐ	Ⓐ	Ⓐ	Ⓐ	Ⓐ	Ⓐ	Ⓐ	Ⓐ	Ⓐ	Ⓐ	Ⓐ	Ⓐ	Ⓐ	Ⓐ	Ⓐ	Ⓐ	Ⓐ
Fishguard Harbour d.	Ⓐ	...	0150	...	...	...	...	0647	...	...	0750	...	...	0954	...	...	...	...	...	...	1329	...	...	...	...	...
Milford Haven d.		0018	|	...	...	...	0555	|	0705	...	|	0908	...	|	...	1108	...	...	...	1308	|	...	...	1508	...	...
Haverfordwest d.		0033	|	...	...	...	0610	|	0720	...	|	0923	...	|	...	1123	...	...	...	1323	|	...	...	1523	...	...
Clarbeston Road d.		0041x	0212x	...	...	...	0618x	0711	0728x	...	0811x	0931x	...	1017x	...	1131x	...	...	...	1331x	|	...	...	1531x	...	...
Pembroke Dock d.		|	|	...	...	...	|	▬	|	0658	|	|	0909	|	...	|	...	1109	...	|	|	1309	...	|	...	1509
Tenby d.		|	|	...	...	...	|		|	0728	|	|	0938	|	...	|	...	1143	...	|	|	1341	...	|	...	1541
Whitland d.		0054	0224	...	...	...	0631	Ⓐ	0741	0755	0824	0944	1007	1032	...	1144	...	1211	...	1344	1404	1409	...	1544	...	1609
Carmarthen a.		0116	0241	...	...	...	0647	A	0755	0815	0843	1003	1024	1049	...	1200	...	1229	...	1400	1421	1430	...	1600	...	1627
Carmarthen d.		...	0303	0503	0547	0615	0650	0730	0801	0817	0900	1006	1031	...	1103	1205	...	1233	1302	1405	1426	1438	1503	1605	...	1631
Llanelli d.		...	0325	0528	0615	0644	0719	0805	0830	0846	0925	1032	1057	...	1131	1230	1245	1259	1330	1430	1448	1503	1532	1630	1645	1657
Swansea a.		...	0347	|	0635	0704	0738	0821	0849	0907	0951	1049	1123	...	1152	1249	1304	1322	1351	1449	|	1523	1551	1649	1702	1722
Swansea 132 d.		...	*0352*	|	0640	0706	0742	0828	0853	0910	0955	1055	...	...	1155	1254	1310	...	1355	1455	|	...	1555	1655	1712	...
Neath 132 d.		...	*0404*	|	0653	0717	0753	0840	0904	0925	1006	1106	...	...	1206	1305	1325	...	1406	1506	|	...	1606	1706	1727	...
Port Talbot 132 d.		...	*0412*	0601	0704	0724	0800	0848	0911	0936	1013	1113	...	...	1213	1312	1336	...	1413	1513	|	...	1613	1713	1738	...
Bridgend 132 d.		...	*0425*	0616	0720	0740	0815	0902	0924	0953	1026	1126	...	...	1226	1325	1353	...	1426	1526	1535	...	1626	1726	1755	...
Cardiff Central 132 a.		...	*0501*	0643	0748	0802	0837	0923	0944	1019	1048	1146	...	...	1248	1347	1415	...	1447	1547	1558	...	1646	1746	1814	...
Manchester Picc. 149 a.		...	...	1014	...	1115	1215	...	1315	...	1415	1515	...	...	1615	1715	...	...	1815	1915	...	...	2021	2106	...	...

	Ⓐ	Ⓐ	Ⓐ	Ⓐ	Ⓐ	Ⓐ	Ⓐ a	Ⓐ b	Ⓐ	Ⓐ	Ⓐ	Ⓐ		⑥	⑥	⑥	⑥	⑥ h	⑥ e	⑥ k	⑥	⑥	⑥	⑥	⑥	⑥
Fishguard Harbour d.	...	...	1908	...	...	...	2050	2105	...	...	...	...	⑥	...	0150	...	...	...	...	...	...	0650	...	...	...	0750
Milford Haven d.	1708	...	|	1912	...	2036	|	|	...	...	...	2318		0018	|	...	...	...	...	...	0555	|	0705	...	...	|
Haverfordwest d.	1723	...	|	1927	...	2051	|	|	...	...	...	2333		0033	|	...	...	...	...	...	0610	|	0720	...	...	|
Clarbeston Road d.	1731x	...	1930	1935x	...	2059x	2112x	2127x	...	...	...	2341x		0041x	0212x	...	...	...	...	...	0618x	0714	0728x	...	...	0811x
Pembroke Dock d.	|	1709	▬	|	*1919*	|	|	|	...	2109	2228	|		|	|	...	...	...	...	...	|	...	|	0657	...	|
Tenby d.	|	1738		|	1957	|	|	|	...	2153	2255	|		|	|	...	...	...	...	...	|	...	|	0727	...	|
Whitland d.	1745	1807	Ⓐ	1948	2027	2112	2126	2141	...	2221	2325	2354		0054	0224	...	...	...	...	...	0631	...	0741	0753	...	0824
Carmarthen a.	1802	1824		2004	2045	2134	2149	2203	...	2239	2344	0016		0116	0241	...	...	...	...	...	0647	...	0755	0815	...	0843
Carmarthen d.	1806	1831	1850	2009	2047	...	...	...	...	2244	...	...		...	0244	0501	0552	0616	0620	0620	0650	...	0801	0815	...	0900
Llanelli d.	1835	1857	1921	2033	2117	...	...	...	2201	2314	...	...		...	0306	0526	0621	0644	0648	0648	0719	...	0830	0845	0855	0928
Swansea a.	1855	1922	1943	2055	2142	...	...	...	2222	2343	...	...		...	0329	|	0643	0704	0708	0708	0738	...	0849	0907	0922	0950
Swansea 132 d.	1858	...	1951	2058	2145	...	...	...	2232	...	...	...		...	*0358*c	|	0644	0707	0711	0729	0744	...	0855	0907	0926	0952
Neath 132 d.	1913	...	2002	2109	2200	...	...	...	2247	...	...	...		...	*0410*c	|	0655	0722	0726	0744	0755	...	0906	0923	0939	1003
Port Talbot 132 d.	1924	...	2009	2116	2211	...	...	...	2258	...	...	...		...	*0418*c	0559	0702	0733	0737	0755	0802	...	0913	0934	0946	1012
Bridgend 132 d.	1940	...	2023	2131	2227	...	...	...	2315	...	...	...		...	*0430*c	0614	0717	0749	0753	0811	0817	...	0928	0952	1004	1027
Cardiff Central 132 a.	2003	...	2046	2205	2256	...	...	...	2340	...	...	...		...	*0452*c	0643	0742	0821	0834f	0838	0844	...	0952	1025d	1034	1052
Manchester Picc. 149 a.	...	...	...	...	...	...	...	...	...	...	...	...		...	...	1016	1115	...	...	...	1215	...	1315	...	...	1415

	⑥ An	⑥	⑥	⑥	⑥	⑥ Am	⑥	⑥	⑥	⑥	⑥	⑥	⑥	⑥	⑥ Ak	⑥ Ar	⑥ p	⑥	⑥	⑥ m	⑥ p	⑥	⑥	⑥	⑥	⑥
Fishguard Harbour d.	...	...	...	0953	...	...	...	...	...	...	1328	...	...	...	...	...	...	...	...	...	...	1900	...	...	...	2100
Milford Haven d.	...	0908	...	|	...	...	1108	...	...	1308	|	...	...	1508	...	...	...	...	1708	...	...	|	1908	...	...	|
Haverfordwest d.	...	0923	...	|	...	...	1123	...	...	1323	|	...	...	1523	...	...	...	...	1723	...	...	|	1923	...	...	|
Clarbeston Road d.	...	0931x	...	1014x	...	...	1131x	...	...	1331x	|	...	...	1531x	...	...	...	...	1731x	...	...	1922	1931x	...	...	2122x
Pembroke Dock d.	...	|	0909p	|	...	0958	|	1109p	...	|	|	1309	...	|	1450	1455	1509	...	|	1625	1712	▬	|	1909	...	|
Tenby d.	...	|	0937p	|	...	1034	|	1141	...	|	|	1340	...	|	1529	1536	1543	...	|	1655	1743	...	|	1951	...	|
Whitland d.	...	0944	1003	1029	...	1105	1144	1209	...	1344	1403	1409	...	1544	1602	1609	1612	...	1745	1726	1811	⑥	1944	2021	...	2136
Carmarthen a.	...	1002	1025	1046	...	1126	1200	1227	...	1400	1419	1428	...	1600	1620	1627	1629	...	1803	1744	1829		2004	2039	...	2159
Carmarthen d.	0950	1004	1025	...	1107	1129	1205	1231	1302	1405	1422	1431	1503	1605	1628	1633	1632	1702	1807	1826	1833	1854	2007	2047		...
Llanelli d.	1018	1031	1051	...	1135	1157	1230	1257	1330	1430	1445	1456	1532	1630	1655	1701	1657	1730	1836	1852	1858	1925	2031	2117	*2138*	...
Swansea a.	1034	1048	1120	...	1156	1219	1249	1322q	1349	1449	|	1522	1551	1649	1714	1717	1722	1749	1856	1921	1920	1947	2051	2142	*2206*	...
Swansea 132 d.	1041	1055	...	...	1158	1222	1253	...	1357	1455	|	...	1555	1658	1722	1728	...	1752	1900	...	...	1952	2055	2143	2220	...
Neath 132 d.	1053	1106	...	...	1209	1234	1304	...	1408	1506	|	...	1606	1707	1734	1740	...	1803	1911	...	...	2003	2106	2159	2235	...
Port Talbot 132 d.	1101	1113	...	...	1216	1242	1311	...	1415	1513	|	...	1613	1714	1742	1748	...	1810	1919	...	...	2010	2113	2210	2246	...
Bridgend 132 d.	1114	1128	...	...	1229	1255	1326	...	1428	1526	1531	...	1628	1729	1755	1801	...	1825	1933	...	...	2024	2126	2226	2302	...
Cardiff Central 132 a.	1135	1148	...	...	1252	1322	1348	...	1452	1551	1558	...	1648	1751	1816	1822	...	1847	1956	...	...	2049	2146	2250	2326	...
Manchester Picc. 149 a.	...	1515	...	...	1615	...	1714	...	1815	1915	...	...	2015	2115	...	...	...	2214	*2349*	...	...	...	...	...	...	...

	⑥	⑥	⑥		⑦	⑦ 🚌	⑦	⑦	⑦	⑦	⑦	⑦	⑦	⑦ A	⑦	⑦	⑦ A	⑦	⑦	⑦ A	⑦	⑦	⑦	⑦	⑦	⑦
Fishguard Harbour d.	...	...	...	⑦	0150	...	...	...	...	...	...	...	...	...	1422	...	...	...	...	...	...	...	...	...	...	...
Milford Haven d.	...	...	2318		|	...	...	...	0928	...	1123	...	1318	...	|	1513	...	...	1732	...	...	...	1938	...	2135	...
Haverfordwest d.	...	...	2333		|	...	...	...	0943	...	1138	...	1331	...	|	1528	...	...	1747	...	...	...	1953	...	2151	...
Clarbeston Road d.	...	...	2341x		|	...	...	...	0952x	...	1147x	...	1340x	...	|	1537x	...	...	1755x	...	...	...	2001x	...	2159x	...
Pembroke Dock d.	2109	2218	|		|	...	...	...	|	...	|	1155	|	...	|	|	...	1625	|	...	...	1900	|	...	|	2145
Tenby d.	2142	2245	|		|	...	...	...	|	...	|	1223	|	...	|	|	...	1653	|	...	...	1928	|	...	|	2213
Whitland d.	2211	2315	2354		0224s	...	...	...	1006	...	1203	1254	1357	...	1457	1554	...	1724	1810	...	...	1959	2017	...	2214	2244
Carmarthen a.	2228	2334	0016		0242	...	...	...	1024	...	1221	1317	1415	...	1514	1611	...	1744	1829	...	...	2016	2036	...	2231	2305
Carmarthen d.	2235	...	...		0245	0250	0840	0940	1030	1053	1224	1320	1425	1458	1540	1616	1655	1747	...	1905	...	2019	...	2115	2234	...
Llanelli d.	2305	...	...		0308s	|	0907	1010	1057	1123	1250	1350	1451	1527	1610	1646	1722	1818	...	1932	1959	2051	...	2141	2304	...
Swansea a.	2330	...	...		|	0350	0927	1036	1116	1147	1313	1415	1513	1543	1635	1708	1739	1846	...	1949	2020	2117	...	2204	2327	...
Swansea 132 d.	...	...	...		|	*0808*	0932	...	1132	*1221*	1342	*1421*	1533	1551	*1651*	1730	1751	*1851*	...	1955	2040	...	...	2210	2331	...
Neath 132 d.	...	...	...		|	*0820*	0943	...	1143	*1233*	1353	*1433*	1544	1603	*1703*	1741	1803	*1903*	...	2007	2051	...	...	2221	2343	...
Port Talbot 132 d.	...	...	...		|	*0827*	0950	...	1150	*1240*	1400	*1440*	1551	1610	*1710*	1748	1810	*1910*	...	2014	2058	...	...	2228	2350	...
Bridgend 132 d.	...	...	...		|	*0840*	1005	...	1205	*1253*	1416	*1453*	1606	1623	*1723*	1803	1823	*1923*	...	2028	2114	...	...	2245	0006	...
Cardiff Central 132 a.	...	...	...		0407	*0905*	1029	...	1234	*1317*	1445	*1517*	1636	1644	*1745*	1832	1845	*1946*	...	2050	2137	...	...	2308	0030	...
Manchester Picc. 149 a.	...	...	...		...	...	1420	...	1615	...	1818	...	2016	...	...	2219	...	...	...	...	...	...	...	...	...	...

A – To London (operated by GW, see Table **132**). Conveys 🍷.

a – May 16 - Sept. 9 and from Oct. 24.
b – Sept. 12 - Oct. 21.
c – Runs 20 minutes later Sept. 17 - Oct. 22.
d – 1018 May 21 - June 18 and from Sept. 17.
e – May 21 - June 18 and Sept. 17 - Oct. 22.
f – 0825 Sept. 17 - Oct. 22.
g – May 21 - Sept. 10 and from Oct. 29.
h – From Oct. 29.
k – June 25 - Sept. 10.
m – May 21 - Sept. 10.
n – Sept. 17 - Oct. 22.
p – From Sept. 17.
q – 1317 June 25 - Sep
r – May 21 - June 18.
s – Calls to set down or
t – May 15 - Sept. 11.
x – Calls on request.

136 CARDIFF - BRISTOL

2nd class

Service May 15 - Sept. 11

km				Ⓐ	Ⓐ	Ⓐ	Ⓐ	Ⓐ	Ⓐ	Ⓐ		Ⓐ	Ⓐ	Ⓐ	Ⓐ	Ⓐ	Ⓐ	Ⓐ		⑥	⑥	⑥	⑥
0	**Cardiff** Central d.	Ⓐ	...	0628	0700	0730	0800	0830	0900	0930	and at the same	1930	2000	2100	2130	2204	2236	2327	⑥	0455	0622	0654	0721
19	Newport d.		...	0642	0715	0744	0815	0844	0915	0944	minutes past	1944	2015	2115	2143	2218	2353	2343		0509	0637	0708	0736
61	**Bristol** T Meads a.		...	0719	0751	0809	0852	0919	0954	1019	each hour until ▽	2017	2053	2151	2222	2304	2337	0033		0554	0719	0751	0822

		⑥	⑥	⑥	⑥	⑥		⑦	⑦	⑦	⑦	⑦	⑦	⑦	⑦	⑦	⑦	⑦	⑦	⑦	⑦	⑦	⑦
Cardiff Central d.	and at the same	1924	1950	2023	2100	2200	⑦	0805	0913	1008	1108	1208	1308	1408	1507	1608	1635	1708	1740	1808	1908	2014	2118
Newport d.	minutes past	1939	2005	2037	2115	2215		0824	0927	1022	1122	1221	1322	1422	1522	1622	1649	1722	1754	1821	1922	2033	2138
Bristol T Meads a.	each hour until ▽	2019	2048	2116	2157	2300		0907	1013	1103	1203	1304	1403	1503	1605	1703	1728	1802	1837	1904	2005	2113	2229

		②–⑤	Ⓐ	Ⓐ	Ⓐ	Ⓐ	Ⓐ	Ⓐ		Ⓐ	Ⓐ	Ⓐ	Ⓐ	Ⓐ	Ⓐ	Ⓐ		⑥	⑥	⑥	⑥	
Bristol T Meads d.	Ⓐ	0137	0554	0619	0650	0716	0720	0754	and at the same	1921	1954	2015	2054	2119	2154	2254	⑥	0137	0650	0721	0754	and at the sa
Newport a.		0215s	0628	0659	0725	0748	0807	0827	minutes past	2001	2027	2047	2126	2158	2235	2339		0203s	0731	0804	0832	minutes pas
Cardiff Central a.		0232	0648	0718	0743	0803	0824	0846	each hour until ▽	2020	2044	2102	2145	2218	2254	2357		0220	0749	0824	0849	each hour unt

	⑥	⑥	⑥	⑥	⑥	⑥	⑥			⑦	⑦	⑦	⑦	⑦	⑦	⑦	⑦	⑦	⑦	⑦	⑦	⑦	⑦	⑦	⑦
Bristol T Meads d.	1921	1954	2010	2054	2129	2157	2255	...	⑦	0848	0948	1048	1147	1248	1348	1416	1448	1548	1612	1648	1748	1848	1948	2048	2148
Newport a.	2002	2029	2049	2130	2210	2238	2335	...		0925	1030	1127	1227	1325	1425	1453	1526	1625	1649	1727	1827	1927	2028	2124	2233
Cardiff Central a.	2021	2048	2104	2146	2230	2257	2355	...		0941	1046	1144	1243	1341	1445	1509	1545	1644	1708	1745	1845	1948	2046	2143	2256

s – Calls to set down only.

▽ – Timings may vary by up to 5 minutes.

BRISTOL - TAUNTON 137

2nd class

		Ⓐ	Ⓐ	ⒶA	Ⓐ	Ⓐ	Ⓐ	Ⓐ	Ⓐ	Ⓐ	Ⓐ	Ⓐ	Ⓐ	Ⓐ	Ⓐ	Ⓐ	Ⓐ	Ⓐ	Ⓐ	Ⓐ	Ⓐ		⑥	⑥	⑥A
Bristol T Meads **132** d.	Ⓐ	0524	0642	0718	0826	0855	0955	1053	1153	1253	1357	1453	1553	1653	1755	1856	1955	2055	2156	2306	2335	⑥	0524	0618	0718
Weston-super-Mare **132** d.		0547	0706	0749	0901	0929	1023	1122	1221	1323	1425	1528	1627	1728	1830	1930	2029	2133	2229	2342	0005**s**		0545	0646	0751
Highbridge ⊖ d.		0557	0717	0800	0911	0940	1034	1133	1232	1334	1436	1538	1638	1739	1841	1940	2039	2144	2240	2354	0016**s**		0555	0657	0802
Bridgwater d.		0605	0725	0808	0919	0948	1042	1141	1240	1342	1444	1546	1646	1747	1849	1948	2047	2152	2248	0002	0024**s**		0603	0705	0810
Taunton **132** a.		0618	0738	0824	0932	1001	1059	1155	1256	1358	1457	1601	1701	1801	1903	2004	2103	2207	2301	0014	0036		0616	0719	0824

	⑥	⑥	⑥	⑥	⑥	⑥	⑥	⑥	⑥	⑥	⑥	⑥	⑥	⑥	⑥		⑦	⑦	⑦	⑦A	⑦	⑦	⑦	⑦	⑦	⑦
tol T Meads **132** d.	0857	0953	1053	1153	1253	1355	1453	1553	1653	1753	1853	1953	2054	2201	2217	⑦	0726	0828	1021	1110**a**	1310	1555	1655	1830	1905	2025
ton-super-Mare **132** d.	0932	1022	1123	1222	1323	1423	1523	1623	1723	1823	1923	2024	2128	2233	2247**s**		0749	0858	1052	1137	1338	1629	1726	1900	1940	2059
bridge ⊖ d.	0944	1033	1134	1233	1334	1434	1535	1634	1734	1834	1934	2034	2139	2244	2258**s**		|	0909	1103	1147	1349	1639	1739	1911	1950	2109
water d.	0952	1041	1142	1241	1342	1442	1543	1642	1742	1842	1942	2042	2147	2252	2305**s**		0805	0917	1111	1155	1357	1647	1744	1919	1958	2117
nton **132** a.	1006	1057	1156	1257	1359	1459	1559	1657	1759	1856	1959	2059	2159	2307	2317		0818	0930	1124	1209	1409	1710	1759	1933	2012	2132

		Ⓐ	Ⓐ	Ⓐ	Ⓐ	Ⓐ	Ⓐ	Ⓐ	Ⓐ	Ⓐ	Ⓐ	Ⓐ	Ⓐ	Ⓐ	Ⓐ	Ⓐ	Ⓐ	Ⓐ	Ⓐ	Ⓐ	Ⓐ		⑥	⑥	⑥	⑥
nton **132** d.	Ⓐ	0512	0602	0634	0654	0712	0836	0938	1007	1104	1207	1307	1410	1457	1607	1706	1808	1917	2030	2129	2245	⑥	0528	0634	0654	0735
water d.		0524	0614	0646	0705	0723	0848	0950	1019	1116	1219	1319	1422	1509	1619	1717	1819	1929	2042	2140	2257		0540	0646	0705	0747
bridge ⊖ d.		0532	0621	0654	0713	0731	0856	0957	1027	1124	1227	1327	1431	1516	1627	1725	1827	1936	2050	2147	2305		0548	0654	0712	0755
ton-super-Mare **132** a.		0543	0632	0704	0724	0742	0909	1008	1038	1134	1238	1338	1441	1527**b**	1637	1737	1838	1947	2100	2159	2315		0559	0705	0724	0805
tol T Meads **132** a.		0620	0709	0741	0757	0825	0943	1042	1110	1212	1309	1412	1513	1612	1711	1812	1913	2020	2135	2232	2351		0634	0742	0758	0840

	⑥	⑥	⑥	⑥	⑥	⑥	⑥	⑥	⑥	⑥	⑥	⑥	⑥	⑥		⑦	⑦c	⑦	⑦	⑦	⑦	⑦	⑦	⑦	⑦	⑦
nton **132** d.	0759	0910	1012	1104	1207	1307	1407	1507	1607	1707	1807	1907	2017	2135	⑦	0835	1008	1136	1334	1519	1658	1719	1818	1856	2025	2136
water d.	0810	0922	1024	1116	1219	1319	1419	1519	1619	1719	1819	1919	2029	2147		0847	1020	1148	1346	1531	1709	1730	1830	1906	2037	2148
bridge ⊖ d.	0817	0930	1032	1124	1227	1327	1427	1527	1627	1727	1827	1927	2037	2155		0855	1028	1155	1353	1538	1717	1737	1837	1913	2045	2155
ton-super-Mare **132** a.	0827	0942	1047	1135	1237	1337	1437	1537	1637	1737	1839	1937	2048	2205		0906	1038	1205	1404	1548	1727	1748	1848	1924	2057	2205
tol T Meads **132** a.	0857	1013	1117	1211	1309	1411	1510	1609	1711	1811	1910	2009	2124	2240		0938	1110	1243	1436	1620	1757	1819	1917	1950	2131	2238

From Gloucester (Table **138**).

a – From Sept. 18.
b – Departs 1543.
c – Runs 10 minutes later from Sept. 18.
s – Calls to set down only.
⊖ – Highbridge and Burnham.

WORCESTER - GLOUCESTER - BRISTOL 138

2nd class

		Ⓐ	ⒶA	ⒶC	Ⓐ	ⒶB	ⒶB	ⒶC	ⒶB	Ⓐ	ⒶD	ⒶB	ⒶC	ⒶB	ⒶB	ⒶC	ⒶD	①–④	Ⓐ	Ⓐ	Ⓐ		⑥A	⑥
Great Malvern d.	Ⓐ	...	...	...	...	...	...	0850	...	1050	...	1251	...	1450	...	1648	...	1850	...	...	...	⑥	...	...
Worcester Shrub Hill d.		0521	...	...	...	0649	*0706*	0906	...	1106	...	1306	...	1506	...	1706	...	1907	...	2146	2228		...	...
Ashchurch for Tewkesbury d.		0540	...	...	*0627*	0705	|	0924	...	1124	...	1324	...	1524	...	1724	...	1924	...	2202	2251		...	...
Cheltenham Spa ◧ d.		0551	...	0624	*0643*	0716	*0729*	0933	...	1133	...	1333	...	1533	...	1733	...	1934	2048	2212	2305		...	0648
Gloucester ◧ a.		0602	...	0634	*0653*	0726	*0738*	0942	...	1145	...	1344	...	1544	...	1744	...	1943	2105	2223	2317		...	0658
Gloucester d.		...	0616	0642	0705	0741	0841	0944	1041	1147	1241	1346	1441	1546	1640	1746	1841	1945	2115	2228	...		0618	0702
Bristol Parkway d.		...	0657	0724	0749	0820	0919	1022	1120	1223	1319	1423	1520	1624	1720	1823	1922	2027	2152	2305	...		0700	0740
Bristol Temple Meads a.		...	0713	0740	0800	0836	0935	1039	1135	1235	1335	1439	1538	1639	1735	1839	1938	2038	2211	2319	...		0713	0755

	⑥B	⑥B	⑥C	⑥B	⑥	⑥D	⑥B	⑥C	⑥B	⑥B	⑥C	⑥D	⑥	⑥	⑥	⑥			⑦A	⑦	⑦	⑦	⑦	⑦	⑦
at Malvern d.	...	...	...	...	1046	...	...	...	1450	...	1650	...	1850	...	2115	...	...	⑦	...	...	...	...	...	...	...
cester Shrub Hill d.	0647	...	0908	...	1106	...	1254	...	1506	...	1706	...	1906	...	2131	2225	...		...	...	1436	1640	1840	2038	...
church for Tewkesbury d.	0703	...	0927	...	1124	...	1310	...	1524	...	1724	...	1924	...	2151	2241	...		...	...	1451	1656	1856	2054	...
ltenham Spa ◧ d.	0713	...	0936	...	1134	...	1320	...	1534	...	1734	...	1934	2102	2201	2251	...		1004	1203	1501	1706	1906	2103	2201
ucester ◧ a.	0725	...	0945	...	1145	...	1332	...	1544	...	1745	...	1945	2112	2211	2301	...		1014	1214	1511	1716	1916	2113	2211
ucester d.	0740	0841	0946	1041	1146	1241	1342	1441	1546	1641	1746	1841	1946	2114	...	...	...		1016	1218	1513	1719	1919	2115	...
stol Parkway d.	0820	0920	1025	1121	1225	1320	1422	1520	1624	1720	1825	1920	2025	2152	...	...	...		1055	1258	1555	1757	1958	2153	...
stol Temple Meads a.	0834	0936	1039	1135	1239	1334	1437	1534	1639	1734	1839	1935	2039	2204	...	...	...		1107**a**	1309	1608	1809	2010	2207	...

		Ⓐ	Ⓐ	ⒶC	ⒶC	ⒶC	Ⓐ	Ⓐ	Ⓐ	Ⓐ	ⒶC	ⒶB	ⒶC	ⒶB	ⒶC	Ⓐ	Ⓐ	Ⓐ	Ⓐ			⑥	⑥	⑥C	⑥C
stol Temple Meads d.	Ⓐ	...	...	0734	0841	0940	1040	1141	1241	1340	1441	1541	1641	1741	1834	1941	2041	...	2211	...	⑥	...	...	0741	0841
stol Parkway d.		...	...	0746	0852	0952	1052	1152	1252	1352	1452	1552	1651	1753	1846	1952	2052	...	2223	...		...	...	0752	0852
ucester a.		...	...	0832	0933	1032	1134	1233	1334	1431	1534	1633	1734	1833	1928	2032	2132	...	2304	...		...	...	0833	0933
ucester ◧ d.		0600	0714	...	0937	...	1136	...	1337	...	1536	...	1737	...	1948	2035	2133	2152	...	...		0550	0715	...	0937
ltenham Spa ◧ a.		0610	0724	...	0946	...	1146	...	1346	...	1546	...	1747	...	2001	2048	2144	2202	...	...		0559	0724	...	0947
church for Tewkesbury a.		0619	0733	...	0955	...	1156	...	1355	...	1556	...	1756	...	2010	...	2153	|	...	...		0608	0733	...	0956
cester Shrub Hill a.		0641	0754	...	1014	...	1213	...	1414	...	1614	...	1816	...	2030	...	2214	2224	...	...		0633	0752	...	1014
at Malvern a.		...	0812	...	1032	...	1233	...	1435	...	1632	...	1836	...	...	...	...	...	...	...		...	...	...	1032

	⑥C	⑥	⑥B	⑥	⑥B	⑥	⑥B	⑥C	⑥C	⑥B	⑥C	⑥	⑥			⑦	⑦		⑦	⑦	⑦	⑦		⑦	⑦
stol Temple Meads d.	0941	1041	1141	1241	1341	1441	1541	1641	1741	1841	1941	2043	2206	...	⑦	0958	1211	...	1441	1641	1837	2041	...	2230	...
stol Parkway d.	0952	1052	1152	1252	1352	1452	1552	1652	1752	1852	1952	2052	2218	...		1007	1222	...	1451	1651	1846	2050	...	2239	...
ucester a.	1032	1132	1233	1335	1433	1533	1633	1733	1833	1933	2033	2134	2301	...		1048	1304	...	1533	1733	1930	2133	...	2321	...
ucester ◧ d.	...	1135	...	1337	...	1537	...	1737	...	1937	2037	2137	...	...		1050	1305	...	1551	1735	1934	2137	...	...	2356
ltenham Spa ◧ a.	...	1147	...	1347	...	1547	...	1747	...	1948	2049	2148	...	...		1100	1316	...	1602	1745	1946	2146	...	...	0007
church for Tewkesbury a.	...	1157	...	1357	...	1556	...	1756	...	1956	...	2157	...	...		...	1325	...	1612	1755	1956	...	...	...	...
cester Shrub Hill a.	...	1215	...	1415	...	1614	...	1815	...	2015	...	2218	...	...		...	1344	...	1629	1815	2022	...	...	...	...
at Malvern a.	...	...	...	1432	...	1632	...	1836	...	2040	...	...	...	...		...	...	...	...	...	...	...	...	...	...

To Taunton (Table **137**).
To/from Weymouth (Table **139**).

C – To/from Westbury (Table **139**).
D – To Frome (Table **139**).
a – From Sept. 18.
◧ – See also Tables **121** and **133**.

BRISTOL - WEYMOUTH 139

2nd class

	Ⓐ	⑥	⚒A	⑦	⑥K	ⒶK	⑥E	a	⑦c	⚒C	⚒D	⚒C	⑥J	⑦c	⑦d	⚒C	ⒶE	⚒D	⑥C	ⒶC	⚒F	⑦	⚒C	⚒F	⚒C		⑥	Ⓐ
Bristol T M **140** d.	*0544*	*0549*	0749	...	0839	0841	k	0906	0925	0949	1049	1149	k	*1310*	1335	1349	...	1448	1538	1544	1649	1743	1749	1849	1949	2048	2310	2320
Bath **140** d.	*0603*	*0607*	0807	...	0857	0859	...	0927	0944	1007	1107	1207	...	*1327*	1354	1407	...	1506	1557	1602	1707	1801	1807	1907	2007	2106	2328	2338
Bradford § **140** d.	*0619*	*0623*	0823	...	0913	0915	...	0941	1000	1023	1123	1223	...	*1340*	1410	1423	...	1522	1613	1618	1723	1816	1823	1923	2023	2123	2343	2354
Trowbridge **140** d.	*0626*	*0629*	0829	...	0919	0921	...	0948	1007	1029	1129	1229	...	*1347*	1416	1429	...	1528	1619	1624	1729	1824	1829	1929	2029	2129	2350	2359
Westbury **140** a.	*0631*	*0636*	0836	...	0926	0928	...	0955	1013	1036	1136	1236	...	*1355*	1422	1436	...	1536	1626	1633	1736	1831	1836	1939	2036	2137	2357	0007
Westbury d.	0646	0647	...	0912	0927	0932	...	1002	1018	1037	...	1237	...	1425	1425	1437	1457	1537	...	...	1738	1831	1840	...	2037	2138	2358	0008
Frome d.	0655	0656	...	0922	0936	0941	...	1016	1031	1046	...	1247	...	1434	1433	1451	1507	1546	...	...	1747	1839	1849	...	2048	2148	0008	0019
Castle Cary d.	0714	0715	...	0940	0953	1000	...	1037	1048	1103	...	1304	...	1451	1450	...	1524	1602	...	...	1805	1858	1906	...	...	2205	...	...
Yeovil Pen Mill d.	0735	0729	...	0956	1007	1014	1033	1053	1103	1117	...	1317	1414	1505	1505	...	1537	1617	...	...	1821	1912	1919	...	...	2221	...	...
Dorchester West d.	0809	0803	...	1030	1040	1048	1100	1133	1141	1154	...	1354	1446	1540	1540	...	...	1658	...	...	1854	1947	1954	...	...	2255	...	...
Weymouth a.	0824	0817	...	1042	1057	1103	1126	1145	1154	1209	...	1409	1508	1554	1554	...	...	1710	...	...	1912**b**	2001	2010	...	...	2313	...	...

	⚒C	Ⓐ	⚒F	⚒	⚒C	⑦	⑥C	Ⓐ	⑦	⑦c	⚒H	⚒F	⑥Jk	⚒C	⚒F	⑦	⑥C	ⒶC	⑥F	⑦	ⒶK	⑥Ek	⚒	⑥a	⑦	ⒶL	⑦	⚒	Ⓐ
ymouth d.	...	0533	...	0638	e	...	0846	0853	...	1105	1110	e	1210	1310	...	1415	1508**g**	1508	1608**a**	1610	...	1656	1728	1828	1756	...	2009	2021	...
chester West d.	...	0545	...	0651	...	...	0859	0906	...	1118	1123	...	1222	1323	...	1428	1521**g**	1521	1623**a**	1623	...	1707	1740	1841	1809	...	2022	2034	...
vil Pen Mill d.	...	0620	...	0730	...	...	0934	0941	...	1154	1205	...	1254	1406	...	1504	1556**g**	1556	1705**a**	1658	...	1734	1818	1919	1844	1927	2057	2106	...
tle Cary d.	...	0644	...	0744	...	...	0948	0955	...	1208	1222	...	...	1420	...	1518	1610**g**	1610	1719**a**	1713	...	—	1832	1933	1859	1939	2110	2118	...
me d.	...	0703	...	0802	...	0935	1007	1015	1140	1227	1239	...	...	1439	...	1537	1629**g**	1629	1738**a**	1731	...	⑥	1857	1958	1918	1956	2129	2138	...
stbury a.	...	0711	...	0811	...	0944	1016	1024	1149	1236	1250**f**	...	...	1450**f**	...	1546	1638**g**	1638	1746**a**	1740	...	F	1916	2009	1927	2005	2139	2151	...
stbury **140** d.	0638	0717	0738	0817	0838	0953	1038	1038	1150	*1256*	1252**f**	1338	...	1451**f**	1538	1547	1638	1642	1746	1741	1738	1746	1917	2014	1934	*2010*	2147	2155	2232
wbridge **140** d.	0644	0723	0744	0823	0844	0959	1044	1044	1156	*1302*	1256	1344	...	1455	1544	1553	1644	1647	1752	1748	1744	1752	1923	2021	1940	*2016*	2155	2202	2238
dford § **140** d.	0650	0729	0750	0829	0850	1005	1050	1050	1202	*1308*	1302	1350	...	1501	1550	1559	1650	1653	1758	1754	1750	1758	1929	2029	1948	*2022*	2201	2208	2244
h **140** a.	0706	0745	0807	0846	0905	1021	1106	1106	1219	*1322*	1320	1406	...	1519	1606	1616	1706	1709	1816	1806	1806	1814	1949	2045	2007	*2034*	2218	2224	2300
stol T M **140** a.	0727	0805	0829	0906	0927	1040	1127	1128	1238	*1341*	1343	1429	...	1537	1629	1635	1728	1731	1837	1831	1828	1837	2009	2105	2029	*2048*	2237	2244	2323

To Cheltenham Spa on Ⓐ (Table **138**).
From/to Gloucester (Table **138**).
To Worcester (also Great Malvern on Ⓐ). See Table **138**.
From/to London Waterloo (Table **140**).
From/to Great Malvern (Table **138**).

G – To Great Malvern on ⑥ (Table **138**).
H – To Gloucester on ⑥ (Table **138**).
J – From/to Yeovil Junction (Table **140**).
K – From Worcester (Table **138**).
L – To Salisbury (Table **140**).

a – May 21 - Sept. 10.
b – 1927 on ⑥ May 21 - Sept. 10.
c – May 15 - Oct. 23.
d – From Oct. 30.
e – Runs 6 minutes later on Ⓐ.

f – 2–3 minutes earlier on ⑥.
g – From Sept. 17.
k – May 21 - Sept. 3.
§ – Bradford on Avon

140 BRISTOL - WESTBURY - SOUTHAMPTON, PORTSMOUTH and LONDON GW,

BRISTOL - WESTBURY - SOUTHAMPTON - PORTSMOUTH

2nd class

km		Ⓐ	Ⓐ	Ⓐ	Ⓐ	Ⓐ	Ⓐ	Ⓐ		Ⓐ	Ⓐ	Ⓐ a	Ⓐ b	⑥	⑥	⑥		⑥	⑥	⑥	⑦	⑦
0	**Bristol** T Meads . 139 d.	...	0544	0722	0822	0922	1022			1922	2022	2123	2204	...	0549	0722		1922	2022	2122	0910	1
19	Bath Spa 139 d.	...	0603	0735	0836	0936	1035		and	1935	2036	2136	2218	...	0607	0735	and	1935	2035	2136	0927	1
34	Bradford on Avon 139 d.	...	0619	0747	0847	0948	1047		at	1947	2047	2148	2230	...	0623	0747	at	1947	2047	2148	0940	1
39	Trowbridge 139 d.	...	0626	0753	0853	0954	1053		the	1953	2053	2155	2236	...	0629	0753	the	1953	2053	2154	0947	1
46	**Westbury** 139 a.	...	0631	0800	0900	1001	1100		same	2000	2100	2203	2244	...	0636	0801	same	2001	2101	2201	0956	1
46	**Westbury** d.	0549	0640	0801	0901	1002	1101		minutes	2001	2101	2203	2244	0601	0643	0801	minutes	2001	2101	2201	0959	1
53	Warminster d.	0557	0648	0809	0909	1010	1109		past	2009	2109	2211	2253	0609	0651	0809	past	2009	2109	2212	1008	1
85	Salisbury d.	0619	0711	0832	0932	1032	1132		each	2032	2132	2232	2314	0632	0724c	0832	each	2032	2132	2233	1032	1
112	Romsey d.	0638	0730	0850	0950	1050	1150		hour	2050	2150	2253	2334	0650	0744	0850	hour	2050	2150	2253	1050	1
123	**Southampton** C a.	0649	0740	0904	1004	1104	1204		until	2104	2202	2304	2346	0702	0802	0903	until	2103	2203	2304	1103	1
147	Fareham a.	0715	0805	0927	1027	1127	1227			2127	2242	2327	0008	0727	0827	0927		2127	2226	2326	1126	1
164	**Portsmouth** & S a.	0738	0824	0946	1046	1146	1246		★	2145	2258	2348	0029	0746	0846	0946	★	2146	2246	2345	1144	1
165	**Portsmouth** H a.	0745	0830	0952	1054	1154	1254			2153	2303	2354	0036	0752	0852	0952		2152	2252	2352	1152	1

	⑦	⑦	⑦	⑦	⑦	⑦	⑦	⑦	⑦	⑦	⑦
Bristol T Meads 139 d.	1110	1210	1413	1510	1611	1710	1810	1847	1910	2015	2125
Bath Spa 139 d.	1126	1222	1427	1527	1624	1728	1827	1900	1926	2027	2138
Bradford on Avon 139 d.	1139	1239	1443	1540	1641	1740	1839	1913	1938	2044	2150
Trowbridge 139 d.	1147	1246	1450	1547	1647	1747	1847	1919	1946	2051	2157
Westbury 139 a.	1159	1254	1457	1554	1658	1754	1854	1929	1953	2058	2204
Westbury d.	1201	1301	1501	1603	1701	1801	1901	1931	1959	2101	2205
Warminster d.	1210	1308	1508	1612	1710	1808	1908	1938	2008	2108	2213
Salisbury d.	1232	1332	1532	1632	1732	1832	1932	2001	2032	2132	2236
Romsey d.	1250	1350	1550	1650	1750	1850	1950	2019	2050	2150	2254
Southampton C a.	1303	1403	1603	1703	1803	1903	2003	2029	2103	2203	2306
Fareham a.	1329	1426	1626	1726	1826	1926	2026	2054	2126	2226	2330
Portsmouth & S a.	...	1444	1644	1744	1844	1944	2047	2115	2143	2243	2348
Portsmouth H a.	...	1452	1652	1752	1853	1952	2052	2126	2151	2251	2356

	Ⓐ	Ⓐ	Ⓐ	Ⓐ	Ⓐ	Ⓐ	Ⓐ		Ⓐ	
Portsmouth H d.		0600	0705	0823	0923	1023	1123		1823	1
Portsmouth & S d.		0604	0709	0827	0927	1027	1127	and	1827	1
Fareham d.		0624	0729	0847	0947	1047	1147	at	1847	1
Southampton C d.		0646	0753	0910	1010	1110	1210	the	1910	2
Romsey d.		0700	0811	0921	1021	1121	1221	same	1921	2
Salisbury d.		0719	0830	0940	1040	1140	1240	minutes	1940	2
Warminster d.		0739	0852	1001	1101	1201	1301	past	2001	2
Westbury a.		0747	0901	1009	1109	1209	1309	each	2009	2
Westbury 139 d.		0753	0909	1010	1110	1210	1310	hour	2010	2
Trowbridge 139 d.		0800	0915	1016	1116	1216	1316	until	2016	2
Bradford on Av'n 139 d.		0806	0921	1022	1122	1222	1322		2022	2
Bath 139 a.		0821	0935	1034	1134	1234	1334	★	2034	2
Bristol T Meads 139 a.		0842	0951	1048	1148	1248	1348		2048	2

	Ⓐ	Ⓐ		⑥	⑥	⑥	⑥		⑥	⑥	⑥	⑦	⑦	⑦	⑦	⑦	⑦	⑦	⑦		⑦	⑦	⑦	⑦	
Portsmouth H d.	2023	2123	...		0600	0723	0823		1823	1923	2023		0908	1108	...	1308	1408	1508	1608	...	1708	1808	1908	2008	2
Portsmouth & S d.	2027	2127	...		0604	0727	0827	and	1827	1927	2027		0912	1112	...	1312	1412	1512	1612	...	1712	1812	1912	2012	2
Fareham d.	2047	2148	...		0628	0747	0847	at	1847	1947	2047		0932	1132	1232	1332	1432	1532	1632	...	1732	1832	1932	2032	2
Southampton Central d.	2110	2222	...		0653	0810	0910	the	1910	2010	2110		0954	1154	1254	1354	1454	1554	1654	...	1754	1854	1954	2054	2
Romsey d.	2121	2234	...		0711	0821	0921	same	1921	2021	2121		1006	1206	1306	1406	1506	1606	1706	...	1806	1906	2006	2106	2
Salisbury d.	2140	2300	...		0730	0840	0940	minutes	1940	2040	2140		1025	1225	1325	1425	1525	1625	1723	...	1825	1925	2025	2125	2
Warminster d.	2201	2320	...		0750	0901	1001	past	2001	2101	2201		1049	1244	1344	1444	1544	1644	1744	...	1844	1944	2044	2144	2
Westbury a.	2209	2331	...		0759	0909	1009	each	2009	2109	2210		1058	1254	1356	1456	1556	1656	1756	...	1856	1957	2056	2156	2
Westbury 139 d.	2210	...	...		0802	0910	1010	hour	2010	2110	2210		1058	1256	1356	1500	1604	1700	1759	...	1857	2000	2100	2200	
Trowbridge 139 d.	2216	...	...		0808	0916	1016	until	2016	2116	2216		1105	1302	1402	1506	1610	1706	1806	...	1902	2006	2106	2206	
Bradford on Avon 139 d.	2222	...	...		0814	0922	1022		2022	2122	2222		1111	1308	1408	1512	1616	1712	1812	...	1908	2012	2112	2212	
Bath 139 a.	2234	...	...		0831	0934	1034	★	2034	2137	2234		1124	1322	1426	1524	1628	1724	1829	...	1925	2025	2125	2225	
Bristol T Meads 139 a.	2250	...	...		0844	0948	1048		2048	2151	2250		1144	1341	1446	1540	1643	1744	1844	...	1939	2039	2141	2241	

BRISTOL - WESTBURY - SALISBURY - LONDON

km		Ⓐ A	⚒	⚒	Ⓐ	⚒	⑦	Ⓐ d	Ⓐ	Ⓐ	⑦	⚒
0	**Bristol** T Meads d.	0518	0851	1249	...	1551	1604	...	...	...	2135	2223
19	Bath Spa d.	|	0907	1307	...	1607	1620	...	...	...	2149	2236
34	Bradford on Avon d.	0542	0921	1319	...	1624	1631	...	...	...	2200	2247
39	Trowbridge d.	0549	0927	1327	...	1630	1637	...	...	...	2206	2253
	Yeovil Pen Mill 113 d.	|	|	|	1544	|	|	1655	1927	2042	|	|
	Castle Cary d.	|	|	|	|	|	|	1707	1939	2054	|	|
	Frome d.	|	|	|	|	|	|	1724	1956	2111	|	|
46	**Westbury** d.	0603	0939	1339	|	1639	1646	1745	2011	2129	2215	2305
53	Warminster d.	|	0946	1346	|	1647	1653	1752	2019	2137	2222	2312
85	**Salisbury** a.	|	1009	1410	1643	1709	1716	1817	2042	2209	2246	2338
	London W'loo 113 a.	0749p	1149	1549	1821	1849	1859	1950	...	...	...	...

	⚒	⚒	⑦	⚒	Ⓐ		⑦		
London W'loo 113 d.	...	0920	1215	1220	1250	...	1815	...	1
Salisbury d.	0640	1052	1355	1352	1424	...	1955	...	2
Warminster d.	0700	1112	1415	1412	1444	...	2015	...	2
Westbury d.	0709	1121	1424	1421	1457	...	2023	...	2
Frome d.	|	|	|	|	1507	...	|	...	
Castle Cary d.	|	|	|	|	1524	...	|	...	
Yeovil Pen Mill 113 a.	|	|	|	|	1537	...	|	...	
Trowbridge d.	0715	1127	1430	1427	...	...	2029	...	2
Bradford on Avon d.	0721	1133	1436	1433	...	...	2035	...	2
Bath a.	0733	1146	1450	1446	...	...	2049	...	2
Bristol T Meads a.	0752	1205	1506	1505	...	...	2105	...	2

A – Train operated by *GW* (Table 115).
a – May 16 - Sept. 9 and from Oct. 24.
b – Sept. 12 - Oct. 21.
c – Arrives 12 minutes earlier.
d – From Yeovil Junction (d. 1648).
p – London Paddington.
★ – Timings may vary by up to 6 minutes

142 EAST CROYDON - MILTON KEYNES

km		Ⓐ	Ⓐ	Ⓐ	Ⓐ	Ⓐ	Ⓐ	Ⓐ	Ⓐ	Ⓐ	Ⓐ	Ⓐ		Ⓐ	Ⓐ	Ⓐ	Ⓐ	Ⓐ	Ⓐ		⑥	⑥
0	**East Croydon** d.		...	...	...	...	...	...	0750	0808	0910	1010		1710	1811	1912	...	...	...	...	...	...
12	Clapham Junction ▶ d.		0503	0530	0555	0620	0638	0739	0819	0839	0939	1039	and at	1739	1839	1939	2039	2139	2239	...	0508	05
18	Kensington Olympia ▶ d.		0514	0544	0607	0630	0649	0750	0831	0850	0950	1050	the same	1750	1850	1950	2050	2150	2250	...	0519	05
20	Shepherd's Bush ▶ d.		|	0547	0610	0633	0652	0753	0834	0853	0953	1053	minutes	1753	1853	1953	2053	2153	2253	...	0522	05
27	Wembley Central d.		0517	0602	0624	0647	0707	0808	0847	0908	1008	1109	past each	1809	1909	2009	2108	|	|	...	|	06
40	Watford Junction 142 d.		0540	0614	0636	0657	0719	0820	0901	0920	1020	1121	hour until	1821	1921	2021	2120	2223	2332	...	0547	06
76	Leighton Buzzard 142 d.		...	0642	...	...	0751	0848	...	0948	1048	1148		1848	1948	2048	2150	...	...	...	...	06
87	Bletchley 142 d.		...	0649	...	...	0758	0855	..	0955	1057	1155	✣	1855	1955	2055	2158	...	...	...	...	06
92	**Milton Keynes** 142 a.		...	0656	...	...	0803	0901	...	1001	1102	1200		1900	2000	2100	2205	...	...	...	...	07

	⑥	⑥	⑥		⑥	⑥	⑥	⑥	⑥	⑥	⑦	⑦	⑦	⑦	⑦	⑦	⑦		⑦	⑦	⑦	
East Croydon d.	...	0610	0710		1710	1810	1910	...	...	...		...	...	...	...	...	...		...	...	...	...
Clapham Junction ▶ d.	0609	0636	0739	and at	1739	1839	1938	2025	2150	2241		0815	0915	1015	1115	1205	1305	and at	1905	2005	2115	22
Kensington Olympia ▶ d.	0620	0647	0750	the same	1750	1852	1948	2036	2201	2251		0826	0926	1026	1126	1216	1316	the same	1916	2016	2125	22
Shepherd's Bush ▶ d.	0623	0650	0753	minutes	1753	1854	1950	2039	2204	2253		0829	0929	1029	1129	1219	1319	minutes	1919	2019	2128	22
Wembley Central d.	0638	0709	0809	past each	1809	1909	|	|	|	|		|	|	|	|	|	|	past each	|	|	|	
Watford Junction 142 d.	0650	0721	0821	hour until	1821	1921	2015	2109	2230	2319		0855	0957	1055	1154	1242	1342	hour until	1942	2042	2153	22
Leighton Buzzard 142 d.	...	0748	0848		1848	...	...	...	...	...		...	...	...	...	...	...		...	...	...	
Bletchley 142 d.	...	0755	0855	✣	1855	...	...	...	...	...		...	...	...	...	...	...	✣	...	...	...	
Milton Keynes 142 a.	...	0800	0900		1900	...	...	...	...	...		...	...	...	...	...	...		...	...	...	

		Ⓐ	Ⓐ	Ⓐ	Ⓐ	Ⓐ	Ⓐ	Ⓐ	Ⓐ		Ⓐ	Ⓐ	Ⓐ	Ⓐ	Ⓐ	Ⓐ	Ⓐ	Ⓐ		⑥	⑥
Milton Keynes 142 d.		...	...	...	0701	0813	...	0913	1013		1713	1813	1915	2013	2113	...	2211	...		...	...
Bletchley 142 d.		...	...	...	0706	0817	...	0917	1017	and at	1717	1817	1920	2017	2117	...	2215	...		...	...
Leighton Buzzard 142 d.		...	...	...	0713	0824	...	0924	1024	the same	1724	1824	1927	2024	2124	...	2222	...		...	...
Watford Junction 142 d.		0554	0653	0725	0738	0852	0915	0952	1052	minutes	1752	1851	1954	2051	2151	2227	2253	2336		0552	0655
Wembley Central d.		0605	0705	0737	0750	0904	0927	1004	1104	past each	1804	1905	2006	2104	|	|	|	|		|	0706
Shepherd's Bush ▶ d.		0622	0719	0756	0804	0919	0944	1019	1119	hour until	1819	1918	2021	2120	2220	2249	2321	0005		0620	0721
Kensington Olympia ▶ d.		0632	0722	0758	0807	0922	0947	1022	1122		1822	1920	2023	2122	2222	2251	2323	0007		0623	0724
Clapham Junction ▶ a.		...	0732	0809	0817	0932	0957	1032	1132	✣	1832	1930	2033	2132	2233	2301	2333	0017		0633	0734
East Croydon a.		...	...	...	0904	1001	...	1101	1201		1903	...	...	...	...	...	2359	...		0656	0801

	⑥		⑥	⑥	⑥	⑥	⑥	⑥	⑥	⑥			⑦	⑦	⑦	⑦		⑦	⑦	⑦	⑦	
Milton Keynes 142 d.	0713		1713	1813	...	1914	...	...	...	...	...		...	...	...	...		...	...	...	...	
Bletchley 142 d.	0717	and at	1717	1817	...	1918	...	...	...	...	...		...	...	...	...	and at	...	...	...	...	
Leighton Buzzard 142 d.	0724	the same	1724	1824	...	1925	...	...	...	...	...		...	...	...	...	the same	...	...	...	...	
Watford Junction 142 d.	0752	minutes	1752	1851	1931	1951	2043	2144	2248	2325	...		0917	1017	1122	1222	minutes	1922	2022	2117	2217	23
Wembley Central d.	0804	past each	1804	1903	1942	|	|	|	|	|	...		|	|	|	|	past each	|	|	|	|	
Shepherd's Bush ▶ d.	0819	hour until	1819	1919	1958	2019	2109	2210	2314	2351	...		0945	1045	1147	1247	hour until	1948	2047	2144	2245	23
Kensington Olympia ▶ d.	0822		1822	1921	2001	2022	2111	2212	2316	2353	...		0947	1047	1149	1250		1950	2049	2147	2247	23
Clapham Junction ▶ a.	0832	✣	1832	1931	2010	2032	2121	2221	2326	0002	...		0958	1058	1159	1259	✣	1959	2059	2200	2257	23
East Croydon a.	0901		1901	2001	...	2101	...	...	...	...	...		...	...	...	...		...	...	...	...	00

✣ – Timings may vary by up to 2 minutes.
▶ – Additional local services run between Clapham Junction and Shepherd's Bush.

LONDON - NORTHAMPTON - BIRMINGHAM and CREWE

LONDON - NORTHAMPTON - BIRMINGHAM

	Ⓐ	Ⓐ	Ⓐ	Ⓐ	Ⓐ	Ⓐ	Ⓐ	Ⓐ	Ⓐ	Ⓐ	Ⓐ	Ⓐ	Ⓐ	Ⓐ	Ⓐ		Ⓐ	Ⓐ	Ⓐ	Ⓐ	Ⓐ	Ⓐ	Ⓐ	Ⓐ
London Euston .... d.	Ⓐ	...	...	...	0534	...	0624	0634	0713	0749	0754	0813	0849	0854	0913	and	1449	1454	1513	1549	1554	1613	1650	1713
Watford Junction .... d.		...	...	...	0555	...	0641	0654	|	0803	0811	|	0903	0911	|	at	1503	1511	|	1603	1611	|	|	|
Leighton Buzzard .... d.		...	...	...	0628	...	0709	0725	0742	|	0836	0842	|	0936	0942	the	|	1536	1542	|	1636	1642	1720	|
Bletchley .... d.		...	...	...	0635	...	0716	0732	0750	|	0843	0850	0924y	0943	0950	same	|	1543	1550	|	1643	1650	1727	|
Milton Keynes .... d.		...	0537	...	0640	...	0721	0737	0754	0825	0849	0854	0928y	0949	0954	minutes	1525	1549	1554	1625	1649	1654	1732	1748
Northampton .... a.		...	0553	...	0656	...	0739	0753	0810	0840	0906	0911	0944y	1006	1010	past	1544	1606	1610	1640	1706	1713	1748	1810
Northampton .... d.		0516	0555	0616	0658	0716	0745	0755	0813	0855	0916	*0925*	0955	...	1016	each	1555	...	1616	1655	1716	...	1755	1819
Rugby .... d.		0538	0617	0638	0720	0738	0804	0817	0835	0917	0938	*0947*	1017	...	1038	hour	1617	...	1638	1717	1738	...	1817	1841
Coventry .... d.		0550	0630	0650	0732	0750	...	0830	0850	0930	0950	*1011*	1030	...	1050	until	1630	...	1650	1730	1750	...	1830	1853
Birmingham Int'l ✈ ... d.		0605	0646	0705	0748	0805	...	0846	0905	0946	1005	*1029*	1046	...	1105	△	1646	...	1705	1746	1805	...	1846	1908
Birmingham New St.. a.		0617	0701	0717	0805	0817	...	0902	0917	1001	1017	*1042*	1101	...	1117		1702	...	1717	1801	1817	...	1901	1920

	Ⓐ	Ⓐ	Ⓐ	Ⓐ	Ⓐ	Ⓐ	Ⓐ	Ⓐ	Ⓐ	Ⓐ	Ⓐ	Ⓐ	Ⓐ	Ⓐ	Ⓐ	Ⓐ	Ⓐ	Ⓐ	Ⓐ		⑥	⑥	⑥	⑥	⑥	⑥
n Euston .... d.	1724	1749	1751	1813	1816	1849	1852	1913	1949	1954	2013	2049	2054	2113	2149	2154	2224	2304	2324	⑥	...	...	0534	...	...	0624
I Junction......... d.	1744	|	1810	|	|	|	|	|	|	2011	|	|	2111	|	|	2215	2241	2329	2341		...	...	0552	...	...	0641
n Buzzard .... d.	1809	1820	|	|	1844	|	1920	1942	2018	2036	2042	2118	2136	2144	2218	2247	2307	0002	0007		...	...	0625	...	...	0709
ey .... d.	1816	|	1841	|	|	|	1927	|	|	2043	2050	|	2143	2152	|	2254	2314	0009	0014		0531	...	0631	...	...	0719
Keynes .... d.	1822	1831	1845	1846	1854	1923	1932	1956	2029	2049	2054	2129	2149	2157	2232	2302	2323	0018	0023		0537	...	0637	...	...	0724
mpton .... a.	1838	1848	1908	1904	1915	1937	1953	2011	2045	2105	2113	2146	2209	2215	2250	2320	2340	0036	0040		0553	...	0653	...	...	0741
mpton .... d.	1839	1857	...	1919	1931	1946	1955	2019	2055	2116	2123	2155	...	2219	2255	...	...	...	...		0555	0616	0655	0716	0737	*0755*
.... d.	1901	1919	...	1941	1956	2005	2017	2041	2117	2138	2142	2217	...	2241	2317	...	...	...	...		0617	0638	0717	0738	0759	*0817*
ry .... d.	1911	1932	...	1953	2011	...	2030	2053	2130	2150	...	2230	...	2253	2330	...	...	...	...		0630	0650	0730	0750	0811	*0830*
gham Int'l ✈... d.	1929	1948	...	2008	2029	...	2046	2108	2146	2205	...	2246	...	2311	2348	...	...	...	...		0646	0705	0746	0805	0829	*0846*
gham New St . a.	1942	2003	...	2020	2042	...	2102	2120	2202	2218	...	2302	...	2322	0004	...	...	...	...		0701	0717	0801	0817	0842	*0901*

	⑥	⑥	⑥	⑥	⑥	⑥	⑥	⑥	⑥		⑥	⑥	⑥	⑥	⑥	⑥	⑥	⑥	⑥	⑥	⑥	⑥	⑥	⑥	⑥
n Euston .... d.	...	0705	0749	0754	...	0849	0854	0913	0949	and	1754	1813	1849	1854	1913	...	1946	2034	2040	2107	2128	2154	2234	2304	2344
d Junction......... d.	...	0726	0803	0811	...	0903	0911	|	1003	at	1811	|	1903	1911	|	...	2002	2050	2101	2124	2144	2214	2250	2324	0003
n Buzzard .... d.	...	0758	|	0836	...	|	0936	0942	|	the	1836	1844	|	1936	1942	...	2034	2118	|	2150	2208	2247	2316	2356	0036
ey .... d.	...	0805	|	0843	...	0924	0943	0950	1024x	same	1843	1852	|	1943	1950	...	2041	2125	2131	2157	2215	2254	2323	0003	0043
Keynes .... d.	...	0810	0825	0849	...	0929	0949	0954	1029x	minutes	1849	1856	1925	1949	1954	...	2049	2133	2140	2206	2224	2303	2331	0011	0051
mpton .... a.	...	0826	0840	0905	...	0944	1006	1013	1045x	past	1906	1913	1944	2006	2011	...	2106	2150	2156	2223	2243	2320	2348	0028	0108
mpton .... d.	0816	0837	0855	0916	0937	0955	...	1016	1055	each	...	1916	1955	...	2022	2055	2116	2159	2216	...	2255	...	...	...	...
.... d.	0838	0859	0917	0938	0959	1017	...	1038	1117	hour	...	1938	2017	...	2044	2117	2138	2221	2238	...	2317	...	...	...	...
ry .... d.	0850	0911	0930	0950	1011	1030	...	1050	1130	until	...	1950	2030	...	2056	2130	2150	2233	2250	...	2330	...	...	...	...
gham Int'l ✈... d.	0905	0929	0946	1005	1029	1046	...	1105	1146	△	...	2008	2046	...	2114	2146	2205	2249	2305	...	2349	...	...	...	...
gham New St . a.	0917	0942	1001	1017	1042	1101	...	1117	1201		...	2020	2102	...	2125	2201	2217	2304	2317	...	0004	...	...	...	...

		⑦	⑦	⑦	⑦	⑦	⑦	⑦	⑦	⑦	⑦	⑦	⑦	⑦	⑦		⑦	⑦	⑦	⑦	⑦	⑦	⑦	⑦	⑦
n Euston .... d.	⑦	0654	0724	0752	0824	0855	0924	0954	1001	1028	1054	1124	1154	1234	1250	and	1934	1950	2034	2106	2130	2200	2228	2258	2334
I Junction......... d.		0713	0745	0810	0845	0914	0945	1010	1019	1046	1114	1142	1214	1250	1306	at	1950	2006	2050	2123	2150	2219	2249	2317	2355
on Buzzard .... d.		0741	0814	0839	0914	0941	1014	1035	1047	1115	1143	1212	1243	1315	1327	the	2015	2027	2115	2149	2219	2247	2318	2350	0028
ey .... d.		0748	0821	0845	0921	0948	1021	1042	|	|	1150	1219	1250	1322	|	same	2022	|	2122	2156	2226	2254	2325	2357	0035
Keynes .... d.		0758	0830	0851	0927	0957	1027	1050	1058	1128	1158	1228	1258	1328	1337	minutes	2028	2037	2128	2204	2234	2303	2333	0005	0043
mpton .... a.		0815	0847	0909	0944	1014	1044	1106	1116	1145	1215	1244	1315	1344	1351	past	2044	2054	2146	2221	2250	2319	2350	0023	0100
mpton .... d.		...	...	0926	1000	...	1100	1108	...	1158	...	1255	...	1355	1402	each	2055	2106	2155	...	2252	2332	...	...	...
.... d.		...	...	0948	1022	...	1122	1130	...	1220	...	1317	...	1417	1424	hour	2117	2128	2217	...	2314	2354	...	...	...
ry .... d.		...	...	1000	1034	...	1134	...	...	1232	...	1330	...	1430	...	until	2130	...	2230	...	2338	0007	...	...	...
gham Int'l ✈... d.		...	...	1009	1052	...	1152	...	...	1250	...	1348	...	1448	...	△	2148	...	2248	...	2356	...	...	...	...
gham New St . a.		...	...	1026	1103	...	1203	...	...	1301	...	1359	...	1459	...		2159	...	2259	...	0007	...	...	...	...

		Ⓐ	Ⓐ	Ⓐ	Ⓐ	Ⓐ	Ⓐ	Ⓐ	Ⓐ	Ⓐ	Ⓐ	Ⓐ	Ⓐ	Ⓐ	Ⓐ	Ⓐ	Ⓐ	Ⓐ	Ⓐ	Ⓐ	Ⓐ		Ⓐ	Ⓐ	Ⓐ
gham New St . d.	Ⓐ	...	...	...	...	...	...	...	0553	...	0614	0654	0714	0733	0754	*0814*	0833	0854	0914	0933	0954	and	1554	...	1633
gham Int'l ✈... d.		...	...	...	...	...	...	...	0605	...	0630	0705	0730	0745	0805	*0830*	0845	0905	0930	0945	1005	at	1605	...	1645
try .... d.		...	...	...	...	...	0557	...	0621	...	0648	0721	0742	0804	0821	*0848*	0900	0925	0948	1000	1021	the	1621	...	1700
.... d.		...	...	...	0516	...	0612	...	0632	*0647*	0659	0732	0753	0815	0839	*0859*	0912	0938	0959	1012	1032	same	1632	...	1716
mpton .... a.		...	...	...	0537	...	0633	...	0654	*0707*	0724	0754	0816	0837	0900	*0920*	0933	0959	1020	1033	1054	minutes	1657	...	1738
mpton .... d.		0415	0449	0505	0546	0618	0638	0700	0710	0732	0738	0805	0825	0847	0905	0925	0950	1005	1025	1050	1105	past	1705	1725	1750
Keynes .... d.		0430	0505	0521	0603	0635	0655	0717	0731	0747	0755	0822	0841	0905	0922	0941	1007	1022	1041	1107	1122	each	1722	1741	1807
ey .... d.		0435	0509	0526	0608	0640	0700	|	|	0752	0800	0827	0846	|	0927	0946	|	1027	1046	|	1127	hour	1727	1746	|
on Buzzard .... d.		0442	0516	0533	0615	0647	0707	0726	0740	0759	0807	0833	0853	|	0933	0953	|	1033	1053	|	1133	until	1733	1753	|
d Junction......... d.		0511	0550	0601	0635	0705	|	|	|	0827	|	|	|	0928	0959	|	1031	1059	|	1131	1159	△	1759	|	1831
n Euston .... a.		0534	0611	0619	0651	0722	0739	0802	0812	0848	0839	0910	0927	0946	1018	1023	1046	1117	1127	1146	1217		1818	1827	1846

	Ⓐ	Ⓐ	Ⓐ	Ⓐ	Ⓐ	Ⓐ	Ⓐ	Ⓐ	Ⓐ	Ⓐ	Ⓐ	Ⓐ	Ⓐ	Ⓐ	Ⓐ	Ⓐ		⑥	⑥	⑥	⑥	⑥	⑥	⑥	⑥	⑥
gham New St . d.	1654	1714	1733	1754	1814	1833	1854	1914	1933	1954	2033	2054	2134	2154	...	2254	⑥	...	...	...	0614	0654	0714	0733	0754	0814
gham Int'l ✈... d.	1705	1726	1745	1805	1830	1845	1905	1930	1945	2005	2045	2105	2145	2205	...	2305		...	...	...	0630	0705	0730	0745	0805	0830
try .... d.	1721	1742	1800	1821	1848	1900	1921	1948	2000	2021	2100	2121	2200	2221	...	2321		...	...	...	0648	0721	0748	0800	0821	0848
.... d.	1732	1756	1812	1832	1859	1918	1932	1959	2015	2032	2114	2132	2212	2232	...	2332		...	...	...	0659	0732	0759	0812	0832	0859
ampton .... a.	1756	1817	1834	1853	1921	1941	1954	2023	2038	2053	2135	2154	2234	2253	...	2354		...	...	...	0720	0754	0820	0836	0857	0920
ampton .... d.	1805	1825	1850	1905	1925	1950	2005	2025	...	2105	2137	2205	...	2255	2335	...		0515	0605	0705	0735	0805	0825	0850	0905	0925
Keynes .... d.	1822	1841	1907	1922	1941	2007	2022	2041	...	2122	2153	2222	...	2313	2353	...		0531	0621	0721	0752	0822	0841	0907	0922	0941
ey .... d.	1827	1846	|	1927	1946	|	2028	2046	...	2127	2158	2227	...	2318	2358	...		0536	0627	0726	0757	0827	0846	|	0927	0946
on Buzzard .... d.	1833	1853	|	1933	1953	|	2035	2053	...	2133	2204	2233	...	2324	0004	...		0543	0633	0733	0803	0833	0853	|	0933	0953
'd Junction......... d.	1859	|	1931	1959	|	2031	2059	|	...	2159	2233	2259	...	2359	0033	...		0616	0701	0759	0828	0859	|	0934	0959	|
n Euston .... a.	1918	1928	1947	2020	2027	2048	2118	2128	...	2222	2252	2321	...	0021	0055	...		0638	0720	0818	0846	0917	0927	0949	1017	1027

	⑥	⑥	⑥	⑥		⑥	⑥	⑥	⑥	⑥	⑥	⑥	⑥	⑥	⑥	⑥	⑥	⑥	⑥z	⑥	⑥	⑥	⑥	⑥	⑥
gham New St . d.	0833	0854	0914	0933	and	1554	1614	1633	1654	1714	1733	1754	1814	1833	1854	1914	1933	1954	...	2033	2054	2134	2154	2214	2254
gham Int'l ✈... d.	0845	0905	0930	0945	at	1605	1630	1645	1705	1731	1745	1805	1830	1845	1905	1930	1945	2005	...	2045	2105	2145	2205	2230	2305
try .... d.	0900	0921	0948	1000	the	1621	1648	1700	1721	1749	1800	1821	1848	1900	1921	1948	2000	2021	...	2100	2121	2200	2221	2248	2321
.... d.	0912	0932	0959	1012	same	1632	1659	1712	1732	1759	1812	1832	1859	1912	1932	1959	2012	2032	2047	2112	2132	2212	2232	2259	2332
ampton .... a.	0934	0954	1020	1034	minutes	1654	1720	1734	1753	1821	1834	1854	1920	1934	1953	2020	2035	2053	2106	2134	2153	2233	2253	2321	2355
ampton .... d.	0950	1005	1025	1050	past	1705	1725	1750	1805	1831	1850	1905	1931	...	2002	2032	...	2102	2120	...	2205	2243	...	2330	...
Keynes .... d.	1007	1022	1041	1107	each	1722	1741	1807	1822	1847	1907	1922	1947	...	2018	2047	...	2118	2134	...	2221	2259	...	2346	...
ey .... d.	|	1027	1046	|	hour	1727	1746	|	1827	1852	|	1927	1952	...	2023	|	...	|	2139	...	2226	2304	...	2351	...
on Buzzard .... d.	|	1033	1053	|	until	1733	1753	|	1833	1859	|	1933	1959	...	2030	2056	...	|	2146	...	2232	2311	...	2358	...
'd Junction......... d.	1031	1059	|	1131	△	1759	|	1831	1859	1927	1931	1959	2027	...	2052	2126	...	2152	2219	...	2307	2346	...	0020	...
on Euston .... a.	1046	1117	1127	1146		1817	1827	1846	1917	1946	1946	2018	2046	...	2112	2146	...	2212	2237	...	2327	0006	...	0040	...

		⑦	⑦	⑦	⑦	⑦	⑦	⑦	⑦	⑦	⑦	⑦	⑦	⑦	⑦		⑦	⑦	⑦	⑦	⑦	⑦	⑦	⑦	⑦
gham New St . d.	⑦	...	...	...	...	...	...	...	0914	...	1014	...	1114	...	1214	and	...	1914	...	...	2014	...	2114	...	2214
gham Int'l ✈... d.		...	...	...	...	...	...	...	0925	...	1025	...	1125	...	1225	at	...	1925	...	...	2025	...	2125	...	2225
try .... d.		...	...	...	...	...	...	...	0944	...	1044	...	1144	...	1244	the	...	1944	...	...	2044	...	2144	...	2244
.... d.		...	...	...	...	...	...	...	0955	...	1055	1120	1155	1220	1255	same	1920	1955	2020	...	2055	2120	2155	...	2255
ampton .... a.		...	...	...	...	...	...	...	1017	...	1117	1141	1217	1241	1317	minutes	1941	2017	2041	...	2117	2141	2217	...	2319
ampton .... d.		...	*0620**	0753	0823	0853	0930	1009	1037	1108	1126	1150	1226	1250	1326	past	1950	2025	2050	...	2129	2155	2226	2300	...
Keynes .... d.		0642	0711	0809	0839	0909	0946	1026	1055	1124	1142	1207	1242	1307	1342	each	2007	2041	2107	2115	2145	2211	2242	2316	...
ley .... d.		0647	0716	0814	0844	0914	0951	1031	1100	1129	1147	|	1247	|	1347	hour	|	2046	|	2120	2150	2216	2246	2321	...
on Buzzard .... d.		0653	0723	0821	0851	0921	0958	1037	1106	1136	1153	1215	1253	1315	1353	until	2015	2052	2115	2126	2156	2222	2253	2327	...
'd Junction......... d.		0725	0754	0853	0922	0952	1029	1105	1137	1206	1218	1240	1318	1335	1418	△	2035	2122	2135	2156	2226	2253	2323	2359	...
on Euston .... a.		0745	0814	0913	0945	1013	1051	1126	1159	1226	1238	1301	1338	1353	1438		2054	2142	2154	2219	2248	2315	2343	0021	...

Trains 11xx and hourly to 17xx do not call at Bletchley and then run 4 minutes earlier to Northampton.
Trains 11xx, 12xx, 13xx and 14xx do not call at Bletchley and then run 4 minutes earlier to Northampton.
From May 28.

* – Connection by 🚌.
△ – Timings may vary by up to 3 minutes.

142 LONDON - NORTHAMPTON - BIRMINGHAM and CREWE

LONDON - CREWE

km		Ⓐ	Ⓐ	Ⓐ	Ⓐ	Ⓐ	Ⓐ	Ⓐ	Ⓐ	Ⓐ	Ⓐ	Ⓐ	Ⓐ	Ⓐ	Ⓐ	Ⓐ	Ⓐ	Ⓐ		⑥	⑥	⑥
0	**London** Euston .... 150 d.	...	...	0624	0746	0846	0946	1046	1146	1246	1346	1446	1546	1646	1746	1849	2013	2049	...	...	...	0624
27	Watford Junction .... 150 d.	...	...	0641	|	|	|	|	|	|	|	|	|	|	|	|	|	|	...	...	...	0641
78	Milton Keynes .... 150 d.	...	...	0721	0819	0919	1019	1119	1219	1319	1419	1519	1619	1719	1819	1923	2054	2129	...	...	...	0724
104	Northampton .... d.	0545	0635	0745	|	|	|	|	|	|	|	|	|	|	|	1946	2123	2155	...	0541	0638	0745
135	Rugby .... 150 d.	0606	0659	0804	0842	0942	1042	1142	1242	1342	1442	1542	1642	1747	1847	2006	2145	2217	...	0602	0658	0804
158	Nuneaton .... d.	0620	0712	0816	0854	0954	1054	1154	1254	1354	1454	1554	1654	1800	1900	2019	2200	|	...	0616	0712	0816
178	Tamworth (Low Level) .... d.	0635	0729	0829	0909	1009	1109	1209	1309	1409	1509	1609	1709	1815	1915	2032	2215	|	...	0629	0729	0829
188	Lichfield Trent Valley .... d.	0641	0735	0835	0917	1017	1117	1217	1317	1417	1517	1617	1717	1822	1922	2038	2222	|	...	0635	0735	0835
217	Stafford .... 150 d.	0700	0755	0855	0942	1042	1142	1242	1339	1442	1542	1642	1742	1842	1942	2057	|	2353	...	0658	0754	0854
231	Stone .... d.	0709	0803	0903	0950	1050	1150	1250	1350	1450	1550	1650	1750	|	|	2105	|	|	...	0707	0803	0903
243	Stoke on Trent .... 150 d.	0721	0812	0912	1002	1102	1202	1302	1402	1502	1602	1702	1802	1907	2002	2113	2250	|	...	0715	0815	0915
268	**Crewe** .... 150 a.	0743	0834	0934	1024	1124	1224	1324	1424	1524	1624	1724	1824	1927	2025	2134	2309	0022	...	0738	0837	0938

	⑥	⑥	⑥	⑥	⑥	⑥	⑥	⑥	⑥	⑥	⑥		⑦	⑦	⑦	⑦	⑦	⑦	⑦	⑦	⑦	⑦	⑦
London Euston .... 150 d.	0846	0946	1046	1146	1246	1346	1446	1546	1646	1746	1846	...	*0752*	0954	1024	1124	1250	1350	1450	1550	1650	1750	1850
Watford Junction .... 150 d.	|	|	|	|	|	|	|	|	|	|	|	...	*0810*	1010	1040	1142	1306	1406	1506	1606	1706	1806	1906
Milton Keynes .... 150 d.	0919	1019	1119	1219	1319	1419	1519	1619	1719	1819	1919	...	*0851*	1050	1120	1228	1337	1437	1537	1637	1737	1837	1937
Northampton .... d.	|	|	|	|	|	|	|	|	|	|	|	...	0940	1108	1140	1302	1402	1502	1602	1702	1802	1902	2002
Rugby .... 150 d.	0942	1042	1142	1242	1342	1442	1542	1642	1742	1842	1942	...	1003	1130	1203	1326	1426	1526	1626	1726	1826	1926	2026
Nuneaton .... d.	0954	1054	1154	1254	1354	1454	1554	1654	1754	1854	1958	...	1016	1143	1216	1340	1440	1540	1640	1740	1840	1940	2040
Tamworth (Low Level) .... d.	1009	1109	1209	1309	1409	1509	1609	1709	1809	1909	2014	...	1030	1157	1230	1355	1455	1555	1655	1755	1855	1955	2055
Lichfield Trent Valley .... d.	1017	1117	1217	1317	1417	1517	1617	1717	1817	1917	2021	...	1037	1204	1237	1401	1501	1601	1701	1801	1901	2001	2101
Stafford .... 150 d.	1042	1142	1242	1342	1442	1538	1642	1742	1844	1942	2044	...	1100	1221	1300	1421	1521	1621	1721	1821	1921	2021	2121
Stone .... d.	1050	1150	1250	1350	1450	1550	1650	1750	1852	1950	|	...	1109	1229	1309	1429	1529	1629	1729	1829	1929	2029	2129
Stoke on Trent .... 150 d.	1102	1202	1302	1402	1502	1602	1702	1802	1902	2002	2102	...	1117	1241	1317	1441	1541	1641	1741	1845	1945	2045	2145
Crewe .... 150 a.	1124	1224	1324	1424	1524	1624	1724	1824	1927	2024	2122	...	1141	1302	1341	1502	1602	1702	1802	1907	2007	2107	2207

	Ⓐ	Ⓐ	Ⓐ	Ⓐ	Ⓐ	Ⓐ	Ⓐ		Ⓐ	Ⓐ	Ⓐ	Ⓐ	Ⓐ	Ⓐ	Ⓐ	Ⓐ		⑥	⑥	⑥	⑥	⑥
Crewe .... 150 d.	0521	0652	0755	0902	1002	1102	1202	...	1302	1402	1502	1602	1702	1802	1902	2010	...	0601	0700	0718	0802	0902
Stoke on Trent .... 150 d.	|	0719	0817	0928	1028	1128	1228	...	1328	1428	1528	1628	1728	1828	1928	2033	...	0624	0722	0738	0828	0928
Stone .... d.	|	|	0825	0936	1036	1136	1236	...	1336	1436	1536	1636	1736	1836	1936	2041	...	|	0731	|	0836	0936
Stafford .... 150 d.	|	0740	0837	0955	1055	1155	1255	...	1355	1455	1555	1655	1755	1855	1951	2100	...	0648	0748	0808	0855	0955
Lichfield Trent Valley .... d.	0607	0757	0854	1013	1113	1213	1313	...	1413	1513	1613	1713	1813	1913	2008	2121	...	0705	0805	0825	0913	1013
Tamworth (Low Level) .... d.	0613	0803	0901	1020	1120	1220	1320	...	1420	1520	1620	1720	1820	1920	2015	2125	...	0711	0811	0831	0920	1020
Nuneaton .... d.	0630	0819	0916	1036	1136	1236	1336	...	1436	1536	1636	1736	1836	1936	2030	2140	...	0727	0827	0847	0936	1036
Rugby .... 150 d.	0647	0834	0932	1053	1153	1253	1353	...	1453	1553	1653	1753	1853	1953	2047	2158	...	0743	0843	0903	0953	1053
Northampton .... d.	0716	|	|	|	|	|	|	...	|	|	|	|	|	|	2107	2217	...	|	|	|	|	|
Milton Keynes .... 150 d.	|	0900	0954	1115	1215	1315	1415	...	1515	1615	1715	1815	1915	2015	...	...	...	0805	0915	0925	1015	1115
Watford Junction .... 150 d.	|	|	|	|	|	|	|	...	|	|	|	|	|	|	...	...	...	|	|	|	|	|
London Euston .... 150 a.	0805	0937	1029	1150	1250	1350	1450	...	1550	1650	1750	1852	1950	2051	...	...	...	0841	0952	1000	1050	1150

	⑥	⑥	⑥	⑥	⑥	⑥	⑥	⑥	⑥a		⑦	⑦	⑦	⑦		⑦	⑦	⑦	⑦		⑦	⑦	⑦
Crewe .... 150 d.	1102	1202	1302	1402	1502	1602	1702	1802	1902	...	0932	1037	1137	1237	...	1337	1432	1537	1637	...	1737	1837	1937
Stoke on Trent .... 150 d.	1128	1228	1328	1428	1528	1628	1728	1828	1928	...	0953	1059	1159	1259	...	1359	1453	1553	1659	...	1759	1859	1959
Stone .... d.	1136	1236	1336	1436	1536	1636	1736	1836	1936	...	1001	1107	1207	1307	...	1407	1501	1607	1707	...	1807	1907	2007
Stafford .... 150 d.	1155	1255	1355	1455	1555	1655	1755	1855	1951	...	1019	1119	1219	1319	...	1419	1519	1619	1719	...	1819	1922	2018
Lichfield Trent Valley .... d.	1213	1313	1413	1513	1613	1713	1813	1913	2008	...	1036	1136	1236	1336	...	1436	1536	1636	1736	...	1836	1939	2036
Tamworth (Low Level) .... d.	1220	1320	1420	1520	1620	1720	1820	1920	2015	...	1043	1143	1243	1343	...	1443	1543	1643	1743	...	1843	1946	2043
Nuneaton .... d.	1236	1336	1436	1536	1636	1736	1836	1936	2031	...	1058	1158	1258	1358	...	1458	1558	1658	1758	...	1858	2001	2058
Rugby .... 150 d.	1253	1353	1453	1553	1653	1753	1853	1952	2047	...	1120	1220	1320	1420	...	1520	1620	1720	1820	...	1920	2020	2120
Northampton .... d.	|	|	|	|	|	|	|	2012	2120	...	1150	1250	1350	1450	...	1550	1650	1750	1850	...	1950	2050	2155
Milton Keynes .... 150 d.	1315	1415	1515	1615	1715	1815	1915	...	2134	...	1207	1307	1407	1507	...	1607	1707	1807	1907	...	2007	2107	2211
Watford Junction .... 150 d.	|	|	|	|	|	|	|	...	2219	...	1240	1335	1435	1535	...	1635	1735	1835	1935	...	2035	2135	2253
London Euston .... 150 a.	1350	1450	1550	1650	1750	1850	1950	...	2237	...	1301	1353	1453	1553	...	1653	1753	1853	1953	...	2054	2154	2315

BIRMINGHAM - CREWE - LIVERPOOL

km		Ⓐ	Ⓐ	Ⓐ	Ⓐ	Ⓐ	Ⓐ	Ⓐ		Ⓐ	Ⓐ	Ⓐ	Ⓐ	Ⓐ	Ⓐ	Ⓐ	Ⓐ	Ⓐ	Ⓐ	⑥	⑥	⑥
0	**Birmingham** New St. d.	...	...	...	0601	0636	0701	0736	and at	1701	1736	1801	1836	1901	1936	2036	2136	2239	2309	...	...	...
19	Wolverhampton .... d.	...	...	...	0620	0654	0720	0754	the same	1720	1754	1820	1854	1920	1954	2054	2154	2305	2336	...	...	...
43	Stafford .... d.	...	...	...	0636	0710	0736	0810	minutes	1736	1810	1836	1910	1945	2010	2110	2210	2321	2353	...	...	...
82	**Crewe** .... d.	0540	0603	0633	0658	0733	0759	0832	past each	1757	1832	1859	1933	2032	2033	2133	2242	2358	0022	0548	0614	0633
118	Runcorn .... d.	0601	0630	0700	0725	0800	0825	0852	hour until	1825	1856	1922	1956	...	2056	2156	2307	...	...	0608	0633	0700
131	**Liverpool** SP ‡ .... d.	0610	0639	0709	0733	0809	0833	0901	★	1834	1905	1931	2005	...	2105	2205	2316	...	...	0617	0642	0709
140	**Liverpool** Lime St .... a.	0621	0649	0721	0746	0821	0844	0911		1844	1916	1942	2016	...	2116	2216	2331	...	...	0627	0652	0721

	⑥	⑥	⑥	⑥	⑥		⑥	⑥	⑥	⑥	⑥	⑥	⑥	⑥	⑥	⑦	⑦	⑦	⑦		⑦	⑦
Birmingham New St. d.	0636	0701	0736	0801	0836	and at	1701	1736	1801	1836	1901	2001	2036	2136	2239	0942	1042	1142	1235	and at	1835	1935
Wolverhampton .... d.	0654	0720	0754	0820	0854	the same	1720	1754	1820	1854	1920	2022	2054	2159	2305	1000	1100	1200	1253	the same	1853	1953
Stafford .... d.	0710	0736	0810	0836	0910	minutes	1736	1810	1836	1910	1936	2038	2110	2216	2321	1017	1117	1217	1309	minutes	1909	2009
Crewe .... d.	0733	0800	0832	0857	0932	past each	1757	1832	1857	1930	1957	2059	2149	2236	2341	1038	1138	1238	1331	past each	1931	2032
Runcorn .... d.	0800	0825	0852	0922	0952	hour until	1825	1852	1922	...	2025	2121	...	...	...	1101	1201	1301	1354	hour until	1954	2054
Liverpool SP ‡ .... d.	0809	0833	0901	0931	1001	★	1833	1901	1931	...	2033	2130	...	...	...	1110	1210	1310	1403	★	2003	2103
Liverpool Lime St .... a.	0821	0844	0911	0942	1011		1844	1911	1942	...	2044	2140	...	...	...	1121	1221	1321	1414		2014	2114

	Ⓐ	Ⓐ	Ⓐ	Ⓐ	Ⓐ	Ⓐ	Ⓐ		Ⓐ	Ⓐ	Ⓐ	Ⓐ	Ⓐ	Ⓐ	Ⓐ	Ⓐ	Ⓐ	Ⓐ	Ⓐ	⑥	⑥	⑥
Liverpool Lime St .... d.	...	...	0630	0704	0734	0804	0834	and at	1704	1734	1804	1834	1912	1934	2004	2034	2134	2234	2334	...	...	0632
Liverpool SP ‡ .... d.	...	...	0640	0715	0744	0815	0844	the same	1715	1744	1815	1844	1922	1944	2015	2044	2144	2246	2346	...	...	0642
Runcorn .... d.	...	...	0648	0723	0752	0823	0852	minutes	1725	1752	1825	1852	1930	1952	2025	2052	2152	2255	2355	...	...	0650
Crewe .... d.	0619	0649	0716	0749	0817	0849	0919	past each	1749	1819	1849	1919	1955	2019	2047	2119	2219	2324	0026	0611	0649	0719
Stafford .... d.	0641	0710	0740	0810	0839	0910	0940	hour until	1810	1843	1910	1939	2016	2039	2110	2139	2240	...	...	0631	0710	0740
Wolverhampton .... a.	0658	0726	0758	0827	0858	0927	0957	★	1827	1859	1928	1957	2032	2056	2127	2157	2259	...	...	0647	0727	0756
Birmingham New St. a.	0720	0750	0818	0848	0918	0948	1018		1848	1918	1948	2018	2050	2118	2148	2218	2326	...	...	0715	0750	0818

	⑥	⑥	⑥		⑥	⑥	⑥	⑥	⑥	⑥	⑥	⑥b	⑥c	⑥d	⑥e	⑦	⑦	⑦		⑦	⑦	⑦
Liverpool Lime St .... d.	0734	0804	0834	and at	1704	1734	1804	1834	1904	1934	2034	2134	2145	2204	2204	...	1134	1234	and at	1934	2034	2134
Liverpool SP ‡ .... d.	0744	0815	0844	the same	1715	1744	1815	1844	1915	1944	2044	2144	2155	2215	|	...	1144	1244	the same	1944	2044	2144
Runcorn .... d.	0752	0825	0852	minutes	1725	1752	1824	1852	1925	1952	2052	2152	2203	2223	|	...	1152	1252	minutes	1952	2052	2152
Crewe .... d.	0819	0849	0919	past each	1749	1822	1849	1919	1951	2019	2118	2224	2230	2247	2356	1021	1219	1319	past each	2019	2119	2222
Stafford .... d.	0840	0910	0940	hour until	1810	1843	1910	1940	2012	2040	2139	2245	...	...	...	1042	1240	1340	hour until	2040	2140	2242
Wolverhampton .... a.	0858	0927	0958	★	1828	1859	1928	1957	2028	2056	2158	2302	...	...	...	1101	1256	1357	★	2057	2157	2259
Birmingham New St. a.	0918	0948	1018		1848	1918	1948	2018	2048	2118	2218	2320	...	...	...	1119	1315	1415		2115	2215	2317

NUNEATON - COVENTRY

From Nuneaton: 2nd class only Journey ± 20 minutes *16 km*

Ⓐ: 0633, 0737, 0833, 1014 and hourly until 2014, 2114, 2214.
⑥: 0644, 0814, 0914, 1014 and hourly until 1814, 1944, 2114, 2214.
⑦: 1236, 1411, 1511, 1611, 1711, 1811, 2011, 2200.

From Coventry:

Ⓐ: 0604, 0704, 0804, 0904, 1042 and hourly until 1842, 1942, 2042, 2142.
⑥: 0615, 0715, 0842, 0942, 1042 and hourly until 1742, 1842, 2015, 2142.
⑦: 1146, 1339, 1439, 1539, 1639, 1739, 1939, 2132.

BEDFORD - BLETCHLEY

From Bedford: 2nd class only Journey ± 44 minutes

Trains call at **Woburn Sands** 30 minutes later:

0625Ⓐ, 0631⑥, 0731⚒, 0831⑥, 0834Ⓐ, 0934⚒, 1055⚒, 1155⚒, 1255⚒, 1355⚒, 1
1555⚒, 1640⚒, 1740⚒, 1823⑥, 1826Ⓐ, 1923⚒, 2055⚒, 2200⚒.

From Bletchley:

Trains call at **Woburn Sands** 11 minutes later:

0531Ⓐ, 0541⑥, 0634⑥, 0642Ⓐ, 0731⚒, 0822Ⓐ, 0839⑥, 1005⚒, 1105⚒, 1201⚒, 1
1401⚒, 1501⚒, 1551⚒, 1651⚒, 1731⑥, 1736Ⓐ, 1831⚒, 2001⚒, 2101⚒.

a – From May 28.
b – Not May 28.
c – May 21 - July 30 and Sept. 17 - Oct. 22.
d – Aug. 6 - Sept. 10 and from Oct. 29.
e – Operated by 🚌 May 21 - July 30 and Sept. 17 - Oct. 22.
‡ – Liverpool South Parkway. 🚌 connections availa to/from Liverpool John Lennon Airport.
★ – Timings may vary by ± 3 minutes.

2nd class

BIRMINGHAM - SHREWSBURY - CHESTER

	⚒	⑥	Ⓐ	⚒A	⑥M	ⒶB	⑥	ⒶL	⚒	ⒶL	⑥	⑥	Ⓐ	⚒	⑥	Ⓐ	⚒	⚒	⚒	ⒶC	⚒	⚒	⑥C	Ⓐ
London Euston **150** d.		...	...	...	...	...	...	...	...	...	...	...	...	...	...	...	...	...	...	1023	...	...	1123	...
Birmingham International ✈ d.		...	...	...	...	...	...	...	...	0709	0709	...	...	0809	0910	0910	1009	...	1110	1133	1209	...	1233	1308
Birmingham New Street d.		...	...	0530	...	...	...	...	0625	0723	0724	...	...	0825	0925	0925	1025	...	1125	1153	1225	...	1253	1325
Wolverhampton d.		...	...	0548	...	...	...	...	0643	0742	0742	...	...	0843	0943	0943	1043	...	1142	1211	1243	...	1311	1343
Telford Central d.		...	...	|	...	...	...	...	0659	0759	0759	...	...	0900	1000	0959	1059	...	1159	1228	1259	...	1328	1400
Wellington d.		...	...	|	...	...	...	...	0706	0805	0805	...	...	0907	1006	1005	1106	...	1205	1235	1306	...	1335	1406
Shrewsbury a.		...	...	|	...	...	...	...	0720	0819	0820	...	...	0920	1018	1021	1119	...	1221	1251	1320	...	1354	1420
Aberystwyth **147** a.		...	...	|	...	...	...	...	0923	|	|	...	...	1120	|	|	1317	...	|	...	1518	...	...	|
Cardiff Central **149** d.		...	...	|	...	...	0520	0508	...	|	|	0716	0721	...	|	|	...	0917	|	...	...	1115	...	|
Shrewsbury d.		0520	0520	|	0610	*0610*	0722	0724	...	0821	0822	0925	0924	...	1022	1023	...	1125	1222	...	...	1324	...	1425
Gobowen d.		0539	0539	|	0630	*0630*	0743	0743	...	0840	0841	0944	0943	...	1042	1044	...	1144	1242	...	...	1343	...	1445
Ruabon d.		0551	0551	|	0642	*0642*	0754	0754	...	0852	0853	0955	0954	...	1054	1056	...	1155	1254	...	...	1354	...	1457
Wrexham General d.		0558	0604	|	0650	0700	0801	0802	...	0900	0901	1002	1002	...	1101	1102	...	1202	1300	...	...	1402	...	1503
Chester a.		0617	0625	0643	0710	0716	0819	0821	...	0919	0918	1020	1021	...	1120	1121	...	1220	1321	...	...	1420	...	1521
Holyhead **165** a.		...	...	0823	...	...	1014	...	...	...	1105	1209	1222	...	1312	1317	...	1414	1508	...	...	1614	...	1716

	⑥	⚒	⑥	Ⓐ	⚒	⚒	⚒	Ⓐ	ⒶL	⑥	Ⓐ✕	⚒	⑥	Ⓐ	Ⓐ	⚒	⚒C	⑥	Ⓐ	Ⓐ	⑥J	ⒶM	⑥	⑥	Ⓐ
don Euston **150** d.	...	...	...	...	...	...	...	...	...	...	...	...	...	...	...	...	1823	...	...	...	...	...	...	...	...
ngham International ✈ d.	1310	1409	...	...	1509	1609	...	...	1709	1709	...	1809	...	...	...	1904	1933	2004	2004	...	...	2104	2109	...	...
ngham New Street d.	1325	1425	...	...	1525	1625	...	...	1725	1725	...	1825	...	...	...	1925	1950	2025	2025	...	...	2125	2125	...	...
erhampton d.	1342	1443	...	...	1542	1643	...	...	1742	1743	...	1843	...	...	...	1943	2019	2043	2043	...	...	2142	2143	...	...
d Central d.	1359	1459	...	...	1558	1659	...	...	1801	1800	...	1859	...	...	...	2000	2036	2059	2059	...	...	2158	2200	...	...
gton d.	1406	1506	...	...	1605	1706	...	...	1806	1807	...	1906	...	...	...	2006	2043	2106	2105	...	...	2206	2206	...	...
wsbury a.	1419	1520	...	...	1620	1720	...	...	1820	1820	...	1919	...	...	...	2020	2055	2120	2118	...	...	2219	2223	...	...
erystwyth **147** a.	|	1720	...	...	|	1917	...	...	|	|	...	2119	...	...	...	|	...	2330	2337	...	...	|	|	...	...
rdiff Central **149** d.	|	...	1315	1321	|	...	1515	1621	|	|	1716	...	1715	...	1821	|	...	...	...	1934	1930	|	|	2055	2117
wsbury d.	1422	...	1528	1526	1624	...	1724	1810	1824	1822	1909	...	1924	1924	2013	2024	...	...	...	2139	2137	2224	2225	2306	2318
wen d.	1442	...	1547	1545	1644	...	1743	|	1843	1842	|	...	1943	1943	|	2043	...	...	...	2158	2156	2243	2244	|	|
on d.	1454	...	1558	1557	1656	...	1754	|	1855	1854	|	...	1954	1954	|	2055	...	...	...	2209	2207	2255	2256	|	|
ham General d.	1500	...	1605	1604	1703	...	1802	|	1905	1902	1943	...	2002	2002	|	2102	...	...	...	2214	2213	2303	2303	|	|
ter a.	1521	...	1624	1624	1721	...	1822	1905	1924	1921	2002	...	2022	2022	2108	2121	...	...	...	2234	2232	2320	2322	0026	0026
yhead **165** a.	1711	...	1819	1821	1917	...	2020	...	...	2131	2145	...	2225	...	...	...	...	...	...	0048	...	...	...	...	...

	Ⓐ	⑥	Ⓐ		⑦	⑦	⑦	⑦	⑦	⑦	⑦	⑦	⑦	⑦	⑦	⑦	⑦	⑦	⑦	⑦C	⑦	⑦	⑦	⑦	⑦
don Euston **150** d.	...	...	...	...		...	...	...	...	...	...	...	...	...	...	...	...	...	...	1900	...	...	...	...	...
ngham International ✈ d.	...	...	...	...		...	0951	1048	1207	1307	...	1407	1507	1607	...	1707	1807	1907	2008	2013	2108	...	2211	2240	2308
ngham New Street d.	2332	2335	2252	...		...	1004	1105	1224	1324	...	1424	1524	1624	...	1724	1824	1924	2024	2027	2124	...	2224	2255	2324
erhampton d.	0002	2354	2327	...		...	1022	1127	1242	1342	...	1443	1543	1643	...	1743	1843	1943	2043	2056	2143	...	2242	2315	2346
d Central d.	0029	0022	|	...		...	1049	1154	1259	1358	...	1459	1559	1659	...	1759	1859	1959	2059	2113	2210	...	2309	|	0013
gton d.	0036	0030	|	...	⑦	...	1057	1201	1305	1404	...	1506	1606	1706	...	1805	1906	2006	2106	2120	2217	...	2316	|	0020
wsbury a.	0052	0043	|	...		...	1109	1215	1324	1418	...	1520	1622	1719	...	1819	1919	2019	2119	2135	2230	...	2332	|	0036
erystwyth **147** a.	▬	▬	|	...		...	1323	|	1523	|	...	1721	|	1922	...	|	2122	|	2317	...	|	...	...	|	...
rdiff Central **149** d.	⑥	Ⓐ	|	...		...	...	|	...	|	1313	...	|	...	1514	|	...	|	▬	...	|	2100	...	|	...
wsbury d.	2333	2337	|	...		1016	...	1217	...	1420	1524	...	1624	...	1730	1820	...	2023	...	...	2232	2319	...	|	...
wen d.	2352	2357	|	...		1035	...	1237	...	1439	1544	...	1643	...	1749	1840	...	2043	⑦	...	|	|	...	|	...
on d.	0004	0009	|	...		1047	...	1249	...	1451	1556	...	1655	...	1801	1851	...	2055		...	|	|	...	|	...
ham General d.	0014	0015	|	...		1054	...	1256	...	1458	1602	...	1706	...	1808	1858	...	2102	2235	...	|	|	...	|	...
ter a.	0033	0035	0037	...		1114	...	1320	...	1518	1622	...	1726	...	1825	1925	...	2121	2255	...	2331	0033	...	0022	...
yhead **165** a.	...	...	0215	...		...	...	...	...	...	1837	...	...	...	2018	2130	...	...	...	...	...	...	...	0220	...

	⚒	⑥	Ⓐ	Ⓐ	⑥	Ⓐ	Ⓐ	ⒶC	⑥	Ⓐ	⚒	⑥C	⑥	Ⓐ✕	Ⓐ	Ⓐ	⑥	⚒	⑥	ⒶL	Ⓐ	Ⓐ	⑥	⚒	⚒
yhead **165** d.		...	...	...	...	...	...	...	0425d	0425	...	...	0522	0533	...	0628	0635	...	0715	...	...	0805	0820	...	0923
ter d.		0422	0422	...	...	0530	0545	...	0612	0618	...	...	0721	0714	...	0819	0819	...	0920	0926	...	1020	1019	...	1130
ham General d.		|	|	...	...	0546	0603	...	0638	0637	...	...	0737	0732	0747	0834	0834	...	0936	0942	...	1036	1035	...	1145
on d.		|	|	...	...	0553	▬	...	0644	0644	...	...	0744	|	0755	0841	0841	...	0943	0949	...	1042	1042	...	1153
wen d.		|	|	...	...	0605	...	...	0657	0656	...	...	0756	|	0807	0853	0853	...	0955	1001	...	1054	1054	...	1205
wsbury a.		|	|	...	...	0627	...	...	0717	0716	...	...	0820	0807	0828	0913	0913	...	1029	1022	...	1114	1114	...	1229
rdiff Central **149** a.		|	|	...	...	|	...	...	0925	0920	...	...	|	0956	▬	1115	1116	...	|	1211	...	1322	1320	...	|
erystwyth **147** d.		|	|	...	...	|	⑥	...	...	...	0530	...	|	...	Ⓐ	...	...	0730	|	...	...	...	...	0930	|
wsbury d.		|	|	0518	0522	0633	0633	0639	...	...	0733	0818	0833	...	0832	...	...	0933	1033	...	1032	...	...	1133	1233
gton d.		|	|	0531	0535	0646	0646	0653	...	...	0746	0832	0846	...	0845	...	...	0946	1046	...	1046	...	...	1146	1246
d Central d.		|	|	0538	0542	0653	0653	0700	...	...	0753	0839	0853	...	0852	...	...	0953	1053	...	1052	...	...	1153	1253
erhampton a.		0539	0539	0558	0601	0711	0711	0717	...	...	0811	0901	0911	...	0910	...	...	1010	1111	...	1109	...	...	1212	1310
ngham New Street a.		0558	0610	0615	0619	0730	0730	0747	...	...	0829	0921	0927	...	0929	...	...	1030	1128	...	1130	...	...	1232	1329
ngham International ✈ a.		...	...	0649	0649	0749	0749	0759	...	...	0849	0939	0950	...	0949	...	...	1050	1150	...	1149	...	...	1250	1350
don Euston a.		...	...	...	...	...	...	0915	...	...	...	1056	...	...	...	...	...	...	...	...	...	...	...	...	...

	⑥	Ⓐ	⚒	⑥	Ⓐ	Ⓐ	⑥	⚒C	⚒	Ⓐ	⑥	⑥	Ⓐ	⚒	⑥	Ⓐ	⚒	⚒	Ⓐ	⑥	ⒶB	⑥	⑥	Ⓐ	ⒶD
yhead **165** d.	1033	1040	...	1123	1127	1232	1238	...	...	1324	1328	1423	1434	...	1523	1544	1650	...	1730	1730	...	...	...	...	...
ter d.	1219	1219	...	1330	1330	1419	1419	...	...	1530	1530	1619	1619	...	1728	1730	1828	...	1917	1928	2022	2026	...	...	2135
ham General d.	1234	1234	...	1346	1346	1434	1434	...	...	1546	1546	1635	1635	...	1744	1748	1845	...	1933	1944	2038	2042	...	...	|
on d.	1241	1241	...	1353	1353	1441	1441	...	...	1553	1553	1642	1642	...	1751	1754	1851	...	1940	1951	*2056*	2049	...	...	|
wen d.	1253	1253	...	1405	1405	1453	1453	...	...	1605	1605	1654	1654	...	1803	1806	1903	...	1952	2002	*2107*	2101	...	...	|
wsbury a.	1313	1314	...	1428	1427	1513	1513	...	...	1629	1629	1714	1714	...	1824	1827	1924	...	2014	2026	*2128*	2121	...	...	|
rdiff Central **149** a.	1530	1510	...	|	|	1715	...	...	...	|	|	1920	1920	...	|	|	2141	...	...	...	...	...	...	...	|
erystwyth **147** d.	...	...	1130	|	|	...	...	...	1330	|	|	...	...	1530	|	|	...	1730	...	...	...	...	1930	1930	|
wsbury d.	...	...	1334	1433	1433	...	...	1524	1533	1633	1633	...	...	1733	1833	1833	...	1932	...	...	...	...	2133	2133	|
gton d.	...	...	1348	1446	1446	...	...	1538	1546	1647	1647	...	...	1746	1846	1846	...	1946	...	...	...	...	2146	2147	|
d Central d.	...	...	1354	1453	1453	...	...	1544	1553	1654	1653	...	...	1753	1853	1853	...	1953	...	...	...	...	2153	2153	|
erhampton a.	...	...	1412	1511	1511	...	...	1601	1610	1709	1708	...	...	1811	1911	1911	...	2011	...	...	...	...	2209	2211	2227
ingham New Street a.	...	...	1432	1528	1530	...	...	1622	1630	1730	1728	...	...	1830	1928	1930	...	2029	...	...	...	...	2228	2233	2250
ingham International ✈ a.	...	...	1449	1550	1549	...	...	1639	1649	1749	1750	...	...	1849	1949	1949	...	2049	...	...	...	...	...	...	...
don Euston a.	...	...	...	...	...	...	...	1756	...	...	...	...	...	...	...	...	...	...	...	...	...	...	...	...	...

	Ⓐ	⑥	⚒		⑦	⑦	⑦	⑦	⑦	⑦	⑦	⑦	⑦C	⑦	⑦	⑦	⑦	⑦	⑦	⑦	⑦	⑦	⑦	⑦	⑦
yhead **165** d.	1921	1921	...		...	...	...	...	...	1020	...	...	...	...	...	...	...	1625	...	...	1825	...	1915e	...	...
ter d.	2121	2120	2228	⑦	0808	...	0922	...	1131	1221	...	1331	...	...	1531	...	1731	1824	...	1926	2027	...	2126	2204	2300
ham General d.	2137	2137	2244		0828	...	0938	...	1148	1238	...	1348	...	...	1548	...	1748	1841	...	1942	|	...	2144	2223	|
on d.	2144	2143	2251		▬	...	0945	...	1154	1245	...	1354	...	...	1554	...	1754	1847	...	1949	|	...	2150	...	|
wen d.	2155	2156	2302		...	...	0957	...	1206	1257	...	1406	...	...	1606	...	1806	1859	...	2000	|	...	2202	...	|
wsbury a.	2216	2217	2323		...	...	1018	...	1227	1318	...	1427	...	...	1627	...	1827	1920	...	2021	|	...	2223	...	0014
rdiff Central **149** a.	|	|	|		...	...	|	...	|	1531	...	|	...	...	|	...	|	2142	...	|	|	...	|	...	...
erystwyth **147** d.	|	|	|		⑦	...	|	0930	|	...	1130	|	...	1330	|	1530	|	...	1730	|	|	1930	|	...	...
wsbury d.	2218	2231	2326		0810	0909	1020	1140	1231	...	1331	1431	1524	1533	1640	1733	1831	...	1931	2023	|	2131	2224	...	...
gton d.	2232	2245	2340		0824	0923	1034	1154	1245	...	1345	1445	1538	1547	1654	1747	1845	...	1945	2037	|	2145	2237	...	...
d Central d.	2238	2251	2347		0831	0930	1040	1200	1251	...	1351	1451	1544	1553	1700	1753	1851	...	1951	2044	|	2151	2245	...	...
erhampton a.	2255	2308	0017		0859	0958	1056	1216	1307	...	1407	1507	1601	1609	1715	1809	1907	...	2008	2111	2129	2207	2314	...	...
ingham New Street a.	2329	2330	...		0915	1014	1113	1232	1323	...	1423	1524	1620	1625	1737	1827	1926	...	2025	2129	2153	2227	...	...	...
ingham International ✈ a.	...	...	...		0932	1032	1131	1302	1357	...	1500	1557	1639	1700	1757	1900	1957	...	2103	2157	2208	2301	...	...	...
don Euston a.	...	...	...		...	...	...	...	...	...	...	...	1757	...	...	...	...	...	...	...	...	...	...	...	...

(12) and 🍷 Birmingham New Street - Crewe - Holyhead (Table **150**).
(12) and 🍷 Wrexham - London Euston and v.v. (Table **150**).
(12) and 🍷 Shrewsbury - London Euston and v.v. (Table **150**).
(12) and 🍷 Bangor - Crewe - Birmingham New Street (Table **150**).
To/from Llandudno Junction (Table **165**).

L – To/from Llandudno (Table **165**).
M – To/from Manchester Piccadilly (Table **160**).

d – From Sept. 17.
e – May 15 - Sept. 11.

146 SHREWSBURY - SWANSEA

2nd class

km		Ⓐ	⑥	Ⓐ	⑥	Ⓐ	⑦	⑥	Ⓐ	⑦	⑥	Ⓐ
0	**Shrewsbury** .... **149** d.	0445	0516	0556	0900	1009	1204	1358	1405	1618	1801	1824
20	Church Stretton **149** d.	0503	0533	0614	0918	1027	1222	1416	1423	1636	1821	1842
32	Craven Arms .... **149** d.	0514	0547	0624	0928	1037	1233	1426	1434	1647	1832	1854
52	Knighton .... d.	0536	0612	0656	0952	1101	1257	1455	1458	1711	1856	1918
84	**Llandrindod** .... a.	0610	0646	0734	1030	1139	1335	1533	1536	1749	1934	1956
84	**Llandrindod** .... d.	▬	0654	0735	1033	1200	1341	1540	1541	1758	1934	1956
110	Llanwrtyd .... d.	Ⓐ	0723	0809	1107	1231	1412	1611	1623	1829	2008	2030
128	Llandovery .... d.	0642	0747	0834	1132	1256	1437	1636	1648	1855	2034	2056
146	Llandeilo .... d.	0703	0808	0856	1154	1318	1459	1658	1710	1916	2055	2117
159	Pantyffynnon .... d.	0721	0825	0913	1211	1335	1516	1715	1727	1934	2113	2135
178	Llanelli .... **135** a.	0741	0845	0933	1235	1358	1537	1735	1747	1959	2133	2155
196	**Swansea** .... **135** a.	0808	0922	1002	1301	1425	1603	1809	1814	2025	2206	2222

	⑥	Ⓐ	Ⓐ	⑥	Ⓐ	⑦	⑥	Ⓐ	⑦	⑥
Swansea .... **135** d.	0431	...	0603	0911	0933	1112	1311	1435	1528	1817
Llanelli .... **135** d.	0450	0520	0625	0934	0954	1132	1332	1453	1548	1840
Pantyffynnon .... d.	0510	0539	0644	0955	1013	1153	1353	1512	1612	1859
Llandeilo .... d.	0529	0559	0706	1015	1033	1213	1413	1532	1632	1919
Llandovery .... d.	0551	0621	0728	1037	1055	1235	1435	1554	1654	1941
Llanwrtyd .... d.	0616	▬	0808	1105	1120	1300	1501	1624	1720	2008
Llandrindod .... a.	0644	Ⓐ	0838	1136	1151	1331	1531	1654	1755	2038
Llandrindod .... d.	0655	0618	0845	1140	1201	1343	1542	1659	1801	2042
Knighton .... d.	0732	0703	0923	1218	1240	1422	1621	1737	1840	2118
Craven Arms .... **149** a.	0753	0727	0946	1240	1302	1444	1642	1759	1902	2140
Church Stretton **149** a.	0806	0742	0958	1253	1317	1457	1655	1812	1917	2153
Shrewsbury .... **149** a.	0822	0757	1014	1309	1332	1512	1711	1828	1933	2209

147 SHREWSBURY - ABERYSTWYTH

2nd class

km		⚒	⚒	⚒	⚒	⚒	⚒	⚒	⚒	⚒	⚒	Ⓐ	⑥	⑥	Ⓐ
	B'mingham N S **145** d.	...	0625	0825	...	1025	1225	1425	1625	...	1825	...	...	2025	2025
0	**Shrewsbury** .... d.	0625	0727	0930	1029	1129	1329	1530	1727	1827	1930	2030	2039	2143	2150
32	Welshpool .... d.	0648	0749	0952	1051	1151	1351	1552	1749	1849	1952	2052	2101	2205	2212
54	Newtown .... d.	0703	0803	1006	1106	1205	1405	1606	1803	1903	2006	2107	2116	2220	2227
63	Caersws .... d.	0710	0810	1013	1113	1212	1412	1613	1810	1910	2013	2114	2123	2227	2234
98	Machynlleth .... a.	0742	0843	1044	1141	1243	1442	1643	1840	1945	2043	2141	2151	2255	2301
98	Machynlleth .... d.	0747	0848	1049	1141	1248	1448	1649	1846	1946	2048	2145	2151	2302	2307
104	Dovey Junction ‡ .... d.	0755	0855	1055	1153	1255	1454	1655	1854	1955	2055	2153	2159	2308	2313
118	Borth .... d.	0805	0905	1105	1203	1305	1504	1705	1904	2005	2105	2203	2209	2318	2323
131	**Aberystwyth** .... a.	0822	0923	1120	1216	1317	1518	1720	1917	2021	2119	2217	2223	2330	2337

km	⑦	⑦a	⑦b	⑦	⑦	⑦	⑦	⑦	⑦	⑦
	B'mingham N S **145** d.	...	🚌	1004	1224	1424	...	1624	...	1824
0	**Shrewsbury** .... d.	0830	0830	1128	1327	1527	1629	1727	1828	1927
32	Welshpool .... d.	0852	0905	1150	1349	1551	1651	1749	1850	1949
54	Newtown .... d.	0906	0930	1204	1403	1605	1705	1803	1904	2003
63	Caersws .... d.	0913	0945	1211	1411	1612	1712	1810	1911	2010
98	Machynlleth .... a.	0945	1025	1245	1447	1643	1741	1840	1940	2044
98	Machynlleth .... d.	0947	1025	1250	1447	1646	1747	1846	1942	2046
104	Dovey Junction ‡ .... d.	0955	|	1258	1455	1654	1755	1854	1954	2054
118	Borth .... d.	1005	1050	1308	1505	1704	1805	1904	2004	2104
131	**Aberystwyth** .... a.	1021	1110	1323	1523	1721	1820	1922	2019	2122

	⚒	⚒	⚒	⚒	⚒	⚒	⚒		⚒	⚒	⚒	Ⓐ	⑥	⑥	Ⓐ
Aberystwyth .... d.	0530	0630	0730	0830	0930	1130	1230	...	1330	1530	1730	1830	1830	1930	1930
Borth .... d.	0541	0641	0741	0841	0941	1141	1241	...	1341	1541	1741	1841	1840	1941	1941
Dovey Junction ‡ .... d.	0552	0653	0753	0858	0952	1153	1257	...	1352	1552	1751	1852	1852	1955	1956
Machynlleth .... a.	0600	0700	0800	0906	0959	1201	1304	...	1358	1559	1759	1859	1859	2002	2003
Machynlleth .... d.	0600	0703	0805	0906	1008	1204	1306	...	1407	1608	1805	1909	1905	2008	2008
Caersws .... d.	0627	0730	0828	0933	1035	1233	1333	...	1434	1631	1828	1932	1928	2031	2031
Newtown .... d.	0634	0737	0839	0940	1042	1240	1340	...	1441	1642	1839	1943	1939	2041	2041
Welshpool .... d.	0649	0752	0854	0955	1056	1255	1354	...	1455	1656	1853	1957	2000	2102	2056
Shrewsbury .... a.	0713	0814	0918	1017	1118	1317	1419	...	1519	1725	1919	2022	2022	2124	2118
B'mingham N S **145** .. a.	0829	...	1030	...	1232	1432	...	...	1630	1830	2029	...	...	2228	2233

⑦	⑦a	⑦b	⑦	⑦	⑦	⑦	⑦	⑦a	⑦b
Aberystwyth .... d.	0930	0930	1030	1130	1330	1433	1530	1730	1730
Borth .... d.	0941	0943	1043	1141	1341	1444	1541	1741	1743
Dovey Junction ‡ .... d.	0953	0953	1056	1151	1351	1457	1553	1752	1753
Machynlleth .... a.	1002	1002	1102	1202	1357	1503	1600	1759	1800
Machynlleth .... d.	1008	1008	1105	1206	1406	1508	1605	1805	1805
Caersws .... d.	1031	1031	1128	1229	1429	1531	1630	1828	1830
Newtown .... d.	1041	1041	1138	1240	1440	1541	1641	1839	1841
Welshpool .... d.	1056	1102	1154	1254	1455	1556	1655	1853	1855
Shrewsbury .... a.	1119	1125	1216	1318	1517	1620	1719	1914	1922
B'mingham N S **145** .. a.	1232	1232	...	1423	1625	...	1827	2023	2025

a – May 15 - Sept. 11.
b – From Sept. 18.
‡ – Trains call on request.
▷ – Additional journeys Machynlleth - Aberystwyth and v.v.:
From Machynlleth at 0453 ⚒, 0545 ⚒, 0647 ⚒, 0850 ⑦, 0947 ⑦, 1049 ⑦, 1400 ⑦, 1800 Ⓐ.
From Aberystwyth at 1830 ⑦, 2030 Ⓑ, 2035 ⑥, 2130 Ⓑ, 2136 ⑥, 2230 ⚒, 2320 ⑦, 2335 ⑥, 2340 ⑦

148 MACHYNLLETH - PWLLHELI

2nd class

km	Ⓐ	Ⓐ	Ⓐ	Ⓐ	Ⓐa	Ⓐb	Ⓐ	Ⓐ	Ⓐ	Ⓐa	Ⓐb	Ⓐ
	Birmingham N S **145** d.	...	...	*0625*	0825	*0825*	1025	1225	1425	1625	*1625*	*1825*
	Shrewsbury **147** ....d.	...	...	*0727*	0930	*0930*	1129	1329	1530	1727	*1727*	*1930*
0	**Machynlleth** .... d.	0507	0643	0852	1055	1055	1251	1456	1655	1900	1900	2130
6	Dovey Junction ‡ .... d.	0513	0649	0858	1101	1101	1257	1502	1701	1906	1906	2136
16	Aberdovey .... d.	0526	0702	0911	1114	1114	1310	1515	1714	1919	1919	2149
22	Tywyn .... a.	0533	0711	0920	1123	1123	1319	1524	1724	1928	1928	2158
22	Tywyn .... d.	0533	0714	0929	1131	1131	1324	1525	1729	1929	1929	2203
37	Fairbourne .... d.	0552	0732	0948	1150	1150	1343	1544	1747	1947	1947	2221
41	**Barmouth** .... a.	0604	0745	0959	1201	1201	1354	1555	1758	1955	1955	2232
41	**Barmouth** .... d.	...	0747	1001	1202	1202	1356	1557	1800	1957	1957	2234
58	Harlech .... a.	...	0811	1025	1226	1226	1420	1621	1824	2015	2015	2258
58	Harlech .... d.	...	0825	1027	1229	1229	1431	1629	1833	2019	2019	2301
67	Penrhyndeudraeth .... d.	...	0838	1040	1242	1242	1444	1642	1846	|	|	2314
69	Minffordd .... **160** d.	...	0842	1044	1245	1245	1448	1645	1849	|	|	2317
72	**Porthmadog** .... **160** d.	...	0850	1052	1253	1253	1456	1653	1857	2039	2039	2325
80	Criccieth .... d.	...	0857	1059	1301	1301	1503	1700	1904	2046	2046	2333
93	**Pwllheli** .... a.	...	0912	1114	1316	1316	1521	1718	1922	2102	2102	2348

⑥	⑥	⑥	⑥	⑥	⑥	⑥	⑥	⑥	⑥
Birmingham N S **145** d.	...	...	*0625*	0825	1025	1225	1425	1625	*1825*
Shrewsbury **147** ....d.	...	...	*0730*	0931	1129	1329	1530	1727	*1930*
Machynlleth .... d.	0507	0643	0853	1055	1252	1456	1655	1900	2130
Dovey Junction ‡ .... d.	0513	0649	0859	1101	1258	1502	1701	1906	2136
Aberdovey .... d.	0526	0702	0912	1114	1311	1515	1714	1919	2149
Tywyn .... a.	0533	0711	0921	1123	1319	1524	1724	1928	2158
Tywyn .... d.	0533	0714	0929	1132	1324	1525	1729	1929	2203
Fairbourne .... d.	0552	0732	0948	1150	1343	1544	1747	1947	2221
Barmouth .... a.	0604	0745	0959	1201	1354	1555	1758	1955	2232
Barmouth .... d.	...	0747	1001	1202	1356	1557	1800	1957	2234
Harlech .... a.	...	0811	1025	1226	1420	1621	1824	2015	2258
Harlech .... d.	...	0825	1027	1229	1431	1629	1833	2019	2301
Penrhyndeudraeth .... d.	...	0838	1040	1242	1444	1642	1846	|	2314
Minffordd .... **160** d.	...	0842	1044	1245	1448	1645	1849	|	2317
Porthmadog .... **160** d.	...	0850	1052	1253	1456	1653	1857	2039	2325
Criccieth .... d.	...	0857	1059	1301	1503	1700	1904	2046	2333
Pwllheli .... a.	...	0913	1114	1316	1520	1716	1919	2101	2348

⑦	⑦c	⑦c
Birmingham N S **145** d.	...	1224
Shrewsbury **147** ....d.	*0830*	1328
Machynlleth .... d.	1010	1453
Dovey Junction ‡ .... d.	1016	1459
Aberdovey .... d.	1029	1512
Tywyn .... a.	1035	1518
Tywyn .... d.	1036	1531
Fairbourne .... d.	1054	1549
Barmouth .... a.	1103	1557
Barmouth .... d.	1104	1559
Harlech .... a.	1130	1625
Harlech .... d.	1132	1625
Penrhyndeudraeth .... d.	1146	1639
Minffordd .... **160** d.	1149	1642
Porthmadog .... **160** d.	1157	1648
Criccieth .... d.	1205	1655
Pwllheli .... a.	1221	1714

Ⓐ	Ⓐ	Ⓐ	Ⓐ	Ⓐ	Ⓐ	Ⓐ	Ⓐ	Ⓐa	Ⓐb	Ⓐ	
Pwllheli .... d.	...	0629	0724	0934	1137	1338	1537	1742	1742	2012	...
Criccieth .... d.	...	0643	0738	0948	1151	1352	1551	1756	1756	2026	...
Porthmadog .... **160** d.	...	0653	0747	0957	1201	1402	1601	1806	1806	2041	...
Minffordd .... **160** d.	...	0657	0752	1001	1205	1406	1605	1810	1810	2045	...
Penrhyndeudraeth .... d.	...	0701	0756	1005	1209	1410	1609	1814	1814	2048	...
Harlech .... a.	...	0715	0809	1020	1224	1425	1624	1827	1827	2102	...
Harlech .... d.	...	0717	0821	1029	1228	1428	1629	1830	1830	2105	...
Barmouth .... a.	...	0742	0845	1054	1253	1453	1654	1855	1855	2130	...
Barmouth .... d.	0646	0746	0852	1101	1255	1455	1656	1857	1857	2132	...
Fairbourne .... d.	0654	0754	0900	1109	1303	1503	1704	1905	1905	2140	...
Tywyn .... a.	0713	0812	0920	1129	1323	1524	1724	1925	1925	2200	...
Tywyn .... d.	0714	0816	0927	1130	1325	1526	1727	1931	1931	2202	...
Aberdovey .... d.	0720	0822	0933	1136	1331	1532	1733	1937	1937	2208	...
Dovey Junction ‡ .... d.	0735	0838	0947	1149	1345	1546	1747	1953	1953	2224	...
Machynlleth .... a.	0743	0845	0954	1157	1352	1554	1755	2001	2001	2231	...
Shrewsbury **147** .... a.	0916	*1017*	1118	1317	1519	1720	*1918*	2118	*2118*	...	...
Birmingham New Str. **145** ... a.	1030	...	1230	1430	1630	1830	*2029*	2233	*2233*	...	...

⑥	⑥	⑥	⑥	⑥	⑥	⑥	⑥	⑥	⑥
Pwllheli .... d.	...	0629	0724	0934	1137	1338	1537	1742	2012
Criccieth .... d.	...	0643	0738	0948	1151	1352	1551	1756	2026
Porthmadog .... **160** d.	...	0653	0747	0958	1201	1402	1601	1806	2041
Minffordd .... **160** d.	...	0657	0752	1002	1205	1406	1605	1810	2046
Penrhyndeudraeth .... d.	...	0701	0756	1006	1209	1410	1609	1814	2049
Harlech .... a.	...	0715	0809	1021	1224	1425	1624	1827	2103
Harlech .... d.	...	0717	0821	1028	1228	1428	1629	1830	2106
Barmouth .... a.	...	0742	0845	1053	1253	1453	1654	1855	2131
Barmouth .... d.	0646	0746	0852	1101	1255	1455	1656	1857	2133
Fairbourne .... d.	0654	0754	0900	1109	1303	1503	1704	1905	2141
Tywyn .... a.	0714	0812	0920	1129	1323	1524	1724	1925	2201
Tywyn .... d.	0715	0816	0927	1130	1325	1526	1727	1931	2203
Aberdovey .... d.	0721	0822	0933	1136	1331	1532	1733	1937	2209
Dovey Junction ‡ .... d.	0736	0838	0947	1151	1345	1546	1747	1952	2225
Machynlleth .... a.	0744	0845	0955	1158	1353	1555	1755	1959	2232
Shrewsbury **147** .... a.	0918	*1017*	1118	1317	1519	1728	*1915*	*2124*	...
Birmingham New Str. **145** ... a.	1030	...	1232	1432	1630	1830	*2029*	*2228*	...

⑦	⑦c	⑦
Pwllheli .... d.	1128	1348
Criccieth .... d.	1141	1402
Porthmadog .... **160** d.	1157	1412
Minffordd .... **160** d.	1202	1416
Penrhyndeudraeth .... d.	1206	1420
Harlech .... a.	1218	1432
Harlech .... d.	1219	1434
Barmouth .... a.	1245	1459
Barmouth .... d.	1248	1501
Fairbourne .... d.	1256	1509
Tywyn .... a.	1316	1527
Tywyn .... d.	1316	1528
Aberdovey .... d.	1322	1535
Dovey Junction ‡ .... d.	1336	1549
Machynlleth .... a.	1346	1559
Shrewsbury **147** .... a.	1517	1719
Birmingham New Str. **145** ... a.	1625	1827

a – May 16 - Sept. 9. b – From Sept. 12. c – May 15 - Sept. 11. ‡ – Trains call on request.

149 CARDIFF - HEREFORD - CREWE - MANCHESTER

2nd class

Most Manchester trains continue to / from destinations on Table **135**

km		Ⓐ	Ⓐ J	Ⓐ	Ⓐ	Ⓐ	Ⓐ	Ⓐ	Ⓐ	Ⓐ	Ⓐ	Ⓐ	Ⓐ	Ⓐ	Ⓐ	Ⓐ	Ⓐ	Ⓐ	Ⓐ	Ⓐ	Ⓐ	Ⓐ ✕	Ⓐ	Ⓐ
0	**Cardiff** Central .... **132** d.	0433	0508	0533	0650	0721	0805	0850	0921	1005	1050	1121	1205	1250	1321	1405	1450	1521	1550	1621	1650	1716	1750	1821
19	Newport .... **132** d.	0452	0528	0558	0704	0736	0819	0905	0936	1019	1104	1136	1219	1304	1336	1419	1504	1536	1604	1635	1704	1731	1804	1835
30	Cwmbrân .... d.	0503	0538	0608	0714	0746	0829	0915	0946	1029	1114	1146	1229	1314	1346	1429	1514	1546	1614	1644	1714	1742	1815	1845
35	Pontypool & New Inn . d.	0509	0544	0614	|	0752	|	|	0952	|	|	1152	|	|	1352	|	|	1552	1619	|	|	1749	1820	|
50	Abergavenny .... d.	0516	0553	0623	0727	0801	0842	0928	1001	1042	1127	1201	1242	1326	1401	1443	1527	1601	1629	1657	1727	1800	1829	1859
89	**Hereford** .... d.	0547	0625	0649	0753	0827	0908	0954	1028	1108	1153	1227	1308	1355	1426	1508	1553	1627	1654	1724	1753	1825	1855	1924
109	Leominster .... d.	0600	0638	0702	0806	|	0921	1007	|	1121	1206	|	1321	1408	|	1521	1606	1640	1707	|	1806	|	1908	|
127	Ludlow .... d.	0611	0649	0713	0817	0848	0932	1018	1049	1132	1217	1248	1332	1419	1447	1532	1617	1651	1718	|	1817	|	1919	1945
138	Craven Arms .... **146** d.	0620	0657	0721	0825	0856	|	1026	1057	|	1225	1256	|	1427	1455	|	1625	|	1727	|	1825	|	1927	|
150	Church Stretton... **146** d.	0629	0706	0730	0834	0905	|	1039	1106	|	1238	1305	|	1436	1504	|	|	1708	1736	|	1841	|	1936	|
170	**Shrewsbury** .... **146** a.	0643	0722	0744	0848	0919	0958	1052	1121	1158	1252	1321	1358	1450	1524	1558	1648	1724	1750	1809	1855	1908	1950	2011
170	**Shrewsbury** .... ¶ d.	0644	0724	0746	0850	0924	1000	1053	1125	1159	1254	1325	1359	1452	1526	1559	1650	1725	1751	1810	1856	1909	1952	2013
200	Whitchurch .... ¶ d.	0704	|	0806	0906	|	|	1112	|	|	1310	|	|	1508	|	|	1710	|	1809	|	1913	|	|	|
223	**Crewe** .... ¶ a.	0724	|	0824	0927	|	1028	1128	|	1228	1328	|	1428	1528	|	1628	1727	|	1827	1843	1933	|	2022	2043
	Chester **145, 160** .... a.	|	0821	|	|	1021	|	|	1220	|	|	1420	|	|	1624	|	|	1821	|	1905	|	2002	|	2108
	Holyhead **145, 160** .. a.	|	...	|	|	1222	|	|	1414	|	|	1614	|	|	1821	|	|	2020	|	...	|	2145	|	...
263	Stockport .... a.	0753	...	0859	0957	...	1058	1158	...	1258	1358	...	1458	1558	...	1659	1758	...	1858	...	2003	...	2050	...
273	**Manchester** P'dilly ..... a.	0808	...	0915	1014	...	1115	1215	...	1315	1415	...	1515	1615	...	1715	1815	...	1915	...	2021	...	2106	...

For continuation of Table and footnotes see next page ▶ ▶ ▶

2nd class

CARDIFF - HEREFORD - CREWE - MANCHESTER

Most Manchester trains continue to / from destinations on Table **135**

	Ⓐ	Ⓐ	Ⓐ	Ⓐ	⑥	⑥	⑥	⑥	⑥	⑥ a	⑥ b	⑥	⑥ a	⑥ b	⑥	⑥	⑥ a	⑥ b	⑥	⑥	⑥ a	⑥ b	⑥	⑥	⑥ a	⑥ b	⑥
ff Central .. **132** d.	1934	2017	2117	2155	0435	0520	0537	0646	0716	0744	0743e	0846	0915	0917	0950	1050	1115	1115	1150	1250	1315	1315	1350	1451	1515	1517	1550
ort **132** d.	1948	2031	2132	2212	0452	0535	0556	0704	0736	0759	0801	0904	0929	0936	1004	1104	1129	1135	1204	1309	1329	1336	1404	1509	1529	1536	1604
rân d.	1958	2041	2143	2224	0503	0545	0608	0714	0746	0809	0814	0914	0950	0946	1019	1119	1140	1146	1214	1319	1340	1346	1414	1519	1540	1546	1614
pool & New Inn d.	2003	2047	|	2230	0509	0551	0613	|	0751	|	|	|	0956	0952	|	|	1144	1150	|	|	1344	1350	|	|	1546	1552	1619
avenny d.	2012	2056	2156	2240	0518	0600	0623	0727	0801	0822	0827	0927	1005	1001	1032	1132	1154	1200	1227	1332	1355	1401	1427	1532	1555	1601	1629
ord d.	2039	2122	2221	2308	0547	0625	0649	0753	0827	0854	0853	0953	1030	1027	1058	1158	1231d	1228	1258	1358	1430d	1426	1458	1558	1630d	1627	1659
nster d.	2052	2135	2234	2321	0600	0638	0702	0806	|	0907	0906	1006	|	|	1111	1211	|	|	1311	1411	|	|	1511	1611	1643	1640	1712
v d.	2103	2146	2245	2332	0611	0649	0713	0817	0848	0918	0917	1017	1051	1048	1122	1222	1252	1249	1322	1422	1451	1447	1522	1622	1654	1651	1723
n Arms **146** d.	2112	2154	2254	2342	0620	0657	0721	0825	0856	|	|	1025	1059	1056	|	1230	1300	1257	|	1430	1459	1455	|	1630	|	|	|
h Stretton . **146** d.	2121	2204	2303	2351	0629	0706	0730	0834	0905	|	|	1034	1108	1105	|	1239	1309	1306	|	1440	1508	1504	|	1639	1708	1705	|
vsbury **146** a.	2137	2218	2317	0007	0643	0722	0744	0851	0921	0944	0943	1048	1123	1121	1148	1252	1323	1320	1348	1455	1523	1523	1548	1653	1722	1719	1749
vsbury **145** ¶ d.	2139	2220	2318	0012	0644	0722	0746	0852	0925	0945	0944	1050	1125	1125	1149	1254	1325	1324	1349	1455	1528	1528	1549	1655	1724	1724	1751
hurch ¶ d.	|	2243	2344	0038	0704	|	0806	0909	|	1002	1001	1106	|	|	1206	|	|	|	1406	|	|	|	1606	|	|	|	1807
e ¶ a.	|	2304	0005	0106	0725	|	0824	0927	|	1023	1023	1125	|	|	1224	1326	|	|	1424	1526	|	|	1624	1726	|	|	1826
ester **145, 160** a.	2234	|	0026	...	|	0819	|	|	1020	|	|	|	1219	1219	|	|	1419	1419	|	|	1624	1624	|	|	1822	1822	|
yhead **145, 160** a.	0048	|	...	...	|	1014	|	|	1209	|	|	|	1413	1413	|	|	1613	1613	|	|	1819	1819	|	|	2018	2018	|
port a.	...	2332	...	...	0754	...	0858	0958	...	1058	1058	1158	...	...	1258	1358	...	...	1458	1558	...	...	1659	1758	...	...	1858
hester P'dilly a.	...	2350	...	...	0810	...	0915	1016	...	1115	1115	1215	...	...	1315	1415	...	...	1515	1615	...	...	1714	1815	...	...	1915

	⑥	⑥ a	⑥ b	⑥	⑥	⑥ L	⑥	⑥ c	⑥ g	⑥	⑦	⑦	⑦	⑦	⑦	⑦	⑦	⑦	⑦	⑦	⑦	⑦	⑦	⑦	⑦	⑦	⑦
ff Central .. **132** d.	1650	1715	1715	1751	1846	1930	2008	2055	2055	2154	...	0830	0917	1034	1135	1235	1313h	1340	1456	1514	1556	1640	1735	1837	1940	2100	2315
ort **132** d.	1704	1729	1735	1810	1904	1948	2026	2110	2114	2209	...	0849	0941	1050	1151	1249	1335	1354	1514	1533	1614	1654	1749	1854	1955	2119	2332
rân d.	1714	1740	1746	1820	1915	1958	2037	2121	2125	2221	...	0859	0951	1102	1205	1304	1347	1409	1524	1545	1624	1709	1804	1909	2010	2130	2343
pool & New Inn d.	|	1746	1752	1825	1920	2003	2042	|	|	2226	...	0905	0957	1108	1211	1310	|	|	|	1551	|	1715	1810	|	2016	2136	2349
avenny d.	1727	1755	1801	1835	1929	2012	2052	2134	2138	2236	...	0914	1008	1118	1222	1320	1400	1422	1538	1602	1637	1725	1820	1922	2026	2146	0001
ord d.	1758	1831d	1827	1900	1955	2039	2120	2200	2204	2303	...	0941	1036	1150	1254	1355	1426	1448	1604	1628	1704	1753	1849	1949	2054	2214	0035
nster d.	1811	|	|	1913	2008	2052	2133	2214	2218	▬	...	0955	1050	1203	1308	1408	|	1501	|	1641	|	1807	1903	2003	2108	2227	...
w d.	1822	1852	1848	1924	2019	2103	2144	2225	2229	...	...	1006	1101	1214	1319	1419	1448	1512	1625	1652	1726	1818	1914	2014	2119	2238	...
n Arms **146** d.	1830	1900	1856	|	2027	2112	2154	2233	2237	...	...	1014	|	1224	|	1428	|	|	|	1700	|	1826	|	2022	2129	2248	...
h Stretton . **146** d.	1839	1909	1905	|	2036	2121	2203	2242	2246	⑥	...	1023	|	1233	|	1437	|	|	|	1709	|	1835	|	2031	2138	2257	...
vsbury **146** a.	1853	1923	1919	1950	2053	2135	2217	2257	2301		...	1037	1130	1248	1348	1451	1521	1538	1651	1723	1752	1849	1941	2045	2200	2314	...
vsbury **145** ¶ d.	1855	1925	1924	1952	2057	2137	2219	2306	2310	2330	0955	1039	1131	1251	1350	1453	1524	1540	1653	1730	1754	1854	1942	2048	*2232*	2319	...
hurch ¶ d.	|	|	|	2008	|	|	2244	2331	2335	2355	|	1100	1158	|	|	|	|	1606	|	|	|	|	2007	|	|	2346	...
e ¶ a.	1926	|	|	2027	|	|	2304	2353	2357	0016	1025	1122	1222	1326	1425	1525	|	1627	1725	|	1825	1924	2028	2121	*2303*	0009	...
ester **145, 160** a.	|	2022	2022	|	|	2232	|	0022	0026	...	|	|	|	|	|	|	1622	|	|	1825	|	|	|	|	*2331*	0033	...
yhead **145, 160** a.	|	2225	2225	|	|	...	|	...	...	...	|	|	|	|	|	|	1837	|	|	2018	|	|	|	|	...	...	...
port a.	1958	...	...	2059	2128	...	2332	...	...	...	1058	|	1258	1359	1500	1558	...	1658	1758	...	1858	1958	2057	2158	...	...	...
hester P'dilly a.	2015	...	...	2115	2214	...	2349	...	...	...	1115	1202	1313	1420	1515	1615	...	1714	1818	...	1913	2016	2113	2219	...	...	...

	Ⓐ	Ⓐ	Ⓐ	Ⓐ	Ⓐ	Ⓐ	Ⓐ ✕	Ⓐ		Ⓐ	Ⓐ	Ⓐ J	Ⓐ	Ⓐ	Ⓐ	Ⓐ	Ⓐ	Ⓐ		Ⓐ	Ⓐ	Ⓐ	Ⓐ	Ⓐ	Ⓐ	Ⓐ	Ⓐ
hester P'dilly d.	...	...	...	...	...	0630	...	0730	...	...	0830	...	0930	...	1030	1130	...	1230	...	1330	...	1430	1530	...	1630	1730	...
port d.	...	...	...	...	...	0639	...	0739	...	...	0839	...	0939	...	1039	1139	...	1239	...	1339	...	1439	1539	...	1639	1739	...
yhead **145, 160** d.	...	...	...	...	0425	|	0533	|	...	0628	|	...	|	0805	|	|	1040	|	...	|	1232	|	|	1434	|	|	1650
ester **145, 160** d.	...	...	...	...	0618	|	0714	|	...	0819	|	0926	|	1020	|	|	1219	|	...	|	1419	|	|	1619	|	|	1828
e ¶ d.	...	0449	...	0555	|	0708	|	0808	...	|	0908	|	1008	|	1108	1208	|	1308	...	1408	|	1508	1608	|	1708	1809	|
hurch ¶ d.	...	0508	...	0616	|	|	|	|	...	|	|	|	|	|	|	|	|	|	...	1428	|	|	1628	|	|	1829	|
vsbury **145** ¶ a.	...	0528	...	0642	0716	0742	0807	0837	...	0913	0937	1022	1037	1114	1137	1237	1314	1337	...	1445	1513	1537	1647	1714	1737	1848	1924
vsbury **146** d.	...	0530	0610	0644	0718	0744	0810	0840	...	0914	0940	1024	1039	1116	1139	1239	1315	1340	...	1450	1515	1540	1650	1716	1740	1850	1925
h Stretton . **146** d.	...	0545	0626	0659	|	0759	|	|	...	0930	|	|	1054	|	1154	|	1330	|	...	1505	1530	|	1706	1731	|	1905	1940
en Arms **146** d.	...	0553	0634	0707	|	0807	|	|	...	0938	|	|	|	1137	|	|	1338	|	...	1513	1538	|	1714	1739	|	1913	1948
w d.	...	0601	0643	0714	0744	0815	|	0906	...	0945	1006	|	1108	1144	1208	1305	1345	1406	...	1520	1546	1606	1721	1746	1806	1920	1956
inster d.	...	0611	0654	0725	0754	0826	|	0916	...	|	1016	|	1118	|	1218	1315	|	1416	...	1531	|	1616	1732	1757	1816	1931	|
ord d.	0526	0641	0710	0745	0811	0842	0858	0933	...	1010	1033	|	1135	1208	1235	1332	1411	1433	...	1551	1611	1633	1751	1814	1833	1948	2022
gavenny d.	0551	0704	0734	0808	0834	0905	|	0958	...	1033	1056	|	1158	1231	1258	1355	1433	1456	...	1614	1634	1656	1814	1837	1856	2011	2045
pool & New Inn d.	0602	0714	0745	0817	0844	|	|	|	...	1043	|	|	|	1242	|	1405	|	|	...	1623	1644	|	1824	|	|	2021	|
brân d.	0607	0719	0750	0822	0849	0917	|	1011	...	1048	1109	|	1211	1247	1311	1410	|	1509	...	1628	1649	1709	1829	1849	1909	2026	2057
ort **132** a.	0619	0729	0800	0837	0900	0934	0940	1022	...	1101	1120	1153	1222	1257	1322	1420	1454	1521	...	1639	1659	1721	1840	1900	1922	2037	2115
ff Central **132** a.	0641	0749	0818	0853	0920	0956	0959	1039	...	1115	1137	1211	1237	1322	1340	1437	1510	1539	...	1657	1715	1739	1858	1920	1943	2103	2138

	Ⓐ	Ⓐ	Ⓐ	Ⓐ	Ⓐ	Ⓐ		⑥	⑥	⑥	⑥	⑥	⑥	⑥	⑥	⑥	⑥	⑥		⑥	⑥	⑥	⑥	⑥	⑥	⑥	⑥
hester P'dilly d.	1830	1930	2030	2136	...	2236	...	...	...	...	...	...	0630	0730	...	0830	0930	...	...	1030	1130	...	1230	1330	...	1430	1530
port d.	1839	1939	2040	2145	...	2244	...	...	...	...	...	...	0639	0739	...	0839	0939	...	...	1039	1139	...	1239	1339	...	1439	1539
yhead **145, 160** d.	|	|	|	|	...	|	...	...	...	...	...	0425k	|	|	0635	|	|	0820	...	|	|	1033	|	|	1238	|	|
ester **145, 160** d.	|	|	|	|	...	|	...	...	...	...	...	0612	|	|	0819	|	|	1019	...	|	|	1219	|	|	1419	|	|
e ¶ d.	1908	2010	2121	2212	...	2314	...	...	0454	...	0555	|	0708	0808	|	0908	1008	|	...	1108	1208	|	1308	1408	|	1509	1608
hurch ¶ d.	1929	2029	2142	2233	...	2334	...	...	0513	...	0616	|	0728	0827	|	|	|	|	...	|	1227	|	|	1427	|	|	1627
vsbury **145** ¶ a.	1955	2048	2208	2301	...	0004	...	...	0533	...	0642	0717	0747	0845	0913	0937	1036	1114	...	1137	1245	1313	1337	1443	1513	1538	1643
vsbury **146** d.	1956	2050	2209	...	2308	...	...	...	0540	0613	0644	0719	0750	0850	0915	0940	1038	1115	...	1140	1250	1315	1340	1445	1515	1540	1645
h Stretton . **146** d.	2011	2105	2224	...	2324	...	...	...	0555	0628	0659	|	0805	0905	|	0955	1054	|	...	1155	1305	1330	|	1500	|	1555	1700
en Arms **146** d.	2019	2113	2232	...	2332	...	...	...	0603	0636	0707	|	0813	0913	|	1003	1102	|	...	1203	1313	1338	|	1508	|	1603	1708
w d.	2027	2120	2240	...	2341	...	...	...	0610	0644	0714	0745	0820	0920	0942	1010	1109	1141	...	1210	1320	1344	1406	1515	1541	1610	1715
inster d.	2037	2131	2250	...	2352	...	...	...	0621	0655	0725	0755	0831	0931	|	1021	1120	|	...	1221	1331	|	1416	1526	|	1621	1726
ford d.	2054	2150	2311	...	0009	...	...	0542	0642	0711	0742	0812	0851	0950	1007	1038	1146	1206	...	1238	1350	1410	1433	1546	1606	1638	1746
gavenny d.	2122	2216	2334	...	0033	...	...	0607	0705	0734	0805	0835	0914	1013	1030	1101	1209	1229	...	1301	1413	1432	1456	1609	1629	1701	1809
pool & New Inn d.	2132	|	2343	...	|	...	...	0618	0715	0744	0814	0845	|	|	1040	|	|	1239	...	|	|	1443	|	|	1639	|	|
brân d.	2137	2228	2348	...	0046	...	...	0623	0720	0749	0819	0850	0926	1025	1045	1113	1221	1244	...	1313	1426	1448	1509	1621	1644	1713	1821
ort **132** a.	2150	2241	2359	...	0059	...	...	0637	0737	0800	0832	0904	0943	1044	1055	1129	1240	1254	...	1328	1442	1505	1521	1643	1654	1733	1839
iff Central .. **132** a.	2206	2304	0022	...	0120	...	...	0655	0757	0821	0853	0925	1003	1103	1116	1157	1301	1320	...	1357	1459	1530	1540	1702	1713	1802	1859

	⑥	⑥	⑥	⑥	⑥	⑥	⑥	⑥	⑥	⑦ 🚌	⑦ m	⑦ n	⑦	⑦	⑦	⑦	⑦	⑦	⑦	⑦	⑦	⑦	⑦	⑦	⑦	⑦	⑦
hester P'dilly d.	...	1630	1730	...	1830	1930	2030	2133	2235	...	...	...	0930	1031	1124	...	1233	1330	1430	1530	1630	1730	...	1830	1930	2030	...
port d.	...	1639	1739	...	1839	1939	2039	2143	2244	...	...	...	0940	1040	1140	...	1243	1340	1440	1539	1639	1739	...	1839	1939	2039	...
lyhead **145, 160** d.	1423	|	|	1650	|	|	|	|	|	...	...	...	|	|	|	1020	|	|	|	|	|	|	1625	|	|	|	...
ester **145, 160** d.	1619	|	|	1829	|	|	|	|	|	...	...	...	|	|	|	1221	|	|	|	|	|	|	1824	|	|	|	2300
e ¶ d.	|	1708	1809	|	1910	2009	2109	2212	2314	...	...	...	1013	1111	1213	|	1313	1413	1510	1613	1713	1813	|	1913	2010	2113	2323
church ¶ d.	|	1727	1828	|	1931	2028	2130	2233	2334	...	...	...	1035	|	|	|	1334	|	|	|	1734	|	|	1934	|	2135	2345
wsbury **145** ¶ a.	1714	1743	1846	1924	1956	2047	2153	2301	0005	...	...	...	1101	1141	1243	1318	1359	1443	1544	1643	1800	1843	1920	2000	2044	2203	0014
wsbury **146** d.	1716	1745	1850	1926	1958	2048	2155	▬	...	0750	...	...	1103	1145	1244	1319	1401	1444	1547	1644	1801	1844	1921	2001	2045	2204	...
ch Stretton . **146** d.	|	1800	1905	1941	2013	2103	2210	...	...	0815	...	...	1119	|	|	1335	|	1500	|	1700	|	|	1937	|	2101	2220	...
en Arms **146** d.	|	1808	1913	1949	2021	2111	2218	...	...	0835	...	...	1127	|	|	1343	|	1508	|	1708	|	|	1945	|	2110	2229	...
ow d.	1742	1815	1920	1955	2028	2119	2226	⑥	...	0855	...	...	1136	1213	1313	1351	1428	1516	1617	1716	1829	1912	1953	2029	2118	2237	...
inster d.	|	1826	1931	|	2039	2129	2237		...	0920	...	...	1147	1223	1324	1402	1439	1526	1628	1726	1839	|	2004	2039	2130	2249	...
eford d.	1807	1843	1951	2021	2056	2146	2253	2315	...	...	1001	1009	1203	1239	1340	1419	1456	1543	1644	1743	1857	1936	2021	2055	2146	2305	...
gavenny d.	1830	1906	2014	2044	2119	2209	2316	2338	...	...	1025	1033	1227	1302	1403	1442	1519	1606	1708	1806	1920	1959	2046	2118	2210	2329	...
ypool & New Inn d.	1840	|	2023	|	2128	|	2325	|	...	...	1035	1043	|	1312	|	1452	|	1616	|	1816	|	|	2056	|	2221	2339	...
brân d.	1845	1918	2028	2057	2133	2222	2330	2350	...	...	1040	1048	1240	1317	1416	1457	1531	1621	1721	1821	1933	2011	2101	2131	2226	2344	...
ort **132** a.	1901	1934	2044	2115	2144	2236	2346	0008	...	...	1051	1059	1251	1330	1431	1507	1550	1631	1735	1831	1948	2026	2115	2149	2236	2354	...
iff Central .. **132** a.	1920	2000	2105	2141	2206	2256	0006	0033	...	...	1113	1117	1313	1350	1453	1531	1610	1655	1756	1854	2006	2026	2142	2210	2259	0020	...

To / from Llandudno (Table **145**).
To Llandudno Junction (Table **145**).

June 25 - Sept. 10.
May 21 - June 18 and from Sept. 17.

c – May 21 - Oct. 22.
d – Arrives 10 minutes earlier.
e – 0750 May 21 - June 18 and Sept 17 - Oct. 22.
g – From Oct. 29.

h – 1322 May 15 - Oct. 23.
k – From Sept. 17.
m – May 15 - June 19 and from Oct. 30.
n – June 26 - Oct. 23.

¶ – Additional journeys Shrewsbury - Whitchurch - Crewe and v.v.: **From Shrewsbury** at 0531Ⓐ, 0544⑥, 0757⑥, 0800Ⓐ, 1018⚒, 1224⚒, 1424⚒, 1624⚒, 1825⑥, 1830Ⓐ, 2032⚒, 2330⑥. **From Crewe** at 0640Ⓐ, 0720⑥, 0734Ⓐ, 0914Ⓐ, 0920⑥, 1120⚒, 1320⚒, 1520⑥, 1522Ⓐ, 1720⚒, 2212⚒, 2314⚒.

150 LONDON - BIRMINGHAM, CHESTER, HOLYHEAD, MANCHESTER and LIVERPOOL

LONDON - BIRMINGHAM - WOLVERHAMPTON

Certain services continue to / from destinations on Tables 145 and 151. For trains via Northampton see Table 142.

km		Ⓐ	Ⓐ	Ⓐ	Ⓐ	Ⓐ	Ⓐ	C	Ⓐ	Ⓐ	Ⓐ	Ⓐ	ⒶD	Ⓐ	Ⓐ	Ⓐ	Ⓐ	Ⓐ	Ⓐ	Ⓐ	Ⓐ	Ⓐ	Ⓐ	①–④
0	**London** Euston .... d.		0620	0643	0703	0723	0743	and	1703	1723	1743	1803	1823	1843	1903	1923	1943	2003	2023	2043	2103	2143	2230	2330
28	Watford Junction .... △ d.		0634	|	|	0737	|	at the	|	1737	|	|	1837	|	|	1937	|	|	2037	|	|	2158	2245	|
80	Milton Keynes .... d.		|	0713	|	|	0813	same	|	|	1813u	|	|	1913	|	|	2013	|	|	2113	2135	2217	2329	0029
133	Rugby .... a.		0712	|	0751	|	|	minutes	1751	|	|	1851	|	|	1951	|	|	2051	|	|	2156	|	2358	0100
151	Coventry .... a.		0722	0742	0802	0822	0842	past	1802	1822	1842	1902	1922	1942	2002	2022	2042	2102	2124	2142	2207	2246	0010	0113
168	Birmingham Int'l ✈ ..... a.		0733	0753	0813	0833	0853	each	1813	1833	1853	1913	1933	1953	2013	2033	2053	2113	2134	2153	2218	2300	0021	0124
182	**Birmingham** New St.. a.		0745	0808	0827	0845	0908	hour	1827	1845	1908	1927	1945	2008	2027	2045	2108	2127	2146	2205	2230	2316	0032	0136
190	Sandwell & Dudley ..... a.		...	0824	...	...	0924	until	...	...	1924	|	1958	2024	...	2058	2124	|	2159	2216	2241	2333	|	|
202	**Wolverhampton** .... a.		...	0836	...	...	0937	☆	...	...	1937	2000	2011	2037	...	2112	2137	2156	2212	2230	2256	2347	0103	0207

	⑥	⑥	⑥	⑥	⑥	⑥	⑥	⑥	E	⑥	⑥	⑥	⑥	⑥D	⑥	⑥	⑥	⑥		⑥		⑥		⑥a
London Euston .... d.		0623	0703	0723	0743	0803	0823	0843	and	1703	1723	1743	1803	1823	1843	1903	1923	1943	...	2025	...	2103	...	2143
Watford Junction .... △ d.		0637	|	0737	|	|	0837	|	at the	|	1737	|	|	1837	|	|	1937	|	...	2040	...	2118	...	2158
Milton Keynes .... d.		|	|	|	0813	|	|	0913	same	|	|	1813	|	|	1913	|	|	2020	...	|	...	2150	...	2230
Rugby .... a.		|	0751	|	|	0851	|	|	minutes	1751	|	|	1851	|	|	1951	|	|	...	|	...	2211	...	2252
Coventry .... a.		0722	0802	0822	0842	0902	0922	0942	past	1802	1822	1842	1902	1922	1942	2002	2022	2050	...	2136	...	2222	...	2302
Birmingham Int'l ✈ .... a.		0733	0813	0833	0853	0913	0933	0953	each	1813	1833	1853	1913	1933	1953	2013	2033	2101	...	2150	...	2233	...	2313
Birmingham New St . a.		0745	0827	0845	0908	0927	0945	1008	hour	1827	1845	1908	1927	1945	2008	2027	2045	2113	...	2204	...	2245	...	2325
Sandwell & Dudley ..... a.		...	...	...	0924	...	...	1024	until	...	1858	1924	1943	1958	2024	2053	2058	|	...	2224	...	2256	...	2336
Wolverhampton .... a.		...	...	...	0937	...	...	1037	☆	...	1911	1937	1956	2011	2037	2109	2112	2138	...	2238	...	2310	...	2350

	⑦	⑦	⑦	⑦	⑦	⑦	⑦	⑦	⑦		⑦	⑦	⑦	⑦	⑦D	⑦	⑦	⑦		⑦	⑦	⑦	⑦	⑦
London Euston .... d.		0850	0950	1050	1150	1220	1240	1300	1320	and	1740	1800	1820	1840	1900	1920	1940	2000	...	2018	2038	2054	2155	2225
Watford Junction .... △ d.		0907	1005	1105	1205	1234	|	|	1334	at the	|	|	1834	|	|	1934	|	|	...	2032	|	2110	2209	2239
Milton Keynes .... d.		0939	1038	1138	1230	|	1313	|	|	same	1813	|	|	1913	|	|	2013	|	...	|	2116	2143	2245	2312
Rugby .... a.		1013	1113	1213	1249	|	|	1351	|	minutes	|	1851	|	|	1952	|	|	2051	...	|	|	2205	2322	2346
Coventry .... a.		1024	1123	1223	1259	1322	1342	1402	1422	past	1844	1902	1922	1942	2003	2022	2042	2103	...	2120	2146	2216	2333	2357
Birmingham Int'l ✈ .... a.		1035	1134	1234	1310	1333	1353	1413	1433	each	1854	1913	1933	1953	2013	2033	2053	2113	...	2131	2157	2227	2344	0008
Birmingham New St . a.		1047	1147	1247	1325	1346	1408	1425	1445	hour	1908	1925	1945	2008	2025	2045	2108	2125	...	2145	2209	2239	2356	0021
Sandwell & Dudley ..... a.		1058	1158	1258	...	1356	1425	...	...	until	1925	1948	...	2024	2035	2056	2124	...	...	2156	2224	2251	|	|
Wolverhampton .... a.		1111	1211	1310	...	1408	1437	...	...	☆	1937	2000	...	2037	2047	2110	2137	...	...	2208	2236	2304	0015	0041

	Ⓐ	Ⓐ	Ⓐ	Ⓐ	Ⓐ	Ⓐ	Ⓐ		Ⓐ	Ⓐ	ⒶD	Ⓐ	Ⓐ	Ⓐ	Ⓐ	Ⓐ	F	Ⓐ	Ⓐ	Ⓐ	Ⓐ	Ⓐ	Ⓐ	Ⓐ
Wolverhampton .... d.		0500	0524	0545	0604	0627	0645	...	0705	...	0724	0745	...	...	0845	...	and	...	1845	...	1945	...	2047	2145
Sandwell & Dudley ..... d.		|	0534	0555	0615	0638	0656	...	0715	...	|	0757	...	...	0855	...	at the	...	1855	...	1955	...	2057	2155
Birmingham New St . d.		0529	0550	0610	0630	0650	0710	...	0730	...	0750	0810	0830	0850	0910	0930	same	1850	1910	1930	2010	2050	2110	2210
Birmingham Intl ✈ ... d.		0540	0600	0620	0640	0700	0720	...	|	0741	0800	0821	0840	0900	0920	0940	minutes	1900	1920	1940	2020	2100	2120	2220
Coventry .... d.		0551	0611	0631	0651	0711	0731	...	|	0752	0811	0831	0851	0911	0931	0951	past	1911	1931	1951	2031	2111	2131	2231
Rugby .... d.		0603	|	|	|	|	|	...	|	|	0823	|	|	0923	|	|	each	1923	|	2003	|	2123	|	2245
Milton Keynes .... d.		0626	0638	0659	|	0740s	|	...	|	|	|	|	0920	|	1000	|	hour	|	2000	|	2100	|	2159	2308
Watford Junction .... ▽ a.		0647	|	|	0737	|	|	...	|	|	|	0916	|	|	|	1039	until	|	|	2041	2119	|	2220	2339
London Euston .... a.		0705	0713	0734	0753	0815	0831	...	0843	0850	0915	0934	0955	1015	1032	1056	☆	2015	2034	2058	2139	2213	2243	0006

	⑥	⑥	⑥	⑥	⑥	⑥	⑥	⑥	⑥	⑥	⑥	⑥	⑥D	⑥	⑥	⑥	F	⑥	⑥	⑥	⑥		⑥a	⑥b
Wolverhampton .... d.		...	0545	0606	0627	0645	0705	0725	0745	...	...	...	0905	...	0945	...	and	...	1845	1945	2045	...	2109	2109
Sandwell & Dudley ..... d.		...	0555	0617	0637	0656	0715	|	0755	...	...	...	|	...	0955	...	at the	...	1855	1955	2055	...	2119	2119
Birmingham New St . d.		0550	0610	0630	0650	0710	0730	0750	0810	0830	0850	0910	0930	0950	1010	1030	same	1850	1910	2010	2110	...	2130	2130
Birmingham Intl ✈ ... d.		0600	0620	0640	0700	0720	0740	0800	0820	0840	0900	0920	0940	1000	1020	1040	minutes	1900	1920	2020	2120	...	2140	2140
Coventry .... d.		0611	0631	0651	0711	0731	0751	0811	0831	0851	0911	0931	0951	1011	1031	1051	past	1911	1931	2031	2131	...	2151	2151
Rugby .... d.		0624	|	|	0723	|	|	0823	|	|	0923	|	|	1023	|	|	each	1923	1943	2043	2143	...	2203	2203
Milton Keynes .... d.		|	0659	|	|	0759	|	|	0859	|	|	0959	|	|	1059	|	hour	|	2007	2105	2205	...	2226	2238
Watford Junction .... ▽ a.		|	0719	0736	|	|	0837	|	|	0939	|	|	1039	|	|	1139	until	|	2034	2135	2234	...	2312	2312
London Euston .... a.		0717	0738	0755	0817	0835	0856	0915	0935	0959	1015	1034	1056	1115	1133	1155	☆	2023	2055	2157	2255	...	2331	2331

	⑦	⑦	⑦	⑦	⑦	⑦	⑦	⑦		⑦	⑦F	⑦	⑦	⑦	⑦	⑦	⑦	⑦	⑦	⑦	⑦	⑦	⑦	⑦
Wolverhampton .... d.		0805	0905	1005	1105	...	1145	...	and	1545	1604	...	1645	...	...	1745	...	...	1845	...	1942	...	2105	2205
Sandwell & Dudley ..... d.		0815	0915	1015	1115	...	1155	...	at the	1555	|	...	1655	...	...	1755	...	...	1855	...	1955	...	2117	2216
Birmingham New St . d.		0830	0930	1030	1130	1150	1210	1230	same	1610	1630	1650	1710	1730	1750	1810	1830	1850	1910	1930	2010	2030	2130	2230
Birmingham Intl ✈ ... d.		0840	0940	1040	1140	1200	1220	1240	minutes	1619	1640	1700	1720	1740	1800	1820	1840	1900	1920	1940	2020	2040	2140	2240
Coventry .... d.		0851	0951	1051	1151	1211	1231	1251	past	1631	1651	1711	1730	1751	1811	1831	1851	1911	1931	1951	2031	2051	2151	2251
Rugby .... d.		0904	1004	1104	1205	1225	|	|	each	|	|	1725	|	|	1825	|	|	1926	|	|	|	2105	2204	2304
Milton Keynes .... d.		0939	1039	1139	1227	|	1301	|	hour	1659	|	|	1759	|	|	1859	|	|	2000	|	2101	2128	2237	2337
Watford Junction .... ▽ a.		1007	1111	1208	|	|	|	1338	until	|	1738	|	|	1838	|	|	1938	|	|	2039	|	2202	2305	0006
London Euston .... a.		1027	1131	1227	1306	1320	1338	1357	☆	1738	1757	1818	1838	1857	1917	1939	1957	2018	2039	2057	2148	2224	2325	0027

LONDON - CHESTER (- HOLYHEAD)

km			ⒶA	Ⓐ	Ⓐ	Ⓐ		Ⓐ	Ⓐ	Ⓐ	Ⓐ	Ⓐ	Ⓐ	Ⓐ		Ⓐ	ⒶG	Ⓐ	Ⓐ			⑥A
0	**London** Euston .... d.	Ⓐ	...	0710	0810	0910	...	1010	1110	1210	1310	1410	1510	1610	...	1710	1810	1910	2010	...	⑥	...
80	Milton Keynes .... d.		...	0741	0843	0941	...	1041	1141	1241	1341	1441	1541	1641u	...	1741u	1841u	1941	2041	...		...
254	Crewe .... d.		0623	0849	0953	1049	...	1149	1249	1352	1449	1549	1649	1749	...	1857	1956	2055	2149	...		0623
288	**Chester** .... a.		0643	0913	1013	1113	...	1213	1313	1416	1513	1613	1713	1808	...	1916	2015	2120	2213	...		0643
	Bangor **160** .... a.		0749	1051	1124	1216	...	1330	1435	1530	1642	1738	1846	1921	...	2028	2125	2229	0013	...		0749
	Holyhead **160** .... a.		0823	1122	1158	1250	...	1414	1508	1614	1716	1821	1917	2020	...	2059	2159	2303	0048	...		0823

	⑥	⑥	⑥		⑥	⑥	⑥		⑥	⑥	⑥		⑥			⑦	⑦		⑦	⑦		⑦
London Euston .... d.	0910	1010	1110	...	1210	1310	1410	...	1510	1610	1710	...	1810	...	⑦	1508	1608	...	1708	1808	...	1908
Milton Keynes .... d.	0941	1041	1141	...	1241	1341	1441	...	1541	1641	1741	...	1841	...		1542	1642	...	1742	1842	...	1942
Crewe .... d.	1049	1156	1249	...	1353	1449	1549	...	1649	1750	1852	...	1949	...		1652	1752	...	1901	1952	...	2055
Chester .... a.	1113	1220	1313	...	1417	1513	1610	...	1713	1810	1912	...	2013	...		1713	1813	...	1919	2013	...	2113
Bangor **160** .... a.	1216	1332	1434	...	1532	1636	1717	...	1841	1921	2024	...	2142	...		...	1947	...	2034	2123	...	2222
Holyhead **160** .... a.	1250	1413	1508	...	1613	1711	1751	...	1913	1955	2058	...	2225	...		...	2018	...	2103	2154	...	2253

		Ⓐ	ⒶG	Ⓐ	Ⓐ		Ⓐ	Ⓐ	Ⓐ	Ⓐ	Ⓐ	Ⓐ		Ⓐ	Ⓐ	Ⓐ	ⒶB			⑥	⑥	⑥
Holyhead **160** .... d.	Ⓐ	0448	0551	0655	0715	...	0855	0923	1040	1127	1252	1358	...	1434	1544	1730	1921	...	⑥	0425	0652	0755
Bangor **160** .... d.		0514	0618	0722	0802	...	0922	1002	1107	1200	1320	1425	...	1504	1623	1809	2020	...		0456	0720	0822
Chester .... d.		0626	0735	0835	0935	...	1035	1135	1235	1335	1435	1535	...	1635	1735	1935	2135	...		0717	0835	0935
Crewe .... a.		0647	0754	0854	0954	...	1054	1154	1254	1354	1454	1554	...	1654	1754	1954	2154	...		0736	0854	0954
Milton Keynes .... a.		|	|	1002	1102	...	1202	1302	1402	1502	1602	1702	...	1802	1901	2104	...	...		0852	1002	1102
London Euston .... a.		0834	0941	1039	1139	...	1239	1339	1439	1538	1639	1739	...	1839	1939	2143	...	...		0930	1039	1138

	⑥	⑥	⑥		⑥	⑥	⑥		⑥	⑥			⑦	⑦	⑦		⑦	⑦	⑦c	⑦d	⑦	⑦
Holyhead **160** .... d.	0923	1033	1123	...	1238	1358	1423	...	1523	1823	...	⑦	0845	1055	1150	...	1250	1355	1430	1530	1625	1730
Bangor **160** .... d.	1002	1105	1202	...	1307	1425	1453	...	1602	1902	...		0913	1122	1217	...	1318	1422	1508	1558	1704	1759
Chester .... d.	1135	1235	1335	...	1435	1535	1635	...	1735	2035	...		1128	1232	1330	...	1433	1533	1735	1735	1835	1935
Crewe .... a.	1154	1254	1354	...	1454	1554	1654	...	1754	2054	...		1147	1252	1350	...	1454	1552	1753	1753	1853	1956
Milton Keynes .... a.	1302	1402	1502	...	1602	1702	1802	...	|	...	...		1304	1405	1503	...	1603	1703	1904	1904	2003	2136
London Euston .... a.	1339	1439	1539	...	1639	1739	1839	...	2005	...	...		1346	1446	1545	...	1644	1744	1944	1944	2044	2228

A – From Birmingham New Street (d. 0530), Wolverhampton (d. 0548) and Stafford (d. 0601).
B – To Wolverhampton (a. 2227) and Birmingham New Street (a. 2250).
C – The 1023 from London continues to Shrewsbury (Table **145**).
D – To / from Shrewsbury (Table **145**).
E – The 1123 from London continues to Shrewsbury (Table **145**).
F – The 1630 from Birmingham New St starts from Shrewsbury (Table **145**) calling at Wolverhampton (d. 1604).

G – Conveys 🛏12 London Euston - Wrexham and v.v. (Table **145**).

a – May 21 - June 18 and from Sept. 17.
b – June 25 - Sept. 10.
c – May 15 - Sept. 11.
d – From Sept. 18.
s – Calls to set down only.

u – Calls to pick up only.

☆ – Timings may vary by up to 5 minutes.
△ – Trains call here to pick up only.
▽ – Trains call here to set down only.
♡ – The 1720Ⓐ from London calls at Milton Ke[ynes] to pick up only.

LONDON - BIRMINGHAM, CHESTER, HOLYHEAD, MANCHESTER and LIVERPOOL 150

LONDON - MANCHESTER

n			Ⓐ	Ⓐ	Ⓐ	Ⓐ	Ⓐ	Ⓐ	Ⓐ	Ⓐ	Ⓐ	Ⓐ	Ⓐ		Ⓐ	Ⓐ	Ⓐ	④-⑤	Ⓐ	Ⓐ	Ⓐ	Ⓐ	Ⓐ	Ⓐ
0	**London** Euston	d.	0616	0636	0655	0720	0735	0800	0820	0840	0900	0920	0940	and at	1800	1820	1840	1857	1900	1920	1940	2000	2040	2100
0	Milton Keynes	d.	0646	|	0727	0750	0806	|	0850	|	|	0950	|	the same	|	1850u	|	|	|	1950	|	|	|	2131
5	Stoke on Trent	d.	0745	|	0825	0848	|	0925	0948	|	1025	1048	|	minutes	1925	1948	|	|	2025	2050	|	2126	|	2228
7	Macclesfield	d.	0802	|	0841	|	|	0941	|	|	1041	|	|	past each	1941	|	|	|	|	2107	|	2142	|	2244
	Crewe	d.	|	0811	|	|	0911	|	|	1011	|	|	1111	hour until	|	|	2018	2033s	|	|	2123	|	2213	|
	Wilmslow	d.	|	0827	|	|	0927	|	|	1027	|	|	1127		|	|	2033	|	|	|	2138	|	2229	|
7	Stockport	d.	0817	0837	0856	0917	0936	0955	1017	1037	1055	1117	1136	☆♡	1956	2016	2043	|	2053	2120	|	2155	2239	2259
6	**Manchester** Piccadilly	a.	0828	0849	0907	0928	0948	1007	1028	1049	1107	1128	1148		2007	2028	2053	2110	2108	2131	2157	2207	2248	2311

		Ⓐe	Ⓐg	Ⓐ	Ⓐ	⑥	⑥	⑥	⑥	⑥	⑥	⑥	⑥	⑥	⑥		⑥	⑥	⑥	⑥	⑥h	⑥	
don Euston	d.	2140	2140	2200	2300	0636	0655	0720	0735	0800	0820	0840	0900	0920	0940	and at	1900	1920	1940	2020	2031	2100	...
n Keynes	d.	|	|	2240	|	|	0727	0750	0806	|	0850	|	|	0950	|	the same	|	1950	|	2105	|	2145	...
e on Trent	d.	2305	2310	|	0121s	|	0825	0848	|	0925	0948	|	1025	1048	|	minutes	2025	2048	|	2205	|	|	...
clesfield	d.	2321	2326	|	0138s	|	0841	|	|	0941	|	|	1041	|	|	past each	2041	|	|	2221	|	|	...
ewe	d.	|	|	0017	|	0811	|	|	0911	|	|	1011	|	|	1111	hour until	|	|	2119	|	2230	2259	...
ilmslow	d.	|	|	...	|	0827	|	|	0927	|	|	1027	|	|	1127		|	|	2134	|	|	2315	...
kport	d.	2339	2342	...	0151s	0837	0856	0917	0937	0955	1017	1037	1056	1117	1137	☆	2056	2120	2145	2236	|	2325	...
chester Piccadilly	a.	2350	2353	...	0202	0849	0907	0928	0949	1007	1028	1049	1107	1128	1149		2107	2131	2153	2251	2305	2338	...

		⑦	⑦	⑦	⑦	⑦	⑦	⑦	⑦	⑦	⑦	⑦		⑦	⑦	⑦	⑦	⑦	⑦	⑦	⑦	⑦	⑦
don Euston	d.	0810	0820	0920	1020	1120	1217	1237	1257	1317	1337	1357	and at	1817	1837	1857	1917	1937	1957	2015	2035	2125	2151
n Keynes	d.	0856	0906	1007	1107	1208	1250	|	|	1350	|	|	the same	1850	|	|	1950	|	|	2048	|	2214	2239
e on Trent	d.	|	1021	1123	1225	1311	1350	|	1426	1450	|	1526	minutes	1950	|	2026	2050	|	2126	2150	|	2329	|
clesfield	d.	|	1038	1139	1242	1328	|	|	1442	|	|	1542	past each	|	|	2042	|	|	2142	|	|	2346	|
rewe	d.	1019	|	|	|	|	|	1413	|	|	1513	|	until	|	2013	|	|	2113	|	|	2221	|	0019s
ilmslow	d.	1034	|	|	|	|	|	1429	|	|	1529	|		|	2029	|	|	2129	|	|	2236	|	|
kport	d.	1044	1052	1153	1256	1342	1419	1439	1456	1520	1539	1556	☆	2019	2039	2057	2119	2139	2159	2219	2246	0001	0041s
chester Piccadilly	a.	1054	1102	1204	1305	1350	1428	1448	1506	1529	1548	1605		2027	2048	2106	2127	2149	2209	2227	2254	0009	0050

m			Ⓐ	Ⓐ	Ⓐ	Ⓐ	Ⓐ	Ⓐ	Ⓐ	Ⓐ	Ⓐ	Ⓐ	Ⓐ	Ⓐ	Ⓐ		Ⓐ	Ⓐ	Ⓐ	Ⓐ	Ⓐ	Ⓐ	Ⓐ
0	**Manchester** Piccadilly	d.	0505	0555	0610	0635	0643	0700	0715	0627	0735	0755	0815	0835	0855	and at	1715	1735	1755	1815	1835	1855	1915
9	Stockport	d.	0513	0603	0618	0643	0651	0707u	0723	0635	0743	0804	0823	0843	0904	the same	1723	1743	1804	1823	1843	1904	1923
20	Wilmslow	d.	|	0611	|	|	0659	|	|	|	|	0811	|	|	0911	minutes	|	|	1811	|	|	1911	|
0	Crewe	d.	0536	0628	|	|	0717	|	|	|	|	0829	|	|	0929	past each	|	|	1829	|	|	1929	|
	Macclesfield	d.	|	|	0631	0656	|	|	|	0648	0756	|	|	0856	|	until	|	1756	|	|	1856	|	1936
	Stoke on Trent	d.	|	|	0648	0712	|	|	0750	0706	0812	|	0850	0912	|		1750	1812	|	1850	1912	|	1952
	Milton Keynes	a.	0651	|	|	|	|	|	0846	|	|	|	0949	|	|	☆	1846	|	1933	1946	|	2031	2048
4	**London** Euston	a.	0729	0808	0823	0846	0854	0900	0924	0934	0952	1019	1030	1053	1108		1924	1943	2008	2024	2042	2106	2126

		Ⓐ	Ⓐ	Ⓐ		⑥	⑥	⑥	⑥	⑥	⑥	⑥	⑥		⑥	⑥	⑥	⑥	⑥	⑥	⑥	⑥	
nchester Piccadilly	d.	1955	2015	2115	...	0525	0555	0610	0635	0655	0715	0735	0755	and at	1715	1735	1755	1815	1835	1855	1935	2035	...
ckport	d.	2004	2023	2123	...	0534	0603	0618	0643	0704	0723	0743	0804	the same	1723	1743	1804	1823	1843	1904	1943	2043	...
ilmslow	d.	2011	|	|	...	0541	0611	|	|	0711	|	|	0811	minutes	|	|	1811	|	|	1911	|	|	...
rewe	d.	2029	|	|	...	0600	0629	|	|	0729	|	|	0829	past each	|	|	1829	|	|	1929	|	|	...
cclesfield	d.	|	2036	2136	...	|	|	0631	0656	|	|	0756	|	until	|	1756	|	|	1856	|	1956	2056	...
ke on Trent	d.	|	2052	2153	...	|	|	0648	0712	|	0750	0812	|		1750	1812	|	1849	1912	|	2012	2112	...
on Keynes	a.	2135	2151	2300	...	0711	0731	|	|	|	0846	|	|	☆	1848	|	|	1945	|	|	2110	2210	...
don Euston	a.	2213	2228	2351	...	0753	0810	0828	0846	0905	0924	0943	1011		1925	1943	2005	2034	2059	2120	2201	2302	...

		⑦	⑦	⑦	⑦	⑦	⑦	⑦	⑦	⑦	⑦	⑦	⑦	⑦	⑦		⑦	⑦	⑦	⑦	⑦	⑦	⑦
nchester Piccadilly	d.	0805	0820	0920	1020	1036	1115	1135	1155	1215	1235	1255	1315	1335	1355	and at	1815	1835	1855	1915	1935	2021	2055
ckport	d.	0814	0828	0928	1029	1046	1124	1144	1205	1223	1243	1305	1322	1342	1405	the same	1822	1842	1904	1922	1941	2027	2103
ilmslow	d.	0822	|	|	1037	|	|	|	1212	|	|	1312	|	|	1412	minutes	|	|	1911	|	|	|	|
rewe	d.	0843	|	|	1055	|	|	|	1230	|	|	1330	|	|	1430	past each	|	|	1929	|	|	|	|
cclesfield	d.	|	0841	0940	|	1057	|	1157	|	|	1257	|	|	1355	|	until	|	1855	|	|	1954	2040	2116
ke on Trent	d.	|	0857	1000	|	1115	1152	1214	|	1251	1314	|	1350	1412	|		1850	1911	|	1950	2011	2057	2133
on Keynes	a.	|	|	1116	|	1221	1250	|	|	1347	|	|	1449	|	|	☆	1948	|	|	2046	|	2203	2246
don Euston	a.	1058	1102	1209	1257	1300	1328	1348	1410	1428	1448	1508	1526	1548	1607		2027	2047	2110	2134	2159	2258	2349

LONDON - LIVERPOOL

m			Ⓐ	Ⓐ	Ⓐ	Ⓐ		Ⓐ	Ⓐ	Ⓐ	Ⓐ	Ⓐ	Ⓐ	Ⓐ	⑥	⑥	⑥	⑥		⑥	⑥
0	**London** Euston	d.	0526	0707	0807	0907	and	1707	1733	1807	1833	1907	2007	2107	0707	0807	0907	1007	and	1607	1633
80	Milton Keynes	d.	0615	|	0838	|	at the	|	|	|	|	|	|	2139	|	|	|	|	at the	|	|
35	Rugby	d.	|	|	|	|	same	|	1823	|	1923	|	|	|	|	|	|	|	same	|	|
55	Nuneaton	d.	0645	|	|	|	minutes	|	|	|	|	|	2103	2208	|	|	|	|	minutes	|	|
45	Stafford	d.	0708	0823	0927	1023	past	1826	1856	1923	1954	|	2127	|	0823	0923	1026	1123	past	1723	1759
54	Crewe	d.	0728	0843	|	1043	each	1844	1916	1943	2016	|	2148	2251	0843	0943	1046	1143	each	1743	|
90	Runcorn	d.	0745	0900	1001	1100	until	1900	1933	2000	2033	2050	2205	2309	0900	1000	1103	1200	until	1800	1832
12	**Liverpool** Lime Street	d.	0805	0921	1021	1121	☆	1921	1952	2021	2054	2108	2225	2334	0921	1021	1121	1221	☆	1821	1852

		⑥	⑥	⑥	⑥	⑥k	⑥h	⑦	⑦	⑦	⑦	⑦		⑦	⑦	⑦	⑦	⑦		⑦	⑦	⑦	⑦	⑦
ndon Euston	d.	1707	1807	1833	1907	2011	2011	0815	0914	1015	1115	1205	...	1305	1405	1505	1605	1705	...	1805	1905	2005	2008	2121
on Keynes	d.	|	|	|	|	|	|	|	|	|	1204	|	...	|	|	|	|	|	...	|	|	|	2041	|
gby	d.	|	|	|	|	2115	2116	|	|	|	|	|	...	|	|	|	|	|	...	|	|	|	|	|
neaton	d.	1803	|	|	2003	|	|	0944	1045	1147	|	|	...	|	|	|	|	1804	...	|	2004	2104	|	2253
fford	d.	1827	1923	1959	2027	2146	2147	1008	1113	1214	1253	1325	...	1425	1525	1625	1726	|	...	1925	2029	|	2133	2318
ewe	d.	1847	1943	|	2047	2206	2214	1030	1135	1234	1315	1345	...	1445	1545	1645	1746	1846	...	1945	2049	2146	2155	2344
ncorn	d.	1904	2000	2031	2105	2224	|	1047	1152	1251	1332	1402	...	1502	1602	1702	1802	1902	...	2002	2106	2203	2212	0004
erpool Lime Street	d.	1925	2021	2054	2125	2246	2333	1105	1209	1308	1351	1420	...	1520	1622	1721	1821	1921	...	2020	2123	2220	2229	0027

		Ⓐ	Ⓐ	Ⓐ	Ⓐ	Ⓐ	Ⓐ		Ⓐ	Ⓐ	Ⓐ	Ⓐ	Ⓐ	Ⓐ	⑥	⑥	⑥	⑥	⑥	⑥	⑥	⑥
erpool Lime Street	d.	0526	0605	0700	0747	0847	0947	and	1547	1647	1747	1847	1948	2049	0547	0645	0720	0747	0847	0947	1047	1147
ncorn	d.	0543	0621	0715u	0803	0903	1003	at the	1603	1703	1803	1903	2004	2105	0603	0701	0737	0803	0903	1003	1103	1203
we	d.	0602	|	|	0823	0925	1022	same	1622	|	1824	1922	2024	2124	|	0720	0757	0822	0924	1022	1122	1222
fford	d.	0622	0654	|	0843	0944	1042	minutes	1642	1736	1843	1942	|	2144	0636	0739	0816	0842	0943	1042	1142	1242
neaton	d.	|	|	|	|	|	|	past	|	|	|	|	2103	2218	0659	|	|	0905	|	|	|	|
gby	d.	0654	|	|	|	|	|	each	|	|	|	|	|	2232	|	|	|	|	|	|	|	|
on Keynes	d.	0714	|	|	|	|	|	until	|	1824	|	|	|	2255	|	|	|	|	|	|	|	|
ndon Euston	a.	0751	0823	0904	1001	1105	1159	☆	1759	1903	2007	2104	2209	2346	0805	0900	0947	1006	1105	1159	1259	1400

		⑥	⑥	⑥	⑥	⑥	⑥	⑥	⑥	⑦	⑦	⑦	⑦	⑦	⑦	⑦	⑦	⑦	⑦	⑦	⑦	⑦	⑦	⑦
erpool Lime Street	d.	1247	1347	1447	1547	1647	1747	1847	1948	0818	0838	0938	1038	1147	1247	1347	1447	1547	1618	1647	1747	1847	1947	2047
ncorn	d.	1303	1403	1503	1603	1703	1803	1903	2004	0835	0854	0954	1054	1203	1303	1403	1503	1603	1634	1703	1803	1903	2003	2103
we	d.	1324	1422	1522	1622	1723	|	1923	2023	0853	0913	1014	1114	1223	1323	1423	1523	1623	1654	1723	1823	1923	2024	2124
fford	d.	1343	1442	1542	1642	1743	1836	1942	2043	|	0933	1034	1136	1244	1344	1444	1544	1644	|	1744	1844	1944	2043	2144
neaton	d.	|	|	|	|	|	|	|	|	|	0956	1057	1159	|	|	|	|	|	|	|	|	|	|	2219
gby	d.	|	|	|	|	|	|	|	|	|	|	|	|	|	|	|	|	|	|	|	|	|	|	2233
ton Keynes	d.	|	|	|	|	|	|	|	|	1021	|	1147	|	|	|	|	|	|	1805	|	|	|	2137	2306
ndon Euston	a.	1503	1559	1659	1759	1907	1959	2117	2215	1108	1137	1232	1313	1404	1504	1604	1705	1803	1844	1904	2005	2103	2228	2354

From June 20.
- May 21 - June 17.
- May 21 - July 30; Sept. 17 - Oct. 22.

k – Aug. 6 - Sept. 10 and from Oct. 29.
s – Calls to set down only.
u – Calls to pick up only.

For explanation of standard symbols see page 4

151 LONDON, BIRMINGHAM and MANCHESTER - PRESTON - EDINBURGH and GLASGOW

TP,

km		⚒	Ⓐ	⚒	⚒	⚒	Ⓐ	⑥	Ⓐ	⚒	⑥	Ⓐ	⑥	⑥ W	⚒	Ⓐ ◐	⑥	⚒	⚒	Ⓐ W	⚒ ◐	⚒	⚒
0	**London Euston** 150 d.		...	...	...	...	...	...	0530	...	0605	...	...	...	0730	0643	...	...	0830	...	0743	...	0930
80	Milton Keynes 150 d.		...	...	...	...	...	...	0623	...	0641	...	...	...	|	0713	...	...	|	...	0813	...	|
	Birmingham New Street 150 d.		...	...	...	0615	...	...	|	...	|	0715	0715	...	|	0815	0815	...	|	...	0915	...	|
	Wolverhampton 150 d.		...	...	...	0637	...	...	|	...	|	0737	0737	...	|	0837	0837	...	|	...	0937	...	|
253	Crewe 150 d.		...	0557	...	0709	...	...	0732	...	0755	0809	0809	...	|	0909	0909	...	|	...	1009	...	|
291	Warrington Bank Quay d.		...	0615	...	0727	...	...	0749	...	0812	0827	0827	...	0914	0927	0927	...	1014	...	1027	...	1114
	Manchester Airport ✈ d.		...	|	0558	|	0700	0700	|	0729	|	|	|	0829	|	|	|	0900	|	...	|	1000	|
	Manchester Piccadilly d.		0500	|	0614	|	0716	0716	|	0745	|	|	|	0846	|	|	|	0916	|	...	|	1016	|
310	Wigan North Western d.		|	0625	0643	0738	0743	0743	0800	0811	0823	0838	0838	|	0925	0938	0938	0943	1025	...	1038	1043	1125
334	**Preston** d.		0542	0640	0658	0753	0758	0758	0815	0826	0837	0853	0853	0932	0941	0954	0953	0958	1041	1029	1053	1058	1141
368	Lancaster d.		0558	0654	0714	0808	0814	0814	0830	0842	0852	0908	0913	0948	0955	1008	1008	1014	1055	1100	1108	1114	1155
398	Oxenholme d.		0612	0709	0728	0822	|	0828	0843	0856	0906	|	|	1004	|	1022	1022	1028	1108	1115	|	|	|
450	Penrith d.		|	0734	0753	|	0851	0853	|	0921	0932	0944	0948	...	1031	|	|	1053	|	...	1145	|	1230
478	Carlisle d.		0652	0751	0811	0901	0910	0911	0922	0938	0948	1001	1003	...	1047	1101	1101	1111	1147	...	1202	1206	1247
519	Lockerbie d.		0711	0810	0830	|	0929	0930	|	0957	|	|	|	...	|	|	|	1130	|	...	|	|	|
	Haymarket a.		|	|	0930s	1013	|	|	|	1057s	|	|	|	...	|	1216	1217	|	|	...	|	1320s	|
641	**Edinburgh** Waverley a.		|	|	0937	1022	|	|	|	1102	|	|	|	...	|	1222	1222	|	|	...	|	1326	|
643	**Glasgow** Central a.		0818	0913	...	...	1029	1029	1036	...	1059	1116	1116	...	1201	...	...	1229	1301	...	1317	...	1401

	Ⓐ ◐	⚒	Ⓐ	⑥	⚒ ◐	⚒	⚒	⚒ ◐	Ⓐ	⑥	⚒	⚒ ◐	⚒	Ⓐ	⑥	⚒ ◐	Ⓐ	⑥	⑥	Ⓐ	⑥ ◐	Ⓐ ◐	⚒
London Euston 150 d.	0843	...	1030	1030	0943	...	1130	1043	...	...	1230	1143	...	1330	1330	1243	...	...	1430	1430	1343	1343	...
Milton Keynes 150 d.	0913	...	|	|	1013	...	|	1113	...	...	|	1213	...	|	|	1313	...	...	|	|	1413	1413	...
Birmingham New Street 150 d.	1015	...	|	|	1115	...	|	1215	...	...	|	1315	...	|	|	1415	...	...	|	|	1515	1515	...
Wolverhampton 150 d.	1037	...	|	|	1137	...	|	1237	...	...	|	1337	...	|	|	1437	...	...	|	|	1537	1537	...
Crewe 150 d.	1109	...	|	|	1207	...	|	1309	...	...	|	1409	...	|	|	1509	...	...	|	|	1609	1609	...
Warrington Bank Quay d.	1127	...	1214	1214	1228	...	1314	1327	...	...	1414	1427	...	1514	1516	1526	...	...	1614	1614	1627	1627	...
Manchester Airport ✈ d.	|	1100	|	|	|	1200	|	|	1300	1300	|	|	1400	|	|	|	1500	1500	|	|	|	|	1600
Manchester Piccadilly d.	|	1116	|	|	|	1216	|	|	1316	1316	|	|	1416	|	|	|	1516	1516	|	|	|	|	1616
Wigan North Western d.	1138	1143	1225	1225	1239	1243	1325	1338	1343	1343	1425	1438	1443	1525	1527	1537	1543	1543	1625	1625	1638	1638	1643
Preston d.	1153	1158	1240	1241	1254	1258	1341	1353	1358	1402	1441	1453	1458	1541	1542	1552	1558	1558	1641	1641	1653	1653	1658
Lancaster d.	1208	1214	|	1255	1309	1314	1355	1408	1414	|	1455	1508	1514	|	1556	1607	1614	1614	1655	1655	1708	1708	1714
Oxenholme d.	1221	1228	|	1308	1324	1328	1408	|	|	|	|	1522	1528	1606	1610	|	1628	1628	|	1709	1722	1722	1728
Penrith d.	|	|	1328	|	|	1353	|	1443	1451	|	1530	|	1553	1631	|	1644	|	1653	1730	1735	|	1747	1753
Carlisle d.	1301	1308	1345	1347	1402	1411	1447	1459	1508	1508	1546	1602	1611	1646	1648	1700	1711	1711	1747	1751	1802	1806	1811
Lockerbie d.	|	1327	|	|	|	1430	|	|	1527	1527	|	|	1630	|	|	|	1730	1730	|	|	|	|	1830
Haymarket a.	1412	|	|	|	|	1534s	|	1616	|	|	|	|	1729s	|	|	1814	|	|	|	|	|	|	1933s
Edinburgh Waverley a.	1422	|	|	|	|	1539	|	1622	|	|	|	|	1736	|	|	1822	|	|	|	|	|	|	1940
Glasgow Central a.	...	1428	1501	1501	1517	...	1601	...	1627	1627	1701	1717	...	1801	1800	...	1830	1830	1901	1915	1916	1923	...

	⚒ ◐	Ⓐ	⑥	Ⓐ	⑥	⚒ ◐	⚒	Ⓐ A	Ⓐ	Ⓐ	⑥	Ⓐ ◐	⑥ ◐	Ⓐ	⚒	Ⓐ ◐	⑥ ◐	Ⓐ	⑤	Ⓐ	⑥	⚒ ◐	Ⓐ
London Euston 150 d.	1443	...	...	1630	1630	1543	...	1633	1657	1730	1730	1643	1643	1757	1830	1743	1743	...	1846	1930	1930	1843	2030
Milton Keynes 150 d.	1513	...	...	|	|	1613	...	|	|	|	|	1713	1713	|	|	1813u	1813	...	|	|	|	1913	|
Birmingham New Street 150 d.	1615	...	...	|	|	1715	...	|	|	|	|	1815	1815	|	|	1915	1915	...	|	|	|	2015	|
Wolverhampton 150 d.	1637	...	...	|	|	1737	...	|	|	|	|	1837	1837	|	|	1937	1937	...	|	|	|	2037	|
Crewe 150 d.	1709	...	...	|	|	1809	...	1820	|	|	|	1909	1909	|	|	2009	2009	...	2042s	|	2105	2116	|
Warrington Bank Quay d.	1727	...	...	1815	1814	1827	...	1837	1850	1914	1914	1927	1927	1950	2014	2027	2027	...	2101s	2116	2123	...	2223
Manchester Airport ✈ d.	|	1700	1700	|	|	|	1800	|	|	|	|	|	|	|	|	|	|	2000	|	|	|	...	|
Manchester Piccadilly d.	|	1715	1716	|	|	|	1816	|	|	|	|	|	|	|	|	|	|	2016	|	|	|	...	|
Wigan North Western d.	1738	|	1743	1826	1825	1838	1843	1848	1901	1925	1925	1938	1938	2001	2025	2038	2038	2043	2112s	2127	2133	...	2234
Preston d.	1753	1758	1758	1843	1841	1853	1858	1902	1915	1941	1941	1953	1954	2015	2041	2053	2057	2058	2131	2142	2149	...	2253
Lancaster d.	1808	1814	1814	1858	1855	1908	1914	...	1930	1955	1955	2008	...	2033	2055	2108	...	2114	...	2157	...	...	...
Oxenholme d.	1823	1828	1828	|	1908	1921	1928	...	1945	2008	2008	|	...	...	2110	2123	...	2128	...	2210	...	...	...
Penrith d.	1848	1853	1853	1932	1934	|	1953	...	2010	|	2034	2045	...	...	2135	|	...	2153	...	2235	...	...	...
Carlisle d.	1904	1911	1911	1948	1951	2001	2011	...	2025	2047	2051	2102	...	...	2150	2202	...	2211	...	2251	...	...	...
Lockerbie d.	|	1930	1930	|	|	|	|	...	2044	|	|	|	...	...	2209	|	...	2230	...	|	...	...	...
Haymarket a.	2013	|	|	|	|	|	2130s	...	|	|	|	2213	...	...	|	|	...	2327s	...	|	...	...	...
Edinburgh Waverley a.	2023	|	|	|	|	|	2138	...	|	|	|	2222	...	...	|	|	...	2336	...	|	...	...	...
Glasgow Central a.	...	2034	2034	2100	2101	2117	...	...	2148	2202	2201	...	...	...	2311	2317	...	...	...	0005	...	...	...

	Ⓐ ◐	Ⓐ	Ⓐ	⑦	⑦ c	⑦	⑦ c	⑦ d	⑦ c	⑦ d	⑦	⑦	⑦	⑦ d	⑦ g	⑦	⑦	⑦	⑦	⑦	⑦	⑦	⑦
London Euston 150 d.	1943	...	2110		...	...	...	...	...	...	...	0845	...	...	...	0945	...	...	1045	...	...	1228	...
Milton Keynes 150 d.	2013	...	|		...	...	...	...	...	...	...	0933	...	...	...	1033	...	...	1133	...	...	|	...
Birmingham New Street 150 d.	2115	...	|		...	0845	0920	0920	...	...	...	|	1020	...	...	|	1120	...	|	1220	...	|	1320
Wolverhampton 150 d.	2137	...	|		...	0904	0938	0938	...	...	...	|	1037	...	...	|	1137	...	|	1237	...	|	1337
Crewe 150 d.	2218	...	2259		...	0937	1009	1009	...	...	1023	1057	1109	...	...	1157	1209	...	1258	1309	...	|	1409
Warrington Bank Quay d.	2235	...	2321		...	0954	1027	1027	...	...	1039	1113	1127	...	...	1214	1227	...	1315	1327	...	1416	1427
Manchester Airport ✈ d.	|	2200	|		0900	|	|	|	1000	1000	|	|	|	1100	1100	|	|	1200	|	|	1300	|	|
Manchester Piccadilly d.	|	2216	|		0916	|	|	|	1016	1016	|	|	|	1116	1116	|	|	1216	|	|	1316	|	|
Wigan North Western d.	2246	2254	2332		0943	1006	1038	1038	1043	1043	1050	1124	1138	1143	1143	1225	1238	1243	1326	1338	1343	1427	1438
Preston d.	2300	2313	2350		1003	1023	1051	1102e	1058	1109e	1112	1139	1153	1158	1159	1240	1253	1258	1342	1353	1358	1442	1453
Lancaster d.	...	2328	...		1019	...	1107	1118	1114	1125	1136	1154	1208	1214	1214	1255	1308	1314	1357	1408	1414	1458	1509
Oxenholme d.	...	...	...		1034	...	1122	1133	1128	1139	...	1208	1224	1228	...	1308	1322	1328	1410	|	1428	|	1524
Penrith d.	...	...	...		1059	...	|	|	|	1204	...	1234	|	|	...	1334	|	1353	1436	1445	1453	1532	|
Carlisle d.	...	...	...		1117	...	1201	1212	1208	1224	...	1249	1303	1308	...	1350	1402	1411	1452	1503	1511	1548	1603
Lockerbie d.	...	...	...		1135	...	|	|	1227	1243	...	|	|	1327	...	|	|	1430	|	|	|	|	|
Haymarket a.	...	...	...		1232s	...	|	|	|	1343s	...	|	1414	|	...	|	|	1527s	|	1614	|	|	|
Edinburgh Waverley a.	...	...	...		1239	...	|	|	|	1348	...	|	1420	|	...	|	|	1534	|	1620	|	|	|
Glasgow Central a.	...	...	...		...	...	1325	1327	1333	...	...	1403	...	1430	...	1503	1516	...	1605	...	1628	1701	1716

	⑦	⑦ ◐	⑦	⑦	⑦ ◐	⑦	⑦	⑦ ◐	⑦	⑦	⑦ ◐	⑦	⑦	⑦ ◐	⑦ h	⑦ k	⑦ ◐m	⑦ ◐p	⑦ r	⑦ t	⑦ ◐	⑦	⑦ ◐
London Euston 150 d.	1328	1240	...	1428	1340	...	1528	1440	...	1628	1540	...	1728	1640	1828	1828	1740	1740	1928	1928	1840	2025	1940
Milton Keynes 150 d.	|	1313	...	|	1413	...	|	1513	...	|	1613	...	|	1713	|	|	1813	1813	|	|	1913	|	2013
Birmingham New Street 150 d.	|	1415	...	|	1515	...	|	1615	...	|	1715	...	|	1815	|	|	1915	1915	|	|	2015	|	2115
Wolverhampton 150 d.	|	1437	...	|	1537	...	|	1637	...	|	1737	...	|	1837	|	|	1937	1937	|	|	2037	|	2137
Crewe 150 d.	|	1509	...	|	1609	...	|	1709	...	|	1809	...	|	1909	|	|	2009	2009	|	|	2110	2213	2217
Warrington Bank Quay d.	1516	1527	...	1616	1627	...	1716	1727	...	1816	1827	...	1917	1927	2016	2016	2027	2027	2116	2113	...	2230	2236
Manchester Airport ✈ d.	|	|	1500	|	|	1600	|	|	1700	|	|	1800	|	|	|	|	|	|	|	|	...	|	|
Manchester Piccadilly d.	|	|	1516	|	|	1616	|	|	1716	|	|	1816	|	|	|	|	|	|	|	|	...	|	|
Wigan North Western d.	1527	1538	1543	1627	1638	1643	1727	1738	1743	1827	1838	1843	1928	1938	2027	2027	2038	2038	2127	2127	...	2241	2247
Preston d.	1542	1553	1558	1642	1653	1658	1742	1753	1758	1842	1853	1858	1942	1953	2042	2042	2053	2053	2142	2142	...	2255	2301
Lancaster d.	1558	1608	1614	1657	1708	1714	1757	1809	1814	1857	1908	1914	1957	2008	2057	2057	2108	2108	2157	2157	...	...	...
Oxenholme d.	1611	|	1628	|	1723	1728	1811	1823	1828	1911	1922	1928	2012	|	2111	2111	2123	2123	2211	2211	...	...	...
Penrith d.	|	1645	|	1732	|	1753	|	1848	1853	1936	|	1953	2037	2047	2136	2136	|	|	2236	2236	...	...	...
Carlisle d.	1649	1702	1708	1748	1803	1811	1849	1904	1917	1953	2001	2011	2051	2104	2152	2152	2202	2202	2252	2252	...	...	...
Lockerbie d.	|	|	1727	|	|	1830	|	|	1936	|	|	2030	|	|	|	|	2221	2221	|	|	...	...	...
Haymarket a.	|	1811	|	|	|	1928s	|	2014	|	|	|	2128s	|	2216	|	|	|	|	|	|	...	...	...
Edinburgh Waverley a.	|	1818	|	|	|	1934	|	2020	|	|	|	2134	|	2223	|	|	|	|	|	|	...	...	...
Glasgow Central a.	1801	...	1828	1900	1916	...	2001	...	2038	2104	2115	...	2202	...	2305	2333	2324	2352	0001	0026	...	...	...

A – To Blackpool North (a. 1931).
W – To Windermere (Table **158**).

b – Aug. 6 - Sept. 10 and from Oct. 29.
c – From June 26.
d – May 15 - June 19.
e – Arrives 11 minutes earlier.
g – June 26 - Sept. 11.
h – May 15 - Aug. 28, Oct. 9, 16 and from Nov. 13.
k – Sept. 4, 11, 18, 25, Oct. 2, 23, 30, Nov. 6.
m – May 15 - June 26, Oct. 9, 16 and from Nov. 13.
p – July 3 - Sept. 25, Oct. 2, 23, 30, Nov. 6.
r – From Nov. 13.
s – Calls to set down only.
t – May 15 - Sept. 25, Oct. 2, 23, 30, Nov. 6.

◐ – Via Table **150**.

GLASGOW and EDINBURGH - PRESTON - MANCHESTER, BIRMINGHAM and LONDON 151

	Ⓐ	⑥	Ⓐ B	Ⓐ	Ⓐ	⑥	⑥ ◐	Ⓐ	⚒	Ⓐ ◐	⑥	⚒ ◐	⚒	⚒	⚒ ◐	⚒	⚒	⑤	⚒ ◐	⚒	⚒
Glasgow Central d.	...	...	...	...	0428	0426	...	0422	0540	...	...	0550	...	0630	...	0709	0735	...	0800	...	0840
Edinburgh Waverley d.	...	...	...	...	|	|	...	|	|	...	...	|	0615	|	0652	|	|	...	|	0812	|
Haymarket d.	...	...	...	...	|	|	...	|	|	...	...	|	0619u	|	0656	|	|	..	|	0816u	|
Lockerbie d.	...	...	...	...	|	|	...	0550	|	...	...	|	|	0725	|	0808	|	...	|	0911	|
Carlisle d.	...	...	...	...	0544	0544	...	0622	0649	...	...	0702	0733	0746	0806	0833	0849	...	0910	0933	0949
Penrith d.	...	...	...	...	0558	0558	...	0642	|	...	...	0717	0748	0800	0821	0848	|	...	|	0948	1003
Oxenholme d.	...	...	...	...	0621	0621	...	0709	0724	...	...	0741	0812	0823	|	0912	0923	...	|	1012	|
Lancaster d.	0513	0538	...	...	0636	0636	...	0724	0738	0658	0658	0756	0827	0838	0857	0927	0938	...	0956	1027	1038
Preston d.	0533	0558	0600	0617	0657	0657	0617	0744	0758	0717	0717	0817	0847	0858	0917	0947	0958	0952	1017	1047	1058
Wigan North Western d.	0545	0609	0611	0628	0709	0709	0628	0756	0809	0728	0728	0828	0859	0909	0928	0959	1009	1004	1028	1059	1109
Manchester Piccadilly a.	|	|	|	|	|	|	|	0827	|	|	|	|	0927	|	|	1027	|	|	|	1127	|
Manchester Airport ✈ a.	|	|	|	|	|	|	|	0847	|	|	|	|	0947	|	|	1047	|	|	|	1147	|
Warrington Bank Quay d.	0556	0620	0622	0639	0719	0719	0639	...	0820	0739	0739	0839	...	0920	0939	...	1020	1016	1039	...	1120
Crewe 150 a.	|	|	0642	0659	|	|	0659	...	|	0758	0758	0858	...	|	0958	...	|	1036	1058	...	|
Wolverhampton 150 a.	|	|	|	0735	|	|	0732	...	|	0833	0831	0933	...	|	1033	...	|	|	1134	...	|
Birmingham New St 150 a.	|	|	|	0801	|	|	0805	...	|	0905	0905	1005	...	|	1105	...	|	|	1205	...	|
Milton Keynes 150 a.	|	0738	|	...	|	|	0858	...	|	0958	...	1058	...	|	1159	...	|	|	1258	...	|
London Euston 150 a.	0758	0817	0834	...	0907	0913	0935	...	1013	1032	...	1134	...	1116	1234	...	1213	1231	1333	...	1313

	Ⓐ ◐	⑥ ◐v	⑥ W	⑥	Ⓐ	Ⓐ W	⚒	⚒ ◐	Ⓐ	⑥	⚒	⚒ ◐	Ⓐ	⑥	⚒	⚒ ◐	Ⓐ	⑥	⚒	⚒ ◐	⚒	⚒	⚒ ◐
Glasgow Central d.	...	...	...	0906	0906	...	0940	1000	...	...	1040	...	1109	1109	1140	1200	...	...	1240	...	1309	1340	1400
Edinburgh Waverley d.	0851	0852	...	|	|	...	|	|	1008	1012	|	1052	|	|	|	|	1212	1212	|	1251	|	|	|
Haymarket d.	0857	0857	...	|	|	...	|	|	1012u	1016u	|	1057	|	|	|	|	1216u	1216u	|	1257	|	|	|
Lockerbie d.	|	|	...	1007	1012	...	|	|	1106	1110	|	|	1207	1207	|	|	1311	1311	|	|	1408	|	|
Carlisle d.	1008	1009	...	1030	1033	...	1049	1111	1133	1133	1149	1208	1231	1231	1249	1311	1333	1333	1349	1408	1430	1449	1510
Penrith d.	|	|	...	1045	1048	...	|	1125	1148	1148	|	|	1247	1247	1303	|	|	1348	|	1422	1445	|	|
Oxenholme d.	1042	1043	1100	1109	|	1113	1123	|	1212	1212	1223	1243	1312	|	|	|	1410	1412	1424	|	1509	1523	1544
Lancaster d.	1057	1057	1117	1124	1124	1131	1138	|	1227	1227	1238	1257	1327	1327	1338	1356	1425	1427	1439	1456	1525	1538	|
Preston d.	1117	1117	1137	1147	1147	1150	1158	1217	1247	1247	1258	1317	1347	1347	1358	1417	1447	1447	1458	1517	1547	1558	1617
Wigan North Western d.	1128	1128	...	|	1159	...	1209	1228	1259	1259	1309	1328	1359	1359	1409	1428	1459	1459	1509	1528	1559	1609	1628
Manchester Piccadilly a.	|	|	...	1227	1227	...	|	|	1327	1327	|	|	1427	1427	|	|	1527	1527	|	|	1627	|	|
Manchester Airport ✈ a.	|	|	...	1247	1247	...	|	|	1347	1347	|	|	1447	1447	|	|	1547	1547	|	|	1647	|	|
Warrington Bank Quay d.	1139	1139	...	...	...	...	1220	1239	...	...	1320	1339	...	...	1420	1439	...	...	1520	1539	...	1620	1639
Crewe 150 a.	1158	1158	...	...	...	...	|	1258	...	...	|	1358	...	...	|	1459	...	...	|	1558	...	|	1658
Wolverhampton 150 a.	1232	1233	...	...	...	...	|	1333	...	...	|	1433	...	...	|	1533	...	...	|	1633	...	|	1733
Birmingham New St 150 a.	1305	1305	...	...	...	...	|	1405	...	...	|	1505	...	...	|	1605	...	...	|	1705	...	|	1805
Milton Keynes 150 a.	1358	1358	...	...	...	...	|	1458	...	...	|	1558	...	...	|	1658	...	...	|	1758	...	|	1858
London Euston 150 a.	1433	1433	...	...	...	...	1412	1534	...	...	1516	1634	...	...	1613	1733	...	...	1715	1834	...	1813	1933

	⚒	⚒	Ⓐ ◐	⑥ ◐	Ⓐ	⑥	Ⓐ	⑥	Ⓐ ◐	⑥ ◐	⚒	Ⓐ	⑥	⑥ W	Ⓐ W	Ⓐ ◐	⑥ ◐	⚒	Ⓐ	⑥	Ⓐ	⑥	⚒
Glasgow Central d.	...	1440	...	...	1509	1509	1540	1540	1600	1600	...	1640	1640	...	...	...	...	1709	1730	1740	1740	1800	...
Edinburgh Waverley d.	1417	|	1451	1452	|	|	|	|	|	|	1612	|	|	...	...	1652	1652	|	|	|	|	|	1813
Haymarket d.	1422u	|	1457	1457	|	|	|	|	|	|	1616u	|	|	...	...	1657	1657	|	|	|	|	|	1817u
Lockerbie d.	1516	|	|	|	1608	1608	|	|	|	|	1710	|	|	...	...	|	|	1808	|	1832	1835	|	1912
Carlisle d.	1540	1549	1608	1608	1630	1630	1648	1649	1710	1710	1733	1753	1752	...	...	1808	1807	1830	1846	1852	1857	1910	1934
Penrith d.	|	|	1621	1622	1645	1645	1703	1703	|	|	1748	1807	|	...	...	|	|	1845	1900	1906	|	|	1949
Oxenholme d.	1616	1624	|	|	1714	1709	|	|	1744	1744	1812	1831	1826	1830	1834	1842	1843	1909	1923	1929	1932	|	2013
Lancaster d.	1630	1638	1657	1657	1729	1725	1737	1738	|	|	1827	1845	1841	1846	1903	1859	1858	1925	1937	1944	1947	1957	2028
Preston d.	1650	1658	1717	1717	1747	1747	1758	1758	1817	1817	1847	1905	1901	1906	1926	1917	1918	1947	1958	2004	2007	2017	2048
Wigan North Western d.	|	1709	1728	1728	1759	1759	1809	1809	1828	1828	1859	1916	1912	...	...	1931	1929	1959	2009	2015	2019	2028	2101
Manchester Piccadilly a.	1729	|	|	|	1829	1827	|	|	|	|	1927	|	|	...	...	|	|	2027	|	|	|	|	2130
Manchester Airport ✈ a.	1747	|	|	|	1847	1847	|	|	|	|	1947	|	|	...	...	|	|	2047	|	|	|	|	2147
Warrington Bank Quay d.	...	1720	1739	1739	...	...	1820	1820	1839	1839	...	1927	1923	...	...	1941	1940	...	2020	2026	2032	2039	...
Crewe 150 a.	...	|	1759	1757	...	...	|	|	1858	1900	...	|	|	...	...	2001	1959	...	2039	2045	2051	2059	...
Wolverhampton 150 a.	...	|	1833	1832	...	...	|	|	1932	1934	...	|	|	...	...	2038	2032	...	|	|	2130	2132	...
Birmingham New St 150 a.	...	|	1905	1905	...	...	|	|	2005	2005	...	|	|	...	...	2105	2105	...	|	|	2154	2155	...
Milton Keynes 150 a.	...	|	1958	2005	...	...	|	|	2058	2104	...	2045	2042	...	...	2158	2204	...	2148	2151	...	...	...
London Euston 150 a.	...	1915	2034	2055	...	...	2012	2019	2139	2157	...	2125	2138	...	...	2243	2255	...	2225	2245	...	...	...

	Ⓐ	⑥	Ⓐ	⑥	Ⓐ	Ⓐ		⑦	⑦	⑦	⑦	⑦	⑦	⑦ ◐	⑦	⑦	⑦ ◐	⑦	⑦	⑦ ◐	⑦	⑦
Glasgow Central d.	1840	1840	...	...	2010	...	...	...	...	...	...	...	0938	...	...	1038	...	1116	1138	1155	...	1238
Edinburgh Waverley d.	|	|	1852	1852	|	2014	...	...	...	...	...	...	|	...	1012	|	1051	|	|	|	1212	|
Haymarket d.	|	|	1856	1856	|	2018u	...	...	...	...	...	...	|	...	1016u	|	1055	|	|	|	1216u	|
Lockerbie d.	|	|	|	|	2105	2112	...	...	...	...	...	...	|	...	1110	|	|	|	|	|	1310	|
Carlisle d.	1949	1948	2007	2009	2126	2135	...	...	...	...	...	...	1049	...	1133	1151	1207	1233	1249	1307	1333	1349
Penrith d.	|	2002	|	2024	2139	|	...	...	...	...	...	...	1103	...	1148	1205	|	1248	|	|	1348	|
Oxenholme d.	2024	2025	2042	2047	2203	2212	...	...	...	...	...	...	1126	...	1212	1229	1243	1312	1323	|	1412	1423
Lancaster d.	2038	2040	2056	2102	2218	2227	...	...	...	...	...	...	1141	1158	1227	1243	1257	1327	1338	1353	1427	1438
Preston d.	2058	2100	2117	2122	2240	2247	...	0856	0956	1015	1058	1117	1201	1217	1247	1304	1317	1347	1358	1417	1447	1458
Wigan North Western d.	2109	2111	2128	2133	2252	2259	...	0907	1009	1028	1109	1128	1212	1228	1259	1315	1328	1359	1409	1428	1459	1509
Manchester Piccadilly a.	|	|	|	|	|	2327	...	|	|	|	|	|	|	|	1327	|	|	1427	|	|	1527	|
Manchester Airport ✈ a.	|	|	|	|	|	2347	...	|	|	|	|	|	|	|	1347	|	|	1447	|	|	1547	|
Warrington Bank Quay d.	2120	2122	2139	2144	2303	...	...	0922	1023	1039	1120	1139	1223	1239	...	1326	1339	...	1420	1439	...	1520
Crewe 150 a.	|	2141	2159	2204	2326	...	...	0941	1043	1059	|	1159	|	1259	...	|	1359	...	|	1458	...	|
Wolverhampton 150 a.	|	2222	2232	2239	...	...	...	|	|	1132	|	1232	|	1332	...	|	1432	...	|	1534	...	|
Birmingham New St 150 a.	|	2248	2257	2259	...	...	...	|	|	1150	|	1250	|	1406	...	|	1506	...	|	1606	...	|
Milton Keynes 150 a.	2240	...	...	...	...	...	...	1107	1207	...	|	...	|	1458	...	|	1558	...	|	1658	...	|
London Euston 150 a.	2339	...	...	...	...	...	...	1206	1246	...	1322	...	1417	1539	...	1521	1639	...	1613	1738	...	1711

	⑦ ◐	⑦	⑦	⑦ ◐	⑦	⑦	⑦ ◐	⑦	⑦	⑦ ◐		⑦	⑦	⑦	⑦	⑦	⑦		⑦	⑦		⑦	⑦
Glasgow Central d.	...	1316	1338	1355	...	1438	...	1516	1538	1557	...	...	1638	...	1716	1738	...	...	1838	...	...	...	2008
Edinburgh Waverley d.	1251	|	|	|	1412	|	1451	|	|	|	...	1612	|	1651	|	|	1812	...	|	1851	...	1957	|
Haymarket d.	1255	|	|	|	1416u	|	1455	|	|	|	...	1616u	|	1655	|	|	1816u	...	|	1856	...	2001u	|
Lockerbie d.	|	|	|	|	1510	|	|	1615	|	|	...	1710	|	|	|	1832	1910	...	|	|	...	2055	2103
Carlisle d.	1407	1435	1449	1511	1533	1549	1607	1636	1649	1709	...	1733	1751	1807	1833	1852	1933	...	1946	2007	...	2117	2124
Penrith d.	1422	|	|	|	1548	|	1622	|	1703	|	...	1748	1805	|	1848	1906	1948	...	|	2022	...	|	2139
Oxenholme d.	|	1512	1523	1545	1612	1623	|	1712	|	1744	...	1812	1828	1842	1912	1929	2012	...	2022	|	...	2153	2203
Lancaster d.	1457	1527	1538	|	1627	1638	1657	1727	1738	|	...	1827	1843	1857	1927	1944	2027	...	2036	2057	...	2208	2218
Preston d.	1517	1547	1558	1617	1647	1658	1717	1747	1758	1817	...	1847	1903	1917	1947	2004	2047	...	2056	2117	...	2228	2238
Wigan North Western d.	1528	1559	1609	1629	1659	1709	1729	1759	1809	1828	...	1859	1914	1928	2001	2015	2059	...	2108	2129	...	2240	2252
Manchester Piccadilly a.	|	1627	|	|	1727	|	|	1827	|	|	...	1927	|	|	2030	|	2127	...	|	|	...	2309	|
Manchester Airport ✈ a.	|	1647	|	|	1747	|	|	1847	|	|	...	1947	|	|	2047	|	2147	...	|	|	...	2326	|
Warrington Bank Quay d.	1539	...	1620	1640	...	1720	1740	...	1820	1839	...	...	1925	1939	...	2026	...	...	2120	2139	...	...	2303
Crewe 150 a.	1559	...	|	1659	...	|	1759	...	|	1858	...	...	|	1959	...	2045	...	...	2139	2159	...	...	2321
Wolverhampton 150 a.	1632	...	|	1732	...	|	1833	...	|	1934	...	...	|	2033	...	|	...	...	2214	2232	...	...	...
Birmingham New St 150 a.	1706	...	|	1805	...	|	1906	...	|	2006	...	...	|	2051	...	|	...	...	2232	2255	...	...	...
Milton Keynes 150 a.	1758	...	|	1858	...	|	1958	...	|	2059	...	...	|	...	...	2152	...	...	...	...	...	...	...
London Euston 150 a.	1838	...	1814	1939	...	1911	2039	...	2013	2148	...	...	2122	...	...	2256	...	...	...	...	...	...	...

From Blackpool North (d. 0525).
From Windermere (Table **158**).

u – Calls to pick up only.
v – From Aug. 13.

◐ – Via Table **150**.

155 CREWE - STOKE - DERBY

2nd class

For other trains Crewe - Stoke on Trent and v.v. see Table **142**

km			Ⓐ	Ⓐ	Ⓐ		Ⓐ	Ⓐ			⑥	⑥	⑥		⑥	⑥		⑦	⑦	⑦	⑦	⑦	⑦	⑦
0	**Crewe** d.	Ⓐ	0607	0658	0807	and at	1907	2045	...	⑥	0607	0707	0807	and at	1907	2045	⑦	1404	1505	1608	1708	1808	1908	2015
24	Stoke on Trent d.		0633	0724	0833	the same	1933	2118	...		0633	0733	0833	the same	1933	2119		1429	1532	1635	1735	1835	1935	2040
33	Blythe Bridge d.		0646	0736	0845	minutes	1945	2130	...		0645	0745	0845	minutes	1945	2131		1441	1544	1647	1747	1847	1947	2052
51	Uttoxeter d.		0658	0749	0858	past each	1958	2142	...		0658	0758	0858	past each	1958	2144		1454	1556	1659	1759	1859	1959	2105
82	**Derby** a.		0726	0818	0928	hour until	2027	2209	...		0728	0828	0928	hour until	2028	2213		1519	1624	1727	1828	1928	2028	2134

		Ⓐ	Ⓐ	Ⓐ		Ⓐ	Ⓐ			⑥	⑥	⑥		⑥	⑥			⑦	⑦	⑦	⑦	⑦	⑦
Derby d.	Ⓐ	0640	0740	0842	and at	1942	2040	...	⑥	0640	0740	0842	and at	1942	2042	...	⑦	1438	1538	1638	1742	1842	1941
Uttoxeter d.		0705	0807	0907	the same	2007	2107	...		0707	0807	0907	the same	2007	2107	...		1503	1603	1703	1806	1906	2006
Blythe Bridge d.		0719	0821	0921	minutes	2021	2121	...		0721	0821	0921	minutes	2021	2121	...		1517	1617	1717	1821	1920	2020
Stoke on Trent a.		0732	0832	0933	past each	2033	2133	...		0734	0832	0933	past each	2033	2133	...		1530	1631	1730	1834	1934	2034
Crewe a.		0800	0902	1004	hour until	2104	2204	...		0800	0902	1004	hour until	2104	2204	...		1600	1700	1802	1902	2003	2100

156 MANCHESTER - PRESTON - BLACKPOOL

2nd Class only

For other trains Manchester - Preston and v.v. see Tables **151** and **157**

km			Ⓐ	Ⓐ	Ⓐ	Ⓐ	Ⓐ		Ⓐ	Ⓐ	Ⓐ	Ⓐ	Ⓐ	Ⓐ	Ⓐ	Ⓐ		⑥	⑥	⑥a	⑥b	⑥	⑥	⑥
0	**Manchester** Airport d.	Ⓐ	0527	0618	0757	0823	0929	and at	1629	1729	1829	1929	2029	2129	2229	2330	⑥	0527	0626	0756	0756	0929	1029	1129
16	**Manchester** Piccadilly d.		0544	0633	0816	0846	0946	the same	1646	1746	1846	1946	2046	2146	2246	2346		0544	0643	0814	0814	0946	1046	1146
34	Bolton d.		0603	0653	0833	0907	1007	minutes	1706	1807	1907	2007	2107	2207	2306	2359s		0603a	0707a	0833	|	1007a	1107a	1207a
66	**Preston** a.		0632	0722	0902	0936	1033	past each	1733	1838	1938	2035	2135	2235	2336	0036s		0633	0739	0902	0910	1035	1135	1235
66	**Preston** d.		0635	0725	0904	0938	1038	hour until	1735	1841	1938	2038	2138	2235	2338	|		0635	0740	0904	0911	1038	1138	1238
94	**Blackpool** North a.		0703	0753	0933	1003	1103	♧	1803	1911	2003	2103	2203	2303	0003	0103		0703	0809	0933	0935	1103	1203	1303

	⑥a	⑥b	⑥	⑥	⑥	⑥	⑥	⑥	⑥	⑥	⑥a		⑦🚌	⑦🚌	⑦c	⑦c	⑦d	⑦c	⑦d	⑦		⑦	⑦	⑦
Manchester Airport d.	1329	1329	1429	1529	1629	1729	1829	1929	2029	2129	2229	⑦	0005	0530	0747	0848	0848	0929	0929	1029	and at	2029	2129	2229
Manchester Piccadilly d.	1346	1346	1446	1546	1646	1746	1846	1946	2046	2146	2246		0030	0555	0801	0903	0903	0946	0946	1046	the same	2046	2146	2246
Bolton d.	1407	|	1507a	1607a	1707a	1807a	1907a	2007a	2107a	2207a	2307		0055s	0620s	0822	0923	|	1007	|	1106c	minutes	2107c	2207c	2307c
Preston a.	1433	1450	1536	1635	1733	1838	1937	2035	2135	2237	2336	▲	0130s	0655s	0852	0952	0959	1036	1039	1136	past each	2134	2238	2345
Preston d.	1438	1454	1538	1637	1738	1841	1938	2038	2138	2238	2338		|	|	0859	1003	1003	1038	1040	1137	hour until	2138	2238	2347
Blackpool North a.	1503	1520	1604	1705	1806	1911	2003	2103	2203	2303	0003		0210	0735	0924	1028	1028	1101	1104	1203	♧	2203	2305	0014

		Ⓐ	Ⓐ	Ⓐ	Ⓐ	Ⓐ			Ⓐ	Ⓐ	Ⓐ	Ⓐ	Ⓐ	Ⓐ	Ⓐ	Ⓐ			⑥	⑥a	⑥	⑥	⑥	⑥
Blackpool North d.	Ⓐ	0337	0446	0635	*0736*	0840	and at	1540	1635	1712	1753	1840	1940	2040	2140	2245	...	⑥	0337	0446	0638	0740	0835	0940
Preston a.		0400	0509	0703	*0803*	0904	the same	1604	1703	1740	1819	1904	2004	2103	2204	2309	...		|	0519	0705	0807	0859	1004
Preston d.		0402	0512	0705	0813	0905	minutes	1609	1705	1743	1821	1909	2009	2105	2205	2310	...		0402u	0512	0707	0809	0905	1012
Bolton d.		0430u	0537	0734	0834	0934	past each	1634	1734	1813	1855	1934	2034	2134	2234	2339	...		0435e	0537	0734a	0834a	0934a	1034a
Manchester Piccadilly a.		0446	0600	0757	0856	0957	hour until	1657	1757	1836	1920	1957	2057	2157	2257	2358	...		0452	0600	0756	0857	0957	1057
Manchester Airport a.		0503	0617	0817	0917	1023	♧	1717	1817	1853	...	2022	2120	2215	2315	0024	...		0508	0617	0817	0922	1022	1123

	⑥b	⑥		⑥	⑥	⑥	⑥	⑥			⑦🚌	⑦🚌	⑦c	⑦		⑦	⑦		⑦	⑦	⑦	⑦	⑦c
Blackpool North d.	1042	1140	and at	1840	1940	2040	2140	2245	...	⑦	0320	0520	0749	0840	...	0940	1040	and at	1740	1840	1940	2040	2140
Preston a.	1106	1204	the same	1904	2003	2104	2204	2309	...		|	|	0813	0904	...	1003	1107	the same	1804	1904	2004	2104	2204
Preston d.	1107	1205	minutes	1911	2005	2105	2205	2310	...		0400u	0600u	0815	0905	...	1005	1109	minutes	1805	1909	2005	2105	2205
Bolton d.	|	1234a	past each	1934a	2034a	2134a	2234a	2339a	...	▲	0435u	0635u	0842	0934d	...	1034d	1134d	past each	1834d	1934d	2034d	2134d	2234d
Manchester Piccadilly a.	1157	1257	hour until	1957	2057	2157	2257	2358a	...		0500u	0700u	0904	0957	...	1057	1156	hour until	1857	1956	2057	2157	2257
Manchester Airport a.	1222	1322	♧	2022	2117	2215	2315	0024a	...		0525	0725	0924	1015	...	1115	1215	♧	1915	2015	2116	2215	2315

a – May 21 - June 11 and from Sept. 17.
b – June 18 - Sept. 10.
c – May 15 - June 12 and from Sept. 18.
d – June 19 - Sept. 11.
e – May 21 - June 11 and from Sept. 17 (calls to pick-up only).
s – Calls to set down only.
u – Calls to pick up only.
▲ – On May 15, June 5, 12 all services start from / terminate Manchester Victoria (please check locally).
♧ – Timings may vary by up to 7 minutes.

157 MANCHESTER - PRESTON - BARROW IN FURNESS

NT,

For other trains Manchester - Preston / Lancaster and v.v. see Tables **151** and **156**.

km			Ⓐ2	Ⓐ	Ⓐ2	Ⓐ2	Ⓐ2	Ⓐ2	Ⓐ2	Ⓐ	Ⓐ2	Ⓐ2	Ⓐ	Ⓐ2	Ⓐ2	Ⓐ2	Ⓐ2	Ⓐ	Ⓐ2	Ⓐ2	Ⓐ	Ⓐ		⑥	⑥2
0	**Manchester** Airport ✈ d.	Ⓐ	...	*0558*	*0729*	...	...	...	...	...	...	...	...	...	...	*1600*	*1629*	...	...	...	...	2200	⑥	*0558*	...
16	**Manchester** Piccadilly d.		...	*0614*	*0745*	0831f	...	...	...	...	...	...	...	...	...	1627	1714f	...	...	...	...	2216		*0614*	...
34	Bolton d.		...	|	|	0852	...	...	...	...	...	...	...		...	...	1649	1731	...	...	...	...	|		|	...
66	**Preston** d.		0519	*0658*	*0826*	0927	1004	1045	...	...	...	...	...	1546	...	...	1728	1805	1847	2008	2109	2147	2313		*0658*	0842
100	Lancaster d.		0542	0733	0848	0947	1025	1105	1219	1320	1437	1533	1602	1648	1721	1748	1826	1903	2028	2129	2203	2329		0733	0902
110	Carnforth d.		0552	0742	0857	0957	1035	1113	1229	1328	1447	1543	1610	1658	1730	1758	1838	1911	2038	2139	2211	2337		0742	0912
119	Arnside d.		0602	0752	0908	1008	1047	1123	1239	1338	1457	1554	1620	1709	1741	1809	1848	1921	2048	2150	2221	2347		0752	0922
124	Grange over Sands d.		0608	0758	0914	1014	1053	1129	1245	1344	1503	1600	1626	1715	1747	1815	1854	1927	2054	2156	2227	2352		0758	0928
140	Ulverston d.		0625	0815	0931	1030	1112	1143	1302	1400	1520	1615	1642	1732	1803	1831	1911	1943	2111	2212	2243	0008		0815	0944
156	**Barrow in Furness** a.		0646	0838	0950	1054	1133	1205	1323	1423	1542	1637	1705	1756	1825	1856	1934	2006	2132	2236	2306	0030		0838	1006

	⑥2	⑥	⑥2	⑥	⑥2	⑥	⑥2	⑥2	⑥	⑥	⑥2	⑥	⑥c	⑥a		⑦b	⑦e	⑦h	⑦	⑦	⑦2		⑦	⑦	⑦2
Manchester Airport ✈ d.	...	...	...	...	...	...	...	...	...	...	...	2000	...	2200	⑦	...	...	1100g	...	...	...	...	...	...	...
Manchester Piccadilly d.	...	...	...	...	...	...	...	...	...	...	...	2016	...	2216		...	...	1116g	...	...	...	...	...	...	...
Bolton d.	...	...	...	...	...	...	...	...	...	...	...	|	...	2234d		...	...	|	...	...	...	...	...	...	...
Preston d.	...	...	...	1407	...	1546	...	...	1745	1908	2003	2058	...	2258		1017	1116	1159	1402	1604	...	...	1747	2004	...
Lancaster d.	1119	1223	1332	1423	1520	1602	1700	1731	1801	1929	2023	2114	2314	2314		1038	1132	1215	1422	1625	1720	...	1803	2024	2103
Carnforth d.	1128	1231	1341	1431	1530	1610	1710	1740	1810	1939	2033	2122	2322	2322		1048	1141	1223	1432	1635	1730	...	1811	2034	2128
Arnside d.	1139	1241	1352	1440	1540	1620	1721	1752	1820	1949	2044	2132	2332	2332		1058	1151	1233	1443	1645	1741	...	1821	2044	2138
Grange over Sands d.	1145	1247	1358	1445	1546	1626	1727	1758	1825	1955	2050	2138	2338	2338		1104	1156	1239	1449	1651	1747	...	1827	2050	2144
Ulverston d.	1201	1303	1414	1458	1603	1642	1744	1816	1842	2012	2106	2154	2354	2354		1121	1212	1255	1505	1708	1802	...	1843	2107	2200
Barrow in Furness a.	1223	1326	1436	1518	1624	1705	1806	1840	1905	2035	2128	2218	0017	0022		1144	1236	1318	1529	1731	1826	...	1906	2130	2224

		Ⓐ	Ⓐ2	Ⓐ2	Ⓐ		Ⓐ2	Ⓐ2	Ⓐ2	Ⓐ2	Ⓐ2	Ⓐ2	Ⓐ2	Ⓐ2	Ⓐ2		Ⓐ2	Ⓐ	Ⓐ2	Ⓐ	Ⓐ2			⑥2	⑥
Barrow in Furness d.	Ⓐ	0435	0523	0615	0648	...	0713	0806	0917	1009	1113	1213	1331	1441	1524	...	1610	1720	1803	2015	2143	...	⑥	0435	0532
Ulverston d.		0451	0539	0634	0707	...	0731	0827	0935	1028	1132	1232	1349	1457	1543	...	1628	1737	1821	2034	2201	...		0451	0547
Grange over Sands d.		0503	0551	0646	0723	...	0745	0845	0951	1044	1148	1247	1405	1509	1559	...	1644	1752	1837	2050	2217	...		0503	0600
Arnside d.		0509	0557	0650	0729	...	0751	0851	0957	1050	1154	1253	1411	1515	1605	...	1650	1758	1843	2056	2223	...		0509	0606
Carnforth d.		0519	0608	0707	0740	...	0803	0905	1009	1108	1206	1305	1423	1525	1617	...	1702	1809	1856	2107	2236	...		0519	0616
Lancaster a.		0531	0616	0718	0748	...	0813	0914	1018	1118	1215	1314	1433	1533	1628	...	1714	1818	1904	2115	2245	...		0531	0623
Preston a.		...	0639	...	0807	...	...	0938	1041	...	1240	...	...	1553	...	...	...	...	1932	2135	2311	...		...	0642
Bolton a.		...	0708	...	0834	...	...	...	...	...	...	...	...	...	...	...	...	...	...	...	...	...		...	0708k
Manchester Piccadilly a.		...	0727	...	0856	...	...	...	...	...	...	...	...	...	...	...	...	...	...	...	...	...		...	0727
Manchester Airport ✈ a.		...	0747	...	0917	...	...	...	...	...	...	...	...	...	...	...	...	...	...	...	...	...		...	0747

	⑥2	⑥2	⑥	⑥2	⑥	⑥2	⑥	⑥2	⑥	⑥2	⑥	⑥2	⑥	⑥2			⑦	⑦2n	⑦	⑦2	⑦2		⑦	⑦	⑦
Barrow in Furness d.	0707	0808	0850	1009	1120	1211	1333	1443	1525	1629	1720	1803	1917	2135	...	⑦	0922	1005	1023	1210	1310	...	1348	1612	1815
Ulverston d.	0726	0826	0907	1028	1137	1229	1352	1503	1541	1647	1737	1821	1936	2153	...		0941	1020	1042	1229	1329	...	1405	1631	1834
Grange over Sands d.	0742	0842	0922	1044	1152	1245	1408	1520	1553	1703	1752	1837	1952	2209	...		0957	1033	1058	1245	1345	...	1419	1647	1850
Arnside d.	0748	0848	0928	1050	1158	1251	1414	1526	1559	1709	1758	1843	1958	2215	...		1003	1039	1104	1251	1351	...	1425	1653	1855
Carnforth d.	0800	0900	0939	1102	1209	1303	1425	1539	1609	1721	1809	1856	2009	2228	...		1014	1049	1115	1304	1404	...	1437	1706	1909
Lancaster a.	0808	0909	0947	1111	1219	1315	1433	1551	1617	1736	1818	1905	2017	2240	...		1023	1101	1123	1312	1415	...	1444	1715	1917
Preston a.	0841	...	1007	...	...	...	1452	...	1637	...	...	1931	2037	2304a	...		1040b	...	1143	1337	...	...	1504	1740	1942
Bolton a.	...	...	...	...	...	...	...	...	...	...	...	...	...	...	...		|	...	|	...	...	...	...	...	...
Manchester Piccadilly a.	...	...	...	...	...	...	...	...	...	...	...	...	...	...	...		1127b	...	1227	...	...	...	...	...	...
Manchester Airport ✈ a.	...	...	...	...	...	...	...	...	...	...	...	...	...	...	...		1147b	...	1247	...	...	...	...	...	...

a – From June 25.
b – From June 26.
c – May 21 - June 18.
d – From Oct. 29.
e – May 15 - June 19.
f – Manchester **Oxford Road**.
g – June 26 - Sept. 11.
h – From June 26.
k – May 21 - June 11 and from Sept. 17.
n – May 15 - Sept. 11.
s – Calls to set down only.
u – Calls to pick up only.

PRESTON - OXENHOLME - WINDERMERE — 158

2nd Class

	Ⓐ	Ⓐ	Ⓐ	Ⓐ	Ⓐ	Ⓐ	Ⓐ	Ⓐ	Ⓐ	Ⓐ	Ⓐ	Ⓐ	Ⓐ	Ⓐ	Ⓐ	Ⓐ	Ⓐ	⑥	⑥	⑥	⑥	⑥ M
Preston d.	...	...	...	...	...	1025	...	...	...	...	...	...	...	...	...	...	...	...	...	...	...	0932
Lancaster d.	0546	...	...	...	...	1100	...	...	...	...	...	...	1821	...	...	...	...	0602	...	...	...	0948
Oxenholme d.	0621	0733	0826	0911	1033	1120	1226	1333	1422	1534	1622	1734	1838	1934	2022	2115	2218	0621	0721	0826	0911	1004
Kendal d.	0626	0737	0830	0915	1037	1125	1230	1337	1426	1538	1626	1738	1843	1938	2026	2119	2222	0626	0725	0830	0915	1009
Windermere a.	0641	0752	0846	0931	1050	1142	1243	1354	1443	1555	1643	1755	1858	1953	2041	2132	2237	0641	0742	0846	0931	1026

	⑥	⑥	⑥	⑥	⑥	⑥	⑥	⑥	⑥	⑥	⑥ b	⑥ f 🚌	⑦ 🚌	⑦ c	⑦ d	⑦	⑦	⑦	⑦	⑦	⑦	⑦	⑦	⑦
Preston d.	1044	...	1248	...	1430	...	1704	...	...	...	...	...	...	1009	...	...	...	...	...	...	...	...	...	...
Lancaster d.	1101	...	1304	...	1500	...	1720	1825	...	...	...	...	...	1026	1128	...	...	...	...	...	...	...	...	...
Oxenholme d.	1120	1226	1321	1417	1519	1634	1737	1842	1934	2022	2115	2120	1040	1043	1145	1227	1335	1421	1535	1621	1733	1841	1927	2016
Kendal d.	1125	1230	1325	1421	1524	1638	1741	1846	1938	2026	2119	2130	1050	1047	1149	1231	1339	1425	1539	1625	1737	1845	1931	2020
Windermere a.	1142	1243	1341	1436	1541	1655	1756	1901	1953	2041	2134	2205	1125	1101	1203	1246	1354	1440	1554	1640	1752	1901	1944	2036

	Ⓐ	Ⓐ	Ⓐ	Ⓐ	Ⓐ	Ⓐ	Ⓐ	Ⓐ	Ⓐ	Ⓐ	Ⓐ	Ⓐ	Ⓐ	Ⓐ	Ⓐ	Ⓐ	Ⓐ	⑥	⑥	⑥	⑥	⑥	⑥
Windermere d.	0645	0756	0850	0947	1056	1147	1247	1358	1458	1600	1649	1803	1906	1958	2050	2140	2245	0657	0747	0850	0937	1040	1147
Kendal d.	0659	0811	0902	1001	1108	1202	1302	1413	1513	1613	1704	1818	1918	2012	2104	2154	2259	0712	0802	0902	0952	1054	1202
Oxenholme a.	0704	0816	0907	1006	1113	1207	1307	1418	1518	1618	1709	1823	1923	2017	2109	2159	2304	0717	0807	0907	0957	1059	1207
Lancaster a.	...	...	...	...	1130	...	...	...	...	...	...	1854	...	...	...	...	2322	...	...	...	1017	1117	...
Preston a.	...	...	...	...	1150	...	...	...	...	...	...	1926e	...	...	...	...	2342	...	...	...	1039	1137	...

	⑥	⑥	⑥	⑥	⑥	⑥	⑥	⑥	⑥	⑥ b	⑥ f 🚌	⑦ 🚌	⑦ c	⑦ c	⑦ d	⑦	⑦	⑦	⑦	⑦	⑦	⑦	⑦	⑦
Windermere d.	1251	1345	1441	1550	1707	1803	1906	1958	2045	2140	2140	1048	1104	1159	1207	1250	1358	1447	1558	1648	1802	1905	1948	2040
Kendal d.	1306	1359	1455	1605	1722	1817	1918	2012	2056	2154	2215	1113	1116	1213	1218	1302	1412	1501	1612	1702	1816	1918	2002	2055
Oxenholme a.	1311	1404	1500	1610	1727	1822	1923	2017	2102	2159	2225	1123	1121	1218	1223	1307	1417	1506	1617	1707	1821	1923	2007	2100
Lancaster a.	1333	...	1517	...	1748	1846	...	...	2121f	2216	2310	...	...	...	...	...	...	...	...	...	1838	...	...	2120
Preston a.	1406	...	1537	...	1811	1906	...	...	...	2237	0001	...	...	...	...	...	...	...	...	...	1858	...	...	2144

M – From Manchester Airport (Table 151).

b – From June 25.
c – From June 26.
d – May 15 - June 19.

e – 1910 May 16 - Sept. 30.
f – May 21 - June 18.
s – Calls to set down only.

BARROW - WHITEHAVEN - CARLISLE — 159

2nd class

	Ⓐ	Ⓐ	Ⓐ	Ⓐ	Ⓐ	Ⓐ	Ⓐ	Ⓐ	Ⓐ	Ⓐ	Ⓐ	Ⓐ	Ⓐ	Ⓐ	Ⓐ	Ⓐ	Ⓐ	Ⓐ		⑥	⑥
Lancaster **151** d.	...	...	...	...	...	...	...	...	...	1219	...	1533	...	...	...	...	...	...	...	...	...
Barrow in Furness d.	...	0546	0651	0744	...	0920	1010	1140	1236	1331	1437	1643	1731	1830	1940	...	2134	...	...	...	0546
Millom d.	...	0621	0719	0812	...	0948	1038	1214	1304	1359	1512	1711	1805	1858	2010	...	2204	...	...	...	0621
Ravenglass for Eskdale 🚂 d.	...	0642	0737	0829	...	1005	1055	1235	1321	1416	1533	1728	1826	1915	...	...	...	...	...	...	0642
Sellafield d.	...	0656	0751	0840	...	1019	1108	1248	1336	1428	1547	1740	1840	1925	...	...	...	...	...	...	0656
Whitehaven d.	0624	0718	0812	...	0904	1037	1128	1310	1356	1454	1612	1800	1915	1944	...	2030	...	2151	...	0622	0718
Workington d.	0642	0739	0831	...	0922	1055	1146	1332	1414	1513	1634	1818	1936	2003	...	2048	...	2211	...	0640	0739
Maryport d.	0650	0749	0839	...	0930	1104	1154	1342	1422	1522	1644	1826	1946	2012	...	2056	...	...	...	0648	0749
Wigton d.	0711	0812	0900	...	0951	1126	1216	1405	1443	1544	1707	1847	2010	2033	...	2117	...	...	...	0709	0812
Carlisle a.	0733	0833	0925	...	1013	1149	1238	1426	1506	1604	1728	1910	2031	2055	...	2139	...	...	...	0731	0833

	⑥	⑥	⑥	⑥		⑥	⑥	⑥	⑥		⑥	⑥	⑥	⑥		⑥	⑥	⑥		⑦	⑦	⑦	⑦
Lancaster **151** d.	...	...	...	...	...	0902	...	1119	...	...	1332	...	1700	...	...	...	...	2023	...	...	...	...	...
Barrow in Furness d.	0655	0741	...	0845	...	1010	1138	1239	1350	...	1452	1533	1810	...	...	1940	...	2130	...	...	...	...	...
Millom d.	0724	0809	...	0919	...	1038	1212	1307	1418	...	1520	1601	1840	...	...	2010	...	2200	...	...	...	...	...
Ravenglass for Eskdale 🚂 d.	0742	0826	...	0940	...	1055	1233	1324	1435	...	1537	1618	...	...	...	...	...	...	...	...	...	...	...
Sellafield d.	0756	0839	...	0954	...	1108	1246	1336	1447	...	1550	1630	...	...	...	...	...	...	...	...	...	...	...
Whitehaven d.	0816	...	0906	1019	...	1128	1308	1355	1507	...	1610	1656	...	1943	...	...	2030	...	...	1233	1433	1633	1933
Workington d.	0834	...	0924	1040	...	1146	1329	1413	1525	...	1628	1714	...	2001	...	...	2048	...	...	1251	1451	1651	1951
Maryport d.	0842	...	0932	1051	...	1154	1340	1421	1533	...	1636	1722	...	2009	...	...	2056	...	...	1259	1459	1659	1959
Wigton d.	0904	...	0953	1114	...	1216	1403	1442	1555	...	1658	1744	...	2030	...	...	2117	...	...	1318	1518	1718	2018
Carlisle a.	0926	...	1015	1137	...	1238	1426	1505	1617	...	1719	1806	...	2053	...	...	2139	...	...	1341	1541	1741	2041

	Ⓐ	Ⓐ	Ⓐ	Ⓐ	Ⓐ	Ⓐ	Ⓐ	Ⓐ	Ⓐ	Ⓐ	Ⓐ	Ⓐ	Ⓐ	Ⓐ	Ⓐ	Ⓐ	Ⓐ	Ⓐ	Ⓐ	Ⓐ		⑥
Carlisle d.	...	0515	...	0737	...	0842	0938	1054	1208	1252	1435	1513	1631	1737	1814	...	1915	2037	...	2200	...	...
Wigton d.	...	0538	...	0755	...	0901	0956	1112	1226	1310	1454	1531	1649	1756	1832	...	1933	2055	...	2218	...	...
Maryport d.	...	0601	0646	0816	...	0925	1017	1133	1247	1331	1517	1552	1710	1820	1853	...	1954	2116	...	2239	...	...
Workington d.	...	0611	0704	0827	...	0935	1028	1144	1258	1342	1528	1604	1721	1831	1904	...	2005	2127	...	2250	...	...
Whitehaven d.	...	0632	0724	0847	...	0956	1048	1205	1318	1403	1549	1623	1741	1852	1925	...	2025	2147	...	2310	...	...
Sellafield d.	...	0653	0742	...	0900	1018	1108	1223	1335	1421	1611	1644	1804	1917	...	...	...	...	...	...	...	...
Ravenglass for Eskdale 🚂 d.	...	0706	0753	...	0910	1031	1118	1233	1345	1431	1624	1655	1814	1930	...	...	...	...	...	...	...	...
Millom d.	0609	0727	0812	...	0929	1052	1136	1252	1404	1450	1645	1715	1835	1951	...	2016	...	...	2209	...	...	0609
Barrow in Furness a.	0642	0803	0845	...	1000	1130	1208	1324	1436	1522	1723	1749	1910	2031	...	2049	...	...	2242	...	...	0641
Lancaster **151** a.	...	0914	...	...	...	...	...	1433	...	1628	...	...	...	...	...	...	...	...	...	...	...	...

	⑥	⑥	⑥	⑥	⑥	⑥	⑥	⑥	⑥	⑥	⑥	⑥	⑥	⑥	⑥	⑥	⑥	⑥		⑦	⑦	⑦	⑦
Carlisle d.	0515	0735	...	0842	0938	1054	1156	1252	1433	1525	1636	1740	1814	1900	...	2015	...	2145	...	1410	1710	1910	2110
Wigton d.	0537	0753	...	0901	0956	1112	1214	1310	1452	1543	1654	1758	1832	1918	...	2032	...	2203	...	1427	1727	1927	2127
Maryport d.	0601	0814	...	0925	1017	1133	1236	1331	1515	1604	1715	1819	1853	1939	...	2052	...	2224	...	1447	1747	1947	2147
Workington d.	0611	0825	...	0935	1028	1144	1248	1342	1526	1616	1726	1830	1904	1950	...	2104	...	2235	...	1459	1759	1959	2159
Whitehaven d.	0632	0845	...	0956	1048	1204	1310	1402	1547	1636	1748	1850	1925	2010	...	2125	...	2255	...	1520	1820	2020	2220
Sellafield d.	0653	...	0905	1018	1108	1222	1329	1419	1612	1656	1808	1911	...	...	...	...	...	...	...	...	...	...	...
Ravenglass for Eskdale 🚂 d.	0706	...	0915	1031	1118	1232	1341	1429	1625	1706	1818	1921	...	...	...	...	...	...	...	...	...	...	...
Millom d.	0726	...	0934	1052	1136	1251	1401	1448	1646	1725	1837	1939	...	...	2016	...	2208	...	...	...	...	...	...
Barrow in Furness a.	0804	...	1005	1132	1208	1325	1435	1520	1723	1757	1911	2013	...	...	2049	...	2241	...	...	...	...	...	...
Lancaster **151** a.	...	...	1111	...	1315	...	1551	...	...	1905	...	...	...	...	...	...	...	...	...	...	...	...	...

🚂 – Ravenglass and Eskdale Railway. ✆ 01229 717171. www.ravenglass-railway.co.uk

160 HOLYHEAD - CHESTER - MANCHESTER

2nd class AW

km			Ⓐ	Ⓐ	Ⓐ	Ⓐ	Ⓐ	Ⓐ	Ⓐ	Ⓐ	Ⓐ	Ⓐ	Ⓐ	Ⓐ	Ⓐ	Ⓐ	Ⓐ	Ⓐ	Ⓐ	Ⓐ	Ⓐ	Ⓐ	Ⓐ	Ⓐ	Ⓐ	Ⓐ
						C	A			C	A			C	A			C		C	A		B		C	
0	**Holyhead** d.	Ⓐ	...	...	...	0425	0448	...	0514	0533	0551	...	...	0628	0655	...	0715	...	...	0805	0855	...	0923	...	1040	...
40	Bangor d.		...	...	...	0457	0514	...	0543	0601	0618	...	...	0706	0722	...	0802	...	...	0902c	0922	...	1002	...	1107	...
	Llandudno ‡ d.		...	...	...	|	|	...	|	|	|	...	0646	|	|	0745	|	0830	...	|	|	0945	|	1044	|	1144
64	Llandudno Junction ‡ d.		...	0438	...	0515	0532	0546	0607	0619	0636	...	0656	0725	0740	0754	0825	0839	0854	0925	0940	0954	1025	1053	1125	1153
71	Colwyn Bay d.		...	0444	...	0521	0538	0552	0613	0627	0642	...	0702	0731	0747	0800	0831	0845	0900	0931	0947	1000	1031	1059	1131	1159
88	Rhyl d.		...	0457	...	0531	0549	0602	0626	0638	0653	...	0715	0741	0758	0813	0841	0856	0913	0941	0958	1013	1041	1112	1141	1212
94	Prestatyn d.		...	0502	...	0537	|	0608	0631	|	0658	...	0721	0747	0804	0819	0847	|	0919	0947	1004	1019	1047	1118	1147	1218
116	Flint d.		...	0516	...	0550	|	0621	0645	0655	0712	...	0735	0800	0817	0832	0900	|	0932	1000	1017	1032	1100	1131	1200	1231
136	**Chester** a.		...	0533	...	0610	0617	0638	0702	0709	0726	...	0753	0815	0831	0850	0914	0923	0950	1015	1031	1050	1115	1149	1216	1249
136	**Chester 150** ♥ d.		0334	0537	0538	...	0626	0640	0712	...	0735	0738	0755	...	0835	0852	0916	...	0952	...	1035	1052	...	1150	...	1250
170	**Crewe 150** ♥ a.		|	0558	|	...	0647	|	|	...	0754	|	0818	...	0854	|	0937	...	|	...	1054	|	...	|	...	|
165	Warrington Bank Quay a.		|	...	0606	...	...	0709	0739	...	...	0808	...	...	...	0918	...	...	1018	...	...	1118	...	1220	...	1318
201	**Manchester** Piccadilly a.		0442	...	0644	...	...	0751	0814	...	...	0854	...	...	...	0952	...	...	1052	...	...	1152	...	1252	...	1352
217	**Manchester** Airport a.		0504	...	...	...	...	...	...	...	...	...	...	...	...	1015	...	...	1115	...	...	1215	...	1315	...	1415

	Ⓐ	Ⓐ	Ⓐ	Ⓐ	Ⓐ	Ⓐ	Ⓐ	Ⓐ	Ⓐ	Ⓐ	Ⓐ	Ⓐ	Ⓐ	Ⓐ	Ⓐ	Ⓐ	Ⓐ	Ⓐ	Ⓐ	Ⓐ	Ⓐ	Ⓐ	Ⓐ	Ⓐ	Ⓐ	Ⓐ
		C	A		B	A			C			B		C		D						B	B			
Holyhead d.	...	1232	1252	1305	1324	1358	...	...	1434	...	...	1544	...	1650	...	1730	...	...	1823	...	...	1921	...	...	2032	...
Bangor d.	...	1307	1320	1332	1404	1425	...	...	1504	...	...	1623	...	1718	...	1809	...	...	1902	...	...	2000	2020	...	2101	...
Llandudno ‡ d.	...	|	|	|	|	|	1440	1508	|	...	1607	|	1705	|	...	|	...	1844	|	1934	...	|	|	2043	|	2145
Llandudno Junction ‡ d.	1253	1325	1339	1350	1429	1443	1449	1517	1527	1618	1625	1646	1715	1737	...	1832	1839	1853	1926	1946	...	2023	2038	2052	2128	2155
Colwyn Bay d.	1259	1331	1345	1358	1435	1450	1455	1523	1533	1624	1631	|	1721	1743	...	|	1845	1859	1932	1954	...	2029	2044	2058	2134	2201
Rhyl d.	1312	1341	1356	1412	1445	1500	1508	1536	1544	1634	1644	|	1733	1753	...	|	1855	1912	1942	2009	...	2039	2055	2111	2147	2216
Prestatyn d.	1318	1347	1401	1418	1451	|	1514	1542	1549	1640	1649	|	1739	1759	...	|	1901	1918	1948	2016	...	2045	2101	2117	2152	2222
Flint d.	1331	1400	1415	1431	1504	|	1527	1555	1603	1653	1703	|	1752	1812	...	|	1914	1931	2001	2030	...	2058	2114	2130	2206	2237
Chester a.	1349	1415	1428	1445	1525	1528	1544	1613	1617	1707	1720	1726	1811	1826	...	1911	1930	1949	2016	2044	...	2116	2128	2147	2222	2255
Chester 150 ♥ d.	1350	...	1435	1447	...	1535	1546	1622	...	...	1722	...	1816	...	1849	...	...	1952	2018	2046	2050	...	2135	2151	2225	2301
Crewe 150 ♥ a.	|	...	1454	|	...	1554	|	|	...	...	|	...	|	...	|	...	...	|	2041	2106	|	...	2154	|	2249	2326
Warrington Bank Quay a.	1418	...	...	1517	...	...	1612	1651	...	...	1752	...	1845	...	1918	...	...	2018	...	...	2119	...	...	2217	...	...
Manchester Piccadilly a.	1452	...	...	1554	...	...	1654	1727	...	...	1826	...	1927	...	1951	...	...	2052	...	...	2153	...	...	2255	...	...
Manchester Airport a.	1515	...	...	...	...	...	...	...	...	...	...	...	...	...	2021	...	...	2121	...	...	...	...	...	...	...	...

		⑥	⑥	⑥	⑥	⑥	⑥	⑥	⑥	⑥	⑥	⑥	⑥	⑥	⑥	⑥	⑥	⑥	⑥	⑥	⑥	⑥	⑥	⑥	⑥	⑥
					d	Cc	c		C	B		C	A		B	A		C	A		B		C		B	
Holyhead d.	⑥	...	...	...	0425	0425	...	...	...	0522	...	0635	0652	...	0715	0755	...	0820	0855	...	0923	...	1033	...	1123	...
Bangor d.		...	...	...	0457	0457	...	...	...	0601	...	0707	0720	...	0802	0822	...	0902	0922	...	1002	...	1105	...	1202	...
Llandudno ‡ d.		...	...	...	|	|	...	...	...	|	0634	|	|	0745	|	|	0845	|	|	0945	|	1044	|	1144	|	1236
Llandudno Junction ‡ d.		...	0438	...	0515	0515	...	0537	...	0624	0644	0725	0738	0754	0825	0840	0854	0925	0940	0954	1025	1053	1125	1153	1225	1253
Colwyn Bay d.		...	0444	...	0521	0521	...	0543	...	0630	0650	0731	0744	0800	0831	0847	0900	0931	0947	1000	1031	1059	1131	1159	1231	1259
Rhyl d.		...	0457	...	0531	0531	...	0556	...	0640	0703	0741	0755	0813	0841	0858	0913	0941	0958	1013	1041	1112	1141	1212	1241	1312
Prestatyn d.		...	0502	...	0537	0537	...	0601	...	0646	0708	0747	0801	0819	0847	0904	0919	0947	1003	1019	1047	1118	1147	1218	1247	1318
Flint d.		...	0516	...	0550	0550	...	0615	...	0659	0721	0800	0815	0832	0900	0917	0932	1000	|	1032	1100	1131	1200	1231	1300	1331
Chester a.		...	0533	...	0604	0604	...	0633	...	0715	0738	0815	0828	0850	0915	0931	0950	1016	1028	1050	1116	1149	1216	1249	1315	1349
Chester 150 ♥ d.		0336	0537	0538	0613	...	0613	0635	0712	...	0740	...	0835	0852	...	0935	0952	...	1035	1052	...	1150	...	1250	...	1350
Crewe 150 ♥ a.		|	0558	|	|	...	|	0659	|	...	|	...	0854	|	...	0954	|	...	1054	|	...	|	...	|	...	|
Warrington Bank Quay a.		|	...	0605	0639	...	0639	...	0738	...	0806	...	...	0918	...	...	1018	...	...	1118	...	1220	...	1318	...	1420
Manchester Piccadilly a.		0441	...	0643	0719	...	0719	...	0818	...	0852	...	...	0952	...	...	1052	...	...	1152	...	1252	...	1352	...	1452
Manchester Airport a.		0504	...	...	...	...	...	...	...	...	0915	...	...	1015	...	...	1115	...	...	1215	...	1315	...	1415	...	1515

	⑥	⑥	⑥	⑥	⑥	⑥	⑥	⑥	⑥	⑥	⑥	⑥	⑥	⑥	⑥	⑥	⑥	⑥	⑥	⑥	⑥		⑦	⑦	⑦	⑦
	C		B	A		C		B		C		D				B								g	g	h
Holyhead d.	1238	...	1328	1358	...	1423	...	1523	...	1650	...	1730	...	1823	...	1921	...	...	2037	...	...	⑦	...	0716	0750	...
Bangor d.	1307	1331	1407	1425	...	1453	...	1602	...	1718	...	1809	...	1902	...	2000	...	...	2106	...	...		...	0743	0828	...
Llandudno ‡ d.	|	|	|	|	1442	|	1544	|	1644	|	1744	|	1844	|	1942	|	2043	...	|	2145	...		...	|	|	...
Llandudno Junction ‡ d.	1325	1356	1425	1443	1451	1516	1553	1625	1653	1736	1753	1832	1853	1926	1951	2023	2052	...	2129	2155	...		...	0800	0851	...
Colwyn Bay d.	1331	1402	1431	1450	1457	1522	1559	1631	1659	1742	1759	1838	1859	1932	1957	2029	2058	...	2135	2201	...		...	0807	0857	...
Rhyl d.	1341	1415	1441	1500	1510	1533	1612	1641	1712	1752	1812	1848	1912	1942	2010	2039	2111	...	2148	2216	...		...	0820	0908	...
Prestatyn d.	1347	1421	1447	|	1516	1538	1618	1647	1718	1758	1818	1854	1918	1948	2016	2045	2117	...	2154	2222	...		...	0825	|	...
Flint d.	1400	1434	1500	|	1529	1552	1631	1700	1731	1811	1831	1907	1931	2001	2029	2058	2130	...	2207	2237	...		...	0839	|	...
Chester a.	1414	1452	1517	1527	1546	1605	1649	1715	1749	1825	1849	1924	1949	2016	2047	2113	2148	...	2223	2255	...		...	0856	0939	...
Chester 150 ♥ d.	...	1453	...	1535	1548	...	1650	...	1750	...	1850	...	1950	2018	2050	...	...	2153	2226	2301	2322		0839	0857	0942	0942
Crewe 150 ♥ a.	...	|	...	1554	|	...	|	...	|	...	|	...	|	2041	|	...	...	|	2250	2326	|		|	0922	|	|
Warrington Bank Quay a.	...	1520	...	...	1617	...	1719	...	1818	...	1920	...	2018	...	2119	...	...	2220	...	...	2350		0908	...	1009	1009
Manchester Piccadilly a.	...	1552	...	...	1652	...	1752	...	1852	...	1952	...	2056	...	2156	...	...	2254	...	...	0022		0942	...	1049	1048
Manchester Airport a.	...	1615	...	...	1715	...	1815	...	1915	...	2016	...	...	...	...	...	...	...	...	...	...		...	...	...	...

	⑦	⑦	⑦	⑦	⑦	⑦	⑦	⑦	⑦	⑦	⑦	⑦	⑦	⑦	⑦	⑦	⑦	⑦	⑦	⑦	⑦	⑦	⑦	⑦	⑦	⑦
			C	A		A		A		A						C				K						
Holyhead d.	...	...	1020	1055	...	1150	...	1250	...	1355	...	1430	...	1540	...	1625	...	1730	...	1825	...	1915	...	...	2035	2140
Bangor d.	...	...	1059	1122	...	1217	...	1318	...	1422	...	1508	...	1608	...	1704	...	1759	...	1904	...	1954	...	...	2114	2209
Llandudno ‡ d.	...	...	|	|	...	|	...	|	...	|	...	|	...	|	...	|	...	|	...	|	...	|	...	...	|	|
Llandudno Junction ‡ d.	...	...	1122	1140	...	1235	...	1336	...	1440	...	1526	...	1635	...	1725	...	1824	...	1924	...	2021	...	...	2137	2227
Colwyn Bay d.	...	...	1128	1146	...	1242	...	1342	...	1446	...	1532	...	1641	...	1731	...	1830	...	1930	...	2027	...	...	2143	2233
Rhyl d.	...	...	1141	1157	...	1253	...	1353	...	1457	...	1545	...	1654	...	1744	...	1843	...	1943	...	2040	...	...	2156	2243
Prestatyn d.	...	...	1146	1203	...	1259	...	1359	...	1503	...	1551	...	1659	...	1749	...	1848	...	1948	...	2146	...	...	2201	2249
Flint d.	...	...	1200	1216	...	|	...	1413	...	|	...	1604	...	1713	...	1803	...	1902	...	2002	...	2100	...	...	2215	2302
Chester a.	...	...	1218	1230	...	1324	...	1426	...	1531	...	1624	...	1734	...	1821	...	1921	...	2019	...	2122	...	...	2232	2316
Chester 150 ♥ d.	1036	1136	...	1232	1236	1330	1336	1433	1436	1533	1536	1636	...	1736	...	...	1836	1924	1936	2027	2036	...	2143	2206	2235	...
Crewe 150 ♥ a.	|	|	...	1252	|	1350	|	1454	|	1552	|	|	...	|	...	...	|	1945	|	2048	|	...	|	|	2259	...
Warrington Bank Quay a.	1103	1203	...	...	1303	...	1403	...	1503	...	1603	1703	...	1803	...	...	1903	...	2003	...	2103	...	2210	2233	...	...
Manchester Piccadilly a.	1137	1240	...	...	1340	...	1441	...	1540	...	1636	1738	...	1840	...	...	1940	...	2040	...	2140	...	2245	2305	...	...
Manchester Airport a.	...	...	...	...	...	...	...	...	...	...	...	...	...	...	...	...	...	...	...	...	...	...	...	...	...	...

LLANDUDNO - BLAENAU FFESTINIOG

km		⚒	⚒	Ⓐ	⑥	⚒	Ⓐ	⑥	⑥	Ⓐ	
0	**Llandudno** d.	...	*0708*	1008	1022	1308	1620	1620	1903	1905	...
5	**Llandudno** Junction d.	0530	0726	1028	1034	1330	1633	1633	1918	1920	...
18	Llanrwst d.	0548	0749	1050	1056	1352	1655	1655	1942	1942	...
24	Betws y Coed d.	0554	0755	1056	1102	1358	1701	1701	1948	1948	...
44	**Blaenau Ffestiniog** d.	0624	0829	1130	1136	1432	1732	1735	2020	2020	...

	⚒	Ⓐ	⑥	⚒	Ⓐ	⑥	Ⓐ	⑥	⚒
Blaenau Ffestiniog d.	0624	0835	0846	1135	1457	1457	1736	1737	2023
Betws y Coed d.	0650	0902	0913	1202	1524	1524	1803	1804	2050
Llanrwst d.	0656	0908	0919	1208	1530	1530	1809	1810	2056
Llandudno Junction a.	0720	0933	0944	1233	1557	1559	1834	1835	2121
Llandudno a.	*0741*	0956	1013	1245	1617	1613	1853	1853	2144

A – To / from London Euston (Table **150**).
B – To / from Birmingham New Street (Table **145** or **150**).
C – To / from Cardiff Central (Tables **145** and **149**).
D – To / from Shrewsbury (Table **145**).
E – (FR Pink service) Apr. 3, 4, 10, 11, 15 – 18, 22 – 25, 29, May 6 – 9, 13 – 16, 20, 23, 27, June 6, 10, 13, 17, 20, 24, 27, Sept. 19, 23, 26, 30, Oct. 2, 3, 7 – 10, 14 – 17, 21, 28 – 30.
F – (FR Blue service) Apr. 1, 2, 5 – 9, 12 – 14, 19 – 21, 26 – 28, 30, May 1 – 5, 10 – 12, 17 – 19, 21, 22, 24 – 26, 28 – 31, June 1 – 5, 7 – 9, 11, 12, 14 – 16, 18, 19, 21 – 23, 25, 26, 28 – 30, July 1 - Sept. 18, Sept. 20 – 22, 24, 25, 27 – 29, Oct. 1, 4 – 6, 11 – 13, 18 – 20, 22 – 28.
G – (WHR Blue service) Apr. 1 – 7, 9 – 14, 16, 17, 19 – 21, 23, 24, 26 – 28, May 3 – 5, 7, 8, 10 – 12, 15, 17 – 19, 22 – 29, June 3 – 9, 11 – 13, 18 – 20, 25 – 27, July 1 – 4, 8 – 10, 15 – 18, 22 – 25, 29 – 31, Sept. 2 – 5, 9 – 29, Oct. 1, 2, 4 – 6, 8, 9, 11 – 13, 16, 18 – 20, 22 – 29.
H – (WHR Yellow service) Apr. 30, May 1, 2, 20, 21, 30, 31, June 1, 25, 14 – 16, 21 – 23, 28 – 30, July 5 – 7, 12 – 14, 19 – 21, 26 – 28, Aug. 1 – 31, Sept. 1, 6, 7, 8.
K – From Birmingham International (Table **145**).

W – To / from Wolverhampton (Table **145**).

b – Runs 15 minutes later on certain dates.
c – Arrives 20 minutes earlier.
d – May 21 - Sept. 10.
e – From Sept. 17.
g – May 15 - Sept. 11.
h – From Sept. 18.

* – Connection by 🚌.
‡ – For full service Llandudno - Llandudno Junction and v.v. see next page.
♥ – For full service Chester - Crewe and v.v. see next page.
△ – Operator: Ffestiniog Railway and Welsh Highland Railways. www.festrail.co.uk. Ffestiniog Railway ✆ 01766 516024. Welsh Highland Railway ✆ 01286 677018

VT 2nd class — MANCHESTER - CHESTER - HOLYHEAD — 160

Ⓐ	① K	②–⑤ B	Ⓐ B	Ⓐ	Ⓐ	Ⓐ	Ⓐ C	Ⓐ	Ⓐ B	Ⓐ	Ⓐ	Ⓐ A	Ⓐ C	Ⓐ	Ⓐ A	Ⓐ B	Ⓐ	Ⓐ C	Ⓐ	Ⓐ B	Ⓐ	Ⓐ C	Ⓐ	Ⓐ B	Ⓐ
hester Airport d.	...	...	...	0533	...	...	...	...	...	...	...	...	...	...	...	...	1036	...	1136	...	1236	...	1336	...	1436
hester Piccadilly d.	...	...	...	0548	...	0650	...	0750	...	0850	0850	...	...	0950	...	...	1052	...	1152	...	1252	...	1352	...	1452
gton Bank Quay d.	...	...	...	0621	...	0725	...	0824	...	0926	0926	...	...	1027	...	...	1126	...	1227	...	1326	...	1426	...	1526
we 150 ♥ d.	0001	0015	0623	|	0654	|	...	|	...	|	|	0953	...	|	1049	...	|	...	|	...	|	...	|	...	|
er 150 ♥ a.	0022	0037	0643	0649	0717	0752	...	0853	...	0953	0953	1013	...	1058	1113	...	1153	...	1255	...	1353	...	1454	...	1553
er d.	0038	0040	0644	0655	0719	0755	0822	0855	0923	0958	1002	1016	1024	1100	1116	1125	1155	1224	1256	1324	1355	1424	1455	1525	1555
d.	0051	0053	0657	0708	0734	0810	0838	0908	0938	|	1018	1029	1039	|	|	1138	1210	1237	1311	1337	1410	1437	1510	1538	1610
atyn d.	0104	0106	0710	0721	0747	0823	0852	0921	0951	|	1031	1042	1053	1124	|	1151	1223	1250	1325	1350	1423	1450	1524	1552	1623
d.	0110	0112	0716	0727	0753	0829	0858	0927	0957	|	1037	1048	1059	1131	1143	1157	1229	1256	1331	1356	1429	1456	1530	1558	1629
n Bay d.	0121	0123	0727	0738	0807	0843	0912	0938	1011	|	1051	1059	1109	|	1154	1211	1243	1307	1345	1407	1443	1507	1544	1608	1643
dno Junction ‡ d.	0128	0129	0733	0744	0816	0851	0918	0944	1018	1036	1058	1106	1116	1146	1201	1218	1248	1313	1351	1413	1450	1513	1550	1620	1650
ndudno ‡ a.	|	|	|	0756	|	...	0926	|	1030	|	1109	|	|	|	|	|	...	|	1403	|	1502	|	1602	|	1702
or d.	0144	0146	0750	...	0838	...	...	1008	...	1053	...	1125	1139	1202	1217	1236	...	1331	...	1437	...	1531	...	1644	...
ead ▽ a.	0220	0215	0823	...	0922	...	...	1036	...	1122	...	1158	1222	1239	1250	1317	...	1414	...	1508	...	1614	...	1716	...

	Ⓐ C	Ⓐ	Ⓐ B	Ⓐ	Ⓐ A	Ⓐ C	Ⓐ	Ⓐ	Ⓐ A	Ⓐ B	Ⓐ	Ⓐ C✕	Ⓐ A	Ⓐ	Ⓐ	Ⓐ A	Ⓐ	Ⓐ	Ⓐ	Ⓐ C	Ⓐ	Ⓐ	⑥	⑥ B	⑥ B	⑥
hester Airport d.	...	1536	...	...	...	...	...	...	...	...	...	...	...	...	...	...	2032	...	2132	...	...	...		...	...	0533
hester Piccadilly d.	...	1552	...	1650	...	...	1719	1750	...	...	1850	...	...	...	1950	...	2050	...	2150	...	2212	2314		...	...	0548
gton Bank Quay d.	...	1626	...	1728	...	...	1752	1824	...	...	1922	...	...	...	2026	...	2126	...	2224	...	2257	2348		...	...	0621
we 150 ♥ d.	...	|	...	|	1749	...	|	|	1857	...	|	...	1956	...	|	2055	|	2136	|	...	|	|		0015	0623	|
er 150 ♥ a.	...	1654	...	1801	1808	...	1822	1853	1916	...	1950	...	2015	...	2053	2120	2155	2158	2251	...	2325	0015		0037	0643	0649
er d.	1627	1655	1725	1803	1810	1824	...	1855	1923	1932	...	2006	2026	2034	...	2124	...	2204	...	2256	...	...		0040	0644	0655
d.	1640	1710	1740	|	1823	1839	...	1910	1936	1947	...	2018	|	2049	...	2137	...	2219	...	2311	...	...		0053	0657	0710
atyn d.	1654	1723	1753	1826	1836	1853	...	1923	1949	2000	...	|	|	2102	...	2150	...	2232	...	2324	...	...		0106	0710	0723
d.	1700	1729	1759	1833	1842	1859	...	1929	1955	2006	...	2035	2053	2108	...	2157	...	2238	...	2330	...	...		0112	0716	0729
n Bay d.	1710	1743	1813	1845	1853	1913	...	1940	2006	2020	...	2047	2104	2122	...	2208	...	2252	...	2344	...	...		0123	0727	0743
dno Junction ‡ d.	1716	1750	1825	1852	1900	1919	...	1950	2013	2030	...	2054	2110	2129	...	2214	...	2259	...	2352	...	...		0129	0733	0750
ndudno ‡ a.	|	1802	|	1904	|	|	...	|	|	2042	...	|	|	|	...	|	...	|	...	|	...	...		|	|	0802
or d.	1739	...	1847	...	1921	1935	...	2015	2029	...	...	2111	2127	2152	...	2231	...	2322	...	0014	...	...		0146	0750	...
ead ▽ a.	1821	...	1917	...	...	2020	...	2042	2059	...	...	2145	2159	2235	...	2303	...	0005	...	0048	...	...		0215	0823	...

	⑥	⑥	⑥ C	⑥	⑥ B	⑥	⑥ C	⑥	⑥ A	⑥ B	⑥	⑥	⑥ C	⑥	⑥ B	⑥	⑥ C	⑥	⑥ B	⑥	⑥ A	⑥ C	⑥	⑥ B	⑥	⑥ A
hester Airport d.	...	...	...	...	...	...	...	0936	...	...	1036	...	...	1136	...	1236	...	1336	...	1436	...	...	1536	...	1636	...
hester Piccadilly d.	...	0650	...	0750	...	0850	...	0952	...	...	1052	...	...	1152	...	1252	...	1352	...	1452	...	...	1552	...	1652	...
gton Bank Quay d.	...	0723	...	0825	...	0926	...	1026	...	...	1126	...	...	1227	...	1326	...	1426	...	1527	...	...	1626	...	1726	...
we 150 ♥ d.	0703	|	...	|	...	|	...	|	1049	...	|	...	...	|	...	|	...	|	...	|	1549	...	|	...	|	1750
er 150 ♥ a.	0723	0750	...	0854	...	0953	...	1053	1113	...	1153	...	...	1255	...	1353	...	1453	...	1554	1610	...	1654	...	1753	1810
er d.	0725	0755	0822	0856	0924	0955	1023	1055	1116	1124	1155	...	1223	1256	1322	1355	1423	1455	1522	1556	1612	1627	1655	1724	1755	1816
d.	0739	0810	0836	0911	0937	1010	1036	1110	|	1139	1210	...	1236	1311	1336	1410	1436	1510	1537	1611	1625	1642	1710	1739	1810	1829
atyn d.	0752	0823	0849	0924	0950	1023	1050	1123	|	1152	1223	...	1250	1325	1349	1423	1450	1523	1550	1624	1638	1655	1724	1752	1823	1842
d.	0758	0829	0855	0930	0956	1029	1056	1129	1143	1158	1229	...	1257	1331	1355	1429	1457	1529	1556	1630	1645	1701	1730	1758	1829	1849
n Bay d.	0809	0843	0906	0944	1007	1043	1106	1143	1154	1209	1243	...	1309	1345	1406	1443	1509	1543	1607	1644	1656	1712	1744	1812	1843	1900
dno Junction ‡ d.	0815	0850	0912	0951	1013	1050	1113	1150	1201	1215	1250	1257	1315	1351	1412	1450	1515	1550	1614	1651	1702	1717	1750	1819	1850	1906
ndudno ‡ a.	|	0902	|	1003	|	1102	|	1202	|	|	|	1307	|	1403	|	1502	|	1602	|	1702	|	|	1803	|	1902	|
or d.	0838	...	0936	...	1031	...	1136	...	1217	1233	1315	...	1333	...	1436	...	1532	...	1637	...	1719	1741	...	1843	...	1923
ead ▽ a.	0921	...	1014	...	1105	...	1209	...	1250	1312	...	...	1413	...	1508	...	1613	...	1711	...	1751	1819	...	1913	...	1955

	⑥ C	⑥	⑥ A	⑥ B	⑥	⑥ C	⑥	⑥	⑥	⑥ C	⑥ 🚌	⑥	⑥	⑥	⑦	⑦ g	⑦ g	⑦ 🚌	⑦	⑦	⑦ A	⑦	⑦	⑦	⑦	⑦
hester Airport d.	...	1736	...	...	1836	...	...	...	2032	...	...	...	...	...		...	...	...	...	...	...	...	...	...	...	...
hester Piccadilly d.	...	1752	...	...	1852	...	1951	...	2050	...	...	2151	2226	2314		...	...	0728	...	0956	...	...	1052	1156	...	1256
gton Bank Quay d.	...	1826	...	...	1926	...	2030	...	|	...	...	2224	2256	2348		...	...	0838	...	1028	...	...	1126	1227	...	1329
we 150 ♥ d.	...	|	1852	...	|	...	|	2100	2128	...	...	|	|	|		...	0827	|	0924	|	1042	1127	|	|	1227	|
er 150 ♥ a.	...	1853	1912	...	1954	...	2057	2121	2158	...	...	2254	2325	0015		...	0849	0938	0947	1059	1102	1150	1154	1255	1252	1358
er d.	1824	1855	1918	1932	...	2032	...	2126	...	2236	...	...	...	...		0620	0900	...	0948	...	1107	1203	...	...	1302	...
d.	1839	1910	1931	1947	...	2047	...	2141	...	2251	...	...	...	...		0633	0913	...	1003	...	|	1218	...	...	1317	...
atyn d.	1852	1923	1945	2000	...	2100	...	2154	...	2305	...	...	...	...		0647	0926	...	1017	...	1130	1231	...	...	1330	...
d.	1858	1929	1951	2006	...	2106	...	2200	...	2311	...	...	...	...		0653	0932	...	1023	...	1137	1237	...	...	1336	...
n Bay d.	1909	1943	2002	2020	...	2119	...	2214	...	2325	...	...	...	...		0703	0943	...	1037	...	1148	1248	...	...	1350	...
dno Junction ‡ d.	1915	1950	2009	2027	...	2126	...	2221	...	2338	2348	...	...	...		0710	0954	...	1043	...	1154	1254	...	...	1357	...
ndudno ‡ a.	|	2002	|	|	...	|	...	|	...	...	|	...	...	...		|	|	...	|	...	|	|	...	...	|	...
or d.	1933	...	2025	2048	...	2143	...	2245	...	...	0013	...	...	...		0726	1012	...	1106	...	1211	1311	...	...	1419	...
ead ▽ a.	2018	...	2058	2131	...	2225	...	2318	...	...	0048	...	...	...		0800	1048	...	1149	...	1240	1342	...	...	1453	...

	⑦	⑦	⑦	⑦	⑦	⑦ C	⑦	⑦	⑦	⑦ g	⑦ h	⑦ C	⑦	⑦	⑦ A	⑦ B	⑦	⑦ A	⑦	⑦ A	⑦	⑦	⑦	⑦	⑦	⑦
hester Airport d.	...	...	...	...	...	...	...	...	...	...	...	...	...	...	...	...	...	...	...	...	...	...	...	...	...	...
hester Piccadilly d.	...	1356	...	1456	...	...	1556	...	1656	...	...	...	...	1756	...	...	1856	...	1956	...	2056	...	2156	...	2256	2325
gton Bank Quay d.	...	1427	...	1528	...	...	1627	...	1727	...	...	...	...	1827	...	...	1930	...	2031	...	2128	...	2226	...	2330	2354
we 150 ♥ d.	1327	|	1427	|	1527	...	|	1627	|	1727	1727	...	1827	|	1901	...	|	1952	|	2055	|	2128	|	2229	|	|
er 150 ♥ a.	1351	1455	1451	1556	1549	...	1655	1649	1755	1750	1749	...	1849	1855	1919	...	1958	2013	2059	2113	2156	2151	2254	2252	2357	0024
er d.	1402	...	1502	...	1602	1636	...	1702	...	...	1802	1829	1852	...	1929	1938	...	2018	...	2117	...	2200	...	2300	...	...
d.	1417	...	1517	...	1617	1651	...	1717	...	...	1817	1844	1907	...	1942	1953	...	2031	...	2130	...	2215	...	2315	...	...
atyn d.	1430	...	1530	...	1630	1704	...	1730	...	...	1830	1857	1921	...	1955	2006	...	2044	...	2143	...	2228	...	2328	...	...
d.	1436	...	1536	...	1636	1710	...	1736	...	...	1836	1903	1927	...	2002	2012	...	2051	...	2150	...	2234	...	2334	...	...
n Bay d.	1450	...	1550	...	1650	1724	...	1750	...	...	1850	1917	1941	...	2013	2026	...	2102	...	2201	...	2248	...	2345	...	...
dno Junction ‡ d.	1457	...	1557	...	1657	1731	...	1757	...	...	1857	1924	1947	...	2019	2033	...	2108	...	2207	...	2255	...	2351	...	...
ndudno ‡ a.	|	...	|	...	|	|	...	|	...	...	|	|	|	...	|	|	...	|	...	|	...	|	...	|	...	...
or d.	1514	...	1619	...	1714	1754	...	1819	...	...	1914	1948	2009	...	2036	2055	...	2125	...	2224	...	2312	...	0014	...	...
ead ▽ a.	1555	...	1653	...	1757	1837	...	1854	...	...	1954	2018	2044	...	2103	2130	...	2154	...	2253	...	2355	...	0049	...	...

CAERNARFON - PORTHMADOG - BLAENAU FFESTINIOG

	🚂 H△	🚂 G△	🚂 EF△	🚂 H△		🚂 G△	🚂 F△	🚂 H△	🚂 EF△	🚂 F△
Blaenau Ffestiniog d.	...	...	1145	...	...	...	1340	...	1505**b**	1720
Minffordd d.	...	...	1240	...	...	...	1450	...	1555**b**	1810
Porthmadog Harbour d.	0940	1045	1255	1300	...	1405	1450	1540	1610**b**	1825
Beddgelert d.	1030	1125	...	1335	...	1445	...	1620	...	...
Rhyd Ddu d.	1055	1155	...	1410	...	1515	...	1645	...	...
Waunfawr d.	1125	1220	...	1440	...	1540	...	1720	...	...
Caernarfon a.	1205	1305	...	1520	...	1620	...	1755	...	...

	🚂 EF△	🚂 F△	🚂 GH△	🚂 EF△		🚂 H△	🚂 F△	🚂 G△	🚂 H△	
Caernarfon d.	...	...	1000	...	...	1310	...	1415	1545	...
Waunfawr d.	...	...	1025	...	...	1340	...	1445	1615	...
Rhyd Ddu d.	...	...	1055	...	...	1410	...	1515	1645	...
Beddgelert d.	...	...	1125	...	...	1435	...	1540	1715	...
Porthmadog Harbour d.	1010	1130	1210	1335	...	1525	1545	1630	1800	...
Minffordd d.	1020	1140	...	1345	...	...	1555	...	...	...
Blaenau Ffestiniog d.	1125	1245	...	1445	...	...	1700	...	...	...

All trains **Chester** - **Crewe**. Journey time ± 23 minutes:
: 0422, 0455, 0537, 0551, 0626Ⓐ, 0635⑥, 0645Ⓐ, 0717⑥, 0735Ⓐ, 0755, 0835, 0855, , 0935, 0955, 1035, 1055 and at the same minutes past each hour until 1535, 1555, , 1655, 1735, 1755, 1855, 1935Ⓐ, 1935⑥**d**, 1955, 2018, 2035⑥, 2046Ⓐ, 2055, 2135Ⓐ, Ⓐ, 2226⑥, 2301. On ⑦: 0756**g**, 0827**g**, 0840**h**, 0857**g**, 0927**g**, 0942**h**, 0957**g**, 1039, **g**, 1128, 1157**g**, 1221, 1232, 1257**g**, 1320**h**, 1330, 1357**g**, 1423**h**, 1433, 1457**g**, 1533, **g**, 1627, 1657**g**, 1722**h**, 1735**h**, 1759**g**, 1835, 1859, 1924, 1935, 1950**h**, 1957**g**, 2027, , 2050**h**, 2057**g**, 2127**g**, 2135**h**, 2150**h**, 2157**g**, 2235, 2300.

All trains **Llandudno Junction** - **Llandudno**. Journey time ± 10 minutes:
: 0540Ⓐ, 0613, 0651, 0731, 0744Ⓐ, 0750⑥, 0817Ⓐ, 0828⑥, 0850⑥, 0918Ⓐ, ⑥, 0948, 1003⑥, 1018Ⓐ, 1028⑥, 1050⑥, 1058Ⓐ, 1126, 1150⑥, 1224⑥, 1235, 1257, , 1428, 1450, 1530⑥, 1550, 1603, 1626⑥, 1650, 1728⑥, 1750, 1826, 1841, 1850, ⑥, 1950⑥, 1955Ⓐ, 2030, 2058Ⓐ, 2132. On ⑦**g**: 1000, 1050, 1125, 1200, 1242, 1258, , 1402, 1500, 1530, 1604, 1639, 1705, 1740, 1831.

♥ – All trains **Crewe** - **Chester**. Journey time ± 23 minutes:
On ⚒: 0001①, 0007②–⑥, 0010① 0015②–⑥, 0623, 0654Ⓐ, 0703⑥, 0711Ⓐ, 0723⑥, 0823, 0849Ⓐ, 0923, 0940Ⓐ, 0949, 1023, 1049 and at the same minutes past each hour until 1823, 1845Ⓐ, 1852⑥, 1857Ⓐ, 1923, 1949⑥, 1956Ⓐ, 2023, 2048Ⓐ, 2055Ⓐ, 2100⑥, 2136, 2149Ⓐ, 2223, 2321⑥, 2330Ⓐ, 2357⑥. On ⑦: 0827**g**, 0924, 0957**g**, 1007**h**, 1042, 1057**g**, 1105**h**, 1127, 1155, 1227, 1254, 1327, 1357**g**, 1427, 1457, 1527, 1557**g**, 1627, 1652, 1727, 1752, 1827, 1901, 1924, 1952, 2027, 2055, 2128, 2157**g**, 2203**h**, 2229, 2306, 2338.

‡ – All trains **Llandudno** - **Llandudno Junction**. Journey time ± 10 minutes:
On ⚒: 0554Ⓐ, 0634⑥, 0646Ⓐ, 0708, 0745, 0802Ⓐ, 0808⑥, 0830Ⓐ, 0845⑥, 0908⑥, 0945, 1008, 1022⑥, 1044, 1108⑥, 1112Ⓐ, 1144, 1208⑥, 1236⑥, 1246, 1308, 1408, 1440Ⓐ, 1442⑥, 1508, 1544⑥, 1607, 1620, 1644⑥, 1705Ⓐ, 1708⑥, 1744⑥, 1808, 1844, 1903⑥, 1905Ⓐ, 1913⑥, 1934Ⓐ, 1942⑥, 2008, 2043⚒, 2111Ⓐ, 2145. On ⑦**g**: 1022, 1107, 1140, 1218, 1319, 1330, 1350, 1420, 1511, 1544, 1616, 1652, 1720, 1805, 1855.

FOR OTHER NOTES SEE PREVIOUS PAGE

GREAT BRITAIN

161 Sleeper trains LONDON - SCOTLAND

All trains in this table convey 🛏 1, 2 cl., 2 (reservation compulsory) ✕ and 🍷.

km		⑦ b	⑦ c	Ⓐ		⑦ b	⑦ c	Ⓐ		
0	**London** Euston **150** d.	2028	2057	2115	...	2139	2328	2350	...	...
28	Watford Junction **150** d.	|	2117u	2133u	...	|	2349u	0010u	...	...
254	Crewe **150 151** d.	|	2336u	2356u	...	|	|	|	...	...
336	Preston **151** d.	|	0035u	0100u	...	|	|	|	...	...
481	Carlisle **151** a.	|	|	|	...	|	0441s	0518s	...	...
625	Motherwell a.	|	|	|	...	0726	0652s	0655s	...	...
646	**Glasgow** Central **151** ◧ a.	|	|	|	...	0759	0720	0720	...	...
646	**Edinburgh** Waverley **151** ◧ a.	|	|	|	...	0540	0721	0721	...	...
	Dundee **224** a.	0611s	0611s	0611s	...	...	...	...	...	...
	Aberdeen **224** ◧ a.	0739	0739	0739	...	...	...	...	...	...
	Perth **221** a.	0539s	0539s	0539s	...	...	...	...	...	...
	Inverness **221** a.	0838	0838	0838	...	...	...	...	...	...
	Fort William **218** a.	0955	0955	0955	...	...	...	...	...	...

	⑦ b	⑦ c	①–④	⑤			Ⓐ	⑦ c
Fort William **218** d.	...	...	...	...	...	...	1950	1900
Inverness **221** d.	...	...	...	...	...	...	2044	2026
Perth **221** d.	...	...	...	...	...	...	2330u	2309u
Aberdeen **224** d.	...	...	...	...	...	...	2143	2143
Dundee **224** d.	...	...	...	...	...	...	2306u	2306u
Edinburgh Waverley **151** d.	2321	2315	2340	2340	...	...	|	|
Glasgow Central **151** d.	2144	2315	2340	2340	...	...	|	|
Motherwell d.	2204u	2330u	0001u	0001u	...	...	|	|
Carlisle **151** d.	|	0144u	0146u	0147u	...	...	|	|
Preston **151** a.	|	|	|	|	...	...	0436s	0444s
Crewe **150 151** a.	|	|	|	|	...	...	0536s	0538s
Watford Junction **150** a.	|	0643s	0643s	0639s	...	...	|	|
London Euston **150** ◧ a.	0746	0707	0707	0707	...	...	0747	0747

b – May 15 - June 19.
c – From June 26.
s – Calls to set down only.
u – Calls to pick up only.
◧ – Sleeping-car passengers may occupy their cabins until 0800 following arrival at these stat

162 PRESTON - LIVERPOOL

2nd class

km		⚒	⑥	Ⓐ	⚒	⚒		⚒	⚒	⚒	⚒	⚒	⚒	⚒	⑦	⑦	⑦		⑦	⑦
0	**Preston** d.	0730	0830	0830	0930	1030	and	1630	1730	1830	1930	2030	2140	2242	...	0925	1025	and	2125	2225
24	Wigan North Western d.	0750	0850	0851	0950	1050	hourly	1650	1750	1850	1950	2050	2202	2304	0847	0946	1046	hourly	2146	2247
38	St Helens Central d.	0807	0905	0907	1006	1106	until	1706	1806	1906	2006	2106	2220	2323	0903	1003	1103	until	2203	2304
57	**Liverpool** Lime Street a.	0836	0927	0932	1032	1129	★	1731	1828	1928	2028	2128	2253	2354	0934	1034	1134	★	2234	2335

	⚒	⚒	⚒	⚒		⚒	⚒	⚒	⚒	⚒	⚒	⚒	⚒	⑦	⑦	⑦		⑦	⑦
Liverpool Lime Street d.	0657	0757	0828	0928	and	1628	1716	1732	1800	1930	2028	2147	2302	0847	0947	1047	and	2047	2147
St Helens Central d.	0717	0815	0849	0949	hourly	1649	1744	1801	1829	1949	2049	2216	2331	0914	1014	1114	hourly	2114	2214
Wigan North Western d.	0731	0831	0903	1003	until	1703	1803	1820	1851	2003	2103	2234	2348	0930	1030	1130	until	2131	2230
Preston a.	0756	0858	0926	1026	★	1726	1830	1851	1916	2026	2131	2302	0013	0953	1053	1153	★	2155	2253

★ – Timings may vary by up to 3 minutes.

163 MANCHESTER and LIVERPOOL local services

2nd class ME

MANCHESTER - CLITHEROE

Journey time: ± 77–85 minutes *57 km*

From Manchester Victoria:

Ⓐ: Trains call at Bolton ± 25 and Blackburn ± 55 minutes later: 0555, 0700, 0752**p**, 0903, 1003, 1103, 1203, 1303, 1403, 1503, 1603, 1635, 1703, 1803, 1903, 2003, 2103, 2203.

⑥: Trains call at Bolton ± 20 and Blackburn ± 52 minutes later: 0555, 0700, 0752**p**, 0903, 1003, 1103, 1203, 1303, 1403, 1503, 1603, 1635, 1703, 1803, 1903, 2003, 2103, 2203.

⑦: Trains call at Bolton ± 18 and Blackburn ± 50 minutes later: 0803**z**, 0903 and hourly until 2103.

From Clitheroe:

Ⓐ: Trains call at Blackburn ± 23 and Bolton ± 54 minutes later: 0645, 0705, 0745, 0946, 1046, 1146, 1245, 1346, 1446, 1528, 1646, 1745, 1810, 1846, 1946, 2045, 2244⑤.

⑥: Trains call at Blackburn ± 24 and Bolton ± 51 minutes later: 0705, 0745, 0825, 1046, 1146, 1245, 1346, 1446, 1528, 1645, 1745, 1803, 1845, 1946, 2045, 2144,

⑦: Trains call at Blackburn ± 24 and Bolton ± 53 minutes later: 0944 and hourly u 2144.

MANCHESTER - BUXTON

Journey time: ± 60–70 minutes *41 km*

From Manchester Piccadilly:

Trains call at Stockport ± 11, Hazel Grove ± 22 and New Mills Newtown ± 31 minutes later.

Ⓐ: 0649, 0749, 0849, 0949, 1049, 1149, 1249, 1349, 1449, 1549, 1621, 1649, 1721, 1749, 1821, 1849, 1949, 2049, 2149, 2310.

⑥: 0649, 0749, 0849, and hourly until 1649, 1721, 1749, 1849, 1949, 2049, 2154, 2310.

⑦: 0856, 0950, 1051, 1149 and hourly until 1949, 2049, 2149, 2249.

From Buxton:

Trains call at New Mills Newtown ± 21, Hazel Grove ± 34 and at Stockport ± 46 minutes

Ⓐ: 0559, 0621, 0648, 0719, 0744, 0822, 0927, 1024, 1124, 1224, 1324, 1424 1524, 1657, 1729, 1757, 1824, 1928, 2024, 2126, 2252.

⑥: 0558, 0622, 0723, 0757, 0821, 0925, 1024 and hourly until 1926, 2024, 2127, 2

⑦: 0818, 0915, 1022, 1122 and hourly until 1922, 2022, 2124, 2222.

MANCHESTER - NORTHWICH - CHESTER

Journey time: ± 90–95 minutes *73 km*

From Manchester Piccadilly:

Trains call at Stockport ± 13, Altrincham ± 28 and Northwich ± 55 minutes later.

⚒: 0618, 0717, 0817, 0917, 1017, 1117, 1217, 1317, 1417, 1517, 1617, 1709Ⓐ, 1717⑥, 1817, 1917, 2017, 2117⑥, 2121Ⓐ, 2217, 2314⑥, 2317Ⓐ.

⑦: 0922, 1122, 1322, 1522, 1722, 1922, 2122.

From Chester:

Trains call at Northwich ± 30, Altrincham ± 55 and Stockport ± 74 minutes later.

⚒: 0600, 0658, 0802, 0857, 0957, 1057, 1179, 1279, 1357, 1459, 1557, 1657, 1804, 2002, 2133, 2248.

⑦: 0903, 1102, 1302, 1502, 1702, 1902, 2102.

MANCHESTER - ST HELENS - LIVERPOOL

Journey time: ± 63 minutes *51 km*

From Manchester Victoria:

Trains call at St Helens Junction ± 30 minutes later.

⚒: 0539, 0602, 0702, 0738, 0802, 0838, 0901 and hourly until 1702, 1738, 1802, 1902, 2002, 2109, 2209, 2309.

⑦: 0859**p**, 1001**p**, 1101**p**, and hourly (note **p** applies to all trains) until 2301**p**.

From Liverpool Lime Street:

Trains call at St Helens Junction ± 28 minutes later.

⚒: 0520, 0620, 0720, 0742, 0820 and hourly until 1620, 1642, 1720, 1739, 1820, 1 2020, 2120, 2220, 2319.

⑦: 0812**p** 0915**p**, and hourly (note **p** applies to all trains) until 2215**p**.

MANCHESTER - WIGAN - SOUTHPORT

Journey time: ± 75 minutes *62 km*

From Manchester Piccadilly:

Trains call at Wigan Wallgate ± 35 minutes later.

Ⓐ: 0641**v**, 0703**v**, 0738**v**, 0810**v**, 0822 and hourly until 1822, 1920, 2020, 2120, 2236.

⑥: 0641**v**, 0703**v**, 0822 and hourly until 1822, 1920, 2020, 2120, 2236.

⑦: 0835, 0935, 1031, 1133, 1231, 1335 and hourly until 2035.

From Southport:

Trains call at Wigan Wallgate ± 30 minutes later.

Ⓐ: 0618, 0649**v**, 0719, 0757**v**, 0820 and hourly until 1620, 1729, 1812, 1917, 2017, 2

⑥: 0618, 0719, 0822, 0920 and hourly until 1620, 1729, 1812, 1917, 2017, 2119**v**, 2

⑦: 0910, 1001 and hourly until 2201.

MANCHESTER AIRPORT - CREWE

Journey time: ± 33 minutes *37 km*

From Manchester Airport:

⚒: 0634, 0730⑥, 0831, 0934, 1034, 1134 and hourly until 1533, 1634, 1733, 1834. Additional later services (and all day on ⑦) available by changing at Wilmslow.

From Crewe:

⚒: 0547, 0711, 0811, 0911 and hourly until 1611, 1711, 1811. Additional later services (and all day on ⑦) available by changing at Wilmslow.

LIVERPOOL - BIRKENHEAD - CHESTER

Journey time: ± 42 minutes *29 km*

From Liverpool Lime Street:

Trains call at Liverpool Central ± 2 minutes and Birkenhead Central ± 9 minutes later.

⚒: 0538, 0608, 0643, 0713, 0743, 0755Ⓐ, 0813, 0820Ⓐ, 0843, 0858⑥, 0913, 0928, 0943, 0958 and every 15 minutes until 1858, 1913 and every 30 minutes until 2343.

⑦: 0813, 0843 and every 30 minutes until 2313, 2343.

From Chester:

Trains call at Birkenhead Central ± 33 minutes and Liverpool Central ± 44* minutes l

⚒: 0555, 0630, 0700, 0722Ⓐ, 0730⑥, 0737Ⓐ, 0752Ⓐ, 0800⑥, 0807Ⓐ, 0815⑥, 0845 and every 15 minutes until 1830, 1900 and every 30 minutes until 2300.

⑦: 0800, 0830 and every 30 minutes until 2300.

LIVERPOOL - SOUTHPORT

Journey time: ± 44 minutes *30 km*

From Liverpool Central:

⚒: 0608, 0623, 0638, 0653, 0708 and every 15 minutes until 2308, 2323, 2338.

⑦: 0808, 0823, 0853, 0923, 0953 and every 15 minutes until 2253, 2308, 2338.

From Southport:

⚒: 0538, 0553, 0608, 0623, 0643, 0658, 0713, 0728, 0738Ⓐ, 0743⑥, 0748Ⓐ, 075 0803Ⓐ, 0813 and every 15 minutes until 2258, 2316.

⑦: 0758, 0828, 0858, 0928, 0958 and every 15 minutes until 2258, 2316.

p – Starts/terminates at Manchester **Piccadilly**, not Victoria.
v – Starts/terminates at Manchester **Victoria**, not Piccadilly.
z – From Aug. 7.
* – Trains FROM Chester call at Liverpool Lime Street, then Liverpool Central.

For explanation of standard symbols see page 4

Most trains 🍸

LONDON - LEICESTER - NOTTINGHAM, DERBY and SHEFFIELD

		②–⑥	⚒	Ⓐ	⑥	Ⓐ	⑥S	⚒	Ⓐ	⑥	Ⓐ	⑥	⑥	Ⓐ	⚒	Ⓐ	Ⓐ	⑥	⚒	⚒	⚒	⚒	⚒	ⒶF	⚒
London St Pancras	d.	0015	...	0545	0545	0632	0637	...	0652	0652	0655	0701	...	0724	0729	...	0752	0757	0801	0815	0826	0829	0856	...	0900
Luton ✈ Parkway	d.	0043	...	ǀ	ǀ	ǀ	ǀ	...	0713	0713	ǀ	ǀ	...	ǀ	0749	...	ǀ	ǀ	ǀ	ǀ	ǀ	0849	ǀ	...	ǀ
Luton	d.	0047	...	0612	0612	0654	0659	...	ǀ	ǀ	0718	0722	...	ǀ	ǀ	...	ǀ	ǀ	0822	ǀ	ǀ	ǀ	ǀ	...	0922
Bedford	d.	0111	...	0627	0627	0709	ǀ	...	ǀ	ǀ	0733	0736	...	ǀ	0804	...	ǀ	ǀ	0837	ǀ	ǀ	0904	ǀ	...	0937
Wellingborough	d.	0131	...	0639	0639	0721	ǀ	...	ǀ	ǀ	0746	0748	...	ǀ	0817	...	ǀ	ǀ	0849	ǀ	ǀ	0917	ǀ	...	0949
Kettering	d.	0143	...	0647	0647	0729	0727	0738	ǀ	ǀ	0756	0758	...	ǀ	0823	0832	ǀ	ǀ	0900	ǀ	ǀ	0923	ǀ	...	1000
Corby	a.	ǀ	...	ǀ	ǀ	ǀ	ǀ	0747	ǀ	ǀ	ǀ	ǀ	...	ǀ	ǀ	0841	ǀ	ǀ	0911	ǀ	ǀ	ǀ	ǀ	0926	1011
Market Harborough	d.	0155	...	0657	0657	0739	0737	...	ǀ	ǀ	0807	0808	...	0816	0834	...	ǀ	ǀ	...	0910	ǀ	0934	ǀ	ǀ	...
Leicester	d.	0210	...	0712	0712	0752	0753	...	0758	0800	0823	0823	0830	0830	0848	...	0901	0901	...	0925	0930	0948	1001	ǀ	...
Loughborough	d.	▬	...	0722	0723	0802	0803	...	0808	0809	0834	0833	0840	0840	0858	...	ǀ	ǀ	...	ǀ	0940	0958	ǀ	ǀ	...
E. Midlands Parkway	d.	...	...	0729	ǀ	ǀ	0811	...	0816	ǀ	0842	0841	0848	0848	ǀ	...	ǀ	ǀ	...	0942	0948	ǀ	ǀ	1031	...
Nottingham	a.	⚒	...	ǀ	ǀ	ǀ	ǀ	...	0832	0829	0854	0854	ǀ	ǀ	0918	...	ǀ	ǀ	...	0955	ǀ	1018	ǀ	ǀ	...
Derby	a.	0627	0721	0745	0745	0817	0823	...	...	...	...	...	0903	0903	...	...	0923	0923	...	...	1003	...	1023	1045	...
Chesterfield	d.	0646	0743	0810	0810	0838	0844	...	...	...	...	...	0927	0927	...	...	0943	0943	...	...	1027	...	1043	...	...
Sheffield	a.	0713	0800	0827	0826	0855	0858	...	...	...	...	...	0940	0941	...	...	0958	0958	...	...	1041	...	1100	...	...

		⚒	⚒	⚒	⚒	⚒	⚒	⚒	⚒	⚒	⚒	⚒	⚒	⚒	⚒	⚒	⚒	⚒	⚒	⚒	⚒	⚒	⚒	⚒	⚒	⚒	⚒
London St Pancras	d.	0915	0926	0929	0958	1000	1015	1026	1029	1058	1101	1115	1126	1129	1158	1201	1215	1226	1229	1258	1301	1315	1326	1329	1358	1401	1415
Luton ✈ Parkway	d.	ǀ	ǀ	0949	ǀ	ǀ	ǀ	ǀ	1049	ǀ	ǀ	ǀ	ǀ	1149	ǀ	ǀ	ǀ	ǀ	1249	ǀ	ǀ	ǀ	ǀ	1349	ǀ	ǀ	ǀ
Luton	d.	ǀ	ǀ	ǀ	ǀ	1022	ǀ	ǀ	ǀ	ǀ	1122	ǀ	ǀ	ǀ	ǀ	1222	ǀ	ǀ	ǀ	ǀ	1322	ǀ	ǀ	ǀ	ǀ	1422	ǀ
Bedford	d.	ǀ	ǀ	1004	ǀ	1037	ǀ	ǀ	1104	ǀ	1137	ǀ	ǀ	1204	ǀ	1237	ǀ	ǀ	1304	ǀ	1337	ǀ	ǀ	1404	ǀ	1437	ǀ
Wellingborough	d.	ǀ	ǀ	1017	ǀ	1049	ǀ	ǀ	1117	ǀ	1149	ǀ	ǀ	1217	ǀ	1249	ǀ	ǀ	1317	ǀ	1349	ǀ	ǀ	1417	ǀ	1449	ǀ
Kettering	d.	ǀ	ǀ	1023	ǀ	1100	ǀ	ǀ	1123	ǀ	1200	ǀ	ǀ	1223	ǀ	1300	ǀ	ǀ	1323	ǀ	1400	ǀ	ǀ	1423	ǀ	1500	ǀ
Corby	a.	ǀ	ǀ	ǀ	ǀ	1111	ǀ	ǀ	ǀ	ǀ	1212	ǀ	ǀ	ǀ	ǀ	1311	ǀ	ǀ	ǀ	ǀ	1412	ǀ	ǀ	ǀ	ǀ	1512	ǀ
Market Harborough	d.	1010	ǀ	1034	ǀ	...	1110	ǀ	1134	ǀ	...	1210	ǀ	1234	ǀ	...	1310	ǀ	1334	ǀ	...	1410	ǀ	1434	ǀ	...	1510
Leicester	d.	1025	1030	1048	1101	...	1125	1130	1148	1201	...	1225	1230	1248	1301	...	1325	1330	1348	1401	...	1425	1430	1448	1501	...	1525
Loughborough	d.	ǀ	1040	1058	ǀ	...	ǀ	1140	1158	ǀ	...	ǀ	1240	1258	ǀ	...	ǀ	1340	1358	ǀ	...	ǀ	1440	1458	ǀ	...	ǀ
E. Midlands Parkway	d.	1042	1048	ǀ	ǀ	...	1142	1148	ǀ	ǀ	...	1242	1248	ǀ	ǀ	...	1342	1348	ǀ	ǀ	...	1442	1448	ǀ	ǀ	...	1542
Nottingham	a.	1055	ǀ	1118	ǀ	...	1155	ǀ	1218	ǀ	...	1255	ǀ	1318	ǀ	...	1355	ǀ	1418	ǀ	...	1455	ǀ	1518	ǀ	...	1555
Derby	a.	...	1103	...	1123	...	...	1203	...	1223	...	...	1303	...	1323	...	...	1403	...	1423	...	...	1503	...	1523	...	...
Chesterfield	d.	...	1127	...	1143	...	...	1227	...	1243	...	...	1327	...	1343	...	...	1427	...	1443	...	...	1527	...	1543	...	...
Sheffield	a.	...	1141	...	1159	...	...	1241	...	1259	...	...	1341	...	1402	...	...	1441	...	1500	...	...	1541	...	1559	...	...

		⚒	⚒	⚒	⚒	⚒	⑥	Ⓐ	⚒	⚒	⚒	⚒	⚒	⑥	Ⓐ	⚒	⑥	Ⓐ	Ⓐ	⑥	Ⓐ	⑥	⑥B	Ⓐ	⚒	Ⓐ	⑥
London St Pancras	d.	1426	1429	1458	1501	1515	1526	1526	1529	1558	1601	1615	1626	1629	1629	1657	1701	1700	1700	1715	1715	1726	1729	1730	1757	1745	1801
Luton ✈ Parkway	d.	ǀ	1449	ǀ	ǀ	ǀ	ǀ	ǀ	1549	ǀ	ǀ	ǀ	ǀ	1649	1649	ǀ	ǀ	ǀ	ǀ	ǀ	ǀ	ǀ	1749	ǀ	ǀ	1808	ǀ
Luton	d.	ǀ	ǀ	ǀ	1522	ǀ	ǀ	ǀ	ǀ	ǀ	1622	ǀ	ǀ	ǀ	1653	ǀ	1722	ǀ	ǀ	ǀ	1740	ǀ	ǀ	ǀ	ǀ	ǀ	1822
Bedford	d.	ǀ	1504	ǀ	1537	ǀ	ǀ	ǀ	1604	ǀ	1637	ǀ	ǀ	1704	1707	ǀ	1737	1737	1737	ǀ	ǀ	ǀ	1804	1804	ǀ	ǀ	1837
Wellingborough	d.	ǀ	1517	ǀ	1549	ǀ	ǀ	ǀ	1617	ǀ	1649	ǀ	ǀ	1717	1719	ǀ	1749	1749	1749	ǀ	ǀ	ǀ	1817	1817	ǀ	1832	1849
Kettering	d.	ǀ	1523	ǀ	1600	ǀ	ǀ	ǀ	1623	ǀ	1700	ǀ	ǀ	1723	1726	ǀ	1800	1806	1814	ǀ	ǀ	ǀ	1823	1823	ǀ	1844	1900
Corby	a.	ǀ	ǀ	ǀ	1611	ǀ	ǀ	ǀ	ǀ	ǀ	1711	ǀ	ǀ	ǀ	ǀ	ǀ	1811	1815	ǀ	ǀ	ǀ	ǀ	ǀ	ǀ	ǀ	ǀ	1911
Market Harborough	d.	ǀ	1534	ǀ	...	1610	ǀ	ǀ	1634	ǀ	...	1710	ǀ	1734	1736	ǀ	...	...	ǀ	1810	1816	ǀ	1834	1834	ǀ	1856	...
Leicester	d.	1530	1548	1601	...	1625	1630	1630	1648	1701	...	1725	1730	1748	1751	1801	...	...	1837	1825	1832	1830	1848	1848	1901	1914	...
Loughborough	d.	1540	1558	ǀ	...	ǀ	1640	1640	1658	ǀ	...	ǀ	1740	1758	1801	ǀ	...	...	1847	ǀ	ǀ	1840	1858	1858	ǀ	1926	...
E. Midlands Parkway	d.	1548	ǀ	ǀ	...	1642	1648	1648	ǀ	ǀ	...	1742	1748	ǀ	ǀ	ǀ	...	...	1856	1842	1850	1848	ǀ	1905	ǀ	1934	...
Nottingham	a.	ǀ	1618	ǀ	...	1655	ǀ	ǀ	1718	ǀ	...	1755	ǀ	1818	1821	ǀ	...	...	ǀ	1855	1909	ǀ	1918	1920	ǀ	1947	...
Derby	a.	1603	...	1623	...	...	1703	1703	...	1723	...	...	1803	...	...	1823	...	...	1913	...	...	1903	...	...	1923	2031	...
Chesterfield	d.	1627	...	1643	...	...	1727	1734	...	1743	...	...	1827	...	...	1843	...	...	1934	...	...	1927	...	...	1943	...	...
Sheffield	a.	1641	...	1659	...	...	1741	1748	...	1800	...	...	1841	...	...	1900	...	...	1950	...	...	1941	...	...	1959	...	...

		ⒶC	⑥	Ⓐ	⑥L	ⒶL	⑥	ⒶB	⑥	Ⓐ	⑥	Ⓐ	⚒	⑥	Ⓐ	⑥	ⒶL	⑥L	ⒶL	Ⓐ	⑥	⚒	⚒	Ⓐ	⑥	⑥	Ⓐ
London St Pancras	d.	1800	1826	1825	1815	1815	1829	1830	1858	1857	1901	1900	1915	1926	1928	1929	1955	1958	1932	2000	2001	2015	2026	2030	2030	2056	2055
Luton ✈ Parkway	d.	ǀ	ǀ	ǀ	ǀ	ǀ	1849	1850	ǀ	ǀ	ǀ	ǀ	ǀ	ǀ	ǀ	1949	ǀ	ǀ	1953	ǀ	ǀ	ǀ	ǀ	2049	2050	ǀ	ǀ
Luton	d.	1822	ǀ	1850	ǀ	ǀ	ǀ	ǀ	ǀ	ǀ	1922	1924	ǀ	ǀ	ǀ	ǀ	ǀ	ǀ	ǀ	2022	2025	ǀ	ǀ	ǀ	ǀ	ǀ	ǀ
Bedford	d.	1837	ǀ	ǀ	ǀ	ǀ	1904	1907	ǀ	ǀ	1937	1940	ǀ	ǀ	ǀ	2004	ǀ	ǀ	2009	2037	2039	ǀ	ǀ	2104	2104	ǀ	ǀ
Wellingborough	d.	1849	ǀ	ǀ	ǀ	1903	1917	1920	ǀ	ǀ	1949	1954	ǀ	ǀ	ǀ	2017	ǀ	ǀ	2022	2049	2051	ǀ	ǀ	2118	2117	ǀ	ǀ
Kettering	d.	1906	ǀ	ǀ	ǀ	1911	1923	1926	ǀ	ǀ	2000	2006	ǀ	ǀ	2019	2023	ǀ	ǀ	ǀ	2101	2100	ǀ	ǀ	2123	2124	ǀ	ǀ
Corby	a.	1916	ǀ	ǀ	ǀ	ǀ	ǀ	ǀ	ǀ	ǀ	2011	2017	ǀ	ǀ	ǀ	ǀ	ǀ	ǀ	ǀ	2112	2111	ǀ	ǀ	ǀ	ǀ	ǀ	ǀ
Market Harborough	d.	...	ǀ	1927	1910	ǀ	1934	ǀ	ǀ	1949	...	...	2010	ǀ	2029	2034	ǀ	ǀ	2038	...	...	2109	ǀ	2134	2134	ǀ	ǀ
Leicester	d.	...	1930	1942	1925	1934	1948	1952	2001	2002	...	...	2025	2030	2045	2048	2102	2105	2053	...	...	2122	2130	2148	2148	2201	2201
Loughborough	d.	...	1940	1953	ǀ	1945	1958	ǀ	ǀ	2013	...	...	ǀ	2040	2055	2058	ǀ	ǀ	2103	...	...	ǀ	2140	2158	2158	ǀ	ǀ
E. Midlands Parkway	d.	...	1948	ǀ	1942	1954	ǀ	2009	ǀ	2021	...	...	2038	2051	2102	ǀ	ǀ	ǀ	ǀ	...	...	2136	2148	ǀ	2207	ǀ	ǀ
Nottingham	a.	...	ǀ	ǀ	1955	2008	2018	2023	ǀ	ǀ	...	...	2055	ǀ	ǀ	2118	ǀ	ǀ	2128	...	...	2150	ǀ	2218	2221	ǀ	ǀ
Derby	a.	...	2003	2015	ǀ	ǀ	...	...	2023	2034	...	...	...	2108	2119	...	2129	2131	ǀ	...	...	...	2205	...	...	2223	2223
Chesterfield	d.	...	2027	2039	2052	2109	...	...	2043	2054	...	...	...	...	...	...	2153	2203	2222	...	...	...	...	...	...	2247	2245
Sheffield	a.	...	2041	2055	2105	2124	...	...	2059	2109	...	...	...	...	...	...	2208	2217	2236	...	...	...	...	...	...	2300	2301

		Ⓐ	⑥	⑥	Ⓐ	⚒		⚒	⚒	⑥	Ⓐ	⑥	Ⓐ	Ⓐ		⑦Y	⑦	⑦	⑦	⑦	⑦	⑦	⑦	⑦	⑦	⑦	⑦
London St Pancras	d.	2100	2101	...	...	2125	...	2130	2200	...	...	2226	2225	2315	⑦	...	0900	0930	1000	1030	1100	1130	1210	1230	1310	1340	1410
Luton ✈ Parkway	d.	ǀ	ǀ	...	...	ǀ	...	2151	ǀ	...	...	2247	2248	ǀ		...	0928	ǀ	1029	ǀ	1129	1159	1231	1253	1331	1402	1431
Luton	d.	2123	2124	...	...	ǀ	...	ǀ	2224	...	...	ǀ	ǀ	2346		...	ǀ	0959	ǀ	1102	1133	1203	1234	1257	1334	1407	ǀ
Bedford	d.	2138	2139	...	...	ǀ	...	2205	2239	...	...	2303	2303	0012	❖	...	0950	1019	1054	1125	1154	1223	1249	1312	1349	1422	1446
Wellingborough	d.	2150	2152	...	...	ǀ	...	2218	2252	...	...	2315	2317	0024		...	1003	1031	1108	1136	1207	1235	1302	1326	1402	1436	1459
Kettering	d.	2157	2202	2206	2211	ǀ	...	2225	2300	2305	2311	2322	2326	0042		...	1010	1038	1116	1143	1215	1242	1309	1334	1409	1443	1506
Corby	a.	ǀ	ǀ	2221	2226	ǀ	...	ǀ	ǀ	2319	2326	ǀ	ǀ	ǀ		...	ǀ	ǀ	ǀ	ǀ	ǀ	ǀ	ǀ	ǀ	ǀ	ǀ	ǀ
Market Harborough	d.	2207	2213	...	...	2218	...	2235	2311	...	...	2332	2337	0052		...	1020	1049	1127	1153	1225	1252	1319	1345	1419	1455	1516
Leicester	d.	2222	2229	...	...	2233	...	2249	2327	...	...	2346	2353	0107		1020	1036	1105	1145	1210	1241	1309	1336	1403	1436	1513	1533
Loughborough	d.	2232	2240	...	...	2243	...	2259	2338	...	...	2356	0004	0119		1030	1046	1115	1156	1220	1251	1319	1346	1414	1446	1524	1543
E. Midlands Parkway	d.	2239	ǀ	...	...	2250	...	2312	2352	...	...	0009	0017	0130		1037	1053	1123	1205	1227	1259	1326	1353	1423	1453	1533	1550
Nottingham	a.	ǀ	ǀ	...	...	2304	...	ǀ	0010	...	...	ǀ	ǀ	0145		ǀ	1108	ǀ	1216	ǀ	1312	ǀ	1407	ǀ	1507	ǀ	1605
Derby	a.	2254	2259	...	...	...	...	2331	...	...	...	0027	0034	0210		1054	...	1143	...	1243	...	1343	...	1442	...	1549	...
Chesterfield	d.	...	...	...	...	...	...	...	...	...	...	...	0056	...		1114	...	1210	...	1312	...	1411	...	1514	...	1612	...
Sheffield	a.	...	...	...	...	...	...	...	...	...	...	...	0112	...		1128	...	1223	...	1328	...	1425	...	1529	...	1629	...

		⑦L	⑦	⑦	⑦	⑦	⑦	⑦	⑦	⑦	⑦	⑦	⑦	⑦	⑦	⑦	⑦	⑦	⑦	⑦	⑦	⑦	⑦L	⑦	⑦	⑦	⑦
London St Pancras	d.	1440	1510	1540	1610	1635	1640	1705	1710	1735	1740	1805	1810	1835	1840	1905	1910	1935	1940	2000	2010	2035	2040	2110	2130	2230	2300
Luton ✈ Parkway	d.	ǀ	1533	ǀ	1631	ǀ	ǀ	ǀ	1731	ǀ	ǀ	ǀ	1831	ǀ	ǀ	ǀ	1931	ǀ	ǀ	ǀ	2031	ǀ	ǀ	2131	ǀ	2251	2327
Luton	d.	1504	ǀ	1604	ǀ	ǀ	1702	ǀ	ǀ	ǀ	1802	ǀ	ǀ	ǀ	1902	ǀ	ǀ	ǀ	2002	ǀ	ǀ	ǀ	2104	ǀ	2152	ǀ	ǀ
Bedford	d.	1519	1548	1619	1646	ǀ	1716	ǀ	1746	ǀ	1816	ǀ	1846	ǀ	1916	ǀ	1946	ǀ	2016	ǀ	2047	ǀ	2120	2146	2206	2313	2351
Wellingborough	d.	1533	1602	1633	1659	ǀ	1729	ǀ	1758	ǀ	1829	ǀ	1858	ǀ	1929	ǀ	1958	ǀ	2029	ǀ	2058	ǀ	2133	2159	2219	2326	0004
Kettering	d.	1541	1611	1641	1706	ǀ	1737	ǀ	1806	ǀ	1837	ǀ	1905	ǀ	1937	ǀ	2005	ǀ	2037	ǀ	2106	ǀ	2141	2206	2227	2333	0012
Corby	a.	ǀ	ǀ	ǀ	ǀ	ǀ	ǀ	ǀ	ǀ	ǀ	ǀ	ǀ	ǀ	ǀ	ǀ	ǀ	ǀ	ǀ	ǀ	ǀ	ǀ	ǀ	ǀ	ǀ	ǀ	ǀ	ǀ
Market Harborough	d.	1552	1622	1652	1716	ǀ	1747	ǀ	1815	ǀ	1847	ǀ	1915	ǀ	1947	ǀ	2015	ǀ	2047	ǀ	2116	ǀ	2152	2216	2237	2343	0022
Leicester	d.	1610	1638	1710	1733	1744	1803	1811	1833	1841	1903	1910	1932	1945	2003	2022	2033	2041	2103	2110	2133	2141	2210	2233	2254	0004	0042
Loughborough	d.	1621	1651	1721	1743	ǀ	1813	ǀ	1843	ǀ	1913	ǀ	1942	ǀ	2013	ǀ	2043	ǀ	2113	2121	2143	2151	ǀ	2247	2304	0014	0052
E. Midlands Parkway	d.	1630	1659	1730	1750	1800	1821	1825	1850	1855	1921	1925	1949	2001	2021	2039	2050	2055	2121	2129	2150	2159	2226	2258	2316	0026	0104
Nottingham	a.	ǀ	1711	ǀ	1805	ǀ	ǀ	1836	1905	ǀ	ǀ	1936	2005	ǀ	ǀ	2051	2105	ǀ	ǀ	2145	2205	ǀ	ǀ	2311	ǀ	0042	ǀ
Derby	a.	1647	...	1747	...	1814	1836	...	...	1908	1937	...	...	2013	2037	...	...	2107	2136	...	...	2211	2240	...	2335	...	0119
Chesterfield	d.	1713	...	1811	...	1837	...	...	...	1934	...	...	...	2037	...	...	...	2129	...	...	...	...	2309	...	2355	...	...
Sheffield	a.	1728	...	1825	...	1851	...	...	...	1950	...	...	...	2051	...	...	...	2143	...	...	...	...	2323	...	0008	...	...

To/from Lincoln (Table **187**).
To/from Melton Mowbray (see panel on page 140).
To/from London St. Pancras (Table **170**).
(12) Derby - Corby - London St Pancras and v.v.
Via Melton Mowbray (see panel on page 140).
To Leeds (Table **171**).
From York (d. 1750) and Doncaster (d. 1813).

S – To Doncaster (a. 0953) and York (a. 1017); continues to Scarborough May 21 - Sept. 10 (a. 1108).
V – From York (d.1750) and Doncaster (d. 1813); starts from Scarborough on ⑥ May 21 - Sept. 10 (d. 1703).
Y – To Doncaster (a. 1152) and York (a. 1215).

e – Arrives 1121.
f – Arrives Kettering 9 minutes after Corby.
❖ – For Kettering - Corby service on ⑦, see next page.

170 SHEFFIELD, DERBY and NOTTINGHAM - LEICESTER - LONDON

Most trains 🍷

		⚒	Ⓐ	Ⓐ	⑥	⑥	Ⓐ	ⒶC	⑥	Ⓐ	⑥	⚒	⑥	Ⓐ	Ⓐ	⑥	Ⓐ	ⒶG	⑥	⑥	Ⓐ	Ⓐ	Ⓐ	⑥	Ⓐ
Sheffield d.	⚒	...	...	...	...	0529	...	...	...	0530	...	...	...	...	0600	0629	...	0629	...	...	...	...	0649	...	...
Chesterfield d.		...	...	...	...	0541	...	...	...	0542	...	...	...	...	0613	0641	...	0640	...	...	...	...	0701	...	...
Derby d.		...	0500	0519	0521	0601	...	...	...	0604	...	...	0621	...	0633	0701	...	0705	...	0721	...	...	0722	...	...
Nottingham d.		...	|	|	|	|	0532	...	0605	|	0632	...	|	0630	|	|	0652	|	0705	|	0710	...	|	0730	0755
E. Midlands Parkway d.		...	0511	|	0535	|	0543	...	|	0617	0643	...	0635	0642	|	|	0704	|	|	0735	0725	...	0733	0743	0804
Loughborough d.		...	0518	|	0542	|	0552	...	0621	0626	|	...	0642	|	0653	|	|	0722	0721	0742	|	...	0741	|	|
Leicester d.		0445	0529	0543	0553	0624	0604	...	0632	0639	0700	...	0653	0659	0706	0724	0719	0736	0732	0753	0742	...	0756	0801	0819
Market Harborough d.		|	0543	0558	0607	|	0620	...	0646	0654	0714	...	|	0713	|	|	0733	|	0746	|	0757	...	|	0815	|
Corby d.		|	|	|	|	|	|	0635	|	|	|	0706	|	|	|	|	|	|	|	|	|	0802	|	|	|
Kettering d.		0505	0554	0608	0617	|	0631	0645	0656	0706	|	0717	0726	0724	0730	|	0743	0759	0756	|	0809	0811	0817	|	|
Wellingborough d.		0517	0602	0616	0624	|	0640	0654	0703	0714	|	...	0734	0732	0738	|	0751	0807	0803	|	|	...	0825	|	|
Bedford d.		0537	|	0630	0638	|	|	0709	0717	|	|	...	0747	|	0755	|	|	|	0817	|	0829	...	|	|	|
Luton d.		|	0625	|	0653	|	|	0724	|	|	|	...	0803	0757	|	|	0815	|	|	|	|	...	|	|	|
Luton ✈ Parkway d.		0554	|	|	|	|	0705	|	0732	0740	|	...	|	|	0811	|	|	|	0832	|	|	...	|	|	|
London St Pancras a.		0628	0649	0708	0718	0729	0731	0748	0756	0807	0814	...	0827	0823	0839	0831	0842	0856	0856	0900	0906	...	0910	0914	0926

	⚒	Ⓐ	⚒B	⑥	Ⓐ	ⒶL	⑥L	⚒	⚒	⚒	⚒	Ⓐ	⑥L	⚒	⚒	⚒	⚒	⚒	⚒	⚒	⚒	⚒	⚒	⚒	⚒
Sheffield d.	0729	...	...	...	0746	0724	0737	...	0829	...	0849	...	0834	...	0929	...	0949	...	...	1029	...	1049	...	...	1129
Chesterfield d.	0741	...	...	...	0759	0737	0750	...	0841	...	0901	...	0847	...	0941	...	1001	...	...	1041	...	1101	...	...	1141
Derby d.	0801	0736	...	0821	0819	|	|	...	0901	...	0921	...	|	...	1001	...	1021	...	...	1101	...	1121	...	...	1201
Nottingham d.	|	|	0805	|	|	0832	0832	...	|	0905	|	0932	0932	...	|	1005	|	1032	...	|	1105	|	1132	...	|
E. Midlands Parkway d.	|	|	|	0835	0835	0843	0843	...	|	|	0935	0943	0943	...	|	|	1035	1043	...	|	|	1135	1143	...	|
Loughborough d.	|	0754	0821	0842	0842	|	|	...	|	0921	0942	|	|	...	|	1021	1042	|	...	|	1121	1142	|	...	|
Leicester d.	0824	0805	0832	0853	0856	0900	0900	...	0924	0932	0953	1000	1000	...	1024	1032	1053	1100	...	1124	1132	1153	1200	...	1224
Market Harborough d.	|	0819	0846	|	|	0914	0914	...	|	0946	|	1014	1014	...	|	1046	|	1114	...	|	1146	|	1214	...	|
Corby d.	|	|	|	|	|	|	|	0916	|	|	|	|	|	1016	|	|	|	|	1116	|	|	|	|	1216	|
Kettering d.	|	0829	0856	|	|	|	|	0926	|	0956	|	|	|	1026	|	1056	|	|	1126	|	1156	|	|	1226	|
Wellingborough d.	|	0842	0903	|	|	|	|	0934	|	1003	|	|	|	1034	|	1103	|	|	1134	|	1203	|	|	1234	|
Bedford d.	|	0905	0917	|	|	|	|	0947	|	1017	|	|	|	1047	|	1117	|	|	1147	|	1217	|	|	1247	|
Luton d.	|	0919	|	|	|	|	|	1003	|	|	|	|	|	1103	|	|	|	|	1203	|	|	|	|	1303	|
Luton ✈ Parkway d.	|	|	0932	|	|	|	|	|	|	1032	|	|	|	|	|	1132	|	|	|	|	1232	|	|	|	|
London St Pancras a.	0933	0945	0956	0959	1006	1017	1014	1026	1030	1056	1100	1114	1114	1126	1130	1156	1201	1214	1226	1231	1256	1300	1314	1326	1331

	⚒	⚒	⚒	⚒	⚒	⚒	⚒	⚒	⚒	⚒	⚒	⚒	⚒	⚒	⚒	⚒	⚒	⚒	⚒	⚒	⑥	Ⓐ	⑥	Ⓐ	⚒
Sheffield d.	1149	...	...	1229	...	1249	...	...	1329	...	1349	...	...	1429	...	1449	...	...	1529	...	1549	1549	...	...	...
Chesterfield d.	1201	...	...	1241	...	1301	...	...	1341	...	1401	...	...	1441	...	1501	...	...	1541	...	1601	1601	...	...	...
Derby d.	1221	...	...	1301	...	1321	...	...	1401	...	1421	...	...	1501	...	1521	...	...	1601	...	1621	1621	...	...	...
Nottingham d.	|	1232	...	|	1305	|	1332	...	|	1405	|	1432	...	|	1505	|	1532	...	|	1605	|	|	1632	1630	...
E. Midlands Parkway d.	1235	1243	...	|	|	1335	1343	...	|	|	1435	1443	...	|	|	1535	1543	...	|	|	1635	1635	1643	1641	...
Loughborough d.	1242	|	...	|	1321	1342	|	...	|	1421	1442	|	...	|	1521	1542	|	...	|	1621	1642	1642	|	|	...
Leicester d.	1253	1300	...	1324	1332	1353	1400	...	1424	1432	1453	1500	...	1524	1532	1553	1600	...	1624	1632	1653	1653	1700	1658	...
Market Harborough d.	|	1314	...	|	1346	|	1414	...	|	1446	|	1514	...	|	1546	|	1614	...	|	1646	|	|	1714	1712	...
Corby d.	|	|	1316	|	|	|	|	1416	|	|	|	|	1516	|	|	|	|	1616	|	|	|	|	|	|	1716
Kettering d.	|	|	1326	|	1356	|	|	1426	|	1456	|	|	1526	|	1556	|	|	1626	|	1656	|	1714	|	|	1726
Wellingborough d.	|	|	1334	|	1403	|	|	1434	|	1503	|	|	1534	|	1603	|	|	1634	|	1703	|	|	|	|	1734
Bedford d.	|	|	1347	|	1417	|	|	1447	|	1517	|	|	1547	|	1617	|	|	1647	|	1717	|	|	|	|	1747
Luton d.	|	|	1403	|	|	|	|	1503	|	|	|	|	1603	|	|	|	|	1703	|	|	|	|	|	1749	1803
Luton ✈ Parkway d.	|	|	|	|	1432	|	|	|	|	1532	|	|	|	|	1632	|	|	|	|	1732	|	|	|	|	|
London St Pancras a.	1400	1414	1427	1430	1456	1459	1514	1527	1531	1556	1559	1614	1627	1632	1656	1700	1715	1726	1730	1756	1800	1807	1814	1815	1826

	Ⓐ	⚒	⑥	Ⓐ	⚒	ⒶE	⑥	⚒	⚒	Ⓐ	⑥	⚒	Ⓐ	⑥	⚒	⚒	Ⓐ	⑥	⑥V	⚒	Ⓐ	⚒	⑥	⑥	Ⓐ
Sheffield d.	1629	...	1649	1649	...	...	...	1729	...	1738	1749	...	...	...	1829	...	1849	...	1849	...	...	1929	...	...	...
Chesterfield d.	1641	...	1701	1701	...	...	...	1741	...	1754	1801	...	...	...	1841	...	1901	...	1901	...	...	1941	...	...	...
Derby d.	1701	...	1721	1721	...	1636	...	1801	...	1821	1821	...	...	...	1901	...	1921	...	1921	...	...	2001	...	...	...
Nottingham d.	|	1705	|	|	1732	|	...	|	1805	|	|	1832	...	...	|	1905	|	...	|	1932	...	|	...	2005	2002
E. Midlands Parkway d.	|	|	1735	1735	1743	1648	...	|	|	1835	1835	1843	...	...	|	|	1935	...	1935	1943	...	|	...	2017	2015
Loughborough d.	|	1721	1742	1742	|	|	...	|	1821	1842	1842	|	...	...	|	1921	1942	...	1942	|	...	|	...	2025	2022
Leicester d.	1724	1732	1753	1753	1800	|	...	1824	1832	1853	1853	1900	...	...	1924	1932	1953	...	1953	2000	...	2024	...	2036	2033
Market Harborough d.	|	1746	|	|	1814	|	...	|	1846	|	|	1914	...	...	|	1946	|	...	|	2014	...	|	...	2049	2047
Corby d.	|	|	|	|	|	1751	1816	|	|	|	|	|	1856	1916	|	|	|	1950	|	|	1953	|	2043	|	|
Kettering d.	|	1756	|	1814	|	1823f	1826	|	1856	|	|	|	1926f	1926	|	1956	|	2026f	2014	|	2026f	|	2126f	2058	2057
Wellingborough d.	|	1803	|	|	|	1834	1834	|	1903	|	|	|	1934	1934	|	2003	|	2034	|	|	2034	|	2134	2107	2104
Bedford d.	|	1817	|	|	|	1847	1847	|	1917	|	|	|	1947	1947	|	2017	|	2047	|	|	2047	|	2147	2121	2118
Luton d.	1811	|	|	|	|	1903	1903	|	|	|	|	|	2003	2003	|	|	|	2103	|	|	2103	|	2203	|	|
Luton ✈ Parkway d.	|	1832	|	|	|	|	|	|	1932	|	|	|	|	|	|	2032	|	|	|	|	|	|	|	2136	2132
London St Pancras a.	1836	1856	1900	1903	1915	1926	1926	1933	1958	2002	2000	2016	2027	2027	2033	2056	2101	2126	2103	2116	2126	2134	2226	2159	2157

	Ⓐ	⑥	⑥	Ⓐ	⑥	⑥	Ⓐ	⚒	Ⓐ	⑥	⑥	Ⓐ	⚒		⑦	⑦	⑦	⑦	⑦	⑦	⑦	⑦	⑦	⑦L	⑦L
Sheffield d.	...	2029	...	2049	...	...	...	2137	2201	2242	2320	2321	2337	⑦	...	...	...	...	0818	...	0925	...	1025	1035	1143
Chesterfield d.	...	2040	...	2101	...	...	...	2153	2213	2256	2332	2345	2353		...	...	...	...	0831	...	0938	...	1037	1048	1155
Derby d.	...	2100	...	2121	...	...	...	|	2234	|	0006	0005	|		0650	...	0751	...	0851	...	0959	...	1057	|	1218
Nottingham d.	2102	|	...	|	2105	2132	2132	2235	...	2328	...	...	0040	✣	|	0729	|	0822	|	0920	|	1030	|	1139e	|
E. Midlands Parkway d.	2114	2113	...	2135	2117	|	|	▬	...	...	...	...	...		0702	0739	0805	0835	0905	0931	1013	1045	1111	1150	1234
Loughborough d.	2122	2120	...	2142	2125	2147	2147	...	...	...	...	...	...		|	|	0813	0843	0912	0940	1020	1053	1119	1159	1242
Leicester d.	2133	2131	...	2153	2137	2158	2158	...	...	...	...	...	...		0720	0755	0825	0855	0924	0954	1032	1108	1130	1213	1256
Market Harborough d.	2147	...	...	|	2150	2212	2212	⚒	...	...	...	...	...		0738	0811	0841	0911	0940	1011	1045	1122	1143	1227	1310
Corby d.	|	...	2143	|	|	|	|	2243	...	...	...	...	...		|	|	|	|	|	|	|	|	|	|	|
Kettering d.	2157	...	2152	|	2200	2223	2223	2252	...	...	...	...	...		0749	0821	0851	0921	0950	1022	1055	1133	1153	1238	1321
Wellingborough d.	2204	...	...	|	2207	2230	2230	...	...	...	...	...	...		0801	0832	0902	0932	1002	1030	1102	1141	1201	1246	1329
Bedford d.	2218	...	...	|	2221	2243	2245	...	...	...	...	...	...		0815	0845	0915	0945	1015	1045	1116	1157	1215	1302	1344
Luton d.	2235	...	...	|	2236	2301	2302	...	...	...	...	...	...		0834	|	0935	|	1035	|	1136	|	1230	|	1401
Luton ✈ Parkway d.	2239	...	...	|	2240	|	|	...	...	...	...	...	...		|	0907	|	1007	|	1106	|	1213	|	1318	|
London St Pancras a.	2305	...	...	2301	2315	2340	2338	...	...	...	...	...	...		0915	0945	1015	1048	1117	1148	1214	1239	1254	1344	1427

	⑦	⑦	⑦	⑦	⑦	⑦	⑦	⑦L	⑦	⑦	⑦	⑦	⑦	⑦	⑦	⑦	⑦	⑦	⑦	⑦V	⑦	⑦	⑦	⑦	⑦
Sheffield d.	1249	...	1343	...	1449	...	...	1529	1550	...	...	...	1649	...	...	...	1750	...	...	1847	...	1928	2026	...	2236
Chesterfield d.	1301	...	1356	...	1501	...	...	1542	1602	...	...	...	1700	...	...	...	1802	...	...	1900	...	1941	2039	...	2248
Derby d.	1322	...	1417	...	1522	...	...	1602	1626	...	...	1657	1723	...	...	1806	1826	...	...	1919	...	2003	2101	...	2323
Nottingham d.	|	1349	|	1452	|	1543	1552	|	|	1645	1650	|	|	1745	1752	|	|	1845	1852	|	1951	|	|	2121	...
E. Midlands Parkway d.	1336	1403	1431	1504	1536	1553	1605	1616	1637	1655	1703	1711	1736	1755	1804	1820	1837	1855	1905	1934	2004	2018	2113	2131	...
Loughborough d.	1344	1412	1439	1512	1543	|	1612	1625	|	|	1711	1719	|	|	1812	1828	|	1902	1912	1942	2011	2027	|	2139	...
Leicester d.	1355	1426	1455	1524	1555	1612	1624	1639	1655	1710	1723	1731	1754	1814	1825	1840	1854	1914	1925	1955	2023	2041	2132	2154	...
Market Harborough d.	1408	1440	1508	1537	|	|	1637	1653	|	|	1736	1744	|	|	1838	1853	|	1927	1938	2008	2036	2055	2146	2208	...
Corby d.	|	|	|	|	|	|	|	|	|	|	|	|	|	|	|	|	|	|	|	|	|	|	|	|	...
Kettering d.	1418	1451	1518	1547	|	|	1647	1703	|	|	1746	1755	|	|	1848	1902	|	1937	1948	2015	2046	2106	2157	2218	...
Wellingborough d.	1426	1459	1525	1554	|	|	1655	1712	|	|	1754	1802	|	|	1855	1910	|	1945	1955	2025	2053	2114	2205	2225	...
Bedford d.	1439	1515	1540	1609	|	|	1709	1728	|	|	1808	1817	|	|	1909	1925	|	1959	2009	2040	2109	2131	2221	2239	...
Luton d.	1454	|	1555	|	1642	|	|	1745	|	|	|	1831	|	|	|	1943	|	2015	|	2054	2123	2146	2237	2254	...
Luton ✈ Parkway d.	|	1531	|	1624	|	|	1725	|	|	|	1824	|	|	|	1924	|	|	|	2024	2058	|	|	|	|	...
London St Pancras a.	1518	1557	1619	1648	1709	1723	1748	1810	1802	1817	1847	1855	1909	1925	1948	2007	2000	2039	2049	2121	2148	2213	2303	2324	...

✣ – **Kettering - Corby** and v.v. trains on ⑦. Journey time: 10 minutes.
From Kettering at 0955, 1055, 1155, 1255, 1355, 1455, 1555, 1650, 1750, 1855, 1950, 2050, 2155.
From Corby at 0930, 1025, 1125, 1220, 1330, 1425, 1525, 1625, 1720, 1820, 1920, 2020, 2125.

← FOR OTHER NOTES SEE PREVIOUS PAGE

CORBY - MELTON MOWBRAY - DERBY

km		Ⓐ	ⒶD	
0	**Corby** d.	0926	1916	...
23	Oakham d.	0947	1936	...
43	**Melton Mowbray** d.	1000	1948	...
81	East Mids Parkway d.	1031	...	...
97	**Derby** a.	1045	...	...

	ⒶD	ⒶE
Derby d.	...	1636
East Mids Parkway d.	...	1648
Melton Mowbray d.	0600	1714
Oakham d.	0612	1727
Corby a.	0635	1751

NOTTINGHAM - SHEFFIELD - HUDDERSFIELD and LEEDS 171

2nd class

NOTTINGHAM - SHEFFIELD - LEEDS

		Ⓐ	⚒	⚒	Ⓐ	⚒	Ⓐ	⚒	Ⓐ	⑥	⚒	⚒	⚒	⚒		⚒	⚒	⚒	Ⓐ	⑥	⚒	⚒	⚒	⑥A
Nottingham .. 170 206 d.	⚒	...	...	0520	...	...	0621	*0639*	0712	0711	...	0817	*0847*	0917	and	*1644*	1717	*1744*	1817	1817	*1847*	1917	...	2016
Langley Mill .... d.		...	...	│	...	...	0640	│	0731	0730	...	0836	│	0936	at	│	1736	*1800*	1836	1836	│	1936	...	2033
Alfreton .... 206 d.		...	...	│	...	...	0648	*0700*	0739	0738	...	0844	*0908*	0944	the	*1705*	1744	*1808*	1844	1844	*1908*	1944	...	2041
Chesterfield ... 170 206 d.		...	...	0549	0626	...	0658	*0710*	0749	0748	...	0855	*0920*	0955	same	*1715*	1755	*1818*	1855	1855	*1920*	1956	...	2052
Sheffield ...... 170 206 a.		...	...	0615	0646	...	0716	*0728*	0804	0811	...	0914	*0937*	1014	minutes	*1737*	1814	*1837*	1914	1914	*1937*	2014	...	2105
Sheffield ...... 192 193 d.		0550	0606	...	0649	0706	0718	0751	0818	0818	0850	0918	0950	1018	past	1750	1818	1850	1922	1916	1952	2018	2106	2126
Meadowhall ... 192 193 d.		0556	0612	...	0655	0712	0725	0757	0825	0825	0856	0924	0956	1024	each	1756	1824	1856	1928	1922	1958	2024	2112	│
Barnsley .... d.		0610	0633	...	0712	0733	0742	0812	0842	0842	0912	0942	1012	1042	hour	1813	1842	1914	1942	1942	2013	2042	2133	│
Wakefield Kirkgate ..... d.		0628	0650	...	0728	0750	0758	0827	0858	0858	0927	0958	1027	1058	until	1832	1858	1932	1958	1958	2028	2058	2153	2202e
Leeds .... a.		0650	0728	...	0751	0825	0819	0849	0919	0919	0949	1017	1049	1118	◇	1851	1925	1952	2017	2018	2049	2118	2229	2217

	ⒶA	⚒A	①–④	⑥	⑥	Ⓐ	ⒶA		⑦	⑦	⑦	⑦	⑦	⑦	⑦	⑦	⑦	⑦	⑦A	⑦	⑦	⑦	⑦	⑦	⑦	⑦A
gham .. 170 206 d.	2033	...	...	2117	...	2114	2146	⑦	...	...	...	1012	1117	1217	1317	1417	1512	1617	...	1717	1817	1917	*1943*	*2015*	2133	...
y Mill .... d.	2050	...	...	2136	...	2141	2203		...	...	...	1036	1136	1236	1336	1436	1536	1636	...	1736	1836	1936	│	*2034*	2157	...
n .... 206 d.	2058	...	...	2144	...	2149	2211		...	...	...	1044	1144	1244	1344	1444	1544	1644	...	1744	1844	1944	*2004*	*2042*	2205	...
rfield .. 170 206 d.	2109	...	...	2155	...	2201	2222		...	...	...	1055	1154	1254	1354	1454	1556	1654	...	1754	1854	1954	*2014*	*2052*	2216	...
eld ...... 170 206 a.	2123	...	...	2214	...	2220	2236		...	...	...	1114	1215	1315	1415	1515	1615	1715	...	1815	1915	2015	*2031*	*2117*	2236	...
eld ...... 192 193 d.	2126	2217	2206	...	2224	...	2253		0839	1017	1039	1117	1216	1317	1417	1517	1617	1718	1734	1817	1917	2017	2039	2136	2239	2331
whall .. 192 193 d.	│	│	2212	...	2231	...	│		0845	1023	1045	1123	1223	1323	1423	1523	1623	1724	│	1823	1923	2023	2045	2142	2245	│
ey .... d.	│	│	2233	...	│	...	│		0910	1037	1110	1137	1237	1337	1437	1537	1637	1738	│	1837	1937	2037	2110	│	2310	│
eld Kirkgate ..... d.	2201e	2246e	2254	...	2320e	...	2323e		0930	1056	1130	1156	1259	1356	1456	1556	1656	1757	1806e	1856	1956	2056	2130	2228e	2330	2358e
.... a.	2218	2305	2330	...	2340	...	2342		1005	1116	1205	1216	1318	1416	1516	1616	1716	1816	1823	1916	2018	2116	2204	2250	0005	0013

		Ⓐ	⑥	Ⓐ	ⒶA	Ⓐ	⑥	Ⓐ	ⒶA	⑥A	⚒	⚒	⑥A	⚒	⚒	⚒		⚒	⚒	⚒	⑥	Ⓐ	⚒	⚒	⚒
.... d.	⚒	...	...	...	0525	...	...	0605	0634	0634	0638	0705	0738	0740	0805	0840	and	1705	1740	1805	1840	1840	1905	1945	2030
ield Kirkgate ..... d.		...	...	...	0538e	0604	...	0621	0647e	0646e	0708	0725	0751e	0756	0823	0856	at	1723	1756	1823	1856	1858	1924	2001	2046
ey .... d.		...	...	*0523*	│	0622	0622	0638	│	│	0726	0742	│	0814	0840	0914	the	1740	1814	1840	1914	1919	1941	2019	2103
whall .. 192 193 d.		...	...	*0545*	│	0642	0643	0652	│	│	0749	0755	│	0831	0854	0930	same	1754	1829	1854	1932	1935	1954	2036	2122
eld ...... 192 193 a.		...	...	*0554*	0620	0655	0651	0700	0722	0722	0758	0805	0821	0840	0902	0937	minutes	1803	1838	1903	1939	1942	2002	2044	2130
eld ...... 170 206 d.		0505	0554	0603	...	...	0703	0703	0724	0737	...	0808	0834	...	0905	...	past	1805	...	1905	...	...	2005	...	*2137*
rfield .. 170 206 d.		0520	0619	0619	...	...	0719	0720	0737	0750	...	0824	0847	...	0922	...	each	1822	...	1922	...	...	2022	...	*2153*
n .... 206 d.		│	0629	0630	...	...	0729	0731	0748	0801	...	0834	0857	...	0932	...	hour	1832	...	1932	...	...	2032	...	*2204*
y Mill .... d.		│	0637	0637	...	...	0737	0739	0757	0809	...	0842	│	...	0940	...	until	1840	...	1940	...	...	2040	...	*2212*
gham .. 170 206 a.		0607	0702	0701	...	...	0755	0757	0823	0825	...	0902	0919	...	1000	...	◇	1900	...	2000	...	...	2100	...	*2235*

	⚒	⚒	Ⓐ	⑥	Ⓐ	⑥		⑦	⑦	⑦	⑦A	⑦	⑦A	⑦	⑦	⑦	⑦	⑦A	⑦	⑦	⑦	⑦	⑦	⑦	⑦	⑦
.... d.	2037	2137	...	...	2237	2244	⑦	...	0834	0905	0950	1002	1050	1105	1205	1305	1405	1434	1505	1605	1705	1803	1905	2022	2145	2217
ield Kirkgate ..... d.	2107	2207	...	...	2310	2300e		...	0903	0921	1003e	1018	1103e	1121	1221	1321	1421	1447e	1521	1622	1722	1822	1921	2051	2200e	2246
ey .... d.	2125	2228	...	...	2331	│		...	0924	0941	│	1038	│	1141	1241	1341	1441	│	1541	1642	1741	1842	1941	2112	│	2312
whall .. 192 193 d.	2148	2248	...	...	2351	2345		...	0944	0957	│	1053	│	1156	1254	1356	1457	│	1557	1657	1758	1857	1954	2133	2246	2336
eld ...... 192 193 a.	2156	2259	...	...	0002	2358		...	0955	1004	1030	1102	1131	1203	1304	1405	1506	1517	1605	1705	1805	1904	2004	2143	2256	2343
eld ...... 170 206 d.	...	...	2337	2338	...	...		0905	...	1007	...	1103	...	1207	1306	1407	1507	...	1607	1707	1807	1907	2007	...	*2330*	...
rfield .. 170 206 d.	...	...	0002	2353	...	...		0921	...	1023	...	1120	...	1223	1323	1423	1523	...	1623	1723	1823	1923	2023	...	*2344*	...
n .... 206 d.	...	...	│	│	...	...		0932	...	1033	...	1130	...	1233	1333	1433	1533	...	1633	1733	1833	1933	2033	...	*2355*	...
y Mill .... d.	...	...	│	│	...	...		0940	...	1041	...	1138	...	1241	1341	1441	1541	...	1641	1741	1841	1941	2041	...	*0002*	...
gham .. 170 206 a.	...	...	0040	0030	...	...		1000	...	1101	...	1158	...	1301	1401	1501	1601	...	1701	1801	1901	1959	2101	...	*0023*	...

SHEFFIELD - HUDDERSFIELD *'The Penistone Line'*

		Ⓐ	⚒	⚒	and at	⚒	⑥	Ⓐ	⑥	Ⓐ	⚒	⚒	⚒	⚒			⑦	⑦	⑦	⑦	⑦	⑦	⑦	⑦
Sheffield .... d.	⚒	0536	0636	0736	the same	1633	1737	1737	1836	1836	1937	2042	2140	2241	...	⑦	0939	1149	1236	1339	1539	1654	1740	1939
Meadowhall .... d.		0542	0642	0842	minutes	1639	1743	1743	1842	1842	1943	2048	2146	2247	...		0945	1155	1242	1345	1545	1700	1747	1945
Barnsley .... d.		0601	0701	0801	past each	1701	1804	1804	1903	1905	2008	2108	2208	2308	...		1006	1216	1306	1406	1606	1715	1810	2006
Penistone .... d.		0618	0718	0818	hour until	1718	1821	1824	1920	1922	2025	2125	2225	2325	...		1023	1233	1323	1423	1623	1732	1827	2023
Huddersfield .... a.		0654	0754	0854	◇	1755	1856	1900	1956	1957	2100	2201	2301	0001	...		1057	1307	1357	1457	1657	1807	1900	2057

		⚒	⚒	⚒	⚒	and at	⚒	Ⓐ	⑥	Ⓐ	⚒	⚒	⚒	⚒			⑦	⑦	⑦	⑦	⑦	⑦	⑦	⑦
ersfield .... d.	⚒	0606	0706	0806	0908	the same	1708	1751	1813	1818	1913	2013	2113	2213	...	⑦	0915	1011	1115	1315	1411	1515	1720	1915
one .... d.		0642	0742	0842	0944	minutes	1744	1831	1844	1849	1949	2052	2149	2249	...		0950	1046	1150	1350	1446	1550	1755	1950
ey .... d.		0658	0758	0858	1001	past each	1801	1848	1901	1906	2006	2112	2206	2306	...		1012	1103	1207	1412	1503	1612	1812	2012
whall .... 192 193 d.		0722	0822	0921	1021	hour until	1822	1906	1920	1925	2024	2131	2225	2327	...		1035	1121	1230	1435	1521	1636	1836	2035
eld .... 192 193 a.		0729	0829	0928	1030	◇	1831	1914	1930	1933	2036	2141	2236	2336	...		1044	1128	1238	1443	1528	1644	1844	2043

From / to London St. Pancras (Table **170**).

e – Wakefield Westgate.

◇ – Timings may vary by up to 5 minutes.

NOTTINGHAM - WORKSOP and MATLOCK 172

2nd class

NOTTINGHAM - WORKSOP *'The Robin Hood Line'*

		⚒	⚒	⑥	Ⓐ	⚒	⚒		⚒	⚒	⚒	⚒	⚒	⚒	⑥			⑦	⑦	⑦	⑦	⑦	⑦	⑦	⑦
Nottingham ..... d.	⚒	0540	0605	0703	0701	0826	0926	and	1726	1755	1855	1955	2055	2205	2305	...	⑦	0807	0942	1128	1328	1525	1653	1829	2025
Mansfield .... d.		0613	0638	0740	0740	0900	0957	hourly	1803	1836	1929	2036	2136	2242	2343	...		0840	1016	1202	1401	1558	1726	1902	2058
Worksop .... a.		0649	0719	0814	0818	0933	1033	until	1837	1908	2005	2109	2208	2314	...	...		...	...	...	...	...	...	...	...

		⚒	⚒	⚒	⚒	⚒		⚒	⚒	⚒	⚒	⚒	⚒	⚒	⚒			⑦	⑦	⑦	⑦	⑦	⑦	⑦	⑦
sop .... d.	⚒	0550	0656	0738	0838	0938	and	1538	1642	1746	1841	1922	2022	2122	2222	...	⑦	...	...	...	...	...	...	...	...
ield .... d.		0621	0729	0810	0910	1010	hourly	1610	1714	1818	1913	1953	2053	2153	2253	...		0855	1033	1217	1415	1612	1739	1921	2110
gham .... a.		0656	0805	0845	0943	1043	until	1643	1746	1852	1948	2030	2125	2226	2326	...		0931	1107	1251	1450	1646	1813	1955	2144

NOTTINGHAM - DERBY - MATLOCK

		⚒	Ⓐ	⑥	⚒	⚒	⚒		⚒	⚒	Ⓐ	⑥			⑦	⑦	⑦	⑦	⑦		⑦	⑦
Nottingham .... 123 d.	⚒	...	0617	0620	0720	0820	0920		1920	2020	*2139*	*2139*	...	⑦	0926	1127	1323	1528	1722	...	1922	2124
Derby .... 123 a.		...	0650	0650	0750	0850	0950	and	1950	2050	*2208*	*2208*	...		0954	1155	1351	1556	1751	...	1950	2153
Derby .... d.		0542	0652	0652	0752	0852	0952	hourly	1952	2052	2215	2216	...		0956	1156	1356	1558	1756	...	1952	2155
Duffield .... ◧ d.		0549	0659	0659	0759	0859	0959	until	1959	2059	2222	2223	...		1003	1204	1403	1605	1803	...	1959	2202
Whatstandwell .... ◧ d.		0604	0714	0714	0814	0914	1014		2014	2114	2237	2239	...		1018	1219	1418	1620	1818	...	2014	2217
Cromford .... d.		0610	0720	0720	0820	0920	1020	★	2020	2120	2243	2245	...		1024	1224	1424	1626	1824	...	2020	2223
Matlock Bath .... ◧ d.		0612	0722	0722	0822	0922	1022		2022	2122	2245	2247	...		1026	1227	1426	1628	1826	...	2022	2225
Matlock .... ◧ a.		0615	0727	0727	0827	0927	1027		2027	2127	2250	2251	...		1030	1230	1430	1632	1830	...	2026	2229

		⚒	⑥	Ⓐ	⚒	⚒	⚒		⚒	⚒	⚒	⚒			⑦	⑦		⑦	⑦	⑦		⑦	⑦
ck .... ◧ d.	⚒	0620	0736	0736	0836	0936	1036		1936	2036	2140	2254	...	⑦	1038	1238	...	1441	1638	1838	...	2038	2244
ck Bath .... ◧ d.		0622	0738	0738	0838	0938	1038	and	1938	2038	2142	2256	...		1040	1240	...	1443	1640	1840	...	2040	2246
ord .... d.		0625	0741	0741	0841	0941	1041	hourly	1941	2041	2141	2259	...		1043	1243	...	1446	1643	1843	...	2043	2249
standwell .... ◧ d.		0630	0746	0746	0846	0946	1046	until	1946	2046	2150	2304	...		1048	1248	...	1451	1648	1848	...	2048	2254
ld .... ◧ d.		0646	0803	0803	0903	1003	1103		2003	2103	2207	2321	...		1105	1305	...	1507	1705	1905	...	2105	2311
.... d.		0655	0811	0811	0911	1011	1111	★	2011	2111	2215	2328	...		1112	1312	...	1515	1712	1912	...	2112	2318
.... 123 d.		*0708*	0813	0813	0913	1013	1113		2013	2113	*2259*	2330	...		1114	1314	...	1516	1714	1914	...	2114	...
gham .... 123 a.		*0738*	0846	0846	0942	1041	1141		2043	2141	*2327*	0002	...		1141	1341	...	1543	1744	1944	...	2141	...

Timings may vary by up to 2 minutes.

◧ – Visitor attractions near these stations:
Duffield: Ecclesbourne Valley Railway (shares National Rail station). ✆ 01629 823076.
Whatstandwell: National Tramway Museum (1.6 km walk). ✆ 01773 854321.
Matlock Bath: Heights of Abraham (short walk to cable car). ✆ 01629 582365.
Matlock: Peak Rail (shares National Rail station). ✆ 01629 580381.

173 LEEDS - SETTLE - CARLISLE — 2nd class

A bus service is currently in operation between Appleby and Carlisle due to emergency engineering works. Timings shown are valid until further notic

km		Ⓐ	⑥	Ⓐ	⑥	⑦		⚒	⚒	⑦	⑥		Ⓐ	⑦	⚒	⑦		⑥	Ⓐ	⚒	Ⓐ A	⑥ A
	London Kings Cross **180** d.	...	...	...	...	...	...	...	...	...	...	...	...	...	...	...	...	...	...	...	1803	1835
0	**Leeds** **176** d.	0529	0619	0849	0849	0900	...	0947	1049	1120	1249	...	1249	1357	1449	1741	...	1750	1806	1919	2039	2055
27	Keighley **176** d.	0556	0642	0912	0912	0929	...	1012	1112	1142	1312	...	1312	1421	1512	1802	...	1813	1829	1942	2057s	2113s
42	Skipton **176** d.	0615	0656	0926	0926	0948	...	1026	1126	1155	1326	...	1326	1435	1526	1815	...	1835	1846	2000	2113	2127
58	Hellifield d.	0626	0708	0940	0940	1002	...	|	1137	|	1340	...	1340	1449	1537	1828	...	1849	1900	2015	...	...
66	**Settle** d.	0636	0715	0950	0950	1011	...	1044	1146	1214	1348	...	1348	1458	1545	1835	...	1857	1908	2024	...	...
76	Horton in Ribblesdale d.	|	0724	0958	0958	1020	...	|	1154	|	1357	...	1357	1507	1553	1844	...	1906	1917	2032	...	...
84	Ribblehead d.	0651	0732	1006	1006	1028	...	|	1202	|	1405	...	1405	1515	1601	1851	...	1914	1925	2042	...	...
99	Garsdale d.	0706	0747	1021	1021	1043	...	|	1217	|	1420	...	1420	1530	1616	1907	...	1929	1940	...	...	...
115	Kirkby Stephen d.	0718	0759	1034	1034	1056	...	1122	1230	1251	1432	...	1432	1543	1629	1919	...	1941	1952	...	...	...
132	Appleby a.	0732	0812	1047	1047	1110	...	1136	1243	1305	1445	...	1445	1556	1641	1931	...	1954	2005	...	...	...
132	Appleby d.	*0742*	*0821*	*1057*	*1055*	*1118*	...	*1144*	*1251*	*1313*	*1454*	...	*1455*	*1605*	*1650*	*1940*	...	*2003*	*2015*	...	...	...
166	Armathwaite d.	*0832*	*0911*	*1147*	*1145*	*1143*	...	|	*1341*	|	*1544*	...	*1545*	*1630*	*1740*	*2005*	...	*2053*	*2105*	...	...	...
182	**Carlisle** a.	*0857*	*0941*	*1212*	*1215*	*1203*	...	*1246*	*1413*	*1413*	*1614*	...	*1615*	*1650*	*1811*	*2025*	...	*2123*	*2135*	...	...	...

	⑥ A	Ⓐ A	⑥	Ⓐ	⑥	Ⓐ	⑦	⑥	⑥	Ⓐ	⑦	Ⓐ	⑥	Ⓐ	⑦	⑥	⚒	⑦	⑥	Ⓐ	Ⓐ	⑥
Carlisle d.	...	...	...	*0502*	*0704*	*0805*	*0912*	*0836*	*1103*	*1106*	*1246*	*1317*	*1334*	*1433*	*1450*	*1516*	*1531*	*1648*	*1719*	*1726*	...	...
Armathwaite d.	...	...	...	*0532*	*0734*	*0835*	*0930*	*0906*	*1133*	*1131*	*1304*	*1347*	*1404*	|	|	|	*1601*	*1706*	*1749*	*1756*	...	...
Appleby a.	...	...	...	*0622*	*0824*	*0925*	*0957*	*0956*	*1223*	*1226*	*1331*	*1437*	*1454*	*1533*	*1550*	*1616*	*1651*	*1733*	*1839*	*1846*	...	...
Appleby d.	...	...	...	0632	0834	0935	1007	1006	1233	1236	1341	1447	1504	1543	1557	1626	1701	1743	1849	1856	...	...
Kirkby Stephen d.	...	...	...	0646	0847	0948	1021	1019	1246	1250	1355	1500	1517	1556	1610	1639	1714	1757	1902	1909	...	...
Garsdale d.	...	...	...	0659	0900	1002	1034	1033	1259	1302	1408	1513	1530	|	|	|	1727	1810	1915	1922	...	...
Ribblehead d.	...	...	0714	0714	0915	1017	1049	1047	1314	1317	1423	1529	1545	|	|	|	1742	1825	1930	1937	2100	2100
Horton in Ribblesdale d.	...	...	0720	0720	0921	1024	1056	1054	1320	1324	1430	1536	1551	|	|	|	1748	1832	1936	1943	2106	2106
Settle d.	...	...	0728	0728	0929	1032	1104	1102	1328	1332	1438	1545	1559	1634	1646	1716	1757	1841	1944	1951	2114	2114
Hellifield d.	...	...	0737	0737	0937	1039	1113	1109	1337	1339	1447	1553	1607	|	|	|	1806	1849	1952	1959	2123	2122
Skipton **176** a.	0655	0655	0753	0753	0952	1054	1129	1124	1355	1356	1504	1608	1622	1654	1707	1738	1823	1904	2007	2015	2138	2140
Keighley **176** a.	0709u	0707u	0807	0807	1007	1107	1139	1137	1407	1407	1515	1621	1637	1707	1718	1750	1837	1915	2018	2025	2202	2203
Leeds **176** a.	0733	0731	0837	0837	1035	1136	1205	1207	1436	1437	1545	1653	1707	1738	1746	1817	1907	1943	2045	2050	2234	*2234*
London Kings Cross **180** a.	0951	0957	...	...	...	...	...	...	...	...	...	...	...	...	...	...	...	...	...	...	...	...

A – (12) and 🍷 London Kings Cross - Skipton and v.v. (Table **180**).   s – Calls to set down only.   u – Calls to pick up only.

174 LEEDS - LANCASTER - HEYSHAM — 2nd class

km	km		Ⓐ	⑥		⑥	Ⓐ		⑦	Ⓐ		⑥	⑦		Ⓐ	⑥		⑦	⑥		Ⓐ	⑦	
0	0	**Leeds** **176** d.	...	0554	...	0819	0818	...	0840	1017	...	1019	1100	...	1316	1350	...	1459	1646	...	1645	1720	...
27	27	Keighley **176** d.	...	0621	...	0843	0841	...	0907	1043	...	1042	1123	...	1340	1413	...	1522	1710	...	1709	1747	...
42	42	Skipton **176** d.	0541	0638	...	0900	0855	...	0926	1100	...	1100	1140	...	1401	1433	...	1538	1724	...	1725	1803	...
58	58	Hellifield d.	0556	0652	...	0914	0910	...	0940	1114	...	1114	1154	...	1415	1448	...	1552	1739	...	1739	1818	...
66	66	Giggleswick d.	0606	0703	...	0925	0920	...	0952	1124	...	1125	1204	...	1425	1459	...	1602	1749	...	1750	1828	...
103	103	Carnforth d.	0643	0739	...	1001	0956	...	1029	1202	...	1202	1240	...	1502	1536	...	1638	1826	...	1827	1904	...
113		**Lancaster** a.	0652	0750	...	1013	1008	...	1038	1211	...	1211	1251	...	1516	1545	...	1647	1838	...	1838	1912	...
120	112	Morecambe a.	*0736*	*0838*	...	1031	1032	...	1055	1243	...	1236	1316	...	1535	1602	...	1714	1858	...	1901	1935	...
127	119	**Heysham** Port a.	...	...	...	...	...	...	...	1301	...	1254	...	...	...	...	...	...	...	...	...	...	...

	Ⓐ	⑥		⑥	Ⓐ		⑦	⑥		Ⓐ	⑦		Ⓐ	⑥		⑦	Ⓐ		⑥	⑦	
Heysham Port d.	...	...	...	...	...	...	...	1315	...	1317	...	...	...	...	...	...	...	...	...	...	...
Morecambe d.	*0610*	*0736*	...	1034	1034	...	1222	1331	...	1333	1446d	...	1619d	1616	...	1736	1908	...	1909	1946	...
Lancaster d.	0707	0823	...	1049	1049	...	1248	1348	...	1349	1429d	...	1605d	1640	...	1750	1924	...	1925	2001	...
Carnforth d.	0718	0833	...	1107	1107	...	1258	1358	...	1359	1500	...	1632	1650	...	1807	1934	...	1935	2011	...
Giggleswick d.	0752	0907	...	1142	1142	...	1332	1433	...	1434	1535	...	1708	1725	...	1846	2009	...	2010	2046	...
Hellifield d.	0803	0919	...	1153	1153	...	1344	1446	...	1444	1546	...	1720	1736	...	1858	2020	...	2020	2057	...
Skipton **176** a.	0821	0936	...	1210	1210	...	1401	1503	...	1503	1603	...	1737	1753	...	1915	2038	...	2037	2114	...
Keighley **176** a.	0836	0950	...	1222	1221	...	1415	1519	...	1520	1616	...	1749	1806	...	1926	2049	...	2048	2126	...
Leeds **176** a.	0904	1020	...	1250	1254	...	1444	1548	...	1547	1646	...	1815	1836	...	1956	2115	...	2116	2154	...

d – Calls at Lancaster, then Morecambe.

175 LEEDS - HARROGATE - YORK — 2nd class

km		⚒	Ⓐ	⑥	Ⓐ	⑥	⑥	Ⓐ	⑥	Ⓐ	⑥	Ⓐ	⚒	⚒		⚒	⚒	Ⓐ	⑥	⚒	⚒	⚒
0	**Leeds** **124 188** d.		0609	0610	0631	0636	0713	0714	0741	0743	0755	0801	0829	0859	and at	1529	1559	1629	1629	1659	1713	1729
29	**Harrogate** d.		0646	0647	0708	0713	0749	0751	0818	0820	0832	0838	0906	0936	the same	1606	1636	1707	1706	1736	1750	1806
36	Knaresborough d.		0654	0657	0718	0723	0759	0759	0826	0829	0843	0849	0915	0947	minutes past each	1615	1647	1715	1714	1747	1801	1814
62	**York** **124 188** a.		0725	0726	0747	0750	0827	0832	0859	0858	...	...	0946	...	hour until	1645	...	1745	1744	...	...	1846

	⚒	⚒	Ⓐ	⚒	⚒	⑥	Ⓐ		⑦	⑦	⑦	⑦		⑦	⑦	⑦		⑦	⑦	⑦		⑦	⑦
Leeds **124 188** d.	1759	1829	1859	1930	2029	2120	2129	...		0954	1054	1154	...	1254	1354	1454	...	1554	1654	1754	...	1854	1954
Harrogate d.	1836	1906	1936	2007	2106	2157	2206	...		1048	1130	1233	...	1333	1429	1533	...	1633	1733	1833	...	1933	2033
Knaresborough d.	1847	1916	1947	2016	2115	2208	2216	...		1057	1141	1245	...	1347	1445	1544	...	1643	1745	1844	...	1945	2044
York **124 188** a.	...	1945	...	2045	2144	...	...	...		1125	1204	1310	...	1413	1509	1609	...	1707	1810	1908	...	2008	2107

	⚒	⑥	Ⓐ	⑥	Ⓐ	Ⓐ	⑥	Ⓐ	⚒	⑥	Ⓐ	⑥	Ⓐ	⚒	⚒	⚒		⚒	⚒	⚒	⚒	⚒
York **124 188** d.		...	...	0652	0649	...	...	...	0754	...	...	0843	0847	0911	...	1011	and at	...	1611	...	1704	1728
Knaresborough d.		0647	0657	0720	0719	0742	0750	0757	0819	0850	0855	0908	0911	0936	1006	1036	the same	1605	1636	1706	1734	1756
Harrogate d.		0656	0707	0729	0740	0751	0759	0806	0829	0859	0904	0918	0921	0945	1015	1045	minutes past each	1614	1645	1715	1744	1805
Leeds **124 188** a.		0733	0746	0806	0816	0830	0836	0840	0908	0936	0937	0955	0957	1022	1052	1122	hour until	1652	1722	1752	1822	1842

	Ⓐ	Ⓐ	⑥	Ⓐ	⚒	⚒	⚒	⑥	Ⓐ		⑦	⑦	⑦	⑦		⑦	⑦	⑦	⑦	⑦		⑦	⑦
York **124 188** d.	...	1805	1811	...	1913	2011	2112	2157	2211	...		1114	1217	1318	...	1418	1517	1617	1718	1817	...	1917	2017
Knaresborough d.	1810	1834	1836	1906	1938	2036	2137	2222	2237	...		1142	1242	1344	...	1442	1542	1641	1743	1842	...	1942	2042
Harrogate d.	1824	1843	1845	1915	1947	2045	2146	2236	2248	...		1153	1253	1353	...	1452	1553	1652	1753	1853	...	1952	2053
Leeds **124 188** a.	1901	1924	1923	1952	2024	2123	2223	2313	2326	...		1228	1330	1430	...	1529	1630	1730	1830	1930	...	2029	2130

Additional trains	⚒A	⑦A	⑦	Ⓐ	⑥	⑥	⑦	Ⓐ	
Leeds d.	1959	2034	2230	2238	2233	2322	2323	2332	...
Harrogate a.	2025	2100	2307	2317	2311	0001	2359	0012	...

Additional trains	⚒	Ⓐ	ⒶA	⑥A	Ⓐ	⑦	⑦	⑦A
Harrogate d.	0605	0625	0734	0813	0815	0953	1053	1707
Leeds a.	0644	0701	0806	0845	0852	1031	1129	1733

A – (12) and 🍷 Harrogate - Leeds - London Kings Cross and v.v. (Table **180**).

176 WEST YORKSHIRE LOCAL SERVICES — 2nd class

BRADFORD FORSTER SQUARE - SKIPTON

Journey: ± 38 minutes

From Bradford Forster Square: Trains call at **Keighley** ± 21 minutes later.

Ⓐ: 0603, 0638, 0715, 0741, 0811, 0841, 0911 and every 30 minutes until 1541, 1612, 1638, 1711, 1738, 1816, 1841, 1908, 1936, 2009, 2109, 2209, 2309.

⑥: 0609, 0709, 0811, 0842, 0911 and every 30 minutes until 1541, 1612, 1637, 1711, 1738, 1811, 1841, 1907, 1936, 2009, 2112, 2202, 2309.

⑦: 1055, 1255, 1455, 1655, 1855, 2055, 2255.

From Skipton: Trains call at **Keighley** ± 13 minutes later.

Ⓐ: 0556, 0626, 0700, 0724, 0800, 0830, 0900 and every 30 minutes until 1430, 14 1530, 1558, 1630, 1700, 1724, 1800, 1830, 1900, 1931, 1954, 2054, 2154.

⑥: 0600, 0704, 0730, 0800, 0831, 0900 and every 30 minutes until 1430, 1458, 15 1600, 1630, 1700, 1728, 1800, 1830, 1900, 1930, 1954, 2057, 2155.

⑦: 0932, 1142, 1342, 1542, 1742, 1942, 2124.

Table continues on next page ►►►

2nd class — WEST YORKSHIRE local services — 176

LEEDS - DONCASTER

ing trains. For faster trains see Table 180.

Journey: ± 50 minutes *48 km*

Leeds:

0620, 0721, 0821, 0921, 1021, 1121, 1221, 1321, 1421, 1521, 1621, 1657, 1721, 1821, 1921, 2022, 2121, 2240.

0621, 0721, 0821, 0921, 1021, 1121, 1221, 1321, 1421, 1521, 1621, 1721, 1821, 1921, 2022, 2121, 2219.

1021, 1221, 1421, 1621, 1821, 2021, 2121.

From Doncaster:

Ⓐ: 0626, 0708, 0726, 0756, 0826, 0926, 1026, 1126, 1226, 1326, 1426, 1526, 1626, 1726, 1826, 1922, 2026, 2127, 2227.

⑥: 0626, 0726, 0827, 0926, 1026, 1126, 1226, 1326, 1426, 1526, 1626, 1726, 1826, 1922, 2026, 2122, 2226.

⑦: 0912, 1112, 1312, 1512, 1712, 1927, 2152.

LEEDS - SKIPTON

lso Tables 173/174

Journey: ± 45 minutes *42 km*

Leeds: Trains call at **Keighley** ± 24 minutes later.

0616, 0657, 0725, 0749, 0825, 0856, 0926, 0956 and every 30 minutes until 1626, 1656, 1726, 1740, 1756, 1826, 1856, 1926, 1956, 2022, 2055, 2126, 2156, 2226, 2256, 2319.

0650, 0750, 0825, 0856, 0926, 0956 and every 30 minutes until 1956, 2026, 2100, 2126, 2204, 2226, 2256, 2319.

0840, 0900, 1009, 1109, 1216 and hourly until 2116, 2220, 2320.

From Skipton: Trains call at **Keighley** ± 13 minutes later.

Ⓐ: 0545, 0614, 0640, 0706, 0718, 0730, 0745, 0813, 0837, 0917, 0947 and every 30 minutes until 1617, 1647, 1715, 1747, 1817, 1847, 1915, 1947, 2022, 2045, 2117, 2217.

⑥: 0545, 0644, 0745, 0816, 0847, 0917, 0947, and every 30 minutes until 1917, 1947, 2022, 2050, 2117, 2149, 2217.

⑦: 0832, 0912, 1012 and hourly until 1612, 1714, 1812, 1922, 2012, 2122, 2212, 2312.

LEEDS - BRADFORD FORSTER SQUARE

eeds - Bradford Interchange see Table 190

Journey: ± 21 minutes *22 km*

Leeds:

0645, 0739, 0810, 0832, 0841, 0910, 0942, 1012, 1040, and every 30 minutes until, 1340, 1540, 1607, 1638, 1709, 1736, 1810, 1837, 1908, 2101.

0710, 0810, 0841, 0910, 0939, 1010, 1040, and every 30 minutes until 1540, 1607, 1638, 1708, 1736, 1810, 1840, 1910, 2158.

0831, 0941 and hourly until 1641, 1745, 1841, 1942, 2041, 2141, 2241.

From Bradford Forster Square:

Ⓐ: 0558, 0630, 0654, 0757, 0826, 0902, 0930, 1000 and every 30 minutes until 1600, 1630, 1701, 1730, 1800, 1830, 1900, 1930.

⑥: 0600, 0658, 0733, 0758, 0826, 0901, 0930, 1000 and every 30 minutes until 1600, 1630, 1701, 1730, 1800, 1831, 1900, 1930.

⑦: 0901, 1003, 1113 and hourly until 1713, 1815, 1913, 2013, 2113, 2213, 2313.

LEEDS - ILKLEY

Journey: ± 30 minutes *26 km*

Leeds:

0600, 0634, 0704, 0729, 0733, 0758, 0835, 0902, and every 30 minutes until 1602, 1632, 1702, 1716, 1732, 1746, 1802, 1832, 1902, 1933, 2007, 2107, 2207, 2315.

0602, 0702, 0758, 0832, 0902, 0932, 1004, 1032 and every 30 minutes until 1832, 1903, 1933, 2007, 2107, 2208, 2315.

0905 and hourly until 2005, 2108, 2215, 2310.

From Ilkley:

Ⓐ: 0602, 0633, 0710, 0737, 0756, 0805, 0816, 0838 and every 30 minutes until 1438, 1510, 1536, 1612, 1638, 1712, 1743, 1804, 1812, 1842, 1910, 1938, 2028, 2118, 2218, 2318.

⑥: 0610, 0710, 0810, 0838, 0910, 0940, 1010, 1038 and every 30 minutes until 1538, 1612, 1638, 1712, 1738, 1812, 1842, 1910, 1938, 2028, 2118, 2224, 2318.

⑦: 0905 and hourly until 2105, 2215, 2315.

HUDDERSFIELD - WAKEFIELD WESTGATE

Journey: ± 33 minutes *25 km*

Huddersfield:

0531, 0631, 0735, 0831, 0931 and hourly until 1931, 2031, 2135.

0640, 0735, 0831, 0931, and hourly until 1931, 2031, 2135.

From Wakefield Westgate:

Ⓐ: 0643, 0744, 0844, and hourly until 1844, 1944, 2050, 2144, 2248.

⑥: 0730, 0844, 0944, and hourly until 1844, 1944, 2050, 2144, 2248.

BRADFORD FORSTER SQUARE - ILKLEY

Journey: ± 31 minutes *22 km*

Bradford Forster Square:

0615, 0642, 0711, 0745, 0816, 0846, and every 30 minutes until 1315, 1346, 1416, 1446, 1516, 1546, 1616, 1643, 1716, 1748, 1811, 1846, 1941 2038, 2140, 2240, 2326.

0615, 0715, 0816, 0846, and every 30 minutes until 1616, 1644, 1716, 1743, 1816, 1846, 1946, 2038, 2140, 2240; 2320.

1027, 1227, 1426, 1627, 1827, 2027, 2237.

From Ilkley:

Ⓐ: 0617, 0652, 0720, 0748, 0824, 0852, 0921, 0951 and every 30 minutes until 1651, 1720, 1751, 1821, 1851, 1921, 2009, 2043, 2143, 2243.

⑥: 0621, 0721, 0821, 0852, 0921, 0951 and every 30 minutes until 1851, 1921, 2009, 2048, 2143, 2243.

⑦: 0925, 1125, 1325, 1525, 1725, 1925, 2130.

2nd class — HULL - BRIDLINGTON - SCARBOROUGH — 177

	⚒	⚒	⚒	⚒		⚒	⚒	⑥		Ⓐ	⚒	Ⓐ	⑥		⑦	⑦	⑦	⑦		⑦	⑦	⑦
Hull △ d.	0653	0814	0947	1114	...	1314	1444	1614	...	1618	1738	1915	1922	...	0925	1025	1205	1405	...	1605	1800	1859
Beverley △ d.	0706	0828	1001	1128	...	1328	1458	1628	...	1632	1752	1929	1936	...	0939	1039	1219	1419	...	1619	1814	1913
Driffield △ d.	0723	0842	1015	1140	...	1340	1512	1643	...	1647	1809	1943	1951	...	0956	1054	1234	1434	...	1634	1826	1928
Bridlington △ a.	0739	0857	1030	1155	...	1353	1527	1658	...	1702	1825	1958	2006	...	1011	1109	1249	1449	...	1649	1839	1946
Bridlington d.	0740	0900	1038	1206	...	1406	1535	1704	...	1704	1835	2003	2019	...	1014	1111	1255	1455	...	1655	1844	...
Filey d.	0802	0922	1100	1228	...	1428	1557	1726	...	1726	1857	2025	2041	...	1036	1133	1317	1517	...	1717	1906	...
Scarborough a.	0821	0940	1118	1246	...	1446	1615	1744	...	1744	1915	2043	2059	...	1054	1151	1335	1535	...	1735	1924	...

		⚒	⚒	⚒	⚒		⚒	⚒	⚒		⚒		⑥	Ⓐ		⑦	⑦	⑦		⑦	⑦	⑦	⑦
borough d.	...	0650	0902	1000	1128	...	1328	1457	1625	...	1757	...	1940	2004	...	...	1111	1206	...	1406	1606	1806	1937
d.	...	0705	0917	1015	1143	...	1343	1512	1640	...	1812	...	1955	2019	...	...	1126	1221	...	1421	1621	1821	1952
lington a.	...	0727	0939	1037	1205	...	1405	1534	1702	...	1834	...	2017	2041	...	...	1148	1243	...	1443	1643	1843	2014
lington △ d.	...	0730	0941	1041	1211	...	1411	1536	1705	...	1841	...	2023	2044	...	0951	1150	1246	...	1446	1646	1856	2016
eld △ d.	...	0747	0957	1057	1224	...	1424	1552	1719	...	1857	...	2039	2100	...	1007	1206	1259	...	1459	1659	1912	2029
erley △ d.	...	0806	1012	1112	1237	...	1437	1607	1731	...	1912	...	2054	2115	...	1022	1221	1312	...	1512	1712	1929	2042
△ a.	...	0822	1028	1128	1253	...	1453	1623	1748	...	1930	...	2110	2131	...	1038	1237	1328	...	1528	1728	1946	2058

All trains Hull - Bridlington and v.v.:

From Hull on ⚒ at 0556, 0620, 0653, 0714, 0752, 0814, 0916, 0947, 1014, and every 30 minutes until 1544, 1614⑥, 1618Ⓐ, 1644, 1714, 1738, 1814, 1915Ⓐ, 1922⑥, 2014, 2148; on ⑦ at 0900, 0925, 1025, 1125, 1205, 1255, 1405, 1500, 1605, 1655, 1715, 1800, 1859.

From Bridlington on ⚒ at 0644, 0712, 0730, 0808, 0905, 0941 and every 30 minutes until 1511, 1536, 1611, 1641, 1705⑥, 1706Ⓐ, 1736, 1815, 1841, 1908Ⓐ, 1911⑥, 2023⑥, 2044Ⓐ, 2128, 2242; on ⑦ at 0951, 1150, 1246, 1346, 1446, 1545, 1646, 1720, 1746, 1816, 1856, 1956, 2016.

2nd class — HULL - YORK — 178

	⚒	⑦	⚒	⚒	⑥	⑦	⚒	⑥	Ⓐ	⑦	⑥	⑦	Ⓐ	⑥	Ⓐ	⑦	Ⓐ	⑥	⑥		Ⓐ	⑦	⚒	⑦	⑦	⑥
Hull .... **181 189** d.	0707	0854	0902	1012	1107	1146	1204	1308	1315	1317	1415	1420	1422	1503	1503	1606	1610	1610	1711	...	1717	1725	1918	1925	2030	2102
Selby .. **181 189** d.	0748	0928	0939	1049	1141	1220	1239	1349	1358	1351	1449	1454	1458	1537	1541	1640	1649	1649	1800	...	1804	1759	1954	2000	2104	2137
York a.	0822	0952	1011	1120	1205	1252	1304	1422	1427	1417	1522	1526	1528	1602	1606	1706	1713	1715	1823	...	1828	1825	2025	2025	2128	2159

	Ⓐ	⑥	⚒	⑥	Ⓐ	⑦	⑥	⚒	⑦	⚒	⚒	⑦	⑥	⑦	Ⓐ	⑦	⑥	Ⓐ	⑦	⚒	⑥	Ⓐ	⑦	⑥	⑦	⑥	Ⓐ
d.	0730	0740	0843	0951	1019	1040	1047	1145	1205	1247	1344	1354	1447	1452	1502	1606	1606	1611	1714	1725	1809	1844	1916	1950	2150	2212	2229
y .. **181 189** d.	0750	0759	0906	1009	1039	1058	1106	1204	1224	1306	1408	1423	1506	1511	1521	1635	1632	1637	1733	1750	1838	1913	1935	2008	2210	2230	2247
.... **181 189** a.	0846	0856	0948	1053	1123	1136	1153	1251	1306	1351	1451	1504	1551	1552	1602	1716	1722	1728	1814	1834	1927	2002	2016	2048	2250	2316	2335

2nd class — LINCOLN - SHEFFIELD — 179

	⚒	⚒	⚒	Ⓐ	⚒		⚒	⑥	⚒	⚒	⚒	⚒	⑥	⚒	⚒	⚒	⚒	⑦	⑦	⑦	⑦	⑦	⑦
Lincoln d.	...	...	0700	...	0825	and at	1523	...	1625	1722	...	1825	...	1943	2027	2127	...	...	1515	1715	1915	2108	...
Gainsborough Lea Rd d.	...	...	0721	...	0846	the same	1546	1619a	1646	1743	...	1846	1932a	2006	2048	2150	...	...	1536	1736	1936	2129	...
Retford d.	...	0701	0740	...	0901	minutes	1601	1636	1701	1758	1814	1903	1954	2019	2103	2205	2245	1450	1551	1751	1951	2144	2224
Worksop ▽ d.	0630	0713	0751	0813	0913	past each	1613	1647	1713	1810	1825	1915	2005	2031	2115	2216	2258	1501	1603	1803	2003	2156	2235
Sheffield ▽ a.	0703	0749	0824	0847	0950	hour until	1648	1723	1748	1833	1858	1953	2039	2105	2145	2251	2333	1535	1635	1835	2035	2228	2308

	⚒	⚒	⚒	⚒	Ⓐ	⑥	⚒	⚒		⚒	⑥	⚒	⚒	⚒	⚒	⚒	⚒	⑦	⑦	⑦	⑦	⑦	⑦
field ▽ d.	0539	0546	0644	0730	0744	0803	0844	0944	and at	1544	1601	1644	1723	1744	1844	1949	2142	1342	1355	1543	1743	1932	2106
sop ▽ d.	0603	0623	0715	0801	0810	0834	0915	1014	the same	1615	1636	1715	1754	1815	1915	2019	2214	1403	1426	1613	1813	2002	2136
rd d.	0613	0637	0725	0811	...	0844	0925	1024	minutes	1625	1646	1725	1808	1825	1925	2029	2228	1413	1437	1624	1824	2013	2148
sborough Lea Rd d.	0628	...	0740	0825	...	0859a	0941	1038	past each	1640	1701a	1740	...	1840	1940	2043	...	1428	...	1638	1838	2027	...
oln a.	0656	...	0807	0853	...	...	1007	1107	hour until	1707	...	1805	...	1906	2007	2114	...	1454	...	1703	1903	2052	...

Gainsborough Central.

▽ – Additional journeys Worksop - Sheffield and v.v: **From Worksop** at 2126⚒, 2328⚒. **From Sheffield** at 2045⚒, 2244⚒.

180 LONDON - LEEDS, YORK, NEWCASTLE and EDINBURGH

Most services convey 🍸

For additional services see Tables **124, 181, 182, 183, 184** and **188**.

km			Ⓐ	Ⓐ	Ⓐ	Ⓐ	Ⓐ	Ⓐ	Ⓐ	Ⓐ	Ⓐ	Ⓐ	Ⓐ	Ⓐ	Ⓐ	Ⓐ	Ⓐ	Ⓐ	Ⓐ	Ⓐ	Ⓐ	Ⓐ	Ⓐ	Ⓐ
					A																	A		
0	**London** Kings Cross d.	Ⓐ	0550	...	...	0615	0630	0700	0705	0708	0730	0735	0800	0806	0830	0835	0900	0903	0908	0930	0935	1000	1003	1008
44	Stevenage d.		0611	...	...	0635	0650	|	|	0728	|	0755	|	|	|	0855	|	|	0929	|	0955	|	|	1029
123	Peterborough d.		0642	...	...	0706	0721	0746	0752	0759	0816	|	|	0853	0916	|	0946	0952	1000	1016	|	|	1051	1101
170	Grantham d.		0702	...	...	0726	0740	|	|	0819	|	0840	|	|	|	0940	|	|	1021	|	1040	|	|	1121
193	Newark North Gate d.		0714	...	...	0738	|	|	|	0831	0844	|	|	|	0944	|	|	|	1033	1044	|	|	|	1135
223	Retford d.		0729	...	...	0754	|	|	|	0846	|	|	|	|	|	|	|	|	1049	|	|	|	|	...
251	Doncaster d.		0745	0615	...	0811	0813	|	0842	0901	0910	0914	|	0942	1010	1014	|	1043	1105	1111	1114	|	1142	...
283	Wakefield Westgate a.		0802	|	...	|	0832	|	0900	|	|	0931	|	1000	|	1031	|	1100	|	|	1131	|	1200	...
299	**Leeds** a.		0818	|	0710	|	0848	|	0917	|	|	0946	|	1015	|	1048	|	1116	|	|	1147	|	1216	...
303	**York** d.		—	0639	0737	0835	...	0855	...	0925	0937	...	0953	...	1035	...	1055	...	1130	1136	...	1154	...	...
351	Northallerton d.		...	|	|	0853	...	|	...	...	|	...	|	...	1054	...	|	...	...	|	...	|	...	...
374	Darlington d.		Ⓐ	0707	0806	0908	...	0923	...	...	1006	...	1021	...	1108	...	1123	...	...	1207	...	1222	...	...
409	Durham a.			0723	0822	0924	...	|	...	...	1022	...	|	...	1124	...	|	...	...	1223	...	|	...	...
432	**Newcastle** a.		0622	0739	0838	0942	...	0951	...	...	1039	...	1049	...	1142	...	1151	...	...	1240	...	1250	...	...
488	Alnmouth a.		0653	0808	|	|	...	|	...	...	1107	...	|	...	...	...	|	...	...	1310	...	|	...	...
540	Berwick upon Tweed a.		0717	0832	0929	1030	...	|	...	...	|	...	1136	...	...	...	1238	...	...	|	...	1337	...	...
632	**Edinburgh** Waverley a.		0807	0921	1020	1114	...	1117	...	...	1209	...	1218	...	...	...	1320	...	...	1413	...	1420	...	...

	Ⓐ	Ⓐ	Ⓐ	Ⓐ	Ⓐ	Ⓐ	Ⓐ	Ⓐ	Ⓐ	Ⓐ	Ⓐ	Ⓐ	Ⓐ	Ⓐ	Ⓐ	Ⓐ	Ⓐ	Ⓐ	Ⓐ	Ⓐ	Ⓐ	Ⓐ	Ⓐ	Ⓐ
							B										A					K		
London Kings Cross d.	1035	1100	1105	1108	1130	1135	1200	1203	1208	1230	1235	1300	1305	1308	1330	1335	1400	1405	1408	1430	1435	1500	1505	1508
Stevenage d.	1055	|	|	1129	|	1156	|	|	1229	|	1255	|	|	1329	|	1355	|	|	1428	|	1455	|	|	1529
Peterborough d.	|	|	1152	1159	1216	|	|	1251	1300	1316	|	1346	1352	1400	1416	|	|	1451	1500	1516	|	|	1551	1600
Grantham d.	1140	|	|	1219	|	1241	|	|	1322	|	1340	|	|	1421	|	1440	|	|	1520	|	1540	|	|	1621
Newark North Gate d.	|	|	|	1231	1244	|	|	|	1334	1344	|	|	|	1434	1444	|	|	|	1534	1544	|	|	|	1633
Retford d.	|	|	|	1246	|	|	|	|	...	|	|	|	|	1449	|	|	|	|	...	|	|	|	|	1649
Doncaster d.	1214	|	1242	1305	1310	1315	|	1342	...	1410	1414	|	1442	1504	1511	1514	|	1542	...	1610	1614	|	1641	1705
Wakefield Westgate a.	1231	|	1300	|	|	1332	|	1400	...	|	1431	|	1459	|	|	1531	|	1559	...	|	1631	|	1659	|
Leeds a.	1248	|	1316	|	|	1348	|	1416	...	|	1448	|	1516	|	|	1548	|	1616	...	|	1648	|	1716	|
York d.	...	1253	...	1329	1336	...	1355	...	...	1435	...	1454	...	1530	1535	...	1555	...	...	1635	...	1654	...	1729
Northallerton d.	...	|	...	...	|	...	|	...	...	1454	...	|	...	...	1554	...	|	...	...	1654	...	|	...	...
Darlington d.	...	1321	...	...	1407	...	1423	...	...	1508	...	1522	...	...	1608	...	1623	...	...	1708	...	1722	...	...
Durham a.	...	|	...	...	1423	...	|	...	...	1524	...	|	...	...	1624	...	|	...	...	1724	...	|	...	...
Newcastle a.	...	1349	...	...	1440	...	1451	...	...	1540	...	1550	...	...	1641	...	1651	...	...	1740	...	1750	...	...
Alnmouth a.	...	|	...	...	1509	...	|	...	...	...	...	|	...	...	|	...	|	...	...	...	...	|	...	...
Berwick upon Tweed a.	...	|	...	...	|	...	1539	...	...	...	...	1638	...	...	1728	...	1739	...	...	...	...	1837	...	...
Edinburgh Waverley a.	...	1517	...	...	1613	...	1622	...	...	...	...	1721	...	...	1812	...	1823	...	...	...	...	1920	...	...

	Ⓐ	Ⓐ	Ⓐ	Ⓐ	Ⓐ	Ⓐ	Ⓐ	Ⓐ	Ⓐ	Ⓐ	Ⓐ	Ⓐ	Ⓐ	Ⓐ	Ⓐ	Ⓐ	Ⓐ	Ⓐ	Ⓐ	Ⓐ	Ⓐ	Ⓐ	Ⓐ	Ⓐ
		A							D		E			F			G			H			J	
London Kings Cross d.	1535	1600	1606	1609	1630	1633	1700	1703	1719	1730	1733	1749	1800	1803	1819	1830	1833	1900	1903	1906	1930	1933	2000	2005
Stevenage d.	1555	|	|	1630	|	1653	|	|	|	|	1755	|	|	|	|	|	1853	|	|	1928	|	1953	|	|
Peterborough d.	|	|	1654	1701	1716	|	|	1750	1808	1817	|	1837	|	1851	1908	1918	|	|	1953	2000	2016	|	|	2051
Grantham d.	1641	|	|	1722	|	1740	|	|	1829	|	1842	1906	|	|	1928	|	1942	|	|	2021	|	2040	|	|
Newark North Gate d.	|	|	|	1736	1744	|	|	|	1841	1846	|	|	|	1922	|	1946	|	|	|	2036	2044	|	|	2120
Retford d.	|	|	|	...	|	1802	|	|	|	|	|	1928	|	|	|	|	2005	|	|	...	|	|	|	|
Doncaster d.	1714	|	1745	...	1810	1818	|	1841	1910	|	1915	1944	|	1950	|	2012	2021	|	2041	...	2110	2114	|	2145
Wakefield Westgate a.	1731	|	1805	...	|	1835	|	1859	...	|	1933	2002	|	2007	|	|	2038	|	2100	...	|	2131	|	2207
Leeds a.	1748	|	1820	...	|	1851	|	1917	...	|	1948	2020	|	2021	|	|	2053	|	2117	...	|	2149	|	2223
York d.	...	1754	...	...	1836	...	1854	...	...	1929	...	...	1951	...	2020	2036	...	2053	...	...	2134	...	2153	...
Northallerton d.	...	|	...	...	1856	...	|	...	...	|	...	...	|	...	2038	|	...	|	...	...	2152	...	|	...
Darlington d.	...	1823	...	...	1910	...	1922	...	...	1957	...	...	2019	...	2053	2105	...	2121	...	...	2207	...	2221	...
Durham a.	...	|	...	...	1926	...	|	...	...	2013	...	...	|	...	2109	2121	...	|	...	...	2223	...	2237	...
Newcastle a.	...	1851	...	...	1942	...	1950	...	...	2029	...	...	2047	...	2125	2137	...	2149	...	...	2239	...	2254	...
Alnmouth a.	...	|	...	...	|	...	|	...	...	|	...	...	|	...	...	2209	...	|	...	...	2311**f**	...	...	...
Berwick upon Tweed a.	...	1939	...	...	|	...	2037	...	...	2117	...	...	|	...	...	|	...	2238	...	...	2336**f**	...	...	...
Edinburgh Waverley a.	...	2022	...	...	2112	...	2122	...	...	2208	...	...	2220	...	...	2315	...	2328	...	...	0026**f**	...	...	...

	Ⓐ	Ⓐ	Ⓐ	Ⓐ			⑥	⑥	⑥	⑥	⑥	⑥	⑥	⑥	⑥	⑥	⑥	⑥	⑥	⑥	⑥	⑥	⑥	⑥
									A											A				
London Kings Cross d.	2100	2135	2200	2330	...	⑥	...	...	...	0615	0700	0703	0730	0800	0803	0830	0900	0903	0930	1000	1003	1030	1100	1103
Stevenage d.	2121	2157	|	|	...		...	...	...	0635	0720	0725	|	|	|	|	|	0923	|	|	|	|	|	1123
Peterborough d.	2152	2228	2247	0017**s**	...		...	...	...	0706	|	0755	0816	|	0849	0916	|	0954	1016	|	1051	1116	|	1154
Grantham d.	|	2249	2309	0045**s**	...		...	...	...	0726	|	0814	|	|	0909	|	|	1015	|	|	1110	|	|	1214
Newark North Gate d.	2220	2302	2321	0057**s**	...		...	...	...	0738	|	0826	|	|	0921	0944	|	1027	|	|	1123	1144	|	1226
Retford d.	|	2319	|	|	...		...	...	...	0754	|	|	0855	|	|	|	|	|	1054	|	|	|	|	|
Doncaster d.	2246	2335	2352	0124**s**	...		...	0610	...	0810	|	0851	0912	|	0951	1012	|	1051	1110	|	1151	1210	|	1251
Wakefield Westgate a.	|	2352	|	|	...		...	|	...	|	|	0907	|	|	1008	|	|	1107	|	|	1207	|	|	1307
Leeds a.	|	0008	|	0234	...		...	|	0710	|	|	0924	|	|	1024	|	|	1125	|	|	1224	|	|	1325
York d.	2312	...	0042	...	...		...	0634	0737	0835	0855	...	0937	0953	...	1036	1053	...	1136	1154	...	1235	1253	...
Northallerton d.	2342	...	0110**s**	...	...		...	0652	|	0853	|	...	|	|	...	1054	|	...	|	|	...	1254	|	...
Darlington d.	2357	...	0124**s**	...	...		...	0707	0806	0908	0923	...	1005	1021	...	1108	1121	...	1205	1222	...	1308	1321	...
Durham a.	0013	...	0143**s**	...	...		...	0723	0822	0924	|	...	1021	|	...	1125	|	...	1221	|	...	1324	|	...
Newcastle a.	0041	...	0214	...	...		0630	0739	0837	0940	0952	...	1037	1049	...	1141	1149	...	1237	1250	...	1340	1349	...
Alnmouth a.	...	...	...	...	...		0657	0808	|	|	|	...	1105	|	...	|	|	...	1306	|	...	|	|	...
Berwick upon Tweed a.	...	...	...	...	...		0721	0832	0931	|	1039	...	|	1139	...	|	1239	...	|	1339	...	|	1439	...
Edinburgh Waverley a.	...	...	...	...	...		0815	0920	1024	1110	1127	...	1212	1227	...	1310	1326	...	1413	1425	...	1510	1527	...

	⑥	⑥	⑥	⑥	⑥	⑥	⑥	⑥	⑥	⑥	⑥	⑥	⑥	⑥	⑥	⑥	⑥	⑥	⑥	⑥	⑥	⑥	⑥	⑥
		B						A											D		E			H
London Kings Cross d.	1135	1200	1203	1230	1300	1303	1330	1400	1403	1430	1500	1503	1530	1600	1603	1630	1700	1703	1710	1730	1735	1800	1803	1808
Stevenage d.	|	|	|	|	|	1324	|	|	|	|	|	1524	|	|	|	|	|	1724	|	|	|	|	|	1829
Peterborough d.	1223	|	1252	1316	|	1354	1416	|	1450	1516	|	1554	1616	|	1651	1716	|	1754	1800	1817	1823	|	1850	1900
Grantham d.	|	|	1315	|	1403	1414	|	|	1511	|	|	1614	|	|	1712	|	|	1814	1821	|	|	|	|	1921
Newark North Gate d.	|	|	1327	1344	|	1426	|	|	1524	1544	|	1626	|	|	1725	1744	|	1826	|	1846	|	|	1918	1935
Retford d.	|	|	|	|	|	|	1455	|	|	|	|	|	1654	|	|	|	|	|	|	|	|	|	1933	...
Doncaster d.	1314	|	1354	1410	|	1452	1512	|	1550	1610	|	1651	1710	|	1751	1810	|	1851	1856	1911	1915	|	1949	...
Wakefield Westgate a.	1331	|	1411	|	|	1508	|	|	1607	|	|	1707	|	|	1808	|	|	1908	...	|	1932	|	2006	...
Leeds a.	1348	|	1429	|	|	1525	|	|	1624	|	|	1725	|	|	1825	|	|	1924	...	|	1948	|	2022	...
York d.	...	1354	...	1435	1456	...	1536	1553	...	1635	1654	...	1735	1752	...	1837	1854	...	...	1936	...	1954	...	...
Northallerton d.	...	|	...	1454	|	...	|	|	...	1654	|	...	|	|	...	1856	|	...	...	|	...	|	...	...
Darlington d.	...	1422	...	1508	1524	...	1605	1621	...	1708	1722	...	1803	1821	...	1910	1922	...	...	2005	...	2022	...	...
Durham a.	...	|	...	1524	|	...	1621	|	...	1724	|	...	1819	|	...	1926	|	...	...	2021	...	|	...	...
Newcastle a.	...	1450	...	1540	1552	...	1637	1649	...	1740	1750	...	1835	1849	...	1942	1950	...	...	2040	...	2050	...	...
Alnmouth a.	...	|	...	|	|	...	1705	|	...	|	|	...	1906	|	...	|	|	...	...	...	...	2124	...	...
Berwick upon Tweed a.	...	1539	...	|	1641	...	|	1739	...	|	1843	...	|	1939	...	|	2037	...	...	...	...	2149	...	...
Edinburgh Waverley a.	...	1624	...	1712	1728	...	1810	1825	...	1911	1928	...	2012	2024	...	2114	2122	...	...	...	...	2237	...	...

A – To/from Aberdeen (Table **222**).
B – To/from Inverness (Table **222**).
C – To/from Glasgow Central (Table **220**).
D – To/from Hull (Table **181**).
E – To/from Harrogate (Table **175**).
F – To/from Skipton (Table **173**).
G – To/from Bradford Forster Square (Table **182**).
H – To/from Lincoln (Table **186**).
J – To/from Sunderland (Table **210**).
K – To/from Stirling (Table **222**)
f – ⑤ only.
s – Calls to set down only.
u – Calls to pick up only.

For explanation of standard symbols see page 4

Most services convey 🍸

LONDON - LEEDS, YORK, NEWCASTLE and EDINBURGH — 180

For additional services see Tables **124, 181, 182, 183, 184** and **188**.

	⑥	⑥	⑥	⑥	⑥	⑥	⑥	⑥
	F			G				
on Kings Cross d.	1835	1900	1904	1930	2000	2030	2100	2200
enage d.	|	|	|	1950	|	|	|	|
borough d.	1924	|	1957	2021	2048	2116	2148	2247
tham d.	|	|	|	2041	|	2136	|	2307
rk North Gate d.	|	|	|	2053	2116	2148	|	2319
rd d.	|	|	|	|	|	2203	|	2334
aster d.	2015	|	2047	2118	2141	2219	|	2349
akefield Westgate a.	2032	|	2104	2134	|	2236	|	0005
eds a.	2047	|	2121	2150	|	2252	|	0023
d.	...	2053	...	...	2206	...	2256	...
allerton d.	...	|	...	...	|	...	2314	...
ngton d.	...	2121	...	...	2235	...	2329	...
am a.	...	|	...	...	2251	...	2345	...
castle a.	...	2151	...	...	2309	...	0003	...
outh a.	...	...	...	...	...	...	...	...
ick upon Tweed a.	...	...	...	...	...	...	...	...
burgh Waverley a.	...	...	...	...	...	...	...	...

⑦	⑦	⑦	⑦	⑦	⑦	⑦	⑦		⑦	⑦	⑦	⑦	⑦	⑦	⑦	⑦	⑦
							A									B	
on Kings Cross d.	...	...	...	0900	0903	0930	1000	...	1003	1020	1030	1100	1103	1120	1130	1200	1203
enage d.	...	...	...	|	0923	|	|	...	|	|	|	|	1123	|	|	|	|
borough d.	...	...	...	|	0954	1016	|	...	1050	1110	1116	|	1154	|	1216	|	1250
tham d.	...	...	...	|	1014	|	|	...	1110	|	|	|	1214	1225	|	|	1310
rk North Gate d.	...	...	...	|	1026	|	|	...	1122	|	1144	|	1226	|	|	|	1322
rd d.	...	...	...	|	|	1055	|	...	|	|	|	|	|	|	1255	|	|
aster d.	...	...	0937	|	1051	1111	|	...	1147	1159	1211	|	1251	|	1311	|	1347
akefield Westgate a.	...	...	|	|	1108	|	|	...	1204	|	|	|	1308	|	|	|	1404
eds a.	...	0830	|	|	1126	|	|	...	1221	|	|	|	1325	|	|	|	1421
d.	...	0900	1001	1049	...	1135	1152	...	...	1223	1235	1251	...	1317	1335	1352	...
allerton d.	...	0918	|	|	...	|	|	...	...	|	1253	|	...	1335	|	|	...
ngton d.	...	0935	1029	1117	...	1203	1221	...	...	1251	1308	1319	...	1350	1403	1421	...
am a.	...	0951	1045	|	...	1219	|	...	...	|	1324	|	...	1406	1419	|	...
castle a.	0915	1006	1101	1145	...	1235	1249	...	...	1322	1340	1347	...	1422	1435	1449	...
outh a.	|	1042	|	|	...	1309	|	...	...	...	|	|	...	|	1508	|	...
ick upon Tweed a.	0959	1107	1148	1232	...	|	1337	...	...	...	|	1434	...	|	|	1537	...
burgh Waverley a.	1045	1158	1232	1316	...	1419	1420	...	...	...	1508	1518	...	1558	1618	1620	...

	⑦	⑦	⑦	⑦	⑦	⑦	⑦	⑦	⑦	⑦	⑦	⑦	⑦	⑦	⑦	⑦	⑦	⑦	⑦	⑦	⑦	⑦	⑦	⑦	⑦	⑦
						A								C				D				E			F	
on Kings Cross d.	1220	1230	1300	1303	1330	1400	1403	1430	1500	1503	1530	1600	1605	1630	1635	1700	1705	1720	1730	1735	1800	1803	1827	1830	1835	1900
nage d.	|	|	|	1323	|	|	|	|	|	1523	|	|	|	|	1655	|	|	|	|	1755	|	|	|	|	1855	|
borough d.	1309	1316	|	1354	1416	|	1452	1516	|	1554	1617	|	1653	1716	|	|	1751	|	1817	|	1846	1851	|	|	|	|
ham d.	|	|	|	1414	|	|	1512	|	|	1614	1638	|	1713	|	1740	|	|	1826	1838	1843	|	|	|	|	1941	|
rk North Gate d.	|	1344	|	1426	|	|	1524	1544	|	1626	|	|	1725	1744	|	|	1819	1838	|	|	|	1920	|	1945	|	|
rd d.	|	|	|	|	1455	|	|	|	|	1642	|	|	|	|	1803	|	|	|	|	|	|	|	|	|	2004	|
aster d.	1358	1411	|	1451	1511	|	1550	1611	|	1658	1712	|	1751	1810	1820	|	1844	1905	1912	1916	|	1948	|	2010	2020	|
kefield Westgate a.	|	|	|	1508	|	|	1607	|	|	1715	|	|	1810	|	1839	|	1901	...	|	1933	|	2005	|	|	2037	|
eds a.	|	|	|	1525	|	|	1625	|	|	1731	|	|	1828	|	1856	|	1918	...	|	1951	|	2023	|	|	2052	|
d.	1423	1435	1453	...	1535	1552	...	1635	1652	...	1736	1749	...	1835	...	1851	...	...	1938	...	1959	...	2026	2036	...	2053
allerton d.	|	1453	|	...	|	|	...	1653	|	...	|	|	...	1853	...	|	...	...	|	...	|	...	|	2055	...	|
ngton d.	1451	1508	1521	...	1603	1621	...	1708	1720	...	1805	1817	...	1908	...	1919	...	...	2006	...	2027	...	2054	2109	...	2122
am a.	1507	1524	|	...	1619	|	...	1724	|	...	1821	|	...	1924	...	|	...	...	2022	...	|	...	2111	2125	...	|
castle a.	1525	1540	1549	...	1635	1649	...	1740	1748	...	1838	1845	...	1943	...	1947	...	...	2038	...	2055	...	2129	2141	...	2150
outh a.	...	|	|	...	1703	|	...	|	|	...	1906	|	...	|	...	|	...	...	2110	...	|	...	...	|	...	2223
ick upon Tweed a.	...	|	1636	...	|	1737	...	|	1835	...	|	1936	...	|	...	2035	...	...	|	...	2143	...	...	2228	...	2248
burgh Waverley a.	...	1709	1720	...	1809	1820	...	1908	1920	...	2013	2020	...	2114	...	2120	...	...	2218	...	2228	...	...	2313	...	2340

	⑦	⑦	⑦	⑦	⑦	⑦	⑦	⑦	⑦	⑦	⑦
		H									
lon Kings Cross d.	1903	1908	1930	1935	2000	2005	2035	2100	2135	2200	2235
enage d.	|	1929	|	1955	|	|	2055	|	2155	|	|
borough d.	1949	2001	2018	2026	2046	2052	2126	2146	2226	2247	2323**s**
tham d.	|	2022	|	2046	|	|	2146	|	2246	|	2344**s**
ark North Gate d.	2017	2036	2047	|	|	|	2158	|	2258	|	2355**s**
ord d.	|	...	|	|	|	2132	|	|	2314	|	|
caster d.	2043	...	2115	2119	|	2148	2223	|	2334	2343	0024**s**
akefield Westgate a.	2100	...	|	2136	|	2206	2239	|	2351	|	|
eds a.	2118	...	|	2152	|	2222	2257	|	0007	|	0130
d.	...	...	2140	...	2157	...	...	2302	...	0035	...
allerton d.	...	...	|	...	|	...	...	2336	...	0106**s**	...
ngton d.	...	...	2219	...	2239	...	...	2351	...	0120**s**	...
am a.	...	...	2235	...	2255	...	...	0007	...	0138**s**	...
castle a.	...	...	2308	...	2327	...	...	0039	...	0210	...
outh a.	...	...	...	...	...	...	...	...	...	...	...
vick upon Tweed a.	...	...	...	...	...	...	...	...	...	...	...
burgh Waverley a.	...	...	...	...	...	...	...	...	...	...	...

Ⓐ	Ⓐ	Ⓐ	Ⓐ	Ⓐ		Ⓐ	Ⓐ	Ⓐ	Ⓐ
									G
Edinburgh Waverley d.	...	...	...	...	...	...	...	...	...
Berwick upon Tweed d.	...	...	...	...	...	...	...	...	...
Alnmouth d.	...	...	...	...	...	...	...	...	...
Newcastle d.	...	...	...	0445	...	...	0525	...	...
Durham d.	...	...	...	0500	...	...	0539	...	...
Darlington d.	...	...	...	0518	...	...	0558	...	...
Northallerton d.	...	...	...	0529	...	...	0609	...	...
York d.	...	...	...	0600	...	...	0631	...	...
Leeds d.	...	0505	0530	|	...	0605	|	0640	0700
Wakefield Westgate d.	...	0518	0544	|	...	0618	|	0653	0713
Doncaster d.	...	0536	0603	0624	...	0636	0654	0712	|
Retford d.	...	0551	|	|	...	0651	|	|	|
Newark North Gate d.	0535	0606	0629	0647	...	0707	|	0737	|
Grantham d.	0547	0618	0641	0700	...	0720	0726	|	|
Peterborough d.	0610	0639	0701	0721	...	0741	0750	|	|
Stevenage a.	|	|	|	|	...	|	|	|	|
London Kings Cross a.	0658	0729	0752	0812	...	0834	0843	0850	0859

	Ⓐ	Ⓐ	Ⓐ	Ⓐ	Ⓐ	Ⓐ	Ⓐ	Ⓐ	Ⓐ	Ⓐ	Ⓐ	Ⓐ	Ⓐ	Ⓐ	Ⓐ	Ⓐ	Ⓐ	Ⓐ	Ⓐ	Ⓐ	Ⓐ	Ⓐ	Ⓐ	Ⓐ	Ⓐ	Ⓐ
	J	H					D	F		E		K								C						
burgh Waverley d.	...	...	...	...	...	0540	...	...	...	...	0548	0626	...	...	0655	0730	...	...	...	0800	0830	...	...	...	0900	0930
vick upon Tweed d.	...	...	...	...	0600	|	...	...	...	...	0634	0710	...	...	|	0812	...	...	...	|	0912	...	...	...	|	1012
nouth d.	...	...	...	...	0621	|	...	...	...	...	0655	|	...	...	|	|	...	...	...	0900	|	...	...	...	|	|
castle d.	0559	...	...	0630	0655	0704	...	...	...	...	0729	0757	...	...	0825	0859	...	...	...	0930	1000	...	...	...	1026	1059
am d.	0612	...	...	0644	0708	|	...	...	←	...	0742	|	...	...	0838	|	...	...	...	0943	|	...	...	...	1039	|
ngton d.	0632	...	...	0703	0725	|	...	...	0731	...	0801	0828	...	...	0857	0928	...	...	...	1001	1029	...	...	...	1058	1128
allerton d.	|	...	...	0715	→	|	...	...	|	...	|	|	...	...	0908	|	...	...	...	|	|	...	...	...	1109	|
d.	0701	...	...	0737	...	|	...	...	0802	...	0831	0857	...	...	0931	0958	...	1003	...	1031	1059	...	...	...	1131	1157
eds d.	|	...	0715	|	...	|	...	0740	|	0817	|	|	0845	0916	|	|	0945	|	1015	|	|	1045	...	1115	|	|
akefield Westgate d.	|	...	0728	|	...	|	...	0753	|	0830	|	|	0858	0929	|	|	0958	|	1028	|	|	1058	...	1128	|	|
caster d.	|	...	0746	|	...	|	0757	0813	|	0848	0855	|	0917	0947	0955	|	1017	1025	1046	1058	|	1117	...	1146	1155	|
ord d.	|	...	|	|	...	|	|	|	0836	|	|	|	|	|	|	|	|	1039	|	|	|	|	...	|	|	|
ark North Gate d.	|	0757	|	|	...	|	0822	0838	|	|	0919	|	|	|	1019	|	|	1054	|	1121	|	|	1154	|	1219	|
tham d.	|	|	0818	|	...	|	0835	|	|	0921	|	|	|	1018	|	|	|	1106	1118	|	|	|	1207	1218	|	|
rborough d.	0812	0827	|	0843	...	|	0902	0907	|	|	0950	|	1009	|	1051	|	1108	1128	|	1152	|	1209	1228	|	1250	|
enage a.	|	0856	0902	|	...	|	|	|	|	1008	|	|	|	1101	|	|	|	1156	1201	|	|	|	1256	1302	|	|
don Kings Cross a.	0906	0924	0929	0937	...	0940	0955	0957	1002	1035	1042	1051	1100	1128	1142	1151	1159	1223	1228	1242	1250	1300	1324	1328	1341	1349

	Ⓐ	Ⓐ	Ⓐ	Ⓐ	Ⓐ	Ⓐ	Ⓐ	Ⓐ	Ⓐ	Ⓐ		Ⓐ	Ⓐ	Ⓐ	Ⓐ	Ⓐ	Ⓐ	Ⓐ	Ⓐ	Ⓐ	Ⓐ	Ⓐ	Ⓐ	Ⓐ	Ⓐ	Ⓐ
					A					B						A										
burgh Waverley d.	...	...	...	1000	1030	...	...	...	...	1130	...	...	...	...	1200	1230	...	...	...	1300	1330	...	...	...	1400	1430
vick upon Tweed d.	...	...	...	|	1112	...	...	...	...	|	...	...	...	...	|	1312	...	...	...	|	1412	...	...	...	|	1512
nouth d.	...	...	...	1100	|	...	...	...	...	|	...	...	...	...	1300	|	...	...	...	|	|	...	...	...	1500	|
castle d.	...	...	...	1130	1200	...	...	...	1225	1257	...	...	...	...	1330	1400	...	...	...	1426	1500	...	...	...	1530	1559
am d.	...	...	...	1143	|	...	...	...	1238	|	...	...	...	...	1343	|	...	...	...	1439	|	...	...	...	1544	|
ngton d.	...	...	...	1201	1229	...	...	...	1257	1328	...	...	...	...	1401	1429	...	...	...	1458	1527	...	...	...	1603	1628
hallerton d.	...	...	...	|	|	...	...	...	1308	|	...	...	...	...	|	|	...	...	...	1509	|	...	...	...	|	|
k d.	...	1203	...	1231	1259	...	...	...	1331	1357	...	...	1402	...	1431	1459	...	...	...	1531	1557	...	1602	...	1633	1657
eeds d.	1145	|	1215	|	|	1245	...	1315	|	|	...	1345	|	1415	|	|	1445	...	1515	|	|	1545	|	1615	|	|
akefield Westgate d.	1158	|	1228	|	|	1258	...	1328	|	|	...	1358	|	1428	|	|	1458	...	1528	|	|	1558	|	1628	|	|
caster d.	1217	1225	1246	1255	|	1317	...	1346	1354	|	...	1417	1425	1446	1455	|	1517	...	1546	1554	|	1617	1625	1646	1656	|
ord d.	|	1240	|	|	|	|	...	|	|	|	...	|	1441	|	|	|	|	...	|	|	|	|	1641	|	|	|
ark North Gate d.	|	1255	|	1319	|	|	1354	|	1417	|	...	|	1456	|	1519	|	|	1552	|	1620	|	|	1656	|	1720	|
ntham d.	|	1307	1318	|	|	|	1406	1418	|	|	...	|	1508	1517	|	|	|	1604	1619	|	|	|	1708	1718	|	|
erborough d.	1307	1328	|	1351	|	1409	1427	|	1452	|	...	1509	1529	|	1552	|	1608	1625	|	1650	|	1709	1730	|	1751	|
enage a.	|	1357	1402	|	|	|	1456	1501	|	|	...	|	1557	1601	|	|	|	1655	1702	|	|	|	1759	1804	|	|
don Kings Cross a.	1358	1425	1428	1442	1451	1459	1524	1527	1544	1551	...	1600	1625	1628	1642	1651	1659	1721	1729	1742	1753	1800	1827	1831	1844	1850

FOR NOTES SEE PREVIOUS PAGE

st Excel service **X1**

🚌 PETERBOROUGH - KINGS LYNN 🚌 — 180a

n **Peterborough** railway station: Journey 75 minutes. Buses call at **Wisbech** bus station ± 39 minutes later.

0704, 0734, 0809 and every 30 minutes until 1109, 1149, 1219 and every 30 minutes until 1449, 1520, 1620, 1650, 1720, 1755, 1833, 1903, 1933, 2033, 2233.

0739, 0809 and every 30 minutes until 1109, 1149, 1219 and every 30 minutes until 1719, 1754, 1833, 1903, 1933, 2033, 2233.

0909, 1009 and hourly until 2009.

le **180a** continues on the next page.

180 EDINBURGH - NEWCASTLE - YORK and LEEDS - LONDON

Most services convey 🍸

For additional services see Tables **124, 181, 182, 183, 184** and **188**.

	Ⓐ	Ⓐ	Ⓐ	Ⓐ	Ⓐ	Ⓐ	Ⓐ	Ⓐ	Ⓐ	Ⓐ	Ⓐ	Ⓐ	Ⓐ	Ⓐ	Ⓐ	Ⓐ	Ⓐ	Ⓐ	Ⓐ			⑥	⑥	⑥
															A				A					
Edinburgh Waverley d.	...	...	...	...	1530	...	...	...	1600	1630	...	...	1700	...	1731	...	1842	1935	2100	...	⑥	...	...	...
Berwick upon Tweed d.	...	...	...	...	1612	...	...	...	|	1712	...	...	|	...	1818	...	1928	2017	2148	...		...	...	...
Alnmouth d.	...	...	...	...	|	...	...	...	|	|	...	...	1800	...	|	...	|	2040	2211	...		...	...	...
Newcastle d.	...	...	...	1625	1659	...	...	...	1726	1759	...	...	1830	...	1906	...	2016	2115	2246	...		...	0445	...
Durham d.	...	...	...	1638	|	...	...	...	1739	|	...	...	1843	...	|	...	2029	2128	2300	...		...	0500	...
Darlington d.	...	...	...	1657	1727	...	...	...	1758	1828	...	...	1901	...	1935	...	2048	2147	2322	...		...	0518	...
Northallerton d.	...	...	...	1709	|	...	...	...	1809	|	...	...	|	...	|	...	|	2158	2348s	...		...	0529	...
York d.	...	...	...	1731	1757	...	1802	...	1831	1857	...	...	1931	...	2005	...	2117	2220	0018	...		...	0601	...
Leeds d.	1645	...	1715	|	|	1745	|	1815	|	|	1845	1916	|	1945	|	2045	|	|	0045	...		0505	|	0605
Wakefield Westgate d.	1658	...	1728	|	|	1758	|	1828	|	|	1858	1929	|	1958	|	2058	|	|	...	...		0518	|	0618
Doncaster d.	1717	...	1746	1755	|	1817	1826	1846	1855	|	1917	1947	1955	2017	2028	2116	2140	2243	...	...		0536	0624	0636
Retford d.	|	...	1800	|	|	|	1840	|	|	|	|	|	|	|	|	2131	|	|	...	...		0550	|	0650
Newark North Gate d.	|	1754	|	1819	|	|	1855	|	1919	|	|	|	2019	|	|	|	2204	2307	...	...		0605	|	0705
Grantham d.	|	1806	1824	|	|	|	1907	1918	|	|	|	2018	|	|	|	2154	2216	2319	...	...		0617	|	0717
Peterborough d.	1809	1828	|	1849	|	1908	1929	|	1951	|	2008	|	2049	2105	2117	2215	2237	2347	...	...		0639	0713	0738
Stevenage a.	|	1857	1907	|	|	|	1958	2003	2019	2025	|	2102	2117	|	2148	2245	2307	0028s	...	...		0707	|	0806
London Kings Cross a.	1900	1925	1935	1943	1950	2000	2025	2028	2046	2052	2059	2128	2142	2156	2213	2311	2335	0103	...	...		0734	0804	0835

	⑥	⑥	⑥	⑥	⑥	⑥	⑥	⑥	⑥	⑥	⑥	⑥	⑥	⑥	⑥	⑥	⑥	⑥	⑥	⑥	⑥	⑥	⑥	⑥
		D		F		G				H	E					C							A	
Edinburgh Waverley d.	...	...	...	...	...	...	...	...	0620	...	...	0655	...	0730	...	0800	0830	...	0900	0930	...	1000	1030	...
Berwick upon Tweed d.	...	...	...	...	...	...	...	...	0706	...	...	|	...	0813	...	|	0913	...	|	1013	...	|	1113	...
Alnmouth d.	...	...	...	...	...	...	...	...	0727	...	...	|	...	|	...	0900	|	...	|	|	...	1100	|	...
Newcastle d.	...	...	0630	...	0655	...	0722	...	0801	...	...	0825	...	0900	...	0930	1000	...	1026	1100	...	1130	1200	...
Durham d.	...	...	0643	...	0708	...	0736	...	|	...	...	0838	...	|	...	0943	|	...	1039	|	...	1143	|	...
Darlington d.	...	...	0702	...	0727	...	0754	...	0829	...	...	0857	...	0929	...	1001	1029	...	1057	1129	...	1201	1229	...
Northallerton d.	...	...	0713	...	|	...	0808	...	|	...	...	0908	...	|	...	|	|	...	1109	|	...	|	|	...
York d.	...	...	0735	...	0757	...	0830	...	0859	...	...	0930	...	0959	...	1031	1059	...	1131	1159	...	1231	1259	...
Leeds d.	0705	...	|	0738	|	0805	|	0840	|	...	0905	|	0940	|	1005	|	|	1105	|	|	1205	|	|	1305
Wakefield Westgate d.	0718	...	|	|	|	0818	|	0854	|	...	0918	|	0953	|	1018	|	|	1118	|	|	1218	|	|	1318
Doncaster d.	0736	0745	0758	0811	0820	0838	0855	0912	|	...	0936	0953	|	|	1037	1055	|	1136	1155	|	1236	1255	|	1336
Retford d.	|	|	|	|	|	0854	|	|	|	...	|	1007	|	|	|	|	|	|	1209	|	|	|	|	|
Newark North Gate d.	0800	|	0822	|	|	0909	0919	|	|	0954	1000	|	|	|	1101	1119	|	1159	|	|	1302	1319	|	1400
Grantham d.	0812	0818	|	0843	|	|	0931	|	|	1006	1014	1030	|	|	1115	|	|	1212	|	|	1314	|	|	1412
Peterborough d.	0833	0840	0851	|	|	0938	0953	1002	1006	1029	1036	1052	1058	|	1136	1151	|	1234	1251	|	1335	1351	|	1433
Stevenage a.	0901	|	|	|	|	|	|	|	|	1100	1107	|	|	|	|	|	|	1302	|	|	|	|	|	1501
London Kings Cross a.	0928	0935	0942	0951	0954	1030	1045	1053	1058	1126	1136	1143	1151	1155	1228	1242	1253	1329	1342	1352	1427	1442	1452	1529

	⑥	⑥	⑥	⑥	⑥	⑥	⑥	⑥	⑥	⑥	⑥	⑥	⑥	⑥	⑥	⑥	⑥	⑥	⑥	⑥	⑥	⑥	⑥	
	B				A															A				
Edinburgh Waverley d.	1130	...	1200	...	1230	...	1300	1330	...	1400	1430	...	1500	1530	...	1600	1630	...	1700	1730	...	1830	1900	⑦
Berwick upon Tweed d.	1213	...	|	...	1313	...	|	1412	...	|	1512	...	|	1612	...	|	1712	...	|	1816	...	1912	1945	
Alnmouth d.	|	...	1300	...	|	...	|	|	...	1500	|	...	|	|	...	|	|	...	1800	|	...	|	2008	
Newcastle d.	1301	...	1330	...	1400	...	1426	1500	...	1530	1559	...	1626	1659	...	1726	1759	...	1830	1904	...	1959	2043	
Durham d.	|	...	1343	...	|	...	1439	|	...	1544	|	...	1639	|	...	1739	|	...	1843	|	...	...	2056	
Darlington d.	1329	...	1401	...	1429	...	1457	1529	...	1603	1628	...	1657	1728	...	1757	1828	...	1902	1933	...	...	2115	
Northallerton d.	|	...	|	...	|	...	1509	|	...	|	|	...	1709	|	...	1809	|	...	|	|	...	...	2128	
York d.	1400	...	1431	...	1459	...	1531	1558	...	1633	1657	...	1731	1758	...	1831	1857	...	1931	2003	...	...	2150	
Leeds d.	|	1405	|	1440	|	1505	|	|	1605	|	|	1705	|	|	1805	|	|	1905	|	|	2005	...	|	
Wakefield Westgate d.	|	1418	|	1453	|	1518	|	|	1618	|	|	1718	|	|	1818	|	|	1919	|	|	2018	...	|	
Doncaster d.	|	1436	1455	1512	|	1536	1555	|	1636	1656	|	1736	1755	|	1839	1855	|	1937	1955	2026	2036	...	2215	
Retford d.	|	|	|	|	|	|	1609	|	|	|	|	|	1809	|	|	|	|	|	|	|	2050	...	...	
Newark North Gate d.	|	1504	1519	|	|	1600	|	|	1659	1720	|	1800	|	|	1903	1919	|	2001	|	|	2105	...	...	
Grantham d.	|	1516	|	|	|	1612	|	|	1711	|	|	1812	|	|	1915	|	|	2013	2027	2058	|	...	...	
Peterborough d.	|	1537	1551	1601	|	1634	1651	|	1733	1751	|	1833	1851	|	1936	1951	|	2034	2051	2121	2134	...	...	
Stevenage a.	|	|	|	|	|	1703	|	|	|	|	|	1901	|	|	|	2019	|	2102	|	2150	|	...	...	
London Kings Cross a.	1555	1629	1643	1653	1656	1731	1744	1751	1825	1842	1852	1929	1942	1952	2028	2046	2051	2129	2142	2218	2225	...	...	

	⑦	⑦	⑦	⑦	⑦	⑦	⑦	⑦	⑦	⑦	⑦	⑦	⑦	⑦	⑦	⑦	⑦	⑦	⑦	⑦	⑦	⑦	⑦	⑦
																					A			
Edinburgh Waverley d.	...	...	...	...	...	...	...	...	0900	0930	...	1000	1030	...	1100	1130	...	...	1200	1220	1230	...	...	1300
Berwick upon Tweed d.	...	...	...	...	...	...	...	...	|	1013	...	|	1112	...	|	1213	...	...	|	|	1313	...	...	|
Alnmouth d.	...	...	...	...	...	...	...	...	|	|	...	1100	|	...	|	|	...	...	1300	|	|	...	...	|
Newcastle d.	...	0755	...	0855	...	0925	1000	...	1029	1100	...	1130	1200	...	1226	1300	...	1315	1330	1352	1400	...	1420	1431
Durham d.	...	0809	...	0908	...	0938	|	...	1042	|	...	1143	|	...	1239	|	...	1328	1343	1405	|	...	1433	|
Darlington d.	...	0827	...	0928	...	0957	1028	...	1101	1130	...	1202	1229	...	1258	1330	...	1348	1401	|	1430	...	1453	1500
Northallerton d.	...	|	...	|	...	1008	|	...	1112	|	...	|	|	...	1310	|	...	1401	|	|	|	...	|	|
York d.	...	0858	...	0958	...	1031	1058	...	1134	1159	...	1232	1259	...	1332	1359	...	1424	1431	1449	1459	...	1523	1530
Leeds d.	0805	|	0905	|	1005	|	|	1105	|	|	1205	|	|	1305	|	|	1405	|	|	|	|	1505	|	|
Wakefield Westgate d.	0818	|	0918	|	1018	|	|	1118	|	|	1218	|	|	1318	|	|	1418	|	|	|	|	1518	|	|
Doncaster d.	0836	|	0937	|	1036	1055	|	1136	1157	|	1236	1255	|	1336	1355	|	1436	1448	1455	|	|	1537	1546	1553
Retford d.	0850	|	|	|	1051	|	|	|	1211	|	|	|	|	|	1409	|	|	|	|	|	|	|	|	1608
Newark North Gate d.	0905	|	1000	|	1106	1119	|	1200	|	|	1259	1319	|	1400	|	|	1459	|	1519	|	|	1600	1609	|
Grantham d.	0917	|	1012	|	1119	|	|	1212	|	|	1311	|	|	1412	|	|	1511	|	|	1540	|	1612	|	|
Peterborough d.	0941	1005	1034	1104	1141	1151	1204	1234	1251	|	1333	1351	|	1434	1451	|	1533	1540	1551	|	|	1634	1642	1651
Stevenage a.	|	|	1104	|	|	|	|	1306	|	|	|	|	|	1503	|	|	|	|	|	|	|	1704	|	|
London Kings Cross a.	1033	1057	1132	1155	1233	1242	1255	1333	1342	1352	1424	1442	1450	1532	1542	1552	1624	1632	1642	1646	1652	1732	1735	1743

	⑦	⑦	⑦	⑦	⑦	⑦	⑦	⑦	⑦	⑦	⑦	⑦	⑦	⑦	⑦	⑦	⑦	⑦	⑦	⑦	⑦	⑦	⑦	⑦
	B			A						E				A										
Edinburgh Waverley d.	1330	...	1400	1430	...	...	...	1500	1530	...	...	1600	1620	1630	...	...	1700	1730	...	1800	...	1830	1900	2000
Berwick upon Tweed d.	1413	...	|	1513	...	...	...	|	1612	...	...	|	|	1713	...	...	|	1816	...	|	...	1912	1946	2047
Alnmouth d.	|	...	1501	|	...	...	...	|	|	...	...	1700	|	|	...	...	|	|	...	1900	...	|	|	2110
Newcastle d.	1500	...	1531	1600	...	1615	...	1627	1659	...	...	1730	1750	1800	...	...	1829	1903	...	1930	...	2001	2033	2145
Durham d.	|	...	1544	|	...	1629	...	1640	|	...	...	1743	|	|	...	...	1842	|	...	1944	...	|	2046	2159
Darlington d.	1531	...	1603	1630	...	1649	...	1659	1728	...	...	1801	1817	1830	...	...	1901	1932	...	2003	...	2029	2105	2219
Northallerton d.	|	...	|	|	...	1700	...	|	|	...	...	|	|	|	...	...	1912	|	...	|	...	|	|	2232
York d.	1601	...	1633	1659	...	1722	...	1731	1759	...	...	1831	1853	1859	...	...	1933	2001	...	2032	...	2059	2135	2306
Leeds d.	|	1616	|	|	1645	|	1716	|	|	1745	1815	|	|	|	1845	1916	|	|	1945	|	2045	|	|	2336
Wakefield Westgate d.	|	1629	|	|	1659	|	1729	|	|	1759	1828	|	|	|	1859	1929	|	|	1959	|	2058	|	|	...
Doncaster d.	|	1647	1656	|	1720	|	1747	1757	|	1819	1846	1855	|	|	1920	1947	1957	|	2020	2055	2116	2125	2158	...
Retford d.	|	|	|	|	|	|	1801	|	|	|	|	|	|	|	|	2001	|	|	|	|	2130	|	|	...
Newark North Gate d.	|	|	1719	|	1745	1803	|	|	|	1844	|	1919	|	|	1946	|	2021	|	2046	2119	|	2149	2221	...
Grantham d.	|	1718	|	|	|	|	1824	1830	|	|	1917	|	1943	|	|	2024	|	2050	|	|	2153	2201	2233	...
Peterborough d.	|	|	1751	|	1814	1832	|	1852	|	1914	|	1950	|	|	2015	|	2051	2110	2115	2151	2214	2223	2255	...
Stevenage a.	|	1801	|	|	|	|	1908	|	|	|	2001	|	|	|	|	2108	|	|	|	|	2244	2253	2333s	...
London Kings Cross a.	1755	1830	1842	1852	1906	1924	1935	1943	1949	2006	2027	2042	2048	2055	2106	2134	2142	2201	2207	2243	2310	2318	2359	...

FOR NOTES SEE PAGE 144

180a KINGS LYNN - PETERBOROUGH

First Excel service

From Kings Lynn bus station: Journey 80 minutes. Buses call at **Wisbech** bus station ± 32 minutes later.

Ⓐ: 0535, 0605, 0635, 0705, 0735, 0806, 0836, 0906, 0936, 1016 and every 30 minutes until 1616, 1656, 1726, 1756, 1901, 2111.

⑥: 0605, 0635, 0705, 0735, 0806, 0836, 0906, 0936, 1016 and every 30 minutes until 1616, 1656, 1726, 1756, 1901, 2111.

⑦: 0741 and hourly until 1841.

LONDON - HULL 181

All trains 🍸

	Ⓐ	⚒		⑦	Ⓐ		⑥	⑦	Ⓐ	⑦	⑥		Ⓐ	⑥ △	Ⓐ △	⑦ △	⑦		⑥	Ⓐ	⑥	⑦	Ⓐ
London Kings Cross ...... 180 d.	0722	0948	...	1048	1148	...	1148	1248	1348	1448	1448	...	1548	1710	1719	1720	1743	...	1748	1850	1948	1950	2030
Grantham ...... 180 d.	0825	1049	...	1147	1249	...	1249	1347	1449	1547	1549	...	1649	1821	1829	1826	1848	...	1849	1952	2052	2051	2132
Retford ...... 180 d.	0851	1110	...	1208	1310	...	1310	1408	1511	1608	1609	...	1711	|	|	|	1908	...	1911	2013	2113	2112	2153
Doncaster ...... 180 a.	0905	1123	...	1222	1324	...	1323	1422	1525	1625	1623	...	1724	1854	1906	1903	1923	...	1924	2026	2126	2126	2206
Selby ...... a.	0922	1139	...	1243	1339	...	1339	1444	1540	1645	1640	...	1740	1911	1925	1921	1945	...	1940	2047	2142	2142	2222
Hull ...... a.	1001	1218	...	1320	1418	...	1418	1521	1616	1722	1725	...	1818	1953	2005	2002	2022	...	2018	2125	2219	2219	2304
Hull ...... d.	...	...	...	...	...	...	...	...	...	...	...	...	...	...	...	...	2030	...	2025	2135	...	...	...
Beverley ...... a.	...	...	...	...	...	...	...	...	...	...	...	...	...	...	...	...	2041	...	2036	2145	...	...	...

		Ⓐ	⑥ △	Ⓐ △	Ⓐ	⑥		⑦	Ⓐ	⑥	⑦	Ⓐ		⑥	⑦	Ⓐ	⑥	⑦		Ⓐ	⑥		⑦	Ⓐ
rley ...... d.	...	0602	...	...	...	...	...	...	...	0955	1053	...	...	...	...	...	...	...	...	...	...	...	...	...
...... a.	...	0613	...	...	...	...	...	...	...	1006	1104	...	...	...	...	...	...	...	...	...	...	...	...	...
...... d.	...	0626	0650	0700	0823	0823	...	0906	1030	1030	1112	1233	...	1331	1436	1513	1530	1632	...	1710	1836	...	1848	1911
/ ...... d.	...	0700	0725	0737	0901	0903	...	0940	1106	1106	1146	1306	...	1405	1510	1547	1605	1706	...	1745	1910	...	1922	1945
caster ...... 180 d.	...	0721	0745	0757	0925	0925	...	1000	1125	1126	1204	1325	...	1426	1528	1605	1624	1727	...	1803	1929	...	1940	2003
ord ...... 180 d.	...	0740	|	|	0939	0939	...	1014	1139	1140	1218	1339	...	1440	1542	1619	1638	1741	...	1817	1943	...	1954	2017
tham ...... 180 d.	...	0803	0818	0835	1001	0959	...	1035	1201	1201	1239	1401	...	1502	1605	1640	1700	1802	...	1839	2006	...	2016	2040
don Kings Cross ...... 180 a.	...	0913	0935	0955	1110	1108	...	1140	1307	1308	1344	1510	...	1608	1714	1745	1806	1915	...	1945	2110	...	2119	2146

Calls to set down only. u – Calls to pick up only. △ – Operated by GR (Table **180**).

LONDON - BRADFORD 182

All trains 🍸

		Ⓐ	Ⓐ	Ⓐ	Ⓐ △	Ⓐ				⑥	⑥	⑥	⑥	⑥ △				⑦	⑦	⑦	⑦		
London Kings Cross ...... 180 d.	Ⓐ	1048	1448	1603	1833	1952	...	...	⑥	1048	1548	1636	1923	1930	...	...	⑦	1236	1550	1845	1922	...	...
Doncaster ...... 180 a.		1222	1622	1735	2020	2122	...	...		1214	1718	1816	2051	2116	...	...		1412	1717	2024	2057	...	...
Pontefract Monkhill ...... a.		1247	1647	|	|	|	...	...		|	|	|	2114	|	...	...		|	|	|	|	...	...
Wakefield Kirkgate ...... a.		1304	1704	1808	2038e	2145	...	...		1242	1742	1844	2131	2134e	...	...		1437	1746	2054	2120	...	...
Mirfield ...... a.		1316	1716	1820	|	2159	...	...		1255	1755	1856	2142	|	...	...		1449	1759	2112	2135	...	...
Brighouse ...... a.		1324	1724	1828	|	2207	...	...		1308	1809	1910	2151	|	...	...		1506	1808	2123	2143	...	...
Halifax ...... 190 a.		1339	1739	1840	|	2223	...	...		1320	1821	1922	2203	|	...	...		1517	1820	2136	2155	...	...
Bradford Interchange ...... 190 a.		1354	1754	1855	2123f	2238	...	...		1337	1838	1938	2219	2220f	...	...		1530	1835	2152	2210	...	...

		Ⓐ △	Ⓐ	Ⓐ	Ⓐ	Ⓐ				⑥	⑥ △	⑥	⑥	⑥				⑦	⑦	⑦	⑦		
dford Interchange ...... 190 d.	Ⓐ	0630f	0655	0752	1021	1433	...	...	⑥	0655	0733f	0851	1021	1521	...	...	⑦	0818	1205	1505	1559	...	...
ax ...... 190 d.		|	0708	0805	1034	1447	...	...		0708	|	0905	1034	1535	...	...		0830	1219	1520	1613	...	...
house ...... d.		|	0719	0816	1048	1503	...	...		0719	|	0915	1048	1549	...	...		0841	1230	1535	1623	...	...
eld ...... d.		|	0727	0824	1057	1513	...	...		0727	|	0924	1057	1557	...	...		0850	1238	1543	1631	...	...
efield Kirkgate ...... d.		0713e	0744	0855	1113	1535	...	...		0743	0818e	0940	1114	1614	...	...		0909	1255	1602	1648	...	...
efract Monkhill ...... d.		|	0801	|	1136	1552	...	...		0800	|	0957	1133	1634	...	...		|	|	|	|	...	...
caster ...... 180 d.		|	0830	0931	1206	1621	...	...		0832	0838	1025	1208	1711	...	...		0942	1321	1627	1713	...	...
don Kings Cross ...... 180 a.		0859	1010	1113	1343	1810	...	...		1006	1030	1156	1343	1844	...	...		1134	1452	1757	1845	...	...

Wakefield Westgate.
Bradford Forster Square.

s – Calls to set down only.
u – Calls to pick up only.

△ – Operated by GR (Table **180**).

LONDON - YORK - SUNDERLAND 183

All trains 🍸

		Ⓐ	Ⓐ	Ⓐ	Ⓐ	Ⓐ				⑥	⑥	⑥	⑥	⑥				⑦	⑦	⑦	⑦		
London Kings Cross ...... 180 d.	Ⓐ	0802	1121	1253	1650	1918	...	...	⑥	0811	1120	1320	1647	1911	...	...	⑦	0948	1348	1647	1822	...	...
York ...... 180 d.		0958	1322	1451	1841	2119	...	...		1019	1319	1519	1842	2101	...	...		1139	1539	1842	2014	...	...
Thirsk ...... d.		1015	1339	1514	1858	2136	...	...		1036	1336	1536	1858	2118	...	...		1155	1556	1901	2030	...	...
Northallerton ...... 180 d.		1024	1347	1524	1907	2146	...	...		1045	1346	1546	1907	2128	...	...		1204	1606	1912	2040	...	...
Eaglescliffe ...... a.		1042	1405	1541	1924	2203	...	...		1104	1404	1604	1925	2146	...	...		1222	1623	1929	2057	...	...
Hartlepool ...... a.		1108	1424	1607	1944	2223	...	...		1123	1423	1623	1944	2206	...	...		1241	1652	1952	2117	...	...
Sunderland ...... a.		1138	1451	1638	2021	2251	...	...		1150	1450	1650	2021	2236	...	...		1308	1721	2020	2151	...	...

		Ⓐ	Ⓐ	Ⓐ	Ⓐ	Ⓐ				⑥	⑥	⑥	⑥	⑥				⑦	⑦	⑦	⑦		
derland ...... d.	Ⓐ	0645	0842	1228	1518	1731	...	...	⑥	0643	0830	1218	1529	1729	...	...	⑦	0920	1212	1412	1812	...	...
tlepool ...... d.		0710	0908	1252	1550	1757	...	...		0710	0855	1245	1553	1754	...	...		0945	1236	1440	1840	...	...
lescliffe ...... d.		0732	0928	1312	1611	1822	...	...		0731	0917	1306	1612	1814	...	...		1005	1304	1504	1904	...	...
thallerton ...... 180 d.		0753	0947	1331	1631	1842	...	...		0752	0943	1327	1631	1832	...	...		1024	1324	1524	1924	...	...
sk ...... d.		0801	0959	1344	1643	1851	...	...		0801	0952	1336	1643	1843	...	...		1033	1333	1533	1933	...	...
k ...... 180 d.		0821	1027	1406	1702	1911	...	...		0820	1012	1356	1702	1902	...	...		1052	1352	1552	1953	...	...
don Kings Cross ...... 180 a.		1020	1230	1610	1906	2105	...	...		1014	1208	1548	1853	2057	...	...		1243	1544	1744	2143	...	...

Calls to set down only. u – Calls to pick up only.

LONDON - PETERBOROUGH 184

		Ⓐ	Ⓐ	Ⓐ	Ⓐ	Ⓐ	Ⓐ	Ⓐ	Ⓐ	Ⓐ	Ⓐ		Ⓐ	Ⓐ	Ⓐ	Ⓐ	Ⓐ	Ⓐ	Ⓐ	Ⓐ	Ⓐ	Ⓐ
London Kings Cross ...... 180 d.	Ⓐ	0035	0135	0522	0622	0635	0722	0735	0810	0822	0835	and at	1522	1535	1622	1640	1650	1710	1713	1740	1743	1810
Finsbury Park ...... d.		0041	0141	0528	0628	0641	0728	0741	|	0828	0841	the same	1528	1541	1628	|	1656	|	1719	|	1749	|
Stevenage ...... 180 d.		0112	0221	0559	0647	0713	0747	0813	|	0847	0913	minutes	1547	1613	1650	|	1717	|	1740	|	1809	|
Huntingdon ...... d.		0150s	0259s	0638	0723	0749	0823	0849	0854	0922	0949	past each	1623	1649	1732	1727	1754	1800	1818	1830	1846	1900
Peterborough ...... 180 a.		0212	0318	0655	0739	0806	0839	0907	0912	0938	1006	hour until ▽	1639	1706	...	1743	1812	1819	1838	1853	1903	1921

	Ⓐ	Ⓐ	Ⓐ	Ⓐ	Ⓐ	Ⓐ	Ⓐ	Ⓐ	Ⓐ	Ⓐ	Ⓐ	Ⓐ	Ⓐ	Ⓐ		⑥	⑥	⑥		⑥	⑥	⑥	⑥	⑥
ndon Kings Cross ...... 180 d.	1813	1840	1843	1910	1922	1952	2010	2022	2110	2122	2210	2222	2301	2322	⑥	0001	0035	0135	...	0522	0622	0635	0722	0735
sbury Park ...... d.	1819	|	1849	|	1928	1958	|	2028	|	2128	|	2228	|	2328		|	0041	0141	...	0528	0628	0641	0728	0741
venage ...... 180 d.	1840	|	1910	|	1948	2019	|	2050	|	2148	|	2247	|	2347		0022	0112	0221	...	0559	0647	0713	0747	0813
ntingdon ...... d.	1918	1927	1947	2002	2024	2057	2053	2126	2156	2224	2256	2323	2347	0023		0057s	0150s	0259s	...	0638	0722	0749	0822	0849
terborough ...... 180 a.	1939	1943	2003	2020	2042	2114	2111	2143	2212	2241	2312	2344	0013	0044		0113	0212	0318	...	0655	0738	0806	0838	0906

	⑥	⑥		⑥	⑥	⑥	⑥	⑥	⑥	⑥	⑥	⑥	⑥	⑥	⑥	⑥		⑥	⑥	⑥	⑥	⑥	⑥
ndon Kings Cross ...... 180 d.	0822	0835	and at	1622	1635	1640	1722	1735	1740	1822	1835	1840	1922	1935	2022	2035	...	2122	2135	2222	2252	2322	2352
sbury Park ...... d.	0828	0841	the same	1628	1641	|	1728	1741	|	1828	1841	|	1928	1941	2028	2041	...	2128	2141	2228	2258	2328	2358
venage ...... 180 d.	0847	0913	minutes	1647	1713	|	1747	1813	|	1847	1913	|	1947	2013	2047	2113	...	2147	2213	2247	2317	2347	0026
ntingdon ...... d.	0922	0949	past each	1722	1749	1727	1822	1849	1827	1922	1949	1927	2022	2049	2122	2149	...	2222	2249	2322	2352	0022	0104s
terborough ...... 180 a.	0938	1006	hour until ▽	1739	1806	1743	1839	1906	1844	1938	2006	1943	2039	2106	2139	2206	...	2238	2307	2340	0013	0043	0125

		⑦	⑦A	⑦	⑦	⑦	⑦	⑦	⑦	⑦	⑦		⑦	⑦	⑦	⑦	⑦	⑦	⑦	⑦	⑦	⑦	⑦	⑦
ndon Kings Cross ...... 180 d.	⑦	0022	0055	0705	0822	0922	1022	1122	1222	1322	1422	...	1522	1622	1710	1722	1810	1822	1840	1922	2022	2122	2222	2322
sbury Park ...... d.		0028	0101	0711	0828	0928	1028	1128	1228	1328	1428	...	1528	1628	|	1728	|	1828	|	1928	2028	2128	2228	2328
venage ...... 180 d.		0057	0133	0746	0847	0947	1047	1147	1247	1347	1447	...	1547	1647	|	1747	|	1847	|	1947	2047	2147	2247	2347
ntingdon ...... d.		0134s	0211s	*0828*	0922	1022	1122	1222	1322	1422	1522	...	1622	1722	1757	1822	1855	1922	1932	2022	2122	2222	2322	0022
terborough ...... 180 a.		0156	0233	*0844*	0939	1039	1138	1240	1339	1439	1539	...	1640	1739	1819	1839	1913	1939	1953	2040	2139	2239	2343	0043

return service and footnotes see next page ▷ ▷ ▷

184 PETERBOROUGH - LONDON

		Ⓐ	Ⓐ	Ⓐ	Ⓐ	Ⓐ	Ⓐ	Ⓐ	Ⓐ	Ⓐ	Ⓐ	Ⓐ	Ⓐ	Ⓐ	Ⓐ	Ⓐ	Ⓐ	Ⓐ	Ⓐ	Ⓐ	Ⓐ	
Peterborough 180 d.	Ⓐ	0325	0410	0510	0540	0549	0615	0632	0655	0715	0706	0726	0732	0746	0816	0846	0919	0930	0946	1016	1046	and at
Huntingdon d.		0340	0425	0525	0555	0603	0630	0646	0710	0733	0724	0740	0750	0802	0831	0901	0934	0945	1001	1034	1101	the same
Stevenage 180 d.		0415	0504	0604	|	0640	0659	0724	0736	0759	0802	|	0828	0832	0907	0937	1003	1021	1036	1110	1136	minutes
Finsbury Park d.		0452s	0538	0623	|	0706	|	0744	|	|	0821	|	0848	|	0928	1000	|	|	1056	1143	1156	past each
London Kings Cross 180 a.		0502	0547	0629	0642	0712	0722	0750	0800	0823	0829	0828	0855	0856	0934	1006	1027	1047	1103	1149	1202	hour until ▽

	Ⓐ	Ⓐ	Ⓐ	Ⓐ	Ⓐ	Ⓐ	Ⓐ	Ⓐ	Ⓐ	Ⓐ	Ⓐ	Ⓐ	Ⓐ			⑥	⑥	⑥	⑥	⑥	⑥	⑥	⑥
Peterborough 180 d.	1646	1721	1754	1821	1846	1916	1946	2016	2044	2123	2146	2224	2244	...	⑥	0325	0416	0516	0546	0616	0646	0716	0746
Huntingdon d.	1701	1742	1812	1841	1900	1935	2000	2034	2100	2137	2200	2239	2258	...		0340	0434	0534	0600	0634	0700	0734	0800
Stevenage 180 d.	1736	1819	1848	1917	1936	2012	2036	2110	2136	2212	2236	2317	2336	...		0415	0510	0610	0636	0710	0736	0810	0836
Finsbury Park d.	1756	1851	1909	1949	1956	2043	2056	2143	2156	2243	2256	2347	2356	...		0453s	0543	0643	0656	0743	0755	0843	0856
London Kings Cross 180 a.	1802	1857	1915	1956	2003	2050	2103	2148	2201	2248	2302	2353	0001	...		0459	0549	0649	0702	0749	0802	0849	0902

	⑥	⑥	⑥	⑥	⑥	⑥	⑥	⑥		⑥	⑥	⑥	⑥	⑥		⑥	⑥	⑥	⑥		⑥	⑥
Peterborough 180 d.	0818	0846	0909	...	0946	1012	1018	1046	and at	1716	1746	1816	1846	1916	...	1946	2016	2046	2116	...	2146	2216
Huntingdon d.	0834	0900	0924	0934	1000	1027	1034	1100	the same	1734	1800	1834	1900	1934	...	2000	2034	2100	2134	...	2200	2234
Stevenage 180 d.	0910	0936	|	1010	1036	|	1110	1136	minutes	1810	1836	1910	1936	2010	...	2036	2110	2136	2210	...	2236	2310
Finsbury Park d.	0945	0956	|	1043	1056	|	1143	1156	past each	1843	1856	1943	1956	2043	...	2056	2143	2156	2243	...	2256	2343
London Kings Cross 180 a.	0951	1002	1011	1049	1102	1115	1149	1202	hour until ▽	1849	1902	1949	2002	2049	...	2102	2149	2202	2249	...	2302	2349

		⑦A	⑦A	⑦	⑦	⑦		⑦	⑦	⑦	⑦	⑦	⑦	⑦	⑦	⑦	⑦	⑦		⑦	⑦	⑦	⑦
Peterborough 180 d.	⑦	0546	0646	0746	0846	0915	...	0946	1015	1046	1115	1146	1246	1346	1446	1546	1646	1746	...	1846	1946	2046	2146
Huntingdon d.		0601	0701	0800	0900	0930	...	1000	1030	1100	1130	1200	1300	1400	1500	1600	1700	1800	...	1900	2000	2100	2200
Stevenage 180 d.		0640	0738	0835	0935	|	...	1035	|	1135	|	1235	1335	1435	1535	1635	1735	1835	...	1935	2035	2135	2235
Finsbury Park d.		0714	0801	0858	0955	|	...	1055	|	1155	|	1255	1355	1455	1555	1655	1755	1855	...	1955	2055	2157	2255
London Kings Cross 180 a.		0723	0811	0904	1001	1016	...	1101	1116	1201	1216	1301	1401	1501	1601	1701	1801	1901	...	2001	2101	2203	2301

A – May 15 - Sept. 11.
s – Calls to set down only.
▽ – Timings may vary by up to 3 minutes.

185 PETERBOROUGH - LINCOLN - DONCASTER

2nd class

km		⑥	Ⓐ	⚒	⚒	⚒	ⒶD	⚒	⑥	Ⓐ	Ⓐ		⚒E	⚒	Ⓐ	⚒	⚒	⑥	ⒶD	⚒	⚒D	⚒	Ⓐ	⑥
0	**Peterborough** d.	...	...	0630	...	0730	...	0833	0932	0935	1040	...	1150	1241	1341	1511	1625	...	...	1732	...	1836	...	...
27	Spalding d.	...	...	0653	...	0753	...	0854	0953	0956	1101	...	1213	1302	1404	1532	1646	...	...	1755	...	1859	...	...
57	Sleaford d.	0650	0653	...	0743	...	0840	0918	1020	1021	1125	...	1241	1326	1429	1614	1718	1754	1756	...	1900	...	2005	2010
91	**Lincoln** a.	0722	0726	...	0815	...	0913	0956	1053	1053	1201	...	1314	1403	1503	1647	1751	1827	1829	...	1932	...	2039	2044

	Ⓐ	⚒	Ⓐ	⑥	⚒	⚒	Ⓐ	Ⓐ	⑥	⚒	Ⓐ	Ⓐ	⑥	⚒	Ⓐ	Ⓐ	⑥	⚒	⑥	Ⓐ	⚒	⚒	⑥	Ⓐ	⚒L
Lincoln d.	0617	...	...	...	0705	0800	0910	1018	1018	1110	1210	1330	1330	1441	1512	1600	1601	...	1715	1718	1810	...	1905	1915	2048
Sleaford d.	0645	...	...	...	0737	0834	0942	1051	1051	1142	1242	1403	1403	1516	1544	1634	1634	...	1747	1753	1842	...	1937	1947	2120
Spalding d.	...	0700	0800	0805	...	0900	1006	1113	1119	1204	1307	1425	1427	1538	...	1656	1657	1808	...	...	...	1959	...	...	...
Peterborough a.	...	0722	0822	0827	...	0925	1030	1134	1143	1228	1330	1446	1450	1602	...	1718	1723	1831	...	...	...	2022	...	...	...

km		ⒶS	⑥	⚒	ⒶP	⑥	⑥	ⒶS	⚒S	
0	**Lincoln** d.	0915	0915	1154	1315	1410	1510	1831	1932	...
26	Gainsborough Lea Road d.	0935	0935	1215	1335	1430	1530	1855	1952	...
60	**Doncaster** a.	1002	1005	1245	1407	1458	1600	1925	2023	...

	⑥	Ⓐ	Ⓐ	⑥	Ⓐ	⑥	⑥	Ⓐ
Doncaster d.	1024	1024	1301	1305	1427	1507	1627	1936
Gainsborough Lea Road d.	1048	1053	1329	1329	1452	1531	1652	2001
Lincoln a.	1110	1116	1354	1354	1515	1557	1719	2023

D – To/from Doncaster (lower panel).
E – To/from Doncaster on Ⓐ (lower panel).
L – To Boston (Table **194**).
P – To/from Peterborough (upper panel).
S – To/from Sleaford (upper panel).

186 GRIMSBY - LINCOLN - NOTTINGHAM

2nd class

km			Ⓐ	Ⓐ	Ⓐ	ⒶA	ⒶB	Ⓐ	Ⓐ	Ⓐ	Ⓐ	Ⓐ	Ⓐ	Ⓐ	Ⓐ	Ⓐ	Ⓐ	Ⓐ	Ⓐ	Ⓐ	Ⓐ	Ⓐ	Ⓐ	Ⓐ	Ⓐ
0	**Grimsby** Town d.	Ⓐ	...	...	0556	...	...	...	0703	...	...	...	0920	...	...	...	1128	...	...	...	1349	...	...	...	1545
47	Market Rasen d.		...	...	0632	...	...	...	0739	...	...	...	0955	...	...	...	1203	...	...	...	1425	...	...	...	1621
71	**Lincoln** a.		...	...	0651	...	...	...	0757	...	...	...	1014	...	...	...	1222	...	...	...	1444	...	...	...	1640
71	**Lincoln** d.		0526	0646	0654	0704	0730	0736	0759	0836	0907	0937	1016	1036	1135	1140	1223	1234	1337	1436	1446	1536	1545	1634	1643
97	Newark North Gate a.		0556	|	0722	|	0755	|	0824	|	0932	|	1040	|	1200	|	1250	|	|	|	1511	|	1611	|	1711
98	Newark Castle ♧ d.		0609	0714	...	0729	...	0806	...	0907	...	1007	...	1107	...	1207	...	1305	1407	1506	...	1608	...	1705	...
126	**Nottingham** ♧ a.		0648	0742	...	0756	...	0835	...	0932	...	1032	...	1132	...	1230	...	1332	1432	1532	...	1632	...	1732	...

	Ⓐ	Ⓐ	Ⓐ	Ⓐ	Ⓐ	Ⓐ	Ⓐ		⑥	⑥A	⑥	⑥	⑥	⑥	⑥	⑥B	⑥	⑥	⑥	⑥	⑥	⑥	⑥	⑥
Grimsby Town d.	...	...	1828	...	...	2124	...	⑥	...	...	...	0650	...	...	...	...	0920	...	...	...	1128	...	...	...
Market Rasen d.	...	...	1904	...	...	2200	...		...	...	...	0726	...	...	...	...	0955	...	...	...	1203	...	...	...
Lincoln a.	...	...	1923	...	...	2219	...		...	...	...	0744	...	...	...	...	1014	...	...	...	1222	...	...	...
Lincoln d.	1818	1835	1925	2031	2140	...	2226		0526	0704	0726	0746	0835	0901	0936	0930	1015	1036	1130	1140	1223	1236	1337	1432
Newark North Gate a.	1846	|	1953	|	|	...	|		0556	|	|	0812	|	0925	|	0953	1044	|	1152	|	1252	|	|	|
Newark Castle ♧ d.	...	1903	...	2058	2207	...	2255		0610	0729	0755	...	0904	...	1007	...	...	1104	...	1204	...	1306	1405	1501
Nottingham ♧ a.	...	1932	...	2129	2239	...	2330		0648	0757	0825	...	0932	...	1032	...	...	1133	...	1229	...	1331	1431	1527

	⑥	⑥	⑥	⑥	⑥	⑥	⑥	⑥	⑥		⑦	⑦	⑦a	⑦b	⑦a	⑦a	⑦	⑦	⑦	⑦a	⑦	⑦	⑦a	⑦b
Grimsby Town d.	...	...	1600	...	...	1828	...	1945	...	⑦	...	...	1403	...	...	...	...	...	...	1825	...	...	2022	...
Market Rasen d.	...	...	1635	...	...	1902	...	2020	...		...	...	1437	...	...	...	...	...	...	1859	...	...	2057	...
Lincoln a.	...	...	1653	...	...	1921	...	2039	...		...	...	1456	...	...	...	...	...	...	1918	...	...	2115	...
Lincoln d.	1526	1635	1655	1725	1830	1924	1939	...	2045		1105	1245	1508	1508	1544	1656	1709	1805	1903	1922	2005	2100	2126	2126
Newark North Gate a.	|	|	1722	|	|	1953	|	...	|		1130	1310	1536	1536	1609	|	1734	|	|	1946	|	2127	2155	2155
Newark Castle ♧ d.	1557	1705	...	1754	1859	...	2004	...	2110		...	...	1550	1550	...	1724	...	1834	1933	...	2035	2140	...	...
Nottingham ♧ a.	1626	1732	...	1831	1926	...	2033	...	2137		...	...	1620	1620	...	1802	...	1911	2005	...	2103	2209	...	...

		Ⓐ	Ⓐ	Ⓐ	Ⓐ	Ⓐ	Ⓐ	Ⓐ	Ⓐ	Ⓐ	Ⓐ	Ⓐ	Ⓐ	Ⓐ	Ⓐ	Ⓐ	Ⓐ	Ⓐ	Ⓐ	Ⓐ	Ⓐ	Ⓐ	Ⓐ	Ⓐ
Nottingham ♧ d.	Ⓐ	...	0554	0653	...	...	0812	0925	...	...	1029	1129	...	1229	...	1329	...	1429	...	1529	...	1627	...	1721
Newark Castle ♧ d.		...	0630	0727	...	...	0840	0952	...	...	1051	1153	...	1253	...	1352	...	1453	...	1553	...	1653	...	1752
Newark North Gate d.		...	|	|	0742	0831	|	|	0957	1050	|	|	1206	|	1302	|	...	|	1528	|	1646	|	1728	|
Lincoln a.		...	0704	0756	0812	0902	0910	1019	1023	1114	1130	1223	1236	1325	1330	1425	...	1524	1555	1625	1713	1718	1800	1826
Lincoln d.		0557	...	...	0815	...	...	...	1025	...	...	...	1237	...	...	...	1437	...	...	...	1722	...	...	...
Market Rasen d.		0613	...	...	0832	...	...	...	1042	...	...	...	1254	...	...	...	1454	...	...	...	1739	...	...	...
Grimsby Town a.		0655	...	...	0912	...	...	...	1122	...	...	...	1335	...	...	...	1534	...	...	...	1818	...	...	...

	Ⓐ	Ⓐ	Ⓐ	Ⓐ	ⒶB	ⒶA	Ⓐ	Ⓐ		⑥	⑥	⑥	⑥	⑥	⑥	⑥	⑥	⑥	⑥	⑥	⑥	⑥	⑥	⑥
Nottingham ♧ d.	1817	...	1919	...	...	2030	2120	2226	⑥	...	0555	0653	...	0811	...	0922	...	1029	1129	...	1229	...	1329	1416
Newark Castle ♧ d.	1853	...	1954	...	...	2054	2154	2257		...	0630	0726	...	0842	...	0950	...	1051	1155	...	1250	...	1350	1441
Newark North Gate d.	|	1935	|	2003	2036	|	|	2310		...	|	|	0820	|	0935	|	1049	|	|	1205	|	1302	|	|
Lincoln a.	1925	2001	2023	2027	2102	2122	2222	2340		...	0703	0757	0855	0909	0959	1016	1117	1127	1228	1236	1321	1330	1424	1512
Lincoln d.	...	2002	...	...	...	...	...	...		0538	...	*0808*	...	...	1006	...	...	...	...	1236	...	...	*1453*	...
Market Rasen d.	...	2019	...	...	...	...	...	...		0554	...	*0825*	...	...	1023	...	...	...	...	1254	...	...	*1510*	...
Grimsby Town a.	...	2056	...	...	...	...	...	...		0636	...	*0913*	...	...	1102	...	...	...	...	1334	...	...	*1550*	...

	⑥	⑥	⑥	⑥	⑥	⑥B	⑥A	⑥	⑥	⑥		⑦b	⑦a	⑦	⑦a	⑦a	⑦	⑦	⑦	⑦	⑦	⑦B	⑦	⑦
Nottingham ♧ d.	1528	1621	1729	...	1822	...	1929	...	2030	2124	⑦	...	...	...	1529	...	1633	...	1726	1836	1935	...	2039	...
Newark Castle ♧ d.	1550	1652	1750	...	1850	...	1953	...	2104	2157		...	...	...	1559	...	1659	...	1801	1859	1958	...	2103	...
Newark North Gate d.	|	|	|	1807	|	1935	|	2032	|	2209		1135	1135	1335	|	1645	|	1755	|	1928	|	2036	|	2210
Lincoln a.	1624	1710	1825	1834	1925	2001	2026	2056	2133	2242		1202	1200	1402	1626	1716	1731	1820	1833	1957	2030	2102	2135	2237
Lincoln d.	...	*1722*	...	1835	...	...	...	2057	...	...		...	1202	...	1627	...	...	1822a	...	...	...	...	...	...
Market Rasen d.	...	*1738*	...	1852	...	...	...	2115	...	...		...	1218	...	1643	...	...	1838a	...	...	...	...	...	...
Grimsby Town a.	...	*1818*	...	1934	...	...	...	...	...	...		...	1253	...	1718	...	...	1913a	...	...	...	...	...	...

A – To/from London St Pancras (Table **170**).
B – To/from London Kings Cross (Table **180**).
a – May 15 - Sept. 11.
b – From Sept. 18.

♧ – Additional journeys Newark Castle - Nottingham and v.v. Journey time: 28–36 minutes.
From Newark Castle at 0642Ⓐ, 0739Ⓐ, 0741⑥, 0841Ⓐ, 0843⑥, 0938⚒, 1047⚒, 1139⚒, 1247⚒, 1347Ⓐ, 1349⑥, 1439⚒, 1547⚒, 1638⑥, 1639Ⓐ, 1739⚒, 1847⑥, 1947⚒.
From Nottingham at 0756⚒, 0854⚒, 0949⚒, 1049⚒, 1154⚒, 1249⚒, 1349⚒, 1453⚒, 1549⚒, 1649⚒, 1852⚒,

THE NORTH EAST and YORKSHIRE - MANCHESTER and LIVERPOOL 188

		Ⓐ	⑥	Ⓐ	⑥	②–⑤	①	⚒	⚒	⚒	⚒	Ⓐ	⚒	⚒	⑥	Ⓐ	⚒	⚒	⚒	⚒	⚒	⚒	⚒	⚒	⚒	Ⓐ	⑥
Newcastle d.	⚒	...	...	...	...	...	...	...	...	...	...	...	...	...	...	...	...	...	0603	...	...	...	...	0706	...	...	...
Durham d.		...	...	...	...	...	...	...	...	...	...	...	...	...	...	...	...	...	0621	...	...	...	...	0719	...	...	...
Middlesbrough d.		...	...	...	...	...	...	...	...	...	...	...	...	...	...	...	0555	...	|	...	0631	...	...	|	0715	...	...
Darlington d.		...	...	...	...	...	...	...	...	...	...	...	...	...	...	...	|	...	0638	...	|	...	...	0736	|	...	...
Northallerton d.		...	...	...	...	...	...	...	...	...	...	...	...	...	...	...	0623	...	0649	...	0659	...	...	|	0743	...	...
Thirsk d.		...	...	...	...	...	...	...	...	...	...	...	...	...	...	...	0631	...	|	...	0710	...	...	|	0755	...	...
Scarborough d.		...	...	...	...	...	...	...	...	...	...	...	...	...	...	...	|	...	|	0630	|	0700	...	|	|	0738	0748
Malton d.		...	...	...	...	...	...	...	...	...	...	...	...	...	...	...	|	...	|	0653	|	0723	...	|	|	0801	0811
York a.		...	...	...	...	...	...	...	...	...	...	...	...	...	...	...	0649	...	0712	0718	0728	0747	...	0810	0813	0826	0836
York d.		0138	0138	0252	0252	0400	0420	...	0521	...	0555	...	0616	...	0640	0645	0652	...	0715	0724	0737	0750	...	0815	0824	0840	0840
Hull d.		|	|	|	|	|	|	...	|	...	|	...	|	0548	|	|	|	0637	|	|	|	|	0735	|	|	|	|
Selby d.		|	|	|	|	|	|	...	|	...	|	...	|	0623	|	|	|	0709	|	|	|	|	0808	|	|	|	|
Leeds a.		0204v	0219	0318x	0333	0441	0446	...	0547	...	0618	...	0640	0647	0704	0708	0717	0733	0741	0750	0804	0820	0832	0840	0851	0904	0904
Leeds d.		0205v	0220	0320x	0335	0449	0449	...	0550	...	0620	0635	0644	0652	0710	0710	0720	0735	0744	0753	0809	0824	0836	0844	0854	0909	0909
Dewsbury d.		|	|	|	|	|	|	...	0601	...	0631	0646	|	|	0721	0721	|	0746	|	|	0820	|	0847	|	|	0920	0920
Huddersfield d.		0243	0256	0358	0411	0526	0526	...	0611	...	0640	0655	0702	0710	0731	0731	0739	0756	0802	0811	0830	0842	0856	0902	0912	0930	0930
Stalybridge d.		|	|	|	|	|	|	...	0630	...	0659	0714	|	0728	0750	0750	0759	0817	|	|	0850	|	0915	|	|	0950	0950
Manchester Victoria d.		|	|	|	|	|	|	...	|	...	|	|	0735	|	|	|	|	|	0835	|	|	|	|	0935	|	|	|
Manchester Piccadilly a.		0346	0329	0458	0443	0557	0557	0607	0645	0707	0714	0730	|	0743	0806	0805	0816	0833	|	0845	0905	0913	0933	|	0945	1005	1005
Manchester Airport ✈ a.		0403	0349	0515	0505	0619	0619	|	0710	|	0742	...	|	0810	|	|	0839	...	|	0910	|	0939	...	|	1010	|	|
Warrington Central a.		...	...	...	...	...	...	0628	...	0728	...	...	|	...	0830	0830	...	...	|	...	0930	...	...	|	...	1030	1030
Liverpool South Parkway a.		...	...	...	...	...	...	|	...	|	...	...	|	...	0847	0847	...	...	|	...	0947	...	...	|	...	1046	1046
Liverpool Lime Street a.		...	...	...	...	...	...	0654	...	0753	...	...	0808	...	0859	0859	...	...	0908	...	0959	...	...	1008	...	1059	1059

	⚒	⚒	⚒	⚒	⚒	⚒	⚒	⚒	⚒	⚒	⚒	⚒	⚒	⚒	⚒	⚒	⚒	⚒	⚒	⚒	⚒	⚒	⚒	⚒	⚒	⚒	⚒	⚒
Newcastle d.	...	...	0806	...	...	...	...	0910	...	...	...	...	1005	...	...	...	...	1110	...	...	...	...	1206	...	...	...	...	1310
Durham d.	...	...	0822	...	...	...	...	0923	...	...	...	...	1021	...	...	...	...	1123	...	...	...	...	1222	...	...	...	...	1323
Middlesbrough d.	...	...	|	0827	...	...	...	|	0927	...	...	...	|	1027	...	...	...	|	1127	...	...	...	|	1227	...	...	...	|
Darlington d.	...	...	0839	|	...	...	...	0940	|	...	...	...	1039	|	...	...	...	1140	|	...	...	...	1239	|	...	...	...	1340
Northallerton d.	...	...	0850	0856	...	...	...	0951	0956	...	...	...	1050	1056	...	...	...	1151	1156	...	...	...	1250	1256	...	...	...	1351
Thirsk d.	...	...	|	0904	...	...	...	|	1004	...	...	...	|	1104	...	...	...	|	1204	...	...	...	|	1304	...	...	...	|
Scarborough d.	...	...	|	|	0850	...	...	|	|	0950	...	...	|	|	1050	...	...	|	|	1150	...	...	|	|	1250	...	...	|
Malton d.	...	...	|	|	0913	...	...	|	|	1013	...	...	|	|	1113	...	...	|	|	1213	...	...	|	|	1313	...	...	|
York a.	...	...	0915	0921	0938	...	...	1014	1021	1038	...	...	1113	1121	1138	...	...	1214	1221	1238	...	...	1313	1321	1338	...	...	1414
York d.	0853	...	0915	0924	0941	0953	...	1016	1024	1041	1053	...	1115	1124	1141	1153	...	1216	1224	1241	1253	...	1315	1324	1341	1353	...	1416
Hull d.	|	0838	|	|	|	|	0938	|	|	|	|	1038	|	|	|	|	1138	|	|	|	|	1238	|	|	|	|	1338	|
Selby d.	|	0910	|	|	|	|	1010	|	|	|	|	1110	|	|	|	|	1210	|	|	|	|	1310	|	|	|	|	1410	|
Leeds a.	0916	0934	0941	0949	1004	1016	1034	1039	1049	1104	1116	1134	1139	1150	1204	1216	1234	1239	1249	1304	1316	1334	1339	1349	1404	1416	1434	1440
Leeds d.	0920	0936	0944	0953	1009	1020	1036	1044	1053	1109	1120	1136	1144	1153	1209	1220	1236	1244	1253	1309	1320	1336	1344	1351	1409	1420	1436	1444
Dewsbury d.	|	0947	|	|	1020	|	1047	|	|	1120	|	1147	|	|	1220	|	1247	|	|	1320	|	1347	|	|	1420	|	1447	|
Huddersfield d.	0940	0956	1002	1011	1030	1040	1056	1102	1111	1130	1140	1156	1202	1211	1230	1240	1256	1302	1311	1330	1340	1356	1402	1409	1430	1440	1456	1502
Stalybridge d.	|	1015	|	|	1050	|	1115	|	|	1150	|	1215	|	|	1250	|	1315	|	|	1350	|	1415	|	|	1450	|	1515	|
Manchester Victoria d.	|	|	1035	|	|	|	|	1135	|	|	|	|	1235	|	|	|	|	1335	|	|	|	|	1435	|	|	|	|	1535
Manchester Piccadilly a.	1013	1032	|	1045	1105	1113	1132	|	1144	1205	1213	1232	|	1244	1305	1313	1332	|	1344	1405	1413	1432	|	1444	1505	1513	1532	|
Manchester Airport ✈ a.	1039	...	|	1110	|	1139	...	|	1210	|	1239	...	|	1310	|	1339	...	|	1410	|	1439	...	|	1510	|	1539	...	|
Warrington Central a.	...	...	|	...	1130	...	...	|	...	1230	...	...	|	...	1330	...	...	|	...	1430	...	...	|	...	1530	...	...	|
Liverpool South Parkway a.	...	...	|	...	1147	...	...	|	...	1247	...	...	|	...	1347	...	...	|	...	1447	...	...	|	...	1547	...	...	|
Liverpool Lime Street a.	...	...	1108	...	1159	...	...	1208	...	1259	...	...	1308	...	1359	...	...	1408	...	1459	...	...	1508	...	1559	...	...	1608

	⚒	⚒	⑥	Ⓐ	⚒	⚒	⚒	⚒	⚒	⚒	⚒	⚒	⚒	⚒	⚒	⚒	⚒	⚒	⚒	⚒	Ⓐ	⑥	⚒	⚒	⚒	⚒	⚒	⚒
Newcastle d.	...	...	...	...	...	1406	...	...	...	...	1508	...	...	...	...	1606	...	...	...	...	1703	1706	...	...	...	1804	...	...
Durham d.	...	...	...	...	...	1422	...	...	...	...	1523	...	...	...	...	1622	...	...	...	...	1719	1722	...	...	...	1822	...	...
Middlesbrough d.	1327	...	...	...	...	|	1427	...	...	...	|	1527	...	...	...	|	1626	...	...	...	|	|	1726	...	...	|	...	1827
Darlington d.	|	...	...	...	...	1439	|	...	...	...	1540	|	...	...	...	1639	|	...	...	...	1736	1739	|	...	...	1839	...	|
Northallerton d.	1356	...	...	...	...	1450	1456	...	...	...	1551	1556	...	...	...	1650	1654	...	...	...	1747	1750	1754	...	...	1850	...	1856
Thirsk d.	1404	...	...	...	...	|	1504	...	...	...	|	1604	...	...	...	|	1702	...	...	...	|	|	1802	...	...	|	...	1904
Scarborough d.	|	1350	...	...	...	|	|	1450	...	...	|	|	1550	...	...	|	|	1650	...	...	|	|	|	1750	1807a	|	...	|
Malton d.	|	1413	...	...	...	|	|	1513	...	...	|	|	1613	...	...	|	|	1713	...	...	|	|	|	1813	|	|	...	|
York a.	1421	1438	...	...	...	1513	1521	1538	...	...	1614	1621	1638	...	...	1713	1720	1738	...	...	1810	1815	1821	1838	|	1913	...	1921
York d.	1424	1441	1453	1453	...	1515	1524	1541	1553	...	1616	1624	1641	1653	...	1715	1722	1741	1753	...	1816	1816	1822	1841	1853	1915	...	1924
Hull d.	|	|	|	|	1438	|	|	|	|	1538	|	|	|	|	1638	|	|	|	|	1738	|	|	|	|	|	|	1849	|
Selby d.	|	|	|	|	1510	|	|	|	|	1610	|	|	|	|	1710	|	|	|	|	1810	|	|	|	|	|	|	1920	|
Leeds a.	1449	1504	1516	1516	1534	1540	1549	1606	1616	1634	1639	1649	1706	1716	1735	1739	1749	1804	1816	1834	1839	1840	1849	1904	1916	1938	1943	1951
Leeds d.	1453	1509	1517	1520	1536	1544	1553	1609	1620	1636	1644	1653	1709	1720	1737	1744	1753	1809	1820	1836	1844	1844	1853	1909	1920	1941	...	1953
Dewsbury d.	|	1520	|	|	1547	|	|	1620	|	1647	|	|	1720	1731	1748	|	|	1820	|	1847	|	|	|	1920	|	1952	...	|
Huddersfield d.	1511	1530	1535	1540	1556	1602	1611	1630	1640	1656	1702	1711	1730	1740	1757	1802	1811	1830	1840	1856	1902	1902	1911	1930	1940	2002	...	2011
Stalybridge d.	|	1550	|	|	1615	|	|	1650	|	1715	|	|	1750	|	1816	|	|	1850	|	1915	|	|	|	1950	|	|	...	|
Manchester Victoria d.	|	|	|	|	|	1635	|	|	|	|	1735	|	|	|	|	1835	|	|	|	|	1935	1935	|	|	|	2035	...	|
Manchester Piccadilly a.	1542	1605	1613	1613	1636	|	1644	1705	1716	1732	|	1746	1805	1817	1833	|	1842	1905	1916	1932	|	|	1943	2005	2014	|	...	2045
Manchester Airport ✈ a.	1610	|	1639	1644	...	|	1712	|	1739t	...	|	1810	|	1839	...	|	1916	|	...	...	|	|	2013	|	...	|	...	2113
Warrington Central a.	...	1630	...	...	...	|	...	1730	...	...	|	...	1830	...	...	|	...	1930	...	...	|	|	...	2030	...	|	...	...
Liverpool South Parkway a.	...	1647	...	...	...	|	...	1747	...	...	|	...	1847	...	...	|	...	1947	...	...	|	|	...	2047	...	|	...	...
Liverpool Lime Street a.	...	1659	...	...	...	1708	...	1759	...	...	1808	...	1859	...	...	1909	...	1959	...	...	2009	2008	...	2059	...	2113	...	...

	⚒	⚒	⚒	⚒	⚒	⚒	Ⓐ	Ⓐ	⑥	Ⓐ	⑥	⚒	⚒	⚒	⚒	⑥	①–④	⑤		⑦ 🚌	⑦	⑦	⑦	⑦	⑦	⑦	⑦	⑦
Newcastle d.	...	1910	...	...	...	...	...	2027	...	...	...	...	...	...	...	2155	2155	2155	⑦	...	...	...	...	...	...	...	...	0800
Durham d.	...	1923	...	...	...	...	...	2045	...	...	...	...	...	...	...	2210	2210	2210		...	...	...	...	...	...	...	...	0813
Middlesbrough d.	...	|	...	1930	...	...	...	|	...	2052	2052	...	...	...	2150	|	|	|		...	...	...	...	...	...	...	...	|
Darlington d.	...	1940	...	|	...	...	...	2102	...	|	|	...	...	...	2219	2227	2227	2227		...	...	...	...	...	...	...	...	0831
Northallerton d.	...	1951	...	1958	...	...	...	2113	...	2120	2120	...	...	...	2230	2238	2238	2238	♣	...	...	...	...	...	...	...	...	0842
Thirsk d.	...	|	...	2006	...	...	...	|	...	2128	2128	...	...	...	2238	|	|	|		...	...	...	...	...	...	...	...	0850
Scarborough d.	1850	|	...	|	1950	...	2045	|	2050	|	|	...	...	2207	|	|	|	|		...	...	...	...	...	...	...	...	|
Malton d.	1913	|	...	|	2013	...	2109	|	2113	|	|	...	...	2230	|	|	|	|		...	...	...	...	...	...	...	...	|
York a.	1938	2014	...	2025	2038	...	2133	2136	2138	2146	2152	...	...	2255	2258	2302	2302	2302		...	...	...	...	...	...	...	...	0909
York d.	1941	2016	...	...	2041	2116	...	2141	2141	2148	...	...	2230	...	...	2306	2306	2306		0130	0400	0512	0612	...	0712	0809	0850	0911
Hull d.	|	|	1959	...	|	|	...	|	|	|	...	2138	|	...	...	|	|	|		|	|	|	|	...	|	|	|	|
Selby d.	|	|	2030	...	|	|	...	|	|	|	...	2212	|	...	...	|	|	|		|	|	|	|	...	|	|	|	|
Leeds a.	2004	2039	2059	...	2104	2139	...	2205	2205	2212	...	2240	2305	...	...	2332	2332	2332		0220	0426	0538	0638	...	0738	0835	0913	0934
Leeds d.	2009	2041	...	...	2109	2141	...	2209	2209	...	...	2241	2309	...	...	2335	2335	2335		0220	0430	0540	0640	...	0740	0840	0916	0944
Dewsbury d.	2020	2052	...	...	2120	2152	...	2220	2220	...	...	2252	2320	...	...	2346	2346	2346		|	|	|	0651	...	0751	0851	0927	|
Huddersfield a.	2030	2102	...	...	2130	2202	...	2230	2230	...	...	2302	2330	...	...	2355	2355	2355		0255	0447	0557	0700	...	0800	0900	0937	|
Huddersfield d.	2030	2102	...	...	2130	2202	...	2230	2230	...	...	2302	2330	...	...	2355	2355	2355		0255	*0500**	*0610**	*0701**	...	*0810**	0903	*0950**	|
Stalybridge d.	2050	|	...	...	2150	|	...	2250	2250	...	...	|	|	...	...	|	|	|		|	|	*0700**	*0800**	...	*0900**	|	|	|
Manchester Victoria d.	|	|	...	...	|	|	...	|	|	...	...	|	|	...	...	|	|	|		|	|	|	|	...	|	0951	|	1048
Manchester Piccadilly a.	2105	2133	...	...	2205	2233	...	2305	2305	...	...	2337	0004	...	...	0027	0028	0041		0355	*0519**	*0720**	*0820**	0912	*0920**	1006	|	|
Manchester Airport ✈ a.	|	2154	...	...	|	2256	...	|	|	...	...	...	...	...	...	0047	0050	0056		0420	*0538**	*0745**	*0845**	|	*0945**	1022	*1105**	|
Warrington Central a.	2130	...	...	...	2230	...	...	2330	2330	...	...	...	...	...	...	...	...	...		...	...	...	...	0933	...	...	...	|
Liverpool South Parkway a.	2147	...	...	...	2245	...	...	2345	2345	...	...	...	...	...	...	...	...	...		...	...	...	...	0949	...	...	...	|
Liverpool Lime Street a.	2159	...	...	...	2256	...	...	2359	2359	...	...	...	...	...	...	...	...	...		...	...	...	...	1001	...	...	...	1125

⑥ June 25 - Sept. 10.
Calls to set down only.
⑥ only.
②–⑤ a. 0219 / d. 0220.
②–⑤ a. 0333 / d. 0335.

♣ – Service on ⑦ valid June 19 - August 21. For service May 15 - June 12 and from August 28 please contact National Rail Enquires on ✆ +44 (0)3457 48 49 50.
* – Connection by 🚌.
▯ – Distances: York (*0 km*) - Malton (*33 km*) - Scarborough (*67 km*).
Hull (*0 km*) - Selby (*34 km*) - Leeds (*83 km*).

188 THE NORTH EAST and YORKSHIRE - MANCHESTER and LIVERPOOL

Service on ⑦ is valid June 19 - August 21. For service on ⑦ May 15 - June 12 and from August 28 please contact National Rail Enquires ✆ +44 (0)3457 48 49

	⑦	⑦	⑦	⑦	⑦	⑦	⑦	⑦	⑦	⑦	⑦	⑦	⑦	⑦	⑦	⑦	⑦	⑦	⑦	⑦	⑦	⑦	⑦	⑦	⑦	⑦
Newcastle d.	...	...	...	...	0906	...	...	...	1004	...	...	...	1110	...	...	...	1206	...	...	...	1310	...	...	...	1405	...
Durham d.	...	...	...	...	0919	...	...	...	1020	...	...	...	1123	...	...	...	1222	...	...	...	1323	...	...	...	1421	...
Middlesbrough d.	...	...	...	...	|	...	...	...	|	1017	...	...	|	...	...	...	|	1228	...	...	|	...	...	...	|	141
Darlington d.	...	...	...	...	0936	...	...	...	1039	|	...	...	1140	...	...	...	1240	|	...	...	1340	...	...	...	1438	|
Northallerton d.	...	...	...	...	0947	...	...	...	1050	1044	...	...	1151	...	...	...	1251	1256	...	...	1351	...	...	...	|	144
Thirsk d.	...	...	...	...	|	...	...	...	|	1052	...	...	|	...	...	...	|	1304	...	...	|	...	...	...	|	145
Scarborough d.	...	...	0853	...	|	...	0953	...	|	|	1053	...	|	...	1153	...	|	|	1253	...	|	...	1353	...	|	|
Malton d.	...	...	0916	...	|	...	1016	...	|	|	1116	...	|	...	1216	...	|	|	1316	...	|	...	1416	...	|	|
York a.	...	...	0941	...	1010	...	1041	...	1113	1111	1141	...	1214	...	1241	...	1314	1322	1341	...	1414	...	1441	...	1512	1517
York d.	...	0928	0945	...	1012	1028	1045	...	1115	1124	1145	...	1216	1224	1245	...	1315	1324	1345	...	1416	1424	1445	...	1515	1524
Hull d.	0835	|	|	0934	|	|	|	...	|	|	|	1137	|	|	|	1237	|	|	|	1339	|	|	|	1429	|	|
Selby d.	0910	|	|	1006	|	|	|	...	|	|	|	1208	|	|	|	1308	|	|	|	1410	|	|	|	1500	|	|
Leeds a.	0938	0953	1008	1032	1036	1051	1108	...	1138	1147	1208	1234	1239	1247	1308	1334	1339	1347	1408	1434	1439	1447	1508	1527	1539	1547
Leeds d.	...	0958	1010	1036	1044	1053	1110	1138	1144	1152	1210	1236	1244	1252	1310	1336	1342	1350	1410	1436	1444	1452	1510	1536	1544	1552
Dewsbury d.	...	1009	1021	1047	|	|	1121	|	|	1203	1221	1247	|	1303	1321	1347	|	1407	1421	1447	|	1503	1521	1547	|	1603
Huddersfield a.	...	|	1029	1056	|	|	1129	1156	|	|	1229	1255	|	|	1329	1356	|	|	1429	1455	|	|	1529	1555	|	|
Huddersfield d.	...	|	*1045**	*1115**	|	|	*1145**	*1215**	|	|	*1245**	*1315**	|	|	*1345**	*1415**	|	|	*1445**	*1515**	|	|	*1545**	*1615**	|	|
Stalybridge d.	...	|	|	*1225**	|	|	|	*1325**	|	|	|	*1425**	|	|	|	*1525**	|	|	|	*1625**	|	|	|	*1725**	|	|
Manchester Victoria d.	...	1056	|	*1305**	1149	1151	|	*1405**	1243	1250	|	*1505**	1342	1350	|	*1605**	1446	1456	|	*1705**	1542	1550	|	*1805**	1642	1650
Manchester Piccadilly a.	...	1132	|	...	|	1206	|	...	|	1307	|	...	|	1406	|	...	|	1510	|	...	|	1606	|	...	|	1706
Manchester Airport ✈ a.	...	1150	*1200**	...	|	1222	*1300**	...	|	1324	*1400**	...	|	1424	*1500**	...	|	1524	*1600**	...	|	1622	*1700**	...	|	1722
Warrington Central d.	...	...	...	...	|	...	...	...	|	...	...	...	|	...	...	...	|	...	...	...	|	...	...	...	|	...
Liverpool South Parkway a.	...	...	...	...	|	...	...	...	|	...	...	...	|	...	...	...	|	...	...	...	|	...	...	...	|	...
Liverpool Lime Street a.	...	...	...	...	1237	...	...	...	1319	...	...	...	1419	...	...	...	1524	...	...	...	1625	...	...	...	1718	...

	⑦	⑦	⑦	⑦	⑦	⑦	⑦	⑦	⑦	⑦	⑦	⑦	⑦		⑦	⑦	⑦	⑦	⑦	⑦	⑦		⑦	⑦	⑦	⑦
Newcastle d.	...	1510	...	...	...	1604	...	...	...	1710	...	...	1804	...	...	...	...	1910	...	2010	...	...	...	...	...	...
Durham d.	...	1523	...	...	...	1620	...	...	...	1723	...	...	1822	...	...	...	...	1923	...	2023	...	...	...	...	...	...
Middlesbrough d.	...	|	...	...	...	|	1624	...	...	|	...	...	|	...	...	1819	...	|	...	|	...	...	2041	...	...	2208
Darlington d.	...	1540	...	...	...	1638	|	...	...	1740	...	...	1840	...	...	|	...	1940	...	2040	...	...	|	...	...	|
Northallerton d.	...	1551	...	...	...	|	1652	...	...	1751	...	...	|	...	...	1847	...	1951	...	2051	...	...	2109	...	...	2237
Thirsk d.	...	|	...	...	...	|	1700	...	...	|	...	...	|	...	...	1859	...	|	...	|	...	...	2117	...	...	2245
Scarborough d.	...	|	...	1553	...	|	|	1653	...	|	...	1753	|	...	...	|	1853	|	1953	|	...	...	|	2138	...	|
Malton d.	...	|	...	1616	...	|	|	1716	...	|	...	1816	|	...	...	|	1916	|	2016	|	...	...	|	2201	...	|
York a.	...	1614	...	1641	...	1711	1723	1741	...	1814	...	1841	1913	...	...	1917	1941	2014	2041	2114	...	...	2142	2226	...	2309
York d.	...	1616	1624	1645	...	1715	1724	1745	...	1816	1824	1845	1915	...	...	1924	1945	2016	2045	2116	...	...	2145	2228	2230	...
Hull d.	1539	|	|	|	1643	|	|	|	1739	|	|	|	|	...	1842	|	|	|	|	|	2049	...	|	|	|	...
Selby d.	1610	|	|	|	1714	|	|	|	1810	|	|	|	|	...	1914	|	|	|	|	|	2120	...	|	|	|	...
Leeds a.	1634	1640	1647	1708	1738	1742	1748	1808	1834	1839	1847	1908	1938	...	1942	1947	2008	2039	2108	2139	2147	...	2208	2251	2305	...
Leeds d.	1636	1644	1652	1710	1739	1744	1752	1810	1836	1844	1852	1910	1944	...	...	1952	2010	2043	2110	2141	...	...	2211	2253	2309	...
Dewsbury d.	1647	|	1703	1721	|	|	1806	1821	1847	|	1903	1921	1955	...	...	2003	2021	2054	2121	2152	...	...	2222	2304	2320	...
Huddersfield a.	1655	|	|	1729	1757	|	|	1829	1857	|	|	1929	|	...	...	|	2029	|	2129	2201	...	...	2230	2312	2327	...
Huddersfield d.	*1715**	|	|	*1745**	*1815**	|	|	*1845**	*1915**	|	|	*1945**	|	...	...	|	*2045**	|	*2145**	*2215**	...	...	2234	2316	2330	...
Stalybridge d.	*1825**	|	|	|	*1925**	|	|	|	*2025**	|	|	|	|	...	...	|	|	|	|	*2305**	...	...	|	|	|	...
Manchester Victoria d.	*1905**	1743	1750	|	*2005**	1844	1854	|	*2105**	1944	1950	|	2043	...	...	2050	|	2144	|	|	...	...	2327	0004	|	...
Manchester Piccadilly a.	...	|	1806	|	...	|	1909	|	...	|	2006	|	|	...	...	2107	|	|	|	*2325**	...	...	...	0021	0004	...
Manchester Airport ✈ a.	...	|	1821	*1900**	...	|	1924	*2000**	...	|	2021	*2100**	|	...	...	2125	*2200**	|	*2300**	*2350**	...	...	...	0035	...	...
Warrington Central d.	...	|	...	...	...	|	...	...	...	|	...	...	|	...	...	...	...	|	...	...	...	...	...	...	...	...
Liverpool South Parkway a.	...	|	...	...	...	|	...	...	...	|	...	...	|	...	...	...	...	|	...	...	...	...	...	...	...	...
Liverpool Lime Street a.	...	1819	...	...	...	1920	...	...	...	2023	...	...	2120	...	...	...	...	2219	...	...	...	...	...	...	...	...

	⚒	②–⑤	⑥	①	⚒	Ⓐ	⑥	⚒	⚒	⚒	⚒	⚒	⚒	⚒	⚒	⚒	⚒	⚒	⚒	⑥ a	⚒	⚒	⚒	⚒	⚒	⚒
Liverpool Lime Street d.		...	...	...	...	...	...	...	...	...	...	...	0612	...	0622	...	...	0712	...	...	0715	...	...	0812	...	0822
Liverpool South Parkway d.		...	...	...	...	...	...	...	...	...	...	...	|	...	0632	...	...	|	...	...	0725	...	...	|	...	0832
Warrington Central d.		...	...	...	...	...	...	...	...	...	...	...	|	...	0645	...	...	|	...	...	0741	...	...	|	...	0845
Manchester Airport d.		0038	0038	0045	...	0422	0425	...	0530	...	...	...	|	0634	|	0706	...	|	0732	...	|	0806	...	|	0834	|
Manchester Piccadilly d.		0053	0055	0100	...	0437	0440	...	0547	...	0615	0626	|	0657	0712	0726	0740	|	0757	...	0811	0826	0841	|	0857	0911
Manchester Victoria d.		|	|	|	...	|	|	...	|	...	|	|	0646	|	|	|	|	0751	|	...	|	|	|	0851	|	|
Stalybridge d.		|	|	|	...	|	|	...	0600	...	0627	|	0658	|	0725	|	0752	|	|	...	0825	|	0854	|	|	0925
Huddersfield d.		|	0125	|	...	0540	0540	...	0618	...	0646	0655	0717	0727	0746	0755	0812	0821	0827	...	0846	0855	0913	0921	0927	0946
Dewsbury d.		|	|	|	...	|	|	...	0627	...	0655	0705	0726	|	0755	0804	0823	|	|	...	0855	|	0923	|	|	0955
Leeds a.		0159	0202	0209	...	0559	0559	...	0642	...	0708	0718	0739	0747	0810	0817	0836	0840	0846	...	0909	0915	0936	0940	0946	1008
Leeds d.		0205	0205	0215	...	0601	0601	...	0643	...	0714	0722	0743	0749	0812	0820	0838	0843	0849	...	0912	0917	0938	0943	0949	1012
Selby d.		|	|	|	...	|	|	...	|	...	|	0742	|	|	|	|	0858	|	|	...	|	|	0958	|	|	|
Hull a.		|	|	|	...	|	|	...	|	...	|	0820	|	|	|	|	0933	|	|	...	|	|	1035	|	|	|
York a.		0244	0242	0243	...	0624	0624	...	0706	...	0737	...	0806	0812	0838	0843	...	0906	0912	...	0936	0940	...	1006	1012	1036
York d.		...	...	...	0600	0626	0626	0640	0708	0718	0740	...	0808	0815	0840	...	...	0908	0915	0920	0940	...	...	1008	1015	1040
Malton d.		...	...	...	|	|	|	0704	|	|	0804	...	|	|	0904	...	...	|	|	0943	1004	...	...	|	|	1104
Scarborough a.		...	...	...	|	|	|	0729	|	|	0829	...	|	|	0930	...	...	|	|	1009	1029	...	...	|	|	1129
Thirsk d.		...	...	...	0616	|	|	...	0725	0734	...	...	|	0831	...	...	...	|	0931	...	...	...	...	|	1031	...
Northallerton d.		...	...	...	0624	0647	0647	...	0733	0742	...	...	0829	0840	...	...	...	0929	0940	...	...	...	...	1029	1040	...
Darlington d.		...	...	...	0640	0700	0700	...	0745	|	...	...	0841	|	...	...	...	0941	|	...	...	...	...	1041	|	...
Middlesbrough a.		...	...	...	0707	|	|	...	|	0817	...	...	|	0912	...	...	...	|	1012	...	...	...	...	|	1112	...
Durham d.		...	...	...	...	0717	0717	...	0801	...	...	...	0857	...	...	...	...	0957	...	...	...	...	...	1057	...	...
Newcastle a.		...	...	...	...	0735	0735	...	0819	...	...	...	0914	...	...	...	...	1015	...	...	...	...	...	1114	...	...

	⚒	⚒	⚒	⚒	⚒	⚒	⚒	⚒	⚒	⚒	⚒	⚒	⚒	⚒	⚒	⚒	⚒	⚒	⚒	⚒	⚒	⚒	⚒	⚒	⚒	⚒
Liverpool Lime Street d.	...	0912	...	0922	...	...	1012	...	1022	...	...	1111	...	1122	...	...	1212	...	1222	...	...	1312	...	1322	...	...
Liverpool South Parkway d.	...	|	...	0932	...	...	|	...	1032	...	...	|	...	1132	...	...	|	...	1232	...	...	|	...	1332	...	...
Warrington Central d.	...	|	...	0945	...	...	|	...	1045	...	...	|	...	1145	...	...	|	...	1245	...	...	|	...	1345	...	...
Manchester Airport d.	...	|	0933	|	1006	...	|	1033	|	1106	...	|	1133	|	1206	...	|	1233	|	1306	...	|	1333	|	1406	...
Manchester Piccadilly d.	0941	|	0957	1011	1026	1041	|	1057	1111	1126	1141	|	1157	1211	1226	1241	|	1257	1311	1326	1341	|	1357	1411	1426	1441
Manchester Victoria d.	|	0951	|	|	|	|	1051	|	|	|	|	1151	|	|	|	|	1251	|	|	|	|	1351	|	|	|	|
Stalybridge d.	0954	|	|	1025	|	1054	|	|	1125	|	1154	|	|	1225	|	1254	|	|	1325	|	1354	|	|	1425	|	1454
Huddersfield d.	1013	1021	1027	1046	1055	1113	1121	1127	1146	1155	1213	1221	1227	1246	1255	1313	1321	1327	1346	1355	1413	1421	1427	1446	1455	1513
Dewsbury d.	1023	|	|	1055	|	1123	|	|	1155	|	1223	|	|	1255	|	1323	|	|	1355	|	1423	|	|	1455	|	1523
Leeds a.	1036	1040	1046	1108	1115	1136	1140	1146	1208	1215	1236	1240	1246	1308	1315	1336	1340	1346	1408	1415	1436	1440	1446	1508	1515	1536
Leeds d.	1038	1043	1049	1112	1117	1138	1143	1149	1212	1217	1238	1243	1249	1312	1317	1338	1343	1349	1412	1417	1438	1443	1449	1512	1517	1538
Selby d.	1058	|	|	|	|	1158	|	|	|	|	1258	|	|	|	|	1358	|	|	|	|	1458	|	|	|	|	1558
Hull a.	1135	|	|	|	|	1235	|	|	|	|	1335	|	|	|	|	1435	|	|	|	|	1535	|	|	|	|	1635
York a.	...	1106	1112	1136	1140	...	1206	1212	1236	1240	...	1306	1312	1336	1340	...	1406	1412	1436	1440	...	1506	1512	1536	1540	...
York d.	...	1108	1115	1140	...	...	1208	1215	1240	...	...	1308	1315	1340	...	...	1408	1415	1440	...	...	1508	1515	1540	...	...
Malton d.	...	|	|	1204	...	...	|	|	1304	...	...	|	|	1404	...	...	|	|	1504	...	...	|	|	1604	...	...
Scarborough a.	...	|	|	1229	...	...	|	|	1329	...	...	|	|	1429	...	...	|	|	1529	...	...	|	|	1629	...	...
Thirsk a.	...	|	1131	...	...	...	|	1231	...	...	...	|	1331	...	...	...	|	1431	...	...	...	|	1531	...	...	...
Northallerton a.	...	1129	1140	...	...	...	1229	1240	...	...	...	1329	1340	...	...	...	1429	1440	...	...	...	1529	1540	...	...	...
Darlington a.	...	1141	|	...	...	...	1241	|	...	...	...	1341	|	...	...	...	1441	|	...	...	...	1541	|	...	...	...
Middlesbrough a.	...	|	1212	...	...	...	|	1312	...	...	...	|	1412	...	...	...	|	1512	...	...	...	|	1612	...	...	...
Durham a.	...	1157	...	...	...	...	1257	...	...	...	...	1357	...	...	...	...	1457	...	...	...	...	1557	...	...	...	...
Newcastle a.	...	1215	...	...	...	...	1317	...	...	...	...	1415	...	...	...	...	1512	...	...	...	...	1615	...	...	...	...

a – ⑥ June 25 - Sept. 10.

* – Connection by 🚌.

LIVERPOOL and MANCHESTER - YORKSHIRE and THE NORTH EAST 188

ervice on ⑦ is valid June 19 - August 21. For service on ⑦ May 15 - June 12 and from August 28 please contact National Rail Enquires ✆ +44 (0)3457 48 49 50.

	⚒	⚒	⚒	⚒	⚒	⚒	⚒	⚒	⚒	⚒	⚒	⚒	⚒	⚒	⚒	⚒	⚒	⚒	⚒	⚒	⚒	⚒	Ⓐ	⚒	⚒	⑥	⚒
pool Lime Street ..... d.	...	1422	...	...	1511	...	1522	...	...	1612	...	1622	...	...	1710	...	1722	...	...	1812	...	1822	...	...	1912	...	1922
pool South Parkway d.	...	1432	...	...	|	...	1532	...	...	|	...	1632	...	...	|	...	1732	...	...	|	...	1832	...	...	|	...	1932
ngton Central........... d.	...	1445	...	...	|	...	1545	...	...	|	...	1645	...	...	|	...	1745	...	...	|	...	1845	...	...	|	...	1945
nchester Airport...... d.	1433	|	1506	...	|	1533	|	1606	...	|	1633	|	1703f	...	|	1733	|	1806t	...	|	1833	|	...	1920	|	...	|
hester Piccadilly ..... d.	1457	1511	1526	1541	|	1557	1611	1626	1641	|	1656	1711	1725	1741	|	1754	1811	1826	1841	|	1857	1911	1926	1943	|	...	2011
nchester Victoria..... d.	|	|	|	|	1551	|	|	|	|	1651	|	|	|	|	1751	|	|	|	|	1851	|	|	|	|	1951	...	|
bridge .... d.	|	1525	|	1554	|	|	1625	|	1654	|	|	1725	1738	1756	|	|	1825	|	1854	|	|	1925	|	|	|	...	2025
ersfield .... d.	1527	1546	1555	1613	1621	1627	1646	1655	1713	1721	1727	1746	1757	1816	1822	1827	1846	1855	1914	1921	1927	1946	1956	2012	2021	...	2046
bury .... d.	|	1555	|	1623	|	|	1655	|	1723	|	|	1755	|	1825	|	|	1855	|	1924	|	|	1956	|	|	|	...	2055
s............................. a.	1546	1608	1615	1636	1640	1646	1708	1715	1736	1742	1746	1808	1816	1838	1843	1846	1908	1916	1937	1942	1946	2009	2017	2031	2042	...	2108
s............................. d.	1549	1612	1617	1638	1643	1649	1712	1717	1740	1744	1749	1812	1818	1841	1845	1849	1912	1917	1939	1943	1949	2012	2020	2033	2043	2105	2112
by............................ d.	|	|	|	1658	|	|	|	|	1801	|	|	|	|	1904	|	|	|	|	2001	|	|	|	2055	|	|	2128	|
l.............................. a.	|	|	|	1735	|	|	|	|	1838	|	|	|	|	1939	|	|	|	|	2041	|	|	|	2135	|	|	2207	|
.... a.	1612	1636	1640	...	1706	1712	1736	1743	...	1807	1814	1836	1844	...	1909	1913	1936	1940	...	2006	2012	2035	...	2058	2107	...	2137
.... d.	1615	1640	...	...	1708	1715	1740	...	...	1809	1816	1840	...	...	1910	1916	1940	...	...	2008	2016	2040	...	...	2109	...	...
ton........................... d.	|	1704	...	...	|	|	1804	...	...	|	|	1904	...	...	|	|	2004	...	...	|	|	2104	...	...	|	...	...
arborough............... a.	|	1729	...	...	|	|	1829	...	...	|	|	1929	...	...	|	|	2029	...	...	|	|	2129	...	...	|	...	...
k .... a.	1631	...	...	...	|	1731	...	...	...	|	1832	...	...	...	|	1933	...	...	...	|	2035	...	...	...	2126	...	...
allerton..................... a.	1640	...	...	...	1729	1740	...	...	...	1830	1840	...	...	...	1932	1941	...	...	...	2029	2043	...	...	...	2134	...	...
gton.......................... a.	|	...	...	...	1741	|	...	...	...	1842	|	...	...	...	1944	|	...	...	...	2041	|	...	...	...	2146	...	...
ddlesbrough............ a.	1712	...	...	...	|	1812	...	...	...	|	1914	...	...	...	|	2014	...	...	...	|	2115	...	...	...	|	...	...
am .... a.	...	...	...	...	1757	...	...	...	...	1858	...	...	...	...	2001	...	...	...	...	2057	...	...	...	...	2202	...	...
castle......................... a.	...	...	...	...	1815	...	...	...	...	1914	...	...	...	...	2020	...	...	...	...	2113	...	...	...	...	2219	...	...

	Ⓐ	Ⓐ	⑥	Ⓐ	Ⓐ	⑥	⚒	⚒	⚒	⚒	⑥	Ⓐ	⑥	⑤	①-④		⑦ 🚌	⑦	⑦	⑦	⑦	⑦	⑦	⑦ 🚌	⑦	⑦	⑦
pool Lime Street ..... d.	...	...	...	2022	...	2022	...	...	2130	...	2230	2230	...	...	...	⑦	...	...	...	...	...	...	...	...	0801	...	...
pool South Parkway d.	...	...	...	2032	...	2032	...	...	2140	...	2240	2240	...	...	...		...	...	...	...	...	...	...	...	|	...	...
ngton Central........... d.	...	...	...	2045	...	2045	...	...	2152	...	2253	2253	...	...	...		...	...	...	...	...	...	...	...	|	...	...
nchester Airport...... d.	...	2020	2020	|	...	|	...	2121	|	2223	|	|	2320	2315	2315		0100	*0335**	*0540**	...	...	*0630**	...	0725	|	...	...
chester Piccadilly ..... d.	...	2042	2042	2111	...	2111	...	2142	2218	2242	2321	2321	2335	2334	2334	♣	0125u	*0400**	*0605**	...	...	*0655**	...	0750u	|	...	0841
nchester Victoria..... d.	...	|	|	|	...	|	...	|	|	|	|	|	2351	2351	2351		|	|	|	...	...	|	...	|	0837	...	0857
bridge .... d.	...	|	|	2125	...	2125	...	|	2231	2254	2334	2334	|	|	|		|	|	|	...	...	*0720**	...	0815	|	...	|
ersfield .... a.	...	2112	2112	2146	...	2146	...	2211	1150	2313	2352	2352	0021	0021	0052		0225	*0500**	*0705**	...	...	*0805**	...	0900	|	...	|
ersfield .... d.	...	2112	2112	2146	...	2146	...	2211	2250	2313	2352	2352	0021	0021	0052		0225	0512	0718	...	...	0818	0852	...	|	...	|
sbury .... d.	...	|	|	2155	...	2155	...	|	2259	2322	|	|	0030	0030s	0102s		|	|	0727	...	...	0827	0901	...	0927	...	0951
s............................. a.	...	2131	2131	2208	...	2208	...	2230	2312	2335	0011	0031	0043	0044	0115		0300	0531	0740	...	...	0840	0914	...	0940	...	1002
s............................. d.	2121	2133	2133	2211	...	2211	2221	2233	2316	2337	0015	0034	0045	0047	0123		0300	0533	0743	...	...	0843	0915	...	0943	0952	1012
by............................ d.	2145	|	|	|	...	|	2243	|	|	|	|	|	|	|	|		|	|	|	...	...	|	|	...	|	1014	|
ll............................. a.	2223	|	|	|	...	|	2319	|	|	|	|	|	|	|	|		|	|	|	...	...	|	|	...	|	1049	|
.... a.	...	2157	2158	2234	...	2236	...	2258	2342	0003	0043	0113	0113	0129	0207		0350	0601	0811	...	...	0906	0938	...	1006	...	1038
.... d.	...	2200	*2212*	2235	2242	...	...	...	...	...	...	...	...	...	...		...	...	...	0847	0857	0908	0942	...	1008	...	1042
lton........................... d.	...	2224	*2236*	|	2306	...	...	...	...	...	...	...	...	...	...		...	...	...	|	0920	|	1006	...	|	...	1106
arborough............... a.	...	2249	*2301*	|	2331	...	...	...	...	...	...	...	...	...	...		...	...	...	|	0945	|	1031	...	|	...	1131
k .... a.	...	...	...	2258	...	...	...	...	...	...	...	...	...	...	...		...	...	...	0903	...	|	...	...	|	...	...
allerton..................... a.	...	...	...	2306	...	...	...	...	...	...	...	...	...	...	...		...	...	...	0911	...	0929	...	...	1029	...	...
ngton.......................... a.	...	...	...	2318	...	...	...	...	...	...	...	...	...	...	...		...	...	...	0925	...	0941	...	...	1041	...	...
ddlesbrough............ a.	...	...	...	|	...	...	...	...	...	...	...	...	...	...	...		...	...	...	0952	...	|	...	...	|	...	...
am .... a.	...	...	...	2334	...	...	...	...	...	...	...	...	...	...	...		...	...	...	...	...	0957	...	...	1057	...	...
castle......................... a.	...	...	...	0008	...	...	...	...	...	...	...	...	...	...	...		...	...	...	...	...	1015	...	...	1114	...	...

	⑦	⑦	⑦	⑦	⑦	⑦	⑦	⑦	⑦	⑦	⑦	⑦	⑦	⑦	⑦	⑦	⑦	⑦	⑦	⑦	⑦	⑦	⑦	⑦	⑦	⑦	⑦
rpool Lime Street ..... d.	...	...	0901	...	...	...	1001	...	...	...	1101	...	...	...	1201	...	...	...	1301	...	...	...	1401	...	...	...	1501
rpool South Parkway d.	...	...	|	...	...	...	|	...	...	...	|	...	...	...	|	...	...	...	|	...	...	...	|	...	...	...	|
ington Central........... d.	...	...	|	...	...	...	|	...	...	...	|	...	...	...	|	...	...	...	|	...	...	...	|	...	...	...	|
anchester Airport...... d.	...	*0830**	|	*0920**	0934	...	|	*1020**	1025	...	|	*1120**	1132	...	|	*1220**	1233	...	|	*1320**	1334	...	|	*1420**	1432	...	|
chester Piccadilly ..... d.	...	|	|	|	0951	...	|	|	1042	...	|	|	1151	...	|	|	1250	...	|	|	1352	...	|	|	1451	...	|
anchester Victoria..... d.	...	|	0936	|	1009	*0913**	1036	|	1110	*1013**	1137	|	1209	*1103**	1237	|	1309	*1203**	1337	|	1409	*1303**	1437	|	1509	*1403**	1536
bridge .... d.	...	*0905**	|	|	|	*0953**	|	|	|	*1053**	|	|	|	*1153**	|	|	|	*1253**	|	|	|	*1353**	|	|	|	*1453**	|
dersfield .... a.	...	*0950**	|	*1035**	|	*1103**	|	*1135**	|	*1203**	|	*1235**	|	*1303**	|	*1335**	|	*1403**	|	*1435**	|	*1503**	|	*1535**	|	*1603**	|
dersfield .... d.	...	1005	|	1046	|	1112	|	1146	|	1213	|	1246	|	1313	|	1346	|	1413	|	1446	|	1513	|	1546	|	1613	|
sbury .... d.	...	1015	|	1055	1101	|	|	1155	1159	1223	|	1255	1301	1322	|	1355	1401	1423	|	1455	1501	1523	|	1555	1559	1623	|
ds............................ a.	...	1030	1040	1109	1114	1132	1140	1209	1212	1236	1241	1309	1314	1334	1340	1409	1414	1436	1440	1509	1514	1536	1539	1609	1613	1636	1640
ds............................ d.	...	1038	1043	1112	1120	...	1143	1212	1220	1238	1243	1312	1318	1337	1343	1412	1418	1438	1443	1512	1520	1538	1542	1612	1618	1638	1643
elby........................... d.	...	1104	|	|	|	...	|	|	|	1301	|	|	|	|	|	|	|	1458	|	|	|	1601	|	|	|	1658	|
ull............................. a.	...	1140	|	|	|	...	|	|	|	1336	|	|	|	1424	|	|	|	1532	|	|	|	1636	|	|	|	1733	|
.... a.	...	...	1106	1139	1143	...	1206	1235	1243	...	1306	1336	1341	...	1406	1439	1441	...	1506	1540	1543	...	1605	1635	1641	...	1706
k .... d.	1052	...	1108	1142	...	...	1208	1242	1254	...	1308	1342	...	...	1408	1442	1456	...	1508	1542	...	...	1608	1642	1655	...	1708
alton.......................... d.	|	...	|	1206	...	...	|	1306	|	...	|	1406	...	...	|	1506	|	...	|	1606	...	...	|	1706	|	...	|
carborough............... a.	|	...	|	1231	...	...	|	1331	|	...	|	1431	...	...	|	1531	|	...	|	1631	...	...	|	1731	|	...	|
sk .... a.	1111	...	|	...	...	...	|	...	1310	...	|	...	...	...	|	...	1513	...	|	...	...	...	|	...	1711	...	|
hallerton.................... a.	1123	...	1129	...	...	...	1229	...	1323	...	1329	...	...	...	1429	...	1526	...	1530	...	...	...	1629	...	1720	...	1729
ngton.......................... a.	|	...	1141	...	...	...	1241	...	|	...	1341	...	...	...	1441	...	|	...	1542	...	...	...	1641	...	|	...	1741
ddlesbrough............ a.	1155	...	|	...	...	...	|	...	1353	...	|	...	...	...	|	...	1607	...	|	...	...	...	|	...	1750	...	|
am .... a.	...	...	1157	...	...	...	1257	...	...	...	1357	...	...	...	1458	...	...	...	1558	...	...	...	1657	...	...	...	1757
castle......................... a.	...	...	1215	...	...	...	1312	...	...	...	1416	...	...	...	1514	...	...	...	1616	...	...	...	1714	...	...	...	1815

	⑦	⑦	⑦	⑦	⑦	⑦	⑦	⑦	⑦	⑦	⑦	⑦	⑦	⑦	⑦	⑦	⑦	⑦	⑦	⑦	⑦	⑦	⑦	⑦ 🚌	⑦	⑦ 🚌	⑦
rpool Lime Street ..... d.	...	...	...	1601	...	...	...	1701	...	...	...	1801	...	...	...	1901	...	...	...	2001	...	...	...	...	2152	...	...
rpool South Parkway d.	...	...	...	|	...	...	...	|	...	...	...	|	...	...	...	|	...	...	...	|	...	...	...	...	|	...	...
ington Central........... d.	...	...	...	|	...	...	...	|	...	...	...	|	...	...	...	|	...	...	...	|	...	...	...	...	|	...	...
anchester Airport...... d.	*1520**	1534	...	|	*1620**	1634	...	|	*1720**	1734	...	|	*1820**	1834	...	|	*1920**	1934	...	|	*2000**	2034	*2025**	2135	|	2235	...
chester Piccadilly ..... d.	|	1551	...	|	|	1650	...	|	|	1750	...	|	|	1852	...	|	|	1952	...	|	|	2052	*2050**	2200u	|	2300u	...
anchester Victoria..... d.	|	1609	*1503**	1637	|	1709	*1603**	1737	|	1809	*1703**	1837	|	1909	...	1937	|	2009	...	2037	|	2109	|	|	2235	|	2332
bridge .... d.	|	|	*1553**	|	|	|	*1653**	|	|	|	*1753**	|	|	|	...	|	|	|	...	|	*2050**	|	*2115**	2225	|	2325	|
dersfield .... a.	*1635**	|	*1703**	|	*1735**	|	*1803**	|	*1835**	|	*1903**	|	*1935**	|	...	|	*2035**	|	...	|	*2135**	|	*2200**	2310	|	0010	0018
dersfield .... d.	1646	|	1713	|	1746	|	1813	|	1846	|	1911	|	1946	|	...	|	2046	|	...	|	2146	|	2212	...	|	...	0021
sbury .... d.	1655	1701	1723	|	1755	1759	1823	|	1855	1901	1921	|	1955	1959	...	|	2055	2102	...	|	2155	2201	2221	...	2327	...	0030
ds............................ a.	1709	1714	1736	1740	1808	1812	1836	1840	1909	1914	1934	1940	2008	2012	...	2040	2108	2114	...	2140	2208	2214	2234	...	2340	...	0043
ds............................ d.	1712	1720	1738	1743	1812	1820	1838	1843	1912	1920	...	1943	2012	2020	2018	2043	2112	2120	2139	2143	2211	2221	2236	...	2351	...	0045
elby........................... d.	|	|	1801	|	|	|	1901	|	|	|	...	|	|	|	2050	|	|	|	2201	|	|	2243	|	...	|	...	|
ull............................. a.	|	|	1834	|	|	|	1936	|	|	|	...	|	|	|	2126	|	|	|	2237	|	|	2319	|	...	|	...	|
k .... a.	1737	1743	...	1806	1835	1843	...	1906	1936	1943	...	2006	2035	2043	...	2106	2137	2143	...	2206	2234	...	2304	...	0022	...	0113
k .... d.	1742	...	...	1808	1842	1855	...	1908	1942	...	...	2008	2042	2100	...	2108	...	...	...	2208	2235	...	...	...	...	...	...
alton.......................... d.	1806	...	...	|	1906	|	...	|	2006	...	...	|	2106	|	...	|	...	...	...	2232	|	...	...	...	...	...	...
carborough............... a.	1831	...	...	|	1931	|	...	|	2031	...	...	|	2131	|	...	|	...	...	...	2257	|	...	...	...	...	...	...
sk .... a.	...	...	...	|	...	1910	...	|	...	...	...	|	...	2116	...	|	...	...	...	...	2258	...	...	...	...	...	...
hallerton.................... a.	...	...	...	1829	...	1923	...	1929	...	...	...	2029	...	2125	...	2129	...	...	...	...	2306	...	...	...	...	...	...
ington.......................... a.	...	...	...	1841	...	|	...	1941	...	...	...	2041	...	|	...	2141	...	...	...	...	2318	...	...	...	...	...	...
iddlesbrough............ a.	...	...	...	|	...	1954	...	|	...	...	...	|	...	2155	...	|	...	...	...	...	|	...	...	...	...	...	...
ham .... a.	...	...	...	1857	...	...	...	1957	...	...	...	2057	...	...	...	2157	...	...	...	...	2334	...	...	...	...	...	...
castle......................... a.	...	...	...	1914	...	...	...	2014	...	...	...	2114	...	...	...	2214	...	...	...	...	0007	...	...	...	...	...	...

①②③④⑥ only.
Calls to set down only.
⑥ only.

u – Calls to pick up only.

* – Connection by 🚌.

♣ – Service on ⑦ is valid June 19 - August 21. For service May 15 - June 12 and from August 28 please contact National Rail Enquires on ✆ +44 (0)3457 48 49 50.

190 LEEDS - HALIFAX - BLACKPOOL and MANCHESTER

2nd class

km	⚒		Ⓐ	⑥	⚒	Ⓐ	⑥	Ⓐ	⚒	⚒	⚒	⚒	⚒	⚒	⚒	⚒	⚒		⚒	⚒	⚒	⚒	⚒	⚒
0	**Leeds**	d.	0508	0535	0557	0608	0618	0623	0651	0708	0718	0723	0751	0805	0818	0823	0851		1805	1818	1823	1851	1905	1919
15	Bradford Interchange	d.	0531	0558	0617	0631	0641	|	0714	0728	0741	|	0814	0826	0841	|	0914	and	1826	1841	|	1914	1926	1942
28	**Halifax**	d.	0544	0611	0629	0644	0654	|	0727	0740	0754	|	0827	0839	0854	|	0927	at	1838	1854	|	1927	1939	1955
	Dewsbury	d.	|	|	|	|	|	0639	|	|	|	0739	|	|	|	0841	|	the	|	|	1841	|	|	|
	Brighouse	d.	|	|	|	|	|	0659	|	|	|	0758	|	|	|	0859	|	same	|	|	1859	|	|	|
42	Hebden Bridge	d.	0559	0627	0645	0659	0710	0717	0742	0752	0805	0817	0842	0852	0906	0917	0942	minutes	1852	1906	1917	1942	1952	2011
49	Todmorden	d.	0607	0634	|	0707	0717	0724	0750	|	0813	0824	0850	|	0913	0924	0950	past	|	1913	1925	1950	|	2018
63	Rochdale	d.	0623	0651	|	0720	0734	0741	0804	|	0825	0841	0900	|	0924	0941	1000	each	|	1924	1941	2000	|	2035
81	**Manchester** Victoria	a.	0647	0717	|	0737	0758	0803	0824	|	0847	0904	0917	|	0942	1004	1020	hour	|	1942	2006	2018	|	2100
63	Burnley Manchester Road	d.	...	...	0705	...	...	...	...	0812	...	...	...	0912	...	...	...	until	1912	...	...	...	2012	...
72	Accrington	d.	...	...	0714	...	...	...	...	0821	...	...	...	0921	...	...	...		1921	...	...	...	2021	...
81	Blackburn	d.	...	...	0723	...	...	...	...	0829	...	...	...	0930	...	...	...	✣	1930	...	...	...	2030	...
100	Preston	156 a.	...	...	0746	...	...	...	...	0854	...	...	...	0947	...	...	...		1949	...	...	...	2047	...
129	**Blackpool** North	156 a.	...	...	0814	...	...	...	...	0923	...	...	...	1015	...	...	...		2017	...	...	...	2115	...

		⚒	⚒	⚒	⚒	⚒		⑦	⑦	⑦	⑦	⑦	⑦	⑦	⑦	⑦	⑦		⑦	⑦	⑦	⑦	⑦
Leeds	d.	2005	2035	2108	2135	2235	...	0818	0851	0908	0953	1008	1053	1108	1151	1208	1251		1908	1951	2008	2052	2108
Bradford Interchange	d.	2026	2058	2128	2158	2258	...	0841	0913	0933	1014	1033	1113	1133	1215	1228	1314	and	1928	2014	2028	2115	2128
Halifax	d.	2039	2111	2140	2211	2311	...	0854	0926	0945	1026	1045	1126	1145	1228	1240	1327	at	1940	2027	2040	2128	2140
Dewsbury	d.	|	|	|	|	|	...	|	|	|	|	|	|	|	|	|	|	the	|	|	|	|	|
Brighouse	d.	|	|	|	|	|	...	|	|	|	|	|	|	|	|	|	|	same	|	|	|	|	|
Hebden Bridge	d.	2052	2126	2154	2226	2326	...	0909	0940	1001	1041	1101	1140	1201	1244	1252	1342	minutes	1952	2042	2052	2144	2152
Todmorden	d.	|	2134	|	2234	2334	...	0917	|	1009	|	1109	|	1209	1251	|	1350	past	|	2050	|	2152	|
Rochdale	d.	|	2150	|	2250	2350	...	0929	|	1021	|	1121	|	1221	1304	|	1403	each	|	2103	|	...	|
Manchester Victoria	a.	|	2215	|	2315	0008	...	0946	|	1043	|	1139	|	1239	1320	|	1420	hour	|	2120	|	...	|
Burnley Manchester Road	d.	2113	...	2214	...	...	...	...	1001	...	1103	...	1201	...	...	1312	...	until	2012	...	2112	...	2212
Accrington	d.	2122	...	2223	...	...	...	...	1009	...	1111	...	1209	...	...	1320	...		2020	...	2120	...	2220
Blackburn	d.	2131	...	2232	...	...	...	...	1018	...	1120	...	1218	...	...	1329	...	✣	2029	...	2129	...	2229
Preston	156 a.	2149	...	2251	...	...	...	...	1041	...	1140	...	1240	...	...	1348	...		2048	...	2147	...	2252
Blackpool North	156 a.	2213	...	2321	...	...	...	...	1108	...	1210	...	1310	...	...	1414	...		2114	...	2216	...	2332

⚒		⚒	⚒	⑥	Ⓐ	⚒	⚒	⚒	⚒	⚒	⚒	⚒	⚒	⚒	⚒	⚒		⚒	⚒	⚒	⚒	⚒	⚒
Blackpool North	156 d.	...	0511	...	...	...	0611	...	...	...	...	0711	...	...	...	0811		...	...	...	1656	...	...
Preston	156 d.	...	0537	...	...	...	0637	...	...	...	...	0737	...	...	...	0836	and	...	...	...	1725	...	...
Blackburn	d.	...	0555	...	...	...	0655	...	...	...	...	0755	...	...	...	0855	at	...	...	...	1753	...	...
Accrington	d.	...	0603	...	...	...	0703	...	...	...	...	0803	...	...	...	0903	the	...	...	...	1801	...	...
Burnley Manchester Road	d.	...	0612	...	...	...	0712	...	...	...	...	0812	...	...	...	0912	same	...	...	...	1812	...	...
Manchester Victoria	d.	0547	|	0608	0612	0636	|	...	0712	0726	0748	|	0816	0826	0848	|	minutes	1708	1725	1745	|	1810	1826
Rochdale	d.	0602	|	0627	0626	0653	|	...	0726	0747	0802	|	0830	0847	0902	|	past	1727	1747	1803	|	1827	1847
Todmorden	d.	0612	|	0644	0643	0710	|	...	0743	0804	0813	|	0841	0904	0913	|	each	1743	1804	1816	|	1842	1904
Hebden Bridge	d.	0619	0634	0651	0650	0717	0734	0739	0750	0811	0820	0834	0848	0911	0920	0934	hour	1750	1811	1822	1834	1849	1911
Brighouse	d.	|	|	|	|	|	|	0756	|	0829	|	|	|	0929	|	|	until	|	1829	|	|	|	1929
Dewsbury	d.	|	|	|	|	|	|	0811	|	0842	|	|	|	0941	|	|		|	1841	|	|	|	1941
Halifax	d.	0637	0648	0709	0707	0734	0748	|	0807	|	0833	0848	0906	|	0933	0947	✣	1807	|	1835	1847	1906	|
Bradford Interchange	d.	0652	0704	0724	0723	0750	0804	|	0823	|	0849	0904	0921	|	0949	1002		1824	|	1852	1903	1922	|
Leeds	a.	0714	0722	0746	0746	0811	0822	0834	0845	0904	0910	0923	0944	1004	1012	1024		1844	1903	1915	1923	1944	2003

		⚒	⚒	⚒	⚒	⚒	⚒	⚒	Ⓐ	⑥	Ⓐ	⑦	⑦	⑦	⑦	⑦		⑦	⑦	⑦	⑦	⑦	⑦
Blackpool North	156 d.	1811	...	...	1911	...	2029	...	...	...	...	...	0911	...	1011	...		...	1911	...	2011	...	2111
Preston	156 d.	1837	...	...	1937	...	2056	...	...	...	...	...	0937	...	1037	...	and	...	1937	...	2037	...	2137
Blackburn	d.	1856	...	...	1955	...	2124	...	...	...	...	...	0955	...	1055	...	at	...	1955	...	2055	...	2155
Accrington	d.	1904	...	...	2003	...	2132	...	...	...	...	...	1003	...	1103	...	the	...	2003	...	2103	...	2203
Burnley Manchester Road	d.	1913	...	...	2012	...	2141	...	...	...	...	...	1012	...	1112	...	same	...	2012	...	2112	...	2212
Manchester Victoria	d.	|	1916	1926	|	2026	|	2126	2226	2254	2321	0915	|	1015	|	1115	minutes	1915	|	2015	|	2115	|
Rochdale	d.	|	1931	1947	|	2047	|	2147	2247	2308	2342	0929	|	1029	|	1129	past	1929	|	2029	|	2129	|
Todmorden	d.	|	1942	2004	|	2104	|	2204	2304	2325	2359	0942	|	1042	|	1142	each	1942	|	2042	|	2142	|
Hebden Bridge	d.	1935	1949	2011	2034	2111	2203	2211	2311	2331	0006	0949	1034	1049	1134	1149	hour	1949	2034	2049	2134	2149	2234
Brighouse	d.	|	|	2029	|	|	|	|	|	|	|	|	|	|	|	|	until	|	|	|	|	|	|
Dewsbury	d.	|	|	2041	|	|	|	|	|	|	|	|	|	|	|	|		|	|	|	|	|	|
Halifax	d.	1949	2007	|	2049	2129	2218	2229	2329	2349	0023	1007	1047	1107	1147	1207	✣	2007	2049	2107	2149	2207	2249
Bradford Interchange	d.	2004	2022	|	2104	2144	2233	2244	2345	0004	0039	1023	1103	1123	1203	1223		2024	2105	2123	2205	2223	2305
Leeds	a.	2026	2044	2103	2126	2206	2253	2309	0006	0026	0057	1044	1122	1144	1224	1244		2044	2122	2144	2226	2246	2324

✣ – Timings may vary by ± 5 minutes.

192 HULL - DONCASTER - SHEFFIELD

2nd classs

km	Ⓐ		Ⓐ	Ⓐ	Ⓐ	Ⓐ	Ⓐ	Ⓐ	Ⓐ	Ⓐ	Ⓐ	Ⓐ	Ⓐ	Ⓐ	Ⓐ	Ⓐ	Ⓐ	Ⓐ	Ⓐ	Ⓐ	⑥	⑥	⑥	⑥
0	**Hull**	181 d.	0520	0641	0803	0857	0957	1057	1156	1257	1357	1457	1557	1657	1743	1757	1857	2003	2057	2220	0520	0640	0803	0857
38	Goole	d.	0547	0717	0830	0924	1024	1124	1223	1324	1424	1524	1624	1725	1821	|	1924	2036	2124	2254	0547	0716	0830	0924
66	**Doncaster**	181 a.	0617	0747	0854	0949	1047	1148	1247	1347	1447	1548	1648	1747	1851	1848	1949	2106	2147	2324	0617	0746	0857	0948
66	**Doncaster**	193 d.	0628	0748	0856	0950	1049	1148	1249	1348	1449	1549	1649	1749	1902	1850	1950	2107	2149	2325	0629	0748	0902	0949
90	Meadowhall	193 d.	0657	0825	0916	1010	1110	1210	1309	1410	1510	1610	1710	1810	1929	1910	2010	2134	2212	2354	0658	0825	0924	1010
96	**Sheffield**	193 a.	0706	0833	0926	1019	1120	1219	1319	1420	1519	1620	1720	1820	1939	1917	2017	2142	2221	0004	0707	0832	0931	1019

		⑥	⑥	⑥	⑥	⑥	⑥	⑥	⑥	⑥	⑥	⑥	⑥	⑥	⑦	⑦	⑦	⑦	⑦		⑦	⑦	⑦	⑦	⑦
Hull	181 d.	1058	1157	1257	1357	1457	1557	1657	1743	1755	1857	2003	2057	2216	0840	1050	1241	1330	1441	...	1532	1637	1732	1835	2001
Goole	d.	1124	1224	1324	1426	1524	1624	1725	1821	|	1924	2036	2124	2250	0908	1118	1314	1402	1509	...	1602	1708	1802	1903	2034
Doncaster	181 a.	1147	1247	1347	1447	1547	1648	1748	1851	1847	1947	2106	2147	2320	0930	1146	1337	1426	1532	...	1627	1731	1831	1934	2059
Doncaster	193 d.	1149	1249	1348	1449	1549	1649	1749	1901	1849	1950	2107	2149	2321	0939	1148	1339	1429	1533	...	1629	1732	1834	1936	2101
Meadowhall	193 d.	1210	1310	1410	1510	1610	1710	1810	1929	1910	2010	2134	2212	2350	1000	1208	1359	1452	1554	...	1654	1754	1853	1957	2128
Sheffield	193 a.	1220	1320	1420	1520	1617	1720	1817	1939	1919	2017	2142	2222	2359	1008	1218	1408	1503	1601	...	1701	1801	1904	2006	2138

Ⓐ		Ⓐ	Ⓐ	Ⓐ	Ⓐ	Ⓐ	Ⓐ	Ⓐ	Ⓐ	Ⓐ	Ⓐ	Ⓐ	Ⓐ	Ⓐ	Ⓐ	Ⓐ	Ⓐ	Ⓐ	Ⓐ	⑥	⑥	⑥	⑥	⑥
Sheffield	193 d.	0529	0741	0841	0941	1041	1141	1241	1341	1441	1541	1641	1741	1753	1841	1944	2000	2115	2234	0529	0741	0841	0941	1041
Meadowhall	193 d.	0535	0747	0847	0947	1047	1147	1247	1347	1447	1547	1647	1747	1759	1847	1950	2006	2121	2240	0535	0747	0847	0947	1047
Doncaster	193 a.	0606	0819	0915	1015	1115	1215	1315	1415	1517	1615	1715	1812	1835	1911	2013	2037	2154	2312	0606	0820	0914	1015	1112
Doncaster	181 d.	0610	0824	0919	1019	1119	1219	1319	1419	1519	1619	1719	1819	1839	1917	2017	2044	2156	2315	0612	0824	0919	1019	1118
Goole	d.	0636	0844	0938	1038	1138	1238	1338	1438	1537	1638	1742	1838	1912	1937	2036	|	2222	2343	0638	0843	0938	1038	1137
Hull	181 a.	0718	0913	1010	1110	1209	1308	1410	1511	1607	1709	1811	1908	1950	2010	2106	2144	2257	...	0720	0915	1010	1110	1209

		⑥	⑥	⑥	⑥	⑥	⑥	⑥	⑥	⑥	⑥	⑥	⑥	⑦	⑦	⑦	⑦	⑦	⑦	⑦	⑦	⑦	⑦	⑦	⑦
Sheffield	193 d.	1241	1341	1441	1541	1641	1741	1753	1841	1944	2000	2115	2233	0845	...	1026	1228	1324	1428	1529	1628	1728	1828	2002	2128
Meadowhall	193 d.	1247	1347	1447	1547	1647	1747	1759	1847	1950	2006	2121	2239	0851	...	1032	1235	1332	1434	1535	1635	1735	1835	2009	2134
Doncaster	193 a.	1316	1416	1516	1614	1712	1813	1837	1913	2015	2036	2154	2309	0922	...	1051	1256	1403	1456	1556	1656	1755	1855	2030	2204
Doncaster	181 d.	1319	1419	1519	1619	1719	1819	1841	1915	2017	2043	2156	2310	0926	1019	1057	1258	1405	1500	1558	1656	1758	1856	2030	2206
Goole	d.	1338	1438	1537	1638	1742	1838	1911	1937	2036	|	2222	2338	0948	1040	1116	1317	1425	1519	1619	1716	1817	1922	2050	2225
Hull	181 a.	1410	1509	1609	1709	1811	1910	1951	2009	2107	2146	2259	...	1021	1118	1150	1354	1455	1557	1652	1748	1851	1956	2122	2257

CLEETHORPES - DONCASTER - SHEFFIELD - MANCHESTER 193

	⚒	①	②–⑥	⚒	⚒	Ⓐ	⑥	⚒	⚒	⚒	⚒	⚒	⚒	⚒	⚒	⚒	⚒	Ⓐ		⑥	⚒	⚒
Cleethorpes d.		...	...	...	...	0504	0504	0620	0726	0826	0926	1026	1126	1226	1326	1426	1526	1626	...	1626	1726	1826
Grimsby Town d.		...	...	...	...	0512	0512	0628	0734	0834	0934	1034	1134	1234	1334	1434	1534	1634	...	1634	1734	1834
Scunthorpe d.		...	...	...	...	0546	0546	0703	0808	0908	1008	1108	1208	1308	1408	1508	1608	1708	...	1708	1808	1908
Doncaster a.		...	...	...	...	0623	0623	0733	0838	0938	1040	1138	1238	1338	1438	1538	1638	1738	...	1738	1838	1938
Doncaster 192 d.		...	...	...	0540	0625	0625	0735	0842	0942	1042	1142	1242	1342	1442	1542	1642	1742	...	1742	1842	1942
Meadowhall 192 d.		...	...	...	0601	0646	0646	0752	0901	1001	1101	1201	1301	1401	1501	1601	1701	1801	...	1801	1901	2001
Sheffield 192 a.		...	...	...	0608	0655	0655	0801	0908	1008	1108	1208	1308	1408	1509	1608	1708	1808	...	1808	1908	2008
Sheffield 206 d.		0325	0325	0511	0611	0708	*0708*	0804	0911	1011	1111	1211	1311	1411	1511	1611	1711	1811	...	1811	1911	2011
Stockport 206 a.		|	|	|	0653	0753	*0753*	0852	0952	1052	1152	1252	1352	1451	1552	1652	1752	1852	...	1851	1952	2052
Manchester Piccadilly 206 a.		0417	0451	0603	0703	0802	*0802*	0901	1002	1102	1202	1303	1402	1501	1601	1702	1801	1902	...	1901	2001	2102
Manchester Airport a.		0442	0512	0628	0727	0826	*0826*	0926	1028	1132	1228	1334	1428	1527	1632	1729	1826	1927	...	1926	2039	2135

	⚒	Ⓐ	⑥		⑦	⑦	⑦	⑦		⑦		⑦	⑦		⑦	⑦	⑦	⑦	⑦	⑦	⑦	⑦	⑦
horpes d.	1926	2026	2026	...		...	...	...	...	0926	...	1026	1126	...	...	1326	1426	1526	1626	1726	1826	1926	2026
sby Town d.	1934	2034	2034	...		...	...	...	...	0934	...	1034	1134	...	...	1334	1434	1534	1634	1734	1834	1934	2034
thorpe d.	2008	2108	2108	...		...	...	...	...	1008	...	1108	1208	...	...	1408	1508	1608	1708	1808	1908	2008	2108
caster a.	2040	2140	2140	...		...	...	...	...	1040	...	1140	1240	...	...	1438	1538	1638	1738	1839	1939	2040	2141
caster 192 d.	2042	2142	2142	...		...	...	...	...	1042	...	1142	1242	...	1342	1442	1542	1642	1742	1842	1942	2042	2142
owhall 192 d.	2109	2159	2159	...		...	...	...	...	1101	...	1201	1301	...	1401	1501	1601	1701	1801	1901	2001	2101	2206
field 192 a.	2119	2207	2207	...		...	...	...	...	1108	...	1208	1308	...	1409	1508	1608	1708	1808	1908	2008	2108	2214
field 206 d.	...	2211	*2224*	...		0751	0911	1011	...	1110	...	1210	1310	...	1411	1511	1611	1711	1811	1911	2011	2111	...
port 206 a.	...	2252	*2324*	...		0832	0953	|	...	1153	...	1252	1353	...	1453	1553	1653	1753	1853	1953	2053	2153	...
chester Piccadilly 206 a.	...	2302	*2340*	...		0841	1003	1103	...	1206	...	1302	1403	...	1503	1603	1703	1803	1903	2003	2103	2203	...
chester Airport a.	...	2323	...	...		0909	1029	1127	...	1229	...	1329	1429	...	1529	1628	1729	1829	1929	2029	2129	2229	...

	⚒	⑥	⑥	Ⓐ	⚒	⚒	⚒	⚒	⚒	⚒	⚒	⚒	⚒	⑥	Ⓐ		⚒	⚒	Ⓐ	⑥		⚒	Ⓐ
chester Airport d.		0550	...	0550	0655	0753	0855	0955	1055	1155	1255	1355	1455	1555	1555	...	1655	1755	1855	1855	...	1955	...
chester Piccadilly 206 d.		0613	...	0613	0720	0820	0920	1020	1120	1220	1320	1420	1520	1620	1620	...	1718	1820	1918	1918	...	2020	...
port 206 d.		0621	...	0621	0728	0828	0928	1028	1128	1228	1328	1428	1528	1628	1628	...	1726	1828	1926	1926	...	2028	...
field 206 a.		0702	...	0702	0810	0908	1008	1109	1208	1308	1408	1508	1608	1709	1709	...	1810	1910	2009	2009	...	2112	...
field 192 d.		...	0709	0712	0812	0910	1010	1110	1210	1310	1410	1510	1610	1710	1710	...	1812	1912	2011	2027	...	...	2134
owhall 192 d.		...	0715	0718	0818	0916	1016	1116	1216	1316	1416	1516	1616	1716	1716	...	1818	1918	2017	2033	...	...	2140
caster 192 a.		...	0739	0737	0837	0935	1036	1135	1235	1335	1435	1535	1635	1737	1737	...	1845	1941	2045	2101	...	...	2202
caster d.		...	0743	0739	0839	0937	1037	1137	1237	1337	1437	1537	1637	1739	1747	...	1847	1948	2046	2107	...	...	2205
thorpe d.		...	0810	0805	0905	1003	1103	1203	1303	1403	1503	1603	1703	1806	1813	...	1915	2015	2112	2133	...	...	2231
sby Town a.		...	0848	0846	0940	1039	1137	1240	1337	1439	1537	1639	1737	1842	1849	...	1948	2048	2148	2209	...	...	2309
thorpes a.		...	0857	0855	0951	1051	1149	1251	1349	1451	1549	1651	1750	1855	1901	...	2000	2101	2200	2221	...	...	2320

	⚒	⑥	Ⓐ	⑥	⚒	Ⓐ			⑦	⑦	⑦	⑦	⑦	⑦	⑦	⑦	⑦	⑦	⑦	⑦	⑦	⑦	⑦
chester Airport d.	...	...	2047	2047	2147	2327	...	⑦	0838	1054	1155	1255	1355	1455	1555	1655	1755	1855	1955	2055	...	2155	2255
chester Piccadilly 206 d.	2043	...	2120	2120	2222	2353	...		0858	1118	1218	1320	1420	1520	1620	1720	1820	1920	2018	2120	...	2216	2316
port 206 d.	2054	...	2128	2128	|	|	...		0906	1127	1228	1328	1428	1528	1627	1727	1828	1928	2027	2127	...	2224	2324
field 206 a.	2135	...	2209	2211	2315	0124	...		0947	1207	1308	1408	1509	1609	1708	1808	1908	2008	2108	2211	...	2306	0006
field 192 d.	...	2152	2210	...	...	...	...		0951	1210	1310	1410	1510	1610	1710	1810	1910	2010	2110	...	2231	...	...
owhall 192 d.	...	2158	2216	...	...	...	...		0958	1216	1316	1416	1516	1616	1716	1816	1916	2016	2116	...	2237	...	...
caster 192 a.	...	2220	2243	...	...	...	...		1028	1235	1335	1435	1535	1635	1735	1835	1935	2035	2135	...	2256	...	...
caster d.	...	2225	2245	...	...	...	...		1029	1237	...	1437	1537	1637	1737	1837	1937	2037	2137	...	2258	...	...
thorpe d.	...	2259	2319	...	...	...	...		1056	1303	...	1503	1603	1703	1803	1903	2003	2103	2203	...	2324	...	...
sby Town a.	...	2335	2355	...	...	...	...		1133	1337	...	1538	1639	1737	1839	1937	2037	2139	2239	...	2358	...	...
thorpes a.	...	2347	0009	...	...	...	...		1143	1349	...	1549	1651	1749	1851	1949	2049	2151	2251	...	0010	...	...

NT *2nd class only*	⚒	⚒	⚒	⑥	⚒	⚒	⑥	⚒	⑥	⚒	⑥	⚒	⚒	⚒	⚒	⚒	⑥	Ⓐ	⑦	⑦	⑦	⑦	⑦	⑦	⑦	⑦
Sheffield ⊙ d.		0620	0712	0814	0914	1014	1114	1214	1314	1414	1514	1614	1714	1814	1914	2035	2224	2248		0914	1114	1314	1514	1714	1914	2214
Grindleford d.		0635	0730	0828	0928	1028	1129	1228	1328	1429	1528	1628	1728	1829	1928	2050	2238	2302		0929	1129	1329	1529	1729	1930	2229
Hathersage d.		0639	0733	0832	0932	1032	1132	1232	1332	1433	1532	1632	1732	1832	1932	2054	2242	2306		0933	1133	1333	1533	1733	1934	2233
Hope d.		0647	0741	0839	0939	1039	1140	1239	1339	1440	1539	1639	1739	1840	1939	2101	2249	2313		0940	1140	1340	1540	1740	1941	2240
Edale d.		0655	0749	0847	0947	1047	1148	1247	1347	1448	1547	1647	1747	1848	1947	2109	2256	2322		0948	1148	1348	1548	1748	1949	2248
Chinley d.		0703	0757	0855	0955	1055	1156	1255	1355	1456	1555	1655	1755	1856	1955	2117	2304	2330		0956	1156	1356	1556	1756	1957	2256
Manchester P'dilly ⊙ a.		0734	0835	0934	1034	1134	1234	1334	1434	1534	1634	1734	1836	1935	2033	2205	2340	2359		1034	1233	1434	1634	1833	2034	2326

2nd class only	⚒	⚒	⑥	Ⓐ	⑥	⚒	⑥	⚒	⑥	⚒	⑥	⚒	⚒	⚒	⚒	⚒	⚒	⚒	⑦	⑦	⑦	⑦	⑦	⑦	⑦	⑦	⑦
chester P'dilly ⊙ d.		0546	0635	0708	0749	0849	0949	1049	1149	1249	1349	1449	1549	1649	1749	1849	2045	2228		0744	0922	1140	1340	1540	1740	1940	2211
ley d.		0614	0714	0748	0823	0923	1025	1123	1225	1323	1425	1523	1623	1723	1823	1923	2120	2253		0823	0959	1217	1417	1617	1817	2017	2243
e d.		0623	0723	0758	0833	0933	1034	1133	1234	1333	1434	1533	1633	1733	1833	1933	2129	2301		0833	1008	1227	1427	1627	1827	2027	2251
e d.		0629	0729	0804	0839	0939	1040	1139	1240	1339	1440	1539	1639	1739	1839	1939	2135	2307		0839	1014	1233	1433	1633	1833	2033	2257
ersage d.		0636	0736	0811	0845	0946	1046	1145	1246	1346	1446	1546	1646	1746	1846	1946	2142	2315		0845	1021	1240	1440	1640	1840	2040	2303
dleford d.		0640	0740	0815	0849	0949	1050	1149	1250	1350	1450	1550	1650	1750	1850	1949	2146	2319		0849	1024	1244	1444	1644	1844	2044	2312
ffield ⊙ a.		0657	0757	0832	0906	1006	1106	1206	1305	1406	1506	1606	1706	1808	1908	2007	2207	2335		0906	1043	1300	1459	1700	1900	2100	2326

Additional journeys on ⑦ May 15 - Oct. 30:
From Sheffield at 1020, 1215, 1415, 1614, 1815.
From Manchester Piccadilly at 0823, 1040, 1240, 1440, 1645.

SKEGNESS - NOTTINGHAM 194

2nd class

	Ⓐ	Ⓐ	Ⓐ	Ⓐ	Ⓐ	Ⓐ	Ⓐ	Ⓐ	Ⓐ	Ⓐ		Ⓐ	Ⓐ	Ⓐ	Ⓐ	Ⓐ	Ⓐ	Ⓐ	Ⓐ	⑥	⑥	⑥	⑥	⑥	⑥	⑥
Skegness d.		...	...	0709	0810	0906	1015	1115	1215	1315	...	1415	1509	1611	1730	1814	1914	2015	2102		...	...	0709	0815	0915	1015
Boston d.		...	0613	0746	0845	0941	1050	1150	1250	1350	...	1450	1544	1648	1805	1848	1949	2050	2137		...	0613	0746	0850	0950	1050
Sleaford d.		...	0635	0811	0907	1003	1112	1212	1312	1413	...	1512	1610	1713	1827	1913	2013	2118	2200		...	0635	0811	0912	1014	1112
Grantham a.		...	0704	0842	0939	1031	1141	1241	1341	1442	...	1541	1641	1742	|	1941	2040	2145	|		...	0707	0842	0941	1043	1141
Grantham 206 d.		0610	0710	0845	0945	1036	1145	1245	1346	1445	...	1545	1645	1745	|	1945	2044	2149	|		0610	0710	0845	0945	1046	1145
Nottingham 206 a.		0654	0753	0920	1021	1114	1222	1323	1422	1523	...	1622	1720	1822	1922	2025	2120	2226	2253		0654	0752	0920	1021	1123	1122

	⑥	⑥c	⑥	⑥	⑥	⑥	⑥c	⑥	⑥	⑥	⑥	⑦	⑦a	⑦a	⑦a	⑦	⑦a	⑦b	⑦	⑦	⑦a	⑦a	⑦b	⑦	⑦	⑦a	⑦b
gness d.	1115	1215	1315	1415	1509	1611	1730	1814	1919	2015	2102		...	1014	1115	...	1227	...	...	1410	1515	1622	1610	1807	1915	2043	...
ton d.	1150	1250	1350	1450	1544	1648	1805	1849	1954	2050	2137		0906	1049	1149	...	1302	1213	...	1445	1552	1657	1650	1842	1950	2118	...
ford d.	1212	1312	1413	1512	1610	1713	1827	1913	2018	2112	2200		0928	1111	1211	...	1324	1235	...	1507	1620	1719	1712	1904	2012	2142	2142
tham a.	1241	1341	1442	1541	1641	1742	|	1941	2045	2143	|		0957	1140	1241	...	|	1304	...	1535	1646	|	1741	1933	2041	2210	2210
tham 206 d.	1245	1346	1445	1545	1645	1745	|	1945	2048	2147	|		1001	1146	1245	1252	|	...	1509	1540	1650	|	1745	1937	2045	2213	2213
ingham 206 a.	1323	1423	1523	1622	1720	1822	1922	2024	2125	2225	2254		1037	1221	1321	1330	1416	...	1539	1617	1722	1811	1820	2012	2120	2249	2249

	Ⓐ	Ⓐ	Ⓐ	Ⓐ	Ⓐ	Ⓐ	Ⓐ	Ⓐ	Ⓐ	Ⓐ	Ⓐ	Ⓐ		Ⓐ	Ⓐ	Ⓐ	Ⓐ	ⒶA	Ⓐ	⑥	⑥	⑥	⑥	⑥		⑥	⑥c
ingham 206 d.		0507	0550	0641	0735	0845	0955	1045	1145	1245	1345	1445	...	1545	1645	1744	1844	...	2051		0510	0550	0641	0731	...	0840	0955
tham 206 a.		0546	0627	0718	0812	0926	|	1123	1219	1323	1423	1522	...	1625	1728	1825	1923	...	2132		0549	0627	0718	0809	...	0923	|
tham d.		▬	0631	0723	0816	0932	|	1127	1225	1327	1427	1526	...	1629	1732	1829	1926	...	2138		▬	0631	0724	0817	...	0930	|
ford d.		Ⓐ	0657	0751	0845	1003	1044	1153	1250	1355	1452	1552	...	1655	1801	1855	1955	2120	2203		⑥	0657	0751	0846	...	0956	1044
ton d.		0625	0725	0818	0912	1026	1111	1219	1315	1421	1517	1620	...	1721	1826	1921	2019	2153	2229		0625	0725	0818	0912	...	1022	1111
gness a.		0703	0805	0856	0949	1100	1150	1258	1354	1500	1556	1659	...	1800	1905	1959	2057	...	...		0703	0805	0856	0948	...	1100	1150

	⑥	⑥	⑥	⑥	⑥c	⑥	⑥	⑥	⑥	⑥A	⑥	⑦	⑦a	⑦a	⑦a	⑦a	⑦		⑦	⑦b	⑦a	⑦	⑦	⑦a	⑦b	⑦a	⑦b
ingham 206 d.	1045	1145	1245	1345	1445	1545	1645	1744	1845	...	2051		...	0900	0941	1109	1157	...	1237	...	1357	1456	1623	1816	1831	1948	1948
tham 206 a.	1123	1219	1325	1423	1522	1625	1728	1825	1923	...	2131		...	|	1015	1144	1229	...	1313	...	1431	1531	1703	1850	1908	2022	2022
tham d.	1127	1225	1329	1427	1526	1629	1732	1829	1926	...	2136		...	|	1020	1150	1233	...	...	1350	1435	1536	1707	1854	1913	2027	2027
ford d.	1153	1250	1355	1452	1552	1655	1801	1855	1955	2121	2201		...	0949	1046	1215	1259	...	...	1416	1508	1602	1736	1920	1941	2052	2055
ton d.	1219	1315	1421	1517	1620	1721	1826	1921	2019	2153	2229		0931	1016	1111	1241	1324	...	...	1445	1532	1629	1802	1950	2010	2120	...
gness a.	1258	1354	1500	1556	1659	1800	1905	1959	2057	...	...		1007	1055	1150	1320	1400	...	...	1524	1611	1708	1838	2026	...	...	...

From Lincoln (Table **185**).

a – May 15 - Sept. 11.
b – From Sept. 18.
c – Subject to alteration July 30 - Sept. 10.

196 LONDON - KINGS LYNN

km			Ⓐ	Ⓐ	Ⓐ	Ⓐ	Ⓐ	Ⓐ	Ⓐ	Ⓐ	Ⓐ	Ⓐ	Ⓐ	Ⓐ	Ⓐ	Ⓐ	Ⓐ	Ⓐ	Ⓐ	Ⓐ	Ⓐ	Ⓐ	Ⓐ
0	**London** Kings Cross 197 d.	Ⓐ	...	0543	0644	0714	0744	0844	0944	1044	1144	1244	1344	1444	1544	1558p	1644	1707p	1714	1744	1814	1807p	1844
93	Cambridge 197 d.		0617	0652	0733	0806	0838	0935	1035	1135	1235	1335	1435	1535	1635	1722	1740	1817	1806	1839	1909	1919	1939
117	Ely d.		0633	0708	0750	0822	0854	0951	1051	1151	1251	1351	1451	1551	1652	1739	1757	1833	1821	1856	1924	1935	1956
142	Downham Market d.		0653	0725	0807	0838	0910	1007	1107	1207	1307	1407	1507	1607	1710	...	1813	1850	...	1912	1939	1952	2012
160	**Kings Lynn** a.		0707	0740	0821	0852	0925	1021	1121	1221	1321	1421	1521	1621	1724	...	1827	1908	...	1927	1954	2010	2026

	Ⓐ	Ⓐ	Ⓐ	Ⓐ	Ⓐ	Ⓐ	Ⓐ	Ⓐ		⑥	⑥	⑥	⑥	⑥	⑥	⑥	⑥	⑥	⑥	⑥	⑥	⑥	⑥
London Kings Cross 197 d.	1944	2014	2044	2114	2144	2214	2244	2314	⑥	...	0644	0744	0844	0944	1044	1144	1244	1344	1444	1544	1644	1744	1814
Cambridge 197 d.	2040	2110	2140	2210	2240	2310	2340	0010		0635	0735	0835	0935	1035	1135	1235	1335	1435	1535	1635	1735	1835	1905
Ely d.	2056	2126	2156	2226	2257	2326	2357	0026		0651	0751	0851	0951	1051	1151	1251	1351	1451	1551	1651	1751	1851	1919
Downham Market d.	2112	2142	2212	2242	...	2342	...	0042		0707	0807	0907	1007	1107	1207	1307	1407	1507	1607	1707	1807	1907	1935
Kings Lynn a.	2126	2156	2226	2256	...	2356	...	0056		0721	0821	0921	1021	1121	1221	1321	1421	1521	1621	1721	1821	1921	1951

	⑥	⑥	⑥	⑥	⑥	⑥	⑥		⑦	⑦	⑦	⑦	⑦	⑦	⑦	⑦	⑦	⑦	⑦	⑦	⑦	⑦	⑦
London Kings Cross 197 d.	1914	1944	2014	2044	2114	2214	2314	⑦	0752	0915	1015	1115	1215	1315	1415	1515	1615	1715	1815	1915	2015	2115	2215
Cambridge 197 d.	2006	2035	2106	2140	2207	2310	0010		0906	1006	1106	1206	1306	1406	1506	1606	1706	1806	1906	2006	2106	2206	2306
Ely d.	2022	2051	2122	2157	2223	2326	0026		0922	1022	1122	1222	1322	1422	1522	1622	1722	1822	1922	2022	2122	2222	2322
Downham Market d.	2038	2108	2138	...	2239	2342	0042		0938	1038	1138	1238	1338	1438	1538	1638	1738	1838	1938	2038	2138	2238	2338
Kings Lynn a.	2053	2121	2153	...	2253	2356	0056		0953	1053	1153	1253	1353	1453	1553	1653	1753	1853	1953	2052	2153	2253	2353

		Ⓐ	Ⓐ	Ⓐ	Ⓐ	Ⓐ	Ⓐ	Ⓐ	Ⓐ	Ⓐ	Ⓐ	Ⓐ	Ⓐ	Ⓐ	Ⓐ	Ⓐ	Ⓐ	Ⓐ	Ⓐ	Ⓐ	Ⓐ	Ⓐ	Ⓐ
Kings Lynn d.	Ⓐ	0455	0519	0551	0610	0617	0651	...	0714	0725	...	0754	0827	0857	...	0954	1054	1154	1254	1354	1454	1554	1636
Downham Market d.		0509	0533	0605	0622	0631	0705	...	0728	0737	...	0808	0841	0911	...	1008	1108	1208	1308	1408	1508	1608	1651
Ely d.		0526	0552	0622	0647	0650	0722	0730	0748	0756	0802	0826	0858	0928	1008	1025	1125	1225	1326	1425	1525	1625	1709
Cambridge 197 a.		0542	0610	0639	0703	0708	0739	0747	0804	0810	0820	0843	0915	0945	1024	1041	1141	1241	1342	1441	1541	1641	1725
London Kings Cross 197 a.		0636	0725p	0737	0807	0825p	0837	0920p	0910	0910	0950p	0945	1013	1043	1132	1135	1238	1335	1435	1535	1636	1738	1833

	Ⓐ	Ⓐ	Ⓐ	Ⓐ	Ⓐ	Ⓐ	Ⓐ	Ⓐ		⑥	⑥	⑥	⑥	⑥	⑥	⑥	⑥	⑥	⑥	⑥	⑥	⑥	⑥
Kings Lynn d.	1736	...	1836	1937	...	2037	2137	2229	⑥	...	0554	0654	0754	...	0854	0930	0954	1054	1154	1254	1354	1454	1554
Downham Market d.	1750	...	1850	1953	...	2051	2151	2243		...	0608	0708	0808	...	0908	0942	1008	1108	1208	1308	1408	1508	1608
Ely d.	1808	1829	1908	2010	2029	2108	2208	2300		0525	0625	0725	0825	0859	0925	0959	1025	1125	1225	1325	1425	1525	1625
Cambridge 197 a.	1824	1843	1924	2026	2043	2124	2224	2316		0541	0641	0741	0841	0913	0941	1014	1041	1141	1241	1341	1441	1541	1641
London Kings Cross 197 a.	1936	1939	2035	2132	2133	2232	2332	0050		0639	0735	0836	0937	1002	1035	1105	1137	1235	1335	1435	1534	1634	1736

	⑥	⑥	⑥	⑥	⑥	⑥	⑥		⑦	⑦	⑦	⑦	⑦	⑦	⑦	⑦	⑦	⑦	⑦	⑦	⑦	⑦	⑦
Kings Lynn d.	1754	1835	1935	2035	2135	2226	2310	⑦	0827	0927	1027	1127	1227	1327	1427	1527	1627	1727	1757	1827	1927	2027	2127
Downham Market d.	1808	1849	1949	2049	2149	2240	2324		0841	0941	1041	1141	1241	1341	1441	1541	1641	1741	1809	1841	1941	2041	2141
Ely d.	1825	1906	2006	2106	2206	2257	2342		0858	0958	1058	1158	1258	1358	1458	1558	1658	1758	1826	1858	1958	2058	2158
Cambridge 197 a.	1841	1922	2022	2122	2222	2313	2359		0915	1015	1115	1215	1315	1415	1515	1615	1715	1815	1840	1915	2015	2115	2215
London Kings Cross 197 a.	1935	2032	2132	2232	2332	0040	...		1009	1108	1209	1308	1408	1508	1609	1709	1808	1909	1936	2009	2109	2209	2311

p – London **Liverpool Street**.

197 LONDON KINGS CROSS - CAMBRIDGE

km			Ⓐ	Ⓐ	Ⓐ	Ⓐ	Ⓐ	Ⓐ	Ⓐ		Ⓐ	Ⓐ	Ⓐ	Ⓐ	Ⓐ	Ⓐ	Ⓐ	Ⓐ	Ⓐ	Ⓐ	Ⓐ	Ⓐ	Ⓐ
0	**London** Kings Cross d.	Ⓐ	0005	0543	0644	0714	0744	0814	0844	and at the same minutes past each hour until ☆	1514	1544	1552	1614	1644	1714	1744	1814	1844	1914	1944	2014	2044
93	**Cambridge** a.		0130	0650	0731	0804	0833	0904	0930		1601	1630	1655	1702	1735	1804	1834	1908	1934	2005	2035	2105	2135

	Ⓐ	Ⓐ	Ⓐ	Ⓐ	Ⓐ		⑥	⑥	⑥	⑥	⑥	⑥		⑥	⑥	⑥	⑥	⑥	⑥	⑥	⑥	⑥	⑥
London Kings Cross d.	2144	2214	2244	2314	2344	⑥	0005	0031	0545	0644	0744	0814	and at the same minutes past each hour until ☆	1744	1814	1844	1914	1944	2014	2044	2114	2144	2214
Cambridge a.	2235	2305	2335	0005	0040		0124	0128	0655	0730	0830	0903		1830	1901	1930	2001	2030	2101	2135	2202	2237	2305

	⑥		⑦	⑦	⑦	⑦	⑦	⑦	⑦	⑦	⑦	⑦		⑦	⑦	⑦	⑦	⑦	⑦	⑦	⑦	⑦	⑦
London Kings Cross d.	2314	⑦	0014	0635	0752	0852	0915	0952	1015	1052	1115	1152	and at the same minutes past each hour until ☆	1815	1852	1915	1952	2015	2052	2115	2152	2215	2252
Cambridge a.	0005		0122	0746	0855	0955	1001	1055	1101	1155	1201	1255		1910	1955	2001	2055	2101	2155	2201	2255	2301	2355

		Ⓐ	Ⓐ	Ⓐ	Ⓐ	Ⓐ	Ⓐ	Ⓐ	Ⓐ	Ⓐ	Ⓐ	Ⓐ	Ⓐ	Ⓐ	Ⓐ	Ⓐ		Ⓐ	Ⓐ	Ⓐ	Ⓐ	Ⓐ	Ⓐ
Cambridge d.	Ⓐ	0514	0545	0615	0645	0715	0745	0815	0850	0920	0927	0950	1015	1047	1115	1147	and at the same minutes past each hour until ☆	1815	1845	1915	1945	2015	2045
London Kings Cross a.		0611	0636	0716	0737	0807	0837	0910	0945	1013	1032	1043	1105	1135	1203	1238		1910	1939	2006	2036	2106	2133

	Ⓐ	Ⓐ	Ⓐ	Ⓐ		⑥	⑥	⑥	⑥	⑥	⑥	⑥	⑥		⑥	⑥	⑥	⑥	⑥	⑥	⑥	⑥	⑥
Cambridge d.	2145	2215	2230	2322	⑥	0545	0647	0715	0747	0815	0847	0915	0947	and at the same minutes past each hour until ☆	1815	1847	1915	1945	2015	2045	2115	2145	2215
London Kings Cross a.	2237	2305	2332	0050		0639	0735	0805	0836	0904	0937	1004	1035		1905	1935	2005	2035	2105	2134	2204	2234	2302

	⑥		⑦	⑦	⑦	⑦	⑦	⑦	⑦	⑦	⑦		⑦	⑦	⑦	⑦	⑦	⑦	⑦	⑦	⑦	⑦	⑦
Cambridge d.	2315	⑦	0628	0728	0828	0920	0928	1020	1028	1120	1128	and at the same minutes past each hour until ☆	1820	1828	1845	1920	1928	2020	2028	2120	2128	2220	2228
London Kings Cross a.	0040		0748	0834	0934	1009	1029	1108	1130	1209	1229		1909	1929	1936	2009	2030	2109	2129	2209	2229	2311	2329

☆ – Timings may vary by up to 3 minutes.

199 LONDON - SOUTHEND and CAMBRIDGE

CC,

Typical off-peak journey time in hours and minutes
READ DOWN ↓ READ UP ↑

Journey times may be extended during peak hours on Ⓐ (0600 - 0900 and 1600 - 1900) and also at weekends.
The longest journey time by any train is noted in the table heading.

LONDON FENCHURCH STREET - SOUTHEND CENTRAL

Longest journey: 1 hour 08 minutes

km	A				A
0	0h00	↓	d.**London** F Street a.	↑	1h04
8	0h09	↓	d.West Ham d.	↑	0h56
12	0h14	↓	d.Barking d.	↑	0h50
39	0h34	↓	d.Basildon d.	↑	0h29
56	0h53	↓	a.**Southend** Central d.	↑	*0h10
63	1h03		a.Shoeburyness d.	↑	0h00

From London Fenchurch Street: 0500⚒/0634⑦ and at least every 30 minutes (every 10 - 20 minutes 0840⚒ - 2010⚒) until 23

From Southend Central*: 0424⚒/0544⑦ and at least every 30 minutes (every 15 minutes 0920⚒ - 2020⚒) until 2249⑦, 2335⚒.

A – During peak hours on Ⓐ (0600 - 0900 and 1600 - 1900) trains may not make all stops.

* – Trains depart Shoeburyness 10 minutes before Southend Central.

☛ On ⑦ passengers for Basildon and Shoeburyness should change at Barking.

LONDON LIVERPOOL STREET - SOUTHEND VICTORIA

Longest journey: 1 hour 14 minutes

km					
0	0h00	↓	d.**London** L Street a.	↑	0h58
6	0h07	↓	d.Stratford d.	↑	0h49
32	0h25	↓	d.Shenfield d.	↑	0h35
53	0h43	↓	d.Rayleigh d.	↑	0h16
64	0h54	↓	a.**Southend** Airport d.	↑	0h05
66	1h01		a.**Southend** Victoria d.		0h00

From London Liverpool Street: 0535⚒/0814⑦ and at least every 30 minutes (every 20 minutes 0635⚒ - 2213⚒) until 2344.

From Southend Victoria: 0400⚒/0749⑦ and at least every 30 minutes (every 20 minutes 0626⚒ - 2130⚒) until 2249⑦/2300⚒.

LONDON LIVERPOOL STREET - CAMBRIDGE

Longest journey: 1 hour 39 minutes

km					
0	0h00	↓	d.**London** L Street a.	↑	1h23
10	0h12	↓	d.Tottenham Hale d.	↑	0h57
36	0h29	↓	d.Harlow Town d.	↑	0h38
48	0h42	↓	d.Bishops Stortford d.	↑	0h28
67	0h54	↓	d.Audley End d.	↑	0h15
89	1h23		a.**Cambridge** d.		0h00

From London Liverpool Street: on Ⓐ at 0528, 0558 and every 30 minutes until 1528 then 1558, 1628, 1643, 1707, 1713, 1737, 1 1807, 1813, 1837, 1843, 1907, 1911, 1928, 1958, 2028 and every 30 minutes until 2258 then 2328, 2358⑤; on ⑥ at 0520, 0558, 0 0658 and every 30 minutes until 2328, 2358; on ⑦ at 0742, 0828, 0857 and at the same minutes past each hour until 2228, 2257.

From Cambridge: on Ⓐ at 0448, 0520, 0548, 0551 and every 30 minutes until 0821 then 0848, 0918, 1004, 1021 and at 04 and 21 min past each hour until 1521 then 1551 and every 30 minutes until 1921, 2004, 2021, 2104, 2121, 2204, 2221, 2251; on ⑥ at 0438, 0521, 0 0621 and at 04 and 21 minutes past each hour until 2221 then 2251; on ⑦ at 0732, 0751 and at the same minutes past each hour until 2

Most Norwich trains convey 🍷

LONDON - HARWICH, IPSWICH and NORWICH

For Rail - Sea - Rail services London - Amsterdam and v.v. via Harwich and Hoek van Holland see Table **15a**.

		Ⓐ P	Ⓐ	Ⓐ	Ⓐ	Ⓐ	Ⓐ C	Ⓐ	Ⓐ	Ⓐ	Ⓐ	Ⓐ	Ⓐ	Ⓐ	Ⓐ		Ⓐ	Ⓐ	Ⓐ	Ⓐ	Ⓐ	Ⓐ	Ⓐ	Ⓐ	Ⓐ
London Liverpool Street d.	Ⓐ	...	...	0600	...	0625	...	0638	0700	0730	0755	...	0830	0900	...	and	1530	1600	...	*1602*	1630	1644	1700	1702	1730
Chelmsford d.		...	...	0630	...	0658	...	0710	|	0803	|	...	0903	|	...	at	1600	|	...	*1634*	|	1715	|	1736	|
Colchester d.		0540	0610	0650	...	0723	...	0743	0751	0823	0847	...	0923	0947	...	the	1621	1647	...	*1704*	1717	1747	|	1801	|
Manningtree d.		0549	0618	0658	0724	0731	...	0751	0759	0831	0855	0900	0931	0955	1000	same	1629	1655	1700	1724	|	1757	|	1809	1827
Harwich International d.		|	0636	|	0741	|	0750	0810	|	|	|	0917	|	|	1017	minutes	|	|	1717	1741	|	1815	|	|	|
Harwich Town a.		|	0641	|	0746	|	|	0815	|	|	|	0922	|	|	1022	past	|	|	1722	1746	|	1822	|	|	|
Ipswich 205 d.		0600	...	0711	...	0744	0820	...	0812	0844	0908	...	0944	1008	...	each	1641	1708	...	...	1736	...	1800	1825	1839
Stowmarket 205 d.		0611	...	0722	...	0755	0834	...	0823	0855	|	...	0955	|	...	hour	1652	1719	...	...	1747	...	|	1836	1850
Diss d.		...	...	0735	...	0808	...	...	0836	0908	0929	...	1008	1029	...	until	1705	1732	...	...	1800	...	1821	1848	1903
Norwich a.		...	...	0754	...	0827	...	...	0855	0927	0948	...	1027	1050	...		1724	1753	...	...	1822	...	1842	1909	1925

	Ⓐ	Ⓐ	Ⓐ	Ⓐ	Ⓐ	Ⓐ	Ⓐ	Ⓐ	Ⓐ	Ⓐ	Ⓐ	Ⓐ	Ⓐ	Ⓐ	Ⓐ	Ⓐ L	Ⓐ	Ⓐ	Ⓐ	Ⓐ	Ⓐ	Ⓐ	Ⓐ	Ⓐ	Ⓐ		⑥ P	⑥
London Liverpool St. d.	...	1750	...	1810	1830	...	1820	1900	...	1930	1932	...	2000	...	2030	...	2100	...	2102	2130	2200	...	2230	...	2330	⑥	...	...
Chelmsford d.	...	|	...	|	|	...	1857	|	...	|	2002	...	|	...	2103r	...	|	...	2134	2203	2228	...	2303	...	0003		...	...
Colchester d.	...	1843	...	1902	1923	...	1930	1947	...	2020	2025	...	2047	...	2119	...	2147	...	2204	2223	2247	...	2323	...	0023		0540	0552
Manningtree d.	1835	1852	1902	1911	1932	1938	1940	1955	2000	2028	2034	2038	2055	2100	2128	...	2156	2200	2212	2232	2255	2300	2332	2336	0032		0549	0600
Harwich Int'l d.	1852	|	1919	|	|	1955	2002	|	2017	|	2054	2055	|	2117	|	2138	|	2217	2228	|	|	2317	|	2353	|		|	0617
Harwich Town a.	1857	|	1924	|	|	2000	...	|	2022	|	...	2100	|	2122	|	|	|	2222	...	|	|	2322	|	2358	|		|	0622
Ipswich 205 d.	...	1904	...	1923	1944	...	...	2008	...	2041	...	...	2108	...	2141	2204	2209	...	...	2245	2308	...	2345	...	0045		0600	...
Stowmarket 205 d.	...	1916	...	1934	1955	...	...	2019	...	2052	...	...	2119	...	2153	...	2220	...	...	2256	...	...	2356	...	0056		0611	...
Diss d.	...	1929	...	1947	2008	...	...	2032	...	2105	...	...	2132	...	2206	...	2233	...	...	2309	...	...	0009	...	0109		...	...
Norwich a.	...	1950	...	2009	2030	...	...	2051	...	2124	...	...	2151	...	2229	...	2253	...	...	2329	...	...	0029	...	0142		...	...

	⑥	⑥	⑥	⑥ C	⑥	⑥	⑥	⑥	⑥	⑥		⑥	⑥	⑥	⑥	⑥	⑥	⑥	⑥ L	⑥	⑥	⑥	⑥	⑥	⑥	⑥	⑥
London Liverpool St. d.	0534	...	0630	...	0638	0700	...	0730	0800	...	and	1900	...	1930	1932	2000	...	2030	...	2100	...	2102	2130	2200	...	2230	...
Chelmsford d.	0610	...	0703	...	0712	|	...	0803	|	...	at	|	...	2003	2007	|	...	2103	...	|	...	2134	2203	2228	...	2303	...
Colchester d.	0640	...	0723	...	0740	0747	...	0823	0847	...	the	1947	...	2023	2032	2047	...	2123	...	2147	..	2204	2223	2248	...	2323	...
Manningtree d.	0648	0700	0731	...	0748	0755	0800	0831	0855	0900	same	1955	2000	2031	2040	2055	2100	2132	...	2155	2200	2212	2232	2256	2300	2332	2336
Harwich Int'l d.	|	0717	|	0750	0809	|	0817	|	|	0917	minutes	|	2017	|	2056	|	2117	|	2138	|	2217	2228	|	|	2317	|	2353
Harwich Town a.	|	0722	|	|	...	|	0822	|	|	0922	past	|	2022	|	...	|	2122	|	|	|	2222	...	|	|	2322	|	2358
Ipswich 205 d.	0700	...	0744	0820	...	0808	...	0844	0908	...	each	2008	...	2044	...	2108	...	2145	2203	2208	...	...	2245	2308	...	2345	...
Stowmarket 205 d.	*0721*	...	0755	0834	...	|	...	0855	|	...	hour	|	...	2055	...	|	...	2156	...	...	...	...	2256	...	...	2356	...
Diss d.	*0734*	...	0808	...	...	0829	...	0908	0929	...	until	2029	...	2108	...	2129	...	2209	...	...	...	...	2309	...	...	0009	...
Norwich a.	*0753*	...	0827	...	...	0850	...	0927	0950	...		2050	...	2127	...	2150	...	2229	...	...	...	...	2329	...	...	0035	...

	⑥		⑦ C	⑦	⑦	⑦	⑦	⑦ P	⑦	⑦	⑦		⑦	⑦	⑦	⑦	⑦	⑦	⑦	⑦	⑦	⑦	⑦	⑦	⑦	⑦	⑦
London Liverpool St. d.	2330	⑦	...	...	0755	0802	0830	...	0902	...	0930	and	1902	...	1930	1932	2002	...	...	2030	2102	...	2130	2202	2230	2302	2330
Chelmsford d.	|		...	...	0836	0843	|	...	0943	...	|	at	1943	...	|	2011	2043	...	...	|	2143	...	|	2243	|	2343	|
Colchester d.	0026		...	0818	0859	0913	0925	0932	1013	...	1025	the	2013	...	2025	2046	2113	...	...	2125	2213	...	2225	2313	2325	0013	0025
Manningtree d.	0035		...	0826	0907	0921	0933	0940	1021	1026	1033	same	2021	2026	2033	2055	2121	...	2126	2134	2221	2226	2234	2321	2334	0021	0034
Harwich Int'l d.	|		0830	0843	0925	|	|	|	|	1043	|	minutes	|	2043	|	2114	|	2110	2143	|	|	2243	|	|	|	|	|
Harwich Town a.	|		|	0848	*0948*	|	|	|	|	1048	|	past	|	2048	|	...	|	|	2148	|	|	2248	|	|	|	|	|
Ipswich 205 d.	0048		0902	...	...	0935	0946	0955	1033	...	1046	each	2033	...	2046	...	2133	2137	...	2147	2233	...	2247	2333	2347	0039	0047
Stowmarket 205 d.	0100		0917	...	...	...	0957	1006	...	...	1057	hour	...	...	2057	...	...	...	...	2158	...	...	2258	...	2358	...	0058
Diss d.	0113		...	...	...	...	1010	...	...	...	1110	until	...	...	2110	...	...	...	...	2211	...	...	2311	...	0011	...	0111
Norwich a.	0138		...	...	...	...	1031	...	...	...	1131		...	...	2131	...	...	...	...	2231	...	...	2331	...	0031	...	0136

		Ⓐ	Ⓐ	Ⓐ	Ⓐ	Ⓐ	Ⓐ	Ⓐ	Ⓐ L	Ⓐ	Ⓐ	Ⓐ	Ⓐ	Ⓐ	Ⓐ	Ⓐ	Ⓐ	Ⓐ	Ⓐ	Ⓐ	Ⓐ	Ⓐ		Ⓐ	Ⓐ	Ⓐ	Ⓐ
Norwich d.	Ⓐ	...	...	0455	0525	...	0555	...	...	0622	0645	...	0703	0740	...	...	...	0800	0830	...	0900	0930	and	1530	...	1600	...
Diss d.		...	...	0514	0544	...	0614	...	...	0640	0704	...	0721	0758	...	...	...	0817	0847	...	0917	0947	at	1547	...	1617	...
Stowmarket 205 d.		...	...	0527	0557	...	0627	...	...	0652	0717	...	0734	|	...	0810	...	0829	|	...	0929	|	the	|	...	1629	...
Ipswich 205 d.		0514	...	0542	0612	...	0642	...	0659	0707	0732	...	0749	0820	...	0826	...	0843	0909	...	0943	1009	same	1609	...	1643	...
Harwich Town d.		|	0524	|	|	0624	|	0652	|	|	|	0716	|	|	0758	|	0828	|	|	0928	|	|	minutes	|	1628	|	1653
Harwich Int'l d.		|	0529	|	|	0629	|	0657	0727	|	|	0721	|	|	0803	|	0833	|	|	0933	|	|	past	|	1633	|	1658
Manningtree d.		0525	0546	0553	0623	0646	0653	0714	...	0718	0743	0738	0759	|	0820	0836	0850	0853	0919	0950	0953	1019	each	1619	1650	1653	1715
Colchester d.		0535	...	0605	0635	...	0705	...	...	0730	|	0754	0810	|	0837	0845	...	0903	0930	...	1003	1030	hour	1630	...	1703	...
Chelmsford d.		0558	...	|	|	...	|	...	...	|	|	0819	|	|	0859	0904	...	0921	|	...	1021	|	until	|	...	1721	...
London Liverpool St. a.		0634	...	0654	0727	...	0758	...	...	0824	0842	0858	0904	0924	0936	0939	...	0958	1019	...	1055	1119		1719	...	1758	...

	Ⓐ	Ⓐ	Ⓐ	Ⓐ	Ⓐ	Ⓐ	Ⓐ	Ⓐ	Ⓐ	Ⓐ	Ⓐ	Ⓐ	Ⓐ	Ⓐ	Ⓐ C	Ⓐ	Ⓐ P	Ⓐ	Ⓐ	Ⓐ	Ⓐ	Ⓐ P	Ⓐ		⑥	⑥	⑥	⑥
Norwich d.	1630	...	1700	1730	...	...	1800	1830	...	1900	1930	...	2000	...	...	2030	...	...	2100	...	2200	...	...	⑥	0500	0530	...	0600
Diss d.	1647	...	1717	1747	...	...	1817	1847	...	1917	1947	...	2017	...	...	2047	...	...	2117	...	2217	...	...		0517	0547	...	0617
Stowmarket 205 d.	|	...	1729	1759	...	...	1829	|	...	1929	|	...	2029	...	2045	|	2114	...	2129	...	2229	2308	...		0529	|	...	0629
Ipswich 205 d.	1709	...	1743	1813	...	...	1843	1909	...	1943	2009	...	2043	...	2101	2109	2128	...	2143	...	2243	2322	...		0543	0609	...	0643
Harwich Town d.	|	1728	|	|	1800	1826	|	|	1928	|	|	2028	|	...	|	|	|	2128	|	2228	|	|	2328		|	|	0628	|
Harwich Int'l d.	|	1733	|	|	1805	1831	|	|	1933	|	|	2033	|	2045	2129	|	|	2133	|	2233	|	|	2333		|	|	0633	|
Manningtree d.	1719	1750	1753	|	1822	1848	1853	1919	1950	1953	2019	2050	2053	2058	...	2119	2138	2150	2153	2250	2253	2332	2350		0553	0619	0650	0653
Colchester d.	1730	...	1803	1830	*1843*	...	1903	1930	...	2003	2030	...	2103	2112	...	2130	2151	...	2203	...	2303	2343	2359		0603	0630	...	0703
Chelmsford d.	|	...	1821	|	*1909*	...	1921	|	...	2021	|	...	2121	2140	...	|	...	...	2221	...	2325	...	...		0621	|	...	0721
London Liverpool St. a.	1819	...	1855	1917	*1945*	...	1955	2020	...	2055	2119	...	2155	2214	...	2219	...	...	2255	...	0006	...	...		0655	0719	...	0755

	⑥	⑥	⑥	⑥	⑥	⑥	⑥	⑥	⑥		⑥	⑥	⑥	⑥	⑥	⑥	⑥	⑥	⑥	⑥ C	⑥	⑥ P	⑥	⑥	⑥	⑥	⑥ P
Norwich d.	...	0630	...	...	0700	0730	...	0800	0830	and	1730	...	1800	1830	...	1900	...	2000	...	...	...	...	...	2100	...	2200	...
Diss d.	...	0647	...	...	0717	0747	...	0817	0847	at	1747	...	1817	1847	...	1917	...	2017	...	...	...	...	...	2117	...	2217	...
Stowmarket 205 d.	...	|	...	...	0729	|	...	0829	|	the	1759	...	1829	|	...	1929	...	2029	...	2045	...	2114	...	2129	...	2229	2308
Ipswich 205 d.	0659	0709	...	...	0743	0809	...	0843	0909	same	1813	...	1843	1909	...	1943	...	2043	...	2101	2109	2128	...	2143	...	2243	2322
Harwich Town d.	|	|	...	0728	|	|	0828	|	|	minutes	|	1828	|	|	1928	|	2028	|	...	|	|	|	2128	|	2228	|	|
Harwich Int'l d.	0727	|	0720	0733	|	|	0833	|	|	past	|	1833	|	|	1933	|	2033	|	2045	2129	|	|	2133	|	2233	|	|
Manningtree d.	...	0719	0733	0750	0753	0819	0850	0853	0919	each	|	1850	1853	1919	1950	1953	2050	2053	2058	...	2119	2138	2150	2153	2250	2253	2332
Colchester d.	...	0730	0743	...	0803	0830	...	0903	0930	hour	1830	...	1903	1930	...	2003	...	2103	2112	...	2130	2149	...	2203	...	2303	2343
Chelmsford d.	...	|	0809	...	0821	|	...	0921	|	until	|	...	1921	|	...	2021	...	2121	2140	...	|	...	...	2221	...	2325	...
London Liverpool St. a.	...	0819	0846	...	0855	0919	...	0955	1019		1919	...	1955	2019	...	2055	...	2155	2214	...	2217	...	...	2301	...	0010	...

		⑦	⑦	⑦	⑦	⑦	⑦	⑦	⑦	⑦	⑦		⑦	⑦	⑦	⑦	⑦ C	⑦	⑦	⑦		⑦ P	⑦	⑦	⑦	⑦	⑦
Norwich d.	⑦	...	0700	...	...	0800	...	...	0900	...	...	and	1900	...	...	...	...	2000	...	...	...	...	2100	...	...	2200	...
Diss d.		...	0717	...	...	0817	...	...	0917	...	...	at	1917	...	...	...	...	2017	...	...	...	...	2117	...	...	2217	...
Stowmarket 205 d.		...	0729	...	...	0829	...	...	0929	...	...	the	1929	...	...	...	2018	2029	...	...	...	2111	2129	...	...	2229	...
Ipswich 205 d.		...	0743	0751	0809	0843	...	0909	0943	...	1009	same	1943	...	2009	...	2036	2043	...	2109	...	2125	2143	...	2209	2243	...
Harwich Town d.		...	|	|	|	|	0853	|	|	0953	|	minutes	1953	1953	|	...	|	|	2053	|	...	|	|	2153	|	|	2253
Harwich Int'l d.		0720	|	0816	|	|	0858	|	|	0958	|	past	|	1958	|	2035	2105	|	2058	|	...	|	|	2158	|	|	2258
Manningtree d.		0733	0753	...	0819	0853	0915	0919	0953	1015	1019	each	|	2015	2019	2048	...	2053	2115	2119	...	2135	2153	2215	2219	2253	2315
Colchester d.		0742	0803	...	0830	0903	...	0930	1003	...	1030	hour	2003	...	2030	2057	...	2103	...	2130	...	2146	2203	...	2230	2303	2324
Chelmsford d.		0804	|	...	0858	|	...	0958	|	...	1058	until	|	...	2058	2115	...	|	...	2158	...	...	|	...	2258	2325	...
London Liverpool St. a.		0859	0904	...	0944	1003	...	1044	1103	...	1144		2103	...	2144	2202	...	2204	...	2240	...	...	2303	...	2340	0007	...

To/from Cambridge (Table **205**).
To/from Peterborough (Table **205**).
To/from Lowestoft (Table **201**).

r – Calls at Chelmsford on ④⑤ only.

201 IPSWICH - LOWESTOFT

km			Ⓐ 2	Ⓐ 2	⑥ 2	Ⓐ 2	⑥ 2	⚒		⚒	Ⓐ 2	⑥ 2	⚒	Ⓐ 2	⑥ 2	⚒	⚒ 2	⚒	⚒H			⑦		
0	**Ipswich** d.	⚒	0620	...	0717	0735	0817	0917	and at	1517	1554	1617	1717	1813	1817	1917	2017	2117	2217	...	⑦	1002	and every	2
17	Woodbridge d.		0637	...	0732	0753	0832	0932	the same	1532	1618	1632	1732	1830	1832	1932	2032	2132	2232	...		1019	**two** hours	2
36	Saxmundham d.		0658	0744	0754	0815	0854	0954	minutes	1554	1640	1654	1754	1851	1854	1954	2054	2154	2254	...		1040	until	2
65	Beccles d.		...	0816	0825	0846	0925	1025	past each	1625	1719	1725	1825	1925	1925	2025	2125	2225	2325	...		1112	☆	2
79	**Lowestoft** a.		...	0833	0843	0906	0943	1043	hour until ☆	1643	1736	1751	1843	1943	1943	2043	2143	2243	2343	...		1130	**m**	2

		ⒶH	⑥	Ⓐ	Ⓐ	⑥	Ⓐ 2	⑥ 2	⚒		⚒	⑥ 2	Ⓐ 2	Ⓐ	⑥	⚒ 2	⚒	⚒ 2	⚒ 2			⑦		
Lowestoft d.	⚒	0525	0607	0614	0641	0707	0727	0807	0907	and at	1507	1607	1607	1702	1707	1807	1907	2007	2107	...	⑦	0805	and every	R
Beccles d.		0541	0625	0630	0657	0725	0743	0825	0925	the same	1525	1625	1625	1725	1725	1825	1925	2025	2125	...		0821	**two** hours	2
Saxmundham d.		0613	0657	0703	0729	0757	0817	0857	0957	minutes	1557	1657	1707	1757	1757	1857	1957	2057	2157	...		0853	until	2
Woodbridge d.		0635	0718	0725	0751	0818	0839	0918	1018	past each	1618	1718	1728	1818	1818	1918	2018	2118	2218	...		0914	☆	2
Ipswich a.		0653	0736	0744	0809	0836	0857	0936	1036	hour until ☆	1636	1736	1746	1836	1836	1936	2037	2136	2236	...		0932	**p**	2

H – To/ from Harwich International (Table **200**).
m – Additional departure from Ipswich at 1907.
p – Additional departure from Lowestoft at 1705.
☆ – The following trains are 2nd class only: From Ipswich at 1017⚒, 1217⚒, 1402⑦, 1417⚒, 1907⑦, 2002⑦; from Lowestoft at 1007⚒, 1205⑦, 1207⚒, 1407⚒, 1705⑦, 1805⑦.

203 NORWICH and IPSWICH local services — 2nd class

NORWICH - GREAT YARMOUTH
Journey time ± 32 minutes *30 km (33 km via Reedh*

From Norwich : Trains noted '**r**' call at **Reedham** 18–21 minutes later.
Ⓐ: 0506, 0613, 0652, 0736**r**, 0809, 0836, 0906**b**, 0936, 1025**b**, 1036, 1136**r**, 1236, 1318**b**, 1336, 1425**b**, 1440, 1536, 1640, 1706, 1736, 1806, 1840, 1933, 2040, 2140, 2300.
⑥: 0530**r**, 0636, 0706, 0736**r**, 0809, 0836, 0906**c**, 0936, 0955**c**, 1025**c**, 1036, 1120**c**, 1136**r**, 1218**c**, 1236, 1318**c**, 1336, 1418**c**, 1436, 1518**c**, 1536, 1640, 1706, 1736, 1806, 1840, 1933, 2040, 2140, 2300.
⑦: 0736**r**, 0845, 0936**r**, 1045, 1136**r**, 1245, 1336**r**, 1445, 1536**r**, 1645, 1736**r**, 1845, 1936**r**, 2045, 2136**r**, 2236.

From Great Yarmouth : Trains noted '**r**' call at **Reedham** 12–14 minutes later.
Ⓐ: 0545, 0624, 0658, 0732, 0817, 0845, 0917, 0952**b**, 1017, 1113**b**, 1117, 1217, 1317, 13 1417, 1517**r**, 1542**b**, 1617, 1717, 1747**r**, 1817, 1847**r**, 1917, 2017, 2117, 2217, 2334**r**
⑥: 0615, 0717, 0745, 0817, 0847, 0917, 0947**c**, 1017, 1042**c**, 1113**c**, 1117, 1155**c**, 1217 1255**c**, 1317, 1355**c**, 1417, 1455**c**, 1512**r**, 1555**c**, 1617, 1717, 1747**r**, 1817, 1847**r**, 19 2017, 2117, 2217, 2334**r**.
⑦: 0817**r**, 0922, 1017**r**, 1122, 1217**r**, 1322, 1417**r**, 1522, 1617**r**, 1722, 1817**r**, 1922, 20 2122, 2217**r**, 2317**r**.

NORWICH - LOWESTOFT
Journey time ± 43 minutes 38

From Norwich : Trains noted '**r**' call at **Reedham** 18–21 minutes later.
Ⓐ: 0536**r**, 0627**r**, 0645**r**, 0755**r**, 0855, 1005**r**, 1058, 1205**r**, 1258, 1405**r**, 1455**r**, 1550**r**, 1658**r**, 1750**r**, 1902**r**, 2005**r**, 2105**r**, 2205**r**, 2240**r**.
⑥: 0540**r**, 0650**r**, 0750**r**, 0855, 1005**r**, 1058, 1205**r**, 1258, 1405**r**, 1458**r**, 1550**r**, 1658**r**, 1750**r**, 1905**r**, 2005**r**, 2105**r**, 2205**r**, 2240**r**.
⑦: 0725, 0805**ar**, 0858**r**, 1005**ar**, 1058**r**, 1205**ar**, 1258**r**, 1405**ar**, 1458**r**, 1605**ar**, 1658**r**, 1805**ar**, 1858**r**, 2005**ar**, 2058**r**.

From Lowestoft : Trains noted '**r**' call at **Reedham** 20–23 minutes later.
Ⓐ: 0542**r**, 0635**r**, 0735**r**, 0747**r**, 0850**r**, 0948**r**, 1057, 1148**r**, 1257, 1348**r**, 1457, 1548 1648**r**, 1748**r**, 1848**r**, 1955**r**, 2057, 2148**r**, 2248**r**, 2330**r**.
⑥: 0638**r**, 0740**r**, 0848**r**, 0948**r**, 1057, 1148**r**, 1257, 1348**r**, 1457, 1548**r**, 1648**r**, 1748 1848**r**, 1955**r**, 2057, 2148**r**, 2248**r**, 2330**r**.
⑦: 0856**ar**, 0946**r**, 1056**ar**, 1146**r**, 1256**ar**, 1346**r**, 1456**ar**, 1546**r**, 1656**ar**, 1746**r**, 185 1946**r**, 2056**ar**, 2146**r**, 2335**r**.

NORWICH - SHERINGHAM (🚂)
Journey time ± 57 minutes 49

From Norwich :
Trains call at **Hoveton and Wroxham** 🚂 ± 15 minutes, and **Cromer** ± 45 minutes later.
⚒: 0510Ⓐ, 0520⑥, 0540Ⓐ, 0545⑥, 0715, 0821, 0945, 1045, 1145, 1245, 1345, 1445, 1545, 1645, 1745, 1855, 1955, 2115, 2245①–④, 2305⑤⑥.
⑦: 0836, 0945, 1036, 1145, 1236, 1345, 1436, 1545, 1636, 1745, 1836, 1945, 2036.

From Sheringham :
Trains call at **Cromer** ± 11 minutes, and **Hoveton and Wroxham** 🚂 ± 39 minutes lat
⚒: 0007⑥, 0621⑥, 0631Ⓐ, 0716, 0822, 0944, 1047, 1144, 1247, 1344, 1447, 154 1649, 1749, 1852, 1956, 2110, 2217, 2347①–④ (also 0553Ⓐ from Cromer).
⑦: 0007, 0942, 1041, 1142, 1241, 1342, 1441, 1542, 1641, 1742, 1841, 1942, 2041, 2

IPSWICH - FELIXSTOWE
Journey time ± 25 minutes 25

From Ipswich :
Ⓐ: 0504, 0604, 0714, 0825, 0857, 0958 and hourly until 2058, then 2228.
⑥: 0558, 0658, 0758, 0858, 0958, 1058 and hourly until 2058, then 2228.
⑦: 0955**a**, 1055 and hourly until 1955.

From Felixstowe :
Ⓐ: 0534, 0636, 0747, 0854, 0928 and hourly until 2128, then 2301.
⑥: 0628, 0728, 0828, 0928, 1028 and hourly until 2128, then 2258.
⑦: 1025**a**, 1125 and hourly until 2025.

a – May 15 - Sept. 11.
b – ①⑤ July 18 - Sept. 9.
c – May 21 - Sept. 10.
r – Via Reedham.

🚂 – Heritage and Tourist railways:
NORTH NORFOLK RAILWAY: Sheringham - Holt and v.v. *8 km*. ✆ 01263 820800. www.nnrailway.co.uk
BURE VALLEY STEAM RAILWAY: Wroxham - Aylsham and v.v. ✆ 01253 833858. www.bvrw.co.uk

205 IPSWICH - CAMBRIDGE and PETERBOROUGH

km			⚒ 2	⚒ C	⚒	Ⓐ	⑥	⑥	Ⓐ	⚒ H	⚒	⚒	⚒	⚒	⚒	⚒	⚒	⚒	⚒	⚒	⚒	⚒	⚒	(
0	**Ipswich** 200 d.	⚒	0510	0600	0616	0654	0720	0800	0803	0820	0920	0958	1020	1120	1158	1220	1320	1358	1420	1520	1558	1620	1720	17
19	Stowmarket 200 d.		0526	0612	0631	0709	0735	0812	0816	0835	0935	1011	1035	1135	1211	1235	1335	1411	1435	1535	1611	1635	1735	18
42	Bury St Edmunds d.		0549	0629	0654	0733	0757	0829	0832	0857	0957	1029	1057	1157	1229	1257	1357	1429	1457	1557	1629	1657	1757	18
65	Newmarket d.		0609	|	0714	0752	0817	|	|	0916	1017	|	1116	1217	|	1316	1417	|	1516	1617	|	1717	1817	
88	**Cambridge** 208 a.		0633	|	0739	0819	0839	|	|	0939	1039	|	1139	1239	|	1339	1439	|	1539	1639	|	1739	1839	
82	Ely 208 d.		...	0656	...	...	...	0858	0858	...	...	1058	...	...	1258	...	...	1458	...	...	1658	...	...	18
108	March 208 d.		...	0714	...	...	...	0916	0916	...	...	1116	...	...	1316	...	...	1516	...	...	1716	...	...	19
132	**Peterborough** 208 a.		...	0737	...	...	...	0939	0939	...	...	1139	...	...	1339	...	...	1539	...	...	1739	...	...	19

	⑥	⚒	Ⓐ	⑥	⚒	⚒	⚒ 2	⚒			⑦ 2	⑦ d	⑦ H	⑦ C	⑦	⑦	⑦	⑦	⑦	⑦	⑦	⑦	⑦	(2
Ipswich 200 d.	1758	1817	1913	1920	1958	2020	2117	2219	...	⑦	0732	0755	0902	0955	1102	1155	1302	1355	1502	1555	1702	1755	1902	21
Stowmarket 200 d.	1811	1832	1928	1935	2011	2035	2133	2235	...		0748	0807	0918	1007	1118	1207	1318	1407	1518	1607	1718	1807	1918	21
Bury St Edmunds d.	1829	1857	1957	1957	2029	2057	2156	2257	...		0811	0824	0941	1024	1141	1224	1341	1424	1541	1624	1741	1824	1941	21
Newmarket d.	|	1916	2017	2017	|	2116	2217	...	...		0831	|	1001	|	1201	|	1401	|	1601	|	1801	|	2001	22
Cambridge 208 a.	|	1939	2039	2039	|	2139	2240	...	...		0857	|	1025	|	1225	|	1425	|	1625	|	1825	|	2024	22
Ely 208 d.	1858	...	...	...	2058	...	...	...	...		...	0852	...	1052	...	1252	...	1452	...	1652	...	1852	...	
March 208 d.	1916	...	...	...	2116	...	...	...	...		...	0908	...	1108	...	1308	...	1508	...	1708	...	1908	...	
Peterborough 208 a.	1939	...	...	...	2139	...	...	...	...		...	0931	...	1131	...	1331	...	1531	...	1731	...	1931	...	

		Ⓐ	Ⓐ 2	⑥ 2	⚒ 2	⚒	⚒		⚒	⚒	⚒	⚒	⚒		⚒	⚒	⚒	⚒		⚒	⚒	⚒	⚒	⚒
Peterborough 208 d.	⚒	...	...	...	...	...	0750	...	...	...	0950	...	...	...	1150	...	...	1350	...	...	...	1550	...	
March 208 d.		...	...	...	...	...	0809	...	...	...	1009	...	...	...	1209	...	...	1409	...	...	...	1609	...	
Ely 208 d.		...	...	...	...	...	0832	...	...	...	1032	...	...	...	1232	...	...	1432	...	...	...	1632	...	
Cambridge 208 d.		...	...	...	0642	0744	|	...	0844	0944	|	1044	1144	...	|	1244	1344	|	...	1444	1544	|	1644	17
Newmarket d.		...	...	...	0702	0805	|	...	0904	1005	|	1104	1205	...	|	1304	1405	|	...	1504	1605	|	1705	18
Bury St Edmunds d.		0531	0621	0623	0723	0824	0858	...	0924	1024	1058	1124	1224	...	1258	1324	1424	1458	...	1524	1624	1658	1725	18
Stowmarket 200 d.		0552	0642	0644	0745	0845	0914	...	0945	1045	1114	1145	1245	...	1314	1345	1445	1514	...	1545	1645	1714	1745	18
Ipswich 200 a.		0607	0700	0702	0802	0902	0928	...	1002	1102	1128	1202	1302	...	1328	1402	1502	1528	...	1602	1702	1728	1804	19

	⚒	⚒	⚒ H	⚒ C	⚒	⚒	⚒ C	⚒ 2			⑦ 2	⑦ d	⑦	⑦	⑦	⑦	⑦	⑦	⑦	⑦	⑦ H	⑦ P	⑦	⑦ 2
Peterborough 208 d.	1750	...	...	1950	...	...	2145	...	...	⑦	...	0950	...	1150	...	1350	...	1547	...	1745	...	1947	...	
March 208 d.	1809	...	...	2009	...	...	2204	...	...		...	1009	...	1209	...	1409	...	1606	...	1804	...	2006	...	
Ely 208 d.	1832	...	...	2032	...	...	2226	...	...		...	1032	...	1232	...	1432	...	1629	...	1829	...	2029	...	
Cambridge 208 d.	|	1844	1944	|	2044	2144	|	2244	...		0912	|	1112	|	1312	|	1512	|	1712	|	1912	|	2112	22
Newmarket d.	|	1904	2005	|	2104	2205	|	2306	...		0934	|	1134	|	1334	|	1534	|	1734	|	1934	|	2134	23
Bury St Edmunds d.	1858	1924	2024	2058	2124	2224	2252	2327	...		0955	1058	1155	1258	1355	1458	1555	1655	1755	1855	1955	2055	2155	23
Stowmarket 200 d.	1914	1945	2045	2114	2145	2245	2308	2348	...		1018	1114	1218	1314	1418	1514	1618	1711	1818	1911	2018	2111	2218	23
Ipswich 200 a.	1928	2004	2100	2128	2202	2302	2322	0005	...		1036	1128	1236	1328	1436	1528	1636	1725	1836	1925	2036	2125	2236	00

C – To/from Colchester (Table **200**).
H – To/from Harwich International (Table **200**).
d – May 15 - Sept. 11.

2nd class — NORWICH - NOTTINGHAM - SHEFFIELD - MANCHESTER - LIVERPOOL — 206

		Ⓐ	Ⓐ	Ⓐ	Ⓐ	Ⓐ	Ⓐ	Ⓐ		Ⓐ	Ⓐ	Ⓐ	Ⓐ	Ⓐ	Ⓐ A		⑥	⑥	⑥	⑥	⑥	⑥
Norwich	207 d.	Ⓐ	…	…	0550	0651	0757	0857		1457	1548	1657	1754	1857	…	⑥	…	…	…	0550	0653	0757
Thetford	207 d.	…	…	…	0623	0719	0824	0924		1524	1623	1727	1824	1924	…		…	…	…	0623	0722	0824
Ely	205, 207, 208 d.	…	…	…	0651	0744	0848	0946	and	1547	1647	1752	1852	1952	…		…	…	…	0648	0748	0848
March	205, 208 d.	…	…	…	0707	0800	0907	|	at	|	|	|	1908	|	…		…	…	…	0707	0804	0905
Peterborough	180, 205, 208 d.	…	…	…	0727	0824	0927	1028	the	1627	1724	1826	1926	2027	2131		…	…	…	0727	0828	0925
Grantham	180 d.	…	…	…	0758	0855	0958	1100	same	1658	1757	1857	1959	2059	|		…	…	…	0758	0859	0953
Nottingham	a.	…	…	…	0840	0926	1035	1134	minutes	1735	1835	1935	2031	2133	2254		…	…	…	0839	0935	1035
Nottingham	171 d.	0521	0639	0747	0847	0947	1047	1147	past	1747	1847	1941	*2114*	*2146*	…		0520	0640	0747	0847	0947	1047
Alfreton	171 d.	|	0700	0810	0908	1008	1108	1208	each	1810	1908	2002	*2149*	*2211*	…		|	0700	0810	0908	1008	1108
Chesterfield	171 d.	0549	0710	0820	0920	1020	1120	1220	hour	1820	1920	2012	*2201*	*2222*	…		0549	0711	0820	0920	1020	1120
Sheffield	171, 193 d.	0620	0732	0840	0940	1040	1140	1240	until	1840	1940	2031	*2220*	*2236*	…		0620	0732	0840	0940	1040	1140
Stockport	193 a.	0722	0824	0924	1025	1125	1224	1325	♤	1924	2025	2124	…	…	…		0722	0824	0925	1025	1125	1224
Manchester Piccadilly	193 a.	0734	0837	0937	1036	1136	1236	1336		1936	2036	2136	…	…	…		0734	0836	0936	1036	1136	1236
Warrington Central	188 a.	0753	0857	0958	1057	1157	1257	1357		1957	2057	…	…	…	…		0753	0857	0957	1057	1157	1257
Liverpool SP ▷	188 a.	0818	0915	1016	1115	1215	1315	1415		2018	2118	…	…	…	…		0818	0915	1015	1115	1215	1315
Liverpool Lime Street	188 a.	0832	0932	1031	1131	1231	1331	1431		2035	2136	…	…	…	…		0831	0931	1031	1131	1231	1331

		⑥		⑥	⑥	⑥	⑥	⑥	⑥		⑦	⑦	⑦	⑦	⑦	⑦	⑦	⑦	⑦	⑦	⑦	⑦	⑦	⑦
ch	207 d.	0857		1457	1552	1654	1750	1857	…	⑦	…	…	…	0939a	1047	…	…	1347	1453	1554	1654	1754	1856	2052
rd	207 d.	0924		1524	1623	1724	1823	1924	…		…	…	…	1006a	1114	…	…	1414	1520	1621	1721	1821	1923	2119
	207 d.	0946	and	1547	1647	1747	1848	1948	…		…	…	…	1038a	1139	…	…	1440	1546	|	1748	1848	1948	2144
	205 d.	|	at	|	|	|	1905	|	…		…	…	…	|	|	…	…	|	1603	|	|	|	|	|
oorough	180 d.	1022	the	1627	1725	1826	1930	2026	2127		…	…	…	1111a	1216	…	1431	1523	1624	1723a	1826	1926	2030	2223b
am	180 d.	1055	same	1656	1759	1858	1957	2058	2202		…	…	…	1153a	1246	…	1506	1555	1656	1755	1856	1957	2102	2255
gham	a.	1134	minutes	1735	1834	1933	2036	2132	2232		…	…	…	1230a	1330	…	1539	1624	1731	1827	1933	2031	2134	2328
gham	171 d.	1147	past	1744	1847	1939	*2117*	…	…		0947	1048	1144	1240	1342	1447	1547	1642	1739	1840	1943	*2133*	…	…
n	171 d.	1208	each	1808	1908	2000	*2144*	…	…		1004	1108	1205	1304	1405	1510	1607	1708	1804	1903	2003	*2205*	…	…
erfield	171 d.	1220	hour	1818	1920	2010	*2155*	…	…		1018	1119	1214	1317	1416	1521	1618	1719	1815	1914	2013	*2216*	…	…
eld	193 d.	1240	until	1837	1940	2032	*2214*	…	…		1041	1139	1237	1338	1437	1543	1639	1744	1836	1935	2035	*2236*	…	…
oort	193 a.	1325	♤	1924	2025	2115	…	…	…		1126	1225	1325	1425	1525	1625	1728	1825	1925	2025	2124	…	…	…
hester Piccadilly	193 a.	1336		1936	2036	2128	…	…	…		1137	1237	1337	1437	1537	1637	1738	1837	1937	2038	2137	…	…	…
gton Central	188 a.	1357		1957	2057	…	…	…	…		1158	1258	1358	1458	1558	1658	1758	1858	1958	…	…	…	…	…
ool SP ▷	188 a.	1415		2015	2120	…	…	…	…		1216	1316	1416	1516	1616	1716	1816	1916	2016	…	…	…	…	…
ool Lime Street	188 a.	1431		2031	2133	…	…	…	…		1230	1330	1430	1530	1630	1730	1830	1930	2030	…	…	…	…	…

			Ⓐ A	Ⓐ A	Ⓐ	Ⓐ	Ⓐ	Ⓐ	Ⓐ		Ⓐ	Ⓐ	Ⓐ	Ⓐ	Ⓐ	Ⓐ		⑥ A	⑥ A	⑥	⑥	⑥	⑥	⑥
ool Lime Street	187 d.	Ⓐ	…	…	…	…	0647	0742	0852		1552	1652	1752	1852	1952	2137	⑥	…	…	…	…	0649	0742	0852
ool SP ▷	188 d.		…	…	…	…	0657	0753	0903		1603	1703	1803	1903	2003	2147		…	…	…	…	0659	0752	0903
gton Central	188 d.		…	…	…	…	0715	0813	0919	and	1619	1719	1819	1919	2019	2203		…	…	…	…	0715	0813	0919
hester Piccadilly	193 d.		…	…	…	…	0742	0843	0943	at	1643	1743	1843	1943	2043	2228		…	…	…	…	0742	0843	0943
oort	193 d.		…	…	…	…	0754	0854	0954	the	1655	1754	1854	1954	2054	2238		…	…	…	…	0754	0854	0954
eld	171 d.		…	…	*0603*	*0724*	0837	0937	1037	same	1745	1852	1937	2041	2137	2337		…	…	*0554*	*0737*	0837	0937	1037
erfield	171 d.		…	…	*0619*	*0737*	0852	0952	1052	minutes	1801	1907	1952	2056	2155	0002		…	…	*0619*	*0750*	0852	0952	1052
n	171 d.		…	…	*0630*	*0748*	0903	1003	1103	past	1811	1918	2003	2108	2205	|		…	…	*0629*	*0801*	0903	1003	1103
gham	171 a.		…	…	*0701*	*0823*	0927	1027	1127	each	1831	1941	2027	2133	2235	0040		…	…	*0702*	*0825*	0927	1027	1127
gham	d.		0456	0610	0752	*0835*	0934	1034	1134	hour	1837	…	2034	…	…	…		0505	0610	0745	0834	0934	1034	1134
am	180 d.		|	|	0828	*0912*	1011	1110	1211	until	1909	…	2110	…	…	…		|	|	0820	0910	1009	1109	1207
oorough	180 d.		0627	0736	0859	*0940*	1045	1141	1242	♤	1942	…	2139	…	…	…		0627	0735	0858	0943	1040	1141	1240
	205 a.		0642	0752	|	|	|	|	|		|	…	|	…	…	…		0642	0750	|	|	|	|	|
	207 a.		0701	0811	0942	*1013*	1118	1213	1314		2015	…	2213	…	…	…		0701	0811	0931	1016	1113	1213	1313
rd	207 a.		0728	0836	1006	*1037*	1143	1238	1338		2038	…	2237	…	…	…		0730	0836	1006	1043	1137	1238	1337
ich	207 a.		0813	0913	1044	*1112*	1215	1313	1413		2113	…	2318	…	…	…		0813	0915	1043	1115	1213	1313	1413

			⑥	⑥	⑥	⑥	⑥	⑥	⑥		⑦ c	⑦ c	⑦	⑦	⑦	⑦	⑦	⑦	⑦	⑦	⑦	⑦	⑦	⑦
pool Lime Street	187 d.		1552	1652	1752	1852	1952	2052	2137	⑦	…	…	…	…	…	1252	1352	1452	1552	1652	1752	1852	1952	2121
pool SP ▷	188 d.		1603	1703	1803	1903	2003	2103	2147		…	…	…	…	…	1303	1403	1503	1603	1703	1803	1903	2003	2131
gton Central	188 d.	and	1619	1719	1819	1919	2019	2119	2203		…	…	…	…	…	1319	1419	1519	1619	1719	1819	1919	2019	2147
hester Piccadilly	193 d.	at	1643	1743	1843	1943	2043	2143	2228		…	…	…	…	1243	1344	1444	1544	1644	1744	1844	1944	2044	2211
oort	193 d.	the	1654	1754	1854	1954	2054	2152	2238		…	…	…	…	1255	1354	1454	1553	1654	1754	1854	1954	2054	2228
ield	171 d.	same	1741	1840	1937	2039	2137	2242	2338		…	1048	…	1241	1348	1441	1539	1643	1740	1839	1940	2040	2140	2330
erfield	171 d.	minutes	1757	1857	1952	2054	2153	2256	2353		…	1104	…	1256	1402	1455	1553	1657	1754	1854	1954	2054	2156	2344
on	171 d.	past	1808	1908	2003	2105	2204	2307	|		…	1114	…	1307	1412	1508	1603	1707	1805	1905	2005	2105	2206	2355
gham	171 a.	each	1829	1930	2027	2133	2234	2328	0030		…	1139	…	1328	1433	1532	1628	1730	1828	1933	2030	2133	2236	0023
gham	d.	hour	1837	…	2034	…	…	…	…		0952	1139	1237	1347	1445	1550	1645	1736	1846	…	2045	…	…	…
ham	180 d.	until	1909	…	2107	…	…	…	…		1029	1223	1314	1422	1520	1622	1721	1817	1928	…	2120	…	…	…
borough	180 d.	♤	1941	…	2140	…	…	…	…		1109	1256	1343	1458	1558	1659	1757	1849	1959	…	2153	…	…	…
n	205 a.		|	…	|	…	…	…	…		1125	|	|	|	|	|	1812	|	|	…	|	…	…	…
	207 a.		2014	…	2213	…	…	…	…		1143	1331	1416	1531	1631	1732	1832	1922	2032	…	2226	…	…	…
ord	207 a.		2038	…	2237	…	…	…	…		1213	1355	1443	1555	1655	1756	1856	1949	2056	…	2250	…	…	…
ich	207 a.		2113	…	2319	…	…	…	…		1253	1428	1521	1635	1726	1830	1929	2026	2137	…	2324	…	…	…

Via Melton Mowbray (Table **208**).

a – Arrives 1712.
b – Arrives 2216.
c – May 15 - Sept. 11.

♤ – Timings may vary by up to 6 minutes.
▷ – Liverpool South Parkway.

CAMBRIDGE - NORWICH — 207

			Ⓐ	⑥	⑥	Ⓐ	⚒	⚒		⚒	⚒	⑥	Ⓐ	⑥	Ⓐ	⑥	Ⓐ	⚒ 2	⚒		⑦	⑦	⑦	⑦
Cambridge	d.	⚒	0605	0607	0700	0704	0812	0912	and at	1712	1812	1912	1925	2012	2020	2112	2115	*2140*	2255	⑦	0852	1052	1152	1252
Ely	206 d.		0620	0622	0716	0719	0828	0927	the same	1728	1828	1928	1940	2028	2037	2128	2130	*2216*	2310		0907	1107	1207	1307
Thetford	206 d.		0644	0647	0743	0747	0853	0951	minutes	1753	1853	1953	2004	2053	2101	2153	2155	*2237*	2334		0934	1134	1231	1334
Wymondham	d.		0711	0714	0813	0816	0915	1015	past each	1815	1915	2015	2027	2115	2124	2215	2217	*2258*	2357		0956	1156	1254	1356
Norwich	206 a.		0727	0728	0830	0830	0930	1030	hour until △	1830	1930	2030	2041	2130	2138	2232	2232	*2319*	0011		1013	1213	1312	1413

		⑦	⑦	⑦	⑦	⑦	⑦	⑦	⑦	⑦
bridge	d.	1352	1452	1552	1652	1752	1852	1952	2152	*2206*
	206 d.	1407	1507	1607	1707	1807	1907	2007	2207	2229
ord	206 d.	1431	1531	1634	1731	1831	1931	2031	2231	2250
ondham	d.	1454	1554	1656	1754	1854	1954	2054	2254	2311
ich	206 a.	1513	1613	1713	1813	1910	2013	2110	2313	2324

			Ⓐ	⑥	Ⓐ	⑥	Ⓐ	⑥	⚒	
Norwich	206 d.	⚒	0533	0537	0633	0640	0737	0740	0840	and at the
Wymondham	d.		0545	0549	0645	0652	0749	0752	0852	same
Thetford	206 d.		0606	0610	0706	0713	0810	0813	0913	minutes
Ely	206 a.		0631	0635	0731	0738	0837	0838	0938	past each
Cambridge	a.		0652	0656	0753	0759	0859	0859	0959	hour until △

		⚒	⑥	Ⓐ	⚒	⚒	⚒	⚒	⑥	Ⓐ		⚒		⑦	⑦	⑦	⑦	⑦	⑦	⑦	⑦	⑦	⑦	⑦	⑦
ich	206 d.	1440	1535	1540	1638	1735	1838	1940	2110	2115	…	2240	⑦	0903	1003	1103	1203	1303	1403	1503	1603	1703	1803	2003	2203
ondham	d.	1452	1547	1552	1650	1747	1850	1952	2122	2127	…	2252		0915	1015	1115	1215	1315	1415	1515	1615	1715	1815	2015	2215
ord	206 d.	1513	1613	1613	1713	1813	1911	2013	2143	2148	…	2313		0936	1036	1136	1236	1336	1436	1536	1636	1736	1836	2036	2236
	206 a.	1538	1638	1638	1738	1839	1938	2039	2210	2216	…	2338		1003	1101	1203	1301	1401	1501	1603	1701	1801	1901	2101	2301
bridge	a.	1559	1659	1659	1759	1859	1959	2059	2229	2235	…	2359		1022	1123	1222	1322	1422	1522	1622	1722	1822	1922	2122	2322

Timings may vary by up to 2 minutes.

208 STANSTED AIRPORT - CAMBRIDGE - PETERBOROUGH - LEICESTER - BIRMINGHAM

km			Ⓐ	Ⓐ	Ⓐ	Ⓐ	Ⓐ	Ⓐ	Ⓐ	Ⓐ	Ⓐ	Ⓐ	Ⓐ	Ⓐ	Ⓐ	Ⓐ	Ⓐ	Ⓐ	ⒶB	Ⓐ		⑥	⑥	⑥	⑥
0	**Stansted Airport**... ▽ d.	Ⓐ	...	0516	0612	0721	0821	0921	1027	1127	1227	1327	1427	1527	1627	1727	1821	1921	...	2021	⑥	...	0525	0627	0727
40	**Cambridge** .... ▽ d.		0515	0555	0656	0801	0901	1001	1101	1201	1301	1401	1501	1601	1701	1801	1901	2001	...	2101		0515	0555	0657	0801
64	Ely .... **205** d.		0530	0610	0712	0815	0915	1015	1115	1215	1315	1415	1515	1615	1715	1815	1915	2015	...	2115		0530	0610	0712	0815
89	March .... **205** d.		0546	0628	0729	0832	0932	1032	1132	1232	1332	1432	1532	1632	1732	1834	1932	2032	...	2132		0546	0628	0729	0832
113	**Peterborough** .... **205** d.		0610	0652	0752	0852	0952	1052	1152	1252	1352	1452	1552	1652	1752	1852	1952	2052	2131	2159		0610	0652	0752	0852
131	Stamford .... d.		0623	0705	0805	0905	1005	1105	1205	1305	1405	1505	1605	1705	1805	1905	2005	2105	2145	2212		0623	0705	0805	0905
154	Oakham .... d.		0637	0719	0819	0919	1019	1119	1219	1319	1419	1519	1619	1719	1819	1919	2019	2119	2201	2226		0635	0719	0819	0919
174	Melton Mowbray......... d.		0648	0730	0830	0930	1030	1130	1230	1330	1430	1530	1630	1730	1830	1930	2030	2130	2212	2237		0646	0730	0830	0930
197	**Leicester** .... d.		0710	0751	0848	0948	1048	1148	1248	1348	1448	1548	1648	1748	1848	1948	2048	2148	...	2255		0710	0748	0848	0948
227	Nuneaton .... d.		0729	0817	0910	1010	1110	1210	1310	1410	1510	1610	1710	1815	1910	2010	2110	2210	...	2314		0729	0810	0910	1010
244	Coleshill Parkway....... d.		0745	0832	0925	1025	1125	1225	1325	1425	1525	1625	1725	1830	1925	2025	2125	2225	...	2329		0747	0825	0925	1025
259	**Birmingham** New St.. a.		0758	0845	0938	1038	1138	1238	1338	1438	1538	1638	1738	1844	1938	2038	2138	2238	...	2342		0803	0838	0938	1038

	⑥	⑥	⑥	⑥		⑥	⑥	⑥	⑥	⑥	⑥	⑥			⑦	⑦	⑦		⑦	⑦	⑦	⑦		⑦	⑦
Stansted Airport... ▽ d.	0927	1027	1127	1227	...	1327	1427	1527	1627	1727	1827	1927	...	⑦	1025	1125	1225	...	1325	1425	1525	1625	...	1725	1825
Cambridge .... ▽ d.	1001	1101	1201	1301	...	1401	1501	1601	1701	1801	1901	2001	...		1100	1200	1300	...	1400	1500	1600	1700	...	1800	1900
Ely .... **205** d.	1015	1115	1215	1315	...	1415	1515	1615	1715	1815	1915	2015	...		1115	1215	1315	...	1415	1515	1615	1715	...	1815	1915
March .... **205** d.	1032	1132	1232	1332	...	1432	1532	1632	1732	1834	1932	2032	...		1132	1232	1332	...	1432	1532	1632	1732	...	1832	1932
Peterborough ..... **205** d.	1052	1152	1252	1352	...	1452	1552	1652	1752	1852	1952	2052	...		1153	1253	1353	...	1453	1553	1653	1753	...	1853	1953
Stamford .... d.	1105	1205	1305	1405	...	1505	1605	1705	1805	1905	2005	2105	...		1206	1306	1406	...	1506	1606	1706	1806	...	1906	2006
Oakham .... d.	1119	1219	1319	1419	...	1519	1619	1719	1819	1919	2019	2119	...		1220	1320	1420	...	1520	1620	1720	1820	...	1920	2020
Melton Mowbray .... d.	1130	1230	1330	1430	...	1530	1630	1730	1830	1930	2030	2130	...		1231	1331	1431	...	1531	1631	1731	1831	...	1931	2031
Leicester .... d.	1148	1248	1348	1448	...	1548	1648	1748	1848	1948	2048	2148	...		1250	1350	1450	...	1550	1650	1750	1850	...	1950	2050
Nuneaton .... d.	1210	1310	1410	1510	...	1610	1710	1810	1910	2010	2110	2210	...		1310	1409	1509	...	1609	1709	1809	1909	...	2010	2110
Coleshill Parkway....... d.	1225	1325	1425	1525	...	1625	1725	1825	1925	2025	2125	2225	...		1325	1425	1525	...	1625	1725	1825	1925	...	2025	2125
Birmingham New St . a.	1238	1338	1438	1538	...	1638	1738	1838	1938	2038	2138	2238	...		1338	1438	1538	...	1638	1738	1838	1938	...	2038	2138

		ⒶA	Ⓐ	ⒶA	Ⓐ	Ⓐ	Ⓐ	Ⓐ	Ⓐ	Ⓐ	Ⓐ	Ⓐ	Ⓐ	Ⓐ	Ⓐ	Ⓐ	Ⓐ	Ⓐ	Ⓐ	Ⓐ			⑥A	⑥	⑥A
Birmingham New St . d.	Ⓐ	...	0519	...	0622	0722	0822	0922	1022	1122	1222	1322	1422	1522	1622	1652	1722	1822	1922	2022	...	⑥	...	0522	...
Coleshill Parkway... △ d.		...	0534	...	0636	0735	0836	0936	1036	1136	1236	1336	1436	1536	1636	1706	1736	1836	1936	2036	...		...	0536	...
Nuneaton .... d.		...	0549	...	0652	0751	0852	0952	1052	1152	1252	1352	1452	1552	1652	1722	1752	1852	1952	2052	...		...	0552	...
Leicester .... d.		...	0615	...	0718	0818	0918	1018	1118	1218	1318	1418	1518	1618	1718	1755	1818	1918	2018	2118	...		...	0615	...
Melton Mowbray .... d.		0536	0632	0653	0735	0835	0935	1035	1135	1235	1335	1435	1535	1635	1735	1813	1835	1935	2035	2135	...		0540	0632	0653
Oakham .... d.		0549	0643	0705	0746	0846	0946	1046	1146	1246	1346	1446	1546	1646	1746	1825	1846	1946	2046	2146	...		0552	0643	0705
Stamford .... d.		0603	0657	0719	0800	0900	1000	1100	1200	1300	1400	1500	1600	1700	1800	1840	1900	2000	2100	2200	...		0608	0657	0719
Peterborough ..... **205** d.		0627	0712	0736	0818	0918	1018	1118	1218	1318	1418	1518	1618	1718	1818	1859	1918	2018	2118	2218	...		0627	0712	0735
March .... **205** d.		0643	0731	0752	0834	0934	1034	1134	1234	1334	1434	1534	1634	1737	1834	1915	1934	2034	2134	2236	...		0643	0731	0751
Ely .... **205** d.		0701	0752	0811	0852	0952	1052	1152	1252	1352	1452	1552	1652	1759	1852	1934	1952	2052	2152	2254	...		0701	0752	0811
Cambridge .... ▽ d.		...	0810	...	0910	1010	1110	1210	1310	1410	1510	1610	1710	1818	1910	1952	2010	2110	2210	2310	...		...	0810	...
Stansted Airport... ▽ a.		...	0839	...	0940	1040	1140	1240	1340	1440	1540	1640	1740	1854	1940	...	2040	2140	2252	...	...		...	0839	...

	⑥	⑥	⑥	⑥	⑥	⑥	⑥	⑥	⑥	⑥	⑥	⑥	⑥	⑥			⑦	⑦	⑦	⑦	⑦	⑦	⑦	⑦	⑦
Birmingham New St . d.	0722	0822	0922	1022	1122	1222	1322	1422	1522	1622	1722	1822	1922	2022	...	⑦	1122	1222	1322	1422	1522	1622	1722	1822	1922
Coleshill Parkway... △ d.	0736	0836	0936	1036	1136	1236	1336	1436	1536	1636	1736	1836	1936	2036	...		1136	1236	1336	1436	1536	1636	1736	1836	1936
Nuneaton .... d.	0752	0852	0952	1052	1152	1252	1352	1452	1552	1652	1752	1852	1952	2052	...		1152	1252	1352	1452	1552	1652	1752	1852	1952
Leicester .... d.	0818	0918	1018	1118	1218	1318	1418	1518	1618	1718	1818	1918	2018	2118	...		1219	1319	1419	1519	1619	1716	1819	1919	2019
Melton Mowbray .... d.	0835	0935	1035	1135	1235	1335	1435	1535	1635	1735	1835	1935	2035	2135	...		1236	1336	1436	1536	1636	1736	1836	1936	2036
Oakham .... d.	0846	0946	1046	1146	1246	1346	1446	1546	1646	1746	1846	1946	2046	2146	...		1247	1347	1447	1547	1647	1748	1848	1948	2048
Stamford .... d.	0900	1000	1100	1200	1300	1400	1500	1600	1700	1800	1900	2000	2100	2200	...		1301	1401	1501	1601	1701	1801	1902	2001	2101
Peterborough ..... **205** d.	0918	1018	1118	1218	1318	1418	1518	1618	1718	1818	1918	2018	2118	2214	...		1318	1418	1518	1618	1718	1818	1918	2018	2118
March .... **205** d.	0934	1033	1134	1234	1334	1434	1534	1634	1737	1834	1934	2034	2134	2229	...		1334	1434	1534	1634	1734	1834	1934	2034	2134
Ely .... **205** a.	0952	1052	1152	1252	1352	1452	1552	1652	1800	1852	1952	2052	2152	2248	...		1352	1452	1552	1652	1752	1852	1952	2052	2152
Cambridge .... ▽ d.	1010	1110	1210	1310	1410	1510	1610	1710	1817	1910	2010	2110	2210	2303	...		1410	1510	1610	1710	1810	1910	2010	2110	2210
Stansted Airport... ▽ a.	1040	1140	1240	1340	1440	1540	1640	1740	1853	1940	2040	2140	2240	...	...		1444	1545	1645	1745	1845	1945	2045	2145	2245

A – [2] Nottingham - Norwich (Table **206**).
B – [2] Peterborough - Nottingham (Table **206**).

△ – 🚌 connections available to the National Exhibition Centre (NEC) and Birmingham International Airport.

☛ **Full service Leicester - Birmingham New Street and v.v.**
From Leicester: On ⚒ at 0549⑥, 0617Ⓐ, 0643Ⓐ, 0649⑥, 0710, 0722Ⓐ, 0748⑥, 0751Ⓐ, 0816, 0848, 0918, 0948 and every 30 minutes until 2018, 2048, 2116Ⓐ, 2118⑥, 2148, 2216⑥, 2227Ⓐ, 2255Ⓐ.
On ⑦ at 1022, 1119, 1219, 1250 and then at 19 and 50 minutes past each hour until 2019, 2050, 2150, 2219.
From Birmingham New Street: On ⚒ at 0519Ⓐ, 0522⑥, 0550Ⓐ, 0552⑥, 0622, 0652, 0722, 0752, 0822, 0852 and every 30 minutes until 1522, 1552, 1609Ⓐ, 1622, 1652, 1709Ⓐ, 1722, 1752, 1822, 1852, 1922, 1952, 2022, 2025Ⓐ, 2052, 2222.
On ⑦ at 0952, 1052, 1122, 1152 and every 30 minutes until 1922, 2022, 2052, 2152.

▽ – **Full service Cambridge - Stansted Airport and v.v.**
From Cambridge: On ⚒ at 0444Ⓐ, 0456⑥, 0517Ⓐ, 0542⑥, 0610⑥, 0632Ⓐ, 0640⑥, 0710⑥, 0740, 0810, 0826⑥, 0910, 0926⑥, 0931Ⓐ, 1010⑥, 1010Ⓐ, 1110, 1126, 1210, 1226, 1310, 1326, 1410, 1426, 1510, 1526, 1610, 1626⑥, 17 1726⑥, 1817⑥, 1818Ⓐ, 1826⑥, 1910, 1926⑥, 2010, 2026⑥, 2110, 2126, 22
On ⑦ at 0739, 0824, 0915, 0924, 1015, 1024, 1115, 1124, 1215, 1224, 1315, 1 1410, 1424, 1510, 1524, 1610, 1624, 1710, 1724, 1810, 1824, 1910, 1924, 2010, 2110, 2124, 2210.
From Stansted Airport: On ⚒ at 0516Ⓐ, 0525⑥, 0612Ⓐ, 0627⑥, 0648⑥, 07 0727⑥, 0748⑥, 0821Ⓐ, 0827⑥, 0905⑥, 0921Ⓐ, 0927⑥, 1005, 1027, 1105, 1205, 1227, 1305, 1327, 1405, 1427, 1505, 1527, 1605, 1627, 1705⑥, 1727, 18 1821Ⓐ, 1827⑥, 1905⑥, 1921Ⓐ, 1927⑥, 2005⑥, 2021Ⓐ, 2027⑥, 2105⑥, 2 2205, 2227, 2257Ⓐ, 2327⑥.
On ⑦ at 0840, 0909, 1009, 1025, 1109, 1125, 1209, 1225, 1309, 1325, 1409, 1 1509, 1525, 1609, 1625, 1709, 1725, 1809, 1825, 1909, 1925, 2009, 2025, 2104, 2209, 2225, 2304.

210 MIDDLESBROUGH - NEWCASTLE

2nd class

km			ⒶA	⚒	⚒	⚒	⚒	⚒	and at	⚒	⚒	⚒	⚒	⚒	⑥	Ⓐ		⑦	⑦	and at	⑦	⑦	⑦
0	**Middlesbrough** .... d.	⚒	...	...	0655	0732	0832	0932	the same	1532	1632	1743	1832	1942	2047	2110	⑦	0931	1032	the same	1632	1742	1831
9	Stockton .... d.		...	...	0706	0743	0843	0943	minutes	1543	1643	1754	1843	1954	2058	2121		0942	1043	minutes	1643	1753	1842
28	Hartlepool .... d.		...	0703	0725	0802	0901	1002	past each	1602	1702	1813	1902	2013	2117	2140		1001	1102	past each	1703	1815	1901
57	Sunderland .... d.		0540	0730	0755	0830	0930	1030	hour until	1630	1730	1843	1929	2039	2142	2211		1028	1128	hour until	1730	1843	1928
77	**Newcastle** .... a.		0556	0751	0816	0852	0951	1053	❖	1652	1751	1907	1955	2104	2204	2232		1048	1148	❖	1748	1908	1952

		Ⓐ	⑥	⚒	⚒	and at	⚒	⚒	⚒	⚒	⚒	Ⓐ	⑥	Ⓐ	⑥	ⒶA		⑦	⑦	and at	⑦	⑦	⑦
Newcastle .... d.	⚒	0600	0600	0700	0730	the same	1630	1653	1730	1830	1930	2030	2033	2118	2130	2300	⑦	1000	1100	the same	1700	1800	1900
Sunderland .... d.		0620	0628	0719	0750	minutes	1650	1715	1752	1851	1951	2051	2055	2138	2151	2320		1021	1121	minutes	1722	1821	1922
Hartlepool .... d.		0646	0653	0745	0815	past each	1715	1739	1818	1915	2017	2115	2122	2203	2215	...		1046	1147	past each	1746	1845	1946
Stockton .... d.		...	...	0804	0833	hour until	1733	1756	1837	1933	2036	2133	2140	2221	2234	...		1104	1205	hour until	1805	1904	2005
Middlesbrough .... a.		...	...	0825	0848	❖	1748	1816	1852	1948	2049	2148	2155	2236	2248	...		1120	1223	❖	1825	1916	2019

A – To/from London Kings Cross (Table **180**).

❖ – Timings may vary by ± 5 minutes.

211 MIDDLESBROUGH and PICKERING - WHITBY

2nd class

km		⚒	⑦A	⚒	⑦A	⑦A	⚒	⑦A	⚒	
0	**Middlesbrough** .... d.	0704	0905	1028	1121	1356	1403	1616	1740	...
46	Grosmont .... d.	0817	1017	1139	1233	1515	1517	1736	1851	...
56	**Whitby** .... a.	0837	1038	1159	1252	1534	1536	1756	1911	...

	⚒	⑦A	⚒	⑦A	⑦A	⚒	⑦A	⚒
Whitby .... d.	0845	1044	1215	1301	1547	1600	1804	1918
Grosmont .... d.	0902	1101	1232	1318	1604	1618	1821	1935
Middlesbrough .... a.	1015	1223	1346	1433	1718	1730	1933	2047

km		🚂	🚂	🚂B	🚂	🚂	🚂	🚂B	🚂	🚂
0	**Pickering** .... d.	...	0925	1000	1100	1200	1300	1400	1500	1610
29	Grosmont .... a.	...	1025	1105	1205	1305	1405	1505	1615	1710
29	Grosmont .... d.	0915	1040	...	...	1315	1430	...	...	1715
39	**Whitby** .... a.	0945	1110	...	...	1345	1500	...	...	1745

	🚂	🚂	🚂B	🚂	🚂	🚂	🚂	🚂
Whitby .... d.	1000	...	...	1245	1400	...	1640	1800
Grosmont .... a.	1025	...	...	1315	1425	...	1705	1825
Grosmont .... d.	1030	1130	1230	1330	1430	1540	1715	...
Pickering .... a.	1140	1240	1340	1440	1540	1650	1820	...

A – May 15 - Oct. 30.
B – July 18 - Sept. 3.

🚂 – May 9 - Oct. 30, 2016. National rail tickets **not** valid. An amended service operates on most ⑦ and on certain other dates and du October - please confirm with operator. The North Yorkshire Moors Railway (✆ 01751 472508. www.nymr.co.uk).

class NT — BISHOP AUCKLAND - DARLINGTON - MIDDLESBROUGH - SALTBURN — 212

	⚒	⚒	Ⓐ	⑥	⚒	⚒	⚒	⚒	⚒	Ⓐ	⑥	⚒	⑦A	⑦		⑦	⑦	⑦		⑦A	⑦
Bishop Auckland d.	0717	0821	0926	0926	1125	1325	1525	1623	1805	1902	1920	2110	0812	1007	...	1207	1507	1708	...	1838	1907
Shildon d.	0722	0826	0931	0931	1130	1330	1530	1628	1810	1907	1925	2115	0817	1012	...	1212	1512	1713	...	1843	1912
Darlington a.	0743	0847	0953	0953	1151	1351	1551	1650	1831	1928	1947	2136	0838	1033	...	1233	1533	1734	...	1904	1933
Darlington ▶ d.	0744	0900	0955	0955	1153	1353	1553	1653	1833	1930	1955	2138	0840	1035	...	1235	1535	1736	...	...	1935
Middlesbrough ▶ d.	0811	0926	1022	1024	1221	1421	1621	1720	1900	1957	2023	2206	0905	1103	...	1303	1603	1803	...	...	2003
Redcar Central ▶ d.	*0907*	0938	1034	1036	1233	1433	1633	1732	1910	2009	*2110*	2218	*1013*	1115	...	1315	1615	1815	...	...	2015
Saltburn ▶ a.	*0926*	0955	1051	1053	1250	1450	1650	1750	1926	2026	*2126*	2235	*1028*	1130	...	1330	1630	1830	...	...	2030

	⚒	⚒	⑥	Ⓐ	⚒	⚒	⚒	⚒	⚒	⚒	⚒	⚒	⚒		⑦A	⑦	⑦	⑦		⑦	⑦A	⑦
urn ▷ d.	...	...	0621	0624	...	0754	0958	1157	1357	1457	1630	1730	1930	...	...	...	1036	1336	...	1536	*1636*	1736
ar Central ▷ d.	...	...	0634	0637	...	0807	1011	1210	1410	1510	1643	1743	1943	...	...	...	1049	1349	...	1549	*1649*	1749
esbrough ▷ d.	0544	...	0647	0650	...	0820	1023	1221	1421	1521	1657	1755	1955	...	...	0850	1102	1402	...	1602	1719	1802
gton ▷ a.	0614	...	0719	0722	...	0851	1053	1252	1452	1552	1726	1825	2026	...	...	0920	1130	1431	...	1631	1747	1831
ngton d.	...	0648	...	...	0749	0851	1054	1254	1454	1554	1728	1832	2032	...	0743	0929	1132	1432	...	1632	1749	1834
n d.	...	0707	...	...	0808	0910	1113	1313	1513	1613	1747	1851	2051	...	0802	0948	1151	1451	...	1651	1808	1853
p Auckland a.	...	0715	...	...	0816	0918	1120	1320	1520	1620	1754	1858	2058	...	0810	0955	1158	1458	...	1658	1815	1900

May 15 - Oct. 30.

▶ – All trains Darlington - Middlesbrough - Redcar - Saltburn:
⚒: 0629, 0658, 0725Ⓐ, 0730⑥, 0823⑥, 0831Ⓐ, 0900, 0931, 0955, 1032, 1053, 1131, 1153, 1232, 1253, 1332, 1353, 1432, 1453, 1531, 1553, 1631, 1653, 1730, 1754Ⓐ, 1800⑥, 1833, 1930, 2032, 2138.
⑦: 0835, 0933, 1035, 1135, 1235, 1335, 1434, 1535, 1635, 1736, 1836, 1935, 2035, 2145.

▷ – All trains Saltburn - Redcar - Middlesbrough - Darlington:
⚒: 0621⑥, 0624Ⓐ, 0710, 0725, 0754, 0830, 0930, 0958, 1030, 1057, 1130, 1157, 1230, 1257, 1330, 1357, 1430, 1457, 1530, 1555, 1630, 1655, 1730, 1757, 1830, 1857, 1930, 2030Ⓐ, 2034⑥, 2130, 2239.
⑦: 0936, 1036, 1146, 1236, 1336, 1436, 1536, 1636, 1736, 1836, 1936, 2042, 2136, 2243.

2nd class — NEWCASTLE - CARLISLE — 213

	⑥	Ⓐ	⚒	⚒	⚒	⚒	⚒	⚒	⚒	⚒	⚒	⚒	⚒	⚒	⚒	⑥	⚒	Ⓐ	⑦	⑦	⑦	⑦
Newcastle d.	0630	0646	0824	0924	1022	1122	1222	1323	1424	1524	1622	1716	1754	1824	1925	2016	2118	2235	0910	1010	1110	1210
MetroCentre d.	0638	0654	0832	0932	1033	1132	1232	1333	1432	1532	1632	1724	1802	1833	1934	2024	2126	2243	0918	1018	1118	1218
Hexham d.	0709	0717	0858	0955	1055	1155	1255	1357	1455	1555	1703	1750	1833	1906	2005	2100	2157	2319	0949	1051	1149	1251
Haltwhistle d.	0732	0740	0921	1013	1118	1214	1318	1416	1518	1616	1726	1813	1855	1925	2028	...	2220	...	1011	1114	1208	1314
Carlisle a.	0807	0815	0959	1049	1159	1250	1359	1451	1559	1653	1803	1852	1935	2000	2104	...	2258	...	1047	1152	1243	1352
Glasgow Central 214 a.	1037	1037	...	...	...	...	...	1737	...	...	...	2139	...	...	...	...	...	...	...	...	...	...

	⑦	⑦	⑦	⑦	⑦		⑦	⑦
astle d.	1310	1410	1510	1610	1710	...	1810	2015
Centre d.	1318	1418	1518	1618	1718	...	1818	2024
am d.	1349	1451	1549	1651	1749	...	1851	2057
histle d.	1408	1510	1611	1710	1808	...	1914	2120
sle a.	1443	1545	1647	1745	1843	...	1952	2158
sgow Central 214 a.	...	...	...	...	...	...	...	...

	⚒	⑥	Ⓐ	⚒	⚒	⚒	Ⓐ	⑥	⚒
Glasgow Central 214 d.	...					0707			
Carlisle d.	...	0625	0628	0718	0828	0943	1025	1025	1133
Haltwhistle d.	...	0657	0700	0750	0900	1011	1057	1057	1201
Hexham d.	0612	0719	0722	0812	0922	1029	1120	1122	1222
MetroCentre d.	0645	0750	0753	0846	0946	1053	1144	1146	1246
Newcastle a.	0655	0807	0807	0901	0959	1106	1157	1159	1259

	⚒	⚒	⚒	⚒	⚒	⚒	Ⓐ	⑥	⚒	⑥	⚒	Ⓐ	⑦	⑦	⑦	⑦	⑦	⑦	⑦	⑦	⑦	⑦	⑦
sgow Central 214 d.	...	...	1212	...	...	...	1612	1612	...	...	...	...	...	...	...	...	...	...	...	...	...	...	...
sle d.	1225	1332	1436	1528	1625	1728	1837	1840	1938	...	2125	...	0859	1001	1105	1201	1305	1407	1508	1601	1705	1801	2012
histle d.	1257	1404	1505	1556	1657	1800	1909	1912	2007	...	2157	...	0931	1033	1133	1233	1333	1435	1536	1633	1733	1833	2040
am d.	1322	1426	1523	1615	1722	1822	1931	1934	2028	2112	2222	2322	0956	1058	1156	1258	1356	1458	1556	1658	1756	1855	2102
Centre d.	1346	1450	1547	1638	1746	1853	2002	2005	2059	2145	2253	2353	1029	1129	1230	1330	1430	1530	1630	1730	1830	1930	2135
castle a.	1400	1503	1558	1651	1759	1907	2011	2018	2113	2158	2306	0004	1041	1141	1241	1341	1441	1541	1641	1741	1841	1942	2148

class — CARLISLE - DUMFRIES - GLASGOW — 214

	⚒	⑥	Ⓐ	⚒	⑥	Ⓐ	⑥	⚒	⑥	⚒	⑦	⑥	⚒	⑦	⚒	⑦	⑥	⚒	⑦	⚒		⑥	⚒	⑦	⚒
Newcastle 213 d.	...	...	...	...	0630	0646	...	...	...	...	...	...	1323	...	...	...	...	...	...	1716	...	...	...	...	...
Carlisle d.	...	0525	0531	0608	0815	0815	0955	1115	1220	1312	1313	1422	1512	1515	1617	1712	1716	1757	1912	1917	...	2022	2112	2126	2310
Gretna Green d.	...	0536	0543	0619	0826	0826	1006	1126	1232	1323	1324	1433	1523	1526	1628	1723	1727	1808	1923	1928	...	2033	2123	2137	2321
Annan d.	...	0545	0553	0627	0834	0834	1014	1134	1240	1331	1332	1441	1531	1534	1636	1731	1735	1816	1931	1937	...	2041	2131	2145	2329
Dumfries d.	0546	0602	0610	0646	0853	0853	1032	1153	1258	1350	1351	1459	1550	1552	1654	1749	1753	1835	1950	1955	...	2059	2150	2203	2347
Auchinleck d.	0634	...	...	0735	0941	0941	...	1241	...	1438	1439	...	1638	...	...	...	...	1923	2038	2044	...	...	2238	...	...
Kilmarnock ▽ d.	0652	...	...	0755	0959	0959	...	1259	...	1458	1457	...	1657	...	...	...	...	1957a	2057	2101	...	...	2257	...	...
Glasgow Central ▽ a.	0732	...	...	0837	1037	1037	...	1335	...	1534	1536	...	1737	...	...	...	...	2037	2135	2139	...	...	2336	...	...

	⚒	⚒	Ⓐ	⑥	⚒	⚒	⑥	⚒	⑦	⑥	⚒	⚒	⑦	⑥	⑦	⚒	⚒	⑥	⑦	⚒	⚒	⑥	Ⓐ	⑥⑦	Ⓐ
gow Central ▽ d.	...	...	...	...	0707	0837	...	1012	...	...	1212	1312	...	...	1512	...	1612	...	...	1742	1912	...	2112	2212	2312
arnock ▽ d.	...	...	...	...	0754	0918	...	1051	...	...	1250	1350	...	...	1553	...	1651	...	...	1826	1951	...	2153	2249	2359
inleck d.	...	...	...	...	0811	0935	...	1108	...	...	1307	1407	...	...	1610	...	1708	...	...	1842	2008	...	2210	2306	0022
fries d.	0458	0618	0743	0743	0901	1025	1102	1158	1300	1314	1357	1457	1501	1602	1700	1707	1758	1841	1901	1933	2100	2213	2300	2356	0115
n d.	0513	0633	0758	0758	0916	1040	1117	1213	1315	1329	1413	1512	1516	1617	1715	1722	1813	1856	1916	1948	2115	2228	2315	0011	...
a Green d.	0522	0642	0807	0807	0925	1049	1126	1222	1324	1338	1421	1521	1525	1626	1724	1731	1822	1905	1925	1957	2124	2237	2324	0020	...
sle a.	0535	0655	0820	0820	0941	1104	1139	1235	1337	1354	1435	1534	1542	1639	1737	1744	1835	1918	1938	2012	2143	2250	2337	0035	...
wcastle 213 a.	...	0901	0959	...	1106	...	...	...	...	...	1558	...	...	...	...	...	2018b	...	...	...	...	...	...	...	...

Arrive 1940. b – 2011 on Ⓐ. ▽ – Frequent additional services are available (half-hourly on ⚒, hourly on ⑦).

2nd class — GLASGOW and KILMARNOCK - STRANRAER — 215

For ⛴ Cairnryan - Belfast and v.v. see Table 2002.

	⚒	⚒	⚒	⚒	⚒	⚒	⑦	⚒	⚒	⑦	⚒	⚒	⑦	⚒	⚒	⚒	⑦	⚒	Ⓐ	⑥	⑦	⚒	B	⚒	A
Glasgow Central 216 d.	...	...	...	...	0807	...	...	...	...	...	...	...	...	1412	...	...	...	1712	1812	...	...	...	2012	...	2212
Kilmarnock 214 a.	...	...	...	...	0849	...	...	...	...	...	...	...	...	1450	...	...	...	1751	1852	...	...	...	2051	...	2251
Kilmarnock d.	...	...	...	0801	0900	...	...	1104	...	...	1303	...	...	1458	...	1700	...	1803	1904	1904	...	...	2104	...	2305
Troon 216 d.	...	...	...	0814	0912	...	...	1116	...	...	1315	...	...	1510	...	1712	...	1818	1916	1916	...	...	2116	...	2317
Ayr 🚌 216 a.	...	...	...	0827	0923	...	...	1130	...	...	1328	...	...	1524	...	1723	...	1828	1927	1927	...	...	2127	...	2330
Ayr d.	0525	0621	0716	0828	0923	1026	1106	1131	1226	1227	1329	1424	1505	1525	1625	1724	1805	1829	1927	1927	1927	2032	2128	2230	2331
Girvan d.	0552	0648	0756	0855	0954	1055	1136	1201	1253	1253	1359	1453	1535	1555	1652	1754	1835	1856	1958	1958	1953	2059	2153	2257	0001
Barrhill d.	...	...	0816	...	1013	...	1155	1220	...	1318	1418	...	1554	1614	...	1813	1854	...	2017	2017	2017	...	...	...	0020
Stranraer a.	...	...	0852	...	1049	...	1231	1256	...	1354	1454	...	1630	1650	...	1849	1930	...	2053	2053	2053	...	...	...	0056

	⚒	⚒	⚒	⚒	⚒	⚒	⚒	⑦	⚒	⑦	⚒		⚒	⑦	⚒	⚒	⚒	⑦	⚒	⚒	⚒	⑦	⑥	Ⓐ	⚒	⚒
nraer d.	...	...	0702	...	0858	...	1106	1041	...	1241	1304	...		1440	1500	...	1659	1740	...	1903	...	1940	2103	2103	...	...
hill d.	...	...	0736	...	0932	...	1140	1116	...	1316	1338	...		1514	1534	...	1733	1814	...	1937	...	2015	2137	2137	...	...
an d.	0557	0653	0754	0900	0951	1100	1159	1134	1300	1334	1357		1500	1533	1553	1658	1752	1833	1901	1956	2104	2033	2157	2157	2230	2302
a.	0627	0721	0823	0928	1020	1128	1229	1202	1328	1402	1429		1528	1601	1626	1726	1820	1901	1929	2026	2132	2101	2225	2225	2309	2330
🚌 216 d.	...	0722	0824	...	1021	...	1229	...	...	...	1430		...	...	1627	1727	1821	...	...	2027	...	...	2226	2226	...	...
on. 216 d.	...	0732	0834	...	1029	...	1238	...	...	...	1441		...	...	1638	1739	1829	...	...	2038	...	...	2239	2239	...	...
arnock a.	...	0749	0852	...	1044	...	1254	...	...	...	1456		...	...	1653	1755	1849	...	...	2055	...	...	2254	2301	...	...
arnock 214 d.	...	...	0857	...	...	...	...	...	...	...	...		...	...	...	...	1857	...	...	...	...	...	...	...	...	...
sgow Central 216 a.	...	...	0938	...	...	...	...	...	...	...	...		...	...	...	...	1937	...	...	...	...	...	...	...	...	...

Runs Ⓐ from Glasgow, ⚒ from Kilmarnock. B – Runs ⑥ from Glasgow, ⚒ from Kilmarnock.

🚌 connections to/from Cairnryan are available from Ayr for pre-booked Rail & Sail ticket holders - www.stenaline.co.uk/rail.

216 GLASGOW - AYR, ARDROSSAN and LARGS

Typical off-peak journey time in hours and minutes
READ DOWN ↓ READ UP ↑

Journey times may be extended during peak hours on Ⓐ (0600 - 0900 and 1600 - 1900) and also at weekends.
The longest journey time by any train is noted in the table heading.

GLASGOW CENTRAL - AYR

Longest journey: 1 hour 04 minutes

km	△				△
0	0h00	↓	**Glasgow** Central......d.	↑	0h49
43	0h25	↓	Kilwinning..................d.	↑	0h22
48	0h29	↓	Irvine.........................d.	↑	0h18
56	0h37	↓	Troon..........................d.	↑	0h11
61	0h41	↓	Prestwick Airport ✈ ..d.	↑	0h07
67	0h52		**Ayr**............................a.		0h00

From Glasgow Central: On ⚒ at 0015②–⑥, 0600, 0630, 0700, 0730, 0745, 0800, 0830, 0838, 0900, 0930, 1000, 1030 and ev minutes until 1500, 1530, 1600, 1627, 1640, 1700, 1705, 1714Ⓐ, 1728Ⓐ, 1730⑥, 1745Ⓐ, 1800, and every 30 minutes until 233 On ⑦ at 0900 and every 30 minutes until 1900, 2000, 2100, 2200, 2300.

From Ayr: On ⚒ at 0513, 0540, 0602, 0620Ⓐ, 0633, 0650, 0705, 0717, 0732Ⓐ, 0740, 0805, 0828, 0850, 0923, 0950 and at the minutes past each hour until 1525, 1548, 1623, 1654, 1706, 1723, 1753, 1805, 1825, 1850, 1915, 1945 and every 30 minutes until 2300.
On ⑦ at 0845 and every 30 minutes until 1945, 2045, 2145, 2300.

△ – Trains at 0015⚒ - 0838⚒ and 1900⚒ - 2330⚒ and all day on ⑦ call additionally at Paisley Gilmour Street.

GLASGOW CENTRAL - ARDROSSAN - LARGS

Longest journey: 1 hour 10 minutes

km					
0	0h00	↓	**Glasgow** Central......d.	↑	0h59
12	0h10		Paisley Gilmour St....d.		0h46
43	0h19	↓	Kilwinning..................d.	↑	0h25
50	0h28		**Ardrossan** Sth Beach..d.		0h17
54	0h49	↓	Fairlie..........................d.	↑	0h05
69	0h56		**Largs**.........................a.		0h00

From Glasgow Central: On ⚒ at 0615, 0715, 0848 and hourly until 1448, 1545⑥, 1548Ⓐ, 1630, 1714⑥, 1722Ⓐ, 1749, 1848, 2045, 2145, 2245, 2315①–④⑥, 2346⑤.
On ⑦ at 0940 and hourly until 2140, 2242.

From Largs: On ⚒ at 0642, 0722Ⓐ, 0742, 0833Ⓐ, 0853⑥, 0953 and hourly until 1553, 1648, 1733, 1852, 1952, 2052, 2152, 22
On ⑦ at 0854 and hourly until 2154, 2300.

218 GLASGOW - OBAN, FORT WILLIAM and MALLAIG

Most services 🍸 2nd class

VALID UNTIL AUGUST 7. For service from August 8 please contact National Rail Enquires ✆ +44 (0)3457 48 49 50.

km		⚒	⚒	⚒ A	Ⓐ Ba	⚒	⚒	⑦ C	⑦		⑦	⚒	Ⓐ Bb		⑦	⑦	⚒	⚒		Ⓐ	⚒	⑦	⑦	⚒
	Edinburgh **220**..........d.	...	...	0450	...	*0645*	*0645*	0808	...	...	*0800*	*0845*	...	...	*1100*	*1100*	*1045*	*1045*	...	...	*1445*	*1630*	*1630*	*1645*
0	**Glasgow** Queen St. ‡..d.	...	0523	0548**u**	...	0821	0821	*0854*	...	...	0941	1022	...	...	1212	1212	1219	1219	...	...	1622	1812	1812	1821
10	Westerton..................d.	...	|	|	...	|	|	|	...	...	|	|	...	...	|	|	|	|	...	...	|	|	|	|
16	Dalmuir.....................d.	...	0539	0604	...	0842	0842	0927**u**	...	...	1016	1056	...	...	1235	1235	1243	1243	...	...	1657	1835	1835	1841
26	Dumbarton Central.......d.	...	0548	0615	...	0851	0851	|	...	...	1025	1105	...	...	1247	1247	1252	1252	...	...	1706	1844	1844	1850
40	Helensburgh Upper .....d.	...	0603	0632	...	0906	0906	0952	...	...	1040	1127	...	...	1306	1306	1307	1307	...	...	1722	1905	1905	1905
51	Garelochhead..............d.	...	0614	0645	...	0917	0917	1003	...	...	1051	1140	...	...	1318	1318	1318	1318	...	...	1733	1916	1916	1916
68	Arrochar & Tarbet........d.	...	0634	0709	...	0936	0936	1023	...	...	1111	1201	...	...	1338	1338	1338	1338	...	...	1757	1936	1936	1936
81	Ardlui.........................d.	...	0652	0724**x**	...	0950	0950	1037	...	...	1127	1214	...	...	1356	1356	1356	1356	...	...	1810	1951	1951	1951
95	**Crianlarich**.................a.	...	0708	0745	...	1006	1006	1053	...	...	1144	1230	...	...	1412	1412	1412	1412	...	...	1826	2007	2007	2007
95	**Crianlarich**.................d.	...	0718	0747	...	1015	1021	1056	...	...	1146	1233	...	...	1418	1424	1418	1424	...	...	1829	2014	2020	2014
	Dalmally.....................d.	...	0749	|	...	1042	|	1122	...	...	1214	1259	...	...	1444	|	1444	|	...	1705	1855	2040	|	2040
	Taynuilt......................d.	...	0811	|	...	1103	|	1142	...	...	1240	1320	...	...	1504	|	1505	|	...	1724	1920	2100	|	2100
162	**Oban**.........................a.	...	0835	|	...	1127	|	1206	...	...	1304	1343	...	...	1527	|	1528	|	...	1747	1943	2124	|	2124
115	Bridge of Orchy...........d.	...	...	0818	...	...	1048	...	...	...	...	...	...	...	...	1449	...	1449	...	...	...	...	2045	...
140	Rannoch......................d.	...	...	0846	...	...	1109	...	...	...	...	...	...	...	...	1512	...	1512	...	...	...	...	2108	...
177	Roy Bridge..................d.	...	...	0931**x**	...	...	1148	...	...	...	...	...	...	...	...	1550	...	1550	...	...	...	...	2146	...
183	Spean Bridge...............d.	...	...	0939	...	...	1155	...	...	...	...	...	...	...	...	1556	...	1556	...	...	...	...	2153	...
197	**Fort William**...............a.	...	...	0955	...	...	1208	...	...	...	...	...	...	...	...	1609	...	1609	...	...	...	...	2206	...
197	**Fort William**...............d.	0830	...	...	1015	...	1212	...	1212	...	...	...	1430	...	...	1619	...	1619	...	...	...	...	2214	...
223	Glenfinnan..................d.	0905	...	...	1122	...	1246	...	1246	...	...	...	1535	...	...	1655	...	1655	...	...	...	...	2247	...
251	Arisaig........................d.	0938	...	...	|	...	1319	...	1319	...	...	...	|	...	...	1727	...	1727	...	...	...	...	2320	...
259	Morar..........................d.	0946	...	...	|	...	1327	...	1327	...	...	...	|	...	...	1736	...	1736	...	...	...	...	2328	...
264	**Mallaig**......................a.	0953	...	...	1225	...	1334	...	1334	...	...	...	1642	...	...	1743	...	1743	...	...	...	...	2335	...

		⚒	⚒	⚒	⚒	⚒	⑦	⑦	Ⓐ	Ⓐ Ba	⑦	⑥		Ⓐ		⚒	⚒	⑦	⑦	⑦ A	⚒	⑦	⚒	Ⓐ A
	Mallaig........................d.	...	0603	...	...	1010	...	1010	...	1410	...	...	...	...	...	1605	...	1605	...	...	1815	1815	...	...
	Morar............................d.	...	0609	...	...	1017	...	1017	...	|	...	...	...	...	...	1612	...	1612	...	...	1822	1822	...	...
	Arisaig..........................d.	...	0619	...	...	1026	...	1026	...	|	...	...	...	...	...	1621	...	1621	...	...	1831	1831	...	...
	Glenfinnan....................d.	...	0651	...	...	1059	...	1059	...	1518	...	...	...	...	...	1654	...	1654	...	...	1904	1904	...	...
	Fort William................a.	...	0725	...	...	1132	...	1132	...	1600	...	...	...	...	...	1728	...	1728	...	...	1937	1937	...	...
	Fort William................d.	...	0744	...	...	1140	...	1140	...	...	...	...	...	...	...	1737	...	1737	...	1900	...	...	...	1950
	Spean Bridge.................d.	...	0757	...	...	1156	...	1156	...	...	...	...	...	...	...	1751	...	1751	...	1920	...	...	...	2010
	Roy Bridge....................d.	...	0804	...	...	1202	...	1202	...	...	...	...	...	...	...	1757	...	1757	...	1927**x**	...	...	...	2017**x**
	Rannoch........................d.	...	0847	...	...	1242	...	1242	...	...	...	...	...	...	...	1838	...	1838	...	2015	...	...	...	2107
	Bridge of Orchy.............d.	...	0907	...	...	1303	...	1303	...	...	...	...	...	...	...	1858	...	1858	...	2048	...	...	...	2135
	Oban...........................d.	0521	|	0857	1211	|	1211	|	1441	...	1611	1611	...	1611	...	|	1811	|	1811	|	...	...	2036	|
	Taynuilt........................d.	0544	|	0920	1235	|	1238	|	1506	...	1635	1634	...	1634	...	|	1833	|	1833	|	...	...	2101	|
	Dalmally.......................d.	0603	|	0940	1300	|	1259	|	1526	...	1656	1654	...	1654	...	|	1856	|	1856	|	...	...	2120	|
	Crianlarich..................a.	0631	0931	1008	1332	1327	1326	1332	1554	...	1725	1722	...	...	...	1922	1927	1922	1927	2118	...	...	2147	2205
	Crianlarich..................d.	0633	0933	1014	1337	1337	1337	1337	1556	...	1731	1724	...	...	...	1932	1932	1932	1932	2119	...	...	2148	2206
	Ardlui............................d.	0651	0951	1029	1355	1355	1355	1355	1611	...	1748	1742	...	...	...	1952	1952	1952	1952	2140**x**	...	...	2204	2227**x**
	Arrochar & Tarbet..........d.	0710	1005	1043	1409	1409	1409	1409	1627	...	1802	1756	...	...	...	2006	2006	2006	2006	2158	...	...	2218	2245
	Garelochhead.................d.	0730	1032	1104	1431	1431	1429	1429	1649	...	1823	1819	...	...	...	2026	2026	2026	2026	2224	...	...	2238	2311
	Helensburgh Upper.........d.	0744	1044	1116	1443	1443	1440	1440	1700	...	1834	1831	...	...	...	2037	2037	2040	2040	2238	...	...	2249	2325
	Dumbarton Central..........a.	0758	1059	1129	1459	1459	1457	1457	1724	...	1847	1854	...	...	...	2054	2054	2053	2053	2252	...	...	2302	2339
	Dalmuir..........................a.	|	1112	1142	1512	1512	1506	1506	1742	...	1856	1912	...	...	...	2111	2111	2105	2105	2304	...	...	2312	2351
	Westerton......................a.	|	|	|	|	|	|	|	|	...	|	|	...	...	...	|	|	|	|	|	...	...	|	|
	Glasgow Queen Street. ‡.......a.	0840	1140	1210	1540	1540	1525	1525	1810	...	1924	1940	...	...	...	2140	2140	2125	2125	2329**s**	...	...	2340	0014**s**
	Edinburgh **220**..............a.	*1008*	*1307*	*1337*	*1707*	*1707*	*1652*	*1652*	*1939*	...	*2050*	*2122*	...	...	...	*2253*	*2253*	*2250*	*2250*	0024	...	...	...	0110

A – 🅁. 🛏2 (limited accommodation), 🛏 1, 2 cl. and 🍸 London - Fort William and v.v. (Table **161**).
B – THE JACOBITE – 🚂. 🅁. National Rail tickets **not** valid. To book ✆ 0845 128 4681 or visit www.westcoastrailways.co.uk.
C – ⑦ June 26 - Aug. 7.

a – May 9 - Oct. 28 (also ⑥⑦ June 18 - Sept. 18).
b – May 16 - Aug. 26.
s – Calls to set down only.
u – Calls to pick up only.
x – Calls on request.

‡ – Glasgow Queen Street Low Level.

219 SCOTTISH ISLAND FERRIES

Caledonian MacBrayne Ltd operates numerous ferry services linking the Western Isles of Scotland to the mainland and to each other. Principal routes – some of which are seasonal – are l below (see also the map on page **92**). Service frequencies, sailing-times and reservations: ✆ +44 (0)800 066 5000; fax +44 (0)1475 635 235; www.calmac.co.uk

Ardrossan – Brodick (Arran)
Ardrossan – Campbeltown (Kintyre)
Barra – Eriskay
Claonaig – Lochranza (Arran)
Colintraive – Rhubodach (Bute)
Fionnphort – Iona (Iona)
Kennacraig – Port Askaig (Islay)
Kennacraig – Port Ellen (Islay)
Kilchoan – Tobermory (Mull)
Largs – Cumbrae (Cumbrae)
Leverburgh (Harris) – Berneray (North Uist)
Lochaline – Fishnish (Mull)
Mallaig – Armadale (Skye)
Mallaig – Eigg, Muck, Rum and Canna
Mallaig – Lochboisdale (South Uist)
Oban – Castlebay (Barra)
Oban – Coll and Tiree
Oban – Colonsay, Port Askaig (Islay) and Kennacraig
Oban – Craignure (Mull)
Oban – Lismore
Portavadie (Cowal & Kintyre) – Tarbert Loch Fyne
Sconser (Skye) – Raasay
Tayinloan – Gigha
Tobermory (Mull) – Kilchoan
Uig (Skye) – Lochmaddy (North U
Uig (Skye) – Tarbert (Harris)
Ullapool – Stornoway (Lewis)
Wemyss Bay – Rothesay (Bute)

SR, XC

EDINBURGH - GLASGOW 220

EDINBURGH - FALKIRK - GLASGOW QUEEN STREET LOW LEVEL

VALID UNTIL AUGUST 7. For service from August 8 please contact National Rail Enquires ✆ +44 (0)345 48 49 50.

	⚒	⚒	⚒	⚒	⚒	⚒	⚒	⚒	⚒	and at	⚒	⚒	⚒	⚒	⚒	⚒	⚒	⚒	⚒	⚒	⚒
Edinburgh Waverley d.	0545	0630	0645	0715	0745	0815	0845	0915	0945	the same	1515	1545	1615	1645	1715	1745	1815	1845	1915	1930	2000
Haymarket d.	0549	0634	0649	0719	0749	0820	0850	0919	0950	minutes	1519	1549	1620	1649	1720	1749	1821	1849	1919	1935	2005
Linlithgow d.	0604	0649	0705	0734	0805	0835	0905	0935	1004	past each	1534	1604	1635	1706	1735	1805	1836	1905	1934	1950	2019
Falkirk High d.	0615	0701	0717	0746	0816	0847	0917	0946	1015	hour until	1545	1615	1646	1719	1747	1817	1848	1916	1945	1959	2030
Glasgow Queen Street L. L. a.	0659	0750	0758	0829	0858	0928	0958	1028	1058	☆	1628	1658	1728	1758	1828	1858	1928	1958	2028	2042	2115

	⚒	⚒	⚒	⚒	⚒	⚒	⚒	⑦	⑦	⑦	⑦	⑦	⑦	and at	⑦	⑦	⑦	⑦		⑦	⑦
ourgh Waverley d.	2030	2100	2130	2200	2230	2300	2330	0800	0830	0900	0930	1000	1030	the same	2100	2130	2200	2230	...	2300	2330
narket d.	2034	2105	2134	2204	2234	2304	2334	0804	0834	0904	0934	1004	1034	minutes	2104	2134	2204	2234	...	2304	2334
ngow d.	2049	2119	2149	2219	2249	2319	2349	0824	0854	0924	0953	1023	1049	past each	2119	2149	2219	2249	...	2319	2349
k High d.	2058	2130	2158	2230	2258	2330	2359	0835	0903	0935	1002	1034	1058	hour until	2130	2158	2230	2258	...	2330	2359
gow Queen Street Low Level a.	2146	2214	2242	2312	2345	0018	0042	0919	0949	1019	1049	1119	1149	☆	2219	2249	2319	2335	...	0007	0037

	⚒	Ⓐ	⚒	⚒	⚒	⚒	⚒	⚒	and at	⚒	⚒	⚒	⚒	⚒	⚒	⚒	⚒	⚒	⚒	⚒	⚒
gow Queen Street Low Level d.	0544	0631	0701	0731	0801	0831	0901	0931	the same	1501	1531	1601	1631	1701	1731	1801	1832	1902	1919	1949	2017
k High d.	0618	0705	0733	0804	0831	0904	0935	1003	minutes	1533	1603	1634	1706	1734	1805	1834	1905	1935	1949	2022	2048
ngow d.	0629	0716	0745	0815	0844	0915	0946	1014	past each	1544	1614	1645	1717	1746	1816	1845	1916	1946	2000	2029	2059
narket ▽ a.	0645	0732	0800	0832	0904	0934	1003	1032	hour until	1602	1631	1701	1734	1802	1833	1903	1932	2001	2021	2049	2116
burgh Waverley a.	0650	0737	0805	0837	0909	0940	1008	1039	☆	1607	1637	1707	1740	1807	1839	1908	1939	2008	2026	2055	2122

	⚒	⚒	⚒	⚒	⚒	⚒	⚒	⑦	⑦		⑦	⑦	⑦	⑦	and at	⑦	⑦	⑦		⑦	⑦
gow Queen Street Low Level d.	2050	2121	2150	2218	2249	2321	2348	0744	0820	...	0852	0922	0952	1022	the same	2152	2222	2252	...	2322	2339
k High d.	2122	2148	2222	2249	2322	2352	0019	0812	0848	...	0922	0952	1022	1052	minutes	-2222	2251	2322	...	2351	0014
ngow d.	2129	2159	2229	2300	2333	0003	0031	0824	0859	...	0929	1002	1029	1102	past each	2229	2302	2329	...	0002	0027
narket ▽ a.	2147	2217	2248	2316	2350	0020	0048	0847	0920	...	0949	1022	1045	1118	hour until	2245	2317	2345	...	0024	0043
burgh Waverley a.	2152	2222	2253	2322	2355	0025	0053	0852	0925	...	0954	1027	1050	1123	☆	2250	2322	2350	...	0029	0049

EDINBURGH - MOTHERWELL - GLASGOW CENTRAL

	Ⓐ	ⒶA	Ⓐ2	ⒶA	Ⓐ2	ⒶA	Ⓐ2	ⒶA	Ⓐ2	ⒶA	Ⓐ2	ⒶA	Ⓐ2	Ⓐ2	ⒶA	ⒶB	ⒶA	Ⓐ2	⑥	⑥	⑥2
Edinburgh Waverley d.	0624	0726	0740	0918	1019	1111	1152	1312	1352	1511	1549	1711	1739	1825	1911	2017	2114	2313	0627	0726	0754
Haymarket d.	|	0730	0746	0924	1024	1116	1158	1317	1357	1516	1553	1717	1746	1830	1916	2022	2119	2317	|	0731	0758
Motherwell a.	0704	0812	0833	1002	1103	1153	1309	1353	1504	1552	1635	1752	1834	1933	1953	2103	2207	0021	0704	0812	0900
Glasgow Central a.	0722	0829	0852	1025	1155	1212	1326	1412	1525	1612	1705	1811	1856	1954	2015	2125	2224	...	0722	0829	0924

	⑥A	⑥2	⑥A	⑥2	⑥A	⑥2	⑥A	⑥2	⑥A	⑥2	⑥2	⑥A	⑥A	⑥2	⑦	⑦A	⑦A	⑦A	⑦A	⑦A	⑦A	⑦B
burgh Waverley d.	0914	1019	1112	1152	1312	1351	1512	1548	1711	1739	1826	1912	2113	2313	1023	1217	1313	1510	1711	1918	2112	2122
narket d.	0920	1024	1116	1158	1316	1357	1516	1553	1716	1746	1831	1916	2118	2317	|	1221	1318	1514	1715	1923	2117	2126
erwell a.	0954	1133	1153	1309	1353	1504	1552	1704	1752	1834	1933	1953	2159	0021	1103	1258	1353	1554	1755	1959	2156	2203
gow Central a.	1015	1155	1212	1325	1412	1525	1612	1723	1811	1854	1954	2012	2220	...	1128	1317	1412	1613	1812	2021	2213	2226

	ⒶA	ⒶB	Ⓐ2	ⒶA	ⒶA	Ⓐ2	ⒶA	Ⓐ2	ⒶA	Ⓐ2	ⒶA		ⒶA	ⒶA	Ⓐ2	Ⓐ		⑥A	⑥B	⑥2	⑥A
gow Central d.	0601	0650	0705	0750	0900	0931	1000	1145	1300	1405	1500	...	1700	1900	1946	2105	...	0601	0650	0703	0750
erwell d.	0617	0706	0721	0805	0915	0959	1116	1202	1316	1427	1516	...	1716	1916	2006	2122	...	0617	0706	0721	0805
narket a.	0657	0748	0829	0851	0957	1049	1155	1249	|	1519	1556	...	1754	1954	2053	|	...	0657	0748	0822	0851
burgh Waverley a.	0701	0752	0834	0855	1001	1054	1159	1254	1358	1524	1600	...	1759	1958	2058	2221	...	0701	0752	0828	0857

	⑥A	⑥2	⑥A	⑥2	⑥A	⑥2		⑥A	⑥2	⑥A	⑥	⑥2	⑥		⑦A	⑦A	⑦A	⑦A		⑦A	⑦A	⑦
gow Central d.	0900	0947	1100	1146	1300	1405	...	1500	1547	1700	1900	1948	2116	...	1055	1200	1348	1455	...	1655	1900	2058
erwell d.	0915	1004	1116	1202	1316	1427	...	1516	1602	1716	1916	2006	|	...	1113	1216	1404	1512	...	1712	1915	2118
narket a.	0957	1112	1154	1250	|	1519	...	1556	1705	1754	1954	2053	2243	...	1151	1256	1442	1552	...	1751	1959	2204
burgh Waverley a.	1001	1117	1159	1258	1357	1524	...	1600	1710	1759	1958	2059	2248	...	1156	1300	1447	1556	...	1755	2005	2208

OTHER SERVICES EDINBURGH - GLASGOW

NBURGH WAVERLEY – SHOTTS – GLASGOW CENTRAL *76 km* Journey time: ±75 minutes (trains marked * ±90 minutes)

n Edinburgh Waverley:

0552*, 0636Ⓐ, 0641⑥, 0655*, 0757, 0825*, 0857, 0926*, 0956 and at the same minutes past each hour until 1555, 1626*, 1657, 1748, 1756*, 1856, 1927*, 2126*, 2256*.

1026*, 1226*, 1426*, 1626*, 1826*, 2026*.

rains call at **Haymarket** 4 minutes later and **Shotts** 38 minutes later (trains marked * 53 utes later).

From Glasgow Central:

⚒: 0006*⑥, 0616*, 0700, 0713*, 0803, 0817*, 0903, 0917*, 1005, 1017*, 1103, 1117* and at the same minutes past each hour until 1503, 1516*, 1603, 1617*, 1703, 1717*, 1803, 1816*, 1903, 1917*, 2116*, 2303*

⑦: 1016*, 1216*, 1416*, 1617*, 1817*, 2017*.

Trains call at **Shotts** 27 minutes later (trains marked * 36 minutes later) and **Haymarket** 59 minutes later (trains marked * 83 minutes later).

NBURGH WAVERLEY – AIRDRIE – GLASGOW QUEEN STREET (Low Level) *71 km* Journey time: ±77 minutes.

ID UNTIL AUGUST 7. For service from August 8 please contact National Rail Enquires ✆ +44 (0)345 48 49 50.

n Edinburgh Waverley:

0607Ⓐ, 0620, 0638, 0649, 0707, 0721, 0737, 0749, 0808, 0822, 0839, 0849, 0911, 0921, 0937, 0951, 1007⑥, 1011Ⓐ, 1022⑥, 1037, 1107 and every 30 minutes until 1640, 1707, 1737, 1807, 1837, 1848, 1921, 1951, 2021, 2051, 2121, 2151, 2221, 2249.

0838, 0906, 0938, 1006, 1040, 1108 and every 30 minutes until 1840, 1940, 2040, 2140, 2240.

ains call at **Haymarket** 4 minutes later, **Bathgate** 27 minutes later and **Airdrie** 52 utes later.

From Glasgow Queen Street Low Level:

⚒: 0547, 0558, 0612Ⓐ, 0638, 0648, 0656Ⓐ, 0658Ⓐ, 0717, 0748, 0816, 0837Ⓐ, 0849, 0918, 0948, 1017, 1047 and every 30 minutes until 1748, 1817, 1848, 1908, 1938, 2008, 2039, 2108, 2138, 2208, 2238Ⓐ.

⑦: 0811, 0845, 0915, 0945, 1015, 1045 and every 30 minutes until 1845, 1945, 2045, 2145.

All trains call at **Airdrie** 27 minutes later, **Bathgate** 48 minutes later and **Haymarket** 74 minutes later.

To/from destinations on Tables **120** and **124**.
To/from London Kings Cross (Table **180**).

☆ – Timings may vary by up ± 5 minutes.

▽ – Trains call to set down only.

EDINBURGH - TWEEDBANK 221

2nd class

	Ⓐa	⑥	Ⓐ	⑥	⚒	⚒	⚒	⚒	⚒	⚒	and at	⚒	⚒	⚒	Ⓐ	⑥	⚒		⚒	⚒	⚒	⚒	⚒
Edinburgh Waverley d.	0543	0555	0622	0625	0651	0723	0753	0824	0854	0924	the same	1524	1552	1623	1651	1654	1720	...	1754	1824	1854	1924	1954
Eskbank d.	0608	0614	0641	0644	0711	0743	0812	0843	0913	0943	minutes	1543	1613	1643	1712	1715	1743	...	1813	1843	1914	1943	2014
Newtongrange d.	0612	0617	0644	0647	0714	0746	0815	0846	0916	0946	past each	1546	1616	1646	1715	1718	1746	...	1816	1846	1917	1946	2017
Galashiels d.	0644	0646	0715	0718	0745	0817	0846	0917	0945	1017	hour until	1617	1645	1717	1746	1749	1817	...	1847	1917	1948	2017	2048
Tweedbank a.	0648	0650	0719	0722	0750	0823	0853	0922	0950	1022	♤	1623	1650	1721	1750	1754	1821	...	1853	1923	1952	2023	2053

	⚒	⚒	⚒	⚒	⑦	⑦	and at	⑦	⑦
burgh Waverley d.	2053	2154	2254	2354	0911	1011	the same	2212	2311
bank d.	2113	2213	2315	0013	0930	1030	minutes	2232	2330
vtongrange d.	2116	2216	2318	0016	0933	1033	past each	2235	2333
ashiels d.	2147	2247	2349	0047	1004	1104	hour until	2306	0004
eedbank a.	2153	2253	2354	0052	1008	1108	♤	2310	0008

	Ⓐ	⑥	⚒	Ⓐ	⑥	Ⓐ	⑥	⚒	⚒	⚒
Tweedbank d.	0520	0530	0559	0628	0629	0658	0700	0728	0758	0828
Galashiels d.	0524	0534	0603	0632	0633	0702	0704	0732	0802	0832
Newtongrange d.	0553	0603	0631	0701	0702	0731	0733	0801	0831	0901
Eskbank d.	0556	0606	0634	0704	0705	0734	0736	0804	0834	0904
Edinburgh Waverley a.	0615	0625	0654	0729	0724	0759	0755	0824	0854	0926

	⚒	Ⓐ	⑥	⚒	⚒	and at	⚒	⚒	Ⓐ	⑥	Ⓐ	⑥	⚒	⚒		⚒	⚒	⚒	⑦	⑦	and at	⑦	⑦
eedbank d.	0859	0928	0931	0959	1029	the same	1729	1800	1828	1832	1859	1903	1929	2029	...	2129	2229	2328	0845	0945	the same	2145	2246
ashiels d.	0903	0932	0935	1003	1033	minutes	1733	1804	1832	1836	1903	1907	1933	2033	...	2133	2233	2332	0849	0949	minutes	2149	2250
vtongrange d.	0931	1001	1004	1031	1102	past each	1802	1832	1901	1905	1931	1935	2002	2102	...	2202	2302	0001	0918	1018	past each	2218	2319
bank d.	0934	1004	1007	1034	1105	hour until	1805	1835	1904	1908	1934	1938	2005	2105	...	2205	2305	0004	0921	1021	hour until	2221	2322
nburgh Waverley a.	0956	1023	1028	1056	1128	♤	1829	1856	1923	1931	1954	1959	2026	2126	...	2226	2328	0026	0940	1040	♤	2240	2341

- Timings may vary by up ± 4 minutes.

222 EDINBURGH and GLASGOW - ABERDEEN and INVERNESS

EDINBURGH and GLASGOW - DUNDEE - ABERDEEN

SERVICE UNTIL AUGUST 7.

From August 8 Glasgow services will revert to serving Glasgow Queen Street. For details please contact National Rail Enquiries ✆ +44 (0)3457 48 49 50.

km		Ⓐ	⚒A	⚒	⚒	⚒	⚒	⚒	⚒2	⚒	⚒	⚒	⚒	⑦	⚒	⚒	⚒	⚒	⑦	Ⓐ	⑥	⑦	Ⓐ	⑥
0	**Edinburgh** Waverley d.	...	...	...	...	0530	...	0633	0700	0728	...	0733	0800	0804	0828	...	0833	0900	0910	0929	0929	0915	...	...
2	Haymarket d.	...	...	...	...	0534	...	0637	0704	0734	...	0737	0805	0808	0832	...	0837	0905	0915	0933	0933	0920	...	...
42	Kirkcaldy d.	...	0520	...	...	0603	...	0706	0736	0803	...	0810	0835	0840	|	...	0907	0934	0950	|	|	1004	...	...
54	Markinch d.	...	|	...	...	0612	...	0715	0747	|	...	0819	0844	|	|	...	0916	0943	|	|	|	1013	...	...
82	Leuchars △ d.	...	0548	...	...	0633	...	|	0808	0826	...	|	0907	0906	0925	...	|	1003	1014	|	1023	1034	...	...
	Glasgow Central d.	...	|	...	...	|	0530	|	|	|	0716	|	|	|	|	0814	|	|	|	|	|	|	0908	0914
	Stirling d.	...	|	...	...	|	0625	|	|	|	0809u	|	|	|	|	0908	|	|	|	|	|	|	1008	1008
	Perth d.	...	|	0600	...	|	0700	0746	|	|	0842	0856	|	|	|	0942	0946	|	|	|	|	|	1040	1040
95	**Dundee** d.	0539	0611	0625	0642	0652	0723	0812	0824	0843	0904	...	0925	0920	0939	1005	...	1019	1029	1034	1037	1052	1102	1102
123	Arbroath d.	0606	0634	0647	0700	0712	0742	...	...	0859	0923	...	...	0936	0958	1021	...	...	1046	1051	1054	1109	1124	1124
145	Montrose d.	0625	0650	0704	0715	0726	0757	...	...	0914	0938	...	...	0950	|	1040	...	...	1102	1105	1108	1124	1144	1138
184	Stonehaven d.	0650	0715	0726	0737	0751	0821	...	...	0935	|	...	...	1010	1034	1101	...	...	1125	1126	1129	1146	1212	1203
210	**Aberdeen** a.	0714	0741	0749	0757	0814	0847	...	...	0955	1017	...	...	1029	1054	1124	...	...	1147	1146	1149	1209	1235	1223

	⑦	⚒	⚒	⚒C	⚒	⚒	⑦	⑦	⚒2	⚒	⑦	⚒	⚒	⑦	⚒	⚒	⚒	⚒	⑦	⑦	⚒	⚒	⑦	⚒
Edinburgh Waverley d.	0932	0934	1000	1028	...	1035	1050	...	1100	1130	1134	...	1136	...	1200	1229	...	1235	1240	...	1300	1328	1331	...
Haymarket d.	0936	0938	1004	1033	...	1041u	1054	...	1104	1135	1138	...	1141	...	1205	1234	...	1241	1245	...	1304	1332	1335	...
Kirkcaldy d.	1009	1010	1035	1104	...	1111u	1123	...	1134	|	1208	...	1211	...	1234	|	...	1310	1313	...	1335	|	1408	...
Markinch d.	1018	1020	1044	|	...	1120	|	...	1143	|	1218	...	1220	...	1243	|	...	1320	|	...	1344	|	1418	...
Leuchars △ d.	|	|	1104	1128	...	|	1147	...	1203	1224	1239	...	|	...	1303	1325	...	|	1337	...	1404	1423	1439	...
Glasgow Central d.	|	|	|	|	1015	|	|	1023	|	|	|	1116	|	1123	|	|	1207b	|	|	1223	|	|	|	1315
Stirling d.	|	|	|	|	1109	|	|	1112	|	|	|	1207	|	1212	|	|	1307	|	|	1312	|	|	|	1408
Perth d.	1050	1052	|	|	1139	1153	|	1143	|	|	|	1237	1252	1247	|	|	1339	1352	|	1343	|	|	|	1438
Dundee d.	...	...	1121	1143	1202	...	1212	1212	1219	1240	1255	1300	...	1310	1319	1339	1402	...	1351	1407	1420	1437	1455	1502
Arbroath d.	...	...	...	1200	1218	...	1228	1228	...	1256	...	1319	...	1326	...	1355	1418	...	1407	1423	...	1454	...	1524
Montrose d.	...	...	...	1216	1233	...	1243	1243	...	|	...	1333	...	1341	...	1410	1433	...	1421	1439	...	|	...	1541
Stonehaven d.	...	...	...	1239	|	...	1304	1304	...	1330	...	|	...	1402	...	1431	1454	...	1445	1500	...	1527	...	|
Aberdeen a.	...	...	...	1303	1313	...	1324	1324	...	1350	...	1417	...	1422	...	1450	1514	...	1505	1520	...	1549	...	1626

	⚒	⑦	⚒	⚒C	⑦C	⚒	⑦	⚒2	⚒	⚒	⑦	⚒	⑦	⚒	⑦	⚒2	⑦	⚒	⚒2	Ⓐ	⑥	⑦	⑦K	⚒2
Edinburgh Waverley d.	1336	1356	1400	1428	1433	...	...	1437	1500	1529	1534	...	...	1535	1550	1600	1601	1627	...	...	...	...	1632	1633
Haymarket d.	1341u	1400	1404	1433	1439	...	...	1442	1504	1533	1538	...	...	1541	1554	1604	1610	1633u	...	...	...	...	1637	1637
Kirkcaldy d.	1410u	1430	1435	1504	1511	...	...	1511	1534	|	1608	...	...	1612	1624	1633	1640	|	...	...	...	...	|	1709
Markinch d.	1419	|	1444	|	|	...	...	1521	1543	|	1618	...	...	1621	1633	1642	1649	|	...	...	...	...	|	1718
Leuchars △ d.	|	|	1504	1529	1536	...	...	|	1603	1625	1639	...	...	|	|	1703	1709	1725	...	...	...	...	|	|
Glasgow Central d.	|	|	|	|	|	1415	1425	|	|	|	|	1507	1523	|	|	|	|	|	1522q	1607	1607	1623	|	|
Stirling d.	|	|	|	|	|	1507	1518	|	|	|	|	|	1612	|	|	|	|	|	1639	|	1706	1712	1722	|
Perth d.	1450	1507	|	|	|	1540	1552	1553	|	|	|	1637	1647	1653	1705	|	|	|	1719	1741	1741	1740	1756	1752
Dundee d.	...	...	1520	1546	1550	1602	1615	...	1620	1639	1655	1700	1710	...	...	1720	1723	1740	1746	1804	1804	1802	...	...
Arbroath d.	...	...	...	1604	1608	1621	1631	...	...	1655	...	1719	1726	...	...	...	1744	1756	1810	1823	1823	1819	...	...
Montrose d.	...	...	...	1620	1624	1636	1645	...	...	1709	...	1733	1741	...	...	...	1800	1812	...	|	|	1836	...	...
Stonehaven d.	...	...	...	1643	1647	|	1707	...	...	1733	...	1755	1805	...	...	...	1822	1837	...	1856	1856	1858	...	...
Aberdeen a.	...	...	...	1707	1708	1715	1727	...	...	1753	...	1815	1825	...	...	...	1843	1901	...	1916	1916	1917	...	...

	⚒2	⑦	⑦	⚒	⚒2	⚒	⑦	⚒	⑦	Ⓐ2	⑦2	⑥D	ⒶD	⑦D	⚒C	⑦C	⚒	⚒	⑦2	⚒2	⚒2	⑦2	ⒶH	⚒
Edinburgh Waverley d.	1700	1704	1734	1736	...	...	...	1743	1750	1800	1805	1811	1810	1813	1833	1836	...	1840	1855	1900	...	1915	1924	1928
Haymarket d.	1704	1708	1738	1743	...	...	...	1747u	1754	1804	1809	1815	1815	1816	1836	1841	...	1846	1859	1904	...	1919	1930	1934
Kirkcaldy d.	1737	1739	1808	|	...	...	...	1816	1823	1840	|	1844	1847	1845	1911	1913	...	1919	|	1934	...	2000	|	|
Markinch d.	1747	|	1818	|	...	...	...	1825	1832	1850	|	1853	1857	1854	|	|	...	1929	2001	1943	...	2009	|	|
Leuchars △ d.	1810	1804	1839	1834	...	...	...	|	|	1911	|	1914	1923	1915	1939	1937	...	|	|	2003	...	2030	|	2029
Glasgow Central d.	|	|	|	|	1622q	1719	1723	|	|	|	|	|	|	|	|	|	1805	|	|	|	1822q	|	|	|
Stirling d.	|	|	|	|	1745	1816	1813	|	|	|	1900	|	|	|	|	|	1907	|	|	|	1936	|	2015	|
Perth d.	|	|	|	|	1825	1855	1845	1857	1904	|	1936	|	|	|	|	|	1943	2001	2033	|	2013	|	...	|
Dundee d.	1826	1818	1855	1849	1853	1918	1909	...	...	1927	...	1930	1936	1931	1953	1952	2005	...	...	2019	2036	2046	...	2043
Arbroath d.	...	1835	...	1905	...	1936	1928	...	...	...	...	1949	1952	1947	2011	2009	2026	...	...	...	...	...	...	2059
Montrose d.	...	1850	...	1922	...	1951	1944	...	...	...	...	2003	2006	2001	2027	2025	2041	...	...	...	...	...	...	2114
Stonehaven d.	...	1912	...	1944	...	2015	2009	...	...	...	...	2024	2027	2023	2050	2048	|	...	...	...	...	...	...	2135
Aberdeen a.	...	1935	...	2007	...	2036	2029	...	...	...	...	2042	2048	2042	2113	2110	2122	...	...	...	...	...	...	2155

	⑦	⚒	⚒2	ⒶD	⑥D	ⒶC	⚒	⚒2	⑦	⚒2	⚒	⚒	⑦	⚒2	⚒	⚒2	⑦2	⑦2	⚒2	Ⓐ2	⑥2	⑦2	⚒2	⚒2
Edinburgh Waverley d.	...	1944	2000	2014	2014	2032	...	2043	2100	2104	2140	...	...	2133	2148	2208	2225	2236	2239	...	...	...	...	2308
Haymarket d.	...	1948	2004	2017	2018	2037	...	2047	2105	2109	2144	...	...	2137	2152	2213	2229	2241	2243	...	...	...	...	2314
Kirkcaldy d.	...	2017	2045	|	2052	2111	...	2117	2135	2149	2212	...	...	|	|	2254	2310	|	2324	...	...	...	...	2355
Markinch d.	...	2026	2054	2102	2102	|	...	2126	2144	2158	|	...	...	|	2256	2303	2319	|	2333	...	...	...	...	0003
Leuchars △ d.	...	|	2115	2127	2128	2139	...	|	2205	2220	2237	...	...	|	|	2328	2340	|	|	...	...	...	...	0024
Glasgow Central d.	1916	|	|	|	|	|	2010c	|	|	|	|	2110	2123	|	|	|	|	|	|	2240	2240	2347q	2351q	|
Stirling d.	2010	|	|	|	|	|	2108	|	|	|	|	2207	2212	2225	|	|	|	2328	|	2336	2336	0029	0056	|
Perth d.	2047	2058	|	|	|	|	2143	2200	|	|	|	2241	2247	2304	2334	|	|	0008	0005	0015	0013	0106	0136	|
Dundee d.	2110	...	2132	2142	2143	2153	2209	...	2221	2240	2251	2303	2310	...	...	2344	2356	...	...	0038	...	...	...	0043
Arbroath d.	2126	...	...	...	...	2211	2227	...	2240	...	2307	2327	2329	...	...	...	...	...	...	...	...	...	...	...
Montrose d.	2141	...	...	...	...	2227	2241	...	2255	...	2322	2341	2344	...	...	...	...	...	...	...	...	...	...	...
Stonehaven d.	2205	...	...	...	...	2250	2302	...	2316	...	2343	0005	0005	...	...	...	...	...	...	...	...	...	...	...
Aberdeen a.	2225	...	...	...	...	2312	2322	...	2339	...	0005	0025	0025	...	...	...	...	...	...	...	...	...	...	...

EDINBURGH and GLASGOW - PERTH - INVERNESS

km		⚒A	⚒	⚒		⑦	⚒	⚒		⑦	⚒	⚒		⑦	⑦	⚒		⑦	⚒K	⑦K	⚒	⑦	⚒	⑥
0	**Edinburgh** Waverley d.	...	*0633*p	0833	...	0932	*0934*p	1035	...	*1035*e	*1136*p	1336	...	1356	...	*1437*p	...	1550	1633	1632	1743	*1750*p	...	1944
2	Haymarket d.	...	*0637*p	0837	...	0936	*0938*p	1041u	...	*1039*e	*1141*p	1341u	...	1400	...	*1442*p	...	1554	1639	1637	1747u	*1754*p	...	1948
42	Kirkcaldy d.	...	*0706*p	0907	...	1009	*1010*p	1111u	...	|	*1211*p	1410u	...	1430	...	*1511*p	...	1624	|	|	1816	*1823*p	...	2017
54	Markinch d.	...	*0715*p	0916	...	1018	*1020*p	1120	...	|	*1220*p	1419	...	|	...	*1521*p	...	1633	|	|	1825	*1832*p	...	2026
	Glasgow Central d.	...	0643	|	...	|	0944	|	...	1046	1125	|	...	|	1414	1432	...	|	|	|	|	1745	1747	|
	Stirling d.	0455	0736	|	...	|	1037	|	...	1140	1237	|	...	|	1507	1537	...	|	1719	1722	|	1840	1842	|
91	**Perth** d.	0539	0810	0947	...	1051	1116	1154	...	1216	1313	1451	...	1511	1546	1617	...	1706	1757	1801	1858	1917	1921	2101
116	Dunkeld & Birnam d.	0600	0830	|	...	1108	1137	|	...	1234	1329	1508	...	1529	|	1634	...	1723	|	|	1918	1933	1938	2118
137	Pitlochry d.	0616	0843	1019	...	1122	1150	1222	...	1247	1342	1521	...	1542	1613	1647	...	1736	1830	1832	1931	1946	1951	2133
148	Blair Atholl d.	0628	0852	1028	...	1132	|	1232	...	|	1352	1530	...	1551	|	1656	...	|	|	|	|	1956	2001	2142
186	Dalwhinnie d.	0659	0917	1056	...	1155	|	1259	...	|	|	1555	...	1622	|	|	...	|	|	|	|	2019	2025	2207
202	Newtonmore d.	0711	0927	|	...	1205	|	1309	...	|	|	|	...	1632	|	1728	...	|	|	|	|	2030	2035	2217
207	Kingussie d.	0719	0936	1109	...	1210	1235	1315	...	1334	1428	1608	...	1637	1656	1733	...	1821	1915	1916	2014	2035	2040	2222
226	Aviemore d.	0743	0950	1123	...	1222	1246	1333	...	1346	1439	1619	...	1649	1710	1744	...	1833	1928	1930	2026	2046	2052	2234
282	**Inverness** a.	0838	1027	1158	...	1259	1329	1411	...	1427	1523	1654	...	1727	1745	1821	...	1927	2006	2008	2101	2124	2127	2310

A – R. 🛏 1, 2 class and (2) London Euston - Aberdeen / Inverness. Departs London previous day. Train stops to set down only. See Table **161**.
B – R. 🛏 1, 2 class and (2) Inverness / Aberdeen - London Euston. Train stops to pick up only. See Table **161**.
C – To / from destinations on Table **180**.
D – To / from destinations on Table **124**.
G – To London (Table **180**). Via Falkirk Grahamston (d. 0542).
H – From London (Table **180**). Via Falkirk Grahamston (d. 1955).
K – From London (Table **180**). Via Falkirk Grahamston (d. 1704).
L – To London (Table **180**). Via Falkirk Grahamston (d. 1047⚒ / 1249⑦).
M – Via Aberdeen (Table **225**).

a – 1711 on Ⓐ.
b – 1213 on ⑥.
c – 2016 on ⑥.
d – 0102 on ⑥.
e – Change at Stirling.
p – Change at Perth.
q – Glasgow Queen Street Low Level.
r – ⑥ only.
s – Stops to set down only.
u – Stops to pick up only.

⊡ – Timings may vary by up to ± 5 minutes.
△ – Frequent 🚌 connections available to / from **St Andrews**. Journey 10 minutes. Operator: Stagecoach (routes 94, 96, 99).

, SR, XC **ABERDEEN and INVERNESS - EDINBURGH and GLASGOW** **222**

ABERDEEN - DUNDEE - GLASGOW and EDINBURGH

ALID UNTIL AUGUST 7. From August 8 Glasgow services will revert to serving Glasgow Queen Street. For details contact National Rail Enquiries ✆ +44 (0)3457 48 49 50.

	ⒶG	Ⓐ2	⚒2	⑥2	Ⓐ	⚒2	⚒	⚒D	⚒2	⚒2	⚒	⚒	⚒	⚒	⑦2	⚒2	⚒	⚒	⚒	⚒2	⚒	⑦2	⑦	⚒
Aberdeen d.	...	...	...	...	...	...	...	...	...	...	0526	0546	...	...	...	...	0633	...	0703	...	...	...	...	0740
Stonehaven d.	...	...	...	...	...	...	...	...	...	...	0545	0602	...	...	...	...	0651	...	0720	...	...	...	...	0756
Montrose d.	...	...	...	...	...	...	...	...	...	...	0610	0624	...	...	...	...	0713	...	0744	...	...	...	...	0817
Arbroath d.	...	...	...	...	...	...	...	...	...	...	0625	0638	...	...	...	...	0727	...	0758	...	...	...	...	0831
Dundee d.	...	...	...	...	...	0553	0605	0632	...	...	0650	0658	0709	0738	0724	...	0752	0817	0821	0829	...	...	0845	0854
Perth d.	...	0513	0518	0536	0614	0619	|	|	0639	0655	0715	|	|	|	|	0802	0813	0841	|	|	0850	0845	0906	0915
Stirling d.	0526	|	0553	|	|	0654	|	|	0715	|	0752	|	|	|	|	|	0843	0915	|	|	|	|	0938	0943
Glasgow Central a.	|	|	0705	|	|	0802	|	|	|	|	0908	|	|	|	|	|	0938	1021q	|	|	|	|	1031	1041
Leuchars △ d.	|	|	...	|	|	...	0618	0646	|	|	...	0712	0723	0751	0737	|	...	...	|	0842	|	|	...	...
Markinch d.	|	0543	...	0606	0646	...	0640	0710	|	0737	...	|	0747	0811	0759	0831	...	...	|	0904	|	0915	...	...
Kirkcaldy d.	|	0553	...	0616	|	...	0649	0720	|	0746	...	0740	0756	0821	0808	0840	...	...	|	0913	0924	0924	...	...
Haymarket a.	0611	0641	...	0703	0752	...	0736	0758	0810	0818	...	0814	0841	0901	0857	0917	...	...	0925	0952	0956	1012	...	...
Edinburgh Waverley a.	0617	0646	...	0708	0800	...	0741	0804	0816	0823	...	0821	0848	0906	0903	0924	...	...	0935	0957	1003	1017	...	...

	⚒C	D	⑦2	⚒	⑦2	⚒L	⚒	⚒	⚒	⑦2	⚒	⚒2	⑦	⚒	⑦C	⚒C	⑦	⚒	⑦L	⚒	⑦	⚒	⚒	⚒	⑦D
rdeen d.	0752	0820	...	...	...	...	...	0842	0907	...	...	...	0924	0936	0947	0952	...	...	...	...	1030	1038	...	1103	1110
ehaven d.	0810	0838	...	...	...	...	...	|	|	...	...	...	0941	0954	1005	1010	...	...	...	...	1047	|	...	1120	1127
trose d.	0833	0859	...	...	...	...	...	0918	0946	...	...	...	1005	1016	1028	1033	...	...	...	...	1108	1114	...	1144	1148
oath d.	0849	0915	...	...	...	...	...	0932	1000	...	...	...	1020	1030	1044	1049	...	...	...	...	1123	1128	...	1158	1204
dee d.	0907	0932	0924	0941	...	...	...	0952	1016	...	1034	...	1046	1052	1103	1107	1120	1130	...	...	1144	1149	1213	1216	1224
erth d.	|	|	|	|	0936	0957	1002	1014	|	1010	|	1102	1108	1114	|	|	|	|	1159	1202	1209	1211	1238	|	|
irling d.	|	|	|	|	|	1029	|	1043	|	1045	|	|	1142	1143	|	|	|	|	1234	|	1243	1241	1312	|	|
lasgow Central a.	|	|	|	|	|	|	|	1137	|	|	|	|	1240	1239	|	|	|	|	|	|	1333	1334	1404	|	|
chars △ d.	0921	0946	0937	0955	|	|	|	...	1029	|	1047	|	...	...	1117	1123	1133	1143	|	|	...	...	...	1229	1237
kinch d.	|	1008	0959	1018	1005	|	1031	...	|	|	1108	1131	...	...	|	|	1155	1204	|	1230	...	...	...	|	1257
caldy d.	0945	1016	1008	1027	|	|	1040	...	|	|	1117	1141	...	...	1139	1147	1204	1213	|	1240	...	...	...	|	1306
market a.	1018	1051	1058	1108	1110	1111	1123	...	1126	1135	1150	1217	...	...	1214	1220	1237	1247	1314	1317	...	...	...	1322	1337
nburgh Waverley a.	1024	1058	1103	1114	1116	1117	1129	...	1131	1141	1157	1222	...	...	1220	1226	1243	1254	1320	1324	...	...	...	1327	1343

	⚒2	⑦	⚒	⑦	⚒	⑦C	⚒	⑦2	⚒	⚒	⑦	⚒	⑦	⚒	⚒	⚒	⑦	⚒	⑦C	⚒	⑦	⑦	⚒	⚒2	⑦
rdeen d.	...	...	...	1129	1142	1147	1206	...	...	...	1229	1240	1247	1309	...	...	1331	1338	1347	1404	...	...	...	...	1431
ehaven d.	...	...	...	1145	|	1205	1224	...	...	...	1246	1256	1306	1325	...	...	1348	1356	1405	1420	...	...	...	...	1448
trose d.	...	...	...	1208	1217	1228	|	...	...	...	1307	1320	1331	1347	...	...	1409	1418	1428	|	...	...	...	...	1509
oath d.	...	...	...	1222	1231	1244	1259	...	...	...	1322	1334	1345	1401	...	...	1424	1432	1444	1457	...	...	...	...	1524
dee d.	1234	...	...	1243	1252	1302	1315	1320	1334	...	1343	1354	1407	1417	1434	...	1445	1454	1502	1516	1515	...	1534	...	1545
erth d.	|	1254	1302	1305	1314	|	|	|	|	1402	1406	1415	|	|	|	1504	1508	1516	|	|	|	1529	|	1600	1608
irling d.	|	|	|	1337	1343	|	|	|	|	|	1438	1443	|	|	|	|	1542	1543	|	|	|	|	|	|	1640
lasgow Central a.	|	|	|	1433	1435	|	|	|	|	|	1530	1534	|	|	|	|	1634	1634	|	|	|	|	|	|	1732
chars △ d.	1247	|	|	...	...	1317	1328	1333	1347	|	...	...	1420	1428	1447	|	...	...	1516	1528	1528	|	1548	|	...
kinch d.	1308	1321	1330	...	...	|	|	1355	1408	1431	...	...	|	|	1508	1532	...	...	|	|	1550	1557	1610	1629	...
caldy d.	1317	1331	1340	...	...	1339	|	1404	1417	1440	...	...	1445	|	1517	1541	...	...	1538	|	1559	1607	1619	1638	...
market a.	1347	1404	1417	...	...	1417	1421	1440	1449	1517	...	...	1518	1526	1552	1617	...	...	1615	1626	1633	1639	1652	1715	...
nburgh Waverley a.	1357	1409	1424	...	...	1423	1427	1445	1454	1523	...	...	1523	1532	1657	1623	...	...	1623	1633	1639	1644	1700	1723	...

	⚒	⚒C	⑦	⑦	⚒	⚒2	⚒2	⚒	⑦	⑦2	⚒2	⑦	⚒	Ⓐ	⑥	⚒	⑦	⚒2	⚒2	⚒	⑦	⑥	ⒶC	⑦2	⚒2
rdeen d.	1439	1452	1511	1528	1533	...	...	1602	...	...	...	1628	...	1627	1637	1709	1710	...	...	1736	1747	1818	1818	...	...
ehaven d.	|	1510	1530	1544	1549	...	...	1619	...	...	...	1645	...	1645u	1655	|	1726	...	...	1752	1804	1836	1836	...	...
trose d.	1515	1533	1551	1609	1610	...	...	|	...	...	...	1706	...	1710	1717	1749	1748	...	...	1817	1828	1859	1859	...	...
oath d.	1529	1549	1605	1623	1624	...	...	1655	...	...	...	1721	...	1726	1731	1803	1801	1819	...	1831	1843	1914	1915	...	...
dee d.	1551	1607	1624	1643	1646	1649	...	1716	...	1720	1726	1742	...	1748	1750	1822	1818	1843	...	1854	1903	1932	1933	1916	...
erth d.	1613	|	|	1705	1711	|	1702	|	1722	|	|	1805	1806	1814	1814	|	|	|	1911	1916	1926	|	|	|	2002
tirling d.	1641s	|	|	1737	1743	|	|	|	|	|	|	1837	|	1843	1843	|	|	|	|	1943	1958	|	|	|	|
lasgow Central a.	1736	|	|	1833	1845	|	|	|	|	|	|	1930	|	1945	1945	|	|	|	|	2037	2057	|	|	|	|
chars △ d.	...	1622	1637	...	...	1702	|	1729	|	1733	1739	...	|	...	...	1835	1831	1856	|	...	...	1946	1947	1929	|
kinch d.	...	|	|	...	...	1723	1731	|	1750	1755	1803	...	1835	...	...	|	|	1917	1944	...	...	|	|	1951	2030
caldy d.	...	1646	1702	...	...	1732	1748	|	1559	1804	1812	...	1844	...	...	|	1856	1926	1953	...	...	2009	2011	2000	2040
market a.	...	1720	1734	...	...	1819	1822	1826	1831	1839	1844	...	1916	...	...	1933	1928	2004	2026	...	...	2044	2045	2048	2115
nburgh Waverley a.	...	1726	1740	...	...	1824	1827	1832	1836	1844	1850	...	1922	...	...	1938	1933	2009	2032	...	...	2048	2050	2053	2120

	⚒	⚒	⑦	⚒2	⚒	⑦	⑦	⚒	⑦	⚒	⚒		⚒		⚒		⑦	⑥	Ⓐ	⚒2	ⒷB	⑦	①–④	⑥	⑤
rdeen d.	1828	1910	1907	...	...	...	1936	1947	2007	2009	2042	...	2105	...	...	...	2128	2131	2131	...	2143	2227	2227	2227	2323
ehaven d.	1849	1926	1924	...	...	...	1952	2005	2026	2025	2058	...	2121	...	...	...	2145	2149	2149	...	2201	2246	2246	2246	2342
trose d.	1912	1950	1945	...	...	...	2014	2027	2050	2046	2120	...	2145	...	...	...	2206	2210	2210	...	2226	2310	2310	2310	0006
oath d.	1926	2004	1959	...	...	...	2028	2041	2104	2100	2134	...	2159	...	...	...	2222	2226	2226	...	2244	2324	2324	2324	0020
dee d.	1949	2020	2022	2043	...	...	2050	2100	2121	2119	2154	...	2216	...	...	...	2239	2243	2243	...	2306	2349	2349	2348	0045
erth d.	2011	|	|	|	2104	2106	2111	2122	|	|	2216	...	|	...	2238	...	|	|	|	2243	|	0012	0012	...	0109
tirling d.	2041	|	|	|	|	|	2143	2149	|	|	2248	...	|	...	2309	...	|	|	|	|	|	...	...	...	...
lasgow Central a.	2153	|	|	|	|	|	2235	2250	|	|	2342	...	|	...	0013	...	|	|	|	|	|	...	...	...	...
chars △ d.	...	2032	2035	2056	|	|	...	...	2134	2132	...	...	2229	...	...	...	2252	2256	2256	|	2325	...	...	...	...
kinch d.	...	|	|	2117	2134	2133	...	...	2157	2154	...	...	2251	...	...	...	2313	2317	2317	2312	|	...	...	...	...
caldy d.	...	|	2101	2126	2144	2142	...	...	2206	2203	...	...	2300	...	...	...	2321	2325	2325	|	2354	...	...	...	...
market a.	...	2128	2133	2211	2217	2214	...	...	2238	2252	...	...	2344	...	...	...	2353	2357	2358	0016	...	...	...	...	...
nburgh Waverley a.	...	2133	2138	2217	2222	2223	...	...	2243	2258	...	...	2349	...	...	...	2358	0005	0007	0022	...	...	...	...	...

INVERNESS - PERTH - GLASGOW and EDINBURGH

km		⚒	⚒M	⚒	⚒L	⚒	⑦L	⚒	⚒	⑦	⑦	⚒	⑦		⚒	⑦	⚒	⑦	⚒		⚒	⑦	⚒	⑦B	ⒶB
0	**Inverness** d.	...	0453	0650	0755	0845	0940	0941	1045	1050	1245	1253	1330	...	1447	1522	1551	1624	1730	...	1846	1851	2015	2026	2044
56	Aviemore d.	...	|	0725	0831	0924	1019	1027	1123	1125	1323	1333	1406	...	1523	1557	1635	1710	1814	...	1928	1930	2106	2115	2131
75	Kingussie d.	...	|	0737	0843	0936	1032	1039	1136	1137	1335	1345	1418	...	1535	1609	1647	1722	1826	...	1940	1942	2118	2129	2151
30	Newtonmore d.	...	|	|	|	0940	1037	|	|	|	1340	1349	|	...	|	|	1651	|	|	...	1945	1946	2122	2135	2157
96	Dalwhinnie d.	...	|	|	|	|	|	1053	|	1151	|	|	|	...	1549	|	|	|	|	...	1957	1958	2134	2150	2211
34	Blair Atholl d.	0712	|	|	|	|	1109	1114	|	|	1411	1420	|	...	|	|	1722	1754	|	...	2018	2019	2156	2215	2238
45	Pitlochry d.	0723	|	0817	0925	1019	1123	1124	1224	1219	1421	1431	1458	...	1619	1649	1732	1804	1906	...	2028	2029	2206	2229	2250
56	Dunkeld & Birnam d.	0736	|	0830	|	|	1137	1137	1237	1234	1434	1443	|	...	1634	1701	1744	1818	1918	...	2041	2041	2218	2243	2304
91	**Perth** d.	0802	|	0850	0957	1053	1159	1202	1302	1254	1454	1504	1529	...	1654	1722	1806	1839	1938	...	2104	2106	2238	2306	2330
44	Stirling d.	|	|	|	1032	1127	1234	|	|	|	1524	|	|	...	1728	|	|	1908	2013	...	|	|	2309	2351	0016
91	**Glasgow** Central a.	|	|	|	|	1231	|	|	|	|	1620	|	|	...	1819	|	|	2006	2108	...	|	|	0013	...	...
	Markinch d.	0831	|	|	|	*1131*p	|	1230	1330	1321	...	1532	1557	...	*1731*p	1750	1835	|	*2030*p	...	2134	2133	*2312*p	...	...
	Kirkcaldy d.	0840	|	0924	|	*1141*p	|	1240	1340	1331	...	1541	1607	...	*1748*p	1759	1844	|	*2040*p	...	2144	2142	|	...	...
	Haymarket a.	0919	0925	0956	1111	*1217*p	1314	1317	1417	1404	...	1617	1639	...	*1820*p	1831	1916	*2008*e	*2115*p	...	2217	2214	*0016*p	...	...
	Edinburgh Waverley a.	0924	0932	1003	1117	*1222*p	1320	1325	1424	1409	...	1623	1644	...	*1829*p	1836	1922	*2013*e	*2120*p	...	2222	2223	*0022*p	...	...

OTHER SERVICES EDINBURGH and GLASGOW - STIRLING

m Edinburgh Waverley to Stirling: *75 km* Journey time: 54 minutes

: 0518, 0633 and every 30 minutes (⊡) until 1933, 2033, 2133, 2233, 2303, 2333.

: 0934, 1035 and hourly until 2135, 2236 (also 1106 and hourly until 1806).

trains call at **Haymarket** 4 minutes later, **Linlithgow** 22 minutes later and **Falkirk** **ahamston** 35 minutes later.

m Glasgow Queen Street Low Level to Stirling: *47 km* Journey time: 57 – 71 minutes

: 0559, 0620, 0652, 0722, 0752, 0822, 0852, 0922, 0951 and every 30 minutes until 2252, 2322, 2351.

: 1002, 1102, 1159, 1259, 1359, 1459, 1602, 1659, 1759, 1859, 1959, 2059, 2159, 2347.

From Stirling to Edinburgh Waverley:

⚒: 0530, 0637, 0717, 0749Ⓐ, 0807 and every 30 minutes (⊡) until 2107, 2207, 2317.

⑦: 0905, 0951, 1110 and hourly until 2210 (also 1046 and hourly until 1646).

Trains call at **Falkirk Grahamston** 17 minutes later, **Linlithgow** 30 minutes later and **Haymarket** 50 minutes later.

From Stirling to Glasgow Queen Street Low Level:

⚒: 0623, 0723, 0757, 0823 and every 30 minutes until 1723, 1751, 1819, 1853, 1923, 1953, 2021, 2053, 2123, 2155, 2223, 2253.

⑦: 0925, 1025, 1125 and hourly until 2125.

◀◀ FOR FOOTNOTES SEE PREVIOUS PAGE

225 INVERNESS - ELGIN - ABERDEEN

🍷 on most trains

km		⚒	⚒	Ⓐ	⚒	⚒	⚒	⚒	⚒	⚒	Ⓐ	⑥	⚒	⚒	⚒	⚒	⚒	⑦	⑦	⑦	⑦	⑦	⑦	
0	**Inverness** d.	0453	0554	...	...	0709	0900	1057	1246	1427	...	...	1529	1714	1813	2004	2133	0959	1233	1529	1713	1800	2103	2
24	Nairn d.	0508	0609	...	...	0725	0916	1114	1301	1442	...	...	1546	1730	1828	2020	2148	1014	1248	1544	1729	1815	2118	2
40	Forres d.	0519	0620	...	...	0737	0927	1125	1312	1453	...	...	1557	1741	1839	2031	2158	1025	1259	1555	1740	1826	2129	2
59	**Elgin** d.	0533	0634	...	...	0752	0952	1141	1330	1509	...	...	1611	1759	1857	2047	2213	1039	1313	1609	1754	1841	2143	2
89	Keith d.	0554	0655	...	...	0813	1011	1202	1349	1530	...	...	1635	1820	1919	...	2234	1100	1334	1631	1815	...	2205	
109	Huntly d.	0609	0711	0746	...	0839	1026	1216	1403	1545	...	...	1650	1847	1942	...	2251	1120	1352	1646	1830	...	2221	
130	Insch d.	0624	0729	0802	...	0857	1048	1235	1419	1603	...	...	1706	1902	1958	...	2306	1136	1408	1702	1851	...	2237	
147	**Inverurie** d.	0637	0743	0816	...	0909	1100	1247	1431	1616	...	...	1719	1915	2010	...	2319	1148	1420	1714	1903	...	2249	
164	Dyce ✈ d.	0651	0759	0829	0907	0921	1113	1302	1443	1630	1639	1705	1735	1929	2024	...	2332	1201	1435	1728	1917	...	2301	
174	**Aberdeen** a.	0702	0811	0845	0918	0933	1125	1313	1455	1641	1650	1716	1746	1940	2035	...	2343	1212	1446	1739	1928	...	2313	

	⚒	⚒	⚒	⚒	⚒	⚒	⚒	⚒	⚒	⚒	Ⓐ	⑥	⑥	Ⓐ	⚒	⚒	⑥ a	⚒ c	Ⓐ b	⑦	⑦	⑦	⑦	
Aberdeen d.	...	...	0614	0715	0819	0849	1013	1200	1338	1527	1619	1644	1721	1726	1822	2014	2156	2156	2156	1000	1300	1522	1801	2
Dyce ✈ d.	...	...	0623	0727	0830	0857	1022	1209	1347	1537	1629	1652	1732	1735	1831	2024	2205	2205	2205	1009	1309	1531	1810	2
Inverurie d.	...	...	0639	0743	0843	...	1034	1221	1359	1549	...	...	1750	1751	1844	2037	2217	2217	2217	1021	1321	1543	1822	2
Insch d.	...	...	0651	0755	0858	...	1047	1234	1412	1602	...	...	1803	1803	1857	2049	2229	2229	2229	1034	1334	1556	1835	2
Huntly d.	...	...	0713	0812	0914	...	1103	1250	1428	1618	...	...	1820	1820	1913	2107	2249	2250	2255	1050	1351	1612	1858	2
Keith d.	...	...	0727	0826	0928	...	1118	1305	1443	1640	...	...	1834	1834	1928	2121	2304	2304	2309	1108	1406	1635	1913	2
Elgin d.	0658	0723	0753	0847	0950	...	1140	1329	1508	1702	...	...	1857	1857	1950	2142	2325	2325	2330	1129	1427	1656	1935	2
Forres d.	0711	0743	0806	0902	1004	...	1153	1342	1522	1716	...	...	1913	1911	2003	2205	2338	2339	2344	1142	1440	1710	1949	2
Nairn d.	0727	0754	0817	0918	1015	...	1204	1353	1545	1731	...	...	1924	1922	2021	2216	2349	2350	2355	1153	1451	1730	2000	2
Inverness a.	0745	0812	0835	0936	1033	...	1222	1414	1603	1749	...	...	1942	1940	2039	2234	0007	0008	0013	1211	1509	1749	2018	2

a – May 16 - Aug. 5. b – May 21 - Aug. 6. c – From Aug. 8.

Other trains **Inverurie - Dyce - Aberdeen**: On ⚒ at 0713, 0815⑥, 0846Ⓐ, 1038, 1133, 1333, 1524, 1638⑥, 1647Ⓐ, 1751, 1845, 1946, 2124; On ⑦ at 1102, 1255, 1458, 1620, 1730, 2

Other trains **Aberdeen - Dyce - Inverurie**: On ⚒ at 0750, 0958, 1103, 1250, 1457, 1552, 1652Ⓐ, 1754, 1912, 2055, 2250; On ⑦ at 1035, 1225, 1426, 1550, 1648, 2035.

226 INVERNESS - THURSO, WICK and KYLE OF LOCHALSH

2nd class

INVERNESS - THURSO and WICK

🍷 on most Wick trains

km		⚒	⚒	⚒	⚒	⑦	⚒
0	**Inverness** ‡ d.	0702	1038	1400	1712	1754	1828
16	Beauly ‡ d.	0717	1053	1415	1727	1809	1843
21	Muir of Ord ‡ d.	0725	1059	1423	1733	1815	1849
30	Dingwall ‡ d.	0740	1112	1437	1747	1831	1905
51	Invergordon ‡ d.	0758	1130	1454	1804	1848	1926
71	Tain ‡ d.	0817	1149	1513	1824	1907	1945
93	Ardgay ‡ d.	0833	1205	1529	1839	1923	2001
108	Lairg d.	0853	1221	1545	...	1942	2017
136	Golspie d.	0918	1246	1610	...	2007	2042
146	Brora d.	0929	1257	1621	...	2018	2053
163	Helmsdale d.	0947	1312	1636	...	2033	2108
201	Forsinard d.	1021	1346	1712	...	2107	2142
237	Georgemas Jcn a.	1045	1410	1736	...	2131	2206
248	**Thurso** a.	1059	1424	1750	...	2145	2220
248	**Thurso** d.	1102	1427	1753	...	2148	2223
237	Georgemas Jcn d.	1114	1439	1805	...	2200	2235
260	**Wick** a.	1131	1456	1822	...	2217	2252

	⚒	⚒	⚒	⑦	⚒	⚒
Wick d.	...	0618	0802	1158	1234	1600
Georgemas Jcn d.	...	0636	0820	1216	1252	1618
Thurso a.	...	0646	0830	1226	1302	1628
Thurso d.	...	0650	0834	1230	1306	1632
Georgemas Jcn d.	...	0703	0847	1243	1319	1645
Forsinard d.	...	0727	0913	1309	1347	1711
Helmsdale d.	...	0800	0946	1342	1421	1744
Brora d.	...	0816	1002	1358	1436	1800
Golspie d.	...	0825	1012	1408	1447	1810
Lairg d.	0628	0852	1038	1433	1512	1836
Ardgay ‡ d.	0645	0907	1054	1449	1530	1852
Tain ‡ d.	0701	0923	1110	1505	1546	1908
Invergordon ‡ d.	0720	0942	1131	1524	1606	1925
Dingwall ‡ d.	0739	1001	1153	1543	1626	1941
Muir of Ord ‡ d.	0752	1014	1205	1555	1638	1952
Beauly ‡ d.	0758	1019	1210	1601	1644	|
Inverness ‡ a.	0813	1034	1225	1616	1701	2010

‡ – Additional trains operate Inverness - Invergordon (- Tain - Ardgay) and v.v.:
From Inverness at 0940⑦T, 1253⑦T, 1450⚒N, 1533⑦N, 2106T, 2333⑤⑥T.
From Invergordon at 0616⚒A, 1055⑦T, 1408⑦T, 1550⚒N, 1631⑦N, 1928⚒A, 2221⚒T, 2223⑦T.

A – From Ardgay.
N – From/to Invergordon.
T – From/to Tain.
a – May 15 - Sept.25.

INVERNESS - KYLE OF LOCHALSH

km		⚒	⚒	⑦	⚒	⚒	⚒	
0	**Inverness** d.	0855	1100	1059	1142	1335	1754	1
16	Beauly d.	0910	1115	1115	1157	1350	1809	1
21	Muir of Ord d.	0916	1121	1121	1206	1356	1815	1
30	Dingwall d.	0929	1132	1134	1218	1411	1829	1
49	Garve d.	0952	1155	1158	...	1433	1853	1
75	Achnasheen d.	1018	1221	1229	...	1500	1920	1
104	Strathcarron d.	1048	1253	1258	...	1530	1949	1
116	Stromeferry d.	1105	1310	1315	...	1547	2006	2
124	Plockton d.	1117	1322	1327	...	1559	2018	2
133	**Kyle of Lochalsh** a.	1130	1335	1340	...	1612	2031	2

	⚒	⑦a	⚒	⚒	⚒	⑦	
Kyle of Lochalsh d.	0612	1020	...	1208	1346	1512	1
Plockton d.	0628	1033	...	1221	1359	1525	1
Stromeferry d.	0640	1045	...	1233	1411	1537	1
Strathcarron d.	0659	1103	...	1252	1430	1556	1
Achnasheen d.	0727	1131	...	1320	1501	1624	1
Garve d.	0754	1157	...	1347	1527	1651	1
Dingwall d.	0817	1220	1245	1410	1550	1714	1
Muir of Ord d.	0830	1232	1258	1422	1603	1726	1
Beauly d.	0835	1237	1303	1427	1608	1732	1
Inverness a.	0850	1252	1318	1442	1623	1747	2

227 🚌 INVERNESS - ULLAPOOL - STORNOWAY

May 23 - October 2, 20

	①-⑥ 🚌	①-⑥ ⛴	⑦a 🚌	⑦a ⛴	①-⑤ 🚌	①-⑤ ⛴	⑦b 🚌	⑦a 🚌	⑦ ⛴	⑥ 🚌	⑥ ⛴
Inverness d.	0810	...	0910	...	1500	...	1540	1610	...	1640	...
Garve d.	0844	...	0944	...	1534	...	1614	1644	...	1714	...
Ullapool a.	0930	...	1030	...	1620	...	1700	1730	...	1800	...
Ullapool d.	...	1030	...	1130	...	1730	...	...	1830	...	1900
Stornoway a.	...	1300	...	1400	...	2000	...	...	2100	...	2130

	①-⑥ ⛴	①-⑥ 🚌	⑦a ⛴	⑦a 🚌	①-⑤ ⛴	①-⑤ 🚌	⑦b ⛴	⑦b 🚌	⑦a ⛴	⑦a 🚌	⑥ ⛴	(
Stornoway d.	0700	...	0800	...	1400	...	1430	...	1500	...	1530	
Ullapool a.	0930	...	1030	...	1630	...	1700	...	1730	...	1800	
Ullapool d.	...	0950	...	1050	...	1650	...	1720	...	1750	...	18
Garve d.	...	1032	...	1132	...	1737	...	1802	...	1832	...	19
Inverness a.	...	1110	...	1210	...	1810	...	1840	...	1910	...	19

a – June 26 - Sept. 4. b – May 29 - June 19 and Sept. 11 - Oct. 2.
☛ Latest passenger check-in for ⛴ is 30 minutes before departure.

Operators: 🚌 Scottish Citylink (service **961**). www.citylink.co.uk. ✆ (0)871 266 3333.
⛴ Caledonian MacBrayne. www.calmac.co.uk. ✆ (0)800 066 5000.

228 🚌 INVERNESS - FORT WILLIAM - OBAN

Valid May 23 - October 2, 20

Service number	19	19	915	919	919	919	919	919	19	19
	①-⑤	⑥		⑦	①-⑥	①-⑥	①-⑥		①-⑥	①-⑥
Inverness bus station d.	0520	0530	...	1045	1115	1245	1445	1645	1830	2015
Fort Augustus d.	0618	0628	...	1143	1218	1343	1543	1743	1931	2116
Invergarry Jct. bus bay A82 d.	0628j	0638j	0948	1153	1233	1353	1553	1753	1943j	2128j
Fort William bus station a.	0710	0720	1030	1235	1315	1435	1635	1835	2020	2205
Service number			918			918		918		
Fort William bus station d.	...	...	1100	...	...	1500	...	1900		
Ballachulish Tourist Office d.	...	...	1127	...	...	1527	...	1927		
Oban Station Road a.	...	...	1227	...	...	1627	...	2027		

Service number	19	919	918	919	919	918	19	19	19C	918	
	①-⑥	①-⑥		⑦			⑥	⑦	①-⑥		①
Oban Station Road d.	...	...	0840	...	...	1240	...	...	...	1640	
Ballachulish Tourist Office d.	...	...	0939	...	...	1339	...	...	...	1739	
Fort William bus station a.	...	...	1008	...	...	1408	...	...	...	1808	
Service number			919 ①-⑥			919 ①-⑥				915	
Fort William bus station d.	0720t	0900	1030	1045	1215	1415	1543	1645	1740	1840	20
Invergarry Jct. bus bay A82 d.	0757t	0937	1108	1123	1253	1453	1620	1723	1831	1919	21
Fort Augustus d.	0809t	0949	1118	1133	1303	1503	1632	1733	1843	...	21
Inverness bus station a.	0920	1050	1216	1231	1401	1601	1733	1831	1944	...	22

r – Departs 1543 on non school days (Service **19**).
t – On ⑥ departs 10 mins later.
j – Picks up on A87 at Invergarry Hotel.

Operator: Scottish Citylink. www.citylink.co.uk. ✆ (0)871 266 3333.

229 ISLE OF MAN RAILWAYS

2016 service ✆ +44 (0)1624 6633

Please confirm all journeys locally as the exact service available may vary from that shown below

km	*Manx Electric Railway*	A	A	A	A	A	A		
0	**Douglas** Derby Castle ‡ d.	0940	1040	1140	1240	1410	1510	...	...
4	Groudle d.	0952	1052	1152	1252	1422	1522	...	...
11	Laxey d.	1010	1110	1210	1310	1440	1540	...	...
29	**Ramsey** a.	1055	1155	1255	1355	1525	1625	...	...

	A	A	A	A	A	A		
Ramsey d.	1110	1210	1340	1440	1540	1640	...	...
Laxey d.	1155	1255	1425	1525	1625	1725	...	...
Groudle d.	1213	1313	1443	1543	1643	1743	...	...
Douglas Derby Castle ‡ a.	1225	1325	1455	1555	1655	1755	...	...

km	*Snaefell Mountain Railway*	B	B	B	B	B	B	B	
0	**Laxey** d.	1015	1115	1215	1315	1400	1455	1545	...
8	**Summit** a.	1045	1145	1245	1345	1430	1525	1615	...

	B	B	B	B	B	B	B	
Summit d.	1120	1225	1325	1425	1510	1605	1655	...
Laxey a.	1150	1255	1355	1455	1540	1635	1725	...

km	*Isle of Man Steam Railway*	C	C	C	C			
0	**Douglas** Railway Station ‡ d.	0950	1150	1350	1550	...	...	...
9	Santon d.	1011	1211	1411	1611	...	...	...
16	Castletown d.	1027	1227	1427	1627	...	...	...
25	**Port Erin** a.	1050	1250	1450	1650	...	...	...

	C	C	C	C			
Port Erin d.	1000	1200	1400	1600	...	...	...
Castletown d.	1027	1227	1427	1627	...	...	...
Santon d.	1047	1247	1447	1647	...	...	...
Douglas Railway Station ‡ a.	1105	1305	1505	1705	...	...	...

A – Mar. 18 - Sept. 30 (also ⑥⑦ in Oct.). Minimum service shown. Additional services operate on most dates. A reduced service operates on ②③④ in Oct.
B – Mar. 24 - Oct. 30 (not Apr. 11, 12, 13, 18, 19, 20, 25, 26, 27, May 3, 4, 10, 11, Oct. 3, 7, 10, 14, 17, 21). Minimum service shown. Additional services operate on most dates June - Septemb
C – Mar. 5 - Nov. 6. **Does not run every day**. Enhanced services with different timetables operate on most ④⑥⑦ in July and ④⑤⑥⑦ in August and on certain other dates.
‡ – 🚌 services **23, 24, 25, 26** connect Derby Castle and the Steam Railway Station.

IRELAND

SEE MAP PAGE 92

:ors: Iarnród Éireann (**IÉ**), www.irishrail.ie Northern Ireland Railways (**NIR**), www.translink.co.uk Bus Éireann, www.buseireann.ie Ulsterbus, www.translink.co.uk and Dublin Area Rapid Transit (**DART**), www.irishrail.ie Most cross-border services are jointly operated.

ıs: **Rail: NIR** services are valid until further notice. **IÉ** services are valid until further notice. **DART** services are valid until further notice.
Bus: Ulsterbus services are valid until further notice. **Bus Éireann** services are valid until further notice.

ervices: Except for *Enterprise* cross-border expresses (for details, see Table **230** below), **all trains** convey *Standard* (2nd) class seating. Most express trains in the Republic of Ireland, as noted in the tables, also have first class accommodation.
On public holiday dates in the **Republic of Ireland**, DART trains run as on Sundays; outer-suburban services to or from Drogheda and Dundalk do not run. Other services may be amended, though most main-line trains run normally. All services are subject to alteration during the Christmas, New Year and Easter holiday periods.

ervices: **Bus Éireann** and **Ulsterbus**: services are shown in detail where there is no comparable rail service; only basic information is given for other routes. Buses do not always call at the rail station, but usually stop nearby. Where possible the stop details are given in the station bank or as a footnote. On longer routes, a change of bus may be required – please check with the driver. At holiday times bus travellers should consult detailed leaflets or seek further information from the operator. **Bus Éireann**: ✆ +353 1 836 6111 (Dublin) or + 353 21 450 8188 (Cork); **Ulsterbus**: ✆ + 028 9033 3000 (Translink, Belfast). **Dublin Busáras** (bus station) is a 5 minute walk from Dublin Connolly station.

The Dublin Tram service (Luas) connects Dublin Connolly and Heuston stations at frequent intervals. Journey time is 14 minutes, depending on traffic conditions. See Dublin City Plan on page 29.

IÉ BELFAST - DUNDALK - DUBLIN 230

Enterprise express trains (***E***) convey Standard (2nd) class and Premium (1st) class seating, 🍸 (Café Bar and trolley service) and ✕ (at-seat meal service in Premium)

	Ⓐ	Ⓐ	⑥	Ⓐ	⚒	⚒	⑥	⚒	⚒	⚒	⚒	⚒	⚒	⚒	⚒	⚒	⚒	⚒	⚒	⑤	⑥	Ⓐ	⚒	⚒	⑥	Ⓐ
						⇊			***E***				***E***			⇊		***E***					***E***			
Belfast Central § d.	...	...	...	...	...	0650	...	0750x	0800	...	...	1010t	1035	...	1210t	1235	1340t	1405	...	...	1540t	1601t	1605	...	1659	1709
Lisburn § d.	...	...	...	...	...	|	...	0801	|	...	...	1032	1049	...	1232	1249	1402	1420	...	...	1602	1612	1620	...	1732	1732
Portadown § d.	...	...	...	*0615*	...	0723	...	0826	0833	...	...	1058	1111	...	1258	1311	1428	1443	...	...	1628	1638	1643	...	1800	1805
Newry d.	...	...	...	0645	...	0744	...	━	0854	...	...	...	1132	...	...	1332	━	1504	...	...	━	━	1704	...	1824	1829
Dundalk d.	0545	0630	0705	0710	...	0802	0815	Ⓐ	0912	0955	1045	...	1150	1240	...	1350	⚒	1522	...	1605	⚒	⚒	1722	...	...	...
Drogheda d.	0609	0654	0729	0736	0800	0824	0839	0835	|	1019	1109	...	1211	1305	...	1411	1417	1543	1605	1630	1700	1730	1743	1800	...	...
Balbriggan d.	0623	0711	0746	0754	0815	|	0854	0851	|	1034	1123	...	|	1320	...	|	1433	|	1621	|	1716	|	|	1815	...	...
Skerries d.	0629	0718	0752	0800	0821	|	0900	0857	|	1040	1129	...	|	1326	...	|	1439	|	1627	|	1722	|	|	1821	...	...
Malahide d.	|	0735	0809	|	0837	|	0915	0912	|	1057	1144	...	|	1341	...	|	1454	|	1642	|	1737	|	|	1838	...	...
Dublin Connolly a.	0659	0758	0830	0835	0858	0904	0931	0930	1000	1115	1200	...	1244	1400	...	1444	1515	1617	1704	1714	1758	1813	1815	1857	...	...

	Ⓐ	⚒	⚒	⚒	⚒	⑦	⑦	⑦	⑦	⑦	⑦
		⇊			w		***E***	⇊	***E***	***E***	***E***
st Central § d.	1801t	1805	1940t	...	2115	...	0900	1105	1305	1605	1905
n § d.	1812	1820	2002	...	|	...	0915	*1032*	*1232*	*1532*	*1832*
lown § d.	1838	1843	2028	...	2144	...	0942	1139	1339	1639	1939
d.	━	1904	━	...	2203	...	1003	1201	1401	1701	2001
alk d.	⚒	1922	⚒	...	2217	0920	1021	1219	1419	1719	2019
eda d.	1850	1943	2005	2205	2236	0945	1042	1241	1441	1740	2041
ggan d.	1905	|	2021	2220	|	1000	|	|	|	|	|
es d.	1911	|	2027	2226	|	1006	|	|	|	|	|
ide d.	1926	|	2042	2241	|	1021	|	|	|	|	|
n Connolly a.	1945	2015	2100	2301	2312	1041	1120	1315	1515	1815	2115

	Ⓐ	⑥	Ⓐ	⚒	⚒	⚒	⚒	⚒	⚒	⚒	⚒	⚒
				E	y	⇊			***E***			***E***
Dublin Connolly d.	...	...	0715	0735	0847	0935	1006	1035	1100	1104	1236	1320
Malahide d.	...	...	0730	|	0907	|	1025	1053	|	1126	1252	|
Skerries d.	...	...	0744	|	0922	|	1040	1108	|	1140	1307	|
Balbriggan d.	...	...	0750	|	0927	|	1045	1113	|	1146	1312	|
Drogheda d.	...	...	0804	0809	0945	1008	1103	1130	1138	1203	1329	1352
Dundalk d.	...	...	...	0832	1010	1032	━	...	1200	1227	━	1417
Newry d.	0655	0720	...	0850	...	1050	⚒	...	1218	...	⚒	1437
Portadown § d.	0720	0745	....	0911	...	1111	1115	...	1240	...	1245	1458
Lisburn § a.	0745	0808	...	*0938*	...	1134	1138	...	|	...	1308	1522
Belfast Central § a.	0806	0840	...	0945	...	1147	1159t	...	1315	...	1329t	1535

	⚒	⑤	⚒	⚒	⚒	⚒	⚒	⚒	Ⓐ	Ⓐ	⑥	⚒	⚒	⚒	⚒	⚒	⚒	⚒	⚒	Ⓐ	⚒	⑦	⑦	⑦	⑦	⑦	⑦
			⇊			***E***								***E***			⇊					***E***	***E***	⇊	***E***	***E***	
n Connolly d.	1336	1445	1520	1550	1621	1650	1651	...	...	1721	1721	1802	1840	1900	1920	2020	2050	...	2137	2237	2337	1000	1200	1400	1600	1900	2122
ide d.	1354	|	|	1609	1639	|	1712	...	...	|	1742	1821	|	|	1939	2038	|	...	2155	2255	2356	|	|	|	|	|	2140
es d.	1408	|	|	1623	1654	|	1726	...	...	1751	1757	1836	1906	|	1953	2053	|	...	2209	2309	0010	|	|	|	|	|	2155
ggan d.	1414	|	|	1629	1659	|	1732	...	...	1756	1802	1847	1912	|	1959	2058	|	...	2215	2315	0016	|	|	|	|	|	2200
eda d.	1431	1527	1552g	1648	1716	|	1749	...	...	1813	1819	1904	1927	1934	2016	2115	2122	...	2231	2332	0032	1032	1232	1432	1632	1932	2220
alk d.	...	1552	1614g	━	━	1745	━	...	...	1837	1845	1928f	...	1955	━	...	2144	...	2256e	2356	*0059*	1055	1255	1455	1655	1955	2243
d.	...	...	1632g	Ⓐ	⑥	1805	⚒	1850	1950	...	...	...	...	2011	⚒	...	2202	...	...	...	...	1113	1313	1513	1713	2013	...
lown § d.	...	...	1653g	1705	1715	1828	1845	1915	2015	...	...	...	...	2031	2045	...	2223	2225	...	...	...	1135	1335	1535	1735	2035	...
n § a.	...	...	|	1730	1738	1852	1908	1938	2038	...	...	...	...	2052	2108	...	|	2248	...	...	...	*1208*	*1408*	*1608*	*1808*	*2108*	...
st Central § a.	...	...	1729j	1739t	1759t	1905	1929t	2010	2110	...	...	...	...	2105	2129t	...	2258	2309t	...	...	...	1208	1408	1608	1808	2108	...

1000 on ⑥.
⑤ only.
Not ⑥.
g – 2–3 minutes later on ⑥.
j – 1727 on ⑥.
t – Belfast **Great Victoria Street**.
w – Conveys 1st and 2nd class.
x – Belfast **Great Victoria Street**. On ⑥ depart 0740.
y – From Rosslare Europort on Ⓐ; from Gorey on ⑥; see table **237**.
⇊ – [2] 🍸 Belfast - Dublin and v.v.
§ – Other local trains run Belfast - Lisburn - Portadown and v.v.

BELFAST - LONDONDERRY and PORTRUSH 231

		Ⓐ	⚒	⚒		⚒	⚒	⚒	⚒			Ⓐ	Ⓐ			⑦	⑦	⑦	⑦	⑦	⑦	⑦		
Belfast GVSt. ★ d.	...	0605	0710	0810	and at the	1910	2010	2110	2240	...		...	...	...	...	0920	1120	1320	1520	1720	1920	2120	...	...
Belfast Central d.	...	0615	0720	0820	same	1920	2020	2120	2250	...		1646	1746	...	...	0930	1130	1330	1530	1730	1930	2130	...	...
Antrim d.	...	0643	0747	0847	minutes	1947	2047	2147	2317	...	addi-	1714	1814	...	...	0957	1157	1357	1557	1757	1957	2157	...	...
Ballymena d.	...	0657	0803	0903	past each	2003	2103	2203	2330	...	tional	1728	1828	...	...	1011	1211	1411	1611	1811	2011	2211	...	...
Coleraine d.	...	0743	0843	0943	hour	2043	2143	2243	0005	...	trains	1810	1910	...	...	1052	1252	1452	1652	1852	2052	2247	...	...
Portrush a.	...	|	|	0955	until	|	2155	|	...	...	→	...	...	...	...	|	|	|	|	|	|	...	...	...
Londonderry a.	...	0825	0925	...		2125	...	2325	...	...		...	...	...	...	1134	1334	1534	1734	1934	2134	...	...	...

	Ⓐ	Ⓐ	⑥	Ⓐ	⑥	Ⓐ	Ⓐ	⑥	⚒	⚒		⚒	⚒	⚒	Ⓐ			⑦	⑦	⑦	⑦	⑦	⑦	⑦	
onderry d.	...	...	...	0605	0635	...	0713	0733	...	0933	and at the	...	1933	...	2133	...	...	...	0942	1142	1342	1542	1742	1942	...
rtrush d.	...	0605	0610	|	|	0705	|	|	0905	|	same	1905	|	2105	|	...	...	...	|	|	|	|	|	|	...
raine d.	0550	0620	0623	0652	0721	0719	0819	0819	0919	1019	minutes	1919	2019	2119	2219	...	...	0828	1028	1228	1428	1628	1828	2028	...
nena d.	0626	0700	0700	0730	0800	0800	0900	0900	1000	1100	past each	2000	2100	2200	2300	...	...	0904	1104	1304	1504	1704	1904	2104	...
n d.	0644	0714	0714	0747	0814	0814	0914	0914	1014	1114	hour	2014	2114	2214	2316	...	...	0918	1118	1318	1518	1718	1918	2118	...
st Central a.	0712	0739	0739	0816	0839	0839	0939	0939	1039	1139	until	2039	2139	2239	2341	...	...	0943	1143	1343	1543	1743	1943	2143	...
st GVSt. ★ a.	0722	0750	0750	0825	0850	0851	0950	0950	1050	1150		2050	2150	2250	...	...	...	0953	1153	1353	1553	1753	1953	2153	...

	Ⓐ	⑥	⚒	⚒	⚒	⚒		⚒	⚒			⑦	⑦	⑦	⑦	⑦	⑦	⑦					
Coleraine d.	0550	0555	0645	0745	0845	0943	and at the same minutes past	2143	2245	...	...	0950	1055	1255	1455	1655	1855	2055	...	...	...	...	...
Portrush a.	0600	0605	0657	0757	0857	0955	each hour	2155	2257	...	...	1002	1107	1307	1507	1707	1907	2107	...	...	...	...	...

	Ⓐ	⑥	⑥	Ⓐ	⚒	⚒		⚒	⚒	Ⓐ	⑥	Ⓐ	⑥			⑦	⑦	⑦	⑦	⑦	⑦	⑦		
ush d.	0605	0610	0703	0705	0803	0905	and at the same minutes past	2003	2105	2203	2223	2303	2305	...	...	1010	1210	1410	1610	1810	2010	2110	...	...
aine a.	0616	0621	0715	0716	0815	0916	each hour	2015	2116	2214	2235	2315	2317	...	...	1022	1222	1422	1622	1822	2022	2122	...	...

Belfast GVSt. (Belfast Great Victoria St.) is the nearest station to Belfast City Centre and the Europa Buscentre is adjacent.

rbus **212** express 🚌 service, Belfast - Londonderry. Journey time: 1 hour 40 minutes.
0630, 0745, 0830, 0900 and every 30 minutes until 1430, 1500 then 1520, 1540, 1600, 1620, 1640, 1700, 1720, 1740, 1800, 1830, 1900, 1930, 2030, 2130, 2300.
0645, 0930, 1030, 1130, 1230, 1330, 1400 and every 30 minutes to 1800, 1830 then 1930, 2030, 2130, 2300.
0830, 1000, 1130, 1330, 1430, 1600, 1730, 1930, 2030, 2130, 2215.

Ulsterbus 212 express 🚌 service, Londonderry - Belfast. Journey time: 1 hour 45 minutes.
Ⓐ: 0520, 0540, 0600, 0620, 0640, 0700, 0720, 0740, 0800, 0830 and every 30 minutes until 1630, 1700 then 1800, 1930, 2100.
⑥: 0700, 0800 and every 30 minutes to 1230, 1300 then 1400, 1500, 1600, 1700, 1800, 1930, 2100.
⑦: 0800, 0900, 1030, 1200, 1330, 1500, 1600, 1700, 1800, 1900.

232 BELFAST - ENNISKILLEN and ARMAGH

Ulsterbus 25

From Belfast ★ to Enniskillen (Bus Stn) (journey time 2 hours 15 mins)

Ⓐ: 0805, 0905 and hourly until 1905, 2005.
⑥: 1005, 1205, 1405, 1505, 1605, 1805, 2005.
⑦: 1605, 2005.

From Enniskillen (Bus Stn) to Belfast ★

Ⓐ: 0725, 0825, and hourly until 1625, 1725, 1825 ◧.
⑥: 0725, 0925, 1125, 1225, 1325, 1525, 1725.
⑦: 1225, 1525, 1725.

From Belfast ★ to Armagh (Bus Stn) (journey time 1 hour 25 mins)

Ⓐ: 0800, 0945, 1045, 1145, 1245, 1345, 1445, 1645, 1715, 1745, 1845, 1945, 2115.
⑥: 1045, 1245, 1445, 1745, 1845, 2005.
⑦: 1335, 1735, 2015, 2200.

From Armagh (Bus Stn) to Belfast ★

Ⓐ: 0630, 0715, 0805, 0905, 1005, 1105, 1205, 1305, 1505, 1605, 1705, 1805.
⑥: 0730, 0905, 1105, 1305, 1605, 1705.
⑦: 1210, 1410, 1610, 1830, 2015.

Buses call at Portadown (Market Street) 40 - 75 minutes from Belfast and Portadown (Norther[n] 20–30 minutes from Armagh (Bus Stn).

◧ – Change at Dungannon; arrive Europa Buscentre 2140. ★ – Europa Buscentre / Great Victoria St. Rail Station.

233 BELFAST - LARNE and BANGOR

From Belfast Central – Ⓐ: 0550, 0655, 0745 **H**, 0855 **H**, and hourly until 1355 **H**, 1455, 1523 **H**, 1555 **H**, 1644, 1714 **H**, 1744, 1825, 1925 **H**, 2025 **H**, 2125 **H**, 2225 **H**, 2325 **H**.
⑥: 0725 **H**, 0825 **H**, and hourly until 2225 **H**, 2325 **H**. ⑦: 0955 **H**, 1155 **H**, 1355 **H**, 1555 **H**, 1755 **H**, 1955 **H**, 2155 **H**.

From Larne Town – Ⓐ: 0558 **S**, 0628 **S**, 0653, 0735 **S**, 0800, 0858 **S**, 0958 **S** and hourly until 1458 **S**, 1553, 1625 **S**, 1706 **S**, 1736, 1828, 1928 **S**, 2028 **S**, 2128 **S**, 2228 **S**.
⑥: 0600 **S**, 0628 **S**, 0728 **S**, 0828 **S** and hourly until 2028 **S**, 2128 **S**, 2228 **S**. ⑦: 0858 **S**, 1058 **S**, 1258 **S**, 1458 **S**, 1658 **S**, 1858 **S**, 2058 **S**.

Trains call at: Carrickfergus 27 - 29 minutes from Belfast and 28 - 31 minutes from Larne and Whitehead 38 - 40 minutes from Belfast, 18 - 21 minutes from Larne.

Trains marked **H** arrive Larne **Harbour** 4 minutes after Larne **Town**. Trains marked **S** depart Larne **Harbour** 3 minutes before Larne **Town**. Journey time Belfast Central - Larne Harbour 57 - 6[…]

A frequent train service operates between Belfast Central and Bangor. Journey time 30–31 minutes. 20 km. Approximate timings from Belfast ①–⑥: 2 per hour at xx12 and xx42 minutes pa[…] hour, ⑦: xx42. Approximate timings from Bangor ①–⑥: 2 per hour at xx27 and xx57 minutes past each hour, ⑦: xx57.

234 DUBLIN - LONDONDERRY

Bus Éireann 33 / Ulsterbus

		A				A				
Dublin Busáras d.	0600	0800	1000	...	1230	1630	1815	...	2200	...
Dublin Airport ✈ △ d.	0620	0820	1020	...	1250	1650	1835	...	2220	...
Monaghan d.	0805	1005	1205	...	1435	1835	2020	...	2340	...
Omagh ▽ a.	0900	1100	1300	...	1530	1930	2115	...	0030	...
Strabane ▽ a.	0930	1130	1330	...	1600	2000	2145	...	0055	...
Londonderry a.	1000	1200	1400	...	1630	2030	2215	...	0120	...

									A
Londonderry d.	0415	...	0700	...	1130	1330	...	1630	2200
Strabane △ d.	0440	...	0730	...	1200	1400	...	1700	2230
Omagh △ d.	0505	...	0800	...	1230	1430	...	1730	2255
Monaghan d.	0600	...	0905	...	1335	1535	...	1835	0000
Dublin Airport ✈ ▽ a.	0745	...	1040	...	1510	1710	...	2010	0130
Dublin Busáras a.	0805	...	1100	...	1530	1730	...	2030	0150

A – May 31 - Sept. 19. △ – Buses call here to pick up only. ▽ – Buses call here to set down only. ☛ The calling point in each town is the bus station unless otherwise ind[icated].

234a DUBLIN - DONEGAL

Bus Éirea[nn]

								⑦				
Dublin Busáras d.	0730	0930	1130	1330	1530	1730	1930	2100	2200	0000	...	...
Dublin Airport ✈ △ d.	0750	0950	1150	1350	1550	1750	1950	|	2220	0020	...	...
Virginia d.	0855	1055	1255	1455	1655	1855	2055	|	2325	0125	...	...
Cavan d.	0925	1125	1325	1525	1725	1925	2125	2250	2350	0150	...	...
Enniskillen d.	1015	1215	1415	1615	1815	2015	2215	2335	0040	0240	...	...
Ballyshannon d.	1100	1300	1500	1700	1900	2100	2300	|	0125	0325	...	...
Donegal ⊡ a.	1120	1320	1520	1720	1920	2120	2320	0035	0145	0345	...	...

Donegal ⊡ d.	...	0100	...	0500	0700	0900	1100	1300	1500	1700	1900
Ballyshannon d.	...	0120	...	0520	0720	0920	1120	1320	1520	1720	1920
Enniskillen d.	...	0205	...	0605	0805	1005	1205	1405	1605	1805	2005
Cavan d.	...	0255	...	0655	0900	1100	1300	1500	1705	1900	2055
Virginia d.	...	0320	...	0725	0925	1125	1325	1525	1730	1925	2125
Dublin Airport ✈ ▽ a.	...	0445	...	0830	1030	1230	1430	1630	1835	2030	2230
Dublin Busáras a.	...	0505	...	0850	1050	1250	1450	1650	1855	2050	2250

● – Dublin **Busáras**. △ – Buses call here to pick up only. ▽ – Buses call here to set down only. ⊡ – Donegal **Abbey Hotel**.

235 LONDONDERRY - GALWAY and GALWAY - CORK

Bus Éireann 51, 64

	⚒									⑤⑦
Londonderry d.	...	...	...	0715	0915	1110	...	1530	1830	...
Letterkenny d.	...	...	...	0755	0957	1150	...	1610	1910	...
Donegal (Abbey Hotel) d.	...	0635	...	0840	1040	1240	...	1655	1955	...
Ballyshannon d.	...	0655	...	0900	1100	1300	...	1715	2015	...
Sligo d.	0600	0740	0800	1000	1200	1400	1600	1815	2105	2115
Ireland West Airport Knock d.	|	...	0905	1105	1305	1500	1705	|	...	|
Knock d.	0724	...	0924	1125	1324	1520	1725	1920	...	2230
Claremorris (Dalton St.) d.	|	...	|	1135	|	1530	1735	|	...	2240
Galway (Bus Station) ✣ a.	0900	...	1045	1240	1445	1635	1840	2040	...	2345

Galway (Bus Station) ✣ d.	...	...	0705	0805		1705	1805	1905	2005
Ennis d.	...	...	0820	0920		1820	1920	2020	2120
Shannon Airport ✈ d.	...	...	0850	0950	and	1850	1950	2050	2150
Limerick (Colbert Rail Station) a.	...	...	0920	1020	hourly	1920	2020	2120	2220
Limerick (Colbert Rail Station) d.	0725	0835	0935	1035	until	1935	2035	...	...
Mallow (Town Park) d.	0830	0940	1040	1140		2040	2140	...	...
Cork a.	0915	1025	1125	1225		2125	2225	...	...

Cork d.	...	...	0725	0825		1725	1825	1925
Mallow (Town Park) d.	...	...	0800	0900		1800	1900	2000
Limerick (Colbert Rail Station) a.	...	...	0910	1010	and	1910	2010	2110
Limerick (Colbert Rail Station) d.	0725	0825	0925	1025	hourly	1925	2025	...
Shannon Airport ✈ d.	0755	0855	0955	1055	until	1955	2055	...
Ennis d.	0825	0925	1025	1125		2025	2125	...
Galway (Bus Station) ✣ a.	0945	1045	1145	1245		2145	2245	...

	⚒	⚒		⚒					
Galway (Bus Station) ✣ d.	0600	...	0845	1030	...	1200	*1410*	1600	1810
Claremorris (Dalton St.) d.	0700	...	|	1135	...	1305	|	|	1911
Knock d.	0710	...	1005	1145	...	1315	*1530*	1725	1921
Ireland West Airport Knock d.	0730	...	1025	1205	...	1335	*1550*	1745	|
Sligo d.	0845	0855	1145	1310	1330	1500	1710	1905	2040
Ballyshannon d.	...	0945	1232	...	1417	1547	1757	1952	...
Donegal (Abbey Hotel) d.	...	1015	1252	...	1437	1607	1817	2012	...
Letterkenny d.	...	1110	1340	...	1525	1655	1905	2100	...
Londonderry a.	...	1145	1420	...	1605	1735	1945	2140	...

✣ – Change buses at Galway. Minimum connection time 45 minutes. ☛ The calling point in each town is the bus station unless otherwise indicated.

236 DUBLIN - SLIGO

km		⚒🍷		⚒🍷	⚒🍷	⚒🍷	⚒🍷	⚒🍷	Ⓐ	Ⓐ	⚒🍷		⑦🍷		⑦🍷		⑦🍷	⑦🍷	⑦🍷		⑦🍷	
0	**Dublin** Connolly d.	0800	...	1105	1305	1505	1600	1705	1715	1805	1905	...	0905	...	1305	...	1505	1600	1705	...	1905	...
26	Maynooth d.	0830	...	1136	1335	1535	1629	1734	1758	1835	1937	...	0932	...	1333	...	1534	1629	1733	...	1933	...
83	Mullingar d.	0910	...	1216	1416	1615	1715	1815	1844	1919	2023	...	1013	...	1413	...	1614	1714	1819	...	2016	...
125	**Longford** d.	0942	...	1247	1445	1646	1745	1846	1916	1950	2052	...	1043	...	1443	...	1644	1750	1849	...	2045	...
143	Dromod d.	1000	...	1259	1457	1658	1759	1901	...	...	2104	...	1056	...	1456	...	1656	1802	1904	...	2057	...
159	Carrick on Shannon d.	1016	...	1314	1513	1713	1815	1918	...	...	2121	...	1113	...	1512	...	1712	1817	1920	...	2114	...
173	Boyle d.	1028	...	1334	1534	1727	1834	1931	...	...	2133	...	1134	...	1534	...	1729	1836	1933	...	2127	...
219	**Sligo** a.	1109	...	1410	1610	1806	1909	2006	...	...	2209	...	1210	...	1610	...	1808	1910	2008	...	2204	...

	Ⓐ	Ⓐ	Ⓐ🍷	⚒🍷	⚒🍷	⚒🍷	⚒🍷	⚒🍷	⚒🍷				⑦🍷		⑦🍷		⑦🍷		⑦🍷		⑦🍷	
Sligo d.	...	...	0545	0700	0900	1100	1300	1500	1800	...	...	...	0900	...	1100	...	1300	...	1500	...	1630	...
Boyle d.	...	...	0617	0733	0933	1136	1333	1533	1834	...	...	...	0933	...	1133	...	1333	...	1533	...	1704	...
Carrick on Shannon d.	...	...	0628	0745	0945	1148	1346	1546	1846	...	...	...	0945	...	1145	...	1345	...	1545	...	1717	...
Dromod d.	...	...	0643	0800	1001	1202	1401	1601	1900	...	...	...	1000	...	1200	...	1400	...	1600	...	1732	...
Longford d.	0540	0615	0657	0815	1016	1217	1416	1616	1919	...	...	...	1015	...	1215	...	1415	...	1615	...	1748	...
Mullingar d.	0614	0649	0726	0845	1047	1253	1453	1652	1959	...	...	...	1051	...	1246	...	1452	...	1652	...	1819	...
Maynooth d.	0657	0730	0810	0933	1128	1334	1534	1733	2040	...	...	...	1131	...	1327	...	1533	...	1733	...	1900	...
Dublin Connolly a.	0736	0818	0847	1000	1158	1404	1604	1803	2108	...	...	...	1203	...	1355	...	1606	...	1800	...	1932	...

236a BALLYBROPHY - ROSCREA - LIMERICK

km		Ⓐ	⚒🍷	⚒		⚒h ◇✕	⚒	⑦ ◇🍷	⑦		
0	**Dublin** Heuston d.	...	0900	...	...	1800	...	1825	...	...	...
107	Ballybrophy d.	...	0958	1005	...	1854	1900	1933	1940	...	...
123	Roscrea d.	...	...	1025	...	...	1921	|	2001	...	...
154	Nenagh d.	0745	...	1105	...	...	2002	|	2040	...	...
199	**Limerick** Colbert a.	0845	...	1204	...	...	2100	2042	2139	...	...

	⚒	⚒h ◇✕		⚒	⚒h ◇✕	⑦	⑦🍷			
Limerick Colbert d.	0630	0740	...	1655	...	1725	1820	...	...	...
Nenagh d.	0739	|	...	1750	...	1822	|	...	...	...
Roscrea d.	0817	|	...	1828	...	1901	|	...	...	...
Ballybrophy d.	0841	0845	...	1851	1855	1924	1927	...	...	...
Dublin Heuston a.	...	0955	...	...	2000	...	2042	...	...	...

h – ✕ on Ⓐ, 🍷 [...]
◇ – Also conveys 1st class.

DUBLIN - ROSSLARE 237

	⚒		⚒ 🍷	Ⓐ	Ⓐ	⚒§ 🍷		⑦	⑦ 🍷	⑦§ 🍷	
Dublin Connolly ▲ d.	0940	...	1336	1637	1736	1838	...	1025	1345	1830	...
Dún Laoghaire ▲ d.	0958	...	1355	1658	1758	1857	...	1041	1402	1847	...
Bray ▲ d.	1017	...	1417	1717	1817	1917	...	1101	1423	1904	...
Wicklow d.	1040	...	1441	1742	1844	1942	...	1126	1446	1929	...
Arklow d.	1108	...	1510	1811	1916	2010	...	1154	1514	1957	...
Gorey d.	1121	...	1522	1824	1945	2023	...	1206	1527	2010	...
Enniscorthy d.	1142	...	1541	1844	2006	2042	...	1225	1546	2029	...
Wexford d.	1202	...	1604	1905	2027	2104	...	1248	1608	2051	...
Rosslare Strand d.	1219	...	1621	1919	...	2121	...	1304	1625	2108	...
Rosslare Europort a.	1226	...	1626	1925	...	2128	...	1310	1632	2115	...

	Ⓐ	Ⓐ y	⑥ y	⚒ 🍷		⚒ 🍷		⚒		⑦ 🍷	⑦ 🍷	⑦	
Rosslare Europort d.	...	0535	...	0720	...	1255	...	1835	...	0940	1420	1835	...
Rosslare Strand d.	...	0540	...	0724	...	1301	...	1841	...	0944	1426	1841	...
Wexford d.	...	0559	...	0743	...	1320	...	1900	...	1003	1445	1900	...
Enniscorthy d.	...	0623	...	0804	...	1341	...	1925	...	1024	1506	1922	...
Gorey d.	0555	0645	0645	0824	...	1401	...	1945	...	1044	1528	1942	...
Arklow d.	0608	0700	0700	0837	...	1413	...	2011	...	1057	1540	1958	...
Wicklow d.	0638	0733	0733	0904	...	1441	...	2038	...	1124	1608	2026	...
Bray ▲ d.	0704	0802	0802	0932	...	1503	...	2102	...	1147	1631	2050	...
Dún Laoghaire ▲ d.	0722	0820	0820	0950	...	1521	...	2122	...	1206	1648	2104	...
Dublin Connolly ▲ a.	0746	0846	0847	1015	...	1545	...	2144	...	1230	1710	2128	...

To Dundalk; see table **230**. § – Does not connect with Ferry: Rosslare - Fishguard. ▲ – Additional surburban trains (*DART*) run Howth - Dublin Connolly - Dún Laoghaire - Bray. Trains run every 10 - 15 minutes on ⚒, every 20 - 30 minutes on ⑦.

LIMERICK - WATERFORD 239

		⚒	⚒			⚒	⚒		
Limerick Colbert d.	...	0855	...	...	...	1745	...	...	...
Limerick Junction d.	...	0921	0945	...	...	1811	1840	...	...
Tipperary d.	...	...	0957	...	...	...	1852	...	...
Cahir d.	...	...	1020	...	...	...	1915	...	...
Clonmel d.	...	...	1037	...	...	...	1932	...	...
Carrick on Suir d.	...	...	1101	...	...	...	1956	...	...
Waterford a.	...	...	1126	...	...	...	2020	...	...

		⚒	⚒			⚒	⚒		
Waterford d.	...	0720	...	...	...	1625	...	...	...
Carrick on Suir d.	...	0745	...	...	...	1650	...	...	...
Clonmel d.	...	0808	...	...	...	1713	...	...	...
Cahir d.	...	0825	...	...	...	1730	...	...	...
Tipperary d.	...	0847	...	...	...	1751	...	...	...
Limerick Junction a.	...	0900	0940	...	...	1805	1834	...	...
Limerick Colbert a.	...	...	1014	...	...	...	1859	...	...

DUBLIN - GALWAY, BALLINA and WESTPORT 240

	⚒	⚒ 🍷	⚒ 🍷	⚒ 🍷	⚒ 🍷	⚒ 🍷	⚒ ◇🍷	⚒ 🍷	⚒ 🍷	⚒h ◇✕	⚒	⚒ ◇🍷	⚒ ◇🍷	⚒ ◇🍷	⚒ 🍷
Dublin Heuston 245 d.	...	0735	0735f	0925	1125	1245	1325	1445	1535	1630	1710	1730	1815	1830	1935
Kildare 245 d.	...	0801	0801f	|	|	|	|	|	|	1659	1739	|	|	|	|
Portarlington 245 d.	...	0814	0814f	1002	1201	1322	1402	1522	1611	|	1756	1811	|	1910	2011
Tullamore d.	...	0830	0830f	1018	1218	1338	1417	1540	1629	1726	1813	1829	1906	|	2030
Athlone d.	0730	0905	0908	1045	1242	1403	1448	1604	1658	1750	1848	1857	1927	1945	2053
Ballinasloe d.	0743	0919	|	1058	1257	|	1501	|	1711	1806	|	1913	|	2000	2108
Athenry 242 d.	0814	0946	|	1117	1318	|	1522	|	1733	1827	|	1932	|	2022	2129
Galway 242 a.	0830	1005	|	1140	1340	|	1540	|	1755	1845	|	1950	|	2040	2150
Roscommon d.	...	...	0931	▬	...	1429	▬	1628	▬	...	1935f	...	1952	▬	...
Castlerea d.	...	...	0946	...	...	1448	...	1647	...	...	1954f	...	2011	...	...
Ballyhaunis d.	...	...	1003	...	...	1502	...	1701	...	...	2008f	...	2025	...	...
Claremorris d.	...	...	1017	⚒	...	1516	⚒	1715	⚒	...	2021f	...	2039	⚒	...
Manulla Junction § d.	...	...	1031	1033	...	1529	1532	1728	1730	...	|	...	2052	2057	...
Ballina a.	...	...	|	1101	...	|	1600	|	1758	...	|	...	|	2125	
Castlebar d.	...	...	1037	...	...	1536	...	1735	...	...	2039f	...	2059	...	...
Westport a.	...	...	1055	...	...	1555	...	1755	...	...	2054f	...	2117	...	...

	⑦ 🍷	⑦	⑦ 🍷	⑦ ◇🍷	⑦ 🍷	⑦ 🍷	⑦ 🍷	⑦ ◇🍷	⑦ ◇🍷	⑦
Dublin Heuston 245 d.	0800	...	1135	1335	1430	1535	1635	1830	1845	2030
Kildare 245 d.	0827	...	1203	1405	|	|	|	1902	1916	|
Portarlington 245 d.	0840	...	1216	1419	1506	|	1714	1915	1929	2109
Tullamore d.	0856	...	1238	1440	1530	1632	1732	1933	1953	2125
Athlone d.	0920	0940	1304	1507	1600	1658	1803	2000	2019	2151
Ballinasloe d.	0936	|	1319	|	1615	|	1817	|	2033	2206
Athenry 242 d.	0959	|	1343	|	1639	|	1843	|	2054	2226
Galway 242 a.	1017	|	1400	|	1707	|	1904	|	2112	2245
Roscommon d.	...	1002	▬	1530	▬	1729	▬	2023	▬	...
Castlerea d.	...	1021	...	1550	...	1748	...	2043	...	...
Ballyhaunis d.	...	1034	...	1604	...	1802	...	2057	...	...
Claremorris d.	...	1048	⑦	1620	⑦	1822	⑦	2111	⑦	...
Manulla Junction § d.	...	1102	1105	1633	1637	1835	1837	2124	2128	...
Ballina a.	...	|	1133	|	1705	|	1905	|	2156	...
Castlebar d.	...	1109	...	1641	...	1843	...	2132	...	...
Westport a.	...	1130	...	1700	...	1900	...	2150	...	...

	Ⓐ	Ⓐ	Ⓐ 🍷	⚒ 🍷	⚒	⚒ ◇🍷	⚒	⚒ 🍷	⚒ 🍷	⚒	⚒ 🍷	⚒ 🍷	⚒	⚒ 🍷	⚒ ◇🍷	Ⓐ
Westport d.	...	...	0525	...	...	0715	...	0945	...	...	1310	...	...	1815	...	...
Castlebar d.	...	...	0537	...	...	0728	...	0957	...	...	1323	...	...	1827	...	...
Ballina d.	...	...	|	...	0705	|	0935	|	...	1300	|	...	1805	|	...	...
Manulla Junction § d.	...	...	|	...	0733	0736	1003	1005	...	1328	1330	...	1833	1835	...	...
Claremorris d.	...	...	0555	...	▬	0750	▬	1020	...	▬	1344	...	▬	1849	...	...
Ballyhaunis d.	...	...	0608	...	...	0804	...	1033	...	...	1357	...	...	1902	...	...
Castlerea d.	...	...	0621	...	⚒h	0818	⚒	1046	...	⚒	1410	...	⚒	1915	...	...
Roscommon d.	...	...	0639	...	◇✕	0838	🍷	1105	...	🍷	1432	...	◇🍷	1934	...	...
Galway 242 d.	...	0530	|	0630	0730	|	0930	|	1130	1330	|	1530	1720	|	1915	2215
Athenry 242 d.	...	0545	|	0644	0745	|	0944	|	1145	1347	|	1550	1736	|	1931	2230
Ballinasloe d.	...	0607	|	|	0805	|	1007	|	1205	1409	|	1615	1807	|	2001	2252
Athlone d.	0520	0625	0705j	0720	0823	0903	1023	1132	1222	1426	1458	1632	1823	2000	2019	2309
Tullamore d.	0543	0649	0727j	0742	0846	0929	1052	1157	1251	1450	1523	1705	1847	2029	2047	...
Portarlington 245 d.	0601	0707	0747j	|	0904	0947	1109	1222	1309	1509	1547	1731	1909	2049	2105	...
Kildare 245 d.	0615	0718	0800j	|	|	|	|	|	|	|	|	|	|	|	|	...
Dublin Heuston 245 a.	0700	0757	0830j	0840	0945	1030	1150	1305	1350	1550	1630	1810	1950	2130	2145	...

	⑦	⑦ 🍷	⑦ 🍷	⑦	⑦ ◇🍷	⑦	⑦ 🍷	⑦ 🍷	⑦	⑦ 🍷
Westport d.	...	0750	...	...	1315	...	1545	...	...	1745
Castlebar d.	...	0803	...	...	1328	...	1558	...	...	1758
Ballina d.	0740	|	...	1305	|	1535	|	...	1735	|
Manulla Junction § d.	0808	0811	...	1333	1336	1603	1606	...	1803	1806
Claremorris d.	▬	0825	...	▬	1350	▬	1620	...	▬	1820
Ballyhaunis d.	...	0839	...	...	1404	...	1634	...	...	1834
Castlerea d.	⑦	0853	...	⑦	1418	⑦	1648	...	⑦	1848
Roscommon d.	🍷	0913	...	🍷	1438	◇🍷	1708	...	🍷	1908
Galway 242 d.	0805	|	1100	1300	|	1505	|	1700	1800	|
Athenry 242 d.	0820	|	1117	1315	|	1520	|	1716	1815	|
Ballinasloe d.	0844	|	1139	1339	|	1542	|	1740	1840	|
Athlone d.	0902	0938	1157	1357	1505	1600	1740	1802	1900	1934
Tullamore d.	0931	1002	1220	1423	1531	1631	1807	1827	1931	2010
Portarlington 245 d.	0949	1020	1238	1441	1549	1653	1826	1845	1950	2028
Kildare 245 d.	1002	|	1253	|	|	1707	1839	1859	|	|
Dublin Heuston 245 a.	1034	1105	1325	1525	1630	1740	1910	1935	2030	2110

An additional journey runs on ⑦: Galway depart 1925, Athenry 1940, Ballinasloe 2000, arrive Athlone 2018. f – ⑤ only. h – ✕ on Ⓐ, 🍷 on ⑥. j – Also runs on ⑥. ◇ – Also conveys [1st class]. § – Passenger transfer point only.

DUBLIN - KILKENNY - WATERFORD 241

	⚒ 🍷	⚒ ◇🍷	⚒ 🍷	⚒ 🍷	⑤	⚒ 🍷	⚒ 🍷	⚒ ◇🍷	Ⓐ	⑦ 🍷	⑦ 🍷	⑦ ◇🍷	⑦ 🍷
Dublin H ◧ .. △ d.	0725	1015	1315	1510	1615	1640	1735	1835	2015	0910	1410	1745	1840
Kildare △ d.	0753	1042	|	1539	|	1717	1806	1905	2101	0940	1439	1814	1908
Athy d.	0813	1059	1358	1556	1702	1735	1825	1923	2116	0957	1458	1832	1927
Carlow d.	0827	1111	1412	1607	1714	1747	1837	1938	2128	1011	1510	1844	1939
Muine Bheag d.	0843	1122	1424	1619	|	1758	1848	1949	...	1025	1521	1858	1951
Kilkenny a.	0901	1140	1441	1636	|	1817	1906	2008	...	1043	1541	1917	2009
Kilkenny d.	0905	1145	1446	1640	|	1821	1910	2013	...	1047	1546	1921	2013
Thomastown d.	0916	1155	1456	1651	|	1831	1921	2023	...	1058	1556	1932	2024
Waterford a.	0940	1220	1525	1715	1810	1900	1946	2048	...	1120	1620	1956	2050

	Ⓐ	⚒ ◇🍷	⚒ 🍷	⚒ 🍷	⚒ 🍷	⚒ 🍷	⚒ ◇🍷	⑤⑥	⚒ 🍷	Ⓐ	⑦ ◇🍷	⑦ 🍷	⑦ 🍷	⑦ 🍷
Waterford d.	...	0605	0710	0750	1100	1305	1450	1600	1825	...	0905	1240	1510	1805
Thomastown d.	...	0624	|	0809	1119	1324	1511	|	1846	...	0924	1259	1529	1824
Kilkenny a.	...	0639	|	0824	1134	1339	1525	|	1900	...	0939	1314	1545	1839
Kilkenny d.	...	0642	|	0828	1141	1343	1530	|	1902	...	0943	1318	1549	1843
Muine Bheag d.	...	0656	|	0846	1155	1357	1545	|	1921	...	0957	1331	1603	1857
Carlow d.	0630	0708	0759	0858	1207	1411	1609	1649	1935	2135	1010	1343	1614	1908
Athy d.	0641	0719	0812	0910	1219	1423	1621	1702	1949	2145	1024	1355	1626	1926
Kildare △ d.	0658	0737	|	0928	1237	1441	1635	|	2009	2200	1042	1416	1644	1945
Dublin H ◧ .. △ a.	0740	0811	0901	1000	1310	1515	1706	1750	2040	2245	1116	1450	1720	2020

◇ – Also conveys [1st class]. ◧ – Full name is **Dublin Heuston**. △ – For additional trains Dublin - Kildare and v.v, see Tables **240**, **245**.

LIMERICK JUNCTION - LIMERICK - GALWAY 242

	⚒	⚒		⚒	⚒	⚒		⑦	⑦	⑦	⑦
Limerick Jct 243 d.	...	0838	...	1340	...	...	...	...	1140	...	...
Limerick ¶ 245 d.	0555	0920	...	1420	1800	1945	...	0900	1220	1555	1815
Ennis 245 d.	0649x	0958	...	1458	1900	2025	...	0940	1304	1635	1857
Gort d.	0712	1020	...	1520	1925	2047	...	1002	1326	1701	1924
Athenry 240 d.	0747	1055	...	1553	1957	2118	...	1033	1357	1732	1955
Galway 240 a.	0805	1113	...	1610	2016	2139	...	1052	1415	1750	2015

	⚒	⚒		⚒	⚒	⚒	⚒	⑦	⑦	⑦	⑦
Galway 240 d.	0620	1030	...	1345	1745	1835	...	0830	1155	1610	1830
Athenry 240 d.	0639	1048	...	1406	1811	1859	...	0850	1215	1633	1851
Gort d.	0716	1118	...	1432	1836	1924	...	0916	1241	1701	1921
Ennis 245 d.	0745	1141	...	1500	1859	1946	2110	0938	1303	1723	1943
Limerick ¶ 245 a.	0825	1220	...	1539	1937	...	2149	1019	1342	1803	2021
Limerick Jct 243 a.	...	...	...	1611	2008	...	...	...	1415	...	...

Arrive 0634. ¶ – Limerick Colbert.

LIMERICK JUNCTION - LIMERICK 243

Shuttle service connecting with main-line trains. *35 km*. Journey time : 25 - 40 minutes. For through services to or from Dublin Heuston see Table **245**.

Limerick Junction ⚒: 0807, 0838, 0940, 1040, 1140, 1240, 1340, 1440, 1540, 1621, 1740, 1813, 1834, 1938, 2044, 2238.
⑦: 1013, 1140, 1335, 1419, 1540, 1618, 1742, 1818, 1942, 2050.

Limerick Colbert ⚒: 0540, 0625, 0725, 0855, 0945, 1045, 1145, 1245, 1345, 1445, 1545, 1645, 1745, 1850, 1940, 2045.
⑦: 0940, 1045, 1245, 1350, 1445, 1545, 1645, 1745, 1845, 1945.

245 DUBLIN - LIMERICK, TRALEE and CORK

km		⚒h ◇✗	⚒	⚒ 🍷	⚒	⚒ 🍷	⚒	⚒ ◇🍷	⚒	⚒ ◇🍷	⚒	⚒h ◇✗	⚒	⚒h ◇✗	⚒	⚒ ◇🍷	⚒	⚒ ◇🍷	⚒ 🍷	⚒	⚒h ◇✗	⚒	⚒h ◇✗	⚒h ◇✗
0	**Dublin Heuston** .. **240** d.	0700	...	0800	...	0900	...	1000	...	1100	...	1200	...	1300	...	1400	...	1500	1525	...	1600	...	1625	1700
48	Kildare **240** d.	|	...	|	...	|	...	|	...	|	...	|	...	|	...	|	...	|	1552	...	|	...	|	|
67	Portarlington **240** d.	|	...	|	...	|	...	|	...	|	...	|	...	|	...	|	...	|	1605	...	|	...	1703	|
82	Portlaoise d.	0742	...	|	...	0943	...	1042	...	1142	...	1242	...	1342	...	1442	...	|	1615	...	|	...	1713	|
107	Ballybrophy d.	|	...	|	...	0958	...	|	...	|	...	|	...	|	...	1458	...	|	1631	...	|	...	1729	|
127	Templemore d.	|	...	0902	...	|	...	|	...	1206	...	|	...	|	...	|	...	|	1643	...	|	...	1740	|
139	Thurles d.	0813	...	0912	...	1015	...	1113	...	1215	...	1313	...	1413	...	1516	...	1609	1653	...	1709	...	1749	|
172	**Limerick Junction** .. § d.	0834**x**	0838	0933**x**	0940	1036**x**	1040	1134**x**	1140	1236**x**	1240	1334**x**	1340	1434**x**	1440	1537**x**	1540	|	|	...	1730**x**	1740	1810	1827
208	**Limerick** ¶ ..... § **242** a.	|	0907	|	1014	|	1113	|	1216	|	1313	|	1414	|	1513	|	1613	|	1740	1800	|	1813	1840	|
**	Ennis **242** a.	|	0957	|	...	|	...	|	1309	|	...	|	1457	|	...	|	1709	|	...	1837	|	...	...	|
208	Charleville d.	|	...	|	...	1057	...	|	...	1257	...	|	...	|	...	|	...	1645	...	...	|	...	...	|
232	**Mallow** **246** d.	0907	...	1007	...	1113	...	1207	...	1313	...	1407	...	1507	...	1611	...	1700	...	...	1803	...	...	1900
	Tralee **246** a.	|	...	|	...	|	...	|	...	|	...	|	...	|	...	|	...	|	...	...	|	...	...	|
266	**Cork** **246** a.	0935	...	1035	...	1145	...	1235	...	1345	...	1435	...	1535	...	1640	...	1730	...	...	1830	...	...	1930

	⚒h ◇✗	⚒	⚒ ◇🍷	⚒h ◇✗	⚒	⚒ ◇🍷	⚒	⚒ ◇	⚒	⑦ ◇🍷	⑦	⑦	⑦ ◇🍷	⑦	⑦ ◇🍷	⑦ ◇🍷	⑦	⑦ ◇🍷	⑦ 🍷	⑦ ◇🍷	⑦ ◇🍷	⑦ 🍷	⑦ ◇🍷	⑦ ◇🍷
Dublin Heuston ... **240** d.	1705	...	1725	1800	...	1900	...	2100	...	0830	...	...	1000	...	1125	1200	...	1300	1325	1400	1500	1525	1600	1700
Kildare **240** d.	|	...	1752	|	...	|	...	|	...	|	...	...	|	...	1151	|	...	|	1351	|	|	1551	|	|
Portarlington **240** d.	|	...	1805	|	...	|	...	|	...	|	...	...	|	...	1204	|	...	|	1404	|	|	1604	|	|
Portlaoise d.	|	...	1815	|	...	1944	...	2142	...	0912	...	...	1042	...	1214	|	...	|	1414	|	|	1614	|	|
Ballybrophy d.	1800	...	1831	1854	...	1959	...	|	...	|	...	...	|	...	1230	|	...	|	1430	|	|	1630	|	|
Templemore d.	1812	...	1843	|	...	2010	...	|	...	|	...	...	|	...	1244	|	...	|	1443	|	|	1643	|	|
Thurles d.	1821	...	1853	1912	...	2019	...	2213	...	0944	...	...	1112	...	1254	1308	...	1408	1453	1508	1608	1653	1708	1808
Limerick Junction ... § d.	|	...	|	1933**x**	1938	2040**x**	2044	2234**x**	2238	1008**x**	1013	...	1137**x**	1140	|	1333**x**	1335	|	|	1531**x**	|	|	1731**x**	|
Limerick ¶ ..... § **242** a.	|	...	1940	|	2009	|	2115	|	2303	|	1038	...	|	1205	1340	|	1400	|	1540	*1613*	|	1741	*1813*	|
Ennis **242** a.	|	...	*2023*	|	2104	|	...	|	...	|	1129	...	|	1257	...	|	*1449*	|	*1635*	|	|	...	*1857***z**	|
Charleville d.	1857	...	...	|	...	2101	...	|	...	1028	...	...	|	...	...	|	...	1445	...	|	|	...	1751	|
Mallow **246** d.	1914	1930	...	2007	...	2116	...	2307	...	1044	...	1050	1210	...	...	1406	...	1502	...	1605	1702	...	1808	1902
Tralee **246** a.	2051	|	...	|	...	|	...	|	...	1220	...	|	|	...	...	|	...	|	...	|	|	...	|	|
Cork **246** a.	...	1955	...	2035	...	2145	...	2335	...	...	...	1112	1235	...	...	1430	...	1530	...	1630	1730	...	1835	1930

	⑦ 🍷	⑦	⑦ ◇🍷	⑦ ◇🍷	⑦	⑦ ◇🍷	⑦ ◇	⑦ 🍷
Dublin Heuston .. **240** d.	1825	...	1900	1905	...	1925	2100	2110
Kildare **240** d.	1854	...	|	|	...	1958	|	2139
Portarlington **240** d.	1907	...	|	1942	...	2011	2135	2152
Portlaoise d.	1918	...	|	|	...	2022	|	2203
Ballybrophy d.	1933	...	|	|	...	2037	|	|
Templemore d.	1946	...	|	|	...	2051	|	|
Thurles d.	1955	...	2008	2021	...	2101	2212	2235
Limerick Junction .. § d.	|	...	|	2047**x**	2050	|	2235**x**	|
Limerick ¶ .... § **242** a.	2042	2050	|	|	2115	2147	|	2320
Ennis **242** a.	...	2129	|	|	▬	...	|	...
Charleville d.	...	...	|	2104	⑦	...	|	...
Mallow **246** d.	...	...	2102	2121	2130	...	2308	...
Tralee **246** a.	...	...	|	2255	|	...	|	...
Cork **246** a.	...	...	2130	...	2155	...	2335	...

	⚒	⚒ 🍷	Ⓐ 🍷	⚒ 🍷	⚒	⚒h ◇✗	⚒	⚒h ◇✗	⚒	⚒h ◇✗	⚒
Cork **246** d.	...	0555	0615	...	...	0700	...	...	0800	...	...
Tralee **246** d.	...	|	|	...	...	|	...	...	|	0700	...
Mallow **246** d.	...	0614	|	...	...	0721	...	...	0825	0836	...
Charleville d.	...	0628	|	...	...	|	...	...	...	0852	...
Ennis **242** d.	...	|	|	...	...	|	0650	...	...	|	0745
Limerick Colbert .. § **242** d.	0540	*0625*	|	0640	0725	|	0730	0740	...	|	0825
Limerick Junction § d.	0607	0650	|	|	0753	0756	...	|	...	0915	...
Thurles d.	0639	|	|	0725	...	0816	...	0826	...	|	...
Templemore d.	0638	|	|	0733	...	|	...	0834	...	|	...
Ballybrophy d.	0650	|	|	0744	...	|	...	0845	...	|	...
Portlaoise d.	0704	|	|	0759	...	|	...	0900	...	|	...
Portarlington **240** d.	0715	|	|	0811	...	|	...	|	...	|	...
Kildare **240** d.	0730	|	|	0823	...	|	...	|	...	|	...
Dublin Heuston **240** a.	0805	0820	0830	0855	...	0930	...	0955	...	1047	...

	⚒	⚒ ◇🍷	⚒	⚒ ◇🍷	⚒	⚒ 🍷	⚒	⚒ 🍷	⚒	⚒h ◇✗	⚒	⚒	⚒ ◇🍷	⚒	⚒ ◇🍷	⚒	⚒h ◇✗	⚒	⚒h ◇✗	⚒	⚒	⚒ ◇🍷	⚒	Ⓐ ◇🍷
Cork **246** d.	...	0920	...	1020	...	1120	...	1230	...	1320	...	...	1420	...	1520	...	1620	...	1720	...	...	1820	...	1920
Tralee **246** d.	...	|	...	|	...	|	...	|	...	|	...	...	|	...	|	...	|	...	|	...	...	|	...	|
Mallow **246** d.	...	0941	...	1041	...	1141	...	1241	...	1341	...	...	1441	...	1541	...	1641	...	1741	...	...	1841	...	1941
Charleville d.	...	|	...	1058	...	|	...	|	...	|	...	...	1458	...	|	...	1658	...	|	...	...	1858	...	|
Ennis **242** d.	...	|	1000	|	...	|	*1141*	|	...	|	1325	...	|	1500	|	...	|	...	|	1720	...	|	1859	|
Limerick ¶ ..... § **242** d.	0945	|	1045	|	1145	|	1245	|	1345	|	1404	1445	|	1545	|	1645	|	1745	|	1759	1850	|	1940	|
Limerick Junction ... § d.	1012	1016	1111	1119	1211	1216	1311	1316	1411	1416	...	1511	1519	1611	1616	1711	1719	1811	1817	...	1916	1919	2008	2015
Thurles d.	...	1036	...	|	...	1236	...	|	...	1436	...	...	1539	...	1636	...	1739	...	1836	...	...	1939	...	2035
Templemore d.	...	|	...	1144	...	|	...	1341	...	|	...	...	|	...	|	...	1748	...	|	...	...	1949	...	|
Ballybrophy d.	...	|	...	|	...	1255	...	|	...	|	...	...	|	...	|	...	|	...	1855	...	...	|	...	|
Portlaoise d.	...	1105	...	|	...	1308	...	1405	...	1505	...	...	|	...	1705	...	1811	...	1908	...	...	2012	...	2105
Portarlington **240** d.	...	|	...	|	...	|	...	|	...	|	...	...	|	...	|	...	|	...	|	...	...	|	...	|
Kildare **240** d.	...	|	...	|	...	|	...	|	...	|	...	...	|	...	|	...	|	...	|	...	...	|	...	|
Dublin Heuston ... **240** a.	...	1155	...	1255	...	1400	...	1455	...	1555	...	...	1655	...	1755	...	1905	...	2000	...	...	2105	...	2155

	⑦ ◇🍷	⑦ ◇🍷	⑦	⑦ ◇🍷	⑦ ◇🍷	⑦ ◇🍷	⑦ ◇🍷	⑦	⑦ ◇🍷	⑦	⑦ ◇🍷	⑦ ◇🍷	⑦ ◇🍷	⑦	⑦ ◇🍷	⑦ ◇🍷	⑦ ◇🍷	⑦	⑦ ◇🍷	⑦ ◇🍷	⑦	⑦ ◇🍷	⑦ ◇🍷	⑦
Cork **246** d.	...	0820	...	...	1020	...	1220	...	1320	...	...	1420	...	...	1520	...	1620	...	1720	...	...	1820	...	...
Tralee **246** d.	...	|	...	...	|	...	|	1150	|	...	...	|	1340	...	|	...	|	...	|	...	...	|	1750	...
Mallow **246** d.	...	0842	...	...	1041	...	1242	1316	1342	...	...	1441	1514	...	1541	...	1641	...	1741	...	...	1842	1922	...
Charleville d.	...	0858	...	...	1057	...	1258	1331	|	...	...	1457	1530	...	|	...	1657	...	|	...	...	1858	|	...
Ennis **242** d.	*0740*	|	0938	...	|	*1135*	|	|	|	1303	...	|	|	...	|	*1515*	|	...	|	*1723*	...	|	|	1900
Limerick ¶ ..... § **242** d.	0825	|	1019	1025	*1045*	1225	*1245*	|	|	1342	1420	|	|	1545	|	1620	|	1745	|	1820	1845	|	|	1945
Limerick Junction ... § d.	|	0917	...	|	1116	|	1317	1352	1415	...	|	|	|	1611	1614	|	|	1811	1814	|	1912	1917	1957	2011
Thurles d.	0909	|	...	1110	1136	1309	1337	1413	1435	...	1505	1533	1609	...	1634	1704	1733	...	1834	1904	...	1937	2018	...
Templemore d.	0918	|	...	1120	|	1318	|	|	|	...	1514	|	|	...	|	1713	|	...	|	1913	...	|	|	...
Ballybrophy d.	0930	|	...	1132	|	1330	|	|	|	...	1528	|	|	...	|	1727	|	...	|	1927	...	|	|	...
Portlaoise d.	0944	|	...	1146	|	1344	|	|	|	...	1544	|	|	...	|	1742	|	...	|	1942	...	|	|	...
Portarlington **240** d.	0955	|	...	1157	|	1355	|	|	|	...	1555	|	1648	...	|	1753	|	...	|	1955	...	|	|	...
Kildare **240** d.	1009	|	...	1211	|	1409	|	|	|	...	1608	|	|	...	|	1807	|	...	|	2009	...	|	|	...
Dublin Heuston ... **240** a.	1040	1050	...	1243	1255	1441	1455	1535	1550	...	1640	1650	1730	...	1750	1840	1850	...	1950	2042	...	2055	2138	...

h – ✗ on Ⓐ, 🍷 on ⑥. **x** – Arr 1 - 2 mins. earlier. **z** – Change at Limerick C. ◇ – Also conveys ①. § – Also Table **243**. ** – Limerick - Ennis: *39 km*. ¶ – Limerick Colb

246 (DUBLIN -) CORK - MALLOW - TRALEE

km		⚒	⚒	⚒	⚒	⚒	⚒	⚒h ◇✗	⚒		⑦	⑦ ◇🍷	⑦	⑦	⑦	⑦	⑦ ◇🍷
0	**Cork** **245** d.	0645	0855	*1020*	*1220*	*1420*	*1655*	*1845*	2055	...	0855	*1020*	1210	1435	*1620*	1845	*2050*
	Dublin **245** d.	|	*0700*	*0900*	*1100*	*1300*	*1500*	1705	*1900*	...	|	0830	*1000*	*1300*	*1500*	*1700*	1905
34	**Mallow** **245** d.	0725	0923	1120	1320	1518	1725	1914	2124	...	0925	1044	1244	1517	1725	1925	2121
66	Millstreet d.	0747	0946	1144	1344	1542	1749	1943	2148	...	0947	1110	1310	1542	1748	1948	2145
100	Killarney d.	0819	1017	1218	1418	1618	1820	2019	2218	...	1014	1140	1340	1622	1825	2026	2218
134	**Tralee** a.	0856	1055	1255	1455	1655	1857	2057	2255	...	1049	1220	1415	1700	1859	2102	2255

	①	②–⑤	⚒h ◇✗	⚒	⚒	⚒	⚒	⚒	⚒		⑦	⑦	⑦ ◇🍷	⑦	⑦	⑦ ◇🍷	⑦
Tralee d.	0450	0555	0700	0905	1105	1305	1505	1705	1905	...	0710	1150	1340	1510	1710	1750	1915
Killarney d.	0522	0627	0736	0937	1138	1337	1538	1737	1938	...	0741	1222	1421	1541	1744	1826	1946
Millstreet d.	0546	0651	0808	1007	1206	1407	1606	1810	2006	...	0807	1249	1448	1607	1810	1854	2012
Mallow **245** d.	0610	0729**z**	0836	1036	1236	1436	1636	1845	2044	...	0843	1316	1514	1635	1844	1922	2045
Dublin **245** a.	*0820*	*0930*	1047	*1255*	*1455*	*1655*	*1905*	*2105*	*2255*	...	*1050*	1535	1730	*1850*	*2055*	2138	|
Cork **245** a.	*0720*	0750	*0915*	*1145*	*1345*	*1535*	*1730*	1907	2105	...	0905	*1430*	*1630*	*1730*	1909	*2030*	2107

h – ✗ on Ⓐ, 🍷 on ⑥. **z** – Arrive 0718. ◇ – Also conveys ①.

CORK - MIDLETON Journey time: 24 minutes *19*

⚒ 0615, 0645 Ⓐ, 0715, 0745 Ⓐ, 0815, 0845 Ⓐ, 0915, 1015, t hourly until 1715, 1745,Ⓐ, 1815, 1915, 2015, 2115, 2215.

† 0815, 0915, 1115, 1215, 1415, 1615, 1715, 1815, 2015.

MIDLETON - CORK

⚒ 0615, 0645, 0715 Ⓐ, 0745, 0815 Ⓐ, 0845, 0915 Ⓐ, 0945, 1 then hourly until 1745, 1815 Ⓐ, 1845, 1945, 2045, 2145, 22

† 0845, 0945, 1145, 1245, 1445, 1645, 1745, 1845, 2045.

CORK - COBH Journey time: 24 minutes *19*

⚒ 0530 Ⓐ, 0600 ⑥, 0630 Ⓐ, 0700, 0730, 0800, 0830 Ⓐ, 0 1000, then hourly until 1600, 1630, 1700, 1730, 1800, 1 1900 Ⓐ, 2000, 2100, 2230.

† 0800, 0900, 1100, 1200, 1300, 1430, 1600, 1700, 1800, 1 2100, 2200.

COBH - CORK

⚒ 0600 Ⓐ, 0630 ⑥, 0700 Ⓐ, 0730, 0800 Ⓐ, 0830, 0900 Ⓐ, 0 1030, then hourly until 1630, 1700, 1730, 1800, 1830, 1 1930 Ⓐ, 2030, 2130, 2300.

† 0830, 0930, 1130, 1230, 1330, 1500, 1630, 1730, 1830, 2 2130, 2230.

FRANCE

SEE MAP PAGES 170/1

ator: Société Nationale des Chemins de Fer Français (SNCF), unless otherwise shown.

'ces: Most trains convey first and second classes of accommodation; many purely local services are second class only (it is not possible to show classes in the tables). *TGV* (*train à grande vitesse*) trains have a bar car in the centre of the train selling drinks and light refreshments. Selected *TGV* trains have an at-seat meal service in first class. On some *Intercité* services refreshments are available from a trolley wheeled through the train. Certain other long-distance trains also have refreshments available (sometimes seasonal or on certain days of the week), but it is not possible to identify these in the tables as this information is no longer supplied. Regional and local trains (outside Paris) are classified *TER* (*Train Express Regional*). Domestic night trains have sleeping accommodation which consists of modern four-berth couchettes (first class) or six-berth couchettes (second class). Women-only compartments are available on request. There are no sleeping cars on domestic trains in France. Note that all luggage placed on luggage racks must be labelled.

ngs: Valid **June 12 - December 10, 2016**, except where shown. Amended services operate on and around public holidays; whilst we try to show holiday variations, passengers are advised to confirm train times locally before travelling during these periods. Public holidays in 2016 are Jan. 1, Easter Monday (Mar. 28), May 1, Ascension Day (May 5), May 8, Whit Monday (May 16), July 14, Aug. 15, Nov. 1, 11, Dec. 25.
Engineering work can often affect schedules; major changes are shown in the tables where possible but other changes may occur at short notice.

ets: **Seat reservations** are **compulsory** for travel by all *TGV* and night trains (also *Intercité* shown with 🅡), and are also available for a small fee on many other long distance trains. Advance reservations are recommended for travel to ski resorts during the winter sports season. **Supplements** (which include the cost of seat reservation) are payable for travel in *TGV*, certain *Intercité* and night trains. All rail tickets (except passes) must be date-stamped before boarding the train using the self-service validating machines (composteurs) at the platform entrances. Note that where two *TGV* units are coupled together, they will often carry different train numbers for reservation purposes.

: The *TGV* services **Lille Europe - Charles de Gaulle ✈ - Marne-la-Vallée - Lyon / Bordeaux / Rennes / Nantes** are shown in the International section (Table **11**).

PARIS - LILLE - TOURCOING — 250

V Nord high-speed trains

For slower trains via Douai see Table **256**. For **Charles de Gaulle ✈ - Lille** see Table **11**. Certain trains continue to Dunkerque, Calais or Boulogne - see Table **265**.

	TGV 7205	TGV 7007	TGV 7511*	TGV 7015	TGV 7021	TGV 7223	TGV 7029	TGV 7033	TGV 7535*	TGV 7043	TGV 7045		TGV 7049	TGV 7053	TGV 7559*	TGV 7061	TGV 7567	TGV 7565	TGV 7065	TGV 7067	TGV 7269	TGV 7571	TGV 7271
	Ⓐ	Ⓐ			①–⑥	①–⑥	⑦				Ⓐ			⑤		Ⓐ	Ⓐ	⑥	⑦	Ⓐ	Ⓑ	⑥	Ⓑ
		J		L	b	b	e				E			Jf		L		u	e	G	⊕	u	⊗
Paris Nord d.	0640	0710	0740	0810	0840	0940	0940	1040	1140	1228r	1313	...	1440	1509	1541	1610	1640	1640	1640	1713	1740	1743	1810
Lille Europe a.	0745	|	0845	|	|	1046	|	|	1246	|	|	...	|	|	1646	|	1746	1746	|	|	1845	1845	|
Lille Flandres 415 a.	...	0818	...	0918	0948	...	1049	1148	...	1341	1425	...	1548	1621	...	1719	...	...	1748	1819	...	...	1918
Roubaix ◇ 415 a.	...	...	...	...	...	...	...	...	...	...	...	...	...	...	...	...	...	...	...	...	...	...	1950
Tourcoing 415 a.	...	...	...	...	...	...	...	...	...	...	...	...	...	...	...	...	...	...	...	...	...	...	1956

	TGV 7277	TGV 7277	TGV 7281	TGV 7083	TGV 7089	TGV 7091	TGV 7093	TGV 7097	TGV 7097	
	⑦	①–⑥	Ⓑ	①–⑥	⑤⑦	①–⑥	⑤⑦	①–⑥	⑦	
	e	b	Lh	b	N	b	w‡	b‡	e	
s Nord d.	1840	1843	1913	1940	2013	2046	2146	2221	2240	...
lle Europe a.	1946	1948	|	|	|	⊡	|	⊡	|	...
Flandres 415 a.	...	...	2020	2048	2120	2210	2248	2339	2348	...
baix ◇ 415 a.	...	...	2043	...	...	...	...	...	...	...
rcoing 415 a.	...	...	2048	...	...	...	...	...	...	...

	TGV 7000	TGV 7206		TGV 7216	TGV 7020		TGV 7229*	TGV 7530	TGV 7030
	Ⓐ	①–⑥		Ⓐ	Ⓐ			Ⓐ	⑥
		b							J
Tourcoing 415 d.	...	0610	...	...	...	...	...	...	...
Roubaix ◇ 415 d.	...	0615	...	...	...	...	...	...	...
Lille Flandres 415 d.	0551	0641	...	...	0741	...	...	...	...
Lille Europe d.	⊡	|	...	0713	|	...	0813	0842	0842
Paris Nord a.	0708	0744	...	0814	0844	...	0914	0944	0944

	TGV 7536*	TGV 7040	TGV 7046	TGV 7546	TGV 7248	TGV 7550	TGV 7254	TGV 7058	TGV 7066	TGV 7070	TGV 7572*	TGV 7074		TGV 7076	TGV 7082	TGV 7288*	TGV 7290		TGV 7292*	TGV 7094	TGV 7294	TGV 7096	TGV 7298	
			Ⓒ	Ⓐ			①–⑥			⑤		Ⓐ					Ⓐ		Ⓒ	⑤	⑦	①–⑥	⑦	
					B		b			Jf		D			E					Jf	e	b‡	e	
rcoing 415 d.	...	...	...	...	1110	...	...	...	...	...	...	...	...	...	...	...	...	...	...	...	2010	...	...	...
baix ◇ 415 d.	...	...	...	...	1115	...	...	...	...	...	...	...	...	...	...	...	...	...	...	...	2015	...	...	...
Flandres 415 d.	...	1011	1111	...	1141	...	...	1511	1611	1641	...	1741	...	1811	1841	...	...	...	...	2041	2041	2120	...	...
lle Europe d.	0913	|	|	1113	|	1313	1413	|	|	|	1713	|	...	|	|	1913	1940	...	2013	|	|	⊡	2213	...
s Nord a.	1014	1114	1214	1214	1244	1414	1514	1614	1714	1744	1814	1844	...	1914	1944	2014	2041	...	2114	2144	2144	2241	2317	...

Daily to July 2; ⚒ July 4 - 23; ⑤ July 29 - Aug. 26; daily from Aug. 28. Starts from Lille on Ⓐ Sept. 26 - Oct. 28.
Ⓐ to July 1; ⑤ July 8 - Aug. 19 (also July 13); ⑤ from Aug. 28.
Ⓐ to July 22; ⑤ July 29 - Aug. 26; Ⓐ from Aug. 29.
Ⓐ to July 15; ⑤ July 22 - Aug. 26; Ⓐ from Aug. 29.
To July 7 / from Aug. 29.

L – To July 2 / from Aug. 29.
N – ⑤⑦ to July 15; ⑦ July 31 - Aug. 28; ⑤⑦ (**w**) from Sept. 2.
b – Not Aug. 15, Nov. 1.
e – Also Aug. 15, Nov. 1.
f – Also Nov. 10; not Nov. 11.
h – Not Nov. 11.
r – 1240 from Aug. 16.
u – Also July 14, Nov. 11.
w – Also Aug. 15, Nov. 1, 10; not Nov. 11.

TGV – 🅡, supplement payable.
⊡ – Via Arras (Table **256**).
◇ – Also calls at Croix Wasquehal.
⊕ – Paris d. 1743 on Ⓐ May 17 - July 15.
⊗ – Depart 1822 on Ⓐ May 17 - July 15.
‡ – Timings may vary.

From July 16 departures from Paris are 3 - 6 minutes later.

* – Train numbers vary as follows:
7229 is numbered **7028** on ⑦.
7288 is numbered **7586/88** on ⑥⑦.
7292 is numbered **7592** on ⑥.
7511 is numbered **7515** on Ⓒ.
7535 is numbered **7035** on ⑦.
7536 is numbered **7036** on ⑦.
7559 is numbered **7059** on ⑥.
7572 is numbered **7072** on ⑦.

PARIS - SOISSONS - LAON — 251

	Ⓐ	⑥	⚒	†	⑥	Ⓐ	Ⓒ	Ⓐ	Ⓐ	Ⓒ	Ⓐ	Ⓐ	⑥	Ⓐ	⑥	†	Ⓐ	Ⓐ	Ⓒ	Ⓐ		Ⓐ	
Paris Nord d.	0601	0618	0705	0813	0813	0834	0946	0955	1158	1326	1326	1446	1446	1530	1627	1631	1631	1750	1746	1850	2008	2116	...
Crépy-en-Valois d.	0653	0658	0742	0857	0907	0909	1025	1033	1237	1359	1403	1535	1535	1609	1706	1716	1714	1829	1825	1928	2045	2154	...
Soissons d.	0723	0727	0811	0932	0939	0938	1053	1102	1306	1429	1432	1604	1604	1640	1733	1743	1743	1903	1857	1958	2114	2223	...
Laon a.	0752	0752	0836	0954	1001	1003	1117	1127	1330	1454	1457	1629	1630	1707	1756	1806	1809	1931	1924	2022	2139	2248	...

	Ⓐ	Ⓐ	⑥	Ⓐ	†	⚒	†	⚒	Ⓒ	Ⓐ	Ⓒ	Ⓐ	Ⓐ	Ⓒ	Ⓐ	Ⓐ	Ⓒ	Ⓐ	Ⓐ	Ⓐ	†	†	⚒	
n d.	0508	0535	0633	0647	0708	0754	0843	0940	1126	1133	1230	1244	1412	1602	1628	1709	1741	1810	1913	2020	2030	2115	2119	...
ssons d.	0534	0601	0702	0714	0733	0822	0909	1006	1152	1159	1256	1311	1438	1629	1653	1735	1805	1836	1938	2046	2055	2138	2145	...
py-en-Valois d.	0602	0629	0734	0742	0802	0852	0941	1034	1221	1227	1324	1338	1506	1657	1722	1803	1837	1904	2007	2114	2126	2205	2213	...
is Nord a.	0640	0710	0812	0826	0850	0927	1017	1112	1300	1300	1412	1417	1542	1742	1810	1840	1913	1939	2042	2158	2200	2257	2257	...

AMIENS - TERGNIER - LAON - REIMS — 252

	⚒	Ⓐ	Ⓐ	Ⓒ	Ⓐ	Ⓑ	⑥	Ⓐ		Ⓐ	†	⚒	Ⓐ	Ⓐ		⚒	Ⓑ	Ⓐ	⑥	Ⓐ	⑤	†		
Amiens d.	0626	0727	0827	0857	...	1227	1327	1457	...	...	1557	1627	...	1727	...	1758	1827	1857	1857	1927	1927	1957	...	...
Ham (Somme) d.	0715	0815	0915	0943	...	1315	1415	1543	...	...	1643	1715	...	1815	...	1843	1915	1943	1943	2015	2015	2043	...	...
Tergnier a.	0732	0832	0932	0956	...	1332	1432	1556	...	...	1656	1732	...	1832	...	1856	1932	1957	1956	2034	2032	2056	...	...
Tergnier d.	0733	0833	0933	1005	1233	1333	1433	1605	...	1657	1705	1733	1804	1833	...	1905	1933	...	2005	...	2033	2105	...	...
Laon a.	0759	0859	0959	1026	1259	1359	1459	1626	...	1719	1726	1759	1826	1859	...	1927	1959	...	2026	...	2059	2126	...	...

	Ⓐ	⚒	Ⓐ	⚒		⚒	†		Ⓐ	†	⚒		Ⓐ			Ⓐ	Ⓐ	Ⓐ	Ⓐ		Ⓒ	Ⓐ	⑤		
n d.	...	0558	0634	0658	...	0734	0834	...	1158	1234	1334	...	1558	...	1658	1734	1758	1834	1858	...	1934	1958	1958	...	...
gnier a.	...	0625	0655	0725	...	0755	0855	...	1227	1255	1355	...	1625	...	1725	1755	1825	1855	1925	...	1955	2025	2025	...	...
gnier d.	0603	0626	0704	0726	...	0804	0905	...	1228	1305	1405	...	1626	...	1726	1805	1826	1905	1926	...	2005	...	2026	...	...
(Somme) d.	0618	0647	0718	0747	...	0817	0919	...	1247	1319	1419	...	1647	...	1747	1819	1847	1919	1947	...	2019	...	2047	...	...
iens a.	0703	0733	0802	0833	...	0902	1003	...	1333	1403	1504	...	1733	...	1833	1902	1933	2002	2033	...	2103	...	2133	...	...

LAON - REIMS

	⚒	ⒶJ	Ⓐ	①g	⑥	†	⚒r	Ⓐ	Ⓐ		△
Laon d.	0636	0715	0745	0810	1032	1202	1320	1659	1730	1832	2031
Reims a.	0725	0750	0828	0844	1106	1249	1407	1737	1810	1919	2106

	D	Ⓐ	ⒸS	†	⑥	Ⓐr	⚒	†	Ⓐ	Ⓐn		Ⓐ
Reims d.	0642	0717	0734	1105	1227	1227	1515	1700	1654	1742	1841	1935
Laon a.	0729	0754	0810	1153	1309	1314	1551	1736	1738	1829	1928	2010

⚒ to June 25; Ⓐ June 27 - Aug. 26; ⚒ from Aug. 28.
To July 1 / from Aug. 29.
July 2 - Aug. 28.

g – Also Aug. 16, Nov. 2; not Aug. 15.
n – July 4 - Aug. 26: d. 1735, a. 1822.
r – Subject to alteration Oct. 23 - Nov. 11, Nov. 27 - Dec. 2.

△ – On Ⓒ July 2 - Aug. 28 Laon d. 2120, Reims a. 2155.

🚐 AMIENS - TGV HAUTE-PICARDIE — 253

ICF 🚐 service

TGV departures and arrivals at TGV Haute-Picardie (Table **11**) have 🚐 connections from / to Amiens and St Quentin. Departs 50 - 60 mins before the train; journey 40 minutes, 🅡.

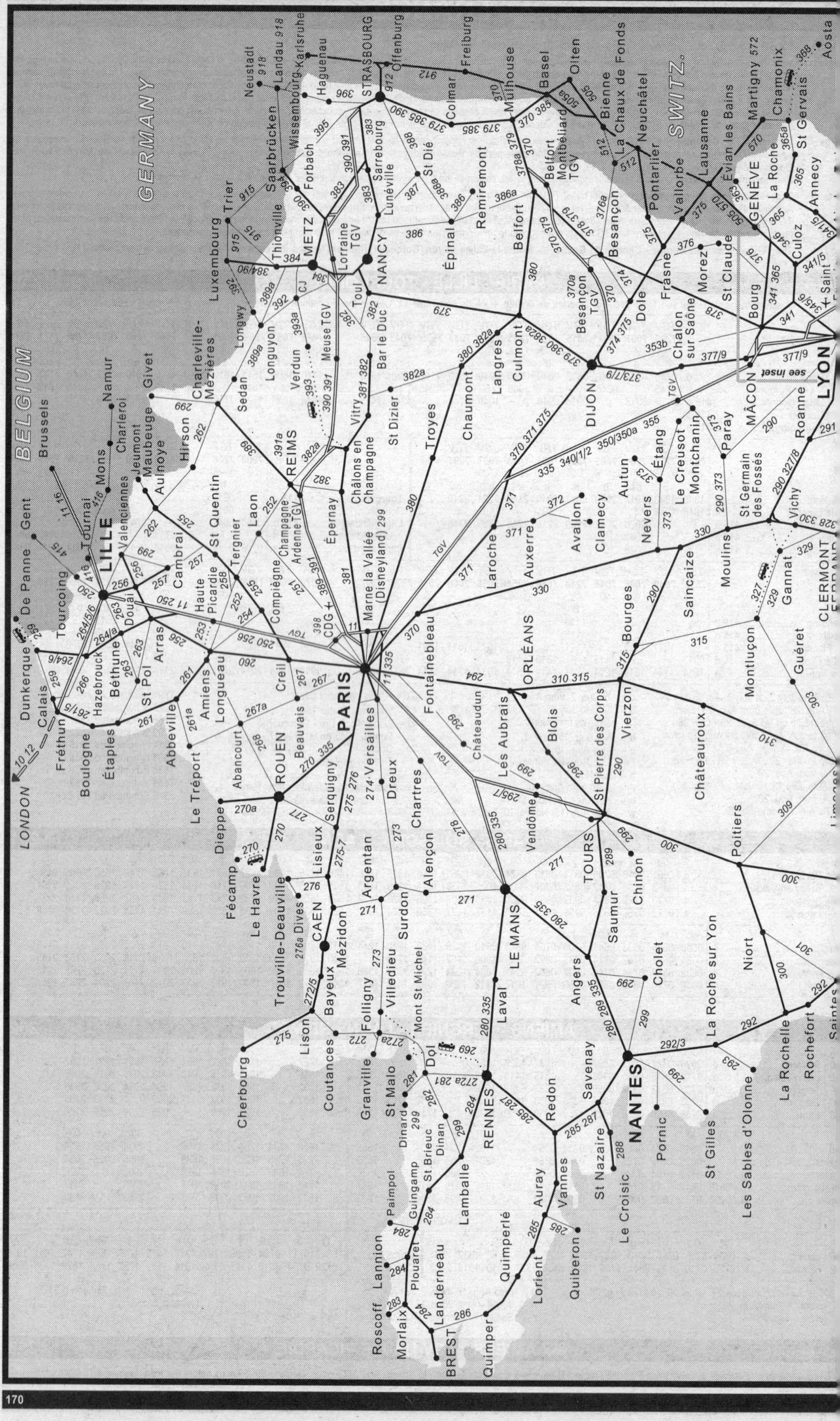

BELGIUM
GERMANY
SWITZ.
LONDON
Brussels
Namur
Charleroi
Mons
Gent
Tournai
De Panne
Dunkerque
Calais
Fréthun
Boulogne
Étaples
Tourcoing
LILLE
Hazebrouck
Béthune
St Pol
Arras
Douai
Valenciennes
Cambrai
Jeumont
Maubeuge
Aulnoye
Hirson
Givet
Charleville-Mézières
Sedan
St Quentin
Tergnier
Laon
Haute Picardie
Amiens
Longueau
Abbeville
Le Tréport
Abancourt
Beauvais
Creil
Compiègne
Champagne Ardenne TGV
REIMS
Épernay
Châlons en Champagne
CDG
Marne la Vallée (Disneyland)
PARIS
Versailles
Dreux
Chartres
Fontainebleau
Luxembourg
Trier
Longwy
Longuyon
Thionville
Saarbrücken
Forbach
METZ
Lorraine TGV
Verdun
Meuse TGV
NANCY
Toul
Bar le Duc
Vitry
St Dizier
Troyes
Chaumont
Langres
Culmont
Lunéville
Sarrebourg
St Dié
Épinal
Remiremont
Belfort
Belfort Montbéliard TGV
Mulhouse
Basel
Colmar
Freiburg
STRASBOURG
Offenburg
Haguenau
Wissembourg
Karlsruhe
Landau
Neustadt
Olten
Bienne
La Chaux de Fonds
Neuchâtel
Pontarlier
Vallorbe
Frasne
Lausanne
Évian les Bains
Martigny
Chamonix
St Gervais
Aosta
Besançon
Besançon TGV
Dole
DIJON
Morez
St Claude
GENÈVE
La Roche
Annecy
Culoz
Bourg
Chalon sur Saône
MÂCON
LYON
see inset
Saint
Le Creusot Montchanin
Étang
Autun
Paray
Roanne
St Germain des Fossés
Vichy
CLERMONT FERRAND
Gannat
Moulins
Nevers
Saincaize
Avallon
Clamecy
Auxerre
Laroche
ORLÉANS
Les Aubrais
Châteaudun
Blois
Bourges
Vierzon
Montluçon
Guéret
Châteauroux
Limoges
St Pierre des Corps
TOURS
Vendôme
Chinon
Saumur
Poitiers
Niort
La Rochelle
Rochefort
Saintes
La Roche sur Yon
Les Sables d'Olonne
St Gilles
Pornic
Cholet
Angers
NANTES
Savenay
St Nazaire
Le Croisic
Redon
Vannes
Auray
Quiberon
Lorient
Quimperlé
Quimper
BREST
Landerneau
Morlaix
Roscoff
Plouaret
Lannion
Guingamp
Paimpol
St Brieuc
Lamballe
Dinan
Dinard
St Malo
Dol
Mont St Michel
RENNES
Laval
LE MANS
Alençon
Surdon
Argentan
Villedieu
Folligny
Granville
Coutances
Lison
Cherbourg
Bayeux
CAEN
Mézidon
Lisieux
Trouville-Deauville
Dives
Le Havre
Fécamp
Dieppe
ROUEN
Serquigny
TGV

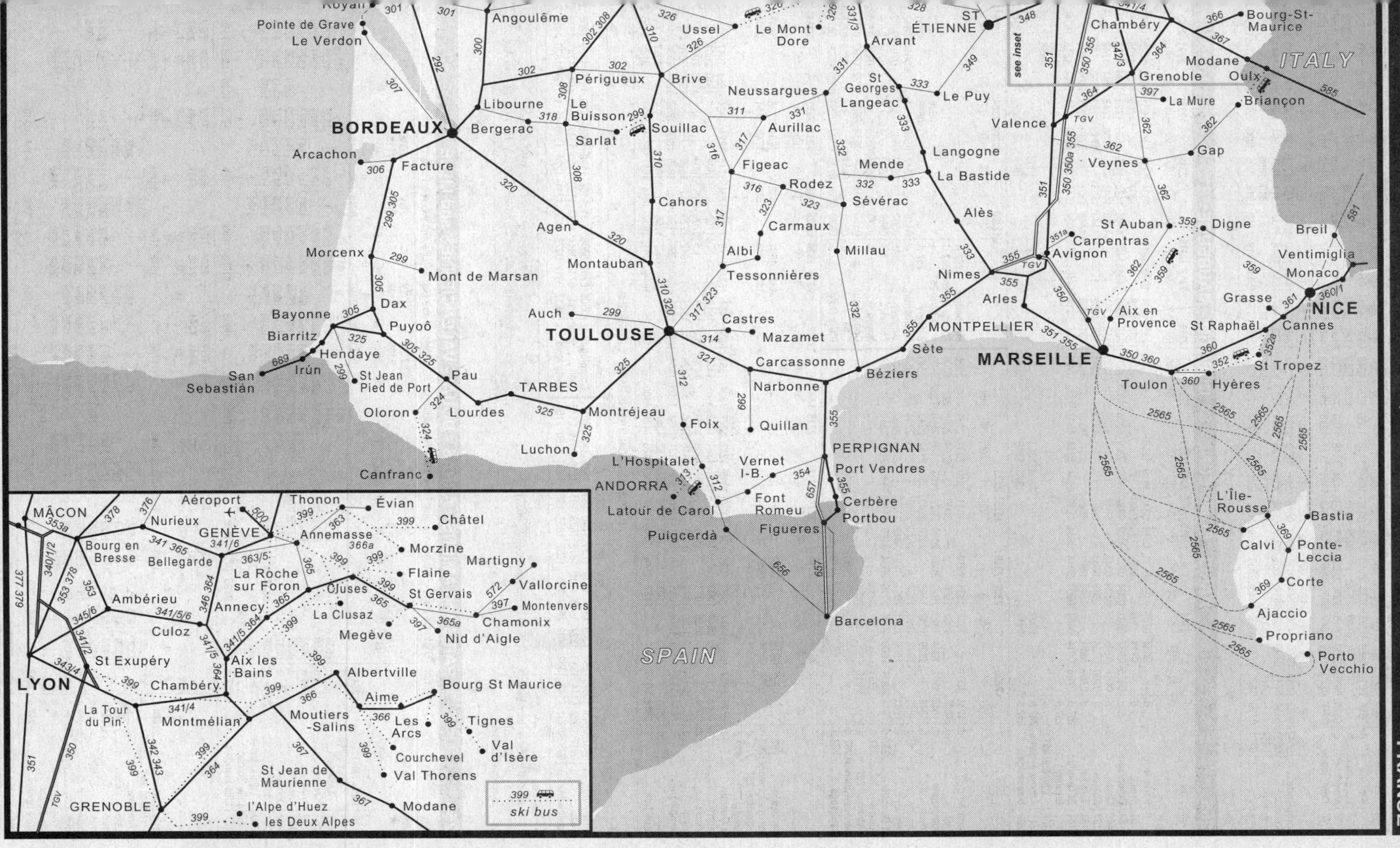
ITALY
SPAIN
Royan
Pointe de Grave
Le Verdon
Angoulême
Ussel
Le Mont Dore
Arvant
ST ÉTIENNE
see inset
Chambéry
Bourg-St-Maurice
Modane
Oulx
Grenoble
La Mure
Briançon
Périgueux
Brive
Neussargues
St Georges Langeac
Le Puy
Valence
Libourne
Le Buisson
Souillac
Aurillac
BORDEAUX
Bergerac
Sarlat
Arcachon
Facture
Figeac
Mende
Langogne
La Bastide
Veynes
Gap
Rodez
Sévérac
Cahors
Carmaux
Agen
Alès
St Auban
Digne
Carpentras
Avignon
Breil
Ventimiglia
Monaco
Morcenx
Albi
Millau
Montauban
Mont de Marsan
Tessonnières
Nimes
Arles
Aix en Provence
Grasse
NICE
Dax
Bayonne
Puyoô
Biarritz
Hendaye
Auch
TOULOUSE
Castres
Mazamet
MONTPELLIER
St Raphaël
Cannes
Sète
MARSEILLE
San Sebastián
Irún
St Jean Pied de Port
Pau
Carcassonne
Béziers
St Tropez
TARBES
Narbonne
Toulon
Hyères
Oloron
Lourdes
Montréjeau
Foix
Quillan
Luchon
PERPIGNAN
Port Vendres
L'Hospitalet
Vernet I-B.
Canfranc
ANDORRA
Font Romeu
Cerbère
Latour de Carol
Portbou
Figueres
Puigcerdà
Barcelona
L'Île-Rousse
Bastia
Calvi
Ponte-Leccia
Corte
Ajaccio
Propriano
Porto Vecchio
MÂCON
Aéroport
Nurieux
Thonon
Évian
GENÈVE
Annemasse
Châtel
Bourg en Bresse
Bellegarde
Morzine
La Roche sur Foron
Flaine
Martigny
Vallorcine
Cluses
St Gervais
Ambérieu
Annecy
Montenvers
La Clusaz
Chamonix
Culoz
Megève
Nid d'Aigle
Aix les Bains
St Exupéry
LYON
Albertville
Chambéry
Bourg St Maurice
Aime
La Tour du Pin
Montmélian
Moutiers -Salins
Les Arcs
Tignes
Val d'Isère
Courchevel
Val Thorens
St Jean de Maurienne
GRENOBLE
l'Alpe d'Huez
les Deux Alpes
Modane
TGV
399 ski bus

254 AMIENS - COMPIÈGNE

km		Ⓐ	Ⓐ	⑥	Ⓐ	†	Ⓐ	⑥	†	Ⓐ	†	⑥	Ⓐ	⑥	†	Ⓐ	Ⓒ	Ⓐ	Ⓐ	Ⓒ	Ⓐ	Ⓐ	†	⑥	Ⓐ	†
0	**Amiens** d.	0550	0619	0659	0733	0735	0855	0914	0932	1054	1118	1126	1230	1246	1330	1443	1619	1640	1703	1733	1752	1817	1835	1926	1931	2020
5	Longueau d.	|	|	|	0740	|	|	0920	0938	|	|	|	1236	1252	1336	|	|	|	1709	1739	|	1825	1843	|	|	2026
36	Montdidier d.	0620	0653	0730	0815	0806	0928	0951	1008	1124	1148	1156	1308	1323	1406	1513	1649	1710	1742	1810	1828	1903	1907	1956	2001	2056
76	**Compiègne** a.	0647	0728	0759	0849	0835	0955	1030	1042	1151	1217	1225	1342	1359	1440	1540	1718	1737	1820	1845	1904	1937	1937	2025	2028	2130

	Ⓐ	Ⓐ	Ⓐ	⑥	†	Ⓐ	Ⓐ	Ⓐ	⑥	†	Ⓐ	⑥	†	Ⓐ	⑥	†	Ⓐ	Ⓒ	Ⓐ	Ⓒ	Ⓐ	Ⓐ	⑥	Ⓐ	†	†
Compiègne d.	0547	0622	0659	0700	0738	0744	0823	0903	0918	0936	1059	1104	1119	1232	1248	1333	1447	1620	1644	1737	1751	1831	1904	1910	1913	2022
Montdidier d.	0621	0654	0741	0729	0807	0814	0855	0929	0952	1009	1125	1131	1147	1307	1322	1407	1514	1648	1711	1811	1827	1904	1931	1937	1941	2057
Longueau a.	0654	|	0818	|	0831	|	|	|	1022	1039	|	|	|	1337	1352	1437	|	|	|	1840	1858	|	|	|	|	2127
Amiens a.	0701	0726	0826	0759	0839	0845	0930	0959	1029	1046	1156	1203	1218	1343	1358	1444	1544	1719	1743	1848	1905	1933	2003	2007	2012	2134

255 PARIS - COMPIÈGNE - ST QUENTIN - MAUBEUGE

km				2301			12303	12305	2307	2309		12311		12313		2317	12315			2319		12321		2321	2323
		⚒	Ⓐ	Ⓐ	⚒	Ⓑ	Ⓐ		Ⓒ	Ⓐ	Ⓑ	⑥	⑥	Ⓐ	†	Ⓐ	†	⑥	Ⓐ	⑥	Ⓐ	Ⓐ	†	⑥	
0	**Paris** Nord d.	...	0634	0707	...	0731	0819	0834	1010	1110	...	1210	...	1225	1234	1310	1319	...	1334	1410	...	1631	1622	1628	1710
51	Creil d.	...	0711	|	...	0803	|	0909	|	|	...	|	...	1305	1308	|	|	...	1407	|	...	1705	1700	1705	|
84	**Compiègne** d.	0625	0732	0801	0804	0827	0902	0932	1100	1200	1235	1301	1304	1328	1328	1408	1405	1404	1428	1459	1635	1728	1726	1728	1800
108	Noyon d.	0647	0745	|	0829	0842	|	0946	|	|	1259	|	1329	1342	1341	|	|	1429	1442	|	1700	1742	1741	1742	|
124	Chauny d.	0700	0754	|	0840	0853	|	0957	|	|	1313	|	1343	1353	1352	|	|	1443	1453	|	1713	1753	1753	1753	|
131	Tergnier d.	0709	0801	|	0849	0901	|	1005	|	|	1319	|	1349	1401	1400	|	|	1449	1501	|	1719	1801	1801	1801	|
154	**St Quentin** 257 d.	0728	0814	0834	0909	0914	0934	1019	1134	1234	1337	1332	1409	1414	1414	1446	1438	1509	1514	1534	1740	1814	1814	1815	1834
181	Busigny 257 d.	...	...	|	...	...	...	...	|	|	...	...	...	...	...	|	...	...	...	|	...	...	...	1834	|
207	*Cambrai* 257 a.	...	...	|	...	...	...	...	|	|	...	...	...	...	...	|	...	...	...	|	...	...	...	1856	|
217	Aulnoye Aymeries 262 a.	...	...	0902	...	...	...	...	1208	1303	...	...	...	...	...	1522	...	...	...	1603	...	...	...	...	1904
229	**Maubeuge** 262 a.	...	...	0919	...	...	...	...	1223	1319	...	...	...	...	...	1537	...	...	...	1618	...	...	...	...	1918

		2325			2327	2329		12331	2333				
	Ⓐ	Ⓐ		Ⓐ	†			Ⓐ	†	Ⓐ	Ⓑ	⑥	§
Paris Nord d.	1734	1801	...	1828	1831	1910	...	1931	2010	2031	2131	2146	2228
Creil d.	1808	|	...	1903	1906	|	...	2006	|	2104	2208	2223	2306
Compiègne d.	1830	1901	1904	1928	1929	2000	2004	2028	2103	2128	2230	2252	2329
Noyon d.	1843	|	1929	1942	1942	|	2029	2042	|	2142	2243	...	2343
Chauny d.	1853	|	1943	1953	1954	|	2043	2053	|	2153	2254	...	2355
Tergnier d.	1901	|	1950	2001	2001	|	2049	2101	|	2201	2302	...	0002
St Quentin 257 d.	1914	1934	2009	2014	2015	2034	2109	2114	2136	2214	2315	...	0015
Busigny 257 d.	...	1951	...	...	2034	|	...	...	|	...	...	...	...
Cambrai 257 a.	...	2015	...	...	2056	|	...	...	|	...	...	...	...
Aulnoye Aymeries 262 d.	...	...	...	...	...	2106	...	...	2206	...	...	...	...
Maubeuge 262 a.	...	...	...	...	...	2119	...	...	2219	...	...	...	...

	12300			12302	2304			2306
	Ⓐ §	†	⑥	Ⓐ	Ⓐ	Ⓐ	Ⓑ	⑥
Maubeuge 262 d.	...	...	...	...	...	...	...	...
Aulnoye Aymeries 262 d.	...	...	...	...	...	...	...	...
Cambrai 257 d.	...	...	...	...	0536	...	...	0607
Busigny 257 d.	...	...	...	...	0608	...	...	0631
St Quentin d.	0446	...	0547	0546	0624	...	0644	0647
Tergnier d.	0502	...	0602	0602	|	...	0701	0702
Chauny d.	0509	...	0609	0609	|	...	0708	0709
Noyon d.	0520	...	0621	0620	|	...	0719	0720
Compiègne d.	0535	0635	0634	0635	0659	0722	0732	0735
Creil d.	0559	0657	0657	|	|	|	0754	0758
Paris Nord a.	0632	0726	0726	0729	0750	0820	0829	0829

		2312	2310			2314		2316	12318		2318	12320		12322		2324	2326	12328	2330		2332	2332			2334
	Ⓑ	⚒	†	Ⓐ	⑥	†	Ⓐ	⚒	Ⓐ	⑥	†	Ⓐ	⑥	⑥	†	†	Ⓐ		†	Ⓐ	Ⓒ	Ⓐ		⚒	†
Maubeuge 262 d.	...	0737	0838	...	...	0938	...	1037	...	...	...	...	...	...	...	1437	1531	...	1632	...	1731	1738	...	...	1947
Aulnoye Aymeries 262 d.	...	0754	0854	...	...	0954	...	1054	...	...	...	...	...	...	...	1454	1548	...	1648	...	1748	1754	...	...	2004
Cambrai 257 d.	...	|	|	...	...	|	...	|	...	...	1206	...	...	...	...	|	|	...	|	...	|	|	...	...	|
Busigny 257 d.	...	|	|	...	...	|	...	|	...	...	1230	...	...	...	...	|	|	...	|	...	|	|	...	...	|
St Quentin d.	0746	0824	0924	0927	0950	1024	1047	1124	1246	1247	1247	1324	1351	1424	1451	1524	1619	1646	1724	1746	1824	1824	1851	1947	2034
Tergnier d.	0802	|	|	0944	1005	|	1101	|	1302	1301	1302	|	1410	|	1510	|	|	1702	|	1802	|	|	1910	2002	|
Chauny d.	0809	|	|	0950	1013	|	1108	|	1309	1308	1309	|	1416	|	1516	|	|	1709	|	1809	|	|	1918	2009	|
Noyon d.	0821	|	|	1000	1024	|	1119	|	1320	1318	1320	|	1429	|	1529	|	1642	1720	|	1820	|	|	1931	2020	|
Compiègne d.	0834	0900	1000	1014	1038	1100	1133	1158	1335	1331	1334	1400	1454	1500	1554	1600	1656	1735	1800	1835	1859	1859	1954	2034	2109
Creil d.	0858	|	|	...	1101	|	1156	|	1357	1352	1357	|	...	|	...	|	|	1758	|	1909	|	|	...	2057	|
Paris Nord a.	0929	0950	1044	...	1132	1144	1226	1250	1432	1423	1426	1450	...	1544	...	1644	1741	1832	1844	1941	1944	1953	...	2129	2153

ADDITIONAL LOCAL TRAINS PARIS - COMPIÈGNE

▽	†	⚒	Ⓐ	Ⓐ	⑥	Ⓐ	⚒	†	⚒	⑥	Ⓐ		†
Paris Nord d.	0837	0843t	1037	1234	1249	1431	1634	1734	1740	1834	1849	1934	2037
Creil d.	0917	0922	1114	1313	1327	1513	1712	1812	1823	1911	1928	2011	2118
Compiègne a.	0953	0951	1148	1352	1402	1550	1751	1852	1851	1950	1955	2050	2154

▽	Ⓐ	Ⓐ		Ⓐ	†	⑥		⑥			Ⓑ
Compiègne d.	0505	0702	0805	1031	1107	1109	1206	1509	1610	1709	1807
Creil d.	0542	0736	0844	1059	1136	1150	1247	1535	1648	1747	1848
Paris Nord a.	0617	0817	0923	1138	1211	1226	1326	1611	1726	1829	1926

t – 0849 on ⑥.
▽ – Additional journeys: from Paris 0637⚒; from Compiègne 0556Ⓐ, 0635†, 0638Ⓐ, 0705⑥, 2004Ⓐ.
§ – Subject to alteration.

Timings may vary by up to 10 minutes.
Subject to alteration on June 25, 26 and ⑥⑦ July 16 - Aug. 14 (also Aug. 15).

256 PARIS and AMIENS - ARRAS - DOUAI - VALENCIENNES and LILLE

For *TGV* trains Paris - Lille and v.v. see Table **250**. For additional *TGV* trains Arras - Douai - Lille and v.v. see Table **11**.

km ★			◇				◇					*TGV* 7105		*TGV* 7107			*TGV* 7111		*TGV* 7113				
		Ⓐ	Ⓐ	⑥	Ⓐ	⚒	Ⓐ	Ⓐ	† v	Ⓐ	⑥	Ⓐ	Ⓐ	⑥ t	⑥ u	† v	Ⓒ	⑥ u	Ⓐ	Ⓑ	⑥ u	Ⓐ	Ⓒ
0	**Paris** Nord 264 d.	...	...	...	...	...	...	...	...	...	...	0743	...	0846	...	...	0946	...	1046	...	...	...	...
	Rouen 268 d.	...	...	...	...	...	...	...	...	0617	...	|	...	|	0817	...	|	...	|	...	...	1117s	...
131	**Amiens** d.	0538	...	...	...	0638	...	...	...	0738	0738	|	0838	|	0938	0938	|	1038	|	1138	...	1238	1238
162	Albert d.	0559	...	...	...	0659	...	...	...	0759	0759	|	0859	|	0959	0959	|	1059	|	1159	...	1301	1259
199	Arras 264 a.	0623	...	...	...	0723	...	...	...	0823	0823	0841	0923	0941	1023	1023	1041	1123	1141	1223	...	1323	1323
199	Arras d.	0625	0647	...	...	0725	0747	...	*0757*	0825	0824	0844	0925	0944	1024	1024	1044	1124	1144	1225	1239	1325	1324
224	Douai a.	0637	|	...	...	0737	|	...	*0826*	0837	0837	0858	0937	0958	1037	1037	1058	1137	1158	1237	1303	1337	1337
224	Douai 257 ▶ d.	0639	|	0644	0708	0739	|	0810	0834	0839	0839	0908	0939	1008	1039	1039	1108	1139	1208	1239	1305	1339	1339
260	Valenciennes ▶ a.	|	|	|	|	|	|	|	|	|	|	0934	|	1034	|	|	1134	|	1234	|	|	|	|
257	**Lille** Europe a.	|	0708	|	|	|	0808	|	|	|	|	...	|	...	|	|	...	|	...	|	|	|	|
257	**Lille** Flandres 257 a.	0658	...	0725	0729	0758	...	0829	0913	0858	0858	...	0958	...	1058	1058	...	1158	...	1258	1330	1358	1358

					TGV 7131		*TGV* 7335		*TGV* 7137	◇		*TGV* 7141	*TGV* 7141		*TGV* 7145	*TGV* 7145		*TGV* 7151		*TGV* 7091		*TGV* 7159	*TGV* 7097
	† v	⑥ u	Ⓐ	Ⓒ v		Ⓐ	⑤ f		Ⓐ	Ⓐ	Ⓑ	Ⓐ	⑦ e	Ⓐ	Ⓐ	Ⓒ J	z	G	Ⓐ	①–⑥ b		⑦ e	①–⑥ b‡
Paris Nord 264 d.	...	...	...	...	1446	...	1546	...	1646	...	...	1746	1743	...	1846	1846	...	1946x	...	2046	...	2146	2221
Rouen 268 d.	...	...	...	...	|	...	|	...	|	...	...	|	|	...	|	|	1817	|	...	|	...	|	|
Amiens d.	...	1338	1438	...	|	1538	|	1638	|	...	1738	|	|	1838	|	|	1938	|	2035	|	...	|	|
Albert d.	...	1359	1459	...	|	1559	|	1659	|	...	1759	|	|	1859	|	|	1959	|	2059	|	...	|	|
Arras 264 a.	...	1423	1523	...	1541	1623	1641	1723	1741	...	1823	1841	1841	1923	1942	1942	2023	2041	2122	2141	...	2241	2312
Arras d.	1408	1424	1525	1523	1544	1625	...	1725	1744	1800	1825	1844	1844	1925	1945	1945	2025	2044	2123	2145	...	2244	2318
Douai a.	1426	1437	1537	1537	1558	1637	...	1737	1758	|	1837	1858	1858	1937	2000	2000	2037	2058	2137	|	...	2259	|
Douai 257 ▶ d.	1428	1439	1539	1539	1608	1639	...	1739	1808	|	1839	1908	1908	1939	2010	2010	2039	2107	2139	|	...	2311	|
Valenciennes ▶ a.	|	|	|	|	1634	|	...	|	1834	|	|	1934	1934	|	2038	2038	|	2134	|	|	...	2337	|
Lille Europe a.	|	|	|	|	...	|	...	|	...	1821	|	...	...	|	...	...	|	...	|	|	...	...	|
Lille Flandres 257 a.	1458	1458	1558	1559	...	1700	...	1758	...	...	1858	...	...	1958	...	...	2058	...	2158	2210	...	...	2339

LILLE and VALENCIENNES - DOUAI - ARRAS - AMIENS and PARIS — 256

ille - Paris: see 250	TGV 7000 Ⓐ	Ⓐ	⑥	TGV 7100 Ⓐ	TGV 7102 Ⓐ	⚒	TGV 7106 B	Ⓐ	⑥	Ⓑ	TGV 7108 ⑦ e	Ⓐ	⑥ u	Ⓐ	Ⓒ v		TGV 7118 Ⓒ	Ⓐ ⊕	⚒	† v	TGV 7124 ①–⑥ b		TGV 7136 D	
landres ..... 257 d.	0551	0602	0602	...	...	0702	...	0731	0802	0802	...	0902	0902	1002	1002	...	...	1102	1202	1202	...	1302	...	...
urope ..... d.	|	|	|	...	...	|	...	|	|	|	...	|	|	|	|	...	...	|	|	|	...	|	...	...
enciennes ..... ▶ d.	|	|	|	0557	0615	|	0713	|	|	|	0815	|	|	|	|	...	1015	|	|	|	1213	|	1415	...
..... 257 ▶ a.	|	0621	0621	0623	0640	0721	0738	0753	0821	0821	0840	0921	0921	1021	1021	...	1040	1121	1221	1221	1239	1321	1440	...
..... d.	|	0623	0623	0635	0651	0723	0750	...	0823	0823	0851	0923	0923	1023	1023	...	1051	1123	1223	1223	1251	1323	1451	...
..... a.	0614	0636	0636	0653	0706	0735	0805	...	0835	0835	0907	0936	0937	1042	1036	...	1106	1136	1235	1236	1307	1335	1505	...
..... 264 d.	0617	0637	0637	0656	0717	0737	0817	...	0837	0837	0917	...	...	...	1038	...	1117	1137	1237	...	1317	1337	1517	...
ert ..... d.	|	0657	0659	|	|	0801	|	...	0901	0901	|	...	...	...	1101	...	|	1159	1301	...	|	1401	|	...
iens ..... a.	|	0717	0721	|	|	0821	|	...	0921	0921	|	...	...	...	1121	...	|	1221	1321	...	|	1421	|	...
ouen 268 ..... a.	|	0832	...	|	|	...	|	...	1044	...	|	...	...	...	...	...	|	1342s	...	...	|	...	|	...
Nord ..... 264 a.	0708	...	...	0747	0808	...	0908	...	...	...	1008	...	...	...	...	...	1208	...	...	...	1408	...	1608	...

		TGV 7142 Ⓑ h	Ⓐ	Ⓐ	⑥ u	◇ Ⓐ		TGV 7148 Ⓑ h	Ⓐ	Ⓐ	Ⓒ z	◇ Ⓐ	Ⓐ		TGV 7154	† w	Ⓐ	Ⓑ n	TGV 7096 ①–⑥ b‡	⑥ u	TGV 7160 ⑦ e	Ⓐ ▷		
landres ..... 257 d.	1602	...	1630	1702	1702	...	...	...	1731	1802	1802	...	1902	...	...	1935	2002	2102	2120	2106	...	2208	...	...
urope ..... d.	|	...	|	|	|	1721	...	...	|	|	|	1838	|	...	...	|	|	|	|	|	...	|	...	...
enciennes ..... ▶ d.	|	1615	|	|	|	|	...	1715	|	|	|	|	|	...	1915	|	|	|	|	|	2115	|	...	...
..... 257 ▶ a.	1621	1640	1650	1721	1721	|	...	1740	1750	1821	1821	|	1921	...	1940	2018	2021	2121	|	2136	2140	2241	...	...
..... d.	1623	1651	1659	1723	1723	|	...	1751	...	1823	1823	|	1923	...	1951	2023	2023	2123	|	2138	2151	2243	...	...
..... a.	1636	1706	1713	1736	1736	1743	...	1806	...	1837	1835	1859	1935	...	2006	2037	2035	2138	2143	2152	2207	2259	...	...
..... 264 d.	1637	1717	...	1737	...	...	...	1817	...	1838	1837	...	1937	...	2017	...	2037	...	2147	...	2217	...	...	...
ert ..... d.	1701	|	...	1801	...	...	...	|	...	1901	1901	...	2001	...	|	...	2101	...	|	...	|	...	...	...
iens ..... a.	1721	|	...	1821	...	...	...	|	...	1924	1921	...	2021	...	|	...	2121	...	|	...	|	...	...	...
ouen 268 ..... a.	...	|	...	1942	...	...	...	|	...	...	2043	...	...	...	|	...	...	...	|	...	|	...	...	...
Nord ..... 264 a.	...	1808	...	...	...	...	...	1908	...	...	...	...	...	...	2108	...	...	...	2238	...	2311	...	...	...

①–⑥ to July 2; ① July 4 - Aug. 22 (also Aug. 16; not Aug. 15);
①–⑥ from Aug. 29 (not Nov. 1).
⑥ (also ⑤ to July 1 / from Sept. 2), also July 14, Nov. 10.
⑥⑦ (also ⑤ to July 1 / from Sept. 2), also July 14, Aug. 15, Nov. 1, 10.
Daily to July 3; ⑦ July 10 - Aug. 28 (also July 14); daily from Aug. 29.
To July 2 / from Aug. 29.

Not Aug. 15, Nov. 1.
Also Aug. 15, Nov. 1.
Also July 13, Nov. 10; not Nov. 11.
Not July 14, Nov. 11.

n – Not Aug. 14.
s – Subject to alteration July 11 - Sept. 2.
t – Also July 14, Nov. 11.
u – Not Aug. 13.
v – Not Aug. 13 - 15.
w – Not Aug. 14.
x – 1943 on ⑦ to July 10.
z – Not Aug. 13, 14.
TGV – 🅁, supplement payable.
▷ – Not May 30 - June 10.

◇ – TER à Grande Vitesse (via high-speed line). Supplement *Grande Vitesse* payable (€3 per day).
⊕ – Subject to alteration Sept. 26 - Oct. 21.
★ – Paris - Arras via high-speed line is *179 km*.
▶ – Additional trains run Douai - Valenciennes (journey 30 - 40 mins).
‡ – Timings may vary.

From July 16 departures from Paris are 6 - 9 minutes later.

LILLE - DOUAI - CAMBRAI - ST QUENTIN — 257

	Ⓐ P	⑥ Pu	Ⓐ	⑥	Ⓐ	Ⓐ	⑥	⚒	Ⓐ	†	⑥	† Pu	†	Ⓐ		⚒	Ⓐ	†	⑥	⑥	Ⓐ	⑥	Ⓐ	⚒
Lille Flandres ..... 256 d.	...	...	...	*0602*	0606	0706	0736	0806	*0902*	0906	1006	...	1110	1136	...	1206	1236	*1302*	*1302*	1406	...	1506	1536	1606
Douai ..... 256 a.	...	...	...	*0621*	0638	0738	0808	0838	*0921*	0938	1038	...	1142	1208	...	1238	1308	*1321*	*1321*	1438	...	1538	1608	1638
Douai ..... d.	...	...	...	0635	0640	0740	0811	0840	0940	0940	1040	...	1144	1211	...	1240	1311	1331	1340	1440	...	1540	1611	1640
Cambrai Ville ..... a.	...	...	...	0713	0713	0813	0844	0913	1013	1013	1113	...	1213	1244	...	1313	1344	1401	1413	1514	...	1613	1643	1713
Cambrai Ville ..... d.	0536	0607	0632	0715	0715	0815	...	0915	...	1015	1115	1206	...	1255	...	1315	...	1403	...	1516	1532	...	...	1715
Caudry ..... d.	0555	0621	0646	0727	0727	0827	...	0927	...	1027	1127	1220	...	1310	...	1327	...	1416	...	1528	1545	...	...	1727
Busigny ..... 255 d.	0608	0631	0658	0736	0737	0837	...	0937	...	1036	1137	1230	...	1320	...	1336	...	1425	...	1537	1555	...	...	1737
St Quentin ..... 255 a.	0622	0645	0718	0757	0757	0857	...	0957	...	1057	1157	1245	...	...	...	1357	...	...	...	1557	1614	...	...	1757
Paris Nord 255 ..... a.	0750	0829	...	...	...	...	...	...	...	...	...	1426	...	...	...	...	...	...	...	...	...	...	...	...

	Ⓐ	Ⓐ	†	Ⓐ	Ⓑ	⑥	Ⓐ	Ⓐ	⑥	Ⓐ	▽
Flandres ..... 256 d.	1636	1706	1706	1736	1806	*1802*	1836	1906	1935	2006	2035
..... 256 a.	1709	1738	1738	1808	1838	*1821*	1908	1938	2017	2038	2118
..... d.	1711	1740	1740	1811	1840	1840	1911	1940	2019	2040	...
rai Ville ..... a.	1743	1813	1813	1843	1913	1913	1943	2013	2052	2113	...
rai Ville ..... d.	...	1815	1815	...	1915	1915	...	2015	2054	2115	...
ry ..... d.	...	1828	1828	...	1928	1927	...	2028	2109	2128	...
ny ..... 255 d.	...	1838	1837	...	1937	1936	...	2037	2119	2137	...
uentin ..... 255 a.	...	1857	1857	...	1957	1957	...	2057	...	2157	...
is Nord 255 ..... a.	...	...	...	...	...	...	...	...	...	...	...

	Ⓐ	Ⓐ	Ⓐ	⚒	Ⓐ	Ⓐ	⑥	Ⓐ	⚒	†
Paris Nord 255 ..... d.	...	...	...	...	...	...	...	...	...	...
St Quentin ..... 255 d.	...	0505	...	0605	...	0705	...	...	0805	...
Busigny ..... 255 d.	...	0526	...	0626	...	0726	0725	...	0826	...
Caudry ..... d.	...	0535	...	0635	...	0735	0735	...	0835	...
Cambrai Ville ..... a.	...	0546	...	0646	...	0746	0746	...	0846	...
Cambrai Ville ..... d.	0506	0548	0617	0648	0717	0748	0748	0817	0848	0848
Douai ..... a.	0536	0620	0649	0720	0749	0820	0820	0850	0920	0920
Douai ..... 256 d.	*0541*	0622	0652	0722	0752	0822	0822	...	0922	0922
Lille Flandres ..... 256 a.	*0621*	0655	0725	0755	0825	0855	0855	...	0955	0955

	Ⓐ	⑥	Ⓐ	Ⓐ	†	⑥	Ⓐ	⑥	†	Ⓐ	Ⓐ	Ⓐ	⑥	Ⓒ	Ⓐ	†		⑥ Pu	Ⓐ	Ⓐ	⑥	†	Ⓐ P	† Pu	
is Nord 255 ..... d.	...	...	...	...	...	...	...	...	...	...	...	...	...	...	...	...	...	1628	...	...	...	...	1801	1831	...
uentin ..... 255 d.	0842	1005	...	1205	1205	1205	...	1405	...	1442	...	1605	1605	...	...	1703	1805	1815	1842	1905	...	1905	1934	2015	2042
ny ..... 255 d.	0903	1025	...	1226	1225	1225	1338	1426	1435	1503	...	1626	1626	...	...	1723	1825	1834	1903	1926	...	1926	1951	2034	2101
ry ..... d.	0912	1035	...	1235	1235	1235	1351	1435	1444	1512	...	1635	1635	...	...	1735	1834	1844	1913	1935	...	1935	2001	2044	2111
rai Ville ..... a.	0924	1046	...	1246	1246	1246	1407	1447	1455	1524	...	1646	1646	...	...	1746	1846	1856	1925	1946	...	1946	2015	2056	2123
rai Ville ..... d.	...	1048	1147	1248	1248	1248	1417	1448	1456	...	1547	1648	1648	1717	1747	1748	1847	...	...	1948	1948	1948	...	...	...
..... a.	...	1120	1220	1320	1319	1320	1450	1521	1529	...	1619	1720	1720	1749	1820	1820	1920	...	...	2020	2020	2020	...	...	...
..... 256 d.	...	1122	1222	1322	1322	*1339*	...	1522	*1539*	...	*1639*	1722	*1739*	1752	1822	1822	1922	...	...	2022	2022	*2039*	...	...	...
Flandres ..... 256 a.	...	1155	1255	1355	1355	*1358*	...	1556	*1559*	...	*1700*	1755	*1758*	1831	1855	1855	1955	...	...	2055	2055	*2058*	...	...	...

For train numbers see Table **255**.
Subject to alteration on June 25, 26 and ⑥⑦ July 16 - Aug. 14 (also Aug. 15).

▽ – Not Aug. 14. Runs one hour later on †.

AMIENS - ST QUENTIN — 258

	Ⓐ	⚒		†	⚒		Ⓐ	Ⓐ		Ⓐ
Amiens ..... d.	0649	0749	...	1049	1249	...	1649	1749	1849	1949
Ham (Somme) ..... d.	0725	0825	...	1125	1325	...	1725	1825	1925	2025
St Quentin ..... a.	0745	0845	...	1145	1345	...	1745	1845	1945	2045

	Ⓐ	⚒	Ⓐ	†		⚒		Ⓐ	⚒	†
St Quentin ..... d.	0616	0716	0816	0916	...	1216	...	1716	1816	2016
Ham (Somme) ..... d.	0637	0737	0837	0937	...	1237	...	1737	1837	2037
Amiens ..... a.	0712	0812	0912	1012	...	1312	...	1812	1912	2112

CALAIS - DUNKERQUE - DE PANNE — 259

	Ⓐ	Ⓐ	⑥	Ⓐ	Ⓐ	⑥	Ⓐ	Ⓐ	Ⓐ	Ⓐ
Calais Ville ..... d.	0541	0643	0712	0741	0812	1241	1300	1612	1741	1841
Gravelines ..... d.	0601	0700	0732	0801	0831	1301	1321	1631	1801	1901
Dunkerque ..... a.	0624	0719	0753	0824	0850	1324	1343	1650	1824	1924

	⚒	Ⓐ	Ⓐ	Ⓐ	⑥	⑥	Ⓐ	Ⓐ	Ⓐ	Ⓐ
Dunkerque ..... d.	0636	0710	0810	1219	1236	1336	1709	1736	1836	1944
Gravelines ..... d.	0700	0731	0830	1244	1300	1400	1728	1800	1902	2017
Calais Ville ..... a.	0719	0747	0847	1305	1319	1419	1744	1819	1921	2036

DUNKERQUE - ADINKERKE (DE PANNE STATION)

ator DK'BUS Marine (route 2B). Journey 40 - 50 minutes. Connects at De Panne station with coastal tram service (Table **406**).

Dunkerque Gare: Ⓐ: 0605, 0701, 0759, 0903, 1003, 1103, 1159, 1256, 1359, 1501, 1557, 1655, 1758, 1903, 2007.
⑥ (also school holidays): 0605, 0701, 0755, 0858, 0959, 1059, 1159, 1302, 1402, 1502, 1558, 1656, 1759, 1903, 2008.
†: 0803, 0903, 1002, 1102, 1202, 1303, 1402, 1502, 1602, 1702, 1802, 1901, 2001.

Adinkerke (De Panne station): Ⓐ: 0712, 0815, 0915, 1015, 1119, 1214, 1315, 1415, 1515, 1616, 1719, 1819, 1915, 2019, 2111.
⑥ (also school holidays): 0715, 0815, 0915, 1015, 1115, 1215, 1315, 1414, 1515, 1615, 1715, 1815, 1915, 2019, 2111.
†: 0915 and hourly to 2015, 2112.

260 PARIS - AMIENS

Trains numbered **2xxx** continue to/from Boulogne (Table **261**).

km		12001 Ⓐ	12003 ⚒	2005 Ⓐ	12007 †	⑥	2009 ⑥	12009 Ⓐ	⚒	†	2011 †	2013 ⚒	⚒	†	12015 Ⓐ	12015 ⑥	†	⑥	2017 Ⓑ	12019 Ⓐ	2021 ⑥	12023 Ⓐ	⑥	2025 Ⓐ	Ⓐ
0	**Paris Nord** d.	0558	0658	0728	0758	0807	0828	0828	0907	0907	0922	1016r	1058	1101	1143	1150	1159	1307	1324	1404	1428	1558	1558	1622	1658
51	Creil d.	0632	0730	0758	0830	0842	|	|	0943	0943	|	|	1137	1146	1215	1223	1229	1345	|	1436	|	|	1629	1656	1730
66	Clermont-de-l'Oise d.	0643	0742	|	0842	0857	|	|	0957	0958	|	|	1156	1200	|	|	1242	1401	|	1447	|	1642	1641	|	1741
81	St Just en Chaussée d.	0653	0752	|	0853	0914	|	|	1009	1014	|	|	1206	1210	|	|	1253	1412	|	1458	|	1653	1652	|	1752
126	Longueau d.	0717	0816	0836	0916	0945	0933	0937	1038	1045	1031	1130	...	1238	1252	1303	1316	1438	1433	1521	1533	1716	1715	1733	1815
131	**Amiens** a.	0722	0821	0840	0922	0950	0938	0943	1043	1050	1038	1135	...	1243	1302	1309	1322	1443	1438	1527	1538	1723	1722	1739	1822

		12027 Ⓐ	2027 Ⓒ	⚒	12029 †	12031 Ⓐ	Ⓐ			2035	12037 ⚒	12039 †		
Paris Nord d.	1658	1728	1728	1749	1802	1807s	1858	1904	1928	2001v	2028	2107	2214
Creil d.	1735	|	|	1830	1833	|	1932	1939	|	2031	|	2143	2252
Clermont-de-l'Oise d.	1752	|	|	1842	1845	|	1942	1955	|	2042	|	2159	2307
St Just en Chaussée d.	1814	|	|	1852	1856	|	1953	2012	|	2053	|	2208	2319
Longueau d.	1846	1840	1835	1915	1922	1934	2015	2044	2033	2116	2134	2238	2349
Amiens a.	1854	1846	1839	1922	1927	1939	2023	2049	2038	2123	2139	2246	2354

	Ⓐz	⚒	12000 Ⓐ		12002 Ⓐ	Ⓐ	12004 ⑥	Ⓐ
Amiens d.	0412	0504	0532	0606	0622	0638	0638	0704
Longueau d.	0418	0510	0539	0612	0629	0645	0646	0710
St Just en Chaussée d.	0450	0540	0603	0640	|	0708	0709	0740
Clermont-de-l'Oise d.	0501	0550	0613	0659	|	0719	0720	0801
Creil d.	0518	0607	0625	0718	|	0730	0731	0819
Paris Nord a.	0556	0650	0656	0759	0732	0802	0802	0856

		12010 Ⓐ	2008 ⑥	2008 Ⓐ	12010 †	Ⓒ	12012 ⑥	2014	12016 Ⓐ	12018 Ⓐ	12020 ⑥	2022 Ⓐ	12024 Ⓐ	†	Ⓒ	2026	12028 Ⓐu	12028 Ⓒ	2030 Ⓑ	12032 Ⓐ	Ⓐ	2034 Ⓒ	Ⓒ	Ⓑ	2036 †
Amiens d.	0738	0818	0825	0838	0838	0910	1038	1121	1222	1238	1322	1410	1538	1536	1606	1623	1711	1738	1823	1835	1917	1923	1937	2038	2122
Longueau d.	0745	0825	0831	0846	0846	0916	1046	1128	1229	1246	1329	1417	1546	1543	1612	1629	1719	1746	1830	1846	1923	1930	1944	2045	2129
St Just en Chaussée d.	0807	|	|	0910	0910	0947	1110	|	|	1310	|	|	1610	1606	1642	|	1744	1810	|	1908	1954	|	2007	2110	|
Clermont-de-l'Oise d.	0818	|	|	0920	0920	0957	1120	|	|	1320	|	|	1620	1617	1658	|	1755	1820	|	1918	2004	|	2018	2120	|
Creil d.	0829	|	|	0931	0931	1020	1131	|	|	1331	|	|	1631	1630	1716	|	1809	1831	|	1930	2020	|	2030	2131	|
Paris Nord a.	0902	0932	0932	1002	1002	1053	1202	1238	1335	1402	1432	1520	1702	1659	1756	1732	1850	1902	1938	2002	...	2032	2102	2159	2232

FOR NOTES SEE TABLE 261

Engineering work: *Timings may vary by a few minutes. Subject to major alteration on June 25, 26 and ⑥⑦ July 16 - Aug. (also Aug. 15). From Oct. 29 departures from Paris may be 3-9 minutes later.*

261 AMIENS - BOULOGNE - CALAIS

For *TGV* service Paris - Étaples / Boulogne / Calais see Table **265**. Faster services Paris - Calais are available by changing at Lille (Tables **250** / **266**) or Hazebrouck (Tables **264** / **266**

km		Ⓐ	Ⓐ	⑥	Ⓐ	Ⓐ	⚒	Ⓐ	†	⚒	⚒	Ⓐ	⑥	2005 Ⓐ	†	†	2009 ⑥	Ⓐ	Ⓐ	⑥	2011 †	†	⚒	2013 ⚒	†
	Paris Nord **260** d.	...	...	...	...	...	...	...	...	...	...	...	...	0728	...	...	0828	...	...	...	0922	...	...	1016r	...
0	**Amiens** d.	...	...	...	...	...	...	0626	...	0713	...	...	0847	0853	...	0947	0951	...	...	...	1051	...	...	1148	...
45	Abbeville d.	...	...	...	...	...	...	0700	...	0756	...	...	0919	0921	...	1019	1019	...	...	...	1119	...	...	1215	...
58	Noyelles sur Mer d.	...	...	...	...	...	...	0708	...	0805	...	...	0928	|	...	1028	1031	...	...	...	1131	...	...	1228	...
85	Rang du Fliers ⊙ d.	...	0544	...	...	...	...	0725	...	0823	...	...	0947	0945	...	1047	1055	⊖	...	⊖	1155	...	...	1252	△
96	Étaples-Le Touquet § d.	...	0552	...	0621	...	0700	0733	...	0832	...	...	0955	0956	...	1055	1106	1121	...	1152	1206	...	1251a	1303	1356
123	**Boulogne** Ville § a.	...	0618	...	0642	...	0726	0758	...	0849	...	...	1009	1016	...	1109	1126	1147	...	1224	1226	...	1311a	1324	1416
123	**Boulogne** Ville d.	0546	0619	0627	0643	0711	0727	0805	0811	0850	0911	0947	1011	...	1048	1111	...	1149	1227	1227	...	1248	1311	...	1418
130	Wimille-Wimereux d.	0554	0627	0635	0653	0720	0735	0812	0819	0857	0920	0955	1019	...	1055	1119	...	1157	1235	1235	...	1256	1320	...	|
140	Marquise-Rinxent d.	0602	0635	0643	0702	0729	0742	0820	0828	0905	0928	1003	1027	...	1103	1128	...	1204	1243	1243	...	1303	1329	...	1429
157	Calais Fréthun **265** d.	0613	0653	0701	0715	0743	0800	0831	0841	0916	0941	1014	1040	...	1114	1140	...	1216	1301	1301	...	1315	1341	...	1441
165	**Calais** Ville **265** a.	0622	0702	0710	0722	0752	0810	0840	0850	0924	0950	1022	1050	...	1123	1150	...	1224	1310	1310	...	1323	1350	...	1448

	⑥	Ⓐ	Ⓐ	⑥	2017 Ⓐ	2017 †	†	⑥	Ⓐ	2021 ⑥	Ⓒ	Ⓐ	Ⓐ	E	†	Ⓐ	⑥	2025 Ⓐ	Ⓐ	Ⓐ	2027 Ⓒ	⑥	Ⓐ	†	Ⓑ
Paris Nord **260** d.	...	...	...	...	1324	1325	...	...	...	1428	...	...	...	...	...	...	...	1622	...	...	1728	...	...	...	...
Amiens d.	...	1347	...	1447	1451	1451	...	...	...	1551	...	...	...	1647	...	...	1747	1752	...	1847	1852	...	...	...	1947
Abbeville d.	...	1419	...	1519	1519	1519	...	...	...	1619	...	...	...	1719	...	...	1819	1819	...	1919	1919	...	...	...	2019
Noyelles sur Mer d.	...	1429	...	1529	|	1531	...	...	...	|	...	...	...	1728	...	...	1828	1831	...	1928	1932	...	...	...	2029
Rang du Fliers ⊙ d.	*1402*	1447	...	1548	1543	1556	...	...	...	1643	...	...	1718	1747	...	⊖	1847	1855	⊖	1947	1956	...	⊖	⊖	2048
Étaples-Le Touquet § d.	1451	1455	...	1555	1554	1606	...	1630	...	1654	...	1658	1727	1755	...	1824	1855	1906	1922	1955	2007	...	2024	2036	2055
Boulogne Ville § a.	1509	...	...	...	1613	1625	...	1648	...	1713	...	1726	1742	1809	...	1850	1911	1926	1946	2010	2026	...	2040	2054	2111
Boulogne Ville d.	1511	...	1611	...	...	...	1648	1650	1711	...	1723	1727	1744	1811	1848	1851	1913	...	1948	2012	...	2036	2043	2056	...
Wimille-Wimereux d.	1519	...	1620	...	...	...	1655	1658	1720	...	1730	1735	1753	1819	1855	1859	1921	...	1956	2021	...	2043	2051	2105	...
Marquise-Rinxent d.	1527	...	1628	...	...	...	1703	1706	1728	...	1738	1743	1801	1828	1902	1907	1929	...	2003	2029	...	2051	2058	2113	...
Calais Fréthun **265** d.	1539	...	1640	...	...	...	1714	1717	1741	...	1749	1801	1814	1840	1913	1931	1941	...	2014	2041	...	2102	2110	2125	...
Calais Ville **265** a.	1548	...	1650	...	...	...	1722	1724	1750	...	1757	1810	1823	1850	1921	1940	1950	...	2023	2050	...	2110	2118	2134	...

	Ⓐ	Ⓐ	2008 ⑥	2008 Ⓐ	⚒	Ⓐ	⑥	Ⓐ	Ⓐ	Ⓐ	Ⓒ	2014 †	⑥	2014 ⑥	2014 Ⓐ	Ⓐ	Ⓐ	Ⓒ	⑥		2022 Ⓐ	⚒	⑥	Ⓐ	⑥
Calais Ville **265** d.	...	0509	...	...	0609	0648	0648	0709	0737	0809	0809	...	0901	...	...	0929	1009	1109	...	...	...	1148	1209	1216	1309
Calais Fréthun **265** d.	...	0519	...	...	0621	0659	0658	0723	0747	0820	0819	...	0910	...	...	0940	1022	1122	...	...	...	1157	1219	1225	1318
Marquise-Rinxent d.	...	0531	...	...	0632	0717	0716	0734	0806	0831	0831	...	0921	...	...	0954	1033	1133	...	...	...	1216	1231	1244	1331
Wimille-Wimereux d.	...	0540	...	...	0640	0725	0724	0741	0815	0839	0839	...	0929	...	...	1002	1041	1141	...	...	...	1224	1239	1251	1340
Boulogne Ville a.	...	0548	...	...	0648	0732	0732	0748	0823	0845	0846	...	0936	...	...	1009	1048	1148	...	...	...	1231	1246	1258	1348
Boulogne Ville § d.	0449	0550	0627	0627	...	0733	...	0750	...	0846	0848	0932	...	0944	0946	...	...	...	1220	...	1228	1233	1248	1300	...
Étaples-Le Touquet § d.	0506	0606	0648	0649	...	0800	...	0806	...	0904	0904	0952	...	1005	1006	...	...	...	1239	...	1248	1259	1305	1316	...
Rang du Fliers ⊙ d.	0515	0615	0659	0700	...	...	...	0815	...	⊖	0913	1003	...	1015	1015	...	...	...	1247	...	1258	⊖	1314	1324	...
Noyelles sur Mer d.	0532	0632	0728	0726	...	...	...	0832	...	...	0932	1028	...	|	└	...	...	...	...	...	|	...	1331	...	...
Abbeville d.	0542	0642	0739	0741	...	...	...	0842	...	...	0942	1040	...	1041	1041	...	...	...	...	...	1323	...	1341	...	...
Amiens a.	0614	0713	0811	0820	...	...	...	0913	...	...	1014	1107	...	1108	1109	...	...	...	...	...	1356	...	1413	...	...
Paris Nord **260** a.	...	...	0932	1002	...	...	...	...	...	...	...	1238	...	1232	1238	...	...	...	...	...	1520	...	...	...	...

	⚒	2026 Ⓐ	2026 ⑥	2026 †	Ⓐ	⚒	†	2030 †	Ⓐ	⑥	2030 Ⓐ	Ⓐ	2034 Ⓒ	Ⓐ	†	Ⓐ	⑥	†	Ⓐ	2036 †	Ⓐ	†	⑥	Ⓐ	Ⓒ
Calais Ville **265** d.	1335	...	...	...	1438	1509	1538	...	1558	1558	...	1648	...	1709	1712	1736	1809	1827	1830	...	1928	2009	2009	2038	2209
Calais Fréthun **265** d.	1343	...	...	...	1448	1522	1547	...	1607	1607	...	1657	...	1720	1720	1745	1819	1837	1840	...	1940	2018	2019	2048	2219
Marquise-Rinxent d.	1354	...	...	...	1458	1533	1559	...	1618	1618	...	1717	...	1734	1731	1803	1832	1852	1852	...	1951	2031	2031	2059	2231
Wimille-Wimereux d.	1402	...	...	...	1506	1541	1607	...	1626	1626	...	1725	...	1741	1739	1811	1840	1900	1900	...	1958	2040	2041	2106	2241
Boulogne Ville a.	1410	...	...	...	1513	1548	1614	...	1633	1633	...	1732	...	1748	1746	1818	1848	1907	1907	...	2005	2048	2048	2113	2248
Boulogne Ville § d.	...	1435	1446	1446	...	1550	1615	1633	1635	...	1646	1733	1733	1750	1747	1819	1902	...	1908	1933	...	...	...	2115	...
Étaples-Le Touquet § d.	...	1454	1505	1506	...	1606	1633	1653	1655	...	1706	1758	1753	1806	1802	1845	1918	...	1926	1953	...	...	...	2133	...
Rang du Fliers ⊙ d.	...	1506	1517	1516	...	1615	△	1704	1702	...	1716	⊖	1804	1815	⊖	1852	1927	...	...	2004	...	...	...	2140	...
Noyelles sur Mer d.	...	1530	|	|	...	1632	...	1729	...	...	|	...	1829	1832	...	...	1945	...	...	2028	...	...	...	...	...
Abbeville d.	...	1543	1542	1541	...	1642	...	1742	...	...	1741	...	1842	1842	...	...	1955	...	...	2041	...	...	...	...	...
Amiens a.	...	1609	1609	1609	...	1713	...	1809	...	...	1809	...	1909	1913	...	...	2026	...	...	2108	...	...	...	...	...
Paris Nord **260** a.	...	1732	1732	1738	...	...	...	1932	...	...	1938	...	2032	...	...	...	...	...	...	2232	...	...	...	...	...

ALSO:	Ⓐ	Ⓐ	Ⓐ	†	Ⓐ	⑥	Ⓐ		⚒	Ⓐ	Ⓑ	⚒	Ⓐ
Amiens d.	0647	0747	0812	0850	0947	1112	1247	1312	1612	1722	1812	1912	2012
Abbeville a.	0732	0820	0856	0922	1020	1156	1320	1357	1656	1807	1857	1957	2057

	⑥	Ⓐb	⚒	⚒	⚒	⑥	Ⓑ	⚒	Ⓐ	Ⓑ
Abbeville d.	0546	0604	0646	0733	0804	1221	1304	1604	1704	1751
Amiens a.	0620	0649	0729	0807	0849	1306	1349	1649	1749	1831

NOTES FOR TABLES 260 / 261

E – Ⓐ from Amiens, ⚒ Boulogne - Calais.
a – Ⓐ only.
b – Also ⑥ July 9 - Aug. 27.
r – 1028 on ⑥; 1019 on Ⓐ to July 15.
s – 1831 from Oct. 31.
u – From Oct. 29 runs in timings shown in next column.
v – 1958 on ⑥.
z – Subject to alteration Sept. 20 - 23.
△ – To / from Lille via Bethune and St Pol (Table **263**).
⊖ – To / from Arras (Table **263**).
⊙ – Rang du Fliers-Verton-Berck.
§ – See also Table **263**.

Weekend engineering work:
Paris - Boulogne and v.v. trains are subject to alterati on June 25, 26 and ⑥⑦ July 16 - Aug. 14 (also Aug. From Oct. 29 departures from Paris may be 3-9 minutes later.

ABBEVILLE - LE TRÉPORT 261a

	🚌	🚌 ⚒	⑦L	†J		⑦L	⑥N	🚌 †	🚌 Ⓐ	🚌 ⑥	🚌 †		🚌 ⚒	🚌 ⚒	⑥		Ⓐ	⑦L	†J	Ⓐ	⑥		🚌 ⑥	🚌 ⑤
Laon 252 ... d.	...	...	...	...	...	0821	0826	...	...	...	...	...	...	...	...	...	...	...	...	...	...	...	...	...
Amiens 261 ... d.	...	...	0847	...	...	|	0939	...	...	...	...	...	...	...	...	...	...	...	...	...	...	...	...	...
Abbeville ... d.	0641	0830	0917	0926	...	1001	1009	1129	1218	1225	1306	...	1407	1529	1627	...	1745	1750	1806	1924	1927	...	2007	2029
Le Tréport ... a.	0745	0937	0950	1006	...	1036	1042	1235	1324	1331	1412	...	1513	1635	1713	...	1836	1836	1852	2014	2013	...	2111	2133

	🚌 ①g		⚒	Ⓐ		⑥	🚌 Ⓐ	🚌 ⑥	🚌 †		🚌 ⚒		🚌 Ⓐ	🚌 †		†	🚌 ⚒	🚌 †		⑥N	⑦L	🚌 ⑥		⑦L	
éport ... d.	0446	...	0638	0745	...	0850	0925	0925	0930	...	1227	...	1629	1629	...	1706	1730	1731	...	1838	1841	1843	...	1927	...
ville ... a.	0532	...	0728	0826	...	0933	1031	1031	1032	...	1331	...	1731	1731	...	1745	1832	1833	...	1912	1914	1945	...	2000	...
ens 261 ... a.	...	...	...	...	...	...	...	...	...	...	...	...	...	...	...	...	...	...	...	1940	|	...	...	2029	...
n 252 ... a.	...	...	...	...	...	...	...	...	...	...	...	...	...	...	...	...	...	...	...	2100	2100	...	...	...	...

To June 26 / from Sept. 4.
⑦ July 3 - Aug. 28 (also July 14, Aug. 15).

N – ⑥ July 2 - Aug. 27.

g – Also Mar. 29, May 6, 17.

LILLE - VALENCIENNES - MAUBEUGE and CHARLEVILLE MÉZIÈRES 262

	⑥	⚒	Ⓐ	Ⓐ	Ⓐ	⑥	Ⓐ	Ⓐ	⑥	⑥	Ⓐ	Ⓐ	⑥	Ⓐ	Ⓐ	Ⓒ	†	⑥	†	†	Ⓐ	⑥	Ⓐ	Ⓐ	⑥	⑥
Lille Flandres ... ▷ d.	0535	*0535*	...	*0535*	0635	0635	0705	0735	0735	...	0805	0835	0835	0905	0935	0935	...	...	1135	...	1201	1201	1235	...	1235	1305
Valenciennes ... ▷ d.	0621	*0620*	...	*0620*	0720	0721	0750	0820	0821	...	0844	0920	0921	0943	1020	1021	...	...	1221	...	1231	1232	1320	...	1321	1349
Aulnoye Aymeries ... a.	0649	*0649*	...	*0649*	0749	0750	0816	0849	0849	...	0910	0949	0949	1009	1049	1049	...	...	1249	...	1253	1253	1349	...	1349	1415
Aulnoye Aymeries ... d.	0652	0701	...	0708	0801	0801	0818	0901	0852	0901	0911	1001	0952	1011	1101	1052	1101	1101	1301	1258	1255	1255	1355	1401	1401	1417
Maubeuge ... a.	0702	|	...	0726	|	|	0834	|	0903	|	0922	|	1003	1022	|	1103	|	|	|	1312	1304	1304	1405	|	|	1430
Jeumont ... a.	0710	|	...	0735	|	|	...	|	0912	|	0931	|	1012	1031	|	1112	|	|	|	1320	|	1312	1413	|	|	1442
Avesnes ... d.	...	0717	...	...	0817	0817	...	0918	...	0917	...	1013	...	...	1113	...	1112	1117	1312	...	*1312**	*1317**	...	1412	1411	...
Hirson ... a.	...	0746	0753	...	0846	0844	...	0946	...	0945	...	1038	...	...	1138	...	1134	1145	1336	...	*1338**	*1345**	...	1438	1434	...
Charleville-Mézières . a.	...	...	0833	...	...	0925	...	...	...	...	...	...	...	...	*1222*	...	1215	...	...	...	...	...	...	...	*1524*	...

	Ⓐ	†	†	Ⓐ	⚒	Ⓐ	Ⓐ	Ⓒ	Ⓐ	Ⓐ	†	⑥	Ⓐ	Ⓐ	Ⓐ	Ⓐ		Ⓒ	†	Ⓐ	⑥	Ⓐ	Ⓐ		Ⓑ	Ⓐ	Ⓐ
Flandres ... ▷ d.	1335	1335	...	1435	...	1535	1605	1635	1701	1635	...	...	1731	1801	1831	...	1835	...	...	1901	...	1935	...	2035	...	2135	...
ciennes ... ▷ d.	1420	1418	...	1520	...	1619	1643	1720	1732	1720	...	...	1802	1831	1902	...	1920	...	...	1931	...	2020	...	2120	...	2220	...
ye Aymeries ... a.	1449	1447	...	1549	...	1649	1709	1749	1753	1749	...	...	|	1853	|	...	1949	...	...	1953	...	2049	...	2149	...	2249	...
ye Aymeries ... d.	1455	1452	1452	1555	1601	1701	1711	1752	1755	1801	1801	1801	|	1855	|	...	2001	...	1958	1955	2017	2055	2101	2155	2201	2255	2301
ubeuge ... a.	1505	1503	|	1605	|	|	1723	1804	1803	|	|	|	|	1903	|	...	|	...	2012	2003	2028	2105	|	2205	|	2305	|
mont ... a.	1513	1512	|	1613	|	|	1735	1812	1812	|	|	|	|	1912	|	...	|	...	2024	2012	2042	2113	|	2213	|	2313	|
nes ... d.	*1512**	...	1503	...	1612	1713	...	...	...	1813	1812	1817	1827	...	1928	...	2013	...	...	...	...	...	2112	...	2212	...	2312
n ... a.	*1538**	...	1527	...	1638	1738	...	...	...	1838	1834	1845	1846	...	1950	1955	2038	2041	...	...	...	...	2138	...	2238	...	2338
eville-Mézières a.	...	...	...	...	...	...	...	...	...	...	1915	...	1924	...	...	2033	...	2119	...	...	...	...	...	...	...	...	...

	Ⓐ	Ⓐ	Ⓐ	⑥	Ⓐ	Ⓐ	⚒	Ⓐ	†	⚒	Ⓐ	⚒	Ⓐ	Ⓐ	Ⓒ	Ⓑ	⑥	Ⓐ	Ⓐ	Ⓐ	⑥	†	Ⓒ	Ⓐ	Ⓐ	⑥	⑥
eville-Mézières d.	...	...	...	...	...	...	...	*0623*	...	...	...	...	...	...	...	...	...	...	...	...	*0939*	...	...	*1042*	...	...	...
n ... d.	...	...	0613	...	...	...	0616	0713	...	...	...	0716	...	0816	0825	...	...	0925	...	*1025**	1027	1101	...	1125	...	1200	...
nes ... d.	...	...	0634	...	...	...	0644	0733	...	...	...	0743	...	0844	0851	...	...	0951	...	*1050**	1050	1126	...	1150	...	1226	...
mont ... d.	0527	0549	|	0618	0623	0648	|	|	0718	0723	0749	|	0827	|	|	0849	0922	|	0949	1049	|	|	1122	|	1149	|	1216
ubeuge ... d.	0536	0558	|	0630	0637	0656	|	|	0730	0737	0758	|	0836	|	|	0857	0931	|	0957	1057	|	|	1130	|	1157	|	1230
ye Aymeries ... a.	0548	0606	|	0642	0648	0704	0659	|	0742	0748	0806	0758	0848	0900	0900	0907	0942	1000	1009	1107	1059	1135	1141	1200	1207	1235	1241
ye Aymeries ... d.	0550	0608	|	0644	0650	0706	0709	|	0744	0750	0808	0811	0850	...	...	0911	0944	...	1011	1111	1113	...	1143	...	1211	...	1243
ciennes ... ▷ d.	0618	0630	0700	0713	0718	0727	0740	0759	0811	0818	0831	0841	0917	...	...	0941	1013	...	1041	1141	1143	...	1210	...	1241	...	1311
Flandres ... ▷ a.	0655	0659	0731	0755	0755	0759	0825	0829	0855	0855	0859	0925	0955	...	...	1025	1055	...	1125	1225	1225	...	1255	...	1325	...	1355

	Ⓐ	⑥	†	†	†	Ⓐ	⚒	†		Ⓐ	Ⓐ	Ⓐ	†	⑥	Ⓒ	Ⓐ	Ⓐ	Ⓐ	†	Ⓐ	Ⓐ	⑥	†	†	⑥	Ⓐ	Ⓐ
eville-Mézières d.	...	1140	...	1320	...	...	...	...	...	...	...	...	*1627*	...	...	...	...	...	...	*1841*	...	1937	...	1940	...	2053	...
n ... d.	1216	1227	1227	1358	...	1425	1525	1535	...	...	1616	...	1718	1725	...	1716	1816	...	*1901**	1925	...	2015	...	2027	2127	2129	...
nes ... d.	1243	1250	1252	1425	...	1450	1550	1559	...	...	1644	...	1744	1751	...	1745	1845	...	*1926**	1950	...	...	...	2050	2150	2154	...
mont ... d.	|	|	|	|	1418	|	|	|	1549	1627	|	1723	|	|	1748	|	|	1849	1917	|	1949	...	2048	|	*2141*	|	2149
ubeuge ... d.	|	|	|	|	1429	|	|	|	1557	1636	|	1737	|	|	1756	|	|	1857	1930	|	1957	...	2056	|	*2149*	|	2157
ye Aymeries ... a.	1300	1259	1302	1435	1442	1500	1600	1608	1607	1648	1700	1748	1759	1800	1807	1800	1900	1907	1946	2000	2007	...	2107	2059	2159	2203	2207
ye Aymeries ... d.	1311	1313	1310	...	1444	*1511*	...	...	1611	1650	1711	1750	...	...	1809	1811	...	1911	1948	...	2011	...	...	2113	2213	...	2211
ciennes ... ▷ d.	1341	1342	1340	...	1513	*1541*	...	...	1641	1718	1741	1818	...	...	1843	1841	...	1941	2013	...	2041	...	...	2142	2243	...	2241
Flandres ... ▷ a.	1425	1425	1425	...	1555	*1625*	...	...	1725	1755	1825	1855	...	...	1925	1925	...	2025	2055	...	2125	...	...	2225	2325	...	2325

ADDITIONAL TRAINS LILLE - VALENCIENNES

	Ⓐ	Ⓐ	Ⓐ	Ⓐ	Ⓒ	Ⓐ	Ⓐ	Ⓐ	†	Ⓐ	⑥	Ⓐ		Ⓐ	Ⓐ	†	⑥	Ⓐ		Ⓐ	Ⓒ	Ⓐ	Ⓒ	Ⓐ	
Flandres ... d.	0512	0812	0912	1012	1035	1112	1205	1212	1235	1312	1335	1412	...	1612	1712	1735	1740	1812	...	1912	1935	2012	2135	2230	...
ciennes ... a.	0600	0855	0955	1055	1125	1201	1241	1255	1325	1355	1418	1455	...	1655	1755	1819	1830	1855	...	1955	2025	2055	2225	2323	...

	⑥	Ⓐ	Ⓐ	Ⓐ	Ⓐ	Ⓐ		Ⓐ	†	Ⓐ	⑥	Ⓐ		⑥	Ⓐ	†	Ⓐ	Ⓒ	Ⓐ		Ⓐ	Ⓐ	⑥		
ciennes ... d.	0434	0440	0605	0703	0804	0905	...	1105	1137	1203	1230	1303	...	1530	1603	1606	1703	1728	1802	...	1903	2005	2005	...	...
Flandres ... a.	0526	0527	0648	0749	0848	0948	...	1148	1227	1248	1321	1348	...	1621	1648	1656	1748	1821	1848	...	1948	2048	2057	...	...

For additional trains see panel below main table.
Change at Aulnoye Aymeries.

Current timings not available. Subject to alteration due to engineering work

BOULOGNE - ST POL - ARRAS / BÉTHUNE 263

	Ⓐ	Ⓐ	⚒	⚒	⚒	⚒	Ⓐ	Ⓐ	†	†	⚒	Ⓐ	⚒	†	Ⓐ	†	Ⓐ	⑥	†	⑥	Ⓐ	†	⑥	Ⓐ
Calais Ville **261** ... d.	...	...	...	...	...	...	0648	0809	...	...	...	...	1148	...	...	...	...	...	1538	...	1648	1712	...	1830
Boulogne Ville ... **261** d.	0404	...	0510	...	0632	...	0733	0846	0903	...	...	...	1233	1343	...	1505	1533	1600	1615	1723	1733	1747	...	1908
Étaples Le Touquet .. **261** d.	0426	...	0537	...	0659	...	0819**z**	0906	0932	...	...	...	1301	1403	...	1523	1601	1631	1635	1759	1800	1804	...	1927
Montreuil ... d.	0438	...	0549	...	0710	...	0831	0918	0944	...	...	...	1312	1414	...	1535	1613	1643	1647	1812	1812	1816	...	1938
Hesdin ... d.	0503	...	0619	...	0739	...	0857	0944	1009	...	...	...	1341	1439	...	1600	1642	1708	1712	1845	1842	1845	...	—
St Pol sur Ternoise ... a.	0528	...	0650	...	0806	...	0926	1010	1032	...	...	...	1410	1502	...	1625	1710	1735	1739	1913	1912	1910	...	†
St Pol sur Ternoise ... d.	0532	0610	0701	0710	0807	0811	...	1012	1034	1040	1110	1210	1412	1504	1510	1627	1712	1737	1741	1915	1914	1912	1920	1927
Arras ... a.	0609	|	0741	|	0847	|	...	1049	1107	|	|	|	1448	1531	|	1658	1752	*1908*	*1908*	1947	1952	1938	|	|
Béthune ... ▷ d.	...	0650	...	0750	...	0850	...	...	...	1120	1150	1250	...	...	1550	...	...	1816	1824	...	...	...	1956	2007
Lille Flandres ... ▷ a.	...	0725	...	0825	...	0925	...	...	...	1203	1225	1325	...	...	1625	...	...	1853	1912	...	...	...	2034	2042

	⚒	⚒	Ⓐ	Ⓐ	Ⓒ	†	⑥	†	⑥	⚒ n	⑥	Ⓐ	Ⓐ	Ⓐ	Ⓐ	Ⓐ	Ⓒ	Ⓐ	Ⓒ	Ⓐ	⑥	†	Ⓐ	Ⓐ	⑥
le Flandres ... ▷ d.	...	...	0836	...	0902	...	...	1135	...	1235	...	...	1536	...	1636	...	...	1736	1742	...	...	...	1836	...	1913
thune ... ▷ d.	...	...	0912	...	0946	...	...	1214	...	1312	...	...	1612	...	1712	...	...	1812	1825	...	...	...	1912	...	1958
s ... d.	...	0617**a**	|	0928	|	0955	0956	|	1228	|	*1328*	1328	|	1628	|	1728	1742**r**	|	|	1828	1828	1828	|	1928	|
l sur Ternoise ... a.	...	0657**a**	0950	1007	1025	1029	1032	1251	1306	1350	*1407*	1407	1650	1707	1750	1808	1814	1850	1903	1908	1905	1907	1950	2006	2035
l sur Ternoise ... d.	0546	0705	...	1014	...	1036	1034	1253	1308	...	1414	1414	...	1714	...	1810	1815	...	...	1916	1917	1923	...	2008	2036
in ... d.	0617	0738	...	1042	...	1103	1100	1320	1344	...	1443	1443	...	1744	...	1844	1843	...	...	1947	1949	1954	...	2035	2101
reuil ... d.	0646	0806	...	1109	...	1129	1125	1345	1410	...	1508	1509	...	1813	...	1910	1908	...	...	2012	2015	2019	...	2101	2124
es Le Touquet ... **261** d.	0700	0817	...	1121	...	1146	1152	1356	1422	...	1520	1519	...	1824	...	1922	1920	...	...	2024	2026	2036	...	2113	2135
ogne Ville ... **261** a.	0726	0843	...	1147	...	1213	1224	1416	1441	...	1539	...	...	1850	...	1946	1948	...	...	2040	2042	2054	...	2133	2153
lais Ville **261** ... a.	0810	...	...	1224	...	...	1310	1448	...	...	...	...	...	1940	...	2023	...	...	...	2118	...	2134	...	...	...

Ⓐ only.
1748 on †.

n – On ⑥ runs through to Boulogne (see next column).
z – Arrive 0800.

▷ – Additional trains run Béthune - Lille and v.v.

264 PARIS and LILLE - DUNKERQUE *High-speed tr*

VIA LILLE For local trains Lille Flandres - Dunkerque see Table 266

km		◇	TGV 7205	TGV 7511	◇	◇		◇	TGV 7567	TGV 7269	TGV 7269	TGV 7571
		Ⓐ	Ⓐ	Ⓐ	†	⚒		Ⓐ	Ⓐ	Ⓐ	⑦	⑥
											e	t
	Paris Nord **250** .. d.	...	0640	0740	...	...	...	...	1640	1743	1740	1743
0	**Lille** Europe .... d.	0712	0750	0850	1150	1250	...	1650	1750	1850	1850	1850
76	**Dunkerque** .... a.	0744	0823	0923	1223	1323	...	1723	1823	1923	1923	1923

	TGV 7214	◇	TGV 7530	◇	TGV 7552		◇	TGV 7288	TGV 7588
	Ⓐ	Ⓐ	Ⓐ	†	①–⑥		Ⓐ	Ⓑ	⑥
					b				t
Dunkerque .... d.	0632	0724	0759	1035	1231	...	1634	1832	1832
Lille Europe .... a.	0703	0754	0832	1106	1306	...	1707	1905	1905
Paris Nord **250** . a.	0814	...	0944	...	1414	...	...	2014	2014

VIA BÉTHUNE For local trains Arras - Béthune - Hazebrouck see Table 264a

km		TGV 7305	TGV 7307	TGV 7311	TGV 7321	TGV 7331	TGV 7337	TGV 7343	TGV 7345	TGV 7351	TGV 7357	
		Ⓐ	⑥	Ⓒ	①–⑥			Ⓐ			⑤	
			t	△	b‡	D			E	F	f	
0	**Paris** Nord...... **256** d.	0743	0846	0946	1246	1446	1646	1816	1846	1946x	2046	...
199	Arras .... **256** d.	0850	0950	1050	1348	1550	1750	1914	1950	2050	2150	...
219	Lens .... d.	0905	1005	1105	1405	1605	1805	1929	2005	2105	2205	...
238	Béthune .... d.	0918	1018	1118	1418	1618	1818	1945	2018	2118	2218	...
272	Hazebrouck .... a.	0939	1039	1139	1439	1639	1839	2009	2039	2139	2239	...
312	**Dunkerque** .... a.	1004	1104	1204	1504	1704	1904	...	2104	2204	2304	...

	TGV 7302	TGV 7304	TGV 7308	TGV 7318	TGV 7336	TGV 7342	TGV 7348	TGV 7354	TGV 7356
	Ⓐ	Ⓐ	⑥					⑦	⑤⑦
			t					e△	n
Dunkerque .... d.	0556	...	0756	0955	1355	1555	1655	...	1956
Hazebrouck .... d.	0620	0653	0820	1019	1419	1619	1719	1918	2020
Béthune .... d.	0643	0725	0843	1042	1442	1642	1742	1942	2043
Lens .... d.	0657	0741	0857	1056	1456	1656	1756	1956	2057
Arras .... **256** d.	0717	0756	0917	1117	1517	1717	1817	2017	2117
Paris Nord... **256** a.	0808	0847	1008	1208	1608	1808	1908	2108	2214

D – Daily to July 3; ⑤⑥⑦ July 8 - Aug. 28 (also July 14), daily from Aug. 31.
E – Ⓑ to June 26; Ⓐ June 27 - Aug. 26; Ⓑ from Aug. 29 (not Nov. 11).
F – ⑤⑥⑦ to July 3; ⑦ July 10 - Aug. 28 (also July 14); ⑤⑥⑦ from Sept. 2 (also Nov. 10).
b – Not Aug. 15, Nov. 1.
e – Also Aug. 15, Nov. 1.
f – Also July 13, Nov. 10; not Nov. 11.
n – Also July 13, Aug. 15, Nov. 1, 10; not Nov. 11.
t – Also July 14, Nov. 11.
x – 1943 on ⑦ to July 10.
TGV –Ⓡ, supplement payable.
◇ – TER à Grande Vitesse (TER GV) via high-speed line (1, 2 c
Supplement *Grande Vitesse* €3 (valid all day).
△ – Subject to alteration Oct. 30 - Nov. 27.
‡ – Not on ⑤ July 8 - Aug. 19.

Most departures from Paris are 3-6 minutes later from July

264a ARRAS - BÉTHUNE - HAZEBROUCK *For TGV trains see Table*

km		Ⓐ	⑥	Ⓐ	Ⓐ	⚒	Ⓐ	⚒	†	Ⓐ	⚒	Ⓒ	Ⓐ	Ⓐ	⑥	⑥	Ⓐ	Ⓐ	†	Ⓐ	⚒	†	Ⓐ	Ⓐ
0	**Arras** .... d.	0604	0623	0622	0657	0723	0804	0822	0856	0904	0923	1056	1204	1222	1225	1256	1257	1323	1356	1456	1604	1556	1617	1651
20	Lens .... d.	0618	0642	0646	0713	0742	0818	0841	0913	0918	0942	1113	1218	1246	1244	1313	1313	1342	1413	1513	1618	1613	1636	1706
39	Béthune .... d.	0634	0703	0705	0733	0800	0835	0900	0931	0935	1001	1131	1235	1304	1303	1331	1335	1401	1431	1531	1636	1631	1655	1728
51	Lillers .... d.	0643	0716	0717	0746	0809	0844	0909	0940	0943	1009	1140	1244	1316	1315	1340	1347	1410	1440	1539	1645	1640	1704	1740
73	**Hazebrouck** .... a.	0659	0736	0740	0806	0826	0900	0925	0956	1000	1026	1156	1300	1336	1334	1356	1406	1426	1456	1556	1703	1656	1719	1759

	Ⓐ	Ⓒ	Ⓐ	Ⓐ	Ⓐ	Ⓐ	Ⓐ	Ⓒ	Ⓒ	Ⓐ	Ⓒ	
Arras .... d.	1722	1756	1757	1822	1904	1923	1957	1955	2056	2137	2156	...
Lens .... d.	1746	1814	1813	1846	1917	1941	2013	2013	2113	2151	2213	...
Béthune .... d.	1805	1831	1831	1907	1934	2000	2030	2031	2131	2206	2231	...
Lillers .... d.	1816	1840	1840	1918	1943	2010	2040	2039	2140	...	2240	...
Hazebrouck .... a.	1836	1856	1859	1937	2000	2026	2056	2056	2156	...	2256	...

	Ⓐ	Ⓐ	⑥	Ⓐ	⑥	Ⓐ d	⑥ d	Ⓐ
Hazebrouck .... d.	0506	0553	0604	0623	0634	0700	0704	0734
Lillers .... d.	0522	0614	0621	0644	0650	0718	0721	0750
Béthune .... d.	0531	0629	0631	0657	0700	0731	0731	0800
Lens .... d.	0549	0649	0649	0714	0722	0750	0749	0821
Arras .... a.	0607	0703	0703	0739	0739	0805	0803	0838

	⚒	Ⓐ	⑥ d	†	Ⓐ	⑥	Ⓐ	⑥	Ⓐ	Ⓑ	⑥	Ⓐ	Ⓐ	Ⓐ	Ⓒ	Ⓐ	Ⓐ	Ⓒ	Ⓐ	Ⓐ	Ⓒ	Ⓐ	Ⓒ	Ⓐ
Hazebrouck .... d.	0834	0934	0934	1004	1034	1134	1201	1234	1253	1434	1434	1501	1604	1634	1634	1653	1723	1734	1800	1823	1834	1901	1934	2001
Lillers .... d.	0850	0950	0950	1021	1050	1150	1218	1253	1314	1450	1450	1518	1621	1651	1651	1713	1744	1751	1816	1847	1850	1918	1951	2017
Béthune .... d.	0900	1000	1000	1031	1101	1200	1228	1304	1328	1501	1500	1528	1631	1701	1701	1728	1758	1801	1827	1900	1901	1928	2002	2027
Lens .... d.	0921	1021	1022	1049	1122	1222	1245	1324	1348	1522	1521	1545	1649	1721	1722	1749	1816	1822	1844	1921	1922	1945	2022	2044
Arras .... a.	0938	1038	1039	1103	1139	1239	1302	1339	1403	1538	1539	1600	1703	1738	1739	1803	1839	1839	1856	1939	1939	1956	2039	2058

d – To/from Dunkerque (Table **266**).

Subject to alteration on ⑥⑦ Oct. 22 - Nov. 26.

265 (PARIS) - LILLE - CALAIS / BOULOGNE *High-speed tr*

For Paris - Boulogne via Amiens see Table **260**. For local trains Lille - Calais see Table **266**. For local trains Calais - Boulogne - Rang du Fliers see Table **261**.

km		TGV 7505		TGV 7513	TGV 7515		🚌	🚌	TGV 7223	TGV 7535		🚌	🚌	TGV 7559	TGV 7559			TGV 7265	TGV 7565		TGV 7569		TGV 7569
		Ⓐ	Ⓐ	Ⓐ	Ⓒ	⚒	†	Ⓒ	①–⑥	①–⑥	⚒	⑥	†	Ⓐ	⑦	Ⓐ	Ⓒ	Ⓐ	⑥	⚒	Ⓐ	Ⓐ	⑦
								§	b	b		§	§		e				t				
	Paris Nord **250** .... d.	0640	...	0740	0740	...	...	...	0940	1140x	...	...	...	1541	1541	...	...	1640	1640	...	1740	...	1740
0	**Lille** Europe .... d.	0755	...	0855	0855	...	...	...	1055	1255	...	...	...	1655	1655	...	...	1755	1755	...	1855	...	1915
99	Calais Fréthun .... a.	0823	...	0923	0923	...	...	...	1122	1323	...	...	...	1723	1723	...	...	1823	1823	...	1923	...	1943
99	Calais Fréthun .... **261** d.	0832	0831	0932	0932	0941	0938	1012	1124	1332	1341	1412	1612	1735	1735	1741	1749	1832	1832	1840	1932	1931	1953
107	**Calais** Ville .... **261** a.	|	0840	|	|	0950	0953	1027	1132	|	1350	1427	1627	|	|	1750	1757	|	|	1850	|	1940	|
133	**Boulogne** Ville .... a.	0853	...	0953	0953	...	...	...	...	1354	...	...	...	1756	1756	...	...	1853	1853	...	1953	...	2014
160	Étaples-Le Touquet .... a.	...	...	...	1012	...	...	...	...	1413	...	...	...	...	|	...	...	1912	...	...	2012	...	...
171	Rang du Fliers ⊙ .... a.	...	...	...	1023	...	...	...	...	1424	...	...	...	...	1822	...	...	1923	...	...	2023	...	...

	TGV 7277	TGV 7277	🚌			🚌	◇	🚌	
	①–⑥	⑦	†	Ⓐ	⑥	Ⓒ	†	†	
	b	e				§			
Paris Nord **250** .... d.	1843	1840	...	...	...	...	...	...	...
Lille Europe .... d.	1955	1955	...	...	...	...	2054	...	...
Calais Fréthun .... a.	2023	2023	...	...	...	...	2123	...	...
Calais Fréthun .... **261** d.	2035	2035	2039	2041	2102	2112	2132	2132	...
Calais Ville .... **261** a.	|	|	2054	2050	2110	2127	|	2157	...
Boulogne Ville .... a.	2056	2056	...	...	...	...	2153	...	...
Étaples-Le Touquet .... a.	...	2114	...	...	...	...	...	...	...
Rang du Fliers ⊙ .... a.	...	2126	...	...	...	...	...	...	...

	TGV 7216	🚌		TGV 7229		🚌	TGV 7537	TGV 7537
	Ⓐ	⑥	Ⓐ	①–⑥		⚒	Ⓐ	⑥
				b				t
Rang du Fliers ⊙ .... d.	...	...	...	0629	...	...	0714	...
Étaples-Le Touquet .... d.	...	...	...	0640	...	...	0725	...
Boulogne Ville .... d.	...	...	...	0700	...	...	0745	0745
Calais Ville .... **261** d.	0617	0702	0709	|	...	0745	|	|
Calais Fréthun .... **261** a.	0626	0717	0722	0721	...	0800	0807	0807
Calais Fréthun .... d.	0629	...	...	0732	...	...	0815	0815
Lille Europe .... a.	0658	...	...	0801	...	...	0845	0845
Paris Nord **250** .... a.	0814	...	...	0914	...	...	1014	1014

		TGV 7546	🚌	🚌			TGV 7551	TGV 7551	TGV 7254	🚌			TGV 7573		🚌	TGV 7586		TGV 7290	🚌	TGV 7292	TGV 7592	🚌	🚌
	Ⓐ	Ⓐ	Ⓒ	†	⑥	Ⓐ	Ⓐ	Ⓒ	①–⑥	Ⓒ		⚒	①–⑥		⑦	⑦	Ⓐ	Ⓐ	Ⓒ	⑦	⑥	Ⓒ	†
			§						b	§			b		e	e				e	t	§	
Rang du Fliers ⊙ .... d.	...	...	...	...	...	...	...	1130	...	...	...	...	1529	...	...	...	...	...	...	1829	...	...	...
Étaples-Le Touquet .... d.	...	...	...	...	...	...	...	1142	...	...	...	...	1541	...	...	...	...	...	...	1840	...	...	...
Boulogne Ville .... d.	...	1001	...	...	...	...	1203	1203	...	...	...	...	1600	...	...	1801	...	1827	...	1900	1903	...	...
Calais Ville .... **261** d.	1009	|	1032	1202	1209	1216	|	|	1327	1432	...	1558	|	...	1800	|	1830	|	1902	|	|	2032	2032
Calais Fréthun .... **261** a.	1022	1023	1047	1217	1218	1224	1223	1223	1335	1447	...	1607	1620	...	1815	1823	1839	1848	1917	1920	1923	2047	2047
Calais Fréthun .... d.	...	1032	...	...	...	...	1232	1232	1337	...	...	...	1632	...	...	1832	...	1900	...	1932	1932	...	...
Lille Europe .... a.	...	1101	...	...	...	...	1301	1301	1406	...	...	...	1701	...	...	1901	...	1930	...	2001	2001	...	...
Paris Nord **250** .... a.	...	1214	...	...	...	...	1414	1414	1514	...	...	...	1814	...	...	2014	...	2041	...	2114	2114	...	...

b – Not Aug. 15, Nov. 1.
e – Also Aug. 15, Nov. 1.
t – Also July 14, Nov. 11.
x – Depart 1142 on ⑥ to July 9.
TGV –Ⓡ, supplement payable.
◇ – TER à Grande Vitesse (TER GV) via high-speed line (1, 2 class). Supplement *Grande Vitesse* payable (€3, valid all day). Reservation not necessary.
⊙ – Full name: Rang du Fliers - Verton - Berck.
§ – Connects with *Eurostar* trains to/from Brussels (Table **10**).
🚌 – TER bus service. Rail tickets valid.

Most departures from Paris are 3-6 minutes later from July 16

ALTERNATIVE ROUTES PARIS - CALAIS
Via Lille (Tables **250** and **266**)
Via Hazebrouck (Tables **264** and **266**)
Via Amiens, Boulogne (Tables **260** and **261**)

al trains

LILLE - DUNKERQUE and CALAIS 266

For trains via high-speed line see Table **264** Lille - Dunkerque and Table **265** Lille - Calais

	Ⓐ	Ⓐ	Ⓐ b	⑥	⑥	Ⓐ	Ⓐ	Ⓐ	⑥	Ⓐ	⑥	Ⓐ	⚒	Ⓐ	Ⓐ	Ⓒ	Ⓐ	†	Ⓐ	Ⓐ	Ⓒ	Ⓒ	Ⓐ	Ⓐ	Ⓒ	Ⓒ
Lille Flandres....... d.	...	...	...	...	...	0615	0635	0645	0645	0700	...	0715	0735	...	0800	0815	0835	...	0845	0900	0935	...	1000	1015	1015	1135
Armentières.......... d.	...	...	...	...	...	|	0649	0701	0659	0713	...	|	0750	...	0814	0829	0849	...	0902	0913	0950	...	1013	|	1029	1150
Hazebrouck.......... d.	0543	0618	0633	0635	0647	0648	0713	0722	0718	0735	0747	0748	0813	0818	0835	0847	0913	0915	0918	0935	1013	1019	1035	1048	1048	1213
Dunkerque....... a.	|	0652	|	|	0720	0720	|	0755	0752	|	0820	0820	|	0852	|	0920	|	|	0952	|	|	1055	|	1120	1120	|
St Omer.............. d.	0557	...	0650	0653	...	...	0726	...	...	0753	...	...	0826	...	0853	...	0926	0929	...	0953	1025	...	1053	...	...	1225
Calais Ville .... a.	0626	...	0727	0726	...	...	0756	...	...	0826	...	...	0856	...	0927	...	0956	0958	...	1026	1056	...	1126	...	...	1256

	Ⓒ	Ⓐ △	Ⓐ	⑥	Ⓐ △	Ⓐ △	Ⓐ	⑥	⚒ △	Ⓐ	⑥	†	⑥	Ⓐ	⑥	Ⓐ △	Ⓐ	Ⓒ	†		Ⓐ	Ⓐ	Ⓐ		Ⓐ	†	⑥
Flandres .... d.	...	1200	1215	1215	1219	1235	1245	1245	...	1315	...	1315	1335	1345	...	1400	...	1435	...	1545	1600	1615	1619	1635	1645	...	...
ntières .... d.	...	1214	|	1229	1234	1249	1302	1258	...	|	...	1329	1350	1402	...	1413	...	1450	...	1559	1613	|	1634	1649	1701	...	...
brouck .... d.	1217	1235	1248	1248	1253	1313	1318	1319	1333	1348	1348	1348	1413	1418	1419	1435	1447	1513	1519	1618	1635	1648	1653	1713	1718	1719	1719
nkerque .... a.	1253	|	1320	1319	|	|	1352	1355	|	1420	1421	1420	|	1452	1455	|	1520	|	1545	1652	|	1720	|	|	1752	1743	1753
mer.............. d.	...	1253	...	...	1305	1326	...	...	1352	...	...	...	1426	...	...	1453	...	1526	...	...	1653	...	1705	1725	...	...	...
is Ville.......... a.	...	1326	...	...	...	1356	...	...	1426	...	...	...	1456	...	...	1526	...	1558	...	...	1725	...	...	1756	...	...	...

	Ⓐ	Ⓐ	Ⓒ	Ⓐ	Ⓐ u	Ⓐ	Ⓐ	Ⓐ	Ⓐ	Ⓐ		Ⓐ	Ⓐ	Ⓐ	†	⑥	Ⓐ	Ⓐ	Ⓐ		†	⑥	†	⚒	Ⓐ	† ⊖	Ⓐ v
Flandres....... d.	1700	1715	1715	1719	...	1735	1745	1800	1815	1819	1835	1845	1900	...	1915	1915	1919	1935	2015	2035	...	...	2115	2115	2215	2300	2312
entières.......... d.	1713	|	1731	1734	...	1749	1802	1813	|	1834	1849	1902	1913	...	1931	1931	1934	1950	|	2049	...	...	2129	2129	2229	2314	2326
brouck .... d.	1735	1748	1748	1753	1806	1812	1817	1835	1848	1853	1913	1918	1935	1947	1949	1948	1953	2018	2048	2113	2119	2118	2148	2148	2247	2335	2349
nkerque .... a.	|	1820	1820	|	1828	|	1852	|	1920	|	|	1952	|	2020	2020	2022	|	2052	2120	|	2145	2152	2211	2220	2320	|	...
mer.............. d.	1753	...	...	1805	...	1826	...	1853	...	1905	1926	...	1953	...	...	...	2005	...	...	2126	...	...	...	...	...	2347	...
is Ville.......... a.	1826	...	...	...	...	1856	...	1926	...	...	1956	...	2026	...	...	...	...	...	...	2156	...	...	...	...	...	0014	...

	Ⓐ	Ⓐ	Ⓐ	Ⓐ	Ⓐ	⑥	Ⓐ	Ⓐ	⑥	Ⓐ	⑥ u	Ⓐ u	Ⓐ	Ⓐ	Ⓐ	⑥	Ⓐ	⑥	Ⓐ	Ⓐ	⑥	Ⓐ	Ⓐ	⑥	Ⓐ	Ⓒ	Ⓐ
is Ville.......... d.	...	0453	...	...	...	...	0534	...	...	0605	...	...	...	...	0634	0635	...	...	0706	...	...	...	0734	0735	...	...	0833
mer.............. d.	...	0523	...	0554	...	...	0607	...	...	0635	...	...	0654	...	0708	0704	...	...	0735	0754	...	...	0808	0808	...	...	0909
ınkerque .... d.	...	|	0507	|	0540	0540	|	0608	0608	|	0630	0637	|	0640	|	|	0708	0708	|	|	0739	0740	|	|	0808	0839	|
ebrouck .... d.	0448	0538	0543	0608	0613	0613	0626	0642	0644	0649	0702	0658	0708	0713	0726	0726	0743	0744	0749	0808	0811	0813	0826	0827	0843	0913	0926
entières.......... d.	0512	...	0600	0627	|	0630	0645	0657	0700	0711	...	...	0726	|	0745	0745	0757	0800	0811	0825	...	|	0845	0844	0857	0930	0945
Flandres .... a.	0525	...	0614	0640	0644	0644	0659	0714	0714	0725	...	...	0740	0744	0759	0759	0814	0814	0825	0840	...	0844	0859	0859	0914	0944	0959

	⑥ u	Ⓐ	†	Ⓐ	Ⓒ	Ⓐ	⑥	†	Ⓐ	Ⓐ	Ⓐ	Ⓒ	⑥	Ⓐ	Ⓐ ▽	Ⓐ	Ⓐ	Ⓐ ▽	⑥	Ⓐ	⑥	†		†	⑥	⑥	Ⓐ ▽
is Ville.......... d.	...	...	...	0906	0906	...	...	...	1036	...	1106	1135	...	...	1206	...	...	1234	1235	...	...	...	...	1335	1338	...	1434
mer.............. d.	...	...	...	0935	0935	...	...	...	1109	...	1135	1209	...	...	1235	1254	...	1308	1306	...	...	...	...	1405	1411	...	1508
ınkerque .... d.	0856	0908	0908	|	|	1040	1039	1039	|	1108	|	|	1208	1213	...	|	1240	|	|	1308	1308	1308	1339	|	|	1439	|
ebrouck .... d.	0932	0943	0942	0949	0949	1113	1113	1108	1126	1143	1149	1225	1244	1248	...	1308	1313	1325	1325	1343	1342	1344	1411	1425	1425	1513	1526
entières.......... d.	...	0957	...	1011	1011	|	1129	1127	1145	1157	1211	1245	1306	1302	...	1325	|	...	1345	1357	1400	1401	...	1445	1445	1530	1545
Flandres .... a.	...	1014	...	1025	1025	1144	1144	1144	1159	1214	1225	1259	1325	1320	...	1340	1344	...	1359	1414	1414	1414	...	1459	1459	1544	1559

	Ⓐ		Ⓐ ▽	Ⓒ	Ⓐ	Ⓐ	Ⓒ	Ⓐ	Ⓐ	Ⓐ	Ⓐ	⑥	†	Ⓐ	Ⓒ	Ⓐ	Ⓒ	Ⓒ	Ⓐ	Ⓒ	Ⓒ	Ⓐ	Ⓐ	Ⓒ	Ⓐ	Ⓐ	Ⓒ
is Ville.......... d.	...	...	1534	1535	...	...	...	1634	...	1706	...	...	...	1733	1735	...	...	...	1834	1835	...	...	1906	1935	...	2034	...
mer.............. d.	...	...	1608	1604	...	...	...	1707	...	1735	...	...	...	1807	1805	...	...	...	1911	1904	...	...	1935	2004	...	2111	...
ınkerque .... d.	1508	1539	|	|	1608	1640	1639	|	1708	|	1740	1740	1740	|	|	1808	1808	1849	|	|	1908	1908	|	|	2008	|	2108
ebrouck .... d.	1543	1611	1626	1626	1643	1713	1709	1726	1743	1748	1813	1811	1812	1826	1823	1843	1844	1921	1926	1925	1939	1942	1949	2025	2043	2126	2142
entières.......... d.	1557	...	1645	1645	1657	|	1727	1745	1757	1810	|	...	...	1845	1843	1857	1900	...	1945	1945	1958	...	2011	2045	2100	2145	2159
Flandres .... a.	1614	...	1659	1659	1714	1744	1744	1759	1814	1825	1844	...	...	1859	1859	1914	1914	...	1959	1959	2014	...	2025	2059	2114	2159	2214

From Bethune, depart 0602.
To/from Arras (Table **264a**).
Subject to alteration Sept. 19 - Oct. 21.

△ – Subject to alteration Oct. 3-7.
▽ – Subject to alteration Oct. 10-14.
⊖ – Subject to alteration.

Subject to alteration on ⑥⑦ Oct. 22 - Nov. 27

PARIS - BEAUVAIS 267

		Ⓐ	⑥	Ⓐ	Ⓐ	⑥	†z	Ⓐ	Ⓒ	Ⓐ			⚒		⑥	Ⓐ	Ⓐ	Ⓒ	Ⓐ	Ⓐ	⑥	Ⓐ	Ⓐ	†	
0	**Paris Nord**................. d.	0605	0631	0635	0735	0801	0801	0850	0901	1001	1101	1201	1301	1401	1601	1605	1635	1701	1705	1735	1801	1805	1835	1844	...
0	**Beauvais** .... a.	0720	0750	0751	0851	0918	0920	1005	1018	1118	1218	1318	1418	1519	1720	1720	1747	1820	1820	1847	1920	1920	1947	2009	...

	⑥	Ⓐ	Ⓐ	⚒	Ⓑ	Ⓒ
s Nord..................... d.	1901	1905	1935	2001	2101	2201
uvais..................... a.	2019	2020	2048	2118	2218	2318

	Ⓐ	Ⓐ	⑥	Ⓐ	Ⓒ	Ⓐ	Ⓐ	Ⓒ	Ⓐ	⚒	†		⚒		⚒
Beauvais .... d.	0513	0540	0540	0613	0627	0640	0713	0737	0740	0840	0937	1037	1137	1237	1337
Paris Nord .... a.	0625	0655	0657	0725	0743	0755	0823	0857	0855	0957	1057	1157	1257	1357	1457

		Ⓐ	⑥	Ⓐ	Ⓐ	Ⓒ	Ⓐ	Ⓐ	Ⓒ	⑥	†M	†L	Ⓐ	Ⓒ	†	†M
uvais..................... d.	1437	1640	1640	1710	1740	1741	1810	1840	1840	1937	1949	1950	2010	2037	2137	2159
s Nord..................... a.	1557	1755	1757	1823	1855	1857	1923	1955	1957	2057	2059	2105	2127	2157	2257	2301

Most trains call at Persan-Beaumont (30 mins from Paris).
CREIL - BEAUVAIS : 14 journeys on Ⓐ, 7 on ⑥, 4 on †.

R NOTES SEE TABLE 267a

Subject to alteration on June 4, 5.

BEAUVAIS - LE TRÉPORT 267a

n		Ⓐ △	† L	† M	⑥	⚒	† M	⚒	Ⓐ	† L	⑥	⑤–⑦ u
	Paris Nord **267** .. d.	...	0801	0801	...	...	...	...	...	...	...	...
0	**Beauvais**............. d.	0740	0926	0926	0924	1234	1752	1759	...	1823	1853	2025
	Rouen ⊖..... **268** d.	|	*0915*	*0915*	*0917r*	|	|	|	...	|	|	|
9	Abancourt ...... **268** d.	0836	1021	1020	1021	1334	1851	1855	1905	1922	1949	2123
3	Eu .... d.	0928	1112	|	1112	1425	1943	...	1956	2013	2041	2214
6	**Le Tréport** .... a.	0932	1116	1109	1116	1430	1947	...	2000	2017	2045	2218

	Ⓐ	⑥	†	⑥	⚒	†	⚒	† M	† L	† M
Le Tréport.......... d.	0529	0643	0731	0847	1205	1238	1720	1800	1758	2001
Eu .... d.	0534	|	|	0852	1210	1243	1725	|	1803	2006
Abancourt ..... **268** d.	0634	0735	0822	0944	1302	1334	1824	1849	1851	2052
Rouen ⊖.... **268** a.	|	|	|	|	|	|	|	*1942*	|	|
Beauvais............. a.	0730	0830	0919	1049	1358	1430	1925	1945	1948	2150
Paris Nord **267** . a.	...	...	...	...	...	...	...	2059	2105	2301

† to June 26/from Sept. 4.
† July 3 - Aug. 28.
⑥ July 9 - Aug. 27.

u – Also holidays.
z – To/from Le Tréport (Table **267a**).

⊖ – Rouen Rive-Droite. See Table **268** for other connections.
△ – Subject to alteration Oct. 10-21.

AMIENS - ROUEN 268

m		① g	Ⓐ	⑥	†	Ⓐ v	Ⓐ △	⑥	†	①–④ n	⑤ f	Ⓑ	⑥	Ⓐ	† M	Ⓐ	Ⓒ	
	Lille Flandres **256**.... d.	...	0602	0802	...	...	1102	...	...	...	...	...	...	1702	...	...	1802	...
0	**Amiens** .... d.	0555	0719	0927	0927	1027	1227	1244	1421	1655	1655	1727	1733	1827	...	1906	1927	...
1	Poix de Picardie .... d.	0614	0737	0946	0944	1044	1245	1305	1439	1718	1717	1745	1755	1845	...	1927	1945	...
2	Abancourt..................... d.	0626	0749	0958	0956	1056	1258	1320	1451	1733	1732	1757	1810	1857	1855	1942	1958	...
3	Serqueux..................... d.	0642	0803	1011	1012	1109	1311	1336	1510	1749	1750	1813	1828	1913	1910	1957	2011	...
21	**Rouen** Rive-Droite...... a.	0724	0832	1044	1044	1142	1342	1423	1542	...	1822	1842	1907	1942	1942	...	2043	...

	Ⓐ	Ⓐ	Ⓐ		⑥		†	⑥ R	Ⓐ ▽	⚒ u		Ⓐ			Ⓐ		⑤	†
ıen Rive-Droite....... d.	...	0617	0717	...	0817	...	0915	0917	1117	1217	...	1617	...	1817	1834	...	1917	1917
queux..................... d.	0611	0647	0747	...	0848	...	0948	0948	1149	1249	...	1649	...	1849	1915	...	1949	1949
ıncourt..................... d.	0628	0703	0802	...	0902	...	1002	1004	1202	1302	...	1703	...	1902	1932	...	2003	2003
x de Picardie............ d.	0643	0715	0814	...	0915	...	1015	...	1215	1314	...	1716	...	1915	...	...	2015	2015
iens .... a.	0705	0732	0832	...	0932	...	1032	...	1232	1332	...	1735	...	1932	...	...	2032	2032
ille Flandres **256**..... a.	...	0858	...	...	1058	...	...	...	1358	...	...	...	...	2058	...	...	...	...

M – † July 3 - Aug. 28.
R – ⑥ July 9 - Aug. 27.

f – Not Nov. 11.
g – Also Aug. 16; not Aug. 15.
n – Not holidays.
u – Subject to alteration on ①–④ July 11 - Sept. 1, Nov. 28 - Dec. 2.
v – Subject to alteration July 11 - Sept. 2, Nov. 28 - Dec. 2.

△ – Subject to alteration July 11 - Sept. 2, Sept. 26 - Oct. 21, Nov. 28 - Dec. 2.
▽ – Subject to alteration July 11 - Sept. 2, Oct. 10-21, Nov. 28 - Dec. 2.

269 🚌 RENNES / DOL - MONT ST MICHEL

By 🚌 Keolis Emera

km	🚌									
			Ⓐ	Ⓒb		S	ⒸW			
0	**Rennes** Gare Routière ⊡ d.	0940	...	...	1135	...	...	1235	1645	...
	Dol (Gare SNCF) d.	|	1040	1115	|	1315	1320	|	|	...
68	**Mont St Michel** a.	1050	1110	1145	1245	1345	1350	1345	1755	...

🚌								
	Ⓐ	Ⓒ			S	W		⑦S
Mont St Michel d.	0905	0935	1105	1435	1605	1610	1730	1840
Dol (Gare SNCF) a.	|	|	|	|	1640	1640	|	1910
Rennes Gare Routière ⊡ a.	1015	1045	1215	1545	...	...	1845	...

b – Runs 5 minutes later July 3 - Aug. 28. S – July 3 - Aug. 28. W – Dec. 12 - July 2. ⊡ – Adjacent to rail station. *Service to Aug. 28, 2016*

Operator: Keolis Emeraude, St Malo. ✆ 02 99 19 70 70. www.keolis-emeraude.com

Connections (not guaranteed) at Rennes or Dol with *TGV* services to / from Paris. Combined rail / bus tickets available from rail stations. Rail passes not valid. At Mont St Michel the coach terminates close to the tourist information office. A free *Passeur* shuttle service operates along the causeway to Mont St Michel itself, allow 25 mins (or 45 mins walk, *2.4 km*). Horse-drawn sh (*Maringotes*) are also available, fee payable.

270 PARIS - ROUEN - LE HAVRE

km								3101		13101		3103	3103	13103	3105	3105		13105	13191	3107	13193			13107
		⚒	⚒	Ⓐ	Ⓐ	⚒	Ⓐ	Ⓐ	⑥	Ⓐ	⑦	⑥	Ⓐ		Ⓒ	Ⓐ		⚒	⑦	Ⓐ	⑥	†	⚒	
							K	J			e	t▷		△	◧			△	n		b			
0	**Paris** St Lazare § d.	...	...	...	...	0611	...	0653	...	0720	...	0750z	0753	0820	0850	0853	...	1020	1036	1050	1050	...	...	1220
57	Mantes la Jolie § d.	...	...	0627	...	0644	...	|	0737	0752	...	|	|	0853	|	|	...	1052	1108	|	|	...	...	1252
79	Vernon-Giverny d.	...	...	0645	...	0706	...	|	0750	0807	...	|	|	0907	|	|	...	1107	1123	|	|	...	...	1307
111	Val de Reuil d.	...	...	0705	...	0727	...	|	0810	0828	...	|	|	0928	|	|	...	1128	1145	|	|	...	...	1328
126	Oissel d.	...	...	0717	...	0736	...	|	0822	0837	...	|	|	0937	|	|	...	1137	1156	|	|	...	...	1337
140	**Rouen** Rive-Droite a.	...	...	0730	...	0750	...	0802	0837	0848	...	0900	0902	0948	1000	1000	...	1148	1207	1200	1200	...	...	1348
140	**Rouen** Rive-Droite d.	0630	0700	...	0740	...	0804	0805	...	...	0904	0903	0905	...	1003	1003	...	...	...	1203	...	1220	1250	...
178	Yvetot d.	0655	0731	...	0807	...	0827	0827	...	...	0927	0925	0927	...	1025	1025	...	...	...	1225	...	1242	1321	...
203	Bréauté-Beuzeville ▲ d.	0713	0751	...	0822	...	0840	0843	...	...	0940	0941	0943	...	1041	1041	...	...	...	1241	...	1256	1340	...
228	**Le Havre** a.	0733	0813	...	0837	...	0855	0858	...	...	0955	0956	0958	...	1056	1056	...	...	...	1256	...	1310	1403	...

	3109	3113	3111	13109	3115	3117		3119	13111		3121		3123	13113	13115	3125		3127	3129	13117	13119			3131
	⚒	⑥	⑤				⑥	⑥	Ⓑ	⑦	Ⓐ	Ⓐ		Ⓒ	Ⓐ		Ⓐ	①–④	⑤	Ⓒ	Ⓐ	⑥	†	Ⓐ
	△	◧t	F	△	△	N		△t	h	e			N	△		△		M	E	△				
Paris St Lazare § d.	1250	1350	1350	1420	1450	1550	...	1620	1620	...	1650	1653	1725	1720	1730	1750	1753	1825	1825	1820	1830	...	...	1850
Mantes la Jolie § d.	|	|	|	1452	|	|	...	1652	1652	...	|	1725	|	1752	|	|	1825	|	|	1852	|	...	...	|
Vernon-Giverny d.	|	|	|	1507	|	|	...	1707	1707	...	|	1747	|	1807	1813	|	1847	|	|	1907	1913	...	...	1936
Val de Reuil d.	|	|	|	1528	|	|	...	1728	1728	...	|	1810	|	1828	1832	|	1910	|	|	1928	1932	...	...	|
Oissel d.	|	|	|	1537	|	|	...	1737	1737	...	|	1819	|	1837	1840	|	1919	|	|	1937	1940	...	...	|
Rouen Rive-Droite a.	1400	1500	1500	1548	1600	1700	...	1748	1748	...	1800	...	1833	1848	1849	1900	...	1933	1933	1948	1949	...	...	2004
Rouen Rive-Droite d.	1403	1503	...	...	1603	1703	1704	1751	...	1804	1803	...	1836	...	...	1903	...	...	1936	...	...	2004	2006	2007
Yvetot d.	1425	1525	...	...	1625	1725	1727	1813	...	1829	1825	...	1859	...	...	1925	...	...	1959	...	...	2031	2032	2029
Bréauté-Beuzeville ▲ d.	1441	1541	...	...	1641	1741	1740	1829	...	1842	1841	...	1915	...	...	1941	...	...	2015	...	...	2045	2048	2045
Le Havre a.	1456	1556	...	...	1656	1756	1755	1844	...	1856	1856	...	1929	...	...	1956	...	...	2029	...	...	2100	2102	2059

	13121	13123	3133	5376	13125	3135	3137	3137	13127	3139	3141	3141	13129	13131
	⑦	Ⓐ		*TGV*	Ⓐ	⑥	①–④		⑤	⑤	⑤	⑦	①–④	⑥
	e		C	♥	J	△t	m	Q	v	v	v	e	D	△t
Paris St Lazare § d.	1920	1930	1950	...	2020	2020	2050	2120	2120	2150	2205	2350	2320x	2350
Mantes la Jolie § d.	1952	|	|	2033	2052	2052	|	2152	2152	|	2237	0022	2352	0022
Vernon-Giverny d.	2007	2013	|	|	2107	2107	2134	2207	2207	|	2252	0036	0007	0037
Val de Reuil d.	2028	2032	|	|	2128	2128	|	2228	2228	|	2312	0058	0028	0058
Oissel d.	2037	2040	|	|	2137	2137	|	2237	2237	|	2322	0107	0037	0107
Rouen Rive-Droite a.	2048	2049	2100	2114	2148	2148	2203	2248	2248	2300	2333	0117	0048	0118
Rouen Rive-Droite d.	...	...	2103	2118	...	2151	2206	2251	...	2303	2336	0120	...	...
Yvetot d.	...	...	2125	|	...	2213	2229	2313	...	2325	2358	0142	...	...
Bréauté-Beuzeville ▲ d.	...	...	2141	|	...	2229	2243	2329	...	2341	0014	0158	...	...
Le Havre a.	...	...	2156	2202	...	2244	2257	2344	...	2356	0028	0213	...	...

		13100	13102	3100	
	Ⓐ	Ⓐ	⑥	Ⓐ	Ⓐ
			△t		
Le Havre d.	...	...	...	0529	...
Bréauté-Beuzeville ▲ d.	...	...	...	0545	...
Yvetot d.	...	...	...	0601	...
Rouen Rive-Droite a.	...	...	...	0623	...
Rouen Rive-Droite d.	0526	0558	0612	0626	...
Oissel d.	0540	0608	0623	|	0639
Val de Reuil d.	0550	0617	0632	|	0650
Vernon-Giverny d.	0611	0639	0653	|	0711
Mantes la Jolie § a.	0631	0656	0705	|	0731
Paris St Lazare § a.	0708	0735	0740	0738	0808

	13106	3104	13108	3102			3106	13110		5316	3108	13112		13114	3110	3112	13116		3114	13118	3116		3118	13120
	Ⓐ	⑥	⑦	Ⓐ	Ⓐ	⑥	Ⓐ	⚒	Ⓐ	*TGV*		⚒	Ⓐ	Ⓑ	⑥	⚒	⑥		⑦		⚒		Ⓐ	
		t▷	d	L				△		♥		J		h	◧t	△	◧t		u	△	△	B	J	△
Le Havre d.	...	0612	...	0629	...	0640	0702	...	0725	0753	0802	...	0903	...	0915	1002	...	...	1102	...	1202	1245	1302	...
Bréauté-Beuzeville ▲ d.	...	0628	...	0646	...	0704	0718	...	0740	|	0818	...	0918	...	0931	1018	...	...	1118	...	1218	1309	1318	...
Yvetot d.	...	0644	...	0702	...	0723	0734	...	0757	|	0834	...	0933	...	0947	1034	...	...	1134	...	1234	1328	1334	...
Rouen Rive-Droite a.	...	0709	...	0725	...	0756	0756	...	0824	0840	0856	...	0957	...	1009	1056	...	...	1156	...	1256	1359	1356	...
Rouen Rive-Droite d.	0658	0712	0712	0728	0712	...	0759	0812	...	0845	0859	0912	...	1012	1012	1059	1112	...	1159	1212	1259	...	1359	1413
Oissel d.	0708	0723	0723	|	0740	...	|	0823	...	|	|	0923	...	1023	1023	|	1123	...	|	1223	|	...	|	1423
Val de Reuil d.	0717	0732	0732	|	0749	...	|	0832	...	|	|	0932	...	1032	1032	|	1132	...	|	1232	|	...	|	1432
Vernon-Giverny d.	0739	0753	0753	|	0811	...	|	0853	...	|	|	0953	...	1053	1053	|	1153	...	|	1253	|	...	|	1453
Mantes la Jolie § a.	0756	0807	0806	|	0831	...	|	0906	...	0930	|	1006	...	1106	1106	|	1206	...	|	1306	|	...	|	1506
Paris St Lazare § a.	0835	0840r	0840	0839	0908	...	0915	0940	...	...	1010r	1040	...	1140	1140	1210	1240	...	1310	1340	1410	...	1510	1540

	3122	3138		13122	3124	13190	13124	13192	3126	3128		13126		3130		13128		13194	3132	3134		13130		3136
	⑤		Ⓐ	⑦	Ⓐ	⑦	Ⓐ	⑥	⑦		Ⓐ	⑦	⑥		⑥	Ⓐ	⑦	⑦		Ⓑ	⑥	⑦		⑦
	v	Y		e		e		◧	e	△		e		P			G	e	△	h		e		e
Le Havre d.	...	1502	...	...	1602	...	...	...	1615	1702	...	...	...	1802	1803	...	1908	...	1915	2002	2000	...	...	2115
Bréauté-Beuzeville ▲ d.	...	1518	...	...	1618	...	...	...	1631	1718	...	...	...	1818	1817	...	|	...	1931	2018	2015	...	...	2131
Yvetot d.	...	1534	...	...	1634	...	...	...	1647	1734	...	...	...	1834	1831	...	|	...	1947	2034	2031	...	...	2147
Rouen Rive-Droite a.	...	1556	...	...	1656	...	...	...	1709	1756	...	...	...	1856	1855	...	1954	...	2009	2056	2053	...	...	2209
Rouen Rive-Droite d.	1555	1559	1612	1612	1659	1659	1712	1712	1712	1759	1812	1812	1823	1859	...	1912	...	1959	2012	2059	...	2110	...	2212
Oissel d.	|	|	1623	1623	|	|	1723	1723	1723	|	1823	1823	1838	|	...	|	...	|	2023	|	...	2123	...	2223
Val de Reuil d.	|	|	1632	1632	|	|	1732	1732	1732	|	1832	1832	1850	|	...	1932	...	|	2032	|	...	2132	...	2232
Vernon-Giverny d.	|	|	1653	1653	|	|	1753	1753	1753	|	1853	1853	1912	|	...	1953	...	|	2053	|	...	2153	...	2253
Mantes la Jolie § a.	|	|	1706	1706	|	|	1806	1805	1806	|	1906	1906	1925	|	...	2006	...	|	2106	|	...	2206	...	2306
Paris St Lazare § a.	1710	1710	1740	1740	1810	1810	1840	1840	1840	1910	1940	1940	...	2010	...	2040	...	2110	2140	2210	...	2240	...	2340

B – ⑥ to July 2; ⚒ July 4 - Aug. 27 (also Sept. 10, 17).
C – Will not run on ⑥ June 25 - Aug. 27; not July 14.
D – To June 30, also Aug. 22 - Sept. 8.
E – ⑤ to July 8 / from Sept. 2 (also Nov. 10; not Nov. 11).
F – ⑤ to July 1 / from Sept. 2 (also Nov. 10; not Oct. 28, Nov. 11).
G – ⑦ Apr. 17 - Sept. 25.
J – To July 1 / from Aug. 29.
K – July 4 - Aug. 26.
L – To July 8 / from Aug. 29.
M – ①–④ to June 30 / from Aug. 29 (also Oct. 31; not Nov. 1).
N – Ⓐ to July 1; ⑤ July 8 - Aug. 26; Ⓐ from Aug. 29.
P – Ⓑ to July 1; ⑤⑦ July 3 - Aug. 28 (also Aug. 15); Ⓑ from Aug. 29.

Q – ⑦ (also ①–④ July 11 - Aug. 11), not July 13, 14.
Y – Aug. 15, 21, 28, Nov. 1, 13 only.
b – ⑥ to June 18 (also July 14, 30, Aug. 13), ⑥ Aug. 27 - Sept. 17.
d – Also Aug. 15, Nov. 1; not June 26, July 10, Aug. 21.
e – Also Aug. 15, Nov. 1.
h – Not July 14, Nov. 11.
m – Not July 11 - Aug. 15.
n – Also Aug. 15, Nov. 1; not June 26, July 10, Aug. 21.
r – 30 - 35 mins later June 25, 26, July 2, 9, 10, 16, 23, Aug. 6, 20, 21.
t – Also July 14.
u – Also Aug. 15; not June 26, July 31, Aug. 21, Sept. 4.
v – Also July 13, Nov. 10; not Nov. 11.

x – 2309 on June 20, 22, 23; 2308 on June 27 - 30.
z – Depart 0709 June 25, July 9, 16, Aug. 20, Oct. 1
TGV – Ⓡ, supplement payable, 🍷.
♥ – To/from Lyon and Marseille (Table **335**).
▲ – 🚌 runs 2 - 8 times per day to Fécamp.
◧ – Subject to alteration from June 25.
▷ – Subject to alteration on Sept. 3, 24.
△ – Subject to alteration June 25, 26, July 2, 9, 16, 23 Aug. 6, 20, 21, Sept. 3, 17, 24, 25, Oct. 1.
§ – Frequent suburban trains run Paris - Mantes-la-J

Service to Oct. 1. Timings may vary from Oct. 2 with earlier departures from Le Havre.

270a ROUEN - DIEPPE

km		⑥	Ⓐ	Ⓐ	Ⓐ	†	⚒		⚒	†	⑥	Ⓐ	⑦S	⑥	⑥	Ⓐ	Ⓐ	Ⓐ		Ⓐr	Ⓐ		Ⓐ	⚒	†
0	**Rouen** Rive-Droite d.	0640	0640	0712	0730	0841	0912	1012	1212	1225	1242	1341	1341	1412	1512	1612	1641	1712	1741	1812	1841	1912	2012	2124	2130
63	**Dieppe** a.	0740	0743	0758	0844	0940	0958	1058	1258	1310	1344	1443	1441	1458	1558	1658	1743	1758	1843	1858	1943	1958	2058	2209	2216

	Ⓐ	⚒	Ⓐ	Ⓐ	Ⓒ	Ⓐ	⚒		⚒	Ⓐ	Ⓒ	Ⓐ	†	Ⓐ	⑥	⑦S	Ⓐ	†	⚒	⑦K	Ⓐ	⚒	†	⑦S	
Dieppe d.	0532	0617	0659	0713	0751	0800	0813	1000	1200	1313	1313	1400	1556	1600	1609	1700	1713	1801	1813	1844	1900	2000	2013	2101	...
Rouen Rive-Droite a.	0616	0719	0748	0819	0835	0848	0919	1048	1248	1419	1419	1448	1642	1647	1655	1746	1819	1847	1919	1929	1948	2048	2113	2146	...

K – ⑦ July 3 - Aug. 28 (also July 14, Aug. 15).
S – ⑦ June 5 - Sept. 11 (also July 14, Aug. 15).
r – Also ⑥ June 4 - Sept. 10.

Timings may vary by a few minutes from Oct. 2.

CAEN - ALENÇON - LE MANS - TOURS 271

	①–⑥ b	Ⓐ	Ⓐ	Ⓐ	①–⑥ b	⑦ e		⑥ d	Ⓐ	⊕				Ⓑ h	⑦ e	①–⑥ b	⑥ 🚌	Ⓐ	⑦ e	Ⓐ	⑥ d	Ⓐ	⑤ f	①–④ m	⑦ e
Caen .... **275/7** d.	...	0535x	...	0600	0726	...	0905	1029	1039	...	1246	...	...	1650	...	...	...	1745	1745	1811	1825	...	2000	2000	2030
Mézidon .... **275/7** d.	...	0550x	...	0615	0741	...	0922	1045	1053	...	1302	...	...	1705	...	...	...	1800	1801	1830	1840	...	2014	2015	2045
Argentan .... **273** d.	...	0614	...	0644	0809	...	0946	1108	1116	...	1326	...	...	1732	...	...	...	1832	1835	1859	1908	...	2040	2043	2108
Surdon .... **273** d.	...	|	...	0654	0818	...	|	1119	1126	...	1336	...	...	|	...	...	...	1842	1846	1909	1918	...	2049	2053	|
Sées .... d.	...	0628	...	0702	0826	...	|	1127	1133	...	1343	...	...	1747	...	...	...	1850	1854	1916	1925	...	2056	2100	2122
Alençon .... d.	...	0642	...	0715	0839	0839	1013	1140	1146	...	1357	...	1624r	1759	...	...	...	1902	1909	1929	1938	...	2108	2112	2135
Le Mans .... a.	...	0729	...	0805	0909	0909	1041	1218	1223	...	1427	...	1712	1831	...	...	...	...	1944	1959	2008	...	...	...	2205
Le Mans .... d.	0625	...	0739	...	...	...	1043	...	...	1240	1438	1638	...	1837	1903	1907	...	...	1947	...	...	2017	...	...	...
Château du Loir .... d.	0656	...	0810	...	...	...	1113	...	...	1311	1507	1710	...	1909	1950	1953	2000	...	2018	...	...	2103	...	...	...
St Pierre des Corps .. a.	|	...	|	...	...	...	1141	...	...	|	1535	|	...	|	|	...	|	...	|	...	...	|	...	...	...
Tours .... a.	0738	...	0838	...	...	...	1153	...	...	1339	1546	1742	...	1938	2025	...	2050	...	2048	...	...	2138	...	...	...

	Ⓐ	Ⓐ	⑥ d	Ⓐ	①–⑥ b	⑦ e	①–⑥ b	⑦ e	Ⓐ	⑥ d	⚒ ⊕	⑥ d	Ⓐ	①–④ m	⑤ f		⑥ d	①–④ m	⑤ f	Ⓐ	Ⓑ h	⑦ e	⑤ f	⑦ e	①–④ m	⑤⑦ w
.... d.	...	*0527*x	...	0634	0750	0907	0908	1022	...	...	1159	1225	1422	...	1519	1654	...	...	...	1729	1822	...	...	1907	...	2121
rre des Corps ... d.	...	|	...	|	|	0922	0922	|	...	...	|	|	|	...	|	|	...	...	...	|	|	...	...	1922	...	|
au du Loir......... d.	...	*0557*x	...	0709	0821	0951	0951	1052	...	...	1229	1307	1453	...	1550	1724	...	...	...	1812	1852	...	...	1952	...	2151
ans.................. a.	...	*0643*x	...	0758	0853	1022	1024	1121	...	...	1259	1357	1523	...	1618	1752	...	...	...	1857	1921	...	...	2021	...	2221
ans.................. d.	0626x	0659	0735	*0859*	...	1034	1036	*1240*	1240	1240	...	...	1531	...	1623	1755	1858	1858	1900	*1931*	...	1958	2003	2025	2029	...
on .... d.	0657	0751	0827	*0947*	...	1104	1107	*1330*	1332	1332	...	...	1612	1722	1722	1829	1928	1928	1936	*2020*	...	2029	2034	2056	2107	...
.... d.	0709	0803	0839	...	...	1116	1119	...	1345	1345	...	...	1625	1735	1735	1842	1940	1941	1949	...	...	2042	2045	2108	2120	...
n.............. **273** d.	0716	0811	0847	...	...	1124	1126	...	1352	1353	...	...	|	1742	1742	1850	1948	1948	1957	...	...	2049	2052	|	2128	...
tan............ **273** d.	0726	0821	0857	...	...	1134	1136	...	1403	1403	...	...	1641	1752	1752	1900	1958	1958	2014	...	...	2059	2101	2122	2137	...
on.......... **275/7** d.	0752	0849	0924	...	...	1158	1159	...	1430	1432	...	...	1707	1821	1821	1924	2025	2027	2048	...	...	2126	2127	|	...	...
.... **275/7** a.	0806	0904	0939	...	...	1212	1213	...	1445	1448	...	...	1723	1836	1836	1939	2040	2043	2104	...	...	2141	2141	2157	...	...

ot Aug. 15, Nov. 1.
lso July 14, Nov. 11.
lso Aug. 15, Nov. 1.
lso July 13, Nov. 10; not Nov. 11.
ot July 14, Nov. 11.

m – Not holidays.
r – 1622 on ⑦, 1641 on ⑥.
w – Also July 13, Aug. 15, Nov. 1, 10; not Oct. 2, Nov. 11.
x – ① (also Aug. 16, Nov. 2; not Aug. 15).

⊕ – Subject to alteration June 6, 7, Oct. 31 - Nov. 25.

Subject to alteration Sept. 20 - 30, Oct. 2

CAEN - COUTANCES - GRANVILLE / RENNES 272

	① J	⚒	⑥	Ⓐ	🚌 Ⓐ K	Ⓐ	Ⓐ	B	🚌 K	J	Ⓐ K	Ⓒ K	Ⓐ		Ⓐ		🚌	⑥ K	† K	⚒	🚌 ⑥	🚌 Ⓐ	⑤ f	A	①–④ m
Caen .... **275** d.	0547	0620	0713	0713	...	0830	0910	0910	...	1110	1110	1110	1210	1238	1335	1411	...	1517	1517	1607	...	...	1710	1729	1735
Bayeux .... **275** d.	0604	0643	0731	0730	...	0852	0928	0926	...	1128	1128	1128	1228	1300	1357	1428	...	1540	1540	1629	...	...	1727	1746	1756
Lison................. **275** d.	0618	0702	0747	0745	...	0910	0944	0941	...	1144	1144	1144	1245	1318	1415	1443	...	1559	1559	1647	...	...	1743	1802	1812
St Lô........................ d.	0633	0715	0800	0800	...	0923	0957	0953	...	1157	1157	1157	1259	1333	1430	1456	...	1612	1612	1700	1706	1732	1757	1815	1825
Coutances .... a.	0653	0735	0820	0820	0857	...	1017	1014	1023	1217	1217	1217	1322	*1416*c	...	1517	1523	1634	1634	...	1743	1802	1817	1836	*1908**
Granville .... a.	*0740*r	*0816*a	*0859**	|	0934	...	...	|	1056	*1256*c	...	1247	*1402**	*1449*c	...	|	1556	1709	1714	...	...	...	*1857**	*1916**	...
Rennes **272a** .... a.	0850	...	...	1005	...	...	...	1157	...	...	...	...	...	...	...	1706	...	...	...	...	...	...	2005	2025	...

	⑤ J	⑤ K	⑤ K	⑤ Jd	①–④ m	⑥ J	Ⓐ	N	†	⑤ f
.... **275** d.	1735	1735	1803	1814	1809	1809	1843	1910	1919	1929
ıx .... **275** d.	1757	1757	1826	1837	1832	1832	1906	1933	1941	1953
.... **275** d.	1815	1815	1845	1856	1851	1851	1924	1951	2000	2011
.... d.	1828	1828	1858	1909	1905	1905	1940	2004	2014	2024
ances .... a.	*1915**	*1914**	1920	1931	1928	1928	...	2024	2035	2044
anville................ a.	*1948**	...	*2002**	...	*2008*v	...	...	...	*2114**	*2123**
nnes **272a**.......... a.	...	...	...	...	...	...	...	...	2220	2228

	⚒	🚌 Ⓐ	🚌 ⑥	⚒	Ⓒ 🚌	Ⓐ J	Ⓐ	Ⓒ J	Ⓒ K	B	Ⓐ	Ⓐ
Rennes **272a**.......d.	...	...	...	...	...	0550	...	...	...	0825	0902	...
Granville.............d.	...	0547	0603	...	...	*0645*n	*0739*v	*0751**	0807	*0932**	*0957**	...
Coutances............d.	0609	0620	0635	*0642*a	0712	0737	0825	0835	0835	1015	1040	...
St Lô ....d.	0632	0657	0712	0722	0749	0759	0847	0857	0857	1035	1100	1225
Lison .... **275** d.	0649	0717	...	0738	0809	0812	0905	0915	0915	1050	1113	1241
Bayeux .... **275** d.	0707	...	...	0756	...	0826	0920	0930	0930	1104	1128	1259
Caen .... **275** a.	0730	...	...	0819	...	0843	0938	0948	0948	1121	1145	1320

	⚒	🚌 Ⓐ K	🚌 ⑤ J	Ⓐ	Ⓒ	Ⓐ	† J	† K		D	🚌 ①–④ Jm	Ⓐ	E	† K	⑤ f	①–④ m	⑤ Jd	† J	⑥ J	①–④ m	⑥ K	† K	⑤ f	⑥ K	†	⑦ Je
nnes **272a**.......... d.	...	...	...	...	...	...	1251	...	...	1455	...	...	...	...	...	...	1630	1648	1648	1654	...	...	1824	1859	1900	2043
anville................ d.	*1149**	1235	1251	...	*1242*v	...	*1342*n	...	...	*1553**	...	...	*1636*s	*1649**	*1651**	*1710**	|	*1754**	*1754**	*1755**	1915	1923	*1919**	*1954**	*1954**	*2132*n
ances .... d.	1234	1312	1324	1334	*1312**	...	1434	1433	*1538*a	1636	1629	...	1719	1734	1734	*1744**	1818	1837	1838	1838	1942	1950	2002	2037	2037	2223
.... d.	1258	...	...	1356	*1349**	1500	1457	1457	1625	1656	1706	1716	1742	1756	1756	1831	1838	1857	1904	1904	2004	2014	2025	2057	2057	2243
.... **275** d.	1311	...	...	1410	1419	1514	1510	1510	1639	1710	...	1730	1756	1810	1810	1844	1851	1911	1918	1918	2017	2027	2040	2111	2111	2257
ıx .... **275** d.	1326	...	...	1425	1435	1528	1525	1525	1657	1724	...	1748	1811	1825	1825	1901	1906	1925	1932	1932	2033	2042	2054	2125	2125	2311
.... **275** a.	1344	...	...	1443	1451	1543	1542	1543	1719	1746	...	1810	1829	1843	1843	1922	1923	1942	1949	1949	2051	2100	2111	2142	2142	2328

NOTES SEE FOOT OF PAGE

COUTANCES / GRANVILLE - DOL - ST MALO / RENNES 272a

•	🚌 Ⓐ J	① J	🚌 Ⓐ	Ⓐ	🚌 ⑥	B	Ⓐ K	Ⓒ K		🚌 J		K	🚌 ⑤	⑤ f		△	A		🚌 †	†		🚌 ⑤	⑤ f	
Caen **272** ....d.	...	0547	...	0713	...	0910	...	...	...	...	1411	...	...	1710	...	...	1729	...	...	1919	...	...	1929	...
Coutances ....d.	...	0654	...	0821	...	1014	...	...	...	...	1519	...	...	1819	...	...	1839	...	...	2038	...	...	2045	...
Granville.......... **273** d.	0645	|	0811	|	1004	|	1042	1110	...	1509	|	1722	1809	|	...	1845	|	...	2020	|	...	2034	|	...
Folligny.............. **273** d.	0705	0717	0831	0841	1024	1034	1054	1121	...	1529	1539	1733	1829	1839	...	1855	1900	...	2040	2058	...	2054	2104	...
Avranches ....d.	...	0733	...	0854	...	1047	1108	1134	...	...	1552	1746	...	1854	...	...	1914	...	...	2112	...	...	2118	...
Pontorson ⊡ ....d.	...	0754	...	0911	...	1105	1126	1152	...	...	1612	1803	...	1913	...	...	1931	...	...	2129	...	...	2135	...
Dol .... **281** a.	...	0814	...	0929	...	1122	1146	1217	...	...	1630	1828	...	1931	...	...	1950	...	...	2147	...	...	2154	...
St Malo........... **281** a.	...	|	...	|	...	|	1209	1235	...	...	|	1845	...	|	...	...	|	...	...	|	...	...	|	...
Rennes............. **281** a.	...	0850	...	1005	...	1157	...	...	...	...	1706	...	...	2005	...	...	2025	...	...	2220	...	...	2228	...

	Ⓐ J	B	🚌 ⑥	Ⓐ	🚌 Ⓐ	Ⓐ K	Ⓒ K	† J	D	🚌 ⑤ J	⑤ Jd	🚌 ⑤ J	† J	⑥ J	🚌 Ⓒ J	①–④ m	🚌 ①–④ J	Ⓒ K	Ⓐ K	⑤ f	🚌 ⑤ J	⑥ K	†	🚌 † J	⑦ Je
ıes .... **281** d.	0550	0825	...	0902	...	...	...	1251	1455	...	1630	...	1648	1648	...	1654	...	...	...	1824	...	1859	1900	...	2043
Malo.......... **281** d.	|	|	...	|	...	1057	1120	|	|	...	|	...	|	|	...	|	...	1735	1750	|	...	|	|	...	|
.... **281** d.	0622	0900	...	0933	...	1121	1143	1324	1527	...	1703	...	1721	1721	...	1728	...	1758	1813	1856	...	1930	1931	...	2116
orson ⊡ ....d.	0639	0916	...	0949	...	1138	1200	1340	1543	...	1719	...	1737	1737	...	1744	...	1815	1830	1912	...	1946	1947	...	2132
nches ....d.	0657	0933	...	1006	...	1154	1216	1357	1600	...	1737	...	1754	1754	...	1801	...	1831	1846	1928	...	2003	2003	...	2149
gny.............. **273** d.	0715	0947	0952	1019	1024	1208	1230	1412	1613	1618	1750	1755	1809	1809	1814	1814	1818	1845	1900	1941	1947	2016	2016	2025	2202
anville.......... **273** a.	*0740**	|	1012	|	1044	1219	1241	*1437**	|	1638	|	1815	|	|	1834	|	1838	1856	1918	|	2007	|	|	2045	*2230**
tances ....a.	0734	1008	...	1039	...	...	...	1432	1633	...	1810	...	1830	1830	...	1833	...	...	...	2001	...	2036	2036	...	2222
en **272** ....a.	0843	1121	...	1145	...	...	...	1542	1746	...	1923	...	1942	1949	...	1949	...	...	...	2111	...	2142	2142	...	2328

ES FOR TABLES 272 AND 272a

①②③④⑥ (also ⑦ to June 26 / from Sept. 4), not July 14.
⑥ (also ⑦ July 3 - Aug. 28), also July 14, Aug. 15.
⑤ (daily July 3 - Aug. 28).
Daily except ⑤ (not on ⑦ July 3 - Aug. 28 or July 14, Aug. 15); also Nov. 11; not Nov. 10.
To July 2 / from Aug. 29.
July 3 - Aug. 28.
①②③④⑥ (not July 13, 14, Aug. 15, Nov. 1, 10).
Ⓐ only. By 🚌.
Ⓒ only. By 🚌.

d – Also Nov. 10; not Nov. 11.
e – Also Nov. 1; not Oct. 30.
f – Also July 13, Nov. 10; not Nov. 11.
m – Not holidays.
n – By 🚌 from Granville (change to train at Folligny, Table **272a**).
r – By 🚌 Folligny (Table **272a**) - Granville.
s – ①②③④⑦ (also holidays). By 🚌.
v – July 3 - Aug. 28. By 🚌.
△ – Train **3450**. For days of running see Table **273**.
⊡ – Pontorson-Mont St Michel (10 km from Mont St Michel).

• – Granville - Folligny is *15 km*.
* – By 🚌.

🚌 Lison - Coutances: 0633Ⓐ **J**, 0722Ⓐ, 0806Ⓐ, 1540⑥, 1840†, 2040Ⓐ, 2140⑤–⑦, 2327Ⓑ.
🚌 Coutances - Lison: 0521Ⓐ, 0712Ⓒ, 1014①–④**m**, 1312Ⓒ, 1630①–④**m**, 1950†. Journey 57 mins.

Subject to alteration Aug. 29 - Sept. 1.
🚌 services from July 3 may vary by a few minutes.

273 PARIS - DREUX - GRANVILLE

TEMPORARILY RELOCATED TO PAGE 223

274 PARIS - VERSAILLES

RER (express Métro) Line C: **Paris Austerlitz** - St Michel Notre Dame - **Versailles Rive Gauche** (for Château). Every 15 - 30 minutes. Journey 40 minutes.

Alternative service: RER Line C: Paris Austerlitz - St Michel Notre Dame - Versailles Chantiers. Journey 39 minutes.

SNCF suburban services: Paris St Lazare - Versailles Rive Droite (journey 28 - 35 minutes); Paris Montparnasse - Versailles Chantiers (journey 12 - 28 minutes). See also Table **278**.

275 PARIS - CAEN - CHERBOURG

For other trains Paris - Lisieux (- Trouville-Deauville) see Table **276**

km		3325 ① g	⚒	Ⓐ	Ⓐ	⚒	Ⓐ J	⚒	⚒	3331 Ⓐ	3301 Ⓐ	Ⓐ		3333 ⑥ ▽t	⑥	3327 T	Ⓐ	3335 Ⓐ	Ⓐ	3303 Ⓒ ▽	3337 Ⓒ ▽	Ⓒ	3305 Ⓐ	Ⓐ	3341 Ⓒ ▽
0	**Paris** St Lazare ▷ d.	0026	...	...	...	...	...	...	...	0645	0707	...	...	0745r	...	0813	...	0845	...	0910	0945	...	1010	...	1145
57	Mantes la Jolie ▷ d.	|	...	...	...	...	...	...	...	|	|	...	...	|	...	|	...	|	...	|	|	...	|	...	|
108	Evreux ▷ d.	0133	...	...	...	...	0609	...	...	0743	|	...	...	0843	...	|	...	0943	...	|	1043	...	|	...	1243
160	Bernay d.	0211	...	...	...	...	0647	...	...	0810	|	...	...	0910	...	|	...	1010	...	|	1110	...	|	...	1310
191	Lisieux 277 d.	0240	...	0610	...	0645	0703	...	0745	0828	|	...	0845	0928	...	|	0945	1028	...	|	1128	...	|	...	1328
216	Mézidon 271 277 d.	|	...	0624	...	0659	0716	...	0759	|	|	...	0859	|	...	|	0959	|	...	|	|	...	|	...	|
239	**Caen** 271 277 a.	0317	...	0644	...	0719	0735	...	0819	0853	0858	...	0919	0953	...	1008	1019	1053	...	1100	1153	...	1200	...	1353
239	**Caen** 272 d.	0320	0557	...	0701	...	...	0801	...	...	0901	0910	...	...	1003	1011	...	...	1103	1104	...	1203	1203	1303	...
269	Bayeux 272 d.	0350	0613	...	0717	...	...	0817	...	...	|	0928	...	...	1019	1028	...	...	1119	1122	...	1219	1221	1319	...
296	Lison 272 d.	0411	0628	...	0732	...	...	0832	...	...	|	0943	...	...	1034	1044	...	...	1134	1137	...	1234	1236	1334	...
314	Carentan d.	0425	0638	...	0742	...	...	0842	...	...	0937	...	...	...	1044	1056	...	...	1144	1149	...	1244	1248	1344	...
343	Valognes d.	0445	0654	...	0758	...	...	0858	...	...	0952	...	...	...	1100	1113	...	...	1200	1204	...	1300	1303	1400	...
371	**Cherbourg** a.	0501	0709	...	0813	...	...	0913	...	...	1008	...	...	...	1115	1129	...	...	1215	1220	...	1315	1319	1415	...

	3307 Ⓐ	3309 ⑥ ▽	Ⓐ	3343 Ⓐ	Ⓐ	3345 ⑤ f	3347 Ⓒ ▽	3311 Ⓐ	Ⓐ	Ⓐ	3313 Ⓒ ▽	d	3349 Ⓐ	3315 Ⓐ	Ⓐ	3351 ▽	3317 Ⓐ u	Ⓒ	3353 Ⓐ	3319 ⑤ f	3321 Ⓒ ▽	3355 ▽	3323 Ⓑ h	3357 ⑥ ▽	3359 ⑤ f
Paris St Lazare ▷ d.	1210	1310	...	1345	...	1410	1445	1510	...	...	1610	...	1645	1710	...	1745s	1810	...	1845	1905	1910	1959x	2045	2045	2145
Mantes la Jolie ▷ d.	|	|	...	|	...	|	|	|	...	...	|	...	|	|	...	|	|	...	|	|	|	2038	|	|	|
Evreux ▷ d.	|	|	...	1443	...	1509	1543	|	...	...	|	...	1743	|	...	1843	|	...	1943	|	|	2106	2140	2143	2243
Bernay d.	|	|	...	1510	...	1536	1610	|	...	...	|	...	1810	|	...	1910	|	...	2010	|	|	2133	2207	2210	2310
Lisieux 277 d.	|	|	1445	1528	...	1554	1628	|	1643	1721	|	1751	1828	|	1845	1928	|	...	2028	|	|	2152	2224	2228	2328
Mézidon 271 277 d.	|	|	1459	|	...	|	|	|	1657	1735	|	1805	|	|	1859	|	|	...	|	|	|	|	|	|	|
Caen 271 277 a.	1400	1500	1519	1553	...	1620	1653	1659	1717	1753	1800	1823	1853	1900	1919	1953	2000	...	2053	2058	2100	2216	2246	2253	2353
Caen 272 d.	1403	1503	...	...	1601	...	...	1702	...	1755	1803	1825	...	1903	...	...	2003	2003	...	2101	2103	...	2249	...	...
Bayeux 272 d.	1421	1521	...	...	1617	...	...	1720	...	1812	1821	1842	...	1921	...	...	2021	2019	...	2118	2121	...	2307	...	...
Lison 272 d.	1436	1536	...	...	1632	...	...	1735	...	1826	1836	1857	...	1936	...	...	2036	2034	...	2134	2136	...	2322	...	...
Carentan d.	1448	1548	...	...	1642	...	...	1747	...	1837	1848	1907	...	1948	...	...	2048	2044	...	2146	2148	...	2334	...	...
Valognes d.	1503	1603	...	...	1658	...	...	1802	...	1851	1903	1921	...	2003	...	...	2103	2100	...	2201	2203	...	2349	...	...
Cherbourg a.	1519	1619	...	...	1713	...	...	1818	...	1907	1919	1937	...	2019	...	...	2119	2115	...	2216	2219	...	0005	...	...

	3330 Ⓐ	3332 ⚒	Ⓐ	3300 Ⓐ ⊕	3334 ▽	⚒ ⊕		Ⓐ ⊕	Ⓒ	3302 ⊕	Ⓐ	Ⓒ	3338 ▽	⚒ ⊕			3340 ⑤ f	3304 ⑥	3304 ①–④ m		† ⊕	3306 ⑤ f⊕	3342 Ⓒ ▽	Ⓐ q	⚒ ⊕
Cherbourg d.	...	...	...	0543	...	0630	...	0719	...	0735	...	...	...	0941	...	...	...	1035	1035	...	1141	1151	...	...	1241
Valognes d.	...	...	...	0601	...	0645	...	0734	...	0752	...	...	...	0956	...	...	...	1052	1052	...	1156	1209	...	...	1256
Carentan d.	...	...	...	0616	...	0701	...	0750	...	0808	...	...	...	1012	...	...	...	1108	1108	...	1212	1224	...	...	1312
Lison 272 d.	...	...	...	0628	...	0712	...	0801	...	0819	0905	0915	...	1023	...	...	...	1119	1119	...	1223	|	...	...	1323
Bayeux 272 d.	...	...	...	0643	...	0729	...	0815	...	0835	0920	0930	...	1037	...	...	...	1135	1135	...	1237	|	...	...	1337
Caen 272 a.	...	...	...	0659	...	0750	...	0831	...	0851	0938	0948	...	1053	...	...	...	1151	1151	...	1253	1259	...	...	1353
Caen 271 277 d.	0507	0607	0634	0702	0742	0752	...	0834	0834	0854	...	...	1007	...	1107	...	1150	1154	1154	...	...	1302	1307	1307	...
Mézidon 271 277 d.	|	|	0654	|	|	0811	...	0854	0854	|	...	...	|	...	1127	...	|	|	|	...	...	|	|	1327	...
Lisieux 277 d.	0534	0634	0708	|	0810	0825	...	0908	0908	|	...	...	1034	...	1141	...	|	|	|	...	...	1334	1334	1341	...
Bernay d.	0553	0653	...	|	0828	...	...	...	...	|	...	...	1053	...	...	...	|	|	|	...	...	1353	1353	...	...
Evreux ▷ d.	0620	0720	...	|	0855	...	...	...	...	|	...	...	1120	...	...	...	|	|	|	...	...	1419	1420	...	...
Mantes la Jolie ▷ a.	|	|	...	|	0922	...	...	...	...	|	...	...	|	...	...	...	|	|	|	...	...	|	|	...	...
Paris St Lazare ▷ a.	0716	0818	...	0858	0957	...	...	...	...	1046	...	...	1216	...	...	...	1345	1345	1345	...	...	1516	1516	...	...

	3324 R	3308 ⊕	Ⓐ	3346 Ⓒ ▽	Ⓐ		3348 ▽	Ⓐ	⚒ ⊕	3312 ⑦ ⊕	3310 Ⓐ ⊕	Ⓐ J	Ⓐ	3314 Ⓐ ⊕	† ⊕	3316 ⑥ ⊕	3350 ⑦ e	⑥ ⊕	Ⓐ ⊕	3318 ⑦ e⊕		3352 ⑦ e	3320 Ⓐ ⊕	Ⓐ	3322 ⑦ ⊕
Cherbourg d.	1253	1335	...	...	...	1541	...	...	1619	1635	1652	...	...	1735	1741	1752	...	1819	1819	1835	...	...	1909	1947	2005
Valognes d.	1311	1352	...	...	...	1556	...	...	1634	1652	|	...	...	1752	1757	1810	...	1834	1834	1852	...	...	1927	2002	2022
Carentan d.	1327	1408	...	...	...	1612	...	...	1650	1708	|	...	...	1808	1812	1825	...	1850	1850	1908	...	...	1942	2018	2038
Lison 272 d.	1339	1419	1514	...	...	1623	...	...	1701	1719	|	...	...	1819	1823	1837	...	1901	1901	1919	...	...	1954	2029	2049
Bayeux 272 d.	1355	1435	1528	...	...	1637	...	...	1715	1735	|	...	...	1835	1837	1852	...	1915	1915	1935	...	...	2009	2043	2105
Caen 272 a.	1411	1451	1543	...	...	1653	...	...	1731	1751	1751	...	...	1851	1853	1908	...	1931	1931	1951	...	...	2025	2059	2121
Caen 271 277 d.	1414	1454	1545	1607	1634	...	1707	1725	1734	1754	1754	1800	1834	1854	...	1911	1907	...	1934	1954	...	2007	2028	...	2124
Mézidon 271 277 d.	|	|	1559	|	1654	...	|	1745	1752	|	|	1819	1854	|	...	|	|	...	1954	|	...	|	|	...	|
Lisieux 277 d.	1441	|	1613	1634	1707	...	1734	1759	1806	|	|	1835	1907	|	...	1936	1934	...	2008	|	...	2034	2052	...	|
Bernay d.	1459	|	...	1653	...	...	1753	...	...	|	|	1854	...	|	...	1953	1953	...	...	|	...	2053	|	...	|
Evreux ▷ d.	1526	|	...	1720	...	...	1820	...	...	|	|	1932	...	|	...	2020	2020	...	...	|	...	2120	|	...	|
Mantes la Jolie ▷ a.	|	|	...	|	...	...	|	...	...	|	|	...	...	|	...	|	|	...	...	|	...	|	|	...	|
Paris St Lazare ▷ a.	1624	1647	...	1816	...	...	1916	...	...	1946	1945	...	...	2046	...	2116	2116	...	...	2145	...	2216	2226	...	2316

LOCAL TRAINS PARIS - EVREUX - SERQUIGNY △

	Ⓐ	Ⓐ	Ⓐ	Ⓐ	Ⓐ	Ⓐ	Ⓐ	Ⓐ	
Paris St Lazare d.	0907	1110	1310	1610	1713	1813	1913	2013	...
Mantes la Jolie d.	0941	1144	1344	1644	1747	1847	1947	2047	...
Evreux a.	1017	1220	1420	1717	1821	1921	2020	2120	...
Serquigny a.	...	1253	...	1754	1856	1956	...	...	...

	Ⓐ	Ⓐ	Ⓐ	Ⓐ	Ⓐ	Ⓐ		Ⓐ
Serquigny d.	...	0604	0704	...	...	1304	...	...
Evreux d.	0539	0639	0739	0844	1139	1339	...	1739
Mantes la Jolie a.	0616	0716	0816	0916	1213	1413	...	1813
Paris St Lazare a.	0652	0755	0855	0954	1248	1448	...	1849

J – To July 1 / from Aug. 29.
R – ⑦ July 3 - Aug. 28 (also Aug. 15, Nov. 1).
T – July 14, 30, Aug. 13, 27, Nov. 11 only.

d – Runs 6 minutes later on ⑤ to July 1 / from Sept. 2.
e – Also aug. 15, Nov. 1.
f – Also July 13, Nov. 10; not Nov. 11.
g – Also Aug. 16, Nov. 2; not Aug. 15, Oct. 31.
h – Not July 14, Nov. 11.
m – Not holidays.
q – On ③ during school term runs 27 minutes later (Caen d. 1334).
r – Depart 0705 on ⑥ Sept. 24 - Oct. 8 (also June 25, July 9, 16, Aug. 20).
s – Depart 1709 on ⑥ June 25 - Aug. 6, ⑥ Sept. 17 - Oct. 15 (also Aug. 20, Oct. 29, Nov. 26).

t – Also July 14, Nov. 11.
u – Runs up to 6 mins earlier on ⑤ July 1 - Aug. 26 (also July 13).
x – Depart 1939 on ⑥ June 25 - Aug. 6, ⑥ Sept. 17 - Oct. 15 (also Aug. 20, Oct. 29, Nov.

▷ – For additional trains see panel below main table (also Table **276**).
△ – Frequent suburban trains run Paris - Mantes-la-Jolie. Additional local trains run Mar la Jolie - Evreux and Evreux - Serquigny.
▽ – Subject to alteration.
⊕ – Runs up to 5 minutes earlier Sept. 20 - Oct. 31.

Timings may vary on certain dates

PARIS - LISIEUX - TROUVILLE DEAUVILLE — 276

			3371		3373	3375		3377		3379		3395	3381			3383		3385			3387	3389	3391	3393
	⚒	Ⓑ h	Ⓐ	⑥ t	Ⓒ n	Ⓐ S	Ⓐ	F	⚒ △	Ⓐ	Ⓒ v	Z	T	Ⓐ		⑤ f	①-④ m	⑤ G	B	b	⑤ G	⑦ Q	⑥ P	Ⓐ
Paris St Lazare ▷ d.	...	...	0745	...	0844	0944	...	1010	...	1145	...	1212	1345	...	...	1545	...	1633	...	...	1810	1820	1845r	1910
Evreux ▷ d.	...	...	0843	...	0943	|	...	1109	...	1243	...	|	1443	...	...	1643	...	|	...	...	|	1919	1943	2012
Bernay ▷ d.	...	...	0910	...	1010	|	...	1136	...	1310	...	|	1510	...	...	1710	...	|	...	...	|	1946	2010	2042
Lisieux ▷ d.	0735	0837	0928	0935	1028	|	1035	1154	1235	1328	1335	|	1528	1535	1635	1728	1735	1823	1835	1935	1950	2006	2028	2102
Pont l'Évêque d.	0748	0850	0940	0948	1040	|	1048	1206	1248	1340	1348	|	1540	1548	1648	1740	1748	1835	1848	1946	2001	2018	2040	2113
Trouville-Deauville a.	0757	0859	0948	0957	1048	1132	1057	1216	1257	1348	1357	1408	1548	1557	1657	1748	1757	1844	1857	1955	2010	2027	2048	2122

		3370				3372	3372					3374	3376		3378			3380	3382	3384				3386	3388
	⚒	Ⓐ	† v	B		Ⓐ J	Ⓐ K	⑥ t	Ⓐ	Ⓒ ⊡v	Ⓐ	E	Ⓐ S	▽	⑦ d		Ⓐ b	Ⓒ u	⑦ V	Ⓐ	†	⑤ f	①-④ m	⑦ H	⑦ R
le-Deauville d.	0700	0711	0738	0808	0959	1111	1110	1154	1204	1259	1404	1411	1415	1604	1638	1704	1807	1811	1853	1911	2004	2012	2020	2029	2057
Évêque d.	0709	0722	0747	0817	1008	1122	1126	1207	1213	1308	1413	1422	1425	1613	1650	1713	1816	1822	|	1922	2013	2021	2029	|	2108
... ▷ d.	0722	0734	0800	0830	1024	1134	1139	1220	1226	1321	1426	1434	1440	1626	1704	1726	1829	1834	|	1934	2029	2034	2042	|	2120
... ▷ d.	...	0753	...	...	...	1153	1158	...	...	...	...	1453	1501	...	1722	...	...	1853	|	1953	...	...	...	|	2139
... ▷ d.	...	0820	...	...	...	1220	1225	...	...	...	...	1520	1528	...	1750	...	...	1920	|	2020	...	...	...	|	2206
St Lazare ▷ a.	...	0918	...	...	...	1316	1324	...	...	...	...	1616	1628	...	1846	...	...	2016	2046	2116	...	...	...	2226	2303

) (also ⑥ July 9 - Aug. 27).
July 3 - Aug. 28 (also July 14, 30, Aug. 13, 15, 27, Nov. 11).
ne 4, 11, 18, July 3, 14, 17, 24, 30, 31, Aug. 7, 13, 14, 27, 28, ept. 3, 10, 17, Oct. 15, 22.
July 1 - Aug. 26 (also July 13).
) July 3 - Aug. 28 (also Aug. 15, Nov. 1).
) to June 24 / from Aug. 29 (also runs July 14, 30, Aug. 13, 27).
) June 27 - Aug. 26.
June 25 - Aug. 27 (also July 14).
July 3 - Aug. 28 (also Aug. 15).
May 1 - Sept. 25 (also Aug. 15; not June 12).
une 27 - Aug. 26.

T – June 4, 18, July 14, 30, Aug. 13, 27, Sept. 3, 17.
V – ⑦ May 29 - Sept. 25 (also Aug. 15; not June 12).
Z – July 14, Oct. 22 only.

b – Not on ⑤ July 8 - Aug. 26; not July 13.
d – Also Aug. 15, Nov. 1; not June 12.
f – Also July 13, Nov. 10; not Nov. 11.
h – Not July 14, Nov. 11.
m – Not holidays or July 13, Nov. 10.
n – Not June 12, Sept. 11, Oct. 29, Nov. 26. On ⑥⑦ Sept. 24 - Oct. 9 (also June 25, 26, July 9, 10, 16, Aug. 20, 21) Paris depart 0805.

r – 1753 on ⑥ June 25 - July 23 (also Aug. 6, 20).
t – Also July 14, Nov. 11.
u – Not June 11, 12, 25, July 2, 9, 16, 23, Aug. 6, 20, Sept. 10, 17, 24, Oct. 1, 8.
v – Not June 12, Sept. 11.
▷ – For other trains see Table **275**.
⊡ – Also runs on ⑤ **f** (depart 1303, arrive 1325).
△ – Runs 5 mins earlier on ⑥ (also July 14, Nov. 11).
▽ – Runs 5 mins earlier on Ⓒ (also June 11, Sept. 10).

TROUVILLE DEAUVILLE - DIVES CABOURG — 276a

Journey 30 minutes

June 25 - Aug. 28

Trouville Deauville: 0833Ⓐ, 0955Ⓐ, 1100Ⓒ, 1143Ⓐ, 1225Ⓒ, 1359Ⓐ**b**, 1407⑥⑦**n**, 1604⑥**t**, 1609Ⓐ, 1645⑦**e**, 1750Ⓐ**c**, 1900⑦**e**, 2005Ⓐ**d**, 2005⑥**t**, 2038⑦**e**, 2111⑥**t**, 2133Ⓐ**k**.
Dives Cabourg: 0620Ⓐ, 0913Ⓐ, 1023Ⓒ, 1032Ⓐ, 1140Ⓒ, 1322, 1523Ⓐ, 1523⑥**t**, 1558⑦**e**, 1710Ⓐ, 1731Ⓒ, 1833Ⓐ, 1951⑦**e**, 2042Ⓐ**d**.

To June 24 / from Aug. 29

Trouville Deauville: 1100⑥, 1106⑦**x**, 1225⑥**E**, 1407⑥**v**, 1417⑦**w**, 1604⑥**D**, 1645⑦**x**, 1900**T**, 2133④⑤**z**.
Dives Cabourg: 0620①**g**, 1140⑥**E**, 1144⑦**x**, 1217⑥**R**, 1322⑥**E**, 1523⑥**D**, 1558⑦**x**, 1731Ⓒ**q**, 1951**T**.

Mar. 26 - June 18; ⑥ Sept. 3 - 24 (also Nov. 11; ot June 11, Sept. 10).
Apr. 23 - June 18; ⑥ Sept. 3 - Oct. 22.
Oct. 29 - Dec. 10.
ov. 1 only.

b – Runs 10 minutes later on ⑤ **f**.
c – Runs 6 minutes later on ⑤ **f**.
d – Runs 15 minutes later on ⑤ **f**.
e – Also Aug. 15.
f – Also July 13.

g – Also Nov. 2; not Oct. 31.
k – Not June 27 - 29.
n – Also Aug. 15; not June 26.
q – Not June 11, Sept. 10.
t – Also July 14.

v – Not June 11, Sept. 10, Oct. 22, 29.
w – Also Oct. 22, 29, Nov. 1, 11.
x – Also Nov. 1.
z – Not Nov. 11.

ROUEN - LISIEUX - CAEN — 277

	Ⓐ	⑥	Ⓐ		Ⓐ	†	⑥		†	Ⓐ	⑥		⑤ f	⑤ f	†	Ⓐ	⑥		⚒	†	Ⓐ	†	
Rouen Rive Droite d.	0604	0704	0704	...	1004	1004	1004	...	1204	1204	1304	...	1504	1604	1604	1704	1704	...	1804	1804	1904	1904	...
Elbeuf-St Aubin d.	0620	0720	0726	...	1020	1020	1020	...	1220	1220	1320	...	1520	1620	1620	1720	1720	...	1820	1820	1920	1920	...
Serquigny d.	0650	|	|	...	|	|	1050	...	1249	1249	1350	...	|	1648	1650	1747	1746	...	1855	1854	|	|	...
Bernay ▷ d.	0657	0752	0800	...	1052	1055	1059	...	1257	1257	1359	...	1552	1656	1659	1756	1754	...	1904	1902	1951	1955	...
Lisieux ▷ d.	0713	0809	0816	...	1109	1111	1116	...	1313	1314	1416	...	1609	1713	1716	1812	1811	...	1920	1919	2009	2011	...
Mézidon **271** ▷ d.	0728	0823	0830	...	1123	1125	1130	...	1328	1329	1429	...	1623	1728	1730	1827	1825	...	1934	1933	2023	2025	...
Caen 271 ▷ a.	0742	0837	0843	...	1137	1138	1143	...	1342	1343	1443	...	1637	1742	1743	1841	1839	...	1948	1947	2037	2038	...

	Ⓐ		⑥	Ⓐ				Ⓐ	Ⓒ		Ⓐ	Ⓒ		Ⓐ	†	⑥		Ⓐ		⑤ f	⑥ S	†		
271 ▷ d.	0553	...	0715	0717	...	1019	...	1215	1215	...	1719	1719	...	1818	1815	1815	...	1919	...	2015	2019	2025	...	...
on **271** ▷ d.	0607	...	0729	0731	...	1033	...	1229	1229	...	1733	1733	...	1833	1829	1829	...	1933	...	2029	2033	2039	...	...
... ▷ d.	0621	...	0743	0745	...	1047	...	1243	1243	...	1747	1747	...	1847	1843	1843	...	1947	...	2043	2047	2053	...	...
y ▷ d.	0638	...	0800	0802	...	1104	...	1300	1300	...	1804	1804	...	1903	1900	1900	...	2004	...	2100	2104	2110	...	...
gny d.	0645	...	0808	0810	...	|	...	1308	1307	...	|	|	...	1911	1907	1908	...	|	...	|	|	|	...	...
-St Aubin d.	0723	...	0837	0837	...	1137	...	1337	1337	...	1837	1837	...	1940	1937	1937	...	2037	...	2137	2137	2143	...	...
n Rive Droite a.	0739	...	0853	0853	...	1153	...	1353	1353	...	1855	1853	...	1956	1953	1953	...	2055	...	2153	2153	2158	...	...

⑤ Apr. 23 - Sept. 3.

f – Also July 13, Nov. 10; not Nov. 11.

▷ – See also Table **275**.

PARIS - CHARTRES - LE MANS — 278

For *TGV* trains Paris - Le Mans via the high-speed line see Table **280**

	Ⓐ	⚒	⚒	Ⓐ	Ⓐ										Ⓐ	Ⓐ	Ⓐ	†	⑥	Ⓑ h	Ⓐ	Ⓐ	Ⓐ	Ⓑ h
Paris Montparnasse **274** d.	0533	0609	0639	0709	0740	0809	0906	1009	1106	1209	1306	1409	1506	1609	1624	1639	1706v	1706	1706	1709	1724	1739	1754	1806
Versailles Chantiers **274** d.	0547	0625	0655	0725	0754	0825	0922	1025	1122	1225	1322	1425	1522	1625	1639	1655	1723*	1722	1722	1726	1739	1754	1809	1822*
Rambouillet d.	0604	0645	0713	0745	0813	0845	0943	1045	1143	1245	1343	1445	1542	1645	1700	1715	|	|	1742	1746	1800	1815	1830	|
Chartres d.	0641	0725	0742	0825	0851	0925	1009	1125	1209	1325	1411	1525	1609	1725	1731	1755	1809	1809	1809	1826	1831	1855	1859	1909
Nogent le Rotrou d.	*0736*	...	0818	...	...	...	1047	...	1247	...	1447	...	1647	*1824*	1824	...	1848	1847	1847	...	1925	...	...	1947
Le Mans a.	*0824*	...	0856	...	...	...	1124	...	1324	...	1524r	...	1724	...	...	...	1925	1924	1924	...	...	...	...	2024

		Ⓐ	Ⓐ		Ⓐ		Ⓑ h		Ⓐ	①⑦
Montparnasse **274** d.	1809	1824	1854	1906	1939	2009	2106	2209	2302	0002
lles Chantiers **274** d.	1825	1840	1910	1922	1954	2025	2122	2225	2321	0017
ouillet d.	1845	1900	1930	1943	2014	2045	2142	2245	2344	0045
res d.	1925	1931	1959	2010	2055	2125	2210	2325	0022	0122
nt le Rotrou d.	...	2024	...	2046	...	...	2247	...	...	...
ans a.	...	...	...	2128	...	...	2324	...	...	...

	Ⓐ	Ⓐ	⑥	Ⓐ	⚒	Ⓐ		Ⓐ	⚒
Le Mans d.	...	0336	...	...	...	...	...	0534	...
Nogent le Rotrou d.	...	0414	...	...	...	0530	...	0614	...
Chartres d.	0404	0452	0452	0534	0604	0627	0632	0652	0702
Rambouillet d.	0446	0519	0518	0616	0646	0701	0714	|	0744
Versailles Chantiers **274** d.	0508	0541	0540	0638	0708	0723	0738	0741*	0808
Paris Montparnasse **274** a.	0520	0553	0553	0650	0720	0736	0750	0753	0820

	Ⓐ	Ⓐ	⑥		Ⓐ	⚒	Ⓐ	⚒	† h										Ⓐ				Ⓑ h	⑦ e
ans d.	0552	...	...	...	0632	...	...	0736	...	...	0936	...	1136	...	1336r	...	1536	...	...	1736	...	1936	...	2136
nt le Rotrou d.	0624	0630	0630	...	0710	...	0733	0814	0811	*0832*	1014	...	1214	...	1416	...	1613	...	...	1814	...	2014	...	2214
res d.	0722	0730	0725	0734	0758	0802	0827	0852	0850	0934	1052	1134	1252	1334	1453	1534	1651	1734	1802	1851	1934	2051	2134	2252
ouillet d.	|	0801	...	0816	0831	0846	0901	0919	0919	1016	1119	1216	1319	1416	1519	1616	1720	1816	1847	1919	2016	2119	2216	2319
lles Chantiers **274** d.	0812*	0823	...	0838	0853	0908	0924	0941	0940	1038	1141	1238	1341	1438	1541	1638	1742	1838	1908	1941	2038	2141	2238	2341
Montparnasse **274** a.	0826	0835	...	0850	0905	0920	0936	0953	0953	1050	1153	1250	1353	1450	1553	1650	1753	1850	1920	1953	2050	2153	2250	2353

Also Aug. 15, Nov. 1.
Not July 14, Nov. 11.
⚒ only.

v – Departs from Montparnasse Vaugirard platforms.

* – Will not convey passengers travelling Paris - Versailles or v.v.

Subject to alteration due to engineering work

280 PARIS - LE MANS - RENNES and NANTES

Trains may be retimed a few minutes earlier owing to engineering work (especially Nantes services)

TGV trains convey 🍷. Many trains continue to destinations in Tables **281**, **284**, **285**, **288** and **293**.
For other trains Massy - Nantes/Rennes and v.v. see Table **11** (Lille services), Table **335** (services via St Pierre des Corps) and Table **391** (Strasbourg services).

km								*TGV* 8801	*TGV* 8903		*TGV* 8603	*TGV* 8603		*TGV* 8807	*TGV* 8081	*TGV* 8809	*TGV* 8053	*TGV* 8091	*TGV* 8911	*TGV* 8611	*TGV* 8813	*TGV* 8715		
		①–⑥	Ⓐ	Ⓐ	⑥	Ⓐ	Ⓐ	Ⓐ	Ⓐ	Ⓐ	Ⓐ	⑥	Ⓐ	①–⑥	Ⓐ	①–⑥	Ⓐ	Ⓒ						†
		h			s						C	s		h		h			H					
0	**Paris** Montparnasse ... d.	...	...	...	...	...	...	0621	0653	...	0704	0708	...	0721	0736	0754	0808	0808	0854	0908	0954	1008	...	...
14	Massy TGV ... d.	...	...	...	...	...	...	|	0705	...	|	|	...	0738	0748	|	|	|	|	|	|	|	...	...
202	**Le Mans** ... d.	0612	0620	0630	0637	0650	0703	0718	|	0731	|	|	0824	0830	|	|	0906	0906	|	|	1052	|	1103	1138
292	Laval ... d.	|	|	0731	0729	|	0753	|	|	|	0841	|	|	|	|	|	0951	0951	|	|	|	|	|	1225
327	Vitré ... d.	|	|	0754	0753	|	0822	|	|	|	|	|	|	|	|	|	|	|	|	|	|	|	|	1250
365	**Rennes** ... a.	|	|	0815	0815	|	0848	|	|	|	0916	0916	|	|	0952	|	1025	1025	|	1113	|	1213	|	1323
251	Sablé ... d.	0639	0648	...	...	0716	...	|	|	0818	...	...	0850	0856	...	|	...	...	|	...	|	...	1129	...
299	Angers St Laud **289** ... a.	0701	0730	...	...	0736	...	0759	|	0853	...	...	0910	0917	...	0928	...	...	1027	...	|	...	1147	...
387	**Nantes 289** ... a.	0750	...	...	...	0820	...	0838	0908	...	...	...	0952	0957	...	1007	...	...	1106	...	1208	...	1231	...

	TGV 8617	*TGV* 8817				*TGV* 8717	*TGV* 8065	*TGV* 8819*	*TGV* 8621	*TGV* 8057	*TGV* 8821*	*TGV* 8623	*TGV* 8059	*TGV* 8629	*TGV* 8823			*TGV* 8825*	*TGV* 8827	*TGV* 8729	*TGV* 8061	*TGV* 8829	*TGV* 8063	*TGV* 8633
					Ⓐ	①–⑥	⑦		⑤	①–④		①–④	⑤	Ⓒ	⑤	⑤	⑤	⚒	⑦	⑥–④	⑤		①–④	⑤†
						h	Ax		z	m		m	z		v	z	z		x	n	z		m	k
Paris Montparnasse ... d.	1108	1154	...	...	...	1208	1208	1221	1307	1341	1354	1408	1408	1408	1421	...	...	1454	1454	1508	1508	1554	1608	1608
Massy TGV ... d.	|	|	...	...	...	|	|	|	|	|	|	|	|	|	|	...	...	|	|	|	|	|	|	|
Le Mans ... d.	1206	|	1215	1223	1301	1306	1306	|	1406	1440	1451	|	|	|	1515	1535	1536	|	1552	|	|	|	|	|
Laval ... d.	1249	|	1302	|	|	|	|	|	|	1523	|	|	1544	1544	...	|	1624	|	|	|	|	|	|	|
Vitré ... d.	1308	|	1327	|	|	|	|	|	|	|	|	|	|	|	...	|	1643	|	|	|	|	|	|	|
Rennes ... a.	1328	|	1400	|	|	1418	1420	|	1520	1558	|	1613	1620	1619	...	|	1702	|	|	1713	1714	|	1812	1812
Sablé ... d.	...	...	...	1315	1324	...	...	1338	...	...	...	...	...	...	...	1557	...	|	|	...	...	|	...	...
Angers St Laud **289** ... a.	...	1328	...	1349	1348	...	...	1359	...	...	1528	...	...	...	...	1619	...	1625	1628	...	...	1726	...	...
Nantes 289 ... a.	...	1407	...	...	1432	...	...	1440	...	...	1607	...	...	...	...	1659	...	1707	1707	...	...	1811	...	...

	TGV 8831				*TGV* 8737*			*TGV* 8833	*TGV* 8747	*TGV* 8743*	*TGV* 8935	*TGV* 8937	*TGV* 8645				*TGV* 8649	*TGV* 8839	*TGV* 8841	*TGV* 8655	*TGV* 8657	*TGV* 8943		
	⑤	⑦	Ⓐ	⑥	Ⓐ	⑦	Ⓐ	Ⓐ	Ⓐ	Ⓒ	⑤	⑦–④	①–④	①–④	⑤	①–④	⑤	Ⓐ		①–④	⑤⑥†	⑤⑥	⑦	Ⓐ
	z	x		s		x					z	d	m	m	z	m	z			m	z	t	x	
Paris Montparnasse ... d.	1623	...	...	...	1641	...	...	1654	1708	1708	1721	1721	1741	...	...	...	1741	1749	1754	1808	1808	1823	...	...
Massy TGV ... d.	|	...	...	...	|	...	...	|	|	|	|	|	|	...	...	...	|	|	|	|	|	|	...	...
Le Mans ... d.	|	1719	1722	1734	1738	1742	1742	1752	|	1806	|	|	|	1821	1823	1825	1839	|	1851	|	|	|	1905	1905
Laval ... d.	|	|	|	|	1822	|	1831	|	|	1850	|	|	1916	|	|	|	1923	|	|	|	|	|	|	|
Vitré ... d.	|	|	|	|	|	|	1848	|	|	|	|	|	|	|	|	|	|	|	|	|	|	|	|	|
Rennes ... a.	|	|	|	|	1858	|	1910	|	1914	1925	|	|	1953	|	|	|	1957	|	|	2014	2014	|	|	|
Sablé ... d.	|	1747	1755	1807	...	1805	...	|	...	...	|	|	...	1844	1846	1856	...	|	|	...	...	|	1935	1941
Angers St Laud **289** ... a.	1757	1816	1826	1837	...	1828	...	1830	...	...	|	|	...	1908	1909	1920	...	|	1930	...	...	|	2005	2006
Nantes 289 ... a.	1837	...	...	...	...	1910	...	1909	...	...	1927	1927	...	1950	1952	...	...	2000	2009	...	...	2032	...	...

	TGV 8067	*TGV* 8845	*TGV* 8945	*TGV* 8977*	*TGV* 8663	*TGV* 8665	*TGV* 8665		*TGV* 8761	*TGV* 8849	*TGV* 8949	*TGV* 8851	*TGV* 8071	*TGV* 8097	*TGV* 8853	*TGV* 8953	*TGV* 8077	*TGV* 8679	*TGV* 8075	*TGV* 8855	*TGV* 8857	*TGV* 8957	*TGV* 8957	*TGV* 8079
	Ⓒ	⑤	①–④		⑤	①–④	⑥⑦	⑦–④		⑦	⑤	①–④	⑤⑥†	⑤	Ⓒ	⑤	①–④	⑤	⑦	①–④	⑦	⑤	⑤	⑦
		z	m		z	E	n	d		x	z	m	z	z		z	m	z	x	m	x	F	Dz	Ax
Paris Montparnasse ... d.	1841	1850	1850	1854	1908	1908	1908	...	1941	1954	1954	1954	2008	2024	2054	2054	2108	2108	2108	2123	2154	2144	2150	2208
Massy TGV ... d.	|	|	|	|	|	|	|	...	|	|	|	|	|	|	|	|	|	|	|	|	|	|	|	|
Le Mans ... d.	|	|	|	1952	2006	2006	2006	2012	|	|	|	2052	2106	2120	|	|	|	|	2206	|	2252	|	2247	|
Laval ... d.	2017	|	|	|	|	|	|	|	|	|	|	|	2149	|	|	|	2244	|	2250	|	|	|	|	2344
Vitré ... d.	2038	|	|	|	|	|	|	|	|	|	|	|	|	|	|	|	|	2259	2311	|	|	|	|	0000
Rennes ... a.	2057	|	|	|	2119	2120	2120	|	2145	|	|	|	2225	2234	|	|	2319	2319	2330	|	|	|	|	0019
Sablé ... d.	...	|	|	2014	...	...	...	2035	...	|	|	|	...	...	|	|	...	...	...	|	|	|	|	...
Angers St Laud **289** ... a.	...	|	|	2036	...	...	...	2058	...	2125	2125	2129	...	...	2224	2224	...	...	...	2311	2329	2333	2329	...
Nantes 289 ... a.	...	2104	2054	2118	...	...	...	2141	...	2204	2204	2208	...	...	2302	2302	...	...	...	2352	0008	0012	0008	...

	TGV 8800	*TGV* 8802	*TGV* 8052	*TGV* 8690	*TGV* 8804	*TGV* 8906	*TGV* 8908	*TGV* 8810	*TGV* 8704	*TGV* 8706	*TGV* 8812		*TGV* 8970	*TGV* 8080		*TGV* 8816	*TGV* 8712			*TGV* 8818	*TGV* 8082	*TGV* 8060	*TGV* 8062	*TGV* 8820
	①	Ⓐ	Ⓐ	Ⓐ	Ⓐ	①	②–⑤	⑥	①	②–⑥	Ⓐ	Ⓐ	Ⓐ	⚒	Ⓐ		Ⓐ	⑥	Ⓐ	Ⓐ	①	②–⑦	⑦	Ⓐ
	w					h	e	s	h	g				s				s			w	y	x	
Nantes 289 ... d.	0453	0518	...	...	0556	0626	0630	0625	...	...	...	0634	0700	...	...	0728	...	...	0739	0756	...	...	...	0900
Angers St Laud **289** ... d.	0536	0558	...	...	0636	|	|	0704	...	...	0714	0718	|	...	...	0807	...	0818	0823	0832	...	...	...	0940
Sablé ... d.	|	0621	...	...	|	|	|	|	...	...	|	0740	|	...	...	|	...	0846	0846	|	...	...	...	|
Rennes ... d.	|	|	0532	0605	|	|	|	|	0635	0635	|	|	|	0704	0713	|	0735	|	|	|	0805	0805	0905	|
Vitré ... d.	|	|	0553	|	|	|	|	|	|	|	|	|	|	|	0732	|	|	|	|	|	|	|	|	|
Laval ... d.	|	|	0615	|	|	|	|	|	0710	0712	|	|	|	|	0751	|	|	|	|	|	0841	0842	|	|
Le Mans ... d.	0622	0650	0702	|	|	|	|	0750	|	|	0801	0806	|	0821	0838	|	0852	0913	0913	|	0926	0926	|	|
Massy TGV ... a.	|	|	|	|	|	|	|	|	|	|	|	...	|	|	...	|	|	...	...	|	|	|	|	|
Paris Montparnasse ... a.	0724	0753	0759j	0819	0823	0837	0837	0845	0853	0853	0857	...	0910	0917	...	0943	0948	...	...	1011	1023	1023	1113	1117

	TGV 8822	*TGV* 8618	*TGV* 8064	*TGV* 8824	*TGV* 8620	*TGV* 8926	*TGV* 8622*	*TGV* 8928		*TGV* 8974	*TGV* 8830		*TGV* 8084		*TGV* 8084	*TGV* 8084	*TGV* 8832	*TGV* 8932	*TGV* 8730	*TGV* 8834	*TGV* 8836	*TGV* 8938	*TGV* 8068	
	Ⓒ	Ⓐ	Ⓐ		Ⓐ	Ⓐ	⑥⑦	Ⓒ	⑦	⑥	Ⓐ	①–⑥	①–④	①–⑥	⑤	Ⓒ	Ⓐ	⑦			⑤	Ⓑ	Ⓑ	Ⓑ
							m		x	s		h	m	h	z			x			v	u	u	u
Nantes 289 ... d.	0855	...	...	1000	...	1105	...	1130	1141	1200	1200	1204	...	...	...	...	1259	1301	...	1400	...	1500	...	1519
Angers St Laud **289** ... d.	0934	...	...	1040	...	1145	...	1209	1223	1238	1240	1246	...	1250	...	...	1338	1340	...	1439	...	|	...	1601
Sablé ... d.	|	...	...	|	...	|	...	|	1247	|	|	1308	...	1330	...	...	|	|	...	|	...	|	...	1625
Rennes ... d.	|	0905	0935	|	1035	|	1105	|	|	|	|	|	1235	|	1235	1305	|	|	1405	|	...	|	1505	|
Vitré ... d.	|	|	|	|	|	|	|	|	|	|	|	|	|	|	|	|	|	|	|	|	...	|	|	|
Laval ... d.	|	|	|	|	1112	|	1141	|	|	|	|	|	1312	|	1312	1341	|	|	|	|	...	|	|	|
Le Mans ... d.	1022	1023	|	|	1157	|	1227	|	1310	1321	|	1333	1357	1402	1406	|	1420	1420	|	1520	1541	|	1622	1648
Massy TGV ... a.	|	|	|	|	|	|	|	|	...	|	|	...	|	...	|	|	|	|	|	|	|	|	|	...
Paris Montparnasse ... a.	1121	1121	1144	1221	1253	1320	1323	1340	...	1418	1420	...	1454	...	1504	1522	1518	1518	1611	1616	1638	1708	1718	...

	TGV 8842*	*TGV* 8646				*TGV* 8752	*TGV* 8844	*TGV* 8944	*TGV* 8976		*TGV* 8846	*TGV* 8088	*TGV* 8088				*TGV* 8660	*TGV* 8880	*TGV* 8980	*TGV* 8848	*TGV* 8762	*TGV* 8762	*TGV* 8762	*TGV* 8670*
			⑤	Ⓐ	Ⓐ		⑤⑥	①–④	⑦	⑦	Ⓐ	Ⓒ	Ⓐ	Ⓐ	⑦	Ⓐ	Ⓑ	⑦	⚒	Ⓑ	Ⓒ	①–④	⑤	Ⓒ
			z				t	m	x	x					x		u	x	s	u		m	z	
Nantes 289 ... d.	1600	...	...	...	...	...	1700	1700	1700	1714	1729	...	...	...	...	1734	...	1800	1800	1830	...	...	...	...
Angers St Laud **289** ... d.	1640	...	1648	...	1704	...	1740	1740	1740	1758	|	...	...	1744	1809	1822	...	1840	1840	|	...	...	...	...
Sablé ... d.	|	...	1718	...	1743	...	|	|	|	1819	|	...	...	1826	1838	1843	...	1904	1904	|	...	...	...	...
Rennes ... d.	|	1605	|	1637	|	1705	|	|	|	|	|	1733	1735	|	|	|	1805	|	|	|	1833	1835	1835	1902
Vitré ... d.	|	|	|	1700	|	|	|	|	|	|	|	|	|	|	|	|	|	|	|	|	1857	1857	1858	|
Laval ... d.	|	1642	|	1720	|	|	|	|	|	|	|	1811	1813	|	|	|	|	|	|	|	|	|	|	|
Le Mans ... d.	|	1726	1747	1806	1811	|	1823	1823	1823	1840	|	|	1856	1858	1909	1904	|	|	|	|	1955	|	|	|
Massy TGV ... a.	|	|	...	...	...	|	|	|	|	...	|	|	|	...	...	...	|	|	|	|	|	|	|	|
Paris Montparnasse ... a.	1814	1822	...	...	...	1911	1920	1920	1920	...	1937	1945	1953	...	...	...	2011	2019	2019	2037	2052	2048	2054	2111

FOR NOTES SEE NEXT PAGE →

NANTES and RENNES - LE MANS - PARIS 280

Trains may be retimed a few minutes earlier owing to engineering work (especially Nantes services)

TGV trains convey 🍷. Many trains continue to destinations in Tables **281**, **284**, **285**, **288** and **293**.
For other trains Nantes / Rennes - Massy see Table **11** (Lille services), Table **335** (services via St Pierre des Corps) and Table **391** (Strasbourg services).

				TGV **8850**	*TGV* **8950**		*TGV* **8982**	*TGV* **8676**		*TGV* **8852**	*TGV* **8952**	*TGV* **8092**	*TGV* **8780**		*TGV* **8854**	*TGV* **8688**	*TGV* **8794**	*TGV* **8682**	*TGV* **8856**	*TGV* **8076**	*TGV* **8958**	*TGV* **8686**	*TGV* **8960**	*TGV* **8796**	
	⑤	①–④	⑤	⑥	Ⓑ	Ⓐ	⑦	⑦		⑤	Ⓒ	Ⓒ	Ⓐ	⑦	①–④	⑦	⑦	Ⓐ	⑤⑦	⑤	⑦	⑦	⑦	⑦	
	z	**m**	**z**	**s**	**u**		**x**	**x**		**r**				**x**	**m**	**x**	**x**		**f**	**z**	**p**	**x**	**x**	**x**	
es 289 .... d.	...	...	1839	1900	1900	1909	1930	...	...	2000	2000	...	...	2011	2030	...	...	...	2100	...	2200	...	2225	...	...
s St Laud **289** ..... d.	1844	1915	1927	1940	1940	1954	|	...	...	2041	2041	...	...	2054	2109	...	...	...	2139	...	|	...	2304	...	...
.... d.	1928	1949	1950	|	|	2017	|	...	...	|	|	...	...	2118	|	...	...	...	|	...	|	...	|	...	...
nnes .... d.	|	|	|	|	|	|	|	1935	...	|	|	2005	2005	|	|	2035	2105	2105	|	2135	|	2205	|	2235	...
é .... d.	|	|	|	|	|	|	|	|	...	|	|	|	|	|	|	2056	|	|	|	|	|	|	|	|	...
al .... d.	|	|	|	|	|	|	|	|	...	|	|	2043	2043	|	|	|	|	|	|	2211	|	|	|	2312	...
ans .... d.	2004	2012	2012	2022	2022	2039	|	2051	...	|	|	|	|	2141	|	|	|	|	2220	2255	|	|	|	|	...
y TGV .... a.	...	...	...	|	|	...	|	|	...	|	|	|	|	...	|	|	|	|	|	|	|	|	|	|	...
Montparnasse .... a.	...	...	...	2119	2119	...	2139	2150	...	2214	2214	2219	2219	...	2241	2241	2310	2310	2319	2353	0005	0011	0038	0053	...

From Apr. 10.
From Apr. 18.
Until May 6.
From May 5.
From May 13.
Not Ⓐ Apr. 4 - 15.
⑤ Apr. 8 - June 10 (not May 6).

Not May 4, 5.
Not May 5, 17.
Also May 4, 16.
Not May 17.
Not May 16.
Arrive 5 minutes later from May 9.
Not Apr. 30, May 5, 7.

m – Not May 4, 5, 16.
n – Not May 4.
p – Also May 16; not May 15.
r – Also May 4; not May 13.
s – Also May 5.
t – Also May 4, 5.
u – Not May 5.
v – Also May 4; not May 6.
w – Also May 17; not May 16.
x – Also May 16.
y – Also May 16; not May 17.
z – Also May 4.

TGV – 🅁, supplement payable, 🍷.

* – Train number variations:
8622 runs as 8624 on ⑦;
8670 runs as 8672 on ⑥;
8737 runs as 8739 on ⑤;
8743 runs as 8745 on †;
8815 runs as 8915 on ⑥;
8819 runs as 8919 on ⑤;
8821 runs as 8921 on ⑦–④;
8825 runs as 8925 on ⑥;
8842 runs as 8942 on ⑤⑥†;
8977 runs as 8979 on ⑥–④.

RENNES - ST MALO 281

TGV trains, 🅁	*TGV* **8081**	*TGV* **8091**	*TGV* **8083**	*TGV* **8085**		*TGV* **8089**	*TGV* **8095**	*TGV* **8099**	*TGV* **8097**
	Ⓐ	Ⓒ	Ⓐ	Ⓒ		Ⓒ	Ⓐ	⑦	⑤
								x	**z**
Paris Montparnasse **280** .... d.	0736	0808	1008	1008	...	1508	1841	1908	2024
Lille Flandres **11** .... d.	|	|	|	|	...	|	|	|	|
Rennes 272 .... d.	0957	1032	1220	1220	...	1723	2058	2128	2241
Dol **272** .... d.	1033	1107	|	1254	...	|	2130	|	2312
St Malo .... a.	1046	1120	1305	1308	...	1805	2145	2210	2328

TGV trains, 🅁	*TGV* **8080**	*TGV* **8082**	*TGV* **8084**	*TGV* **8084**	*TGV* **8084**		*TGV* **8088**	*TGV* **8088**	*TGV* **8092**
	⚒	①	①–④	⑤	Ⓒ		Ⓐ	Ⓒ	Ⓒ
	s	**w**	**m**	**z**					
St Malo .... d.	0605	0707	1144	1144	1215	...	1637	1638	1910
Dol **272** .... d.	0620	0722	|	|	|	...	1653	1655	1925
Rennes 272 .... a.	0654	0759	1229	1229	1259	...	1729	1727	1959
Lille Flandres **11** .... a.	|	|	|	|	|	...	|	|	|
Paris Montparnasse **280** . a.	0917	1023	1454	1504	1522	...	1953	1945	2219

Local services below are subject to minor alteration May 30 - June 19

	⚒	⚒	⑦	Ⓐ	Ⓒ	Ⓐ	⑥	⚒	⑤	Ⓒ	Ⓐ	Ⓐ	Ⓐ	†	Ⓐ	†	⑥	Ⓐ	Ⓐ	⑤	⑥	†	①–④	⑤	†	⚒
			x																	**z**			**m**	**z**		**h**
es 272 ...... d.	0630	0730	0930	0940	1130	1245	1300	1440	1535	1635	1637	1700	1730	1733	1800	1831	1830	1835	1908	1930	1940	1945	2005	2028	2030	2208
272 .... d.	0712	0811	1011	1022	1212	1328	1345	1519	1613	1713	1720	1741	1811	1814	1845	1909	1916	1913	1949	2008	2019	2026	2045	2109	2106	2248
alo .... a.	0733	0830	1025	1035	1225	1346	1403	1533	1626	1726	1737	1755	1831	1828	1904	1923	1934	1926	2003	2022	2032	2040	2059	2122	2119	2302

	Ⓐ	Ⓐ	⚒	Ⓐ		⑥	Ⓐ	⑥	Ⓐ	③	†	⚒		†	Ⓐ	⑤	Ⓒ	Ⓐ	Ⓐ	†	Ⓐ	†	Ⓐ		†	
																z									**h**	
alo .... d.	0547	0617	0647	0717	0750	0845	0927	0947	0948	1217	1247	1247	1449	1546	1547	1647	1718	1720	1747	1750	1820	1827	1846	1953	2047	...
272 .... d.	0601	0635	0700	0735	0804	0858	0941	1001	1003	1236	1301	1306	1503	1600	1601	1701	1732	1738	1806	1808	1835	1841	1902	2008	2102	...
es 272 ...... a.	0641	0719	0744	0819	0844	0941	1019	1039	1043	1320	1341	1349	1537	1642	1636	1736	1808	1819	1849	1850	1915	1916	1945	2043	2137	...

Not May 15.
Not May 4, 5, 16.

s – Also May 5.
w – Also May 17; not May 16.

x – Also May 16.
z – Also May 4.

DOL - DINAN 282

	Ⓐ	⑥		⑥	Ⓐ		†	⑥	Ⓒ	Ⓐ	Ⓐ	†	†	Ⓐ	⑤⑥
					q	**j**									**z**
Dol .... d.	0701	0820	...	1305	1425	1430	1428	1525	1725	1730	1850	1920	2112	2136	2252
Dinan .... a.	0724	0843	...	1328	1448	1453	1451	1555	1756	1758	1920	1943	2134	2159	2314

	Ⓐ	⚒		⑥		Ⓐ			⑥			Ⓐ	⑥		†	
						n	**p**			**m**						
n .... d.	0628	0730	...	0924	...	1215	1227	...	1433	1622	...	1805	1856	...	2032	...
.... a.	0656	0757	...	0954	...	1243	1255	...	1456	1645	...	1828	1919	...	2055	...

j – June 22, 29.
m – Not May 23 - 27, May 30 - June 3.
n – June 20 - July 1.
p – Daily Apr. 3 - May 22, June 4 - 19 (also May 28, 29, June 25, 26, July 2).
q – Apr. 4 - May 20, June 6 - July 1 (not June 22, 29).
z – Also May 4.

MORLAIX - ROSCOFF 283

laix - St Pol de Leon (*21* km) - **Roscoff** (*28* km). Journey 30 minutes (38 mins by 🚌). 🚌 journeys serve Roscoff port at sailing times.

n Morlaix: 0808🚌Ⓐ, 0840🚌Ⓐ, 1025⚒, 1110🚌⑥, 1151†, 1309⚒, 1526†, 1530🚌⑥, 1625🚌①–④**s**, 1715🚌⑤, 1810🚌①–④, 1820🚌Ⓒ, 2005🚌⑤, 2010🚌†, 2110🚌①–④, 2140🚌⑤.

n Roscoff: 0630🚌Ⓐ, 0755🚌Ⓐ, 0820🚌⑥, 1120⚒, 1125🚌†, 1320†, 1330🚌⚒, 1416⑥, 1511Ⓐ, 1630🚌⑥, 1649†, 1710🚌①–④, 1830🚌Ⓐ, 1935🚌†, 2040🚌⑤.

Schooldays only.

284 RENNES - ST BRIEUC - MORLAIX - BREST

Trains may be retimed a few minutes earlier owing to engineering work

km	*TGV* trains convey 🍷												*TGV* 8603	*TGV* 8603					*TGV* 8611					*TGV* 8617	*TGV* 8617		*TGV* 8627
		Ⓐ	Ⓐ	Ⓐ	⑥	Ⓐ	①	Ⓐ	⑥	Ⓐ	Ⓐ	⑥	Ⓐ	⑥	†	†	⑥	⑥		Ⓑ	⑥	⚒	⑥	①–⑥	⑦		①–④
			L				w						C	✤s		u			✤					✤v	✤x		✤n
	Paris Mont. **280** d.	...	...	...	...	...	...	...	...	...	...	...	0704	0708	...	...	...	...	0908	...	...	...	...	1108	1108	...	1208
0	**Rennes** d.	...	...	...	...	0612	...	0620	0640	0700	0720	0830	0920	0920	0957	...	1042	...	1117	...	...	...	1238	1332	1332	1349	1428
80	Lamballe **299** d.	...	...	...	...	0652	...	0723	0745	|	0809	0907	1000	0959	1035	...	1121	...	|	...	...	...	1315	|	1412	1447	|
101	**St Brieuc 299** d.	...	...	...	0651	0705	...	0737	0800	0746	0823	0919	1013	1012	1048	...	1133	...	1207	...	1223	...	1327	1422	1427	1502	1516
132	Guingamp d.	...	...	...	0709	0721	...	...	...	|	...	0939	1030	1030	1106	...	1151	...	1225	1234	1243	...	1347	1440	1446	▬	1534
158	Plouaret-Trégor d.	...	0619	...	0724	0736	0742	...	...	|	...	0953	|	|	1121	1134	1205	1216	|	1250	1301	...	1401	1457	1502	1508	|
175	Lannion a.	...	|	...	|	|	0759	...	...	|	...	|	|	|	|	1151	|	1233	|	1307	1318	...	|	|	|	1529	|
189	Morlaix d.	0614	0637	0725	0745	0800	...	...	...	0830	...	1012	1102	1101	1140	...	1223	...	1254	...	...	1305	1420	1516	1521	...	1604
215	Landivisiau d.	0628	0657	0741	0801	0815	...	...	...	|	...	1027	|	|	1155	...	1239	...	|	...	...	1329	1435	|	|	...	|
230	Landerneau **286** d.	0638	0709	0751	0814	0828	...	...	...	|	...	1037	|	|	1205	...	1248	...	|	...	...	1341	1445	1541	1545	...	|
248	**Brest 286** a.	0653	0724	0809	0826	0840	...	...	...	0902	...	1049	1133	1132	1217	...	1301	...	1326	...	...	1359	1457	1553	1556	...	1638

			TGV 8621							*TGV* 8623		*TGV* 8629															
	Ⓒ	Ⓐ	⑤	⑥	⑤	①–④	Ⓐ	⑤	⑤	①–④	⑤	Ⓒ	Ⓐ	†	Ⓒ	⑥	①–④	⑤	⑤	⑤	①–④	⑤	†	†	Ⓒ	Ⓐ	①–④
			✤z		z	m		z	z	✤m	z	✤					m	z	z	z	m	z					Lm
Paris Mont. **280** d.	...	...	1307	...	...	...	...	...	...	1408	...	1408	...	...	...	...	...	...	...	...	...	...	...	...	...	...	...
Rennes d.	1435	...	1524	...	...	...	...	1600	...	1617	1623	1623	...	...	...	...	...	1650	...	1655	1710	1720	1729	...	1737	1744	...
Lamballe **299** d.	1513	...	1604	...	...	...	...	1638	...	|	1707	1703	...	...	...	...	1713	1728	...	1757	1806	1807	1807	...	1838	1823	...
St Brieuc 299 d.	1526	...	1617	...	...	...	...	1651	...	1709	1719	1716	...	...	...	1730	1733	1741	...	1812	1820	1819	1820	...	1852	1835	...
Guingamp d.	1543	...	1636	...	...	...	...	1708	...	1727	...	1734	...	...	...	1752	1800	1759	...	...	...	...	1835	...	...	1852	...
Plouaret-Trégor d.	1557	...	|	1603	1617	1635	...	1722	1729	|	...	1749	...	1758	...	1811	1818	1813	1835	...	...	...	1850	1856	...	1906	1924
Lannion a.	|	...	|	1620	1634	1652	...	|	1746	|	...	|	...	1815	...	1828	1834	|	1852	...	...	...	|	1913	...	|	1941
Morlaix d.	1615	1630	1706	...	...	...	1720	1741	...	1757	...	1808	1808	...	1817	...	...	1831	...	...	...	...	1907	...	...	1925	...
Landivisiau d.	1630	1646	|	...	...	...	1744	1757	...	|	...	|	1827	...	1838	...	...	1847	...	...	...	...	1922	...	...	1941	...
Landerneau **286** d.	1640	1656	|	...	...	...	1756	1807	...	|	...	|	1837	...	1847	...	...	1857	...	...	...	...	1932	...	...	1950	...
Brest 286 a.	1654	1708	1738	...	...	...	1814	1819	...	1828	...	1840	1852	...	1905	...	...	1910	...	...	...	...	1946	...	...	2002	...

	TGV 8633							*TGV* 8647	*TGV* 8643						*TGV* 8645	*TGV* 8649	*TGV* 8691	*TGV* 8655	*TGV* 8655	*TGV* 8657			*TGV* 8663	*TGV* 8665	*TGV* 8665	*TGV* 8667	*TGV* 8679
	⑤†	①–④	①–④	†	⑥	⑥	Ⓐ	⑤	①–④	⑤	⑤	Ⓐ	†	†	①–④	⑤	⑤	①–④	①–④	⑤⑥†	Ⓐ	†	⑤	⑥⑦	①–④	⑤	⑤
	✤k	m	m					✤z	✤m	z	z				m	✤z	✤z	Dv	✤B	✤z			✤z	✤n	E	z	✤z
Paris Mont. **280** d.	1608	...	...	...	...	...	...	1712	1708	...	...	...	...	...	1741	1741	1741	1808	1808	1808	...	...	1908	1908	1908	1908	2108
Rennes d.	1817	1826	...	1838	1845	...	1849	|	1922	1927	...	1935	1940	...	1956	2001	2007	2018	2018	2018	2033	...	2123	2124	2124	2128	2323
Lamballe **299** d.	|	1902	...	1937	1924	...	1942	|	|	2006	...	2027	2016	...	2036	|	2048	|	|	|	2124	...	|	2204	2204	2212	|
St Brieuc 299 d.	1908	1914	1922	1947	1936	...	1953	2008	2012	2019	...	2038	2029	...	2049	|	2101	2108	2110	2108	2135	...	2213	2219	2219	2223	0013
Guingamp d.	1926	1932	1943	...	1952	...	...	|	2030	2037	...	...	2046	...	...	|	2117	|	2128	2126	...	2143	2231	2236	2236	...	0030
Plouaret-Trégor d.	|	|	1959	...	2006	2013	...	|	|	2051	2057	...	2100	2108	...	|	2133	|	2143	|	...	2200	2246	2252	2252	...	|
Lannion a.	|	|	2015	...	|	2030	...	|	|	|	2114	...	|	2125	...	|	2150	|	|	|	...	2217	|	|	|	...	|
Morlaix d.	1955	2001	...	...	2024	...	...	|	2059	2111	...	...	2119	...	...	2129	...	|	2201	2156	...	...	2304	2310	2310	...	0059
Landivisiau d.	|	|	...	...	2041	...	...	|	|	|	...	...	2135	...	...	|	...	|	|	|	...	...	|	|	|	...	|
Landerneau **286** d.	2020	|	...	...	2051	...	...	|	|	2133	...	...	2145	...	...	|	...	|	2226	|	...	...	2329	2334	2334	...	|
Brest 286 a	2031	2034	...	...	2103	...	...	2119	2130	2145	...	...	2157	...	...	2200	...	2217	2237	2228	...	...	2340	2345	2345	...	0130

	TGV 8690		*TGV* 8612	*TGV* 8610									*TGV* 8618	*TGV* 8618				*TGV* 8620				*TGV* 8622	*TGV* 8624				
	Ⓐ		⑥	Ⓐ	Ⓐ	⑥	Ⓐ	Ⓐ	Ⓐ	Ⓐ	⚒	①	⑥	Ⓐ	Ⓐ	Ⓐ	Ⓐ	Ⓐ	⑥	⑦	⑥	⑥	⑦	⑥	†	⑥	Ⓐ
		G	✤s				L					w	✤s	✤				✤A		x	s	✤s	✤x				
Brest 286 d.	...	...	0446	0445j	0525	...	...	0542	...	0635	...	...	0638	0642	0702	0752	...	0819	0802	...	...	0842	0849	1022	1034	...	...
Landerneau **286** d.	...	...	|	|	0536	...	...	|	...	0647	...	...	0654	0656	0719	0804	...	|	0819	...	...	|	|	1034	1045	...	...
Landivisiau d.	...	...	|	|	0547	...	...	|	...	0657	...	...	|	|	0732	0814	...	|	0831	...	...	|	|	|	1055	...	...
Morlaix d.	...	...	0520	0515j	0602	...	...	0613	...	0713	...	...	0717	0721	0755	0830	...	0851	0854	...	...	0916	0922	1057	1110	...	...
Lannion d.	...	0508	|	|	▬	...	0558	|	...	▬	0656	0714	|	|	...	...	0836	|	▬	0906	0908	|	|	|	|	...	...
Plouaret-Trégor d.	...	0524	|	|	...	...	0613	0631	...	†	0711	0730	|	|	...	...	0852	|	...	0922	0925	0935	|	|	1128	...	...
Guingamp d.	...	0540	0549	0550j	Ⓐ	...	...	0645	0702	0726	0731	...	0747	0750	...	...	0908	0922	Ⓒ	0938	...	0950	0952	1126	1142	...	...
St Brieuc 299 d.	0508	...	0607	0609	0616	0633	...	0703	0725	0742	0751	...	0805	0809	...	...	...	0940	0936	...	...	1009	1010	1144	1159	1236	1237
Lamballe **299** d.	0522	...	0620	|	0628	0644	...	0715	0740	0754	...	...	|	|	...	...	...	|	0951	...	...	|	|	1157	1211	1248	1251
Rennes a.	0559	...	0659	0659	0725	0745	...	0753	0840	0850	...	...	0855	0859	...	...	...	1025	1048	...	...	1055	1055	1236	1250	1340	1345
Paris Mont. **280** a.	0819	...	0917	0917	...	...	...	...	...	...	...	...	1117	1121	...	...	...	1253	...	...	...	1323	1323	...	...	...	...

				TGV 8634						*TGV* 8646						*TGV* 8660									*TGV* 8672	*TGV* 8670	*TGV* 8668
	Ⓐ	⑦	⑥	Ⓑ	⑤	⚒		†	⑥		Ⓐ	Ⓒ	①–④	⑤	⑦–④	Ⓑ	†	†	⑤	①–④	⑥	⑤	①–④	⑤	⑥	⑦	Ⓐ
	F	x		✤u	z					✤			m	z	n	✤u	q		z	m		z	m	z	✤s	✤x	✤
Brest 286 d.	...	...	1135	1146	1204	1230	...	1308	...	1345	1433	1432	1525	...	...	1541	...	1600	...	...	...	...	...	1630	1648	1654	1700
Landerneau **286** d.	...	...	1147	|	1215	1247	...	1325	...	|	1444	1443	1536	...	...	|	...	1611	...	...	...	...	...	1641	|	|	|
Landivisiau d.	...	...	1157	|	1225	1300	...	1338	...	|	1454	1453	1546	...	...	|	...	1621	...	...	...	...	...	1651	|	|	|
Morlaix d.	...	...	1214	1219	1241	1323	...	1401	...	1418	1511	1510	1603	...	...	1614	...	1637	...	...	...	...	...	1706	1721	|	|
Lannion d.	1204	1213	|	|	|	...	1401	...	1432	|	|	|	▬	1554	1605	|	1627	|	...	...	1658	1658	1703	|	|	|	|
Plouaret-Trégor d.	1221	1230	1231	1237	1258	...	1418	...	1448	|	1529	1528	...	1611	1622	1633	1644	1655	...	...	1714	1715	1720	1724	|	|	|
Guingamp d.	...	...	1245	1253	1313	...	1434	...	...	1448	1543	1542	†	...	...	1648	...	1709	...	...	1730	...	1735	1740	1750	1754	|
St Brieuc 299 d.	...	...	1302	1312	1330	...	1453	...	...	1507	1601	1558	1607	...	...	1707	...	1726	1725	1732	...	...	1755	1759	1808	1813	1814
Lamballe **299** d.	...	...	1314	|	1342	...	...	...	...	1521	1614	1610	1621	...	...	1720	...	1738	1739	1744	...	...	...	1813	1821	|	|
Rennes a.	...	...	1353	1359	1421	...	...	...	...	1559	1653	1650	1720	...	...	1759	...	1817	1836	1823	...	...	...	1854	1900	1857	1900
Paris Mont. **280** a.	...	...	...	1611	...	...	...	...	...	1822	...	...	...	...	...	2011	...	...	...	...	...	...	...	...	2111	2111	2111

				TGV 8676										*TGV* 8688				*TGV* 8696	*TGV* 8682					*TGV* 8686			
	†	①–④	⚒	⑦	Ⓐ	Ⓐ	⑤	†	Ⓐ	⑦		①–④	⑤	⑦	†	⑤⑥	⑤⑥	⑦	Ⓐ	†	Ⓐ	⑤	†	⑦	†	†	†
		m		✤x			z			x		Lm	z	✤x		z	z	✤x	✤			z		✤x	q		
Brest 286 d.	...	...	1704	1714	...	1717	...	1729	1737	...	...	1800	1800	1815	...	...	1834	...	1850	1905	1933	...	...	1948	...	2102	...
Landerneau **286** d.	...	...	1718	|	...	1732	...	1740	1748	...	...	1817	1817	|	...	...	1845	...	|	1916	1951	...	...	2001	...	2113	...
Landivisiau d.	...	...	1728	|	...	1745	...	1750	1758	...	...	1829	1830	|	...	...	1855	...	|	1926	2003	...	...	|	...	|	...
Morlaix d.	...	...	1742	1748	...	1800	...	1806	1813	...	...	1852	1853	1848	...	...	1911	...	1923	1942	2018	...	...	2024	...	2136	...
Lannion d.	1729	1735	|	|	...	...	1757	|	|	1820	...	|	...	|	...	1900	|	1918	|	|	...	2028	2036	|	2131	|	2228
Plouaret-Trégor d.	1747	1753	1805	|	...	...	1814	1824	1831	1836	...	1912	...	|	...	1917	1929	|	|	2000	...	2045	2053	|	2148	2154	2245
Guingamp d.	1802	1808	...	1819	...	...	1828	1838	1845	1854	...	...	...	1918	...	...	1943	1947	1952	2014	...	...	...	|	...	2208	...
St Brieuc 299 d.	...	1827	...	1836	1832	...	1849	1855	1902	1914	...	...	...	1941	1945	...	2000	2005	2011	2031	...	...	...	2108	...	2225	...
Lamballe **299** d.	...	...	...	1849	1846	...	...	1907	1914	...	...	...	...	|	2001	...	2012	2019	|	2043	...	...	...	|	...	2237	...
Rennes a.	...	...	...	1925	1940	...	...	1945	1953	...	...	...	...	2029	2053	...	2050	2059	2059	2121	...	...	...	2155	...	2316	...
Paris Mont. **280** a.	...	...	...	2150	...	...	...	...	...	...	...	...	...	2241	...	...	...	2310	2310	...	...	...	...	0011	...	...	...

A – Not Apr. 16 - May 1.
B – Until May 3.
C – From Apr. 18.
D – From May 9.
E – From May 5.
F – Not Apr. 5 - 15.
G – ① Apr. 11 - May 2; Ⓐ May 6 - July 1.
L – Lannion - Brest and v.v.

j – Not ②③④⑤ Apr. 5 - May 4.
k – Not Apr. 30, May 5, 7.
m – Not May 4, 5, 16.
n – Not May 4.
q – Not May 15.
s – Also May 5.
u – Not May 5.
v – Not May 16.

w – Also May 17; not May 16.
x – Also May 16.
z – Also May 4.

TGV – R, supplement payable, 🍷.

✤ – Subject to minor retiming Brest - Rennes and v.v. until April 10 (service may run ear

RENNES and NANTES - QUIMPER 285

Trains may be retimed a few minutes earlier owing to engineering work

										TGV					TGV					TGV				
										8705					8711					8715				
	Ⓐ	Ⓐ	Ⓐ	Ⓐ	⑥	Ⓐ	①	②–⑤		Ⓐ	†	⑥	⑥		Ⓒ	Ⓐ	Ⓐ		⑥		⑥	Ⓐ	⑥	Ⓐ
							w	e		A						D	C				s			
Paris Mont **280** d.	...	...	...	...	...	...	...	...	...	0704	...	...	...	...	0808	...	...	...	...	1008	...	...	...	...
Rennes 287 d.	...	0626	...	0641	0654	0723	...	...	...	0924	0930	0930	...	...	1029	1040	...	...	1127	1217	...	...	...	1343
Nantes ◧ d.	...	|	0612	|	|	|	0730	0738	...	|	|	|	0920	...	|	|	1029	...	|	|	1227	1253	1312	|
Savenay ◧ d.	...	|	0636	|	|	|	0752	0802	...	|	|	|	|	...	|	|	1051	...	|	|	1249	1315	1336	|
Redon **287** ◧ d.	...	0707	0712	0735	0735	0759	0827	0836	...	|	1005	1007	1012	...	1107	1127	1127	...	1202	1253	1316	1343	1403	1419
Vannes d.	0634	...	0741	0807	0804	0825	...	...	...	1024	1031	...	1038	...	1134	1156	1156	...	1232	1319	1344	...	...	1445
Auray d.	0648	...	0753	0818	0817	|	...	...	...	1038	1043	...	1049	...	1148	1209	1209	...	1244	1333	1357	...	...	1458
Lorient d.	0718	...	0814	0843	0836	0851	...	...	...	1056	1102	...	1109	...	1207	1230	1230	...	1306	1352	1418	...	...	1516
Quimperlé d.	0733	...	0826	...	0848	|	...	...	...	|	1114	...	1121	...	|	1242	1242	...	1318	1406	1430	...	...	...
Quimper a.	0802	...	0853	...	0915	0926	...	...	...	1130	1142	...	1147	...	1242	1309	1309	...	1346	1435	1457	...	...	...

	TGV		TGV																TGV						
	8717		8723																8729						
	①–⑥		⑤		①–④	⑤	⑤	⑦	⑤	①–④	⑤	①–④		⑥	†	⑤		①–④	⑥–④	⑤	⑤	†	①–④	⑤	Ⓑ
	h		z		m	z	z	x	z	m	z	m		⊖	⊖	z		m	n	z	z		m	z	
ris Mont **280** d.	1208	...	1346	...	...	...	...	...	...	...	...	...	...	...	...	...	...	...	1508	...	...	...	...	...	...
nes **287** d.	1422	...	|	...	...	1610	...	...	...	1635	1638	...	...	...	...	1654	...	...	1717	1727	...	...	...	...	1756
ntes ◧ d.	|	1520	|	...	...	|	1620	1620	...	|	|	1620	...	1659	1659	|	...	...	|	|	1702	1723	1724	1725	|
venay ◧ d.	|	|	|	...	...	|	1641	1642	...	|	|	1642	...	|	|	|	...	...	|	|	1736	1745	1747	1747	|
on **287** ◧ d.	|	1604	|	...	...	1649	1708	1710	...	1715	1716	1720	...	1743	1742	1733	...	...	|	1803	1805	1810	1821	1821	1836
es d.	1522	1633	1652	...	1708	1720	...	...	1741	...	1739	1745	...	1809	1810	1800	...	1802	1819	1830	...	...	...	...	1905
y d.	1535	1646	1706	...	1720	1732	...	...	1754	...	...	1758	...	|	|	1812	...	1816	1834	...	...	...	...	...	1918
nt d.	1558	1707	1724	...	1750	1753	...	...	1823	...	...	1817	...	1836	1837	1835	...	1841	1854	...	...	...	...	...	1940
nperlé d.	|	1719	|	...	1805	1805	...	...	1837	...	...	|	...	|	|	1847	...	1852	|	...	...	...	...	...	1952
nper a.	1631	1747	1758	...	1834	1832	...	...	1904	...	...	1852	...	1910	1911	1914	...	1923	1930	...	...	...	...	...	2020

					TGV	TGV		TGV	TGV	TGV				TGV			TGV			TGV	TGV	TGV	TGV	TGV	
					8739	8737		8747	8745	8743				8759			8757			8761	5237	5237	8777	8779	
	⑥	⑥	⑤	Ⓐ	⑤	①–④		Ⓐ	⑦	⑥	†	⑤	①–④	①–④	①–④	†	⑤	⑦			①–④	⑤⑦	⑤		
			z		z	m			x	s		z	m	m	m		z	x			♥m	♥x		K	
ris Mont **280** d.	...	...	...	...	1641	1641	...	1708	1708	1708	...	...	...	1808	...	...	1858	...	...	1941	...	...	2024	2208	...
nes **287** d.	1756	...	...	...	1901	1901	...	1918	1929	1929	...	...	...	2022	2029	2032	|	...	...	2149	2203	2203	2238	0027	...
ntes ◧ d.	|	1741	1805	1821	|	|	...	|	|	|	1940	1950	2000	|	|	|	|	2043	...	|	|	|	|	|	...
venay ◧ d.	|	1803	|	1843	|	|	...	|	|	|	2002	2018	2026	|	|	|	|	2105	...	|	|	|	|	|	...
on **287** ◧ d.	1837	1842	1853	1911	1939	1939	...	|	|	2007	2030	2045	2054	|	2117	2108	|	2131	...	2227	2240	2240	2314	|	...
es d.	...	1912	1922	...	2006	2004	...	2017	2030	2032	...	...	...	2123	2146	2134	2201	...	...	2252	2306	2306	2341	0129	...
y d.	...	1925	1934	...	2020	...	...	2032	2043	2046	...	...	...	|	...	2146	2214	...	...	2305	2320	2319	2355	0142	...
nt d.	...	1946	1954	...	2040	...	...	2053	2101	2106	...	...	...	2150	...	2205	2233	...	...	2325	2336	2338	0013	0159	...
nperlé d.	...	1958	2006	...	|	...	...	2107	|	2119	...	...	...	|	...	2217	|	...	...	2340	...	2351	|	...	...
nper a.	...	2025	2033	...	2115	...	...	2135	2134	2147	...	...	...	2224	...	2247	2307	...	...	0009	...	0020	0047	...	...

	TGV	TGV	TGV									TGV						TGV	TGV		TGV	TGV	TGV		
	8704	8706	8712									8718						5272	5272		8720	8722	8724		
	①	②–⑥	Ⓐ	Ⓐ	Ⓐ	①	Ⓐ	⑥	⑥	Ⓐ	Ⓐ	①–⑥	Ⓐ	⑥	Ⓐ	Ⓐ		②–⑤	①⑥	Ⓐ	Ⓐ	⑥	⑦	†	Ⓐ
	h	g				w			s			h			E			♥e	♥b	B	B	s	x	⊖	F
nper d.	0418	...	0524	...	0531	...	...	...	...	0612	...	0635	0650	0710	...	0717	...	...	0739	0754	0809	0839	0839	0927	0928
nperlé d.	|	...	|	...	0559	...	...	...	...	|	...	0706	0719	0736	...	0744	...	...	0810	0823	0839	0910	0910	|	0955
nt d.	0455	0500	0601	...	0610	...	...	...	...	0645	...	0721	0734	0749	...	0757	...	0824	0824	0838	0854	0925	0925	1002	1008
y d.	0514	|	|	...	0631	...	...	...	...	0702	...	0741	0805	0807	...	0817	...	0843	0843	0904	0914	0945	0945	|	1029
es d.	0527	0527	0628	...	0643	...	0654	0703	...	0715	...	0755	0815	0820	...	0837	...	0857	0857	0918	0928	0959	0959	1029	1041
on **287** d.	0552	0554	|	0648	0713	0720	0725	0734	0741	0745	0750	0820	...	0847	0851	0907	...	0923	0923	...	|	|	|	1055	1112
avenay ◧ d.	|	|	|	0724	|	0749	|	|	0810	|	0818	|	...	|	0922	|	...	|	|	...	|	|	|	|	1140
antes ◧ a.	|	|	|	0745	|	0812	|	|	0831	|	0840	|	...	|	0945	|	...	|	|	...	|	|	|	1141	1201
nes **287** ◧ a.	0629	0629	0730	...	0753	...	0821	0814	...	0825	...	0859	...	0923	...	0942	...	0959	0959	...	1029	1059	1059	...	...
aris Mont **280** a.	0853	0853	0948	...	...	...	...	...	...	...	...	1121	...	...	...	...	...	...	...	...	1253	1323	1323	...	...

			TGV											TGV								TGV	TGV	TGV	
			8730											8752								8762	8762	8762	
	⑥	Ⓒ		†	①–④	⑤	①–④	Ⓐ	⑤	⑥	⑦	⑥	⑦		Ⓐ	⑦	†	⑤	†	†	Ⓐ	①–④	Ⓒ	⑤	Ⓐ
	⊖				m	z	m		z	s	x	s	x			x	q	z				m		z	
nper d.	0949	1038	1142	1221	1232	1238	...	1248	1317	1331	1335	...	...	1431	1512	...	...	1544	1547	...	...	1617	1617	1617	1627
nperlé d.	|	1105	|	1248	1259	1306	...	1317	1344	1358	1402	...	...	1501	1539	...	...	1611	1615	...	...	|	|	|	1656
ent d.	1023	1118	1219	1300	1312	1318	...	1332	1357	1410	1415	...	...	1517	1552	...	...	1631	1627	...	...	1656	1656	1656	1711
ay d.	|	1137	1240	1320	1331	1337	...	1358	1414	1432	1437	...	...	1539	1614	...	...	1653	1650	...	...	1716	1716	1716	1736
nes d.	1050	1149	1254	1333	1344	1350	...	1411	1427	1444	1449	...	...	1553	1626	...	1648	1705	1702	...	...	1731	1730	1730	1749
on **287** d.	1119	1215	1320	1402	1418	1418	1423	...	1503	1518	1520	1523	1526	1622	1657	1657	1718	1736	1736	1741	1743	|	|	|	...
avenay ◧ d.	|	|	|	|	|	|	1449	...	1526	|	|	1546	1549	|	1722	1729	|	|	|	1807	1810	|	|	|	...
antes ◧ a.	1200	|	|	1447	|	|	1511	...	1550	|	|	1608	1611	|	1745	1750	|	|	|	1828	1833	|	|	|	...
nes **287** ◧ a.	...	1250	1355	...	1453	1453	...	...	...	1553	1553	...	...	1659	...	...	1753	1812	1811	...	...	1829	1827	1829	...
aris Mont **280** a.	...	...	1611	...	...	...	...	...	...	...	...	...	...	1911	...	...	...	...	...	...	...	2048	2052	2054	...

				TGV					TGV	TGV				TGV				TGV			TGV		TGV		
				8774					8776	8780				8794				8790			8798		8796		
	†	Ⓐ	①–④	⑦	⑦	Ⓐ	⑥		⑦	Ⓐ	⑦	⑤	①–④	⑦	①–④	①–④	⑤	⑤	†	†	⑦	⑤	⑦	†	
	q		m	x	x		s		x		x	z	m	x	m	m	z	z			x	z	x	q	
nper d.	1632	...	1715	1715	...	1722	1738	...	1748	1748	1757	1800	1807	1834	1835	...	...	1845	1918	...	1947	2003	...	2035	...
nperlé d.	1659	...	|	|	...	1750	1805	...	|	|	1825	1828	1836	1905	1902	...	...	|	1945	...	|	2030	...	2103	...
ent d.	1712	...	1750	1751	...	1805	1818	...	1825	1825	1839	1839	1851	1920	1915	...	...	1922	1958	...	2024	2042	2059	2117	...
ay d.	1733	...	|	1811	...	1833	1836	...	1845	1845	1858	1901	1917	1940	1932	...	...	1942	2020	...	2044	2103	2120	2136	...
nes d.	1746	...	1818	1825	...	1846	1849	...	1859	1859	1911	1913	1930	1954	1944	...	...	1957	2033	...	2058	2114	2133	2149	...
on **287** d.	1816	1841	1847	1852	1857	...	1919	...	|	|	1938	1940	...	2020	2018	2022	2036	|	2105	2113	|	2145	|	2217	...
avenay ◧ d.	|	1908	|	|	1926	...	|	...	|	|	|	|	...	|	|	2048	2102	|	|	2140	|	2211	|	|	...
antes ◧ a.	|	1931	|	|	1948	...	|	...	|	|	|	|	...	|	|	2110	2125	|	|	2204	|	2233	|	|	...
nes **287** ◧ a.	1853	...	1920	1929	...	...	1953	...	|	1959	2018	2015	...	2055	2053	...	...	2055	2139	...	2159	...	2230	2251	...
aris Mont **280** a.	...	...	...	2150	...	...	...	...	2205	2219	...	...	...	2310	...	...	...	2310	...	...	0011	...	0053	...	...

Not May 9-20.
Not May 23 - June 3.
Apr. 4-15, May 3 - July 1.
Apr. 4 - May 6, May 23 - July 1.
Apr. 4-15, Apr. 25 - July 1.
Apr. 4-15, Apr. 25 - May 20, June 6 - July 1.
⑤ Apr. 8 - June 10 (not May 6).

b – Also May 5, 17; not May 16.
e – Not May 5, 17.
g – Not May 17.
h – Not May 16.
m – Not May 4, 5, 16.
n – Not May 4.
q – Not May 15.
s – Also May 5.
w – Also May 17; not May 16.
x – Also May 16.
z – Also May 4.

TGV –Ⓡ, supplement payable, 🍷.

⊖ – To/from Brest (Table **286**).
◧ – See also **287** Nantes - Redon, **287/8** Nantes - Savenay.
♥ – From/to Lille Europe/Le Mans (Table **11**).

AURAY - QUIBERON: runs in Summer only

286 BREST - QUIMPER

km		Ⓐ	† N	⑥ N	Ⓐ M	Ⓒ		Ⓒ	Ⓐ M		Ⓒ	⑤ z		†	Ⓐ		⑥
0	**Brest 284** d.	0725	0747	0813	0945	0954	...	1140	1210	...	1607	1609	...	1720	1723	...	2026
18	Landerneau **284** d.	0737	|	|	0957	1006	...	1152	1222	...	1619	1621	...	1732	1736	...	2042
72	Châteaulin d.	0838	|	|	1058	1107	...	1253	1323	...	1721	1722	...	1838	1838	...	2143
102	**Quimper** a.	0907	0922	0947	1126	1135	...	1321	1351	...	1750	1751	...	1906	1905	...	2210

CAT 🚌 *31*, journey approx 90 minutes.
From **Brest** : 0700Ⓐ, 0930†, 1000⚒, 141 1445⚒, 1600⑤, 1805Ⓐ.
From **Quimper**: 0710Ⓐ, 1135⑤, 1245†, 1255⚒, 1640⚒, 1730Ⓐ, 1740†.

	Ⓐ	⑥		†	Ⓐ M		J	⑥	†	Ⓐ		⑥ N	† N	⑤ z		† k	
Quimper d.	0600	0647	...	0824	1028	...	1444	1757	1808	1808	...	1912	1913	1926	...	2030	...
Châteaulin d.	0628	0715	...	0859	1100	...	1512	1825	1836	1840	...	|	1942	1954	...	2058	...
Landerneau **284** d.	0732	0819	...	1001	1202	...	1614	1927	1938	1941	...	|	2041	2051	...	2200	...
Brest 284 a.	0745	0832	...	1014	1215	...	1627	1940	1951	1955	...	2048	2054	2104	...	2213	...

J – ⑥⑦ until May 1; daily from May 2.
M – From May 2.
N – To/from Nantes (Table **285**).
k – Not May 15.
z – Also May 4.

287 RENNES - REDON - NANTES

km		Ⓐ	① g	Ⓐ	⑥ s	Ⓐ	Ⓐ H	Ⓐ K	Ⓒ	Ⓐ	⑥ s	①–④ m	⑤ z	⑥ s	⑦ n	⑤ z	⑦ n	①–④ m	⑤ z	⑥	†	Ⓐ	†	Ⓐ	Ⓐ
0	**Rennes** § d.	...	...	0710	...	...	...	0854	1000	1208	1229	...	1415	...	...	1535	...	1641	1647	1700	...	...	1729	1745	...
72	Redon § a.	...	...	|	...	...	...	|	|	|	|	...	|	...	...	|	...	|	|	|	...	...	|	|	...
72	Redon ◇ d.	0648	0720	|	0741	0750	0851	|	|	|	|	1423	|	1523	1526	|	1657	|	|	|	1741	1743	|	|	1841
106	Savenay ◇ d.	0724	0749	|	0810	0818	0922	|	|	|	|	1449	|	1546	1549	|	1729	|	|	|	1807	1810	|	|	1908
145	**Nantes** ◇ a.	0745	0812	0826	0831	0840	0945	1009	1115	1323	1349	1511	1529	1608	1611	1650	1750	1806	1805	1815	1828	1833	1845	1900	1931

	⑥	Ⓐ	†	⑥	①–④ m	†	①–④ m	⑤ z	†	
Rennes § d.	1815	1831	1858	1920	1928	1948	...	...	...	...
Redon § a.	1855	1917	1937	|	|	|	...	...	...	...
Redon ◇ d.	1901	1926	1945	|	|	|	2022	2036	2113	...
Savenay ◇ d.	1928	1954	2013	|	|	|	2048	2102	2140	...
Nantes ◇ a.	1950	2015	2034	2035	2044	2105	2110	2125	2204	...

	Ⓐ	① g	②–⑤ p	⑥ s	Ⓐ J	⑦ n	⑥ s		Ⓐ
Nantes ◇ d.	0651	0730	0738	0756	0917	1007	1008	...	1229
Savenay ◇ d.	0715	0752	0802	|	0940	1029	1030	...	|
Redon ◇ a.	0743	0827	0836	|	1007	1055	1055	...	|
Redon § d.	0753	...	...	|	1013f	1101	1101	...	|
Rennes § a.	0838	...	...	0914	1050f	1151	1151	...	1345

	Ⓐ	⑥	Ⓐ	⑥ b	⑤ z	①–④ m	⑤ z	⑦ n	①–④ m	⑤ z	†	①–④ m	⑤ z	†	Ⓐ	Ⓐ		†	⑤ z	①–④ m	⑤ z	⑦ n	①–④ m	⑥
Nantes ◇ d.	1253	1312	1440	1503	1600	1601	1620	1620	1648	1702	1723	1724	1725	1758	1759	1821	1925	1940	1950	2000	2025	2043	2126	2126
Savenay ◇ d.	1315	1336	|	|	|	|	1641	1642	|	1736	1745	1747	1747	|	|	1843	|	2002	2018	2026	2047	2105	|	2147
Redon ◇ a.	1343	1403	|	|	|	|	1708	1710	|	1805	1810	1821	1821	|	|	1911	|	2030	2045	2054	2112	2131	|	2215
Redon § d.	...	...	|	|	|	|	...	...	|	...	...	...	...	|	|	...	|	...	...	...	2119	...	|	2229
Rennes § a.	...	...	1557	1617	1715	1716	...	...	1805	...	...	...	...	1912	1913	...	2044	...	...	...	2154	...	2240	2306

H – Not Apr. 18 - 22.
J – Not Apr. 25 - May 5.
K – Not Apr. 18 - May 20.
f – Not May 23 - June 3.
g – Also May 17; not May 16.
m – Not May 4, 5, 16.
n – Also May 16.
p – Not May 17.
s – Also May 5.
z – Also May 4.
◇ – For other trains Redon - Nantes s Table **285**, for Savenay - Nantes s Tables **285** and **288**.
§ – For other trains see Table **285**.

288 NANTES - ST NAZAIRE - LE CROISIC

Trains may be retimed a few minutes earlier owing to engineering work

km	*TGV* trains convey 🍷	Ⓐ	Ⓐ	Ⓐ	Ⓐ	⚒	*TGV* **8903** Ⓐ		Ⓐ	*TGV* **8911** r	Ⓐ		G	⑤ z	*TGV* **8915** ⑥ s	Ⓐ		*TGV* **8919** ⑤ z	⑥ s	⑤ z	*TGV* **8921** ⑦–④ d	Ⓐ	①–④ m	*TGV* **8925** ⑥ s
	Paris Mont **280** d.	...	...	...	...	...	0653	...	...	0854	...	...	...	...	1054	...	...	1221	...	...	1354	...	...	1454
0	**Nantes 285/7** d.	0616	0642	0656	0753	0800	0913	...	1008	1110	1202	1223	1234	1234	1307	1312	...	1444	1531	1604	1611	1643	1702	1709
39	Savenay **285/7** d.	0648	0706	0720	0820	0834	|	...	1029	|	1233	1244	1308	1308	|	1347	...	|	1606	1636	|	1704	1735	|
64	**St Nazaire** d.	0710	0726	0739	0835	0859	0945	...	1045	1146	1249	1301	1331	1332	1343	1403	...	1520	1625	1650	1648	1728	1749	1745
79	Pornichet d.	...	...	0753	...	0910	...	...	1058r	|	...	1312r	...	1342f	1355	...	...	|	1636	1700	|	1741	...	|
83	La Baule Escoublac d.	...	...	0800	...	0915	...	...	1104r	1202	...	1321r	...	1349f	1404	...	...	1537	1643	1706	1706	1748	...	1801
90	**Le Croisic** a.	...	...	0815	...	0926	...	...	1117r	1211	...	1333r	...	1359f	1417	...	...	1546	1659	1717	1715	1802	...	1810

	⑥ s	Ⓐ	①–④ m	⑤ z	⑥ s	⑦ x	①–④ m	*TGV* **8935** ⑤ z	*TGV* **8937** ⑦–④ d		①–④ m	*TGV* **8943** ⑤⑥ t	⑦ x	*TGV* **8945** ①–④ m	①–④ m		*TGV* **5230** ⑤† ♥u	*TGV* **8949** ⑤ z	⑦–④ d	⑤ z	*TGV* **8953** ⑤ z	⑦ x	⑤⑥ t	*TGV* **8957** ⑤ Dz
Paris Mont **280** d.	...	...	...	...	...	...	...	1721	1721	...	...	1823	...	1850	...	...	...	1954	...	...	2054	...	...	2150
Nantes 285/7 d.	1729	1734	1839	1841	1841	1900	1909	1932	1932	...	2006	2036	2034	2058	2131	...	2154	2208	2222	2222	2306	2325	2325	0012
Savenay **285/7** d.	1753	1809	1913	1916	1917	1923	1943	|	|	...	2031	|	2059	|	2158	...	|	|	2249	2249	|	2346	2354	|
St Nazaire d.	1808	1829	1928	1929	1940	1939	2018	2010	2006	...	2045	2112	2120	2134	2212	...	2229	2245	2302	2303	2343	0002	0008	0048
Pornichet d.	1819	...	1939	...	1950	1950	2031	2022	...	...	...	|	2132	|	2223	...	2242	2257	...	2314	|	0013	0019	|
La Baule Escoublac d.	1826	...	1949	...	1958	1957	2040	2030	...	...	...	2128	2140	2151	2227	...	2249	2304	...	2321	2359	0020	0026	0104
Le Croisic a.	1839	...	2002	...	2011	2010	2052	2044	...	...	...	2137	2152	2200	2238	...	2303	2317	...	2333	0008	0033	0037	0113

	① g	*TGV* **8906** ① h	*TGV* **8908** ②–⑤ e	Ⓐ	⑥ s		Ⓐ	⑥ s	Ⓐ	Ⓒ	Ⓐ	Ⓐ	Ⓐ		*TGV* **5270** ①⑥ ♥c	*TGV* **8926** Ⓐ	*TGV* **8928** Ⓒ		Ⓐ	Ⓐ	*TGV* **8932** ⑦ x		Ⓐ	*TGV* **8938** Ⓑ u
Le Croisic d.	0441	...	...	...	0547	...	0610	...	0634	0710	...	0730	0828	...	0850	0957	1024	...	1036r	...	1147	1219r	...	...
La Baule Escoublac d.	0454	...	...	...	0557	...	0624	...	0647	0722	...	0744	0841	...	0904	1009	1036	...	1049r	...	1201	1231r	...	...
Pornichet d.	0501	...	...	...	0602	...	0632	...	0654	0729	...	0751	0846	...	0911	|	|	...	1057r	...	1207	1238r	...	...
St Nazaire d.	0512	0542	0546	0557	0613	...	0644	0649	0705	0741	0742	0807	0858	...	0924	1025	1051	...	1107	1210	1221	1248	1352	1419
Savenay **285/7** d.	0526	0558	|	0616	0626	...	0659	0709	0729	0755	0757	0824	0912	...	|	|	|	...	1122	1224	|	1311	1408	|
Nantes 285/7 a.	0550	0620	0620	0649	0648	...	0720	0743	0750	0820	0820	0848	0934	...	1000	1059	1124	...	1143	1245	1255	1345	1440	1454
Paris Mont **280** a.	...	0837	0837	...	...	...	...	...	...	...	...	...	...	...	...	1320	1340	...	...	...	1518	...	...	1708

	①–④ m	*TGV* **8942** ⑤⑥† z	Ⓑ u		*TGV* **8944** ①–④ m	Ⓐ	⑥ s	Ⓐ	⑦ x		*TGV* **8950** Ⓑ u	①–④ m	Ⓐ	*TGV* **8952** Ⓒ	Ⓐ	①–④ m	⑤ z	⑦ x	Ⓐ		*TGV* **8958** ⑦ p		*TGV* **8960** ⑦ x	⑤ z
Le Croisic d.	...	1451	1520	...	1552	...	1628	...	1651	...	1746	...	1815	1854	...	1933	1939	2020	...	...	2052	...	2112	...
La Baule Escoublac d.	...	1502	1536	...	1603	...	1644	...	1705	...	1801	...	1827	1906	...	1947	1951	2032	...	...	2103	...	2126	...
Pornichet d.	...	|	1542	...	|	...	1651	...	1712	...	1808	...	1834	|	...	1952	1956	2038	...	...	|	...	2133	...
St Nazaire d.	1458	1518	1552	...	1621	1631	1701	1701	1724	...	1821	1829	1846	1921	1924	2002	2008	2050	2116	...	2121	...	2146	2214
Savenay **285/7** d.	1513	|	1609	...	|	1648	1714	1726	1740	...	|	1848	1915	|	1940	|	2025	2110	2134	...	|	...	|	2231
Nantes 285/7 a.	1545	1554	1630	...	1654	1714	1741	1758	1812	...	1854	1917	1945	1954	2005	2036	2046	2136	2201	...	2154	...	2219	2252
Paris Mont **280** a.	...	1814	...	...	1920	...	...	...	...	...	2119	...	...	2214	...	...	...	...	...	...	0005	...	0038	...

D – Until May 6.
F – From May 13.
G – ①②③④⑥ (not May 5, 9, 16, 17).
c – Also May 17; not Apr. 9, May 16.
d – Not May 4, 5.
e – Not May 5, 17.
f – Not Apr. 15.
g – Also May 17; not May 16.
h – Not May 16.
m – Not May 4, 5, 16.
p – Also May 16; not May 15.
r – Not Ⓐ Apr. 4 - 15.
s – Also May 5.
t – Also May 4, 5.
u – Not May 5.
x – Also May 16.
z – Also May 4.

TGV –Ⓡ, supplement payable, 🍷.

♥ – To/from Lille Europe (Table 1

NANTES - ANGERS - TOURS 289

For other *TGV* trains Nantes - Angers - Lyon (via Massy) see Table **335**

	TGV 5304 ① L	TGV 5302 ②–④ J	Ⓐ	4402 ⑥ B	4402 ⑥ A	Ⓐ	© W	Ⓐ P	Ⓐ		TGV 5322 ♠ M	4406 ⑦ j		TGV 5328 Ⓐ	⑤ g	①–④ x	14408 ⑤⑦ S	©	Ⓐ	Ⓐ	† c	⑦ dj	⑥ B	⑥ Zh	⑦ dj
Nantes 280 d.	0448	0456	...	0608	0622	0713	0916	...	1118	...	1252	1347	...	1454	...	1615	1618	...	1652	1818	1845	1910	2018	2025	2214
Angers St Laud **280** d.	0530	0536	0632	0654	0704	0800	1001	1053	1201	1254	1333	1429	...	1534	1551	1700	1700	1735	1750	1901	1932	1952	2101	2114	2258
Saumur d.	0558	|	0708	0727	0727	0822	1023	1127	1222	1327	|	1452	...	1558	1627	1722	1724	1808	1815	1924	1955	2013	2123	2138	2320
St Pierre des Corps a.	0628	0627	|	|	|	0851	1054	|	1256	|	1428	|	...	1628	|	1754	1755	|	|	1955	|	|	2154	2217	|
Tours a.	|	|	0747	0800	0800	|	|	1218	|	1419	|	1524	...	|	1717	1805	1807	1849	1854	|	2038	2055	|	|	2351
St Pierre des Corps a.	|	|	...	0824	0824	|	|	...	|	...	|	1549	...	|	...	...	...	...	...	|	...	...	|	|	...
Orléans **296** a.	◐	◐	...	|	|	1005	1157	...	1408	...	◐	|	...	◐	...	...	...	...	...	2057	...	...	2257	2321	...
Lyon Part Dieu **290** a.	0930	0930	...	1334	1334	...	...	...	...	...	1730	2106	...	1930	...	...	...	...	...	...	...	...	...	...	...

	Ⓐ	Ⓐ	© V	TGV 5352 Ⓐ P	TGV 5352 Ⓐ N		Ⓐ P	Ⓐ	⚒ h	©	Ⓐ	⑥	†	TGV 5368		X	Ⓐ	† s	† X	Ⓐ	⑤ g	TGV 5380 ♣		4506 4507 ⑤–⑦ G	
on Part Dieu **290** d.	...	...	...	0630	0630	...	...	...	...	...	...	...	...	1428	...	...	...	...	...	...	...	1830	...	1533	...
léans **296** d.	...	0706	0705	◐	◐	...	...	1127	...	...	...	...	...	◐	...	1706	...	...	1804	...	...	◐	...	|	...
ierre des Corps d.	...	|	|	|	|	...	...	|	...	...	...	...	...	|	...	|	...	...	|	...	...	|	...	2108	...
s d.	0714	|	|	|	|	...	0912	|	1246	1512	1612	1612	1612	|	...	|	1740	1842	|	1842	2112	|	...	2140	...
ierre des Corps d.	|	0806	0806	0933	|	...	|	1239	|	|	|	|	|	1733	...	1806	|	|	1905	|	|	2132	...	|	...
mur d.	0753	0837	0837	|	|	...	1009	1317	1338	1552	1653	1653	1653	|	...	1837	1842	1923	1939	1939	2153	2207	...	2216	...
rs St Laud **280** d.	0819	0900	0900	1025	1025	...	1038	1338	1411	1615	1717	1720	1718	1825	...	1901	1915	1948	2001	2016	2218	2232	...	2239	...
tes 280 a.	0902	0940	0940	1102	1102	...	...	1417	...	1655	1802	1800	1802	1903	...	1942	...	...	2044	...	...	2308	...	2320	...

NOTES SEE BELOW. Additional services operate Saumur - Tours and v.v. *Frequent connecting services are available St Pierre des Corps - Tours and v.v. (journey time 5 minutes).*

TOURS - BOURGES - NEVERS - MOULINS - LYON 290

Local service liable to alteration around public holidays. For faster *TGV* trains Nantes / Tours - Massy - Lyon and v.v. see Table **335**

	Ⓐ	Ⓐ	U	Ⓐ	⚒ h		4412 Ⓐ	4402 ⑥ B	4402 ⑥ A	E	16840 U			4406 ⑦ j	4416 ①–⑥ D	Ⓑ a	Ⓐ	Ⓐ	⑥ h	Ⓑ s	Ⓐ	⑦ y		
Nantes **289** d.	...	...	...	...	...	...	...	0608	0622	...	...	...	...	1347	...	...	...	...	...	...	...	...	...	...
Tours d.	...	...	...	0558	0658	...	0817	0817	0817	0958	1157	1358	...	1544	1544	...	...	...	1700	1700	1758	1758	1858	2045
St Pierre des Corps d.	...	...	...	0605	0705	...	0826	0827	0827	1005	1204	1405	...	1551	1551	...	...	...	1706	1706	1805	1805	1905	2052
Orléans **315** d.	...	0607	...	|	|	...	|	|	|	|	|	|	...	|	|	1614	1614	1715	|	|	|	|	|	|
Vierzon **315** d.	...	0657	...	0728	0828	...	0929	0929	0929	1128	1323	1528	...	1652	1652	1707	1707	1807	1828	1828	1928	1928	2028	2221
Bourges **315** d.	...	0730	...	0746	0847	...	0948	0948	0948	1146	1342	1547	...	1714	1714	1726	1730	1830	1847	1847	1951	1951	2047	2239v
Saincaize a.	...	|	...	...	|	...	|	|	|	...	|	|	...	|	|	...	|	|	|	|	|	|	|	...
Nevers a.	...	0821	...	...	0925	...	1024	1024	1024	...	1419	1625	...	1751	1751	...	1821	1921	1925	1925	2038	2038	2127	...
Nevers d.	0523	...	0830	...	0930	...	1037	1037	1037	...	1426	...	...	1804	1804	...	...	...	...	1926	...	...	...	...
Dijon **373** a.	|	...	|	...	1148	...	|	|	|	...	|	...	...	|	|	...	...	...	...	2148	...	...	...	...
Saincaize d.	0531	...	0838	...	...	...	1046	1047	1047	...	|	...	...	1814	1814	...	...	...	...	...	...	...	...	...
Moulins-sur-Allier d.	0601	...	0904	...	...	...	1113	1114	1114	...	1457	...	...	1843	1843	...	...	...	...	...	...	...	...	...
Digoin d.	0647	...	0945	...	...	...	|	|	|	...	1540	...	...	|	|	...	...	...	...	...	...	...	...	...
Paray le Monial d.	0704	...	0957	...	...	...	|	|	|	...	1552	...	...	|	|	...	...	...	...	...	...	...	...	...
St Germain des Fossés **328** d.	|	...	|	...	...	...	1138	1138	1138	...	|	...	...	1909	1909	...	...	...	...	...	...	...	...	...
Roanne **328** d.	|	...	|	...	...	...	1220	1220	1220	...	|	...	...	1956	1956	...	...	...	...	...	...	...	...	...
Lyon Part Dieu **328** a.	|	...	1152	...	...	...	1326	1334	1334	...	1752	...	...	2106	2106	...	...	...	...	...	...	...	...	...
Lyon Perrache **328** a.	0902	...	1205	...	...	...	1340	1348	1348	...	1805	...	...	2118	2118	...	...	...	...	...	...	...	...	...

	②–⑤ u	Ⓐ	Ⓐ	Ⓐ	©	Ⓐ	K	⚒ Ch	4504 ⑥	4504 Ⓐ F	⑤ g		16848 16850 U		Ⓐ	Ⓐ	Ⓑ	Ⓐ	4506 ⑤–⑦ G	4516 ①–④ H	† a	©	Ⓐ	Ⓐ Y	Ⓐ M
n Perrache **328** d.	...	...	...	...	...	...	...	...	0842	0900	...	...	1145	...	...	...	...	...	1521	1521	...	1743	1810	...	...
n Part Dieu **328** d.	...	...	...	...	...	...	...	...	0854	0912	...	...	1158	...	...	...	...	...	1533	1533	...	1754	|	...	...
nne **328** d.	...	...	...	...	...	...	...	...	1012	1024	...	...	|	...	...	...	...	...	1647	1647	...	|	|	...	...
Germain des Fossés **328** d.	...	...	...	...	...	...	...	...	1059	1117	...	...	|	...	...	...	...	...	1735	1735	...	|	|	...	...
aray le Monial d.	...	...	...	...	...	...	...	...	|	|	...	...	1353	...	...	...	...	...	|	|	...	2000	2026	...	...
igoin d.	...	...	...	...	...	...	...	...	|	|	...	...	1403	...	...	...	...	...	|	|	...	2010	2035	...	...
ulins-sur-Allier d.	...	...	...	...	...	...	...	...	1135	1140	...	...	1452	...	...	...	...	...	1802	1804	...	2059	2119	2120	2120
ncaize d.	...	...	...	...	...	...	...	...	1205	1210	...	...	|	...	...	...	...	...	1834	1835	...	2129**e**	...	2151	2151
ijon **373** d.	...	...	...	...	...	...	0712**b**	...	|	|	...	...	|	...	...	...	1608	...	|	|	...	|	...	|	|
ers a.	...	...	...	...	...	...	0929	...	1215	1220	...	...	1527	...	...	...	1829	...	1845	1845	...	2137**e**	...	2158	2158
ers d.	...	0535	0635	0640	0735	0740	0935	...	1230	1233	...	...	1534	1635	1639	1739	1835	1840	1904	1904	1935	...	...	...	...
ncaize d.	...	|	|	|	|	|	|	...	|	|	...	...	|	|	|	|	|	|	|	|	|	...	...	...	...
rges **315** d.	...	0615	0714	0733	0814	0833	1015	1214	1310	1312	1514	...	1614	1714	1733	1833	1914	1933	1944	1944	2014	...	...	...	...
zon **315** d.	0534	0634	0734	0755	0834	0855	1035	1234	1331	1331	1534	...	1634	1734	1755	1855	1934	1955	2006	2006	2034	...	...	...	...
rléans **315** a.	|	|	|	0845	|	0945	|	|	|	|	|	...	|	|	1845	1946	|	2045	|	|	|	...	...	...	...
Pierre des Corps a.	0658	0755	0855	...	0955	...	1154	1355	1436	1430	1707	...	1754	1855	...	...	2055	...	2105	2105	2155	...	...	...	...
rs a.	0706	0802	0902	...	1002	...	1201	1402	1443	1437	1714	...	1801	1904	...	...	2102	...	2113	2113	2202	...	...	...	...
antes **289** a.	...	...	...	...	...	...	...	...	...	...	...	...	...	...	...	...	...	...	2320	...	...	...	...	...	...

TES FOR TABLES 289 AND 290

July 9 - Aug. 28 (also July 14).
June 18 - July 2.
June 18 - Aug. 27.
Also July 14; not Aug. 15.
Daily June 18 - Sept. 18 (also June 12).
June 13 - Aug. 26 (also July 14).
Also July 13, Aug. 15; not June 12.
Not July 13, Aug. 15.
June 14 - 30.
June 18 - 26, July 2 - Aug. 28 (also June 12; not June 21, 23, 24).
June 13 - 27.
June 13 - July 8 (not June 27, 30, July 1).
Aug. 16 - 26.
June 13 - Aug. 12.
Also July 13, Aug. 15; not Aug. 14.

U – Not June 12.
V – June 12 - July 2.
W – Not Aug. 15.
X – Not Aug. 14.
Y – July 11 - Aug. 26.
Z – July 9 - Aug. 27.

a – Not July 14, Aug. 14.
b – ⚒ (also July 14).
c – June 12 - 26.
d – July 3 - Aug. 28.
e – Not June 12 - July 10.
g – Also July 13.
h – Also July 14.
j – Also Aug. 15.
s – Not July 14.
u – Not July 15.

v – † (not July 14).
x – Not July 13, 14, Aug. 15.
y – Also Aug. 15; not Aug. 14.
z – ① only.

♠ – To / from Marseille (Table **335** / **350**).
♣ – From Montpellier (Table **355**).
◐ – Via Massy.

Frequent connecting services are available St Pierre des Corps - Tours and v.v. (journey time 5 minutes).

ROANNE - ST ÉTIENNE 291

km		Ⓐ	Ⓐ A	⑥ B	Ⓐ	Ⓐ A	⚒		Ⓐ A		Ⓐ A	J			Ⓐ	Ⓐ A	Ⓑ	E	Ⓐ			H		⑦ C
0	**Roanne** d.	0524	0554	0624	0631	0652	0722	...	0824	0854	0954	1054	...	1224	1354	1454	1554	1654	1724	...	1822	1922	...	2024
80	**St Étienne** Châteaucreux a.	0637	0707	0737	0744	0805	0835	...	0937	1007	1107	1207	...	1337	1507	1607	1707	1807	1837	...	1935	2035	...	2137

	Ⓐ A	⚒		⚒	B	Ⓐ A	⚒		Ⓐ A			D	Ⓐ		Ⓐ A		F		G	Ⓐ		B	
Étienne Châteaucreux d.	0550	0622	...	0723	0823	0853	0953	...	1153	1223	...	1453	1553	...	1719	1653	1753	...	1819	1853	1953	2053	...
anne a.	0703	0735	...	0836	0936	1006	1106	...	1306	1336	...	1606	1706	...	1832	1806	1906	...	1932	2006	2106	2206	...

Until July 15.
Until July 16.
Until July 10.

D – Daily June 12 - July 16; ⚒ July 18 - Aug. 27.
E – Daily June 12 - July 16; ⑥ July 23 - Aug. 20 (also Aug. 27, 28).
F – ⚒ June 13 - July 22; Ⓐ July 25 - Aug. 26.

G – Daily June 12 - July 16; ⑥ July 23 - Aug. 27.
H – Daily June 12 - July 16; † July 17 - Aug. 28.
J – Daily June 12 - July 16; Ⓐ July 18 - Aug. 26.

292 NANTES - LA ROCHELLE - BORDEAUX

km				13899					3831			3835	3835							3837				
		Ⓐ	Ⓐ	⚒	Ⓐ ◇		Ⓐ					⑥ h	Ⓑ q		Ⓐ	Ⓐ ◇						①–④ x		
0	**Nantes** ▷ d.	...	...	...	...	...	...	...	0810	...	...	1210	1217	...	...	...	...	...	...	1705	...	...	...	
77	La Roche sur Yon ▷ d.	...	...	...	...	...	...	...	0901	...	...	1254	1301	...	...	...	...	...	...	1749	...	...	...	
113	Luçon d.	...	...	...	...	...	...	...	0942	...	...	1335	1342	...	...	...	...	...	...	1830	...	...	...	
	La Rochelle Porte Dauphine d.	...	...	...	...	...	...	...	|	...	...	|	|	...	...	...	...	1803	...	|	...	2035	...	
180	**La Rochelle** d.	...	...	0555	0633	0812	0947	...	1055	1144	...	1455	1455	...	...	1631	1741	1810	...	1944	...	2042	...	2
209	Rochefort d.	...	...	0622	0655	0834	1009	...	1116	1206	...	1516	1516	...	...	1659	1804	1839	...	2005	...	2113	...	2
253	Saintes d.	0515	0605	0702	0731	0906	1042	...	1149	1239	...	1549	1549	...	1742	1735	1845	1918	...	2037	...	2143	...	2
376	**Bordeaux** St Jean a.	0700	0741	0848	...	1037	...	...	1311	1410	...	1711	1711	...	1922	...	2024	...	...	2159	...	...	...	

								3842				3854			3856			3888	13898			
	Ⓐ	⑥ h	Ⓐ	Ⓐ	Ⓐ ◇		Ⓐ	Ⓒ		Ⓐ			◇			Ⓐ		①–④ y	⑤⑦ t		⑤	⑦–④
Bordeaux St Jean d.	...	...	...	...	...	...	0755	0823	1000	1255	...	...	1451	...	...	1655	1710	1745	1851	1851	...	2055	2055
Saintes d.	0530	0602	0619	0702	0742	...	0922	0950	1123	1422	1517	...	1610	1744	...	1822	1859	1925	2035	2035	...	2222	2221
Rochefort d.	0600	0641	0658	0738	0818	...	0954	1022	1155	1454	1549	...	1642	1819	...	1855	...	...	2107	2107	...	2254	...
La Rochelle d.	0629	0710	0727	0800	0843	...	1016	1044	1219	1516	1611	...	1705	1841	...	1920	...	...	2132	2135	...	2316	...
La Rochelle Porte Dauphine a.	0635	0716	0733	...	...	...	...	...	|	...	...	...	|	...	...	|	...	...	...	...	...	...	...
Luçon d.	...	...	...	...	...	...	...	...	1331	...	...	...	1815	...	...	2029	...	...	...	...	...	...	...
La Roche sur Yon ▷ d.	...	...	...	...	...	...	...	...	1416	...	...	...	1901	...	...	2111	...	...	...	...	...	...	...
Nantes ▷ a.	...	...	...	...	...	...	...	...	1458	...	...	...	1947	...	...	2153	...	...	...	...	...	...	...

ADDITIONAL TRAINS LA ROCHELLE - ROCHEFORT

	Ⓐ	⑥ h	Ⓐ	①–⑥ k			B q	A k	Ⓐ	⑤⑥ h
La Rochelle Pte Dauphine d.	0650	0723	0740	0850	1230	1406	1606	1706	1829	2019
La Rochelle d.	0657	0730	0747	0857	1237	1413	1613	1713	1836	2026
Rochefort a.	0725	0758	0815	0926	1306	1441	1641	1741	1904	2055

	Ⓐ	①–⑥ k	①–⑥ k			Ⓐ		Ⓐ	
Rochefort d.	0756	0851	1051	...	1319	1610	1710	1749	1
La Rochelle d.	0826	0921	1121	...	1349	1640	1740	1818	2
La Rochelle Pte D'phine a.	0832	0927	1127	...	1355	1646	1746	1824	2

A – Daily June 12 - July 2; ①-⑥ July 4 - Aug. 20; daily Aug. 22 - 28.
B – Ⓐ June 13 - 24; Ⓑ June 27 - Aug. 28.

h – Also July 14.
k – Not Aug. 15.
q – Not July 14.
t – Also Aug. 15; not Aug. 14.

x – Not July 13, 14, Aug. 15.
y – Not July 14, Aug. 15.
z – Also July 13; not July 14.

◇ – To / from Angoulême (Table **301**).
▷ – See also Table **293**.

293 NANTES - LES SABLES D'OLONNE

km								*TGV* 8971			*TGV* 8975												*TGV* 8979	*TGV* 8977		
		Ⓐ	Ⓐ	Ⓐ A	E	Ⓐ S	Ⓒ			S	S	①–⑥ F		Ⓐ A	Ⓐ A	Ⓐ S	⚒ h	Ⓐ A	Ⓐ A	Ⓐ S	G	①–④ C x	⑥–④ m	⑤ g	⑦ D	⑤
	Paris Mont. **280** d.	...	...	...	...	...	...	0854	...	...	1154	...	...	...	...	...	...	...	...	...	...	...	1854	1854	...	
0	**Nantes** ▷ d.	0625	0725	0743	0825	0917	1025	1117	1225	1325	1418	1425	1625	1725	1743	1743	1825	1843	1925	2025	2025	2043	2130	2131	2143	22
77	La Roche sur Yon ▷ a.	0715	0815	0836	0915	1005	1115	1157	1315	1415	1457	1515	1715	1815	1836	1836	1915	1936	2015	2115	2115	2136	2212	2213	2235	23
77	La Roche sur Yon d.	0717	0817	...	0917	1006	1128	1200	1317	1417	1500	1517	1717	1817	...	1838	1917	...	2017	...	2117	...	2215	2216	...	23
114	**Les Sables d'Olonne** a.	0749	0849	...	0949	1033	1200	1224	1349	1449	1524	1549	1749	1849	...	1908	1949	...	2049	...	2149	...	2240	2241	...	23

		TGV 8970								*TGV* 8974	*TGV* 8972							*TGV* 8976		*TGV* 8980			*TGV* 8982			
	Ⓐ	Ⓐ A	Ⓐ	Ⓐ	Ⓐ		Ⓐ	①–⑥ k	⑦ D	⑥ h	Ⓑ S q	S	Ⓐ A	⑥ h	Ⓑ q	⚒ F	Ⓐ S	⑦ D	Ⓑ q	H	Ⓐ		J	Ⓐ A		S
Les Sables d'Olonne d.	...	0543	...	0617	...	0717	0817	0917	1017	1042	1042	1107	1117	1232	1317	1517	1532	1543	1617	1642	...	1717	1810	1817	1917	20
La Roche sur Yon a.	...	0608	...	0648	...	0748	0848	0948	1048	1107	1107	1148	1148	1300	1348	1548	1600	1606	1648	1706	...	1748	1833	1848	1948	20
La Roche sur Yon ▷ d.	0526	0610	0626	0650	0726	0750	0850	0950	1050	1109	1109	1150	1150	1302	1350	1550	1602	1609	1650	1709	1726	1750	1836	1850	1950	20
Nantes ▷ a.	0616	0650	0716	0743	0816	0843	0943	1043	1143	1150	1150	1242	1242	1349	1443	1643	1649	1650	1743	1750	1816	1843	1921	1943	2043	2
Paris Mont. **280** a.	...	0906	...	...	...	...	...	...	...	1418	1420	...	...	...	...	...	...	1920	...	2019	...	...	2139	...	...	

A – June 13 - July 1.
C – June 13 - 30.
D – June 12 - 26.
E – Daily June 12 - July 1; Ⓒ July 2 - Aug. 28.
F – June 13 - July 2.
G – ⑤⑥† June 12 - July 3; ⒸJuly 9 - Aug. 28.
H – ⚒ June 13 - July 2; daily July 3 - Aug. 28.
J – ⑦ June 12 - July 3; daily July 4 - Aug. 28.
S – July 3 - Aug. 28.

g – Also July 13.
h – Also July 14.
j – Also Aug. 15.
k – Not Aug. 15.
m – Not July 13.
q – Not July 14.
x – Not July 13, 14, Aug. 15.

TGV – Ⓡ, supplement payable, 🍸.

▷ – For additional trains see Table **292**.

294 PARIS - LES AUBRAIS - ORLÉANS

km		Ⓐ	⚒ h			f		e				⚒ h	⑤ A		Ⓑ q	Ⓐ					Ⓐ		Ⓒ	①- x
0	**Paris** Austerlitz ▷ d.	0626	0826	0926	...	1126	...	1326	...	1526	...	1626	1656	...	1726	1756	...	1826	...	1926	2026	...	2126	23
119	Les Aubrais-Orléans ▷ a.	0725	0925	1025	...	1225	...	1425	...	1625	...	1725	1755	...	1825	1855	...	1925	...	2025	2125	...	2225	00
121	**Orléans** a.	0732	0932	1032	...	1232	...	1432	...	1632	...	1732	1802	...	1832	1902	...	1932	...	2032	2132	...	2232	00

	⚒ h	Ⓐ	Ⓐ	Ⓐ		Ⓐ	⚒ h			⚒ h		⚒ h		⑤† z		⚒ h	B q				† q	⚒ h	
Orléans d.	0458	0558	0628	0659	...	0728	0828	...	0928	1132	...	1328	1528	1628	...	1728	1828	...	1928	...	2035	2128	...
Les Aubrais-Orléans ▷ d.	0505	0605	0635	0706	...	0735	0835	...	0935	1139	...	1335	1535	1635	...	1735	1835	...	1935	...	2042	2135	...
Paris Austerlitz ▷ a.	0604	0704	0734	0807	...	0834	0934	...	1034	1238	...	1434	1634	1734	...	1834	1934	...	2034	...	2141	2234	...

LOCAL TRAINS

km		Ⓐ	⚒	† q		⚒ e	Ⓐ		Ⓐ	
0	**Paris** Austerlitz § d.	0551	0651	1022	...	1222	1622	1722	1822	1935
56	Étampes § d.	0625	0726	1056	...	1256	1655	1758	1857	2011
88	Toury d.	0652	0754	1124	...	1326	1718	1825	1926	2035
119	Les Aubrais-Orléans a.	0720	0822	1153	...	1354	1748	1850	1954	2058
121	**Orléans** a.	0726	0832	1201	...	1400	1754	1856	2000	2104

	Ⓐ	⑥ h	Ⓐ	⑦ j	⑥ h	Ⓐ e	Ⓐ		Ⓐ
Orléans d.	0624	0739	0755	1014	1235	1247	1724	1825	19
Les Aubrais-Orléans d.	0630	0745	0801	1020	1241	1253	1730	1831	19
Toury d.	0702	0817	0829	1048	1310	1310	1758	1859	20
Étampes § d.	0731	0844	0850	1117	1336	1336	1831	1931	20
Paris Austerlitz § a.	0804	0915	0920	1149	1407	1407	1903	2003	21

A – Until July 1.
B – ⑤† June 12 - July 3; † July 10 - Aug. 28.

e – Not June 23, 27, 28.
f – Not June 23, 24, 27, 28.
h – Also July 14.
j – Also Aug. 15.
q – Not July 14.
x – Not July 13, 14, Aug. 15.
z – Also July 13; not July 14.

◇ – For days of running see Table **315**.
▷ – For *Intercités* trains (Ⓡ) Paris - Les Aubrais-Orléans and v see Table **310**; for other trains see Table **296** and **315**.
§ – Suburban trains run Paris Austerlitz - Étampes and v.v. approx. every 30 minutes (journey 55 minutes).

PARIS - TOURS 295

TGV trains via high-speed line. For other trains see Table 296.
Trains may be retimed a few minutes owing to engineering work

TGV trains convey 🍸	*TGV* 8403	*TGV* 8301 ①–⑥ k	*TGV* 8341	*TGV* 8407 8471	*TGV* 8411	*TGV* 8303	*TGV* 8413 Qm	*TGV* 8415 ①–④ x	*TGV* 8433	*TGV* 8321 ⑤ g	*TGV* 8323 Ⓐ	*TGV* 8437	*TGV* 8325 Ck	*TGV* 8327 Ez	*TGV* 8327 Dx	*TGV* 8331 Ⓐ	*TGV* 8445 Ⓒ	*TGV* 8333 Fm	*TGV* 8481 ①–④ x	*TGV* 8335 Gn	*TGV* 8353 ①–④ P	*TGV* 8457 ⑤† c	*TGV* 8337 ⑤ g	*TGV* 8355 ⑤† z
Paris Montparnasse ... d.	0641	0716	0746	0846	1046	1216	1246	1404	1446	1516	1616	1646	1732	1816	1819	1837	1846	1916	1946	2016	2036	2046	2116	2201
Massy-TGV ... d.	0653	|	|	|	|	|	|	|	|	|	|	|	1744	|	|	|	|	|	|	|	|	|	|	|
Vendôme-Villiers TGV. d.	|	0802	|	|	|	1302	|	|	|	1602	1702	|	1823	1902	|	1925	|	2002	|	2102	2122	|	2202	|
St Pierre des Corps ... a.	0745	0822	0845	0945	1145	1322	1345	1507	1545	1620	1722	1745	1845	1921	1921	1944	1945	2020	2045	2122	2140	2145	2222	2300
St Pierre des Corps ... d.	...	0825	...	...	...	1325	...	...	...	1623	1725	...	1852	1924	1924	1951	...	2023	...	2125	...	...	2225	...
Tours ... a.	...	0830	...	...	...	1330	...	...	...	1628	1730	...	1857	1929	1929	1956	...	2028	...	2130	...	...	2230	...

	TGV 8340 ① y	*TGV* 8300 Ⓐ a	*TGV* 8302 ①–④ J	*TGV* 8302 Ah	*TGV* 8342 Hg	*TGV* 8342 Lb	*TGV* 8306 B	*TGV* 8402 ⑦ j	*TGV* 8308 ①–⑥ k	*TGV* 8410	*TGV* 8310 Ⓒ	*TGV* 8310 Ⓐ	*TGV* 8430	*TGV* 8432	*TGV* 8320 ⑤† z	*TGV* 8322	*TGV* 8436	*TGV* 8324 Ⓐ	*TGV* 8326 ⑤† z	*TGV* 8350 M	*TGV* 8328 ⑤ K	*TGV* 8350 N	*TGV* 8330 ⑦ j	*TGV* 8444 8472	*TGV* 8448 ⑤† c
s ... d.	...	0611	0649	0649	...	...	0735	...	0800	...	1131	1201	...	...	1631	1731	...	1831	1931	...	2031	...	2130	...	...
erre des Corps ... a.	...	0616	0654	0654	...	...	0740	...	0805	...	1136	1206	...	...	1636	1736	...	1836	1936	...	2036	...	2135	...	...
erre des Corps ... d.	0600	0619	0657	0657	0714	0717	0743	0815	0817	1014	1139	1209	1414	1614	1639	1739	1815	1839	1939	2012	2039	2057	2139	2214	2314
ôme-Villiers TGV.. d.	|	0639	0719	0719	0737	|	|	|	0839	|	1201	1231	|	|	1701	1801	|	1901	2001	|	2101	|	2202	|	|
y-TGV ... a.	|	|	|	0802	|	|	|	|	|	|	|	|	|	|	|	|	|	|	|	|	|	|	|	|	|
Montparnasse ... a.	0704	0729	0809	0815	0827	0827	0841	0913	0923	1117	1245	1315	1513	1713	1745	1845	1915	1945	2045	2115	2145	2201	2245	2314	0015

⑤⑥ June 17 - July 2; ①–⑥ July 4 - Aug. 27.
Ⓐ June 13 - July 18; ⑤ July 22 - Aug. 19; Ⓐ Aug. 22 - 26.
Ⓐ June 13 - July 13; ①–④ July 18 - Aug. 18; Ⓐ Aug. 22 - 26.
Ⓐ June 13 - July 1; ①–④ July 4 - Aug. 25.
Ⓒ June 12 - July 3; ⑤† July 8 - Aug. 28.
①–⑥ June 13 - July 2; ⑤⑥ July 8 - Aug. 27.
⑦ June 12 - July 3; ⑦–④ July 4 - Aug. 25.
Ⓐ June 13 - July 1; ⑤ July 8 - Aug. 26.
June 13 - 30.
Until July 1 and from Aug. 26.
Ⓒ June 12 - July 3; ⑥–④ July 4 - Aug. 25; Ⓒ Aug. 27 - 28.

M – Until July 2.
N – July 3 - Aug. 28.
P – Until June 30 and from Aug. 22.
Q – ⑤ June 17 - July 1; ⑤⑥ July 8 - Aug. 27.

a – Not Aug. 8 - 11.
b – Not July 13.
c – Not July 14.
g – Also July 13.
h – Also July 14.
j – Also Aug. 15.
k – Not Aug. 15.

m – Also July 13, 14.
n – Not July 13, 14.
x – Not July 13, 14, Aug. 15.
y – Also Aug. 16; not Aug. 15.
z – Also July 13; not July 14.

TGV –Ⓡ, supplement payable, 🍸.

☛ *Frequent connecting services are available St Pierre des Corps - Tours and v.v. (journey time 5 minutes).*

ORLÉANS - BLOIS - TOURS 296

For fast *TGV* services Paris - Tours and v.v. see Table 295. Certain trains continue to / from Le Croisic (Table 288)

	Ⓐ	⚒ h	⑥ Kh	Ⓒ J	⑦ Nj	Ⓐ	Ⓐ	⚒ h		Ⓐ	Ⓑ q		Ⓒ	Ⓒ	Ⓐ	Ⓐ		⑥ h	Ⓒ	Ⓐ	⚒ h	⑥ h	Ⓐ a
Paris Austerlitz **294** ... d.	...	...	...	...	...	...	...	...	...	...	0737	...	...	1036	...	...	...	...	...	...	...	1236	1259
Orléans ... d.	...	0642	0702	0705	0705	0706	0710	0742	...	0801	|	0842	1042	|	1127	1135	...	1225	1242	1244	...	|	|
Les Aubrais-Orléans ... d.	...	|	|	|	|	|	|	|	...	|	0837	|	|	1136	|	|	...	|	|	|	...	1336	1400
Beaugency ... d.	...	0700	0717	0720	0721	0721	0732	0800	...	0830	|	0900	1100	|	1142	1153	...	1254	1300	1304	...	|	|
Blois ... d.	0636	0719	0734	0735	0737	0738	0753	0819	...	0857	0903	0919	1119	1203	1204	1214	...	1314	1319	1325	1332	1403	1427
Amboise ... d.	0658	0738	0750	0750	0751	0753	0813	0837	...	...	0919	0937	1138	1219	1221	1233	...	...	1338	1347	1355	1419	1444
St Pierre des Corps ... a.	0714	0750	0804	0804	0803	0804	0827	0849	...	...	0935	0949	1149	1231	1238	1248	...	...	1349	1402	1415	1431	1456
Tours ... a.	0721	0757	|	|	|	|	0834	0859	...	...	0942	0957	1157	1238	|	1255	...	...	1357	1409	1422	1438	1503
Nantes **289** ... a.	...	...	0951	0940	0955	0940	...	...	...	...	...	...	...	...	1417	...	...	...	...	...	...	...	...

		Ⓐ			Ⓐ	† q	Ⓐ		† p	Ⓑ q	⚒ h		①–④ x	⑤ g	⑥⑦ h		Ⓐ	Ⓐ				Ⓑ q		⑤⑥† g
ris Austerlitz **294** ... d.	...	...	...	...	...	...	...	...	...	...	...	1737	...	...	...	...	...	1837	...	...	...	...	...	2307
ans ... ▷ d.	1442	1542	1642	1706	1709	1740	1742	...	1804	...	1810	|	1842	1845	1847	...	1910	|	1942	...	2042	2142	...	|
Aubrais-Orléans ... ▷ d.	|	|	|	|	|	|	|	...	|	...	|	1836	|	|	|	...	|	1936	|	...	|	|	...	0010
gency ... d.	1500	1600	1700	1721	1738	1809	1801	...	1820	...	1839	|	1900	1904	1905	...	1939	|	2000	...	2100	2200	...	|
... d.	1519	1619	1719	1738	1756	1827	1821	...	1837	1844	1857	1903	1919	1924	1924	...	1957	2003	2019	...	2119	2219	...	0036
oise ... d.	1537	1637	1738	1752	...	...	1839	...	1852	1909	...	1919	1938	1943	1942	...	...	2019	2037	...	2137	2239	...	0052
erre des Corps ... a.	1550	1650	1750	1804	...	...	1851	...	1903	1926	...	1931	1950	1955	1955	...	...	2031	2050	...	2150	2250	...	0103
s ... a.	1557	1657	1757	|	...	...	1901	...	|	1933	...	1938	2004	2004	2002	...	...	2038	2057	...	2157	2257	...	0110
ntes **289** ... a.	...	...	...	1942	...	...	...	...	2041	...	...	...	...	...	...	...	...	...	...	...	...	...	...	...

	Ⓐ	Ⓐ	⚒ h	⚒ h	Ⓐ		Ⓐ	Ⓐ	⚒ h	Ⓐ	Ⓒ		Ⓐ	Ⓒ	Ⓒ	Ⓐ	Ⓒ k		Ⓒ	Ⓐ	⑥	⑥ h	Ⓐ	Ⓐ
ntes **289** ... d.	...	...	...	...	...	...	...	...	...	...	...	...	0713	...	...	...	0916	...	...	...	...	...	1118	...
s ... d.	0503	...	0603	0620	...	...	0628	0703	...	0750	0805	...	|	0920	1003	1003	|	...	1120	1118	1203	...	|	1239
erre des Corps ... d.	0510	...	0610	0627	...	...	0635	0710	...	0757	0811	...	0857	0927	1010	1010	1056	...	1127	1126	1210	...	1258	1246
oise ... d.	0521	...	0621	0640	...	...	0649	0722	...	0808	0823	...	0908	0938	1022	1022	1109	...	1138	1140	1221	...	1309	1257
... d.	0542	0603	0642	0657	0703	...	0714	0742	0803	0828	0843	...	0926	0957	1042	1044	1126	...	1157	1214	1242	1255	1328	1336
gency ... d.	0600	0621	0700	|	0722	...	...	0800	0822	0847	0901	...	0945	|	1100	1105	1142	...	|	|	1300	1322	1346	1358
Aubrais-Orléans ... a.	|	|	|	0724	|	...	...	|	|	|	|	...	|	1024	|	|	|	...	1224	1245	|	|	|	|
ans ... a.	0618	0651	0718	|	0751	...	...	0818	0851	0905	0919	...	1005	|	1118	1124	1157	...	|	|	1318	1351	1408	1420
ris Austerlitz **294** ... a.	...	...	...	0823	...	...	...	...	...	...	...	...	...	1123	...	...	...	...	1323	1346	...	...	...	...

		⑤† z	Ⓐ	Ⓐ h	† q	Ⓐ	Ⓐ	Ⓑ q		⚒ h	⚒ h		Ⓐ		Ⓐ	Ⓑ q		A	⑥ J	⑦ Nj		⑥ K	Ⓐ	
ntes **289** ... d.	...	...	...	...	...	...	...	...	...	...	...	...	...	...	1818	...	...	2016	2018	2025	...	2025	...	...
s ... d.	1403	1503	1520	1603	1620	...	1627	1704	1719	...	1728	1803	1828	1910	|	2103	...	|	|	|	...	|	2213	...
erre des Corps ... d.	1410	1510	1527	1610	1627	...	1635	1710	1727	...	1735	1810	1835	1917	1957	2110	...	2158	2156	2219	...	2220	2220	...
oise ... d.	1422	1521	1538	1622	1638	...	1652	1721	1739	...	1752	1822	1852	1931	2009	2121	...	2209	2208	2231	...	2232	2231	...
... d.	1441	1542	1557	1642	1657	1703	1714	1742	1759	1803	1814	1842	1914	1950	2027	2142	...	2227	2225	2248	...	2250	2252	...
gency ... d.	1500	1600	|	1700	|	1730	...	1800	|	1830	...	1900	...	2008	2042	2200	...	2242	2241	2303	...	2306	2310	...
Aubrais-Orléans ... a.	|	|	1622	|	1724	|	...	|	1824	|	...	|	...	|	|	|	...	|	|	|	...	|	|	...
ans ... a.	1518	1618	|	1718	|	1759	...	1819	|	1858	...	1919	...	2026	2057	2218	...	2257	2257	2318	...	2321	2328	...
ris Austerlitz **294** ... a.	...	...	1723	...	1823	...	...	...	1923	...	...	...	...	...	...	...	...	...	...	...	...	...	...	...

June 12 - 26.
Until July 2.
From July 9.
From July 3.

a – Not June 23, 27, 28.
g – Also July 13.
h – Also July 14.
j – Also Aug. 15.
k – Not Aug. 15.

p – Not Aug. 14.
q – Not July 14.
x – Not July 13, 14, Aug. 15.
z – Also July 13; not July 14.

☛ *Frequent connecting services are available St Pierre des Corps - Tours and v.v. (journey time 5 minutes).*

ANGERS - CHOLET

Journey 45 - 50 minutes *60 km*

Angers depart: 0645Ⓐ, 0721Ⓐ, 0745⚒**c**, 0938**A**, 1155**B**, 1202⑦**j**, 1250Ⓐ**C**, 1303⑥**c**, 1548**D**, 1638**E**, 1721Ⓐ**J**, 1741Ⓐ. 1843Ⓐ, 1845⑥**c**, 1938Ⓑ**d**, 2047①–⑥**k**, 2147⑤**a**, 2248**F**, 2043⑦**j**, 2308①–④**H**.

Cholet depart: 0615Ⓐ, 0638①–⑥**k**, 0656Ⓐ, 0717⑥**c**, 0738Ⓐ, 0832⑦**j**, 0843①–⑥**k**, 0945**C**, 1103⑥**c**, 1243⑥**c**, 1245Ⓐ**C**, 1352**G**, 1646Ⓑ**J**, 1733Ⓐ, 1737Ⓒ, 1838Ⓐ, 1843⑦**j**, 1939⑥**c**, 1953Ⓑ**d**, 2146⑦**j**.

BAYONNE - ST JEAN PIED DE PORT

50 km

			L				L		N	
Bayonne ... d.	0745	...	1110	...	1455	...	1806	...	2110	...
Cambo les Bains ... d.	0808	...	1133	...	1518	...	1834	...	2133	...
St Jean Pied de Port ... a.	0843	...	1208	...	1554	...	1912	...	2208	...
	K								**M**	
St Jean Pied de Port ... d.	0610	...	0920	...	1341	...	1651	...	1917	...
Cambo les Bains ... d.	0649	...	0955	...	1416	...	1726	...	1952	...
Bayonne ... a.	0715	...	1017	...	1438	...	1748	...	2014	...

BORDEAUX - MONT DE MARSAN

147 km

	⚒	Ⓐ				⚒						Ⓑ
Bordeaux ... **305** d.	...	0623	0858	1058	...	1258	1558	...	1730	...	...	2158
Morcenx ... **305** d.	0655	0736	1003	1203	...	1403	1703	...	1834	1959	...	2303
Mont de Marsan ... a.	0724	0759	1026	1227	...	1427	1726	...	1859	2028	...	2327
	Ⓐ	⚒	⚒		⚒					Ⓐ	†	†
Mont de Marsan ... d.	0533	0603	0733	1033	1233	...	1433	1633	1801	1832	1933	2033
Morcenx ... **305** d.	0558	0633	0759	1058	1258	...	1458	1658	1831	1901	1957	2105
Bordeaux ... **305** a.	0702	...	0902	1202	1402	...	1602	1802	...	2006	2102	...

CARCASSONNE - LIMOUX - QUILLAN

km		🚌 ⚒	⚒	🚌 †	⚒	⚒	🚌	⚒	⚒	🚌 †	⚒
0	Carcassonne ... d.	0709	0719	0940	1037	1238	1337	1600	1736	1847	1908
26	Limoux ... a.	0738	0751	1018	1109	1311	1410	1633	1808	1925	1940
54	Quillan ... a.	0818	...	1058	*1158*r	1347	1450	*1722*r	...	2005	2016

	⚒	⚒	🚌 †	⚒	🚌 †	⚒	⚒	🚌 †	⚒	🚌 ⚒	🚌 †
Quillan ... d.	0603	...	0805	*1027*r	1103	1358	*1553*r	1624	...	1817	2005
Limoux ... d.	0639	0803	0845	1117	1145	1433	1645	1708	1818	1900	2045
Carcassonne ... a.	0712	0836	0918	1150	1223	1507	1718	1745	1851	1937	2117

CHARLEVILLE MÉZIÈRES - GIVET

Journey 60 - 80 minutes *64 km*

Charleville Mézières depart: 0557**Xy**, 0643**Xy**, 0743Ⓐ**J**, 0841**Y**, 0955**Z**, 1049†**d**, 1240⚒**T**, 1336**p**, 1500Ⓑ, 1635**qj**, 1730**r**, 1821Ⓐ**J**, 1850**s**, 1938**qj**, 2025Ⓐ**J**, 2055**qj**.

Givet depart: 0447**Xy**, 0531**Xy**, 0600**Z**, 0614Ⓐ**J**, 0640**p**, 0725**Xy**, 0924Ⓐ**J**, 1050**J**, 1229**Z**, 1401⚒**R**, 1442**Yj**, 1542**t**, 1712**qj**, 1758**s**, 1913**qj**.

DINARD - ST MALO

🚌: 7 - 10 times per day (fewer on †), journey 24 minutes. Operator: TIV. *11 km*

⛴: *Le Bus de Mer* passenger ferry operates 12 - 17 times daily from April to September. Journey time 10 minutes. Operator: Compagnie Corsaire.

LILLE - LENS

Journey 40 - 47 minutes *39 km*

Lille Flandres depart: Ⓐ: 0615, 0642, 0715, 0719, 0819, 0919, 1219, 1242, 1318, 1542, 1619, 1642, 1655, 1715, 1719, 1742, 1815, 1819, 1842, 1915, 1919, 2019, 2119; ⑥: 0645, 0742, 0919**b**, 1019**b**, 1118**b**, 1219**b**, 1318**b**, 1518**b**, 1619**b**, 1719**b**, 1819**b**, 1919**b**, 2018**b**; †: 1019**n**, 1118**n**, 1318**n**, 1519**n**, 1619**n**, 1719**h**, 1819**h**, 1919**h**, 2018**h**.

Lens depart: Ⓐ: 0454, 0554, 0639, 0654, 0709, 0736, 0740, 0754, 0810, 0836, 0854, 1110, 1210, 1254, 1546, 1639, 1709, 1736, 1754, 1854, 2010; ⑥: 0454, 0554, 0654, 0740, 0754, 0839, 0954**b**, 1054**b**, 1154**b**, 1254**b**, 1354**b**, 1454**b**, 1554**b**, 1654**b**, 1754**b**, 1854**b**, 1954**b**; †: 0838**n**, 1054**n**, 1254**n**, 1454**n**, 1654**n**, 1754**n**, 1854**h**, 1954**h**.

NANTES - CHOLET

Journey 45 - 68 minutes *65 km*

Nantes depart: 0635Ⓐ🚌, 0816Ⓐ, 0835Ⓐ🚌, 0925Ⓒ🚌, 1030⑥🚌, 1216⑥**c**, 1316Ⓑ**d**, 1355⑤⑦🚌, 1405⑥🚌, 1425⑤🚌, 1620Ⓐ🚌, 1716Ⓐ, 1730🚌, 1815Ⓐ🚌, 1816⑦**j**, 1916①–⑥**k**, 1945⑦🚌.

Cholet depart: 0633Ⓐ, 0645Ⓐ🚌, 0730⑥🚌, 0733Ⓐ, 0833⑥**c**, 1025🚌, 1233⑦**j**, 1245⚒🚌, 1545⑤🚌, 1558⑤⑦🚌, 1633Ⓐ, 1745Ⓐ🚌, 1800⑦🚌, 1833Ⓐ, 1933⑦**j**, 2030🚌.

🚌 *times subject to alteration.*

NANTES - PORNIC

Valid July 3 - Aug. 28

km		Ⓐ	⑦j	⑦j	Ⓐ	⑥c	Ⓒ	Ⓐ	Ⓐ	Ⓐ	⑤a	Ⓐ	⑦j
0	Nantes ... d.	0923	1000	1125	1132	1224	1421	1622	1747	1828	1942	2133	2204
	Ste Pazanne . d.	0952	1029	1155	1204	1252	1455	1656	1818	1902	2015	2203	2233
60	Pornic ... a.	1021	1057	1223	1233	1320	1524	1724	1848	1930	2044	2232	2300

	Ⓐ	Ⓐ	⑦j	⑦j	Ⓐ		Ⓐ	⑦j	⑦j	⑥c	Ⓐ	⑦j
Pornic ... d.	0617	0708	0846	1124	1134	1539	1748	1746	1827	1846	1940	2049
Ste Pazanne ... d.	0647	0738	0915	1156	1204	1608	1819	1814	1905	1925	2017	2126
Nantes ... a.	0720	0808	0945	1226	1235	1645	1847	1845	1935	1949	2042	2150

NANTES - ST GILLES CROIX DE VIE

Valid July 3 - Aug. 28

km		Ⓐ	⚒c	⑦j	⑥c	⑦j	⑥c	Ⓐ	Ⓐ	⑦j	⚒c
0	Nantes ... d.	0702	1011	1019	1123	1238	1332	1309	1421	1621	1721
	Ste Pazanne ... d.	0733	1040	1051	1152	1309	1403	1339	1457	1651	1752
87	St Gilles Croix ... a.	0814	1124	1130	1232	1348	1442	1420	1537	1730	1834

	⚒c	⑦j	Ⓐ	⑤a
Nantes ... d.	1849	2030	2109	2223
Ste Pazanne ... d.	1923	2059	2138	2252
St Gilles Croix ... a.	2006	2140	2217	2332

	Ⓐ	Ⓐ	⑥c
St Gilles Croix ... d.	0535	0629	0725
Ste Pazanne ... d.	0614	0709	0814
Nantes ... a.	0645	0743	0845

	⑥c	Ⓐ	⑥c	⑦j	⑦j	Ⓐ	⑥c	⚒c	Ⓑj	⑥c	⑦j
St Gilles Croix ... d.	0836	0938	0958	1011	1228	1233	1240	1321	1610	1628	1655
Ste Pazanne ... d.	0915	1017	1046	1050	1308	1313	1319	1410	1650	1708	1736
Nantes ... a.	0945	1050	1116	1115	1338	1347	1350	1440	1718	1740	1807

Services call at Challans approx 1 hour after leaving Nantes.

PARIS - CHÂTEAUDUN - VENDÔME - TOURS

km		Ⓐf	⚒		Ⓐ	⚒		Ⓐ	†m	Ⓐ	
0	Paris Austerlitz ... d.	...	...	0810	1010	...	1357	1610	...	1810	1910
134	Châteaudun ... d.	...	0643	0946	1149	1206	1523	1748	1834	1947	2048
178	Vendôme ... d.	0624	0724	...	...	1248	1602	...	1914	...	2127
248	Tours ... a.	0725	0825	...	...	1348	...	...	2022	...	...

	Ⓐ	⚒c		⚒	Ⓐ		⑤†v	Ⓑd	⑤a	†k	⚒
Tours ... d.	...	...	...	1242	...	...	1536	...	1736	...	1836
Vendôme ... d.	0536	...	...	1345	...	1621	1705	...	1838	1917	1939
Châteaudun ... d.	0616	0715	1211	1425	1604	1702	1743	1802	1917	1957	2018
Paris Austerlitz ... a.	0750	0850	1335	...	1745	1838	...	1931	...	2131	...

PARIS - DISNEYLAND (Marne la Vallée - Chessy)

32

Trains run approximately every 15 minutes 0500 - 2400 on RER Line A: Paris Châtelet les Halles - Paris Gare de Lyon - Marne la Vallée Chessy (for Disneyland

Operator: RATP. For *TGV* services serving Marne la Vallée see Tables **11** and **391**.

Journey 39 minutes.

ROYAN - POINTE DE GRAVE ⛴

Subject to alteration

Apr. 3 - July 2 and **Sept. 1 - 27**:

From Royan: 0750, 0930, 1100, 1230, 1400, 1545, 1715, 1900, 2030.

From Pointe de Grave (Le Verdon): 0715, 0855, 1025, 1155, 1325, 1510, 1640, 1825,

July 3 - Aug. 31: approx every 40 - 50 minutes 0715 - 2115 (0630 - 2030 from Pointe de Gr

Sept. 28 - Feb. 1 ❦:

From Royan: 0745Ⓐ, 0830Ⓒ, 1000Ⓐ, 1015Ⓒ, 1200, 1500, 1715, 1915.

From Pointe de Grave: 0715Ⓐ, 0800Ⓒ, 0930Ⓐ, 0945Ⓒ, 1130, 1430, 1645, 1845.

❦ – Oct. 16 - Nov. 1 the 1715 sailing from Royan is replaced by sailings at 1615 and 1 the 1645 sailing from Pointe de Grave is replaced by sailings at 1545 and 1715.

Sailing time approx 20 minutes. ✆ 05 56 73 37 73. www.transgironde.fr

ST BRIEUC - DINAN

km		ⒶJ	ⒶS	⑥	†Q	K	†Q	⚒T	⚒S	†S
0	St Brieuc ... **284** d.	0650	0652	0717	1237	1318	1715	1718	1722	1735
21	Lamballe ... **284** d.	0707	0709	0735	1254	1334	1731	1734	1739	1754
62	Dinan ... a.	0743	0744	0809	1329	1410	1833	1809	1816	1830

	Ⓐ	⑥	ⒶP	Ⓐ	Ⓒ	ⒶJ	W	⑥R	⑤J	⚒S
Dinan ... d.	0626	0657	0749	1102	1141	1610	1816	1820	1824	1828
Lamballe ... **284** d.	0703	0731	0824	1134	1215	1646	1852	1856	1900	1905
St Brieuc ... **284** a.	0719	0747	0836	1150	1231	1701	1908	1912	1916	1921

SOUILLAC - SARLAT 🚌

30 k

Souillac (rail station) depart: 0645Ⓐ, 0910⑥, 1500, 1836†, 2235⑤.

Sarlat (rail station) depart: 1142, 1310③, 1638①②④⑤, 1712③⑥, 1720†, 1815①②④

Service by 🚌 (Trans Périgord Ligne 06). Journey 41 minutes. Subject to alteration during school holidays.

TOULOUSE - AUCH

88 k

Toulouse Matabiau depart: 0624Ⓐ, 0724, 1224, 1424Ⓐ, 1624Ⓐ, 1724, 1824, 2024.

Auch depart: 0606Ⓐ, 0706, 0806Ⓐ, 0906, 1106, 1406, 1706, 1806, 1906.

Journey 90 minutes.

TOURS - CHINON

49 k

Tours depart: 0743Ⓐ, 0915⚒**Uc**, 1236⚒**Uc**, 1515**h**, 1642Ⓐ, 1732Ⓐ, 1851**h**, 2014

Chinon depart: 0625Ⓐ, 0652⚒**c**, 0749Ⓐ, 0839Ⓐ, 1138⚒**Uc**, 1355**Vh**, 1609Ⓐ, 1738 1829Ⓑ**m**, 2019†**m**.

Journey 45 - 50 minutes (70 - 80 minutes by 🚌).

VALENCIENNES - CAMBRAI

40 k

Valenciennes depart: 0604Ⓐ, 0626⑥, 0631Ⓐ, 0733Ⓐ, 0759⑥, 1006Ⓐ, 1206Ⓐ, 122 1259⑥, 1306Ⓐ, 1703Ⓐ, 1726Ⓐ, 1731Ⓐ, 1804Ⓐ, 1904Ⓐ, 2023†.

Cambrai depart: 0612Ⓐ, 0644⑥, 0650Ⓐ, 0712Ⓐ, 0744⑥, 0750Ⓐ, 0950⑥, 1112Ⓐ, 1212Ⓐ, 1215⑥, 1312Ⓐ, 1351⑥, 1712Ⓐ, 1745†, 1751⑥, 1812Ⓐ, 1912Ⓐ, 1922†.

Journey 40 - 50 minutes.

- **A** – ①–⑥ June 13 - July 2, July 23 - Aug. 27 (not Aug. 15).
- **B** – ①–⑥ June 13 - July 2, July 23 - Aug. 27 (also July 9, 16; not Aug. 15).
- **C** – Not July 2 - 24.
- **D** – Daily June 12 - July 2; Ⓐ July 4 - Aug. 28.
- **E** – ⑥ June 18 - July 2; Ⓒ July 3 - Aug. 28.
- **F** – ⑤⑦ June 12 - July 1; ⑦ July 3 - Aug. 28 (also Aug. 15).
- **G** – Daily June 12 - July 3; ⑥⑦ July 9 - 17; daily July 23 - Aug. 28.
- **H** – Until June 30.
- **J** – Until July 1.
- **K** – ⚒ (daily July 3 - Aug. 28).
- **L** – ⚒ (daily June 27 - Aug. 28).
- **M** – † (daily July 3 - Aug. 28).
- **N** – ⑤† (daily July 3 - Aug. 28).
- **P** – Not July 16 - Aug. 15.
- **Q** – June 12 - 26.
- **R** – June 18 - July 2.
- **S** – July 3 - Aug. 28.
- **T** – June 13 - July 2.
- **U** – Not July 17 - 22.
- **V** – Not July 18 - 22.
- **W** – ①–④ June 13 - 30.
- **X** – ⚒ June 13 - July 2; ① July 4 - Aug. 27.
- **Y** – Ⓑ June 12 - July 1; † July 3 - Aug. 28.
- **Z** – ⚒ June 13 - July 2; ⑥ July 9 - Aug. 27.
- **a** – Also July 13.
- **b** – Not Aug. 13.
- **c** – Also July 14.
- **d** – Not July 14.
- **f** – Not July 15.
- **h** – Not Aug. 14.
- **j** – Also Aug. 15.
- **k** – Not Aug. 15.
- **m** – Not July 14, Aug. 14.
- **n** – Not Aug. 14, 15.
- **p** – Daily June 12 - July 3; ⑥⑦ July 9 - Aug. 21 (also Aug. 15, 27, 28).
- **q** – Daily June 12 - July 3; ⑤⑥⑦ July 8 - Aug. 2
- **r** – ⑥–④ June 12 - July 2; ⑤⑥ July 8 - Aug. 27
- **s** – Ⓐ June 13 - July 1; ⑤ July 8 - Aug. 26.
- **t** – Ⓑ June 12 - July 3; ⑤⑦ July 10 - Aug. 21 (also Aug. 15, 28).
- **v** – Also July 13; not July 14, 15, Aug. 14.
- **y** – Also Aug. 16; not Aug. 15.

PARIS - POITIERS - LA ROCHELLE and BORDEAUX 300

Certain *TGV* services continue to Toulouse (Table **320**), Hendaye, Irún or Tarbes (Table **305**) or Arcachon (Table **306**).
Trains may be retimed a few minutes owing to engineering work

TGV trains convey 🍷			*TGV* 8401		*TGV* 8501		*TGV* 8403	*TGV* 8371	*TGV* 8531	*TGV* 8341		*TGV* 8573	*TGV* 8407 8471	*TGV* 5200		*TGV* 8503	*TGV* 8373	*TGV* 8473 8533	*TGV* 8411	*TGV* 5202	*TGV* 5450	*TGV* 5202	*TGV* 5450	
	Ⓐ	⚒ h	⚒ h	⚒ h	①–⑥ k	Ⓐ			①–⑥ k		† q				Ⓒ t					Ⓐ	Ⓐ	Ⓒ	Ⓒ	①–⑥ tk
Lille Europe **11** d.	...	...	...	...	...	...	...	...	...	...	...	...	...	0717	...	...	...	...	...	0921	...	0921	...	...
Strasbourg **391** d.	...	...	...	...	...	...	...	...	...	...	...	...	...	|	...	...	...	...	...	|	0812	|	0812	...
Charles de Gaulle ✈ d.	...	...	...	...	...	...	...	...	...	...	...	...	...	0819	...	...	...	...	...	1016	|	1016	|	...
Marne la Vallee - Chessy d.	...	...	...	...	...	...	...	...	...	...	...	...	...	0833	...	...	...	...	...	1032	1032	1032	1032	...
Paris Montparnasse **295** d.	...	...	0602	...	0628	...	0641	0712	0728	0746	...	0828	0846	|	...	0928	1012	1028	1046	|	|	|	|	...
Massy TGV **295** d.	...	...	|	...	|	...	0653	|	|	|	...	|	|	0908	...	|	|	|	|	1108	1108	1108	1108	...
Vendôme-Villiers TGV d.	...	...	|	...	|	...	|	|	|	|	...	|	|	|	...	|	|	|	|	|	|	|	|	...
Tours d.	...	0615	|	...	|	...	|	|	|	|	...	|	|	|	...	|	|	|	|	|	|	|	|	...
St Pierre des Corps **295** d.	...	|	|	...	|	...	0749	|	|	0849	...	|	0949	1005	...	|	|	|	1149	1203	1203	1203	1203	...
Châtellerault d.	...	0709	|	...	|	0756	0819	|	|	0917	...	|	|	|	...	|	|	|	|	|	|	|	|	...
Futuroscope ⊖ d.	...	0722	|	...	|	0819	|	|	|	0934	...	|	|	|	...	|	|	|	|	|	|	1241	1241	...
Poitiers a.	...	0729	0740	...	|	0828	0834	0852	|	0943	...	|	1032	1042	...	|	1152	|	1231	1242	1242	|	|	...
Poitiers ▷ d.	0608	...	0743	0755	|	...	0837	0855	|	...	0955	|	1035	1045	1055	|	1155	|	1234	1245	1245	|	|	1254
Niort d.	0707	...	|	0843	|	...	|	0941	|	...	1043	|	|	|	1143	|	1241	|	|	|	|	|	|	1350
La Rochelle a.	0755t	...	|	0924t	|	...	|	1021t	|	...	1124t	|	|	|	1223	|	1321r	|	|	|	|	|	|	1429
Angoulême ▷ d.	...	...	0837	...	|	...	0928	...	|	...	...	|	1125	1138	...	|	...	|	1328	1338	1338	1338	1338	...
Libourne **302** ▷ d.	...	...	|	...	|	...	1010	...	|	...	...	|	1209	|	...	|	...	|	1410	|	|	|	|	...
Bordeaux St Jean **302** ▷ a.	...	...	0936	...	0942	...	1032	...	1042	...	...	1142	1232	1237	...	1242	...	1342	1432	1437	1437	1437	1437	...

	TGV 8507 8535		*TGV* 8375	*TGV* 8505 8537	*TGV* 8413	*TGV* 8381	*TGV* 8415	*TGV* 8417	*TGV* 8591		*TGV* 8433	*TGV* 5452	*TGV* 8383			*TGV* 8511	*TGV* 8435	*TGV* 8385				*TGV* 8437	*TGV* 5222	*TGV* 5456	*TGV* 8387
	Gg				Em	⑤† z	①–④ x	⑤⑥† g		Ⓐ t		S		t	Ⓐ		Ⓐ	⑤† z	Ⓐ	Ⓐ				Ⓒ S	⑥–④ x
ille Europe **11** d.	...	...	...	...	...	...	...	...	...	...	...	...	...	...	...	...	...	...	...	...	...	...	1445f	...	...
trasbourg **391** d.	...	...	...	...	...	...	...	...	...	...	...	1231	...	...	...	...	...	...	...	...	...	...	|	1431	...
arles de Gaulle ✈ d.	...	...	...	...	...	...	...	...	...	...	...	|	...	...	...	...	...	...	...	...	...	...	1621	|	...
ne la Vallee - Chessy d.	...	...	...	...	...	...	...	...	...	...	...	1433	...	...	...	...	...	...	...	...	...	...	1633	1633	...
Montparnasse **295** d.	1128	...	1212	1228	1246	1312	1404	1404	1428	...	1446	|	1512	...	...	1528	1604	1612	...	...	...	1646	|	|	1712
TGV **295** d.	|	...	|	|	|	|	|	|	|	...	|	1508	|	...	...	|	|	|	...	...	...	|	1708	1708	|
ôme-Villiers TGV d.	|	...	|	|	|	|	|	|	|	...	|	|	|	...	...	|	|	|	...	...	...	|	|	|	|
rs d.	|	1228	|	|	|	|	|	|	|	...	|	|	|	...	1628	|	|	|	...	1722	...	|	|	|	|
erre des Corps **295** d.	|	|	|	|	1349	|	1511	|	|	...	1549	1604	|	...	|	|	|	|	...	|	...	1749	1802	1802	|
llerault d.	|	1311	|	|	|	|	|	|	|	...	1620	|	|	...	1716	|	|	|	1743	1808	...	|	|	|	|
oscope ⊖ d.	|	1332	|	|	|	|	|	|	|	...	|	|	|	...	1729	|	|	|	1805	1820	...	|	|	|	|
ers a.	|	1341	1352	|	1431	1452	|	1540	|	...	|	1642	1652	...	1737	|	1740	1752	1815	1828	...	1831	1842	1842	1852
ers ▷ d.	|	...	1355	|	1434	1455	|	1543	|	1630	|	1645	1655	1730	...	|	1743	1755	...	...	1830	1834	1845	1845	1855
rt d.	|	...	1441	|	|	1545	|	|	|	1721	|	|	1741	1830	...	|	|	1841	...	...	1930	|	|	|	1941
Rochelle a.	|	...	1521r	|	|	1621t	|	|	|	1803	|	|	1821t	1913	...	|	|	1921t	...	...	2011t	|	|	|	2021t
ulême ▷ d.	|	...	...	|	1528	...	1640	1637	|	...	1728	1735	...	...	...	|	1837	...	...	...	...	1928	1938	1938	...
rne **302** ▷ d.	|	...	...	|	1610	...	|	|	|	...	1810	|	...	...	...	|	|	...	...	...	...	2010	|	|	...
eaux St Jean **302** ▷ a.	1442	...	...	1542	1632	...	1736	1736	1742	...	1832	1837	...	...	...	1842	1936	...	...	...	...	2032	2037	2037	...

	TGV 8593		*TGV* 8351	*TGV* 8441 8479	*TGV* 8391	*TGV* 8391	*TGV* 8513		*TGV* 8445	*TGV* 8445	*TGV* 5240	*TGV* 5454	*TGV* 8393	*TGV* 8395	*TGV* 8449 8515	*TGV* 8481		*TGV* 8453		*TGV* 8397		*TGV* 8455	*TGV* 8353	*TGV* 8457	*TGV* 8355
			Ⓐ		Dx	⑤ C		Ⓐ	Ⓐ	Ⓒ			①–⑥ k	⑦ j	Ⓐ	①–④ x	† h	⑤	⑦–④ q	⑤ g	⑤ g	Fq	①–④ Ax	⑤† q	⑤† z
ille Europe **11** d.	...	...	...	...	...	...	...	...	...	...	1709f	...	...	...	...	...	...	...	...	...	...	...	...	...	...
trasbourg **391** d.	...	...	...	...	...	...	...	...	...	...	|	1631	...	...	...	...	...	...	...	...	...	...	...	...	...
arles de Gaulle ✈ d.	...	...	...	...	...	...	...	...	...	...	1809	|	...	...	...	...	...	...	...	...	...	...	...	...	...
rne la Vallee - Chessy d.	...	...	...	...	...	...	...	...	...	...	1833	1833	...	...	...	...	...	...	...	...	...	...	...	...	...
Montparnasse **295** d.	1728	...	1732	1804	1812	1812	1828	...	1837	1846	|	|	1912	1912	1928	1946	...	2004	...	2012	...	2028	2036	2046	2201
y TGV **295** d.	|	...	1744	|	|	|	|	...	|	|	1908	1908	|	|	|	|	...	|	...	|	...	|	|	|	|
ôme-Villiers TGV d.	|	...	1823	|	1858	|	|	...	1925	|	|	|	|	|	|	|	...	|	...	|	...	|	2122	|	|
rs d.	|	1828	|	|	|	|	|	...	|	|	|	|	|	|	|	|	2028	|	...	|	...	|	|	|	|
erre des Corps **295** d.	|	|	1849	|	|	|	|	...	1948	1949	2003	2003	|	|	|	2049	|	|	...	|	...	|	2143	2149	2304
llerault d.	|	1912	1919	|	|	|	|	1953	2021	2021	|	|	|	|	|	2120	2116	|	...	|	...	|	|	2221	|
oscope ⊖ d.	|	1924	|	1941	|	|	|	2014	|	|	|	|	|	|	|	|	2128	|	...	|	...	|	|	|	|
ers a.	|	1932	1939	|	1952	1952	|	2023	|	|	2041	2041	2052	2052	|	2134	2135	2140	...	2152	...	|	2226	|	2346
ers ▷ d.	|	...	...	|	1955	1955	|	...	|	|	2044	2044	2055	2055	|	2137	...	2143	2155	2155	2208	|	...	|	...
rt d.	|	...	...	|	2041	2041	|	...	|	|	|	|	2141	2141	|	|	...	|	2243	2241	2303	|	...	|	...
Rochelle a.	|	...	...	|	2117t	2122	|	...	|	|	|	|	2221t	2221r	|	|	...	|	2330t	2321t	2344t	|	...	|	...
ulême ▷ d.	|	...	...	2037	...	...	|	...	2128	2128	2138	2138	...	...	|	2225	...	2237	...	...	...	|	...	2328	...
rne **302** ▷ d.	|	...	...	|	...	...	|	...	2210	2210	|	|	...	...	|	...	...	|	...	...	...	|	...	0010	...
eaux St Jean **302** ▷ a.	2042	...	...	2136	...	...	2142	...	2232	2232	2237	2237	...	...	2242	...	...	2336	...	...	...	2342	...	0032	...

LOCAL TRAINS ANGOULÊME - BORDEAUX and v.v.

	Ⓐ B	Ⓐ	⚒	†	⚒	†	⑥	⚒	Ⓐ	†
ulême d.	...	0605	0705	1005	...	...	...	1805	1900	2005
ras **302** d.	0535	0656	0754	1054	1235	1433	1732	1855	1948	2055
rne **302** d.	0547	0709	0808	1106	1248	1446	1744	1908	2000	2107
eaux St Jean **302** a.	0623	0735	0832	1132	1323	1523	1821	1932	...	2132

	Ⓐ	†	†	⚒		Ⓐ	Ⓒ			
Bordeaux St Jean **302** d.	0628	0828	0929	1140	...	1337	1440	1727	1840	2040
Libourne **302** d.	0654	0854	1007	1216	...	1417	1518	1750	1918	2119
Coutras **302** d.	0707	0907	1021	1229	...	1429	1531	1803	1931	2131
Angoulême a.	0800	0956	...	...	...	1517	...	1855	...	...

Until June 30 and from Aug. 22.
Until July 1.
From July 8.
Ⓐ June 13 - July 1; ①–④ July 4 - Aug. 25.
⑤ June 17 - July 1; ⑤⑥ July 8 - Aug. 27.
⑤† June 12 - July 3; † July 10 - Aug. 28.
⑤ (also Ⓒ July 3 - Aug. 28).
July 3 - Aug. 28.

Lille **Flandres**.
Also July 13.
Also July 14.
Not Aug. 15.
Not July 14.
Not June 12-26.
Not June 12-19.
Not July 13, 14, Aug. 15.
Also July 13; not July 14.

TGV – Ⓡ, supplement payable, 🍷.

⊖ – Not for journeys to/from Poitiers or Châtellerault.
▷ – For local trains Angoulême - Bordeaux see below main table. For local trains Poitiers - Angoulême see panel on next page.

Frequent connecting services are available Tours - St Pierre des Corps and v.v. (journey time 5 minutes).

300 BORDEAUX and LA ROCHELLE - POITIERS - PARIS

Certain *TGV* services start from Toulouse (Table **320**), Hendaye or Tarbes (Table **305**) or Arcachon (Table **306**).
Trains may be retimed a few minutes owing to engineering work

TGV trains convey 🍷	*TGV* 8340	*TGV* 8342	*TGV* 8342		*TGV* 8400		*TGV* 8370	*TGV* 8370	*TGV* 8402	*TGV* 8402		*TGV* 8404 8470			*TGV* 8406			*TGV* 8372	*TGV* 5260	*TGV* 5441		*TGV* 8410	*TGV* 8410	*TGV* 8500
	① y	Jm	Hg	Ⓐ	Ⓐ	Ⓐ	Ⓐ	⑥ h	⑦ j	①–⑥ k	⚒ h	Ⓐ	Ⓐ	⑥ h	①–⑥ k	Ⓐ	† q	M			Ⓐ	①–⑥ k	⑦ j	①–⑥ k
Bordeaux St Jean **302** .... ▷ d.	...	...	...	...	0516	...	...	...	0528	0528	...	0618	...	...	0623	...	...	...	0723	0723	...	0728	0728	0819
Libourne **302** ▷ d.	...	...	...	...	|	...	...	...	0553	0553	...	|	...	...	|	...	...	...	|	|	...	0753	0753	|
Angoulême ▷ d.	...	...	...	...	0615	...	...	...	0635	0635	...	|	...	...	0725	...	...	...	0826	0826	...	0836	0836	|
La Rochelle d.	...	...	...	...	|	...	0524r	0533s	|	|	...	|	...	0631s	|	0642t	...	0734t	|	|	0755t	|	|	|
Niort d.	...	...	...	...	|	...	0613	0615	|	|	...	|	...	0719	|	0730	...	0822	|	|	0837	|	|	|
Poitiers ▷ a.	...	...	...	...	|	...	0704	0704	|	|	...	|	...	0809	0814	0824	...	0904	0914	0914	0921	|	|	|
Poitiers d.	0515	0624	0624	0627	|	0633	0707	0707	|	|	0728	|	0800	...	0817	...	0854	0907	0917	0917	...	|	|	|
Futuroscope ⊖ d.	|	|	|	0635	|	0643	|	|	|	|	0736	|	0810	...	|	...	0902	|	|	|	...	|	|	|
Châtellerault d.	|	0642	0642	0646	|	0707	|	|	0742	0742	0747	|	0828	...	|	...	0915	|	|	|	...	0942	0947	|
St Pierre-des-Corps **295** a.	0556	0710	0710	|	|	...	|	|	0811	0811	|	|	...	...	|	...	...	|	0957	0957	...	1010	1015	|
Tours a.	|	|	|	0732	|	...	|	|	|	|	0832	|	...	...	|	...	...	|	|	|	...	|	|	|
Vendôme-Villiers TGV d.	|	|	0737	...	|	...	|	|	|	0839	...	|	...	...	|	...	...	|	|	|	...	|	|	|
Massy TGV **295** a.	|	|	|	...	|	...	|	|	|	|	...	|	...	...	|	...	...	|	1052	1052	...	|	|	|
Paris Montparnasse **295** a.	0704	0827	0827	...	0833	...	0848	0849	0913	0923	...	0933	...	...	0957	...	...	1049	|	|	...	1113	1117	1136
Marne la Vallee - Chessy .. a.	...	...	...	...	...	...	...	...	...	...	...	...	...	...	...	...	...	...	1127	1127	...	...	...	...
Charles de Gaulle ✈ a.	...	...	...	...	...	...	...	...	...	...	...	...	...	...	...	...	...	...	1145	|	...	...	...	...
Strasbourg **391** a.	...	...	...	...	...	...	...	...	...	...	...	...	...	...	...	...	...	...	|	1328	...	...	...	...
Lille Europe **11** a.	...	...	...	...	...	...	...	...	...	...	...	...	...	...	...	...	...	...	1301f	...	...	...	...	...

	TGV 8412	*TGV* 8530	*TGV* 8374	*TGV* 5264	*TGV* 5264	*TGV* 5447		*TGV* 8510	*TGV* 5442 5443	*TGV* 8380	*TGV* 8430		*TGV* 8540		*TGV* 8580	*TGV* 8432	*TGV* 8382	*TGV* 8434	*TGV* 8514		*TGV* 5266	*TGV* 5266	*TGV* 5445	*TGV* 8436
	Ⓐ			Ⓐ	Ⓒ	① Sy	⑥ h		S					①–⑥ k						Ⓐ	⑥–④	⑤⑦		
Bordeaux St Jean **302** .... ▷ d.	0823	0918	...	0923	0923	0923	...	1118	1123	...	1128	...	1218	...	1318	1328	...	1424	1518	...	1523	1523	1523	1528
Libourne **302** ▷ d.	|	|	...	|	|	|	...	|	|	...	1153	...	|	...	|	1353	...	|	|	...	|	|	|	1553
Angoulême ▷ d.	0925	|	...	1026	1026	1026	...	|	1226	...	1235	...	|	...	|	1435	...	1525	|	...	1626	1626	1626	1635
La Rochelle d.	|	|	0935t	|	|	|	...	|	|	1133t	|	...	|	1232t	|	|	1435t	|	|	...	|	|	|	|
Niort d.	|	|	1020	|	|	|	...	|	|	1221	|	...	|	1314	|	|	1520	|	|	...	|	|	|	|
Poitiers ▷ a.	1014	|	1104	1114	1114	1114	...	|	1314	1307	|	...	|	1406	|	1524	1604	|	|	...	1713	1713	1713	1723
Poitiers d.	1017	|	1107	1117	1117	1117	1233	|	1317	1310	|	1334	|	...	|	1527	1607	|	|	1638	1716	1716	1716	1726
Futuroscope ⊖ d.	|	|	|	|	|	|	1243	|	|	|	1333	1342	|	...	|	|	|	|	|	1648	1725	1725	1725	|
Châtellerault d.	|	|	|	|	|	|	1303	|	|	|	|	1354	|	...	|	|	|	1629	|	1709	|	|	|	1742
St Pierre-des-Corps **295** a.	|	|	|	1156	1156	1156	...	|	1355	|	1410	|	|	...	|	1610	|	|	|	...	1758	1758	1758	1811
Tours a.	|	|	|	|	|	|	...	|	|	|	|	1455	|	...	|	|	|	|	|	...	|	|	|	|
Vendôme-Villiers TGV d.	|	|	|	|	|	|	...	|	|	|	|	...	|	...	|	|	|	|	|	...	|	|	|	|
Massy TGV **295** a.	|	|	|	1252	1252	1252	...	|	1452	|	|	...	|	...	|	|	|	|	|	...	1852	1852	1852	|
Paris Montparnasse **295** a.	1157	1233	1249	|	|	|	...	1439	|	1449	1513	...	1533	...	1633	1713	1749	1757	1833	...	|	|	|	1915
Marne la Vallee - Chessy .. a.	...	...	...	|	1327	|	...	...	1527	...	...	...	...	...	...	...	...	...	...	...	1927	1927	1927	...
Charles de Gaulle ✈ a.	...	...	...	1331	1341	|	...	...	|	...	...	...	...	...	...	...	...	...	...	...	1941	1941	|	...
Strasbourg **391** a.	...	...	...	|	|	1553	...	...	1728	...	...	...	...	...	...	...	...	...	...	...	|	|	2145	...
Lille Europe **11** a.	...	...	...	1430	1437	...	...	...	...	...	...	...	...	...	...	...	...	...	...	...	2109	2111	...	...

	TGV 8384	*TGV* 8440 8476			*TGV* 8582	*TGV* 8386	*TGV* 5284	*TGV* 5449	*TGV* 5284	*TGV* 8350		*TGV* 8516	*TGV* 8350		*TGV* 8442 8478	*TGV* 8584	*TGV* 8390		*TGV* 8444 8472	*TGV* 8392	*TGV* 8518	*TGV* 8392	*TGV* 8448	*TGV* 8394
			Ⓑ q	Ⓐ		⑤ g	Ⓒ	⑦ S	Ⓐ	K			S	Ⓐ						⑤		⑦ j	⑤† q	⑦ j
Bordeaux St Jean **302** .... ▷ d.	...	1623	...	...	1718	...	1723	1723	1723	...	...	1818	...	...	1823	1918	...	...	1928	...	2018	...	2028	...
Libourne **302** ▷ d.	...	|	...	...	|	...	|	|	|	...	...	|	...	...	|	|	...	...	1952	...	|	...	2053	...
Angoulême ▷ d.	...	1726	...	...	|	...	1826	1826	1825	...	...	|	...	...	1926	|	...	...	2035	...	|	...	2135	...
La Rochelle d.	1635t	|	1646t	...	|	1735u	|	|	|	...	1752t	|	...	1832t	|	|	1935t	1950t	|	2020u	|	2035t	|	2109t
Niort d.	1720	|	1733	...	|	1820	|	|	|	...	1834	|	...	1921	|	|	2020	2032	|	2105	|	2120	|	2151
Poitiers ▷ a.	1804	1814	1828	...	|	1904	|	|	1910	...	1928	|	...	2007	2014	|	2104	2117	2124	2149	|	2204	2224	2232
Poitiers d.	1807	1817	...	1836	|	1907	|	|	1913	1917	1932	|	1950	...	2017	|	2107	...	2127	2152	|	2207	2227	2235
Futuroscope ⊖ d.	|	|	...	1846	|	|	1921	1921	|	1927	1943	|	2005	...	|	|	|	...	|	|	|	|	|	|
Châtellerault d.	|	|	...	1909	|	|	|	|	|	1941	2012	|	2022	...	|	|	|	...	|	|	|	|	|	|
St Pierre-des-Corps **295** a.	|	|	...	...	|	|	1956	1956	1958	2009	|	|	2053	...	|	|	|	...	2210	|	|	|	2310	|
Tours a.	|	|	...	...	|	|	|	|	|	|	2045n	|	|	...	|	|	|	...	|	|	|	|	|	|
Vendôme-Villiers TGV d.	|	|	...	...	|	|	|	|	|	|	...	|	|	...	|	|	|	...	|	|	|	|	|	|
Massy TGV **295** a.	|	|	...	...	|	|	2052	2052	2052	|	...	|	|	...	|	|	|	...	|	|	|	|	|	|
Paris Montparnasse **295** a.	1949	1957	...	...	2033	2049	|	|	|	2115	...	2133	2201	...	2157	2233	2249	...	2314	2329	2333	2344	0015	0019
Marne la Vallee - Chessy .. a.	...	...	...	...	...	...	2127	2127	2127	...	...	...	...	...	...	...	...	...	...	...	...	...	...	...
Charles de Gaulle ✈ a.	...	...	...	...	...	...	2141	|	2146	...	...	...	...	...	...	...	...	...	...	...	...	...	...	...
Strasbourg **391** a.	...	...	...	...	...	...	|	2328	|	...	...	...	...	...	...	...	...	...	...	...	...	...	...	...
Lille Europe **11** a.	...	...	...	...	...	...	2244	...	2251	...	...	...	...	...	...	...	...	...	...	...	...	...	...	...

LOCAL TRAINS ANGOULÊME - POITIERS and v.v.

	Ⓐ	①–⑥ k	Ⓐ	⑦ j		①–⑥ k	Ⓑ q	Ⓐ	
Angoulême d.	0624	0731	0840	0943	...	1240	1643	1743	1843
Ruffec d.	0658	0758	0906	1010	...	1306	1710	1810	1909
Poitiers a.	0743	0843	0950	1047	...	1350	1748	1847	1947

	Ⓐ			①–⑥ k		Ⓐ	Ⓑ q	
Poitiers d.	0620	0750	...	1306	...	1610	1718	1808
Ruffec d.	0700	0836	...	1354	...	1654	1804	1857
Angoulême a.	0727	0904	...	1420	...	1722	1830	1922

H – Ⓐ June 13 - July 1; ⑤ July 8 - Aug. 5.
J – Ⓒ June 12 - July 3; ⑥–④ July 4 - Aug. 25; Ⓒ Aug. 27 - 28.
K – Until July 2.
M – Ⓑ June 12 - July 3; daily July 4 - Aug. 28.
S – July 3 - Aug. 28.

f – Lille **Flandres**.
g – Also July 13.
h – Also July 14.
j – Also Aug. 15.
k – Not Aug. 15.
m – Not July 13.
n – Ⓑ (not July 14).
q – Not July 14.
r – Not June 12 - 26.
s – Not June 18.
t – Not June 12 - 19.
u – Not June 17.
y – Also Aug. 16; not Aug. 15.

TGV – Ⓡ, supplement payable, 🍷.

▷ – For local trains Bordeaux - Angoulême see panel on previous page. For local trains Angoulême - Poitiers see below main table.

⊖ – Not for journeys to/from Poitiers or Châtellerault.

Frequent connecting services are available St Pierre des Corps - Tours and v.v. (journey time 5 minutes).

ANGOULÊME - SAINTES - ROYAN 301

	Ⓐ	Ⓐ ◇	Ⓐ	Ⓐ	Ⓐ J	⑥ A	⑦ S	S	K	S		⚒ Hh	Ⓐ J					◇	Ⓐ	①–⑥ k	①–⑥ k	Ⓑ q	Ⓐ	⑦ j
Paris Austerlitz ◐ d.	...	...	...	...	...	...	...	...	...	...	...	...	...	...	...	...	...	...	...	...	...	...	...	...
Angoulême d.	...	0638	...	0732	...	...	...	0937	0937	...	...	1141	1231	...	1400	...	...	1643	...	...	1738	...	1843	1844
Cognac d.	...	0720	...	0815	...	...	...	1016	1016	...	...	1225	1314	...	1439	...	...	1722	...	...	1821	...	1923	1922
Niort d.	...	|	0628	|	0731	...	...	|	|	1013	...	|	|	1254	|	1507	...	|	...	1726	|	1818	|	|
Saintes a.	...	0740	0747	0834	0834	...	...	1036	1036	1113	...	1245	1334	1357	1459	1607	...	1742	...	1832	1840	1925	1942	1941
Saintes d.	0735	...	0759	...	...	0930	0954	...	1101	1115	...	1251	...	1359	1505	1614	...	...	1751	...	1846	...	1949	2016
Royan a.	0804	...	0828	...	...	0959	1023	...	1130	1144	...	1320	...	1428	1534	1643	...	...	1822	...	1917	...	2018	2045

	⑥ h	⑤ g		Ⓑ q	⑤† q	①–④ x	⑤⑦ z	①–④ x		⑤ g
ris Austerlitz ◐ d.	...	...	...	...	...	...	...	...	...	...
oulême d.	1949	1953	...	2041	2141	2141	...	...	...	2241
ac d.	2029	2040	...	2122	2220	2220	...	...	...	2321
rt d.	|	|	...	|	|	|	2155	...	...	|
tes a.	2049	2059	...	2141	2240	2240	2255	←	...	2341
tes d.	2056	2105	...	2146	...	→	2257	2300	...	2348
an a.	2125	2134	...	2215	...	...	2326	2329	...	0017

	Ⓐ	Ⓐ	①–⑥ k	⑥ h		Ⓐ	Ⓐ ◇	Ⓐ	Ⓒ	Ⓐ
Royan d.	...	0602	0627	...	...	0658	...	0811	0831	0840
Saintes a.	...	0631	0656	...	...	0727	...	0842	0859	0909
Saintes d.	0616	0637	0706	0712	...	...	0732	...	0911	0911
Niort a.	|	|	0815	|	...	...	|	...	1010	1010
Cognac d.	0635	0655	...	0731	...	...	0750	...	...	...
Angoulême a.	0718	0739	...	0811	...	...	0829	...	...	...
Paris Austerlitz ◐ a.	...	...	...	...	...	...	...	...	...	...

		①–⑥ k	Ⓐ h		G	D	①–④ E	F	D		Ⓐ	⑦ j	Ⓐ ◇				Ⓐ	⑦ j	⑤ g	⑤ g	⑦ j		①–④ Cx	⑥ A	⑤† B
an d.	1029	...	1327	...	1433	1538	...	1538	...	...	1659	1659	...	...	1805	...	1900	1916	...	...	1942	...	2030	2213	2224
tes a.	1058	...	1356	...	1502	1607	...	1607	...	...	1728	1728	...	...	1834	...	1928	1945	...	...	2011	...	2059	2242	2253
tes d.	1105	1252	1400	...	1508	1615	1615	1616	1616	...	...	1736	1737	1841	1841	...	1933	2013	2015	2019	2019	...	...	...	...
rt a.	|	|	1459	...	|	1713	1713	|	|	...	...	|	|	|	1956	...	|	2111	2113	|	|	...	...	...	...
ac d.	1124	1313	...	...	1527	...	...	1636	1636	...	...	1755	1757	1859	...	...	1952	...	...	2039	2039	...	...	...	...
oulême a.	1207	1351	...	...	1607	...	...	1719	1719	...	...	1835	1837	1943	...	...	2030	...	...	2120	2120	...	...	...	...
ris Austerlitz ◐ a.	...	...	...	...	...	...	...	...	...	...	...	...	...	...	...	...	...	...	...	...	...	...	...	...	...

July 9 - Aug. 27 (also July 14).
July 3 - Aug. 28 (also July 13; not July 14).
July 4 - Aug. 25.
⑤⑦ (daily July 3 - Aug. 28).
June 13 - 30.
①②③④⑥ June 13 - July 2 (not July 13).

G – Ⓑ (daily July 3 - Aug. 28).
H – July 4 - Aug. 27.
J – Until July 1.
K – Until July 2.
S – July 3 - Aug. 28.

g – Also July 13.
h – Also July 14.
j – Also Aug. 15.
k – Not Aug. 15.
q – Not July 14.

x – Not July 13, 14, Aug. 15.
z – Also July 13, Aug. 15.

◇ – To / from La Rochelle (Table **292**).
◐ – See Table **300** for *TGV* connections at Niort or Angoulême.
• – Distance from Saintes.

BORDEAUX - PÉRIGUEUX - BRIVE and LIMOGES 302

	Ⓐ	Ⓒ	⚒	4490 C	4492 ⑥	Ⓐ	†	4480	Ⓐ	⚒	Ⓐ	Ⓑ			Ⓐ J	⚒	†	Ⓑ	Ⓐ	Ⓐ	†	Ⓐ	Ⓐ		†
Bordeaux St Jean **300** d.	0558	...	0700	0735	0910	0835	1035	1100	...	1234	1400	...	1600	...	1634	1700	...	1735	1800	1836	1835	...	1935	2035	2200
Libourne **300** d.	0622	...	0726	0800	|	0901	1059	1123	...	1259	1427	...	1626	...	1659	1725	...	1759	1826	1902	1901	...	1959	2102	2226
Coutras **300** d.	0634	...	0735	0810	|	0919	1111	1135	...	1310	1437	...	1635	...	1711	1736	...	1811	1835	1914	1911	...	2011	2112	2235
Mussidan d.	0703	...	0804	0836	|	0945	1137	1156	...	1336	1507	...	1704	...	1737	1807	...	1837	1904	1940	1937	...	2040	2139	2304
Périgueux a.	0727	...	0833	0858	1021	1006	1159	1215	...	1357	1532	...	1728	...	1758	1832	...	1900	1928	2000	1958	...	2101	2201	2328
Périgueux ▷ d.	0737	0737	...	0900	1023	...	...	1221	1313	1402	...	1550	...	1735	...	1840	1840	...	...	...	2004	2005	...	...	...
Brive la Gaillarde ▷ a.	|	|	...	0954	1113	...	...	|	|	|	...	|	...	|	...	|	|	...	...	...	|	|	...	...	...
Ussel **326** a.	|	|	...	1157	1309	...	...	|	|	|	...	|	...	|	...	|	|	...	...	...	|	|	...	...	...
Thiviers d.	0802	0802	...	...	...	...	...	1243	1345	1422	...	1610	...	1801	...	1913	1913	...	...	...	2025	2028	...	...	...
Limoges ▷ a.	0843	0843	...	...	...	...	...	1320	1432	1459	...	1655	...	1858	...	1958	1958	...	...	...	2110	2118	...	...	...

	Ⓐ	⚒	Ⓐ	Ⓐ		⚒	†	†	⚒			Ⓒ		Ⓐ	Ⓑ	Ⓐ	⑥	Ⓐ	†	4581	4591 Dq	Ⓐ J	†	†	Ⓐ	
oges ▷ d.	...	...	...	0603	...	...	...	1103	1103	1222	...	1431	...	1520	...	...	...	1711	1715	1803	...	...	2011	...	2014	...
iers d.	...	...	...	0649	...	...	...	1147	1150	1312	...	1519	...	1611	...	...	...	1800	1800	1846	...	...	2101	...	2108	...
ssel **326** d.	...	...	...	|	...	...	...	|	|	|	...	|	...	|	...	...	...	|	|	|	1626	...	|	...	|	...
rive la Gaillarde ▷ d.	...	...	...	|	...	...	0907	|	|	|	1304	|	...	|	...	...	...	|	|	|	1813	...	|	2029	|	...
gueux ▷ a.	...	...	...	0717	...	...	1000	1210	1212	1339	1359	1547	...	1639	...	...	...	1822	1822	1908	1909	...	2121	2124	2128	...
gueux d.	0556	0633	0702	0733	0833	1002	1002	...	1235**r**	...	1405	...	1604	...	1702	1803	1828	1828	1828	1929	1911	2007	...	2127	...	...
sidan d.	0617	0657	0723	0757	0857	1023	1023	...	1258**r**	...	1426	...	1625	...	1723	1824	1857	1857	1857	1948	1932	2028	...	2150	...	...
tras **300** d.	0647	0726	0750	0826	0926	1049	1050	...	1326**r**	...	1452	...	1652	...	1750	1851	1926	1926	1926	2021	|	2055	...	2217	...	...
urne **300** d.	0700	0736	0800	0837	0936	1100	1100	...	1339**r**	...	1502	...	1702	...	1800	1901	1936	1936	1936	2036	2004	2105	...	2228	...	...
deaux St Jean **300** a.	0727	0801	0827	0902	1001	1127	1127	...	1402**r**	...	1528	...	1727	...	1826	1926	2001	2001	2001	2100	2028	2130	...	2255	...	...

ADDITIONAL TRAINS PÉRIGUEUX - BRIVE

	Ⓐ	Ⓐ	⑥	A	Ⓐ	†	⑥	⑤†	⚒	Ⓑ
gueux d.	0623	0740	0750	1050	1306	1354	1454	1639	1811	2005
e la Gaillarde a.	0722	0834	0844	1148	1405	1449	1549	1736	1919	2100

	Ⓐ	⑥	Ⓐ	Ⓐ		†	Ⓐ	K		⑤
Brive la Gaillarde d.	0613	0708	0732	1116	...	1505	1705	1808	...	2012
Périgueux a.	0718	0801	0828	1212	...	1559	1758	1907	...	2113

ADDITIONAL TRAINS PÉRIGUEUX - LIMOGES

	Ⓐ	Ⓐ	⚒		Ⓐ	Ⓒ	†		⑤† g	
gueux d.	0448	0623	0840	...	1055	1115	1402	...	2212	...
iers d.	0509	0648	0901	...	1115	1151	1422	...	2233	...
oges a.	0553	0736	0946	...	1155	1239	1459	...	2314	...

	⑥	Ⓐ	Ⓐ		⚒	Ⓐ		Ⓑ	⑥	Ⓑ
Limoges d.	0603	0722	0853	...	1734	1842	...	2103	2203	2308
Thiviers d.	0649	0801	0935	...	1824	1935	...	2147	2248	2353
Périgueux a.	0717	0821	0955	...	1856	2002	...	2207	2307	0012

Ⓒ June 12 - July 3; daily July 4 - Aug. 28.
⑤ June 17 - July 1; Ⓐ July 4 - Aug. 28.
⑤⑦ June 12 - July 3; Ⓑ July 4 - Aug. 28.
Until July 1.
①②③④⑥ June 13 - July 2.

g – Also July 13.
q – Not Aug. 14.
r – Not June 18.

▷ – See below main table for additional trains Périgueux - Brive and Périgueux - Limoges.

LIMOGES - MONTLUÇON 303

🚌 service subject to alteration

n		Ⓐ	B	Ⓒ		A	Ⓐ 🚌		Ⓒ	Ⓐ 🚌
0	**Limoges** d.	0811	0957	1011	...	1211	1340	...	1611	...
8	Guéret d.	0918	1103	1117	...	1318	1445	...	1718	1725
6	**Montluçon** d.	1020	1204	1216	...	1420	1545	...	1820	1834

	Ⓐ 🚌	A		Ⓐ 🚌	B	Ⓒ	Ⓐ		Ⓒ
Montluçon d.	0715	1134	...	1435	1455	1534	1634	...	1834
Guéret d.	0826	1236	...	1530	1557	1636	1736	...	1936
Limoges a.	...	1342	...	1645	1707	1742	1842	...	2042

①②③④ June 13 - 16, June 27 - Aug. 25 (not July 13).
①②③④ June 20 - 23 (also July 13).

305 BORDEAUX - TARBES, HENDAYE and IRÚN

For night train Paris - Tarbes - Hendaye - Irún see top of next page.

km	All *TGV* convey 🍷	Ⓐ	Ⓐ	Ⓐ J	Ⓐ	⚒	Ⓐ	Ⓐ J		H	⚒	⑥ U	*TGV* 8571 ①–⑥ k		† q	† q	*TGV* 8531 ①–⑥ k	Ⓐ v	Ⓐ F		*TGV* 8573	⚒	K	K
	Paris M'parnasse **300** d.	...	...	...	...	...	...	...	...	...	...	...	0628	...	...	...	0728	...	...	...	0828	...	...	...
0	**Bordeaux** St Jean d.	...	...	...	...	...	...	0645	0747	...	...	0930	0951	...	0947	...	1051	...	...	...	1151	...	1251	1251
109	Morcenx d.	...	...	...	...	...	...	0746	0843	...	...	1025	|	...	1043	...	|	...	...	...	|	...	1348	1348
148	Dax a.	...	...	...	...	...	...	0806	0903	...	...	1046	1058	...	1103	...	1200	...	...	...	1259	...	1407	1407
148	Dax d.	0602	0642	0650	0712	0742	0811	0815	0908	0912	1012	1051	1101	...	1108	1112	1203	1209	1229	...	1302	1312	1412	1416
179	Puyoô **325** d.	|	|	0708	|	|	0829	|	|	0930	|	|	|	...	|	1130	|	1227	1248	...	|	|	|	1434
193	Orthez **325** d.	|	|	0719	|	|	0839	|	|	0940	|	|	|	...	|	1140	|	1237	1259	...	1331	|	|	1444
233	Pau **325** d.	|	|	0745	|	|	0904	|	|	1006	|	|	1151	...	|	1207	|	1302	1325	...	1357	|	|	1510
272	Lourdes **325** d.	|	|	...	|	|	...	|	|	...	|	|	1223	...	|	1236	|	...	...	...	1432	|	|	...
293	**Tarbes 325** a.	|	|	...	|	|	...	|	|	...	|	|	1240	...	|	1251	|	...	...	...	1448	|	|	...
199	**Bayonne 325** d.	0647	0728	...	0801	0828	...	0846	0940	...	1058	1128	...	...	1159	...	1235	...	...	...	...	1358	1443	...
209	Biarritz **325** d.	0656	0737	...	0810	0837**v**	...	0855	0949	...	1107	1138	...	...	1208	...	1247	...	...	...	...	1407	1451	...
222	St Jean de Luz **325** d.	0708	0751	...	0822	0851**v**	...	0909	1001	...	1121	1152	...	...	1221	...	1300	...	...	...	...	1421	1504	...
235	Hendaye **325** a.	0721	0804	...	0834	0904**v**	...	0922	1014	...	1134	1205	...	...	1235	...	1310	...	...	...	...	1434	1517	...
237	**Irún 325** a.	...	0811**v**	...	...	0911**v**	...	...	1021**s**	...	...	1212	...	...	1242**s**	...	1318	...	...	...	...	1441**v**	...	...

	Ⓐ	K	*TGV* 8577 ⑤ g	*TGV* 8535 Ⓒ s	K	Ⓐ J		*TGV* 8537 ⑥–④ m	*TGV* 8537 ⑤	Ⓐ	Ⓐ J	Ⓐ		Ⓐ		*TGV* 8541 A	*TGV* 8591	⑥			*TGV* 8543 B	*TGV* 8593	D	*TGV* 8545 ⑤ Th
Paris M'parnasse **300** d.	...	...	1128	1128	...	...	...	1228	1228	...	...	...	...	...	...	1428	1428	...	...	...	1728	1728	...	1928
Bordeaux St Jean d.	1445	1445	1451	1451	...	...	...	1551	1551	...	...	...	1645	...	...	1751	1751	...	1847	...	2047	2047	...	2251
Morcenx d.	1539	1539	|	|	...	...	...	|	|	...	...	...	1747	...	...	|	|	...	1950	...	|	|	...	|
Dax a.	1558	1558	1602	1600	←	...	...	1700	1700	...	...	...	1807	...	...	1900	1900	...	2010	...	2159	2159	...	2358
Dax d.	1600	→	1605	1603	1612	1642	...	1703	1703	1712	1742	1812	1816	1842	...	1904	1908	1912	2015	2019	2203	2207	2212	0001
Puyoô **325** d.	|	...	|	|	1631	|	...	|	|	|	|	1831	|	|	...	|	|	|	|	2036	|	|	|	|
Orthez **325** d.	|	...	|	|	1641	|	...	|	|	|	|	1841	|	|	...	|	1938	|	|	2047	|	2236	|	|
Pau **325** d.	|	...	1653	|	1705	|	...	|	|	|	|	1905	|	|	...	|	2003	|	|	2116	|	2303	|	|
Lourdes **325** d.	|	...	1729	|	...	|	...	|	|	|	|	...	|	|	...	|	2037	|	|	2143	|	2337**t**	|	|
Tarbes 325 a.	|	...	1744	|	...	|	...	|	|	|	|	...	|	|	...	|	2053	|	|	2158	|	2353**t**	|	|
Bayonne 325 d.	1632	...	...	1635	...	1727	...	1735	1735	1758	1826	...	1848	1928	...	1936	...	1958	2047	...	2235	...	2258	0033
Biarritz **325** d.	1641	...	...	1646	...	1737	...	1746	1746	1807	...	...	1858	1937	...	1947	...	2007	2056	...	2246	...	...	0046
St Jean de Luz **325** d.	1653	...	...	1659	...	1751	...	1801	1801	1821	...	...	1911	1951	...	2000	...	2021	2109	...	2259	...	...	0058
Hendaye **325** a.	1706	...	...	1710	...	1804	...	1810	1810	1834	...	...	1923	2004	...	2011	...	2034	2121	...	2310	...	...	0109
Irún 325 a.	...	...	...	...	...	...	...	1818	1818	...	...	...	...	2011**v**	...	...	...	2041**v**	...	...	...	...	...	...

	⚒	⚒	Ⓐ	Ⓐ	Ⓐ J	*TGV* 8561 ①–⑥ k	*TGV* 8530	Ⓐ	⑥		Ⓐ	Ⓐ	Ⓐ j	Ⓐ	Ⓒ	Ⓐ	Ⓐ J	Ⓐ J	*TGV* 8540		*TGV* 8581	⚒ v		*TGV* 8542 M
Irún 325 d.	...	...	...	...	...	...	...	0644**v**	...	...	...	...	...	...	...	0837**v**	...	...	...	...	...	1137	1220**s**	...
Hendaye **325** d.	...	0505	...	0600	...	...	0645	0650	...	...	0726	...	0756	...	...	0844	0920	...	0945	...	...	1144	1226	1245
St Jean de Luz **325** d.	...	0518	...	0613	...	...	0659	0705	...	...	0739	...	0809	...	...	0857	0933	...	0959	...	...	1157	1239	1259
Biarritz **325** d.	...	0531	...	0626	...	...	0713	0718	...	...	0751	...	0822	...	...	0911	0945	...	1013	...	...	1209	1251	1313
Bayonne 325 d.	...	0542	...	0637	0702	...	0725	0730	0732	...	0801	...	0831	...	...	0922	0955	...	1025	...	...	1219	1301	1325
Tarbes 325 d.	0430**e**	|	...	|	|	0610	|	|	|	...	|	0707	...	...	0807	|	|	...	|	...	1017	|	|	|
Lourdes **325** d.	0446**e**	|	...	|	|	0627	|	|	|	...	|	0723	...	...	0823	|	|	...	|	...	1041	|	|	|
Pau **325** d.	0515	|	0626	|	|	0701	|	|	|	...	|	0752	...	0852	0853	|	|	0955	|	...	1108	|	|	|
Orthez **325** d.	0539	|	0650	|	|	0725	|	|	|	...	|	0818	...	0919	0919	|	|	1019	|	...	1134	|	|	|
Puyoô **325** d.	0550	|	0700	|	|	|	|	|	|	...	|	0829	...	0930	0930	|	|	1030	|	...	|	|	|	|
Dax a.	0608	0614	0718	0722	0748	0751	0754	0815	0818	...	0847	0852	...	0948	0948	0952	1041	1048	1055	...	1159	1248	1345	1355
Dax d.	...	0619	...	0727	...	0800	0800	...	...	...	...	0857	...	...	0957	0957	...	...	1100	...	1202	1253	...	1400
Morcenx d.	...	0639	...	0748	...	|	|	...	...	...	...	0916	...	...	1017	1018	...	...	|	...	|	1313	...	|
Bordeaux St Jean a.	...	0745	...	0845	...	0909	0909	...	...	...	...	1015	...	...	1115	1115	...	...	1209	...	1309	1409	...	1509
Paris M'parnasse **300** a.	...	...	...	...	...	1233	1233	...	...	...	...	...	...	...	...	...	...	...	1533	...	1633	...	...	1833

	s	Ⓐ J	⑤†	*TGV* 8544 Ⓑ q	*TGV* 8583	Ⓐ	⑤†	Ⓑ	B	*TGV* 8585	Ⓐ	Ⓑ	①–④ n	⑤†		*TGV* 8546 C	Ⓐ	⚒	⚒	*TGV* 8548 ⑦ s	*TGV* 8587 ⑦ j	†	†	⚒ v
Irún 325 d.	1337	...	...	...	...	1540**v**	...	...	...	...	...	...	...	...	...	...	...	...	1839**v**	...	...	...	...	2023
Hendaye **325** d.	1344	1344	...	1445	...	1546	...	...	1624	...	...	...	1720	1722	...	1745	...	...	1846	1845	...	...	1944	2030
St Jean de Luz **325** d.	1357	1358	...	1458	...	1559	...	...	1637	...	...	...	1733	1735	...	1800	...	...	1900	1859	...	...	1957	2043
Biarritz **325** d.	1411	1411	...	1511	...	1612	...	...	1649	...	...	...	1745	1748	...	1814	...	...	1913	1913	...	...	2011	2055
Bayonne 325 d.	1422	1422	1502	1523	...	1621	...	...	1700	...	1732	...	1755	1758	...	1825	1832	...	1924	1925	...	...	2021	2105
Tarbes 325 d.	|	|	|	|	1416	...	1541	...	|	1614	|	...	...	|	...	|	|	...	|	|	1822	...	|	|
Lourdes **325** d.	|	|	|	|	1440	...	1600	...	|	1638	|	...	...	|	...	|	|	...	|	|	1841	...	|	|
Pau **325** d.	|	|	|	|	1509	...	1631	1631	|	1705	|	1726	...	|	...	|	|	1858	|	|	1910	1952	|	|
Orthez **325** d.	|	|	|	|	|	...	1659	1659	|	1730	|	1750	...	|	...	|	|	1922	|	|	|	2019	|	|
Puyoô **325** d.	|	|	|	|	|	...	1710	1710	|	|	|	1800	...	|	...	|	|	1932	|	|	|	2030	|	|
Dax a.	1452	1452	1548	1552	1556	...	1728	1728	1732	1756	1818	1822	...	1830	...	1855	1918	1950	1954	1954	1958	2049	2053	2149
Dax d.	1457	1457	...	1602	1602	...	...	...	1737	1759	...	...	...	1835	...	1900	...	...	1959	2004	2004	...	2058	...
Morcenx d.	1518	1518	...	|	|	...	...	...	1757	|	...	...	...	1856	...	|	...	...	2019	|	|	...	2117	...
Bordeaux St Jean a.	1615	1615	...	1711	1711	...	...	...	1900	1909	...	...	...	2000	...	2009	...	...	2120	2113	2113	...	2216	...
Paris M'parnasse **300** a.	...	...	...	2033	2033	...	...	...	...	2233	...	...	...	...	...	2333	...	...	...	0033	0033	...	...	...

A – ⑤ June 17 - July 1; ①⑤⑥ July 4 - Aug. 27 (also July 13, 14, Aug. 16; not Aug. 15).
B – Ⓑ June 12 - July 3; daily July 4 - Aug. 28.
C – ⑥⑦ June 12 - July 3; ①②③④⑥⑦ July 4 - Aug. 28 (not July 13).
D – Ⓑ (daily July 3 - Aug. 27).
E – ①–⑥ June 13 - 25; daily June 27 - Aug. 28.
F – June 27 - July 1.
G – ⑥ July 16 - Aug. 27 (also July 2).
H – June 12 - 19, July 2 - Aug. 28.
J – Until July 1.
K – Ⓐ (daily July 3 - Aug. 28).
L – Ⓐ June 13 - 17, July 4 - Aug. 26.
M – ②③④⑤⑦ June 12 - July 17; ②⑤⑥⑦ July 19 - Aug. 28 (also July 9, 16, Aug. 15; not July 6, 7, Aug. 16).
T – July 8 - Aug. 26.
U – July 9 - Aug. 27.

e – ① only (also Aug. 16; not Aug. 15).
g – Also July 13.
h – Also July 14.
j – Also Aug. 15.
k – Not Aug. 15.
m – Not July 13.
n – Not July 14, Aug. 15.
q – Not July 14.
s – July 3 - Aug. 28.
t – ⑤⑥⑦ June 12 - 19; daily June 20 - July 3; ⑤⑥⑦ July 8 - Aug. 14; daily Aug. 15 - (also July 13, 14).
v – From July 4.

TGV –🅁, supplement payable, 🍷.

PARIS - HENDAYE - IRÚN NIGHT TRAIN 305 (contd)

NIGHT TRAIN **PARIS - IRÚN**

1, 2 cl. and (2) (reclining). *Timings and dates may vary.*

	4053	4055		4052	4054
	R	R		R	R
	A	B		Y	Z
ris Austerlitz .... d.	2152	2152	Irún .... d.	...	...
s Aubrais-Orléans .... d.	2252	2252	**Hendaye** .... d.	1924	1924
rbes .... a.	0551	0551	St Jean de Luz .... d.	1940	1940
urdes .... a.	0608	0608	Biarritz .... d.	1954	1954
u .... a.	0635	0635	**Bayonne** .... d.	2006	2006
hez .... a.	0700	0700	Dax .... d.	2059	2059
x .... a.	0728	0728	Orthez .... d.	2133	2133
yonne .... a.	0836	0836	Pau .... d.	2202	2202
arritz .... a.	0848	0848	Lourdes .... d.	2228	2228
Jean de Luz .... a.	0903	0903	**Tarbes** .... d.	2246	2246
ndaye .... a.	0914	0914	Les Aubrais-Orléans .... a.	0610	0608
n .... a.	0925	0925	**Paris** Austerlitz .... a.	0720	0720

A – ①⑦ June 12-27, Sept. 4 - Oct. 16.
B – ⑤ June 17-24; daily July 1 - Sept. 3; ⑤ Sept. 9 - Oct. 14 (not Sept. 23).
Y – ①⑤ June 13-27, Sept. 5-26 (also Oct. 3, 10, 14).
Z – † June 12-26; daily July 7 - Sept. 4; ⑦ Sept. 11 - Oct. 16.

Note: some night services are expected to be withdrawn during the currency of this timetable.

BORDEAUX - ARCACHON 306

TGV Trains

n	*TGV services,* R	*TGV* 8471		*TGV* 8473	*TGV* 8473		*TGV* 8477		*TGV* 8479	
				⑦			©		⑤	
		B		C	D		T		g	
	Paris Montparnasse **300** .... d.	0846	...	1028	1028	...	1128	...	1804	...
0	**Bordeaux** St Jean .... d.	1235	...	1355	1355	...	1455	...	2141	...
0	Facture Biganos .... d.	1259	...	1419	1419	...	1519	...	2206	...
6	La Teste .... a.	|	...	|	|	...	|	...	2218	...
9	**Arcachon** .... a.	1313	...	1443	1443	...	1543	...	2223	...

TGV services, R	*TGV* 8470		*TGV* 8476	*TGV* 8476		*TGV* 8478		*TGV* 8472	
	①			⑥⑦				⑦	
	A		S	C		E		j	
Arcachon .... d.	0533	...	1530	1533	...	1719	...	1839	...
La Teste .... d.	|	...	|	|	...	|	...	1845	...
Facture Biganos .... d.	0549	...	1546	1551	...	1743	...	1858	...
Bordeaux St Jean .... a.	0613	...	1609	1613	...	1807	...	1923	...
Paris Montparnasse **300** . a.	0933	...	1957	1957	...	2157	...	2314	...

Local services

	Ⓐ	G	Ⓐ J		Ⓐ J	⚒	©		Ⓐ					Ⓐ		Ⓐ		Ⓐ		Ⓐ J				H	⑤
deaux St Jean .... d.	0635	0705	0735	0805	0835	0905	1005	1105	1242	1305	1405	1505	1605	1635	1705	1735	1805	1835	1905	1935	2005	2105	2205	2305	2355
ture Biganos .... d.	0704	0735	0805	0835	0905	0935	1035	1135	1312	1335	1435	1535	1635	1705	1735	1805	1835	1905	1935	2005	2035	2135	2235	2335	0025
achon .... ⊖ a.	0727	0757	0827	0857	0927	0957	1057	1157	1335	1357	1457	1557	1657	1727	1757	1827	1857	1927	1957	2027	2057	2157	2257	2357	0047

	F	⚒	Ⓐ J	⚒	Ⓐ	G	Ⓐ						Ⓐ		©			Ⓐ J		Ⓐ		Ⓐ J		G	†
achon .... ⊖ d.	0513	0549	0621	0634	0648	0704	0734	0804	0904	1004	1104	1204	1234	1304	1404	1504	1604	1634	1704	1734	1804	1834	1904	2004	2104
ture Biganos .... d.	0535	0611	0643	0656	0710	0726	0756	0826	0926	1026	1126	1226	1256	1326	1426	1526	1626	1656	1726	1756	1826	1856	1926	2026	2126
deaux St Jean .... a.	0605	0641	0713	0725	0740	0755	0825	0855	0955	1055	1155	1255	1325	1355	1455	1555	1655	1725	1755	1825	1855	1925	1955	2055	2155

June 20-27.
⑤⑥⑦ June 12 - July 2; Ⓐ July 4 - Aug. 26.
June 12-26.
June 18 - July 2; daily July 3 - Aug. 28.
© June 12 - July 3; daily July 4 - Aug. 28.
Ⓐ June 13 - July 1; ① July 4 - Aug. 22 (also Aug. 16; not Aug. 15).
⚒ June 13-25; daily June 27 - Aug. 28.

H – ⑤† June 17 - July 1; daily July 3 - Aug. 28.
J – Until July 1.
S – July 2 - Aug. 28.
T – July 3 - Aug. 28.
g – Also July 13.
j – Also Aug. 15.

TGV – R, supplement, 🍷.
⊖ – Trains also call at La Teste, 4-5 mins from Arcachon.

BORDEAUX - LE VERDON - POINTE DE GRAVE 307

Valid April 3 - July 2

m		Ⓐ	Ⓐ	Ⓐ	©	Ⓐ	⑥	Ⓐ		Ⓐ	
									z		z
0	**Bordeaux** St Jean...... d.	0641	0711	0811	0911	1011	1111	1211	1611	1711	1811
19	Blanquefort .... d.	0708	0748	0847	0946	1047	1147	1247	1648	1748	1848
35	Margaux .... d.	0727	0810	0909	1009	1109	1209	1308	1710	1810	1910
57	Pauillac .... d.	0747	0832	0928	1030	1130	1230	1329	1731	1831	1931
76	Lesparre .... d.	0801	0847	0944	1045	1144	1244	1344	1745	1846	1946
02	Soulac sur Mer .... d.	...	0906	...	1104	...	...	...	...	1906	2006
09	**Le Verdon** .... a.	...	0914	...	1112	...	...	...	...	1913	2013
12	Pointe de Grave..... ▷ a.	...	...	...	...	...	...	...	...	...	...

	Ⓐ	©	Ⓐ	⑥	Ⓐ		Ⓐ		Ⓐ	
						z				z
Pointe de Grave ..... ▷ d.	...	...	...	...	...	...	...	...	...	...
Le Verdon .... d.	0625	0747	...	0947	...	1147	...	1552c	1647	1747c
Soulac sur Mer .... d.	0632	0754	...	0954	...	1154	...	1559c	1654	1754c
Lesparre .... d.	0651	0814	0814	1014	1114	1214	1414	1620	1714	1814
Pauillac .... d.	0706	0831	0831	1029	1129	1229	1429	1635	1730	1830
Margaux .... d.	0728	0853	0853	1053	1153	1253	1453	1655	1754	1854
Blanquefort .... d.	0747	0914	0914	1114	1214	1314	1514	1715	1815	1915
Bordeaux St Jean ...... a.	0819	0949	0949	1149	1249	1349	1549	1749	1849	1949

Valid July 3 - August 28

m		Ⓐ						Ⓐ		Ⓐ	†
0	**Bordeaux** St Jean ⊖ d.	0711	0811	0911	1111	1311	1611	1711	1811	1941	1941
19	Blanquefort .... d.	0748	0847	0946	1147	1347	1648	1748	1848	2016	2016
35	Margaux .... d.	0810	0909	1009	1209	1409	1710	1810	1910	2035	2035
57	Pauillac .... d.	0832	0927	1030	1230	1430	1731	1831	1931	2055	2055
76	Lesparre .... d.	0847	...	1045	1245	1445	1746	1845	1946	2111	2110
02	Soulac sur Mer .... d.	0907	...	1105	1305	1505	1806	...	2006	2133	...
09	**Le Verdon** .... a.	0914	...	1112	1312	1512	1813	...	2013	2141	...
12	Pointe de Grave..... ▷ a.	0919	...	1117	1317	1517	1818	...	...	...	...

	⚒	Ⓐ								
Pointe de Grave ..... ▷ d.	...	...	...	0942	...	1142	1342	...	1642	1842
Le Verdon .... d.	...	0625	0747	0947	...	1147	1347	...	1647	1847
Soulac sur Mer .... d.	...	0632	0754	0954	...	1154	1354	...	1654	1854
Lesparre .... d.	0614	0651	0814	1014	...	1214	1414	...	1714	1914
Pauillac .... d.	0629	0706	0831	1029	...	1229	1429	...	1730	1930
Margaux .... d.	0648	0728	0853	1053	...	1253	1453	...	1754	1954
Blanquefort .... d.	0709	0749	0914	1114	...	1314	1514	...	1815	2015
Bordeaux St Jean ⊖ .a.	0749	0819	0949	1149	...	1349	1549	...	1849	2049

© only.
Not May 7.

▷ – For ferry schedule Pointe de Grave - Royan see Table **299**.

PÉRIGUEUX - LE BUISSON - AGEN 308

km		①	Ⓐ				Ⓐ	⚒	Ⓐ		⑤†
		G		H						A	
0	**Périgueux** .... d.	0505	0757	0952	...	1223	1452	1730	1830	1913	1913
40	Les Eyzies .... d.	0535	0828	1022	...	1255	1522	1810	1905	1948	1948
57	Le Buisson .... d.	0552	0849	1039	...	1310	1539	1830	1920	2003	2004
08	Monsempron Libos .... d.	0639	0933	1123	...	1355	1624	1914	...	...	2052
52	**Agen** .... a.	0719	1007	1158	...	1428	1704	1948	...	...	2128

	Ⓐ	⚒	†	Ⓐ		Ⓑ	†	⑥		⑤
		⊖								J
Agen .... d.	...	...	...	0728	1117	1431	...	1631	1836	2046
Monsempron Libos ..... d.	...	...	...	0802	1153	1505	...	1706	1915	2123
Le Buisson .... d.	0638	0720	0847	0848	1238	1550	1727	1752	2007	2211
Les Eyzies .... d.	0654	0735	0902	0903	1254	1607	1742	1809	2023	2227
Périgueux .... a.	0729	0810	0937	0939	1329	1635	1817	1840	2052	2258

- ①②③④⑥ (not July 14, Aug. 15).
- June 13-27.
- ©June 12-26; daily July 2 - Aug. 28.
- Until July 1.

⊖ – Runs 7 minutes later throughout on ⑥.

309 LIMOGES - ANGOULÊME and POITIERS

km		J	Ⓐ		⑥		⚒v	†x		Ⓑ	⑥v	⑤g	†
0	**Limoges** ..... d.	0529	0553	...	0926	...	1210	1220	...	1711	1750	1821	1840
122	**Angoulême**. a.	0731	0805	...	1130	...	1417	1424	...	1914	1953	2023	2050

	Ⓐ	L		A	z		†y	B		Ⓐ	Ⓒv	⑤g	
Angoulême d.	0546	0748	...	1203	1230	...	1448	1703	...	1820	1857	1937	2
Limoges ..... a.	0752	0942	...	1400	1424	...	1645	1858	...	2042	2102	2141	2

km		Ⓐ		Ⓒ	Ⓐ	Ⓐ	Ⓐ			Ⓐ	G	H	⑤g
0	**Limoges** ..... d.	0604	0807	1206	1208	1302	1407	1607	1805	2007	2029	2040	2229
139	**Poitiers** .... a.	0755	0956	1356	1356	1507	1556	1756	1959	2156	2213	2229	0012

	Ⓐ	⚒	†	⚒	Ⓐ	Ⓑ		Ⓐ		⚒	H	G	
Poitiers .... d.	0559	0804	1004	1204	1251	1404	1604	1653	1804	2004	2130	2148	2
Limoges ..... a.	0755	0955	1157	1357	1457	1555	1757	1858	1957	2155	2318	2341	(

A – ①②④⑤⑥ June 13 - Aug. 27 (also July 13; not June 18).
B – Ⓑ June 12 - 26; Ⓐ June 27 - Aug. 19; Ⓑ Aug. 22 - 26.
F – ⑦ June 19 - Aug. 28 (also Aug. 15; not Aug. 14).
G – ⑦ June 12 - July 3.
H – † July 10 - Aug. 28.
J – ①⑤ June 13 - July 1.
L – ⚒ June 13 - July 2; ①⑥ July 4 - Aug. 27 (not Aug. 15).

g – Also July 13.
v – Not June 18.
x – Not June 12, 19.
y – Not June 19.
z – Not July 13.

310 PARIS - LIMOGES - TOULOUSE

For faster TGV services Paris - Agen - Toulouse and v.v. see Table 320

km		⚒	Ⓐ	Ⓐ		⚒ h	⑥	Ⓐ	★ 3601 Ⓐ	⚒ h	★ 3611 ⑥ h	★ 3611 Ⓐ	★ 3613 † q		★ 3621	Ⓐ	★ 3631	★ 3701 ①⑤ ☆k	Ⓒ	★ 3703 Ⓒ ☆	★ 3633 D	★ 3635 ⑤† g	⑤ g	★ 3637 ⑤⑥† g	
	Lille Europe .... d.	...	...	...	...	...	...	...	...	...	...	...	...	...	...	...	...	...	...	...	...	...	...	...	
0	**Paris** Austerlitz **294 315** d.	...	...	...	...	...	...	...	0641	...	0752	0752	0752	...	0841	...	0941	0929	...	1029	1052	1152	...	1241	
	Orléans 315 .... d.	...	...	...	...	...	...	0650	|	0750	|	|	|	...	|	...	|	|	1050	|	|	|	...	|	1:
119	Les Aubrais-Orléans **294 315** d.	...	...	...	...	...	...	|	|	|	0848	0848	0848	...	|	...	1039	1030	|	1131	|	|	...	|	
200	Vierzon **315** .... d.	...	...	...	...	0649	...	0749	0810	0849	|	|	|	...	1010	...	|	|	1155	|	|	1318	...	|	1
236	Issoudun .... d.	...	...	...	...	0714	...	0814	0829	0912	|	|	|	...	|	...	|	|	1217	|	|	|	...	1427	1
263	Châteauroux .... d.	...	...	...	...	0732	...	0832	0845	0932	0949	0949	0949	...	1041	...	|	1137	1235	1248c	1254	1349	...	1444	1
294	Argenton sur Creuse .... d.	...	...	...	...	0749	...	0849	|	0949	|	|	|	...	1058	...	|	|	1252	|	|	|	...	|	
341	La Souterraine .... d.	...	...	...	...	0818	...	...	0923	...	|	|	|	...	1124	...	|	|	...	|	|	|	...	1523	
400	**Limoges** .... a.	...	...	...	...	0854	...	...	0954	...	1054	1054	1054	...	1154	...	1254	1245	...	1409	1358	1454	...	1554	
400	**Limoges** .... d.	...	...	0540	...	▬	0907	...	0957	...	1057	1057	1057	...	1157	...	1257	1249	...	1413	1401	1457	...	...	
459	Uzerche .... d.	...	...	0617	...	...	0956	...	|	...	1134	1134	1134	...	1234	...	|	|	...	|	|	1534	...	...	
499	**Brive la Gaillarde** .... a.	...	...	0644	...	...	1024	...	1057	...	1159	1159	1159	...	1300	...	1357	1350	...	1512	1500	1600	...	...	
499	**Brive la Gaillarde** .... d.	...	0557	...	0702	...	...	...	...	...	1202	1202	1202	...	...	1306	1400	1407	...	1515	...	...	1702	...	
536	Souillac .... d.	...	0625	...	0731	⚒	...	...	...	...	|	|	1231	...	...	1335	1427	|	...	|	...	...	1731	...	
559	Gourdon .... d.	...	0642	...	0747		...	...	...	...	|	|	1248	...	...	1350	1446	|	...	|	...	...	1747	...	
600	Cahors .... d.	0612	0712	...	0812	0900	...	...	...	...	1309	1312	1318	...	...	1420	1516	1525	...	1625	...	...	1812	...	
639	Caussade .... d.	0638	0738	...	0839	0926	...	...	...	...	|	|	1344	...	...	1444	1541	|	...	|	...	...	1837	...	
662	Montauban **320** .... d.	0657	0757	...	0857	0945	...	...	...	...	1348	1351	1400	...	...	1500	1557	1606	...	1704	...	...	1852	...	
713	**Toulouse** Matabiau **320** a.	0735	0835	...	0935	1023	...	...	...	...	1415	1418	1426	...	...	1538	1623	1632	...	1731	...	...	1935	...	
	Portbou **355** .... a.	...	...	...	...	...	...	...	...	...	...	...	...	...	...	...	...	...	...	...	...	...	...	...	

	N	★ 3643	Ⓐ	Ⓐ	Ⓐ	★ 3651 Ⓐ	† e	Ⓐ		Ⓒ	★ 3655 Ⓐ	Ⓐ	★ 3661 ⑤⑦ b	★ 3669 ①–④ x	Ⓐ	★ 3665 Ⓒ		Ⓐ	★ 3667	★ 3663 ⑤ g	★ 3681	*TGV* 5248 L	3731 ♦ 🅁	3751 ♦ 🅁 P	37 🅁
Lille Europe .... d.	...	...	...	...	...	...	...	...	...	...	...	...	...	...	...	...	...	...	...	...	...	1800	...	...	
Paris Austerlitz **294 315** d.	...	1352	...	...	...	1552	...	...	...	...	1652	...	1752	1752	...	1811	...	...	1841	1913	1941	|	2139	2252	22
Orléans 315 .... d.	...	|	...	...	...	|	...	...	...	1650	|	...	|	|	...	|	...	1850	|	|	|	|	|	|	
Les Aubrais-Orléans **294 315** d.	...	1448	...	...	...	|	...	...	...	|	|	...	|	|	...	|	...	|	|	2012	|	2042	2240	2357	23
Vierzon **315** .... d.	...	|	...	...	1649	1718	...	...	1733	1749	|	1821	|	1918	1933	1937	...	1949	2010	2056	2107	2116	2320	|	
Issoudun .... d.	...	|	...	...	1713	|	...	...	1754	1812	|	1842	|	|	1953	|	...	2012	2029	|	|	|	|	|	
Châteauroux .... d.	...	1549	...	...	1732	1749	...	...	1809	1832	1846	1908	1950	1950	2008	2008	...	2030	2045	2126	2138	2148	|	|	
Argenton sur Creuse .... d.	...	|	...	...	1757	|	...	...	1824	1903	|	1926	|	|	2024	2027	...	...	|	2145	2155	|	|	|	
La Souterraine .... d.	...	|	...	...	▬	|	...	...	1853	1932f	1924	1955	|	|	2053	2053	...	...	2124	2210	2221	2229	|	|	
Limoges .... a.	...	1654	...	...	†	1854	...	...	1937	...	1954	...	2054	2054	2138	2124	...	...	2154	2240	2252	2300	0053	|	
Limoges .... d.	...	1657	1707	1807	1837	1857	...	1907	...	...	...	...	2057	2057	...	2127	...	...	...	2243	2255	2303	0106	|	
Uzerche .... d.	...	|	1756	1856	1926	1933	...	1959	...	...	...	...	2134	2134	...	2204	...	...	...	2320	|	|	|	|	
Brive la Gaillarde .... a.	...	1755	1824	1924	1954	1959	...	2027	...	...	...	...	2159	2159	...	2229	...	...	...	2345	2355	0006	|	|	
Brive la Gaillarde .... d.	1731	1758	...	...	...	...	2004	...	...	...	...	...	2202	2202	...	2232	...	...	...	2348	...	...	|	|	
Souillac .... d.	1800	1827	...	...	...	...	2033	...	...	...	...	...	2230	2230	...	2259	...	...	...	0018	...	...	|	|	04
Gourdon .... d.	1815	1845	...	...	...	...	2048	...	...	...	...	...	2249	2249	...	2318	...	...	...	0034	...	...	|	|	04
Cahors .... d.	1840	1916	...	...	...	...	2114	...	...	...	...	...	2318	2318	...	2348	...	...	...	0102	...	...	|	0510	05
Caussade .... d.	1907	1942	...	...	...	...	2140	...	...	...	...	...	...	...	...	|	...	...	...	|	...	...	|	|	05
Montauban **320** .... d.	1926	1958	...	...	...	...	2158	...	...	...	...	...	...	...	...	|	...	...	...	|	...	...	|	0608	06
Toulouse Matabiau **320** a.	2005	2024	...	...	...	...	2235	...	...	...	...	...	...	...	...	0050	...	...	...	0203	...	...	|	0645	06
Portbou **355** .... a.	...	...	...	...	...	...	...	...	...	...	...	...	...	...	...	...	...	...	...	...	...	...	0810	...	

	★ 3600 Ⓐ	Ⓐ	★ 3604 Ⓐ	⚒ h	★ 3602 Ⓒ	⚒ h	★ 3606 Ⓐ	Ⓐ	⚒ h		*TGV* 5296 M	⚒ h	⚒	★ 3612 † q	★ 3610 ①–⑥ k		★ 3620 ①–⑥ k		Ⓐ	★ 3630	★ 3700 ☆H	★ 3634 ⑤⑥ a	★ 3632 ⑦ j	Ⓑ q	Ⓒ
Cerbère **355** .... d.	...	...	...	...	...	...	...	...	...	...	...	...	...	...	...	...	...	...	...	...	...	...	...	...	
Toulouse Matabiau **320** d.	...	...	...	...	...	...	...	...	...	...	...	...	...	...	...	0619	0640	...	0725	1044	1050	...	...	...	12
Montauban **320** .... d.	...	...	...	...	...	...	...	...	...	...	...	...	...	...	...	0658	0708	...	0804	1112	1119	...	...	...	13
Caussade .... d.	...	...	...	...	...	...	...	...	...	...	...	...	...	...	...	0715	|	...	0820	1128	|	...	...	...	13
Cahors .... d.	...	...	...	...	...	...	...	...	...	...	...	...	...	...	0644	0742	0749	...	0848	1155	1204	...	...	...	13
Gourdon .... d.	...	...	...	...	...	...	...	...	...	...	...	...	...	...	0711	0810	|	...	0918d	1222	|	...	...	...	
Souillac .... d.	...	...	...	...	...	...	...	...	...	...	...	...	...	...	0728	0826	|	...	0936d	1239	|	...	...	...	
Brive la Gaillarde .... a.	...	...	...	...	...	...	...	...	...	...	...	...	...	...	0757	0853	0900	...	1001d	1308	1312	...	...	...	
Brive la Gaillarde .... d.	...	...	0457	...	0457	...	...	0604	...	...	0704	...	0733	0800	0800	▬	0903	...	▬	1311	1318	...	1357	...	
Uzerche .... d.	...	...	0523	...	0523	...	...	0633	...	...	|	...	0802	0826	0826	...	|	...	...	|	|	...	1424	...	
Limoges .... a.	...	...	0600	...	0600	...	...	0721	...	...	0804	...	0850	0902	0903	...	1002	...	...	1411	1419	...	1503	...	
Limoges .... d.	0503	...	0603	...	0603	...	0706	...	0723	...	0807	...	...	0905	0906	...	1005	...	...	1414	1422	1506	1506	...	
La Souterraine .... d.	0535	...	|	0607	0636	...	0738	...	0808	...	0837	...	...	|	|	...	1037	...	⑥	|	|	1537	1537	...	
Argenton sur Creuse .... d.	|	...	|	0636	|	←	|	...	0836	...	|	0910	...	|	|	Ⓐ	1101	...	h	|	|	|	|	1610	
Châteauroux .... d.	0613	0629	0710	0700	0715	0718	0817	...	0853	...	0920	0929	...	1012	1011	1107	1119	...	1229	|	1527	1616	1616	1629	
Issoudun .... d.	0630	0649	|	→	0730	0736	|	...	0907	...	|	0948	...	|	|	1124	|	...	1249	|	|	1630	1631	1647	
Vierzon **315** .... d.	0651	0716	0742	...	0750	0800	0849	...	0927	...	0953	1015	...	|	|	1209	|	...	1316	|	|	1651	1651	1716	
Les Aubrais-Orléans **294 315** a.	|	|	|	...	|	|	|	...	...	...	1027	|	...	1111	1111	|	1220	...	|	1621	1637	|	|	|	
Orléans 315 .... a.	|	0810	|	...	|	0854	|	...	...	...	|	1109	...	|	|	1257	|	...	1410	|	|	|	|	1810	
Paris Austerlitz **294 315** a.	0819	...	0907	...	0918	...	1018	...	...	...	|	...	...	1207	1207	...	1318	...	...	1718	1738	1818	1818	...	
Lille Europe .... a.	...	...	...	...	...	...	...	...	...	...	1308	...	...	...	...	...	...	...	...	...	...	...	...	...	

FOR NOTES SEE NEXT PAGE

TOULOUSE - LIMOGES - PARIS 310

For faster TGV services Toulouse - Agen - Paris and v.v. see Table 320

		★ 3640			★ 3652	★ 3660			★ 3664		★ 3672				★ 3680			★ 3690						3752	3750	3730
				⑤	⑦	①–⑥		⚒	⑦	Ⓐ	⑦	Ⓐ		⚒	Ⓑ	⑤	Ⓑ		Ⓑ	Ⓑ	Ⓐ	Ⓒ	Ⓐ	♦	♦	♦
					j	k			j		j		T		q	g			e					🅁 Q	🅁 P	🅁
bère 355	d.	...	...	...	...	...	...	...	...	...	...	...	...	...	...	...	...	...	...	...	...	...	...	...	...	2005
ouse Matabiau 320	d.	...	...	1325	1334	...	...	...	...	...	1434	...	1444	...	...	1544	...	1634	1725	...	1825	1925	1927	2230	2230	0049
uban 320	d.	...	...	1404	1402	...	...	...	...	...	1502	...	1525	...	...	1631	...	1702	1804	...	1904	2004	2006	2259	2312	|
sade	d.	...	...	1417	1418	...	...	...	...	...	1518	...	1540	...	...	1646	...	1718	1821	...	1920	2019	2023	2316	|	|
rs	d.	...	...	1443	1445	...	...	...	...	...	1545	...	1604	...	...	1712	...	1745	1848	...	1947	2047	2049	2345	2353	|
don	d.	...	...	1513	1513	...	...	...	...	...	1613	...	1629	...	...	1742	...	1813	1918	...	2016	2116	...	0013	|	|
ac	d.	...	...	1531	1531	...	...	...	...	...	1631	...	1644	...	...	1759	...	1831	1935	...	2032	2132	...	0031	|	|
la Gaillarde	a.	...	...	1555	1600	...	...	...	...	...	1700	...	1711	...	...	1825	...	1903	2001	...	2057	2157	...	|	|	|
la Gaillarde	d.	1459	...	▬	1603	1603	...	...	...	1650	1703	...	...	1736	1800	...	1836	1906	...	2009	...	...	...	|	|	|
che	d.	1525	...	...	|	|	...	...	...	1718	|	...	...	1805	1825	...	1905	|	...	2038	...	...	...	|	|	|
ges	a.	1603	...	Ⓑ q	1703	1703	...	...	...	1755	1803	...	...	1854	1903	...	1954	2004	...	2126	...	...	...	|	|	|
ges	d.	1606	...	1623	1706	1706	...	1723	1736	...	1806	...	...	...	1906	...	...	2007	...	...	...	...	...	|	|	|
outerraine	d.	|	...	1708	|	1737	...	1808	1808	...	|	...	...	...	1937	...	...	|	...	...	...	...	...	|	|	|
nton sur Creuse	d.	|	...	1736	|	1801	...	1836	1832	...	|	1910	...	...	|	...	...	|	...	...	...	...	...	|	|	|
eauroux	d.	1713	1729	1753	1811	1819	...	1853	1850	...	1911	1929	...	...	2015	...	...	2115	...	...	...	...	...	|	|	|
dun	d.	|	1747	1807	|	|	...	1907	1906	...	|	1947	...	...	2031	...	...	|	...	...	...	...	...	|	|	|
on 315	d.	|	1814	1827	|	1851	...	1927	1927	...	|	2016	...	...	2051	...	...	2147	...	...	...	...	...	|	|	0543
ubrais-Orléans 294 315	a.	|	|	...	1911	|	...	...	|	...	2011	|	...	...	|	...	...	2220	...	...	...	...	...	0535	0535	0620
léans 315	a.	|	1910	...	|	|	...	...	|	...	|	2110	...	...	|	...	...	|	...	...	...	...	...	|	|	|
Austerlitz 294 315	a.	1907	...	...	2007	2019	...	...	2053	...	2107	...	...	...	2218	...	...	2318	...	...	...	...	...	0652	0652	0723
e Europe	a.	...	...	...	...	...	...	...	...	...	...	...	...	...	...	...	...	...	...	...	...	...	...	...	...	...

NOTES (LISTED BY TRAIN NUMBER):

– Not Oct. 22, 29, 30, 31: ▬ 1,2 cl., (2) (reclining) Cerbère - Paris; ▬ 1,2 cl., (2) (reclining) Latour de Carol (**3970**) - Toulouse - Paris. Train number **3732** July 1 - Sept. 4.
– Not Oct. 22, 29, 30, 31: ▬ 1,2 cl., (2) (reclining) Paris - Portbou; ▬ 1,2 cl., (2) (reclining) Paris - Toulouse (**3971**) Latour de Carol. Train number **3733** July 1 - Sept. 4.
-3 – ▬ 1,2 cl. and (2) (reclining) Paris - Toulouse and v.v. Conveys (to / from Brive) portions Paris - Rodez / Albi and v.v. on dates in Table **316**.

: some night services are expected to be withdrawn during the currency of this timetable.

July 2, Aug. 13 only.
①⑤⑥⑦ June 12 - Aug. 28 (also July 14).
④⑤⑥† (also July 13).
①⑤⑥⑦ (also Aug. 16; not Aug. 15).
①②③④⑦ (not July 13).
①②③④ (not July 13, 14, Aug. 15, Oct. 31, Nov. 10).
⑤⑥† (also July 13, Nov. 10; not Oct. 22, 29, 30).
①②③④⑥ (not July 13, 14, Aug. 15).

a – Also July 13, 14.
b – Also July 13, Aug. 15.
c – Depart 1300 on July 2, Aug. 13.
d – ① (also Aug. 16; not Aug. 15).
e – Not Aug. 14.
f – † (not July 14).
g – Also July 13.
h – Also July 14.
j – Also Aug. 15.
k – Not Aug. 15.
q – Not July 14.
x – Not July 13, 14, Aug. 15.

TGV – 🅁, supplement payable, 🍸.
★ – *Intercités* service, 🅁.
☆ – Also conveys couchettes and reclining seats for daytime use (also vending machines).

BRIVE - AURILLAC 311

		Ⓐ	⑥	⚒	†		⑥	†	Ⓑ	⑥
Brive la Gaillarde 316	d.	1130	1211	1403	1422	...	1801	1803	2216	2244
St Denis-près-Martel **316**	d.	1156	1242	1430	1454	...	1834	1834	2242	2310
Aurillac	a.	1321	1406	1553	1619	...	2001	1958	0006	0034

		Ⓐ	⚒	Ⓒ	Ⓐ		†	† V	⚒	
Aurillac	d.	0515	0700	1049	1112	...	1456	1553	1557	1710
St Denis-près-Martel **316**	d.	0637	0824	1213	1237	...	1629	1723	1721	1835
Brive la Gaillarde 316	a.	0705	0850	1242	1303	...	1654	1749	1746	1900

July 10 - Aug. 21.

TOULOUSE - LATOUR DE CAROL 312

		3971 🅁 P				Ⓒ					
Paris Austerlitz **310**	d.	2139	...	...	...	...	...	...	...	...	...
Toulouse Matabiau	d.	0501	0648	0848	1048	1348	1448	1647	1748	1848	1948
Pamiers	d.	0549	0750	0950	1150	1450	1550	1750	1850	1950	2050
Foix	a.	0600	0803	1003	1202	1504	1602	1802	1904	2002	2104
Foix	d.	0602	0805	1005	1205	1506	1605	1805	1906	2005	2106
Ax les Thermes	d.	0651	0849	1049	1249	1543	1649	1849	1943	2049	2143
L'Hospitalet ⊖	d.	0724	0921	1115	1321	...	1721	1921	...	2118	...
Latour de Carol	a.	0751	0947	1136	1347	...	1747	1947	...	2139	...

		Ⓐ				Ⓐ	Ⓐ	Ⓒ				3970 🅁 P
Latour de Carol	d.	0525	...	0721	0921c	...	1321	1321	...	1721	1921	2020
L'Hospitalet ⊖	d.	0552	...	0752	0951c	...	1347	1351	...	1751	1951	2050
Ax les Thermes	d.	0620	0723	0820	1020	1123	1415	1420	1523	1820	2020	2121
Foix	a.	0704	0802	0904	1104	1203	1458	1504	1603	1904	2104	2212
Foix	d.	0705	0804	0905	1105	1204	1459	1505	1604	1905	2105	2214
Pamiers	d.	0721	0821	0921	1121	1221	1517	1521	1621	1921	2121	2230
Toulouse Matabiau	a.	0817	0917	1017	1217	1317	1617	1617	1717	2017	2217	2314
Paris Austerlitz **310**	a.	...	...	...	...	...	...	...	...	...	...	0723

▬ 1,2 cl. and (2) (reclining) Paris (**3732/3**) - Toulouse - Latour de Carol and v.v.

c – Ⓒ only.

⊖ – Full name: Andorre-L'Hospitalet. For 🚌 connections to / from Andorra see Table **313**.

: some night services are expected to be withdrawn during the currency of this timetable.

ANDORRA 🚌 313

🚌							⊖		
orre-L'Hospitalet (Gare)	d.	0745	...	1945	...	...	and	...	...
de la Casa	d.	0810	...	2000	...	0845	hourly	2045	...
eu ⊙	d.	0825	...	2025	...	0855	until	2055	...
orra la Vella	a.	0910	...	2105	...	0940	...	2140	...

🚌							⊖		
Andorra la Vella	d.	0545	...	1700	...	0745	and	1945	...
Soldeu ⊙	d.	0610	...	1735	...	0825	hourly	2025	...
Pas de la Casa	d.	0640	...	1815	...	0840	until	2040	...
Andorre-L'Hospitalet (Gare)	a.	0710	...	1930	...	...	...	...	...

Also calls at Canillo, Encamp and Escaldes.
Additional journeys operated by Cooperativa Interurbana (service L4) run from Andorra hourly 0720 - 2020, from Pas de la Casa at 0715 then hourly 0820 - 2120.

Operator: La Hispano Andorrana, Av. Santa Coloma, entre 85 - 87, Andorra la Vella, ✆ + 376 821 372. www.andorrabus.com. Subject to cancellation when mountain passes are closed by snow.
Additional service: approx hourly (5 per day on ⑦) Escaldes - Andorra la Vella - Sant Julià de Lòria - Seu d'Urgell (Spain).

TOULOUSE - CASTRES - MAZAMET 314

		Ⓐ	Ⓐ	⚒	†			Ⓐ	Ⓐ	Ⓐ			
Toulouse ◇	d.	0543	0643	0750	0839	1144	1343	1544	1643	1722	1742	1847	2043
Castres	a.	0655	0758	0901	0952	1251	1452	1654	1750	1833	1853	1957	2155
Mazamet	a.	0721	0824	0927	1014	1318	1518	1716	1817	1859	1920	2024	2217

		Ⓐ	Ⓐ	Ⓐ		Ⓐ	Ⓑ	⚒			Ⓐ	
Mazamet	d.	0532	0555	0636	0740	0843	1032	1232	1433	1731	1821	1939
Castres	d.	0554	0617	0659	0802	0905	1054	1255	1456	1754	1857	2001
Toulouse ◇	d.	0701	0730	0806	0909	1012	1201	1401	1602	1905	2005	2112

◇ – Toulouse Matabiau.

315 PARIS - VIERZON - BOURGES - MONTLUÇON

km				3903				3909								3913	3915						3917	3921
		Ⓐ ⊖	⚒ m	⚒ m	⑥	E	C	A	Ⓐ	Ⓑ ⊖s	Ⓐ	Ⓐ	Ⓐ ⊖	⚒ m		G	⑤ y		①–④ w	† q	Ⓐ	Ⓑ q		⑤⑦ z
0	**Paris** Austerlitz 310 d.	...	...	0707	...	...	...	1154	...	...	...	...	...	...	...	1707	1707	...	...	...	...	...	1907	2107
	Orléans 310 d.	0607	0715	|	...	0913	...	|	1450	1614	...	1650	1715	1750	...	|	|	1815	...	...	1915	1950	|	|
119	Les Aubrais-Orléans 310 d.	|	|	0808	...	|	...	1325	|	|	...	|	|	|	...	1808	1808	|	...	...	|	|	2008	2208
178	Salbris d.	0644	0751	0835	...	0950	...	|	1529	1653	...	1729	1753	1829	...	1835	1835	1853	...	...	1952	2029	2035	2235
200	Vierzon 310 ▷ d.	0657	0805	0852	0902	1004	1018	1403	1545	1707	...	1744	1807	1844	...	1852	1852	1907	1923	...	2006	2044	2052	2252
232	**Bourges** ▷ a.	0726	0826	0911	|	1025	|	1421	1613	1726	...	1811	1826	...	...	1911	1911	1927	|	...	2026	...	2111	2311
	Bourges d.	...	...	...	|	...	|	...	...	...	1729	...	...	...	...	...	1929	...	|	1930	...	...	2128	...
•291	St Amand-Montrond-Orval d.	...	...	...	0957	...	1111	...	...	...	1823	...	...	...	...	...	2018	...	2021	2020	...	...	2215	...
•341	**Montluçon** a.	...	...	...	1031	...	1145	...	...	...	1904	...	...	...	...	...	2053	...	2055	2103	...	...	2250	...

						3904					3908		3916	3914			3920		3918					3924
	Ⓐ	Ⓐ	⑥ m	Ⓐ	⚒	⚒ m	Ⓐ	⑥	⚒ ⊖m	Ⓐ ⊖	B	D	† q	①–⑥ p	Ⓐ	Ⓐ ⊖	† q	⊖	⚒ m	Ⓐ	Ⓐ ⊖	⑤ g	①–④ w	† s
Montluçon d.	...	...	...	...	0536	...	...	0613	...	...	0844	1035	...	...	...	...	1651	...	1710	1735	...	1911	1914	1906
St Amand-Montrond-Orval d.	...	...	...	...	0609	...	0627	0650	...	...	0920	1110	...	...	...	...	1727	...	1746	1835	...	1944	1947	1942
Bourges a.	...	...	...	...	|	...	0714	|	...	...	1011	|	...	...	...	...	1812	...	1832	1921	...	|	|	2030
Bourges ▷ d.	...	...	...	0633	|	0649	...	|	0733	0833	1030	|	1349	1549	1633	1733	1829	1833	1849	...	1933	|	|	2049
Vierzon 310 ▷ d.	0550	0616	0650	0656	0702	0709	...	0742	0755	0855	1049	1159	1409	1609	1655	1755	1848	1855	1909	...	1955	2038	2039	2108
Salbris d.	0602	0631	0704	0709	...	0725	...	...	0809	0909	|	...	1425	1625	1709	1809	|	1909	1925	...	2009	...	...	2122
Les Aubrais-Orléans 310 a.	|	|	|	|	...	0752	...	...	|	|	1121	...	1452	1650	|	|	1921	|	1952	...	|	...	...	2147
Orléans 310 a.	0640	0710	0740	0745	...	|	...	...	0845	0945	|	...	|	|	1745	1845	|	1946	|	...	2045	...	...	|
Paris Austerlitz 310 a.	...	...	...	...	...	0853	...	...	...	...	1219	...	1553	1752	...	...	2019	...	2053	...	...	...	...	2246

LOCAL TRAINS VIERZON - BOURGES (see also Table **290**)

	Ⓐ	⑥ m	Ⓐ	⚒ m	J		K				Ⓐ
Vierzon d.	0618	0657	0740	0840	1040	...	1240	1440	1640	1840	1940
Bourges a.	0646	0726	0808	0908	1108	...	1308	1508	1708	1907	2008

	Ⓐ		Ⓐ	H		⚒ m	Ⓐ	Ⓐ		Ⓐ
Bourges d.	0654	0752	0852	1052	...	1252	1452	1552	1652	1750
Vierzon a.	0721	0820	0920	1120	...	1320	1520	1620	1720	1820

A – ①②③④ June 23 - 28.
B – Not June 13 - 15, 23, 24, 27, 28.
C – Ⓒ June 12 - 19; daily June 23 - Aug. 28 (not June 29, 30).
D – ⑥ June 18 - 25; ⚒ June 29 - Aug. 27 (also July 14).
E – Not June 20 - 22, 29, 30.
G – ①②③④⑦ (not June 13, 14).
H – Ⓐ June 16 - 22, June 29 - Aug. 26 (not June 21).
J – June 13 - 17, 23 - 28, July 1 - Aug. 28.
K – ⚒ June 11 - 18, June 23 - Aug. 27 (also July 14; not June 29, 30).

g – Also July 13.
m – Also July 14.
p – Not Aug. 15.
q – Not July 14.
s – Not July 14, Aug. 14.
w – Not July 13, 14, Aug. 15.
y – Also July 13; not July 15.
z – Also July 13, Aug. 15; not Aug. 14.

⊖ – To / from Nevers (Table **290**).
▷ – For additional trains see below main table.
• – Via Bourges (Montluçon is 327 km direct).

316 BRIVE - FIGEAC - RODEZ

km		3755 A 🅁		⚒	Ⓑ	Ⓐ		Ⓐ		Ⓑ p
	Paris Austerlitz 310 d.	2252	...	...	...	...	...	...	...	...
0	**Brive la Gaillarde** 311 d.	0345	...	0608	0732	1124	1328	1616	1825	2225
27	St Denis-près-Martel 311 d.	0410	...	0633	0758	1150	1354	1647	1859	2249
45	Rocamadour-Padirac d.	0426	...	0648	0814	1205	1409	1702	1914	2304
53	Gramat d.	0435	...	0655	0822	1212	1417	1708	1920	2311
88	Figeac 317 d.	0506	...	0723	0850	1240	1445	1735	1952	2339
94	Capdenac 317 d.	0514	...	0733	0857	1249	1453	1742	2001	2346
109	Viviez-Decazeville d.	0530	...	0747	0911	1304	1507	1757	2016	0000
161	**Rodez** 323 a.	0617	...	0832	0955	1349	1551	1842	2101	0045
227	Carmaux 323 a.	0737f	...	...	...	...	...	...	...	...
244	**Albi** 323 a.	0758f	...	...	...	...	...	...	...	...

	⚒	†	Ⓐ						3
Albi 323 d.	...	...	...	...	...	...	...	...	20
Carmaux 323 d.	...	...	...	...	...	...	...	...	2
Rodez 323 d.	0631	0825	1022	1218	1421	1624	1753	...	2
Viviez-Decazeville d.	0717	0912	1106	1305	1508	1710	1841	...	2
Capdenac 317 d.	0732	0927	1122	1322	1525	1727	1901	...	2
Figeac 317 d.	0738	0934	1129	1330	1532	1736	1913	...	2
Gramat d.	0806	1002	1157	1400	1600	1805	1944	...	0
Rocamadour-Padirac d.	0815	1009	1206	1410	1607	1813	1951	...	0
St Denis-près-Martel 311 d.	0830	1024	1222	1429	1622	1829	2007	...	0
Brive la Gaillarde 311 a.	0856	1049	1245	1453	1647	1854	2031	...	0
Paris Austerlitz 310 a.	...	...	...	...	...	...	...	...	0

A – 🛏 1, 2 cl. and (2) (reclining) Paris (**3751/3**) - Brive - Rodez. Runs Paris - Brive (**3757**) - Rodez - Albi on ⑤; also July 13; not July 15 (from Paris).
B – 🛏 1, 2 cl. and (2) (reclining) Rodez - Brive (**3750/2**) - Paris. Runs Albi (**3756**) - Rodez - Brive - Paris on ⑦ (also Aug. 15; not Aug. 14).

e – ⑦ (also Aug. 15; not Aug. 14).
f – ⑥ (also July 14; not July 16).
p – Not Aug. 14.

Note: some night services are expected to be withdrawn during the currency of this timetable.

317 AURILLAC - FIGEAC - TOULOUSE

km		Ⓐ			Ⓐ				k	⑤ g
	Clermont Ferrand 331 d.	...	...	...	...	...	1034y	...	...	...
0	**Aurillac** d.	...	0646d	0855d	...	...	1255	1653	1832	2117
65	Figeac 316 d.	0606	0805	1004	1204	...	1405	1806	1947	2230
71	Capdenac 316 d.	0614	0814	1014	1212	...	1415	1815	...	...
100	Villefranche de Rouergue d.	0641	0844	1044	1239	...	1442	1844	...	...
117	Najac d.	0656	0859	1058	1254	...	1456	1859	...	...
170	Gaillac 323 d.	0742	0949	1143	1340	...	1543	1948	...	...
224	**Toulouse** Matabiau 323 a.	0830	1030	1221	1421	...	1623	2029	...	...

	⚒	① m	②–⑤ p	†	⚒			Ⓐ	
Toulouse Matabiau 323 d.	...	0533	0654	0857	0857	1303	1704	1811	1
Gaillac 323 d.	...	0611	0742	0937	0937	1340	1742	1852	1
Najac d.	...	0657	0828	1028	1028	1426	1828	1939	2
Villefranche de Rouergue d.	...	0713	0843	1043	1043	1443	1843	1954	2
Capdenac 316 d.	0547	0740	0911	1112	1112	1513	1912	2021	2
Figeac 316 d.	0558	0747	0917	1119	1120	1522	1919	2031	2
Aurillac a.	0726	...	...	...	1229	1632	2031f	2140	22
Clermont Ferrand 331 a.	...	...	...	...	...	1905j	...	...	

c – Ⓒ only.
d – ⚒ only.
f – ⑤ (also July 13).
g – Also July 13.
j – Not July 4 - Aug. 25.
k – ①②③④⑥⑦ (not July 13, Aug. 14).
m – Also Aug. 16; not Aug. 15.
p – Not Aug. 16.
y – Not July 4 - Aug. 26.

318 BORDEAUX - LIBOURNE - BERGERAC - SARLAT

km		① K	Ⓐ	⚒				Ⓐ	Ⓒ		⚒	Ⓐ J				Ⓐ	Ⓐ		Ⓐ		⑥–④	⑤		
0	**Bordeaux** St Jean ▷ d.	...	0605	0705	...	0805	...	...	1005	...	1205	1305	1405	...	1605	1705	...	1805	1905	...	2005	2005	...	22
37	Libourne ▷ d.	...	0631	0732	...	0831	...	1031	1031	...	1235	1334	1431	...	1631	1735	1757	1835	1932	...	2031	2031	...	22
77	Ste Foy la Grande d.	...	0710	0810	...	0909	...	1109	1109	...	1309	1412	1511	...	1709	1810	1836	1909	2009	...	2109	2109	...	23
99	**Bergerac** a.	...	0730	0830	...	0928	...	1128	1128	...	1329	1433	1529	...	1728	1829	1857	1928	2029	...	2129	2128	...	23
99	**Bergerac** d.	0550	0733	...	...	0931	...	1132	1130	...	...	...	1532	...	1729	...	...	1930	...	...	...	2130	...	
135	Le Buisson d.	0627	0820	...	...	1018	...	1217	1218	...	...	...	1618	...	1820	...	...	2018	...	...	...	2205	...	
168	**Sarlat** a.	0658	0850	...	...	1046	...	1246	1246	...	...	...	1646	...	1850	...	...	2046	...	...	...	2235	...	

	Ⓐ J	Ⓐ	⚒	Ⓐ J		Ⓐ	†	⚒			Ⓐ J			Ⓐ	Ⓒ			Ⓑ			Ⓐ		A
Sarlat d.	...	...	...	...	...	0607	...	0707	...	0909	...	...	1105	...	1325	...	1505	...	...	1705	...	...	1909
Le Buisson d.	...	...	...	...	...	0641	...	0737	...	0938	...	...	1136	...	1356	...	1535	...	...	1736	...	...	1938
Bergerac a.	...	...	...	...	...	0728	...	0829	...	1029	...	...	1226	...	1429	...	1629	...	...	1829	...	...	2028
Bergerac d.	0536	0612	0628	0703	...	0732	0832	0833	...	1032	1132	...	1229	1436	1432	...	1632	1730	...	1832	1932	...	2032
Ste Foy la Grande d.	0555	0630	0649	0725	...	0751	0852	0852	...	1052	1151	...	1250	1455	1454	...	1652	1750	...	1852	1951	...	2052
Libourne ▷ a.	0627	0703	0725	0803	...	0824	0929	0929	...	1129	1226	...	1327	1527	1528	...	1727	1829	...	1926	2026	...	2129
Bordeaux St Jean ▷ a.	0655	0731	0755	...	...	0855	0955	0955	...	1155	1255	...	1355	...	1555	...	1755	1855	...	1955	2055	...	2155

A – ⑤† June 12 - July 1; daily July 3 - Aug. 28.
J – Until July 1.
K – Until June 27.
▷ – See also Tables **300** and **302**.

BORDEAUX - TOULOUSE 320

For Paris - Toulouse via Limoges see Table 310

	Ⓐ		⚒	4655 4654 ★	4657 4656 ★	*TGV* 8501 ①–⑥ k	4659 4658 ★		*TGV* 8503	4663 4662 ★	4665 4664 ★ ⑤g	4665 4664 ★ B	4665 4664 ★ Ⓒ	*TGV* 8507 ⑤ g	*TGV* 6857	*TGV* 8505 ⑥–④ m		4667 4666 ★ ⑤†y	Ⓐ	4669 4668 ★ r	*TGV* 8511		*TGV* 8513	*TGV* 8515 ⑤ g
Paris M'parnasse **300** d.	...	...	...	...	...	0628	...	...	0928	...	...	...	...	1128	...	1228	...	...	...	...	1528	...	1828	1928
Nantes **292** d.	...	...	...	...	...	|	...	...	|	...	...	...	...	|	...	|	...	...	...	...	|	...	|	|
Bordeaux St Jean d.	...	...	...	0731	0931	0947	1047	...	1247	1331	1440	1447	1447	1447	1538	1547	...	1644	...	1731	1847	...	2147	2247
Marmande d.	...	...	...	|	|	|	|	...	|	1410	|	|	|	|	|	|	...	|	...	1810	|	...	|	|
Agen d.	0625	0725	0825	0840	1040	1051	|	1225	1353	1441	|	|	|	1553	1642	1652	1714	|	1825	1841	1953	2025	2254	2352
Montauban d.	0714	0814	0912	0918	1118	1129	|	1314	1432	|	|	|	|	1631	1719	1729	1811	|	1913	1918	2032	2114	2332	0029
Toulouse Matabiau a.	0740	0840	0940	0944	1144	1155	1252	1355	1457	1544	1649	1649	1649	1657	1744	1755	1840	1845	1940	1944	2057	2140	2359	0055
Narbonne **321** a.	...	...	...	1100	1301	...	|	...	...	1701	|	|	|	...	1901	...	...	|	...	2101	...	...	...	...
Montpellier **355** a.	...	...	...	1200	1401	...	1459	...	...	1801	1857	1857	1857	...	1959	...	...	2057	...	2205	...	...	...	...
Marseille **355** a.	...	...	...	1350	1550	...	1642	...	...	1950	2042	2042	2042	...	...	...	...	2235	...	2351	...	...	...	...
Nice **360** a.	...	...	...	...	...	...	1937	...	...	...	2337	...	2337	...	...	...	...	...	...	...	...	...	...	...

	TGV 8500 ①–⑥ k	Ⓐ		*TGV* 8510	*TGV* 8512 ⑦ j		*TGV* 6809	4754 4755 ★	*TGV* 8514		4756 4757 ★		*TGV* 8516	4760 4761 ★			*TGV* 8518	4762 4763 ★		Ⓐ	4764 4765 ★		4768 4769 ★	
ice **360** d.	...	...	...	...	...	...	...	...	...	...	...	...	...	1024	...	...	...	...	...	...	...	...	1424f	...
arseille **355** d.	...	...	...	...	...	...	...	0818	...	...	1018	...	...	1318	...	...	...	1410	...	...	1518	...	1718	...
ontpellier **355** d.	...	...	...	...	...	...	0856	1003	...	...	1158	...	...	1458	...	...	...	1559	...	...	1658	...	1858	...
arbonne **321** d.	...	...	...	...	...	...	0958	1101	...	...	1301	...	...	|	...	...	...	1658	...	...	|	...	|	...
louse Matabiau d.	0604	0611	0722	0904	1104	...	1117	1220	1304	1322	1421	...	1604	1712	1722	...	1804	1817	...	1822	1912	1922	2112	...
tauban d.	0632	0640	0751	0932	1132	...	1144	|	1332	1349	1447	...	1632	|	1751	...	1832	1844	...	1851	|	1951	|	...
n d.	0710	0735	0837	1010	1209	...	1221	1321	1410	1437	1525	...	1710	|	1837	...	1910	1921	...	1937	|	2037	|	...
mande d.	|	...	...	|	|	...	|	1351	|	...	1555	...	|	|	...	...	|	1952	...	...	|	...	|	...
deaux St Jean a.	0813	...	...	1113	1312	...	1322	1429	1512	...	1632	...	1813	1913	...	...	2012	2029	...	...	2113	...	2313	...
Nantes **292** a.	|	...	...	|	|	...	...	...	|	...	...	...	|	...	...	...	|	...	...	...	...	...	...	...
aris M'parnasse **300** a.	1136	...	...	1439	1633	...	...	...	1833	...	...	...	2133	...	...	...	2333	...	...	...	...	...	...	...

Local services BORDEAUX - AGEN and v.v.

	Ⓐx	Ⓐk	Ⓐ		Ⓐ	⑥		Ⓑ			Ⓑ
deaux d.	0552	0638	0710	1052	1252	1252	1452	1652	1752	1855	2052
mande d.	0640	0740	0756	1140	1340	1352	1540	1740	1844	1944	2140
n a.	0715	0819	0830	1215	1415	1426	1615	1816	1919	2020	2215

	⚒	ⒶJ	⑥	Ⓐ	Ⓐ	†		⑥	Ⓐ		Ⓑ	Ⓑ		†
Agen d.	0447	0535	0610	0629	0745	0845	1045	1229	1245	1445	1643	1737	1845	1947
Marmande d.	0522	0611	0648	0707	0821	0921	1121	1305	1321	1521	1718	1813	1921	2021
Bordeaux a.	0608	0700	0754	0758	0908	1008	1210	1408	1408	1608	1808	1924	2008	2108

NOTES SEE TABLE 321 BELOW

TOULOUSE - CARCASSONNE - NARBONNE 321

	3731 🅁 ♦	*TGV* 6863 ♦	Ⓐ	⚒		4655 4654 ★	Ⓐ	*TGV* 6859	4657 4656 ★	Ⓐ	4659 4658 ★	Ⓒ	*TGV* 6861	4663 4662 ★	Ⓐ	4665 4664 ★ ⑤g	4665 4664 ★ B	4665 4664 ★ Ⓒ		*TGV* 6857		4667 4666 ★ ⑤†y	Ⓐ	4669 4668 ★ r
Paris Austerlitz **310** d.	2139	...	...	...	...	...	...	...	...	...	...	...	...	...	...	...	...	...	...	...	...	...	...	...
Bordeaux **320** d.	|	...	...	...	...	0731	...	...	0931	...	1047	...	...	1331	...	1440	1447	1447	...	1538	...	1644	...	1731
Toulouse Matabiau d.	|	0554	...	0715	0815	0949	1015	1049	1149	1215	1257	1315	1449	1549	1555	1654	1654	1654	1658	1749	1815	1850	1855	1949
Castelnaudary d.	0506	|	...	0752	0905	|	1105	|	|	1305	|	1405	|	|	1636	|	|	|	1736	|	1905	|	1936	|
Carcassonne d.	0525	|	0643	0816	0927	1032	1127	1134	1233	1327	|	1427	1534	1633	1658	|	|	|	1758	1834	1927	|	1958	2033
Lézignan d.	0545	|	0702	0835	0945	|	1145	|	|	1345	|	1444	|	|	1715	|	|	|	1815	|	1945	|	2015	|
Narbonne a.	0558	0700	0716	0849	0957	1100	1157	1201	1301	1357	|	1457	1601	1701	1728	|	|	|	1828	1901	1957	|	2028	2101
Montpellier **355** a.	|	0758	0830	...	...	1200	...	1259	1401	...	1459	...	1701	1801	...	1857	1857	1857	1933	1959	...	2057	...	2205
Marseille **355** a.	|	|	...	...	...	1350	...	|	1550	...	1642	...	|	1950	...	2042	2042	2042	...	|	...	2235	...	2351
Nice **360** a.	|	|	...	...	...	...	...	|	...	...	1937	...	|	...	...	2337	...	2337	...	|	...	...	...	...
Lyon Part Dieu **350** a.	|	0950	...	...	...	...	...	1454	...	...	...	...	1850	...	...	...	...	...	...	2150	...	...	...	...
Perpignan **355** a.	0712	...	...	...	...	...	...	...	...	...	...	...	...	...	...	...	...	...	...	...	...	...	...	...
Cerbère **355** a.	0800	...	...	...	...	...	...	...	...	...	...	...	...	...	...	...	...	...	...	...	...	...	...	...
Portbou **355** a.	0810	...	...	...	...	...	...	...	...	...	...	...	...	...	...	...	...	...	...	...	...	...	...	...

	Ⓐ	Ⓐ	⚒	*TGV* 6809	4754 4755 ★	*TGV* 6813		4756 4757 ★	Ⓐ	4760 4761 ★		Ⓐ	4762 4763 ★	Ⓐ	Ⓒ C	4764 4765 ★		A	4768 4769 ★	*TGV* 6817	4766 4767 ★ ⑤†z	3730 🅁 ♦	*TGV* 6824 H	*TGV* 6824 ⑦ a
erbère **355** d.	...	...	...	...	...	...	...	...	...	...	...	...	...	...	...	...	...	...	...	...	...	2005	...	...
erpignan **355** d.	...	...	...	...	...	...	...	...	...	...	...	...	...	...	...	...	...	...	...	...	...	2055	...	...
yon Part Dieu **350** d.	...	...	...	0706	...	0936	...	...	...	...	...	...	...	...	...	...	...	...	...	1810	...	|	1936	1936
lice **360** d.	...	...	...	|	...	|	...	...	...	1022	...	...	...	...	...	...	...	...	1424f	|	...	|	|	|
larseille **355** d.	...	...	...	|	0818	|	...	1018	...	1318	...	...	1410	...	...	1518	...	...	1718	|	1918	|	|	|
lontpellier **355** d.	...	...	0613	0856	1003	1127	...	1158	...	1458	...	...	1559	1620	...	1658	...	...	1858	2005	2103	|	2130	2137
bonne d.	0632	0702	0732	0958	1101	1227	1232	1301	1500	|	1602	1632	1658	1732	1732	|	1804	1917	|	2104	2201	2213	2228	2232
ignan d.	0645	0715	0745	|	|	|	1245	|	1514	|	1615	1645	|	1745	1745	|	1817	1930	|	|	|	2228	|	|
cassonne d.	0704	0734	0804	1029	1132	1259	1304	1331	1536	|	1635	1709	1729	1804	1804	|	1836	1949	|	2135	2232	2249	2259	2301
stelnaudary d.	0724	0755	0824	|	|	|	1324	|	1556	|	1656	1729	|	1824	1824	|	1856	2009	|	|	|	2310	|	|
ulouse Matabiau a.	0804	0845	0904	1112	1215	1340	1404	1416	1645	1707	1745	1808	1812	1904	1904	1907	1945	2058	2107	2217	2316	2337	2341	2343
Bordeaux **320** a.	...	...	...	1322	1429	...	...	1632	...	1913	...	...	2029	...	...	2113	...	...	2313	...	...	|	...	...
Paris Austerlitz **310** a.	...	...	...	...	...	...	...	...	...	...	...	...	...	...	...	...	...	...	...	...	...	0723	...	...

ADDITIONAL LOCAL TRAINS

	Ⓐ	Ⓐ		Ⓐ	Ⓒ	ⒶJ	Ⓐ	Ⓐ	Ⓐ	
ulouse Matabiau d.	...	0615	0655	...	...	...	...	1715	1755	1955
stelnaudary d.	0555	0705	0736	...	...	...	...	1805	1836	2045
rcassonne d.	0617	0727	0756	1011	1113	1727	1823	1826	1858	2106
zignan d.	0634	0745	...	1032	1132	1745	1842	...	1915	...
rbonne a.	0647	0757	...	1045	1145	1757	1855	...	1928	...

	Ⓐ		Ⓐ	Ⓐ	Ⓒ			Ⓒ	Ⓐ	ⒶJ	
Narbonne d.	...	...	0808	0908	1009	...	...	...	1708	1832	...
Lézignan d.	...	...	0821	0921	1022	...	...	...	1721	1845	...
Carcassonne d.	0602	0636	0840	0944	1042	1202	...	1536	1740	1904	...
Castelnaudary d.	0624	0656	...	...	...	1224	...	1556	...	...	...
Toulouse Matabiau a.	0704	0745	...	...	...	1304	...	1645	...	...	...

– **NOTES FOR TABLES 320/1** (LISTED BY TRAIN NUMBER):

30 – Not Oct. 22, 29, 30, 31: 🛏 1,2 cl., 🚃2 (reclining) Cerbère - Paris. Train number **3732** July 1 - Sept. 4.

31 – Not Oct. 22, 29, 30, 31: 🛏 1,2 cl., 🚃2 (reclining) Paris - Portbou. Train number **3733** July 1 - Sept. 4.

te: some night services are expected to be withdrawn during the currency of this timetable.

63 – 🚃12 🍷 Toulouse - Montpellier - Lyon - Dijon - Nancy.

- Daily June 12 - 24; Ⓐ June 27 - Aug. 26.
- ①②③④ (not July 13, 14, Aug. 15).
- June 25 - Aug. 28.
- ①②③④⑥ (not July 13).
- Until July 1.

a – Also June 17, 24, July 1, 8, 15.
f – ①⑥† (also July 15, Aug. 16).
g – Also July 13.
j – Also Aug. 15.
k – Not Aug. 15.
m – Not July 13.
r – Not June 18.
x – Also July 15, Aug. 16; not Aug. 15.
y – Also July 13; not July 14, Aug. 14.
z – Also July 13, Aug. 15; not Aug. 14.

TGV – 🅁, supplement payable, 🍷.

★ – *Intercités* service, 🅁.

323 TOULOUSE - ALBI - RODEZ - MILLAU

km																								
		Ⓐ			R	S		Ⓐ				Ⓐ	Ⓐ		Ⓐ		Ⓐ		Ⓐ	†		⚒	P🅁	
0	**Toulouse** Matabiau .... 317 d.	0607	0727	0915	1006	...	1116	1231	1307	1412	...	1638	1713	1737	1752	...	1814	1837	1914	1914	...	1928	...	2
54	Gaillac .... 317 d.	0647	0812	1004	1051	1052	1158	1318	1358	1500	...	1725	1757	1823	1841	...	1905	1922	2003	2003	...	2019	...	2
75	**Albi Ville** .... d.	0704	0826	1024	...	1108	1216	1338	1418	1514	...	1744	1819	1837	1902	...	1924	1935	2024	2025	...	2035	2053	2
92	Carmaux .... d.	0722	0843	1039	...	1124	1233	1354	1433	1533	...	1802	...	1854	1918	...	...	1952	...	2041	...	2051	2112	2
158	**Rodez** .... a.	0823	0946	...	...	1221	1332	...	...	1632	...	...	...	1952	...	...	...	2049	...	2138	...	2150	2209	2

	Ⓐ	⚒	Ⓐ		Ⓐ	P🅁						Ⓐ		Ⓐ				Ⓐ				†	
Rodez .... d.	...	...	...	...	0622	0644	0739**d**	0837	...	1026	...	1224	...	...	1435	...	1638	1730	...	1845	...	2055	2
Carmaux .... d.	0522	0558	0618	0646	0723	0739	0844	0933	...	1125	1143	1321	...	1457	1532	1650	1736	1827	...	1953	...	2203	2
Albi Ville .... d.	0538	0614	0634	0705	0741	0758	0901	0949	...	1141	1200	1340	...	1515	1548	1706	1753	1845	...	2009	...	2220	2
Gaillac .... 317 d.	0556	0632	0657	0725	0756	...	0919	1003	...	1158	1221	1358	...	1534	1601	1725	1808	1905	...	2031	...	2233	2
Toulouse Matabiau .... 317 a.	0646	0719	0743	0820	0836	...	1002	1043	...	1237	1310	1437	...	1619	1641	1817	1850	1954	...	2118	...	2314	2

km										
			⑥		Ⓑ		⑥	Ⓐ		†
		T								n
0	**Rodez** .... d.	0624	0635	...	1351	...	1715	1916	...	2038
44	Sévérac-le-Château **332** . d.	0707	0718	...	1435	...	1758	1959	...	2130
74	**Millau 332** .... a.	0739	0750	...	1507	...	1830	2031	...	2202

	①	Ⓑ		©		⑤	①–④		①–④	
	z					g	w		w	
Millau 332 .... d.	0455	0907	...	1523	...	1629	1753	...	2046	2
Sévérac-le-Château **332**. d.	0527	0939	...	1554	...	1707	1823	...	2116	2
Rodez .... d.	0608	1020	...	1635	...	1748	1906	...	2159	2

P – 🛏 1, 2 cl. and 🪑2 (reclining) Paris - Brive - Rodez - Albi and v.v. For days of running see Table **316**.
Note: some night services are expected to be withdrawn during the currency of this timetable.
R – ①⑤ (not Aug. 15).
S – ①⑤ (also July 13, Aug. 16; not Aug. 15).
T – ②③④⑤ (not Aug. 16).

d – ⚒ only.
g – Also July 13.
n – Not Aug. 14.
w – Not July 13, 14, Aug. 15.
z – Also Aug. 16; not Aug. 15.

324 PAU - OLORON - CANFRANC

36 km	S			D	R		Q	⑤†		⑤K
Pau .... d.	0730	0920	...	1225	1407	1533	1710	1834	1855	2025	2150
Oloron-Ste-Marie ..... a.	0806	0956	...	1301	1443	1609	1746	1910	1931	2101	2226

	①p	C	⑥q	†r	T		F	©L	Ⓐ			Q	⑤
Oloron-Ste-Marie .. d.	0639	0646	0722	0802	0812	1005	1310	1321	1450	1616	1753	1935	1
Pau .... a.	0715	0722	0758	0838	0848	1041	1346	1357	1526	1652	1829	2011	2

🚌 OLORON - CANFRANC (rail tickets valid). Canfranc buses continue to / from Somport, 11 mins beyond Canfranc. 🚌 subject to confirmation

54 km	Ⓐ						Ⓑ	Y	⑤
Oloron-Ste-Marie .... d.	0815	...	1005	...	1450	...	1810	1920	1940
Bedous (Gare) .... d.	0848	...	1038	...	1523	...	1843	1953	2013
Urdos (Douane) 🏛 .... d.	0910	...	1100	...	1545	...	1905	2015	2035
Canfranc (Gare) .... 670 a.	0928	...	1118	...	1603	...	...	...	...

	Ⓐ	Ⓐ	©	Ⓐ		†	Y	⑤
Canfranc (Gare) .... 670 d.	...	1141	1151	1321	...	1626	1806	1811
Urdos (Douane) 🏛 .... d.	0650	1158	1208	1338	...	1643	1823	1828
Bedous (Gare) .... d.	0713	1221	1231	1401	...	1706	1846	1851
Oloron-Ste-Marie .... a.	0749	1257	1307	1437	...	1742	1922	1927

C – ②–⑤ June 14 - July 1; Ⓐ July 4 - Aug. 26 (also Aug. 15; not Aug. 16).
D – Daily June 12 - 25; ⚒ July 26 - Aug. 27.
F – Ⓐ June 13 - 24; daily June 26 - Aug. 28.
K – Until June 24.
L – Until June 25.

Q – ①②③④⑥ (not July 14, Aug. 15).
R – Ⓐ June 13 - July 1; ⚒ July 2 - Aug. 27.
S – Ⓐ June 13 - July 1; daily July 3 - Aug. 28.
T – Ⓐ June 13 - 24; Ⓑ June 26 - Aug. 28.
Y – ①②③④⑥ only.

a – Not June 24.
p – June 13 - 27 (also Aug. 16).
q – June 18 - 25.
r – June 12 - 19.

325 TOULOUSE - TARBES - PAU - BAYONNE - HENDAYE

km									**14143**		**14145**						**14151**					**14155**			
		Ⓐ	Ⓐ	⑥	Ⓐ					Ⓐ				⚒	Ⓐ	⑤		†	⑤		Ⓐ				
						A				h						J								B	
0	**Toulouse** Matabiau .... d.	...	...	...	0600	...	0731	0931	1031	...	1231	1241	...	1441	...	1600	1613	...	...	1736	1806	1831	1941	...	20
91	St Gaudens .... d.	...	...	...	0718	...	0828	1027	1121	...	|	1354	...	1554	...	1654	1712	...	...	1830	1903	|	2054	...	21
104	Montréjeau .... d.	...	...	...	0728	...	0838	1037	|	...	1328	1404	...	1604	...	1704	|	...	...	1840	1913	|	2104	...	22
121	Lannemezan .... d.	...	...	...	0740	...	0850	1049	|	...	|	1416	...	1617	...	1716	|	...	...	1852	1925	1938	2116	...	22
158	**Tarbes** .... 305 d.	...	0628	0635	0808	...	0919	1117	1205	1305	1404	1445	...	1645	...	1745	1757	...	...	1922	1951	2004	2145	...	22
179	Lourdes .... 305 d.	...	0647	0651	0824	...	...	...	1223j	1320	1421j	1503f	...	1703	...	...	1814	...	...	1942	...	2021	2205	...	23
218	**Pau** .... 305 d.	0614	0721	0730	0851	0936	...	...	1251j	1348	1449j	1533f	...	1730	1736	...	1843	1936	1937	2011	...	2049	2232	2246	
258	Orthez .... 305 d.	0638	0745	0800	...	1000	...	...	1314j	...	1513j	...	...	...	1800	...	1907	2000	2001	...	...	2114	...	2310	
272	Puyoô .... 305 d.	0649	0756	0813	...	1011	...	...	|	...	|	...	...	...	1811	...	|	2011	2011	...	...	|	...	2321	
323	**Bayonne** § .... 305 a.	0737	0837	0858	...	1058	...	...	1358j	...	1556j	...	...	...	1858	...	1954	2059	2051	...	...	2156	...	2358	
323	**Bayonne** § .... 305 d.	...	...	...	...	...	...	...	...	...	...	...	...	...	...	...	2021	...	...	...	...	...	...	...	
333	Biarritz § .... 305 d.	...	...	...	...	...	...	...	...	...	...	...	...	...	...	...	2031	...	...	...	...	...	...	...	
346	St Jean de Luz .... 305 d.	...	...	...	...	...	...	...	...	...	...	...	...	...	...	...	2043	...	...	...	...	...	...	...	
359	Hendaye .... 305 a.	...	...	...	...	...	...	...	...	...	...	...	...	...	...	...	2053	...	...	...	...	...	...	...	
361	**Irún** .... 305 a.	...	...	...	...	...	...	...	...	...	...	...	...	...	...	...	...	...	...	...	...	...	...	...	

									14340	**14240**	**14140**			**14144**				**14148**	**14148**			**14150**		
	Ⓐ	©	⑥	Ⓑ	①		Ⓐ	⚒	†	⑥	Ⓐ		Ⓐ			Ⓐ		⑤			Ⓑ		†	
					m	K								j		j				Ⓑ				
Hendaye .... 305 d.	...	...	...	...	...	...	...	...	...	0656	0656	...	...	...	...	...	...	...	1456e	...	...	...	...	
St Jean de Luz .... 305 d.	...	...	...	...	...	...	...	...	...	0711	0711	...	...	...	...	...	...	...	1508e	...	...	...	...	
Biarritz § .... 305 d.	...	...	...	...	...	...	...	...	...	0724	0724	...	...	...	...	...	...	...	1522e	...	...	...	...	
Bayonne § .... 305 a.	...	...	...	...	...	...	...	...	...	0733	0733	...	...	...	...	...	...	...	1531e	...	...	...	...	
Bayonne § .... 305 d.	...	...	...	...	...	...	0608	0704	0805	0805	0805	...	...	1203	...	1411	...	...	1603	...	1724	1802	2002	
Puyoô .... 305 d.	...	...	...	...	...	...	0646	0745	|	|	|	...	...	|	...	1448	...	...	|	...	1806	|	2048	
Orthez .... 305 d.	...	...	...	...	...	...	0657	0756	|	|	|	...	...	|	...	1459	...	...	1652	...	1817	1854	2059	
Pau .... 305 d.	...	...	0549	0555	0706	...	0727	0823	0913	0915	0919	0955k	1214n	1317	...	1525	1550f	...	1716	1753	1847	1918	2133	
Lourdes .... 305 d.	0528	0520	0618	0626	0734	...	0803	...	0944	0944	0948	1026k	1242n	1348	...	...	1619f	...	1742	1822	1921	1945	2206	
Tarbes .... 305 d.	0543	0535	0635	0642	0800	0820	0821	...	1000	1000	1004	1042	1300	1405	1520	...	1635	1800	1800	1841	1938	2003	2222	
Lannemezan .... d.	0610	0602	0703	0710	0827	0847	...	...	|	|	|	1110	1328	1431	1547	...	1704	|	|	1910	...	2027	...	
Montréjeau .... d.	0623	0614	0716	0722	0839	0859	...	...	|	|	|	1122	1340	|	1559	...	1717	|	|	1923	...	|	...	
St Gaudens .... d.	0633	0624	0725	0732	0848	0909	...	...	1044	1043	1047	1132	1350	|	1609	...	1726	1842	1842g	1932	...	|	...	
Toulouse Matabiau .... a.	0730	0735	0830	0830	1001	1021	...	...	1132	1132	1134	1230	1446	1542	1722	...	1829	1930	1932g	2030	...	2141	...	

TOULOUSE - LUCHON *For connections Toulouse - Montréjeau see also main table.*

	🚌 ⚒	Ⓐ	🚌	🚌	🚌 ⚒	🚌 ⚒	Ⓐ		🚌	Ⓐ		🚌
Paris Aust. **310** ..... d.	...	...	...	...	...	...	...	...	...	...	...	...
Toulouse Mat. .... d.	...	0741	...	...	...	...	1630	1700	...	1741	1900	...
St Gaudens .... d.	...	0855	...	...	...	...	1739	1818	...	1851	2018	...
Montréjeau .... d.	0800	0904	0932	1121	1420	1608	1750	1826	1853	1859	2026	2111
Luchon .... ◐ a.	0852	...	1022	1213	1509	1700	...	...	1945	...	...	2203

	Ⓐ	Ⓐ	Ⓐ	🚌 ⚒	🚌		🚌 †	🚌 ⚒	🚌 ⚒		🚌 ⑥	🚌 ©
Luchon .... d.	...	...	...	0841	0941	...	1223	1454	1605	...	1740	18
Montréjeau .... d.	0523	0557	0641	0935	1035	1155	1317	1548	1655	1804	1834	19
St Gaudens .... d.	0532	0606	0650	...	...	1204	...	...	...	1813	...	
Toulouse Mat. ...... a.	0647	0723	0759	...	...	1322	...	...	...	1922	...	
Paris Aust. **310** . a.	...	...	...	...	...	...	...	...	...	...	...	

A – Ⓐ June 13 - 24; daily July 9 - Aug. 28 (also July 3).
B – ⑤† June 12 - July 3; daily July 4 - Aug. 28.
J – Until July 1.
K – ②③④⑤⑥ (not Aug. 16).

e – † only.
f – ⑤ (also July 13).
g – Daily **except** ⑤.
h – Not Ⓐ June 20 - 24.

j – Not Ⓐ June 13 - 24.
k – Not Ⓐ June 27 - July 8.
m – Also Aug. 16; not Aug. 15.
n – Not Ⓐ June 27 - July 1.

◐ – Luchon - Montréjeau is *35* km.
§ – 🚌 services available to / from Biarritz town.

BRIVE LA GAILLARD and LIMOGES - USSEL - CLERMONT FERRAND 326

BRIVE - USSEL

		4490		🚌	4492					
	Ⓐ		Ⓒ	Ⓐ	⑥		Ⓑ		†	
		F			u	◇	t		t	
Bordeaux 302 d.	...	0735	...	...	0910	...	...	...	...	...
Brive la Gaillarde ▷ d.	0620	0957	1019	1107	1116	1346	1710	1832	1920	...
Tulle ▷ d.	0652	1039z	1050	1147	1154r	1417	1751r	1910	1951	...
Meymac d.	0747	1145	1145	1255	1256	1511	1845	2008	2044	...
Ussel a.	0758	1157	1157	1317	1309	1523	1858	2019	2057	...

							4591			
	Ⓐ	⑥				⑤⑦		①-④	⑥	Ⓑ
		k		⊖		d	E	w	k	t
Ussel d.	0545	0935	...	1205	...	1545	1626	1631	1716	1954
Meymac d.	0558	0948	...	1218	...	1559	1641	1644	1729	2007
Tulle ▷ d.	0656	1046	...	1315	...	1703r	1749r	1745r	1827	2107
Brive la Gaillarde ▷ a.	0725	1111	...	1340	...	1729	1811	1812	1853	2133
Bordeaux 302 a.	...	...	...	...	...	...	2028	...	...	...

LIMOGES - USSEL ⊠

	①							Ⓐ	Ⓑ	
	g								t	
Limoges d.	0557	...	1001	...	1319	...	1802	1937	2109	...
Meymac d.	0732	...	1132	...	1454	...	1938	2109	2237	...
Ussel a.	0744	...	1143	...	1506	...	1950	2121	2249	...

	Ⓐ	⑥							⑤⑦	
		k	M				B		d	
Ussel d.	0632	0702	0813	1031	1219	...	1353	...	1603	1754
Meymac d.	0645	0715	0826	1045	1232	...	1406	...	1616	1807
Limoges a.	0819	0849	0959	1223	1402	...	1536	...	1747	1947

🚌 USSEL and LE MONT DORE - CLERMONT FERRAND 🚌

	🚌	🚌	🚌	🚌	🚌	🚌	🚌	🚌	🚌	🚌	🚌	🚌	🚌	🚌	🚌
	⚒	⚒	†			⑥		Ⓒ		⑤⑦		⑤	⑤	†	Ⓑ
							E			f	H	v	v		
Ussel d.	0818	...	1008	...	1207	1319	...	1511	...	...	...	...	1915	...	2033
Eygurande-Merlines d.	0838	...	1028	...	1227	1339	...	1531	...	...	...	...	1935	...	2053
Le Mont Dore d.	|	0843	|	1045	|	|	1454	|	1535	1730	1745	1930	|	2048	|
La Bourboule d.	|	0851	|	1053	|	|	1502	|	1542	1738	1753	1938	|	2056	|
Laqueuille d.	0858	0903	1048	1105	1247	1359	1515	1550	1556	1750	1805	1950	1955	2108	2113
Clermont Ferrand a.	...	1003	...	1229	1347	1459	...	...	1722	*1909*	1910	...	2055	...	2213

	🚌	🚌	🚌	🚌	🚌	🚌	🚌	🚌	🚌	🚌	🚌	🚌	🚌	🚌	🚌
			†		①-⑥			⚒	⚒			Ⓐ	⑤	⑤	†
			n		⊡	G	E			D			v	v	
Clermont Ferrand d.	1010	...	*1246*	1305	...	1424	...	1600	...	*1738*e	1804	1948	...	*2119*	*2145*
Laqueuille d.	1110	1115	1351	1424	1436	1524	1529	1700	1705	1859	1904	2048	2053	2214	2240
La Bourboule a.	|	1127	|	1438	|	|	1542	|	1719	1911	|	2100	|	2226	2252
Le Mont Dore a.	|	1133	|	1445	|	|	1549	|	1726	1919	|	2108	|	2234	2300
Eygurande-Merlines d.	1130	...	1411	...	1456	1544	...	1720	...	...	1924	...	2111	...	...
Ussel a.	1150	...	1431	...	1516	1604	...	1740	...	...	1944	...	2131	...	...

)②③④⑥ (also Nov. 11; not July 13, 14, Aug. 15, Nov. 1, 10).
🚌 runs 7 minutes later on †.
⑦ to June 26; Ⓑ July 1 - Aug. 31 (not Aug. 14); ⑤⑦ from Sept. 2 (also Oct. 20, 24–27, 31, Nov. 1, 2, 10; not Nov. 11).
) to June 24; Ⓐ July 1 - Aug. 31; ⑤ from Sept. 2 (also Oct. 20, 24–27, 31, Nov. 2; not Nov. 11).
⑦ to June 26; Ⓑ July 1 - Aug. 28 (not July 14, Aug. 15); ⑤⑦ from Sept. 2 (also Nov. 10; not Nov. 11).
)②③④⑥ (not July 13, 14, Aug. 15, Nov. 1, 10).

M – ① to June 27; Ⓐ July 4 - Aug. 26; ① from Aug. 29 (also Nov. 2).
d – Also July 13, 14, Aug. 15, Nov. 1, 10; not Nov. 11.
e – *1726* on ⑥; *1745* on †. By train to Volvic, then 🚌 (d. 1809 **D**).
f – Also July 13, 14, Aug. 15, Nov. 1, 10.
g – Also Nov. 2; not July 4 - Aug. 22.
k – Also Nov. 11.
n – Also Aug. 31, Nov. 2, 12; not Nov. 11.
r – Arrives 10–15 minutes earlier.
t – Not Nov. 11.
u – Also Nov. 11; not Nov. 12. On June 4, July 2 departs Bordeaux 0852, Brive 1107, Tulle 1145, Meymac 1301, arrives Ussel 1314.
v – Also July 13, Nov. 10; not Nov. 11.
w – Not July 4 - Aug. 31, Oct. 10–13, 20–31, Nov. 1, 2, 10.
z – Arrives 1020.

◇ – Subject to alteration Oct. 10–13, Nov. 7–10, 14–17.
⊖ – Subject to alteration Nov. 7–10, 14–17.
⊠ – Subject to alteration on Sept. 5 - Oct. 28.
⊡ – ①-⑥ (not July 14, Aug. 15, Nov. 1, 12). Runs 13 minutes **earlier** on ⑥ (also Nov. 11).
▷ – Additional local trains run Brive - Tulle and v.v.

MONTLUÇON - LYON 327

For other rail journeys via Riom - Châtel-Guyon see Tables **328** and **329**. Services Vichy - Lyon and v.v. are subject to alteration Oct. 29 - Nov. 1.

	🚌		🚌		🚌		🚌		🚌	
	①g	⚒	⚒	⊡	Ⓐ	Ⓐd			†	⑦w
Montluçon 329 d.	0503	...	0721	...	0950	...	1600	...	1834	...
Gannat 329 d.	0621	...	0841	...	|	...	|	...	|	...
St Germain des Fossés d.	|	...	|	...	1115	1138	|	...	|	...
Vichy **330** d.	0646	0659	0910	0929	...	|	|	...	2009	2028
Roanne 328 d.	...	0749	...	1016	...	1220	1810	1845	...	2116
Lyon Part Dieu 328 a.	...	0856	...	1120	...	1326	...	|	...	2219
Lyon Perrache 328 a.	...	0917	...	1131	...	1340	...	2020	...	2229

	◇	🚌		🚌		🚌		🚌		🚌
	Ⓐd	Ⓐ				⑤⑦j		A		⑤⑦j
Lyon Perrache 328 d.	0900	...	1000	...	1629	...	1729	...	2029	...
Lyon Part Dieu 328 d.	0912	...	1012	...	1640	...	1740	...	2040	...
Roanne 328 d.	1024	...	1130	1230	1745	...	1847	...	2145	...
Vichy **330** d.	|	...	...	|	1831	1845	1933	2004	2231	2245
St Germain des Fossés d.	1107	1136	...	|	...	|	...	|	...	|
Gannat 329 d.	...	|	...	|	...	|	...	2034	...	2315
Montluçon 329 a.	...	1302	...	1435	...	2012	...	2152	...	0034

Runs 9 minutes **earlier** on †.
Not Oct. 31.

g – Also Aug. 16, Sept. 1, Nov. 2, 3; not Aug. 15.
j – Also July 13, 14, Aug. 15, Nov. 1, 10.
w – Also July 14, Aug. 15.

⊡ – Subject to alteration on ①-⑤ Oct. 10–28.
◇ – Subject to alteration Oct. 17–21 and from Nov. 28.

CLERMONT FERRAND - LYON 328

Timings of services from Clermont Ferrand to Lyon may vary by up to 4 minutes until July 10. Services Clermont Ferrand - Lyon and v.v. are subject to alteration Oct. 29 - Nov. 1.

	⚒	Ⓐn	⊡	⊕	⊕	Ⓑr		Ⓑr	⑦w	
Clermont Ferrand ★ d.	0626	0701	0857	1157	1357	1457	1657	1757	1957	...
Riom - Châtel-Guyon ★ d.	0636	|	0907	1207	1406	1507	1706	1806	2006	...
Vichy **330** d.	0659	|	0929	1229	1428	1528	1729	1828	2028	...
St Germain des Fossés d.	|	|	|	|	|	|	|	|	|	...
Roanne **290** ▶ d.	0749	|	1016	1316	1516	1616	1816	1916	2116	...
Lyon Part Dieu **290** ▶ a.	0856	0918	1120	1420	1620	1720	1920	2020	2219	...
Lyon Perrache **290** ⊠ a.	0917	0930	1131	1435	1631	1733	1935	2031	2229	...

	⚒		⊗					ⒶL	
Lyon Perrache **290** ⊠ d.	0629	...	1129	1429	1629	1729	1829	1929	2029
Lyon Part Dieu **290** ▶ d.	0640	...	1140	1440	1640	1740	1840	1940	2040
Roanne **290** ▶ d.	0745	...	1245	1545	1745	1847	1943	|	2145
St Germain des Fossés d.	|	...	|	|	|	|	|	|	|
Vichy **330** d.	0832	...	1333	1632	1832	1934	2030	|	2232
Riom - Châtel-Guyon ▷ d.	0859	...	1359	1658	1858	2000	2055	|	2258
Clermont Ferrand ▷ a.	0908	...	1408	1707	1907	2010	2104	2158	2308

CLERMONT FERRAND - ST ÉTIENNE

	🚌		🚌	🚌	🚌				🚌	
	⚒	Ⓐ		Ⓐ✤	Ⓒ✤	Ⓐ⊙	⚒	†		Ⓐ
Clermont Ferrand d.	0700	0902	0925	1050	1250	1414	1622	1739	1920	1937
Thiers d.	0815	0950	|	1154	1354	1459	1705	1822	|	2024
Montbrison d.	|	...	|	1330	1530	1614	...	1937	|	...
St Étienne Châteaucreux a.	0956	...	1110	1419	1619	1652	...	2008	2105	...

			🚌			🚌	🚌		🚌
	⚒	⚒		Ⓐ⊙	†	⚒✤		Ⓐ	Ⓒ✤
St Étienne Châteaucreux d.	...	...	0720	0808	1216	1216	1720	...	1800
Montbrison d.	...	...	|	0848	1257	1302	|	...	1855
Thiers d.	0706	0759	|	0959	1412	1427	|	1929	2022
Clermont Ferrand a.	0752	0854	0905	1046	1455	1542	1905	2014	2132

From July 4.
Not Oct. 10–31.
To Lyon Perrache (not Part-Dieu).
Not Nov. 11.
Also July 14, Aug. 15.

⊡ – Subject to alteration on ①-⑤ Oct. 10–28.
⊗ – Subject to alteration on ①-⑤ Oct. 10–28, Nov. 10, 12, 14–18, 21–25.
⊕ – Subject to alteration Oct. 17–21 and ①-⑤ from Nov. 28.
⊙ – Subject to alteration on ①-⑤ July 4 - Aug. 26 and ①-⑤ Oct. 17 - Nov. 4.
⊠ – Services may not run to / from Lyon Perrache Nov. 11–13.
✤ – Subject to confirmation.
▷ – See also Tables **329** and **330**.

▶ – Other trains Roanne - Lyon Part Dieu (journey 73–95 minutes):
From Roanne at 0503 Ⓐ, 0603, 0625 Ⓐ, 0706 ⚒, 0718 †, 0728 ⚒, 0831 ⚒, 0931, 1131, 1245 **p**, 1445 Ⓐ **p**, 1645 ⚒ **p**, 1745 Ⓑ **p** and 1845 **p**.
From Lyon Part Dieu at 0612 ⚒, 0712, 0812 ⚒, 1012, 1212, 1412 Ⓐ, 1512 ⚒, 1612, 1712 ⚒, 1812, 1912 Ⓐ, 2012 Ⓑ and 2112.

MONTLUÇON - CLERMONT FERRAND 329

	⑥	Ⓐ	Ⓐ		Ⓐ			Ⓑ		†
				E	⊙	⊙				
Montluçon 327 d.	...	0600	0700	0828	1036	1221	...	1703	1844	1936
Commentry d.	...	0612	0711	0840	1047	1235	...	1716	1857	1948
Gannat **327** d.	0703	0706	0802	0926	1133	1327	1626	1804	1949	2043
Riom - Châtel-Guyon ▷ d.	0729	0732	0825	0944	1153	1346	1651	1831	2009	2101
Clermont Ferrand ▷ a.	0742	0743	0836	0953	1202	1356	1702	1840	2019	2110

	Ⓐ	①		⚒		Ⓑ	⚒	Ⓑ	⑤	†
		g		⊗	⊖				f	
Clermont Ferrand ▷ d.	0603	0634	0747	1218	1401	1648	1746	1910	2004	2012
Riom - Châtel-Guyon ▷ d.	0613	0644	0759	1230	1413	1702	1758	1923	2015	2022
Gannat **327** d.	0630	0707	0820	1249	1437	1727	1824	1950	2034	2042
Commentry d.	0721	0811	0909	1344	...	1818	1917	2041	2125	2132
Montluçon 327 a.	0734	0823	0920	1355	...	1829	1927	2051	2135	2143

①⑥⑦ (also July 14, 15, Aug. 16, Nov. 1, 2, 11).
Also July 13, Nov. 10; not Nov. 11.
Also July 15, Aug. 16, Nov. 2; not Aug. 15.

⊗ – Subject to alteration on ①-⑤ Sept. 26 - Oct. 7, Oct. 17–21 and ①-⑤ from Nov. 28.
⊙ – Subject to alteration on ①-⑤ Sept. 26 - Oct. 7.

⊖ – Subject to alteration on ①-⑤ Oct. 10–21 and ①-⑤ from Nov. 14.
▷ – See also Tables **328** and **330**.

330 PARIS - NEVERS - CLERMONT FERRAND

Warning! Subject to alteration June 11, 12, Oct. 29 - Nov. 1.

km							5951		5955				5959	5963			5967		5971	5973		5977	5979	5983
							🄡★		🄡★				🄡★	🄡★			🄡★		🄡★	🄡★		🄡★	🄡★	🄡★
		⚒	⚒J	Ⓐ	⚒	Ⓑ	①–⑥	⚒		⚒	⚒	Ⓐ			E	Ⓐ	⑤	Ⓐ		ⒶJ	Ⓑ	ⒶJ	B	A
		z					b	♠		⊙	D⊙	⊙					f							
0	**Paris** Bercy ▶ d.	...	...	...	...	...	0700	...	0900	...	...	...	1300	1400	...	...	1500	...	1600	1700	...	1800	1800	1900
254	**Nevers** ▶ d.	...	...	...	0700	...	0859	...	1059	...	...	...	1459	1559	...	...	1659	...	1759	1859	...	|	1959	2059
314	Moulins sur Allier d.	0602	0639	0709	0742	0812	0928	...	1128	1212	1308	1411	1528	1628	1642	1712	1728	1740	1828	1929	1937	|	2028	2128
355	St Germain des Fossés ▷ d.	0627	0708	0739	0809	0838	|	1140	|	1238	1337	1438	|	|	1709	1739	|	1807	|	|	2001	|	|	|
365	Vichy ▷ d.	0635	0717	0748	0817	0846	0955	1149	1155	1247	1345	1447	1555	1655	1717	1747	1755	1815	1855	1956	2009	|	2055	2155
406	Riom - Châtel-Guyon ▷ d.	0700	0744	0814	0842	0912	1022	1215	1222	1314	1411	1514	1623	1723	1742	1812	1822	1841	1922	2023	2036	|	2122	2223
420	**Clermont Ferrand** ▷ a.	0709	0753	0823	0851	0920	1031	1226	1231	1323	1422	1523	1632	1732	1750	1821	1831	1850	1931	2032	2047	2108	2131	2232

SEE NOTE ⊠	5948	5950	5954		5958			5962		5966			5970	5974		5978			5982			5986		5990
	🄡★	🄡★	🄡★		🄡★			🄡★		🄡★			🄡★	🄡★		🄡★			🄡★			🄡★		🄡★
	①	②–⑤	ⒶJ	Ⓐ	⑥	Ⓐ	⚒		⑥	①–⑥	⚒	⚒		⑦	Ⓐ		Ⓐ	Ⓐ	Ⓑ		⚒J	⑦		
	g	w			k					b		⊗	⊗	e		⊗			h	D		e		❦
Clermont Ferrand ▷ d.	0528	0532	0559	0612	0632	0640	0743	0832	0842	1032	1042	1242	1332	1432	1542	1628	1641	1710	1728	1742	1812	1832	1842	1932
Riom - Châtel-Guyon ▷ d.	0538	0542	|	0621	0642	0650	0752	0842	0851	1042	1051	1251	1343	1442	1551	1643	1651	1719	1742	1751	1821	1843	1851	1943
Vichy ▷ d.	0601	0605	|	0644	0705	0712	0814	0905	0914	1105	1114	1314	1405	1505	1614	1705	1714	1742	1805	1814	1844	1905	1914	2005
St Germain des Fossés ▷ d.	0610	|	|	0652	|	0721	0822	|	0922	|	1122	1322	|	|	1622	|	1722	1750	|	1822	1853	|	1922	|
Moulins sur Allier d.	0631	0631	|	0719	0731	0749	0846	0931	0948	1131	1150	1348	1431	1531	1650	1731	1750	1815	1831	1849	1918	1931	1950	2031
Nevers ▶ d.	0701	0701	|	0755	0801	...	0918	1001	...	1201	...	...	1501	1601	...	1801	...	...	1901	...	...	2001	...	2101
Paris Bercy ▶ a.	0857	0857	0901	...	0957	...	...	1157	...	1357	...	...	1657	1757	...	1957	...	...	2057	...	...	2157	...	2257

STOPPING TRAINS PARIS - NEVERS

km			5901	5905		5909		5911	5915	5917	5919	5921
			Ⓐ			⚒		Ⓐ	Ⓐ	Ⓒ	Ⓐ	⑦
				⊕	⊙	m						e
0	**Paris** Bercy d.	...	0715	0915	...	1415	...	1705	1805	1804	1905	2004
119	Montargis d.	...	0816	1016	...	1514j	...	1812	1912	1912	2012	2112
155	Gien d.	...	0837	1037	...	1536j	...	1835	1935	1934	2034	2135
196	Cosne d.	0739	0900	1100	1236	1600	1745	1859	1959	1958	2058	2159
228	La Charité d.	0805	0920	1120	1301	1620	1811	1916	2016	2017	2118	2216
254	**Nevers** d.	0833	0940	1140	1325	1642	1834	1938	2038	2038	2138	2238

	5900	5904	5906	5908			5910	5912	5914		5916
	Ⓐ	Ⓐ	⑥	Ⓐ	Ⓐ	⑥		Ⓐ	⑦	⚒	
			k					⊗	e		
Nevers d.	0455	0555	0624	0724	0835	0935	1024	1421	1624	1635	1824
La Charité d.	0518	0618	0644	0745	0859	0955	1044	1442	1647	1659	1845
Cosne d.	0534	0634	0703	0805	0923	1017	1104	1501	1703	1724	1905
Gien d.	0558	0658	0726	0828	...	...	1129	1525	1727	...	1928
Montargis d.	0622	0721	0748	0851	...	...	1153	1548	1751	...	1951
Paris Bercy a.	0732	0832	0849	0949	...	...	1249	1649	1849	...	2049

A – ①②③④⑥⑦ (also Nov. 11; not July 13, Nov. 10).
B – ⑦ to June 26; Ⓑ July 3 - Aug. 28 (not July 14); ⑦ from Sept. 4.
D – From / to Dijon (Table **373**).
E – Daily to July 3; Ⓒ July 9 - Aug. 21; daily from Aug. 27.
J – To July 2 and from Aug. 29.

b – Not Aug. 15.
e – Also Aug. 15.
f – Also July 13, Nov. 10; not Nov. 11.
g – Also Aug. 16, Nov. 2; not Aug. 15, Oct. 31.

h – Not July 14, Nov. 11, Dec. 1.
j – On ⑤⑥ (also July 13, 14, Nov. 10) departs Montargis 1518, Gien 1538.
k – Also July 14, Nov. 11.
m – Also July 14.
w – Not July 14, Aug. 16, Nov. 1, 2, 11.
z – Runs 3 minutes later until July 9.

★ – *INTERCITÉS*. 🄡.
▶ – For additional trains see below main table.
▷ – See also Tables **328** and **329**.

⊠ – Northbound timings Clermont - Moulins may vary by up to 7 m until July 10 (earlier departures possible).
♠ – Runs 15 minutes **earlier** on ⑥.
⊕ – Subject to alteration on ①–⑤ Oct. 10 – 21 and ①–⑤ from No
⊙ – Subject to alteration Oct. 10 – 14, Nov. 14 – 18, 21 – 25.
⊗ – Subject to alteration Oct. 17 – 21, Nov. 28 – 30, Dec. 1, 2, 5 – 9.
❦ – On Ⓐ to July 18 departs Clermont 1849, Riom 1901, Vichy 19 Moulins 1958, Nevers 2034, arrives Paris 2231. On Ⓐ July 1 and Ⓐ Aug. 29 - Nov. 18 departs Clermont 1900, Riom 1910, Vichy 1933, Moulins 2000, Nevers 2029, arrives Paris 2231.

331 CLERMONT FERRAND - NEUSSARGUES - AURILLAC

Warning! Subject to alteration Aug. 1 – 26 (services between Neussargues and Aurillac are subject to alteration July 4 - Aug. 26).

km		⚒			⑤		Ⓐ	†	⚒	†	Ⓐ	⑤	†
			T⊡	z	B							f	w
0	**Clermont Ferrand** ‡ d.	0558	1034	1303	...	1648	1748	1757	1843	1957	2004	2123	2144
36	Issoire ‡ d.	0627	1102	1329	...	1718	1816	1825	1911	2025	2032	2151	2211
61	Arvant ‡ d.	0646	1121	1349	...	1737	1838	1845	1930	2045	2053	2211	2230
85	Massiac-Blesle d.	0707	1142	1410	...	1757	1901	1906	1951	2106	2113	2232	2251
111	**Neussargues** a.	0728	1201	1430	...	1817	1922	1925	2011	2125	2133	2251	2310
111	**Neussargues** d.	0730	1202	*1438*	1613	1818	1926	1926	2014	2126	2134	2252	2311
120	Murat (Cantal) d.	0740	1211	*1447*	1622	1827	1935	1935	2023	2137	2143	2301	2319
131	Le Lioran d.	0751	1223	*1458*	1635	1839	1951	1947	2034	2149	2154	2313	2330
168	**Aurillac** a.	0823	1252	*1528*	1707	1908	2020	2019	2104	2220	2224	2343	0001

	⚒	Ⓐ					Ⓐ	Ⓐ
		◇	◇		z	T⊗		
Aurillac d.	0552	0755	1027	1328	...	1639	1744	1918
Le Lioran d.	0624	0826	1100	1401	...	1710	1815	1949
Murat (Cantal) d.	0635	0838	1111	1413	...	1721	1829	2001
Neussargues a.	0643	0847	1119	1421	...	1731	1838	2009
Neussargues d.	0644	0848	1120	...	1437	1733	1839	2010
Massiac-Blesle d.	0707	0909	1143	...	1458	1758	1900	2031
Arvant ‡ d.	0726	0932	1204	...	1518	1818	1921	2051
Issoire ‡ d.	0744	0953	1223	...	1537	1836	1940	2110
Clermont Ferrand ‡ a.	0818	1020	1253	...	1602	1905	2008	2139

B – ⑤ (not Nov. 11). To Brive (Table **311**).
T – To / from Toulouse (Table **317**).

f – Also Nov. 10; not July 8 - Aug. 26, Nov. 11.
w – Also ⑤ July 8 - Aug. 26.
z – Not July 25 - Aug. 19, Aug. 22 – 26, Aug. 29 - Sept. 2.

⊡ – Not July 4 - Aug. 26. Subject to alteration ①–⑤ Sept. 26 - Oct. 7 and ①–⑤ Nov. 7 – 25.

⊗ – Not July 4 - Aug. 25.
◇ – Subject to alteration ①–⑤ Nov. 7
‡ – See also Table **333**.

332 (CLERMONT FERRAND) - NEUSSARGUES - MILLAU - BÉZIERS

km		🚌			🚌		🚌				
		⚒	⚒	⚒	⚒	⚒	⚒			⑤	†
			z	z		z		x	z	d	w
0	**Clermont Ferrand 331** d.	...	...	...	...	...	...	...	*1303*	...	...
111	**Neussargues 331** d.	...	...	...	...	...	...	...	1436	...	...
130	St Flour ⊖ d.	...	...	...	...	...	...	...	1459	...	...
168	St Chély d'Apcher d.	...	...	...	...	1131	...	...	1540	1631	...
201	Marvejols d.	...	...	...	...	1207	...	...	1616	1707	...
243	Sévérac le Château d.	...	...	...	...	1300	...	...	1703	1757	...
273	Millau ⊙ d.	...	0600	...	...	1330	...	...	1738	1827	2102
352	Bédarieux △ d.	0619	0717	0844	1315	1446	1625	1734	1854	1941	2221
394	**Béziers** △ a.	0714	0750	0918	1400	1520	1710	1808	1928	2015	2255

					🚌	🚌			
	⚒	⚒		⑤	⚒	⚒			⑦
	z	z	z	d			x	A	v▽
Béziers △ d.	0642	0800	0937	...	1215	1530	1644	1818	1856
Bédarieux △ d.	0718	0834	1010	...	1300	1615	1719	1855	1940
Millau ⊙ d.	0837	...	1127	1345	...	...	...	2013	2053
Sévérac le Château d.	0905	...	1159	1413	...	...	...	...	2128
Marvejols d.	0952	...	1248	1459	...	...	...	...	2219
St Chély d'Apcher d.	1026	...	1325	1535	...	...	...	...	2253
St Flour ⊖ d.	...	...	1405	...	...	...	...	...	...
Neussargues 331 a.	...	...	1425	...	...	...	...	...	...
Clermont Ferrand 331 a.	...	...	*1602*	...	...	...	...	...	...

km		🚌	🚌	🚌		🚌	🚌	🚌	🚌	🚌	🚌
		Ⓐt		⚒	⑤d			⑤f	Ⓑ	⑤⑥j	Ⓑs
	Clermont Ferrand 331 d.	*0647*r	*1034*r	1050	...	1645	*1648*r	*1648*r	*1748*q	1945	2125
	Massiac-Blesle 331 d.	0758	1155	|	...	|	1804	1804	1910	|	|
	St Flour ⊖ d.	0824	1219	|	...	|	1829	1829	1935	|	2240
	St Chély d'Apcher d.	...	...	1220	...	1820	...	1856	...	2120	2310
0	Marvejols ● d.	...	...	1300	1720	1900	...	1934	...	2200	2350
35	**Mende** ● a.	...	...	1340	1807	1945	...	|	...	2245	0035
	Millau a.	...	...	...	...	...	...	2101	...	...	...

	🚌	🚌	🚌	🚌	🚌	🚌	🚌		🚌
	⚒	⚒			†	ⒶE	⑥k	⑤d	Ⓐ
Millau d.	...	...	...	...	...	...	...	...	...
Mende ● d.	...	0640	...	0945	1445	1515	1545	1615	...
Marvejols ● d.	...	0730	...	1040	1540	1605	1635	1702	...
St Chély d'Apcher d.	...	0806	...	1127	1623	1640	1710	...	...
St Flour ⊖ d.	0632	0835	1108	|	1650	1715	1745	...	1825
Massiac-Blesle 331 a.	0657	|	1132	|	|	|	|	...	1850
Clermont Ferrand 331 a.	*0818*r	1000	*1253*r	1305	1810	1839	1910	...	*2008*r

A – ①②③④⑥⑦ to July 24 / from Sept. 3 (also July 8, 15, 22, Aug. 19 – 21, 26 – 28, Oct. 21, 28, Nov. 11; not Oct. 19, Nov. 10).
B – ②–⑤ (not July 14, 15, 26 – 29, Aug. 2 – 19, Nov. 1, 2, 11).
D – ①–④ (also July 8, 9, 15, 16, 22, 23, Aug. 19, 20, 26, 27, Oct. 21, 28; not July 14, 25, 26, 27, 28, Aug. 1 – 18, Oct. 19, Nov. 1, 10).
E – Ⓐ to Nov. 18 (not July 25 - Aug. 26).
G – ⚒ July 4 – 23; ⚒ Aug. 20 – 27.

d – Also Oct. 19, Nov. 10; not July 8 - Aug. 26, Oct. 21, 28, Nov. 11.
f – ⑤ (also July 13, Nov. 10; not Nov. 11).
j – Also July 13, Nov. 10; not July 15, Nov. 11. Runs 10 – 15 minutes later on ⑥.
k – ⑥ (⚒ July 25 - Aug. 27 and from Nov. 21).
q – Connection by train. Departs *1757* on †. Subject to alteration Aug. 1 – 18.
r – Connection by train. Subject to alteration on certain dates (see Table **331**).
s – 20 minutes later on † to June 26 / from Sept. 4. 25 minutes later July 3 - Aug. 28.

t – Change from train to bus at Arvant (d. 0741).
u – Not July 3 - Aug. 28, Oct. 23, 30.
v – Also Nov. 2; not July 3 - Aug. 28, Oct. 23, 30.
w – Not July 31, Aug. 7, 14.

x – Not July 25 - Aug. 18, Aug. 2 Aug. 29 - Sept. 1.
z – Not July 25 - Aug. 19, Aug. 2 Aug. 29 - Sept. 2.

⊖ – St Flour - Chaudes Aigues.
▽ – From Montpellier (Table **355**).
● – Other rail services Marvejols - Mende and v.v.: **From Marvejols** at 0700 **B**, 1353 **G** an 2228 ⑦ **v**. **From Mende** at 1114 **G**, 1730 **D** and 2125 ⑦ **u**.
△ – Additional 🚌 journeys Bédarieux - Béziers and v.v.: **From Bédarieux** at 0715 †, 12 and 1610 †. **From Béziers** at 1049 †, 1445 †, 1730 ⚒ and 2045 ⑤ **f**.
⊙ – Additional SNCF 🚌 service Millau - Montpellier (journey 85 – 125 minutes): **From Mil** 0700 ⚒, 0730 †, 1000, 1515 and 1716. **From Montpellier** 1005, 1205, 1805 ⚒ and 2

☛ *Bus services in this table are operated on behalf of SNCF. Rail tickets valid.*

CLERMONT FERRAND - LE PUY EN VELAY and NIMES — 333

Warning! Services from/to Clermont Ferrand are subject to alteration Aug. 1–12.

			🚌		🚌			🚌	🚌			🚌		🚌				🚌		🚌			🚌		
	Ⓐ	Ⓐ	Ⓐ ♠	Ⓐ	Ⓐ	⑦ s	⑥	⑥			⊙				⑤⑦ z	◧			⚒	①–④ h❖	⑤ f	⑥	⑤ b	†	Ⓐ w
Clermont Ferrand ▷ d.	...	0545	...	0647	...	...	0732	...	...	...	0949	...	1250	...	...	...	1642	...	1757	1854	1855	1950	*2004**	2118	2127
Issoire ▷ d.	...	0613	...	0715	...	...	0800	...	...	...	1017	...	1319	...	...	...	1709	...	1825	1929	1923	2030	*2032**	2146	2205
Arvant ▷ d.	...	0632	...	0736	...	...	0820	...	...	...	1037	...	1341	...	...	...	1728	...	1845	2002	1943	2050	2055	2205	2226
Brioude d.	...	0643	...	0746	...	...	0829	...	...	...	1048	...	1352	1355	...	...	1737e	...	1854	2014	1952	2058	2110	2215	2235
St Georges d'Aurac d.	...	0709	...	0805	...	...	0847	...	...	...	1112	...	|	|	...	...	1759	1802	1917	2039	2016	...	|	2238	...
Langeac d.	...	|	...	0813	0819	...	0855	0859	...	...	|	...	1420	|	...	...	1808	|	|	|	|	...	2148	|	...
Le Puy en Velay a.	...	0755	...	|	0905	...	|	0945	...	...	1200	...	|	1503	...	...	|	1854	2005	2134	2101	...	2234	2326	...
Langogne d.	...	▬	...	0936	...	...	1021	...	1232	...	...	...	1545	...	...	...	1940	...	...	...	...	...	...	...	...
Mende d.	0450	⑥p	0838	|	...	*0840*	|	...	|	1147	...	1445	|	...	1650	1832	|	...	...	...	...	...	...	...	...
La Bastide-St Laurent d.	0605	0706	0948	0959	...	0959	1040	...	1257	1307	...	1553	1606	...	1805	1942	2009	...	...	...	...	...	...	...	...
Grand Combe la Pise d.	0709	0808	...	1057	...	1057	1138	...	...	1407	...	...	1708	...	1909	...	2107	...	...	...	...	...	...	...	...
Alès a.	0724	0824	...	1112	...	1112	1152	...	...	1424	...	...	1724	...	1924	...	2122	...	...	...	...	...	...	...	...
Alès ▶ d.	0726	0826	...	1114k	...	1114	1159	...	...	1426	...	...	1726	...	1926	...	2126	...	...	...	...	...	...	...	...
Nimes 355 ▶ a.	0758	0858	...	1146k	...	1146	1231	...	...	1458	...	...	1758	...	1958	...	2158	...	...	...	...	...	...	...	...

						🚌		🚌		🚌		🚌			🚌		🚌	🚌				🚌		🚌		🚌
	⑥	① g	②–⑤ d	⚒ ⊙	① m	† n	⊠	♣	⑥	Ⓐ ❖				ⒶD		C		Ⓑ	Ⓐ	†	Ⓑ	⑤ b	◇		⑤ v	⑤ v
s 355 ▶ d.	...	...	...	...	0715	...	0812	...	...	...	1218	...	...	1315	...	1413	...	...	...	...	1658	...	1811r	...	2118	...
▶ a.	...	...	...	...	0750	...	0843	...	...	...	1250	...	...	1348	...	1443	...	...	...	...	1735	...	1845r	...	2150	...
d.	...	...	...	...	0752	...	0845	...	...	...	1252	...	...	1350	...	1445	...	...	...	...	1745	...	1852	...	2155	...
Combe la Pise d.	...	...	...	...	0809	...	0900	...	...	...	1307	...	...	1409	...	1501	...	...	...	...	1806	...	1907	...	2210	...
stide-St Laurent d.	...	...	...	...	0913	...	0958	1001	...	...	1415	1417	...	1523	...	1605	1612	...	...	...	1912	...	2013j	2013	2313	2321
nde a.	...	...	...	...	|	...	|	1111	...	...	1523	|	...	|	...	|	1720	...	...	...	|	...	2121	|	...	|
gne d.	...	...	...	...	0932	...	1023	...	...	...	...	1441	...	1546	...	1624	...	...	...	...	1937	...	...	2038	...	2346
Puy en Velay d.	...	0526	0617	0808	...	1101	|	...	1210	1207	...	...	1606	|	1654	|	...	1910	...	1954	|	2026	...	...	...	...
ac d.	...	|	|	|	...	|	1148	...	|	|	...	...	|	1710	|	1747	...	|	...	|	2103	2112	...	...	...	...
orges d'Aurac d.	...	0616	0705	0856	...	|	1156	...	1259	1302	...	...	1655	1718	1747	1757	...	|	...	2043	2111	|	...	...	...	...
de d.	0630	0641	0725	0916	...	1204	1214	...	1319	1324	...	...	1716	1738	...	1821	...	2018	...	2103	2129	2150	...	...	...	...
t. ▷ d.	0638	0649	0738	0924	...	...	1223	...	1331	1336	...	...	1725	1747	...	1830	...	2035	2051	2113	2139	2201	...	...	...	...
e ▷ d.	0659	0710	0758	0945	...	...	1242	...	1351	1412	...	...	1746	1807	...	1849	...	...	2110	2133	2158	...	...	...	...	...
ont Ferrand ▷ a.	0738	0742	0827	1015	...	...	1310	...	1419	1444	...	...	1815	1834	...	1916	...	...	2137	2200	2226	...	...	...	...	...

Ⓒ (daily July 23 - Aug. 28 and from Nov. 19).
Ⓐ to Nov. 18 (not July 25 - Aug. 26).
Ⓐ July 25 - Aug. 26; ①–⑤ from Nov. 21.

Also July 13, Nov. 10; not Nov. 11.
Not July 14, Aug. 16, Nov. 1, 2, 11.
1741 on Ⓐ to July 22 and Ⓐ Aug. 29 - Nov. 18.
Also July 13, Oct. 31, Nov. 10; not Nov. 11.
Also Aug. 16, Nov. 2; not Aug. 15.
Not July 13, 14, Aug. 15, Oct. 31, Nov. 1, 10.
Arrives 2008.
Not Oct. 10 - Nov. 4. 5 minutes later July 4 - Aug. 26.
Also Nov. 3; not July 4 - Aug. 29, Oct. 24, 31.
Also Aug. 31, Nov. 2.
Also Nov. 11; not July 9 - Aug. 27, Oct. 22, 29, Nov. 12.

r – 5 minutes later on ⑦ (not July 3 - Aug. 28, Oct. 23, 30).
s – Also July 14, Aug. 15.
v – Also Oct. 19, Nov. 10; not July 8 - Aug. 26, Oct. 21, 28, Nov. 11.
w – Not July 4 - Aug. 26.
z – Also July 14, Aug. 15, Oct. 19, Nov. 1, 10; not July 8, 15, 22, 29, Aug. 5, 12, 19, 26, Oct. 21, 28.

* – Connection is by train.
◧ – By train on ⑤ (also Oct. 19, Nov. 10; not July 8 - Aug. 26, Oct. 21, 28, Nov. 11); by 🚌 on other dates.
⊠ – Subject to alteration on ①–⑤ Oct. 3–21.
⊙ – Subject to alteration on Ⓐ Nov. 7–25.
¶ – Subject to alteration on ①–⑤ Oct. 24 - Nov. 4.

♠ – Also ⑥ July 9 - Aug. 27. Operated by train July 4 - Aug. 27 (Mende d. 0840, La Bastide a. 0949).
♣ – Operated by train on ⚒ July 4 - Aug. 27 (La Bastide d. 1006, Mende a. 1112).
❖ – Subject to confirmation.
◇ – From Narbonne and Montpellier on Ⓐ (Table **355**).
Δ – Distance from La Bastide.
▷ – See also Table **331**.
▶ – Other trains Alès - Nimes (journey time 32–40 minutes): **From Alès** at 0600 Ⓐ, 0628 Ⓐ, 0656, 0758 ⚒, 0826, 0926 Ⓐ ¶, 1226 Ⓐ, 1257, 1526, 1641 Ⓐ, 1821 Ⓐ and 1926.
From Nimes at 0618 Ⓐ, 0655 Ⓐ, 0715 ⚒, 0746 Ⓐ, 0918 Ⓐ ¶, 1018 ¶, 1123 Ⓐ ¶, 1318 Ⓐ **E**, 1413, 1518 Ⓐ, 1618, 1733 ⚒, 1918 Ⓐ and 2118.

LYON - MASSY - LE MANS - RENNES and NANTES — 335

services

For slower services via Bourges see Table **290**. For Lille - Massy - Rennes/Nantes see Table **11**. For Strasbourg - Massy - Rennes/Nantes see Table **391**.

	TGV **5352** Ⓐ		*TGV* **5350** ⊡	*TGV* **5365** ⑥ d⊡		*TGV* **5368** ⊙	*TGV* **5394** ⑥ B	*TGV* **5393** ⑥ B	*TGV* **5372** ⊖	*TGV* **5371** ⊖		*TGV* **5380** ⊗	*TGV* **5387** ⊗r	
rseille St Charles **350** d.	...	...	0844	0844	...	1244	...	...	1444	1444	...	...	...	...
gnon TGV **350** d.	...	...	0914	0914	...	1321	...	...	1521	1521	...	...	...	...
Montpellier **355** d.	...	...	|	|	...	|	...	...	|	|	...	1627t	1627t	...
ence TGV **355** d.	...	...	0949	0949	...	|	...	...	|	|	...	1749	1749	...
Bourg St Maurice **366** d.	...	...	|	|	...	|	1148	1148	|	|	...	|	|	...
Perrache d.	0616	...	|	|	...	|	|	|	|	|	...	|	|	...
Part Dieu d.	0630	...	1030	1030	...	1428	|	|	1630	1630	...	1830	1830	...
y TGV d.	0839	...	1238	1238	...	1638	1805	1805	1838	1838	...	2039	2049	...
St Pierre des Corps a.	0930h	...	|	|	...	1729	|	|	|	|	...	2129	|	...
ans **280** a.	|	...	1328	1328	...	|	1852	1852	1928	1928	...	|	2136	...
nnes 280 a.	|	...	1444k	|	...	|	|	2021	|	2100	...	|	2252	...
ur a.	|	...	...	|	...	|	|	...	|	...	...	2204	...	...
rs St Laud **280** a.	1022	...	...	1414	...	1822	1936	...	2010	...	...	2229	...	...
es 280 a.	1102	...	...	1453	...	1903	2014	...	2048	...	...	2308	...	...

	TGV **5304** ① g	*TGV* **5302** ②–④ w	*TGV* **5308** ⑥ A	*TGV* **5310** ⑥ A	*TGV* **5312** ⊡	*TGV* **5314** ⊡	*TGV* **5326** ◇	*TGV* **5318** ◇	*TGV* **5322** ⊕	*TGV* **5328** Ⓐ	*TGV* **5346** ☆	*TGV* **5342** ⑤⑦ z	*TGV* **5344** ⑤⑦ z	
es 280 d.	0454j	0456	0558	...	0705	...	0908	...	1252	1454	...	1905	...	...
rs St Laud **280** d.	0533j	0536	0637	...	0743	...	0946	...	1333	1534	...	1944	...	...
ur d.	0558	|	|	...	|	...	|	...	|	1558	...	|	...	...
nnes 280 d.	|	|	|	0557	|	0710	|	0910	|	|	1610	|	1910	...
ans **280** d.	|	|	0745	0745	0833	0833	1033	1033	|	|	1732	2033	2033	...
St Pierre des Corps d.	0631	0630	|	|	|	|	|	|	1432	1631	|	|	|	...
y TGV d.	0725	0725	0837	0837	0925	0925	1125	1125	1525	1725	1825	2124	2124	...
Part Dieu a.	0930	0930	|	|	1130	1130	1330	1330	1730	1930	2030	2330	2330	...
Perrache a.	0943	0943	|	|	|	|	|	|	|	1943	|	2343c	2343c	...
Bourg St Maurice **366** a.	...	...	1412	1412	|	|	|	|	|	...	|	...	...	...
ence TGV **355** a.	...	...	...	...	|	|	1412	1412	1810	...	2110	...	...	...
Montpellier **355** a.	...	...	...	...	|	|	1530	1530	|	...	|	...	...	...
gnon TGV **350** a.	...	...	...	...	1242	1242	...	...	1844	...	2145	...	...	...
rseille St Charles **350** a.	...	...	...	...	1322	1322	...	...	1916	...	2216	...	...	...

YON - ROUEN	*TGV* **5376** ♥	
arseille **350** d.	1543	...
ignon TGV **350** d.	1614	...
lence TGV **355** d.	1649	...
n Part Dieu d.	1730	...
sy-Palaiseau a.	1937	...
ailles Chantiers a.	1955	...
es la Jolie a.	2030	...
en Rive Droite a.	2114	...
Havre **270** a.	2206	...

ROUEN - LYON	*TGV* **5316** ♠	
Le Havre **270** d.	0753	...
Rouen Rive Droite d.	0845	...
Mantes la Jolie d.	0933	...
Versailles Chantiers d.	1006	...
Massy-Palaiseau d.	1024	...
Lyon Part Dieu a.	1226	...
Valence TGV **355** a.	1309	...
Avignon TGV **350** a.	1344	...
Marseille **350** a.	1420	...

A – ⑥ Dec. 26 - Mar. 19.
B – ⑥ Jan. 2 - Mar. 26.

c – ⑦ to June 26; ⑤⑦ July 3 - Aug. 28 (also July 13, Aug. 15); ⑦ from Sept. 4.
d – Also July 14, Nov. 11.
g – Also Nov. 2; not July 4 - Aug. 22, Oct. 31.
h – Not Aug. 16 - Oct. 28.
j – Until June 27 departs Nantes 0448, Angers 0530.
k – 1447 on ⑥ (also July 14, Nov. 11).
r – Not Oct. 15.
t – 1630 on ①–④ to June 30.
w – Not July 5 - Aug. 25, Nov. 1, 2, 10.
z – Also July 13, Aug. 15, Nov. 1, 10; not Nov. 11.

TGV – 🅁, supplement payable, 🍷.

⊡ – Subject to alteration on Oct. 1, 8, 9, 15, 30, 31, Nov. 26.
⊙ – Subject to alteration on Oct. 1, 8, Nov. 26.
⊖ – Subject to alteration on Oct. 15, 29, 30, 31, Nov. 26.
⊗ – Subject to alteration on Oct. 29, 30, 31, Nov. 26.
◇ – Subject to alteration on Oct. 1, 8, 9, 15, 29, 30, 31, Nov. 26.
⊕ – Subject to alteration on Sept. 25, Oct. 1, 2, 8, 29, 30, 31, Nov. 26.
☆ – Subject to alteration on Oct. 1, 8, 15, 29, 30, 31, Nov. 26.
♥ – Subject to alteration July 18 - Aug. 5, Sept. 11, 30, Oct. 1, 2, 8, 15, 29, 30, 31, Nov. 18, 19, 20, 26, Dec. 2, 3, 4. Terminates at Versailles on July 8, 9. Terminates at Rouen on Sept. 2, 3, 10, 17, 23, 24.
♠ – Subject to alteration on July 9, 10, 18–31, Aug. 1–5, Sept. 18, Oct. 1, 2, 3, 8, 9, 16, 30, 31, Nov. 19, 20, 21, 26, Dec. 3, 4, 5. On June 25, July 2, 16, Aug. 6, 13, 20, 27 arrives Valence 1312, Avignon 1347, Marseille 1421. Starts from Rouen on Sept. 3, 4, 11, 24, 25.

Timings at Marseille, Avignon Valence and Montpellier may vary by a few minutes until June 5. Please check your reservation for confirmed timings.

340 PARIS - LYON

TGV Suc

For Charles de Gaulle ✈ - Marne la Vallée - Lyon see Table **11**. For Paris - Lyon St Exupéry ✈ see Table **342**. Most trains not serving Lyon Perrache continue to/from other destinati

km	SEE NOTE ⊠	TGV 6601	TGV 6641	TGV 6603	TGV 6681	TGV 6643	TGV 6605	TGV 6605		TGV 6607	TGV 6609	TGV 6611	TGV 6613	TGV 6615	TGV 6685	TGV 6617	TGV 6657	TGV 6619	TGV 6621	TGV 6659	TGV 6623	TGV 6687	TGV 6663	TGV 6627
		Ⓐ	Ⓐ	①–⑥	①–⑥	Ⓐ	Ⓑ	⑥									⑤			Ⓐ				
			n	b	b	J	h	k									y			J			E	
0	**Paris** Gare de Lyon ..... **341** d.	0550	0629	0659	0659	0729	0753	0753	...	0859	0959	1059	1153**v**	1259	1259	1353	1429	1459	1553	1619	1657	1657	1729	1753
303	Le Creusot TGV .... d.	0712	|	|	|	|	0917	0915	...	|	|	|	1313	|	|	1514	|	|	1714	|	|	|	|	1914
363	Mâcon Loché TGV .... **341** a.	|	|	|	|	|	|	0933	...	|	|	|	|	|	|	|	|	|	|	|	|	|	|	|
427	**Lyon** Part-Dieu .... a.	0756	0826	0856	0856	0926	0956	1000	...	1056	1156	1256	1356	1456	1456	1556	1624	1656	1756	1817	1856	1856	1926	1956
432	**Lyon** Perrache .... a.	0809	0843	0909	...	0939	1009	1013	...	1109	1209	1309	1409	1509	...	1609	1637	1714	1809	...	1909	...	1939	2009

SEE NOTE ⊠	TGV 6689	TGV 6629	TGV 6669	TGV 6631	TGV 6633	TGV 6635	TGV 6635	
		⑤⑥			Ⓑ	⑤⑦	⑦	
		t	H		h	u	d	
Paris Gare de Lyon ...... **341** d.	1857	1857	1929	1958	2059	2159	2159	...
Le Creusot TGV .... d.	|	|	|	2119	|	|	|	...
Mâcon Loché TGV .... **341** a.	|	|	|	2137	|	|	|	...
Lyon Part-Dieu .... a.	2056	2056	2126	2203	2256	2356	2356	...
Lyon Perrache .... a.	...	2109	2139	2219	2309	...	0009	...

SEE NOTE ⊠	TGV 6640	TGV 6602	TGV 6642	TGV 6644	TGV 6604	TGV 6690	TGV 6648	TGV 6608	TGV 6610	TGV 6612	TGV 6612
	①	Ⓐ		①–④	①–⑥	①–⑥					①–⑤
	g		A	r	b	b	D			P	Q
Lyon Perrache .... d.	0521	0551	0621	0638	0646	...	0721	0751	0851	0951	0951
Lyon Part-Dieu .... d.	0534	0604	0634	0652	0704	0704	0734	0804	0904	1004	1004
Mâcon Loché TGV .... **341** d.	0601	0631	|	|	|	|	|	0832	|	|	1033
Le Creusot TGV .... d.	0623	0652	|	|	|	|	|	0853	|	1046	1055
Paris Gare de Lyon ... **341** a.	0743	0813	0831	0849	0901	0901	0931	1015	1104	1207	1215

SEE NOTE ⊠	TGV 6692	TGV 6616	TGV 6616	TGV 6618	TGV 6694	TGV 6620	TGV 6622	TGV 6624	TGV 6624	TGV 6664	TGV 6626	TGV 6668	TGV 6696	TGV 6628	TGV 6638	TGV 6696	TGV 6630	TGV 6632	TGV 6674	TGV 6674	TGV 6634	TGV 6634	TGV 6672	TGV 6676
		Ⓐ	Ⓒ						②–⑤	Ⓑ		⑤⑦	Ⓐ		Ⓐ			Ⓑ	⑦	⑥	⑤⑦	①–④	⑤	⑦
								L	s	B		x	J§		J	N		h	e		w	m	f	
Lyon Perrache .... d.	...	1121	1151	1247	...	1351	1451	1551	1551	1621	1651	1716	...	1751	...	...	1846**z**	1951	2016	2016	2051	2119**c**	2151	2151
Lyon Part-Dieu .... d.	1104	1134	1204	1305	1305	1404	1504	1604	1604	1634	1704	1734	1734	1804	1834	1904	1904	2004	2034	2034	2104	2137	2204	2204
Mâcon Loché TGV .... **341** d.	|	|	|	|	|	|	|	|	1630	|	|	|	|	|	|	|	|	|	|	|	|	|	|	2231
Le Creusot TGV .... d.	|	|	|	|	|	1445	|	1646	1651	|	|	|	|	1846	|	|	|	2046	|	2115**j**	|	|	2246	2252
Paris Gare de Lyon ...... **341** a.	1301	1331	1401	1501	1501	1607	1701	1807	1812	1831	1901	1933	1933	2007	2031	2101	2101	2207	2232	2238	2301	2332	0017‡	0013

A – Ⓐ to July 4; ① July 11 - Aug. 22 (also Aug. 16; not Aug. 15); Ⓐ from Aug. 29.
B – Ⓑ to July 1 / from Aug. 29 (not Nov. 11).
D – Daily to July 3; Ⓒ July 9 - Aug. 21; daily from Aug. 27.
E – Ⓐ to July 1; ⑤ July 8 - Aug. 19 (also July 13); Ⓐ from Aug. 26.
G – Ⓑ to July 1; ⑤ July 8 - Aug. 26 (also July 13); Ⓑ from Aug. 29 (not Nov. 11).
H – Ⓑ to July 3; ⑤⑦ July 8 - Aug. 21 (also July 13, Aug. 15); Ⓑ from Aug. 26 (not Nov. 11).
J – To July 1 and from Aug. 29.
L – ①⑥⑦ (also Nov. 1, 2, 11; runs daily July 2 - Aug. 29).
N – ⑥⑦ (also Nov. 11; daily July 2 - Aug. 28).
P – Daily to Oct. 19; ⑥⑦ from Oct. 22 (also Nov. 11).
Q – ①–⑤ from Oct. 20 (not Nov. 11).

b – Not Aug. 15, Nov. 1.
c – 2117 on Nov. 1, 10.
d – Also July 8, 13, 15, 22, 29, Aug. 15, Dec. 9; not Aug. 28, Nov. 13.
e – Also July 14; not July 24 - Aug. 14.
f – Also July 13, Nov. 10; not Nov. 11.
g – Also Nov. 2; not July 4 - Aug. 22, Oct. 31.
h – Not July 14, Nov. 11.
j – Not Aug. 27.
k – Also July 14, Nov. 11.
m – Not July 13, 14, Aug. 1 – 15. May arrive Paris up to 15 minutes later until July 28.
n – Not July 4 - Aug. 31.
r – Not July 4 - Aug. 25, Nov. 1, 10.

s – Not July 5 - Aug. 26, Nov. 1, 2, 11.
t – Also July 13, 14, Nov. 10.
u – Also July 13, Aug. 15, Nov. 1, 10; not Nov. 11.
v – 1149 on Oct. 3, Nov. 7, 21, Dec. 5.
w – Also July 13, Aug. 15; not Nov. 11.
x – Also July 14, Oct. 31, Nov. 1; not ⑦ July 3 - Aug. 28, No
y – Also Nov. 10; not July 8 - Aug. 26, Nov. 11.
z – 1851 on Ⓐ to July 1 / from Aug. 29.

TGV –🅁, supplement payable, 🍸.

§ – Not Oct. 31.
‡ – Arrival time may vary by a few minutes.
⊠ – Subject to alteration Aug. 13 – 15. Services may not rur to / from Lyon Perrache Nov. 11 – 13.

341 PARIS - GENÈVE, CHAMBÉRY and ANNECY

TGV tr

km	SEE NOTE ❖	TGV 9241	TGV 9761	TGV 6467	TGV 6933	TGV 9763	TGV 9765	TGV 9765	TGV 6937	TGV 6503	TGV 6939	TGV 6939	TGV 9245	TGV 6407	TGV 9773	TGV 6941	TGV 6941	TGV 6941	TGV 9249	TGV 9775	TGV 9777	TGV 6947
			①–⑤	⑦	Ⓑ	⑥⑦	⑦	①–⑤		⑥				⑥		⑤					Ⓑ	
		M❦	a	P	h	c	e	a		k	N	T	M❦	H	Q	W	u	B	M❦		h	u
0	**Paris** Gare de Lyon .... **340 366** d.	0628**j**	0707	0711	0748	0811	0911	0917	0949	1011	1027	1041	1041	1149	1211	1219	1245	1245	1441	1511	1611	1645
363	Mâcon Loché TGV .... **340** d.	|	|	|	0927	|	|	|	1127	|	|	|	|	1327	|	1359	1423	1423	|	|	|	1823
406	Bourg-en-Bresse .... **365** d.	|	0900	|	0949	1003	1102	|	1149	1205	|	|	|	|	1404	|	|	|	|	|	1804	|
	Lyon St Exupéry TGV ✈ .... **342** d.	◧	|	|	|	|	|	|	|	|	|	1236	1236	|	|	|	|	|	1637	|	|	|
439	Nurieux Brion .... a.	|	|	|	|	|	|	|	|	|	|	|	|	|	|	|	|	|	|	|	|	|
470	Bellegarde .... **346** a.	|	0947	0948	|	1058	1151	|	|	1300	|	|	|	|	1457	|	|	|	|	1747	1858	|
503	**Genève** .... **346** a.	|	1016	⊙	|	1127	1216	1215	|	⊖	|	|	|	|	1527	|	|	|	|	1816	1927	|
532*	Chambéry .... **366** a.	0939	...	...	|	...	...	...	|	...	|	1338	1338	1504	...	1541	1538	|	1739	...	...	1938
532*	Chambéry .... **345 364** d.	...	...	...	|	...	...	...	|	...	|	1348	...	...	...	1551	1548	|	...	...	...	1948
546*	Aix les Bains .... **345 364** a.	...	...	...	1050	...	...	...	1251	...	1318	1358	...	...	...	1529**z**	1558	1551	...	...	...	1958
585*	**Annecy** .... **345 364** a.	...	...	...	1129	...	...	...	1329	...	1416	1429	...	...	...	1629	1629	1633	...	...	...	2029

SEE NOTE ❖	TGV 9781	TGV 6511	TGV 6951	TGV 6951	TGV 9785	TGV 9789	TGV 6953
		⑤	Ⓑ			⑤	⑤
		g	uv	Y		v	f
Paris Gare de Lyon .... **340 366** d.	1811	1815	1845	1845	1911	2011	2019
Mâcon Loché TGV .... **340** d.	|	|	2023	2023	|	|	2157
Bourg-en-Bresse .... **365** d.	|	|	|	|	2104	2204	2221
Lyon St Exupéry TGV ✈ .... **342** d.	|	|	|	|	|	|	|
Nurieux Brion .... a.	2030	|	|	|	|	|	|
Bellegarde .... **346** a.	2058	2111	|	|	2151	2251	|
Genève .... **346** a.	2127	⊖	|	|	2220	2320	|
Chambéry .... **366** a.	...	...	2138	|	...	...	2338
Chambéry .... **345 364** d.	...	...	2148	|	...	...	|
Aix les Bains .... **345 364** a.	...	...	2158	2152	...	...	2324**z**
Annecy .... **345 364** a.	...	...	2229	2229	...	...	...

SEE NOTE ❖	TGV 6960	TGV 9760	TGV 9764	TGV 9764	TGV 6962	TGV 6962	TGV 9768	TGV 6964	TGV 6964
	①–⑥	①–⑥	①–⑥	⑦	①–⑥				
	us	b	b	e	su	X		D	E
Annecy .... **345 364** d.	0531	...	...	...	0730	0730	...	0931	0931
Aix les Bains .... **345 364** d.	0601	...	...	...	0801	0846**y**	...	1008	1034**y**
Chambéry .... **345 364** a.	0612	...	...	...	0812	0812	...	|	1010
Chambéry .... **366** d.	0622	...	...	...	0822	0829	...	|	1022
Genève .... **346** d.	|	0614	0742	0742	|	|	0942	|	|
Bellegarde .... **346** d.	|	0643	0810	0810	|	|	1010	|	|
Nurieux Brion .... d.	|	0709	|	0834	|	|	|	|	|
Lyon St Exupéry TGV ✈ .... **342** a.	|	|	|	|	|	|	|	|	|
Bourg-en-Bresse .... **365** d.	|	0736	0859	0902	|	|	|	|	|
Mâcon Loché TGV .... **340** d.	|	|	|	|	|	|	|	|	|
Paris Gare de Lyon .... **340 366** a.	0917	0927	1049	1050	1117	1134	1249	1310	1336

SEE NOTE ❖	TGV 9240	TGV 9770	TGV 9244	TGV 6972	TGV 9772	TGV 9774	TGV 6482	TGV 6508	TGV 6976	TGV 6976	TGV 9776	TGV 6976	TGV 9778	TGV 6980	TGV 6980	TGV 6506	TGV 9780	TGV 6486	TGV 6414	TGV 6984	TGV 9248	TGV 9784
		①–⑤			⑥⑦	①–⑤	⑥	⑦	①–⑥		⑤–⑦		①–④	Ⓑ		⑦	Ⓑ	⑥	⑥	Ⓑ	⑤–⑦	
	M❦	a	M		d	a	P	e	u	L	r	♥	mR	uv	G	t	h	P	H	h	M❦	
Annecy .... **345 364** d.	...	...	...	1231	...	...	...	...	1531	1531	...	1611	...	1731	1731	...	...	...	...	1831	...	...
Aix les Bains .... **345 364** d.	...	...	1310**y**	1310	...	...	...	...	1601	1630**y**	...	1649	...	1801	1831**y**	...	...	...	...	1908	...	...
Chambéry .... **345 364** a.	...	...	|	|	...	...	...	...	1612	1609	...	|	...	1812	1808	...	...	...	...	|	...	...
Chambéry .... **366** d.	1024	...	1252	|	...	...	...	...	1623	1618	...	|	...	1822	1818	...	...	...	1850	|	1855	...
Genève .... **346** d.	|	1142	|	|	1342	1442	⊙	⊖	|	|	1630	|	1742	|	|	⊖	1830	⊙	|	|	|	1942
Bellegarde .... **346** d.	|	1210	|	|	1410	1510	1503	1503	|	|	1659	|	1809	|	|	1818	1900	1900	|	|	|	2010
Nurieux Brion .... d.	|	|	|	|	|	|	|	|	|	|	|	|	|	|	|	|	|	|	|	|	|	|
Lyon St Exupéry TGV ✈ .... **342** a.	1123	|	|	|	|	|	|	|	1723	|	|	|	|	|	|	|	|	|	|	|	◧	|
Bourg-en-Bresse .... **365** d.	|	|	1413	1413	|	1559	1556	1556	|	|	1757	|	1858	|	|	1935	|	1956	2012	2013	|	|
Mâcon Loché TGV .... **340** d.	|	|	1434	1434	|	|	|	|	|	|	|	|	|	|	|	1955	|	|	2034	2034	|	|
Paris Gare de Lyon .... **340 366** a.	1320	1452	1612	1612	1649	1749	1749	1749	1919	1934	1949	2011	2049	2115	2120	2133	2149	2149	2211	2212	2232‡	2251

A – ①②③④⑥ to June 22; daily from Sept. 1.
B – ①②③④⑥⑦ June 23 - Aug. 31 (also June 24; not July 14).
D – ①②③④⑥ July 4 - Aug. 31 (also June 10, 12, 17, 19, 24, 25, July 1; not July 13, Aug. 15).
E – ⑤⑦ July 3 - Aug. 28 (also June 23, 26 – 30, July 2, 13, Aug. 15). Timings may vary.
G – Ⓐ July 18 - Aug. 26.
H – ⑥ July 9 - Aug. 27. To / from Modane (Table **367**).
L – ①–⑥ July 16 - Aug. 27 (also June 25, July 2, 9, 10, 14, 24, Aug. 7, 14, 21; not Aug. 15, 24).
M – 12 Paris - Modane - Torino - Milano and v.v. (Table **44**). Special 'global' fares payable.

N – Until July 2. On June 25 Paris d. 1019.
P – ⑥ July 9 - Aug. 27.
Q – To Lausanne (a. 1615) on ①–④ (not July 13, 14, Aug. 15, Nov. 1, 10).
R – From Lausanne (d. 1638).
T – From Sept. 1.
W – ⑤ July 8 - Aug. 19 (not July 29, Aug. 12).
X – ①–⑥ June 23 – 30 (also Aug. 29 – 31).
Y – Ⓑ June 23 - July 1 (also Aug. 29 – 31).
a – Not July 14, Aug. 15, Nov. 1, 11.
b – Not Aug. 15, Nov. 1.
c – Also July 14, Aug. 15, Nov. 1, 11.
d – Also July 14, Aug. 15, Nov. 1.
e – Also Aug. 15, Nov. 1.

f – Also July 13, Nov. 10; not Nov. 11.
g – Also July 13; not Oct. 28, Nov. 4, 11.
h – Not July 14, Nov. 11.
j – 0624 on Ⓒ from Sept. 10.
k – Also ⑦ July 3 - Aug. 28; also July 14.
m – Not July 13, 14, Aug. 15, Nov. 1, 10.
r – Also July 13, 14, Aug. 15, Nov. 1, 10.
s – Not Nov. 1.
t – Also Aug. 15, Nov. 1; not Aug. 14, Nov. 13.
u – Not June 23 - Aug. 31.
v – Not Nov. 11.
y – Calls after Chambéry.
z – Calls before Chambéry.

TGV –🅁, supplement payable,
‡ – 2231 on ⑤; 2238 on ⑥.
♥ – Runs on June 19, July 3, 17 Aug. 15, 28 only.
⊖ – To / from Évian (Table **363**)
⊙ – To / from St Gervais (Table
❦ – **Service from Sept. 1**. See Table **44** for service to Aug
❖ – Services via Bourg en Bres are subject to alteration No 11 – 13.
◧ – Via Lyon Part Dieu.
* – Via St Exupéry TGV (Paris Aix via Bourg is *511* km).

PARIS - LYON ST EXUPÉRY ✈ - GRENOBLE 342

Shows complete service Paris - Lyon St Exupéry ✈ and v.v. Journeys not serving Grenoble continue to destinations in other tables.

All trains convey 🍸	TGV 6901 ①–④ m	TGV 6905 ①–⑥ b	TGV 6191 ①–⑥ b	TGV 6105	TGV 6911 Ⓐ	TGV 6911 ©	TGV 9245 N	TGV 6917	TGV 6193 B		TGV 9249 N	TGV 6919		TGV 6921 J	TGV 6923 Ⓑ h	TGV 6195 Ⓑ h	TGV 6195 ⑥ k		TGV 6925 L	TGV 6927	TGV 6197		TGV 6929 ⑤⑦ w
Paris Gare de Lyon ... d.	0641	0741	0741	0837	0941	0945	1041	1141	1141	...	1441	1441z	...	1641	1741	1741	1745	...	1849	1941	1941	...	2045
Lyon St Exupéry ✈ ... a.	0834	0934	0934	1029	1134	1139	1233	1334	1334	...	1633	1633	...	1834	1933	1933	1940	...	2048	2134	2134	...	2240
Lyon St Exupéry ✈ ... d.	0837	0938	...	...	1138	1143	...	1338	...	...	...	1641	...	1837	1937	...	...	...	2052	2138	...	...	2243
Grenoble ... a.	0942	1042	...	...	1242	1247	...	1442	...	...	...	1745	...	1942	2042	...	...	...	2154	2242	...	...	2346

	TGV 6900 ①–④ m	TGV 6902 Ⓐ		TGV 6904 ①–⑥ b		TGV 6906 ①–⑥ D		TGV 6908	TGV 9240 N		TGV 6910		TGV 6120 d	TGV 6920 ① g	TGV 6920 E		TGV 6976 ①–⑥ r	TGV 6922 © x	TGV 6922 Ⓐ	TGV 6198 ©		TGV 6924		TGV 6928 ⑦
ble ... d.	0516	0616	...	0716	...	0816	...	1016	...	...	1316	...	...	1505	1516	...	...	1716	1716	...	...	1916	...	2116
t Exupéry ✈ ... a.	0621	0721	...	0821	...	0921	...	|	...	...	1422	...	...	1608	1620	...	...	|	1819	...	...	2020	...	2221
t Exupéry ✈ ... d.	0626	0726	...	0826	...	0926	...	|	1126	...	1425	...	1538	1613	1625	...	1726	|	1822	1924	...	2025	...	2226
Gare de Lyon ... a.	0819	0919	...	1019	...	1119	...	1315	1320	...	1619	...	1730	1811	1819	...	1919	2015	2019	2119	...	2219	...	0019

aily to Sept. 18; © from Sept. 24 (also Oct. 10–14).
)–⑥ to July 1 / from Aug. 29 (not Nov. 1).
)③④⑤⑦ to July 1 / from Aug. 30 (not Nov. 2, 11).
o July 2 / from Aug. 29.
) to July 1; ⑤ July 8 - Aug. 26 (also July 13); Ⓐ from Aug. 29.
rom Sept. 1.

b – Not Aug. 15, Nov. 1.
d – Not July 9, 14, 16, 23, 30, Aug. 6, 13, 20, 27.
g – Also Nov. 2; not July 4 - Aug. 22.
h – Not July 14, Nov. 11.
k – Also July 14.
m – Not June 4 - Aug. 25, Nov. 1, 10.

r – Not June 23 - Aug. 31.
w – Also July 13, Aug. 15, Nov. 1, 10; not Nov. 11.
x – Also calls at Mâcon Loché TGV (d. 1839).
z – 1427 on ①②③④⑥ to June 22, June 27, 29, 30, July 2, ⑤⑦ July 3 - Aug. 28 (also July 13, Aug. 15).

TGV – Ⓡ, supplement payable, 🍸.

LYON - GRENOBLE 343

	⊡	Ⓐ		Ⓐ		Ⓐ	Ⓐ	©	Ⓐ ⊕	⊗				Ⓐ	©	Ⓐ		Ⓐ		Ⓐ		Ⓐ		Ⓐ	
Lyon Part-Dieu .... 344 d.	0612	0642	0712	0744	0814	0844	0914	0914	0944	1014	1114	1214	1314	1314	1344	1414	1444	1514	1544	1614	1644	1714	1744	1814
Bourgoin-Jallieu ... 344 d.	0639	0709	0739	0812	0841	0911	0940	0941	1011	1040	1141	1241	1341	1341	1411	1440	1511	1541	1611	1643	1712	1742	1811	1840
La Tour du Pin ..... 344 d.	0650	0720	0750	0823	0850	0921	0950	0950	1021	1051	1150	1250	1351	1350	1421	1451	1521	1550	1622	1653	|	1752	1822	1849
Voiron ... d.	0721	0753	0822	0853	0921	0952	1022	1022	1052	1123	1222	1322	1422	1422	1452	1523	1552	1622	1653	1724	1751	1822	1852	1922
Grenoble ... a.	0738	0808	0838	0908	0938	1008	1038	1038	1108	1138	1238	1338	1438	1438	1508	1538	1608	1638	1708	1740	1808	1838	1908	1938

	Ⓐ	Ⓐ	©	Ⓐ		◧	⑦ ●	Ⓐ ⊖	⑥ 🚌	🚌	
Part-Dieu ..... 344 d.	1842	1914	1914	1944	2014	2114	2212	2215	2206	2314	...
in-Jallieu .... 344 d.	1912	1940	1942	2011	2041	2143	2241	2243	2257	0005	...
ır du Pin ...... 344 d.	|	1950	1951	2022	2050	2152	2251	2253	|	|	...
... d.	1951	2022	2022	2052	2122	2223	2322	2322	|	|	...
ble ... a.	2008	2038	2038	2108	2138	2238	2338	2339	0005	0110	...

	⊡	Ⓐ		Ⓐ		Ⓐ	©	Ⓐ	Ⓐ
Grenoble ... d.	0522	0550	0622	0650	0720	0750	0822	0822	0852
Voiron ... d.	0539	0608	0639	0708	0738	0808	0839	0838	0909
La Tour du Pin ... 344 d.	0609	0639	0708	0739	0806	0839	0908	0909	0939
Bourgoin-Jallieu ... 344 d.	0619	0650	0719	0750	0818	0850	0918	0921	0949
Lyon Part-Dieu ... 344 a.	0644	0718	0746	0818	0846	0918	0946	0946	1016

	©	Ⓐ	Ⓐ		⊗		Ⓐ		©	Ⓐ	Ⓐ		Ⓐ	©	Ⓐ	Ⓐ		Ⓐ		Ⓐ		🚌	Ⓑ △	⑥ 🚌
ble ... d.	0922	0920	0952	1022	1122	1222	1252	1320	1422	1422	1452	1522	1550	1622	1622	1650	1720	1752	1822	1852	1922	1947	2022	2138	2123
... d.	0939	0937	1009	1039	1139	1239	1309	1337	1438	1438	1509	1539	1608	1639	1639	1708	1738	1809	1839	1909	1939	|	2039	2155	2153
ır du Pin ...... 344 d.	1008	1009	1039	1108	1208	1309	1339	1409	1508	1509	1539	1609	1639	1708	1709	1739	1809	1837	1908	1939	2008	|	2109	2224	2233
oin-Jallieu ... 344 d.	1018	1020	1049	1118	1218	1319	1349	1420	1519	1520	1549	1619	1650	1718	1720	1750	1821	1847	1918	1949	2018	|	2119	2235	2248
Part-Dieu ..... 344 a.	1044	1046	1114	1144	1244	1344	1414	1446	1546	1546	1614	1644	1720	1746	1746	1820	1846	1915	1946	2014	2044	2116	2146	2305	2335

⚒ to Sept. 12; ① from Sept. 19 (also Oct. 11–15, 8–22, 29, Nov. 2, Dec. 6–10; not Oct. 31).
Subject to alteration Sept. 20 - Oct. 14.
Subject to alteration on ①–⑤ Sept. 26 - Oct. 14.

◧ – Subject to alteration on Sept. 3.
● – Also July 14, Aug. 15, Nov. 11. Subject to alteration on Sept. 18, Oct. 16, Nov. 27.
⊕⊖ – Subject to alteration Sept. 12–30, Oct. 3–7, 24–27, 31, Nov. 2 - Dec. 2.
△ – Subject to alteration on ①–⑤ Sept. 12 - Dec. 2 (runs as normal on Oct. 28, Nov. 1).

Subject to alteration on Oct. 29, 30, 31

LYON - CHAMBÉRY 344

Subject to alteration June 23 - Aug. 31 (see note ✣). Subject to alteration Oct. 29, 30, 31. Certain journeys continue to/from Bourg St Maurice (Table **366**) or Modane (Table **367**).

	⚒	⚒	9241 ★			Ⓐ	©		©	Ⓐ	⚒		Ⓐ					Ⓐ	▲					
Lyon Part Dieu .... 343 d.	0650	0750	0831	0850	0950	1030	1050	1150	1250	1250	1350	1450	1550	1650	1750	1850	1950	2050	2150	...	...	...	...	...
Bourgoin-Jallieu ... 343 d.	0719	0817	|	0919	1017	|	1117	1217	1317	1319	1417	1519	1617	1719	1817	1919	2017	2119	2217	...	...	...	...	...
La Tour du Pin ..... 343 d.	0730	0829	|	0930	|	a	1129	|	1329	1330	|	1530	|	1730	|	1930	|	2130	|	...	...	...	...	...
Chambéry ... a.	0816	0916	0940	1016	1116	1158	1216	1316	1416	1416	1516	1617	1716	1816	1916	2016	2118	2216	2316	...	...	...	...	...

	⚒	⚒		Ⓐ	©	⑥	Ⓐ							Ⓐ	†	†	Ⓐ	9248 ⑥⑦ ★	9248 ⑤ ★	Ⓑ	⑥	9250 ①–④ ★		† w	⚒ ◇
ıbéry ... d.	0544	0644	0744	0844	0944	1044	1144	1207	1244	1344	1444	1544	1644	1744	1744	1844	1844	1855	1855	1943	1944	2020	...	2044	2044
ır du Pin ...... 343 d.	0628	|	0829	|	1028	|	1228	|	|	1427	|	1627	|	1827	1829	|	|	|	|	2030	2028	|	...	|	|
oin-Jallieu .... 343 d.	0639	0744	0839	0944	1039	1144	1239	|	1344	1439	1544	1639	1744	1839	1839	1943	1944	|	|	2043	2039	|	...	2144	2144
Part Dieu ..... 343 a.	0710	0810	0910	1010	1110	1210	1310	1326	1410	1510	1610	1710	1810	1910	1910	2010	2010	2028	2032	2110	2110	2131	...	2210	2216

Via Aix les Bains (Table 345).
Not Nov. 11. Subject to alteration on Sept. 18, Oct. 16, Nov. 27.
Not June 26, July 3, 10, 17, 24.

Subject to alteration Sept. 12–15, Oct. 24–27, 31 and ①–④ Nov. 2–17.
Subject to alteration on ①–⑤ Sept. 12 - Oct. 7, Oct. 24–27, 29, 31, Nov. 2–4, 7–18, 21–25, 28–30, Dec. 1, 2.

★ – *TGV* service. Ⓡ and supplement payable. ⑫ and 🍸 Paris - Lyon - Modane - Milano and v.v.

✣ – **June 23 - Aug. 31** services between Lyon and Chambéry are retimed and diverted, not calling at Bourgoin-Jallieu or La Tour du Pin. During this period through trains run from Lyon Part Dieu at 0702 Ⓐ, 0744 ⚒, 0846, 0945 Ⓑ, 0950 ⑥, 1050 ©, 1252, 1339 ⚒, 1450 Ⓐ, 1454 ©, 1543 Ⓐ, 1646, 1738 ⚒, 1750 †, 1850, 1944, 2040 Ⓐ and 2130 **z**; from Chambéry at 0552 ⚒, 0640 ⚒, 0730 †, 0844 ⚒, 0850 †, 0944 Ⓐ, 1037 ©, 1207 ⑥, 1247, 1340, 1449, 1533, 1650, 1744 Ⓑ, 1844 †, 1849 Ⓐ, 1940 ⑥, 1943 Ⓑ, 2044 † and 2047 ⚒. Other journeys are possible via Aix les Bains (Tables **345** and **364**).

LYON - AIX LES BAINS - ANNECY 345

	Ⓐ	🚌 Ⓐ	⚒ r	⚒	🚌 †	⚒	Ⓐ	🚌 Ⓐ	©	Ⓐ	Ⓐ r		🚌 Ⓐ		🚌 Ⓐ	Ⓐ		Ⓐ r		Ⓐ	r		
Lyon Part Dieu .... 344 346 d.	...	0608	...	0708	0708	0808	0908	1008	1008	1030	...	1208	1308	1408	1508	...	1608	...	1708	1808	...	1908	2108
Ambérieu ... 346 d.	0611	|	0713	0734	|	0834	0934	|	1034	|	1213	1234	|	1434	|	1611	1634	...	1734	1834	1913	1934	2134
Culoz ... 346 d.	0649	|	0753	0804	|	|	|	|	|	|	1253	|	|	|	|	1651	|	1749	|	|	1950	|	2205
Aix les Bains ... a.	0708	|	0811	0820	0835	0918	1018	|	1118	1145	1312	1318	|	1518	|	1709	1718	1808	1818	1918	2009	2018	2221
Aix les Bains ... 364 d.	0710	|	0813	0832	0835	0925	1025	|	1125	1147	1314	1325	|	1525	|	1710	1728	1810	1825	1925	2010	2025	2228
Chambéry ... 344 364 a.	0722	|	0827	|	|	|	|	|	|	1158	1326	|	|	|	|	1721	|	1822	|	|	2022	|	|
Annecy ... 364 a.	...	0759	...	0902	0910	1007	1107	1159	1207	...	...	1407	1459	1607	1659	...	1807	...	1907	2000	...	2107	2300

	Ⓐ r	Ⓐ	⚒	Ⓐ		🚌 Ⓐ	⑥	🚌 †	Ⓐ	Ⓐ	©	🚌 Ⓐ	⚒ r	🚌 Ⓐ			Ⓐ r			Ⓐ	Ⓐ r		🚌 Ⓐ	† ♥
cy ... 364 d.	...	0600	0653	...	0753	0900	0953	1000	1053	...	1153	1200	...	1300	1353	1553	...	1653	...	1753	...	1853	2000	2053
ambéry ... 344 364 d.	0535	|	|	0734	|	|	|	|	|	1124	|	|	1235	|	|	|	1635	|	1734	|	1834	|	|	|
s Bains ... 364 a.	0547	0635	0735	0745	0831	|	1035	1030	1130	1135	1235	|	1247	|	1435	1635	1647	1726	1746	1835	1846	1935	|	2135
s Bains ... d.	0549	0642	0742	0747	0838	|	1042	1030	1144	1144	1242	|	1248	|	1442	1642	1649	1740	1748	1842	1848	1942	|	2142
... 346 d.	0608	|	|	0808	|	|	|	|	|	|	|	|	1307	|	|	|	1709	1757	1808	|	1908	|	|	|
rieu ... 346 d.	0646	0728	0828	0846	0928	|	1128	|	1228	1228	1328	|	1346	|	1528	1728	...	1828	1846	1928	1946	2028	|	2228
Part Dieu ... 344 346 a.	...	0752	0852	...	0952	1052	1152	1210	1252	1252	1352	1352	...	1452	1552	1752	...	1852	...	1952	...	2052	2152	2252

Not July 18–22, 25–29, Aug. 1–5, 8–12, 16–19, 22–26.

♥ – On Oct. 2, Nov. 6, 20, Dec. 4 departs Aix les Bains 2138, arrives Lyon 2307 (not calling at Ambérieu).

346 LYON - BELLEGARDE - GENÈVE

km		①-⑤ n	①-⑤ n	⑥	①-⑤ n	①-⑥	⑥⑦ t⊗	①-⑤ a		①-⑤ n			TGV 9750 N	①-⑤ n		Ⓑ △	①-⑤ n			①-⑤ n	①-⑤ n	⑤ f△	⑥ k
0	**Lyon Perrache** d.	...	...	...	...	0625	0823	...	1023	...	1223	1423	...	...	...	...	...	...	...	...	...	...	...
4	**Lyon Part Dieu** 345 d.	...	...	...	...	0636	0834	0834	1034	...	1234	1436	1534	...	1635	1734	...	...	1836	...	...	2034	2024
54	Ambérieu 345 d.	...	...	...	...	0701	0858	0858	1100	...	1258	1501	|	...	1701	1802	...	...	|	...	...	2059	2058
106	Culoz 345 d.	...	...	...	...	0732	0931	0931	1133	...	1332	1535	|	...	1737	1836	...	...	1932	...	...	2133	2135
139	Bellegarde 341 364 d.	0553	0623	0653	0723	0801	1001	1001	1201	1249	1401	1601	1650	1723	1805	1902	1921	1934	2001	2027	2127	2159	2205
172	**Genève** 341 364 a.	0627	0657	0727	0757	0827	1027	1027	1227	1327	1427	1627	1716	1757	1830	...	1957	2000	2027	2101	2201	...	2232

	①-⑤ n	①-⑥ a	①-⑥ n	①-⑥ a‡△					z	①-⑤ n	TGV 9756 N				①-⑤ n	①-⑤ n			† △	①-⑤ n	①-⑤ n		①-⑤ n
Genève 341 364 d.	0503	...	0558	...	0730	...	0930	...	1130	1203	1242	1330	...	1530	1603	1703	1730	...	...	1803	1903	1930	2017
Bellegarde 341 364 d.	0535	0552	0631	0655	0757	...	0958	...	1158	1235	1311	1357	...	1558	1635	1735	1758	...	1855	1835	1935	1957	2051
Culoz 345 d.	...	0617	...	0721	0823	...	1026	...	1223	...	|	1425	...	1626	...	...	1826	...	1926	...	...	2025	...
Ambérieu 345 d.	...	0654	...	0755	0858	...	1058	...	1258	...	|	1458	...	1658	...	...	1858	...	2002	...	...	2058	...
Lyon Part Dieu 345 a.	...	0724	...	0823	0922	...	1124	...	1322	...	1426	1522	...	1724	...	...	1924	...	2032	...	...	2122	...
Lyon Perrache a.	...	...	...	...	0934	...	1135	...	1334	...	...	...	...	...	...	...	...	...	...	...	...	2135	...

N – (12) Genève - Lyon - Marseille - Nice and v.v. (Table **350**).
R – ①②③④⑦ (also June 25, July 2, 9, 16, 23, 30, Aug. 6, 13, 20, 27, Nov. 11; not Nov. 10).

a – Not July 14, Aug. 15, Nov. 1, 11.
f – Not Aug. 19 - Sept. 23, Nov. 11.
k – Not June 25 - Aug. 27.

n – Not Aug. 1.
t – Also July 14, Aug. 15, Nov. 1, 11.
v – Not July 13, Aug. 14, Oct. 31, Nov. 10.
z – Not ①-⑤ Nov. 28 - Dec. 9.

⊗ – Subject to alteration on May 15, 22, 29.
‡ – Subject to alteration on June 25.

TGV – Ⓡ, supplement payable, 🍷.

△ – To/from Évian les Bains (Table **363**) and/or St Gervais (Table **365**).

Certain services are subject to alteration Nov. 10

348 LYON - ST ÉTIENNE

TGV trains (Paris) - Lyon - St Étienne

		TGV 6681 ①-⑥ b		TGV 6685		TGV 6687		TGV 6689	
Paris Gare de Lyon **340** d.	...	0659	...	1259	...	1657	...	1857	...
Lyon Part-Dieu d.	...	0905	...	1505	...	1905	...	2105	...
St Étienne Châteaucreux a.	...	0947	...	1547	...	1947	...	2147	...

		TGV 6691 ①-⑥ b		TGV 6693		TGV 6695		TGV 6697 Ⓐ J
St Étienne Châteaucreux d.	...	0613	...	1013	...	1213	...	1642
Lyon Part-Dieu a.	...	0658	...	1058	...	1259	...	1728
Paris Gare de Lyon **340** a.	...	0901	...	1301	...	1501	...	1933

Local Trains Lyon - St Étienne

km		⚒	⚒	⑥	Ⓐ △	Ⓐ		Ⓐ		Ⓒ	Ⓐ	Ⓐ	Ⓐ		⚒	Ⓐ			Ⓐ		⚒	Ⓐ		
0	**Lyon** Part-Dieu d.	...	0624	...	...	0654	0705	...	0724	...	...	0754	...	0824	...	0854	0924	...	0954	1024	...	1054	1124	...
	Lyon Perrache d.	0540	|	0633	0640	|	|	0710	|	0733	0740	|	0810	|	0833	|	|	0933	|	|	1033	|	|	1133
22	Givors Ville d.	0558	0641	0658	0658	0711	|	0728	0741	0758	0758	0811	0828	0841	0858	0911	0941	0958	1011	1041	1058	1111	1141	1158
47	St Chamond d.	0617	0700	0717	0717	0730	|	0747	0800	0817	0817	0830	0847	0900	0917	0930	1000	1017	1030	1100	1117	1130	1200	1217
59	**St Étienne** ⊙ a.	0626	0709	0726	0726	0739	0747	0756	0809	0826	0826	0839	0856	0909	0926	0939	1009	1026	1039	1109	1126	1139	1209	1226

			⚒	Ⓐ			Ⓐ		⚒	Ⓐ			Ⓐ	Ⓐ		⑥	Ⓐ	Ⓐ	⚒	Ⓐ △		Ⓒ	Ⓐ	Ⓐ	Ⓐ △
Lyon Part-Dieu d.	1206	1224	...	1254	1324	...	1354	1424	...	1454	1524	...	1554	...	1624	...	...	1654	1706	...	1724	...	...	1754	...
Lyon Perrache d.	|	|	1233	|	|	1333	|	|	1433	|	|	1533	|	1603	|	1633	1640	|	|	1710	|	1733	1740	|	1810
Givors Ville d.	|	1241	1258	1311	1341	1358	1411	1441	1458	1511	1541	1558	1611	1628	1641	1658	1658	1711	|	1728	1741	1758	1758	1811	1828
St Chamond d.	|	1300	1317	1330	1400	1417	1430	1500	1517	1530	1600	1617	1630	1647	1700	1717	1725	1731	|	1747	1800	1817	1817	1830	1847
St Étienne ⊙ a.	1247	1309	1326	1339	1409	1426	1439	1509	1526	1539	1609	1626	1639	1656	1709	1726	1738	1741	1746	1756	1809	1826	1826	1839	1856

	⑥	Ⓐ	Ⓐ	Ⓐ △		Ⓐ		⚒	Ⓑ	¶	Ⓑ h ‡
Lyon Part-Dieu d.	...	...	1854	...	1924	...	1954	2024	...	2124	2225	2323
Lyon Perrache d.	1833	1840	|	1910	|	1933	|	|	2033	|	|	|
Givors Ville d.	1858	1858	1911	1928	1941	1958	2011	2041	2058	2141	2245	2342
St Chamond d.	1917	1917	1930	1947	2000	2017	2030	2100	2117	2200	2303	0001
St Étienne ⊙ a.	1926	1926	1939	1956	2009	2026	2039	2109	2126	2209	2312	0010

	Ⓐ	Ⓐ	⚒	Ⓐ	Ⓐ	Ⓐ		Ⓐ △	⑥
St Étienne ⊙ d.	0520	0534	0550	0604	0620	0634	0650	0704	0704
St Chamond d.	0529	0543	0559	0613	0629	0643	0700	0713	0713
Givors Ville d.	0548	0602	0618	0632	0648	0702	0718	0732	0732
Lyon Perrache a.	|	0627	|	0657	|	0720	|	0750	0757
Lyon Part-Dieu a.	0606	...	0636	...	0706	...	0736	...	...

	Ⓐ	Ⓐ		△	⚒	Ⓐ	Ⓐ		⚒	Ⓐ			Ⓐ		⚒	Ⓐ			Ⓐ		⚒	Ⓐ			⊗
St Étienne ⊙ d.	0720	0734	0750	0804	0813	0820	0834	0850	0904	0920	0950	1004	1020	1050	1104	1120	1150	1204	1220	1250	1304	1320	1350	1404	1413
St Chamond d.	0729	0743	0759	0813	|	0829	0843	0859	0913	0929	0959	1013	1029	1059	1113	1129	1159	1213	1229	1259	1313	1329	1359	1413	|
Givors Ville d.	0748	0802	0818	0831	|	0848	0902	0918	0932	0948	1018	1031	1048	1118	1131	1148	1218	1231	1248	1318	1331	1348	1418	1431	|
Lyon Perrache a.	|	0820	|	0850r	|	|	0927	|	0957	|	|	1057	|	|	1157	|	|	1257	|	|	1357	|	|	1457	|
Lyon Part-Dieu a.	0806	...	0836	...	0854	0906	...	0936	...	1006	1036	...	1106	1136	...	1206	1236	...	1306	1336	...	1406	1436	...	1454

		⚒	Ⓐ			Ⓐ	Ⓐ △		Ⓐ △	⑥	Ⓐ	Ⓐ		Ⓐ △	Ⓒ	Ⓐ	Ⓐ △		Ⓐ	⑥	Ⓑ	Ⓐ			Ⓑ
St Étienne ⊙ d.	1450	1504	1520	1550	1604	1620	1634	1650	1704	1704	1720	1734	1750	1804	1804	1820	1834	1850	1904	1904	1913	1920	2004	2020	2120
St Chamond d.	1459	1513	1529	1600	1613	1629	1643	1700	1713	1713	1729	1743	1759	1813	1813	1830	1843	1900	1913	1913	|	1929	2013	2029	2129
Givors Ville d.	1518	1532	1548	1618	1631	1648	1702	1718	1732	1731	1748	1802	1818	1832	1831	1848	1902	1918	1932	1932	|	1948	2031	2048	2148
Lyon Perrache a.	|	1557	|	|	1657	|	1720	|	1750	1757	|	1820	|	1850	1857	|	1920	|	1950	1957	|	|	2057	|	|
Lyon Part-Dieu a.	1536	...	1606	1636	...	1706	...	1736	...	...	1806	...	1836	...	...	1906	...	1936	...	...	1954	2006	...	2106	2206

J – To July 1 and from Aug. 29.
L – ⑥⑦ (also Nov. 11; daily July 2 - Aug. 28).

b – Not Aug. 15, Nov. 1.
d – Also July 17, 24, 31, Aug. 14, Sept. 4, 11, 25, Oct. 2.
h – Not July 14, Aug. 15, Nov. 1, 11.

r – 0857 on Ⓒ.

TGV – Ⓡ, supplement payable, 🍷.

⊙ – St Étienne Châteaucreux.
⊗ – Subject to alteration Oct. 10 – 15.

¶ – Subject to alteration on July 14, Sept. 18, Oct. 16, Nov. 27.
‡ – Subject to alteration on Sept. 18, Oct. 9, 16, Nov. 20, 27, Dec.
△ – Timings may vary by up to 5 minutes on Ⓐ July 18 - Aug. 26.

Certain services are subject to alteration Aug. 13 – 15, Oct. 29 – 31, Nov. 10 – 13

349 ST ÉTIENNE - LE PUY

km		Ⓐ	⚒			⚒		e		Ⓐ			Ⓐ	⚒		Ⓐ							
	Lyon Part Dieu **348** d.	...	...	...	...	...	...	1206	...	1454	...	...	...	1706	...	...	...	...	...	...	...	...	...
0	**St Étienne** Châteaucreux d.	0531	0648	...	0846	1010	...	1251	...	1543	1553	...	1711	1748	1748	1845	...	2010	...	2157	...	...	...
15	Firminy a.	0547	0709	...	0902	1025	...	1309	...	1603	1609	...	1727	1805	1805	1900	...	2032	...	2219	...	...	...
88	**Le Puy en Velay** a.	0721	0827	...	1022	1138	...	1428	...	...	1720	...	1844	1917	1917	2017	...	2144	...	2328	...	...	...

	Ⓐ		Ⓐ	Ⓐ	⚒	Ⓐ					n			Ⓑ k				†					
Le Puy en Velay d.	0430	...	...	0556	0639	0740	0834	...	1032	...	1232	...	1615	1728	...	1935	...	2107	...	...	...	...	...
Firminy d.	0541	...	0645	0708	0755	0858	0948	...	1148	...	1354	...	1726	1854	...	2053	...	2217	...	...	...	...	...
St Étienne Châteaucreux a.	0603	...	0709	0731	0810	0913	1005	...	1205	...	1410	...	1742	1910	...	2109	...	2233	...	...	...	...	...
Lyon Part Dieu **348** a.	...	...	0754	0820p	0854	...	...	...	...	...	1454t	...	...	1954	...	...	...	...	...	...	...	...	...

e – Not Oct. 30, 31, Nov. 11, 12.
k – Not Oct. 30, 31, Nov. 11.

n – Not Oct. 29 – 31, Nov. 11, 12.
p – Lyon **Perrache**.

t – Subject to alteration Oct. 10 – 15.

PARIS / LYON - AVIGNON - MARSEILLE - TOULON - NICE

For *TGV* trains Paris - Valence Ville - Avignon Centre see Table **351**. Certain Paris - Toulon trains continue to Hyères (Table **360**).

SERVICE FROM JUNE 6. *Services via Lyon are subject to alteration Aug. 13, 14, 15, Oct. 29, 30, 31.*

All *TGV* trains are 🄡	*TGV* **6805** Ⓐ ⊖	*TGV* **6805** Ⓒ ⊖		*TGV* **6101** Ⓐ		*TGV* **6171**	*TGV* **5102**	*TGV* **6103**	*TGV* **6890** C A		*TGV* **6105**	*TGV* **9810**	*TGV* **5110**		*TGV* **6173**		*TGV* **6820**	*TGV* **6886** B	*TGV* **6107**		*TGV* **5312** N ⊗	*TGV* **6175**
Brussels Midi **11** d.	...	...	...	...	...	...	...	...	...	...	...	0710	...	...	...	...	...	...	...	...	...	...
Lille Europe **11** d.	...	...	...	...	...	...	0537	...	...	...	...	|	0654f	...	...	...	...	...	...	...	...	...
Charles de Gaulle ✈ **11** d.	...	...	...	...	...	...	0658j	...	...	...	...	0831	0831	...	...	...	...	...	...	...	...	...
Marne la Vallée-Chessy § **11** d.	...	...	...	...	...	...	0711	...	...	...	...	0843	0843	...	...	...	...	...	...	...	...	...
Paris Gare de Lyon ▶ d.	...	...	...	0607	...	0719	|	0737	...	...	0837	|	|	...	0921	...	...	...	0937	...	...	1019
Metz **379** d.	...	...	...	|	...	|	|	|	...	...	|	|	|	...	|	...	0600	...	|	...	...	|
Strasbourg **379** ⊠ d.	...	...	...	|	...	|	|	|	...	...	|	|	|	...	|	...	|	...	|	...	...	|
Dijon **379** d.	...	...	...	|	...	|	|	|	...	...	|	|	|	...	|	...	0921	0921	|	...	...	|
Genève **346** d.	...	...	...	|	...	|	|	|	...	...	|	|	|	...	|	...	|	|	|	...	...	|
Lyon Part Dieu ▶ d.	0636	0702	...	|	...	|	0906	|	...	...	|	1036	1036	...	|	...	1106	1106	|	...	1136	|
Lyon St Exupéry ✈ ▶ d.	|	|	...	|	...	|	|	|	...	...	1031	|	|	...	|	...	|	|	|	...	|	|
Valence TGV ▶ d.	0712	|	...	0827	...	|	|	|	1006	...	|	1114	1114	...	|	...	|	|	|	...	|	|
Avignon TGV d.	0747	0808	...	0902	...	1000	1011	1019	1041	...	1124	1148	1148	...	|	...	1212	1212	1220	...	1245	1259
Aix en Provence TGV d.	0809	0833	...	0925	...	|	1034	1042	1104	...	|	|	|	...	1217	...	1234	1234	1242	...	1308	|
Marseille St Charles a.	0821	0846	...	0941	...	|	1046	1054	1117	...	1154	1216	1216	...	|	...	1246	1246	1254	...	1322	|
Marseille St Charles **360** d.	0831	0900	...	...	...	|	...	...	...	...	...	...	...	...	|	...	1300	...	...	...	...	|
Toulon **360** a.	0912	0943	...	...	...	1108	...	...	...	...	...	...	...	...	1308	...	1341	...	...	...	...	1408
Les Arcs-Draguignan **360** a.	0948	1019	...	...	...	1144	...	...	...	...	...	...	...	...	|	...	1418	...	...	...	...	1444
St Raphaël-Valescure **360** a.	1005	1036	...	...	...	|	...	...	...	...	...	...	...	...	1359	...	1438	...	...	...	...	1501
Cannes **360** a.	1035	1103	...	...	...	1223	...	...	...	...	...	...	...	...	1424	...	1503	...	...	...	...	1526
Antibes **360** a.	1046	1117	...	...	...	1235	...	...	...	...	...	...	...	...	1435	...	1515	...	...	...	...	1536
Nice **360** a.	1106	1140	...	...	...	1255	...	...	...	...	...	...	...	...	1455	...	1537	...	...	...	...	1556

	TGV **9801**	*TGV* **6109**	*TGV* **5316** H	*TGV* **6165** K	*TGV* **9877** E X	*TGV* **6111**	*TGV* **9877** G X		*TGV* **9826**	*TGV* **5164**	*TGV* **6163** K	*TGV* **6113** J	*TGV* **9756**	*TGV* **6837** ◇	*TGV* **6115** Ⓑ q	*TGV* **6177** V	*TGV* **9828**	*TGV* **6145**	*TGV* **6179** L	*TGV* **6117**	*TGV* **5322** N ⊕	*TGV* **6169** ①–④ m	*TGV* **6119** ⑤⑦ d
ssels Midi **11** d.	0817	...	...	...	...	...	...	...	1031	...	...	...	...	...	...	...	1217	...	...	...	...	...	...
e Europe **11** d.	0902	...	...	...	...	...	...	...	|	1043	...	...	...	...	...	...	1303	...	...	...	...	...	...
arles de Gaulle ✈ **11** d.	0958	...	...	...	...	...	...	...	1158	1158	...	...	...	...	...	...	1358	...	...	...	...	...	...
rne la Vallée-Chessy § **11** d.	1011	...	...	...	...	...	...	...	1211	1211	...	...	...	...	...	...	1411	...	...	...	...	...	...
Gare de Lyon ▶ d.	|	1037	...	1119	...	1137	...	...	|	|	1237	1237	...	...	1415	1419	|	1437	1519	1537	...	1615	1615
tz **379** d.	|	|	...	|	0811	|	0811	...	|	|	|	|	...	...	|	|	|	|	|	|	...	|	|
asbourg **379** ⊠ d.	|	|	...	|	0906	|	0906	...	|	|	|	|	...	1112	|	|	|	|	|	|	...	|	|
on **379** d.	|	|	...	|	|	|	|	...	|	|	|	|	...	|	|	|	|	|	|	|	...	|	|
nève **346** d.	|	|	...	|	|	|	|	...	|	|	|	|	1242	|	|	|	|	|	|	|	...	|	|
Part Dieu ▶ d.	1206	|	1236	|	1306	|	1308	...	1406	1406	|	|	1436	1536	|	|	1606	|	|	|	1736	|	|
on St Exupéry ✈ ▶ d.	|	|	|	|	|	|	|	...	|	|	|	|	|	|	|	|	|	|	|	|	|	|	|
ice TGV ▶ d.	|	|	1312	|	|	|	1350	...	1442	1442	|	|	1513	1613	|	|	|	|	|	|	1813	|	|
non TGV d.	1311	1319	1347	1400	1410	1419	1427	...	|	|	|	1520	1548	1648	|	|	1712	1720	1800	1820	1847	|	|
n Provence TGV d.	1334	1342	|	|	1434	1443	1450	...	1532	1532	1540	1543	|	|	|	1718	1734	1743	|	1843	|	|	|
eille St Charles a.	1346	1354	1420	|	1446	1454	1502	...	1546	1546	1551	1554	1618	1716	1720	|	1746	1754	|	1854	1916	1920	1920
eille St Charles **360** d.	...	...	...	|	...	...	...	...	...	...	1602	...	1631	...	...	|	1801	...	|	...	...	1931	1931
on **360** a.	...	...	...	1508	...	...	...	...	...	...	|	...	1713	...	...	1809	1844	...	1909	...	...	2014	2014
Arcs-Draguignan **360** a.	...	...	...	|	...	...	...	...	...	...	1718	...	|	...	...	|	1921	...	|	...	...	|	...
aphaël-Valescure **360** a.	...	...	...	1558	...	...	...	...	...	...	1736	...	1807	...	...	1858	1937	...	1958	...	...	2109	...
es **360** a.	...	...	...	1623	...	...	...	...	...	...	1802	...	1832	...	...	1924	2003	...	2023	...	...	2137	...
es **360** a.	...	...	...	1635	...	...	...	...	...	...	1816	...	1842	...	...	1935	2015	...	2035	...	...	2149	...
360 a.	...	...	...	1654	...	...	...	...	...	...	1835	...	1905	...	...	1955	2037	...	2055	...	...	2210	...

	TGV **6815**	*TGV* **6121** Ⓑ q		*TGV* **6181**	*TGV* **5134**	*TGV* **6123**		*TGV* **6183** ⑤–⑦ r	*TGV* **6153** ①–④ m	*TGV* **9580** ♣	*TGV* **6127**	*TGV* **5346** R ⊖	*TGV* **6187** ⑤ y		*TGV* **6129**	*TGV* **6892** D A	*TGV* **5124**	*TGV* **6131** ②–④ ♥	*TGV* **6827** Ⓒ T	*TGV* **6827** Ⓐ J	*TGV* **6131** S		*TGV* **6137** ⑤⑦ p
ssels Midi **11** d.	...	...	...	...	...	...	...	...	...	...	...	...	...	...	...	...	...	...	...	...	...	...	...
e Europe **11** d.	...	...	...	...	1554	...	...	...	...	...	...	...	...	...	...	...	1826	...	...	...	...	...	...
arles de Gaulle ✈ **11** d.	...	...	...	...	1656	...	...	...	...	...	...	...	...	...	...	...	1928	...	...	...	...	...	...
rne la Vallée-Chessy § **11** d.	...	...	...	...	1711	...	...	...	...	...	...	...	...	...	...	...	1941	...	...	...	...	...	...
Gare de Lyon ▶ d.	...	1637	...	1719	|	1737	...	1819	1819	...	1837	...	1919	...	1937	...	|	2019	...	...	2037	...	2137
tz **379** d.	...	|	...	|	|	|	...	|	|	...	|	...	|	...	|	...	|	|	...	...	|	...	|
asbourg **379** ⊠ d.	...	|	...	|	|	|	...	|	|	1615	|	...	|	...	|	...	|	|	1803	1836	|	...	|
on **379** d.	1612z	|	...	|	|	|	...	|	|	|	|	...	|	...	|	...	|	|	|	|	|	...	|
nève **346** d.	|	|	...	|	|	|	...	|	|	|	|	...	|	...	|	...	|	|	|	|	|	...	|
Part Dieu ▶ d.	1806	|	...	|	1906	|	...	|	|	2006	|	2036	|	...	|	...	2136	|	2206	2206	|	...	|
on St Exupéry ✈ ▶ d.	|	|	...	|	|	|	...	|	|	|	|	|	|	...	|	...	|	|	|	|	|	...	|
ice TGV ▶ d.	|	|	...	1932	|	|	...	|	|	|	|	2113	|	...	|	2157	|	|	|	|	|	...	|
non TGV d.	1912	1920	...	|	2012	2019	...	|	|	2111	2120	2148	2200	...	2219	2235	2243	2302	2312	2312	2322	...	0023
n Provence TGV d.	1935	1943	...	|	2034	2042	...	2117	2117	2134	2143	|	|	...	2242	2258	2306	2325	2334	2334	2346	...	0047
eille St Charles a.	1946	1954	...	|	2046	2054	...	|	|	2146	2154	2216	|	...	2254	2310	2318	2338	2349	2349	2358	...	0059
eille St Charles **360** d.	2000	...	...	|	...	...	...	|	|	...	...	...	|	...	2306	...	...	...	...	...	...	...	...
on **360** a.	2043	...	...	2108	...	...	...	2208	2208	...	...	...	2308	...	2349	...	...	...	...	...	...	...	...
Arcs-Draguignan **360** a.	2121	...	...	2145	...	...	...	|	...	...	...	...	|	...	...	...	...	...	...	...	...	...	...
aphaël-Valescure **360** a.	2138	...	...	|	...	...	...	2258	...	...	...	...	2357	...	...	...	...	...	...	...	...	...	...
es **360** a.	2205	...	...	2223	...	...	...	2323	...	...	...	...	0024	...	...	...	...	...	...	...	...	...	...
es **360** a.	2217	...	...	2234	...	...	...	2335	...	...	...	...	0036	...	...	...	...	...	...	...	...	...	...
360 a.	2237	...	...	2255	...	...	...	2355	...	...	...	...	0055	...	...	...	...	...	...	...	...	...	...

From Annecy (see panel).
From Basel (Table **379**).
⑥ July 2 - Aug. 27 (also July 14, Oct. 29, Nov. 11; not July 16).
⑦ July 3 - Aug. 28 (also Aug. 15, Nov. 1, 13; not Aug. 14).
②③④⑦ to June 30; ②③ July 5 - Aug. 31 (also July 28); ②③④⑦ Sept. 4 - Oct. 27; ②③④⑤⑦ from Oct. 30.
Subject to alteration on July 6, Sept. 4, Oct. 2, 30.
①⑤⑥ to June 27; ①④⑤⑥⑦ July 1 - Sept. 3 (not July 28); ①⑤⑥ Sept. 5 - Oct. 29; ①⑥ from Oct. 31. Subject to alteration on ① from Oct. 31.
(12) Le Havre - Rouen - Lyon - Marseille (Table **335**).
Subject to alteration on July 9, 10, 18 – 31, Aug. 1 – 5, Sept. 18, Oct. 1, 2, 3, 8, 9, 16, Nov. 19, 20, 21, 26, Dec. 3, 4, 5.
To July 2 and from Aug. 29.
July 3 - Aug. 28.
Daily to Aug. 28; ⑤⑥ from Sept. 2 (also Nov. 10).
From Nantes via Massy TGV (Table **335**).
From Rennes via Massy TGV (Table **335**).
①⑤⑥⑦.
Runs daily July 2 - Aug. 28.
To Ventimiglia (Table **360**).
From Luxembourg from July 3 (Table **379**). Departs Metz 0743 until July 2.

d – Also July 13, Aug. 15, Nov. 1, 10; not Nov. 11.
f – Lille **Flandres**.
j – 0656 until June 11.
m – Not July 13, 14, Aug. 15, Nov. 1, 10.
p – Not July 3, 10, 17, 24, 31, Aug. 7, 14, 21, 28, Nov. 11.
q – Not Nov. 11; runs daily July 3 - Sept. 2.
r – Also July 13, 14, Aug. 15, Nov. 1, 10.
y – Not June 17, 24, Nov. 11.
z – 1609 from Aug. 29.

TGV – 🄡, supplement payable, 🍸.

♥ – Subject to alteration on July 13, 14, Aug. 16, Nov. 1, 2, 10.
◇ – Subject to alteration on Nov. 11, 12.
⊗ – Subject to alteration on Oct. 1, 8, 9, 15, Nov. 26.
⊕ – Subject to alteration on Sept. 25, Oct. 1, 2, 8, Nov. 26.
⊖ – Subject to alteration on Oct. 1, 8, 15, Nov. 26.
⊠ – Strasbourg departures may be up to 4 minutes earlier on ①–⑤ Aug. 16 - Sept. 30 and ①–⑤ from Nov. 21.
▶ – For Paris to Lyon see Table **340** (for Paris to St Exupéry ✈ see Table **342**). For additional trains from Paris and Lyon to Valence TGV see Table **355**. For Lyon to Valence Ville see Table **351**.
◧ – Lyon Part Dieu - Valence TGV is 104 km.

ANNECY - MARSEILLE

	TGV **6890** C	*TGV* **6892** D
Annecy d.	0726	1931
Aix les Bains d.	0757	2001
Chambéry d.	0811	2016
Grenoble d.	0905	2056
Valence TGV a.	1001	2154
Marseille (see above) a.	1117	2310

♣ – From Frankfurt (Main), Table **47**.
§ – Station for Disneyland Paris.

Additional low-cost 'Ouigo' TGV trains run from Marne la Vallée-Chessy – see Table **350a**

350 NICE - TOULON - MARSEILLE - AVIGNON - LYON / PARIS

TGV Méditerr

For *TGV* trains Avignon Centre - Valence Ville - Paris see Table **351**. Certain Toulon - Paris trains start from Hyères (Table **360**).

SERVICE FROM JUNE 6. *Services via Lyon are subject to alteration on Aug. 13, 14, 15, Oct. 29, 30, 31.*

All *TGV* trains are Ⓡ	*TGV* 6102	*TGV* 6136	*TGV* 9854	*TGV* 6150	*TGV* 6898	*TGV* 6898	*TGV* 6106	*TGV* 5144*		*TGV* 6894	*TGV* 9582	*TGV* 6108	*TGV* 5350	*TGV* 6112	*TGV* 9860	*TGV* 9860	*TGV* 6172		*TGV* 6114	*TGV* 6814	*TGV* 6188	
	Ⓐ	①–④		Ⓐ	Ⓐ	Ⓒ				C		①–⑥			Ⓒ	Ⓐ						
		t			J	T				A	♣	b	R⊗								K	
Nice 360 d.	...	...	...	...	...	...	...	...	...	...	...	...	...	...	0602	0602	0702	...	...	0724	0804	...
Antibes 360 d.	...	...	...	...	...	...	...	...	...	...	...	...	...	...	0626	0626	0722	...	...	0743	0823	...
Cannes 360 d.	...	...	...	...	...	...	...	...	...	...	...	...	...	...	0641	0641	0733	...	...	0758	0835	...
St Raphaël-Valescure 360 d.	...	...	...	...	...	...	...	...	...	...	...	...	...	...	0708	0708	|	...	...	0825	0859	...
Les Arcs-Draguignan 360 d.	...	...	...	...	...	...	...	...	...	...	...	...	...	...	0727	0727	0813	...	...	0841	|	...
Toulon 360 d.	...	...	...	0545	...	...	...	...	...	...	...	0742j	...	...	0816	0816	0850	...	...	0917	0950	...
Marseille St Charles 360 a.	...	...	...	|	...	...	...	...	...	...	...	0829	...	...	0859	0859	|	...	...	0959	|	...
Marseille St Charles d.	0524	0606	0614	|	0644	0644	0706	0714	...	0755	0814	0840	0844	0906	0914	0914	|	...	1006	1014	|	...
Aix en Provence TGV d.	0539	0620	0628	0641	|	|	0720	0728	...	0809	0829	|	|	0920	0929	0929	|	...	1020	1029	|	...
Avignon TGV d.	0601	0642	|	0704	0715	0715	0742	|	...	0831	0851	|	0914	0942	0951	0951	1001	...	1042	|	1101	...
Valence TGV ▶ d.	|	|	0720	|	0749	0749	|	|	...	0904	|	|	0949	|	|	|	|	...	|	1124	|	...
Lyon St Exupéry ✈ ▶ d.	|	|	|	|	|	|	|	|	...	...	|	|	|	|	|	|	|	...	|	|	|	...
Lyon Part Dieu ▶ a.	|	|	0754	|	0824	0824	|	0850	...	...	0954	|	1024	|	1054	1054	|	...	|	1158	|	...
Genève **346** a.	|	|	|	|	|	|	|	|	...	...	|	|	...	|	|	|	|	...	|	|	|	...
Dijon **379** a.	|	|	|	|	|	0956	|	|	...	...	|	|	...	|	|	|	|	...	|	1352	|	...
Strasbourg **379** ⊠ a.	|	|	|	|	1147	1217	|	|	...	...	1344	|	...	|	|	|	|	...	|	...	|	...
Metz **379** a.	|	|	|	|	...	...	|	|	...	...	...	|	...	|	|	|	|	...	|	...	|	...
Paris Gare de Lyon ▶ a.	0841	0923	|	0942	...	...	1023	|	...	...	...	1145	...	1223	|	|	1241	...	1323	...	1341	...
Marne la Vallée-Chessy § **11** a.	...	...	0947	...	...	...	...	1048	...	...	...	...	...	...	1248	1248	...	...	...	...	...	...
Charles de Gaulle ✈ **11** a.	...	...	1001	...	...	...	...	1102	...	...	...	...	...	...	1302	1302	...	...	...	...	...	...
Lille Europe **11** a.	...	...	1107r	...	...	...	...	1158r	...	...	...	...	...	...	1405r	1427r	...	...	...	...	...	...
Brussels Midi **11** a.	...	...	1151	...	...	...	...	...	...	...	...	...	...	...	1459r	1516r	...	...	...	...	...	...

	TGV 5184	*TGV* 9866	*TGV* 6174	*TGV* 5368	*TGV* 6874	*TGV* 6118	*TGV* 9750	*TGV* 6176	*TGV* 9750	*TGV* 6120	*TGV* 5192	*TGV* 6170	*TGV* 5372	*TGV* 6122	*TGV* 6864	*TGV* 6885		*TGV* 5376	*TGV* 6124	*TGV* 9898	*TGV* 6178	
			V	N⊖				△		u		K	N			B		H		X	L	
Nice 360 d.	0924	...	1004	...	...	...	1055	1104	...	...	...	1202	...	...	1223	...	...	...	...	...	1359	...
Antibes 360 d.	0943	...	1024	...	...	...	1114	1123	...	...	...	1221	...	...	1245	...	...	...	...	...	1419	...
Cannes 360 d.	0953	...	1036	...	...	...	1126	1134	...	...	...	1234	...	...	1257	...	...	...	...	...	1430	...
St Raphaël-Valescure 360 d.	1020	...	1101	...	...	...	1154	1200	...	...	...	1301	...	...	1322	...	...	...	...	...	1455	...
Les Arcs-Draguignan 360 d.	1035	...	|	...	...	...	|	|	...	...	...	|	...	...	1338	...	...	...	...	...	1512	...
Toulon 360 d.	1116	...	1149	...	...	...	1246	1251	←	...	...	1351	...	...	1416	...	...	...	1450	...	1551	...
Marseille St Charles 360 a.	1159	...	|	...	...	...	1331	|	1331	...	...	|	...	...	1500	...	...	...	1534	...	|	...
Marseille St Charles d.	1214	1214	|	1244	1244	1306	→	|	1346	1406	1414	|	1444	1506	1514	1514	...	1543	1548	1614	|	...
Aix en Provence TGV d.	1229	1229	|	1259	1259	1320	...	|	1403	1420	1429	|	1459	1520	1529	1529	...	|	1603	1629	|	...
Avignon TGV d.	1251	1251	1300	1321	1321	1342	...	1401	1426	1442	1451	1502	1521	1542	1551	1551	...	1614	|	1652	1701	...
Valence TGV ▶ d.	|	|	|	|	|	|	...	|	|	|	|	|	|	|	|	|	...	1649	1657	|	|	...
Lyon St Exupéry ✈ ▶ d.	|	|	|	|	|	|	...	|	|	1538	|	|	|	|	|	|	...	|	|	|	|	...
Lyon Part Dieu ▶ a.	1354	1354	|	1424	1424	|	...	|	1528	|	1554	|	1624	|	1654	1654	...	1724	|	1754	|	...
Genève **346** a.	|	|	|	...	|	|	...	|	1716	|	|	|	...	|	|	|	...	...	|	|	|	...
Dijon **379** a.	|	|	|	...	|	|	...	|	...	|	|	|	...	|	1839	1839	...	...	|	|	|	...
Strasbourg **379** ⊠ a.	|	|	|	...	1857	|	...	|	...	|	|	|	...	|	|	...	...	...	|	2147	|	...
Metz **379** a.	|	|	|	...	...	|	...	|	...	|	|	|	...	|	2157	...	...	...	|	2247	|	...
Paris Gare de Lyon ▶ a.	|	|	1541	...	...	1623	...	1641	...	1730	|	1745	...	1823	...	...	...	...	1915	...	1941	...
Marne la Vallée-Chessy § **11** a.	1548	1548	...	...	...	...	...	...	...	...	1748	...	...	...	...	...	...	...	...	...	...	...
Charles de Gaulle ✈ **11** a.	1602	1602	...	...	...	...	...	...	...	...	1802	...	...	...	...	...	...	...	...	...	...	...
Lille Europe **11** a.	1701r	1701r	...	...	...	...	...	...	...	...	1944f	...	...	...	...	...	...	...	...	...	...	...
Brussels Midi **11** a.	...	1752r	...	...	...	...	...	...	...	...	...	...	...	...	...	...	...	...	...	...	...	...

	TGV 9882	*TGV* 6184		*TGV* 6130	*TGV* 5180*		*TGV* 6168	*TGV* 6896	*TGV* 6132	*TGV* 6180		*TGV* 6134	*TGV* 6806		*TGV* 6186	*TGV* 6140	*TGV* 6140		*TGV* 6144			
				Ⓑ				D							⑦	⑤	⑦		⑦			
				p				A				S				F						
Nice 360 d.	...	1502	...	...	...	...	1551	...	...	1702	...	...	1724	...	1804	...	...	...	...	...	...	...
Antibes 360 d.	...	1521	...	...	...	...	1610	...	...	1721	...	...	1743	...	1823	...	...	...	...	...	...	...
Cannes 360 d.	...	1533	...	...	...	...	1622	...	...	1732	...	...	1756	...	1835	...	...	...	...	...	...	...
St Raphaël-Valescure 360 d.	...	1559	...	...	...	...	1648	...	...	|	...	...	1822	...	1901	...	...	...	...	...	...	...
Les Arcs-Draguignan 360 d.	...	|	...	...	...	...	1704	...	...	1809	...	...	1839	...	|	...	...	...	...	...	...	...
Toulon 360 d.	...	1650	...	...	...	...	1746	...	...	1850	...	...	1917	...	1951	...	...	...	...	...	...	...
Marseille St Charles 360 a.	...	|	...	...	...	...	1829	...	...	|	...	...	1959	...	|	...	...	...	...	...	...	...
Marseille St Charles d.	1714	|	...	1806	1814	...	1840	1848	1906	|	...	2006	2014	...	|	2025	2032	...	2106	...	...	...
Aix en Provence TGV d.	1729	|	...	1820	1829	...	|	1906	1920	|	...	2020	2029	...	|	2039	2047	...	2120	...	...	...
Avignon TGV d.	1751	1800	...	1842	1852	...	|	1927	1942	2001	...	2042	2051	...	2059	2102	2110	...	2142	...	...	...
Valence TGV ▶ d.	|	|	...	|	|	...	|	2000	|	|	...	|	2125	...	|	|	|	...	|	...	...	...
Lyon St Exupéry ✈ ▶ d.	|	|	...	|	|	...	|	...	|	|	...	|	|	...	|	|	|	...	|	...	...	...
Lyon Part Dieu ▶ a.	1854	|	...	|	1954	...	|	...	|	|	...	|	2200	...	|	|	|	...	|	...	...	...
Genève **346** a.	|	|	...	|	|	...	|	...	|	|	...	|	...	...	|	|	|	...	|	...	...	...
Dijon **379** a.	|	|	...	|	|	...	|	...	|	|	...	|	...	...	|	|	|	...	|	...	...	...
Strasbourg **379** ⊠ a.	|	|	...	|	|	...	|	...	|	|	...	|	...	...	|	|	|	...	|	...	...	...
Metz **379** a.	|	|	...	|	|	...	|	...	|	|	...	|	...	...	|	|	|	...	|	...	...	...
Paris Gare de Lyon ▶ a.	|	2041	...	2123	|	...	2145	...	2223	2242	...	2323	...	...	2341	2342	2349	...	0023	...	...	...
Marne la Vallée-Chessy § **11** a.	2048	...	...	...	2148	...	...	...	...	...	...	...	...	...	...	...	...	...	...	...	...	...
Charles de Gaulle ✈ **11** a.	2102	...	...	...	2202	...	...	...	...	...	...	...	...	...	...	...	...	...	...	...	...	...
Lille Europe **11** a.	2203r	...	...	...	2308z	...	...	...	...	...	...	...	...	...	...	...	...	...	...	...	...	...
Brussels Midi **11** a.	2256	...	...	...	...	...	...	...	...	...	...	...	...	...	...	...	...	...	...	...	...	...

A – To Annecy (see panel).
B – To Basel (Table **379**).
C – ⑥ July 2 - Aug. 27 (also July 14, Oct. 29, Nov. 11; not July 16).
D – ⑦ July 3 - Aug. 28 (also Aug. 15, Nov. 1, 13; not Aug. 14).
F – ⑤ July 8 - Aug. 26 (also July 13; not July 15).
H – (12) Marseille - Lyon - Rouen - Le Havre (Table **335**). Subject to alteration July 18 - Aug. 5, Sept. 30, Oct. 1, 2, 8, 15, Nov. 18, 19, 20, 26, Dec. 2, 3, 4.
J – To July 2 and from Aug. 29.
K – July 3 - Aug. 28.
L – Daily to Sept. 11; ⑥⑦ from Sept. 17 (also Nov. 11).
N – To Nantes via Massy TGV (Table **335**).
R – To Rennes via Massy TGV (Table **335**).
S – Ⓑ to July 3; ⑤⑦ July 8 - Aug. 21 (also July 13, Aug. 15); Ⓑ from Aug. 26 (not Nov. 11).
T – Runs daily July 2 - Aug. 28.
V – From Ventimiglia (Table **360**).
X – To Luxembourg from July 3 (Table **379**). Arrives Metz 2318 until July 2.

b – Not Aug. 15, Nov. 1.
f – Lille **Flandres**.
j – 0748 on ⑥ to July 2 / from Sept. 3 (also Nov. 11).

p – Not Nov. 11; runs daily July 3 - Sept. 2.
r – Arrives up to 9 minutes earlier from July 16.
t – Also ⑦ July 3 - Aug. 28; not July 13, 14, Nov. 1, 10.
u – Not July 9, 14, 16, 23, 30, Aug. 6, 13, 20, 27.
z – 2328 on Ⓐ to July 15. 2304 from July 16. On July 14 arrives Lille **Flandres** 2312.

TGV – Ⓡ, supplement payable, 🍸.

⊗ – Subject to alteration on Oct. 1, 8, 9, 15, Nov. 26.
⊖ – Subject to alteration on Oct. 1, 8, Nov. 26.
¶ – Subject to alteration on Oct. 15, Nov. 26.
△ – Subject to alteration on Oct. 4, Nov. 8, Dec. 6.
* – **5144** is combined with **9862** Lyon - Lille. **5180** is combined with **5186** Lyon - Lille.
⊠ – Strasbourg arrivals may be up to 3 minutes later on ①–⑤ Aug. 16 - Sept. 30 and ①–⑤ from Nov. 21.
♣ – To Frankfurt (Main) Hbf, Table **47**.
▶ – For Lyon - Paris see Table **340** (for St Exupéry ✈ - Paris see Table **342**). For additional trains Valence TGV - Lyon and Paris see Table **355**. For Valence Ville - Lyon see Table **351**.
§ – Station for Disneyland Paris.

MARSEILLE - ANNECY

	TGV 6894 C
Marseille (see above) d.	0755
Valence TGV d.	0907
Grenoble a.	1000
Chambéry a.	1042
Aix les Bains a.	1055
Annecy a.	1130

Additional low-cost 'Ouigo' TGV trai[n] run to Marne la Vallée-Chessy – see Table **350a**

Ⓐ – Mondays to Fridays, except holidays   Ⓑ – Daily except Saturdays   Ⓒ – Saturdays, Sundays and holidays

OUIGO LOW-COST TGV — 350a

Low-cost *TGV* services branded **Ouigo**, internet booking only through www.ouigo.com, special conditions apply. For normal *TGV* services see Tables **350** and **355**.

	TGV	*TGV*		*TGV*	*TGV*	*TGV*	*TGV*		*TGV*	*TGV*		*TGV*	*TGV*		*TGV*	*TGV*	*TGV*	*TGV*	*TGV*	*TGV*			
	6299	**6299**		**6258**	**6250**	**6258**	**6254**		**6252**	**6258**		**6260**	**6262**		**6264**	**6266**	**6268**	**6272**	**6270**	**6272**			
	B	**A**		⑤	⑥⑦	①	②–④		①–⑤	⑥⑦		⑥	⑤⑦		①	②–④	②–④	⑤	①	⑦			
. la Vallée § d.	...	...	...	0914	0948	1020	1114	...	1222	1222	...	1748	1752	...	1909	1926	2018	2035	2042	2048	...	...	...
n Part Dieu a.	...	...	...	|	|	|	|	...	|	|	...	|	|	...	2100	|	2208	|	|	|	...	...	...
n Perrache d.	0536	0605	...	|	|	|	|	...	|	|	...	|	|	...	...	|	...	|	|	|	...	...	...
St Exupéry ✈ d.	|	|	...	1115	1135	1211	1302	...	1409	1409	...	1936	1948	...	...	2113	...	2234	2231	2237	...	...	...
ce TGV d.	|	|	...	|	|	|	|	...	|	|	...	|	2014	...	...	2139	...	2301	2257	2303	...	...	...
on TGV d.	0717	0709	...	|	1233	|	|	...	1503	|	...	|	|	...	...	|	...	|	|	|	...	...	...
Provence TGV d.	0742	0732	...	|	|	|	|	...	|	|	...	2050	|	...	...	2229	...	2356	2354	2357	...	...	...
ille St Charles a.	0754	0744	...	|	1302	|	|	...	1532	|	...	2102	|	...	...	2243	...	0008	0006	0009	...	...	...
es a.	...	...	...	1220	...	1313	1405	...	...	1515	...	...	2056	...	...	...	...	...	...	...	...	...	...
tpellier a.	...	...	...	1254	...	1351	1435	...	...	1546	...	...	2126	...	...	...	...	...	...	...	...	...	...

	TGV	*TGV*	*TGV*	*TGV*	*TGV*	*TGV*	*TGV*		*TGV*	*TGV*	*TGV*	*TGV*	*TGV*	*TGV*	*TGV*	*TGV*	*TGV*	*TGV*	*TGV*		*TGV*		
	6276	**6278**	**6276**	**6280**	**6282**	**6284**	**6296**		**6286**	**6286**	**6294**	**6294**	**6290**	**6290**	**6288**	**6288**	**6292**	**6292**	**6294**		**6298**		
	⑤	⑦	⑥	①	②–④	①–⑥	⑦		⑦	⑥	⑤	①	**D**	④**E**	⑤	①	**G**	**H**	⑥⑦		⑥¶		
tpellier d.	...	...	...	...	...	...	...	...	...	...	1338	1437	1510	1519	...	...	...	...	1638	...	...	...	...
es d.	...	...	...	...	...	...	...	...	...	...	1405	1504	1540	1555	...	...	...	...	1710	...	...	...	...
eille St Charles d.	0520	...	0606	0622	...	0825	0835	...	1340	1340	|	|	|	|	1606	1609	1609	1622	|	...	2144	...	...
Provence TGV d.	|	...	|	|	...	0840	|	...	1355	1355	|	|	|	|	1621	|	|	|	|	...	|	...	...
on TGV d.	0552	...	0637	0655	...	|	0906	...	|	|	|	|	|	|	|	1643	1643	1700	|	...	|	...	...
ce TGV d.	|	...	|	|	...	|	|	...	|	|	1450	1554	1633	1642	|	|	|	|	1757	...	|	...	...
St Exupéry ✈ d.	0652	...	0731	0754	...	0949	1000	...	1512	|	1517	1622	1659	1711	1751	1753	1753	1753	1825	...	|	...	...
n Perrache d.	|	0713	|	|	0834	|	|	...	|	|	|	|	|	|	|	|	|	|	|	...	2321	...	...
e la Vallée § a.	0838	0911	0916	0940	1034	1134	1145	...	1701	1701	1701	1809	1844	1900	1938	1938	1938	1938	2013	...	...	...	...

TOURCOING - NANTES, RENNES and LYON

	TGV	*TGV*	*TGV*	*TGV*
	7632	**7608**	**7612**	**7602**
	①–⑥	⑦		
oing d.	0829	...	1126	1949
Haute-Picardie d.	0915	...	1214	|
es de Gaulle ✈ d.	0949	...	1250	2103
e la Vallée § d.	1003	...	1303	|
n Part Dieu a.	|	...	|	2308
n Perrache d.	|	0807	|	...
/ TGV d.	1038	1038	1338	...
ans a.	1127	1127	1428	...
nnes a.	|	|	1544	...
s St Laud a.	1208	1210	...	...
es a.	1246	1246	...	...

	TGV	*TGV*	*TGV*	*TGV*
	7600	**7630**	**7610**	**7604**
			Ⓑ	⑥
Nantes d.	...	1408	...	...
Angers St Laud d.	...	1446	...	...
Rennes d.	...	|	1810	1810
Le Mans d.	...	1533	1929	1929
Massy TGV d.	...	1625	2025	2026
Lyon Part Dieu a.	...	|	|	2222
Lyon Perrache d.	0734	|	|	...
Marne la Vallée § d.	|	1701	2059	...
Charles de Gaulle ✈ d.	0948	1715	2113	...
TGV Haute-Picardie a.	|	|	2147	...
Tourcoing a.	1051	1827	2226	...

A – ①⑤⑥⑦ (not Sept. 16, 23, 24, 30, Oct. 1, 7, 8, 28, Nov. 4, 11, 18, 25, 26, Dec. 2, 3). Subject to alteration on Oct. 30, 31.
B – Sept. 16, 23, 24, 30, Oct. 1, 7, 8, 28, Nov. 4, 11, 18, 25, 26, Dec. 2, 3 only.
D – ②–④ (not July 7, 14, 21, 28, Aug. 4, 11, 18, 25).
E – ④ July 7 - Aug. 25.
G – ②–④ to Sept. 8.
H – ②–④ from Sept. 13.

¶ – Subject to alteration on Oct. 29.
§ – Marne la Vallée - Chessy (station for Disneyland Paris). Journey from central Paris is approximately 40 minutes on RER Line A.

__Ouigo__ services : internet booking only; special conditions apply. Timings may vary by a few minutes (please check when booking).

351 LYON - VALENCE - AVIGNON - MARSEILLE

km	All *TGV* trains are [R]	⚒	⚒	⚒		⚒	17705			*TGV* 6191 ①–⑥ b	17709	①–⑤ J	⚒ q	17713 q	q	①–⑤ J	*TGV* 6193 C	17717 q	17717 ①–⑤ J		17721		⚒	17725
	Paris Gare de Lyon ▲ d.	...	...	...	...	...	...	...	...	0741	...	...	...	...	...	...	1141	...	...	...	...	...	...	...
	Lyon St Exupéry TGV ✈ d.	...	...	...	...	...	...	...	...	0942	...	...	...	...	...	...	1342	...	...	...	...	...	...	...
	Lyon Perrache ▷ d.	...	...	0540	...	...	...	...	...	|	...	...	...	...	...	...	|	...	...	...	...	...	...	...
0	**Lyon** Part-Dieu ▷ d.	...	...	|	...	0620	0720	...	0820	|	0920	1010	1020	1120	1220	1231	|	1320	1331	1420	1520	...	1620	1720
32	Vienne ▷ d.	...	...	0603	...	0640	0741	...	0840	|	0941	|	1040	1141	1240	|	|	1341	|	1440	1541	...	1640	1741
87	Tain-l'Hermitage-Tournon ▷ d.	...	...	0641	...	0719	0814	...	0918	|	1014	|	1118	1214	1318	|	|	1414	|	1520	1614	...	1718	1814
105	**Valence** Ville ▷ a.	...	...	0652	...	0731	0826	...	0931	1011	1025	|	1128	1225	1328	|	1411	1425	|	1531	1625	...	1728	1825
105	**Valence** Ville d.	0612	0632	...	0702	...	0829	0932	...	1014	1028	|	1132	1228	1332	|	1414	1428	|	...	1628	1702	1732	1828
150	Montélimar d.	0635	0701	...	0731	...	0850	1001	...	1038	1050	1158z	1201	1250	1401	1414z	1437	1450	1517z	...	1650	1731	1801	1850
202	Orange d.	0706	0735	...	0805	...	0924	1035	...	1103	1124	1235z	1235	1323	1435	1449z	1503	1524	1555z	...	1724	1805	1835	1925
230	**Avignon** Centre a.	0729	0801	...	0828	...	0938	1058	...	1118	1138	1258	1258	1338	1458	1512	1516	1538	1612	...	1738	1828	1858	1940
230	**Avignon** Centre ▷ d.	0731	...	...	...	...	0941	...	...	1121v	1141	...	...	1341	...	...	1519	1541	1615	...	1741	...	...	...
265	Arles **355** ▷ d.	0749	...	...	...	...	1002	...	...	1143v	1202	...	...	1402	...	...	1538	1601	1634	...	1802	...	...	...
299	Miramas **355** ▷ d.	0809	...	...	...	...	1018	...	...	1203v	1218	...	...	1418	...	...	1557	1618	1652	...	1818	...	...	...
328	Vitrolles (for ✈) ⊖ **355** ▷ d.	0825	...	...	...	...	1036	...	...	...	1236	...	...	1436	...	...	...	1636	1711	...	1836	...	...	...
351	**Marseille** St Charles **355** ▷ a.	0844	...	...	...	...	1050	...	...	...	1250	...	...	1450	...	...	...	1650	1727	...	1850	...	...	...

	⑤ d A			*TGV* 6195 Ⓑ h	*TGV* 6195 ⑥ k	17729		*TGV* 6197		⑤ f
Paris Gare de Lyon ▲ d.	...	...	...	1741	1745	...	...	1941	...	...
Lyon St Exupéry TGV ✈ d.	...	...	...	1941	1943	...	...	2142	...	...
Lyon Perrache ▷ d.	...	1740	...	|	|	...	...	|	...	...
Lyon Part-Dieu ▷ d.	...	|	1820	|	|	1920	2020	|	2120	2220
Vienne ▷ d.	...	1803	1840	|	|	1941	2040	|	2139	2240
Tain-l'Hermitage-Tournon ▷ d.	...	1841	1918	|	|	2014	2120	|	2220	2320
Valence Ville ▷ a.	...	1852	1928	2011	2013	2025	2131	2211	2231	2331
Valence Ville d.	1852	1902	1932	2014	2016	2028	...	2214	...	...
Montélimar d.	1918	1931	2001	2036	2042	2050	...	2238	...	...
Orange d.	1951	2005	2035	2102	2111	2124	...	|	...	...
Avignon Centre a.	2005	2028	2058	2118	2127	2138	...	2316	...	...
Avignon Centre ▷ d.	...	...	...	2121	2130	2141	...	...	...	...
Arles **355** ▷ d.	...	...	...	2140	2149	2200	...	...	...	...
Miramas **355** ▷ d.	...	...	...	2158	2207	2218	...	...	...	...
Vitrolles (for ✈) ⊖ **355** ▷ d.	...	...	...	...	...	2236	...	...	...	...
Marseille St Charles **355** ▷ a.	...	...	...	...	...	2250	...	...	...	...

	Ⓐ	*TGV* 6192 Ⓐ	⚒	17702 ①⑥ p	17702 ⚒		Ⓐ	⚒
Marseille St Charles **355** ▷ d.	...	...	...	0510	...	...	...	...
Vitrolles (for ✈) ⊖ **355** ▷ d.	...	...	...	|	...	...	...	...
Miramas **355** ▷ d.	...	...	...	0540	...	...	...	...
Arles **355** ▷ d.	...	...	...	0558	...	...	...	...
Avignon Centre ▷ a.	...	...	...	0615	...	...	...	...
Avignon Centre d.	...	0534	0538	0618	0618	0633	0633	0703
Orange d.	...	|	0601	0634	0634	0655	0655	0725
Montélimar d.	0529	0615	0637	0708	0708	0731	0731	0801
Valence Ville a.	0558	0638	0705	0730	0730	0758	0758	0828
Valence Ville ▷ d.	0608	0641	0708	0733	0733	...	0808	0831
Tain-l'Hermitage-Tournon ▷ d.	0619	|	0719	0745	0745	...	0819	0841
Vienne ▷ d.	0658	|	0758	0819	0819	...	0858	0920
Lyon Part-Dieu ▷ a.	|	|	|	0840	0840	...	|	0940
Lyon Perrache ▷ a.	0720	|	0820	...	...	...	0920	...
Lyon St Exupéry TGV ✈ a.	...	|	...	...	...	...	...	...
Paris Gare de Lyon ▲ a.	...	0911	...	...	...	...	...	...

	TGV 6194 ①–⑤ G⊙	17706 q	17706 ①–⑤ z	17706 ①–⑤ H	*TGV* 6194 D◇	17704 ♥	17704 ①–⑤ H	17714 q	*TGV* 6196 E	⚒ ⊗		17716	17718			Ⓐ	†	*TGV* 6198 Ⓐ ¶	*TGV* 6198 Ⓒ	17724	† A			Ⓑ
Marseille St Charles **355** ▷ d.	...	0710	0710	0710	...	0910	0910	1110	...	...	...	1310	1510	...	...	...	...	...	...	1710	...	...	...	1902
Vitrolles (for ✈) ⊖ **355** ▷ d.	...	0725	0725	0725	...	0926	0925	1125	...	...	...	1325	1525	...	...	...	...	...	...	1725	...	...	...	1918
Miramas **355** ▷ d.	0714	0743	0743	0743	0803	0943	0943	1143	...	...	...	1343	1543	...	...	...	...	1700	1700	1743	...	...	...	1937
Arles **355** ▷ d.	0734	0800	0800	0800	0823	1000	1000	1200	...	...	...	1400	1600	...	...	...	...	1721	1720	1800	...	...	...	1955
Avignon Centre ▷ a.	0751	0818	0818	0818	0839	1018	1018	1218	...	...	...	1418	1618	...	...	...	...	1737	1737	1818	...	...	...	2015
Avignon Centre d.	0754	0821	0821	0830	0842	1021	1026	1221	1242	...	1303	1421	1621	...	1703	1726	...	1740	1740	1821	1843	1900	1933	2017
Orange d.	0811	0837	0837	|	0858	1037	|	1237	1300	...	1325	1437	1637	...	1725	1749	...	1758	1758	1837	1858	1923	1955	2030
Montélimar d.	0840	0910	0910	|	0925	1109	|	1310	1326	...	1401	1510	1710	1728t	1801	1831	1852t	1824	1824	1910	1931	1958	2031	2102
Valence Ville a.	0901	0931	|	|	0947	1131	|	1331	1347	...	1428	1531	1732	1756t	1828	1858	1916t	1845	1845	1931	1953	2025	2058	2124
Valence Ville ▷ d.	0904	0934	|	|	0950	1134	|	1334	1350	1429	...	1534	1735	1808	1831	...	1921	1848	1848	1934	...	2033	2101r	...
Tain-l'Hermitage-Tournon ▷ d.	|	0945	|	|	|	1145	|	1345	|	1440	...	1545	1746	1819	1841	...	1933	|	|	1945	...	2044	2112r	...
Vienne ▷ d.	|	1019	|	|	|	1219	|	1419	|	1521	...	1619	1819	1858	1920	...	2008	|	|	2019	...	2122	2151r	...
Lyon Part-Dieu ▷ a.	|	1040	1102	1129	|	1240	1310	1440	|	1540	...	1640	1840	|	1940	...	2030	|	|	2040	...	2142	|	...
Lyon Perrache ▷ a.	|	...	...	...	|	...	...	...	|	...	...	...	...	1920	...	...	...	|	|	...	...	...	2212r	...
Lyon St Exupéry TGV ✈ a.	|	...	...	...	|	...	...	...	|	...	...	...	...	...	...	...	...	|	1919	...	...	...	...	...
Paris Gare de Lyon ▲ a.	1130	...	...	...	1215	...	...	...	1615	...	...	...	...	...	...	...	...	2111	2119	...	...	...	...	...

ADDITIONAL TRAINS LYON - VALENCE

	Ⓐ	Ⓐ	⚒⊗	Ⓐ		Ⓐ	Ⓐ	Ⓑ	Ⓐ	
Lyon Perrache d.	0640	0740	1340	1540	1640	1710	1810	1840	1910	1940
Lyon Part Dieu d.	|	|	|	|	|	|	|	|	|	|
Vienne d.	0703	0803	1403	1603	1703	1731	1833	1903	1931	2003
Tain-l'Hermitage-Tournon d.	0741	0841	1441	1641	1741	1810	1911	1941	2010	2041
Valence Ville a.	0752	0852	1452	1652	1752	1822	1922	1952	2022	2052

	Ⓐ	⚒	†	⚒	Ⓐ⊗	⊗	Ⓑ	⚒	Ⓑ
Valence Ville d.	0538	0629	0708	0738	1029	1229	1508	1608	1708
Tain-l'Hermitage d.	0549	0639	0719	0750	1039	1239	1519	1619	1719
Vienne d.	0628	0719	0758	0828	1119	1319	1558	1658	1758
Lyon Part Dieu a.	|	0740	|	|	1140	1340	|	|	|
Lyon Perrache a.	0650	...	0820	0850	...	...	1620	1720	1820

ADDITIONAL TRAINS AVIGNON - MARSEILLE

	Ⓐ	Ⓐ	⚒	Ⓐ		⚒	Ⓐ		L		⊕	Ⓐ		Ⓐ		Ⓐ	Ⓐ			Ⓐ		Ⓐ	
Avignon Centre d.	0542	0546	0617	0641	0647	0710	0805	0755	0947	1217	1217	1417	1419	1512	1617	1720	1717	1805	1747	1817	1847	1905	1917
Arles **355** d.	0600	|	|	0700	|	|	0824	|	|	1235	|	1436	|	1530	|	1739	|	1825	|	|	|	1924	|
Cavaillon d.	|	0622	0652	|	0723	0753	|	0824	1021	|	1253	|	1453	|	1653	|	1753	|	1823	1853	1921	|	1953
Salon de Provence d.	|	0644	0715	|	0745	0815	|	0846	1043	|	1315	|	1515	|	1715	|	1815	|	1844	1915	1936	|	2015
Miramas **355** d.	0622	0655	0726	0720	0756	0826	0844	0857	1054	1256	1326	1457	1524	1551	1724	1758	1826	1845	1855	1926	1946	1944	2024
Vitrolles (for ✈) ⊖ **355** d.	0644	0718	0743	|	0819	0849	0902	0920	1116	1319	1349	1519	...	1612	...	...	1849	...	1919	1949	...	|	...
Marseille St Charles **355** a.	0700	0745	0801	0750	0845	0914	0924	0945	1144	1351	1408e	1545	...	1631	...	...	1910	...	1938	2008	...	2019	...

	Ⓐ	Ⓐ		Ⓐ	Ⓐ		Ⓐ		Ⓐ⊕	T	⊡			Ⓐ			Ⓐ	Ⓐ	Ⓐ		Ⓐ		Ⓐ
Marseille St Charles **355** d.	...	...	...	0630	0652	...	0745	0831	0852	1017	...	1217	1252	1417	...	1552	1617	...	1652	1759	1810	1852	1929
Vitrolles (for ✈) ⊖ **355** d.	...	...	...	0647	0713	...	0801	0850	0913	1042	...	1242	1312	1442	...	1613	1642	...	1713	1815	1826	1912	1953
Miramas **355** d.	0622	0638	0706	0708	0736	0806	0822	0913	0936	1105	1136	1305	1337	1505	1536	1636	1705	1721	1736	1838	1842	1936	2016
Salon de Provence d.	0633	|	0715	|	0745	0815	...	|	0945	|	1145	|	1346	|	1545	1645	1714	|	1746	1847	|	1945	2025
Cavaillon d.	0655	|	0737	|	0807	0837	...	|	1007	|	1207	|	1407	|	1607	1707	1737	|	1807	1909	|	2007	2046
Arles **355** d.	|	0700	|	0728	|	|	...	0933	|	1126	|	1325	|	1526	|	|	|	1746	|	|	1900	|	|
Avignon Centre a.	0730	0718	0811	0747	0841	0911	...	0952	1042	1145	1241	1344	1441	1545	1642	1741	1811	1806	1841	1943	1918	2041	2121

A – From / to Annecy (Table **364**).
C – Daily to Sept. 18; Ⓒ from Sept. 24 (also Oct. 10 – 14).
D – Daily to Sept. 18; ⑥⑦ from Sept. 24 (also Oct. 10 – 14, 17 – 19).
E – Daily to Oct. 16; Ⓒ from Oct. 22.
G – ①–⑤ from Oct. 20.
H – ①–⑤ Sept. 19 - Oct. 7.
J – ①–⑤ Sept. 19 - Oct. 7 and ①–⑤ Nov. 21 - Dec. 2.
L – ⚒ to Sept. 24; ⑥ Oct. 1 - Nov. 26.
T – ⑥⑦ (daily Sept. 24 - Oct. 16). Departs Marseille 1023 on ①–⑤ Sept. 26 - Oct. 14. Arrives Avignon 1154 on Sept. 26, Oct. 3, 10, 12.

b – Not Aug. 15, Nov. 1.
d – Also July 13, Nov. 10; not Nov. 11.
e – 1414 until June 5.
f – Also July 13; not Nov. 11.

h – Not July 14, Nov. 11.
k – Also July 14.
p – Not Aug. 15.
q – Not Sept. 19 – 23, 26 – 30, Oct. 3 – 7, Nov. 21 – 25, 28 – 30, Dec. 1, 2.
r – ⚒ only.
t – ⑦ (not July 3 - Aug. 28, Oct. 23, 30).
v – Ⓐ from Oct. 17.
z – ①–⑤ Nov. 21 - Dec. 2.

TGV – [R], supplement payable, 🍷.

⊙ – Also calls at Mâcon-Loché TGV (d. 0954).
◇ – Also calls at Mâcon-Loché TGV (d. 1037).
¶ – Also calls at Mâcon-Loché TGV (d. 1935).
♥ – Not ①–⑤ Sept. 19 - Oct. 7. Does not run Avignon - Lyon on ①–⑤ Nov. 21 - Dec. 2.

⊗ – Subject to alteration on ①–⑤ Sept. 19 - Oct. 7 and ①–⑤ Nov. Dec. 2.
⊕ – Subject to alteration June 6 – 10, Oct. 10 – 14, 17 – 21, 24 – 28, N 21 – 25, 28 – 30, Dec. 1, 2, 5 – 9.
⊡ – Subject to alteration June 6 – 10, Oct. 10 – 14, 17 – 21, 24 – 28, N 21 – 25, 28 – 30, Dec. 1 – 10.
◧ – Subject to alteration on Sept. 18, Oct. 16, 30, Nov. 11, 27.
▲ – For *TGV* services via high-speed line see Table **340** Paris - Lyo Table **350** Paris - Avignon - Marseille, Table **355** Paris - Montpe
▷ – For additional trains Lyon - Valence Ville and Avignon - Marseil see below main table.
⊖ – Vitrolles Aéroport Marseille-Provence ✈. A shuttle bus runs to t airport terminal (journey 5 minutes) connecting with trains.

Services from / to Lyon Perrache are subject to alteration Nov. 10 –

AVIGNON TGV - AVIGNON CENTRE - CARPENTRAS 351a

	Ⓐ		Ⓐ		⊡	⊡		⊡		Ⓒ	⊡				Ⓐ			Ⓐ		Ⓐ				
Avignon TGV........ ◇ d.	0627	0657	0727	0757	0857	0957	...	1157	1257	1342	...	1427	...	1557	1627	1657	1727	1757	1827	1857	1927	2043	...	2227
Avignon Centre .... ◇ d.	0636	0707	0736	0807	0907	1007	...	1207	1307	1351	1351	1436	...	1607	1636	1707	1736	1807	1836	1907	1936	2052	...	2236
Carpentras ....a.	0706	0737	0806	0836	0936	1036	...	1236	1336	1420	1420	1506	...	1636	1706	1736	1806	1836	1906	1936	2006	2120	...	2305

	Ⓐ		Ⓐ		Ⓐ		Ⓐ			⊡	⊡	Ⓐ⊡	Ⓒ		⊡		Ⓐ		Ⓐ		Ⓐ		Ⓐ		
ɛntras..................d.	0520	...	0624	0652	0722	0752	0822	0854	...	1046	1156	1254	1254	...	1452	1554	1622	1652	1722	1752	1822	1852	1922	1952	...
ıon Centre ..... ◇ d.	0547	...	0657	0727	0757	0827	0858	0924	...	1116	1227	1324	1327	...	1527	1627	1657	1727	1757	1827	1857	1927	1959	2027	...
ıon TGV......... ◇ a.	0552	...	0703	0733	0803	0833	0903	...	...	1122	1233	...	1333	...	1533	1633	1703	1733	1803	1834	1904	1933	2005	2032	...

Journeys to / from Carpentras are subject to alteration on ①–⑤ Sept. 19 - Oct. 7.

◇ – **Full service** Avignon TGV - Avignon Centre and v.v.:
From Avignon TGV at 0627 Ⓐ, 0657, 0727, 0757, 0827, 0857, 0908, 0957, 1008, 1027, 1107 Ⓐ, 1128, 1157, 1210, 1226 Ⓐ, 1227 Ⓒ, 1257, 1308, 1327, 1342 Ⓒ, 1410, 1427, 1457, 1508, 1527, 1557, 1627, 1657, 1710 Ⓐ, 1727, 1740, 1757, 1807 Ⓒ, 1810 Ⓐ, 1827, 1840, 1857, 1927, 1957, 2025, 2043, 2124, 2201, 2227, 2257 and 2327. **From Avignon Centre** at 0547 Ⓐ, 0627, 0657, 0727, 0757, 0827, 0844 Ⓐ, 0847 Ⓒ, 0858, 0914, 0957, 1044 Ⓐ, 1101, 1116, 1147, 1157, 1227, 1244, 1301, 1327 Ⓒ, 1347, 1357, 1427, 1444, 1457, 1527, 1557, 1627, 1644, 1657 Ⓐ, 1716, 1727, 1745, 1757, 1815 Ⓐ, 1817 Ⓒ, 1827, 1857, 1927, 1946, 1959, 2027, 2125, 2147, 2227 and 2257.

TOULON - ST TROPEZ 352

routes 7801/2

'oulon Gare Routière (adjacent to railway station) → Hyères → Le Lavandou → **St Tropez** Gare Routière. *84 km.*

ce April 2 - July 5 (journey 2 hrs 5 mins - 2 hrs 15 mins).
Toulon: 0550 ⚒, 0620 ⚒**d**, 0650 ⚒, 0720 ⚒**d**, 0810, 0900 ⚒**d**, 1030 ⚒, 1210**d**, 1300, 1415, 1530 ⚒**d**, 1630, 1730, 1815**d** and 2100 Ⓒ.
St Tropez at 0600 ⚒**d**, 0640 ⚒, 0845, 1040, 1110 ⚒**d**, 1230 ⚒**d**, 1230, 1440, 1630**d**, 1700 ⚒, 1730 ⚒**d**, 1830 ⚒**d** and 1930.

Direct (not via Le Lavandou), journey 1 hr 40 mins - 2 hrs.

ator: Groupement SUMA, 13340 Rognac ✆ (in France) 0 810 006 177 www.varlib.fr

ST RAPHAEL - ST TROPEZ 352a

route 7601

t Raphael Gare Routière (adjacent to railway station) → St Aygulf → Ste Maxime → Grimaud → Port Grimaud (certain journeys) → **St Tropez** Gare Routière. *35 km.*

ce April 2 - July 5 (journey 1 hr 10 mins - 1 hr 35 mins).
St Raphael: 0600, 0750, 0915, 1100, 1300, 1340, 1500, 1615, 1745, 1915 and 2040.
St Tropez: 0600, 0730, 0925, 1100, 1230, 1330, 1515, 1630, 1730, 1900 and 2100.

ator: Groupement SUMA, 13340 Rognac ✆ (in France) 0 810 006 177 www.varlib.fr

LYON - BOURG EN BRESSE 353

also Table ***378***

ervices Lyon - Bourg en Bresse and v.v. are subject to alteration June 27 - Aug. 26 (services via Ambérieu are unaffected). Lyon services are subject to alteration on Nov. 11, 12, 13.

	Ⓐn ⊖	Ⓐ	⚒	Ⓐn	Ⓐ	⚒	Ⓐ	Ⓐn ⊙		Ⓐ	⚒	Ⓐ	Ⓐn ⊖		Ⓐ	Ⓐn ⊖	⚒	Ⓐ	Ⓐn ⊖		Ⓐ	⚒	⑦	⚒	
Lyon Perrache..........d.	...	0608	0708	...	0808	1008	1108	...	1208	1308	1408	1508	...	1608	1655	...	1708	1755	...	1808	1855	1908	1955	2008	2108z
Lyon Part Dieu ....d.	...	0620	0720	...	0820	1020	1120	...	1220	1320	1420	1520	...	1620	1708	...	1720	1808	...	1820	1908	1920	2008	2020	2120z
Ambérieu ....d.	0652	|	|	0805	|	|	|	1305	|	|	|	|	1705	|	|	1805	|	|	1905	|	|	|	2044	|	|
Bourg en Bresse .....a.	0716	0729	0829	0828	0929	1129	1229	1328	1329	1429	1529	1629	1728	1729	1757	1828	1829	1857	1928	1929	1957	2029	2102	2129	2230

	⚒	Ⓐ	⚒	Ⓐ	Ⓐn ⊖	⚒		Ⓐ	⚒		Ⓐ		Ⓐ	Ⓐn	⚒	Ⓐ		Ⓐn	⚒		Ⓐn ⊖	Ⓐ	Ⓐn ⊖		Ⓐn ⊖	Ⓑ
g en Bresse...... d.	0531	0601	0631	0703	0734	0743	0731	0803	0831	0844	0844	1031	1131	1224r	1231	1331	1431	1624	1631	1731	1733	1831	1834	1931	1934	2031
ıbérieu................ a.	|	|	|	|	0757	0802	|	|	|	0900	0900	|	|	1250	|	|	|	1650	|	|	1757	|	1857	|	1958	|
Part Dieu.......... a.	0639	0710	0739	0752	...	0830	0839	0852	0939	0926	0926	1139	1239	...	1339	1439	1539	...	1739	1839	...	1939	...	2039	...	2139
Perrache .... a.	0651	0722	0751	0803	...	0847	0851	0903	0951	...	0947	1151	1251	...	1352	1451	1551	...	1751	1851	...	1950	...	2051	...	2151

Not July 18 - Aug. 26.
1221 Aug. 29 - Sept. 30, Oct. 17–28, Nov. 28 - Dec. 2.
5 minutes later on ⑤† (also Oct. 31, Nov. 10).

⊙ – Aug. 29 - Sept. 30, Oct. 17–28, Nov. 28 - Dec. 2 departs Ambérieu 1307, arrives Bourg en Bresse 1335.

⊖ – To / from Mâcon Ville (Table **353a**).
∆ – Ambérieu - Bourg en Bresse: *31* km.

MÂCON - BOURG EN BRESSE 353a

	Ⓐn	🚌 Ⓒd	Ⓐn	🚌	Ⓐn	🚌	Ⓐn	Ⓐn	Ⓐn	🚌 Ⓒd
Mâcon Ville.................d.	0704	0727	0757	0927	1304	1457	1704	1804	1904	2057
Bourg en Bresse.........a.	0732	0829	0827	1029	1334	1559	1731	1832	1932	2130
Ambérieu ***353***..........a.	0757	...	...	...	...	...	1757	1857	1958	...

	Ⓐn	🚌	Ⓐn	🚌	Ⓐn	🚌 Ⓒd	Ⓐn	Ⓐn	Ⓐn	🚌 Ⓒd
Ambérieu ***353***.......d.	0652	...	...	...	...	...	1705	1805	1905	...
Bourg en Bresse......d.	0717	0938	1228	1338	1628	1638	1729	1829	1930	1938
Mâcon Ville.............a.	0741	1041	1258	1441	1658	1741	1758	1858	1959	2041

ional journeys by 🚌: from Mâcon Ville at 1057 Ⓐ, 1657 Ⓒ**d**, 1757 Ⓒ**d** and 1957 Ⓐ; from Bourg en Bresse at 0638 Ⓐ and 1038 Ⓐ.

Runs daily July 16 - Aug. 28.

n – Not July 18 - Aug. 26.

DIJON - BOURG EN BRESSE 353b

ject to alteration Nov. 11–13

	Ⓐ		Ⓒ		C		Ⓐ		
Dijon..............................d.	0633	...	0833	...	1245	...	1736	1844	...
St Jean de Losne ....d.	0705	...	0905	...	1316	...	1806	1914	...
Louhans ....d.	0744	...	0944	...	1354	...	1845	1953	...
Bourg en Bresse...............a.	0816	...	1016	...	1426	...	1917	2025	...

	Ⓐ			D				†	
Bourg en Bresse...............d.	0530	0632	...	1142	...	1737	...	1840	...
Louhans...............................d.	0603	0705	...	1215	...	1813	...	1912	...
St Jean de Losne..................d.	0637	0745	...	1254	...	1847	...	1949	...
Dijon ....a.	0703	0815	...	1326	...	1914	...	2014	...

Daily to June 19; Ⓒ June 25 - Aug. 21; daily from Aug. 27 (not Oct. 31, Nov. 2, 3, 4, 7–10).
⚒ to June 18; ⑥ June 25 - Aug. 20; ⚒ from Aug. 27 (not Oct. 31, Nov. 2, 3, 4, 7–10).

PERPIGNAN - VILLEFRANCHE - LATOUR DE CAROL 354

	⚒	r	r	r	Ⓐ		Ⓑ	
Perpignan.............................. d.	0726	0826	1226	1426	1646	1746	1846	1946
Prades-Molitg les Bains ....d.	0811	0911	1309	1509	1731	1831	1931	2031
Villefranche-Vernet les Bains ....a.	0819	0919	1317	1517	1739	1839	1939	2039

	⚒		Ⓐ	r	r	r		Ⓑ
Villefranche-Vernet les Bains ....d.	0625	0725	0825	1125	1325	1525	1745	1845
Prades-Molitg les Bains..............d.	0633	0733	0833	1133	1333	1533	1753	1853
Perpignan..................................a.	0713	0813	0913	1213	1413	1613	1833	1933

VILLEFRANCHE - LATOUR DE CAROL *Petit Train Jaune* Narrow gauge, 2nd class. In summer most trains include open sightseeing carriages.

	S	A	S	n	S	†B	A	S
Villefranche-Vernet les Bains ....d.	0855	0930	0958	1343t	1541	1547	1747	1749
Mont Louis la Cabanasse................d.	1025	1050	1130	1505	1709	1715	1859	1913
Font Romeu-Odeillo-Via..................d.	1046	1116	1157	1525	1728	1734	1920	1940
Bourg Madame ....d.	...	1213	1255	...	...	...	2015	2036
Latour de Carol............................a.	...	1231	1311	...	...	...	2031	2052

	A	S	S	n⊙	S	A	S	†B
Latour de Carol ....d.	0814	0828	...	...	1513	1535	...	...
Bourg Madame ....d.	0832	0848	...	...	1534	1553	...	...
Font Romeu-Odeillo-Via..................d.	0934	1000	1106	1540	1645	1651	1750	1751
Mont Louis la Cabanasse................d.	0959	1032	1136	1610	1715	1713	1818	1815
Villefranche-Vernet les Bains.......a.	1114	1149	1255	1729	1834	1829	1934	1931

Sept. 26 - Oct. 2 and from Oct. 15.
† from Oct. 2 (not Oct. 9).
Until Sept. 25.

n – Not Oct. 3–14.
r – Not Oct. 17–21, 24–28.
t – 1350 from Sept. 26.

⊙ – From Sept. 26 Font Romeu d. 1556, Mont Louis d. 1617, Villefranche a. 1736.

355 PARIS - MONTPELLIER - PERPIGNAN - PORTBOU

SERVICE FROM JUNE 6. *Subject to alteration on Nov. 12, 19. Services from or via Lyon are subject to alteration on Aug. 13, 14, 15, Oct. 29, 30, 31.*

km		Ⓐ	3731 Q [R]	Ⓐ	⚒	⚒	Ⓐ	4250 4251 R [R]	Ⓐ	Ⓐ	⚒	Ⓐ	†	⑥	Ⓐ	Ⓐ ☆	Ⓐ	⊗	*TGV* 6809		*TGV* 9730 ■	*TGV* 6201 Ⓐ J	*TGV* 6201 ①–⑥ L
	Brussels Midi **11** d.	...	...	...	...	...	...	...	...	...	...	...	...	...	...	...	...	...	...	...	...	...	...
	Lille Europe **11** d.	...	...	...	...	...	...	...	...	...	...	...	...	...	...	...	...	...	...	...	...	...	...
	Charles de Gaulle ✈ **11** d.	...	...	...	...	...	...	...	...	...	...	...	...	...	...	...	...	...	...	...	...	...	...
	Marne la Vallée § **11** d.	...	...	...	...	...	...	...	...	...	...	...	...	...	...	...	...	...	...	...	...	...	...
0	**Paris** Gare de Lyon ▶ d.	...	2139a	...	...	...	...	...	...	...	...	...	...	...	...	...	...	...	...	...	...	0607	0607
	Dijon **379** d.	...	|	...	...	...	...	...	...	...	...	...	...	...	...	...	...	...	...	...	...	|	|
	Lyon Part Dieu ▶ d.	...	|	...	...	...	...	...	...	...	...	...	...	...	...	...	...	...	0706	...	...	|	|
527	Valence TGV ▶ d.	...	|	...	...	...	...	...	...	...	...	...	...	...	...	...	...	...	0743	...	...	0820	0820
	Nice **360** d.	...	|	...	...	...	...	...	...	...	...	...	...	...	...	...	...	...	|	...	...	|	|
Δ128	**Marseille** St Charles **351** d.	...	|	...	...	...	...	...	...	...	...	...	...	...	0558	...	...	...	|	0718	0805	|	|
Δ105	Vitrolles Aéroport Marseille ‡ d.	...	|	...	...	...	...	...	...	...	...	...	...	...	0616	...	...	...	|	0737	|	|	|
Δ76	Miramas **351** d.	...	|	...	...	...	...	...	...	...	...	...	...	...	0634	...	...	...	|	0753	|	|	|
Δ42	Arles **351** d.	...	|	...	...	...	...	...	...	...	...	...	...	...	0654	...	...	...	|	0813	|	|	|
Δ49	**Avignon** Centre d.	...	◐	...	...	...	...	...	...	...	0612r	0638	...	...	|	...	0712	0738	|	|	0843v	|	|
Δ28	Tarascon-sur-Rhône d.	...	|	...	...	...	...	...	...	...	0625r	0652	...	...	0705	...	0725	0752	|	0823	|	|	|
686	**Nimes** d.	...	|	0506	...	0543	...	0608	0612	0643	0647	0712	0712	...	0722	0743	0747	0812	0829	0843	0904	0908	0908
712	Lunel d.	...	|	0524	...	0559	...	|	0630	0659	0706	0730	0730	...	...	0759	0806	0830	|	0859	|	|	|
736	**Montpellier** a.	...	|	0539	...	0610	...	0634	0645	0710	0729	0747	0747	...	...	0814	0830	0845	0852	0914	0930	0935	0935
736	**Montpellier** d.	...	|	0547j	...	0613	...	0638	0649	0713	...	0750	0750	0750	...	0820	...	0849	0856	0920r	0933	...	0942
756	Frontignan d.	...	|	0558j	...	0631	...	|	0701	0732	...	0802	0802	0802	...	0832	...	0901	|	0931r	|	...	|
763	Sète d.	...	|	0606j	...	0636	...	0655	0709	0738	...	0809	0809	0809	...	0839	...	0909	0915	0938r	|	...	1000
786	Agde d.	...	|	0619j	...	0653	...	0711	0722	0755	...	0822	0822	0822	...	0853	...	0922	|	0951r	|	...	1016
807	Béziers d.	...	|	0631j	...	0711	...	0726	0734	0811	...	0836	0836	0836	...	0912	...	0935	0941	1010r	1015	...	1029
833	**Narbonne** a.	...	0558	0650	...	0729	...	0742	0755g	0829	...	0851	0851	0851	...	0927	...	0950	0956	1025r	1031	...	...
833	**Narbonne** d.	...	0628	0657	0657	0732	0734	0746	0802g	...	...	0857	0857	0857	...	...	...	0957	0958	...	1034	...	...
	Carcassonne **321** a.	...	|	|	|	0802	|	|	|	...	...	|	|	|	...	...	...	|	1026	...	|	...	...
	Toulouse **321** a.	...	|	|	|	0904	|	|	|	...	...	|	|	|	...	...	...	|	1112	...	|	...	...
	Bordeaux **320** a.	...	|	|	|	...	|	|	|	...	...	|	|	|	...	...	...	|	1322x	...	|	...	...
854	Port la Nouvelle d.	...	|	0710	0710	...	0746	|	0814g	...	...	0910	0910	0910	...	...	...	1010	...	...	|	...	...
896	**Perpignan** a.	...	0712	0740	0740	...	0815	0819	0840	...	...	0940	0940	0940	...	...	...	1040	...	...	1106	...	...
896	**Perpignan** d.	0620	0716	0745	0745	...	...	0823	0845	...	...	...	0945	0945	...	...	...	1045	...	...	...	...	...
918	Argelès sur Mer d.	0635	0735	0802	0802	...	...	0843	0902	...	...	...	1002	1002	...	...	...	1102	...	...	...	...	...
923	Collioure d.	0640	0742	0807	0807	...	...	0849	0907	...	...	...	1007	1007	...	...	...	1107	...	...	...	...	...
926	Port Vendres d.	0644	0747	0811	0811	...	...	0855	0911	...	...	...	1011	1011	...	...	...	1111	...	...	...	...	...
931	Banyuls sur Mer d.	0649	0754	0816	0816	...	...	0901	0916	...	...	...	1016	1016	...	...	...	1116	...	...	...	...	...
938	Cerbère **657** a.	0654	0800	0822	0822	...	...	0908	0922	...	...	...	1022	1022	...	...	...	1122	...	...	...	...	...
940	**Portbou** **657** a.	...	0810	...	...	...	...	...	...	...	...	...	...	...	...	...	...	1128	...	...	...	...	...

	4754 4755 ★ ◇	*TGV* 9711 P ♥		*TGV* 5104	*TGV* 6813 ⊡	*TGV* 6035 ①–⑥ E	*TGV* 6069 N	Ⓐ		*TGV* 6839 S	4756 4757 ★	Ⓒ K	*TGV* 6207 ⑥ H	†	⚒	*TGV* 6207 G	Ⓐ J	Ⓐ	*TGV* 9713 ♠	D	Ⓐ	Ⓐ K	*TGV* 9812
Brussels Midi **11** d.	...	...	...	...	...	...	...	...	...	...	...	...	...	...	...	...	...	...	...	...	...	...	0817
Lille Europe **11** d.	...	...	...	0537	...	...	...	...	...	...	...	...	...	...	...	...	...	...	...	...	...	...	0902
Charles de Gaulle ✈ **11** d.	...	...	...	0658y	...	...	...	...	...	...	...	...	...	...	...	...	...	...	...	...	...	...	0958
Marne la Vallée § **11** d.	...	...	...	0711	...	...	...	...	...	...	...	...	...	...	...	...	...	...	...	...	...	...	1011
Paris Gare de Lyon ▶ d.	...	0715	...	|	...	0807	0807	...	...	...	...	...	0915	...	...	0925	...	...	1007	...	...	...	|
Dijon **379** d.	...	|	...	|	...	|	|	...	...	0835	...	...	|	...	...	|	...	...	|	...	...	...	|
Lyon Part Dieu ▶ d.	...	|	...	0910	0936	|	|	...	...	1006	...	...	|	...	...	|	...	...	|	...	...	...	1210
Valence TGV ▶ d.	...	|	...	0950	1013	1021	1021	...	...	|	...	...	|	...	...	|	...	...	1221	...	...	...	1249
Nice **360** d.	...	|	...	|	|	|	|	...	...	|	...	...	|	...	...	|	...	...	|	...	...	...	|
Marseille St Charles **351** d.	0818	|	...	|	|	|	|	...	...	|	1018	...	|	...	...	|	...	...	|	1150	...	1150	|
Vitrolles Aéroport Marseille ‡ d.	|	|	...	|	|	|	|	...	...	|	|	...	|	...	...	|	...	...	|	1205	...	1205	|
Miramas **351** d.	|	|	...	|	|	|	|	...	...	|	|	...	|	...	...	|	...	...	|	1222	...	1222	|
Arles **351** d.	0906	|	...	|	|	|	|	...	...	|	|	...	|	...	...	|	...	...	|	1242	...	1242	|
Avignon Centre d.	|	|	0938	|	|	|	|	...	...	|	|	...	|	1138	1138	|	...	1212	|	|	...	|	|
Tarascon-sur-Rhône d.	|	|	0952	|	|	|	|	...	...	|	|	...	|	1158	1158	|	...	1225	|	1252	...	1252	|
Nimes d.	0932	1008	1012	1036	1058	1109	1108	...	...	1120	1125	...	1206	1215	1215	1219	...	1247	1308	1312	...	1312	1336
Lunel d.	|	|	1030	|	|	|	|	...	...	|	|	...	|	1232	1232	|	...	1306	|	1330	...	1330	|
Montpellier a.	0958	1034	1045	1106	1124	1136	1134	...	...	1146	1153	...	1232	1247	1247	1250	...	1330	1334	1347	...	1347	1404
Montpellier d.	1003	1037	1049	...	1127	1140	1138	1151	...	...	1158	1205	1239	1250	1250	...	1306	...	1337	1351	...	1351	...
Frontignan d.	|	|	1101	...	|	|	|	1202	...	...	|	1217	|	1302	1302	...	1323	...	|	1402	...	1409	...
Sète d.	1019	|	1109	...	1145	1159	1155	1209	...	...	1215	1224	1259	1309	1309	...	1329	...	|	1409	...	1416	...
Agde d.	|	|	1122	...	|	1215	1210	1222	...	...	|	1237	1315	1322	1322	...	1344	...	|	1422	...	1433	...
Béziers d.	1044	|	1135	...	1209	1227	1234	1235	...	...	1242	1250	1330	1335	1335	...	1359	...	1416	1435	...	1448	...
Narbonne a.	1058	1132	1150	...	1224	...	1250	1250	...	...	1258	1305	1343	1350	1350	...	1420	...	1432	1450	...	1505	...
Narbonne d.	1101	1135	1157	...	1227	...	1253	1257	1257	...	1301	...	1346	1357	1357	...	...	...	1435	1457	...	1508	...
Carcassonne **321** a.	1129	|	|	...	1256	...	|	|	|	...	1329	...	|	|	|	...	...	...	|	|	...	|	...
Toulouse **321** a.	1215	|	|	...	1340	...	|	|	|	...	1416	...	|	|	|	...	...	...	|	|	...	|	...
Bordeaux **320** a.	1429	|	|	...	...	...	|	|	|	...	1632t	...	|	|	|	...	...	...	|	|	...	|	...
Port la Nouvelle d.	...	|	1210	...	...	...	|	1310	1310	...	...	...	|	1410	1410	...	...	...	|	1510	...	1521	...
Perpignan a.	...	1207	1240	...	...	...	1328	1340	1340	...	...	...	1419	1440	1440	...	...	...	1508	1540	...	1550	...
Perpignan d.	...	...	1245¦	...	...	...	...	...	...	...	...	...	...	*1445*	1445	...	...	...	...	...	1545	...	...
Argelès sur Mer d.	...	...	1302¦	...	...	...	...	...	...	...	...	...	...	*1502*	1502	...	...	...	...	...	1602	...	...
Collioure d.	...	...	1307¦	...	...	...	...	...	...	...	...	...	...	*1507*	1507	...	...	...	...	...	1607	...	...
Port Vendres d.	...	...	1311¦	...	...	...	...	...	...	...	...	...	...	*1511*	1511	...	...	...	...	...	1611	...	...
Banyuls sur Mer d.	...	...	1316¦	...	...	...	...	...	...	...	...	...	...	*1516*	1516	...	...	...	...	...	1616	...	...
Cerbère **657** a.	...	...	1322¦	...	...	...	...	...	...	...	...	...	...	*1522*	1522	...	...	...	...	...	1622	...	...
Portbou **657** a.	...	...	1328¦	...	...	...	...	...	...	...	...	...	...	...	1528	...	...	...	...	...	...	...	...

D – Daily to July 3; Ⓒ July 9 - Aug. 21; daily from Aug. 27.
E – ①–⑥ to July 2 / from Aug. 29 (not Nov. 1).
G – Daily to July 8; Ⓑ July 10 - Aug. 28 (not July 14); ⑥ from Sept. 3 (also Nov. 11).
H – ⑥ July 9 - Aug. 27 (also July 14).
J – To July 1 and from Aug. 29.
K – July 2 - Aug. 28.
L – ①–⑥ July 4 - Aug. 27 (not Aug. 15).
N – July 3 - Aug. 28.
P – June 2 - Aug. 28.
Q – 🛏 1, 2 cl. and (2) (reclining) Paris Austerlitz - Toulouse - Narbonne - Portbou. **Service may be withdrawn from July 1**.
R – For days of running see Table **379**. 🛏 1, 2 cl. Luxembourg - Metz - Portbou; 🛏 1, 2 cl. Strasbourg - Portbou. **Service may be withdrawn from July 1**.
S – From Strasbourg (Table **379**).

a – Paris **Austerlitz**.
g – 4–5 minutes earlier from Oct. 31.
j – 2–4 minutes later from Oct. 31.
r – Ⓐ only.
t – Not Oct. 22.
v – Avignon **TGV**. Also calls at Aix en Provence (d. 0821).
x – Not Sept. 19–23, 26–30, Oct. 23.

y – 0656 until June 11.

TGV – [R], supplement payable, 🍷.

☆ – Also runs on ⑥ Nimes - Montpellier.
⊡ – Subject to alteration on ①–⑤ Sept. 19–30.
⊗ – Subject to alteration Perpignan - Portbou on ①–⑤ Sept. 19–30.
◇ – Subject to alteration Sept. 19–23, 26–30, Oct. 23.
¦ – 9–12 minutes later on ①–⑤ Sept. 19–30.
★ – *INTERCITÉS*. [R].
♠ – To Barcelona (Table **13**).
■ – (12) Marseille - Barcelona - Madrid.
◐ – Via Limoges and Toulouse (Table **310**).
Δ – Distance from Nimes. Marseille to Nimes via Avignon TGV is *135 km*.
§ – Marne la Vallée - Chessy (station for Disneyland Paris).
‡ – Vitrolles Aéroport Marseille-Provence. A shuttle bus runs to the airport terminal (journey time 5 minutes). For additional trains see Table **351**.
▶ – For additional trains from Paris and Lyon to Valence TGV see Table **350**. For Lyon to Valence Ville see Table **351**.

Additional low-cost 'Ouigo' TGV trains run from Marne la Vallée-Chessy in the eastern suburbs of Paris. See Table **350a**.

PARIS - MONTPELLIER - PERPIGNAN - PORTBOU 355

SERVICE FROM JUNE 6. *Subject to alteration on Nov. 12, 19. Services from or via Lyon are subject to alteration on Aug. 13, 14, 15, Oct. 29, 30, 31.*

		4760 4761 ★	TGV 5318 5326 △	TGV 6211	Ⓐ	Ⓒ K	4762 4763 ★	Ⓐ	Ⓐ	TGV 9743 ♠		4764 4765 ★	Ⓐ	Ⓐ	TGV 9715 ♠	Ⓑ	⑦ e	Ⓐ J	Ⓐ J	C	Ⓐ		4768 4769 ★	TGV 9879 ♣
sels Midi 11 d.	...	...	...	...	...	...	...	...	...	...	...	...	...	...	...	...	...	...	...	...	...	...	...	...
Europe 11 d.	...	...	...	...	...	...	...	...	...	...	...	...	...	...	...	...	...	...	...	...	...	...	...	...
es de Gaulle ✈ 11 d.	...	...	...	...	...	...	...	...	...	...	...	...	...	...	...	...	...	...	...	...	...	...	...	...
e la Vallée § 11 d.	...	...	...	...	...	...	...	...	...	...	...	...	...	...	...	...	...	...	...	...	...	...	...	...
Gare de Lyon ▶ d.	...	...	...	1207	...	...	...	...	...	...	...	...	...	...	1407	...	...	...	...	...	...	...	...	...
on 379 d.	...	...	...	|	...	...	...	...	...	...	...	...	...	...	|	...	...	...	...	...	...	...	...	1532
Part Dieu ▶ d.	...	...	1336	|	...	...	...	...	...	1423	...	...	...	...	|	...	...	...	...	...	...	...	...	1710
e TGV ▶ d.	...	...	1415	1422	...	...	...	...	...	1503	...	...	...	...	1621	...	...	...	...	...	...	...	...	1749
ce 360 d.	...	1024	|	|	...	...	...	...	...	|	...	...	...	...	|	...	...	...	...	...	...	...	1424z	|
eille St Charles 351 d.	...	1318	|	|	...	...	1410	...	...	|	...	1518	...	...	|	...	...	...	1618	1618	...	...	1718	|
es Aéroport Marseille ‡ d.	...	|	|	|	...	...	|	...	...	|	...	|	...	...	|	...	...	...	1637	1633	...	...	|	|
mas 351 d.	...	|	|	|	...	...	|	...	...	|	...	|	...	...	|	...	...	...	1653	1654	...	...	|	|
351 d.	...	|	|	|	...	...	1502	...	...	|	...	|	...	...	|	...	...	...	1713	1712	...	...	|	|
ignon Centre d.	1338	|	|	|	...	...	|	...	...	|	1538	|	...	...	|	1638r	...	...	|	|	1712	1738	|	|
scon-sur-Rhône d.	1352	|	|	|	...	...	|	...	...	|	1552	|	...	...	|	1652r	...	...	1722	1721	1725	1752	|	|
d.	1412	|	1504	1508	1512	...	1528	...	1543	1548	1612	|	...	1643	1708	1712	...	...	1743	1743	1747	1812	|	1835
d.	1430	|	|	|	1530	...	|	...	1559	|	1630	|	...	1659	|	1730	...	...	1759	1759	1813	1830	|	|
ellier a.	1445	1453	1530	1536	1545	...	1554	...	1615	1622	1645	1653	...	1715	1735	1745	...	...	1815	1815	1826	1845	1853	1902
ellier d.	1449	1458	...	1543	1549	1549	1559	...	1620	1625	1649	1658	1705	1720	1738	1749	1800	1805	1820	1820	...	1849	1858	...
nan d.	1501	|	...	|	1601	1601	|	...	1631	|	1701	|	1722	1732	|	1801	1813	1822	1832	1837	...	1901	|	...
d.	1509	|	...	1602	1609	1609	1616	...	1639	|	1709	|	1728	1740	|	1809	1820	1828	1840	1844	...	1909	|	...
d.	1522	|	...	1619	1622	1622	|	...	1652	|	1722	|	1743	1756	|	1822	1834	1844	1857	1859	...	1922	|	...
s d.	1535	|	...	1631	1636	1636	1640	...	1709	1716	1735	|	1803	1811	|	1835	1846	1901	1911	1916	...	1935	|	...
nne a.	1550	|	...	▬	1651	1651	1655	...	1726	1732	1750	|	1819	1827	1831	1850	...	1920	1927	1933	...	1950	|	...
nne d.	1557	|	...	...	1658	...	1658	1718	1732	1735	1757	|	1821	...	1834	1857	...	...	...	...	...	1957	|	...
assonne 321 a.	|	|	...	...	|	...	1727	|	1802	|	|	|	|	...	|	|	...	...	...	...	...	|	|	...
ouse 321 a.	|	1707	...	...	|	...	1812	|	1904b	|	|	1907	|	...	|	|	...	...	...	...	...	|	2107	...
eaux 320 a.	|	1913j	...	...	|	...	2029t	|	...	|	|	2113t	|	...	|	|	...	...	...	...	...	|	2313t	...
Nouvelle d.	1610	...	...	...	1711	...	...	1730	...	|	1810	...	1833	...	|	1910	...	...	...	...	...	2010	...	...
nan a.	1640	...	...	...	1740	...	...	1759	...	1806	1840	...	1902	...	1908	1940	...	...	...	...	...	2040	...	...
nan d.	1645f	...	...	1711	1745	...	...	...	...	...	1845	...	...	...	...	1945	...	...	...	...	...	...	...	...
s sur Mer d.	1702f	...	...	1728	1802	...	...	...	...	...	1902	...	...	...	...	2002	...	...	...	...	...	...	...	...
re d.	1707f	...	...	1733	1807	...	...	...	...	...	1907	...	...	...	...	2007	...	...	...	...	...	...	...	...
endres d.	1711f	...	...	1737	1811	...	...	...	...	...	1911	...	...	...	...	2011	...	...	...	...	...	...	...	...
s sur Mer d.	1716f	...	...	1742	1816	...	...	...	...	...	1916	...	...	...	...	2016	...	...	...	...	...	...	...	...
e 657 a.	1722f	...	...	1748	1822	...	...	...	...	...	1922	...	...	...	...	2022	...	...	...	...	...	...	...	...
ou 657 a.	...	...	...	1754	...	...	...	...	...	...	1928	...	...	...	...	...	...	...	...	...	...	...	...	...

	Ⓐ	Ⓐ	TGV 6231 ♥		Ⓐ	TGV 6817		TGV 6215 Q		Ⓑ	4766 4767 ⑤⑦ p★	TGV 5119	TGV 6824 A ⊙	TGV 6824 ⑤⑦ s⊙	TGV 6217 B	TGV 6217 ⑤⑦	TGV 9836	TGV 9836 ⑤⑦ v	TGV 6219 Ⓑ h	TGV 6219 ⑤ d		TGV 6221 ❖	TGV 6225 ⑤⑦ w	TGV 5137 ⑦ n
sels Midi 11 d.	...	...	...	...	...	...	...	...	...	...	...	...	...	...	...	...	1617	1617	...	...	...	...	...	...
Europe 11 d.	...	...	...	...	...	...	...	...	...	...	...	1554	...	...	...	...	1703	1703	...	...	...	...	...	2002
les de Gaulle ✈ 11 d.	...	...	...	...	...	...	...	...	...	...	...	1656	...	...	...	...	1758	1758	...	...	...	...	...	2117
ne la Vallée § 11 d.	...	...	...	...	...	...	...	...	...	...	...	1711	...	...	...	...	1811	1811	...	...	...	...	...	2130
Gare de Lyon ▶ d.	...	...	1607	...	...	...	...	1707	...	...	...	|	...	...	1807	1807	|	|	1915	1915	...	2015	2107	|
ion 379 d.	...	...	|	...	...	...	...	|	...	...	...	|	1734	1734	|	|	|	|	|	|	...	|	|	|
n Part Dieu ▶ d.	...	...	|	...	...	1810	...	|	...	...	...	1910	1936	1936	|	|	2010	2010	|	|	...	|	|	2333
ce TGV ▶ d.	...	...	1821	...	...	1849	...	1921	...	...	...	1950	2014	|	2022	2029	2049	2049	|	|	...	2229	2322	0010
ce 360 d.	...	...	|	...	...	|	...	|	...	...	...	|	|	|	|	|	|	|	|	|	...	|	|	|
seille St Charles 351 d.	...	1738	|	...	...	|	1818	|	...	...	1918	|	|	|	|	|	|	|	|	|	...	|	|	|
lles Aéroport Marseille ‡ d.	...	1753	|	...	...	|	1837	|	...	...	|	|	|	|	|	|	|	|	|	|	...	|	|	|
mas 351 d.	...	1811	|	...	...	|	1853	|	...	...	|	|	|	|	|	|	|	|	|	|	...	|	|	|
s 351 d.	...	1832	|	...	...	|	1913	|	...	...	2006	|	|	|	|	|	|	|	|	|	...	|	|	|
vignon Centre d.	1812	|	|	1838	1838	|	|	|	1938	1938	|	|	|	|	|	|	|	|	|	|	2138r	|	|	|
ascon-sur-Rhône d.	1825	1841	|	1852	1852	|	1922	|	1952	1952	|	|	|	|	|	|	|	|	|	|	|	|	|	|
s d.	1846	1855	1907	1912	1912	1936	1943	2008	2009	2012	2032	2036	2100	2103	2106	2113	2136	2136	2206	2206	2212	2314	0009	0057
d.	1912	...	|	1930	1930	|	1959	|	...	2030	|	|	|	|	|	|	|	|	|	|	2230	|	|	|
ellier a.	1926	...	1935	1946	1946	2002	2015	2035	...	2045	2058	2102	2126	2129	2134	2140	2204	2204	2234	2234	2246	2341	0056	0124
ellier d.	1929	...	1941	1950	1950	2005	2020	▬	...	2049	2103	...	2128	2133	2141	2144	...	2206	2238	2238	2250x	...	...	...
gnan d.	1946	...	|	2002	2002	|	2032	...	...	2101	|	...	|	|	|	|	...	|	|	|	2301x	...	...	...
d.	1952	...	1958	2009	2009	|	2040	...	...	2109	2120	...	|	|	2158	2202	...	2224	2255	2255	2309x	...	...	...
d.	2008	...	2014	2022	2022	|	2056	...	...	2122	|	...	|	|	2214	2219	...	2239	2311	2311	2322x	...	...	...
s d.	2023	...	2029	2035	2035	2043	2112	...	...	2135	2144	...	2216	2215	2231	2235	...	2252	2323	2325	2335x	...	...	...
nne a.	2041	...	2045	2050	2050	2101	2127	⑥	...	2150	2158	...	2230	2230	2245	2249	...	2310	...	2340	2353x	...	...	...
nne d.	...	...	2047	...	2057	2104	...	2157	...	2157	2201	...	2233	2233	2248	2252	...	2311	...	2342	...	...	...	...
cassonne 321 a.	...	...	|	...	|	2133	...	|	...	|	2229	...	2301	2300	|	|	...	|	...	|	...	...	...	...
louse 321 a.	...	...	|	...	|	2217	...	|	...	|	2316	...	2345	2345	|	|	...	|	...	|	...	...	...	...
deaux 320 a.	...	...	|	...	|	...	...	|	...	|	...	...	...	...	|	|	...	|	...	|	...	...	...	...
Nouvelle d.	...	...	|	...	2110	...	...	2210	...	2210	...	...	...	...	|	|	...	|	...	|	...	...	...	...
gnan a.	...	...	2120	...	2140	...	...	2240	...	2240	...	...	...	...	2320	2325	...	2344	...	0019	...	...	...	...
gnan d.	...	...	...	...	2145	...	...	...	...	...	...	...	...	...	...	...	...	...	...	...	...	...	...	...
s sur Mer d.	...	...	...	...	2202	...	...	...	...	...	...	...	...	...	...	...	...	...	...	...	...	...	...	...
ure d.	...	...	...	...	2207	...	...	...	...	...	...	...	...	...	...	...	...	...	...	...	...	...	...	...
endres d.	...	...	...	...	2211	...	...	...	...	...	...	...	...	...	...	...	...	...	...	...	...	...	...	...
ls sur Mer d.	...	...	...	...	2216	...	...	...	...	...	...	...	...	...	...	...	...	...	...	...	...	...	...	...
re 657 a.	...	...	...	...	2222	...	...	...	...	...	...	...	...	...	...	...	...	...	...	...	...	...	...	...
ou 657 a.	...	...	...	...	...	...	...	...	...	...	...	...	...	...	...	...	...	...	...	...	...	...	...	...

①②③④⑥ (not July 13).
①②③④⑥.
Ⓒ (daily July 2 - Aug. 28).
To July 1 and from Aug. 29.
July 2 - Aug. 28.
July 3 - Aug. 28.
Ⓐ (daily July 3 - Sept. 2).
1859 on ⑤ (also July 13, Nov. 10).
Also July 13, Nov. 10; not Nov. 11.
⑦ (also Nov. 2; not July 3 - Aug. 28, Oct. 23, 30). Runs 5–6 minutes earlier on Nov. 2. To St Chély d'Apcher (Table **332**).
⑤ (also July 13, Oct. 31, Nov. 10; not Nov. 11).
Not Nov. 11; runs daily July 3 - Sept. 2.
Not Sept. 19, Oct. 22.
Not June 19.
Also July 13, Aug. 15, Nov. 1, 10; not Aug. 14, Nov. 11.
Ⓐ only.
Also July 13.
Not Oct. 22.
Also Aug. 15, Nov. 1, 10; not Nov. 11.
Also July 13, Nov. 1, 10; not Nov. 11. Subject to alteration on June 19.

x – Not ⑤ June 3 - July 1, ⑤ Aug. 5 - Oct. 28.
z – ①⑥⑦ (also July 14, 15, Aug. 16, Nov. 1, 2, 11).

TGV – Ⓡ, supplement payable, 🍷.

★ – *INTERCITÉS*. Ⓡ.
♠ – To Barcelona (Table **13**).
♣ – (12) Luxembourg - Metz - Strasbourg - Montpellier (Table **379**).
⊙ – From Nancy (Table **379**). Timings may vary by up to 6 minutes Nimes - Toulouse (please check your reservation for confirmed timings).
♥ – July 3 - Aug. 28 runs as **9717** and continues to Barcelona (Table **13**).
❖ – On ①–④ runs up to 5 minutes later Valence - Montpellier. Subject to alteration on June 18, 19.
△ – From Nantes and Rennes (Table **335**). Subject to alteration on Oct. 1, 8, 9, 15, Nov. 26
§ – Marne la Vallée - Chessy (station for Disneyland Paris).
‡ – Vitrolles Aéroport Marseille-Provence. A shuttle bus runs to the airport terminal (journey time 5 minutes). For additional trains see Table **351**.
▶ – For Paris to Lyon see Table **340**. For additional trains from Paris and Lyon to Valence TGV see Table **350**. For Lyon to Valence Ville see Table **351**.

Additional low-cost 'Ouigo' TGV trains run from Marne la Vallée-Chessy in the eastern suburbs of Paris. See Table **350a**.

355 CERBÈRE - PERPIGNAN - MONTPELLIER - PARIS

SERVICE FROM JUNE 6. *Subject to alteration on Nov. 12, 19. Services from or via Lyon are subject to alteration on Aug. 13, 14, 15, Oct. 29, 30, 31.*

		TGV 6202	*TGV* 6202			*TGV* 6230			*TGV* 9862	*TGV* 9862		*TGV* 6204	*TGV* 6204							*TGV* 6869				*TGV* 5166
		Ⓐ	Ⓐ	Ⓐ	Ⓐ	①–⑥		Ⓐ		①⑥	Ⓐ			Ⓐ	Ⓐ		⚒	Ⓐ	Ⓒ		Ⓒ	Ⓐ	Ⓐ	
		J				b	✣		L	r		G		K	J	H		J		⊙				
Cerbère	d.	...	...	...	...	...	...	...	...	...	...	...	...	...	...	...	...	...	...	...	...	0537	...	...
Banyuls sur Mer	d.	...	...	...	...	...	...	...	...	...	...	...	...	...	...	...	...	...	...	...	...	0544	...	...
Port Vendres	d.	...	...	...	...	...	...	...	...	...	...	...	...	...	...	...	...	...	...	...	...	0549	...	...
Collioure	d.	...	...	...	...	...	...	...	...	...	...	...	...	...	...	...	...	...	...	...	...	0553	...	...
Argelès sur Mer	d.	...	...	...	...	...	...	...	...	...	...	...	...	...	...	...	...	...	...	...	...	0558	...	...
Perpignan	a.	...	...	...	...	...	...	...	...	...	...	...	...	...	...	...	...	...	...	...	...	0614	...	...
Perpignan	d.	...	...	...	...	...	...	...	...	0515	...	0540	...	0535	0544	...	...	...	0603	...	...	0619	...	...
Port la Nouvelle	d.	...	...	...	...	...	...	...	...	|	...	|	...	0606	0614	...	...	...	0634	...	...	0651	...	...
Bordeaux **320**	d.	...	...	...	...	...	...	...	...	|	...	|	...	|	|	...	...	...	|	...	...	|	...	...
Toulouse **321**	d.	...	...	...	...	...	...	...	...	|	...	|	...	|	|	...	...	...	|	0554	...	|	...	...
Carcassonne **321**	d.	...	...	...	...	...	...	...	...	|	...	|	...	|	|	...	...	...	|	|	...	|	0643	...
Narbonne	a.	...	...	...	...	...	...	...	...	0549	...	0614	...	0618	0627	...	...	...	0646	0700	...	0705	0716	...
Narbonne	d.	...	...	0430	...	...	0532	...	...	0552	0601	0617	...	0622	0631	0631	...	0640	0649	0702	...	0708	0720	...
Béziers	d.	0427	...	0447	...	...	0547	...	...	0608	0616	0633	...	0639	0646	0646	...	0659	0708	0716	...	0724	0737	...
Agde	d.	0443	...	0500	...	...	0558	...	...	0622	0630	0648	...	0651	0658	0658	...	0714	0723	|	←	0737	0751	...
Sète	d.	0501	...	0514	...	...	0612	...	...	0638	0646	0704	...	0708	0712	0712	...	0730	0738	|	0745	0751	0807	...
Frontignan	d.	|	...	0520	...	...	0618	...	...	|	0651	|	...	0713	0718	0718	...	0737	→	|	0751	0757	0813	...
Montpellier	a.	0520	...	0532	...	...	0630	...	...	0653	0709	0718	...	0730	0730	0730	...	0755	...	0800	0809	0809	0830	...
Montpellier	d.	0527	0527	0534	...	0626	0633	0638	0656n	0657	0713	0725	0725	0734	0733	...	0739	...	...	0803	0813	0813	0834	0856
Lunel	d.	|	|	0550	...	|	0648	0654	|	|	0732	|	|	0749	0749	...	0755	...	...	|	0832	0832	0850	|
Nimes	d.	0556	0556	0606	0649	0655	0706	0722	0726	0726	0751	0755	0755	0803	0803	...	0822	...	...	0830	0851	0851	0903	0926
Tarascon-sur-Rhône	d.	|	|	0622	0709	|	0722	0742	|	|	0808	|	|	...	...	...	0842	...	...	|	0908	0908	...	|
Avignon Centre	a.	|	|	|	0723g	|	|	0755	|	|	0821	|	|	...	...	...	0855	...	...	|	0921	0921	...	|
Arles **351**	d.	|	|	0632	...	|	0732	...	|	|	...	|	|	...	...	...	...	...	...	|	...	...	...	|
Miramas **351**	d.	|	|	0652	...	|	0752	...	|	|	...	|	|	...	...	...	...	...	...	|	...	...	...	|
Vitrolles Aéroport Marseille ‡	d.	|	|	0709	...	|	0809	...	|	|	...	|	|	...	...	...	...	...	...	|	...	...	...	|
Marseille St Charles **351**	a.	|	|	0727	...	|	0828	...	|	|	...	|	|	...	...	...	...	...	...	|	...	...	...	|
Nice **360**	a.	|	|	...	...	|	...	...	|	|	...	|	|	...	...	...	...	...	...	|	...	...	...	|
Valence TGV	d.	0643	0643	...	...	0741	...	...	0818	0818	...	|	|	...	...	...	...	...	...	0913	...	...	...	1015
Lyon Part Dieu	a.	|	|	...	...	|	...	...	0854	0854	...	|	|	...	...	...	...	...	...	0950	...	...	...	1050
Dijon **379**	a.	|	|	...	...	|	...	...	|	|	...	|	|	...	...	...	...	...	...	1130	...	...	...	|
Paris Gare de Lyon	a.	0853	0853	...	...	0953	...	...	|	|	...	1045	1045	...	...	...	...	...	...	...	...	...	...	|
Marne la Vallée § **11**	a.	...	...	...	...	...	...	...	1048	1048	...	...	...	...	...	...	...	...	...	...	...	...	...	1248
Charles de Gaulle ✈ **11**	a.	...	...	...	...	...	...	...	1102	1102	...	...	...	...	...	...	...	...	...	...	...	...	...	1302
Lille Europe **11**	a.	...	...	...	...	...	...	...	1158c	1158c	...	...	...	...	...	...	...	...	...	...	...	...	...	1427z
Brussels Midi **11**	a.	...	...	...	...	...	...	...	1252v	1252v	...	...	...	...	...	...	...	...	...	...	...	...	...	...

			TGV 9700	*TGV* 6206		*TGV* 6878			*TGV* 6208	*TGV* 9734	*TGV* 6234	4655 4654		*TGV* 9702		*TGV* 6859			*TGV* 6210	*TGV* 6210		4657 4656	*TGV* 6882	
					Ⓐ		Ⓐ					★			Ⓐ		Ⓐ	Ⓐ			Ⓐ	★		Ⓒ
			D♠	E		♣				♠	T	⊗	◇	♠			◇		N	P		⊗	S	K
Cerbère	d.	0637	...	...	0707	...	0737	...	...	...	...	...	0937	...	...	...	1037	...	...	...	...	...	...	...
Banyuls sur Mer	d.	0644	...	...	0714	...	0744	...	...	...	...	...	0944	...	...	...	1044	...	...	...	...	...	...	...
Port Vendres	d.	0649	...	...	0719	...	0749	...	...	...	...	...	0949	...	...	...	1049	...	...	...	...	...	...	...
Collioure	d.	0652	...	...	0722	...	0752	...	...	...	...	...	0952	...	...	...	1053	...	...	...	...	...	...	...
Argelès sur Mer	d.	0658	...	...	0727	...	0758	...	...	...	...	...	0958	...	...	...	1058	...	...	...	...	...	...	...
Perpignan	a.	0714	...	...	0743	...	0814	...	...	...	...	...	1014	...	...	...	1114	...	...	...	...	...	...	...
Perpignan	d.	0719	0736	0740	0745	...	0819	0819	...	0847	0936	...	1019	1053	...	...	...	1119	...	...	...	...	...	...
Port la Nouvelle	d.	0750	|	|	0815	...	0850	0850	...	|	|	...	1050	|	...	...	...	1150	...	...	...	...	...	...
Bordeaux **320**	d.	|	|	|	|	...	|	|	...	|	|	0731	|	|	...	...	...	|	...	...	...	0931	...	...
Toulouse **321**	d.	|	|	|	|	...	|	|	...	|	|	0949	|	|	...	1049	...	|	...	...	...	1149	...	...
Carcassonne **321**	d.	|	|	|	|	...	|	|	...	|	|	1032	|	|	...	1134	...	|	...	...	...	1233	...	...
Narbonne	a.	0803	0811	0814	0827	...	0903	0903	...	0922	1010	1100	1103	1127	...	1201	...	1203	...	...	...	1301	...	...
Narbonne	d.	0809	0814	0817	0832	...	0909	0909	...	0925	1013	1103	1109	1130	...	1204	...	1209	...	...	1240	1304	...	1309
Béziers	d.	0825	0831	0833	0846	...	0924	0924	...	0941	1030	1120	1125	|	...	1219	...	1225	1233	...	1259	1320	...	1325
Agde	d.	0838	0845	0848	0858	...	0937	0937	...	|	1044	|	1138	|	...	|	...	1238	1248	...	1314	|	...	1338
Sète	d.	0852	0901	0904	0912	...	0952	0952	...	|	1100	1144	1152	|	...	1244	...	1252	1304	...	1330	1344	...	1352
Frontignan	d.	0857	|	|	0918	...	0957	0957	...	|	|	|	1157	|	...	|	...	1258	|	...	1336	|	...	1359
Montpellier	a.	0909	0924	0920	0931	...	1009	1009	...	1024	1123	1200	1209	1221	...	1259	...	1309	1319	...	1355	1401	...	1411
Montpellier	d.	0913	0928	0925	...	0958	1013	1013	1024	1031	1127	1205	1213	1224	1228	1304	...	1313	1325	1325	...	1405	1412	...
Lunel	d.	0932	|	|	...	|	1032	1032	|	|	|	|	1232	|	1253	|	...	1331	|	|	...	|	|	...
Nimes	d.	0951	0955	0955	...	1027	1051	1051	1055	1059	1155	1234	1251	1254	1316	1333	...	1351	1355	1355	...	1434	1443	...
Tarascon-sur-Rhône	d.	1008	|	|	...	|	1108	1108	|	|	|	|	1308	|	1336	|	...	1408	|	|	...	|	|	...
Avignon Centre	a.	|	|	|	...	|	1121	1121	|	|	|	|	1321	|	1348	|	...	1421	|	|	...	|	|	...
Arles **351**	d.	1019	|	|	...	|	...	...	|	|	|	1259	...	|	...	|	...	...	|	|	...	1458	|	...
Miramas **351**	d.	1039	|	|	...	|	...	...	|	|	|	|	...	|	...	|	...	...	|	|	...	|	|	...
Vitrolles Aéroport Marseille ‡	d.	1054	|	|	...	|	...	...	|	|	|	|	...	|	...	|	...	...	|	|	...	|	|	...
Marseille St Charles **351**	a.	1112	|	|	...	|	...	...	|	|	|	1350	...	|	...	|	...	...	|	|	...	1550	|	...
Nice **360**	a.	...	|	|	...	|	...	...	|	|	|	...	...	|	...	|	...	...	|	|	...	...	|	...
Valence TGV	d.	...	|	|	...	1115	...	...	1141	1149	|	...	...	1341	...	1420	...	...	|	|	...	...	1529	...
Lyon Part Dieu	a.	...	|	|	...	1150	...	...	|	1226	|	...	...	|	...	1454	...	...	|	|	...	...	1604	...
Dijon **379**	a.	...	|	|	...	1338	...	...	|	...	|	...	...	|	...	...	...	...	|	|	...	...	1738	...
Paris Gare de Lyon	a.	...	1245	1245	...	...	...	...	1353	...	1445	...	...	1553	...	...	...	...	1645	1645	...	...	...	...
Marne la Vallée § **11**	a.	...	...	...	...	...	...	...	...	...	...	...	...	...	...	...	...	...	...	...	...	...	...	...
Charles de Gaulle ✈ **11**	a.	...	...	...	...	...	...	...	...	...	...	...	...	...	...	...	...	...	...	...	...	...	...	...
Lille Europe **11**	a.	...	...	...	...	...	...	...	...	...	...	...	...	...	...	...	...	...	...	...	...	...	...	...
Brussels Midi **11**	a.	...	...	...	...	...	...	...	...	...	...	...	...	...	...	...	...	...	...	...	...	...	...	...

D – July 4 - Aug. 28.
E – To July 2 and from Aug. 29.
G – Daily to July 2; ⑥ July 9 - Aug. 27; daily from Aug. 29.
H – ⚒ to July 2; ⑥ July 9 - Aug. 27; ⚒ from Aug. 29.
J – To July 1 and from Aug. 29.
K – July 2 - Aug. 28.
L – ②③④⑤⑦ (also Aug. 15, Oct. 31; not July 14, Aug. 16, Nov. 2, 11).
N – July 3 - Aug. 28.
P – Daily to Aug. 28; ⑦ from Sept. 4 (also Nov. 1).
S – To Strasbourg (Table **379**).
T – Runs on July 10, 24, Aug. 7, 14, 15, 21, 28 only.

b – Not Aug. 15, Nov. 1.
c – 2 minutes earlier from July 16.
g – 0725 Aug. 29 - Sept. 9.
n – 0658 on ⑦ (also Aug. 15, Nov. 1).
r – Also July 14, Aug. 16, Nov. 2, 11; not Aug. 15, Oct. 31.
v – 1243 on ⑥⑦ (also July 14, Aug. 15, Nov. 1, 11).
z – 1405 on Ⓒ to July 10; 1403 on Ⓒ from July 16; 1421 on Ⓐ from July 18.

TGV –🅁, supplement payable.

◇ – Subject to alteration Cerbère - Perpignan on ①–⑤ Sept. 19 – 30.
⊗ – Subject to alteration on Oct. 23.
✣ – Runs 28 – 35 minutes later on June 19.
⊙ – To Nancy (Table **379**). Timings Toulouse - Montpellier may vary by up to 5 minute (please check your reservation for confirmed timings). Departs Toulouse 10 – 11 minutes earlier on ②–⑤ July 19 - Sept. 30 (also Sept. 19, 26; not Aug. 16).
♠ – From Barcelona (Table **13**).
♣ – 🅃 Montpellier - Strasbourg - Metz - Luxembourg (Table **379**). Subject to alterat on ①–⑤ Sept. 19 – 30, ①–⑤ Oct. 10 – 28 and ①–⑤ Nov. 14 - Dec. 2.
★ – *INTERCITÉS*. 🅁.
‡ – Vitrolles Aéroport Marseille-Provence. A shuttle bus runs to the airport terminal (journey time 5 minutes). For additional trains see Table **351**.
§ – Marne la Vallée - Chessy (station for Disneyland Paris).

Additional low-cost 'Ouigo' TGV trains run to Marne la Vallée-Chessy in the eastern suburbs of Paris. See Table **350a**.

CERBÈRE - PERPIGNAN - MONTPELLIER - PARIS

SERVICE FROM JUNE 6. *Subject to alteration on Nov. 12, 19. Services from or via Lyon are subject to alteration on Aug. 13, 14, 15, Oct. 29, 30, 31.*

	TGV 6212 N	TGV 6212	TGV 9868	4659 4658 ★ ⊗		TGV 6214 T			TGV 9704 ♠	TGV 5380 5387 A△	TGV 5380 5387 B△	Ⓐ d		Ⓐ	TGV 6861		TGV 6218 D	TGV 6218 Ⓑ C	Ⓐ ☆	⚒	TGV 5186	4663 4662 ★ ⊖	Ⓒ	Ⓐ
ère d.	...	...	...	...	1237	...	...	...	...	...	...	...	...	...	...	1437	...	...	...	...	...	...	1537	...
ls sur Mer d.	...	...	...	...	1244	...	...	...	...	...	...	...	...	...	...	1444	...	...	...	...	...	...	1544	...
'endres d.	...	...	...	...	1249	...	...	...	...	...	...	...	...	...	...	1449	...	...	...	...	...	...	1549	...
ure d.	...	...	...	...	1252	...	...	...	...	...	...	...	...	...	...	1453	...	...	...	...	...	...	1552	...
es sur Mer d.	...	...	...	...	1258	...	...	...	...	...	...	...	...	...	...	1458	...	...	...	...	...	...	1558	...
gnan a.	...	...	...	...	1314	...	...	...	...	...	...	...	...	...	...	1514	...	...	...	...	...	...	1614	...
gnan d.	1240	...	...	...	1319	1337	...	1419	1451r	...	...	...	...	...	...	1519	1540	...	...	...	...	...	1619	1619
a Nouvelle d.	|	...	...	...	1350	|	...	1450	|	...	...	...	...	...	...	1550	|	...	...	...	...	...	1650	1650
deaux **320** d.	|	...	...	1047	|	|	...	|	|	...	...	...	...	...	...	|	|	...	...	...	...	1331	|	|
louse **321** d.	|	...	...	1257	|	|	...	|	|	...	...	...	...	...	1449	|	|	...	...	...	...	1549	|	|
cassonne **321** d.	|	...	...	|	|	|	...	|	|	...	...	...	...	...	1534	|	|	...	...	...	...	1633	|	|
nne a.	1314	...	...	|	1403	1411	...	1503	1525r	...	...	...	...	...	1601	1603	1614	...	...	...	...	1701	1703	1703
nne d.	1317	...	...	|	1409	1414	...	1509	1528r	...	...	1532	...	...	1604	1609	1617	...	1632	...	...	1704	1709	1709
's d.	1334	1334	...	|	1425	1431	...	1525	|	...	...	1547	...	...	1620	1625	1633	...	1646	...	...	1719	1725	1725
d.	1348	1348	...	|	1438	1445	...	1538	|	...	...	1558	...	...	|	1638	1648	...	1658	...	...	|	1738	1738
d.	1404	1404	...	|	1452	1501	...	1552	|	...	...	1612	...	...	1644	1652	1704	...	1712	...	...	1743	1752	1752
gnan d.	|	|	...	|	1457	|	...	1557	|	...	...	1617	...	...	|	1657	|	...	1718	...	...	|	1757	1759
pellier a.	1420	1420	...	1459	1509	1524	...	1610	1619	...	...	1628	...	...	1701	1709	1720	...	1731	...	...	1801	1809	1811
pellier d.	1425	1425	1457	1504	1513	1528	...	1613	1623q	1627	1630	1632	1632	1638	1706	1713	1724	1724	1734	1738	1757	1805	1812	1814
d.	|	|	|	|	1532	|	...	1632	|	|	|	1648	1648	1703	|	1732	|	|	1750	1801	|	|	1832	1832
s d.	1455	1455	1526	|	1551	1555	...	1651	1655	1658	1700	1706	1706	1721	1735	1751	1755	1755	1803	1821	1826	1835	1851	1851
ascon-sur-Rhône d.	|	|	|	|	1608	|	...	1708	|	|	|	1721	1721	1742	|	1808	|	|	...	1842	|	|	1908	1908
vignon Centre a.	|	|	|	|	1621	|	...	1721	|	|	|	|	|	1754	|	1821	|	|	...	1854	|	|	1921	1921
es **351** d.	|	|	|	|	...	|	...	...	|	|	|	1732	1732	...	|	...	|	|	...	...	|	1859	...	...
amas **351** d.	|	|	|	|	...	|	...	...	|	|	|	1753	1753	...	|	...	|	|	...	...	|	|	...	...
olles Aéroport Marseille ‡ d.	|	|	|	|	...	|	...	...	|	|	|	1813	1813	...	|	...	|	|	...	...	|	|	...	...
'seille St Charles **351** a.	|	|	|	1642	...	|	...	...	|	|	|	1834	1834	...	|	...	|	|	...	...	|	1950	...	...
lice **360** a.	|	|	|	1937	...	|	...	...	|	|	|	...	...	...	|	...	|	|	...	...	|	...	...	...
ce TGV d.	1541	1541	1615	...	...	|	...	...	1741	1749	1749	...	...	...	|	...	1841	1841	...	...	1915	...	...	...
on Part Dieu a.	|	|	1650	...	...	|	...	...	|	1824	1824	...	...	...	1850	...	|	|	...	...	1950	...	...	...
ijon **379** a.	|	|	|	...	...	|	...	...	|	...	...	...	...	...	...	...	|	|	...	...	|	...	...	...
Gare de Lyon a.	1753	1753	|	...	...	1845	...	...	1953	...	...	...	...	...	...	...	2053	2053	...	...	|	...	...	...
rne la Vallée § **11** a.	...	...	1848	...	...	...	...	...	...	...	...	...	...	...	...	...	...	...	...	...	2148	...	...	...
arles de Gaulle ✈ **11** a.	...	...	1902	...	...	...	...	...	...	...	...	...	...	...	...	...	...	...	...	...	2202	...	...	...
e Europe **11** a.	...	...	1959j	...	...	...	...	...	...	...	...	...	...	...	...	...	...	...	...	...	2308x	...	...	...
ssels Midi **11** a.	...	...	2043	...	...	...	...	...	...	...	...	...	...	...	...	...	...	...	...	...	...	...	...	...

	TGV 6220			4665 4664 ★		TGV 6222 ♥	Ⓒ	Ⓐ	TGV 9724 ■	TGV 6857	Ⓑ	TGV 6224 ⑤ f	TGV 6224 ⑦		4667 4666 ⑤⑦ w★	Ⓐ	①–④ m		TGV 6228 ⑦		4669 4668 ★ ◇		4350 4351 R 🅁	3730 Q 🅁
ère d.	...	...	...	...	1637	...	...	...	...	...	1737	...	...	...	...	1837	1837	...	...	...	...	1937	1944	2005
uls sur Mer d.	...	...	...	...	1644	...	...	...	...	...	1744	...	...	...	...	1844	1844	...	...	...	...	1944	1953	2014
Vendres d.	...	...	...	...	1649	...	...	...	...	...	1749	...	...	...	...	1849	1849	...	...	...	...	1949	2000	2021
ure d.	...	...	...	...	1653	...	...	...	...	...	1753	...	...	...	...	1852	1852	...	...	...	...	1952	2005	2026
ès sur Mer d.	...	...	...	...	1658	...	...	...	...	...	1758	...	...	...	...	1858	1858	...	...	...	...	1958	2012	2033
gnan a.	...	...	...	...	1714	...	...	...	...	...	1814	...	...	...	...	1914	1914	...	...	...	...	2014	2031	2051
gnan d.	...	...	...	...	1719	1749	...	...	1815	...	1819	...	1838	...	...	...	1919	1919	...	...	...	2019	2035	2055
a Nouvelle d.	...	...	...	...	1750	|	...	...	|	...	1850	...	|	...	...	...	1950	1950	...	...	...	2050	|	|
rdeaux **320** d.	...	...	...	1447p	|	|	...	...	|	1538t	|	...	|	...	1644	...	|	|	...	...	1731	|	|	|
ulouse **321** d.	...	...	...	1654	|	|	1658	1658	|	1749	|	...	|	...	1850	...	|	|	...	...	1949	|	|	|
rcassonne **321** d.	...	...	...	|	|	|	1758	1758	|	1834	|	...	|	...	|	...	|	|	...	...	2033	|	|	|
onne a.	...	...	...	|	1803	1823	1828	1828	1854	1901	1904	...	1913	...	|	...	2003	2003	...	...	2101	2103	2113	2143
onne d.	...	1720	...	|	1809	1826	1832	1832	1857	1904	1909	...	1916	...	|	...	2009	2009	...	...	2104	2109	2117	2213
rs d.	1734	1738	...	|	1825	1842	1848	1848	1913	1920	1925	...	1932	...	|	...	2025	2025	...	...	2120	2125	2133	|
d.	1748	1752	...	|	1838	|	1900	1900	|	|	1938	...	1947	...	|	...	2038	2038	...	...	|	2137	2146	|
d.	1803	1809	...	|	1852	|	1915	1915	|	1943	1952	...	2003	...	|	...	2052	2052	...	...	2148	2152	2202	|
ignan d.	|	1814	...	|	1859	|	1921	1921	|	|	1957	...	|	...	|	...	2057	2057	...	...	|	2157	|	|
pellier a.	1818	1831	...	1857	1909	1920	1933	1933	1954	1959	2009	...	2017	...	2057	...	2109	2109	...	...	2205	2209	2222	|
pellier d.	1825	1834	...	1902	1913	1925	1939	1939	1958	2004	2013	2024	2024	...	2102	...	2113	2113	2126	...	2210	2213	2225	|
d.	|	1850	...	|	1932	|	1955	2004	|	|	2032	|	|	...	|	...	2132	2132	|	...	|	2232	|	|
s d.	1855	1906	...	|	1951	1955	2008	2021	2025	2033	2048	2054	2054	...	|	...	2148	2148	2155	...	2239	2248	2253	|
rascon-sur-Rhône d.	|	1922	...	|	2008	|	...	2042	|	|	...	|	|	...	|	...	...	...	|	...	|	...	...	◐
Avignon Centre a.	|	|	...	|	2021	|	...	2054	2043v	|	...	|	|	...	|	...	...	...	|	...	|	...	...	|
es **351** d.	|	1932	...	|	...	|	...	...	|	|	...	|	|	...	|	...	...	...	|	...	2304	...	...	|
amas **351** d.	|	1951	...	|	...	|	...	...	|	|	...	|	|	...	|	...	...	...	|	...	|	...	...	|
rolles Aéroport Marseille ‡ d.	|	2008	...	|	...	|	...	...	|	|	...	|	|	...	|	...	...	...	|	...	|	...	...	|
rseille St Charles **351** a.	|	2026	...	2042	...	|	...	...	2120	|	...	|	|	...	2235	...	...	...	|	...	2351	...	...	|
Vice **360** a.	|	...	...	2337z	...	|	...	...	...	|	...	|	|	...	...	...	...	...	|	...	...	...	...	|
ce TGV d.	1941	...	...	...	...	|	...	...	...	|	...	2141	2143	...	...	...	...	...	2241	...	...	...	...	|
on Part Dieu a.	|	...	...	...	...	|	...	...	...	2150	...	|	|	...	...	...	...	...	|	...	...	...	...	|
Dijon **379** a.	|	...	...	...	...	|	...	...	...	...	...	|	|	...	...	...	...	...	|	...	...	...	...	|
Gare de Lyon a.	2153	...	...	...	...	2245y	...	...	...	...	...	2353	2353	...	...	...	...	...	0053	...	...	...	...	0723a
rne la Vallée § **11** a.	...	...	...	...	...	...	...	...	...	...	...	...	...	...	...	...	...	...	...	...	...	...	...	...
arles de Gaulle ✈ **11** a.	...	...	...	...	...	...	...	...	...	...	...	...	...	...	...	...	...	...	...	...	...	...	...	...
e Europe **11** a.	...	...	...	...	...	...	...	...	...	...	...	...	...	...	...	...	...	...	...	...	...	...	...	...
ussels Midi **11** a.	...	...	...	...	...	...	...	...	...	...	...	...	...	...	...	...	...	...	...	...	...	...	...	...

⑤–⑦ to June 26; daily from July 1.
①–④ to June 30.
Ⓑ (not July 4 - Aug. 28, Nov. 11). Subject to alteration on June 5, 19, July 3.
Daily July 4 - Aug. 28. Subject to alteration on July 16, 17, 30, 31.
July 3 - Aug. 28.
🛏 1, 2 cl. and (2) (reclining) Cerbère - Narbonne - Toulouse - Paris Austerlitz. **Service may be withdrawn from July 1**.
For days of running see Table **379**. 🛏 1, 2 cl. Cerbère - Metz - Luxembourg; 🛏 1, 2 cl. Cerbère - Strasbourg. **Service may be withdrawn from July 1**.
Runs on July 10, 24, Aug. 7, 14, 15, 21, 28 only.

Paris **Austerlitz**.
Runs daily June 27 - Sept. 2.
Also July 13, Nov. 10; not Nov. 11.
1956 from July 16.
Not July 13, 14, Aug. 15, Nov. 1, 10.
Not Oct. 22. 1440 on ⑤ (also July 13, Oct. 31, Nov. 10).
1626 on ①–④ to June 30.
6 minutes earlier Aug. 29 - Sept. 11.
Not Oct. 22.
Avignon **TGV** station. Also calls at Aix en Provence TGV (a. 2105).
Also July 13, Aug. 15, Nov. 1, 10; not Aug. 14, Nov. 11.

x – 2328 on Ⓐ to July 15; 2304 July 16 - Nov. 13 and from Nov. 19; Nov. 14 – 18 arrives Lille **Flandres** 2307.
y – 2246 on ⑥ to Aug. 27; 2255 on ⑥ from Sept. 3 (also Nov. 11).
z – ⑤–⑦ (also July 13, 14, Aug. 15, Oct. 31, Nov. 1, 10).

TGV – 🅁, supplement payable.

⊗ – Subject to alteration on Sept. 19 – 23, 26 – 30, Oct. 23.
◇ – Subject to alteration on June 18, Oct. 22.
⊖ – Subject to alteration on Oct. 22.
♠ – From Barcelona (Table **13**).
♥ – June 2 - Aug. 28 runs as **9706** and starts from Barcelona (Table **13**).
■ – (12) Madrid - Barcelona - Marseille.
◐ – Via Toulouse and Limoges (Table **310**).
★ – *INTERCITÉS*. 🅁.
△ – To Nantes and Rennes (Table **335**). Subject to alteration on Nov. 26.
☆ – To Mende (Table **333**).
‡ – Vitrolles Aéroport Marseille-Provence. A shuttle bus runs to the airport terminal (journey time 5 minutes). For additional trains see Table **351**.
§ – Marne la Vallée - Chessy (station for Disneyland Paris).

Additional low-cost 'Ouigo' TGV trains run to Marne la Vallée-Chessy in the eastern suburbs of Paris. See Table **350a**.

359 NICE - ANNOT - DIGNE

2nd class

km	CP ▲					
0	**Nice** (Gare CP) d.	0655	0925	1305	1715	1813
	Plan du Var d.	0741	0957	1341	1757	1854
41	Villars sur Var d.	0801	1017	1401	1818	1915
58	Puget Théniers d.	0821	1038	1421	1839	1937
64	Entrevaux d.	0830	1046	1429	1847	1945
78	Annot d.	0851	1106	1449	1908	2001
96	Thorame Haute d.	0915	1130	1512	1932	...
106	St André les Alpes d.	0927	1144	1523	1945	...
150	**Digne** a.	1020	1239	1620	2041	...

CP ▲	⚒	†				
Digne d.	...	...	0715	1045	1425	1735
St. André les Alpes d.	...	...	0812	1143	1524	1830
Thorame Haute d.	...	...	0824	1156	1536	1842
Annot d.	0540	0750	0850	1219	1600	1910
Entrevaux d.	0558	0810	0908	1238	1619	1929
Puget Théniers d.	0606	0822	0916	1246	1627	1938
Villars sur Var d.	0627	0842	0937	1306	1648	1957
Plan du Var d.	0649	0903	0958	1328	1710	2018
Nice (Gare CP) a.	0731	0940	1030	1400	1745	2057

TRAIN DES PIGNES steam train, 20

⑦ May 8 - Oct. 30 ⊠

Puget Théniers 1055 → Annot 1205
Annot 1500 → Puget Théniers 1540

Also calls at Entrevaux

www.traindespignes.fr

🚌 ★	🚌 v	🚌	🚌	🚌
Digne △ d.	0735	1100	1330	1640
Digne (Gare) d.	0745	1110	1340	1650
Manosque-Gréoux d.	0850	1215	1445	1800
Aix en Provence TGV a.	0950	1315	1545	1900
Aéroport Marseille ✈ a.	1005	1330	1600	1915

🚌 ★	🚌 ⚒	🚌	🚌	🚌 z
Aéroport Marseille ✈ d.	0920	1255	1530	1820
Aix en Provence TGV d.	0950	1325	1600	1850
Manosque-Gréoux a.	1055	1430	1705	1955
Digne (Gare) a.	1155	1530	1805	2050
Digne △ a.	1205	1540	1815	2055

🚌 ☆	🚌 ⚒	🚌		🚌 ⑥
Digne △ d.	0700	1430	...	2000
Digne (Gare) d.	|	1435	...	2003
Château Arnoux. a.	0725	1503	...	2029
Sisteron (Gare) a.	0742	1520	...	2045
Veynes (Gare) a.	...	1620	...	2140

🚌 ☆	🚌		🚌 n
Veynes (Gare) d.	0645	...	1245
Sisteron (Gare) d.	0745	...	1345
Château Arnoux d.	0800	...	1400
Digne (Gare) a.	0828	...	1428
Digne △ a.	0830	...	1430

n – Not May 1.
v – Additional journey: 0500 ⚒.
z – Additional journey: 2035 (2100 from Aix TGV).

△ – Gare Routière (bus station).
▲ – Narrow gauge railway, operated by Chemins de Fer de Provence (CP).
☆ – LER route 33, operated by Autocars Payan or SCAL. SNCF rail tickets valid. For rail connections see **362**.

★ – LER (Lignes Express Régionales) Rou operated by Autocars Payan. Combine tickets 🚌 + TGV available.
⊠ – Also July 15, 22, 29, Aug. 12, 19, 26. An amended service runs on June 19.

360 MARSEILLE - TOULON - NICE - VENTIMIGLIA

SERVICE FROM JUNE 6. *Services from or via Lyon are subject to alteration on Aug. 13, 14, 15, Oct. 29, 30, 31.*

km	All *TGV* trains are 🅁	139 🅁 ♥	17471 Ⓐ	5773 🅁 B		17473 Ⓐ	4283 4282 🅁 A	4251 4283 🅁 A	17475	*TGV* 6805 Ⓐ	*TGV* 6805 Ⓒ	*TGV* 6171	145 D🅁 ♥	145 🅁 ♥		*TGV* 6173	*TGV* 6155	17483	*TGV* 6820	*TGV* 6175	*TGV* 6165 K	17487
	Brussels Midi **11** d.	...	...	...	...	...	...	...	...	...	...	...	...	...	...	...	...	...	...	...	...	...
	Lille Europe **11** d.	...	...	...	...	...	...	...	...	...	...	...	...	...	...	...	...	...	...	...	...	...
	Paris Gare de Lyon **350** ▶ d.	...	...	2122a	...	...	...	...	...	...	...	0719	...	...	...	0921	0921	...	...	1019	1119	...
	Strasbourg **379** d.	...	...	|	...	...	2012	...	...	...	...	|	...	...	...	|	|	...	...	|	|	...
	Metz **379** d.	...	...	|	...	...	|	2037	...	...	...	|	...	...	...	|	|	...	0600	|	|	...
	Dijon **379** d.	...	...	|	...	...	|	|	...	...	...	|	...	...	...	|	|	...	0921	|	|	...
	Genève **346** d.	...	...	|	...	...	|	|	...	...	...	|	...	...	...	|	|	...	|	|	|	...
	Lyon Part-Dieu **350** d.	...	...	|	...	...	|	|	...	0636	0702	|	...	...	...	|	|	...	1106	|	|	...
	Bordeaux **320** d.	...	...	|	...	...	|	|	...	|	|	|	...	...	...	|	|	...	|	|	|	...
	Toulouse **321** d.	...	...	|	...	...	|	|	...	|	|	|	...	...	...	|	|	...	|	|	|	...
	Montpellier **355** d.	...	...	|	...	...	|	|	...	|	|	|	...	...	...	|	|	...	|	|	|	...
0	**Marseille** St Charles ▶ d.	...	0531	|	...	0631	0658	0658	0729	0831	0900	|	1131	...	...	|	|	1231	1300	|	|	1431
67	**Toulon** ▶ a.	...	0614	0640	...	0714	0745	0745	0812	0912	0943	1108	1216	...	...	1308	1308	1314	1343	1408	1508	1515
67	**Toulon** ▶ d.	...	0617	0643	0651	0717	0748	0748	0815	0916	0947	1112	1218	...	1221	1312	1320	1316	1347	1411	1512	1517
	Hyères ▶ a.	...	|	|	|	|	|	|	|	|	|	|	|	...	|	|	1335	|	|	|	|	|
100	Carnoules d.	...	0637	|	0721	0736	|	|	0836	|	|	|	|	...	1252	|	...	1336	|	|	|	1536
135	Les Arcs-Draguignan ▷ d.	...	0657	0720	0749	0755	0824	0824	0857	0950	1022	1147	|	...	1319	|	...	1355	1423	1446	|	1555
162	St Raphaël-Valescure ▷ d.	...	0716	0742	...	0813	0842	0842	0916	1009	1039	|	1311	...	...	1402	...	1413	1441	1504	1601	1613
195	**Cannes** ▷ d.	...	0740	0808	...	0839	0908	0908	0942	1039	1107	1227	1335	...	...	1428	...	1439	1507	1529	1627	1639
206	Antibes ▷ d.	...	0750	0819	...	0850	0919	0919	0952	1049	1120	1238	1347	...	...	1438	...	1448	1518	1539	1638	1649
229	**Nice** Ville ▷ a.	...	0808	0838	...	0908	0937	0937	1005	1106	1140	1255	1402	...	...	1455	...	1506	1537	1556	1654	1707
229	**Nice** Ville ▷ d.	0808	0813	...	...	...	...	...	...	...	...	...	1406	1406	...	...	...	...	...	...	...	...
245	Monaco-Monte Carlo ▷ a.	0823	0837	...	...	...	...	...	...	...	...	...	1421	1421	...	...	...	...	...	...	...	...
252	Menton ▷ a.	|	0849	...	...	...	...	...	...	...	...	...	|	|	...	...	...	...	...	...	...	...
262	**Ventimiglia** ▷ a.	0845	0905	...	...	...	...	...	...	...	...	...	1442	1442	...	...	...	...	...	...	...	...

360	147 🅁 ♥	*TGV* 6163 K	J	K	*TGV* 9756	Ⓐ	4659 4658 ★ ⊗	*TGV* 6177	17491 Ⓑ		*TGV* 9828		*TGV* 6179 S	17495	Ⓐ	*TGV* 6169 ①–④ m	*TGV* 6815	*TGV* 6181	*TGV* 6159 L	17499	4665 4664 ⑤–⑦ w★	*TGV* 6183 ⑤–⑦ z
Brussels Midi **11** d.	...	...	...	...	...	...	...	...	...	...	1217	...	...	...	...	...	...	...	...	...	...	...
Lille Europe **11** d.	...	...	...	...	...	...	...	...	...	...	1303	...	...	...	...	...	...	...	...	...	...	...
Paris Gare de Lyon **350** ▶ d.	...	1237	...	...	...	...	...	1419	...	...	|	...	1519	...	...	1615	...	1719	1719	...	...	1819
Strasbourg **379** d.	...	|	...	...	...	...	...	|	...	...	|	...	|	...	...	|	...	|	|	...	...	|
Metz **379** d.	...	|	...	...	...	...	...	|	...	...	|	...	|	...	...	|	...	|	|	...	...	|
Dijon **379** d.	...	|	...	...	...	...	...	|	...	...	|	...	|	...	...	|	1612r	|	|	...	...	|
Genève **346** d.	...	|	...	...	1242	...	...	|	...	...	|	...	|	...	...	|	|	|	|	...	...	|
Lyon Part-Dieu **350** d.	...	|	...	...	1436	...	...	|	...	...	1606	...	|	...	...	|	1806	|	|	...	...	|
Bordeaux **320** d.	...	|	...	...	|	...	1047	|	...	...	|	...	|	...	...	|	|	|	|	...	1447v	|
Toulouse **321** d.	...	|	...	...	|	...	1257	|	...	...	|	...	|	...	...	|	|	|	|	...	1654	|
Montpellier **355** d.	...	|	...	...	|	...	1504	|	...	...	|	...	|	...	...	|	|	|	|	...	1902	|
Marseille St Charles ▶ d.	...	1602	...	...	1631	...	1700	|	1731	...	1801	...	|	1831	...	1931	2000	|	|	2031	2100	|
Toulon ▶ a.	...	|	...	...	1713	...	1744	1809	1815	...	1844	...	1909	1914	...	2014	2043	2108	2108	2113	2143	2208
Toulon ▶ d.	...	|	1624	1627	1716	1720	1747	1812	1817	1826	1847	...	1912	1917	1920	2018	2047	2112	2120	2116	2146	2212
Hyères ▶ a.	...	|	|	|	|	|	|	|	|	|	|	←	|	|	|	|	|	|	2134	|	|	|
Carnoules d.	...	|	1657	1704	|	1751	|	|	1836	1858	|	1907	|	1936	1951	|	|	|	...	2136	|	|
Les Arcs-Draguignan ▷ d.	...	1721	1726	1733	|	1818	1824	|	1856	→	1924	1935	|	1956	2018	|	2124	2148	...	2155	2224	|
St Raphaël-Valescure ▷ d.	...	1739	...	...	1810	...	1841	1901	1913	...	1940	...	2001	2014	...	2113	2141	|	...	2213	2241	2301
Cannes ▷ d.	...	1806	...	...	1835	...	1907	1928	1939	...	2007	...	2027	2039	...	2141	2209	2227	...	2239	2307	2327
Antibes ▷ d.	...	1819	...	...	1845	...	1918	1938	1952	...	2018	...	2038	2050	...	2152	2220	2237	...	2250	2318	2338
Nice Ville ▷ a.	...	1835	...	...	1905	...	1937	1955	2011	...	2037	...	2055	2106	...	2210	2237	2255	...	2306	2337	2355
Nice Ville ▷ d.	1807	...	...	...	...	...	...	1959	...	...	...	...	...	...	...	...	...	...	...	...	...	...
Monaco-Monte Carlo ▷ a.	1823	...	...	...	...	...	...	2014	...	...	...	...	...	...	...	...	...	...	...	...	...	...
Menton ▷ a.	|	...	...	...	...	...	...	2025	...	...	...	...	...	...	...	...	...	...	...	...	...	...
Ventimiglia ▷ a.	1843	...	...	...	...	...	...	2040	...	...	...	...	...	...	...	...	...	...	...	...	...	...

A – 🛏 1, 2 cl. Luxembourg - Metz - Nice; 🛏 1, 2 cl. Strasbourg - Nice. For days of running see Table **379**. **Service may be withdrawn from July 1**.
B – TRAIN BLEU – 🛏 1, 2 cl., (2) (reclining) Paris Austerlitz - Nice. **Service may be withdrawn from July 1**.
C – Daily to July 3; ⑥⑦ from July 9.
D – ①–⑤ from July 4.
J – To July 2 and from Aug. 29.
K – July 3 - Aug. 28.
L – ⑤⑦ to June 26; daily July 1 - Aug. 28; ⑤⑦ from Sept. 2 (also Nov. 1, 10; not Nov. 11).
S – Daily to Aug. 28; ⑥⑦ from Sept. 2 (also Nov. 10).

a – Paris **Austerlitz**.
f – Not June 17, 24, Nov. 11.
m – Not July 13, 14, Aug. 15, Nov. 1, 10.

r – 1609 from Aug. 29.
v – Not Oct. 22. 1440 on ⑤ (also July 13, Oct. 31, Nov. 10).
w – ⑤–⑦ (also July 13, 14, Aug. 15, Oct. 31, Nov. 1, 10).
z – Also July 13, 14, Aug. 15, Nov. 1, 10.

TGV –🅁, supplement payable, 🍸.

⊗ – Subject to alteration Sept. 19 – 23, 26 – 30, Oct. 23.
▷ – For local trains Les Arcs - Cannes - Nice - Ventimiglia see Table **361**.
▶ – For complete *TGV* service Paris - Marseille - Toulon see Table **350**. For local trains Marseille - Toulon - Hyères see separate panel on next pa
★ – *INTERCITÉS*. 🅁.
♥ – International service to Italy. Operated by *Thello*. See Table **90**.

VENTIMIGLIA - NICE - TOULON - MARSEILLE

SERVICE FROM JUNE 6. *Services to or via Lyon are subject to alteration on Aug. 13, 14, 15, Oct. 29, 30, 31.*

All *TGV* trains are Ⓡ	Ⓐ	⑥	Ⓐ		*TGV* 6108 ⑥ p	17470 Ⓐ	Ⓐ	*TGV* 9860 Ⓒ	*TGV* 9860 Ⓐ		17474	*TGV* 6172	*TGV* 6814	*TGV* 6158 K	*TGV* 6188 K		17478	*TGV* 5184	*TGV* 6174	4760 4761 ★		*TGV* 9750	*TGV* 6176	*TGV* 6170 K
miglia ▷ d.	...	...	...	...	...	...	...	...	...	...	...	...	...	...	...	...	...	...	0918	...	...	...	...	...
on ▷ d.	...	...	...	...	...	...	...	...	...	...	...	...	...	...	...	...	...	...	0931	...	...	...	...	...
aco-Monte Carlo ▷ d.	...	...	...	...	...	...	...	...	...	...	...	...	...	...	...	...	...	...	0942	...	...	...	...	...
Ville ▷ a.	...	...	...	...	...	...	...	...	...	...	...	...	...	...	...	...	...	...	0958	...	...	...	...	...
Ville ▷ d.	...	...	...	...	...	0555	...	0602	0602	...	0655	0702	0724	...	0804	...	0858	0924	1004	1024	...	1055	1104	1202
es ▷ d.	...	...	...	...	...	0613	...	0626	0626	...	0713	0722	0743	...	0823	...	0917	0943	1024	1044	...	1114	1123	1221
nes ▷ d.	...	...	...	...	...	0625	...	0641	0641	...	0724	0733	0758	...	0835	...	0928	0953	1036	1055	...	1126	1134	1234
aphaël-Valescure ▷ d.	...	...	...	...	...	0649	...	0708	0708	...	0750	|	0825	...	0859	...	0953	1020	1101	1120	...	1154	1200	1301
Arcs-Draguignan ▷ d.	0549	0556	0618	0641	...	0705	0711	0727	0727	0741	0805	0813	0841	...	|	...	1009	1035	|	1137	1141	|	|	|
oules d.	0617	0623	0645	0709	...	0724	0739	|	|	0809	0824	|	|	...	|	...	1028	|	|	|	1209	|	|	|
ères ▶ d.	|	|	|	|	0729	|	|	|	|	|	|	|	|	0918	|	...	|	|	|	|	|	|	|	|
on ▶ a.	0646	0655	0715	0738	0744	0742	0808	0812	0812	0838	0842	0846	0913	0933	0944	...	1046	1112	1146	1213	1239	1243	1248	1347
on ▶ d.	0649	0657	0720	...	0748	0745	...	0816	0816	...	0845	0850	0917	0950	0950	...	1050	1116	1149	1216	...	1246	1251	1351
eille St Charles ▶ a.	0742	0744	0811	...	0829	0833	...	0859	0859	...	0929	|	0959	|	|	...	1133	1159	|	1259	...	1331	|	|
ntpellier **355** a.	...	...	...	...	|	...	...	|	|	...	...	|	|	|	|	...	...	|	|	1453	...	|	|	|
ulouse **321** a.	...	...	...	...	|	...	...	|	|	...	...	|	|	|	|	...	...	|	|	1707	...	|	|	|
rdeaux **320** a.	...	...	...	...	|	...	...	|	|	...	...	|	|	|	|	...	...	|	|	1913j	...	|	|	|
Part-Dieu **350** a.	...	...	...	...	|	...	...	1054	1054	...	...	|	1158	|	|	...	...	1354	|	...	...	1528	|	|
nève **346** a.	...	...	...	...	|	...	...	|	|	...	...	|	|	|	|	...	...	|	|	...	...	1716	|	|
on **379** a.	...	...	...	...	|	...	...	|	|	...	...	|	1352	|	|	...	...	|	|	...	...	...	|	|
tz **379** a.	...	...	...	...	|	...	...	|	|	...	...	|	...	|	|	...	...	|	|	...	...	...	|	|
asbourg **379** a.	...	...	...	...	|	...	...	|	|	...	...	|	...	|	|	...	...	|	|	...	...	...	|	|
Gare de Lyon **350** ▶ a.	...	...	...	...	1145	...	...	|	|	...	...	1241	...	1341	1341	...	...	|	1541	...	...	...	1641	1745
e Europe **11** a.	...	...	...	...	...	...	...	1405r	1427r	...	...	...	...	...	...	...	...	1701r	...	...	...	...	...	...
ussels Midi **11** a.	...	...	...	...	...	...	...	1459r	1516r	...	...	...	...	...	...	...	...	...	...	...	...	...	...	...

	142 Ⓡ ♥	*TGV* 6864	Ⓐ	*TGV* 6124	17486	*TGV* 6178 D	4768 4769 ★ H	*TGV* 6184	17488 Ⓐ	*TGV* 6168			144 Ⓡ ♥	17490	*TGV* 6180	*TGV* 6806	17494 Ⓑ	*TGV* 6186 ⑦	17498		4382 4383 Ⓡ A	4382 4350 Ⓡ A	5774 Ⓡ B	160 Ⓡ ♥
timiglia ▷ d.	1121	...	...	...	...	...	...	...	...	...	...	...	1518	...	...	...	1651	...	...	...	...	...	...	1921
on ▷ d.	|	...	...	...	...	...	...	...	...	...	...	...	|	...	...	...	1709	...	...	...	...	...	...	|
aco-Monte Carlo ▷ d.	1148	...	...	...	...	...	...	...	...	...	...	...	1544	...	...	...	1721	...	...	...	...	...	...	1947
Ville ▷ a.	1204	...	...	...	...	...	...	...	...	...	...	...	1600	...	...	...	1743	...	...	...	...	...	...	2004
Ville ▷ d.	...	1223	...	...	1350	1359	1424	1502	1526	1551	...	...	...	1658	1702	1724	1746	1804	1850	...	1903	1903	2000	2006
es ▷ d.	...	1245	...	...	1413	1419	1440	1521	1544	1610	...	...	...	1713	1721	1743	1815	1823	1913	...	1923	1923	2019	2027
nes ▷ d.	...	1257	...	...	1424	1430	1451	1533	1557	1622	...	...	...	1725	1732	1756	1825	1835	1926	...	1935	1935	2029	2040
aphaël-Valescure ▷ d.	...	1322	...	...	1450	1455	1517	1559	1621	1648	...	...	...	1750	|	1822	1850	1901	1950	...	2002	2002	2054	2104
Arcs-Draguignan ▷ d.	...	1338	1342	...	1506	1512	1533	|	1637	1704	1741	...	...	1806	1809	1839	1906	|	2006	...	2019	2019	2110	|
oules d.	...	|	1410	...	1525	|	|	|	1655	|	1809	...	...	1825	|	|	1926	|	2025	...	|	|	|	|
ères ▶ d.	...	|	|	1434	|	|	|	|	|	|	|	...	...	|	|	|	|	|	|	...	|	|	|	|
on ▶ a.	...	1412	1440	1447	1543	1548	1613	1646	1713	1742	1838	...	...	1843	1847	1913	1943	1947	2043	...	2055	2055	2146	2157
on ▶ d.	...	1416	...	1450	1546	1551	1616	1650	1716	1746	...	...	...	1846	1850	1917	1946	1951	2046	...	2058	2058	2149	2159
seille St Charles ▶ a.	...	1500	...	1534	1629	|	1659	|	1759	1829	...	...	...	1929	|	1959	2029	|	2129	...	2141	2141	|	2242
ontpellier **355** a.	...	|	...	|	...	|	1853	|	...	|	...	...	...	...	|	|	...	|	...	...	|	|	|	...
oulouse **321** a.	...	|	...	|	...	|	2107	|	...	|	...	...	...	...	|	|	...	|	...	...	|	|	|	...
ordeaux **320** a.	...	|	...	|	...	|	2313v	|	...	|	...	...	...	...	|	|	...	|	...	...	|	|	|	...
Part-Dieu **350** a.	...	1654	...	|	...	|	...	|	...	|	...	...	...	...	|	2200	...	|	...	...	|	|	|	...
enève **346** a.	...	|	...	|	...	|	...	|	...	|	...	...	...	...	|	...	...	|	...	...	|	|	|	...
jon **379** a.	...	1839	...	|	...	|	...	|	...	|	...	...	...	...	|	...	...	|	...	...	|	|	|	...
etz **379** a.	...	2157	...	|	...	|	...	|	...	|	...	...	...	...	|	...	...	|	...	...	|	0827	|	...
rasbourg **379** a.	...	...	...	|	...	|	...	|	...	|	...	...	...	...	|	...	...	|	...	...	0850z	...	|	...
s Gare de Lyon **350** ▶ a.	...	...	...	1915	...	1941	...	2041	...	2145	...	...	...	...	2242	...	...	2341	...	...	...	...	0738a	...
lle Europe **11** a.	...	...	...	...	...	...	...	...	...	...	...	...	...	...	...	...	...	...	...	...	...	...	...	...
ussels Midi **11** a.	...	...	...	...	...	...	...	...	...	...	...	...	...	...	...	...	...	...	...	...	...	...	...	...

LOCAL TRAINS MARSEILLE - TOULON - HYÈRES

n			Ⓐ	⚒		⚒		Ⓐ			Ⓐ	Ⓒ			Ⓐ		Ⓐ			Ⓐ		Ⓐ	Ⓐ		
0	**Marseille** d.	...	0535	0603	0635	0703	0735	0805	0835	0935	1003	1035	...	1135	1203	1235	1304	1335	1435	1503	1535	1607	1619	1635	1704
7	Cassis • d.	...	0558	0627	0658	0726	0758	0828	0858	0958	1027	1058	...	1158	1226	1258	1328	1358	1458	1527	1558	1630	|	1658	1728
7	La Ciotat d.	...	0606	0635	0705	0734	0805	0836	0905	1005	1034	1106	...	1205	1233	1305	1335	1406	1505	1535	1605	1637	1646	1705	1735
1	Bandol d.	...	0618	0647	0718	0747	0817	0849	0918	1018	1047	1118	...	1218	1246	1318	1348	1419	1518	1547	1618	1649	|	1718	1748
7	**Toulon** a.	...	0636	0704	0734	0804	0833	0904	0934	1034	1104	1134	...	1234	1302	1334	1404	1436	1534	1604	1634	1703	1709	1734	1805
7	**Toulon** d.	0605	...	0706	0736	0806	0835	...	0936	1036	...	1136	...	1236	...	1336	...	...	1536	1606	1637	1705	...	1737	1807
7	**Hyères** a.	0623	...	0725	0755	0825	0855	...	0955	1055	...	1155	...	1255	...	1355	...	...	1555	1625	1657	1725	...	1757	1825

				Ⓐ					n		
seille d.	1735	1804	1835	1905	1935	2005	2035	2101	2145	2235	...
sis • d.	1758	1827	1858	1928	1958	2028	2058	2125	2209	2259	...
Ciotat d.	1805	1834	1905	1936	2005	2036	2105	2133	2217	2307	...
dol d.	1818	1847	1918	1949	2018	2049	2117	2146	2229	2319	...
lon a.	1834	1904	1934	2006	2034	2104	2134	2204	2246	2335	...
lon d.	1836	...	1936	...	2036	...	2136	...	...	...	...
res a.	1855	...	1956	...	2056	...	2159	...	...	...	...

	Ⓐ		Ⓐ	Ⓐ		Ⓐ		Ⓑ q	⑥ w	Ⓐ
Hyères ⊡ d.	...	...	0533	...	0602	0633	0700	...	...	0733
Toulon a.	...	...	0553	...	0621	0653	0720	...	...	0753
Toulon d.	0500	0524	0555	0614	0623	0655	0723	0750	0752	0755
Bandol d.	|	0541	0612	0630	0639	0711	0740	|	|	0812
La Ciotat d.	0521	0553	0625	0643	0652	0723	0752	0814	0814	0825
Cassis • d.	|	0601	0632	0651	0659	0731	0759	|	|	0833
Marseille a.	0550	0625	0655	0711	0723	0755	0823	0841	0841	0855

		Ⓐ					Ⓐ		Ⓐ							Ⓐ		Ⓐ							
res ⊡ d.	0802	...	0902	...	...	1102	...	1202	...	1302	1402	...	...	...	1602	1634	1702	1728	1802	...	1902	2002	...	...	...
lon a.	0822	...	0922	...	...	1122	...	1222	...	1322	1422	...	...	...	1622	1653	1722	1748	1822	...	1922	2022	...	...	...
lon d.	0825	0854	0925	...	1054	1125	1154	1225	1254	1325	1425	1454	...	1554	1625	1655	1725	1756	1825	1854	1925	2025	...	2124	2219
dol d.	0842	0911	0941	...	1111	1142	1211	1241	1311	1341	1441	1511	...	1611	1641	1712	1741	1813	1841	1911	1941	2041	...	2141	2235
Ciotat d.	0854	0924	0954	...	1124	1155	1224	1254	1323	1353	1454	1523	...	1623	1654	1724	1753	1825	1853	1923	1953	2053	...	2153	2248
sis • d.	0901	0932	1001	...	1132	1203	1231	1301	1330	1401	1501	1531	...	1631	1701	1731	1801	1837	1901	1931	2001	2100	...	2201	|
seille a.	0925	0955	1025	...	1155	1225	1255	1325	1355	1425	1525	1555	...	1655	1725	1755	1825	1900	1925	1955	2025	2125	...	2225	2316

🛏 1, 2 cl. Nice - Metz - Luxembourg; 🛏 1, 2 cl. Nice - Strasbourg. For days of running see Table **379**. **Service may be withdrawn from July 1**.

TRAIN BLEU – 🛏 1, 2 cl., (2) (reclining) Nice - Paris Austerlitz. **Service may be withdrawn from July 1**.

Daily to Sept. 11; ⑥⑦ from Sept. 17 (also Nov. 11).

①⑥⑦ (also July 14, 15, Aug. 16, Nov. 1, 2, 11).

July 3 - Aug. 28.

Paris **Austerlitz**.

Not Sept. 19, Oct. 22.

Not June 18, 21.

Also Nov. 11; not July 9 - Aug. 27.

Not Nov. 11.

2–6 minutes earlier from July 16.

Not Oct. 22.

Also Nov. 11.

0832 on the mornings of ⑥⑦.

TGV – Ⓡ, supplement payable, 🍷.

▷ – For local trains Ventimiglia - Nice - Cannes - Les Arcs see Table **361**.

▶ – For complete *TGV* service Toulon - Marseille - Paris see Table **350**. For local trains Hyères - Toulon - Marseille see separate panel below main table.

★ – *INTERCITÉS*. Ⓡ.

♥ – International service from Italy. Operated by *Thello*. See Table **90**.

• – Cassis station is located 4 km from Cassis town.

361 LES ARCS - ST RAPHAEL - CANNES - NICE - MONACO - VENTIMIGLIA *Local tr*

For TGV / Intercités / night trains over this route see Table **360**

km		①–⑤	Ⓑ ⊗		Ⓐ		①–⑤		①–⑤ ⊗	Ⓑ	⑥		①–⑤		①–⑤	Ⓐ ◇	①–⑤		①–⑥			Ⓐ ◇			
0	**Les Arcs-Draguignan** .. d.	...	...	...	...	...	...	...	0542	...	...	0604	...	...	0635	0657	...	...	0706	...	0735	0755	...	...	...
23	Fréjus d.	...	...	...	...	...	...	...	0556	...	...	0618	...	...	0648	|	...	...	0720	...	0749	|	...	...	...
27	St Raphaël-Valescure d.	...	...	...	...	...	...	...	0559	...	...	0622	...	...	0652	0716	...	...	0724	...	0752	0813	...	...	...
31	Boulouris sur Mer d.	...	...	...	...	...	...	...	0604	...	...	0626	...	...	0656	|	...	...	0729	...	0757	|	...	...	...
	Grasse d.	...	...	...	...	...	...	...	|	0614	...	|	...	...	|	|	...	0720	|	0749	|	|	...	0822	...
60	**Cannes** d.	...	0516	...	0545	...	...	0617	0631	0640	0640	0654	...	0709	0731	0740	...	0746	0758	0813	0831	0839	...	0848	...
69	Juan les Pins d.	...	0526	...	0554	...	...	0627	0641	0649	0649	0703	...	0719	0741	|	...	0755	0809	0823	0840	|	...	0857	...
71	Antibes d.	...	0529	...	0557	...	0617	0630	0644	0652	0652	0706	...	0722	0744	0750	←	0758	0813	0826	0843	0850	←	0900	0913
80	Cagnes sur Mer d.	...	0540	...	0608	...	0628	0641	0654	0704	0703	0713	...	0734	0800	|	0801	0809	0829	0837	0900	|	0901	0911	0928
94	**Nice** Ville a.	...	0600	...	0626	...	0647	0659	0713	0721	0721	0728	...	0750	→	0808	0818	0825	0846	0855	→	0908	0917	0928	0946
94	**Nice** Ville d.	0526	0603	0603	0630	0630	0650	0703	0717	0726	0725	...	0741	0754	...	0813	0821	0828	0850	0859	...	...	0920	0931	0949
99	Villefranche sur Mer d.	0534	0611	0611	0638	0638	0658	0711	0725	0734	0733	...	0748	0802	...	|	0831	0837	0858	0907	...	...	0928	0939	0957
101	Beaulieu sur Mer d.	0537	0614	0614	0642	0642	0702	0714	0728	0737	0736	...	0752	0805	...	|	0834	0840	0902	0910	...	...	0931	0943	1001
104	Eze d.	0541	0618	0618	0645	0645	|	0719	|	0741	0740	...	|	|	...	0828	|	0844	|	0914	...	...	|	0946	|
110	**Monaco-Monte Carlo** d.	0551	0628	0628	0656	0656	0712	0728	0742	0751	0751	...	0802	0814	...	0840	0847	0854	0912	0925	...	...	0942	0957	1012
114	Cap Martin-Roquebrune d.	0557	0633	0633	0701	0701	|	0733	|	0757	0756	...	|	|	...	0845	|	0900	|	0930	...	...	|	1002	|
117	Menton d.	0604	0640	0640	0708	0708	0722	0740	0753	0804	0803	...	0813	0826	...	0851	0858	0907	0922	0937	...	...	0953	1008	1023
127	**Ventimiglia** a.	0618	0654	0654	0722	0722	...	0754	...	0817	0817	...	...	0840	...	0905	...	0921	...	0950	...	...	1007	...	1036

	◇						①–⑤	⑥⑦	H			①–⑤	⑥⑦	①–⑤	⑥⑦				◇				①–⑤		
Les Arcs-Draguignan d.	0857	...	0900	...	...	1000	...	...	...	...	...	...	...	...	...	...	1302	...	1355	...	...	...	...	...	...
Fréjus d.	|	...	0915	...	...	1014	...	...	...	...	...	...	...	...	...	...	1316	...	|	...	...	...	...	...	...
St Raphaël-Valescure d.	0916	...	0919	...	...	1018	...	...	...	...	...	...	...	...	...	...	1321	...	1413	...	...	...	...	...	...
Boulouris sur Mer d.	|	...	0923	...	...	1023	...	...	...	...	...	...	...	...	...	...	1325	...	|	...	...	...	...	...	...
Grasse d.	|	0920	|	...	1020	|	...	...	...	1125	...	...	1221	...	...	1324	|	...	|	1422	...	...	...	1522	...
Cannes d.	0942	0946	0956	1008	1045	1058	1112	1113	...	1151	1208	...	1247	...	1329	1350	1358	1405	1439	1449	...	1511	...	1549	1611
Juan les Pins d.	|	0955	...	1019	1055	1109	1122	1125	...	1200	1218	...	1257	...	1338	1400	...	1415	|	1458	...	1522	...	1558	1622
Antibes d.	0952	0958	...	1023	1058	1112	1125	1129	...	1203	1221	...	1300	...	1342	1403	...	1419	1448	1501	...	1525	...	1601	1626
Cagnes sur Mer d.	|	1009	...	1034	1109	1121	1136	1140	...	1214	1234	...	1311	...	1354	1414	...	1431	|	1512	...	1535	...	1612	1637
Nice Ville a.	1005	1027	...	1050	1127	1134	1155	1156	...	1232	1250	...	1329	...	1412	1434	...	1447	1506	1532	...	1552	...	1630	1651
Nice Ville d.	...	1031	...	1055	1130	...	...	1200	1230	1240	1254	1319	1333	1343	1415	1437	...	1451	...	1536	1549	1556	1619	1634	1655
Villefranche sur Mer d.	...	1039	...	1103	1138	...	...	1208	1238	1248	1302	1326	1341	1350	1423	1445	...	1459	...	1544	1556	1604	1626	1642	1703
Beaulieu sur Mer d.	...	1042	...	1106	1141	...	...	1211	1241	1251	1305	1329	1344	1354	1426	1448	...	1503	...	1547	1559	1607	1629	1645	1706
Eze d.	...	1046	...	1110	1146	...	...	1216	1245	1255	1309	|	1348	1358	1430	1452	...	1508	...	1551	|	1611	|	1650	1710
Monaco-Monte Carlo d.	...	1057	...	1121	1156	...	...	1226	1255	1305	1320	1340	1359	1410	1442	1501	...	1519	...	1602	1610	1622	1640	1700	1720
Cap Martin-Roquebrune d.	...	1102	...	1126	1201	...	...	1231	1301	1311	1325	|	1404	1415	1447	1507	...	1525	...	1607	|	1627	|	1705	1726
Menton d.	...	1108	...	1133	1208	...	...	1238	1307	1317	1332	1350	1411	1422	1455	1514	...	1532	...	1615	1620	1634	1652	1712	1733
Ventimiglia a.	...	...	...	1147	1222	...	...	1252	...	...	1345	...	1424	1437	1509	1527	...	1545	...	1628	...	1647	1705	1725	1746

	◇			¶	①–⑤		①–⑤		①–⑥		①–⑤ r				Ⓑ ◇				◇				⑤–⑦	◇	⑤–⑦
Les Arcs-Draguignan d.	1555	...	...	1600	...	...	...	...	1658	...	...	...	1800	...	1856	...	1900	...	1956	...	...	...	...	2155	...
Fréjus d.	|	...	...	1614	...	...	...	...	1712	...	...	...	1815	...	|	...	1914	...	|	...	...	...	...	|	...
St Raphaël-Valescure d.	1613	...	...	1619	...	...	...	...	1717	...	...	...	1819	...	1913	...	1919	...	2014	...	...	...	...	2213	...
Boulouris sur Mer d.	|	...	...	1623	...	...	...	...	1721	...	...	...	1823	...	|	...	1923	...	|	...	...	...	...	|	...
Grasse d.	|	...	1621	|	...	...	...	1721	|	...	...	1820	|	...	|	1920	|	...	|	2022	2124	...	2208	|	←
Cannes d.	1639	...	1647	1658	...	1708	...	1747	1756	1812	...	1846	1859	1916	1939	1946	1959	2017	2039	2048	2148	2218	2230	2239	2242
Juan les Pins d.	|	...	1656	1708	...	1719	...	1756	1806	1823	...	1856	1908	1928	|	1956	2008	2028	|	2057	2158	2228	→	|	2252
Antibes d.	1649	←	1659	1711	...	1722	1743	1759	1809	1826	1840	1859	1911	1932	1952	1959	2011	2032	2050	2100	2201	2231	...	2250	2255
Cagnes sur Mer d.	|	1659	1710	1718	...	1734	1758	1810	1817	1838	1854	1910	1918	1947	|	2010	2018	2046	|	2111	2212	2247	...	|	2306
Nice Ville a.	1707	1718	1728	1733	...	1750	1816	1826	1831	1855	1914	1928	1933	2002	2011	2028	2033	2102	2106	2129	2230	2302	...	2306	2324
Nice Ville d.	...	1721	1732	...	1748	1753	1820	1830	...	1859	1918	1932	...	2006	...	2032	...	2105	...	2132	2234	2305	...	...	2327
Villefranche sur Mer d.	...	1729	1740	...	1755	1801	1829	1839	...	1907	1926	1940	...	2014	...	2040	...	2113	...	2139	2242	2313	...	...	2335
Beaulieu sur Mer d.	...	1732	1743	...	1759	1805	1832	1842	...	1911	1929	1943	...	2018	...	2043	...	2116	...	2142	2245	2316	...	...	2338
Eze d.	...	|	1747	...	|	1809	|	1846	...	1915	|	1947	...	2022	...	2047	...	2120	...	2146	2249	2320	...	...	2342
Monaco-Monte Carlo d.	...	1742	1758	...	1810	1829j	1844	1855	...	1926	1940	1958	...	2032	...	2058	...	2130	...	2155	2259	2329	...	...	2352
Cap Martin-Roquebrune d.	...	|	1803	...	|	1835	|	1901	...	1932	|	2003	...	2038	...	2103	...	2135	...	2200	2305	2334	...	...	2357
Menton d.	...	1752	1810	...	1820	1842	1855	1906	...	1939	1950	2010	...	2045	...	2110	...	2140	...	2207	2310	2341	...	...	0004
Ventimiglia a.	...	...	1823	...	...	1855	1908	...	...	1953	2004p	2023	...	2058	...	2123	...	...	...	2220	...	2354k	...	...	0017

km		①–⑤ D ⊗	①–⑤ ⊗	Ⓐ ◇	①–⑤ ⊗	⑦ m		⑥⑦		◇		②–⑤			①–⑤			①–⑤	①–⑤	◇		①–⑤		①–⑤	
	Ventimiglia d.	...	...	...	0517	...	...	0538	...	...	0609	...	...	0634	...	0710	0718	...	...	...	0805	...	0830	...	0901
	Menton d.	...	...	...	0530	...	...	0552	0552	...	0626	0635	...	0651	0705	0727	0738	0748	0809	...	0822	0838	0848	0909	0915
	Cap Martin-Roquebrune d.	...	...	...	0537	...	...	0558	0558	...	0633	|	...	0657	|	0734	|	0754	|	...	0829	|	0854	|	0922
	Monaco-Monte Carlo d.	...	...	...	0543	...	...	0603	0603	...	0640	0649	...	0705	0718	0741	0750	0802	0821	...	0836	0850	0902	0921	0928
	Eze d.	...	...	...	0552	...	...	0612	0612	...	0649	|	...	0714	|	0750	|	0812	|	...	0845	|	0910	|	0937
	Beaulieu sur Mer d.	...	...	...	0555	...	...	0616	0616	...	0653	0700	...	0717	0726	0754	0801	0816	0830	...	0849	0859	0914	0930	0941
	Villefranche sur Mer d.	...	...	...	0559	...	...	0619	0619	...	0656	0703	...	0721	0729	0757	0804	0820	0833	...	0852	0903	0918	0933	0945
	Nice Ville a.	...	...	...	0605	...	...	0626	0626	...	0703	0711	...	0728	0736	0804	0812	0827	0840	...	0859	0910	0925	0940	0952
	Nice Ville d.	0515	0526	0555	0608	0610	0624	0629	0629	0655	0706	...	0728	0732	0739	0808	0816	0831	...	0858	0902	...	0929	...	0955
	Cagnes sur Mer d.	0531	0543	|	0625	0625	0637	0645	0645	|	0724	...	0739	0749	0756	0825	0834	0849	...	|	0919	...	0946	...	1011
	Antibes d.	0544	0559	0613	0638	0638	0645	0658	0658	0713	0735	...	0749	0801	0809	0838	0848	0903	...	0917	0932	...	0958	...	1029
	Juan les Pins d.	0547	0603	|	0641	0641	0649	0701	0701	|	0738	...	0752	0804	0812	0841	0851	...	...	|	0935	...	1001	...	1033
0	**Cannes** d.	0605j	0611	0625	0651	0651	0658	0712	0712	0724	0746	...	0804	0814	0821	0849	0906	...	...	0928	0943	...	1012	...	1041
17	Grasse a.	0631	...	|	0714	0714	|	0738	0738	|	...	...	|	0840	...	...	0937	...	...	|	...	...	1038	...	...
	Boulouris sur Mer d.	...	...	|	...	...	0734	...	...	|	...	...	0838	...	...	...	...	...	...	|	...	...	...	...	...
	St Raphaël-Valescure d.	...	...	0649	...	...	0739	...	...	0750	...	...	0843	...	...	...	...	...	...	0953	...	...	...	...	...
	Fréjus d.	...	...	|	...	...	0743	...	...	|	...	...	0847	...	...	...	...	...	...	|	...	...	...	...	...
	Les Arcs-Draguignan a.	...	...	0703	...	...	0756	...	...	0803	...	...	0900	...	...	...	...	...	...	1007	...	...	...	...	...

		①–⑤	⑥⑦	⑥⑦	①–⑤	t			⑥⑦			◇					Ⓐ ◇			①–④	⑤				◇
Ventimiglia d.	0933	...	1011	1032	1032	1102	...	...	1208	1208	...	...	1306	...	...	1409	...	1432	1455	...	1528	...	...	1549	...
Menton d.	0949	...	1028	1049	1049	1119	...	1150	1225	1225	1251	...	1323	...	1346	1427	...	1449	1512	1541	1545	...	1551	1606	...
Cap Martin-Roquebrune d.	0955	...	1034	1056	1056	1126	...	1157	1232	1232	1257	...	1330	...	1353	1433	...	1455	1519	|	|	...	1557	|	...
Monaco-Monte Carlo d.	1003	...	1041	1103	1104	1134	...	1204	1239	1239	1305	...	1337	...	1402	1440	...	1503	1527	1553	1557	...	1604	1618	...
Eze d.	1011	...	1050	1112	1112	1145	...	1213	1248	1248	1313	...	1346	...	1412	1449	...	1512	1537	|	|	...	1614	|	...
Beaulieu sur Mer d.	1015	...	1054	1116	1116	1149	...	1217	1252	1252	1317	...	1350	...	1416	1452	...	1515	1542	1602	1607	...	1618	1627	...
Villefranche sur Mer d.	1019	...	1058	1119	1119	1152	...	1220	1255	1255	1321	...	1353	...	1420	1456	...	1519	1545	1605	1610	...	1621	1630	...
Nice Ville a.	1026	...	1106	1126	1126	1200	...	1228	1302	1302	1328	...	1400	...	1428	1503	...	1526	1552	1612	1618	...	1629	1638	...
Nice Ville d.	1032	1109	1109	1130	1130	1206	1227	1231	1306	...	1332	1350	1403	...	1432	1506	1526	1530	1555	...	...	1628	1633	1642	1658
Cagnes sur Mer d.	1050	1125	1126	1147	1147	1221	1240	1249	1323	...	1349	|	1420	...	1449	1521	|	1547	1613	...	...	1640	1648	1700	|
Antibes d.	1103	1138	1138	1200	1200	1234	1249	1302	1336	...	1402	1413	1433	...	1502	1533	1544	1559	1625	...	...	1649	1700	1716	1713
Juan les Pins d.	1106	1141	1141	1203	1203	1237	1252	1305	1339	...	1405	|	1436	...	1505	1536	|	1602	1628	...	...	1652	1703	...	|
Cannes d.	1117	1150	1150	1214	1214	1245	1302	1316	1348	...	1416	1424	1445	1502	1516	1545	1557	1613	1637	...	...	1705	1714	...	1725
Grasse a.	1143	...	...	1239	|	...	|	1342	...	...	1441	|	...	|	1541	...	|	1638	...	...	...	|	1739	...	|
Boulouris sur Mer d.	...	...	...	...	1240	...	1337	...	...	...	...	|	...	1537	...	...	|	...	...	...	...	1739	...	...	|
St Raphaël-Valescure d.	...	...	...	...	1245	...	1343	...	...	...	...	1450	...	1543	...	...	1621	...	...	...	...	1744	...	...	1750
Fréjus d.	...	...	...	...	1249	...	1347	...	...	...	...	|	...	1547	...	...	|	...	...	...	...	1747	...	...	|
Les Arcs-Draguignan a.	...	...	...	...	1302	...	1400	...	...	...	...	1504	...	1600	...	...	1635	...	...	...	...	1800	...	...	1804

FOR NOTES SEE NEXT PAGE

al trains

VENTIMIGLIA - MONACO - NICE - CANNES - ST RAPHAEL - LES ARCS 361

For TGV / Intercités / night trains over this route see Table **360**

		①-⑥		Ⓑ ◇	①-⑤ ⊖	⑥⑦	①-⑤			◇		①-⑤		①-⑤					⑥⑦	h	h	⑥⑦ d	⑥⑦		⑥⑦
imiglia d.	...	...	1634	1651	1701	1701	...	1738	...	...	1808	...	1833	1851	...	1936	2014	2052	2052	...	...	...	2209e	2235	2235
ton d.	1642	...	1651	1709	1717	1717	1740	1754	1806	...	1825	1836	1850	1908	1921	1953	2027	2109	2109	...	...	...	2229	2252	2252
Martin-Roquebrune d.	|	...	1657	|	1724	1724	|	1801	|	...	1832	|	1856	|	1927	2000	2034	2115	2115	...	...	...	2236	2258	2258
aco-Monte Carlo d.	1654	...	1705	1721	1730	1730	1750	1807	1819	...	1839	1849	1904	1920	1934	2007	2040	2123	2123	...	2213	2213	2243	2306	2306
d.	|	...	1714	|	1738	1738	|	1816	|	...	1849	|	1913	|	1943	2016	2049	2133	2133	...	2222	2222	2252	2316	2316
ulieu sur Mer d.	1703	...	1717	1731	1742	1742	1800	1819	1829	...	1853	1859	1916	1930	1948	2020	2053	2137	2137	...	2226	2226	2256	2320	2320
ranche sur Mer d.	1706	...	1721	1735	1745	1745	1803	1823	1832	...	1857	1903	1920	1933	1951	2023	2056	2140	2140	...	2229	2229	2259	2323	2323
Ville a.	1713	...	1728	1743	1752	1752	1810	1829	1840	...	1904	1910	1927	1940	1958	2031	2103	2147	2147	...	2237	2237	2306	2330	2330
Ville d.	...	1728	1732	1746	1755	▬	1813	1832	1844	1850	1908	...	1931	...	2012	2034	2107	2151	2151	2213	...	2241	2310	...	2334
es sur Mer d.	...	1742	1747	1804	1813	...	1827	1848	1900	|	1925	...	1948	...	2031	2052	2124	2207	2207	2227	...	2258	2327	...	2351
es d.	...	1750	1759	1815	1827	...	1836	1900	1915	1913	1938	...	2000	...	2046	2108	2137	2220	2220	2243	...	2311	2340	...	0003
les Pins d.	...	1753	1802	|	...	⑥⑦	1839	1903	...	|	1941	...	2003	...	2049	2112	2140	2223	2223	2246	...	2314	2343	...	0006
nes d.	...	1804	1813	1825	...	1859	1859j	1913	...	1926	1949	...	2015	...	2059	2123	2149	2232	2235	2255	...	2325	2353	...	0015
asse a.	...	|	1838	|	...	|	|	1938	...	|	...	...	2040	...	2122	|	...	...	2258	...	...	2348	...	...	...
ouris sur Mer d.	...	1838	...	|	...	1938	1938	...	...	|	...	...	...	...	...	2158	...	...	...	...	...	...	...	...	...
aphaël-Valescure d.	...	1844	...	1850	...	1943	1943	...	...	1950	...	...	...	...	...	2204	...	...	...	...	...	...	...	...	...
us d.	...	1848	...	|	...	1947	1947	...	...	|	...	...	...	...	...	2207	...	...	...	...	...	...	...	...	...
Arcs-Draguignan a.	...	1901	...	1904	...	2000	2000	...	...	2004	...	...	...	...	...	2220	...	...	...	...	...	...	...	...	...

Runs daily Cannes - Grasse.
①-⑤ (daily June 27 - Sept. 2).

Not June 4, 11, 17, 24. Also runs Monaco - Cannes on ⑤ from July 1.
2212 on ⑥.
Not June 3, 10, 17, 24.

j – Arrives 9–12 minutes earlier.
k – ⑤-⑦ (also July 14, Aug. 15, Nov. 1).
m – Also ⑥ from July 2.
p – ①-④ only.
r – Also runs on ⑥ Nice - Menton.
t – Not June 23.

⊗ – Subject to alteration on July 14, Nov. 1, 11.
¶ – Subject to alteration on June 12, 17, 22, 26, 27.
⊖ – Runs up to 5 minutes **earlier** on Aug. 15, Nov. 1.
◇ – To / from Marseille (Table **360**).

BRIANÇON - GRENOBLE, LYON and MARSEILLE 362

n		②-⑤ e	①⑥ g	① w	②-⑤ r	②-⑤ p	① d	Ⓒ	Ⓐ ⊗	h	Ⓐ	k	Ⓐ	⊕	🚌 ⚒				⑥	†	Ⓐ		🚌 Ⓐ		5790 [R] D‡
0	**Briançon** d.	...	...	0443	...	...	...	0534	0600	...	0652	0757	...	0940	1115	...	1340	1458	1550	1551	1605	1724	1810	...	2027
3	L'Argentière les Écrins d.	...	...	0458	...	...	...	0549	0615	...	0708	0813	...	0956	1135	...	1358	1513	1606	1606	1620	1739	1830	...	2046
8	Montdauphin-Guillestre d.	...	...	0509	...	...	...	0600	0626	...	0719	0824	...	1008	1150	...	1409	1524	1617	1617	1632	1751	1845	...	2059
5	Embrun d.	...	...	0522	...	...	...	0613	0640	...	0733	0840	...	1023	1225	...	1424	1538	1632	1632	1646	1806	1920	...	2116
2	**Gap** a.	...	...	0553	...	...	...	0643	0713	...	0803	0919	...	1053	1310	...	1454	1611	1703	1703	1717	1836	1957	...	2151
2	**Gap** d.	0520	0520	0556	...	...	...	0646	0715	...	...	0922	...	1055	...	...	1456	1614	1706	1706	...	1839	...	...	2155
9	Veynes-Dévoluy a.	0541	0541	0615	...	...	...	0706	0734	...	...	0951	...	1114	...	...	1517	1637	1727	1727	...	1902	...	...	2220
9	Veynes-Dévoluy d.	0553	0553	0618	0618	...	0637	0710	0741	0758	...	0954	...	1117	...	...	1520	1640	1729	1729	...	1905	...	...	2225
2	Die d.	|	|	0715	0715	...	|	0806	0838	|	...	|	...	1217	...	...	|	1742	|	|	...	|	...	...	2327
9	Crest d.	|	|	0749	0750	...	|	0839	0911	|	...	|	...	1253	...	...	|	1815	|	|	...	|	...	...	0003
4	**Valence** Ville **364** a.	|	|	0816	0816	...	|	0906	0939	|	...	|	...	1321	...	...	|	1841	|	|	...	|	...	...	0030
	Valence TGV a.	|	|	0828	0828	...	|	0917	0950	|	...	|	...	1338	...	...	|	1901	|	|	...	|	...	...	|
	Paris Austerlitz a.	|	|	...	...	...	|	...	...	|	...	|	...	...	...	...	|	...	|	|	...	|	...	...	0738
9	Sisteron d.	0633	0634	...	...	0721	0721	...	...	0841	...	1041	1238	...	...	...	1601	...	1812	1812	...	1947	...	...	...
6	Château Arnoux - St Auban d.	0646	0648	...	...	0734	0734	...	...	0854	...	1054	1251	...	...	...	1614	...	1828	1828	...	2002	...	...	...
9	Manosque-Gréoux d.	0711	0714	...	...	0800	0800	...	...	0918	...	1120	1316	...	...	...	1637	...	1904	1908t	...	2030	...	...	...
8	Aix en Provence ▷ d.	0800	0800	...	...	0842	0843	...	...	1001	...	1204	1402	...	...	...	1720	...	1959	1959	...	2121	...	...	...
5	**Marseille** St Charles ▷ a.	0836	0836	...	...	0915	0915	...	...	1033	...	1233	1433	...	...	...	1753	...	2032	2032	...	2150	...	...	...

	Ⓐ	5789 [R] D§	① g	⑥	Ⓐ	h	Ⓐ	⚒		Ⓐ	Ⓒ	Ⓒ	Ⓐ	Ⓐ			⑤	①-④ m	⑤†	①-④	Ⓑ	⑤	⑤⑦	Ⓑ	🚌 ①-④
seille St Charles ▷ d.	...	...	0636	0645	...	0844	0951	...	...	1245	1245	...	...	...	...	1646	...	1736	1734y	...	1845	1845	...	...	...
en Provence ▷ d.	...	...	0718	0718	...	0920	1040	...	...	1320	1320	...	...	...	...	1719	...	1821	1821	...	1919	1919	...	...	...
osque-Gréoux d.	...	...	0803	0803	...	1002	1123	...	...	1401	1401	...	...	...	...	1802	...	1900	1902	...	2005	2005	...	...	...
teau Arnoux - St Auban d.	...	...	0826	0826	...	1026	1147	...	...	1425	1424	...	...	...	...	1827	...	1925	1929	...	2031	2031	...	...	...
eron d.	...	...	0842	0842	...	1040	1200	...	...	1438	1438	...	...	...	...	1841	...	1938	1946	...	2045	2045	...	...	...
Paris Austerlitz d.	...	2122	|	|	...	|	...	...	...	|	|	...	...	...	...	|	...	...	|	...	|	|	...	...	...
alence TGV d.	...	|	|	|	...	|	...	1011	...	|	|	1426	...	...	1632	|	1801	...	|	1825	|	|	2030	2030	...
alence Ville **364** d.	...	0405	|	|	...	|	...	1021	...	|	|	1436	...	...	1641	|	1812	...	|	1836	|	|	2040	2040	...
rest d.	...	0435	|	|	...	|	...	1054	...	|	|	1506	...	...	1706	|	1843	...	|	1905	|	|	2105	2105	...
d.	...	0511	|	|	...	|	...	1133	...	|	|	1540	...	...	1745	|	1919	...	|	1938	|	|	2140	2140	...
nes-Dévoluy a.	...	0612	0923	0924	...	1122	...	1234	...	1519	1519	1636	...	...	1837	1935	2013	...	2028	2035	2126	2126	2235	2235	...
nes-Dévoluy d.	...	0619	0926	0927	...	1125	...	1236	...	1522	1522	1639	...	...	1839	1950	2016	...	2031	...	2129	2129	2238	2238	...
a.	...	0641	0947	0947	...	1146	...	1256	...	1541	1541	1701	...	...	1902	2010	2036	...	2051	...	2150	2150	2257	2257	...
d.	0607	0644	...	0950	1058	1149	...	1259	...	1544	1544	1704	1731	1837	1905	2012	2039	...	...	...	...	2153	2300	...	2310
brun d.	0641	0734	...	1024	1131	1222	...	1333	...	1618	1631t	1735	1807	1909	1938	2044	2114	...	...	...	...	2226	2333	...	2345
tdauphin-Guillestre d.	0657	0753	...	1040	1146	1237	...	1347	...	1633	1646	1752	1822	1923	1953	2058	2129	...	...	...	...	2240	2347	...	0001
gentière les Écrins d.	0709	0812	...	1051	1156	1248	...	1359	...	1644	1658	1803	1832	1934	2004	2109	2140	...	...	...	...	2251	2357	...	0015
ançon a.	0723	0831	...	1107	1211	1303	...	1414	...	1659	1712	1817	1847	1948	2019	2123	2154	...	...	...	...	2306	0011	...	0035

GAP - GRENOBLE *Subject to alteration June 6 - July 1 and Sept. 19 - Oct. 7*

m		⚒	Ⓒ	Ⓐ		L				
0	**Gap** d.	*0520*	0720	0728	...	1148	1329	1724	1929	...
7	Veynes-Dévoluy d.	0546	0749	0749	...	1211	1351	1747	1951	...
7	St Georges de Commiers d.	0720	0920	0920	...	1346	1522	1920	2123	...
6	**Grenoble** a.	0744	0944	0944	...	1408	1544	1944	2145	...

	L					Ⓐ	Ⓒ			⑥
Grenoble d.	0809	1009	1209	1409	...	1609	1609	...	1809	1809
St Georges de Commiers d.	0833	1031	1231	1434	...	1631	1631	...	1832	1832
Veynes-Dévoluy d.	1010	1209	1407	1612	...	1803	1803	...	2004	2005
Gap a.	1030	1229	1427	1636	...	1823	1831	...	...	2025

LOCAL TRAINS MARSEILLE - AIX EN PROVENCE (see note ⊠) Journey time: 33–45 minutes

m Marseille at 0536, 0636 **E**, 0656 ⚒, 0719 Ⓐ, 0734, 0805 Ⓐ, 0816, 0856 Ⓐ, 0925 **h**, 6 **h**, 1216, 1256 Ⓐ, 1336, 1406 Ⓐ, 1416, 1456 Ⓐ, 1526, 1536, 1603 Ⓐ, 1614, 1654 Ⓐ, 0, 1805 ⚒, 1816, 1856, 1936, 2036, 2136, 2216 and 2256 **s**.

From Aix en Provence at 0540 Ⓐ, 0619 ⚒, 0640 Ⓐ, 0700, 0720 ⚒, 0740, 0820 **z**, 0900, 0921 Ⓐ, 0940, 1140 **h**, 1220, 1300, 1322 **k**, 1340, 1420, 1500 Ⓐ, 1540, 1620, 1639 Ⓐ, 1700, 1740, 1801 Ⓐ, 1820, 1840 Ⓐ, 1920, 2021 ⚒, 2100, 2140 Ⓐ and 2240 **s**.

Conveys 🛏 1, 2 cl. and 2 (reclining).
Subject to confirmation from July 1.
②③④⑤⑦.
⚒ (daily to Sept. 18).

Also July 15, Aug. 16, Nov. 2, 12; not Aug. 15.
Not July 14, Nov, 1, 11.
Not Aug. 15.
Not Oct. 23, Dec. 4.
Not Oct. 23.
Not July 14, Aug. 15, Nov. 1.
Not July 14, 15, Aug. 16, Nov. 1, 2, 11.
Also ① July 4 - Aug. 29.
Not ①-⑤ Sept. 26 - Oct. 7.
Arrives 13–14 minutes earlier.
Not July 4 - Aug. 29.
1739 on †.

z – Not Oct. 2, 9, 23, Nov. 6, Dec. 4.

⊗ – Subject to alteration Veynes-Dévoluy - Valence on ①-⑤ Sept. 19 - Oct. 7 and ①-⑤ Nov. 21 - Dec. 2.
⊕ – Subject to alteration on ①-⑤ Sept. 19 - Oct. 7 and ①-⑤ Nov. 21 - Dec. 2.
⊠ – Services are subject to alteration late evening on Dec. 3 and on the morning of Dec. 4.
▷ – For other local trains see panel below main table.
◇ – Gare SNCF (rail station).
§ – Train number **5793** on † (daily July 1 - Aug. 31).
‡ – Train number **5792** on † (daily July 1 - Aug. 31).

Services Marseille - Veynes - Briançon and v.v. are subject to alteration on Sept. 10, 11

🚌 BRIANÇON - OULX

[R]				⑤-⑦	
Briançon ◇ d.	0700	0925	...	1445	1625
Oulx ◇ a.	0805	1030	...	1550	1730

[R]					
Oulx ◇ d.	1145	...	1605	...	1945
Briançon ◇ a.	1245	...	1710	...	2045

Operator: 05 voyageurs ✆ +33 (0) 4 92 502 505
www.05voyageurs.com

363 BELLEGARDE - ANNEMASSE - ÉVIAN LES BAINS

Trains from Lyon / Bellegarde may divide at Belllegarde and / or Annemasse - take care to travel in the correct portion. For connections Paris - Bellegarde and v.v. see Table **341**.

km									*TGV* 6503												*TGV* 6511		
		①–⑤	Ⓐ	⚒				①–⑤					①–⑤	Ⓐ	①–⑤		①–⑤	Ⓑ		⑤	⑤	⑤	
				▲		▲		§▲	§▲	E	§		§			◇				V	f	k	
	Paris Gare de Lyon **341** d.	...	...	...	...	...	...	...	...	1011	...	...	...	...	...	...	...	...	...	...	...	1815	...	
	Lyon Part-Dieu **346** d.	...	...	*0636*	...	*0834*	...	...	*1034*	|	*1234*	...	*1436*	...	...	...	*1635*	...	1734	*1836*	...	|	2034	2
0	**Bellegarde** **365** d.	...	0709	0809	...	1009	...	...	1209	1317	1409	...	1609	...	...	...	1809	...	1908	2009	...	2118	2209	2
38	Annemasse **365** a.	...	0747	0844	...	1044	...	...	1244	1400	1444	...	1645	...	...	...	1844	...	1946	2044	...	2202	2244	2
38	Annemasse d.	0715	0749	0853	...	1053	...	1220	1253	1419	1453	...	1653	1716	1753	1821	1853	1920	1956	2053	2127	2212	2253	2
68	Thonon les Bains d.	0744	0825	0931	...	1131	...	1249	1331	1457	1531	...	1726	1747	1831	1851	1931	1950	2029	2131	2153	2237	2331	2
77	**Évian les Bains** a.	0752	...	0939	...	1139	...	1256	1338	1505	1539	...	1734	1755	1838	1859	1939	1959	2036	2139	2202	2245	2338	2

												TGV 6508				*TGV* 6506	*TGV* 6504						
	⚒	⚒	①–⑤	①–⑤	①–⑤	Ⓒ					①–⑤	⑦			①–⑤	⑦	⑥	†	†	①–⑤			
		¶						▲		§▲	§▲	d	§▲	§	n§	e	R		G				
Évian-les-Bains d.	0502	0521	0621	0654	0715	0800	0821	...	1021	...	1221	1302	1314	1421	1621	1656	1656	1717	1715	1737	1802	1821	...	2
Thonon-les-Bains d.	0510	0532	0632	0703	0724	0808	0832	0832	1032	...	1230	1310	1329	1432	1632	1706	1707	1729	1726	1750	1811	1832	...	2
Annemasse a.	0542	0606	0706	0733	0804	0836	0906	0906	1106	...	1306	1339	1352	1507	1706	1736	1733	1758	1806	1816	1839	1907	...	2
Annemasse **365** d.	0545	0617	0717	...	...	...	0917	0917	1117	...	1315	...	1406	1517	1717	...	1746	1813	1817	...	...	1915	...	2
Bellegarde **365** a.	0620	0650	0749	...	...	...	0950	0950	1150	...	1350	...	1458	1550	1750	...	1815	1853	1850	...	...	1950	...	2
Lyon Part-Dieu **346** a.	...	0823	*0922*	...	...	...	*1124*	*1124*	*1322***z**	...	*1522*	...	|	*1724*	*1924*	...	|	|	2032	...	...	*2122*	...	
Paris Gare de Lyon **341** a.	...	...	...	...	...	...	...	...	...	...	...	...	1749	...	...	...	2133	2149	...	...	...	...	...	

D – ①②③④⑥⑦ (also Nov. 11; not July 13, ①–④ Aug. 16 - Sept. 22, Nov. 10).
E – ⑥ to June 25; ⑥⑦ July 2 - Sept. 3 (also July 14); ⑥ from Sept. 10 (not Nov. 12).
G – Not Oct. 2, 9. To Grenoble (Tables **365** and **364**).
R – ⑥ July 9 - Aug. 27.
V – ⑤ (also July 13, Nov. 10; not Sept. 30, Oct. 7, 14, Nov. 11). From Valence (Tables **364** and **365**).

d – Also Aug. 15, Nov. 1.
e – Also Aug. 15, Nov. 1; not Aug. 14.
f – Also July 13, Nov. 10. Subject to alteration on Oct. 28, Nov. 4.
k – Not Aug. 19 - Sept. 23, Nov. 11.
n – Not Aug. 15, Nov. 1.
r – *2024* on ⑥ to June 18 / from Sept. 3.
t – Not ①–④ Aug. 16 - Sept. 22.
z – Not ①–⑤ Nov. 28 - Dec. 9.

TGV – Ⓡ, supplement payable, 🍷.

§ – Subject to alteration on ①–⑤ Sept. 26 - Oct. 14.
¶ – Subject to alteration on June 25.
▲ – Does not run Thonon - Évian and v.v. on July 4 – 8, 11 – 13 ①–⑤ Sept. 12 - Oct. 21 and Ⓐ from Nov. 2.
◇ – Change trains at Annemasse on ⑥.

Services are subject to alteration Nov. 10 – 13

364 GENÈVE and ANNECY - CHAMBÉRY - GRENOBLE - VALENCE

Warning! Until July 2 timings Chambéry - Grenoble and v.v. may vary by up to 6 minutes (earlier departures possible) and many trains do not call at Montmélian.

km		Ⓐ	⚒	Ⓐ	⚒			⚒	⚒				Ⓒ	Ⓐ	⑥			Ⓐ	Ⓒ							
										⊗						⊗❦	⊗	⊗		♥				❦	r	
0	**Genève** **341 346** d.	...	...	...	...	...	...	...	0700	...	...	...	...	...	...	1000	...	...	...	1200	...	...	...	1500	...	
33	Bellegarde **341 346** d.	...	...	...	...	...	...	...	0726	...	...	...	...	...	...	1026	...	...	...	1226	...	...	...	1526	...	
66	Culoz **346** d.	...	...	...	...	...	...	...	|	...	...	...	...	...	...	|	...	...	...	|	...	...	...	|	...	
	Annecy **341 345** d.	...	...	...	0539	...	...	0639	|	0747	...	0839	0839	0939	0953	|	1039	...	1139	|	1245	1339	1439	|	...	15
88	Aix les Bains **341 345** d.	...	...	...	0626	...	...	0726	0806	0825	...	0926	0926	1026	1035	1107	1126	...	1226	1307	1326	1426	1526	1608	...	16
102	**Chambéry** **341 345** a.	...	...	...	0636	...	...	0736	0816	0835	...	0936	0936	1037	...	1117	1136	...	1236	1317	1336	1436	1536	1618	...	16
102	**Chambéry** ⊠ d.	...	0540	*0553*r	0640	...	0653	0740	0818**k**	0838	0853	...	0940	...	...	1120	1140	1240	1240	1320	1340	1440	1540	1620	1624	16
116	Montmélian ⊠ d.	...	0551	*0606*r	0651	...	0706	0751	|	0850	0906	...	0951	...	...	|	1151	1251	1251	|	1351	1451	1551	|	1634	16
165	**Grenoble** ⊠ a.	...	0627	*0655*r	0727	...	0755	0827	0904**k**	0927	0955	...	1027	...	...	1204	1227	1327	1327	1404	1427	1527	1627	1704	1723	17
165	**Grenoble** d.	0602	0630	0707	0730	0730	...	0830	...	0930	...	...	1030	...	...	1207	1230	1330	1330	...	1430	1530	1630	1707	...	17
242	Romans-Bourg de Péage d.	0701	0727	0758	0827	0827	...	0927	...	1027	...	...	1127	...	...	1258	1327	1427	1427	...	1527	1627	1727	1758	...	18
249	Valence TGV ⊙ a.	0708	0734	0804	0834	0834	...	0934	...	1034	...	...	1134	...	...	1304	1334	1434	1437	...	1534	1636	1734	1804	...	18
259	**Valence** Ville ⊙ a.	0718	0744	0815	0844	0844	...	0944	...	1044	...	...	1144	...	...	1315	1344	1444	1448	...	1544	1646	1744	1815	...	18

	Ⓑ		①–⑤	⑤		⚒			
		b		f			⊡		E
Genève **341 346** d.	...	...	1642	1642	...	...	...	1842	...
Bellegarde **341 346** d.	...	...	1709	1709	...	...	...	1910	...
Culoz **346** d.	...	...	1746	1746	...	...	...	1946	...
Annecy **341 345** d.	1639	...	|	|	1739	...	1839	|	1939
Aix les Bains **341 345** d.	1726	...	1805	1805	1825	...	1926	2007	2025
Chambéry **341 345** a.	1736	...	1815	1815	1836	...	1936	2017	2036
Chambéry ⊠ d.	1740	1753	1817**k**	1817	1840	...	1940	2020	2040
Montmélian ⊠ d.	1751	1806	|	|	1851	...	1951	|	2051
Grenoble ⊠ a.	1827	1855	1904**k**	1904	1927	...	2027	2104	2127
Grenoble d.	1830	...	...	1907	1930	1942	2030	...	...
Romans-Bourg de Péage d.	1927	...	...	1958	2027j	2058	2127	...	...
Valence TGV ⊙ a.	1934	...	...	2004	2034j	2104	2134	...	...
Valence Ville ⊙ a.	1944	...	...	2015	2044j	2115	2144	...	...

	①–⑤	⚒	⚒	Ⓐ	Ⓐ	⚒	①–⑥	⚒	Ⓐ			
			r			k	❖				❦	
Valence Ville ⊙ d.	...	...	...	...	...	...	...	0524	0615	...	0644	
Valence TGV ⊙ d.	...	...	...	...	...	...	...	0534	0625	...	0657	
Romans-Bourg de Péage d.	...	...	...	...	...	...	...	0543	0632	...	0705	
Grenoble a.	...	...	...	...	...	...	...	0648**p**	0729	...	0751	
Grenoble ⊠ d.	0507	...	0538	...	0632	0638	0654	0700	0732	0732	0754	
Montmélian ⊠ d.	0544	...	0625	...	0710	0725	|	0753	0810	0810	|	
Chambéry ⊠ a.	0554	...	0635	...	0720	0735	0739	0803	0819	0819	0838	
Chambéry **341 345** d.	0557	0622	...	0644	0723	...	0742	...	0822	0822	0841	
Aix les Bains **341 345** d.	0610	0636	...	0656	0736	...	0755	...	0835	0835	0854	0
Annecy **341 345** a.	|	0715	...	0745	0815	...	|	...	0915	0915	|	1
Culoz **346** d.	0632	...	...	...	...	...	|	...	...	...	|	
Bellegarde **341 346** a.	0700	...	...	...	...	...	0831	...	...	...	0932	
Genève **341 346** a.	0729	...	...	...	...	...	0900	...	...	...	1000	

	Ⓐ	Ⓑ	†	Ⓐ		Ⓐ																	Ⓑ			
	r				⊗		◇	●		⊗	⊗	⊗❦	⊗	⊗		❦		E					A		S	
Valence Ville ⊙ d.	...	...	...	0715	0815	0915	1015	...	...	1215	1316	1344	1415	1515	1615	1644	...	1715	1744	...	1815	1915	2015	2115	2115	22
Valence TGV ⊙ d.	...	...	...	0725	0825	0925	1025	...	...	1225	1325	1357	1425	1525	1625	1657	...	1725	1757	...	1825	1925	2025	2125	2125	22
Romans-Bourg de Péage d.	...	...	...	0732	0832	0932	1032	...	...	1232	1332	1405	1432	1532	1632	1705	...	1732	1805	...	1832	1932	2032	2132	2132	22
Grenoble a.	...	...	...	0829	0929	1029	1129	...	...	1329	1429	1451	1529	1629	1729	1751	...	1829	1851	...	1929	2029	2129	2229	2229	23
Grenoble ⊠ d.	0806	...	0838	...	0932	...	1132	1154	1232	1332	1432	1454	1532	1632	1732	1754	1806	1832	...	1906	1932	2032	2132	...	2232	
Montmélian ⊠ d.	0857	...	0925	...	1010	...	1210	|	1310	1410	1510	|	1611	1710	1810	|	1856	1910	...	1956	2010	2110	2210	...	2310	
Chambéry ⊠ a.	0906	...	0935	...	1019	...	1219	1238	1319	1419	1519	1538	1619	1719	1819	1839	1906	1919	...	2006	2019	2119	2219	...	2319	
Chambéry **341 345** d.	...	0923	...	...	1022	...	1222	1241	1322	1422	1522	1541	1622	1722	1823	1841	...	1922	...		2023	2122	2222	...	...	
Aix les Bains **341 345** d.	...	0936	...	...	1036	...	1236	1255	1335	1435	1535	1554	1636	1735	1836	1854	...	1936	...	...	2035	2136	2235	...	...	
Annecy **341 345** a.	...	1015	...	...	1115	...	1315	|	1415	1515	1615	|	1715	1815	1915	|	...	2015	...	...	2115	2215	2315	...	...	
Culoz **346** d.	...	...	...	...	...	...	...	|	...	...	...	|	...	...	...	|	...	...	...	...	...	...	...	...	...	
Bellegarde **341 346** a.	...	...	...	...	...	...	...	1332	...	...	...	1632	...	...	...	1932	...	...	...	...	...	...	...	...	...	
Genève **341 346** a.	...	...	...	...	...	...	...	1400	...	...	...	1700	...	...	...	2000	...	...	...	...	...	...	...	...	...	

A – To / from Avignon on dates in Table **351**. Does not run Grenoble - Annecy on June 5, 12, 19.
E – To / from Évian les Bains on dates in Table **363**.
S – ⑥ to July 2; Ⓒ from July 9 (not July 17, Aug. 7, 21).

b – Not ①–⑤ July 18 - Aug. 26.
f – Also July 13, Nov. 10.
j – 3–5 minutes later on ⑦ (also Aug. 15, Nov. 1).
k – From July 4.
p – Connects with train in previous column.
r – Not July 17 - Aug. 28.
v – 5 minutes earlier until July 2.

⊗ – Subject to alteration on ①–⑤ Sept. 26 - Oct. 7.
◇ – Subject to alteration on ①–⑤ Sept. 19 - Oct. 7 and ①–⑤ Nov. 21 - Dec. 2.

⊠ – Until July 2 timings Chambéry - Grenoble and v.v. may vary by up to 6 minute (earlier departures possible) and many trains do not call at Montmélian.
♥ – Until July 2 calls additionally at Montmélian (d. 1336) and arrives Grenoble 142
❖ – Until July 2 departs Grenoble 0638 and calls additionally at Montmélian (d. 072
● – Until July 2 departs Grenoble 1137 and calls additionally at Montmélian (d. 122
❦ – Until July 2 does not run Valence - Chambéry and v.v.
⊡ – Does not run Grenoble - Valence on Sept. 3.
⊙ – 🚌 runs 2 – 3 times per hour.

Certain services Chambéry - Grenoble and v.v. do not run on July 4, 5

*See Table **350** for TGV services Annecy - Valence - Marseille*

GENÈVE AÉROPORT ✈ - CHAMBÉRY - GRENOBLE 364a

service operated by Aerocar, www.aerocar.fr. Journey 1 hr to Chambéry (Gare), 2 hrs 15 m to Grenoble (Gare Routière). Rail tickets not valid. Reduced service on May 1.

ve Aéroport (Secteur International): depart 1030, 1300, 1530, 1800 and 2030.

oble: depart 0600, 0830, 1100, 1330 and 1530 (from Chambéry 60 minutes later).

PARIS / ANNECY - LA ROCHE SUR FORON - ST GERVAIS 365

Trains from Lyon / Bellegarde may convey portions for Évian les Bains. For connections Genève Eaux-Vives - Annemasse / La Roche sur Foron see Table **366a**.

Warning! All services Annecy - La Roche sur Foron and v.v. are subject to alteration Sept. 26 - Oct. 14.

TGV trains convey 🍸							*TGV*	*TGV*				*TGV*				*TGV*				*TGV*			
		5705 **5594**					**9761**	**6467**				**9765**				**6472**				**9773**			
	①–⑥	B	Ⓐ		①–⑥	⚒	©	Ⓐ	⑥			Ⓐ	⑦			⑥			Ⓐ				
		[R] ◇							E		⊗	⊗	e		⊗		G		⊗			⊗	
Paris Gare de Lyon .... **341** d.	...	2225a	...	...	...	...	...	0707	0711	...	...	...	0911	...	...	...	1011	...	...	...	1211	...	...	...
Bourg en Bresse .... **341** d.	...	|	...	...	...	...	...	|	|	...	...	...	1102	...	...	...	1205	...	...	...	1404	...	...	...
Lyon Perrache **346** .... d.	...	|	...	...	0625	...	...	|	|	0823c	...	...	|	1023	...	...	|	1223	...	...	|	1423	...	...
Lyon Part-Dieu **346** .... d.	...	|	...	...	0636	...	...	|	|	0834	...	...	|	1034	...	...	|	1234	...	...	|	1436	...	...
Bellegarde .... **341** a.	...	△	...	...	0759	...	...	0947	0948	0958	...	...	1148	1158	...	...	1300	1357	...	...	1457	1559	...	...
Bellegarde .... **363** d.	...	|	...	...	...	0809	...	...	0951	...	1009	...	...	...	1209	...	1317	...	1409	...	...	...	1609	...
Annemasse .... **363** a.	...	|	...	...	...	0844	...	...	1024	...	1044	...	...	...	1244	...	1400	...	1444	...	...	...	1644	...
Annemasse .... ▷ d.	0650	|	...	...	...	0850	...	...	1034	...	1050	...	...	...	1250	...	1412	...	1450	...	...	...	1650	...
Annecy .... ★ ▷ d.	|	0659	0732	...	...	|	0932	...	|	...	|	1132	...	...	|	1332	|	...	|	1532	...	...	|	1732
La Roche sur Foron ... ★ ▷ a.	0707	0736	0807	...	...	0907	1007	...	|	...	1107	1207	...	...	1307	1407	|	...	1507	1607	...	...	1707	1807
La Roche sur Foron .... d.	0712	0800	0812	...	...	0912	1012	...	|	...	1112	1212	...	...	1312	1412	|	...	1512	1612	...	...	1712	1812
Cluses (Haute-Savoie) .... d.	0737	0825	0837	...	...	0937	1037	...	1108	...	1137	1237	...	...	1337	1437	1454	...	1537	1636	...	...	1737	1837
Sallanches Megève .... d.	0750	0839	0850	...	...	0951	1051	...	1127	...	1151	1250	...	...	1351	1450	1512	...	1551	1650	...	...	1751	1850
St Gervais .... a.	0756	0844	0856	...	...	0956	1056	...	1133	...	1156	1256	...	...	1356	1456	1520	...	1556	1656	...	...	1756	1856

	TGV			*TGV*				*TGV*	
	9775			**9777**				**9785**	
				Ⓑ	Ⓑ				⑤
				k					d
s Gare de Lyon ..... **341** d.	1511	...	...	1611	...	...	...	1911	...
g en Bresse .... **341** d.	|	...	...	1804	...	...	...	2104	...
on Perrache **346** .... d.	|	...	...	|	...	...	...	|	...
on Part-Dieu **346** .... d.	|	1635	...	|	1734	1836	...	|	2034
garde .... **341** a.	1747	1802	...	1858	1902	1957	...	2151	2159
garde .... **363** d.	...	...	1809	...	1908	...	2009	...	2209
masse .... **363** a.	...	...	1844	...	1946	...	2044	...	2244
masse .... ▷ d.	...	...	1850	...	1950	...	2050	...	2250
necy .... ★ ▷ d.	...	...	|	...	|	...	|	...	|
oche sur Foron ..... ★ ▷ a.	...	...	1907	...	2009	...	2107	...	2307
oche sur Foron .... d.	...	...	1912	...	2012	...	2112	...	2312
es (Haute-Savoie) .... d.	...	...	1937	...	2037	...	2137	...	2337
nches Megève .... d.	...	...	1951	...	2051	...	2150	...	2350
ervais .... a.	...	...	1956	...	2056	...	2156	...	2356

				TGV				*TGV*			
				9764				**9768**			
	⚒								Ⓐ		
	¶									⊗	v
St Gervais .... d.	0504	0604	...	...	0703	0804	...	...	0904	1004	...
Sallanches Megève .... d.	0509	0609	...	...	0708	0809	...	...	0909	1009	...
Cluses (Haute-Savoie) ...... d.	0523	0623	...	...	0722	0823	...	...	0923	1023	...
La Roche sur Foron .... a.	0546	0647	...	...	0746	0847	...	...	0947	1047	...
La Roche sur Foron. ★ ▷ d.	0552	0653	...	...	0752	0853	...	...	0952	1053	...
Annecy .... ★ ▷ a.	|	|	...	...	0829	|	...	...	1029	|	...
Annemasse .... ▷ a.	0610	0710	...	...	...	0910	...	...	...	1110	...
Annemasse .... **363** d.	0617	0717	...	...	...	0917	...	...	...	1117	...
Bellegarde .... **363** a.	0650	0749	...	...	...	0950	...	...	...	1150	...
Bellegarde .... **341** d.	0655	...	0757	0810	...	...	0958	1010	...	...	1158
Lyon Part-Dieu **346** ...... a.	0823	...	0922	|	...	...	1124	|	...	...	1322
Lyon Perrache **346** .... a.	...	...	0934	|	...	...	1135	|	...	...	1334
Bourg en Bresse .... **341** d.	...	...	...	0859r	...	...	...	|	...	...	...
Paris Gare de Lyon .. **341** a.	...	...	...	1049r	...	...	...	1249	...	...	...

	TGV				*TGV*	*TGV*				*TGV*				*TGV*	*TGV*			*TGV*			*TGV*				
	9770				**9772**	**6482**				**9776**				**9778**	**6486**			**9780**			**9784**		**5598** **5708**		**5596** **5706**
	Ⓐ	©			©	⑥	Ⓐ			⑤–⑦				①–④	⑥	Ⓐ	†	Ⓑ				Ⓑ	⑥⑦	Ⓑ	D
			⊗			E	⊗	⊗		s		⊗		m	E			k					[R] ◇		[R] ◇
ervais .... d.	...	1104	1204	...	...	1239	1304	1404	...	...	1504	1604	...	...	1658	1704	1704	...	1804	...	...	1904	1913	2004	2041
nches Megève .... d.	...	1109	1209	...	...	1247	1309	1409	...	...	1509	1609	...	...	1706	1709	1710	...	1809	...	...	1909	1923	2009	2052
es (Haute-Savoie) .... d.	...	1123	1223	...	...	1306	1323	1423	...	...	1523	1623	...	...	1720	1723	1723	...	1823	...	...	1923	1944	2023	2110
oche sur Foron .... a.	...	1147	1247	...	...	|	1347	1447	...	...	1547	1647	...	...	|	1747	1747	...	1847	...	...	1947	2004	2047	2132
oche sur Foron ..... ★ ▷ d.	...	1152	1253	...	...	|	1352	1453	...	...	1552	1653	...	...	|	1752	1753	...	1853	...	...	1952	2025	2053	2152
nnecy .... ★ ▷ a.	...	1229	|	...	...	|	1429	|	...	...	1629	|	...	...	|	1829	|	...	|	...	...	2029	2102	|	2222
emasse .... ▷ a.	...	...	1310	...	...	1349	...	1510	...	...	...	1710	...	...	1757	...	1810	...	1910	...	...	...	|	2110	|
emasse .... **363** d.	...	...	1317	...	...	1406	...	1517	...	...	...	1717	...	...	1813	...	1817	...	1915	...	...	...	|	2131t	|
garde .... **363** a.	...	...	1350	...	...	1458	...	1550	...	...	...	1750	...	...	1853	...	1850	...	1950	...	...	...	|	2203t	|
garde .... **341** d.	1210	...	...	1357	1410	1503	...	...	1558	1659	...	...	1758	1809	1900	...	1855	1900	...	1957	2010	...	▽	...	▽
on Part-Dieu **346** .... a.	|	...	...	1522	|	|	...	...	1724	|	...	...	1924	|	|	...	2032	|	...	2122	|	...	|	...	|
on Perrache **346** .... a.	|	...	...	...	|	|	...	...	...	|	...	...	...	|	|	...	...	|	...	2135	|	...	|	...	|
g en Bresse .... **341** d.	|	...	...	...	|	1556	...	...	...	1757	...	...	...	1858	1956	...	...	|	...	...	|	...	|	...	|
s Gare de Lyon ..... **341** a.	1452	...	...	...	1649	1749	...	...	...	1949	...	...	...	2049	2149	...	...	2149	...	...	2251	...	0619a	...	0619a

ANNECY - ANNEMASSE direct services

	⚒		Ⓐ	⚒ ⊗		⚒	Ⓐ	Ⓑ	Ⓐ	⑤f A
ecy .... ★ d.	0632	...	0932	1032	...	1432	1632	1832	1932	2032
oche sur Foron .... ★ a.	0707	...	1007	1107	...	1507	1707	1907	2007	2108
oche sur Foron .... d.	0710	...	...	1110	...	1510	1710	1910	2010	2110
emasse .... a.	0726	...	...	1126	...	1526	1726	1926	2026	2125

	Ⓐ	⚒	Ⓐ	⚒ ⊗		Ⓑ	†w A		Ⓑ
Annemasse .... d.	0633	0830	...	1233	...	1633	1827	...	2033
La Roche sur Foron .... a.	0649	0846	...	1249	...	1649	1843	...	2049
La Roche sur Foron ...... ★ d.	0652	0852	1208	1252	...	1652	1852	...	2052
Annecy .... ★ a.	0729	0929	1240	1329	...	1729	1930	...	2129

(12) Grenoble - Chambéry - Annecy - Évian les Bains and v.v. See Tables **363** and **364**.
⑤–⑦ to June 26; daily July 1 - Sept. 4; ⑤–⑦ from Sept. 9 (also Nov. 1, 10).
⑤ to June 24; ①–⑤ July 1 - Sept. 2; ⑤ from Sept. 9 (also Nov. 1, 10).
⑥ July 9 - Aug. 27.
⑥ July 9 - Aug. 27 (also July 14).

Paris **Austerlitz**.
© only.
Not Aug. 19 - Sept. 23, Nov. 11.
Also Aug. 15, Nov. 1.
Also July 13, Nov. 10; not Sept. 30, Oct. 7, 14, Nov. 11.
Not July 14, Nov. 11.
Not July 13, 14, Aug. 15, Nov. 1, 10.
On ⑦ (also Aug. 15, Nov. 1) Bourg en Bresse d. 0902, Paris a. 1050.
Also July 13, 14, Aug. 15, Nov. 1, 10.
Not ①–④ Aug. 16 - Sept. 22.
Not ①–⑤ Nov. 28 - Dec. 9.
Not Oct. 2, 9.

TGV – [R], supplement payable, 🍸.

▷ – For other trains Annemasse - La Roche sur Foron - Annecy see panel below main table.
◇ – 🛏 1,2 cl. and (2) (reclining). **Service may be withdrawn from July 1.**
△ – Via Aix les Bains (a. 0553).
▽ – Via Aix les Bains (d. 2203 ⑥⑦, 2304 **D**).
⊗ – Subject to alteration on ①–⑤ Sept. 26 - Oct. 14.
¶ – Subject to alteration on June 25.
★ – Services between Annecy and La Roche sur Foron are subject to alteration Sept. 26 - Oct. 14.
• – Annecy to La Roche sur Foron is 39 km.

Services are subject to alteration Nov. 10 – 13

ST GERVAIS - CHAMONIX 365a

Many journeys continue to / from Le Châtelard or Martigny (Table **572**).

St Gervais ..... d.	0705	0805	0905	1005	...	1205	1305	1405	1605	and	2105
Les Houches .. d.	0733	0833	0933	1033	...	1233	1333	1433	1633	hourly	2133
Chamonix ...... a.	0750	0850	0950	1050	...	1250	1350	1450	1650	until	2150

Chamonix .. d.	0714	0814	0914	1014	...	1214	1314	1414	1614	and	2014
Les Houches d.	0732	0832	0932	1032	...	1232	1332	1432	1632	hourly	2032
St Gervais .. a.	0757	0857	0957	1057	...	1257	1357	1457	1657	until	2057

366 (PARIS) - CHAMBÉRY - ALBERTVILLE - BOURG ST MAURICE

For Paris - Chambéry see Table 341. *Warning! Train timings at Chambéry, Montmélian and St Pierre d'Albigny may vary by up to 6 minutes until July 2 (earlier departures possible,*

km										TGV 6429													
		🚌 Ⓐ	Ⓐ	🚌 Ⓐ	🚌 Ⓐ	⊗	🚌 Ⓐ	Ⓐ ⊗	⑥	⑥ D	🚌 Ⓐ	⊗	Ⓐ	🚌 Ⓐ	⚒		Ⓐ	⚒ n	🚌 Ⓐ		🚌 ⚒	🚌 ⑤⑦ v	
0	**Paris Gare de Lyon** 341 d.	...	...	...	...	...	...	...	...	0845	...	...	...	...	...	...	...	...	...	...	...	...	...
	Lyon Part Dieu 344 d.	...	...	...	...	...	...	...	0950	|	...	1150n	...	...	...	1550r	...	1750	...	...	...	...	...
	Aix les Bains d.	...	...	...	...	...	...	...	|	|	...	|	...	...	...	|	...	|	...	...	...	...	...
532	**Chambéry** 367 ▷ d.	0601	0704	...	0800	0929	0950	1129	1129	1200	1230	1329	1531	...	1629	1729	1830	1929	1950	2031	2125	2245	...
545	Montmélian 367 ▷ d.	0619	0714	...	0819	0940	|	1141	1141	|	|	1341	1541	...	1641	1741	1841	1941	|	2041	2143	|	...
557	St Pierre d'Albigny 367 ▷ d.	0637	0722	...	0834	0949	|	1149	1150	|	|	1350	1549	...	1649	1749	1849	1950	|	2049	2158	|	...
580	Albertville a.	0715	0744	...	0859	1014	1040	1214	1215	1234	1320	1414	1614	...	1714	1814	1914	2014	2040	2114	2223	2335	...
580	Albertville d.	0715	0754	...	0859	1021	1040	1221	1222	1248	1320	1421	...	1620	1721	1821	1921	2021	2040	2121	2223	2335	...
608	**Moûtiers-Salins** d.	0743	0817	0855	0929	1050	1110	1250	1248	1314	1350	1450	...	1655	1750	1850	1950	2050	2110	2150	2258	0010	...
623	Aime la Plagne d.	0758	...	0910	0944	1107	|	1307	1307	1332	|	1507	...	1715	1807	1907	2007	2105	|	2206	|	0025	...
630	Landry d.	0808	...	0920	0954	1115	|	1315	1316	1342	|	1516	...	1725	1815	1914	2014	2114	|	2214	|	0035	...
637	**Bourg St Maurice** a.	0820	...	0932	1006	1122	1140	1322	1324	1349	1420	1524	...	1735	1822	1922	2022	2122	2145	2222	2338	0050	...

																TGV 6436							5708
	🚌 Ⓐ	🚌 Ⓐ	⚒ E	⚒ n	🚌 Ⓐ		🚌 †	🚌 Ⓐ	Ⓐ	🚌 Ⓐ	⊗	⚒ ⊗	⊗	🚌 Ⓐ	Ⓐ	⑥ D	⚒	†	🚌 Ⓐ	†	⚒	🚌 ⑤⑦ v	🅁 ◇ ⑥⑦
Bourg St Maurice d.	...	0418	0521	0538	0620	0638	0710	0805	...	0905	1038	1238	1438	1520	...	1615	1638	1638	1740	1838	1838	1940	2024
Landry d.	...	|	0529	0546	|	0646	0717	0817	...	0912	1046	1246	1446	1527	...	1625	1646	1648	1747	1846	1846	1947	2034
Aime la Plagne d.	...	|	0536	0553	|	0654	0726	0826	...	0921	1054	1254	1454	1536	...	1636	1654	1657	1756	1854	1854	1956	2044
Moûtiers-Salins d.	0436	0448	0551	0608	0650	0708	0755	0845	0855	0945	1114	1314	1514	1600	...	1653	1713	1713	1820	1914	1914	2020	2107
Albertville a.	0511	0523	0613	0630	0720	0738	0840	...	0916	1020	1138	1338	1539	1635	...	1720	1738	1738	1855	1938	1939	2055	2138
Albertville d.	0511	0523	0620	0645	0720	0745	0840	...	0925	1020	1145	1345	1546	...	1645	1734	1745	1745	1855	1945	1947	2055	2158
St Pierre d'Albigny 367 ▷ d.	0531	|	0646	0712	|	0812	0908	...	0949	1050	1212	1412	1612	...	1712	|	1812	1812	1925	2012	2012	2115	|
Montmélian 367 ▷ d.	0546	0606	0654	0720	|	0820	0923	...	1000	1105	1220	1420	1620	...	1720	|	1820	1821	1940	2021	2020	2130	|
Chambéry 367 ▷ a.	0612	0634	0704	0729	0812	0829	0950	...	1009	1124	1233	1429	1629	...	1729	1810	1829	1829	2006	2029f	2029	2150	2230
Aix les Bains a.	0631	...	0719	|	...	|	...	...	...	...	...	...	...	...	|	|	...	|	...	|	...	...	|
Lyon Part Dieu 344 a.	...	...	...	0910	...	1010p	...	...	...	...	...	...	...	...	1910t	|	...	2010t	...	2210‡	...	...	|
Paris Gare de Lyon 341 a.	...	...	...	...	...	...	...	...	...	...	...	...	...	...	...	2115	...	...	...	...	...	...	0619a

D – ⑥ July 9 - Aug. 27.
E – June 23 - Aug. 31.

a – Paris **Austerlitz**.
f – 2034 on Nov. 1.
n – Not June 23 - Aug. 31.
p – Ⓐ only. 1014 June 23 - Aug. 31.
r – Ⓐ only. 1543 June 23 - Aug. 31.
t – 3–5 minutes later June 23 - Aug. 31.

v – Also July 13, Aug. 15, Nov. 1, 10; not Aug. 14, Nov. 11.

TGV – 🅁, supplement payable, 🍸.

♠ – ⑤–⑦ to June 26; daily July 1 - Sept. 4; ⑤–⑦ from Sept. 9 (also Nov. 1, 10).
♣ – ⑤ to June 24; ①–⑤ July 1 - Sept. 2; ⑤ from Sept. 9 (also Nov. 1, 10).
◇ – 🛏 1, 2 cl., (2) (reclining). **Service may be withdrawn from July 1**.
⊗ – Subject to alteration on ①–⑤ Oct. 3 – 21.
‡ – Not Nov. 11. Arrives 2212 June 26 - Aug. 28. Subject to alteration on Sept. 18, Oct. 16, Nov. 27.

▷ – Train timings at Chambéry, Montmélia and St Pierre d'Albigny may vary by u 6 minutes until July 2 (earlier departur possible).

Subject to alteration on Oct. 29, 30, 31

366a 🚌 GENÈVE - ANNEMASSE

🚌 **TPG route 61 Genève Cornavin railway station - Annemasse rail station** Journey time: 34 – 43 minutes *TER tickets valid between Genève Rieu and Annema*

From Genève Cornavin Ⓐ: 0650 and every 15 minutes until 1920 then 1936, 1951, 2008, 2025, 2051, 2121, 2151, 2221.
⑥: 0636 and every 30 minutes until 2136. ⑦ and holidays: 0843 and every 30 minutes until 2143.

From Annemasse Ⓐ: 0620 and every 15 minutes until 1535 then 1549, 1603, 1618, 1633, 1648, 1703, 1718, 1732, 1747, 1802, 1817, 1833, 1850, 1907, 1925, 1944, 2007, 2035, 2105, 2
⑥: 0551 and every 30 minutes until 2051. ⑦ and holidays: 0757 and every 30 minutes until 2057.

🚌 GENÈVE EAUX VIVES - ANNEMASSE - ANNECY

SNCF 🚌 service	🚌	🚌 ⚒	🚌	🚌	🚌	🚌	🚌 ©	🚌	🚌 Ⓐ	🚌	🚌
Genève Eaux-Vives d.	0648	0848	1045	1048	1248	1448	1648	1725	1800	1925	2115
Annemasse ▷ a.	0708	0908	|	1108	1308	1508	1708	|	|	|	2135
La Roche sur Foron ▷ a.	0741	0941	1120	1141	1341	1541	1741	1800	1845	2000	2200
Annecy ▷ a.	...	...	1155	...	...	...	...	1835	...	...	2235

	🚌 ⚒	🚌	🚌 Ⓐ	🚌 ©	🚌	🚌	🚌	🚌	🚌 ⚒ ⊠	🚌
Annecy ▷ d.	0615	0700	...	...	...	...	...	...	1640	...
La Roche sur Foron ▷ d.	0650	0735	0812	0812	1012	1212	1412	1612	1715	1812
Annemasse ▷ d.	|	|	|	0847	1042	1242	1442	1647	|	1847
Genève Eaux-Vives a.	0740	0825	0858	0912	1102	1302	1502	1702	1805	1912

⊠ – Runs 15 minutes **earlier** on ⑥.

▷ – See also Table **365**.

367 CHAMBÉRY - MODANE

Warning! Timings may vary by up to 13 minutes until July 2 (earlier departures possible).

km					TGV 9241	TGV 9241						TGV 9245			TGV 6407				TGV 9249					
		⚒	Ⓐ	🚌 Ⓐ	Ⓐ M❄	© M❄	⊡		©	Ⓐ		M❄	©	Ⓐ	⑥ D		Ⓐ	⚒	M❄	⚒			⑤† w	Ⓑ
	Paris Gare de Lyon 341 d.	...	...	...	0628f	0624f	...	...	...	...	...	1041	...	...	1149	...	...	...	1441	...	...	...	...	...
	Lyon St Exupéry ✈ 342 d.	...	...	...	|	|	...	...	...	...	...	1236	...	...	|	...	...	...	1637	...	...	...	...	...
	Lyon Part Dieu 344 d.	...	...	...	0831	0831	...	...	1050	...	...	|	1250b	...	|	...	1450	...	|	...	...	...	...	...
0	**Chambéry** 366 d.	0636	0736	0826	0942	0944	1043	...	1235	1236	...	1344	1436	1450	1509	...	1636	1736	1744	...	1836	1936	2036	2136
14	Montmélian 366 d.	0646	0746	|	|	|	1053	...	1245	1246	...	|	1446	1500	|	...	1645	1746	|	←	1846	1946	2046	2145
26	St Pierre d'Albigny 366 d.	0654	0754	|	|	|	1107	...	1253	1253	...	|	1454	1508	|	...	1653	1753	|	1800	1854	1954	2054	2153
61	St Avre la Chambre d.	0725	0824	0947	|	|	1139	...	1324	1325	...	|	1525	1541	1553	...	1725	→	|	1832	1925	2025	2124	2224
71	St Jean de Maurienne ⊖ d.	0732	0832	1002	|	|	1150	...	1332	1333	...	|	1533	1551	1606	...	1733	...	1827	1840	1933	2032	2132	2231
83	St Michel-Valloire d.	0742	0841	1022	|	|	1204	...	1342	1342	...	|	1542	1600	1619	...	1742	...	|	1849	1942	2042	2141	2241
99	**Modane** a.	0755	0855	1040	1045	1050	1217	...	1356	1355	...	1450	1556	1614	1637	...	1757	...	1847	1902	1956	2055	2155	2255

						TGV 9240					TGV 9244								TGV 6414	TGV 9248	TGV 9248			TGV 9250
	⚒	Ⓐ	⑥	🚌 Ⓐ		M❄	A	▲			M	🚌 Ⓐ	G	E		⚒ △	†	Ⓐ	⑥ D	⑤ M❄	⑥⑦ M❄	⑥	Ⓑ	①–④ M❄
Modane d.	0604	0704	0704	0804	...	0910	0940	0956	...	1122	1149	1234	...	1402	...	1604	1601k	1704	1733	1752	1752	1804	1804	1917
St Michel-Valloire d.	0618	0717	0718	0824	...	|	0954	1010	...	1140	|	1254	...	1415	...	1618	1616k	1717	1749	|	|	1818	1818	|
St Jean de Maurienne ⊖ d.	0628	0727	0729	0839	...	0932	1007	1022	...	1150	|	1309	1423	1428	...	1630	1627k	1728	1801	|	|	1828	1828	|
St Avre la Chambre d.	0636	0735	0737	0849	...	|	1024	1029	...	1157	|	1319	1430	1436	...	1637	1635k	1736	1811	|	|	1836	1836	|
St Pierre d'Albigny 366 d.	0706	0803	0807	|	...	|	1100	1100	...	1226	|	1359	1505	1505r	...	1708	1706	1806	|	|	|	1906	1906	|
Montmélian 366 d.	0714	0811	0815	|	...	|	1110	1110	...	1234	|	1414	1514	1514r	...	1715	1715	1814	|	|	|	1914	1915	|
Chambéry 366 a.	0723	0823	0825	0957	...	1015	1126	1119	...	1245	1249	1434	1529	1523r	...	1723	1725	1823	1847	1852	1852	1923	1925	2015
Lyon Part Dieu 344 a.	...	...	1010	...	...	|	...	...	...	...	|	...	...	...	...	...	1910c	...	|	2032	2028	...	2110	2131
Lyon St Exupéry ✈ 342 a.	...	...	...	...	...	1123	...	...	...	...	|	...	...	...	...	...	...	...	|	|	|	...	...	|
Paris Gare de Lyon 341 a.	...	...	...	...	...	1320	...	...	...	...	1612	...	...	...	...	...	...	...	2211	2231	2232j	...	...	2332

A – ①–⑤ June 6 - July 1.
D – ⑥ July 9 - Aug. 27.
E – From July 3.
G – Until July 2.
M – (12) and 🍸 Paris - Torino - Milano and v.v. (Table 44). 🅁, special 'global' fares payable.

b – 1252 June 25 - Aug. 28.
c – 1914 June 26 - Aug. 28.
f – 0629 until Sept. 5.

j – 2238 on ⑥.
k – 3 minutes later from Sept. 4.
r – 5–7 minutes later on ①–⑤ Nov. 14 - Dec. 2.
w – Also July 13, Nov. 10.

TGV – 🅁, supplement payable, 🍸.

❄ – Subject to alteration until Aug. 31 (see Table **44**).
✣ – Subject to alteration on ①–④ until June 23.
△ – Subject to alteration until June 3.

⊡ – Timings may vary by up to 6 minutes on ①–⑤ Sept. 26 - Oc and ①–⑤ Nov. 14 - Dec. 2. On ③ July 6 - Sept. 21 (also Oct 26, Nov. 2, 9, Dec. 7) St Jean de Maurienne a. 1147, d. 1212, St Michel-Valloire d. 1222, Modane a. 1237.
▲ – Not ①–⑤ June 6 - July 1. Subject to alteration on ①–⑤ Aug. Nov. 10 and Nov. 14 – 18.
⊖ – 🚌 calls at Arvan not rail station.

Subject to alteration Oct. 29, 30, 31

/SAVDA 🚐 CHAMONIX - MONT BLANC TUNNEL - COURMAYEUR 368

🚐, journey 45 minutes. Reservation compulsory by 1700 on previous day through SAT, Chamonix station ✆ +33 (0) 450 530 115 or SAVDA, Aosta bus station ✆ +39 0165 367 032.

19 - Apr. 10: From Chamonix (Avenue de Courmayeur) at 0830, 0930, 1100, 1500, 1615, 1730. From Courmayeur (Piazzale Monte Bianco) at 0815, 0945, 1200, 1400, 1615, 1730.

11 - July 1: From Chamonix (Avenue de Courmayeur) at 0830, 1145, 1530, 1715. From Courmayeur (Piazzale Monte Bianco) at 0945, 1045, 1545, 1700.

2 - Sept. 4: From Chamonix (Avenue de Courmayeur) at 0830, 1030, 1230, 1430, 1600, 1800. From Courmayeur (Piazzale Monte Bianco) at 0900, 1100, 1200, 1400, 1600, 1800.

'DA 🚐 COURMAYEUR - PRÉ ST DIDER - AOSTA

mayeur △ ....d.	0645	0735	0835	0935	and	1935	2035	2135	...	...
t Didier .... **586** d.	0653	0743	0843	0943	hourly	1943	2043	2143	...	...
a ⊡ .... **586** a.	0745	0835	0935	1035	until	2035	2135	2235	...	...

Aosta ⊡ .... **586** d.	0645	0745	0845	0945	1045	1145	1245	1335	1445	and	2145
Pré St Didier ... **586** d.	0737	0837	0937	1037	1137	1237	1337	1427	1537	hourly	2237
Courmayeur △ ...... a.	0745	0845	0945	1045	1145	1245	1345	1436	1545	until	2245

P. le Monte Bianco.

⊡ – Autostazione (bus station).

CORSICAN RAILWAYS 369

row gauge. 2nd class.

SERVICE UNTIL JUNE 26

	Ⓐ	Ⓐ	⑥	Ⓐ	†	⑥	⑥	Ⓐ	†	⑥	Ⓐ	Ⓐ	⑥	†	Ⓐ	†	⑥	⑥	Ⓐ	Ⓐ	⑥	†c	Ⓐ	Ⓐ
Bastia .... ▷ d.	0603	0617	0649	0754	0927	0944	...	0945	1043	1127	1130	1509	1523	1531	1638	1648	1648	...	1654	...	1754	1816	1832	1925
Biguglia .... ▷ d.	0618	|	0704	0809	0942	0959	...	1000	1058	1142	1144	1522	1538	1546	1654	1703	1703	...	|	...	1809	1833	1848	1940
Casamozza .... ▷ d.	0632	0641	0719	0824	0956	1013	...	1015	1114	1155	1158	1537	1553	1600	1708	1718	1717	...	1719	...	1823	1850	1904	1954
Ponte Leccia .... a.	...	0718	0753	0901	1031	1047	...	1050	1149	1229	1232	1611	1627	1635	...	1753	1751	...	1754	...	▬	1924	1941	...
Ponte Leccia .... d.	...	0720	0754	0907	1035	1051	1100	1059	1156	1230	1233	1612	1628	1640	...	1801	1759	1805	1759	1816	...	1925	1942	...
Ile Rousse .... ▶ d.	...	|	|	|	|	|	1215	1215	1312	|	|	|	|	|	...	1917	|	1920	|	1935	...	|	|	...
Calvi .... ▶ a.	...	|	|	|	|	|	1250	1250	1347	|	|	|	|	|	...	1952	|	1955	|	2010	†b	|	|	...
Corté .... d.	...	0803	0833	0944	1115	1128	...	...	...	1308	1311	1649	1709	1719	...	...	1843	...	1838	...	1904	1959	2016	...
Vivario .... d.	...	0835	0905	1020	1147	1200	...	...	...	1340	1343	1724	1739	1751	...	...	1913	...	1910	...	1936	...	...	...
Vizzavona .... d.	...	0853	0926	1038	1205	1220	...	...	...	1358	1401	1746	1800	1812	...	...	1931	...	1928	...	1954	...	...	...
Mezzana .... △ d.	...	0943	1013	1128	1252	1307	...	...	...	1445	1448	1835	1847	1859	...	...	2018	...	2015	...	2041	...	...	...
Ajaccio .... △ a.	...	1001	1031	1146	1310	1325	...	...	...	1503	1506	1853	1905	1917	...	...	2036	...	2033	...	2059	...	...	...

	Ⓐ	⑥	Ⓐ	⑥	†	Ⓐ	Ⓐ	Ⓐ	⑥	†	Ⓐ	⑥	⑥	†	Ⓐ	⑥	†	⑥	⑥	Ⓐ	Ⓐ	†	Ⓐ	⑥	†b
cio .... △ d.	...	...	...	...	...	0602	...	...	0633	...	0812	...	0815	0915	1106	1109	...	...	1513	...	1523	1520	1633	1644	1700
zana .... △ d.	...	...	...	...	...	0621	...	...	0652	...	0831	...	0834	0934	1128	1128	...	...	1532	...	1542	1539	1652	1703	1719
avona .... d.	...	...	...	...	...	0712	...	...	0744	...	0925	...	0927	1025	1219	1221	...	...	1623	...	1633	1630	1747	1758	1813
io .... d.	...	...	...	...	...	0728	...	...	0800	...	0941	...	0943	1041	1235	1237	...	...	1638	...	1649	1646	1803	1813	1829
é .... d.	...	0608	0621	...	...	0802	...	...	0834	...	1018	...	1015	1116	1309	1310	...	...	1712	...	1723	1720	1839	1845	1858
lvi .... ▶ d.	...	|	|	...	...	|	...	0700	|	0835	|	0845	|	|	|	|	1440	1545	|	1545	|	|	|	|	▬
Rousse .... ▶ d.	...	|	|	...	...	|	...	0737	|	0912	|	0921	|	|	|	|	1517	1621	|	1622	|	|	|	|	...
e Leccia .... a.	...	0642	0655	...	...	0836	...	0854	0908	1029	1052	1038	1049	1150	1343	1344	1634	1738	1746	1739	1757	1754	1913	1919	...
e Leccia .... d.	...	0643	0656	...	...	0837	...	0909	0910	1036	1056	...	1054	1154	1344	1345	1639	...	1754	...	1800	1759	1914	1920	Ⓐ
amozza .... ▷ d.	0641	0720	0736	0806	0851	0916	0934	0946	0946	1115	1131	...	1129	1230	1419	1421	1717	...	1829	...	1835	1835	1955	1955	2000
glia .... ▷ d.	0657	0734	0752	0820	0905	|	0948	1000	0959	1128	1144	...	1142	1244	1431	1434	1730	...	1842	...	1848	1849	|	2008	2014
ia .... ▷ a.	0712	0750	0812	0836	0920	0938	1004	1014	1013	1142	1157	...	1156	1258	1444	1448	1744	...	1856	...	1901	1903	2017	2022	2029

Not Apr. 24, May 1, 5, 15.   **c** – Not May 15.

Additional journeys Bastia - Casamozza and v.v.: **From Bastia** at 0624 Ⓐ, 0717 Ⓐ, 0729 ⑥, 0810 †, 0815 ⑥, 0820 Ⓐ, 0845 ⑥, 0856 Ⓐ, 1020 Ⓐ, 1035 ⑥, 1213 †, 1215 ⚒, 1325 Ⓐ, 1335 ⑥, 1449 Ⓐ, 1505 ⑥, 1605 Ⓐ, 1626 ⑥, 1717 Ⓐ, 1756 Ⓐ and 1923 ⑥. **From Casamozza** at 0719 Ⓐ, 0810 Ⓐ, 0857 Ⓐ, 0902 ⑥, 0959 ⑥, 1116 ⑥, 1054 Ⓐ, 1250 †, 1301 ⑥, 1316 Ⓐ, 1405 Ⓐ, 1409 ⑥, 1523 Ⓐ, 1552 ⑥, 1639 Ⓐ, 1718 Ⓐ, 1720 ⑥, 1757 Ⓐ, 1838 ⑥, 1850 Ⓐ and 2010 ⑥.

△ – **Additional journeys** Ajaccio - Mezzana and v.v.: **From Ajaccio** at 0637 Ⓐ, 0715 ⑥, 0723 Ⓐ, 1215 ⚒, 1715 ⚒, 1815 ⚒ and 1925 Ⓐ. **From Mezzana** at 0700 Ⓐ, 0745 ⑥, 0746 Ⓐ, 1330 Ⓐ, 1335 ⑥, 1740 ⚒, 1900 Ⓐ, 1912 ⑥ and 1948 Ⓐ.

▶ – **Additional journeys** Ile Rousse - Calvi and v.v.: **From Ile Rousse** at 0900 Ⓐ, 0930 ⑥, 1020 †, 1100 Ⓐ, 1130 ⑥, 1220 †, 1400 ⚒, 1620 †, 1630 ⚒, 1820 † and 1830 ⚒. **From Calvi** at 0800 ⚒, 0920 †, 1000 Ⓐ, 1030 ⑥, 1120 †, 1305 ⚒, 1500 ⚒, 1520 †, 1720 † and 1730 ⚒.

PARIS - DREUX - GRANVILLE 273

Temporarily relocated from page 179

	E		3411 Ⓐ		3413 Ⓒ		16511 ⑦e	Ⓐ		3421		3431	3435 ⑤f	⑥		3441 Ⓐ	3443 Ⓒ		3445 ⑤f	Ⓐ	Ⓐ	3451 Ⓐ	3453 Ⓒ	
Paris Montparnasse ⊖ d.	...	...	0738	...	0850	...	0927	0927	...	1055	...	1355	1528	1527	...	1643	1655	...	1713	...	1813	1943	1955	...
Versailles Chantiers . ▲ d.	...	...	|	...	0902	...	|	|	...	|	...	|	|	|	...	|	|	...	|	...	1827	|	2007	...
Dreux .... ▶ d.	0515	...	0825	...	0938	...	1014	1014	...	|	...	1443	|	1614	...	|	|	...	|	1819	1914	2044	2044	...
Verneuil sur Avre .... d.	0544	...	0845	...	0957	...	1044	1036	...	1158	...	1503	|	1642	...	1801	1800	...	|	1847	1936	2104	2103	...
L'Aigle .... d.	0601	...	0858	...	1011	...	1102	1049	...	1211	...	1516	1640	1659	...	1814	1814	...	1840	1904	1950	2117	2117	...
Surdon .... **271** d.	0628	...	0919	...	1032	...	1132	1118	...	|	...	1537	|	1724	...	1835	1836	...	1901	1929	2015	2138	2138	...
Argentan .... **271** d.	0638	...	0931	...	1043	...	1142	1127	...	1242	...	1548	1711	1734	...	1847	1848	...	1913	1939	2025	2149	2148	...
Briouze .... d.	0657	...	0947	...	1100	...	1158	...	...	|	...	1605	|	...	...	|	|	...	1929	...	...	2205	2205	...
Flers .... d.	0708	...	0958	...	1110	...	1209	...	...	1305	...	1616	1734	...	...	1910	1913	...	1942	...	...	2216	2215	...
Vire .... d.	0724	...	1015	...	1127	...	1225	...	...	1322	...	1632	1751	...	...	1927	1930	...	1958	...	...	2232	2232	...
Villedieu les Poêles ...... d.	0742	...	1030	...	1142	...	1241	...	...	1337	...	1647	1806	...	...	1942	1946	...	2014	...	...	2247	2247	...
Folligny .... **272** d.	0752	...	1040	...	1152	...	1251	...	...	|	...	|	|	...	...	|	|	...	2024	...	...	|	|	...
Granville .... **272** a.	0803	...	1051	...	1203	...	1302	...	...	1355	...	1704	1824	...	...	1959	2004	...	2034	...	...	2305	2304	...

	Ⓐ	16510 ①g	Ⓐ	⑥	†	3410 ⑥	3410 Ⓐ	3412 †Q	3412 †P		3420	⑥	3430 ⚒Q	3430 ⚒P	Ⓐ	3432 †	3440	3444 †Q	3444 †P	E	3450 M	13272 †	3450 L	3454 †P	3454 †Q
nville .... **272** d.	...	0448	...	...	...	0553	0555	0640	0655	...	0900	...	1147	1154	...	1356	1503	1700	1705	1710	1750	...	1845	1954	1955
gny .... **272** d.	...	|	...	...	...	|	|	|	|	...	|	...	|	|	...	|	|	|	|	1721	1800	...	1856	2005	2006
dieu les Poêles .... d.	...	0506	...	...	...	0610	0613	0657	0714	...	0918	...	1206	1213	...	1414	1521	1719	1724	1730	1811	...	1906	2015	2015
.... d.	...	0522	...	...	...	0625	0628	0712	0730	...	0934	...	1221	1228	...	1430	1536	1734	1740	1749	1825	...	1922	2031	2030
s .... d.	...	0538	...	...	...	0643	0644	0729	0746	...	0951	...	1238	1245	...	1447	1553	1752	1757	1805	1843	...	1939	2048	2047
uze .... d.	...	0549	...	...	...	0654	0655	0740	0758	...	|	...	1249	1256	...	1458	|	1803	1808	1816	1854	...	1950	2059	2058
entan .... **271** d.	0453	0606	0606	0603	0630	0712	0712	0759	0816	...	1017	1154	1308	1315	1357	1516	1619	1821	1825	1836	1912	1926	2009	2117	2117
don .... **271** d.	0503	0616	0616	0613	0640	0722	0722	0809	0826	...	1027	1204	1318	1325	1407	1527	|	|	|	...	1922	1936	2019	|	|
gle .... d.	0527	0641	0641	0637	0707	0742	0741	0829	0847	...	1048	1228	1338	1346	1435	1548	1645	1847	1853	...	1942	2003	2041	2145	2142
neuil sur Avre .... d.	0544	0655	0655	0650	0721	0755	0754	0843	0900	...	1101	1244	1351	1359	1448	1601	1658	|	|	...	1955	2016	2055	2158	2155
ux .... ▶ d.	0612	0720	0720	0713	0743	0815	0813	0903	0921	...	|	1313	1411	1420	1512	|	|	|	|	...	2016	2039	2116	2219	2214
sailles Chantiers .. ▲ a.	...	0803	0803	|	|	|	|	|	|	...	|	|	|	|	|	|	|	|	|	...	|	2119	|	2254	2255
s Montparnasse ⊖ a.	...	0816	0816	0805	0835	0905	0916	1006	1006	...	1205	1405	1505	1505	1605	1705	1805	2006	2006	...	2107	2131	2205	2307	2307

Ⓐ to July 4; ①⑤ July 8 - Aug. 26 (also July 13, 15, Aug. 16; not Aug. 15); Ⓐ from Aug. 29.
Not dates in note **M**.
①–⑤ July 5 - Nov. 25 (not July 14, 15, Aug. 15, Nov. 1, 11).
To July 4 / from Sept. 10.
July 5 - Sept. 9.

e – Also Aug. 15, Nov. 1; not Aug. 14, Oct. 30.
f – Also July 13, Nov. 10; not Nov. 11.
g – Also Aug. 16, Nov. 2; not Aug. 15.
▲ – Local travel between Paris and Versailles is not permitted on some trains (see Table **274** for local services).
▶ – Suburban trains run Paris - Versailles - Dreux approx hourly.

⊖ – Most trains use **Vaugirard** platforms (5 - 10 mins walk from Montparnasse main concourse).

Timings may vary by a few minutes

370 PARIS - DIJON - BESANÇON - MULHOUSE - BASEL *TGV Rhin-Rh*

For *TGV* trains Lyon - Dijon - Mulhouse - Strasbourg see Table **379**. For *TGV* trains Paris - Dijon - Dole - Lausanne see Table **375**.
Local services: Tables **371** Paris - Dijon, **374** Dijon - Besançon, **378** Besançon - Belfort, **370b** Belfort - Mulhouse.

km		*TGV* 6701	*TGV* 9203	*TGV* 6747		*TGV* 9211	*TGV* 6703	*TGV* 9213		*TGV* 9215	*TGV* 6755	*TGV* 6755	*TGV* 6741	*TGV* 9219	*TGV* 6759	*TGV* 9589	*TGV* 9223	*TGV* 9225	*TGV* 6757	*TGV* 6707		*TGV* 5130	*TGV* 6709
		Ⓐ	①–⑥	Ⓒ							Ⓐ	⑦	⑤			Ⓑ							
			b	⊙		⊗	⊗	u⊗		‡		J	Jw	⊡	¶	h	⊡	B⊡	H	⊡		♥⊡	G
	Lille Europe **11** d.	...	...	...	...	...	...	...	...	...	...	...	...	...	...	...	...	...	...	...	...	1900f	...
0	**Paris** Gare de Lyon **375** d.	0653	0723	0853	...	1023	1123	1223	...	1423	1453	1453	1523	1623	1653	1723	1823	1823	1853	1923	...	|	2023
212	Montbard d.	0759	|	1000	...	|	|	|	...	|	1600	1600	|	|	1759	|	|	|	2000	|	...	2109	|
287	**Dijon** **375** a.	0833	|	1034	...	1159	1258	1359	...	|	1634	1634	1657	|	1834	1857	1958	1958	2034	2057	...	2143	2157
287	**Dijon** **375** d.	0837	|	1037	...	1201	1302	1402	...	|	1637	...	...	|	1837	1901	2001	2001	2037	2101	...	2153	2201
333	Dole **375** a.	|	|	|	...	|	|	|	...	|	|	...	...	|	|	|	|	|	2100	|	...	|	|
364	**Besançon TGV** ⊖ d.	0908	|	1108	...	|	1331	|	...	|	1708	...	...	|	1908	1931	|	|	|	2131	...	2224	2231
377	Besançon Viotte a.	|	|	1120	...	|	|	|	...	|	1720	...	...	|	1920	|	|	|	2128	|	...	|	|
446	Belfort Montbéliard TGV d.	0933	0941	...	...	|	1355	|	...	1641	...	...	...	1841	...	1955	|	|	...	2155	...	2248	2255
491	Mulhouse **385** d.	0955	1006	...	...	1306	1417	1507	...	1706	...	...	...	1907	...	2023	2106	2106	...	2217	...	2310	2317
	Freiburg (Brsg) Hbf a.	...	|	...	...	|	...	|	...	|	...	...	...	|	...	2111§	|	|	...	...	...	...	...
525	**Basel** **385** a.	...	1026	...	...	1326	...	1526	...	1726	...	...	...	1926	...	...	2126	2126	...	...	...	...	...
	Zürich HB **510** a.	...	1126	...	...	1426	...	1626	...	...	...	...	...	2026	...	...	2226	...	...	...	...	...	...

	TGV 6750	*TGV* 6700	*TGV* 5152	*TGV* 6745	*TGV* 9588	*TGV* 9206	*TGV* 6704	*TGV* 9210	*TGV* 9214		*TGV* 6704	*TGV* 9218		*TGV* 9222	*TGV* 6706	*TGV* 6706	*TGV* 6784	*TGV* 9226	*TGV* 6708	*TGV* 6765	*TGV* 6765	*TGV* 9230	*TGV* 6708
	Ⓐ				①–⑥		Ⓒ				Ⓐ				Ⓐ	⑦	⑦	Ⓑ	Ⓒ	⑦	Ⓐ		Ⓐ
		D	♠	◧⊙	m	⊗	⊗	⊗	B			‡		⊡	s	Jn	n	h	⊡	e		⊡	
Zürich HB **510** d.	...	...	...	...	...	0734	...	0934	...	...	...	1134	...	1334	...	...	...	1534	...	...	...	...	...
Basel **385** d.	...	...	...	...	...	0834	...	1034	1034	...	...	1234	...	1434	...	...	...	1634	...	...	...	1834	...
Freiburg (Brsg) Hbf d.	...	...	...	...	0654§	|	...	|	|	...	...	|	...	|	...	...	...	|	...	...	...	|	...
Mulhouse **385** d.	...	0542	0551	...	0742	0856	0940	1056	1056	...	1158	1257	...	1456	1537	1542	...	1656	1742	...	...	1859	1942
Belfort Montbéliard TGV d.	...	0607	0617	...	0808	0921	1005	|	|	...	1223	1323	...	|	1603	1608	...	|	1808	...	...	1924	2008
Besançon Viotte d.	0533	|	|	0638	|	|	|	|	|	...	|	|	...	|	|	|	...	|	|	1837	1837	|	|
Besançon TGV ⊖ d.	|	0630	0641	0652	0832	|	1030	|	|	...	1249	|	...	|	1626	1632	...	|	1831	1851	1851	|	2032
Dole **375** d.	0559	|	|	|	|	|	|	|	|	...	|	|	...	|	|	|	...	|	|	|	|	|	|
Dijon **375** a.	0622	0658	0711	0719	0858	|	1058	1158	1158	...	1316	|	...	1558	1655	1658	...	1758	1858	1922	1922	|	2058
Dijon **375** d.	0625	0702	0714	0725	0902	|	1102	1201	1201	...	1319	|	...	1601	1658	1702	1725	1801	1901	1925	1925	|	2102
Montbard d.	0703	|	0750	0803	|	|	|	|	|	...	1404	|	...	|	1735	|	1803	|	|	2003	|	|	|
Paris Gare de Lyon **375** a.	0807	0837	|	0907	1037	1137	1237	1337	1337	...	1507	1537	...	1737	1838	1838	1907	1937	2037	2107	2107	2138	2237
Lille Europe **11** a.	...	...	1002v	...	...	...	...	...	...	...	...	...	...	...	...	...	...	...	...	...	...	...	...

LOCAL TRAINS MULHOUSE - FREIBURG *Subject to alteration July 19 - Sept. 17*

km		①–⑤ a	⑥⑦ c	①–⑤ a		①–⑤ a	①–⑤ a	⑥⑦ c		
0	**Mulhouse** d.	0632	0831	0831	1023	1251	1434	1534	1751	1923
19	Neuenburg d.	0658	0851	0851	1043	1311	1504	1604	1812	1944
22	Müllheim (Baden) a.	0702	0856	0856	1047	1316	1509	1609	1817	1949
22	Müllheim (Baden) **912** d.	*0707*	0857	*0906*	*1055*	*1323*	1510	1609	*1823*	*1955*
51	**Freiburg** (Brsg) Hbf **912** a.	*0736*	0916	*0934*	*1122*	*1344*	1529	1628	*1844*	*2021*

	①–⑤ a		⑥⑦ c			①–⑤ a		
Freiburg (Brsg) Hbf **912** d.	*0628*	0915	0926	...	*1115*	*1315*	1645	*1815*j
Müllheim (Baden) **912** a.	*0654*	0934	0944	...	*1134*	*1336*	1704	*1834*
Müllheim (Baden) d.	0707	...	0945	0945	1140	1340	1705	1839
Neuenburg d.	0711	...	0950	0950	1145	1345	1710	1844
Mulhouse a.	0730	...	1011	1011	1205	1406	1730	1904

B – [12] Bern - Basel - Paris and v.v.
D – ①–⑥ to July 4; ①⑥ July 9 - Aug. 22 (also July 14, Aug. 16; not Aug. 15); ①–⑥ from Aug. 27 (not Nov. 1).
G – Ⓑ to July 3; ⑤⑦ July 8 - Aug. 21 (also July 13, Aug. 15); Ⓑ from Aug. 26 (not Nov. 11).
H – Ⓑ to July 1; Ⓐ July 4 - Aug. 26; Ⓑ from Aug. 29 (not Nov. 11).
J – To July 1 and from Sept. 2.

a – Not Oct. 3, Nov. 1.
b – Not Aug. 15, Nov. 1.
c – Also Oct. 3, Nov. 1.
e – Also Aug. 15, Nov. 1.
f – Lille **Flandres**.

h – Not July 14, Nov. 11.
j – *1811* July 16 - Aug. 28.
m – Not July 15, Nov. 12.
n – Also Nov. 1.
p – 2033 on ⑥.
r – Also July 13, Aug. 15, Nov. 10; not Nov. 11.
s – Also ⑦ July 3 - Aug. 28; also Aug. 15.
u – Not July 4 – 7.
v – 0958 from July 16.
w – Also Nov. 10; not Nov. 11.

TGV – Ⓡ, supplement payable, 🍸.

⊡ – Subject to alteration on Oct. 8, 15.
¶ – Subject to alteration on Oct. 1, 8, 15.
⊙ – Subject to alteration on Oct. 9, 16.
⊗ – Subject to alteration on Oct. 9, 16, Nov. 5, 6.
‡ – Subject to alteration on Oct. 8, 15, Nov. 5, 6.
§ – Subject to alteration July 19 - Sept. 17.
◧ – Departures are 1 – 2 minutes earlier Oct. 3 - Nov
♥ – Also calls at Charles de Gaulle ✈ (d. 1958) and Marne la Vallée-Chessy (d. 2011).
♠ – Also calls at Marne la Vallée-Chessy (a. 0849) a Charles de Gaulle ✈ (a. 0903).
⊖ – Full name: Besançon Franche-Comté TGV.

370a BESANÇON VIOTTE - BESANÇON FRANCHE-COMTÉ TGV *Local connecting servic*

km		⚒				Ⓐ	Ⓒ			Ⓐ					Ⓑ			Ⓒ			Ⓐ	
0	Besançon Viotte d.	0605	0735	0806	...	0953	1005	...	1143	1223	1303	1336	1430	...	1603	...	1736	1806	1849	1930	2007	2100
13	Besançon Franche-Comté TGV a.	0620	0750	0822	...	1008	1020	...	1156	1238	1318	1354	1445	...	1616	...	1749	1821	1904	1945	2022	2115

	Ⓐ	⑥	⑦e	A	Ⓒ	Ⓐ	Ⓒ	Ⓐ		Ⓐ				Ⓑ		ⒸL	ⒸN			Ⓐ	z	⑥
Besançon Franche-Comté TGV d.	0650	0708	0823	0839	0855	0915	1040	1104	1222	1301	1338	1427	1502	1640	1821	1845	1849	1946	2022	2039	2138	2231
Besançon Viotte a.	0705	0723	0837	0854	0909	0929	1055	1119	1239	1318	1353	1445	1517	1655	1835	1903	1904	2001	2037	2054	2152	2245

A – ①–⑥ (not Aug. 15, Nov. 1). **L** – From July 3. **N** – Until July 2. **e** – Also Aug. 15, Nov. 1. **z** – Not Aug. 31, Sept. 1, 5, 6, 7, 26, 27, 28.

371 PARIS - SENS - AUXERRE and DIJON *Local Servic*

For *TGV* services Paris - Dijon see Table **370**. Certain Paris - Auxerre trains continue to / from destinations in Table **372**.
WARNING! Certain services are subject to alteration on June 11, 12, Oct. 1, 2, 8, 9, 15, 16, 29, 30, Nov. 5, 6, 11, 12.

km		Ⓐ	⚒	Ⓐ	Ⓐ		⚒			Ⓒ		Ⓑ	⚒	Ⓐ	Ⓑ		Ⓐ	Ⓒ	Ⓑ		Ⓐ	Ⓒ	†	Ⓐ	
							△♥	⊗	◇♥		♥	⊡													
0	**Paris** Bercy d.	...	...	0613	...	0738	0838	0926	1038	...	1238	...	1338	1438	...	1538	1631	1638	...	1731v	1831	1838	...	...	1931v
113	Sens d.	...	0617	0719	...	0834	0934	1034	1134	...	1334	...	1434	1534	...	1634	1734	1734	...	1834	1934	1934	...	...	2034
147	Joigny d.	...	0647	0748	...	0850	0950	1050	1150	...	1350	...	1450	1550	...	1650	1750	1750	...	1850	1950	1950	...	...	2050
	Auxerre d.	0532	|	|	*0738*	|	|	|	|	*1139*	|	*1337*	|	|	1536a	|	|	|	1728	|	|	|	*1940*	*1945*	|
156	Laroche Migennes a.	0549	0655	0755	*0752*	0858	0956	1058	1156	*1152*	1356	*1352*	1458	1556	1553a	1658	1756	1756	1744	1858	1957	1956	*1954*	*2001*	2058
156	Laroche Migennes d.	0602	0701	0759	0800	0901	1003e	1101	1158	1201	1406	1401	1501	1606	1601	1701	1806	1758	1801	1901	*2003*y	1959h	2005	2008	2101
175	**Auxerre** a.	|	|	0813	|	|	1017e	|	1213	|	1419	|	|	1620	|	|	1819	1814	|	|	*2018*y	2014h	|	|	|
197	Tonnerre d.	0629	0726	...	0827	0927	...	1127	...	1231	...	1428	1527	...	1628	1727	...	...	1828	1927	...	...	2032	2036	2127
243	Montbard d.	0654	0752	...	0852	0953	...	1153	...	1300	...	1453	1553	...	1653	1753	...	...	1853	1953	...	...	2058	2101	2153
315	**Dijon** a.	0730	0829	...	0932	1030	...	1235	...	1335	...	1530	1630	...	1733	1830	...	...	1933	2030	...	...	2133	2138	2230
	Lyon Part Dieu **377** a.	...	1044	...	...	1244	...	1444	...	...	...	...	1844	...	...	2048	...	...	...	2244t	...	...	...	...	...

	Ⓐ	Ⓐ	⑥	⚒	Ⓑ		⚒	⚒	⚒			Ⓐ	Ⓒ		Ⓒ	Ⓐ			Ⓑ				Ⓐ	†	
										⊗	⊙														
Lyon Part Dieu **377** d.	...	...	...	...	...	...	0512g	...	...	0716	...	...	...	...	1116	1116	...	1316	...	...	1516	...	...	...	1716
Dijon d.	...	...	...	0529	0629	...	0729	0829	...	0929	...	1207	1229	...	1329	1331	...	1529	1629	...	1729	1829	...	...	1929
Montbard d.	...	...	...	0607	0706	...	0807	0906	...	1007	...	1302	1306	...	1407	1419	...	1607	1706	...	1807	1906	...	...	2007
Tonnerre d.	...	...	...	0633	0731	...	0833	0932	...	1033	...	1331	1331	...	1433	1444	...	1633	1731	...	1833	1931	...	...	2033
Auxerre d.	0446	*0532*	0546	|	|	0738k	|	|	0946	|	1139	|	|	1337	|	|	1536c	|	|	1737	|	|	1945	1940	|
Laroche Migennes a.	0500	*0549*	0600	0656	0757	0752k	0856	0957	1000	1056	1152	1357	1357	1352	1456	1505	1553c	1656	1757	1752	1856	1957	2001	1954	2056
Laroche Migennes d.	0502	0559	0602	0701	0807	0802	0901	1015r	1002	1101	1202	*1406*	*1406*	1402	1501	1506	1601	1701	*1806*a	1802	1901	2009r	2004	2004	2101
Auxerre a.	|	|	|	|	0822	|	|	1030r	|	|	|	*1419*	*1419*	|	|	|	|	|	*1819*a	|	|	2026r	|	|	|
Joigny d.	0509	0609	0609	0708	...	0809	0909	...	1010	1109	1209	...	...	1409	1509	1513	1609	1709	...	1809	1909	...	2012	2013	2109
Sens d.	0527	0627	0627	0725	...	0827	0926	...	1027	1126	1227	...	...	1427	1526	1530	1627	1726	...	1827	1926	...	2040	2040	2126
Paris Bercy a.	0628	0728	0722	0828	...	0922	1022	...	1136	1222	1322	...	...	1522	1622	1622	1722	1823	...	1922	2022	...	2148	2148	2222

CONTINUED ON NEXT PAGE (including other stopping services Paris Gare de Lyon - Laroche Migennes - Auxerre).

PARIS - SENS - AUXERRE and DIJON — 371 (contd.)

…CAL TRAINS PARIS - LAROCHE MIGENNES For faster trains see the main part of Table **371** on the previous page. See **WARNING** note on previous page for important information.

			♥	♥		†	⚒♥				Ⓐ	Ⓒ	Ⓐ	Ⓐ	Ⓒ	Ⓐ	Ⓐ	Ⓒ	Ⓐ	Ⓐ		Ⓒ		w	
Paris Gare de Lyon .. d.	0649z	0749	0849	1049	1149	1249	1249	1349	1449	1549	1619	1649	1700	1719	1749	1800	1819	1849	1900	1919	1949	2049	2149	2238b	2249
Melun.......... d.	0715z	0815	0915	1115	1215	1315	1315	1415	1515	1615	1645	1715	|	1745	1815	|	1845	1915	|	1945	2015	2115	2215	|	2315
Fontainebleau-Avon .. d.	0728z	0827	0928	1128	1227	1328	1328	1427	1528	1627	1658	1728	|	1757	1828	|	1857	1928	|	1957	2028	2128	2229	|	2327
Montereau.......... d.	0750	0845	0950	1150	1245	1350	1350	1445	1550	1645	1720	1750	1752	1820	1850	1850	1920	1950	1950	2015	2050	2150	2245	|	2345
Sens.......... d.	0838f	...	1038f	1220	...	1420	1438f	...	1638f	...	1749	1838f	1819	1849	1938f	1919	1949	2038f	2019	...	2138f	2219	...	2349	...
Joigny.......... d.	0905	...	1106	1248	...	1448	1506	...	1705	...	1817	1905	1848	1918	2005	1948	2018	2105	2048	...	2205	2248	...	0018	...
Laroche Migennes... a.	0913	...	1113	1255	...	1455	1513	...	1713	...	1825	1913	1855	1925	2013	1955	2025	2113	2055	...	2213	2255	...	0025	...

		Ⓐ	⑥	Ⓐ	Ⓐ	Ⓒ	Ⓐ	⑥	†	Ⓐ	Ⓐ		♥		♥			†	⚒		†	⚒	Ⓐ	Ⓒ		
…che Migennes ... d.	0404	0504	0504	0534	0604	0604	0634	0647	...	0704	...	0747	1007	...	1207	...	1407	1447	...	1547	1647	...	1747	1807	...	...
…y.......... d.	0411	0511	0511	0541	0611	0611	0641	0654	...	0711	...	0754	1014	...	1214	...	1414	1454	...	1554	1654	...	1754	1814	...	...
.... d.	0440	0540	0540	0610	0640	0640	0710	0740f	...	0740	...	0840f	1040	...	1240	...	1440	1540f	...	1640f	1740f	...	1840f	1842	...	...
…ereau.......... d.	0511	0610	0612	0642	0710	0710	0742	0812	0812	0810	0819	0912	1112	1212	1312	1412	1512	1612	1612	1712	1812	1812	1912	1912	2012	2112
…ainebleau-Avon ... d.	0529	|	0630	0700	|	0727	0800	0831	0830	|	0836	0931	1131	1230	1331	1430	1531	1631	1630	1731	1831	1830	1931	1931	2030	2130
…n.......... d.	0546	|	0643	0715	|	0743	0814	0844	0843	|	0849	0944	1144	1243	1344	1443	1544	1644	1643	1744	1844	1843	1944	1944	2043	2143
…s Gare de Lyon ... a.	0611	0700	0711	0741	0800	0811	0841	0911	0911	0909	0917	1011	1211	1311	1411	1511	1611	1711	1715	1813	1911	1915	2013	2013	2111	2211

ADDITIONAL LOCAL TRAINS LAROCHE MIGENNES - AUXERRE

	⑥	⚒	†	⚒				⚒§	†	D	E
…che Migennes ..... d.	0031	0706	0903	0908	1106	1511	1704	1908	1914	2106	2108
…rre.......... a.	0044	0723	0916	0921	1123	1528	1721	1921	1932	2123	2121

	⑥	Ⓐ	◧	⊖			Ⓐ	†	⚒	⚒‡	†
Auxerre.......... d.	0636	0637	0836	1037	1436	1636	1824	1830	1837	2036	2037
Laroche Migennes.. a.	0654	0653	0854	1051	1454	1654	1842	1844	1851	2054	2051

①–④ (not July 13, 14, Aug. 15, Nov. 1, 10).
⑤–⑦ (also July 13, 14, Aug. 15, Nov. 1, 10).
Ⓐ only.
Paris **Bercy**.
Ⓒ only.
3 minutes later on ⑥.
Arrives 18–20 minutes earlier.
① only.
3 minutes later on †.
On † Auxerre d. 0746, Laroche a. 0800.

r – ⑥ only.
t – Ⓑ only. Change trains at Dijon on ⑤ (also July 13, Nov. 10).
v – 7 minutes later on Ⓒ.
w – Not June 11, 12, Oct. 2, 28, 29, 30, Nov. 20, 27.
y – 5 minutes later July 4 - Aug. 26.
z – 4–5 minutes earlier until July 10.
◇ – On Ⓒ runs 3–8 minutes later Sens - Auxerre.
◧ – On ⑥ Auxerre d. 0837, Laroche a. 0851.
⊖ – On ⑥ Auxerre d. 1036, Laroche a. 1054.
‡ – 2–3 minutes earlier on Ⓐ July 4 - Aug. 26.

⊡ – On †: Laroche d. 1402, Tonnerre d. 1433, Montbard d. 1501, Dijon a. 1536.
§ – On Ⓐ July 4 - Aug. 26 Laroche d. 1906, Auxerre a. 1923.
△ – Subject to alteration on Ⓐ to July 8.
⊗ – Subject to alteration June 6–10, 13–17, July 18–22, Aug. 8–12, Sept. 19–23, 26–30, Oct. 10–14, 24–28, Nov. 14–18, 21–25, Dec. 5–9.
⊙ – Subject to alteration on ①–⑤ Oct. 3–21.
♥ – Subject to alteration Oct. 10–14.

AUXERRE - CLAMECY / AVALLON — 372

…		Ⓐ ⊖	†	⚒ ⊙	⑥	Ⓒ	⑥	♥	Ⓐ	Ⓐ K	†	⑥	Ⓐ J	†	Ⓐ ♣	⑤–⑦ E
	Paris Bercy **371** .... ▲ d.	0613	...	...	0838	1038	1038	1238	1438	1631	1638	...	...	...	...	...
	Laroche Migennes **371** . ▲ d.	0759	0903	0908	1006	1206	1206	1406	1606	1806	1758	1908	1908	1914	2003	2108
…)	**Auxerre**.......... d.	0815	0918	0923	1022	1222	1222	1421	1622	1829	1831	1923	1923	1941	2025	2123
…7	Cravant-Bazarnes .... d.	0832	0934	0939	1039	1238	1238	1438	1638	1845	1846	1939	1939	1956	2042	2139
…3	Clamecy.......... a.	|	1011	1014	|	1313	1315	|	1713	|	|	2014	|	2030	2118	|
…6	Corbigny.......... a.	|	1049	...	|	...	1353	|	...	|	|	...	|	2109	2156	|
…1	Sermizelles-Vézelay .... d.	0854	...	...	1102	...	...	1500	...	1908	1907	...	2002	...	...	2202
…5	**Avallon**.......... a.	0906	...	...	1114	...	...	1512	...	1919	1919	...	2013	...	...	2213

	Ⓐ	⚒	⑥	Ⓑ ♠	⊙		⑥			†	⑥	Ⓐ K	Ⓐ J	†	Ⓐ K	†
…llon.......... d.	0545	...	0745	0945	...	...	1245	...	1644	...	...	...	...	...	1936	1945
…nizelles-Vézelay .... d.	0558	...	0758	0958	...	...	1258	...	1658	...	...	...	...	...	1949	1958
…orbigny.......... d.	|	0606	|	|	...	...	|	...	|	1657	1705	...	...	...	|	|
…amecy.......... d.	|	0645	|	|	1046	...	|	...	|	1736	1744	1737	1745	1847	|	|
…vant-Bazarnes.......... d.	0620	0722	0820	1020	1122	...	1320	...	1720	1813	1821	1813	1821	1923	2012	2020
…erre.......... a.	0635	0736	0835	1035	1137	...	1335	...	1735	1828	1835	1827	1835	1938	2028	2035
…aroche Migennes **371** .. ▲ a.	0653	0752	0851	1051	1152	...	1352	...	1752	1844	1851	1851	1851	1954	2051	2051
…aris Bercy **371** .... ▲ a.	...	0922	...	...	1322	...	1522	...	1922	...	...	...	...	2148	...	...

E – ⑤–⑦ (also July 13, 14, Aug. 15, Nov. 1, 10).
J – To July 1 and from Aug. 29.
K – July 4 - Aug. 26.

⊖ – Subject to alteration Nov. 28 - Dec. 2.
⊙ – Subject to alteration on ①–⑤ Oct. 3–21.
♥ – Subject to alteration Oct. 10–14.
♠ – Subject to alteration Oct. 3–7, 10–14, Nov. 28 - Dec. 2.
♣ – Runs 4–5 minutes later July 4 - Aug. 26.
▲ – See **WARNING** note for Table **371** on page 224 for important information regarding services from / to Paris.

DIJON - ÉTANG - AUTUN and NEVERS — 373

…bject to alteration on Oct. 1, 2

…m		Ⓐ ♥	Ⓐ	①–⑥ b	Ⓑ	⚒ ⊖	¶	⚒	Ⓑ w	⚒	Ⓐ	†	
0	**Dijon**.......... **377** d.	...	0612	0712	0812	1012	1212	1412	1608	1712	1812	1812	1912
…7	Beaune .... **377** d.	...	0631	0733	0831	1031	1231	1431	1627t	1731	1831	1831	1931
…1	**Montchanin**.......... d.	...	0659	0800	0859	1102	1259	1459	1700	1759	1859	1859	1959
…9	Le Creusot .... d.	...	0705	0806	0905	1109	1305	1505	1707	1806	1905	1905	2005
…1	Étang .... d.	0605	0721	0821	0921	1125	1321	1521	1721	1821	1925	1921	2021
…6	**Autun**.......... a.	|	|	|	|	|	|	|	|	|	1944	|	|
…9	Decize.......... d.	0647	0804	0904	1004	1207	1404	1604	1804	1904	...	2004	2104
…6	**Nevers**.......... a.	0719	0829	0929	1029	1232	1430	1629	1829	1929	...	2029	2129
	Bourges **290** .... a.	...	...	1013‡	...	...	...	...	1912	...	...	...	...
	Vierzon **290** .... a.	...	...	1033‡	...	...	...	...	1932	...	...	...	...
	Tours **290** .... a.	...	...	1201‡	...	...	...	...	2102	...	...	...	...

	① g	②–⑤ v	⚒	Ⓑ	①–⑥ b	⑦ e	§	Ⓐ		Ⓑ	⑥	Ⓐ ♥	Ⓑ n⊖
…ours **290**.......... d.	...	...	...	...	0658	...	...	...	...	...	...	...	1700
…ierzon **290**.......... d.	...	...	...	...	0828	...	...	...	...	...	...	...	1828
…ourges **290**.......... d.	...	...	...	...	0847	...	...	...	...	...	...	...	1847
…**ers**.......... d.	0530	...	0630	0730	0930	0930	1130	1330	1530	1730	1830	1846	1926
…ize.......... d.	0557	...	0657	0757	0956	0957	1157	1357	1557	1757	1857	1918	1953
…**utun**.......... d.	*0611*	0611	|	|	|	|	|	|	|	|	|	|	|
…ng.......... d.	0640	0640	0740	0840	1040	1040	1240	1440	1640	1840	1940	2000	2036
…Creusot.......... d.	0655	0655	0755	0855	1055	1055	1255	1455	1655	1855	1955	...	2052
…**ntchanin**.......... d.	0703	0703	0803	0903	1103	1103	1303	1503	1703	1903	2003	...	2102
…une.......... **377** d.	0728	0728	0828	0928	1128	1128	1328	1528	1728	1928	2028	...	2128
…**on**.......... **377** a.	0748	0748	0848	0948	1148	1148	1348	1548	1748	1948	2048	...	2148

CONNECTIONS CHALON - MONTCHANIN

km		Ⓐ	⚒	⚒¶	Ⓑ	⚒	Ⓑ	
0	**Chalon sur Saône** ....d.	...	0710	1410	1610	1710	1810	1910
15	Chagny..........d.	0622	0722	1422	1622	1722	1822	1922
44	**Montchanin** ....a.	0649	0749	1449	1649	1749	1849	1949

	Ⓐ	⚒	Ⓐ	§	Ⓐ	Ⓑ	Ⓑ	⑥
Montchanin .... ★ d.	0711	0811	0911	1111	1511	1711	1911	2011
Chagny.......... ★ d.	0737	0837	0937	1137	1537	1737	1937	2037
Chalon sur Saône ★ a.	0749	0849	0949	1149	1549	1749	1949	2049

CONNECTIONS ÉTANG - AUTUN ⊡

	Ⓐ	⚒	⊠	🚌 ⚒	⑥	Ⓑ	🚌 ⚒	Ⓑ	Ⓐ♥	🚌 ⚒	†
Étang.....d.	0725	0825	1325	1525	1645	1725	1825	1845	2003	2041	2045
Autun.....a.	0743	0843	1343	1546	1703	1743	1846	1903	2021	2102	2103

	Ⓐ♥	⚒	🚌 ⚒	⚒	⚒	🚌 ⚒		Ⓑ	🚌 ⑥	🚌 Ⓐ	†
Autun.....d.	0545	0632	0709	0757	1217	1249	1617	1817	1909	1949	1958
Étang.....a.	0603	0650	0730	0815	1235	1310	1635	1835	1930	2010	2016

CONNECTIONS MONTCHANIN - PARAY LE MONIAL - MOULINS SUR ALLIER

…m		Ⓐ	⑥	⚒◧		⚒	Ⓑ	⚒	Ⓑ	
	Dijon (see above).......... d.	...	...	1012	...	...	...	...	...	...
0	**Montchanin**.......... d.	0708	0808	1106	1308	1507	1708	1808	1908	2008
…5	Montceau les Mines.......... d.	0721	0822	1121	1321	1519	1722	1822	1922	2022
…0	Paray le Monial.......... **290** d.	0751	0851	1158	1351	1544	1751	1851	1951	2051
…1	Digoin.......... **290** d.	...	...	1210	...	...	...	...	...	...
…7	**Moulins sur Allier** .... **290** a.	...	...	1256	...	...	...	...	...	...
	Clermont Ferrand **330** .... a.	...	...	1422	...	...	...	...	...	...

	Ⓐ	⚒			⚒		Ⓑ	⑥	Ⓑ◇
Clermont Ferrand **330**.....d.	...	...	...	...	...	...	...	...	1742r
Moulins sur Allier...... **290** d.	...	...	...	...	...	...	...	...	1903
Digoin.......... **290** d.	...	...	...	...	...	...	...	...	1948
Paray le Monial.......... **290** d.	0609	0709	1009	...	1409	1609	1809	1909	1959
Montceau les Mines.......... d.	0639	0739	1039	...	1439	1639	1839	1939	2040
Montchanin .... d.	0652	0752	1052	...	1452	1652	1852	1952	2054
Dijon (see above) .... a.	...	...	...	...	...	...	...	...	2148n

Not Aug. 15, Nov. 1.
Also Aug. 15, Nov. 1.
Not Aug. 15.
Not July 14, Nov. 11.
1739 until July 10.
①②③④⑦ (not July 13, Nov. 10).
Not July 14, Aug. 16, Nov. 1, 2, 11.
- Not Nov. 11.

◧ – Subject to alteration Oct. 10–14, 29, 31, Nov. 14–18, 21–25.
¶ – Subject to alteration on ①–⑤ Nov. 28 - Dec. 9.
§ – Subject to alteration on ①–⑤ Nov. 14–25.
‡ – Subject to alteration June 6–10, 13–17, 21, 23, 24, 27–30, July 1, Sept. 19–23, 26–30, Oct. 1–7, 10–14, 17–21, 23, 30, 31, Nov. 22, 25.
◇ – Subject to alteration on Oct. 30, 31, Nov. 1.
⊖ – Conveys (12) Dijon - Montchanin - Clermont Ferrand and v.v. See panel below main table.

♥ – (2) Autun - Étang - Nevers and v.v.
⊠ – By 🚌 on † (arrives Autun 1346).
★ – Additional journeys Montchanin - Chagny - Chalon: Montchanin d. 0651 ⑥ and 1811 ⑥.
⊡ – Additional 🚌 journeys: **From Étang** at 0745 ⚒, 1445 Ⓐ and 1925 †. **From Autun** at 1209 †, 1506 Ⓐ, 1749 ⚒ and 1849 †.

374 DIJON - DOLE - BESANÇON

Local Serv

For *TGV* services see Table **370** (Paris - Dijon - Besançon - Basel) and Table **379** (Strasbourg - Besançon - Dijon).

km		Ⓐ		Ⓑ	Ⓐ		⚒			Ⓐ		Ⓐ	Ⓐ	Ⓐ	d						w			⊗	
0	**Dijon** 375 d.	0509	0613	0641	0709	0713	0741	0809	1009	1109	1213	1241	1349	1509	1609	1613	1646	1711	1741	1813	1841	1913	2009	2109	2
32	Auxonne d.	0529	0640	0701	0729	0740	0801	0829	1029	1129	1240	1301	1409	1529	1631	1640	1706	1740	1800	1840	1902	1941	2029	2129	2
46	Dole 375 d.	0540	0650	0710	0739	0750	0810	0839	1039	1138	1250	1310	1418	1538	1641	1650	1716	1750	1809	1850	1912	1951	2039	2139	2
91	**Besançon** Viotte a.	0605	0726	0737	0805	0826	0837	0905	1105	1205	1327	1337	1445	1605	1713	1726	1742	1826	1838	1927	1938	2026	2105	2205	2
	Belfort 378 a.	0726	0856	...	...	...	...	...	...	...	...	...	...	...	...	1856	...	1956	...	...	...	...	...	...	

	Ⓐ		⚒		Ⓐ	⚒			Ⓐ				Ⓐ			Ⓐ	Ⓒ		Ⓐ	w				†	
Belfort 378 d.	...	...	...	...	...	...	0604	...	...	...	...	...	...	...	...	...	...	...	...	...	1704	...	...	...	
Besançon Viotte d.	0514	0556	0607	0625	0656	0713	0733	0756h	0856	0956	1233	1356	1456	1556	1633	1656	1723	1733	1756	1823	1833	1933	2023	2121	2
Dole 375 d.	0542	0622	0632	0701	0722	0750j	0811	0822	0922	1022	1311	1422	1522	1622	1711	1722	1748	1811	1822	1848	1911	2011	2050	2150	2
Auxonne d.	0551	0631	0641	0710	0731	0759	0820	0831	0931	1031	1320	1431	1531	1631	1719	1731	1757	1820	1831	1857	1920	2020	2059	2159	2
Dijon 375 a.	0610	0651	0707	0743	0751	0818	0847	0851	0953	1051	1347	1451	1551	1651	1747	1751	1818	1847	1851	1917	1947	2047	2118	2218	2

d – ⑤–⑦ (also July 14, Aug. 15, Nov. 1, 10, 11).
h – 0754 on ① (also July 15, Aug. 16, Nov. 2; not Aug. 15).
j – Arrives 0740.
w – Not Ⓐ July 4 - Aug. 26.
⊗ – Subject to alteration on Aug. 31, Sept. 1.

375 PARIS - DIJON - LAUSANNE and NEUCHÂTEL

km						*TGV* 9261					*TGV* 9269		*TGV* 9773	*TGV* 9271				*TGV* 9273			*TGV* 9277	*TGV* 9277		
		①–⑤ d⊖	⚒	Ⓐ	Ⓐ	‡			⚒	†	‡	⊗	①–④ m	⑦ h	①–⑤ ⊙⊖	Ⓐ		◇			①–⑥ b◇	⑦ e		
0	**Paris** Gare de Lyon 370 d.	...	...	...	...	0757	...	...	...	...	1157	...	1211	1357	...	...	...	1557	...	...	1757	1757	...	
287	**Dijon** 370 a.	...	...	...	...	0928	...	...	...	...	1332	...	|	1528	...	...	...	1729	...	...	1929	1929	...	
287	**Dijon** 374 d.	...	*0509*a	...	*0641*	0931	...	1009	...	...	1334t	...	|	1531	...	...	1711	1732	...	1913	1932	1932	...	
333	Dole 374 376 d.	...	0614	...	0715	0959	...	1037	1118	1118	1401	...	|	1556	...	...	1748	1758	1814	1949	1958	1959	...	2
365	Mouchard 376 d.	...	0645	...	0740	|	...	...	1143	1143	|	...	|	|	...	...	...	|	1844	...	2015	|	...	2
389	Andelot 376 d.	...	0704	...	...	|	...	...	1203	1205	|	...	◐	|	...	...	...	|	1905	...	|	|	...	
410	Frasne d.	0538	0720	0817	...	1042	1055	...	1217	1219	1443	1455	|	1641	1715	1802	...	1842	1920	...	2043	2043	2052	
426	Pontarlier 🏛 a.	|	0735	0833	...	|	1106	...	1233	1235	|	1506	|	|	1725	1818	...	|	1936	...	|	|	2103	
490	**Neuchâtel 511** a.	|	...	...	...	|	1154	...	...	...	|	1554	|	|	...	...	...	|	...	...	|	|	2154	
434	Vallorbe 🏛 a.	0557	...	...	...	1057	...	...	...	...	1457	...	|	1657	...	...	...	1857	...	...	2057	2057	...	
480	**Lausanne** a.	...	...	...	...	1137	...	...	...	...	1537	...	1615	1737	...	...	...	1937	...	...	2137	2137	...	

				TGV 9260			*TGV* 9264					*TGV* 9268		*TGV* 9270	*TGV* 9270	*TGV* 9778					*TGV* 9272	*TGV* 9272		
	①–⑤ d⊖	Ⓐ	Ⓐ	①–⑥ b	Ⓐ		§	⚒				¶	①–⑤ ⊙⊖	⑤ f	⑦ e	①–④ m	Ⓐ				①–⑥ b◇	⑦ e	⑤⑦ z	
Lausanne d.	...	...	...	0623	...	...	0823	...	...	...	...	1223	...	1623	1623	1638	...	...	...	...	1823	1823	...	
Vallorbe 🏛 d.	...	...	...	0700	...	...	0900	...	...	...	...	1300	1652	1700	1701	|	...	...	...	...	1901	1900	...	
Neuchâtel 511 d.	...	...	...	|	0806	...	|	...	...	...	1206	|	|	|	|	|	...	...	...	1806	|	|	...	
Pontarlier 🏛 d.	0524	0555	...	|	0742	0855	|	1128	...	...	1256	|	|	|	|	|	1742	1828	...	1849	|	|	...	
Frasne d.	0534	0612	...	0715	0758	0906	0916	1145	...	...	1307	1316	1710	1718	1716	|	1758	1847	...	1900	1916	1916	...	
Andelot 376 d.	...	0625	...	|	...	...	|	1204	1204	...	...	|	...	|	|	◐	...	1902	...	...	|	|	...	
Mouchard 376 d.	...	0647	...	0743	...	...	|	1221	1221	...	...	|	...	|	|	|	...	1919	...	...	|	|	2121	
Dole 374 376 d.	...	0710	0722	0801	...	...	0958	1245	1245	1311	...	1402	...	1800	1759	|	...	1941	2011	...	1958	1959	2145	2
Dijon 374 a.	...	...	0751	0822	...	...	1024	...	...	1347	...	1425	...	1822	1822	|	...	...	2047	...	2022	2022	...	2
Dijon 370 d.	...	...	...	0825	...	...	1027	...	...	...	...	1428	...	1825	1825	|	...	...	...	...	2025	2025	...	
Paris Gare de Lyon 370 a.	...	...	...	1003	...	...	1203	...	...	...	...	1603	...	2003	2003	2049	...	...	...	...	2159	2203	...	

a – Ⓐ only.
b – Not Aug. 15, Nov. 1.
d – Not Aug. 1.
e – Also Aug. 15, Nov. 1.
f – Also July 13, Nov. 10; not Nov. 11.
h – Also Aug. 15, Nov. 1; not Nov. 6.
m – Not July 13, 14, Aug. 15, Nov. 1, 10.
t – 1336 on Ⓐ.
z – Also July 13, 14, Aug. 15, Oct. 31, Nov. 1, 10.
‡ – Subject to alteration on Oct. 9, 16, Nov. 5, 6.
§ – Subject to alteration on July 8, 12, 13, Oct. 9, 16, Nov. 5, 6.
¶ – Subject to alteration on Oct. 8, 15, Nov. 5, 6.
⊙ – Runs 18–19 minutes later on Aug. 15, Nov. 1. Subject to alteration Oct. 17–20, 24–27.
⊗ – Subject to alteration Sept. 26–30.
◇ – Subject to alteration on Oct. 8, 15.
◐ – Via Genève (Table **341**).
⊖ – 🚌12 Pontarlier - Frasne - Vallorbe and v.v.
TGV – *TGV Lyria*, 🄱, supplement payable, 🍸. Special 'global' fares including the reservation fee are payable for international journ

☛ See Table **970** for other *TGV* services Paris - Dijon and v.v.

376 DOLE / BESANÇON - MOREZ - ST CLAUDE

km		Ⓐ				p	⑤ v	Ⓐ s		⑤⑦ z	🚌 ⊖	🚌 ⑤⑦ c
0	**Dole** 375 d.	...	*0614*r	...	1014	*1118*	...	...	1814	...	...	*2014*t
	Besançon 378 d.	0601	|	1004	|	|	1640	1751	|	...	...	|
32	Mouchard 375 378 d.	0640	*0645*r	1034	1039	*1143*	1712	1820	1844	...	...	2044
56	Andelot 375 d.	...	0709	...	1101	1207	1735	...	1902	1910	1910	|
70	Champagnole d.	...	0740	...	1118	1221	1749	...	...	1923	1930	2126
105	Morez d.	...	0832	...	1212	1313	1844	...	...	2015	2017	2208
128	**St Claude** a.	...	0859	...	1240	1340	1912	...	...	2041	2057	2248

	① g	A	Ⓐ			⑤ f	①–④ n	🚌 Ⓐ		⑤⑦ z	①
St Claude d.	0444	0620	...	0954	...	1510	1551	...	1725	1725	
Morez d.	0516	0652	...	1029	...	1545	1626	...	1757	1757	
Champagnole d.	0603	0738	...	1147j	...	1631	1712	1740	1846	1846	
Andelot 375 d.	0619	0758	...	1158	...	1647	...	1800	1857	1909	
Mouchard 375 378 a.	0637	0816	0841	*1220*	1225	1705	...	1830	*1918*	1925	1
Besançon 378 a.	|	|	0910	|	1255	1738	...	|	|	1956	1
Dole 375 a.	*0710*	0845	...	*1245*	...	*1804*b	...	1917	*1941*	...	

ST CLAUDE - OYONNAX - BOURG EN BRESSE

km		⚒‡	⚒‡	🚌 †	🚌 ⚒	🚌 ⚒	Ⓐu	🚌 Ⓒ	🚌	🚌 Ⓐ	†¶	🚌
0	**St Claude** d.	0556	0647	0807	0810	1025	1247	1345	1610	1710	1745	1825
32	Oyonnax d.	0632	0724	0852	0855	1110	1324	1430	1655	1755	1823	1910
45	Brion Montréal § d.	0648	0740	0912	0920	1135	1341	1455	1720	1820	1838	1935
48	Nurieux Brion ◧ d.	0651	0744	0917	0927	|	1344	|	1727	1827	1842	|
81	**Bourg en Bresse** a.	0727	0822	1010	1020	1220	1422	1540	1820	1920	1922	2020
	Lyon P. Dieu 353 a.	0830	...	...	...	...	...	...	...	...	...	...

	🚌 Ⓐ	🚌 ⚒	🚌 Ⓒ	Ⓐ	🚌	🚌 ⑦	🚌 ⚒	🚌	Ⓑ¶		🚌
Lyon P. Dieu 353 d.	...	...	...	...	...	...	...	...	...	...	
Bourg en Bresse d.	0610	0740	1030	1038	1240	1335	1340	1605	1719	1821	19
Nurieux Brion ◧ d.	0701	|	|	1120	1336	|	|	|	1800	1901	20
Brion Montréal § d.	0708	0825	1113	1124	1343	1420	1425	1650	1804	1904	20
Oyonnax d.	0733	0850	1138	1139	1408	1440	1450	1715	1824	1920	21
St Claude a.	0809	0926	1214	1216	1444	1516	1526	1751	1902	1958	21

A – ⚒ to July 2; ⑥ July 9 - Aug. 20; ⚒ from Aug. 27 (not Oct. 20, 21, 24–28, 31, Nov. 2).
b – Connection by 🚌 from Mouchard.
c – Also July 14, Aug. 15, Nov. 1; not Aug. 14.
f – Also Oct. 31, Nov. 10; not Oct. 14, 21, Nov. 11.
g – Also July 15, Aug. 16, Nov. 2; not Aug. 15.
j – Arrives 1115.
m – Not July 13, 14, Aug. 15, Oct. 31, Nov. 1, 10.
n – Not July 4 - Aug. 25, Oct. 10–31, Nov. 1, 2, 10.
p – Not ①–⑤ Oct. 10–21.
r – ⚒ only.
s – Not July 4 - Aug. 26.
t – By train Dole - Mouchard.
u – Not Oct. 10–21.
v – Also Nov. 10; not Nov. 11.
z – Also July 13, 14, Aug. 15, Oct. 31, Nov. 1, 10.
⊖ – ①②③④⑥ (not July 13, 14, Aug. 15, Oct. 31, Nov. 1, 10).
‡ – Subject to alteration on Nov. 12.
¶ – Subject to alteration on Nov. 11.
◧ – For *TGV* connection Paris - Nurieux Brion and v.v. see Table 34
§ – Brion Montréal la Cluse.

376a BESANÇON - LE LOCLE - LA CHAUX DE FONDS

Subject to alteration July 4 - Aug. 26

km		①–⑤ a	①–⑤ a		Ⓐ	⑥ ⊡		⊗	Ⓐ	
0	**Besançon** Viotte d.	...	...	...	0700	0728	0935	1400	1725	1932
67	Morteau d.	0510	0618	0729	0828	0959	1102	1528	1857	2102
80	Le Locle 512 d.	0529	0639	0750	...	...	1140	1551	...	2121
88	**La Chaux de Fonds** 512 a.	0537	0648	0759	...	...	1147	1558	...	2128

	①–⑤ a		①–⑤ a		⚒ ⊗				Ⓐ	
La Chaux de Fonds 512 d.	0543	...	0656	0809	...	...	1608	1701	...	21
Le Locle 512 d.	0551	...	|	0817	...	...	1618	1711	...	
Morteau d.	0610	0633	0721	0837	1234	...	1637	1731	1936	22
Besançon Viotte a.	...	0801	...	1008	1401	...	1801	1903	2105	

a – Not July 14, Aug. 15.
⊡ – Includes a long stop at Le Valdahon (a. 0817, d. 0920).
⊗ – Subject to alteration Oct. 24–28.

al Services — DIJON - CHALON SUR SAÔNE - LYON — 377

For *TGV* services Dijon - Lyon and Paris - Dijon - Chalon sur Saône see Table **379**.

Certain services are subject to alteration on June 11, 12, Oct. 1, 2, 8, 9, 15, 16, 29, 30, Nov. 5, 6.

	Ⓐ		Ⓐ	†	⚒ s	Ⓐ		Ⓐ	⊗	Ⓐ		Ⓐ	†	⚒		Ⓐ	⊡	Ⓐ	⑥	†	Ⓐ	† ⊡	⚒	
Paris Bercy **371** d.	...	...	...	...	...	...	0738	...	0926	...	...	...	...	1338	...	...	1538	...	...	...	1731z	1738	...	...
Dijon **373** d.	0540	0640	0740	0840	0843	0942	1040	1140	1240	1345	1440	1540	...	1640	1640	1743	1848	1943	1950	2015	2040	2040	2050	2212
Beaune **373** d.	0600	0700	0800	0900	0902	1001	1100	1200	1300	1403	1500	1600	...	1700	1700	1802	1908	2001	2020	2052	2100	2100	2120	2241
Chagny d.	0612	0712	0812	0912	0913	1011	1112	1212	1312	1414	1512	1612	...	1712	1712	1812	1920	2012	2033	2104	2112	2112	2133	2253
Chalon sur Saône d.	0623	0723	0823	0923	0924	1023	1123	1223	1323	1426	1523	1623	...	1723	1723	1823	1931	2023	2043	2119	2123	2124	2143	2307
Mâcon Ville d.	0656	0756	0856	0956	0957	1056	1156	1256	1356	1459	1556	1656	1658	1756	1756	1856	2003	2056	...	...	2156	2156	...	...
Villefranche sur Saône ⊖ d.	0721	0821	0921	1021	1021	1121	1221	1321	1421	1524	1621	1721	1721	1821	1821	1922	2026	2121	...	...	2221	2221	...	...
Lyon Part Dieu a.	0744	0844	0944	1044	1044	1144	1244	1344	1444	1547	1644	1744	1744	1844	1844	1944	2048	2144	...	...	2244	2244	...	...
Lyon Perrache a.	...	...	...	...	...	...	...	...	...	...	...	...	...	...	...	...	2101	...	...	...	...	2257	...	...

	Ⓐ	Ⓒ	⚒ h	① g	Ⓐ	Ⓐ	⊗		Ⓐ	Ⓐ			Ⓐ		Ⓐ		Ⓐ		Ⓐ		Ⓐ		Ⓐ		⊡
n Perrache d.	...	...	...	0500	0604	...	...	...	...	0905	...	...	...	...	...	...	...	...	...	...	...	...	...	...	2104
n Part Dieu d.	...	...	...	0512	0616	...	0716	...	0816	0916	0916	...	1016	1116	1216	1316	1416	1516	1616	1716	1816	1916	2016	...	2116
franche sur Saône ⊖ d.	...	...	...	0537	0641	...	0741	...	0841	0941	0941	...	1041	1141	1241	1341	1441	1541	1641	1741	1841	1941	2041	...	2139
on Ville d.	...	...	0602	0602	0706	0735	0806	...	0906	1006	1006	...	1106	1206	1306	1406	1506	1606	1706	1806	1906	2006	2106	...	2202
lon sur Saône d.	0556	0607	0635	0635	0739	0817	0839	0913	0939	1039	1039	1117	1139	1239	1339	1439	1539	1639	1739	1839	1939	2039	2139	...	...
gny d.	0605	0617	0645	0645	0749	0827	0849	0922	0949	1049	1049	1127	1149	1249	1349	1449	1549	1649	1749	1849	1949	2049	2149	...	...
une **373** d.	0615	0629	0656	0656	0800	0839	0900	0941	1000	1100	1100	1139	1200	1300	1400	1500	1600	1700	1800	1900	2000	2100	2200	...	...
n **373** a.	0639	0658	0715	0715	0819	0910	0919	1011	1019	1119	1119	1210	1219	1319	1419	1519	1619	1719	1819	1919	2019	2119	2219	...	...
aris Bercy **371** a.	...	...	1022	1022	...	...	1222	...	...	...	...	...	...	1622	...	1823	...	2022	...	2222	...	...	...	...	...

Additional local trains DIJON - CHALON SUR SAÔNE and MÂCON - LYON ◇

	⚒	⚒		Ⓐ		Ⓐ		Ⓐ	Ⓐ		
n d.	0646	0725	0820	1050	1221	1450	1625	1650	1722	1750	1825
une d.	0716	0753	0853	1120	1250	1520	1653	1720	1748	1820	1853
gny d.	0728	0803	0903	1133	1303	1533	1703	1733	1804	1833	1903
lon sur Saône a.	0743	0818	0918	1143	1318	1543	1718	1743	1818	1843	1918

	Ⓐ	⚒	Ⓐ		⚒	Ⓐ			Ⓐ	Ⓑ	
Chalon sur Saône d.	0617	0717	0742	1242	1417	1617	1642	1717	1742	1814	1914
Chagny d.	0627	0727	0757	1255	1427	1627	1657	1727	1757	1829	1929
Beaune d.	0639	0739	0806	1306	1439	1639	1706	1739	1806	1840	1941
Dijon a.	0710	0810	0834	1334	1510	1710	1734	1810	1834	1910	2010

	Ⓐ	⚒⊡	Ⓐ	Ⓐ	⑥	Ⓐ	Ⓐ	⊡	Ⓐ	⊡
on Ville d.	0602	0635	0725	0735	0735	0825	0835	1235	1735	1835
franche sur Saône ⊖ d.	0636	0706	0750	0806	0807	0850	0906	1306	1806	1906
n Part Dieu a.	0701	|	0814	|	|	0914	|	|	|	|
n Perrache a.	...	0735	0826	0835	0840	0926	0935	1335	1835	1935

	Ⓐ	△	Ⓐ	Ⓐ	Ⓐ	⚒⊡	Ⓐ	Ⓐ	⊡	Ⓐ
Lyon Perrache d.	0726	0825	1325	1625	1633	1725	1734	1825	1925	2204
Lyon Part Dieu d.	|	|	|	|	1646	|	1746	|	|	2216
Villefranche sur Saône ⊖ d.	0755	0855	1355	1655	1710	1755	1810	1855	2000	2239
Mâcon Ville a.	0825	0925	1425	1725	1734	1825	1834	1925	2030	2302

Not Aug. 15.
Not Aug. 16, Nov. 2.
From Sens (Table **371**).
Change trains at Dijon on ⑤ (also July 13, Nov. 10).

⊡ – Subject to alteration on Nov. 11, 12.
△ – Subject to alteration on Nov. 11, 12, 13.
⊗ – Subject to alteration on June 6 – 17, July 18 – 22, Aug. 8 – 12, Sept. 19 – 23, 26 – 30, Oct. 1, 2, 9 – 14, 16, 24 – 30, Nov. 5, 6, 14 – 18, 21 – 25, Dec. 5 – 9.

◇ – Certain trains continue beyond Lyon to / from Valence.
⊖ – Villefranche is also served by 🚌 service to Mâcon Loché TGV station, connecting with *TGV* trains to / from Paris (Tables **340/1**).

cal Services — LYON - LONS-LE-SAUNIER - BESANÇON - BELFORT — 378

For *TGV* services Lyon - Besançon Franche-Comté TGV - Belfort Montbéliard TGV - (Strasbourg) via high-speed line see Table **379**.

	†	⚒	⚒	Ⓐ	Ⓐ	Ⓐ		Ⓐ	Ⓒ				⚒	*TGV* **6874** s	Ⓒ	Ⓐ	Ⓐ			Ⓐ	Ⓑ	Ⓐ	Ⓒ	⑤† f
Lyon Perrache .... **353** d.	...	...	...	...	...	...	0717	...	...	...	...	...	...	...	...	...	...	...	1617	1617	1712	1815	1817	2113
Lyon Part-Dieu .... **353** d.	...	...	...	...	...	...	0734	0941	0941	...	...	...	...	1432	...	...	...	...	1630	1630	1730	1830	1830	2125
Ambérieu **353** d.	...	...	...	...	...	...	|	|	|	...	...	...	...	|	...	...	...	...	|	|	1757	1859	1859	|
Bourg-en-Bresse.. **353** d.	...	...	...	...	...	0717	0816	1021	1020	...	...	...	...	1517	...	...	...	...	1719	1719	1817	1919	1919	2232
Lons-le-Saunier d.	...	0544	0613	0646n	...	0800	0859	1101	1100	...	...	1218	1501	1559	1605	1605	1701	1713	1801	1801	1857	2001	2002	2312
Mouchard d.	...	0627	0702	0722n	0802	0841	0937	1138	1140	...	1225	1302	1538	|	1641	1642	1737	1802	1841	1841	...	2042	2041	...
Besançon Viotte a.	...	0710	0742	0753n	0846	0910	1009	1209	1209	...	1255	1342	1609	1654	1709	1709	1809	1844	1909	1909	...	2109	2109	...
Besançon Viotte ... ▷ d.	0711	0712	...	0810	...	...	1011	1211j	...	1232	...	...	...	1657	...	1711	1811n	...	...	1911	...	...	2115	...
Montbéliard ▷ d.	0808	0808	...	0908	...	...	1110	1309j	...	1341	...	...	...	|	...	1809	1908n	...	...	2010	...	...	2213	...
Belfort ▷ a.	0824	0824	...	0924	...	...	1125	1324j	...	1356	...	...	...	1727z	...	1825	1924n	...	...	2025	...	...	2228	...

	⚒	Ⓐ	Ⓐ		Ⓐ	⚒	†		⚒		*TGV* **6837** s				⑥	Ⓐ	†	Ⓑ	Ⓐ		⑥	Ⓐ	Ⓐ		
fort ▷ d.	...	...	0504	...	0636n	0736	...	...	0936	...	1232z	1204	...	1336	1536	1536	1536	...	1636	...	...	1734	...	1838	1937
ntbéliard ▷ d.	...	...	0518	...	0653n	0751	...	...	0953	...	|	1218	...	1352	1553	1553	1552	...	1653	...	...	1749	...	1853	1952
sançon Viotte ▷ a.	...	...	0620	...	0749n	0849	...	...	1049	...	1259	1328	...	1449	1649	1649	1649	...	1749	...	...	1849	...	1951	2050
sançon Viotte d.	...	0601	...	0651	0750	0851	0851	1004	1052	1218	1302	...	1351	1451	1651	1651	1651	1727	1751n	1817	1850	1851	1925	1953	...
uchard d.	...	0642	...	0720	0821	0920	0921	1034	1121	1300	|	...	1423	1521	1722	1720	1721	1806	1822n	1900	1923	1923	2005	2023	...
ns-le-Saunier d.	0600	0730	...	0758	0859	1001	1001	...	1200	1344	1400	...	1500	1602	1800	1802	1802	...	1900n	1944	2001	2001	...	2102	...
urg-en-Bresse... **353** d.	0642	...	...	0844	...	1045t	1045	...	...	...	1442	...	...	1646	...	1843	1846	...	...	...	...	...	...	2146	...
bérieu **353** d.	|	...	...	0902	...	|	|	...	...	...	|	...	...	|	...	...	|	...	...	...	...	...	...	|	...
on Part-Dieu..... **353** a.	0731	...	...	0926	...	1126	1126	...	...	...	1526	...	...	1727	...	...	1927	...	...	...	...	...	...	2230	...
on Perrache .... **353** a.	0743	...	...	0947a	...	1139	1139	...	...	...	...	...	...	1739	...	...	1940	...	...	...	...	...	...	2243	...

ADDITIONAL LOCAL TRAINS BESANÇON - BELFORT

	Ⓐ J	Ⓐ	Ⓑ		Ⓐ					Ⓐ
Dijon **374** d.	...	0509	...	0613	...	...	...	1613	1711	...
sançon Viotte d.	0530	0608	0632	0732	1311	1511	1632	1732	1832	2011
ntbéliard d.	0640	0711	0741	0842	1408	1608	1741	1842	1942	2108
fort a.	0655	0726	0756	0856	1424	1624	1756	1856	1956	2124

		Ⓐ	Ⓐ	Ⓐ	†	Ⓐ					⚒
Belfort d.	0604	0704	0804	0836	0936	1136	1304	1704	1819	2036	2136
Montbéliard d.	0618	0718	0818	0853	0953	1153	1318	1718	1833	2053	2151
Besançon Viotte a.	0728	0828	...	0952	1051	1251	1428	1828	1943	2152	...
Dijon **374** a.	0847	...	...	...	...	...	...	1947	...	...	...

To July 1 / from Aug. 29.
– [12] Strasbourg - Lyon - Marseille and v.v. See also Table **379**. On ①–⑤ Oct. 3 – 14 service is diverted and does not call at Bourg-en-Bresse, Lons-le-Saunier or Besançon.

a – Ⓐ only.
f – Also Oct. 31, Nov. 10; not July 1 - Aug. 26, Nov. 11.
j – 4 minutes later on ① (also July 15, Aug. 16, Nov. 2).
n – Not July 4 - Aug. 26.
t – 1041 on ①–⑤ Aug. 29 - Sept. 30, Oct. 17 – 21, 24 – 28, Nov. 28 - Dec. 2.

z – Belfort Montbéliard TGV station (see Table **379**).
▷ – For additional trains Besançon - Belfort and v.v. see below main table.

Services from / to Lyon are subject to alteration on Nov. 11, 12, 13

Local trains BELFORT - MULHOUSE — 378a

	Ⓐ		Ⓐv	⚒	Ⓐ	Ⓒ	Ⓐv	Ⓐv	Ⓒ	Ⓐv	Ⓐ	Ⓐ	Ⓒ	Ⓐ	Ⓒ	Ⓐv	Ⓐv	Ⓐ	v	Ⓐ	†	Ⓐ	⚒v	†	Ⓐ	⚒v	†
lfort d.	0529	0558	0631	0700	0732	0737	0806	0906	1004	1006	1106	1206	1211	1303	1404	1406	1506	1606	1706	1736	1754	1806	1841	1855	1906	2006	2042
irch d.	0550	0618	0652	0721	0752	0757	0827	0927	1025	1027	1127	1227	1235	1327	1425	1427	1526	1627	1727	1758	1820	1829	1905	1921	1927	2026	2106
lhouse a.	0609	0636	0710	0740	0810	0815	0839	0939	1039	1039	1139	1239	1246	1339	1439	1439	1539	1639	1739	1809	1839	1840	1917	1939	1939	2039	2119

km		Ⓐ		Ⓐv	Ⓐ		Ⓐv		Ⓐv	Ⓒ	Ⓐ			Ⓐv	Ⓐ	†	⚒v	Ⓐv	Ⓐ	v	Ⓐ	Ⓐ	⚒v	†	Ⓐ	v	Ⓐ🚌
0	**Mulhouse** d.	0620	0650	0723	0801	0823	0923	...	1023	1123	1220	1315	...	1423	1523	1559	1619	1651	1720	1750	1823	1851	1922	1928	2020	2056	2204
16	Altkirch d.	0632	0702	0735	0815	0835	0935	...	1035	1135	1235	1334	...	1435	1538	1618	1638	1708	1740	1809	1839	1910e	1939	1947	2038	2110	2229
19	**Belfort** a.	0653	0726	0757	0837	0856	0956	...	1058	1156	1256	1355	...	1456	1558	1639	1659	1729	1800	1829	1859	1932e	1959	2011	2059	2130	2321

– 8 minutes later July 4 - Aug. 26.

v – Not Ⓐ July 18 - Aug. 26.

379 LUXEMBOURG - METZ - STRASBOURG - DIJON - LYON

TGV serv…

km		*TGV* 6839	*TGV* 6820	*TGV* 6886	*TGV* 9877 C	*TGV* 9877 D	*TGV* 9877 A	*TGV* 9877 B	*TGV* 6837 ◇	*TGV* 9879 L	*TGV* 9879 P	*TGV* 6815	*TGV* 6783 ⑤ h	*TGV* 6825 W T	*TGV* 6825 ⑤⑦ sT		*TGV* 9580 F	*TGV* 6783 ⑥ k	*TGV* 6827 Ⓒ H	6…
	Luxembourg 384 d.	...	...	...	...	...	0724	0724	...	1044	1124	...	...	...	...	...	...	...	...	
	Thionville 384 d.	...	...	...	...	...	0747	0747	...	1114	1147	...	...	...	...	...	...	...	...	
	Metz 384 d.	...	0600	...	0743	0743	0811	0811	...	1141	1211	...	...	...	...	...	...	...	...	
	Strasbourg 383 a.	...	|	...	0901	0901	0901	0901	...	1301	1301	...	...	...	...	...	...	...	...	
0	**Strasbourg** ⊕ 383 385 ⊕ d.	0635	|	...	0906	0906	0906	0906	1112	1309	1309	...	...	...	...	...	1615	...	1803	1
65	Colmar 385 d.	|	|	...	0933	0933	0933	0933	|	1337	1337	...	...	...	...	...	|	...	1833	
	Basel 385 d.	|	|	0732	|	|	|	|	|	|	|	...	...	...	...	...	|	...	|	
106	**Mulhouse** 370 d.	|	|	0756	1006	1006	1006	1006	1207	1407	1407	...	...	...	...	...	1708	...	1906	
151	Belfort Montbéliard TGV 370 d.	0737	|	0821	1033	1032	1033	1032	1232	1432	1432	...	...	...	...	...	1735	...	1932	1
233	**Besançon TGV** ⊖ 370 d.	0800	|	0845	1057	1057	1057	1057	1302v	1455	1455	...	...	...	...	...	1759	...	1958	2
	Nancy d.	|	0644	|	|	|	|	|	|	|	|	...	...	1512t	1512t	...	|	...	|	
	Toul d.	|	0705	|	|	|	|	|	|	|	|	...	...	|	|	...	|	...	|	
	Neufchâteau d.	|	0731	|	|	|	|	|	|	|	|	...	...	|	|	...	|	...	|	
	Culmont Chalindrey d.	|	0823	|	|	|	|	|	|	|	|	...	...	|	|	...	|	...	|	
	Paris Gare de Lyon **370** d.	|	|	|	|	|	|	|	⊙	|	|	...	1453	|	|	...	|	1653	|	
310	**Dijon** 370 a.	0828	0907	0911	|	|	|	|	|	1523	1523	...	1634	1727t	1727t	...	|	1834	2026	
310	**Dijon** 377 d.	0835	0921	0921	|	|	|	|	|	1532	1532	1612j	1644	1734	1734	1750	|	1844	2033	
347	Beaune 377 d.	|	|	|	|	|	|	|	|	|	|	1633j	1705	|	|	1820	|	1904	|	
377	**Chalon sur Saône** 377 d.	|	0956	0956	|	|	|	|	|	|	|	1652j	1724	|	|	1843	1855f	1925	|	
435	Mâcon Ville 377 d.	|	|	|	1220	1220	1220	1220	|	|	|	1721	...	1847	1847	...	|	...	|	
507	**Lyon** Part Dieu 377 a.	1002	1056	1056	1256	1256	1256	1256	1526	1702	1702	1756	...	1930	1930	...	1956	...	2201	2
	Lyon Perrache a.	|	|	|	|	|	|	|	|	|	|	|	...	|	|	...	|	...	|	
	Valence TGV **350** a.	|	|	|	|	1345	|	1345	1610	1744	1744	|	...	2011	|	...	|	...	|	
	Avignon TGV **350** a.	|	1209	1209	1407	1424	1407	1424	1645	|	|	1909	...	|	|	...	2108	...	2309	2
	Aix en Provence TGV **350** a.	|	1231	1231	1431	1447	1431	1447	|	|	|	1932	...	|	|	...	2131	...	2331	2
	Marseille **350** a.	|	1246	1246	1446	1502	1446	1502	1716	|	|	1946	...	|	|	...	2146	...	2349	2
	Toulon **350** a.	|	1341	...	...	...	...	...	...	|	|	2043	...	|	|	...	...	...	...	
	Nice **360** a.	|	1537	...	...	...	...	...	...	|	|	2237	...	|	|	...	...	...	...	
	Nimes **355** a.	1117	...	...	...	...	...	...	...	1832	1832	...	...	2057	2100	...	...	...	...	
	Montpellier **355** a.	1146	...	...	...	...	...	...	...	1902	1902	...	...	2126	2129	...	...	...	...	

km		*TGV* 6898 Ⓐ J	*TGV* 6898 Ⓒ H	*TGV* 6869 T	*TGV* 9582 F		*TGV* 9896 P⊡	*TGV* 9896 L	*TGV* 6814	*TGV* 6874	*TGV* 6784 ⑦ e	*TGV* 6882	*TGV* 6885	*TGV* 6864	*TGV* 9898 P	*TGV* 9898 L
	Montpellier **355** d.	...	...	0803z	...	...	0958	0958	...	...	...	1412	...	...	...	...
	Nimes **355** d.	...	...	0830	...	...	1027	1027	...	...	...	1443	...	...	...	...
	Nice **360** d.	...	...	|	...	...	|	|	0724	...	...	|	...	1223	...	...
	Toulon **350** d.	...	...	|	...	...	|	|	0917	...	...	|	...	1416	...	...
	Marseille **350** d.	0644	0644	|	0814	...	|	|	1014	1244	...	|	1514	1514	1614	1614
	Aix en Provence TGV **350** d.	|	|	|	0829	...	|	|	1029	1259	...	|	1529	1529	1629	1629
	Avignon TGV **350** d.	0715	0715	|	0851	...	|	|	|	1321	...	|	1551	1551	1652	1652
	Valence TGV **350** d.	0749	0749	0916	|	...	1115	1115	1124	|	...	1529	|	|	|	|
	Lyon Perrache d.	|	|	|	|	...	|	|	|	|	...	|	|	|	|	|
0	**Lyon** Part Dieu 377 d.	0834	0834	0954	1004	...	1204	1204	1208	1432	...	1608	1704	1704	1804	1804
72	Mâcon Ville 377 d.	|	|	1031	|	...	|	|	1245	|	...	|	|	|	1841	1841
130	**Chalon sur Saône** 377 d.	|	|	|	1108	1117	|	|	1315	|	1635	|	1806	1806	|	|
160	Beaune 377 d.	|	|	|	|	1139	|	|	1333	|	1655	|	|	|	|	|
197	**Dijon** 377 a.	|	0956	1130	|	1210	1338	1338	1352	|	1715	1738	1839	1839	|	|
197	**Dijon** 370 d.	|	1003	1140t	|	...	1346	1346	...	|	1725	1745	1847	1851	|	|
	Paris Gare de Lyon **370** a.	|	|	|	|	...	|	|	...	⊙	1907	|	|	|	|	|
274	Culmont Chalindrey d.	|	|	|	|	...	|	|	...	|	...	|	|	1944	|	|
348	Neufchâteau d.	|	|	|	|	...	|	|	...	|	...	|	|	2032	|	|
392	Toul a.	|	|	|	|	...	|	|	...	|	...	|	|	2055	|	|
425	**Nancy** a.	|	|	1352t	|	...	|	|	...	|	...	|	|	2117	|	|
	Besançon TGV ⊖ 370 d.	1020	1033	...	1205	...	1413	1413	...	1657v	...	1814	1917	|	2004	2004
	Belfort Montbéliard TGV 370 d.	1044	1057	...	1230	...	1437	1437	...	1730	...	1837	1943	|	2027	2027
	Mulhouse 370 d.	|	1122	...	1257	...	1502	1502	...	1804	...	|	2008	|	2101r	2101r
	Basel 385 a.	|	|	...	|	...	|	|	...	|	...	|	2027	|	|	|
	Colmar 385 d.	|	1149	...	|	...	1529	1529	...	|	...	|	...	|	2121	2121
	Strasbourg ⊕ 385 ⊕ a.	1147	1217	...	1344	...	1555	1555	...	1857	...	1943	...	|	2147	2147
	Strasbourg 383 d.	...	...	...	...	...	1559	1559	...	...	...	...	...	|	2200	2200
	Metz 383 384 a.	...	...	...	...	...	1648	1716	...	...	...	...	...	2157	2247	2318
	Thionville 384 a.	...	...	...	...	...	1711	1746	...	...	...	...	...	...	2311	...
	Luxembourg 384 a.	...	...	...	...	...	1735	1816	...	...	...	...	...	...	2324	...

NIGHT TRAINS ❦

STRASBOURG - NICE / CERBÈRE — 1, 2 cl. only ❦

	4283 4282 Ⓡ❦ ⑤–⑦	4283 4250 Ⓡ❦ ⑤–⑦
Strasbourg d.	2012	2012
Sélestat d.	2037	2037
Colmar d.	2051	2051
Mulhouse d.	2124	2124
Belfort d.	2216	2216
Besançon-Viotte d.	2326	2326
Avignon Centre a.	0521	|
Arles a.	0543	|
Marseille St Charles a.	0633	|
Toulon a.	0745	|
Nice **360** a.	0937	|
Nimes a.	...	0605
Montpellier a.	...	0634
Narbonne **355** a.	...	0742
Perpignan **355** a.	...	0819
Cerbère **355** a.	...	0908

	4382 4383 Ⓡ❦ ⑤–⑦	4350 4382 Ⓡ❦ ⑤–⑦
Cerbère **355** d.	...	1944
Perpignan **355** d.	...	2035
Narbonne **355** d.	...	2117
Montpellier d.	...	2225
Nimes d.	...	2256
Nice **360** d.	1903	|
Toulon d.	2058	|
Marseille St Charles d.	2201	|
Arles d.	2251	|
Avignon Centre d.	2313	|
Besançon-Viotte a.	0522	0522
Belfort a.	0631	0631
Mulhouse a.	0724x	0724x
Colmar a.	0800x	0800x
Sélestat a.	0814x	0814x
Strasbourg a.	0850x	0850x

LUXEMBOURG - NICE / CERBÈRE — 1, 2 cl. only ❦

	4251 4283 Ⓡ❦ ⑤–⑦	4251 4250 Ⓡ❦ ⑤–⑦
Luxembourg d.	1928	1928
Thionville d.	2008	2008
Metz d.	2037	2037
Nancy d.	2140	2140
Toul d.	2204	2204
Neufchâteau d.	2234	2234
Avignon Centre a.	0521	|
Arles a.	0543	|
Marseille St Charles a.	0633	|
Toulon a.	0745	|
Nice **360** a.	0937	|
Nimes a.	...	0605
Montpellier a.	...	0634
Narbonne **355** a.	...	0742
Perpignan **355** a.	...	0819
Cerbère **355** a.	...	0908

	4382 4351 Ⓡ❦ ⑤–⑦	435… 435… Ⓡ ⑤–…
Cerbère **355** d.	...	194…
Perpignan **355** d.	...	203…
Narbonne **355** d.	...	211…
Montpellier d.	...	222…
Nimes d.	...	225…
Nice **360** d.	1903	|
Toulon d.	2058	|
Marseille St Charles d.	2201	|
Arles d.	2251	|
Avignon Centre d.	2313	|
Neufchâteau a.	0622	062…
Toul a.	0655	065…
Nancy a.	0723	072…
Metz a.	0827	082…
Thionville a.	0852	085…
Luxembourg a.	0935	093…

A – ②③ July 5 - Aug. 31 (also July 28); ②③④⑦ Sept. 4 - Oct. 27; ②③④⑤⑦ from Oct. 30. Subject to alteration on July 6, Sept. 4, Oct. 2, 30.
B – ①④⑤⑥⑦ July 3 - Sept. 3 (not July 28); ①⑤⑥ Sept. 5 - Oct. 29; ①⑥ from Oct. 31. Subject to alteration on ① from Oct. 31.
C – ②③④⑦ June 7 - June 30.
D – ①⑤⑥ June 6 - July 2.
F – (12) Frankfurt - Strasbourg - Marseille and v.v. (Table **47**).
H – Runs daily July 2 - Aug. 28.
J – To July 1/ from Aug. 29.
L – Until July 2.
P – From July 3.
T – To/ from Toulouse (Table **321**).
W – ①②③④⑥ (not July 13).

e – Also Nov. 1; not Aug. 14.
f – 1900 from Aug. 29.
h – Also Nov. 10; not July 8, Nov. 11.
j – From Aug. 29 departs Dijon 1609, Beaune 1630, Chalon 1653.
k – Also July 14, Nov. 11; not Oct. 1, 8, 15.
r – Arrives 2050.
s – Also July 13. Subject to alteration on Sept. 23, 30, Nov. 18, 25.
t – Not ①–⑤ Sept. 19 – 30, ①–⑤ Nov. 14 – 25.
v – Besançon **Viotte** (on ①–⑤ Oct. 3 – 14 calls at Besançon TGV).
x – On ⑥⑦ arrives Mulhouse 0722, Colmar 0752, Sélestat 0807, Strasbourg 0832.

z – Departs 0801 on certain dates from Sept. 10.

TGV – Ⓡ, supplement payable, 🍸.

◇ – Subject to alteration on Nov. 11, 12.
⊡ – Subject to alteration on ①–⑤ Sept. 19 – 30, ①–⑤ Oct. 10 – 28 and ①–⑤ Nov. 14 - Dec. 2.
⊕ – Strasbourg departures may be up to 4 minutes earli… arrivals may be up to 4 minutes later on ①–⑤ Aug. 1… Sept. 30 and ①–⑤ from Nov. 21.
❦ – Subject to confirmation. **Service may be withdrawn from July 1.**
⊙ – Via Lons le Saunier and Bourg en Bresse (Table 37…
⊖ – Full name: Besançon Franche-Comté TGV.

PARIS - TROYES - BELFORT 380

'arning! Engineering work in the Chaumont area affects services on Ⓐ July 18 - Aug. 30 (also on July 23, 24, Aug. 28). Please confirm timings locally for journeys during this period. Certain afternoon / evening services are scheduled to run as normal on ⑤ July 29 - Aug. 26 and these are indicated in the relevant footnotes.

		1539	40407	11641	1643	11643	1643	1647	1647	1645		11649	1741	11743	1745	1749	11747	1747	11749	11841	1843	11847	11941	11943
	⚒	Ⓐ	Ⓐ	⚒	⑥	Ⓐ	†	Ⓐ	Ⓐ	⑥						†		⑥	Ⓐ			Ⓑ		⑦
									D				⊗		B		A			E	E		E	w
Paris Est ... d.	...	...	...	0642	0742	0742	0742	0842	0842	0912	...	1212	1312	1412	1512	1642	1642	1642	1712	1812	1842	1942	2042	2212
Nogent sur Seine ... d.	...	...	0651	0741	|	0840	0842	|	|	1013	...	1311	|	1511	|	|	1742	1742	1819	1914	|	2044	2141	2313
Romilly sur Seine ... d.	...	...	0703	0754	|	0853	0856	|	|	1026	...	1325	|	1525	|	|	1756	1756	1833	1927	|	2058	2154	2327
Troyes ... d.	...	0527	0724	0816	0910	0913	0918	1005	1007	1048	...	1346	1439	1546	1640	1810	1819	1819	1855	1950	2011	2119	2216	2348
Bar sur Aube ... d.	...	0553	0757	0852	|	...	|	...	|	|	...	1418	|	1619	|	1845	1854	1854	...	2025	|	...	2248	...
Chaumont ... **382** d.	...	0616	0818	0917	1001	...	1009	...	1057	1135	...	1440	1530	1642	1731	1911	1918	1918	...	2051	2103	...	2311	...
Langres ... **382** d.	...	0637	...	0937	|	...	|	...	|	|	...	1500	|	1702	|	1932	1940	1940	...	2112	|	...	2330	...
Culmont Chalindrey ... **382** d.	...	0647	...	0945	|	...	|	...	|	|	...	1508	|	1713	1758	1948	1949	1950	...	2120	|	...	2338	...
Dijon ... **382** a.	...	0747	...	...	|	...	|	...	|	|	...	...	|	...	|	|	...	|	...	...	|	...	...	...
Vesoul ... d.	0839	...	...	...	1104	...	1112	...	1206	1235	1239	...	1633	...	1837	2026	...	2029	...	...	2206	...	...	...
Lure ... **386a** d.	0856	...	...	...	1123	...	1132	...	1226	...	1256	...	1653	...	1857	2047	...	2049	...	...	2225	...	...	...
Belfort ... **386a** a.	0925	...	...	...	1144	...	1152	...	1252	...	1325	...	1714	...	1917	2108	...	2109	...	...	2246	...	...	...

	11640	11642	11644	40404	1942	1646	11742	11942	1742	11944		1840	1543	11842	1842	1844	11946	1848	11948	1946	1944	1545	1545		
	⚒	Ⓐ	Ⓐ	Ⓐ	⑥	Ⓐ	†	⚒				Ⓒ		Ⓐ	⑥	†				†		①–④	⑤	Ⓐ	†
							z		⊕	★								B	E		G	m	v		
rt ... **386a** d.	...	...	...	...	0459	0512	...	...	0820	...	1235	1320	...	...	...	1442	...	1648	...	1757	1806	...	...	1838	2035
... **386a** d.	...	...	...	...	0520	0533	...	...	0842	...	1303	1341	...	...	...	1503	...	1709	...	1819	1827	...	...	1906	2103
ul ... d.	...	...	...	...	0539	0552	...	...	0902	...	1321	1400	...	...	1521	1522	...	1729	...	1840	1846	...	...	1924	2121
on ... **382** d.	...	...	...	...	|	|	...	...	|	...	▬	|	1405r	...	|	|	1551r	|	...	|	|	1857	1857	...	...
ont Chalindrey ... **382** d.	...	...	0525	0610	0619	|	0644	0817	|	1047	...	|	1453	...	|	|	1644	|	1817	1916	1927	1951	1952	...	...
'res ... **382** d.	...	...	0535	0619	0629	|	0654	0826	|	1056	...	|	1503	...	|	|	1653	|	1826	1926	|	2003	2003	...	...
mont ... **382** d.	...	...	0558	0639	0651	0657	0716	0847	1003	1117	**11746**	1503	1524	...	1625	1625	1715	1833	1847	1946	1956	2022	2026	...	...
ur Aube ... d.	...	...	0620	0701	0712	|	0739	0909	|	1138		|	1545	...	|	|	1738	|	1909	2007	|	...	2048	...	...
es ... d.	0512	0602	0655	0732	0745	0742	0814	0945	1050	1212	1412	1550	1616	1712	1712	1711	1812	1920	1942	2041	2042	...	2118	...	...
lly sur Seine ... d.	0535	0625	0717	...	0806	0803	0836	1005	|	1233	1434	|	...	1733	1733	1733	1833	|	2003	2104	|	...	...	...	...
nt sur Seine ... d.	0548	0638	0730	...	0818	0817	0850	1017	|	1247	1448	|	...	1747	1747	1746	1847	|	2017	2117	|	...	...	...	...
s Est ... a.	0646	0746	0831	...	0916	0916	0946	1116	1216	1346	1546	1716	...	1846	1846	1846	1946	2046	2116	2216	2216	...	...	...	...

Ⓐ to July 15 / from Aug. 31 (also ⑤ July 29 - Aug. 26).
Ⓑ to July 17 / from Aug. 31 (also ⑤† July 29 - Aug. 28).
June 6 - July 1, Sept. 5–16, Oct. 31, Nov. 2–4 only.
Daily to July 17 / from Aug. 31 (also ⑤⑥† July 29 - Aug. 28).
⚒ to July 6 / from Aug. 31 (also ⑤⑥ July 29 - Aug. 27).

m – Not July 13, 14, Aug. 15, Oct. 31, Nov. 1, 10.
r – Not June 20–24; not Ⓐ Sept. 19 - Nov. 25.
v – Also Oct. 31, Nov. 10; not Nov. 11.
w – Also Aug. 15, Nov. 1; not Aug. 14.
z – Subject to alteration on Nov. 20, 27.

⊗ – Does not run Troyes - Belfort July 18–29, Ⓐ Aug. 1–30, ①–⑤ Sept. 19–30, Ⓐ Oct. 17 - Nov. 4, ①–⑤ from Nov. 21.
⊕ – Does not run Belfort - Troyes July 18–29, Ⓐ Aug. 1–31.
★ – Does not run Culmont - Chaumont Oct. 24–28. Does not run Culmont - Troyes on ①–⑤ Sept. 19 - Oct. 21.

PARIS - CHÂLONS EN CHAMPAGNE - BAR LE DUC 381

									2777						2785				2787				
	Ⓐ	Ⓐ	Ⓐ	Ⓒ	Ⓐ	⑥	†			Ⓐ		Ⓐ			Ⓐ	Ⓐ	⑤		⑦	Ⓒ	Ⓐ	⑤	†
	⊖	⊕			◇			▽	♥	◧					♥	n	v	k	e♥			f	
Paris Est ... d.	0636	0736	0836	0836	1036	1036	1036	1236	1428	1436	1636	1736	...	1836	1928	1936	1936	...	2028	2036	2136	2136	2236
Château Thierry ... d.	0724	0824	0924	0924	1124	1124	1124	1324	|	1524	1724	1831	...	1931	|	2031	2031	...	|	2124	2224	2224	2324
Épernay ... **382** d.	0752	0852	0948	0952	1151	1151	1152	1352	|	1552	1752	1859	...	1959	|	2059	2059	...	|	2152	2252	2252	2352
Champagne-Ardenne TGV . d.	|	|	|	|	|	|	|	|	1519	|	|	|	...	|	2010	|	|	...	2111	|	|	|	|
Châlons en Champagne 382 d.	0810	0910	1008	1010	1210	1210	1208	1410	1542	1610	1810	1914	1924j	2016	2036	2114	2116	2121	2134	2208	2308	2310	0008
Vitry le François ... **382** d.	0828	0928	...	1028	1228	1228	...	1428	1602	1628	1828	...	1941	2034	2056	...	2133	2142	2154	...	...	2328	...
St Dizier ... **382** a.	0846	*0954*	...	*1054*	*1251*	1246	...	1446	|	1646	*1906*z	...	1959	2052	|	...	2152	2200	|	...	...	*2354*	...
Bar le Duc ... **382** a.	...	0952	...	1052	1252	...	...	...	1626	...	1852	...	...	...	2120	...	...	...	2219	...	...	2352	...

					2778															2784				
	Ⓐ	⚒	⑥	Ⓐ	①–⑥	Ⓐ	②–⑤	E	†	⑥	⑥	Ⓐ	†	Ⓐ		Ⓐ		Ⓑ			Ⓐ	†	①–④	
					b♥		c					◧		d	⊗	◇	■			♥			m	
e Duc ... **382** d.	...	...	...	...	0611	...	...	...	...	...	0937	...	...	...	1133	1333	...	...	...	1713	...	...	...	1937
Dizier ... **382** d.	...	...	0553	0609	|	0636	...	0738	0930	0933	|	0937	...	1122	|	|	1537	...	1650	|	1737	1837	1937	|
le François ... **382** d.	...	...	0614	0628	0637	0658	...	0759	0950	0952	1002	0958	...	1142	1158	1358	1558	...	1710	1739	1758	1858	1956	2003
ons en Champagne . **382** d.	0516	0613	0632	0643	0655	0716	0815	0817	1007	...	1020	1016	1016	...	1216	1416	1616	1716	1728	1757	1816	1916	...	2021
ampagne-Ardenne TGV .. d.	|	|	...	...	0718	|	|	|	...	...	|	|	|	...	|	|	|	|	...	1821	|	|	...	|
nay ... **382** d.	0535	0633	...	...	|	0732	0833	0833	...	...	1038	1037	1037	...	1232	1432	1632	1733	...	|	1832	1932	...	2037
eau Thierry ... d.	0601	0701	...	...	|	0801	0901	0901	...	...	1102	1101	1101	...	1301	1501	1701	1801	...	|	1901	2001	...	2101
s Est ... a.	0653	0753	...	...	0801	0853	0953	0953	...	...	1153	1153	1153	...	1353	1553	1753	1853	...	1901	1953	2053	...	2153

①⑥⑦ (also July 14, Aug. 16, Nov. 1, 11).
Not Aug. 15.
Not July 14, Aug. 16, Nov. 1, 2, 11.
Not Oct. 3–14, Dec. 5–9.
Also Aug. 15.
Also July 13, Oct. 31, Nov. 10; not Nov. 11.
1922 on ⑥ Sept. 24 - Oct. 29.
Not Oct. 1, 8, 15, 22, 29.

m – Not July 13 - Aug. 30, Oct. 31, Nov. 1, 10.
n – Not Oct. 31.
v – Also July 13, Nov. 10; not Nov. 11.
z – *1852* on †; *1856* on ⑥.

♥ – *TGV train*, 🅁, supplement payable. 🍸. Subject to alteration from Aug. 29.
◇ – Subject to alteration Sept. 19 - Oct. 21. Does not run Châlons - Bar le Duc and v.v. Oct. 24–28, Nov. 2–25, Dec. 5–9.
⊕ – Does not run Châlons - Bar le Duc Sept. 19 - Oct. 21, Dec. 5–9.

⊖ – Does not run Châlons - St Dizier Oct. 3–14.
◧ – Subject to alteration Sept. 19 - Oct. 21.
▽ – Subject to alteration on ①–⑤ Sept. 19 - Oct. 21. Does not run Châlons - St Dizier Dec. 5–9.
⊗ – Subject to alteration on Ⓐ Sept. 19 - Oct. 21. Does not run Bar le Duc - Châlons on Dec. 5–9.
■ – Does not run St Dizier - Châlons on ①–⑤ Sept. 19 - Oct. 21, Dec. 5–9.
* – *188 km* via high-speed line.

REIMS - BAR LE DUC - METZ / NANCY 382

SERVICE UNTIL AUGUST 28. See Table **381** for services Paris Est - Épernay - Châlons en Champagne - Bar le Duc and v.v.

	Ⓐ	⚒	⚒	Ⓐ	Ⓒ	Ⓐ	⑥	Ⓐ	Ⓐ	†	Ⓐ	⑥	Ⓑ	Ⓐ	⑥	⚒	Ⓐ	Ⓐ	†	†	Ⓐ	†	⑥	†
								B																
Reims ... **382a** ♠ d.	...	...	...	0612	0743	...	...	...	...	...	...	...	...	...	...	...	...	1642	...	...	...	...	1740	1840
Épernay ... **381** ♠ d.	...	...	...	0644	0819	...	...	...	...	...	...	...	...	...	...	1612a	...	1714	...	...	...	...	1827	1927
Châlons en C. ★ **381 382a** d.	...	...	...	0704	0841	...	...	...	...	...	...	...	...	...	...	1633a	...	1734	...	...	...	...	1844	1943
Vitry le François .. **381 382a** d.	...	...	...	0723	0858	...	...	...	...	...	...	...	...	...	...	1650a	...	1756	...	...	...	...	1859	1958
Bar le Duc ... **381** ♥ d.	0554	0716	0726	0754	0924	1003	1113	1126	1213	1222	1257	1426	1526	1626	1713	1719	1726	1822	1826	1857	1903	1913	1924	2026
Metz ... ♥ a.	|	0814	|	|	|	|	|	|	|	|	1354	|	|	|	|	1817	|	|	|	1954	|	|	|	|
Commercy ... d.	0614	...	0745	0814	0944	1023	1138	1146	1238	1242	...	1446	1546	1646	1738	...	1746	1844	1846	...	1923	1938	1947	2046
Toul ... d.	0629	...	0759	0829	0958	1036	1157	1201	1257	1256	...	1501	1601	1701	1757	...	1801	1902	1901	...	1938	1957	2004	2105
Nancy ... a.	0654	...	0825	0854	1021	1100	1225	1225	1325	1320	...	1525	1625	1725	1825	...	1825	1928	1925	...	2002	2025	2028	2131

	Ⓐ	⑥	⚒		Ⓐ	Ⓒ	Ⓐ	Ⓐ	Ⓒ	Ⓐ	⑥	†	Ⓐ	Ⓐ	⑥	Ⓑ	†	Ⓐ	⑥	Ⓐ	†		Ⓑ	⑤
																		⊙				D		
cy ... d.	0632	0634	0834	1032	1234	1234	1334	...	1434	1534	1607	1607	1632	1707	1734	1734	...	...	...	1834	1834	1934	2034	2034
... d.	0651	0658	0858	1051	1258	1259	1359	...	1458	1559	1630	1634	1658	1732	1758	1758	...	...	...	1858	1900	1959	2058	2058
mercy ... d.	0705	0712	0912	1105	1312	1318	1418	...	1512	1612	1645	1652	1712	1751	1812	1812	...	...	...	1912	1919	2018	2112	2112
etz ... ♥ d.	|	|	|	|	|	|	|	1406	|	|	|	|	|	|	|	|	1739	1835	1836	|	|	|	|	|
le Duc ... **381** ♥ d.	0725	0732	0932	1125	1336	1342	1442	1503	1533	1632	1705	1716	1732	1815	1833	1833	1835	1936	1932	1932	1942	2042	2132	2134
le François ... **381 382a** d.	0750	...	...	...	...	...	...	1531	1602	...	...	...	...	...	1901	1901	...	...	...	...	...	...	...	2201
lons en C. ★ .. **381 382a** d.	0808	...	...	...	...	...	...	1550	1621	...	...	...	...	...	1918	1921	...	...	...	...	...	...	...	2216
rnay ... **381** ♠ d.	0830	...	...	...	...	...	...	1605	1645	...	...	...	...	...	1940	2005j	...	...	...	...	...	...	...	2241
ns ... **382a** ♠ a.	0900	...	...	...	...	...	...	...	1714h	...	...	...	...	...	2007	2038	...	...	...	...	...	...	...	...

Until July 15.
⚒ to July 16; ⑥ from July 23.
Ⓐ only.
1710 on ⑥.
Arrives 1940.
Not July 4 - Aug. 26.

⊙ – July 25 - Aug. 26 departs Metz 1826, arrives Bar le Duc 1921.
★ – Châlons en Champagne.
♥ – **Additional journeys** Metz - Bar le Duc - Metz (journey 56–61 minutes): **From Metz** at 0826 Ⓐ and 1235 ⑥.

♠ – Other trains Épernay - Reims and v.v. (journey 20–43 minutes). Timings may vary by a few minutes until July 2 (please check locally). **From Épernay** at 0622 Ⓐ **r**, 0649 ⚒, 0724 Ⓐ, 0725 ⑥, 0800, 0905 ⚒, 1003 Ⓐ **r**, 1155, 1240 ⚒, 1410, 1603 Ⓑ, 1605 ⑥, 1634 Ⓐ, 1730 Ⓐ, 1804, 1830 Ⓐ, 1907 ⚒, 2111 Ⓐ, 2156 Ⓒ and 2355 †. **From Reims** at 0500 Ⓐ, 0649 ⚒, 0709 Ⓐ, 0730 Ⓐ, 0825 ⚒, 0922 Ⓐ **r**, 0950, 1154 †, 1234, 1340 ⑥, 1356 Ⓐ, 1548, 1646 †, 1735 Ⓐ, 1800 Ⓐ, 1835 Ⓐ, 1932 Ⓐ, 2040 Ⓑ and 2142 ⚒.

382a REIMS - CHÂLONS EN CHAMPAGNE - DIJON

See Table **382** for other trains Reims - Vitry le François and v.v.
Warning! Engineering work in the Chaumont area affects services on Ⓐ July 18 - Aug. 31 (also July 23, 24, Aug. 28, Sept. 24, 25). Please confirm timings locally for journeys on these

km		⑥w	Ⓑ◇	❖	⑤f	Ⓐn	†	⑥	Ⓐ		z
0	**Reims** d.	0727	0731	1311	1509	1640	1733	1733z	1749	1833z	2042
58	**Châlons en Champ.** 381 d.	0805	0814	1355	1548	1721	1814	1817	1826	1924	2121
91	Vitry le François 381 d.	0825	0833	1415	1607	1744	1833	1837	1847	1941	2142
120	St Dizier 381 d.	0844	0854	1436	1628	1805	1854	1856	1906	1959	2202
193	Chaumont 380 d.	0928	0937	1519	1714	1852	1938	...	...	...	2246
227	Langres 380 d.	0949	0958	1541	1735	1915	1959	...	...	...	2308
238	Culmont Chalindrey 380 d.	0959	1009	1550	1745	1924	2009	...	...	...	2316
315	**Dijon** 380 a.	1046	1102	1636	1835	...	2102	...	...	...	...

	⑥	Ⓐ	⚒	Ⓐ	Ⓒ		⑤†s		Ⓑ
Dijon 380 d.	...	...	...	...	...	1405r	...	...	...
Culmont Chalindrey 380 d.	...	...	0533	0658	...	1453	...	...	...
Langres 380 d.	...	...	0544	0707	...	1503	...	...	...
Chaumont 380 d.	...	...	0606	0727	1130	1522	1528j	...	1734
St Dizier 381 d.	0553	0609	0654	0816	1214	...	1615	1650	1843
Vitry le François 381 d.	0614	0628	0719	0836	1235	...	1635	1710	1906
Châlons en Champ. 381 d.	0634	0646	0740	0856	1255	...	1656	1736	1927
Reims a.	0717	0728	0820	0936	1330z	...	1732	1815z	2004

f – Also July 13, Oct. 31, Nov. 10; not Nov. 11.
j – Not July 13.
n – Not July 13, 15.
r – Not June 20 – 24, Ⓐ Sept. 19 - Nov. 25.
s – Also July 13, Oct. 31, Nov. 10.
v – 3 – 8 minutes later on ⑥.
w – Subject to alteration on July 16.
z – Subject to alteration on Sept. 24, Oct. 1, 8, 15, 22, 29.
◇ – Subject to alteration Reims - Chaumont on Oct. 3 – 7, 10 – 14, 24
❖ – Subject to alteration Reims - Chaumont on July 7, 8, 11 – 13, Sept. 19 – 30, Oct. 17 – 21, 24, 25. Subject to alteration Reims - St Dizier on Oct. 3 – 7, 10 – 14, Dec. 5 – 9.

383 METZ and NANCY - STRASBOURG

For high-speed *TGV* services to / from southern France see Table **379**. *WARNING! Timings may vary by up to 12 minutes to July 2 and from Oct. 31.*

km		Ⓐ	⑥	Ⓐ	⚒ w	⚒	⚒	Ⓑ	Ⓐ	Ⓒ	⚒ ⊠	**1001** Ⓒ ★[R]	†	†	**2507** ⑦ e♥	Ⓐ	⚒	⑥	Ⓑ	Ⓐ	⑥	Ⓐ	†	†	†	Ⓐ
0	**Metz** ▶ d.	...	...	...	0629	...	0747	...	0933	0943	...	...	1047	...	...	...	1247	...	...	...	...	...	1547	...	1643	1643
	Paris Est d.	...	...	...	|	...	|	...	|	|	...	0735	|	...	1013	...	|	...	...	...	...	...	|	...	|	|
Δ	**Nancy** 387 d.	...	...	0612	|	0716	|	0816	|	|	1016	1028	|	1116	1150	1216	|	1316	1416	...	1516	1611	|	1613	|	|
	Lunéville 387 d.	...	...	0630	|	0733	|	0833	|	|	1034	|	|	1133	|	1234	|	1332	1433	...	1533	1628	|	1630	|	|
88	Sarrebourg ▶ d.	0608	0630	0653	|	0757	0851	0857	|	|	1057	|	1151	1157	1232	1259	1351	1355	1457	1547	1557	1652	1651	1656	|	|
91	Réding d.	0613	0633	0657	0719	|	...	0901a	1021	1030	|	|	...	|	|	|	...	1359	1501a	1551	|	1656a	...	|	1731	1733
114	Saverne d.	0630	0649	0712	0737	0815	...	0915	1037	1046	1115	|	...	1215	1249	1315	...	1414	1514	1607	1613	1710	...	1712	1746	1747
159	**Strasbourg** a.	0705	0732	0741	0811	0845	...	0945	1110	1115	1145	1144	...	1245	1312	1346	...	1443	1545	1641	1643	1741	...	1742	1816	1815

	⚒	Ⓐ	†	Ⓐ	Ⓑ	⚒	⑥	Ⓐ	†	†	†	**2583** Ⓑ h♥
Metz ▶ d.	...	1747	...	...	1843	...	1934	*1950*	1949	...	2047	...
Paris Est d.	...	|	...	...	|	...	|	|	|	...	|	1913
Nancy 387 d.	1716	|	1814	1816	|	1916	|	|	|	2016	|	2048
Lunéville 387 d.	1733	|	1831	1834	|	1934	|	|	|	2033	|	|
Sarrebourg ▶ d.	1759	1851	1855	1859	|	1957	2029	2055	2051	2057	|	2128
Réding d.	|	...	|	|	1933j	|	|	|	...	|	2137	|
Saverne d.	1814	...	1913	1915	1948j	2015	2046	2111	...	2115	2152	2145
Strasbourg a.	1845	...	1944	1945	2016	2045	2115	2145	...	2144	2219	2209

	2584 ①–⑥ b♥	Ⓐ	Ⓐ	Ⓐ	Ⓐ	⚒	⑥	†	Ⓐ	†
Strasbourg d.	0540	0615	...	0640	0715	0743r	0815	0816	0819	0946
Saverne d.	0607	0644	...	0710	0744	0812	0844	0845	0848	1015
Réding d.	|	|	...	0727	|	0827	|	|	|	1029
Sarrebourg ▶ d.	0624	0659	0702	|	0800	|	0900	0903	0907	|
Lunéville 387 d.	0649	0725	|	|	0826	|	0926	0926	0930	|
Nancy 387 a.	0709	0744	|	|	0844	|	0944	0944	0948	|
Paris Est a.	0846	...	|	|	...	|	...	...	...	|
Metz ▶ a.	...	...	0752	0815	...	0915	...	...	...	1115

	Ⓒ	⚒ v	⑥	Ⓐ ❖		†	Ⓐ	⑥	**1002** †◧ ★[R]	**2545** ⑦ e♥	Ⓑ	†	**1002** ⑥ ★[R]	⑥	Ⓐ	⑥	†	Ⓐ	†	Ⓐ	⑥	†	Ⓐ	Ⓐ	⑥	†
Strasbourg d.	1015n	...	1143	1144	1215	1240	1415	1515	1530	1546	1614	...	1642	1716	1719	...	1749	1751	1819	1819	1849	1846	1919	...	1949	1949
Saverne d.	1044n	...	1213	1212	1245	1312	1446	1544	|	1615	1645	...	|	1745	1749	...	1824	1828t	1848	1848	1918	1919	1949	...	2018	2019
Réding d.	|	...	1227	1227	|	1327	|	|	|	|	|	...	|	1759z	|	...	1839	1844t	|	1903	1932	|	2003	...	|	|
Sarrebourg ▶ d.	1059n	1109	|	|	1303	|	1504	1600	|	1631	1703	1715	|	1803	1807	1815	|	|	1906	1907	|	1942	2007	2011	2036	2034
Lunéville 387 d.	1126	|	|	|	1326	|	1526	1626	|	|	1725	|	|	1826	1830	|	|	|	1929	1930	|	|	2030	|	2059	2101
Nancy 387 a.	1144	|	|	|	1344	|	1544	1644	1643	1711	1744	|	1755	1844	1851	|	|	|	1947	1948	|	|	2048	|	2117	2118
Paris Est a.	...	|	|	|	...	|	...	...	1935	1846	...	|	2103	...	...	|	|	|	...	...	|	|	...	|	...	...
Metz ▶ a.	...	1211	1313	1315	...	1415	...	...	...	...	...	1817	...	...	...	1917	1925	1933t	...	...	2028	2031	...	2104	...	...

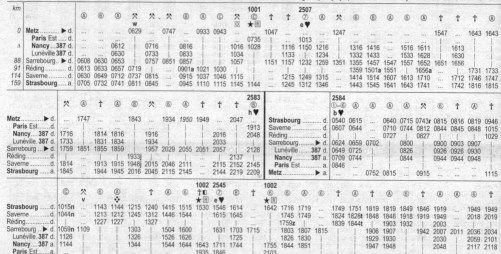

a – Ⓐ from July 4.
b – Not Aug. 15.
e – Also Aug. 15.
h – Not July 14.
j – 2 minutes earlier on †.
n – 4 minutes later on ⑥.
r – 0745 on ⑥.
t – 12 – 17 minutes **earlier** until July 1.
v – 25 minutes later on Ⓐ.
w – 2 – 5 minutes later on ⑥.
z – From July 9.
♥ – *TGV* train, [R], 🍷. Subject to alteration from Aug. 29.
★ – *INTERCITÉS 100% ÉCO.* Low-cost service via the classic route.
◧ – On July 14, Aug. 15, Nov. 1, 11 departs Strasbourg 1522, arrives Nancy 1653, Paris 1938.
Δ – Nancy - Sarrebourg: *80* km.
⊠ – Runs 61 – 66 minutes **earlier** on ①–⑤ until July
❖ – Runs 64 – 68 minutes later until July 1.
▶ – Additional journeys Metz - Sarrebourg and v.v. **From Metz** at 0610 Ⓐ, 1617 Ⓐ, 1717 Ⓐ and 181 **From Sarrebourg** at 0634 Ⓐ, 0636 ⑥, 0734 Ⓐ, 1209 †, 1409 ⑥, 1634 Ⓐ, 1743 Ⓐ and 1854 Ⓐ t

384 LUXEMBOURG - METZ - NANCY

Subject to alteration from Augus

For *TGV* trains Luxembourg - Metz - Paris see Table **390**. For long distance trains to Lyon and southern France see Table **379**.

km		Ⓐ	Ⓐ	⚒	Ⓐ		Ⓐ		⚒	ⒶJ		ⒶJ	†	⑥	ⒶJ		⊡	ⒶJ			⑥	
0	**Nancy** d.	0528	0620	0650	0720	0750	0820	0828	0850	0920	0950	1020	1028	1050	1120	1150	and at the same	2020	2050	2150	2250	...
28	Pont-à-Mousson d.	0553	0636	0706	0736	0806	0836	0853	0906	0936	1006	1036	1053	1106	1136	1206	minutes past	2036	2106	2206	2306	...
37	Pagny sur Moselle d.	0602	0643	0713	0743	0813	0843	0902	0913	0843	1013	1043	1102	1113	1143	1213	each hour until	2043	2113	2213	2313	...
57	**Metz** a.	0621	0658	0728	0758	0828	0858	0921	0928	0958	1028	1058	1121	1128	1158	1228		2058	2128	2228	2328	...

	Ⓐ	⚒	Ⓐ		Ⓐ		ⒶJ	⚒	†	Ⓐ		ⒶJ	⚒	ⒶJ		ⒶJ	⊠		ⒶJ		Ⓑ	Ⓒ
Metz d.	0602	0632	0702	0732	0802	0832	0902	0932	0939	1002	1032	1102	1132	1202	1232	1302	and at the same	1932	2002	2032	2132	2232
Pagny sur Moselle d.	0616	0646	0716	0746	0817	0846	0916	0946	0959	1016	1046	1116	1146	1216	1246	1316	minutes past	1946	2016	2046	2146	2246
Pont-à-Mousson d.	0623	0653	0723	0753	0824	0853	0923	0953	1006	1023	1053	1123	1153	1223	1253	1323	each hour until	1953	2023	2053	2153	2253
Nancy a.	0641	0711	0740	0811	0840	0911	0940	1011	1032	1041	1111	1140	1211	1240	1311	1340		2011	2040	2111	2211	2311

(NANCY -) METZ - LUXEMBOURG ⊖

km		Ⓐ	⚒	Ⓐ	⚒	Ⓐ		⚒	Ⓐ	†	⚒				Ⓐ	Ⓒ	Ⓐ		⑤f	D	Ⓒ	Ⓐ	Ⓐ	Ⓒ	Ⓐ
	Nancy ★ d.	...	...	0620	...	0720	0750z	0850k	...	0950	1050k	1150	1250	1350	1450	...	...	1550	...	...	1650	1650	1720	1750	...
0	**Metz** d.	0533	0633	0703	0733	0803	0833	0933	1025	1033	1133	1233	1333	1433	1533	1542	1603	1633	1701	1703	1733	1733	1803	1832	1833
18	Hagondange d.	0545	0645	0715	0745	0815	0845	0945	1045	1045	1145	1245	1345	1445	1545	1602	1616	1645	1713	1715	1745	1745	1815	1845	1845
30	Thionville d.	0557	0657	0727	0757	0828	0857	0957	1057	1057	1157	1257	1357	1457	1557	1617	1634	1656	1733j	1727	1757	1803j	1827	1857	1857
64	**Luxembourg** a.	0623	0723	0753	0823	0853	0923	1023	1123	1123	1223	1323	1423	1523	1623	1647	1702	1723	1802	1753	1823	1832	1853	1923	1923

		⚒		⑥	Ⓑ	Ⓒ	Ⓐ	Ⓒ	⑤⑥	
Nancy ★ d.	1850z	...	1950z	2050	...	2150	...	...	...	...
Metz d.	1933	1946	2033	2133	2146	2233	2246	2316	2316	...
Hagondange d.	1945	2002	2045	2145	2202	2245	2302	2332	2332	...
Thionville d.	1957	2017	2057	2157	2217	2257	2317	2343	2347	...
Luxembourg a.	2023	2047	2123	2223	2247	2323	2347	...	0017r	...

	Ⓐ	⑥	Ⓐ	Ⓐ	⑥	ⒶJ	Ⓐ		①g	E	Ⓒ
Luxembourg d.	0513	0538	0543	0613	0629	0644	0708	0738	0759	0808	0813
Thionville d.	0546	0604	0615	0646	0702	0716	0735	0805	0831	0835	0846
Hagondange d.	0557	0616	0626	0657	0713	0727	0746	0816	0842	0846	0857
Metz a.	0614	0627	0643	0714	0730	0744	0757	0827	0854	0857	0914
Nancy ★ a.	...	0711	...	...	0811	...	0840	0911z	...	...	...

	Ⓐ	ⒶJ		Ⓒ	Ⓐ			Ⓒ	Ⓐ	†	⚒		Ⓐ		Ⓐ		Ⓐ		ⒶJ		Ⓐ	Ⓑ	Ⓐ	Ⓒ	Ⓐ
Luxembourg d.	0838	...	0938	1013	1038	1138	1238	1338	1338	1413	1438	1538	1608	1638	1657	1738	1813	1838	1908	1938	2008	2013	2113	2138	2213
Thionville d.	0908	0935	1005	1046	1105	1205	1305	1404	1404	1444	1505	1605	1635	1705	1736j	1805	1846	1905	1935	2005	2035	2046	2146	2205	2246
Hagondange d.	0919	0946	1016	1059	1116	1216	1316	1416	1416	1455	1516	1616	1646	1716	1748	1816	1857	1916	1946	2016	2046	2057	2157	2216	2257
Metz a.	0931	0957	1027	1118	1128	1228	1328	1428	1432	1512	1527	1627	1657	1727	1758	1827	1914	1927	1957	2027	2057	2114	2214	2227	2314
Nancy ★ a.	...	1041	1111	...	...	1311	1411	1511	...	...	1611k	1711z	...	1811	...	1911	...	2011	...	2111z	...	...	...	2311	...

D – ①–④ (not July 13, 14, 18 – 28, Aug. 1 – 25).
E – ②–⑤ (not July 14, Aug. 16).
J – To July 15 / from Aug. 29.
f – Also July 13, 14; not July 22 - Aug. 26.
g – Also July 14, Aug. 16; not Aug. 15.
j – Arrives 8 – 10 minutes earlier.
k – ⑥ only.
r – Thionville - Luxembourg is subject to alteration on July 8.
z – Ⓒ only.
⊡ – The 1620, 1720, 1820 and 1920 from Nancy also run on Ⓐ July 18 - Aug
⊠ – Metz d. 1831 (not 1832). The 1702, 1802 and 1902 from Metz also run on Ⓐ July 18 - Aug. 26.
★ – See panel above for full service Nancy - Metz and v.v.
⊖ – French holiday dates apply.

STRASBOURG - MULHOUSE - BASEL 385

For *TGV* trains Paris - Strasbourg - Colmar see Table **390**. For *TGV* trains Luxembourg - Metz - Strasbourg - Mulhouse - Lyon - Marseille / Montpellier see Table **379**.

	Ⓐ	Ⓐ	Ⓐ	⑥	Ⓐ	Ⓐ	†	⑥	Ⓐ	Ⓐ	Ⓒ	Ⓐ		Ⓐ	Ⓒ		⚒	†			Ⓐ	Ⓒ	⑥⑦
Strasbourg d.	...	0518	0551	0547	0621	0651k	0650	0651	0721	0751	0751	0821	...	0851	0951	0951	...	1051	1151	1151	...	1251	1351	1351	...
Sélestat d.	...	0538	0610	0614	0640	0710	0710	0711	0740	0810	0816	0840	...	0910	1010	1016	...	1110	1210	1216	...	1310	1410	1416	...
Colmar d.	...	0550	0623	0626	0653	0723	0723	0723	0753	0823	0828	0853	...	0923	1023	1028	...	1123	1223	1228	...	1323	1423	1428	...
Mulhouse ▷ d.	0546	0616	0646	0654	0716	0746	0746	0746	0816	0846	0855	0916	0919	0946	1046	1055	1119	1146	1245	1255	1319	1346	1446	1455	1519
Basel ▷ a.	0609	0639	0709	*0750*	0739	0809	0820	0820	0839	0909	...	0939	0950	1009	1109	...	1150	1209	1309	...	1350	1409	1509	...	1550

	Ⓐ	†	Ⓐ	⑥	Ⓑ		Ⓐ	⑥	Ⓑ		Ⓑ	⑥	Ⓐ	①–⑤	†		†	Ⓐ	⚒	†	⚒	†	†	⑤⑥ f	①–④ m
bourg d.	1451	1521	1551	1551	1551	1621	1651	1721	1745	1751	1821	1851	1851	1921	...	1921	1951	2021	2051	2121	2121	2221	2221	2251	2321	2321
tat d.	1510	1540	1610	1610	1616	1640	1710	1740	1810	1810	1840	1912	1916	1940	...	1940	2010	2040	2117	2140	2146	2246	2248	2310	2346	2349
ar d.	1523	1553	1621	1623	1627	1653	1723	1753	1821	1823	1853	1924	1927	1953	...	1953	2023	2053	2131	2153	2159	2259	2301	2323	2359	0003
ouse ▷ d.	1546	1616	1646	1646	1653	1716	1746	1816	1849	1846	1916	1946	1955	2014	2019	2016	2046	2116	2154	2216	2220	2320	2324	2344	0020	0026
▷ a.	1609	1639	1709	1709	...	1739	1809	1839	...	1909	1939	2009	...	...	2050	2039	2109	2139	...	2239	...	...	...	...	...

	Ⓐ	⑥	Ⓐ	Ⓐ	Ⓐ		Ⓐ	Ⓒ	Ⓐ	Ⓐ			Ⓐ	Ⓐ	Ⓒ	Ⓐ			Ⓒ	Ⓐ			†	⑥	Ⓐ	⑥⑦
▷ d.	...	...	0521	0537	...	0621	0651	...	0721	0751	0821	0839	0851	...	...	0921	1021	1039	...	1121	1221	1321	...	...	1421	1439
ouse ▷ d.	0458	0533	0545	0600	0616	0646	0716	0735	0746	0816	0846	0910	0916	0923	0935	0946	1046	1110	1135	1146	1246	1346	1434	1435	1446	1510
ar d.	0519	0559	0604	0629	0644	0707	0737	0802	0807	0837	0907	...	0936	0958	1002	1006	1107	...	1202	1207	1307	1407	1501	1502	1507	...
tat d.	0532	0611	0616	0642	0657	0719	0749	0813	0819	0849	0919	...	0947	|	1013	1017	1119	...	1214	1219	1319	1419	1513	1514	1519	...
bourg a.	0558	0637	0636	0709	0724	0739	0809	0840	0839	0909	0939	...	1008	1034	1039	1037	1139	...	1239	1239	1339	1439	1540	1539	1539	...

	†	⚒	Ⓐ		①–⑥ ⊙	Ⓐ	⑥	Ⓑ	Ⓑ		①–⑥	Ⓐ	⑥	Ⓑ	Ⓑ	⑤†	†		⚒	Ⓐ	†	⑥	①–⑤	⑤ f	①–④ m	†
l ▷ d.	...	1521	1551	1621	1639	1651	...	1721	1751	1821	1839	1851	...	1921	1951	1951	...	2021	2021	2039	2121	...	2239	...	...	...
ouse ▷ d.	1532	1546	1616	1646	1710	1716	1735	1746	1816	1846	1910	1916	1935	1946	2014	2016	2035	2044	2046	2116	2146	2235	2310	2330	2335	2338
ar d.	1558	1606	1637	1706	...	1737	1802	1806	1837	1906	...	1937	2002	2007	...	2037	2102	...	2107	2136	2207	2301	...	2358	0002	0006
stat d.	1610	1619r	1649	1719r	...	1749	1814	1819	1849	1919	...	1950	2014	2019	...	2049	2114	...	2119	2148	2219	2313	...	0013	0015	0020
bourg a.	1636	1639	1709	1739	...	1809	1839	1839	1909	1939	...	2009	2039	2039	...	2109	2139	...	2139	2214	2239	2339	...	0040	0042	0048

Not Nov. 11.
Not ①–⑤ July 18 - Aug. 26.
0646 on Sept. 10.
Not July 14, Aug. 15, Nov. 1.
2 minutes earlier on ⑥.

Runs 4 minutes later on July 14, Aug. 15, Nov. 1, 11.
Subject to alteration on ①–③ Nov. 14 - Dec. 7.

▷ – **Other local trains** Mulhouse - Basel and v.v. (journey 31 minutes):
From Mulhouse at 0449①–⑤**h**¶, 0549①–⑤, 0619①–⑥, 0649①–⑤**h**, 0719, 0749Ⓐ, 0819①–⑤**h**, 1056①–⑤**h**, 1219①–⑤**h**, 1419①–⑥**h**, 1549①–⑤, 1619①–⑥, 1649①–⑤**h**, 1719①–⑥, 1749①–⑤, 1819**h**, 1849①–⑤, 1919①–⑥ and 1949Ⓑ**h**.
From Basel at 0609①–⑤**h**¶, 0639①–⑤, 0709①–⑥, 0739①–⑤**h**, 0809①–⑥, 0903①–⑤**h**, 1139①–⑤**h**, 1239, 1339①–⑤**h**, 1539①–⑥, 1609①–⑤**h**, 1709①–⑤, 1739**h**, 1809①–⑤, 1909Ⓑ**h**, 1939①–⑤, 2039⑥⑦ and 2139①–⑤**h**.

NANCY - ÉPINAL - REMIREMONT 386

Subject to alteration from August 29

	Ⓐ	Ⓐ	Ⓐ	⚒ n	⚒	⊗	Ⓑ ⊗	Ⓐ ⊗	⑥	†	Ⓐ ⊗	⚒ ⊗	⊗	⚒ ⊗	Ⓒ	⑥	2571 ♥	Ⓐ	⚒	Ⓒ	Ⓐ	Ⓐ		Ⓐ n	
Paris Est **390** d.	...	...	...	...	...	...	...	...	...	...	...	...	...	...	...	...	1228	...	...	...	...	...	...	...	...
Nancy d.	0520	0555	0620	0655	0720	0820	0855	0920	0920	1020	1022	1120	1220	1255	1320	1320	1403	1420	1420	1520	1555	1620	1620	1655	1720
Épinal a.	0613	0648	0713	0748	0813	0913	0948	1013	1013	1113	1115	1213	1313t	1348	1413	1413	1444	1513	1513	1613	1648	1713	1713	1748	1813
Épinal d.	...	...	0720	...	0820	0920	...	1020	...	1120	...	1220	1320	...	...	1420	1447	1520	...	1620	...	1720	...	...	1820
Remiremont a.	...	...	0750	...	0850	0950	...	1050	...	1150	...	1250	1350	...	...	1450	1508	1550	...	1650	...	1750	...	...	1850

		⚒	Ⓐ n		2573 Ⓐ ♥	2573 Ⓒ ♥	Ⓑ		⑥	Ⓐ	†
Paris Est **390** d.	...	...	...	...	1810	1810	...	...	...	...	...
Nancy d.	1755	1820	1855	1920	1955	1951	2020	2120	2205	2220	2255
Épinal a.	1848	1913	1953	2013	2036	2037	2113	2213	2304	2313	2354
Épinal d.	...	1920	...	2020	2039	2040	...	2220	...	...	...
Remiremont a.	...	1950	...	2050	2100	2102	...	2250	...	...	...

	Ⓐ	Ⓐ n	⚒	Ⓐ ⊙	2574 Ⓐ ♥	⚒		⚒	Ⓐ	⚒	Ⓐ
Remiremont d.	...	0511	...	...	0600	0615	...	...	0711	...	...
Épinal a.	...	0540	...	...	0619	0642	...	...	0740	...	...
Épinal d.	0502	0546	0546	0551	0621	0646	0646	0708	0746	0746	0808
Nancy a.	0602	0640	0640	0650	0704	0740	0740	0802	0840	0840	0902
Paris Est **390** a.	...	...	...	...	0846	...	...	...	...	...	...

		Ⓐ n	2576 Ⓒ ♥	⑥	Ⓐ ⊗	Ⓒ	Ⓐ n	⑥	Ⓐ ⊗	⊗	⊗	Ⓐ n	Ⓑ	2578 ①–⑥ b♥		Ⓐ	2580 ⑦ e♥	⚒	Ⓐ n	Ⓑ			Ⓐ n	⑥	†	Ⓐ
Remiremont d.	0811	...	0857	...	1011	1033	...	...	...	1211	1411	1511	...	1600	1615	...	1658	1711	...	1811	...	1911	...	...	...	...
Épinal a.	0840	...	0917	...	1040	1102	...	...	...	1240	1440	1540	...	1619	1642	...	1717	1740	...	1840	...	1940	...	...	...	...
Épinal d.	0846	0908	0920	0946	1046	1104	1108	1142	1146	1246j	1446	1546	1546	1622	1646	1708	1720	1746	1808	1846	1908	1946	2008	2046	2146	2208
Nancy a.	0940	1002	1002	1040	1140	1202	1202	1240	1240	1340	1540	1640	1640	1704	1740	1802	1803	1840	1902	1940	2002	2040	2102	2140	2240	2302
Paris Est **390** a.	...	...	1146	...	...	...	...	...	...	...	...	...	...	1845z	...	...	1945	...	...	...	...	...	...	...	...	...

Not Aug. 15
Also Aug. 15.
1242 on †.
Not Ⓐ July 18 - Aug. 26.
1316 on ⑥.

z – 1850 on ⑥ (also July 14).

♥ – *TGV* train, Ⓡ, 🍸, supplement payable.
⊗ – Subject to alteration on ①–⑤ Aug. 16 – 26.
⊙ – July 18 - Aug. 26 Épinal d. 0554, Nancy a. 0647.

ÉPINAL - BELFORT 386a

km		⚒	Ⓑ		Ⓐ n	🚌 B	⑥	†	†	⚒
0	**Épinal** d.	0627	0959	...	1455	1455	1455	1500	1849	1858
8	Luxeuil les Bains d.	0712	1042	...	1538	1620	1538	1543	1942	1944
6	Lure **380** d.	0726	1056	...	1552	1655	1551	1557	1955	1957
8	**Belfort** **380** a.	0758	1128	...	1616	1749	1618	1623	2025	2028

	Ⓐ m	A	n	🚌 B		Ⓑ	†	Ⓐ D	⚒ r
Belfort **380** d.	0601	0605	1101	1100	...	1704	2001	2032	2035
Lure **380** d.	0632	0634	1132	1156	...	1735	2032	2100	2103
Luxeuil les Bains d.	0646	0647	1146	1220	...	1748	2045	2113	2117
Épinal a.	0733	0733	1233	1340	...	1835	2133	2158	2202

July 20, 21, 22, 26, Oct. 12, 13, Nov. 25 only.
Aug. 16 – 19, 22 – 26, Sept. 19 – 23, 26 – 30, Oct. 17 – 21, 24 – 28, 31, Nov. 2 – 4, 21 – 25, 28 – 30, Dec. 1, 2, 5 – 9.
Ⓐ Oct. 17 - Nov. 3.

m – Not July 20, 21, 22, 26, Oct. 12, 13, Nov. 25.
n – Not Aug. 16 – 19, 22 – 26, Sept. 19 – 23, 26 – 30, Oct. 17 – 21, 24 – 28, 31, Nov. 2 – 4, 21 – 25, 28 – 30, Dec. 1, 2, 5 – 9.
r – Not Oct. 17 – 21, 24 – 28, 31, Nov. 1, 2, 3.

387 NANCY - LUNÉVILLE - ST DIÉ

Subject to alteration from Augu

km											2591									2593				
		Ⓐ ⊗	Ⓐ		Ⓐ ⊗	⑥	Ⓒ	Ⓐ			⚒	⑦e ♥	Ⓐ ⊗	†	Ⓐ		Ⓐ	⑥	Ⓐ	Ⓐ ♥	⑥	†	Ⓐ ⊗	Ⓐ ◇
	Paris Est **390** d.	...	...	...	...	...	...	...	...	...	...	1410	...	...	...	...	...	...	...	...	1810	...	...	...	...
0	**Nancy** 383 d.	0545	0650	0750	0850	0853	0953	1027	1250	1411	1550	1551	1650	1653	1711	1750	1850	1850	1911	1931	1955	1954	1955	...	2152
33	Lunéville 383 d.	0604	0711	0811	0911	0914	1014	1048	1311**h**	1429	1611	1614	1710	1713	1729	1811	1911	1911	1930	2006	2012	2014	2016	2030	2214
84	**St Dié** a.	0703	0753	0853	0953	0953	1104	1146	1353	1528	1653	1642	1753	1804	1829	1853	1953	2000	2027	...	2044	2053	2055	2122	2252

						2596	2596														2598				
	Ⓐ	⑥	Ⓐ	Ⓐ	†	Ⓐ ♥	⑥z ♥	Ⓐ	⑥	Ⓐ	⊗	Ⓐ	Ⓒ	Ⓐ	Ⓒ	Ⓐ	†	⚒ ⊗	Ⓐ	⑥	⑦e ♥	⑥	Ⓐ	†	Ⓐ
St Dié d.	0507	0607	0607	0631	0651	0713	0719	0731	0803	0807	0907	1031	1107	1207	1300	1431	1604	1607	1631	1707	1716	1804	1807	1900	1931
Lunéville 383 d.	0546	0645	0652	0728	0738	|	|	0829	0853	0849	0949	1130	1149	1249	1352	1530	1649	1649	1729	1749	1747	1851	1849	1949	2030
Nancy 383 a.	0605	0705	0714	0748	0757	0809	0806	0848	0913	0913	1010	1148	1210	1310	1412	1548	1708	1708	1748	1808	1807	1910	1908	2015	2048
Paris Est **390** a.	...	...	...	...	...	0946	0949	...	...	...	...	...	...	...	...	...	...	...	...	...	1945	...	...	...	...

e – Also Aug. 15.
h – 1314 on †.
t – On Ⓒ Lunéville d. 2051, Nancy a. 2112.
z – Also runs on July 14 (departs St Dié 0718).
♥ – *TGV* train, Ⓡ, 🍸, supplement payable.
◇ – Until July 1 departs Nancy 2154, Lunéville 2213.
⊗ – Not Ⓐ July 18 - Aug. 27.

388 STRASBOURG - ST DIÉ

km		Ⓐ	⑥	†	Ⓐ	Ⓐ	⑥	†	Ⓐ	⑥	Ⓑ
0	**Strasbourg** ‡d.	0655	0855	0955	0955	1205	1255	1355	1555	1755	1755
9	Entzheim Aéroport ✈ ‡d.	0705	0904	1006	1004	1213	1304	1406	1604	1804	1805
19	Molsheim d.	0714	0912	1016	1012	1221	1313	1417	1615	1812	1814
87	**St Dié** a.	0841	1033	1125	1131	1351	1437	1529	1736	1927	1929

	Ⓐ D	Ⓑ	⑥	⚒	Ⓐ	⑥	†	†	Ⓐ	⑥
St Dié d.	0734	0857**k**	0908	1212**j**	1538	1610	1653	1755	1800	1832
Molsheim d.	0846	1010**k**	1020	1338**j**	1704	1724	1805	1921	1917	1957
Entzheim Aéroport ✈ ‡d.	0854	1018**k**	1028	1345**j**	1712	1732	1815	1930	1924	2005
Strasbourg ‡a.	0901	1026	1039	1353	1721	1740	1826	1940	1932	2015

D – To July 15 and from Aug. 29.
j – On ⑥ St Dié d. 1215, Molsheim d. 1334, Entzheim d. 1342.
k – On † St Dié d. 0856, Molsheim d. 1005, Entzheim d. 1015.
‡ – Trains run between Strasbourg and Entzheim Aéroport (300 metres terminal) approx. 3 per hour on Ⓐ, 2 per hour on ⑥, 1 per hour on

388a ST DIÉ - ÉPINAL

km		Ⓐ¶	⑥	Ⓐ	⑥	Ⓐ¶	†	⑥	Ⓐ	Ⓒ⊖	Ⓐ¶	⑥	†
0	**St Dié** d.	0613*	0635	0733	1043	1215*	1403	1447	1648	1723	1833	2023	2030
60	**Épinal** a.	0714	0735	0833	1145	1315	1503	1547	1750	1823	1933	2123	2129

	Ⓐ	Ⓐ¶	⑥	Ⓐ¶	Ⓒ	†	⑥	Ⓐ¶	Ⓐ	⑥
Épinal d.	0610	0730*	0800	1210	1235	1543	1555	1645	1830	1835
St Dié a.	0714	0835	0900	1315	1335	1643	1655	1750	1935	1935

⊖ – Runs 7 minutes later on †.
¶ – By 🚌 July 18 - Aug. 27 (journey time 1 hr 40 minutes).
* – July 18 - Aug. 27 🚌 departs up to 24 minutes earlier.

389 PARIS - REIMS - CHARLEVILLE MÉZIÈRES - SEDAN

Subject to alteration on July

km						*TGV* 2709		*TGV* 2713	*TGV* 2715				*TGV* 2733			*TGV* 2743						*TGV* 2747		*TGV* 2751	*TGV* 2753
		Ⓐ ◇	Ⓐ	⑥ q	Ⓐ	①–⑥ b⊗	⊡	①–⑥ b	⑦ e	①⑤ g	⑥	△		●	Ⓐ ⊖			Ⓐ	Ⓒ		Ⓐ	Ⓑ h	Ⓑ	N	⑤ f
0	**Paris** Est d.	...	...	...	...	0758	...	0928	0928	...	...	...	1308	...	...	1528	...	...	...	...	...	1728	...	1828	1828
136	Champ. Ardenne TGV § d.	...	...	...	...	|	0937	|	|	...	...	...	|	...	...	|	...	1640	1640	1700**n**	...	|	...	|	|
147	**Reims** § a.	...	...	...	...	0844	0949	1014	1014	...	...	...	1354	...	...	1616	...	1646	1648	1708**n**	...	1816	...	1916	1916
147	**Reims** d.	0610	0705	0710	0740	0848	0951	...	1018	1130	1130	1232	...	1400	1500	...	1622	1650	1652	1718	1752	...	1826	1921	1921
186	Rethel d.	0632	0728	0732	0804	0911	1012	...	1041	1153	1153	1255	...	1424	1521	...	1645	1715	1715	1743	1818	...	1852	1943	1943
235	**Charleville-Mézières** a.	0704	0758	0805	0836	0938	1039	...	1108	1220	1220	1326	...	1452	1549	...	1713	1745	1745	1816	1844	...	1924	2010	2011
255	**Sedan** a.	0732	0820	0932	0903**p**	1004	1404	...	...	...	1255	1350**c**	...	1524	1615	...	1737*	1814	1814	1845	...	...	1948	2037	...

	TGV 2785		*TGV* 2757			*TGV* 2787		*TGV* 2759		*TGV* 2765
	Ⓐ	①–④ m	⑤⑦ r	⑤⑦ r	⑤ v	⑦ e	⑦ e	R	R	⑤⑦ r
Paris Est d.	1928	...	1958	...	...	2028	...	2058	...	2128
Champ. Ardenne TGV § d.	2007	2019	|	...	2052	2108	2116	|	...	|
Reims § a.	...	2029	2044	...	2058	...	2128	2145	...	2214
Reims d.	...	2031	...	2054	2128	...	2130	...	2154	2218
Rethel d.	...	2056	...	2118	2153	...	2153	...	2220	2241
Charleville-Mézières a.	...	2123	...	2144	2219	...	2219	...	2247	2308
Sedan a.	...	...	...	2206**p**	2241	...	2241	...	2310	2335

		TGV 2706		*TGV* 2778		*TGV* 2712	*TGV* 2714	*TGV* 2716		
	Ⓐ	Ⓐ	⚒	①–⑥ b	⚒	Ⓐ	Ⓐ	⑥ k	Ⓐ	
Sedan d.	...	...	0529	...	0602	...	0652	...	0702	0733**z**
Charleville-Mézières d.	0541	...	0601	...	0624	...	0718	...	0736	0801
Rethel d.	0608	...	0630	...	0657	...	0748	...	0808	0832
Reims a.	0632	...	0653	...	0721	...	0808	...	0831	0856
Reims § d.	...	0645	0655	...	...	0745	0813	0813	...	0900
Champ. Ardenne TGV § d.	...	|	0707	0718	...	|	|	|	...	0913
Paris Est a.	...	0731	...	0801	...	0831	0901	0901	...	...

			TGV 2722		*TGV* 2724	*TGV* 2726			*TGV* 2738			*TGV* 2750			*TGV* 2752	*TGV* 2754		*TGV* 2784		*TGV* 2756		*TGV* 2760	*TGV* 2762		
	Ⓐ	⑥	Ⓐ ⊗	†	⑦ e	⑥ k	L	Ⓑ △	Ⓑ h	⑥	Ⓑ	⑥ k	Ⓐ	†	Ⓐ	⑦ e	⚒		Ⓑ	⑤⑦ r		R	⑤⑦ r		j
Sedan d.	0806**p**	0815	1019	1025	...	1052	1116**x**	1211**x**	...	1448	1450**t**	...	1537**y**	1547	...	...	1633	...	1702**p**	...	1746	...	...	1914	2028
Charleville-Mézières d.	0840	0840	1048	1047	...	1118	1138	1240	...	1515	1516	...	1558	1608	...	1618	1700	...	1723	...	1814	...	...	1939	2049
Rethel d.	0911	0909	1117	1114	...	1147	1206	1312	...	1544	1545	...	1630	1636	...	1648	1730	...	1758	...	1847	...	...	2009	2118
Reims a.	0932	0930	1139	1136	...	1209	1229	1340	...	1604	1609	...	1655	1705	...	1709	1751	...	1824	...	1912	...	...	2028	2140
Reims § d.	...	...	1145	...	1145	1216	...	...	1415	...	...	1618	1700	1717	1713	1714	1753	...	...	1845	1918	1915	1945	...	...
Champ. Ardenne TGV § d.	...	...	|	...	|	|	...	...	|	...	...	|	1712	1725	|	|	1805	1821	...	|	1926	|	|	...	...
Paris Est a.	...	...	1231	...	1231	1302	...	...	1501	...	...	1704	...	...	1801	1801	...	1901	...	1931	...	2001	2031	...	...

J – To July 1 and from Aug. 29.
L – Ⓒ (daily July 9–31, Aug. 20 - Sept. 11, Sept. 24 - Oct. 2 and from Oct. 22). On Ⓐ Sedan d. 1114, Charleville d. 1139, Rethel d. 1208, Reims a. 1228.
N – ①②③④⑥⑦ (also Nov. 11; not July 13, Nov. 10).
R – ①②③④⑥ (also Nov. 11; not July 13, Aug. 15, Nov. 1, 10).
S – Ⓐ to Nov. 25 (not July 4 - Aug. 26, Oct. 3–7).
T – Not Oct. 3–7, Nov. 28–30, Dec. 1, 2, 5–9.

b – Not Aug. 15, Nov. 1.
c – Ⓒ only.
e – Also Aug. 15, Nov. 1.
f – Also July 13, Nov. 10; not Nov. 11.
g – ①⑤ from July 4 (also July 13, Nov. 2, 10; not Aug. 1–19, Sept. 12–23, Oct. 3–21, Nov. 11).
h – Not July 14, Nov. 11.
j – Not ①–⑤ Aug. 22 - Sept. 1.
k – Also July 14, Nov. 11.
m – Not July 13, 14, Aug. 15, Oct. 31, Nov. 1, 10.
n – Not ⑥.
p – Not July 3 - Aug. 28.
q – Not July 16, 23, 30, Aug. 27, Sept. 3, Nov. 5.
r – Also July 13, Aug. 15, Nov. 1, 10; not Nov. 11.
t – Not Sept. 5–9, 12–16, 19–23, Dec. 7.
v – Also July 13, 14, Oct. 31, Nov. 10.
x – Not Sept. 5–9, 26–30, Dec. 7.
y – Not Dec. 7.
z – 0710 on ⑥ to July 2/from Sept. 3. 0726 on Ⓐ July 4 - Aug.
TGV – Ⓡ, supplement payable, 🍸.
* – 1734 on †.
◇ – Runs 16–20 minutes later on ②–⑤.
⊗ – Subject to alteration Reims - Sedan and v.v. on ①–⑤ until Ju
⊖ – Subject to alteration Aug. 1–19. Terminates at Charleville Sept. 5–16.
⊡ – Subject to alteration on ①–⑤ to July 8, ①–⑤ Sept. 5 - Oct. Nov. 14–18, 25, 29, 30, Dec. 5–9.
△ – Subject to alteration on ①–⑤ to July 8, Aug. 1–5, 8–12, 16– Sept. 12–16, 19–23, Oct. 3–7, 10–14, 17–21.
● – Subject to alteration on ①–⑤ to July 1, Aug. 1–5, 8–12, 16– Sept. 5–9, 12–16, 19–23.
§ – For full service see Table **391a**.

389a CHARLEVILLE MÉZIÈRES - LONGWY and METZ

Subject to alteration on July 16, August 13–15

km		Ⓐ ◇	Ⓐ G	⑥ t	⑥	†		
	Reims **389** d.	0610	0705	0710**q**	1400	1400	1622	1946
0	**Charleville-Mézières** 389 d.	0711	0806	0812	1459	1459	1719	2046
20	Sedan 389 a.	0732	0820	0832**r**	1524	1524	1737**v**	2106
20	Sedan d.	0734	0822	0834**r**	1526	1526	1738**v**	2108
69	Montmédy d.	0805	0853	0905**r**	1557	1601	1809**v**	2138
91	Longuyon 392 d.	0823	0906	0921	1610	1616	1824	2159
107	**Longwy** 392 a.	|	...	|	|	|	|	2211
	Hayange d.	0853	...	0951	1640	1651	1853	...
	Thionville a.	|	...	|	|	|	1902	...
170	**Metz** a.	0918	...	1018	1718	1718	...	...

	Ⓐ	Ⓒ	Ⓐ H	⑥		
Metz d.	...	...	...	1300	1728	...
Thionville d.	...	...	...	|	|	1910
Hayange d.	...	...	...	1326	1755	1917
Longwy 392 d.	0540	0643	...	|	|	|
Longuyon 392 d.	0559	0701	0930	1357	1824	1945
Montmédy d.	0614	0715	0945	1414	1842	1958
Sedan a.	0648	0746	1015	1446	1912	2026
Sedan 389 d.	0702	0815**k**	...	1448	1914	2028
Charleville-Mézières 389 a.	0731	0835**k**	...	1506	1934	2044
Reims **389** a.	0831	0930**k**	...	1604	2028	2140**j**

G – From Oct. 17 (also July 15
H – From Oct. 17 (not Dec. 1, 6
j – Not ①–⑤ Aug. 22 - Sept.
k – ⑥ only.
q – Not July 16, 23, 30, Aug. 2 Sept. 3.
r – 2–5 minutes earlier on Ju 16, 23, 30, Aug. 27, Sept.
t – Not Oct. 22, 29, Nov. 5.
v – 3 minutes earlier on †.
◇ – 15–21 minutes later on ②-

PARIS - STRASBOURG - COLMAR

For other connecting trains Strasbourg - Colmar and v.v., see Table **385**

TGV trains: 🅁, 🍸 *ICE* trains: 🅁, ✕	*ICE* **9571**	*TGV* **9561** ①–⑥	*TGV* **2407** ♠	*TGV* **2365**		*ICE* **9573** Ⓑ	*TGV* **9593** ⑥		*TGV* **2421**	*TGV* **9575**	*TGV* **2371** Ⓑ h	*ICE* **9563**	*TGV* **9577** Ⓑ ⊙	*TGV* **2443**	*TGV* **2457** Ⓑ h	*TGV* **9579**	*TGV* **2377**	*TGV* **2583** Ⓑ h		*TGV* **2465**		*TGV* **2471** ⑤⑦ w
Paris Est d.	0637	0720	0744	0925	...	1042	1042	...	1255	1353	1454	1520	1555	1655	1725	1755	1855	1913	...	2040	...	2155
Strasbourg a.	0826	0907	0949	1111	...	1237	1238	...	1447	1541	1642	1708	1742	1850	1917	1952	2041	2209	...	2230	...	2342
Strasbourg 385 d.	0831	0913	...	1116	...	1246	1246	...	...	1546	1646	1713	1747	...	...	2007	2046	...	...	...	...	...
Stuttgart Hbf **931** a.	0952	|	...	|	...	1409	1409	...	...	1709	|	|	1909	...	...	2149	|	...	...	...	...	...
Frankfurt Hbf **912** a.	...	1058j	...	|	...	...	...	...	...	...	|	1858j	...	...	...	...	|	...	...	...	...	...
Sélestat 385 ■ a.	...	...	...	|	...	...	...	...	...	...	|	...	...	...	...	...	2104	...	...	...	...	...
Colmar 385 ■ a.	...	...	...	1143	...	...	...	...	...	...	1711	...	...	...	...	...	2119	...	...	...	...	...

	TGV **2404** Ⓐ	*TGV* **2350** ①–⑥ b	*TGV* **2410** Ⓐ	*TGV* **2352** ⑦ e	*TGV* **9578** ①–⑥	*ICE* **9568** Ⓑ	*TGV* **9576** ⊙	*ICE* **9566** ⑥		*ICE* **9574**	*TGV* **2358** ⚒	*TGV* **2358** †	*TGV* **2430**	*TGV* **2440** Ⓑ h	*ICE* **9572** Ⓑ	*TGV* **9592** ⑥	*TGV* **2450**		*TGV* **2364** Ⓑ h♥	*TGV* **9560**	*TGV* **9570**	*TGV* **2470** ⑤ f	*TGV* **2474** ⑦ e
nar 385 ■ d.	...	0637	...	0710	...	...	...	...	...	...	1242	1256	...	...	...	...	...	...	1744	...	...	...	...
stat 385 ■ d.	...	0653	...	0723	...	...	...	...	...	...	|	|	...	...	...	...	...	...	|	...	...	...	...
ankfurt Hbf **912** d.	...	|	...	|	...	0658k	...	0856k	...	...	|	|	...	...	...	...	...	...	|	1657k	..	...	...
uttgart Hbf **931** d.	...	|	...	|	0649	|	0849	|	...	1049	|	|	...	...	1449	1449	...	...	|	|	1849	...	...
sbourg 385 a.	...	0713	...	0741	0813	0847	1012	1047	...	1213	1307	1322	...	...	1612	1612	...	...	1812	1911	2013	...	...
sbourg d.	0646	0718	0746	0746	0821	0859	1016	1102	...	1227	1312	1327	1447	1546	1634	1634	1658	...	1816	1918	2019	2057	2139
s Est a.	0835	0907	0935	0935	1024	1049	1205	1253	...	1419	1505	1516	1635	1735	1833	1833	1850v	...	2013	2132	2224	2248	2335

PARIS - METZ - LUXEMBOURG

For other connecting trains Metz - Luxembourg and v.v., see Table **384**

TGV trains: 🅁, 🍸	*TGV* **2803** ①–⑥ b		*TGV* **2809** z	*TGV* **2809** ⑤		*TGV* **2815**		*TGV* **2817** ⑤⑦ w	*TGV* **2617** Y		*TGV* **2827** ①–④ m	*TGV* **2831** ⑤–⑦ t		*TGV* **2621** Ⓑ h	*TGV* **2833**	*TGV* **2635** Ⓑ h	*TGV* **2839**		*TGV* **2643** ①–⑥ b	*TGV* **2843** ⑦ e		*TGV* **2647** ⑤⑦ w
Paris Est d.	0740	...	0840	0840	...	1029	...	1340	1340	...	1440	1540	...	1640	1740	1840	1940	...	2040	2040	...	2140
Champagne-Ardenne TGV d.	|	...	|	|	...	1112	...	|	|	...	|	|	...	|	|	|	|	...	|	|	...	|
Meuse TGV a.	|	...	|	|	...	|	...	|	|	...	|	|	...	|	|	|	|	...	|	|	...	|
Metz a.	0904	...	1004	1005	...	1204	...	1503	1504	...	1604	1703	...	1804	1904	2004	2105	...	2204	2204	...	2304
Metz 384 d.	0909	...	1009	1010	...	1208	...	1508	...	...	1609	1708	...	...	1909	...	2109	...	...	2209	...	...
Thionville 384 a.	0927	...	1029	1029	...	1227	...	1527	...	...	1627	1727	...	...	1927	...	2127	...	...	2227	...	...
Luxembourg 384 a.	0953	...	1054	1054	...	1253	...	1553	...	...	1653	1753	...	...	1953	...	2153	...	...	2253	...	...

	TGV **2650** Ⓐ	*TGV* **2853** Ⓐ	*TGV* **2654** ⑦ p	*TGV* **2855** ①–⑥ b		*TGV* **2861** ⑦ d	*TGV* **2861** ①⑥ c	*TGV* **2660** ②–⑤ u		*TGV* **2865**		*TGV* **2869**		*TGV* **2672**	*TGV* **2676** ⑤–⑦ t		*TGV* **2881** Ⓑ h		*TGV* **2682** ①–④ m	*TGV* **2877** ⑤–⑦ t	*TGV* **2891** Ⓐ	*TGV* **2684** ⑦ e	*TGV* **2893** ⑦ e
embourg 384 d.	...	0605	...	0640	...	0809	0809	...	...	1009	...	1309	...	...	...	...	1709	...	...	1809	1859	...	2003y
nville 384 d.	...	0628	...	0703	...	0831	0832	...	...	1033	...	1333	...	...	...	...	1732	...	...	1832	1925	...	2026y
z 384 a.	...	0646	...	0721	...	0850	0851	...	...	1051	...	1351	...	...	...	...	1750	...	...	1851	1947	...	2044
z d.	0623	0650	0725	0726	...	0855	0856	0856	...	1056	...	1356	...	1556	1656	...	1755	...	1850	1856	1951	1956	2049
se TGV d.	|	0720	|	|	...	|	|	|	...	|	...	|	...	|	|	...	1825	...	|	|	|	|	|
npagne-Ardenne TGV a.	|	|	|	|	...	|	|	|	...	|	...	|	...	|	|	...	|	...	1937	|	2038	|	2136
s Est a.	0750	0820	0850	0850	...	1020	1020	1020	...	1220	...	1520	...	1720	1820	...	1924	...	2020	2020	2122	2120	2220

PARIS - NANCY

Certain trains continue beyond Nancy to Épinal and Remiremont (Table **386**) or to Lunéville and St Dié (Table **387**).

TGV trains: 🅁, 🍸	*TGV* **2501** ① g	*TGV* **2407**	*TGV* **2503**		*TGV* **2505** ①–⑥ b	*TGV* **2507** ⑦ eS	*TGV* **2815**		*TGV* **2571**	*TGV* **2591** ⑦ e	*TGV* **2509** Ⓐ	*TGV* **2777** B	*TGV* **2513** ⑥ d	*TGV* **2515** Ⓑ h	*TGV* **2517** Ⓐ	*TGV* **2573**	*TGV* **2583** Ⓑ hS	*TGV* **2785** Ⓐ B	*TGV* **2595** ⑦ e	*TGV* **2519** ①–⑥ b	*TGV* **2787** ⑦ eB	*TGV* **2521** ⑤⑦ w
Paris Est d.	0710	0744	0810	...	1013	1013	1029	...	1228	1410	1410	1428	1513	1610	1713	1810	1913	1928	2010	2010	2028	2113
Champagne-Ardenne TGV d.	0752	0829	|	...	|	|	1109	...	|	|	|	1511	|	1652	|	|	|	2007	|	|	2108	|
Meuse TGV d.	|	0853	0912	...	|	|	...	...	|	1512	1512	...	|	|	|	1913	|	...	2112	2112	...	|
Nancy a.	0847	...	0948	...	1143	1143	...	...	1359	1547	1548	...	1644	1747	1845	1947	2044	...	2147	2148	...	2244

	TGV **2531** ① g	*TGV* **2778** ①–⑥ bB	*TGV* **2584** ①–⑥ bS	*TGV* **2533** ⑦ e	*TGV* **2596** ⑥ ⊗	*TGV* **2597** Ⓐ	*TGV* **2535** Ⓐ	*TGV* **2577** Ⓒ	*TGV* **2537**	*TGV* **2541**	*TGV* **2543** Ⓐ	*TGV* **2579** ①–⑥ b★	*TGV* **2545** ⑦ eS	*TGV* **2784** B	*TGV* **2581** ⑦ e	*TGV* **2547** ①–⑥ b	*TGV* **2364** Ⓑ h	*TGV* **2682** ①–④ m	*TGV* **2549** ⑤⑥ q	*TGV* **2890** Ⓐ	*TGV* **2551** Ⓑ h	*TGV* **2892** ⑦ e	*TGV* **2553** ⑦ e
cy d.	0613	...	0716	0811	0813	0816	1011	1016	1224	1430	1611	1711	1716	...	1812	1816	...	...	1916	...	2016	...	2116
se TGV d.	|	...	|	0849‡	0849	|	|	|	1301	|	|	|	|	...	|	|	...	...	|	...	|	...	|
npagne-Ardenne TGV d.	|	0718	|	|	|	|	1107	|	|	|	1708	|	|	1821	|	|	1932	1940	|	2041	|	2139	|
s Est a.	0746	0801	0846	0949	0949	0946	1150	1146	1401	1602	1750	1845	1846	1901	1945	1946	2013	2020	2046	2122	2146	2220	2246

PARIS - SAARBRÜCKEN (- FRANKFURT)

Timings valid July 3 - December 10 (see also note ▶)

TGV trains: 🅁, 🍸 *ICE* trains: 🅁, ✕	*TGV* **9551**		*ICE* **9553**		*ICE* **9555** Ⓑ		*ICE* **9557** Ⓑ	*TGV* **9559** ⑥	
Paris Est d.	0906	...	1301	...	1710	...	1906	1906	...
Lorraine TGV d.	|	...	1418	...	|	...	|	|	...
Forbach 🏛 a.	1045	...	|	...	|	...	2047	2047	...
Saarbrücken Hbf a.	1055	...	1457	...	1857	...	2057	2057	...
Frankfurt (Main) Hbf **919** ▶ a.	1258	...	1658	...	2058	...	2258	2258	...

	ICE **9558** ①–⑤	*ICE* **9586** ⑥	*ICE* **9556** ①–⑤	*ICE* **9554** ⑥	*ICE* **9554** ⑦	*TGV* **9552** Ⓑ	*TGV* **9552** ⑥		*ICE* **9550** Ⓑ
Frankfurt (Main) Hbf **919** ▶ d.	0558	0658	0856	1058	1058	1258	1258	...	1858
Saarbrücken Hbf d.	0800	0902	1101	1307	1307	1501	1501	...	2101
Forbach 🏛 d.	0811	0913	|	|	1318	|	1512	...	2112
Lorraine TGV d.	|	|	|	|	|	|	1544¦	...	2144
Paris Est a.	0951	1053	1251	1454	1458	1650	1658¦	...	2259

To / from Bar le Duc (Table **381**).
To / from Strasbourg via Sarrebourg (Table **383**).
①②③④⑥ (not July 13, Aug. 15).

Not Aug. 15.
Also Aug. 16.
Also July 14.
Also Aug. 15.
Also July 13.
Also Aug. 16; not Aug. 15.
Not July 14.
26 – 35 minutes later July 16 - Aug. 28.
8 – 31 minutes **earlier** July 16 - Aug. 28.

m – Not July 13, 14, Aug. 15.
p – Not July 3, Aug. 15.
q – Also July 13, 14.
t – Also July 13, 14, Aug. 15.
u – Not July 14, Aug. 16.
v – 1905 on ⑥ (also July 3).
w – Also July 13, Aug. 15.
y – 4 minutes earlier on July 10.
z – Not ⑤.

TGV – 🅁, supplement payable, 🍸.
ICE – 🅁, supplement payable, ✕.

‡ – 0846 on Aug. 15.
¦ – From Sept. 3 departs Lorraine 15454, arrives Paris 1701.
⊗ – Also runs on July 14 (departs Nancy 0811, Meuse 0846).
♠ – Also calls at Champagne-Ardenne TGV (d. 0829) and Meuse TGV (d. 0856).
♥ – Also calls at Champagne-Ardenne TGV (a. 1929).
★ – On ⑥ (also July 14) calls additionally at Meuse TGV (d. 1751) and arrives Paris 1850.
▶ – Frankfurt timings are subject to alteration July 16 - Aug. 28 (arrivals are 18 – 21 minutes later, departures 13 – 21 minutes earlier).
■ – Journeys to / from Sélestat and Colmar are subject to alteration Aug. 16 – 28.
⊙ – To / from München (Table **32**).

391 STRASBOURG - NORTHERN and WESTERN FRANCE

SERVICE FROM JUL

SEE NOTE ⊠	TGV 9890	TGV 5487	TGV 5470	TGV 5450	TGV 5450	TGV 5422	TGV 5452	TGV 5424	TGV 5424	TGV 5456	TGV 5488	TGV 9894	TGV 9894	TGV 5454
				Ⓐ	Ⓒ			⑥	Ⓑ	Ⓒ	Ⓑ	Ⓑ	⑥	
	d	A	r		s		B	k	h	B	h	m		w
Strasbourg d.	0608	0731	0731	0812	0812	1000	1231	1244	1244	1431	1510	1510	1510	1631
Lorraine TGV d.	0646	0812	0812	0858	0858	1037	1310	1321	1322	1509	1548	1548	1552	1711
Meuse TGV d.	|	|	|	0924	0924	1058	|	|	|	|	|	|	|	|
Champagne-Ardenne TGV d.	0725f	0900	0900	0950	0950	1130	1353	1401	1404	1549	1632	1632	1631	1754
Paris Charles de Gaulle ✈ a.	0757f	|	|	|	|	1201	|	1433	1436	|	1703	1703	1704	|
Lille Europe a.	0856	|	|	|	|	...	|	1528v	1537t	|	|	1758z	1758z	|
Brussels Midi/Zuid a.	0943	|	|	|	|	...	|	...	...	|	|	1845z	1843z	|
Marne la Vallée - Chessy § a.	...	0928	0928	1025	1025	...	1428	...	...	1623	1728	...	...	1826
Massy TGV a.	...	1005	1005	1105	1105	...	1505	...	...	1705	1803	...	...	1905
Le Mans a.	...	1057	1057	|	|	...	|	...	...	|	1857	...	...	|
Angers a.	...	1139	|	|	|	...	|	...	...	|	1941	...	...	|
Nantes a.	...	1218	|	|	|	...	|	...	...	|	2019	...	...	|
Laval a.	...	...	1149	|	|	...	|	...	...	|	...	...	...	|
Rennes a.	...	...	1228	|	|	...	|	...	...	|	...	...	...	|
St Pierre des Corps a.	...	...	...	1159	1159	...	1600	...	...	1758	...	...	...	1959
Futuroscope a.	...	...	...	|	1238	...	|	...	...	|	...	...	...	|
Poitiers a.	...	...	...	1242	|	...	1642	...	...	1842	...	...	...	2041
Angoulême a.	...	...	...	1335	1335	...	1732	...	...	1935	...	...	...	2135
Bordeaux St Jean a.	...	...	...	1437	1437	...	1837	...	...	2037	...	...	...	2237

SEE NOTE ⊠	TGV 9870		TGV 5478	TGV 5441	TGV 5406	TGV 5406	TGV 5446	TGV 5442	TGV 9874	TGV 5480	TGV 5460	TGV 5416	TGV 5445	TGV 5449
			①–⑥		Ⓐ	Ⓒ	①							⑦
			c	q			D	B		A	b		w	E
Bordeaux St Jean d.	...	...	...	0723	...	...	0923	1123	...	...	...	...	1523	1723
Angoulême d.	...	...	...	0826	...	...	1026	1226	...	...	...	...	1626	1826
Poitiers d.	...	...	...	0917	...	...	1117	1317	...	...	...	...	1716	|
Futuroscope d.	...	...	...	|	...	...	|	|	...	...	...	...	1725	1921
St Pierre des Corps d.	...	...	...	1001	...	...	1200	1359	...	...	...	...	1802	2000
Rennes d.	...	...	...	|	...	...	|	|	...	...	1433	...	|	|
Laval d.	...	...	...	|	...	...	|	|	...	...	1511	...	|	|
Nantes d.	...	...	0735	|	...	...	|	|	...	1433	|	...	|	|
Angers d.	...	...	0814	|	...	...	|	|	...	1513	|	...	|	|
Le Mans d.	...	...	0857	|	...	...	|	|	...	1602	1602	...	|	|
Massy TGV d.	...	...	0955	1055	...	...	1255	1455	...	1656	1656	...	1855	2055
Marne la Vallée - Chessy § d.	...	...	1031	1131	...	...	|	1536	...	1731	1731	...	1946p	2135
Brussels Midi/Zuid d.	0717	...	|	|	...	...	|	|	1517	|	|	...	|	|
Lille Europe d.	0802	...	|	|	...	...	|	|	1602	|	|	1800	|	|
Paris Charles de Gaulle ✈ d.	0859	...	1058p	|	1246	1323	1352p	|	1659	|	|	1859	|	|
Champagne-Ardenne TGV a.	0929	...	1129	1202	1315	1352	1426	1605	1729	1759	1759	1929	2017	2203
Meuse TGV a.	|	...	|	|	1342	1419	|	|	|	|	|	|	2044	|
Lorraine TGV a.	1009	...	1216	1244	1402	1439	1512	1648	1813	1846	1846	2014	2105	2248
Strasbourg a.	1049	...	1305	1328	1441	1518	1553	1728	1901	1928	1928	2058	2145	2328

A – Daily July 3 - Aug. 28; ⑤–⑦ from Sept. 2 (als Nov. 1, 10).
B – July 3 - Aug. 28 only.
D – ① July 4 - Aug. 22 (also Aug. 16; not Aug. 1
E – ⑦ July 3 - Aug. 28 (also Aug. 15).

b – Not Oct. 1, 8, 15, Nov. 26.
c – Not Aug. 15, Oct. 1, 8, 15, Nov. 1, 26.
d – Not Oct. 31, Nov. 13.
f – 5 minutes later on ① (also Aug. 16, Nov. 2; not Aug. 15).
h – Not July 14, Nov. 11.
k – Also July 14, Nov. 11.
m – Not July 14.
p – Arrives 16 – 21 minutes earlier.
q – Not Oct. 1, 8, 9, Nov. 26.
r – Not Oct. 1, 8, 9, 15, Nov. 26.
s – Not Nov. 26.
t – 1545 until July 15.
v – 1540 on July 9; 1545 on July 14.
w – Not Oct. 1, 8, Nov. 26.
z – Until July 15 arrrives Lille 1804, Brussels 1901

TGV – Ⓡ, supplement payable, 🍸.

⊠ – Service from July 3. See May edition for servi to July 2.
§ – Station for Disneyland Paris.

CONNECTING 🚌 SERVICES (✆ 03 87 78 67 09 for further details).
Bus services connect with the trains in Table **391** on the following routes: Nancy - Lorraine TGV (journey 35 minutes); Metz - Lorraine TGV (journey 25 minutes); Verdun - Meuse TGV (journey 25 minutes).

391a REIMS - CHAMPAGNE ARDENNE TGV

Certain trains continue to / from destinations in Table **389**

	⚒	⑥	ⒶD						s				p	ⒷJ	ⒷH	⚒	†			w	Ⓐ	⑦e	
Châlons en Champagne **382** d.	...	...	0646	...	...	...	...	...	...	...	...	...	...	...	...	...	...	...	...	...	...	...	
Reims d.	0655	0732	0734	0837	0900	1010	1045	1147	1237	1330	...	1502	1607	1632	1635	1700	1717	1753	1918	2000	2015	2050	2
Champagne-Ardenne TGV a.	0707	0743	0746	0845	0913	1018	1053	1155	1245	1338	...	1510	1615	1640	1645	1712	1725	1805	1926	2008	2025	2100	2

	⚒	Ⓑz	⑥				t			J		Ⓑ	Ⓐ	⑥k	Ⓑh		Ⓑ	⑥	⑤f	E	⑦e	†p	(
Champagne-Ardenne TGV d.	0800	0904	0905	0937	1050	1120	1211	1327	1416	1520	1640b	1700	1720	1809	1812	1947	2019	2025	2052	2052	2116	2150	2
Reims a.	0808	0918	0913	0949	1057	1128	1223	1335	1424	1528	1648	1708	1728	1821	1823	1955	2029	2037	2058	2104	2128	2159	2
Châlons en Champagne **382** a.	...	0956	...	...	...	...	1326r	...	...	...	...	...	...	...	...	...	...	...	...	...	...	...	

D – From St Dizier (Table **382a**).
E – ①–④ (not July 13, 14, Aug. 15, Oct. 31, Nov. 1, 10).
G – ⑦ July 3 - Aug. 28 (also Aug. 15).
H – Until July 1.
J – From July 3.

b – 1638 to June 11 (also July 16).
e – Also Aug. 15, Nov. 1.
f – Also July 13, 14, Oct. 31, Nov. 10.
h – Not July 14, Nov. 11.
k – Also July 14, Nov. 11.

p – Not July 3 - Aug. 28.
r – Not Sept. 12 – 16, 24, Oct. 1, 8, 12, 15, 17 – 22, 29, Nov. 2 – 4, 7 – 10, 14 – 18, 21 – 25.
s – From June 12.

t – Not Ⓒ July 30 - Aug. 28.
w – 3 minutes earlier June 12 - Ju
z – On ⑦ Sept. 25 - Oct. 30 depa Champagne-Ardenne 0910 ar terminates at Reims (a. 0923).

392 LONGWY - NANCY / LUXEMBOURG

Longwy - Nancy

km		Ⓐ	⚒ z	①–⑤ G	Ⓒ n	①–⑤ G	Ⓒ	⑦ cv	ⒶE 🚌	Ⓐ D	† ◇
0	**Longwy** 389a d.	0534	0646	0841	1045	1233	1638	...	1828	1856	1943
16	Longuyon 389a d.	0548	0701	0854	1058	1247	1652	...	1855	1909	1956
57	Conflans-Jarny d.	0622	0734	0927	1131	1323	1725	1928	1953	1941	2030
91	Pagny sur Moselle 384 d.	|	|	|	|	|	|	|	2036	|	|
100	Pont-à-Mousson 384 d.	0700	0812	1000	1203	1400	1758	2002	*2053**	2016	2105
128	**Nancy** 384 a.	0720	0835	1020	1220	1420	1818	2019	*2111**	2036	2124

	Ⓐ D	Ⓐ	ⒶE 🚌	⑥ b	Ⓒ n	①–⑤ G	⑦ w	Ⓐ		
Nancy 384 d.	0554	0820	...	0839	1239	1439	1639	1738	1839	1
Pont-à-Mousson 384 d.	0613	0836	...	0858	1258	1458	1658	1758	1858	2
Pagny sur Moselle 384 d.	|	0842	0849	|	|	|	|	|	|	
Conflans-Jarny d.	0652	...	0932	0938	1337	1537	1737	1837t	1938	2
Longuyon 389a d.	0727	...	1030	1013	1412	1612	1812	1912t	2013	
Longwy 389a a.	0739	...	1057	1025	1424	1624	1824	1925t	2025	

Longwy - Luxembourg

km		①–⑤ a	①–⑤ a	①–⑤ a	⑥	①–⑤ a	①–⑥ a	①–⑤ a	①–⑤ d	①–⑤ a	⑥
0	**Longwy** d.	0617	0647	0714	0728	0747	0817	0847	1317	1843	1907
8	Rodange 🏛 d.	0626	0655	0726	0736	0756	0826	0856	1326	1852	1915
27	**Luxembourg** a.	0648	0718	0748	0827	0818	0848	0918	1348	1911	2012

	①–⑥ a	⑥	①–⑤ a	①–⑤ d	①–⑤ a	①–⑤ a	①–⑤ a	①–⑤ a	①–⑥ a	①–⑤ a	①
Luxembourg d.	0615	0715	0741	1215	1615	1645	1715	1745	1812	1845	1
Rodange 🏛 d.	0639	0739	0809	1239	1639	1709	1739	1809	1839	1909	1
Longwy a.	0647	0746	0816	1246	1646	1716	1746	1816	1846	1916	1

D – From Aug. 29.
E – Until Aug. 26.
G – ①–⑤ from Nov. 28.

a – Not June 23, Aug. 15, Nov. 1.
b – Also Nov. 28, 29, 30, Dec. 1, 2, 5 – 10.
c – Also Nov. 11; not July 10 - Aug. 21, Oct. 23, 30.
d – Not June 23, Aug. 15, Oct. 17 – 28, Nov. 1 – 25.
f – Not July 8 - Aug. 26, Oct. 21, 28, Nov. 11.

n – Not Nov. 1.
t – 1 – 2 minutes earlier Nov. 14 – 25.
v – From / to Verdun (Table **393a**).
w – Also July 14, Nov. 1, 11.
z – Not ①–⑤ Aug. 1 - Oct. 14. Until July 2 departs Longwy 0622, Longuyon 0636, Conflans-Jarny 0722, Pont-à-Mousson 0759, arrives Nancy 0820.
* – By train Pagny - Nancy.

◇ – Runs 7 – 12 minutes later from Nov. 1.

LONGWY - METZ 🚌 service (journey 55 minutes):
From Longwy at 0450 Ⓐ, 0645 Ⓐ, 0745, 0945 ⚒, 124 1445 ⑤ f, 1645 Ⓐ, 1827 Ⓐ and 1930.
From Metz at 0631 Ⓐ, 0820 Ⓐ, 0920 ⚒, 1025 †, 1220 1520 ⑤ f, 1620 Ⓐ, 1820 ⚒, 2020 Ⓐ, 2120 † and 2220 ⚒

393 🚌 CHÂLONS EN CHAMPAGNE - VERDUN

km		Ⓐ 🚌	Ⓒ 🚌	Ⓐ 🚌	🚌	Ⓐ 🚌	† 🚌	Ⓒ 🚌	Ⓐ 🚌	
0	**Châlons en Champagne** d.	0820	1020	1220	1420	1820	1930	2030	2040	...
62	Ste Menehould Médiathèque d.	0923	1123	1323	1523	1923	2033	2133	2143	...
107	**Verdun** a.	1008	1208	1408	1608	2008	2118	2218	2228	...

	Ⓐ 🚌	Ⓒ 🚌		Ⓐ 🚌	🚌		Ⓐ 🚌		
Verdun d.	0542	0612	...	1017	1212	...	1517	...	1
Ste Menehould Médiathèque d.	0627	0657	...	1102	1257	...	1602	...	1
Châlons en Champagne a.	0730	0800	...	1205	1400	...	1705	...	2

VERDUN - METZ 393a

ject to alteration on July 16, 17

	⑥	Ⓐ	Ⓐ	⊗	Ⓐ	Ⓐs	Ⓐb	⑥	Ⓐ	⑦jN	†
Verdun .... d.	...	0639	0739**h**	1039	1239**x**	1439**t**	1639	1639	1815	1851	1939
Conflans-Jarny ..... d.	0633	0717	0815	1115	1315	1515	1715	1715	1850	1927	2018
Hagondange . **384** d.	0711	|	0849	1149	1348	1549	1742	1749	|	...	|
Metz .... **384** a.	0724	0756	0901	1204	*1419*	1601	*1758*	1801	1931	...	2059

	Ⓐ	Ⓐ	⑥	Ⓐm	Ⓐn	Ⓒz	Ⓐ▲	†	Ⓐ	⑥	⑤fN
Metz .... **384** d.	0604	*0846*v	0855	1045	1237	1255	1637	1642*	1821	1855	...
Hagondange **384** d.	|	0910	0910	1110	1251	1310	1651	1700*	|	1910	...
Conflans-Jarny .. d.	0642	0943	0943	1143	1323	1343	1723	1735*	1859	1943	2037
Verdun .... a.	0721	1019**k**	1019	1219**r**	1359**t**	1419	1759	*1819*	1932	2019	2111

To/from Nancy (Table **392**).

From Aug. 29.
Not July 8 - Aug. 26, Oct. 21, 28, Nov. 11.
Not Sept. 19 - Oct. 14.
Also Nov. 11; not July 10 - Aug. 21, Oct. 23, 30.
Not Sept. 19 - Nov. 2.

m – Not June 6, 13, Sept. 26 - Nov. 2.
n – Not June 6, 13, Sept. 26 - Oct. 28.
r – Not Sept. 19–23, Nov. 3, 4.
s – Not Sept, 26 - Oct. 28.
t – Not July 4–13, 18–29, Aug. 1 - Sept. 23, Oct. 31, Nov. 2.
v – *0833* July 18 - Aug. 26.
x – Not July 4 - Nov. 2.

z – Not July 14–17, Oct. 22 - Nov. 5.

⊗ – Subject to alteration on ①–⑤ July 4 - Nov. 2 (also June 6, 13, Oct. 22, 23, 29, 30, Nov. 5).
▲ – Runs 4–9 minutes earlier on June 22, 23, 29, July 1 - Sept. 2, Oct. 24–31.
* – Runs 5–10 minutes earlier from Oct. 2.

METZ - FORBACH - SAARBRÜCKEN 394

ject to alteration from August 29

	Ⓐv	⑥	Ⓐ	⚒v		Ⓒ 🚌	Ⓐ		Ⓒ	Ⓐ	⚒	Ⓐ	Ⓒ	⑥	Ⓐv	Ⓒ	Ⓐ	Ⓒ	Ⓐ	Ⓐ	†	⚒	⑥ 🚌	†	†	Ⓐ
Metz .... ▶ d.	0538	0608	0638	0738	0838	...	0938	1038	1238	1238	1338	1538	1538	1638	1638	1737	1738	1838	1838	1938	1938	2038	...	2138	2238	2238
St Avold ...... ▶ d.	0610	0639	0710	0810**z**	0910	...	1010	1110**z**	1313	1312	1410	1610	1613	1710	1710	1811	1810	1910	1910	2010	2012	2110	...	2212	2310	2310
Forbach ...... ▶ a.	0626	0655	0726	0826	0926	...	1026	1126	1326	1326	1426	1626	1626	1726	1726	1824	1826	1926	1926	2026	2026	2126	...	2227	2326	2326
Forbach .... d.	*0632*	0659	*0732*	*0832***a**	0930**a**	0932	*1032*	1130	1330	*1332*	*1432***z**	*1632*	*1634***k**	*1733**	*1732*	*1832**	*1832*	1930	*1932*	*2032*	*2034*	*2132***a**	2131	...	2330	*2345*
Saarbrücken .. a.	*0642*	0709	*0742*	*0842***a**	0940**a**	1007	*1042*	1140	1340	*1342*	*1442***z**	*1642*	*1644***k**	*1808**	*1742*	*1907**	*1842*	1940	*1942*	*2042*	*2044*	*2142***a**	2206	...	2340	*2355*

	Ⓐ	⑥		⚒	Ⓐ	Ⓒ	Ⓐv	Ⓐ	Ⓒ	Ⓐ		⑥	⚒	†	Ⓐ	⑥	Ⓑ	Ⓐ	Ⓒ	Ⓒ	Ⓐ	Ⓒ 🚌		⑥ 🚌	Ⓒ	Ⓐv	Ⓐ
rbrücken .... d.	*0446*	0451	...	*0616***a**	*0716*	0721	*0816*	0921	*0948**	*1116*	1221**a**	1321	*1416*	1421	*1516*	1521	*1616*	*1716*	1721	*1748**	*1816*	1848	*1916***a**	1948	...	*2016*	*2116*
ach .... a.	*0456*	0501	...	*0626***a**	*0726*	0731	*0826*	0931	*1023**	*1126*	1231**a**	1331	*1426*	1431	*1526*	1531	*1626*	*1726*	1731	*1823**	*1826*	1923	*1926***a**	2023	...	*2026*	*2126*
ach .... ▶ d.	0503	0503	...	0633	0733	0733	0833	0933	1033	1133	1233	1333	1433	1433	1533	1533	1633	1733	1733	1833	1833	...	1933	...	2033	2033	2133
vold .... ▶ d.	0518	0518	...	0646	0748	0748	0848	0948	1047	1148	1246	1348	1448**r**	1449	1548	1548	1648**t**	1748	1748	1846	1848	...	1948	...	2046	2048	2148
: .... ▶ a.	0550	0550	...	0720	0820	0820	0920	1020	1120	1220	1320	1420	1520	1522	1620	1620	1721	1820	1820	1921	1920	...	2020	...	2121	2120	2220

Ⓐ only.
⑥ only.
1446 on ⑥.
1646 on †.
Not Ⓐ July 18 - Aug. 26.
2–3 minutes later on ⑥.

* – By 🚌.

▶ – Additional journeys Metz - Forbach and v.v.:
From Metz at 0704 Ⓐ, 1813 Ⓐ, 1709 Ⓐ, 1904 Ⓐ v and 2138 †.
From Forbach at 0607 Ⓐ, 0707 Ⓐ, 0801 Ⓐ and 1807 Ⓐ v.

METZ - SARREGUEMINES Journey: 59–66 minutes.
From Metz at 0734 Ⓐ, 1234 ⚒ v, 1634 Ⓐ, 1734 ⑥, 1834 Ⓐ and 2034 Ⓑ v.
From Sarreguemines at 0605 ⑥, 0611 Ⓐ, 0726 Ⓐ, 1526 Ⓐ v, 1620 ⑥, 1721 †, 1726 Ⓐ and 1926 Ⓐ v.

STRASBOURG - SAARBRÜCKEN 395

Valid July 3 - October 28 (see May edition for service to July 2). Services between Sarreguemines and Saarbrücken are subject to alteration July 21–24, Aug. 6, 7.

n		Ⓐf	Ⓐ	⑥	Ⓐ	†	⑥	Ⓐw	Ⓐnw	†	⚒w	†	Ⓐnw	⑥	Ⓐ	Ⓐ	†	Ⓐn	⑥	Ⓐ	†	Ⓐ	⑥	†	Ⓐ
0	**Strasbourg** .... d.	0545	0645	0737	0747	0845	0945	0947	1149	1245	1245	1445	1445	1541	1547	1643	1645	1713	1745	1747	1815	1847	1941	1945	1947
1	Diemeringen .... d.	0643	0744	0836	0849	0941	1044	1045	1247	1343	1344	1541	1544	1640	1645	1741	1742	1816	1843	1850	1911	1945	2040	2041	2045
7	Sarreguemines 🏛.. ▲ d.	0705	0805	0902	0911	1002	1105	1107	1311	1405	1405	1602	1605	1702	1707	1803	1804	1837	1904	1911	1933	2007	2102	2103	2107
5	**Saarbrücken Hbf** .. ▲ a.	...	...	0922	0929	1020	...	...	1327	...	...	...	...	1722	...	...	...	...	...	...	...	...	2122	...	...

	Ⓐ	Ⓐ	⑥	Ⓐn	Ⓐ	†	⑥	Ⓐw	⑥	⑥	†	Ⓐw	†	⑥	Ⓐw	⑥	Ⓐn	Ⓐ	Ⓐn	†	†	Ⓐ	⑥	†	Ⓐ
rbrücken Hbf ... ▲ d.	...	...	...	...	...	0654	...	...	...	0954	...	0954	1154	...	...	...	1354w	...	...	...	...	...	1744	...	...
eguemines 🏛... ▲ d.	0518	0610	0616	0640	0714	0717	0719	0816	0817	1016	1017	1019	1217	1218	1219	1416	1419	1515	1612	1617	1717	1719	1809	1817	1819
neringen .... d.	0539	0631	0637	0701	0735	0738	0740	0837	0838	1037	1038	1040	1238	1239	1240	1437	1439	1536	1633	1638	1738	1740	1830	1838	1840
sbourg .... a.	0638	0737	0737	0807	0838	0838	0838	0937	0937	1137	1137	1139	1338	1339	1339	1537	1539	1637	1734	1737	1837	1839	1930	1937	1939

SAARBAHN LIGHT RAIL SERVICE **S1 SARREGUEMINES - SAARBRÜCKEN** ⊖

	⚒	Ⓐ	⚒	Ⓐ				
eguimes (Bahnhof) .... d.	0516	0546	0616	0646	0716	hourly ◐	2316	0016
rbrücken Hbf .... a.	0545	0615	0645	0715	0745	until	2345	0045

	⚒	Ⓐ	⚒	Ⓐ	⚒	Ⓐ			
Saarbrücken Hbf .... d.	0440	0510	0540	0610	0640	0710	0740	hourly ◧	2340
Sarreguimes (Bahnhof) ...... a.	0510	0540	0610	0640	0710	0740	0810	until	0010

5 minutes later Oct. 3–28.
Not July 18 - Aug. 26.
Subject to alteration on ①–⑤ from Oct. 3.

◐ – Every 30 minutes 0716 - 0916 and 1216 - 2116 on Ⓐ, 0816 - 1816 on ⑥, 1216 - 1816 on †.
◧ – Every 30 minutes 0740 - 0840 and 1140 - 2040 on Ⓐ, 0740 - 1740 on ⑥, 1140 - 1740 on †.

▲ – For additional light rail service Sarreguemines - Sarrbrücken see below main table.
⊖ – Operated by Saarbahn (www.saarbahn.de). In Saarbrücken also serves city centre.

STRASBOURG - WISSEMBOURG 396

Service from July 3 (see May edition for service to July 2).

n		⚒	Ⓐ	⑥	⑥	†	Ⓐ	⑥	Ⓐn	⑥	Ⓐ	†	⑥	Ⓐn	†	⑥	Ⓐ	†	⚒	†	Ⓐn	Ⓐ	†	Ⓐ	Ⓑ	⑥
0	**Strasbourg** .... d.	0619	0735	0751	0851	0921	0935	1055	1121	1205	1251	1251	1351	1405	1451	1551	1621	1651	1721	1721	1751	1821	1851	1851	1921	1951
4	Haguenau .... d.	0641	0811	0827	0913	0944	0958	1118	1150	1231	1314	1315	1415	1429	1515	1615	1644	1716	1743	1757	1817	1848	1916	1916	1946	2014
6	**Wissembourg** ... **918** a.	0717	0841	0853	0941	1010	1025**b**	1144	1217**b**	1309	1346**b**	1341	1441	1456**b**	1541	1641	1710	1742	1816	1823	1854	1914	1942	1953	2020	2046

	Ⓐ	Ⓐ	⑥	Ⓐ	⑥	†	Ⓐ	⑥	⑥	Ⓐ	†	†	Ⓐn	⑥	Ⓒ	Ⓐ	⑥	Ⓐn	†	Ⓐ	⑥	Ⓐ	⑥	†	Ⓐn	†
sembourg ..... **918** d.	0607	0641	0641	0730	0737	0844	0848	0948	1037	1040**c**	1047	1147	1230**c**	1237	1348	1402**c**	1548	1551**c**	1647	1741	1744	1821	1837	1838	1920	2049
uenau .... d.	0644	0714	0720**r**	0804	0808	0915	0917	1015	1104	1106	1115	1214	1301	1303	1415	1429	1615	1618	1714	1817	1813	1847	1903	1913	1947	2115
sbourg .... a.	0711	0741	0743**r**	0830	0830	0938	0945	1038	1138	1141	1138	1237	1324	1338	1437	1453	1637	1645	1737	1845	1837	1910	1937	1937	2009	2138

By 🚌 from Haguenau Sept. 19–30 (arrives up to 32 minutes later).
By 🚌 to Haguenau Sept. 19–30 (departs up to 38 minutes **earlier**).

n – Not July 18 - Aug. 26.
r – 5 minutes earlier from Nov. 5.

☛ Additional services run Strasbourg - Haguenau and v.v.

397 PRIVATE TOURIST RAILWAYS

MER DE GLACE - TRAIN DE MONTENVERS

✆ 04.50.53.22.75. www.compagniedumontblanc.fr

From Chamonix (200 metres from SNCF station) to Montenvers 'Mer de Glace' (altitude 1913 metres). Journey 20 minutes. **No service Sept. 26 - Oct. 14.**

A cable car takes visitors to the ice grotto inside the glacier

Dec. 19 - Mar. 18: from Chamonix 1000 - 1600, returning until 1630. Runs every 20–30 mins.
Mar. 19 - Apr. 30: from Chamonix 1000 - 1630, returning until 1700. Runs every 20–30 mins.
May 1 - July 8: from Chamonix 0830 - 1630 ‡, returning until 1700. Runs every 20–30 mins.
July 9 - Aug. 28: from Chamonix 0800 - 1800, returning until 1830. Runs every 20–30 mins.
Aug. 29 - Sept. 11: from Chamonix 0830 - 1700 ‡, returning until 1730. Runs every 20–30 mins.
Sept. 12 – 25: from Chamonix 0830 - 1630 ‡, returning until 1700. Runs every 20–30 mins.
Oct. 15–31: from Chamonix 1000 - 1600, returning until 1630. Runs every 30–60 mins.
Nov. 1 - Dec. 17: 1000, 1200, 1400, 1500, 1600, returning 1130, 1330, 1430, 1530, 1630.

‡ – Departure from Chamonix at 0900 (also 0930 return service) runs if sufficient demand.

PANORAMIQUE DES DÔMES

Electric rack railway from the foot to the summit of Le puy de Dôme. Journey: 15 minutes. No service on ①② until Mar. 15, Mar. 16–18, Oct. 10–14. www.panoramiquedesdomes.fr

Until Mar. 13 and Nov. 16 - Dec. 16: Hourly departures 1000 - 1700, returning 1030 - 1730. **Mar. 19 - July 1 and Sept. 5 - Oct. 2**: Departures every 40 minutes 0900 - 1900, returning 0920 - 1920. **July 2 - Sept. 4**: Departures every 20 minutes 0900 - 2040, returning 0920 - 2100. **Oct. 3 - Nov. 13 and Dec. 17–31**: Departures every 40 minutes 1000 - 1800, returning 1020 - 1820.

TRAMWAY DU MONT BLANC

The highest rack railway in France. www.compagniedumontblanc.fr
✆ 04.50.53.22.75.

Winter season : Dec. 19, 2015 - Apr. 17, 2016

Runs from St Gervais Le Fayet (opposite SNCF station) to Bellevue (altitude 1794 me Journey 60 minutes.

Mondays to Fridays (not school holidays):
Depart St Gervais : 0900, 1100, 1310, 1430.
Depart Bellevue : 1000, 1200, 1430, 1620 (to Feb. 5), 1650 (from Feb. 6).

Saturdays and Sundays (also school holidays):
Depart St Gervais : 0900, 1000, 1100, 1310, 1410, 1510.
Depart Bellevue : 1000, 1100, 1200, 1410, 1510, 1620 (to Feb. 5), 1650 (from Feb. 6).

Summer season : June 11 - Sept. 11, 2016 *(may run until Sept. 18 – please ch*

From St Gervais Le Fayet (opposite SNCF station) to Nid d'Aigle (altitude 2372 metres). Journey 70–80 minutes.

June 11 - July 8 and Aug. 29 - Sept. 11:
Depart St Gervais : 0820, 0930, 1030, 1100, 1220, 1330, 1430, 1510.
Depart Nid d'Aigle : 0935, 1040, 1155, 1225, 1335, 1445, 1600, 1700.

July 9 - Aug. 28:
Depart St Gervais : 0720, 0830, 0930, 1000, 1110, 1220, 1330, 1400, 1520, 1630, 1740.
Depart Nid d'Aigle : 0835, 0940, 1050, 1125, 1230, 1340, 1455, 1610, 1640, 1750, 1900.

398 PARIS - PARIS AÉROPORTS

See page 31 for plan of central Pa

CHARLES DE GAULLE - PARIS

VAL shuttle train : air terminals - RER / TGV station.

Roissyrail (RER line B) : Aéroport Charles de Gaulle 2 TGV - Paris Châtelet les Halles. Frequent service 0450 - 2400.

Journey time from Charles de Gaulle :

Gare du Nord	35 minutes
Châtelet les Halles ★	38 minutes
St Michel Notre Dame	40 minutes
Antony (for Orly , see middle panel)	58 minutes

★ Cross - platform interchange with *RER* for Gare de Lyon.

ORLY - PARIS (*VAL + RER B*)

VAL light rail : Orly Sud - Orly Ouest - Antony (7 minutes). Frequent service ① - ⑤: 0600 - 2230; ⑦: 0700 - 2300. Cross platform interchange with RER line B (below).

RER line B : Antony - Paris. Frequent service 0510 - 0010.

Journey time from Antony :

St Michel Notre Dame	20 minutes
Châtelet les Halles ☆	25 minutes
Gare du Nord	29 minutes

☆ Interchange with *RER* for Gare de Lyon.

ORLY - PARIS (*Orlyrail*)

🚌 : Orly (Ouest and Sud) - Pont de Rungis Aéroport d' station. Frequent shuttle service.

RER line C : Pont de Rungis Aéroport d'Orly - Paris. E 15 minutes approx. 0500 - 2330 (0530 - 2400 from Par

Journey time from Pont de Rungis Aéroport d'Orly :

Paris Austerlitz	24 minut
St Michel Notre Dame	27 minute
Musée d'Orsay	31 minute
Champ de Mars Tour Eiffel	39 minut

Delfzijl
Leer
Harlingen
Leeuwarden
Groningen
Veendam
Texel
Den Helder
Stavoren
Enkhuizen
see inset below
Emmen
Meppel
Alkmaar
Hoorn
Kampen
Zwolle
Marienberg
Zandvoort
AMSTERDAM
Almelo
Bad Bentheim
Haarlem
Leiden
Osnabrück
Deventer
Hengelo
DEN HAAG
UTRECHT
Amersfoort
Enschede
Hoek van Holland
Zutphen
Ede
Münster
ROTTERDAM
Arnhem
Winterswijk
Dordrecht
Emmerich
's-Hertogenbosch
Nijmegen
Breda
Vlissingen
Roosendaal
Tilburg
Dortmund
Knokke
Eindhoven
Venlo
Duisburg
Zeebrugge
Breskens
Blankenberge
Noorderkempen
ANTWERPEN
Turnhout
Oostende
St-Niklaas
Lier
Roermond
BRUGGE
Eeklo
Hamont
De Panne
Dendermonde
Mechelen
Genk
Sittard
Heerlen
Köln
GENT
Hasselt
Lichtervelde
Poperinge
Maastricht
Dunkerque
Oudenaarde
BRUSSELS
Leuven
Kerkrade
Aachen
Ieper
Ronse
Landen
Welkenraedt
Kortrijk
Geraardsbergen
Eupen
LONDON
Mouscron
LIÈGE
Verviers
Halle
Lille
Tournai
Spa
NAMUR
La Louvière
GERMANY
Quiévrain
Mons
Binche
Charleroi
Marloie
Jemelle
Gouvy
Troisvierges
PARIS
Quévy
Erquelinnes
Dinant
Couvin
Libramont
Wiltz
Kautenbach
Bertrix
Diekirch
Ettelbruck
Trier
Arlon
Wasserbillig
Virton
FRANCE
Athus
LUXEMBOURG
Rodange
Bettembourg
Longwy
LUXEMBOURG
Local services are shown in Table 449
Metz
Alkmaar
Hoorn
Zwolle
Lelystad
IJmuiden
Haarlem
Zandvoort aan Zee
Sloterdijk
AMSTERDAM
Centraal
Almere
Schiphol
Zuid
Weesp
Hilversum
Amersfoort
Leiden
Alphen
DEN HAAG
UTRECHT
Delft
Gouda
Hoek van Holland
ROTTERDAM
Europoort
Geldermalsen
Tiel
Dordrecht

BELGIUM and LUXEMBOURG

Operators: **Belgium**: Nationale Maatschappij der Belgische Spoorwegen / Société Nationale des Chemins de fer Belges (NMBS / SNCB). www.belgianrail.be
Luxembourg: Société Nationale des Chemins de fer Luxembourgeois (CFL). www.cfl.lu

Services: All trains convey first and second classes of seating accommodation unless otherwise indicated. Most trains shown in our tables are classified *IC* (InterCity). Trains for more different destinations are sometimes linked together for part of their journey and passengers should be careful to board the correct portion of the train. The line nu used by Belgian Railways in their public timetables are shown as small numbers in the table headings.

Timings: Valid **December 13, 2015 - December 10, 2016**. Local train services may be amended on and around the dates of public holidays (see page 2), and passengers are adv confirm train times locally if planning to travel during these periods.

Reservations: Seat reservations are not available for journeys wholly within Belgium or Luxembourg. Reservations are compulsory for international journeys on *Thalys* or *ICE* trains (for t see the International section).

Supplements: Supplements are not payable for journeys in Belgium or Luxembourg. However, a higher level of fares is payable on *Thalys* trains (timings shown in the International se

Dutch-language forms of some **French-language** Belgian names

Aarlen = **Arlon**
Aat = **Ath**
Bergen = **Mons**
Doornik = **Tournai**
Duinkerke = **Dunkerque** (France)
Hoei = **Huy**
Luik = **Liège**
Moeskroen = **Mouscron**
Namen = **Namur**
Nijvel = **Nivelles**
Rijsel = **Lille** (France)
's Gravenbrakel = **Braine le Comte**
Wezet = **Visé**

French-language forms of some **Dutch-language** Belgian names

Anvers = **Antwerpen**
Audenarde = **Oudenaarde**
Bruges = **Brugge**
Courtrai = **Kortrijk**
Dixmude = **Diksmuide**
Furnes = **Veurne**
Gand = **Gent**
Hal = **Halle**
La Panne = **De Panne**
Lierre = **Lier**
Louvain = **Leuven**
Malines = **Mechelen**
Menin = **Menen**
Ostende = **Oostende**
Renaix = **Ronse**
Roulers = **Roeselare**
Saint Nicolas = **Sint Niklaas**
Saint Trond = **Sint Truiden**
Termonde = **Dendermonde**
Tirlemont = **Tienen**
Tongres = **Tongeren**
Ypres = **Ieper**

Some other places outside Belgium

Aken / Aix la Chapelle = **Aachen**
Keulen / Cologne = **Köln**
Londen / Londres = **London**

400 OOSTENDE - BRUSSELS - LIÈGE - VERVIERS - EUPEN

Lines 50a, 3

For *Thalys* trains Paris - Oostende and Paris - Brussels - Liège - Köln see Tables **16 / 21**. For *ICE* trains Brussels - Köln - Frankfurt see Tables **20 / 21**.

km			Ⓐ		Ⓐ		Ⓐ	Ⓐ ♠		Ⓐ		Ⓐ ⊡			Ⓐ		Ⓐ		Ⓐ		Ⓐ		Ⓐ	△
0	**Oostende** ▶ d.	...	...	0440	...	0540	...	...	0640r	...	0740	...		1640	...	1740	...	1840	...	1940	...	2040	...	2140
22	Brugge ▷ d.	...	...	0457	...	0557	...	...	0657r	...	0757	...		1657	...	1757	...	1857	...	1957	...	2057	...	2157
	Kortrijk **410** d.	...	0415	|	0515	|	0615	0640	|	0715	|	0815	and	|	1715	|	1815	|	1915	|	2015	|	2115	|
62	Gent Sint-Pieters ▷ d.	...	0453	0523	0553	0623	0653	0714	0723	0753	0823	0853	at	1723	1753	1823	1853	1923	1953	2023	2053	2123	2153	2223
114	**Brussels** Midi / Zuid ▷ a.	...	0524	0554	0624	0654	0724	0746	0754	0824	0854	0924	the	1754	1824	1854	1924	1954	2024	2054	2124	2154	2225	2254
114	**Brussels** Midi / Zuid d.	...	0527	0556	0627	0656	0727	0748	0756	0827	0856	0927	same	1756	1827	1856	1927	1956	2027	2056	2127	2156	2227	2256
116	Brussels Central d.	...	0531	0600	0631	0700	0731	0752	0800	0831	0900	0931	minutes	1800	1831	1900	1931	2000	2031	2100	2131	2200	2231	2300
118	Brussels Nord d.	...	0535	0607	0637	0707	0737	0756	0807	0837	0907	0938	past	1807	1838	1907	1935	2007	2035	2107	2135	2207	2235	2307
148	Leuven d.	...	...	0627	0658	0728	0800	...	0828	0853	0928	0957	each	1828	1857	1928	...	2028	...	2128	...	2228	...	2328
221	**Liège** Guillemins a.	...	...	0702	0730	0801	0833	...	0901	...	1001	1030	hour	1901	1930	2001	...	2101	...	2201	...	2301	...	0022
221	**Liège** Guillemins d.	...	...	0704	0733	0804	0836	...	0904	...	1004	1033	until	1904	1933	2004	...	2104	...	2204	...	2304	...	0024
241	Pepinster **438** d.	...	...	|	0753	|	0854	...	|	...	|	1053		|	1953	|	...	|	...	|	...	|	...	|
245	**Verviers** Central **438** d.	...	...	0723	0801	0823	0902	...	0923	...	1023	1101		1923	2001	2023	...	2123	...	2223	...	2323	...	0045
258	Welkenraedt **438** d.	0637	...	0737	0815	0837	0914	...	0937	...	1037	1113		1937	2013	2037	...	2137	...	2235	...	2335	...	0057
264	**Eupen** a.	0644	...	0744	...	0844	...	...	0944	...	1044	...		1944	...	2044	...	2144	...	...	...	...	...	...

	Ⓐ	△	Ⓐ		Ⓐ		Ⓐ		Ⓐ		Ⓐ ⊙			Ⓐ		Ⓐ		Ⓐ •	•	Ⓐ	•	•	△	
Eupen d.	...	...	...	...	...	0617	...	0717	...	0817	...		1617	...	1717	...	1817	...	1917	...	2017	2117	2222	
Welkenraedt **438** d.	...	...	...	0524	0547	0626	0647	0726	0745	0826	0847		1626	1647	1726	1747	1826	...	1926	...	2026	2126	2231	
Verviers Central **438** d.	...	...	...	0537	0600	0639	0700	0739	0800	0839	0900	and	1639	1700	1739	1800	1839	...	1939	...	2039	2139	2244	
Pepinster **438** d.	...	...	...	|	0607	|	0707	|	0807	|	0907	at	|	1707	|	1807	|	...	|	...	|	|	|	
Liège Guillemins a.	...	...	...	0555	0625	0656	0725	0756	0825	0856	0925	the	1656	1725	1756	1825	1856	...	1956	...	2056	2156	2303	
Liège Guillemins d.	...	0440	...	0600	0630	0701	0730	0801	0830	0901	0930	same	1701	1730	1801	1830	1901	...	2001	...	2101	2201	2308	A
Leuven d.	...	0534	...	0635	0703	0734	0803	0834	0903	0934	1003	minutes	1734	1803	1834	1903	1934	...	2034	...	2134	2234	0001	L
Brussels Nord d.	0521	0555	0621	0655	0721	0756	0825	0856	0921	0955	1021	past	1755	1821	1855	1921	1955	2021	2052	2121	2152	2252	0019	S
Brussels Central d.	0525	0559	0625	0659	0725	0800	0829	0900	0925	0959	1025	each	1759	1825	1859	1925	1959	2025	2056	2125	2156	2256	0023	O
Brussels Midi / Zuid a.	0529	0603	0629	0703	0729	0804	0833	0904	0929	1003	1029	hour	1803	1829	1903	1929	2003	2029	2100	2129	2200	2300	0027	
Brussels Midi / Zuid ▷ d.	0531	0606	0633	0706	0733	0806	0835	0906	0933	1006	1033	until	1806	1833	1906	1933	2006	2033	2104	2133	2204	2304	0029	
Gent Sint-Pieters ▷ d.	0609	0640	0709	0740	0809	0840	0909	0940	1009	1040	1109		1840	1909	1940	2009	2040	2109	2140	2209	2240	2340	0109	
Kortrijk **410** a.	0644	|	0744	|	0844	|	0944	|	1044	|	1144		|	1944	|	2044	|	2144	|	2244	|	|	|	
Brugge ▷ d.	...	0705	...	0805	...	0905	...	1005	...	1105	...		1905	...	2005	...	2105	...	2205	...	2305	0005	0134	
Oostende ▶ a.	...	0720	...	0820	...	0920	...	1020	...	1120	...		1920	...	2020	...	2120	...	2220	...	2320	0020	0149	

r – Runs 2 minutes earlier on Ⓐ.
♠ – From Poperinge (Table **410**). An additional journey runs one hour later.
♥ – To Poperinge (Table **410**). An additional journey runs one hour later.
▶ – For Oostende - Brugge see also Tables **407** and **410**.
△ – Via Landen (Table **430**) between Leuven and Liège (not high-speed line).
▷ – For Brugge - Gent - Brussels see also Table **405**.
⊡ – Train from Kortrijk at 1015 terminates at Leuven.
⊙ – There are no trains from Welkenraedt at 1047 or 1347 (instead they start from Leuven at 1203 and 1503).
• – On Ⓐ dep. 2 - 3 mins later from Brussels Nord / Cent / Midi.

For slower trains Brussels - Liè Landen see Table **430.**
For Aachen change at Verviers Welkenraedt (Table **438**).

401 BRUSSELS - BRUSSELS NATIONAAL ✈

Line

FROM BRUSSELS MIDI / ZUID TO AIRPORT

	hour	minutes past	hour	minutes past	hour	minutes past
Ⓐ	**04**	10 40 51	**11**	11 14 24 40 45 51	**18**	11 14 24 40 45 51
	05	11 14 40 45 51	**12**	09 14 24 40 45 51	**19**	11 14 24 40 45 51
	06	06 14 40 45 51	**13**	11 14 24 40 45 51	**20**	11 14 24 40 45 51
	07	06 14 24 40 45 51	**14**	11 14 24 40 45 51	**21**	11 14 24 40 51
	08	09 14 24 40 45 51	**15**	11 14 24 40 45 51	**22**	11 14 24 51
	09	11 14 24 40 45 51	**16**	06 14 24 40 45 51	**23**	11 14 24
	10	06 14 24 40 45 51	**17**	11 14 24 40 45 51		
	hour	minutes past	hour	minutes past	hour	minutes past
Ⓒ	**04**	51	**11**	09 14 24 43 45 51	**18**	09 14 24 43 45 51
	05	09 43 45 51	**12**	09 14 24 43 45 51	**19**	09 14 24 43 45 51
	06	09 24 43 45 51	**13**	09 14 24 43 45 51	**20**	09 14 24 43 45 51
	07	09 14 24 43 45 51	**14**	09 14 24 43 45 51	**21**	09 14 24 43 51
	08	09 14 24 43 45 51	**15**	09 14 24 43 45 51	**22**	09 14 24 51
	09	09 14 24 43 45 51	**16**	09 14 24 43 45 51	**23**	09 14 51
	10	09 14 24 43 45 51	**17**	09 14 24 43 45 51		

All services call at Brussels Central 4 minutes later and Brussels Nord 10 minutes later. Journey time to airport: from Brussels Midi / Zuid 20 - 27 mins, from Brussels Centraal 16 - 23 minutes, from Brussels Nord 10 - 17 minutes.

FROM AIRPORT TO BRUSSELS MIDI / ZUID

	hour	minutes past	hour	minutes past	hour	minutes past
Ⓐ	**04**	41	**11**	13 26 30 41 52 59	**18**	13 26 30 41 52
	05	13 26 30 41	**12**	13 26 30 41 52 59	**19**	13 26 30 41 52
	06	13 26 30 41	**13**	13 26 30 41 52 59	**20**	13 26 30 41 52
	07	13 26 30 41 59	**14**	10 26 30 41 52 59	**21**	13 26 30 41 52
	08	13 26 31 41 52 59	**15**	13 26 30 41 52 59	**22**	13 26 30 41 52
	09	13 26 30 41 52 59	**16**	13 26 30 41 52 59	**23**	26 30 41 52 59
	10	13 26 30 41 52 59	**17**	13 26 30 41 52 59		
	hour	minutes past	hour	minutes past	hour	minutes past
Ⓒ			**11**	13 26 31 42 52 57	**18**	13 26 31 42 52
	05	26 31 42	**12**	13 26 31 42 52 57	**19**	13 26 31 42 52
	06	13 26 31 42 57	**13**	13 26 31 42 52 57	**20**	13 26 31 42 52
	07	13 26 31 42 57	**14**	13 26 31 42 52 57	**21**	13 26 31 42 52
	08	13 26 31 42 52 58	**15**	13 26 31 42 52 57	**22**	13 26 31 42 52
	09	13 26 31 42 52 57	**16**	13 26 31 42 52 57	**23**	31 42 52
	10	13 26 31 42 52 57	**17**	13 26 31 42 52 57	**00**	30

All services call at Brussels Nord (11 - 18 minutes from airport), Brussels Centraal (16 - minutes from airport) and Brussels Midi / Zuid (21 - 28 minutes from airport).
Airport is referred to as Brussels Airport, Brussels Nat. Luchthaven or Brussels Nat. Aér

EUROPEAN QUARTER: from Brussels Luxembourg every 30 mins 0654Ⓐ – 2254Ⓐ, from Airport every 30 mins 0547Ⓐ – 2147Ⓐ. Journey 19 mins. Also calls at Brussels Schuman.

FOR DIRECT SERVICES TO AND FROM BRUSSELS AIRPORT SEE THE FOLLOWING TABLES:

Aalst **411**, Antwerpen **420 / 432**, Brugge **405**, De Panne **411**, Denderleeuw **411**, Gent **405**, Hasselt **432**, Kortrijk **407**, Leuven **430 / 432**, Mechelen **432**, Mons **422**, Namur **440**, Tournai **4**

ZEEBRUGGE - BRUGGE 402

50a

		Ⓐ	Ⓐ	Ⓐ	Ⓐ		Ⓐ	Ⓐ	Ⓐ	Ⓐ	Ⓐ	Ⓐ	Ⓐ			Ⓒ	Ⓒ	Ⓒ	Ⓒ	Ⓒ	Ⓒ	Ⓒ	
Zeebrugge Strand .... d.	Ⓐ	...	...	...	...	and	...	...	...	...	...	...	...	...	Ⓒ	0806	1006	1206	1406	1606	1806	2006	...
Zeebrugge Dorp .... d.		0706	0732	0806	0906	hourly	1506	1606	1632	1706	1806	1906	2006	...		|	|	|	|	|	|	|	...
Brugge .... a.		0726	0752	0826	0926	until	1526	1626	1652	1726	1826	1926	2026	...		0826	1026	1226	1426	1626	1826	2026	...

		Ⓐ	Ⓐ	Ⓐ	Ⓐ		Ⓐ	Ⓐ	Ⓐ	Ⓐ	Ⓐ	Ⓐ				Ⓒ	Ⓒ	Ⓒ	Ⓒ	Ⓒ	Ⓒ	Ⓒ		
ıe .... d.	Ⓐ	0634	0708	0734	0834	and	1534	1634	1716	1734	1834	1934	...	...	Ⓒ	0734	0934	1134	1334	1534	1734	1934	...	...
·ugge Dorp .... a.		0654	0724	0754	0854	hourly	1554	1654	1736	1754	1854	1954	...	...		|	|	|	|	|	|	|	...	...
·ugge Strand .... a.		...	...	...	...	until	...	...	...	...	...	...	...	...		0754	0954	1154	1354	1554	1754	1954	...	...

trains continue beyond Brugge as stopping services to Gent (not shown). Change at Brugge for Brussels and faster service to Gent (Tables **400**/**405**).

KNOKKE and BLANKENBERGE - BRUGGE - GENT - BRUSSELS 405

50a

For additional trains Brugge - Gent - Brussels see Table **400**

	Ⓐ	Ⓐ		Ⓐ	Ⓐ	Ⓒ	Ⓐ	Ⓐ	Ⓒ	Ⓐ	Ⓐ		Ⓐ	Ⓐ		Ⓐ ◇			Ⓐ			
Knokke .... d.	...	...	...	...	0536	...	...	0636	...	0657	...	0736	0757	...	0836	...	and	1936	...	2036	...	...
Blankenberge .... d.	...	...	...	...	0542r	...	...	0642r	...	|	0715	0742r	|	...	0842r	...	at	1942r	...	2042r	2142	2242
Brugge .... a.	...	...	...	...	0559	...	...	0659	...	0719	0729	0759	0819	...	0859	...	the	1959	...	2059	2155	2255
Brugge .... d.	0408	0432	0508	0532	0608	0608	0631	0708	0708	...	0732	0808	...	0832	0908	0932	same	2008	2032	2108	...	...
Gent Sint-Pieters .... d.	0437	0507	0538	0607	0638	0638	0705	0738	0738	...	0805	0838	...	0907	0938	1007	minutes	2038	2107	2138	...	...
Brussels Midi / Zuid .... a.	0509	0538	0609	0638	0709	0709	0736	0809	0809	...	0836	0909	...	0938	1009	1038	past	2109	2138	2209	...	...
Brussels Central .... a.	0515	0543	0615	0643	0715	0715	0743	0814	0815	...	0843	0915	...	0943	1015	1043	each	2115	2143	2215	...	...
Brussels Nord .... a.	0520	0548	0620	0648	0720	0720	0748	0819	0820	...	0848	0920	...	0948	1020	1048	hour	2120	2148	2220	...	...
Brussels Nationaal ✈ ... a.	...	0601	...	0701	...	...	0801	...	...	...	0901	...	...	1001	...	1101	until	...	2201	...	...	...

	Ⓐ △	Ⓐ	Ⓒ	Ⓐ	Ⓒ		Ⓐ		Ⓐ			Ⓐ		Ⓐ	Ⓐ	Ⓒ	Ⓐ		Ⓐ	Ⓒ		Ⓐ	Ⓐ
sels Nationaal ✈ ... d.	...	...	...	...	...	...	0759	...	0859	...	and	1959	...	2059	...	...	2159	...	2259	...		1459	...
sels Nord .... d.	...	0540	...	0640	...	0739	0812	0839	0912	0940	at	2012	2040	2112	2140	2140	2212	2240	2312	2340		1512	...
sels Central .... d.	...	0544	...	0644	...	0743	0816	0843	0916	0944	the	2016	2044	2116	2144	2144	2216	2244	2316	2344	A	1516	...
sels Midi / Zuid .... d.	...	0551	...	0651	...	0751	0822	0851	0922	0951	same	2022	2051	2122	2151	2151	2222	2251	2324	2351	L	1522	...
Sint-Pieters .... d.	...	0625	...	0725	...	0825	0900	0925	1000	1025	minutes	2100	2125	2200	2225	2225	2300	2325	0000	0025	S	1600	...
ıe .... a.	...	0652	...	0752	...	0852	0929	0952	1029	1052	past	2129	2152	2229	2252	2252	2329	2352	0029	0052	O	1629	...
ıe .... d.	0602	0702	0702	0802	0802	0902	...	1002	...	1102	each	...	2202	...	...	2302	...	...	...	...		1639	1739
nkenberge .... a.	0618s	0718s	0718s	0818s	0818s	0918s	...	1018s	...	1118s	hour	...	2218s	...	...	2318s	...	...	...	...		1646s	|
ke .... a.	0623	0723	0723	0823	0823	0923	...	1023	...	1123	until	...	2223	...	...	2323	...	...	...	...		1701	1801

Portion from Blankenberge attaches to main train at Brugge.
Portion for Blankenberge detaches from main train at Brugge (depart Brugge xx05 and 1631).

• – Blankenburg - Brugge: *15 km*.
◇ – 1732 journey starts from Blankenberge (d. 1715).
△ – An additional train runs one hour earlier.

*Knokke / Blankenberge trains continue beyond Brussels Nord to / from Leuven, Hasselt and Genk (Table **430**).*

KNOKKE - OOSTENDE - DE PANNE (Coastal Tramway) 406

Lijn 'Kusttram'

KKE railway station - **OOSTENDE** railway station *Journey 65 mins*

10 - Mar. 25: 0458⚒, 0558, 0658⚒, 0728, 0743Ⓐ, 0758⚒, 0823, 0858⚒, 0923 and 20 minutes until 1923, 2027, 2127, 2227, 2327.

26 - June 30: 0458⚒, 0558, 0658, 0728, 0743Ⓐ, 0758⚒, 0823, 0838⚒, 0853, 0908 and 15 minutes until 1938, 2003, 2027, 2127, 2227, 2327.

at Heist (+6 mins), Zeebrugge (+13 mins), Blankenberge (+25 mins).

TENDE railway station - **DE PANNE** railway station *Journey 79 mins*

10 - Mar. 25: 0505⚒, 0605⚒, 0700⚒, 0710, 0735, 0805⚒, 0820, 0835, 0850, 0910 and 20 minutes until 1830, 1900, 1930, 2030, 2130, 2230, 2330.

26 - June 30: 0505⚒, 0605⚒, 0700⚒, 0710, 0735, 0750⚒, 0805, 0820, 0835, 0850, 0930 and every 15 minutes until 1830, 1900, 1930, 2000, 2030, 2130, 2230, 2330.

at Middelkerke (+23 mins), Nieuwpoort (+41 mins), Koksijde (+60 mins).

DE PANNE railway station - **OOSTENDE** railway station *Journey 79 mins*

Nov. 10 - Mar. 25: 0419⚒, 0519⚒, 0619, 0712, 0737⚒, 0809, 0829⚒, 0849, 0909 and every 20 minutes until 1729, 1752, 1811, 1824, 1844, 1917, 1942, 2017, 2117, 2217, 2317.

Mar. 26 - June 30: 0419⚒, 0519⚒, 0619, 0712, 0737⚒, 0809, 0824, 0839⚒, 0854, 0909 and every 15 minutes until 1754, 1811, 1824, 1839, 1854, 1917, 1942, 2017, 2117, 2217, 2317.

Calls at Koksijde (+19 mins), Nieuwpoort (+38 mins), Middelkerke (+56 mins).

OOSTENDE railway station - **KNOKKE** railway station *Journey 65 mins*

Nov. 10 - Mar. 25: 0455⚒, 0545⚒, 0645⚒, 0715⚒, 0745, 0827, 0855, 0910, 0930, 0950 and every 20 minutes until 1830, 1900, 1930, 2030, 2130, 2230, 2330.

Mar. 26 - June 30: 0455⚒, 0545⚒, 0645⚒, 0715, 0725Ⓐ, 0745, 0810, 0827, 0840, 0855, 0915 and every 15 minutes until 1900, 1930, 2000, 2030, 2130, 2230, 2330.

Calls at Blankenberge (+37 mins), Zeebrugge (+47 mins), Heist (+58 mins).

me journeys run Knokke - Oostende - De Panne and v.v. In July and August daytime frequency is enhanced to every 10 minutes. Timings may vary at Christmas and New Year.
ections with rail services are available at Knokke (Table **405**), Zeebrugge (Table **402**), Blankenberge (Table **405**), Oostende (Tables **400/07/10**) and De Panne (Table **411**).

OOSTENDE - BRUGGE - KORTRIJK - BRUSSELS 407

s 66, 89

For direct trains Oostende - Brugge - Brussels via Gent (also Kortrijk - Gent - Brussels) see Table **400**. For direct trains Brugge - Brussels - Brussels Nationaal ✈ see Table **405**

		Ⓐ	Ⓐ	Ⓐ	Ⓐ	Ⓐ	Ⓐ N	Ⓐ	Ⓐ	Ⓐ	Ⓐ		Ⓐ	Ⓐ	Ⓐ		Ⓒ	Ⓒ	Ⓒ	Ⓒ		Ⓒ	Ⓒ
Oostende .... ▷ d.	Ⓐ	...	...	...	...	0546	0634	0646	...	0746	0846		1946	2046	2146	Ⓒ	...	...	...	0646		1946	2046
Brugge .... ▷ d.		...	...	...	...	0605	0658	0705	...	0805	0905		2005	2105	2205		...	...	...	0706		2006	2106
Torhout .... d.		...	...	...	...	0621	0712	0721	...	0821	0921		2021	2121	2221		...	...	...	0721		2021	2121
Lichtervelde .... a.		...	...	...	...	0625	|	0725	...	0825	0925		2025	2125	2225		...	...	...	0725		2025	2125
Lichtervelde .... d.		...	...	...	...	0635	|	0735	...	0835	0935		2035	2135	2235		...	...	...	0735		2035	2135
Roeselare .... d.		...	...	...	...	0643	0723	0743	...	0843	0943	and	2043	2143	2243		...	...	...	0742	and	2042	2142
Kortrijk .... a.		...	...	...	...	0704	0741	0804	...	0904	1004		2104	2204	2304		...	...	...	0802		2102	2202
Kortrijk .... d.		0511	0544	0611	0644	0711	0744	0815	0811	0911	1011	hourly	2111	2211	...		0506	0607	0706	0806	hourly	2106	...
Oudenaarde .... d.		0531	0605	0632	0705	0732	0805	|	0832	0932	1032		2132	2232	...		0524	0625	0725	0825		2125	...
Zottegem .... d.		0546	0619	0645	0719	0745	0819	◇	0845	0945	1045	until	2145	2245	...		0540	0640	0740	0840	until	2140	...
Denderleeuw .... d.		0604	0639	0704	0742	0804	0843	|	0904	1004	1104		2204	2304	...		0604	0704	0804	0904		2204	...
Brussels Midi / Zuid .... a.		0621	0659	0721	0800	0821	0901	0924	0921	1021	1121		2221	2321	...		0621	0721	0821	0921		2221	...
Brussels Central .... a.		0627	0706	0727	0806	0827	0906	0930	0927	1027	1127		2227	2327	...		0627	0727	0827	0927		2227	...
Brussels Nord .... a.		0632	0711	0732	0811	0832	0911	0935	0932	1032	1132		2232	2332	...		0632	0732	0832	0932		2232	...
Brussels Nationaal ✈ . a.		...	...	0747	...	0847	...	...	0947	1047	1147		2247	2347	...		0647	0747	0847	0947		2247	...

		Ⓐ	Ⓐ	Ⓐ	Ⓐ		Ⓐ	Ⓐ	Ⓐ	Ⓐ	Ⓐ	Ⓐ	Ⓐ	Ⓐ	Ⓐ	Ⓐ	Ⓐ		Ⓒ	Ⓒ		Ⓒ	Ⓒ	Ⓒ ♡
sels Nationaal ✈ .. d.	Ⓐ	...	...	0513	0613		1613	...	1713	...	1813	...	1913	2013	2113	2213	...	Ⓒ	...	0613		1913	2013	2113
sels Nord .... d.		...	...	0528	0628		1628	1649	1728	1749	1828	1921	1928	2028	2128	2228	2315		...	0628		1928	2028	2128
sels Central .... d.		...	...	0532	0632		1632	1653	1732	1753	1832	1925	1932	2032	2132	2232	2319		...	0632		1932	2032	2132
ssels Midi / Zuid ..... d.		...	...	0539	0639		1638	1702	1738	1800	1839	1933	1939	2039	2139	2239	2327		...	0639		1939	2039	2139
derleeuw .... d.		...	...	0559	0659		1659	1724	1759	1824	1859	|	1959	2059	2159	2259	2347		...	0700		2000	2100	2200
egem .... d.		...	...	0616	0716	and	1716	1743	1816	1843	1916	⊡	2016	2116	2216	2316	0015		...	0722	and	2022	2122	2222
enaarde .... d.		...	...	0631	0731		1731	1757	1831	1857	1931	|	2031	2131	2231	2331	0031		...	0737		2037	2137	2237
rijk .... a.		...	...	0648	0748	hourly	1748	1816	1848	1914	1948	2044	2048	2148	2248	2348	...		...	0754	hourly	2054	2154	2254
rijk .... d.		0456	0556	0656	0756		1756	...	1856	...	1956	2056	...	2156	...	...	...		0658	0758		2058	...	...
selare .... d.		0518	0618	0718	0818	until	1818	...	1918	...	2018	2118	...	2218	...	...	...		0718	0818	until	2118	...	...
ervelde .... a.		0525	0625	0725	0825		1825	...	1925	...	2025	2125	...	2225	...	...	...		0725	0825		2125	...	...
ervelde .... d.		0535	0635	0735	0835		1835	...	1935	...	2035	2135	...	2235	...	...	...		0735	0835		2135	...	...
out .... d.		0540	0640	0740	0840		1840	...	1940	...	2040	2140	...	2240	...	...	...		0740	0840		2140	...	...
ge .... ▷ d.		0557	0657	0757	0857		1857	...	1957	...	2057	2157	...	2257	...	...	...		0757	0857		2157	...	...
tende .... ▷ a.		0613	0713	0813	0913		1913	...	2013	...	2113	2213	...	2313	...	...	...		0813	0913		2213	...	...

Not Dec. 19 - Jan. 2, Mar. 26 - Apr. 9, May 6, June 25 - Aug. 28, Oct. 31. Runs Ⓐ Oostende - Kortrijk.

◇ – Via Gent (arrive 0850, Table **400**).
⊡ – Via Gent (depart 2009, Table **400**).

▷ – See also Tables **400** and **410**.
♡ – Also at 2213.

410 POPERINGE - KORTRIJK - GENT - ANTWERPEN

Lines 69, 7

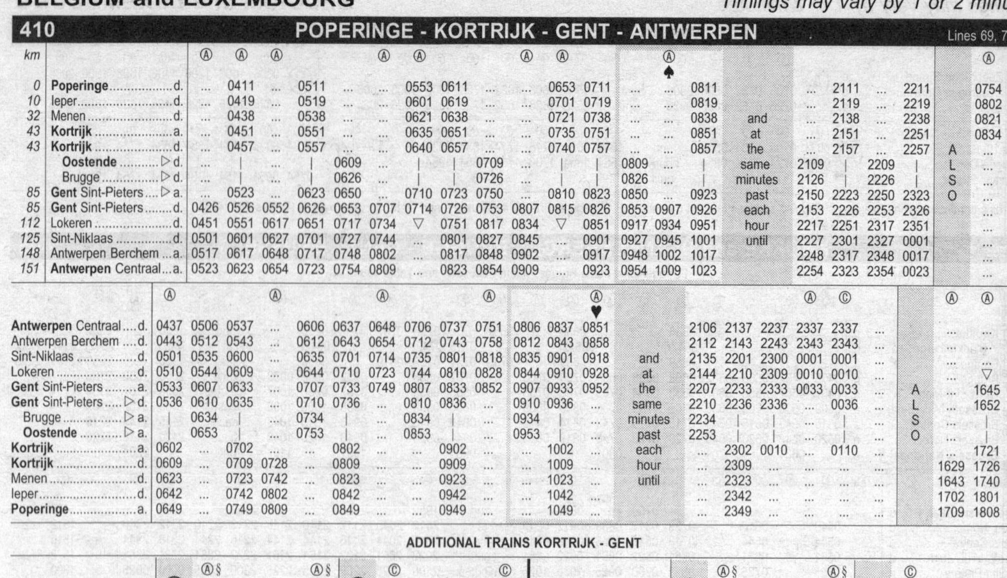

km		Ⓐ	Ⓐ	Ⓐ			Ⓐ	Ⓐ			Ⓐ	Ⓐ			Ⓐ ♠								
0	**Poperinge** d.	...	0411	...	0511	...	...	0553	0611	...	...	0653	0711	...	...	0811		...	2111	...	2211		0754
10	Ieper d.	...	0419	...	0519	...	...	0601	0619	...	...	0701	0719	...	...	0819		...	2119	...	2219		0802
32	Menen d.	...	0438	...	0538	...	...	0621	0638	...	...	0721	0738	...	...	0838	and	...	2138	...	2238		0821
43	**Kortrijk** a.	...	0451	...	0551	...	...	0635	0651	...	...	0735	0751	...	...	0851	at	...	2151	...	2251		0834
43	**Kortrijk** d.	...	0457	...	0557	...	...	0640	0657	...	...	0740	0757	...	...	0857	the	...	2157	...	2257	A	...
	Oostende ▷ d.	...	|	...	|	0609	...	|	|	0709	...	|	|	0809	...	|	same	2109	|	2209	|	L	...
	Brugge ▷ d.	...	|	...	|	0626	...	|	|	0726	...	|	|	0826	...	|	minutes	2126	|	2226	|	S	...
85	**Gent** Sint-Pieters ▷ a.	...	0523	...	0623	0650	...	0710	0723	0750	...	0810	0823	0850	...	0923	past	2150	2223	2250	2323	O	...
85	**Gent** Sint-Pieters d.	0426	0526	0552	0626	0653	0707	0714	0726	0753	0807	0815	0826	0853	0907	0926	each	2153	2226	2253	2326		...
112	Lokeren d.	0451	0551	0617	0651	0717	0734	▽	0751	0817	0834	▽	0851	0917	0934	0951	hour	2217	2251	2317	2351		...
125	Sint-Niklaas d.	0501	0601	0627	0701	0727	0744	...	0801	0827	0845	...	0901	0927	0945	1001	until	2227	2301	2327	0001		...
148	Antwerpen Berchem a.	0517	0617	0648	0717	0748	0802	...	0817	0848	0902	...	0917	0948	1002	1017		2248	2317	2348	0017		...
151	**Antwerpen** Centraal a.	0523	0623	0654	0723	0754	0809	...	0823	0854	0909	...	0923	0954	1009	1023		2254	2323	2354	0023		...

	Ⓐ			Ⓐ			Ⓐ			Ⓐ			Ⓐ ♥					Ⓐ	Ⓒ			Ⓐ	Ⓐ
Antwerpen Centraal d.	0437	0506	0537	...	0606	0637	0648	0706	0737	0751	0806	0837	0851		2106	2137	2237	2337	2337	...		...	...
Antwerpen Berchem d.	0443	0512	0543	...	0612	0643	0654	0712	0743	0758	0812	0843	0858		2112	2143	2243	2343	2343	...		...	...
Sint-Niklaas d.	0501	0535	0600	...	0635	0701	0714	0735	0801	0818	0835	0901	0918	and	2135	2201	2300	0001	0001	...		...	...
Lokeren d.	0510	0544	0609	...	0644	0710	0723	0744	0810	0828	0844	0910	0928	at	2144	2210	2309	0010	0010	...		...	▽
Gent Sint-Pieters a.	0533	0607	0633	...	0707	0733	0749	0807	0833	0852	0907	0933	0952	the	2207	2233	2333	0033	0033	...	A	...	1645
Gent Sint-Pieters ▷ d.	0536	0610	0635	...	0710	0736	...	0810	0836	...	0910	0936	...	same	2210	2236	2336	...	0036	...	L	...	1652
Brugge ▷ a.	|	0634	|	...	0734	|	...	0834	|	...	0934	|	...	minutes	2234	|	|	...	|	...	S	...	|
Oostende ▷ a.	|	0653	|	...	0753	|	...	0853	|	...	0953	|	...	past	2253	|	|	...	|	...	O	...	|
Kortrijk a.	0602	...	0702	...	...	0802	...	...	0902	...	...	1002	...	each	...	2302	0010	...	0110	...		...	1721
Kortrijk d.	0609	...	0709	0728	...	0809	...	...	0909	...	...	1009	...	hour	...	2309	...	...	...	...		1629	1726
Menen d.	0623	...	0723	0742	...	0823	...	...	0923	...	...	1023	...	until	...	2323	...	...	...	...		1643	1740
Ieper d.	0642	...	0742	0802	...	0842	...	...	0942	...	...	1042	...		...	2342	...	...	...	...		1702	1801
Poperinge a.	0649	...	0749	0809	...	0849	...	...	0949	...	...	1049	...		...	2349	...	...	...	...		1709	1808

ADDITIONAL TRAINS KORTRIJK - GENT

		Ⓐ§		Ⓐ§		Ⓒ		Ⓒ
Kortrijk d.	Ⓐ	0415	hourly	2215	Ⓒ	0521	hourly	2221
Gent Sint-Pieters a.		0450	until	2250		0554	until	2254

		Ⓐ§		Ⓐ§		Ⓒ	
Gent Sint-Pieters d.	Ⓐ	0609	hourly	2309	Ⓒ	0606	hourly
Kortrijk a.		0644	until	2344		0639	until

♠ – Last journey is at 1707Ⓐ (also 1810Ⓐ).
♥ – Last journey is at 1851Ⓐ.
▽ – To/from Brussels (Table **400**).
▷ – See also Table **400**.
§ – Most journeys continue to/from Brussels (Table 4

411 DE PANNE - GENT - AALST - DENDERLEEUW - BRUSSELS

Lines 7

For direct trains Gent - Brussels see Tables **400** and **405** (faster journeys may be available by changing at Gent)

km		Ⓐ	△	△					Ⓐ ◧	Ⓐ
0	**De Panne** § d.	...	0452	0552	0652		2052		0525	0725
5	Veurne d.	...	0501	0601	0701		2101		0533	0733
20	Diksmuide d.	...	0513	0613	0713		2113		0545	0745
39	Lichtervelde d.	...	0530	0630	0730	and	2130		0602	0802
56	Tielt d.	...	0542	0642	0742		2142	A	0614	0814
86	**Gent** Sint-Pieters a.	...	0606	0706	0806	hourly	2206	L	0641	0840
86	**Gent** Sint-Pieters d.	0513	0613	0713	0813		2213	S	0644	...
114	Aalst d.	0542	0642	0742	0842	until	2242	O	|	...
121	Denderleeuw d.	0553	0653	0753	0853		2253		|	...
144	**Brussels** Midi / Zuid a.	0612	0712	0812	0912		2312		0715	...
146	Brussels Central a.	0617	0717	0817	0917		2317		0720	...
148	Brussels Nord a.	0622	0722	0822	0922		2322		0725	...
160	**Brussels Nationaal** ✈ a.	0635	0735	0835	0935		2335		...	...

	Ⓐ			▽	◧		Ⓐ	Ⓐ
Brussels Nationaal ✈ d.	...	0526		2026	2126		...	...
Brussels Nord d.	...	0538		2038	2138		...	1634
Brussels Central d.	...	0542		2042	2142		...	1638
Brussels Midi / Zuid d.	...	0548	and	2048	2148		...	1644
Denderleeuw d.	...	0610		2110	2210	A	...	|
Aalst d.	...	0620	hourly	2120	2220	L	...	|
Gent Sint-Pieters a.	...	0649		2148	2248	S	...	1715
Gent Sint-Pieters d.	0555	0655	until	2154	...	O	1620	1719
Tielt d.	0619	0719		2219	...		1647	1746
Lichtervelde d.	0632	0732		2232	...		1700	1800
Diksmuide d.	0648	0749		2249	...		1715	1816
Veurne d.	0701	0801		2301	...		1726	1827
De Panne § a.	0708	0808		2308	...		1734	1834

△ – On Ⓒ starts from Gent.
▽ – 2026 journey terminates at Gent on Ⓒ.
◧ – An additional journey runs one hour later.
§ – De Panne railway station is situated in Adinkerke. Connection available into the coastal tramway (Table **406**).

Trains continue beyond Brussels to/from Leuven and Landen (Table ***430****).*

ADDITIONAL TRAINS Gent - Aalst - Denderleeuw - Brussels Midi - Brussels Nord:
From Gent hourly 0540 - 2140 (also 0440Ⓐ).
From Brussels Nord hourly 0607 - 2207 (also 2307Ⓐ); from Brussels Midi 11 minutes later.
On Ⓐ most trains continue beyond Brussels to/from Hasselt and Tongeren (Table **431**).

412 GENT - OUDENAARDE - RONSE

Line

km			Ⓐ		Ⓐ		Ⓒ		Ⓒ
0	**Gent** St-Pieters d.	Ⓐ	0600	and	2100	Ⓒ	0800	every	2000
25	Oudenaarde a.		0629	hourly	2129		0829	**two**	2029
25	Oudenaarde d.		0637	until	2137		0840	hours	2040
39	**Ronse** a.		0648	△	2148		0851	until	2051

		Ⓐ		Ⓐ		Ⓒ	
Ronse d.	Ⓐ	0511	and	221	Ⓒ	0709	every
Oudenaarde a.		0522	hourly	2222		0720	**two**
Oudenaarde d.		0531	until	2231		0731	hours
Gent St-Pieters a.		0559	▽	2259		0759	until

△ – Also at 1628Ⓐ, 1728Ⓐ, 1828Ⓐ.
▽ – Also at 0548Ⓐ, 0649Ⓐ, 0749Ⓐ.
Most trains continue beyond Gent to/from Eeklo (Table ***413****).*

413 GENT - EEKLO

Line

km			Ⓐ		Ⓐ		Ⓒ		Ⓒ
0	**Gent** St-Pieters d.	Ⓐ	0612	hourly	2112	Ⓒ	0812	every	2012
7	Gent Dampoort d.		0622	until	2122		0822	**two**	2022
27	**Eeklo** a.		0647	△	2147		0847	hours	2047

		Ⓐ		Ⓐ		Ⓒ	
Eeklo d.	Ⓐ	0514	hourly	2214	Ⓒ	0714	every
Gent Dampoort d.		0539	until	2239		0739	**two**
Gent St-Pieters a.		0547	▽	2247		0747	hours

△ – Also at 1732Ⓐ.
▽ – 0714Ⓐ journey runs at 0708Ⓐ. Additional journey runs at 1649Ⓐ.
Most trains continue beyond Gent to/from Ronse (Table ***412****).*

414 GENT - MECHELEN - LEUVEN

Line

For Mechelen - Leuven via Brussels Nationaal ✈ see Table **432**

km			Ⓐ	Ⓐ	Ⓐ △	Ⓐ	Ⓐ	Ⓐ	Ⓐ		Ⓐ	Ⓐ	Ⓐ	Ⓐ			Ⓒ	Ⓒ	Ⓒ	Ⓒ		Ⓒ	Ⓒ
0	**Gent** St-Pieters d.	Ⓐ	0420	...	...	0520	0600	...	0620	and at the same	2100	...	2120	2200	...	Ⓒ	...	0700	...	0800	and at the same	...	2200
30	Dendermonde d.		0501	0525	...	0601	0626	...	0701	minutes	2126	...	2201	2226	...		...	0728	...	0828	minutes	...	2228
57	Mechelen d.		0528	0548	0621	0628	0648	0721	0728	past each	2148	2221	2228	2248	...		0736	0754	0836	0854	past each	2236	2254
82	**Leuven** a.		...	0618	0647	...	0718	0747	...	hour until	2218	2247	...	2318	...		0805	...	0905	...	hour until	2305	...

		Ⓐ	Ⓐ	Ⓐ	Ⓐ ▽	Ⓐ	Ⓐ	Ⓐ		Ⓐ	Ⓐ	Ⓐ	Ⓐ		Ⓒ	Ⓒ	Ⓒ	Ⓒ	Ⓒ		Ⓒ	Ⓒ	Ⓒ
Leuven d.	Ⓐ	0510	0542	...	0613	0642	...	0713	and at the same	2142	...	2213	2242	Ⓒ	...	...	0655	...	0755	and at the same	...	2055	2155
Mechelen d.		0536	0614	0632	0639	0714	0732	0739	minutes	2214	2232	2239	2314		0606	0706	0724	0806	0824	minutes	2106	2124	2224
Dendermonde d.		...	0637	0705	...	0737	0805	...	past each	2237	2305	...	2335		0634	0734	...	0834	...	past each	2134	...	...
Gent St-Pieters a.		...	0700	0740	...	0800	0840	...	hour until	2300	2340	...	...		0700	0800	...	0900	...	hour until	2200	...	...

△ – Also at 0708Ⓐ, 0809Ⓐ.
▽ – Also at 0622Ⓐ, 0722Ⓐ, 0828Ⓐ.

75

LILLE - MOUSCRON - KORTRIJK - (GENT - ANTWERPEN) 415

Lille - Mouscron is subject to alteration on French and Belgian public holidays

	Ⓐ	⑥	⚒			⚒	†			Ⓒ	Ⓐ	Ⓒ	Ⓐ	⑥	†		†	Ⓐ	⑥		⚒	†		Ⓑ	⑥
Lille Flandres ▷ d.	0708	0708	0808	0908	1008	1108	1108	1208	1308	1403	1408	1508	1608	1603	1608	1708	1803	1808	1808	1908	2008	2008	2108	2208	2208
Roubaix ▷ d.	0718	0721	0818	|	1018	1118	|	1218	|	1417	1418	|	1618	1618	1618	1718	1818	1818	1820	1918	2018	|	2118	2218	2218
Tourcoing 🚊 ▷ d.	0722	0725	0822	|	1022	1122	|	1222	|	1422	1422	|	1622	1622	1622	1722	1822	1822	1824	1922	2022	|	2122	2222	2222
Mouscron a.	0728	0731	0828	0928	1032	1128	1128	1230	1324	1428	1428	1528	1628	1628	1628	1732	1828	1828	1830	1928	2028	2028	2130	2228	2228
Mouscron d.	0739	0739	0839	0939	1039	1139	1139	1239	1339	1439	1439	1539	1639	1639	1639	1739	1839	1839	1839	1939	2039	2039	2139	2239	2239
Kortrijk a.	0747	0747	0847	0947	1047	1147	1147	1247	1347	1447	1447	1547	1647	1647	1647	1747	1847	1847	1847	1947	2047	2047	2147	2247	2247
Gent Sint-P. **410** a.	...	0823	0923	1023	1123	1223	1223	1323	1423	1523	1523	1623	...	1723	1723	1823	...	...	1923	2023	2123	2123	2223	...	2323
Antwerpen **410** a.	...	0923	1023	1123	1223	1323	1323	1423	1523	1623	1623	1723	...	1823	1823	1923	...	...	2023	2123	2223	2223	2323	...	0023

	⚒	Ⓐ	⑥	⚒	†			Ⓒ			Ⓐ	Ⓒ				Ⓐ	Ⓒ	Ⓑ	⑥		⚒	†		⚒	†	
twerpen **410** d.	...	...	0537	...	0637	0737	...	0837	...	1037	1137	...	1237	1337	...	1437	1437	...	1537	1637	1737	...	1837	1937	...	...
nt Sint-P. **410** d.	...	...	0636	...	0736	0836	...	0936	...	1136	1236	...	1336	1436	...	1536	1536	...	1636	1736	1836	...	1936	2036	...	...
rijk d.	0613	0713	0713	0813	0813	0913	...	1013	1113	1213	1313	1313	1413	1513	...	1613	1613	1713	1713	1813	1913	1913	2013	2113	2113	...
scron a.	0621	0721	0721	0821	0821	0921	...	1021	1121	1221	1321	1321	1421	1521	...	1621	1621	1721	1721	1821	1921	1921	2021	2121	2121	...
scron d.	0631	0730	0729	0830	0830	0930	...	1030	1130	1230	1331	1330	1430	1530	...	1630	1630	1730	1730	1830	1930	1930	2030	2130	2130	...
coing 🚊 ▷ a.	|	0735	0734	0835	0835	0935	...	|	|	1235	|	1335	|	1535	...	1635	1635	1735	1735	1835	1935	1935	|	|	|	...
aix ▷ a.	|	0740	0739	0840	0840	0940	...	|	|	1240	|	1339	|	1540	...	1639	1639	1739	1739	1840	1939	1939	|	|	|	...
Flandres ▷ a.	0650	0750	0754	0850	0850	0950	...	1050	1150	1250	1350	1350	1450	1550	...	1650	1653	1750	1750	1850	1950	1950	2050	2150	2150	...

Frequent services Lille Flandres - Lille Europe - Roubaix and Tourcoing are operated by the Lille *VAL* métro (Line 2) or by tram. For *TGV* trains see Table **250**.

*Between Kortrijk and Antwerpen these trains are attached to Poperinge - Kortrijk - Gent - Antwerpen trains (Table **410**).*

es 78, 118

LILLE - TOURNAI - MONS 416

		Ⓐ	Ⓐ	Ⓐ	Ⓐ	Ⓐ	Ⓐ	Ⓐ ◇	Ⓐ ◇	Ⓐ ◇	Ⓐ	Ⓐ ◇	Ⓐ ◇	Ⓐ	Ⓐ ◇	Ⓐ ◇	Ⓐ ◇	Ⓐ	Ⓐ ◇	Ⓐ ◇	Ⓐ ◇	Ⓐ	Ⓐ	Ⓐ
Lille Flandres § d.	Ⓐ	...	0608	...	0708	...	0731	0808	0908	1008	...	1208	1308	...	1508	1608	1708	1736	1808	1908	2008	...	...	2208
Mouscron **417** d.		0524	|	0624	|	0718	|	|	|	|	...	|	|	...	|	|	|	|	|	|	|	...	...	|
Tournai **417** a.		0541	0638	0641	0739	0735	0758	0838	0938	1033	...	1238	1333	...	1533	1638	1738	1810	1839	1933	2033	...	...	2233
Tournai d.		0544	...	0644	...	0744	...	0844	0944	1044	1144	1244	1344	1444	1544	1644	1744	...	1844	1944	2044	2144	2224	...
Saint-Ghislain d.		0606	...	0706	...	0806	...	0906	1006	1106	1206	1306	1406	1506	1606	1706	1806	...	1906	2006	2108	2208	2256	...
Mons a.		0614	...	0714	...	0814	...	0914	1014	1114	1214	1314	1414	1514	1614	1714	1814	...	1914	2014	2116	2216	2308	...
Charleroi Sud **425** a.		0649	...	0749	...	0849	...	0949	1049	1149	1249	1349	1449	1549	1649	1749	1849	...	1949	2049	2149	2249	...	...
Namur **425** a.		0722	...	0822	...	0922	...	1022	1122	1222	1322	1422	1522	1622	1722	1822	1922	...	2022	2122	2222	2322	...	...

		Ⓐ	Ⓐ	Ⓐ ◇	Ⓐ ◇	Ⓐ	Ⓐ ◇	Ⓐ ◇	Ⓐ ◇	Ⓐ ◇	Ⓐ ◇	Ⓐ ◇	Ⓐ ◇	Ⓐ ◇	Ⓐ ◇	Ⓐ	Ⓐ	Ⓐ	Ⓐ	Ⓐ	Ⓐ ◇	Ⓐ ◇	Ⓐ	Ⓐ	Ⓐ
amur **425** d.	Ⓐ	...	...	...	0538	...	0638	0738	0838	0938	1038	1138	1238	1338	1438	...	1538	...	1638	...	1738	1838	1938	2038	2138
harleroi Sud **425** d.		...	...	...	0611	...	0711	0811	0911	1011	1111	1211	1311	1411	1511	...	1611	...	1711	...	1811	1911	2011	2111	2211
s d.		0452	...	0552	0645	...	0745	0845	0945	1045	1145	1245	1345	1445	1545	...	1645	...	1745	...	1845	1945	2045	2145	2245
t-Ghislain d.		0505	...	0605	0654	...	0754	0854	0954	1054	1154	1254	1354	1454	1554	...	1654	...	1754	...	1854	1954	2054	2154	2254
rnai a.		0536	...	0636	0715	...	0815	0915	1015	1115	1215	1315	1415	1515	1615	...	1715	...	1815	...	1915	2015	2115	2215	2315
rnai **417** d.		...	0622	0647	0722	0809	0822	0922	1022	1122	1222	1322	...	1522	1622	1649	1720	1724	1819	1822	1922	2022	2122	...	...
uscron **417** a.		...	|	|	|	|	|	|	|	|	|	|	...	|	|	|	1738	|	1837	|	|	|	|	...	...
Flandres § a.		...	0651	0721	0751	0835	0851	0951	1051	1151	1251	1351	...	1551	1651	1723	...	1751	...	1851	1951	2051	2151	...	...

		Ⓒ	Ⓒ	Ⓒ		Ⓒ	Ⓒ	Ⓒ	
scron **417** d.	Ⓒ	0613	0713	0813		2013	2113	2213	...
rnai **417** d.		0630	0730	0830	and	2030	2130	2230	...
t-Ghislain d.		0701	0801	0901	hourly	2101	2202	2301	...
s a.		0712	0812	0912	until	2112	2213	2314	...
harleroi Sud **425** a.		0749	0849	0949		2149	2249	...	...
amur **425** a.		0827	0927	1027		2227	2327	...	...
ège Guillemins **442** a.		0918	1018	1118		2318	...	...	...

		Ⓒ	Ⓒ	Ⓒ	Ⓒ		Ⓒ	Ⓒ	
Liège Guillemins **442** d.	Ⓒ	...	...	0642	0742		1942	2042	...
Namur **425** d.		...	0633	0733	0833	and	2033	2133	...
Charleroi Sud **425** d.		0611	0711	0811	0911	hourly	2111	2211	...
Mons d.		0648	0748	0848	0948	until	2148	2248	...
Saint-Ghislain d.		0701	0801	0901	1001	△	2201	2301	...
Tournai **417** a.		0730	0830	0930	1030		2230	2331	...
Mouscron **417** a.		0747	0847	0947	1047		2247	2349	...

		⑥	⑥	Ⓒ	▽	Ⓒ	⑥	†	Ⓒ
Flandres § d.	Ⓒ	0649	0749	0849	and hourly	1949	2049	2056	2149
rnai a.		0721	0821	0921	until	2021	2121	2121	2221

		⑥	⑥	Ⓒ		Ⓒ	Ⓒ	Ⓒ	
Tournai d.	Ⓒ	0636	0736	0836	and hourly	1936	2036	2144	...
Lille Flandres § a.		0708	0809	0908	until	2008	2108	2208	...

Mouscron arrivals at 1247, 1347, 1447, 1647, 1747, 2047, 2147 are 9 minutes later on ⑦.
1649 departs 1651 on ⑥.

◇ – Change trains at Tournai.
§ – 🚊 between Lille and Tournai = Blandain.

Between Lille and Tournai a Sunday service applies on May 8 and July 14; subject to alteration on July 21.

es 94, 60

KORTRIJK - MOUSCRON - TOURNAI - BRUSSELS - SINT NIKLAAS 417

For direct trains Kortrijk - Brussels see Table **400** (via Gent) and Table **407** (via Oudenaarde)

1			Ⓐ	Ⓐ	Ⓐ	Ⓐ	Ⓐ	Ⓐ	Ⓐ	Ⓐ	Ⓐ	Ⓐ	Ⓐ	Ⓐ	Ⓐ		Ⓐ	Ⓐ	Ⓐ		Ⓒ		Ⓒ
0	**Kortrijk** d.	Ⓐ	...	...	...	...	...	...	...	...	0639	...	...	0739	...		2039	...	2139	Ⓒ	...		...
3	Mouscron **416** d.		...	...	...	...	0548	0608	...	...	0649	0709	...	0748	...		2048	...	2148		...		...
2	**Tournai** **416** d.		0444	0508	0544	0601	0609	0629	0644	0657	0710	0729	0744	0809	0844	and	2109	2144	2209		0544		2244
0	Leuze d.		0456	0521	0556	0613	0621	0641	0656	0709	0722	0741	0756	0821	0856	at	2121	2156	2221		0556		2256
0	Ath d.		0508	0534	0608	0625	0634	0653	0708	0721	0734	0753	0808	0834	0908	the	2134	2208	2234		0608	and	2308
0	Halle d.		0538	0603	0638	|	0703	|	0738	|	0803	|	0838	0903	0938	same	2203	2238	2303		0638		2338
6	**Brussels** Midi / Zuid a.		0548	0614	0648	0700	0715	0727	0748	0759	0815	0827	0848	0915	0948	minutes	2215	2248	2315		0648	hourly	2348
6	**Brussels** Midi / Zuid d.		0551	0617	0651	0703	0718	0730	0751	0803	0818	0830	0851	0918	0951	past	2218	2251	2318		0651		2351
8	Brussels Central d.		0555	0621	0655	0707	0722	0733	0755	0807	0822	0834	0855	0922	0955	each	2222	2255	2322		0655	until	2355
0	Brussels Nord d.		0602	0628	0702	0711	0728	0738	0802	0811	0828	0838	0902	0928	1002	hour	2228	2302	2328		0701		0001
2	**Brussels Nationaal** ✈ a.		0620	|	0720	...	|	...	0820	...	|	...	0920	|	1020	until	|	2320	|		0718		0018
4	Dendermonde a.		...	0655	...	...	0755	...	...	...	0855	...	...	0955	...		2255	...	0015		...		...
8	Lokeren **410** a.		...	0721	...	...	0821	...	...	...	0921	...	...	1021	...		2321	...	...		...		...
1	**Sint-Niklaas** **410** a.		...	0736	...	...	0836	...	...	...	0936	...	...	1036	...		2336	...	...		...		...

		Ⓐ	Ⓐ	Ⓐ	Ⓐ	Ⓐ		Ⓐ	Ⓐ	Ⓐ	Ⓐ	Ⓐ	Ⓐ		Ⓐ	Ⓐ	Ⓐ	Ⓐ			Ⓒ		Ⓒ
-Niklaas **410** d.	Ⓐ	...	...	0524	...	0624		...	1924	...	2024	...	2124		...	...	...	...	...	Ⓒ	...		...
eren **410** d.		...	...	0539	...	0639		...	1939	...	2039	...	2139		...	...	...	...	...		...		...
dermonde d.		...	...	0604	...	0704	and	...	2004	...	2104	...	2204		...	...	...	...	...		...		...
russels Nationaal ✈ d.		0441	0541	|	0641	|	at	1941	|	2041	|	2141	|		...	...	...	...	...		0542		2242
ssels Nord d.		0501	0601	0634	0701	0734	the	2001	2034	2101	2134	2201	2234	A	1550	1617	1649	1717	...		0601	and	2301
ssels Central d.		0505	0605	0638	0705	0738	same	2005	2038	2105	2138	2205	2238	L	1554	1621	1653	1721	...		0605		2305
ssels Midi / Zuid a.		0509	0609	0642	0709	0742	minutes	2009	2042	2109	2142	2209	2242	S	1558	1625	1657	1725	...		0609	hourly	2309
ssels Midi / Zuid d.		0512	0612	0645	0712	0745	past	2012	2045	2112	2145	2212	2245	O	1600	1627	1659	1727	...		0613		2313
e d.		0523	0623	0658	0723	0758	each	2023	2058	2123	2158	2223	2258		|	|	|	|	...		0623	until	2323
d.		0554	0654	0729	0754	0829	hour	2054	2129	2154	2226	2254	2329		1639	1704	1739	1804	...		0654		2354
ze d.		0605	0705	0738	0805	0838	until	2105	2138	2205	...	2305	2338		1648	1713	1748	1813	...		0705		0005
rnai **416** d.		0616	0716	0753	0816	0853		2116	2153	2216	...	2316	2351		1702	1728	1802	1827	...		0716		0016
uscron **416** d.		...	...	0812	...	0912		...	2212	...	...	...	...		...	1747	...	1846	...		...		...
rtrijk a.		...	...	0821	...	0921		...	2221	...	...	...	...		...	...	...	...	...		...		...

420 ROOSENDAAL - ANTWERPEN - BRUSSELS - CHARLEROI

Lines 12, 25,

For *Thalys* services Paris - Brussels - Antwerpen - Amsterdam see Table **18**. For additional trains Antwerpen - Brussels Nationaal ✈ see Table **432**.

km	Ⓐ		Ⓐ	Ⓐ	Ⓐ	Ⓐ	Ⓐ	Ⓐ	Ⓐ	Ⓐ	Ⓐ	Ⓐ	Ⓐ	Ⓐ	Ⓐ ♥	Ⓐ ◇	Ⓐ	Ⓐ	Ⓐ		Ⓐ ◇	Ⓐ	Ⓐ
0	**Roosendaal**	d.	...	...	...	...	...	...	...	...	...	...	...	...	...	0747	...	...	...		2047	...	...
8	Essen 🛃	d.	...	...	0507	...	...	...	0607	...	...	...	0707	...	...	|	...	0807	...	and	|	...	2107
26	Kapellen	d.	...	...	0523	...	...	...	0623	...	...	...	0723	...	...	|	...	0823	...	at	|	...	2123
41	**Antwerpen** Centraal	a.	...	...	0537	...	...	...	0637	...	...	...	0737	...	...	0815	...	0837	...	the	2115	...	2137
41	**Antwerpen** Centraal	d.	0454	...	0539	0554	0609	0625	0639	0654	0709	0725	0739	0754	0809	0817	0825	0839	0854	same	2117	2125	2139
43	Antwerpen Berchem	d.	0500	...	0544	0600	0614	0631	0644	0700	0714	0731	0744	0800	0814	0823	0831	0844	0900	minutes	2123	2131	2144
65	Mechelen	d.	0515	...	0604	0615	0634	0645	0704	0715	0734	0745	0804	0815	0834	0838	0845	0904	0915	past	2138	2145	2204
	Brussels Nationaal ✈	a.	|	...	|	|	|	|	|	|	|	|	|	|	|	0849	|	|	|	each	2149	|	|
85	Brussels Nord	d.	0532	0602	0624	0632	0654	0702	0724	0732	0756	0802	0825	0832	0854	0907	0902	0924	0932	hour	2207	2202	2224
87	Brussels Central	d.	0536	0606	0628	0636	0658	0706	0728	0736	0800	0806	0829	0836	0858	0911	0906	0928	0936	until	2211	2206	2228
89	**Brussels** Midi / Zuid	a.	0540	0610	0632	0640	0702	0710	0732	0740	0804	0810	0833	0840	0902	0915	0910	0932	0940		2215	2210	2232
89	**Brussels** Midi / Zuid	d.	0543	0613	...	0643	...	0713	...	0743	...	0813	...	0843	...	...	0913	...	0943		...	2213	...
118	Nivelles	d.	0611	0641	...	0711	...	0741	...	0811	...	0841	...	0911	...	...	0941	...	1011		...	2241	...
144	**Charleroi** Sud	a.	0636	0706	...	0736	...	0806	...	0836	...	0906	...	0936	...	...	1006	...	1036		...	2306	...

		Ⓐ ◇	Ⓐ	Ⓐ	Ⓐ ◇	Ⓐ ⊡	Ⓐ	Ⓐ ⊡	Ⓒ	Ⓒ	Ⓒ	Ⓒ	Ⓒ	Ⓒ	Ⓒ	Ⓒ ◇	Ⓒ		Ⓒ	Ⓒ ◇	Ⓒ	Ⓒ	Ⓒ ◇
Roosendaal	d.	2147	...	...	2247	...	...	...	...	...	...	...	...	...	...	0747	...		...	2147	...	...	2247
Essen 🛃	d.	|	...	2207	|	...	...	...	...	...	...	...	...	...	...	|	...	and	...	|	...	...	|
Kapellen	d.	|	...	2223	|	...	...	...	...	...	...	...	...	...	...	|	...	at	...	|	...	...	|
Antwerpen Centraal	a.	2215	...	2237	2315	...	...	...	...	...	...	...	...	...	...	0815	...	the	...	2215	...	...	2315
Antwerpen Centraal	d.	2217	2225	2239	2317	2305	2325	0010	...	0540	0609	0640	0709	0740	0809	0817	0840	same	2209	2217	2240	2309	2317
Antwerpen Berchem	d.	2223	2231	2244	2323	2310	2331	0015	...	0545	0614	0645	0714	0745	0814	0823	0845	minutes	2214	2223	2245	2314	2323
Mechelen	d.	2238	2245	2304	2338	2348	2345	0048	...	0604	0634	0704	0734	0804	0834	0838	0904	past	2234	2238	2304	2334	2338
Brussels Nationaal ✈	a.	2249	|	|	2349	|	|	|	...	|	|	|	|	|	|	0849	|	each	|	2249	|	|	2349
Brussels Nord	d.	2307	2302	2324	0007	0014	0002	0119	0555	0624	0655	0724	0755	0824	0855	0907	0924	hour	2255	2307	2324	2355	0007
Brussels Central	d.	2311	2306	2328	0011	0018	0006	|	0559	0628	0659	0728	0759	0828	0859	0911	0928	until	2259	2311	2328	2359	0011
Brussels Midi / Zuid	a.	2315	2310	2332	0015	0022	0010	0130	0603	0632	0703	0732	0803	0832	0903	0915	0932		2303	2315	2332	0003	0015
Brussels Midi / Zuid	d.	...	...	...	...	0025	...	...	0606	△	0706	△	0806	△	0906	...	△		2306	...	...	...	...
Nivelles	d.	...	...	...	...	0105	...	...	0634	...	0734	...	0834	...	0934	...	...		2334	...	...	...	...
Charleroi Sud	a.	...	...	...	...	0132	...	...	0657	...	0757	...	0857	...	0957	...	...		2357	...	...	...	...

		Ⓐ	Ⓐ	Ⓐ ⊡	Ⓐ ◇	Ⓐ	Ⓐ	Ⓐ	Ⓐ	Ⓐ ◇	Ⓐ	Ⓐ	Ⓐ	Ⓐ	Ⓐ ◇	Ⓐ		Ⓐ	Ⓐ	Ⓐ	Ⓐ ◇	Ⓐ	Ⓐ
Charleroi Sud	d.	...	...	0428	...	...	...	0524	...	...	0554	...	0624	...	...	0654		...	1924	...	...	1954	2024
Nivelles	d.	...	...	0456	...	...	...	0550	...	...	0620	...	0650	...	...	0720		...	1950	...	...	2020	2050
Brussels Midi / Zuid	a.	...	...	0535	...	...	...	0617	...	...	0647	...	0717	...	...	0747	and	...	2017	...	...	2047	2117
Brussels Midi / Zuid	d.	0450	0527	0539	0545	0550	0557	0620	0627	0645	0650	0657	0720	0727	0745	0750	at	1957	2020	2027	2045	2050	2120
Brussels Central	d.	0454	0531	0543	0549	0554	0601	0624	0631	0649	0654	0701	0724	0731	0749	0754	the	2001	2024	2031	2049	2054	2124
Brussels Nord	d.	0500	0537	0550	0555	0600	0607	0630	0637	0655	0700	0707	0730	0737	0755	0800	same	2007	2030	2037	2055	2100	2130
Brussels Nationaal ✈	d.	|	|	|	0611	|	|	|	|	0711	|	|	|	|	0811	|	minutes	|	|	|	2111	|	|
Mechelen	d.	0517	0559	0621	0625	0617	0629	0648	0659	0725	0717	0729	0748	0759	0825	0817	past	2029	2048	2059	2125	2117	2148
Antwerpen Berchem	d.	0531	0617	0651	0639	0631	0647	0702	0717	0739	0731	0747	0802	0817	0839	0831	each	2047	2102	2117	2139	2131	2202
Antwerpen Centraal	a.	0535	0621	0655	0643	0635	0651	0706	0721	0743	0735	0751	0806	0821	0843	0835	hour	2051	2106	2121	2143	2135	2206
Antwerpen Centraal	d.	...	0623	...	0645	...	...	...	0723	0745	...	...	...	0823	0845	...	until	...	...	2123	2145	...	...
Kapellen	d.	...	0636	...	|	...	...	...	0736	|	...	...	...	0836	|	...		...	...	2136	|	...	...
Essen 🛃	a.	...	0653	...	|	...	...	...	0753	|	...	...	...	0853	|	...		...	...	2153	|	...	...
Roosendaal	a.	...	...	...	0711	...	...	...	...	0811	...	...	...	...	0911	...		...	...	...	2211	...	...

		Ⓐ	Ⓐ	Ⓐ	Ⓐ	Ⓐ	Ⓐ	Ⓐ ⊡	Ⓒ ◇	Ⓒ	Ⓒ	Ⓒ ◇	Ⓒ	Ⓒ		Ⓒ ◇	Ⓒ	Ⓒ	Ⓒ	Ⓒ	Ⓒ	Ⓒ
Charleroi Sud	d.	2054	2124	...	2154	2224	...	...	...	0503	...	...	0603	...		...	2003	...	2103	...	2203	...
Nivelles	d.	2120	2150	...	2220	2250	...	2256	...	0528	...	...	0628	...		...	2028	...	2130	...	2228	...
Brussels Midi / Zuid	a.	2147	2217	...	2247	2318	...	2335	...	0554	△	...	0654	△	and	...	2054	△	2155	△	2255	△
Brussels Midi / Zuid	d.	2150	2220	2227	2250	2320	2327	2339	0545	0557	0628	0645	0657	0728	at	2045	2057	2128	2157	2228	2257	2328
Brussels Central	d.	2154	2224	2231	2254	2324	2331	2343	0549	0601	0632	0649	0701	0732	the	2049	2101	2132	2201	2232	2301	2332
Brussels Nord	d.	2200	2230	2237	2300	2328	2337	2349	0555	0608	0638	0655	0708	0738	same	2055	2108	2138	2208	2238	2308	2338
Brussels Nationaal ✈	d.	|	|	|	|	|	|	|	0611	|	|	0711	|	|	minutes	2111	|	|	|	|	|	|
Mechelen	d.	2217	2248	2259	2317	...	2359	0021	0625	0629	0658	0725	0729	0758	past	2125	2129	2158	2229	2258	2329	2358
Antwerpen Berchem	d.	2231	2302	2317	2330	...	0017	0051	0639	0647	0716	0739	0747	0816	each	2139	2147	2216	2247	2316	2347	0016
Antwerpen Centraal	a.	2235	2306	2321	2335	...	0021	0055	0643	0651	0720	0743	0751	0820	hour	2143	2151	2220	2251	2320	2351	0020
Antwerpen Centraal	d.	...	...	2323	...	...	...	...	0645	...	...	0745	...	...	until	2145	...	...	...	...	...	...
Kapellen	d.	...	...	2336	...	...	...	...	|	...	...	|	...	...		|	...	...	...	...	...	...
Essen 🛃	a.	...	...	2353	...	...	...	...	|	...	...	|	...	...		|	...	...	...	...	...	...
Roosendaal	a.	...	...	...	...	...	...	...	0711	...	...	0811	...	...		2211	...	...	...	...	...	...

LOCAL TRAINS ROOSENDAAL - ANTWERPEN

		Ⓐ			
Roosendaal	d.	0653	0724	and	2224
Essen 🛃	d.	0710	0733	hourly	2233
Kapellen	d.	0731	0753	until	2253
Antwerpen Cent.	a.	0749	0810		2310

					Ⓒ
Antwerpen Cent.	d.	0550	and	2050	2150
Kapellen	d.	0608	hourly	2108	2208
Essen 🛃	d.	0630	until	2130	2230
Roosendaal	a.	0637		2137	2237

ANTWERPEN - NOORDERKEMPEN

		◧	◧	
Antwerpen Centraal	d.	0640	hourly	2140
Noorderkempen	a.	0655	until	2155

		◐	◐	
Noorderkempen	d.	0605	hourly	2
Antwerpen Centraal	a.	0620	until	2

Noorderkempen station is situated on the high-speed line, 2 km from Brecht

♥ – No journey at 2109.
◧ – 0640 and 0740 run on Ⓐ only. No journeys at 1140 or 1340.
◐ – 0605 and 0705 run on Ⓐ only. No journeys at 1105 or 1305.
⊡ – Local train.

⊙ – Local train. Runs night of ⑥/⑦ and night of ⑦/①.
△ – To/from Binche via La Louvière (Table **423**).
◇ – *Benelux* train from/to Amsterdam via Schiphol ✈, Rotterdam, Den Haag (Table **18**).

ADDITIONAL TRAINS:
Brussels Midi - Charleroi Sud: 1618Ⓐ, 1655Ⓐ, 1718Ⓐ, 1755Ⓐ (from Brussels Nord 10 mins earli
Charleroi - Brussels Nord: 0611Ⓐ, 0647Ⓐ, 0709Ⓐ

421 CHARLEROI - MARIEMBOURG - COUVIN

Line 1

km			Ⓐ	Ⓐ	Ⓐ	Ⓐ	Ⓐ		Ⓐ	Ⓐ	Ⓐ	Ⓐ	Ⓐ	Ⓐ	Ⓐ	Ⓐ	Ⓒ	Ⓒ	Ⓒ	Ⓒ	Ⓒ	Ⓒ	Ⓒ	Ⓒ
0	**Charleroi** Sud	d.	0555	0706	0814	0914	and		1614	1650	1720	1735	1814	1914	2014	2140	0815	1015	1215	1415	1615	1815	2015	2215
18	Berzée	d.	0619	0729	0832	0932	hourly		1632	1713	1739	1758	1832	1932	2032	2203	0838	1038	1238	1438	1638	1838	2038	2238
22	Walcourt	d.	0625	0736	0837	0937	until		1637	1719	1744	1804	1837	1937	2037	2209	0846	1046	1246	1446	1646	1846	2046	2246
35	Philippeville	d.	0639	0750	0850	0950			1650	1734	1757	1819	1850	1950	2050	2223	0900	1100	1300	1500	1700	1900	2100	2300
48	Mariembourg ▲	d.	0650	0801	0901	1001			1701	1745	1809	1829	1901	2001	2101	2234	0911	1111	1311	1511	1711	1911	2111	2311
53	**Couvin**	a.	0658	0809	0909	1009			1709	1753	1817	1837	1909	2009	2109	2242	0919	1119	1319	1519	1719	1919	2119	2319

		Ⓐ	Ⓐ	Ⓐ	Ⓐ	Ⓐ	Ⓐ		Ⓐ	Ⓐ	Ⓐ	Ⓐ	Ⓐ	Ⓐ	Ⓐ	Ⓒ	Ⓒ	Ⓒ	Ⓒ	Ⓒ	Ⓒ	Ⓒ	Ⓒ
Couvin	d.	0434	0459	0544	0618	0642	0750		1450	1550	1629	1757	1850	1950	2051	0639	0839	1039	1239	1439	1639	1839	2039
Mariembourg ▲	d.	0444	0509	0554	0628	0653	0800	and	1500	1600	1639	1807	1900	2000	2101	0649	0849	1049	1249	1449	1649	1849	2049
Philippeville	d.	0455	0520	0605	0640	0704	0811	hourly	1511	1611	1651	1820	1911	2011	2112	0703	0903	1103	1303	1503	1703	1903	2103
Walcourt	d.	0509	0534	0618	0654	0719	0823	until	1523	1626	1705	1832	1923	2023	2126	0718	0918	1118	1318	1518	1718	1918	2118
Berzée	d.	0516	0539	0622	0658	0724	0828		1528	1631	1711	1836	1928	2028	2131	0724	0924	1124	1324	1524	1724	1924	2124
Charleroi Sud	a.	0540	0603	0640	0717	0748	0846		1546	1655	1735	1854	1946	2046	2155	0745	0945	1145	1345	1545	1745	1945	2145

▲ – Service available on certain dates Mariembourg - Treignes and v.v. Some trains operated by steam locomotive.
Operator: Chemin de Fer à Vapeur des 3 Vallées (CFV3V), Chaussée de Givet 49-51, 5660 Mariembourg. www.cfv3v.com

BRUSSELS - MONS - QUIÉVRAIN 422

s 96, 97

For additional trains Brussels - Halle - Braine-le-Comte see Table **423**

		Ⓐ	Ⓐ ◇	Ⓐ	Ⓐ ◇	Ⓐ		Ⓐ ◇	Ⓐ	Ⓐ ◇	Ⓐ	Ⓐ ◇	Ⓐ	Ⓐ ◇	Ⓐ	Ⓐ ◇	Ⓐ			Ⓒ		Ⓒ
Brussels Nationaal ✈ .... d.	Ⓐ	0530	...	0630	...	0730		...	1930	...	2030	...	2130	...	2230	...	2330	...	Ⓒ	0531		2231
Brussels Nord .... d.		0543	0613	0643	0713	0743	and	1913	1943	2013	2043	2113	2143	2213	2243	2313	2343	...		0543		2243
Brussels Central .... d.		0547	0617	0647	0717	0747	at	1917	1947	2017	2047	2117	2147	2217	2247	2317	2347	...		0547	and	2247
Brussels Midi / Zuid .... d.		0553	0624	0653	0724	0753	the	1924	1953	2024	2053	2124	2153	2224	2253	2324	2353	...		0554	hourly	2254
Halle .... d.		|	0634	|	0734	|	same	1934	|	2034	|	2134	|	2234	|	2334	|	...		|	until	|
Braine-le-Comte .... d.		0616	0647	0716	0747	0816	minutes	1947	2016	2047	2116	2147	2216	2247	2316	2347	0016	...		0616		2316
Soignies .... d.		0622	0653	0722	0753	0822	past	1953	2022	2053	2122	2153	2222	2253	2322	2353	0022	...		0622		2322
Mons .... a.		0640	0711	0740	0811	0840	each	2011	2040	2111	2140	2211	2240	2311	2340	0011	0040	...		0640		2340
Mons .... d.		...	0714	...	0814	...	hour	2014	...	2114	...	2214	...	2314	...	...	...	...		...		...
Saint-Ghislain .... a.		...	0728	...	0828	...	until	2028	...	2128	...	2228	...	2328	...	...	...	...		...		...
Quiévrain .... a.		...	0747	...	0847	...		2047	...	...	...	...	...	...	...	...	...	...		...		...

		Ⓐ	Ⓐ ◇	Ⓐ	Ⓐ ◇	Ⓐ	Ⓐ ◇	Ⓐ	Ⓐ ◇	Ⓐ		Ⓐ ◇	Ⓐ	Ⓐ ◇	Ⓐ	Ⓐ				Ⓒ		Ⓒ	
évrain .... d.	Ⓐ	...	...	...	0513	...	0613	...	0713	...		1913	...	2013	...	...	...	...	Ⓒ	...		...	...
t-Ghislain .... d.		...	...	...	0532	...	0632	...	0732	...	and	1932	...	2032	...	...	...	...		...		...	...
ns .... a.		...	...	...	0546	...	0646	...	0746	...	at	1946	...	2046	...	...	...	...		...		...	...
ns .... d.		0422	0449	0520	0549	0620	0649	0720	0749	0820	the	1949	2020	2049	2122	2222	...	...		0520		2220	...
gnies .... d.		0441	0507	0538	0607	0638	0707	0738	0807	0838	same	2007	2038	2107	2141	2241	...	...		0538		2238	...
ne-le-Comte .... d.		0449	0514	0546	0614	0646	0714	0746	0814	0845	minutes	2014	2045	2114	2149	2249	...	...		0546	and	2246	...
e .... d.		|	0528	|	0628	|	0728	|	0828	|	past	2028	|	2128	|	|	...	...		|	hourly	|	...
ssels Midi / Zuid .... a.		0509	0536	0604	0636	0704	0736	0804	0837	0909	each	2036	2109	2136	2209	2309	...	...		0606	until	2306	...
ssels Central .... a.		0514	0542	0609	0642	0709	0742	0812	0842	0914	hour	2042	2114	2142	2214	2314	...	...		0612		2312	...
ssels Nord .... a.		0519	0547	0614	0647	0714	0747	0817	0847	0919	until	2047	2119	2147	2219	2319	...	...		0617		2317	...
ssels Nationaal ✈ .... d.		0532	...	0628	...	0729	...	0831	...	0932		...	2132	...	2232	2332	...	...		0629		2329	...

From / to Liège via Landen (Table **430**).

MONS - QUIÉVRAIN LOCAL TRAINS ON Ⓒ: From Mons hourly 0654Ⓒ - 2054Ⓒ, from Quiévrain hourly 0737Ⓒ - 2137Ⓒ.

BRUSSELS - LA LOUVIÈRE - BINCHE 423

es 96, 108

For additional trains Brussels - Halle - Braine-le-Comte see Table **422**

n			Ⓐ		Ⓐ	Ⓐ	Ⓐ		Ⓒ		Ⓒ
)	**Brussels** Nord .... d.	Ⓐ	0619		2019	2119	2219	Ⓒ	0624		2224
2	Brussels Central .... d.		0623		2023	2123	2223		0628		2228
4	**Brussels** Midi / Zuid .... d.		0630	and	2030	2130	2230		0635	and	2235
)	Halle .... d.		0641	hourly	2041	2141	2241		0644	hourly	2244
3	Braine-le-Comte .... d.		0658	until	2058	2158	2258		0700	until	2300
)	**La Louvière** Centre ... a.		0720		2120	2220	2320		0721		2321
5	La Louvière Sud .... a.		0726		2126	2226	2326		0726		2326
4	**Binche** .... a.		0740		2140	...	...		0746		2346

		Ⓐ		Ⓐ		Ⓒ	Ⓒ		Ⓒ
Binche .... d.	Ⓐ	0520		2120	Ⓒ	0521	0614		2214
La Louvière Sud .... d.		0534		2134		0534	0634		2234
La Louvière Centre .... d.		0540	and	2140		0539	0639	and	2239
Braine-le-Comte .... d.		0603	hourly	2203		0602	0702	hourly	2302
Halle .... d.		0621	until	2221		0617	0717	until	2317
Brussels Midi / Zuid . a.		0630		2230		0625	0725		2325
Brussels Central .... a.		0636		2236		0631	0731		2331
Brussels Nord .... a.		0641		2241		0636	0736		2336

Ⓐ trains run beyond Brussels to / from Turnhout (Table **434**). On Ⓒ trains run beyond Brussels to / from Antwerpen (Table **420**).

BRUSSELS - GERAARDSBERGEN 424

es 94, 123

n			Ⓐ		Ⓐ		Ⓒ		Ⓒ
0	**Brussels** Nord .... d.	Ⓐ	0442		2042	Ⓒ	0742		2042
2	Brussels Centraal .... d.		0446	and	2046		0746	and	2046
4	**Brussels** Midi / Zuid . d.		0453	hourly	2053		0753	hourly	2053
8	Halle .... d.		0504	until	2104		0804	until	2104
3	Edingen .... d.		0515		2115		0815		2115
9	**Geraardsbergen** ..... a.		0535		2135		0835		2135

		Ⓐ		Ⓐ		Ⓒ		Ⓒ
Geraardsbergen .... d.	Ⓐ	0424		2024	Ⓒ	0724		2024
Edingen .... d.		0446	and	2046		0746	and	2046
Halle .... d.		0458	hourly	2058		0758	hourly	2058
Brussels Midi / Zuid .. a.		0507	until	2107		0807	until	2107
Brussels Centraal .... a.		0513		2113		0813		2113
Brussels Nord .... a.		0518		2118		0818		2118

MONS - CHARLEROI - NAMUR 425

es 118, 130

n			Ⓐ	Ⓐ	Ⓐ	Ⓐ ♡	Ⓐ	Ⓐ ◇	Ⓐ		Ⓐ	Ⓐ	Ⓐ	Ⓐ	Ⓐ	Ⓐ		Ⓒ	Ⓒ ♡	Ⓒ ♡		Ⓒ ♡	Ⓒ ♡
	Tournai 416 .... d.	Ⓐ	...	...	...	0544	...	0644	...	and at	1944	...	2044	...	2144	...	Ⓒ	...	0630	0730		2030	2130
0	**Mons** .... d.		0437	...	0537	0617	0638	0717	0737	the	2017	2037	2118	2137	2218	2237		0615	0715	0815		2115	2215
0	La Louvière Sud .... d.		0454	...	0554	0633	0654	0733	0754	same	2033	2054	2133	2154	2233	2254		0631	0731	0831	and	2131	2231
1	**Charleroi** Sud .... d.		0514	0552	0614	0652	0714	0752	0814	minutes	2052	2114	2152	2214	2252	2312		0651	0751	0851	hourly	2151	2251
6	Tamines .... d.		0527	0603	0627	0703	0727	0803	0827	past	2103	2127	2203	2227	2303	...		0704	0804	0904	until	2204	2304
1	Jemeppe-sur-Sambre .... d.		0535	|	0635	|	0735	|	0835	each	|	2135	|	2235	|	...		0712	0812	0912		2212	2312
8	**Namur** .... a.		0550	0622	0650	0722	0750	0822	0850	hour	2122	2150	2222	2250	2322	...		0727	0827	0927		2227	2327
	Liège Guillemins 442 .... a.		0642	...	0742	...	0842	...	0942	until	...	2242	...	...	...	...		0818	0918	1018		2318	...

		Ⓐ	Ⓐ	Ⓐ	Ⓐ	Ⓐ	Ⓐ	Ⓐ ◇		Ⓐ	Ⓐ	Ⓐ	Ⓐ	Ⓐ			Ⓒ ♡	Ⓒ ♡	Ⓒ ♡		Ⓒ ♡	Ⓒ ♡	Ⓒ
iège Guillemins 442 ..... a.	Ⓐ	...	...	...	0518	...	0618	...	and at	2018	...	2118	...	2218	...	Ⓒ	...	...	0642		1942	2042	2142
mur .... d.		...	0510	0538	0610	0638	0710	0738	the	2110	2138	2210	2238	2310	...		...	0633	0733		2033	2133	2233
neppe-sur-Sambre .... d.		...	0525	|	0625	|	0725	|	same	2125	|	2225	|	2325	...		...	0648	0748	and	2048	2148	2248
mines .... d.		...	0534	0558	0634	0658	0734	0758	minutes	2134	2158	2234	2258	2334	...		...	0657	0757	hourly	2057	2157	2257
arleroi Sud .... d.		0448	0548	0611	0648	0711	0748	0811	past	2148	2211	2248	2309	2346	...		0611	0711	0811	until	2111	2211	2310
Louvière Sud .... d.		0508	0608	0628	0708	0728	0808	0828	each	2208	2228	2308	...	...	...		0631	0731	0831		2131	2231	...
ns .... a.		0522	0622	0642	0722	0742	0822	0842	hour	2222	2242	2322	...	...	...		0645	0745	0845		2145	2245	...
Tournai 416 .... a.		...	...	0715	...	0815	...	0915	until	...	2315	...	...	...	...		0730	0830	0930		2230	2330	...

- Certain journeys run from / to Mouscron (Table **416**).

♡ – From / to Mouscron (Table **416**).

MONS - QUEVY 426

e 96

m		Ⓐ	Ⓐ		Ⓐ	Ⓐ§	Ⓐ§	Ⓐ	Ⓐ	Ⓐ
0	Mons .... d.	0721	0821	hourly	1621	1728	1809	1818	1921	2021
8	Quevy .... a.	0736	0836	until	1636	1743	1826	1833	1936	2036

	Ⓐ	Ⓐ‡	Ⓐ‡	Ⓐ	Ⓐ	Ⓐ	Ⓐ		Ⓐ
Quévy .... d.	0524	0601	0615	0655	0724	0755	0824	hourly	1924
Mons .... a.	0539	0617	0632	0711	0739	0810	0839	until	1939

From Brussels (depart Brussels Midi 1636 and 1715).

‡ – To Brussels (arrive Brussels Midi 0704 and 0719).

No service on Ⓒ.

CHARLEROI - ERQUELINNES 427

e 130a

m			Ⓐ		Ⓐ		Ⓒ		Ⓒ
0	**Charleroi** Sud .... d.	Ⓐ	0655	and	1955	Ⓒ	0614	every	2014
4	Thuin .... d.		0712	hourly	2012		0629	**two**	2029
6	Lobbes .... d.		0718	until	2018		0635	hours	2035
29	**Erquelinnes** .... a.		0734		2034		0653	until	2053

		Ⓐ		Ⓐ		Ⓒ		Ⓒ
Erquelinnes .... d.	Ⓐ	0504	and	2004	Ⓒ	0704	every	2104
Lobbes .... d.		0521	hourly	2021		0724	**two**	2124
Thuin .... d.		0523	until	2023		0727	hours	2127
Charleroi Sud .... a.		0543		2043		0745	until	2145

mont (France) is approximately 2 km from Erquelinnes station (for Jeumont - Lille see Table **262**).

430 BRUSSELS - LANDEN - HASSELT, GENK and LIÈGE

Lines 36

For direct services Brussels - Liège via high-speed line see Table **400**. For other services Brussels - Hasselt on Ⓐ (via Aarshot) see Table **431**.

km			Ⓐ ♡	Ⓐ	Ⓐ •	Ⓐ ♡	Ⓐ △	Ⓐ •		Ⓐ ♡	Ⓐ △	Ⓐ •	Ⓐ ♡	Ⓐ △	Ⓐ b	Ⓐ △	Ⓐ b		Ⓐ	Ⓐ	Ⓐ	Ⓐ	Ⓐ
0	**Brussels** Midi / Zuid d.	Ⓐ	0512	0514	0539	0612	0614	0639		2112	2114	2139	2212	2214	2256	2314	0021		1548	1603	1634	1706	1734
2	Brussels Central d.		0516	0518	0543	0616	0618	0643	and	2116	2118	2143	2216	2218	2300	2318	0025		1552	1607	1638	1710	1738
4	Brussels Nord d.		0522	0525	0549	0622	0625	0649	at	2122	2125	2149	2222	2225	2307	2325	0032		1602	1614	1645	1716	1745
33	**Brussels Nationaal ✈** d.		|	0538	|	|	0638	|	the	|	2138	|	|	2238	|	2338	|	A	|	|	|	|	|
33	Leuven d.		0543	0553	0610	0643	0653	0710	same	2143	2153	2210	2243	2253	2328	2353	0050	L	1621	1634	1703	1737	1803
64	Tienen d.		0555	0607	0623	0655	0707	0723	minutes	2155	2207	2223	2255	2307	2340	0009	0102	S	1638	1647	1716	1750	1816
64	Landen d.		0607	0621	0634	0707	0721	0734	past	2207	2221	2234	2307	2321	2351	0024	0113	O	1653	1659	1729	1801	1829
75	Sint-Truiden d.		0616	...	|	0716	...	|	each	2216	...	|	2316	...	|	...	|		1704	|	1745	|	1845
92	**Hasselt** a.		0630	...	|	0730	...	|	hour	2230	...	|	2330	...	|	...	|		1721	|	1803	|	1903
108	Genk a.		0652	...	|	0752s	...	|	until	2252	...	|	...	...	|	...	|		...	|	...	|	1924
103	**Liège** Guillemins a.		...	...	0706	...	...	0806		...	...	2306	...	...	0022	...	0144		...	1734	...	1835	...

		Ⓒ ♡	Ⓒ	Ⓒ ♡	Ⓒ	Ⓒ △	Ⓒ ♡	Ⓒ	Ⓒ △		Ⓒ ♡	Ⓒ	Ⓒ △	Ⓒ ♡	Ⓒ	Ⓒ △	Ⓒ ♡	Ⓒ	Ⓒ △	Ⓒ ♡	Ⓒ △	Ⓒ b	Ⓒ △
Brussels Midi / Zuid d.	Ⓒ	0612	...	0712	...	0714	0812	...	0814		1912	...	1914	2012	...	2014	2112	...	2114	2212	2214	2256	2314
Brussels Central d.		0616	...	0716	...	0718	0816	...	0818	and	1916	...	1918	2016	...	2018	2116	...	2118	2216	2218	2300	2318
Brussels Nord d.		0622	...	0722	...	0724	0822	...	0824	at	1922	...	1924	2022	...	2024	2122	...	2124	2222	2224	2307	2324
Brussels Nationaal ✈ d.		|	...	|	...	0738	|	...	0838	the	|	...	1938	|	...	2038	|	...	2138	|	2238	|	2338
Leuven d.		0643	...	0743	...	0751	0843	...	0853	same	1943	...	1951	2043	...	2053	2143	...	2151	2243	2253	2328	2351
Tienen d.		0655	...	0755	...	...	0855	...	0907x	minutes	1955	...	...	2055	...	2107	2155	...	...	2255	2307	2340	...
Landen d.		0707	0712	0807	0812	...	0907	0912	0921x	past	2007	2012	...	2107	2112	2121	2207	2212	...	2307	2321	2351	...
Sint-Truiden d.		0716	|	0816	|	...	0916	|	...	each	2016	|	...	2116	|	...	2216	|	...	2316	...	|	...
Hasselt a.		0730	|	0830	|	...	0930	|	...	hour	2030	|	...	2130	|	...	2230	|	...	2330	...	|	...
Genk a.		0752	|	0852	|	...	0952	|	...	until	2052	|	...	2152	|	...	2252	|	...	2352	...	|	...
Liège Guillemins a.		...	0752	...	0852	...	...	0952	...		...	2052	...	...	2152	...	...	2252	...	...	...	0022	...

		Ⓐ △	Ⓐ ♡	Ⓐ b	Ⓐ •	Ⓐ △	Ⓐ ♡	Ⓐ •	Ⓐ △		Ⓐ ♡	Ⓐ •	Ⓐ	Ⓐ b			Ⓐ	Ⓐ	Ⓐ	Ⓐ	Ⓐ		Ⓐ
Liège Guillemins d.	Ⓐ	...	...	0440	0454	...	...	0554	...		...	2154	...	2308	...		...	...	0624	...	0724	...	...
Genk d.		...	...	|	|	...	0508r	|	...	and	2108	|	...	|	...		...	0533	|	0624	|	...	1537
Hasselt d.		...	0430	|	|	...	0530	|	...	at	2130	|	...	|	...		...	0557	|	0657	|	...	1558
Sint-Truiden d.		...	0445	|	|	...	0545	|	...	the	2145	|	...	|	...	A	...	0616	|	0716	|	...	1616
Landen d.		0439	0455	0510	0527	0539	0555	0627	0639	same	2155	2227	2239	2338	...	L	0604	0630	0659	0730	0759	...	1630
Tienen d.		0454	0506	0521	0539	0554	0606	0639	0654	minutes	2206	2239	2254	2349	...	S	0617	0643	0711	0743	0811	...	1643
Leuven d.		0509	0519	0534	0552	0609	0619	0652	0709	past	2219	2252	2309	0001	...	O	0630	0659	0725	0759	0825	...	1655
Brussels Nationaal ✈ a.		0523	|	|	|	0623	|	|	0723	each	|	|	2323	|	...		|	|	|	|	|	...	...
Brussels Nord a.		0536	0538	0552	0611	0636	0638	0711	0736	hour	2238	2311	2336	0017	...		0646	0716	0744	0816	0843	...	...
Brussels Central a.		0541	0543	0558	0616	0641	0643	0716	0741	until	2243	2316	2341	0022	...		0652	0721	0750	0821	0848	...	...
Brussels Midi / Zuid a.		0546	0548	0603	0621	0646	0648	0721	0746		2248	2321	2346	0027	...		0657	0726	0755	0826	0853	...	...

		Ⓒ △	Ⓒ b	Ⓒ △	Ⓒ △	Ⓒ ♡	Ⓒ △	Ⓒ	Ⓒ ♡	Ⓒ △	Ⓒ	Ⓒ ♡	Ⓒ △		Ⓒ	Ⓒ ♡	Ⓒ △	Ⓒ	Ⓒ ♡	Ⓒ	Ⓒ ♡	Ⓒ b	
Liège Guillemins d.	Ⓒ	...	0440	...	...	...	...	0708	...	...	0808	...	...		2008	...	...	2108	...	2208	...	2308	...
Genk d.		...	|	...	...	...	...	|	0708	...	|	0808	...	and	|	2008	...	|	2108	|	2204	|	...
Hasselt d.		...	|	...	...	0630	...	|	0730	...	|	0830	...	at	|	2030	...	|	2130	|	2230	|	...
Sint-Truiden d.		...	|	...	...	0645	...	|	0745	...	|	0845	...	the	|	2045	...	|	2145	|	2245	|	...
Landen d.		...	0510	0539	...	0655	0739	0748	0755	...	0848	0855	0939z	same	2048	2055	...	2148	2155	2248	2255	2338	...
Tienen d.		...	0521	0554	...	0706	0754	...	0806	...	...	0906	0954z	minutes	...	2106	...	...	2206	...	2306	2349	...
Leuven d.		0509	0534	0609	0709	0719	0809	...	0819	0909	...	0919	1009	past	...	2119	2209	...	2219	...	2319	0001	...
Brussels Nationaal ✈ a.		0522	|	0622	0722	|	0822	...	|	0922	...	|	1022	each	...	|	2222	...	|	...	|	|	...
Brussels Nord a.		0536	0552	0636	0736	0738	0836	...	0838	0936	...	0938	1036	hour	...	2138	2236	...	2238	...	2338	0017	...
Brussels Central a.		0541	0558	0641	0741	0743	0841	...	0843	0941	...	0943	1041	until	...	2143	2241	...	2243	...	2343	0022	...
Brussels Midi / Zuid a.		0546	0603	0646	0746	0748	0846	...	0848	0946	...	0948	1046		...	2148	2246	...	2248	...	2348	0027	...

b – From / to Brugge and Oostende (Table **400**).
r – 1308 departs at 1301.
s – 1312 from Brussels terminates at Hasselt.
x – Extends beyond Leuven to Landen every **two** hours (even hours from Brussels).

z – Every **two** hours from Landen 0939 - 1939.
♡ – From / to Brugge and Gent, Table **405** (most trains also from / to Knokke and Blankenberge).
△ – From / to Gent via Aalst, Table **411** (most trains also from / to De Panne).

• – From / to Mons (Table **422**).

ADDITIONAL JOURNEYS HASSELT - GENK:
From Hasselt: 0716Ⓐ, 1616Ⓐ, 1716Ⓐ, 1816Ⓐ.
From Genk: 0725Ⓐ, 0837Ⓐ, 0925Ⓐ, 1625Ⓐ, 1725Ⓐ, 1825

431 BRUSSELS - AARSCHOT - HASSELT - TONGEREN

Line

No service on Ⓒ via this route. For other trains Brussels - Hasselt (via Landen) see Table **430**.

km			Ⓐ	Ⓐ		Ⓐ	Ⓐ	Ⓐ	
	Gent **411** ▷ d.	Ⓐ	0440	0540		1940	2040	2140	...
0	**Brussels** Midi / Zuid d.		0545	0645		2045	2145	2245	...
2	Brussels Central d.		0549	0649	and	2049	2149	2249	...
4	Brussels Nord d.		0555	0655	hourly	2055	2155	2255	...
46	Aarschot **432** d.		0621	0721	until	2121	2221	2321	...
63	Diest **432** d.		0634	0734		2134	2234	2334	...
84	**Hasselt** **432** a.		0649	0749		2149	2249	2349	...
110	Tongeren **435** a.		0723	0823		2223	...	...	...

		Ⓐ	Ⓐ	Ⓐ		Ⓐ	Ⓐ
Tongeren **435** d.	Ⓐ	...	0537	0637		2037	2137
Hasselt **432** d.		0511	0611	0711		2111	2211
Diest **432** d.		0527	0627	0727	and	2127	2227
Aarschot **432** d.		0541	0641	0741	hourly	2141	2241
Brussels Nord a.		0605	0705	0805	until	2205	2305
Brussels Central a.		0610	0710	0810	▽	2210	2310
Brussels Midi / Zuid a.		0615	0715	0815		2215	2315
Gent **411** ▷ a.		0720	0820	0920		2320	0020

▽ – There is no 0937 departure from Tongeren (starts from Hasselt at 1011). On 1937 from Tongeren change trains at Hasselt.

▷ – Gent to Brussels is via Aalst and Denderleeuw (shown in footnote on Table **411**).

432 ANTWERPEN - BRUSSELS NATIONAAL ✈ - AARSCHOT - HASSELT

Lines 35, 36c,

For Antwerpen - Hasselt via Mol see Table **434**. For additional trains Brussels Nationaal ✈ - Leuven see Table **430**.

km	*Via Airport*		Ⓐ		Ⓐ		Ⓒ ♠	♠	Ⓒ ♠	Ⓒ ♠
0	**Antwerpen** Centraal ▷ d.	Ⓐ	0445		2245	Ⓒ	0536		1936	2236
24	Mechelen ▷ d.		0507		2307		0556	and	1956	2256
40	**Brussels Nationaal ✈** ▷ d.		0521	and	2321		0610	every	2010	2310
59	Leuven d.		0543	hourly	2343		0634	**two**	2034	2334
75	Aarschot d.		0555	until	2355		0647	hours	2047	2347
92	Diest d.		0608		0008		0706	until	2106	0006
113	**Hasselt** a.		0622		0022		0723		2123	0023

		Ⓐ		Ⓐ		Ⓒ ♥	Ⓒ ♥	♥
Hasselt d.	Ⓐ	0438		2238	Ⓒ	...	0637	
Diest d.		0453		2253		...	0654	and
Aarschot d.		0507	and	2307		...	0715	every
Leuven d.		0526	hourly	2326		0536	0736	**two**
Brussels Nationaal ✈ ▷ a.		0539	until	2339		0550	0750	hours
Mechelen ▷ a.		0553		2353		0604	0804	until
Antwerpen Centraal ▷ a.		0615		0015		0624	0824	

km	*Via Lier*		Ⓐ		Ⓐ		Ⓒ		Ⓒ	Ⓒ ◇
0	**Antwerpen** Centraal d.	Ⓐ	0631		2231	Ⓒ	0631		1931	2031
14	Lier d.		0649	and	2249		0649		1949	2049
41	Aarschot d.		0712	hourly	2312		0717	and	2017	2117
57	**Leuven** a.		0724	until	2324	◧	|	hourly	|	|
59	Diest d.		...		...		0730	until	2030	2130
80	**Hasselt** a.		...		...		0744		2044	2144
	Tongeren **435** a.		...		...		0814		2114	2214
	Liège Guillemins **435** a.		...		...		0851		2151	...

		Ⓐ		Ⓐ		Ⓒ	Ⓒ	
Liège Guillemins **435** d.	Ⓐ	...		...	Ⓒ	...	0609	
Tongeren **435** d.		...		...		...	0646	
Hasselt d.		...		...		0616	0716	and
Diest d.		...		...	◧	0631	0731	hourly
Leuven d.		0636	and	2036		|	|	until
Aarschot d.		0650	hourly	2050		0650	0750	
Lier d.		0713	until	2113		0712	0812	
Antwerpen Centraal a.		0729		2129		0729	0829	

♠ – Antwerpen - Leuven runs **hourly** 0436 - 2236.
♥ – Leuven - Antwerpen runs **hourly** 0536 - 2336.

◧ – On Ⓒ local trains run hourly Antwerpen - Aarschot - Leuven (journey 63 mins): from Antwerpen 0646 - 2246, from Leuven 0611 - 2211.

◇ – Also at 2131 to Tongeren, 2231 to Hasselt.
▷ – For additional trains see Table **420**.

15 BRUSSELS and ANTWERPEN - LIER - TURNHOUT / HASSELT / HAMONT 434

		Ⓐ	Ⓐ	Ⓐ	Ⓐ	Ⓐ	Ⓐ	Ⓐ	Ⓐ		Ⓐ	Ⓐ	Ⓐ	Ⓐ	Ⓐ	Ⓐ	Ⓐ	Ⓐ	Ⓐ	Ⓐ	Ⓐ	
Brussels Midi / Zuid ▷ d.	Ⓐ	...	...	...	0633	...	...	0733	...		...	1933	...	...	2033	...	...	2133	...	2233	...	...
Brussels Centraal ▷ d.		...	...	...	0637	...	...	0737	...		...	1937	...	...	2037	...	...	2137	...	2237	...	...
Brussels Nord ▷ d.		...	...	...	0643	...	...	0743	...	and	...	1943	...	...	2043	...	...	2143	...	2243	...	...
Mechelen ▷ d.		...	...	...	0704	...	...	0804	...	at	...	2004	...	...	2104	...	...	2204	...	2304	...	...
Antwerpen Centraal d.		...	0609	0648	|	0709	0748	|	0809	the	1948	|	2009	2048	|	2109	2148	|	2225	|	2325	...
Antwerpen Berchem d.		...	0615	0653	|	0715	0753	|	0815	same	1953	|	2015	2053	|	2115	2153	|	2230	|	2330	...
Lier d.		...	0627	0704	0722	0727	0804	0822	0827	minutes	2004	2022	2027	2104	2122	2127	2204	2222	2246	2322	2346	...
Herentals d.		...	0642	0722	0738	0742	0822	0838	0842	past	2022	2038	2042	2122	2138	2142	2222	2238	2309	2338	0009	...
Turnhout a.		...	|	0738	0753	|	0838	0853	|	each	2038	2053	|	2138	2153	|	2238	2253	|	2353	|	...
Geel d.		...	0654	...	...	0754	...	...	0854	hour	...	...	2054	...	...	2154	...	...	2321	...	0021	...
Mol a.		0607	0702	...	...	0802	...	...	0902	until	...	...	2102	...	...	2202	...	...	2329	...	0029	...
Hasselt a.		0652	0752r	...	...	0852r	...	...	0952r		...	...	2152r	...	...	2252r	...	...	|	...	...	...
Overpelt a.		...	0726	...	...	0826	...	...	0926		...	...	2126	...	...	2226	...	...	2346	...	...	...
Neerpelt a.		...	0728	...	...	0828	...	...	0928		...	...	2128	...	...	2228	...	...	2348	...	...	...
Hamont a.		...	0737	...	...	0837	...	...	0937		...	...	2137	...	...	2237	...	...	...	...	...	...

		Ⓐ	Ⓐ	Ⓐ	Ⓐ	Ⓐ	Ⓐ	Ⓐ	Ⓐ	Ⓐ	Ⓐ	Ⓐ		Ⓐ	Ⓐ	Ⓐ	Ⓐ	Ⓐ	Ⓐ	Ⓐ	Ⓐ	
Hamont d.	Ⓐ	...	...	...	0528	...	...	0621	...	...	0721	...		...	1921	...	...	2021	...	2121	...	...
Neerpelt d.		...	...	...	0537	...	...	0630	...	...	0730	...		...	1930	...	...	2030	...	2130	...	...
Overpelt d.		...	...	...	0540	...	...	0633	...	...	0733	...	and	...	1933	...	...	2033	...	2133	...	...
Hasselt d.		...	...	...	|	...	...	0608s	...	...	0708s	...	at	...	1908s	...	...	2008s	...	2108s	2208	...
Mol d.		0458	...	...	0558	...	...	0658	...	...	0758	...	the	...	1958	...	...	2058	...	2158	2253	...
Geel d.		0506	...	...	0606	...	...	0706	...	...	0806	...	same	...	2006	...	...	2106	...	2206	...	...
Turnhout d.		|	0500	0522	|	0607	0622	|	0707	0722	|	0807	minutes	1922	|	2007	2022	|	2107	|	...	...
Herentals d.		0520	0524	0541	0620	0624	0641	0720	0724	0741	0820	0824	past	1941	2020	2024	2041	2120	2124	2220	...	...
Lier d.		0535	0540	0557	0635	0640	0657	0735	0740	0757	0835	0840	each	1957	2035	2040	2057	2135	2140	2235	...	...
Antwerpen Berchem a.		0545	|	0607	0645	|	0707	0745	|	0807	0845	|	hour	2007	2045	|	2107	2145	|	2245	...	...
Antwerpen Centraal a.		0551	|	0612	0651	|	0712	0751	|	0812	0851	|	until	2012	2051	|	2112	2151	|	2251	...	...
Mechelen ▷ d.		...	0559	...	...	0659	...	...	0759	...	...	0859		...	...	2059	...	...	2159	...	...	...
Brussels Nord ▷ a.		...	0617	...	...	0717	...	...	0817	...	...	0917		...	...	2117	...	...	2217	...	...	...
Brussels Central ▷ a.		...	0622	...	...	0722	...	...	0822	...	...	0922		...	...	2122	...	...	2222	...	...	...
Brussels Midi / Zuid ▷ a.		...	0627	...	...	0727	...	...	0827	...	...	0927		...	...	2127	...	...	2227	...	...	...

		Ⓒ	Ⓒ	Ⓒ	Ⓒ		Ⓒ	Ⓒ	Ⓒ △	Ⓒ ▽
erpen C. d.	Ⓒ	0609	0709	0752	0809		1952	2009	2052	2109
erchem d.		0615	0715	0758	0815	and	1958	2015	2058	2115
d.		0627	0727	0810	0827	at	2010	2027	2110	2127
tals d.		0642	0742	0832	0842	the	2032	2042	2132	2142
nhout a.		|	|	0847	|	same	2047	|	2147	|
d.		0654	0754	...	0854	minutes	...	2054	...	2154
a.		0702	0802	...	0902	past	...	2102	...	2202
sselt a.		0752r	|	...	0952x	each	...	2152x	...	|
elt a.		0726	0826	...	0926	hour	...	2126	...	2226
elt a.		0728	0828	...	0928	until	...	2128	...	2228
nt a.		0737	0837	...	0937		...	2137	...	2237

		Ⓒ ⊙	Ⓒ ⊡	Ⓒ	Ⓒ	Ⓒ		Ⓒ	Ⓒ	Ⓒ	Ⓒ	Ⓒ
Hamont d.	Ⓒ	...	...	...	...	0821		...	2021	...	2121	...
Neerpelt d.		0630	...	0730	...	0830	and	...	2030	...	2130	...
Overpelt d.		0633	...	0733	...	0833	at	...	2033	...	2133	...
Hasselt d.		|	...	|	...	0808z	the	...	2008z	...	|	...
Mol d.		0658	...	0758	...	0858	same	...	2058	...	2158	...
Geel d.		0706	...	0806	...	0906	minutes	...	2106	...	2206	...
Turnhout d.		|	0713	|	0813	|	past	2013	|	2113	|	2213
Herentals d.		0720	0730	0820	0830	0920	each	2030	2120	2130	2220	2230
Lier d.		0735	0752	0835	0852	0935	hour	2052	2135	2152	2235	2252
Ant. Berchem a.		0745	0802	0845	0902	0945	until	2102	2145	2202	2245	2302
Antwerpen C. a.		0751	0808	0851	0908	0951		2108	2151	2208	2251	2308

Portion for Hasselt is detached from main train at Mol (departs Mol xx07; Hamont portion departs xx10).
Portion from Hasselt attaches to main train at Mol (arrives Mol xx53; Hamont portion arrives xx49).
Portion for Hasselt runs every **two** hours (from Antwerpen 0809, 1009, 1209, 1409, 1609, 1809, 2009).
Portion from Hasselt runs every **two** hours (from Hasselt 0808, 1008, 1208, 1408, 1608, 1808, 2008).
See also Table **420**.

△ – Also at 2152, 2252, 2352.
▽ – Also at 2209, 2309.
⊡ – Also at 0613.
⊙ – Also at 0458 from Mol and 0530 from Neerpelt.

On Ⓐ Turnhout trains run beyond Brussels to / from Binche (Table ***423****).*

34 LIÈGE - HASSELT 435

		Ⓐ ◇		Ⓐ ◇		Ⓒ ♡		Ⓒ ♡
Liège Guillemins d.	Ⓐ	0722	and	2122	Ⓒ	0609	and	2109
Tongeren 431 d.		0758	hourly	2158		0646	hourly	2146
Hasselt 431 a.		0822	until	2222		0710	until	2210

		Ⓐ ◇		Ⓐ ◇		Ⓒ ♡		Ⓒ ♡	Ⓒ ♡	Ⓒ ♡
Hasselt 431 d.	Ⓐ	0638	and	2038	Ⓒ	0550	and	2050	2150	2250
Tongeren 431 d.		0703	hourly	2103		0615	hourly	2115	2214	2314
Liège Guillemins a.		0738	until	2138		0651	until	2151	...	...

From / to Maastricht (Table **436**).

♡ – Most journeys on Ⓒ run beyond Hasselt to / from Antwerpen (Table **432**).

40 LIÈGE - MAASTRICHT 436

		Ⓐ	Ⓐ	Ⓐ ◇	Ⓐ ◇		Ⓐ ◇	Ⓐ ◇	Ⓐ				⑥	Ⓒ	Ⓒ	Ⓒ		Ⓒ	Ⓒ			
Liège Guillemins d.	Ⓐ	0609	0640	0740	0840	and	2040	2140	2240	...	...	Ⓒ	0610	0709	0810	0910	and	2110	2210	...	...	...
Visé d.		0627	0658	0758	0858	hourly	2058	2158	2258	...	...		0628	0728	0828	0928	hourly	2128	2228	...	...	...
Maastricht a.		0642	0713	0813	0913	until	2113	2213	2313	...	...		0643	0743	0843	0943	until	2143	2243	...	...	...

		Ⓐ	Ⓐ ◇	Ⓐ ◇	Ⓐ ◇		Ⓐ ◇	Ⓐ	Ⓐ				⑥	Ⓒ	Ⓒ	Ⓒ		Ⓒ	Ⓒ				
tricht d.	Ⓐ	...	0648	0748	0848	and	2048	2148	2248	...	...	Ⓒ	0718	0818	0918	1018	and	2218	2318	...	...	...	...
d.		0615	0703	0803	0903	hourly	2103	2203	2303	...	...		0733	0833	0933	1033	hourly	2233	2333	...	...	...	...
e Guillemins a.		0633	0720	0820	0920	until	2120	2220	2320	...	...		0750	0850	0950	1050	until	2250	2350	...	...	...	...

To / from Hasselt (Table **435**).

s 37, 44 SPA - VERVIERS - AACHEN 438

For international trains Brussels - Aachen and beyond see Tables **20** / **21**.

	Ⓐ	Ⓐ	Ⓐ				Ⓐ	Ⓒ	Ⓒ
Spa Géronstère d.	...	0605	0646	0746		1946	2046	2046	2146
Spa d.	...	0608	0650	0750	and	1950	2050	2050	2150
Pepinster d.	...	0627	0712	0812	hourly	2012	2112	2112	2212
Verviers Central a.	...	0634	0718	0818	until	2018	2118	2118	2218
Verviers Central 400 d.	...	...	0726	0826		2026	2126	2126	2226
Welkenraedt 🏛 400 d.	0642	...	0742	0842		2042	2140	2142	2240
Aachen Hbf a.	0656	...	0756	0856		2056	...	2156	...

						Ⓐ	Ⓒ	Ⓒ
Aachen Hbf d.	...	0704a	0804		2004	2104	2104	2204
Welkenraedt 🏛 400 d.	0620	0720	0820	and	2020	2118	2120	2218
Verviers Central 400 a.	0634	0734	0834	hourly	2034	...	2134	...
Verviers central d.	0642	0742	0842	until	2042	...	2142	...
Pepinster d.	0651	0751	0851		2051	...	2151	...
Spa a.	0710	0810	0910		2110	...	2210	...
Spa Géronstère a.	0714	0814	0914		2114	...	2214	...

Ⓐ only.

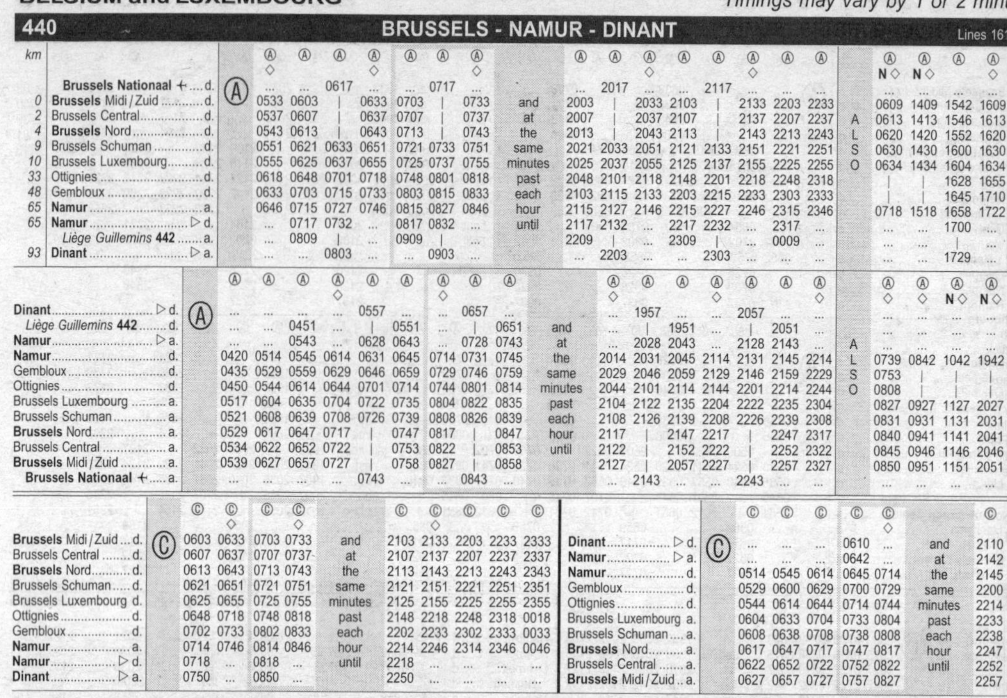

440 BRUSSELS - NAMUR - DINANT

Lines 16

km		Ⓐ ◇	Ⓐ	Ⓐ	Ⓐ ◇	Ⓐ	Ⓐ	Ⓐ ◇
	Brussels Nationaal ✈ d.	...	...	0617	...	...	0717	...
0	**Brussels** Midi/Zuid d.	0533	0603	|	0633	0703	|	0733
2	Brussels Central d.	0537	0607	|	0637	0707	|	0737
4	**Brussels** Nord d.	0543	0613	|	0643	0713	|	0743
9	Brussels Schuman d.	0551	0621	0633	0651	0721	0733	0751
10	Brussels Luxembourg d.	0555	0625	0637	0655	0725	0737	0755
33	Ottignies d.	0618	0648	0701	0718	0748	0801	0818
48	Gembloux d.	0633	0703	0715	0733	0803	0815	0833
65	**Namur** a.	0646	0715	0727	0746	0815	0827	0846
65	**Namur** ▷ d.	...	0717	0732	...	0817	0832	...
	Liège Guillemins **442** a.	...	0809	|	...	0909	|	...
93	**Dinant** ▷ a.	...	...	0803	...	...	0903	...

and at the same minutes past each hour until

	Ⓐ	Ⓐ	Ⓐ ◇	Ⓐ	Ⓐ	Ⓐ ◇	Ⓐ	Ⓐ
Brussels Nationaal ✈ d.	...	2017	...	...	2117	...	...	...
Brussels Midi/Zuid d.	2003	|	2033	2103	|	2133	2203	2233
Brussels Central d.	2007	|	2037	2107	|	2137	2207	2237
Brussels Nord d.	2013	|	2043	2113	|	2143	2213	2243
Brussels Schuman d.	2021	2033	2051	2121	2133	2151	2221	2251
Brussels Luxembourg d.	2025	2037	2055	2125	2137	2155	2225	2255
Ottignies d.	2048	2101	2118	2148	2201	2218	2248	2318
Gembloux d.	2103	2115	2133	2203	2215	2233	2303	2333
Namur a.	2115	2127	2146	2215	2227	2246	2315	2346
Namur ▷ d.	2117	2132	...	2217	2232	...	2317	...
Liège Guillemins **442** a.	2209	|	...	2309	|	...	0009	...
Dinant ▷ a.	...	2203	...	...	2303	...	...	...

ALSO

	Ⓐ N◇	Ⓐ N◇	Ⓐ	Ⓐ ◇
Brussels Nationaal ✈ d.	...	...	...	...
Brussels Midi/Zuid d.	0609	1409	1542	1609
Brussels Central d.	0613	1413	1546	1613
Brussels Nord d.	0620	1420	1552	1620
Brussels Schuman d.	0630	1430	1600	1630
Brussels Luxembourg d.	0634	1434	1604	1634
Ottignies d.	|	|	1628	1655
Gembloux d.	|	|	1645	1710
Namur a.	0718	1518	1658	1722
Namur ▷ d.	...	...	1700	...
Liège Guillemins **442** a.	...	...	|	...
Dinant ▷ a.	...	...	1729	...

	Ⓐ	Ⓐ	Ⓐ	Ⓐ ◇	Ⓐ	Ⓐ	Ⓐ ◇	Ⓐ	Ⓐ
Dinant ▷ d.	...	...	...	...	0557	...	...	0657	...
Liège Guillemins **442** d.	...	...	0451	...	|	0551	...	|	0651
Namur ▷ a.	...	...	0543	...	0628	0643	...	0728	0743
Namur d.	0420	0514	0545	0614	0631	0645	0714	0731	0745
Gembloux d.	0435	0529	0559	0629	0646	0659	0729	0746	0759
Ottignies d.	0450	0544	0614	0644	0701	0714	0744	0801	0814
Brussels Luxembourg a.	0517	0604	0635	0704	0722	0735	0804	0822	0835
Brussels Schuman a.	0521	0608	0639	0708	0726	0739	0808	0826	0839
Brussels Nord a.	0529	0617	0647	0717	|	0747	0817	|	0847
Brussels Central a.	0534	0622	0652	0722	|	0753	0822	|	0853
Brussels Midi/Zuid a.	0539	0627	0657	0727	|	0758	0827	|	0858
Brussels Nationaal ✈ a.	...	...	...	...	0743	...	...	0843	...

and at the same minutes past each hour until

	Ⓐ ◇	Ⓐ	Ⓐ	Ⓐ ◇	Ⓐ	Ⓐ	Ⓐ ◇
Dinant ▷ d.	...	1957	...	...	2057	...	...
Liège Guillemins **442** d.	...	|	1951	...	|	2051	...
Namur ▷ a.	...	2028	2043	...	2128	2143	...
Namur d.	2014	2031	2045	2114	2131	2145	2214
Gembloux d.	2029	2046	2059	2129	2146	2159	2229
Ottignies d.	2044	2101	2114	2144	2201	2214	2244
Brussels Luxembourg a.	2104	2122	2135	2204	2222	2235	2304
Brussels Schuman a.	2108	2126	2139	2208	2226	2239	2308
Brussels Nord a.	2117	|	2147	2217	|	2247	2317
Brussels Central a.	2122	|	2152	2222	|	2252	2322
Brussels Midi/Zuid a.	2127	|	2057	2227	|	2257	2327
Brussels Nationaal ✈ a.	...	2143	...	...	2243	...	...

ALSO

	Ⓐ ◇	Ⓐ ◇	Ⓐ N◇	Ⓐ N◇
Dinant ▷ d.	...	...	...	...
Liège Guillemins **442** d.	...	...	...	...
Namur ▷ a.	...	...	...	...
Namur d.	0739	0842	1042	1942
Gembloux d.	0753	|	|	|
Ottignies d.	0808	|	|	|
Brussels Luxembourg a.	0827	0927	1127	2027
Brussels Schuman a.	0831	0931	1131	2031
Brussels Nord a.	0840	0941	1141	2041
Brussels Central a.	0845	0946	1146	2046
Brussels Midi/Zuid a.	0850	0951	1151	2051
Brussels Nationaal ✈ a.	...	...	...	...

	Ⓒ	Ⓒ ◇	Ⓒ	Ⓒ ◇		Ⓒ	Ⓒ ◇	Ⓒ	Ⓒ	Ⓒ
Brussels Midi/Zuid d.	0603	0633	0703	0733	and	2103	2133	2203	2233	2333
Brussels Central d.	0607	0637	0707	0737	at	2107	2137	2207	2237	2337
Brussels Nord d.	0613	0643	0713	0743	the	2113	2143	2213	2243	2343
Brussels Schuman d.	0621	0651	0721	0751	same	2121	2151	2221	2251	2351
Brussels Luxembourg d.	0625	0655	0725	0755	minutes	2125	2155	2225	2255	2355
Ottignies d.	0648	0718	0748	0818	past	2148	2218	2248	2318	0018
Gembloux d.	0702	0733	0802	0833	each	2202	2233	2302	2333	0033
Namur a.	0714	0746	0814	0846	hour	2214	2246	2314	2346	0046
Namur ▷ d.	0718	...	0818	...	until	2218	...	...	...	...
Dinant ▷ a.	0750	...	0850	...		2250	...	...	...	...

	Ⓒ	Ⓒ	Ⓒ	Ⓒ ◇	Ⓒ		Ⓒ
Dinant ▷ d.	...	...	...	0610	...	and	2110
Namur ▷ a.	...	...	...	0642	...	at	2142
Namur d.	0514	0545	0614	0645	0714	the	2145
Gembloux d.	0529	0600	0629	0700	0729	same	2200
Ottignies d.	0544	0614	0644	0714	0744	minutes	2214
Brussels Luxembourg a.	0604	0633	0704	0733	0804	past	2233
Brussels Schuman a.	0608	0638	0708	0738	0808	each	2238
Brussels Nord a.	0617	0647	0717	0747	0817	hour	2247
Brussels Central a.	0622	0652	0722	0752	0822	until	2252
Brussels Midi/Zuid a.	0627	0657	0727	0757	0827		2257

N – Not Dec. 19 - Jan. 2, Mar. 26 - Apr. 9, May 6, June 25 - Aug. 28, Oct. 31.
◇ – To/from Luxembourg or other destinations in Table **445**.
▷ – See also Table **448**.

442 NAMUR - LIÈGE

Line

km		Ⓐ	Ⓐ	Ⓐ	Ⓐ ◇	Ⓐ	Ⓐ ◇		Ⓐ	Ⓐ ◇	Ⓐ	Ⓐ ◇	Ⓐ ◇	
	Mons **425** d.	0437	...	0537	...	0637	...	and at	1937	...	2037	...	...	...
	Charleroi Sud **425** d.	0514	...	0614	...	0714	...	the same	2014	...	2114	...	...	...
0	**Namur** d.	0553	0617	0653	0717	0753	0817	minutes	2053	2117	2153	2217	2317	...
20	Andenne d.	0607	0631	0707	0731	0807	0831	past	2107	2131	2207	2231	2331	...
31	Huy d.	0619	0645	0719	0745	0819	0845	each	2119	2145	2219	2245	2345	...
60	**Liège** Guillemins a.	0642	0709	0742	0809	0842	0909	hour	2142	2209	2242	2309	0009	...
63	Liège Palais a.	0651	0718	0751	0818	0851	0918	until	2151	2218	2251	2318	0018	...

	Ⓒ	Ⓒ	Ⓒ ▽	Ⓒ ▽		Ⓒ ▽	Ⓒ ▽
Mons **425** d.	...	0615	0715	0815		1915	2015
Charleroi Sud **425** d.	...	0651	0751	0851	and	1951	2051
Namur d.	0629	0729	0829	0929	hourly	2029	2129
Andenne d.	0643	0743	0843	0943	until	2043	2143
Huy d.	0655	0755	0855	0955		2055	2155
Liège Guillemins a.	0718	0818	0918	1018		2118	2218
Liège Palais a.	0727	0827	0927	1027		2127	2227

	Ⓐ ◇	Ⓐ	Ⓐ ◇	Ⓐ	Ⓐ ◇	Ⓐ	Ⓐ ◇		Ⓐ	Ⓐ ◇	Ⓐ	Ⓐ	Ⓐ	
Liège Palais d.	0442	0509	0542	0609	0642	0709	0742	and at	2009	2042	2109	2142	2209	...
Liège Guillemins d.	0451	0518	0551	0618	0651	0718	0751	the same	2018	2051	2118	2151	2218	...
Huy d.	0516	0542	0616	0642	0716	0742	0816	minutes	2042	2116	2142	2216	2242	...
Andenne d.	0527	0551	0627	0651	0727	0751	0827	past	2051	2127	2151	2227	2251	...
Namur a.	0543	0607	0643	0707	0743	0807	0843	each	2107	2143	2207	2243	2307	...
Charleroi Sud **425** a.	...	0646	...	0746	...	0846	...	hour	2146	...	2246	...	2346	...
Mons **425** a.	...	0722	...	0822	...	0922	...	until	2222	...	2322	...	...	...

	Ⓒ ▽	Ⓒ ▽	Ⓒ ▽	Ⓒ ▽		Ⓒ ▽	Ⓒ
Liège Palais d.	0633	0733	0833	0933		2033	2133
Liège Guillemins d.	0642	0742	0842	0942	and	2042	2142
Huy d.	0705	0805	0905	1005	hourly	2105	2205
Andenne d.	0716	0816	0916	1016	until	2116	2216
Namur a.	0731	0831	0931	1031		2131	2231
Charleroi Sud **425** a.	0809	0909	1009	1109		2209	2310
Mons **425** a.	0845	0945	1045	1145		2245	...

◇ – From/to Brussels (Table **440**).
▽ – From/to Mouscron via Tournai (Table **416**).

On Ⓐ June 27 - Aug. 26 the 0642 train from Liège extends to Oostende (a. 1016) and the 2118 arrival at Liège starts from Oostende (d. 1735).

On Ⓒ trains continue beyon Liège to/from Liers.

445 (BRUSSELS) - NAMUR - LUXEMBOURG

Line

km		Ⓐ	Ⓐ	Ⓐ N		B					B		Ⓐ N		Ⓐ		Ⓐ			Ⓐ	s	s	A	
	Brussels Midi/Zuid **440** d.	...	0533	0609	0633	0733	0833	0933	1033	1133	1233	1333	1409	1433	...	1533	1609	1633	1733	1809	1833	1933	2033	2133
	Brussels Central **440** d.	...	0537	0613	0637	0737	0837	0937	1037	1137	1237	1337	1413	1437	...	1537	1613	1637	1737	1813	1837	1937	2037	2137
	Brussels Nord **440** d.	...	0543	0620	0643	0743	0843	0943	1043	1143	1243	1343	1420	1443	...	1543	1620	1643	1743	1820	1843	1943	2043	2143
	Brussels Luxembourg **440** d.	...	0555	0634	0655	0755	0855	0955	1055	1155	1255	1355	1434	1455	...	1555	1634	1655	1755	1834	1855	1955	2055	2155
0	**Namur** d.	0550	0650	0720	0750	0850	0950	1050	1150	1250	1350	1450	1520	1550	1622	1650	1726	1750	1850	1920	1950	2050	2150	2250
29	Ciney d.	0613	0713	|	0813	0913	1013	1113	1213	1313	1413	1513	|	1613	1646	1713	1748	1813	1913	|	2013	2113	2213	2313
52	Marloie d.	0629	0729	|	0829	0929	1029	1129	1229	1329	1429	1528	|	1629	1701	1729	1803	1829	1929	|	2029	2129	2229	2329
58	Jemelle d.	0635	0735	|	0835	0935	1035	1135	1235	1335	1435	1535	|	1635	1707	1735	1809	1835	1935	|	2035	2135	2235	2335
90	Libramont d.	0657	0757	0817	0857	0957	1057	1157	1257	1357	1457	1557	1617	1657	1729	1757	1831	1857	1957	2017	2057	2157	2257	2357
137	Arlon ▷ d.	0730	0830	0854	0931	1030	1130	1231	1333	1433	1532	1633	1652	1730	...	1833	1902	1931	2033	2052	2130	2233	2330	0028
165	**Luxembourg** ▷ a.	0750	0850	0914	0951	1050	1150	1251	1353	1453	1552	1653	1712	1750	...	1853	...	1951	2053	2112	2150	2253	2350	...

	Ⓐ	Ⓐ	Ⓐ	Ⓒ u	Ⓐ	u	Ⓐ			Ⓐ N									B	⑦ R	Ⓐ N			B
Luxembourg ▷ d.	...	...	0510	...	...	0610	0648	0707	0810	0848	0910	1009	1107	1210	1309	1407	1510	1607	1709	...	1746	1809	1910	2009
Arlon ▷ d.	...	0432	0532	...	0557	0632	0710	0732	0832	0910	0932	1032	1132	1232	1332	1432	1532	1632	1732	1800	1810	1832	1932	2032
Libramont d.	...	0504	0604	...	0629	0704	0744	0804	0904	0944	1004	1104	1204	1304	1404	1504	1604	1704	1804	1832	1844	1904	2004	2104
Jemelle d.	0426	0526	0626	0626	0653	0726	|	0826	0926	|	1026	1126	1226	1327	1426	1526	1626	1726	1826	1853	|	1928	2026	2126
Marloie d.	0433	0533	0633	0633	0659	0733	|	0833	0933	|	1033	1133	1233	1333	1433	1533	1633	1733	1833	1900	|	1934	2033	2133
Ciney d.	0448	0548	0648	0648	0714	0748	|	0848	0948	|	1048	1148	1248	1348	1448	1548	1648	1748	1848	1915	|	1948	2048	2148
Namur a.	0510	0610	0710	0710	0736	0810	0840	0910	1010	1040	1110	1210	1310	1410	1510	1610	1710	1810	1910	1937	1940	2010	2110	2210
Brussels Luxembourg **440** a.	0604	0704	0804	0804	0827	0904	0927	1004	1104	1127	1204	1304	1404	1504	1604	1704	1804	1904	2004	2028	2027	2104	2204	2304
Brussels Nord **440** a.	0617	0717	0817	0817	0840	0917	0941	1017	1117	1141	1217	1317	1417	1517	1617	1717	1817	1917	2017	2041	2041	2117	2217	2317
Brussels Central **440** a.	0622	0722	0822	0822	0845	0922	0946	1022	1122	1146	1222	1322	1422	1522	1622	1722	1822	1922	2022	2049	2046	2122	2222	2322
Brussels Midi/Zuid **440** a.	0627	0727	0827	0827	0850	0927	0951	1027	1127	1151	1227	1327	1427	1527	1627	1727	1827	1927	2027	2054	2051	2127	2227	2327

A – Terminates at Arlon on ⑦ and holidays.
B – (12) Brussels - Luxembourg - Basel and v.v. (Table **43**).
C – On Ⓒ terminates at Jemelle.
N – Not Dec. 19 - Jan. 2, Mar. 26 - Apr. 9, May 6, June 25 - Aug. 28, Oct. 31.
R – Also May 5, 16, Nov. 1, 11; not Dec. 20, 27, Mar. 27, Apr. 3, June 26 - Aug. 28.
s – From Oostende on Ⓒ June 25 - Aug. 28 (d. 1712 and 1806).
u – To Oostende on Ⓒ June 25 - Aug. 28 (a. 0944 and 1045).

▷ – ADDITIONAL TRAINS ARLON - LUXEMBOURG (journey 20-30 minutes):
From Arlon: 0537Ⓐ, 0607Ⓐ, 0632, 0652Ⓐ, 0707Ⓐ, 0730Ⓒ, 0737Ⓐ, 0753Ⓐ, 080 0830Ⓒ, 0837Ⓐ, 0854Ⓐ, 0907Ⓐ, 1107Ⓐ, 1237Ⓐ, 1307Ⓐ, 1507Ⓐ, 1637Ⓐ, 165 1707Ⓐ, 1740Ⓐ, 1807Ⓐ, 1837Ⓐ, 1911Ⓐ, 1937Ⓐ, 2107Ⓐ.
From Luxembourg: 0519Ⓐ, 0555Ⓐ, 0626Ⓐ, 0654Ⓐ, 0723Ⓐ, 0752Ⓐ, 0825Ⓐ, 0852Ⓐ, 1023Ⓐ, 1153Ⓐ, 1223Ⓐ, 1323Ⓐ, 1423Ⓐ, 1623Ⓐ, 1638Ⓐ, 1656Ⓐ, 172 1734Ⓐ, 1756Ⓐ, 1823Ⓐ, 1838Ⓐ, 1853Ⓐ, 2024Ⓐ, 2051Ⓐ, 2207Ⓐ, 2307Ⓐ, 235

LIÈGE - GOUVY - CLERVAUX - LUXEMBOURG 446

…43/L10

	Ⓐ	Ⓐ	Ⓒ			Ⓐ N										Ⓐ N		Ⓐ			Ⓐ			
Liège Guillemins .. **447** d.	...	...	...	0608	...	0728	0808	...	1008	...	1208	...	1408	...	1608	1629	...	1708	1808	...	1908	2008	...	2208
Rivage **447** d.	...	...	...	0630	...	0751	0830	...	1030	...	1230	...	1430	...	1630	1653	...	1731	1830	...	1931	2030	...	2230
Aywaille d.	...	...	...	0639	...	0759	0839	...	1039	...	1239	...	1439	...	1639	1701	...	1739	1839	...	1939	2039	...	2239
Trois-Ponts d.	...	...	...	0701	...	0822	0901	...	1101	...	1301	...	1501	...	1701	1729	...	1802	1901	...	2002	2101	...	2301
Vielsalm d.	...	...	...	0713	...	0834	0913	...	1113	...	1313	...	1513	...	1713	1741	...	1814	1913	...	2014	2113	...	2313
Gouvy d.	0525	0625	...	0726	...	0844	0926	...	1126	...	1326	...	1526	...	1726	1751	...	1824	1926	...	2024	2126	...	2324
Troisvierges d.	0536	0636	0636	0736	0836	...	0936	1036	1136	1236	1336	1436	1536	1636	1736	...	1836	...	1936	2036	...	2136	2236	...
Clervaux d.	0545	0645	0645	0745	0845	...	0945	1045	1145	1245	1345	1445	1545	1645	1745	...	1845	...	1945	2045	...	2145	2245	...
Kautenbach d.	0602	0702	0702	0802	0902	...	1002	1102	1202	1302	1402	1502	1602	1702	1802	...	1902	...	2002	2102	...	2202	2302	...
Ettelbruck d.	0617	0717	0717	0817	0917	...	1017	1117	1217	1317	1417	1517	1617	1717	1817	...	1917	...	2017	2117	...	2217	2317	...
Mersch d.	0628	0728	0728	0828	0928	...	1028	1128	1228	1328	1428	1528	1628	1728	1828	...	1928	...	2028	2128	...	2228	2328	...
Luxembourg a.	0646	0746	0742	0842	0942	...	1042	1142	1242	1342	1442	1542	1642	1742	1842	...	1942	...	2042	2142	...	2242	2342	...

	Ⓐ	Ⓐ		Ⓐ N												Ⓐ		Ⓐ							⑦
…mbourg d.	...	...	...	...	0618	0718	0818	0918	1018	1118	1218	1318	1418	1518	1618	1645	1718	1745	1818	1918	2018	2118	2218	2318	0018
…ch d.	...	...	...	...	0633	0733	0833	0933	1033	1133	1233	1333	1433	1533	1633	1703	1733	1803	1833	1933	2033	2133	2233	2333	0033
…ruck d.	...	...	...	...	0644	0744	0844	0944	1044	1144	1244	1344	1444	1544	1644	1714	1744	1814	1844	1944	2044	2144	2244	2344	0044
…nbach d.	...	...	...	...	0700	0800	0900	1000	1100	1200	1300	1400	1500	1600	1700	1730	1800	1830	1900	2000	2100	2200	2300	0000	0100
…aux d.	...	...	...	...	0717	0817	0917	1017	1117	1217	1317	1417	1517	1617	1717	1747	1817	1847	1917	2017	2117	2217	2317	0017	0117
…vierges d.	...	...	...	...	0724	0826	0924	1026	1124	1226	1324	1426	1524	1626	1724	1756	1826	1856	1924	2026	2124	2226	2324	0024	0124
… d.	0507	0547	0639	0707	...	0839	...	1039	...	1239	...	1439	...	1639	...	1805	1839	1905	...	2039	...	2239	...	...	...
…alm d.	0518	0558	0649	0718	...	0849	...	1049	...	1249	...	1449	...	1649	...	...	1849	...	...	2049	...	2249	...	...	...
…Ponts d.	0529	0609	0701	0729	...	0901	...	1101	...	1301	...	1501	...	1701	...	...	1901	...	...	2101	...	2301	...	...	...
…ille d.	0551	0631	0723	0751	...	0923	...	1123	...	1323	...	1523	...	1723	...	...	1923	...	...	2123	...	2323	...	...	...
…e **447** d.	0600	0640	0732	0800	...	0932	...	1132	...	1332	...	1532	...	1732	...	...	1932	...	...	2132	...	2332	...	...	...
…Guillemins ... **447** a.	0623	0701	0754	0823	...	0954	...	1154	...	1354	...	1554	...	1754	...	...	1954	...	...	2154	...	2354	...	...	...

…Not Dec. 14-17, 21-31, Jan. 1-3, Mar. 28 - Apr. 8, June 27 - Aug. 26.

…TIONAL TRAINS TROISVIERGES - CLERVAUX - LUXEMBOURG:
…Troisvierges hourly 0406Ⓐ - 2206Ⓐ. From Luxembourg hourly 0645Ⓐ - 2245Ⓐ.

CONNECTIONS KAUTENBACH - WILTZ (journey 12 minutes):
From Kautenbach: on Ⓐ every 30 minutes 0602 - 2302; on Ⓒ 0602, 0702, hourly 0804 - 2204.
From Wiltz: on Ⓐ every 30 minutes 0416 - 2246; on Ⓒ 0546, 0646, 0746, hourly 0842 - 2242.

LIÈGE - MARLOIE 447

…43

	Ⓐ	Ⓐ		Ⓐ	Ⓒ S		Ⓐ		Ⓐ		Ⓐ		Ⓐ k	Ⓐ		Ⓐ		Ⓐ					
Liège Guillemins **446** d.	0614	0714	0814	0914	0914	1014	1114	1214	1314	1414	1514	1614	1649	1714	1814	1914	2014	2114	2214	...	...	...	...
Rivage **446** d.	0641	0741	0841	0941	0941	1041	1141	1241	1341	1441	1541	1641	1718	1741	1841	1941	2041	2141	2241	...	...	...	...
Barvaux d.	0704	0804	0904	1004	1004	1104	1204	1304	1404	1504	1604	1704	1740	1804	1904	2004	2104	2204	2304	...	...	...	...
Marloie a.	0722	0822	0922	1022	1022	1122	1222	1322	1422	1522	1622	1722	1800	1822	1922	2022	2122	2222	2322	...	...	...	...

	Ⓐ	Ⓐ	Ⓐ n	Ⓐ		Ⓐ		Ⓐ		Ⓐ		Ⓐ		Ⓐ		Ⓐ		Ⓐ	Ⓒ					
…oie d.	0438	0538	0613	0638	0738	0838	0938	1038	1138	1238	1338	1438	1538	1638	1738	1838	1938	2038	2138	...	...	...	...	...
…aux d.	0456	0556	0631	0656	0756	0856	0956	1056	1156	1256	1356	1456	1556	1656	1756	1856	1956	2056	2156	...	...	...	...	...
…ge **446** d.	0519	0619	0654	0719	0819	0919	1019	1119	1219	1319	1419	1519	1619	1719	1819	1919	2019	2119	2219	...	...	...	...	...
…Guillemins **446** a.	0546	0646	0723	0746	0846	0946	1046	1146	1246	1346	1446	1546	1646	1746	1846	1946	2046	2146	2246	...	...	...	...	...

…June 25 - Aug. 28.

k – To Jemelle, arrive 1811.

n – From Jemelle, depart 0606.

ARDENNES LOCAL SERVICES 448

…s 154, 166, 165

		Ⓒ	Ⓐ							Ⓐ	
Namur **440** d.	0552	0618	0632	0752	0952	1152	1352	1551	1752	1857	1951
Dinant **440** d.	0621	0650	0703	0821	1021	1221	1421	1619	1821	1929	2019
Houyet d.	0639	...	...	0839	1039	1239	1439	1637	1839	1947	2037
Beauraing d.	0647	...	...	0847	1047	1247	1447	1645	1847	1955	2045
Bertrix a.	0726	...	...	0926	1126	1326	1527	1724	1926	2034	2124
Bertrix d.	0733	...	...	0933	1133	1333	1534	1731	1933	...	2131
Libramont a.	0741	...	...	0941	1141	1341	1542	1739	1941	...	2139

		Ⓐ					Ⓐ			Ⓐ
Libramont d.	...	...	0719	0919	1119	1319	1516	...	1719	1916	2210
Bertrix a.	...	...	0728	0928	1128	1328	1525	...	1728	1925	2219
Bertrix d.	0535	0626	0735	0935	1135	1335	1532	1605	1735	1932	—
Beauraing d.	0613	0705	0813	1013	1213	1413	1609	1642	1813	2009	...
Houyet d.	0621	0713	0821	1021	1221	1421	1617	1650	1821	2017	**d**
Dinant **440** d.	0640	0732	0840	1040	1240	1440	1636	1708	1840	2036	2140
Namur **440** a.	0708	0801	0908	1108	1308	1508	1704	...	1908	2104	2209

	Ⓐ					§	Ⓐ			Ⓒ
Libramont d.	...	0809	1009	1209	1409	1609	1715	1809	2009	2209
Bertrix a.	...	0818	1018	1218	1418	1618	1724	1818	2018	2218
Bertrix d.	...	0821	1021	1221	1421	1621	1738	1824	2021	2221
Florenville d.	...	0834	1034	1234	1434	1634	1751	1837	2034	2234
Virton a.	...	0852	1052	1252	1452	1652	1808	1855	2052	2252
Virton d.	0709	0909**a**	1109**a**	1309**a**	1509**a**	1654**a**	1809	1909**a**	2109**a**	...
Athus ▷ d.	0730	0932**a**	1132**a**	1332**a**	1532**a**	1732**a**	1832	1932**a**	2132**a**	...
Arlon a.	0744	0946**a**	1146**a**	1346**a**	1546**a**	1746**a**	1846	1946**a**	2146**a**	...

		Ⓐ	Ⓐ N							Ⓐ		Ⓐ
Arlon d.	...	...	0645	0711**a**	0914**a**	1114**a**	1314**a**	1514**a**	1714**a**	1814	1914**a**	2112
Athus ▷ d.	...	...	0701	0737**a**	0931**a**	1131**a**	1331**a**	1531**a**	1731**a**	1831	1931**a**	2137
Virton a.	...	...	0721	0757**a**	0952**a**	1152**a**	1352**a**	1552**a**	1752**a**	1852	1952**a**	2157
Virton d.	0608	0700	0722	0808	1008	1208	1408	1608	1808	...	2008	2208
Florenville d.	0625	0717	0739	0825	1025	1225	1425	1625	1825	...	2025	2225
Bertrix a.	0639	0731	0752	0839	1039	1239	1439	1639	1839	...	2039	2239
Bertrix d.	0642	0737	0753	0842	1042	1242	1442	1642	1842	...	2042	2242
Libramont a.	0651	0746	0802	0851	1051	1251	1451	1651	1851	...	2051	2251

…Not Dec. 14-17, 21-31, Jan. 1-3, Mar. 28 - Apr. 8, June 27 - Aug. 26.

a – Ⓐ only.
d – On Ⓒ Dinant d. 2210, Namur a. 2242.

▷ – For connections Athus - Luxembourg see Table **449**.
§ – Arrives Athus at 1714.

LUXEMBOURG – local services 449

…erator: CFL

		⚒				
…mbourg d.	0454	0524	0554	every 30 mins on ⚒	2354	...
…bruck d.	0534	0604	0634	hourly on ⑦	0034	...
…rch a.	0539	0609	0639	(every 30 mins from 1154)	0039	...

	⚒	⚒	⚒			
Diekirch d.	0421	0451	0521	0551	every 30 mins on ⚒	2251
Ettelbruck d.	0427	0457	0527	0557	hourly on ⑦	2257
Luxembourg a.	0506	0536	0606	0636	(every 30 mins from 1251)	2336

		⚒				
…mbourg d.	...	0523	0553	every 30 mins on ⚒	2353	...
…nge d.	...	0545	0615	hourly on ⑦	0015	...
…ange d.	...	0552	0622	(every 30 mins from 1153)	0022	...
…s (Belgium) ▷ a.	...	0556	0626		0026	...

	⚒	⚒	⚒			
Athus (Belgium) ▷ d.	0504	0534	0604	0634	every 30 mins on ⚒	2234
Rodange d.	0510	0540	0610	0640	hourly on ⑦	2240
Pétange d.	0517	0547	0617	0647	(every 30 mins from 1134)	2247
Luxembourg a.	0537	0607	0637	0707		2307

…embourg → Bettembourg → Esch-sur-Alzette → Pétange → **Rodange** (journey 12 … to Bettembourg, 20 mins to Esch, 45-50 mins to Pétange, 50-55 mins to Rodange):
…535Ⓐ, 0605⚒, 0620 and every 15 minutes to 1950 then every 30 minutes to 2350.
…620 and hourly to 1220 then every 30 minutes to 2350 then 0050.

…embourg → **Wasserbillig** (journey 35-42 minutes):
…3Ⓐ**t**, 0612, 0631Ⓐ**t**, 0651Ⓐ**t**, 0710Ⓒ, 0731**t**, 0751Ⓐ, 0810, 0831**t**, 0910, 0931**t** and at …same minutes past each hour until 1610, 1631**t**, 1659Ⓐ**t**, 1710, 1731**t**, 1759Ⓐ**t**, 1810, …**t**, 1859Ⓐ**t**, 1910, 1931**t**, 2010, 2031**t**, 2110, 2131**t**, 2210, 2231**t**, 2310, 2331**t**.

…embourg → **Kleinbettingen** (journey 18-19 minutes):
…0555, 0623, approx every 30 mins to 2051 (not 0923, 1123, 1523, 1923) also 2119, 2215.
…0544, 0653 and hourly to 2153, 2254, 2358.

…embourg → Dudelange → **Volmerange-les-Mines** (journey 14 minutes):
…4⚒, 0734⚒ and approx every 30 mins to 2334⚒
…† runs only to Dudelange Usines, hourly 0634-1234, every 30 mins 1234-2334).

Rodange → Pétange → Esch-sur-Alzette → Bettembourg → **Luxembourg** (5-7 mins to Pétange, 26-32 mins to Esch, 39-45 mins to Bettembourg, 50-55 mins to Luxembourg):
⚒: at 06, 15, 36, 45 minutes past most hours 0536-1915, then every 30 mins to 2245.
†: 0645 and hourly to 1145 then every 30 minutes to 2345.

Wasserbillig → **Luxembourg** (journey 35-42 minutes):
0434Ⓐ, 0508, 0554Ⓐ**t**, 0608, 0627Ⓐ**t**, 0639Ⓐ, 0654**t**, 0708, 0735Ⓐ**t**, 0754, 0808Ⓐ**t**, 0808Ⓒ, 0854**t**, 0908, 0954**t**, 1008, 1054**t** and at the same minutes past each hour until 2208, 2254**t**, 2308.

Kleinbettingen → **Luxembourg** (journey 18-19 minutes):
Ⓐ: 0446 and approx every 30 mins to 2246 (not 1016, 1216, 2016, 2216).
Ⓒ: 0614, 0723 and approx hourly to 2323.

Volmerange-les-Mines → Dudelange → **Bettembourg** (journey 14 minutes):
0609⚒ and approx every 30 mins to 2339⚒.
(on † runs only from Dudelange Usines, hourly 0617-1217, every 30 mins 1217-2347).

…To/from Trier (Table **915**).

▷ – For connections to/from Arlon see Table **448**.

NETHERLANDS

SEE MAP PAGE

Operator: **NS** – Nederlandse Spoorwegen (unless otherwise indicated) www.ns.nl

Services: Trains convey first- and second-class seated accommodation, unless otherwise indicated in the tables. Some trains consist of portions for two or more destinations, and passe should be careful to join the correct part of the train. The destination of each train portion is normally indicated beside the entrance doors. Train numbers of internal services a announced or displayed on stations and are therefore not indicated in these tables. Sleeping cars (🛏) and couchettes (▬) are conveyed on international night trains or

Timings: Valid **December 13**, 2015 - **December 10**, 2016.

Holidays: Unless otherwise indicated, services marked ⚒ do not run on ⑦ or on Dec. 25, 26, Jan. 1, Mar. 28;
those marked Ⓐ do not run on ⑥⑦ or on Dec. 25, Jan. 1, Mar. 28, Apr. 27, May 5, 16;
those marked † run on ⑦ and on Dec. 25, 26, Jan. 1, Mar. 28;
those marked Ⓒ run on ⑥⑦ and on Dec. 25, Jan. 1, Mar. 28, Apr. 27, May 5, 16.
No trains, other than international services, will run between ± 2000 hours on Dec. 31 and ± 0200 on Jan. 1.

Tickets: A nationwide smartcard system called *OV-chipkaart* is used for all public transport in the Netherlands. Personalised and anonymous cards are available (€7.50) which ca loaded and topped up with travel credit. Disposable single use cards can also be purchased from ticket machines and ticket offices for full fare single / return journeys and day (a €1 supplement is payable for single use cards). You must always check-in and check-out your OV-chipkaart for each journey. Alternatively, e-tickets for full fare single and journeys may be purchased on-line and printed yourself.

Supplements: A supplement is payable for journeys on *Intercity direct* services (except for local journeys Amsterdam - Schiphol and Rotterdam - Breda), also for internal journeys on *IC* trains between Amsterdam and Arnhem. In both cases the single journey supplement is €2.30. Supplements may be purchased from special Supplement Pillars (using y OV-chipkaart) or from ticket machines.

450 AMSTERDAM - DEN HAAG - ROTTERDAM - ROOSENDAAL - VLISSINGEN

km		C	A	◧	C	C◧	Ⓐ	⚒	⚒	Ⓐ	Ⓐ	⚒	Ⓐ	⚒	⚒◧		Ⓑh	Ⓐ		◧	Ⓐ		◧	Ⓐ
0	**Amsterdam** Centraal ★ d.	0027	0027	0028	0057	0058	...	0527	0528	0557	0558	...	0612	0627	0628	...	0642	0642	0657	0658	0712	0727	0728	0742
5	Amsterdam Sloterdijk ★ d.	0032	0032	0035	0102	0105	...	0532	0535	0602	0605	...	0617	0632	0635	...	0647	0647	0702	0705	0717	0732	0735	0747
17	**Schiphol** ✈ ★ d.	|	|	0046	|	0116	...	|	0546	|	0616	...	|	|	0646	...	|	|	|	0716	|	|	0746	|
	Haarlem d.	0044	0044	|	0114	|	...	0544	|	0614	|	...	0628	0644	|	...	0658	0658	0714	|	0728	0744	|	0758
44	Leiden Centraal a.	0103	0104	0102	0133	0132	...	0603	0602	0633	0632	...	0648	0703	0702	...	0718	0718	0733	0732	0748	0803	0802	0818
44	Leiden Centraal d.	0105	0107	0105t	0135	0135	...	0605	0605	0635	0635	...	0650	0705	0705	...	0720	0720	0735	0735	0750	0805	0805	0820
	Den Haag Centraal 471 a.	0117	|	|	0147	|	...	0617	|	0647	|	...	|	0717	|	...	|	|	0747	|	|	0817	|	|
60	**Den Haag** HS 18 471 d.	...	0123	0117t	...	0147	...	▬	0619	...	0649	...	0704	...	0719	...	0734	0734	...	0749	0804	...	0819	0834
68	Delft 471 d.	...	...	...	...	...	...	...	0625	...	0655	...	0710	...	0725	...	0740	0740	...	0755	0810	...	0825	0840
78	Schiedam Centrum d.	...	...	...	...	...	...	Ⓐ	0633	...	0703	...	0718	...	0733	...	0748	0748	...	0803	0818	...	0833	0848
82	**Rotterdam** Centraal 18 471 d.	...	...	...	...	...	...	0611	0641	...	0711	0711	0725	...	0741	0741	0753	0755	...	0811	0825	...	0841	0855
102	Dordrecht 18 471 d.	...	...	...	...	...	...	0627	0657	...	0727	0727	0741	...	0757	0757	...	0811	...	0827	0841	...	0857	0911
140	**Roosendaal** 18 d.	...	...	...	...	...	0622	0652	0722	...	0752	0752	...	...	0822	0822	...	...	...	0852	...	...	0922	...
153	Bergen op Zoom d.	...	...	...	...	...	0631	0701	0731	...	0801	0801	...	...	0831	0831	...	...	...	0901	...	...	0931	...
190	Goes d.	...	...	...	...	...	0702	0732	0802	...	0832	0832	...	...	0902	0902	...	...	...	0932	...	...	1002	...
209	Middelburg d.	...	...	...	...	...	0716	0746	0816	...	0846	0846	...	...	0916	0916	...	...	...	0946	...	...	1016	...
215	**Vlissingen** a.	...	...	...	...	...	0724	0754	0824	...	0854	0854	...	...	0924	0924	...	...	...	0954	...	...	1024	...

	◧	⚒		◧	⚒		◧	⚒		◧	⚒		◧	⚒		◧	⚒		◧			◧		
Amsterdam Centraal ★ d.	0758	0812	0827	0828	0842	0857	0858	0912	0927	0928	0942	0957	0958	1012	1027	1028	1042	1057	1058	1112	1127	1128	1142	
Amsterdam Sloterdijk ★ d.	0805	0817	0832	0835	0847	0902	0905	0917	0932	0935	0947	1002	1005	1017	1032	1035	1047	1102	1105	1117	1132	1135	1147	
Schiphol ✈ ★ d.	0816	|	|	0846	|	|	0916	|	|	0946	|	|	1016	|	|	1046	|	|	1116	|	|	1146	|	
Haarlem d.	|	0828	0844	|	0858	0914	|	0928	0944	|	0958	1014	|	1028	1044	|	1058	1114	|	1128	1144	|	1158	and
Leiden Centraal a.	0832	0848	0903	0902	0918	0933	0932	0948	1003	1002	1018	1033	1032	1048	1103	1102	1118	1133	1132	1148	1203	1202	1218	the
Leiden Centraal d.	0835	0850	0905	0905	0920	0935	0935	0950	1005	1005	1020	1035	1035	1050	1105	1105	1120	1135	1135	1150	1205	1205	1220	
Den Haag Centraal 471 a.	|	|	0917	|	|	0947	|	|	1017	|	|	1047	|	|	1117	|	|	1147	|	|	1217	|	|	sam
Den Haag HS 18 471 d.	0849	0904	...	0919	0934	...	0949	1004	...	1019	1034	...	1049	1104	...	1119	1134	...	1149	1204	...	1219	1234	minu
Delft 471 d.	0855	0910	...	0925	0940	...	0955	1010	...	1025	1040	...	1055	1110	...	1125	1140	...	1155	1210	...	1225	1240	pas
Schiedam Centrum d.	0903	0918	...	0933	0948	...	1003	1018	...	1033	1048	...	1103	1118	...	1133	1148	...	1203	1218	...	1233	1248	
Rotterdam Centraal 18 471 d.	0911	0925	...	0941	0955	...	1011	1025	...	1041	1055	...	1111	1125	...	1141	1155	...	1211	1225	...	1241	1255	eac
Dordrecht 18 471 d.	0927	0941	...	0957	1011	...	1027	1041	...	1057	1111	...	1129	1141	...	1157	1211	...	1227	1241	...	1257	1311	
Roosendaal 18 d.	0952	...	...	1022	...	...	1052	...	...	1122	...	...	1152	...	...	1222	...	...	1252	...	...	1322	...	hou
Bergen op Zoom d.	1001	...	...	1031	...	...	1101	...	...	1131	...	...	1201	...	...	1231	...	...	1301	...	...	1331	...	unt
Goes d.	1032	...	...	1102	...	...	1132	...	...	1202	...	...	1232	...	...	1302	...	...	1332	...	...	1402	...	
Middelburg d.	1046	...	...	1116	...	...	1146	...	...	1216	...	...	1246	...	...	1316	...	...	1346	...	...	1416	...	
Vlissingen a.	1054	...	...	1124	...	...	1154	...	...	1224	...	...	1254	...	...	1324	...	...	1354	...	...	1424	...	

		◧			◧			◧			◧			◧			◧			◧		◧		
Amsterdam Centraal ★ d.	1957	1958	2012	2027	2028	2042	2057	2058	2112	2127	2128	2142	2157	2158	2212	2227	2228	...	2257	2258	2327	2328	...	2357
Amsterdam Sloterdijk ★ d.	2002	2005	2017	2032	2035	2047	2102	2105	2117	2132	2135	2147	2202	2205	2217	2232	2235	...	2302	2305	2332	2335	...	0002
Schiphol ✈ ★ d.	|	2016	|	|	2046	|	|	2116	|	|	2146	|	|	2216	|	|	2246	...	|	2316	|	2346	...	|
Haarlem d.	2014	|	2028	2044	|	2058	2114	|	2128	2144	|	2158	2214	|	2228	2244	|	...	2314	|	2344	|	...	0014
Leiden Centraal a.	2033	2032	2048	2103	2102	2118	2133	2132	2148	2203	2202	2218	2233	2232	2248	2303	2302	...	2333	2332	0003	0002	...	0033
Leiden Centraal d.	2035	2035	2050	2105	2105	2120	2135	2135	2150	2205	2205	2220	2235	2235	2250	2305	2305	...	2335	2335	0005	0005	...	0035
Den Haag Centraal 471 a.	2047	|	|	2117	|	|	2147	|	|	2217	|	|	2247	|	|	2317	|	...	2347	|	0017	|	...	0047
Den Haag HS 18 471 d.	...	2049	2104	...	2119	2134	...	2149	2204	...	2219	2234	...	2249	2304	...	2319	...	...	2349	...	0019	...	...
Delft 471 d.	...	2055	2110	...	2125	2140	...	2155	2210	...	2225	2240	...	2255	2310	...	2325	...	...	2355	...	0025	...	...
Schiedam Centrum d.	...	2103	2118	...	2133	2148	...	2203	2218	...	2233	2248	...	2303	2318	...	2333	...	...	0003	...	0033	...	...
Rotterdam Centraal 18 471 d.	...	2111	2125	...	2141	2155	...	2211	2225	...	2241	2255	...	2311	2325	...	2341	...	...	0011	...	0041	...	...
Dordrecht 18 471 d.	...	2127	2141	...	2157	2211	...	2227	2241	...	2257	2311	...	2327	2341	...	2357	...	...	0026	...	0057	...	...
Roosendaal 18 d.	...	2152	...	...	2222	...	...	2252	...	...	2322	...	...	2352	...	...	0021	...	...	...	...	0130	...	...
Bergen op Zoom d.	...	2201	...	...	2231	...	...	2301	...	...	2331	...	...	0001	...	...	...	...	...	...	...	...	...	...
Goes d.	...	2232	...	...	2302	...	...	2332	...	...	0002	...	...	0032	...	...	...	...	...	...	...	...	...	...
Middelburg d.	...	2246	...	...	2316	...	...	2346	...	...	0016	...	...	0046	...	...	...	...	...	...	...	...	...	...
Vlissingen a.	...	2254	...	...	2324	...	...	2354	...	...	0024	...	...	0054	...	...	...	...	...	...	...	...	...	...

A – ①–⑤ (also Dec. 26, 27, Jan. 2; not Apr. 28, May 6, 17).
C – ⑥⑦ (also Apr. 28, May 6, 17; not Dec. 26, 27, Jan. 2).

h – Also Dec. 26; not Apr. 27, May 5, 16.
t – ①②③⑥⑦ (also Apr. 28, May 6).

◧ – From Lelystad, Leeuwarden or Groningen (Table **460**).
★ – **Additional trains** Amsterdam Centraal - Schiphol ✈ at 0013, 0513 ⚒, 0543 ⚒, 0613, 0643 and at 13 and 43 minutes past each hour until 2313, 2343.

☛ For NIGHT NETWORK **Amsterdam** – **Schiphol** – **Den Haag** – **Rotterdam**, see Table **454**.
For INTERNATIONAL SERVICES **Amsterdam** – **Den Haag** – **Rotterdam** – **Roosendaal** – **Antwerp** **Brussels**, see Table **18**.

451 AMSTERDAM - ROTTERDAM - BREDA

Intercity direct services via the high-speed line. Supplement payable (except for local journeys Amsterdam - Schiphol and Rotterdam - Breda).

km		910	1012	912	1014	914	1016	916	1018	918	1020	920	1022	922	1024	924	1026	926	1028	928	1030	930	1032
		⚒	⚒	⚒	⚒	b	⚒	b	⚒		⚒		⚒		⚒		⚒		⚒		⚒		
0	**Amsterdam** Centraal d.	0555	0610	0625	0640	0655	0710	0725	0740	0755	0810	0825	0840	0855	0910	0925	0940	0955	1010	1025	1040	1055	1110
17	**Schiphol** ✈ d.	0609	0625	0639	0655	0709	0725	0739	0755	0809	0825	0839	0855	0909	0925	0939	0955	1009	1025	1039	1055	1109	1125
70	**Rotterdam** Centraal a.	0636	0651	0706	0721	0736	0751	0806	0821	0836	0851	0906	0921	0936	0951	1006	1021	1036	1051	1106	1121	1136	1151
70	**Rotterdam** Centraal d.	0639	...	0709	...	0739	...	0809	...	0839	...	0909	...	0939	...	1009	...	1039	...	1109	...	1139	...
117	**Breda** a.	0702	...	0732	...	0802	...	0832	...	0902	...	0932	...	1002	...	1032	...	1102	...	1132	...	1202	...

	1034	934	1036	936	1038	938		1064	964	1066	966	1068	968	1070	970	1072	972		974	1076	
Amsterdam Centraal d.	1140	1155	1210	1225	1240	1255	and at the same	1910	1925	1940	1955	2010	2025	2040	2055	2110	2125	...	2155	2225	...
Schiphol ✈ d.	1155	1209	1225	1239	1255	1309	minutes past	1925	1939	1955	2009	2025	2039	2055	2109	2125	2139	...	2209	2239	...
Rotterdam Centraal a.	1221	1236	1251	1306	1321	1336	each hour until	1951	2006	2021	2036	2051	2106	2121	2137	2151	2206	...	2236	2306	...
Rotterdam Centraal d.	...	1239	...	1309	...	1339		...	2009	...	2039	...	2109	...	2139	...	2209	...	2239	...	...
Breda a.	...	1302	...	1332	...	1402		...	2032	...	2102	...	2132	...	2202	...	2232	...	2302	...	...

b – Not Jan. 1.

For explanation of standard symbols, see page 4

VLISSINGEN - ROOSENDAAL - ROTTERDAM - DEN HAAG - AMSTERDAM 450

	Ⓐ◧	Ⓐ	⑥k◧	Ⓐ◧	⚒	Ⓐ	Ⓐ◧	⚒◧	⚒	Ⓐ	†◧	Ⓐ◧	⚒◧		Ⓐ	†◧	Ⓐ◧	⚒◧		Ⓐ	†◧	⚒◧		⚒
Vlissingen d.	...	...	...	...	...	...	...	...	...	...	...	...	...	...	...	...	0536	...	...	...	...	0606	...	...
Middelburg d.	...	...	...	...	...	...	...	...	...	...	...	...	...	...	...	...	0543	...	...	...	...	0613	...	...
Goes d.	...	...	...	...	...	...	...	...	...	...	...	...	...	...	...	...	0558	...	...	...	...	0628	...	...
Bergen op Zoom d.	...	...	...	...	...	...	0527	...	...	...	...	0557	...	...	...	...	0627	...	...	...	...	0657	...	...
Roosendaal 18 d.	...	...	...	...	...	...	0540	...	...	...	...	0611	...	...	...	...	0640	0640	...	...	...	0710	...	...
Dordrecht 18 471 d.	...	...	...	...	...	0550	0605	0605	...	0620	0634	0635	0635	...	0650	0704	0705	0705	...	0720	0734	0735	...	0750
Rotterdam Centraal 18 471 d.	0522	...	0551	0552	...	0607	0622	0622	...	0637	0652	0652	0652	...	0707	0722	0722	0722	...	0737	0752	0752	...	0807
Schiedam Centrum d.	0526	...	0556	0556	...	0611	0626	0626	...	0641	0656	0656	0656	...	0711	0726	0726	0726	...	0741	0756	0756	...	0811
Delft 471 d.	0534	...	0604	0604	...	0619	0634	0634	...	0649	0704	0704	0704	...	0719	0734	0734	0734	...	0749	0804	0804	...	0819
Den Haag HS 18 471 d.	0543	...	0613	0613	...	0628	0643	0643	...	0658	0713	0713	0713	...	0728	0743	0743	0743	...	0758	0813	0813	...	0828
Den Haag Centraal 471 d.	|	0544	|	|	0614	|	|	|	0644	|	|	|	|	0714	|	|	|	|	0744	|	|	|	0814	|
Leiden Centraal a.	0555	0555	0625	0625	0625	0640	0655	0655	0655	0710	0725	0725	0725	0725	0740	0755	0755	0755	0755	0810	0825	0825	0825	0840
Leiden Centraal d.	0557	0557	0627	0627	0627	0642	0657	0657	0657	0712	0727	0727	0727	0727	0742	0757	0757	0757	0757	0812	0827	0827	0827	0842
Haarlem d.	|	0617	|	|	0647	0702	|	|	0717	0732	|	|	|	0747	0802	|	|	|	0817	0832	|	|	0847	0902
Schiphol ✈ ★ d.	0614	|	0644	0644	|	|	0714	0714	|	|	0744	0744	0744	|	|	0814	0814	0814	|	|	0844	0844	|	|
Amsterdam Sloterdijk ★ d.	0625	0626	0655	0655	0656	0711	0725	0725	0726	0741	0755	0755	0755	0756	0811	0825	0825	0825	0826	0841	0855	0855	0856	0911
Amsterdam Centraal ★ a.	0632	0632	0702	0702	0702	0717	0732	0732	0732	0747	0802	0802	0802	0802	0817	0832	0832	0832	0832	0847	0902	0902	0902	0917

	†◧	⚒◧		⚒	◧		⚒	◧		⚒	◧		⚒	◧		⚒		◧			◧			
ingen d.	...	0636	...	...	0706	...	...	0736	...	...	0806	...	...	0836	...	...	...	0906	...	...	0936	...	...	and at
elburg d.	...	0643	...	...	0713	...	...	0743	...	...	0813	...	...	0843	...	...	...	0913	...	...	0943	...	...	the
s d.	...	0658	...	...	0728	...	...	0758	...	...	0828	...	...	0858	...	...	...	0928	...	...	0958	...	...	same
en op Zoom d.	...	0727	...	...	0757	...	...	0827	...	...	0857	...	...	0927	...	...	...	0957	...	...	1027	...	...	minutes
sendaal 18 d.	...	0740	...	...	0810	...	...	0840	...	...	0910	...	...	0940	...	...	...	1010	...	...	1040	...	...	past
recht 18 471 d.	0804	0805	...	0820	0835	...	0850	0905	...	0920	0935	...	0950	1005	...	1020	...	1035	...	1050	1105	...	1120	each
erdam Centraal 18 471 d.	0822	0822	...	0837	0852	...	0907	0922	...	0937	0952	...	1007	1022	...	1037	...	1052	...	1107	1122	...	1137	hour
edam Centrum d.	0826	0826	...	0841	0856	...	0911	0926	...	0941	0956	...	1011	1026	...	1041	...	1056	...	1111	1126	...	1141	until
471 d.	0834	0834	...	0849	0904	...	0919	0934	...	0949	1004	...	1019	1034	...	1049	...	1104	...	1119	1134	...	1149	
Haag HS 18 471 d.	0843	0843	...	0858	0913	...	0928	0943	...	0958	1013	...	1028	1043	...	1058	...	1113	...	1128	1143	...	1158	
n Haag Centraal 471 d.	|	|	0844	|	|	0914	|	|	0944	|	|	1014	|	|	1044	|	...	|	1114	|	|	1144	|	
en Centraal a.	0855	0855	0855	0910	0925	0925	0940	0955	0955	1010	1025	1025	1040	1055	1055	1110	...	1125	1125	1140	1155	1155	1210	
en Centraal d.	0857	0857	0857	0912	0927	0927	0942	0957	0957	1012	1027	1027	1042	1057	1057	1112	...	1127	1127	1142	1157	1157	1212	
arlem d.	|	|	0917	0932	|	0947	1002	|	1017	1032	|	1047	1102	|	1117	1132	1132	|	1147	1202	|	1217	1232	
phol ✈ ★ d.	0914	0914	|	|	0944	|	|	1014	|	|	1044	|	|	1114	|	|	|	1144	|	|	1214	|	|	
erdam Sloterdijk ★ d.	0925	0925	0926	0941	0955	0956	1011	1025	1026	1041	1055	1056	1111	1125	1126	1141	1141	1155	1156	1211	1225	1226	1241	
terdam Centraal ★ a.	0932	0932	0932	0947	1002	1002	1017	1032	1032	1047	1102	1102	1117	1132	1132	1147	1147	1202	1202	1217	1232	1232	1247	

	◧			◧			◧			◧												②	G	E	
ingen d.	1906	...	...	1936	...	...	2006	...	...	2036	...	...	2106	...	...	2136	...	...	2206	...	...	2236	2236	2236	2306
elburg d.	1913	...	...	1943	...	...	2013	...	...	2043	...	...	2113	...	...	2143	...	...	2213	...	...	2243	2243	2243	2313
s d.	1928	...	...	1958	...	...	2028	...	...	2058	...	...	2128	...	...	2158	...	...	2228	...	...	2258	2258	2258	2328
en op Zoom d.	1957	...	...	2027	...	...	2057	...	...	2127	...	...	2157	...	...	2227	...	...	2257	...	...	2327	2327	2327	2357
sendaal 18 d.	2010	...	...	2040	...	...	2110	...	...	2140	...	...	2210	...	...	2240	...	...	2310	...	...	2340	2340	2340	0007
recht 18 471 d.	2035	...	2050	2105	...	2120	2135	...	2150	2205	...	...	2235	...	...	2305	...	...	2335	...	...	0005	0005	0005	...
erdam Centraal 18 471 d.	2052	...	2107	2122	...	2137	2152	...	2207	2222	...	...	2252	...	...	2322	...	...	2352	...	...	0022	0022	0022	...
edam Centrum d.	2056	...	2111	2126	...	2141	2156	...	2211	2226	...	...	2256	...	...	2326	...	...	2356	...	...	0026	0026	0026	...
471 d.	2104	...	2119	2134	...	2149	2204	...	2219	2234	...	...	2304	...	...	2334	...	...	0004	...	...	0034	0034	0034	...
Haag HS 18 471 d.	2113	...	2128	2143	...	2158	2213	...	2228	2243	...	...	2313	...	...	2343	...	...	0013	...	...	0043	0043	0043	...
n Haag Centraal 471 d.	|	2114	|	|	2144	|	|	2214	|	|	2244	...	|	2314	...	|	2344	...	|	0014	...	|	|	|	...
en Centraal a.	2125	2125	2140	2155	2155	2210	2225	2225	2240	2255	2255	...	2325	2325	...	2355	2355	...	0025	0025	...	0055	0055	0055	...
en Centraal d.	2127	2127	2142	2157	2157	2212	2227	2227	2242	2257	2257	...	2327	2327	...	2357	2357	...	0027	0027	...	0057	0057	0057	...
arlem d.	|	2147	2202	|	2217	2232	|	2247	2302	|	2317	...	|	2347	...	|	0017	...	|	0047	...	|	|	|	...
phol ✈ ★ d.	2144	|	|	2214	|	|	2244	|	|	2314	|	...	2344	|	...	0014	|	...	0044	|	...	|	0114	0120	...
terdam Sloterdijk ★ d.	2155	2156	2211	2225	2226	2241	2255	2256	2311	2325	2326	...	2355	2356	...	0025	0026	...	0055	0056	...	0122	0123	0129	...
terdam Centraal ★ a.	2202	2202	2217	2232	2232	2247	2302	2302	2317	2332	2332	...	0002	0002	...	0032	0032	...	0102	0103	...	0128	0130	0136	...

①③④ (not Mar. 28, Apr. 27, May 5, 16).
⑤–⑦ (also Mar. 28, Apr. 27, May 5, 16).

Also Apr. 27, May 5, 16; not Dec. 26.

◧ – To Lelystad, Leeuwarden or Groningen (Table **460**).
★ – **Additional trains** Schiphol ✈ - Amsterdam Centraal at 0029, 0529 Ⓒ, 0544 Ⓐ, 0559, 0629, 0659 and at 29 and 59 minutes past each hour until 2329, 2359.

☛ For NIGHT NETWORK **Rotterdam** – **Den Haag** – **Schiphol** – **Amsterdam**, see Table **454**.
For INTERNATIONAL SERVICES **Brussels** – **Antwerpen** – **Roosendaal** – **Rotterdam** – **Den Haag** – **Amsterdam**, see Table **18**.

BREDA - ROTTERDAM - AMSTERDAM 451

Intercity direct services via the high-speed line. Supplement payable (except for local journeys Breda - Rotterdam and Schiphol - Amsterdam).

	1003 ⚒		905 ⚒	1007 ⚒	907 ⚒	1007 †	1009 ⚒	909	1011 ⚒	911	1013 ⚒	913	1015 ⚒	915	1017 ⚒	917	1019 ⚒	919	1021 ⚒	921	1023 ⚒	923	1025 ⚒	925	1027	927
da d.	...	...	0627	...	0657	...	...	0727	...	0757	...	0827	...	0857	...	0927	...	0957	...	1027	...	1057	...	1127	...	1157
erdam Centraal a.	...	...	0651	...	0721	...	...	0751	...	0821	...	0851	...	0921	...	0951	...	1021	...	1051	...	1121	...	1151	...	1221
erdam Centraal d.	0624	...	0654	0709	0724	0724	0739	0754	0809	0824	0839	0854	0909	0924	0939	0954	1009	1024	1039	1054	1109	1124	1139	1154	1209	1224
iphol ✈ a.	0650	...	0720	0734	0750	0750	0804	0820	0834	0850	0904	0920	0934	0950	1004	1020	1034	1050	1104	1120	1134	1150	1204	1220	1234	1250
sterdam Centraal a.	0708	...	0736	0751	0808	0808	0821	0836	0851	0908	0921	0936	0951	1008	1021	1036	1051	1108	1121	1136	1151	1208	1221	1236	1251	1308

	1029	929	1031	931	1033	933		1063	963	1065	965	1067	967		969		971							
da d.	...	1227	...	1257	...	1327	and at the same	...	2057	...	2127	...	2157	...	2227	...	2257	...	...	...	...	...	...	...
erdam Centraal a.	...	1251	...	1321	...	1351	minutes past	...	2121	...	2151	...	2221	...	2251	...	2321	...	...	...	...	...	...	...
erdam Centraal d.	1239	1254	1309	1324	1339	1354	each hour until	2109	2124	2139	2154	2209	2224	...	2254	...	2324	...	...	...	...	...	...	...
iphol ✈ a.	1304	1320	1334	1350	1404	1420		2134	2150	2204	2220	2234	2250	...	2320	...	2350	...	...	...	...	...	...	...
sterdam Centraal a.	1321	1336	1351	1408	1421	1436		2151	2208	2221	2236	2251	2308	...	2336	...	0008	...	...	...	...	...	...	...

UTRECHT - AMSTERDAM - ROTTERDAM - EINDHOVEN Night Network 454

	⑥⑦	⑥⑦	L	④⑤	③	③	H	④⑤	③	③	H	④⑤	③	③	H	④⑤	③	③	P	†
cht Centraal d.	...	...	...	...	...	0058	0058	0059	...	0207	0207	0207	...	0307	0307	0307	...	0407	0407	0503
sterdam Centraal d.	...	...	0045	0045	...	0145	0145	0145	...	0245	0245	0245	...	0345	0345	0345	...	0445	0445	0545
phol ✈ d.	...	...	0103	0103	0200	|	0203	0203	0300	|	0303	0303	0400	|	0403	0403	0500	|	0503	0602
en Centraal d.	...	...	0123	0123	0215	0223	0223	0223	0315	0324	0323	0323	0415	0423	0423	0423	0515	0523	0523	0619
Haag HS d.	...	...	0138	0145	...	0237	0238	0244	...	0337	0338	0344	...	0437	0438	0444	...	0537	0538	0636
t d.	...	...	0146	|	...	0243	0246	|	...	0343	0346	|	...	0443	0446	|	...	0543	0546	0644
terdam Centraal d.	0002	0102	0159	0225	...	0256	0259	0325	...	0356	0357	0426	...	0456	0457	0526	...	0556	0559	0656
drecht d.	0017	0117	...	...	...	...	...	...	...	...	...	...	...	...	...	...	...	...	...	...
da d.	0035	0135	...	...	...	...	...	...	...	...	...	...	...	...	...	...	...	...	...	...
urg d.	0055	0155	...	...	...	...	...	...	...	...	...	...	...	...	...	...	...	...	...	...
dhoven a.	0118	0218	...	...	...	...	...	...	...	...	...	...	...	...	...	...	...	...	...	...

		④⑤	H	③	③	④⑤	⑥⑦	①②	③	③	④⑤	⑥⑦	⑦	E	③	③	④⑤	H	③	③		④⑤	L		†
dhoven d.	...	...	...	...	...	...	0030	...	...	...	...	0130	0130	...	...	...	...	...	...	...	...	...	...	...	...
urg d.	...	...	...	...	...	...	0102	...	...	...	...	0202	0202	...	...	...	...	...	...	...	...	...	...	...	...
da d.	...	...	...	...	...	...	0119	...	...	...	...	0219	0219	...	...	...	...	...	...	...	...	...	...	...	...
drecht d.	...	...	...	...	...	...	0141	...	...	...	...	0241	0241	...	...	...	...	...	...	...	...	...	...	...	...
terdam Centraal d.	...	0052	0102	0102	...	0132	0202	0202	0202	...	0232	0255	0302	0302	0302	...	0332	0402	0402	...	...	0432	0502	...	0602
t d.	...	0104	0114	0114	...	|	0214	0214	0214	...	|	...	0314	0314	0314	...	|	0414	0414	...	...	|	0514	...	0614
Haag HS d.	...	0124	0123	0123	...	0223	0223	0223	0223	...	0323	...	0323	0323	0323	...	0423	0423	0423	...	...	0523	0523	...	0625
en Centraal d.	...	0138	0138	0140	0143	0238	0238	0239	0240	0243	0338	...	0338	0338	0340	0343	0438	0438	0440	0443	...	0542	0538	...	0646
phol ✈ d.	...	0200	0200	|	0159	0300	0300	0300	|	0259	0400	...	0400	0400	|	0359	0500	0500	|	0459	...	0602	0602	...	0704
sterdam Centraal a.	0117	0214	0214	0214	...	0314	0314	0314	0314	...	0414	...	0414	0414	0414	...	0514	0514	0514	...	...	0619	0619	...	0719
cht Centraal a.	0151	0257	0251	0246	...	0357	0351	0351	0346	...	0457	...	0454	0451	0446	...	0557	0554	0548	...	...	...	0649c	...	...

E – ①②⑥.
H – ①②⑥⑦.
L – ①②③⑥⑦.
P – Daily except ③.

c – ⑥⑦ (also Mar. 28, Apr. 27, May 16).

457 ALMERE - UTRECHT

km		Ⓐ	Ⓐ	Ⓐ		Ⓐ			⚒			⚒						
0	**Almere** Buiten d.	0602	0632	0702	0732	0802	0832	...	0902	0932	and at the same	2002	2032	...	2132	2232	2332	...
6	**Almere** Centrum d.	0609	0639	0709	0739	0809	0839	...	0909	0939	minutes past	2009	2039	...	2139	2239	2339	...
26	Naarden-Bussum d.	0627	0657	0727	0757	0827	0857	...	0927	0957		2027	2057	...	2157	2257	2357	...
32	Hilversum d.	0633	0703	0733	0803	0833	0903	...	0933	1003	each hour until	2033	2103	...	2203	2303	0003	...
49	**Utrecht** Centraal a.	0650	0720	0750	0820	0850	0920	...	0950	1020		2050	2120	...	2220	2320	0020	...

	A	⑥⑦c			Ⓐ	⚒	Ⓐ		⚒			⚒						
Utrecht Centraal d.	0010	0040	...	...	0610	0640	0710	...	0740	0810	and at the same	1840	1910	...	2010	2110	2210	2310
Hilversum d.	0028	0058	...	...	0628	0658	0728	...	0758	0828	minutes past	1858	1928	...	2028	2128	2228	2328
Naarden-Bussum d.	0033	0103	...	...	0633	0703	0733	...	0803	0833		1903	1933	...	2033	2133	2233	2333
Almere Centrum d.	0051	0121	...	...	0651	0721	0751	...	0821	0851	each hour until	1921	1951	...	2051	2151	2251	2351
Almere Buiten a.	0057	0127	...	...	0656	0726	0756	...	0826	0856		1926	1956	...	2056	2156	2256	2356

A – ②③⑥⑦ (also Ap
May 6; not Mar. 2

c – Also Apr. 28, May
not Dec. 26, 27, Ja

460 DEN HAAG - SCHIPHOL - AMSTERDAM - ALMERE - ZWOLLE

km		Ⓐ	Ⓐ	⑥k	Ⓐ	Ⓐ R	⚒	†	Ⓐ R	⑥k R	Ⓐ	†	Ⓐ B	⑥k D	Ⓐ	⚒ B	† D	⚒	⚒ V	† D	⚒	⚒ V	† D
0	**Den Haag** Centraal 450 d.	...	...	...	...	...	...	...	...	...	...	...	...	...	0703	...	...	0733a	...	...	0803	...	...
	Den Haag HS 450 d.	...	...	...	...	0543	...	...	0613	0613	...	...	0643	0643	|	0713	0713	|	0743	0743	|	0813	0813
15	Leiden Centraal 450 d.	...	...	...	...	0557	...	...	0627	0627	...	...	0657	0657	0716	0727	0727	0746a	0757	0757	0816	0827	0827
42	**Schiphol** ✈ 450 d.	...	...	...	...	0614	...	...	0644	0644	0703	...	0714	0714	0733	0744	0744	0803	0814	0814	0833	0844	0844
51	**Amsterdam** Zuid d.	...	...	...	...	|	...	...	|	|	0712	...	|	|	0742	|	|	0812	|	|	0842	|	|
56	Duivendrecht d.	...	...	...	...	|	...	...	|	|	0717	...	|	|	0747	|	|	0817	|	|	0847	|	|
	Amsterdam Sloterdijk 450 d.	...	...	...	...	0625	...	...	0655	0655	|	...	0725	0725	|	0755	0755	|	0825	0825	|	0855	0855
	Amsterdam Centraal 450 d.	...	...	...	0607	0637	0637	...	0707	0707	|	0737	0737	0737	|	0807	0807	|	0837	0837	|	0907	0907
80	**Almere** Centrum d.	...	...	...	0630	0700	0700	...	0730	0730	0734	0800	0800	0800	0804	0830	0830	0834	0900	0900	0904	0930	0930
104	**Lelystad** Centrum d.	0543	0613	0643	0649	0719	0719	0743	0745	0749	0749	0819	0815	0819	0819	0845	0849	0849	0915	0919	0919	0945	0949
154	**Zwolle** a.	0615	0645	0715	0715	0745	0745	0815	...	0815	0815	0850	...	0845	0845	...	0915	0915	...	0945	0945	...	1015
	Leeuwarden **482** a.	|	0756	|	|	0856	0856	|	...	|	|	0956	...	0956	0956	...	|	|	...	1056	1056	...	|
	Groningen **482** a.	0724	...	0829	0814	...	...	0914	...	0914	0914	...	...	...	...	...	1014	1014	...	...	...	...	1114

	⚒ V	† D	⚒	⚒ V	† V	⚒	V		V			V		V		V		V		V ◇	V	V
Den Haag Centraal 450 d.	...	...	0903	...	...	0933	...	1003	...	1033		...	2003	...	2033	...	2103	...	2133	...	...	...
Den Haag HS 450 d.	0843	0843	|	0913	0913	|	0943	|	1013	|	and at	1943	|	2013	|	2043	|	2113	|	2143	2213	2243
Leiden Centraal 450 d.	0857	0857	0916	0927	0927	0946	0957	1016	1027	1046		1957	2016	2027	2046	2057	2116	2127	2146	2157	2227	2257
Schiphol ✈ 450 d.	0914	0914	0933	0944	0944	1003	1014	1033	1044	1103	the same	2014	2033	2044	2103	2114	2133	2144	2203	2214	2244	2314
Amsterdam Zuid d.	|	|	0942	|	|	1012	|	1042	|	1112		|	2042	|	2112	|	2142	|	2212	|	|	|
Duivendrecht d.	|	|	0947	|	|	1017	|	1047	|	1117	minutes	|	2047	|	2117	|	2147	|	2217	|	|	|
Amsterdam Sloterdijk 450 d.	0925	0925	|	0955	0955	|	1025	|	1055	|		2025	|	2055	|	2125	|	2155	|	2225	2255	2325
Amsterdam Centraal 450 d.	0937	0937	|	1007	1007	|	1037	|	1107	|	past each	2037	|	2107	|	2137	|	2207	|	2237	2307	2337
Almere Centrum d.	1000	1000	1004	1030	1030	1034	1100	1104	1130	1134		2100	2104	2130	2134	2200	2204	2230	2234	2300	2330	0000
Lelystad Centrum d.	1015	1019	1019	1045	1049	1049	1115	1119	1145	1149	hour until	2115	2119	2145	2149	2215	2219	2245	2249	2319	2349	0019
Zwolle a.	...	1045	1045	...	1115	1115	...	1145	...	1215		...	2145	...	2215	...	2245	...	2315	2345	0015	0045
Leeuwarden **482** a.	...	1156	1156	...	|	|	...	1256	...	|		...	2256	...	|	...	2356	...	|	0056	|	...
Groningen **482** a.	...	...	...	...	1214	1214	...	...	...	1314		...	...	...	2314	...	...	...	0026	...	0130	...

	⑥z		Ⓐ V	Ⓐ	Ⓐ V	Ⓐ	Ⓐ V	Ⓐ	⑥k V	⚒ V	Ⓐ	⚒	⚒ V	⑥k	Ⓐ	† V	V	⚒	† V	V		†	⚒
Groningen **482** d.	0029	...	...	...	...	...	...	0530r	0546	...	...	...	...	0634	0646	0646	...	...	...	...	...	0734	0746
Leeuwarden **482** d.	|	...	...	...	...	0503	...	|	|	...	0603	...	...	|	|	|	...	0703	0703	...	...	|	|
Zwolle d.	0135	...	...	0545	...	0615	...	0645	0645	...	0715	0715	...	0745	0745	0745	...	0815	0815	...	...	0845	0845
Lelystad Centrum d.	0203	...	0544	0611	0614	0641	0644	0711	0714	0714	0741	0741	0744	0811	0811	0814	0814	0841	0844	0844	...	0911	0911
Almere Centrum d.	0219	...	0602	0627	0632	0657	0702	0727	0732	0732	0757	0757	0802	0827	0827	0832	0832	0857	0902	0902	...	0927	0927
Amsterdam Centraal 450 a.	0239	...	0623	|	0653	|	0723	|	0753	0753	|	|	0823	|	|	0853	0853	|	0923	0923	...	|	|
Amsterdam Sloterdijk 450 a.	...	...	0635	|	0705	|	0735	|	0805	0805	|	|	0835	|	|	0905	0905	|	0935	0935	...	|	|
Duivendrecht d.	...	...	|	0644	|	0714	|	0744	|	|	0814	0814	|	0844	0844	|	|	0914	|	|	...	0944	0944
Amsterdam Zuid d.	...	...	|	0650	|	0720	|	0750	|	|	0820	0820	|	0850	0850	|	|	0920	|	|	...	0950	0950
Schiphol ✈ 450 a.	...	...	0645	0656	0715	0726	0745	0756	0815	0815	0826	0826	0845	0856	0856	0915	0915	0926	0945	0945	...	0956	0956
Leiden Centraal 450 a.	...	...	0702	0713	0732	0743	0802	0813	0832	0832	0843	0843	0902	0913	0913	0932	0932	0943	1002	1002	...	1013	1013
Den Haag HS 450 a.	...	...	0717	|	0747	|	0817	|	0847	0847	|	|	0917	|	|	0947	0947	|	1017	1017	...	|	|
Den Haag Centraal 450 a.	...	...	...	0726	...	0756	...	0826	...	...	0857	0857	...	0927	0926	...	...	0957	...	...	...	1027	1027

		V		V			V		V		V		V		S	D	S	R			⑤⑥ f	
Groningen **482** d.	...	...	0846	...		...	...	1846	...	...	...	1946	...	...	...	2046	...	2146	...	2246	2246	...
Leeuwarden **482** d.	0803	...	|	...	and at	1803	...	|	...	1903	...	|	...	2003	...	|	2103	|	2203	|	|	...
Zwolle d.	0915	...	0945	...		1915	...	1945	...	2015	...	2045	...	2115	...	2145	2215	2245	2315	2345	2345	...
Lelystad Centrum d.	0941	0944	1011	1014	the same	1941	1944	2011	2014	2041	2044	2111	2114	2141	2144	2214	2244	2314	2344	0014	0014	...
Almere Centrum d.	0957	1002	1027	1032		1957	2002	2027	2032	2057	2102	2127	2132	2157	2202	2232	2302	2332	0002	0032	0032	...
Amsterdam Centraal 450 a.	|	1023	|	1053	minutes	|	2023	|	2053	|	2123	|	2153	|	2223	2253	2323	2353	0024	0053	0053	...
Amsterdam Sloterdijk 450 a.	|	1035	|	1105		|	2035	|	2105	|	2135	|	2205	|	2235	2305	2335	0005	0035	...	0105	...
Duivendrecht d.	1014	|	1044	|	past each	2014	|	2044	|	2114	|	2144	|	2214	|	|	|	|	|	...	|	...
Amsterdam Zuid d.	1020	|	1050	|		2020	|	2050	|	2120	|	2150	|	2220	|	|	|	|	|	...	|	...
Schiphol ✈ 450 a.	1026	1045	1056	1115	hour until	2026	2045	2056	2115	2126	2145	2156	2215	2226	2245	2315	2345	0015	0045	...	0115	...
Leiden Centraal 450 a.	1043	1102	1113	1132		2043	2102	2113	2132	2143	2202	2213	2232	2243	2302	2332	0002	0032	0102	...	0132	...
Den Haag HS 450 a.	|	1117	|	1147		|	2117	|	2147	|	2217	|	2247	|	2317	2347	0017	0047	0117v	...	0147	...
Den Haag Centraal 450 a.	1057	...	1127	...		2057	...	2127	...	2157	...	2227	...	2257	...	...	...	...	...	...	...	...

Other stopping trains **Amsterdam** - **Zwolle**

km			A	Z 🚌	⑥⑦c	Ⓐ	Ⓐ	Ⓐ	⑥k	Ⓐ	⚒	⚒	†		⚒	†							
0	**Amsterdam** Centraal d.	0010	0010	...	0040	...	...	0540	...	0610	...	0640	...	0710	0710	0737	0740	0810	0840		2210	2240	2310
14	Weesp d.	0027	0029	0035	0059	...	...	0559	...	0629	...	0659	...	0729	0729	|	0759	0829	0859	and every	2229	2259	2329
30	**Almere** Centrum d.	...	0043	0109	0113	...	...	0613	...	0643	...	0713	...	0743	0743	0800	0813	0843	0913	30 minutes	2243	2313	2343
36	Almere Buiten d.	...	0049	0119	0119	...	...	0619	...	0649	...	0719	...	0749	0749	|	0819	0849	0919		2249	2319	2349
54	**Lelystad** Centrum d.	...	0102	0151	0132	0543	0613	0634	0643	0704	0704	0734	0743	0802	0804	0819	0834	0904	0934	until	2304	2334	0004
75	Dronten d.	...	...	...	...	0555	0625	0646	0655	0716	0716	0746	0755	...	0816	0831	0846	0916	0946		2316	2346	0016
88	Kampen Zuid d.	...	...	...	...	0604	0634	0654	0704	0724	0724	0754	0804	...	0824	0840	0854	0924	0954		2324	2354	0024
104	**Zwolle** a.	...	...	...	...	0615	0645	0705	0715	0735	0735	0805	0815	...	0835	0850	0905	0935	1005		2335	0005	0035

	⑥⑦c		Ⓐ		Ⓐ		Ⓐ		Ⓐ		⚒		⚒									
Zwolle d.	0035	...	...	...	0525	...	0555	...	0625	...	0655	...	0725	...	0755	0825		2155	2225	2255	2325	...
Kampen Zuid d.	0045	...	...	...	0535	...	0605	...	0635	...	0705	...	0735	...	0805	0835		2205	2235	2305	2335	...
Dronten d.	0054	...	...	...	0543	...	0613	...	0643	...	0713	...	0743	...	0813	0843	and every	2213	2243	2313	2343	...
Lelystad Centrum d.	0106	...	0504	0527	0557	0557	0627	0627	0657	0657	0727	0727	0757	0757	0827	0857	30 minutes	2227	2257	2327	2357	...
Almere Buiten d.	|	...	0517	0540	0610	0610	0640	0640	0710	0710	0740	0740	0810	0810	0840	0910		2240	2310	2340	0010	...
Almere Centrum d.	0121	...	0524	0547	0617	0617	0647	0647	0717	0717	0747	0747	0817	0817	0847	0917	until	2247	2317	2347	0017	...
Weesp a.	|	...	0538	0601	0631	0631	0701	0701	0731	0731	0801	0801	0831	0831	0901	0931		2301	2331	0001	0031	...
Amsterdam Centrum a.	0142	...	0601	0620	0650	0650	0720	0720	0750	0750	0820	0820	0850	0850	0920	0950		2320	2350	0021	0050	...

A – ②③⑥⑦ (also Apr. 28, May 6; not Mar. 29).
B – From Bergen op Zoom (Table **450**).
D – From / to Dordrecht (Table **450**).
R – From / to Rotterdam (Table **450**).
S – To Roosendaal (Table **450**).
V – From / to Vlissingen (Table **450**).
Z – ①④⑤ (not Apr. 28, May 6).

a – Ⓐ only.
c – Also Apr. 28, May 6, 17; not Dec. 26, 27, Jan. 2.
f – Also Apr. 27, May 5, 16; not Dec. 25, 26, Jan. 1.
k – Also Apr. 27, May 5, 16; not Dec. 26.
r – 0534 on ①④⑤.
v – Mornings of ①②③⑥⑦ (also Apr. 28, May 6).
z – Not Dec. 26, Jan. 2.

◇ – Change trains at Lelystad Centrum on ③ (not Apr. 27).

HAARLEM - ALKMAAR - HOORN 461

	Ⓐ	Ⓐ	⚒	Ⓐ	⑥k	Ⓐ	Ⓒ	Ⓐ	⑥k													
Haarlem ... d.	...	...	0624a	0654	0654	0724	0724k	0754	0754	0824	0854	❖	1854	1924	1954	2024	2054	2124	2154	2224	2254	2324	2354
Beverwijk ... d.	...	...	0640a	0710	0710	0740	0740k	0810	0810	0840	0910	and every	1910	1940	2010	2040	2110	2140	2210	2240	2310	2340	0010
Castricum ... 466 d.	...	*0622*	0656a	0726	0729	0756	0759k	0826	0829	0859	0929	30 minutes	1929	1959	2029	2059	2129	2159	2229	2259	2329	2359	0029
Alkmaar ... 466 a.	...	*0633*	0707a	0737	0740	0807	0810k	0837	0840	0910	0940	until	1940	2010	2040	2110	2140	2210	2240	2310	2340	0010	0040
Alkmaar ... 466 d.	0614	0644	0714	0744	0744	0814	0814	0844	0844	0914	0944		1944	2014	...	2114	...	2214	...	2314	...	0014	...
Heerhugowaard ... 466 d.	0622	0652	0722	0752	0752	0822	0822	0852	0852	0922	0952		1952	2022	...	2122	...	2222	...	2322	...	0022	...
Hoorn ... a.	0639	0709	0739	0809	0809	0839	0836	0909	0909	0939	1009		2009	2039	...	2139	...	2239	...	2339	...	0039	...

	Ⓐ	Ⓐ	⚒	⚒		⚒		⚒														
rn ... d.	0550	0620	0650	0720	0750	0820	0850	0920	0950	1020	1050		1920	1950	...	...	2050	...	2150	...	2250	...	2350
hugowaard ... 466 d.	0607	0636	0706	0736	0806	0836	0906	0936	1006	1036	1106	and every	1936	2006	...	...	2106	...	2206	...	2306	...	0006
naar ... 466 a.	0616	0645	0715	0746	0816	0846	0915	0945	1015	1045	1115	30 minutes	1945	2015	...	...	2115	...	2215	...	2315	...	0015
naar ... 466 d.	0621	0651	0721	0751	0821	0851	0921	0951	1021	1051	1121	until	1951	2021	...	2051	2121	2151	2221	2251	2321	2351	0021
ricum ... 466 d.	0632	0702	0732	0802	0832	0902	0932	1002	1032	1102	1132		2002	2032	...	2102	2132	2202	2232	2302	2332	0002	0032
erwijk ... d.	0647	0717	0747	0817	0847	0917	0947	1017	1048	1117	1147		2017	2047	...	2117	2147	2217	2247	2317	2347	0017	0047
rlem ... a.	0704	0734	0804	0834	0904	0934	1004	1034	1104	1134	1204		2034	2104	...	2134	2204	2234	2304	2334	0004	0034	0104

Ⓐ only. k – ⑥ (also Apr. 27, May 5, 16; not Dec. 26). ❖ – Certain Castricum departures may be 1 minute earlier.

SCHIPHOL and AMSTERDAM - ENKHUIZEN 462

		⑥⑦c			Ⓐ	Ⓐ	Ⓐ	Ⓐ	Ⓒ	Ⓐ	Ⓐ	⑥k	Ⓐ										
Amsterdam Centraal ... 466 d.	0009	0009	...	...	...	0600	0639	...	0700	0709	...	0730	0739	...	0809	...	0839	and at	...	2309	...	2339	...
Schiphol ✈ ... d.	|	|	...	...	0610	|	|	0640	|	|	0710	|	|	0740	|	0810	|	the same	2240	|	2310	|	2340
Amsterdam Sloterdijk ... 466 d.	0015	0015	...	...	0621	0606	0645	0651	0706	0715	0721	0737	0745	0751	0815	0821	0845	minutes	2251	2315	2321	2345	2351
Zaandam ... 466 d.	0021	0021	...	...	0627	0612	|	0657	0712	|	0727	0744	|	0757	|	0827	|	past each	2257	|	2327	|	2357
Hoorn ... d.	0049	0050	...	...	0654	0642	0712	0724	0744	0742	0754	0814	0814	0824	0844	0854	0914	hour until	2324	2344	2354	0014	0024
Enkhuizen ... a.	...	0120	...	...	...	0707	0737	...	0808	0807	...	0838	0838	...	0908	...	0938		...	0008	...	0038	...

	Ⓐr	⚒r		Ⓐ	Ⓐ	Ⓐ	⚒	⚒	Ⓐ	⚒	⚒	⚒	⚒											
huizen ... d.	0440	...	...	...	0524	...	0554	...	0624	...	...	0654	...	0724	...	0754	...	and at	2224	...	2254	...	2324	2354
rn ... d.	0506	0506	...	0536	0550	0606	0620	0636	0650	0650	0706	0720	0736	0750	0806	0820	0836	the same	2250	2306	2320	2336	2350	0020
ndam ... 466 d.	0533	0533	...	0602	|	0632	|	0702	|	|	0732	|	0802	|	0832	|	0902	minutes	|	2332	|	0002	0016	0046
terdam Sloterdijk ... 466 a.	0539	0539	...	0608	0615	0638	0645	0708	0715	0715	0738	0745	0808	0815	0838	0845	0908	past each	2315	2338	2345	0008	0023	0052
chiphol ✈ ... a.	0550	0550	...	0620	|	0650	|	0720	|	|	0750	|	0820	|	0850	|	0920	hour until	|	2350	|	0020	|	|
sterdam Centraal ... 466 a.	...	...	...	...	0623	...	0653	...	0723	0723	...	0753	...	0823	...	0853	...		2323	...	2353	...	0031	0100

Also Apr. 28, May 6, 17; not Dec. 26, 27, Jan. 2. k – Also Apr. 27, May 5, 16; not Dec. 26. r – Timings may be up to 5 minutes later on ①–③ (not Apr. 27, May 16).

LEIDEN - ALPHEN - UTRECHT and GOUDA 463

	Ⓐ	⚒	⚒							
Leiden Centraal ... d.	0552	0622	0652	0722	0752	and every	2322	2352	0022	...
Alphen a/d Rijn ... d.	0607	0637	0707	0737	0807	30 minutes	2337	0007	0037	...
Woerden ... d.	0624	0654	0724	0754	0824	until	2354	0024	0054	...
Utrecht Centraal ... a.	0634	0704	0734	0804	0834		0004	0034	0104	...

	Ⓐ	⚒	⚒						
Utrecht Centraal ... d.	0555	0625	0655	0725	0755	and every	2325	2355	0025
Woerden ... d.	0606	0636	0706	0736	0806	30 minutes	2336	0006	0036
Alphen a/d Rijn ... d.	0623	0653	0723	0753	0823	until	2353	0023	0053
Leiden Centraal ... a.	0637	0707	0737	0807	0837		0007	0037	0107

	Ⓐ	Ⓐ	Ⓐ	⑥k	Ⓐ	Ⓒ	Ⓐ	Ⓒ	Ⓐ	Ⓒ	Ⓐ	Ⓒ						Ⓒ	Ⓐ	Ⓒ	Ⓐ	
Leiden Centraal ... d.	0608	0638	0708	...	0738	...	0808	...	0838	...	0908	...	...	...	and every	...	...	...	1508	...	1538	and at the same
Alphen a/d Rijn ... ★ d.	0623	0653	0723	0738	0753	0808	0823	0838	0853	0908	0923	0938	1008	1038	30 minutes	1408	1438	1508	1523	1538	1553	minutes past
Gouda ... ★ a.	0643	0713	0743	0758	0813	0828	0843	0858	0913	0928	0943	0958	1027	1058	until	1427	1458	1528	1543	1558	1613	each hour until

	Ⓒ	Ⓐ	Ⓒ	Ⓐ	Ⓒ					
len Centraal ... d.	...	1838	...	1908	...	...	...	and every	...	...
en a/d Rijn ... d.	1838	1853	1908	1923	1938	2008	2038	30 minutes	0008	0038
da ... a.	1858	1913	1928	1943	1958	2027	2058	until	0028	0058

	Ⓐ	Ⓐ	⑥k	Ⓐ	⑥k	Ⓐ	Ⓒ	Ⓐ	Ⓒ	Ⓐ	Ⓒ
Gouda ... d.	0617	0647	0702	0717	0732	0747	0802	0817	0832	0847	0902
Alphen a/d Rijn ... a.	0636	0706	0721	0736	0751	0806	0821	0836	0851	0906	0921
Leiden Centraal ... a.	0651	0721	...	0751	...	0821	...	0851	...	0921	...

	Ⓐ	Ⓒ						Ⓒ	Ⓐ	Ⓒ	Ⓐ		Ⓒ	Ⓐ	Ⓒ	Ⓐ	Ⓒ					
da ... d.	0917	0932	1002	1032	and every	1402	1432	1502	1517	1532	1547	and at the same	1832	1847	1902	1917	1932	2002	2032	and every	0002	0032
en a/d Rijn ... d.	0936	0951	1021	1051	30 minutes	1421	1451	1521	1536	1551	1606	minutes past	1851	1906	1921	1936	1951	2021	2051	30 minutes	0021	0051
len Centraal ... a.	0951	...	...	...	until	...	...	...	1551	...	1621	each hour until	...	1921	...	1951	...	...	...	until	...	...

Also Apr. 27, May 5, 16; not Dec. 26. ★ – **Additional trains** Alphen - Gouda at 0553 Ⓐ and 0708 ⑥ **k**.

AMSTERDAM - GOUDA - ROTTERDAM 465

	Ⓐ	⚒	⚒	⚒					
Amsterdam Centraal ... d.	0547	0617	0647	0717	0747	0817		2317	2347
Amsterdam Amstel ... d.	0555	0625	0655	0725	0755	0825	and every	2325	2355
Duivendrecht ... d.	0559	0629	0659	0729	0759	0829	30 minutes	2329	2359
Breukelen ... d.	0619	0649	0719	0749	0819	0849	until	2349	0019
Woerden ... d.	0628	0658	0728	0758	0828	0858		2358	0028
Gouda ... d.	0641	0711	0741	0811	0841	0911		0011	0041
Rotterdam Alexander ... d.	0653	0723	0753	0823	0853	0923		0023	0053
Rotterdam Centraal ... a.	0704	0734	0804	0834	0904	0934		0034	0104

	Ⓐ	Ⓐ	⚒	⚒					
Rotterdam Centraal ... d.	0525	0555	0625	0655	0725	0755		2255	2325
Rotterdam Alexander ... d.	0535	0605	0635	0705	0735	0805	and every	2305	2335
Gouda ... d.	0549	0619	0649	0719	0749	0819	30 minutes	2319	2349
Woerden ... d.	0602	0632	0702	0732	0802	0832	until	2332	0002
Breukelen ... d.	0610	0640	0710	0740	0810	0840		2341	0010
Duivendrecht ... d.	0629	0659	0729	0759	0829	0859		2359	0029
Amsterdam Amstel ... d.	0633	0703	0733	0803	0833	0903		0003	0033
Amsterdam Centraal ... a.	0642	0712	0742	0812	0842	0912		0012	0042

For fast trains **Amsterdam** - **Rotterdam**, see Table **450**. For other trains **Gouda** - **Rotterdam**, see Table **481**.

AMSTERDAM - ALKMAAR - DEN HELDER 466

			Ⓐf	Ⓐ	Ⓐ	⚒	Ⓐ	⑥k	†					†	⚒									
Nijmegen 468 ... d.	...	...	...	...	...	...	...	...	...	0534a	0612v	0642v	0712	0737	0742	0812	0842	0912		2042	2112	2142	2212
Arnhem 468 ... d.	...	...	...	...	...	...	...	...	...	0601a	0631v	0701v	0731	0801	0801	0833	0901	0931		2101	2131	2201	2233
Amsterdam Centraal ... 459 d.	0017	...	0517	...	0612	...	0642	0647	0648	0712	0742	0812	0842	0912	0912	0942	1012	1042	and every	2212	2242	2312	2342
Amsterdam Sloterdijk ... 459 d.	0024	...	0523	...	0618	...	0648	0653	0654	0718	0748	0818	0848	0918	0918	0948	1018	1048	30 minutes	2218	2248	2318	2348
Zaandam ... 459 d.	0030	...	0530	...	0625	...	0655	0700	0701	0725	0755	0825	0855	0925	0925	0955	1025	1055	until	2225	2255	2325	2355
Castricum ... 461 d.	0049	...	0552	...	0637	...	0707	0722	0722	0737	0807	0837	0907	0937	0937	1007	1037	1107		2237	2307	2337	0007
Alkmaar ... 461 d.	0102	...	0603	0620	0650	0650	0720	0733	0733	0750	0820	0850	0920	0950	0950	1020	1050	1120		2250	2320	2350	0020
Heerhugowaard ... 461 d.	0110	...	...	0628	0658	0658	0728	...	...	0758	0828	0858	0928	0958	0958	1028	1058	1128		2258	2328	2358	0028
Den Helder ... a.	0139z	...	...	0656	0726	0726	0756	...	...	0826	0856	0926	0956	1026	1026	1056	1126	1156		2326	2355	0032	0056

	⚒w	Ⓐ		Ⓐ	Ⓐ	Ⓒ	⚒	⊡	⊡	⊡	⊡	⊡	⊡									⚒	†	
Helder ... d.	...	0504	...	0534	0604	...	0634	0704	0734		1704	1734	1804	1834	1904	1934	2004	2034	2104	2134	2204	2304	2304	2356
rhugowaard ... 461 d.	...	0530	...	0600	0630	...	0700	0730	0800		1730	1800	1830	1900	1930	2000	2030	2100	2130	2200	2230	2330	2330	0022
maar ... 461 d.	0456	0542	0556	0612	0642	0656	0712	0742	0812	and every	1742	1812	1842	1911	1941	2011	2041	2111	2141	2211	2241	2341	2341	0031
tricum ... 461 d.	0507	0550	0607	0620	0650	0707	0720	0750	0820	30 minutes	1750	1820	1850	1921	1951	2021	2051	2121	2151	2221	2251	2351	2351	0042
ndam ... 459 d.	0533	0605	0630	0635	0705	0730	0735	0805	0835	until	1805	1835	1905	1935	2005	2035	2105	2135	2205	2235	2305	0005	0005	0103
sterdam Sloterdijk ... 459 d.	0539	0612	0638	0642	0712	0738	0742	0812	0842		1812	1842	1912	1942	2012	2042	2112	2142	2212	2242	2312	0012	0012	0108
sterdam Centraal ... 459 a.	0545	0618	0644	0648	0718	0744	0749	0818	0848		1818	1848	1918	1948	2018	2048	2118	2148	2218	2248	2318	0018	0018	0114
rnhem 468 ... a.	...	0728	...	0758	0828	...	0858	0928	0958		1928	1958	2028	2058	2128	2158	2229	2259	2329	2359	0029	0130	0132	...
ijmegen 468 ... a.	...	0747	...	0817	0847	...	0917	0947	1017		1947	2017	2047	2117	2147	2217	2247	2317	2347	0019	0048	0149p	0153	...

Ⓐ only.
Runs 3–4 minutes later on ①.
Also Apr. 27, May 5, 16; not Dec. 26.
p – 0210 on the mornings of ④⑤ (by 🚌 from Arnhem).
v – ⚒ only.
w – Runs 3–6 minutes later on ①–③ (not Apr. 27, May 16).
z – *0221* on the mornings of ②③ (not Mar. 29, May 17; by 🚌 from Heerhugowaard).
⊡ – Timings on † may vary by 1–2 minutes.

468 AMSTERDAM and SCHIPHOL ✈ - ARNHEM - NIJMEGEN

km		A	①m	④⑤j	Ⓐ	Ⓐ	Ⓐ	Ⓐ	⚒	Ⓐ	⚒	⚒	Ⓐ	⚒	†	⚒		⚒		⚒		⚒		⚒
0	**Amsterdam** Centraal ... **470** d.	0023	0023	...	...	...	*0529*	...	...	0623	...	0653	...	0723	...	...	0753	...	0823	...	0853	...	0923	...
6	Amsterdam Amstel .... **470** d.	0030	0030	...	...	...	*0537*	...	...	0630	...	0700	...	0730	...	...	0800	...	0830	...	0900	...	0930	...
	Schiphol ✈ .... **470** d.	|	|	...	...	...	|	...	...	|	...	|	0700	|	...	0730	|	0800	|	0830	|	0900	|	0930
	Amsterdam Zuid ...... **470** d.	|	|	...	...	...	|	...	...	|	...	|	0709	|	...	0739	|	0809	|	0839	|	0909	|	0939
39	**Utrecht** Centraal .... **470** a.	0050	0050	...	...	...	*0612*	...	...	0650	...	0720	0733	0750	...	0803	0820	0833	0850	0903	0920	0933	0950	1003
39	**Utrecht** Centraal ....d.	0053	0053	...	0553	0608	0623	0638	0653	0653	0708	0723	0738	0753	0753	0808	0823	0838	0853	0908	0923	0938	0953	1008
79	Ede-Wageningen ....d.	0118	0118	...	0617	0632	0647	0702	0717	0717	0732	0747	0802	0817	0818	0832	0847	0902	0917	0932	0947	1002	1017	1032
96	**Arnhem** ....a.	0130	0132	🚌	0628	0643	0658	0713	0728	0728	0743	0758	0813	0828	0829	0843	0859	0913	0929	0943	0959	1013	1029	1043
96	**Arnhem** .... **475** d.	0134t	0137	0139	0634	0649	0704	0719	0734	0734	0749a	0804	0819	0834	0834	0849a	0904	0919	0934	0949	1004	1019	1034	1049
114	**Nijmegen** .... **475** a.	0149t	0153	0210	0647	0702	0717	0732	0747	0747	0802a	0817	0832	0847	0847	0902a	0917	0932	0947	1002	1017	1032	1047	1102

	⚒		⚒		⚒																		
Amsterdam Centraal .... **470** d.	...	1023	...	1053	...	1123	...	1153	...	1223	...	1253	...	1323		...	2053	...	2123	2153	2223	2253	2323
Amsterdam Amstel .... **470** d.	...	1030	...	1100	...	1130	...	1200	...	1230	...	1300	...	1330	and at	...	2100	...	2130	2200	2230	2300	2330
Schiphol ✈ .... **470** d.	1000	|	1030	|	1100	|	1130	|	1200	|	1230	|	1300	|	the same	2030	|	2100	|	|	|	|	|
Amsterdam Zuid .... **470** d.	1009	|	1039	|	1109	|	1139	|	1209	|	1239	|	1309	|		2039	|	2109	|	|	|	|	|
Utrecht Centraal .... **470** a.	1033	1050	1103	1120	1133	1150	1203	1220	1233	1250	1303	1320	1333	1350	minutes	2103	2120	2133	2150	2220	2250	2320	2350
Utrecht Centraal .... d.	1038	1053	1108	1123	1138	1153	1208	1224	1238	1254	1308	1323	1338	1353	past each	2108	2123	2138	2153	2223	2253	2323	2353
Ede-Wageningen .... d.	1102	1117	1132	1147	1202	1217	1232	1247	1302	1317	1332	1347	1402	1417	hour until	2132	2147	2202	2218	2248	2318	2348	0018
Arnhem .... a.	1113	1129	1143	1159	1213	1229	1243	1258	1313	1328	1343	1358	1413	1428		2143	2158	2213	2229	2259	2329	2359	0029
Arnhem .... **475** d.	1119	1134	1149	1204	1219	1234	1249	1304	1319	1334	1349	1404	1419	1434		2149	2204	2219	2234	2304	2334	0004	0034
Nijmegen .... **475** a.	1132	1147	1202	1217	1232	1247	1302	1317	1332	1347	1402	1417	1432	1447		2202	2217	2232	2247	2317	2347	0019	0048

km		Ⓐ	Ⓐ	⚒	Ⓐ	Ⓐ	⚒	†	⚒	⚒	†	⚒		⚒	†	⚒	⚒		⚒		⚒		⚒	
	Nijmegen .... **475** d.	...	...	...	0534	...	0612	...	0627a	0642	...	0657a	0712	0727a	0737	0742	0757a	0812	0827a	0842	0857a	0912	0927	0942
	Arnhem .... **475** a.	...	...	...	0553	...	0626	...	0640a	0656	...	0710a	0726	0740a	0756	0756	0810a	0826	0840a	0856	0910a	0926	0940	0956
	Arnhem ....d.	...	0546	...	0601	0616	0631	...	0646	0701	...	0716	0731	0746	0801	0801	0816	0833	0846	0901	0916	0931	0946	1001
	Ede-Wageningen ....d.	...	0556	...	0611	0626	0641	...	0656	0711	...	0726	0741	0756	0811	0811	0826	0843	0856	0911	0926	0941	0956	1011
	Utrecht Centraal ....a.	...	0622	...	0637	0652	0707	...	0722	0737	...	0752	0807	0822	0838	0837	0852	0909	0922	0938	0952	1008	1022	1038
0	**Utrecht** Centraal .... **470** d.	0558	0628	0640	0640	0658	0710	0710	0728	0740	0740	0758	0810	0828	0840	0840	0858	0910	0928	0940	0958	1010	1028	1040
36	**Amsterdam** Zuid ...... **470** d.	0623	0653	|	|	0723	|	|	0753	|	|	0823	|	0853	|	|	0923	|	0953	|	1023	|	1053	|
45	**Schiphol** ✈ .... **470** a.	0629	0659	|	|	0729	|	|	0759	|	|	0829	|	0859	|	|	0929	|	0959	|	1029	|	1059	|
	Amsterdam Amstel ...... **470** d.	...	...	0658	0658	...	0728	0731	...	0758	0801	...	0828	...	0858	0858	...	0928	...	0958	...	1028	...	1058
	Amsterdam Centraal ... **470** a.	...	...	0707	0707	...	0737	0738	...	0807	0808	...	0837	...	0907	0907	...	0937	...	1007	...	1037	...	1107

		⚒						❖															⑤⑥f
Nijmegen .... **475** d.	1012	1027	1042	1057	1112	1127	1142		1857	1912	1927	1942	1957	2012	2027	2042	2112	2142	2212	2242	2312	...	2342
Arnhem .... **475** a.	1026	1040	1056	1110	1126	1140	1156	and at	1910	1926	1940	1956	2010	2026	2040	2056	2126	2156	2226	2256	2326	...	2356
Arnhem .... d.	1033	1046	1101	1116	1131	1146	1201	the same	1916	1933	1946	2001	2016	2031	2046	2101	2131	2201	2233	2301	2331	...	0001
Ede-Wageningen .... d.	1043	1056	1111	1126	1141	1156	1211		1926	1943	1956	2011	2026	2041	2056	2111	2141	2211	2243	2311	2341	...	0011
Utrecht Centraal .... a.	1109	1122	1138	1152	1207	1222	1237	minutes	1952	2007	2022	2037	2052	2107	2122	2138	2208	2238	2309	2338	0008	...	0038
Utrecht Centraal .... **470** d.	1110	1128	1140	1158	1210	1228	1240	past each	1958	2010	2028	2040	...	2110	•...	2140	2210	2240	2310	2340	...	0025	0040
Amsterdam Zuid .... **470** d.	|	1153	|	1223	|	1253	|	hour until	2023	|	2053	|	...	|	...	|	|	|	|	|	...	|	|
Schiphol ✈ .... **470** a.	|	1159	|	1229	|	1259	|		2029	|	2059	|	...	|	...	|	|	|	|	|	...	|	|
Amsterdam Amstel .... **470** d.	1128	...	1158	...	1228	...	1258		...	2028	...	2058	...	2128	...	2158	2228	2258	2328	2358	...	0044	0001
Amsterdam Centraal .... **470** a.	1137	...	1207	...	1237	...	1307		...	2037	...	2107	...	2137	...	2207	2237	2307	2337	0007	...	0054	0109

A – ②–⑦ (not Dec. 26, 27, Jan. 2, Mar. 29).

a – Ⓐ only.
f – Also Apr. 27, May 5, 16; not Dec. 25, 26, Jan. 1.
j – Not Apr. 28, May 6.
m – Also Dec. 26, 27, Jan. 2, Mar. 29.

t – ②③⑥⑦ (also Apr. 28, May 6; not Dec. 26, 27, Jan. 2, Mar. 29).

❖ – The 1212, 1412 and 1612 from Nijmegen depart Arnhem and Ede-Wageningen 2 minutes la

☛ Many trains from / to Amsterdam Centraal start from / continue to Den Helder (Table **466**).
For INTERNATIONAL TRAINS **Amsterdam – Arnhem – Köln**, see Table **28**.

470 AMSTERDAM and SCHIPHOL ✈ - EINDHOVEN - SITTARD - MAASTRICHT and HEERLEN

km		Ⓐ	Ⓐ	⚒	Ⓐ		Ⓐ	⚒	Ⓐ		⚒		⚒	†										
0	**Amsterdam** Centraal . **468** d.	...	...	...	...	...	0608	...	0638	...	0708	...	0738	...	0808	0838	0908	0938	1008	1038		2208	2238	2307
6	Amsterdam Amstel ..... **468** d.	...	...	...	...	...	0615	...	0645	...	0715	...	0745	...	0816	0845	0915	0945	1015	1045		2215	2245	2314
39	**Utrecht** Centraal .... **468** a.	...	...	...	...	...	0634	...	0704	...	0734	...	0804	...	0835	0904	0934	1004	1034	1104	and at	2234	2304	2335
39	**Utrecht** Centraal ....d.	...	...	...	...	...	0637	...	0707	...	0737	...	0807	0808	0837	0907	0937	1007	1037	1107	the same	2237	2307	2337
87	's-Hertogenbosch ....d.	...	*0540*	...	*0610*	...	0707	...	0737	...	0807	...	0837	0837	0907	0937	1007	1037	1107	1137		2307	2337	0007
119	**Eindhoven** ....a.	...	*0609*	...	*0639*	...	0726	...	0756	...	0826	...	0856	0856	0926	0956	1027	1057	1126	1156	minutes	2326	2356	0026
119	**Eindhoven** ....d.	...	0631	...	0701	...	0731	0731	0801	0801	0831	0831	0901	0901	0931	1001	1031	1101	1131	1201	past each	2331	0001	...
148	Weert ....d.	...	0648	...	0718	...	0748	0748	0818	0818	0848	0848	0918	0918	0948	1018	1048	1118	1148	1218	hour until	2348	0018	...
172	Roermond ....d.	...	0702	0707	0732	0737	0802	0802	0832	0832	0902	0902	0932	0932	1002	1032	1102	1131	1202	1232		0002	0032	...
196	Sittard ....a.	...	0717	0726	0747	0756	0817	0817	0847	0847	0917	0917	0947	0947	1017	1047	1117	1147	1217	1247		0017	0047	...
196	Sittard ....d.	0634	0720	0734	0750	0804	0820	0820	0850	0850	0920	0920	0950	0950	1020	1050	1120	1150	1220	1250		0020	0050	...
218	**Maastricht** ....a.	0654	0735	0754	0804	0824	0834	0834	0904	0904	0934	0934	1004	1004	1034	1104	1134	1204	1234	1304		0034	0104	...

	Ⓐ	Ⓐ	Ⓐ	⚒	Ⓐ	⚒	⚒		⚒															
Maastricht ....d.	...	...	0527	...	0557	...	0627	...	0657	...	0727	0757		1927	1957	2027	2057	2127	2157	2227	...	2257	...	...
Sittard ....a.	...	...	0542	...	0612	...	0642	...	0712	...	0742	0812	and at	1942	2012	2042	2112	2142	2212	2242	...	2312	...	...
Sittard ....d.	...	...	0543	...	0613	...	0643	...	0713	...	0743	0813		1943	2013	2043	2113	2143	2213	2243	...	2313	...	...
Roermond ....d.	...	...	0559	...	0629	...	0659	...	0729	...	0759	0829	the same	1959	2029	2059	2129	2159	2229	2259	...	2329	...	...
Weert ....d.	...	...	0613	...	0643	...	0713	...	0743	...	0813	0843		2013	2043	2113	2143	2213	2243	2313	...	2343	...	...
Eindhoven ....a.	...	...	0629	...	0659	...	0729	...	0759	...	0829	0859	minutes	2029	2059	2129	2159	2229	2259	2329	...	2359	...	...
Eindhoven ....d.	0531	0601	0631	...	0701	0701	0731	0731	0801	0801	0831	0901	past each	2031	2101	2131	2201	2231	2301	2331	...	...	0017	...
's-Hertogenbosch ....d.	0553	0623	0653	...	0723	0723	0753	0753	0823	0823	0853	0923	hour until	2053	2123	2153	2223	2253	2323	2353	...	...	0044	...
Utrecht Centraal ....a.	0621	0651	0721	...	0751	0751	0821	0821	0851	0851	0921	0951		2121	2151	2221	2251	2321	2351	0021	...	...	...	...
Utrecht Centraal .... **468** d.	0625	0655	0725	0725	0755	0755	0825	0825	0855	0855	0925	0955		2125	2155	2225	2255	2325	2355	0025	...	...	...	...
Amsterdam Amstel .... **468** d.	0643	0713	0743	0743	0813	0813	0843	0843	0913	0913	0943	1013		2143	2213	2243	2315	2344	0014	0044	...	...	...	...
Amsterdam Centraal ... **468** a.	0652	0722	0752	0752	0822	0822	0852	0852	0922	0922	0952	1022		2152	2222	2252	2323	2353	0024	0054	...	...	...	...

km			Ⓐ		Ⓐ	⚒	Ⓐ	⚒																
0	**Schiphol** ✈ .... **468** d.	...	...	...	0616	...	0646	0646	0716	0746		1716	1746	1816	1846	1916	1946	2016	2046	2116	2146	2216	2246	2316
9	**Amsterdam** Zuid .... **468** d.	...	...	...	0624	...	0654	0654	0724	0754	and at	1724	1754	1824	1854	1924	1954	2024	2054	2124	2154	2224	2254	2324
45	**Utrecht** Centraal .... **468** a.	...	...	...	0648	...	0718	0718	0748	0818	the same	1748	1818	1848	1918	1948	2018	2048	2118	2148	2218	2248	2318	2348
45	**Utrecht** Centraal .... ¶ d.	...	...	...	0653	...	0723	—	0753	0823		1753	1823	1853	1923	1953	2023	—	—	—	—	—	...	...
93	's-Hertogenbosch .... ¶ d.	...	*0640*	...	0724	...	0754	...	0824	0854	minutes	1824	1854	1924	1954	2024	2054	...	...	...	...	...	...	...
125	**Eindhoven** .... ¶ d.	...	0716	...	0746	0746	0816	0816	0846	0916	past each	1846	1916	1943	2013	2043	2113	...	...	...	...	...	...	...
154	Weert .... ¶ d.	...	0732	...	0802	0802	0832	0832	0902	0932	hour until	1902	1932	—	—	—	—	...	...	...	...	...	...	...
178	Roermond .... ¶ d.	...	0747	...	0817	0817	0847	0847	0917	0947		1917	1947	...	...	...	...	...	...	...	...	...	...	...
202	Sittard .... ¶ d.	0719	0806	0819	0836	0836	0906	0906	0936	1006		1936	2006	2049	2119	2149	2219	2249	2319	2349	0019	0049	...	...
221	**Heerlen** ....a.	0741	0821	0841	0851	0851	0921	0921	0951	1021		1951	2021	2104	2141	2204	2241	2304	2341	0004	0041	0104	...	...

	Ⓐ	Ⓐ	Ⓐ	Ⓐ	⚒	⚒			⚒																
Heerlen ....d.	...	...	0544	0614	...	0644	...	0647	0714	...	0744	0814	0844		1814	1844	1917r	1947	2025	2047	2125	2147	2225	2247
Sittard ....¶ d.	...	...	0600	0630	...	0700	...	0709	0730	...	0800	0830	0900	and at	1830	1900	1939	2009	2039	2109	2139	2209	2239	2309
Roermond ....¶ d.	...	...	0615	0645	...	0715	...	...	0745	...	0815	0845	0915	the same	1845	1915	—	—	—	—	—	—	...	...
Weert ....¶ d.	...	...	0629	0659	...	0729	...	...	0759	...	0829	0859	0929		1859	1929	...	...	...	...	...	...	...	...
Eindhoven ....¶ d.	...	0618	0648	0718	0718	0748	0748	...	0818	0818	0848	0918	0948	minutes	1918	1948	...	...	...	...	...	...	...	...
's-Hertogenbosch ....¶ d.	0609	0639	0709	0739	0739	0809	0809	...	0839	0839	0909	0939	1009	past each	1939	2009	...	...	...	...	...	...	...	...
Utrecht Centraal ....¶ a.	0637	0707	0737	0807	0807	0837	0837	...	0907	0907	0937	1007	1037	hour until	2007	2037	...	...	...	...	...	...	...	...
Utrecht Centraal .... **468** d.	0643	0713	0743	0813	0813	0843	0843	...	0913	0913	0943	1013	1043		2013	2043	2113	2143	2213	2243	2313	2343	...	...
Amsterdam Zuid .... **468** d.	0706	0736	0806	0836	0836	0906	0906	...	0936	0936	1006	1036	1106		2036	2106	2136	2206	2236	2306	2336	0006	...	...
Schiphol ✈ .... **468** a.	0712	0742	0812	0842	0842	0912	0912	...	0942	0942	1012	1042	1112		2042	2112	2142	2212	2242	2312	2342	0012	...	...

r – 1924 on ©.

¶ – See also Amsterdam - Maastricht panel above.

For traffic arrangements on Dutch holiday dates, see page 248

DEN HAAG - EINDHOVEN - VENLO 471

	Ⓐ	Ⓐ		Ⓐ	Ⓐ		Ⓐ	⚒	⚒	⚒												
Den Haag Centraal 450 d.	...	...	...	0513	...	...	0552	...	0622	0652	...	...	0722	0752	and every	2122	2152	...	2222	...	...	2252
Den Haag HS 450 d.	...	...	...	0519	...	...	0558	...	0628	0658	...	...	0728	0758	30 minutes	2128	2158	...	2228	...	...	2258
Delft 450 d.	...	...	...	0529	...	...	0605	...	0635	0705	...	...	0735	0805	until	2135	2205	...	2235	...	...	2305
Rotterdam Centraal 450 451 d.	...	...	...	0543	0548	...	0618	0618	0648	0718	...	...	0748	0818		2148	2218	...	2248	...	...	2318
Dordrecht 450 d.	...	...	...	...	0602	...	0632	0632	0702	0732	...	...	0802	0832		2202	2232	...	2302	...	...	2332
Breda 450 451 475 d.	...	...	...	...	0621	...	0651	0651	0721	0751	...	...	0821	0851		2221	2251	...	2321	...	...	2351
Tilburg 475 d.	0551	...	...	...	0637	...	0707	0707	0737	0807	...	...	0837	0907		2237	2307	...	2337	...	...	0007
Eindhoven a.	0622	...	...	...	0659	...	0729	0729	0759	0829	...	...	0859	0929		2259	2329	...	2359	...	...	0029
Eindhoven d.	...	0632	...	...	0702	...	0732	0732	0802	0832	0832	...	0902	0932		2302	2332	...	...	0015	...	0032
Helmond d.	...	0642	...	...	0712	...	0742	0742	0812	0842	0842	...	0912	0942		2312	2342	...	...	0028	...	0042
Venlo a.	...	0710	...	...	0740	...	0810	0810	0840	0910	0910	...	0940	1010		2340	0010	...	...	...	...	0110

	Ⓐ	Ⓐ	Ⓐ	Ⓐ	⚒	⚒											
... d.	...	...	0549	0619	...	0649	...	0719	0749	0819	0849	and every	2119	2149	2219	2249	2319
ınd d.	...	...	0619	0649	...	0719	...	0749	0819	0849	0919	30 minutes	2149	2219	2249	2319	2349
oven a.	...	...	0628	0658	...	0728	...	0758	0828	0858	0928	until	2158	2228	2258	2328	2358
ıoven d.	0531	0601	0631	0701	0701	0731	0731	0801	0831	0901	0931		2201	2231	2301	2331	...
g 475 d.	0555	0625	0655	0725	0725	0755	0755	0825	0855	0925	0955		2225	2255	2325	2355	...
450 451 475 d.	0609	0639	0709	0739	0739	0809	0809	0839	0909	0939	1009		2239	2309	2340	0009	...
echt 450 d.	0629	0659	0729	0759	0759	0829	0829	0859	0929	0959	1029		2259	2329	2359	0029	...
rdam Centraal 450 451 a.	0641	0711	0741	0811	0811	0841	0841	0911	0941	1011	1041		2311	2341	0011	0041	...
450 a.	0655	0725	0755	0825	0825	0855	0855	0925	0955	1025	1055		2325	2355	0025	*0100*	...
ıaag HS 450 a.	0702	0732	0802	0832	0832	0902	0902	0932	1002	1032	1102		2332	0002	0032	*0111*	...
ıaag Centraal 450 a.	0707	0737	0807	0837	0837	0907	0907	0937	1007	1037	1107		2337	0007	0037	*0117*y	...

y – Mornings of ①③⑥⑦ (also Mar. 29, Apr. 28, May 6, 17).

☛ For NIGHT NETWORK **Amsterdam – Den Haag – Rotterdam – Eindhoven**, see Table **454**.

MAASTRICHT - HEERLEN - KERKRADE 472

…rated by **Veolia** (NS tickets valid)

	Ⓐ	Ⓐ	⚒	⚒									Ⓐn		Ⓐn	⚒		⚒	z	⊡	z
Maastricht d.	0513	0541	0611	0641	0711	0741	and every	2311	2341	0011	0041	A	0702	and every	0932	1002	and every	1232	1302	and every	2232
Valkenburg d.	0526	0554	0624	0654	0724	0754	30 minutes	2324	2354	0024	0054	L	0713	30 minutes	0943	1013	30 minutes	1243	1313	30 minutes	2243
Heerlen d.	0543	0613	0643	0713	0743	0813	until	2343	0013	0041	0111	S	0724	until	0954	1024	until	1254	1324	until	2254
Kerkrade Centrum a.	0556	0626	0656	0726	0756	0826		2356	0026	...	...	O	...		...	...		...	...		...

	Ⓐ	Ⓐ	Ⓐ	⚒	⚒										Ⓐn		Ⓐn	⚒		⚒	z	⊡	z
rade Centrum d.	...	...	0559	...	0629	0659v	0729	0759	and every	2329	2359	0029	A	...	and every	...	...	and every	...	...	and every	...
en d.	0514	0544	0614	0614	0644	0714	0744	0814	30 minutes	2344	0014	0044	L	0630	30 minutes	0900	0930	30 minutes	1200	1230	30 minutes	2200
nburg d.	0530	0600	0630	0630	0700	0730	0800	0830	until	0000	0030	0059	S	0641	until	0911	0941	until	1211	1241	until	2211
tricht a.	0545	0615	0645	0645	0715	0745	0815	0845		0015	0045	0112	O	0652		0922	0952		1222	1252		2222

Not Dec. 24–31, Feb. 8, 9. v – ⚒ only. z – Not Dec. 25, Mar. 27. ⊡ – Last trains on Dec. 24, 31, Jan. 1: From Maastricht at 1802, from Heerlen at 1730.

HEERLEN - AACHEN 473

	A	E							
Heerlen d.	0556	0656	0756	0856	and	2156	2256	...	...
Herzogenrath 🚌 802 a.	0610	0710	0810	0910	hourly	2210	2310	2329	...
Aachen Hbf 802 a.	*0631*r	*0731*t	*0831*j	*0931*	until	*2231*	*2331*f	2345	...

	A	E						
Aachen Hbf 802 d.	*0602*r	*0702*	...	*0802*	and	*2202*	*2237*	*2302*y
Herzogenrath 🚌 802 d.	0622	0722	...	0822	hourly	2222	2251	2322
Heerlen a.	0635	0735	...	0835	until	2235	...	2335

①–⑤ (not Dec. 25, Jan. 1, Mar. 28, Apr. 27, May 5, 16).
①–⑥ (not Dec. 25, 26, Jan. 1, Mar. 28).
f – Until June 11.
j – 0845 on ⑦ from June 12 (also Oct. 3, Nov. 1).
r – Not Mar. 25, May 26, Oct. 3, Nov. 1.
t – Not Mar. 25, May 5, 16, 26, Oct. 3, Nov. 1. 0745 on ⑥ from June 18.
y – ⑤⑥ to June 4 (also Mar. 24, 27, May 4, 15, 25); daily from June 10.

ROOSENDAAL - 's-HERTOGENBOSCH - NIJMEGEN - ARNHEM - ZWOLLE 475

	Ⓐ	Ⓐ	Ⓐ	⚒	Ⓐ	⚒	†	⑥k	Ⓐ	†	⚒	Ⓒ	Ⓐ											
Roosendaal d.	...	...	...	...	0520	...	...	...	0550	...	0620	0645	0650	0720	0750	0820	0850	and every	2120	2150	2220	...	2250	2320
Breda 472 d.	...	...	...	...	0540	...	...	...	0610	...	0640	0704	0710	0740	0810	0840	0910	30 minutes	2140	2210	2240	...	2310	2340
Tilburg 472 d.	...	...	...	...	0555	...	...	...	0625	...	0655	0725	0725	0755	0825	0855	0925	until	2155	2225	2255	...	2325	2355
's-Hertogenbosch d.	...	...	*0526*	...	0614	...	...	...	0644	...	0714	0744	0744	0814	0844	0914	0944		2214	2244	2314	...	2344	0010
Oss d.	...	...	*0543*	...	0626	...	...	...	0656	...	0726	0756	0756	0826	0856	0926	0956		2226	2256	2326	...	2356	...
Nijmegen a.	...	...	*0606*	...	0642	...	...	...	0712	...	0742	0812	0812	0842	0912	0942	1012		2242	2312	2342	...	0012	...
Nijmegen 468 d.	...	...	0618	...	0648	0648	...	*0712*	0718	*0737*	0748	0818	0818	0848	0918	0948	1018		2248	2318	2348	0003	0019	...
Arnhem 468 a.	...	...	0637	...	0707	0707	...	*0726*	0737	*0756*	0807	0837	0837	0907	0937	1007	1037		2307	2337	0008	0021	0039	...
Arnhem d.	...	0557	0640	...	0710	0710	0729	0740	0740	0810	0810	0840	0840	0910	0940	1010	1040		2310	2340	...	0024	...	...
Dieren d.	...	0618	0651	...	0721	0721	0749	0751	0751	0821	0821	0851	0851	0921	0951	1021	1051		2321	2351	...	0042	...	...
Zutphen d.	0604	0634	0704	0704	0734	0734	0804	0804	0804	0834	0834	0904	0904	0934	1004	1034	1104		2334	0004	...	0054	...	...
Deventer d.	0617	0647	0717	0717	0747	0747	0817	0817	0817	0847	0847	0917	0917	0947	1017	1047	1117		2347	0017	...	...	...	...
Zwolle a.	0641	0711	0741	0741	0811	0811	0841	0841	0841	0911	0911	0941	0941	1011	1041	1111	1141		0011	0041	...	...	...	...

	Ⓐ	Ⓐ	Ⓐ	Ⓐ	⚒	Ⓐ	⚒		⚒		⚒									†	⚒				
le d.	...	...	...	...	...	...	...	...	0619a	...	0649a	...	0719v	0749	0819	0849	and every	2119	2149	2219	2219	2249	...	2319	2349
nter d.	...	...	...	...	...	...	...	...	0644a	...	0714a	...	0744v	0814	0844	0914	30 minutes	2144	2214	2244	2244	2314	...	2344	0014
ıen d.	...	...	...	0548	...	0606	...	...	0658	...	0728	...	0758	0828	0858	0928	until	2158	2228	2258	2258	2328	...	2358	0028
n d.	...	...	...	0600	...	0617	...	...	0708	...	0738	...	0808	0838	0908	0938		2208	2238	2308	2308	2338	...	0008	0038
em a.	...	...	...	0620	...	0636	...	...	0720	...	0750	...	0820	0850	0920	0950		2220	2250	2320	2320	2350	...	0020	0050
em 468 d.	...	...	0552	0622	...	0638	0652	...	0722	...	0752	0752	0822	0852	0922	0952		2222	2252	2322	2322	2352	*0004*	*0034*	...
egen 468 a.	...	...	0612	0642	...	0656	0712	...	0742	...	0812	0812	0842	0912	0942	1012		2242	2312	2342	2342	0012	*0019*	*0048*	...
egen d.	...	...	0617	0647	...	▬	0717	...	0747	...	0817	0817	0847	0917	0947	1017		2247	2317	2347	2347	...	0023	...	...
d.	...	...	0633	0703	...	...	0733	...	0803	...	0833	0833	0903	0933	1003	1033		2303	2333	0003	0003	...	0046	...	...
ertogenbosch d.	...	0617	0647	0717	0717	...	0747	0747	0817	0817	0847	0847	0917	0947	1017	1047		2317	2347	0016	0017	...	0104	...	...
rg 472 d.	*0555*	0636	0706	0736	0736	...	0806	0806	0836	0836	0906	0906	0936	1006	1036	1106		2336	0006	0032	0036	...	...	...	...
a 472 d.	0620	0650	0720	0750	0750	0750	0820	0820	0850	0850	0920	0920	0950	1020	1050	1120		2350	0020	0052	0057	...	...	...	...
sendaal a.	0638	0708	0738	0808	0808	0808	0838	0838	0908	0908	0940	0940	1008	1040	1108	1138		0008	0038	0110	0115	...	...	...	...

Ⓐ only. k – Also Apr. 27, May 5, 16; not Dec. 26. v – ⚒ only.

ARNHEM and ZUTPHEN - WINTERSWIJK 476

…rated by **Arriva** (NS tickets valid) 2nd class only

Arnhem - Winterswijk

	S		Ⓐ	Ⓐ	Ⓐ	⑥k	†	Ⓐ	Ⓐ	Ⓒ	Ⓐ															
Arnhem d.	0005	...	0600	0630	0730	0731	0735	0800	0830	0835	0900	0932r	1032r	1131	1233r	1331	1433r	1531	1633r	1731	1833r	1931	2035z	2136	2235	2335
Zevenaar d.	0019	...	0614	0644	0744	0749	0749	0815	0844	0849	0915	0947r	1047r	1147r	1247r	1347r	1447r	1547r	1647r	1747r	1847r	1947r	2049	2149	2249	2349
Doetinchem d.	0037	...	0634	0704	0804	0807	0807	0834	0907	0907	0937	1007	1107	1207	1307	1407	1507	1607	1707	1807	1907	2007	2107	2207	2307	0007
Winterswijk a.	0110	...	0707	0737	0837	0840	0840	0910	0940	0940	1010	1040	1140	1240	1340	1440	1540	1640	1740	1840	1940	2040	2140	2240	2343	0042

	⑦w		Ⓐ	Ⓐ	Ⓐ	Ⓒ	Ⓐ	Ⓐ	Ⓒ	Ⓐ															Ⓐ
erswijk d.	0020	...	0517	0547	0647	0650	0717	0747	0750	0817	0850	0950	1050	1150	1250	1350	1450	1550	1650	1750	1850	1950	2050	2150	2250	2320
inchem d.	0053	...	0550	0620	0720	0723	0750	0820	0823	0850	0923	1023	1123	1223	1323	1423	1523	1623	1723	1823	1923	2023	2123	2223	2323	2353
naar d.	0111	...	0609	0639	0739	0741	0809	0839	0841	0909	0941	1041	1141	1241	1341	1441	1541	1641	1741	1841	1941	2041	2141	2241	2341	0011
em a.	0127	...	0623	0654	0754	0757	0824	0854	0856	0924	0957	1057	1157	1257	1357	1457	1557	1657	1757	1857	1957	2057	2157	2257	2357	0027

Zutphen - Winterswijk

	S		Ⓐ	⑥k	Ⓐ	Ⓐ	Ⓒ				
Zutphen d.	0006	...	0702	0706	0732	0802	0806	0906	and	2306	...
Ruurlo d.	0022	...	0718	0722	0747	0818	0822	0922	hourly	2322	...
Winterswijk a.	0040	...	0736	0740	0806	0836	0840	0940	until	2340	...

	Ⓐ	Ⓐ	⑥k	Ⓐ	Ⓐ	Ⓒ				⑥k
Winterswijk d.	0616	0646	0650	0716	0746	0750	0850	and	2250	2350
Ruurlo d.	0634	0704	0708	0734	0804	0808	0908	hourly	2308	0008
Zutphen a.	0650	0720	0724	0750	0820	0824	0924	until	2324	0024

②–⑦ (not Dec. 26, 27, Jan. 2, Mar. 29).
k – Also Apr. 27, May 5, 16; not Dec. 26.
r – 2–3 minutes later on Ⓒ.
w – Also Apr. 28, May 6, 17; not Dec. 27.
z – 2034 on ③ (not Apr. 27).
☛ Additional trains run on both routes on ⚒.

477 NIJMEGEN - VENLO - ROERMOND

Operated by **Veolia** (NS tickets

km		Ⓐh	Ⓐh	⚒d	⚒d						
0	**Nijmegen** ....d.	0538	0608	0638	0708	0738	0808	and every 30 minutes until	2238	2308	2338
24	Boxmeer..........d.	0600	0630	0700	0730	0800	0830		2300	2330	0000
39	Venray..............d.	0615	0645	0715	0745	0815	0845		2315	2345	0015
61	**Venlo** ....d.	0634	0704	0734	0804	0834	0904		2334	0004	0031
84	**Roermond** ....a.	0657	0727	0757	0827	0857	0927		2357	0027	...

	⚒	⚒							
Roermond.....d.	...	0606a	0636a	0706v	0736v	0806	0836	and every 30 minutes until	2236
Venlo ....d.	0600	0630	0700	0730	0800	0830	0900		2300
Venray...........d.	0617	0647	0717	0747	0817	0847	0917		2317
Boxmeer.........d.	0630	0700	0730	0800	0830	0900	0930		2330
Nijmegen ......a.	0652	0722	0752	0822	0852	0922	0952		2352

☛ Additional journeys: **Venlo** → **Roermond** at 0534 Ⓐ, 0604 Ⓐ; **Nijmegen** → **Venlo** at 0008; **Venlo** → **Nijmegen** at 0530 Ⓐ; **Roermond** → **Venlo** at 2336, 0006, 0036.

a – Ⓐ only. d – Runs daily Venlo - Roermond. h – Also runs on ⑥ Venlo - Roermond. v – ⚒ only.

478 ARNHEM - TIEL - GELDERMALSEN - UTRECHT and 's-HERTOGENBOSCH

km		Ⓐ	Ⓐ	Ⓐ	Ⓐ	Ⓐ	⚒	⚒	⚒														
0	**Tiel**..........d.	...	0551	...	0618	...	0648	...	0718	...	0748	...	0818	...	and at the same minutes past each hour until	1948	...	2018	...	...	2048	...
	's-Hertogenbosch..d.	0532	|	0602	|	0632	|	0702	|	0732	|	0802	|	0832		|	2002	|	2032	...	|	2102
12	Geldermalsen ....a.	0548	0603	0618	0630	0648	0700	0718	0730	0748	0800	0818	0830	0848		2000	2018	2030	2048	...	2100	2118
38	**Utrecht** Centraal.........a.	0618	0632	0648	0702	0718	0733	0748	0803	0818	0833	0848	0903	0918		2033	2048	2103	2118	...	2133	2148

Tiel...........d.	...	2148	...	2218	2248	...	2318	2348	...	0018	...
's-Hertogenbosch...d.	2132	|	2202	|	|	2302	|	|	0002	|	...
Geldermalsen ....a.	2148	2200	2218	2230	2300	2318	2330	2400	0018	0030	...
Utrecht Centraal.........a.	2218	2233	2248	2303	2333	2348	0003	0033	0048	0103	...

km		Ⓐ	Ⓐ	Ⓐ		Ⓐ	Ⓐ	⚒
0	**Utrecht** Centraal..................d.	0527	0542	0557	...	0612	0627	0642
26	Geldermalsen ....d.	0553	0610	0623	...	0640	0653	0710
48	**'s-Hertogenbosch** ....a.	|	0625	|	...	0655	|	0725
	Tiel ....a.	0605	...	0635	...	...	0705	...

Utrecht Centraal..........d.	0712	0727	0742	0757	and at the same minutes past each hour until	1912	1927	1942	1957	2012	2027	2042	2057	2112	2127	2142	2157	2227	2242	2257	2327	2342
Geldermalsen ....d.	0740	0753	0810	0823		1940	1953	2010	2023	2040	2053	2110	2123	2140	2153	2210	2223	2253	2310	2323	2353	0010
's-Hertogenbosch...a.	0755	|	0825	|		1955	|	2025	|	2055	|	2125	|	2155	|	2225	|	|	2325	|	|	0025
Tiel.........................a.	...	0805	...	0835		...	2005	...	2035	...	2105	...	2135	...	2205	...	2235	2305	...	2335	0005	...

ARNHEM - TIEL and v.v. Operated by ***Arriva*** (NS tickets valid). 2nd class only. *44 km.* Journey time: 39 – 40 minutes.

From Arnhem: 0629 Ⓐ, 0659 Ⓐ, 0729 Ⓐ, 0759 Ⓐ, 0829 ⚒, 0929, 1029, 1129, 1229, 1329, 1429, 1459 Ⓐ, 1529, 1559 Ⓐ, 1629, 1659 Ⓐ, 1729, 1759 Ⓐ, 1829, 1929, 2029, 2129, 2229,

From Tiel: 0615 Ⓐ, 0645 Ⓐ, 0715 Ⓐ, 0745 ⚒, 0815 Ⓐ, 0845, 0945, 1045, 1145, 1245, 1345, 1445, 1515 Ⓐ, 1545, 1615 Ⓐ, 1645, 1715 Ⓐ, 1745, 1815 Ⓐ, 1845, 1945, 2045, 2145, 22

479 DORDRECHT - GELDERMALSEN

Operated by **Arriva** (NS tickets valid); 2nd class

km											
0	**Dordrecht** ....d.	0606r	0636r	0706r	0736r	0806r	0838	0908	and every 30 minutes until	2338	0008
10	Sliedrecht ....d.	0618r	0648r	0718r	0748r	0818r	0850	0920		2350	0020
24	Gorinchem.........d.	0639	0709	0739	0809	0839	0909	0939		0009	0039
49	**Geldermalsen**..a.	0703	0733	0803	0833	0903	0933	1003		0033	0103

	Ⓐ	Ⓒ							
Geldermalsen d.	0639	0639k	0709	0739	0809	0839	0909	and every 30 minutes until	2339
Gorinchem.....d.	0704	0706	0734r	0804r	0834r	0906	0936		0006
Sliedrecht.......d.	0719	0721	0749r	0819r	0849r	0921	0951		0021
Dordrecht .....a.	0731	0733	0801r	0831r	0901r	0933	1003		0033

k – ⑥ (also Apr. 27, May 5, 16; not Dec. 26).
r – 2 minutes later on Ⓒ.

☛ Additional journeys: **Dordrecht** → **Geldermalsen** at 0441 Ⓐ, 0506 Ⓐ, 0508 ⑥ **k**, 0536 Ⓐ and 0538
Geldermalsen → **Dordrecht** at 0039, 0109, 0539 Ⓐ and 0609 ⚒.

480 AMSTERDAM and SCHIPHOL ✈ - AMERSFOORT - DEVENTER - ENSCHEDE

SCHIPHOL ✈ - AMSTERDAM CENTRAAL - AMERSFOORT

km		Ⓐ	Ⓐ	Ⓐ	⚒	z	⚒	Ⓐ		⚒						❖							D
0	**Schiphol** ✈..................d.	...	...	...	0559	...	0629	...	0659	...	0729	...	0759	...	0829	and at the same minutes past each hour until	...	2229	...	2259	2329	2359	2359
17	**Amsterdam** Centraal......d.	0601	0552	0631	0622	0701	0652	0731	0722	0801	0752	0831	0822	0901	0852		2301	2252	2331	2322	2352	0022	0022
31	Weesp.........................d.	|	0614	|	0644	|	0714	|	0744	|	0814	|	0844	|	0914		|	2314	|	2344	0014	0039	0044
40	Naarden-Bussum ....d.	|	0621	|	0651	|	0721	|	0751	|	0821	|	0851	|	0921		|	2321	|	2351	0021	...	0051
46	Hilversum ....d.	0622	0631	0652	0701	0722	0731	0752	0801	0822	0831	0852	0901	0922	0931		2322	2331	2352	0001	0031	...	0101
53	Baarn............................d.	|	0636	|	0706	|	0736	|	0806	|	0836	|	0906	|	0936		|	2336	|	0006	0036	...	0106
62	**Amersfoort** ....a.	0635	0644	0705	0715	0735	0745	0805	0815	0835	0845	0905	0915	0935	0945		2335	2345	0005	0015	0047	...	0115

		Ⓐ	Ⓐ	Ⓐ		Ⓐ		⚒		⚒		⚒										⑤⑥f	
Amersfoort ....d.	0451	0546	0616	0626	0646	0656	0716	0726	0746	0756	0816	0826	0846	0856	0916	0926	and at the same minutes past each hour until	2246	2256	2316	2326	2346	2356
Baarn ....d.	0458	0553	0623	|	0653	|	0723	|	0753	|	0823	|	0853	|	0923	|		2253	|	2323	|	2353	|
Hilversum ....d.	0505	0601	0631	0639	0701	0709	0731	0739	0801	0809	0831	0839	0901	0909	0931	0939		2301	2309	2331	2342	0001	0009
Naarden-Bussum ....d.	0514	0610	0640	|	0710	|	0740	|	0810	|	0840	|	0910	|	0940	|		2310	|	2340	|	0010	|
Weesp..............................a.	0522	0617	0647	|	0717	|	0747	|	0817	|	0847	|	0917	|	0947	|		2317	|	2347	|	0017	|
Amsterdam Centraal ......a.	0540	0638	0708	0700	0738	0730	0808	0800	0838	0830	0908	0900	0938	0930	1008	1000		2338	2330	0010	0003	0038	0031
Schiphol ✈.....................a.	0600v	0700	0730	...	0800	...	0830	...	0900	...	0930	...	1000	...	1030	...		2400	...	0030	...	...	...

SCHIPHOL ✈ - AMSTERDAM ZUID - AMERSFOORT - ENSCHEDE

km		Ⓐ	Ⓐ	⚒H	⚒	⚒	H			H			H				H			H			H	
0	**Schiphol** ✈.........d.	0537	0607	...	0637	0707	...	0737	0807	...	0837	0907	...	0937	and at the same minutes past each hour until	2107	...	2137	2207	...	2237	2307	...	2337
9	Amsterdam Zuid ...d.	0545	0615	...	0645	0715	...	0745	0815	...	0845	0915	...	0945		2115	...	2145	2215	...	2245	2315	...	2345
14	Duivendrecht.........d.	0551	0621	...	0651	0721	...	0751	0821	...	0851	0921	...	0951		2121	...	2151	2221	...	2251	2321	...	2351
37	Hilversum ....d.	0608	0638	...	0708	0738	...	0808	0838	...	0908	0938	...	1008		2138	...	2208	2238	...	2308	2338	...	0008
53	**Amersfoort** ....d.	0623	0650	0653	0723	0750	0753	0823	0850	0853	0923	0950	0953	1023		2150	2153	2223	2250	2253	2323	2350	2353	0020
96	Apeldoorn ....d.	0648	...	0718	0748	...	0818	0848	...	0918	0948	...	1018	1048		...	2218	2248	...	2318	2348	...	0018	...
111	**Deventer** ....d.	0700	...	0731	0800	...	0831	0900	...	0931	1000	...	1031	1100		...	2231	2300	...	2331	0000	...	0031	...
149	Almelo .... **492** d.	0726	...	0756	0826	...	0856	0926	...	0956	1026	...	1056	1126		...	2256	2326	...	2356	0026	...	0056	...
164	**Hengelo** .... **492** d.	0738	...	0808	0838	...	0908	0938	...	1008	1038	...	1108	1138		...	2308	2338	...	0008	0038	...	0108	...
172	**Enschede** ..... **492** a.	0745	...	0815	0845	...	0915	0945	...	1015	1045	...	1115	1145		...	2315	2345	...	0015	0045	...	0115	...

	ⒶH	Ⓐ	Ⓐ	ⒶH	⚒H	Ⓐ	⚒	⚒H	H	⚒	⚒		H				H			H			U
Enschede .... **492** d.	0446	...	0516	0546	...	...	0616	0646	...	...	0716	...	0746	...	0816	and at the same minutes past each hour until	2046	...	2116	2146	...	2216	2246
Hengelo.................. **492** d.	0454	...	0524	0554	...	...	0624	0654	...	...	0724	...	0754	...	0824		2054	...	2124	2154	...	2224	2254
Almelo .... **492** d.	0506	...	0536	0606	...	...	0636	0706	...	...	0736	...	0806	...	0836		2106	...	2136	2206	...	2236	2306
Deventer.........................d.	0532	...	0602	0632	0632	...	0702	0732	0732	...	0802	0802	0832	...	0902		2132	...	2202	2232	...	2302	2332
Apeldoorn.........................d.	0543	...	0613	0643	0643	...	0713	0743	0743	...	0813	0813	0843	...	0913		2143	...	2213	2243	...	2313	2343
Amersfoort......................d.	0607	0610	0640	0707	0707	0710	0740	0807	0807	0810	0840	0840	0907	0910	0940		2207	2210	2240	2307	2310	2340	0007
Hilversum ....d.	...	0623	0653	...	...	0723	0753	...	...	0823	0853	0853	...	0923	0953		...	2223	2253	...	2323	2353	...
Duivendrecht ....d.	...	0640	0710	...	...	0740	0810	...	...	0840	0910	0910	...	0940	1010		...	2240	2310	...	2340	0010	...
Amsterdam Zuid ....d.	...	0646	0716	...	...	0746	0816	...	...	0846	0916	0916	...	0946	1016		...	2246	2316	...	2346	0016	...
Schiphol ✈.......................a.	...	0653	0723	...	...	0753	0823	...	...	0853	0923	0923	...	0953	1023		...	2253	2323	...	2353	0023	...

Through trains AMSTERDAM CENTRAAL - DEVENTER - HENGELO

	A♥	z♥	Ⓐ	♥	Ⓐ	♥	Ⓐ	♥	Ⓐ	♥	Ⓐ	♥	Ⓐ	⚒m	⑦t♥
Amsterdam Centraal.......d.	0502	0701	0801	0901	1001	1101	1201	1301	1401	1501	1601	1701	1801	1901	1901
Hilversum ....d.	0526	0722	0822	0922	1022	1122	1222	1322	1422	1522	1622	1722	1822	1922	1922
Amersfoort.......................d.	0538	0737	0837	0937	1037	1137	1237	1337	1437	1537	1637	1737	1837	1937	1937
Apeldoorn..........................a.	0602	0802	0902	1002	1102	1202	1302	1402	1502	1602	1702	1802	1902	2002	2002
Deventer...........................a.	0614	0815	0913	1015	1113	1215	1313	1415	1513	1615	1713	1815	1913	2013	2015
Almelo ....a.	0640	0843	...	1043	...	1243	...	1443	...	1643	...	1843	...	2043	2043
Hengelo ....a.	0652	0856	...	1056	...	1256	...	1456	...	1656	...	1856	...	2056	2056

	Ⓐ	Ⓐ	①j♥	A♥	Ⓐ	♥	Ⓐ	♥	Ⓐ	♥	Ⓐ	♥	Ⓐ	♥	n♥
Hengelo ....d.	...	...	0803	0903	...	1103	...	1303	...	1503	...	1703	...	1903	2103
Almelo ....d.	...	...	0816	0916	...	1116	...	1316	...	1516	...	1716	...	1916	2116
Deventer...........................d.	0648	0748	0848	0948	1048	1148	1248	1348	1448	1548	1648	1748	1818	1948	2148
Apeldoorn..........................d.	0700	0800	0900	1000	1100	1200	1300	1400	1500	1600	1700	1800	1830	2000	2200
Amersfoort.......................a.	0724	0824	0924	1024	1124	1224	1324	1424	1524	1624	1724	1824	1854	2024	2224
Hilversum ....a.	0738	0838	0938	1038	1138	1238	1338	1438	1538	1638	1738	1838	1908	2038e	2238
Amsterdam Centraal.......a.	0800	0900	1000	1100	1200	1300	1400	1500	1600	1700	1800	1900	1930	2100e	2300

A – ①–⑥ (not Dec. 25, 26, Jan. 1, Mar. 28, May 16).
B – ①②⑦ (not May 16).
D – ③–⑥ (also May 16).
H – From / to Den Haag (Table **481**).
U – 🚌12 Enschede - Utrecht (- Den Haag ⑤⑥ **f**).
e – Not Dec. 31.
f – Also Apr. 27, May 5, 16; not Dec. 25, 26, Jan. 1.
j – Also Mar. 29, May 17; not Mar. 28, May 16.
m – Not May 16.
n – Not Dec. 24, 31.
t – Also Mar. 28, May 16; not Mar. 27, May 15.
v – ⚒ only.
z – Not Dec. 25, Jan. 1.
❖ – On Ⓐ the 1629 from Schiphol departs Amsterdam Centraal 1649.
♥ – *IC* service to / from Germany via Bad Bentheim. Conveys 🍸. See Table **22** for further details.

For traffic arrangements on Dutch holiday dates, see page 248

ROTTERDAM and DEN HAAG - UTRECHT - ZWOLLE 481

	Ⓐ	Ⓐ	⚒	Ⓐ	Ⓐ	⚒	Ⓐ	Ⓐ	⚒	⚒	⚒	⚒▷	⑥k	Ⓐ	⚒	⚒		⚒▷	⑥k	Ⓐ	⚒		⚒▷	
Rotterdam Centraal d.	...	...	...	...	0605	...	0620	...	...	...	0635	0650	...	...	...	0705	...	0720	...	...	...	0735	0750	...
Rotterdam Alexander d.	...	...	...	...	0613	...	0628	...	...	...	0643	0658	...	...	...	0713	...	0728	...	...	...	0743	0758	...
Den Haag Centraal d.	...	0554	...	0609	|	...	|	0624	...	0639	|	|	0653	0654	0709	|	...	|	0723	0724	0739	|	|	0754r
Gouda d.	...	0612	...	0627	0624	...	0639	0642	...	0657	0654	0709	0713	0712	0727	0724	...	0739	0743	0742	0757	0754	0809	0812
Utrecht Centraal a.	...	0631	...	0646	0643	...	0658	0701	...	0716	0713	0728a	0731	0731	0746	0743	...	0758a	0801	0801	0816	0813	0828a	0831
Utrecht Centraal d.	0620	0636	0636	...	0650	0650	0706	0706	0706	...	0720	...	0736	0736	...	0750	...	...	0806	0806	...	0820	...	0836
Amersfoort a.	0634	0650	0650	...	0704	0704	0720	0720	0720	...	0734	...	0750	0750	...	0804	...	...	0820	0820	...	0834	...	0850
Amersfoort d.	0637	0653	0653	...	0707	0707	...	...	...	...	0737	...	0753	0753	...	0807	0807	...	...	...	...	0837	...	0853
Deventer **480** a.	|	0729	0729	...	|	|	...	...	...	...	|	...	0829	0829	...	|	|	...	...	...	...	|	...	0929
Enschede **480** a.	|	0815	0815	...	|	|	...	...	...	...	|	...	0915	0915	...	|	|	...	...	...	...	|	...	1015
Zwolle a.	0712	...	...	...	0742	0742	...	...	...	...	0812	...	...	...	...	0842	0842	...	...	...	...	0912	...	...
Leeuwarden **482** a.	0828	...	...	...	|	|	...	...	...	...	0917	...	...	...	...	|	|	...	...	...	...	1017	...	...
Groningen **482** a.	...	...	...	...	0844	0844	...	...	...	...	...	...	...	...	...	0944	0944	...	...	...	...	...	...	...

	⚒		⚒▷		⚒		⚒▷			⚒		⚒▷		⚒		⚒▷		⚒		⚒▷		⚒		⚒▷	
rdam Centraal d.	...	0805	0820	...	...	0835	0850	...	...	...	0905	0920	...	...	0935	0950	...	...	1005	1020	...	...	1035	1050	...
rdam Alexander d.	...	0813	0828	...	...	0843	0858	...	...	...	0913	0928	...	...	0943	0958	...	...	1013	1028	...	...	1043	1058	...
n Haag Centraal d.	0809	|	|	0824r	0839	|	|	0854r	...	0909	|	|	0924r	0939	|	|	0954r	1009	|	|	1024r	1039	|	|	1054r
a d.	0827	0824	0839	0842	0857	0854	0909	0912	...	0927	0924	0939	0942	0957	0954	1009	1012	1027	1024	1039	1042	1057	1054	1109	1112
cht Centraal a.	0846	0843	0858a	0901	0916	0913	0928a	0931	...	0946	0943	0958a	1001	1016	1013	1028a	1031	1046	1043	1058a	1101	1116	1113	1128a	1131
cht Centraal d.	...	0850	...	0906	...	0920	...	0936	...	...	0950	...	1006	...	1020	...	1036	...	1050	...	1106	...	1120	...	1136
rsfoort a.	...	0904	...	0920	...	0934	...	0950	...	...	1004	...	1020	...	1034	...	1050	...	1104	...	1120	...	1134	...	1150
rsfoort d.	...	0907	...	...	...	0937	...	0953	...	...	1007	...	...	...	1037	...	1053	...	1107	...	...	...	1137	...	1153
venter 480 a.	...	|	...	...	...	|	...	1029	...	...	|	...	...	...	|	...	1129	...	|	...	...	...	|	...	1229
schede 480 a.	...	|	...	...	...	|	...	1115	...	...	|	...	...	...	|	...	1215	...	|	...	...	...	|	...	1315
le a.	...	0942	...	...	...	1012	...	...	...	...	1042	...	...	...	1112	...	...	...	1142	...	...	...	1212	...	...
euwarden 482 a.	...	|	...	...	...	1117	...	...	...	...	|	...	...	...	1217	...	...	...	|	...	...	...	1317	...	...
oningen 482 a.	...	1044	...	...	...	...	...	...	...	...	1144	...	...	...	...	...	...	...	1244	...	...	...	...	...	...

			▶				▶					▶				▶								
rdam Centraal d.	...	1105	1120	...	...	1135	1150	...		...	2005	2020	...	...	2035	2050	...	2105	...	2135	...	2205	...	2235
rdam Alexander d.	...	1113	1128	...	...	1143	1158	...		...	2013	2028	...	...	2043	2058	...	2113	...	2143	...	2213	...	2243
n Haag Centraal d.	1109	|	|	1124r	1139	|	|	1154r	and at	2009	|	|	2024r	2039	|	|	2054r	|	2124r	|	2154r	|	2224r	|
a d.	1127	1124	1139	1142	1157	1154	1209	1212		2027	2024	2039	2042	2057	2054	2109	2112	2124	2142	2154	2212	2224	2242	2254
cht Centraal a.	1146	1143	1158a	1201	1216	1213	1228a	1231	the same	2046	2043	2058a	2101	2116	2113	2128a	2131	2143	2201	2213	2231	2243	2301	2313
cht Centraal d.	...	1150	...	1206	...	1220	...	1236		...	2050	...	2106	...	2120	...	2136	2150	2206	2220	2236	2250	2306	2320
rsfoort a.	...	1204	...	1220	...	1234	...	1250	minutes	...	2104	...	2120	...	2134	...	2150	2204	2220	2234	2250	2304	2320	2334
rsfoort d.	...	1207	...	...	...	1237	...	1253	past each	...	2107	...	...	...	2137	...	2153	2207	...	2237	2253	2307	...	2337
venter 480 a.	...	|	...	...	...	|	...	1329	hour until	...	|	...	...	...	|	...	2229	|	...	|	2329	|	...	|
schede 480 a.	...	|	...	...	...	|	...	1415		...	|	...	...	...	|	...	2315	|	...	|	0015	|	...	|
le a.	...	1242	...	...	...	1312	...	...		...	2142	...	...	...	2212	...	...	2242	...	2312	...	2342	...	0012
euwarden 482 a.	...	|	...	...	...	1417	...	...		...	|	...	...	...	2318	...	...	|	...	0017	...	|	...	...
oningen 482 a.	...	1344	...	...	...	...	...	...		...	2244	...	...	...	...	...	...	2344	...	...	...	0045	...	...

			⚒				
rdam Centraal d.	...	2305	2305	...	2335	...	0005
rdam Alexander d.	...	2313	2313	...	2343	...	0013
n Haag Centraal d.	2254r	|	|	2324r	|	2354r	|
a d.	2312	2324	2324	2342	2354	0012	0024
cht Centraal a.	2331	2343	2343	0001	0013	0031	0044
cht Centraal d.	2336	2350	2350	0006	0020	0036	0050
rsfoort a.	2350	0004	0004	0020	0034	0050	0104
rsfoort d.	2353	0007	0007	...	...	...	0107c
venter 480 a.	0029	|	|	...	...	...	|
schede 480 a.	0115	|	|	...	...	...	|
le a.	...	0048	0048	...	...	...	0142c
euwarden 482 a.	...	...	|	...	...	...	|
oningen 482 a.	...	...	0200	...	...	...	0253e

km		Ⓐ	Ⓐ	Ⓐ	Ⓐ	Ⓐ	Ⓐ	Ⓐ	Ⓐ	⚒	⚒⊙	⚒	⚒
	Groningen **482** d.	...	...	...	...	...	...	...	...	...	...	...	...
	Leeuwarden **482** d.	...	...	...	...	...	...	...	...	...	...	...	...
	Zwolle d.	...	...	...	...	...	...	...	0548	...	...	...	...
	Enschede **480** d.	...	...	...	...	0446	...	...	|	...	...	...	...
	Deventer **480** d.	...	...	...	...	0532	...	...	|	...	...	...	...
	Amersfoort a.	...	...	...	...	0607	...	...	0622	...	...	...	...
	Amersfoort d.	...	...	...	...	0610	0610	...	0626	0640a	...	...	...
	Utrecht Centraal a.	...	...	...	...	0624	0624	...	0641	0654a	...	...	...
0	**Utrecht** Centraal d.	0559	0602	0614	0617	0629	0632	0644	0647	0659	0702a	0714	0717
32	Gouda d.	0619	0622	0634	0637	0649	0652	0704	0707	0719	0722	0734	0737
60	**Den Haag** Centraal a.	0637	|	0652	|	0707	|	0722	|	0737	|	0752	|
	Rotterdam Alexander d.	...	0631	...	0646	...	0701	...	0716	...	0731	...	0746
	Rotterdam Centraal a.	...	0640	...	0655	...	0711	...	0725	...	0740	...	0755

	Ⓐ	⚒	⚒⊙	⚒	⚒	⚒	⚒⊙	⚒		⚒		⚒⊙	⚒			⚒⊙	⚒	Ⓒ	Ⓐ		⚒⊙	⚒	†	⚒	
oningen 482 d.	0502j	...	...	...	...	...	...	...	...	0604	...	...	...	...	...	...	...	0704	0716	...	...	...	...	...	...
euwarden 482 d.	|	...	...	...	0542a	...	...	...	...	|	...	...	...	0642h	...	...	...	|	|	...	...	...	0734	0744	...
le d.	0618	...	...	...	0648	...	...	...	...	0718	...	...	...	0748	...	...	...	0818	0818	...	...	...	0848	0848	...
schede 480 d.	|	0546a	...	...	|	...	...	...	...	|	0646v	...	...	|	...	...	...	|	|	0746	...	...	|	|	...
eventer 480 d.	|	0632	...	...	|	...	...	...	...	|	0732	...	...	|	...	...	...	|	|	0832	...	...	|	|	...
rsfoort a.	0652	0707	...	...	0722	...	...	...	...	0752	0807	...	...	0822	...	...	...	0852	0852	0908	...	...	0922	0922	...
rsfoort d.	0656	0710	...	...	0726	0740	...	...	...	0756	0810	...	...	0826	0840	...	...	0856	0856	0910	...	...	0926	0926	0940
cht Centraal a.	0711	0724	...	...	0741	0754	...	...	...	0811	0824	...	...	0841	0854	...	...	0911	0911	0924	...	...	0941	0941	0954
cht Centraal d.	0717	0729	0732a	0744	0747	0759	0802a	0814	0817	0817	0829	0832a	0844	0847	0859	0902a	0914	0917	0917	0929	0932a	0944	0947	0947	0959
da d.	0737	0749	0752	0804	0807	0819	0822	0834	0837	0837	0849	0852	0904	0907	0919	0922	0934	0937	0937	0949	0952	1004	1007	1007	1019
en Haag Centraal a.	|	0807	|	0822	|	0837	|	0852	|	|	0907	|	0922	|	0937	|	0952	|	|	1007	|	1022	|	|	1037
rdam Alexander d.	0746	...	0801	...	0816	...	0831	...	0846	0846	...	0901	...	0916	...	0931	...	0946	0946	...	1001	...	1016	1016	...
rdam Centraal a.	0755	...	0810	...	0825	...	0840	...	0855	0855	...	0910	...	0925	...	0940	...	0955	0955	...	1010	...	1025	1025	...

	⚒⊙	⚒			⚒⊙	⚒			⚒⊙				⊖				⊖				⊖			
oningen 482 d.	...	...	0816	...	...	...	...	...	...	...	0916	...	...	...	...	...	...	...	1016	...	...		...	...
euwarden 482 d.	...	...	|	...	...	...	0844	...	...	...	|	...	...	...	0944	...	...	...	|	...	...		...	1744
lle d.	...	...	0918	...	...	...	0948	...	...	...	1018	...	...	...	1048	...	...	...	1118	...	...	and at	...	1848
schede 480 d.	...	...	|	0846	...	...	|	...	...	...	|	0946	...	...	|	...	...	...	|	1046	...		...	|
eventer 480 d.	...	...	|	0932	...	...	|	...	...	...	|	1032	...	...	|	...	...	...	|	1132	...	the same	...	|
rsfoort a.	...	...	0952	1007	...	...	1023	...	...	...	1052	1107	...	...	1122	...	...	...	1152	1207	...		...	1922
rsfoort d.	...	...	0956	1010	...	...	1026	1040	...	...	1056	1110	...	...	1126	1140	...	...	1156	1210	...	minutes	...	1926
cht Centraal a.	...	...	1011	1024	...	...	1041	1054	...	...	1111	1124	...	...	1141	1154	...	...	1211	1224	...	past each	...	1941
cht Centraal d.	1002a	1014	1017	1029	1032a	1044	1047	1059	1102a	1114	1117	1129	1132a	1144	1147	1159	1202a	1214	1217	1229	1232a	hour until	1944	1947
da d.	1022	1034	1037	1049	1052	1104	1107	1119	1122	1134	1137	1149	1152	1204	1207	1219	1222	1234	1237	1249	1252		2004	2007
en Haag Centraal a.	|	1052	|	1107	|	1122	|	1137	|	1152	|	1207	|	1222	|	1237	|	1252	|	1307	|		2022	|
rdam Alexander d.	1031	...	1046	...	1101	...	1116	...	1131	...	1146	...	1201	...	1216	...	1231	...	1246	...	1301		...	2016
rdam Centraal a.	1040	...	1055	...	1110	...	1125	...	1140	...	1155	...	1210	...	1225	...	1240	...	1255	...	1310		...	2025

		⊖				⊖																		⑤⑥f	
oningen 482 d.	...	...	...	1805z	...	...	...	...	...	1916	...	...	...	2016	...	...	...	2116	...	...	...	2216	...	...	...
euwarden 482 d.	...	...	...	|	...	...	...	1844	...	|	...	1944	...	|	...	2044	...	|	...	2144	...	|	...	...	2234
lle d.	...	...	...	1918	...	...	...	1948	...	2018	...	2048	...	2118	...	2148	...	2218	...	2248	...	2318	...	...	2348
nschede 480 d.	...	...	...	|	1846	...	...	|	...	|	1946	|	...	|	2046	|	...	|	2146	|	...	|	2246	2246	|
eventer 480 d.	...	...	...	|	1932	...	...	|	...	|	2032	|	...	|	2132	|	...	|	2232	|	...	|	2332	2332	|
rsfoort a.	...	...	...	1952	2007	...	...	2022	...	2052	2107	2122	...	2152	2207	2222	...	2252	2307	2322	...	2352	0007	0007	0022
rsfoort d.	1940	...	...	1956	2010	...	...	2026	2040	2056	2110	2126	2140	2156	2210	2226	2240	2256	2310	2326	2340	2356	0010	0010	0026
cht Centraal a.	1954	...	...	2011	2024	...	...	2041	2054	2111	2124	2141	2154	2211	2224	2241	2254	2311	2324	2341	2354	0011	0024	0024	0041
cht Centraal d.	1959	2002a	2014	2017	2029	2032a	2044	2047	2059	2117	2129	2147	2159	2217	2229	2247	2259	2317	2329	2347	2359	0017	...	0029	...
da d.	2019	2022	2034	2037	2049	2052	2104	2107	2119	2137	2149	2207	2219	2237	2249	2307	2319	2337	2349	0007	0019	0037	...	0049	...
en Haag Centraal a.	2037	|	2052	|	2107	|	2122	|	2137	|	2207	|	2237	|	2307	|	2337	|	0007	|	0037	|	...	0107	...
rdam Alexander d.	...	2031	...	2046	...	2101	...	2116	...	2146	...	2216	...	2246	...	2316	...	2346	...	0016	...	0046	...	...	...
rdam Centraal a.	...	2040	...	2055	...	2110	...	2125	...	2155	...	2225	...	2255	...	2325	...	2355	...	0025	...	0055	...	...	...

Ⓐ only.
⑥⑦ (also Apr. 28, May 6, 17; not Dec. 26, 27, Jan. 2).
⑥ (not Dec. 26, Jan. 2).
Also Apr. 27, May 5, 16; not Dec. 25, 26, Jan. 1.
⚒ only. 0634 on ⑥**k**.

j – 0504 on ①④⑤.
k – Also Apr. 27, May 5, 16; not Dec. 26.
r – Departs 1 minute **earlier** on Ⓒ.

▷ – On Ⓐ attached to train in following column at Utrecht. On ⑥**k** attached to train in following column at Gouda. See also note ♥.

v – ⚒ only.
z – 1816 on Ⓒ.

▶ – On Ⓐ attached to train in following column at Utrecht. On Ⓒ attached to train in following column at Gouda. See also note ♥.
⊙ – On Ⓐ detached from train in the preceding column at Utrecht. On ⑥**k** detached from train in the preceding column at Gouda. See also note ♥.
⊖ – On Ⓐ detached from train in the preceding column at Utrecht. On Ⓒ detached from train in the preceding column at Gouda. See also note ♥.
♥ – Through coaches may only run to/from Deventer or Amersfoort.

482 ZWOLLE - GRONINGEN and LEEUWARDEN

km		⑥j	Ⓐ	Ⓐ	ⒶL	Ⓐ	Ⓐ	⑥k	Ⓐ	⚒L	Ⓐ	⑥kL	Ⓐ	⚒	Ⓐ		Ⓐ			⑥k	Ⓐ	†L	
	Rotterdam Centraal **481** d.	0005	...	...	...	...	...	...	...	...	...	...	...	...	...	0605a	0522	...	...	0551	...	...	0635v
	Utrecht Centraal **481** d.	0050	...	...	...	...	...	...	...	...	...	...	...	0620a	...	0650v	|	...	...	|	...	...	0720v
	Amersfoort **481** d.	0107	...	...	...	...	...	...	...	...	...	...	...	0637a	...	0707v	|	...	...	|	...	...	0737v
	Den Haag Centraal **460** d.	|	...	...	...	...	...	...	...	...	...	...	...	|	...	|	0543h	...	...	0613h	...	...	|
	Schiphol + **460** d.	|	...	...	...	...	...	...	...	...	...	...	...	|	...	|	0614	...	...	0644	0703	...	|
	Amsterdam Zuid **460** d.	|	...	...	...	...	...	...	...	...	...	...	...	|	...	|	|	...	...	|	0712	...	|
	Amsterdam Centraal **460** d.	|	...	...	...	...	...	...	...	...	...	...	0607	|	...	|	0637	0637v	...	0707	|	...	|
	Zwolle **460 481** a.	0142	...	...	...	...	...	...	...	...	...	...	0715	0712a	...	0742v	0745	0745v	...	0815	0815	...	0812v
0	**Zwolle** d.	0145	0545	0553	0616	0623	0626	0645	0647	0653	0656	0716	0717	0723	0726	0747	0753	0753	0756	0817	0817	0817	0823
27	Meppel d.	0202	0601	0609	0632	0638	0642	0701	|	0709	0713	0732	|	0738	0743	|	0809	0809	0813	|	|	|	|
	Steenwijk d.	|	|	0618	|	0647	|	|	|	0718	|	|	|	0747	|	|	0818	0818	|	|	|	|	0847
	Heerenveen d.	|	|	0634	|	0704	|	|	|	0734	|	|	|	0804	|	|	0834	0834	|	|	|	|	0900
	Leeuwarden a.	|	|	0656	|	0728	|	|	|	0756	|	|	|	0828	|	|	0856	0856	|	|	|	|	0917
47	Hoogeveen d.	0214	0613	...	0643	...	0654	0713	|	...	0724	0743	|	...	0754	|	...	...	0824	|	|	|	...
77	Assen d.	0233	0632	...	0701	...	0714	0732	0727	...	0744	0801	0757	...	0814	0827	...	...	0844	0857	0857	0857	...
104	**Groningen** a.	0253	0652	...	0724	...	0734	0752	0744	...	0804	0829	0814	...	0834	0844	...	...	0904	0914	0914	0914	...

		Ⓐ	⑥k	†	⚒	†	⚒				†	⚒	⚒	†	⚒				†	⚒	⚒	†	⚒
Rotterdam Centraal **481** d.	0705v	...	0622	...	...	0652	...	0735	...	0805	0722	...	...	0752	...	0835	...	0905	0822	...	...	0852	...
Utrecht Centraal **481** d.	0750v	...	|	...	...	|	...	0820	...	0850	|	...	...	|	...	0920	...	0950	|	...	...	|	...
Amersfoort **481** d.	0807	...	|	...	...	|	...	0837	...	0907	|	...	...	|	...	0937	...	1007	|	...	...	|	...
Den Haag Centraal **460** d.	|	0703	0643h	...	...	0713h	0733a	|	...	|	0743h	0803	...	0813h	0833	|	...	|	0843h	0903	...	0913h	0933
Schiphol + **460** d.	|	0733	0714	...	...	0744	0803	|	...	|	0814	0833	...	0844	0903	|	...	|	0914	0933	...	0944	1003
Amsterdam Zuid **460** d.	|	0742	|	...	...	|	0812	|	...	|	|	0842	...	|	0912	|	...	|	|	0942	...	|	1012
Amsterdam Centraal **460** d.	|	|	0737	0737	...	0807	|	|	...	|	0837	|	...	0907	|	|	...	|	0937	|	...	1007	|
Zwolle **460 481** a.	0842	0845	0845	0850	...	0915	0915	0912	...	0942	0945	0945	...	1015	1015	1012	...	1042	1045	1045	...	1115	1115
Zwolle d.	0847	0853	0853	0853	0856	0917	0917	0923	0926	0947	0953	0953	0956	1017	1017	1023	1026	1047	1053	1053	1056	1117	1117
Meppel d.	|	0909	0909	0909	0913	|	|	|	0942	|	1009	1009	1013	|	|	|	1042	|	1109	1109	1113	|	|
Steenwijk d.	|	0918	0918	0918	|	|	|	0947	|	|	1018	1018	|	|	|	1047	|	|	1118	1118	|	|	|
Heerenveen d.	|	0934	0934	0934	|	|	|	1000	|	|	1034	1034	|	|	|	1100	|	|	1134	1134	|	|	|
Leeuwarden a.	|	0956	0956	0956	|	|	|	1017	|	|	1056	1056	|	|	|	1117	|	|	1156	1156	|	|	|
Hoogeveen d.	|	...	...	...	0924	|	|	...	0954	|	...	...	1024	|	|	...	1054	|	...	...	1124	|	|
Assen d.	0927	...	...	...	0944	0957	0957	...	1014	1027	...	...	1044	1057	1057	...	1114	1127	...	...	1144	1157	1157
Groningen a.	0944	...	...	...	1004	1014	1014	...	1034	1044	...	...	1104	1114	1114	...	1134	1144	...	...	1204	1214	1214

				⚒◐																D		⚒
Rotterdam Centraal **481** d.	...	1005	...	...	...	1035	...	and at the same minutes past each hour until	2005	...	...	...	2035	...	2105	...	...	2135	2205	2122	2152	2305
Utrecht Centraal **481** d.	...	1050	...	...	...	1120	...		2050	...	...	...	2120	...	2150	...	...	2220	2250	|	|	2350
Amersfoort **481** d.	...	1107	...	...	...	1137	...		2107	...	...	...	2137	...	2207	...	...	2237	2307	|	|	0007
Den Haag Centraal **460** d.	...	|	1003	...	1033	|	...		|	2003	...	2033	|	...	|	2103	2133	|	|	2143h	2213h	|
Schiphol + **460** d.	...	|	1033	...	1103	|	...		|	2033	...	2103	|	...	|	2133	2203	|	|	2214	2244	|
Amsterdam Zuid **460** d.	...	|	1042	...	1112	|	...		|	2042	...	2112	|	...	|	2142	2212	|	|	|	|	|
Amsterdam Centraal **460** d.	...	|	|	...	|	|	...		|	|	...	|	|	...	|	|	|	|	|	2237	2307	|
Zwolle **460 481** a.	...	1142	1145	...	1215	1212	...		2142	2145	...	2215	2212	...	2242	2245	2315	2312	2342	2345	0015	0048
Zwolle d.	1126	1147	1153	1156	1217	1223	1226		2147	2153	2156	2217	2223	2226	2247	2253	2317	2323	2347	2353	0017	0049
Meppel d.	1142	|	1209	1213	|	|	1242		|	2209	2213	|	2238	2242	|	2309	2332	|	|	0009	0033	0104
Steenwijk d.	|	|	1218	|	|	1247	|		|	2218	|	|	2247	|	|	2318	|	2347	|	0018	|	|
Heerenveen d.	|	|	1234	|	|	1300	|		|	2234	|	|	2300	|	|	2334	|	0000	|	0034	|	|
Leeuwarden a.	|	|	1256	|	|	1317	|		|	2256	|	|	2318	|	|	2356	|	0017	|	0056	|	|
Hoogeveen d.	1154	|	...	1224	|	...	1254		|	...	2224	|	...	2254	|	...	2344	...	|	...	0045	0115
Assen d.	1214	1227	...	1244	1257	...	1314		2227	...	2244	2257	...	2314	2327	...	0002	...	0027	...	0103	0133
Groningen a.	1234	1244	...	1304	1314	...	1334		2244	...	2304	2314	...	2334	2344	...	0026	...	0045	...	0130	0200

km		⑥j	Ⓐ	Ⓐ	Ⓐ	Ⓐ	⑥k	Ⓐ	⚒	Ⓐ	⑥k	Ⓐ	⑥k	Ⓐ	†	Ⓐ	⚒	†	Ⓒ	Ⓐ	⚒	†	⚒
	Groningen d.	0029	...	0502t	...	0530t	0546	...	0604	0623	...	...	0634	0646	0646	0653	...	...	0704	0716	0723	...	...
	Assen d.	0047	...	0524	...	0552t	0602	...	0625	0644	...	...	0655	0702	0702	0714	...	...	0725	0732	0744	...	...
	Hoogeveen d.	|	...	0544	...	0614	|	...	0644	0703	...	...	0714	|	|	0733	...	...	0744	|	0803	...	...
0	**Leeuwarden** d.	|	0503	|	0542	|	|	0603	|	|	0634	0642	|	|	|	|	0703	0703	|	|	|	0734	0744
29	Heerenveen d.	|	0525	|	0559	|	|	0625	|	|	0656	0659	|	|	|	|	0725	0725	|	|	|	0756	0801
53	Steenwijk d.	|	0540	|	0612	|	|	0640	|	|	0712	0712	|	|	|	|	0740	0740	|	|	|	0812	0814
67	Meppel d.	|	0551	0557	0622	0626	|	0651	0657	0716	0722	0722	0727	|	|	0746	0751	0751	0757	|	0816	0822	|
94	**Zwolle** a.	0129	0608	0613	0638	0643	0643	0708	0713	0733	0738	0738	0743	0743	0743	0803	0808	0808	0813	0813	0833	0838	0838
	Zwolle **460 481** d.	0135	0615	0618	0648	0645	0645	0715	0718	...	0748	0748	0745	0745	0745	...	0815	0815	0818	0818	...	0848	0848
	Amsterdam Centraal **460** a.	0239	|	|	|	|	0753	|	|	...	|	|	|	|	0853	...	|	0923	|	|	...	|	|
	Amsterdam Zuid **460** a.	...	0719	|	|	0749	|	0819	|	...	|	|	0849	0849	|	...	0919	|	|	|	...	|	|
	Schiphol + **460** a.	...	0726	|	|	0756	0815	0826	|	...	|	|	0856	0856	0915	...	0926	0945	|	|	...	|	|
	Den Haag Centraal **460** a.	...	0756	|	|	0826	0847h	0857	|	...	|	|	0927	0926	0947h	...	0957	1017h	|	|	...	|	|
	Amersfoort **481** a.	...	...	0652	0722	...	|	...	0752	...	0822	0822	...	...	|	...	...	|	0852	0852	...	0922	0922
	Utrecht Centraal **481** a.	...	...	0711	0741	...	|	...	0811	...	0841	0841	...	...	|	...	...	|	0911	0911	...	0941	0941
	Rotterdam Centraal **481** a.	...	...	0755	0825	...	0908	...	0855	...	0925	0925	...	...	1008	...	...	1038	0955	0955	...	1025	1025

	⚒	⚒◧													Ⓐ	Ⓒ						
Groningen d.	0746	0753	...	0816	0823	...	0846	and at the same minutes past each hour until	1716	1723	...	1746	1753	...	1805	1816	1823	...	1846	1853	...	1916
Assen d.	0802	0814	...	0832	0844	...	0902		1732	1744	...	1802	1814	...	1825	1832	1844	...	1902	1914	...	1932
Hoogeveen d.	|	0833	...	|	0903	...	|		|	1803	...	|	1833	...	1844	|	1903	...	|	1933	...	|
Leeuwarden d.	|	|	0803	|	|	0844	|		|	|	1744	|	|	1803	|	|	|	1844	|	|	1903	|
Heerenveen d.	|	|	0825	|	|	0901	|		|	|	1801	|	|	1825	|	|	|	1901	|	|	1925	|
Steenwijk d.	|	|	0840	|	|	0914	|		|	|	1814	|	|	1840	|	|	|	1914	|	|	1940	|
Meppel d.	|	0846	0851	|	0916	|	|		|	1816	|	|	1846	1851	1857	|	1916	|	|	1946	1951	|
Zwolle a.	0843	0903	0908	0913	0933	0938	0943		1813	1833	1838	1843	1903	1908	1913	1913	1933	1938	1943	2003	2008	2013
Zwolle **460 481** d.	0845	...	0915	0918	...	0948	0945		1818	...	1848	1845	...	1915	1918	1918	...	1948	1945	...	2015	2018
Amsterdam Centraal **460** a.	|	...	|	|	...	|	|		|	...	|	|	...	|	|	|	...	|	|	...	|	|
Amsterdam Zuid **460** a.	0949	...	1019	|	...	|	1049		|	...	|	1949	...	2019	|	|	...	|	2049	...	2119	|
Schiphol + **460** a.	0956	...	1026	|	...	|	1056		|	...	|	1956	...	2026	|	|	...	|	2056	...	2126	|
Den Haag Centraal **460** a.	1027	...	1057	|	...	|	1127		|	...	|	2027	...	2057	|	|	...	|	2127	...	2157	|
Amersfoort **481** a.	...	...	...	0952	...	1023	...		1852	...	1922	...	...	...	1952	1952	...	2022	...	...	...	2052
Utrecht Centraal **481** a.	...	...	...	1011	...	1041	...		1910	...	1941	...	...	...	2011	2011	...	2041	...	...	...	2111
Rotterdam Centraal **481** a.	...	...	...	1055	...	1125	...		1955	...	2025	...	...	...	2055	2055	...	2125	...	...	...	2155

																			⑤⑥r	⑤⑥r	⊡	⑤⑥r
Groningen d.	...	1946	1953	...	2016	2023	...	2046	2053	...	2116	2123	...	2146	...	2216	2223	...	2246	2246	...	2323	2325
Assen d.	...	2002	2014	...	2032	2044	...	2102	2114	...	2132	2144	...	2202	...	2232	2244	...	2302	2302	...	2344	2346
Hoogeveen d.	...	|	2033	...	|	2103	...	|	2133	...	|	2203	...	|	...	|	2303	...	|	|	...	0003	0006
Leeuwarden d.	1944	|	|	2003	|	|	2044	|	|	2103	|	|	2144	|	2203	|	|	2234	|	|	2325	|	|
Heerenveen d.	2001	|	|	2025	|	|	2101	|	|	2125	|	|	2201	|	2225	|	|	2256	|	|	2347	|	|
Steenwijk d.	2014	|	|	2040	|	|	2114	|	|	2140	|	|	2214	|	2240	|	|	2312	|	|	0003	|	|
Meppel d.	|	|	2046	2051	|	2116	|	|	2146	2151	|	2216	|	|	2251	|	2316	2322	|	|	0013	0016	0018
Zwolle a.	2038	2043	2103	2108	2113	2133	2138	2143	2203	2208	2213	2233	2238	2243	2308	2313	2333	2338	2343	2343	0029	0033	0034
Zwolle **460 481** d.	2048	2045	...	2115	2118	...	2148	2145	...	2215	2218	...	2248	2245	2315	2318	...	2348	2345	2345	...	...	0035
Amsterdam Centraal **460** a.	|	|	...	|	|	...	|	2253	...	2323	|	...	|	2353	0023	|	...	|	0053	0053	...	...	0142
Amsterdam Zuid **460** a.	|	2149	...	2219	|	...	|	|	...	|	|	...	|	|	|	|	...	|	...	|	...	...	...
Schiphol + **460** a.	|	2156	...	2226	|	...	|	2315	...	2345	|	...	|	0015	0045	|	...	|	...	0115	...	...	...
Den Haag Centraal **460** a.	|	2227	...	2257	|	...	|	2347h	...	0017h	|	...	|	0047h	0117‡	|	...	|	...	0147h	...	...	...
Amersfoort **481** a.	2122	...	...	...	2152	...	2222	|	...	|	2252	...	2322	|	...	2352	...	0022	...	...	...	...	...
Utrecht Centraal **481** a.	2141	...	...	...	2211	...	2241	|	...	|	2311	...	2341	|	...	0011	...	0041	...	...	...	...	...
Rotterdam Centraal **481** a.	2225	...	...	...	2255	...	2325	0008	...	0038	2355	...	0025	0108	...	0055	...	...	...	...	...	...	...

D – Change trains at Lelystad on ③ (not Apr. 27). See Table **460**.
L – From Lelystadt (Table **460**).
a – Ⓐ only.
h – Den Haag **HS**.
j – Not Dec. 26, Jan. 2.
k – Also Apr. 27, May 5, 16; not Dec. 26.
t – 2–4 minutes later on ①④⑤.
r – Also Apr. 27, May 5, 16; not Dec. 25, 26, Jan. 1
v – ⚒ only.
‡ – Mornings of ①②③⑥⑦ (also Apr. 28, May 6). Den Haag **HS**.
⊡ – ①②③④⑦ (also Dec. 25, 26, Jan. 1; not Apr. 27, May 5, 16).
◐ – The 1556, 1656, 1756, 1856, 1955 and 2056 from Zwolle run dai
◧ – The 1553 and 1653 from Groningen run daily.

For traffic arrangements on Dutch holiday dates, see page 248

OLDENZAAL - HENGELO - ZUTPHEN 488

rated by **Syntus** (NS tickets valid) 2nd class only

				Ⓐ	Ⓐ	⚒	⚒				⚒				⚒				Ⓐ					
Oldenzaal d.	0003	0033	...	0603	0633	0703	0733	...	...	0803	0833	0833	and at	2003	2033	2033	...	2103	2133	2133	2203	2233	2303	2333
Hengelo a.	0013	0043	...	0613	0643	0713	0743	...	...	0813	0843	0843	the same	2013	2043	2043	...	2113	2143	2143	2213	2243	2313	2343
Hengelo d.	0016	0046	...	0616	0646	0716	0746	...	...	0816	0846	...	minutes	2016	2046	...	...	2116	2146	...	2216	...	2316	...
Goor d.	0031	0100	...	0631	0701	0731	0801	0801	...	0831	0901	...	past each	2031	2101	...	...	2131	2201	...	2231	...	2331	...
Lochem d.	0039	...	...	0639	0709	0739	0809	0809	...	0839	0909	...	hour until	2039	2109	...	...	2139	2209	...	2239	...	2339	...
Zutphen a.	0052	...	...	0653	0723	0753	0823	0823	...	0853	0923	...		2053	2123	...	...	2153	2223	...	2253	...	2353	...

			Ⓐ	Ⓐ	Ⓐ	⚒	Ⓐ	⚒	⚒			⚒				⚒			Ⓐ						
hen d.	0006	...	...	...	0608	...	0636	...	0706	...	0736	0806	...	and at	1936	2006	...	2036	2106	...	2136	...	2236	...	2336
em d.	0019	...	...	...	0621	...	0651	...	0721	...	0751	0821	...	the same	1951	2021	...	2051	2121	...	2151	...	2251	...	2351
d.	0029	...	0530	0600	0630	0630	0700	0700	0730	0730	0800	0830	...	minutes	2000	2030	...	2100	2130	...	2200	...	2300	...	0000
gelo a.	...	...	0544	0614	0644	0644	0714	0714	0744	0744	0814	0844	...	past each	2014	2044	...	2114	2144	...	2214	...	2314	...	0014
gelo d.	...	...	0548	0618	0648	0648	0718	0718	0748	0748	0818	0848	0848	hour until	2018	2048	2048	2118	2148	2148	2218	2248	2318	2348	0018
nzaal a.	...	...	0558	0628	0658	0658	0728	0728	0758	0758	0828	0858	0858		2028	2058	2058	2128	2158	2158	2228	2258	2328	2358	0028

ZWOLLE - ENSCHEDE 492

	Ⓐ	Ⓐ	⚒	⚒						
Zwolle d.	0549	0619	0649	0719	0749	0819	and	1949	2019	...
Raalte d.	0605	0635	0705	0735	0805	0835	every 30	2005	2035	...
Nijverdal d.	0616	0646	0716	0746	0816	0846	minutes	2016	2046	...
Almelo 480 a.	0630	0700	0730	0800	0830	0900	until	2030	2100	...
Hengelo 480 a.	0645	0715	0745	0815	0845	0915		2045	2115	...
Enschede 480 a.	0657	0727	0757	0828	0857	0927		2057	2157	...

	Ⓐ	Ⓐ	Ⓐ	⚒	⚒					
Enschede 480 d.	*0446*	*0516*	0604	0634	0704	0734	0804	and	1904	1934
Hengelo 480 d.	0516	0546	0616	0646	0716	0746	0816	every 30	1916	1946
Almelo 480 d.	0531	0601	0631	0701	0731	0801	0831	minutes	1931	2001
Nijverdal d.	0545	0615	0645	0715	0745	0815	0845	until	1945	2015
Raalte d.	0554	0624	0654	0724	0754	0824	0854		1954	2024
Zwolle a.	0611	0641	0711	0741	0811	0841	0911		2011	2041

ZWOLLE - EMMEN 493

erated by **Arriva** (NS tickets valid)

	Ⓐ	⚒	Ⓐ						⚒	⚒
Zwolle d.	0620	0650	0720	0750	0820	and at	2220	2250	2320	2350
Ommen d.	0638	0708	0738	0808	0838	the same	2238	2308	2338	0008
Mariënberg d.	0645	0715	0745	0815	0845	minutes	2245	2315	2345	0015
Coevorden d.	0700	0734	0800	0834	0900	past each	2300	2334	0000	0036
Emmen a.	0715	0753	0815	0853	0915	hour until	2315	2353	0015	0053

	Ⓐ	Ⓐ	⚒	⚒						⚒	⚒
Emmen d.	0540	0615	0638	0715	0738	0815	and at	2215	2238	2315	2338
Coevorden d.	0559	0631	0659	0731	0759	0831	the same	2231	2259	2331	2359
Mariënberg d.	0616	0646	0716	0746	0816	0846	minutes	2246	2316	2346	0016
Ommen d.	0623	0653	0723	0753	0823	0853	past each	2253	2323	2353	0023
Zwolle a.	0640	0710	0740	0810	0840	0910	hour until	2310	2340	0010	0040

Not Dec. 26, 27, Jan. 2, Mar. 29. **w** – Also Apr. 28, May 6, 17; not Dec. 27.

☛ Other journeys Zwolle - Emmen and v.v.: **From Zwolle** at 0020 ②–⑦ **n**, 0056 ⑦ **w** and 0550 Ⓐ. **From Emmen** at 0020 ②–⑦ **n** and 0512 Ⓐ.

LEEUWARDEN - GRONINGEN 494

erated by **Arriva** (NS tickets valid)

			Ⓐ	Ⓐ	⑥k	Ⓐ	⚒	Ⓐ	Ⓐ	⚒		Ⓐ	⚒		⚒	⚒		⚒	⚒			⚒	❖
Leeuwarden d.	0024	...	0551	0618	0621	0643	0651	0721	0743	0751	0821	0843	0851	0921	0943	0951	1021	1043	1051	1121	1143	1151	and at the same
Buitenpost d.	0047	...	0616	0645	0645	0659	0716	0745	0759	0816	0845	0859	0916	0945	0959	1016	1045	1059	1116	1145	1159	1216	minutes past
Groningen a.	0109	...	0640	0710	0710	0718	0740	0810	0818	0840	0910	0918	0940	1010	1018	1040	1110	1118	1140	1210	1218	1240	each hour until

			⚒						†		
uwarden d.	1821	1843	1851	1921	1943	2021	2043	2121	2143	2224	2324
enpost d.	1845	1859	1916	1945	1959	2045	2059	2145	2159	2247	2347
ningen a.	1910	1918	1940	2010	2018	2110	2118	2210	2218	2309	0009

			Ⓐ	⚒	Ⓐ	Ⓐ	⑥k	Ⓐ	Ⓐ		⚒
Groningen d.	0029	...	0548	0621	0641	0649	0651	0721	0741	0749r	0821
Buitenpost d.	0051	...	0611	0645	0659	0715	0715	0745	0759	0815	0845
Leeuwarden a.	0116	...	0637	0710	0716	0740	0740	0812	0816	0840	0910

	Ⓐ		⚒	⚒		⚒	⚒		†	⚒		⚒		†	⚒	⚒		†	⚒	⚒				
ningen d.	0841	0849r	0921	0941	0951	1021	1041	1051	1121	1121	and at the same	1841	1851	1921	1921	1941	1951	2021	2021	2041	2051	2127	2227	2327
enpost d.	0859	0915	0945	0959	1015	1045	1059	1115	1139	1145	minutes past	1859	1915	1939	1945	1959	2015	2039	2045	2059	2115	2149	2249	2349
uwarden a.	0916	0940	1010	1016	1040	1110	1116	1140	1200	1210	each hour until	1916	1940	2000	2010	2016	2040	2100	2110	2116	2140	2214	2314	0014

Also Apr. 27, May 5, 16; not Dec. 26. **r** – 2 minutes later on Ⓒ. ❖ – On Ⓐ Leeuwarden d. 1550 / 1650 (not 1551 / 1651).

GRONINGEN - BAD NIEUWESCHANS - LEER 495

erated by **Arriva** (NS tickets valid)

			Ⓐ	⑥k	Ⓐ	⑥k	Ⓐ	Ⓐ	⑥k		⚒		⚒			⚒				⚒		
Groningen 498 d.	0023	...	0506	0546	0549	0613	0620	0650	0652	0722	0752	0822	0852	and at the same	1822	1852	1922	2022	2122	2122	2222	2322
Hoogezand-Sappemeer **498** d.	0038	...	0521	0601	0604	0628	0635	0705	0707	0737	0807	0837	0907	minutes past	1837	1907	1937	2037	2137	2137	2237	2337
Winschoten d.	0057	...	0540	0620	0623	0648	0700	0730	0730	0800	0830	0900	0926	each hour until	1900	1926	2000	2100	2156	2200	2300	2356
Bad Nieuweschans a.	0106	...	0550	...	...	0657	0710	0740	0740	0810	0840	0910	...		1910	...	2010	2110	...	2210	2310	0005

			Ⓐ	⑥k	Ⓐ	Ⓐ	Ⓐ	Ⓒ	⚒	Ⓒ		†	⚒	⚒			⚒				⚒		
Nieuweschans d.	0010	0110	...	...	...	0645	0715	0719k	0749	0819	...	...	0849	...	0949	and at the same	...	1949	2049	2149	2219	2249	2319
schoten d.	0019	0119	0555	0625	0628	0658	0727	0731	0801	0831	0831	0901	0901	0931	1001	minutes past	1931	2001	2101	2201	2231	2301	2330
gezand-Sappemeer **498** d.	0038	0138	0614	0647	0647	0717	0746	0750	0820	0850	0850	0919	0920	0950	1020	each hour until	1950	2020	2120	2220	2250	2320	2350
ningen a.	0056	0155	0630	0704	0703	0734	0803	0807	0837	0907	0907	0937	0937	1007	1037		2007	2037	2137	2237	2307	2337	0007

service to / from Leer (operates until further notice). Dutch holiday dates apply (see page 248). See panel above for rail connections Groningen - Winschoten and v.v.

🚌	Ⓐ	⚒	⚒	†	⚒	†	⚒	†	⚒	†		⚒	†			⊠	⚒							
ningen d.	...	...	...	*0656**	...	*0750**	...	*0850**	...	*0952**	and at	...	*1852**	*1952**	*2052**	A	0630	0830	1030	1230	1430	1630	1830	2030
lbroek d.	...	...	...	0722	...	0819	...	0919	...	1019	the same	...	1919	2019	2119	L	|	|	|	|	|	|	|	|
schoten d.	...	0632	0732	0740	0832	0837	0932	0937	1032	1037	minutes	1932	1937	2037	2137	S	|	|	|	|	|	|	|	|
Nieuweschans 🏛 d.	0552	0647	0747	0755	0847	0852	0947	0952	1047	1052	past each	1947	1952	2052	2152	O	|	|	|	|	|	|	|	|
r a.	0630	0725	0825	0833	0925	0930	1025	1030	1125	1130	hour until	2025	2030	2130	2230		0725	0925	1125	1325	1525	1725	1925	2125

🚌	Ⓐ	⚒	⚒	†	⚒		†	⚒			†	⚒	†	⚒		⊠	⚒							
r d.	0630	0730	0830	0926	0930	and at	1826	1830	1926	2026	2122	2130	2222	2230	...	A	0730	0930	1130	1330	1530	1730	1930	2130
Nieuweschans 🏛 a.	0708	0808	0908	1004	1008	the same	1904	1908	2004	2104	2200	2208	2300	2308	...	L	|	|	|	|	|	|	|	|
schoten a.	0723	0823	0923	1019	1023	minutes	1919	1923	2019	2119	2215	2223	2315	2323	...	S	|	|	|	|	|	|	|	|
lbroek a.	...	...	...	1037	...	past each	1937	...	2037	2137	2233	...	2333	...	...	O	|	|	|	|	|	|	|	|
ningen a.	...	...	...	*1107**	...	hour until	*2007**	...	*2107**	*2207**	*2302**	...	*0002**	...	...		0825	1025	1225	1425	1625	1825	2025	2225

⑥ (also Apr. 27, May 5, 16; not Dec. 26). * – Connection by train to / from Zuidbroek. ⊠ – Additional fast 🚌 services.

LEEUWARDEN - STAVOREN 496

erated by **Arriva** (NS tickets valid); 2nd class only

	Ⓐ	Ⓐ	⑥k	Ⓐ	⚒z	Ⓐ	⑥k	†	Ⓐ	⚒	Ⓐ	⑥k	†	Ⓐ	⚒	⚒	†	Ⓐ	⚒	⚒	†	Ⓐ	⚒	
Leeuwarden d.	0531	0600	0612	0621	0641	0701	0701	0708	0721	0741	0801	0801	0808	0821	0841	0901	0908	0923	0943	1003	1008	1023	0943	and at the same
Sneek a.	0550	0619	0631	0640	0700	0720	0720	0727	0740	0800	0820	0822	0827	0840	0902	0922	0927	0942	1002	1022	1027	1042	1002	minutes past
Sneek d.	0551	0622	0632	0653	...	0724	0730	...	...	...	0828	0830	0830	...	...	0930	0930	...	...	1030	1030	...	...	each hour until
Stavoren a.	0618	0649	0659	0720	...	0751	0757	...	...	...	0855	0857	0857	...	...	0957	0957	...	...	1057	1057	...	...	

	⚒	†	Ⓐ	⚒	Ⓐ					⑤⑥f		
uwarden d.	1803	1808	1823	1843	1903	1923	2023	2123	2223	2223	2323	...
ek a.	1822	1827	1842	1902	1922	1941	2041	2141	2242	2242	2342	...
ek d.	1830	1830	...	...	...	1943	2043	2143	...	2243	...	...
voren a.	1857	1857	...	...	...	2009	2109	2209	...	2309	...	...

	Ⓐ	Ⓐ	Ⓐ	⚒	†	Ⓐ	⑥k		Ⓐ	⚒	†
Stavoren d.	...	...	0623	...	...	0654	0704	...	0725	...	...
Sneek a.	...	...	0651	...	...	0722	0730	...	0752	...	...
Sneek d.	0615	0635	0655	0715	0732	0735	0735	...	0756	0815	0832
Leeuwarden a.	0636	0656	0716	0736	0753	0756	0756	...	0816	0836	0853

	Ⓐ	⑥k	Ⓐ	⚒	†	⚒	Ⓐ		⚒	†	⚒	Ⓐ	⚒		Ⓒ	Ⓐ									⑤⑥f
voren d.	0802	0804	...	...	0904	0904	...	and at the same	...	1804	1804	...	...	...	1909	1917	...	2014	...	2114	...	2214	...	...	2314
ek a.	0828	0830	...	...	0930	0930	...	minutes past	...	1830	1830	...	...	...	1935	1943	...	2039	...	2139	...	2239	...	...	2339
ek d.	0834	0834	0857	0917	0932	0937	0957	each hour until	1817	1832	1837	1857	1917	1936	1936	1953	...	2041	...	2141	...	2242	...	2347	2347
uwarden a.	0856	0856	0918	0938	0953	0958	1018		1838	1853	1858	1918	1938	1956	1956	2012	...	2100	...	2200	...	2301	...	0006	0006

Also Apr. 27, May 5, 16; not Dec. 25, 26, Jan. 1. **k** – Also Apr. 27, May 5, 16; not Dec. 26. **z** – 2 minutes later on ⑥ (also Apr. 27, May 5, 16).

497 ROTTERDAM - HOEK VAN HOLLAND

km				Ⓐ	⚒	Ⓐ	⚒	Ⓐ		Ⓐ		Ⓐ					
0	**Rotterdam** Centraal .... d.	0002	...	0532	0602	0617	0632	0647	0702	0717	0732	0747	0802	0832	and every 30 minutes until	2302	2332
4	Schiedam Centrum .... d.	0007	...	0537	0607	0622	0637	0652	0707	0722	0737	0752	0807	0837		2307	2337
10	Vlaardingen Centrum .... d.	0015	...	0545	0615	0630	0645	0700	0715	0730	0745	0800	0815	0845		2315	2345
27	**Hoek van Holland** Haven .... a.	0032	...	0602	0632	0647	0702	0717	0732	0747	0802	0817	0832	0902		2332	0002

			Ⓐ	Ⓐ	Ⓐ	⚒	Ⓐ	⚒	Ⓐ		Ⓐ					
Hoek van Holland Haven .... d.	0026	...	0556	0626	0641	0656	0711	0726	0741	0756	0811	0826	0856	and every 30 minutes until	2326	2356
Vlaardingen Centrum .... d.	0043	...	0613	0643	0658	0713	0728	0743	0758	0813	0828	0843	0913		2343	0013
Schiedam Centrum .... a.	0051	...	0621	0651	0707	0721	0737	0751	0807	0821	0837	0851	0921		2351	0021
Rotterdam Centraal .... a.	0057**n**	...	0627	0657	0712	0727	0742	0757	0812	0827	0842	0857	0927		2357	0027

n – 0103 on ⑤ (not M

498 OTHER BRANCH LINES

ALMELO – MARIËNBERG Operated by **Arriva** (NS tickets valid)

From Almelo:
0618 Ⓐ, 0648 Ⓐ, 0718 Ⓐ, 0748 ⚒, 0818 Ⓐ, 0848, 0948, 1048, 1148, 1248, 1318 ⚒, 1348, 1418 ⚒, 1448, 1518 ⚒, 1548, 1618 ⚒, 1648, 1718 ⚒, 1748, 1818 ⚒, 1848, 1948, 2048, 2148, 2248 and 2357.

19 km. Journey time: 22 – 23 minutes.

From Mariënberg:
0553 Ⓐ, 0623 Ⓐ, 0653 Ⓐ, 0723 ⚒, 0753 Ⓐ, 0823, 0853 Ⓐ, 0923, 1023, 1123, 1223, 1 1353 ⚒, 1423, 1453 ⚒, 1523, 1553 ⚒, 1623, 1653 ⚒, 1723, 1753 ⚒, 1823, 1923, 2023, 2 2223 and 2323.

AMERSFOORT – EDE-WAGENINGEN Operated by **Connexxion** (NS tickets valid)

From Amersfoort:
0011 **H**, 0041 ⑦ **c**, 0111 ⑦ **c**, 0511 Ⓐ, 0541 **P**, 0611 **P**, 0641 **P**, 0711, 0741, 0811, 0841 and every 30 minutes until 2341.
All trains call at Barneveld Centrum (17 minutes from Amersfoort)

34 km. Journey time: 37 – 38 minutes.

From Ede-Wageningen:
0025, 0055 **H**, 0125 ⑦ **c**, 0155 ⑦ **c**, 0555 Ⓐ, 0625 **P**, 0655 **P**, 0725 **P**, 0755, 0825, 0855 and every 30 minutes until 2355.
All trains call at Barneveld Centrum (20 minutes from Ede-Wageningen)

APELDOORN – ZUTPHEN Operated by **Arriva** (NS tickets valid)

From Apeldoorn:
0006, 0636 Ⓐ, 0706 Ⓐ, 0736 Ⓐ, 0806 ⚒, 0836, 0906 and every 30 minutes until 2336.

18 km. Journey time: 19 – 20 minutes.

From Zutphen:
0606 Ⓐ, 0636 Ⓐ, 0706 Ⓐ, 0736 ⚒, 0806, 0836 and every 30 minutes until 2336.

GRONINGEN – DELFZIJL Operated by **Arriva** (NS tickets valid)

From Groningen:
0033, 0514 Ⓐ, 0544 Ⓐ, 0548 ⑥ **k**, 0614 Ⓐ, 0618 Ⓒ, 0644 Ⓐ, 0648 **S**, 0714 Ⓐ, 0718 Ⓒ, 0744 Ⓐ, 0748 ⑥ **k**, 0818, 0848 ⚒ and at 18 and 48 ⚒ minutes past each hour until 1718, 1748 ⚒; then 1818, 1848 Ⓐ, 1918, 2018, 2048 ④ **d**, 2118, 2226 and 2326.

38 km. Journey time: 37 – 39 minutes.

From Delfzijl:
0008, 0113, 0525 ① **m**, 0555 Ⓐ, 0625 Ⓐ, 0630 ⑥ **k**, 0655 Ⓐ, 0700 Ⓒ, 0725 Ⓐ, 0730 **S**, 0756 Ⓐ, 0800 Ⓒ, 0830 ⚒, 0900, 0930 ⚒ and at 00 and 30 ⚒ minutes past each hour u 1800, 1830 ⚒; then 1900, 1930 Ⓐ, 2000, 2100, 2200 and 2308.

GRONINGEN – VEENDAM 🚂 Operated by **Arriva** (NS tickets valid)

From Groningen:
0008, 0456 Ⓐ, 0535 Ⓐ, 0606 ⚒, 0635 Ⓐ, 0656 †, 0708 ⚒, 0738 ⚒, 0750 †, 0808 ⚒, 0838 ⚒, 0850 †, 0908 ⚒, 0938 ⚒, 0952 † and at 08 ⚒, 38 ⚒ and 52 † minutes past each hour until 1808 ⚒, 1838 ⚒, 1852 †; then 1908 ⚒, 1952, 2052, 2152 and 2250.
All trains call at Hoogezand-Sappemeer (15 minutes from Groningen)

29 km. Journey time: 29 – 32 minutes.

From Veendam:
0048, 0530 Ⓐ, 0615 Ⓐ, 0646 ⚒, 0716 Ⓐ, 0730 †, 0746 ⚒, 0818 ⚒, 0830 †, 0848 ⚒, 09 0935 †, 0948 ⚒ and at 18 ⚒, 35 † and 48 ⚒ minutes past each hour until 1918 ⚒, 1935 1948 ⚒; then 2035, 2135, 2230 and 2330.
All trains call at Hoogezand-Sappemeer (15 minutes from Veendam)

LEEUWARDEN – HARLINGEN Haven ¶ Operated by **Arriva** (NS tickets valid)

From Leeuwarden:
0538 Ⓐ, 0603 ⚒, 0638 Ⓐ, 0703 ⚒, 0738, 0803, 0838, 0903, 0946 ⚒, 1021, 1046 ⚒, 1121, 1146, 1221, 1246 ⚒, 1321, 1346, 1421, 1446, 1521, 1546 ⚒, 1621, 1646, 1721, 1746 ⚒, 1821, 1846, 1921, 1946, 2021, 2125, 2225 and 2325.

26 km. Journey time: 25 – 26 minutes. 2nd class.

From Harlingen Haven:
0607 Ⓐ, 0632 ⚒, 0707 Ⓐ, 0732 ⚒, 0807, 0832, 0907, 0950 ⚒, 1015, 1050 ⚒, 1115, 11 1215, 1250 ⚒, 1315, 1350, 1415, 1450, 1515, 1550 ⚒, 1615, 1650, 1715, 1750 ⚒, 1815, 1 1915, 1950, 2015, 2050, 2154, 2254 and 2354.

ZWOLLE – KAMPEN

From Zwolle:
0549 Ⓐ, 0619 Ⓐ, 0649 ⚒, 0719 ⚒, 0749 ⚒, 0819, 0849 ⚒ and at 19 and 49 ⚒ minutes past each hour until 1219, 1249 ⚒; then 1319, 1349 and every 30 minutes until 2349.

13 km. Journey time: 10 minutes.

From Kampen:
0003, 0603 Ⓐ, 0633 Ⓐ, 0703 ⚒, 0733 ⚒, 0803 ⚒, 0833 and at 03 ⚒ and 33 minutes pa each hour until 1303 ⚒, 1333; then 1403, 1433 and every 30 minutes until 2333.

H – ④–⑦ (not Dec. 26, 27, Jan. 2, 3, May 7).
P – ①–⑥ (not Dec. 25, 26, Jan. 1, Mar. 28, May 5, 16).
S – ⑥ to Apr. 23 (not Dec. 26); Ⓒ Apr. 27 - Sept. 25; ⑥ from Oct. 1.
c – Also Apr. 28, May 6, 17; not Dec. 27.
d – Not May 5.
k – Also Apr. 27, May 5, 16; not Dec. 26.
m – Not Mar. 28, May 16.
¶ – For ⛴ to / from Terschelling and Vlieland. All trains also call at Harlingen (station for the town centre), 3 minutes from Harlingen Ha
🚂 – Station for *Museumspoorlijn S.T.A.R.* Steam trains operate to / from Stadskanaal on ⑦ May - September. www.stadskanaalrail.nl

498a AMSTERDAM - ZANDVOORT AAN ZEE

km		Ⓐ	⚒	⚒	Ⓒ	Ⓐ	Ⓒ	Ⓐ		Ⓒ	Ⓐ							⊠					
0	**Amsterdam** Centraal..... **450** d.	*0527*	*0557***a**	*0627*	*0642***h**	0649	0719**k**	0719	0734	0749**k**	0749	0819	0849	0919	0949	1019	1049	and every 30 minutes until	2219	2249	2319	2349	0
19	Haarlem.......................... **450** d.	0548	0618	0649	0709	0714	0739	0744	0753	0809	0814	0839**r**	0909**r**	0941	1009	1039	1109		2239	2309	2341	0009	0
27	**Zandvoort** aan Zee.............. a.	0558	0628	0659	0719	0724	0749	0754	...	0819	0824	0849**r**	0919**r**	0951	1019	1049	1119		2249	2319	2351	0019	0

				Ⓐ	⚒	⚒																		
Zandvoort aan Zee............. d.	0029	0055	...	0609	0639	0709	0739	0809	and every 30 minutes until	2309	2339	2359	...	...	...	...	...	...	...	...	...	...	...
Haarlem........................ **450** a.	0040	0105	...	0620	0650	0720	0750	0820		2320	2350	0010	...	...	...	...	...	...	...	...	...	...	...
Amsterdam Centraal.... **450** a.	*0103*	...	...	0640	0710	0740	0810	0840		2340	0010	*0032*	...	...	...	...	...	...	...	...	...	...	...

a – Ⓐ only.
h – † only.
k – ⑥ (also Apr. 27, May 5, 16; not Dec. 26).
r – 5 minutes later on Ⓐ.
⊠ – Certain trains run 2 minutes later Haarlem - Zandvoort.

499 OTHER 🚌 and ⛴ LINES

ALKMAAR – LEEUWARDEN 🚌 *Arriva Qliner* route **350**

From Alkmaar rail station:
On Ⓐ at 0521, 0621, 0735, 0835, 0939, 1039, 1139, 1239, 1339, 1435, 1535, 1630, 1730, 1839, 1939, 2039 and 2139.
On ⑥ at 0639 and hourly until 2139. On † at 0839 and hourly until 2239.

Journey time: 1 hr 54 m – 2 hrs 10 m

From Leeuwarden bus station:
On Ⓐ at 0602, 0720, 0820 and hourly until 1820; then 1921, 2022, 2122 and 2222.
On ⑥ at 0720 and hourly until 1820; then 1921, 2022, 2122 and 2222.
On † at 0820 and hourly until 1820; then 1921, 2022, 2122 and 2222.

DEN HELDER – TEXEL ⛴ *TESO*: ✆ +31 (0)222 36 96 00

🚌 route **33**: Den Helder rail station (departs 18 minutes before ships sail) to Havenhoofd.
From Den Helder Havenhoofd: 0630 ⚒, 0730 ⚒ **d**, 0830 and hourly until 2030; 2130 **n**.

Journey time: 20 minutes

From Texel ('t Horntje ferryport): 0600 ⚒, 0700 ⚒ **d**, 0800 and hourly until 2000; 2100 **n**.
🚌 route **33**: Den Helder Havenhoofd to rail station (journey: 7 minutes).

ENKHUIZEN – STAVOREN ⛴ *Rederij V & O* ▲: ✆ +31 (0)228 32 66 67

From Enkuizen Spoorhaven: 0830 **A**, 1230 **B**, 1530 **C**, 1630 **B**.

Journey time: ± 90 minutes

From Stavoren: 1010 **A**, 1410 **B**, 1710 **C**, 1810 **B**.

VLISSINGEN – BRESKENS ⛴ *Westerschelde Ferry* ▲ Journey time: 20 minutes
0603 Ⓐ, 0703 Ⓐ, 0803, 0903 and hourly until 2103; then 2203 Ⓐ.
Additional sailings operate June - August.

BRESKENS ferryport **– BRUGGE** rail station 🚌 *Connexxion* **42** Journey time: 80 minutes
0632 Ⓐ, 0732 ⚒, 0832 ⚒, 0932, 1032 and hourly until 1932; then 2032 ⚒.

BRUGGE rail station **– BRESKENS** ferryport 🚌 *Connexxion* **42** Journey time: 80 minu
0705 ⚒, 0805 ⚒, 0905, 1005 and hourly until 2005; then 2105 ⚒.

BRESKENS – VLISSINGEN ⛴ *Westerschelde Ferry* ▲ Journey time: 20 minutes
0633 Ⓐ, 0733 Ⓐ, 0833, 0933 and hourly until 2133; then 2233 Ⓐ.
Additional sailings operate June - August.

A – Daily Apr. 26 - Oct. 2 (also Apr. 16, 17, 23, 24); ⑥⑦ Oct. 8 – 23 (also Oct. 18 – 21).
B – Daily May 1 - Sept. 30.
C – Apr. 16, 17, 23, 24, 26 – 30, Oct. 1, 2, 8, 9, 15, 16, 18 – 23.
d – Runs daily Mar. 29 - Oct. 1.
n – Not Dec. 31.
▲ – Conveys foot passengers, cycles and mopeds only.

For traffic arrangements on Dutch holiday dates, see page 248

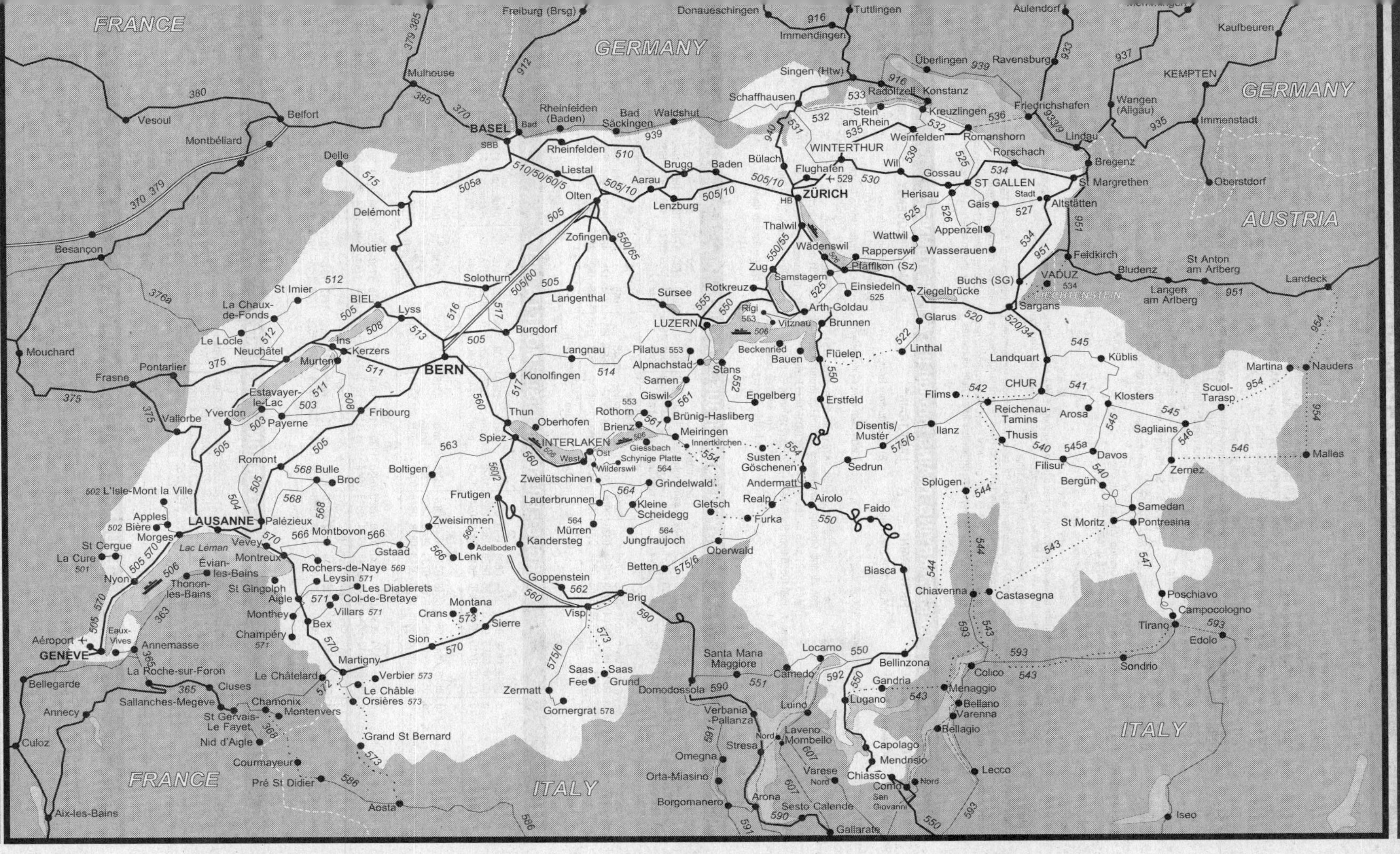

For list of Scenic Rail Routes in Switzerland see contents page

SWITZERLAND

Operators: There are numerous operators of which Schweizerische Bundesbahnen (SBB)/Chemins de fer Fédéraux (CFF)/Ferrovie Federali Svizzere (FFS) is the principal: www.sbl Bus services are provided by PostAuto/Autopostale (PA): www.postauto.ch. Table headings show the operators' initials; abbreviations used in the European Rail Timetable

AB	Appenzeller Bahnen	MOB	Montreux - Oberland Bernois	SMC	Sierre - Montana - Crans
BLM	Bergbahn Lauterbrunnen - Mürren	MThB	Mittelthurgau Bahn	SNCF	Société Nationale des Chemins de Fer Fran
BLS	BLS Lötschbergbahn	MVR	Montreux - Vevey Riviera	SOB	Schweizerische Südostbahn
BOB	Berner Oberland Bahnen	NStCM	Nyon-St Cergue-Morez	THURBO	an alliance of MThB and SBB
BRB	Brienz - Rothorn Bahn	PA	PostAuto / Autopostale / AutoDaPosta	TMR	Transports de Martigny et Régions
CGN	Compagnie Générale de Navigation	PB	Pilatus Bahn	TPC	Transports Publics du Chablais
CP	CarPostal Suisse	RA	RegionAlps	TPF	Transports Publics Fribourgeois
FART	Ferrovie Autolinee Regionali Ticinesi	RB	Rigi Bahnen	URh	Untersee und Rhein
FS	Ferrovie dello Stato	RBS	Regionalverkehr Bern - Solothurn	WAB	Wengernalpbahn
GGB	Gornergrat Bahn	RhB	Rhätische Bahn	ZB	Zentralbahn
JB	Jungfraubahn	RM	Regionalverkehr Mittelland	ZSG	Zürich Schifffahrtsgesellschaft
MBC	Morges - Bière - Cossonay	SBB	Schweizerische Bundesbahnen		
MIB	Meiringen - Innertkirchen Bahn	SBS	Schweizerische Bodensee-Schifffahrtsgesellschaft		
MGB	Matterhorn Gotthard Bahn	SGV	Schifffahrtsgesellschaft des Vierwaldstättersees		

Services: All trains convey first and second class seating except where shown otherwise in footnotes or by a '1' or '2' in the train column. For most local services you must be in posses of a valid ticket before boarding your train.

Train Categories:
- *TGV* French high-speed **Train à Grande Vitesse**;
- *ICE* German high-speed **InterCity Express** train;
- *RJ* Austrian high-speed **Railjet** train;
- *EC* **EuroCity** quality international express train;
- *IC* **InterCity** quality internal express train;
- *ICN* **InterCity Neigezug** high-speed tilting train;
- *IR* **InterRegio** fast inter-regional trains;
- *RE* **RegioExpress** semi-fast regional trains.

Catering: ✕ – Restaurant; (✕) – Bistro; (🍸) – Bar coach; 🍸 – Minibar.
Details of catering is shown in the tables where known, but as a general guide *ICE, RJ, EC* and *ICN* trains convey ✕ or (✕), *IC* services convey ✕ or (🍸), and *TGV* and *IR* tr convey (🍸) or 🍸. Catering facilities may not be open for the whole journey and may vary from that shown.

Timings: Valid until **December 10, 2016** unless otherwise stated in the table.

Supplements: *TGV, ICE* and *RJ* high-speed trains may be used for internal Swiss journeys without supplement. For international journeys *TGV* services are priced as 'global' fare, and trains serving Italy are subject to the payment of a supplement; both types require compulsory reservation for international travel.

Reservations: Seat reservations may be made on all *TGV, ICE, RJ, EC, IC* and *ICN* trains. Reservation is recommended for travel in first class panorama cars. Fares in Switzerland calculated according to distance and many Swiss railways use artificially inflated tariff-kilometres. Distances shown in tables below, however, are actual kilometres.

CAR-CARRYING TRAINS through the ALPINE TUNNELS

TUNNEL	CAR TERMINALS	FIRST TRAIN*	LAST TRAIN*	NORMAL FREQUENCY	INFORMATION ✆
FURKA:	Oberwald - Realp	0535 (0605 from Realp)	2135 (2205 from Realp)	every 60 minutes (every 30 minutes on ①⑤⑥⑦).	027 927 76 66, 027 927 76 7
LÖTSCHBERG:	Kandersteg - Goppenstein	0550	2350 (2320 from Goppenstein)	every 30 minutes, more frequent 0805–2120 on ⑤⑥⑦ and mid-June – mid-Oct.	0900 55 33 33
OBERALP:	Andermatt - Sedrun	Dec. 13 - Mar. 28: 0950, 1450, 1828 (from Andermatt); 0731, 1150, 1725 (from Sedrun) Mar. 29 until Oberalppass opening: 0828, 1728 (from Andermatt); 0731, 1731 (from Sedrun)			027 927 77 07, 027 927 77 4
SIMPLON:	Brig - Iselle (Italy)	0445 (0521 from Iselle)	2336 (0018 from Iselle)	9–10 services per day	0900 300 300
VEREINA:	Selfranga (Klosters) - Sagliains	0520 (0550 from Sagliains)	2050 (2120 from Sagliains) Dec. - Apr. services continue for a further 2 hours	every 30 minutes 0620–1920	081 288 37 37

* – Not necessarily daily.

501 NYON - ST CERGUE - LA CURE

Narrow gauge 2nd class only NStC

km		Ⓐj	⚒	⚒		Ⓐj							⚒		⚒		⚒		Ⓐj					
0	**Nyon** d.	0522	0552	0622	0652	0722	0752	0822	and at the same minutes past each hour until	1452	1522	1552	1622	1652	1722	1752	1822	1852	1922	1952	2052	2152	2322	0C
19	St Cergue d.	0601	0631	0701	0731	0759	0831	0859		1531	1559	1631	1659	1731	1759	1831	1859	1931	1959	2031	2131	2226	2356	01
27	La Cure a.	0614	0644	0714	0744	...	0844	...		1544	...	1644	...	1744	...	1844	...	1944	...	2044	2144	...	...	

	Ⓐj		Ⓐj	⚒	⚒		Ⓐj								⚒		⚒			Ⓐj				
La Cure d.	...	...	0616	0648	0716	0748	...	0848	...	and at the same minutes past each hour until	1548	...	1648	...	1748	...	1848	1948	...	2048	...	...	
St Cergue d.	0533	0604	0633	0704	0733	0804	0833	0904	0933		1604	1633	1704	1733	1804	1833	1904	2004	2033	2104	2233	...	00
Nyon a.	0608	0638	0708	0738	0808	0838	0908	0938	1008		1638	1708	1738	1808	1838	1908	1938	2038	2108	2138	2308	...	00

j – Not Sept. 19. k – ⑥⑦ (not Dec. 26, 27, Jan. 2, 3, Mar. 26).

502 MORGES - BIÈRE and L'ISLE MONT LA VILLE

Narrow gauge 2nd class only MB

km		⚒	⚒		⚒		⚒								X⚡			Ⓐ	Ⓐ	Ⓐ	Ⓐ	Ⓐ	Ⓐ
0	**Morges** d.	0609	0639	0709	0739	0809	0839	0909	1009	and hourly until	2209	2309	...	0009	0116	...	Additional services on Ⓐ	1139	1239	1639	1739	1839	19
12	Apples a.	0628	0658	0728	0758	0828	0858	0928	1028		2228	2328	...	0028	0133	...		1158	1258	1658	1758	1858	19
19	**Bière** a.	0640	0710	0740	0810	0840	0910	0940	1040		2240	2340	...	0040	0144	...		1210	1310	1710	1810	1910	20

	⚒	⚒		⚒		⚒						X			Ⓐ	Ⓐ	Ⓐ	Ⓐ	Ⓐ	Ⓐ	
Bière d.	0518	0548	0618	0648	0718	0748	0818	0918	and hourly until	2318	...	0018	...	Additional services on Ⓐ	1048	1148	1548	1648	1748	1848	...
Apples d.	0530	0600	0630	0700	0730	0800	0830	0930		2330	...	0030	...		1100	1200	1600	1700	1800	1900	...
Morges a.	0548	0618	0648	0718	0748	0818	0848	0948		2348	...	0048	...		1118	1218	1618	1718	1818	1918	...

km			Ⓐ	Ⓒ	Ⓐ	Ⓐ	Ⓒ	Ⓐ		Ⓐ	Ⓒ	Ⓐ											X	X⚡
0	Apples d.	0556	0630	0630	0700	0730	0730	0800	0930	1130	1130	1200	1230	1430	1630	1730	1830	1930	2030	2230	2330	...	0030	0134
11	L'Isle Mont la Ville d.	0610	0643	0644	0713	0743	0744	0813	0944	1143	1144	1213	1244	1444	1644	1744	1844	1944	2044	2244	2344	...	0044	0148

		Ⓐ	Ⓒ	Ⓐ	Ⓐ	Ⓒ	Ⓐ		Ⓐ	Ⓒ	Ⓐ										X		X
L'Isle Mont la Ville d.	0614	0645	0712	0715	0745	0812	0815	1012	1145	1212	1215	1312	1512	1712	1812	1912	2012	2112	2312	...	0012	...	0112
Apples a.	0628	0658	0726	0728	0758	0826	0828	1026	1158	1226	1228	1326	1526	1726	1826	1926	2026	2126	2326	...	0026	...	0126

X – ⑥⑦ (not Dec. 26, 27, Jan. 2, 3, Mar. 26). ⚡ – Supplement payable.

503 YVERDON - FRIBOURG

SB

km		Ⓐ	Ⓐ	Ⓐ								K	L
0	**Yverdon** d.	0504	0604	0633	0704	and hourly until	1904	2003	2103	2203	2303	0048	0208
18	Estavayer-le-Lac d.	0520	0620	0649	0720		1920	2020	2120	2220	2320	0104	0224
28	Payerne d.	0530	0630	0700	0730		1930	2030	2130	2230	2329	0114	0234
50	**Fribourg** a.	0556	0656	0726	0756		1956	2056	2156	2257	...	...	...

	Ⓐ	Ⓐ	Ⓐ						G	⑤
Fribourg d.	...	0535	0601	0704	and hourly until	2004	2104	2204	2304	23
Payerne d.	0530	0602	0630	0730		2030	2130	2230	2330	00
Estavayer-le-Lac d.	0539	0610	0639	0739		2039	2139	2239	2339	00
Yverdon a.	0555	0628	0655	0755		2055	2157	2257	2357	00

G – ①②③④⑦ only. L – ⑥ Dec. 26, Jan. 2. Additional services operate on Ⓐ.
K – ⑥⑦ (also Dec. 25, Jan. 1, Mar. 25, 28, May 5, 16, Aug. 1).

504 LAUSANNE - PALÉZIEUX - PAYERNE

SB

km						▲				Z
0	**Lausanne 505** d.	0524	0624	0724	0824	and hourly until	2124	...	2324	0253
21	Palézieux **505** d.	0540	0640	0740	0840		2140	...	2346	0315
38	Moudon d.	0600	0700	0800	0900		2200	...	0006	...
58	Payerne **511** a.	0621	0722	0819	0919		2219	...	0025	...

						▲		
Payerne **511** d.	0540	0640	0738	...	0840	and hourly until	2240	...
Moudon d.	0559	0659	0759	...	0859		2259	...
Palézieux **505** d.	0618	0718	0818	...	0918		2318	...
Lausanne 505 a.	0636	0736	0836	...	0936		2336	...

Z – ⑥⑦ (also Jan. 1). ▲ – Times vary by ± 2 minutes on some journeys.

GENÈVE - LAUSANNE - BERN / BIEL - ZÜRICH 505

	IR 2155	*IR* 2155	*IR* 2355 10355	*IC* 703	*ICN* 1507	*IR* 2159	*ICN* 507	*IR* 2357	*IR* 2505	*IC* 805	*RE* 3859	*IC* 705	*ICN* 1509	*IR* 2161	*ICN* 509	*IR* 2359	*IR* 2507	*RE* 3861	*IC* 1411	*ICN* 1511	*IC* 707	*IR* 2163	*RE* 3107
	y	z						Ⓐ		R									Ⓐ				
Genève Aéroport ✈ 570 d.	...	...	...	...	...	...	...	...	...	...	...	...	...	...	...	...	...	...	...	...	...	...	...
Genève 570 d.	...	...	...	...	...	...	...	...	...	...	...	...	...	...	...	...	...	...	...	...	0542	...	0549
Nyon 570 d.	...	...	...	...	...	...	...	...	...	...	...	...	...	...	...	...	...	...	...	...	|	...	0605
Morges 570 d.	...	...	...	...	...	...	...	...	...	...	...	...	...	...	...	...	...	...	...	...	|	...	0626
Lausanne 570 a.	...	...	...	...	...	...	...	...	...	...	...	...	...	...	...	...	...	...	...	...	0618	...	0639
Lausanne d.	...	...	...	...	...	...	...	...	0445	...	...	...	...	...	0543	...	0545	...	...	0615	0620	...	0642
Yverdon d.	...	...	...	...	...	...	...	...	|	...	...	...	...	...	0606	...	|	...	...	0639	|	...	|
Neuchâtel d.	...	...	...	...	...	...	...	...	|	...	...	...	...	...	0626	...	|	...	...	0659	|	...	|
Palézieux 504 d.	...	...	...	...	...	...	...	...	0501	...	...	...	...	...	|	...	0601	...	...	|	|	...	0658
Romont 568 d.	...	...	...	...	...	...	...	...	0516	...	...	...	...	...	|	...	0616	...	...	|	|	...	0721r
Fribourg 508 568 d.	...	...	...	...	...	...	...	...	0534	...	...	0604	...	...	|	...	0634	...	...	|	0704	...	0739a
Bern 568 a.	...	...	...	...	...	...	...	...	0556	...	...	0626	...	...	|	...	0656	...	...	|	0726	...	...
Bern 560 d.	0421	0421	0440	0529p	...	...	...	0539	0600	0602	0607	0632	...	0634	|	0639	0700	0707	0711	|	0732	0734	...
Biel / Bienne a.	|	|	|	|	...	...	...	|	|	|	|	|	...	|	0642	|	|	|	|	0715	|	|	...
Biel / Bienne d.	|	|	|	|	0516	...	0543	|	|	|	|	|	0616	|	0644	|	|	|	|	0717	|	|	...
Burgdorf d.	|	|	0454	|	|	...	|	0553	|	|	0621	|	|	|	|	0653	|	0721	|	|	|	|	...
Langenthal d.	|	|	0513	|	|	...	|	0612	|	|	0641	|	|	|	|	0712	|	0741	|	|	|	|	...
Solothurn d.	|	|	|	|	0533	...	0601	|	|	|	|	|	0633	|	0701	|	|	|	|	0734	|	|	...
Olten a.	0446	0500	0525	0555	0557	...	0618	0624	|	0628	0652	|	0657	0700	0718	0724	|	0754	|	0757	|	0800	...
Olten d.	0448	0501	0535	0557	0559	0602	0620	...	|	0631	▬	|	0659	0702	0720	0730	|	▬	|	0759	|	0802	...
Aarau d.	0459	0512	0547	|	|	0615	0632	...	|	|	0653	|	|	0715	0732	|	|	0753	|	|	|	0815	...
Lenzburg d.	0506	0519	0554	|	|	|	|	...	|	|	0700	|	|	|	|	|	|	0800	|	|	|	|	...
Brugg d.	|	|	|	|	|	0630	|	...	|	|	|	|	|	0730	|	|	|	|	|	|	|	0830	...
Baden a.	|	|	|	|	|	0638	|	...	|	|	|	|	|	0738	|	|	|	|	|	|	|	0838	...
Zürich HB 560 a.	|	|	0620	0628	0630	0654	0656	...	|	0702	0722	0728	0730	0754	0756	0805	|	0822	0813	0830	0828	0854	...
Zürich Flughafen ✈ 530/5 a.	0532	0546	...	0642	0649	...	...	...	|	0718	...	0742	0749	...	...	...	|	...	...	0849	0842	...	...
St Gallen 530 a.	...	...	...	0735	0748	...	...	...	|	...	...	0835	0848	...	...	...	|	...	...	0948	0935	...	...
Luzern a.	...	...	...	...	...	...	...	...	0700	...	...	...	...	...	...	...	0800	...	...	...	...	...	...

	IR 2361	*IR* 2509	*ICN* 511	*RE* 3863	*ICN* 1513	*IC* 709	*IR* 2165	*RE* 3109	*IR* 2363	*IR* 2511	*ICN* 513	*RE* 3865	*ICN* 1515	*IC* 711	*IR* 2167	*RE* 3111	*IR* 2365	*IR* 2513	*ICN* 515	*RE* 3867	*ICN* 1517	*IC* 713	*IR* 2169
Genève Aéroport ✈ 570 d.	...	0551	0603	...	...	0633	...	...	...	0703	0706	...	...	0733	...	...	...	0803	0806	...	...	0833	...
Genève 570 d.	...	0600	0612	...	...	0642	...	0649	...	0712	0715	...	...	0742	...	0749	...	0812	0815	...	...	0842	...
Nyon 570 d.	...	0614	0625	...	...	|	...	0705	...	|	|	...	...	|	...	0805	...	|	|	...	...	|	...
Morges 570 d.	...	0630	0642	...	...	|	...	0726	...	|	0742	...	...	|	...	0826	...	|	0842	...	...	|	...
Lausanne 570 a.	...	0642	|	...	...	0718	...	0739	...	0748	|	...	...	0818	...	0839	...	0848	|	...	...	0918	...
Lausanne d.	...	0647	|	...	0715	0720	...	0742	...	0750	|	...	0815	0820	...	0842	...	0850	|	...	0915	0920	...
Yverdon d.	...	|	0707	...	0739	|	...	|	...	|	0807	...	0839	|	...	|	...	|	0907	...	0939	|	...
Neuchâtel d.	...	|	0727	...	0759	|	...	|	...	|	0827	...	0859	|	...	|	...	|	0927	...	0959	|	...
Palézieux 504 d.	...	0703	|	...	|	|	...	0758	...	|	|	...	|	|	...	0858	...	|	|	...	|	|	...
Romont 568 d.	...	|	|	...	|	|	...	0813	...	|	|	...	|	|	...	0913	...	|	|	...	|	|	...
Fribourg 508 568 d.	...	0734	|	...	|	0804	...	...	...	0834	|	...	|	0904	...	...	...	0934	|	...	|	1004	...
Bern 568 a.	...	0756	|	...	|	0826	...	...	...	0856	|	...	|	0926	...	...	...	0956	|	...	|	1026	...
Bern 560 d.	0739	0800	|	0807	|	0832	0834	...	0839	0900	|	0907	|	0932	0934	...	0939	1000	|	1007	|	1032	1034
Biel / Bienne a.	|	|	0743	|	0815	|	|	...	|	|	0843	|	0915	|	|	...	|	|	0943	|	1015	|	|
Biel / Bienne d.	|	|	0746	|	0817	|	|	...	|	|	0846	|	0917	|	|	...	|	|	0946	|	1017	|	|
Burgdorf d.	0753	|	|	0821	|	|	|	...	0853	|	|	0921	|	|	|	...	0953	|	|	1021	|	|	|
Langenthal d.	0812	|	|	0841	|	|	|	...	0912	|	|	0941	|	|	|	...	1012	|	|	1041	|	|	|
Solothurn d.	|	|	0801	|	0834	|	|	...	|	|	0901	|	0934	|	|	...	|	|	1001	|	1034	|	|
Olten a.	0824	|	0818	0854	0857	|	0900	...	0824	|	0918	0954	0957	|	1000	...	1024	|	1018	1054	1057	|	1100
Olten d.	0830	|	0820	▬	0859	|	0902	...	0930	|	0920	▬	0959	|	1002	...	1030	|	1020	▬	1059	|	1102
Aarau d.	|	|	0832	0853	|	|	0915	...	|	|	0932	0953	|	|	1015	...	|	|	1032	1053	|	|	1115
Lenzburg d.	|	|	|	0900	|	|	|	...	|	|	|	1000	|	|	|	...	|	|	|	1100	|	|	|
Brugg d.	|	|	|	|	|	|	0930	...	|	|	|	|	|	|	1030	...	|	|	|	|	|	|	1130
Baden a.	|	|	|	|	|	|	0938	...	|	|	|	|	|	|	1038	...	|	|	|	|	|	|	1138
Zürich HB 560 a.	0905	|	0856	0922	0930	0928	0954	...	1005	|	0956	1022	1030	1028	1054	...	1105	|	1056	1122	1130	1128	1154
Zürich Flughafen ✈ 530/5 a.	...	|	...	...	0949	0942	...	...	...	|	...	...	1049	1042	...	...	...	|	...	...	1149	1142	...
St Gallen 530 a.	...	|	...	...	1048	1035	...	...	...	|	...	...	1148	1135	...	...	...	|	...	...	1248	1235	...
Luzern a.	...	0900	...	...	...	...	...	...	...	1000	...	...	...	...	...	...	...	1100	...	...	...	...	...

	RE 3113	*IR* 2367	*IR* 2515	*ICN* 517	*RE* 3869	*ICN* 1519	*IC* 715	*IR* 2171	*RE* 3115	*IR* 2369	*IR* 2517	*ICN* 519	*RE* 3871	*ICN* 1521	*IC* 717	*IR* 2173		*RE* 3117	*IR* 2371	*IR* 2519	*ICN* 521	*RE* 3873	*ICN* 1523	*IC* 719
Genève Aéroport ✈ 570 d.	...	...	0903	0906	...	...	0933	...	...	...	1003	1006	...	...	1033	...	...	...	...	1103	1106	...	...	1133
Genève 570 d.	0849	...	0912	0915	...	...	0942	...	0949	...	1012	1015	...	...	1042	...	...	1049	...	1112	1115	...	...	1142
Nyon 570 d.	0905	...	|	|	...	...	|	...	1005	...	|	|	...	...	|	...	...	1105	...	|	|	...	...	|
Morges 570 d.	0926	...	|	0942	...	...	|	...	1026	...	|	1042	...	...	|	...	...	1126	...	|	1142	...	...	|
Lausanne 570 a.	0939	...	0948	|	...	...	1018	...	1039	...	1048	|	...	...	1118	...	...	1139	...	1148	|	...	...	1218
Lausanne d.	0942	...	0950	|	...	1015	1020	...	1042	...	1050	|	...	1115	1120	...	...	1142	...	1150	|	...	1215	1220
Yverdon d.	|	...	|	1007	...	1039	|	...	|	...	|	1107	...	1139	|	...	...	|	...	|	1207	...	1239	|
Neuchâtel d.	|	...	|	1027	...	1059	|	...	|	...	|	1127	...	1159	|	...	...	|	...	|	1227	...	1259	|
Palézieux 504 d.	0958	...	|	|	...	|	|	...	1058	...	|	|	...	|	|	...	...	1158	...	|	|	...	|	|
Romont 568 d.	1013	...	|	|	...	|	|	...	1113	...	|	|	...	|	|	...	...	1213	...	|	|	...	|	|
Fribourg 508 568 d.	...	...	1034	|	...	|	1104	...	...	...	1134	|	...	|	1204	...	...	...	...	1234	|	...	|	1304
Bern 568 a.	...	...	1056	|	...	|	1126	...	...	...	1156	|	...	|	1226	...	...	...	...	1256	|	...	|	1326
Bern 560 d.	...	1039	1100	|	1107	|	1132	1134	...	1139	1200	|	1207	|	1232	1234	...	...	1239	1300	|	1307	|	1332
Biel / Bienne a.	...	|	|	1043	|	1115	|	|	...	|	|	1143	|	1215	|	|	...	...	|	|	1243	|	1315	|
Biel / Bienne d.	...	|	|	1046	|	1117	|	|	...	|	|	1146	|	1217	|	|	...	...	|	|	1246	|	1317	|
Burgdorf d.	...	1053	|	|	1121	|	|	|	...	1153	|	|	1221	|	|	|	...	...	1253	|	|	1321	|	|
Langenthal d.	...	1112	|	|	1141	|	|	|	...	1212	|	|	1241	|	|	|	...	...	1312	|	|	1341	|	|
Solothurn d.	...	|	|	1101	|	1134	|	|	...	|	|	1201	|	1234	|	|	...	...	|	|	1301	|	1334	|
Olten a.	...	1124	|	1118	1154	1157	|	1200	...	1224	|	1218	1254	1257	|	1300	...	...	1324	|	1318	1354	1357	|
Olten d.	...	1130	|	1120	▬	1159	|	1202	...	1230	|	1220	▬	1259	|	1302	...	...	1330	|	1320	▬	1359	|
Aarau d.	...	|	|	1132	1153	|	|	1215	...	|	|	1232	1253	|	|	1315	...	...	|	|	1332	1353	|	|
Lenzburg d.	...	|	|	|	1200	|	|	|	...	|	|	|	1300	|	|	|	...	...	|	|	|	1400	|	|
Brugg d.	...	|	|	|	|	|	|	1230	...	|	|	|	|	|	|	1330	...	...	|	|	|	|	|	|
Baden a.	...	|	|	|	|	|	|	1238	...	|	|	|	|	|	|	1338	...	...	|	|	|	|	|	|
Zürich HB 560 a.	...	1205	|	1156	1222	1230	1228	1254	...	1305	|	1256	1322	1330	1328	1354	...	...	1405	|	1356	1422	1430	1428
Zürich Flughafen ✈ 530/5 a.	...	...	|	...	...	1249	1242	...	...	...	|	...	...	1349	1342	...	...	...	...	|	...	...	1449	1442
St Gallen 530 a.	...	...	|	...	...	1348	1335	...	...	...	|	...	...	1448	1435	...	...	...	...	|	...	...	1548	1535
Luzern a.	...	...	1200	...	...	...	...	...	...	...	1300	...	...	...	...	...	...	...	...	1400	...	...	...	...

To Romanshorn (Table **535**).

a – Ⓐ only.
p – Depart 0515 on dates in note **z**.
r – Arrive 0713.

y – Daily (not Feb. 8, 15, 29, Apr. 30, May 1, 2, 9, 23, 30, 31, June 1-3, 6-10, Aug. 8, 15, Sept. 5, 26-30, Oct. 3-7, 15-17, 30, 31, Nov. 14, 28, Dec. 5).
z – Feb. 8, 15, 29, Apr. 30, May 1, 2, 9, 23, 30, 31, June 1-3, 6-10, Aug. 8, 15, Sept. 5, 26-30, Oct. 3-7, 15-17, 30, 31, Nov. 14, 28, Dec. 5.

505 GENÈVE - LAUSANNE - BERN / BIEL - ZÜRICH

	IR 2175	RE 3119	IR 2373	IR 2521	ICN 523	RE 3875	ICN 1525	IC 721	IR 2177	RE 3121	IR 2375	IR 2523	ICN 525	RE 3877	ICN 1527	IC 723	IR 2179	RE 3123	IR 2377	IR 2525	ICN 527	RE 3879	IC 1429
																							Ⓐ
Genève Aéroport ✈ .... 570 d.	...	...	...	1203	1206	...	...	1233	...	...	...	1303	1306	...	...	1333	...	...	...	1403	1406	...	...
Genève .... 570 d.	...	1149	...	1212	1215	...	...	1242	...	1249	...	1312	1315	...	...	1342	...	1349	...	1412	1415	...	...
Nyon .... 570 d.	...	1205	...	|	|	...	...	|	...	1305	...	|	|	...	...	|	...	1405	...	|	|	...	...
Morges .... 570 d.	...	1226	...	|	1242	...	...	|	...	1326	...	|	1342	...	...	|	...	1426	...	|	1442	...	...
Lausanne .... 570 a.	...	1239	...	1248	|	...	...	1318	...	1339	...	1348	|	...	...	1418	...	1439	...	1448	|	...	...
Lausanne .... d.	...	1242	...	1250	|	...	1315	1320	...	1342	...	1350	|	...	1415	1420	...	1442	...	1450	|	...	...
Yverdon .... d.	...	|	...	|	1307	...	1339	|	...	|	...	|	1407	...	1439	|	...	|	...	|	1507	...	...
Neuchâtel .... d.	...	|	...	|	1327	...	1359	|	...	|	...	|	1427	...	1459	|	...	|	...	|	1527	...	...
Palézieux .... 504 d.	...	1258	...	|	|	...	|	|	...	1358	...	|	|	...	|	|	...	1458	...	|	|	...	...
Romont .... 568 d.	...	1313	...	|	|	...	|	|	...	1413	...	|	|	...	|	|	...	1513	...	|	|	...	...
Fribourg .... 508 568 d.	...	...	...	1334	|	...	|	1404	...	...	...	1434	|	...	|	1504	...	...	...	1534	|	...	...
Bern .... 568 a.	...	...	...	1356	|	...	|	1426	...	...	...	1456	|	...	|	1526	...	...	...	1556	|	...	...
Bern .... 560 d.	1334	...	1339	1400	|	1407	|	1432	1434	...	1439	1500	|	1507	|	1532	1534	...	1539	1600	|	1607	1611
Biel / Bienne .... a.	|	...	|	|	1343	|	1415	|	|	...	|	|	1443	|	1515	|	|	...	|	|	1543	|	|
Biel / Bienne .... d.	|	...	|	|	1346	|	1417	|	|	...	|	|	1446	|	1517	|	|	...	|	|	1546	|	|
Burgdorf .... d.	|	...	1353	|	|	1421	|	|	|	...	1453	|	|	1521	|	|	|	...	1553	|	|	1621	|
Langenthal .... d.	|	...	1412	|	|	1441	|	|	|	...	1512	|	|	1541	|	|	|	...	1612	|	|	1641	|
Solothurn .... d.	|	...	|	|	1401	|	1434	|	|	...	|	|	1501	|	1534	|	|	...	|	|	1601	|	|
Olten .... a.	1400	...	1424	|	1418	1454	1457	|	1500	...	1524	|	1518	1554	1557	|	1600	...	1624	|	1618	1654	|
Olten .... d.	1402	...	1430	|	1420	▬	1459	|	1502	...	1530	|	1520	▬	1559	|	1602	...	1630	|	1620	▬	|
Aarau .... d.	1415	...	|	|	1432	1453	|	|	1515	...	|	|	1532	1553	|	|	1615	...	|	|	1632	1653	|
Lenzburg .... d.	|	...	|	|	|	1500	|	|	|	...	|	|	|	1600	|	|	|	...	|	|	|	1700	|
Brugg .... d.	1430	...	|	|	|	|	|	|	1530	...	|	|	|	|	|	|	1630	...	|	|	|	|	|
Baden .... a.	1438	...	|	|	|	|	|	|	1538	...	|	|	|	|	|	|	1638	...	|	|	|	|	|
Zürich HB .... 560 a.	1454	...	1505	|	1456	1522	1530	1528	1554	...	1605	|	1556	1622	1630	1628	1654	...	1705	|	1656	1722	1713
Zürich Flughafen ✈ **530/5** . a.	...	...	...	|	...	...	1549	1542	...	...	...	|	...	...	1649	1642	...	...	...	|	...	...	...
St Gallen **530** .... a.	...	...	...	|	...	...	1648	1635	...	...	...	|	...	...	1748	1735	...	...	...	|	...	...	...
Luzern .... a.	...	...	...	1500	...	...	...	...	...	...	...	1600	...	...	...	...	...	...	...	1700	...	...	...

	IC 725	IR 2181	RE 3125	IR 2379	IR 2527	ICN 529	RE 3881	IC 1431	ICN 1531	IC 727	IR 2183	RE 3127	IR 2381	IR 2529	ICN 531	RE 3883	ICN 1533	IC 729	IR 2185	RE 3129	IR 2383	IR 2531	ICN 533
								Ⓐ															
Genève Aéroport ✈ .... 570 d.	1433	...	...	...	1503	1506	...	...	...	1533	...	...	...	1603	1606	...	...	1633	...	...	...	1703	1706
Genève .... 570 d.	1442	...	1449	...	1512	1515	...	...	...	1542	...	1549	...	1612	1615	...	...	1642	...	1649	...	1712	1715
Nyon .... 570 d.	|	...	1505	...	|	|	...	...	...	|	...	1605	...	|	|	...	...	|	...	1705	...	|	|
Morges .... 570 d.	|	...	1526	...	|	1542	...	...	...	|	...	1626	...	|	1642	...	...	|	...	1726	...	|	1742
Lausanne .... 570 a.	1518	...	1539	...	1548	|	...	...	...	1618	...	1639	...	1648	|	...	...	1718	...	1739	...	1748	|
Lausanne .... d.	1520	...	1542	...	1550	|	...	...	1615	1620	...	1642	...	1650	|	...	1715	1720	...	1742	...	1750	|
Yverdon .... d.	|	...	|	...	|	1607	...	...	1639	|	...	|	...	|	1707	...	1739	|	...	|	...	|	1807
Neuchâtel .... d.	|	...	|	...	|	1627	...	...	1659	|	...	|	...	|	1727	...	1759	|	...	|	...	|	1827
Palézieux .... 504 d.	|	...	1558	...	|	|	...	...	|	|	...	1658	...	|	|	...	|	|	...	1758	...	|	|
Romont .... 568 d.	|	...	1613	...	|	|	...	...	|	|	...	1713	...	|	|	...	|	|	...	1813	...	|	|
Fribourg .... 508 568 d.	1604	...	...	...	1634	|	...	...	|	1704	...	...	...	1734	|	...	|	1804	...	...	...	1834	|
Bern .... 568 a.	1626	...	...	...	1656	|	...	...	|	1726	...	...	...	1756	|	...	|	1826	...	...	...	1856	|
Bern .... 560 d.	1632	1634	...	1639	1700	|	1707	1711	|	1732	1734	...	1739	1800	|	1807	|	1832	1834	...	1839	1900	|
Biel / Bienne .... a.	|	|	...	|	|	1643	|	|	1715	|	|	...	|	|	1743	|	1815	|	|	...	|	|	1843
Biel / Bienne .... d.	|	|	...	|	|	1646	|	|	1717	|	|	...	|	|	1746	|	1817	|	|	...	|	|	1846
Burgdorf .... d.	|	|	...	1653	|	|	1721	|	|	|	|	...	1753	|	|	1821	|	|	|	...	1853	|	|
Langenthal .... d.	|	|	...	1712	|	|	1741	|	|	|	|	...	1812	|	|	1841	|	|	|	...	1912	|	|
Solothurn .... d.	|	|	...	|	|	1701	|	|	1734	|	|	...	|	|	1801	|	1834	|	|	...	|	|	1901
Olten .... a.	|	1700	...	1724	|	1718	1754	|	1757	|	1800	...	1824	|	1818	1854	1857	|	1900	...	1924	|	1918
Olten .... d.	|	1702	...	1730	|	1720	▬	|	1759	|	1802	...	1830	|	1820	▬	1859	|	1902	...	1930	|	1920
Aarau .... d.	|	1715	...	|	|	1732	1753	|	|	|	1815	...	|	|	1832	1853	|	|	1915	...	|	|	1932
Lenzburg .... d.	|	|	...	|	|	|	1800	|	|	|	|	...	|	|	|	1900	|	|	|	...	|	|	|
Brugg .... d.	|	1730	...	|	|	|	|	|	|	|	1830	...	|	|	|	|	|	|	1930	...	|	|	|
Baden .... a.	|	1738	...	|	|	|	|	|	|	|	1838	...	|	|	|	|	|	|	1938	...	|	|	|
Zürich HB .... 560 a.	1728	1754	...	1805	|	1756	1822	1810	1830	1828	1854	...	1905	|	1856	1922	1930	1928	1954	...	2005	|	1956
Zürich Flughafen ✈ **530/5** . a.	1742	...	...	...	|	...	...	...	1849	1842	...	...	...	|	...	...	1949	1942	...	...	...	|	...
St Gallen **530** .... a.	1835	...	...	...	|	...	...	...	1948	1935	...	...	...	|	...	...	2048	2035	...	...	...	|	...
Luzern .... a.	...	...	...	...	1800	...	...	...	...	...	...	...	...	1900	...	...	...	...	...	...	...	2000	...

	ICN 1535	IC 731	IR 2187	RE 3131	IR 2385	IR 2533	ICN 535	RE 3887	ICN 1537	IC 733	IR 2189	IR 2387	RE 3133	IR 2535	ICN 537	RE 3889	ICN 1539	IC 735	IR 2191	IR 2389	RE 3135	IR 2537	ICN 539
																	‡	‡					‡
Genève Aéroport ✈ .... 570 d.	...	1733	...	...	...	1803	1806	...	...	1833	...	...	...	1903	1906	...	...	1933	...	...	...	2003	2006
Genève .... 570 d.	...	1742	...	1749	...	1812	1815	...	...	1842	...	...	1849	1912	1915	...	...	1942	...	...	1949	2012	2015
Nyon .... 570 d.	...	|	...	1805	...	|	|	...	...	|	...	...	1905	|	|	...	...	|	...	...	2005	|	|
Morges .... 570 d.	...	|	...	1826	...	|	1842	...	...	|	...	...	1926	|	1942	...	...	|	...	...	2026	|	2042
Lausanne .... 570 a.	...	1818	...	1839	...	1848	|	...	...	1918	...	...	1939	1948	|	...	...	2018	...	...	2039	2048	|
Lausanne .... d.	1815	1820	...	1842	...	1850	|	...	1915	1920	...	...	1942	1950	|	...	2015	2020	...	...	2042	2050	|
Yverdon .... d.	1839	|	...	|	...	|	1907	...	1939	|	...	...	|	|	2007	...	2039	|	...	...	|	|	2107
Neuchâtel .... d.	1859	|	...	|	...	|	1927	...	1959	|	...	...	|	|	2027	...	2059	|	...	...	|	|	2127
Palézieux .... 504 d.	|	|	...	1858	...	|	|	...	|	|	...	...	1958	|	|	...	|	|	...	...	2058	|	|
Romont .... 568 d.	|	|	...	1913	...	|	|	...	|	|	...	...	2013	|	|	...	|	|	...	...	2113	|	|
Fribourg .... 508 568 d.	|	1904	...	...	...	1934	|	...	|	2004	...	...	...	2034	|	...	|	2104	...	...	...	2134	|
Bern .... 568 a.	|	1926	...	...	...	1956	|	...	|	2026	...	...	...	2056	|	...	|	2126	...	...	...	2156	|
Bern .... 560 d.	|	1932	1934	...	1939	2000	|	2007	|	2032	2034	2039	...	2100	|	2107	|	2132	2134	2138	...	2200	|
Biel / Bienne .... a.	1915	|	|	...	|	|	1943	|	2015	|	|	|	...	|	2043	|	2115	|	|	|	...	|	2143
Biel / Bienne .... d.	1917	|	|	...	|	|	1946	|	2017	|	|	|	...	|	2046	|	2117	|	|	|	...	|	2146
Burgdorf .... d.	|	|	|	...	1953	|	|	2021	|	|	|	2053	...	|	|	2121	|	|	|	2154	...	|	|
Langenthal .... d.	|	|	|	...	2012	|	|	2041	|	|	|	2112	...	|	|	2141	|	|	|	2212	...	|	|
Solothurn .... d.	1934	|	|	...	|	|	2001	|	2034	|	|	|	...	|	2101	|	2134	|	|	|	...	|	2201
Olten .... a.	1957	|	2000	...	2024	|	2018	2054	2057	|	2100	2124	...	|	2118	2154	2157	|	2200	2225	...	|	2218
Olten .... d.	1959	|	2002	...	2030	|	2020	▬	2059	|	2102	...	...	|	2120	▬	2159	|	2202	...	...	|	2220
Aarau .... d.	|	|	2015	...	|	|	2032	2053	|	|	2115	...	...	|	2132	2153	|	|	2215	...	...	|	2232
Lenzburg .... d.	|	|	|	...	|	|	|	2100	|	|	|	...	...	|	|	2200	|	|	|	...	...	|	|
Brugg .... d.	|	|	2030	...	|	|	|	|	|	|	2130	...	...	|	|	|	|	|	2230	...	...	|	|
Baden .... a.	|	|	2038	...	|	|	|	|	|	|	2138	...	...	|	|	|	|	|	2238	...	...	|	|
Zürich HB .... 560 a.	2030	2028	2054	...	2105	|	2056	2122	2130	2128	2154	...	...	|	2156	2222j	2230t	2228t	2254	...	...	|	2256v
Zürich Flughafen ✈ **530/5** . a.	2049	...	...	...	...	|	...	...	2149	...	...	...	...	|	...	...	2249	...	...	...	...	|	...
St Gallen **530** .... a.	2148	...	...	...	...	|	...	...	2248	...	...	...	...	|	...	...	2348	...	...	...	...	|	...
Luzern .... a.	...	...	...	...	...	2100	...	...	...	...	...	...	...	2200	...	...	...	...	...	...	...	2300	...

R – To Romanshorn (Table **535**).

j – 4 minutes later Jan. 4 - Mar. 10.
t – 8 minutes later Jan. 4 - Mar. 10.
v – 10 minutes later Jan. 4 - Mar. 10.

‡ – Train number variations Jan. 4 - Mar. 10: 539 runs as 10539; 735 runs as 10735; 1539 runs as 10549.

GENÈVE - LAUSANNE - BERN / BIEL - ZÜRICH 505

	RE 3891	ICN 1541	IC 737	IR 2193	RE 3137	IR 2539	IC 839	ICN 541	RE 3893	ICN 1543	IC 739	RE 3139	IR 2541	IC 841	ICN 543	RE 3241	ICN 1545	IR 2543	IC 843	ICN 1547	RE 3143	RE 3147	IR 2503
			‡								‡						D		g				h
ve Aéroport ✈ ... 570 d.	...	...	2033	...	...	...	...	2102	...	...	2133	...	...	...	...	...	...	...	...	...	2340	0022	...
ve ... 570 d.	...	...	2042	...	2049	2100	...	2112	...	...	2142	2149	...	...	...	2219	...	...	...	...	2349	0031	...
... 570 d.	...	...	|	...	2105	2114	...	2125	...	...	|	2205	...	...	...	2235	...	...	...	...	0005	0047	...
es ... 570 d.	...	...	|	...	2126	2130	...	2142	...	...	|	2226	...	...	...	2256	...	...	...	...	0026	0108	...
anne ... 570 a.	...	...	2118	...	2139	2142	...	|	...	...	2218	2239	...	...	...	2309	...	...	...	...	0039	0121	...
anne ... d.	...	2115	2120	...	...	2145	...	|	...	2215	2220	...	2245	...	...	—	2315	2347	...	0015	...	...	0130
erdon ... d.	...	2139	|	...	...	|	...	2207	...	2239	|	...	|	...	...	...	2339	|	...	0039	...	...	|
uchâtel ... d.	...	2159	|	...	...	|	...	2227	...	2259	|	...	|	...	...	...	2359	|	...	0059	...	...	|
ieux ... 504 d.	...	|	|	...	...	2201	...	|	...	|	|	...	2301	...	...	...	|	0003	...	|	...	...	0146
ont ... 568 d.	...	|	|	...	...	2216	...	|	...	|	|	...	2316	...	...	...	|	0018	...	|	...	...	0201
urg ... 508 568 d.	...	|	2204	...	...	2234	...	|	...	|	2304	...	2334	...	...	RE	|	0036	...	|	...	...	0218
... 568 a.	...	|	2226	...	...	2256	...	|	...	|	2326	...	2356	...	...	**3895**	|	0101	...	|	...	...	...
... 560 d.	2207	|	2232	...	...	2300	2302	|	2307	|	2332	...	...	0002	...	0007	|	...	0104	|	...	...	...
el / Bienne ... a.	|	2215	|	...	...	|	|	2243	|	2315	|	...	...	|	...	|	0015	...	|	0115	...	...	...
el / Bienne ... d.	|	2217	|	...	...	|	|	2246	|	2317	|	...	...	|	2346	|	...	...	|	...	...	...	...
dorf ... d.	2223	|	|	...	...	|	|	|	2323	|	|	...	...	|	|	0023	...	...	|	...	...	...	...
enthal ... d.	2242	|	|	...	...	|	|	|	2342	|	|	...	...	|	|	0042	...	...	|	...	...	...	...
othurn ... d.	|	2234	|	...	...	|	|	2305	|	2334	|	...	...	|	0005	|	...	...	|	...	...	...	...
... a.	2255	2257	2258	...	...	|	2328	2330	2355	2357	2358	...	...	0028	0030	0055	...	...	0130	...	...	...	...
... d.	—	...	2300	2302	...	|	2330	2335	—	...	0000	...	...	0033	0035	...	...	...	0133	...	...	...	...
... d.	2253	...	|	2315	...	|	|	2347	2353	...	0012	...	...	|	0047	...	...	...	0145	...	...	...	...
nzburg ... d.	2300	...	|	|	...	|	|	|	0000	...	|	...	...	|	0053	...	...	...	|	...	...	...	...
... d.	|	...	|	2330	...	|	|	|	|	...	|	...	...	|	|	...	...	...	|	...	...	...	...
n ... a.	|	...	|	2338	...	|	|	|	|	...	|	...	...	|	|	...	...	...	|	...	...	...	...
ch HB ... 560 a.	2322j	...	2331v	2354	...	|	0001	0010	0022n	...	0035x	...	...	0104	0112	...	...	...	0207	...	...	...	...
rich Flughafen ✈ 530/5 ... a.	...	...	...	...	...	|	...	...	...	...	...	...	...	...	...	...	...	...	...	...	...	...	...
Gallen 530 ... a.	...	...	...	...	...	|	...	...	...	...	...	...	...	...	...	...	...	...	...	...	...	...	...
zern ... a.	...	...	...	...	...	2400	...	...	...	...	...	...	...	...	...	...	...	...	...	...	...	...	...

	RE 3102	IR 2504	ICN 504	RE 3104	IC 702	ICN 1504	RE 3856	IR 2506	ICN 1606	RE 3106	IR 2354	IC 704	ICN 1506	RE 3858	IR 2508	IR 2356	ICN 508	IR 2158	RE 3108	ICN 1508	IC 706	RE 4808	IC 1408
							Ⓐ		D														Ⓐ
Luzern ... d.	...	...	...	...	...	...	...	...	...	...	...	...	...	...	0600	...	...	...	...	...	...	...	...
St Gallen 530 ... d.	...	...	...	...	...	...	...	...	...	...	...	...	...	...	|	...	...	...	...	...	0509	...	...
Zürich Flughafen ✈ 530/5 . d.	...	...	...	...	...	...	...	...	...	...	...	...	...	...	|	...	...	...	...	...	0613	...	...
Zürich HB ... 560 d.	...	...	...	...	...	...	...	...	...	...	...	0519	...	...	|	0555	0603	0606	...	0630	0632	0638	0647
Baden ... d.	...	...	...	...	...	...	...	...	...	...	...	|	...	...	|	|	|	0622	...	|	|	|	|
Brugg ... d.	...	...	...	...	...	...	...	...	...	...	...	|	...	...	|	|	|	0632	...	|	|	|	|
Lenzburg ... d.	...	...	...	...	...	...	...	...	...	...	...	0540	...	...	|	|	|	|	...	|	|	0658	|
Aarau ... d.	...	...	...	...	...	...	...	...	...	...	...	0548	...	...	|	|	0629	0646	...	|	|	0705	|
Olten ... a.	...	...	...	...	...	...	...	...	...	...	...	0557	...	...	|	0626	0638	0657	...	0700	|	...	|
Olten ... d.	...	...	...	...	...	...	0506	...	...	...	0536	0602	0602	0606	|	0636	0640	0659	...	0702	|	...	|
Solothurn ... d.	...	...	...	...	...	...	|	...	...	...	|	|	0626	|	|	|	0658	|	...	0726	|	...	|
Langenthal ... d.	...	...	...	...	...	...	0518	...	...	...	0549	|	|	0618	|	0648	|	|	...	|	|	...	|
Burgdorf ... d.	...	...	...	...	...	...	0538	...	...	...	0607	|	|	0638	|	0707	|	|	...	|	|	...	|
Biel / Bienne ... a.	...	...	...	...	...	...	|	...	...	...	|	|	0643	|	|	|	0713	|	...	0743	|	...	|
Biel / Bienne ... d.	...	...	0516	...	...	0545	|	...	0616	...	|	|	0645	|	|	|	0716	|	...	0745	|	...	|
Bern ... 560 a.	...	...	|	...	...	|	0553	...	|	...	0621	0628	|	0653	0700	0721	|	0726	...	|	0728	...	0750
Bern ... 568 d.	...	0459	|	...	0534	|	...	0604	|	...	...	0634	|	...	0704	...	|	...	...	|	0734	...	...
Fribourg ... 508 568 d.	...	0521	|	...	0556	|	...	0626	|	...	...	0656	|	...	0726	...	|	...	...	|	0756	...	...
Romont ... 568 d.	...	0539	|	...	|	|	...	|	|	0647	...	|	|	...	|	...	|	...	0747	|	|	...	...
Palézieux ... 504 d.	...	0554	|	...	|	|	...	|	|	0702	...	|	|	...	|	...	|	...	0802	|	|	...	...
Neuchâtel ... d.	...	|	0534	...	|	0603	...	|	0634	|	...	|	0703	...	|	...	0734	...	|	0803	|	...	...
Yverdon ... d.	...	|	0553	...	|	0622	...	|	0653	|	...	|	0722	...	|	...	0753	...	|	0822	|	...	...
Lausanne ... a.	...	0610	|	...	0640	0645	...	0710	|	0717	...	0740	0745	...	0810	...	|	...	0817	0845	0840	...	...
Lausanne ... 570 d.	0521	0612	|	0621	0642	...	...	0712	|	0721	...	0742	...	...	0812	...	|	...	0821	...	0842	...	...
Morges ... 570 d.	0534	|	0618	0634	|	...	...	|	0718	0734	...	|	...	...	|	...	0818	...	0834	...	|	...	...
Nyon ... 570 d.	0555	|	|	0655	|	...	...	|	|	0755	...	|	...	...	|	...	|	...	0855	...	|	...	...
Genève ... 570 a.	0611	0648	0645	0711	0718	...	...	0748	0745	0811	...	0818	...	...	0848	...	0845	...	0911	...	0918	...	...
Genève Aéroport ✈ ... 570 a.	0620	0657	0654	...	0727	...	...	0757	0754	...	...	0827	...	...	0857	...	0854	...	...	...	0927	...	...

	RE 3860	IR 2510	IR 2358	ICN 510	IR 2160	RE 3110	ICN 1510	IC 708	RE 4810	IC 1410	RE 3862	IR 2512	IR 2360	ICN 512	IR 2162	RE 3112	ICN 1512	IC 710	RE 4812	IR 2514	IR 2362	ICN 514	IR 2164
										Ⓐ													
Luzern ... d.	...	0700	...	...	...	...	...	...	...	...	...	0800	...	...	...	...	...	...	...	0900	...	...	...
St Gallen 530 ... d.	...	|	...	...	...	...	0612	0625	...	...	...	|	...	...	...	...	0712	0725	...	|	...	...	...
Zürich Flughafen ✈ 530/5 . d.	...	|	...	...	...	...	0713	0718	...	...	...	|	...	...	...	...	0813	0818	...	|	...	...	...
Zürich HB ... 560 d.	...	|	0655	0703	0706	...	0730	0732	0738	0749	...	|	0755	0803	0806	...	0830	0832	0838	|	0855	0903	0906
Baden ... d.	...	|	|	|	0722	...	|	|	|	|	...	|	|	|	0822	...	|	|	|	|	|	|	0922
Brugg ... d.	...	|	|	|	0732	...	|	|	|	|	...	|	|	|	0832	...	|	|	|	|	|	|	0932
Lenzburg ... d.	...	|	|	|	|	...	|	|	0758	|	...	|	|	|	|	...	|	|	0858	|	|	|	|
Aarau ... d.	...	|	|	0729	0746	...	|	|	0805	|	...	|	|	0829	0846	...	|	|	0905	|	|	0929	0946
Olten ... a.	...	|	0726	0738	0757	...	0800	|	...	|	...	|	0826	0838	0857	...	0900	|	—	|	0926	0938	0957
Olten ... d.	0706	|	0736	0740	0759	...	0802	|	...	|	0806	|	0836	0840	0859	...	0902	|	0906	|	0936	0940	0959
Solothurn ... d.	|	|	|	0758	|	...	0826	|	...	|	|	|	|	0858	|	...	0926	|	|	|	|	0958	|
Langenthal ... d.	0718	|	0748	|	|	...	|	|	...	|	0818	|	0848	|	|	...	|	|	0918	|	0948	|	|
Burgdorf ... d.	0738	|	0807	|	|	...	|	|	...	|	0838	|	0907	|	|	...	|	|	0938	|	1007	|	|
Biel / Bienne ... a.	|	|	|	0813	|	...	0843	|	...	|	|	|	|	0913	|	...	0943	|	|	|	|	1013	|
Biel / Bienne ... d.	|	|	|	0816	|	...	0845	|	...	|	|	|	|	0916	|	...	0945	|	|	|	|	1016	|
Bern ... 560 a.	0753	0800	0821	|	0826	...	|	0828	...	0850	0853	0900	0921	|	0926	...	|	0928	0953	1000	1021	|	1026
Bern ... 568 d.	...	0804	...	|	...	...	|	0834	...	...	...	0904	...	|	...	...	|	0934	...	1004	...	|	...
Fribourg ... 508 568 d.	...	0826	...	|	...	...	|	0856	...	...	...	0926	...	|	...	...	|	0956	...	1026	...	|	...
Romont ... 568 d.	...	|	...	|	...	0847	|	|	...	...	...	|	...	|	...	0947	|	|	...	|	...	|	...
Palézieux ... 504 d.	...	|	...	|	...	0902	|	|	...	...	...	|	...	|	...	1002	|	|	...	|	...	|	...
Neuchâtel ... d.	...	|	...	0834	...	|	0903	|	...	...	...	|	...	0934	...	|	1003	|	...	|	...	1034	...
Yverdon ... d.	...	|	...	0853	...	|	0922	|	...	...	...	|	...	0953	...	|	1022	|	...	|	...	1053	...
Lausanne ... a.	...	0910	...	|	...	0917	0945	0940	...	...	...	1010	...	|	...	1017	1045	1040	...	1110	...	|	...
Lausanne ... 570 d.	...	0912	...	|	...	0921	...	0942	...	...	...	1012	...	|	...	1021	...	1042	...	1112	...	|	...
Morges ... 570 d.	...	|	...	0918	...	0934	...	|	...	...	...	|	...	1018	...	1034	...	|	...	|	...	1118	...
Nyon ... 570 d.	...	|	...	|	...	0955	...	|	...	...	...	|	...	|	...	1055	...	|	...	|	...	|	...
Genève ... 570 a.	...	0948	...	0945	...	1011	...	1018	...	...	...	1048	...	1045	...	1111	...	1118	...	1148	...	1145	...
Genève Aéroport ✈ ... 570 a.	...	0957	...	0954	...	...	...	1027	...	...	...	1057	...	1054	...	...	...	1127	...	1157	...	1154	...

From / to Delémont (Table **505a**).

g – ⑥⑦ (also Jan. 1; not Mar. 26).
h – ⑥⑦ (also Jan. 1, Aug. 1; not Dec. 26, Mar. 26).
j – 4 minutes later Jan. 4 - Mar. 10.
n – 4 minutes later Jan. 5 - Mar. 11.
v – 10 minutes later Jan. 4 - Mar. 10.
x – 8 minutes later Jan. 5 - Mar. 4.

‡ – Train number variations Jan. 4 - Mar. 10: 737 runs as 10737; 739 runs as 10739.

505 ZÜRICH - BIEL / BERN - LAUSANNE - GENÈVE

	RE 3114	*ICN* 1514	*IC* 712	*RE* 4814	*IR* 2516	*IR* 2364	*ICN* 516	*IR* 2166	*RE* 3116	*ICN* 1516	*IC* 714	*RE* 4816	*IR* 2518	*IR* 2366	*ICN* 518	*IR* 2168	*RE* 3118	*ICN* 1518	*IC* 716	*RE* 4818	*IR* 2520	*IR* 2368	*ICN* 520
Luzern d.	...	...	...	...	1000	...	...	...	...	...	...	...	1100	...	...	...	...	...	...	...	1200	...	...
St Gallen **530** d.	...	0812	0825	...	|	...	...	...	...	0912	0925	...	|	...	...	...	...	1012	1025	...	|	...	...
Zürich Flughafen + **530/5** d.	...	0913	0918	...	|	...	...	...	...	1013	1018	...	|	...	...	...	...	1113	1118	...	|	...	...
Zürich HB **560** d.	...	0930	0932	0938	|	0955	1003	1006	...	1030	1032	1038	|	1055	1103	1106	...	1130	1132	1138	|	1155	1203
Baden d.	...	|	|	|	|	|	|	1022	...	|	|	|	|	|	|	1122	...	|	|	|	|	|	|
Brugg d.	...	|	|	|	|	|	|	1032	...	|	|	|	|	|	|	1132	...	|	|	|	|	|	|
Lenzburg d.	...	|	|	0958	|	|	|	|	...	|	|	1058	|	|	|	|	...	|	|	1158	|	|	|
Aarau d.	...	|	|	1005	|	|	1029	1046	...	|	|	1105	|	|	1129	1146	...	|	|	1205	|	|	1229
Olten a.	...	1000	|	▬	|	1026	1038	1057	...	1100	|	▬	|	1126	1138	1157	...	1200	|	▬	|	1226	1238
Olten d.	...	1002	|	1006	|	1036	1040	1059	...	1102	|	1106	|	1136	1140	1159	...	1202	|	1206	|	1236	1240
Solothurn d.	...	1026	|	|	|	|	1058	|	...	1126	|	|	|	|	1158	|	...	1226	|	|	|	|	1258
Langenthal d.	...	|	|	1018	|	1048	|	|	...	|	|	1118	|	1148	|	|	...	|	|	1218	|	1248	|
Burgdorf d.	...	|	|	1038	|	1107	|	|	...	|	|	1138	|	1207	|	|	...	|	|	1238	|	1307	|
Biel / Bienne a.	...	1043	|	|	|	|	1113	|	...	1143	|	|	|	|	1213	|	...	1243	|	|	|	|	1313
Biel / Bienne d.	...	1045	|	|	|	|	1116	|	...	1145	|	|	|	|	1216	|	...	1245	|	|	|	|	1316
Bern **560** a.	...	|	1028	1053	1100	1121	|	1126	...	|	1128	1153	1200	1221	|	1226	...	|	1228	1253	1300	1321	|
Bern **568** d.	...	|	1034	...	1104	...	|	...	...	|	1134	...	1204	...	|	...	...	|	1234	...	1304	...	|
Fribourg **508 568** d.	...	|	1056	...	1126	...	|	...	...	|	1156	...	1226	...	|	...	...	|	1256	...	1326	...	|
Romont **568** d.	1047	|	|	...	|	...	|	...	1147	|	|	...	|	...	|	...	1247	|	|	...	|	...	|
Palézieux **504** d.	1102	|	|	...	|	...	|	...	1202	|	|	...	|	...	|	...	1302	|	|	...	|	...	|
Neuchâtel d.	|	1103	|	...	|	...	1134	...	|	1203	|	...	|	...	1234	...	|	1303	|	...	|	...	1334
Yverdon d.	|	1122	|	...	|	...	1153	...	|	1222	|	...	|	...	1253	...	|	1322	|	...	|	...	1353
Lausanne a.	1117	1145	1140	...	1210	...	|	...	1217	1245	1240	...	1310	...	|	...	1317	1345	1340	...	1410	...	|
Lausanne **570** d.	1121	...	1142	...	1212	...	|	...	1221	...	1242	...	1312	...	|	...	1321	...	1342	...	1412	...	|
Morges **570** d.	1134	...	|	...	|	...	1218	...	1234	...	|	...	|	...	1318	...	1334	...	|	...	|	...	1418
Nyon **570** d.	1155	...	|	...	|	...	|	...	1255	...	|	...	|	...	|	...	1355	...	|	...	|	...	|
Genève **570** a.	1211	...	1218	...	1248	...	1245	...	1311	...	1318	...	1348	...	1345	...	1411	...	1418	...	1448	...	1445
Genève Aéroport + **570** a.	...	...	1227	...	1257	...	1254	...	...	...	1327	...	1357	...	1354	...	...	...	1427	...	1457	...	1454

	RE 3120	*ICN* 1520	*IC* 718	*RE* 4820	*IR* 2522		*IR* 2370	*ICN* 522	*IR* 2172	*RE* 3122	*ICN* 1522	*IC* 720	*RE* 4822	*IR* 2524	*IR* 2372	*ICN* 524	*IR* 2174	*RE* 3124	*ICN* 1524	*IC* 722	*RE* 4824	*IR* 2526	*IR* 2374
Luzern d.	...	...	...	...	1300	...	...	...	...	...	...	...	...	1400	...	...	...	...	...	...	...	1500	...
St Gallen **530** d.	...	1112	1125	...	|	...	...	...	...	...	1212	1225	...	|	...	...	...	...	1312	1325	...	|	...
Zürich Flughafen + **530/5** d.	...	1213	1218	...	|	...	...	...	...	...	1313	1318	...	|	...	...	...	...	1413	1418	...	|	...
Zürich HB **560** d.	...	1230	1232	1238	|	...	1255	1303	1306	...	1330	1332	1338	|	1355	1403	1406	...	1430	1432	1438	|	1455
Baden d.	...	|	|	|	|	...	|	|	1322	...	|	|	|	|	|	|	1422	...	|	|	|	|	|
Brugg d.	...	|	|	|	|	...	|	|	1332	...	|	|	|	|	|	|	1432	...	|	|	|	|	|
Lenzburg d.	...	|	|	1258	|	...	|	|	|	...	|	|	1358	|	|	|	|	...	|	|	1458	|	|
Aarau d.	...	|	|	1305	|	...	|	1329	1346	...	|	|	1405	|	|	1429	1446	...	|	|	1505	|	|
Olten a.	...	1300	|	▬	|	...	1326	1338	1357	...	1400	|	▬	|	1426	1438	1457	...	1500	|	▬	|	1526
Olten d.	...	1302	|	1306	|	...	1336	1340	1359	...	1402	|	1406	|	1436	1440	1459	...	1502	|	1506	|	1536
Solothurn d.	...	1326	|	|	|	...	|	1358	|	...	1426	|	|	|	|	1458	|	...	1526	|	|	|	|
Langenthal d.	...	|	|	1318	|	...	1348	|	|	...	|	|	1418	|	1448	|	|	...	|	|	1518	|	1548
Burgdorf d.	...	|	|	1338	|	...	1407	|	|	...	|	|	1438	|	1507	|	|	...	|	|	1538	|	1607
Biel / Bienne a.	...	1343	|	|	|	...	|	1413	|	...	1443	|	|	|	|	1513	|	...	1543	|	|	|	|
Biel / Bienne d.	...	1345	|	|	|	...	|	1416	|	...	1445	|	|	|	|	1516	|	...	1545	|	|	|	|
Bern **560** a.	...	|	1328	1353	1400	...	1421	|	1426	...	|	1428	1453	1500	1521	|	1526	...	|	1528	1553	1600	1621
Bern **568** d.	...	|	1334	...	1404	...	...	|	...	...	|	1434	...	1504	...	|	...	...	|	1534	...	1604	...
Fribourg **508 568** d.	...	|	1356	...	1426	...	...	|	...	...	|	1456	...	1526	...	|	...	...	|	1556	...	1626	...
Romont **568** d.	1347	|	|	...	|	...	...	|	...	1447	|	|	...	|	...	|	...	1547	|	|	...	|	...
Palézieux **504** d.	1402	|	|	...	|	...	...	|	...	1502	|	|	...	|	...	|	...	1602	|	|	...	|	...
Neuchâtel d.	|	1403	|	...	|	...	...	1434	...	|	1503	|	...	|	...	1534	...	|	1603	|	...	|	...
Yverdon d.	|	1422	|	...	|	...	...	1453	...	|	1522	|	...	|	...	1553	...	|	1622	|	...	|	...
Lausanne a.	1417	1445	1440	...	1510	...	...	|	...	1517	1545	1540	...	1610	...	|	...	1617	1645	1640	...	1710	...
Lausanne **570** d.	1421	...	1442	...	1512	...	...	|	...	1521	...	1542	...	1612	...	|	...	1621	...	1642	...	1712	...
Morges **570** d.	1434	...	|	...	|	...	...	1518	...	1534	...	|	...	|	...	1618	...	1634	...	|	...	|	...
Nyon **570** d.	1455	...	|	...	|	...	...	|	...	1555	...	|	...	|	...	|	...	1655	...	|	...	|	...
Genève **570** a.	1511	...	1518	...	1548	...	...	1545	...	1611	...	1618	...	1648	...	1645	...	1711	...	1718	...	1748	...
Genève Aéroport + **570** a.	...	...	1527	...	1557	...	...	1554	...	...	...	1627	...	1657	...	1654	...	...	...	1727	...	1757	...

	IR 2176	*RE* 3126	*ICN* 1526	*IC* 724	*RE* 4826	*IR* 2528	*IR* 2376	*ICN* 528	*IR* 2178	*RE* 3128	*ICN* 1528	*IC* 726	*RE* 4828	*IR* 2530		*IR* 2378	*ICN* 530	*IR* 2180	*RE* 3130	*ICN* 1530	*IC* 728	*RE* 4830	*IR* 2532
Luzern d.	...	...	...	...	...	1600	...	...	...	...	...	...	...	1700	...	...	...	...	...	...	...	...	1800
St Gallen **530** d.	...	...	1412	1425	...	|	...	...	...	...	1512	1525	...	|	...	...	...	...	...	1612	1625	...	|
Zürich Flughafen + **530/5** d.	...	...	1513	1518	...	|	...	...	...	...	1613	1618	...	|	...	...	...	...	...	1713	1718	...	|
Zürich HB **560** d.	1506	...	1530	1532	1538	|	1555	1603	1606	...	1630	1632	1638	|	...	1655	1703	1706	...	1730	1732	1738	|
Baden d.	1522	...	|	|	|	|	|	|	1622	...	|	|	|	|	...	|	|	1722	...	|	|	|	|
Brugg d.	1532	...	|	|	|	|	|	|	1632	...	|	|	|	|	...	|	|	1732	...	|	|	|	|
Lenzburg d.	|	...	|	|	1558	|	|	|	|	...	|	|	1658	|	...	|	|	|	...	|	|	1758	|
Aarau d.	1546	...	|	|	1605	|	|	1629	1646	...	|	|	1705	|	...	|	1729	1746	...	|	|	1805	|
Olten a.	1557	...	1600	|	▬	|	1626	1638	1657	...	1700	|	▬	|	...	1726	1738	1757	...	1800	|	▬	|
Olten d.	1559	...	1602	|	1606	|	1636	1640	1659	...	1702	|	1706	|	...	1736	1740	1759	...	1802	|	1806	|
Solothurn d.	|	...	1626	|	|	|	|	1658	|	...	1726	|	|	|	...	|	1758	|	...	1826	|	|	|
Langenthal d.	|	...	|	|	1618	|	1648	|	|	...	|	|	1718	|	...	1748	|	|	...	|	|	1818	|
Burgdorf d.	|	...	|	|	1638	|	1707	|	|	...	|	|	1738	|	...	1807	|	|	...	|	|	1838	|
Biel / Bienne a.	|	...	1643	|	|	|	|	1713	|	...	1743	|	|	|	...	|	1813	|	...	1843	|	|	|
Biel / Bienne d.	|	...	1645	|	|	|	|	1716	|	...	1745	|	|	|	...	|	1816	|	...	1845	|	|	|
Bern **560** a.	1626	...	|	1628	1653	1700	1721	|	1726	...	|	1728	1753	1800	...	1821	|	1826	...	|	1828	1853	1900
Bern **568** d.	...	...	|	1634	...	1704	...	|	...	...	|	1734	...	1804	...	...	|	...	...	|	1834	...	1904
Fribourg **508 568** d.	...	...	|	1656	...	1726	...	|	...	...	|	1756	...	1826	...	...	|	...	...	|	1856	...	1926
Romont **568** d.	...	1647	|	|	...	|	...	|	...	1747	|	|	...	|	...	...	|	...	1847	|	|	...	|
Palézieux **504** d.	...	1702	|	|	...	|	...	|	...	1802	|	|	...	|	...	...	|	...	1902	|	|	...	|
Neuchâtel d.	...	|	1703	|	...	|	...	1734	...	|	1803	|	...	|	...	...	1834	...	|	1903	|	...	|
Yverdon d.	...	|	1722	|	...	|	...	1753	...	|	1822	|	...	|	...	...	1853	...	|	1922	|	...	|
Lausanne a.	...	1717	1745	1740	...	1810	...	|	...	1817	1845	1840	...	1910	...	...	|	...	1917	1945	1940	...	2010
Lausanne **570** d.	...	1721	...	1742	...	1812	...	|	...	1821	...	1842	...	1912	...	...	|	...	1921	...	1942	...	2012
Morges **570** d.	...	1734	...	|	...	|	...	1818	...	1834	...	|	...	|	...	...	1918	...	1934	...	|	...	|
Nyon **570** d.	...	1755	...	|	...	|	...	|	...	1855	...	|	...	|	...	...	|	...	1955	...	|	...	|
Genève **570** a.	...	1811	...	1818	...	1848	...	1845	...	1911	...	1918	...	1948	...	...	1945	...	2011	...	2018	...	2048
Genève Aéroport + **570** a.	...	...	...	1827	...	1857	...	1854	...	...	...	1927	...	1957	...	...	1954	...	...	...	2027	...	...

a – Ⓐ only.
m – ① (not Aug. 1).
r – Arrive 0713.
v – 10 minutes later Jan. 4 - Mar. 10.
w – ⑥⑦ (also Jan. 1, Aug. 1; not Dec. 26, Mar. 26).

ZÜRICH - BIEL / BERN - LAUSANNE - GENÈVE 505

	ICN 532	IR 2182	RE 3132	ICN 1532	IC 730	RE 4832	IR 2534	IR 2382	ICN 534	IR 2184	RE 3134	ICN 1534	IC 732	RE 4834	IR 2536	IR 2384	ICN 536	IR 2186	ICN 1536	IC 734	RE 4836	IR 2538	IR 2386	ICN 538
ern d.	...	...	...	...	...	...	1900	...	...	...	...	...	...	...	2000	...	...	...	...	...	...	2100	...	...
allen 530 d.	...	...	...	1712	1725	...	│	...	...	...	...	1812	1825	...	│	...	...	...	1912	1925	...	│	...	...
ch Flughafen ✈ 530/5 d.	...	...	...	1813	1818	...	│	...	...	...	...	1913	1918	...	│	...	...	...	2013	2018	...	│	...	...
HB 560 d.	1803	1806	...	1830	1832	1838	│	1855	1903	1906	...	1930	1932	1938	│	1955	2003	2006	2030	2032	2038	│	2055	2103
d.	│	1822	...	│	│	│	│	│	│	1922	...	│	│	│	│	│	│	2022	│	│	│	│	│	│
d.	│	1832	...	│	│	│	│	│	│	1932	...	│	│	│	│	│	│	2032	│	│	│	│	│	│
zburg d.	│	│	...	│	│	1858	│	│	│	│	...	│	│	1958	│	│	│	│	│	│	2058	│	│	│
d.	1829	1846	...	│	│	1905	│	│	1929	1946	...	│	│	2005	│	│	2029	2046	│	│	2105	│	│	2129
a.	1838	1857	...	1900	│	▬	│	1926	1938	1957	...	2000	│	▬	│	2026	2038	2057	2100	│	▬	│	2126	2138
d.	1840	1859	...	1902	│	1906	│	1936	1940	1959	...	2002	│	2006	│	2036	2040	2059	2102	│	2106	│	2136	2140
thurn d.	1858	│	...	1926	│	│	│	│	1958	│	...	2026	│	│	│	│	2058	│	2126	│	│	│	│	2158
nthal d.	│	│	...	│	│	1918	│	1948	│	│	...	│	│	2018	│	2048	│	│	│	│	2118	│	2149	│
orf d.	│	│	...	│	│	1938	│	2007	│	│	...	│	│	2038	│	2107	│	│	│	│	2138	│	2209	│
/Bienne a.	1913	│	...	1943	│	│	│	│	2013	│	...	2043	│	│	│	│	2113	│	2143	│	│	│	│	2213
/Bienne d.	1916	│	...	1945	│	│	│	│	2016	│	...	2045	│	│	│	│	2116	│	2145	│	│	│	│	...
560 a.	│	1926	...	│	1928	1953	2000	2021	│	2026	...	│	2028	2053	2100	2121	│	2126	│	2128	2153	2200	2226	...
568 d.	│	...	...	│	1934	...	2004	...	│	...	...	│	2034	...	2104	...	│	...	│	2134	...	2204	...	...
rg 508 568 d.	│	...	...	│	1956	...	2026	...	│	...	...	│	2056	...	2126	...	│	...	│	2156	...	2226	...	...
nt 568 d.	│	...	1947	│	│	...	│	...	│	...	2047	│	│	...	2144	...	│	...	│	│	...	2244	...	...
eux 504 d.	│	...	2002	│	│	...	│	...	│	...	2102	│	│	...	2159	...	│	...	│	│	...	2259	...	...
châtel d.	1934	...	│	2003	│	...	│	...	2034	...	│	2103	│	...	│	...	2134	...	2203	│	...	│	...	...
rdon d.	1953	...	│	2022	│	...	│	...	2053	...	│	2122	│	...	│	...	2153	...	2222	│	...	│	...	...
nne a.	│	...	2017	2045	2040	...	2110	...	│	...	2117	2145	2140	...	2215	...	│	...	2245	2240	...	2315	...	...
nne 570 d.	│	...	2021	...	2042	...	2112	...	│	...	2121	...	2142	...	...	...	│	...	...	2242	...	...	...	...
s 570 d.	2018	...	2034	...	│	...	│	...	2118	...	2134	...	│	...	...	...	2218	...	...	│	...	...	...	...
570 d.	│	...	2055	...	│	...	│	...	│	...	2155	...	│	...	...	...	2233	...	...	│	...	...	...	...
ve 570 a.	2045	...	2111	...	2118	...	2148	...	2145	...	2211	...	2218	...	...	...	2247	...	...	2318	...	...	...	...
e Aéroport ✈ 570 a.	2054	...	...	...	2127	...	2157	...	2154	...	...	...	2227	...	...	...	2256	...	...	2327	...	...	...	...

	IR 2188	ICN 1538	IC 736	RE 4838	IR 2540	IC 836	IR 2544	IR 2388	ICN 540	IR 2190	IC 738	RE 4840	IR 2542	IC 838	IR 2502	IR 2390	ICN 542	IR 2192	IC 740	RE 4842	IC 842	IR 2194	IR 2392	IC 844
						R								R	y								g	g
ern d.	...	...	...	...	2200	...	...	...	...	...	...	...	2300	...	...	...	...	...	...	...	...	...	...	...
allen 530 d.	...	2012	...	...	│	...	...	...	...	...	...	...	│	...	...	...	...	...	...	...	...	...	...	...
ch Flughafen ✈ 530/5 d.	...	2113	...	...	│	2140	...	...	...	...	...	...	│	2240	...	...	...	...	...	...	...	...	...	...
HB 560 d.	2106	2130	2132	2138	│	2202	...	...	2203	2206	2232j	2238	│	2302	...	...	2303	2306	2332j	2338	0002	0006	...	0102
d.	2122	│	│	│	│	│	...	...	│	2222	│	│	│	│	...	...	│	2322	│	│	│	0022	...	│
d.	2132	│	│	│	│	│	...	...	│	2232	│	│	│	│	...	...	│	2332	│	│	│	0030	...	│
zburg d.	│	│	│	2158	│	│	...	...	│	│	│	2258	│	│	...	...	│	│	│	2358	│	...	...	│
d.	2146	│	│	2205	│	│	...	...	2229	2246	│	2305	│	│	...	...	2329	2346	│	0005	│	...	...	│
a.	2157	2200	│	...	│	2232	...	...	2238	2257	2302	▬	│	2332	...	...	2338	2357	0002	...	0032	...	...	0132
d.	2159	2202	│	...	│	2235	...	2237	2240	...	2304	...	│	2335	...	2337	2340	...	0004	...	0035	...	0037	0135
thurn d.	│	2226	│	...	│	│	...	│	2257	...	│	...	│	│	...	│	0005	...	│	...	│	...	│	│
nthal d.	│	│	│	...	│	│	...	2249	│	...	│	...	│	│	...	2349	│	...	│	...	│	...	0049	│
orf d.	│	│	│	...	│	│	...	2309	│	...	│	...	│	│	...	0009	│	...	│	...	│	...	0109	│
/Bienne a.	│	2243	│	...	│	│	...	│	2314	...	│	...	│	│	...	│	0022	...	│	...	│	...	│	│
/Bienne d.	│	2245	│	...	│	│	...	│	2316	...	│	...	│	│	...	│	0025t	...	│	...	│	...	│	│
560 a.	2226	│	2228	...	2300	2302	...	2326	│	...	2331	...	2400	0002	...	0023	│	...	0031	...	0102	...	0123	0202
568 d.	...	│	2234	...	...	...	2308	...	│	...	...	...	...	...	0008	...	│	...	...	...	...	...	...	...
rg 508 568 d.	...	│	2255	...	...	...	2330	...	│	...	...	...	...	...	0032	...	│	...	...	...	...	...	...	...
nt 568 d.	...	│	▬	...	...	...	2350	...	│	...	...	...	...	...	0050	...	│	...	...	...	...	...	...	...
eux 504 d.	...	│	...	...	...	...	0005	...	│	...	...	...	...	...	0105	...	│	...	...	...	...	...	...	...
châtel d.	...	2303	*RE*	...	...	...	│	...	2334	...	...	*RE*	...	...	│	...	0042t	...	...	...	...	...	...	...
rdon d.	...	2322	**3238**	...	...	...	│	...	2353	...	...	**3240**	...	...	│	...	0102t	...	...	...	...	...	...	...
nne a.	...	2345		...	...	...	0021	...	0015	...	...		...	...	0121	...	0122t	...	...	...	...	...	...	...
nne 570 d.	...	...	2351	...	...	...	...	...	...	...	...	0051	...	...	...	...	...	...	...	...	...	...	...	...
s 570 d.	...	...	0004	...	...	...	...	...	...	...	...	0104	...	...	...	...	...	...	...	...	...	...	...	...
570 d.	...	...	0025	...	...	...	...	...	...	...	...	0125	...	...	...	...	...	...	...	...	...	...	...	...
ve 570 a.	...	...	0041	...	...	...	...	...	...	...	...	0143	...	...	...	...	...	...	...	...	...	...	...	...
e Aéroport ✈ 570 a.	...	...	0050t	...	...	...	...	...	...	...	...	...	...	...	...	...	...	...	...	...	...	...	...	...

From Romanshorn (Table **535**).

g – ⑥⑦ (also Jan. 1; not Mar. 26).
j – Depart 2 minutes **earlier** Jan. 4 - Mar. 10.

t – ⑥⑦ (not Dec. 26, 27, Jan. 2, 3, Mar. 26).
y – ①⑥⑦ (also Jan. 1; not Dec. 26, Mar. 26).

BIEL - BASEL 505a

	ICN 1607	RE 3159	ICN 1609		RE 3161	ICN 1611	RE 3163		ICN 1613	RE 3165		ICN 1615	RE 3167	and at the same	ICN 1641	RE 3193		ICN 1545 L		RE 3151 h			
Biel/Bienne 515 d.	0549	0619	0649	...	0719	0749	0819	...	0849	0919	...	0949	1019	minutes	2249	2319	...	0019	...	0119	...	...	...
Moutier 515 d.	0608	0639	0708	...	0739	0808	0839	...	0908	0939	...	1008	1039	past each	2308	2339	...	0038	...	0139	...	...	...
Delémont 515 d.	0623	0648	0723	...	0748	0823	0848	...	0923	0948	...	1023	1048	hour	2318	2348	...	0048	...	0148	...	...	...
Basel a.	0653	...	0753	...	...	0853	...	...	0953	...	...	1053	...	until	2353	...	...	...	...	...	...	...	...

	RE 3154	ICN 1606 G	RE 3156	ICN 1608	RE 3158	ICN 1610	RE 3160	and at the same	ICN 1628	RE 3178	ICN 1630	RE 2230 Ⓐ	RE 3180	ICN 1632	RE 2232 Ⓐ	RE 3182	ICN 1634	RE 3184	ICN 1636	RE 3186	ICN 1638	RE 3188	ICN 1640	ICN 1642
d.	...	*0457*	...	0603	...	0703	...	minutes	1603	...	1703	1716	...	1803	1816	...	1903	...	2003	...	2103	...	2203	2303
ont 515 d.	0512	0542	0612	0642	0712	0742	0812	past each	1642	1712	1742	1800	1812	1842	1900	1912	1942	2012	2042	2112	2142	2212	2242	2337
er 515 d.	0523	0552	0623	0652	0723	0752	0823	hour	1652	1723	1752	...	1823	1852	...	1923	1952	2023	2052	2123	2152	2223	2252	...
Bienne 515 d.	0541	0610	0640	0710	0741	0810	0841	until	1710	1741	1810	...	1841	1910	...	1941	2010	2041	2110	2141	2210	2241	2310	...

To Genève Aéroport (Table **505**).
From Lausanne (Table **505**).

h – ⑥⑦ (also Dec. 25, Jan. 1, Mar. 25).

506 SWISS LAKES

LAC LÉMAN

June 19 - September 4 — Operator:

⚒															⚒												
...	...	...	...	...	1015	...	...	1440	1450	...	...	1900	...	d. Genève ⊗ ... a.	...	...	...	1440	...	...	...	1750	1835	...	...	...	221
...	...	...	...	...	1101	...	...	|	1535	...	...	1958	...	d. Coppet ... d.	...	...	...	1350	...	...	...	1700	|	...	...	...	211
...	...	...	...	...	1135	...	...	1615	|	...	...	|	...	d. Nyon ... d.	...	...	...	1240	...	...	...	1630	1715	...	...	...	|
...	...	...	...	...	1205	...	...	1640	1615	...	...	2032	2037	d. Yvoire ... d.	...	...	...	1310n	...	...	...	1600	1650	...	...	2029	2034
...	...	...	...	...	|	...	...	...	|	...	...	▬	|	d. Thonon-les-Bains ... d.	...	...	...	|	...	...	...	|	▬	...	...	|	...
0700	0820	1005	1145	1315	|	1445	1615	...	|	1800	1920	2045	|	d. Évian-les-Bains ... d.	0655	0815	1000	|	1135	1305	1435	|	1605	1750	1915	|	...
|	|	|	|	|	1315	|	|	...	1727	|	|	|	2153	d. Morges ... d.	|	|	|	1119	|	|	|	1439	|	|	|	1929	...
0735	0855	1040	1220	1350	1351	1520	1650	...	1802	1835	1955	2120	2227	a. Lausanne-Ouchy ... d.	0620	0740	0925	1045	1100	1230	1400	1405	1530	1715	1840	1855	...

0920	0930	1100	1230	...	1415	1530	...	1810	...	d. Lausanne-Ouchy ... a.	1040	1220	1352	...	1520	...	1745	1833	...
|	1032	1205	|	1405	1522	|	1605	1857	1900	d. Vevey-Marché ... d.	0955	1135	1251	1400	1435	1600	1640	1745	1850
|	1037	1210	|	1410	|	|	1610	|	|	d. Vevey-La Tour ... d.	|	|	|	|	|	|	|	|	|
|	1101	1240	|	1440	1546	|	1640	1917	|	d. Montreux ... d.	0933	1113	1229	|	1415	|	1616	1720	1830
|	1108	1247	|	1447	|	|	1647	...	|	d. Territet ... d.	|	|	|	|	|	|	|	|	|
|	1116	1255	|	1455	1556	|	1655	...	|	d. Château-de-Chillon ... d.	|	1100	|	|	1403	|	1603	1705	1815
|	1124	1303	|	1503	...	|	1703	...	|	d. Villeneuve ... d.	|	1050	|	|	1355	|	...	1657	1806
1010	|	|	1320	|	...	1620	|	...	|	d. St Gingolph ... d.	|	|	1200	1338	|	1538	...	|	1740
1025	1145	1325	1333	1525	...	1635	1725	...	1920	d. Bouveret ... d.	0910	1025	1145	1325	1333	1525	...	1635	1725
...	1200	1338	...	1538	...	...	1738	...	...	a. St Gingolph ... d.	...	1010	...	...	1320	...	...	1620	...

THUNERSEE

March 25 - October 16 — Operator:

p		L	Ⓒq		Ⓒq	T	p	Z	q	p	X		Ⓒq	L	p			Z	Ⓒq	T	q	p	p
0840	0940	1010	1040	1140	1240	1240	1340	1440	1540	1540	1840	d. Thun ... a.	1220	1220	1320	1420	1620	1715	1720	1720	1820	1820	2020
0851	0951	|	1051	1151	1251	1251	1351	1451	1551	1551	1851	d. Hünibach ... d.	1209	1209	1309	1409	1609	|	1709	1709	1809	1809	2009
0903	1003	|	1103	1203	1303	1303	1403	1503	1603	1603	1903	d. Oberhofen ... d.	1157	1157	1257	1357	1557	|	1657	1657	1757	1757	1957
0916	1016	|	1116	1216	1316	1316	1416	|	1616	1616	1916	d. Gunten ... d.	1144	1144	1244	1344	1544	|	1644	1644	1744	1744	1944
0928	1028	1038	1126	1228	1328	1328	1428	1538	1628	1628	1928	d. Spiez ... d.	1134	1134	1234	1334	1534	1636	1634	1634	1734	1734	1934
0940	1040	|	...	1240	1340	1340	1440	|	1640	1640	1940	d. Faulensee ... d.	...	1120	1220	1320	1520	1610	1620	1620	1720	1720	1920
0955	1055	|	...	1255	1355	1355	1455	1554	|	1655	1955	d. Merligen ... d.	...	1105	1205	1305	1505	1555	1605	1605	1705	1705	1905
1002	1102	1057	...	1302	1402	1402	1502	...	1657	1702	2002	d. Beatenbucht ... d.	...	1058	1158	1258	1458	...	1558	1558	1658	1658	1858
1049	1149	...	...	1349	1449	1449	1549	...	...	1749	...	a. Interlaken West ... d.	...	...	1110	1210	1410	...	1510	1510	...	1610	1810

VIERWALDSTÄTTERSEE

May 28 - September 11 — Operator:

		S	†S		S			S				M		S					†S			S		S		S	M		
0812	...	0912	0940	1012	1112	...	1212	1312	1412	1512	1612	1712	1812	1912	d. Luzern (Bahnhofquai) a.	1047	1147	1247	1230	1347	...	1447	1547	1647	1747	1847	1905	1947	204
0822	...	0922	0950	1022	1122	...	1222	1322	1422	1522	1622	1722	1822	1922	d. Verkehrshaus Lido .. d.	1035	|	1235	|	1335	...	1435	1535	1635	1735	1835	|	1935	203
|	...	|	|	|	|	...	|	|	|	|	|	|	|	|	d. Kehrsiten-Bürgenstock d.	|	1120	|	|	|	...	|	|	|	|	|	1836	|	|
0843	...	0943	|	1043	1143	...	1243	1343	1443	1543	1643	1743	1843	1943	d. Hertenstein ... d.	1014	|	1214	|	1314	...	1414	1514	1614	1714	1814	|	1914	201
0853	...	0953	1024	1053	1153	...	1253	1353	1453	1553	1653	1753	1853	1953	d. Weggis ... d.	1005	1105	1205	|	1305	...	1405	1505	1605	1705	1805	|	1905	200
0910	...	1010	1040	1110	1210	...	1310	1410	1510	1610	1710	1809	1910	2010	d. Vitznau ... d.	0949	1049	1149	|	1249	...	1349	1449	1549	1649	1749	1811	1849	194
0927	...	1027	1123	1127	1227	...	1327	1427	1527	1627	1800	...	1926	2031	d. Beckenried ... d.	...	1000	1132	1135	1232	...	1332	1432	1532	1632	1732	...	1832	193
0945	...	1045	...	1145	1245	...	1345	1445	1545	1645	1817	...	...	...	d. Gersau ... d.	...	0942	1114	...	1214	...	1314	1414	1514	1614	1714	...	1814	...
1002	...	1102	...	1202	1302	...	1402	1502	1602	1702	1834	...	...	...	d. Treib ... d.	...	0927	1057	...	1157	...	1257	1357	1457	1557	1657	...	1757	...
1011	1020	1111	...	1211	1311	1320	1411	1511	1611	1711	1841	...	...	...	d. Brunnen ... d.	...	0919	1049	...	1149	1220	1249	1349	1449	1549	1649	...	1749	...
1021	1031	1121	...	1221	1321	1331	1421	1521	1621	1721	...	...	...	...	d. Rütli ... d.	...	...	1036	...	1136	|	1236	1336	1436	1536	1636	...	1736	...
1032	|	|	...	|	1332	|	|	1532	|	1732	...	...	...	...	d. Sisikon ... d.	...	...	1024	...	|	1202	1224	|	|	|	|	...	|	...
1039	|	|	...	|	1339	|	|	1539	|	|	...	...	...	...	d. Tellsplatte ... d.	...	...	1016	...	|	1155	1216	|	|	|	|	...	1714	...
|	1047	1135	...	1235	|	1347	1435	|	1635	1744	...	...	...	...	d. Bauen ... d.	...	...	1006	...	1121	|	|	1321	1421	1521	1621	...	1724t	...
|	1055	1143	...	1243	|	1355	1443	|	1643	1751	...	...	...	...	d. Isleten-Isenthal ... d.	...	...	0958	...	1112	1146	|	1312	1412	1512	1612	...	|	...
1055	1107	1155	...	1255	1355	1420	1455	1555	1655	1803	...	...	...	...	a. Flüelen ... d.	...	...	0946	...	1100	1119	1200	1300	1400	1500	1600	...	1700	...

									S			M	S											S			M
0838	0840	0938	1000	1038	1150	1238	1338	1400	1438	1550	1600	1712	1912	d. Luzern (Bahnhofquai) ... a.	1153	1028	1047	1218	1328	1358	1516	1547	1628	1745	1802	1810	1905
|	0850	0948	1010	1048	1200	1248	1348	1410	1448	1600	1610	1722	1922	d. Verkehrshaus Lido ... d.	|	1016	1035	1206	1316	|	1501	|	1616	|	1750	1759	|
|	|	|	1053	|	|	|	|	1453	|	|	1704	|	|	a. ..Küssnacht am Rigi ... d.	1055	|	|	|	|	|	|	1455	|	|	1706	|	|
|	|	|	...	1123	|	|	|	...	1523	1634	...	1836	2112	d. Kehrsiten-Bürgenstock ... d.	...	|	|	|	|	|	|	...	|	|	...	|	1836
|	0911	|	...	1131	|	|	1409	...	1531	1643	...	...	...	d. Kehrsiten Dorf ... d.	...	|	0911	1146	|	|	1424	...	1556	|	...	1722	...
|	...	1016	...	1146	|	|	1424	...	1548	1658	...	...	...	d. Hergiswil ... d.	...	|	...	1131	1247	|	1409	...	1541	1710	...	|	...
|	...	1025	...	|	1226	1314	1433	...	1558	1708	...	...	...	d. Stansstad ... d.	...	0951	...	1122	1238	1326	|	...	1531	1700	...	1710	...
|	...	|	...	|	|	|	|	...	|	...	...	...	...	d. Hergiswil ... d.	...	|	...	|	|	|	|	...	|	|	...	...	...
0925	...	1046	...	1210	1250	1335	1455	...	1621	...	...	...	...	a. Alpnachstad ... d.	...	0930	...	1100	1217	1305	1345	...	1510	1637	...	...	...

ZÜRICHSEE

May 1 - September 30 — Operator:

A	A			A			A	A			A			A			A	A	A
0805	0930	1030	1130	1230	1330	1430	1530	1630	1730	d. Zürich (Bürkliplatz) ... a.	1325	1425	1525	1625	1725	1825	1855	1925	2025
0836	|	1100	|	1300	|	1500	|	1700	|	d. Erlenbach ... d.	1253	|	1453	|	1653	|	|	1853	|
|	1000	|	1200	|	1400	|	1600	|	1800	d. Thalwil ... d.	|	1355	|	1555	|	1755	1825	|	1955
|	1007	|	1207	|	1407	|	1607	|	1807	d. Oberrieden ... d.	|	1346	|	1546	|	1746	1816	|	1946
0917	|	1142	|	1342	|	1542	|	1742	1859	d. Wädenswil ... d.	1212	|	1412	|	1612	|	|	1812	|
1005	1120	1225	1315	1425	1520	1625	1720	1825	1946	a. Rapperswil ... d.	1130	1235	1330	1435	1530	1635	1700	1730	1835

BRIENZERSEE

March 25 - August 28 — Operator:

C	⑦J	Q	C	J	Q	J	B	⑥K		C	⑦J	Q	C	J	Q	J	B
0907	1025	1107	1207	1307	1407	1507	1607	1907	d. Interlaken Ost ... a.	1153	1253	1353	1453	1553	1653	1753	1853
0925	1025	1125	1225	1325	1425	1525	1625	1925	d. Bönigen ... d.	1135	1235	1335	1435	1535	1635	1735	1835
0951	1044	1151	1244	1351	1451	1544	1651	1951	d. Iseltwald ... d.	1110	1217	1310	1417	1510	1610	1717	1810
1009	1109	1209	1309	1409	1509	1609	1709	2009	d. Giessbach ... d.	1051	1151	1251	1351	1451	1551	1651	1751
1020	1120	1220	1320	1420	1520	1620	1720	2020	a. Brienz ... d.	1040	1140	1240	1340	1440	1540	1640	1740

A – From June 1.
B – From May 14.
C – From Apr. 9.
J – From June 19.
K – From June 18.
L – ⑦ May 14 - Oct. 16. Normally operated by historic Steamship.
M – Daily. Normally operated by historic Steamship on ⚒.
Q – Daily. Normally operated by historic Steamship on Ⓒ from May 14 (daily from May 30).
S – Normally operated by historic Steamship.
T – May 14 - Oct. 16. Normally operated by historic Steamship.
X – ②③④⑤⑥ May 14 - Oct. 26. Normally operated by historic Steamship.
Z – May 5-8, June 26 - Aug. 28, Sept. 4, 11, 18.

n – Via Nyon.
p – May 14 - Oct. 16.
q – Mar. 25 - May 13.
t – Via Tellsplatte.

⊗ – Genève has landing stages at: Mont-Blanc, Jardin-Anglais, Pâquis and Eaux-
Services do not call at all landing stages.

Operators:
BLS – Schifffahrt Berner Oberland: ✆ +41 (0)33 334 52 11. (www.bls.ch)
CGN – Compagnie Générale de Navigation: ✆ +41 (0)848 811 848. (www.c
SGV – Schifffahrtsgesellschaft Vierwaldstättersee: ✆ +41 (0)41 367 67 67. (www.lakelucerne.ch)
ZSG – Zürichsee Schifffahrtsgesellschaft: ✆ +41 (0)44 487 13 33. (www.zs

508 FRIBOURG - MURTEN - INS

km		⚒	⚒	†	▲		▲			⑤⑥
0	Fribourg **505** ... d.	0500	0530	0600	0630	and at the	2130	...	2230	2330
22	Murten ... d.	0530	0600	0630	0700	same minutes	2200	...	2300	0000
32	Ins **511** ... a.	0540	0610	0640	0710	past each	2210	...	2310	0010
45	Neuchâtel **511** ... a.	...	0624	...	0724	hour until	2224	...	...	...

	⚒		▲		▲			
Neuchâtel **511** ... d.	...	0636d	0736	and at the	2136		2236	...
Ins **511** ... d.	0548	0648	0748	same minutes	2148	...	2248	2320
Murten ... d.	0601	0701	0801	past each	2201	...	2301	2333
Fribourg **505** ... a.	0630	0730	0830	hour until	2230	...	2330	0001

d – ⚒ only.

▲ – Departures from Fribourg at 1030, 1130; from Neuchâtel at 0936, 1036 do not operate Fribourg - Murten and v.v. on O

BASEL - ZÜRICH 510

Via Lenzburg

	IC 557	EC 191 Mq	IR 2247 p	ICE 1251	IC 559	IR 2259	IC 761 Ⓐ	ICE 1253 Ⓒ	ICE 1255 Ⓐ	IC 561 Ⓒ	EC 193 M	ICE 3 ♦	IC 563	IR 2263	ICE 271 H	IC 565	IR 2265	IC 767	TGV 9203 ♦	IC 567 y	IR 2267	IC 769 m	IC 207 Fn	IC 569	IR 2269	IC 771	IC 571	IR 2271
Basel SBB d.	0533	0547	0547	0607	0633	0647	0707	0707	0733	0733	0747	0807	0833	0847	0907	0933	0947	1007	1033	1033	1047	1107	1107	1133	1147	1207	1233	1247
Liestal d.	|	0557	0557	|	|	0657	|	|	|	|	0757	|	|	0857	|	|	0957	|	|	|	1057	|	|	|	1157	|	|	1257
Aarau d.	|	0624	0624	|	|	0724	|	|	|	|	0824	|	|	0924	|	|	1024	|	|	|	1124	|	|	|	1224	|	|	1324
Lenzburg d.	|	0631	0631	|	|	0731	|	|	|	|	0831	|	|	0931	|	|	1031	|	|	|	1131	|	|	|	1231	|	|	1331
Zürich HB a.	0626	0652	0652	0700	0726	0752	0800	0800	0826	0826	0852	0900	0926	0952	1000	1026	1052	1100	1126	1126	1152	1200	1200	1226	1252	1300	1326	1352
St Gallen **530** a.	|	0818	0818	...	|	...	...	|	|	|	1018	...	|	1118	|	|	1218	...	...	...	1318	...	....	|	...	...	|	1518
Chur **520** a.	0752	...	...	...	0852	...	...	0922	0952	0952	...	...	1052	...	1122	1152	...	...	...	...	...	...	...	1352	...	...	1452	...

	ICE 71 H	TGV 9211 P	IR 2273	IC 775	IC 575	IR 2275	ICE 73 ♦	ICE 1173 ♦	TGV 9213 P	IR 2277	EC 9 H	IC 579	IR 2279	ICE 75 ♦	ICE 1175 ♦	IC 581	IR 2281	IC 783	IC 583	IR 2283	ICE 77 K	TGV 9219 P	IR 2285	IC 787	IC 587 Ⓐ	ICE 1261 Ⓒ	IR 2287
SBB d.	1307	1333	1347	1407	1433	1447	1507	1507	1533	1547	1607	1633	1647	1707	1707	1733	1747	1807	1833	1847	1907	1933	1947	2007	2033	2033	2047
l d.	|	|	1357	|	|	1457	|	|	|	1557	|	|	1657	|	|	|	1757	|	|	1857	|	|	1957	|	|	|	2057
d.	|	|	1424	|	|	1524	|	|	|	1624	|	|	1724	|	|	|	1824	|	|	1924	|	|	2024	|	|	|	2124
urg d.	|	|	1431	|	|	1531	|	|	|	1631	|	|	1731	|	|	|	1831	|	|	1931	|	|	2031	|	|	|	2131
h HB a.	1400	1426	1452	1500	1526	1552	1600	1600	1626	1652	1700	1726	1752	1800	1800	1826	1852	1900	1926	1952	2000	2026	2052	2100	2126	2126	2152
Gallen **530** a.	|	...	1618	...	|	1718	...	...	...	1818	...	|	...	...	...	|	2018	...	|	2118	...	...	2218	...	|	...	2318
ur **520** a.	1522	...	...	...	1652	...	...	...	...	...	...	1852	...	...	...	1952	...	...	2052r	...	...	...	...	...	2252t	...	...

	ICE 79 H	TGV 9223 Pj	TGV 9723 Pk	IR 2289 j	IR 10289 k	IC 791 j	IC 10791 k	IR 2291 j	IR 10291 k	IC 793 j	IC 10793 k
SBB d.	2107	2133	2133	2147	2147	2207	2207	2247	2247	2307	2307
l d.	|	|	|	2157	2157	|	|	2257	2257	|	|
d.	|	|	|	2224	2224	|	|	2324	2324	|	|
urg d.	|	|	|	2231	2231	|	|	2331	2331	|	|
h HB a.	2200	2226	2226	2252	2258	2300	2304	2352	2358	2400	0004
Gallen **530** a.	...	...	...	0018	0018	...	...	...	...	...	
ur **520** a.	...	...	...	...		...	...	...	...	...	...

	IR 2252	ICE 78 H	IR 2254	IC 556	IC 760	IR 2256	TGV 9206 P	ICE 76 K	IR 2258	IC 560	IC 764
Chur **520** d.	...	...	...	0509d	...	...	...	...	...	0709	...
St Gallen **530** a.	...	...	...	|	...	0542	...	...	...	|	...
Zürich HB d.	0508	0600	0608	0634	0700	0708	0734	0800	0808	0834	0900
Lenzburg d.	0528	|	0628	|	|	0728	|	|	0828	|	|
Aarau d.	0536	|	0636	|	|	0736	|	|	0836	|	|
Liestal d.	0601	|	0701	|	|	0801	|	|	0901	|	|
Basel SBB a.	0612	0652	0712	0727	0752	0812	0827	0852	0912	0927	0952

	IR 2260	TGV 9210 Pv	IC 562 w	ICE 74 K	IR 2262	IC 564	EC 8 H	IR 2264	TGV 9218 P		ICE 72 H	IR 2266	IC 568	IC 772	IR 2268	TGV 9222 P	ICE 70 H	IR 2270	IC 572	IC 776 m	IC 206 Fn	IR 2272	TGV 9226 ♦	IC 590 x	IC 778	IR 2274	IC 576
ur **520** d.	...	...	0809	...	...	0909	...	...	...	...	1039	...	1109	...	...	...	1239	...	1309	...	...	...	...	...	...	...	1509
Gallen **530** a.	0742	...	|	...	0842	|	...	0942	...	...	|	...	|	...	1142	...	|	1242	|	...	...	1342	...	...	...	1442	|
h HB d.	0908	0934	0934	1000	1008	1034	1100	1108	1134	...	1200	1208	1234	1300	1308	1334	1400	1408	1434	1500	1500	1508	1534	1534	1600	1608	1634
urg d.	0928	|	|	|	1028	|	|	1128	|	...	|	1228	|	|	1328	|	|	1428	|	|	|	1528	|	|	|	1628	|
d.	0936	|	|	|	1036	|	|	1136	|	...	|	1236	|	|	1336	|	|	1436	|	|	|	1536	|	|	|	1636	|
l d.	1001	|	|	|	1101	|	|	1201	|	...	|	1301	|	|	1401	|	|	1501	|	|	|	1601	|	|	|	1701	|
SBB a.	1012	1027	1027	1052	1112	1127	1152	1212	1227	...	1252	1312	1327	1352	1412	1427	1452	1512	1527	1552	1552	1612	1627	1627	1652	1712	1727

	ICE 272 ♦	ICE 1172 ♦	ICE 292 ♦	IR 2276	IC 578	ICE 1256 Ⓒ	IC 782 Ⓐ	IR 2278	IC 580	ICE 4 F	IR 2280	IC 582	IC 786	IR 2282	IC 584		ICE 1260	EC 192 M	ICE 1262 Ⓒ	ICE 1258 Ⓐ	IC 790	IR 2286	IC 792	IR 2288	IR 2292	IR 2296 z	
ur **520** d.	...	...	...	...	1609	1639	...	...	1709	...	...	1809	...	...	1909	...	...	...	...	2009	...	...	...	...	...	...	...
Gallen **530** a.	...	...	...	...	|	|	...	1642	|	...	1742	|	...	1842	|	...	...	1942	...	|	...	2042	...	...	...	...	...
h HB d.	1700	1700	1700	1708	1734	1800	1800	1808	1834	1900	1908	1934	2000	2008	2034	...	2100	2108	2134	2134	2200	2208	2300	2308	0008	0108	...
urg d.	|	|	|	1728	|	|	|	1828	|	|	1928	|	|	2028	|	...	|	2128	|	|	|	2228	|	2328	0028	0128	...
d.	|	|	|	1736	|	|	|	1836	|	|	1936	|	|	2036	|	...	|	2136	|	|	|	2236	|	2336	0036	0136	...
l d.	|	|	|	1801	|	|	|	1901	|	|	2001	|	|	2101	|	...	|	2201	|	|	|	2301	|	0001	0101	0201	...
SBB a.	1752	1752	1752	1812	1827	1852	1852	1912	1927	1952	2012	2027	2052	2112	2127	...	2152	2212	2227	2227	2252	2312	2352	0012	0112	0212	...

Via Baden

	IR 2055	IR 1957	IR 2057	IR 1959	IR 2059	IR 1961	IR 2061	IR 1963	IR 2063	IR 1965	IR 2065	IR 1967	IR 2067	IR 1969	IR 2069	IR 1971	IR 2071	IR 1973	IR 2073	IR 1975	IR 2075	IR 1977	IR 2077	IR 1979	IR 2079
Basel SBB d.	0437	0513	0537	0613	0637	0713	0737	0813	0837	0913	0937	1013	1037	1113	1137	1213	1237	1313	1337	1413	1437	1513	1537	1613	1637
Rheinfelden d.	0449	0525	0549	0625	0649	0725	0749	0825	0849	0925	0949	1025	1049	1125	1149	1225	1249	1325	1349	1425	1449	1525	1549	1625	1649
Brugg d.	0520	0600	0620	0700	0720	0800	0820	0900	0920	1000	1020	1100	1120	1200	1220	1300	1320	1400	1420	1500	1520	1600	1620	1700	1720
Baden d.	0529	0608	0629	0708	0729	0808	0829	0908	0929	1008	1029	1108	1129	1208	1229	1308	1329	1408	1429	1508	1529	1608	1629	1708	1729
Zürich HB a.	0549	0624	0649	0724	0749	0824	0849	0924	0949	1024	1049	1124	1149	1224	1249	1324	1349	1424	1449	1524	1549	1624	1649	1724	1749
Zürich Flug ✈ **530/5** a.	0604	...	0704	...	0804	...	0904	...	1004	...	1104	...	1204	...	1304	...	1404	...	1504	...	1604	...	1704	...	1804

	IR 1981	IR 2081	IR 1983	IR 2083	IR 1985	IR 2085	IR 1987	IR 1989	IR 1991	IR 1993	IR 1995
SBB d.	1713	1737	1813	1837	1913	1937	2013	2113	2213	2313	0013
felden d.	1725	1749	1825	1849	1925	1949	2025	2125	2225	2325	0025
d.	1800	1820	1900	1920	2000	2020	2100	2200	2300	0000	0100
n d.	1808	1829	1908	1929	2008	2029	2108	2208	2308	0008	0108
h HB a.	1824	1849	1924	1949	2024	2049	2124	2224	2324	0024	0124
ich Flug ✈ **530/5** a.	...	1904	...	2004	...	2104	...	...	...	...	...

	IR 1956	IR 2058	IR 1958	IR 2060	IR 1960	IR 2062	IR 1962	IR 2064	IR 1964	IR 2066
Zürich Flug ✈ **530/5** d.	...	0556	...	0656	...	0756	...	0856	...	0956
Zürich HB d.	0536	0609	0636	0709	0736	0809	0836	0909	0936	1009
Baden d.	0552	0633	0652	0733	0752	0833	0852	0933	0952	1033
Brugg d.	0602	0642	0702	0742	0802	0842	0902	0942	1002	1042
Rheinfelden d.	0635	0713	0734	0810	0834	0910	0934	1010	1034	1110
Basel SBB a.	0650	0731	0747	0824	0847	0924	0947	1024	1047	1124

	IR 1966	IR 2068	IR 1968	IR 2070	IR 1970	IR 2072	IR 1972	IR 2074	IR 1974	IR 2076	IR 1976	IR 2078	IR 1978	IR 2080	IR 1980	IR 2082	IR 1982	IR 2084	IR 1984	IR 2086	IR 1986	IR 2088	IR 1988	IR 1990	IR 1992	
ich Flug ✈ **530/5** d.	...	1056	...	1156	...	1256	...	1356	...	1456	...	1556	...	1656	...	1756	...	1856	...	1956	...	2056	...	...	...	...
h HB d.	1036	1109	1136	1209	1236	1309	1336	1409	1436	1509	1536	1609	1636	1709	1736	1809	1836	1909	1936	2009	2036	2109	2136	2236	2336	...
n d.	1052	1133	1152	1233	1252	1333	1352	1433	1452	1533	1552	1633	1652	1733	1752	1833	1852	1933	1952	2033	2052	2133	2152	2252	2352	...
d.	1102	1142	1202	1242	1302	1342	1402	1442	1502	1542	1602	1642	1702	1742	1802	1842	1902	1942	2002	2042	2102	2142	2202	2302	0002	...
felden d.	1134	1210	1234	1310	1334	1410	1434	1510	1534	1610	1634	1710	1734	1810	1834	1910	1934	2010	2034	2110	2134	2210	2234	2334	0034	...
l SBB a.	1147	1224	1247	1324	1347	1424	1447	1524	1547	1624	1647	1724	1747	1824	1847	1924	1947	2024	2047	2124	2147	2224	2247	2347	0047	...

NOTES (LISTED BY TRAIN NUMBER)

- [12] and ✕ Karlsruhe - Basel - Zürich.
- ①–⑥ (not Dec. 25, 26, Jan. 1, Mar. 26, 28, May 16, Oct. 3): [12] and ✕ Kiel - Hamburg - Basel - Zürich.
- ①–⑥ (not Dec. 25, 26, Jan. 1, Mar. 26, 28, May 16, Oct. 3): [12] and ✕ Hamburg - Basel - Zürich.
- – Ⓐ (also May 5, Aug. 1; not Dec. 24, 31, Oct. 3): [12] and ✕ Zürich - Basel - Hamburg.
- – ⑦ (also Mar. 28, May 16, Oct. 3; not Mar. 27, May 15, Oct. 2): [12] and ✕ Zürich - Basel - Berlin Ost.
- – ⑥ (also Dec. 24, 25, 31, Jan. 1, Mar. 25, 27, May 15, Oct. 2): [12] and ✕ Zürich - Basel - Hamburg.
- – ⑦ (also Dec. 25, 26, Jan. 1, Mar. 26, 28, May 16, Oct. 3): [12] and ✕ Hamburg - Basel - Zürich.
- – ⑦ (also Dec. 25, 26, Jan. 1, Mar. 26, 28, May 16, Oct. 3): [12] and ✕ Kiel - Hamburg - Basel - Zürich.
- – ①–⑥ (not Mar. 28, May 16, Aug. 15, Nov. 1): [12] and (🍸) Paris Lyon - Basel - Zürich.
- – Ⓑ (not Dec. 25, Jan. 1, May 5, July 14, Nov. 11): [12] and (🍸) Zürich - Basel - Paris Lyon.

- [12] and ✕ Frankfurt (Main) - Basel - Zürich and v.v.
- [12] and ✕ Hamburg - Basel - Zürich / Chur and v.v.
- [12] and ✕ Kiel - Hamburg - Basel - Zürich and v.v.
- [12] and ✕ München - St Gallen - Basel and v.v.
- [12] and (🍸) Paris Lyon - Basel - Zürich and v.v.

- d – ⚒ only.
- j – Dec. 13 - Jan. 3, Mar. 11 - Dec. 10.
- k – Jan. 4 - Mar. 10.
- m – Dec. 13 - June 11.
- n – June 12 - Dec. 10.
- p – Jan. 1.
- q – Not Jan. 1.
- r – By connecting train on ⑥ (not Dec. 26, Jan. 2).
- t – By connecting train on ⑤⑥⑦ (also Mar. 28, May 5, 16, Aug. 1).
- v – Apr. 3 - July 1, Aug. 29 - Dec. 10.
- w – Dec. 13 - Apr. 2, July 2 - Aug. 28.
- x – ⑥ (also Dec. 25, Jan. 1, May 5, July 14, Nov. 11).
- y – ⑦ (also Mar. 28, May 16, Aug. 15, Nov. 1).
- z – ⑥⑦ (also Aug. 1).

511 BERN - PAYERNE and NEUCHÂTEL

km																		n						
0	**Bern** d.	0553	...	...	0653	0708	...	...	and at	2053	2108	...	...	...	2153	2208	...	...	2253	2308	...	2337	0008	...
22	Kerzers ▲ d.	0610	0634	...	0710	0731	0734	...	the same	2110	2131	2134	...	...	2210	2231	2234	...	2310	2331	2334	0003	0034	0036
	Murten d.	|	0643	0703	|	|	0743	0803	minutes	|	|	2143	2203	...	|	|	2243	2303	|	|	2343	|	|	0045
	Avenches d.	|	0649**d**	0711	|	|	...	0811	past each	|	|	...	2211	...	|	|	...	2311	|	|	2350	|	|	...
	Payerne **504** a.	|	0657**d**	0723	|	|	...	0823	hour	|	|	...	2223	...	|	|	...	2323	|	|	0002	|	|	...
30	Ins **508** d.	0617	...	...	0717	0738	...	...	until	2117	2138	...	...	...	2217	2238	...	...	2317	2338	...	0013	0041	...
43	**Neuchâtel 508** a.	0627	...	...	0727	0757	...	...		2127	2157	...	...	...	2227	2257	...	...	2327	2357	...	0026	0056	...

km																								
	Neuchâtel 508 d.	0536	...	0601	0633	...	...	0701	0733	...	...	0801	0833	and at	...	...	2201	2233	...	2301	...	2333	...	0009
	Ins **508** d.	0552	...	0617	0643	...	...	0717	0743	...	...	0817	0843	the same	...	...	2217	2243	...	2317	...	2343	...	0025
0	Payerne **504** d.	|	0556**d**	|	|	0634	0701**d**	|	|	0734	...	|	|	minutes	2134	...	|	|	2236	|	...	|	...	|
11	Avenches d.	|	0609**d**	|	|	0648	0710**d**	|	|	0748	...	|	|	past each	2148	...	|	|	2248	|	...	|	...	|
18	Murten d.	|	0617	|	|	0656	0717	|	|	0756	0817	|	|	hour	2156	2217	|	|	2256	|	2317	|	...	|
26	Kerzers ▲ d.	0600	0626	0630	0649	...	0726	0730	0749	...	0826	0830	0849	until	...	2226	2230	2249	...	2324	2330	2349	...	0032
	Bern a.	0626	...	0652	0707	...	...	0752	0807	...	...	0852	0907		...	...	2252	2307	...	...	2352	0012	...	...

d – ⚒ only.
m – ⑥⑦ (also Dec. 25, Jan. 1, Mar. 25, 28, May 5, 16, Aug. 1).
n – ①②③④⑦ (also Dec. 25, 26, Jan. 1, 2, Mar. 25).

▲ – **Rail service KERZERS - LYSS and v.v.**: *17 km*, journey 20 minutes.
From **Kerzers**: 0606 and hourly until 2306. From **Lyss**: 0535 and hourly until 2335, then 0009.

512 BIEL and NEUCHÂTEL - LA CHAUX DE FONDS - LE LOCLE

km																								
0	**Biel / Bienne** d.	0547	...	0647	...	...	0747	...	and at	1847	...	...	1947	...	...	...	2047	...	2147	...	2247	...	...	2347
28	St Imier d.	0613	...	0713	...	...	0813	...	the same	1913	...	...	2017	...	...	...	2117	...	2217	...	2317	...	...	0017
	Neuchâtel d.	|	0600	|	0700	...	|	0800	minutes	|	1900	...	|	2000	...	2100	|	...	|	2200	|	2300	...	|
44	La Chaux de Fonds d.	0628	0631	0728	0731	...	0828	0831	past each	1928	1931	...	2034	2037	...	2131	2134	...	2234	2237	2334	2337	...	0034
52	**Le Locle** a.	...	0639	...	0739	...	...	0839	hour until	...	1939	...	...	2045	...	2139	...	...	...	2245	...	2345	...	...

km																								
0	**Le Locle** d.	0521	...	0621	...	0721	...	...	0821	...	and at	1921	...	...	2021	...	...	2113	...	2221	...	...	2321	...
8	La Chaux de Fonds a.	0529	0532	0629	0632	0729	0732	...	0829	0832	the same	1929	1932	...	2029	2044	...	2121	2144	2229	2244	...	2329	2344
37	**Neuchâtel** a.	0600	|	0700	|	0800	|	...	0900	|	minutes	2000	|	...	2100	|	...	2200	|	2300	|	...	2400	|
	St Imier d.	...	0545	...	0645	...	0745	...	...	0845	past each	...	1945	...	...	2100	...	...	2200	...	2300	...	...	0000
	Biel / Bienne a.	...	0612	...	0712	...	0812	...	...	0912	hour until	...	2012	...	...	2140	...	...	2240	...	2340	...	...	0040

Additional services operate.

513 BERN - BIEL

km		Ⓐ						and at the																	
0	**Bern** d.	0500	0530	0600	0613	0630	0643	same minutes	2000	2013	2030	2043	...	2100	2113	2130	2200	2213	2232	2300	2313	2332	0013	0015
23	Lyss d.	0522	0552	0622	0630	0652	0700	past each	2022	2030	2052	2100	...	2122	2130	2152	2222	2230	2254	2322	2330	2354	0030	0037
34	**Biel / Bienne** a.	0535	0605	0635	0638	0705	0708	hour until	2035	2038	2105	2108	...	2135	2138	2205	2235	2238	2307	2335	2338	0007	0038	0050

							and at the																
Biel / Bienne d.	0518	...	0552	0554	0622	0624	same minutes	1952	1954	2022	2024	...	2052	2054	2122	2124	2154	2222	2224	2254	2322	2324	2354
Lyss d.	0531	...	0601	0607	0631	0637	past each	2001	2007	2031	2037	...	2101	2107	2131	2137	2207	2231	2237	2307	2331	2337	0007
Bern a.	0554	...	0617	0630	0647	0700	hour until	2017	2030	2047	2100	...	2117	2130	2147	2200	2230	2247	2300	2330	2347	2400	0030

y – ⑥⑦ (also Jan. 1; not Mar. 26).

514 BERN - LUZERN via Langnau

For faster services Bern - (Olten -) Luzern see Tables 505 / 565

km													
0	**Bern** d.	0536**a**	0612	0636	0712	and at	2136	2212	2236	2312	2342	0012
21	Konolfingen d.	0552**a**	0634	0652	0734	the same	2152	2234	2252	2334	2356	0034
38	Langnau d.	0605	0652	0705	0752	minutes	2205	2252	2305	2352	0008	0052
75	Wolhusen d.	0645	...	0745	...	past each	2245	...	2345	...	...	...
96	**Luzern** a.	0703	...	0803	...	hour until	2303	...	0010	...	...	...

Luzern d.	0557	...	and at	2057	...	2157	2216	...	...	2316
Wolhusen d.	0615	...	the same	2115	...	2215	2240	...	...	2344
Langnau d.	0653	0707	minutes	2153	2207	2253	...	2307	0008	0021
Konolfingen d.	0707	0725	past each	2207	2225	2307	...	2325	0026	...
Bern a.	0726	0748	hour until	2226	2248	2326	...	2348	0049	...

a – Ⓐ only.

Additional services operate.

515 DELÉMONT - DELLE

km										
0	**Biel / Bienne** **505a** d.	0619	...	0719	and at	2119	...	2219	2319	...
24	Moutier **505a** d.	0639	...	0739	the same	2139	...	2239	2339	...
35	Delémont **505a** d.	0650	...	0750	minutes	2150	...	2250	2350	...
63	Porrentruy d.	0722	...	0822	past each	2222	...	2322	0017	...
75	Delle ▲ a.	0740	...	0840	hour until	2240	...	2340	...	...

Delle ▲ d.	...	0519	0619	...	0719	and at	2019	...
Porrentruy d.	0435	0542	0642	...	0742	the same	2042	...
Delémont **505a** d.	0512	0612	0712	...	0812	minutes	2112	...
Moutier **505a** a.	0522	0622	0722	...	0822	past each	2122	...
Biel / Bienne **505a** a.	0541	0640	0741	...	0841	hour until	2141	...

▲ – 🚌 connection available Delle - Belfort Montbéliard TGV and v.v.

516 BERN - SOLOTHURN

Narrow gauge. F

km		⚒	⚒				and at the same																
0	**Bern** RBS d.	0513	0550	...	0605	0635	minutes past	1905	1935	...	2005	...	2035	2105	2141	...	2211	2241	2311	2341	...	0011
34	Solothurn a.	0556	0627	...	0642	0712	each hour until	1942	2012	...	2042	...	2112	2142	2223	...	2253	2323	2353	0023	...	0053

						and at the same															
Solothurn d.	0519	0549	...	0619	0649	minutes past	1919	1949	...	2019	...	2049	2119	...	2135	2208	...	2238	2308	...	2338	...
Bern RBS a.	0556	0626	...	0656	0726	each hour until	1956	2026	...	2056	...	2126	2156	...	2220	2250	...	2320	2350	...	0020	...

y – ⑥⑦ only.

Additional services operate on Ⓐ.

SOLOTHURN - BURGDORF - THUN 517

Solothurn d.	0545	0645	0745	0845	...	0945	1016	...		1845	1916	...	...	2016	...	2116	...	2216	...	2316	...	...	...
Biberist Ost d.	0550	0650	0750	0850	...	0950	1021	...	and at	1850	1921	...	...	2021	...	2121	...	2221	...	2321	...	...	...
Burgdorf a.	0612	0712	0812	0912	...	1012	1045	...	the same	1912	1945	...	...	2045	...	2145	...	2245	...	2345	...	...	...
Burgdorf d.	0626	0726	0826	0926	...	1026	*1049*	...	minutes	1926	*1949*	...	...	*2049*	...	*2149*	...	*2249*	...	*2349*	...	...	...
Hasle-Rüegsau d.	0638	0738	0838	0938	...	1038	*1057*	1102	past each	1938	*1957*	2002	...	*2057*	2101	*2157*	2201	*2257*	2301	*2357*	0001	...	...
Konolfingen a.	0700	0800	0900	1000	...	1100	...	1122	hour	2000	...	2022	...	...	2122	...	2222	...	2322	...	0022	...	...
Konolfingen d.	0701	0801	0901	1001	...	1101	...	1135	until	2001	...	2035	...	...	2136	...	2236	...	2336	...	0036	...	...
Thun a.	0719	0819	0919	1019	...	1119	...	1156		2019	...	2056	...	...	2156	...	2256	...	2356	...	0056	...	...

	Ⓐ																							
d.	0532	0639	0739	0839	0939	...	1039	1103	...		1839	1903	...	...	1939	2009	...	2109	...	2209	...	2309	...	0009
ngen a.	0553	0658	0758	0858	0958	...	1058	1124	...	and at	1858	1924	...	...	1958	2030	...	2130	...	2230	...	2330	...	0030
ngen d.	0600	0700	0800	0900	1000	...	1100	1136	...	the same	1900	1936	...	...	2000	2036	...	2136	...	2236	...	2336	...	0036
Rüegsau d.	0622	0722	0822	0922	1022	...	1122	1156	*1202*	minutes	1922	1956	*2002*	...	2022	2057	*2102*	2157	*2202*	2257	*2302*	2357	*0002*	0057
rf a.	0632	0732	0832	0932	1032	...	1132	...	*1211*	past each	1932	...	*2011*	...	2032	...	*2111*	...	*2211*	...	*2311*	...	*0011*	0106
rf d.	0646	0746	0846	0946	1046	...	1146	...	1215	hour	1946	...	2015	...	...	...	2115	...	2215	...	2315	...	0015	...
Ost a.	0706	0806	0906	1006	1106	...	1206	...	1236	until	2006	...	2036	...	...	...	2136	...	2236	...	2336	...	0036	...
urn a.	0713	0813	0913	1013	1113	...	1213	...	1243		2013	...	2043	...	...	...	2143	...	2243	...	2343	...	0043	...

Additional services operate

ZÜRICH - SARGANS - CHUR 520

	RE 4857	*RE* 5059	*IC* 557	*RJ* 161 W	*IC* 911	*RE* 5061	*IC* 559	*IC* 913 Ⓐ	*ICE* 1253 Ⓒ	*RE* 5063	*ICE* 1255 Ⓐ	*IC* 561	*EC* 163 T		*RE* 5065	*IC* 563	*ICE* 271 G	*RE* 5067	*IC* 565	*RJ* 165 B	*RE* 5069	*IC* 567	*IC* 921	*RE* 5071
Basel SBB 510 d.	...	...	...		...	...	0633	...	0707	...	0733	0733	...	...	...	0833	0907	...	0933	...	...	...	...	...
Zürich HB d.	...	0612	0637	0640	0707	0712	0737	0807	0807	0812	0837	0837	0840	...	0912	0937	1007	1012	1037	1040	1112	1137	1207	1212
Thalwil d.	...	0621	|	|	|	0721	|	|	|	0821	|	|	|	...	0921	|	|	1021	|	|	1121	|	|	1221
Wädenswil d.	...	0632	|	|	|	0732	|	|	|	0832	|	|	|	...	0932	|	|	1032	|	|	1132	|	|	1232
Pfäffikon d.	...	0641	|	|	|	0741	|	|	|	0841	|	|	|	...	0941	|	|	1041	|	|	1141	|	|	1241
Ziegelbrücke d.	...	0659	|	|	|	0759	|	|	|	0859	|	|	|	...	0959	|	|	1059	|	|	1159	|	|	1259
Sargans 534 d.	0627	0723	0733	0737	0803	0823	0833	0903	0903	0923	0933	0933	0937	...	1023	1033	1103	1123	1133	1137	1223	1233	1303	1323
Buchs 534 a.	|	|	|	0748	|	|	|	|	|	|	|	|	0948	...	|	|	|	|	|	1148	|	|	|	|
Landquart d.	0640	0734	0743	...	0813	0834	0843	0913	0913	0934	0943	0943	...	...	1034	1043	1113	1134	1143	...	1234	1243	1313	1334
Chur 540 a.	0649	0743	0752	...	0822	0843	0852	0922	0922	0943	0952	0952	...	...	1043	1052	1122	1143	1152	...	1243	1252	1322	1343

	IC 569	*RJ* 167 W	*RE* 5073	*IC* 571	*ICE* 71 G	*RE* 5075	*IC* 573	*RJ* 169 W		*RE* 5077	*IC* 575	*IC* 929	*RE* 5079	*IC* 577	*RJ* 361 W	*RE* 5081	*IC* 579	*ICE* 1175 x	*IC* 933 y	*ICE* 75 z		*RE* 5083	*IC* 581	*RJ* 363 N	*RE* 5085
l SBB 510 d.	1133	...	...	1233	1307	...	...	...	...	...	1433	...	...	...	...	...	1633	1707	...	1707	...	...	1733	...	...
HB d.	1237	1240	1312	1337	1407	1412	1437	1440	...	1512	1537	1607	1612	1637	1640	1712	1737	1807	1807	1807	...	1812	1837	1840	1912
d.	|	|	1321	|	|	1421	|	|	...	1521	|	|	1621	|	|	1721	|	|	|	|	...	1821	|	|	1921
swil d.	|	|	1332	|	|	1432	|	|	...	1532	|	|	1632	|	|	1732	|	|	|	|	...	1832	|	|	1932
n d.	|	|	1341	|	|	1441	|	|	...	1541	|	|	1641	|	|	1741	|	|	|	|	...	1841	|	|	1941
rücke d.	|	|	1359	|	|	1459	|	|	...	1559	|	|	1659	|	|	1759	|	|	|	|	...	1859	|	|	1959
ns 534 d.	1333	1337	1423	1433	1503	1523	1533	1537	...	1623	1633	1703	1723	1733	1737	1823	1833	1903	1903	1903	...	1923	1933	1937	2023
s 534 a.	|	1348	|	|	|	|	|	1548	...	|	|	|	|	|	1748	|	|	|	|	|	...	|	|	1948	|
uart d.	1343	...	1434	1443	1513	1534	1543	...	...	1634	1643	1713	1734	1743	...	1834	1843	1913	1913	1913	...	1934	1943	...	2034
40 a.	1352	...	1443	1452	1522	1543	1552	...	...	1643	1652	1722	1743	1752	...	1843	1852	1922	1922	1922	...	1943	1952	...	2043

	IC 593 n	*IC* 583 p	*RE* 5087	*IC* 585	*RE* 5089	*IC* 597 m	*IC* 587 j	*RE* 5091	*RE* 5093	*RE* 5095 k
l SBB 510 d.	...	1833	...	...	...	...	2033	...	...	...
HB d.	1937	1937	2012	2037	2112	2137	2137	2212	2312	0020
d.	|	|	2021	|	2121	|	|	2221	2321	0028
swil d.	|	|	2032	|	2132	|	|	2232	2332	0037
n d.	|	|	2041	|	2141	|	|	2241	2341	|
rücke d.	|	|	2059	|	2159	|	|	2259	0000	|
ns 534 d.	2033	2033	2124	2133	2224	2233	2233	2324	0028	0117
ns 534 a.	|	|	|	|	|	|	|	|	|	|
uart d.	2043	2043	2135	2143	2235	2243	2243	2336	0038	0128
540 a.	2052	2052	2144	2152	2243	2252	2252	2345	0047	0136

	IC 556 ⚒	*RE* 5056	*IC* 558	*RE* 5058	*IC* 912 Ⓐ	*IC* 560	*RE* 5060		*IC* 562	*RE* 5062
Chur 540 d.	0509	0516	0609	0616	0639	0709	0716	...	0809	0816
Landquart d.	0519	0525	0619	0625	0649	0719	0725	...	0819	0825
Buchs 534 d.	|	|	|	|	|	|	|	...	|	|
Sargans 534 d.	0528	0537	0628	0637	0658	0728	0737	...	0828	0837
Ziegelbrücke d.	|	0600	|	0700	|	|	0800	...	|	0900
Pfäffikon d.	|	0619	|	0719	|	|	0819	...	|	0919
Wädenswil d.	|	0629	|	0729	|	|	0829	...	|	0929
Thalwil d.	|	0639	|	0739	|	|	0839	...	|	0939
Zürich HB a.	0623	0648	0723	0748	0753	0823	0848	...	0923	0948
Basel SBB 510 a.	0727	...	...	...	...	0927	...	...	1027e	...

	IC 916	*IC* 564	*RE* 5064		*RJ* 360 N	*IC* 566	*RE* 5066		*ICE* 72 G	*IC* 568	*RE* 5068		*RJ* 362 W	*IC* 570	*RE* 5070	*ICE* 70 G		*IC* 572	*RE* 5072	*RJ* 160 W	*IC* 574		*RE* 5074	*IC* 928	*IC* 576
540 d.	0839	0909	0916	...	...	1009	1016	...	1039	1109	1116	...	...	1209	1216	1239	...	1309	1316	...	1409	...	1416	1439	1509
uart d.	0849	0919	0925	...	...	1019	1025	...	1049	1119	1125	...	...	1219	1225	1249	...	1319	1325	...	1419	...	1425	1449	1519
ns 534 d.	|	|	|	...	1012	|	|	...	|	|	|	...	1212	|	|	|	...	|	|	1412	|	...	|	|	|
ns 534 d.	0858	0928	0937	...	1025	1028	1037	...	1058	1128	1137	...	1225	1228	1237	1258	...	1328	1337	1425	1428	...	1437	1458	1528
rücke d.	|	|	1000	...	|	|	1100	...	|	|	1200	...	|	|	1300	|	...	|	1400	|	|	...	1500	|	|
n d.	|	|	1019	...	|	|	1119	...	|	|	1219	...	|	|	1319	|	...	|	1419	|	|	...	1519	|	|
swil d.	|	|	1029	...	|	|	1129	...	|	|	1229	...	|	|	1329	|	...	|	1429	|	|	...	1529	|	|
d.	|	|	1039	...	|	|	1139	...	|	|	1239	...	|	|	1339	|	...	|	1439	|	|	...	1539	|	|
HB a.	0953	1023	1048	...	1120	1123	1148	...	1153	1223	1248	...	1320	1323	1348	1353	...	1423	1448	1520	1523	...	1548	1553	1623
l SBB 510 a.	...	1127	...	...	...	...	...	...	1253	1327	...	...	...	...	...	1453	...	1527	...	...	...	...	...	...	1727

	RE 5076	*RJ* 162 B	*IC* 578	*RE* 5078	*ICE* 1256		*IC* 580	*RE* 5080	*EC* 164 T	*IC* 582	*RE* 5082	*IC* 936		*IC* 584	*RE* 5084	*RJ* 166 W	*ICE* 1258 v	*IC* 590 y		*RE* 5086	*IC* 588 †	*RE* 5088	*RJ* 168 W	*RE* 5090	
540 d.	1516	...	1609	1616	1639	...	1709	1716	...	1809	1816	1839	...	1909	1916	...	2009	2009	...	2016	2109	2116	...	2216	...
uart d.	1525	...	1619	1625	1649	...	1719	1725	...	1819	1825	1849	...	1919	1925	...	2019	2019	...	2025	2119	2123	...	2223	...
ns 534 d.	|	1612	|	|	|	...	|	|	1812	|	|	|	...	|	|	2012	|	|	...	|	|	|	2212	|	...
ns 534 d.	1537	1625	1628	1637	1658	...	1728	1737	1825	1828	1837	1858	...	1928	1937	2025	2028	2028	...	2037	2128	2137	2225	2237	...
rücke d.	1600	|	|	1700	|	...	|	1800	|	|	1900	|	...	|	2000	|	|	|	...	2100	|	2200	|	2300	...
on d.	1619	|	|	1719	|	...	|	1819	|	|	1919	|	...	|	2019	|	|	|	...	2119	|	2219	|	2319	...
swil d.	1629	|	|	1729	|	...	|	1829	|	|	1929	|	...	|	2029	|	|	|	...	2129	|	2229	|	2329	...
d.	1639	|	|	1739	|	...	|	1839	|	|	1939	|	...	|	2039	|	|	|	...	2139	|	2239	|	2339	...
HB a.	1648	1720	1723	1748	1753	...	1823	1848	1920	1923	1948	1953	...	2023	2048	2120	2123	2123	...	2148	2223	2248	2320	2348	...
l SBB 510 a.	...	...	1827	...	1853y	...	1927	...	...	2027	...	...	...	2127	...	...	2227	...	...	...	...	...	...	...	...

Additional services SARGANS - BUCHS and v.v.

ns d.	0500	0536	0600	0636	and at the same minutes past each hour until	2200	2236	2300	0000
a.	0512	0544	0612	0644		2212	2244	2312	0012

Buchs d.	0615	0648	0715	0748	and at the same minutes past each hour until	2315	2348	0015	0048
Sargans a.	0624	0659	0724	0759		2324	2359	0024	0059

[12] and ✕ Budapest - Wien - Zürich and v.v.
[12] and ✕ Hamburg / Frankfurt - Basel - Zürich - Chur.
[12] and ✕ Innsbruck - Zürich and v.v.
TRANSALPIN – [12] and ✕ Zürich - Graz and v.v.
[12] and ✕ Wien - Salzburg - Zürich and v.v.

e – Dec. 13 - Apr. 2, Aug. 2 - 28.
j – ①–④ (not Mar. 28).
k – ⑥⑦ (also Jan. 1; not Dec. 26, 27, Mar. 26).
m – ⑤–⑦ (also Mar. 28).
n – ⑥ (not Dec. 26, Jan. 2).

p – Ⓑ (also Dec. 26, Jan. 2).
v – ①–⑥ (not Mar. 28).
x – Dec. 25, 26, Jan. 1, Mar. 26, May 16, Oct. 3.
y – ⑦ (also Mar. 28).
z – ①–⑥ (not Dec. 25, 26, Jan. 1, Mar. 26, 28, May 16, Oct. 3).

522 ZIEGELBRÜCKE - LINTHAL

km											
	Zürich HB ....d.	...	...	...	0643		1743	...	...	...	...
0	Ziegelbrücke ....d.	0430	0530	0630	0730	and	1830	1903	and	2303	0003
11	Glarus ....d.	0444	0544	0644	0744	hourly	1844	1918	hourly	2318	0018
16	Schwanden ....d.	0500	0600	0700	0800	until	1900	1929	until	2329	0025
27	Linthal ....▲ a.	0517	0617	0717	0817		1917	1946		2346	...

	Ⓐ								
Linthal ....▲ d.	0443	0543		1843	...	1946	2011		2311
Schwanden ....d.	0504	0607	and	1907	...	2007	2033	and	2333
Glarus ....d.	0513	0616	hourly	1916	...	2016	2043	hourly	2343
Ziegelbrücke ....a.	0526	0629	until	1929	...	2029	2056	until	2356
Zürich HB ....a.	0617	0717		2017	...	...	...		...

h – Also Aug. 15.

▲ – 🚌 service **Linthal - Flüelen** Bahnhof (Table **550**) and v.v. operates **June 25 - September 25, 2016** o Klausenpass. Ⓡ. Journey time: ± 2 hours 45 minutes. **NO WINTER SERVICE**.
From **Linthal**: 0827Ⓒ **h**, 0927, 1027, 1527, 1727Ⓒ **h**. From **Flüelen**: 0600Ⓒ **h**, 0730, 0930, 1500Ⓒ **h**,
Operator: PostAuto Zentralschweiz, Luzern. ✆ (Luzern) 058 448 06 22, fax: 058 667 34 33.

525 ARTH GOLDAU - ST GALLEN - ROMANSHORN

SBB,

km				2561 S		Ⓐ	Ⓒ	2563 S			2565 S		2567 S			2591 S			2593 S			2595 S	
	Luzern **550** ....d.	...	...	...	...	...	...	...	...	...	...	...	0740	...		1940	...	...	...	...	...	...	...
0	**Arth Goldau** ....d.	...	...	...	...	*0519*	...	...	...	*0619*	...	...	0814	...		2014	...	2113	...	...	2213	...	...
20	Biberbrugg ◐ ....● d.	...	...	...	...	0550	0553	...	...	0653	...	...	0837	...		2037	...	2137	...	...	2237	...	...
26	Samstagern ◐ ....● d.	...	...	...	...	0601	0601	...	...	0701	...	...	|	...	and at	|	...	2145	...	...	2245	...	...
34	Pfäffikon ....● d.	...	...	...	...	0617	0617	...	...	0717	...	...	0854	...	the same	2054	...	2157	...	...	2257	...	...
38	Rapperswil ....● a.	...	...	...	...	0622	0622	...	...	0722	...	...	0859	...	minutes	2102	...	2202	...	...	2302	...	...
38	Rapperswil ....d.	...	...	0603	...	...	...	0703	...	...	0803	...	0903	...	past each	2103	...	...	2203	...	...	2303	...
66	Wattwil ....d.	...	0559	0628	0629	...	...	0728	0729	...	0828	0829	0928	0929	hour	2128	2129	...	2228	...	...	2328	...
89	Herisau ....d.	...	0624	0647	0654	...	...	0747	0754	...	0847	0854	0947	0954	until	2147	2154	...	2247	...	...	2349	...
97	**St Gallen** ....a.	...	0633	0655	0704	...	...	0755	0804	...	0855	0904	0955	1004		2155	2204	...	2255	...	...	2357	...
97	**St Gallen 532** ....d.	0635	...	...	0704	...	...	...	0804	...	...	0904	...	1004		...	2204	...	...	2305	...	...	0004
119	**Romanshorn 532** ....a.	0700	...	...	0730	...	...	...	0830	...	...	0930	...	1030		...	2230	...	...	2330	...	...	0030

		2560 S	Ⓒ	Ⓐ		2562 S				2564 S			2588 S		2590 S		2592 S		2594 S		2596 S	
Romanshorn 532 ....d.	...	...	...	...	0530	...	...	...	0630	...		1830	...	1930	...	2030	...	2130	...	2230	...	2330
St Gallen 532 ....a.	...	...	...	...	0555	...	...	...	0655	...		1855	...	1955	...	2055	...	2155	...	2255	...	2355
St Gallen ....d.	...	...	...	...	0556	0605	...	...	0656	0705		1856	1905	1956	2005	2056	2105	...	2205	...	2305	...
Herisau ....d.	...	0513	...	...	0606	0613	...	...	0706	0713	and at	1906	1913	2006	2013	2106	2113	...	2213	...	2313	...
Wattwil ....d.	...	0533	...	...	0630	0633	...	...	0730	0733	the same	1930	1933	2030	2033	2130	2133	...	2233	...	2333	...
Rapperswil ....a.	...	0557	...	...	...	0657	...	...	...	0757	minutes	...	1957	...	2057	...	2157	...	2257	...	2357	...
Rapperswil ....● d.	0544	...	0636	0636	...	...	0659	...	...	0759	past each	...	1959	...	*2057*	...	*2157*	...	*2257*	...	*0003*	...
Pfäffikon ....● d.	0549	...	0642	0642	...	...	0704	...	...	0805	hour	...	2005	...	*2102*	...	*2202*	...	*2302*	...	*0007*	...
Samstagern ◐ ....● d.	0559	...	0654	0658	...	...	0714	...	...	|	until	...	|	...	*2113*	...	*2213*	...	*2313*	...	*0019*	...
Biberbrugg ◐ ....● d.	0616	...	0702	0705	...	...	0721	...	...	0821		...	2021	...	*2121*	...	*2221*	...	*2321*	...	...	...
Arth Goldau ....a.	0641	...	...	...	...	...	0743	...	...	0844		...	2044	...	*2146*	...	*2246*	...	*2346*	...	...	...
Luzern **550** ....a.	...	...	...	...	...	...	...	...	...	0920		...	2120	...	...	...	...	...	...	...	...	...

km		Ⓐ			and at					
0	**Wädenswil** ....d.	0541	0609	0634	the same	2209	2234	2309	2334	0015
6	Samstagern ....● d.	0549	0617	0642	minutes	2217	2242	2317	2342	0023
11	Biberbrugg ....● d.	0558	0625	0651	past each	2225	2251	2325	2351	0031
17	**Einsiedeln** ....● a.	0605	0632	0658	hour until	2232	2258	2332	2358	0038

	Ⓐ			and at				
Einsiedeln ....● d.	0454	0525	0558	the same	2225	2258	2325	...
Biberbrugg ....● d.	0501	0532	0607	minutes	2232	2307	2332	...
Samstagern ....● d.	0510	0541	0617	past each	2241	2317	2341	...
Wädenswil ....a.	0518	0549	0625	hour until	2249	2325	2349	...

S – VORALPEN EXPRESS – 🚃 Luzern / Arth Goldau / Rapperswil - St Gallen and v.v. Also conveys (🍸) on most services.

t – ⑥⑦ (also Jan 1, Mar. 25, 28, May 5, 6, 16, Aug. 1, Nov. 1; not Dec. 26).

w – ⑤⑥ (also Dec. 31, Mar. 24, 27, May 4, 5, 15, July 31; not Dec. 25).

◐ – For service to Einsiedeln – see panel.

● – Additional services run Einsiedeln - Biberbrugg - Sams - Pfäffikon - Rapperswil and v.v.

* – Operated by SOB, except Rapperswil - Wattwil (SBB)

526 GOSSAU - APPENZELL - WASSERAUEN

Narrow gaug

km		⚒																					🚌 j		
0	**Gossau** ....d.	0547	0647	0747	0851	0951	1051	1121	1151	1221	1251	1321	1421	1521	1551	1621	1721	1751	1851	...	1951	2051	...	2151	2251
5	Herisau ....a.	0554	0654	*0754	0858	0958	1058	1128	1158	1228	1258	1328	1428	1528	1558	1628	1728	1758	1858	...	1958	2058	...	2158	2258
5	Herisau ....d.	0554a	0658	0758	0858	0958	1058	1128	1158	1228	1258	1328	1428	1528	1558	1628	1728	1758	1858	...	1958	2058	...	2158	2258
15	Urnäsch ....d.	0610a	0713	0813	0913	1013	1113	1143	1213	1243	1313	1343	1443	1543	1613	1643	1743	1813	1913	...	2013	2113	...	2213	2313
26	**Appenzell** ....d.	0631a	0731	0831	0931	1031	1131	1201	1231	1301	1330	1401	1501	1601	1631	1701	1803	1831	1932	...	2030	2130	2132	2230	2330
32	**Wasserauen** ....a.	0642a	0742	0842	0942	1042	1142	1212	1242	1312	...	1412	1512	1612	1642	1712	1814	1842	1942	...	*2042*y	...	2142	...	...

																						🚌 j	
Wasserauen ....d.	...	...	0648a	0748	0848	0948	1048	1148	1218	1248	1318	...	1418	1518	1618	1648	1718	1818	1848	...	*1942*y	*2042*y	2142	...
Appenzell ....d.	0530a	0630	0700a	0800	0900	1000	1100	1200	1230	1300	1330	1400	1430	1530	1630	1700	1730	1830	1900	1930	2000	2100	2153	2200
Urnäsch ....d.	0545a	0645	0715a	0815	0915	1015	1115	1215	1245	1315	1345	1415	1445	1545	1645	1715	1745	1845	1915	1945	2015	2115	...	2215
Herisau ....a.	0600a	0700	0730a	0830	0930	1030	1130	1230	1300	1330	1400	1430	1500	1600	1700	1730	1800	1900	1930	2000	2030	2130	...	2230
Herisau ....d.	0601	0701	0731	0831	0931	1031	1131	1231	1301	1331	1401	1431	1501	1601	1701	1731	1801	1901	1931	2001	2031	2131	...	2231
Gossau ....a.	0607	0707	0737	0837	0937	1037	1137	1237	1307	1337	1407	1437	1507	1607	1707	1737	1807	1907	1937	2007	2037	2137	...	2237

a – Ⓐ only. j – May 1 - Oct. 30. y – Connection by 🚌. Additional services operate May 1 - Oct. 30.

527 ST GALLEN - APPENZELL

Narrow gauge rack railwa

km		⚒	⚒	Ⓐ			⚒			and			Ⓐ								Ⓐ		🚌	🚌	🚌 y	🚌 z
0	**St Gallen** ....d.	0608	0638a	0704	0738d	0808	0838	0908	0938	every	1608	1638	1708	1722	1740	1810	1840	1910	1940	2010	2110	2140	2230	2330	0030	0135
7	Teufen ....d.	0624	0654a	0724	0754d	0824	0854	0924	0954	30	1624	1654	1724	1738	1756	1826	1856	1926	1956	2026	2126	2156	2242	2342	0042	0147
14	Gais ▲ ....d.	0640	0710	0740	0810	0840	0910	0940	1010	mins.	1640	1710	1740	1750	1812	1842	1912	1942	2012	2042	2142	2212	2252	2352	0052	0157
20	**Appenzell** ..a.	0651	0721	0751	0821	0851	0921	0951	1021	until	1651	1721	1751c	1759	1823	1853	1923	1953	2023	2053	2153	2223	2302	0002	0102	0207

	⚒	Ⓐ	⚒	Ⓐ		⚒				and				Ⓒ	Ⓐ						Ⓐ		🚌	🚌	🚌
Appenzell ....d.	0515	0608	0638	0701	0708c	0738	0808	0838	0908	every	1538	1608	1638	1708	1708	1738	1810	1840	1910	1940	2010	2040	2105	2155	2249
Gais ▲ ....d.	0527	0620	0650	0711	0720	0750	0820	0850	0920	30	1550	1620	1650	1720	1725	1750	1822	1852	1922	1952	2022	2052	2114	2204	2258
Teufen ....d.	0540	0633	0703	0723	0733	0803	0833	0903	0933	mins.	1603	1633	1703	1733	1738	1805	1835	1905	1935	2005	2035	2105	2124	2214	2308
St Gallen ....a.	0558	0651	0721	0740	0751	0821	0851	0921	0951	until	1621	1651	1721	1753	1758	1823	1853	1923	1953	2023	2053	2123	2137	2228	2321

a – Ⓐ only.
c – Ⓒ only.
d – ⚒ only.
k – ⑤⑥ (also Dec. 31, Mar. 24, 27, May 4, 5, 15, July 31, Oct. 31; not Dec. 25).
y – ⑥⑦ (also Jan. 1, Mar. 25, 28, May 5, 6, 16, Aug. 1, Nov. 1; not Dec. 26).
z – ⑥⑦ (also Jan. 1, Mar. 25, 28, May 5, 6, 16, Aug. 1, Nov. 1; not Dec. 26). Supplement payable.

▲ – Rail service **Gais - Altstätten Stadt** and v.v. *8 km*. Journey time: 19 - 22 minutes. **Operator**
From **Gais**: 0621Ⓐ, 0721 and hourly until 1821, then 1921🚌, 2021🚌.
From **Altstätten Stadt**: 0648Ⓐ, 0748 and hourly until 1848, then 1948🚌, 2048🚌.
A bus connects Altstätten Stadt with Altstätten SBB station (Table **534**). Journey time: 6 minutes.

529 ZÜRICH - ZÜRICH FLUGHAFEN ✈

Journey time: 9 - 13 minutes

From **Zürich** HB:
0502, 0514, 0533, 0544, 0546, 0552, 0601, 0607, 0609, 0614, 0616, 0633, 0637, 0639, 0644, 0646, 0652, 0707, 0714, 0716, 0733, 0737, 0739, 0744, 0746, 0752, then 10 - 13 trains per hour until 2052, then 2107, 2109, 2114, 2116, 2137, 2139, 2144, 2146, 2207, 2209, 2214, 2216, 2237, 2239, 2244, 2246, 2307, 2309, 2314, 2316, 2337, 2344, 2346, 0014, 0017.

From **Zürich** Flughafen:
0500, 0533, 0540, 0556, 0601, 0603, 0606, 0610, 0613, 0631, 0633, 0636, 0640, 0643, 0656, 0701, 0703, 0706, 0710, 0713, 0718, 0731, 0733, 0736, 0740, 0743, 0756, then 10 - 13 trains per hour until 2056, then 2101, 2103, 2106, 2110, 2113, 2131, 2133, 2136, 2140, 2201, 2203, 2210, 2213, 2231, 2233, 2236, 2240, 2301, 2303, 2313, 2331, 2333, 2336, 2343, 0003, 0005, 0013, 0033, 0043.

ZÜRICH - ST GALLEN 530

	IC 701	IR 2255	IC 703	ICN 1507	IR 2247 h	EC 191 Mj	IC 705 F	ICN 1509	IR 2251	IC 707	ICN 1511	EC 193 M	IC 709	ICN 1513	IR 2263	IC 711	ICN 1515	IR 2265	IC 713	ICN 1517	IR 2267	IC 715	ICN 1519
Genève Aéroport ✈ **505** d.	...	...	...	...	...	...	...	...	...	...	...	...	0633	...	...	0733	...	...	0833	...	...	0933	...
Genève **505** d.	...	...	...	...	...	...	...	...	...	0542	...	...	0642	...	...	0742	...	...	0842	...	...	0942	...
Lausanne **505** d.	...	...	...	...	...	...	...	...	...	0620	0615	...	0720	0715	...	0820	0815	...	0920	0915	...	1020	1015
Biel **505** d.	...	...	...	0516	...	...	...	0616	...	|	0717	...	|	0817	...	|	0917	...	|	1017	...	|	1117
Bern **505** d.	...	...	0515	|	...	...	0632	|	...	0732	|	...	0832	|	...	0932	|	...	1032	|	...	1132	|
Basel **510** d.	...	...	|	|	0547	0547	|	|	...	|	|	0747	|	|	0847	|	|	0947	|	|	1047	|	|
Zürich HB **535** d.	0533	0609	0633	0639	0709	0709	0733	0739	0809	0833	0839	0909	0933	0939	1009	1033	1039	1109	1133	1139	1209	1233	1239
Zürich Flughafen ✈ **535** d.	0544	0621	0644	0652	0721	0721	0744	0752	0821	0844	0851	0921	0944	0951	1021	1044	1051	1121	1144	1151	1221	1244	1251
Winterthur **535** d.	0559	0637	0659	0707	0737	0737	0759	0807	0837	0859	0907	0937	0959	1007	1037	1059	1107	1137	1159	1207	1237	1259	1307
Wil **539** d.	0618	0655	|	0723	0755	0755	|	0823	0855	|	0923	0955	|	1023	1055	|	1123	1155	|	1223	1255	|	1323
Gossau d.	0638	0710	|	0740	0810	0810	|	0840	0910	|	0940	1010	|	1040	1110	|	1140	1210	|	1240	1310	|	1340
St Gallen a.	0648	0718	0735	0748	0818	0818	0835	0848	0918	0935	0948	1018	1035	1048	1118	1135	1148	1218	1235	1248	1318	1335	1348

	EC 195 M	IC 717	ICN 1521	IR 2271	IC 719	ICN 1523	IR 2273	IC 721	ICN 1525	IR 2275	IC 723	ICN 1527	IR 2277	IC 725	ICN 1529	IR 2249 w	EC 197 Mx	IC 727	ICN 1531	IR 2281	IC 729	ICN 1533	IR 2283	ICN 1535
nève Aéroport ✈ **505** d.	...	1033	...	...	1133	...	...	1233	...	...	1333	...	...	1433	...	...	...	1533	...	...	1633	...	...	...
nève **505** d.	...	1042	...	...	1142	...	...	1242	...	...	1342	...	...	1442	...	...	...	1542	...	...	1642	...	...	...
usanne **505** d.	...	1120	1115	...	1220	1215	...	1320	1315	...	1420	1415	...	1520	1515	...	...	1620	1615	...	1720	1715	...	1815
iel **505** d.	...	|	1217	...	|	1317	...	|	1417	...	|	1517	...	|	1617	...	...	|	1717	...	|	1817	...	1917
n **505** d.	...	1232	|	...	1332	|	...	1432	|	...	1532	|	...	1632	|	...	...	1732	|	...	1832	|	...	|
Basel **510** d.	...	|	|	1247	|	|	1347	|	|	1447	|	|	1547	|	|	...	...	|	|	1747	|	|	1847	|
h HB **535** d.	1309	1333	1339	1409	1433	1439	1509	1533	1539	1609	1633	1639	1709	1733	1739	1809	1809	1833	1839	1909	1933	1939	2009	2039
h Flughafen ✈ **535** d.	1321	1344	1351	1421	1444	1452	1521	1544	1551	1621	1644	1651	1721	1744	1751	1821	1821	1844	1851	1921	1944	1951	2021	2051
rthur **535** d.	1337	1359	1407	1437	1459	1507	1537	1559	1607	1637	1659	1707	1737	1759	1807	1837	1837	1859	1907	1937	1959	2007	2037	2107
39 d.	1355	|	1423	1455	|	1523	1555	|	1623	1655	|	1723	1755	|	1823	1855	1855	|	1923	1955	|	2023	2055	2123
au d.	1410	|	1440	1510	|	1540	1610	|	1640	1710	|	1740	1810	|	1840	1910	1910	|	1940	2010	|	2040	2110	2140
allen a.	1418	1435	1448	1518	1535	1548	1618	1635	1648	1718	1735	1748	1818	1835	1848	1918	1918	1935	1948	2018	2035	2048	2118	2148

	IR 2285	ICN 1537	IR 2287	ICN 10549 p	ICN 1539 q	IR 10289 p	IR 2289 q		IR 2293
nève Aéroport ✈ **505** d.	...	...	...	...	...	...	...	...	...
nève **505** d.	...	...	...	...	...	...	...	...	...
usanne **505** d.	...	1915	...	2015	2015	...	...	...	...
iel **505** d.	...	2017	...	2117	2117	...	...	...	...
n **505** d.	...	|	...	|	|	...	...	...	...
Basel **510** d.	1947	|	2047	|	|	2147	2147	...	...
h HB **535** d.	2109	2139	2209	2239	2239	2309	2309	2337	0017
h Flughafen ✈ **535** d.	2121	2151	2221	2252	2252	2321	2321	2348	0028
rthur **535** d.	2137	2207	2237	2307	2307	2337	2337	0003	0043
39 d.	2155	2223	2255	2323	2323	2355	2355	*0025*	0101
au d.	2210	2240	2310	2340	2340	0010	0010	*0041*	0120
allen a.	2218	2248	2318	2348	2348	0018	0018	*0051*	0129

	IC 706	IR 2256	ICN 1510	IC 708	IR 2250	ICN 1512	IC 710	IR 2260	ICN 1514
St Gallen d.	0509	0542	0612	0625	0642	0712	0725	0742	0812
Gossau d.	0518	0550	0620	|	0650	0720	|	0750	0820
Wil **539** d.	0539	0608	0640	|	0708	0740	|	0808	0840
Winterthur **535** d.	0558	0628	0658	0703	0728	0758	0803	0828	0858
Zürich Flughafen ✈ **535** d.	0613	0643	0713	0718	0743	0813	0818	0843	0913
Zürich HB **535** a.	0623	0653	0723	0727	0753	0823	0827	0853	0923
Basel **510** a.	|	0812	|	|	...	|	|	1012	|
Bern **505** a.	0728	...	|	0828	...	|	0928	...	|
Biel **505** a.	|	...	0843	|	...	0943	|	...	1043
Lausanne **505** a.	0840	...	0945	0940	...	1045	1040	...	1145
Genève **505** a.	0918	...	...	1018	...	...	1118	...	...
Genève Aéroport ✈ **505** a.	0927	...	...	1027	...	...	1127	...	...

	IC 712	IR 2262	ICN 1516	IC 714	IR 2264	ICN 1518	IC 716	EC 196 M	ICN 1520	IC 718	IR 2268		ICN 1522	IC 720	IR 2270	ICN 1524	IC 722	IR 2272		ICN 1526	IC 724	IR 2274	ICN 1528	IC 726
allen d.	0825	0842	0912	0925	0942	1012	1025	1042	1112	1125	1142	...	1212	1225	1242	1312	1325	1342	...	1412	1425	1442	1512	1525
au d.	|	0850	0920	|	0950	1020	|	1050	1120	|	1150	...	1220	|	1250	1320	|	1350	...	1420	|	1450	1520	|
39 d.	|	0908	0940	|	1008	1040	|	1108	1140	|	1208	...	1240	|	1308	1340	|	1408	...	1440	|	1508	1540	|
rthur **535** d.	0903	0928	0958	1003	1028	1058	1103	1128	1158	1203	1228	...	1258	1303	1328	1358	1403	1428	...	1458	1503	1528	1558	1603
ch Flughafen ✈ **535** a.	0918	0943	1013	1018	1043	1113	1118	1143	1213	1218	1243	...	1313	1318	1343	1413	1418	1443	...	1513	1518	1543	1613	1618
ch HB **535** a.	0927	0953	1023	1027	1053	1123	1127	1153	1223	1227	1253	...	1323	1327	1353	1423	1427	1453	...	1523	1527	1553	1623	1627
Basel **510** a.	|	1112	|	|	1212	|	|	...	|	|	1412	...	|	|	1512	|	|	1612	...	|	|	1712	|	|
n **505** a.	1028	...	|	1128	...	|	1228	...	|	1328	...	...	|	1428	...	|	1528	...	...	|	1628	...	|	1728
iel **505** a.	|	...	1443	|	...	1243	|	...	1343	|	...	...	1443	|	...	1543	|	...	...	1643	|	...	1743	|
usanne **505** a.	1140	...	1245	1240	...	1345	1340	...	1445	1440	...	...	1545	1540	...	1645	1640	...	...	1745	1740	...	1845	1840
nève **505** a.	1218	...	...	1318	...	...	1418	...	...	1518	...	...	...	1618	...	...	1718	...	...	...	1818	...	...	1918
nève Aéroport ✈ **505** a.	1227	...	...	1327	...	...	1427	...	...	1527	...	...	...	1627	...	...	1727	...	...	...	1827	...	...	1927

	EC 194 M	ICN 1530	IC 728	IR 2278	ICN 1532	IC 730	IR 2280		ICN 1534	IC 732	IR 2282	ICN 1536	IC 734	EC 192 M	ICN 1538		IR 2286	ICN 1540	IR 2248 y	EC 190 Mk	RE 23094	IR 2292	IR 2294	
allen d.	1542	1612	1625	1642	1712	1725	1742	...	1812	1825	1842	1912	1925	1942	2012	...	2042	2112	2142	2142	2212	2242	2342	...
au d.	1550	1620	|	1650	1720	|	1750	...	1820	|	1850	1920	|	1950	2020	...	2050	2120	2150	2150	2220	2250	2350	...
39 d.	1608	1640	|	1708	1740	|	1808	...	1840	|	1908	1940	|	2008	2040	...	2108	2140	2208	2208	2240	2308	0008	...
rthur **535** d.	1628	1658	1703	1728	1758	1803	1828	...	1858	1903	1928	1958	2003	2028	2058	...	2128	2158	2228	2228	2258	2328	0028	...
ch Flughafen ✈ **535** a.	1643	1713	1718	1743	1813	1818	1843	...	1913	1918	1943	2013	2018	2043	2113	...	2143	2213	2243	2243	2313	2343	0043	...
ch HB **535** a.	1653	1723	1727	1753	1823	1827	1853	...	1923	1927	1953	2023	2027	2053	2123	...	2153	2223	2253	2253	2323	2353	0053	...
Basel **510** a.	...	|	|	1912	|	|	2012	...	|	|	2112	|	|	2212	|	...	2312	...	...	...	...	0112	...	...
n **505** a.	...	|	1828	...	|	1928	...	...	|	2028	...	|	2128	...	|	...	...	...	...	...	...	...	...	...
iel **505** a.	...	1843	|	...	1943	|	...	...	2043	|	...	2143	|	...	2243	...	...	...	...	...	...	...	...	...
usanne **505** a.	...	1945	1940	...	2045	2040	...	...	2145	2140	...	2245	2240	...	2345	...	...	...	...	...	...	...	...	...
nève **505** a.	...	...	2018	...	...	2118	...	...	...	2218	...	...	2318	...	...	...	...	...	...	...	...	...	...	...
nève Aéroport ✈ **505** a.	...	...	2027	...	...	2127	...	...	...	2227	...	...	2327	...	...	...	...	...	...	...	...	...	...	...

From / to Fribourg.
From / to München.

h – Jan. 1 only.
j – Not Jan. 1.
k – Not Dec. 24, 31.
p – Jan. 4 - Mar. 10.
q – Dec. 13 - Jan. 3, Mar. 11 - Dec. 10.
w – Dec. 24 only.
x – Not Dec. 24.
y – Dec. 24, 31 only.

WINTERTHUR - SCHAFFHAUSEN 531

					and at the same minutes past each hour until										...								...	
Winterthur d.	0542	0606	0619	0642		1806	1819	1842	1906	1919	1942	2006	2019	2042	...	2106	2119	2142	2206	2242	2306	2342	...	0012
Schaffhausen a.	0613	0638	0646	0713		1838	1846	1913	1938	1946	2013	2038	2046	2113	...	2138	2146	2213	2238	2313	2338	0013	...	0041

						Ⓐ		Ⓐ			Ⓐ					and at the same minutes past each hour until								
ffhausen d.	0514	0521	0546	0614	0621	0631	0646	0700	0714	0721	0731	0746	0814	0821	0846		2014	2021	2046	2121	2146	2221	2246	2321	2346
rthur a.	0541	0554	0619	0641	0654	0659	0719	0729	0741	0754	0759	0819	0841	0854	0919		2041	2054	2119	2154	2219	2254	2319	2354	0023

3, THURBO*

SCHAFFHAUSEN - ROMANSHORN - RORSCHACH 532

Temporarily relocated to page 280

533 SCHAFFHAUSEN - KREUZLINGEN

Valid Mar. 25 - Oct. 16, 2016 (no winter service)

	✕A		✕C		✕A		✕A		
Schaffhausen d.	0910	...	1110	...	1318	...	1518	...	...
Stein am Rhein d.	1115	...	1315	...	1523	...	1723		
Kreuzlingen Hafen a.	1355	...	1555	...	1805	...	2005y	...	...

	✕A		✕B		✕A		✕D	
Kreuzlingen Hafen d.	0900	...	1100	...	1427	...	1627	...
Stein am Rhein d.	1130	...	1330	...	1657	...	1857	...
Schaffhausen a.	1245	...	1445	...	1815	...	2015y	...

A – © Mar. 25 - Apr. 10; daily Apr. 18 - Oct. 3.
B – © Mar. 25 - Apr. 10; daily Apr. 17 - Oct. 16.
C – † Mar. 27 - June 19; daily June 25 - Sept. 11, Oct. 4 - 16 (also Mar. 25, May 26, Sept. 18, 25).
D – † Mar. 25 - June 19 (also May 26, Sept. 18, 25, Oct. 2, 3).
y – Not Aug. 13.

534 WIL - ST GALLEN - BUCHS - CHUR

km		*RE* 4857 R	*RE* 4859 R	*RE* 4861 R	*EC* 191 Mj	*RE* 4863 R	*RE* 4865 R	*EC* 193 B	*RE* 4867 R	*RE* 4869 R	*RE* 4871 R	*RE* 4873 R	*EC* 195 M	*RE* 4875 R	*RE* 4877 R		*RE* 4879 R	*RE* 4881 R	*RE* 4883 R	*EC* 197 Mn	*RE* 4885 R	*RE* 4889 R	*IC* 585			
	Wil 530 d.	500	0601	0701	0755	0801	0901	0955	1001	1101	1201	1301	1355	1401	1501	...	1601	1701	1801	1855	1901	2001	...	2101	2201	2301
0	**St Gallen** d.	0526	0626	0726	0820	0826	0926	1020	1026	1126	1226	1326	1420	1426	1526	...	1626	1726	1826	1920	1926	2026	...	2126	2226	2326
16	Rorschach d.	0540	0640	0740	|	0840	0940	|	1040	1140	1240	1340	|	1440	1540	...	1640	1740	1840	|	1940	2040	...	2140	2240	2340
27	**St Margrethen** d.	0547	0647	0747	0840	0847	0947	1040	1047	1147	1247	1347	1440	1447	1547	...	1647	1747	1847	1940	1947	2047	...	2147	2247	2347
39	Altstätten **527** d.	0600	0700	0800	...	0900	1000	...	1100	1200	1300	1400	...	1500	1600	...	1700	1800	1900	...	2000	2100	...	2200	2300	0000
65	**Buchs 520** ⊖ d.	0615	0715	0815	...	0915	1015	...	1115	1215	1315	1415	...	1515	1615	...	1715	1815	1915	...	2015	2115	...	2215	2315	0015
81	Sargans **520** ⊖ d.	0627	0727	0827	...	0927	1027	...	1127	1227	1327	1427	...	1527	1627	...	1727	1827	1927	...	2027	2124	2133	2224	2324	0024
93	Landquart **520** a.	0638	0736	0836	...	0936	1036	...	1136	1236	1336	1436	...	1536	1636	...	1736	1836	1936	...	2036	...	2141	*2246*	*2346*	...
107	**Chur 520** a.	0649	0748	0848	...	0948	1048	...	1148	1248	1348	1448	...	1548	1648	...	1748	1848	1948	...	2048	...	2152	*2256*	*2356*	...

	IC 556 ⚒	*RE* 4858 R	*RE* 4860 R	*RE* 4862 R	*RE* 4864 R	*RE* 4866 R	*EC* 196 M	*RE* 4868 R	*RE* 4870 R	*RE* 4872 R	*RE* 4874 R	*RE* 4876 R	*EC* 194 M	*RE* 4878 R	*RE* 4880 R	*RE* 4882 R	*RE* 4884 R	*EC* 192 B	*RE* 4886 R	*RE* 4888 R	*EC* 190 Mk	*RE* 5088		*RE* 5090		
Chur 520 d.	0509	...	0612	0712	0812	0912	...	1012	1112	1212	1312	1412	...	1512	1612	1712	1812	...	1912	2012	...	2116	...	2216	...	*2231*
Landquart **520** d.	0519	...	0622	0722	0822	0922	...	1022	1122	1222	1322	1422	...	1522	1622	1722	1822	...	1922	2022	...	2123	...	2223	...	*2239*
Sargans **520** ⊖ d.	0527	0536	0636	0736	0836	0936	...	1036	1136	1236	1336	1436	...	1536	1636	1736	1836	...	1936	2036	...	2132	2136	2232	2236	2300
Buchs 520 ⊖ d.	...	0545	0645	0745	0845	0945	...	1045	1145	1245	1345	1445	...	1545	1645	1745	1845	...	1945	2045	...	...	2145	...	2245	2315
Altstätten **527** d.	...	0601	0701	0801	0901	1001	...	1101	1201	1301	1401	1501	...	1601	1701	1801	1901	...	2001	2101	...	...	2201	...	2301	2338
St Margrethen d.	...	0613	0713	0813	0913	1013	1020	1113	1213	1313	1413	1513	1520	1613	1713	1813	1913	1920	2013	2113	2120	...	2213	...	2313	2352
Rorschach d.	...	0620	0720	0820	0920	1020	|	1120	1220	1320	1420	1520	|	1620	1720	1820	1920	|	2020	2120	|	...	2220	...	2320	0002
St Gallen a.	...	0634	0734	0834	0934	1034	1041	1134	1234	1334	1434	1534	1541	1634	1734	1834	1934	1941	2034	2134	2141	...	2234	...	2334	0020
Wil 530 a.	...	0658	0758	0858	0958	1058	1106	1158	1258	1358	1458	1558	1606	1658	1758	1858	1958	2006	2058	2158	2206	...	2258	...	2358	...

⊖ – services to **VADUZ (LIECHTENSTEIN)**

[line 11]	Ⓐ	Ⓐ	Ⓐ																		
Feldkirch (Bahnhof) d.	...	...	...	...	0624a	0654	0724	0754	and at the same minutes past each hour until	1724	1754	1824	1854	1924	1954	2024	2054	2124	2154	2224	2254
Schaan (Bahnhof) d.	0515	0530	0600	0630	0700	0730	0800	0830		1800	1830	1900	1930	2000	2030	2100	2130	2200	2230	2300	2330
Vaduz Post d.	0524	0541	0611	0641	0711	0741	0811	0841		1811	1841	1908	1941	2008	2041	2108	2141	2208	2241	2308	2338
Sargans (Bahnhof) a.	0554	0612	0642	0712	0742	0812	0842	0912		1842	1912	...	2012	...	2112	...	2212	...	2312f	...	...

[line 11]	Ⓐ	Ⓐ																			
Sargans (Bahnhof) d.	...	...	0544a	0614a	0644	0714a	0744	0814	and at the same minutes past each hour until	1844	1914	1944	...	2044	...	...	2144	...	...	2244	...
Vaduz Post d.	0520	0548	0618	0648	0718	0748	0818	0848		1918	1948	2018	2048	2118	2148	...	2218	2248	...	2318	...
Schaan (Bahnhof) d.	0530	0600	0630	0700	0730	0800	0830	0900		1930	2000	2030	2100	2130	2200	...	2230	2300	...	2328	...
Feldkirch (Bahnhof) a.	0606	0636	0706	0736	0806	0836	0906	0936		2006	2036	2106	2136	2206	2236	...	2306	2336	...	...	...

[line 12] **Buchs** (Bahnhof) - **Vaduz** (Post) and v.v. Journey time: ± 15 minutes. **Service shown operates on Ⓐ only**. Regular services also operate between Buchs and Schaan. Operator: LIEmobil, Postplatz 7, FL-9494 Schaan. ✆ +423 237 94 94, fax +423 237 94 99, (www.liemobil.li).

From **Buchs**: 0630, 0700, 0730, 0750, 1200, 1230, 1300, 1630, 1700, 1730, 1800.
From **Vaduz**: 0639, 0709, 0739, 0749, 1209, 1239, 1309, 1639, 1709, 1739, 1809, 18

B – (12) and ✕ Basel - Zürich - München and v.v.
M – (12) and ✕ Zürich - München and v.v.
R – RHEINTAL EXPRESS.
a – Ⓐ only.
f – ⑤⑥ (also Feb. 4, 8; not Dec. 25, Jan. 1, Mar. 25).
j – Not Jan. 1.
k – Not Dec. 24, 31.
n – Not Dec. 24.

535 ZÜRICH - KONSTANZ and ROMANSHORN

km		*IC* 803	*IR* 2107	*IC* 805	*IR* 2109	*IC* 807	*IR* 2111	*IC* 809	*IR* 2113	*IC* 811	*IR* 2115	*IC* 813	*IR* 2117	*IC* 815	*IR* 2119	*IC* 817	*IR* 2121	*IC* 819	*IR* 2123	*IC* 821	*IR* 2125	*IC* 823	*IR* 2127	*IC* 825	*IR* 2129	*IC* 827
	Brig **560** d.	...	...	...	...	0546	...	0649	...	0749	...	0849	...	0949	...	1049	...	1149	...	1249	...	1349	...	1449	...	1549
	Bern **505 560** d.	...	...	0602	...	0702	...	0802	...	0902	...	1002	...	1102	...	1202	...	1302	...	1402	...	1502	...	1602	...	1702
0	**Zürich** HB **530** d.	0607	0637	0707	0737	0807	0837	0907	0937	1007	1037	1107	1137	1207	1237	1307	1337	1407	1437	1507	1537	1607	1637	1707	1737	1807
10	**Zürich** Flug ✈ **530** d.	0618	0648	0718	0748	0818	0848	0918	0948	1018	1048	1118	1148	1218	1248	1318	1348	1418	1448	1518	1548	1618	1648	1718	1748	1818
30	Winterthur **530** d.	0635	0705	0735	0805	0835	0905	0935	1005	1035	1105	1135	1205	1235	1305	1335	1405	1435	1505	1535	1605	1635	1705	1735	1805	1835
46	Frauenfeld d.	0647	0717	0747	0817	0847	0917	0947	1017	1047	1117	1147	1217	1247	1317	1347	1417	1447	1517	1547	1617	1647	1717	1747	1817	1847
64	Weinfelden **539** ▲ d.	0700	0730	0800	0830	0900	0930	1000	1030	1100	1130	1200	1230	1300	1330	1400	1430	1500	1530	1600	1630	1700	1730	1800	1830	1900
	Kreuzlingen ▲ a.	|	0750	|	0850	|	0950	|	1050	|	1150	|	1250	|	1350	|	1450	|	1550	|	1650	|	1750	|	1850	|
	Konstanz ▲ a.	|	0754	|	0854	|	0954	|	1054	|	1154	|	1254	|	1354	|	1454	|	1554	|	1654	|	1754	|	1854	|
86	**Romanshorn** a.	0718	...	0818	...	0918	...	1018	...	1118	...	1218	...	1318	...	1418	...	1518	...	1618	...	1718	...	1818	...	1918

	IC 829	*IR* 2133	*IC* 831	*IR* 2135	*IC* 833	*IR* 2137	*IC* 835	*IR* 2139 ‡	*IC* 837	*RE* 2145	*IC* 845 Y
Brig **560** d.	1649	...	1749	...	1849	...	1949	...	...	...	...
Bern **505 560** d.	1802	...	1902	...	2002	...	2102	...	2202	...	...
Zürich HB **530** d.	1907	1937	2007	2037	2107	2137	2207	2237	2307	2337	0008
Zürich Flug ✈ **530** d.	1918	1948	2018	2048	2118	2148	2218	2248	2318	2348	0021
Winterthur **530** d.	1935	2005	2035	2105	2135	2205	2235	2305	2335	0005	0036
Frauenfeld d.	1947	2017	2047	2117	2147	2217	2247	2317	2347	0017	0047
Weinfelden **539** ▲ d.	2000	2030	2100	2130	2200	2230	2300	2330	0000	0030	0058
Kreuzlingen ▲ a.	|	2050	|	2150	|	2250	|	2350	|	0050	|
Konstanz ▲ a.	|	2054	|	2154	|	2254	|	2354	|	0054	|
Romanshorn a.	2018	...	2118	...	2218	...	2318	...	0018	...	0116

	IR 2106	*IC* 806	*IR* 2108	*IC* 808	*IR* 2110	*IC* 810	*IR* 2112	*IC* 812	*IR* 2114	*IC* 814
Romanshorn d.		0538	...	0638	...	0741	...	0841	...	0941
Konstanz ▲ d.	0503	|	0603	|	0703	|	0803	|	0903	|
Kreuzlingen ▲ d.	0507	|	0607	|	0707	|	0807	|	0907	|
Weinfelden **539** ▲ d.	0529	0559	0629	0659	0729	0759	0829	0859	0929	0959
Frauenfeld d.	0542	0612	0642	0712	0742	0812	0842	0912	0942	1012
Winterthur **530** d.	0555	0625	0655	0725	0755	0825	0855	0925	0955	1025
Zürich Flughafen ✈ **530** a.	0608	0638	0708	0738	0808	0838	0908	0938	1008	1038
Zürich HB **530** a.	0621	0651	0721	0751	0821	0851	0921	0951	1021	1051
Bern **505 560** a.	...	0758	...	0858	...	0958	...	1058	...	1158
Brig **560** a.	...	0911	...	1011	...	1111	...	1211	...	1311

km		*IC* 816	*IR* 2118	*IC* 818	*IR* 2120	*IC* 820	*IR* 2122	*IC* 822	*IR* 2124	*IC* 824	*IR* 2126	*IC* 826	*IR* 2128	*IC* 828	*IR* 2130	*IC* 830	*IR* 2132	*IC* 832	*IR* 2134	*IC* 834	*IR* 2136	*IC* 836	*IR* 2138 ‡	*IC* 838	*RE* 2144	*IC* 840
	Romanshorn d.	1041	...	1141	...	1241	...	1341	...	1441	...	1541	...	1641	...	1741	...	1841	...	1941	...	2041	...	2141	...	2241
0	**Konstanz** ▲ d.	|	1103	|	1203	|	1303	|	1403	|	1503	|	1603	|	1703	|	1803	|	1903	|	2003	|	2103	|	2203	|
1	Kreuzlingen ▲ d.	|	1107	|	1207	|	1307	|	1407	|	1507	|	1607	|	1707	|	1807	|	1907	|	2007	|	2107	|	2207	|
24	Weinfelden **539** ▲ d.	1059	1129	1159	1229	1259	1329	1359	1429	1459	1529	1559	1629	1659	1729	1759	1829	1859	1929	1959	2029	2059	2129	2159	2229	2259
	Frauenfeld d.	1112	1142	1212	1242	1312	1342	1412	1442	1512	1542	1612	1642	1712	1742	1812	1842	1912	1942	2012	2042	2112	2142	2212	2242	2312
	Winterthur **530** d.	1125	1155	1225	1255	1325	1355	1425	1455	1525	1555	1625	1655	1725	1755	1825	1855	1925	1955	2025	2055	2125	2155	2225	2258	2325
	Zürich Flug ✈ **530** a.	1138	1208	1238	1308	1338	1408	1438	1508	1538	1608	1638	1708	1738	1808	1838	1908	1938	2008	2038	2108	2138	2208	2238	2311	2338
	Zürich HB **530** a.	1151	1221	1251	1321	1351	1421	1451	1521	1551	1621	1651	1721	1751	1821	1851	1921	1951	2021	2051	2121	2151	2221	2251	2323	2351
	Bern **505 560** a.	1258	...	1358	...	1458	...	1558	...	1658	...	1758	...	1858	...	1958	...	2058	...	2158	...	2302	...	0002	...	...
	Brig **560** a.	1411	...	1511	...	1611	...	1711	...	1811	...	1911	...	2011	...	2111	...	...	...	...	...	...	...	...	...	...

Y – ⑥⑦ (also Jan. 1; not Mar. 26).
‡ – Runs as *RE* train on ⑦–④ (also Mar. 25; not Dec. 31).

▲ – Additional services operate **Weinfelden - Konstanz and v.v.** journey time: 30 – 36 minutes. A change of trains may be necessary at Kreuzlingen. *Subject to alteration Mar. 1 - Dec. 10 owing to engineering*

From **Weinfelden**: 0528Ⓐ, 0602, 0628Ⓐ, 0702, 0735Ⓐ, 0802, 0902, 1002, 1102, 1202, 1302, 1402, 1502, 1602, 163
1702, 1735Ⓐ, 1802, 1835Ⓐ, 1902, 1935Ⓐ, 2002, 2102, 2202, 2302, 0002.

From **Konstanz**: 0521, 0550Ⓐ, 0621, 0648Ⓐ, 0721, 0748Ⓐ, 0821, 0921, 1021, 1121, 1221, 1321, 1421, 1521, 154
1621, 1648Ⓐ, 1721, 1748Ⓐ, 1821, 1848Ⓐ, 1921, 2021, 2121, 2221, 2321.

ROMANSHORN - FRIEDRICHSHAFEN car ferry service 536

Journey time: 41 minutes. ✕ available 0836 - 2036 from Romanshorn; 0841 - 2041 from Friedrichshafen. 🍸 on other sailings. Operator: SBS ✆ 071 466 78 88

Romanshorn: 0936 and hourly until 1636.
Friedrichshafen: 0941 and hourly until 1641.

Services shown operate daily. Additional hourly service available on certain dates from 0536 - 0836 and 1736 - 2036 from Romanshorn; 0541 - 0841 and 1741 - 2041 from Friedrichshafen.

WEINFELDEN - WIL 539

RBO

	Ⓐ		Ⓐ		Ⓐ		Ⓐ			and	
Weinfelden 535 d.	0502	0532	0602	0632	0702	0732	0802	...	0832	hourly	2332
Wil 530 a.	0529	0555	0629	0655	0729	0755	0829	...	0855	until	2355

	Ⓐ		Ⓐ		Ⓐ		Ⓐ		and		
Wil 530 d.	0531	0601	0631	0701	0731	0801	0831	0901	hourly	2301	0001
Weinfelden 535 a.	0557	0625	0657	0725	0757	0825	0857	0925	until	2325	0025

Additional services operate on Ⓐ:
Weinfelden depart 1602, 1702, 1802, 1902; Wil depart 1631, 1731, 1831, 1931.

CHUR - ST MORITZ 540

Narrow gauge

For *Glacier Express* services see Table **575**

	2⚒	⚒		△		951 ♦🅁✓	△	961 ♦🅁✓		△	△	△	△	△	△		△	△	△	△	△		K
Chur 575 d.	0502	...	0658	0758	...	0832	0858	...	...	0958	1058	1158	1258	1358	1458	...	1558	1658	1758	1858	1958	2056	...
Reichenau-Tamins **575** d.	0514	...	0710	0808	...	|	0908	...	...	1008	1108	1208	1308	1408	1508	...	1608	1708	1808	1908	2008	2107	...
Thusis d.	0541	...	0730	0830	...	|	0930	...	...	1030	1130	1230	1330	1430	1530	...	1630	1730	1830	1930	2030	2133	...
Tiefencastel d.	0558	...	0747	0847	...	0918	0947	...	...	1047	1147	1247	1347	1447	1547	...	1647	1747	1847	1947	2047	2149r	...
Davos Platz d.	|	...	|	|	...	|	|	0953	...	|	|	|	|	|	|	...	|	|	|	|	|	|	...
Filisur 545a d.	0613	...	0802	0902	...	0933u	1002	1016u	...	1102	1202	1302	1402	1502	1602	...	1702	1802	1902	2002	2102	2205r	...
Bergün / Bravuogn d.	0630	...	0814	0914	...	0947u	1014	1029u	...	1114	1214	1314	1414	1514	1614	...	1714	1814	1914	2014	2114	2217r	...
Preda d.	0645x	...	0830	0930	...	|	1030	|	...	1130	1230	1330	1430	1530	1630	...	1730	1830	1930	2030	2130	2233r	...
Samedan a.	0700	...	0845	0945	...	|	1045	1109u	...	1145	1245	1345	1445	1545	1645	...	1745	1846	1946	2046	2147	2248r	...
Samedan 546 d.	...	0712	0851	0951	...	|	1051	...	...	1151	1251	1351	1451	1551	1651	...	1751	1851	1951	2051	2151	2251r	2333
Pontresina **546/7** a.	...	|	|	|	...	1019	|	...	...	|	|	|	|	|	|	...	|	|	|	|	|	|	|
Celerina **546/7** d.	...	0715	0854	0954	...	...	1054	...	...	1154	1254	1354	1454	1554	1654	...	1754	1854	1954	2054	2154	2254r	2336
St Moritz 546/7 a.	...	0719	0903	1003	...	...	1103	...	...	1203	1303	1403	1503	1603	1703	...	1803	1903	2003	2103	2203	2258r	2341

	M	Ⓐ	⚒	†	△	△	△	△	△	△	△	△	△	△		950 ♦🅁✓	△	960 ♦🅁✓		△	△		
ritz 546/7 d.	0503	...	0541	0603	0702	0757	0857	0957	1057	1157	1257	1357	1457	1557	...	...	1657	...	...	1757	1857	1957	...
na **546/7** d.	0506	...	0544	0606	0705	0800	0900	1000	1100	1200	1300	1400	1500	1600	...	...	1700	...	...	1800	1900	2000	...
tresina **546/7** d.	|	...	|	|	|	|	|	|	|	|	|	|	|	|	...	1621s	|	1722s	...	|	|	|	...
dan 546 a.	0510	...	0548	0611	0709	0809	0909	1009	1109	1209	1309	1409	1509	1609	...	|	1709	1727s	...	1809	1909	2009	...
dan d.	...	0511v	0550	0612	0717	0817	0917	1017	1117	1217	1317	1417	1517	1617	...	|	1717	|	...	1817	1917	2017	...
d.	...	|	0603	0624	0730	0830	0930	1030	1130	1230	1330	1430	1530	1630	...	|	1730	|	...	1830	1930	2030	...
n / Bravuogn d.	...	0537v	0619	0641	0747	0847	0947	1047	1147	1247	1347	1447	1547	1647	...	1704s	1747	1804s	...	1847	1948	2048	...
r 545a d.	...	0554v	0635	0656	0801	0901	1001	1101	1201	1301	1401	1501	1601	1701	...	1717s	1801	1818s	...	1901	2001	2101	...
os Platz a.	...	|	|	|	|	|	|	|	|	|	|	|	|	|	...	|	|	1846	...	|	|	|	...
castel d.	...	0610v	0651	0711	0815	0915	1015	1115	1215	1315	1415	1515	1615	1715	...	1731s	1815	...	...	1915	2015	2116	...
s d.	...	0627	0710	0728	0833	0933	1033	1133	1233	1333	1433	1533	1633	1733	...	1749s	1833	...	...	1933	2033	2133	...
enau-Tamins **575** d.	...	0652	|	0752	0853	0953	1053	1153	1253	1353	1453	1553	1653	1753	...	|	1853	...	...	1953	2053	2156	...
575 a.	...	0705	0742	0805	0903	1003	1103	1203	1303	1403	1503	1603	1703	1803	...	1820	1903	...	...	2003	2103	2209	...

NOTES (LISTED BY TRAIN NUMBER)

– BERNINA EXPRESS – 🚃12 [panorama car] and 🍸 Tirano - Pontresina - Chur and v.v.
– BERNINA EXPRESS – May 5 - Oct. 23: 🚃12 [panorama car] and 🍸 Tirano - Davos and v.v.

May 17 - Oct. 16: 🚃12 Klosters - St Moritz.
⚒ May 17 - Oct. 15: St Moritz - Klosters.

Daily Dec. 13 - Mar. 6; ⑤⑥ Mar. 11 - Nov. 19; daily Nov. 20 - Dec. 10 (also Mar. 24, 27, May 4, 5, 15, July 31).
Stops to set down only.
Stops to pick up only.

v – Ⓐ Dec. 14 - Mar. 4; ①–⑤ Nov. 21 - Dec. 9.
x – Stops only on request.

△ – Conveys 🚃12 [panorama car] Dec. 13 - Mar. 28, 🅁, ✓.
✓ – Supplement payable.

Catering (✕ and / or 🍸) available on most services.

CHUR - AROSA 541

Narrow gauge

	⚒						and				q
Chur d.	0508	0620	0808	0908	...	1008	and	1908	2006	2106	2300
Langwies d.	0549	0706	0849	0949	...	1049	hourly	1949	2044	2143	2340x
Arosa a.	0609	0723	0909	1009	...	1109	until	2009	2103	2206	2358

	⚒	Ⓐ	Ⓒ							t	
Arosa d.	0548	0625	0648	0748	...	0848	and	1948	2108	0003	...
Langwies d.	0604	0641	0704	0804	...	0904	hourly	2004	2123	0018x	...
Chur a.	0651	0723	0751	0851	...	0951	until	2051	2207	0059	...

Runs daily. Operated by 🚌 ①–④ Mar. 29 - Nov. 17 (not May 5, 16, Aug. 1).
Runs daily. Operated by 🚌 ②–⑤ Mar. 30 - Nov. 18 (not May 6, 17, Aug. 2).

x – Stops only on request.

🚌 CHUR - FLIMS 542

Chur (Postautostation) - **Flims** Dorf (Post), ± 35 minutes, and **Flims** Waldhaus (Caumasee), ± 40 minutes.

Chur:
0603⚒, 0638Ⓐ, 0658, 0758 and hourly until 1758, then 1828Ⓐ, 1858, 1928Ⓐ, 2000, 2100, 2200, 2300.

From **Flims** Waldhaus (± 5 minutes from Flims Dorf):
0516⚒, 0613, 0700Ⓐ, 0714, 0814, 0914 and hourly until 1914, then 2013, 2113, 2213, 2313.

Additional services available

🚌 ST MORITZ and TIRANO - CHIAVENNA - LUGANO 543

RhB *

					P🅁	B🅁				
oritz, Bahnhof § d.	0725	0908	1108r	1208	1220	...	1408	1508	1708	1914
lana, Post § d.	0737	0921	1121	1221	1232u	...	1421	1521	1721	1926
Segl Maria, Posta § d.	0744	0929	1129	1229	1239u	...	1429	1529	1729	1933
a, Posta § d.	0756	0944	1144	1244	1250u	...	1444	1554	1744	1945
asegna 🏛 § d.	0835	1028	1228	1328	1327u	...	1528	1638	1828	2024
ano, Stazione d.	|	|	|	|	|	1420	|	|	|	|
enna, Stazione § d.	0858	1051	1251	1351	1410	|	1551	1701	1851	2047
ggio d.	...	...	...	...	1505x	|	...	...	...	...
no, Stazione ◐ a.	...	...	...	...	1620s	1730	...	...	...	...
no, Autosilo Balestra a.	...	...	...	...	1630	...	...	...	...	...

				h	g	B🅁	Q🅁				
Lugano, Autosilo Balestra d.	...	...	...	...	...	...	1145	...	...	...	...
Lugano, Stazione ◐ d.	...	...	...	...	...	1000	1205u	...	...	...	...
Menaggio d.	...	...	...	...	...	|	1255x	...	...	...	...
Chiavenna, Stazione § d.	0708	0908	1108	1308	1308	|	1420	1408	1608	1708	1915
Tirano, Stazione d.	|	|	|	|		1300	|	|	|	|	|
Castasegna 🏛 § d.	0728	0928	1128	1328	1328	...	1436s	1428	1628	1728	1933
Maloja, Posta § d.	0814	1014	1214	1413	1414	...	1510s	1514	1714	1814	2014
Sils / Segl Maria, Posta § d.	0827	1027	1227	1424	1427	...	1521s	1527	1727	1827	2027
Silvaplana, Post § d.	0836	1036	1236	1431	1436	...	1529s	1536	1736	1836	2036
St Moritz, Bahnhof § a.	0851	1051	1251	1439	1451	...	1545	1551	1751	1851	2051

Bernina Express service. Runs Mar. 25 - Oct. 23.
Palm Express service. Runs ⑤⑥⑦ (daily Dec. 21 - Jan. 3, June 13 - Oct. 23).
Palm Express service. Runs ①⑥⑦ (daily Dec. 22 - Jan. 4, June 14 - Oct. 24).

Dec. 13 - June 10, Oct. 24 - Dec. 10.
June 11 - Oct. 23.
Depart 1116 June 11 - Oct. 23.
Stops to set down only.
Stops to pick up only.
Calls only if advance reservation is made.

§ – Additional services operate June 11 - Oct. 23 St Moritz - Chiavenna and v.v.
◐ – 🏛 is at Gandria.

* – Operators:
Tirano - Lugano: RhB, Reservation: ✆ (081) 288 65 65;
St Moritz - Chiavenna - Lugano: PA, Reservation: ✆ St Moritz (058) 341 34 92; fax (058) 667 49 81.

544 🚌 CHUR - BELLINZONA and CHIAVENNA

km			S	Bj	Bh	B		S	B	Bh		B	Bh		B	B		B	S	Bh		B		Ⓡ✗g
0	**Chur** Postautostation **540**	d.	...	...	0808	0813	0913	...	...	1008	1113	...	1208	1313	...	1408	1513	...	1608	...	1713	...	1808	...	...
40	Thusis Bahnhof **540** ⊡	d.	0735	...	0835	0840	0940	0935	...	1035	1140	1135	1235	1340	1335	1435	1540	1535	1635	...	1740	1735	1835	1935	2250
64	Splügen Post	d.	0809	0820	0904	0904	1004	1009	1020	1104	1204	1209	1304	1404	1409	1504	1604	1609	1704	1715	1804	1809	1904	2009	2330
	San Bernardino Posta	a.	0829	|	0923	0923	1023	1029	|	1123	1223	1229	1323	1423	1429	1523	1623	1629	1723	|	1823	1829	1923	2029	...
	Chiavenna Stazione ◐	a.	|	1015	|	|	|	|	1215	|	|	|	|	|	|	|	|	|	|	1910	|	|	|	|	...
179	**Bellinzona** Stazione	a.	*0950*	...	1020	1013	1113	*1150*	...	1220	1313	*1350*	1420	1513	*1550*	1620	1713	*1750*	1820	...	1913	*1950*	2020	*2150*	...

		Ⓐ		S		B	B		Bh	B		Bh	B		B	S	B		Bh	S	B		B	Ⓡ✗g
Bellinzona Stazione	d.	...	*0707*	...	*0807*	0845	0940	*1007*	1045	1140	*1207*	1245	1340	*1407*	1445	...	1540	*1607*	1645	...	1740	*1807*	1845**r**	...
Chiavenna Stazione ◐	d.	...	|	0750	|	|	|	|	|	|	|	|	|	|	|	1440	|	|	|	1640	|	|	|	...
San Bernardino Posta	d.	0600	0823	|	0923	0935	1031	1123	1135	1231	1323	1335	1431	1523	1535	|	1631	1723	1735	|	1831	1923	1940	...
Splügen Post	d.	0622	0845	0940	0945	0953	1051	1145	1153	1251	1345	1353	1451	1545	1553	1630	1651	1745	1753	1830	1851	1945	1958	2351
Thusis Bahnhof **540** ⊙	d.	0705	0925	...	1025	1020	1125	1225	1220	1325	1425	1420	1525	1625	1620	...	1725	1825	1820	...	1925	2025	2025	0018
Chur Postautostation **540**	a.	...	...	...	...	1045	1150	...	1245	1350	...	1445	1550	...	1645	...	1750	...	1845	...	1950	...	2050	...

B – San Bernardino Route Express. Ⓡ.
S – Splügen Pass service. Runs June 4 - Oct. 9. Supplement payable.
g – ⑤⑥ (also Mar. 24, May 4; not Dec. 25, 26, Jan. 1, 2, Mar. 25).
h – June 4 - Oct. 23.
j – Dec. 13 - June 3, Oct. 24 - Dec. 10.
n – ⑥⑦ (also Mar. 25, May 5; not Dec. 26, 27, Jan. 2, 3, Mar. 26).
r – Depart 1850 on ⚒.
⊙ – Stops to set down only.
⊡ – Stops to pick up only.
◐ – 🚌 is at Splügen Pass.
✗ – Supplement payable.
Reservations: ✆ Chur (058) 386 31 66; Thusis (058) 341 34

545 CHUR - LANDQUART - KLOSTERS - DAVOS / SCUOL TARASP

Narrow gauge.

km			Ⓐ	⚒	Ⓐ						L				L		A			❖ L		❖ L			
	Chur 520/534	d.	...	...	*0601*	...	...	*0731*	...	...	...	*0831*	...	...	...	*0931*	...	*1031*	...	...		...	*1731*	...	*1831*
	Landquart 520/534	a.	...	...	*0609*	...	...	*0739*	...	...	...	*0839*	...	...	...	*0939*	...	*1039*	...	...	and at	...	*1739*	...	*1839*
0	**Landquart**	d.	0512	0534	0620	0647	...	0747	0749	...	0821	0847	0849	...	0921	0947	0949	1047	1049	1121	the same	1721	1747	1749	1847
21	Küblis	d.	0535**x**	0605	0645	0712	...	0810	0814	...	0844	0910	0914	...	0944	1010	1014	1110	1114	1144	minutes	1744	1810	1814	1910
30	Klosters Dorf	d.	0553**x**	0618	0658	0724	...	0821	|	...	|	|	|	...	|	1021	|	1121	|	|	past each	|	1821	|	1921
32	**Klosters** Platz 🚗	d.	0559	0629	0703	0734	...	0829	0833	...	0859	0929	0933	...	0959	1029	1033	1129	1133	1159	hour	1800	1829	1833	1929
	Sagliains **546** 🚗 §	a.	|	0653	|	0752	...	|	0851	...	...	|	0951	...	...	|	1051	|	1151	...	until	...	|	1851	|
	Ardez	a.	|	0705	|	0807**t**	...	|	0903	...	...	|	1003	...	...	|	1103	|	1203	...		...	|	1903	|
	Scuol-Tarasp 546	a.	|	0716	|	0819**t**	...	|	0915	...	...	|	1015	...	...	|	1115	|	1215	...		...	|	1915	|
47	Davos Dorf	d.	0621	...	0723	...	...	0850	...	...	...	0950	...	...	...	1050	...	1150	...	...		...	1850	...	1950
50	**Davos** Platz **545a**	a.	0633	...	0730	...	...	0856	...	...	...	0956	...	...	...	1056	...	1156	...	...		...	1856	...	1956

								m		
Chur 520/534	d.	...	*1931*	...	*2031*	...	*2131*	...	*2231*	...
Landquart 520/534	a.	...	*1939*	...	*2039*	...	*2139*	...	*2239*	...
Landquart	d.	1921	1947	...	2048	...	2147	...	2247	...
Küblis	d.	1944	2013	...	2113	...	2213	...	2313	...
Klosters Dorf	d.	|	2025	...	2125	...	2225	...	2325	...
Klosters Platz 🚗	d.	2001	2030	2034	2130	2134	2230	2234	2330	...
Sagliains **546** 🚗 §	a.	|	|	2052	|	2152	|	2252	|	...
Ardez	a.	|	|	2107**r**	|	2212**t**	|	2312	|	...
Scuol-Tarasp 546	a.	|	|	2119**r**	|	2219**t**	|	2319	|	...
Davos Dorf	d.	2021	2051	...	2151	...	2251	...	2351	...
Davos Platz **545a**	a.	2029	2057	...	2157	...	2257	...	2357	...

		⚒		Ⓐ							
Davos Platz **545a**	d.	0500	0600	0626	...	0700	0730	...	0802	...	0902
Davos Dorf	d.	0503	0603	0629	...	0703	0733	...	0806	...	0906
Scuol-Tarasp 546	d.	|	|	|	...	|	|	0741**j**	|	0841	|
Ardez	d.	|	|	|	...	|	|	0748**j**	|	0848	|
Sagliains **546** 🚗 §	d.	|	|	|	...	|	|	0803	|	0903	|
Klosters Platz 🚗	d.	0528	0628	0654	...	0728	0758	0825	0831	0925	0931
Klosters Dorf	d.	0530	0630	0658	...	0730	|	|	0833	|	0933
Küblis	d.	0543	0643	0710	...	0743	0813	0839	0850	0939	0950
Landquart	a.	0613	0713	0737	...	0813	0836	0910	0913	1010	1013
Landquart 520/534	d.	...	*0718*	...	...	*0818*	...	...	*0918*	...	*1018*
Chur 520/534	a.	...	*0726*	...	...	*0826*	...	...	*0926*	...	*1026*

km						❖ L			L			L						h	m		h	m		
	Davos Platz **545a**	d.		...	1502	...	...	1602	...	...	1702	...	...	1802	...	1902	2000	...	...	...	2100	...	...	2150	...
	Davos Dorf	d.	and at	...	1506	...	...	1606	...	...	1706	...	...	1806	...	1906	2003	...	...	...	2103	...	...	2154	...
0	**Scuol-Tarasp 546**	d.	the same	1441	|	...	1541	|	...	1641	|	...	1741	|	1841	|	|	1941	2032	2041	|	2132	2141	|	...
	Ardez	d.	minutes	1448	|	...	1548	|	...	1648	|	...	1748	|	1848	|	|	1948	2040	2048	|	2140	2148	|	...
17	Sagliains **546** 🚗 §	d.	past each	1503	|	...	1603	|	...	1703	|	...	1803	|	1903	|	|	2003	2051	2103	|	2151	2201	|	2203
39	**Klosters** Platz 🚗	d.	hour	1525	1531	1557	1625	1631	1657	1725	1731	1757	1825	1831	1925	1931	2027	2029	*2122*	2122	2129	...	...	2217	2223
	Klosters Dorf	d.	until	|	1533	|	|	1633	|	|	1733	|	|	1833	|	1933	...	2031	...	...	2131	...	...	...	2225
	Küblis	d.		1539	1550	1613	1639	1650	1713	1739	1750	1813	1839	1850	1939	1950	...	2044	...	...	2146	...	...	...	2239
	Landquart	a.		1610	1613	1636	1710	1713	1736	1810	1813	1836	1910	1913	2010	2013	...	2113	...	...	2213	...	...	...	2305
	Landquart 520/534	d.		...	*1618*	...	...	*1718*	...	...	*1818*	...	...	*1918*	...	*2018*	...	*2118*	...	...	*2218*	...	...	...	...
	Chur 520/534	a.		...	*1626*	...	...	*1726*	...	...	*1826*	...	...	*1926*	...	*2026*	...	*2126*	...	...	*2226*	...	...	...	...

A – AQUALINO – (12) Disentis/Mustér - Scuol-Tarasp.
L – (12) Landquart - St Moritz and v.v.
h – May 17 - Oct. 16.
j – 4–5 minutes **earlier** May 17 - Oct. 16.
m – Dec. 13 - May 16, Oct. 17 - Dec. 10.
r – 4–5 minutes later May 17 - Oct. 16.
t – By connecting train May 17 - Oct. 16 (4–6 minutes later).
x – Stops only on request.
z – ⑤⑥ (also Mar. 24, May 4; not Mar. 25).
❖ – Every two hours.
§ – Sagliains station can only be used for changing trains.
🚗 – Car-carrying shuttle available (see page 2

545a DAVOS - FILISUR

Narrow gauge.

For *Glacier Express* services see Table 575

km			⚒				961 ◆					
0	**Davos** Platz **545**	d.	0605	0731	0831	0931	0953	0931	and hourly	1931	2031	...
16	**Filisur 540**	a.	0630	0756	0856	0956	1015	0956	until	1956	2056	...

		⚒				960 ◆		
Filisur 540	d.	0634	0804	and hourly	1804	1819	1904	2004
Davos Platz **545**	a.	0658	0829	until	1829	1846	1929	2029

960/1 – BERNINA EXPRESS – May 5 - Oct. 23: (12) [panorama car] and 🍷 Tirano - Davos and v.v. Ⓡ ✗.
✗ – Supplement payable.

546 PONTRESINA / ST MORITZ - SCUOL TARASP

Narrow gauge.

Valid May 17 - Oct. 16. For service to May 16 and from Oct. 17 – see page 576

km			⚒	⚒	⚒	⚒	†				⚒			❖ L				❖ L			L			L	
0	**Pontresina 540/7**	d.	...	0535	...	...	0601	...	...	0702	...	...	0802	...		...	1402	...	...	1502	...	...	1602	...	...
	St Moritz 540/7	d.	0503	|	*0541*	0602	|	0603	0702	|	0723	0757	|	0849**r**	and at	1357	|	1445	1457	|	1538	1557	|	1645	1657
5	Samedan **540**	a.	0510	0542	*0548*	0608	0607	0611	0709	0708	0729	0809	0808	0857	the same	1409	1408	1457	1509	1508	1545	1609	1608	1657	1709
5	Samedan	d.	0511	...	0600	0609	0608	...	...	0713	0730	...	0813	0858	minutes	...	1413	1458	...	1513	1545	...	1613	1658	...
15	Zuoz	d.	0524	...	0613	0622	0622	...	...	0727	0743	...	0827	0910	past each	...	1427	1510	...	1527	1559	...	1627	1710	...
32	Zernez ⊖	d.	0544	...	0635	—	0642	...	...	0747	...	...	0847	0929	hour	...	1447	1529	...	1547	1628	...	1647	1729	...
38	Susch	d.	0552	...	0641	⚒	0648	...	...	0753	...	...	0853	0935	until	...	1453	1535	...	1553	1634	...	1653	1735	...
40	Sagliains **545** §	a.	0558	...	0651	0653	0657	...	...	0802	...	...	0902	|		...	1502	|	...	1602	|	...	1702	|	...
	Klosters Platz **545**	a.	0623	...	...	|	0723	...	...	|	...	...	|	0955		...	|	1555	...	|	1655	...	|	1755	...
57	**Scuol-Tarasp 545**	a.	...	...	...	0716	...	...	...	0824	...	...	0924	...		...	1524	...	...	1624	...	...	1724	...	...

L – (12) St Moritz - Landquart.
r – Subsequent departures at 1045, 1245, 1445.
❖ – Every two hours.
§ – Sagliains station can only be used for changing trains.
⊖ – For 🚌 service **Zernez - Malles and v.v.** – see next page.

PONTRESINA / ST MORITZ - SCUOL TARASP 546

ow gauge. RhB

Valid May 17 - Oct. 16. For service to May 16 and from Oct. 17 – see page 576

resina 540/7 d.	...	1802	...	1902	2002	...	2102	...	2202	...
Moritz 540/7 d.	1757	|	1857	|	|	1957	|	2057	|	2157
edan 540 a.	1809	1808	1909	1908	2008	2009k	2108	2109k	2208	2209k
edan d.	...	1813	...	1913	2011	▬	2111	▬	2211	...
d.	...	1827	...	1927	2024	...	2124	...	2224	...
ez ⊖ d.	...	1847	...	1947	2044	...	2144	...	2244	...
h d.	...	1853	...	1953	2050	...	2150	...	2253	...
ains 545 § a.	...	1902	...	2002	2059	2103	2159	2203	|	...
sters Platz 545 a.	...	|	...	|	...	|	...	|	|	...
l-Tarasp 545 a.	...	1924	...	2024	...	2119	...	2223	2321	...

	⚒	Ⓐ		⚒						
Scuol-Tarasp 545 d.	0541	...	...	0600	0636j	...	0736	...	0832	...
Klosters Platz 545 d.	|	0530	...	|	|	...	|	...	|	...
Sagliains 545 § d.	0601	|	...	|	0658	...	0756	0758	0854	...
Susch d.	...	0553	...	0621	0702	...	▬	0802	0900	...
Zernez ⊖ d.	...	0602	...	0637	0713	...	...	0813	0908	...
Zuoz d.	...	0622	0634d	0657	0733	0757d	...	0833	0927	...
Samedan a.	...	0633	0646d	0710	0747	0811d	...	0847k	0942	...
Samedan 540 d.	...	0635	0648	0712	0749	0812	0851	0849	0948	0951
St Moritz 540/7 a.	...	0643	|	0719	|	0819	0903	|	|	1003
Pontresina 540/7 a.	...	...	0655	...	0756	...	...	0856	0955	...

		L		❖ L				❖ L		
l-Tarasp 545 d.	...	0932	...	...	1032	...	and at	...	1632	...
sters Platz 545 d.	0901	|	...	1001	|	...	the same	1601	|	...
ains 545 § d.	|	0954	...	|	1054	...	minutes	|	1654	...
h d.	0918	1000	...	1017	1100	...	past each	1617	1700	...
ez ⊖ d.	0929	1008	...	1027	1108	...	hour	1627	1708	...
d.	0953	1027	...	1046	1127	...	until	1646	1727	...
edan a.	1006	1042	...	1058	1142	...		1658	1742	...
edan 540 d.	1009	1048	1051	1100	1148	1151		1700	1748	1751
Moritz 540/7 a.	1016	|	1103	1109	|	1203		1709	|	1803
resina 540/7 a.	...	1055	...	...	1155	...		...	1755	...

			L									z	⑤⑥	
l-Tarasp 545 d.	1732	...	...	1832	...	1932	...	2032	...	2132	...	...	2241	...
sters Platz 545 d.	|	...	1801	|	...	|	...	|	...	|	...	...	|	...
ains 545 § d.	1754	...	|	1854	...	1954	...	2054	...	2151	2154	...	2300	...
h d.	1800	...	1817	1900	...	2000	...	2100	...	...	2200	...	...	...
ez ⊖ d.	1808	...	1827	1908	...	2008	...	2108	...	...	2208	...	...	...
d.	1827	...	1846	1927	...	2030	...	2130	...	...	2230	...	...	...
edan a.	1842	...	1858	1942	...	2043	...	2143	...	...	2243	...	...	...
edan 540 d.	1848	1851	1900	1948	1951	...	2051	2148	2151	...	2248	2251	...	...
Moritz 540/7 a.	|	1903	1909	|	2003	...	2103	|	2203	...	|	2258	...	...
resina 540/7 a.	1855	...	...	1955	...	...	...	2155	...	...	2255	...	...	...

[12] Landquart - St Moritz.
⚒ only.
Connection on ⚒.
Connects with train in previous column.
⑤⑥ (also July 31).

❖ – Every two hours.
§ – Sagliains station can only be used for changing trains.

⊖ – 🚌 service **Zernez - Malles and v.v.** (journey ±1 h 35 minutes):
From **Zernez**: 0715, 0815, 0915, 1015, 1032, 1115, 1215, 1315, 1415, 1515, 1615, 1715.
From **Malles / Mals** bahnhof: 0610, 0657⚒, 0803, 0903, 1003, 1103, 1203, 1303, 1403, 1503, 1545, 1603, 1703, 1803, 1903.
Operator: AutoDaPosta (PA); ✆ +41 (0)81 856 10 90.

ST MORITZ - TIRANO 547

row gauge. RhB

	🚌					△		973 ♦🅁⚡	🚌 w		951 ♦🅁⚡		▷	961 ♦🅁⚡		🚌 w		△	△	▽▷		975 ♦🅁⚡	△	▷
St Moritz d.	...	...	...	...	0748	0848	...	0930	...	0948	...	...	1048	...	...	...	1148	1248	1348	1448	...	1512	1548	1648
Celerina Staz ⊡ d.	...	...	...	...	0751	0851	...	|	...	0951	...	...	1051	...	...	...	1151	1251	1351	1451	...	|	1551	1651
Pontresina a.	...	...	...	...	0758	0858	...	|	...	0958	...	...	1058	...	...	...	1158	1258	1358	1458	...	|	1558	1658
Pontresina 540 d.	...	...	...	0704d	0808	0904	...	0941u	...	1008	1021	...	1104	1117u	...	...	1208	1304	1408	1504	...	1521u	1608	1704
Morteratsch ⊡ d.	...	...	...	0712d	0817	0912	...	|	...	1016	|	...	1112	|	...	...	1216	1312	1416	1512	...	|	1616	1712
Bernina Diavolezza ⊡ d.	...	...	...	0719d	0825	0919	...	|	...	1023	|	...	1119	|	...	...	1223	1319	1423	1519	...	|	1623	1719
Bernina Lagalb ⊡ d.	...	...	...	0721d	0828	0921	...	|	...	1025	|	...	1121	|	...	...	1225	1321	1425	1521	...	|	1625	1721
Ospizio Bernina d.	...	...	...	0729d	0837	0929	...	|	...	1033	|	...	1129	|	...	...	1233	1329	1433	1529	...	1551	1633	1729
Alp Grüm d.	...	...	...	0745d	0853	0942	...	1013s	...	1051	1057s	...	1142	1157s	...	...	1251	1342	1451	1542	...	1601	1651	1742
Poschiavo a.	...	...	...	0826d	0935	1022	...	1112s	...	1132	1200	...	1222	1248s	...	...	1332	1422	1532	1622	...	1648s	1732	1822
Poschiavo d.	0610	0620	0736	0833	0938	1023	...	|	1134	1136v	1208	...	1223	|	...	1334	1336v	1423	1536	1623	...	|	1736	1823
Le Prese d.	0616	0627x	0744x	0840	0946	1029	...	1131s	1139	1143v	1216s	...	1229	1301s	...	1339	1343v	1429	1543	1629	...	1701s	1743	1829
Miralago ⊡ d.	0620	0632	0749	0844	0952	1034	...	|	1142	1147v	|	...	1234	|	...	1342	1347v	1434	1547	1634	...	|	1747	1834
Brusio ⊡ d.	0624	0639	0757	0851	1000	1041	...	|	1146	1154v	|	...	1241	|	...	1346	1354v	1441	1554	1641	...	|	1754	1841
Campocologno 🏛 d.	0629	0650	0807	0908	1012	1049	...	|	1151	1203v	|	...	1249	|	...	1351	1403v	1449	1603	1649	...	|	1803	1849
Tirano a.	0638	0703	0823	0916	1021	1100	...	1200	1157	1219v	1245	...	1300	1332	...	1357	1419v	1500	1619	1700	...	1732	1819	1900

		🚌			🚌	Ⓐ		🚌 h	🚌	
oritz d.	1748	...	...	1848	...	1948	2020	...	...	...
rina Staz ⊡ d.	1751	...	...	1851	...	1951	2023	...	...	...
tresina a.	1758	...	...	1858	...	1958	2030	m	...	...
tresina 540 d.	1808	...	...	1908	...	2014	...	2057	...	...
eratsch ⊡ d.	1816	...	...	1916	...	2022	...	|	...	...
ina Diavolezza ⊡ d.	1823	...	...	1923	...	2029	...	|	...	...
ina Lagalb ⊡ d.	1825	...	...	1925	...	2031	...	|	...	...
zio Bernina d.	1833x	...	...	1933x	...	2038x	...	|	...	...
Grüm d.	1851	...	...	1951	...	2054	...	|	...	...
chiavo a.	1932	...	...	2032	...	2132	...	2133	...	...
chiavo d.	...	1934	...	...	2034	...	...	...	2134	...
rese d.	...	1939	...	...	2039	...	...	...	2139	...
lago ⊡ d.	...	1943	...	...	2043	...	...	...	2143	...
io ⊡ d.	...	1946	...	...	2046	...	...	...	2146	...
pocologno 🏛 d.	...	1952	...	...	2052	...	...	...	2152	...
no a.	...	1959	...	...	2059	...	...	...	2159	...

	⚒	†	🚌				△	▽▷		976 ♦🅁⚡
Tirano d.	...	...	0655	...	0740	...	0900	0940	...	1003
Campocologno 🏛 d.	...	...	0702	...	0752	...	0908	0952	...	|
Brusio ⊡ d.	...	...	0706	...	0759	...	0915	0959	...	|
Miralago ⊡ d.	...	...	0711	...	0805	...	0920	1005	...	|
Le Prese d.	...	...	0714	...	0810	...	0925	1010	...	1041u
Poschiavo a.	...	...	0730	...	0820	...	0935	1020	...	1048
Poschiavo d.	0627	...	...	0732	0825	...	0937	1024	...	1049
Alp Grüm d.	0704x	...	...	0815	0905	...	1014	1105	...	1125s
Ospizio Bernina d.	0713x	...	...	0824	0914	...	1021	1114	...	1148s
Bernina Lagalb ⊡ d.	0721	...	...	0832	0921	...	1029	1121	...	|
Bernina Diavolezza ⊡ d.	0723	...	...	0834	0924	...	1031	1124	...	|
Morteratsch ⊡ d.	0732	...	...	0844	0936	...	1039	1136	...	|
Pontresina 540 a.	0749	...	...	0858	0950	...	1052	1150	...	1224s
Pontresina d.	0801	0801	...	0901	1001	...	1101	1201	...	|
Celerina Staz ⊡ d.	0806	0806	...	0906	1006	...	1106	1206	...	|
St Moritz a.	0811	0811	...	0911	1011	...	1111	1211	...	1236

	△	▷	🚌 w	△	◇	🚌 w		974 ♦🅁⚡	950 ♦🅁⚡				960 ♦🅁⚡		△			🚌 h				🚌	🚌	🚌	
no d.	1100	1140v	1159	1300	1340v	1359	...	1403	1426	...	1500	...	1512	...	1540	1700	1740	...	...	1900	1940	2002	2102	2202	...
pocologno 🏛 d.	1108	1152v	1205	1308	1352v	1405	...	|	|	...	1508	...	|	...	1552	1708	1752	...	...	1909	1952	2010x	2110x	2210x	...
sio ⊡ d.	1115	1159v	1209	1315	1359v	1409	...	|	|	...	1515	...	|	...	1559	1715	1759	...	...	1917	1959	2016	2116	2216	...
lago ⊡ d.	1120	1205v	1213	1320	1405v	1413	...	|	|	...	1520	...	|	...	1605	1720	1805	...	...	1924	2005	2019	2119	2219	...
rese d.	1125	1210v	1216	1325	1410v	1416	...	1441u	1455u	...	1525	...	1539u	...	1610	1725	1810x	...	...	1929x	2010x	2023x	2123x	2223x	...
chiavo a.	1135	1220v	1221k	1335	1420v	1421k	...	|	|	...	1535	...	1547	...	1620	1735	1820	...	...	1940	2020	2029	2129	2229	...
chiavo d.	1137	1224	...	1337	1424	...	...	1449u	1509u	...	1537	...	1557	...	1624	1737	1824	1905	...	...	...	...	...	...	...
Grüm d.	1214	1305	...	1414	1505	...	...	1524u	1544u	...	1614	...	|	...	1705	1814	1905	|	...	...	...	...	...	...	...
izio Bernina d.	1221	1314	...	1421	1514	...	...	1533u	|	...	1621	...	1650u	...	1714	1821	1911x	|	...	...	...	...	...	...	...
ina Lagalb ⊡ d.	1229	1321	...	1429	1521	...	...	|	|	...	1629	...	|	...	1721	1829	1920	|	...	...	...	...	...	...	...
ina Diavolezza ⊡ d.	1231	1324	...	1431	1524	...	...	|	|	...	1631	...	|	...	1724	1831	1923	|	...	...	...	...	...	...	...
teratsch ⊡ d.	1239	1336	...	1439	1536	...	...	|	|	...	1639	...	|	...	1736	1839	1931	|	...	...	...	...	...	...	...
tresina 540 a.	1252	1350	...	1452	1550	...	...	1602s	1616s	...	1652	...	1719s	...	1750	1852	1950	2000	...	...	...	...	...	...	...
tresina d.	1301	1401	...	1501	1601	...	...	|	...	...	1701	...	...	...	1801	1901	2001	n	...	...	...	...	...	...	...
rina Staz ⊡ d.	1306	1406	...	1506	1606	...	...	|	...	...	1706	...	...	...	1806	1906	2006	...	...	...	...	...	...	...	...
oritz a.	1311	1411	...	1511	1611	...	...	1620	...	...	1711	...	...	...	1811	1911	2012	...	...	...	...	...	...	...	...

NOTES (LISTED BY TRAIN NUMBER)

1 – BERNINA EXPRESS – [12] [panorama car] and 🍸 Tirano - Chur and v.v.
1 – BERNINA EXPRESS – May 5 - Oct. 23: [12] [panorama car] and 🍸 Tirano - Davos and v.v.
4 – BERNINA EXPRESS – May 5 - Oct. 23: [12] [panorama car] and 🍸 Tirano - St Moritz and v.v.
6 – BERNINA EXPRESS – May 5 - Oct. 23: [12] [panorama car] and 🍸 Tirano - St Moritz and v.v.

d – ⚒ only.
h – ⑤⑥⑦ (also Mar. 24, 28, May 4, 5, 16, Aug. 1).
k – Connects with train in previous column.
m – From Samedan (d. 2050).
n – To Samedan (a. 2008).
s – Stops to set down only.
u – Stops to pick up only.
v – May 5 - Oct. 23.
w – Dec. 13 - May 4, Oct. 24 - Dec. 10.
x – Stops only on request.

△ – Conveys [12] [panorama car] Dec. 13 - Mar. 28, 🅁, ⚡.
▽ – Conveys [12] [panorama car] Dec. 13 - May 4, Oct. 24 - Dec. 10, 🅁, ⚡.
▷ – Conveys open panorama car July 1 - Aug. 31, 🅁, ⚡. Subject to good weather.
◇ – Conveys open panorama car Poschiavo - St Moritz July 1 - Aug. 31, 🅁, ⚡. Subject to good weather.
⊡ – Request stop.
⚡ – Supplement payable.

550 LUZERN and ZÜRICH - LOCARNO, CHIASSO and MILANO

SBB

	RE 25509	RE 25511		ICN 659	IR 2409		ICN 861	IR 2311	2567	EC 13		ICN 863	IR 2313	2569	EC 153	IR 2413	ICN 865	IR 2315	2571	EC 15	ICN 667	IR 2417	2573	ICN 869	IR 2319
									(🍷) S	✕ ◧				(🍷) S	🍷 ◧	g			(🍷) S	✕ ◧			(🍷) S		W
Basel SBB **565** d.	...	...	...	0504	...	...	...	0604	...	...	...	...	0704	...	...	...	...	0804	...	...	0904	...	...	...	1004
Olten **565** d.	...	...	...	0530	...	...	...	0630	...	...	...	...	0730	...	...	...	...	0830	...	...	0930	...	...	...	1030
Luzern 565 d.	...	...	...	0618	...	...	...	0718	0740	...	...	...	0818	0840	0846	...	...	0918	0940	...	1018	...	1040	...	1118
Küssnacht am Rigi d.	...	...	...	|	...	...	...	|	0758	...	...	...	|	0858	|	...	...	|	0958	...	|	...	1058	...	|
Zürich HB d.	...	...	...	|	0609	...	0709	|	|	0732	...	0809	|	|	|	0832	0909	|	|	0932	|	1009	|	1109	|
Zug d.	...	...	...	|	0631	...	0731	|	|	0800	...	0831	|	|	|	0900	0931	|	|	1000	|	1031	|	1131	|
Arth-Goldau a.	...	...	...	0644	0646k	...	0746	0744k	0811	0814	...	0846	0844k	0911	0916	0914	0946	0944k	1011	1014	1044	1046k	1111	1146	1144k
Arth-Goldau d.	...	...	...	0650	0652	...	0750	0752	...	0817	...	0850	0852	—	0917	0922	0950	0952	—	1017	1050	1052	—	1150	1152
Schwyz d.	...	...	...	|	0700	...	|	0800	...	|	...	|	0900	...	|	|	|	1000	...	|	|	1100	...	|	1200
Brunnen d.	...	...	...	|	0704	...	|	0804	...	|	...	|	0904	...	|	|	|	1004	...	|	|	1104	...	|	1204
Flüelen d.	...	...	...	|	0714	...	|	0814	...	|	...	|	0914	...	|	|	|	1014	...	|	|	1114	...	|	1214
Erstfeld d.	...	...	...	|	0723	...	|	0823	...	|	...	|	0923	...	|	|	|	1023	...	|	|	1123	...	|	1223
Göschenen d.	...	...	...	|	0748	...	|	0848	...	|	...	|	0948	...	|	1010	|	1048	...	|	|	1148	...	|	1248
Airolo d.	...	0615	...	|	0759	...	|	0859	...	|	...	|	0959	...	|	1020	|	1059	...	|	|	1159	...	|	1259
Faido d.	...	0633	...	|	0817	...	|	0917	...	|	...	|	1017	...	|	1037	|	1117	...	|	|	1217	...	|	1317
Biasca d.	0556j	0656	...	|	0837	...	|	0937	...	|	...	|	1037	...	|	1058	|	1137	...	|	|	1237	...	|	1337
Bellinzona a.	0610j	0710	...	0825	0851	...	0925	0951	...	0955	...	1025	1051	...	1055k	1111	1125	1151	...	1155k	1225	1251	...	1325	1351
Bellinzona ▲ d.	0614	0714	0803	0826	0852	0903	0926	0952	...	0956	1003	1026	1052	1103	1056	1113	1126	1152	1203	1156	1226	1252	1303	1326	1352
Locarno 551 ▲ a.	|	|	|	|	0913	|	|	1013	...	|	|	|	1113	|	|	|	|	1213	|	|	|	1313	|	|	1413
Lugano a.	0642	0742	0833	0850	...	0933	0950	...	...	1023	1033	1050	...	1133	1123	1140	1150	...	1233	1223	1250	...	1333	1350	...
Lugano d.	0643	0743	0833	...	...	0933	...	...	...	1025	1033	...	...	1133	1125	1141	...	...	1233	1225	...	...	1333	...	...
Capolago-Riva San Vitale d.	|	|	0847	...	...	0947	...	...	...	|	1047	...	...	1147	|	|	...	...	1247	|	...	...	1347	...	...
Mendrisio d.	0658	0758	0854	...	...	0954	...	...	...	|	1054	...	...	1154	|	1159	...	...	1254	|	...	...	1354	...	...
Chiasso a.	0705	0805	0903	...	...	1003	...	...	...	1048	1103	...	...	1203	1148	1208	...	...	1303	1248	...	...	1403	...	...
Chiasso 🛃 § d.	0708	0808	...	...	...	...	...	...	...	1052	...	...	...	...	1152	...	...	...	...	1252	...	...	...	...	...
Como San Giovanni § a.	0712	0812	...	...	...	...	...	...	...	1056	...	...	...	...	1158	...	...	...	...	|	...	...	...	...	...
Milano Centrale § a.	0750	0850	...	...	...	...	...	...	...	1135	...	...	...	...	1250	...	...	...	...	1335	...	...	...	...	...

	EC 17	ICN 671	IR 2421	2577	ICN 873	IR 2323	2579	EC 19	ICN 675	IR 2425	2581	ICN 877	IR 2327	2583	EC 21	RE 25533	ICN 679	IR 2429	2585	ICN 881	IR 2331	2587	EC 23	ICN 683	IR 2433
	🍷 ◧		T	(🍷) S		V	(🍷) S	✕ ◧			(🍷) S			(🍷) S	✕ ◧	j			(🍷) S			(🍷) S	✕ ◧		
Basel SBB **565** d.	...	1104	...	...	...	1204	...	...	1304	...	...	...	1404	...	...	...	1504	...	...	...	1604	...	...	1704	...
Olten **565** d.	...	1130	...	...	...	1230	...	...	1330	...	...	...	1430	...	...	...	1530	...	...	...	1630	...	...	1730	...
Luzern 565 d.	...	1218	...	1240	...	1318	1340	...	1418	...	1440	...	1518	1540	...	...	1618	...	1640	...	1718	1740	...	1818	...
Küssnacht am Rigi d.	...	|	...	1258	...	|	1358	...	|	...	1458	...	|	1558	...	...	|	...	1658	...	|	1758	...	|	...
Zürich HB d.	1132	|	1209	|	1309	|	|	1332	|	1409	|	1509	|	|	1532	...	|	1609	|	1709	|	|	1732	|	1809
Zug d.	1200	|	1231	|	1331	|	|	1400	|	1431	|	1531	|	|	1600	...	|	1631	|	1731	|	|	1800	|	1831
Arth-Goldau a.	1214	1244	1246k	1311	1346	1344k	1411	1414	1444	1446k	1511	1546	1544k	1611	1614	...	1644	1646k	1711	1746	1744k	1811	1814	1844	1846k
Arth-Goldau d.	1217	1250	1252	—	1350	1352	—	1417	1450	1452	—	1550	1552	—	1617	...	1650	1652	—	1750	1752	—	1817	1850	1852
Schwyz d.	|	|	1300	...	|	1400	...	|	|	1500	...	|	1600	...	|	...	|	1700	...	|	1800	...	|	|	1900
Brunnen d.	|	|	1304	...	|	1404	...	|	|	1504	...	|	1604	...	|	...	|	1704	...	|	1804	...	|	|	1904
Flüelen d.	|	|	1314	...	|	1414	...	|	|	1514	...	|	1614	...	|	...	|	1714	...	|	1814	...	|	|	1914
Erstfeld d.	|	|	1323	...	|	1423	...	|	|	1523	...	|	1623	...	|	...	|	1723	...	|	1823	...	|	|	1923
Göschenen d.	|	|	1348	...	|	1448	...	|	|	1548	...	|	1648	...	|	...	|	1748	...	|	1848	...	|	|	1948
Airolo d.	|	|	1359	...	|	1459	...	|	|	1559	...	|	1659	...	|	...	|	1759	...	|	1859	...	|	|	1959
Faido d.	|	|	1417	...	|	1517	...	|	|	1617	...	|	1717	...	|	...	|	1817	...	|	1917	...	|	|	2017
Biasca d.	|	|	1437	...	|	1537	...	|	|	1637	...	|	1737	...	|	...	|	1837	...	|	1937	...	|	|	2037
Bellinzona a.	1355k	1425	1451	...	1525	1551	...	1555	1625	1651	...	1725	1751	...	1755k	...	1825	1851	...	1925	1951	...	1955	2025	2051
Bellinzona ▲ d.	1356	1426	1452	1503	1526	1552	1603	1556	1626	1652	1703	1726	1752	1803	1756	1814	1826	1852	1903	1926	1952	2003	2056	2026	2056
Locarno 551 ▲ a.	|	|	1513	|	|	1613	|	|	|	1713	|	|	1813	|	|	|	|	1913	|	|	2013	|	|	|	|
Lugano a.	1423	1450	...	1533	1550	...	1633	1623	1650	...	1733	1750	...	1833	1823	1841	1850	...	1933	1950	...	2033	2023	2050	2128
Lugano d.	1425	...	...	1533	...	...	1633	1625	1654j	...	1733	...	...	1833	1825	1842	...	...	1933	...	...	2033	2025	...	2130
Capolago-Riva San Vitale d.	|	...	...	1547	...	...	1647	|	|	...	1747	...	...	1847	|	|	...	...	1947	...	...	2047	|	...	2146
Mendrisio d.	|	...	...	1554	...	...	1654	|	1710j	...	1754	...	...	1854	|	1858	...	...	1954	...	...	2054	|	...	2154
Chiasso a.	1448	...	...	1603	...	...	1703	1648	1718j	...	1803	...	...	1903	1848	1905	...	...	2003	...	...	2103	2048	...	2204
Chiasso 🛃 § d.	1452	...	...	...	...	...	...	1652	...	...	...	...	...	...	1852	1908	...	...	...	...	...	...	2052	...	...
Como San Giovanni § a.	1456	...	...	...	...	...	...	|	...	...	...	...	...	...	|	1912	...	...	...	...	...	...	2056	...	...
Milano Centrale § a.	1535	...	...	...	...	...	...	1735	...	...	...	...	...	...	1935	1950	...	...	...	...	...	...	2135	...	...

	ICN 885	IR 2335	2591	EC 25	ICN 689	IR 2437	ICN 889	IR 2339	IR 2241	IR 2441	RE 2443
			(🍷) S	✕ ◧							
Basel SBB **565** d.	...	1804	...	...	1904	...	...	2004	...	...	...
Olten **565** d.	...	1830	...	...	1930	...	...	2030	...	...	...
Luzern 565 d.	...	1918	1940	...	2018	...	...	2118	2218	...	...
Küssnacht am Rigi d.	...	|	1958	...	|	...	...	|	|	...	...
Zürich HB d.	1909	|	|	1932	|	2009	2109	|	|	2209	2309
Zug d.	1931	|	|	2000	|	2031	2131	|	|	2231	2331
Arth-Goldau a.	1946	1944k	2011	2014	2044	2046k	2146	2144k	2245	2246	2346
Arth-Goldau d.	1950	1952	—	2017	2050	2052	2150	2152	...	2254	...
Schwyz d.	|	2000	...	|	|	2100	|	2200	...	|	...
Brunnen d.	|	2004	...	|	|	2104	|	2204	...	|	...
Flüelen d.	|	2014	...	|	|	2114	|	2214	...	|	...
Erstfeld d.	|	2023	...	|	|	2123	|	2225	...	2317	...
Göschenen d.	|	2048	...	|	|	2148	|	—	...	2342	...
Airolo d.	|	2059	...	|	|	2159	|	...	...	2352	...
Faido d.	|	2117	...	|	|	2217	|	...	...	0009	...
Biasca d.	|	2137	...	|	|	2237	|	...	...	0030	...
Bellinzona a.	2125	2151	...	2155k	2225	2251	2325	...	...	0043	...
Bellinzona ▲ d.	2126	2152	2203	2156	2226	2256	2326	2333	...	0044	...
Locarno 551 ▲ a.	|	2213	|	|	|	|	|	|	...	|	...
Lugano a.	2150	...	2233	2223	2250	2328	2350	0003	...	0115	...
Lugano d.	...	...	2233	2225	2250	2330	2350	0003	...	0116	...
Capolago-Riva San Vitale d.	...	...	2247	|	|	2346	|	0017	...	0132	...
Mendrisio d.	...	...	2254	|	2308	2354	0008	0024	...	0141	...
Chiasso a.	...	...	2303	2248	2315	0004	0015	0033	...	0151	...
Chiasso 🛃 § d.	...	...	...	2252	...	...	...	...	...	...	...
Como San Giovanni § a.	...	...	...	2256	...	...	...	...	...	...	...
Milano Centrale § a.	...	...	...	2335	...	...	...	...	...	...	...

	IR 2310	ICN 860	IR 2314	ICN 862		IR 2414	ICN 668		IR 2316
Milano Centrale § d.	...	...	...	...	...	...	...	...	...
Como San Giovanni § d.	...	...	...	...	...	...	...	...	...
Chiasso 🛃 § a.	...	...	...	...	...	...	...	...	...
Chiasso d.	...	0444	...	0546	0558	0611	0641	0658	0710
Mendrisio d.	...	0452	...	0554	0606	0620	0650	0706	0720
Capolago-Riva San Vitale d.	...	|	...	|	0610	|	|	0710	|
Lugano a.	...	0508	...	0607	0626	0635	0705	0726	0735
Lugano d.	...	0510	...	0610	0627	0637	0710	0727	0737
Locarno 551 ▲ d.	...	|	0547	|	|	|	|	|	|
Bellinzona ▲ a.	...	0532	0605	0633	0656	0705	0733	0756	0805
Bellinzona d.	...	0534	0606	0634	—	0706	0734	—	0806
Biasca d.	...	|	0621	|	...	0721	|	...	0821
Faido d.	...	|	0642	|	...	0742	|	...	0842
Airolo d.	...	|	0700	|	...	0800	|	...	0900
Göschenen d.	...	|	0711	|	...	0811	|	...	0911
Erstfeld d.	0627	|	0736	|	...	0836	|	...	0936
Flüelen d.	0636	0653	0744	|	...	0844	|	...	0944
Brunnen d.	0650	|	0755	|	**2564**	0855	|	**2566**	0955
Schwyz d.	0655	|	0759	|	(🍷)	0859	|	(🍷)	0959
Arth-Goldau a.	0706	0709k	0807	0809k	S	0906	0909k	S	1007
Arth-Goldau d.	0714	0713	0814	0813	0848	0913	0914	0948	1014
Zug d.	|	0729	|	0829	|	0929	|	|	|
Zürich HB a.	|	0751	|	0851	|	0951	|	|	|
Küssnacht am Rigi d.	|	...	|	...	0900	...	|	1000	|
Luzern 565 a.	0741	...	0841	...	0920	...	0941	1020	1041
Olten **565** a.	0827	...	0927	...	...	...	1027	...	1127
Basel SBB **565** a.	0855	...	0955	...	...	...	1055	...	1155

S – VORALPEN EXPRESS – [12] Luzern - Arth Goldau - Rapperswil - St Gallen and v.v.
T – [12] Zürich - Locarno. Dec. 13 - Apr. 15, Oct. 24 - Dec. 10 runs as WILHELM TELL EXPRESS Flüelen - Locarno ([1] [R]).
V – [12] Basel - Locarno. Apr. 16 - Oct. 23 runs as WILHELM TELL EXPRESS Flüelen - Locarno ([1] [R]).
W – [12] Basel - Locarno. May 28 - Sept. 11 runs as WILHELM TELL EXPRESS Flüelen - Locarno ([1] [R]).

g – ⑥ Dec. 19 - Oct. 29 (also Mar. 25, May 5; not Dec. 26, Jan. 2).
j – Ⓐ Dec. 14 - Dec. 7 (also Mar. 25, Dec. 9; not Jan. 6, May 26, June 29, Aug. 15, Nov. 1).
k – Connects with train in previous column(s).

◧ – Supplement payable in Italy and for international journeys.

▲ – For additional services Locarno - Bellinzona and v.v. – see panel on page 277.
§ – For additional services Chiasso - Como San Giovanni - Milano Porta Garibaldi and v see panel on page 277.

MILANO, CHIASSO and LOCARNO - ZÜRICH and LUZERN — 550

BB

		IR 2418	ICN 672		EC 12 🍴 ◧	IR 2320 W	ICN 870		IR 2422 T	ICN 676		EC 14 🍴 ◧	IR 2324 V	ICN 874		IR 2426	ICN 680		EC 16 🍴 ◧	IR 2328	ICN 878		IR 2430	ICN 684	
Milano Centrale § d.	...	...	...	...	0825	...	...	...	...	...	...	1025	...	...	...	...	...	...	1225	...	...	...	...	...	...
Como San Giovanni § d.	...	...	...	...	0903	...	...	...	...	...	...	1103	...	...	...	...	...	...	|	...	...	...	...	...	...
Chiasso 🏛 § a.	...	...	...	...	0908	...	...	...	...	...	...	1108	...	...	...	...	...	...	1308	...	...	...	...	...	...
Chiasso d.	0758	...	...	0858	0912	...	...	0958	...	...	1058	1112	...	...	1158	...	...	1258	1312	...	...	1358	...	...	1458
Mendrisio d.	0806	...	...	0906	|	...	...	1006	...	...	1106	|	...	...	1206	...	...	1306	|	...	...	1406	...	...	1506
Capolago-Riva San Vitale d.	0810	...	...	0910	|	...	...	1010	...	...	1110	|	...	...	1210	...	...	1310	|	...	...	1410	...	...	1510
Lugano a.	0826	...	...	0926	0932	...	...	1026	...	...	1126	1132	...	...	1226	...	...	1326	1332	...	...	1426	...	...	1526
Lugano d.	0827	...	0910	0927	0934	...	1010	1027	...	1110	1127	1134	...	1210	1227	...	1310	1327	1334	...	1410	1427	...	1510	1527
Locarno 551 ▲ d.	|	0847	|	|	|	0947	|	|	1047	|	|	|	1147	|	|	1247	|	|	|	1347	|	|	1447	|	|
Bellinzona ▲ a.	0856	0905	0933	0956	0959	1005	1033	1056	1105	1133	1156	1159	1205	1233	1256	1305	1333	1356	1359	1405	1433	1456	1505	1533	1556
Bellinzona d.	▬	0906	0934	▬	1000	1006	1034	▬	1106	1134	▬	1200	1206	1234	▬	1306	1334	▬	1400	1406	1434	▬	1506	1534	▬
Biasca d.	...	0921	|	...	|	1021	|	...	1121	|	...	|	1221	|	...	1321	|	...	|	1421	|	...	1521	|	...
Faido d.	...	0942	|	...	|	1042	|	...	1142	|	...	|	1242	|	...	1342	|	...	|	1442	|	...	1542	|	...
Airolo d.	...	1000	|	...	|	1100	|	...	1200	|	...	|	1300	|	...	1400	|	...	|	1500	|	...	1600	|	...
Göschenen d.	...	1011	|	...	|	1111	|	...	1211	|	...	|	1311	|	...	1411	|	...	|	1511	|	...	1611	|	...
Erstfeld d.	...	1036	|	...	|	1136	|	...	1236	|	...	|	1336	|	...	1436	|	...	|	1536	|	...	1636	|	...
Flüelen d.	...	1044	|	...	|	1144	|	...	1244	|	...	|	1344	|	...	1444	|	...	|	1544	|	...	1644	|	...
Brunnen d.	**2568**	1055	|	**2570**	|	1155	|	**2572**	1255	|	**2574**	|	1355	|	**2576**	1455	|	**2578**	|	1555	|	**2580**	1655	|	**2582**
Schwyz d.	(🍸)	1059	|	(🍸)	|	1159	|	(🍸)	1259	|	(🍸)	|	1359	|	(🍸)	1459	|	(🍸)	|	1559	|	(🍸)	1659	|	(🍸)
Arth-Goldau a.	**S**	1107	1109**k**	**S**	1143**k**	1207	1209**k**	**S**	1307	1309**k**	**S**	1343**k**	1407	1409**k**	**S**	1507	1509**k**	**S**	1543**k**	1607	1609**k**	**S**	1707	1709**k**	**S**
Arth-Goldau d.	1048	1113	1114	1148	1145	1214	1213	1248	1313	1314	1348	1345	1414	1413	1448	1513	1514	1548	1545	1614	1613	1648	1713	1714	1748
Zug d.	|	1129	|	|	1201	|	1229	|	1329	|	|	1401	|	1429	|	1529	|	|	1601	|	1629	|	1729	|	|
Zürich HB a.	|	1151	|	|	1228	|	1251	|	1351	|	|	1428	|	1451	|	1551	|	|	1628	|	1651	|	1751	|	|
Küssnacht am Rigi d.	1100	...	|	1200	...	|	...	1300	...	|	1400	...	|	...	1500	...	|	1600	...	|	...	1700	...	|	1800
Luzern 565 a.	1120	...	1141	1220	...	1241	...	1320	...	1341	1420	...	1441	...	1520	...	1541	1620	...	1641	...	1720	...	1741	1820
Olten **565** a.	...	...	1227	...	...	1327	...	...	...	1427	...	...	1527	...	...	...	1627	...	...	1727	...	...	...	1827	...
Basel SBB **565** a.	...	...	1255	...	...	1355	...	...	...	1455	...	...	1555	...	...	...	1655	...	...	1755	...	...	...	1855	...

	EC 18 🍴 ◧	IR 2332	ICN 882	IR 2432 h		EC 158 🍸 ◧	IR 2434	ICN 688	RE 25524 j		EC 20 🍸 ◧	IR 2336	ICN 886	RE 25526 j		IR 2438	ICN 692		EC 22 🍴 ◧	IR 2340	ICN 890		IR 2442	ICN 696		EC 24 🍴 ◧
Milano Centrale § d.	1425	...	...	...	...	1510	...	...	1610	...	1625	...	...	1710	...	...	...	...	1825	...	...	...	...	...	...	2025
Como San Giovanni § d.	|	...	...	...	...	1601	...	...	1647	...	|	...	...	1747	...	...	...	...	|	...	...	...	...	...	...	2103
Chiasso 🏛 § a.	1508	...	...	...	...	1608	...	...	1652	...	1708	...	...	1752	...	...	...	...	1908	...	...	...	...	...	...	2108
Chiasso d.	1512	...	...	1544	1558	1612	...	...	1655	1658	1712	...	...	1755	1758	...	...	1858	1912	...	...	1958	...	...	2058	2112
Mendrisio d.	|	...	...	1552	1606	|	...	...	1702	1706	|	...	...	1802	1806	...	...	1906	|	...	...	2006	...	...	2106	|
Capolago-Riva San Vitale d.	|	...	...	|	1610	|	...	...	|	1710	|	...	...	|	1810	...	...	1910	|	...	...	2010	...	...	2110	|
Lugano a.	1532	...	...	1607	1626	1632	...	...	1718	1726	1732	...	...	1818	1826	...	...	1926	1932	...	...	2026	...	...	2126	2132
Lugano d.	1534	...	1610	1614	1627	1634	...	1710	1719	1727	1734	...	1810	1819	1827	...	1910	1927	1934	...	2010	2027	...	2110	2127	2134
Locarno 551 ▲ d.	|	1547	|	|	|	|	1647	|	|	|	|	1747	|	|	|	1847	|	|	|	1947	|	|	2047	|	|	|
Bellinzona ▲ a.	1559	1605	1633	1641	1656	1659	1705	1733	1747	1756	1759	1805	1833	1847	1856	1905	1933	1956	1959	2005	2033	2056	2105	2133	2156	2159
Bellinzona d.	1600	1606	1634	1643	▬	1700	1706	1734	...	▬	1800	1806	1834	...	▬	1906	1934	▬	2000	2006	2034	...	2106	2134	...	2200
Biasca d.	|	1621	|	1657	...	|	1721	|	...	...	|	1821	|	...	...	1921	|	...	|	2021	|	...	2121	|	...	|
Faido d.	|	1642	|	1719	...	|	1742	|	...	...	|	1842	|	...	...	1942	|	...	|	2042	|	...	2142	|	...	|
Airolo d.	|	1700	|	1737	...	|	1800	|	...	...	|	1900	|	...	...	2000	|	...	|	2100	|	...	2200	|	...	|
Göschenen d.	|	1711	|	1748	...	|	1811	|	...	...	|	1911	|	...	...	2011	|	...	|	2111	|	...	2211	|	...	|
Erstfeld d.	|	1736	|	|	...	|	1836	|	...	...	|	1936	|	...	...	2036	|	...	|	2136	|	...	2236	|	...	|
Flüelen d.	|	1744	|	1824	...	|	1844	|	...	...	|	1944	|	...	...	2044	|	...	|	2144	|	...	2244	|	...	|
Brunnen d.	|	1755	|	|	**2584**	|	1855	|	...	**2586**	|	1955	|	...	**2588**	2055	|	*RE*	|	2155	|	...	2255	|	...	|
Schwyz d.	|	1759	|	|	(🍸)	|	1859	|	...	(🍸)	|	1959	|	...	(🍸)	2059	|	**2338**	|	2159	|	...	2259	|	...	|
Arth-Goldau a.	1743**k**	1807	1809**k**	1842	**S**	1839**k**	1907	1909**k**	...	**S**	1943**k**	2007	2009**k**	...	**S**	2107	2109**k**		2143**k**	2207	2209**k**	...	2307	2309**k**	...	2343
Arth-Goldau d.	1745	1814	1813	1845	1848	1841	1913	1914	...	1948	1945	2014	2013	...	2048	2113	2114	2148	2145	2214	2213	...	2313	2314	...	2345
Zug d.	1801	|	1829	1901	|	|	1929	|	...	|	2001	|	2029	...	|	2129	|	|	2201	|	2229	...	2329	|	...	0001
Zürich HB a.	1828	|	1851	1928	|	|	1951	|	...	|	2028	|	2051	...	|	2151	|	|	2228	|	2251	...	2351	|	...	0028
Küssnacht am Rigi d.	...	|	...	...	1900	|	...	|	...	2000	...	|	...	...	2100	...	|	2200	...	|	...	...	...	|	...	...
Luzern 565 a.	...	1841	...	...	1920	1913	...	1941	...	2020	...	2041	...	...	2120	...	2141	2220	...	2241	...	...	...	2341	...	...
Olten 565 a.	...	1927	...	...	...	...	...	2027	...	...	...	2127	...	...	...	...	2227	...	...	2327	...	...	...	0027	...	...
Basel SBB 565 a.	...	1955	...	...	...	...	...	2055	...	...	...	2155	...	...	...	...	2259	...	...	2359	...	...	...	0102	...	...

Additional services **BELLINZONA - LOCARNO and v.v.**:

Bellinzona d.	0500 0530	and at the same minutes past each hour until	2300 2330	0000	...	0054	...
Locarno a.	0526 0556		2326 2356	0026	...	0116	...

Locarno d.	0534	0604 0634	and at the same minutes past each hour until	2304 2334	0016 0046 0121
Bellinzona a.	0559	0629 0659		2329 2359	0040 0110 0143

Additional services **MILANO PORTA GARIBALDI - COMO SAN GIOVANNI - CHIASSO and v.v.** (2nd class only): Operator: Trenord

	♠			♠				
Milano Porta Garibaldi d.	0609	0639	and at the same minutes past each hour until	2309	...	0039	...
Monza d.	0626	0656		2326	...	0056	...
Como San Giovanni d.	0708	0738		0008	...	0138	...
Chiasso a.	0717	0747		0017	...	0147	...

			♣			♣			
Chiasso d.	0513	0613	0643	and at the same minutes past each hour until	2113	2143	2213	2240	2313
Como San Giovanni d.	0522	0622	0652		2122	2152	2222	2246	2322
Monza d.	0602	0702	0732		2202	2232	2302	2332	0002
Milano Porta Garibaldi a.	0621	0721	0751		2221	2251	2321	2351	0021

VORALPEN EXPRESS – [12] St Gallen - Rapperswil - Arth Goldau - Luzern.

[12] Locarno - Zürich. Dec. 13 - Apr. 15, Oct. 24 - Dec. 10 runs as WILHELM TELL EXPRESS Locarno - Flüelen ([1] [R]).

[12] Locarno - Basel. Apr. 16 - Oct. 23 runs as WILHELM TELL EXPRESS Locarno - Flüelen ([1] [R]).

[12] Locarno - Basel. May 28 - Sept. 11 runs as WILHELM TELL EXPRESS Locarno - Flüelen ([1] [R]).

⑦ June 12 - Oct. 30 (also Mar. 28, May 16).

Ⓐ Dec. 14 - Dec. 7 (also Mar. 25, Dec. 9; not Jan. 6, May 26, June 29, Aug. 15, Nov. 1).

Connects with train in previous column(s).

♠ – Services at 0809, 1009 and 2009 from Milano Porta Garibaldi arrive Chiasso at 0920, 1120 and 2120 respectively.

♣ – Services at 10xx, 14xx and 20xx depart Chiasso at 1040, 1440 and 2040; Como San Giovanni at 1046, 1446 and 2046.

◧ – Supplement payable in Italy and for international journeys.

▲ – For additional services Locarno - Bellinzona and v.v. – see panel above.

§ – For additional services Chiasso - Como San Giovanni - Milano Porta Garibaldi and v.v. – see panel above.

* – Other distances: Arth-Goldau *0*, Küssnacht am Rigi *12 km*, Luzern *28 km*.

LOCARNO - DOMODOSSOLA — 551

RT

			C 🍸	V 🍸	C 🍸	V 🍸	V 🍸	🍸	V 🍸q	C	C
Locarno 550 d.	0647	0749	0849	1049	1149	1249	1449	1549	1649	1748	1848
Camedo 🏛 d.	0724	0824	0924	1124**u**	1224	1324**u**	1524**u**	1624	1724	1824	1924
Re d.	0740	0840**x**	0940**x**	1140**x**	1240**x**	1340**x**	1540**x**	1640	1740**x**	1840**x**	1940
S. M. Maggiore § d.	0753	0853**x**	0953**x**	1153**x**	1253**x**	1353**x**	1553**x**	1653	1753**x**	1853**x**	1953
Domodossola 590 a.	0836	0936	1036	1236	1336	1436	1636	1736	1836	1936	2036

		🍸q	C 🍸	V 🍸	V 🍸		V 🍸	Y 🍸	C 🍸	C	C
Domodossola 590 d.	0530**a**	0825	0925	1025	1125	1240	1325	1525	1625	1725	2025
S. M. Maggiore § d.	0612**a**	0910**x**	1010**x**	1110**x**	1210**x**	1324	1410**x**	1610**x**	1710**x**	1810	2109
Re d.	0625	0922**x**	1022**x**	1122**x**	1222**x**	1339	1422**x**	1622**x**	1722**x**	1822	2122
Camedo 🏛 d.	0639	0940	1040	1140	1240	1355	1440	1640	1740	1840	2138
Locarno 550 a.	0720	1019	1119	1219	1319	1432	1519	1719	1819	1919	2215

CENTOVALLI EXPRESS.

TRENO PANORAMICO VIGEZZO VISION – Conveys panorama car (supplement payable).

Daily. Runs Apr. 3 - Oct. 9 as TRENO PANORAMICO VIGEZZO VISION – Conveys panorama car (supplement payable).

a – Ⓐ Dec. 14 - Dec. 7 (also Jan. 2, Mar. 25, Dec. 9; not Jan. 6, May 26, June 29, Aug. 15, Nov. 1).

q – Apr. 3 - Oct. 9.

u – Stops to pick up only.

x – Stops only on request.

§ – Full name is Santa Maria Maggiore.

552 LUZERN - STANS - ENGELBERG

Narrow gauge rack railway.

km		E		E				E			E		🚌			🚌			🚌			🚌		T
0	**Luzern 561** d.	0505	0527	0610	0627	0657	and at	1910	1927	1957	2010	2027	...	2057	2127	...	2157	2227	...	2257	2327	...	EXTRA	0836
9	Hergiswil **561** d.	0517	0540	|	0640	0710	the same	|	1940	2010	|	2040	...	2110	2140	...	2210	2240	...	2310	2340	...	SERVICES	0847
11	Stansstad d.	0520	0544	|	0644	0714	minutes	|	1944	2014	|	2044	...	2114	2144	...	2214	2244	...	2314	2344	...	▶▶▶	0851
15	Stans d.	0524	0548	0624	0648	0719	past each	1924	1948	2019	2024	2048	...	2119	2148	...	2219	2248	...	2319	2348	...		0854
19	Dallenwil d.	0530	0552	0629	0652	...	hour until	1929	1952	...	2029	2052	2055	...	2152	2155	...	2252	2255	...	2352	2355		|
34	**Engelberg** ⊡ a.	0554	...	0653	...	...		1953	...	...	2053	...	2116	...	...	2216	...	...	2316	...	...	0016		0921

		🚌		E				E			E		🚌			🚌			🚌				T
Engelberg ⊡ d.	...	0535	...	0601	...	...	and at	2001	...	...	2101	...	2130	...	...	2230	...	...	2330	...	...		1631
Dallenwil d.	0504	0558	0604	0629	...	0704	the same	2029	...	2104	2129	...	2153	2204	...	2253	2304	...	2353	0004	...	EXTRA	|
Stans d.	0510	...	0610	0634	0640	0710	minutes	2034	2040	2110	2134	2140	...	2210	2240	...	2310	2340	...	0010	0040	SERVICES	1704
Stansstad d.	0514	...	0614	|	0644	0714	past each	|	2044	2114	|	2144	...	2214	2244	...	2314	2344	...	0014	0044	▶▶▶	1707
Hergiswil **561** d.	0518	...	0618	|	0648	0718	hour until	|	2048	2118	|	2148	...	2218	2248	...	2318	2348	...	0018	0048		1710
Luzern 561 a.	0531	...	0632	0649	0702	0732		2049	2102	2132	2149	2202	...	2232	2302	...	2332	0002	...	0032	0102		1724

E – LUZERN - ENGELBERG EXPRESS. Conveys panorama car.
T – Ⓒ Dec. 13 - Mar. 28, July 2 - Oct. 30 (also Dec. 28 - 31).

⊡ – Station for Titlis, accessible by cable car s
(including the world's first revolving cable

553 MOUNTAIN RAILWAYS IN CENTRAL SWITZERLAND

2nd class only.

km			p			and		p	q	
0	Arth-Goldau d.	0800	0910	...	1010	hourly	1610	1710	1810	...
9	Rigi Kulm a.	0845	0947	...	1047	until	1647	1747	1847	...

		p			and		p	q
Rigi Kulm d.	0900	1004	...	1104	hourly	1704	1804	1904
Arth-Goldau a.	0948	1048	...	1148	until	1748	1848	1948

December 13 - April 15 and October 24 - December 10

km			and			g						
0	Rigi Kulm d.	1000	hourly	1400	...	1430	...	1500	1600	...	1700	...
7	Vitznau a.	1040	until	1440	...	1539	...	1540	1640	...	1740	...

				f✗			and		n	
Vitznau d.	0915	1015	1115	1116	...	1215	hourly	1615	1740	...
Rigi Kulm a.	0947	1047	1147	1242	...	1247	until	1647	1812	...

April 16 - May 27 and September 12 - October 23

						🚂			and		⑤⑥
Rigi Kulm d.	1000	1100	1200	1300	1400	1430	...	1500	hourly	2000	2240
Vitznau a.	1040	1140	1240	1340	1440	1539	...	1540	until	2040	2320

					🚂✗			and		
Vitznau d.	0915	1015	1115	...	1116	...	1215	hourly	1915	...
Rigi Kulm a.	0947	1047	1147	...	1242	...	1247	until	1947	...

May 28 - September 11

		†	⚒				🚂		and		
Rigi Kulm d.	1000	1057	1100	1200	1300	1400	1430	1500	hourly	2000	2240
Vitznau a.	1040	1140	1140	1240	1340	1440	1539	1540	until	2040	2320

			†		🚂✗		and			
Vitznau d.	0915	1015	1050	1115	1116	1215	hourly	1915	...	2205
Rigi Kulm a.	0947	1047	1122	1147	1242	1247	until	1947	...	2237

ALPNACHSTAD - PILATUS KULM. Narrow gauge rack railway. *5 km*. Journey time: 30 minutes uphill, 40 minutes downhill. **Operator**: PB, ✆ 041 329 11 11.
Services run daily **early May - November 20** (weather permitting). **No winter service** (December - April).

From **Alpnachstad**: 0810 **j**, 0850, 0935, 1015, 1055, 1135, 1220, 1300, 1345, 1425, 1505, 1550, 1630 **j**, 1710 **j**, 1750 **k**.

From **Pilatus Kulm**: 0845 **j**, 0930, 1010, 1050, 1130, 1215, 1255, 1340, 1420, 1500, 1625, 1705 **j**, 1745 **j**, 1845 **k**.

BRIENZ - BRIENZER ROTHORN. Narrow gauge rack railway. *8 km*. Most services operated by 🚂. Journey time: 55 – 60 minutes uphill, 60 – 70 minutes downhill.
Operator: BRB, ✆ 033 952 22 22. Service valid **June 4 - October 23**, and is subject to weather conditions on the mountain and demand. Extra trains may run at busy times. **No winter se**

From **Brienz**: 0730 **h**, 0836, 0940, 1000③, 1045, 1145, 1258, 1358, 1458, 1636.

From **Brienzer Rothorn**: 0830 **h**, 0938, 1115, 1220, 1328, 1428, 1528, 1628, 1740.

f – Jan. 30, Feb. 27 only. Operated by 🚂. (✗).
g – Jan. 31, Feb. 28 only. Operated by 🚂.
h – ⑦ Sept. 4 - 25.
j – Until Oct. 29.
k – June 19 - Aug. 21.
n – Daily Dec. 19 - Mar. 13; Ⓒ Mar. 19 - Apr. 10; daily Oct. 24 - Dec. 10 (also Dec. 13).
p – Daily Dec. 19 - Mar. 13; Ⓒ Mar. 19 - May 1; daily May 2 - Oct. 30; ⑥⑦ Nov. 5 - Dec. 4 (also Dec. 13, Nov. 1, Dec. 8, 10).
q – ⑤ Dec. 18 - Apr. 29; ⑤⑥⑦ Apr. 30 - June 26; daily June 27 - Sept. 4; ⑤⑥⑦ Sept. 9 - Nov. 4; ⑤ Nov. 11 - Dec. 9 (also Dec. 24, 31, Mar. 24, May 4, 25).
w – ⑤⑥ (not Apr. 16).
x – ⑤⑥ Dec. 26 - Mar. 12, Oct. 28 - Dec. 10.
🚂 – June 5, 19, July 3, 17, Aug. 1, Sept. 4, 18. Reservations: ✆ 041 399 87
✗ – Supplement payable (CHF 20)
♧ – Subject to favourable weather conditions.

554 🚌 MEIRINGEN - ANDERMATT

Service June 25 - Oct. 16 (no winter service)

	Ⓡ						Ⓒ				
Meiringen Bahnhof d.	...	0850	0925	...	...	1050	1055	1325	1330	1520	...
Steingletscher, Susten d.	...	0944	|	1000	...	|	1149	|	1430	|	...
Susten Passhöhe d.	...	...	|	1010	...	|	...	|	1440	|	...
Göschenen Bahnhof d.	...	...	|	1049	...	|	...	|	1519	|	...
Grimsel Passhöhe d.	0912	...	1100	|	...	1204	...	1439	|	1634	...
Gletsch Post d.	0922	...	1110	|	...	1215	...	1450	|	1645	...
Oberwald Bahnhof a.	0937	...	1125	|	...	1230	...	1505	|	1700	...
Oberwald Bahnhof d.	...	...	...	|	1220	...	...	...	|	...	1704
Gletsch Post d.	...	...	...	|	1233	...	...	...	|	...	1720
Furka Passhöhe d.	...	...	...	|	1407	...	...	...	|	...	1743
Realp Post d.	...	...	...	|	1433	...	...	...	|	...	1809
Andermatt Bahnhof a.	...	...	...	1104	1452	...	...	...	1534	...	1828

			Ⓡ			Ⓒ				
Andermatt Bahnhof d.	...	...	...	0830	...	...	...	...	1539	1559
Realp Post d.	...	...	...	0842	...	...	...	...	1551	|
Furka Passhöhe d.	...	...	...	0906	...	...	...	...	1615	|
Gletsch Post d.	...	...	...	1005	...	...	...	...	1645	|
Oberwald Bahnhof a.	...	...	...	1020	...	...	...	...	1700	|
Oberwald Bahnhof d.	...	...	0845	...	1030	...	1250	1530	...	|
Gletsch Post d.	...	...	0857	...	1046	...	1302	1542	...	|
Grimsel Passhöhe d.	...	...	0911	...	1125	...	1330	1610	...	|
Göschenen Bahnhof d.	0910	...	...	...	|	...	|	|	...	1615
Susten Passhöhe d.	0945	...	...	...	|	...	|	|	...	1650
Steingletscher, Sustend.	0950	1000	...	...	|	1150	|	|	...	1720
Meiringen Bahnhof a.	...	1050	...	...	1225	1240	1434	1714	...	1810

Reservations: ✆ +41 (0)58 448 20 08.

555 ZÜRICH FLUGHAFEN ✈ - ZÜRICH - LUZERN

All trains *IR*

km																Ⓐ			Ⓐ					
0	**Zürich** Flughafen ✈ **530/5** d.	...	...	...	...	...	...	...	0847	...	and at	1547	...	...	...	1647	...	...	1747	...	...	1847	...	1947
10	**Zürich** HB **530/5** d.	0535	0604	0635	0704	0735	0804	0835	0904	0935	the same	1604	1635	...	1639	1704	1735	1739	1804	1835	...	1904	1935	2004
22	Thalwil d.	0545	0614	0645	0714	0745	0814	0845	0914	0945	minutes	1614	1645	...	|	1714	1745	|	1814	1845	...	1914	1945	2014
39	Zug d.	0602	0629	0702	0729	0802	0829	0902	0929	1002	past each	1629	1702	...	1712	1729	1802	1812	1829	1902	...	1929	2002	2029
49	Rotkreuz d.	0610	|	0710	|	0810	|	0910	|	1010	hour	|	1710	...	1721	|	1810	1821	|	1910	...	|	2010	|
67	**Luzern** a.	0625	0649	0725	0749	0825	0849	0925	0949	1025	until	1649	1725	...	1739	1749	1825	1839	1849	1925	...	1949	2025	2049

									x✗	y✗	y✗
Zürich Flughafen ✈ **530/5** d.	2047	...	...	...	...	...	...	...	...	...	...
Zürich HB **530/5** d.	2104	2135	2204	2235	2304	2335	...	0008	0135	0235	0335
Thalwil d.	2114	2145	2214	2245	2314	2345	...	0017	|	|	|
Zug d.	2129	2202	2229	2302	2329	0002	...	0035	0155	0255	0355
Rotkreuz d.	|	2210	|	2310	|	0010	...	0046	0202	0302	0402
Luzern a.	2149	2225	2249	2325	2349	0025	...	0107	0225	0325	0425

				Ⓐ				Ⓐ
Luzern d.	0455	0528	0610	0620	0635	...	0710	0720
Rotkreuz d.	0513	0548	|	0636	0648	...	|	0736
Zug d.	0526	0558	0631	0647	0658	...	0731	0747
Thalwil d.	0542	0615	0646	|	0715	...	0746	|
Zürich HB **530/5** a.	0555	0625	0656	0720	0725	...	0756	0820
Zürich Flughafen ✈ **530/5** a.	0613	...	...	...	...	...	0813	...

																							x	y✗
Luzern d.	0810	0835	and at	1510	1535	...	1610	1635	1710	1735	1810	1835	1910	1935	2010	2035	2110	2135	2210	2235	2310	2335	0035	0135
Rotkreuz d.	|	0848	the same	|	1548	...	|	1648	|	1748	|	1848	|	1948	|	2048	|	2148	|	2248	|	2348	0048	0146
Zug d.	0831	0858	minutes	1531	1558	...	1631	1658	1731	1758	1831	1858	1931	1958	2031	2058	2131	2158	2231	2258	2331	2358	0058	0153
Thalwil d.	0846	0915	past each	1546	1615	...	1646	1715	1746	1815	1846	1915	1946	2015	2046	2115	2146	2215	2246	2315	2346	0015	0116	0211
Zürich HB **530/5** a.	0856	0925	hour	1556	1625	...	1656	1725	1756	1825	1856	1925	1956	2025	2056	2125	2156	2225	2256	2325	2356	0025	0125	0225
Zürich Flughafen ✈ **530/5** a.	0913	...	until	1613	...	...	1713	...	1813	...	1913	...	2013	...	...	...	...	...	...	...	...	...	...	...

x – ⑥⑦ (also Jan. 1, Mar. 25, 28, May 5, 6, 16, Aug. 1).
y – ⑥⑦ (also Jan. 1, Mar. 25, 28, May 5, 6, 16, Aug. 1; not Dec. 26).
✗ – Supplement payable.

BASEL - BERN - INTERLAKEN and BRIG

	IC	*IC*	*IC*	*IC*	*IC*	*EC*	*IC*	*IC*	*IC*	*IC*	*IC*	*IC*	*IC*	*IC*	*IC*	*IC*	*IC*	*IC*	*IC*	*IC*	*IC*	*ICE*	*IC*	*EC*
	955	**802**	**1057**	**957**	**804**	**51**	**959**	**806**	**1061**	**961**	**808**	**1063**	**963**	**810**	**1065**	**965**	**812**	**1067**	**967**	**814**	**1069**	**275**	**816**	**57**
						◧												**D**				◆		◧
Romanshorn **535** d.	...	...	...	...	...	...	...	0538	...	...	0638	...	...	0741	...	...	0841	...	...	0941	...	...	1041	...
Zürich Flug ✈ **535** d.	...	...	...	...	...	...	...	0640	...	...	0740	...	...	0840	...	...	0940	...	...	1040	...	...	1140	...
Zürich HB **505** d.	...	...	...	...	0602	...	...	0702	...	...	0802	...	...	0902	...	...	1002	...	...	1102	...	...	1202	...
Basel SBB d.	...	...	0524	0559	|	0631	0659	|	0731	0759	|	0831	0859	|	0931	0959	|	1031	1059	|	1131	1159	|	1231
Olten d.	...	...	0557	0629	|	0657	0729	|	0757	0829	|	0857	0929	|	0957	1029	|	1057	1129	|	1157	1229	|	1257
Bern **505** a.	...	...	0624	0656	0658**k**	0724	0756	0758**k**	0824	0856	0858**k**	0924	0956	0958**k**	1024	1056	1058**k**	1124	1156	1158**k**	1224	1256	1258**k**	1324
Bern d.	0604	0606	0634	0704	0706	0734	0804	0806	0834	0904	0906	0934	1004	1006	1034	1104	1106	1134	1204	1206	1234	1304	1306	1334
Thun d.	0623	0625	0654	0723	0725	0754	0823	0825	0854	0923	0925	0954	1023	1025	1054	1123	1125	1154	1223	1225	1254	1323	1325	1354
Spiez a.	0632	0634	0702	0732	0734	0802	0832	0834	0902	0932	0934	1002	1032	1034	1102	1132	1134	1202	1232	1234	1302	1332	1334	1402
Spiez ▲ d.	0633	0636	0703	0733	0736	0805	0833	0836	0903	0933	0936	1005	1033	1036	1103	1133	1136	1205	1233	1236	1303	1333	1336	1405
Interlaken West ▲ d.	0652	|	0723	0752	|	*0824*	0852	|	0923	0952	|	*1024*	1053	|	1123	1153	|	*1224*	1252	|	1323	1353	|	*1424*
Interlaken Ost ▲ a.	0657	|	0728	0757	|	*0828*	0857	|	0928	0957	|	*1028*	1057	|	1128	1157	|	*1228*	1257	|	1328	1357	|	*1428*
Visp d.	...	0703	...	...	0803	0832	...	0903	...	...	1003	1032	...	1103	...	...	1203	1232	...	1303	...	...	1403	1432
Brig a.	...	0711	...	...	0811	0840	...	0911	...	...	1011	1040	...	1111	...	...	1211	1240	...	1311	...	...	1411	1440
Milano C **590** a.	...	...	...	...	...	1035	...	...	...	...	...	...	...	...	...	...	...	...	...	...	...	...	...	1637

	IC	*IC*	*IC*	*EC*	*IC*	*IC*	*IC*	*IC*	*IC*	*IC*	*IC*	*IC*	*IC*	*IC*		*EC*	*ICE*	*IC*	*IC*	*IC*	*IC*	*IC*	*ICE*	*IC*	*IC*
	971	**818**	**1073**	**7**	**820**	**1075**	**975**	**822**	**1077**	**977**	**824**	**1079**	**979**	**826**		**59**	**371**	**828**	**1083**	**983**	**830**	**1085**	**373**	**1087**	**1089**
				H												◧	**B**						**B**	①–⑥	⑦
Romanshorn **535** d.	...	1141	...	...	1241	...	...	1341	...	...	1441	...	...	1541	...	...	...	1641	...	...	1741	...	...	...	...
Zürich Flug ✈ **535** d.	...	1240	...	...	1340	...	...	1440	...	...	1540	...	...	1640	...	...	...	1740	...	...	1840	...	...	...	...
Zürich HB **505** d.	...	1302	...	...	1402	...	...	1502	...	...	1602	...	...	1702	...	...	...	1802	...	...	1902	...	...	...	...
Basel SBB d.	1259	|	1331	1359	|	1431	1459	|	1531	1559	|	1631	1659	|	...	1731	1759	|	1831	1859	|	1931	1959	2031	2031
Olten d.	1329	|	1357	1429	|	1457	1529	|	1557	1629	|	1657	1729	|	...	1757	1829	|	1857	1929	|	1957	2029	2057	2057
Bern **505** a.	1356	1358**k**	1424	1456	1458**k**	1524	1556	1558**k**	1624	1656	1658**k**	1724	1756	1758**k**	...	1824	1856	1858**k**	1924	1956	1958**k**	2024	2056	2124	2124
Bern d.	1404	1406	1434	1504	1506	1534	1604	1606	1634	1704	1706	1734	1804	1806	...	1834	1904	1906	1934	2004	2006	2034	2107	2134	2134
Thun d.	1423	1425	1454	1523	1525	1554	1623	1625	1654	1723	1725	1754	1823	1825	...	1854	1923	1925	1954	2023	2025	2054	2126	2154	2154
Spiez a.	1432	1434	1502	1532	1534	1602	1632	1634	1702	1732	1734	1802	1832	1834	...	1902	1932	1934	2002	2032	2034	2102	2135	2202	2202
Spiez ▲ d.	1433	1436	1503	1533	1536	1605	1633	1636	1703	1733	1736	1805	1833	1836	...	1905	1933	1936	2003	2033	2036	2105	2136	2205	2205
Interlaken West ▲ d.	1453	|	1523	1553	|	*1624*	1652	|	1723	1753	|	*1824*	1852	|	...	*1924*	1952	|	2023	2050	|	|	2153	|	|
Interlaken Ost ▲ a.	1457	|	1528	1557	|	*1628*	1657	|	1728	1757	|	*1828*	1857	|	...	*1928*	1957	|	2028	2054	|	|	2157	|	|
Visp d.	...	1503	...	...	1603	1632	...	1703	...	...	1803	1832	...	1903	...	1932	...	2003	...	...	2103	2132	...	2232	|
Brig a.	...	1511	...	...	1611	1640	...	1711	...	...	1811	1840	...	1911	...	1940	...	2011	...	...	2111	2140	...	2240	2301
Milano C **590** a.	...	...	...	...	...	...	...	...	...	...	...	...	...	...	...	2137	...	...	...	...	...	...	...	...	...

	IC	*IC*	*TGV*	*IC*	*IC*	*IC*	*IC*	*IC*	*IC*	
	987	**1091**	**9225**	**989**	**1093**	**1095**	**1097**	**991**	**993**	
			(🍷) **P**		①–⑥	⑦			**w**	
Romanshorn **535** d.	...	...	...	...	...	...	...	...	...	...
Zürich Flug ✈ **535** d.	...	...	...	...	...	...	...	...	...	...
Zürich HB **505** d.	...	...	...	...	...	...	...	...	...	...
Basel SBB d.	2059	2131	2136	...	...	...	2231	...	...	...
Olten d.	2129	2157	2202	...	...	...	2257	...	...	...
Bern **505** a.	2156	2224	2250	...	...	...	2326	...	...	...
Bern d.	2207	...	2302	2308	2234	2234	2339	0008	0108	...
Thun d.	2226	...	|	2327	2254	2254	0000	0029	0133	...
Spiez a.	2235	...	|	2336	2302	2302	0009	0038	0143	...
Spiez ▲ d.	2236	...	|	2337	2305	2305	...	0038	0143	...
Interlaken West ▲ d.	2252	...	2349	2356	|	|	...	0053	0200	...
Interlaken Ost ▲ a.	2257	...	2353	0001	**f**	**f**	...	0100	0205	...
Visp d.	...	...	...	...	2335	|	...	...	...	...
Brig a.	...	...	...	...	2344	0011	...	...	...	...
Milano C **590** a.	...	...	...	...	...	...	...	...	...	...

	IC	*IC*	*IC*	*ICE*	*IC*	*IC*	*IC*	*IC*	*IC*	*IC*
	956	**805**	**1056**	**372**	**807**	**1058**	**960**	**809**	**1060**	**962**
				B						
Milano C **590** d.	...	...	...	...	...	...	...	...	...	...
Brig d.	...	...	...	...	0546	...	...	0649	0720	...
Visp d.	...	...	...	...	0554	...	...	0657	0728	...
Interlaken Ost ▲ d.	...	...	0521	0600	**f**	0627	0700	|	*0729*	0800
Interlaken West ▲ d.	...	...	0526	0605	|	0632	0705	|	*0733*	0805
Spiez ▲ a.	...	...	0548	0621	0624	0652	0721	0724	0753	0821
Spiez d.	0520	...	0550	0622	0625	0654	0722	0725	0754	0822
Thun d.	0530	...	0601	0633	0636	0704	0733	0736	0804	0833
Bern a.	0552	...	0623	0652	0654**k**	0723	0752	0754**k**	0823	0852
Bern **505** d.	0604	0602	0636	0704	0702	0736	0804	0802	0836	0904
Olten d.	0632	0631	0705	0732	|	0805	0832	|	0905	0932
Basel SBB a.	0659	|	0729	0759	|	0829	0859	|	0929	0959
Zürich HB **505** a.	...	0702	...	...	0758	...	...	0858	...	...
Zürich Flug ✈ **535** a.	...	0716	...	...	0816	...	...	0916	...	...
Romanshorn **535** a.	...	0818	...	...	0918	...	...	1018	...	...

	IC	*TGV*	*IC*	*IC*	*IC*	*EC*	*ICE*	*IC*	*IC*	*IC*	*IC*	*IC*	*EC*	*IC*	*IC*	*IC*	*IC*	*EC*	*IC*	*IC*	*IC*	*ICE*	*IC*	*IC*
	811	**9214**	**1062**	**964**	**813**	**50**	**278**	**815**	**1066**	**968**	**817**	**1068**	**6**	**819**	**1070**	**972**	**821**	**52**	**974**	**823**	**1074**	**376**	**825**	**1076**
		(🍷) **P**				◧	**B**						**H**					◧				◆		**D**
Milano C **590** d.	...	...	...	...	...	0723	...	...	...	...	...	...	...	...	...	...	...	1123	...	...	...	...	...	...
Brig d.	0749	...	...	...	0849	0920	...	0949	...	...	1049	1120	...	1149	...	...	1249	1320	...	1349	...	...	1449	1520
Visp d.	0757	...	...	...	0857	0928	...	0957	...	...	1057	1128	...	1157	...	...	1257	1328	...	1357	...	...	1457	1528
Interlaken Ost ▲ d.	|	...	0830	0900	|	*0929*	1000	|	1030	1100	|	*1129*	1200	|	1230	1300	|	*1329*	1400	|	1430	1500	|	*1529*
Interlaken West ▲ d.	|	...	0835	0905	|	*0933*	1005	|	1035	1105	|	*1133*	1205	|	1235	1305	|	*1333*	1405	|	1435	1505	|	*1533*
Spiez ▲ a.	0824	...	0852	0921	0924	0953	1021	1024	1052	1121	1124	1153	1221	1224	1252	1321	1324	1353	1421	1424	1452	1521	1524	1553
Spiez d.	0825	...	0854	0922	0925	0954	1022	1025	1054	1122	1125	1154	1222	1225	1254	1322	1325	1354	1422	1425	1454	1522	1525	1554
Thun d.	0836	...	0904	0933	0936	1004	1033	1036	1104	1133	1136	1204	1233	1236	1304	1333	1336	1404	1433	1436	1504	1533	1536	1604
Bern a.	0854**k**	...	0923	0952	0954**k**	1023	1052	1054**k**	1123	1152	1154**k**	1223	1252	1254**k**	1323	1352	1354**k**	1423	1452	1454**k**	1523	1552	1554**k**	1623
Bern **505** d.	0902	0910	0936	1004	1002	1036	1104	1102	1136	1204	1202	1236	1304	1302	1336	1404	1402	1436	1504	1502	1536	1604	1602	1636
Olten d.	|	|	1005	1032	|	1105	1132	|	1205	1232	|	1305	1332	|	1405	1432	|	1505	1532	|	1605	1632	|	1705
Basel SBB a.	|	1023	1029	1059	|	1129	1159	|	1229	1259	|	1329	1359	|	1429	1459	|	1529	1559	|	1629	1659	|	1729
Zürich HB **505** a.	0958	...	...	...	1058	...	...	1158	...	...	1258	...	...	1358	...	...	1458	...	...	1558	...	...	1658	...
Zürich Flug ✈ **535** a.	1016	...	...	...	1116	...	...	1216	...	...	1316	...	...	1416	...	...	1516	...	...	1616	...	...	1716	...
Romanshorn **535** a.	1118	...	...	...	1218	...	...	1318	...	...	1418	...	...	1518	...	...	1618	...	...	1718	...	...	1818	...

	IC	*IC*	*IC*	*IC*	*IC*	*IC*	*IC*	*IC*	*IC*	*IC*	*IC*	*IC*	*IC*	*IC*	*EC*	*ICE*	*IC*	*IC*	*ICE*	*IC*	*IC*	*IC*	*IC*	*IC*	*IC*
	978	**827**	**1078**	**980**	**829**	**1080**	**982**	**831**	**1082**	**984**	**833**	**1084**	**986**	**835**	**56**	**336**	**837**	**1088**	**338**	**990**	**1090**	**1096**	**992**	**1092**	**1094**
															◧						①–⑥			⑦	**v**
Milano C **590** d.	...	...	...	...	...	...	...	...	...	...	...	...	...	...	1823	...	...	...	...	...	...	...	...	...	...
Brig d.	...	1549	...	...	1649	1720	...	1749	...	...	1849	1920	...	1949	2020	...	...	2120	...	...	2220	...	...	2226	...
Visp d.	...	1557	...	...	1657	1728	...	1757	...	...	1857	1928	...	1957	2028	...	...	2128	...	...	2228	...	...	|	...
Interlaken Ost ▲ d.	1600	|	1630	1700	|	*1729*	1800	|	1830	1900	|	*1929*	2000	|	|	2100	...	|	...	2200	|	...	2300	|	2333
Interlaken West ▲ d.	1605	|	1635	1705	|	*1733*	1805	|	1835	1905	|	*1933*	2005	|	|	2105	...	|	...	2205	|	...	2305	|	2338
Spiez ▲ a.	1621	1624	1652	1721	1724	1753	1821	1824	1852	1921	1924	1953	2021	2024	2053	2121	...	2153	...	2221	2253	...	2321	2322	2356
Spiez d.	1622	1625	1654	1722	1725	1754	1822	1825	1854	1922	1925	1954	2022	2025	2054	2122	...	2154	...	2222	2254	...	2322	2325	2357
Thun d.	1633	1636	1704	1733	1736	1804	1833	1836	1904	1933	1936	2004	2033	2036	2104	2133	...	2204	...	2233	2304	...	2333	2336	0007
Bern a.	1652	1654**k**	1723	1752	1754**k**	1823	1852	1854**k**	1923	1952	1954**k**	2023	2052	2054**k**	2123	2152	...	2223	...	2252	2323	...	2352	2354	0026
Bern **505** d.	1704	1702	1736	1804	1802	1836	1904	1902	1936	2004	2002	2036	2104	2102	2136	...	2202	...	2236	...	...	2336	...	...	...
Olten d.	1732	|	1805	1832	|	1905	1932	|	2005	2032	|	2105	2132	|	2205	...	2230	...	2307	...	...	0007	...	...	...
Basel SBB a.	1759	|	1829	1859	|	1929	1959	|	2029	2059	|	2129	2159	|	2229	...	|	...	2330	...	...	0033	...	...	...
Zürich HB **505** a.	...	1758	...	...	1858	...	...	1958	...	...	2058	...	...	2158	...	...	2301	...	...	...	...	...	...	...	...
Zürich Flug ✈ **535** a.	...	1816	...	...	1916	...	...	2016	...	...	2116	...	...	2216	...	...	2316	...	...	...	...	...	...	...	...
Romanshorn **535** a.	...	1918	...	...	2018	...	...	2118	...	...	2218	...	...	2318	...	...	0018	...	...	...	...	...	...	...	...

NOTES (LISTED BY TRAIN NUMBER)

– [12] and ✕ (Berlin ①–⑤ **h** -) Frankfurt - Basel - Interlaken.
– [12] and ✕ Interlaken - Basel - Frankfurt (- Hamburg ⑤⑦ July 17 - Aug. 28, train number **396**).
[12] and ✕ Interlaken - Basel - Berlin and v.v.
[12] and ✕ Basel - Brig - Domodossola and v.v.
[12] and ✕ Interlaken - Basel - Hamburg and v.v.
[12] and (🍷) Paris Lyon - Basel - Bern / Interlaken and v.v.

f – Via Frutigen.
h – Not Dec. 24, 31.
k – Connects with train in previous column.
v – ⑤⑥ (also Dec. 31; not Mar. 25).
w – ⑥⑦ (also Jan. 1; not Mar. 26).

◧ – Supplement payable for journeys from / to Italy.

561 LUZERN - INTERLAKEN

Narrow gauge rack railway.

km																							
		Ⓐ	Ⓐ	L		L			L				L			L			L			L	
0	**Luzern 552** d.	...	...	...	0542	0605	0612	0642	0705	0712	0742		1705	1712	1742	1805	1812	1842	1905	1912	1942	2005	2012
9	Hergiswil **552** d.	...	...	...	0554	|	0624	0654	|	0724	0754		|	1724	1754	|	1824	1854	|	1924	1954	|	2024
13	Alpnachstad d.	...	...	...	0559	|	0629	0659	|	0729	0759		|	1729	1759	|	1829	1859	|	1929	1959	|	2029
15	Alpnach Dorf d.	...	...	...	0601	|	0631	0701	|	0731	0801	and at	|	1731	1801	|	1831	1901	|	1931	2001	|	2031
21	Sarnen d.	...	...	...	0609	0624	0641	0709	0724	0741	0809	the same	1724	1741	1809	1824	1841	1909	1924	1941	2009	2024	2041
23	Sachseln d.	...	...	...	0613	0628	0645	0713	0728	0745	0813	minutes	1728	1745	1813	1828	1845	1913	1928	1945	2013	2028	2045
29	Giswil d.	...	...	...	0621	0638	0654	0721	0738	0754	0821	past each	1738	1754	1821	1838	1854	1921	1938	1954	2021	2038	2054
36	Lungern d.	...	...	...	—	0652	...	—	0752	...	—	hour	1752	...	—	1852	...	...	1952	—	...	2052	—
40	Brünig Hasliberg d.	...	...	...	...	0704	...	...	0804	...	...	until	1804	...	...	1904	...	...	2004	...	...	2104	...
45	**Meiringen ●** a.	...	...	...	...	0716	...	...	0816	...	...		1816	...	...	1916	...	...	2016	...	...	2116	...
45	**Meiringen ●** d.	0515	0545	0614	0651	0722	...	0751	0822	...	0851		1822	...	1851	1922	...	...	...	2020	...	...	2120
58	**Brienz** d.	0527	0558	0628	0702	0733	...	0802	0837	...	0902		1837	...	1902	1935	...	...	...	2033	...	...	2132
65	Oberried d.	0537	0609	0639	0712	0744	...	0812	|	...	0912		|	...	1912	1944	...	...	...	2043	...	...	2142
74	**Interlaken** Ost a.	0550	0621	0651	0724	0754	...	0824	0855	...	0924		1855	...	1924	1955	...	...	...	2055	...	...	2155

	L								
Luzern 552 d.	2105	2112	2142	2212	2242	2312	2342	0012	0042
Hergiswil **552** d.	|	2124	2154	2224	2254	2324	2354	0024	0054
Alpnachstad d.	|	2129	2159	2229	2259	2329	2359	0029	0059
Alpnach Dorf d.	|	2131	2201	2231	2301	2331	0001	0031	0101
Sarnen d.	2124	2141	2209	2241	2309	2341	0009	0041	0109
Sachseln d.	2128	2145	2213	2245	2313	2345	0013	0045	0113
Giswil d.	2138	2154	2221	2254	2321	2354	0021	0054	0121
Lungern d.	2152	—	...	—	...	...	...	...	...
Brünig Hasliberg d.	2204	...	...	...	...	...	...	...	...
Meiringen ● a.	2216	...	...	y	...	...	...	...	...
Meiringen ● d.	...	2220	...	2320	...	...	...	...	...
Brienz d.	...	2232	...	2332	...	...	...	...	...
Oberried d.	...	2242	...	2342	...	...	...	...	...
Interlaken Ost a.	...	2255	...	2355	...	...	...	...	...

				L		Ⓐ		L	Ⓐ
Interlaken Ost d.	...	...	...	...	...	0554	...	...	0627
Oberried d.	...	...	...	...	...	0608	...	...	0640
Brienz d.	...	...	...	...	...	0618	...	...	0650
Meiringen ● a.	...	...	...	...	...	0631	...	...	0703
Meiringen ● d.	...	...	...	0542	...	...	...	0642	—
Brünig Hasliberg d.	...	...	...	0552	...	...	...	0652	...
Lungern d.	...	...	...	0605	...	...	...	0705	...
Giswil d.	0505	0537	0605	0622	0637	...	0705	0722	0737
Sachseln d.	0513	0545	0613	0629	0645	...	0713	0729	0745
Sarnen d.	0517	0549	0617	0635	0649	...	0717	0735	0749
Alpnach Dorf d.	0524	0554	0624	|	0654	...	0724	|	0754
Alpnachstad d.	0529	0559	0629	|	0659	...	0729	|	0759
Hergiswil **552** d.	0534	0604	0634	|	0704	...	0734	|	0804
Luzern 552 a.	0547	0617	0647	0655	0717	...	0747	0755	0817

	L			L				L				L			L						z
Interlaken Ost d.	0704	...	0733	0804	...	0833		1804	...	1833	...	1904	...	1933	2004	...	2106	...	2206	...	2306	0006
Oberried d.	0714	...	0745	|	...	0844		|	...	1844	...	|	...	1946	2015	...	2118	...	2218	...	2318	0017
Brienz d.	0725	...	0754	0825	...	0854		1825	...	1854	...	1925	...	1957	2025	...	2130	...	2230	...	2330	0027
Meiringen ● a.	0736	...	0807	0836	...	0907	and at	1836	...	1907	...	1936	...	2009	2036	...	2142	...	2242	...	2342	0039
Meiringen ● d.	0742	...	—	0842	...	—	the same	1842	...	—	...	1942	...	—	2042	...	—	...	—	...	—	...
Brünig Hasliberg d.	0752	...	...	0852	...	...	minutes	1852	...	...	...	1952	...	...	2052	...	...	...	...	...	...	...
Lungern d.	0805	...	...	0905	...	...	past each	1905	...	...	...	2005	...	...	2105	...	...	...	...	...	...	...
Giswil d.	0822	0837	0905	0922	0937	1005	hour	1922	1937	2005	...	2022	2037	2105	2122	2137	2205	2237	2305	2337	0005	...
Sachseln d.	0829	0845	0913	0929	0945	1013	until	1929	1945	2013	...	2029	2045	2113	2129	2145	2213	2245	2313	2345	0013	...
Sarnen d.	0835	0849	0917	0935	0949	1017		1935	1949	2017	...	2035	2049	2117	2135	2149	2217	2249	2317	2349	0017	...
Alpnach Dorf d.	|	0854	0924	|	0954	1024		|	1954	2024	...	|	2054	2124	|	2154	2224	2254	2324	2354	0024	...
Alpnachstad d.	|	0859	0929	|	0959	1029		|	1959	2029	...	|	2059	2129	|	2159	2229	2259	2329	2359	0029	...
Hergiswil **552** d.	|	0904	0934	|	1004	1034		|	2004	2034	...	|	2104	2134	|	2204	2234	2304	2334	0004	0034	...
Luzern 552 a.	0855	0917	0947	0955	1017	1047		1955	2017	2047	...	2055	2117	2147	2155	2217	2247	2317	2347	0017	0047	...

L – LUZERN - INTERLAKEN EXPRESS. Conveys [12] [panorama car] (reservation recommended). Also conveys (✕) on most services.

q – ⑥⑦ May 7 - Aug. 21 (also May 5, 16).
y – ⑤⑥ (not Dec. 25, 26, Jan. 1, 2, Mar. 25).
z – ⑥⑦ (not Dec. 26, 27, Jan. 2, 3, Mar. 26).

● – Rail service **Meiringen - Innertkirchen** and v.v. Narrow gauge. 2nd class only. *5 km*. Journey time: 11 minutes. **Operator**: MIB.

From **Meiringen**: 0612Ⓐ, 0634Ⓐ, 0656, 0718, 0745, 0815, 0845, 0945, 1045, 1115, 1145, 1215, 1315, 1345, 1415 **q**, 1445, 1515 **q**, 1545, 1615, 1645, 1715Ⓐ, 1745, 1815Ⓐ, 1845, 1945, 2145, 2245 **y**.

From **Innertkirchen**: 0558Ⓐ, 0623Ⓐ, 0629Ⓒ, 0645Ⓐ, 0707, 0729, 0802, 0827, 0902, 1002, 1102, 1202, 1227, 1302, 1327, 1402, 1427 **q**, 1502, 1527 **q**, 1602, 1627, 1702, 1727Ⓐ, 1802, 18[illegible] 1902, 2002, 2102, 2202 **y**.

562 SPIEZ - BRIG (via Lötschberg pass)

km									*IC* 1093	*IC* 1095	
			T		and at				①–⑥	⑦	
	Bern d.	...	...	0739	the same	1939	...	...	2234	2234	...
0	**Spiez** d.	0612	0712	0812	minutes	2012	2112	2212	2305	2305	0012
14	Frutigen ● d.	0625	0725	0825	past each	2025	2125	2225	2317	2317	0025
31	Kandersteg 🚗 d.	0642	0742	0842	hour	2042	2142	2242	|	2335	0042
48	Goppenstein 🚗 d.	0657	0757	0857	until	2057	2157	2257	|	2348	0053
74	**Brig** a.	0723	0823	0923		2123	2223	2323	2344	0011	0120

		IC 807							
		R			and at				
Brig d.	0516	0546	...	0636	the same	1736	1836	1936	2036
Goppenstein 🚗 d.	0542	|	...	0701	minutes	1801	1901	2001	2101
Kandersteg 🚗 d.	0554	|	←	0713	past each	1813	1913	2013	2113
Frutigen ● d.	0609	0612	0630	0730	hour	1830	1930	2030	2130
Spiez a.	→	0624	0644	0744	until	1844	1944	2044	2144
Bern a.	...	0654	0720	0820		1920	...	...	...

♦ – **NOTES** (LISTED BY TRAIN NUMBER)

R – [12] Brig - Romanshorn.
T – From Thun.

🚗 – Car-carrying shuttle available (see page 260).

● – 🚌 **SERVICE FRUTIGEN - ADELBODEN and v.v.:**
20 km, journey ±32 minutes. Operator: AFA, 3715 Adelboden. ✆ +41 (0)33 673 74 74, fax +41 (0)33 673 74 7[illegible]

From **Frutigen:** 0615Ⓐ, 0631, 0700Ⓐ, 0731, 0800, 0831, 0900Ⓒ, 0931, 1000Ⓒ, 1031, 1131 and hourly until 1631, then 170[illegible] 1731, 1800, 1831, 1900Ⓐ, 1931, 2031, 2131, 2231, 2331.

From **Adelboden** (Post): 0535Ⓐ, 0550, 0622Ⓐ, 0650, 0725, 0750, 0825Ⓒ, 0850, 0925Ⓒ, 0950, 1050 and hourly until 155[illegible] then 1625, 1650, 1725, 1750, 1825Ⓐ, 1850, 1950, 2050, 2150, 2225.

532 SCHAFFHAUSEN - ROMANSHORN - RORSCHACH

SBB, THURB[illegible]

km																								
																					X	Y		
0	**Schaffhausen 939/40** d.	...	...	...	...	0503	...	0531	...	0601	...		2031	...	2101	...	2131	2201	...	2231	2301	2301	...	2331
20	Stein am Rhein d.	...	...	...	...	0527	...	0557	...	0627	...		2057	...	2127	...	2157	2227	...	2257	2327	2327	...	2357
46	**Kreuzlingen** d.	0500	...	0530	...	0600	...	0630	...	0700	...	and at	2130	...	2200	...	2230	2300	...	2330	0000	0000	...	0026
47	Kreuzlingen Hafen d.	0502	...	0532	...	0602	...	0632	...	0702	...	the same	2132	...	2202	...	2232	2302	...	2332	0002	0002	...	...
65	**Romanshorn** a.	0526	...	0556	...	0626	...	0656	...	0726	...	minutes	2156	...	2226	...	2256	2326	...	2356	0026	0026	...	...
65	**Romanshorn** d.	0530	0531	0600	0601	0630	0631	0700	0701	0730	0731	past each	2200	2201	2230	2231	2300	2330	2331	*0001*	0030	...	0031	...
	St Gallen **525** a.	0555	|	0624	|	0655	|	0724	|	0755	|	hour	2224	|	2255	|	2324	2355	|	|	0055	...	|	...
73	Arbon a.	...	0540	...	0610	...	0640	...	0710	...	0740	until	...	2210	...	2240	...	...	2340	*0010*	...	...	0040	...
79	Rorschach Hafen a.	...	0547	...	0617	...	0647	...	0717	...	0747		...	2217	...	2247	...	...	2347	*0017*	...	...	0047	...
80	**Rorschach** a.	...	0550	...	0620	...	0650	...	0720	...	0750		...	2220	...	2250	...	...	2350	*0020*	...	...	0050	...

Rorschach d.	...	...	0508	...	0538	...	0608	...	0638	...		2108	...	2138	...	2208	...	2238	...	2308	...	2338	...	0008
Rorschach Hafen d.	...	...	0510	...	0540	...	0610	...	0640	...		2110	...	2140	...	2210	...	2240	...	2310	...	2340	...	0010
Arbon d.	...	...	0517	...	0547	...	0617	...	0647	...	and at	2117	...	2147	...	2217	...	2247	...	2317	...	2347	...	0017
St Gallen **525** d.	...	...	|	...	|	0535	|	0604	|	0635	the same	|	2104	|	2135	|	2204	|	2235	|	2305	|	2335	|
Romanshorn a.	...	...	0528	...	0557	0600	0628	0630	0658	0700	minutes	2128	2130	2158	2200	2228	2230	2258	2300	2328	2330	2358	2400	0028
Romanshorn d.	...	0502	...	0532	...	0602	...	0632	...	0702	past each	...	2132	...	2202	...	2232	...	2302	...	2332	...	0002	...
Kreuzlingen Hafen d.	...	0524	...	0554	...	0624	...	0654	...	0724	hour	...	2154	...	2224	...	2254	...	2324	...	2354	...	0024	...
Kreuzlingen d.	0500	0530	...	0600	...	0630	...	0700	...	0730	until	...	2200	...	2230	...	2300	...	2330	...	0000	...	0027	...
Stein am Rhein d.	0530	0600	...	0630	...	0700	...	0730	...	0800		...	2230	...	2300	...	2330	...	0003	...	0030	...	...	...
Schaffhausen 939/40 a.	0556	0626	...	0656	...	0726	...	0756	...	0826		...	2256	...	2326	...	2356	...	0030	...	0054	...	...	...

X – ⑤⑥ (also Dec. 31, Mar. 24, 27, May 4, 5, 15, July 31, Oct. 31; not Dec. 25).
Y – Daily **except** days / dates in note **X**.

* – SBB Romanshorn - Rorschach; THURBO Schaffhausen - Romanshorn.

✕ – Restaurant (✕) – Bistro (🍸) – Bar coach 🍸 – Minibar

SPIEZ - ZWEISIMMEN 563

Boltigen - Zweisimmen and v.v. replaced by 🚌 (from 2000 hrs) Aug. 28 - Sept. 9

					Ⓒ											Ⓐ	Ⓒ	Ⓐ	Ⓒ		Ⓐ	Ⓐ	Ⓒ
Interlaken Ost **560** d.	...	...	...	...	...	...	0908	...	...	...	...	...	...	1308	...	...	...	1508	1508	...	...	...	...
Spiez 560 d.	0605	0712	0736	0818	0846	0912	0936	1018	1112	1136	1218	1312	...	1336	1418	1512	1512	1536	1536	1618	1641	1712	1712
Erlenbach im Simmental d.	0624	0729	0750	0833	|	0929	0950	1033	1129	1150	1233	1329	...	1350	1433	1529	1529	1550	1550	1633	1655	1729	1729
Boltigen d.	0642	0746	0810	0850	0911	0946	1010	1050	1146	1210	1250	1346	...	1410	1450	1546	1546	1608	1610	1650	1711	1746	1746
Zweisimmen a.	0653	0757	0819	0859	0920	0957	1019	1059	1157	1219	1259	1357	...	1419	1459	1556	1557	1617	1619	1659	1720	1756	1757

	Ⓐ	Ⓒ		Ⓐ					
erlaken Ost **560** d.	1708	1708	...	...	...	...	...	...	...
z 560 d.	1736	1736	1818	1841	1912	2012	2107	2207	2340
bach im Simmental d.	1750	1750	1833	1855	1929	2029	2121	2221	2355
gen d.	1808	1810	1850	1911	1946	2046	2140	2240	0013
simmen a.	1817	1819	1859	1920	1957	2057	2150	2250	0023

	Ⓐ		Ⓐ		Ⓐ					
Zweisimmen d.	0538	0557	0633	0701	0738	...	0801	0903	0938	1001
Boltigen d.	0546	0606	0642	0710	0746	...	0810	0910	0946	1010
Erlenbach im Simmental d.	0603	0625	0657	0729	0803	...	0832	0930	1003	1032
Spiez 560 a.	0618	0640	0712	0747	0818	...	0847	0947	1018	1047
Interlaken Ost **560** a.	...	...	...	...	...	...	...	...	...	...

										Ⓐ	Ⓒ	Ⓒ			Ⓐ	Ⓒ								
simmen d.	1103	1138	1201	1303	1338	1401	1503	1538	...	1600	1601	1629	1703	1738	1800	1801	...	1903	2001	2106	...	2206	2306	...
gen d.	1110	1146	1210	1310	1346	1410	1510	1546	...	1608	1610	1636	1710	1746	1808	1810	...	1910	2010	2115	...	2215	2315	...
bach im Simmental d.	1130	1203	1232	1330	1403	1432	1530	1603	...	1626	1632	1655	1730	1803	1826	1832	...	1929	2030	2134	...	2234	2334	...
z 560 a.	1147	1218	1247	1347	1418	1447	1547	1618	...	1641	1647	1710	1747	1818	1841	1847	...	1945	2045	2149	...	2249	2352	...
erlaken Ost **560** a.	...	1249	...	...	1449	...	...	1649	...	...	...	...	...	1849	...	...	...	...	...	...	...	...	...	...

INTERLAKEN - KLEINE SCHEIDEGG - JUNGFRAUJOCH 564

row gauge rack railway. BOB, WAB, JB

					m	v			m	m			m	m			m	m			m	m			m	
Interlaken Ost d.	0635	0635	0705	0705	0735	0735	0805	0805	0835	0835	0905	0905	0935	0935	1005	1005	1035	1035	1105	1105	1135	1135	1205	1205	1235	1305
Wilderswil ▲ d.	0640	0640	0710	0710	0740	0740	0810	0810	0840	0840	0910	0910	0940	0940	1010	1010	1040	1040	1110	1110	1140	1140	1210	1210	1240	1310
Zweilütschinen d.	0646	0647	0716	0717	0746	0747	0816	0817	0846	0847	0916	0917	0946	0947	1016	1017	1046	1047	1116	1117	1146	1147	1216	1217	1246	1316
Lauterbrunnen ● a.	0655	|	0725	|	0755	|	0825	|	0855	|	0925	|	0955	|	1025	|	1055	|	1125	|	1155	|	1225	|	1255	1325
change trains		|		|		|		|		|		|		|		|		|		|		|		|		
Lauterbrunnen d.	0707	|	0737	|	0807	|	0837	|	0907	|	0937	|	1007	|	1037	|	1107	|	1137	|	1207	|	1237	|	1307	1337
Wengen a.	0721	|	0751	|	0821	|	0851	|	0921	|	0951	|	1021	|	1051	|	1121	|	1151	|	1221	|	1251	|	1321	1351
Wengen d.	0724	|	0754	|	0824r	|	0854	|	0924r	|	0954	|	1024r	|	1054	|	1124r	|	1154	|	1224r	|	1254	|	1324r	1354
Grindelwald a.	|	0709	|	0739	|	0809	|	0839	|	0909	|	0939	|	1009	|	1039	|	1109	|	1139	|	1209	|	1239	|	|
change trains	|		|		|	k	|		|	k	|		|	k	|		|	k	|		|	k	|		|	|
Grindelwald d.	|	0717	|	0747	|	0817	|	0847	|	0917	|	0947	|	1017	|	1047	|	1117	|	1147	|	1217	|	1247	|	|
Grindelwald Grund d.	|	0725	|	0755	|	0825	|	0855	|	0925	|	0955	|	1025	|	1055	|	1125	|	1155	|	1225	|	1255	|	|
Kleine Scheidegg a.	0750	0750	0820	0820	0850r	0850	0920	0920	0950r	0950	1020	1020	1050r	1049	1120	1120	1150r	1150	1220	1220	1250r	1250	1320	1320	1350r	1420

				m			m	m			m	m			v			y	y		r						
rlaken Ost d.	1305	1405	1405	1435	1505	1505	1535	1535	1605	1605	1635	1635	1705	1705	1735	1805	1805	1835	1835	1905	1935	2002	2005	2102	2105	2202	2205
erswil ▲ d.	1310	1410	1410	1440	1510	1510	1540	1540	1610	1610	1640	1640	1710	1710	1740	1810	1810	1840	1840	1910	1940	2007	2010	2107	2110	2207	2210
lütschinen d.	1317	1416	1417	1447	1516	1517	1546	1547	1616	1617	1646	1647	1716	1717	1746	1816	1817	1846	1847	1917	1946	2013	2016	2113	2116	2213	2216
erbrunnen ● a.	|	1425	|	|	1525	|	1555	|	1625	|	1655	|	1725	|	1755	1825	|	1855	|	|	1955	2022	|	2122	|	2222	|
change trains	|		|	|		|		|		|		|		|			|		|	|			|		|		|
terbrunnen d.	|	1437	|	|	1537	|	1607	|	1637	|	1707	|	1737	|	1807	1837	|	1907	|	|	2007	2030	|	2130	|	2230	|
gen a.	|	1451	|	|	1551	|	1621	|	1651	|	1721	|	1751	|	1821	1851	|	1921	|	|	2021	2044	|	2144	|	2244	|
gen d.	|	1454	|	|	1554	|	1624r	|	1654	|	1724j	|	1754r	|	1824j	1854j	|	...	|	|	...	...	|	...	|	...	|
indelwald a.	1339	|	1439	1509	|	1539	|	1609	|	1639	|	1709	|	1739	|	|	1839	...	1909	1939	...	...	2039	...	2135	...	2235
change trains		|		k	|		|	k	|		|	j	|	r	|	|			r	j							
indelwald d.	1347	|	1447	1517	|	1547	|	1617	|	1647	|	1717	|	1747	|	|	1847	...	1917	1947	...	...	...	...	...	...	...
indelwald Grund d.	1355	|	1455	1525	|	1555	|	1625	|	1655	|	1725	|	1755	|	|	1852	...	1922	1952	...	...	...	...	...	...	...
ne Scheidegg a.	1420	1520	1520	1550	1620	1620	1650r	1650	1720	1720	1750j	1750	1820r	1820	1850j	1920j	...	...	...	...	...	...	...	...	...	...	...

																		k				k				k	
ne Scheidegg d.	...	...	...	...	...	...	...	...	...	...	...	...	0801	0803	0831	0833	0901r	0903	0931	0933	1001r	1003	1031	1033	1101r	1103	1131
indelwald Grund d.	...	...	...	...	...	...	...	0708	...	0738	...	0808	|	0838	|	0908	|	0938	|	1008	|	1038	|	1108	|	1138	|
indelwald a.	...	...	...	...	...	...	...	0712	...	0742	...	0812	|	0842	|	0912	|	0942	|	1012	|	1042	|	1112	|	1142	|
change trains			⚒							v			|	m	|		|	m	|		|	m	|		|	m	|
indelwald d.	0519	...	0547	...	0619	...	...	0719	...	0749	...	0819	|	0849	|	0919	|	0949	|	1019	|	1049	|	1119	|	1149	|
gen a.	|	...	|	...	|	...	...	|	...	|	...	|	0830	|	0900	|	0930r	|	1000	|	1030r	|	1100	|	1130r	|	1200
gen d.	|	0512	|	0605	|	0642	0703	|	0733	|	0803	|	0833	|	0903	|	0933	|	1003	|	1033	|	1103	|	1133	|	1203
terbrunnen a.	|	0529	|	0622	|	0659	0721	|	0751	|	0821	|	0851	|	0921	|	0951	|	1021	|	1051	|	1121	|	1151	|	1221
change trains	|		|		|			|	m	|		|	m	|		|	m	|		|	m	|		|	m	|	
terbrunnen ● d.	|	0533	|	0633	|	0703	0733	|	0803	|	0833	|	0903	|	0933	|	1003	|	1033	|	1103	|	1133	|	1203	|	1233
ilütschinen d.	0537	0543	0611	0643	0643	0713	0743	0743	0813	0813	0843	0843	0913	0913	0943	0943	1013	1013	1043	1043	1113	1113	1143	1143	1213	1213	1243
erswil ▲ d.	0543	0549	0617	0649	0649	0719	0749	0749	0819	0819	0849	0849	0919	0919	0949	0949	1019	1019	1049	1049	1119	1119	1149	1149	1219	1219	1249
rlaken Ost a.	0549	0554	0622	0654	0654	0724	0754	0754	0824	0824	0854	0854	0924	0924	0954	0954	1024	1024	1054	1054	1124	1124	1154	1154	1224	1224	1254

							k				k				k				k			r			j		
ne Scheidegg d.	1133	1231	1233	1331	1333	1401r	1403	1431	1433	1501r	1503	1531	1533	1601r	1603	1631	1633	1701r	1703	1731	1733	1833	1831r	1931j	1933	...	...
rindelwald Grund d.	1208	|	1308	|	1408	|	1438	|	1508	|	1538	|	1608	|	1638	|	1708	|	1738	|	1808	1908	|	|	2008	...	...
rindelwald a.	1212	|	1312	|	1412	|	1442	|	1512	|	1542	|	1612	|	1642	|	1712	|	1742	|	1812	1912	|	|	2012	...	...
change trains		|		|		|	m	|		|	m	|		|	m	|		|	v	|			|	|			
rindelwald d.	1219	|	1319	|	1419	|	1449	|	1519	|	1549	|	1619	|	1649	|	1719	|	1749	|	1819	1919	|	|	2019	2119	...
ngen a.	|	1300	|	1400	|	1430r	|	1500	|	1530r	|	1600	|	1630r	|	1700	|	1730r	|	1800	|	|	1900r	2000j	|	|	...
ngen d.	|	1303	|	1403	|	1433	|	1503	|	1533	|	1603	|	1633	|	1703	|	1733	|	1803	|	|	1903	2003	|	|	2103
terbrunnen a.	|	1321	|	1421	|	1451	|	1521	|	1551	|	1621	|	1651	|	1721	|	1751	|	1821	|	|	1921	2021	|	|	2120
change trains	|		|		|	m	|		|	m	|		|	m	|		|	v	|		|	|			|	|	
terbrunnen ● d.	|	1333	|	1433	|	1503	|	1533	|	1603	|	1633	|	1703	|	1733	|	1803	|	1833	|	|	1933	2033	|	|	2133
ilütschinen d.	1243	1343	1343	1443	1443	1513	1513	1543	1543	1613	1613	1643	1643	1713	1713	1743	1743	1813	1813	1843	1843	1943	1944	2044	2043	2140	2144
erswil ▲ d.	1249	1349	1349	1449	1449	1519	1519	1549	1549	1619	1619	1649	1649	1719	1719	1749	1749	1819	1819	1849	1849	1949	1950	2050	2049	2146	2150
rlaken Ost a.	1254	1354	1354	1454	1454	1524	1524	1554	1554	1624	1624	1654	1654	1724	1724	1754	1754	1824	1824	1854	1854	1954	1954	2054	2054	2150	2154

At times of heavy snowfall (November 1 - April 30) the Eigergletscher - Jungfraujoch service is subject to cancellation

n				q		q		q			q		q		q			q			j	q	j	j
0	**Kleine Scheidegg** d.	0800	0830	0900	0930	1000	1030	1100	1130	...	1200	1230	1300	1330	1400	1430	...	1500	1530	...	1600	1630	1700	1730
2	Eigergletscher d.	0810	0840	0910	0940	1010	1040	1110	1140	...	1210	1240	1310	1340	1410	1440	...	1510	1540	...	1610	1640	1710	1740
9	**Jungfraujoch** a.	0852	0922	0952	1022	1052	1122	1152	1222	...	1252	1322	1352	1422	1452	1522	...	1552	1622	...	1652	1722	1752	1822

	q		q		q		q		q			q		q		q			j	q	j	j	
gfraujoch d.	0900	0930	1000	1030	1100	1130	1200	1230	1300	...	1330	1400	1430	1500	1530	1600	...	1630	1700	1730	1800	1830	...
rgletscher d.	0940	1010	1040	1110	1140	1210	1240	1310	1340	...	1410	1440	1510	1540	1610	1640	...	1710	1740	1810	1832	1902	...
ne Scheidegg a.	0950	1020	1050	1120	1150	1220	1250	1320	1350	...	1420	1450	1520	1550	1620	1650	...	1720	1750	1820	1842	1912	...

May 14 - Sept. 4.
Dec. 19 - Apr. 3, Apr. 23 - Oct. 23.
Dec. 19 - Apr. 3, May 14 - Oct. 23.
Apr. 2 - Dec. 10.
Dec. 19 - Oct. 23.
June 11 - Oct. 9.
Daily Dec. 14 - Apr. 9; ①–⑥ Apr. 11 - 23; daily Apr. 24 - Oct. 29; ①–⑥ Oct. 31 - Dec. 10.
⚒ Dec. 14 - May 21; daily May 22 - Sept. 10; ①–⑥ Sept. 12 - Dec. 10 (also May 15, 16).
Additional services available Dec. 19 - Apr. 3, May 14 - Oct. 23.
Via Wengen (*28 km* via Grindelwald).

k – Dec. 19 - Dec. 10.

● – Cableway operates **Lauterbrunnen - Grütschalp**, and narrow gauge railway **Grütschalp - Mürren**, *total: 5 km*. **Operator**: BLM. Journey time: 20 minutes allowing for the connection.
From **Lauterbrunnen**: 0613, 0631, 0701, 0731, 0801, 0838, 0908, and every 30 minutes◆ until 1908, then 1938, 2031 **n**.
From **Mürren**: 0606, 0636, 0706, 0736, 0806, 0828, 0858, and every 30 minutes◆ until 1858, then 1928, 2006 **n**.

Cableway operates **Mürren - Schilthorn and v.v. Dec. 13 - Apr. 17, Apr. 23 - Nov. 13, Dec. 10**.
From **Mürren**: 0810, 0840, 0910 and every 30 minutes until 1610. From **Schilthorn**: 0903, 0933, 1003 and every 30 minutes until 1703. Additional services available Apr. 23 - Nov. 13. Operator: Schilthornbahn, ✆ +41 33 826 00 07.

▲ – Narrow gauge rack railway operates **May 28 - Oct. 23 Wilderswil - Schynige Platte**. *7 km*. Journey time: 52 minutes. **Operator**: BOB. Service may be reduced in bad weather.
From **Wilderswil**: 0725, 0805 **s**, 0845, 0925, 1005, 1045, 1125, 1205, 1245, 1325, 1405, 1445, 1525, 1605, 1645.
From **Schynige Platte**: 0821, 0901 **s**, 0941, 1021, 1101, 1141, 1221, 1301, 1341, 1421, 1501, 1541, 1621, 1701, 1753.

565 BASEL, OLTEN and BERN - LUZERN

km		ICN 659	IR 2457	RE 4709	IR 2505	IR 2311	IR 2459	RE 4711	IR 2507	IR 2313	IR 2461	RE 4713	IR 2509	IR 2315	IR 2463	RE 4715		IR 2511	ICN 667	IR 2465	RE 4717	IR 2513	IR 2319	IR 2467	RE 4719	IR 2515
		G	Ⓐ			L				L				L					G				L			
	Genève Aéroport ✈ **505** d.	...	...	...	...	...	...	...	...	...	...	...	0551	...	...	...	...	0703	...	...	...	0803	...	...	...	0903
	Genève **505** d.	...	...	...	...	...	...	...	...	...	...	...	0600	...	...	...	...	0712	...	...	...	0812	...	...	...	0912
	Lausanne **505** d.	...	...	...	0445	...	...	...	0545	...	...	...	0647	...	...	...	...	0750	...	...	...	0850	...	...	...	0950
0	**Basel** SBB d.	0504	...	...	|	0604	0617	...	|	0704	0717	...	|	0804	0817	...	...	|	0904	0917	...	|	1004	1017	...	|
14	Liestal d.	|	...	...	|	|	0627	...	|	|	0727	...	|	|	0827	...	...	|	|	0927	...	|	|	1027	...	|
21	Sissach d.	|	...	...	|	|	0633	...	|	|	0733	...	|	|	0833	...	...	|	|	0933	...	|	|	1033	...	|
39	**Olten** a.	0528	...	...	|	0628	0647	...	|	0728	0747	...	|	0828	0847	...	...	|	0928	0947	...	|	1028	1047	...	|
39	**Olten** d.	0530	0549	0606	|	0630	0649	0706	|	0730	0749	0806	|	0830	0849	0906	...	|	0930	0949	1006	|	1030	1049	1106	|
	Bern d.	|	|	|	0600	|	|	|	0700	|	|	|	0800	|	|	|	...	0900	|	|	|	1000	|	|	|	1100
47	Zofingen d.	|	0558	0613	0628	|	0658	0713	0728	|	0758	0813	0828	|	0858	0913	...	0928	|	0958	1013	1028	|	1058	1113	1128
69	Sursee d.	|	0611	0632	0641	|	0711	0732	0741	|	0811	0832	0841	|	0911	0932	...	0941	|	1011	1032	1041	|	1111	1132	1141
95	**Luzern** a.	0605	0630	0655	0700	0705	0730	0755	0800	0805	0830	0855	0900	0905	0930	0955	...	1000	1005	1030	1055	1100	1105	1130	1155	1200

	IR 2469	RE 4721	IR 2517	IR 2323	IR 2471	RE 4723	IR 2519	ICN 675	IR 2473	RE 4725	IR 2521		IR 2327	IR 2475	RE 4727	IR 2523	ICN 679	IR 2477	RE 4729	IR 2525	IR 2331	IR 2479	RE 4731	IR 2527	ICN 683	IR 2481
				L				G					L				G				L				G	
Genève Aéroport ✈ **505** d.	...	...	1003	...	...	...	1103	...	...	...	1203	...	...	...	...	1303	...	...	...	1403	...	...	...	1503	...	...
Genève **505** d.	...	...	1012	...	...	...	1112	...	...	...	1212	...	...	...	...	1312	...	...	...	1412	...	...	...	1512	...	...
Lausanne **505** d.	...	...	1050	...	...	...	1150	...	...	...	1250	...	...	...	...	1350	...	...	...	1450	...	...	...	1550	...	...
Basel SBB d.	1117	...	|	1204	1217	...	|	1304	1317	...	|	...	1404	1417	...	|	1504	1517	...	|	1604	1617	...	|	1704	1717
Liestal d.	1127	...	|	|	1227	...	|	|	1327	...	|	...	|	1427	...	|	|	1527	...	|	|	1627	...	|	|	1727
Sissach d.	1133	...	|	|	1233	...	|	|	1333	...	|	...	|	1433	...	|	|	1533	...	|	|	1633	...	|	|	1733
Olten a.	1147	...	|	1228	1247	...	|	1328	1347	...	|	...	1428	1447	...	|	1528	1547	...	|	1628	1647	...	|	1728	1747
Olten d.	1149	1206	|	1230	1249	1306	|	1330	1349	1406	|	...	1430	1449	1506	|	1530	1549	1606	|	1630	1649	1706	|	1730	1749
Bern d.	|	|	1200	|	|	|	1300	|	|	|	1400	...	|	|	|	1500	|	|	|	1600	|	|	|	1700	|	|
Zofingen d.	1158	1213	1228	|	1258	1313	1328	|	1358	1413	1428	...	|	1458	1513	1528	|	1558	1613	1628	|	1658	1713	1728	|	1758
Sursee d.	1211	1232	1241	|	1311	1332	1341	|	1411	1432	1441	...	|	1511	1532	1541	|	1611	1632	1641	|	1711	1732	1741	|	1811
Luzern a.	1230	1255	1300	1305	1330	1355	1400	1405	1430	1455	1500	...	1505	1530	1555	1600	1605	1630	1655	1700	1705	1730	1755	1800	1805	1830

	IR 2529	IR 2335	IR 2483	RE 4735	IR 2531	ICN 689	IR 2485	RE 4737	IR 2533	IR 2339	IR 2487	RE 4739	IR 2535	IR 2341	IR 2489	RE 4741	IR 2537	IR 2343	IR 2491	RE 4743	IR 2539	IR 2345	IR 2493	RE 4745		IR 2347
		L				C				E																
Genève Aéroport ✈ **505** d.	1603	...	...	...	1703	...	...	...	1803	...	...	...	1903	...	...	...	2003	...	...	...	...	...	...	...	...	...
Genève **505** d.	1612	...	...	...	1712	...	...	...	1812	...	...	...	1912	...	...	...	2012	...	...	...	2100	...	...	...	...	...
Lausanne **505** d.	1650	...	...	...	1750	...	...	...	1850	...	...	...	1950	...	...	...	2050	...	...	...	2145	...	...	...	...	...
Basel SBB d.	|	1804	1817	...	|	1904	1917	...	|	2004	2017	...	|	2104	2117	...	|	2202	2217	...	|	2302	2317	...	...	0002
Liestal d.	|	|	1827	...	|	|	1927	...	|	|	2027	...	|	|	2127	...	|	2211	2227	...	|	2311	2327	...	...	0011
Sissach d.	|	|	1833	...	|	|	1933	...	|	|	2033	...	|	|	2133	...	|	|	2233	...	|	|	2333	...	...	|
Olten a.	|	1828	1847	...	|	1928	1947	...	|	2028	2047	...	|	2128	2147	...	|	2228	2247	...	|	2328	2347	...	...	0028
Olten d.	|	1830	1849	1906	|	1930	1949	2006	|	2030	2049	2106	|	2130	2149	2206	|	2230	2249	2307	|	2330	...	0007	...	0033
Bern d.	1800	|	|	|	1900	|	|	|	2000	|	|	|	2100	|	|	|	2200	|	|	|	2300	|	...	|	...	|
Zofingen d.	1828	|	1858	1913	1928	|	1958	2013	2028	|	2058	2113	2128	|	2158	2213	2228	|	2256	2314	2328	|	...	0014	...	0040
Sursee d.	1841	|	1911	1932	1941	|	2011	2032	2041	|	2111	2132	2141	|	2211	2232	2241	|	...	2332	2341	|	...	0034	...	0054
Luzern a.	1900	1905	1930	1955	2000	2005	2030	2055	2100	2105	2130	2155	2200	2205	2230	2255	2300	2305	...	2355	2400	0005	...	0056	...	0114

km (via hsl)		RE 4706	IR 2456	IR 2456	IR 2306	IR 2508	RE 4708	IR 2458	IR 2308	IR 2510	RE 4710	IR 2460	IR 2310	IR 2512	RE 4712	IR 2462	IR 2314	IR 2514	RE 4714	IR 2464	ICN 668	IR 2516	RE 4716	IR 2466	IR 2316	IR 2518
			Ⓐ	Ⓒ									E				L				C				C	
	Luzern d.	0456	0530	...	0554	0600	0605	0630	0654	0700	0705	0730	0754	0800	0805	0830	0854	0900	0905	0930	0954	1000	1005	1030	1054	1100
	Sursee d.	0521	0548	...	|	0618	0626	0648	|	0718	0726	0748	|	0818	0826	0848	|	0918	0926	0948	|	1018	1026	1048	|	1118
0	Zofingen d.	0543	0602	...	|	0632	0643	0702	|	0732	0743	0802	|	0832	0843	0902	|	0932	0943	1002	|	1032	1043	1102	|	1132
63	**Bern** a.	|	|	...	|	0700	|	|	|	0800	|	|	|	0900	|	|	|	1000	|	|	|	1100	|	|	|	1200
	Olten a.	0552	0610	...	0627	|	0652	0710	0727	|	0752	0810	0827	|	0852	0910	0927	|	0952	1010	1027	|	1052	1110	1127	|
	Olten d.	...	0612	0612	0630	|	...	0712	0730	|	...	0812	0830	|	...	0912	0930	|	...	1012	1030	|	...	1112	1130	|
	Sissach d.	...	0627	0627	|	|	...	0727	|	|	...	0827	|	|	...	0927	|	|	...	1027	|	|	...	1127	|	|
	Liestal d.	...	0633	0633	|	|	...	0733	|	|	...	0833	|	|	...	0933	|	|	...	1033	|	|	...	1133	|	|
	Basel SBB a.	...	0644	0644	0655	|	...	0744	0755	|	...	0844	0855	|	...	0944	0955	|	...	1044	1055	|	...	1144	1155	|
	Lausanne **505** a.	...	...	...	...	0810	...	...	...	0910	...	...	...	1010	...	...	...	1110	...	...	...	1210	...	...	...	1310
	Genève **505** a.	...	...	...	...	0848	...	...	...	0948	...	...	...	1048	...	...	...	1148	...	...	...	1248	...	...	...	1348
	Genève Aéroport ✈ **505** a.	...	...	...	...	0857	...	...	...	0957	...	...	...	1057	...	...	...	1157	...	...	...	1257	...	...	...	1357

	IR 2468	ICN 672	IR 2520	RE 4720	IR 2470	IR 2320		IR 2522	RE 4722	IR 2472	ICN 676	IR 2524	RE 4724	IR 2474	IR 2324		IR 2526	RE 4726	IR 2476	ICN 680	IR 2528	RE 4728	IR 2478	IR 2328	IR 2530	RE 4730
		G				L					G				L					G				L		
Luzern d.	1130	1154	1200	1205	1230	1254	...	1300	1305	1330	1354	1400	1405	1430	1454	...	1500	1505	1530	1554	1600	1605	1630	1654	1700	1705
Sursee d.	1148	|	1218	1226	1248	|	...	1318	1326	1348	|	1418	1426	1448	|	...	1518	1526	1548	|	1618	1626	1648	|	1718	1726
Zofingen d.	1202	|	1232	1243	1302	|	...	1332	1343	1402	|	1432	1443	1502	|	...	1532	1543	1602	|	1632	1643	1702	|	1732	1743
Bern a.	|	|	1300	|	|	|	...	1400	|	|	|	1500	|	|	|	...	1600	|	|	|	1700	|	|	|	1800	|
Olten a.	1210	1227	|	1252	1310	1327	...	|	1352	1410	1427	|	1452	1510	1527	...	|	1552	1610	1627	|	1652	1710	1727	|	1752
Olten d.	1212	1230	|	...	1312	1330	...	|	...	1412	1430	|	...	1512	1530	...	|	...	1612	1630	|	...	1712	1730	|	...
Sissach d.	1227	|	|	...	1327	|	...	|	...	1427	|	|	...	1527	|	...	|	...	1627	|	|	...	1727	|	|	...
Liestal d.	1233	|	|	...	1333	|	...	|	...	1433	|	|	...	1533	|	...	|	...	1633	|	|	...	1733	|	|	...
Basel SBB a.	1244	1255	|	...	1344	1355	...	|	...	1444	1455	|	...	1544	1555	...	|	...	1644	1655	|	...	1744	1755	|	...
Lausanne **505** a.	...	...	1410	...	...	...	...	1510	...	...	...	1610	...	...	...	...	1710	...	...	...	1810	...	...	...	1910	...
Genève **505** a.	...	...	1448	...	...	...	...	1548	...	...	...	1648	...	...	...	...	1748	...	...	...	1848	...	...	...	1948	...
Genève Aéroport ✈ **505** a.	...	...	1457	...	...	...	...	1557	...	...	...	1657	...	...	...	...	1757	...	...	...	1857	...	...	...	1957	...

	ICN 684	IR 2532	RE 4732	IR 2482	IR 2332	IR 2534	RE 4734	IR 2484	ICN 688	IR 2536	RE 4736	IR 2486	IR 2336	IR 2538	RE 4738	IR 2488	ICN 692	IR 2540	RE 4740	IR 2490	IR 2340	IR 2542	RE 4742	ICN 696	RE 4744	IR 2344
	G				L				G				L				G				L			G		q
Luzern d.	1754	1800	1805	1830	1854	1900	1905	1930	1954	2000	2005	2030	2054	2100	2105	2130	2154	2200	2205	...	2254	2300	2305	2354	0005	0049
Sursee d.	|	1818	1826	1848	|	1918	1926	1948	|	2018	2026	2048	|	2118	2126	2148	|	2218	2226	...	|	2318	2326	|	0026	0108
Zofingen d.	|	1832	1843	1902	|	1932	1943	2002	|	2032	2043	2102	|	2132	2143	2202	|	2232	2243	2302	|	2332	2343	|	0043	0121
Bern a.	|	1900	|	|	|	2000	|	|	|	2100	|	|	|	2200	|	|	|	2300	|	|	|	2400	|	|	|	|
Olten a.	1827	|	1852	1910	1927	|	1952	2010	2027	|	2052	2110	2127	|	2152	2210	2227	...	2252	2310	2327	...	2352	0027	0052	0128
Olten d.	1830	|	...	1912	1930	|	...	2012	2030	|	...	2112	2130	|	...	2212	2233	...	...	2312	2333	...	...	0035	...	0137
Sissach d.	|	|	...	1927	|	|	...	2027	|	|	...	2127	|	|	...	2227	|	...	...	2327	|	...	...	|	...	|
Liestal d.	|	|	...	1933	|	|	...	2033	|	|	...	2133	|	|	...	2233	2248	...	...	2333	2349	...	...	0052	...	0153
Basel SBB a.	1855	|	...	1944	1955	|	...	2044	2055	|	...	2144	2155	|	...	2244	2259	...	...	2344	2359	...	...	0102	...	0202
Lausanne **505** a.	...	2010	...	...	...	2110	...	...	...	2215	...	...	...	2315	...	...	...	...	...	...	...	...	...	...	...	...
Genève **505** a.	...	2048	...	...	...	2148	...	...	...	...	...	...	...	...	...	...	...	...	...	...	...	...	...	...	...	...
Genève Aéroport ✈ **505** a.	...	...	...	...	...	2157	...	...	...	...	...	...	...	...	...	...	...	...	...	...	...	...	...	...	...	...

C – 🚃12 Basel - Chiasso and v.v.
E – 🚃12 Basel - Erstfeld and v.v.
G – 🚃12 Basel - Lugano and v.v.
L – 🚃12 Basel - Locarno and v.v.

q – ⑥⑦ (also Jan. 1; not Mar. 26).

rrow gauge. MOB — LENK - ZWEISIMMEN - MONTREUX — 566

	Ⓐ		Ⓐ				Ⓒ		Ⓒ										Ⓐ		Ⓐ					⑤⑥
Lenk d.	0611	0634	0703	0737	0837	0937	1003	1037	1103	1137	1237	1303	1337	1437	1537	1603	1637	1737	1803	1842	1903	1937	2037	2132	2232	2326
Zweisimmen a.	0629	0652	0721	0755	0855	0955	1021	1055	1121	1155	1255	1321	1355	1455	1555	1621	1655	1755	1821	1900	1921	1955	2055	2150	2250	2344

							2111				3115	2217	2119			3123			2127	2229		2131				
											🍸	(✗)	🍸			🍸			(✗)	🍸						
		Ⓒ	Ⓐ	Ⓐ	Ⓒ		G				G	C	G★			G			C	G	Ⓐ	G★				
Zweisimmen d.	0411	0505	0505	0608	0617	0700	0825	0905	1005	...	1025	1105	1225	1305	1405	1425	...	1505	1625	1705	1724	1825	1905	2005	2102	2200
Saanenmöser d.	0426	0519	0519	0622	0631	0714	0839	0919	1019	...	1039	1119	1239	1319	1419	1439	...	1519	1639	1719	1738	1839	1919	2019	2116	2213
Schönried d.	0431	0524	0524	0626	0635	0719	0843	0924	1024	...	1043	1124	1243	1324	1424	1443	...	1524	1643	1724	1743	1843	1924	2024	2121	2218
Gstaad d.	0440	0533	0533	0635	0644	0730	0853	0937	1034	...	1053	1137	1253	1337	1434	1453	...	1537	1653	1737	1752	1853	1937	2037	2130	2232
Saanen d.	0444	0537	0537	0639	0648	0735	0858	0942	1038	...	1058	1142	1258	1342	1438	1458	...	1542	1658	1742	1756	1858	1942	2042	2135	2236
Rougemont d.	0450	0555	0555	0644	0653	0741	0903	0948	1044	...	1103	1148	1303	1348	1444	1503	...	1548	1703	1748	...	1903	1948	2048	2141	2241
Château d'Oex d.	0503	0607	0607	0703	0703	0806t	0913	1006	...	...	1113	1206	1313	1406	...	1513	...	1606	1713	1806	...	1913	2006	2101	2152	2251
Montbovon d.	0522	0623	0623	0723	0723	0826	0928	1026	...	...	1128	1226	1328	1426	...	1528	...	1626	1728	1826	...	1928	2026	2116	2208	...
Les Avants § d.	0543	0644	0644	0744	0744	0847	0948	1047	...	...	1148	1247	1348	1447	...	1548	...	1647	1748	1847	...	1948	2051	2135	2228	...
Chamby ⊙ § d.	0551	0651	0651	0751	0751	0855	0955	1055	...	...	1155	1255	1355	1455	...	1555	...	1655	1755	1855	...	1955	2058	2142	2235	...
Chernex § d.	0600	0658	0658	0758	0758	0904	1004	1104	...	...	1204	1304	1404	1504	...	1604	...	1704	1804	1904	...	2004	2103	2147	2241	...
Montreux § a.	0610	0707	0707	0807	0807	0913	1013	1113	...	...	1213	1313	1413	1513	...	1613	...	1713	1813	1913	...	2013	2111	2158	2249	...

						2112		2216	2118	3118			2124			3126		2228	2128			2234					
								(✗)	(🍸)	🍸			🍸			(✗)			🍸								
	Ⓐ	Ⓐ	Ⓒ			G		C	[R]T	G★			G			C		G	G★	Ⓐ		G					
treux § d.	...	...	...	0537	0638	0744	...	0844	0857	0944	...	1044	1144	...	1244	1344	...	1444	1544	...	1644	1744	...	1844	1944	2112	2212
rnex § d.	...	...	...	0548	0648	0753	...	0853	|	0953	...	1053	1153	...	1253	1353	...	1453	1553	...	1653	1753	...	1853	1953	2121	2221
mby ⊙ § d.	...	...	...	0556	0653	0758	...	0858	|	0958	...	1058	1158	...	1258	1358	...	1458	1558	...	1658	1758	...	1858	1958	2126	2226
Avants § d.	...	...	...	0604	0701	0807	...	0907	|	1007	...	1107	1207	...	1307	1407	...	1507	1607	...	1707	1807	...	1907	2007	2134	2239
tbovon d.	...	0521	0548	0622	0722	0828	...	0927	0946	1028	...	1127	1228	...	1327	1428	...	1527	1628	...	1727	1827	...	1927	2029	2154	2259
teaux d'Oex d.	...	0539	0606	0639	0737	0843	...	0944	...	1043	...	1144	1243	...	1344	1443	...	1544	1643	...	1744	1844	...	1944	2045	2213	2315
gemont d.	...	0549	0616	0653	0750	0853	...	0959	...	1053	1111	1159	1253	...	1359	1453	1511	1559	1653	...	1759	1903	...	2005	2057	2224	2327
nen d.	0500	0554	0621	0659	0756	0859	...	1005	...	1059	1117	1205	1259	...	1405	1459	1517	1605	1659	1800	1805	1908	...	2010	2103	2229	2333
aad d.	0505	0559	0625	0703	0803	0905	...	1023j	...	1105	1123	1223j	1305	...	1423j	1505	1523	1623j	1705	1811	1823j	1923j	...	2023r	2115r	2233	2339
önried d.	0513	0607	0635	0711	0812	0914	...	1032	...	1114	1132	1232	1314	...	1432	1514	1532	1632	1714	1820	1832	1932	...	2032	2122	2241	2347
nenmöser d.	0518	0611	0639	0715	0817	0918	...	1038	...	1118	1138	1238	1318	...	1438	1518	1538	1638	1718	1825	1838	1938	...	2038	2126	2246	2351
isimmen a.	0535	0625	0653	0729	0834	0932	...	1052	...	1132	1152	1252	1332	...	1452	1532	1552	1652	1732	1841	1852	1955	...	2052	2142	2300	0005

	Ⓐ		Ⓐ				Ⓒ		Ⓒ				Ⓐ							Ⓐ		Ⓐ					⑤⑥
isimmen d.	0550	0611	0634	0703	0803	0903	0937	1003	1037	1103	1137	1203	1237	1303	1403	1503	1537	1603	1703	1737	1803	1824	1903	2003	2103	2200	2306
k a.	0608	0629	0652	0721	0821	0921	0956	1021	1056	1121	1156	1221	1256	1321	1421	1521	1556	1621	1721	1756	1821	1842	1921	2021	2121	2218	2324

ADDITIONAL SERVICES LES AVANTS - MONTREUX and v.v. (2nd class only):

	Ⓐ	Ⓐ	Ⓐ		Ⓐ		Ⓐ	Ⓐ			
Avants d.	0620	0718	0813	...	1319	...	1713	1813	...	2320	...
mby ⊙ d.	0629	0725	0820	...	1326	...	1720	1820	...	2327	...
rnex d.	0634	0731	0832	...	1332	...	1732	1832	...	2332	...
ntreux a.	0646	0741	0841	...	1341	...	1741	1841	...	2342	...

	Ⓐ	Ⓐ	Ⓐ		Ⓐ	Ⓐ	Ⓐ	Ⓐ			
Montreux d.	0549	0610	0715	...	1215	1615	1715	1815	2150	2250	2345
Chernex d.	0558	0619	0730	...	1224	1624	1724	1824	2159	2259	2355
Chamby ⊙ d.	0603	0627	0735	...	1229	1629	1729	1829	2204	2304	2400s
Les Avants a.	0610	0634	0742	...	1236	1636	1736	1836	2211	2311	0007

GOLDEN PASS CLASSIC – [12] and (✗).
GOLDEN PASS PANORAMIC – conveys [12] [panorama car].
TRAIN DU CHOCOLAT – ①②③④ May 2 - June 30; daily July 1 - Aug. 31; ①③④ Sept. 1 - Oct. 27. Conveys [1] only.

j – Arrive 12–14 minutes earlier.
r – Arrive 8–9 minutes earlier.
s – Stops to set down only.
t – Arrive 16 minutes earlier.

★ – Also conveys VIP accommodation. [R]
⊙ – Chamby is a request stop.

rrow gauge. 2nd class only. TPF — MONTBOVON - BULLE - PALÉZIEUX, BROC and BERN — 568

Replacement 🚌 service owing to engineering work: Montbovon - Gruyères and v.v. Oct. 15 - Nov. 20; Châtel-St Denis - Palézieux and v.v. July 9 - Aug. 23.

	⚒		Ⓐ		⚒	†		Ⓐ	Ⓐ	Ⓒ			♣			♣						
Montbovon d.	...	...	0540	...	0640	...	...	0723	...	0740	...	...	0840	...		1840	...	...	1940	...	2040	...
Gruyères d.	...	...	0558	...	0658	...	...	0745	...	0758	...	...	0858	...	and at	1858	...	...	1958	...	2058	...
Bulle ▲ a.	...	...	0608	...	0708	...	...	0753	...	0808	...	...	0908	...	the same	1908	...	...	2008	...	2108	...
Bulle d.	0513	0554	0612	0613	0712	0712	0733	...	0812	0812	0833	...	0912	0933	minutes	1912	1933	...	...	2033	...	2118
Châtel-St Denis d.	0539	0629	|	0643	|	|	0759	...	|	|	0859	...	|	0959	past each	|	1959	...	...	2059	...	2144
Palézieux a.	0550	0640	|	0655	|	|	0810	...	|	|	0910	...	|	1010	hour until	|	2010	...	...	2110	...	2155
Broc-Fabrique a.	...	...	0624	...	0724	0724	...	...	0824	0824	...	...	0924	...		1924	...	...	...	...	...	...

	Ⓐ	⚒	⚒	Ⓐ			Ⓐ		Ⓐ	Ⓒ												
Broc-Fabrique d.	...	...		0636	...		0736		...	0736	...	0836		...	1836	...	1936	...	...	...	...	...
Palézieux d.	...	...	0605	|	...	0646	|	0706	...	|	0746	|	and at	1746	|	1846	|	1946	2046	2115	2205	...
Châtel-St Denis d.	...	...	0618	|	...	0700	|	0722	...	|	0800	|	the same	1800	|	1900	|	2000	2100	2128	2218	...
Bulle a.	...	...	0644	0648	...	0727	0748	0749a	...	0748	0827	0848	minutes	1827	1848	1927	1948	2027	2127	2153	2243	...
Bulle ▲ d.	0450	0552	...	...	0652	...	...	...	0753	0753	...	0852	past each	...	1852	...	1952	...	...	...	...	...
Gruyères d.	0457	0559	...	...	0659	...	...	...	0800	0800	...	0859	hour until	...	1859	...	1959	...	...	...	...	...
Montbovon a.	0518	0620	...	...	0720	...	...	...	0821	0821	...	0920		...	1920	...	2020	...	...	...	...	...

BULLE - FRIBOURG - BERN and v.v.: Operator: TPF

			and at									
Bulle d.	0552	0620	the same	1852	1920	1952	2020	2052	2120	2220	2320	...
Romont d.	0611	0638	minutes	1911	1938	2011	2038	2111	2138	2238	2338	...
Fribourg **505** d.	0629	0655	past each	1929	1955	2028	2055	2129	2155	2255	2355	...
Bern 505 a.	0651	...	hour until	1951	...	...	...	2151	...	...	...	...

			and at						g
Bern 505 d.	...	0609	the same	...	2009	...	...	...	...
Fribourg **505** d.	0604	0631	minutes	2004	2031	2104	2204	2304	0006
Romont d.	0623	0649	past each	2023	2049	2123	2223	2323	0024
Bulle a.	0642	0708	hour until	2042	2108	2142	2242	2342	0041

Ⓐ only.
②–⑥ (not Dec. 26, Jan. 2, Mar. 26, 29, May 6, 17, Aug. 2).

♣ – On 1540 Ⓐ departure, change trains at Bulle.

Operator: Transports Publics Fribourgeois (TPF), ✆ +41 26 351 02 00, fax +41 26 351 02 90.

rrow gauge rack railway. 2nd class only. MVR — MONTREUX - CAUX - ROCHERS DE NAYE — 569

Caux - Rochers de Naye and v.v.: no service during bad weather

Montreux d.	0547	0644	0744	...	0817	0917	1017	1117	...	1217	1317	1417	1517	...	1617	1717	...	1817	1917	2017	...	2117	...	2217
Glion ▲ d.	0558	0655	0755	...	0830	0930	1030	1130	...	1230	1330	1430	1530	...	1630	1730	...	1830	1928	2028	...	2128	...	2228
Caux a.	0607	0704	0804	...	0842	0942	1042	1142	...	1242	1342	1442	1542	...	1642	1742	...	1841	1937	2037	...	2137	...	2237
Rochers de Naye a.	...	...	...	...	0911	1011	1111	1211	...	1311	1411	1511	1611	...	1711t	1811t	...	...	...	...	...	...	...	...

chers de Naye d.	...	...	...	...	0916	1016	...	1116	1216	...	1316	1416	...	1516	1616	...	1716t	1816t	...	...	...	...	...	...
ux d.	0612	0712	0812	...	0946	1046	...	1146	1246	...	1346	1446	...	1546	1646	...	1746	1846	...	1948	2048	2148	...	...
on ▲ d.	0625	0725	0829	...	0959	1059	...	1159	1259	...	1359	1459	...	1559	1659	...	1759	1859	...	2001	2101	2201	...	...
ntreux a.	0637	0737	0841	...	1011	1111	...	1211	1311	...	1411	1511	...	1611	1711	...	1811	1911	...	2013	2113	2213	...	...

May 5 - Oct. 9.

▲ – Funicular railway operates **Glion** - **Territet** and v.v. (no service Oct. 24 - 28): From **Glion** and **Territet**: 0515, 0530, 0545, 0557, 0615, 0630, 0645, 0700 and every 15 minutes until 2100, then 2120, 2145, 2220, 2245, 2320, 2350, 0020, 0050, 0130⑥⑦.
Operator: MVR, ✆ 021 989 81 90.

570 GENÈVE - LAUSANNE - SION - BRIG

For *TGV Lyria* services Paris - Lausanne - Montreux - Brig and v.v. – see Table 42

km		IR 1705	IR 1805	IR 1707	EC 35	IR 1807	IR 1709	IR 1809	IR 1711	EC 37	IR 1811	IR 1713	IR 1813	IR 1715	IR 1815	IR 1717	IR 1817	IR 1719	IR 1819	IR 1721	IR 1821	IR 1723	EC 39	IR 1823	IR 1725
					✕ ◧					✕ ◧V													✕ ◧		
0	Genève Aéroport ✈ **505** d.	...	...	...	...	...	0621	0651	0721	...	0751	0821	0851	0921	0951	1021	1051	1121	1151	1221	1251	1321	...	1351	1421
6	**Genève 505** d.	...	0453	0530	0539	0609	0630	0700	0730	0739	0800	0830	0900	0930	1000	1030	1100	1130	1200	1230	1300	1330	1339	1400	1430
27	Nyon **505** d.	...	0507	0544	|	|	0644	0714	0744	|	0814	0844	0914	0944	1014	1044	1114	1144	1214	1244	1314	1344	|	1414	1444
53	Morges **505** d.	...	0525	0600	|	|	0700	0730	0800	|	0830	0900	0930	1000	1030	1100	1130	1200	1230	1300	1330	1400	|	1430	1500
66	**Lausanne 505** a.	...	0539	0612	0615k	0648	0712	0742	0812	0815k	0842	0912	0942	1012	1042	1112	1142	1212	1242	1312	1342	1412	1415k	1442	1512
66	**Lausanne** ▲ d.	...	0547	0621	0618	0650	0717	0750	0821	0818	0850	0917	0950	1017	1050	1117	1150	1217	1250	1317	1350	1421	1418	1450	1517
84	Vevey ▲ d.	...	0601	0635	|	0704	0731	0804	0835	|	0904	0931	1004	1031	1104	1131	1204	1231	1304	1331	1404	1435	|	1504	1531
92	**Montreux** ▲ d.	...	0607	0642	0636	0710	0738	0810	0842	0836	0910	0938	1010	1038	1110	1138	1210	1238	1310	1338	1410	1442	1436	1510	1538
105	Aigle d.	...	0618	0653	|	0721	0749	0821	0853	|	0921	0949	1021	1049	1121	1149	1221	1249	1321	1349	1421	1453	|	1521	1549
114	Bex d.	...	|	|	|	|	0756	|	|	|	|	0956	|	1056j	|	1156	|	1256	|	1356	|	|	|	|	1556
118	St Maurice d.	...	0629	|	|	0732	|	0832	|	|	0932	|	1032	|	1132	|	1232	|	1332	|	1432	|	|	1532	|
133	Martigny d.	0610	0640	0712	|	0743	0810	0843	0912	|	0943	1010	1043	1110	1143	1210	1243	1310	1343	1410	1443	1512	|	1543	1610
158	**Sion** d.	0625	0655	0727	0713	0758	0825	0858	0927	0913	0958	1025	1058	1125	1158	1225	1258	1325	1358	1425	1458	1527	1513	1558	1625
174	Sierre d.	0635	0705	0737	|	0808	0835	0908	0937	|	1008	1035	1108	1135	1208	1235	1308	1335	1408	1435	1508	1537	|	1608	1635
184	Leuk d.	0643	0713	|	|	|	0843	|	|	|	|	1043	|	|	|	1243	|	1343	|	1443	|	|	|	|	1643
203	Visp d.	0655	0725	0755	|	0825	0855	0925	0955	|	1025	1055	1125	1155	1225	1255	1325	1355	1425	1455	1525	1555	|	1625	1655
212	**Brig** a.	0702	0732	0802	0740	0832	0902	0932	1002	0940	1032	1102	1132	1202	1232	1302	1332	1402	1432	1502	1532	1602	1540	1632	1702
	Milano Centrale **590** a.	...	...	...	0935	...	...	...	...	1135	...	...	...	...	...	...	...	...	...	...	...	...	1735	...	...

	IR 1727	IR 1827	IR 1729	IR 1729	IR 1927	IR 1829	IR 1929	IR 1731	IR 1731	IR 1931	IR 1831	IR 1733	EC 41	IR 1833	IR 1735	IR 1835	IR 1737	IR 1837	IR 1739	IR 1839	IR 1741	IR 1841	RE 3591	IR 1743
			Ⓐ	Ⓒ	Ⓐ		Ⓐ	Ⓐ	Ⓒ	Ⓐ			✕ ◧										⑥⑦	
Genève Aéroport ✈ **505** d.	1521	1551	1630	1621	1621	1651	1657	1730	1721	1721	1751	1821	...	1851	1921	1951	2021	2100	2121	2151	2221	2251	...	*2310*
Genève 505 d.	1530	1600	1639	1630	1630	1700	1707	1739	1730	1730	1800	1830	1839	1900	1930	2000	2030	2109	2130	2200	2230	2300	...	*2319*
Nyon **505** d.	1544	1614	|	1644	1644	1714	|	|	1744	1744	1814	1844	|	1914	1944	2014	2044	|	2144	2214	2244	2314	...	*2335*
Morges **505** d.	1600	1630	|	1700	1700	1730	1734	|	1800	1800	1830	1900	|	1930	2000	2030	2100	|	2200	2230	2300	2330	...	*2356*
Lausanne 505 a.	1612	1642	1715	1712	1712	1742	1751	1815	1812	1812	1842	1912	1915k	1942	2012	2042	2112	2148	2212	2242	2312	2342	...	*0009*
Lausanne ▲ d.	1617	1650	1717	1717	1721	1750	1756	1817	1817	1821	1850	1921	1918	1950	2017	2050	2117	2150	2220	2250	2320	...	2350	0025
Vevey ▲ d.	1631	1704	|	1731	1735	1804	1810	|	1831	1835	1904	1935	|	2004	2031	2104	2131	2204	2234	2304	2334	...	0004	0039
Montreux ▲ d.	1638	1710	1735	1738	1742	1810	1817	1835	1838	1842	1910	1942	1936	2010	2038	2110	2138	2210	2241	2310	2341	...	0011	0045
Aigle d.	1649	1721	1746	1749	1753	1821	1828	1846	1849	1853	1921	1953	|	2021	2049	2121	2149	2221	2252	2321	2352	...	0022	0056
Bex d.	1656	|	|	1756	1800t	|	1835	|	1856	1900t	|	2000	|	|	2056	|	2156r	|	2259	2328t	2359	...	0029	0103
St Maurice d.	|	1732	|	|	1807t	1832	1841	|	|	1907t	1932	|	|	2032	|	2132	|	2232	2305	2334t	0005	...	0034	0109
Martigny d.	1710	1743	1805	1810	1818t	1843	...	1905	1910	1918t	1943	2014	|	2043	2110	2143	2210r	2242	2316	2345t	0016	...	...	0120
Sion d.	1725	1758	1820	1825	1833t	1858	...	1920	1925	1933t	1958	2029	2013	2058	2125	2158	2225r	...	2331	2358t	0031	...	...	0133
Sierre d.	1735	1808	1830	1835	...	1908	...	1930	1935	...	2008	2039	|	2108	2135	2208	2235r	...	2341	...	0041	...	...	...
Leuk d.	1743	|	1838	1843	...	|	...	1938	1943	...	|	2047	|	|	2143	|	2243r	...	2349	...	0049	...	...	...
Visp d.	1755	1825	1850	1855	...	1925	...	1950	1955	...	2025	2059	|	2125	2155	2225	2255r	...	0001	...	0101	...	...	...
Brig a.	1802	1832	1857	1902	...	1932	...	1957	2002	...	2032	2106	2040	2132	2202	2232	2302r	...	0008	...	0108	...	...	...
Milano Centrale **590** a.	...	...	...	...	...	...	...	...	...	...	...	...	2235	...	...	...	...	...	...	...	...	...	...	...

	IR 1702	IR 1804	IR 1704	IR 1904	IR 1806	IR 1806	IR 1706	IR 1906	IR 1706	IR 1908	IR 1808	IR 1808	IR 1708	IR 1810	IR 1710	IR 1812	IR 1712	IR 1814	IR 1714	EC 32	IR 1816	IR 1716	IR 1818	IR 1718
				Ⓐ	Ⓒ	Ⓐ	Ⓐ	Ⓐ	Ⓒ	Ⓐ	Ⓒ	Ⓐ								✕ ◧				
Milano Centrale **590** d.	...	...	...	...	...	...	...	...	...	...	...	...	...	...	...	...	...	...	...	0825	...	...	...	...
Brig d.	...	0422	...	...	0524	0528	0549	...	0558	...	0624	0628	0658	0727	0758	0827	0858	0927	0958	1020	1027	1058	1127	1158
Visp d.	...	0429	...	...	0531	0535	0557	...	0606	...	0631	0635	0706	0734	0806	0834	0906	0934	1006	|	1034	1106	1134	1206
Leuk d.	...	0440	...	...	0542	0546	0607	...	0616	...	0642	0646	0716	|	0816	|	0916	|	|	|	|	1116	|	1216
Sierre d.	...	0448	...	...	0550	0554	0615	...	0624	...	0650	0654	0724	0750	0824	0850	0924	0950	1021	|	1050	1124	1150	1224
Sion d.	0428	0459	0531	0551	0601	0605	0627	0636	0636	...	0701	0705	0736	0801	0836	0901	0936	1001	1033	1049	1101	1136	1201	1236
Martigny d.	0442	0512	0545	0607	0614	0618	0641	0653	0650	...	0714	0718	0750	0814	0850	0914	0950	1014	1047	|	1114	1150	1214	1250
St Maurice d.	0453	0523	0556	0618	0625	0629	0652	|	|	...	0725	0729	|	0825	|	0925	|	1025	|	|	1125	|	1225	|
Bex d.	0459	0529	0602	0627	|	|	0659	|	0705	0727	|	|	0805	|	0905	|	1005	|	|	|	|	1205	|	1305
Aigle d.	0506	0537	0609	0634	0637	0641	0706	0712	0712	0734	0737	0741	0812	0837	0912	0937	1012	1037	1106	|	1137	1212	1237	1312
Montreux ▲ d.	0517	0548	0620	0645	0648	0652	0717	0723	0723	0745	0748	0752	0823	0848	0923	0948	1023	1048	1117	1124	1148	1223	1248	1323
Vevey ▲ d.	0524	0555	0627	0652	0655	0659	0724	|	0730	0752	0755	0759	0830	0855	0930	0955	1030	1055	1124	|	1155	1230	1255	1330
Lausanne ▲ a.	0539	0610	0642	0707	0710	0714	0739	0742	0745	0807	0810	0814	0845	0910	0945	1010	1045	1110	1139	1142k	1210	1245	1310	1345
Lausanne 505 d.	0548	0618	0648	0709	0718	0718	0748	0745	0748	0809	0818	0818	0848	0918	0948	1018	1048	1118	1148	1145	1218	1248	1318	1348
Morges **505** d.	0559	0629	0659	0720	0729	0729	0759	|	0759	0820	0829	0829	0859	0929	0959	1029	1059	1129	1159	|	1229	1259	1329	1359
Nyon **505** d.	0615	0645	0715	|	0745	0745	0815	|	0815	|	0845	0845	0915	0945	1015	1045	1115	1145	1215	|	1245	1315	1345	1415
Genève 505 a.	0630	0700	0730	0751	0800	0800	0830	0821	0830	0851	0900	0900	0930	1000	1030	1100	1130	1200	1230	1221	1300	1330	1400	1430
Genève Aéroport ✈ **505** a.	0639	0709	0739	0800	0809	0809	0839	0830	0839	0900	0909	0909	0939	1009	1039	1109	1139	1209	1239	...	1309	1339	1409	1439

	IR 1720	IR 1822	IR 1722	EC 34	IR 1824	IR 1724	IR 1826	IR 1726	IR 1828	IR 1728	IR 1830	IR 1730	IR 1832	IR 1732	EC 36	IR 1834	IR 1734	IR 1836	IR 1736	EC 42	IR 1838	RE 3586	IR 1840	RE 3590
				✕ ◧											✕ ◧					✕ ◧V		⑤⑥		⑥⑦
Milano Centrale **590** d.	...	...	...	1225	...	...	...	...	...	...	...	...	...	...	1725	...	...	...	...	1925	...	...	...	...
Brig d.	1258	1327	1358	1420	1427	1458	1527	1558	1627	1658	1727	1758	1827	1858	1918	1927	1958	2027	2058	2118	2127	...	2227	...
Visp d.	1306	1334	1406	|	1434	1506	1534	1606	1634	1706	1734	1806	1834	1906	|	1934	2006	2034	2106	|	2134	...	2234	...
Leuk d.	1316	|	|	|	|	1516	|	1616	|	1716	|	1816	|	|	|	|	2016	|	|	|	|	...	|	...
Sierre d.	1324	1350	1421	|	1450	1524	1550	1624	1650	1724	1750	1824	1850	1921	|	1950	2024	2050	2121	|	2150	...	2250	...
Sion d.	1336	1401	1433	1449	1501	1536	1601	1636	1701	1736	1801	1836	1901	1933	1949	2001	2036	2101	2133	2149	2201	...	2301	...
Martigny d.	1350	1414	1447	|	1514	1550	1613	1650	1714	1750	1814	1850	1914	1947	|	2014	2050	2114	2147	|	2214	...	2314	...
St Maurice d.	|	1425	|	|	1525	|	1625	|	1725	|	1825	|	1925	|	|	2025	|	2125	|	|	2225	2255	2325	0039
Bex d.	1405	|	|	|	|	1605	|	1705	|	1805	|	1905	|	|	|	|	2105	|	|	|	|	2300	|	0044
Aigle d.	1412	1437	1506	|	1537	1612	1637	1712	1737	1812	1837	1912	1937	2006	|	2037	2112	2137	2206	|	2237	2307	2337	0050
Montreux ▲ d.	1423	1448	1517	1524	1548	1623	1648	1723	1748	1823	1848	1923	1948	2017	2024	2048	2123	2148	2217	2224	2248	2318	2348	0102
Vevey ▲ d.	1430	1455	1524	|	1555	1630	1655	1730	1755	1830	1855	1930	1955	2024	|	2055	2130	2155	2224	|	2255	2325	2355	0108
Lausanne ▲ a.	1445	1510	1539	1542k	1610	1645	1710	1745	1810	1845	1910	1945	2010	2039	2042k	2110	2145	2210	2239	2242	2310	2339	0010	0122
Lausanne 505 d.	1448	1518	1548	1545	1618	1648	1718	1748	1818	1848	1918	1948	2018	2048	2045	2118	2148	2221	2248	2245	2321	*2351*	0025	...
Morges **505** d.	1459	1529	1559	|	1629	1659	1729	1759	1829	1859	1929	1959	2029	2059	|	2129	2159	2234	2259	|	2334	*0004*	0038	...
Nyon **505** d.	1515	1545	1615	|	1645	1715	1745	1815	1845	1915	1945	2015	2045	2115	|	2145	2215	2252	2315	|	2352	*0025*	0056	...
Genève 505 a.	1530	1600	1630	1621	1700	1730	1800	1830	1900	1930	2000	2030	2100	2130	2121	2200	2230	2307	2330	2321	0007	*0041*	0111	...
Genève Aéroport ✈ **505** a.	1539	1609	1639	...	1709	1739	1809	1839	1909	1939	2009	2039	2109	2139	...	2209	2239	2316	2339	...	0016	...	0122	...

▲ – Local services **Lausanne - Montreux - Villeneuve and v.v.**

Lausanne d.	0600	0636	0700	0736	and at	2000	2036	2100	2200	2300	0000
Vevey d.	0622	0653	0722	0753	the same	2022	2053	2122	2222	2322	0022
Montreux d.	0631	0702	0731	0802	minutes	2031	2102	2131	2231	2331	0031
Territet d.	0632	|	0732	|	past each	2032	|	2132	2232	2332	0032
Veytaux-Chillon d.	|	0704	|	0804	hour until	|	2104	|	|	|	|
Villeneuve a.	0637	0708	0737	0808		2037	2108	2137	2237	2337	0037

Villeneuve d.	0523	0549	0623	0651	and at	2023	2051	2123	2223
Veytaux-Chillon d.	|	0551	|	0653	the same	|	2053	|	|
Territet d.	0525	|	0626	|	minutes past	2026	|	2126	2226
Montreux d.	0528	0554	0628	0656	each	2028	2056	2128	2228
Vevey d.	0538	0604	0638	0706	hour until	2038	2106	2138	2238
Lausanne a.	0559	0624	0659	0723		2059	2123	2159	2259

♦ – **NOTES** (LISTED BY TRAIN NUMBER)

V – (12) and ✕ Genève - Milano - Venezia and v.v.

j – Dec. 13 - May 1.
k – Connects with train in previous column.
r – 4 minutes later from May 2.
t – 2–3 minutes later from May 2.

◧ – Supplement payable for journeys from/to Italy.

class only — Local services from VEVEY, AIGLE and BEX — 571

Y - BLONAY: Narrow gauge. *6 km*. Journey time: 14 – 16 minutes. **Operator**: MVR.

Vevey: 0610⚒, 0629Ⓐ, 0640Ⓒ, 0648Ⓐ, 0710⚒, 0729Ⓐ, 0740Ⓒ, 0748Ⓐ, 0810⚒, 0829Ⓐ, 0840Ⓒ, 0848Ⓐ, 0910⚒, 0940, 1010⚒, 1040, 1110⚒, 1140, 1210⚒, 1240, 1310⚒, 1340, 1410⚒, 1440, 1510⚒, 1540, 1610⚒, 1629Ⓐ, 1640Ⓒ, 1648Ⓐ, 1710⚒, 1729Ⓐ, 1740Ⓒ, 1748Ⓐ, 1810⚒, 1829Ⓐ, 1840Ⓒ, 1848Ⓐ, 1910⚒, 1940, 2010⚒, 2040, 2140, 2240, 2340, 0045⑥⑦.

From **Blonay**: 0534⚒, 0604, 0631Ⓐ, 0634⑥, 0650Ⓐ, 0704, 0731Ⓐ, 0734⑥, 0750Ⓐ, 0804, 0831Ⓐ, 0834⑥, 0850Ⓐ, 0904, 0934⚒, 1004, 1034⚒, 1104, 1134⚒, 1204, 1234⚒, 1304, 1334⚒, 1404, 1434⚒, 1504, 1534⚒, 1604, 1631Ⓐ, 1634⑥, 1650Ⓐ, 1704, 1731Ⓐ, 1734⑥, 1750Ⓐ, 1804, 1831Ⓐ, 1834⑥, 1850Ⓐ, 1904, 1934⚒, 2004, 2104, 2204, 2304, 0004⑥⑦.

E - LEYSIN: Narrow gauge rack railway. *6 km*. Journey time: 29 – 39 minutes. **Operator**: TPC.

Aigle: 0547Ⓐ, 0608Ⓐ, 0623Ⓒ, 0655Ⓒ, 0723Ⓐ, 0755, 0855 and hourly until 2255.

From **Leysin** Grand Hotel: 0522, 0619Ⓐ, 0640Ⓐ, 0655Ⓒ, 0755, 0852 and hourly until 2252, then 2327.

E - LES DIABLERETS: Narrow gauge. *23 km*. Journey time: 45 – 55 minutes. **Operator**: TPC.

Aigle: 0602, 0706, 0827, 0925, 1056, 1156 and hourly until 1856, then 2056, 2156.

From **Les Diablerets**: 0609, 0710, 0807, 0936, 1136, 1236, 1333, 1436 and hourly until 1836, then 1908, 2039, 2204.

E - CHAMPÉRY: Narrow gauge rack railway. 2nd class only. **Operator**: TPC. Additional services operate Aigle - Monthey Ville and v.v.

	⚒			⚒				⚒		⚒		⚒					⚒								⑥h	
Aigle .... d.	0511	0622	0725	0755	0824	0924	1023	1058	1124	1154	1224	1254	1324	1423	1524	1624	1654	1724	1824	1923	2024	2123	2223	2324	...	2355
Monthey Ville .. d.	0541	0644	0750	0814	0851	0950	1054	1117	1151	1213	1251	1313	1350	1451	1554	1651	1713	1751	1850	1951	2050	2150	2242	2343	2351	0014
Champéry ...... a.	0614	0720	0823	...	0924	1023	1127	...	1224	...	1324	...	1423	1524	1627	1724	...	1824	1923	2024	2123	2223	...	...	0024	...

		Ⓐ		⚒				⚒		⚒		⚒						⚒		⚒							⑦g
npéry ....d.	...	...	0554	0631a	0700d	0803	0904	...	1003	...	1107	...	1204	1304	1403	1504	1607	...	1704	...	1804	1903	2004	2103	2203	2230	0026
ney Ville ...d.	0544	0606	0646	0709	0747	0846	0946	1007	1042	1123	1146	1223	1246	1346	1442	1546	1646	1723	1747	1823	1847	1942	2046	2142	2242	2308	0101
................a.	0604	0626	0707	0731	0807	0906	1006	1027	1102	1143	1206	1243	1306	1406	1502	1606	1706	1743	1807	1843	1907	2002	2106	2202	2302	2328	...

- VILLARS-SUR-OLLON: *12 km*. Journey time: 40 – 46 minutes. All trains call at Bex (Place du Marché), and Bévieux (*3 km* and 4 minutes from Bex). **Operator**: TPC.

Bex: 0631, 0720, 0803, 0909, 1007, 1115, 1203, 1303, 1403, 1509, 1603, 1703, 1803, 1907, 2003, 2107.

From **Villars**: 0534, 0624, 0714, 0813, 0903, 1000, 1108, 1213, 1313, 1356, 1503, 1556, 1713, 1813, 1901, 2013, 2101.

ARS-SUR-OLLON - COL-DE-BRETAYE: *5 km*. Journey time: 18 – 20 minutes. **Operator**: TPC.

Villars:
13 - 18, Apr. 11 - June 10, Sept. 20 - Dec. 10: 0900, 1100**j**, 1200, 1300**j**, 1500**j**, 1600.
19 - Apr. 10: 0810, 0830, 0900, 0930 and every 30 minutes until 1730.
11 - Sept. 19: 0815, 0900, 1000 and hourly until 1700.

From **Col-de-Bretaye**:
Dec. 13 - 18, Apr. 11 - June 10, Sept. 20 - Dec. 10: 0930, 1130**j**, 1230, 1330**j**, 1530**j**, 1630.
Dec. 19 - Apr. 10: 0840, 0855, 0925, 0955 and every 30 minutes until 1725, then 1815.
June 11 - Sept. 19: 0837, 0930, 1030 and hourly until 1730.

Ⓐ only. **d** – ⚒ only. **g** – Also Aug. 2. **h** – Also Aug. 1. **j** – Dec. 13 - 18, May 14 - June 10, Sept. 20 - Oct. 30 (also Dec. 10).

class only. SNCF, TMR — MARTIGNY - CHAMONIX — 572

Vallorcine - Chamonix (- St Gervais) and v.v. is subject to alteration. *Narrow gauge rack railway. A change of train may be necessary at Vallorcine.*

			Ⓐ	Ⓒ																			♣	♣y
Martigny .... d.	0602	...	...	...	0651	0745	0845	0945	1045	...	1145	1245	1345	1445	1545	...	1645	1745	1845	1945	2045	2145	2245	2343
Salvan .... d.	0616	...	...	...	0705	0759	0859	0959	1059	...	1159	1259	1359	1459	1559	...	1659	1759	1859	1959	2059	2159	2259	2359
Les Marécottes .... d.	0620	...	...	...	0709	0803	0903	1003	1103	...	1203	1303	1403	1503	1603	...	1703	1803	1903	2003	2103	2203	2303	0003
Finhaut .... d.	0633	...	...	...	0722	0816	0916	1016	1116	...	1216	1316	1416	1516	1616	...	1716	1816	1916	2016	2116	2216	2316s	0015s
Le Châtelard Frontière 🏛 .... d.	0642	...	...	...	0732	0826	0926	1026	1126	...	1226	1326	1426	1526	1626	...	1726	1826	1926	2026	2126	2226	2326	0025
Vallorcine .... a.	...	...	...	...	...	0833	0933	1033	1133r	...	1233r	1333	1433r	1533r	1633	...	1733	1833	1933	2033r	...	...	...	...
Vallorcine .... d.	...	0638	0707	0738	...	0838	0938	1038	1138	1207	1238	1338	1438	1538	1638	1707	1738	1838	1938	2038	...	...	...	...
Argentière Haute Savoie .... d.	...	0653	0724	0753	...	0853	0953	1053	1153	1224	1253	1353	1453	1553	1653	1724	1753	1853	1953	2053	...	...	...	...
Les Tines .... d.	...	0703	0734	0803	...	0903	1003	1103	1203	1234	1303	1403	1503	1603	1703	1734	1803	1903	2003	2103	...	...	...	...
Chamonix .... a.	...	0710	0742	0810	...	0910	1010	1110	1210	1242	1310	1410	1510	1610	1710	1742	1810	1910	2010	2110	...	...	...	...
St Gervais **365a** .... a.	...	0757	0857	0857	...	0957	1057	...	1257	...	1357	1457	...	1657	1757	...	1857	1957	2057	...	...	...	...	...

	Ⓐ		Ⓐ																				♣	
Gervais **365a** .... d.	...	...	...	...	0705	0805	0905	1005	...	...	1205	...	1305	1405	...	...	1605	1705	1805	1905	...	...	...	...
nonix .... d.	...	...	0620	...	0754	0854	0954	1054	1120	1154	1254	...	1354	1454	1554	1620	1654	1754	1854	1954	...	...	...	...
Tines .... d.	...	...	0633	...	0804	0904	1004	1104	1133	1204	1304	...	1404	1504	1604	1633	1704	1804	1904	2004	...	...	...	...
ntière Haute Savoie .... d.	...	...	0641	...	0813	0913	1013	1113	1141	1213	1313	...	1413	1513	1613	1641	1713	1813	1913	2013	...	...	...	...
rcine .... a.	...	...	0700	...	0830	0930	1030	1130	1200	1230	1330	...	1430	1530	1630	1700	1730	1830	1930	2030	...	...	...	...
rcine .... d.	...	...	...	...	0843	0943	1043	1143r	...	1243r	1343	...	1443r	1543	1643r	...	1743	1843	1943	2043r	...	...	...	...
hâtelard Frontière 🏛 .... d.	0526	0647	...	0750	0850	0950	1050	1150	...	1250	1350	...	1450	1550	1650	...	1750	1850	1950	2050	2150	2250	2331	...
aut .... d.	0536	0657	...	0800	0900	1000	1100	1200	...	1300	1400	...	1500	1600	1700	...	1800	1900	2000	2100	2200	2300	2341	...
Marécottes .... d.	0549	0709	...	0812	0912	1012	1112	1212	...	1312	1412	...	1512	1612	1712	...	1812	1912	2012	2112	2212	2312	2353	...
an .... d.	0553	0714	...	0817	0917	1017	1117	1217	...	1317	1417	...	1517	1617	1717	...	1817	1917	2017	2117	2217	2318	2359	...
igny .... a.	0613	0733	...	0836	0936	1036	1136	1236	...	1336	1436	...	1536	1636	1736	...	1836	1936	2036	2136	2236	2337	0018	...

Dec. 13 - Mar. 27, June 11 - Sept. 11.
Stops to set down only.
y – ⑤⑥ only.
♣ – Runs only by prior reservation ✆ 027 764 12 71.

SION VALLEY RESORTS — 573

TIGNY - ORSIÈRES▲ and LE CHÂBLE: *19 km*. Journey time: 26 minutes to both resorts. ▲ – A change of train is necessary at Sembrancher. **Operator**: RA.

Martigny: 0609Ⓐ, 0716, 0816, 0916, 1016, 1145, 1222, 1316, 1416, 1516, 1645, 1722, 1816, 1916, 2016, 2116, 2318⑤⑥.

From **Orsières and Le Châble**: 0532Ⓐ, 0640, 0710Ⓐ, 0745Ⓒ, 0810, 0910, 1010, 1110, 1218, 1310, 1410, 1510, 1610, 1718, 1810, 1910, 2045, 2242⑤⑥.

HÂBLE - VERBIER: 🚌 service. Journey time: ± 25 minutes. **Operator**: PA.

Le Châble Gare: 0645⚒, 0715†, 0750⚒, 0855, 0955, 1055†, 1255, 1355, 1455⚒, 1610, 1715, 1755⚒, 1806†, 1900, 1955, 2055, 2149**w**.
Verbier Post: 0610⚒, 0715⚒, 0740†, 0840⚒, 0925, 1025, 1230, 1330, 1430⚒, 1525, 1640, 1740, 1835, 1930, 2020, 2120**w**.

TIGNY - AOSTA: 🚌 service via Grand St Bernard tunnel. Service runs daily throughout the year (**not Dec. 25**). Journey time: ± 1 hour 45 minutes. **Operator**: TMR / SAVDA.

Martigny Gare: 0825, 1830. From **Aosta** Stazione: 1100, 1600. *Timings subject to alteration.*

- CRANS-SUR-SIERRE: 🚌 service. Journey time: ± 45 minutes. **Operator**: PA.

Sion Gare: 0645⚒, 0745, 0840⚒, 1000, 1045⚒, 1150, 1230⚒ 1345, 1510Ⓒ**y**, 1540Ⓐ**z**, 1650⚒, 1710†, 1810, 1910.

From **Crans-sur-Sierre** Post: 0643, 0740⚒, 0835, 0930⚒, 1050, 1135⚒, 1245, 1335⚒, 1545, 1635, 1805, 61905.

RE - CRANS-SUR-SIERRE - MONTANA: 🚌 service. Principal stop in **Crans-sur-Sierre** is Hotel Scandia (± 40 minutes from Sierre, ± 8 minutes from Montana. **Operator**: SMC.

Sierre Gare: 0745, 0845, 0945⚒, 1045⚒, 1140, 1200⚒, 1231⚒, 1340, 1440⚒, 1546, 1650Ⓐ**z**, 1715, 1745, 1845⚒, 1945, 2045, 2215.

From **Montana** Gare: 0602⚒, 0622Ⓐ**z**, 0632, 0736†, 0839⚒, 0958, 1037⚒, 1133⚒, 1226, 1334⚒, 1435, 1558, 1603Ⓐ**z**, 1646, 1733⚒, 1833, 1907, 2058.

G - SAAS-FEE: 🚌 service. Journey time: 50 – 70 minutes. All services call at **Visp** (Bahnhof Süd) ± 20 minutes from Brig, and **Saas Grund** (Post) ± 10 minutes from Saas Fee.

Brig (Bahnhof): 0420, 0545, 0615, 0645 and every 30 minutes until 1045, then 1115, 1140, 1215, 1250, 1315, 1345 and every 30 minutes until 1845, then 1945, 2045, 2215.

From **Saas-Fee**: 0530, 0600, 0630, 0700, 0730, 0752, 0822, 0852, 0922, 0952 and every 30 minutes until 1852, then 1930, 2030.

rator: PA. Seat reservation recommended on Ⓒ from Saas Fee to Brig. ✆ 058 454 26 16.

Dec. 19 - Apr. 10.
Not Dec. 26, Jan. 2, Mar. 19.
Also Mar. 25; not May 26, Aug. 15, Nov. 1, Dec. 8.

575 GLACIER EXPRESS MGB, R

Glacier Express through services (compulsory reservation). **No service Oct. 24 - Dec. 10, 2016.** For local services see Table 576. Narrow gauge railway (part rack).

km		WINTER SERVICE ▶▶▶	902 ⊡ ✕		SUMMER SERVICE ▶▶▶	900 ★ T ✕	902 ★ ✕	904 ★ S ✕	
0	**Zermatt** d.		0852	...		0752	0852	0952	...
21	St Niklaus △ d.		|	...		|	|	1027	...
36	Visp △ d.		|	...		|	|	|	...
45	**Brig** △ d.		1018	...		0918	1018	1118	...
62	Fiesch △ d.		1042	...		0942	1042	1142	...
86	Oberwald △ d.	Dec. 13	1111	...	May 5	1011	1111	1211	...
113	**Andermatt** a.	to	1149	...	to	1049	1149	1249	...
113	**Andermatt** d.	May 4	1154	...	Oct. 23	1054	1154	1254	...
142	**Disentis / Mustér** a.		1255	...		1155	1255	1355	...
142	**Disentis / Mustér** d.		1327	...		1227	1327	1427	...
201	**Chur** ▽ a.		1434	...		1334	1434	1534	...
228	Thusis ▽ a.		1528	...		1428	1528	1628	...
242	Tiefencastel ▽ a.		1547	...		1447	1547	1647	...
252	**Filisur 545a** ▽ a.		1600	...		1500	1600	1700	...
	Davos Platz **545a** a.		|	...		|	|	|	...
285	**Samedan 546** ▽ a.		1645	...		1545	1645	1745	...
288	Celerina **546/7** ▽ a.		1654	...		1554	1654	1754	...
290	**St Moritz 546/7** a.		1703	...		1603	1703	1803	...

	WINTER SERVICE ▶▶▶	903 ⊡ ✕		SUMMER SERVICE ▶▶▶	901 ★ S ✕	903 ★ ✕	905 ★ T ✕
St Moritz 546/7 d.		0857	...		0757	0857	0957
Celerina **546/7** △ d.		0900	...		0800	0900	1000
Samedan 546 △ d.		0917	...		0817	0917	1017
Davos Platz **545a** d.		|	...		|	|	|
Filisur 545a △ d.		1001	...		0901	1001	1101
Tiefencastel △ d.	Dec. 13	1015	...	May 5	0915	1015	1115
Thusis △ d.	to	1033	...	to	0933	1033	1133
Chur △ d.	May 4	1126	...	Oct. 23	1026	1126	1226
Disentis / Mustér a.		1227	...		1127	1227	1327
Disentis / Mustér d.		1237	...		1137	1237	1337
Andermatt a.		1350	...		1250	1350	1450
Andermatt d.		1354	...		1308	1408	1508
Oberwald ▽ a.		1418	...		|	1436	1536
Fiesch ▽ a.		1510	...		1410	1510	1610
Brig ▽ a.		1540	...		1440	1540	1640
Visp ▽ a.		1553	...		1453	1553	1653
St Niklaus ▽ a.		|	...		1524	|	|
Zermatt a.		1710	...		1610	1710	1810

All Glacier Express trains convey (12) [panorama cars]. Reservations can be made at any Swiss station. Reservations for ✕ are obligatory in advance: RhB, ✆ 081 288 65 65. Meals are served between 1100 and 1330 at your seat. Further information: www.glacierexpress.ch

S – June 11 - Sept. 18.
T – May 5 - Oct. 9.

△ – Calls to pick up only.
▽ – Calls to set down only.

⊡ – Ⓡ (reservation fee including supplement: 13
★ – Ⓡ (reservation fee including supplement: 33
* – For operators see foot of page.

576 ZERMATT - BRIG - ANDERMATT (- GÖSCHENEN) - DISENTIS - CHUR local services MGB, R

Narrow gauge railway (part rack). For *Glacier Express* through services see Table 575

ZERMATT - BRIG

km													
0	**Zermatt** d.	0537	0613	0637	0813		1813	1837	1913	1937	2013	2113	2213
8	Täsch d.	0548x	0625	0648x	0825	and	1825	1848	1925	1948	2025	2125	2223
21	St Niklaus d.	0613	0650	0713	0850	every	1850	1913	1950	2013	2050	2150	2244
29	Stalden-Saas d.	0635	0710	0735	0910	hour	1910	1935	2010	2035	2110	2210	2304
36	Visp a.	0645	0721	0745	0921	until	1921	1945	2021	2045	2121	2221	2313
36	Visp d.	0650	0725	0750	0925	△	1925	1950	2025	2050	2125	2225	2318
45	**Brig** a.	0702	0737	0802	0937		1937	2002	2037	2102	2137	2237	2327

										①-⑥	⑦
Brig d.	0520	0552	0627	0652	0727		1827	1952	2052	2227	2308
Visp a.	0531	0603	0638	0703	0738	and	1838	2003	2103	2238	2318
Visp d.	0533	0608	0641	0708	0741	every	1841	2008	2108	2241	2323
Stalden-Saas d.	0542	0618	0651	0718	0751	hour	1851	2018	2118	2249	2331
St Niklaus d.	0559	0636	0713	0736	0813	until	1913	2036	2136	2305	2347
Täsch d.	0621	0700	0736	0800	0836	▽	1936	2100x	2200x	2325x	0007
Zermatt a.	0633	0713	0750	0813	0850		1950	2113	2213	2336	0018

VISP - BRIG - ANDERMATT

km										①-⑥	⑦	
	Visp d.	...	0708	0808		1908	...	2008	2108	2238	2255	...
0	**Brig** d.	0623	0723	0823	and	1923	...	2023	2123	2250	2312	...
7	Mörel d.	0633	0733	0833	every	1933	...	2033	2133	2300	2320	...
10	Betten d.	0639	0739	0839	hour	1939	...	2039	2139	2306	2326	...
17	Fiesch d.	0656	0756	0856	until	1956	...	2056	2155	2322	2343	...
41	Oberwald 🚘 d.	0744	0844	0944		2044	...	2137	2237z	...	...	...
59	Realp ▲ 🚘 § d.	0805	0905	1005		2105	...	...	...	...	...	...
68	**Andermatt** a.	0820	0920	1020		2120	...	...	...	...	...	...

									①-⑥	⑦
Andermatt d.	...	...	0737	0837		1837	1937	2025	...	...
Realp ▲ 🚘 § d.	...	...	0750	0850	and	1850	1950	2036	...	...
Oberwald 🚘 d.	*0612z*	0712	0812	0912	every	1912	2012	2056	*2250z*	*2250z*
Fiesch d.	0656	0756	0856	0956	hour	1956	2056	2131	2326	2346
Betten d.	0715	0815	0915	1015	until	2015	2115	2147	2344	0004
Mörel d.	0722	0822	0922	1022		2022	2122	2157	2351	0011
Brig a.	0733	0833	0933	1033		2033	2133	2206	0001	0021
Visp a.	0750	0850	0950	1050		2050	2150	...	...	...

ANDERMATT - GÖSCHENEN

km												
0	**Andermatt** d.	0638	0725	0748	0828	0848	and hourly until	1828	1848	1948	2048	2128
4	**Göschenen** a.	0652	0740	0803	0842	0903		1842	1903	2003	2103	2142

Göschenen d.	0714	0753	0814	0853	and hourly until	1814	1853	1914	2014	2114
Andermatt a.	0724	0804	0824	0904		1824	1904	1924	2023	2124

ANDERMATT - DISENTIS

km		🚌Ⓐ	🚌		w◇		w◇		w◇			w◇				w◇								🚌	🚌v	
0	**Andermatt** 🚘 d.	...	...	0728	0755	0828	0855	0928	0955	...	1028	1055	1128	1228	1328	1355	...	1428	1528	1628	1728	1828	...	...	...	
10	Oberalppass d.	...	...	0750	0814	0850	0914	0950	1014	...	1050	1114	1150	1250	1350	1414	...	1450	1550	1650	1750	1850	...	...	...	
19	Sedrun 🚘 d.	0616	0705	0816	...	0916	...	1016	...	...	1116	...	1216	1316	1416	...	...	1516	1616	1716	1816	1916	...	2001	2101	2
29	**Disentis / Mustér** a.	0634	0725	0836	...	0936	...	1036	...	...	1136	...	1236	1336	1436	...	...	1536	1636	1736	1836	1936	...	2021	2119	2

	🚌	n	r												w◇					🚌	🚌		🚌v	🚌v	
Disentis / Mustér d.	0640	0708	0714	0814	0914	...	1014	1114	1214	...	1314	1414	1514	...	...	1614	1714	1814	...	1922	2022	...	2122	2222	(
Sedrun 🚘 d.	0650	0731	0731	0831	0931	...	1031	1131	1231	...	1331	1431	1531	...	...	1631	1731	1831	...	1939	2039	...	2139	2239	0
Oberalppass d.	...	0753	0753	0853	0953	...	1053	1153	1253	...	1353	1453	1553	...	1625	1653	1753	1853	...	...	...	...	...	...	
Andermatt 🚘 a.	...	0822	0822	0922	1022	...	1122	1222	1322	...	1422	1522	1622	...	1654	1722	1822	1922	...	...	...	...	...	...	

DISENTIS - CHUR

km			⚒								
0	**Disentis / Mustér** d.	0544	0615	0644	0744	and	1744	1844	1944	2044	...
12	Trun d.	0600	0629	0700	0800	every	1800	1900	2000	2100	...
30	Ilanz d.	0624	0653	0724	0824	hour	1824	1924	2024	2123	...
49	Reichenau-Tamins d.	0649	0716x	0749	0849	until	1849	1949	2049	2149	...
59	**Chur** a.	0702	0732	0802	0901		1901	2001	2101	2202	...

	⚒								
Chur d.	0609	0654	0756	0856	and	1856	1956	2059	2259
Reichenau-Tamins d.	0621	0703	0805	0905	every	1905	2005	2113	2311
Ilanz d.	0654	0733	0833	0933	hour	1933	2033	2140	2333
Trun d.	0714	0754	0854	0954	until	1954	2054	2158	2351
Disentis / Mustér a.	0730	0811	0911	1011		2011	2111	2217	0009

n – Dec. 13 - May 4, Oct. 24 - Dec. 10.
q – ⑥⑦ Dec. 19 - Mar. 27.
r – May 5 - Oct. 23.
v – Dec. 13 - Mar. 28.
w – Dec. 19 - Mar. 28.
x – Stops only on request.
z – Connection by 🚌.

◇ – Subject to favourable weather conditions.
§ – Realp is a request stop.
△ – Additional services Zermatt - Visp: 0737, 0837, and hourly until 1737.
▽ – Additional services Visp - Zermatt: 0808, 0908, and hourly until 1908.

▲ – 🚂 service (summer only, not daily) runs Realp - Furka - Gletsch - Obe and v.v. Operator: Dampfbahn Furka-Bergstrecke ✆ 0848 000 144.
🚘 – Car-carrying shuttle available (see page 260).
* – For operators see foot of page.

578 ZERMATT - GORNERGRAT Narrow gauge rack railway. G

Journey 33 minutes uphill, 44 minutes downhill, *9 km. Services are liable to be suspended in bad weather*

Dec. 13 - Apr. 17, June 11 - Oct. 16, Nov. 26 - Dec. 10:
From Zermatt: 0700, 0800, 0824, 0848, 0912*, 0936*, 1000*, 1024*, 1048*, 1112*, 1136, 1200, 1224, 1248, 1312, 1336, 1400, 1424, 1448, 1512, 1536, 1600, 1624, 1724, 1824**m**, 1924
From Gornergrat: 0735, 0843, 0907, 0931, 0955, 1019, 1043, 1107, 1131, 1155, 1219, 1243, 1307, 1331, 1355, 1419, 1443, 1507, 1531, 1555, 1619, 1638, 1718, 1818, 1918**m**, 2007**p**.

Apr. 18 - June 10, Oct. 17 - Nov. 25:
From Zermatt: 0700**r**, 0824, 0936**q**, 1024, 1136, 1224, 1336, 1424, 1536**q**, 1624, 1724**q**, 1824**q**.
From Gornergrat: 0735**r**, 0931, 1019**q**, 1131, 1219, 1331, 1419, 1531, 1619**q**, 1718, 1818**q**, 1918**q**.

m – Dec. 13 - Apr. 17, June 11 - Oct. 16.
p – Dec. 13 - Apr. 10, June 18 - Sept. 18.
q – Apr. 18 - June 10, Oct. 17 - 30.
r – Daily Apr. 18 - June 10, Oct. 17 - 30; ①-⑤ Oct. 31 - Nov. 25 (not Nov. 1).
* – Duplicated by non-stop journeys Dec. 20 - Ap (journey time 29 minutes).

* – Operators: MGB, Zermatt - Andermatt / Göschenen - Disentis; RhB, Disentis - Chur.

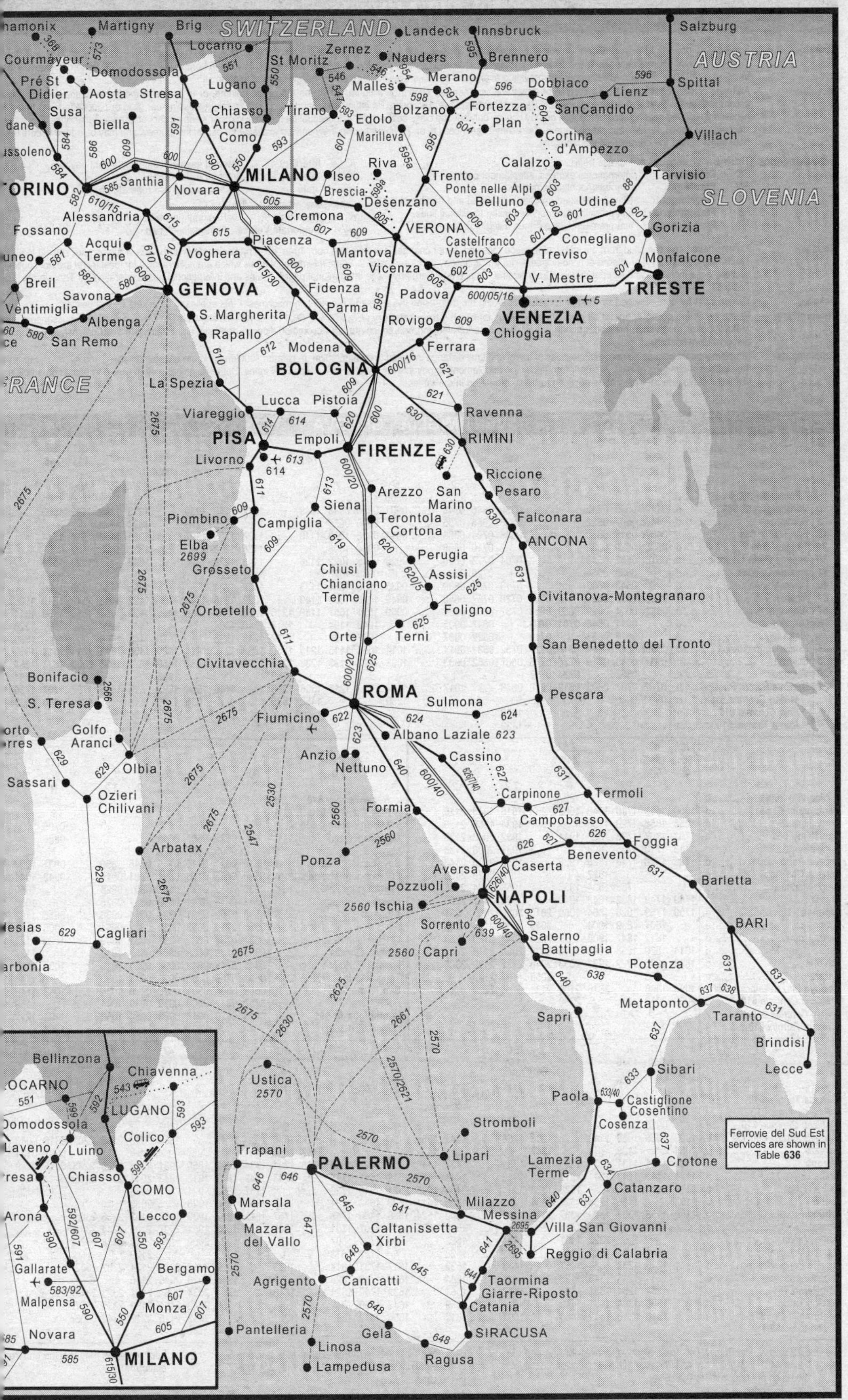

A list of Scenic Rail Routes appears elsewhere in the timetable – see Contents page

ITALY

Operator: Services are operated by Trenitalia, a division of Ferrovie dello Stato Italiane S.p.a. (FS), unless otherwise noted: www.trenitalia.com.
Trenord is a joint venture between Trenitalia and Ferrovie Nord Milano (LeNord) that operates local services, mainly in the Lombardia region: www.trenord.it. Nuovo Tras Viaggiatori (NTV) is an open-access operator providing alternative services over the high-speed network: www.italotreno.it.

Services: All trains convey First and Second classes of travel unless otherwise shown by a figure "2" at the top of the column, or in a note in the Table heading. Four class accommodation is available on Frecciarossa (*FR*) services: Executive, Business, Premium and Standard class. Overnight sleeping car (🛏) or couchette (▬) trains c necessarily convey seating accommodation or may convey only second class seats - refer to individual footnotes. Excelsior sleeping cars offer en-suite facilities. Descriptic sleeping and couchette cars appear on page 8. Refreshment services (✕ or 🍷) where known, may only be available for part of the journey, and may be added to or taken from trains during the currency of the timetable.

Train Categories: There are 8 categories of express train:

EC	**EuroCity**	international express; supplement payable.
EN	**EuroNight**	international night express.
FA	**Frecciargento**	tilting trains used on both high-speed and traditional lines.
FB	**Frecciabianca**	fast premium fare services using traditional lines.
FR	**Frecciarossa**	fast premium fare services using high-speed lines.
IC	**InterCity**	internal day express; supplement payable.
ICN	**InterCity Notte**	internal night express.
ITA	**.italo**	high-speed service (operated by NTV).

Other services are classified:

R	**Regionale**	Regional (local) train.
RV	**Regionale Veloce**	Fast regional train.

Timings: Timings have been compiled from the latest information received. Minor changes are expected from **June 12**. In particular, days and dates of running are subject to altera Trains may be cancelled or altered at holiday times – for public holiday dates see page 2. Some international trains which are not available for local travel are not shown i section; these include some sleeper services from Austria, France and Germany – see International pages. Trains and international buses operating via Tarvisio are sho Table **88**.

Tickets: Tickets must be date-stamped by the holder before boarding the train using the self-service validating machines – this applies to all tickets except passes.

Reservations: Reservations are **compulsory** for all journeys by services for which a **train category** (*EC, EN, FA, FB, FR, IC, ICN*) is shown in the timing column and passengers boa without a prior reservation may be surcharged. Reservations for sleeping and couchette car accommodation on domestic night trains are valid only when presented personal identification.

Supplements Supplements are calculated according to class of travel and total distance travelled (minimum 10km, maximum 3000km), and are payable on all *EC* and *IC* trains, regardle the number of changes of train. A higher fare (including supplement) is payable for travel by *FA*, *FB* and *FR* trains. Some trains are only available to passengers holding distance tickets and the restrictions applying to these are noted in the tables.

580 VENTIMIGLIA - GENOVA

km		*IC* 655 ⚒		Ⓐ 2	⚒ 2	Ⓐ 2	*IC* 505	2	2		*EC* 139 🍷 N	2	2	*IC* 745	Ⓒ	2	2	*IC* 1539 †	Ⓒ	2	2	*EC* 143 🍷 Nz	*EC* 145 🍷 Ny	Ⓒ
	Nice Ville **360/1** d.	...	...	...	...	...	...	...	...	...	0808	...	...	...	...	...	...	...	...	...	...	1406	1406	...
0	**Ventimiglia 🏛 581** d.	0440t	0500	0515	...	...	0630	0646	0748	...	0901	0910	0948	1049	...	1110	1148	1250	...	1313	1348	1502	1502	...
5	Bordighera d.	0448t	0507	0522	...	...	0638	0655	0755	...	|	0920	0955	1101	...	1120	1155	1258	...	1323	1355	|	|	...
16	**San Remo 581** d.	0457t	0515	0530	...	...	0648	0704	0803	...	0914	0928	1003	1110	...	1128	1203	1307	...	1331	1403	1514	1514	...
24	Taggia-Arma d.	0503t	0520	0536	...	...	|	0710	0808	...	|	0934	1008	|	...	1135	1208	1313	...	1336	1408	|	|	...
39	Imperia Porto Maurizio d.	0516t	0532	0549	...	...	0704	0723	0820	...	0928	0945	1022	1126	...	1148	1220	1326	...	1348	1421	1528	1528	...
41	Imperia Oneglia d.	|	0536	0554	...	...	|	0729	0824	...	|	0949	1028	|	...	1152	1227	|	...	|	1427	|	|	...
46	Diano Marina d.	|	0543	0602	...	...	0713	0736	0830	...	0936	0955	1034	1135	...	1158	1234	|	...	1355	1434	1536	1536	...
61	Alassio d.	0535t	0558	0623	...	0650	0729	0757	0850	...	0949	1025	1051	1149	...	1222	1248	1348	...	1422	1448	1549	1549	1608
67	**Albenga** d.	0542t	0604	0629	0650	0658	0737	0804	0856	...	0959	1031	1057	1159	1210	1228	1257	1359	1406	1428	1454	1559	1559	1614
76	Loano d.	|	0611	0648	0701	0709	|	0817	0903	...	|	1043	1104	|	1218	1240	1304	|	1414	1440	1504	|	|	1626
79	Pietra Ligure d.	|	0616	0654	|	0713	|	0822	0907	...	|	1047	1108	|	1222	1248	1308	|	1418	1447	1508	|	|	1630
85	Finale Ligure Marina d.	0559t	0623	0701	0710	0724	0752	0831	0914	...	1014	1058	1115	1215	1230	1258	1315	1414	1429	1458	1515	1614	1614	1637
108	**Savona** d.	0617	0645	0719	0726	0745	0807	0852	0933	...	1033	1122	1133	1233	1248	1322	1333	1432	1450	1522	1533	1633	1633	1654
120	Varazze d.	|	0653	|	0734	0757	|	...	|	...	|	...	|	|	1259	...	|	|	1458	...	|	|	|	1701
151	**Genova** Piazza Principe .. § a.	0702	0737	0803	0812	0840	0848	...	1017	...	1107	...	1216	1306	1328	...	1416	1504	1532	...	1616	1707	1707	1730
	Milano Centrale **610** a.	0900	0940	...	...	...	|	...	...	...	1250	...	...	1450	1535	...	...	1650	1735	...	...	1850	1850	1937
	Pisa Centrale **610** a.	...	...	...	...	...	1056	...	...	...	...	...	...	...	...	...	...	...	...	...	...	...	...	...
	Roma Termini **610** a.	...	...	...	...	...	1433	...	...	...	...	...	...	...	...	...	...	...	...	...	...	...	...	...

	IC 681 Ⓐ	*IC* 1537 Ⓒ	T2	2	*EC* 147 🍷 N	2	T2	2	2	
Nice Ville **360/1** d.	...	...	...	...	1807	...	...	...	...	...
Ventimiglia 🏛 581 d.	1650	1650	1710	1748	1902	...	1916	1948	2110	...
Bordighera d.	1658	1658	1720	1755	|	...	1924	1955	2120	...
San Remo 581 d.	1707	1707	1728	1803	1914	...	1932	2003	2128	...
Taggia-Arma d.	1713	1713	1735	1808	|	...	1937	2008	2135	...
Imperia Porto Maurizio d.	1726	1726	1748	1820	1928	...	1950	2020	2148	...
Imperia Oneglia d.	|	|	|	1827	|	...	|	2028	2152	...
Diano Marina d.	|	|	1756	1834	1936	...	1958	2034	2158	...
Alassio d.	1749	1749	1822	1848	1949	...	2022	2047	2223	...
Albenga d.	1759	1759	1828	1854	1959	2010	2028	2053	2231	...
Loano d.	|	1807	1839	1904	|	2019	2039	2104	2249	...
Pietra Ligure d.	|	1812	1847	1908	|	2023	2047	2108	2254	...
Finale Ligure Marina d.	1814	1820	1858	1915	2016	2030	2058	2115	2303	...
Savona d.	1833	1835	1922	1933	2033	2048	2122	2133	2326	...
Varazze d.	|	1843	...	|	|	2056	...	2146	...	...
Genova Piazza Principe .... § a.	1906	1906	...	2016	2106	2134	...	2224	...	...
Milano Centrale **610** a.	2050	2050	...	...	2250	...	...	...	...	...
Pisa Centrale **610** a.	...	...	...	...	...	...	...	...	...	...
Roma Termini **610** a.	...	...	...	...	...	...	...	...	...	...

	Ⓐ 2	2	2	⚒ 2	† 2	T2		*EC* 142 🍷 N	Ⓒ 2
Roma Termini **610** d.	...	...	...	...	...	...	...	...	...
Pisa Centrale **610** d.	...	...	...	...	...	...	...	...	...
Milano Centrale **610** d.	...	...	...	...	...	...	...	0705	...
Genova Piazza Principe ... § d.	...	0522	0607	0646	...	...	...	0856	...
Varazze d.	...	0605	0653	0729	...	...	...	|	...
Savona d.	0515	0621	0710	0745	0745	0850	...	0931	1027
Finale Ligure Marina d.	0530	0636	0728	0801	0801	0911	...	0943	1041
Pietra Ligure d.	0536	0642	0736	0807	0807	0920	...	|	1050
Loano d.	0541	0648	0741	0812	0812	0925	...	|	1055
Albenga d.	0548	0702	0801	0824	0824	0938	...	0956	1102
Alassio d.	0555	0711	0808	0832	0832	0951	...	1006	1109
Diano Marina d.	0624	0733	0833	0851	0851	1009	...	1023	1121
Imperia Oneglia d.	0636	0739	0839	0857	0857	1015	...	|	1127
Imperia Porto Maurizio d.	0640	0748	0843	0904	0904	1019	...	1034	1131
Taggia-Arma d.	0653	0759	0855	0921	0921	1030	...	|	1144
San Remo 581 d.	0658	0804	0901	0929	0929	1036	...	1049	1149
Bordighera d.	0707	0812	0909	0939	0939	1044	...	|	1159
Ventimiglia 🏛 581 a.	0719	0820	0918	0953	0953	1055	...	1101	1212
Nice Ville **360/1** a.	...	...	...	...	...	...	...	1204	...

	⑥	*IC* 660 Ⓐ	*IC* 1536 Ⓒ	2	2	Ⓒ 2	*EC* 144 🍷 N		2	Ⓒ 2	2	2	2		*EC* 160 🍷 N		2	2	*IC* 676	2	*IC* 518	*IC* 690	2	2
Roma Termini **610** d.	...	...	...	...	...	...	...	...	...	...	...	...	...	...	...	...	...	...	...	...	1557	...	...	...
Pisa Centrale **610** d.	...	...	...	...	...	...	...	...	...	...	...	...	...	...	...	...	...	...	...	...	1903	...	...	...
Milano Centrale **610** d.	...	0910	0910	...	...	...	1110	...	...	...	...	...	...	1425	1510	...	...	...	1705	...	|	2000	...	...
Genova Piazza Principe .... § d.	1003	1058	1058	1143	...	1203	1258	...	1343	1354	...	1543	...	1626	1658	...	1743	...	1858	1943	2135	2201	2316	0043
Varazze d.	1051	|	1123	|	...	1247	|	...	|	1432	...	|	...	1712	|	←	|	...	|	|	|	|	0002	0131
Savona d.	1108	1131	1131	1227	1250	1304	1331	...	1427	1440	1450	1627	1650	1725	1731	1734	1827	1850	1931	2026	2206	2233	0015	0149
Finale Ligure Marina d.	1124	1143	1143	1241	1312	1320	1343	...	1441	1455	1512	1641	1712	→	1743	1749	1841	1912	1943	2041	2219	2245r	...	...
Pietra Ligure d.	1132	|	1150	1251	1320	1328	|	...	1450	1505	1521	1648	1726	...	|	1757	1850	1921	|	2050	|	|	...	...
Loano d.	1137	|	1156	1256	1325	1334	|	...	1455	1511	1526	1653	1731	...	|	1802	1855	1926	|	2055	|	|	...	...
Albenga d.	1150	1158	1204	1303	1337	1345	1356	...	1502	1524	1538	1700	1743	...	1757	1815	1902	1938	1957	2102	2236	2300r	...	...
Alassio d.	...	1208	1212	1310	1350	...	1406	...	1509	1535	1551	1707	1751	...	1806	...	1909	1951	2007	2109	2244	2309r	...	...
Diano Marina d.	...	|	|	1322	1407	...	1424	...	1522	...	1609	1721	1807	...	1823	...	1922	2009	|	2122	2258	2323r	...	...
Imperia Oneglia d.	...	|	|	1328	1413	...	|	...	1528	...	|	1727	1813	...	|	...	1928	|	|	2129	|	|	...	...
Imperia Porto Maurizio d.	...	1233	1233	1334	1417	...	1433	...	1532	...	1617	1731	1817	...	1833	...	1932	2017	2034	2134	2307	2332r	...	...
Taggia-Arma d.	...	1244	1246	1346	1428	...	|	...	1544	...	1628	1743	1828	...	|	...	1944	2028	2046	2146	|	|	...	...
San Remo 581 d.	...	1251	1254	1351	1434	...	1447	...	1551	...	1634	1749	1834	...	1848	...	1951	2034	2054	2151	2323	2347r	...	...
Bordighera d.	...	1300	1304	1401	1442	...	|	...	1559	...	1642	1759	1842	...	|	...	1959	2042	2104	2159	2335	2357r	...	...
Ventimiglia 🏛 581 a.	...	1310	1316	1412	1453	...	1501	...	1612	...	1656	1812	1853	...	1901	...	2012	2055	2115	2212	2342	0005r	...	...
Nice Ville **360/1** a.	...	...	...	...	...	...	1600	...	...	...	...	...	...	...	2006	...	...	...	...	...	...	...	...	...

N – 🚃12 and 🍷 Marseille / Nice - Ventimiglia - Genova - Milano and v.v. Trains **143** ①–⑤ from July 4; **147** daily until July 3, ⑥⑦ from July 4; **160** daily, operate from / to Marseille.
T – From / to Torino.

r – Not ①⑦ Jan. 10 - Feb. 22, ① May 2 - June 6.
t – Not ①② Jan. 11 - Feb. 23, ② May 3 - June 7.
y – Until July 3.
z – From July 4.

§ – Local services may use the undergro platforms.

VENTIMIGLIA and NICE - CUNEO ◦ 581

class only

	d	e				z									e	d				e			
Ventimiglia d.	...	...	...	...	...	...	...	...	1037	...	...	...	...	...	...	...	...	...	1837	...	...	...	...
Nice Ville d.	...	0543	...	...	0735	0833	...	0923**z**	|	...	1240**z**	...	1500**z**	...	1637	...	1723	...	|	1803	...	1905	1951
Sospel d.	...	0635	...	...	0825	0928	...	1012**z**	|	...	1330**z**	...	1551**z**	...	1727	...	1817	...	|	1858	...	1957	2041
Breil sur Roya a.	...	0647	...	...	0837	0940	...	1024**z**	1108	...	1342**z**	...	1603**z**	...	1739	...	1829	...	1908	1910	...	2009	2053
Breil sur Roya d.	...	...	...	...	0842	...	...	1029	1109	...	1344	...	1608	...	...	...	...	...	1917	...	...	...	...
Tende d.	...	...	...	...	0939	...	...	1124	1201	...	1439	...	1704	...	...	...	...	...	2009	...	...	...	...
Limone 🏛 d.	0640	...	0732	0932	...	...	1132	...	1232	1332	...	1532	...	1732	...	1840	...	1932	2040	...	2132	...	...
Cuneo a.	0719	...	0811	1011	...	...	1211	...	1311	1411	...	1611	...	1811	...	1919	...	2011	2115	...	2211	...	...
Fossano **582** a.	...	...	0835	1035	...	...	1235	...	...	1435	...	1635	...	1835	...	...	...	2035	...	...	2235	...	...

	f	e		f	d	Ⓑ	z															d	
Fossano **582** d.	...	...	...	...	...	...	...	0725	...	0925	...	1125	...	...	1325	...	...	...	1525	...	1725	...	1925
Cuneo d.	...	...	0550	...	0641	...	...	0750	0841	0950	...	1150	...	...	1350	1441	...	...	1550	...	1750	1841	1950
Limone 🏛 d.	...	...	0628	...	0719	...	...	0830	0919	1028	...	1228	...	...	1428	1517	...	...	1628	...	1828	1919	2028
Tende d.	...	...	...	...	...	...	...	0859	...	...	1001	...	1202	1447	...	1544	...	1712	...	...	...	...	...
Breil sur Roya a.	...	...	...	...	...	...	...	0954	...	...	1058	...	1252	1537	...	1638	...	1802	...	...	...	...	...
Breil sur Roya d.	0540	0621	...	0704	...	0733	0851	0955	...	...	1101**z**	...	1254**z**	1539**z**	...	1642	1650	1804	...	1920	...	...	...
Sospel d.	0553	0635	...	0717	...	0745	0903	|	...	...	1114**z**	...	1306**z**	1551**z**	...	|	1702	1817	...	1932	...	...	...
Nice Ville a.	0640	0724	...	0807	...	0837	0954	|	...	...	1203**z**	...	1356**z**	1641**z**	...	|	1754	1906	...	2023	...	...	...
Ventimiglia a.	...	...	...	...	...	...	...	1027	...	...	...	...	...	...	...	1720	...	...	...	...	...	...	...

①–⑥ (not Italian public holidays).
①–⑤ (not French public holidays).

f – ①–⑥ (not French public holidays).

z – Not Apr. 4 - 8, 11 - 15.

TORINO - CUNEO and SAVONA 582

t trains 2nd class only

			†A	V			†A		⚒	†A														
Torino Porta Nuova d.	0525	...	0610	0625	...	...	0655	0725	...	0750	...	0825	...	0925	...	1025	...	1125	...	1225	...	...	1325	...
Savigliano d.	0603	...	0654	0703	...	...	0739	0803	...	0837	...	0903	...	1003	...	1103	...	1203	...	1303	...	...	1403	...
Fossano d.	0612	0622	0703	0713	0725	...	0748	0812	0822	0847	...	0913	0925	1012	1022	1113	1125	1212	1222	1313	1325	...	1412	1422
Cuneo a.	0636	|	|	|	0749	...	|	0836	|	|	...	|	0949	1036	|	|	1149	1236	|	|	1349	...	1436	|
Mondovi d.	...	0640	0715	0728	...	...	0800	...	0840	0902	...	0928	...	...	1040	1128	...	...	1240	1328	...	...	...	1440
Ceva d.	...	0700	0729	0743	...	...	0817	...	0900	0921	...	0943	...	...	1100	1143	...	...	1300	1342	...	...	...	1500
Savona a.	...	0752**d**	0818	0836	...	...	0911	...	...	1004	...	1036	...	...	...	1236	...	...	...	1436	...	...	...	...

										Ⓐ	Ⓐ						⚒							
no Porta Nuova d.	1425	...	1525	...	1625	...	1725	...	...	1750	...	1825	...	...	1855	1925	1955	2025	...	...	2125	...	2325	...
gliano d.	1503	...	1603	...	1703	...	1803	...	...	1829	...	1903	...	...	1931	2003	2032	2103	...	...	2203	...	0014	...
ano d.	1513	1525	1612	1622	1713	1725	1812	1822	...	1837	1845	1913	1925	...	1941	2012	2041	2113	2125	...	2212	2217	0022	...
ineo a.	|	1549	1636	|	|	1749	1836	|	...	1901	|	|	1949	...	|	2036	|	|	2150	...	2236	|	0046	...
dovi d.	1528	...	...	1640	1728	...	...	1840	...	...	1858	1928	...	...	1956	...	2100	2128	...	...	...	2235	...	...
d.	1543	...	...	1700	1743	...	...	1900	...	...	1912	1943	...	...	2018	...	2120	2143	...	...	...	2253	...	...
na a.	1636	...	...	...	1836	...	...	...	...	...	...	2036	...	...	2112	...	...	2236	...	...	...	...	...	...

	Ⓐ		†	⚒			⚒	⚒				⚒							⚒					
na d.	...	...	...	...	...	0530	...	...	...	...	...	...	...	0730	0808**d**	...	...	0930	...	...	...	1130	...	...
d.	...	...	0502	0520	...	0617	...	0650	...	0700	...	...	...	0817	0900	...	...	1017	1100	...	...	1217	1300	...
dovi d.	...	...	0522	0540	...	0632	...	0706	...	0720	...	...	...	0832	0920	...	...	1032	1120	...	...	1232	1320	...
ineo d.	0421	0524	|	|	0612	|	0654	|	...	|	0724	0751	0812	|	|	0924	1012	|	|	1124	1212	|	|	1324
ano d.	0441	0544	0540	0558	0635	0644	0714	0723	...	0738	0744	0814	0835	0844	0938	0944	1035	1044	1138	1144	1235	1244	1338	1344
gliano d.	0449	0552	...	...	...	0652	0722	0733	...	...	0752	0822	...	0852	...	0952	...	1052	...	1152	...	1252	...	1352
no Porta Nuova a.	0535	0635	...	...	...	0735	0805	0815	...	...	0835	0905	...	0935	...	1035	...	1135	...	1235	...	1335	...	1435

										†A		V	†A				†A		V			†A		V
na d.	...	1328	...	...	...	...	1530	...	...	1635	...	1730	1754	...	1800**d**	...	1845	...	1930	...	...	2028	...	2130
d.	...	1417	...	1500	...	...	1617	1700	...	1736	...	1817	1837	...	1900	...	1938	...	2017	2100	...	2115	...	2217
dovi d.	...	1432	...	1520	...	...	1632	1720	...	1750	...	1832	1851	...	1920	...	1953	...	2032	2120	...	2133	...	2232
ineo d.	1412	|	...	|	1524	1612	|	|	1724	|	1812	|	|	...	|	1924	|	2012	|	|	2124	|	2212	|
ano d.	1435	1444	...	1538	1544	1635	1644	1738	1744	1803	1835	1844	1903	...	1938	1944	2011	2035	2044	2138	2144	2155	2235	2244
gliano d.	...	1452	...	...	1552	...	1652	...	1752	1812	...	1852	1912	...	...	1952	2020	...	2052	...	2152	2205	...	2252
no Porta Nuova a.	...	1535	...	...	1635	...	1735	...	1835	1850	...	1935	1955	...	...	2035	2110	...	2135	...	2235	2250	...	2335

From Apr. 24.
From / to Ventimiglia.

d – ⚒ only.

MILANO MALPENSA AEROPORTO ✈ 583

Nord

		X			X				
no Centrale d.	0525	0555	and at the same minutes past each hour until	1925	1955	2025	2125	2225	2325
no Porta Garibaldi d.	0535	0605		1935	2005	2035	2135	2235	2335
no Bovisa d.	0542	0612		1942	2012	2042	2142	2242	2342
pensa Aeroporto ✈ a.	0616	0646		2016	2046	2116	2216	2316	0016

			X			X			
Malpensa Aeroporto ✈ d.	0543	...	0613	0643	and at the same minutes past each hour until	2113	2143	...	2243	...
Milano Bovisa a.	0618	...	0648	0718		2148	2218	...	2318	...
Milano Porta Garibaldi a.	0624	...	0654	0724		2154	2224	...	2324	...
Milano Centrale a.	0635	...	0705	0735		2205	2235	...	2335	...

All services below operate as *Malpensa Express*. Special fare payable.

no Cadorna d.	0427	0457	...	0527	0557	and each hour until	2227	2257	...	2327
no Bovisa d.	0433	0503	...	0533	0603		2233	2303	...	2333
pensa Aeroporto ✈ a.	0504	0534	...	0604	0634		2304	2334	...	0004

Malpensa Aeroporto ✈ d.	0526	0556	...	0626	0656	and each hour until	2326	2356	...	0026
Milano Bovisa a.	0556	0626	...	0656	0726		2356	0026	...	0056
Milano Cadorna a.	0603	0633	...	0703	0733		0003	0033	...	0103

Malpensa Express. Special fare payable.

Operator: Ferrovie Nord Milano (LeNord), Piazzale Cadorna 14, 20123 Milano.
✆ + 39 02 85 111, fax: + 39 02 85 11 708, www.trenord.it

584 TORINO - OULX - BARDONECCHIA

2nd class

For Italy-France services via Oulx and Modane – see Table 44

km		⚒	⚒	†	⚒	⚒		⚒	†	⚒	⚒		⚒	†	⚒	⚒		⚒	†	⚒	⚒		⚒	†
0	**Torino** Porta Nuova d.	0445	0515	0545	0545	0615	0645	0715	0745	0745	0815	0845	0915	0945	0945	1015	1045	1115	1145	1145	1215	1245	1315	1345
46	Bussoleno d.	0543	0559	0632	0643	0659	0743	0759	0832	0843	0859	0943	0959	1032	1043	1059	1143	1159	1232	1243	1259	1343	1359	1432
	Susa a.	0553	|	|	0653	|	0753	|	|	0853	|	0953	|	|	1053	|	1153	|	|	1253	|	1353	|	|
76	Oulx-Claviere-Sestriere ▲ d.	...	0628	0701	...	0728	...	0828	0901	...	0928	...	1028	1101	...	1128	...	1228	1301	...	1328	...	1428	1501
87	Bardonecchia ♣ d.	...	0641	0714	...	0741	...	0841	0914	...	0941	...	1041	1114	...	1141	...	1241	1314	...	1341	...	1441	1514

km		⚒		⚒	†	⚒	⚒		⚒	†	⚒	⚒		⚒	†	⚒	⚒			⚒	†	⚒	⚒	
	Torino Porta Nuova d.	1415	1445	1515	1545	1545	1615	1645	1715	1745	1745	1815	1845	1915	1945	1945	2015	2045	...	2115	2145	2145	2215	2245
0	Bussoleno d.	1459	1543	1559	1632	1643	1659	1743	1759	1832	1843	1859	1943	1959	2032	2043	2059	2143	...	2159	2232	2243	2259	2342
8	Susa a.	|	1553	|	|	1653	|	1753	|	|	1853	|	1953	|	|	2053	|	2153	...	|	|	2253	|	...
	Oulx-Claviere-Sestriere ▲ d.	1528	...	1628	1701	...	1728	...	1828	1901	...	1928	...	2028	2101	...	2128	...	...	2228	2301	...	2328	...
	Bardonecchia ♣ d.	1541	...	1641	1714	...	1741	...	1841	1914	...	1941	...	2041	2114	...	2141	...	...	2241	2314	...	2341	...

	⚒	†	⚒	†	⚒	⚒	⚒	⚒	†	⚒		⚒	⚒	†		⚒		⚒	⚒	†	⚒		⚒	⚒
Bardonecchia ♣ d.	...	...	...	0509	0521	...	0621	...	0648	0721	...	0821	...	0848	...	0921	...	1021	...	1048	1121	...	1221	...
Oulx-Claviere-Sestriere ▲ d.	...	...	...	0522	0534	...	0634	...	0701	0734	...	0834	...	0901	...	0934	...	1034	...	1101	1134	...	1234	...
Susa d.	...	0439	0509	|	|	0609	|	0709	|	|	0809	|	0909	|	...	|	1009	|	1109	|	|	1209	|	1309
Bussoleno d.	0419	0449	0519	0549	0601	0619	0701	0719	0728	0801	0819	0901	0919	0928	...	1001	1019	1101	1119	1128	1201	1219	1301	1319
Torino Porta Nuova a.	0515	0545	0615	0645	0645	0715	0745	0815	0815	0845	0915	0945	1015	1015	...	1045	1115	1145	1215	1215	1245	1315	1345	1415

	⚒		⚒	⚒	†	⚒		⚒	⚒	†	⚒			⚒	⚒	†	⚒		⚒	⚒	†	⚒		⚒
Bardonecchia ♣ d.	1321	...	1421	...	1448	1521	...	1621	...	1648	1721	...	...	1821	...	1848	1921	...	2021	...	2048	2121	...	2221
Oulx-Claviere-Sestriere ▲ d.	1334	...	1434	...	1501	1534	...	1634	...	1701	1734	...	...	1834	...	1901	1934	...	2034	...	2101	2134	...	2234
Susa d.	|	1409	|	1509	|	|	1609	|	1709	|	|	...	1809	|	1909	|	|	2009	|	2109	|	|	2209	|
Bussoleno d.	1401	1419	1501	1519	1528	1601	1619	1701	1719	1728	1801	...	1819	1901	1919	1928	2001	2019	2101	2119	2128	2201	2219	2301
Torino Porta Nuova a.	1445	1515	1545	1615	1615	1645	1715	1745	1815	1815	1845	...	1915	1945	2015	2015	2045	2115	2145	2215	2215	2245	2317	2345

▲ – Station for the resorts of Cesana, Claviere and Sestriere.

♣ – A cross-border 🚌 service is available Bardonecchia - Modane (Table 3 and v.v.: 4 services on ⚒, 3 on †. See www.bardonecchia.it

585 TORINO - MILANO

For high-speed services – see Table 600. For Italy-France *TGV* service – see Table 44. *FB* services convey 🍷

km			*FB* 9707 Ⓐ T		*FB* 9709		*FB* 9713		*FB* 9717 Ⓒ			*FB* 9723			*FB* 9727		*ICN* 795 ♦		*FB* 9733		*FB* 9737 T			9
0	**Torino** Porta Nuova **586** d.	0454	0540	0554	0610	0650	0710	0754	0805	0854	1054	1110	1154	1254	1310	...	1335	1354	1410	1450	1510	1554	1654	1
6	**Torino** Porta Susa **586** d.	0505	0549u	0605	0619u	0701	0719u	0805	0817u	0905	1105	1119u	1205	1305	1319u	...	1348u	1405	1419u	1501	1519u	1605	1705	1
29	Chivasso **586** d.	0520	|	0620	|	0716	|	0820	|	0920	1120	|	1220	1320	|	...	|	1420	|	1516	|	1620	1720	
60	Santhià d.	0537	|	0637	|	0733	|	0837	|	0937	1137	|	1237	1337	|	...	|	1437	|	1532	|	1637	1737	
79	Vercelli d.	0549	0629	0649	0657	0745	0757	0849	0857	0949	1149	1157	1249	1349	1357	...	1425	1449	1457	1545	1557	1649	1749	1
101	Novara d.	0604	0643	0704	0713	0802	0813	0904	0913	1004	1204	1213	1304	1404	1413	...	1443	1504	1513	1602	1613	1704	1804	1
153*	**Milano** Centrale **605** a.	0646	0716	0746	0754	0842	0846	0946	0954	1046	1246	1254	1346	1446	1450	...	1542g	1546	1550	1642	1646	1746	1846	1
	Venezia SL **605** a.	...	0958v	...	1040	...	1140	...	1228v	...	...	1540	...	...	1740	...	...	...	1840	...	1928v	...	...	2

		2 Ⓐ	*FB* 9753				*ICN* 797 ♦	2	
Torino Porta Nuova **586** d.	1754	1820	1840	1854	1954	2054	2125	2154	2254
Torino Porta Susa **586** d.	1805	1829	1849u	1905	2005	2105	2140u	2205	2305
Chivasso **586** d.	1820	1842	|	1920	2020	2120	|	2220	2320
Santhià d.	1837	1903	|	1937	2037	2137	|	2237	2337
Vercelli d.	1849	1916	1929	1949	2049	2149	2222	2249	2349
Novara d.	1904	1937	1943	2004	2104	2204	2238	2304	0004
Milano Centrale **605** a.	1946	2020g	2022	2046	2146	2246	2315g	2346	0046
Venezia SL **605** a.	...	...	2310	...	...	...	...	...	...

			2 Ⓐ	*ICN* 798 ♦			*FB* 9702		9
Venezia SL **605** d.	...	...	...	...	...	...	0620	...	0
Milano Centrale d.	0518	0618	0640g	0713g	0718	0818	0910	0918	1
Novara d.	0558	0658	0718	0805	0758	0858	0948	0958	1
Vercelli d.	0613	0713	0736	0821	0813	0913	1001	1013	1
Santhià d.	0624	0724	0747	|	0824	0924	|	1024	
Chivasso **586** d.	0643	0743	0812	|	0843	0943	|	1043	
Torino Porta Susa **586** a.	0658	0758	0829	0910s	0858	0958	1040s	1058	12
Torino Porta Nuova **586** a.	0710	0810	0840	0920	0910	1010	1050	1110	1

		FB 9712			*FB* 9716 T		*ICN* 794 ♦		*FB* 9726		*FB* 9728		*FB* 9732				*FB* 9740		*FB* 9746			⚒	2 ①
Venezia SL **605** d.	...	0850	...	...	1132v	...	...	...	1320	...	1420	...	1520	...	...	...	1720	...	1820	...	...	...	...
Milano Centrale d.	1118	1140	1218	1318	1410	1418	1444g	1518	1610	1618	1710	1718	1810	1818	...	1913	2006	2015	2110	2115	2218	2318	0018
Novara d.	1158	1219	1258	1358	1448	1458	1521	1558	1648	1658	1748	1758	1848	1858	...	1953	2048	2055	2148	2155	2258	2358	0058
Vercelli d.	1213	1234	1313	1413	1501	1513	1536	1613	1701	1713	1801	1813	1901	1913	...	2010	2101	2110	2201	2210	2313	0013	0113
Santhià d.	1224	|	1324	1424	|	1524	|	1624	|	1724	|	1824	|	1924	...	2021	|	2121	|	2221	2324	0024	0126
Chivasso **586** d.	1243	|	1343	1443	|	1543	|	1643	|	1743	|	1843	|	1943	...	2039	|	2140	|	2240	2343	0043	0147
Torino Porta Susa **586** a.	1258	1315s	1358	1458	1540s	1558	1630s	1658	1740s	1758	1840s	1858	1940s	1958	...	2053	2140s	2155	2240s	2255	2358	0058	0203
Torino Porta Nuova **586** a.	1310	1325	1410	1510	1550	1610	1640	1710	1750	1810	1850	1910	1950	2010	...	2105	2150	2207	2250	2307	0010	0110	0215

♦ – **NOTES** (LISTED BY TRAIN NUMBER)

794 – 🛏 1, 2 cl., 🛌 2 cl. (4 berth) and 🚃(2) Reggio di Calabria - Milano - Torino.
795 – 🛏 1, 2 cl., 🛌 2 cl. (4 berth) and 🚃(2) Torino - Milano - Reggio di Calabria. Train number **1595** on ①.
797/8 – 🛏 1, 2 cl., 🛌 2 cl. (4 berth) and 🚃(2) Salerno - Napoli - Milano - Torino and v.v.

T – 🚃(12) and 🍷 Torino - Milano - Venezia Mestre - Trieste and v.v.
g – Milano **Porta Garibaldi**.
u – Stops to pick up only.
s – Stops to set down
v – Venezia **Mestre**.
* – Milano Porta Garibaldi: *149 km*.

586 TORINO - AOSTA - PRÉ SAINT DIDIER

Most trains 2nd class o

km							†	⚒	†	⚒	⚒		⚒	†	⚒			⚒				⚒		†	⚒	
0	**Torino** Porta Nuova **585** d.	...	0530	...	0730	0830	0930	1130	1130	...	1230	1330	1430	1430	...	...	1630	...	1730	...	1830	...	1930	2030	...	2
6	**Torino** Porta Susa **585** d.	...	0539	...	0739	0839	0939	1139	1139	...	1239	1339	1439	1439	...	...	1639	...	1739	...	1839	...	1939	2039	...	2
29	Chivasso **585** d.	0525	0605	...	0805	0905	1005	1205	1205	1225	1305	1405	1505	1505	1525	...	1705	...	1805	1825	1905	...	2005	2105	2125	2
62	Ivrea a.	0607	0638	...	0831	0931	1031	1231	1231	1307	1331	1431	1531	1531	1607	...	1731	...	1831	1907	1931	...	2031	2131	2207	2
62	Ivrea d.	0616	...	0647	0837	0937	1038	1237	1247	1312	1341	1447	1537	1547	...	1643	1747	1800	1847	1912	1947	2000	2047	2138	2212	2
79	Pont Saint Martin d.	0629	...	0700	0849	0949	1050	1249	1300	1332	1354	1500	1550	1600	...	1656	1800	1829	1900	1929	2000	2029	2100	2150	2229	2
91	Verrès d.	0644	...	0715	0900	0959	1106	1300	1315	1346	1415	1515	1600	1615	...	1715	1815	1844	1915	1944	2015	2044	2115	2200	2244	0
104	Chatillon-Saint Vincent d.	0703	...	0726	0912	1010	1117	1311	1326	1402	1426	1526	1611	1626	...	1726	1826	1903	1926	2003	2026	2103	2126	2212	2303	0
129	**Aosta** a.	0723	...	0753	0933	1031	1138	1333	1353	1423	1453	1553	1635	1653	...	1753	1853	1923	1953	2023	2053	2123	2153	2234	2323	0

		⚒						⚒	†		⚒			⚒		†	⚒				⚒				
Aosta d.	0518	0540	0628	...	0728	0828	1034	1134	1140	1228	...	1340	1428	1503	1528	1628	1640	1705	1728	1828	1859	1928	2028	2128	
Chatillon-Saint Vincent d.	0539	0603	0649	...	0749	0849	1055	1155	1203	1249	...	1401	1449	1526	1549	1649	1701	1726	1749	1849	1926	1949	2049	2149	
Verrès d.	0550	0615	0700	...	0800	0900	1106	1206	1216	1300	...	1415	1500	1536	1600	1700	1715	1737	1800	1900	1944	2000	2100	2200	
Pont Saint Martin d.	0601	0629	0713	...	0813	0913	1116	1220	1232	1313	...	1429	1513	1550	1613	1713	1730	1801	1813	1913	2000	2013	2113	2213	
Ivrea a.	0614	0644	0726	...	0826	0926	1128	1235	1244	1326	...	1444	1526	1608	1626	1728	1744	1816	1826	1926	2014	2026	2126	2226	
Ivrea d.	0623	0650	0732	0750	0834	0934	1134	1250	1250	1334	1434	1450	1534	...	1634	1734	1750	...	1834	1934	...	2034	2134	...	22
Chivasso **585** a.	0656	07357	0756	0837	0856	0956	1156	13357	1337	1356	1456	1537	1556	...	1656	1756	1837	...	1856	1956	...	2056	2156	...	23
Torino Porta Susa **585** a.	0724	...	0824	0858	0924	1024	1224	...	...	1424	1524	...	1624	...	1724	1824	...	...	1924	2024	...	2124	2224	...	23
Torino Porta Nuova **585** a.	0735	...	0835	0910	0935	1035	1235	...	...	1435	1535	...	1635	...	1735	1835	...	...	1935	2035	...	2135	2235	...	00

km		
0	Aosta d.	*NO SERVICE*
32	Pré Saint Didier ▲ a.	*UNTIL FURTHER NOTICE*

Pré Saint Didier ▲ d.	*NO SERVICE*
Aosta a.	*UNTIL FURTHER NOTICE*

▲ – A connecting 🚌 service is available Pré Saint Didier - Courmayeur and v.v. (see Table 3

BRIG - STRESA - MILANO 590

		♠	⚒	2	♠	2 ⚒	EC 35 🍷 ◧	♠	EC 51 🍷 ◧	2	EC 37 🍷 ◧V	2		♠	2	♠	EC 57 🍷 ◧	2	EC 39 🍷 ◧	♠	2	♠	2	EC 59 🍷 ◧	©	EC 41 🍷 ◧
Genève **570**	d.	...	...	...	...	...	0539	...	...	...	0739	...	...	...	...	...	...	...	1339	...	...	...	...	...	...	1839
Lausanne **570**	d.	...	...	...	...	...	0618	...	...	...	0818	...	...	...	...	...	...	...	1418	...	...	...	...	...	...	1918
Basel **560**	d.	...	...	...	...	...	|	...	0631	...	|	...	...	...	...	...	1231	...	|	...	...	...	...	1731	...	|
Bern **560**	d.	...	...	...	...	...	|	...	0734	...	|	...	...	...	...	...	1334	...	|	...	...	...	...	1834	...	|
Brig 🏛	d.	...	...	...	...	...	0744	...	0844	...	0944	...	...	...	...	...	1444	...	1544	...	...	...	...	1944	...	2044
Domodossola 🏛 §	a.	...	...	...	...	...	0812	...	0912	...	1012	...	...	...	...	...	1512	...	1612	...	...	...	...	2012	...	2112
Domodossola 551	d.	0453	0553	0603	0651	0720	0817	0853	0917	0958	1017	1158	...	1253	1358	1453	1517	1558	1617	1653	1758	1853	1958	2017	2053	2117
Verbània-Pallanza	d.	0513	0613	0629	0713	0743	|	0913	|	1024	|	1224	...	1313	1424	1513	|	1624	|	1713	1824	1913	2024	|	2113	|
Baveno	d.	|	|	0634	|	|	|	|	|	1029	|	1229	...	|	1429	|	|	1629	|	|	1829	|	2029	|	|	|
Stresa	d.	0521	0621	0639	0721	0751	0840	0921	0940	1035	|	1235	...	1321	1435	1521	1540	1635	1640	1721	1835	1921	2035	|	2121	2140
Arona	d.	0535	0635	0701	0735	0806	|	0935	|	1106	|	1306	...	1335	1506	1535	|	1706	|	1735	1906	1935	2106	|	2135	|
Gallarate ▲	d.	0558	0658	0731	0758	0834	|	0958	|	1134	1104	1334	...	1358	1534	1558	|	1734	|	1758	1934	1958	2134	2105	2158	|
Rho Fiera Milano	d.	0619	0719	0800	0823	0900	|	1019	|	1200	|	1400	...	1419	1600	1619	|	1800	|	1819	2000	2019	2200	|	2219	|
Milano Porta Garibaldi	a.	|	|	0811	|	0911	|	|	|	1211	|	1411	...	|	1611	|	|	1811	|	|	2011	|	2211	|	|	|
Milano Centrale	a.	0631	0731	...	0835	...	0937	1031	1037	...	1137	...	...	1431	...	1631	1637	...	1737	1831	...	2031	...	2137	2231	2237

		2	EC 50 🍷 ◧	♠	EC 32 🍷 ◧	2	♠		EC 52 🍷 ◧	2	EC 34 🍷 ◧	♠	2	♠	2	EC 36 🍷 ◧	♠	EC 56 🍷 ◧	2	⚒	EC 42 🍷 ◧V		2	♠ 2 ⚒	♠	♠ 2 ⚒	♠ 2
no Centrale	d.	...	0723	0729	0823	...	0829	0929	1123	...	1223	1329	...	1529	...	1723	1729	1823	...	1829	1923	1929	...	...	2129	...	...
no Porta Garibaldi	d.	0612	|	|	|	0749	|	|	|	1149	|	|	1349	|	1549	|	|	|	1749	|	|	|	1949	2049	|	2149	2249
Fiera Milano	d.	0622	|	0740	|	0759	0840	0940	|	1159	|	1340	1359	1540	1559	|	1740	|	1759	1840	|	1940	1959	2059	2140	2159	2259
arate ▲	d.	0649	0757	0802	|	0826	0902	1002	|	1226	|	1402	1426	1602	1626	|	1802	|	1826	1902	1957	2002	2026	2126	2202	2226	2326
a	d.	0721	|	0823	|	0854	0923	1023	|	1254	|	1423	1454	1623	1654	|	1823	|	1854	1923	|	2023	2054	2154	2223	2254	2354
sa	d.	0742	|	0838	0921	0916	0938	1038	1221	1316	1321	1438	1516	1638	1716	1821	1838	1921	1916	1938	|	2038	2116	...	2238	...	...
eno	d.	0746	|	|	|	0921	|	|	|	1321	|	|	1521	|	1721	|	|	|	1921	|	|	|	2121	...	|	...	...
ània-Pallanza	d.	0751	|	0845	|	0926	0945	1045	|	1326	|	1445	1526	1645	1726	|	1845	|	1926	1945	|	2045	2126	...	2245	...	...
odossola 551	a.	0820	0843	0907	0943	1002	1007	1107	1243	1402	1343	1507	1602	1707	1802	1843	1907	1943	2002	2007	2043	2107	2202	...	2307	...	...
odossola 🏛 §	d.	...	0848	...	0948	...	...	...	1248	...	1348	...	...	...	...	1848	...	1948	...	...	2048	...	...	...	...	...	...
🏛	a.	...	0916	...	1016	...	...	...	1316	...	1416	...	...	...	...	1916	...	2016	...	...	2116	...	...	...	...	...	...
Bern **560**	a.	...	1023	...	|	...	...	...	1423	...	|	...	...	...	...	|	...	2123	...	...	|	...	...	...	...	...	...
Basel **560**	a.	...	1129	...	|	...	...	...	1529	...	|	...	...	...	...	|	...	2229	...	...	|	...	...	...	...	...	...
usanne **570**	a.	...	...	...	1142	...	...	...	...	...	1542	...	...	...	...	2042	...	...	...	...	2242	...	...	...	...	...	...
enève **570**	a.	...	...	...	1221	...	...	...	...	...	1621	...	...	...	...	2121	...	...	...	...	2321	...	...	...	...	...	...

Additional services BRIG - DOMODOSSOLA and v.v.

			Ⓐ	⑥h			Ⓒ	B	⑥		Ⓐ		
0	**Brig**	d.	0607	0840	0940	1044	1145	1244	1344	1644	1745	1844	0026
8	Iselle di Trasquera §	d.	0625	|	|	|	1203	|	|	|	1803	1902	0044
2	**Domodossola**	a.	0643	0907	1008	1112	1222	1312	1412	1712	1822	1920	0102

			Ⓐ		⚒		⑥	⑥	B	⑥		
Domodossola	d.	0356	0456	0615	0655	1048	1148	1258	1448	1548	1648	1748
Iselle di Trasquera §	d.	0418	0518	0638	0717	|	|	1320	|	|	|	|
Brig	a.	0433	0533	0652	0732	1116	1216	1335	1516	1616	1716	1816

IC service. (12) and ✕ Basel - Brig - Domodossola and v.v.
(12) and 🍷 Genève - Milano - Venezia Santa Lucia and v.v.

Also Mar. 25, May 5.
Operates during school terms only.

🅁 inclusive of supplement.

♠ – Operator: Trenord.
§ – Ticket point is **Iselle**.

▲ – 🚌 service **Gallarate - Milano Malpensa Aeroporto and v.v.**: *Subject to alteration*
From **Gallarate**: 0555Ⓐ, 0631⚒, 0720, 0800⚒, 0825, 0900Ⓐ, 0930, 0955Ⓐ, 1100, 1205⚒, 1240**k**, 1320**k**, 1355, 1435Ⓐ, 1605, 1705, 1810.
From **Malpensa** ✈ Terminal 1: 0534Ⓐ, 0605⚒, 0645, 0715⚒, 0756, 0829Ⓐ, 0900, 0930Ⓐ, 1030, 1130⚒, 1215⚒**k**, 1250⚒**k**, 1313**k**, 1353Ⓐ**k**, 1530, 1628, 1738, 1845Ⓐ, 1950Ⓐ.
Journey time 25 minutes. Operator: S.A.C.O. ✆ 0331 25 84 11.

DOMODOSSOLA and ARONA - NOVARA 591

d class only

n			⚒	⚒	⚒	⚒		⚒	†	†		†	⚒			⚒	†	⚒	†		⚒	⚒		†	⚒		†
0	**Domodossola**	d.	0520	...	0620	...	0648	0800	...	...	...	...	...	1245	...	1343	...	...	...	1543	...	...	1747	...	...	1848	...
8	Omegna	d.	0614	...	0657	...	0752	0850	...	...	...	...	...	1337	...	1444	...	...	...	1641	...	...	1842	...	...	1940	...
4	Pettenasco	d.	0621	...	0704	...	0759	0856	...	...	...	...	...	1343	...	|	...	...	...	1648	...	...	1849	...	...	1947	...
7	Orta-Miasino	d.	0626	...	0712	...	0804	0904	...	...	...	...	...	1351	...	1453	...	...	...	1653	...	...	1854	...	...	1952	...
0	Borgomanero	d.	0641	...	0724	...	0815	0917	...	...	...	...	...	1406	...	1504	...	...	...	1704	...	...	1905	...	...	2004	...
	Arona	d.	|	0648	|	0748	|	|	0915	1115	...	1315	1348	|	...	|	1515	1548	1715	|	1748	1848	|	1915	1948	|	2115
	Oleggio	d.	|	0712	|	0812	|	|	0932	1132	...	1332	1412	|	...	|	1532	1612	1732	|	1812	1912	|	1932	2012	|	2132
0	**Novara**	a.	0716	0732	0754	0832	0842	0945	0948	1148	...	1348	1432	1437	...	1535	1548	1632	1748	1740	1832	1932	1943	1948	2032	2039	2148

n			⚒		⚒	⚒	†	†	†		⚒	†	⚒		⚒	†	Ⓐ	⚒			†	Ⓐ	⚒		⚒	†	
0	**Novara**	d.	0546	0645	0650	0750	0812	1012	1212	1223	1345	1412	1423	1516	1523	1612	1619	1723	1734	...	1812	1818	1823	1915	1923	2012	...
7	Oleggio	d.	|	|	0713	0813	0826	1026	1226	|	|	1426	1441	|	1541	1626	|	1741	|	...	1826	|	1841	|	1941	2026	...
7	**Arona**	a.	|	|	0739	0839	0845	1045	1245	|	|	1445	1512	|	1612	1645	|	1812	|	...	1845	|	1912	|	2012	2045	...
	Borgomanero	d.	0621	0725	...	...	...	...	...	1249	1420	...	...	1552	...	...	1650	...	1811	...	...	1851	...	1950	...	...	...
	Orta-Miasino	d.	0645	0740	...	...	...	...	...	1306	1432	...	...	1608	...	...	1711	...	1826	...	...	1911	...	2006	...	...	...
	Pettenasco	d.	0649	0744	...	...	...	...	...	1311	1436	...	...	1612	...	...	1715	...	1831	...	...	1915	...	2011	...	...	...
	Omegna	d.	0656	0751	...	...	...	...	...	1318	1443	...	...	1619	...	...	1722	...	1843	...	...	1922	...	2018	...	...	...
3	**Domodossola**	a.	0748	0849	...	...	...	...	...	1417	1542	...	...	1714	...	...	1804	...	1938	...	...	2004	...	2114	...	...	...

d class only

Local services NOVARA - ALESSANDRIA and v.v.

m				⚒		⚒	†	⚒	⚒	⚒	†	†
0	Novara ▲	d.	0608	0708	0808	0908	1408	1423	1608	1708	1908	2008
67	Alessandria ▲	a.	0715	0815	0915	1015	1515	1532	1715	1815	2015	2125

		♠†			⚒			♠⚒		⚒	
Alessandria ▲	d.	0645	...	1245	1345	1645	1745	1845	1945	2045	...
Novara ▲	a.	0753	...	1353	1453	1753	1853	1957	2053	2153	...

♠ – Operator: Trenord.
▲ – Additional journeys available by changing trains at Mortara (25 km from Novara).

BELLINZONA - LUINO - MILANO MALPENSA ✈ 592

erator: Trenord. 2nd class only

n						IR 2319 B		IR 2323 B		IR 2327 B	
0	**Bellinzona 550**	d.	0554	0754	...	1352	...	1552	...	1752	...
9	Cadenazzo	d.	0608	0808	...	1400	1408	1600	1608	1800	1808
27	Pino-Tronzano 🏛	d.	0628	0828	...	...	1428	...	1628	...	1828
0	**Luino 608**	d.	0645	0845	...	...	1445	...	1645	...	1845
5	Laveno Mombello	d.	0705	0900	1300	...	1500	...	1700	...	1900
6	Gallarate	d.	0746	0946	1346	...	1546	...	1746	...	1946
1	**Milano** Malpensa Aeroporto ✈	a.	0811	1011	1411	...	1611	...	1811	...	2011

					IR 2332 B		IR 2336 B		IR 2340 B	
Milano Malpensa Aeroporto ✈	d.	0750	1150	350	...	1550	...	1750	...	1950
Gallarate	d.	0819	1215	1419	...	1619	...	1819	...	2019
Laveno Mombello	d.	0901	1252	1501	...	1701	...	1901	...	2101
Luino 608	d.	0918	...	1518	...	1715	...	1918	...	2118
Pino-Tronzano 🏛	d.	0932	...	1532	...	1732	...	1932	...	2132
Cadenazzo	d.	0956	...	1552	1559	1752	1759	1952	1958	2154
Bellinzona 550	a.	1005	...	...	1605	...	1805	...	2005	2204

(12) Basel - Locarno and v.v. Operator: SBB/CFF/FFS.

Additional services operate Bellinzona - Cadenazzo - Luino and v.v.

593 MILANO - COLICO - TIRANO

Operator: Trer

km																								
			2		2							2		2		2	2			2				2	2
							†C		Ⓒ										⚒						
0	**Milano** Centrale ▷ d.	...	0620	...	0720	0722p	0820	0920	1020	1220	1252p	1320	1352p	1420	1452p	1552p	1620	1720	1752p	1820	1920	2020	2120	2252
12	Monza ▷ d.	...	0632	...	0732	0739	0832	0932	1032	1232	1309	1332	1409	1432	1509	1609	1632	1732	1809	1832	1932	2032	2132	2309
50	Lecco ▷ d.	...	0702	0718	0802	0815	0902	1002	1102	1302	1353	1402	1453	1502	1553	1653	1702	1802	1853	1902	2002	2102	2202	2353
72	Varenna-Esino d.	...	0724	0753	0824	0853	0924	1024	1124	1324	...	1424	...	1524	...	...	1724	1824	...	|	2024	2124	2236	...
75	Bellano-Tartavalle Terme d.	...	0729	0758	0829	0858	0929	1029	1129	1329	...	1429	...	1529	...	...	1729	1829	...	1929	2029	2129	2241	...
89	**Colico** ▲ a.	...	0747	0824	0847	0923	0947	1047	1147	1347	...	1447	...	1547	...	...	1747	1847	...	1947	2047	2147	2258	...
130	Sondrio a.	0533	0820	0910d	0920	...	1020	1120	1220	1420	...	1520	...	1620	...	...	1820	1921	...	2020	2120	2221	2334	...
156	**Tirano** ♣ a.	0607	0852	...	0952	...	1052	1205	1252	1452	...	1552	...	1652	...	...	1852	...	...	2052	2152	...	...	...

	2	2	2					2			2		2	2			2		2		2			2
											⚒		⚒				⚒		†C		⚒			
Tirano ♣ d.	...	...	...	0612	0712	...	0908	...	1108	1208	...	1308	...	...	1508	1608	...	1708	...	1808	...	1908	2008	...
Sondrio d.	0432	0532	...	0641	0741	...	0941	...	1141	1241	...	1341	...	...	1541	1641	...	1741	...	1841	1847	1941	2041	2122
Colico ▲ d.	0503	0603	...	0716	0816	...	1016	...	1216	1316	...	1416	...	...	1616	1716	...	1816	1837	1916	1937	2016	2116	2200
Bellano-Tartavalle Terme d.	0518	0618	...	0732	0832	...	1032	...	1232	1332	...	1432	...	...	1632	1732	...	1832	1901	1932	2001	2032	2132	2215
Varenna-Esino d.	0523	0623	...	0737	0837	...	1037	...	1237	1337	...	1437	...	...	1637	1737	...	1837	1906	1937	2006	2037	2137	2220
Lecco ▽ d.	0549	0652	0707	0759	0901	1007	1101	1207	1301	1401	1437	1501	1537	1607	1701	1801	1837	1901	1946	2001	2045	2101	2201	2243
Monza ▽ a.	0622	0724	0749	0824	0926	1049	1126	1249	1326	1426	1519	1526	1619	1649	1726	1826	1919	1926	2019	2026	...	2126	2226	2315
Milano Centrale ▽ a.	0640	0738	0808p	0838	0940	1108p	1140	1308p	1340	1440	1538p	1540	1638p	1708p	1740	1840	1938p	1940	2038p	2040	...	2140	2240	2330

▲ – **COLICO - CHIAVENNA and v.v.:** 2nd class o

km																								
			†	⚒	⚒	†	⚒		†C		⚒		⚒		⚒			⚒	†		⚒		🚌†	⚒
0	Colico d.	0548	0706	0706	0810	0810	0845	...	0925	1004	1045	1204	1245	1404	1445	...	1604	1645	1730	1804	1852	2004	2100	2114
27	Chiavenna a.	0618	0730	0737	0834	0840	0916	...	0955	1034	1116	1234	1316	1434	1516	...	1634	1716	1755	1834	1922	2034	2135	2144

	🚌Ⓐ		⚒	†	⚒		⚒		⚒			⚒		⚒		†	⚒		†C		⚒	†	⚒	
Chiavenna d.	0512	0626	0704	0738	0745	...	0844	0926	1044	1126	...	1244	1326	1444	1526	1638	1644	1726	1805	...	1848	1926	1932	...
Colico a.	0548	0656	0735	0802	0809	...	0915	0956	1115	1156	...	1315	1356	1515	1556	1702	1715	1756	1835	...	1919	1956	2002	...

C – †: [12] Milano - Colico - Chiavenna and v.v.
d – ⚒ only.
p – Milano **Porta Garibaldi**.
▷ – Local trains run Milano Porta Garibaldi - Lecco hourly 0652 - 2152.
▽ – Local trains run Lecco - Milano Porta Garibaldi hourly 0607 - 2207.

♣ – 🚌 **TIRANO - EDOLO and v.v.**

	⚒	⚒		⚒	⑥	Ⓐ
Tirano Stazione d.	0840	1040	...	1435	1635	1700
Aprica S Pietro a.	0920	1120	...	1515	1720	1745
Edolo a.	0945	1145	...	1540	1745	1810

	⚒	⚒	⚒	⚒	⚒	
Edolo d.	0615	0915	1115	1515	1715	...
Aprica S Pietro d.	0650	0940	1140	1540	1740	...
Tirano Stazione a.	0730	1020	1220	1620	1820	...

♣ – For 🚌 service Tirano - Edolo and v.v. – see panel.
Operator: Automobilistica Perego (AP): ✆ (0342) 701 200; fax (0342) 704 400.

595 INNSBRUCK - BOLZANO / BOZEN - VERONA - BOLOGNA

km																										
			FA 9461	FA 9463			FA 9465				§							EC 1289	EC 81						FA 9477	EC 85
		2	🍷	🍷	2	2	🍷	2	2	2	2	2	2	2	2	2	2	✕	✕	2	2	2	2	2	🍷	✕
				♦	⚒	⚒		⚒M		M		Ⓐ	M	Ⓐ	Ⓒ	ⒸM	M	♠f	♠a			M		M		♠
	München Hbf **951** d.	...	...	...	...	...	...	...	...	...	...	...	...	...	...	...	...	0738	0738	...	...	...	...	...	...	0938
0	**Innsbruck** Hbf ▲ d.	...	...	...	...	...	...	...	...	...	0622	...	...	...	...	...	...	0927	0927	...	...	...	...	...	...	1127
37	**Brennero / Brenner** 🏛 ▲ a.	...	...	...	...	...	...	...	...	...	0659	...	...	...	...	...	...	|	|	...	...	...	...	...	...	|
37	**Brennero / Brenner** 🏛 d.	...	...	...	...	...	...	0536	0608	0638	0702	...	0738	0808	...	0838	0938	|	|	...	...	1038	...	1138	...	|
60	Vipiteno / Sterzing d.	...	...	...	...	...	...	0555	0627	0657	0723	...	0757	0827	...	0857	0957	|	|	...	...	1057	...	1157	...	|
78	Fortezza / Franzensfeste d.	...	...	...	0540	...	...	0613	0645	0715	0739	0745	0815	0845	...	0915	1015	1041	1046	...	...	1115	...	1215	...	1246
89	Bressanone / Brixen d.	...	...	...	0549	...	...	0623	0655	0725	0749	0755	0825	0855	...	0925	1025	1050	1056	...	...	1125	...	1225	...	1256
99	Chiusa / Klausen d.	...	...	...	0557	...	...	0631	0703	0733	0758	0803	0833	0903	...	0933	1033	|	|	...	...	1133	...	1233	...	|
127	**Bolzano / Bozen** a.	...	...	...	0621	...	...	0655	0729	0759	0823	0829	0859	0929	...	0959	1059	1115	1127	...	...	1159	...	1259	...	1327
										2			2⑥	2Ⓒ		2Ⓒ	2									
127	**Bolzano / Bozen** d.	0500	0516	...	0624	0636	0716	...	0731	0736	...	0831	0831	...	0936	1031	...	1117	1131	...	1136	...	1231	...	1316r	1331
143	Ora / Auer d.	0512	|	...	0637	0655	|	...	0743	0755	...	0843	0843	...	0955	1043	...	|	|	...	1155	...	1243	...	|	|
165	Mezzocorona d.	0525	|	...	0654	0716	|	...	0756	0816	...	0856	0856	...	1016	1056	...	|	|	...	1216	...	1256	...	|	|
182	**Trento** 595a d.	0537	0547	...	0710	0733	0747	...	0810	0833	...	0910	0910	...	1033	1110	...	1150	1204	...	1233	...	1310	...	1347r	1404
206	Rovereto d.	0551	0602	...	0725	0747	0802	...	0825	0847	...	0925	0925	...	1047	1125	...	|	1219	...	1247	...	1325	...	1402r	1419
274	**Verona** Porta Nuova **605** a.	0640	0644	...	0814	0854	0844	...	0914	0951	...	1014	1014	...	1151	1214	...	1237	1256	...	1351	...	1414	...	1444r	1458
274	**Verona** Porta Nuova d.	0701	0652	0752	...	...	0852	...	...	...	...	...	...	1026	...	...	1226	1239	1313	1326	...	...	1426	...	1452	1515
388	**Bologna** Centrale a.	0825	0742	0842	...	...	0942	...	...	...	...	...	...	1150	...	...	1355	|	1407	1450	...	...	1554	...	1542	1620
	Milano Centrale **615** a.	...	|	|	...	...	|	...	...	...	...	...	...	...	...	...	...	|	...	...	...	...	...	...	|	...
	Venezia S L **605** a.	...	|	|	...	...	|	...	...	...	...	...	...	...	...	...	...	1356	...	...	...	...	...	...	|	...
	Firenze SMN **620** a.	...	0825c	0925c	...	...	1025c	...	...	...	...	...	...	...	...	...	...	...	...	...	...	...	...	...	1625c	...
	Roma Termini **620** a.	...	0945	1045	...	...	1145	...	...	...	...	...	...	...	...	...	...	...	...	...	...	...	...	...	1745	...

				FA 9481	EC 87		FA 9483					FA 9485	EC 89						EC 83				ICN 763		§	EN 485
	2	2	2	🍷	✕	2	🍷	2	2	2	2	🍷	✕	2	2	2	2	2	✕	2	2	2		2	2	
	M		M		♠	⚒	♦	M		Ⓐ	M		♠		M		Ⓐ	M	♠	M		M	♦			♦
München Hbf **951** d.	...	...	...	...	1138	...	...	...	...	...	...	...	1338	...	...	...	...	...	1538	...	...	...	...	...	...	2108
Innsbruck Hbf ▲ d.	...	...	...	...	1327	...	...	...	...	...	...	...	1527	...	...	...	...	...	1727	...	...	...	...	...	2100	2305
Brennero / Brenner 🏛 ▲ a.	...	...	...	...	|	...	...	...	...	...	...	...	|	...	...	...	...	...	|	...	...	...	...	...	2137	|
Brennero / Brenner 🏛 d.	1238	1308	1338	...	|	...	...	1438	1508	...	1538	...	|	...	1638	1708	...	1738	|	1838	1908	1938	...	...	2143	|
Vipiteno / Sterzing d.	1257	1327	1357	...	|	...	...	1457	1527	...	1557	...	|	...	1657	1727	...	1757	|	1857	1927	1957	...	...	2202	|
Fortezza / Franzensfeste d.	1315	1345	1415	...	1446	...	...	1515	1545	...	1615	...	1646	...	1715	1745	...	1815	1846	1915	1945	2015	...	...	2220	|
Bressanone / Brixen d.	1325	1355	1425	...	1456	...	...	1525	1555	...	1625	...	1656	...	1725	1755	...	1825	1856	1925	1955	2025	...	...	2230	0040
Chiusa / Klausen d.	1333	1403	1433	...	|	...	...	1533	1603	...	1633	...	|	...	1733	1803	...	1833	|	1933	2003	2033	...	...	2238	|
Bolzano / Bozen a.	1359	1429	1459	...	1527	...	...	1559	1629	...	1659	...	1727	...	1759	1829	...	1859	1927	1959	2029	2059	...	...	2303	0107
			2Ⓐ					2			2Ⓐ				2Ⓐ			2Ⓐ		2		2Ⓐ			2	
Bolzano / Bozen d.	...	1431	1436	1516	1531	...	...	1536	1631	1636	1704	1716	1731	1736	1806	1831	1836	1906	1931	1936	2031	2036	2130	2136	2308	0109
Ora / Auer d.	...	1443	1455	|	|	...	...	1555	1643	1655	1720	|	|	1755	1822	1843	1855	1922	|	1955	2043	2055	2144	2155	2324	|
Mezzocorona d.	...	1456	1516	|	|	...	...	1616	1656	1716	1740	|	|	1816	1842	1856	1916	1942	|	2016	2056	2116	2200	2216	2344	|
Trento 595a d.	...	1510	1533	1547	1604	...	...	1633	1710	1733	1758	1747	1804	1833	1855	1910	1933	1955	2004	2033	2110	2133	2216	2233	2357	0143
Rovereto d.	...	1525	1547	1602	1619	...	...	1647	1725	1747	1812	1802	1819	1847	1910	1925	1947	2010	2019	2047	2125	2147	2232	2247e	...	|
Verona Porta Nuova **605** a.	...	1614	1654	1644	1658	...	...	1751	1814	1854	...	1844	1858	1951	...	2014	2051	2108	2056	2151	2214	2251	2316	2348e	...	0237
Verona Porta Nuova d.	...	1626	...	1652	1700	1707	1752	...	1826	...	...	1852	...	...	...	2104	...	...	...	...	...	...	2336	...	...	0305
Bologna Centrale a.	...	1754	...	1742	|	1854	1842	...	1954	...	...	1942	...	...	...	2225	...	...	...	...	...	...	|	...	...	0420
Milano Centrale **615** a.	...	...	...	|	|	...	|	...	...	...	...	|	...	...	...	...	...	...	...	...	...	...	|	...	...	...
Venezia S.L. **605** a.	...	...	...	|	1810	...	|	...	...	...	...	|	...	...	...	...	...	...	...	...	...	...	|	...	...	|
Firenze SMN **620** a.	...	...	...	1825c	...	...	1925c	...	...	...	...	2025c	...	...	...	...	...	...	...	...	...	...	|	...	...	0607
Roma Termini **620** a.	...	...	...	1948	...	...	2045	...	...	...	...	2145	...	...	...	...	...	...	...	...	...	...	0600	...	...	0922

♦ – **NOTES** (LISTED BY TRAIN NUMBER)

485 – LUPUS – 🛏 1, 2 cl. (Excelsior), 🛏 1, 2 cl., ▬ 2 cl. and [2] München - Bologna (**235**) - Roma. Supplement payable.
763 – 🛏 1, 2 cl., ▬ 2 cl. (4 berth) and [2] Bolzano - Roma.
9463 – [12] and 🍷 Brescia - Verona - Roma.
9483 – [12] and 🍷 Brescia - Verona - Roma.

D – APUS – 🛏 1, 2 cl. (Excelsior), 🛏 1, 2 cl. and ▬ 2 cl. München (**485**) - Verona (**480**) - Milano. Supplement payable.

M – To Merano. See Table **597**.
a – Ⓐ only.
c – Firenze **Campo di Marte**.
e – † only.
f – Ⓒ only.
r – ⑤⑥⑦ only.

§ – Operated by *SAD* (for contact details see Table 59
♠ – Also available to passengers without reservati
Operator within Italy: LeNord.
▲ – For additional trains Innsbruck - Brennero / Brenne see page 293. Austrian holiday dates apply Innsbru Brennero / Brenner.

BOLOGNA - VERONA - BOLZANO / BOZEN - INNSBRUCK 595

	2 ⚒	2 ⚒	2 †	§ 2	2 ⚒	ICN 764 ♦	2 ⚒	2 ⚒	2	2	2	2	2 Ⓐ	EC 88 ✕ ♠	FA 9460 🍷	2 ⒸM	2 †	EC 80 ✕ ♠	FA 9462 🍷	2	2	2	FA 9464 🍷 ♦	EC 84 ✕ ♠	FA 9466 🍷	2 ⚒	2
na Termini **620** d.	...	...	...	...	...	2300	...	...	...	...	...	...	...	...	0645	...	...	...	0845	...	...	...	0945	...	1045	...	...
nze SMN **620** d.	...	...	...	...	...	|	...	...	...	...	...	...	...	...	0803c	...	...	...	1003c	...	...	...	1103c	...	1203c	...	...
ezia SL **605** d.	...	...	...	...	...	|	...	...	...	...	...	...	...	...	|	...	...	...	|	...	...	...	|	...	|	...	...
no Centrale **615** d.	...	...	...	...	...	|	...	...	...	...	...	...	...	...	|	...	...	...	|	...	...	...	|	...	|	...	...
na Centrale d.	...	...	...	...	...	|	...	...	...	0613	...	0710	...	...	0845	...	...	...	1045	...	1010f	...	1145	1152	1245	...	1210
a Porta Nuova **605** a.	...	...	...	...	...	0530	...	...	...	0752	...	0832	...	...	0937	...	...	...	1137	...	1132f	...	1237	1247	1337	...	1332
a Porta Nuova d.	...	...	...	...	0525	0552	0609	0709	0750	▬	0809	...	0850	0904	0945r	...	0950	1102	1145	1109d	1150	1209	▬	1304	1345	1309	1350
eto d.	...	...	...	...	0613	0657	0714	0814	0839	...	0914	...	0937	0943	1026r	...	1039	1143	1226	1211d	1239	1314	...	1343	1426	1411	1439
o **595a** d.	...	0602	...	...	0630	0714	0732	0832	0854	...	0932	...	0952	0959	1041r	...	1054	1159	1241	1225	1254	1332	...	1359	1441	1425	1454
ocorona d.	...	0617	...	...	0644	0727	0746	0846	0905	...	0946	...	1005	|	|	...	1105	|	|	1239	1305	1346	...	|	|	1439	1505
Auer d.	...	0636	...	...	0706	0745	0806	0906	0919	...	1006	...	1020	|	|	...	1119	|	|	1300	1319	1406	...	|	|	1500	1519
no / Bozen a.	...	0652	...	...	0724	0805	0822	0922	0930	...	1022	...	1039	1031	1114r	...	1130	1231	1314	1322	1330	1422	...	1431	1514	1522	1530
		2⚒M			2M		2M		|	2M				|			2M	|	▬ 2M		|		2M	|	▬ 2M		|
no / Bozen d.	0601	0701	0701	0732	0801	...	0901	...	0932	1001	...	...	...	1034	...	1101	1201	1234	1301	...	1332	...	1401	1434	1501	...	1532
a / Klausen d.	0626	0726	0726	0755	0826	...	0926	...	0955	1026	...	...	...	|	...	1126	1226	|	1326	...	1355	...	1426	|	1526	...	1555
anone / Brixen d.	0635	0735	0735	0804	0835	...	0935	...	1004	1035	...	...	...	1104	...	1135	1235	1304	1335	...	1404	...	1435	1504	1535	...	1604
zza / Franzensfeste d.	0645	0745	0745	0815	0845	...	0945	...	1015	1045	...	...	...	1115	...	1145	1245	1315	1345	...	1415	...	1445	1515	1545	...	1615
no / Sterzing d.	0703	0803	0803	0833	0903	...	1003	...	1033	1103	...	...	...	|	...	1203	1303	|	1403	...	1433	...	1503	|	1603	...	1633
nero / Brenner 🏛 a.	0722	0822	0822	0852	0922	...	1022	...	1052	1122	...	...	...	|	...	1222	1322	|	1422	...	1452	...	1522	|	1622	...	1652
nero / Brenner 🏛 ▲ d.	...	...	...	0902	...	...	...	...	...	...	...	...	...	|	...	...	...	|	...	...	...	...	...	|	...	...	...
ruck Hbf ▲ a.	...	...	...	0938	...	...	...	...	...	...	...	...	...	1232	...	...	...	1432	...	...	...	...	...	1632	...	...	...
nchen Hbf **951** a.	...	...	...	...	...	...	...	...	...	...	...	...	...	1421	...	...	...	1624	...	...	...	...	...	1821	...	...	...

	2 M	2	EC 86 ✕ ♠	2 Ⓐ	2	2 Ⓐ	2	EC 188 ✕ ♠a	EC 1288 ✕ ♠f	2 M	2 Ⓐ	2	2	2	§ 2	FA 9478 🍷	2	2	FA 9480 🍷	§ 2	2 Ⓐ	FA 9482 🍷 ♦	2	2	2	EN 484 ♦	EN 481 484 D
ma Termini **620** d.	...	...	...	...	...	...	...	...	...	...	...	...	...	...	...	1645	...	...	1745	...	...	1845	...	...	...	1904	...
enze SMN **620** d.	...	...	...	...	...	...	...	...	...	...	...	...	...	...	...	1803c	...	...	1903c	...	...	2003c	...	...	...	2214	...
nezia SL **605** d.	...	...	1350	...	...	...	...	...	1550	...	...	...	...	...	...	|	...	...	|	...	...	|	...	...	...	|	...
ano Centrale **615** d.	...	...	|	...	...	...	...	...	|	...	...	...	...	...	...	|	...	...	|	...	...	|	...	...	...	|	2105
gna Centrale d.	...	...	|	...	1410	...	...	1552	|	...	...	1610	...	...	...	1845	1810	...	1945	...	...	2045	2010	2110	...	2345	|
na Porta Nuova **605** a.	...	...	1500	...	1532	...	...	1645	1700	...	...	1732	...	...	...	1937	1932	...	2037	...	...	2137	2132	2240	...	0036	2240
na Porta Nuova d.	...	1409	1502	...	1550	...	1609	1702	1702	...	1709	1750	...	1809	...	1945	1950	2009	2045	...	2109	...	2150	...	2250	0111	0111
reto d.	...	1514	1543	1550	1639	1650	1714	1743	1743	...	1814	1839	...	1914	...	2026	2039	2111	2126	...	2214	...	2239	...	2339	|	|
o **595a** d.	...	1532	1559	1605	1654	1705	1732	1759	1759	...	1832	1854	...	1932	...	2041	2054	2125	2141	...	2232	...	2254	...	2352	|	|
ocorona d.	...	1546	|	1616	1705	1716	1746	|	|	...	1846	1905	...	1946	...	|	2105	2139	|	...	2246	...	2305	...	...	|	|
Auer d.	...	1606	|	1636	1719	1736	1806	|	|	...	1906	1919	...	2006	...	|	2119	2200	|	...	2306	...	2319	...	...	|	|
ano / Bozen a.	...	1622	1631	1652	1730	1752	1822	1831	1831	...	1922	1930	...	2022	...	2114	2130	2222	2214	...	2322	...	2332	...	...	|	|
			|	2M	|	2M	|	|	|			|					|									|	|
ano / Bozen d.	1601	...	1634	1701	1732	1801	1824a	1834	1834	1901	...	1932	2002	...	2032	...	2132	...	...	2232	...	...	...	...	...	|	|
sa / Klausen d.	1626	...	|	1722	1755	1826	1847a	|	|	1926	...	1955	2026	...	2055	...	2155	...	...	2256	...	...	...	...	...	|	|
anone / Brixen d.	1635	...	1704	1730	1804	1835	1856a	1904	1904	1935	...	2004	2035	...	2104	...	2204	...	...	2305	...	...	...	...	...	|	|
zza / Franzensfeste d.	1645	...	1715	1745	1815	1845	1905a	1915	1915	1945	...	2015	2045	...	2115	...	2215	...	...	2314	...	...	...	...	...	|	|
no / Sterzing d.	1703	...	|	1803	1833	1903	1923a	|	|	2003	...	2033	2103	...	2133	...	2233	...	...	...	...	...	...	...	...	|	|
nero / Brenner 🏛 a.	1722	...	|	1822	1852	1922	1944a	|	|	2022	...	2052	2122	...	2151	...	2252	...	...	...	...	...	...	...	...	|	|
nero / Brenner 🏛 ▲ d.	...	...	|	...	...	...	...	|	|	...	...	...	...	...	2154	...	...	...	...	...	...	...	...	...	...	|	|
ruck Hbf ▲ a.	...	...	1832	...	...	...	...	2032	2032	...	...	...	...	...	2230	...	...	...	...	...	...	...	...	...	...	0431	0431
nchen Hbf **951** a.	...	...	2021	...	...	...	...	2221	2221	...	...	...	...	...	...	...	...	...	...	...	...	...	...	...	...	0633	0633

INNSBRUCK - BRENNERO / BRENNER and v.v. stopping services: 2nd class only

	⚒					⚒															⚒			
Innsbruck Hbf d.	0522	0552	0622	0652	0752	0822	0852	0952	1052	1152	...	1252	1352	1452	1552	1652	1752	...	1852	1952	2100	2200	2257	2352	...
Matrei d.	0540	0610	0640	0710	0810	0840	0910	1010	1111	1210	...	1310	1411	1510	1610	1710	1811	...	1910	2010	2118	2218	2315	0010	...
Steinach in Tirol d.	0545	0615	0645	0715	0815	0845	0915	1015	1116	1215	...	1315	1416	1515	1615	1715	1816	...	1915	2015	2123	2223	2320	0015	...
Brennero / Brenner 🏛 a.	0602	0632	0659	0732	0832	0902	0932	1032	1132	1232	...	1332	1432	1532	1632	1732	1832	...	1932	2032	2137	2240	2337	0032	...

		⚒			⚒																				
nero / Brenner 🏛 d.	0528	0558	0628	...	0658	0728	0828	0902	0928	...	1028	1128	1228	1328	...	1428	1528	...	1628	1728	...	1828	1928	...	2128	2304
ach in Tirol d.	0547	0617	0647	...	0717	0746	0846	0917	0947	...	1047	1147	1247	1347	...	1447	1547	...	1647	1747	...	1847	1947	...	2147	2323
ei d.	0551	0621	0651	...	0721	0750	0850	0921	0951	...	1051	1151	1251	1351	...	1451	1551	...	1651	1751	...	1851	1951	...	2151	2327
ruck Hbf a.	0608	0638	0708	...	0739	0808	0908	0938	1008	...	1108	1208	1308	1408	...	1508	1608	...	1708	1808	...	1908	2008	...	2208	2344

NOTES (LISTED BY TRAIN NUMBER)

– 🛏 1,2 cl., ▬ 2 cl. (4 berth) and (2) Roma - Bolzano.
– LUPUS – 🛏 1,2 cl. (Excelsior), 🛏 1,2 cl., ▬ 2 cl. and (2) Roma (**234**) - Bologna - München. Supplement payable.
– (12) and 🍷 Roma - Verona - Brescia.
– (12) and 🍷 Roma - Verona - Brescia.

APUS – 🛏 1,2 cl. (Excelsior), 🛏 1,2 cl. and ▬ 2 cl. Milano (**481**) - Verona (**484**) - München. Supplement payable.
From Merano. See Table **597**.

Ⓐ only.
Firenze **Campo di Marte**.
⚒ only.
Ⓒ only.
⑤⑥⑦ only.

§ – Operated by *SAD* (for contact details see Table **598**).
♠ – Also available to passengers without reservation. Operator within Italy: LeNord.
▲ – For additional trains Brennero / Brenner - Innsbruck – see panel above. Austrian holiday dates apply Brennero / Brenner - Innsbruck.

TRENTO - MALÉ - MARILLEVA 595a

ntino Trasporti

	†	⚒	⚒	†	⚒	⚒	⚒	†	⚒	⚒	†	⚒	⚒	†	⚒	⚒	†	⚒	†	⚒	⚒	†	⚒	⚒	†	⚒	⚒	†
Trento **595** d.	0609	0612	0710	0810	0812	0931	1027	1041	1106	1202	1230	1243	1324	1342	1342	1454	1509	1554	1625	1634	1718	1723	1727	1809	1835	1836	1932	1933
Malé d.	0743	0752	0859	0944	0953	1107	1205	1217	1250	1347	1405	1421	1452	1518	1524	1638	1645	1736	1801	1810	1839	1858	1905	1935	2009	2012	2104	2105
Marilleva d.	0758	...	0914	0959	1008	1122	1220	1232	1306	1405	1420	...	...	1533	1541	1653	1700	1751	...	...	1855	...	...	...	...	...	...	...

	⚒	†	⚒	⚒	⚒	⚒	†	⚒	†	⚒	†	⚒	⚒	†	⚒	⚒	⚒	†	⚒	†	⚒	†	⚒	⚒	†	⚒	†	
leva d.	...	...	0613	...	0658	...	0816	0927	1017	1023	...	1138	1233	1300	1347	1424	...	1445	...	1618	1621	1715	1718	1808	...	1942	...	...
d.	0528	0556	0630	0644	0716	0823	0832	0943	1034	1039	1148	1154	1252	1316	1407	1440	1509	1502	1530	1635	1639	1732	1735	1825	1829	1958	2001	...
to **595** a.	0700	0730	0748	0826	0907	1002	1006	1121	1208	1216	1324	1338	1436	1450	1545	1621	1630	1639	1705	1811	1823	1908	1916	2005	2004	2132	2135	...

Operator: Trentino Trasporti Esercizio S.p.a, Via Innsbruck 65, 38121 Trento.
✆ +39 0 461 821000, fax +39 0 461 031407.

596 FORTEZZA / FRANZENSFESTE - S. CANDIDO / INNICHEN - LIENZ

2nd class

km		Ⓐ	Ⓐ						Ⓐ	Ⓒ	A		A		A		A				Ⓐ		Ⓐ	
0	**Fortezza / Franzensfeste** d.	0547	0617	0650	0750	0850	0950	1050	1120	1150	1220	1250	1320	1350	1420	1450	1520	1550	1650	1750	1820	1850	1920	1950
33	Brunico / Bruneck d.	0630	0700	0730	0830	0930	1030	1130	1200	1230	1300	1330	1400	1430	1500	1530	1600	1630	1730	1830	1900	1930	2000	2030
61	Dobbiaco / Toblach d.	0706	0736	0806	0906	1006	1106	1206	1236	1306	1336	1406	1436	1506	1536	1606	1636	1706	1806	1906	1936	2006	2036	2106
65	**S. Candido / Innichen** a.	0710	0740	0810	0910	1010	1110	1210	1240	1310	1340	1410	1440	1510	1540	1610	1640	1710	1810	1910	1940	2010	2040	2110
65	**S. Candido / Innichen** 🏛 d.	0716	...	0816	0916	1016	1116	1216	...	1316	...	1416	...	1516	...	1616	...	1716	1816	1916	...	2016	...	...
78	Sillian 🏛 d.	0730	...	0830	0930	1030	1130	1230	...	1330	...	1430	...	1530	...	1630	...	1730	1830	1930	...	2030	...	...
108	**Lienz 971** a.	0809	...	0909	1009	1109	1209	1309	...	1409	...	1509	...	1609	...	1709	...	1809	1909	2009	...	2109	...	...

	Ⓐ	⚒		Ⓐ				A			A	Ⓐ	Ⓒ	Ⓐ		A		A						
Lienz 971 d.	...	...	0550	...	0650	0750	0850	...	0950	1050	...	...	1150	...	1250	...	1350	...	1450	1550	1650	1750	1850	1950
Sillian d.	...	...	0630	...	0730	0830	0930	...	1030	1130	...	...	1230	...	1330	...	1430	...	1530	1630	1730	1830	1930	2030
S. Candido / Innichen 🏛 a.	...	...	0643	...	0743	0843	0943	...	1043	1143	...	...	1243	...	1343	...	1443	...	1543	1643	1743	1843	1943	2043
S. Candido / Innichen 🏛 d.	0521	0550	0650	0720	0750	0850	0950	1020	1050	1150	1220	1250	1250	1320	1350	1420	1450	1520	1550	1650	1750	1850	1950	2050
Dobbiaco / Toblach d.	0526	0555	0655	0725	0755	0855	0955	1025	1055	1155	1225	1255	1255	1325	1355	1425	1455	1525	1555	1655	1755	1855	1955	2055
Brunico / Bruneck d.	0600	0631	0731	0801	0831	0931	1031	1101	1131	1231	1301	1331	1331	1401	1431	1501	1531	1601	1631	1731	1831	1931	2031	2131
Fortezza / Franzensfeste a.	0634	0710	0810	0840	0910	1010	1110	1140	1210	1310	1340	1410	1410	1440	1510	1540	1610	1640	1710	1810	1910	2010	2110	2210

A – Daily until Apr. 3; Ⓐ Apr. 4 - June 10.

Operators:
SAD Fortezza - S. Candido; *ÖBB* S. Candido - Lienz.

597 BOLZANO / BOZEN - MERANO / MERAN

2nd class

km		⚒	⚒		⚒		⚒§		⚒	Ⓐ	Ⓒ	⚒§			⚒		⚒§		⚒				⚒§	
	Brennero **595** d.	...	...	0536**d**	...	0638	0702	0738	...	...	0838	...	0938	...	...	1038	...	1138	...	1238	...	1338	...	1438
0	**Bolzano / Bozen** d.	0547	0626	0657	0735	0801	0835	0901	0935	1001	1001	1035	1101	...	1135	1201	1235	1301	1335	1401	...	1501	1535	1601
32	Merano / Meran a.	0633	0707	0743	0815	0845	0915	0945	1014	1045	1045	1115	1145	...	1215	1245	1315	1345	1415	1445	...	1545	1615	1645

		⚒§		⚒§		⚒§			§	
Brennero **595** d.	1538	...	1638	...	1738	...	1838	1938	...	...
Bolzano / Bozen d.	1701	1735	1801	1835	1901	1935	2001	2101	2203	...
Merano / Meran a.	1745	1815	1845	1914	1944	2014	2044	2144	2247	...

	⚒	⚒		⚒		⚒		⚒§	Ⓒ
Merano / Meran d.	0602	0635	0713	0745	0816	0846	0916	0946	1016
Bolzano / Bozen a.	0648	0720	0759	0826	0859	0926	0959	1026	1059
Brennero **595** a.	0822	...	0922	...	1022	...	1122	...	1222

		⚒§		⚒			⚒§		⚒		⚒§			⚒§		⚒§		⚒§		§		⚒§	†	⚒
Merano / Meran d.	1116	1146	1216	1246	...	1316	1346	1416	1446	1516	1546	...	1616	1646	1716	1746	1816	1846	1916	1946	...	2046	2046	2146
Bolzano / Bozen a.	1159	1226	1259	1326	...	1359	1426	1459	1526	1559	1626	...	1659	1726	1759	1826	1859	1926	1957	2027	...	2126	2126	2227
Brennero **595** a.	1322	...	1422	...	...	1522	...	1622	...	1722	...	...	1822	...	1922	...	2022	...	...	2151	...	...	...	...

d – ⚒ only.

§ – Operated by SAD (for contact details see Table **598**).

Additional services operate on ⚒.

598 MERANO / MERAN - MALLES / MALS

2nd class only

km		⚒									
0	Merano / Meran d.	0538	0638	0716	and hourly until	1916	1946	2046	2146	2250	...
60	Malles / Mals **546 / 954** a.	0654	0754	0838		2038	2055	2155	2255	2358	...

	⚒								
Malles / Mals **546 / 954** d.	0520	0542	0616	0720	and hourly until	1820	1920	2020	2120
Merano / Meran a.	0630	0654	0732	0843		1943	2039	2139	2239

Additional services operate.

Trains call at Silandro / Schlanders 46–54 minutes after leaving Merano, 24–28 minutes after leaving Malles.

Ferrovia della Val Venosta Operator: Servizi Autobus Dolomiti (SAD), Via Conciapelli 60, I-39100 Bolzan ✆ +39 0471 97 12 59, fax +39 0471 97 00 42.

599 ITALIAN LAKES (LAGO MAGGIORE, GARDA, COMO)

Lago Maggiore: ⛴ services link Arona, Stresa, Baveno, Laveno, Luino and Locarno throughout the year on an irregular schedule.
Operator: Navigazione sul Lago Maggiore, P. le Baracca 1, 28041 Arona, Italy. ✆ +39 (0)322 233 200, fax: +39 (0)322 249 530. www.navigazionelaghi.it

Lago di Garda: ⛴ services link Desenzano, Peschiera, Garda, Salo, Gardone and Riva, (April to September only), on an irregular schedule.
Operator: Navigazione sul Lago di Garda, Piazza Matteotti 1, 25015 Desenzano del Garda, Italy. ✆ +39 (0)30 914 9511, fax: +39 (0)30 914 9520. www.navigazionelaghi.it

Lago di Como: ⛴ services link Como, Bellagio, Menaggio, Varenna, Bellano and Colico (April to September only) on an irregular schedule.
Operator: Navigazione Lago di Como, Via Per Cernobbio 18, 22100 Como, Italy. ✆ +39 (0)31 579 211, fax: +39 (0)31 570 080. www.navigazionelaghi.it

Hydrofoil service **March 20 - May 28, 2016**:

	⚒		†	⚒	⚒	†	⚒	†	⚒	⚒	
Como d.	0733	0900	1110	1225	1330	1400	1420	1615	1710	1810	1920
Tremezzo d.	0819**r**	0939	1153	1302	1419	1445	1457	1652	1746	1857	1957
Bellagio d.	0813**r**	0946	1200	1309	1439**r**	1452	1504	1658	1752	1904	2003
Menaggio d.	0808	0954	1208	1314	1430	1500	1509	1704	1758	1919	2009
Bellano d.	...	1004	1218	...	1455	1516	...	1713	1807	...	2021
Colico a.	...	1034	1251	...	1528	1549	...	1740	...	...	2044

	⚒	⚒	†	⚒		⚒	†	⚒		†
Colico d.	0606	...	0707	...	1035	...	1356	...	1604	1741
Bellano d.	0630	...	0738	...	1106	...	1424	...	1644	1806
Menaggio d.	0641	0703	0748	0808	1117	1316	1435	1511	1654	1814
Bellagio d.	0647	0712	0757	0814	1127	1330	1442	1525	1704	1820
Tremezzo d.	0653	0718	0803	0820	1134	1336	1448	1531	1710	1826
Como a.	0730	0805	0850	0857	1220	1412	1525	1607	1800	1905

r – Via Menaggio.

599a LAKE GARDA 🚌 services

Valid from Sept. 14, 2

Desenzano FS → Salo *+0h33* → Gardone *+0h38* → Maderno *+0h46* → Toscolano *+0h49* → Gargnano *+1h00* → Limone *+1h32* → **Riva** *+1h50*.
Route LN027. From Desenzano: 0600, 0810, 1135, 1330, 1620, 1830.

Subject to alteration.

Verona PN → **Peschiera** FS *+0h51* → Lazise + *1h13* → Bardolino *+1h25* → **Garda** *+1h35*.
Route 164. From Verona: 0820⚒, 0850†, 1020⚒, 1050†, 1220⚒, 1320, 1420⚒, 1620, 1750⚒, 1850.

Verona PN → Lazise *+0h58* → Bardolino *+1h08* → **Garda** *+1h13*.
Route 163. From Verona: 0720⚒, 1020⚒, 1250⚒, 1410⚒, 1620⚒, 1850⚒, 1920⚒.

Garda → Torri del Benaco *+0h14* → Porto Brenzone *+0h35* → Malcesine + *0h46* → Torbole *+1h06* → **Riva** *+1h18*
Route 184. From Garda: 0625⚒, 0735, 0935⚒, 1005†, 1135⚒, 1205†, 1315⚒, 1335†, 1415⚒, 1435, 1535⚒, 1635⚒, 1735, 1835†, 1905⚒, 2005.

Services from Verona Porta Nuova bus station, and Peschiera and Desenzano railway stations (Table **605**).

Operator: Azienda Transporti Verona s.r.l., Lungadige Galtarossa 5, 37133 Verona. ✆ 045 8057811, fax 045 8057800.

Riva → Limone *+0h18* → Gargnano *+0h50* → Toscolano *+1h01* → Maderno *+ 1h0* Gardone *+1h12* → Salo *+1h17* → **Desenzano** FS *+1h50*.
Route LN027. From Riva: 0540, 0810, 0910, 1245, 1510, 1710.

Subject to alteration.

Garda → Bardolino *+0h10* → Lazise *+0h22* → **Peschiera** FS *+0h44* → **Verona P** *+1h32*.
Route 164. From Garda: 0620⚒, 0720⚒, 0820⚒, 1020, 1320†, 1520⚒, 1620†, 1720, 1820.

Garda → Bardolino *+0h05* → Lazise *+0h15* → **Verona PN** *+1h05*.
Route 163. From Garda: 0550⚒, 0720⚒, 0820⚒, 1305⚒, 1415⚒, 1620⚒.

Riva → Torbole *+0h15* → Malcesine + *0h35* → Porto Brenzone *+0h48* → Torri de Benaco *+1h09* → **Garda** *+1h22*.
Route 184. From Riva: 0510⚒, 0610, 0710⚒, 0810, 0910, 1110⚒, 1210†, 1240⚒, 13 1330⚒, 1430⚒, 1510†, 1610⚒, 1710, 1810.

Additional local services run serving the lakeside resorts.

Other operators: Brescia Transporti ✆ 030 44061, fax 030 3754505; Trentino Transporti ✆ 0461 821000, fax 0461 031407.

ator: Trenitalia

Trenitalia high-speed services

All trains 🅁 and 🍸

km		FR 9601	FR 9501 ⚒t A	FR 9605 Ⓐ	FA 9401 9490	FA 9403 ⚒	FR 9503 9505 ⚒t	FA 9461 Y	FR 9607	FR 9507 M	FR 9509	FR 9609 Ⓐ	FR 9561 Ⓐ	FR 9593 R	FA 9463 B	FR 9611 Ⓐ	FA 9407	FR 9513	FR 9613 Ⓐ	FR 9563 9565	FA 9465 Y	FR 9615	FA 9411 T	FA 9413 U	FR 9517	FR 9567
0	**Venezia** Santa Lucia ♣ d.	...	...	...	...	0606	...	...	...	...	...	...	...	...	...	...	0725	...	...	...	...	...	...	...	...	...
9	**Venezia** Mestre ♣ d.	...	...	...	0537	0618	...	...	...	...	...	...	...	...	...	...	0737	...	...	...	...	...	0837	0847	...	...
37	Padova d.	...	...	...	0553	0632	...	...	...	...	...	...	...	...	...	...	0753	...	...	...	...	...	0853	0903	...	...
	Torino Porta Nuova d.	...	...	...	|	|	...	...	0550	...	...	...	0620	...	...	...	|	0700	...	0720	...	0750	|	|	0810	0820
	Torino Porta Susa d.	...	...	...	|	|	...	...	0600	...	...	...	0630	...	...	...	|	0710	...	0730	...	0800	|	|	0822	0830
	Verona Porta Nuova d.	...	...	...	|	|	...	0652	|	...	...	...	|	...	0752	...	|	|	...	|	0852	|	|	|	|	|
	Milano Centrale a.	...	...	...	|	|	...	|	0650	...	...	...	0715g	...	|	...	|	0800	...	0815g	|	0850	|	|	0910	0915g
	Milano Centrale d.	...	...	0608	|	|	0615	|	0700	0542	0720	0730	0718g	0750	|	0800	|	0820	0830	0818g	|	0900	|	|	0920	0918g
	Milano Rogoredo d.	...	...	|	|	|	|	|	0709	|	|	|	0735	|	|	|	|	|	|	0835	|	|	|	|	|	0935
	Reggio Emilia AV d.	...	...	0656	|	|	0703	|	|	|	|	|	0811	0834	|	|	|	|	|	0911	|	|	|	|	|	1011
160	**Bologna** Centrale ❖ d.	...	0600	|	0653	|	0725	0745	|	0755	0825	0835	0840	0855	0845	|	0853	0925	0935	0940	0945	|	0953	1003	1025	1040
—	**Firenze** SMN a.	...	0641	|	0730	|	0759	0825c	|	0830	0859	|	0915	...	0925c	|	0930	0959	|	1015	1025c	|	1030	1040	1059	1115
0	**Firenze** SMN d.	...	0650	|	0738	|	0808	0827c	|	0839	0908	|	0924	...	0927c	|	0938	1008	|	1024	1027c	|	1038	1048	1108	1124
257	**Roma** Tiburtina a.	...	0824	|	0858	0918	0928	|	0948	0958	1028	|	1043	...	|	|	1058	1128	|	1143	|	|	1158	1208	1228	1243
261	**Roma** Termini a.	...	0835	0910	0910	0930	0940	0945	0959	1010	1040	1029	1055	...	1045	1055	1110	1140	1129	|	1145	1155	1210	1220	1240	1245
	Roma Termini d.	0735	0848	0920	0920	...	0953	...	1010	...	1053	1040	...	...	...	...	1125	1153	1140	|	...	...	...	...	1253	1255
	Roma Fiumicino ✈ a.	|	|	|	0952	...	|	...	|	...	|	|	...	...	...	...	|	|	|	|	...	...	...	...	|	...
	Napoli Centrale a.	0845	0955	1032	...	...	1100	...	1120	...	1200	1150	...	...	...	...	1235	1300	1248	1253	...	...	...	...	1400	...
	Salerno a.	...	...	...	...	...	1154	...	...	...	...	...	...	...	...	...	...	...	...	1340	...	...	...	...	...	...

	FR 9619	FA 9415 9492	FR 9521 9523	FR 9623 Ⓐ	FR 9419	FR 9525	FR 9627 Ⓐ	FA 9423	FR 9529	FR 9631 Ⓐ	FR 9427		FR 9533	FR 9635 q	FA 9431	FR 9583 ⑤w	FR 9537	FR 9569 9571 Ⓑq	FA 9477 Y	FR 9639	FR 9435	FA 9437	FR 9541 9543	FR 9573	FR 9641 Ⓑq	FR 9643 Ⓑq	FR 9439 9441
zia Santa Lucia ♣ d.	...	0925	...	...	1025	...	...	1125	...	...	1225	...	...	...	1325	...	...	...	...	...	1425	1435	...	...	...	...	1525
zia Mestre ♣ d.	...	0937	...	...	1037	...	...	1137	...	...	1237	...	...	...	1337	...	...	...	...	...	1437	1447	...	...	...	...	1537
va d.	...	0953	...	...	1053	...	...	1153	...	...	1253	...	...	...	1353	...	...	...	...	...	1453	1503	...	...	...	...	1553
rino Porta Nuova d.	...	|	...	0950	|	...	...	|	...	1150	|	...	...	...	|	...	...	1320	...	...	|	|	...	1420	...	...	|
rino Porta Susa d.	...	|	...	1000	|	...	...	|	...	1200	|	...	...	...	|	...	...	1330	...	...	|	|	...	1430	...	...	|
erona Porta Nuova d.	...	|	...	|	|	...	...	|	...	|	|	...	...	...	|	...	...	|	1452	...	|	|	...	|	...	...	|
o Centrale a.	...	|	...	1050	|	...	...	|	...	1250	|	...	...	...	|	...	...	1415g	|	...	|	|	...	1515g	...	...	|
o Centrale d.	1000	|	1021	1100	|	1120	1200	|	1220	1300	|	...	1320	1400	|	1405	1420	1418g	|	1500	|	|	1520	1518g	1530	1600	|
ano Rogoredo d.	|	|	|	|	|	|	|	|	|	|	|	...	|	|	|	|	|	1435	|	|	|	|	|	1535	|	|	|
io Emilia AV d.	|	|	|	|	|	|	|	|	|	|	|	...	|	|	|	|	|	1511	|	|	|	|	|	1611	|	|	|
gna Centrale ❖ d.	|	1053	1125	|	1153	1225	|	1253	1325	|	1353	...	1425	|	1453	1510	1525	1540	1545	|	1553	1603	1625	1640	1635	|	1653
ze SMN a.	|	1130	1159	|	1230	1259	|	1330	1359	|	1430	...	1459	|	1530	1545	1559	1615	1625c	|	1630	1640	1659	1715	|	|	1730
ze SMN d.	|	1138	1208	|	1238	1308	|	1338	1408	|	1438	...	1508	|	1538	1554	1608	1624	1627c	|	1638	1648	1708	1724	|	|	1738
na Tiburtina a.	|	1258	1328	|	1358	1428	|	1458	1528	|	1558	...	1628	|	1658	1713	1728	1743	|	|	1758	1808	1828	1843	|	|	1858
Termini a.	1255	1310	1340	1355	1410	1440	1455	1510	1540	1555	1610	...	1640	1655	1710	1725	1740	|	1745	1755	1810	1820	1840	1855	1828	1855	1910
Termini d.	1305	1320	1353	...	1425	1453	...	...	1553	...	1625	...	1650	1705	...	...	1753	|	...	...	...	...	1850	...	1840	...	1923
ma Fiumicino ✈ a.	|	1352	|	...	|	|	...	...	|	...	|	...	|	|	...	...	|	|	...	...	...	...	|	...	|	...	|
li Centrale a.	1415	...	1500	...	1535	1602	...	...	1700	...	1735	...	1800	1815	...	...	1900	1855	...	...	...	...	2000	...	1950	...	2035
no a.	...	...	1550	...	...	...	...	...	...	...	...	...	...	...	...	...	...	1942	...	...	...	...	2047	...	...	...	2124

	FR 9585 ⑤w	FR 9545	FR 9645 Ⓑq	FA 9481 Y	FR 9647	FR 9443	FA 9445	FR 9549 9551	FR 9575	FA 9483 B	FR 9591 N	FR 9651	FA 9447	FR 9553	FR 9653 Ⓑq	FA 9485 Y	FR 9555 Ⓑq A	FR 9655	FR 9451	FR 9587 ⑤w	FR 9557	FR 9657 Ⓑq	FR 9659 Ⓑq	FA 9455	FR 9559	FR 9663 †q	
zia Santa Lucia ♣ d.	...	...	...	...	...	1625	1635	...	...	...	...	...	1725	...	...	...	...	...	1825	...	...	...	...	1925	...	...	...
zia Mestre ♣ d.	...	...	...	...	...	1637	1647	...	...	...	...	...	1737	...	...	...	...	...	1837	...	...	...	...	1937	...	...	...
va d.	...	...	...	...	...	1653	1703	...	...	...	...	...	1753	...	...	...	...	...	1853	...	...	...	...	1953	...	...	...
rino Porta Nuova d.	...	...	...	...	1550	|	|	...	1620	...	...	...	|	...	...	...	...	1750	|	...	1810	...	...	|	1910	1950	...
rino Porta Susa d.	...	...	...	...	1600	|	|	...	1630	...	...	...	|	...	...	...	...	1800	|	...	1822	...	...	|	1922	2000	...
erona Porta Nuova d.	...	...	...	1652	|	|	|	...	|	1752	...	...	|	...	...	1852	...	|	|	...	|	...	...	|	|	|	...
o Centrale a.	...	...	...	|	1650	|	|	...	1715g	|	...	...	|	...	...	|	...	1850	|	...	1910	...	...	|	2010	2050	...
o Centrale d.	1605	1620	1630	|	1700	|	|	1720	1718g	|	1740	1800	|	1820	1830	|	1850	1900	|	1905	1920	1930	2000	|	2020	2100	...
ano Rogoredo d.	|	|	|	|	1709	|	|	|	1735	|	|	|	|	|	|	|	|	|	|	|	|	|	|	|	|	|	...
io Emilia AV d.	|	|	|	|	|	|	|	|	1813	|	1826	|	|	|	|	|	1938	|	|	|	|	|	|	|	|	|	...
gna Centrale ❖ d.	1710	1725	1735	1745	|	1753	1803	1825	1840	1845	1855	|	1853	1925	1935	1945	2005	|	1953	2010	2025	2035	|	2053	2125	|	...
ze SMN a.	1745	1759	|	1825c	|	1830	1840	1859	1915	1925c	...	|	1930	1959	|	2025c	2040	|	2030	2045	2059	|	|	2130	2159	|	...
ze SMN d.	1754	1808	|	1827c	|	1838	1848	1908	1924	1927c	...	|	1938	2008	|	2027c	...	|	2038	2054	2108	|	|	2138	2208	|	...
na Tiburtina a.	|	1928	|	|	1948	1958	2008	2028	2043	|	...	|	2058	2128	|	|	...	|	2158	|	2228	|	|	2258	2328	|	...
Termini a.	1920	1940	1929	1948	1958	2010	2020	2040	2055	2045	...	2055	2110	2140	2129	2145	...	2155	2210	2220	2240	2229	2255	2310	2340	2355	...
Termini d.	1933	1953	1940	...	...	2025	...	2053	...	...	...	2105	...	2153	...	...	...	2205	...	...	...	2240	...	...	...	...	...
ma Fiumicino ✈ a.	|	|	|	...	...	|	...	|	...	...	...	|	...	|	...	...	...	|	...	...	...	|	...	...	...	...	...
li Centrale a.	2040	2100	2050	...	...	2135	...	2200	...	...	...	2215	...	2300	...	...	...	2315	...	...	...	2350	...	...	...	...	...
no a.	...	...	...	...	...	...	...	2247	...	...	...	...	...	...	...	...	...	...	...	...	...	...	...	...	...	...	...

Also calls at Arezzo – see Table **620**.
From Brescia – see Table **605**.
Via Modena – see Table **615**.
To Ancona – see Table **630**.
To Bari – see Table **631**.

T – From Trieste – see Table **601**.
U – From Udine – see Table **601**.
Y – From Bolzano – see Table **595**.

c – Firenze **Campo di Marte**.
g – Milano **Porta Garibaldi**.
q – Not Mar. 27, Apr. 24.
t – Not Mar. 28, Apr. 25, June 2.
w – Not June 3.

♣ – Local journeys are not permitted Venezia Santa Lucia - Mestre and v.v.
❖ – Most services use underground platforms 16 – 19; allow a minimum of 10 minutes for connecting services from / to the main station.

erator: Nuovo Trasporto Viaggiatori (NTV)

Italo high-speed services

Club, Prima, Smart XL and Smart class

rains 🅁

Trenitalia tickets and passes not valid

www.italotreno.it

	ITA 9991 h ①-⑤	ITA 9901 g ①-⑤	ITA 9961 9963	ITA 9993	ITA 9903	ITA 9965 h	ITA 9905 9907	ITA 9967	ITA 9981	ITA 9909	ITA 9913 9915	ITA 9917	ITA 9995 ①-⑥	ITA 9921	ITA 9969 y	ITA 9983	ITA 9923	ITA 9925 9927	ITA 9973 j	ITA 9985	ITA 9929 9931	ITA 9975	ITA 9999	ITA 9933 9935	ITA 9977	ITA 9939	ITA 9989	ITA 9941 k Ⓑ
no Porta Nuova d.	...	...	...	...	...	...	0725d	...	...	...	0925	...	...	1120b	...	...	...	1325	...	...	1520	...	...	...	1700	...	...	...
no Porta Susa d.	...	...	...	...	...	...	0735d	...	...	...	0935	...	...	1130b	...	...	...	1335	...	...	1530	...	...	...	1712	...	...	...
no Centrale d.	...	0635	0715	...	0740	0815	0835	0915	...	0935	1035	1135	...	1235	1315	...	1335	1435	1615	...	1635	1715	...	1745	1815	1835	...	2035
no Rogoredo d.	...	0645	|	...	0752	|	0845	0924	...	0945	1045	1145	...	1245	1324	...	1345	1445	|	...	1645	|	...	|	|	1845	...	2045
io Emilia ⊖ d.	...	0723	|	...	|	|	0923	|	...	1023	1123	1223	...	1323	|	...	1423	1523	|	...	1723	|	...	|	|	1923	...	2123
nezia Santa Lucia d.	...	|	|	...	|	|	|	|	0900	|	|	|	...	|	|	1300	|	|	|	1600	|	|	...	|	|	|	1900	|
nezia Mestre d.	...	|	|	...	|	|	|	|	0912	|	|	|	...	|	|	1312	|	|	|	1612	|	|	...	|	|	|	1912	|
dova d.	...	|	|	...	|	|	|	|	0928	|	|	|	...	|	|	1328	|	|	|	1628	|	|	...	|	|	|	1928	|
Brescia d.	0546	|	|	0646	|	|	|	|	|	|	|	|	...	|	|	|	|	|	|	|	|	|	...	|	|	|	|	|
Verona Porta Nuova d.	0637	|	|	0737	|	|	|	|	|	|	|	|	1237	|	|	|	|	|	|	|	|	|	1737	|	|	|	|	|
gna Centrale ❖ d.	0730	0750	|	0830	0850	|	0950	|	1028	1050	1150	1250	1330	1350	|	1428	1450	1550	|	1728	1750	|	1830	1850	|	1950	2028	2150
nze SMN d.	0813	0833	|	0913	0933	|	1033	|	1113	1133	1233	1333	1413	1433	|	1513	1533	1633	|	1813	1833	|	1913	1933	|	2033	2113	2233
a Tiburtina a.	0933	0953	|	1033	1053	|	1153	1204	1233	1253	1353	1453	1533	1553	1604	1633	1653	1753	|	1933	1953	|	2033	2053	|	2153	2233	2353
a Termini a.	0945	1005	1010	1045	1105	1110	1205	1215	1245	1305	1405	1505	1545	1605	1615	1645	1705	1805	1910	1945	2005	2010	2045	2105	2110	2205	2245	0005
a Termini d.	...	...	1023	1057	1115	...	1215	...	...	1315	1415	1515	...	...	...	...	1715	1815	1920	1958	2015	...	2058	2115f	2120	...	2255	...
oli Centrale a.	...	...	1130	1205	1224	...	1322	...	...	1428	1530	1630	...	...	...	...	1823	1925	2030	2105	2125	...	2205	2225f	2230	...	0005	...
no a.	...	...	1232	...	...	...	1416	...	...	...	1617	...	...	...	...	...	...	2016	...	...	2220	...	...	2317f	...	...	...	...

Ⓑ only.
①–⑥ only.
⑤ only.

g – Not Mar. 28.
h – Not Mar. 28, Apr. 25.
j – Not Mar. 27.

k – Not Mar. 27, Apr. 24.
y – ①④⑤⑥⑦ only.
⊖ – Reggio Emilia Mediopadana.

❖ – Most services use underground platforms 16 – 19; allow a minimum of 10 minutes for connecting services from / to the main station.

600 HIGH-SPEED SERVICES – northbound

All trains [R] and 🍷 — **Trenitalia high-speed services** — Operator: Tren

km		FR 9596 ⚒	FR 9500 ⚒ A	FR 9600 ⚒	FR 9502 ⚒	FR 9592 N	FR 9504 ⚒	FR 9602 Ⓐ	FA 9460 Y	FA 9402	FR 9606	FR 9566	FR 9608 Ⓐ	FR 9508	FA 9406		FR 9610	FR 9512 9514	FA 9408	FA 9462 Y	FR 9410 9412	FR 9614	FA 9464 B	FR 9568 9570 ⚒	FR 9414	FR 9618 Ⓐ
	Salerno d.	...	...	...	...	...	...	...	...	...	...	...	...	...	...	...	...	0612	...	...	0636	...	...	0717	...	...
	Napoli Centrale d.	...	...	...	...	...	...	...	...	...	...	...	0610	...	...	...	0640	0700	...	...	0730	0740	...	0805	0830	0840
	Roma Fiumicino ✈ d.	...	...	...	...	...	...	...	...	...	...	...	|	...	...	...	|	|	...	...	|	|	...	|	|	|
	Roma Termini a.	...	...	...	...	...	...	...	...	...	...	...	0720	...	...	...	0750	0810	...	...	0840	0850	...	|	0940	0947
	Roma Termini d.	...	...	0600	...	...	0620	0630	0645	0650	0700	0705	0730	0720	0750	...	0800	0820	0835	0845	0850	0900	0945	|	0950	1000
	Roma Tiburtina d.	...	...	|	...	...	0629	|	|	0700	0707	0715	|	0729	0800	...	|	0829	0845	|	0900	|	|	0915	1000	|
	Firenze SMN a.	...	...	|	...	...	0751	|	0801c	0822	|	0836	|	0851	0922	...	|	0951	1007	1001c	1022	|	1101c	1036	1122	|
	Firenze SMN d.	...	0653	|	0730	...	0800	|	0803c	0830	|	0845	|	0900	0930	...	|	1000	1015	1003c	1030	|	1103c	1045	1130	|
0	**Bologna** Centrale ✣ d.	...	0731	|	0808	0810	0838	0828	0845	0910	|	0923	0928	0938	1010	...	|	1038	1055	1045	1110	|	1145	1123	1210	|
	Reggio Emilia AV d.	...	0752	|	|	0837	|	|	|	|	|	0944	|	|	|	...	|	|	|	|	|	|	|	1144	|	|
	Milano Rogoredo a.	...	|	|	|	|	|	|	|	|	0947	1022	|	|	|	...	|	|	|	|	|	|	|	1222	|	|
	Milano Centrale a.	...	0840	0855	0910	0920	0942	0929	|	|	0959	1042g	1029	1040	|	...	1055	1140	|	|	|	1155	|	1242g	|	1255
	Milano Centrale d.	0800	...	0905	...	...	...	...	|	|	...	1045g	...	...	|	...	1105	...	|	|	|	...	|	1245g	|	...
114	**Verona** Porta Nuova a.	|	...	|	...	...	...	...	0937	|	...	|	...	...	|	...	|	...	|	1137	|	...	1237	|	|	...
	Torino Porta Susa a.	0848	...	0952	...	...	...	...	...	|	...	1130	...	...	|	...	1152	...	|	...	|	...	...	1330	|	...
	Torino Porta Nuova a.	0900	...	1005	...	...	...	...	...	|	...	1140	...	...	|	...	1205	...	|	...	|	...	...	1340	|	...
	Padova d.	...	...	...	...	...	...	...	...	1009	...	...	...	...	1109	...	...	...	1154	...	1209	...	...	...	1309	...
	Venezia Mestre ♣ a.	...	...	...	...	...	...	...	...	1023	...	...	...	...	1123	...	...	...	1208	...	1223	...	...	...	1323	...
	Venezia Santa Lucia ♣ a.	...	...	...	...	...	...	...	...	1035	...	...	...	...	1135	...	...	...	1220	...	1235	...	...	...	1335	...

	FR 9520	FA 9416	FA 9466 Y	FR 9418	FR 9622 ⚒	FR 9524 9526	FA 9491 9422		FR 9626 Ⓐ	FR 9528	FA 9426	FR 9630 Ⓐ	FR 9532	FR 9430	FR 9634 Ⓑ	FR 9536	FR 9584 ⑤w	FA 9434		FR 9638	FR 9574 9576 Ⓑq	FR 9540	FR 9640 Ⓑq	FA 9493 9438	FR 9642 Ⓑ	FR 9578
Salerno d.	...	...	...	...	...	0914	...	...	...	...	...	...	...	...	...	...	...	...	...	...	1312	...	...	...	...	...
Napoli Centrale d.	0900	...	...	0930	0940	1000	...	...	...	1100	...	...	1200	1230	...	1300	...	...	...	...	1405	1400	1410	...	1440	...
Roma Fiumicino ✈ d.	|	...	...	|	|	|	1108	...	...	|	...	...	|	|	...	|	...	...	...	...	|	|	|	1508	|	...
Roma Termini a.	1010	...	...	1040	1050	1110	1140	...	...	1210	...	...	1307	1337	...	1410	...	...	...	...	|	1510	1520	1540	1547	...
Roma Termini d.	1020	1035	1045	1050	1100	1120	1150	...	1200	1220	1250	1300	1320	1350	1400	1420	1429	1450	...	1500	|	1520	1530	1550	1600	1605
Roma Tiburtina d.	1029	1045	|	1100	|	1129	1200	...	|	1229	1300	|	1329	1400	|	1429	1439	1500	...	|	1515	1529	|	1600	|	1615
Firenze SMN a.	1151	1207	1201c	1222	|	1251	1322	...	|	1351	1422	|	1451	1522	|	1551	1602	1622	...	|	1636	1651	|	1722	|	1736
Firenze SMN d.	1200	1215	1203c	1230	|	1300	1330	...	|	1400	1430	|	1500	1530	|	1600	1611	1630	...	|	1645	1700	|	1730	|	1745
Bologna Centrale ✣ d.	1238	1255	1245	1310	|	1338	1410	...	|	1438	1510	|	1538	1610	|	1638	1650	1710	...	|	1723	1738	1728	1810	|	1823
Reggio Emilia AV d.	|	|	|	|	|	|	|	...	|	|	|	|	|	|	|	|	|	|	...	|	1744	|	|	|	|	1844
Milano Rogoredo a.	|	|	|	|	|	|	|	...	|	|	|	|	|	|	|	|	|	|	...	|	1822	|	|	|	|	1922
Milano Centrale a.	1340	|	|	|	1355	1440	|	...	1455	1540	|	1555	1640	|	1655	1740	1750	|	...	1755	1842g	1842	1829	|	1855	1942g
Milano Centrale d.	...	|	|	|	1405	...	|	...	...	1550	|	...	...	|	1705	...	...	|	...	1805	1845g	1900	...	|	...	1945g
Verona Porta Nuova a.	...	|	1337	|	|	...	|	...	...	|	|	...	...	|	|	...	...	|	...	|	|	|	...	|	...	|
Torino Porta Susa a.	...	|	...	|	1452	...	|	...	...	1636	|	...	...	|	1752	...	...	|	...	1852	1930	1948	...	|	...	2030
Torino Porta Nuova a.	...	|	...	|	1505	...	|	...	...	1650	|	...	...	|	1805	...	...	|	...	1905	1940	2000	...	|	...	2040
Padova d.	...	1354	...	1409	...	...	1509	...	...	...	1609	...	...	1709	...	...	...	1809	...	...	...	...	...	1909	...	...
Venezia Mestre ♣ a.	...	1408	...	1423	...	...	1523	...	...	...	1623	...	...	1723	...	...	...	1823	...	...	...	...	...	1923	...	...
Venezia Santa Lucia ♣ a.	...	1420	...	1435	...	...	1535	...	...	...	1635	...	...	1735	...	...	...	1835	...	...	...	...	...	1935	...	...

	FR 9644 Ⓑq	FA 9440 9449 T	FA 9478 Y	FA 9442 U	FR 9646	FR 9548 9550	FA 9444 Ⓑq	FR 9648 Ⓑq	FA 9480 Y	FR 9446	FR 9650	FR 9580		FR 9552	FR 9652 Ⓑq	FA 9482 B	FR 9450	FR 9654	FR 9556 9558	FR 9594 R	FR 9560 M	FA 9454	FR 9660 Ⓑq	FR 9562 Ⓑq	FR 9564 Ⓑq A	FR 9662 †q
Salerno d.	...	...	...	...	...	1512	...	...	...	...	...	...	...	...	...	...	...	...	1712	...	...	...	...	...	...	...
Napoli Centrale d.	1505	...	...	...	...	1600	...	1605	...	1630	1640	...	...	1700	1710	...	...	...	1800	...	...	...	1840	1900	1930	1940
Roma Fiumicino ✈ d.	|	...	...	...	...	|	...	|	...	|	|	...	...	|	|	...	...	...	|	...	...	...	|	|	|	|
Roma Termini a.	1615	...	...	...	...	1710	...	1715	...	1740	1750	...	...	1810	1820	...	...	...	1907	...	...	...	1948	2010	2040	2050
Roma Termini d.	1630	1635	1645	1650	1700	1720	1730	1730	1745	1750	1800	1805	...	1820	1830	1845	1850	1900	1920	...	1935	1950	2000	2020	2050	2100
Roma Tiburtina d.	|	1645	|	1700	1707	1729	1739	|	|	1800	|	1815	...	1829	|	|	1900	|	1929	...	1945	2000	|	2029	2100	|
Firenze SMN a.	|	1807	1801c	1822	|	1851	|	|	1901c	1922	|	1936	...	1951	|	2001c	2022	|	2051	...	2107	2122	|	2151	2235	|
Firenze SMN d.	|	1815	1803c	1830	|	1900	|	|	1903c	1930	|	1945	...	2000	|	2003c	2030	|	2100	...	2116	2130	|	2200	...	|
Bologna Centrale ✣ d.	1828	1855	1845	1910	|	1938	|	1928	1945	2010	|	2023	...	2038	2028	2045	2110	|	2138	2140	2155	2210	|	2238	...	|
Reggio Emilia AV d.	|	|	|	|	|	|	|	|	|	|	|	2044	...	|	|	|	|	2118	|	2206	|	|	|	|	...	|
Milano Rogoredo a.	|	|	|	|	1947	|	|	|	|	|	|	2122	...	|	|	|	|	|	|	|	|	|	|	|	...	|
Milano Centrale a.	1929	|	|	|	1959	2040	|	2029	|	|	2055	2142g	...	2140	2129	|	|	2202	2240	2250	2345	|	2255	2340	...	2355
Milano Centrale d.	...	|	|	|	2010	...	|	...	|	|	...	2145g	...	...	...	|	|	2212	...	...	...	|	...	...	...	...
Verona Porta Nuova a.	...	|	1937	|	|	...	|	...	2037	|	...	|	...	...	...	2137	|	|	...	...	...	|	...	...	...	...
Torino Porta Susa a.	...	|	...	|	2059	...	|	...	...	|	...	2230	...	...	...	...	|	2302	...	...	...	|	...	...	...	...
Torino Porta Nuova a.	...	|	...	|	2110	...	|	...	...	|	...	2240	...	...	...	...	|	2312	...	...	...	|	...	...	...	...
Padova d.	...	1954	...	2009	...	...	2029	...	...	2109	...	...	...	...	...	...	2209	...	...	...	...	2309	...	...	...	...
Venezia Mestre ♣ a.	...	2008	...	2021	...	...	2042	...	...	2123	...	...	...	...	...	...	2223	...	...	...	...	2323	...	...	...	...
Venezia Santa Lucia ♣ a.	...	...	...	...	...	...	2054	...	...	2135	...	...	...	...	...	...	2235	...	...	...	...	2335	...	...	...	...

A – Also calls at Arezzo – see Table **620**.
B – To Brescia – see Table **605**.
M – Via Modena – see Table **615**.
N – From Ancona – see Table **630**.
R – From Bari – see Table **631**.
T – From Trieste – see Table **601**.
U – To Udine – see Table **601**.
Y – To Bolzano – see Table **595**.
c – Firenze **Campo di Marte**.
g – Milano **Porta Garibaldi**.
q – Not Mar. 27, Apr. 24.
w – Not June 3.
♣ – Local journeys are not permitted Venezia Santa Lu Mestre and v.v.
✣ – Most services use underground platforms 16 – allow a minimum of 10 minutes for connecting serv from / to the main station.

Club, Prima, Smart XL and Smart class — ***Italo* high-speed services** — Operator: Nuovo Trasporto Viaggiatori (N

All trains [R] — *Trenitalia* tickets and passes not valid — www.italotren

	ITA 9900 ①-⑤	ITA 9990 h ①-⑤	ITA 9960 h	ITA 9902	ITA 9980	ITA 9962 g	ITA 9904	ITA 9964	ITA 9908 9910	ITA 9982 9984	ITA 9912 y	ITA 9914 9916	ITA 9966	ITA 9992	ITA 9922	ITA 9986	ITA 9996	ITA 9928 9930	ITA 9968	ITA 9932	ITA 9970	ITA 9934 9936	ITA 9972 9974	ITA 9940	ITA 9998 Ⓑ	ITA 9988	ITA 9976 9978	9
Salerno d.	...	...	...	...	...	...	...	...	0737	0805c	...	0936	...	...	...	...	...	1334	...	...	...	1525	1604e	...	...	...	1759	
Napoli Centrale d.	...	...	...	0625	...	0655	0720	0745	0825	0850c	...	1027	...	...	...	1255	1355	1423	1455	...	...	1625	1650e	1725	1755	...	1845	1
Roma Termini a.	...	...	...	0735	...	0805	0830	0855	0935	1005c	...	1135	...	...	...	1402	1502	1530	1605	...	...	1735	1758e	1835	1902	...	2000	2
Roma Termini d.	0545	0715	0715	0745	0815	0815	0845	0915	0945	1015	1045	1145	1310	1315	1345	1415	1515	1545	1615	1645	1715	1745	1815	1845	1915	1945	2010	2
Roma Tiburtina d.	0553	0725	|	0755	0825	|	0855	|	0955	1025	1055	1155	1318	1325	1355	1425	1525	1555	|	1655	|	1755	|	1855	1925	1955	2018	2
Firenze SMN d.	0725	0854	|	0925	0954	|	1025	|	1125	1154	1225	1325	|	1454	1525	1554	1654	1725	|	1825	|	1925	|	2025	2054	2125	|	2
Bologna Centrale ✣ d.	0803	0933	|	1003	1035	|	1103	|	1203	1235	1303	1403	|	1533	1603	1635	1733	1803	|	1903	|	2003	|	2103	2133	2205	|	2
Verona Porta Nuova a.	|	1023	|	|	|	|	|	|	|	|	|	|	|	1623	|	|	1823	|	|	|	|	|	|	|	2223	|	|	
Brescia a.	|	...	|	|	|	|	|	|	|	|	|	|	|	...	|	|	1917	|	|	|	|	|	|	|	2310	|	|	
Padova a.	|	...	|	|	1132	|	|	|	|	1332	|	|	|	...	|	1732	...	|	|	|	|	|	|	|	...	2302	|	
Venezia Mestre a.	|	...	|	|	1148	|	|	|	|	1348	|	|	|	...	|	1748	...	|	|	|	|	|	|	|	...	2318	|	
Venezia Santa Lucia a.	|	...	|	|	1200	|	|	|	|	1400	|	|	|	...	|	1800	...	|	|	|	|	|	|	|	...	2330	|	
Reggio Emilia ⊖ d.	0824	...	|	1024	...	|	1124	|	1224	...	1324	1424	|	...	1624	...	...	1824	|	1924	|	2024	|	2124	...	...	|	2
Milano Rogoredo a.	0905	...	|	1103	...	|	1203	|	1303	...	1403	1503	1558	...	1703	...	...	1903	|	2003	|	2103	|	2203	...	...	2258	0
Milano Centrale a.	0917	...	1010	1115	...	1110	1215	1210	1315	...	1415	1515	1610	...	1715	...	...	1917	1910	2017	2010	2115	2110	2215	...	...	2310	0
Torino Porta Susa a.	1013	...	...	1215	...	...	...	...	1413	...	...	1613	...	...	...	...	...	...	...	2113	...	2213	...	...	...	...	...	
Torino Porta Nuova a.	1025	...	...	1227	...	...	...	...	1425	...	...	1625	...	...	...	...	...	...	...	2125	...	2225	...	...	...	...	...	

c – ⑥⑦ (also Mar. 28, Apr. 25).
e – ⑦ (not Mar. 27).
g – Not Mar. 28.
h – Not Mar. 28, Apr. 25.
n – Not Apr. 24.
y – ①④⑤⑥⑦ (not Mar. 27).
⊖ – Reggio Emilia Mediopadana.
✣ – Most services use underground platforms 16 – 19; allow a minir of 10 minutes for connecting services from / to the main station.

VENEZIA - UDINE - TRIESTE

Venezia - Trieste direct services

	2 Ⓐ	IC 735				FB 9707 ⒶT		FB 9717 ⒸT					IC 589 ♦				FB 9737 T		FA 9449 ♦	FB 9741 M	IC 593 ♦	FB 9747 M	
Roma Termini **616** d.	...	...	...	...	...	...	...	...	...	...	...	...	1030	...	...	...	...	...	1635	...	1540		...
Venezia Santa Lucia **605** d.	...	...	0641	0741	0941	...	1041	...	1241	1341	1441	1541	|	1641	1741	1841	...	1941	|	...	|	...	2241
Venezia Mestre **605** d.	...	0550	0653	0753	0953	1020	1053	1247	1253	1353	1453	1553	1646	1653	1753	1853	1949	1953	2021	2046	2138	2155	2253
S. Dona di Piave-Jesolo ◧ d.	...	0617	0717	0817	1017	1046	1117	1305	1317	1417	1517	1617	1708	1717	1817	1917	|	2017	|	|	2216	|	2317
Portogruaro-Caorle d.	0607	0635	0737	0837	1037	1104	1137	1321	1337	1437	1537	1637	1730	1737	1837	1937	2029	2037	|	2129	2234	|	2337
Latisana-Lignano-Bibione d.	0618	0648	0748	0848	1048	1114	1148	1330	1348	1448	1548	1648	1740	1748	1848	1948	|	2048	|	|	2244	|	2348
S. Giorgio di Nogaro d.	0630	0700	0800	0900	1100	|	1200	|	1400	1500	1600	1700	|	1800	1900	2000	|	2101	|	|	|	|	0000
Cervignano-Aquileia-Grado d.	0639	0709	0809	0909	1109	1131	1209	1346	1409	1509	1609	1709	1800	1809	1909	2009	|	2110	|	|	2301	|	0009
Monfalcone d.	0653	0723	0823	0923	1123	1145	1223	1359	1423	1523	1623	1723	1816	1823	1923	2023	2059	2123	|	2159	2314	|	0023
Trieste Centrale ⊗ a.	0720	0746	0846	0946	1146	1208	1246	1422	1446	1546	1646	1746	1839	1846	1946	2046	2122	2151	2146	2222	2337	2319	0046

	2	2 ⚒			FB 9790 M	FB 9710 T	FA 9404 ♦		IC 584 ♦			FB 9716 T		IC 594 ♦					FB 9748 M					IC 734
ste Centrale ⊗ d.	...	...	0515	0610	0616	0638	0652	0715	0721	0815	0915	0938	1215	1302	1315	1415	1515	1615	1702	1715	1815	1915	2115	2206
falcone d.	...	...	0539	0638	|	0703	|	0739	0746	0839	0939	1003	1239	1327	1339	1439	1539	1639	1727	1739	1839	1939	2139	2230
ignano-Aquileia-Grado d.	...	...	0551	0651	|	|	|	0751	0758	0851	0951	|	1251	1337	1351	1451	1551	1651	1737	1751	1851	1951	2151	2242
orgio di Nogaro d.	...	...	0600	0700	|	|	|	0800	|	0900	1000	|	1300	|	1400	1500	1600	1700	|	1800	1900	2000	2200	2251
ana-Lignano-Bibione d.	...	...	0613	0713	|	|	|	0813	0821	0913	1013	|	1313	1351	1413	1513	1613	1713	1751	1813	1913	2013	2213	2304
ogruaro-Caorle d.	0413	0538	0624	0724	|	0733	|	0824	0832	0924	1024	1033	1324	1401	1424	1524	1624	1724	1801	1824	1924	2024	2224	2315
ona di Piave-Jesolo ◧ d.	0436	0601	0642	0742	|	|	|	0842	0850	0942	1042	|	1342	1419	1442	1542	1642	1742	1817	1842	1942	2042	...	2337
ezia Mestre **605** a.	0511	0636	0708	0808	0740	0814	0824	0908	0912	1008	1108	1114	1408	1452	1508	1608	1708	1808	1842	1908	2008	2108	...	0005
ezia Santa Lucia **605** a.	0525	0650	0720	0820	...	...	|	0920	|	1020	1120	...	1424	|	1520	1620	1720	1820	...	1920	2020	2120	...	...
oma Termini **616** a.	...	...	...	...	...	...	1210	...	1520	...	...	...	...	2036	...	...	...	...	...	...	...	...	...	...

Venezia - Trieste via Udine

	Ⓐ	2 Ⓐ	ICN 774 ♦	2 Ⓐ	2 ⚒		⚒	2 †	2 †	2 ⚒	2 ⚒	†		FB 9720 ♦	2 †	2 Ⓒz		2 Ⓒ			2 ⚒	⚒	2	
Venezia Santa Lucia d.	0504	0515	0536	0602	0615	...	0704	...	0715	0715	0804	0804	...	...	...	0915	1004	1115	1204	...	1215	1304	1315	1404
Venezia Mestre d.	0516	0529	|	0616	0629	...	0716	...	0729	0729	0816	0816	...	0913	...	0929	1016	1129	1216	...	1229	1316	1329	1416
Treviso Centrale d.	0536	0554	0614	0636	0654	...	0736	...	0754	0754	0836	0836	...	0930	...	0954	1036	1154	1236	...	1254	1336	1354	1436
Conegliano **603** d.	0555	0622	0637	0655	0722	...	0755	...	0822	0822	0855	0855	...	0948	...	1022	1055	1222	1255	...	1322	1355	1422	1455
Sacile d.	0607	0638	0656	0707	0738	...	0807	...	0838	0838	0907	0907	...	|	...	1038	1107	1238	1307	...	1338	1407	1438	1507
Pordenone d.	0617	0650	0706	0717	0750	...	0817	...	0850	0850	0917	0917	...	1007	...	1050	1117	1250	1317	...	1350	1417	1450	1517
Udine a.	0653	0730	0740	0753	0830	...	0853	...	0930	0930	0953	0953	...	1035	...	1130	1153	1330	1353	...	1430	1453	1530	1553
Udine d.	0655	0736	0755	...	...	...	0855	0909	...	0932	...	0955	...	...	1109	...	1155	...	1355	...	...	...	...	1555
Gorizia Centrale ♣ d.	0719	0807	0828	...	...	...	0919	0940	...	1003	...	1019	...	...	1140	...	1219	...	1419	...	...	...	...	1619
Monfalcone d.	0740	0831	0855	...	...	...	0940	1004	...	1027	...	1040	...	...	1204	...	1240	...	1440	...	...	...	...	1640
Trieste Centrale ⊗ a.	0803	0900	0920	...	...	...	1003	1033	...	1056	...	1103	...	...	1233	...	1303	...	1503	...	...	...	...	1703

	Ⓐy	2	2	EC 30 ♦		2 Ⓐ	2 Ⓐ	†	Ⓐ		2 †	2		2 Ⓐ	Ⓐ	2 †	2 ⚒	2		FA 9442 ♦	FB 9744 ♦	2			
ezia Santa Lucia d.	1504	...	1515	1555	1604	...	1615	1704	1704	...	...	1715	1804	1815	1904	1904	...	1915	2004	...	...	2115	2204	2304	...
ezia Mestre d.	1516	...	1529	1607	1616	...	1629	1716	1716	...	...	1729	1816	1829	1916	1916	...	1929	2016	2040	...	2129	2216	2316	...
iso Centrale d.	1536	...	1554	1630	1636	...	1654	1736	1736	...	...	1754	1836	1854	1936	1936	...	1954	2036	2056	2128	2154	2236	2336	...
egliano **603** d.	1555	...	1622	|	1655	...	1722	1755	1755	...	...	1822	1855	1922	1955	1955	...	2022	2055	2115	2146	2222	2255	2355	...
le d.	1607	...	1638	|	1707	...	1738	1807	1807	...	...	1838	1907	1938	2007	2007	...	2038	2107	|	2156	2238	2307	0007	...
enone d.	1617	...	1650	1707	1717	...	1750	1817	1817	...	...	1850	1917	1950	2017	2017	...	2050	2117	2136	2205	2250	2317	0017	...
ne a.	1653	...	1730	1742	1753	...	1830	1853	1853	...	...	1930	1953	2030	2053	2053	...	2130	2153	2205	2230	2330	2353	0053	...
ne d.	1655	1709	...	...	1755	1809	...	...	1855	...	1909	...	1955	...	...	2120	2120	...	2155	...	...	...	2355	...	...
zia Centrale ♣ d.	1719	1740	...	...	1819	1840	...	...	1919	...	1931	...	2019	...	...	2151	2151	...	2219	...	...	...	0026	...	...
falcone d.	1740	1804	...	...	1840	1904	...	...	1940	...	1952	...	2040	...	...	2215	2215	...	2240	...	...	...	0049	...	...
ste Centrale ⊗ a.	1803	1833	...	...	1903	1933	...	...	2003	...	2015	...	2103	...	...	2244	2244	...	2303	...	...	...	0118	...	...

	Ⓐ	FB 9705 ♦		2	FA 9413 ♦	⚒	2 ⚒	2 ⚒		2 †	2 ⚒		2 †	Ⓐy			EC 31 ♦	2	Ⓐ	2 †	⑥	FB 9729 ♦	2 ⚒	2 ⚒	
ste Centrale ⊗ d.	...	...	...	...	...	0527	0557	0622	0657	0727	0727	0857	0927	...	...	1057	...	...	1127	1127	...	...	...	1227	1257
falcone d.	...	...	...	...	...	0557	0627	0646	0721	0757	0757	0921	0957	...	...	1121	...	...	1157	1157	...	...	...	1257	1321
zia Centrale ♣ d.	...	...	...	...	...	0619	0649	|	0742	0819	0819	0942	1019	...	...	1142	...	...	1219	1219	...	...	...	1319	1342
ne a.	...	...	...	...	...	0651	0721	0721	0805	0851	0851	1005	1051	...	...	1205	...	...	1251	1251	...	...	...	1351	1405
ne d.	0507	0550	0607	0631	0655	0701	0731	...	0807	0907	...	1007	...	1107	...	1207	1218	1231	1307	...	1307	1325	1331	...	1407
denone d.	0542	0619	0642	0710	0729	0740	0810	...	0842	0942	...	1042	...	1142	...	1242	1251	1310	1342	...	1342	1354	1410	...	1442
le d.	0552	0632	0652	0724	|	0752	0824	...	0852	0952	...	1052	...	1152	...	1252	|	1324	1352	...	1352	|	1424	...	1452
egliano **603** d.	0605	0649	0705	0740	0755	0805	0840	...	0905	1005	...	1105	...	1205	...	1305	|	1340	1405	...	1405	1413	1440	...	1505
iso Centrale d.	0625	0710	0725	0807	0815	0825	0907	...	0925	1025	...	1125	...	1225	...	1325	1332	1407	1425	...	1425	1432	1507	...	1525
ezia Mestre a.	0644	...	0744	0832	0837	0844	0932	...	0944	1044	...	1144	...	1244	...	1344	1353	1432	1444	...	1444	1449	1532	...	1544
ezia Santa Lucia a.	0656	...	0756	0846	...	0900	0946	...	0956	1056	...	1156	...	1256	...	1356	1405	1446	1456	...	1456	...	1546	...	1556

	2	Ⓐ	2 Ⓒ	2 Ⓐy	2 Ⓐ			2	2 Ⓒ	Ⓐy	2 Ⓐ	2 Ⓐ		2	2 Ⓒ	Ⓐy	†	2 Ⓑ				ICN 771 ♦		2	
ste Centrale ⊗ d.	...	1327	1327	...	1427	1457	...	...	1527	...	...	1630	1657	...	1727	1757	...	...	1857	1927	2031	2040	...	2222	...
falcone d.	...	1357	1357	...	1457	1521	...	...	1557	...	...	1700	1721	...	1757	1821	...	...	1921	1957	2057	2106	...	2246	...
zia Centrale ♣ d.	...	1419	1419	...	1519	1542	...	...	1619	...	...	1722	1742	...	1819	1842	...	...	1942	2019	2119	2131	...	2308	...
ne a.	...	1451	1451	...	1551	1605	...	...	1651	...	...	1754	1805	...	1851	1905	...	...	2005	2051	2151	2156	←	2340	...
ne d.	1431	1507	...	1531	...	1607	...	1631	...	1707	1731	...	1807	1831	...	1907	1907	1931	2007	...	→	2158	2207	...	...
denone d.	1510	1542	...	1610	...	1642	...	1710	...	1742	1810	...	1842	1910	...	1942	1942	2010	2042	...	...	2233	2242	...	...
le d.	1524	1552	...	1624	...	1652	...	1724	...	1752	1824	...	1852	1924	...	1952	1952	2024	2052	...	...	2243	2252	...	...
egliano **603** d.	1540	1605	...	1640	...	1705	...	1740	...	1805	1840	...	1905	1940	...	2005	2005	2040	2105	...	...	2255	2305	...	...
iso Centrale d.	1607	1625	...	1707	...	1725	...	1807	...	1825	1907	...	1925	2007	...	2025	2025	2107	2125	...	...	2314	2325	...	...
ezia Mestre a.	1632	1644	...	1732	...	1744	...	1832	...	1844	1932	...	1944	2032	...	2044	2044	2132	2144	...	...	|	2344	...	...
ezia Santa Lucia a.	1646	1656	...	1746	...	1756	...	1846	...	1856	1946	...	1956	2046	...	2058	2058	2146	2156	...	...	2348	2356	...	...

NOTES (LISTED BY TRAIN NUMBER)

– [12] and ✕ Wien - Villach - Udine - Venezia and v.v.
– [12] Trieste - Venezia Mestre (**585**) - Roma.
– [12] Roma (**588**) - Venezia Mestre - Trieste.
– [12] Roma (**592**) - Venezia Mestre - Trieste.
– [12] Trieste - Venezia Mestre (**595**) - Roma.
4 – 🛏 1, 2 cl., 🛏 2 cl. (4 berth) and [2] Trieste (**770/5**) - Udine - Venezia - Roma and v.v.
4 – [12] and 🍷 Trieste - Venezia Mestre (**9411**) - Roma.
3/42 – [12] and 🍷 Udine - Venezia Mestre - Roma and v.v.
9 – [12] and 🍷 Roma (**9440**) - Venezia Mestre - Trieste.
5/44 – [12] and 🍷 Udine - Treviso (**9706/43**) - Vicenza - Milano and v.v.
0/29 – [12] and 🍷 Udine - Venezia Mestre (**9701/30**) - Milano and v.v.

M – [12] and 🍷 Milano - Trieste and v.v.
T – [12] and 🍷 Torino - Milano - Trieste and v.v.

y – Not Mar. 24 - 29.
z – Also Mar. 24, 25, 29.

◧ – A frequent 🚌 service operates 0600 - 1930 to Lido di Jesolo; 1 – 2 per hour, journey time 35 minutes.

♣ – Line **1** 🚌 service operates between Gorizia Centrale and Nova Gorica (Slovenia; bus stop 100 metres from station on Italian side) stations. Total journey time ± 20 minutes.

⊗ – 🚋 service **Trieste** (Piazza Oberdan) - **Villa Opicina** (Stazione Trenovia) and v.v. *Linea Tranviaria.* Operator: Trieste Trasporti S.p.A.
From **Trieste**: 0711, 0731, 0751 and every 20 minutes until 2011.
From **Villa Opicina**: 0700, 0720, 0740 and every 20 minutes until 2000.
Walking times: Trieste Centrale railway station - Piazza Oberdan ± 10 minutes; Villa Opicina Stazione Trenovia - Villa Opicina railway station ± 20 minutes.

602 VICENZA - TREVISO

2nd class only except where sh

km		⚒		⚒		†					⚒			⚒			⚒	⚒					FB 9743 ♦
0	**Vicenza** d.	0614	0714	0814	...	0914	...	...	1214	...	1314	1414	...	1514	...	1614	1714	1814	...	1914	2014	...	2026
24	Cittadella d.	0639	0739	0839	...	0939	...	...	1239	...	1339	1439	...	1539	...	1639	1739	1839	...	1939	2039	...	2052
36	Castelfranco Veneto d.	0655	0755	0855	...	0955	...	...	1255	...	1355	1455	...	1555	...	1655	1755	1855	...	1955	2055	...	2108
60	**Treviso** Centrale a.	0721	0821	0921	...	1021	...	...	1321	...	1421	1521	...	1621	...	1721	1821	1921	...	2021	2121	...	2126

	⚒	⚒		FB 9706 ♦			⚒		†			⚒			⚒			⚒			⚒		
Treviso Centrale d.	0539	0639	...	0712	...	0739	0839	...	0939	...	...	1239	1339	...	1439	1539	...	1639	1739	...	1839	...	2039
Castelfranco Veneto d.	0607	0707	...	0731	...	0807	0907	...	1007	...	...	1307	1407	...	1507	1607	...	1707	1807	...	1907	...	2107
Cittadella d.	0621	0721	...	0743	...	0821	0921	...	1021	...	...	1321	1421	...	1521	1621	...	1721	1821	...	1921	...	2121
Vicenza a.	0646	0746	...	0803	...	0846	0946	...	1046	...	...	1346	1446	...	1546	1646	...	1746	1846	...	1946	...	2146

♦ – NOTES (LISTED BY TRAIN NUMBER)

9706 – 🚃12 and 🍸 Udine (**9705**) - Treviso - Milano.
9743 – 🚃12 and 🍸 Milano - Treviso (**9744**) - Udine.

603 CONEGLIANO and PADOVA - BELLUNO and CALALZO

2nd class

km		⚒	⚒	⚒			†	⚒	Ⓐ	Ⓒ	Ⓐ	H	Ⓒ			†	⚒		⚒	⚒	⚒	⚒			⚒	
0	**Conegliano 601** d.	0641	...	...	0741	...	...	...	0841	0841	...	0941	...	...	1241	...	...	...	1341	...	...	1441	...	...	...	1641
14	Vittorio Veneto d.	0702	...	...	0802	...	...	...	0902	0902	...	1002	...	...	1302	...	...	...	1402	...	...	1502	...	...	...	1702
	Padova d.	|	0507	...	|	...	0723	0707	|	|	...	|	...	0907	|	1107	1125	...	|	1207	...	|	1307	...	1407	|
	Castelfranco Veneto d.	|	0536	...	|	...	0752	0736	|	|	...	|	...	0936	|	1136	1152	...	|	1236	...	|	1336	...	1436	|
	Montebelluna d.	|	0553	...	|	...	0806	0753	|	|	...	|	...	0953	|	1153	1206	...	|	1253	...	|	1353	...	1453	|
	Feltre d.	|	*0639*	...	|	...	0839	*0839*	|	|	...	|	...	*1039*	|	*1239*	1239	...	|	*1339*	...	|	*1439*	...	*1539*	|
	Belluno d.	|	*0715*	0730	|	0830	0910	*0915*	|	|	0930	|	1030	*1115*	|	*1315*	1315	1330	|	*1415*	1430	|	*1515*	1530	*1615*	|
41	Ponte nelle Alpi-Polpet a.	0731	...	0738	0831	0828	0919	...	0931	0931	0938	1031	1038	...	1331	...	...	1338	1431	...	1438	1531	...	1538	...	1731
41	Ponte nelle Alpi-Polpet § d.	0739	...	0739	0839	0839	0920	...	0939	0939	0939	1039	1039	...	1339	...	...	1339	1439	...	1439	1539	...	1539	...	1739
	Belluno § a.	0747	...	|	0847	|	|	...	0947	|	|	1047	|	...	1347	...	...	|	1447	...	|	1547	...	|	...	1747
78	**Calalzo ▲** a.	...	...	0827	...	0927	1010	...	...	1027	1027	...	1127	...	...	...	...	1427	...	...	1527	...	...	1627	...	...

		⚒				Ⓑ	Ⓑ				
Conegliano 601 d.	...	1741	1841	...	...	...	...	...	2041	...	2141
Vittorio Veneto d.	...	1802	1902	...	...	...	...	...	2102	...	2202
Padova d.	...	|	|	1707	...	1807	...	1907	|	2107	|
Castelfranco Veneto d.	...	|	|	1736	...	1836	...	1936	|	2136	|
Montebelluna d.	...	|	|	1753	...	1853	...	1953	|	2153	|
Feltre d.	...	|	|	*1839*	...	*1939*	...	*2039*	|	*2239*	|
Belluno d.	1730	|	|	*1915*j	1930	*2015*	2030	*2115*	|	*2315*	|
Ponte nelle Alpi-Polpet a.	1738	1831	1931	...	1938	...	2038	...	2131	...	2231
Ponte nelle Alpi-Polpet § d.	1739	1839	1939	...	1939	...	2039	...	2139	...	2239
Belluno § a.	|	1847	1947	...	|	...	|	...	2147	...	2247
Calalzo ▲ a.	1827	...	...	...	2027	...	2127	...	...	...	...

	⚒	⚒		⚒		⚒		⚒	
Calalzo ▲ d.	...	...	...	0628	...	...	0728	...	...
Belluno § d.	0520	...	0620	|	...	0720	|	...	0820
Ponte nelle Alpi-Polpet § a.	0528	...	0628	0708	...	0728	0808	...	0828
Ponte nelle Alpi-Polpet d.	0533	...	0633	0710	...	0733	0810	...	0833
Belluno d.	|	*0534*	|	0718	*0734*	|	0818	0844	|
Feltre d.	|	*0613*	|	...	*0813*	|	...	0923	|
Montebelluna d.	|	0707	|	...	0907	|	...	0957	|
Castelfranco Veneto d.	|	0725	|	...	0925	|	...	1010	|
Padova a.	|	0753	|	...	0953	|	...	1034	|
Vittorio Veneto d.	0601	...	0701	...	...	0801	...	...	0901
Conegliano 601 a.	0618	...	0718	...	...	0818	...	...	0918

km					⚒	⚒	⚒				⚒	⚒	Ⓑ	Ⓑ	⑥		⚒	Ⓑ		H Ⓐ	Ⓒ	†				
0	**Calalzo ▲** d.	...	...	...	1228	...	...	1328	...	...	...	...	1528	...	1628	...	...	1728	...	...	1740	1758	1828	...	...	1928
	Belluno § d.	...	1020	...	|	...	1320	|	...	1420	...	1520	|	...	|	...	1720	|	...	1820	|	|	|	...	1920	|
37	Ponte nelle Alpi-Polpet § a.	...	1028	...	1308	...	1328	1408	...	1428	...	1528	1608	...	1708	...	1728	1808	...	1828	1825	1842	1908	...	1928	2008
37	Ponte nelle Alpi-Polpet d.	...	1033	...	1310	...	1333	1410	...	1433	...	1533	1610	...	1710	...	1733	1810	...	1833	1833	1843	1910	...	1933	2010
44	**Belluno** d.	*1034*	|	*1234*	1318	1334	|	1418	*1434*	|	*1534*	|	1618	*1634*	1718	*1734*	|	1818	*1834*	|	|	1853	1918	*1934*	|	2018
75	Feltre d.	*1113*	|	*1313*	...	1413	|	...	*1513*	|	*1613*	|	...	*1713*	...	*1813*	|	...	*1913*	|	|	1932	...	*2013*	|	...
110	Montebelluna d.	1207	|	1407	...	1457	|	...	1607	|	1707	|	...	1807	...	1907	|	...	2007	|	|	2017	...	2107	|	...
127	Castelfranco Veneto d.	1225	|	1425	...	1510	|	...	1625	|	1725	|	...	1825	...	1925	|	...	2025	|	|	2032	...	2125	|	...
158	**Padova** a.	1253	|	1453	...	1534	|	...	1653	|	1753	|	...	1853	...	1953	|	...	2053	|	|	2100	...	2153	|	...
	Vittorio Veneto d.	...	1101	...	...	...	1401	...	...	1501	...	1601	...	...	...	...	1801	...	...	1901	1901	...	...	...	2001	...
	Conegliano 601 a.	...	1118	...	...	...	1418	...	...	1518	...	1618	...	...	...	...	1818	...	...	1918	1918	...	...	...	2018	...

H – Not Mar. 24, 25, 29.
j – Arrive 1923 on †.
§ – See other direction of table for further connections.
▲ – Full name of station is Calalzo-Pieve di Cadore-Cortina.

604 VAL GARDENA / GRÖDNERTAL and CORTINA 🚌 services

Service **445/446**	⚒										
S. Candido / Innichen d.	...	0839	...	1039	...	1339	...	1539	...	1739	...
Dobbiaco / Toblach ♣ d.	0705	0849	0905	1049	1105	1349	1405	1549	1605	1749	1805
Cortina a.	0755	...	0955	...	1155	...	1455	...	1655	...	1855

Service **445/446**	⚒									
Cortina d.	0805	...	1005	...	1305	...	1505	...	1705	...
Dobbiaco / Toblach ♣ d.	0850	0910	1050	1110	1350	1410	1550	1610	1750	1810
S. Candido / Innichen a.	...	0920	...	1120	...	1420	...	1620	...	1820

♣ – Dobbiaco bus station. Services also call at Dobbiaco railway station en route between Dobbiaco town and Cortina (5 minutes from town stop).

Service 350	⚒										
Bolzano / Bozen ♦ d.	0644	0826	...	1126	...	...	1526	...	1726	...	1926
Ponte Gardena / Waidbruck d.	0715	0857	1057	1157	1257	1357	1557	1657	1757	1857	1957
Ortisei / St Ulrich ▲ d.	0747	0927	1127	1227	1327	1427	1627	1727	1827	1927	2027
Santa / St Cristina ▲ d.	0800	0940	1140	1240	1340	1440	1640	1740	1840	1940	2040
Selva / Wolkenstein ▲ d.	0808	0948	1148	1248	1348	1448	1648	1748	1848	1948	2048
Plan ▲ a.	0812	0952	1152	1252	1352	1452	1652	1752	1852	1952	2052

Service 350	⚒									
Plan ▲ d.	0604	0704	0834	0904	1034	1304	1334	1504	1704	1734
Selva / Wolkenstein ▲ d.	0607	0707	0837	0907	1037	1307	1337	1507	1707	1737
Santa / St Cristina ▲ d.	0616	0716	0846	0916	1046	1316	1346	1516	1716	1746
Ortisei / St Ulrich ▲ d.	0631	0731	0901	0931	1101	1331	1401	1531	1731	1801
Ponte Gardena / Waidbruck d.	0659	0759	0931	0959	1131	1359	1431	1559	1759	1831
Bolzano / Bozen ♦ a.	0730	0830	1002	...	...	1430	...	1630	...	1902

♦ – Bolzano / Bozen town. Services also call at railway station (2 minutes from town stop).
▲ – Extra buses run Ortisei/St Ulrich - Plan and v.v. in summer.

Valid until December 10, 2016.
Operator: Servizi Autobus Dolomiti, Via Conciapelli 60, 39100, Bolzano / Bozen. ✆: + 39 0471 450111 Fax: + 39 0471 970042.

🚌 service **30 Cortina - Calalzo.** 35 km. Journey time: 55 minutes.
Valid September 16, 2015 - June 8, 2016.

From **Cortina Autostazione** (Bus Station):
0535⚒, 0625⚒, 0635†, 0650⚒, 0800†, 0830, 0930⚒, 1115, 1220⚒, 1235†**z**, 1240⚒, 1315⚒, 1402, 1505, 1615⚒, 1705⚒, 1725†, 1755⚒, 1940⚒, 1940†**p**, 2010⚒, 2010†**z**.

Operator: Dolomitibus, via Col Da Ren 14, 32100, Belluno, Italy.
✆ +39 00 437 217 111, fax +39 00 437 940 522.

From **Calalzo Stazione** (FS rail station):
0625⚒, 0658, 0730†**x**, 0740⚒, 0820, 0945, 1100⚒, 1215⚒, 1215†**y**, 131
1310†**p**, 1400⚒, 1400†**z**, 1455, 1615, 1740⚒, 1850†, 1900⚒, 2045.

p – Not Dec. 6 - Mar. 28. x – Dec. 20 - Feb. 14. y – Dec. 20 - Mar. 13. z – Dec. 6 - Mar. 28.

MILANO - VERONA - VENEZIA 605

					FA 9463	FB 9701	FR 9703		FB 9707	FB 9709		FR 9711	FB 9713		FR 9715	FB 9717	FR 9791	EC 1289	FR 9719	EC 37		FR 9721	FB 9723
	2 Ⓐ		⚒	†	🍷 R	🍷 ♦	🍷		🍷 Ⓐ T	🍷 V		🍷 Ⓐ	🍷 V	Ⓐ	🍷	🍷 T Ⓒ	🍷 Ⓒ	✕ ♦	🍷 §	🍷 ♦		🍷	🍷 V
Milano Centrale d.	...	...	...	...	...	0635	0705	...	0735	0805	...	0835	0905	...	0935	1005	1035	...	1135	1205	...	1235	1305
Milano Lambrate d.	...	...	...	...	...	│	│	...	│	│	...	│	│	...	│	│	│	...	│	│	...	│	│
Treviglio d.	...	...	...	...	...	│	│	...	│	│	...	│	│	...	│	│	│	...	│	│	...	│	│
Brescia d.	...	...	0629	...	0710	0723	0753	...	0823	0853	...	0923	0953	...	1023	1053	1123	...	1223	1253	...	1323	1353
Desenzano-Sirmione **599a** d.	...	...	0652	...	│	0738	│	...	│	0908	...	│	1008	...	│	│	│	...	1238	│	...	1338	│
Peschiera del Garda **599a** ‡ d.	...	...	0701	...	│	│	0814	...	0844	│	...	0944	│	...	1044	1114	1144	...	│	1314	...	│	1414
Verona Porta Nuova **599a** a.	...	...	0719	...	0744	0758	0828	...	0858	0928	...	0958	1028	...	1058	1128	1158	...	1258	1328	...	1358	1428
Verona Porta Nuova **595** d.	0521	0621	0721	0721	...	0800	0830	0821	0900	0930	0921	1000	1030	1021	1100	1130	1200	1239	1300	1330	1321	1400	1430
Vicenza d.	0602	0702	0802	0802	...	0826	0856	0902	0926	0956	1002	1026	1056	1102	1126	1156	1226	1311	1326	1356	1402	1426	1456
Padova **616** d.	0621	0721	0821	0821	...	0844	0914	0921	0944	1014	1021	1044	1114	1121	1144	1214	1244	1328	1344	1414	1421	1444	1514
Venezia Mestre **616** a.	0636	0736	0836	0836	...	0858	0928s	0936	0958	1028s	1036	1058s	1128s	1136	1158s	1228	1258s	1344	1358s	1428	1436	1458s	1528s
Venezia Mestre **616** d.	0638	0738	0838	0838	...	...	│	0938	1020	│	1038	│	│	1138	│	1247	│	1346	│	1430	1438	│	│
Venezia Santa Lucia **616** a.	0648	0748	0848	0848	...	...	0940	0948	│	1040	1048	1110	1140	1148	1210	│	1310	1356	1410	1440	1448	1510	1540
Trieste Centrale **601** a.	...	...	...	...	...	...	...	...	1208	...	...	...	...	...	...	1422	...	...	...	...	...	...	...

		FB 9725		FB 9727		EC 87	FB 9733		FA 9483	FR 9735		FB 9737	FR 9739	FB 9741		FB 9743	FB 9745	FB 9747		FR 9749	FB 9753			EN 481
	Ⓐ	🍷		🍷 V		✕ ♦◨	🍷 V		🍷 R	🍷		🍷 T	🍷 §	🍷	2	🍷 ♦	🍷 V	🍷	2 ⚒	🍷	🍷 V			♦
no Centrâle d.	...	1405	...	1505	...	...	1605	...	...	1635	...	1705	1735	1805	...	1835	1905	1935	...	2005	2035	...	...	2105
no Lambrate d.	...	│	...	│	...	...	│	...	...	│	...	│	│	│	...	│	│	│	...	│	│	...	...	│
glio d.	...	│	...	│	...	...	│	...	...	│	...	│	│	│	...	│	│	│	...	│	│	...	...	│
cia d.	...	1453	...	1553	...	...	1653	...	1710	1723	...	1753	1823	1853	...	1923	1953	│	...	2053	2123	...	...	2154u
enzano-Sirmione **599a** d.	...	1508	...	│	...	...	1708	...	│	1738	...	│	1838	1908	...	│	2008	│	...	│	│	...	...	2212u
hiera del Garda **599a** ‡ d.	...	│	...	1614	...	...	│	...	│	│	...	1814	│	│	...	1944	│	│	...	2114	2144	...	...	2223u
na Porta Nuova **599a** a.	...	1528	...	1628	...	...	1728	...	1744	1758	...	1828	1858	1928	...	1958	2028	2048	...	2128	2158	...	...	2240u
na Porta Nuova **595** d.	1421	1530	1521	1630	1621	1700	1730	1721	...	1800	1821	1830	1900	1930	1921	2000	2030	2050	2042	2130	2200	2221	...	2330u
nza d.	1502	1556	1602	1656	1702	1727	1756	1802	...	1826	1902	1856	1926	1956	2002	2024	2056	│	2138	2156	2226	2302	...	0003u
ova **616** d.	1521	1614	1621	1714	1721	1744	1814	1821	...	1844	1921	1914	1944	2014	2021	...	2114	│	2205	2214	2244	2321	...	0024u
ezia Mestre **616** a.	1536	1628s	1636	1728s	1736	1758	1828s	1836	...	1858s	1936	1928	1958s	2028	2036	...	2128s	2145	2241	2228s	2258s	2336	...	0043u
ezia Mestre **616** d.	1538	│	1638	│	1738	1801	│	1838	...	│	1938	1949	│	2046	2038	...	│	2155	2243	│	│	2338	...	...
ezia Santa Lucia **616** a.	1548	1640	1648	1740	1748	1810	1840	1848	...	1910	1948	│	2010	│	2048	...	2140	│	2255	2240	2310	2348	...	...
este Centrale **601** a.	...	...	...	...	...	...	...	...	...	...	...	2122	...	2222	...	...	...	2319	...	...	...	...	...	...

	EN 480	FB 9700		FB 9702	FR 9704	FB 9706		FB 9790	FR 9708		FB 9710	FB 9712	FR 9792		FR 9714		FA 9464	FB 9716	FR 9718		FR 9722		FB 9726	EC 86
	♦	🍷	2	🍷 V	🍷 §	🍷 ♦		🍷	🍷 §Ⓐ		🍷 T	🍷 V	🍷 §Ⓒ		🍷		🍷 R	🍷 T	🍷	Ⓐ	🍷		🍷 V	✕ ♦◨
ieste Centrale **601** d.	...	...	...	...	...	...	...	0616	...	...	0638	...	...	...	...	...	...	0938	...	...	...	...	...	...
ezia Santa Lucia **616** d.	...	0540	0612	0620	0650	...	0712	│	0750	0812	│	0850	0950	...	1050	1112	...	│	1150	1212	1250	1312	1320	1350
ezia Mestre **616** a.	...	│	0622	│	│	...	0722	0740	│	0822	0814	│	│	...	│	1122	...	1114	│	1222	│	1322	│	1400
ezia Mestre **616** d.	0522s	0552u	0624	0632u	0702u	...	0724	0750	0802u	0824	0832	0902u	1002u	...	1102u	1124	...	1132	1202u	1224	1302u	1324	1332u	1402
ova **616** d.	0539s	0607	0640	0648	0718	...	0740	│	0818	0840	0848	0918	1018	...	1118	1140	...	1148	1218	1240	1318	1340	1348	1418
nza d.	0600s	0625	0659	0705	0735	0805	0759	│	0835	0859	0905	0935	1035	...	1135	1159	...	1205	1235	1259	1335	1359	1405	1435
na Porta Nuova **595** a.	0635s	0650	0739	0730	0800	0830	0839	0843	0900	0939	0930	1000	1100	...	1200	1239	...	1230	1300	1339	1400	1439	1430	1500
na Porta Nuova **599a** d.	0715s	0652	...	0732	0802	0832	...	0845	0902	...	0932	1002	1102	...	1202	...	1250	1232	1302	...	1402	...	1432	...
hiera del Garda **599a** ‡ d.	0730s	0707	...	0748	│	0848	...	│	│	...	0948	│	1118	...	│	...	│	│	1318	...	│	...	1448	...
enzano-Sirmione **599a** d.	0741s	0716	...	│	0823	│	...	│	0923	...	│	1023	│	...	1223	...	│	1253	│	...	1423	...	│	...
cia d.	0801s	0734	...	0809	0839	0909	...	│	0939	...	1009	1039	1139	...	1239	...	1328	1309	1339	...	1439	...	1509	...
iglio d.	│	│	...	│	│	│	...	│	│	...	│	│	│	...	│	...	...	│	│	...	│	...	│	...
no Lambrate d.	│	│	...	│	│	│	...	│	│	...	│	│	│	...	│	...	...	│	│	...	│	...	│	...
no Centrale a.	0912	0825	...	0855	0925	0955	...	1000	1025	...	1055	1125	1225	...	1325	...	...	1355	1425	...	1525	...	1555	...

		FB 9728	FB 9730		FB 9732	EC 1288			EC 42		FR 9738		FB 9740	FR 9742		FB 9746		FB 9748		FR 9750		FA 9482		
	⚒	🍷 V	🍷 ♦		🍷 V	✕ ♦	†	⚒	🍷 ♦		🍷		🍷 V	🍷		🍷 V		🍷		🍷	Ⓐ	🍷 R		
ieste Centrale **601** d.	...	...	...	...	...	...	...	...	...	...	...	...	...	...	...	...	...	1702	...	...	...	...	...	...
ezia Santa Lucia **616** d.	1412	1420	...	1512	1520	1550	1612	1612	1620	...	1650	1712	1720	1750	1812	1820	...	│	1912	1950	2012	...	2112	...
ezia Mestre **616** a.	1422	│	...	1522	│	1600	1622	1622	1630	...	│	1722	│	│	1822	│	...	1842	1922	│	2022	...	2122	...
ezia Mestre **616** d.	1424	1432u	1502	1524	1532u	1602	1624	1624	1632	...	1702u	1724	1732u	1802u	1824	1832u	...	1902	1924	2002u	2024	...	2124	...
ova **616** d.	1440	1448	1518	1540	1548	1618	1640	1640	1648	...	1718	1740	1748	1818	1840	1848	...	1918	1940	2018	2040	...	2140	...
nza d.	1459	1505	1535	1559	1605	1635	1659	1659	1705	...	1735	1759	1805	1835	1859	1905	...	1935	1959	2035	2059	...	2159	...
ona Porta Nuova **595** a.	1539	1530	1600	1639	1630	1700	1739	1739	1730	...	1800	1839	1830	1900	1939	1930	...	2000	2039	2100	2139	...	2239	...
ona Porta Nuova **599a** d.	...	1532	1602	...	1632	...	...	1744	1732	...	1802	...	1832	1902	...	1932	...	2002	...	2102	...	2150	...	...
hiera del Garda **599a** ‡ d.	...	│	│	...	1648	...	...	1802	1748	...	│	...	1848	1918	...	│	...	2018	...	│	...	│	...	...
enzano-Sirmione **599a** d.	...	1553	1623	...	│	...	...	1811	│	...	1823	...	│	│	...	1953	...	│	...	2123	...	│	...	...
cia d.	...	1609	1639	...	1709	...	...	1834	1809	...	1839	...	1909	1939	...	2009	...	2039	...	2139	...	2228	...	...
iglio d.	...	│	│	...	│	...	...	...	│	...	│	...	│	│	...	│	...	│	...	│	...	...	...	...
no Lambrate d.	...	│	│	...	│	...	...	...	│	...	│	...	│	│	...	│	...	│	...	│	...	...	...	...
no Centrale a.	...	1655	1725	...	1755	...	...	...	1855	...	1925	...	1955	2025	...	2055	...	2125	...	2225	...	...	...	...

ANO - VERONA and v.v. local services :

Operator: Trenord

					Ⓐ	†																		
no Centrale d.	0625	0725	0825	...	0850	0925	...	1125	1225	1325	1425	...	1525	1625	1725	1825	...	1925	2025	...	2125	2225	...	0015
no Lambrate d.	0633	0733	0833	...	0900	0933	...	1133	1233	1333	1433	...	1533	1633	1733	1833	...	1933	2033	...	2133	2233	...	0022
iglio d.	0656	0756	0856	...	0926	0956	...	1156	1256	1356	1456	...	1556	1656	1756	1856	...	1956	2056	...	2156	2256	...	0049
cia d.	0735	0835	0935	...	1016	1035	...	1235	1335	1435	1535	...	1635	1735	1835	1935	...	2035	2135	...	2235	2335	...	0135
enzano-Sirmione **599a** d.	0751	0851	0951	...	...	1051	...	1251	1351	1451	1551	...	1651	1751	1851	1951	...	2051	2151	...	2251	2351	...	0151
hiera del Garda **599a** ‡ d.	0801	0901	1001	...	...	1101	...	1301	1401	1501	1601	...	1701	1801	1901	2001	...	2101	2201	...	2301	0001	...	0201
ona Porta Nuova **599a** a.	0820	0920	1020	...	...	1120	...	1320	1420	1520	1620	...	1720	1820	1920	2020	...	2120	2220	...	2320	0020	...	0220

			Ⓐ														†							
ona Porta Nuova **599a** d.	0540	0640	0655	0740	...	0836	0940	...	...	1236	1340	1440	1540	...	1640	1740	1810	1840	...	1940	2040	...	2140	...
hiera del Garda **599a** ‡ d.	0555	0655	0712	0755	...	0852	0955	...	...	1252	1355	1455	1555	...	1655	1755	1825	1855	...	1955	2055	...	2155	...
enzano-Sirmione **599a** d.	0605	0705	0721	0805	...	0902	1005	...	...	1302	1405	1505	1605	...	1705	1805	1835	1905	...	2005	2105	...	2205	...
cia d.	0625	0725	0740	0825	...	0925	1025	1244	...	1325	1425	1525	1625	...	1725	1825	1855	1925	...	2025	2125	...	2225	...
iglio d.	0702	0802	0813	0902	...	1002	1102	1332	...	1402	1502	1602	1702	...	1802	1902	1932	2002	...	2102	2202	...	2302	...
no Lambrate d.	0728	0828	0837	0928	...	1028	1128	1358	...	1428	1528	1628	1728	...	1828	1928	1958	2028	...	2128	2228	...	2328	...
no Centrale a.	0735	0835	0845	0935	...	1035	1135	1405	...	1435	1535	1635	1735	...	1835	1935	2005	2035	...	2135	2235	...	2335	...

NOTES (LISTED BY TRAIN NUMBER)

2 – [12] and 🍷 Genève - Milano - Venezia and v.v. Ⓡ inclusive of supplement.

– [12] and ✕ Venezia - Verona - München and v.v. Operator within Italy: LeNord.

– 🛏 1, 2 cl., ▬ 2 cl. and [2] Wien (**235**) - Venezia Mestre - Milano; 🛏 1, 2 cl. and ▬ 2 cl. München (**485**) - Verona - Milano.

– 🛏 1, 2 cl., ▬ 2 cl. and [2] Milano - Venezia Mestre (**234**) - Wien; 🛏 1, 2 cl. and ▬ 2 cl. Milano - Verona (**484**) - München.

8/9 – Ⓒ: [12] and ✕ Venezia - Verona - München and v.v. Operator within Italy: LeNord.

– [12] and 🍷 Milano - Venezia Mestre (**9720**) - Udine.

– [12] and 🍷 Udine (**9705**) - Treviso - Milano.

– [12] and 🍷 Udine (**9729**) - Venezia Mestre - Milano.

– [12] and 🍷 Milano - Treviso (**9744**) - Udine.

R – [12] and 🍷 Roma - Brescia and v.v.

T – [12] and 🍷 Trieste - Venezia Mestre - Milano - Torino and v.v.

V – [12] and 🍷 Torino - Milano - Venezia and v.v.

s – Stops to set down only.

u – Stops to pick up only.

§ – *Frecciabianca (FB)* until Apr. 30, *Frecciasrossa (FR)* from May 1.

♠ – Operator: Trenord.

◨ – Also available to passengers without reservation. Operator within Italy: LeNord.

‡ – Station for Gardaland Park. Free shuttle bus available.

607 MILANO LOCAL SERVICES

Operator: Tren

MILANO - BERGAMO: Some services 2nd class only

km							Ⓐ	Ⓒ	Ⓐ	Ⓒ													
0	**Milano** Centrale ◇ d.	0540	0610	0710	0810	0910	1010	1010	1110	1110	...	1210	1310	1410	1510	1610	1710	...	1810	1910	2010	2110	2210	2340
56	**Bergamo** a.	0628	0658	0758	0858	0958	1058	1103	1158	1203	...	1258	1358	1458	1558	1658	1758	...	1858	1958	2058	2158	2258	0050

				Ⓐ				Ⓒ	Ⓐ	Ⓒ	Ⓐ												
Bergamo d.	0500	0602	0702	0735	...	0802	0902	0957	1002	1057	1102	...	1202	1302	1402	1502	1602	1702	...	1802	1902	2002	2102	2202
Milano Centrale ◇ a.	0550	0650	0750	0830	...	0850	0950	1050	1050	1150	1150	...	1250	1350	1450	1550	1650	1750	...	1850	1950	2050	2150	2250

Additional trains run approximately hourly Milano Porta Garibaldi - Bergamo via Monza, journey 64 minutes, *43 km*.

MILANO - COMO LAGO: *46 km* Journey: 52 – 65 minutes 2nd class only

From **Milano** Cadorna: 0613⚒, 0643, 0713⚒, 0743, 0800Ⓐ, 0843, 0900, 0943, 1043, 1143, 1213⚒, 1243, 1313⚒, 1343, 1400†, 1413Ⓐ, 1443, 1513Ⓐ, 1543, 1613Ⓐ, 1643, 1700Ⓐ, 1713⚒, 1743, 1800Ⓐ, 1813, 1843, 1900Ⓐ, 1913⚒, 1943, 2013⚒, 2043, 2113Ⓐ, 2143, 2243.

From **Como Nord Lago**: 0546⚒, 0616, 0635Ⓐ, 0646⚒, 0716, 0735Ⓐ, 0746⚒, 0816, 0835⚒, 0916, 0935Ⓐ, 1016, 1116, 1216, 1246⚒, 1316, 1346⚒, 1416, 1446Ⓐ, 1516, 1546Ⓐ, 1616, 1646Ⓐ, 1716, 1746, 1816, 1835†, 1846⚒, 1916, 1946, 2016, 2046⚒, 2116.

A reduced service operates in August.

MILANO - VARESE - LAVENO: *72 km* Journey: 87 – 107 mins 2nd class only

From **Milano** Cadorna: 0609⚒, 0639, 0709Ⓐ, 0752, 0852, 0939, 1039, 1139, 1209⚒, 1352, 1439Ⓒ, 1452Ⓐ, 1539, 1609Ⓐ, 1652, 1722Ⓐ, 1752, 1822Ⓐ, 1852, 1922Ⓒ, 1939Ⓒ, 2022Ⓐ, 2039Ⓒ.

From **Laveno-Mombello** F N: 0538Ⓐ, 0608⚒, 0638, 0708⚒, 0738, 0808Ⓐ, 0838, 09… 1038, 1138, 1238, 1308⚒, 1338, 1438, 1538, 1638, 1738, 1808Ⓐ, 1838, 1938, 2…

Additional journeys run Milano Cadorna - Varese (journey 63 minutes).

A reduced service operates in August.

MILANO - LUINO: *91 km* 2nd class only

	Ⓐ									Ⓐ	Ⓐ		
Milano P Garibaldi d.	*0632*	*0732*	0806	*1132*	*1232*	*1332*	*1432*	*1532*	*1632*	1806	1906	*2032*	2236
Gallarate **590** d.	0719	0819	0842	1215	1319	1419	1519	1619	1719	1842	1942	2119	2307
Laveno-Mombello d.	0801	0901	0922	1252	1401	1501	1601	1701	1801	1922	2022	2201	2341
Luino 592 a.	0816	0915	*0958*j	*1329*j	1416	1515	1616	1715	1816	1941	2041	2216	2359

	Ⓒ	Ⓐ	Ⓐ	Ⓒ		†							
Luino 592 d.	0604	0619	0720	0744	0845	1044	1344	1445	1544	1645	1744	1944	2045
Laveno-Mombello d.	0620	0642	0736	0800	0900	1100	1400	1500	1600	1700	1800	2000	2100
Gallarate **590** a.	0652	0718	0805	0841	0941	1141	1441	1541	1641	1741	1841	2041	2141
Milano P Garibaldi a.	0728	0757	0844	*0928*	*1028*	*1228*	*1528*	*1628*	*1728*	*1828*	*1928*	*2128*	2228

Additional journeys are available by changing at Gallarate.

MILANO - CREMONA - MANTOVA:

km											
0	**Milano** C d.	0620	0820	1020	1220	...	1420	1620	1715	1820	1915
60	Codogno d.	0702	0902	1102	1302	...	1502	1702	1758	1902	1958
88	Cremona d.	0732	0930	1130	1330	...	1530	1730	1820	1930	2020
151	**Mantova** a.	0814	1010	1210	1410	...	1610	1810	1910	2019	2110

Mantova d.	0518	0610	0641	0850	1050	1250	1450	1650	1850	2050
Cremona d.	0617	0656	0732	0930	1130	1330	1530	1730	1930	2130
Codogno a.	0638	0717	0752	0952	1152	1352	1552	1752	1952	2152
Milano Centrale a.	0730	0810	0840	1040	1240	1440	1640	1840	2040	2240

j – Connection by 🚌.

BRESCIA - EDOLO: 2nd class only

km		⚒	†							Ⓐ		
0	**Brescia** d.	0555	0707	0907	1107	...	1307	1507	1707	1758	...	1907
103	Edolo a.	0834	0907	1107	1307	...	1507	1707	1907	2018	...	2107

	⚒	⚒								†	
Edolo d.	0554	0647	0754	0954	1154	...	1354	1554	1754	1954	...
Brescia a.	0754	0903	0954	1154	1354	...	1554	1754	1954	2200	...

For 🚌 Edolo - Tirano see Table **593**.

609 Local services in NORTHERN and CENTRAL ITALY

2nd class o…

ALESSANDRIA - ACQUI TERME: *34 km* Journey 28 – 38 minutes

From **Alessandria**: 0643, 0743, 0938, 1043⚒, 1143, 1343, 1543, 1743, 1943.

From **Acqui Terme**: 0646⚒, 0737, 0942, 1137, 1337, 1437⚒, 1537, 1737, 1937.

BOLOGNA - PORRETTA TERME: *59 km* Journey 60 – 72 minutes

From **Bologna** Centrale: 0552⚒§, 0630⚒, 0704, 0804⚒, 0904⚒§, 0904†, , 1004⚒, 1104, 1204⚒§, 1204†, 1304, 1404, 1504, 1604§, 1704, 1734, 1804, 1834Ⓐ, 1904Ⓐ, 1904Ⓒ§, 1934Ⓐ§, 2004, 2104, 2204.

From **Porretta Terme**: 0500⚒, 0550, 0608, 0640, 0718⚒§, 0718†, 0750⚒, 0822, 0922⚒, 1022⚒§, 1022†, 1122⚒, 1222, 1322, 1422⚒§, 1422†, 1522, 1622, 1722§, 1821, 1921, 2021Ⓐ, 2021Ⓒ§, 2050Ⓐ, 2122Ⓐ§.

CAMPIGLIA - PIOMBINO: *16 km* Journey 22 – 30 minutes

From **Campiglia Marittima**: 0556⚒, 1008**p**, 1336⚒, 1533, 1640, 1736**q**, 1806, 1839**r**.

From **Piombino Marittima**: 0632⚒, 0915Ⓒ, 0920Ⓐ, 1053**p**, 1140**s**, 1527⚒, 1608, 1724, 1812**q**, 1845.

GENOVA - ACQUI TERME: *58 km* Journey 65 – 81 minutes

From **Genova** Piazza Principe: 0612Ⓐ, 0714, 0921, 1021⚒, 1121, 1221Ⓐ, 1321, 1421Ⓐ, 1621, 1721Ⓐ, 1821, 1921, 2043.

From **Acqui Terme**: 0520Ⓐ, 0610, 0703⚒, 0740Ⓐ, 0917, 1117, 1217, 1317, 1417Ⓐ, 1617, 1717Ⓐ, 1817, 2040.

PORRETTA TERME - PISTOIA: *40 km* Journey 60 – 75 minutes

From **Porretta Terme**: 0655⚒, 0717, 0926⚒, 1022**n**, 1324, 1524, 1824.

From **Pistoia**: 0600, 0825⚒, 0921**n**, 1222, 1422, 1721, 1926.

ROVIGO - CHIOGGIA:

km		⚒	m	⚒	Ⓑ	†	⚒	⚒	†	⚒	Ⓑ	Ⓐk	
0	**Rovigo** d.	0615	0715	0815	0915	1115	1315	1415	1515	1615	1715	1815	1915
25	Adria d.	0642	0742	0842	0942	1142	1342	1442	1542	1642	1742	1842	1942
57	**Chioggia** a.	0725	0825	0925	1025	1225	1425	1525	1625	1725	1825	1925	2025

	⚒k	⚒		Ⓑ	⚒	†	⚒	Ⓐ		Ⓐ	Ⓐk	⑥
Chioggia d.	0535	0635	0735	0935	1235	1335	1435	1535	1735	1835	1935	2035
Adria d.	0614	0714	0814	1014	1314	1414	1514	1614	1814	1914	2014	2114
Rovigo a.	0645	0745	0845	1045	1345	1445	1545	1645	1845	1945	2045	2145

SANTHIÀ - BIELLA S. PAOLO: *27 km* Journey 20 – 35 minutes

From **Santhià**: 0548⚒, 0648⚒, 0748⚒, 0751†, 0848⚒, 0948⚒, 0951†, 1148⚒, 1151†, 1248⚒, 1348⚒, 1351†, 1448⚒, 1548⚒, 1551†, 1648⚒, 1748⚒, 1751†, 1848⚒, 1913Ⓐ, 1948⚒, 1951†, 2048⚒, 2051†, 2148⚒, 2151†.

From **Biella S. Paolo**: 0548⚒, 0648, 0718Ⓐ, 0748⚒, 0848, 0948⚒, 1048†, 1148⚒, 1248, 1348⚒, 1448, 1548⚒, 1648, 1748⚒, 1848†, 1943†, 1948⚒, 2048, 2148⚒.

k – Not Mar. 24 - 29.
m – Daily except ④ (not Mar. 25, 26,29).
n – † from May 1.
p – Ⓒ until Mar. 20; ⑥ Mar. 26 - May 21.
q – Ⓐ (also † from Mar. 27).
r – † from Mar. 27 (also ⑥ from May 28).
s – † from Mar. 27 (also June 11).

SIENA - GROSSETO:

km		⚒	†	⚒	†	⚒	†	⚒	⚒	†	†	⚒	
0	**Siena** d.	0555	0748	0809	0946	1215	1245	1327	1545	1552	1740	1746	1843
29	Buonconvento d.	0630	0818	0839	1011	1240	1311	1352	1610	1616	1814	1812	1909
102	**Grosseto** a.	0734	0920	0941	1120	1340	1417	1510	1722	1722	1920	1921	2009

	⚒	†	⚒		⚒	†		†	⚒	⚒		
Grosseto d.	0500	0500	0610	0719	0952	1002	...	1322	1336	1500	1632	1755
Buonconvento d.	0555	0559	0719	0817	1059	1105	...	1432	1443	1611	1732	1910
Siena a.	0622	0625	0744	0840	1132	1132	...	1500	1511	1636	1806	1935

TRENTO - BASSANO DEL GRAPPA: *97 km* Journey 120 – 130 minutes

From **Trento**: 0505⚒‡, 0605, 0705⚒, 0805, 0905‡, 1005⚒‡, 1105, 1205⚒, 1305, 140… 1505⚒‡, 1505†, 1605⚒, 1705, 1805⚒, 1905‡.

From **Bassano del Grappa**: 0502Ⓐ, 0625⚒‡, 0725‡, 0825⚒, 0925, 1025⑥, 1125⚒, 1125†‡, 1225⚒‡, 1325, 1425⚒‡, 1525, 1625⚒, 1725†, 1825⚒‡, 1925, 2025⚒, 2…

All services stop at Levico Terme and Borgo Valsugana Centro (*31/44 km*, ± 50/65 minutes from Trento, respectively).

VENEZIA - BASSANO DEL GRAPPA:

km		⚒							
0	**Venezia** Santa Lucia d.	0556	0656	0756	...	0856	and	2056	...
9	Venezia Mestre d.	0608	0708	0808	...	0908	hourly	2108	...
45	Castelfranco Veneto d.	0646	0746	0846	...	0946	until	2146	...
64	**Bassano del Grappa** a.	0707	0807	0907	...	1007		2207	...

Bassano del Grappa d.	0523	0623	0723	...	0823	and	2023	...
Castelfranco Veneto d.	0546	0646	0746	...	0846	hourly	2046	...
Venezia Mestre a.	0622	0722	0822	...	0922	until	2122	...
Venezia Santa Lucia a.	0634	0734	0834	...	0934		2134	...

Additional services operate on ⚒.

VERONA PORTA NUOVA - MANTOVA: *37 km* Journey 45 – 50 minutes

From **Verona** PN: 0630⚒, 0730⚒, 0830⚒, 0930, 1230⚒, 1330, 1430⚒, 1530, 1630⚒, 1… 1830⚒, 1930, 2030⚒, 2130†.

From **Mantova**: 0628⚒, 0728⚒, 0828, 0928⚒, 1228, 1328⚒, 1428, 1528⚒, 1628, 172… 1828, 1928⚒, 2028.

MANTOVA - MODENA: *Services operated by TPER on some days*

km		⚒		⚒						⚒		
0	**Mantova** d.	0535	0628	0730	0830	0930	1130	1330	1530	1630	1730	1930
19	Suzzara d.	0554	0654	0756	0856	0956	1156	1356	1556	1656	1756	1956
61	**Modena** a.	0645	0740	0840	0942	1046	1242	1442	1642	1740	1842	2042

	⚒			†	⚒		⚒		⚒			
Modena d.	0605	0707	0907	1107	1209	1307	1409	1507	1609	1707	1907	2007
Suzzara d.	0655	0755	0955	1155	1255	1355	1455	1555	1655	1755	1955	2055
Mantova d.	0716	0816	1016	1216	1316	1416	1516	1616	1716	1816	2016	2116

‡ – Operator: *TTE* ✆ contact centre 0461 821000; www.tteservizio.it
§ – Operator: *TPER*. Trenitalia tickets valid.

TORINO and MILANO - GENOVA - PISA 610

	2 ⚒	IC 501 ♦	2	FB 9761 🍷	2	2	FB 9763 🍷	2	2 †	2	IC 651		IC 503 2	⚒	2	EC 141 🍷 ♦	IC 505 ♦	2	2		2	IC 657 ♦	IC 1533 ♦	2	2 ⚒
Torino Porta Nuova **615** d.	...	...	...	...	...	...	...	...	...	0530	...	...	0605	...	0630	...	...	...	...	...	0730	...	...	...	...
Asti **615** d.	...	...	...	...	...	...	...	...	...	0607	...	...	0641	...	0707	...	...	...	...	...	0807	...	...	...	...
Alessandria **615** d.	...	...	...	...	...	...	...	...	...	0631	...	...	0702	...	0731	...	...	...	...	...	0831	...	...	...	...
Novi Ligure d.	...	...	...	...	...	...	...	...	...	0644	...	...	0718	...	0744	...	...	...	...	...	0844	...	...	...	...
Milano Centrale d.	...	...	...	...	...	...	...	...	...	|	0610	...	|	0625	|	0705	...	...	0645	0725	|	0810	0810	...	...
Milano Rogoredo d.	...	...	...	...	...	...	...	...	...	|	|	...	|	0638	|	|	...	...	|	0738	|	|	|	...	...
Pavia d.	...	...	...	...	...	...	...	...	...	|	0635	...	|	0659	|	0735	...	...	|	0759	|	0835	0835	...	...
Voghera **615** d.	...	...	...	...	...	...	...	...	...	|	|	...	|	0714	|	0751	...	...	|	0814	|	0851	0851	...	...
Tortona **615** d.	...	...	...	...	...	...	...	...	...	|	0659	...	|	0725	|	|	...	...	|	0825	|	|	|	...	...
Genova Piazza Principe a.	...	...	...	...	...	...	...	...	...	0730	0744	...	0803	0818	0830	0840	...	...	|	0909	0928	0944	0944	...	...
Genova Piazza Principe d.	...	...	...	0549	...	0606	0705	0711	...	0732	0747	...	...	0820	...	...	0851	...	|	0912	0930	0947	0947	...	...
Genova Brignole d.	...	...	0500	0558u	...	0615	0713u	0720	...	0738	0756	...	...	0826	...	...	0900	...	|	0921	0938	0956	0956	1035	...
S. Margherita-Portofino d.	...	...	0530	|	...	0647	|	0759	...	...	0820	...	...	...	...	...	|	...	|	0955	...	1022	1022	|	...
Rapallo d.	...	...	0534	|	...	0652	0736	0803	...	...	0825	...	...	...	...	...	0922	...	w	0959	...	1027	1027	1106	...
Chiavari d.	...	...	0542	|	...	0701	0745	0811	...	...	0834	...	...	...	...	...	0931	...	|	1007	...	1036	1036	1115	...
Sestri Levante d.	...	0505	0551	|	...	0710	|	0820	...	...	0842	...	...	...	...	...	|	...	|	1030	...	1044	1044	1124	...
Levanto d.	...	0522	0615	|	...	0730	|	0840	...	...	0857	...	...	...	...	...	|	...	|	▬	...	1100	1100	1148	...
Monterosso d.	...	0528	0620	|	...	0735	|	0845	...	...	0903	...	...	...	...	...	|	...	|	...	...	1106	1106	|	...
Riomaggiore d.	...	|	0635	|	...	|	|	0859	...	...	|	...	...	...	...	...	|	...	|	2	...	|	|	|	...
La Spezia Centrale d.	0443	0544	0644	0650	0707	0750	0818	0908	0913	...	0923	...	...	...	...	...	1006	1020	|	F	...	1123	1123	1210	1215
Sarzana d.	0459	0557	...	|	0728	...	|	0924d	0931	...	|	...	...	...	...	...	|	1035	1043	1056	...	|	|	...	1228
Carrara-Avenza d.	0507	0606	...	|	0738	...	|	0931d	0939	...	|	...	...	...	...	...	|	1043	1052	1106	...	|	1141	...	1236
Massa Centro d.	0513	0614	...	|	0745	...	0839	0937d	0946	...	0945	...	...	...	...	...	1028	1049	1100	1112	...	1145	1148	...	1242
Viareggio d.	0530	0628	...	|	0806	...	0852	1006d	1011	...	1000	...	...	...	...	...	1041	1109	1124	1132	...	1200	1209	...	1259
Pisa Centrale **611** a.	0551	0644	...	0730	0827	...	0908	1038d	1038	...	1017	...	...	...	...	...	1056	1139	1145	1200	...	1217	1223	...	1322
Livorno Centrale **611** a.	...	0701	...	0744	...	...	0925	...	...	...	1035	...	...	...	...	...	1119	...	...	...	...	1235	1240	...	...
Roma Termini **611** a.	...	1018o	...	1003	...	...	1203	...	...	...	...	...	...	...	...	...	1433	...	...	...	...	...	...	...	...

	2	IC 659 Ⓐ V	IC 1535 Ⓒ V	FB 9773 🍷	2	2	2	EC 143 🍷 ♦	IC 511 ♦	2	IC 665	2		2	2	FB 9777 🍷	2 †	2 Ⓐ	2	IC 669	IC 515 2 ⚒	2		EC 159 🍷 ♦	FB 9781 🍷	2
Torino Porta Nuova **615** d.	0820	...	...	...	...	...	1030	...	1050	1130	...	...	...	...	1230	...	...	...	1330	...	1405	...	...	...	1520	1530
Asti **615** d.	0904	...	...	...	...	...	1107	...	1128	1207	...	...	...	...	1307	...	...	...	1407	...	1443	...	...	...	1600	1607
Alessandria **615** d.	0931	...	...	...	...	...	1131	...	1152	1231	...	...	...	...	1331	...	...	...	1431	...	1502	...	...	...	1616	1631
Novi Ligure d.	0944	...	...	...	...	...	1144	...	|	1244	...	...	...	...	1344	...	...	...	1444	...	1516	...	...	...	|	1644
Milano Centrale d.	|	0910	0910	...	...	...	|	1110	|	|	1210	...	1225	...	|	1310	...	...	|	1405	|	...	1425	1510	|	|
Milano Rogoredo d.	|	|	|	...	...	...	|	|	|	|	|	...	1238	...	|	|	...	...	|	1416u	|	...	1438	|	|	|
Pavia d.	|	0935	0935	...	...	...	|	1135	|	|	1235	...	1259	...	|	1338	...	...	|	1435	|	...	1459	1535	|	|
Voghera **615** d.	|	|	|	...	...	...	|	1151	|	|	|	...	1314	...	|	|	...	...	|	1451	|	...	1514	1551	|	|
Tortona **615** d.	|	0959	0959	...	...	...	|	|	|	|	1259	...	1325	...	|	|	...	...	|	|	|	...	1525	|	|	|
Genova Piazza Principe a.	1030	1042	1042	...	...	...	1230	1242	1235	1330	1344	...	1418	...	1430	1455	...	...	1530	1544	1550s	...	1610	1642	1654	1730
Genova Piazza Principe d.	1032	...	...	1212	...	...	1232	...	1238	1332	1347	...	1420	...	1432	1502	...	...	1532	1547	1553s	...	...	...	1659	1732
Genova Brignole d.	1040	...	...	1221u	...	1235	1238	...	1247	1338	1356	...	1427	1435	1438	1511	...	...	1538	1556	1559	1635	...	...	1708	1738
S. Margherita-Portofino d.	...	...	...	|	...	|	...	...	|	▬	1421	...	...	|	...	|	...	...	...	|	...	|	...	...	|	...
Rapallo d.	...	...	...	|	...	1314	...	...	1309	...	1426	...	...	1506	...	1537	...	...	...	1625	...	1706	...	...	1737	...
Chiavari d.	...	...	...	|	...	1323	...	...	1318	...	1436	...	...	1515	...	1546	...	...	...	1634	...	1715	...	...	1746	...
Sestri Levante d.	...	...	...	|	...	1333	...	...	1326	...	1444	...	...	1524	...	|	...	...	...	1644	...	1724	...	...	|	...
Levanto d.	...	...	...	|	...	1348	...	...	|	...	1501	...	...	1548	...	|	...	...	...	1700	...	1748	...	...	|	...
Monterosso d.	...	...	...	|	...	|	...	...	|	...	1507	...	...	|	...	|	...	...	...	1706	...	|	...	...	|	...
Riomaggiore d.	...	...	...	|	...	|	...	...	|	2	|	...	...	|	...	|	...	...	...	|	...	|	...	...	|	...
La Spezia Centrale d.	...	...	...	1314	1319	1410	...	...	1357	1414	1521	1540	...	1610	...	1618	1640	1715	...	1721	...	1810	...	...	1818	...
Sarzana d.	...	...	...	|	1334	...	...	...	|	1429	...	1600	...	...	...	|	1700	1730	...	...	...	...	...	...	|	...
Carrara-Avenza d.	...	...	...	|	1342	...	...	...	1414	1439	...	1608	...	...	...	|	1708	1738	...	...	...	...	...	...	|	...
Massa Centro d.	...	...	...	1333	1348	...	...	...	1421	1445	...	1614	...	...	...	1639	1714	1744	...	...	...	...	...	...	1839	...
Viareggio d.	...	...	...	|	1406	...	...	...	1436	1502	...	1633	...	...	...	1652	1733	1803	...	...	...	...	...	...	1852	...
Pisa Centrale **611** a.	...	...	...	1355	1427	...	...	...	1452	1526	...	1651	...	...	...	1707	1751	1825	...	...	...	...	...	...	1908	...
Livorno Centrale **611** a.	...	...	...	1409	...	...	...	...	1507	...	...	...	...	...	...	1724	...	...	...	...	...	...	...	...	1925	...
Roma Termini **611** a.	...	...	...	1632	...	...	...	...	1803	...	...	...	...	...	...	2003	...	...	...	...	...	...	...	...	2203	...

	IC 673	Ⓒ S	Ⓐ	2	IC 675 V	FB 9787 9789 ♦		2	IC 679	IC 519 2		2	2	IC 521 2 Ⓑ y	IC 685	2 ⑤	2	ICN 1699 ♦	IC 689	ICN 1963 ♦	2	A	IC 687	2	ICN 799 ♦	
Torino Porta Nuova **615** d.	...	...	...	...	...	...	...	1730	...	1805	...	...	1830	1840	...	...	1930	2010	...	...	...	...	...	2130	2155	...
Asti **615** d.	...	...	...	...	...	...	...	1807	...	1843	...	...	1907	1921	...	...	2007	2051	...	...	...	...	...	2207	2236	...
Alessandria **615** d.	...	...	...	...	...	...	...	1831	...	1902	...	...	1931	1947	...	...	2031	2113	...	...	...	...	...	2231	2259	...
Novi Ligure d.	...	...	...	...	...	...	...	1844	...	1916	...	...	1944	|	...	...	2044	|	...	...	...	...	...	2244	|	...
Milano Centrale d.	1605	1625	1625	...	1705	...	1705	|	1805	|	1825	...	|	|	1905	1857g	|	|	2005	2010	...	2025	2110	|	|	...
Milano Rogoredo d.	1616u	1638	1638	...	1716u	...	|	|	1816u	|	1838	...	|	|	1916u	|	|	|	2012u	|	...	2038	|	|	|	...
Pavia d.	1635	1659	1659	...	1735	...	|	|	1835	|	1859	...	|	|	1935	|	|	|	2032	2038	...	2059	2135	|	|	...
Voghera **615** d.	1651	1714	1714	...	1751	...	|	|	1851	|	1914	...	|	|	1951	|	|	|	2049	2056	...	2114	2151	|	|	...
Tortona **615** d.	|	1725	1725	...	|	...	|	|	1902	|	1925	...	|	|	|	|	|	|	|	2108	...	2125	|	|	|	...
Genova Piazza Principe a.	1744	1814	1818	...	1842	...	|	1930	1944	1952s	2019	...	2030	2035s	2044	|	2130	2204	2145	2153	...	2214	2240	2330	2350	...
Genova Piazza Principe d.	1747	...	1820	...	...	1852	|	1932	1947	1954s	2021	...	2032	2037s	2047	|	2132	2207	...	2156	...	...	2243	2332	2353	...
Genova Brignole d.	1756	...	1827	1835	...	1900u	|	1938	1956	2001	2027	2035	2038	2043	2056	|	2138	2216	...	2205	2238	...	2252	2338	0002	...
S. Margherita-Portofino d.	1820	...	...	|	...	|	|	...	2020	...	...	|	...	...	|	|	▬	|	...	|	2321	...	2315	...	|	...
Rapallo d.	1825	...	...	1906	...	|	w	...	2026	...	...	2106	...	...	2127	w	...	2247	...	|	2325	...	2320	...	0028	...
Chiavari d.	1836	...	...	1915	...	|	|	...	2036	...	...	2115	...	...	2136	|	...	2257	...	|	2334	...	2329	...	0038	...
Sestri Levante d.	1844	...	...	1924	...	|	|	...	2044	...	...	2124	...	...	2144	|	...	|	...	|	2345	...	2341	...	|	...
Levanto d.	1900	...	...	1944	...	|	|	...	2101	...	...	2148	...	...	|	|	...	|	...	|	0006	...	2357	...	|	...
Monterosso d.	1906	...	...	|	...	|	|	...	2107	...	...	|	...	...	|	|	...	|	...	|	0011	...	0003	...	|	...
Riomaggiore d.	|	...	...	|	...	|	|	...	|	...	...	|	...	...	|	|	2	|	...	|	0026	...	|	...	|	...
La Spezia Centrale d.	1923	...	...	2010	...	2006	|	...	2123	...	...	2210	...	...	2223	|	2226	2347	...	2309	0035	...	0018	...	0127	...
Sarzana d.	|	...	...	...	...	|	2043	...	|	...	...	...	...	...	2235	2229	2241	|	...	|	...	...	...	...	|	...
Carrara-Avenza d.	1941	...	...	...	...	|	2051	...	|	...	...	...	...	...	2243	2236	2249	|	...	|	...	...	...	...	|	...
Massa Centro d.	1949	...	...	...	...	2026	2057	...	2145	...	...	...	...	...	2250	2243	2256	|	...	|	...	...	...	...	|	...
Viareggio d.	2002	...	...	...	...	|	2118	...	2200	...	...	...	...	...	2303	2304	2317	|	...	2343	...	...	...	...	|	...
Pisa Centrale **611** a.	2017	...	...	...	...	2049	2138	...	2217	...	...	...	...	...	2317	2322	2337	0041	...	2359	...	...	...	...	0216	...
Livorno Centrale **611** a.	2035	...	...	...	...	|	2155	...	2235	...	...	...	...	...	2335	2340	...	0110	...	0016j	...	...	...	...	0237j	...
Roma Termini **611** a.	...	...	...	...	...	2259	...	...	...	...	...	...	...	...	...	...	...	0520o	...	...	...	...	...	...	0554o	...

NOTES (LISTED BY TRAIN NUMBER)

[12] and 🍷 Milano - Genova (**142**) - Nice.
[12] and 🍷 Milano - Genova (**144**) - Nice.
[12] and 🍷 Milano - Genova (**160**) - Ventimiglia - Nice - Marseille.
⚒: [12] Sestri Levante - Napoli.
[12] Ventimiglia - Genova - Roma.
[12] Torino - Salerno.
Ⓐ: [12] Milano - Livorno - Grosseto.
Not Jan. 7 - 16, 26 - 30: 🛏 1,2 cl., ▬ 2 cl. (4 berth) and [2] Torino - Napoli - Salerno. Train number **35099** on Feb. 6.
– Ⓒ: [12] Milano - Livorno - Grosseto.

1699 – Jan. 7 - 16, 26 - 30: 🛏 1,2 cl., ▬ 2 cl. (4 berth) and [2] Torino - Napoli - Salerno.
1963 – 🛏 1,2 cl., 🛏 1,2 cl. (T2) and ▬ 2 cl. (4 berth) Milano - Genova - Siracusa; 🛏 1,2 cl. and ▬ 2 cl. (4 berth) Milano - Messina (**1965**) - Palermo. Runs as train number **35063** on ②-⑤ Jan. 5 - Feb. 26; **35163** on Feb. 6.
9787/9 – [12] and 🍷 Genova (**9787**) - Pisa (**9788**) - Firenze (**9789**) - Roma.

A – To Albenga.
F – [2] Bergamo - Fidenza - Aulla - Pisa.
S – To Savona.
V – To Ventimiglia.

d – ⚒ only.
g – Milano **Porta Garibaldi**.
j – Not Feb. 7.
o – Roma **Ostiense**.
s – Stops to set down only.
u – Stops to pick up only.
w – Via Fidenza and Aulla.
y – Not Mar. 27, Apr. 24, and days before holidays.

610 PISA - GENOVA - MILANO and TORINO

km				ICN 796			IC 652	IC 500	IC 656		IC 502				IC 658		ICN 1962		IC 662		IC 504		FB 9758 9760		
		2				2		2			2	2	2	2		2		2		2	2	2		2	2
				♦				⚒	⚒	V		Ⓐ	†	Ⓐ			♦						♦		
	Roma Termini **611** d.	...	...	0006o	...	...	...	...	...	...	...	...	...	...	...	...	...	...	...	...	...	...	0615	...	...
	Livorno Centrale d.	...	...	0309	...	...	...	...	...	...	...	...	...	...	0524	...	0543s	0552	0624	...	...	...	|	...	...
	Pisa Centrale d.	...	...	0326	...	...	...	...	...	...	...	...	...	...	0542	...	0600s	0610	0642	...	...	...	0828	...	...
	Viareggio d.	...	...	|	...	...	...	...	...	...	...	...	...	...	0557	...	0617s	0628	0657	...	...	...	|	...	...
	Massa Centro d.	...	...	|	...	...	...	...	...	...	...	...	...	...	0612	...	|	0645	0709	...	...	...	0851	...	...
	Carrara-Avenza d.	...	...	|	...	...	...	...	...	...	...	...	...	...	|	...	|	0651	0716	...	...	...	|	...	...
	Sarzana d.	...	...	|	...	...	...	...	...	...	...	...	...	...	|	...	|	0701	0724	...	...	...	|	...	...
	La Spezia Centrale d.	...	...	0425	...	...	0459	...	...	...	...	0538	0600	0625	0638	...	0656s	|	0738	0745	...	...	0913	...	...
	Riomaggiore d.	...	...	|	...	...	|	...	...	...	...	0547	0608	|	|	...	|	|	|	|	...	...	|	...	...
	Monterosso d.	...	...	|	...	...	0517	...	...	...	...	0602	0623	|	0654	...	|	|	|	|	...	...	|	...	...
	Levanto d.	...	...	|	...	...	0524	...	...	...	...	0607	0628	0642	0700	...	|	|	0757	0805	...	...	|	...	...
	Sestri Levante d.	...	0432	|	...	...	0540	...	...	...	...	0634	0659	0659	0716	...	|	|	0814	0820	...	...	|	...	0955
	Chiavari d.	...	0443	0512	...	...	0552	...	...	...	...	0644	0708	0708	0724	...	|	|	0824	0830	...	...	|	...	1006
	Rapallo d.	...	0451	0521	...	...	0601	...	...	...	...	0655	0717	|	0733	...	|	w	0833	0838	...	...	|	...	1017
	S. Margherita-Portofino d.	...	0455	|	...	...	0607	...	...	...	...	0659	0721	|	0739	...	|	|	|	|	...	...	|	...	1021
	Genova Brignole d.	0522	0536	0555	...	0622	0635	0655	...	...	0750	0756	0757	0745	0809	0822	0830s	|	0909	0915	...	...	1013s	1022	1108
	Genova Piazza Principe a.	0528	0542	0601	...	0628	0641	0703	...	...	|	0802	0803	0751	0815	0828	0839s	|	0915	...	...	...	1021	1028	1114
0	**Genova** Piazza Principe d.	0530	0544	0606	...	0630	0644	0708	0721	0750	0808u	...	...	...	0818	0830	0842s	|	0918	...	0924	0930	...	1030	...
72	Tortona **615** d.	|	0632	|	...	|	|	|	|	0832	|	...	...	...	0859	|	0922s	|	|	...	|	|	...	|	...
89	Voghera **615** d.	|	0643	|	...	|	0734	|	0808	0843	|	...	...	...	0911	|	0935s	|	1008	...	|	|	...	|	...
115	Pavia d.	|	0701	|	...	|	0751	|	0825	0901	|	...	...	...	0927	|	0958s	|	1025	...	|	|	...	|	...
144	**Milano** Rogoredo a.	|	0720	|	...	|	0810s	|	0846s	0920	|	...	...	...	|	|	|	|	|	...	|	|	...	|	...
154	**Milano** Centrale a.	|	0735	|	...	|	0823	|	0900	0940	|	...	...	...	0955	|	1045	1020	1055	...	|	|	...	|	...
	Novi Ligure d.	0614	...	|	...	0714	...	0741	...	...	0841	...	...	...	...	0914	...	...	...	...	|	1014	...	1114	...
	Alessandria **615** d.	0631	...	0657	...	0731	...	0757	...	...	0857	...	...	...	...	0931	...	...	...	...	1010	1031	...	1131	...
	Asti **615** d.	0654	...	0723	...	0754	...	0818	...	...	0918	...	...	...	...	0954	...	...	...	...	1029	1054	...	1154	...
	Torino Porta Nuova **615** a.	0730	...	0810	...	0830	...	0855	...	...	0955	...	...	...	...	1030	...	...	...	...	1110	1130	...	1230	...

	FB 9764	IC 666		IC 746						IC 670			IC 1540		IC 510			IC 674		IC 512	FB 9772	EC 146			
	🍷		2		2	2			2		2	2		2					2	2	🍷	🍷	2	2	
				V			Ⓐ	ⒸA					†V		♦	ⒸA	ⒶS		†	⚒		♦			Ⓐ
Roma Termini **611** d.	0657	...	...	...	...	...	...	...	...	...	...	...	...	...	0957	...	...	...	...	...	1157	...	...	...	...
Livorno Centrale d.	0932	...	...	...	...	...	...	...	...	1124	...	...	...	...	1245	...	...	1324	1419	...	1431	...	...	...	...
Pisa Centrale d.	0949	...	...	...	...	...	...	...	1105	1142	...	1234	...	...	1303	...	...	1342	1435	...	1448	...	...	...	...
Viareggio d.	1005	...	...	...	...	...	...	...	1122	1200	...	1254	...	...	1318	...	...	1402	1454	...	1504	...	...	...	...
Massa Centro d.	1019	...	...	...	...	...	...	...	1143	1212	...	1312	...	...	1331	...	...	1414	1512	...	1518	...	...	...	...
Carrara-Avenza d.	|	...	...	...	...	...	...	...	1149	1219	...	1318	...	...	1339	...	...	|	1518	...	|	...	...	...	...
Sarzana d.	|	...	...	...	...	...	...	...	1157	|	...	1326	...	...	|	...	...	|	1531	...	|	...	...	...	...
La Spezia Centrale d.	1041	1027	...	...	...	1150	...	...	1220	1238	...	1341	...	1350	1357	...	...	1438	1550	...	1539	...	...	1550	...
Riomaggiore d.	|	|	...	...	...	|	...	...	...	|	...	...	...	|	|	...	...	|	—	...	|	...	...	|	...
Monterosso d.	|	1054	...	...	...	|	...	...	...	1254	...	...	...	...	...	...	...	1454	...	...	|	...	...	|	...
Levanto d.	|	1102	...	...	...	1207	...	...	...	1301	...	...	...	1407	|	...	...	1501	...	...	|	...	...	1608	...
Sestri Levante d.	|	1118	...	...	...	1221	...	...	...	1316	...	...	...	1421	1430	...	...	1516	...	...	|	...	...	1622	...
Chiavari d.	1115	1127	...	...	...	1230	...	...	...	1324	...	...	...	1430	1438	...	...	1524	...	...	1611	...	...	1630	...
Rapallo d.	1124	1136	...	...	...	1240	...	...	...	1333	...	...	...	1440	1447	...	...	1533	...	...	1620	...	...	1640	...
S. Margherita-Portofino d.	|	|	...	...	...	|	...	...	...	1339	...	...	...	|	|	...	...	1539	2	...	|	...	...	|	...
Genova Brignole d.	1150	1209	1222	...	1322	1325	1336	...	...	1409	1422	...	...	1525	1513	...	...	1609	1622	1640	1652	...	1722	1725	...
Genova Piazza Principe a.	1156	1215	1228	...	1328	...	1342	...	...	1415	1428	...	...	...	1521	...	...	1615	1628	|	1658	...	1728	...	...
Genova Piazza Principe d.	1159	1218	1230	1322	1330	...	1344	1344	...	1418	1430	...	1520	...	1524	1544	1544	1618	1630	1649u	1703	1723	1730	...	1744
Tortona **615** d.	|	|	|	|	|	...	1432	1432	...	|	|	...	|	...	|	1632	1632	1700	|	|	|	|	|	...	1832
Voghera **615** d.	|	1308	|	1408	|	...	1443	1443	...	1508	|	...	1608	...	|	1643	1643	|	|	|	|	1810	|	...	1843
Pavia d.	|	1325	|	1425	|	...	1501	1501	...	1525	|	...	1625	...	|	1701	1701	1725	|	|	1818	1826	|	...	1901
Milano Rogoredo a.	|	|	|	|	|	...	1520	1520	...	|	|	...	|	...	|	1720	1720	|	|	|	|	|	|	...	1920
Milano Centrale a.	|	1350	|	1450	|	...	1535	1535	...	1550	|	...	1650	...	|	1735	1735	1750	|	|	1847	1850	|	...	1937
Novi Ligure d.	|	...	1314	...	1414	...	...	...	...	...	1514	...	...	...	|	...	...	...	1714	1722	...	...	1814	...	...
Alessandria **615** d.	1244	...	1331	...	1431	...	...	...	...	...	1531	...	...	...	1612	...	...	...	1731	1736	...	...	1831	...	...
Asti **615** d.	1302	...	1354	...	1454	...	...	...	...	...	1554	...	...	...	1636	...	...	...	1754	1800	...	...	1854	...	...
Torino Porta Nuova **615** a.	1340	...	1430	...	1530	...	...	...	...	...	1630	...	...	...	1720	...	...	...	1830	1840	...	...	1930	...	...

	IC 680	FB 9774		IC 682	IC 1538				IC 1534	IC 684					EC 148	IC 518				FB 9782		FB 9784			IC 522
		🍷	2			2	2	2			2		2	2	🍷		2	A	2	🍷	2	🍷	2	2	
				ⒶV	ⒸV			⑦z	♦	♦		F			♦	♦		Ⓑy					Ⓒ		♦
Roma Termini **611** d.	...	1357	...	...	...	...	...	...	...	...	...	...	...	...	...	1557	...	...	...	1657	...	1827	...	...	1941o
Livorno Centrale d.	...	1615	...	...	...	...	...	1703	1718	1724	...	...	...	...	...	1846	...	...	...	1931	...	2047	...	...	2236
Pisa Centrale d.	...	1629	...	...	...	1634	...	1720	1736	1742	...	1822	1834	...	...	1903	...	...	1909	1948	2042	2101	...	...	2253
Viareggio d.	...	|	...	...	...	1655	...	1736	1753	1800	...	1840	1856	...	...	1919	...	...	1926	2004	2102	|	...	...	2310
Massa Centro d.	...	1652	...	...	...	1712	...	1754	1814	1814	...	1858	1913	...	...	1932	...	...	1946	2017	2119	|	...	...	2323
Carrara-Avenza d.	...	|	...	...	...	1718	...	1759	1821	|	...	1904	1919	...	...	|	...	...	1952	|	2130	|	...	...	2331
Sarzana d.	...	|	...	...	...	1726	...	1807	|	|	...	1914	1926	...	...	|	...	...	1959	|	2143	|	...	...	2340
La Spezia Centrale d.	1640	1715	...	...	...	1741r	1750	|	1838	1838	...	...	1947	1950	...	1955	...	...	|	2039	2158	2143	2150	2310	0008
Riomaggiore d.	|	|	...	...	...	...	|	|	|	|	...	...	...	|	...	|	...	...	|	|	...	|	|	2319	|
Monterosso d.	1656	|	...	...	...	...	|	|	1854	1854	...	...	...	|	...	|	...	...	|	|	...	|	|	2335	0024
Levanto d.	1703	|	...	...	...	...	1807	|	1901	1901	...	...	...	2006	...	|	...	...	|	|	...	|	2207	2340	0031
Sestri Levante d.	1719	|	...	...	...	...	1821	|	1916	1916	...	...	...	2022	...	|	...	...	|	|	...	|	2221	0005	0049
Chiavari d.	1727	|	...	...	...	...	1830	|	1924	1924	...	...	...	2038	...	2033	...	...	|	2113	...	|	2230	0014	...
Rapallo d.	1736	|	...	...	...	...	1840	w	1933	1933	...	...	...	2047	...	2042	...	...	w	2122	...	|	2240	0025	...
S. Margherita-Portofino d.	1742	|	...	...	...	...	|	|	1941	1941	...	...	...	|	...	|	...	...	|	|	...	|	|	0029	...
Genova Brignole d.	1804	1809s	1822	...	...	...	1925	|	2009	2009	2022	...	...	2125	...	2126	2122	...	|	2147s	...	2236s	2325	0123	...
Genova Piazza Principe a.	1811	1816	1828	...	...	...	...	|	2015	2015	2028	...	...	...	...	2132	2128	...	|	2157	...	2244	...	...	...
Genova Piazza Principe d.	1819	...	1830	1922	1922	...	...	|	2018	2018	2030	...	...	...	2122	...	2130	2146	|	...	...	...	...	...	...
Tortona **615** d.	1900	...	|	2000	2000	...	...	|	|	|	|	...	...	...	|	...	|	2232	|	...	...	...	...	...	...
Voghera **615** d.	|	...	|	|	|	...	...	|	2108	2108	|	...	...	...	2208	...	|	2243	|	...	...	...	...	...	...
Pavia d.	1925	...	|	2025	2025	...	...	|	2125	2125	|	...	...	...	2225	...	|	2301	|	...	...	...	...	...	...
Milano Rogoredo a.	|	...	|	|	|	...	...	|	|	|	|	...	...	...	|	...	|	2320	|	...	...	...	...	...	...
Milano Centrale a.	1950	...	|	2050	2050	...	...	2133g	2150	2150	|	...	...	...	2250	...	|	2335	2320	...	...	...	...	...	...
Novi Ligure d.	...	...	1914	...	...	...	...	...	...	...	2114	...	...	...	...	...	2214	...	...	...	...	...	...	...	...
Alessandria **615** d.	...	...	1931	...	...	...	...	...	...	...	2131	...	...	...	...	...	2231	...	...	...	...	...	...	...	...
Asti **615** d.	...	...	1954	...	...	...	...	...	...	...	2154	...	...	...	...	...	2254	...	...	...	...	...	...	...	...
Torino Porta Nuova **615** a.	...	...	2030	...	...	...	...	...	...	...	2230	...	...	...	...	...	2340	...	...	...	...	...	...	...	...

♦ – **NOTES** (LISTED BY TRAIN NUMBER)

140 – [12] and 🍷 Nice (**139**) - Genova - Milano.

146 – [12] and ✕ (Marseille, ①–⑤ from July 4, train **143/5** -) Nice - Genova - Milano.

148 – [12] and 🍷 (Marseille, daily until July 3, ⑥⑦ from July 4, train **147** -) Nice - Ventimiglia - Genova - Milano.

510 – [12] Salerno - Torino.

518 – [12] Roma - Ventimiglia.

522 – Ⓑ (not days before holidays): [12] Napoli - Sestri Levante.

684 – Ⓐ: [12] Grosseto - Livorno - Milano.

796 – 🛏 1, 2 cl., ▬ 2 cl. (4 berth) and [2] Salerno - Napoli - Torino. Train number **35796** on ① (Roma Termini d. 0011, not Ostiense).

1534 – Ⓒ: [12] Grosseto - Livorno - Milano.

1962 – 🛏 1,2 cl., 🛏 1,2 cl. (T2) and ▬ 2 cl. (4 berth) Siracusa - Genova - Milano; 🛏 1,2 cl. and ▬ 2 cl. (4 berth) Palermo (**1964**) - Messina - Milano. Runs as number **1584** on ①.

9758/60 – [12] and 🍷 Roma (**9758**) - Firenze (**9759**) - Pisa (**9760**) - Genova.

A – From Albenga.
F – [2] Pisa - Aulla - Fidenza - Bergamo.
S – From Savona.
V – From Ventimiglia.

g – Milano **Porta Garibaldi**.
o – Roma **Ostiense**.
r – Arrive 1746 on Ⓐ.

s – Stops to set down only.
w – Via Aulla and Fidenza.
y – Not Mar. 27, Apr. 24, and d before holidays.
z – Also Mar. 28, Apr. 25; not Mar. 27, Apr. 24.

PISA - ROMA 611

	ICN 1963 ♦	ICN 1699 ♦	ICN 799 ♦	2 ⚒	2 ⚒	IC 1571 ♦		IC 501 ♦	FB 9761 🍷		FB 9763 🍷	IC 505 ♦		IC 1533 Ⓒ	IC 657 Ⓐ	FB 9773 🍷		IC 511 ♦	2		FB 9777 🍷		FB 9781 🍷	2	2 Ⓑy
Torino P N **610** d.	...	2010	2155	...	...	...	...	...	...	...	...	...	...	...	...	...	...	1050	...	...	...	...	1520	...	...
Milano Centrale **610** d.	2010	|	|	...	...	...	...	...	...	...	...	...	...	0810	0810	...	...	|	...	...	1310	...	|	...	...
Genova P P **610** d.	2156	2207	2353	...	...	...	...	...	0549	...	0705	0851	...	0947	0947	1212	...	1238	...	...	1502	...	1659	...	...
Pisa Centrale **610** d.	0002	0051	0221	...	...	...	0545	0647	0732	0745	0911	1106	1145	1226	1220	1357	1343	1455	...	1545	1710	1745	1911	1945	2150
Livorno Centrale d.	0016	0120	0240j	...	...	0527	0603	0703	0746	0803	0927	1121	1203	1255	1255	1411	1400	1509	...	1603	1726	1803	1927	2003	2209
Rosignano d.	...	|	|	...	...	|	0620	|	|	0820	|	|	1220	|	|	|	1416	|	...	1620	|	1820	|	2020	2230
Cecina d.	...	|	|	...	...	0549	0629	0728	|	0829	|	1144	1229	1323	1326	|	1424	|	...	1629	|	1829	1949	2029	2238
Campiglia Marittima d.	...	|	|	...	...	0611	0650	0747	|	0851	1003	|	1251	1341	1350	|	1452	1544	...	1651	1801	1851	|	2051	2306
Follonica d.	...	|	|	...	...	0624	0700	0758	|	0902	|	1207	1302	1352	1401	|	1503	1556	...	1702	|	1902	|	2102	2318
Grosseto d.	...	0257	0357	0419	0523	0650	0728	0819	0838	0930	1029	1230	1330	1425	1433	1503	1530	1617	1629	1730	1827	1930	2027	2130	2343
Orbetello-Monte Argentario d.	...	|	|	0444	0549	0709	0751	0838	|	0953	|	|	1353	...	...	|	1553	|	1655	1753	|	1953	|	2153	...
Tarquinia d.	...	|	|	0518	0622	|	0827	|	|	1029	|	|	1429	...	...	|	1629	|	1729	1829	|	2029	|	2229	...
Civitavecchia d.	...	0425	0500	0532	0636	0750	0842	0918	|	1044	1118	1323	1444	...	...	1551	1644	1708	1743	1844	1918	2044	2118	2244	...
S. Marinella d.	...	|	|	0539	0643	|	0849	|	|	1051	|	|	1451	...	...	|	1651	|	1750	1851	|	2051	|	2251	...
Ladispoli-Cerveteri d.	...	|	|	0555	0700	|	0905	|	|	1105	|	|	1505	...	...	|	1705	|	1805	1905	|	2105	|	2305	...
Roma Ostiense a.	...	0520	0554	0633	0739	0834	0936	1018	|	1139	|	1420s	1536	...	...	|	1736	1752	1838	1936	|	2136	|	2336	...
Roma Termini **640** a.	...	|	|	0648	0750	0845	0948	|	1003	1150	1203	1433	1548	...	...	1632	1747	1803	1848	1948	2003	2148	2203	2348	...
Napoli Centrale **640** a.	...	0817	0817	...	...	1103	...	1229	...	...	...	...	...	...	...	...	...	2029	...	...	...	...	...	...	...

	ICN 1962 ♦	2 ⚒	2 †	2	2	FB 9764 🍷	IC 510 ♦		FB 9772 🍷		FB 9774 🍷	IC 1534 Ⓒ	IC 684 § Ⓐ		IC 518 ♦		FB 9782 🍷	FB 9784 🍷		IC 522 ♦	IC 1572 ♦		2	2 †	ICN 796 ♦	ICN 1696 ♦
poli Centrale **640** d.	...	...	...	...	...	...	0731	...	...	...	...	...	...	...	...	...	...	...	...	1731	1731	...	...	...	2146	2211
a Termini **640** d.	...	...	...	...	0612	0657	0957	1012	1157	1212	1357	...	...	1412	1557	1612	1657	1827	1812	|	|	2012	2112	2212	|	|
a Ostiense d.	...	...	...	...	0623	|	1007	1023	|	1223	|	...	...	1423	1607u	1623	|	|	1823	1941	1941	2023	2121	2223	0006	0033
poli-Cerveteri d.	...	...	...	...	0651	|	|	1051	|	1251	|	...	...	1451	|	1651	|	|	1855	|	|	2051	2155	2300	|	|
rinella d.	...	...	...	...	0706	|	|	1107	|	1307	|	...	...	1506	|	1706	|	|	1910	|	|	2106	2211	2315	|	|
avecchia d.	...	...	...	...	0715	0741	1047	1115	1241	1315	1439	...	...	1515	1647	1715	1741	1908	1924	2023	2023	2115	2220	2324	0053	0133
inia d.	...	...	...	...	0729	|	|	1129	|	1328	|	...	...	1528	|	1728	|	|	1937	|	|	2128	2233	2336	|	|
ello-Monte Argentario d.	...	0602	...	...	0801	|	|	1202	|	1400	|	...	...	1600	|	1800	|	|	2009	2102	2102	2200	2306	0009	|	|
seto d.	...	0628	0647	0738	0826	0833	1139	1227	1333	1427	1524	1604	1610	1625	1739	1825	1832	1954	2033	2121	2121	2227	2330	0034	0153	0244
nica d.	...	0652	0710	0810	0859	|	1158	1254	|	1453	|	1624	1631	1653	1759	1857	|	|	2057	2141	2141	2253	...	...	|	|
piglia Marittima d.	...	0704	0722	0825	0908	|	1209	1305	1357	1504	|	1636	1642	1704	|	1906	1856	|	2108	2151	2151	2304	...	...	|	|
a d.	...	0729	0746	0850	0930	0911	|	1327	|	1527	|	1655	1700	1727	1823	1928	|	|	2128	2210	2210	2327	...	...	|	|
nano d.	...	0737	0754	0858	0939	|	|	1336	|	1536	|	|	|	1736	|	1936	|	|	2136	|	|	2336	...	...	|	|
rno Centrale d.	0540s	0755	0812	0919	1001	0932	1245	1358	1431	1558	1615	1718	1724	1758	1846	1958	1931	2047	2158	2236	2239	2358	...	...	0309j	0404
Centrale **610** a.	0557s	0811	0829	0939	1018	0946	1300	1415	1445	1615	1627	1733	1739	1815	1900	2015	1945	2059	2215	2250	...	0015	...	...	0323	0418
nova P P **610** a.	0839	...	...	...	...	1156	1521	...	1658	...	1816	2015	2015	...	2132	...	2157	2244	...	...	...	...	...	...	0601	0723
ano Centrale **610** a.	1045	...	...	...	...	|	|	...	1847	...	...	2150	2150	...	...	...	...	...	...	...	...	...	...	...	|	|
Torino P N **610** a.	...	...	...	...	...	1340	1720	...	...	...	...	...	...	...	...	...	...	...	...	...	...	...	...	...	0810	0925

NOTES (LISTED BY TRAIN NUMBER)

- ⚒: [12] Sestri Levante - Napoli.
- [12] Ventimiglia - Genova - Roma.
- [12] Salerno - Torino.
- [12] Torino - Salerno.
- [12] Roma - Genova - Ventimiglia.
- Ⓑ: [12] Napoli - Sestri Levante.
- Not Jan. 7 - 16, 26 - 30: 🛏 1,2 cl., ▬ 2 cl. (4 berth) and [2] Salerno - Napoli - Torino. Train number **35796** on ①; **35096** on Feb. 6.
- Not Jan. 7 - 16, 26 - 30: 🛏 1,2 cl., ▬ 2 cl. (4 berth) and [2] Torino - Napoli - Salerno. Train number **35099** on Feb. 6.
- †: [12] Livorno - Napoli.
- ⑥ (also Mar. 27, Apr. 24, and days before holidays): [12] Napoli - Livorno.
- Jan. 7 - 16, 26 - 30: 🛏 1,2 cl., ▬ 2 cl. (4 berth) and [2] Salerno - Napoli - Torino.
- Jan. 7 - 16, 26 - 30: 🛏 1,2 cl., ▬ 2 cl. (4 berth) and [2] Torino - Napoli - Salerno.
- 🛏 1,2 cl., 🛏 1,2 cl. (T2) and ▬ 2 cl. (4 berth) Siracusa - Genova - Milano; 🛏 1,2 cl. and ▬ 2 cl. (4 berth) Palermo (**1964**) - Messina - Milano. Runs as train number **1584** on ①.
- 🛏 1,2 cl., 🛏 1,2 cl. (T2) and ▬ 2 cl. (4 berth) Milano - Genova - Siracusa; 🛏 1,2 cl. and ▬ 2 cl. (4 berth) Milano - Messina (**1965**) - Palermo. Runs as train number **35063** ②–⑤ Jan. 5 - Feb. 26; **35163** on Feb. 6.

j – Not Feb. 7.
s – Stops to set down only.
u – Stops to pick up only.
y – Not Mar. 27, Apr. 24, and days before holidays.
§ – Train number **35684** Jan. 11 - Feb. 14; runs 6 - 7 minutes earlier Grosseto - Cecina.

PARMA and FIDENZA - SARZANA and LA SPEZIA 612

st services 2nd class only

	⚒						B		⚒		⚒		⚒		⚒						⚒	⑤		⚒	⚒	†
Milano Centrale d.	...	...	...	...	...	0645	...	...	...	...	...	...	...	...	...	...	...	...	...	1705	...	1857g	...	...	...	...
Parma d.	...	...	0517	0625	0748	|	...	...	1228	1256	...	1344	...	1442	...	1549	1645	...	1747	|	1947	|	2057	2140	2240	2240
Fidenza d.	...	...	|	|	|	0824	0913	...	|	|	...	|	...	|	...	|	|	...	|	1830	|	2030	|	|	|	|
Fornovo d.	...	...	0534	0648	0813	0843	0930	...	1249	1322	...	1407	...	1506	...	1612	1708	...	1812	1851	2014	2047	2124	2208	2309	2310
Borgo Val di Taro d.	...	0544	0605	0725	0846	0931	0959	...	1322	1359	...	1444	...	1549	...	1644	1747	...	1848	1936	2045	2135	2157	2240	2342	2343
Pontremoli d.	0545	0601	0627	0743	0903	0953	1018	1216	1342	1416	1421	1503	1542	1607	1621	1700	1803	1822	1903	1957	2101	2152	2213	2255	2357	2359
Aulla Lunigiana d.	0608	0623	0657	0813	0922	1021	1035	1238	1410	...	1443	1522	1610	...	1643	1721	...	1843	1922	2027	2121	2211	2231	...	...	0019
S. Stefano di Magra d.	0615	0631	0704	0820	0930	1028	1042	1246	1416	...	1451	1531	1616	...	1651	1729	...	1851	1929	2034	2130	2219	2238	...	...	0026
Sarzana a.	|	0638	|	|	|	1042	1055	1255	|	...	1459	|	|	...	1659	|	...	1900	|	2042	|	2227	|	...	...	|
Pisa C **611** a.	|	0736	|	|	|	1145	1200	1345	|	...	1551	|	|	...	1751	|	...	1951	|	2138	|	2322	|	...	...	|
Livorno **611** a.	|	...	|	|	|	...	...	...	|	...	...	|	|	...	...	|	...	...	|	2155	|	2340	|	...	...	|
La Spezia Centrale a.	0631	...	0722	0838	0946	...	...	...	1432	...	...	1550	1633	...	...	1746	...	...	1947	...	2148	...	2258	...	...	0042

		⚒				⚒	⚒			⚒			⚒		⚒		⚒	⚒	⚒	⑦p		B	⚒				G
pezia Centrale d.	...	...	0540	0615	...	0810	0927	1012	1226	...	1325	1419	...	...	1527	1610	...	...	1729	...	1809	...	1927	...	2012	...	2103
Livorno **611** d.	...	...	|	|	0552	|	|	|	|	...	|	|	...	...	|	|	...	...	|	1703	|	...	|	...	|	...	|
Pisa C **611** a.	...	...	|	|	0610	|	|	|	|	...	|	|	1405	...	|	|	1605	...	|	1720	|	1822	|	1909	|	2006	|
rzana d.	...	...	|	|	0701	|	|	|	|	...	|	|	1457	...	|	|	1657	...	|	1807	|	1915	|	1959	|	2058	|
efano di Magra d.	...	...	0551	0631	0711	0829	0945	1030	1242	...	1343	1436	1509	...	1544	1629	1712	...	1747	1815	1828	1926	1943	2015	2029	2109	2118
Lunigiana d.	...	...	0558	0638	0718	0838	0952	1038	1249	...	1351	1443	1516	...	1551	1637	1718	...	1754	1823	1836	1932	1950	2025	2038	2116	2126
emoli d.	0413	0556	0627	0658	0740	0858	1015	1058	1308	1351	1413	1501	1539	1550	1612	1656	1739	1750	1820	1844	1858	1952	2015	2042	2057	2139	2148
Val di Taro d.	0429	0613	0641	0714	0800	0914	...	1114	1323	1407	...	1516	...	1607	...	1711	...	1807	...	1859	1914	2008	...	2057	2114	...	2205
ovo d.	0504	0649	0715	0744	0843	0953	...	1147	1402	1446	...	1550	...	1644	...	1746	...	1848	...	1936	1946	2047	...	2131	2148	...	2241
denza a.	|	|	|	|	0903	|	...	|	|	|	...	|	...	|	...	|	...	|	...	2000	|	2103	...	2156	|	...	|
a a.	0530	0710	0735	0805	|	1013	...	1206	1428	1510	...	1613	...	1710	...	1804	...	1913	...	|	2004	...	...	|	2209	...	2305
ano Centrale a.	...	...	...	...	1020	...	...	...	...	...	...	...	...	...	...	...	...	...	...	2133g	...	...	...	2320	...	...	...

[2] Bergamo - Pisa and v.v.
[2] Genova - La Spezia - Parma.

g – Milano **Porta Garibaldi**.
p – Also Mar. 28, Apr. 25; not Mar. 27, Apr. 24.
* – Fidenza - Fornovo is *25 km*.

613 FIRENZE - SIENA, PISA, PISA AEROPORTO ✈ and LIVORNO

Most services 2nd class

Pisa Centrale - Pisa Aeroporto and v.v. is currently closed for construction work (see footnote)

km		⚒		⚒					⚒	1239 ♦			FB 9759 ♦				⚒		⚒	⚒				
0	**Firenze** SMN **614** d.	0430	0535	...	0608	0620	0653	0700	...	0711	0728	...	0738c	0753	0810	0828	0910	0928	0953	1010	1028	1053	1100	1110
34	Empoli d.	0506	0601	0621	0645	0650	0730	0722	0726	|	0758	0806	|	0827	0840	0858	0940	0958	1027	1040	1058	1127	|	1140
	Poggibonsi ▲ d.	|	|	0702	|	0724j	|	|	0811	|	|	0848	|	|	0915	|	1015	|	|	1115	|	|	|	1215
	Siena 609 619 a.	|	|	0731	|	0747j	|	|	0840	|	|	0915	|	|	0938	|	1038	|	|	1138	|	|	|	1238
81	**Pisa** Centrale **614** ¶ d.	0555	0637	...	0732	...	0809	0752	...	0834	0837	...	0826	0903	...	0932	...	1032	1103	...	1132	1203	1153	...
	Pisa Aeroporto ✈ ¶ a.	|	|	...	...	...	|	|	...	|	|	...	...	...	...	|	...	|	...	...	|	...	|	...
101	**Livorno** Centrale a.	0616	0651	...	...	...	0826	0808	...	0850	0851	...	...	...	...	0948	...	1048	...	...	1148	...	1208	...

km		⚒	⚒					⚒	⚒	⚒		†				⚒			⚒			Ⓑ	⑥	⚒
	Firenze SMN **614** d.	...	1153	1210	1228	...	1253	1300	1310	1328	...	1338	1353	1410	1428	...	1453	1500	1510	1528	...	1538	1546	1610
0	Empoli d.	1208	1227	1240	1258	1308	1327	|	1340	1358	1408	1413	1427	1440	1458	1508	1527	|	1540	1558	1608	1613	1626	1640
38	Poggibonsi ▲ d.	1249	|	1315	|	1349	|	|	1415	|	1449	|	|	1514	|	1549	|	|	1615	|	1649	|	|	1715
63	**Siena 609 619** a.	1314	|	1338	|	1414	|	|	1438	|	1515	|	|	1537	|	1614	|	|	1638	|	1714	|	|	1738
	Pisa Centrale **614** ¶ d.	...	1304	...	1332	...	1403	1401	...	1432	...	1509	1503	...	1532	...	1603	1553	...	1632	...	1659	1703	...
	Pisa Aeroporto ✈ ¶ a.	...	...	...	|	...	...	|	...	|	...	|	...	...	|	...	...	|	...	|	...	...	...	...
	Livorno Centrale a.	...	...	...	1348	...	...	1416	...	1448	...	1526	...	...	1548	...	...	1612	...	1648	...	...	...	...

	⚒		⚒				Ⓐ							⚒			⚒	⚒					
Firenze SMN **614** d.	...	1653	1700	1710	1728	1738	1753	1810	1828	1853	1900	1910	1928	...	1953	2010	2028	...	2038	2053	2128	...	2157
Empoli d.	1708	1727	|	1740	1758	1813	1827	1840	1858	1927	|	1940	1958	2008	2027	2040	2058	2108	2113	2127	2158	2208	2233
Poggibonsi ▲ d.	1749	|	|	1815	|	|	|	1915	|	|	|	2015	|	2049	|	2115	|	2152	|	|	|	2250	|
Siena 609 619 a.	1814	|	|	1838	|	|	|	1938	|	|	|	2038	|	2114	|	2144	|	2216	|	|	|	2314	|
Pisa Centrale **614** ¶ d.	...	1803	1753	...	1832	1858	1904	...	1932	2003	1949	...	2032	...	2103	...	2128	...	2158	2205	2232j	...	2327
Pisa Aeroporto ✈ ¶ a.	...	...	|	...	|	|	...	...	|	...	...	...	|	...	...	...	...	...	...	|	|	...	|
Livorno Centrale a.	...	...	1808	...	1846	1912	...	...	1948	...	...	...	2048	...	...	...	...	...	...	2224	2248j	...	2344

km			⚒		⚒		⚒	⚒	†	⚒	⚒	†	⚒			⚒					⚒	†	⚒	⚒
	Livorno Centrale d.	...	0500	0519	...	0612	...	...	...	...	0710	...	...	0730	0743	...	0812	...	0852	...	0912	0912	...	1012
0	Pisa Aeroporto ✈ ¶ d.	...	|	|	...	|	...	...	...	...	|	...	...	|	|	...	|	...	|	...	|	|	...	|
2	**Pisa** Centrale **614** ¶ d.	0415	0519	0539	...	0629	...	...	...	...	0732	0732	...	0754	0801	...	0832	...	0912	...	0932	0932	...	1032
	Siena 609 619 d.	|	|	|	0543	|	0625	0613	0636	0636	|	|	0702	|	|	0732	|	0818	|	0847	|	|	0918	|
	Poggibonsi ▲ d.	|	|	|	0606	|	|	0648	0658	0659	|	|	0728	|	|	0805	|	0846	|	0909	|	|	0946	|
	Empoli d.	0453	0602	0618	0645	0659	0709	0723	0735	0750	0804	0804	0820	0832	0847	0852	0904	0921	|	0940	1004	1017	1021	1104
	Firenze SMN **614** a.	0527	0638	0652	0721	0727	0734	0752	0802	0827	0832	0832	0855	0907	0922	...	0932	0950	1000	1005	1032	1046	1050	1132

	⚒	⚒		⚒	⚒				⚒							⚒		⚒	⚒	Ⓒ			⚒	
Livorno Centrale d.	...	...	1112	...	...	...	1212	...	...	1252	1312	...	...	1343	1412	...	...	1452	1512	...	...	1608	...	...
Pisa Aeroporto ✈ ¶ d.	...	...	|	...	...	...	|	...	...	|	|	...	...	|	|	...	...	|	|	...	...	|	...	...
Pisa Centrale **614** ¶ d.	1112	...	1132	...	1154	...	1232	...	1254	1312	1332	...	1354	1401	1432	...	1454	1512	1532	1554	...	1632	...	1654
Siena 609 619 d.	|	1041	|	1118	|	1141	|	1218	|	|	|	1318	|	|	|	1418	|	|	|	|	1518	|	1618	|
Poggibonsi ▲ d.	|	1112	|	1146	|	1212	|	1246	|	|	|	1346	|	|	|	1446	|	|	|	|	1546	|	1646	|
Empoli d.	|	1152	1204	1221	1232	1252	1304	1321	1332	|	1404	1421	1432	1447	1504	1521	1532	|	1604	1632	1621	1704	1721	1732
Firenze SMN **614** a.	1200	...	1232	1250	1307	...	1332	1350	1407	1400	1432	1450	1507	1524	1532	1550	1607	1600	1632	1712	1650	1732	1750	1807

			Ⓑ	⑥	Ⓑ						⚒	†		EN 1232/4 ♦	⚒		Ⓐ			⚒	FB 9788 ♦			
Livorno Centrale d.	1712	...	...	...	...	...	1812	...	...	1852	...	...	...	1920	...	...	...	...	2012	...	...	...	...	2112
Pisa Aeroporto ✈ ¶ d.	|	...	...	...	...	...	|	...	...	|	...	...	...	|	...	...	...	...	|	...	...	...	...	|
Pisa Centrale **614** ¶ d.	1732	...	1754	1754	1801	...	1832	...	1854	1912	...	...	1932	1946	...	1954	2001	...	2032	2038	2051	...	2101	2132
Siena 609 619 d.	|	1719	|	|	|	1741	|	1818	|	|	1841	1847	|	|	1918	|	|	1941	|	|	|	2018	|	|
Poggibonsi ▲ d.	|	1746	|	|	|	1812	|	1846	|	|	1912	1912	|	|	1946	|	|	2012	|	|	|	2046	|	|
Empoli d.	1804	1821	1832	1836	1847	1852	1904	1921	1932	|	1952	1952	2004	|	2021	2033	2047	2052	2104	2111	|	2121	2147	2204
Firenze SMN **614** a.	1832	1850	1907	1915	1922	...	1932	1950	2007	2000	...	...	2032	2044	2050	2107	2122	...	2132	2142	2140c	2150	2222	2232

♦ – NOTES (LISTED BY TRAIN NUMBER)

1232/4 – ④⑥ Mar. 19 - Oct. 15 (also Mar. 28, May 16, Aug. 15): 🛏 1, 2 cl. (T2), ▬ 2 cl. and (2) Livorno - Pisa - Firenze (**1236/8**) - Wien.

1239 – ③⑤ Mar. 18 - Oct. 14; also Mar. 27, May 15, Aug. 14 (from Wien): 🛏 1, 2 cl. (T2), ▬ 2 cl. and (2) Wien - Firenze (**1239**) - Pisa - Livorno.

9759 – (12) and 🍸 Roma (**9758**) - Firenze (**9759**) - Pisa (**9760**) - Genova.

9788 – (12) and 🍸 Genova (**9787**) - Pisa (**9788**) - Firenze (**9789**) - Roma.

c – Firenze **Campo di Marte**.

j – 5–7 minutes later on ⚒.

▲ – Poggibonsi-S. Gimignano.

¶ – Pisa Centrale - Pisa Aeroporto and v.v. has closed for conversion into an auton[...] metro route (due to open September 2016). Currently a shuttle 🚌 service ope[...] every 10 minutes between 0600 and 2400. Journey time: ±8 minutes.

Operator: Pisa Mover.

614 FIRENZE - LUCCA - VIAREGGIO and PISA

Most services 2nd class

km		⚒	⚒	⚒	⚒			⚒		†	⚒						†	Ⓐ					
0	**Firenze** SMN **613** d.	...	0510	...	...	...	0603	...	0710	...	...	0738	0810	...	0910	...	1010	...	...	1210	...	and at	1610
17	Prato Centrale d.	...	0533	...	...	...	0623	...	0729	...	...	0759	0831	...	0931	...	1031	...	...	1231	...	the same	1631
34	Pistoia d.	...	0551	...	...	...	0640	...	0745	...	...	0816	0844	...	0944	...	1044	...	...	1244	...	minutes	1644
47	Montecatini Centro d.	...	0604	...	...	...	0658	...	0801	...	...	0832	0901	...	1001	...	1101	...	...	1301	...	past each	1701
78	Lucca ⊡ d.	0537	0646	0652	0708	0742	0755	0813	0830	0842	0850	0923	0930	0942	1030	1042	1130	1242	1312	1330	1342	hour	1730
101	**Viareggio** a.	|	0707	|	|	|	|	|	0850	|	|	...	0950	|	1053	|	1150	|	|	1350	|	until	1750
	Pisa Centrale **613** ⊡ a.	0602	...	0716	0741	0813	0825	0842	...	0913	0916	...	...	1013	...	1109	...	1313	1343	...	1413		...

		†	⚒							⚒		
Firenze SMN **613** d.	1710	...	...	1810	...	1910	...	2010	...	2110	2210	...
Prato Centrale d.	1731	...	...	1831	...	1931	...	2031	...	2131	2231	...
Pistoia d.	1744	...	...	1844	...	1944	...	2044	...	2144	2246	...
Montecatini Centro d.	1801	...	...	1901	...	2001	...	2101	...	2200	2301	...
Lucca ⊡ d.	1830	1831	1842	1930	1942	2030	2042	2130	2142	2249	2330	...
Viareggio a.	1850	|	|	1950	|	2050	|	2150	|	2309	2350	...
Pisa Centrale **613** ⊡ a.	...	1901	1913	...	2014	...	2113	...	2213	...	...	...

	⚒		⚒	⚒		
Pisa Centrale **613** ⊡ d.	...	0525	...	0613	...	...
Viareggio d.	...	|	0545	|	0628	0710
Lucca ⊡ d.	0505	0559	0609	0639	0648	0727
Montecatini Centro d.	0533	...	0641	...	0715	0753
Pistoia d.	0551	...	0708	...	0732	0812
Prato Centrale d.	0611	...	0727	...	0747	0827
Firenze SMN **613** a.	0637	...	0750	...	0806	0850

km		⚒																			⚒		
0	**Pisa** Centrale **613** ⊡ d.	...	0750	...	0850	...	0950	...	1020	...	1250	...	1343	...	1450	...	and at	1950	...	2050	...	2150	...
	Viareggio d.	...	|	0810	|	0910	|	1010	|	1207	|	1310	|	1410	|	1510	the same	|	2010	|	2110	|	2210
24	Lucca ⊡ d.	0740	0823	0831	0920	0931	1017	1031	1047	1231	1317	1331	1409	1431	1517	1531	minutes	2017	2031	2117	2131	2217	2231
	Montecatini Centro d.	0821	...	0857	...	0957	...	1057	...	1257	...	1357	...	1457	...	1557	past each	...	2057	...	2157	...	2257
	Pistoia d.	0841	...	0912	...	1012	...	1112	...	1312	...	1412	...	1512	...	1612	hour	...	2112	...	2212	...	2312
	Prato Centrale d.	0900	...	0929	...	1030	...	1128	...	1329	...	1430	...	1529	...	1629	until	...	2129	...	2229	...	2329
	Firenze SMN **613** a.	0922	...	0950	...	1100	...	1150	...	1350	...	1450	...	1550	...	1650		...	2150	...	2250	...	2350

⊡ – Additional services operate Lucca - Pisa Centrale and v.v. on ⚒.

MILANO and TORINO - BOLOGNA — 615

For high-speed services – see Table 600

		FR 9507 🍷	A	P	IC 583 ♦	R	2	IC 605 T	IC 1589 ♦		FB 9803 🍷C		2	A	A		FB 9807 🍷C		IC 1545 ♦	A	FB 9809 🍷T		FB 9811 🍷C		A
Milano Centrale d.	0515	0542	...	0620	0650	...	0645	0710	0645	0715	0735	...	...	...	...	0920	...	...	1000	...	1035	1120	1135	...	...
Milano Rogoredo d.	0527	|	...	|	0702u	...	0700	0722u	0656u	0727	|	...	...	...	...	0932	...	...	1012u	...	|	1132	|	...	...
Torino P N **610** d.	|	|	...	|	|	...	|	|	|	|	|	...	...	...	...	|	0832	...	|	...	|	|	|	...	...
Asti **610** d.	|	|	...	|	|	...	|	|	|	|	|	...	...	...	...	|	0908	...	|	...	|	|	|	...	...
Alessandria **610** d.	|	|	...	|	|	...	|	|	|	|	|	...	...	...	...	|	0924	...	|	...	|	|	|	...	...
Tortona **610** d.	|	|	...	|	|	...	|	|	|	|	|	...	...	...	...	|	|	...	|	...	|	|	|	...	...
Voghera **610** d.	|	|	...	|	|	0700	|	|	|	|	|	...	0804	...	...	|	|	...	|	...	|	|	|	...	...
Piacenza d.	0609	0629	0652	0715	0745	0752	0759	0810	0739	0814	0820	←	0844	0852	0952	1014	1020	←	1048	1052	1120	1214	1220	←	1252
Fidenza d.	0632	|	0715	0739	0803	0815	0821	0827	0809	0841	|	0843	...	0915	1015	1041	|	1043	1105	1115	|	1241	|	1243	1315
Parma d.	0646	0658	0730	0754	0816	0830	...	0840	0823	→	0846	0856	...	0930	1030	→	1046	1056	1121	1130	1146	→	1246	1256	1330
Reggio Emilia d.	0704	0715	0747	0810	0833	0847	...	0855	0839	...	0900	0914	...	0947	1047	...	1100	1114	1138	1147	1200	...	1300	1314	1347
Modena d.	0721	0730	0801	0826	0850	0901	...	0924	0856	...	0915	0932	...	1001	1101	...	1115	1132	1153	1201	1215	...	1315	1332	1401
Bologna Centrale **620** a.	0802	0752	0828	0902	0914	0928	...	0954	0933	...	0938	1008	...	1028	1128	...	1138	1208	1219	1228	1238	...	1338	1408	1428
Roma Termini **620** a.	...	1010	...	...	1317t	...	...	...	1311t	...	...	...	...	...	...	...	...	...	...	...	...	...	...	...	...

	FB 9813 🍷C	2	R		FB 9815 🍷C		A	IC 597 ♦	A		IC 613 E	FB 9819 🍷B		ICN 795 ♦	2	A	R	2		FB 9823 🍷E		IC 599 ♦	2	A		FB 9825 🍷A
no Centrale d.	1235	...	...	1320	1335	...	...	1450	...	1520	1510	1535	...	1544g	...	...	...	1705	1720	1735	...	1743	...	...	1815	1835
no Rogoredo d.	|	...	...	1332	|	...	...	1501u	...	1532	1522u	|	...	|	...	...	...	1717	1732	|	...	1801u	...	...	1827	|
rino P N **610** d.	|	...	...	|	|	...	...	|	...	|	|	|	...	|	...	...	...	|	|	|	...	|	...	...	|	|
ti **610** d.	|	...	...	|	|	...	...	|	...	|	|	|	...	|	...	...	...	|	|	|	...	|	...	...	|	|
essandria **610** d.	|	...	...	|	|	...	...	|	...	|	|	|	...	|	...	...	...	|	|	|	...	|	...	...	|	|
rtona **610** d.	|	1252	...	|	|	...	...	|	...	|	|	|	...	|	...	...	...	|	|	|	...	|	...	...	|	|
oghera **610** d.	|	1303	...	|	|	...	...	|	...	|	|	|	...	|	1607	...	...	|	|	|	...	|	1807	...	|	|
enza d.	1320	1342	1346	1414	1420	←	1452	1545	1552	1614	1610	1620	←	1630	1647	1652	1752	1805	1814	1820	←	1845	1847	1852	1909	1922
nza d.	|	...	1415	1441	|	1443	1515	1603	1615	1641	1627	|	1643	|	...	1715	1815	1826	1841	|	1843	1903	...	1915	1931	|
na d.	1346	...	1430	→	1446	1456	1530	1616	1630	→	1640	1646	1656	1705	...	1730	1830	...	→	1846	1856	1916	...	1930	→	1948
gio Emilia d.	1400	...	1447	...	1500	1514	1547	1633	1647	...	1655	1700	1714	1722	...	1747	1847	...	...	1900	1914	1933	...	1947	...	2002
ena d.	1415	...	1501	...	1515	1532	1601	1650	1701	...	1724	1715	1732	1741	...	1801	1901	...	...	1915	1932	1950	...	2001	...	2017
ogna Centrale **620** a.	1438	...	1528	...	1538	1608	1628	1714	1728	...	1746	1738	1808	|	...	1828	1928	...	...	1938	2008	2014	...	2028	...	2038
oma Termini **620** a.	...	...	...	...	...	...	...	2118t	...	...	...	...	...	2313t	...	...	...	...	...	...	...	...	...	...	...	...

		R	2⑤		FB 9829 🍷A	ICN 765 ♦		ICN 755 ♦	2		ICN 757 ♦	§ 2	ICN 797 ♦
no Centrale d.	...	...	1857g	1920	1935	1950	...	2050	...	2120	...	2215	2317g
no Rogoredo d.	...	...	1918	1932	|	|	...	|	...	2132	...	2228	|
rino P N **610** d.	...	...	|	|	|	|	...	|	...	|	2020	|	|
ti **610** d.	...	...	|	|	|	|	...	|	...	|	2101	|	|
essandria **610** d.	...	...	|	|	|	|	...	|	...	|	2122	|	|
rtona **610** d.	...	1850	|	|	|	|	...	|	...	|	2139	|	|
oghera **610** d.	...	1903	|	|	|	|	2007	|	...	|	2153	|	|
enza d.	←	1952	2006	2014	2020	|	2052	2134	2152	2214	2230	2305	0011
nza d.	1933	2015	2028	2043	|	|	2115	|	2215	2242	|	|	|
na d.	1956	2030	...	2056	2046	|	2130	2206	2230	2257	|	2332	0101
gio Emilia d.	2016	2047	...	2114	2100	|	2147	2224	2247	...	|	2347	|
ena d.	2034	2101	...	2134	2115	|	2201	2240	2301	...	|	0001	|
ogna Centrale **620** a.	2108	2128	...	2208	2138	2155	2230	2305	2328	...	2347	0030	|
oma Termini **620** a.	...	...	...	...	...	...	...	...	...	...	...	...	0717t

	ICN 1580 ♦	ICN 798 ♦	ICN 758 ♦					ICN 752 ♦
Roma Termini **620** d.	...	2343t	...	...	...	...	...	...
Bologna Centrale **620** d.	0357	|	0432	0500	...	0528	0552	0620
Modena d.	|	|	|	0524	...	0555	0625	0645
Reggio Emilia d.	|	|	|	0538	...	0610	0642	0702
Parma d.	|	0521	|	0553	0610	0627	0705	0724
Fidenza d.	|	|	|	0607	0624	0639	0726	|
Piacenza d.	0516	0602	|	0638	0650	0706	0755	0816
Voghera **610** d.	0550	|	|	0718	|	|	|	|
Tortona **610** d.	0603	|	|	...	|	|	|	|
Alessandria **610** d.	0624	|	|	...	|	|	|	|
Asti **610** d.	0646	|	|	...	|	|	|	|
Torino P N **610** a.	0740	|	|	...	|	|	|	|
Milano Rogoredo a.	...	|	|	...	0733	0746	0838	|
Milano Centrale a.	...	0711g	0712	...	0745	0800	0850	0930

	2	FB 9802 🍷A	A	ICN 754 ♦			FB 9804 🍷A	A	FB 9806 🍷E	A	2	IC 580 ♦		A	IC 604 E	FB 9810 🍷B	A	ICN 794 ♦		R	2	FB 9814 🍷C	A		A	FB 9818 🍷C
oma Termini **620** d.	...	...	...	...	...	...	...	...	...	...	...	...	...	...	...	...	...	0639t	...	...	...	...	...	...	...	...
ogna Centrale **620** d.	...	0705	0728	0734	...	0752	0818	0828	0918	0928	...	0946	0952	1028	1105	1118	1128	1142	1152	1228	...	1318	1328	1352	1428	1518
ena d.	...	0725	0756	|	...	0825	0840	0856	0941	0956	...	1007	1025	1056	1136	1141	1156	1217	1225	1256	...	1341	1356	1425	1456	1541
gio Emilia d.	...	0738	0810	|	...	0842	0853	0910	0954	1010	...	1021	1042	1110	1201	1154	1210	1234	1242	1310	...	1354	1410	1442	1510	1554
na d.	...	0753	0825	|	...	0905	0908	0925	1010	1025	...	1036	1105	1125	1218	1210	1225	1256	1305	1325	...	1410	1425	1505	1525	1610
nza d.	...	|	0837	|	0905	0923	|	0937	|	1037	...	1054	1117	1137	1230	|	1237	|	1326	1337	...	|	1437	1517	1537	|
enza d.	0817	0824	0905	0911	0930	0950	0937	1005	1041	1105	1115	1119	1150	1205	1252	1241	1305	1328	1350	1405	1423	1441	1505	1550	1605	1641
oghera **610** d.	0855	|	...	0942	|	|	|	...	|	...	1155	|	|	...	|	|	...	|	|	...	1504	|	...	|	...	|
rtona **610** d.	0908	|	...	0953	|	|	|	...	|	...	...	|	|	...	|	|	...	|	|	...	1516	|	...	|	...	|
essandria **610** d.	...	|	...	1015	|	|	|	...	|	...	...	|	|	...	|	|	...	|	|	...	...	|	...	|	...	|
sti **610** d.	...	|	...	1041	|	|	|	...	|	...	...	|	|	...	|	|	...	|	|	...	...	|	...	|	...	|
orino P N **610** a.	...	|	...	1120	|	|	|	...	|	...	...	|	|	...	|	|	...	|	|	...	...	|	...	|	...	|
no Rogoredo a.	...	0859s	...	...	1007	1033	1014s	...	|	...	...	1204s	1233	...	1332s	|	...	|	1433	...	...	|	...	1633	...	|
no Centrale a.	...	0910	...	...	1020	1045	1025	...	1125	...	...	1215	1245	...	1345	1325	...	1442g	1445	...	...	1525	...	1645	...	1725

	A	2		R	IC 590 ♦	FB 9822 🍷T	A	2		FB 9824 🍷C	R	IC 1546 ♦	IC 612 T	FB 9826 🍷C	A			IC 596 ♦	2	P	FB 9830 🍷C	A	IC 1588 ♦	FR 9560 🍷	R
Roma Termini **620** d.	...	...	...	...	1240t	...	...	...	...	...	...	...	...	...	...	...	...	1639t	...	...	...	...	1710t	1935	...
Bologna Centrale **620** d.	1528	...	1552	1628	1646	1718	1728	...	1752	1818	1828	1840	1905	1918	1928	1952	2028	2046	...	2052	2118	2128	2135	2155	2219
Modena d.	1556	...	1625	1656	1707	1741	1756	...	1825	1841	1856	1910	1936	1941	1956	2025	2056	2108	...	2116	2141	2156	2203	2217	2245
Reggio Emilia d.	1610	...	1642	1710	1721	1754	1810	...	1842	1854	1910	1924	2001	1954	2010	2042	2110	2122	...	2132	2154	2210	2217	2231	2258
Parma d.	1625	...	1705	1725	1736	1810	1825	...	1905	1910	1925	1940	2018	2010	2025	2105	2125	2138	...	2149	2210	2225	2235	2247	2325
Fidenza d.	1637	...	1717	1737	1754	|	1837	...	1923	|	1937	1954	2030	|	2037	2126	2137	2154	2158	2205	|	2237	2249	|	...
Piacenza d.	1705	1715	1750	1805	1819	1841	1909	1915	1950	1941	2005	2019	2052	2041	2105	2150	2205	2219	2226	2232	2241	2305	2311	2317	...
Voghera **610** d.	...	1755	|	...	|	|	...	1955	|	|	...	|	|	|	...	|	...	|	|	|	|	...	|	|	...
Tortona **610** d.	...	...	|	...	|	|	...	...	|	|	...	|	|	|	...	|	...	|	|	|	|	...	|	|	...
Alessandria **610** d.	...	...	|	...	|	|	...	...	|	2044	...	|	|	|	...	|	...	|	|	|	|	...	|	|	...
Asti **610** d.	...	...	|	...	|	|	...	...	|	2102	...	|	|	|	...	|	...	|	|	|	|	...	|	|	...
Torino P N **610** a.	...	...	|	...	|	|	...	...	|	2140	...	|	|	|	...	|	...	|	|	|	|	...	|	|	...
Milano Rogoredo a.	...	...	1833	...	1906s	|	...	...	2033	...	...	2104s	2134s	|	...	2233	...	2304s	2308	2315	|	...	2353s	|	...
Milano Centrale a.	...	...	1845	...	1917	1925	...	...	2045	...	...	2115	2145	2125	...	2245	...	2315	2320	2325	2325	...	0005	2345	...

NOTES (LISTED BY TRAIN NUMBER)

– [12] Terni - Milano.
– [12] Milano - Napoli.
– [12] Napoli - Milano.
– [12] Napoli - Milano.
– [12] Milano - Napoli.
– [12] Milano - Terni.
– 🛏 1, 2 cl., ▬ 2 cl. (4 berth) and [2] Lecce - Bologna - Milano.
– ①–⑥: 🛏 1, 2 cl., ▬ 2 cl. (4 berth) and [2] Lecce - Bologna - Torino.
– 🛏 1, 2 cl., ▬ 2 cl. (4 berth) and [2] Milano - Bologna - Lecce.
– 🛏 1, 2 cl., ▬ 2 cl. (4 berth) and [2] Torino - Bologna - Lecce.
– 🛏 1, 2 cl., ▬ 2 cl. (4 berth) and [2] Lecce - Bologna - Milano.
– 🛏 1, 2 cl., ▬ 2 cl. (4 berth) and [2] Milano - Bologna - Lecce.
– 🛏 1, 2 cl., ▬ 2 cl. (4 berth) and [2] Reggio di Calabria - Milano - Torino.
– 🛏 1, 2 cl., ▬ 2 cl. (4 berth) and [2] Torino - Milano - Reggio di Calabria. Train number **1595** on ①.
– 🛏 1, 2 cl., ▬ 2 cl. (4 berth) and [2] Torino - Milano - Napoli - Salerno.

798 – 🛏 1, 2 cl., ▬ 2 cl. (4 berth) and [2] Salerno - Napoli - Milano - Torino.
1545 – ⑥ (also June 2; not June 4, and days before holidays): [12] Milano - Lecce.
1546 – ⑦ (also Mar. 28, Apr. 25; not Mar. 27, Apr. 24): [12] Lecce - Milano.
1580 – ⑦: 🛏 1, 2 cl., ▬ 2 cl. (4 berth) and [2] Lecce - Bologna - Torino.
1588 – ⑦ (also Mar. 28, Apr. 25; not Mar. 27, Apr. 24): [12] Reggio di Calabria - Milano.
1589 – ⑥ (not June 4): [12] Milano - Reggio di Calabria.

A – From / to Ancona.
B – From / to Bari.
C – From / to Lecce.
E – From / to Pescara.
P – ⑥⑦ (also Mar. 28, Apr. 25; not Mar. 27, Apr. 24): [2] Milano - Pescara and v.v.

R – From / to Rimini.
T – From / to Taranto.

g – Milano **Porta Garibaldi**.
s – Stops to set down only.
t – Roma **Tiburtina**.
u – Stops to pick up only.

§ – Operator: *TPER*. Trenitalia tickets valid.

616 VENEZIA - BOLOGNA

For additional high-speed trains Venezia - Padova - Bologna - Roma see Table **600** (only trains calling at Rovigo or Ferrara are included below)

km		*EN* 235 ♦	*EN* 1237 ♦	*FA* 9401	⚒		*FB* 9801 ♦		*FA* 9411 T		*IC* 585 ♦							*FB* 9817 ♦	*IC* 595 ♦			*FA* 9447				
0	**Venezia** Santa Lucia **605**. d.	...	...	...	...	0642	0657	0742	...	0842	...	1042	1142	...	1242	1342	1442	1457	...	1542	1642	1725	1742	1842	1942	2142
9	**Venezia** Mestre **605** .... d.	0311	...	0537	0554	0654	0709u	0754	0837	0854	0929	1054	1154	...	1254	1354	1454	1509u	1514	1554	1654	1737u	1754	1854	1954	2154
37	Padova **605** .... d.	|	0418	0553	0610	0710	0724	0810	0853	0910	0945	1110	1210	...	1310	1410	1510	1524	1532	1610	1710	1753	1810	1910	2010	2210
81	Rovigo .... d.	|	0445	0613	0650	0750	0746	0850	|	0950	1022	1150	1250	...	1350	1450	1550	1546	1600	1650	1750	|	1850	1950	2050	2248
113	Ferrara .... d.	0408	0506	|	0712	0811	0803	0911	0925	1011	1042	1211	1311	...	1411	1511	1611	1603	1621	1711	1811	1825	1910	2014	2111	...
160	**Bologna** Centrale .... a.	0434	0541	0650	0743	0840	0835	0940	0950	1040	1108	1240	1340	...	1441	1540	1640	1633	1645	1740	1840	1850	1940	2044	2140	...
	Roma Termini **600 620**. a.	0922	...	0910	...	...	...	...	1210	...	1520	...	...	...	...	...	...	...	2036	...	...	2110	...	...	...	...

	ICN 774 ♦	⚒			*FA* 9402			*FA* 9408			*FB* 9816 ♦		*IC* 588 ♦					*FA* 9442 U		*IC* 592 ♦		*FB* 9828 ♦		*FA* 9454	*EN* 1236/8 ♦	*EN* 234 ♦
Roma Termini **600 620** .. d.	2235	...	...	...	0650	...	...	0835	...	...	...	...	1030	...	...	...	...	1650	...	1540	...	...	...	1950	...	1904
Bologna Centrale .... d.	0318	0620	0720	0820	0910	0920	1018	1055	1220	1320	1416	1427	1452	1520	1618	1718	1820	1910	1920	1952	...	2016	2120	2210	2223	2320
Ferrara .... d.	0349	0651	0751	0851	0932	0951	1051	|	1251	1351	1443	1457	1518	1551	1651	1751	1851	|	1951	2018	...	2043	2151	2232	2256	2348
Rovigo .... d.	0411	0710	0810	0910	|	1010	1110	1132	1310	1410	1500	1515	1534	1610	1710	1810	1910	1946	2010	2035	...	2100	2210	|	2319	|
Padova **605** .... d.	0450	0751	0851	0951	1009	1051	1147	1154	1347	1451	1532	1551	1602	1651	1751	1851	2000	2009	2051	2102	...	2132	2251	2309	2347	|
Venezia Mestre **605** .... a.	0508	0806	0906	1006	1023s	1106	1203	1208s	1403	1506	1548s	1606	1619	1706	1806	1906	2014	2021	2106	2118	...	2148s	2306	2323s	...	0045
Venezia Santa Lucia **605** .. a.	0520	0818	0918	1018	1035	1118	1218	1220	1418	1518	1600	1618	...	1718	1818	1918	2026	...	2118	...	...	2200	2318	2335	...	...

♦ – NOTES (LISTED BY TRAIN NUMBER)

234 – 🛏 1, 2 cl., ▬ 2 cl. and [2] Roma - Venezia Mestre - Villach - Wien.
235 – 🛏 1, 2 cl., ▬ 2 cl. and [2] Wien - Villach - Venezia Mestre - Roma.
585 – [12] Trieste (**584**) - Venezia Mestre - Roma.
588 – [12] Roma - Venezia Mestre (**589**) - Trieste.
592 – [12] Roma - Venezia Mestre (**593**) - Trieste.
595 – [12] Trieste (**594**) - Venezia Mestre - Roma.
771 – 🛏 1, 2 cl., ▬ 2 cl. (4 berth) and [2] Trieste (**770**) - Udine - Venezia - Roma.
774 – 🛏 1, 2 cl., ▬ 2 cl. (4 berth) and [2] Roma - Venezia - Udine (**775**) - Trieste.
1236/8 – ④⑥ Mar. 19 - Oct. 15 (also Mar. 28, May 16): 🛏 1, 2 cl. (T2), ▬ 2 cl. and [2] Livorno (**1232/4**) - Pisa - Firenze - Wien.
1237 – ③⑤ Mar. 18 - Oct. 14; also Mar. 27, May 15 (from Wien): 🛏 1, 2 cl. (T2), ▬ 2 cl. and [2] Wien - Firenze (**1239**) - Pisa - Livorno.

9801 – [12] and 🍸 Venezia - Bologna - Lecce.
9816 – [12] and 🍸 Lecce - Bologna - Venezia.
9817 – [12] and 🍸 Venezia - Bologna - Lecce.
9828 – [12] and 🍸 Lecce - Bologna - Venezia.

T – To/from Trieste (Table **601**).
U – To/from Udine (Table **601**).
s – Stops to set down only.
u – Stops to pick up only.

619 SIENA - CHIUSI-CHIANCIANO TERME

2nd class o

km		⚒	†	†	⚒	†		⚒	⚒	⚒	†	⚒		†	⚒	⚒		⚒	†	⚒		⚒	†	⚒
0	Siena **609 613** .... d.	0554	0600	0802	0804	1002	...	1215	1328	1357	1402	1443	...	1602	1604	1655	...	1743	1802	1815	...	1927	2002	2024
89	Chiusi-Chianciano Terme **620** ..... a.	0715	0721	0927	0923	1127	...	1330	1448	1523	1523	1615	...	1727	1719	1820	...	1851	1927	1942	...	2053	2127	2142

	⚒	⚒	†		⚒	⚒	†		⚒	†	⚒		†	⚒	⚒	†	⚒		†	⚒	⚒	†	⚒	
Chiusi-Chianciano Terme **620** ...... d.	0430	0600	0627	...	0645	0707	0830	...	0914	1030	1045	...	1230	1348	1510	1630	1706	...	1830	1840	1955	2030	2147	...
Siena **609 613** .... a.	0546	0723	0745	...	0750	0826	0950	...	1035	1150	1157	...	1350	1519	1632	1750	1836	...	1950	2003	2122	2150	2259	...

BOLOGNA - FIRENZE (- PERUGIA - FOLIGNO) - ROMA — 620

For high-speed services – see Table 600

	ICN 763 ◆	ICN 771 ◆	ICN 797 ◆	⚒	IC 581 ⚒	EN 235 ◆	EN 1237 ◆	FR 9501 ⚒		2 ⚒			IC 583	IC 1589 ◆			IC 585 ◆		2		2	2	IC 595 ◆	2
Milano Centrale **615** d.	...	...	2317g	...	...	...	...	...	...	...	...	...	0650	0645	...	...	...	...	...	...	...	...	...	...
Bologna Centrale **615** d.	...	0217	|	...	...	0508	0546	0600	...	...	...	...	0918	0937	...	...	1118	...	...	...	...	...	1648	...
Prato Centrale d.	...	|	|	...	...	|	|	|	...	...	...	...	1004	1044	...	...	1208	...	...	...	...	...	1732	...
Firenze S M Novella d.	...	|	|	...	...	0607	0653	0641	...	...	...	...	1011r	1052r	...	...	1217r	...	...	...	...	...	1745r	...
Firenze S M Novella d.	...	|	|	...	0550	0625	...	0650	0640	0734	0802	0904	1014r	1055r	1113	1213	1220r	1313	1413	1513	1613	1713	1748r	...
Arezzo d.	...	0425	|	...	0630	0705	...	0725	0743	0855	0913	1007	1102	|	1216	1316	1302	1416	1516	1616	1716	1816	1828	...
Castiglion Fiorentino d.	...	|	|	...	|	|	...	|	0755	0907	0924	1020	|	|	1227	1327	|	1427	1527	1627	1727	1827	|	...
Terontola-Cortona d.	...	0445	|	0609	0650	|	...	|	0808	0921	0941	1036	|	|	1240	1341	|	1440	1541	1640	1741	1840	1847	...
Passignano sul Trasimeno d.	...	|	|	|	|	|	...	|	|	|	0950	|	|	|	|	1349	|	|	1550	|	1750	|	|	...
Perugia 625 d.	...	|	|	|	|	|	...	|	|	|	1021	|	|	|	|	1423	|	|	1627	|	1825	|	|	...
Assisi **625** d.	...	|	|	|	|	|	...	|	|	|	1050	|	|	|	|	1447	|	|	1649	|	1853	|	|	...
Foligno **625** a.	...	|	|	|	|	|	...	|	|	|	1106	|	|	|	|	1501	|	|	1703	|	1916	|	|	...
Castiglione del Lago d.	...	|	|	0617	|	|	...	|	0815	0930	...	1043	|	|	1247	...	|	1447	...	1647	...	1847	|	←
Chiusi-Chianciano Terme **619** d.	...	0507	|	0629	0710	0736	...	|	0831	0943	...	1058	1145	1207	1259	...	1345	1459	...	1659	...	1858	1904	1935
Orvieto d.	0500	|	|	0657	0731	0802	...	|	0859	...	...	1124	1210	|	1325	...	1410	1525	...	1725	...	→	1927	2001
Orte **625** d.	|	|	0644	0731	|	|	...	|	0943	...	...	1200	1245	|	1400	...	1445	1600	...	1800	...	...	1956	2040
Roma Tiburtina **625** a.	|	|	0717	0809	|	|	...	0824	1049	...	...	1237	1317	1311	1435	...	|	1642	...	1837	...	...	|	2113
Roma Termini **625 640** a.	0600	0635	|	0821	0826	0922	...	0835	...	...	...	1248	|	|	1446	...	1520	1656	...	1850	...	...	2036	2126
Napoli Centrale **640** a.	...	...	0938	...	...	...	...	0955	...	...	...	...	1529	1547	...	...	...	...	...	...	...	...	...	...

	2	IC 597 ◆		ICN 795 ◆		FR 9555 Ⓑq		IC 599 ◆	
Milano Centrale **615** d.	...	1450	...	1544g	...	1850	...	1743	...
Bologna Centrale **615** d.	...	1718	...	|	...	2005	...	2018	...
Prato Centrale d.	...	1808	...	1910	...	|	...	2108	...
Firenze S M Novella d.	...	1817r	...	1929c	...	2040	...	2120	...
Firenze S M Novella d.	1813	1820r	1913	1932c	2013	2049	2113	2142	...
Arezzo d.	1916	1902	2017	|	2116	2122	2216	2224	...
Castiglion Fiorentino d.	1927	|	2029	|	2127	...	2227	|	...
Terontola-Cortona d.	1941	1924	2042	|	2141	...	2240	2249	...
Passignano sul Trasimeno d.	1950	|	|	|	2152	...	|	|	...
Perugia 625 d.	2027	|	|	|	2221	...	|	2318	...
Assisi **625** d.	2053	|	|	|	2242	...	|	2339	...
Foligno **625** a.	2110	|	|	|	2257	...	|	2350	...
Castiglione del Lago d.	...	|	2049	|	...	...	2247	...	...
Chiusi-Chianciano Terme **619** d.	...	1945	2101	|	...	...	2259	...	...
Orvieto d.	...	2010	2127	|	...	...	2325	...	...
Orte **625** d.	...	2049	2202	|	...	...	2358	...	...
Roma Tiburtina **625** a.	...	2118	2243	2313	...	...	0032	...	...
Roma Termini **625 640** a.	...	|	2254	...	...	...	0045	...	...
Napoli Centrale **640** a.	...	2330	...	...	...	...	...	...	...

	FR 9500 ⚒	2 ⚒	2 ⚒	IC 580 ◆			ICN 794 ◆			
Napoli Centrale **640** d.	...	...	...	...	...	...	0421	...	...	...
Roma Termini **625 640** d.	...	...	...	...	0603	...	|	0728	...	0858
Roma Tiburtina **625** d.	...	...	...	...	0612	...	0639	0737	...	0908
Orte **625** d.	...	...	...	...	0647	...	|	0811	...	0942
Orvieto d.	...	...	...	...	0721	...	|	0844	...	1015
Chiusi-Chianciano Terme **619** d.	...	0543	...	...	0758t	...	|	0909	...	1058v
Castiglione del Lago d.	...	0556	...	...	0809	...	|	0920	...	1109
Foligno **625** d.	...	|	0515	0555	|	...	|	|	0912	|
Assisi **625** d.	...	|	0530	0608	|	...	|	|	0925	|
Perugia 625 d.	...	|	0600	0635	|	...	|	|	0952	|
Passignano sul Trasimeno d.	...	|	0636	|	|	...	|	|	1024	|
Terontola-Cortona d.	...	0604	0656	0710	0819	...	|	0927	1036	1119
Castiglion Fiorentino d.	...	0618	0710	|	0831	...	|	0940	|	1131
Arezzo d.	0615	0632	0725	0732	0844	...	|	0953	1100	1145
Firenze S M Novella a.	0644	0738	0835	0806	0948	...	1006c	1057	1157	1250
Firenze S M Novella d.	0653	...	...	0821	...	...	1008c	...	...	...
Prato Centrale d.	|	...	...	0837	...	...	1030	...	...	...
Bologna Centrale **615** a.	0728	...	...	0942	...	...	1138	...	...	...
Milano Centrale **615** a.	0840	...	...	1215	...	...	1442g	...	...	...

		IC 588 ◆		IC 590 ◆					IC 592 ◆		IC 596		IC 1588 ◆		EN 1236/8 ◆	IC 598 Ⓑy	EN 234 ◆			⚒	FR 9564 Ⓑq	ICN 774 ◆	ICN 764 ◆	ICN 798 ◆
Napoli Centrale **640** d.	...	...	...	1031	...	...	...	...	...	...	1431	...	1452	...	...	...	...	...	...	...	1930	...	...	2132
Roma Termini **625 640** d.	...	1030	...	|	...	1300	...	1458	1540	...	|	...	|	1712	...	1816	1904	...	2005	...	2050	2235	2300	|
Roma Tiburtina **625** d.	...	|	1110	1240	...	1309	...	1507	|	...	1639	...	1710	1722	...	|	|	...	2015	...	2100	|	|	2343
Orte **625** d.	...	1110	1147	1314	...	1347	...	1542	1617	...	1715	...	|	1756	...	1854	|	...	2045	...	|	|	2341	0018
Orvieto d.	...	1145	1221	1345	...	1421	...	1616	1645	...	1745	...	1811	1829	...	1923	2012	...	2118	...	|	|	0011	|
Chiusi-Chianciano Terme **619** d.	...	1210	1258t	1410	...	1458t	...	1658v	1710	...	1810	...	1835	1858	...	1946	2044	...	2145	...	|	0007	...	|
Castiglione del Lago d.	...	|	1309	|	...	1509	...	1709	|	...	|	...	|	1909	...	|	|	...	2156	...	|	|	...	|
Foligno **625** d.	1108	|	|	|	1303	|	1503	|	|	1708	|	...	|	|	...	|	|	1903	|	2050	|	|	...	|
Assisi **625** d.	1122	|	|	|	1317	|	1517	|	|	1721	|	...	|	|	...	|	|	1917	|	2110	|	|	...	|
Perugia 625 d.	1144	|	|	|	1339	|	1539	|	|	1744	|	...	|	|	...	|	|	1941	|	2134	|	|	...	|
Passignano sul Trasimeno d.	1212	|	|	|	1408	|	1609	|	|	1810	|	...	|	|	...	|	|	2009	|	2206	|	|	...	|
Terontola-Cortona d.	1222	|	1319	|	1419	1519	1619	1719	1730	1819	1830	...	1853	1919	...	2004	|	2019	2203	2218	|	0025	...	|
Castiglion Fiorentino d.	1234	|	1331	|	1431	1531	1631	1731	|	1831	|	...	|	1931	...	|	|	2031	2216	...	|	|	...	|
Arezzo d.	1245	1255	1344	1455	1444	1544	1644	1744	1755	1844	1855	...	1916	1944	...	2026	2115	2044	2228	...	2202	0047	...	|
Firenze S M Novella a.	1348	1336r	1448	1536r	1548	1648	1753	1848	1836r	1951	1936r	...	2005r	2048	...	2111	2156	2148	2328	...	2235	0144c	...	|
Firenze S M Novella d.	...	1339r	...	1539r	...	...	...	...	1839r	...	1939r	...	2008r	...	2105	...	2214	...	...	...	...	0147c	...	|
Prato Centrale d.	...	1352	...	1552	...	...	...	...	1852	...	1952	...	2026	...	|	...	|	...	...	...	...	|	...	|
Bologna Centrale **615** a.	...	1443	...	1640	...	...	...	...	1948	...	2038	...	2127	...	2218	...	2308	...	...	...	...	0313	...	|
Milano Centrale **615** a.	...	...	...	1917	...	...	...	...	...	...	2315	...	0005	...	...	...	...	...	...	...	...	...	...	0711g

NOTES (LISTED BY TRAIN NUMBER)

– 🛏 1, 2 cl., ▬ 2 cl. and [2] Roma - Venezia Mestre - Villach - Wien; 🛏 1, 2 cl., ▬ 2 cl. and [2] Roma - Bologna (**484**) - München.
– 🛏 1, 2 cl., ▬ 2 cl. and [2] Wien - Villach - Venezia Mestre - Roma; 🛏 1, 2 cl., ▬ 2 cl. and [2] München (**485**) - Bologna - Roma.
99 – [12] Terni - Milano and v.v.
– [12] Trieste (**584**) - Venezia Mestre - Roma.
95 – [12] Roma - Venezia Mestre (**589/594**) - Trieste and v.v.
– [12] Napoli - Firenze - Milano.
– [12] Roma - Venezia Mestre (**593**) - Trieste.
– [12] Milano - Firenze - Napoli.
/4 – 🛏 1, 2 cl., ▬ 2 cl. (4 berth) and [2] Bolzano - Roma and v.v.
– 🛏 1, 2 cl., ▬ 2 cl. (4 berth) and [2] Trieste (**770**) - Udine - Venezia - Roma.
– 🛏 1, 2 cl., ▬ 2 cl. (4 berth) and [2] Roma - Venezia - Udine (**775**) - Trieste.
– 🛏 1, 2 cl., ▬ 2 cl. (4 berth) and [2] Reggio di Calabria - Milano - Torino.
– 🛏 1, 2 cl., ▬ 2 cl. (4 berth) and [2] Torino - Milano - Reggio di Calabria. Train number **1595** on ①.

797/8 – 🛏 1, 2 cl., ▬ 2 cl. (4 berth) and [2] Salerno - Napoli - Milano - Torino and v.v.
1236/8 – ④⑥ Mar. 19 - Oct. 15 (also Mar. 28, May 16): 🛏 1, 2 cl. (T2), ▬ 2 cl. and [2] Livorno (**1232/4**) - Pisa - Firenze - Wien.
1237 – ③⑤ Mar. 18 - Oct. 14; also Mar. 27, May 15 (from Wien): 🛏 1, 2 cl. (T2), ▬ 2 cl. and [2] Wien - Firenze (**1239**) - Pisa - Livorno.
1588 – ⑦ (also Mar. 28, Apr. 25; not Mar. 27, Apr. 24): [12] Reggio di Calabria - Milano.
1589 – ⑥ (not June 4): [12] Milano - Reggio di Calabria.

c – Firenze **Campo di Marte**.
g – Milano **Porta Garibaldi**.
q – Not Mar. 27, Apr. 24.
r – Firenze **Rifredi**.
t – Arrive 9 – 13 minutes earlier.
v – Arrive 14 – 18 minutes earlier.
y – Not Mar. 27, Apr. 24, and days before holidays.

FERRARA and BOLOGNA - RAVENNA - RIMINI — 621

d class only except where shown

For express services Bologna - Faenza - Rimini and v.v. – see Table 630

n		⚒	9851 R	⊙	⊙	⊙	⊙ ⚒		⚒	⊙ ⚒	⚒	⊙ †		⊙ ⚒	⚒		⊙ ⚒	†h	†n	†h		⚒	⚒	⊙	
0	**Ferrara** d.	...	...	0516	...	0545	0609	...	...	0710	...	0816	...	0817	...	...	0922	0939	1004	...	...	...	...	1215	...
	Bologna Centrale **630** d.	...	...	|	...	|	|	...	0650	|	...	|	0754	|	0852	0906	|	|	|	1006	1106	...	1206	|	...
	Imola d.	...	...	|	...	|	|	...	0712	|	...	|	0826	|	0914	0936	|	|	|	1033	1136	...	1235	|	...
	Castelbolognese-Riolo Terme d.	...	...	|	...	|	|	...	0719	|	...	|	0832	|	|	0942	|	|	|	1038	1142	...	1242	|	...
	Lugo d.	...	...	|	...	|	|	...	0734	|	...	|	0847	|	0931	0958	|	|	|	1056	1200	...	1300	|	...
4	**Ravenna** a.	...	...	0619	...	0702	0724	...	0805	0830	...	0921	0917	0925	0951	1030	1030	1052	1114	1118	1227	...	1327	1329	...
4	**Ravenna** d.	0525	0607	...	0628	...	...	0752	...	...	0836	...	0924	0934	...	...	...	1053	1116	1119	...	1245	...	...	1336
5	Cervia-Milano Marittima d.	0537	|	...	0650	...	...	0811	...	...	0900	...	0943	0958	...	...	...	1114	1134	1138	...	1307	...	...	1400
3	Cesenatico d.	0545	|	...	0657	...	...	0817	...	...	0906	...	0949	1005	...	...	...	1132	1142	1145	...	1313	...	...	1410
4	**Rimini 630** a.	0604	0641	...	0727	...	...	0850	...	...	0932	...	1015	1027	...	...	...	1200	1216	1217	...	1345	...	...	1447

FOR NOTES SEE NEXT PAGE →

621 FERRARA and BOLOGNA - RAVENNA - RIMINI

2nd class only except where sh

For express services Bologna - Faenza - Rimini and v.v. – see Table 630

	⚒		⚒	⊙ ⚒	⊙		⚒	⚒j				⚒		⊙ ⚒			⚒	⊙				⊙		
Ferrara d.	...	...	...	1309	1423	...	...	...	1615	...	...	...	...	1701	...	...	...	1814	...	...	...	2050	...	...
Bologna Centrale **630** d.	1252	1306	...	|	|	1406	1506	...	|	1606	...	1652	...	|	1706	...	1752	|	1806	1906	2006	|	...	2116
Imola d.	1314	1336	...	|	|	1436	1536	...	|	1636	...	1714	...	|	1734	...	|	|	1838	1936	2036	|	...	2146
Castelbolognese-Riolo Terme d.	|	1342	...	|	|	1442	1542	...	|	1642	...	|	...	|	1742	...	1817	|	1844	1942	2042	|	...	2152
Lugo d.	1331	1358	...	|	|	1458	1600	...	|	1700	...	1731	...	|	1800	...	1831	|	1858	1958	2058	|	...	2208
Ravenna a.	1351	1427	...	1441	1530	1527	1627	...	1723	1727	...	1751	...	1814	1827	...	1851	1926	1928	2027	2127	2150	...	2237
Ravenna d.	...	...	1435	...	...	1532	...	1635	...	...	1735	...	...	...	...	1835	...	...	1935	...	...	...	2155	...
Cervia-Milano Marittima d.	...	...	1502	...	...	1554	...	1654	...	...	1754	...	...	...	...	1857	...	...	1956	...	...	...	2213	...
Cesenatico d.	...	...	1508	...	...	1603	...	1702	...	...	1803	...	...	...	...	1904	...	...	2006	...	...	...	2220	...
Rimini 630 a.	...	...	1535	...	...	1630	...	1730	...	...	1835	...	...	...	...	1935	...	...	2034	...	...	...	2248	...

km				⚒			⊙		⊙ ⚒	⚒	⚒	⊙ ⚒		⊙ †	⊙	⚒	⊙	†	⚒	†	†	⊙ ⚒		
	Rimini 630 d.	...	0520	...	...	0614	...	0658	...	0736	...	...	0820	...	0900	...	...	...	...	1036	...	...	...	1230
	Cesenatico d.	...	0544	...	...	0642	...	0724	...	0801	...	...	0852	...	0935	...	...	...	...	1104	...	...	...	1300
	Cervia-Milano Marittima d.	...	0550	...	...	0651	...	0730	...	0812	...	...	0859	...	0942	...	...	...	...	1113	...	...	...	1306
	Ravenna a.	...	0606	...	...	0712	...	0751	...	0827	...	...	0921	...	1003	...	...	...	...	1140	...	...	...	1325
0	**Ravenna** d.	0503	...	0621	0628	...	0726	0755	0753	...	0833	0849	0931	0932	...	1009	1032	1131	1133	...	1143	1227	1233	...
28	Lugo d.	0528	...	|	0657	...	|	0815	|	...	0901	|	0958	|	...	1031	|	1200	1200	...	|	|	1300	...
42	Castelbolognese-Riolo Terme d.	0544	...	|	0714	...	|	|	|	...	0916	|	1014	|	...	|	|	1214	1216	...	|	|	1316	...
50	Imola d.	0551	...	|	0721	...	|	|	|	...	0923	|	1021	|	...	1046	|	1221	1223	...	|	|	1323	...
84	**Bologna** Centrale **630** a.	0621	...	|	0743	...	|	0854	|	...	0954	|	1053	|	...	1108	|	1251	1254	...	|	|	1354	...
	Ferrara a.	...	...	0736	...	...	0847	...	0914	...	...	1005	...	1053	...	...	1142	...	...	...	1250	1348	...	...

	⊙	⚒	⚒	⊙ ⚒		⊙	⚒j	⚒		⊙		†h	⚒	⊙ ⚒	⚒			⊙	⚒		†	⚒	9852 R	⊙
Rimini 630 d.	...	1318	...	...	1418	...	1508	...	...	1632	...	1703	...	...	1733	...	1837	...	1939	...	2037	2037	2117	...
Cesenatico d.	...	1350	...	...	1451	...	1535	...	...	1701	...	1732	...	...	1802	...	1905	...	2006	...	2105	2105	|	...
Cervia-Milano Marittima d.	...	1359	...	...	1501	...	1541	...	...	1708	...	1740	...	...	1808	...	1912	...	2012	...	2113	2121	|	...
Ravenna a.	...	1418	...	...	1523	...	1604	...	...	1733	...	1759	...	...	1826	...	1929	...	2028	...	2131	2137	2153	...
Ravenna d.	1341	...	1431	1453	1533	1540	...	1633	1733	1735	...	1801	1809	1824	...	1831	1931	1957	...	2033	...	...	...	2200
Lugo d.	|	...	1458	|	1600	|	...	1700	1800	|	...	1823	1831	|	...	1858	1958	|	...	2058	...	...	...	|
Castelbolognese-Riolo Terme d.	|	...	1514	|	1616	|	...	1716	1816	|	...	1836	|	|	...	1914	2014	|	...	2114	...	...	...	|
Imola d.	|	...	1521	|	1623	|	...	1723	1822	|	...	1842	1846	|	...	1920	2021	|	...	2122	...	...	...	|
Bologna Centrale **630** a.	|	...	1554	|	1654	|	...	1754	1854	|	...	1908	1908	|	...	1954	2054	|	...	2154	...	...	...	|
Ferrara a.	1501	...	...	1611	...	1651	...	...	...	1849	...	...	...	1936	...	...	...	2109	...	...	...	...	...	2300

R – *FB* train. (12) and 🍸 Roma - Rimini - Ravenna and v.v.

h – From June 5.
j – Until May 28.
n – Until June 2.

⊙ – Operated by *TPER*. Trenitalia tickets valic

622 ROMA AIRPORTS ✈

ROMA FIUMICINO AIRPORT ✈

Leonardo Express rail service Roma Termini - Roma Fiumicino ✈. *31 km* Journey time: 32 minutes. Special fare payable.

From **Roma** Termini: 0535, 0605, 0635, 0705, 0735, 0805, 0835, 0850, 0905, 0935, 1005, 1035, 1050, 1105, 1135, 1205, 1220, 1235, 1250, 1305, 1335, 1405, 1435, 1450, 1505, 1535, 1605, 1620, 1635, 1650, 1705, 1735, 1750, 1805, 1820, 1835, 1905, 1935, 2005, 2035, 2105, 2135, 2205, 2235.

From **Roma Fiumicino**: 0623, 0653, 0723, 0753, 0823, 0853, 0923, 0938, 0953, 1023, 1
1123, 1138, 1153, 1223, 1253, 1308, 1323, 1338, 1353, 1423, 1453, 1523, 1538, 1553, 1
1653, 1708, 1723, 1738, 1753, 1823, 1838, 1853, 1908, 1923, 1953, 2023, 2053, 2123, 2
2223, 2253, 2323.

Additional rail service (2nd class only) operates from Roma Tiburtina **and** Roma Ostiense - Roma Fiumicino ✈. *39 km* Journey times: Tiburtina - ✈ ± 45 minutes; Ostiense - ✈ ± 30 minu

From **Roma** Tiburtina (Ostiense 15 minutes later): ◐
0501, 0546⚒, 0601, 0616Ⓐ, 0631, 0646Ⓐ, 0701, 0716Ⓐ, 0731, 0746⚒, 0801, 0816⚒, 0831, 0846Ⓐ, 0901, 0916⚒, 0931, 0946Ⓐ, 1001, 1016Ⓐ, 1031, 1046Ⓐ, 1101, 1116Ⓐ, 1131⚒, 1146Ⓐ, 1201⚒, 1216Ⓐ, 1231⚒, 1246Ⓐ, 1301, 1316Ⓐ, 1331, 1346⚒, 1401, 1416Ⓐ, 1431, 1446Ⓐ, 1501, 1516Ⓐ, 1531, 1546Ⓐ, 1601, 1616⚒, 1631, 1646⚒, 1701, 1716⚒, 1731, 1746Ⓐ, 1801, 1816Ⓐ, 1831, 1846Ⓐ, 1901, 1916Ⓐ, 1931, 2001, 2031, 2101, 2146, 2201.

From **Roma Fiumicino** ✈: ◐
0557, 0627, 0642⚒, 0657, 0712Ⓐ, 0727, 0742Ⓐ, 0757, 0812Ⓐ, 0827, 0842Ⓐ, 085
0912⚒, 0927⚒, 0942Ⓐ, 0957⚒, 1012⚒, 1027, 1042Ⓐ, 1057, 1112Ⓐ, 1127, 1142Ⓐ, 1
1212Ⓐ, 1227, 1242Ⓐ, 1257, 1312Ⓐ, 1327, 1342Ⓐ, 1357, 1412⚒, 1427, 1442⚒, 1
1512Ⓐ, 1527, 1542Ⓐ, 1557, 1612Ⓐ, 1627, 1642Ⓐ, 1657, 1712⚒, 1727, 1742⚒, 1
1812⚒, 1827, 1842Ⓐ, 1857, 1912Ⓐ, 1927, 1942Ⓐ, 1957, 2012Ⓐ, 2042, 2112, 2142, 2
2242.

ROMA CIAMPINO AIRPORT ✈

Frequent services operate Roma Termini - Ciampino and v.v., journey approximately 15 minutes. There is a 🚌 service between Ciampino station and airport.

◐ – A reduced service operates in July and August.

623 ROMA - ANZIO and ALBANO LAZIALE

ROMA - ANZIO *57 km* Journey time: 56–68 minutes. 2nd class only. All services continue to Nettuno (*3 km* and 4–6 minutes from Anzio).

From **Roma** Termini:
⚒: 0507, 0607, 0714, 0821, 0942, 1042, 1142, 1242, 1342, 1406Ⓐ, 1442, 1542, 1642, 1742, 1806Ⓐ, 1842, 1906Ⓐ, 1942, 2042, 2136.
†: 0714, 0821, 0942, 1142, 1342, 1442, 1642, 1842, 1942, 2136.

From **Anzio**:
⚒: 0451, 0559, 0635, 0703Ⓐ, 0735, 0800, 0912, 1014, 1112, 1212, 1312, 1412, 151
1514Ⓐ, 1612, 1630Ⓐ, 1712, 1812, 1917, 2012, 2113Ⓐ, 2202.
†: 0635, 0735, 0912, 1014, 1312, 1512, 1712, 1812, 2012, 2202.

ROMA - ALBANO LAZIALE *29 km* Journey time: 40–58 minutes. 2nd class only.

From **Roma** Termini: 0542⚒, 0721, 0821, 0900⚒, 1221, 1321⚒, 1421, 1521⚒, 1621, 1721⚒, 1821, 1921⚒, 2021, 2121⚒.

From **Albano Laziale**: 0629⚒, 0700⚒, 0743⚒, 0838, 1023, 1144⚒, 1343, 1443⚒, 15
1643⚒, 1743, 1843⚒, 1943, 2043⚒, 2140⚒, 2145†.

All trains call at Marino Laziale and Castel Gandolfo approximately 35 and 40 minutes from Roma, 7 and 15 minutes from Albano Laziale respectively.

624 ROMA - PESCARA

2nd class o

km		†	⚒	⚒	†	⚒	⚒	⚒	†	⚒		⚒	†	⚒	⑥	Ⓑ	†	⚒	⚒	⚒	†	⚒	†	⚒
0	**Roma** Tiburtina § ▲ d.	...	...	...	0742	0742	...	1033	...	1233	...	...	1433	1433	1527	1533	1633	1630	1733	1833	1833	1933	1933	1938
40	Tivoli ▲ d.	...	...	...	0833	0832	...	1124	...	1308	...	...	1510	1510	1613	1614	1703	1723	1828	1906	1907	2019	2019	2036
108	Avezzano d.	0615	0612	0730	0941	0944	...	1256	1300	1409	...	...	1613	1617	1720	1720	1804	1823	1935	2011	2019	2127	2130	2200
172	Sulmona **627** d.	0747	0747	0844	1049	1049	1230	1410	1410	1536	...	1613	1728	1740	...	...	1913	1931	...	2126	2121	...	...	...
226	Chieti a.	0840	0854	0936	1127	1128	1337	1516	1510	1627	...	1708	1812	1832	...	...	2004	2016	...	2212	2212	...	...	...
240	**Pescara** Centrale a.	0858	0910	0955	1145	1145	1400	1540	1525	1650	...	1732	1836	1850	...	...	2020	2032	...	2230	2230	...	...	...

	⚒		⚒			⚒		Ⓐ	⑥	†	⚒	Ⓐ	⚒	⚒	†	Ⓐ	⑥	†	⚒	†	†	⚒		Ⓐ
Pescara Centrale d.	...	...	...	...	0615	0701	0922	...	...	...	...	1146	1334	1406	1410	...	...	1610	1655	...	1800	1846	1912	1957
Chieti d.	...	...	...	...	0628	0718	0940	...	...	...	...	1202	1353	1422	1425	...	...	1624	1712	...	1816	1901	1931	2014
Sulmona **627** d.	...	...	...	0557	0724	0825	1025	...	...	...	...	1259	1448	1513	1513	...	...	1727	1811	...	1912	2002	2035	2119
Avezzano d.	0508	0530	0629	0654	0814	0920	1121	1259	1259	1307	1425	1430	...	1615	1614	1721	1721	1840	1907	1910	2018	2100	...	...
Tivoli ▲ d.	0614	0640	0736	0759	0921	1022	1225	1417	1417	1416	1555	...	...	1722	1728	1827	1827	...	2020	2018	2131	2203	...	...
Roma Tiburtina § ▲ a.	0700	0731	0830	0845t	0959	1059	1259	1459	1515	1459	1654	...	...	1759	1759	1859	1912	...	2059	2059	2225t	2255t	...	...

t – Roma **Termini**.

§ – Roma Tiburtina **Piazzale Est**.
▲ – Additional services operate Roma Tiburtina (Piazzale Est) - Tivoli and v.v., journey 60–75 minutes.

ROMA - PERUGIA and ANCONA 625

	2 Ⓐ	2 ⚒	2 ⚒	IC 580 T	2 †	2 ⚒		⚒		IC 534	⚒	2 ⚒			IC 540		Ⓐ	FB 9852 R	2 ⚒	Ⓑ p		⚒	IC 546 Ⓑ y		
Roma Termini **620** d.	...	...	...	...	...	...	0545	0653	0758	0935	1128	1158	1328	1423	1535	1558	1700	1738	...	1758	1835	1858	1958	2058	2240
Roma Tiburtina **620** d.	...	...	...	...	...	...	0555	0702	0807	|	1137	1208	1337	1432	|	1607	1710	|	...	1807	1845	1907	2008	2109	2249
Orte **620** d.	...	...	...	...	...	...	0634	0739	0840	1011	1211	1240	1410	1506	|	1640	|	|	...	1840	1917	1941	2037	2141	2321
Terni d.	...	...	...	0505	...	...	0654	0800	0901	1029	1235	1305	1432	1526	1629	1704	1802	1827	...	1902	1943	2006	2054	2204	2339
Spoleto d.	...	...	...	0532	...	...	0716	0831	0933	1055	1259	1329	1457	1550	1656	1733	1825	|	...	1932	2008	2029	2121	2226	...
Foligno a.	...	...	...	0553	...	...	0740	0853	0949	1113	1319	1350	1516	1607	1715	1752	1844	1858	...	1953	2029	2048	2136	2242	...
Foligno d.	...	...	0545	0555	0622	0640	0742	...	0953	1115	1321	*1416*	1518	1609	1717	1754	...	1900	...	1955	2031	2050	2138	2244	...
Spello d.	...	...	|	|	|	|	|	...	|	|	|	|	|	1614	|	|	...	|	...	2001	|	2059	|	|	...
Assisi d.	...	...	|	0608	|	|	|	...	1008	|	|	|	|	1622	|	|	...	|	...	2010	|	2110	2151	|	...
Perugia Ponte SG ▲ d.	...	...	|	0623	|	|	|	...	1018	|	|	|	|	1635	|	|	...	|	...	2021	|	2124	2202	|	...
Perugia 620 a.	...	...	|	0633	|	|	|	...	1028	|	|	|	|	1652	|	|	...	|	...	2032	|	2132	2213	|	...
Fabriano d.	0500	0600	0646	...	0713	0732	0847	...	...	1205	1414	*1522*	1621	...	1806	1846	...	1940	1945	...	2122	...	...	2333	...
Jesi d.	0539	0641	0733	...	0758	0828	0924	...	...	1236	1501	*1605*	1704	...	1836	1922	...	2008	2028	...	2156	...	...	0010	...
Falconara Marittima **630** d.	0555	0700	0749	...	0818	0845	0940	...	...	1250	1523	*1625*	1721	...	1850	1941	...	2019	2046	...	2210	...	...	0025	...
Ancona 630/2 a.	0604	0712	0802	...	0834	0858	0955	...	...	1300	1535	*1638*	1735	...	1859	1951	...	...	2054	...	2222	...	...	0040	...

	⚒		⚒ q	2 ⚒	IC 531 ⚒	†	IC 533	2 Ⓐ	FB 9851 R			2 ⚒	Ⓐ	2 ⚒		⚒	IC 541	2 ⚒		2			2 ⚒	2	IC 599 T
Ancona 630/2 d.	...	0350	...	0505	...	...	0625	0651	...	0845	...	...	...	1250	1344	...	1532	1545	...	1733	1815	1942	2015	2130	...
Falconara Marittima **630** d.	...	0403	...	0513	...	...	0639	0701	0739	0855	...	...	...	1305	1354	...	1542	1556	...	1745	1824	1951	2025	2139	...
Jesi d.	...	0415	...	0526	...	...	0656	0720	0751	0910	...	...	...	1323	1409	...	1554	1614	...	1801	1848	2004	2041	2153	...
Fabriano d.	...	0451	...	0604	...	...	0731	0808	0825	0949	...	...	...	1412	1450	...	1627	1710	...	1855	1939	2038	2120	2235	...
Perugia 620 d.	...	|	0554	|	0640	0712	|	...	|	|	1105	1226	1348	|	|	1556	|	|	1810	...	|	|	...	|	2318
Perugia Ponte SG ▲ d.	...	|	0603	|	0651	0721	|	...	|	|	1114	1235	1357	|	|	1605	|	|	1819	...	|	|	...	|	2328
Assisi d.	...	|	0618	|	0703	0732	|	...	|	|	1130	1246	1412	|	|	1619	|	|	1831	...	|	|	...	|	2339
Spello d.	...	|	0628	|	|	0741	|	...	|	|	1141	1255	1424	|	|	1632	|	|	1840	...	|	|	...	|	|
Foligno a.	...	0537	0634	0700	0715	0748	0818	...	0901	1039	1146	1301	1434	1512	1543	1638	1714	*1830*	1846	...	2029	2134	...	2334	2350
Foligno d.	...	0539	0636	...	0717	0749	0820	...	0903	1041	1148	...	1436	1514	1545	1640	1716	...	1848	...	2031	2136	...	...	2354
Spoleto d.	...	0555	0653	...	0733	0809	0836	...	|	1057	1206	...	1458	1532	1605	1658	1734	...	1904	...	2048	2152	...	...	0011
Terni d.	0540	0625	0732	...	0758	0833	0900	...	0936	1122	1235	...	1524	1604	1628	1728	1800	...	1927	...	2118	2225	...	...	0035
Orte **620** d.	0600	0651	0801	...	0816	0854	0918	...	|	1149	1305	...	1547	1627	1657	1749	|	...	1949	...	2140	2246	...	...	...
Roma Tiburtina **620** a.	0630	0723	0836	...	0844	0926	|	...	|	1221	1337	...	1618	...	1724	1818	|	...	2016	...	2209	2318	...	...	...
Roma Termini **620** a.	0640	0737	0850	...	0856	0939	0956	...	1022	1235	1356	...	1633	...	1742	1835	1902	...	2030	...	2225	2330	...	...	...

[12] and 🍷 Ravenna - Rimini - Roma and v.v.
[12] Terni - Perugia - Milano and v.v.

p – Not Mar. 27, Apr. 24.
q – Not Mar. 28, Apr. 25.
y – Not Mar. 27, Apr. 24, and days before holidays.

▲ – Perugia Ponte San Giovanni.

ROMA - CASERTA - NAPOLI and FOGGIA 626

	2 ⚒	2 ⚒	2 ⚒	2 ⚒	2 ⚒	2 †	FA 9351 🍷	IC 703 2	2 †	2 ⚒	2 †	2 ⚒	2 ⚒	2	FA 9355 🍷	IC 705 T	2	2 †	2 ⚒	2 Ⓐ	2	FA 9357 🍷	2	2	ICN 789 ♦
Roma Termini d.	...	...	...	0535	...	0621	0805	0728	1014	1014	...	1235	...	1242	1445	1606	...	1642	1642	1707	1742	1800	1807	1942	2358
Cassino d.	0510	0550	...	0736	0747	0827	|	0912	1227	1245	1317	1406	1438	1441	|	|	1838	1845	1858	1844	1940	|	1946	2140	0140
Vairano-Caianello d.	0541	0621	0715	...	0819	...	|	0935	...	...	1350	1430	1510	...	|	|	1910	1918	1928	...	...	|	2008	...	|
Caserta d.	0625	0705	0800	...	0904	...	0915	1011	...	...	1434	1512	1555	...	1603	1801	1955	2000	2014	...	...	1914	2045	...	0236
Napoli Centrale a.	0707	0746	0841	...	0945	...	|	|	...	...	1515	|	1636	...	|	|	2036	...	...	...	...	|	...	...	|
Benevento d.	...	...	...	...	...	...	0952	1059	...	...	...	1615	...	...	1640	1848	...	...	...	...	...	1952	...	...	0324
Foggia 631 a.	...	...	...	...	...	...	1056	1223	...	...	...	...	...	...	1741	2018	...	...	...	...	...	2056	...	...	0449
Bari Centrale **631** a.	...	...	...	...	...	...	1204	1400	...	...	...	...	...	...	1849	2143	...	...	...	...	...	2204	...	...	0621
Lecce **631** a.	...	...	...	...	...	...	1328	...	...	...	...	...	...	...	2013	...	...	...	...	...	...	2328	...	...	0810

	2 ⚒	ICN 788 ♦	2 ⚒	2 ⚒	2	2 ⚒	2 ⚒	2	FA 9350 🍷	2	2 ⚒	2 ⚒	2 ⚒	2 ⚒	2 ⚒	FA 9354 🍷	2 †	2 †	2 Ⓐ	2 ⚒	2	IC 704 2	2 Ⓐ	IC 710 R	FA 9358 🍷
Lecce **631** d.	...	2230	...	...	...	...	...	...	0550	...	...	...	...	...	...	1150	...	...	...	...	...	...	...	...	1650
Bari Centrale **631** d.	...	0015	...	...	...	...	...	...	0714	...	...	...	...	...	...	1314	...	...	...	...	...	1555	...	1705	1814
Foggia 631 d.	...	0200	...	...	...	...	...	...	0822	...	...	...	...	...	...	1422	...	...	...	...	...	1741	...	1827	1922
Benevento d.	...	0321	0520	...	...	...	0632	...	0925	...	...	...	...	...	...	1525	...	...	...	...	...	1900	...	1948	2031
Napoli Centrale d.	...	|	|	0450	...	...	|	0750	|	...	1150	1250	...	...	...	|	1550	...	1656	1750	...	|	1950	|	|
Caserta d.	0410	0413	0611	0530	0610	0630	0730	0830	1010	...	1230	1330	1350	...	1530	1602	1630	...	1736	1830	...	1958	2030	2037	2110
Vairano-Caianello d.	0455	|	|	0613	0646	0713	0808	0912	|	...	1312	1416	1433	...	1613	|	1713	...	1816	1912	...	2025	2112	|	|
Cassino d.	0530	|	|	...	0711	0745	0837	0947	|	1025	1347	...	1505	1622	1648	|	1747	1822	1853	1947	2020	2048	2147	|	|
Roma Termini a.	...	0634	0827	...	0848	...	1013	...	1120	1227	...	...	...	1820	...	1720	...	2020	...	...	2241	2220	...	2300	2220

NOTES (LISTED BY TRAIN NUMBER)

- ⑦ (also Mar. 28, June 2; not Mar. 27, May 29): 🛏 1, 2 cl., ▬ 2 cl. (4 berth) and [2] Lecce - Roma.
- ⑤ (from Roma): 🛏 1, 2 cl., ▬ 2 cl. (4 berth) and [2] Roma - Lecce.

R – ⑦ (also Mar. 28, Apr. 25; not Mar. 27, Apr. 24): [12] Taranto - Roma.
T – ⑤ (also June 2; not June 3): [12] Roma - Taranto.

ROMA and NAPOLI - CAMPOBASSO - TERMOLI 627

class only

	⚒		⚒		⚒	⚒	†			⚒	⚒	†	⚒		⚒	†	⚒	Ⓑ n		†	🚌		⚒	†	⚒
Roma Termini d.	...	...	...	0615	...	...	...	0907	...	...	...	...	1307	...	...	1435	1435	...	...	1740	...	...	1935	2014	2035
Cassino d.	...	...	...	0742	...	...	...	1033	...	...	...	...	1445	...	...	1602	1603	...	...	|	...	...	|	|	|
Napoli Centrale d.	...	...	...	|	...	...	...	|	...	...	1210	...	|	1410	...	|	|	...	1713	|	...	1930	|	|	|
Caserta d.	...	...	...	|	...	0805	0837	|	...	...	1245	...	|	1440	...	|	|	...	1745	|	...	2004	|	|	|
Vairano-Caianello d.	...	...	...	|	...	0850	0922	|	...	...	1320	...	|	1516	...	|	|	...	1821	|	...	2040	|	|	|
Isernia d.	...	...	0646	0828	...	0934	1012	1116	...	...	1408	...	1528	1557	...	1641	1650	...	1901	1949	...	2126	2148	2226	2238
Carpinone ♣ d.	...	...	0657	0839	...	|	|	1128	...	...	1420	...	1540	1610	...	|	|	...	1913	2000	...	2138	|	|	|
Campobasso ▲ a.	0600	0648	0751	0924	0940	1036	1110	1212	1218	1414	1519	1525	1633	1709	1720	1742	1749	1828	2007	2052	2100	2227	2243	2325	2331
Termoli a.	0743	0834	...	...	1115	...	...	...	1409	1553	...	1708	...	...	1908	...	...	2009	...	...	2245	...	...	...	...

	⚒		⚒	⚒	†	⚒			⚒	†			⚒	†	⚒	⚒	†	⚒	⚒			⚒		🚌	🚌
Termoli d.	...	...	...	...	...	0549	0649	...	...		...	1220	...	...	1317	...	...	1500	...	1616	...	1728	...	1855	2045
Campobasso ▲ d.	0513	0550	0628	0653	0727	0740	0825	0836	1232	1232	1316	1400	1415	1421	1501	1528	1621	1642	1650	1753	1758	1918	1938	2040	2230
Carpinone ♣ d.	0554	|	0716	|	0811	...	...	0926	1315	1317	1359	...	|	|	...	1613	1712	...	1736	...	1845	...	|	...	...
Isernia d.	0607	0644	0727	0745	0825	...	...	0937	1328	1330	1411	...	1510	1515	...	1627	1724	...	1749	...	1858	...	2033	...	...
Vairano-Caianello d.	0648	|	0809	|	0909	...	...	|	|	1412	1459	...	|	|	...	1718	|	...	|	...	1949	...	|	...	...
Caserta a.	0715	|	0846	|	0937	...	...	|	|	1449	1534	...	|	|	...	1756	|	...	|	...	2025	...	|	...	...
Napoli Centrale a.	0752	|	0925	|	1008	...	...	|	|	...	1608	...	|	|	...	...	|	...	|	...	2100	...	|	...	...
Cassino a.	...	0726	...	|	...	...	...	1017	1416	...	...	...	1549	1557	...	...	1804	...	1829	...	...	...	2115	...	...
Roma Termini a.	...	0853	...	0959	...	...	...	1147	...	...	...	...	1727	1727	...	...	1934	...	1953	...	...	...	2254	...	...

🚌 SULMONA - CASTEL DI SANGRO - CARPINONE

	⚒	⚒		⚒	⚒	⚒
ona **624** d.	...	...	1110	...	...	1932
el di Sangro d.	0615	0805	1210	1240	1830	2032
inone a.	0718	0908	...	1343	1933	...

	⚒	⚒	⚒	⚒		⚒
Carpinone d.	...	0653	0853	1433	...	2038
Castel di Sangro d.	0610	0758	0958	1538	1710	2143
Sulmona **624** a.	0720	...	...	...	1820	...

▲ – 🚌 **CAMPOBASSO - BENEVENTO and v.v.:** (*67 km*, journey time 70 minutes).
From Campobasso: 0620⚒, 1305⚒, 1416⚒, 1750⚒.
From Benevento: 0640⚒, 0740⚒, 1420⚒, 1740⚒.

Not Mar. 27, Apr. 24, and days before holidays.

629 SARDINIA

Some trains 2nd class

km																											
		⚒		⚒	⚒	†	†	†	⚒	†	⚒	†	⚒	⚒	⚒	†	†	†	⚒	†	⚒	⚒	†	⚒	⚒	⚒	†
0	**Cagliari** d.	...	...	...	...	...	...	...	0623	0624	...	...	0722	0825	...	...	...	0914	0918	1013	1040	...	1113	1122	...	1222	1222
17	Decimomannu d.	...	...	...	...	...	...	...	0637	0638	...	...	0737	0839	...	...	...	0929	0932	1032	|	...	1132	1141	...	1237	1238
95	**Oristano** d.	...	...	...	...	...	...	...	0727	0730	...	...	0829	0929	...	...	...	1030	1038	1129	1130	...	1229	1244	...	1329	1330
154	Macomer d.	...	...	...	...	...	...	...	0817	0815	...	...	...	1017	...	...	...	1122	1127	...	1217	...	...	▬	...	▬	1421
214	Ozieri-Chilivani a.	...	...	...	...	...	...	...	0855	0858	...	...	...	1055	...	...	...	▬	...	...	|	...	...	⚒	...	...	1505
214	Ozieri-Chilivani d.	...	...	0652	0656	0757	0805	...	0858	0906	0900	0904	...	...	1100	1101	1105	...	...	...	|	...	...	1336	...	⚒	1507
	Sassari d.	...	0650	|	0743	0843	|	0848	|	0945	0939	|	...	...	1139	|	1145	...	...	...	1328	1333	...	1415	...	1426	|
	Porto Torres a.	...	0705	|	0756	...	|	0901	|	...	...	|	...	...	...	|	...	...	...	...	...	1348	...	...	...	1441	|
	Porto Torres M a.	...	0708	|	0759	...	|	0905	|	...	...	|	...	...	...	|	...	...	...	...	...	1351	...	...	...	1444	|
285	Olbia a.	0645	...	0750	...	...	0908	...	0950	...	...	1000	...	...	...	1201	...	1300	...	...	...	...	...	...	1430	...	1602
306	Golfo Aranci a.	0708	...	...	...	...	...	...	...	...	...	...	...	...	...	...	...	1325	...	...	...	...	...	...	1455	...	...

km																											
		⚒	⚒		⚒	⚒	⚒	†	†	⚒		†	⚒	⚒	†	†	†	⚒	†	⚒	†	⚒	†	⚒	⚒	⚒	
	Cagliari d.	...	...	...	1322	1425	...	1413	...	1522	...	1638	1640	...	...	...	1713	1722	1822	1840	...	...	1913	...	1922	🚌	2035
	Decimomannu d.	...	...	...	1338	1439	...	1428	...	1537	...	|	|	...	...	...	1732	1741	1837	|	...	...	1932	...	1941	...	2050
	Oristano d.	1334	...	...	1431	1529	...	1531	...	1629	...	1730	1730	...	...	...	1829	1846	1930	1930	...	...	2029	...	2044	2050	2149j
	Macomer d.	1426	...	...	1520	1617	...	1629	...	...	...	1815	1817	...	...	...	...	...	2022	2017	...	...	...	2032	...	2158	...
	Ozieri-Chilivani a.	1509	...	...	...	1655	...	1711	...	...	...	1853	1855	...	...	...	...	...	2106	|	...	...	...	2115	...	...	...
0	Ozieri-Chilivani d.	1514	1514	...	...	1702	1700	1719	1716	...	...	1900	1858	1900	1905	2006	...	...	2108	|	2108	2120	...	...	...	...	...
47	**Sassari** d.	|	1553	...	...	1741	|	1758	|	...	...	1946	|	1939	|	2050	...	...	|	2128	2148	2200	...	...	...	...	...
66	Porto Torres a.	|	...	...	...	1753	|	1810	|	...	...	...	|	...	|	...	...	...	|	...	...	...	...	...	...	...	...
67	Porto Torres M a.	|	...	...	...	1757	|	1814	|	...	...	...	|	...	|	...	...	...	|	...	...	...	...	...	...	...	...
	Olbia a.	1619	...	1626	...	...	1756	...	1814	...	...	...	1951	...	2002	...	...	...	2203	...	...	...	...	...	...	...	...
	Golfo Aranci a.	...	...	1651	...	...	...	...	...	...	...	...	...	...	...	...	...	...	...	...	...	...	...	...	...	...	...

		⚒	⚒	⚒	⚒	†	⚒	⚒	⚒	†	†	⚒		⚒	†	⚒	†	†	⚒	⚒	⚒	†	†	⚒	⚒	⚒
Golfo Aranci d.	...	🚌	...	🚌	...	...	...	...	...	...	...	...	...	0715	...	...	...	...	...	...	...	...	...	...	...	...
Olbia d.	...	...	...	...	...	...	...	0600	...	0651	...	...	...	0738	...	0800	0802	...	...	1000	...	1002	...	...	...	...
Porto Torres M d.	...	...	...	...	...	...	...	|	...	|	...	...	0718	▬	...	|	|	...	0952	|	...	|	1001	...	...	...
Porto Torres d.	...	...	...	...	...	...	...	|	...	|	...	...	0721	⚒	...	|	|	...	0955	|	...	|	1004	...	...	...
Sassari d.	...	...	...	...	...	...	0610	|	0640	|	0715	...	0736	0815	0816	|	|	0917	1010	|	1015	|	1018	...	1215	...
Ozieri-Chilivani a.	...	...	...	...	...	...	0649	0651	|	0751	0754	...	...	0853	0855	0855	0901	1004	...	1053	1051	1059	1056	...	1254	...
Ozieri-Chilivani d.	...	...	...	...	...	...	...	0654	|	...	0801	...	...	...	...	0858	0903	...	...	...	1058	...	1104	...	...	...
Macomer d.	...	0525	...	0620	...	...	...	0738	0753	...	0848	...	...	...	...	0938	0946	...	...	...	1138	...	1147	...	...	1339
Oristano d.	0530	0620	0628	0725	0730	0730	...	...	0835	...	0930	0930	...	...	...	1020	1030	...	...	...	1221	...	1230	1330	...	1430
Decimomannu d.	0629	...	0719	...	0821	0828	...	...	|	...	1018	1030	...	...	...	|	1129	...	...	...	1309	...	1327	1421	...	1521
Cagliari a.	0643	...	0735	...	0837	0841	...	...	0927	...	1031	1051	...	...	...	1110	1144	...	...	...	1323	...	1343	1437	...	1537

	†	⚒	†		†	†	⚒	⚒	⚒	⚒	†	⚒	⚒	†	†		⚒	†	⚒	⚒	⚒	†	†	†		†
Golfo Aranci d.	...	...	...	1335	...	...	...	...	...	...	...	1525	...	...	...	1731	...	...	...	...	...	...	...	...	...	...
Olbia d.	...	...	...	1359	1401	...	1410	...	...	...	...	1550	1600	...	1614	1755	...	...	...	1800	...	...	1852	...	...	2007
Porto Torres M d.	...	1400	...	...	|	...	|	...	...	1552	...	▬	|	...	|	...	...	...	...	|	1813	1850	|	...	...	|
Porto Torres d.	...	1403	...	...	|	...	|	...	...	1555	...	⚒	|	...	|	...	...	...	...	|	1816	1853	|	...	...	|
Sassari d.	...	1418	...	...	|	1422	|	1430	...	1610	...	1615	|	1629	|	...	1651	...	1815	|	1831	1908	|	1921	2025	|
Ozieri-Chilivani a.	...	...	...	...	1503	1500	1510	1508	...	...	...	1653	1655	1708	1714	...	1733	...	1853	1855	...	...	1958	2001	2103t	2106
Ozieri-Chilivani d.	...	...	...	...	...	1508	...	1515	...	...	...	...	1658	...	...	...	1741	...	...	1858	...	...	...	2009	...	...
Macomer d.	...	...	...	...	...	1546	...	1554	1638	...	1731	...	1738	...	...	...	1836	...	...	1938	...	...	...	2057	...	...
Oristano d.	1430	...	1530	...	...	1630	...	1634	1730	...	1830	...	1821	...	...	...	1930	1930	...	2021	...	...	...	2143	...	...
Decimomannu d.	1530	...	1629	...	...	1723	...	|	1829	...	1930	...	1909	...	...	...	2030	2030	...	2109	...	...	...	2241	...	...
Cagliari a.	1552	...	1650	...	...	1738	...	1725	1849	...	1945	...	1923	...	...	...	2052	2052	...	2123	...	...	...	2255	...	...

km																										
		⚒	⚒	⚒	Ⓐ					⚒	⚒	Ⓑ	Ⓑ	⚒	⚒	Ⓑ	Ⓑ	⚒	⚒			⚒	⚒	⚒	⚒	
0	**Cagliari** d.	0526	0545	...	0615	0645	...	0745	...	0845	...	0945	...	1045	...	1145	...	1245	...	1345	...	1418	...	1445	...	1545
17	Decimomannu d.	0541	0604	...	0635	0705	...	0804	...	0904	...	1004	...	1105	...	1204	...	1304	...	1404	...	1432	...	1504	...	1604
46	Villamassargia a.	0601	0629	0639	0701	0729	0734	0829	0834	0929	0934	1029	1034	1129	1134	1229	1234	1329	1334	1429	1434	1457	1502	1529	1534	1629
	Carbonia Serbariu a.	|	0652	|	|	|	0751	0847	|	|	0951	1047	|	|	1150	1247	|	|	1350	1447	|	|	1525	|	1550	1647
55	**Iglesias** a.	0611	...	0648	0712	0739	...	...	0843	0939	...	...	1043	1139	...	...	1243	1339	...	...	1443	1506	...	1539	...	...

	Ⓑ	Ⓑ			Ⓐ	Ⓐ				🚌	
Cagliari d.	1645	...	1745	...	1845	...	1945	...	2045	...	...
Decimomannu d.	1704	...	1804	...	1904	...	2004	...	2105	...	...
Villamassargia a.	1729	1734	1829	1834	1929	1934	2029	2034	2129	2135	...
Carbonia Serbariu a.	|	1750	1847	|	|	1950	2047	|	|	2158	...
Iglesias a.	1739	...	...	1843	1939	...	...	2043	2138	...	...

	⚒	⚒	⚒	†	⚒				Ⓐ	
Iglesias d.	0554	0626	...	0630	0654	...	0722	...	0754	0819
Carbonia Serbariu d.	|	|	0616	|	|	0710	|	...	|	|
Villamassargia d.	0603	0633	0638	0638	0703	0726	0731	...	0803	0826
Decimomannu d.	0632	...	0702	0703	0732	...	0755	...	0831	...
Cagliari a.	0651	...	0723	0723	0750	...	0812	...	0850	...

km																											
		⚒	⚒	Ⓑ	Ⓑ	⚒	⚒	Ⓑ	Ⓑ	⚒	⚒		†	⚒		⚒	⚒	⚒			Ⓑ	Ⓑ			Ⓐ	Ⓐ	
	Iglesias d.	...	0922	1019	...	...	1122	1219	...	...	1322	1419	...	...	...	...	1522	1554	1619	...	...	1722	1819	...	...	1922	2019
0	**Carbonia** Serbariu d.	0910	|	|	1010	1110	|	|	1210	1310	|	|	1410	1410	...	1510	|	|	|	1610	1710	|	|	1810	1910	|	|
23	Villamassargia d.	0926	0931	1026	1031	1126	1131	1226	1231	1326	1331	1426	1431	1431	...	1526	1531	1602	1626	1631	1726	1731	1826	1831	1926	1931	2026
	Decimomannu d.	...	0955	...	1055	...	1156	...	1255	...	1355	...	1454	1500	...	...	1555	1631	...	1655	...	1755	...	1855	...	1955	...
	Cagliari a.	...	1015	...	1115	...	1214	...	1315	...	1413	...	1512	1519	...	...	1612	1645	...	1716	...	1812	...	1915	...	2013	...

j – Arrive 10 minutes later on †.

t – Arrive 2112 on ⚒.

Narrow gauge services on Sardinia are operated by ARST Gestione FdS, Via Zagabria 54, 09129 Cagliari. ✆ +39 070 4098 1, fax +39 070 4098 220, www.arst.sardegna.it.

Regular services operate on the following routes to differing frequencies: Monserrato Gottardo - Isili (*71 km*); Macomer - Nuoro (*61 km*); Sassari - Alghero (*30 km*); Sassari - Sorso (*11 km*). Tram connections are available at Monserrato Gottardo to / from Cagliari (Repubblica).

Additionally, summer only tourist services operate on the following routes: Sassari - Te (*91 km*); Tempio - Palau Marina (*59 km*); Macomer - Bosa Marina (*46 km*); Mandas - Ar (*159 km*); Isili - Sorgono (*83 km*). See www.treninoverde.com.

MILANO - BOLOGNA - RIMINI - ANCONA

	2 ⚒	2 ⚒	2 †	2	FB 9851 🍷 ◆	2 ⚒			IC 603	FB 9801 🍷 ◆		FR 9593 🍷	P	FB 9803 🍷	2	IC 605 ◆	Ⓒ	Ⓐ	FB 9807 🍷		IC 607	FB 9809 🍷 ◆	IC 1545 ◆		FB 9811 🍷
Torino Porta Nuova **615** d.	...	...	...	...	...	...	...	...	...	...	...	...	...	...	...	...	...	...	0832	...	...	...	...	...	...
Milano Centrale **600/15** d.	...	...	...	...	...	...	...	...	...	...	...	0750	0620	0735	...	0710	...	...	|	...	...	1035	1000	...	1135
Bologna Centrale d.	...	...	...	0500	...	...	0635	0735	0800	0842	0835	0858	0911	0942	0935	0958	1035	1035	1142	1135	1200	1242	1223	1235	1342
Imola d.	...	...	...	0526	...	...	0701	0801	|	|	0901	|	0945	|	1001	|	1101	1101	|	1201	|	|	|	1301	|
Castelbolognese-Riolo Terme d.	...	...	...	0532	...	...	0709	0809	|	|	0909	|	|	|	1009	|	1109	1109	|	1209	|	|	|	1309	|
Faenza d.	...	...	...	0538	...	...	0716	0816	0825	|	0916	|	0954	|	1016	1025	1116	1124	|	1216	1225	|	1256	1316	|
Forlì d.	...	...	...	0547	...	...	0727	0827	0836	|	0927	|	1003	|	1027	1036	1127	1142	|	1227	1236	|	1306	1327	|
Cesena d.	...	...	...	0602	...	...	0742	0842	0848	|	0945	|	1014	|	1042	1048	1142	1205	|	1244	1248	|	1328	1342	|
Rimini 621 ● ⊖ d.	0547	0610	0628	0629	0644	0720	0803	0903	0910	0936	1005	0957	1042	1036	1103	1110	1203	1232	1236	1315	1310	1336	1352	1403	1436
Riccione d.	0558	0620	0636	...	|	0730	0813	0911	0919	|	1014	|	1052	|	...	1119	1213	1242	|	1325	1319	|	1400	1413	|
Cattolica-Gabicce d.	0606	0629	0643	...	|	0739	0823	0918	|	|	1023	|	1059	|	...	|	1223	1255	|	1335	|	|	|	1423	|
Pesaro d.	0617	0640	0654	...	0702	0751	0834	0929	0938	0958	1034	|	1111	1058	...	1138	1234	1309	1258	1347	1335	1358	1415	1434	1455
Fano d.	0625	0648	0705	...	|	0759	0842	0937	0947	|	1042	|	|	|	...	1147	1242	1317	|	1355	1344	|	1424	1442	|
Senigallia d.	0640	0702	0724	...	|	0813	0857	0952	0959	|	1057	|	1130	|	...	1159	1257	1331	|	1410	1358	|	1438	1457	|
Falconara Marittima **625** d.	0654	0717	0738	...	0729	0828	0907	1002	|	|	1108	|	|	|	...	|	1308	1347	|	1429	|	|	|	1508	|
Ancona 625 a.	0707	0729	0748	...	...	0843	0919	1012	1018	1029	1119	1042	1150	1129	...	1218	1319	1400	1329	1442	1414	1429	1459	1519	1529
Pescara Centrale **631** a.	...	0935	0950	...	...	...	...	...	1159	1140	...	1151	1345	1240	...	1352	...	...	1440	...	1552	1540	1656	...	1640
Bari Centrale **631** a.	...	...	...	...	...	...	...	...	1511	1432	...	1425	...	1521	...	1700	...	...	1721	...	1900	1821	2026	...	1930
Lecce **631** a.	...	...	...	...	...	...	...	...	1706	1555	...	...	...	1648	...	...	...	...	1848	...	...	...	2215	...	2055

		IC 609	FB 9813 🍷		FB 9815 🍷		IC 611	EC 85 ✕ ◆	FB 9817 🍷 ◆		FB 9819 🍷		IC 613		FR 9591 🍷	FB 9823 🍷		FB 9825 🍷		FB 9829 🍷	2	ICN 765 ◆	ICN 755 ◆	ICN 757 ◆		
rino Porta Nuova **615** d.	...	...	...	...	...	...	...	...	...	...	...	...	...	...	...	...	...	...	...	...	...	...	...	2020	...	...
no Centrale **600/15** d.	...	...	1235	...	1335	...	...	...	...	...	1535	...	1510	...	1740	1735	...	1835	...	1935	...	1950	2050	|	...	...
gna Centrale d.	1335	1400	1442	1435	1542	1535	1600	1625	1642	1635	1742	1735	1758	1835	1858	1942	1935	2042	2035	2142	2135	2200	2310	2352	0030	...
a d.	1401	|	|	1501	|	1601	|	|	|	1701	|	1801	|	1901	|	|	2001	|	2101	|	2201	|	|	|	0100	...
elbolognese-Riolo Terme d.	1409	|	|	1509	|	1609	|	|	|	1709	|	1809	|	1909	|	|	2009	|	2109	|	2209	|	|	|	0109	...
za d.	1416	1425	|	1516	|	1616	1625	|	|	1716	1807	1816	1825	1916	|	2007	2016	2107	2116	|	2216	2234	2337	|	0117	...
d.	1427	1436	|	1527	|	1627	1636	|	|	1727	1817	1827	1836	1927	1931	2017	2027	2117	2127	|	2227	2246	2348	|	...	...
na d.	1442	1448	|	1542	|	1642	1648	|	|	1742	1829	1842	1848	1945	|	2029	2043	2129	2142	|	2242	2300	0002	|	...	...
ni 621 ● ⊖ d.	1503	1510	1536	1603	1636	1712	1710	1729	1736	1803	1848	1903	1910	2005	1956	2048	2110	2148	2203	2236	2320	2330	0025	0058	...	...
one d.	1510	1519	|	1613	|	1723	1719	...	|	1813	|	1911	1919	2014	|	|	...	|	2213	|	...	|	|	|	...	...
lica-Gabicce d.	1517	|	|	1623	|	1733	|	...	|	1823	|	1923	|	2023	|	|	...	|	2223	|	...	|	|	|	...	...
ro d.	1528	1535	1558	1634	1658	1745	1735	...	1758	1834	1910	1939	1938	2034	2017	2110	...	2210	2234	2258	...	0000	|	|	...	...
d.	1536	1544	|	1642	|	...	1744	...	|	1842	|	1951	1947	2042	|	|	...	|	2242	|	...	|	|	|	...	...
gallia d.	1550	1558	|	1657	|	...	1758	...	|	1857	|	2005	1959	2057	|	|	...	|	2257	|	...	|	|	|	...	...
onara Marittima **625** d.	1604	|	|	1708	|	...	|	...	|	1908	|	2021	|	2108	|	|	...	|	2308	|	...	|	|	|	...	...
ona 625 a.	1625	1614	1629	1719	1729	...	1814	...	1829	1919	1941	2031	2018	2119	2046	2141	...	2241	2319	2329	...	0048	0131	0206	...	...
Pescara Centrale **631** a.	...	1752	1740	...	1840	...	1952	...	1940	...	2057	...	2152	...	...	2258	...	...	...	...	...	0228	0313	0340	...	...
Bari Centrale **631** a.	...	2100	2021	...	2121	...	2259	...	2221	...	2338	...	...	...	...	...	...	...	...	...	...	0611	0644	0654	...	...
Lecce **631** a.	...	2256	2148	...	2248	...	...	...	2348	...	...	...	...	...	...	...	...	...	...	...	...	0915	0830	0852	...	...

	ICN 1580 ◆	ICN 758 ◆	ICN 752 ◆		FB 9802 🍷	ICN 754 ◆		FR 9592 🍷	FB 9804 🍷		FB 9806 🍷		Ⓐ	IC 604	Ⓒ		FB 9810 🍷	EC 84 ✕ ◆		IC 606		FB 9814 🍷		FB 9816 🍷 ◆	IC 608	
Lecce **631** d.	1835	1825	2120	...	...	2210	...	...	...	...	...	...	...	...	...	...	...	...	...	...	...	0603	...	0703	0620	...
Bari Centrale **631** d.	2030	2133	2309	...	...	0001	...	...	...	...	...	...	...	...	...	...	0530	...	...	0555	...	0730	...	0830	0755	...
Pescara Centrale **631** d.	0008	0105	0235	...	...	0323	...	...	...	...	0600	...	...	0710	...	...	0811	...	...	0904	...	1011	...	1111	1104	...
ona 625 d.	0139	0231	0406	0435	0500	0510	0533	0610	0620	0640	0716	0740	0825	0841	0850	...	0922	...	...	1036	1040	1122	1140	1222	1236	1240
onara Marittima **625** d.	|	|	|	0444	|	|	0541	|	|	0651	|	0753	0834	|	0901	...	|	...	...	|	1051	|	1151	|	|	1251
gallia d.	|	|	|	0457	|	|	0551	|	|	0705	|	0805	0844	0859	0911	...	|	...	...	1054	1101	|	1205	|	1254	1301
d.	|	|	|	0512	|	|	0606	|	|	0721	|	0820	0858	0912	0925	...	|	...	...	1107	1115	|	1221	|	1307	1315
ro d.	|	|	|	0520	0528	0543	0615	0636	0649	0729	0745	0828	0906	0922	0934	...	0955	...	...	1117	1124	1155	1229	1255	1317	1324
lica-Gabicce d.	|	|	|	0534	|	|	0626	|	|	0740	|	0839	0917	|	0945	...	|	...	...	|	1135	|	1240	|	|	1335
one d.	|	|	|	0547	|	|	0633	|	|	0749	|	0847	0926	0939	0954	...	|	...	...	1134	1144	|	1249	|	1334	1344
ni 621 ● ⊖ d.	0245	0324	0459	0600	0550	0610	0645	0654	0709	0800	0806	0857	0940	0951	1007	...	1017	1035	1041	1147	1157	1217	1300	1317	1347	1357
na d.	|	|	|	0618	0607	0628	0711	|	0725	0816	0824	0916	1001	1009	1025	...	|	|	1108	1207	1216	|	1318	|	1407	1416
d.	|	|	|	0631	0620	0640	0724	0718	0736	0827	0836	0927	1023	1021	1036	...	|	|	1123	1219	1227	|	1329	|	1419	1427
nza d.	|	|	|	0642	0629	0650	0735	|	0746	0838	0846	0937	1034	1031	1046	...	|	|	1133	1229	1237	|	1339	|	1429	1438
elbolognese-Riolo Terme d.	|	|	|	0649	|	|	0743	|	|	0844	|	0944	1044	|	1058	...	|	|	1140	|	1244	|	1345	|	|	1444
a d.	|	|	|	0656	|	|	0756	|	|	0856	|	0956	1056	|	1104	...	|	|	1146	|	1256	|	1356	|	|	1456
gna Centrale a.	0352	0427	0615	0722	0701	0727	0821	0807	0814	0921	0914	1021	1121	1101	1129	...	1114	1147	1221	1300	1321	1314	1421	1412	1500	1521
no Centrale **600/15** a.	|	0712	0930	...	0910	|	...	0920	1025	...	1125	...	...	1345	...	...	1325	...	...	...	...	1525	...	...	...	...
rino Porta Nuova **615** a.	0740	...	...	...	...	1120	...	...	...	...	...	...	...	...	...	...	...	...	...	...	...	...	...	...	...	...

	FB 9818 🍷	2	2 ⚒	IC 610		FB 9822 🍷 ◆			FB 9824 🍷	IC 1546 ◆	IC 612 ◆		FB 9826 🍷		FB 9828 🍷 ◆	P	IC 614		FB 9830 🍷	FR 9594 🍷	2	2 ⚒	FB 9852 🍷 ◆		2	
Lecce **631** d.	0803	...	...	0820	...	...	...	...	1103	1005	...	...	1203	...	1303	...	...	...	1403	...	...	...	...	...	...	...
Bari Centrale **631** d.	0930	...	...	0955	...	1130	...	...	1230	1142	1155	...	1330	...	1430	...	1355	...	1530	1615	...	...	...	...	...	...
Pescara Centrale **631** d.	1211	...	...	1304	...	1411	...	...	1511	1445	1504	...	1611	...	1711	1620	1704	...	1811	1848	...	...	...	...	...	...
ona 625 d.	1322	...	1337	1436	1440	1522	...	...	1622	1617	1636	1640	1722	...	1822	1810	1836	1840	1922	1956	...	1947	...	2040	2240	...
onara Marittima **625** d.	|	...	1349	|	1451	|	...	...	|	|	|	1651	|	...	|	1818	|	1851	|	|	...	2004	2029	2051	2249	...
gallia d.	|	...	1404	1454	1501	|	...	...	|	1632	1654	1704	|	...	|	1833	1854	1904	|	|	...	2020	|	2104	2301	...
d.	|	...	1418	1507	1515	|	...	...	|	1645	1707	1718	|	...	|	1851	1907	1918	|	|	...	2034	|	2118	2315	...
ro d.	1355	...	1427	1517	1524	1555	...	...	1655	1701	1717	1727	1758	1817	1855	1901	1917	1927	1955	|	...	2042	2053	2127	2323	...
lica-Gabicce d.	|	...	1438	|	1535	|	...	...	|	|	|	1738	|	1828	|	1912	|	1938	|	|	...	2053	|	2138	2334	...
ione d.	|	...	1446	1534	1544	|	...	...	|	1717	1734	1745	|	1837	|	1919	1934	1945	|	|	...	2101	|	2145	2341	...
ni 621 ● ⊖ d.	1417	1444	1458	1547	1557	1617	1644	...	1717	1727	1747	1757	1817	1847	1917	1927	1947	1957	2017	2042	2050	2112	2115	2157	2355	...
na d.	|	1509	...	1607	1616	|	1709	...	|	1744	1807	1816	|	1912	|	1944	2007	2016	|	|	2111	...	...	2216	...	...
d.	|	1527	...	1619	1627	|	1727	...	|	1757	1819	1827	|	1926	|	1956	2019	2027	|	|	2125	...	...	2227	...	...
nza d.	|	1537	...	1629	1638	|	1736	...	|	1807	1829	1837	|	1937	|	2007	2029	2037	|	|	2135	...	...	2238	...	...
elbolognese-Riolo Terme d.	|	1544	...	|	1644	|	1744	...	|	|	|	1844	|	1945	|	|	|	2044	|	|	2142	...	...	2244	..	...
a d.	|	1556	...	|	1656	|	1756	...	|	|	|	1856	|	1956	|	2017	|	2056	|	|	2148	...	...	2256	...	...
gna Centrale a.	1514	1621	...	1700	1721	1714	1821	...	1814	1833	1901	1921	1914	2021	2012	2047	2100	2121	2114	2137	2214	...	...	2321	...	...
no Centrale **600/15** a.	1725	...	...	...	...	1925	...	...	|	2115	2145	...	2125	...	...	2325	...	...	2325	2250	...	...	...	...	...	...
rino Porta Nuova **615** a.	...	...	...	...	...	...	...	...	2140	...	...	...	...	...	...	...	...	...	...	...	...	...	...	...	...	...

NOTES (LISTED BY TRAIN NUMBER)

- ⑥⑦ June 18 - Sept. 11: [12] and ✕ Rimini - Bologna - München. Also available to passengers without reservation. Operator within Italy: LeNord.
- ⑤⑥ June 17 - Sept. 10: [12] and ✕ München - Bologna - Rimini. Also available to passengers without reservation. Operator within Italy: LeNord.
- – [12] Milano - Bologna - Bari - Taranto.
- – [12] Taranto - Bari - Milano.
- – 🛏 1, 2 cl., ▬ 2 cl. (4 berth) and [2] Lecce - Bologna - Milano.
- – ①–⑥: 🛏 1, 2 cl., ▬ 2 cl. (4 berth) and [2] Lecce - Bologna - Torino.
- – 🛏 1, 2 cl., ▬ 2 cl. (4 berth) and [2] Milano - Bologna - Lecce.
- – 🛏 1, 2 cl., ▬ 2 cl. (4 berth) and [2] Torino - Bologna - Lecce.
- – 🛏 1, 2 cl., ▬ 2 cl. (4 berth) and [2] Lecce - Bologna - Milano.
- – 🛏 1, 2 cl., ▬ 2 cl. (4 berth) and [2] Milano - Bologna - Lecce.

1545 – ⑥ (also June 2; not June 4, and days before holidays): [12] Milano - Lecce.
1546 – ⑦ (also Mar. 28, Apr. 25; not Mar. 27, Apr. 24): [12] Lecce - Milano.
1580 – ⑦: 🛏 1, 2 cl., ▬ 2 cl. (4 berth) and [2] Lecce - Bologna - Torino.
9801 – [12] and 🍷 Venezia - Bologna - Lecce.
9809 – [12] and 🍷 Milano - Bari - Taranto.
9816 – [12] and 🍷 Lecce - Bologna - Venezia.
9817 – [12] and 🍷 Venezia - Bologna - Lecce.
9822 – [12] and 🍷 Taranto - Bari - Milano.
9828 – [12] and 🍷 Lecce - Bologna - Venezia.
9851/2 – [12] and 🍷 Ravenna - Rimini - Roma and v.v.

P – ⑥⑦ (also Mar. 28, Apr. 25; not Mar. 27, Apr. 24): [2] Milano - Pescara and v.v.

⊖ – Connections may be available to service(s) in previous column(s).
● – For 🚌 service Rimini - San Marino and v.v. – see page 312.

631 ANCONA - BARI - LECCE

km		2 ⚒	2	2 ⚒	ICN 765 ♦	ICN 789 ♦	ICN 755 ♦	ICN 757 ♦	ICN 765 ♦		2 ⚒	2 ⚒	2	FA 9351 🍷	2 ⚒	2 ⚒	2 ⚒	IC 703 2	2 ⚒	FB 9801 🍷 ♦	FR 9593 🍷	2	IC 603	FB 9803 🍷
	Torino Porta Nuova **615** d.	...	...	...	...	...	...	2020	...	...	...	...	...	...	...	...	...	...	...	...	...	...	...	...
	Milano Centrale **615/30** d.	...	...	...	1950	...	2050	|	...	...	...	...	...	...	...	...	...	...	...	...	0750	...	...	0735
	Bologna Centrale **615/30** d.	...	...	...	2200	...	2310	2352	...	...	...	...	...	...	...	...	...	...	...	0842	0858	...	0800	0942
0	**Ancona 625/30** d.	...	...	...	0051	...	0134	0209	...	...	...	...	...	...	...	...	...	...	...	1032	1045	...	1021	1132
43	Civitanova Marche-Montegranaro d.	...	...	...	|	...	|	|	...	...	...	...	...	...	...	...	...	...	...	|	|	...	1042	|
85	S. Benedetto del Tronto d.	...	...	...	|	...	|	|	...	...	...	...	...	...	...	...	...	...	...	|	|	...	1116	|
146	**Pescara** Centrale a.	...	...	...	0228	...	0313	0340	...	...	...	...	...	...	...	...	...	...	...	1140	1151	...	1159	1240
146	**Pescara** Centrale d.	...	...	...	0233	...	0315	0342	...	...	...	...	...	...	...	...	...	...	...	1143	1154	...	1201	1243
236	Termoli d.	...	...	...	|	...	|	|	...	...	...	...	...	...	...	...	...	...	...	1231	1242	...	1255	1331
	Roma Termini **626** d.	...	...	...	|	2358	|	|	...	...	...	...	...	0805	...	...	...	0728	...	|	|	...	|	|
323	**Foggia 626** a.	...	...	...	0449	0449	0515	0535	...	...	...	...	...	1056	...	...	...	1223	...	1315	1325	...	1352	1415
323	**Foggia** d.	...	...	...	0453	0504	0519	0539	...	...	0606	0710	...	1105	...	...	...	1238	...	1318	1328	...	1355	1418
391	Barletta d.	...	...	...	0527	0537	0554	0615	...	...	0650	0754	...	1136	...	...	...	1310	...	1351	|	...	1428	1447
446	**Bari** Centrale a.	...	...	...	0611	0621	0644	0654	←	...	0740	0844	...	1204	...	...	...	1400	...	1432	1425	...	1511	1521
446	**Bari** Centrale ▲ d.	0500	0542	0610	0641	0625	0648	0658	0641	...	0744	0846	0940	1208	1215	1257	1332	...	1415	1436	...	1442	1515	1525
	Gioia del Colle ▲ d.	|	|	|	→	|	|	|	0717	...	|	|	|	|	|	|	|	...	|	|	...	|	|	|
	Taranto 637/8 ▲ a.	|	|	|	...	|	|	|	0755	...	|	|	|	|	|	|	|	...	|	|	...	|	|	|
487	Monopoli d.	0534	0616	0638	...	0649	0712	0727	|	...	0820	0915	1014	|	1241	1331	1400	...	1442	|	...	1516	1545	|
501	Fasano d.	0542	0624	0646	...	0700	0723	0740	|	...	0829	0923	1022	|	1249	1339	|	...	1451	|	...	1524	1604	|
521	Ostuni d.	0555	0637	0657	...	0714	0739	0754	|	...	0840	0936	1035	|	|	1350	|	...	1503	|	...	1537	1619	|
557	**Brindisi** ♣ d.	0620	0702	0717	...	0737	0803	0820	0850	...	0906	1003	1058	1303	1320	1411	1440	...	1535	1530	...	1603	1642	1619
596	**Lecce** a.	0652	0735	0745	...	0810	0830	0852	0915	...	0935	1034	1130	1328	1345	1443	1505	...	1615	1555	...	1634	1706	1648

	2 ⚒	P	IC 605	FB 9807 🍷	2	FB 9809 🍷	IC 607	FA 9355 🍷	FB 9811 🍷	2	IC 1545 ♦	FB 9813 🍷	IC 1545 ♦	2 ⚒	IC 609	FB 9815 🍷	IC 705 ⑤y	FA 9357 🍷	FB 9817 🍷 ♦	2	IC 611	FB 9819 🍷	IC 613	FB 9823 🍷
Torino Porta Nuova **615** d.	...	...	...	0832	...	...	...	...	...	...	...	...	...	...	...	...	...	...	...	...	...	...	...	...
Milano Centrale **615/30** d.	...	0620	0710	|	...	1035	...	...	1135	...	1000	1235	...	...	...	1335	...	...	...	...	...	1535	1510	1735
Bologna Centrale **615/30** d.	...	0911	0958	1142	...	1242	1200	...	1342	...	1223	1442	...	...	1400	1542	...	...	1642	...	1600	1742	1758	1942
Ancona 625/30 d.	...	1152	1221	1332	...	1432	1417	...	1532	...	1501	1629	...	...	1617	1732	...	...	1832	...	1817	1944	2021	2144
Civitanova Marche-Montegranaro d.	...	1227	1242	|	...	|	1443	...	|	...	1529	|	...	...	1643	|	...	...	|	...	1843	|	2042	|
S. Benedetto del Tronto d.	...	1256	1316	|	...	|	1516	...	|	...	1558	|	...	...	1716	|	...	...	|	...	1916	2023	2116	2223
Pescara Centrale a.	...	1345	1352	1440	...	1540	1552	...	1640	...	1656	1740	...	...	1752	1840	...	...	1940	...	1952	2057	2152	2258
Pescara Centrale d.	...	...	1354	1443	...	1543	1554	...	1643	...	1700	1743	...	...	1754	1843	...	...	1943	...	1954	2100	...	...
Termoli d.	...	...	1447	1531	...	1631	1647	...	1731	...	1759	1831	...	...	1847	1931	...	...	2031	...	2047	2148	...	...
Roma Termini **626** d.	...	...	|	|	...	|	|	1445	|	...	|	|	...	...	|	|	1606	1800	|	...	|	|	...	...
Foggia 626 a.	...	...	1535	1615	...	1715	1735	1741	1821	...	1851	1915	...	...	1935	2015	2018	2056	2115	...	2135	2232	...	...
Foggia d.	...	...	1538	1618	...	1718	1738	1750	1824	...	1854	1918	...	...	1938	2018	2036	2105	2118	...	2138	2235	...	...
Barletta d.	...	...	1610	1647	...	1747	1810	1818	1852	...	1930	1947	←	...	2010	2047	2110	2136	2147	...	2210	2304	...	...
Bari Centrale a.	...	...	1700	1721	...	1821	1900	1849	1930	...	2026	2021	2026	...	2100	2121	2143	2204	2221	...	2259	2338	...	...
Bari Centrale ▲ d.	1635	...	1715	1725	1815	1836	...	1853	1934	1945	→	2025	2030	2040	2104	2125	2201	2208	2225	2240	...	...	...	...
Gioia del Colle ▲ d.	|	...	1747	|	|	1908	...	|	|	|	...	|	|	|	|	|	2232	|	|	|	...	...	...	...
Taranto 637/8 ▲ a.	|	...	1820	|	|	1942	...	|	|	|	...	|	|	|	|	|	2310	|	|	|	...	...	...	...
Monopoli d.	1706	...	...	|	1850	...	...	|	|	2019	...	|	2058	2114	2130	|	...	|	|	2314	...	...	...	...
Fasano d.	1715	...	...	|	1859	...	...	|	|	2027	...	|	2108	2123	2142	|	...	|	|	2322	...	...	...	...
Ostuni d.	1726	...	...	|	1912	...	...	|	|	2040	...	|	2123	2137	2154	|	...	|	|	2335	...	...	...	...
Brindisi ♣ d.	1747	...	...	1819	1934	...	...	1948	2030	2105	...	2119	2147	2201	2231	2219	...	2303	2319	2357	...	...	...	...
Lecce a.	1820	...	...	1848	2005	...	...	2013	2055	...	...	2148	2215	2233	2256	2248	...	2328	2348	0030	...	...	...	...

	FB 9806 🍷	IC 604	FB 9810 🍷	IC 606	2 ⚒	2	FA 9350 🍷	FB 9814 🍷	IC 608	2 ⚒	FB 9816 🍷 ♦	2 ⚒	FB 9818 🍷	IC 610	2 ⚒	FB 9822 🍷	IC 1546 🍷 ♦	2 ⚒		IC 612	2 ⚒	FB 9824 🍷	FA 9354 🍷	FB 9826 🍷
Lecce d.	...	...	...	...	0450	0508	0550	0603	0620	0610	0703	0710	0803	0820	0810	...	1005	1000	...	...	1040	1103	1150	1203
Brindisi ♣ d.	...	...	...	...	0522	0536	0611	0626	0642	0646	0726	0739	0826	0842	0845	...	1029	1031	...	...	1109	1126	1211	1226
Ostuni d.	...	...	...	...	0544	0600	|	|	0704	0715	|	|	|	0904	0914	...	1050	1052	...	...	1131	|	|	|
Fasano d.	...	...	...	...	0558	0615	|	|	0717	0729	|	0810	|	0917	|	...	1103	1104	...	...	1145	|	|	|
Monopoli d.	...	...	...	...	0607	0623	|	|	0727	0738	|	0820	|	0927	0934	...	1114	1113	...	...	1153	|	|	|
Taranto 637/8 ▲ d.	...	...	...	...	|	|	|	|	|	|	|	|	|	|	|	1010	|	|	...	1025	|	|	|	|
Gioia del Colle ▲ d.	...	...	...	...	|	|	|	|	|	|	|	|	|	|	|	1041	|	|	...	1059	|	|	|	|
Bari Centrale ▲ a.	...	...	...	...	0643	0700	0710	0726	0751	0812	0826	0848	0926	0951	1000	1115	1139	1153	...	1130	1238	1226	1310	1326
Bari Centrale d.	...	...	0530	0555	0645	...	0714	0730	0755	0814	0830	...	0930	0955	...	1130	1142	...	...	1155	1240	1230	1314	1330
Barletta d.	...	...	0602	0643	0732	...	0745	0802	0843	0917	0902	...	1002	1043	...	1202	1224	...	...	1243	1326	1302	1345	1402
Foggia a.	...	...	0633	0717	...	...	0813	0833	0917	1000	0933	...	1033	1117	...	1233	1252	...	...	1317	1410	1333	1413	1433
Foggia 626 d.	...	...	0636	0720	...	...	0822	0836	0920	...	0936	...	1036	1120	...	1236	1254	...	...	1320	...	1336	1422	1436
Roma Termini **626** a.	...	...	|	|	...	...	1120	|	|	...	|	...	|	|	...	|	|	...	...	|	...	|	1720	|
Termoli d.	...	...	0722	0810	...	...	...	0922	1010	...	1022	...	1122	1210	...	1322	1353	...	...	1410	...	1422	...	1522
Pescara Centrale a.	...	...	0808	0902	...	...	...	1008	1102	...	1108	...	1208	1302	...	1408	1443	...	...	1502	...	1508	...	1608
Pescara Centrale d.	0600	0710	0811	0904	...	...	...	1011	1104	...	1111	...	1211	1304	...	1411	1445	...	...	1504	...	1511	...	1611
S. Benedetto del Tronto d.	0630	0745	0840	0940	...	...	...	|	1141	...	|	...	|	1340	...	|	1520	...	...	1541	...	|	...	|
Civitanova Marche-Montegranaro d.	|	0810	|	1006	...	...	...	|	1210	...	|	...	|	1406	...	|	1545	...	...	1610	...	|	...	|
Ancona 625/30 a.	0713	0838	0919	1033	...	...	...	1119	1233	...	1219	...	1319	1433	...	1519	1614	...	...	1633	...	1619	...	1719
Bologna Centrale **615/30** a.	0914	1101	1114	1300	...	...	...	1314	1500	...	1412	...	1514	1700	...	1714	1833	...	...	1901	...	1814	...	1914
Milano Centrale **615/30** a.	1125	1345	1325	...	...	...	...	1525	...	...	...	...	1725	...	...	1925	2115	...	...	2145	...	|	...	2125
Torino Porta Nuova **615** a.	...	...	...	...	...	...	...	...	...	...	...	...	...	...	...	...	...	...	...	...	...	2140	...	...

♦ – **NOTES** (LISTED BY TRAIN NUMBER)

755 – 🛏 1, 2 cl., ▬ 2 cl. (4 berth) and (2) Milano - Bologna - Lecce.
757 – 🛏 1, 2 cl., ▬ 2 cl. (4 berth) and (2) Torino - Bologna - Lecce.
765 – 🛏 1, 2 cl., ▬ 2 cl. (4 berth) and (2) Milano - Bologna - Lecce.
789 – ⑤ (from Roma): 🛏 1, 2 cl., ▬ 2 cl. (4 berth) and (2) Roma - Lecce.
1545 – ⑥ (also June 2; not June 4, and days before holidays): (12) Milano - Lecce.
1546 – ⑦ (also Mar. 28, Apr. 25; not Mar. 27, Apr. 24): (12) Lecce - Milano.
9801 – (12) and 🍷 Venezia - Bologna - Lecce.
9816 – (12) and 🍷 Lecce - Bologna - Venezia.
9817 – (12) and 🍷 Venezia - Bologna - Lecce.

P – ⑥⑦ (also Mar. 28, Apr. 25; not Mar. 27, Apr. 24): (2) Milano - Pescara and v.v.

y – Also June 2; not June 3.

▲ – For additional services Bari - Taranto and v.v. – see page 313.
♣ – For additional services Brindisi - Taranto and v.v. – see panel.
● – For 🚌 service Rimini - San Marino and v.v. – see panel.

BRINDISI - TARANTO
No service on

	⚒	⚒		⚒		⚒	⚒		⚒	
Brindisi d.	0654	0749	...	1050	...	1515	1650	...	1809	20
Francavilla Fontana **636** d.	0723	0819	...	1120	...	1546	1720	...	1838	20
Taranto a.	0755	0853	...	1148	...	1619	1748	...	1913	20

	⚒	⚒	⚒		⚒		⚒	⚒	⚒
Taranto d.	0554	0614	0859	...	1249	...	1457	1649	1849
Francavilla Fontana **636** d.	0620	0640	0925	...	1316	...	1523	1717	1915
Brindisi a.	0651	0718	0957	...	1347	...	1556	1753	1954

● – 🚌 service **RIMINI - SAN MARINO and v.v.**: **Valid Sept. 15, 2015 - June 6, 20**
27 km, journey 50 – 55 minutes.

From **Rimini** (FS railway station): 0810, 0925, 1040, 1155⚒, 1215†, 1310⚒, 1425, 15
1655, 1810, 1925⚒.

From **San Marino**: 0645⚒, 0800, 0915, 1030, 1145⚒, 1215†, 1300⚒, 1415, 1530, 16
1800, 1915⚒.

Operator: BonelliBus s.a.s., Via Murano 47838, Riccione ✆ +39 0541 662 069.

LECCE - BARI - ANCONA 631

	IC	*FB*			*FB*		*IC*	*FR*		*IC*				*FA*			*ICN*	*ICN*		*ICN*	*ICN*	*ICN*	
	614	**9828**			**9830**		**704**	**9594**		**710**				**9358**			**1580**	**758**		**752**	**754**	**788**	
	2		🍷	2	2	🍷	2	2	🍷	2		2	2	2	🍷	2	2			2			
			♦	⚒	†		⚒			⚒	†y		⚒	⚒		⚒	⚒	♦	♦		♦	♦	♦
e ... d.	1210	...	1303	1323	1340	1403	1355	...	...	1430	...	1510	1610	1630	1650	1710	1835	1835	1825	1955	2120	2210	2230	...
isi ♣ ... d.	1238	...	1326	1348	1410	1426	1430	...	...	1500	...	1542	1633	1652	1711	1739	1858	1904	1851	2025	2148	2238	2255	...
i ... d.	1300	...	|	1409	1432	|	1459	...	...	1522	...	1606	1655	|	|	1803	1919	1928	|	2049	2211	2301	2317	...
o ... d.	1314	...	|	1420	1446	|	1513	...	...	1536	...	1620	1707	1722	|	1817	1931	1943	|	2103	2226	2316	2330	...
oli ... d.	1322	...	|	1430	1455	|	1522	...	...	1544	...	1628	1717	1731	|	1827	1940	1955	|	2111	2237	2327	2340	...
anto 637/8 ▲ d.	|	...	|	|	|	|	|	...	...	|	1540	|	|	|	|	|	|	|	1949	|	|	|	|	...
ia del Colle ▲ d.	|	...	|	|	|	|	|	...	...	|	1612	|	|	|	|	|	|	|	2023	|	|	|	|	...
Centrale ▲ a.	1358	...	1426	1508	1545	1526	1600	...	...	1620	1649	1705	1753	1800	1810	1905	2015	2026	2108	2150	2305	2357	0010	...
Centrale ... d.	...	1355	1430	...	...	1530	...	1555	1615	...	1705	...	...	...	1814	...	...	2030	2133	...	2309	0001	0015	...
ta ... d.	...	1443	1502	...	...	1602	...	1648	|	...	1737	...	...	...	1845	...	...	2121	2221	...	2357	0034	0103	...
ia ... a.	...	1517	1533	...	...	1633	...	1725	1711	...	1810	...	...	...	1913	...	...	2200	2302	...	0037	0111	0145	...
a 626 ... d.	...	1520	1536	...	...	1636	...	1741	1714	...	1827	...	...	...	1922	...	...	2203	2306	...	0041	0115	0200	...
na Termini **626** ... a.	...	|	|	...	...	|	...	2220	|	...	2300	...	...	...	2220	...	...	|	|	...	|	|	0634	...
oli ... d.	...	1610	1622	...	...	1722	...	...	1758	...	...	...	...	...	...	...	...	2304	|	...	|	|	...	...
ara Centrale ... a.	...	1702	1708	...	...	1808	...	...	1845	...	...	...	...	...	...	...	...	0005	0103	...	0233	0321	...	...
ara Centrale ... d.	...	1704	1711	...	...	1811	...	...	1848	...	...	...	...	...	...	...	...	0008	0105	...	0235	0323	...	...
nedetto del Tronto ... d.	...	1741	|	...	...	|	...	...	|	...	...	...	...	...	...	...	...	|	|	...	|	|	...	...
nova Marche-Montegranaro ... d.	...	1810	|	...	...	|	...	...	|	...	...	...	...	...	...	...	...	|	|	...	|	|	...	...
na 625/30 ... a.	...	1833	1819	...	...	1919	...	...	1953	...	...	...	...	...	...	...	...	0135	0227	...	0402	0507	...	...
ogna Centrale **615/30** ... a.	...	2100	2012	...	...	2114	...	...	2137	...	...	...	...	...	...	...	...	0352	0427	...	0615	0727	...	...
ano Centrale **615/30** ... a.	...	...	...	...	...	2325	...	...	2250	...	...	...	...	...	...	...	...	|	0712	...	0930	|	...	...
Torino Porta Nuova **615** ... a.	...	...	...	...	...	...	...	...	...	...	...	...	...	...	...	...	...	0740	...	...	...	1120	...	...

BARI - TARANTO and v.v. local services: 2nd class only

	⚒	⚒		⚒	†		⚒		⚒	⚒		†	⚒		†	⚒		⚒			⚒		†	⚒
Bari ... d.	0530	0624	...	0715	0815	...	1020	...	1308	1335	...	1443	1510	...	1600	1615	...	1744	1815	...	1932	...	2040	2050
Gioia del Colle ... d.	0610	0706	...	0802	0856	...	1101	...	1342	1418	...	1524	1543	...	1640	1657	...	1817	1855	...	2013	...	2123	2140
Taranto ... a.	0650	0746	...	0843	0938	...	1143	...	1415	1500	...	1603	1624	...	1720	1734	...	1856	1950	...	2056	...	2207	2221

	⚒	⚒		†	⚒		⚒	⚒		†		⚒		⚒	†	⚒		⚒		†	⚒	⚒	†		⚒
to ... d.	0525	0609	...	0630	0630	...	0720	0814	...	1040	...	1220	...	1345	1352	1433	...	1537	...	1700	1700	1911	1910	...	2000
del Colle ... d.	0601	0650	...	0709	0713	...	0759	0853	...	1119	...	1301	...	1425	1431	1511	...	1617	...	1739	1739	1942	1950	...	2037
... a.	0640	0732	...	0751	0755	...	0841	0933	...	1200	...	1351	...	1506	1519	1543	...	1658	...	1811	1812	2025	2033	...	2125

NOTES (LISTED BY TRAIN NUMBER)

🛏 1, 2 cl., 🛌 2 cl. (4 berth) and (2) Lecce - Bologna - Milano.
①–⑥: 🛏 1, 2 cl., 🛌 2 cl. (4 berth) and (2) Lecce - Bologna - Torino.
🛏 1, 2 cl., 🛌 2 cl. (4 berth) and (2) Lecce - Bologna - Milano.
⑦ (also Mar. 28, June 2; not Mar. 27, May 29): 🛏 1, 2 cl., 🛌 2 cl. (4 berth) and (2) Lecce - Roma.
– ⑦: 🛏 1, 2 cl., 🛌 2 cl. (4 berth) and (2) Lecce - Bologna - Torino.
– (12) and 🍷 Lecce - Bologna - Venezia.

Also Mar. 28, Apr. 25; not Mar. 27, Apr. 24.

▲ – For additional services Bari - Taranto and v.v. – see panel.
♣ – For additional services Brindisi - Taranto and v.v. – see page 312.

PAOLA - COSENZA - SIBARI 633

class only

	⚒		†	⚒	⚒	⚒	⚒		†		©	†	⚒			⚒	⚒	⚒	†	⚒	⚒				⚒	†	⚒
Napoli Centrale **640** ... d.	...	...	...	...	...	...	...	...	...	...	0650	...	...	...	0855	...	...	...	...	...	...	...	1225	...	...	...	...
Paola 640 ... d.	0529	...	0619	0657	...	0728	0843	0919	0937	...	1051	1135	1218	...	1256	1313	...	1416	1427	1429	1529	...	1620	1629	...	...	...
Cosenza ... d.	|	0600	|	|	0730	|	|	|	|	...	|	|	|	1250	|	|	1402	|	|	|	|	...	|	|	1730	1734	1820
Castiglione Cosentino ... a.	0543	0606	0633	0711	0736	0741	0857	0937	0951	...	1105	1150	1233	1256	1310	1327	1408	1430	1441	1443	1543	...	1634	1643	1736	1739	1826
Castiglione Cosentino ... d.	0544	0606	0634	0712	0736	0743	0900	0939	0952	...	1106	1151	1234	1256	1311	1328	1408	1431	1442	1444	1544	...	1635	1644	1736	1739	1826
Cosenza 640 ... a.	0552	|	0642	0719	|	0750	0907	0945	1000	...	1114	1158	1242	|	1319	1336	|	1437	1450	1450	1550	...	1643	1650	|	|	|
Sibari 637 ... a.	...	0703	...	...	0832	...	...	...	...	...	...	...	...	1351	...	...	1503	...	...	...	...	...	...	...	1840	1836	1925

	⚒	†						
oli Centrale **640** ... d.	...	...	...	...	...	...	1923	...
a 640 ... d.	1831	1849	1929	2029	2130	2210	2305	...
senza ... d.	|	|	|	|	|	|	|	...
glione Cosentino ... a.	1844	1903	1943	2043	2143	2224	2320	...
glione Cosentino ... d.	1845	1904	1944	2044	2143	2225	2321	...
senza 640 ... a.	1853	1912	1950	2050	|	2233	2328	...
i 637 ... a.	...	...	...	...	2257	...	...	...

	⚒		⚒	⚒	†	⚒	†	⚒	†	⚒	⚒	†	⚒
Sibari 637 ... d.	...	...	...	0549	...	0630	0640	...	...	...	...	0800	0835
Cosenza 640 ... d.	0540	0554	0630	|	0639	|	|	0737	0746	0814	0853	|	|
Castiglione Cosentino ... a.	0545	0600	0636	0649	0645	0721	0730	0742	0752	0820	0859	0853	0927
Castiglione Cosentino ... d.	0545	0600	0636	0650	0645	0722	0731	0742	0752	0820	0859	0854	0928
Cosenza ... a.	|	|	|	0658	|	0727	0736	|	|	|	|	0901	0936
Paola 640 ... a.	0600	0617	0653	...	0700	...	...	0758	0808	0837	0916	...	...
Napoli Centrale **640** ... a.	...	1010	...	...	...	...	...	...	...	...	...	...	...

	†	⚒		†		©	⚒	⚒	⚒		⚒	†	⚒	⚒	⚒	†		⚒	†		⚒	†	†	⚒		†	
Sibari 637 ... d.	...	...	...	...	...	...	1240	...	...	...	...	...	1510	...	...	1622	...	1657	...	...	1859	...	1914	...	...	...	...
Cosenza 640 ... d.	1010	1139	1231	1308	...	1324	|	1339	1439	1502	1539	1552	|	1639	1705	|	1739	|	1752	1900	|	1955	|	2005	2045	2135	...
Castiglione Cosentino ... a.	1016	1145	1237	1314	...	1330	1339	1345	1445	1508	1545	1558	1604	1645	1711	1717	1745	1751	1758	1906	1952	2001	2007	2011	2051	2144	...
Castiglione Cosentino ... d.	1016	1145	1237	1314	...	1330	1340	1345	1445	1508	1545	1558	1605	1645	1711	1718	1745	1752	1758	1906	1953	2001	2008	2011	2051	2144	...
Cosenza ... a.	|	|	|	|	...	|	1348	|	|	|	|	|	1613	|	|	1725	|	1800	|	|	2001	|	2015	|	|	|	...
Paola 640 ... a.	1033	1200	1254	1331	...	1347	...	1400	1502	1525	1600	1615	...	1700	1727	...	1802	...	1815	1923	...	2018	...	2028	2108	2159	...
Napoli Centrale **640** ... a.	...	...	...	...	...	1740	...	...	...	1920	...	...	...	...	...	...	...	...	...	2310	...	...	...	...	...	...	...

CATANZARO LIDO - LAMEZIA TERME 634

class only

	⚒	⚒	⚒	†		⚒	†	⚒	⚒
Catanzaro Lido **637** ... d.	0550	0630	0750	0825	1350	1544	1749	1750	1948
Catanzaro ... d.	0558	0638	0758	0833	1358	1552	1757	1758	1956
Lamezia Terme Centrale **640** ... a.	0632	0720	0832	0912	1432	1625	1835	1832	2030

	⚒	⚒	†	⚒		⚒	⚒	†	⚒
Lamezia Terme Centrale **640** ... d.	0655	0855	0922	0955	1455	1700	1900	1900	2138
Catanzaro ... d.	0730	0929	1001	1029	1530	1734	1937	1938	2212
Catanzaro Lido **637** ... a.	0738	0937	1009	1037	1538	1743	1944	1947	2220

636 FERROVIE DEL SUD EST services

Valid until further notice. No service

Line 1: BARI - TARANTO

km																								
0	Bari Centrale ♣ d.	...	...	...	...	...	...	0610	0625	0655	0715	0759	0814	0907	0948	1026	1052	...	1142	...	1200	1243	...	1250
1	Bari Sud Est d.	0425	...	...	0525	0529	...	0614	0629	0658	0719	0802	0817	0910	0952	1030	1056	...	1146	...	1204	1247	...	1254
4	Mungivacca d.	0430	...	...	0531	0534	...	0619	0635	0703	0724	0807	0822	0916	0957	1035	1101	...	1151	...	1210	1252	...	1259
	Casamassima d.	|	...	...	0558	|	...	0646	|	0730	|	0834	|	0942	|	1101	|	...	1217	...	|	1321	...	|
43	Putignano d.	0525	...	...	0625	0632	...	0715	0740	0757	0825	0903	0917	1008	1052	1130	1156	...	1246	...	1309	1348	...	1404
78	Martina Franca **2** d.	0602	0606	0651	...	0714	0743	...	0820	...	0907	...	0957	...	1131	...	1234	1238	...	1325	1346	...	1414	1448
113	Taranto ♣ a.	...	0644	0730	...	...	0823	...	...	...	...	...	...	...	...	...	...	1317	...	1405	...	...	1454	...

km																								
	Bari Centrale ♣ d.	1342	1424	1428	...	1515	1522	1600	1608	...	...	1655	1710	...	1745	...	1830	1835	1920	1935	2036	2040	...	2118
	Bari Sud Est d.	1346	1428	1432	...	1519	1525	1604	1612	...	...	1659	1713	...	1749	...	1834	1839	1924	1939	2039	2043	...	2122
0	Mungivacca d.	1351	1434	1437	...	1524	1530	1610	1617	...	...	1704	1719	...	1754	...	1839	1844	1929	1944	2045	2048	...	2127
20	Casamassima d.	|	1503	|	...	1551	|	1637	|	...	...	|	1746	...	|	...	1906	|	1956	|	2111	|	...	|
44	Putignano d.	1454	1532	1538	...	1620	1625	1705	1712	...	...	1754	1812	1816	1844	1855	1935	1934	2024	2034	2138	2135	2140	2213
	Martina Franca **2** d.	1534	...	1618	1639	...	1725	...	1752	1822	...	...	...	1852	...	1930	...	...	...	2111	...	...	2230	...
	Taranto ♣ a.	...	...	...	1717	...	...	...	...	1900	...	...	...	...	...	...	...	...	...	...	...	...	...	...

Taranto ♣ d.	...	...	...	...	...	...	...	...	...	...	...	0650	...	0743	...	...	0836	...	...	...	...	...	...
Martina Franca **2** d.	...	...	0508	...	0549	0618	0641	...	...	0723	...	0731	...	0833	...	...	0915	0925	1010	...	...	1140	...
Putignano d.	0457	0501	0546	0548	0630	0655	0735	0648	0734	0806	0822	...	0835	0915	0925	0931	...	1009	1051	1051	1115	1220	1221
Casamassima d.	|	0528	|	0616	|	|	|	0716	0802	|	0850	...	|	|	|	0959	...	|	|	1119	|	|	1249
Mungivacca d.	0544	0553	0634	0643	0716	0734	0833	0743	0830	0856	0917	...	0925	0950	1015	1025	...	1057	1131	1145	1204	1309	1316
Bari Sud Est a.	0550	0558	0639	0648	0723	0740	0840	0748	0836	0902	0924	...	0932	0957	1020	1032	...	1103	1136	1152	1211	1316	1321
Bari Centrale ♣ a.	0552	0600	0641	0650	0725	0742	0842	0750	0838	0904	0926	...	0934	0959	1022	1034	...	1105	1138	1154	1213	1318	1323

Taranto ♣ d.	...	...	...	1323	...	...	1412	...	...	...	...	1529	...	...	...	...	1726	...	...	...	1922	...	...
Martina Franca **2** d.	...	...	1315	1404	1415	...	1453	1500	...	...	1546	1608	1631	...	1720	...	1806	1837	...	...	2001	2020	2115
Putignano d.	1311	1403	1405	...	1455	1453	...	1540	1539	1625	1629	...	1717	1719	1807	1856	...	1917	1955	2059	...	2100	2150
Casamassima d.	1339	1432	|	...	|	1521	...	|	1607	1653	|	...	|	1747	|	1924	...	|	|	2127	...	|	...
Mungivacca d.	1406	1459	1455	...	1542	1548	...	1629	1634	1721	1716	...	1807	1813	1854	1951	...	2004	2044	2152	...	2147	...
Bari Sud Est a.	1412	1505	1501	...	1549	1554	...	1636	1640	1727	1723	...	1814	1819	1901	1958	...	2010	2050	2157	...	2152	...
Bari Centrale ♣ a.	1414	1507	1503	...	1551	1556	...	1638	1642	1729	1725	...	1816	1821	1903	2000	...	2012	2052	2159	...	2154	...

Line 2: MARTINA FRANCA - LECCE

km																								
0	Martina Franca **1** d.	0523	0621	0727	...	...	0828	...	...	1025	...	1145	...	1242	...	1349	...	1454	...	...	1623	...	...	1829
41	Francavilla Fontana ♣ d.	0605	0707	0811	...	...	0911	...	...	1104	...	1225	...	1325	...	1432	...	1537	...	...	1701	...	...	1910
92	Novoli **3** d.	0712	0815	0907	0921	...	1004	1017	1149	1202	...	1323	...	1418	1512	1529	...	1630	1643	...	1752	1808	...	2003
103	Lecce **5** ♣ a.	0724	0827	0919	0933	...	1016	1026	1201	1211	...	1335	...	1427	1524	1541	...	1642	1652	...	1804	1820	...	2015

Lecce **5** ♣ d.	0528	0617	0655	...	0759	0857	0950	...	1028	1119	1244	...	1307	1341	1431	...	1619	1659	...	1833	...	1902	2040
Novoli **3** d.	0538	0626	0715	...	0818	0918	0959	...	1038	1129	1254	...	1316	1352	1442	...	1636	1708	...	1843	...	1911	2103
Francavilla Fontana ♣ d.	0632	...	0810	...	0912	1010	...	...	1130	1224	1356	...	...	1501	1538	...	1729	...	...	1937	...	...	...
Martina Franca **1** a.	0716	...	0851	...	0952	1048	...	...	1208	1305	1440	...	...	1544	1621	...	1811	...	...	2017	...	...	...

Line 3: NOVOLI - GAGLIANO

km												
0	Novoli **2** d.	0628	0716	0818	1001	1042	1321	1441	1710	1914	2101	...
25	Nardò Centrale **5** d.	0659	0745	0847	1030	1116	1350	1511	1740	1945	2143	...
49	Casarano **4** d.	0728	0813	0918	1059	1144	1419	1540	1808	2013	...	...
74	Gagliano Leuca **6** a.	0802	0846	0951	1132	1218	1452	1613	1841	2046	...	...

Gagliano Leuca **6** d.	...	0642	0737	0847	1013	1151	1243	1333	1504	1633	1842
Casarano **4** d.	0603	0716	0815	0917	1047	1224	1317	1407	1539	1707	1916
Nardò Centrale **5** d.	0631	0746	0848	0944	1118	1252	1351	1439	1608	1738	1946
Novoli **2** a.	0659	0813	0915	1012	1147	1320	1415	1510	1635	1805	2013

Line 4: CASARANO - GALLIPOLI

km		S										
0	Casarano **3** d.	0717	0735	0817	1010	...	1259	1422	...	1541	1647	...
22	Gallipoli **5** a.	0742	0801	0842	1035	...	1324	1447	...	1606	1712	...

				S							
Gallipoli **5** d.	0536	0645	0736	0745	0915	...	1226	1335	1500	1619	...
Casarano **3** a.	0601	0710	0802	0810	0940	...	1251	1401	1525	1644	...

Foggia, Napoli, Roma **626/631**
Bari
Brindisi **631**
Putignano
Casamassima
Martina Franca
Brindisi **631**
Bari **631**
631
Novoli
Lecce
Francavilla Fontana
Taranto
Zollino
Otran
Nardò Centrale
Maglie
Gallipoli
Casarano
Gagliano Leuc
FSE lines (with Line No.)
Trenitalia lines (with Table No.)

Line 5: LECCE - GALLIPOLI

km							S	S		S								S	S			S	S	
0	Lecce **2** ♣ d.	0554	0612	0655	0758	0936	0937	0956	1044	1052	1140	...	1300	1341	1432	1530	1653	1705	1726	1752	1859	2016	2051	2104
19	Zollino **6** d.	0617	0636	0723	0825	1009	0955	1011	1111	1118	1210	...	1327	1414	1455	1553	1718	1721	1741	1818	1924	2033	2106	2128
36	Nardò Centrale **3** d.	...	0700	0748	0850	1031	1012	...	1129	1136	1230	...	1351	1436	1513	...	1741	1739	...	1838	1947	...	...	2147
53	Gallipoli **4** a.	...	0717	0806	0908	1049	1025	...	1148	1155	1250	...	1409	1454	1531	...	1759	1752	...	1856	2005	...	...	2205

							S	S						S				S	S	S		S	S
Gallipoli **4** d.	0611	0637	0724	0826	...	0924	0940	...	1108	...	1225	1328	1412	1531	1546	...	1717	1723	...	...	1922	...	2117
Nardò Centrale **3** d.	0634	0702	0746	0849	...	0945	0954	...	1128	...	1246	1349	1437	1551	1607	...	1739	1739	...	...	1944	...	2131
Zollino **6** d.	0700	0722	0806	0908	0924	1006	1012	1035	1147	1112	1307	1408	1457	1610	1625	1608	1759	1754	1804	1906	2004	2131	2148
Lecce **2** ♣ a.	0725	0742	0829	0931	0947	1029	1027	1050	1211	1135	1311	1430	1520	1633	1648	1631	1823	1809	1819	1923	2027	2146	2203

Line 6: ZOLLINO - GAGLIANO

km						S	S										S	S				S		S
0	Zollino **5** d.	0618	0728	0823	1008	1013	...	1116	...	1205	1326	1412	1502	1554	...	1720	1742	...	1819	...	1928	2034	...	2107
10	Maglie **7** d.	0633	0750	0837	1023	1022	1024	1134	...	1219	1352	1437	1520	1611	...	1739	1751	1753	1834	...	1949	2043	...	2119
47	Gagliano Leuca **3** a.	0728	0844	0932	1117	...	1056	1228	...	1314	1446	1530	1613	1704	...	1832	...	1825	1927	...	2042	...	...	2151

							S	S									S	S			S	S	S
Gagliano Leuca **3** d.	0540	0611	0654	0812	0858	...	0951	...	1001	1154	...	1242	1330	1457	1633	...	1720	...	1854	...	...	2046	...
Maglie **7** d.	0642	0705	0749	0908	0952	...	1023	1025	1056	1250	...	1350	1438	1553	1741	...	1752	1754	1948	...	1856	2118	2120
Zollino **5** d.	0655	0718	0802	0921	1005	...	...	1034	1109	1303	...	1404	1451	1607	1754	...	...	1803	2001	...	1905	...	2129

Line 7: MAGLIE - OTRANTO

km						S								S	S
0	Maglie **6** d.	0643	0751	0856	1025	1026	1135	...	1249	1343	1439	1612	1737	1755	2044
18	Otranto a.	0709	0817	0922	1051	1041	1201	...	1315	1409	1505	1638	1803	1810	2059

				S							S		S
Otranto d.	0715	0828	0924	1006	1059	1220	1316	1410	1522	1706	1735	1805	1840
Maglie **6** a.	0741	0854	0950	1021	1125	1246	1342	1436	1548	1732	1750	1831	1855

S – Peak summer only (nominally early July - late Aug.).

♣ – Connections into *Trenitalia* services possible.

Operator: Ferrovie Del Sud Est E Servizi Automobilistici S.R.L., Sede via Giovanni Amendola, 106/D, 70126 Bari ✆ +39 080 546 2111, fax +39 080 546 2376. Call centre ✆ 800 079 090.

class only — REGGIO DI CALABRIA - SIBARI - TARANTO — 637

	🚌			🚌				🚌						🚌						🚌	*IC* 562/3				🚌
	⚒	⚒	⚒	⚒	⚒		⚒	⚒	⚒	†	⚒	⚒	†	⚒	⚒	†	Ⓐ	†	⚒	⚒		⚒	⚒	⚒	⚒
Reggio di Calabria Centrale **640** d.	...	...	...	...	...	...	0510	...	0605	0627	...	0738	0750	...	...	1010	1027	...	...	...	1155	1218	...	1325	...
Melito di Porto Salvo d.	...	...	...	...	...	...	0533	...	0638	0702	...	0800	0828	...	...	1049	1100	...	...	...	1221	1253	...	1353	...
Locri d.	...	...	...	...	...	...	0614	...	0747	0805	...	0847	0940	...	...	1154	1204	...	...	...	1314	1406	...	1503	...
Siderno d.	...	...	...	...	...	...	0619	...	0753	0811	...	0853	0947	...	...	1200	1210	...	...	...	1322	1412	...	1509	...
Roccella Jonica d.	...	...	...	...	...	0600	0631	...	0805	0823	...	0908	1000	...	...	1212	1222	...	...	...	1342	1423	...	1522	...
Soverato d.	...	...	...	...	...	0654	0714	...	0849	0909	...	0940	1053	...	...	1304	...	...	...	...	1420	1501	...	...	...
Catanzaro Lido a.	...	...	...	...	...	0712	0727	...	0910	0927	...	0956	1112	...	...	1323	...	...	...	...	1434	1517	...	...	...
Catanzaro Lido **634** d.	...	...	0535	...	0637	...	0729	...	...	...	1000	...	...	...	1223	...	...	1348	1351	...	1436	...	1603	...	...
Crotone d.	...	...	0623	...	0721	...	0814	...	...	...	1046	...	...	...	1323	...	...	1439	1448	...	1535	...	1649	...	...
Rossano d.	...	...	0737	...	0850	...	0910	...	...	...	1214	...	...	...	1439	...	...	1552	1603	...	1641	...	1758	...	...
Corigliano Calabro d.	...	...	0750	...	0859	...	0918	...	...	...	1222	...	...	...	1448	...	...	1600	1611	...	1653	...	1807	...	...
Sibari 633 a.	...	...	0805	...	0911	...	0930	...	...	...	1235	...	...	...	1500	...	...	1612	1624	...	1706	...	1819	...	...
Sibari d.	0500	0545	...	...	...	...	...	1003	...	...	...	...	...	1403	...	...	...	...	...	1648	1709	...	...	...	1843
Trebisacce d.	0514	0603	...	...	...	...	...	1017	...	...	...	...	...	1417	...	...	...	...	...	1702	1735	...	...	...	1857
Metaponto **638** d.	0632	0702	...	0900	...	...	...	1135	...	...	...	...	...	1530	...	...	...	...	...	1820	1835	...	...	...	2015
Taranto 631/8 a.	0727	...	...	0940	...	...	...	1245	...	...	...	...	...	1640	...	...	...	...	...	1915	1907	...	...	...	2110

	†	⚒	⚒	†	⚒	⚒	†	⚒	†
gio di Calabria Centrale **640** d.	...	1428	1538	1526	1702	...	1808	1808	2012
o di Porto Salvo d.	...	1501	1604	1607	1735	...	1848	1842	2045
d.	...	1601	1651	1718	1834	...	1946	1952	2152
no d.	...	1607	1657	1725	1844	...	1952	1958	2158
ella Jonica d.	...	1624	1717	1740	1857	...	2005	2010	2210
rato d.	...	1712	1751	1828	1933	...	...	2056	...
nzaro Lido a.	...	1730	1805	1848	1947	...	...	2124	...
nzaro Lido **634** d.	1635	...	1811	...	...	1955	...	...	...
one d.	1722	...	1854	...	...	2051	...	...	...
ano d.	1843	...	1955	...	...	2154	...	...	...
liano Calabro d.	1852	...	2005	...	...	2203	...	...	...
ri 633 a.	1906	...	2022	...	...	2215	...	...	...
ri d.	...	...	...	...	...	...	...	...	...
sacce d.	...	...	...	...	...	...	...	...	...
ponto **638** d.	...	...	...	...	...	...	...	...	...
nto 631/8 a.	...	...	...	...	...	...	...	...	...

								🚌	
	⚒	⚒	⚒	⚒	†	⚒	†	⚒	†
Taranto 631/8 d.	...	...	...	...	...	...	...	0515	...
Metaponto **638** d.	...	...	...	...	...	...	...	0627	...
Trebisacce d.	...	...	...	...	...	...	...	0743	...
Sibari 633 a.	...	...	...	...	...	...	...	0757	...
Sibari d.	...	...	...	0558	...	0735	...	▬	...
Corigliano Calabro d.	...	...	...	0609	...	0749	...	...	...
Rossano d.	...	...	...	0617	...	0757	...	...	...
Crotone d.	...	...	...	0722	...	0904	...	...	...
Catanzaro Lido a.	...	...	...	0805	...	0945	...	...	...
Catanzaro Lido **634** d.	...	0540	0605	0808	0810	...	1008	...	1123
Soverato d.	...	0553	0619	0829	0830	...	1022	⚒	1137
Roccella Jonica d.	0534	0630	0705	0909	0923	...	1057	1110	1213
Siderno d.	0545	0641	0717	0919	0933	...	1108	1122	1225
Locri d.	0550	0646	0722	0924	0939	...	1113	1127	1231
Melito di Porto Salvo d.	0658	0738	0833	1020	1044	...	1215	1238	1333
Reggio di Calabria Centrale **640** a.	0734	0804	0903	1042	1122	...	1246	1310	1400

				IC 558/9			🚌	🚌						🚌					🚌					🚌	🚌
	⚒	⚒	Ⓐ		†	⚒	⚒	⚒	†	⚒	⚒	⚒	†	⚒	⚒	⚒	†	⚒	⚒	†	⚒	⚒	⚒	⚒	⚒
nto 631/8 d.	...	...	...	0820	...	...	0835	0900	...	...	...	...	...	1235	...	...	...	...	1425	...	...	...	...	1755	1915
ponto **638** d.	0715	...	...	0856	...	...	0915	0957	...	...	...	...	...	1313	...	...	...	...	1517	...	...	...	...	1852	2012
sacce d.	0813	...	...	0945	...	...	...	1116	...	...	...	...	...	...	...	...	...	...	1625	...	...	...	...	2008	2126
ri 633 a.	0829	...	...	1000	...	...	...	1135	...	...	...	...	...	...	...	...	...	...	1640	...	...	...	...	2022	2140
ri d.	...	0935	...	1002	1034	1057	...	▬	...	...	1323	...	...	...	1552	...	...	1635	...	1718	...	1845	1930	...	...
liano Calabro d.	...	0947	...	1020	1046	1109	...	...	...	...	1335	...	...	...	1612	...	...	1654	...	1731	...	1858	1943	...	...
ano d.	...	0955	...	1032	1056	1117	...	...	...	...	1343	...	...	...	1620	...	...	1703	...	1739	...	1906	1956	...	...
one d.	...	1112	...	1145	1211	1228	...	...	...	...	1447	...	...	...	1730	...	...	1820	...	1855	...	2018	2115	...	...
nzaro Lido a.	...	1159	...	1244	1258	1320	...	⚒	...	...	1540	...	...	...	1809	...	...	1915	...	1941	...	2107	...	...	...
nzaro Lido **634** d.	...	...	...	1246	...	...	...	1345	1419	1521	...	1620	1630	...	1811	...	1915	...	...	...	2000	2108	...	...	...
rato d.	...	...	...	1303	...	...	...	1402	1443	1535	...	1633	1647	...	1825	...	1934	...	...	...	2017	2122	...	...	...
ella Jonica d.	...	...	1305	1343	...	...	...	1444	1532	1608	...	1716	1739	...	1856	1910	2025	...	...	...	2105	2200	...	...	...
no d.	...	...	1323	1359	...	...	...	1454	1543	1621	...	1726	1752	...	1908	1922	2037	...	...	...	...	...	...	...	...
d.	...	...	1329	1407	...	...	...	1504	1548	1627	...	1731	1757	...	1913	1927	2043	...	...	...	...	...	...	...	...
o di Porto Salvo d.	...	...	1436	1501	...	...	...	1602	1656	1725	...	1832	1906	...	1959	2027	2152	...	...	...	...	...	...	...	...
gio di Calabria Centrale **640** a.	...	...	1510	1530	...	...	...	1634	1736	1752	...	1906	1949	...	2026	2100	2220	...	...	...	...	...	...	...	...

class only — NAPOLI - POTENZA - TARANTO — 638

		IC 701								*IC* 707		
	⚒		†	⚒	⚒	⚒	⚒			§	⚒	†
Roma T **640** d.	...	0626	...	...	...	...	...	...	...	1526	...	...
Napoli C **640** d.	...	0845	...	...	...	...	...	...	1617	1750	...	...
Salerno d.	0606	0924	0957	...	1400	1510	...	1605	1659	1824	1955	2000
Battipaglia **640** d.	0622	0939	1013	...	1415	1525	...	1624	1720	1840	2011	2016
Potenza Centrale d.	0755	1059	1146	1429	1538	1653	1715	1810	1848	2004	2142	2143
Metaponto **637** d.	...	1218	...	1607	...	...	1847	...	2007	2124	...	...
Taranto 637 a.	...	1253	...	1645	...	...	1922	...	2045	2156	...	...

			IC 700			*IC* 702						
		⚒	§				⚒	⚒	⚒	†	⚒	
Taranto 637 d.	...	0517	0805	0941	...	1400	1420	...	...	...	...	...
Metaponto **637** d.	...	0556	0839	1016	...	1433	1459	...	...	...	...	...
Potenza Centrale d.	0717	0730	1000	1147	1327	1558	1639	1709	1858	1928	2104	...
Battipaglia **640** d.	0841	...	1124	1312	1459	1721	...	1839	2029	2102	2233	...
Salerno d.	0857	...	1138	1327	1518	1737	...	1855	2043	2118	2247	...
Napoli C **640** a.	...	...	1215	1405	...	1810	...	...	...	...	...	...
Roma T **640** a.	...	...	1434	...	...	2034	...	...	...	...	...	...

§ – Also conveys 1st class.

umvesuviana Ferrovia — 2nd class only — NAPOLI - SORRENTO, BAIANO and SARNO — 639

Napoli P. Garibaldi ▲ d.	0611	0642	0711	0741	0813	0841	0911	and	1311	1343	1411	1441	1513	1541	1611	1641	1711	1743	1811	1841	1913	1941	2011	and	2141	...
Ercolano Scavi d.	0628	0652	0728	0758	0823	0858	0928	every	1328	1353	1428	1458	1523	1558	1628	1658	1728	1753	1828	1858	1923	1958	2028	every	2158	...
Pompei S. Villa Misteri d.	0647	0705	0747	0817	0836	0917	0947	30	1347	1406	1447	1517	1536	1617	1647	1717	1747	1806	1847	1917	1936	2017	2047	30	2217	...
Castellammare d.	0657	0715	0757	0827	0846	0927	0957	minutes	1357	1416	1457	1527	1546	1627	1657	1727	1757	1816	1857	1927	1946	2027	2057	minutes	2227	...
Sorrento a.	0717	0732	0817	0847	0903	0947	1017	until	1417	1433	1517	1547	1603	1647	1717	1747	1817	1833	1917	1947	2003	2047	2117	until	2247	...

ento d.	0601	0625	0722	0755	0826	0852	0907	0937	1037	and	1307	1325	1356	1422	1455	1526	1607	1637	1707	1725	1756	1822	1855	1926	2007	2037	2107	2137
ellammare d.	0621	0645	0739	0815	0845	0909	0927	0957	1057	every	1327	1345	1415	1439	1515	1545	1627	1657	1727	1745	1815	1839	1915	1945	2027	2057	2127	2156
ei S. Villa Misteri d.	0631	0655	0748	0825	0853	0918	0937	1007	1107	30	1337	1356	1423	1448	1525	1553	1637	1707	1737	1755	1823	1848	1925	1953	2037	2107	2137	2205
ano Scavi d.	0649	0713	0807	0843	0906	0937	0955	1025	1125	minutes	1355	1414	1436	1507	1543	1606	1655	1725	1755	1813	1836	1907	1943	2006	2055	2125	2155	2222
li P. Garibaldi ▲ a.	0707	0731	0826	0901	0916	0956	1013	1043	1143	until	1413	1431	1446	1526	1601	1616	1713	1743	1813	1831	1846	1926	2001	2016	2113	2143	2213	2239

OLI (Porta Nolana) ▲ - **BAIANO and v.v.** Journey 60 minutes.

Napoli: 0618, 0648⚒, 0718, 0748, 0818, 0918, 1018, 1118, 1148⚒, 1218, 1318, 1418, 1448⚒, 1518, 1618, 1718, 1748Ⓐ, 1818, 1848, 1918, 1948.

From **Baiano:** 0602, 0632⚒, 0700, 0730, 0802, 0832, 0902, 0932, 1002, 1102, 1202, 1302, 1332⚒, 1402, 1502, 1602, 1632⚒, 1702, 1802, 1902, 1932Ⓐ, 2002.

OLI (Porta Nolana) ▲ - **SARNO and v.v.** Journey 65 minutes. All services call at Poggiomarino (49 minutes from Napoli, 12 minutes from Sarno).

Napoli: 0632, 0651 **p**, 0722, 0802, 0902, 1002, 1102, 1132⚒, 1202, 1302, 1402, 1432⚒, 1502, 1602, 1702, 1732Ⓐ, 1802, 1832, 1932, 2002 **p**.

From **Sarno:** 0619, 0649, 0719, 0759, 0819, 0849, 0949, 1049, 1149, 1249, 1349, 1449, 1549, 1619⚒, 1649, 1749, 1849, 1919Ⓐ, 1949.

To Poggiomarino only.

Services originate / terminate at Napoli Porta Nolana station (journey time: 1 – 2 minutes).

ator: Circumvesuviana Ferrovia ✆ +39 081 77 22 444, fax +39 081 77 22 450.

A reduced service operates in peak summer.

Frequent 🚌 services operate along the Amalfi Coast between Sorrento and Salerno. Up to 20 services on ⚒, less frequent on †. Change of buses at Amalfi is necessary. Operator: SITA, Via G. Pastore 28/30, 84131 Salerno. ✆ +39 089 3866 701, fax +39 089 3856 494.

640 ROMA - NAPOLI - COSENZA and REGGIO DI CALABRIA

For high-speed services – see Table 600

km		2	2	2	2	ICN 1699 ♦	ICN 799 ♦	2 ⚒	IC 701 ♦	2	ICN 797 ♦	IC 723 ♦	IC 721 K	2	2 ⚒	FB 9873 🍷 ⚒	IC 1571 ♦	2 ⚒	IC 551	2 ⚒	2 ⚒	2 †	2 ⚒	2
	Torino PN **610** d.	...	...	...	...	2010	2155	...	...	...	2125	...	...	...	...	...	...	...	...	...	...	...	...	...
	Milano C **615** d.	...	...	...	...	|	|	...	...	...	2317g	...	...	...	...	...	...	...	...	...	...	...	...	...
	Venezia SL **616** d.	...	...	...	...	|	|	...	...	...	|	...	...	...	...	...	...	...	...	...	...	...	...	...
	Bologna C **620** d.	...	...	...	...	|	|	...	...	...	|	...	...	...	...	...	...	...	...	...	...	...	...	...
0	**Roma** Termini **620** d.	...	...	...	0536	0557o	0557o	...	0626	...	0725t	0726	0726	...	0814	0849	0900	...	0926	...	...	...	...	...
62	Latina d.	...	...	...	0612	0637	0637	...	0657	...	|	0757	0757	...	0850	|	0931	...	0957	...	...	...	...	...
129	Formia-Gaeta d.	...	...	...	0702	0717	0717	...	0734	...	|	0834	0834	...	0936	|	1008	...	1034	...	...	...	...	...
195	Aversa d.	...	...	...	0748	0758	0758	...	0809	...	|	0909	0909	...	1025	|	1043	...	1109	...	...	...	...	...
	Caserta **626** d.	...	...	...	|	|	|	...	|	...	|	|	|	...	|	|	|	...	|	...	...	...	...	...
214	**Napoli** Centrale **626** a.	...	...	...	0812	0817	0817	...	0829	...	0938	0929	0929	...	1044	1036	1103	...	1129	...	...	...	...	...
214	**Napoli** Centrale d.	0540	0650	0725	...	0835	0835	...	0845	0855	0955	0950	0950	...	...	1046	▬	...	1145	...	...	1207	...	1225
268	Salerno d.	0637	0736	0806	...	0912	0912	...	0924	0937	1032	1029	1029	...	...	1120	...	...	1222	...	...	1247	...	1308
288	Battipaglia **638** d.	0653	0752	0824	...	...	...	...	0937	0952	...	|	|	...	...	|	...	...	1237	...	...	1305	...	1323
318	Agropoli-Castellabate d.	0716	0814	0848	...	...	...	...	...	1014	...	|	|	...	...	|	...	...	1253	...	...	1327	...	1348
349	Ascea d.	0743	0841	0914	...	...	...	...	...	1041	...	|	|	...	...	|	...	...	|	...	...	1351	...	1419
395	Sapri d.	0825	0925	1000	...	...	...	...	...	1120	...	1141	1141	...	...	1237	...	1242	1345	1348	...	1431	...	1501
407	Maratea d.	...	0943	...	...	...	...	...	...	1133	...	|	|	...	...	|	2	1258	1355	1404	...	1442	...	1511
455	Belvedere Marittimo d.	...	1016	...	...	...	...	...	...	1208	...	|	|	...	...	|	⚒	1335	|	1439	...	1519	...	1547
	Cosenza **633** d.	...	|	...	...	...	...	1139		|	...	|	|	...	...	|	1339	|	|	|	1439	|	1539	|
489	Paola **633** d.	...	1051	...	...	...	...	1210	...	1256	...	1231	1231	1306	...	1330	1410	1416	1445	1510	1521	1550	1610	1620
	Cosenza **633** a.	...	1114c	...	...	...	...	|	...	1319	...	|	|	|	...	|	|	1437	|	...	|	...	|	1643
546	**Lamezia Terme** Centrale a.	...	...	...	...	...	...	1244	...	...	...	1259	1259	1340	...	1355	1444	...	1517	...	1553	...	1644	...
546	**Lamezia Terme** Centrale **634** d.	...	...	...	...	...	...	1246	...	...	...	1302	1302	1342	...	1358	1446	...	1520	...	1555	...	1646	...
616	Gioia Tauro d.	...	...	...	...	...	...	1324	...	...	...	|	|	1420	...	1436	1526	...	1602	...	1636	...	1734	...
652	Villa S. Giovanni **641** a.	...	...	...	...	...	...	1355	...	...	...	1405	1405	1451	...	1459	1557	...	1628	...	1707	...	1805	...
652	Villa S. Giovanni d.	...	...	...	...	...	...	1357	...	...	...	1425	1425	1453	...	1502	1559	...	1631	...	1709	...	1807	...
667	**Reggio di Calabria** C **637** a.	...	...	...	...	...	...	1413	...	...	...	|	|	1509	...	1515	1616	...	1648	...	1726	...	1822	...
	Siracusa **641** a.	...	...	...	...	...	...	...	...	...	...	|	1829	...	...	...	...	...	...	...	...	...	...	...
	Palermo C **641** a.	...	...	...	...	...	...	...	...	...	...	1900	...	...	...	...	...	...	...	...	...	...	...	...

km		2 n	IC 727 ♦	IC 729 L	2	IC 553	2 ⚒	2	IC 583	2 ⚒	2 ⚒	IC 1589 ♦	2 ⑥	FB 9877 🍷	2	2 ⑥	IC 555	2	2	IC 707 ♦	IC 705 ♦	IC 561	2	FA 9377/9 🍷
	Torino PN **610** d.	...	...	...	...	...	...	...	...	...	...	...	...	...	...	...	...	...	...	...	...	...	...	...
	Milano C **615** d.	...	...	...	...	...	...	...	0650	...	...	0645	...	...	...	...	...	...	...	...	...	...	...	...
	Venezia SL **616** d.	...	...	...	...	...	...	...	|	...	...	|	...	...	...	...	...	...	...	...	...	...	...	...
	Bologna C **620** d.	...	...	...	...	...	...	...	0918	...	...	0937	...	...	...	...	...	...	...	...	...	...	...	...
	Roma Termini **620** d.	1106	1126	1126	...	1226	...	1236	1322t	...	...	1314t	1336	1356	...	...	1426	...	1436	1526	1606	1626	1636	1730
	Latina d.	1143	1157	1157	...	1257	...	1312	1357	...	...	1404	1413	|	...	...	1457	...	1512	1557	|	1657	1718	|
	Formia-Gaeta d.	1241	1234	1234	...	1334	...	1359	1434	...	...	1444	1509	|	...	...	1534	...	1603	1634	|	1734	1807	|
	Aversa d.	1321	1309	1309	...	1409	...	1448	1509	...	...	1523	1554	|	...	...	1609	...	1651	1709	|	1809	1858	|
	Caserta **626** d.	|	|	|	...	|	...	|	|	...	...	|	|	|	...	...	|	...	|	|	1758	|	|	|
	Napoli Centrale **626** a.	1343	1329	1329	...	1429	...	1510	1529	...	...	1547	1616	1541	...	...	1629	...	1715	1729	...	1829	1918	1845
	Napoli Centrale d.	...	1345	1345	1350	1448	...	...	...	...	1530	1605	...	1551	...	...	1645	1715	...	1750	...	1850	...	1855
	Salerno d.	...	1424	1424	1436	1526	...	...	...	...	1612	1653	...	1628	...	1703	1729	1757	...	1824	...	→	...	1928
	Battipaglia **638** d.	...	|	|	1452	1540	...	...	...	...	1628	|	...	|	...	1725	1743	1815	...	1838	...	...	...	|
	Agropoli-Castellabate d.	...	|	|	1517	1556	...	...	...	...	1656	|	...	|	...	1747	1800	1838	...	...	...	...	...	|
	Ascea d.	...	|	|	1542	|	...	...	...	...	1725	1739	...	|	...	1811	1827	1903	...	...	...	...	...	|
	Sapri d.	...	1532	1532	1624	1640	...	...	...	1745	1809	1816	...	1732	...	1850	1905	1943	...	...	...	...	...	|
	Maratea d.	...	|	|	...	|	...	...	...	1758	...	|	...	|	...	...	|	...	...	...	...	...	...	|
	Belvedere Marittimo d.	...	|	|	...	|	...	...	...	1833	...	|	...	|	...	...	|	...	...	...	...	...	...	|
	Cosenza **633** d.	...	|	|	...	|	1639	...	...	|	...	|	...	|	1739	...	|	...	...	...	...	...	...	|
	Paola **633** d.	...	1624	1624	...	1740	1710	...	...	1903	...	1915	...	1821	1812	...	2001	...	...	...	...	...	...	2106
	Cosenza **633** a.	...	|	|	...	|	|	...	...	...	...	|	...	|	|	...	|	...	...	...	...	...	...	|
	Lamezia Terme Centrale a.	...	1652	1652	...	1811	1744	...	...	...	...	1946	...	1848	1855	...	2032	...	...	...	...	...	...	2132
	Lamezia Terme Centrale **634** d.	...	1655	1655	...	1814	1746	...	...	...	...	1949	...	1851	1857	...	2035	...	...	...	...	...	...	2135
	Gioia Tauro d.	...	|	|	...	1854	1824	...	...	...	...	2033	...	1931	1936	...	2116	...	...	...	...	...	...	|
	Villa S. Giovanni **641** a.	...	1800	1800	...	1921	1855	...	...	...	...	2058	...	1953	2007	...	2143	...	...	...	...	...	...	2227
	Villa S. Giovanni d.	...	1820	1820	...	1924	1857	...	...	...	...	2101	...	1956	2009	...	2146	...	...	...	...	...	...	2230
	Reggio di Calabria C **637** a.	...	|	|	...	1945	1913	...	...	...	...	2120	...	2013	2026	...	2203	...	...	...	...	...	...	2243
	Siracusa **641** a.	...	2245	|	...	...	...	...	...	...	...	...	...	...	...	...	...	...	...	...	...	...	...	...
	Palermo C **641** a.	...	...	2300	...	...	...	...	...	...	...	...	...	...	...	...	...	...	...	...	...	...	...	...

km		2	IC 591	2	IC 511 ♦	2 †	2 Ⓐ	2 Ⓑ	2	2 ⚒	IC 597 ♦	ICN 1955 ♦	ICN 1957 D	ICN 1959 ♦	ICN 1961 C	ICN 795 ♦	2 ⚒	ICN 789 ♦	2 †	2 †	2	ICN 1963 ♦	ICN 1965 A	ICN 35063 ♦
	Torino PN **610** d.	...	...	...	1050	...	...	...	...	...	...	...	...	...	...	1335	...	...	...	...	...	...	...	...
	Milano C **615** d.	...	...	...	|	...	...	...	...	...	1450	...	...	...	...	1544g	...	...	...	...	...	2010	2010	2010
	Venezia SL **616** d.	...	...	...	|	...	...	...	...	...	|	...	...	...	...	|	...	...	...	...	...	|	|	|
	Bologna C **620** d.	...	...	...	|	...	...	...	...	...	1718	...	...	...	...	|	...	...	...	...	...	|	|	|
0	**Roma** Termini **620** d.	...	1726	...	1826	1836	1836	...	1931	2056	2122t	2131	2131	2226	2226	2317t	...	2358	...	...	...	|	|	|
	Latina d.	...	1757	...	1857	1916	1916	...	2006	2132	2157	2205	2205	2301	2301	|	...	|	...	...	...	|	|	|
	Formia-Gaeta d.	...	1834	...	1934	2006	2007	...	2042	2220	2234	2244	2244	2340	2340	|	...	|	...	...	...	|	|	|
	Aversa d.	...	1909	...	2009	2052	2058	...	|	2302	2309	|	|	|	|	|	...	|	...	...	...	|	|	|
216	Caserta **626** d.	...	|	...	|	|	|	...	2139	|	|	|	|	|	|	|	...	0232	...	...	...	|	|	|
	Napoli Centrale **626** a.	...	1929	...	2029	2113	2118	...	2220	2324	2330	2337	2337	|	|	|	...	▬	...	...	...	|	|	|
	Napoli Centrale d.	1923	1950	2028	2053	...	...	2122	...	...	...	2358	2358	|	|	|	...		...	...	...	|	|	|
287	Salerno d.	2006	2027	2111	2130	...	...	2205	...	...	...	|	|	|	|	0221	...	...	...	...	0551	0556s	0556s	0616s
—	Battipaglia **638** d.	2021	...	2129	...	...	...	2222	...	...	...	|	|	|	|	|	...	...	...	...	0610	0616s	0616s	0628s
	Agropoli-Castellabate d.	2041	...	2153	...	...	...	2241	...	...	...	|	|	|	|	|	...	...	...	...	0632	0637s	0637s	0647s
	Ascea d.	2108	...	2218	...	...	...	2302	...	...	...	|	|	|	|	|	...	...	...	...	0657	0703s	0703s	0713s
	Sapri d.	2149	...	2255	...	...	...	2340	...	...	...	|	|	|	|	0343	...	...	...	...	0747	0735s	0735s	0742s
	Maratea d.	2201	...	...	...	...	...	...	...	...	...	|	|	|	|	|	...	2	...	...	0759	0749s	0749s	0755s
	Belvedere Marittimo d.	2232	...	...	...	...	...	...	...	...	...	|	|	|	|	|	...	⚒	...	...	0832	|	|	|
	Cosenza **633** d.	|	...	...	...	...	...	...	...	...	...	|	|	|	|	|	...	0620	0639	...	|	|	|	|
0	Paola **633** d.	2305	...	...	...	...	...	...	...	...	...	|	|	|	|	0441	0525	0651	0710	0818	0903	0839s	0839s	0841s
26	Cosenza **633** a.	2328	...	...	...	...	...	...	...	...	...	|	|	|	|	|	|	|	|	|	...	|	|	|
	Lamezia Terme Centrale a.	...	...	...	...	...	...	...	...	...	...	|	|	|	|	0516	0600	0725	0744	0855	...	0916s	0916s	0917s
	Lamezia Terme Centrale **634** d.	...	...	...	...	...	...	...	...	...	...	|	|	|	|	0519	0602	0727	0746	0857	...	0919s	0919s	0920s
	Gioia Tauro d.	...	...	...	...	...	...	...	...	...	...	|	|	|	|	0700	0643	0805	0824	0940	...	1004s	1004s	1004s
	Villa S. Giovanni **641** a.	...	...	...	...	...	...	...	...	...	...	0425	0425	0520	0520	0735	0715	0836	0855	1011	...	1040s	1040s	1040s
	Villa S. Giovanni d.	...	...	...	...	...	...	...	...	...	...	0445	0445	0540	0540	0738	0717	0838	0857	1013	...	1105s	1105s	1105s
	Reggio di Calabria C **637** a.	...	...	...	...	...	...	...	...	...	...	|	|	|	|	0805	0741	0858	0914	1030	...	|	|	|
	Siracusa **641** a.	...	...	...	...	...	...	...	...	...	...	0936	|	1025	|	...	...	...	...	...	...	1548	|	1548
	Palermo C **641** a.	...	...	...	...	...	...	...	...	...	...	...	1002	...	1046	...	...	...	...	...	...	...	1639	...

FOR NOTES SEE PAGE 318

REGGIO DI CALABRIA and COSENZA - NAPOLI - ROMA 640

For high-speed services – see Table 600

				IC 582			IC 510	ICN 1960	ICN 1958						IC 590			IC 550		FA 9372/4	IC 550		IC 700		
	2	2	2		2	2					2	2	2	2		2	2		2	🍷				2	2
	①–⑥	①–⑥	⑦		⑦	⚒	♦	♦	W						♦	⚒	⚒		⚒				♦		①–⑥
ermo C 641 d.	...	...	...	...	...	...	...	...	2110	...	...	...	...	...	...	...	...	...	...	...	...	...	...	...	...
iracusa 641 d.	...	...	...	...	...	...	...	2145	│	...	...	...	...	...	...	...	...	...	...	...	...	...	...	...	...
o di Calabria C 637 d.	...	...	...	...	...	...	...	│	│	...	...	...	...	...	...	...	0510	0610	0619	0637	...	...	...	0709	...
. Giovanni 641 a.	...	...	...	...	...	...	...	0200	0200	...	...	...	...	...	...	...	0525	0626	0634	0650	...	...	...	0724	...
. Giovanni d.	...	...	...	...	...	...	...	0230	0230	...	...	...	...	...	...	...	0527	0629	0636	0653	...	...	...	0726	...
Tauro d.	...	...	...	...	...	...	...	│	│	...	...	...	...	...	...	...	0559	0652	0704	│	...	...	...	0759	...
zia Terme Centrale a.	...	...	...	...	...	...	...	│	│	...	...	...	...	...	...	...	0638	0732	0742	0748	...	...	...	0835	...
zia Terme Centrale 634 d.	...	...	...	...	...	...	...	│	│	...	...	...	...	...	...	...	0640	0735	0754	0751	...	...	...	0837	...
enza 633 d.	...	...	...	...	...	...	...	│	│	...	...	...	...	0554	...	0630	│	│	│	│	...	...	...	│	...
633 d.	...	...	...	...	...	...	...	│	│	...	...	...	...	0620	...	0656	0718	0813	0843	0823	...	...	...	0919	...
enza 633 a.	...	...	...	...	...	...	...	│	│	...	...	...	...	│	...	│	...	│	0907	│	...	...	...	0945	...
dere Marittimo d.	...	...	...	...	...	...	...	│	│	...	...	...	...	0647	...	0727	...	│	...	│	...	...	...	...	...
ea d.	...	...	...	...	...	...	...	│	│	...	...	...	...	0725	...	0808	...	0902	...	│	...	...	...	...	...
d.	...	...	...	...	...	0438	...	│	│	...	0547	0610	0645	0739	...	0822	...	0912	...	│	...	...	...	...	...
d.	...	...	...	...	...	0514	...	│	│	...	0624	0644	0717	0821	...	...	...	│	...	│	...	...	...	...	...
oli-Castellabate d.	...	...	...	...	...	0540	...	│	│	...	0650	0710	0739	0847	...	...	...	│	...	│	←	...	...	...	...
aglia 638 d.	...	...	...	...	...	0603	...	│	│	...	0711	0737	0759	0911	...	...	...	1011	...	│	1013	...	1124	...	...
o d.	...	...	...	0531	...	0621	0630	0640s	0640s	...	0729	0755	0820	0930	...	...	...	→	...	0952	1033	...	1138	...	...
i Centrale a.	...	...	...	0608	...	0701	0707	0718s	0718s	...	0808	0834	0900	1010	...	...	...	...	...	1025	1115	...	1215	...	...
i Centrale 626 d.	0512	0517	0532	0631	0636	...	0731	0739s	0739s	...	...	...	...	...	1031	...	...	...	...	1035	1131	...	1231	...	1239
erta 626 d.	│	│	│	│	│	...	│	│	│	...	...	...	...	...	│	...	...	...	...	│	│	...	│	...	│
a d.	0529	0542	0550	0648	0654	...	0748	│	│	...	...	...	...	...	1048	...	...	...	...	│	1148	...	1248	...	1258
a-Gaeta d.	0611	0631	0638	0722	0740	...	0822	0831s	0831s	...	...	...	...	...	1122	...	...	...	...	│	1222	...	1322	...	1349
d.	0652	0720	0722	0759	0825	...	0859	0910s	0910s	...	...	...	...	...	1159	...	...	...	...	│	1259	...	1359	...	1438
Termini 620 a.	0734	0806	0806	0834	0904	...	0937	0951	0951	...	...	...	...	...	1237	...	...	...	...	1147	1334	...	1434	...	1524
ogna C 620 a.	...	...	...	...	...	...	│	...	...	...	...	...	...	...	1640	...	...	...	...	...	...	...	...	...	...
ezia SL 616 a.	...	...	...	...	...	...	│	...	...	...	...	...	...	...	│	...	...	...	...	...	...	...	...	...	...
no C 615 a.	...	...	...	...	...	...	│	...	...	...	...	...	...	...	1917	...	...	...	...	...	...	...	...	...	...
ino PN 610 a.	...	...	...	...	...	...	1720	...	...	...	...	...	...	...	...	...	...	...	...	...	...	...	...	...	...

	IC 552	FB 9872	IC 596	IC 1588				IC 556			IC 728	IC 722		IC 1572	IC 522				IC 702				IC 724	IC 730	
		🍷			2	2	2		2				2			2	2	2	2	2	2	2			2
				♦	†n	⚒					♦	N		♦	♦	...	⚒	⚒	♦				♦	P	
ermo C 641 d.	...	...	...	...	...	...	...	...	...	...	0700	...	...	...	...	...	...	...	...	...	...	...	...	1005	...
iracusa 641 d.	...	...	...	...	...	...	...	...	...	...	│	0720	...	...	...	...	...	...	...	...	...	...	1025	│	...
o di Calabria C 637 d.	0810	0840	...	0925	...	...	...	1005	...	...	│	│	...	...	...	...	1219	1319	...	...	...	1419	│	│	...
. Giovanni 641 a.	0825	0852	...	0938	...	...	...	1019	...	...	1125	1125	...	...	...	...	1234	1334	...	...	...	1434	1425	1425	...
. Giovanni d.	0828	0855	...	0941	...	...	...	1022	...	...	1155	1155	...	...	...	...	1236	1336	...	...	...	1436	1455	1455	...
Tauro d.	0852	0918	...	1009	...	...	...	1047	...	...	│	│	...	...	...	...	1309	1409	...	...	...	1509	│	│	...
zia Terme Centrale a.	0932	0957	...	1052	...	...	...	1127	...	...	1253	1253	...	...	...	...	1345	1445	...	...	...	1545	1556	1556	...
zia Terme Centrale 634 d.	0935	1000	...	1055	...	...	...	1130	...	...	1256	1256	...	...	...	...	1347	1447	...	...	...	1547	1559	1559	...
enza 633 d.	│	│	...	│	...	...	...	│	...	...	│	│	...	...	...	1324c	│	│	...	...	1502	│	│	│	...
633 d.	1011	1028	...	1135	...	...	...	1211	1230	...	1330	1330	...	...	...	1350	1429	1529	...	...	1528	1629	1631	1631	...
enza 633 a.	│	│	...	│	...	...	...	│	│	...	│	│	...	...	...	│	1450	1550	...	...	│	1650	│	│	...
dere Marittimo d.	│	│	...	│	...	...	...	│	1257	...	│	│	...	...	...	1421	...	...	...	...	1558	...	│	│	...
ea d.	│	│	...	│	...	...	...	│	1336	...	│	│	...	...	...	1458	...	...	...	...	1643	...	│	│	...
d.	1107	1116	...	1228	...	...	1250	1313	1347	...	1420	1420	...	...	...	1513	...	...	...	...	1655	...	1720	1720	...
d.	│	│	...	1300	...	...	1330	1346	1426	...	│	│	...	...	...	1554	...	...	...	...	1730	...	│	│	←
oli-Castellabate d.	1157	│	...	│	...	...	1356	1405	1454	...	│	│	...	...	...	1619	...	...	...	...	1756	...	│	│	1756
aglia 638 d.	1222	│	...	│	...	...	1428	1421	1519	...	│	│	...	...	...	1644	...	...	1721	...	→	...	│	│	1820
o d.	1237	1229	...	1351	...	...	1446	1438	1545	...	1536	1536	...	...	...	1702	...	...	1737	...	...	...	1836	1836	1843
i Centrale a.	1315	1305	...	1433	...	...	1525	1515	1623	...	1615	1615	...	...	...	1740	...	...	1810	...	...	...	1912	1912	1920
i Centrale 626 d.	1331	1319	1431	1452	1442	1446	...	1531	...	...	1631	1631	1638	1731	1731	...	...	...	1831	1839	...	...	1931	1931	...
erta 626 d.	│	│	│	│	│	│	...	│	...	...	│	│	│	│	│	...	...	...	│	│	...	...	│	│	...
a d.	1348	│	1448	1510	1500	1505	...	1548	...	...	1648	1648	1702	1748	1748	...	...	...	1848	1904	...	...	1948	1948	...
a-Gaeta d.	1422	│	1522	1548	1558	1557	...	1622	...	...	1722	1722	1757	1822	1822	...	...	...	1922	2001	...	...	2022	2022	...
d.	1459	│	1559	1625	1644	1644	...	1659	...	...	1759	1759	1844	1859	1859	...	...	...	1959	2047	...	...	2059	2059	...
Termini 620 a.	1534	1504	1637t	1706t	1727	1724	...	1734	...	...	1834	1834	1924	1939o	1939o	...	...	...	2034	2129	...	...	2134	2134	...
ogna C 620 a.	...	...	2038	2127	...	...	...	...	...	...	...	...	...	...	...	...	...	...	...	...	...	...	...	...	...
ezia SL 616 a.	...	...	│	│	...	...	...	...	...	...	...	...	...	...	...	...	...	...	...	...	...	...	...	...	...
no C 615 a.	...	...	2315	0005	...	...	...	...	...	...	...	...	...	...	...	...	...	...	...	...	...	...	...	...	...
ino PN 610 a.	...	...	...	...	...	...	...	...	...	...	...	...	...	...	...	...	...	...	...	...	...	...	...	...	...

		IC 560	IC 710		ICN 798	FB 9878			ICN 796	ICN 1696						ICN 1962	ICN 1964					ICN 788	ICN 794	ICN 1956	ICN 1954
	2			2		🍷	2	2			2	2	2	2	2			2	2		2				
			♦		♦	⑥y	†	⚒	♦	♦		⚒			⚒	♦	Z		⚒			♦	♦	♦	X
ermo C 641 d.	...	...	...	...	...	...	...	...	...	...	...	...	...	...	...	...	1254	...	...	...	...	...	...	...	1830
iracusa 641 d.	...	...	...	...	...	...	...	...	...	...	...	...	...	...	...	1335	│	...	...	...	...	...	...	1910	│
o di Calabria C 637 d.	...	1505	...	...	...	1600	...	...	...	...	...	1619	1719	...	...	│	│	1819	1919	...	...	...	2135	│	│
. Giovanni 641 a.	...	1517	...	...	...	1612	...	...	...	...	...	1634	1734	...	...	1815	1815	1834	1934	...	...	...	2152	2335	2335
. Giovanni d.	...	1520	...	...	...	1615	...	...	...	...	...	1636	1736	...	...	1845	1845	1836	1936	...	...	...	2155	0005	0005
Tauro d.	...	1548	...	...	...	│	...	...	...	...	...	1709	1809	...	...	1921	1921	1909	2009	...	...	...	2237	│	│
zia Terme Centrale a.	...	1628	...	...	...	1718	...	...	...	...	...	1748	1845	...	...	2007	2007	1945	2045	...	...	...	0009	│	│
zia Terme Centrale 634 d.	...	1631	...	...	...	1721	...	...	...	...	...	1750	1847	...	...	2010	2010	1947	2047	...	...	...	0012	│	│
enza 633 d.	...	│	...	...	...	│	...	...	...	...	...	│	│	1900	2005	│	│	│	│	...	...	...	│	│	│
633 d.	...	1709	...	...	...	1750	1725	...	...	...	...	1831	1929	1926	2031	2047	2047	2029	2119	...	...	...	0052	│	│
enza 633 a.	...	│	...	...	...	│	│	...	...	...	...	1853	1950	│	│	│	│	2050	...	...	...	...	│	│	│
dere Marittimo d.	...	│	...	...	...	│	1751	...	...	...	...	...	...	1954	2059	│	│	...	...	...	...	...	│	│	│
ea d.	...	1754	...	...	...	│	1832	...	...	...	...	...	...	2032	2135	2143	2143	...	...	...	...	...	│	│	│
d.	1729	1807	...	...	...	1839	1852	1852	...	...	2010	...	...	2045	2148	2156	2156	...	...	...	...	...	0153	│	│
d.	1809	│	...	...	...	│	1927	1927	...	...	2052	...	...	2123	...	2228	2228	...	...	...	...	...	│	│	│
oli-Castellabate d.	1833	1903	...	...	...	│	1950	1950	...	...	2120	...	...	2149	...	2254	2254	...	...	...	...	...	│	│	│
aglia 638 d.	1857	1923	...	...	...	│	2012	2012	...	...	2144	...	...	2214	...	2315	2315	...	...	...	...	...	│	│	│
o d.	1917	1937	...	...	2038	1946	2032	2032	2052	2116	2202	...	...	2232	...	2333	2333	...	...	...	...	...	0325	│	│
i Centrale a.	1955	2015	...	...	2115	2020	2110	2110	2130	2155	2240	...	...	2310	...	│	│	...	...	...	...	...	0405	│	│
i Centrale 626 d.	...	2031	...	2045	2132	2036	...	...	2146	2211	...	...	...	...	...	│	│	...	...	...	0404	...	0421	│	│
erta 626 d.	...	│	2037	│	│	│	...	...	│	│	...	...	...	...	...	│	│	...	...	...	│	0413	│	│	│
a d.	...	2053	│	2103	│	│	...	...	2205	2230	...	...	...	...	...	│	│	...	...	...	0427	│	0440	│	│
a-Gaeta d.	...	2128	│	2155	│	│	...	...	2243	2308	...	...	...	...	...	│	│	...	...	...	0511	│	0518	0548s	0548s
d.	...	2205	│	2243	│	│	...	...	2321	2346	...	...	...	...	...	│	│	...	...	...	0547	│	0554	0630s	0630s
Termini 620 a.	...	2241	2300	2324	2339t	2221	...	...	0003o	0028o	...	...	...	...	...	│	│	...	...	...	0627	0634	0631t	0713	0713
ogna C 620 a.	...	...	...	...	│	...	...	...	│	│	...	...	...	...	...	│	│	...	...	...	...	...	1138	...	...
ezia SL 616 a.	...	...	...	...	│	...	...	...	│	│	...	...	...	...	...	│	│	...	...	...	...	...	│	...	...
no C 615 a.	...	...	...	...	0711g	...	...	...	│	│	...	...	...	...	...	1045	1045	...	...	...	...	...	1442g	...	...
ino PN 610 a.	...	...	...	...	0920	...	...	...	0810	0925	...	...	...	...	...	...	...	...	...	...	...	...	1640	...	...

FOR NOTES SEE PAGE 318

641 VILLA SAN GIOVANNI - MESSINA - SIRACUSA and PALERMO

km				ICN 1957	ICN 1955				ICN 1961	ICN 1959						ICN 1963		ICN 1965	ICN 1965					IC 721
			2 ⚒	2 ⚒	D	♦	2 ⚒	2 Ⓑ	2 ⚒	C	♦	2	2 ⚒	2 Ⓐ	2 ⚒	2 ⚒	♦	2 ⚒	A	B	2 Ⓐ	2 ⚒	2	2	K
0	**Villa S. Giovanni 640** ▲	d.	...	...	0445	0445	...	...	...	0540	0540	...	...	...	...	...	1105	...	1105	1105	...	...	...	...	1425
9	**Messina** Centrale ▲	a.	...	...	0610	0610	...	...	...	0710	0710	...	...	...	...	...	1245	...	1245	1245	...	...	...	...	1530
9	**Messina** Centrale	d.	0500	0510	0635	0640s	0655	0703	0720	0735s	0745	0915	1115	1122	1220	1230	1310s	1318	1320	1320	1355	1435	1423	1546	1555
	Taormina-Giardini	d.	│	0552	│	0731s	0756	│	0805	│	0827	0957	1154	│	1319	│	1353s	1405	│	│	│	1539	│	│	1636
	Giarre-Riposto **644**	d.	│	0610	│	0748s	0826	│	0818	│	0842	1011	1210	│	1339	│	1407s	1419	│	│	│	1603	│	│	1652
	Catania Centrale	a.	│	0631	│	0818s	0855	│	0840	│	0904	1033	1233	│	1408	│	1432s	1441	│	│	│	1628	│	│	1719
	Catania Centrale	d.	│	0635	│	0825s	...	│	0842	│	0907	1035	1235	│	...	│	1436s	1507	│	│	│	...	│	│	1722
	Augusta	d.	│	0724	│	0913s	...	│	0927	│	1001	1119	1319	│	...	│	1524s	1557	│	│	│	...	│	│	1810
	Siracusa 648	a.	│	0742	│	0936s	...	│	0948	│	1025	1140	1340	│	...	│	1548	1625	│	│	│	...	│	│	1829
45	Milazzo	d.	0521	...	0657s	...	...	0722	...	0757s	...	...	...	1157	...	1300	...	...	1343s	1343s	1415	...	1454	1618	...
174	Cefalù	d.	0702	...	0847s	...	...	0909	...	0953s	...	...	...	1402	...	1507	...	...	1527s	1527s	1635	...	1709	1838	...
204	Termini Imerese **645/7**	d.	0732	...	0932s	...	...	0927	...	1018s	...	...	...	1429	...	1534	...	...	1611s	1611s	1705	...	1736	1902	...
241	**Palermo** C **645/7**	a.	0800	...	1002	...	...	0951	...	1046	...	...	...	1500	...	1601	...	...	1639	1639	1729	...	1800	1930	...

								IC 729	IC 727		
		2 Ⓐ	2	2 ⚒	2	2	2	L	♦	2	2
Villa S. Giovanni 640 ▲	d.	...	...	...	...	...	...	1820	1820	...	...
Messina Centrale ▲	a.	...	...	...	...	...	...	1930	1930	...	...
Messina Centrale	d.	1713	1715	1725	1825	...	1910	1955	2005	2020	2120
Taormina-Giardini	d.	│	1757	│	1929	...	│	│	2045	2124	2232
Giarre-Riposto **644**	d.	│	1811	│	1947	...	│	│	2102	2144	2251
Catania Centrale	a.	│	1833	│	2014	...	│	│	2126	2213	2320
Catania Centrale	d.	│	1835	│	...	2036	│	│	2129	...	...
Augusta	d.	│	1933	│	...	2120	│	│	2222	...	...
Siracusa 648	a.	│	1952	│	...	2140	│	│	2245	...	...
Milazzo	d.	1736	...	1758	...	...	1932	2017	...	...	...
Cefalù	d.	1906	...	2007	...	...	2116	2206	...	...	...
Termini Imerese **645/7**	d.	1936	...	2035	...	...	2138	2230	...	...	...
Palermo C **645/7**	a.	2000	...	2100	...	...	2204	2300	...	...	...

								IC 722	IC 728	
		2 ⚒	2 ⚒	2 Ⓐ	2	2 ⚒	2 ⚒	N	♦	2
Palermo C **645/7**	d.	...	...	0508	...	0606	...	...	0700	0804
Termini Imerese **645/7**	d.	...	...	0535	...	0634	...	...	0732	0830
Cefalù	d.	...	...	0600	...	0701	...	...	0757	0851
Milazzo	d.	...	...	0739	...	0843	...	...	0937	1040
Siracusa 648	d.	...	0515	│	...	│	0640	0720	│	│
Augusta	d.	...	0535	│	...	│	0702	0741	│	│
Catania Centrale	a.	...	0617	│	...	│	0758	0838	│	│
Catania Centrale	d.	0510	0619	│	0633	│	0800	0841	│	│
Giarre-Riposto **644**	d.	0534	0640	│	0653	│	0830	0906	│	│
Taormina-Giardini	d.	0552	0659	│	0716	│	0850	0922	│	│
Messina Centrale	a.	0655	0753	0800	0830	0903	0940	0956	1000	1104
Messina Centrale ▲	d.	...	...	...	...	...	...	1015	1015	...
Villa S. Giovanni 640 ▲	a.	...	...	...	...	...	...	1125	1125	...

km			IC 730	IC 724				ICN 1964	ICN 1962												ICN 1956	ICN 1954			ICN 1960
			P	♦	2 ⚒	2 ⚒	2 ⚒	Z	♦	2	2 ⚒	2 ⚒	2	2	2 Ⓐ	2	2 ⚒	2	2	2 Ⓐ	♦	X	2 ⚒	2	♦
	Palermo C **645/7**	d.	1005	...	...	1108	...	1254	...	1306	...	1405	1506	...	1606	...	...	...	1705	1805	...	1830	...	2008	...
	Termini Imerese **645/7**	d.	1031	...	...	1137	...	1323u	...	1334	...	1437	1535	...	1632	...	...	...	1733	1832	...	1902u	...	2032	...
	Cefalù	d.	1055	...	...	1206	...	1352u	...	1401	...	1506	1602	...	1652	...	...	...	1803	1907	...	1926u	...	2055	...
	Milazzo	d.	1229	...	...	1411	...	1555u	...	1609	...	1657	1803	...	1829	...	...	...	2013	2037	...	2126u	...	2236	...
0	**Siracusa 648**	d.	│	1025	...	│	1253	│	1335	│	1415	│	│	1615	│	...	1714	1820	│	│	1910	│	2010	│	2145
31	Augusta	d.	│	1046	...	│	1320	│	1400	│	1435	│	│	1634	│	...	1728	1841	│	│	1934	│	2032	│	2206
87	**Catania** Centrale	a.	│	1136	...	│	1407	│	1447	│	1523	│	│	1719	│	...	1834	1925	│	│	2019	│	2124	│	2251
87	**Catania** Centrale	d.	│	1139	1220	│	1411	│	1456	│	1525	│	│	1721	│	1745	1836	1927	│	│	2026	│	2127	│	2254
117	Giarre-Riposto **644**	d.	│	1205	1253	│	1431	│	1522	│	1545	│	│	1743	│	1813	1900	1947	│	│	2051	│	2156	│	2318
135	Taormina-Giardini	d.	│	1220	1319	│	1448	│	1539	│	1601	│	│	1757	│	1834	1919	2000	│	│	2107	│	2216	│	2333
182	**Messina** Centrale	a.	1255	1300	1430	1445	1537	1620	1625	1643	1647	1717	1830	1844	1855	1945	2000	2045	2051	2101	2150	2155	2300	2300	0015
182	**Messina** Centrale ▲	d.	1315	1315	...	...	...	1640	1640	...	...	...	...	...	...	...	...	...	...	...	2210	2210	...	...	0035
191	**Villa S. Giovanni 640** ▲	a.	1425	1425	...	...	...	1815	1815	...	...	...	...	...	...	...	...	...	...	...	2335	2335	...	...	0200

♦ – **NOTES FOR TABLES 640/641**

501 – ⚒: [12] Sestri Levante - Napoli.
510 – [12] Salerno - Torino.
511 – [12] Torino - Salerno.
522 – ⑥ (not Mar. 27, Apr. 24, and days before holidays): [12] Napoli - Sestri Levante.
590 – [12] Napoli - Firenze - Milano.
597 – [12] Milano - Firenze - Napoli.
700 – [12] Taranto - Roma.
701 – [2] Roma - Taranto.
702 – [2] Taranto - Roma.
705 – ⑤ (also June 2; not June 3): [12] Roma - Taranto.
707 – [12] Roma - Taranto.
710 – ⑦ (also Mar. 28, Apr. 25; not Mar. 27, Apr. 24): [12] Taranto - Roma.
723 – [12] Roma - Palermo; [12] Roma - Messina (**721**) - Siracusa.
724 – [12] Siracusa - Roma; [12] Palermo (**730**) - Messina - Roma.
727 – [12] Roma - Siracusa; [12] Roma - Messina (**729**) - Palermo.
728 – [12] Palermo - Roma; [12] Siracusa (**722**) - Messina - Roma.
788 – ⑦ (also Mar. 28, June 2; not Mar. 27, May 29): 🛏 1,2 cl., ▬ 2 cl. (4 berth) and [2] Lecce - Roma.
789 – ⑤ (from Roma): 🛏 1,2 cl., ▬ 2 cl. (4 berth) and [2] Roma - Lecce.
794 – 🛏 1,2 cl., ▬ 2 cl. (4 berth) and [2] Reggio di Calabria - Milano - Torino.
795 – 🛏 1,2 cl., ▬ 2 cl. (4 berth) and [2] Torino - Milano - Reggio di Calabria. Train number **1595** on ①.
796 – Not Jan. 7-16, 26-30: 🛏 1,2 cl., ▬ 2 cl. (4 berth) and [2] Salerno - Napoli - Torino. Train number **35796** on ①; **35096** on Feb. 6.
797 – 🛏 1,2 cl., ▬ 2 cl. (4 berth) and [2] Torino - Milano - Napoli - Salerno.
798 – 🛏 1,2 cl., ▬ 2 cl. (4 berth) and [2] Salerno - Napoli - Milano - Torino.
799 – Not Jan. 7-16, 26-30: 🛏 1,2 cl., ▬ 2 cl. (4 berth) and [2] Torino - Napoli - Salerno. Train number **35099** on Feb. 6.
1571 – †: [12] Livorno - Napoli.
1572 – ⑥ (also Mar. 27, Apr. 24, and days before holidays): [12] Napoli - Livorno.
1588 – ⑦ (also Mar. 28, Apr. 25; not Mar. 27, Apr. 24): [12] Reggio di Calabria - Milano.
1589 – ⑥ (not June 4): [12] Milano - Reggio di Calabria.
1696 – Jan. 7-16, 26-30: 🛏 1,2 cl., ▬ 2 cl. (4 berth) and [2] Salerno - Napoli - Torino.
1699 – Jan. 7-16, 26-30: 🛏 1,2 cl., ▬ 2 cl. (4 berth) and [2] Torino - Napoli - Salerno.

1955 – 🛏 1,2 cl. and ▬ 2 cl. (4 berth) Roma - Siracusa; 🛏 1,2 cl. ▬ 2 cl. (4 berth) Roma - Messina (**1957**) - Palermo.
1956 – 🛏 1,2 cl. and ▬ 2 cl. (4 berth) Siracusa - Roma; 🛏 1,2 cl. ▬ 2 cl. (4 berth) Palermo (**1954**) - Messina - Roma.
1959 – 🛏 1,2 cl. and ▬ 2 cl. (4 berth) Roma - Siracusa; 🛏 1,2 cl. ▬ 2 cl. (4 berth) Roma - Messina (**1961**) - Palermo. Train number **1559** (
1960 – 🛏 1,2 cl. and ▬ 2 cl. (4 berth) Siracusa - Roma; 🛏 1,2 cl. ▬ 2 cl. (4 berth) Palermo (**1958**) - Messina - Roma.
1962 – 🛏 1,2 cl., 🛏 1,2 cl. (T2) and ▬ 2 cl. (4 berth) Siracusa - Genova - Mil 🛏 1,2 cl. and ▬ 2 cl. (4 berth) Palermo (**1964**) - Messina - Milano. Ru train number **1584** on ①.
1963 – Not ②–⑤ Jan. 5 - Feb. 26: 🛏 1,2 cl., 🛏 1,2 cl. (T2) and ▬ 2 cl. (4 Milano - Genova - Siracusa; 🛏 1,2 cl. and ▬ 2 cl. (4 berth) Milano - Me (**1965**) - Palermo. Runs as train number **35163** on Feb. 6.
35063 – ②–⑤ Jan. 5 - Feb. 26: 🛏 1,2 cl., 🛏 1,2 cl. (T2) and ▬ 2 cl. (4 berth) Mi Genova - Siracusa; 🛏 1,2 cl. and ▬ 2 cl. (4 berth) Milano - Messina (1 Palermo.

A – Not ②–⑤ Jan. 5 - Feb. 26: 🛏 1,2 cl. and ▬ 2 cl. (4 berth) Milano (1 Genova - Messina - Palermo.
B – ②–⑤ Jan. 5 - Feb. 26: 🛏 1,2 cl. and ▬ 2 cl. (4 berth) Milano (**35063**) - Ge Messina - Palermo.
C – 🛏 1,2 cl. and ▬ 2 cl. (4 berth) Roma (**1959**) - Messina - Palermo.
D – 🛏 1,2 cl. and ▬ 2 cl. (4 berth) Roma (**1955**) - Messina - Palermo.
K – [12] Roma (**723**) - Messina - Siracusa.
L – [12] Roma (**727**) - Messina - Palermo.
N – [12] Siracusa - Messina (**728**) - Roma.
P – [12] Palermo - Messina (**724**) - Roma.
W – 🛏 1,2 cl. and ▬ 2 cl. (4 berth) Palermo - Messina (**1960**) - Roma.
X – 🛏 1,2 cl. and ▬ 2 cl. (4 berth) Palermo - Messina (**1956**) - Roma.
Z – 🛏 1,2 cl. and ▬ 2 cl. (4 berth) Palermo - Messina (**1962**) - Genova - Mila

c – Ⓒ only.
g – Milano **Porta Garibaldi**.
n – Not May 1.
o – Roma **Ostiense**.
s – Stops to set down only.
t – Roma **Tiburtina**.
u – Stops to pick up only.
y – Not Mar. 27, Apr. 24, and before holidays.

▲ – Through trains are conveyed by ⛴ Villa S. Giovanni - Messina and v.v. See **Table 2695** for other available sailings.

644 CATANIA - RANDAZZO - RIPOSTO

Ferrovia Circume

Winter service valid until June 19. No service on †

km			⚒	⚒	⚒	⚒	⚒	⚒	⚒	⚒	⚒	⚒	⚒	⚒	⚒	⚒
0	**Catania** ▲	d.	...	0536	0658	0751	0923	1126	1228	1342	1505	1638	1728	1843	1939	2009
20	Paternò	d.	...	0609	0734	0827	0957	1201	1305	1417	1540	1712	1804	1919	2015	2044
36	Adrano N.	d.	...	0638	0802	0855	1030	1230	1333	1446	1610	1739	1832	1947	2042	...
52	Bronte	d.	...	0704	0825	0921	1053	1254	1357	1509	1633	1803	1857	2011	...	...
71	Randazzo	a.	...	0737	0853	0949	1121	1322	1425	1537	1701	1831	1926	2038	...	...
71	Randazzo	d.	0632	0748	...	...	1123	1324	...	...	1706	...	...	...	...	...
109	Giarre **640**	a.	0746	0853	...	...	1226	1429	...	...	1812	...	...	...	...	...
111	**Riposto**	a.	0750	0857	...	...	1230	1433	...	...	1816	...	...	...	...	...

		⚒	⚒	⚒	⚒	⚒	⚒	⚒	⚒	⚒	⚒	⚒	⚒	⚒
Riposto	d.	...	...	...	0634	0910	...	...	1240	...	1406	1455	...	...
Giarre **640**	d.	...	...	...	0639	0915	...	...	1245	...	1411	1500	...	...
Randazzo	a.	...	...	...	0745	1019	...	...	1351	...	1520	1605	...	...
Randazzo	d.	0520	0612	0705	0821	1023	1224	1327	...	1439	...	...	1730	1853
Bronte	d.	0548	0641	0736	0850	1053	1253	1356	...	1508	...	...	1804	1922
Adrano N.	d.	0611	0705	0801	0913	1115	1317	1420	...	1533	...	...	1833	1948
Paternò	d.	0640	0733	0828	0940	1143	1346	1447	...	1601	...	...	1900	2015
Catania ▲	a.	0713	0807	0901	1013	1215	1420	1521	...	1633	...	...	1933	2047

▲ – Catania Borgo station. The Metropolitana di Catania operates a metro service Borgo - Porto and v.v. (3.8 km) via Catania Centrale station. Weekdays only, every 15 minutes 0700–

PALERMO and AGRIGENTO - CATANIA 645

class only except where shown

	⚒	⚒	⚒	⚒				⚒		⚒y	⚒	⚒	⚒y	⚒		⚒	Ⓐ					⚒	
Palermo Centrale **647** d.	...	0500	...	...	...	0736	...	0938	...	...	...	1338	...	...	...	...	1538	...	1736	...	...	...	1938
Termini Imerese **647** d.	...	0525	...	...	...	0759	...	|	...	...	...	|	...	...	...	...	|	...	1759	...	...	...	|
Roccapalumba-Alia **647** d.	...	|	...	0640	...	|	...	|	...	...	...	|	...	1435	...	1549	|	...	|	...	...	1949	|
Agrigento Centrale **647** d.	...	|	0505	|	...	|	...	|	...	...	1254	|	1357	|	...	|	|	...	|	...	1912	|	|
Aragona-Caldare **647** d.	...	|	0522	|	...	|	...	|	...	...	1311	|	1416	|	...	|	|	...	|	...	1930	|	|
Canicattì **648** d.	...	|	0601	|	...	|	...	|	...	...	1349	|	1452	|	...	|	|	...	|	...	2008	|	|
Caltanissetta Xirbi **648** a.	...	0626	|	0740	...	0900	...	1100	...	...	|	1500	|	1537	...	1641	1700	...	1900	...	|	2047	2100
Caltanissetta Centrale **648** d.	0525	|	0635	0756	0800	|	...	|	...	1357	1415	|	1521	1555	...	1657	|	1757	|	...	2033	2104	|
Caltanissetta Xirbi **648** d.	0534	0627	...	...	0809	0901	...	1101	...	1407	...	1501	...	...	...	...	1701	1805	1901	...	2043	...	2101
Enna d.	0607	0647	...	...	0842	0921	...	1121	...	1442	...	1521	...	...	...	...	1721	1842	1921	...	...	...	2121
Catania Centrale ♣ a.	0733	0750	...	...	1005	1025	...	1225	...	1605	...	1625	...	...	...	...	1825	2005	2026	...	...	...	2225

	⚒	⚒	⚒	⚒y			⚒		⚒	⚒	⚒	⚒		Ⓐ	⚒	⚒	⚒y						
Catania Centrale ♣ d.	...	...	0503	...	0737	0849	0932	...	...	...	1338	1449	...	1532	...	...	1649	1732	...	...	1849	1932	...
Enna d.	...	...	0606	...	0841	1011	1041	...	...	...	1441	1611	...	1641	...	...	1811	1841	...	...	2011	2041	...
Caltanissetta Xirbi **648** a.	...	...	0626	...	0900	1035	1100	...	...	...	1500	1634	...	1700	...	...	1836	1900	...	...	2038	2100	...
Caltanissetta Centrale **648** d.	0500	0558	|	0645	|	1044	|	...	1305	1409	|	1644	...	|	1732	1745	1900	|	...	1930	2053	|	...
Caltanissetta Xirbi **648** d.	0515	|	0627	|	0901	...	1101	...	1320	1424	1501	...	...	1701	|	1801	...	1901	...	|	...	2101	...
Canicattì **648** d.	|	0633	|	0720	|	...	|	...	|	|	|	...	...	|	1813	|	...	|	...	2012	...	|	...
Aragona-Caldare **647** d.	|	0705	|	0751	|	...	|	...	|	|	|	...	...	|	1847	|	...	|	...	2046	...	|	...
Agrigento Centrale **647** a.	|	0725	|	0808	|	...	|	...	|	|	|	...	...	|	1905	|	...	|	...	2104	...	|	...
Roccapalumba-Alia **647** d.	0615	...	|	...	|	...	|	...	1415	1529	|	...	...	|	...	1908	...	|	...	...	...	|	...
Termini Imerese **647** d.	...	...	0727	...	1006	...	|	...	...	...	|	...	...	|	...	...	...	2006	...	...	...	|	...
Palermo Centrale **647** a.	...	...	0752	...	1029	...	1227	...	...	...	1627	...	...	1827	...	...	...	2029	...	...	...	2227	...

Not Mar. 24-29.

PALERMO - TRAPANI 646

class only

	⚒	⚒	⚒	⚒		🚌 ⚒	⚒	🚌 †	†	🚌 †	🚌 ⚒	†	⚒	⚒y	⚒	🚌 ⚒	⚒	🚌 ⚒	🚌 †		🚌 ⚒		🚌	
Palermo Centrale d.	...	...	...	...	...	0600	...	0705	...	1002	1007	...	...	...	...	1257	...	*1439*t	1510	...	*1639*t	...	1843	...
Fiera d.	...	...	...	...	...	|	...	|	...	|	|	...	...	...	...	|	...	1510	|	...	1712	...	|	...
Piraineto d.	...	...	...	...	...	0721	0745	0825	0835	1123	1128	1135	...	...	...	1417	...	1621	1621	1715	1823	1915	2003	...
Castellammare del Golfo d.	...	...	...	...	...	...	0831	...	0914	...	...	1216	1225	...	...	1549	...	...	...	1755	...	2001	...	2116
Alcamo Diramazione d.	...	...	...	...	...	...	0839	...	0921	...	...	1223	1233	...	1534	1600	...	...	...	1802	...	2016	...	2124
Castelvetrano d.	0530	0619	0640	0722	0830	...	0920	...	0958	...	...	1300	1316	1400	1611	1655	1713	...	...	1838	...	2052	...	2205
Mazara del Vallo d.	0550	0639	0706	0748	0856	...	0939	...	1018	...	...	...	1336	1419	1630	...	1735	...	...	1858	...	2111	...	...
Marsala d.	0613	0658	0729	0808	0914	...	0956	...	1035	...	...	...	1356	1446	1648	...	1758	...	...	1915	...	2128	...	...
Trapani a.	0644	0739	0755	0841	0943	...	1020	...	1105	...	...	...	1430	1520	1716	...	1825	...	...	1940	...	2200	...	...

	⚒	⚒	†	🚌 †	🚌 ⚒	⚒	⚒	†	🚌 †	⚒y	⚒	⚒y		⚒	🚌 ⚒	🚌 †		🚌 †	🚌 ⚒	Ⓐz		⚒y		
Trapani d.	...	0543	0543	...	...	...	0800	0825	...	1200	1240	1342	...	1435	...	...	1601	...	...	1726	1830	1945	2035	...
Marsala d.	...	0612	0612	...	...	...	0837	0904	...	1234	1313	1422	...	1513	...	...	1627	...	...	1757	1856	2018	2106	...
Mazara del Vallo d.	...	0640	0640	...	...	...	0855	0927	...	1253	1337	1442	...	1534	...	...	1650	...	...	1815	1918	2041	2131	...
Castelvetrano d.	0500	0700	0701	...	0705	...	0921	0959	...	1315	1359	1505	1538	1555	...	...	1710	...	...	1835	1938	2110	2155	...
Alcamo Diramazione d.	0540	...	0738	...	0806	...	0959	1037	...	...	1440	...	1621	...	...	...	1803	...	...	...	2015	...	...	...
Castellammare del Golfo d.	0547	...	0745	...	0817	...	1006	1045	...	...	...	...	1628	...	...	...	1811	...	...	...	2023	...	...	...
Piraineto d.	...	...	0825	0833	0955	...	...	1125	1130	...	...	...	1707	...	1715	1815	1855	1915	1915	...	...	...	...	...
Fiera a.	...	...	...	|	1106	1132	...	...	|	...	...	...	...	...	1825	|	...	|	2026	...	...	...	...	...
Palermo Centrale a.	...	...	...	0944	...	1157	...	...	1246	...	...	...	...	...	*1857*t	1926	...	2026	*2057*t	...	...	...	...	...

Connection by train.　y – Not Mar. 24-29.　z – Not days before holidays.

PALERMO - AGRIGENTO 647

class only

	⚒	⚒y		⚒y	Ⓐy			⚒	⚒			
Palermo Centrale **645** d.	0548	0743	0841	1143	1243	1343	1443	1543	1643	1743	1841	2022
Termini Imerese **645** d.	0617	0814	0907	1209	1309	1411	1509	1609	1710	1810	1908	2050
Roccapalumba-Alia **645** d.	0647	0843	0941	1239	1341	1442	1540	1643	1739	1844	1940	2123
Aragona-Caldare **645** d.	0740	0937	1034	1335	1435	1536	1635	1735	1836	1936	2034	2209
Agrigento C **645** a.	0758	0954	1052	1354	1452	1554	1654	1754	1854	1954	2052	2226

	⚒	⚒y			Ⓐy	⚒y	⚒	⚒	†			
Agrigento C **645** d.	0520	0614	0814	1014	1214	1314	1414	1514	1610	1714	1814	2014
Aragona-Caldare **645** d.	0537	0632	0833	1035	1232	1334	1435	1535	1634	1734	1835	2033
Roccapalumba-Alia **645** d.	0624	0723	0921	1121	1321	1424	1523	1624	1727	1825	1923	2122
Termini Imerese **645** d.	0654	0749	0951	1152	1352	1453	1553	1653	1754	1852	1951	2152
Palermo C **645** a.	0722	0816	1016	1216	1416	1516	1616	1716	1822	1916	2016	2216

Not Mar. 24-29.

SIRACUSA - GELA - CALTANISSETTA 648

class only

	⚒	⚒	⚒ 🚌	⚒ 🚌	⚒	⚒ 🚌	⚒	⚒	⚒ 🚌	⚒
Siracusa 640 d.	...	1010	...	...	1356	...	1425	1735	...	1922
Pozzallo d.	...	1113	...	...	1508	...	1530	1846	...	2031
Modica d.	0515	1200	...	1415	1604	...	...	1926	1932	2110
Ragusa d.	0543	1223	...	1441	1630	...	...	...	2002	...
Vittoria d.	0622	1309	...	1541	1721	...	...	...	2042	...
Gela 645 d.	...	1340	1457	1631	1748	1748	...	...	2130	...
Licata d.	...	...	1542	1721	...	1838	...	...	...	...
Canicattì **645** d.	...	...	1638	1805	...	1922	...	...	...	...
Caltanissetta C **645** d.	...	...	1728	1858	...	2003	...	...	...	...

	⚒	⚒	⚒	⚒	⚒ 🚌	⚒	⚒ 🚌	⚒	⚒ 🚌	⚒
Caltanissetta C **645** d.	...	...	...	...	0500	...	1120	...	1419	...
Canicattì **645** d.	...	...	...	...	0541	...	1205	...	1505	...
Licata d.	...	...	...	...	0621	...	1250	...	1550	...
Gela 645 d.	...	...	...	...	0700	...	1324	1426	1640	1758
Vittoria d.	...	...	0638	...	0748	...	...	1457	...	1829
Ragusa d.	...	...	0727	...	0828	...	...	1541	...	1918
Modica d.	0541	0612	0748	0821	0858	...	...	1601	...	1938
Pozzallo d.	0614	0644	...	0854	...	1540	...	...	...	2010
Siracusa 640 a.	0717	0747	...	0957	...	1645	...	...	...	2115

MALTA

ent bus services throughout Malta and Gozo are operated by Malta Public Transport www.publictransport.com.mt. Travellers will also find useful information on the unofficial website www. bybus.com.

PRINCIPAL BUS SERVICES 649

es from Valletta: **X4** Airport - Hal Far, **1** L'Isla (Senglea), **2/4** Birgu (Vittoriosa), **3** Birgu - Smart City - Rinella - Kalkara, **13-15** Sliema - San Giljan (St Julian's), **13** Bahar ic-Caghaq, **31/45/48** a - Bugibba (**45** via Qawra seafront), **31/43/45** Naxxar, **41/42** Mosta - St Paul's Bay - Mellieha - Ghadira - Cirkewwa (for Gozo ferry), **44** Ghajn Tuffieha (Golden Bay), **49** Armier Bay (summer), Rabat / Mdina, **52/56** Dingli, **61** Zebbug, **62** Siggiewi, **71/73** Zurrieq, **72** Qrendi, **74** Hagar Qim - Blue Grotto, **80/82/X4** Birzebbuga, **81/85** Marsaxlokk, **91-93** Marsaskala, **94** Xghajra.

routes: **X1** Airport - Cirkewwa, **X2** Airport - Sliema, **X3** Airport - Rabat - Bugibba, **186** Bugibba - Ta' Qali - Rabat, **202** Sliema - Naxxar - Mosta - Rabat, **203** Sliema - Naxxar - Mosta - Bugibba, liema - San Giljan - Bugibba, **221** Bugibba - Mellieha - Cirkewwa, **222** Sliema - St Paul's Bay - Mellieha - Cirkewwa, **223** Bugibba - Ghajn Tuffieha, **225** Sliema - St Paul's Bay - Ghajn Tuffieha.

: routes from Rabat (Victoria): **301/303** Mgarr (for Cirkewwa ferry), **302** Ramla, **305** Sannat, **306/330** Xlendi, **307** Xaghra, **308** Ta' Pinu - Ghasri, **309** Zebbug, **310** Marsalforn, **311** Dwejra.

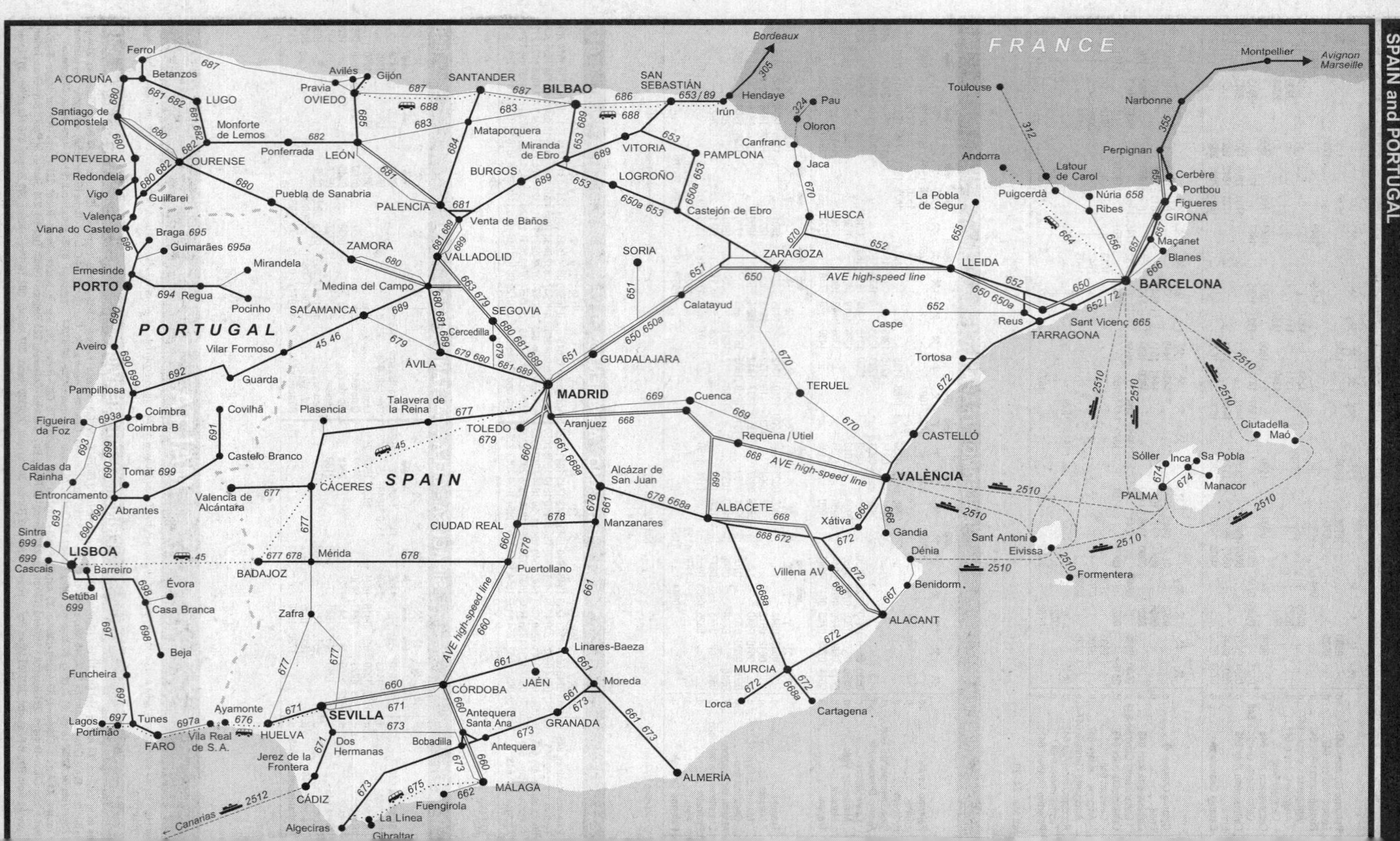
FRANCE
SPAIN
PORTUGAL
Bordeaux
Montpellier
Avignon Marseille
Ferrol
Betanzos
A CORUÑA
Avilés
Gijón
Pravia
OVIEDO
SANTANDER
BILBAO
SAN SEBASTIÁN
Hendaye
Irún
Pau
Oloron
Toulouse
Narbonne
LUGO
Santiago de Compostela
Monforte de Lemos
Ponferrada
LEÓN
Mataporquera
Miranda de Ebro
VITORIA
PAMPLONA
Canfranc
Jaca
Andorra
Latour de Carol
Perpignan
Cerbère
Portbou
Figueres
GIRONA
Maçanet
Blanes
BARCELONA
PONTEVEDRA
Redondela
Vigo
Guillarei
Valença
Viana do Castelo
OURENSE
Puebla de Sanabria
PALENCIA
BURGOS
LOGROÑO
Castejón de Ebro
HUESCA
La Pobla de Segur
Puigcerdà
Núria 658
Ribes
Braga 695
Guimarães 695a
Venta de Baños
Mirandela
ZAMORA
VALLADOLID
SORIA
ZARAGOZA
LLEIDA
Ermesinde
PORTO
694 Regua
Pocinho
Medina del Campo
SALAMANCA
SEGOVIA
Cercedilla
Calatayud
Caspe
Reus
TARRAGONA
Sant Vicenç 665
Aveiro
Vilar Formoso
ÁVILA
GUADALAJARA
Tortosa
TERUEL
AVE high-speed line
Guarda
Pampilhosa
Coimbra
Coimbra B
Figueira da Foz
Covilhã
Plasencia
Talavera de la Reina
MADRID
Cuenca
Aranjuez
TOLEDO 679
Requena / Utiel
CASTELLÓ
Ciutadella
Maó
Castelo Branco
Caldas da Rainha
Tomar 699
Entroncamento
Abrantes
Valencia de Alcántara
CÁCERES
Alcázar de San Juan
VALÈNCIA
Sóller
Inca
Sa Pobla
Manacor
PALMA
ALBACETE
Xàtiva
Gandia
CIUDAD REAL
Manzanares
Sant Antoni
Eivissa
Formentera
Dénia
Sintra 699
Cascais 699
LISBOA
Barreiro
BADAJOZ
Mérida
Puertollano
Villena AV
Benidorm
Évora
Setúbal 699
Casa Branca
Beja
Zafra
ALACANT
Linares-Baeza
Funcheira
JAÉN
Moreda
MURCIA
CÓRDOBA
Lorca
Cartagena
Lagos
Portimão
Tunes
FARO
Vila Real de S.A.
Ayamonte
HUELVA
SEVILLA
Antequera Santa Ana
GRANADA
Dos Hermanas
Bobadilla
Antequera
Jerez de la Frontera
ALMERÍA
CÁDIZ
MÁLAGA
Fuengirola
La Línea
Gibraltar
Algeciras
Canarias

SPAIN

ator: **Renfe Operadora** – unless otherwise indicated. www.renfe.es

ces: On long-distance trains first class is known as *Preferente* and second class as *Turista*. Unless otherwise indicated (by '2' in the train column or (2) in the notes), all trains convey both first- and second-class seating accommodation.

🍸 indicates a buffet car (*cafeteria*) or a mobile trolley service. ✕ indicates a full restaurant car service or the availability of hot meals served from the buffet car. Meals are served free of extra charge, on Mondays to Fridays, to holders of *Preferente* tickets on all *AVE* and *Euromed* trains. Note that catering services may not be available throughout a train's journey, particularly in the case of trains with multiple origins / destinations.

🛏 indicates coaches equipped with couchettes: for occupancy of these a standard supplement is payable in addition to the normal *Turista* fare. 🛏 indicates sleeping-cars with single, double, and 3- or 4-berth compartments. The *Turista* fare is payable plus a sleeping-car supplement corresponding to the type and standard of accommodation. ***Trenhotel*** services additionally convey *Gran Clase* accommodation: *de luxe* single- and double-occupancy compartments with *en suite* shower and toilet. *Preferente* fare is payable for travel in *Gran Clase* plus a sleeping-car supplement corresponding to the type and standard of accommodation.
Local (*Media Distancia*) and suburban (*Cercanias*) trains are shown without an indication of category except for some fast ***Media Distancia*** (*MD*).

categories:
Altaria (*Alta*): Talgo trains which can change gauge and run on the high-speed lines as well as the broad-gauge system.
Alta Velocidad Española (*AVE*): High-speed trains running on the standard-gauge lines.
Alvia: High-speed gauge-changing trains.
Avant (*Av*): Medium-distance high-speed trains on the standard-gauge lines.
Euromed (*Em*): *AVE*-like trains running on the broad-gauge Barcelona - València - Alacant route.
Intercity (*IC*): *Alvia*-like trains offering *Turista* class only.
Media Distancia (*MD*): Medium distance regional trains.
Reginal Exprés (*RE*): Medium distance regional trains.
Talgo: Quality express trains using light, articulated stock.
Train à Grande Vitesse (*TGV*): French High-speed trains.
Trenhotel (*Hotel*): Quality night express trains (see Services, above).

rvations: Reservations are compulsory for all journeys by services for which a train category (e.g. *AVE*, *RE*) is shown in the timing column. Advance purchase of tickets is also available for travel by services for which a train number is shown.

lements: Higher fares, incorporating a supplement, are payable for travel by *Altaria, Alvia, AVE, Euromed, InterCity, Talgo, TGV* and *Trenhotel* services.

ngs: Timings have been compiled from the latest information supplied by operators.

gh-speed services — MADRID - ZARAGOZA - BARCELONA — 650

	AVE	*AVE*	*AVE*	*Av*	*AVE*	*AVE*	*AVE*	*AVE*	*AVE*	*AVE*	*AVE*	*AVE*	*AVE*	*AVE*	*AVE*	*AVE*	*AVE*	*AVE*	*AVE*	*AVE*	*AVE*	*AVE*	*AVE*	*Av*	*AVE*
	3263	**3053**	**3061**	**8087**	**3463**	**3063**	**3071**	**3271**	**3483**	**3073**	**3073**	**3081**	**3283**	**3083**	**3293**	**3093**	**3103**	**3993**	**3943**	**3113**	**3123**	**9724**	**3141**	**8167**	**3143**
	①–⑤	①④⑤	①–④		⑥⑦	①–⑤	①–⑤	①–④	⑥⑦	①–⑤	⑥⑦	①–⑤	①–④		②③							**19725** **M**	Ⓑ	Ⓑ	Ⓑ
Sevilla **660** d.	...	...	...	...	...	...	...	...	...	...	...	...	...	...	...	...	...	...	0850	...	...	...	...	...	...
Málaga **660** d.	...	...	...	...	...	...	...	...	...	...	...	...	...	...	...	...	...	0840	|	...	...	...	...	...	...
Madrid Puerta de Atocha d.	...	0550	0610	...	0620	0630	0700	0720	...	0730	0730	0800	0820	0830	0900	0930	1030	|	|	1130	1230	1325	1400	...	1430
Guadalajara - Yebes d.	...	|	|	...	|	|	|	|	...	0754	0754	|	|	|	|	|	|	|	|	|	|	1350	|	...	|
Calatayud d.	...	|	|	...	0716	0726	|	|	...	|	|	|	|	|	|	|	|	|	|	1226	|	|	|	...	1526
Zaragoza Delicias d.	0620	0706	|	...	0742	0752	|	|	0800	0852	0852	|	0936	0946	1016	1046	1146	1236	1236	1252	1346	1452	|	...	1552
Lleida d.	0705	0750	|	0800	0826	|	|	|	0855	0937	0937	|	|	|	|	1131	|	1322	1322	1337	1431	|	|	1600	|
Camp de Tarragona d.	0735	0819	|	0832	0854	|	|	|	0923	1005	1005	|	|	1045x	|	1159	|	1351	1351	1405	|	1547	|	1632	|
Barcelona Sants a.	0810	0855	0840	0908	0929	0920	0930	0950	0958	1040	1040	1030	1105	1115z	1145	1234	1315	1425	1425	1440	1530	1624	1630	1708	1721
Girona **657** a.	...	...	...	...	1023	...	1023	...	...	...	1128	...	...	...	...	1322	...	...	...	1529f	1618v	1723	...	...	1815
Figueres Vilafant **657** a.	...	...	...	...	1040	...	1040	...	...	...	1145	...	...	...	...	1339	...	...	...	1545f	1635v	1740	...	...	1832

	AVE	*AVE*	*AVE*	*Av*	*AVE*	*AVE*	*Av*	*AVE*	*Av*	*AVE*	*AVE*	*AVE*	*AVE*	*AVE*	*AVE*	*AVE*	*AVE*	*Av*	*AVE*	*AVE*	*AVE*	*AVE*	*AVE*			
	3151	**3153**	**3161**	**8187**	**3163**	**3163**	**3563**	**3171**	**3793**	**3991**	**3941**	**3173**	**3181**	**3945**	**3183**	**3183**	**3191**	**8207**	**3193**	**3201**	**3203**	**3211**	**3593**			
	①–⑤		Ⓑ		①–⑤	⑥⑦	④⑤⑦	Ⓑ	⑤⑦				Ⓑ	⑦	⑥	Ⓑ	Ⓑ			Ⓑ		Ⓑ	**10831** Ⓑ			
villa **660** d.	...	...	...	...	...	...	...	...	...	...	1450	...	...	1555	...	...	...	...	...	...	...	...	1848	...	...	...
álaga **660** d.	...	...	...	...	...	...	...	...	...	1435	|	...	...	|	...	...	...	...	...	...	...	...	|	...	...	...
rid Puerta de Atocha d.	1500	1530	1600	...	1630	1630	1635	1700	...	|	|	1730	1800	|	1830	1830	1900	...	1930	2000	2030	2125	2130	...	...	...
dalajara - Yebes d.	|	|	|	...	|	|	|	|	...	|	|	1754	|	|	|	|	|	...	|	|	2054	|	2155	...	...	...
tayud d.	|	1626	|	...	|	|	|	|	...	|	|	|	|	|	|	|	|	...	|	|	|	|	2235	...	...	...
goza Delicias d.	|	1652	|	...	1746	1746	1756	|	1805	1831	1831	1852	|	1935	1946	1946	|	...	2046	|	2152	|	2300	...	...	...
a d.	|	1737	|	1800	|	|	...	|	1848	1918	1918	1937	|	|	|	|	|	2040	2131	|	2237	|	...	...	...	...
p de Tarragona d.	|	1805	|	1832	1844x	1844x	...	|	1916	1947	1947	2005	|	2039	2045	2045	|	2112	2206	|	2305	|	...	...	...	...
elona Sants a.	1730	1840	1830	1908	1915z	1915z	...	1930	1951	2022	2022	2040	2030	2115	2120	2120	2130	2148	2240	2230	2340	2355	...	...	...	...
rona **657** a.	...	1928	...	...	2003z	...	...	...	...	...	...	...	...	...	2208	...	2218	...	...	...	...	...	...	...	...	...
gueres Vilafant **657** a.	...	1945	...	...	2020z	...	...	...	...	...	...	...	...	...	2225	...	2235	...	...	...	...	...	...	...	...	...

	AVE	*AVE*	*AVE*	*AVE*	*AVE*	*AVE*	*AVE*	*AVE*	*AVE*	*AVE*	*AVE*	*AVE*	*AVE*	*AVE*	*AVE*	*AVE*	*Av*	*AVE*	*AVE*	*AVE*	*AVE*	*AVE*	*AVE*	*AVE*	*Av*	*AVE*
	3252	**3772**	**3062**	**3260**	**3462**	**3270**	**3072**	**3070**	**3662**	**3082**	**3082**	**3080**	**3940**	**3990**	**3092**	**3092**	**8096**	**3102**	**3112**	**3122**	**9731**	**3132**	**3142**	**3152**	**3562**	**3150**
	①–④	**10830** ①–⑥	①–⑥	①–⑤	①–④	①–④		①–④	①–⑤	①–⑤	⑥⑦	①–⑥			①–⑥	⑦					**19730** **M**	①–⑥			⑤⑦	①–⑤
gueres Vilafant **657** d.	...	...	...	...	...	...	...	...	0630	0655	...	...	...	...	0755	...	...	0855	...	...	1143	...	...	...	...	...
rona **657** d.	...	...	...	...	...	...	...	...	0646	0711	...	...	...	...	0811	...	...	0911	...	...	1200	...	...	...	...	...
elona Sants d.	0550	...	0605	0625	0640	0700	0705	0725	0740	0800	0800	0825	0830	0830	0900	0900	0910	1000	1100	1200	1250	1325	1400	1500	1515	1525
p de Tarragona d.	|	...	0638	|	|	|	|	0757	|	0833	0833	|	0905	0905	|	|	0947	1033	|	1233	1322	|	1433	|	1548	|
a d.	|	...	0704	|	|	|	|	|	|	0859	0859	|	0934	0934	|	|	1018	1059	|	1259	|	|	1459	|	1614	|
goza Delicias d.	|	0705	0748	|	0806	|	0831	|	|	0943	0943	|	1020	1020	1026	1026	...	1143	1226	1343	1425	1451	1543	1626	1655	|
tayud d.	|	0732	|	|	|	|	|	|	|	1008	1008	|	|	|	|	|	...	|	|	|	|	|	1608	|	...	|
dalajara - Yebes d.	|	0813	0845	|	|	|	|	|	|	|	|	|	|	|	|	|	...	1243	|	1443	|	|	|	|	...	|
rid Puerta de Atocha a.	0820	0840	0915	0855	0925	0930	0950	1001	1010	1110	1110	1055	|	|	1145	1145	...	1310	1345	1510	1545	1610	1710	1745	...	1755
álaga **660** a.	...	|	...	...	...	...	...	...	...	...	...	...	|	1424	...	...	...	...	...	...	...	...	...	...	...	...
villa **660** a.	...	1135	...	...	...	...	...	...	...	...	...	...	1402	...	...	...	...	...	...	...	...	...	...	...	...	...

	AVE	*AVE*	*AVE*	*AVE*	*Av*	*AVE*	*AVE*	*AVE*	*AVE*	*AVE*	*Av*	*AVE*	*Av*	*AVE*	*AVE*	*AVE*	*AVE*	*AVE*	*Av*	*AVE*	*AVE*	*AVE*	*AVE*			
	3942	**3992**	**3162**	**3162**	**8166**	**3160**	**3946**	**3172**	**3172**	**3170**	**3792**	**3182**	**8186**	**3180**	**3180**	**3192**	**3190**	**3202**	**8206**	**3212**	**3412**	**3610**	**3222**			
			①–⑥	⑦	Ⓑ	Ⓑ	⑤	①–⑥	⑦	Ⓑ	**10792** ④⑤⑦			①–⑤	⑦		Ⓑ			⑤⑦	**A**	⑤⑦				
gueres Vilafant **657** d.	...	...	1455	...	...	...	...	...	1545	...		1655	...	...	1720	1755	...	...	...	...	...	...	...	...	...	...
rona **657** d.	...	...	1511	...	...	...	...	...	1601	...	...	1711	...	...	1736	1811	...	...	...	...	...	...	...	...	...	...
elona Sants d.	1550	1550	1600	1600	1605	1625	1632	1700	1700	1725	...	1800	1805	1825	1825	1900	1925	2000	2010	2100	2115	2125	2150	...	...	...
p de Tarragona d.	1623	1623	1633	1633	1642	|	1705	1732x	1732x	|	...	1833	1842	|	|	1932	|	2033	2047	2133	|	|	2223	...	...	...
a d.	1649	1649	1659	1659	1713	|	|	|	|	|	...	1859	1913	|	|	1958	|	2059	2118	2159	|	|	2250	...	...	...
goza Delicias d.	1733	1733	1743	1743	...	|	1804	1826z	1826z	|	1900	1943	...	|	|	2041	|	2143	...	2243	2243	|	2335	...	...	...
tayud d.	|	|	1808	1808	...	|	|	|	|	|	|	2008	...	|	|	|	|	|	...	|	|	|	...	...	...	...
dalajara - Yebes d.	|	|	|	|	...	|	|	|	|	|	|	|	...	|	|	|	|	2243	...	|	|	|	...	...	...	...
rid Puerta de Atocha a.	|	|	1910	1910	...	1855	|	1945z	1945z	1955	2030	2110	...	2055	2055	2200	2155	2310	...	0002	0002	2355	...	...	...	...
álaga **660** a.	|	2140	...	...	...	...	|	...	...	...	...	...	...	...	...	...	...	...	...	...	...	...	...	...	...	...
villa **660** a.	2115	...	...	...	...	...	2143	...	...	...	...	...	...	...	...	...	...	...	...	...	...	...	...	...	...	...

①②③④⑥.
To / from Marseille (Table **13**).
f – ①–⑤.
v – Not ⑥.
x – June 12 - Sept. 11.
z – 5 minutes later June 12 - Sept. 11.
☛ *AVE* trains convey ✕ and 🍸. *Avant* trains (*Av*) are *Turista* class only.

650a MADRID – LOGROÑO, PAMPLONA / IRUÑA, HUESCA – BARCELONA

	IC 635 ①–⑥	IC 10655 ⑥ y	Alvia 533 K	Alvia 433 F	Alvia 601 ①–⑤	IC 631 ①–⑥ B	Alvia 603 ⑥	Alvia 605 Ⓑ	IC 633 ⑦ B	Alvia 661 ①–⑥ G	AVE 3363 ⑤⑦	IC 10657 ⑦ b	Alvia 621 625 J	Alvia 537 K	Alvia 437 Ⓑ F	Alvia 609	Alvia 613 ⑤	Alvia 613 ④⑦ b	Alvia 701 Ⓑ	AVE 3393	Alvia 801 Ⓑ	
Madrid Puerta de Atocha ... d.	...	...	...	...	0735	...	0940	1135	...	...	1605	...	...	...	...	1505	1735	1735	1835	1905	1935	...
Guadalajara - Yebes ... d.	...	...	...	...	|	...	1007	1202	...	...	|	...	...	...	...	1532	|	|	1901	1928	|	...
Calatayud ... d.	...	...	...	...	|	...	1055	1250	...	...	|	...	...	...	...	1620	|	|	1948	2007	|	...
Logroño **653** ... a.	...	...	...	0904	|	1021	|	|	1434	...	|	...	...	...	1753	|	|	|	2158	|	|	...
Pamplona / Iruña **653** ... a.	0625	0812	0913	|	1038	|	1252	1440	|	1447	|	1625	1724	1754	|	1826	2043	2043	...	|	2240	...
Zaragoza Delicias ... d.	0810	1003	1113	1113	...	1215	...	...	1628	1637	1727	1811	1918	1952	1952	...	...	...	...	2034	...	...
Huesca **670** ... a.	|	|	|	|	...	|	...	...	|	|	1810	|	|	|	|	...	...	...	...	2118	...	...
Lleida ... d.	0900	1056	1203	1203	...	1313	...	...	1722	1732	...	|	2013	2051	2051	...	...	...	...	...	...	...
Camp de Tarragona ... d.	0930	1127	1238	1238	...	1343	...	...	1753	1813	...	1924	2050	2128	2128	...	...	...	...	...	...	...
Barcelona Sants ... a.	1010	1205	1320	1320	...	1420	...	...	1835	1850	...	2000	2125	2209	2209	...	...	...	...	...	...	...

	Alvia 802 ①–⑤	AVE 3272	Alvia 702 ①–⑥	Alvia 800 ① b	Alvia 600 ⑥	Alvia 534 K	Alvia 434 ①–⑥ F	Alvia 602 Ⓑ	Alvia 622 626 J	IC 10560 ⑥ b	Alvia 606	Alvia 664 G	IC 632 B	Alvia 612 ⑦	Alvia 612 ⑤ b	Alvia 530 K	Alvia 430 F	AVE 3592 ⑤⑦	Alvia 610 Ⓑ	IC 562 ①–⑤ w	IC 562 ⑦	
Barcelona Sants ... d.	...	...	...	...	...	0730	0730	...	0930	1005	...	1210	1410	...	...	1530	1530	...	...	1840	1930	...
Camp de Tarragona ... d.	...	...	...	...	...	0808	0808	...	1007	1043	...	1248	1447	...	...	1608	1608	...	...	1918	2008	...
Lleida ... d.	...	...	...	...	...	0844	0844	...	1037	1115	...	1322	1517	...	...	1639	1639	...	...	1950	2041	...
Huesca **670** ... d.	...	0815	...	...	...	|	|	...	|	|	...	|	|	...	...	|	|	1935	...	|	|	...
Zaragoza Delicias ... d.	...	0900	...	...	...	0934	0934	...	1128	1204	...	1414	1608	...	...	1729	1729	2020	...	2102	2134	...
Pamplona / Iruña **653** ... d.	0635	|	...	0810	0900	1117	|	1130	1315	1354	1535	1606	|	1807	1807	1922	|	|	1935	2244	2328	...
Logroño **653** ... d.	|	|	0735	|	|	...	1123	|	...	...	|	...	1750	|	|	...	1936	|	|	...	...	...
Calatayud ... d.	|	0925	0936	|	1101	...	...	1324	...	...	|	...	...	|	|	...	...	|	2134	...	...	...
Guadalajara - Yebes ... d.	|	1005	1022	|	1150	...	...	1412	...	...	|	...	...	|	|	...	...	|	2224	...	...	...
Madrid Puerta de Atocha ... a.	0945	1035	1050	1120	1218	...	...	1440	...	...	1838	...	...	2125	2125	...	...	2140	2253	...	...	...

B – (12) Valladolid - Barcelona and v.v. (Tables **653, 689**).
F – (12) Bilbao - Barcelona and v.v. (Table **653**).
G – (12) Gijón - Barcelona and v.v. (Table **685**).
J – (12) Vigo / A Coruña - Barcelona and v.v. (Table **680**).
K – (12) Irún - Barcelona and v.v. (Table **653**).
b – From / to Irún (Table **653**).
w – To Vitoria / Gasteiz on ⑤ (Table 6
y – From Vitoria / Gasteiz (Table 653

651 MADRID - SORIA and ZARAGOZA

km	For high-speed trains see Tables **650** and **650a**	2 Ⓐ		2 Ⓒ		2 Ⓐ H	2 Ⓐ	2 Ⓒ	2 Ⓒ		2 Ⓐ		2 ⑤	2 ⑤	2 w		2	2 Ⓐ A	2 ⑦	2 Ⓐ	2 Ⓐ B	
0	**Madrid** Chamartín ... d.	...	...	...	...	0715	0745	0814	0915	...	...	...	1432	1540	1545	...	1900	1935	2002	2007	...	...
55	Guadalajara ... d.	...	...	...	...	0756	0823	0854	0959	...	...	...	1509	1624	1638	...	1940	2025	2038	2117	2125	...
138	Sigüenza ... d.	...	...	...	...	0858	0915	0944	1102	...	...	...	1612	1713	1740	...	2032	2128	2142	...	2228	...
248	**Soria** ... a.	...	...	...	...	|	1042	1110	|	...	...	...	...	1840	|	...	2158	...	...	...	...	...
178	Arcos de Jalón ... d.	0650	...	0850	...	0936	...	...	1140	...	...	...	...	...	1814	...	...	...	...	...	...	...
241	Calatayud ... d.	0736	...	0936	...	1016	...	...	1221	...	1321	...	...	...	1859	...	...	...	...	...	...	...
339	**Zaragoza** Delicias ♣ ... a.	0855	...	1101	...	1114	...	...	1325	...	1438	...	...	...	2011	...	...	...	...	...	...	...

For high-speed trains see Tables **650** and **650a**	2 Ⓐ		2 Ⓐ		2 Ⓒ		2 f		2 H	2 ⑤	2 Ⓑ	2 ⑦		2		2 ⑦		2				
Zaragoza Delicias ♥ ... d.	...	...	...	...	...	...	0857	...	1359	...	1620	...	...	...	...	...	...	2036	...	...	...	...
Calatayud ... d.	...	...	...	...	...	...	1018	...	1458	...	1742	...	...	...	...	...	...	2157	...	...	...	...
Arcos de Jalón ... d.	...	...	...	...	...	...	1104	...	1535	...	...	...	...	...	...	...	...	2244	...	...	...	...
Soria ... d.	...	...	0750	...	0845	...	|	...	|	...	...	1657	...	1906	...	...	...	...	...	...	...	...
Sigüenza ... d.	0650	...	0914	...	1009	...	1140	...	1612	1700	...	1817	...	2033	...	2150	...	...	...	...	...	...
Guadalajara ... d.	0800	...	1005	...	1056	...	1244	...	1716	1758	...	1907	...	2126	...	2248	...	...	...	...	...	...
Madrid Chamartín ... a.	0913	...	1045	...	1136	...	1329	...	1807	1837	...	1948	...	2206	...	2327	...	...	...	...	...	...

A – Jan. 11 - June 17.
B – June 20 - Sept. 9.
H – To / from Barcelona (Table **652**).
f – From Lleida on Ⓐ (Table **652**).
w – To Lleida (Table **652**).
♥ – All services call 7 – 8 minutes earlier at Zaragoza **Goya** and 5 minutes earlier at Zaragoza **Port**
♣ – All services call 4 – 5 minutes later at Zaragoza **Portillo** and 6 – 8 minutes later at Zaragoza **Go**

652 ZARAGOZA - BARCELONA

km	For high-speed trains see Tables **650** and **650a**	2 ⚒	2	2	2	*Hotel* **921**¶ G🍸	2	2 Ⓐ	2	2	2	2 ⑥	2 ⑦	2	2 Ⓐ	2 Ⓒ	2	2	2 Ⓐ	2 ⚒	2 ⑦	2	2
	Madrid Chamartín **651** ... d.	...	...	...	...	...	...	...	...	...	...	...	...	...	0715	...	...	...	...	...	...	...	...
0	**Zaragoza** Delicias ♣ ... d.	...	...	...	...	0632	...	0610	...	...	...	0857	1027	...	1116	1116	...	...	1515	...	...	1630	2005
114	Caspe ... d.	...	...	...	...	|	0715	|	...	...	...	|	|	...	1300	1300	...	...	|	...	...	1803	2141
★	Lleida ... d.	...	...	...	0715	0730	|	0820	...	...	...	1121	1237	1310	|	|	1545	...	1727	1748	1748	|	—
239	Reus ... d.	0537	0643	0732	|	|	0917	...	1110	1210	1307	...	...	1437	1455	1455	1714	1839	...	|	|	2007	2118
257	Tarragona ... **672** d.	0552	0700	0747	|	0804t	0935	...	1125	1225	1324	...	...	1455	1517	1517	1729	1859	...	|	|	2029	2134
282	Sant Vicenç de Calders ... **672** d.	0615	0719	0810	0845	|	0954	...	1145	1245	1345	...	...	1517	1542	1542	1747	1920	...	1913	1923	2047	2200
342	**Barcelona** Sants ... **672** a.	0717	0805	0905	0935	0849	1036	...	1235	1340	1435	...	...	1606	1636	1636	1835	2008	...	2005	2017	2135	2302
345	Barcelona Pass. de Gràcia ... a.	0723	0811	0914	0944	...	1045	...	1244	1345	1444	...	...	1614	1645	1645	1844	2014	...	2012	2023	2142	2307
350	**Barcelona** França ... a.	0733	0819	0922	0952	...	1055	...	1252	1353	1453	...	...	1623	1656	1656	1852	2023	...	2020	2032	2151	2316

For high-speed trains see Tables **650** and **650a**	2 Ⓐ	2 Ⓐ	2	2 Ⓒ	2 ⑥	2	2	2	2	2	2	2	2	2 ⑦	2 Ⓐ	2	2	2	2	2	2 Ⓑ	2	*Hotel* **922**¶ G🍸
Barcelona França ... d.	...	...	0617	...	...	0650	0717	0847	0946	1147	...	1317	1347	...	...	1547	1648	1717	1847	1850	1947	2018	...
Barcelona Pass. de Gràcia ... d.	...	...	0626	...	...	0659	0726	0856	0956	1156	...	1326	1355	...	...	1556	1656	1726	1855	1859	1958	2026	...
Barcelona Sants ... **672** d.	...	...	0633	...	...	0706	0733	0903	1003	1203	...	1333	1403	...	...	1603	1703	1733	1903	1906	2003	2033	2020
Sant Vicenç de Calders .. **672** d.	...	...	0718	...	...	0807	0818	0948	1047	1248	...	1417	1446	...	...	1648	1746	1818	1947	2004	2048	2118	|
Tarragona ... **672** d.	...	...	0739	...	...	|	0839	1009	1108	1308	...	1437	1507	...	...	1708	1808	1838	|	2036	2109	2138	2103t
Reus ... d.	...	...	0754	...	...	|	0855	1027	1123	1326	...	1454	1529	...	...	1724	1827	1853	|	2050	2125	2153	|
Lleida ... d.	...	0625	...	...	1025	0955	...	|	...	1455	1515	...	1646	1803	1836	|	1953	|	2111	...	...	...	2142
Caspe ... d.	0652	|	...	0951	|	...	...	1224	...	...	|	...	...	|	|	1933	...	2053	...	...	...	...	|
Zaragoza Delicias ♥ ... a.	0822	0857	...	1124	1253	...	...	1358	...	...	1729	...	...	2031	2044	2105	...	...	...	...	...	...	2238
Madrid Chamartín **651** ... a.	...	1329	...	...	...	...	...	1807	...	...	...	...	...	...	...	...	...	...	...	...	...	...	...

G – Ⓑ: GALICIA *Trenhotel* – 🛏, (1) (reclining) Barcelona - A Coruña and Vigo and v.v.
t – **Camp** de Tarragona.
¶ – Via high speed line.
★ – Leida - Reus: *90 km.* Zaragoza - Lleida: *189 km.* Lleida - Sant Vicenç: *106 km.*
♥ – All trains (except *Hotel* **922**) call 5 – 8 minutes earlier at Zaragoza **Goya** and 3 – 5 minutes e at Zaragoza **Portillo**.
♣ – All trains (except *Hotel* **921**) call 4 – 5 minutes later at Zaragoza **Portillo** and 6 – 8 minutes at Zaragoza **Goya**.

ZARAGOZA - IRÚN and BILBAO 653

			Alvia	Alvia	Alvia	Alvia	Alvia	Alvia	IC		Alvia			IC	Alvia		Alvia		Alvia	Alvia				IC	Alvia	Alvia		Hotel
	18071	16071	601	603	534	434	622	605	10560	18021	664	18073	16015	632	609	18023	530	16017	430	613	18075	16027	18077	562	701	801	18079	922
	2	2				B	626			2	A	2	2	V		2		2			2	2	2	S			2	G 🍷
	①–⑥	①–⑤	①–⑤	⑥			J	Ⓑ	⑥							⑤		①–⑥		④⑤⑦		⑦		Ⓑ	Ⓑ	Ⓑ	⑤⑥⑦	¶
Barcelona Sants **652** d.	...	...	...	...	0730	0730	0930	...	1005	...	1210	...	...	1410	...	...	1530	...	1530	...	...	...	...	1840	...	...	...	2020
Madrid PA ‡ **650a** d.	...	...	0735	0940	|	|	|	1135	|	...	|	...	...	|	1505	...	|	...	|	1735	...	...	...	|	1835	1935	...	|
Zaragoza Delicias d.	0625	...	|	|	0934	0934	1128	|	1204	1259	1414	1435	...	1608	|	1652	1729	...	1729	|	1742	...	1921	2102	|	|	2109	2250
Castejón de Ebro ★ d.	0729	0730	0945	1159	1028	1031	1224	|	1259	1407	|	1540	...	1702	|	1748	1833	...	1845	|	1849	1852	2031	|	|	|	2215	0014
Pamplona / Iruña d.	0837	|	1038	1252	1119	|	1317	1440	1356	1517	1608	|	1642	|	1826	1859	1924	1930	|	2044	|	2005	2138	2244**a**	|	2240	|	|
Altsasu **689** d.	0918**t**	|	...	...	1150	|	|	...	|	...	|	|	1718**t**	|	...	...	1953	2004**t**	|	|	|	2046**t**	...	|	|	...	|	|
Vitoria / Gasteiz **689** d.	0950	|	...	...	|	|	1410	...	|	...	1702	|	1753	|	...	...	|	2037	|	|	|	2118	...	2337**r**	|	...	|	|
San Seb / Don ✣ d.	|	|	...	...	1305	|	|	...	1550	...	|	|	|	|	...	...	2112	...	|	2227**x**	|	|	...	...	|	...	|	|
Irún **689** a.	|	|	...	...	1328	|	|	...	1611	...	|	|	|	|	...	...	2135	...	|	2245**x**	|	|	...	...	|	...	|	|
Logroño 650a d.	|	0829	...	...	...	1125	|	...	...	...	|	1635	|	1751	...	...	...	...	1938	...	1945	|	...	...	2158	...	2312	0102
Miranda de Ebro **689** d.	1016	...	...	...	...	1225	1431	...	...	...	1722	...	1820	1851	...	...	...	...	2032	...	...	2143	...	...	...	...	...	...
Bilbao Abando **689** a.	...	...	...	...	...	1404	...	...	...	...	...	...	...	...	...	...	...	...	2209	...	...	...	...	...	...	...	...	...

		IC		Alvia	Alvia	Alvia		IC	Alvia	Alvia	Alvia		Alvia	IC		Alvia	Alvia	IC			Alvia	Alvia	Alvia	Alvia	Alvia				Hotel
	18068	635	18072	802	800	702	18074	10655	600	533	433	16019	602	631	18076	661	606	10657	18070	18029	621	537	437	612	610	16111	16011	18078	921
	2		2		11616		2					2		V	2	A			2	2	625	M	P			2	2	2	G 🍷
	①–⑤	①–⑤	①–⑤	①–⑤	①	①–⑥		⑥	⑥				Ⓑ			①–⑥		⑦	⑤⑥⑦	b	J			⑤⑦	Ⓑ	①–⑥	⑦	❦	¶
ao Abando **689** d.	...	...	...	...	...	...	...	...	...	...	0630	...	...	...	...	...	...	...	...	...	...	...	1520	...	...	...	...	...	...
nda de Ebro **689** d.	...	...	...	...	...	...	...	...	...	...	0805	0940	...	0921	...	1325	...	...	...	1501	1605	...	1652	...	...	...	...	...	...
roño 650a d.	...	...	0615	...	...	0735	...	...	...	...	0904	|	...	1021	1415	|	...	...	1642	|	|	...	1753	...	...	...	...	2018	0403
689 d.	...	...	|	...	0605	|	...	...	...	0710	|	|	...	|	|	|	...	1420	|	|	|	1552	|	1600**r**	...	...	...	|	|
Seb / Don ✣ d.	...	...	|	...	0624	|	...	...	...	0728	|	|	...	|	|	|	...	1437	|	|	|	1610	|	1619**r**	...	...	...	|	|
oria / Gasteiz **689** d.	...	...	|	...	|	|	...	0718	...	|	|	1005	...	|	|	1350	...	|	|	1530	1627	|	|	|	...	1900	1921	|	|
asu **689** d.	...	...	|	...	|	|	...	|	...	0842	|	1038**t**	...	|	|	|	...	|	|	1601**t**	|	1722	|	|	...	1931**t**	1952**t**	|	|
nplona / Iruña d.	...	0625	|	0635	0810	|	0743**z**	0812	0900	0913	|	1110	1130	|	|	1447	1535	1625	|	1638	1724	1754	|	1807	1935	2015	2026	|	|
ejón de Ebro d.	0605	0717	0720**e**	0725	|	|	0850	|	0952	1010	1010	...	|	1114	1510	|	|	|	1741	1744	1818	1854	1854	|	|	2121	2123	2121	0456
goza Delicias a.	0715	0807	0836	|	|	|	0956	1000	|	1110	1110	...	|	1212	1611	1635	|	1808	...	1851	1916	1950	1950	|	|	2229	2217	2229	0629
adrid PA ‡ **650a** a.	...	|	...	0945	1120	1050	...	|	1218	|	|	...	1440	|	...	|	1838	|	...	...	|	|	|	2125	2253	...	...	...	|
rcelona Sants **652** a.	...	1010	...	...	...	...	...	1205	...	1320	1320	...	...	1420	...	1850	...	2000	...	...	2125	2209	2209	...	...	...	...	...	0849

[12] Barcelona - Gijón and v.v. (Table **685**).
①–⑥ (daily June 21 - Sept. 13).
Ⓑ: GALICIA *Trenhotel* – 🛏, [1] (reclining) Barcelona - A Coruña and Vigo and v.v.
[12] 🍷 Barcelona - Vigo / A Coruña and v.v. (Table **680**).
Ⓑ (daily June 20 - Sept. 12).
On ⑦ departs Barcelona 1930, Zaragoza 2134, arrives Pamplona 2328.
[12] Barcelona - Valladolid and v.v. (Tables **650a, 689**). On ⑦ *IC* **631** runs as *IC* **633**, departs Miranda de Ebro 1337, Logroño 1434, Castejón de Ebro 1527, arrives Zaragoza 1626, Barcelona 1835.

a – Arrival time.
b – From Burgos Rosa de Lima on ①–⑥ (Table **689**).
e – Arrive 0709.
r – ⑤ only.
t – Altsasu Pueblo (*230 km*).
x – ④⑦.
z – ①–⑤.

❦ – On ⑦ runs 13 - 18 minutes earlier.
¶ – Via high speed line.
★ – Calatayud - Castejón: *140 km*.
‡ – Full name is Madrid Puerta de Atocha.
✣ – Full name is San Sebastián / Donostia.

LLEIDA - LA POBLA DE SEGUR 655

C 2nd class

Timings subject to confirmation until new timetable, below, commences

	①–⑤		①–⑥	⑦	A	⑦		①–⑥		
Lleida d.	0715	...	0910	0910	1030	1040	...	1730	...	2030
Balaguer d.	0744	...	0939	0939	1100	1109	...	1759	...	2059
Tremp d.	...	...	1044	...	|	1214	...	...	...	...
La Pobla de Segur a.	...	...	1100	...	1230	1230	...	...	...	...

	①–⑤		⑦		①–⑥		①–⑥	⑦	A	
La Pobla de Segur d.	...	...	...	...	1256	...	...	1730	1730	...
Tremp d.	...	...	...	...	1311	...	...	1745	|	...
Balaguer d.	0800	...	1000	...	1416	...	1810	1850	1900	2105
Lleida a.	0830	...	1030	...	1446	...	1839	1920	1930	2134

New timetable from a date to be announced

	Ⓐ			A	†	Ⓐ		⑥	†	①–④	⑤	
Lleida d.	0525	0620	0750	1030	1045	1045	1305	1505	1715	1730	1930	...
Balaguer d.	0550	0644	0819	1100	1114	1114	1329	1529	1739	1754	1954	...
Tremp d.	0648	...	0917	|	1212	1212	...	1627	1837	1852	2052	...
La Pobla de Segur a.	0701	...	0930	1230	1225	1225	...	1640	1850	1905	2105	...

	Ⓐ	Ⓑ	⑥	Ⓑ	Ⓑ	⑥	A	Ⓒ	①–④	⑥	Ⓑ	⑤
La Pobla de Segur d.	0710	1005	1300	...	1530	...	1730	1900	1930	...	...	2120
Tremp d.	0722	1017	1312	...	1542	...	|	1912	1942	...	...	2132
Balaguer d.	0820	1115	1410	1410	1640	1640	1900	2010	2040	2145	2200	2230
Lleida a.	0845	1140	1435	1435	1705	1705	1930	2035	2105	2210	2225	2255

Tren dels Llacs: ⑥ Apr. 2 - July 9, Aug. 20 - Oct. 29.

BARCELONA - PUIGCERDÀ - LATOUR DE CAROL 656

d class

	Ⓐ ✣	Ⓐ	Ⓐ	Ⓐ	Ⓒ	Ⓐ	Ⓒ	Ⓐ	Ⓒ	Ⓐ	Ⓐ	Ⓒ	Ⓐ	Ⓒ	Ⓐ	Ⓐ	Ⓒ	Ⓐ	Ⓒ	Ⓐ	Ⓒ	Ⓐ	Ⓒ	Ⓐ	Ⓒ	Ⓐ
Barcelona Sants d.	...	0511	0602	0622	0701	0701	0749	0752	0936	0951	1022	1109	1122	1207	1233	1303	1317	1402	1408	1501	1510	1549	1623	1702	1717	1732
La Sagrera-Meridiana d.	...	0524	0615	0636	0714	0714	0802	0805	0949	1004	1035	1122	1135	1220	1246	1316	1330	1415	1421	1514	1523	1602	1637	1715	1730	1745
Sant Andreu Arenal d.	...	0526	0617	0639	0717	0716	0804	0807	0951	1006	1037	1124	1137	1222	1248	1318	1332	1417	1423	1516	1525	1604	1639	1717	1732	1747
Granollers - Canovelles d.	...	0556	0645	0706	0743	0744	0833	0837	1017	1033	1108	1153	1209	1248	1315	1347	1406	1444	1450	1542	1550	1633	1708	1741	1759	1817
Vic d.	...	0638	0722	0743	0816	0824	0914	0924	1051	1115	1147	1232	1252	1326	1353	1426	1445	1519	1521	1617	1623	1714	1755	1813	1832	1900
Torelló d.	...	...	0736	0805	0831	...	0927	0938	1105	1129	1202	1246	1305	1340	1408	1441	1501	1535	1536	1632	1636	1730	1809	1827	1847	1916
Ripoll d.	...	...	0801	0829	0856	...	0953	1006	1130	1156	1228	1313	1330	1404	1436	1513	1531	1559	1600	1658	1700	1757	1835	1856	1914	1942
Ribes de Freser **658** a.	...	...	...	0847	0914	...	1013	1023	1147	1214	...	...	...	1421	1458	...	1548	...	...	1715	1718	...	...	1916	1931	...
La Molina a.	...	...	...	0912	0947	...	...	...	1212	1240	...	...	...	1448	1523	...	...	...	...	1740	1751	...	...	1949	1958	...
Puigcerdà a.	0801	...	...	0934	1007	...	...	...	1232	1259	...	...	...	1508	1542	...	...	...	...	1800	1811	...	...	2007	2017	...
Latour de Carol 🏛 **312** a.	0807	...	...	0940	1013	...	...	...	1238	1305	...	...	...	1514	1548	...	...	...	...	1806	1817	...	...	...	...	...

	Ⓐ	Ⓐ	Ⓒ	Ⓐ	Ⓒ	Ⓐ	Ⓐ	Ⓐ	Ⓒ	Ⓐ	
celona Sants d.	1827	1857	1857	2012	2015	2054	2102	2132	2207	2230	...
Sagrera-Meridiana d.	1840	1910	1910	2025	2028	2107	2115	2145	2220	2243	...
nt Andreu Arenal d.	1842	1912	1912	2027	2030	2109	2117	2147	2222	2245	...
ollers - Canovelles d.	|	1939	1941	2054	2055	2139	2145	2217	2251	2312	...
d.	1935	2017	2019	2128	2131	2218	2223	2256	2328	2349	...
lló d.	|	2036	2033	2143	2145	...	...	...	...	...	...
ll d.	2010	2102	2059	2208	2210	...	...	...	...	...	...
s de Freser **658** a.	|	2119	2116	...	...	...	...	...	...	...	...
olina a.	|	2143	2141	...	...	...	...	...	...	...	...
cerdà a.	2106	2201	2200	...	...	...	...	...	...	...	...
ur de Carol 🏛 **312** a.	...	...	...	...	...	...	...	...	...	...	...

			Ⓐ	Ⓒ	Ⓐ	Ⓐ	Ⓒ	Ⓐ	Ⓐ	Ⓒ	Ⓐ
Latour de Carol 🏛 **312** d.	...	...	...	...	...	...	...	...	...	...	...
Puigcerdà d.	...	...	...	...	...	0617	0652	0729	...	...	...
La Molina d.	...	...	...	...	...	|	0710	0747	...	...	...
Ribes de Freser **658** d.	...	...	...	...	...	|	0735	0812	...	...	...
Ripoll d.	...	...	0625	...	...	0713	0753	0830	...	...	0913
Torelló d.	...	...	0651	...	...	|	0817	0854	...	...	0940
Vic d.	0548	0641	0705	0723	0726	0750	0831	0908	0925	0917	0955
Granollers - Canovelles d.	0625	0720	0744	0801	0803	|	0902	0942	1002	0956	1034
Sant Andreu Arenal a.	0651	0750	0809	0830	0832	0843	0930	1010	1029	1024	1059
La Sagrera-Meridiana a.	0654	0753	0812	0833	0835	0847	0933	1013	1032	1027	1102
Barcelona Sants a.	0707	0806	0825	0846	0850	0902	0946	1026	1045	1040	1115

	Ⓒ	Ⓒ	Ⓐ	Ⓐ	Ⓒ	Ⓐ	Ⓒ	Ⓐ	Ⓒ	Ⓒ	Ⓐ	Ⓐ	Ⓒ	Ⓐ	Ⓐ	Ⓒ	Ⓒ	Ⓐ	Ⓒ	Ⓐ	Ⓐ	Ⓒ		Ⓒ	Ⓐ	Ⓐ	Ⓒ
ur de Carol 🏛 **312** d.	...	0848	0850	...	...	...	...	1048	1113	...	...	1334	1347	...	...	...	...	...	...	...	1713	1652	...	1859	1852	...	...
cerdà d.	...	0855	0856	...	...	...	...	1055	1120	...	...	1341	1354	...	...	...	...	...	...	...	1720	1659	...	1906	1859	...	...
olina d.	...	0913	0915	...	...	...	...	1113	1138	...	...	1359	1412	...	...	...	...	...	...	...	1739	1717	...	1924	1917	...	...
s de Freser **658** d.	...	0938	0944	...	...	1103	1111	1137	1205	...	...	1423	1439	...	...	...	1640	...	...	...	1805	1744	...	1951	1943	...	...
ll d.	0919	0956	1004	1036	...	1121	1129	1155	1223	1407	1342	1441	1457	...	1604	...	1658	1705	...	...	1823	1802	1906	2009	2004	2104	...
lló d.	0946	1020	1028	1102	...	1149	1156	1222	1247	1431	1410	1507	1522	...	1631	...	1724	1732	...	...	1848	1828	1933	2035	2035	2130	...
d.	1001	1034	1041	1117	1121	1203	1211	1236	1301	1446	1425	1521	1536	1601	1646	1650	1739	1746	1806	1823	1902	1846	1949	2051	2049	2145	2140
ollers - Canovelles d.	1044	1110	1115	1155	1201	1243	1256	1312	1332	1529	1505	1558	1608	1640	1727	1728	1817	1826	1850	1904	1938	1918	2033	2123	2124	2227	2219
nt Andreu Arenal a.	1112	1135	1141	1221	1230	1310	1328	1339	1357	1557	1536	1627	1638	1708	1754	1757	1851	1851	1918	1937	2009	1942	2058	2150	2151	2253	2247
Sagrera-Meridiana a.	1115	1138	1144	1223	1233	1312	1331	1342	1400	1600	1538	1630	1638	1711	1756	1800	1854	1853	1921	1940	2012	1945	2101	2153	2154	2256	2250
celona Sants a.	1128	1150	1157	1236	1246	1325	1344	1355	1412	1613	1551	1644	1650	1724	1809	1813	1907	1906	1934	1954	2025	1958	2114	2206	2207	2309	2303

Timing subject to confirmation. Please check locally.

657 BARCELONA - GIRONA - FIGUERES - PORTBOU / PERPIGNAN

Reservations are not compulsory on *Media Distancia* (*MD*) services on the Barcelona - Girona - Portbou - Cebère route. All stopping services convey 2nd class only

km	km		*MD* 15900 Ⓐ	*TGV* 9700 34700* G P	Ⓐ	⑥	Ⓐ	*AVE* 9734 34735* L	*MD* 15056 Ⓒ	*MD* 15076 Ⓐ	Ⓒ	Ⓐ	*TGV* 9702 P	*AVE* 3071 3463*	*MD* 15908 Ⓒ	*MD* 15094 Ⓐ	Ⓒ	*AVE* 3073 34073* ⑥⑦	Ⓐ	*MD* 15078 Ⓐ	*MD* 15078 Ⓒ	*AVE* 3093 34093*	*MD* 15004 Ⓐ	Ⓒ	
		Madrid ⊠ **630** d.	...	...	...	...	...	...	...	...	...	...	...	0700**x**	...	...	...	0730	...	...	...	0930	...	...	
0	*0*	**Barcelona** Sants **666** d.	0556	0610	0616	0646	0716	0720	0746	0822	0846	0916	0925	0945	0949	1016	1046	1050	1116	1146	1146	1244	1246	1246	1
3		Barcelona P de G ❖ d.	0601	|	0620	0650	0720	|	0751	0827	0850	0920	|	|	0954	1021	1050	|	1120	1151	1151	|	1251	1250	1
31		Granollers Centre d.	|	|	0646	0716	0752	|	|	|	0917	0946	|	|	|	|	1116	|	1146	|	|	|	|	1316	1
72		Maçanet - Massanes **666** d.	0651	|	0722	0752	0832	|	0843	0919	0957	1022	|	|	1049	1113	1152	|	1222	1243	1243	|	1343	1353	1
86		Caldes de Malavella d.	0702	|	0733	0803	0843	|	0854	0930	1007	1033	|	|	1100	1124	1203	|	1233	1254	1253	|	1353	1403	1
102	*95*	**Girona** d.	0713	0651	0748	0818	0858	0801	0905	0941	1023	1049	1006	1026	1111	1135	1218	1130	1248	1305	1305	1324	1404	1419	1
118		Flaçà d.	0726	|	0802	0832	0912	|	0915	0954	1038	1104	|	|	1124	1148	1232	|	1302	1318	1318	|	1417	1434	1
143		Figueres § d.	0744	|	0827	0857	0937	|	0937	1013	1102	1129	|	|	1143	1207	1257	|	1327	1336	1337	|	1437	1458	1
	129	Figueres Vilafant § d.	...	0708	|	|	|	0818	|	|	|	|	1023	1040	|	|	|	1145	|	...	|	1339	...	|	
162		Llançà d.	...	|	0842	0912	0952	|	0950	1026	1116	1143	|	...	1156	1220	1312	...	1342	...	1350	...	...	1512	1
169		**Portbou** 🏛 **355** a.	...	|	0852	0922	1002	|	0957	1033	1126	1153	|	...	1203	1227	1323	...	1352	...	1357	...	...	1521	1
171		**Cerbère** 🏛 **355** a.	...	|	0857	0927	1007	|	...	...	1130	1157	|	...	...	...	1327	...	1357	...	...	...	...	1526	1
	177	**Perpignan** **355** a.	...	0731	...	...	...	0843	...	...	...	...	1046	...	...	...	...	...	...	...	...	...	...	...	

	TGV 9704 P	*MD* 15910 ⑤⑦	*MD* 15096 ①–⑥	*AVE* 3113 34113* ①–⑤		*AVE* 3123 34123* Ⓑ	*MD* 15098	*TGV* 9706 C P		*AVE* 9724 19725* M	*TGV* 3143 34143 Ⓑ	*MD* 15080 Ⓐ	*MD* 15082 Ⓐ	*MD* 15922 Ⓒ	*AVE* 9726 34727* E T	*MD* 15084 Ⓐ	*AVE* 3153 34153*		*AVE* 3163 31163* ①–⑤	*AVE* 31399* ⑦	*MD* 15086 Ⓐ	*MD* 15088 Ⓒ	*MD* 15006 Ⓑ	*AVE* 3191 31191* ❦	*M* 15
Madrid ⊠ **630** d.	...	...	...	1130	...	1230	...	...	...	1325	1430	...	...	...	...	...	1530	...	1630	...	...	...	...	1900	
Barcelona Sants **666** d.	1317	1346	1416	1450	1516	1540	1616	1620	1716	1645	1737	1746	1816	1819	1830	1846	1850	1916	1925**z**	1945	1946	2016	2046	2140	2
Barcelona P de G ❖ d.	|	1351	1421	|	1520	|	1621	|	1720	|	|	1751	1821	1824	|	1851	|	1920	|	|	1951	2021	2051	|	2
Granollers Centre d.	|	|	|	|	1546	|	|	|	1746	|	|	|	|	|	|	|	|	1947	|	|	|	|	|	|	
Maçanet - Massanes **666** d.	|	1443	1513	|	1622	|	1713	|	1822	|	|	1843	1913	1920	|	1945	|	2026	|	|	2043	2113	2157	|	2
Caldes de Malavella d.	|	1454	1524	|	1633	|	1724	|	1833	|	|	1854	1924	1931	|	1956	|	2037	|	|	2054	2124	2206	|	2
Girona d.	1358	1505	1535	1531	1648	1620	1735	1701	1848	1726	1817	1905	1935	1942	1911	2007	1930	2054	2005**z**	2025	2105	2135	2217	2220	2
Flaçà d.	|	1518**t**	1548	|	1702	|	1748	|	1902	|	|	1918	1948	1955	|	2020	|	2108	|	|	2118	2148	2229	|	2
Figueres § d.	|	1537**t**	1607	|	1727	|	1806	|	1927	|	|	1937	2006	2013	|	2038	|	2130	|	|	2138	2206	2246	|	2
Figueres Vilafant § d.	1415	|	|	1545	|	1635	...	1718	|	1743	1832	|	...	...	1928	...	1945	|	2020**z**	2040	...	...	...	2235	
Llançà d.	|	1550**t**	1620**f**	...	1742	...	...	|	1942	|	...	1950	...	...	|	...	...	2145	...	...	...	...	...	...	
Portbou 🏛 **355** a.	|	1557**t**	1627**f**	...	1751	...	...	|	1952	|	...	1957	...	...	|	...	...	2155	...	...	...	...	...	...	
Cerbère 🏛 **355** a.	|	...	...	...	1757	...	...	|	1957	|	...	...	...	...	|	...	...	...	...	...	...	...	...	...	
Perpignan **355** a.	1440	...	...	...	...	....	...	1742	...	1806	...	...	...	...	1951	...	...	...	...	...	...	...	...	...	

	MD 15010 Ⓐ	*MD* 15046 ①–⑥	*AVE* 3662 34662* ①–⑤	*AVE* 3082 31082* ①–⑤	*MD* 15060 Ⓐ	*MD* 15060 Ⓒ	*MD* 15062 Ⓐ	①–⑥	*AVE* 3092 31092* ①–⑥	*MD* 15064 ⑦	*MD* 15066 ①–⑥	*AVE* 3102 31102*		*MD* 15068	*AVE* 9729 34728* B T		*AVE* 9731 19730* M	*MD* 15070	*TGV* 9711 C P		*MD* 15090	*MD* 15002	*AVE* 3162 31162* ①–⑥		*T* 97 34
Perpignan **355** d.	...	...	...	...	...	...	...	...	...	...	...	...	...	...	1000	...	1117	...	1212	...	...	...	...	...	1
Portbou 🏛 **355** d.	...	...	...	...	0623	...	...	0703	...	...	...	...	0833	...	|	1033	|	1127	|	1235	1327	...	...	1433	
Llançà d.	...	...	...	...	0630	...	...	0712	...	...	...	...	0842	...	|	1042	|	1135	|	1244	1335	...	...	1442	
Figueres Vilafant § d.	...	...	0630	0655	|	...	...	|	0755	...	...	0855	|	...	1026	|	1143	|	1239	|	|	...	1455	|	1
Figueres § d.	0544	0555	|	|	0643	0643	0713	0728	|	0749	0819	|	0858	0949	|	1058	|	1149	|	1300	1349	1419	|	1458	
Flaçà d.	0600	0615	|	|	0659	0659	0729	0750	|	0805	0835	|	0920	1005	|	1120	|	1205	|	1323	1405	1435	|	1520	
Girona d.	0614	0629	0646	0711	0713	0713	0743	0806	0811	0819	0849	0911	0936	1019	1043	1136	1200	1219	1256	1339	1419	1449	1511	1536	1
Caldes de Malavella d.	0624	0640	|	|	0724	0724	0754	0820	|	0829	0859	|	0950	1029	|	1150	|	1229	|	1353	1429	1459	|	1550	
Maçanet - Massanes **666** d.	0635	0651	|	|	0735	0735	0805	0831	|	0839	0909	|	1001	1039	|	1201	|	1239	|	1404	1439	1509	|	1601	
Granollers Centre d.	|	|	|	|	|	|	|	0905	|	|	|	|	1035	|	|	1235	|	|	|	1437	|	|	|	1635	
Barcelona P de G ❖ a.	0735	0749	|	|	0835	0835	0905	0934	|	0935	1005	|	1105	1135	|	1305	|	1335	|	1505	1535	1605	|	1705	
Barcelona Sants **666** a.	0739	0753	0725	0750	0839	0839	0909	0939	0850	0939	1009	0950	1109	1139	1121	1309	1238	1339	1334	1509	1539	1609	1550	1709	16
Madrid ⊠ **630** a.	...	...	1010	1110	...	...	...	...	1145	...	...	1310	...	...	...	...	1545	...	...	...	...	...	1910	...	

	AVE 3172 ⑦	*MD* 15072	Ⓑ	*AVE* 3182 34182*	*AVE* 3180 ⑦	⑥	*MD* 15018 Ⓐ	*MD* 15018 ⑦	*AVE* 3192	*MD* 15092 Ⓐ	*MD* 15092 Ⓒ	Ⓐ	*MD* 15918 ⑦	*AVE* 9743 34742* L	*MD* 15074 Ⓑ	*MD* 15920 ⑥	⑦	*TGV* 9715 P	Ⓐ	Ⓒ	*MD* 15000 Ⓐ	*AVE* 3222 34222*	*TGV* 9717 A P	*MD* 15904 Ⓐ	
Perpignan **355** d.	...	...	...	...	...	...	...	...	...	...	...	...	...	1809	...	...	...	1913	...	...	...	...	2125	...	
Portbou 🏛 **355** d.	...	1527**j**	1603	...	...	1633	...	...	...	...	1727	1733	1757	|	...	...	1839	|	1903	1941	...	...	|	2028	2
Llançà d.	...	1535**j**	1612	...	...	1642	...	...	...	...	1735	1742	1805	|	...	...	1848	|	1912	1950	...	...	|	2036	20
Figueres Vilafant § d.	1545	|	|	1655	1720	|	...	...	1755	...	|	|	|	1836	...	...	|	1939	|	|	...	2045	2150	|	
Figueres § d.	|	1549	1628	|	|	1658	1719	...	|	...	1749	1758	1819	|	1849	1856	1904	|	1928	2006	2029	|	|	2050	2
Flaçà d.	|	1605	1650	|	|	1720	1735	...	|	...	1805	1820	1835	|	1905	1912	1926	|	1950	2030	2045	|	|	2106	2
Girona d.	1601	1619	1706	1711	1736	1736	1749	1749	1811	1819	1819	1836	1849	1853	1919	1926	1942	1956	2006	2046	2059	2101	2207	2119	2
Caldes de Malavella d.	|	1629	1720	|	|	1750	1759	1759	|	1829	1829	1850	1859	|	1929	1936	1956	|	2020	2100	2109	|	|	2129	2
Maçanet - Massanes **666** d.	|	1639	1731	|	|	1801	1809	1809	|	1839	1839	1901	1909	|	1939	1946	2007	|	2031	2111	2119	|	|	2139	2
Granollers Centre d.	|	|	1805	|	|	1835	|	|	|	|	|	1935	|	|	|	|	|	|	2105	2145	|	|	|	|	22
Barcelona P de G ❖ a.	|	1735	1835	|	|	1905	1905	1905	|	1935	1935	2004	2005	|	2035	2042	2105	|	2135	2215	2215	|	|	2235	22
Barcelona Sants **666** a.	1640	1739	1839	1750	1815	1909	1909	1909	1850	1939	1939	2009	2009	1931	2039	2046	2109	2034	2139	2219	2219	2140	2246	2239	22
Madrid ⊠ **630** a.	1945**z**	...	...	2110	2055	...	...	...	2200	...	...	...	...	...	...	...	...	...	...	...	...	...	...	...	

A – July 3 - Aug. 28.
B – June 2 - Sept. 26.
C – June 2 - Aug. 28.
E – June 2 - Sept. 25.
G – July 4 - Aug. 28.

L – To/from Lyon (Table **13**).
M – To/from Marseille (Table **13**).
P – To/from Paris (Table **13**).
T – To/from Toulouse (Table **13**).
f – ⑥ only.

j – Ⓒ only.
t – ⑦ only.
x – 0620 on ⑥⑦.
z – 3 - 5 minutes later June 12 - Sept. 11.

⊠ – Madrid Puerta de Atocha.
❦ – On ⑥, as train number **3183**, depart Madrid 18 Barcelona 2130, Girona 2210, arrive Figueres 2
* – Train number for *Turista class (classified Av)*.
❖ – Barcelona Passeig de Gràcia.

§ – **FIGUERES VILAFANT - FIGUERES BUS STATION (150m from Figueres).** *5 km.* By 🚌. Journey time: 15 - 20 minutes.

From **Figueres Vilafant**: 0835 Ⓐ, 1020, 1050, 1125, 1150, 1255, 1345, 1550 Ⓐ, 1645 Ⓑ, 1725, 1830, 1935, 1955, 2035 Ⓐ, 2240.

From **Figueres Bus Station**: 0600 Ⓐ, 0625 Ⓐ, 0725 ⚒, 0815, 0945, 1030, 1105, 1 1425 ⚒, 1515 ⑦, 1625, 1740, 1810, 1845, 1915, 2015, 2205.

658 VALL DE NÚRIA 2nd class

Ribes Enllaç - **Ribes** Vila - **Queralbs** - **Núria** rack railway

HIGH SEASON:

⑥⑦ (daily July 15 - Sept. 11), also Apr. 1, May 1, 20, June 24, Nov. 1:

From **Ribes** Enllaç: 0735 **v**, 0830 **n**, 0920 and hourly until 1730, also 1840 **c**.
From **Núria**: 0830, 0920 **n**, 1020 and hourly until 1820, also 1930 **c**.

LOW SEASON:

①–⑤ (except dates above). No service from Nov. 4 (resumes early December)

From **Ribes** Enllaç: 0730 **v**, 0910, 1110, 1250, 1440, 1630, 1820 ⑤
From **Núria**: 0820, 1000, 1200, 1345, 1530, 1720, 1910 ⑤.

Journey times **Ribes** – **Queralbs** (*6 km*) 24 minutes, **Ribes** – **Núria** (*12 km*) 44 minutes.

Ferrocarrils de la Generalitat de Catalunya (FGC) ✆ +34 972 73 20 20. www.valldenuria.cat

c – ⑤ (also July 27, Aug. 3 - 31, Sept. 1, 7, 11).
n – Ski season only, also ⑥⑦ in June and July (daily July 29 - Sept. 1).
v – From Ribes Vila.

659 AEROPORT BARCELONA 2nd cla

Local rail service *Cercanías* (suburban) line **R2 Nord**. *14km*

Aeroport - Barcelona Sants – Barcelona Passeig de Gràcia

Journey time: 19 minutes Sants, 26 minutes Passeig de Gràcia

From Aeroport del Prat:

0542, 0608, 0638, 0708, 0738 and every 30 minutes until 2208, 2238, 2308, 2

From Barcelona Sants:

0513, 0535, 0609, 0639, 0709 and every 30 minutes until 2139, 2209, 2239, 2

MADRID - CÓRDOBA - SEVILLA and MÁLAGA 660

Buses replace trains between Antequera - Santa Ana and Granada until June 2016

	Av 2260	AVE 2070	AVE 2270	AVE 2072	AVE 2072	AVE 2080	AVE 2082	Alvia 2084	Alta 9366	AVE 2090	AVE 3982	AVE 2092	Alvia 2294	Alvia 2094	AVE 2100	AVE 2102	AVE 2110	Alvia 2114	AVE 3940	AVE 3990	AVE 2112	AVE 2120	AVE 3944	AVE 3994	AVE 2130	AVE 2122	Alvia 2134	AVE 2140
	①-⑤	①-⑤	①-④	①-⑤	⑥⑦	①-⑥	①-④			10830	①-⑥		2494		①-⑥	①-⑤							①-⑥	①⑤⑦				
	D❦	D	D							Z	V		Q	R				A					J	J	C			
Barcelona Sants **650** . d.	...	...	...	...	...	...	...	...	...	...	...	...	...	...	...	...	...	...	0830	0830	...	...	0940	0940	...	...	...	...
Madrid Puerta de Atocha d.	0620	0700	0730	0720	0735	0800	0825	0830	0835	0900	...	0935	0945	0945	1000	1035	1100	1105	|	|	1135	1200	|	|	1300	1300	1330	1400
Ciudad Real .... d.	0720	|	|	|	|	|	|	0922	0937	0951	1021	1026	|	|	|	|	|	|	1213	1213	|	|	|	|	1351	1351	1421	|
Puertollano .... d.	0738	|	|	|	|	|	|	0937	0953	1007	1037	1044	|	|	|	|	|	|	1229	1229	|	|	|	|	1407	1407	1435	|
Córdoba .... d.	0830	0844	|	0902	0917	0944	|	1020	1039	1052	1121	1127	1132	1132	1144	|	1244	|	1319	1330	1324	1344	1406	1406	1452	1505	1517	1544
Sevilla .... a.	0916	0930	0950	|	|	1030	|	1106	|	1135	1205	|	|	1225	1230	|	1330	|	1402	|	|	1430	1455	|	1540	|	1605	1630
Cádiz **671** .... a.	...	...	...	|	|	...	|	1238	|	...	...	|	|	1400	...	|	...	1510	...	|	|	...	...	|	...	|	1740	...
Huelva **671** .... a.	...	...	...	|	|	...	|	...	|	...	...	|	1320	...	...	|	...	...	...	|	|	...	...	|	...	|	...	...
Puente Genil - Herrera ¶ a.	...	...	...	0923	0938	...	|	...	|	...	...	|	...	...	...	|	...	...	...	1351	|	...	...	1439	...	1526	...	...
Antequera - Santa Ana § a.	...	...	...	0937	0952	...	|	...	1117	...	...	1155	...	...	...	|	...	...	...	1402	1352	...	...	1452	...	1539	...	...
Algeciras **673** .... a.	...	...	...	|	|	...	|	...	1348	...	...	|	...	...	...	|	...	...	...	|	|	...	...	|	...	|	...	...
Granada **673** .... a.	...	...	...	*1130*¦	*1130*¦	...	|	...	...	...	...	*1330*¦	...	...	...	|	...	...	...	*1610*¦	|	...	...	*1630*¦	...	|	...	...
Málaga María Zambrano . a.	...	...	...	1035	1020	...	1045	...	...	...	...	1222	...	...	...	1255	...	...	...	1424	1417	...	...	1516	...	1605	...	...

	AVE 2142	AVE 2142	AVE 2150	Alta 9330	AVE 2152	AVE 2160	Alvia 2164	AVE 2360	AVE 2162	AVE 2170	AVE 2172	AVE 2180	Alvia 2384	AVE 2182	AVE 3942	AVE 3992	AVE 3974	Alvia 2184	AVE 2190	AVE 3946	AVE 2390	AVE 2192	AVE 2200	AVE 2202	Av 2410	AVE 2212			
	Ⓑ	⑥	Ⓑ		④⑤⑦			④⑤⑦					Ⓑ	Ⓑ			①⑤⑦		Ⓑ	⑤						⑤⑦			
			D	◐				M									E	B			H				❦				
rcelona Sants **650** .. d.	...	...	...	...	...	...	...	...	...	...	...	...	...	...	1550	1550	...	...	...	1632	...	...	...	...	...	...	...	...	...
d Puerta de Atocha d.	1435	1435	1500	1505	1535	1600	1615	1630	1635	1700	1735	1800	1805	1830	|	|	...	1835	1900	|	1930	1930	2035	2035	2125	2120	...	...	...
d Real........ d.	|	|	|	|	|	|	|	|	|	1751	1826	|	|	|	1936	1936	1942	|	1951	|	|	|	2126	2126	2219	|	...	...	...
ıllano .... d.	|	|	|	|	|	|	|	|	|	1807	1842	|	|	|	|	|	1957	|	2007	|	|	|	2142	2142	2234	|	...	...	...
oba .... d.	1619	1619	|	1708	|	1744	|	1814	1819	1852	1925	1944	1952	|	2030	2040	2045	2016	2052	2056	2114	2114	2227	2227	2324	|	...	...	...
villa .... a.	|	|	1720	|	|	1830	|	1900	|	1935	|	2030	|	|	2115	|	|	2106	2135	2143	2205	|	2315	|	0010	|	...	...	...
ádiz **671** .... a.	|	|	...	|	|	...	2010	...	|	...	|	...	|	|	...	|	|	2239	...	...	...	|	...	|	...	|	...	...	...
luelva **671** .... a.	|	|	...	|	|	...	...	...	|	...	|	...	2145	|	...	|	|	...	...	...	...	|	...	|	...	|	...	...	...
e Genil - Herrera ¶. a.	|	|	...	|	|	...	...	...	|	...	1946	...	...	|	...	2104	2110	...	...	...	...	|	...	2302	...	|	...	...	...
uera - Santa Ana §. a.	1654	1654	...	1753	|	...	...	...	|	...	1959	...	...	|	...	2117	2125	...	...	...	...	|	...	2315	...	|	...	...	...
eciras **673** .... a.	|	|	...	2030	|	...	...	...	|	...	|	...	...	|	...	|	|	...	...	...	...	|	...	|	...	|	...	...	...
anada **673** .... a.	*1820*¦	|	...	...	|	...	...	...	|	...	*2130*¦	...	...	|	...	*2300*¦	*2300*¦	...	...	...	...	|	...	|	...	|	...	...	...
ga María Zambrano . a.	1718	1718	...	...	1806	...	...	...	1907	...	2025	...	...	2053	...	2140	2151	...	...	...	...	2218	...	2340	...	2343	...	...	...

	Av 2261	AVE 2063	AVE 2061	AVE 2073	AVE 2471	AVE 2271	AVE 2071	AVE 2273	AVE 2083	AVE 2081	AVE 3993	AVE 3943	Alvia 2285	AVE 2093	AVE 2091	Alvia 2085	AVE 3971	AVE 2101	AVE 2113	Alta 9367	Alvia 2205	AVE 2111	AVE 2123	Alvia 2115	AVE 2121	AVE 2131	AVE 2143	AVE 2141	
	①-⑤	①-④	①-⑤	①-④	⑥⑦	①-④	①-⑥						①-⑤		①-⑥		⑤⑥				⑥			A	Ⓑ				
	D★	D	D	D	P	D		R					D				U											W	
ga María Zambrano . d.	...	0620	...	0710	...	...	...	0730	0800	...	0840	...	...	0900	...	...	0945	...	1055	...	...	...	1205	...	...	...	1405	...	...
anada **673** .... d.	...	|	...	|	...	...	...	|	*0655*¦	...	*0645*¦	...	...	|	...	...	*0830*¦	...	*1000*¦	...	...	...	|	...	...	...	|	...	...
eciras **673** .... d.	...	|	...	|	...	...	...	|	|	...	|	...	...	|	...	...	|	...	|	0843	...	...	|	...	...	...	|	...	...
quera - Santa Ana §. d.	...	0644	...	|	...	...	...	0754	0823	...	0902	...	...	0926	...	...	1008	...	1123	|	...	...	|	...	...	...	1429	...	...
te Genil - Herrera ¶. d.	...	0657	...	|	...	...	...	0807	|	...	0916	...	...	|	...	...	1021	...	|	|	...	...	|	...	...	...	1442	...	...
Huelva **671** .... d.	...	|	...	|	...	...	...	|	|	...	|	...	0800	|	...	...	|	...	|	|	1025	...	|	...	...	...	|	...	...
Cádiz **671** .... d.	...	|	...	|	...	...	...	|	|	...	|	...	|	|	...	0815	|	...	|	|	|	...	|	1050	...	...	|	...	...
villa .... d.	0610	|	0645	|	0700	0715	0745	|	|	0845	|	0850	|	|	0945	0950	|	1045	|	|	|	1145	|	|	1245	1345	|	1445	...
oba .... d.	0653	0722	0729	|	0750	0803	|	0832	0856	0929	0944	0944	0950	0959	1028	1042	1051	1129	1156	1202	1218	1229	1256	|	1328	|	1506	1529	...
ollano .... d.	0744	|	|	|	0841	0845	|	|	|	|	|	|	|	1041	1110	1125	1135	|	|	|	|	|	|	|	1413	|	1548	|	...
ad Real........ d.	0759	|	|	|	0858	0859	|	|	|	|	1041	1041	|	1057	1124	1140	1149	|	|	|	|	|	|	|	1427	|	1603	|	...
id Puerta de Atocha a.	0857	0905	0915	0938	1002	0955	1005	1015	1040	1115	|	|	1140	1150	1220	1236	...	1315	1340	1405	1410	1415	1440	1455	1520	1605	1655	1715	...
rcelona Sants **650** .. a.	...	...	...	...	...	...	...	...	...	...	1425	1425	...	...	...	...	...	...	...	...	...	...	...	...	...	...	...	...	...

	AVE 3991	AVE 3941	AVE 2153	Alvia 2135	AVE 2151	AVE 3995	AVE 3945	AVE 2163	AVE 2163	AVE 2361	AVE 2161	Alvia 2155	AVE 3973	AVE 2173	Alvia 2365	Alta 9331	AVE 2171	AVE 2183	AVE 3981	AVE 2181	IC 2375	Alvia 2175	AVE 2391	AVE 2193	AVE 2191	AVE 2203	Alvia 2195	Av 2411	AVE 2213
			④⑤⑦			①⑤⑦	⑦	Ⓑ	⑥	④⑤⑦			⑦		⑦			Ⓑ	Ⓑ	10381									⑤⑦
										M		R	F			★			V	ⒷZ	G		H				B	★	X
ga María Zambrano . d.	1435	...	1500	...	...	1535	...	1555	1555	...	...	...	1635	1700	...	...	...	1810	...	...	...	...	...	1905	...	2005	...	...	2120
anada **673** .... d.	*1245*¦	...	|	...	...	*1400*¦	...	*1500*¦	|	...	...	...	*1520*¦	|	...	...	...	|	...	...	...	...	...	|	...	*1900*¦	...	...	|
eciras **673** .... d.	|	...	|	...	...	|	...	|	|	...	...	...	|	|	...	1503	...	|	...	...	...	...	...	|	...	|	...	...	|
quera - Santa Ana §. d.	1500	...	|	...	...	1557	...	1623	1623	...	...	...	1658	1724	...	1733	...	|	...	...	...	...	...	1929	...	2030	...	...	|
te Genil - Herrera ¶. d.	1513	...	|	...	...	1611	...	|	|	...	...	...	1711	1737	...	|	...	|	...	...	...	...	...	|	...	2044	...	...	|
Huelva **671** .... d.	|	...	|	...	...	|	...	|	|	...	...	...	|	|	1620	|	...	|	...	...	1820	...	...	|	...	|	...	...	|
Cádiz **671** .... d.	|	...	|	1330	...	|	...	|	|	...	...	1505	|	|	|	|	...	|	...	...	|	1728	...	|	...	|	1855	...	|
villa .... d.	|	1450	|	1500	1545	|	1555	|	|	1625	1645	1643	|	|	|	|	1745	|	1830	1845	|	|	1915	|	1945	|	2036	2100	|
oba .... d.	1542	1542	|	1554	1629	1641	1641	1656	1656	1710	1729	1731	1740	1802	1810	1815	1829	1900	1914	1929	2009	|	|	2001	2029	2110	2127	2149	2208
ollano .... d.	1625	1625	|	1637	|	|	|	|	|	1752	|	|	1823	|	|	1919	|	|	1957	|	|	|	|	|	|	2153	|	2239	|
ad Real........ d.	1639	1639	|	1653	|	|	|	|	|	1806	|	|	1837	|	|	1936	|	|	2010	|	|	|	|	|	|	2208	|	2255	|
id Puerta de Atocha a.	|	|	1740	1748	1815	|	|	1841	1841	1903	1915	1920	...	1945	2001	2035	2015	2045	...	2113	2159	2127	2135	2145	2215	2306	2314	2350	2355
rcelona Sants **650** .. a.	2022	2022	...	...	...	2115	2115	...	...	...	...	...	...	...	...	...	...	...	...	...	...	...	...	...	...	...	...	...	...

④⑤⑦ (daily June 12 - Sept. 11).
⑤⑦ (④⑤⑦ June 12 - Sept. 11).
①④⑤⑦.
Not July 25 - Sept. 4.
①⑤⑦ (From València, dep. 1715).
⑦ (To València, arr. 2101).
Ⓑ June 12 - Sept. 4.
③④⑤⑦ (not July 20 - Sept. 4).
July 13 - Sept 12.
Not July 20 - Sept. 4.

P – ⑥⑦ (daily July 25 - Sept. 4).
Q – Runs 55 minutes later July 25 - Sept 4.
R – July 25 - Sept 4.
U – ⑤⑥ (To València (arr. 1411).
V – From / to València (Table **668**).
W – ①④⑤⑦ (not July 25 - Sept. 4).
X – ⑤⑦ (Ⓑ July 25 - Sept. 4).
Z – From / to Zaragoza (Table **660**).

¶ – ± *8 km* from Puente Genil.

§ – ± *17 km* from Antequera.
‡ – Antequera - Ciudad.
★ – Also calls at Villanueva de CLP (⊠), 23 - 24 mins. after departing Córdoba.
◐ – Also calls at Villanueva de CLP (⊠), 100 mins. after departing Madrid.
❦ – Also calls at Villanueva de CLP (⊠), 25 - 28 mins. after departing Puertollano.
⊠ – Full name: Villanueva de Córdoba-Los Pedroches.
¦ – 🚌 Antequera-Santa Ana - Granada and v.v. Subject to alteration.

☛ All trains convey 🍸. *AVE* trains also convey ✕.

rista class; 🍸 — Málaga – Córdoba – Sevilla — *Avant* high-speed shuttle services

	8654	8664	8664	8694	8714	8744	8764	8784	8804
	①-⑤	①-⑤			①-⑤		①-⑤		
ga María Zambrano .... d.	...	0645	...	0915	...	1415	1615	1820	2015
quera - Santa Ana § .... d.	...	0711	...	0941	...	1441	1641	1844	2041
te Genil - Herrera ¶ .... d.	...	0725	...	0955	...	1455	1655	1858	2055
oba .... a.	...	0750	...	1020	...	1520	1720	1922	2120
oba .... d.	0650	0755	0755	1025	1300	1525	1725	1930	2125
la .... a.	0735	0840	0840	1110	1345	1610	1810	2015	2210

	8075	8085	8095	8095	8125	8155	8175	8195	8215	
	①-⑤	①-⑤	⑥⑦				①-⑤			
Sevilla .... d.	0650	0800	0920	0920	1250	1540	1755	1935	2135	...
Córdoba .... a.	0735	0845	1005	1005	1335	1625	1840	2020	2220	...
Córdoba .... d.	0740	0850	1010	...	1340	1630	1845	2025	...	...
Puente Genil - Herrera ¶ .... d.	0803	0913	1033	...	1403	1653	1908	2048	...	...
Antequera - Santa Ana § .... d.	0817	0927	1047	...	1417	1707	1922	2102	...	...
Málaga María Zambrano .... a.	0845	0955	1115	...	1445	1735	1950	2130	...	...

± *17 km* from Antequera.

¶ – ± *8 km* from Puente Genil.

rista class; 🍸 — Madrid – Puertollano — *Avant* high-speed shuttle services

		8260		8080		8100			8130	8140		8150		8170	8180	8190	8200		8220					
		①-⑤		①-⑥						①-⑤		①-⑥			①-⑤		Ⓑ							
id Puerta de Atocha ...... d.	...	0640	...	0805	...	1015	...	...	1315	1415	...	1545	...	1715	1815	1915	2015	...	2215	...	...	...	...	...
ad Real ...... d.	...	0736	...	0901	...	1111	...	...	1411	1511	...	1641	...	1812	1911	2011	2111	...	2311	...	...	...	...	...
tollano ...... a.	...	0753	...	0918	...	1128	...	...	1428	1528	...	1658	...	1828	1928	2028	2128	...	2328	...	...	...	...	...

		8261		8271	8471	8081		8101		8121			8151	8161	8171	8181	8191		8211					
		①-⑤		①-⑤	①-⑤	①-⑥							①-⑥	①-⑤		⑦								
tollano ...... d.	...	0625	...	0700	0750	0815	...	1015	...	1215	...	...	1515	1615	1715	1815	1915	...	2115	...	...	...	...	...
ad Real ...... d.	...	0642	...	0717	0807	0832	...	1032	...	1232	...	...	1532	1632	1732	1832	1932	...	2132	...	...	...	...	...
id Puerta de Atocha ...... a.	...	0742	...	0813	0903	0928	...	1128	...	1329	...	...	1628	1728	1828	1928	2028	...	2228	...	...	...	...	...

661 MADRID - GRANADA, ALMERÍA and MÁLAGA

For other trains Madrid – Córdoba – Granada / Málaga and v.v. via the AVE high-speed line, see Table **660**

km		MD	MD		Talgo	MD		MD	MD	MD	Talgo	MD	Talgo	MD		MD		MD		MD	Hotel	
		17008	**13079**		**276**	**18030**		**18170**	**13083**	**13035**	**697**	**13073**	**278**	**18032**		**18034**		**18036**		**17000**	**897**	
		2	2		🍷	2		2	2	2	🍷	2	🍷	2		2		2		2	🍴	
		①–⑤												①–⑤		Ⓑ					❦	
		J	**E**					**C**	**E**	**E**	**N**	**E**		**J**							**R**	
0	**Madrid** Chamartín **668a 669** d.	...	...	...	0800	0916	...	1258	...	...	...	...	1434	1545	...	1720	...	1918	...	2114	...	...
8	**Madrid** Atocha Cercanías **668a 669** d.	0713	...	...	0819	0929	...	1310	...	...	...	...	1453	1559	...	1734	...	1932	...	2128	...	...
57	Aranjuez **668a 669** d.	0751	...	...	|	1004	...	1342	...	...	...	...	|	1634	...	|	...	2010	...	2207	...	...
	Barcelona Sants **672** d.	|	...	...	|	|	...	|	...	...	0927	...	|	|	...	|	...	|	...	|	2000	...
	València Nord **668** d.	|	...	...	|	|	...	|	...	...	1252	...	|	|	...	|	...	|	...	|	2340	...
157	Alcázar de San Juan **678** d.	0840	...	...	0937	1101	...	1435	...	...	1550	...	1614	1723	...	1854	...	2101	...	2301	0248	...
206	Manzanares **678** d.	...	...	...	|	1125	...	1459	...	...	1613	...	1637	1747	...	1918	...	2124	...	...	|	...
323	Linares - Baeza a.	...	...	...	1117	1249	...	...	...	...	1735	...	1756	1911	...	2039	...	2241	...	...	0455	...
323	Linares - Baeza d.	...	...	...	1119	1250	...	...	...	...	1737	...	1801	1912	...	2040	...	2242	...	...	0505	...
441	Moreda d.	...	...	...	|	|	...	...	...	...	|	...	1933	|	...	|	...	|	...	...	|	...
499	**Granada** **673** a.	...	...	...	|	|	...	...	...	...	|	...	|	|	...	|	...	|	...	...	0755	...
466	Guadix **673** d.	...	...	...	1309	|	...	...	...	...	|	...	1956	|	...	|	...	|	...	...	...	...
565	**Almería** **673** a.	...	...	...	1422	|	...	...	...	...	|	...	2114	|	...	|	...	|	...	...	...	...
¶	**Jaén** d.	...	0637	...	...	1333	...	...	1430	1650	|	1830	...	1955	...	2125	...	2325	...	...	...	...
371	Andújar d.	...	0720	...	...	...	...	...	1514	1737	1817	1913	...	...	...	...	...	...	...	...	...	...
450	**Córdoba** a.	...	0810	...	...	...	...	...	1610	1828	1905	2007	...	...	...	...	...	...	...	...	...	...

	MD		MD		MD	Talgo	MD	Talgo	MD	MD	MD		MD	MD	MD	MD	Talgo		MD	Hotel		
	18047		**18031**		**18033**	**277**	**13001**	**694**	**18171**	**13003**	**17041**		**18035**	**13009**	**18037**	**13011**	**279**		**13017**	**894**		
	2		2		2	🍷	2	🍷	2	2	2		2	2	2	2	🍷		🍷	🍴		
	①–⑤		①–⑤				①–⑤			⑥⑦										❦		
	J		**J**				**J E**	**N**		**H E**	**C**			**E**		**T**			**E**	**R**		
Córdoba d.	...	...	...	...	...	...	0906	0950	...	1002	...	...	...	1451	...	1626	...	...	2105	...	...	...
Andújar d.	...	...	...	...	...	...	0959	1040	...	1056	...	...	...	1544	...	1720	...	...	2157	...	...	...
Jaén d.	...	...	0610	...	0830	...	1049	|	...	1143	...	...	1520	1629	1718	1811	...	...	2245	...	...	...
Almería **673** d.	...	...	|	...	|	0730	...	|	...	...	...	...	|	...	|	...	1536	...	...	...	...	...
Guadix **673** d.	...	...	|	...	|	0848	...	|	...	...	...	...	|	...	|	...	1654	...	...	...	...	...
Granada **673** d.	...	...	|	...	|	|	...	|	...	...	...	...	|	...	|	...	|	...	...	2130	...	...
Moreda d.	...	...	|	...	|	0910	...	|	...	...	...	...	|	...	|	...	|	...	...	|	...	...
Linares - Baeza a.	...	...	0650	...	0912	1040	...	1117	...	...	...	...	1602	...	1800	...	1859	...	...	2341	...	...
Linares - Baeza d.	...	...	0651	...	0913	1045	...	1120	...	...	...	...	1603	...	1801	...	1900	...	...	2353	...	...
Manzanares **678** d.	...	...	0807	...	1032	|	...	1237	...	...	1520	...	1723	...	1921	...	2019	...	...	|	...	...
Alcázar de San Juan **678** d.	0527	...	0832	...	1055	1223	...	1315	1355	...	1546	...	1745	...	1946	...	2044	...	...	0140	...	...
València Nord **668** a.	|	...	|	...	|	|	...	1602	|	...	|	...	|	...	|	...	|	...	...	0410	...	...
Barcelona Sants **672** a.	|	...	|	...	|	|	...	1939	|	...	|	...	|	...	|	...	|	...	...	0839	...	...
Aranjuez **668a 669** d.	0621	...	0918	...	1143	|	...	...	1447	...	1643	...	1830	...	2032	...	|	...	...	...	...	...
Madrid Atocha Cercanías **668a 669** a.	0656	...	0959	...	1214	1343	...	...	1526	...	1717	...	1905	...	2109	...	2213	...	...	...	...	...
Madrid Chamartín **668a 669** a.	...	...	1013	...	1228	1358	...	...	1541	...	1731	...	1919	...	2122	...	2227	...	...	...	...	...

C – To / from Ciudad Real (Table **678**).
E – To / from Cádiz (Table **671**).
H – ⑥⑦ (also May 2).
J – ①–⑤ (not May 2).

N – TORRE DEL ORO – 12 🍷 Barcelona - Córdoba - Sevilla and v.v. (Tables **668a**, **671**, **672**).
R – ALHAMBRA *Trenhotel* – 🛏, 1 (reclining) Barcelona - Granada and v.v. **Service currently suspended**.
T – Daily from Sevilla. From Cádiz on ①–⑤ (not May 2). Table **671**.

❦ – Service currently suspended.
¶ – Linares - Jaen: *59 km*. Jaen - Andújar: 5

662 MÁLAGA - TORREMOLINOS - FUENGIROLA

2nd c

km					❦						
0	**Málaga** María Zambrano d.	0523	0558	0633	0653	and	2133	2203	2233	2303	2333	...
8	Málaga Aeropuerto ✈ d.	0532	0607	0642	0702	every	2142	2212	2242	2312	2342	...
16	**Torremolinos** d.	0543	0618	0653	0713	20	2153	2223	2253	2323	2353	...
20	Benalmádena d.	0554	0629	0704	0724	mins.	2204	2234	2304	2334	0004	...
31	**Fuengirola** a.	0606	0641	0716	0736	until	2216	2246	2316	2346	0016	...

				❦						
Fuengirola d.	0610	0645	0720	0740	and	2220	2250	2320	2350	0020
Benalmádena d.	0624	0659	0734	0754	every	2234	2304	2334	0004	0034
Torremolinos d.	0633	0708	0743	0803	20	2243	2313	2343	0013	0043
Málaga Aeropuerto ✈ d.	0644	0719	0754	0814	mins.	2254	2324	2354	0024	0054
Málaga María Zambrano a.	0652	0727	0802	0822	until	2302	2332	0002	0032	0102

❦ – 0653, 0733, 0813 from Málaga and 0740, 0820, 0900 from Fuengirola do not run on ⑥⑦.

663 MADRID - VALLADOLID

High-speed services. For Avant high-speed services, see Table **679**.

km		*Alvia*	*Alvia*	*Alvia*	*Alvia*	*Alvia*	*AVE*	*Alvia*	*Alvia*	*Alvia*	*Alvia*	*Alvia*	*Alvia*	*Alvia*	*Alvia*	*Alvia*	*Alvia*	*Alvia*	*IC*	*Alvia*	*Alvia*	*Alvia*	*Alvia*	*AVE*				
		4071	**4275**	**4073**	**4087**	**4087**	**4099**	**4111**	**4143**	**4149**	**4541**	**4141**	**4345**	**4145**	**4143**	**4167**	**4167**	**4179**	**4177**	**4377**	**4181**	**4193**	**4197**	**4209**				
		①–⑥	①–⑤	①–⑥		①–⑥	**4299**			Ⓑ	⑥	Ⓑ	⑦	①–⑤	⑤		Ⓑ	Ⓑ	⑤	⑦	**4381**		①–④					
							L	**V**		**L**			**F**	**F**	2			2 **P**	2 **Q**	2 **Q**			**T**	**L**				
	Alacant Terminal **668** d.	...	...	...	...	...	...	...	1035**c**	...	...	...	1020	...	...	...	...	...	...	...	1445	...	...	...	...	...	...	...
0	**Madrid** Chamartín d.	0705	0720	0745	0800	0800	0930	1105	1420	1440	1440	1450	1500	1500	1525	1605	1605	1730	1740	1740	1830	1900	1915	2025	...	...	...	...
68	Segovia AV d.	|	0750	|	0830	0830	0958	1137	|	1508	|	|	1531	1531	|	1635	1635	1758	|	|	|	1929	|	|	...	...	...	...
	A Coruña **680** a.	|	|	|	|	|	|	|	|	|	|	|	2052	2052	|	|	|	|	|	|	|	|	|	|	...	...	...	...
	Pontevedra **680** a.	|	1353	|	|	|	|	|	|	|	|	|	...	...	|	|	|	|	|	|	|	|	|	|	...	...	...	...
180	**Valladolid** ⊠ a.	0808	...	0843	0916	0916	1033	1214	1520	1541	1539	1549	...	...	1626	1721	1721	1833	1848	1848	1930	2005	2023	2119	...	...	...	...
	Gijón Cercanías **681** a.	1158	...	|	|	|	...	1604	|	...	1938	1922	...	...	|	|	|	...	...	...	2322**r**	|	...	...	...	...	...	...
	Santander **681** a.	...	...	1209	|	|	...	...	1815	...	...	...	...	...	1947	|	|	...	...	...	...	2312	...	...	...	...	...	...
	Bilbao Abando **689** a.	...	...	...	|	1304	...	...	...	...	...	...	...	...	...	|	2116	...	...	...	...	...	...	...	...	...	...	...
	Hendaye **689** a.	...	...	...	1355	...	...	...	...	...	...	...	...	...	...	2158	...	...	...	...	...	...	...	...	...	...	...	...

	AVE	*Alvia*	*Alvia*	*Alvia*	*Alvia*	*Alvia*	*Alvia*	*Alvia*	*Alvia*	*AVE*	*Alvia*	*Alvia*	*Alvia*	*Alvia*	*Alvia*	*Alvia*	*AVE*	*AVE*	*IC*	*Alvia*	*AVE*	*Alvia*	*Alvia*	*AVE*	*Alvia*	*Alvia*	*Alvia*	*Alvia*
	4078	**4088**	**4076**	**4072**	**4070**	**4270**	**4092**	**4086**	**4086**	**4128**	**4084**	**4584**	**4064**	**4110**	**4142**	**4140**	**4178**	**4188**	**4176**	**4162**	**4198**	**4166**	**4166**	**4398**	**4354**	**4180**	**4380**	**4208**
	①–⑤	①–⑤	①–⑤	①–⑤	①–⑥	⑦	⑥⑦		①–⑥	①–⑤	①–⑤	⑥	①–⑤				Ⓑ	⑥	⑦	⑦	⑥		Ⓑ	⑦	Ⓑ	①–⑤	⑦	⑦
	L	2 **P**	**T**							2 **L**			**F**			**V**	**L**	2 **L**	2 **Q**		**L**			**L**				2 **P**
Irún **689** d.	...	...	...	...	...	...	...	0840	...	...	...	...	...	...	...	...	...	...	...	...	...	1615	...	...	...	...	...	...
Bilbao Abando **689** d.	...	...	...	...	...	...	...	|	0920	...	...	...	...	...	...	...	...	...	...	...	...	|	1700	...	...	...	...	...
Santander **681** d.	...	...	...	0705	...	...	0910	|	|	...	...	...	...	...	1400	...	...	...	...	1610	...	|	|	...	...	...	...	...
Gijón Cercanías **681** d.	...	...	...	|	0700	0700	|	|	|	...	...	...	...	1100	|	1425	...	...	...	|	...	|	|	...	...	1800	1810	...
Valladolid ⊠ d.	0811	0910	0916	1011	1035	1055	1216	1311	1311	1341	...	...	...	1450	1704	1813	1836	1901	1914	1930	2005	2050	2050	2106	...	2145	2145	2156
Pontevedra **680** d.	|	|	|	|	|	|	|	|	|	|	0818	0818	...	|	|	|	|	|	|	|	|	|	|	|	1546	|	|	|
A Coruña **680** d.	|	|	|	|	|	|	|	|	|	|	|	|	0715	|	|	|	|	|	|	|	|	|	|	|	|	|	|	|
Segovia AV d.	|	0947	|	1051	|	|	1256	1359	1359	1421	|	|	1237	|	|	1853	1915	1941	|	|	|	2137	2137	2145	2216	|	|	|
Madrid Chamartín a.	0910	1015	1030	1121	1138	1158	1326	1428	1428	1448	1504	1506	1306	1557	1807	1926	1942	2008	2027	2040	2110	2206	2206	2214	2245	2253	2253	2303
Alacant Terminal **668** a.	...	...	...	1512	...	...	1715	...	...	...	...	1846	...	1936	...	...	...	...	...	...	...	...	...	...	...	...	...	...

F – To / from Ferrol (Table **682**).
L – To / from Leon (Table **681**).
P – To / from Ponferrada (Tables **681**, **682**).
Q – To / from Irún (Table **689**).
T – To and from Vitoria / Gasteiz (Table **689**).

V – From / to Castelló de la Plana and València on dates shown in Table **668**.

c – 1020 on ⑦.
r – 2305 on ⑤.

⊠ – Full name is Valladolid Campo Grande.
☛ All trains convey 🍷. *AVE* trains also convey 🍴.

BARCELONA - ANDORRA 664

Barcelona Nord bus station: 0630*, 0700, 0730*, 1030, 1500, 1700*, 1900.
Andorra la Vella bus station: 0600, 0815*, 1100, 1500, 1700*, 1915.
ey 3 hr 15 min (* 4 hours). Operator: Alsina Graells, Barcelona (ALSA) ✆ (+34) 91 327 05 40.

Barcelona Airport ✈ (T1 and T2): 0730, 1100, 1300, 1500, 1730, 2000, 2300.
Barcelona Sants railway station: 0615, 0815, 1145, 1345, 1545, 1815, 2045, 2345.
Andorra la Vella bus station: 0615, 0815, 1115, 1315, 1515, 1815, 2015, 2215.
ey 3 hours (3 hrs 30 mins to / from Barcelona ✈). Operator: Autocars Nadal ✆ +376 805 151.

2nd class BARCELONA - SITGES - SANT V de CALDERS 665

Local rail service **Barcelona - Sitges - Sant Vicenç de Calders**.
From Barcelona Sants: 0606, 0636 and every 30 minutes until 2206; then 2306.
From Sant Vicenç: 0600, 0615 ⚒, 0632 Ⓐ, 0643 Ⓐ, 0658, 0732, 0751, 0816, 0831, 0903, 0933 and every 30 minutes until 2103, 2133 Ⓐ, then 2200.

Additional trains operate **Barcelona - Sitges** and v.v.
Journey times: **Barcelona – Sitges** (*34 km*) 30 minutes, **Barcelona – Sant Vicenç** (*60 km*) 57 minutes.

class BARCELONA - MATARÓ, BLANES and MAÇANET 666

Cercanías (suburban) line **R1**. For faster services Barcelona - Maçanet via Granollers, see Table **657**.

oximate journey times (in mins) to / from **Barcelona** Sants: Mataró (46), Arenys de Mar (57), Calella (69), Pineda de Mar (73), Malgrat de Mar (79), Blanes (84), Maçanet-Massanes (97).

elona Sants – **Mataró** and v.v. *35 km*
4–6 trains per hour.
From Barcelona 0546–2354; from Mataró 0450–2313.
2–4 trains per hour.
From Barcelona 0612–0010; from Mataró 0457–2220.

Barcelona Sants – **Blanes** *67 km*
0612, 0642 and every 30 mins. until 2042, then 2112 Ⓒ, 2124 Ⓐ, 2142 Ⓒ, 2154 Ⓐ, 2213 Ⓒ, 2224 Ⓐ.
Blanes - Barcelona Sants
Ⓐ: 2 trains per hour, 0617–2115, 2155
Ⓒ: 2 trains per hour; 0603–2103, 2144.

Barcelona Sants – Blanes – **Maçanet-Massanes** *82 km*
Ⓐ: 0546 and hourly until 2045, 2124, 2154.
Ⓒ: 0612 and hourly until 2012, then 2042, 2142.
Maçanet-Massanes – Blanes – **Barcelona** Sants
Ⓐ: 0605, 0636, 0704, 0734, 0804 and hourly until 2103
Ⓒ: 0620, 0650, 0720 and hourly until 2020, then 2130.

class ALACANT - BENIDORM - DÉNIA 667

◐ *By tram (route L1)*									
ant Luceros ⊙ .....d.	...	0541	0611	every	1711	1811	1841	1941	2041
ampello.....d.	...	0609	0639	hour	1739	1839	1909	2009	2109
la Joiosa.....d.	0612	0635	0705	◐	1805	1905	1935	2035	2135
dorm.....a.	0630	0653	0723	until	1823	1923	1953	2053	2153
By train (route L9)									
dorm.....d.	0636	...	0736		1836	...	1959	2059	2159
.....d.	0650	...	0750	every	1850	...	2013	2113	2211
e.....d.	0712	...	0812	hour	1912	...	2035	2135	...
.....d.	0739	...	0839	until	1939	...	2101	2201	...
a.....a.	0753	...	0853		1953	...	2115	2215	...

By train (route L9)									
Dénia.....d.	...	...	0604		1804	1904	...	2026	...
Gata.....d.	...	...	0619	every	1819	1919	...	2041	...
Calpe.....d.	...	...	0646	hour	1846	1948	...	2111	...
Altea.....d.	0616	...	0708	until	1908	2014	...	2134	2216
Benidorm.....a.	0629	...	0721		1921	2027	...	2147	2229
✤ *By tram (route L1)*									
Benidorm.....d.	0635	0705	0735	every	1935	2035	2135	2205	2235
La Vila Joiosa.....d.	0653	0723	0753	hour	1953	2053	2153	2223	2253
El Campello.....d.	0723	0753	0823	✤	2023	2123	2223	2253	...
Alacant Luceros ⊙.....a.	0751	0821	0851	until	2051	2151	2251	2321	...

Alacant - Benidorm runs every 30 minutes 0541 - 2141 (also 2319, 0119 night of ④⑤⑥ June 30 - Sept. 1).
Benidorm - Alacant runs every 30 minutes 0635 - 2205 (also 0113, 0313 night of ④⑤⑥ June 30 - Sept. 1).
± 400 m from Alacant Renfe station.

Operator: Tram Metropolitano / FGV ✆ 900 72 04 72
www.fgvalicante.com

MADRID - ALBACETE, ALACANT and VALÈNCIA 668

		AVE	*AVE*		*AVE*	*AVE*	*AVE*	*AVE*	*AVE*	*MD*	*AVE*	*AVE*	*AVE*	*AVE*	*AVE*	*Alvia*	*AVE*	*AVE*	*Talgo*	*AVE*	*Alvia*	*AVE*	*AVE*	*MD*	*Alvia*	*AVE*
	18024	**5270**	**5072**	**18018**	**5070**	**5080**	**5290**	**5092**	**5090**	**14404**	**5302**	**5100**	**5102**	**5310**	**5320**	**4072**	**5122**	**5120**	**694**	**5340**	**4092**	**5142**	**5150**	**14406**	**4584**	**5162**
	①–⑤	①–⑤	①–⑥	⑥⑦		①–⑥	⑦		①–⑥	①–⑥		⑦			⑦	①–⑤	⑥	①–⑤	🍸		⑥⑦	①–⑤			⑥	
	B	**c**			**D**			**L**	**c**		**N**		**L**	✤		**S**		**c**	**T**		**S**				**H**	**R**
Madrid Puerta de Atocha d.	...	0645	0745	...	0740	0840	0910	0930	0940	...	1010	1040	1045	1110	1210	1215	1230	1240	...	1410	1420	1445	1540	...	1555	1625
Cuenca Fernando Zóbel .. d.	...	0737	0842	...	|	0936	1002	|	|	...	1103	|	1142	1202	1302	1325	|	|	...	|	1526	1542	1636	...	1657	|
Requena / Utiel..... d.	...	0811	|	...	|	|	1036	|	|	...	|	|	|	1236	|	|	|	|	...	1529	|	|	|	...	|	|
Albacete..... d.	0806	|	0918	0918	|	|	|	1056	|	1100	1139	|	1218	|	|	1405	1356	|	1420	|	1605	1618	|	1650	1740	|
Villena AV..... d.	|	|	0953	|	|	|	|	|	|	|	1214	|	1253	|	|	1449	1431	|	|	|	1652	1653	|	|	1824	|
Alacant Terminal..... a.	|	|	1014	|	|	|	|	1146	|	|	1235	|	1314	|	|	1512	1452	|	|	|	1715	1714	|	|	1846	1834
Xátiva..... d.	0928	|	...	1039	|	|	|	...	|	1206	...	|	...	|	|	...	...	|	1524	|	...	...	|	1757	...	...
València Joaquín Sorolla.§ a.	|	0839	...	|	0922	1029	1104	...	1124	|	...	1222	...	1304	1359	...	...	1422	|	1554	...	...	1729	|	...	...
València Nord.....§ a.	1011	...	...	1115	...	...	...	...	...	1245	...	...	...	...	...	...	...	...	1602	...	...	...	...	1837	...	...
Sagunt..... a.	...	...	...	...	...	...	...	...	...	...	...	...	...	...	...	...	...	...	|	...	...	...	...	...	...	...
Castelló de la Plana **672** a.	...	...	...	...	...	...	...	...	...	...	...	...	...	...	...	...	...	...	1703	...	...	...	...	...	...	...

	AVE	*Alvia*	*AVE*	*IC*	*AVE*	*AVE*	*AVE*	*AVE*	*Alvia*	*AVE*	*AVE*	*AVE*	*Hotel*
	5160	**4110**	**5170**	**5036**	**5172**	**5180**	**5392**	**5190**	**4140**	**3981**	**5212**	**5410**	**894**
	Ⓑ		Ⓑ	Ⓑ					Ⓑ	Ⓑ	Ⓑ		✕
		G				**J**			**G**	**P**			**Z**❋
rid Puerta de Atocha . d.	1640	1645	1740	1748	1745	1840	1920	1940	2010	...	2105	2110	...
nca Fernando Zóbel ... d.	|	1752	|	|	|	|	2017	|	|	2130	2202	2203	...
uena / Utiel..... d.	|	|	|	|	|	|	|	|	|	|	|	2238	...
acete..... d.	|	1831	|	2012	1911	|	2053	|	|	|	2238	|	0236
ena AV..... d.	|	1914	|	|	|	|	2128	|	|	|	2313	|	|
cant Terminal..... a.	|	1936	|	|	2001	|	2149	|	|	|	2334	|	|
a..... d.	|	...	|	2115	...	|	...	|	|	|	...	|	|
ncia Joaquín Sorolla..§ a.	1822	...	1922	|	...	2022	...	2122	2210	2224	...	2304	|
ncia Nord.....§ a.	...	...	...	2153	...	...	...	...	|	...	...	...	0410
unt..... a.	...	...	...	...	...	...	...	...	2247	...	...	...	|
stelló de la Plana **672** . a.	...	...	...	...	...	...	...	...	2320	...	...	...	0519

	AVE	*AVE*	*IC*	*AVE*	*AVE*	*AVE*	*AVE*	*Alvia*	*AVE*
	5261	**5063**	**5035**	**5071**	**5081**	**3982**	**5073**	**4111**	**5281**
	①–⑤	①–⑤	①–⑤		①–⑥	①–⑥	①–⑥	①–⑥	⑦
	c			**D**		**P**		**G**	
Castelló de la Plana **672**. d.	...	...	...	...	...	...	...	0717	...
Sagunt..... d.	...	...	...	...	...	...	...	0743	...
València Nord.....§ d.	...	...	...	...	...	...	...	|	...
València Joaquín Sorolla § d.	0645	...	0620	0710	0800	0807	...	0820	0840
Xátiva..... d.	|	...	0659	|	|	|	...	|	|
Alacant Terminal..... d.	|	0615	|	|	|	|	0720	|	|
Villena AV..... d.	|	0636	|	|	|	|	|	|	|
Albacete..... d.	|	0712	0803	|	|	|	0810	|	|
Requena / Utiel..... d.	0708	|	|	|	0823**y**	|	|	|	0903
Cuenca Fernando Zóbel . d.	0743	0748	|	|	0855	0902	|	|	0939
Madrid Puerta de Atocha. a.	0838	0845	1020	0851	0948	...	0935	1020	1033

	AVE	*AVE*	*AVE*	*Alvia*	*Alvia*	*Alvia*	*AVE*	*AVE*	*Talgo*	*MD*	*AVE*	*Alvia*	*AVE*	*AVE*	*AVE*	*AVE*		*AVE*	*AVE*	*AVE*	*AVE*	*AVE*	*AVE*	*Alvia*	*MD*	*Hotel*	*AVE*
	5091	**5083**	**5301**	**4143**	**4345**	**4143**	**5321**	**5123**	**697**	**14405**	**5141**	**4181** **4381**	**5151**	**5161**	**5163**	**5171**	**18027**	**5181**	**5183**	**5193**	**5391**	**5201**	**5211**	**5203**	**14407**	**897**	**5213**
	①–⑥			⑦	⑦	①–⑥			🍸		Ⓑ			Ⓑ				Ⓑ			①–⑥	⑦			Ⓑ	✕	⑦
		Q	**E**	**S**	**F**	**S**		**U**	**T**			**G**		**b**			**A**			**R**	**b**	**c**				**Z**❋	
stelló de la Plana **672** . d.	...	...	...	...	...	...	...	...	1158	...	...	...	...	...	...	...	...	...	...	...	...	...	...	...	...	2236	...
unt..... d.	...	...	...	...	...	...	...	...	|	...	...	...	...	...	...	...	...	...	...	...	...	...	...	...	...	|	...
ncia Nord.....§ d.	...	...	...	...	...	...	...	...	1255	1345	...	...	...	...	...	...	1730	...	...	...	...	...	...	...	2045	2340	...
ncia Joaquín Sorolla..§ d.	0915	...	1040	...	...	...	1240	...	|	|	1410	...	1510	1615	...	1710	|	1810	...	...	1940	2015	2110	...	|	|	...
a..... d.	|	...	|	...	...	...	|	...	1337	1426	|	...	|	|	...	|	1806	|	...	...	|	|	|	...	2124	|	...
cant Terminal..... d.	|	0840	|	1020	1020	1035	|	1240	|	|	|	1445	|	|	1610	|	|	|	1810	1905	|	|	|	2010	|	|	2115
ena AV..... d.	|	0901	|	1043	1043	1058	|	1301	|	|	|	1508	|	|	1631	|	|	|	|	|	|	|	|	2031	|	|	|
acete..... d.	|	0937	|	1125	1125	1140	|	1337	1439	1534	|	1553	|	|	1707	|	1924	|	1900	|	|	|	|	2107	2232	0125	|
uena / Utiel..... d.	|	|	1103**e**	|	|	|	|	|	...	...	|	|	1533	|	|	|	...	|	|	|	|	|	2133	|	...	...	|
nca Fernando Zóbel ... d.	|	1013	1138	1204	1204	|	|	1413	...	...	|	1630	1607	|	1743	|	...	|	|	|	|	|	2207	2143	...	...	|
rid Puerta de Atocha ... a.	1056	1110	1233	1310	1310	1320	1421	1510	...	...	1548	1735	1703	1756	1838	1851	...	1951	2025	2116	2124	2156	2303	2241	...	...	2323

To Ciudad Real on ⑦ Table **678**.
From Ciudad Real on ① Table **678**.
①–④ (①–⑤ July 18 - Sept. 11).
Daily (not ①–⑥ June 24 - Sept. 10).
To Ferrol (Table **682**).
From / to Gijón (Table **685**).
From Pontevedra (Table **680**).
Daily (not ⑥ July 23 - Sept. 10).
June 1 - Sept. 11.
Sept. 12 - Dec. 10.

P – From / to Sevilla (Table **660**).
Q – From Sept. 12 runs 25 mins. later as Train **5293.**
R – ⑤⑦ (Ⓑ June 12 - Sept. 11).
S – From / to Santander (Table **684**).
T – TORRE DEL ORO – 🚃12 🍸 Barcelona - Sevilla and v.v. (Table **672**).
U – ①–⑤ (daily June 1 - Sept. 11).
Z – ALHAMBRA *Trenhotel* – 🛏, 🚃1 (reclining) Barcelona - Granada and v.v. **Service currently suspended**.

b – Not July 18 - Sept. 11.
c – Not July 17 - Sept. 11.
e – Not ⑥⑦.
y – ⑥ only.
§ – Free 🚌 between València Joaquín Sorolla and València Nord, 0615 - 2330, every ± 10 minutes.
* – Albacete - Xátiva - València: *203 km*.
❋ – Service currently suspended.
✤ – Train **5310** runs ①–⑤. On ⑥ **5110** departs Madrid 1140 and runs 30 mins later.

Cercanías (suburban) line **C1**: **València - Gandia** and v.v. *62 km* 2nd class. Journey time: 54 - 60 minutes.

n **València** Nord
0611, 0641 and every 30 mins. until 1941; then 1956, 2033, 2041, 2111, 2141, 2211, 2241.
0641, 0741 and hourly until 2241.

From **Gandia**
Ⓐ: 0605, 0640, 0655, 0710, 0725, 0755, 0825 and every 30 mins. until 2225.
Ⓒ: 0655, 0755 and hourly until 2055; then 2225.

668a MADRID - CARTAGENA

km		18024	*Alta* 220	*Alta* 222	*Talgo* 694	*Alta* 228	*MD* 18040	*IC* 10146	*Alta* 224	*MD* 18042	*Alta* 226
		①–⑤ w	①–⑤		A	C		⑤ B		Ⓑ	Ⓑ
0	**Madrid** Chamartín ‡ d.	...	0713	0900	...	1234	1419	1555	1629	1818	1900
8	**Madrid** Atocha C ◧ ‡ d.	...	0730	0921	...	1251	1432	1609	1648	1832	1919
57	Aranjuez ‡ d.	...	|	|	...	|	1509	1649	|	1908	|
157	Alcázar de San Juan ‡ d.	0645	0849	|	1315	1404	1604	|	|	2000	2034
288	**Albacete** d.	0805	0947	1132	1418	1502	1715	1827	1856k	2106	2135
354	Hellín d.	...	1023	|		|	...	|	|	...	2215
466	Murcia **672** d.	...	1144	1326		1645	...	2006	2050	...	2331
531	**Cartagena** **672** a.	...	...	1412		1728	...	...	2138	...	0017

	MD 18047	*MD* 18041	*MD* 18049	*Alta* 221	*Alta* 223	*Talgo* 697	*Alta* 229	*MD* 18043	*Alta* 225	*IC* 10418	18027
	①–⑤	①–⑤	⑥⑦	①–⑤		A	Ⓑ			⑦ D	w
Cartagena **672** d.	...	...	...	0530	0850	...	1215t	...	1600		...
Murcia **672** d.	...	...	...	0610	0936	...	1258	...	1647	1713	...
Hellín d.	...	...	...	|	1049	...	|	...	|	|	...
Albacete d.	0412f	0605	0730c	0753	1129	1430	1446	1740	1834q	1858	1946
Alcázar de San Juan ‡ d.	0527	0711	0837	|	1235	1535	|	1851	1929q	1955	2106
Aranjuez ‡ d.	0621	0807	0933	|	|	...	|	1948	|	2042	...
Madrid Atocha C ◧ ‡ a.	0656	0844	1008	1008	1402	...	1704	2020	2045	2125	...
Madrid Chamartín ‡ a.	...	0858	1022	1025	1416	...	1718	2034	2100	2140	...

A – TORRE DEL ORO – [12] 🍸 Sevilla - Alcázar - Albacete - Barcelona and v.v. (Tables **661**, **671**, **672**).
B – ⑤: [2] Madrid - Murcia - Aguilas (arrive 2150).
C – Ⓑ (daily Aug. 1 - 29).
D – ⑦: [2] Aguilas (depart 1533) - Murcia - Madrid.

c – ⑥ only.
f – ① only.
k – Not ⑤.
q – Not ⑦.

t – ⑦ only.
w – To / from València Nord (Table
‡ – See also Table **661**.
◧ – Madrid **Atocha Cercanías**.

669 MADRID - CUENCA - VALÈNCIA

2nd c

km		18160	18160	18160	18162	18162	14162	18164	18164	18768
		①–⑤	⑦	⑥	①–⑤	⑦	⑦	①–④	⑤⑥⑦	⑤
0	**Madrid** Chamartín d.	*0554*	...	...	*1207*	...	...	*1548*	...	...
8	**Madrid** Atocha Cercanías d.	*0608*	0620	0800	*1221*	1242	...	*1602*	1630	1754
16	Villaverde Bajo **677** d.	*0616*	0630	0808	*1229*	1250	...	*1610*	1640	1803
57	Aranjuez **661 668a** a.	*0652*	0700	0836	*1305*	1318	...	*1649*	1708	1832
	change trains on certain services		|	|		|			|	|
57	Aranjuez **661 668a** d.	0702	0702	0837	1328	1328	...	1709	1709	1833
209	**Cuenca** d.	0918	0918	1044	1537	1537	1740	1915	1915	2048
335	Requena d.	1155	1155	1303	1756	1756	2010	2139	2139	...
407	**València** Nord a.	1320	1320	1430	1924	1924	2147	2301	2301	...

	18161	18161	18163	18163		18765	18165	18165
	⑥⑦	①–⑤	⑤⑦	①–④		⑦	⑤⑥⑦	①–④
València Nord d.	0638	0638	0950	0950	...	...	1454	1454
Requena d.	0818	0818	1125	1125	...	...	1639	1639
Cuenca d.	1045	1045	1410	1410	...	1745	1914	1914
Aranjuez **661 668a** a.	1246	1246	1614	1614	...	1953	2114	2114
change trains on certain services	|					|	|	
Aranjuez **661 668a** d.	1247	*1312*	1615	*1630*	...	1954	2116	*2132*
Villaverde Bajo **677** a.	1314	*1348*	1649	*1706*	...	2026	2149	*2208*
Madrid Atocha Cercanías a.	1323	*1356*	1657	*1714*	...	2035	2158	*2216*
Madrid Chamartín a.	...	*1410*	...	*1728*	...	...	...	*2230*

670 VALÈNCIA - TERUEL - ZARAGOZA - HUESCA - CANFRANC

2nd class (except *AVE* tra

km		Ⓒ	Ⓐ	Ⓒ	18500	*MD* 18502		*MD* 18504	*AVE* 3363	*AVE* 3393	Ⓐ	*MD* 18506	14530
								C	⑤⑦				A
0	**València** Nord d.	...	...	...	...	0917	...	1220	...	...	...	1735	1911
34	Sagunt d.	...	...	...	...	0950	...	1254	...	...	...	1810	1946
65	Segorbe d.	...	...	...	...	1017	...	1322	...	...	...	1839	2022
171	**Teruel** d.	...	...	...	0630	1157	...	1503	...	...	...	2029	2218
242	Calamocha d.	...	...	...	0719	|	...	1547	...	...	...	2111	...
305	Cariñena d.	...	...	...	0817	1339	...	1637	...	...	...	2205	...
	Madrid ◇ **650** d.	...	...	...	|	|	...	|	1605	1905	...	|	...
359	**Zaragoza** Delicias d.	0640	0840	0847	0905	1420	1541	1718	1727	2034	2140	2252	...
361	**Zaragoza** Portillo d.	0643	0843	0851	0910	1424	1545	1722	|	|	2143	2255	...
363	**Zaragoza** Goya d.	0645	0845	0855	0914	1428	1549	1726	|	|	2145	2257	...
417	Tardienta d.	0727	0932	0936	...	...	1629	...	|	2105	2227	...	...
439	**Huesca** d.	0748	0953	0959	...	...	1652	...	1810	2118	2242	...	...
474	Ayerbe d.	0831	1036	1047	...	...	1738	...	...	...	...	...	...
533	Sabiñánigo d.	0937	1143	1157	...	...	1841	...	...	...	...	...	...
549	Jaca d.	0953	1159	1214	...	...	1902	...	...	...	...	...	...
574	**Canfranc 324** a.	1026	1232	...	...	...	1937	...	...	...	...	...	...

	Ⓐ	14531	*MD* 18511	*AVE* 3272	Ⓐ	*MD* 18523	Ⓒ	*MD* 18515	18517	Ⓒ	*AVE* 3592
		B				w					⑤⑦
Canfranc 324 d.	...	...	...	...	0600	...	0845	...	...	...	...
Jaca d.	...	...	...	...	0635	...	0920	...	...	1610	...
Sabiñánigo d.	...	...	...	...	0650	...	0934	...	...	1625	...
Ayerbe d.	...	...	...	...	0757	...	1045	...	...	1737	...
Huesca d.	0640	...	...	0815	0845	...	1138	...	...	1827	1935
Tardienta d.	0656	...	...	0827	0859	...	1152	...	...	1842	|
Zaragoza Goya d.	0738	...	0806	|	0940	1058	1234	1703	1923	1935	|
Zaragoza Portillo d.	0740	...	0809	|	0942	1101	1236	1706	1925	1939	|
Zaragoza Delicias d.	0744	...	0814	0900	0945	1107	1240	1710	1932	1943	2020
Madrid ◇ **650** a.	...	...	|	1035	...	|	...	|	|	...	2140
Cariñena d.	...	...	0905	...	...	1154	...	1757	2022	...	...
Calamocha d.	...	...	0958	...	...	1253	...	1856	2129	...	...
Teruel d.	...	0705	1044	...	...	1336	...	1937	2219	...	...
Segorbe d.	...	0854	1216	...	...	1510	...	2127	...	...	...
Sagunt d.	...	0929	1247	...	...	1541	...	2158	...	...	...
València Nord a.	...	1002	1316	...	...	1622	...	2227	...	...	...

A – ②④⑥⑦. B – ①③⑤⑦. C – From Cartagena on ①–⑤ and from Murcia on ⑥ (Table **672**). w – To Cartagena (Table **672**). ◇ – Madrid Puerta de Atoc

671 CÓRDOBA - SEVILLA - HUELVA and CÁDIZ

km		*MD* 13000	*MD* 13002	*MD* 13030	*MD* 13099	*MD* 13079	*MD* 13037	*MD* 13020	*Alvia* 2084	*Alvia* 2294 2494	*Alvia* 2094	*MD* 13008	*Alvia* 2114	*MD* 13010	*MD* 13032	*Alvia* 2134	*MD* 13014	*MD* 13039	*MD* 13083	*Alvia* 2164	*MD* 13035	*Talgo* 697	*MD* 13394	*Alvia* 2384	*MD* 13095	*MD* 13073
		2	2	2	2	2	2	2				2		2	2		2	2	2		2		2		2	2
		①–⑤	①–⑥		⑥⑦	J	①–⑤			Q	R	①–⑤	A		①–⑤				J		J	G		Ⓑ		J
	Madrid PA ✣ **660** d.	...	...	...	...	...	...	...	0830	0945	0945	...	1105	...	...	1330	...	...	...	1615	...	...	...	1805	...	...
0	**Córdoba** **660** d.	...	...	0700t	...	0812	...	0908	1020	1132	1132	...	|	...	1400	1517	...	...	1612	|	1830	1910	...	1952	...	2010
51	Palma del Río d.	...	...	0729t	...	0845	...	0940	|	|	|	...	|	...	1431	|	...	...	1643	|	1905	|	...	|	...	2042
129	**Sevilla** **660** a.	...	...	0821t	...	0937	...	1029	1106	|	1225	...	|	...	1520	1605	...	...	1730	|	1956	2025	...	|	...	2128
129	**Sevilla** **673** § d.	0640	0745	0830	0845	0945	1000	1045	1109	|	1227	1245	|	1445	1545t	1608	1645	1700	1745	|	2010	...	2045	|	2050	2150
204	La Palma del Condado d.	|	|	|	0949	|	1108	|	|	1254	|	|	|	|	|	|	|	1758	|	|	|	...	|	2120	2149	|
244	**Huelva** a.	|	|	|	1020	|	1138	|	|	1320	|	|	|	|	|	|	|	1834	|	|	|	...	|	2145	2218	|
145	Dos Hermanas **673** § d.	0654	0758	0843	...	0958	...	1058	|	...	|	1258	|	1500	1559t	|	1658	...	1758	|	2023	...	2058	...	...	2203
162	Utrera § d.	0705	|	0854	...	|	...	1108	|	...	|	1308	|	|	1609t	|	|	...	1808	|	|	...	2109	...	...	2213
224	Aeropuerto de Jerez ▲ d.	0739	|	0929	...	|	...	1143	|	...	|	1345	|	1540	|	|	1741	...	1844	|	|	...	|	...	...	2248
236	Jerez de la Frontera ▲ d.	0746	0846	0936	...	1047	...	1151	1204	...	1321	1353	1432	1548	1651t	1705	1749	...	1852	1934	2113	...	2148	...	...	2256
251	Puerto de Santa María d.	0756	0855	0946	...	1057	...	1200	1213	...	1331	1402	1442	1558	1700t	1714	1758	...	1901	1943	2122	...	2157	...	...	2305
270	San Fernando - Bahía Sur d.	0809	0911	1002	...	1112	...	1214	1228	...	1348	1418	1459	1615	1714t	1729	1813	...	1917	1958	2137	...	2212	...	...	2321
285	**Cádiz** a.	0826	0923	1013	...	1126	...	1226	1238	...	1400	1430	1510	1627	1726t	1740	1825	...	1930	2010	2150	...	2223	...	...	2335

	MD 13001	*MD* 13041	*Talgo* 694	*MD* 13003	*Alvia* 2285	*Alvia* 2085	*MD* 13005	*MD* 13007	*Alvia* 2205	*Alvia* 2115	*MD* 13009	*MD* 13011	*Alvia* 2135	*MD* 13393	*MD* 13013	*MD* 13043	*Alvia* 2115	*MD* 13015	*Alvia* 2365	*Alvia* 2175	*IC* 2375	*MD* 13017	*MD* 13031	*MD* 13049	*Alvia* 2195	*MD* 13019
	2 J	2		2	D		2	2	H		2	2 J		2	2	2		2				2	2	2		2
	①–⑤		G	M	①–⑤			①–⑤	⑥	A	J				①–⑤		R		⑦		C	J			B	
Cádiz d.	0540	...	...	0630	...	0815	0840	0940	...	1050	1140	1240t	1330	1412	1440	...	1505	1540	...	1728	...	1740	1840	...	1855	1940
San Fernando - Bahía Sur d.	0553	...	...	0641	...	0827	0851	0951	...	1102	1151	1251t	1342	1423	1451	...	1518	1551	...	1740	...	1751	1851	...	1907	1951
Puerto de Santa María d.	0608	...	...	0656	...	0840	0905	1006	...	1116	1206	1306t	1355	1436	1506	...	1535	1606	...	1754	...	1805	1905	...	1921	2006
Jerez de la Frontera ▲ d.	0617	...	...	0705	...	0850	0914	1015	...	1126	1215	1315t	1405	1445	1515	...	1545	1615	...	1805	...	1814	1914	...	1931	2015
Aeropuerto de Jerez ▲ d.	0624	...	...	0713	...	|	|	1023	...	|	1223	|	|	|	1523	...	|	1623	...	|	...	1822	1921	...	|	|
Utrera § d.	0702	...	...	0751	...	|	|	|	...	|	|	1356t	|	1525	|	...	|	1700	...	|	...	|	|	...	|	2102
Dos Hermanas **673** § d.	0712	...	...	0801	...	|	1005	1107	...	|	1306	1406t	|	1535	1606	...	|	1710	...	|	...	1906	2005	...	|	2112
Huelva d.	|	0655	...	|	0800	|	|	|	1025	|	|	|	|	|	|	1500	|	|	1620	|	1820	|	|	1900	|	|
La Palma del Condado d.	|	0725	...	|	0824	|	|	|	1047	|	|	|	|	|	|	1530	|	|	1647	|	1844	|	|	1930	|	|
Sevilla **673** § a.	0728	0825	...	0816	|	0947	1020	1120	|	|	1320	1420t	1458	1549	1620	1627	1640	1725	|	|	|	1920	2017	2030	2033	2128
Sevilla **660** d.	0740	...	0835	0838	|	0950	...	...	|	|	1330	1503	1500	...	...	...	1643	1735	|	|	|	1940	2030	...	2036	...
Palma del Río d.	0828	...	|	0926	|	|	...	...	|	|	1415	1551	|	...	...	...	|	1824	|	|	|	2027	2117	...	|	...
Córdoba **660** a.	0904	...	0945	1000	0948	1040	...	...	1216	|	1449	1624	1552	...	...	...	1729	1587	1810	|	2009	2102	2148	...	2125	...
Madrid PA ✣ **660** a.	...	...	...	...	1140	1233	...	...	1410	1455	...	...	1748	...	...	...	1920	...	2001	2127	2159	...	...	...	2314	...

A – ④⑤⑦ (daily June 12 - Sept. 11).
B – ⑤⑦ (④⑤⑦ June 12 - Sept. 11).
C – Ⓑ June 12 - Sept. 4.
D – Until July 24 and from Sept. 5.
G – TORRE DEL ORO – [12] 🍸 Barcelona - València - Córdoba - Sevilla and v.v. (Tables **661**, **668a**, **672**).
H – ⑥ (①–⑥ July 26 - Sept. 4).
J – From / to Jaén (Table **661**).

M – To Jaén on ⑥⑦ (Table **661**).
Q – Runs 55 minutes later July 25 - Sept 4.
R – July 25 - Sept 4.
t – ①–⑤.

✣ – Madrid Puerta de Atocha.
§ – Frequent suburban services operate Sevilla - Utrera and v.v.
▲ – Additional suburban services operate Jerez de la Frontera - Aeropuerto de Jerez and v.v.: depart Aeropuerto 0720 Ⓐ, 0820 Ⓒ, 1325, 1920; depart Jerez 0657 Ⓐ, 0757 Ⓒ, 1257, 1857.

BARCELONA - VALÈNCIA - ALACANT - CARTAGENA 672

	MD 14123	Alvia 4111				Em 1071	Em 1081		Talgo 697	Em 1101		Talgo 1111			Talgo 463			MD 18523	Em 1341	Talgo 165			Em 1161	
	2	①-⑥	2 ①-⑤	2 ⑥	2 ①-⑥	①-⑥		2			2		2 Ⓑ	2	♀	2	2	Ⓡ 2	Ⓑ		2 ⑤	2		2 ①-⑤
		G							T					✣				p						
Barcelona França d.	...	...	...	...	0548	0630	0730	0747	0904	0930	0919	...	...	1047	...	...	1247	...	1330	...	...	1446	1530	1618
Barcelona Passeig de Gràcia d.	...	...	...	...	0556	|	|	0756	|	|	0927	...	...	1055	...	...	1256	...	|	...	...	1456	|	1626
Barcelona Sants 652 d.	...	...	...	...	0603	0700	0800	0803	0927	1000	0933	1100	...	1103	1200	...	1303	...	1400	1500	...	1503	1600	1633
Sant Vicenç de Calders 652 d.	...	...	...	...	0648	|	|	0848	|	|	1019	|	...	1147	|	...	1346	...	|	|	...	1547	|	|
Altafulla - Tamarit d.	...	...	...	...	0658	|	|	0859	|	|	1030	|	...	1158	|	...	1356	...	|	|	...	1558	|	|
Tarragona 652 d.	...	...	...	...	0707	0754	0856	0909	1027	1055	1041	1155	...	1207	1254	...	1405	...	1502	1556	...	1608	1657	1724
Port Aventura d.	...	...	...	...	0720	|	|	0918	|	|	1049	|	...	1216	|	...	1413	...	|	|	...	1616	|	1732
Salou d.	...	...	...	...	0724	|	|	0923	1039	|	1052	1206	...	1219	1307	...	1417	...	|	1607	...	1620	|	1736
Tortosa d.	...	...	0645	0751	|	|	|	|	|	|	|	|	...	|	|	1325	|	...	|	|	...	|	|	|
L'Aldea - Amposta d.	...	...	0658	0806	0807	|	|	1006	1107	|	1138	1242	...	1302	1335	1337	1502	...	|	1634	...	1710	|	1815
Tortosa a.	...	...	|	|	0817	|	|	1015	|	|	1149	|	...	1312	|	|	1512	...	|	|	...	1720	|	1824
Vinaròs d.	...	...	0720	0828	...	|	|	...	1122	|	1227	1259	...	...	1350	1401	...	...	|	1650	...	...	|	...
Benicarló - Peñíscola d.	...	...	0726	0833	...	|	|	...	1129	|	1233	1304	...	...	1355	1407	...	...	|	1656	...	...	|	...
Benicàssim d.	...	...	0804	0914	...	|	|	...	|	|	1310	1334	...	...	1419	1444	...	...	|	1723	...	...	|	...
Castelló de la Plana d.	...	0717	0815	0922	...	0919	1012	...	1158	1217	1319	1346	...	...	1427	1453	...	...	1627	1734	...	...	1818	...
València Nord a.	...	0814r	0913	1025	...	1012r	1109r	...	1247	1308r	1418	1440	...	...	1525	1553	...	...	1727r	1828	...	...	1918r	...
València Nord 668 d.	0717	0820r	...	...	...	1025r	...	...	1252	1318r	...	1450k	1502	...	1535	...	...	1635	...	1838	1705	...	1932r	...
Xàtiva 668 d.	0753	|	...	...	...	|	...	...	1332	|	...	1529k	1539	...	1615	...	...	1711	...	1913	1744	...	|	...
Madrid P de Atocha 668 a.	|	1020	...	...	...	|	...	...	|	|	...	|	|	...	|	...	...	|	...	|	|	...	|	...
Sevilla 671 a.	|	...	...	...	...	|	...	...	2025	|	...	|	|	...	|	...	...	|	...	|	|	...	|	...
Elda - Petrer d.	0840	...	...	...	...	|	...	...	...	|	...	1623k	1632	...	1657	...	...	1757	...	1954	1839	...	|	...
Alacant a.	0908	...	...	...	...	1202	...	...	...	1455	...	1658k	1704	...	1727	...	...	1823	...	2020	1914	...	2108	...
Alacant ¦ d.	0916	...	...	...	...	...	...	...	...	...	...	...	...	...	1745	...	...	1830	...	2035	...	...	...	...
Murcia 668a ¦ a.	1043	...	...	...	...	...	...	...	...	...	...	...	...	...	1859	...	...	1941	...	2147	...	...	...	...
Lorca Sutullena ¦ a.	...	...	...	...	...	...	...	...	...	...	...	...	...	...	2006	...	...	|	...	|	...	...	...	...
Cartagena 668a ¦ a.	...	...	...	...	...	...	...	...	...	...	...	...	...	...	...	...	...	2033	...	2245	...	...	...	...

	Talgo 1171		Em 11571 1571	Em 1181		Em 1191	Talgo 1391		Hotel 897		
		2	Ⓑ		2	Ⓑ		2	✗ A❦	2	
Barcelona França d.	...	...	...	1730	1748	...	...	1917	...	2046	...
Barcelona Passeig de Gràcia d.	...	...	...	|	1756	...	...	1925	...	2056	...
Barcelona Sants 652 d.	1700	...	1730	1800	1803	1900	1930	1933	2000	2103	...
Sant Vicenç de Calders 652 d.	|	...	|	|	1848	|	|	2017	|	2147	...
Altafulla - Tamarit d.	|	...	|	|	1900	|	|	2029	|	2159	...
Tarragona 652 d.	1755	...	1820	1855	1909	1955	2025	2040	2059	2208	...
Port Aventura d.	|	...	|	|	1923	|	2033	2050	|	2219	...
Salou d.	1807	...	|	|	1927	|	2038	2055	2116	2223	...
Tortosa d.	|	1840	|	|	|	|	|	|	|	|	...
L'Aldea - Amposta d.	1845	1857	|	|	2017	|	2115	2142	|	2306	...
Tortosa a.	|	|	|	|	2028	|	|	2151	|	2316	...
Vinaròs d.	1901	1919	|	|	...	|	2131	...	|	...	...
Benicarló - Peñíscola d.	1913	1923	|	|	...	|	2137	...	|	...	...
Benicàssim d.	1940	2007	|	|	...	|	2205	...	|	...	...
Castelló de la Plana d.	1952	2020	1944	2017	...	2127	2214	...	2236	...	...
València Nord a.	2043	2123	2039r	2109r	...	2222r	2312	...	2325	...	...
València Nord 668 d.	2055	...	...	2119r	...	...	...	...	2340	...	...
Xàtiva 668 d.	2131	...	...	|	...	...	...	...	|	...	...
Granada 661 a.	|	...	...	|	...	...	...	...	0755	...	...
Elda - Petrer d.	2219	...	...	|	...	...	...	...	...	...	...
Alacant a.	2247	...	...	2257	...	...	...	...	...	...	...
Alacant ¦ d.	2302	...	...	...	...	...	...	...	...	...	...
Murcia 668a ¦ a.	0008	...	...	...	...	...	...	...	...	...	...
Cartagena 668a ¦ a.	...	...	...	...	...	...	...	...	...	...	...

		Hotel 894	Em 1262		Em 11472 1472		Em 1282	
	2 ①-⑤	✗ A❦	①-⑤	2	①-⑥	2		2
Cartagena 668a ¦ d.	...	...	...	...	...	...	...	...
Murcia 668a ¦ d.	...	...	...	...	...	...	...	...
Alacant ¦ a.	...	...	...	...	...	...	...	...
Alacant d.	...	...	...	...	...	...	0640	...
Elda - Petrer d.	...	...	...	...	...	...	|	...
Granada 661 d.	...	2130	...	...	...	...	|	...
Xàtiva 668 d.	...	|	...	...	...	...	|	...
València Nord 668 a.	...	0410	...	...	...	...	0812r	...
València Nord d.	...	0425	0620r	...	0726r	...	0822r	0815
Castelló de la Plana d.	...	0521	0710	...	0818	...	0917	0935
Benicàssim d.	...	|	|	...	|	...	|	0943
Benicarló - Peñíscola d.	...	|	|	...	|	...	|	1020
Vinaròs d.	...	|	|	...	|	...	|	1026
Tortosa d.	0605	|	|	0748	|	0918	|	|
L'Aldea - Amposta d.	0616	|	|	0800	|	0930	|	1050
Tortosa a.	|	|	|	|	|	|	|	1102
Salou d.	0656	0650	|	0843	|	1014	|	...
Port Aventura d.	0659	|	|	0845	|	1017	|	...
Tarragona 652 d.	0711	0705	0837	0856	0932	1027	1042	...
Altafulla - Tamarit d.	|	|	|	0904	|	1035	|	...
Sant Vicenç de Calders 652 d.	|	|	|	0917	|	1049	|	...
Barcelona Sants 652 a.	0809	0839	0940	1005	1040	1140	1146	...
Barcelona Passeig de Gràcia a.	0815	...	|	1014	...	1145	|	...
Barcelona França a.	0823	...	1008	1023	...	1153	1207	...

		Talgo 1102	Em 1112	①-⑤	MD 18504	Talgo 460		Talgo 1142	Em 1152		Em 1162		Talgo 694	Talgo 264			Em 1182	Em 1192		Talgo 1202	Talgo 1212	MD 14202		Alvia 4140
	2			2	①-⑥ 2f	♀	2		Ⓑ	2		2	T		2	2	⊠	Ⓑ	2 Ⓑ	①-⑥	⑦	2	2 Ⓑ	Ⓑ G
Cartagena 668a ¦ d.	...	...	...	...	0740z	...	...	...	...	...	...	...	...	1255	...	...	...	...	...	...	...	1638	...	...
Lorca Sutullena ¦ d.	...	...	...	...	|	0828	...	...	...	...	...	...	...	|	...	...	...	...	...	...	...	|	...	...
Murcia 668a ¦ d.	...	0630k	...	...	0838	0934	...	...	...	...	...	...	...	1354	...	...	...	...	...	...	1647	1735	...	...
Alacant ¦ a.	...	0744k	...	...	0955	1052	...	...	...	...	...	...	...	1502	...	...	...	...	...	...	1804	1846	...	...
Alacant d.	...	0800	0913	...	1003	1108	...	...	...	...	1353	...	...	1516	...	...	1610	...	...	1838	1838	1856	1930	...
Elda - Petrer d.	...	0828	...	...	1032	1137	...	...	...	...	|	...	...	1540	...	...	|	...	...	1905	1905	1925	2004	...
Sevilla 671 d.	...	|	...	...	|	|	...	...	...	...	|	...	0835	|	...	...	|	...	...	|	|	|	|	...
Madrid P de Atocha 668 d.	...	|	...	...	|	|	...	...	...	...	|	...	|	|	...	...	|	...	...	|	|	|	|	2010
Xàtiva 668 d.	...	0917	...	...	1120	1216	...	...	...	...	|	...	1524	1620	...	...	|	...	...	1945	1945	2014	2059	|
València Nord 668 a.	...	0955	1043r	...	1156	1251	...	...	...	...	1536r	...	1602	1658	...	...	1749r	...	...	2021	2021	2048	2139	2210r
València Nord d.	...	1005	1053r	...	...	1303	...	1345	1450r	1445	1544r	...	1610	1711	...	1648	1756r	1847r	2005	2035	2035	...	...	2220r
Castelló de la Plana d.	...	1101	1145	...	...	1359	...	1439	1546	1601	1641	...	1703	1804	...	1800	1851	1943	2105	2129	2129	...	...	2320
Benicàssim d.	...	1108	|	...	...	1407	...	1447	|	1610	|	...	|	1812	...	1808	|	|	2113	2136	2136	...	...	...
Benicarló - Peñíscola d.	...	1137	|	...	...	1432	...	1519	|	1651	|	...	1734	1839	...	1851	|	|	2149	2204	2204	...	...	...
Vinaròs d.	...	1143	|	...	...	1437	...	1525	|	1656	|	...	1740	1845	...	1857	|	|	2155	2210	2210	...	...	...
Tortosa d.	1049	|	|	1345	...	|	1554	|	|	|	|	1725	|	|	1850	1936	|	|	|	|	|	...	...	...
L'Aldea - Amposta d.	1059	1158	|	1355	...	1453	1605	1541	|	1721	|	1735	1755	1902	1903	1950	|	|	2220	2227	2227	...	...	...
Tortosa a.	|	|	|	|	...	|	|	|	|	1736	|	|	|	|	|	|	|	|	2235	|	|	...	...	...
Salou d.	1140	1225	|	1431	...	1527	1645	1619	|	...	|	1818	1828	1951	1943	2039	|	|	...	2258	2258	...	...	...
Port Aventura d.	1143	1229	|	1434	...	|	1647	|	|	...	|	1821	|	|	1947	2041	|	|	...	|	|	...	...	...
Tarragona 652 d.	1154	1240	1312	1445	...	1539	1658	1639	1713	...	1803	1830	1841	2004	1957	2100	2027	2108	...	2310	2310	...	...	...
Altafulla - Tamarit d.	|	|	|	|	...	|	1706	|	|	...	|	1838	|	|	2005	2108	|	|	...	|	|	...	...	...
Sant Vicenç de Calders 652 d.	1216	|	|	|	...	|	1718	|	|	...	|	1849	|	|	2017	2118	|	|	...	|	|	...	...	...
Barcelona Sants 652 a.	1305	1340	1409	1539	...	1640	1805	1740	1810	...	1910	1935	1939	2110	2105	2205	2137	2210	...	2359	2359	...	...	...
Barcelona Passeig de Gràcia a.	1313	...	|	1545	...	...	1814	...	...	...	|	1944	|	...	2111	2214	|	|	...	...	...	...	...	...
Barcelona França a.	1322	...	1435	1553	...	...	1822	...	...	...	1937	1953	2005	...	2120	2222	2208	2238	...	...	...	...	...	...

Murcia – Cartagena

	Ⓐ	Ⓐ		Alta 222	Ⓐ	Alta 228	Ⓐ	MD 18523	Alta 224	Talgo 165	Alta 226	
	2	2	2	m	2	Cm	2	p2	m		Ⓑm	
Murcia d.	0745	0950	1150	1326	1443	1645	1745	1948	2050	2202	2331	...
Cartagena a.	0834	1040	1240	1412	1536	1728	1840	2033	2138	2245	0017	...

	Alta 221	MD 18504	Alta 223		Alta 229	Talgo 264	Ⓐ	Alta 225	MD 14202	Alta 227	Ⓐ	Ⓐ	Ⓒ
	Ⓐm	Ⓐf	m	2	⑦m		2	m	2	Ⓑm	2	2	2
Cartagena d.	0530	0740	0850	1050	1215	1255	1438	1600	1638	1820	1938	2110	2205
Murcia a.	0608	0830	0934	1140	1256	1340	1528	1645	1726	1902	2030	2205	2257

ALHAMBRA *Trenhotel* – 🛏, ▭ (reclining) Barcelona - Granada and v.v. **Service currently suspended.**

Ⓑ (daily Aug. 1-29).

To/from Gijón (Tables **681**, **685**).

June 22 - Sept. 12.

TORRE DEL ORO – ▭ ♀ Barcelona - Sevilla and v.v. (Tables **661**, **668a**, **671**).

To Zaragoza (Table **670**).

k – ①-⑥.

m – From/to Madrid (Table **668a**).

p – From Zaragoza (Table **670**).

r – València **Joaquín Sorolla**. Free 🚌 to València Nord.

x – Also ⑥ Aug. 1-29.

y – Also Mar. 25, May 2.

z – ①-⑤.

✣ – On ①-⑤ runs 16 - 28 minutes later and does not call at Sant Vicenç de Calders and Altafulla - Tamarit.

¦ – Additional local trains operate between these stations.

❦ – Service currently suspended.

673 SEVILLA and ALGECIRAS - MÁLAGA, GRANADA and ALMERÍA 2nd

For trains **Sevilla** – **Málaga** and v.v. via **Córdoba**, see Table **660**. **Buses replace trains between Antequera - Santa Ana and Granada until further notice**

km		MD 13920	MD 13063	MD 13900	Alta 9367		MD 13902	MD 13922	MD 13065	MD 13904	MD 13906 ⑤⑦	Alta 9331	MD 13924	MD 13061	MD 13077	MD 13908	MD 13926		MD 13910	
0	**Sevilla** ¶ d.	0635	...	0740	...	...	1100	1145	...	1308	1510	...	1555	...	...	1725	1756	...	2005	...
15	Dos Hermanas ¶ d.	0650u	...	0754u	...	...	1114u	1159u	...	1322u	1524u	...	1612u	...	...	1739u	1812u	...	2019u	...
	Algeciras d.	|	0615	|	0843	...	|	|	1145	|	|	1503	|	...	1530	|	|	...	|	...
	San Roque - La Línea d.	|	0630	|	0858	...	|	|	1201	|	|	1518	|	...	1546	|	|	...	|	...
	Ronda d.	|	0753	|	1009	...	|	|	1336	|	|	1631	|	1650	1713	|	|	...	|	...
167	Bobadilla **661** d.	|	0846	0919	|	...	1243	|	1429	1448	1645	|	|	1739	1801	1905	|	...	2145	...
236	**Málaga** M. Zambrano **661** a.	|	|	1015	|	...	1336	|	|	1547	1736	|	|	1850	|	1955	|	...	2236	...
	Antequera - Santa Ana § a.	0817	0856	...	|	...	...	1336	1440	...	...	1733	1737	...	1811	...	1940	...	...	...
	Madrid Pta de Atocha **660** a.	|	|	...	1405	...	...	|	|	...	...	2035	|	...	|	...	|	...	...	...
183	Antequera - Ciudad d.	*0836*¦	*0915*¦	...	...	...	...	*1356*¦	*1459*¦	...	...	...	*1757*¦	...	*1828*¦	...	*2000*¦	...	...	...
290	**Granada** **661** d.	*1002*¦	*1055*¦	...	...	...	...	*1512*¦	*1610*¦	...	...	...	*1915*¦	...	*1945*¦	...	*2116*¦	...	...	...
372	Guadix **661** d.	1111	...	...	...	...	...	1621	...	...	...	...	2019	...	...	...	2224	...	...	...
471	**Almería** **661** a.	1223	...	...	...	...	...	1746	...	...	...	...	2136	...	...	...	2343	...	...	...

km		MD 13062	MD 13901	MD 13941	MD 13057	Alta 9366	MD 13903	MD 13943		MD 13064	MD 13905		MD 13907	Alta 9330	MD 13076	MD 13945	MD 13909 ⑤⑦	MD 13911	MD 13947	
0	**Almería** **661** d.	...	...	0615	...	...	...	0900	...	...	...	...	...	...	...	1500	...	...	1815	...
99	Guadix **661** d.	...	...	0735	...	...	...	1014	...	...	...	...	...	...	...	1616	...	...	1939	...
181	**Granada** d.	*0645*¦	...	*0843*¦	...	...	...	*1124*¦	...	*1245*¦	...	...	...	...	*1700*¦	*1732*¦	...	...	*2056*¦	...
288	Antequera - Ciudad d.	*0750*¦	...	*0955*¦	...	...	...	*1236*¦	...	*1402*¦	...	...	...	...	*1807*¦	*1841*¦	...	...	*2202*¦	...
	Madrid Pta de Atocha **660** d.	|	...	|	...	0835	...	|	...	|	...	...	...	1505	|	|	...	...	|	...
	Antequera - Santa Ana § d.	0818	...	1018	...	1118	...	1259	...	1440	...	...	...	1754	1840	1902	...	...	2225	...
	Málaga M. Zambrano **661** d.	|	0740	|	1005	|	1040	|	...	|	1408	...	1648	|	|	|	1900	2005	|	...
304	Bobadilla **661** d.	0826	0835	|	1104	|	1129	|	...	1452	1502	...	1747	|	1847	|	1956	2057	|	...
376	Ronda d.	0918	|	|	1156	1221	|	|	...	1546	|	...	|	1858	1940	|	|	|	|	...
468	San Roque - La Línea d.	1045	|	|	...	1335	|	|	...	1725	|	...	|	2016	2102	|	|	|	|	...
480	**Algeciras** a.	1100	|	|	...	1348	|	|	...	1740	|	...	|	2030	2117	|	|	|	|	...
456	Dos Hermanas ¶ a.	...	1002s	1147s	...	...	1252s	1423s	...	...	1626s	...	1917s	...	...	2028s	2118s	2226s	2352s	...
471	**Sevilla** ¶ a.	...	1019	1207	...	...	1310	1443	...	...	1641	...	1933	...	...	2044	2135	2241	0008	...

s – Calls to set down only.
u – Calls to pick up only.
§ – ± *17 km* from Antequera.
¦ – 🚌 Antequera-Santa Ana - Antequera-Ciudad - Granada and v.v. Until further notice.
¶ – Frequent suburban services run Sevilla - Dos Hermanas and v.v.

674 PALMA DE MALLORCA - INCA - SA POBLA and MANACOR SFM 2nd c

For services between Inca and sa Pobla, and Inca and Manacor change at Enllaç (5 *km* from Inca, 34 *km* from Palma)

km		Ⓐ	Ⓐ ◧		Ⓐ	Ⓒ	Ⓐ ◧		Ⓐ	Ⓒ	Ⓐ ◧		Ⓐ	Ⓒ	Ⓐ		and at the same minutes past each hour until		Ⓐ	Ⓒ	Ⓐ		Ⓐ	Ⓒ	Ⓒ
0	**Palma** d.	0545	0607	0615**x**	0635	0640	0650	0715**x**	0735	0740	0750	0815**x**	0835	0840	0855	0915**x**		2015**x**	2035	2040	2055	2115**x**	2135	2140	2210
7	Marratxi d.	0600	0615	0623	0643	0655	0658	0723	0743	0754	0758	0823	0843	0854	0903	0923		2023	2043	2054	2103	2123	2143	2154	2225
29	**Inca** d.	0625	0632	0644	0704	0720	0715	0744	0804	0815	0815	0844	0904	0915	0923	0944		2044	2104	2115	2123	2144	2204	2215	2250
*****	sa Pobla a.	0642	...	|	*0723*	0736	...	|	*0823*	*0834*	...	|	*0923*	*0934*	...	|		|	*2123*	*2134*	...	|	*2223*	*2234*	|
64	**Manacor** a.	...	...	*0718*	...	...	...	*0818*	...	...	...	*0916*	...	...	...	*1016*		*2116*	...	...	...	*2216*	...	...	2320

	Ⓐ	Ⓐ ◧		Ⓐ	Ⓐ ◧		Ⓐ	Ⓒ	Ⓐ ◧		Ⓐ	Ⓒ	Ⓐ		Ⓐ	Ⓒ	and at the same minutes past each hour until	Ⓐ		Ⓐ	Ⓒ	Ⓐ		Ⓐ	Ⓒ
Manacor d.	...	...	*0623*	...	*0659*	*0723*	...	...	...	*0823*	...	...	...	*0923*	...	...		...	*2023*	...	...	...	*2123*	...	...
sa Pobla d.	...	...	|	*0656*	|	|	*0756*	*0807*	...	|	*0856*	*0907*	...	|	*0956*	*1007*		...	|	*2056*	*2107*	...	|	*2156*	*2207*
Inca d.	0621	0650	0656	0716	0733	0756	0816	0827	0833	0856	0916	0927	0936	0956	1016	1027		2036	2056	2116	2127	2136	2156	2216	2227
Marratxi d.	0645	0707	0716	0736	0750	0816	0836	0847	0850	0916	0936	0947	0956	1016	1036	1047		2056	2116	2136	2147	2156	2216	2236	2247
Palma a.	0653	0715	0724**z**	0744	0758	0824**z**	0844	0901	0858	0924**z**	0944	1001	1004	1024**z**	1044	1101		2104	2124**z**	2144	2201	2204	2224**z**	2253	2301

x – 5 minutes earlier on Ⓒ.
z – 7 minutes later on Ⓒ.
◧ – Incaexprés.
*** – *19 km* Inca - sa Pobla.
Operator: Serveis Ferroviaris de Mallorca (SFM) ✆ +34 971 752 245

PALMA DE MALLORCA - SÓLLER *28 km* Journey time: 55 minutes. **Operator**: Ferrocarril de Sóller (FS) ✆ +34 971 752 051.

Nov. - Mar.: 1030, 1250, 1510, 1800. Apr. - Oct.: 1010, 1050, 1215, 1330, 1510, 1930.

SÓLLER - PALMA DE MALLC

Nov. - Mar.: 0900, 1140, 1400, 1700. Apr. - Oct.: 0900, 1050, 1215, 1400,

A connecting tram service operates **Sóller - Port de Sóller**. *5 km*. Journey time: 15–20 minutes. Not all services shown.

From Sóller: 0800, 0900, 1000, 1100, 1200, 1300, 1400, 1500, 1600, 1700, 1800, 1900.
From Port de Sóller: 0830, 0930, 1025, 1130, 1230, 1325, 1430, 1530, 1630, 1730, 1830, 1930.

675 🚌 MÁLAGA and ALGECIRAS - LA LÍNEA (for Gibraltar)

There are no cross-border 🚌 services: passengers to / from Gibraltar must cross the frontier on foot (walking-time about 5 minutes) and transfer to / from Gibraltar local 🚌 services

🚌 **MÁLAGA** bus stn – **LA LÍNEA** bus station (for **Gibraltar**)

From Málaga: 0700, 1130 ▽, 1400, 1630, 1915 ⑦.
From La Línea: 0850, 1030, 1630 ▽, 1900, 2045 ⑦.

Journey time: 3 hours. Operator: Automóviles Portillo, Málaga ✆ (+34) 902 020 052.

▽ – Journey operated by Alsina Graells (see Table **664** for contact details).

🚌 **ALGECIRAS** bus station - **LA LÍNEA** bus station (for **Gibraltar**) Route M-120

From Algeciras: Ⓐ: 0700 and every 30 minutes until 2130, also 2230.
⑥: every 45 mins 0700 – 2115, also 2230. †: every 45 mins 0800 – 2130, also 2230.
From La Línea: Ⓐ: 0700, 0745 and every 30 minutes until 2215, also 2315.
⑥: every 45 mins 0700 – 2200, also 2315. †: 0700, 0845 then every 45 mins until 2215, also

Journey time: 45 mins. Operator: Transportes Generales Comes SA, Algeciras ✆ (+34) 902 45C

676 🚌 SEVILLA - AYAMONTE - FARO - LAGOS DAMA

	Summer				Ⓐ	Ⓒ		Ⓐ	†	⑥	Ⓐ	Winter	Ⓐ	Ⓒ	⚒		⑥	Ⓐ		†	Ⓐ	⑥	†
Sevilla ⊖ d.	July 1 -	0730	0930	1130	*1230*	*1330*	1530	1800	1900	2000	2030	Sept. 1 -	0730	*0730*	0930	1130	1300	*1300*	1530	*1630*	*1730*	1730	1900
Huelva d.	Aug. 31	0900	1100	1300	1400	1500	1700	1930	2030	2130	2200	June 30,	0900	0900	1100	1300	1430	1530	1700	1900	1900	1900	2030
Ayamonte a.		1015	1215	1415	1500	1600	1815	2045	2145	2245	2315	2016	1000	1000	1200	1400	1530	1630	1800	2000	2000	2000	2130

	Summer	⚒	Ⓑ		⚒	Ⓐ	⑥	†	Ⓐ	⑦		Winter	⚒	Ⓐ			Ⓐ	⑥	†	Ⓐ	⑥	⑥	Ⓑ
Ayamonte d.	June 28 -	0640	0830	0930	1145	1400	1515	1615	1715	1730	1945	Sept. 1 -	0645	0830	0930	1145	1400	1500	1515	1545	1615	1715	1730
Huelva d.	Aug. 31	0740	0930	1030**z**	1245	1500	1645	1715	1815	1830	2045	June 30,	0745	0945	1030	1245	1500	1600	1615	1645	1715	1815	1830
Sevilla ⊖ a.		0910	*1115*	1215**z**	*1515*	1645	1815	1845	1945	*2015*	2215	2016	0915	*1115*	1215	*1415*	*1645*	1715	1745	1815	1845	1945	*2045*

⛴ **Ayamonte - Vila Real de Santo António Guadiana** Journey time: 10 minutes. ✆ (+34) 959 470 617. Sept. 16 - Mar. 31: hourly (from Ayamonte 1000 - 1900 ⚒, 1100 - 1700, 18 Apr. 1 - June 30: hourly (from Ayamonte 1000 - 2000 ⚒, 1100 - 1700, 1815 †). July 1 - Sept. 15: every 30 mins (from Ayamonte 0930 - 2100 ⚒, 1000 - 1900, 2015 †).

INTERNATIONAL 🚌 SERVICE Joint EVA △ / DAMAS ☆ service *for international journeys only* No service Dec. 25, Jan. 1

	→ Winter Sept. 7 - June 30, 2016			→ Summer June 27 - Sept. 6				
Sevilla, Plaza de Armas ⊖ d.		0730	1615		0730	0930	1400	1615
Huelva d.		0845	1730		0845	1100	1515	1730
Ayamonte 🏛 ES d.		0930	|		|	1200	|	
Vila Real de Santo António 🏛 PT a.		|	1740		|	|	|	1740
Faro, Av. da República a.		0955	1855		0920	1240	1550	1855
Albufeira, Alto dos Caliços a.		1040	1940		1000	1325	1630	1940
Portimão, Largo do Dique a.		1115	2015		|	1400	|	2015
Lagos, Rossio de S. João a.		1145	2045		1045	1430	1715	2045

	→ Winter Sept. 7 - June 30, 2016			→ Summer June 27 - Sept. 6			
Lagos, Rossio de S. João d.		0630	1345		0700	0630	1230
Portimão, Largo do Dique d.		0700	1415		|	0700	|
Albufeira, Alto dos Caliços d.		0735	1450		0745	0735	1315
Faro, Av. da República d.		0820	1535		0825	0820	1355
Vila Real de Santo António 🏛 PT d.		0935	|		|	0935	|
Ayamonte 🏛 ES a.		|	1800		|	|	|
Huelva a.		1145	1850		|	1145	1630
Sevilla, Plaza de Armas ⊖ a.		1300	2000		1145	1300	1745

r – 30 minutes later on ⚒.
z – 30 minutes later on Ⓒ.
☆ – DAMAS, Huelva ✆ +34 959 256 900. www.damas-sa.es
△ – EVA, Faro ✆ +351 289 899 700. www.eva-bus.com
⊖ – Sevilla Plaza de Armas bus station (± 2 km from Santa Justa rail station).
ES – Spain (Central European Time).
PT – Portugal (West European Time).
Huelva bus station is ± 1 km from the rail station.
Ayamonte bus station is ± 1.5 km from the ferry termir

MADRID - CÁCERES - BADAJOZ 677

	MD 13084					17905	17014	17028	MD 17900	MD 17902		17702			MD 17012	MD 17194		17018		17706		
	2	2	2	2	2	2	2	2	2	2	2	2	2	2	2	2		2		2		
	①–⑥	Ⓐ	Ⓐ	Ⓒ		Ⓐ	①–⑥	T	⑤⑥⑦	①–④			Ⓐ	Ⓑ				Ⓑ				
Madrid Chamartín d.	...	...	...	...	...	...	...	...	...	...	...	...	...	...	...	1604	...	...	...	...	...	...
Madrid Atocha Cercanías d.	...	...	...	...	...	...	0807	...	1018	1018	...	1228	...	...	1430	1623	...	1827	...	2043	...	...
Villaverde Bajo **669** d.	...	...	...	...	...	...	|	...	|	|	...	1236	...	...	|	|	...	|	...	2051	...	...
Talavera de la Reina d.	...	...	...	...	...	...	0937	...	1154	1154	...	1408	...	...	1614	1755	...	2004	...	2218	...	...
Navalmoral de La Mata d.	...	...	...	...	...	...	1016	...	1230	1230	...	...	...	...	1652	1833	...	2039	...	...	...	...
Plasencia a.	...	...	...	...	...	...	1107	...	1310	1310	...	...	...	...	1740	|	...	2123	...	...	...	...
Plasencia d.	...	...	...	...	...	0708	1110	...	1313	1313	...	...	...	...	1743z	|	...	2126	...	...	...	...
Cáceres d.	...	0650	...	0805	...	0818	1219	1220	1416	1416	...	...	1640	...	1843z	2003	...	2235	...	...	...	...
San Vicente de Alcántara d.	...	|	...	|	...	|	|	1333	|	|	...	...	|	...	...	|	...	...	...	...	...	...
Valencia de Alcántara d.	...	|	...	|	...	|	|	1348	|	|	...	...	|	...	...	|	...	...	...	...	...	...
Mérida a.	...	0746	...	0901	...	0921	1317	...	1517	1517	...	...	1733	...	...	2100	...	...	...	...	...	...
Mérida **678** d.	...	0754	0754	0910	0910	...	1320	...	1522	1522	1524	...	1741	1751	...	2105	...	...	...	...	...	...
Badajoz **678** a.	...	|	0841	|	1006	...	1405	...	|	|	1603	...	|	1842	...	2145	...	...	...	...	...	...
Zafra d.	...	0843	...	0959	...	...	...	...	1615	1614	...	...	1829	...	...	...	...	...	...	...	...	...
Sevilla a.	...	1133	...	1247	...	...	...	...	|	...	...	...	...	...	...	...	...	...	...	...	...	...
Fregenal de la Sierra d.	...	...	...	...	...	...	...	...	1655	...	...	...	...	...	...	...	...	...	...	...	...	...
Jabugo-Galaroza d.	0735	...	...	...	...	...	...	...	1738	...	...	...	...	...	...	...	...	...	...	...	...	...
Huelva a.	0932	...	...	...	...	...	...	...	1934	...	...	...	...	...	...	...	...	...	...	...	...	...

	17703	17705	17021		MD 17197	MD 17199		17707		17026	17709	17029		MD 17907	MD 2 17907		MD 17025				MD 13089		
	2	2	2	2	2	2		2	2	2	2	2	2	2	2		2		2	2	2		
	Ⓐ	Ⓒ	①–⑥	Ⓐ	Ⓐ	Ⓒ		Ⓐ	Ⓐ		Ⓒ	T		⑤⑥⑦	①–④		Ⓑ				Ⓑ		
va d.	...	...	...	...	...	...	...	...	...	...	...	...	...	1055	...	...	...	...	...	...	1940	...	...
go-Galaroza d.	...	...	...	...	...	...	...	...	...	...	...	...	...	1252	...	...	...	...	...	...	2133	...	...
enal de la Sierra d.	...	...	...	...	...	...	...	...	...	...	...	...	...	1335	...	...	...	...	...	...	...	...	...
villa d.	...	...	...	...	...	...	...	...	...	...	...	...	...	|	...	...	...	...	...	1720	...	...	...
d.	...	...	...	0655	...	...	...	...	...	...	...	...	...	1418	1418	...	...	...	...	2002	...	...	...
dajoz **678** d.	...	...	...	|	0717	0845	...	...	1225	...	...	...	1425	|	|	...	1705	...	2010	|	...	...	...
a **678** a.	...	...	...	0742	0753	0922	...	...	1311	...	...	...	1510	1507	1507	...	1744	...	2055	2053	...	...	...
a d.	...	...	...	...	0758	0928	...	...	...	1316	...	...	...	1518	1518	...	1750	...	...	2101	...	...	...
lencia de Alcántara d.	...	...	...	...	|	|	...	...	...	|	...	1425	...	|	|	...	|	...	...	|	...	...	...
n Vicente de Alcántara d.	...	...	...	...	|	|	...	...	...	|	...	1439	...	|	|	...	|	...	...	|	...	...	...
res d.	...	...	0715	...	0854	1025	...	...	...	1416	...	1557	...	1616	1616	...	1850	...	...	2200	...	...	...
sencia a.	...	...	0821	...	|	|	...	...	...	1529	...	...	...	1718	1718	...	2004	...	...	...	...	...	...
sencia d.	...	...	0825	...	|	|	...	...	...	1531	...	...	...	1721	1721	...	2007	...	...	...	...	...	...
lmoral de La Mata d.	...	...	0907	...	1020	1152	...	...	...	1616	...	...	...	1801	1801	...	2049	...	...	...	...	...	...
vera de la Reina d.	0650	0840	0940	...	1056	1234	...	1510	...	1657	1755	...	...	1840	1840	...	2124	...	...	...	...	...	...
verde Bajo **669** a.	0814	1008	|	...	|	|	...	1636	...	|	1918	...	...	|	|	...	|	...	...	...	...	...	...
rid Atocha Cercanías a.	0827	1018	1107	...	1226	1353	...	1646	...	1828	1927	...	...	2009	2009	...	2258	...	...	...	...	...	...
rid Chamartín a.	...	...	...	...	1242	1411	...	...	...	...	...	...	...	...	...	...	...	...	...	...	...	...	...

Not ②. z – ⑤ only. * – Madrid - Cáceres via Plasencia *363 km*.

ALCÁZAR DE SAN JUAN - BADAJOZ 678

	MD 17042					MD 18183	MD 18170	MD 18330	MD 18083	18027 A
	2	2		2	2	2	2	2	2	2
					Ⓑ	h	f		k	⑦
Madrid AC § **661 668** d.	...	...	...	...	...	...	1310	...	...	...
Albacete **668a** d.	...	...	...	...	...	1148	|	...	1842	1926
Alcázar de San Juan **661** d.	0715	...	...	...	...	1300	1435	1610	1954	2050
Manzanares **661** d.	0740	...	...	...	...	1325	1500	1633	2021	2117
Ciudad Real **660** d.	0820	...	...	...	...	1406	1546	1720	2102	2157
Puertollano **660** d.	...	...	...	1140	...	...	...	1751	...	...
Cabeza del Buey d.	...	0720x	...	1323	1545z	...	...	1949	...	...
Mérida **677** d.	...	0910	...	1524	1751	...	...	2145	...	...
Badajoz **677** a.	...	1006	...	1603	1842	...	...	2227	...	...

	18024 B	MD 18081	MD 18331		MD 17041	MD 18181				MD 17043
	2	2	2		2	2	2		2	2
	①	j			f	g				
Badajoz **677** d.	...	...	0656	...	...	...	1425	...	2010	...
Mérida **677** d.	...	...	0750	...	...	...	1520	...	2104	...
Cabeza del Buey d.	...	...	0935	...	...	...	1707	...	2256	...
Puertollano **660** d.	...	...	1118	...	...	...	1854	...	...	...
Ciudad Real **660** d.	0536	1012	1158	...	1440	1625	...	...	...	2222
Manzanares **661** d.	0614	1052	1243	...	1520	1712	...	...	...	2300
Alcázar de San Juan **661** a.	0642	1117	1309	...	1545	1735	...	...	...	2327
Albacete **668a** a.	0805	1227	...	...	|	1847	...	...	...	...
Madrid AC § **661 668** a.	...	...	...	...	1717	...	...	...	...	...

⑦: 2 València - Albacete - Ciudad Real (Table **668**).
①: 2 Ciudad Real - Albacete - València (Table **668**).

From / to Madrid **Chamartin** (Table **661**).

g – To Alacant (arrive 2032).
h – From Alacant (depart 1012).
j – To Alacant (arrive 1400).
k – From Alacant (depart 1705).

x – ①–⑥.
z – ⑦ only.

§ – Madrid Atocha Cercanías.

679 MADRID - TOLEDO, SEGOVIA, VALLADOLID, SALAMANCA and EL ESCORIAL

2nd c

km		Av 8062 ①–⑤	Av 8072 ①–⑤	Av 8082	Av 8292	Av 8102	Av 8312	Av 8322		Av 8132	Av 8142 ①–⑤	Av 8152	Av 8162 ①–⑤	Av 8172	Av 8182 ①–⑤	Av 8192		Av 8212				
0	**Madrid** Puerta de Atocha d.	0650	0750	0850	0920	1020	1120	1220	...	1350	1450	1550	1650	1750	1850	1950	...	2150	...	...	...	...
75	**Toledo** a.	0723	0823	0923	0953	1051	1153	1253	...	1423	1523	1623	1723	1823	1923	2023	...	2223	...	...	...	...

	Av 8063 ①–⑤	Av 8273 ①–⑤	Av 8073 ①–⑤	Av 8283 ①–⑤		Av 8093	Av 8103		Av 8123	Av 8133		Av 8153	Av 8163 ①–⑤	Av 8173	Av 8183	Av 8193	Av 8203	Av 8213				
Toledo d.	0625	0650	0725	0755	...	0925	1025	...	1225	1325	...	1525	1618	1725	1825	1920	2025	2130	...	...	...	...
Madrid Puerta de Atocha a.	0658	0723	0758	0828	...	0958	1058	...	1258	1358	...	1558	1651	1758	1858	1953	2058	2203	...	...	...	...

km	km		Av 8069 ①–⑤	Av 8079 ①–⑤	Alvia 4899	Av 8109		Av 8129	Alvia 4929 ①–⑤	Av 34149 Ⓑ	Av 8159 ⑤	Av 8359	Alvia 4969	IC 10167	Av 8169 ①–⑤	Av 8179	Av 8189 A	Av 8199 ①–⑤	Av 8209	Av 34209 Ⓑ	Alvia 4909	Av 8219
0	0	**Madrid** Chamartín d.	0640	0730	0855	1015	...	1200	1245	1440	1510	1540	1555	1605	1635	1700	1840	1925	2000	2025	2035	2130
68	68	**Segovia** AV d.	0708	0758	0923	1043	...	1228	1313	1508	1538	1608	1623	1635	1703	1728	1908	1952	2028	|	2103	2158
180		**Valladolid** a.	0745	0835	|	1120	...	1305	|	1541	1615	1645	|	1721	1740	1805	1945	...	2105	2119	|	2235
	230	**Salamanca** a.	...	...	1031	...	...	...	1421	...	...	...	1731	...	...	...	...	...	...	...	2211	...

	Av 8058 ①–⑤	Av 8068 ①–⑤	Av 8078 ①–⑤	Alvia 4868 ①–⑤	Av 8278	Av 34078 ①–⑤	Av 8088 ①–⑤	Alvia 4898 ⑥⑦	Av 8098 ⑥⑦	Av 8108 ①–⑤	Alvia 4918 ①–⑤	IC 10086	Av 8148	Av 8158	Alvia 4958		Av 8178	Av 34178 Ⓑ	Alvia 4988	Av 8198	Av 8208	
Salamanca d.	...	...	...	0650	...	...	...	0845	...	...	1050	...	...	...	1530	...	...	...	1820	...	...	...
Valladolid d.	...	0645	0715	|	0750	0811	0845	|	0935	1050	|	1311	1410	1520	|	...	1745	1836	|	1946	2035	...
Segovia AV d.	0700	0722	0752	0759	0827	|	0922	0954	1012	1127	1159	1359	1447	1557	1639	...	1822	1912	1929	2023	2112	...
Madrid Chamartín a.	0728	0750	0820	0826	0855	0907	0950	1021	1040	1155	1226	1428	1515	1625	1706	...	1850	1939	1956	2051	2140	...

km		①–⑤	⑥⑦	⑥⑦	①–⑤	⑥⑦		⑤	⑥⑦	①–⑤	⑥⑦
0	**Madrid** Chamartín d.	...	0845	*1015*	*1116*	*1216*	...	*1547*	*1616*	*1846*	*1916*
58	Cercedilla d.	0700	0947	1132	1230	1332	...	1700	1732	2000	2032
100	**Segovia** a.	0737	1024	1208	1307	1409	...	1736	1808	2039	2110

	①–⑤	⑥⑦	⑥⑦			⑤	⑥⑦	①–⑤	⑥⑦
Segovia d.	0750	1050	1250	1450	...	1750	1850	2050	2120
Cercedilla a.	0828	1128	1326	1527	...	1826	1926	2127	2157
Madrid Chamartín a.	*0935*	*1234*	*1435*	*1635*	...	*1935*	*2036*	*2235*	2254

km		MD 18601 ①–⑤	MD 18921 ⑥⑦	MD 18903	MD 18905 ①–⑤	MD 18907	MD 18913	MD 18909	MD 18911 Ⓑ		
0	**Madrid** Chamartín ◧ d.	0733	0830	1108	1335	1530	1757	1930	2110	...	...
122	Ávila ◧ d.	0908	0958	1239	1506	1714	1930	2108	2238	...	...
233	**Salamanca** a.	1036	1120	1353	1614	1825	2043	2217	2344	...	...

	MD 18920 ①–⑤	MD 18910 ①–⑥	MD 18900	MD 18912	MD 18902	MD 18904	MD 18906 ①–⑤	MD 18006	MD 18908
Salamanca d.	...	0548	0758	0945	1228	1644	1738	...	1958
Ávila ◧ d.	0555	0655	0906	1055	1339	1812	1849	1900	2106
Madrid Chamartín ◧ a.	0743	0832	1038	1224	1509	1952	...	2052	2238

MADRID ATOCHA CERCANÍAS - VILLALBA - EL ESCORIAL. *45 km.* Line C8. Journey time: Villalba, 53 minutes; El Escorial, 66-67 minutes. Depart 14 minutes later from Madrid Cham arrive 15 minutes earlier at Madrid Charmartín. Additional services operate.

From **Madrid Atocha Cercanías**: 0621 Ⓐ, 0635 Ⓒ, 0651 Ⓐ, 0709 Ⓐ, 0723 Ⓐ, 0737 Ⓒ, 0750 Ⓐ, 0835 Ⓒ, 0839 Ⓐ, 0935 Ⓒ, 0941 Ⓐ, 1036, 1135, 1235, 1335, 1407 Ⓐ, 1436 Ⓒ, 145 1521 Ⓐ, 1536 Ⓒ, 1547 Ⓐ, 1635, 1715 Ⓐ, 1736 Ⓒ, 1745 Ⓐ, 1827 Ⓐ, 1836 Ⓒ, 1847 Ⓐ, 1920, 1936, Ⓒ, 1944 Ⓐ, 2036 Ⓐ, 2042 Ⓒ, 2139, 2236, 2334.

From **El Escorial**: 0548, 0616 Ⓒ, 0631 Ⓐ, 0658 Ⓐ, 0706 Ⓐ, 0716 Ⓒ, 0736 Ⓐ, 0802 Ⓐ, 0817 Ⓒ, 0831 Ⓐ, 0915, 1015, 1115, 1215, 1315, 1414, 1515, 1601 Ⓐ, 1615 Ⓒ, 1624 Ⓐ, 1713, 1858 Ⓐ, 1912 Ⓐ, 1915 Ⓒ, 1930 Ⓐ, 1959 Ⓐ, 2013 Ⓒ, 2029 Ⓐ, 2115, 2215.

A – ①②③④⑥.

Av – ***Avant*** high-speed services. Single class.

MD – Medium Distance Plus.

◧ – See also Tables **680**, **681**, **689**.

MADRID - ZAMORA - VIGO, PONTEVEDRA and A CORUÑA 680

For services to / from A Coruña via León, see Table 682

Additional connections between Vigo and Ourense can be made by changing trains at Santiago de Compostela

	12512 R ①–⑤ 2	Av 9470 2 ①–⑤	MD 9072 R 2	12480 R 2	Av 9480 2	12584 2 ①–⑤	MD 9082 R 2	12526 R 2	MD 9112 R 2	Hotel 922 🍸 G	12586 R ①–⑤ 2	12528 R 2	Alvia 4275 ①–⑤	2 h	Av 9520 2	MD 9132 R 2	12960 R 2	Alvia 4095 ①–⑥ b	MD 9142 R ①–⑤ 2	Av 9550 2 ①–⑤	12538 R 2	MD 9162 R 2	MD 9172 R 2	
Madrid Chamartín. **681 689** d.	...	...	...	...	...	...	...	...	...	...	...	...	0715	...	...	...	...	0915	...	...	...	...	...	...
Segovia AV........... **663 679** d.	...	...	...	...	...	...	...	...	...	...	...	...	0745	...	...	...	...	|	...	...	...	...	...	...
Irún **689**...................d.	...	...	...	...	...	...	...	...	...	...	...	...	|	...	...	...	...	|	...	...	...	...	...	...
Barcelona Sants **652**.........d.	...	...	...	...	...	...	...	...	...	2020	...	...	◧	...	...	...	...	◧	...	...	...	...	...	...
Miranda de Ebro **681 689** .d.	...	...	...	...	...	...	...	...	...	|	...	...	|	...	...	...	...	|	...	...	...	...	...	...
Medina AV .... **681 689** d.	...	...	...	...	...	...	...	...	...	|	...	...	0815	...	...	...	...	|	...	...	...	...	...	...
Zamora ....d.	...	...	...	...	...	...	...	...	...	|	...	...	0853	...	...	...	...	1044	...	...	...	...	...	...
Puebla de Sanabria.............d.	...	...	...	...	...	...	...	...	...	|	...	...	|	...	...	...	...	|	...	...	...	...	...	...
Ourense...........................d.	...	0650	...	...	0755	...	...	...	...	0938	...	...	1148	1208	1210	...	1330	1336	...	1530	...	...	...	...
Guillarei ....d.	...	|	...	...	|	...	...	...	...	1109	...	...	1251	1333	|	...	|	|	...	|	...	...	...	...
Vigo Urzáiz ....d.	0513**c**	|	0640	0658**c**	|	0725**c**	0850	0945**c**	1115	|	1210**c**	1230**c**	|	|	|	1340	|	|	1435	|	1510**c**	1635	1715	...
Redondela AV ....d.	0526**r**	|	0648	0711**r**	|	0737**r**	|	0958**r**	|	1130	1222**r**	1243**r**	1310**r**	1357**r**	|	1348	|	|	|	|	1521**r**	|	|	...
Vigo Guixar...................a.	|	◧	|	|	◧	|	|	|	|	1141	|	|	1320	1412	◧	|	|	◧	|	◧	|	|	|	...
Pontevedra....................d.	0544	|	0659	0729	|	0758	0905	1017	1130	...	1243	1302	1353	...	|	1401	|	|	1450	|	1542	1650	1730	...
Vilagarcía de Arousa.........d.	0602	|	0716	0747	|	...	0920	1035	1145	...	...	1320	...	...	|	1418	|	|	1505	|	1600	1705	1745	...
Santiago de Compostela .....d.	0648	0730	0742	0828	0835	...	0942	1122	1207	...	...	1405	...	...	1250	1444	1515	1417	1527	1610	1644	1727	1807	...
A Coruña ....a.	0727	0758	0813	...	0903	...	1010	1158	1235	...	...	1442	...	...	1318	1512	...	1448	1555	1638	1721	1755	1835	...

	Alvia 4325 q	Av 9570 R 2	12588 2 ①–⑤	MD 9182 R 2	12488 R 2	IC 283 2 B	IC 283 2 🍸 A	Alvia 4145 4345 Ⓑ b d	MD 9192 R 2	Av 9590 2	12554 R 2	Alvia 4165	2 h	Alvia 622 🍸 P	Alvia 626 🍸 Q	MD 9212 R 2	12560 2 Ⓑ	RE 18322 2 J	Alvia 4185	Hotel 751 ✕ C Ⓑ	Hotel 851 ✕ D Ⓑ				
d Chamartín ..**681 689** d.	1305	...	...	...	...	...	...	1500	...	...	...	1625	...	...	...	...	...	...	1850	2214	2214	...	...	...	...
ia AV.............**663 679** d.	1337	...	...	...	...	...	...	1531	...	...	...	|	...	...	...	...	...	...	|	|	|	...	...	...	...
689...........................d.	|	...	...	...	...	...	0915	|	...	...	...	|	...	...	...	...	...	...	|	|	|	...	...	...	...
elona Sants **652** ....d.	◧	...	...	...	...	...	|	◧	...	...	...	◧	...	0930	0930	...	...	...	◧	|	|	...	...	...	...
nda de Ebro **681 689** .. d.	|	...	...	...	...	1140	1140	|	...	...	...	|	...	1432	1432	...	...	...	|	|	|	...	...	...	...
a AV.............**681 689** d.	1408	...	...	...	...	|	|	1602	...	...	...	|	...	|	|	...	...	1805**x**	|	0028**x**	0028**x**	...	...	...	...
ra ....d.	1441	...	...	...	...	|	|	1636	...	...	...	1752	...	|	|	...	...	1858	2019	|	|	...	...	...	...
a de Sanabria ....d.	1556	...	...	...	...	|	|	1755	...	...	...	|	...	|	|	...	...	2024	2135	|	|	...	...	...	...
nse..............................d.	1742	1800	...	...	...	1913	1918	1939	...	2010	...	2045	2100	2125	2112	...	...	...	2319	|	0655	...	...	...	...
arei...............................d.	...	|	...	...	...	2027	|	|	...	|	...	|	2218	|	|	...	...	...	|	|	0759	...	...	...	...
jo Urzáiz......................d.	...	|	1725**c**	1815	1820**c**	|	|	|	1935	|	2030**c**	|	|	|	|	2135	...	...	|	|	|	...	...	...	...
ondela AV ....d.	...	|	1739**r**	|	1833**r**	2051**r**	|	|	|	|	2043**r**	|	2239**r**	2252	|	2143	...	...	|	|	0819**r**	...	...	...	...
jo Guixar ....a.	...	◧	|	|	|	2104	◧	◧	|	◧	|	2214	2249	2303	◧	|	...	...	|	|	0830	...	...	...	...
tevedra.........................d.	...	|	1801	1830	1852	...	|	|	1950	|	2102	2246	...	...	|	2156	...	...	|	|	0924	...	...	...	...
jarcía de Arousa ....d.	...	|	...	1845	1914	...	|	|	2005	|	2122	...	...	...	|	2213	...	...	|	|	...	...	...	...	...
ago de Compostela......d.	...	1840	...	1907	1956	...	2001	2021	2027	2050	2207	...	...	...	2152	2239	2255	...	2359	|	...	...	...	...	...
ruña..............................a.	...	1908	...	1935	...	...	2033	2052	2055	2118	2243	...	...	...	2222	2307	2331	...	...	0841	...	...	...	...	...

	RE 18321 2 J	Alvia 4344 ①–⑤	Alvia 4254 ⑥⑦	12411 R ①–⑤ 2	Av 9071 2 ①–⑤	12585 2 ①–⑤	MD 9073 R 2	Alvia 4064 ①–⑤ b	2 h	Alvia 621 🍸 R	Alvia 625 🍸 S	Alvia 4484 4584 ①–⑥ y	MD 9083 R 2	MD 9093 R 2	Av 9581 2	IC 280 2 🍸 A	IC 280 2 B	12421 R 2	MD 9113 R ①–⑤ 2	Av 9111 2	Alvia 4114 q	MD 9123 R 2	MD 12587 2 ①–⑤	
A Coruña ....d.	...	...	...	0538	0630	...	0700	0715	...	...	0805	...	0800	0900	0910	0930	...	1000	1100	1140	...	1200	...	...
Santiago de Compostela .....d.	...	0515	0600	0617	0700	...	0730	0748	...	...	0834	...	0830	0930	0939	1006	...	1042	1130	1210	...	1230	...	...
Vilagarcía de Arousa ....d.	...	|	|	0654	|	...	0756	|	...	...	|	...	0850	0950	|	|	...	1120	1150	|	...	1250	...	...
Pontevedra.....................d.	...	|	|	0714	|	0805	0813	|	...	...	|	0818	0906	1006	|	|	...	1138	1206	|	...	1306	1350	...
Vigo Guixar ....d.	...	|	|	|	◧	|	|	◧	0705	0745	◧	0849	|	|	◧	◧	0916	|	|	◧	...	|	|	...
Redondela AV ....d.	...	|	|	0733**r**	|	0823**r**	|	|	0716**r**	0756	|	0901**r**	|	|	|	|	0927	1156**r**	|	|	...	|	1408**r**	...
Vigo Urzáiz ....d.	...	|	|	0744**c**	|	0835**c**	0833	|	|	|	|	|	0920	1020	|	|	|	1209**c**	1220	|	...	1320	1420**c**	...
Guillarei ....d.	...	|	|	...	|	...	...	|	0735	|	|	0920	...	...	|	|	0947	...	...	|	...	...	...	...
Ourense ....d.	...	0555	0640	...	0738	...	...	0829	0855	0916	0916	1027	...	...	1016	1113	1113	...	...	1248	1303	...	...	...
Puebla de Sanabria.............d.	0702	0733	0818	...	...	...	...	1007	...	|	|	|	...	...	...	|	|	...	...	...	1451	...	...	...
Zamora ....d.	0826	0850	0940	...	...	...	...	1130	...	|	|	1333	...	...	...	|	|	...	...	...	1616	...	...	...
Medina AV .... **681 689** d.	0919**x**	|	|	...	...	...	...	1205	...	|	|	|	...	...	...	|	|	...	...	...	1655	...	...	...
Miranda de Ebro **681 689** a.	...	|	|	...	...	...	...	|	...	1603	1603	|	...	...	...	1842	1842	...	...	...	|	...	...	...
Barcelona Sants **652** ....a.	...	◧	◧	...	...	...	...	◧	...	2125	2125	◧	...	...	...	|	...	...	...	...	◧	...	...	...
Hendaye **689** ....a.	...	|	|	...	...	...	...	|	...	...	...	|	...	...	...	2115	...	...	...	...	|	...	...	...
Segovia AV........... **663 679** d.	...	|	|	...	...	...	...	1237	...	...	...	|	...	...	...	...	...	...	...	...	1725	...	...	...
Madrid Chamartín. **681 689** a.	...	1023	1109	...	...	...	...	1306	...	...	...	1504	...	...	...	...	...	...	...	...	1754	...	...	...

	MD 9133 R 2	12453 R 2	Av 9141 2 ①–⑤	12455 R 2	Alvia 4134 🍸 b	MD 9153 R 2	2 h	Av 9161 2	Alvia 4354 🍸 Ⓑ	MD 12431 R 2	12967 R 2	Hotel 921 🍸 G	MD 9173 R 2	12589 2 ①–⑤	MD 9183 R 2	12441 R 2	Av 9201 2	Hotel 852 ✕ Ⓑ D	12459 R 2	MD 9213 R 2	12461 R 2	Hotel 752 ✕ Ⓑ C	MD 12561 R Ⓑ 2		
ruña...............................d.	1300	1315	1400	...	1440	1500	...	1630	...	1545	...	...	1700	...	1800	1908	2000	...	...	2100	...	2225	2210	...	...
ago de Compostela......d.	1330	1357	1430	1435	1512	1530	...	1700	...	1627	1725	...	1730	...	1830	1950	2030	...	2040	2132	2200	|	2248	...	...
jarcía de Arousa ....d.	1355	1433	|	1516	|	1550	...	|	...	1704	|	...	1750	...	1850	2033	|	...	2118	2158	2241	|	...	...	...
ntevedra........................d.	1412	...	|	1534	|	1606	...	|	1546	1722	|	...	1806	1840	1906	2054	|	2128	2136	2216	2259	|	...	...	...
'igo Guixar ....d.	|	...	◧	|	◧	|	1430	◧	1619	|	|	1755	|	|	|	|	◧	2215	|	|	|	|	...	...	...
ondela AV ....d.	1422	...	|	1554**r**	|	|	1443**r**	|	1630**r**	1740**r**	|	1805	|	1858**r**	|	2115**r**	|	2226**r**	2156**r**	2228	2319**r**	|	...	...	...
go Urzáiz.......................d.	1429	...	|	1607**c**	|	1620	|	|	|	1753**c**	|	|	1820	1910**c**	1920	2126**c**	|	|	2209**c**	2236	2332**c**	|	...	...	...
illarei..............................d.	...	...	|	...	|	...	1504	|	1647	...	|	1825	...	...	...	...	|	2251	...	...	...	|	...	...	...
nse................................d.	...	...	1508	...	1550	...	1629	1738	1753	...	1911	1933	...	...	...	...	2108	2359	...	...	...	|	...	...	...
la de Sanabria ....d.	...	...	...	...	|	...	...	...	1947	...	...	|	...	...	...	...	...	|	...	...	...	|	...	...	...
ora ....d.	...	...	...	...	1844	...	...	...	2108	...	...	|	...	...	...	...	...	|	...	...	...	|	...	...	...
ia AV.............**681 689** d.	...	...	...	...	|	...	...	...	2144	...	...	|	...	...	...	...	...	0650**x**	...	...	...	0650**x**	...	...	...
anda de Ebro **681 689** . a.	...	...	...	...	|	...	...	...	|	...	...	|	...	...	...	...	...	|	...	...	...	|	...	...	...
rcelona Sants **652** ....a.	...	...	...	...	◧	...	...	...	◧	...	...	0849	...	...	...	...	...	|	...	...	...	|	...	...	...
ndaye **689**.....................a.	...	...	...	...	|	...	...	...	|	...	...	...	...	...	...	...	...	|	...	...	...	|	...	...	...
via AV............**663 679** d.	...	...	...	...	|	...	...	...	2216	...	...	...	...	...	...	...	...	|	...	...	...	|	...	...	...
id Chamartín ..**681 689** a.	...	...	...	...	2017	...	...	...	2245	...	...	...	...	...	...	...	...	0925	...	...	...	0925	...	...	...

CAMINO DE SANTIAGO – 2 🍸 Irún / Hendaye - Miranda de Ebro - A Coruña and v.v.

CAMINO DE SANTIAGO – 2 Bilbao - Miranda de Ebro - Ourense - Vigo and v.v.

Ⓑ: ATLÁNTICO *Trenhotel* – 🛏, 2 Madrid - A Coruña - Ferrol and v.v.

Ⓑ: RÍAS GALLEGAS *Trenhotel* – 🛏, 2 Madrid - Pontevedra and v.v.

Ⓑ: GALICIA *Trenhotel* – 🛏, 1 (reclining) Barcelona - Vigo and v.v.

2 Valladolid - Medina del Campo - Puebla de Sanabria and v.v. (Table **689**).

③⑤⑦ 12 🍸 Barcelona - Ourense - Vigo ✣.

①②④⑥ 12 🍸 Barcelona - Ourense - A Coruña ✣.

①④⑥ 12 🍸 Vigo - Ourense - Barcelona ✣.

②③⑤⑦ 12 🍸 A Coruña - Ourense - Barcelona ✣.

b – To / from Ferrol (Table **682**).

c – Vigo **Guixar**.

d – From Alacant on ⑦ (Table **668**).

h – To / from León (Table **682**).

q – To / from Lugo (Table **682**).

r – Redondela **de Galica**.

x – Medina del Campo.

y – To Alacant on ⑥ (Table **668**).

◐ – Via Lugo (Table **682**).

◧ – Via high-speed line.

* – *153 km* Madrid - Medina del Campo via high-speed line.

§ – *636 km* Madrid - Santiago de Compostela via high-speed line. *697 km* Madrid - A Coruña via high-speed line.

✣ – On days of indirect service, connections are available between Ourense and Vigo / A Coruña and v.v. in the same timings.

681 MADRID - LEÓN

km	km via HSL			Alvia	Alvia		AVE	Alvia	IC	IC	Alvia	Alvia	AVE	Alvia	Alvia	Alvia	MD	Alvia	Alvia	MD	Alvia	AVE	Hotel	Hotel
				4071	4073	18101	4099	4111	283	283	4143	622	4149	4541	4141	664	18003	4179	4181	18005	4193	4209	751	922
				①–⑥	①–⑥		4299		2 🍷	2		626	Ⓑ	⑥	Ⓑ		2	Ⓑ	4381	2			Ⓑ	
			2			2		P	B	K	E	L						2	m				C	G
0	0	**Madrid** Chamartín .... 680 689 d.	...	0705	0745	...	0930	1105	...	...	1420	...	1440	1440	1450	...	1630	1730	1830	1835	1900	2025	2214	...
121		Ávila .... 680 689 d.	...	◧	◧	...	◧	◧	...	...	◧	...	◧	◧	◧	...	1759	◧	◧	2009	◧	◧	2341	...
207		Medina del Campo .. 680 689 d.	...	|	|	...	|	|	...	...	|	...	|	|	|	...	1845	|	|	2054	|	|	0028	...
249	180	**Valladolid** C. Grande .... 689 d.	0615	0810	0845	0955	1035	1216	...	...	1522	...	1543	1541	1551	...	1913	1835	1932	2120	2007	2121	0057	...
286		Venta de Baños .... 689 d.	0650	|	|	1027	|	|	...	...	|	...	|	|	|	...	1938	|	|	2147	|	|	0125	...
		Barcelona Sants **652** .... d.	|	|	|	|	|	|	...	...	|	0930	|	|	|	1210	|	|	|	|	|	|	|	2020
		Irún **689** .... d.	|	|	|	|	|	|	0915	...	|	|	|	|	|	|	|	|	|	|	|	|	|	|
		Bilbao Abando **689** .... d.	|	|	|	|	|	|	|	0942	|	|	|	|	|	|	|	|	|	|	|	|	|	|
		Miranda de Ebro .... 689 d.	|	|	|	|	|	|	1140	1140	|	1432	|	|	|	1723	|	|	|	|	|	|	|	|
		Burgos Rosa de Lima . 689 d.	|	|	|	|	|	|	1233	1233	|	1525	|	|	|	1816	|	|	|	|	|	|	|	0249
297	233	Palencia .... 689 d.	0705	0838	0917	1038	1102	1243	1323	1323	1552	1613	1610	|	|	1906	1949	1902	1959	2158	2039	2148	0138	0342
		Santander **684** .... a.	|	|	1209	1341	|	|	|	|	1815	|	|	|	|	|	|	|	|	|	2312	|	|	|
420	345	**León** .... a.	0831	0921	...	...	1145	1330	1428	1428	...	1721	1653	1651	|	2014	2102	1945	2043e	2307	...	2231	0246	0450
		Gijón Cercanías **685** .... a.	1138	1158	...	...	...	1604	|	|	...	|	...	1938	1922	2300x	...	|	2322z	...	...	...	|	|
		Ponferrada **682** .... a.	...	...	...	...	...	...	1612	1612	...	1852	...	...	...	...	...	2133	...	...	...	...	0431	0649
		Vigo Guixar **682** .... a.	...	...	...	...	...	...	|	2104	...	2303	...	...	...	...	...	...	...	...	...	...	|	1141
		A Coruña **682** .... a.	...	...	...	...	...	...	2033	...	...	2222	...	...	...	...	...	...	...	...	...	...	0841	1114
		Ferrol **682** .... a.	...	...	...	...	...	...	...	...	...	...	...	...	...	...	...	...	...	...	...	...	1025	...

	MD	AVE	Alvia	Alvia	AVE	Alvia	Alvia	Alvia	AVE	Alvia	Alvia	IC	IC	Alvia	MD	Alvia	AVE		AVE		Alvia	Alvia	Alvia	Hotel	Hotel
	18002	4078	4088	4072	4288	4070	661	4092	4128	4110	625	280	280	4142	18006	4140	4178	18104	4198		4180	4380	4192	921	752
	2	①–⑤	①–⑤	①–⑤	⑥⑦	4270	①–⑥	⑥⑦	①–⑤		621	2 🍷	2		2		Ⓑ	2	⑥	✣	①–⑤	⑦	Ⓑ		Ⓑ
			2	E				E		m	L	B	K			P				2				G	C
Ferrol **682** .... d.	...	...	...	...	...	...	...	...	...	...	...	...	...	...	...	...	...	...	...	...	...	...	...	...	2040
A Coruña **682** .... d.	...	...	...	...	...	...	...	...	...	...	0805	0930	...	...	...	...	...	...	...	...	...	...	...	1749	2225
Vigo Guixar **682** .... d.	...	...	...	...	...	...	...	...	...	...	0745	|	0916	...	...	...	...	...	...	...	...	...	...	1755	|
Ponferrada **682** .... d.	...	...	0611	...	...	...	...	...	...	...	1128	1344	1344	...	...	...	...	...	...	...	...	...	...	2222	0236
Gijón Cercanías **685** .... d.	...	...	|	...	...	0700	0750	...	...	1100	|	|	|	...	...	1425	...	...	...	1627t	1800	1810	...	|	|
León .... d.	0650	0700	0750	...	0840	0931j	1020	...	1230	1336	1310	1544	1544	...	1550	1659	1725	...	1850	1945	2031	|	...	0012	0425
Santander **684** .... d.	|	|	|	0705	|	|	|	0910	|	|	|	|	|	1400	|	|	|	1538	|	|	|	|	1900	|	|
Palencia .... 689 d.	0800	0744	0834	0935	0924	|	1136	1140	1314	1420	1419	1655	1655	1628	1702	1743	1809	1844	1935	2109	2115	2115	2131	0124	0536
Burgos Rosa de Lima ... 689 d.	|	|	|	|	|	|	1230	|	|	|	1508	1746	1746	|	|	|	|	|	|	|	|	|	|	0217	|
Miranda de Ebro .... 689 a.	|	|	|	|	|	|	1323	|	|	|	1603	1842	1842	|	|	|	|	|	|	|	|	|	|	|	|
Bilbao Abando **689** .... a.	|	|	|	|	|	|	|	|	|	|	|	|	2032	|	|	|	|	|	|	|	|	|	|	|	|
Hendaye **689** .... a.	|	|	|	|	|	|	|	|	|	|	|	2115	...	|	|	|	|	|	|	|	|	|	|	|	|
Barcelona Sants **652** .... a.	|	|	|	|	|	|	1850	|	|	|	2125	...	...	|	|	|	|	|	|	|	|	|	|	0849	|
Venta de Baños .... 689 d.	0813	|	|	|	|	|	...	|	|	|	...	...	...	|	1717	|	|	1855	|	2122	|	|	|	...	0548
Valladolid C. Grande .... 689 d.	0843	0811	0910	1011	0951	1035v	...	1216	1341	1450	...	...	...	1704	1747	1813	1836	1927	2005	2156	2145	2145	2207	...	0618
Medina del Campo .... 680 689 a.	0909	|	|	|	|	|	...	|	|	|	...	...	...	|	1812	|	|	...	|	...	|	|	|	...	0648
Ávila .... 680 689 a.	0943	◧	◧	◧	◧	◧	...	◧	◧	◧	...	...	...	◧	1858	◧	◧	...	◧	...	◧	◧	◧	...	0738
Madrid Chamartín .... 680 689 a.	1140	0910	1015	1121	1047	1138v	...	1326	1448	1557	...	...	...	1807	2052	1926	1942	...	2110	...	2253	2253	2310	...	0925

☛ **FOR NOTES**, SEE TABLE **682** BELOW.

682 LEÓN - VIGO, FERROL and A CORUÑA

km		MD	MD	Hotel	Hotel	MD		Alvia	Alvia	MD	MD	IC	IC	Alvia	MD	Alvia		MD	Alvia	Alvia	MD	Alvia	Hotel	Hotel
		37064	12641	922	922	12741		4134	4095	12685	12687	283	283	4325	12691	4145		37752	626	622	12647	4179	751	851
		2	2	🍷		2	2		①–⑥	2	2	2 🍷	2		2	4345	2	2			2	2	Ⓑ	Ⓑ
		①–⑤	①–⑤	G	G	⑥⑦		A	A			B	K	M		Ⓑ A g		Ⓑ	L	L	R	Ⓑ	C	D
	Madrid Chamartín ‡ d.	...	...	...	...	...	...	...	0915	...	...	...	...	1305	...	1500	...	...	...	...	...	1730	2214	2214
	Barcelona Sants ... ‡ d.	...	...	2020	2020	...	...	...	|	...	...	...	...	|	...	|	...	...	0930	0930	...	|	|	|
	Irún .... ‡ d.	...	...	|	|	...	...	...	|	...	...	0915	...	|	...	|	...	...	|	|	...	|	|	|
	Bilbao Abando .... ‡ d.	...	...	|	|	...	...	...	|	...	...	|	0942	|	...	|	...	...	|	|	...	|	|	|
0	**León** .... d.	...	...	0505	0505	...	0710	...	|	...	...	1443	1443	|	...	|	1700	...	1726	1726	...	1950	0301	0301
52	Astorga .... d.	...	...	0541	0541	...	0754	...	|	...	...	1515	1515	|	...	|	1733	...	1756	1756	...	2026	0335	0335
128	**Ponferrada** .... d.	...	...	0651	0651	...	0910	...	|	...	...	1614	1614	|	...	|	1834	...	1853	1853	...	2133	0432	0432
238	Monforte de Lemos .... a.	...	...	0822	0822	...	1105	...	|	...	...	1749	1749	1831	...	|	2016	...	2022	2022	...	...	0559	0559
238	Monforte de Lemos .... d.	...	0730	0835	0842	0900	1110	...	|	...	...	1805	1805	1833	...	|	2021	...	2027	2027	2042	...	0614	0615
285	Ourense .... 680 d.	...	|	|	0938	|	1208	...	1336	...	...	1918	1913	1752	...	1939	2100	...	2112	2125	1950	...	|	0655
416	**Vigo** Guixar .... 680 a.	...	|	|	1141	|	1412	...	|	...	...	|	2104	|	...	|	2249	...	|	2303	|	...	|	0830
309	Lugo .... d.	...	0824	0935	...	0956	...	...	|	...	...	|	...	1926	1945	|	...	...	|	...	2134	...	0710	...
445	**Ferrol** .... d.	0555	|	|	...	|	...	1325	|	1718	1915	▲	...	...	|	|	...	2040	▲	...	|	...	|	...
402	Betanzos - Infesta .... d.	0641	0950	1052	...	1127	...	1408	1526	1811	2004	|	...	...	2056	2127	...	2225f	|	...	2246	...	0818	...
428	**A Coruña** .... 680 a.	0705	1016	1114	...	1151	...	1430	1448	1835	2030	2033	...	...	2125	2059	...	2207	2222	...	2315	...	0841	...
445	**Ferrol** .... a.	...	...	...	...	...	...	...	1604	...	...	...	...	...	...	2209	...	...	...	...	...	...	1025	...

	Alvia		MD	MD	Alvia	Alvia	Alvia	MD	MD	Alvia	IC	IC	MD	Alvia	MD		Alvia	MD	Hotel	Hotel	MD	MD	Hotel	Hotel
	4088		12644	12680	4064	621	625	37751	12686	4114	280	280	12682	4134	12684		4095	12696	921	921	12642	37145	752	852
	2	2	2	2	A			2	2		2 🍷	2	2		2	2	A	2		🍷	2	12692	Ⓑ	Ⓑ
	①–⑤		R	①–⑥	①–⑤	L	L	①–⑥		M	B	K	⑥⑦	A			①–⑥		G	G		2	C	D
Ferrol .... d.	...	...	...	...	0555	...	...	...	...	...	...	...	...	1325	...	...	...	...	...	...	...	...	2040	...
A Coruña .... 680 d.	...	...	0638	0706	0715	...	0805	0845	0920	...	0930	...	1050	1440	1431	...	1458	1720	...	1749	1930	2059	2225	...
Betanzos - Infesta .... d.	...	...	0708	0738	0641	...	|	0947f	0949	...	|	...	1123	1408	1459	...	1526	1751	...	1811	2001	2127	2249	...
Ferrol .... a.	...	...	|	0820	|	...	▲	1025	|	...	▲	...	1207	|	1545	...	1604	1838	...	|	|	2209	|	...
Lugo .... d.	...	...	0826	...	|	...	|	...	1056	1110	|	...	▬	|	▬	...	...	...	...	1924	2135	...	2356	...
Vigo Guixar .... 680 d.	...	0705	|	...	|	0745	|	...	...	|	|	0916	...	|	*Alvia*	1430	...	...	1755	|	|	...	|	2215
Ourense .... 680 d.	...	0858	1020	...	0829	0916	0916	...	...	1303	1113	1113	...	1550	**4208**	1630	...	...	1933	|	|	...	|	2359
Monforte de Lemos .... a.	...	0946	0929	...	|	0953	0953	...	...	1203	1150	1150	...	|	2	1720	...	...	2013	2021	2228	...	0048	0038
Monforte de Lemos .... d.	...	0951	...	...	|	0958	0958	...	...	1206	1208	1208	2	|	⑦	1726	...	...	2041	2041	...	...	0108	0108
Ponferrada .... d.	0611	1144	...	...	|	1128	1128	...	...	|	1344	1344	1755	|	1855	1925	...	...	2222	2222	...	...	0236	0236
Astorga .... d.	0708	1247	...	...	|	1228	1228	...	...	|	1453	1453	1920	|	1957	...	...	...	2325	2325	...	...	0332	0332
León .... a.	0745	1323	...	...	|	1302	1302	...	...	|	1528	1528	2017	|	2035	...	...	...	2357	2357	...	...	0410	0410
Bilbao Abando .... ‡ a.	|	...	...	...	|	|	|	...	...	|	|	2032	...	|	|	...	...	...	|	|	...	...	|	|
Hendaye .... ‡ a.	|	...	...	...	|	|	|	...	...	|	2115	...	...	|	|	...	...	...	|	|	...	...	|	|
Barcelona Sants .... ‡ a.	|	...	...	...	|	2125	2125	...	...	|	...	...	...	|	|	...	...	...	0849	0849	...	...	|	|
Madrid Chamartín .. ‡ a.	1015	...	...	...	1306	...	...	...	...	1754	...	...	...	2017	2303	...	...	...	...	...	...	...	0925	0925

A – [12] Madrid - Zamora - Ourense - A Coruña - Betanzos - Ferrol and v.v. (Table **680**).
B – CAMINO DE SANTIAGO – [2] 🍷 Irún / Hendaye - Monforte de Lemos - Santiago - A Coruña and v.v.
C – Ⓑ: ATLÁNTICO *Trenhotel* – 🛏, [1] (reclining) Madrid - A Coruña - Ferrol and v.v.
D – Ⓑ: RÍAS GALLEGAS *Trenhotel* – 🛏, [2] Madrid - Vigo - Pontevedra and v.v.
E – [12] Alacant - Madrid - Santander and v.v.
G – Ⓑ: GALICIA *Trenhotel* – 🛏, [1] (reclining) Barcelona - A Coruña and Vigo and v.v.
K – CAMINO DE SANTIAGO – [2] Bilbao - Monforte de Lemos - Vigo and v.v.
L – [12] 🍷 Barcelona - A Coruña and Vigo and v.v. For days of running see Table **680**.
M – [12] Madrid - Zamora - Ourense - Monforte de Lemos - Lugo and v.v. (Table **680**).
P – From / to Castelló de la Plana and València on dates shown in Table **668**.
R – Routeing is A Coruña - Lugo - Monforte de Lemos - Ourense and v.v., with connections at Ourense to and from Madrid (Table **680**).

e – Not ⑤.
f – Betanzos - **Cidade**.
g – From Alicant on ⑦.
j – ⑦ only.
m – From / to Alacant (Table **668**).
t – ①–⑥.
v – 20 minutes later on ⑦.
x – Not ⑥.
z – 2305 on ⑤.

▲ – Via Santiago (Table **680**).
‡ – See Table **681**.
◧ – Via high-speed line (Table **663**).
✣ – On ⑦ runs 4 - 11 mi[nutes] later.

683 LEÓN - BILBAO

FEVE narrow-ga[uge]

1350 ✣ →	1410 →	1445 →	1535 →	1636 →	1717 →	1801 →	1935 →	2044 →	2130
León	San Feliz	La Vecilla	Cistierna	Guardo	Vado Cervera	Mataporquera	Espinosa	Balmaseda	**Bilbao** Concordia
2200 ✣	← 2138	← 2059	← 2018	← 1921	← 1841	← 1800	← 1623	← 1520	← 1430

✣ – Journey may be by 🚌 between León and Asunción-Universidad y León, due to construction of a new tunnel.

PALENCIA - SANTANDER 684

	Alvia 4073		Alvia 4143	Alvia 4153			Alvia 4193		
	①–⑥			⑤	2	⑤			
		2	A	2	C	2			
Madrid Chamartín **681 689** d.	0745	...	1420	1525	...	...	1900	...	...
Valladolid C G **681 689** d.	0845	0955	1522	1628	1654	1829	2007	...	...
Palencia d.	0917	1038	1552	1706	1736	1915	2039	...	...
Aguilar de Campoo d.	1030	1152	|	1805	1750	2028	2132	...	...
Mataporquera **683** ‡ d.	|	1201	|	1815	1901	2042	|	...	...
Reinosa § d.	1053	1216	|	1831	1917	2058	2157	...	...
Torrelavega § d.	1145	1312	1751	1921	2020	2153	2246	...	...
Santander § a.	1209	1341	1815	1947	2102	2222	2312	...	...

		Alvia 4072	Alvia 4092		Alvia 4142		Alvia 4162	Alvia 4192	
	⑥⑦	①–⑤	⑥⑦	①–⑤			⑦	Ⓑ	
	2	A	A	2		2	2		
Santander § d.	0700	0705	0910	0919	1400	1538	1610	1900	...
Torrelavega § d.	0729	0729	0934	0953	1424	1609	1633	1923	...
Reinosa § d.	0823	0816	1021	1056	|	1702	1729	2010	...
Mataporquera **683** ‡ d.	0838	|	|	1112	|	1723	1745	|	...
Aguilar de Campoo d.	0848	0838	1047	1122	|	1733	1754	2032	...
Palencia a.	1001	0933	1138	1234	1626	1843	1854	2129	...
Valladolid C G **681 689** a.	1047	1006	1211	1320	1659	1927	1928	2202	...
Madrid Chamartín **681 689** a.	...	1121	1326	...	1807	...	2040	2310	...

From / to Alacant (Table **668**). **C** – ①②③④⑥⑦. ‡ – Narrow gauge station is 600 metres. § – Additional local services operate between these stations.

LEÓN - OVIEDO - GIJÓN 685

		Alvia 4071	Alvia 4111	Alvia 4541	Alvia 4141	Alvia 4171	Alvia 664	Alvia 4381	Alvia 4181
	2	①–⑥		⑥	Ⓑ	⑤		⑤	
	Y		V			2	A	C	C Z
Barcelona Sants **681** d.	...	...	...	...	...	...	1210	...	...
Madrid Chamartín **681** d.	...	0705	1105	1440	1450	1715	|	1830	1830
León d.	0836	0926	1335	1656	|	|	2019	|	2048
Pola de Lena § a.	1033	|	1508	|	|	|	2155**x**	|	|
Oviedo ▽ § a.	1106	1128	1536	1905	1850	2117	2227**x**	2233	2253
Gijón Cercanias § a.	1138	1158	1604	1938	1922	2150	2300**x**	2305	2322

	Alvia 4070	Alvia 661	Alvia 4110	Alvia 4140	Alvia 4160	2	Alvia 4180	Alvia 4380	
		①–⑥			⑦	①–⑥	①–⑤	⑦	⑦
		A	C	W	2	Y			
Gijón Cercanias § d.	0700	0750	1100	1425	1626	1627	1800	1810	2025
Oviedo ▽ § d.	0727	0816	1127	1451	1653	1658	1827	1837	2055
Pola de Lena § d.	|	0845	1158	1520	|	1735	|	|	2127
León a.	|	1015	1331	1654	|	1940	2026	|	2352
Madrid Chamartín **681** a.	1138**f**	|	1557	1926	2106	...	2253	2253	...
Barcelona Sants **681** a.	...	1850	...	...	...	...	...	...	...

(12) Gijón - Barcelona and v.v. (Table **681**). From / to Alacant (Table **668**).
V – From Castelló de la Plana and València on ①–⑥ (Table **668**).
W – To València and Castelló de la Plana on Ⓑ (Table **668**).
Y – From / to Valladolid (Table **681**).
Z – ①②③④⑥⑦.
f – 1158 on ⑦.
x – Not ⑥.

OVIEDO – AVILÉS and v.v. *Renfe Cercanías* (suburban) service. *31 km.* Journey time: ± 38 minutes. **Additional services on** Ⓐ.
From Oviedo: Approximately 1 train each hour 0550 Ⓐ, 0616 Ⓐ, then 0716 until 2216. **From Avilés**: Approximately 1 train each hour 0641 Ⓐ, 0741 Ⓐ, then 0841 until 2311.

GIJÓN – OVIEDO – POLA de LENA and v.v. *Renfe Cercanías* (suburban) service. *63 km.* Journey time: ± 78 minutes.
From Pola de Lena: Approximately 1–2 trains each hour from 0630 until 2200. **From Gijón**: Approximately 1–2 trains each hour from 0600 until 2230.

SAN SEBASTIÁN - BILBAO 686

koTren (narrow gauge)

	Ⓐ	Ⓐ	Ⓒ					
Sebastián ⊡ Amara d.	0550	0650	...	0750	0850		1950	2050
ıtz d.	0620	0720	...	0820	0920		2020	2120
aia d.	0629	0729	...	0829	0929	and	2029	2129
d.	0711	0811	0811	0911	1011	hourly	2111	2211
ngo d.	0742	0842	0842	0942	1042	until	2142	2241
ao Bolueta ⊖ a.	0818	0918	0918	1018	1118		2218	...
ao Atxuri § a.	0822	0922	0922	1022	1122		2222	...

	Ⓐ	Ⓐ	Ⓒ					
Bilbao Atxuri § d.	...	0600	...	0700	0800		2000	2100
Bilbao Bolueta ⊖ d.	...	0603	...	0703	0803		2003	2103
Durango d.	0540	0640	...	0740	0840	and	2040	2140
Eibar d.	0614	0714	...	0814	0914	hourly	2114	2214
Zumaia d.	0700	0800	0800	0900	1000	until	2200	...
Zarautz d.	0708	0808	0808	0908	1008		2208	...
San Sebastián ⊡ Amara a.	0738	0838	0838	0938	1038		2238	...

San Sebastián / Donostia. Metro interchange.
§ – Bilbao Atxuri ⇆ Bilbao Concordia: ± *1000 m*. Linked by tram approx every 10 minutes, journey 6 minutes. Bilbao Concordia is adjacent to Bilbao Abando (*Renfe*).
Operator: EuskoTren. 2nd class, narrow gauge. Distance: San Sebastian - Bilbao *108* km.

BILBAO - SANTANDER - OVIEDO - FERROL 687

E (narrow gauge)

		Ⓐ			Ⓐ					
ao Concordia § d.	...	...	...	0800	...	1300	...	...	1930	...
ón d.	...	0715	...	0943	...	1440	...	...	2112	...
d.	...	0726	...	0955	...	1451	...	...	2124	...
ander a.	...	0825	...	1101	...	1600	...	...	2225	...
ander ▽ d.	...	...	0910	...	...	...	1610	...	...	...
elavega ▽ d.	...	...	0937	...	...	...	1637	...	...	...
ezón de la Sal ▽ d.	...	...	1007	...	...	...	1707	...	...	...
uera d.	...	...	1049	...	...	...	1749	...	...	...
es d.	0740	...	1121	...	1420	...	1826	...	...	...
desella d.	0821	...	1200	...	1500	...	1905	...	...	...
do a.	1037	...	1410	...	1713	...	2109	...	...	...

					Ⓐ			Ⓐ		
Oviedo d.	...	...	0835	...	1045	...	1535	...	1855	...
Ribadesella d.	...	...	1041	...	1256	...	1746	...	2104	...
Llanes d.	...	...	1121	...	1333	...	1826	...	2141	...
Unquera d.	...	...	1151	...	...	...	1855	...	...	...
Cabezón de la Sal ▽ d.	...	...	1233	...	...	...	1936	...	...	...
Torrelavega ▽ d.	...	...	1303	...	...	...	2005	...	...	...
Santander ▽ a.	...	...	1333	...	...	...	2033	...	...	...
Santander d.	0800	...	...	1400	...	1900	...	2045	...	...
Treto d.	0858	...	...	1507	...	2001	...	2144	...	...
Marrón d.	0910	...	...	1519	...	2013	...	2155	...	...
Bilbao Concordia § a.	1053	...	...	1658	...	2158	...	...	...	...

					Ⓐ					
do △ d.	...	...	0730	...	...	...	...	...	1430	...
jón Sanz Crespo △ d.	...	0701	|	0931	...	...	1131	1421	|	1831
ilés △ d.	...	0740	|	1018	...	...	1218	1500	|	1918
ia △ d.	...	0812	0833	1048	...	...	1248	1529	1534	1948
ca d.	...	...	1004	...	...	...	...	...	1708	...
a d.	...	...	1034	...	...	...	...	...	1739	...
deo d.	0655	...	1134	...	...	1500	...	...	1840	...
ro d.	0803	...	1244	...	...	1609	...	...	1948	...
ueira d.	0843	...	1324	...	1505	1650	...	...	2028	...
ol a.	1000	...	1444	...	1624	1810	...	...	2144	...

							Ⓐ			
Ferrol d.	...	...	0820	...	1045	...	1300	1530	...	1905
Ortigueira d.	...	...	0938	...	1204	...	1420	1649	...	2027
Viveiro d.	...	...	1018	...	1245	...	...	1729	...	2106
Ribadeo d.	...	...	1130	...	1353	...	...	1841	...	2215
Navia d.	...	...	1226	...	...	...	...	1939	...	...
Luarca d.	...	...	1256	...	...	...	...	2011	...	...
Pravia △ d.	0848	1148	1429	1448	...	1648	...	2151	2155	...
Avilés △ d.	0926	1226	|	1526	...	1726	...	|	2229	...
Gijón Sanz Crespo △ a.	1008	1308	|	1608	...	1808	...	|	2309	...
Oviedo △ a.	...	...	1530	...	...	...	...	2253	...	...

Additional trains run Santander - Cabezón de al Sal and v.v.
Additional trains run Oviedo / Gijón - Pravia and v.v.
§ – Bilbao Concordia is adjacent to Bilbao Abando (*Renfe*).
Operator: FEVE. 2nd class, narrow gauge.

IRÚN - BILBAO - SANTANDER - GIJÓN 688

SA ★

🚌	▽ ①–⑥			♡ Ⓑ	♡ ⑥	①–⑥	⑦				♡ Ⓑ	⑥		♡ Ⓑ		♡	⑤⑦					⊖ ⑤⑦		⑦	
RENFE rail station d.	...	...	...	0645	...	0745	...	...	0845	...	...	...	1100	...	1345	1445	...	...	1615	...	1830	...	2045	2115	2355
Sebastián / Donostia d.	...	...	...	0710	...	0810	...	...	0910	...	...	...	1125	...	1410	1510	...	...	1640	...	1855	...	2110	2140	0020
ao TermiBus d.	0600	...	0700	0830	0830	0930	0930	1000	1030	1130	1230	1230	1330	1430	1530	1630	1730	1730	1800	1845	2030	2115	2230	2300	0145
ander d.	0715	0830	0830	0950	0950	1100	1115	1130	1215	1300	1350	1400	1530	1550	1700	1750	1900	1900	1930	2015	2200	2235	2350	0020	0330
do a.	1000*	1145	...	1205	1205	...	...	...	1530	...	1605	...	1845	1805	...	2005	2145	...	2230	2230	...	0050	...	...	0600
n a.	0930	1215	...	1230	1230	...	...	...	1600	...	1635	...	1915	1835	...	2030	2215	...	2300	2300	...	0120	...	...	0700

🚌		①–⑥			①–⑥	♡	♡ ①–⑥	⑤	⑦	①–⑥	♡ ①–⑥		⑤⑦	♡			⑥	♡ Ⓑ				▽ Ⓑ	⑤⑦	▽ ⑤	▽ ⑦
n d.	0014	...	...	...	...	0715	...	...	0815	0815	0915	1130	...	1315	...	1515	1545	1630	...	1715	...	1915	2015	2115	2115
do d.	0100	...	...	...	...	0745	...	...	0845	0845	0945	|	...	1345	...	|	1615	1700	...	1745	...	1945	2045	2145	2145
ander d.	0345	0600	0700	0800	0930	1005	1200	...	1200	1230	1200	1400	1545	1605	1700	1900	1900	1920	...	2030	2100	2205	2340	0005	2359
ao TermiBus d.	0515	0730	0840	0930	1100	1120	1315	1400	1400	1415	1315	1530	1745	1720	1830	2045	2030	2035	2045	2200	2230	2320	...	0120	0115
Sebastián / Donostia a.	0640	0845	1000	...	1210	1230	...	1510	1600	1615	...	...	1855	1830**z**	1940	2155	...	2145**r**	2155	2310	...	...	...	...	0225
RENFE rail station a.	0700	0915	1030	...	1240	1305	...	1545	1630	1645	...	...	1925	1905**z**	2010	2225	...	2220**r**	2225	2340	...	...	...	...	0300

Clase Supra+ luxury coach.
Clase Supra Economy luxury coach.
Supra+ on ⑤, *Supra Economy* on ⑦.
r – ①–④ only.
z – ⑥ only.
* – Calls after Gijon.
★ – ALSA: ✆ +34 913 270 540 www.alsa.es
Frequent services operate Bilbao - Santander and Oviedo - Gijón.

689 MADRID and SALAMANCA - BILBAO and IRÚN

km △		2 ①–⑤	RE 16001 2	Hotel 310 ✕ B	MD 18316 ①–⑥	IC 631 ①–⑥	16019 2 N	17227 2	17201 2 ①–⑤	RE 18302 2	Alvia 4087	Alvia 4087 ①–⑥	MD 18001 w2 ①–⑤	RE 18321 2 Y	17203 2 ⑥⑦	MD 18324 ⑦	IC 633 ⑦	Alvia 661 A ①–⑥	MD 18061 2	18029 2 Z	2	Alvia 621 625 Q
0	**Madrid** Chamartín 680 681 d.	...	...	...	...	...	...	...	...	...	0800	0800	0633	...	...	...	...	...	0905	...	...	...
121	Ávila 680 681 d.	...	...	...	...	...	...	...	0700	...	|	|	0808	...	0905	...	...	...	1038	...	...	...
	Salamanca d.	...	...	0456	0600	...	...	...	|	0712	◧	◧	|	...	|	0954	...	...	|	...	...	...
207	Medina del Campo 680 681 d.	...	...	0600	0639	...	...	0655	0748	0802	|	|	0856	0920	0954	1042	...	...	1125	...	...	...
250	**Valladolid** Campo Grande 681 d.	...	...	0629	0705	0716	...	0730	0815	0830	0918	0918	0925	0955	1022	1108	1132	...	1150	...	1220	...
286	Venta de Baños 681 d.	...	...	|	...	|	...	...	...	...	|	|	...	...	...	...	|	...	1215	...	1300	...
298	Palencia 681 d.	...	...	|	...	|	...	...	...	...	|	|	...	...	...	...	|	1136	1229	...	1313	1419
371	**Burgos** Rosa de Lima 681 d.	...	...	0748	...	0821	...	...	...	...	1028	1028	...	...	...	...	1240	1230	1320	1405j	...	1508
460	Miranda de Ebro 653 d.	0720	0830	0848	...	0921	0940	...	...	...	1128	1135	...	...	...	...	1337	1325	1417	1501	...	1605
565	**Bilbao** Abando 653 a.	|	|	|	...	|	|	...	...	...	|	1304	...	...	...	...	|	|	|	|	...	|
494	Vitoria / Gasteiz 653 d.	0747	0902	0912	...	|	1005	...	...	...	1151	...	...	...	...	...	|	1350	1440	1530	...	1627
	Barcelona Sants **653** a.	...	|	|	...	1420	|	...	...	...	|	...	...	...	...	...	1835	1850	|	|	...	2125
537	Altsasu 653 d.	...	0931	|	...	...	1038n	...	...	...	|	...	...	...	...	...	...	...	1509	1601n	...	...
624	**San Sebastián / Donostia** ▲ 653 d.	...	1049	1055	...	...	...	...	...	...	1326	...	...	...	...	...	...	...	1629	...	...	...
641	**Irún** ▲ 653 a.	...	1113	1117s	...	...	...	...	...	...	1348s	...	...	...	...	...	...	...	1651	...	...	...
643	Hendaye ▲ 653 a.	...	...	1128	...	...	...	...	...	...	1355	...	...	...	...	...	...	...	...	...	...	...

	MD 18063 2 Ⓑ	MD 18063 2 ⑥	MD 18306 2	IC 280 2 D	IC 280 2 E	17221 2	MD 18314 2	16111 Z2 ①–⑥	16011 Z2 ⑦	RE 18009 2 ⑤	Alvia 4167	Alvia 4167 g Ⓑ	IC 4177 2 ⑤	Alvia 4377 ⑦	Alvia 4197 ①–④	MD 18065 2 Ⓑ	RE 18312 2	MD 18007 2 Ⓑ	Hotel 921 🍸 G			
Madrid Chamartín 680 681 d.	1220	1220	...	...	...	...	...	...	...	1541	1605	1605	1740	1740	1915	1710	...	2030	...	...	...	...
Ávila 680 681 d.	1405	1405	...	...	...	1510	...	...	...	1641	|	|	|	|	|	1850	...	2156	...	...	...	...
Salamanca d.	|	|	1405	...	...	|	1555	...	...	|	◧	◧	◧	◧	◧	|	2040	|	...	...	...	...
Medina del Campo 680 681 d.	1452	1452	1504	...	...	1559	1635	...	...	1734	|	|	|	|	|	1938	2135	2242	...	...	...	...
Valladolid Campo Grande 681 d.	1517	1517	1529	...	...	1632	1703	...	...	1806	1723	1723	1850	1850	2025	2006	2209	2307	...	...	...	...
Venta de Baños 681 d.	1542	1542	1605	...	...	...	...	...	...	1834	|	|	|	|	|	2034	...	2335	...	...	...	...
Palencia 681 d.	1557	1557	1617	1655	1655	...	...	...	...	|	|	|	|	|	|	2050	...	2347	0124	...	...	...
Burgos Rosa de Lima 681 d.	1645	1652	...	1746	1746	...	...	...	...	1927	1833	1833	1959	1959	2134	2143	...	...	0217	...	...	...
Miranda de Ebro 653 d.	1741	1747	...	1850	1858	...	...	...	...	2027	1935	1948	2054	2054	2230	2239	...	...	|	...	...	...
Bilbao Abando 653 a.	|	|	...	|	2032	...	...	...	...	|	|	2116	|	|	|	|	...	...	|	...	...	...
Vitoria / Gasteiz 653 d.	1802	1807	...	1911	...	...	...	1900	1921	2050	1956	...	2117	2117	2252	2300	...	...	|	...	...	...
Barcelona Sants **653** a.	|	|	...	|	...	...	...	|	|	...	|	...	|	|	...	...	...	...	0849	...	...	...
Altsasu 653 d.	1829	1836	...	1934	...	...	...	1931n	1952n	...	|	...	|	|	...	...	...	...	...	...	...	...
San Sebastián / Donostia ▲ 653 d.	1949	2000	...	2051	...	...	...	...	...	...	2130	...	2252	2250	...	...	...	...	...	...	...	...
Irún ▲ 653 a.	2011	2022	...	2109s	...	...	...	...	...	...	2151s	...	2310	2312t	...	...	...	...	...	...	...	...
Hendaye ▲ 653 a.	...	...	...	2115	...	...	...	...	...	...	2158	...	...	...	...	...	...	...	...	...	...	...

km		Hotel 922 G 🍸	MD 18000 2 ①–⑥	RE 18300 2 ①–⑤	Alvia 4076 ②–⑤	Alvia 4056 K ①	MD 18304 2	MD 18010 2 ①–⑥	17218 2	16000 2 ①–⑥	18071 Z2 ①–⑥	Alvia 4086	Alvia 4086 k ①–⑥	IC 283 2 E	IC 283 2 D	MD 18308 2	MD 18004 2	18070 2 ①–⑥	MD 18012 2 ①–⑥	MD 18012 2 ⑦	Alvia 622 Q	2 ①–⑤
0	**Irún** ▲ 653 d.	...	...	...	...	0450	...	...	...	0600	...	0840	...	...	0915	...	...	...	1050	1050	...	...
17	**San Sebastián / Donostia** ▲ 653 d.	...	...	...	...	0510	...	...	...	0619	...	0857	...	...	0933	...	...	...	1108	1108	...	...
104	Altsasu 653 d.	...	...	...	...	|	...	...	...	0736	0918n	|	...	...	1046	...	...	...	1227	1227	...	...
	Barcelona Sants **653** d.	2020	...	...	...	|	...	...	...	|	|	|	...	...	|	...	...	...	|	|	0930	...
147	Vitoria / Gasteiz 653 d.	|	...	...	0645	0645	...	0745	...	0803	0950	1033	...	...	1108	...	...	...	1257	1257	1410	1430
	Bilbao Abando 653 d.	|	...	...	|	|	...	|	...	...	|	|	0920	0942	|	...	...	...	|	|	|	|
180	Miranda de Ebro 681 d.	|	...	...	0706	0706	...	0806	...	...	1016	1058	1058	1140	1140	...	...	1245	1317	1317	1432	1457
270	**Burgos** Rosa de Lima 681 d.	0249	...	...	0800	0800	...	0903	...	...	...	1156	1156	1233	1233	...	...	1347	1414	1414	1525	...
353	Palencia 681 d.	0339	0625	...	|	|	...	1002	...	...	...	|	|	1321	1321	1335	...	...	1506	1512	1611	...
355	Venta de Baños 681 d.	...	0638	...	|	|	...	1013	...	...	...	|	|	...	...	1348	...	...	1517	1523	...	...
391	**Valladolid** Campo Grande 681 d.	...	0708	0735	0916	0916	0940	1039	1205	...	...	1311	1311	...	...	1419	1435	...	1544	1550	...	...
434	Medina del Campo 680 681 d.	...	0733	0812	|	|	1007	1105	1243	...	...	|	|	...	...	1448	1511	...	1610	1616	...	...
511	**Salamanca** a.	...	|	0903	◧	◧	1046	|	|	...	...	◧	◧	...	...	1548	|	...	|	|	...	...
	Ávila 680 681 d.	...	0821	...	|	|	...	1155	1334	...	...	|	|	...	...	...	1600	...	1700	1705	...	...
	Madrid Chamartín 680 681 a.	...	1010	...	1030	1030	...	1330	...	...	...	1428	1428	...	...	...	1731	...	1840	1845	...	...

	2	RE 18322 2 Y	MD 18014 2	RE 18318 2	IC 4176 2 ⑦	Alvia 664 A	17200 2	RE 18008 2 ⑦	16015 2 N	Alvia 4166	Alvia 4166 Ⓑ	IC 632	MD 18310 2	17226 2	Hotel 313 ✕ C	16017 2 N ①–⑥	16027 2 b ⑦	RE 16004 2				
Irún ▲ 653 d.	...	...	1350	...	1450	...	...	...	...	1615	...	...	...	...	1850	...	...	1937	...	...	...	...
San Sebastián / Donostia ▲ 653 d.	...	...	1408	...	1509	...	...	...	...	1633	...	...	...	...	1910	...	...	1957	...	...	...	...
Altsasu 653 d.	...	...	1527	...	|	...	...	...	1718n	|	...	...	...	...	|	2004n	2046n	2116	...	...	...	...
Barcelona Sants **653** d.	...	...	|	...	|	1210	...	...	|	|	...	1410	...	...	|	|	|	|	...	...	...	...
Vitoria / Gasteiz 653 d.	...	...	1557	...	1644	1702	...	1715	1753	1809	...	|	...	...	2046	2037	2118	2150	...	...	...	...
Bilbao Abando 653 d.	...	...	|	...	|	|	...	|	|	|	1700	|	...	...	|	...	|	|	...	...	...	...
Miranda de Ebro 681 d.	...	...	1617	...	1705	1723	...	1739	1820	1835	1835	1856	...	...	2108	...	2143	2215	...	...	...	...
Burgos Rosa de Lima 681 d.	...	...	1714	...	1759	1816	...	1838	...	1933	1933	1948	...	...	2200	...	...	...	...	...	...	...
Palencia 681 d.	1638	...	1806	...	|	1904	...	|	...	|	|	|	...	...	|	...	...	...	...	...	...	...
Venta de Baños 681 d.	1652	...	1817	...	|	...	...	1929	...	|	|	|	...	...	|	...	...	...	...	...	...	...
Valladolid Campo Grande 681 d.	1735	1740	1845	1905	1914	...	2030	2005	...	2050	2050	2058	2135	2230	2310	...	...	...	...	...	...	...
Medina del Campo 680 681 d.	...	1804	1912	1933	|	...	2107	2038	...	|	|	...	2210	2306	0011	...	...	...	...	...	...	...
Salamanca a.	...	...	|	2021	◧	...	|	|	...	◧	◧	...	2252	...	0057	...	...	...	...	...	...	...
Ávila 680 681 d.	...	...	2000	...	|	...	2157	2133	...	|	|	...	...	...	...	...	...	...	...	...	...	...
Madrid Chamartín 680 681 a.	...	...	2144	...	2027	...	...	2330	...	2206	2206	...	...	...	...	...	...	...	...	...	...	...

A – 12 Gijón - Barcelona and v.v. (Table **685**).
B – SUD EXPRESSO / SUREX *Trenhotel* – 🛏 *Gran Clase / Gran Classe* (1, 2 berths), 🛏 *Preferente* (1, 2 berths), 🛏 *Turista* (4 berths), 2 ✕ Lisboa (**310**) - Vilar Formoso (**311**) - Salamanca - Hendaye (Table **46**).
C – SUREX / SUD EXPRESSO *Trenhotel* – 🛏 *Gran Clase / Gran Classe* (1, 2 berths), 🛏 *Preferente* (1, 2 berths), 🛏 *Turista* (4 berths), 2 ✕ Irún (**312**) - Salamanca - Vilar Formoso (**313**) - Lisboa (Table **46**).
D – CAMINO DE SANTIAGO – 2 A Coruña - Palencia - Miranda de Ebro - Irún / Hendaye and v.v.
E – CAMINO DE SANTIAGO – 2 Vigo - Palencia - Miranda de Ebro - Bilbao and v.v.
G – Ⓑ (daily June 20 - Sept. 19; not Dec. 24, 31): GALICIA *Trenhotel* – 🛏, 1 (reclining) 🍸 Barcelona - A Coruña and Vigo and v.v.
K – ① June 27 - Aug. 29.
N – To / from Pamplona (Table **653**).
Q – 12 Vigo / A Coruña - Palencia - Barcelona and v.v. (Table **680**).
Y – 2 Puebla de Sanabria - Medina del Campo - Valladolid and v.v. (Table **680**).
Z – To / from Pamplona and Zaragoza (Table **653**).

b – From / to Castejón de Ebro a[illegible] Pamplona / Iruña (Table **653**).
g – Daily June 20 - Oct. 17.
j – ①–⑥.
k – Daily June 21 - Oct. 18.
n – Altsasu Pueblo.
s – Calls to set down only.
t – June 28 - Aug. 30.
w – Not Oct. 12, Dec. 8, 25.

◧ – Via high-speed line (Table 6[illegible]
△ – Via Ávila.

▲ – **SAN SEBASTIÁN** - **IRÚN** and v.v. ***Renfe Cercanías*** (suburban) service. *17 km.* Journey time: ± 23 minutes
From San Sebastián: Approximately 2 - 3 trains each hour from 0630 until 2300. **From Irún**: Approximately 2 - 3 trains each hour from 0522 until 22[illegible]

▲ – **SAN SEBASTIÁN** (Amara) - **IRÚN** (Colón, near Renfe station) - **HENDAYE** (SNCF station) and v.v. ***EuskoTren*** (narrow-gauge) service. *22 km.* Journey time: ± 37 minutes
From San Sebastián: 0555 Ⓐ, 0615 Ⓑ, 0645 Ⓐ, 0715, 0745 and every 30 mins until 2145, also 2315 ⑥ **s**. On ⑦ also 0015, 0115 **s**, 0215, 0315 **s**, 0415, 0515 **s**.
From Hendaye (A): 0647 Ⓐ, 0703 Ⓐ, 0733 Ⓐ, 0803, 0833 and every 30 mins until 2233. On ⑦ also 0003 **s**, 0103, 0203 **s**, 0303, 0403 **s**, 0503.
A – 4 minutes later from Irún. **s** – Summer only (late-June to mid-Sept).

PORTUGAL

SEE MAP PAGE 320

ator: **CP** – Comboios de Portugal (www.cp.pt).

categories: ***Alfa Pendular*** – *AP* – high-quality tilting express trains. ***Intercidades*** – *IC* – high-quality express trains linking the main cities of Portugal to Lisboa and Porto. ***Interregional*** – *IR* – 'semi-fast' links usually calling at principal stations only. ***Celta*** – International services between Porto and Vigo. ***Regional*** and ***Suburbano*** – local stopping trains (shown without train numbers).

Higher fares are payable for travel by *AP* and *IC* trains, also the international **Sud Expresso** service (Lisboa - Hendaye / Irún - Lisboa), and there is an additional supplement for travel by *AP* trains. The **Lusitania** *Hotel Train* service (Lisboa - Madrid and v.v.) is shown in Table **46**, special fares apply.

ces: All services shown with a train number convey first and second class accommodation (on *Alfa Pendular* trains termed, respectively, *Conforto* and *Turística*) unless otherwise indicated. *Regional* and *Suburbano* trains convey second-class seating only.

AP, *IC*, *IR* and international trains convey a buffet car (*carruagem-bar*) and there is an at-seat service of meals to passengers in 1st class on *AP* and certain *IC* trains. Sleeping (🛏) and couchette (▬) cars are of the normal European types described on page 8.

rvations: Reservations are **compulsory** for travel by *AP*, *IC* and international trains. Seat reservation is not normally available on other services.

ngs: Timings shown are the most recent available. Amendments to timetables may come into effect at short notice, especially during the Christmas and New Year period.

LISBOA - COIMBRA - PORTO 690

eservations compulsory on *AP* and *IC* trains. For local trains Entroncamento - Coimbra / Coimbra - Aveiro see Table **699**. Local trains Aveiro - Porto run approx hourly.

	IR	*AP*	*AP*	*IC*	*AP*	*IC*	*IC*	*AP*	*IC*	*AP*	*IC*	*AP*	*IC*	*AP*	*AP*	*IC*	*AP*	*IC*	*AP*	*IC*	*AP*		**310**	*IC*
	823	**121**	**131**	**521**	**141**	**511**	**721**	**182**	**523**	**125**	**513**	**133**	**525**	**135**	**127**	**621**	**184**	**515**	**137**	**723**	**129**		**335**	**527**
		Ⓐ		①–⑥						⚒				Ⓑ								Ⓑ	**S**	
			△	**n**	☆	◇	△				◇	△		**h** △		☆‡		◇	△	△			[R]	
Faro **697** d.	...	...	...	...	...	...	...	0700	...	...	...	...	...	...	...	...	1505	...	...	...	...	...	...	...
Lisboa S Apolónia ▷ d.	...	0600	0700	0730	0800	0830	0930	|	1130	1200	1330	1400	1530	1600	1700	1730	|	1830	1900	1930	2000	...	2125	2200
Lisboa Oriente ▷ d.	...	0609	0709	0739	0809	0839	0939	1009	1139	1209	1339	1409	1539	1609	1709	1739	1809	1839	1909	1939	2009	...	2134	2209
Vila Franca de Xira ▷ d.	...	|	|	0752	|	0852	0952	|	1152	|	1352	|	1552	|	|	1752	|	1852	|	1952	|	...	|	2222
Santarém ▷ d.	...	|	|	0813	0839	0913	1013	|	1213	|	1413	|	1613	|	|	1813	|	1913	|	2013	2039	...	|	2243
Entroncamento ▷ d.	...	|	|	0831	0856	0932	1031	|	1231	|	1432	|	1631	|	|	1831	|	1932	|	2031	2056	2140	2230	2301
Fátima ⊙ d.	...	|	|	|	|	0948	|	|	|	|	1448	|	|	|	|	|	|	1948	|	|	|	2201	|	|
Caxarias ⊖ d.	...	|	|	|	|	0955	1051	|	|	|	1455	|	|	|	|	1850	|	1955	|	|	|	2210	2249	2321
Pombal d.	...	|	|	0905	0926	1011	1107	|	1305	|	1511	|	1705	|	|	1907	|	2011	|	2105	2126	2233	2306	2337
Alfarelos d.	...	|	|	|	|	1025	|	|	1319	|	1525	|	1719	|	|	|	|	2025	|	|	|	2256	|	|
Coimbra B ▶ d.	0520	0745	0845	0930	0950	1039	1133	1145	1332	1345	1539	1545	1732	1745	1845	1932	1945	2039	2045	2130	2150	2319	2332	0003
Pampilhosa d.	0533	|	|	|	|	1050	|	|	1343	|	1550	|	1743	|	|	|	|	2050	|	|	|	2330	...	|
Aveiro d.	0601	0812	0912	1001	1016	...	1201	1212	1402	1412	...	1612	1802	1812	1912	2000	2012	...	2112	2201	2216	2359	...	0031
Espinho d.	0633	|	|	1024	1036	...	1224	|	1424	|	...	|	1824	|	|	2024	|	...	|	2224	2236	0028	...	0054
Vila Nova de Gaia d.	0645	0838	0939	1034	1046	...	1234	1238	1433	1438	...	1639	1833	1839	1938	2034	2038	...	2139	2235	2245	0040	...	0103
Porto Campanhã ▽ a.	0650	0844	0946	1039	1052	...	1246	1244	1439	1444	...	1646	1839	1846	1944	2041	2044	...	2146	2246	2252	0045	...	0109

		313	*AP*	*AP*	*IC*	*AP*	*IC*	*IC*	*AP*	*IC*	*AP*	*IC*	*AP*	*IC*	*IC*	*AP*	*AP*	*IC*	*AP*	*AP*	*IC*	*IC*	*AP*	*IR*	
		332	**180**	**130**	**520**	**120**	**510**	**620**	**122**	**720**	**124**	**522**	**132**	**512**	**722**	**186**	**126**	**524**	**140**	**134**	**514**	**526**	**136**	**822**	
	①–⑥	**S**			①–⑥	①–⑥			⚒		Ⓑ												Ⓑ		
		[R]		△	**n**	**n**	◇	☆		△	**b**		△	◇	△				☆	△	◇		**h** △		
o Campanhã ▽ d.	0130	...	0547	0647	0652	0745	...	0852	0947	1052	1147	1252	1347	...	1452	1547	1647	1652	1745	1847	...	1952	2047	2155	...
Nova de Gaia d.	0135	...	0552	0652	0657	0750	...	0857	0952	1057	1152	1257	1352	...	1457	1552	1652	1657	1750	1852	...	1957	2052	2201	...
nho d.	0146	...	|	|	0707	0800	...	0908	|	1107	|	1307	|	...	1507	|	|	1707	1800	|	...	2007	|	2212	...
ro d.	0218	...	0621	0721	0731	0821	...	0932	1021	1129	1221	1331	1421	...	1529	1621	1721	1731	1821	1921	...	2031	2121	2245	...
pilhosa d.	0247	...	|	|	|	|	0907	|	|	1146	|	|	|	1510	1546	|	|	|	|	|	2010	|	|	2314	...
nbra B ▶ d.	0258	0447	0646	0746	0800	0846	0921	0959	1046	1157	1246	1357	1446	1521	1557	1646	1746	1757	1846	1946	2021	2057	2146	2325	...
elos d.	0312	|	|	|	|	|	0934	|	|	1210	|	|	|	1534	1610	|	|	|	|	|	2034	|	|	...	...
bal d.	0332	0522	|	|	0826	0910	0949	1024	|	1226	|	1423	|	1549	1626	|	|	1823	1910	|	2049	2123	|	...	...
arias ⊖ d.	0352	0543	|	|	|	|	1005	1040	|	|	|	1439	|	1605	|	|	|	1839	|	|	2105	2139	|	...	...
na ⊙ d.	0359	|	|	|	|	|	1012	|	|	|	|	|	|	1612	|	|	|	|	|	|	2112	|	|	...	...
oncamento ▷ d.	0415	0606	|	|	0858	0939	1027	1059	|	1258	|	1458	|	1627	1658	|	|	1858	1939	|	2127	2158	|	...	...
arém ▷ d.	0439	|	|	|	0916	0955	1046	1117	|	1316	|	1516	|	1646	1716	|	|	1916	1955	|	2146	2216	|	...	...
Franca de Xira ▷ d.	0518	|	|	|	0939	|	1109	1139	|	1339	|	1539	|	1709	1739	|	|	1939	|	|	2209	2239	|	...	...
oa Oriente ▷ a.	0535	0720	0823	0922	0952	1031	1122	1152	1222	1352	1422	1552	1622	1722	1752	1823	1922	1952	2031	2122	2222	2252	2322	...	...
oa S Apolónia ▷ a.	0543	0730	|	0930	1000	1040	1130	1200	1230	1400	1430	1600	1630	1730	1800	|	1930	2000	2040	2130	2230	2300	2330	...	...
ro **697** a.	...	...	1123	...	...	...	...	...	...	...	...	...	...	...	...	2123	...	...	...	...	...	...	...	...	...

SUD EXPRESSO / LUSITANIA – see Tables **46** / **692**. International journeys only.

Not public holidays.
Not ⑦ if the following day is a public holiday. Not ⑤ if it is a public holiday.
Not ① if it is a public holiday. Not ⑥ if the day before is a public holiday. (runs June 11).

20 km from Fátima (full name of station is Chão de Maçãs - Fátima).
Lisboa - Guarda and v.v. (Table **692**).

☆ – Lisboa - Porto - Guimarães and v.v. (Table **695a**).
△ – Lisboa - Porto - Braga and v.v. (Table **695**).
▷ – For other fast trains see Table **691**, for local trains see Table **699**.
▽ – Local services run Porto Campanhã - Porto São Bento.
▶ – Local trains run Coimbra B - Coimbra and v.v.
⊖ – 🚌 available Caxarias - Fátima. See www.rodotejo.pt for details.
‡ – Departs Lisboa 5 minutes earlier on ⑤.

LISBOA - ENTRONCAMENTO - COVILHÃ 691

				IC		*IC*			*IC*	
				541		**543**			**545**	
	Ⓐ		⚒							
Lisboa Sta Apolónia ▷ d.	0545	...	0645	0815	*0945*	1315	1615	*1745*	1915	1945
Lisboa Oriente ▷ d.	0553	...	0653	0823	*0953*	1323	1623	*1753*	1923	1953
Vila Franca de Xira ▷ d.	0611	...	0711	0838	*1011*	1338	1639	*1811*	1938	2011
Santarém ▷ d.	0655	...	0755	0905	*1055*	1405	1706	*1855*	2005	2055
Entroncamento ▷ a.	0719	...	0819	0925	*1119*	1425	1726	*1919*	2025	2119
Entroncamento d.	▬	0748	...	0926	1152	1426	1727	1943	2026	*2154*
Abrantes d.	...	0820	...	0950	1224	1450	1758	2021	2050	*2235*
Ródão d.	...	0928	...	1042	1323	1548	1904	2126	2142	...
Castelo Branco a.	⚒	0957	...	1105	1352	1611	1948	2154	2206	...
Castelo Branco d.	0625	1000	...	1106	1420	1612	1951	...	2207	...
Fundaõ d.	0713	1048	...	1142	1513	1648	2039	...	2243	...
Covilhã a.	0729	1104	...	1156	1529	1702	2055	...	2257	...

		IC					*IC*		*IC*	
		540					**542**		**544**	
	①–⑥			Ⓐ						
Covilhã d.	*0450***r**	0731	0850	...	...	*1300*	1431	...	1831	1841
Fundaõ d.	*0506***r**	0746	0906	...	...	*1316*	1446	...	1846	1857
Castelo Branco a.	*0553***r**	0820	0953	...	...	*1404*	1521	...	1920	1944
Castelo Branco d.	0556	0821	1009	...	...	*1408*	1522	*1817*	1921	...
Ródão d.	0624	0845	1042	...	...	*1436*	1548	*1845*	1945	...
Abrantes d.	0723	0937	1141	...	...	*1541*	1639	*1946*	2037	...
Entroncamento a.	0800	1006	1216	...	...	*1611*	1703	*2015*	2106	...
Entroncamento ▷ d.	0808	1007	...	1238	1342	1638	1704	2042	2107	...
Santarém ▷ d.	0827	1026	...	1302	1406	1702	1726	2106	2126	...
Vila Franca de Xira ▷ d.	0856	1055	...	1347	1447	1747	1755	2147	2155	...
Lisboa Oriente ▷ a.	0911	1111	...	1405	1505	1805	1811	2205	2211	...
Lisboa Sta Apolónia ▷ a.	0920	1120	...	1413	1513	1813	1820	2213	2220	...

① (not public holidays).

▷ – For other fast trains see Table **690**, for local trains see Table **699**.

(LISBOA -) COIMBRA - GUARDA - VILAR FORMOSO 692

	IC			*IC**					*IC**	*IN*
	511			**513**					**515**	**311**
						Ⓑ		Ⓑ		**S** [R]
Lisboa Sta Apolónia **690** d.	0830	...	...	1330	...	...	...	...	1830	2125
Lisboa Oriente **690** d.	0839	...	...	1339	...	...	...	...	1839	2134
Coimbra ▶ d.	*1014*	...	1221	*1453*	...	1624	1824	2014	|	|
Coimbra B d.	1039	...	1227	1539	...	1630	1828	2017	2039	2332
Pampilhosa d.	1050	...	1242	1550	...	1648	1848	...	2050	|
Santa Comba Dão d.	1122	...	1317	1622	...	1726	1937	...	2122	0016
Nelas d.	1144	...	1342	1644	...	1800	2008	...	2144	|
Mangualde d.	1152	...	1351	1652	...	1810	2018	...	2152	0046
Guarda a.	1251	1305	1501	1751	1805	1921	2128	...	2251	0144
Vilar Formoso 🏛 a.	...	1348	...	...	1848	...	...	...	...	0220

	IN		*IC*			*IC**				*IC**
	312		**510**			**512**				**514**
	S [R]	⚒		⑦**h**			⚒**b**	⑦**z**	⚒**b**	
Vilar Formoso 🏛 d.	0150	...	*0615***r**	0917	...	...	...	*1530*	1710	...
Guarda d.	0223	0500	0707	1000	1010	1309	1625	1625	1755	1809
Mangualde d.	0324	0559	0804	...	1118	1408	1733	1733	...	1908
Nelas d.	|	0609	0812	...	1128	1416	1744	1744	...	1916
Santa Comba Dão d.	0355	0636	0834	...	1202	1437	1812	1812	...	1937
Pampilhosa d.	|	0718	0907	...	1242	1510	1851	1851	...	2010
Coimbra B a.	0447	0731	0921	...	1256	1520	1902	1903	...	2020
Coimbra ▶ a.	|	0736	*0946***a**	...	1302	*1551***a**	1908	*1914*	...	*2041***a**
Lisboa Oriente **690** a.	0720	...	1122	...	...	1722	...	2142	...	2222
Lisboa Sta Apolónia **690** a.	0730	...	1130	...	...	1730	...	2150	...	2230

SUD EXPRESSO / LUSITANIA – see Tables **46** / **690**.
Ⓐ only.
①–⑥ (if ① is a public holiday runs previous day instead).

h – Also public holidays if they fall on ①–④ or ⑥.
r – ⚒ only.
z – If the following day is a public holiday runs ① instead.

▶ – Local trains run Coimbra B - Coimbra and v.v.
* – On ⑤ **513** and **515** are numbered **517** and **519**; on ⑦ **512** and **514** are numbered **516** and **518**.

693 LISBOA - CALDAS DA RAINHA - FIGUEIRA DA FOZ / COIMBRA *Linha do C*

km										
				Ⓐ	◇				△	◇
	Lisboa Santa Apolonia d.	...	0541	...	...	1150	1350	1630	...	...
0	**Lisboa** Rossio ▷ d.	...	|	*0701*	*0831*	|	|	|	*1731*	*1831*
7	Entrecampos ▷ d.	...	0555	|	|	1201	1401	1641	|	|
9	Sete Rios ▷ d.	...	0558	|	|	1204	1404	1644	|	|
22	Agualva - Cacém ⊙ ▷ d.	...	0613	*0727*	*0857*	1221	1421	1700	*1757*	*1857*
26	Mira Sintra - Meleças ▷ a.	...	0617	*0730*	*0900*	1226	1426	1704	*1800*	*1900*
26	Mira Sintra - Meleças d.	...	0618	0735	0925	1227	1427	1705	1835	1930
72	Torres Vedras d.	0619	0715	0835	1023	1326	1525	1813	1936	2030
95	Bombarral d.	0644	0741	0859	1047	1354	1547	1836	2001	...
114	**Caldas da Rainha** a.	0706	0803	0921	1109	1416	1609	1858	2023	...
	Leiria (below) a.	...	0929	...	...	1529	...	2029	...	...

	Ⓐ			Ⓐ			▽	
Leiria (below) d.	...	...	...	...	*1009*	1213	*1509*	...
Caldas da Rainha d.	...	0606	0721	0816	1116	1316	1616	1730
Bombarral d.	...	0627	0742	0838	1137	1338	1637	1750
Torres Vedras d.	0603	0651	0807	0904	1159	1400	1659	1814
Mira Sintra - Meleças a.	0705	0753	0915	...	1301	1501	1758	1913
Mira Sintra - Meleças ▷ d.	*0710*	0754	*0930*	...	1302	1502	*1810*	*1930*
Agualva - Cacém ⊙ ▷ a.	*0713*	0757	*0933*	...	1306	1506	*1813*	*1933*
Sete Rios ▷ a.	|	0813	|	...	1323	1523	|	|
Entrecampos ▷ a.	|	0816	|	...	1327	1527	|	|
Lisboa Rossio ▷ a.	*0739*	|	*0959*	...	|	|	*1839*	*1959*
Lisboa Santa Apolónia a.	...	0830	...	...	1341	1541	...	...

km		*IR* 801			*IR* 803			*IR* 805		
		①–⑥								
	Lisboa S Apolónia (above) d.	...	...	0541	...	...	1150	*1350*	...	1630
0	**Caldas da Rainha** d.	0615	...	0830	1115	...	1430	1615	...	1930
13	São Martinho do Porto d.	0623	...	0842	1123	...	1442	1623	...	1942
47	Marinha Grande d.	0652	...	0920	1152	...	1520	1652	...	2020
57	Leiria d.	0700	...	0929	1200	...	1529	1700	...	2029
110	Verride d.	0748	0756	...	1248	1249	...	1748	1749	...
104	Bifurcação de Lares ▽ a.	|	0803	...	|	1256	...	|	1756	...
111	**Figueira da Foz** a.	|	0815	...	|	1309	...	|	1809	...
118	Alfarelos ▽ d.	0756	...	...	1256	...	...	1756	...	...
138	**Coimbra** B ▽ a.	0810	...	...	1310	...	...	1810	...	...

			IR 802			*IR* 804		
Coimbra B ▽ d.	...	...	0851	...	...	1351	...	...
Alfarelos ▽ d.	...	...	0905	...	...	1405	...	...
Figueira da Foz d.	...	0858	|	...	1358	|	...	1858
Bifurcação de Lares ▽ d.	...	0911	|	...	1411	|	...	1911
Verride d.	...	0918	0921	...	1418	1421	...	1918
Leiria d.	0713	...	1009	1213	...	1509	1813	...
Marinha Grande d.	0723	...	1019	1223	...	1519	1823	...
São Martinho do Porto d.	0756	...	1046	1256	...	1546	1856	...
Caldas da Rainha a.	0808	...	1055	1308	...	1555	1908	...
Lisboa S Apol. (above) a.	...	...	*1341*	1541	...	...	2142	...

▷ – For suburban services see Table **699** (including connections from / to Oriente).
▽ – See Table **693a**.
⊙ – Connections to / from Lisboa Rossio every 20 - 30 minutes (see Table **699**).
◇ – On Ⓐ there is a connection 20 minutes later Lisboa Rossio - Mira Sintra-Meleças.
△ – On Ⓐ there is a connection 30 minutes later Lisboa Rossio - Mira Sintra-Meleças.
▽ – On Ⓒ connection Mira Sintra-Meleças - Lisboa Rossio runs 20 minutes later.

693a FIGUEIRA DA FOZ - COIMBRA

km																								
		⚒	⚒	Ⓐ																				
0	**Figueira da Foz** d.	0558	0658	0740	...	0858	...	0958	1058	...	1158	1258	...	1358	1458	1558	...	1658	1758	...	1858	1958	...	2
8	Bifurcação de Lares d.	0611	0711	0750	...	0911	...	1011	1111	...	1211	1311	...	1411	1511	1611	...	1711	1811	...	1911	2011	...	2
20	Verride d.	0620	0720	0757	...	0920	...	1020	1120	...	1220	1320	...	1420	1520	1620	...	1720	1820	...	1920	2020	...	2
28	Alfarelos d.	0633	0733	0806	0812	0938	1031	1033	1133	1212	1238	1333	1412	1433	1538	1633	1704	1738	1838	1903	1933	2038	2119	2
47	**Coimbra** B a.	0700	0800	0824	0832	1005	1052	1104	1200	1232	1305	1400	1432	1500	1605	1700	1725	1805	1905	1924	2000	2105	2142	2
49	**Coimbra** a.	0710	0814	0837	0841	1014	1103	1113	1210	1241	1314	1410	1441	1510	1614	1710	1735	1814	1914	1938	2010	2114	2157	2

		⚒	⚒											Ⓐ			Ⓑ		Ⓐ			Ⓑ	
Coimbra d.	0017	0523	0553	0659	0814	0853	0953	1014	1159	1253	1314	1359	1453	1559	1614	1659	1756	1814	1900	1914	1953	2014	2232
Coimbra B d.	0026	0531	0601	0707	0822	0901	1001	1022	1207	1301	1322	1407	1501	1607	1622	1707	1807	1822	1908	1922	2001	2022	2242
Alfarelos d.	0055	0606	0636	0736	0844	0938	1036	1044	1236	1336	1344	1436	1536	1636	1644	1736	1836	1844	1932	1944	2036	2044	2311
Verride d.	0106	0619	0649	0756	...	0949	1049	...	1249	1349	...	1449	1549	1649	...	1749	1849	...	1940	...	2049	...	2323
Bifurcação de Lares d.	0114	0626	0656	0803	...	0956	1056	...	1256	1356	...	1456	1556	1656	...	1756	1856	...	|	...	2056	...	2330
Figueira da Foz a.	0126	0639	0709	0815	...	1009	1109	...	1309	1409	...	1509	1609	1709	...	1809	1909	...	1955	...	2109	...	2342

For main line trains calling at Alfarelos see Table **690**. Other trains: Coimbra - Alfarelos Table **699**, Figueira da Foz - Bifurcação de Lares Table **693**.

694 PORTO - RÉGUA - POCINHO

km				*IR* 861	*IR* 863	*IR* 865	*IR* 867	*IR* 869	*IR* 871	*IR* 875	
			⚒								
0	**Porto** São Bento d.	0625	...	...	0910	...	...	1510	...	1925	...
3	**Porto** Campanhã d.	0630	...	0715	0915	1115	1315	1515	1715	1930	2156
12	Ermesinde d.	0642	...	0727	0927	1127	1327	1527	1727	1941	2205
50	Caíde d.	0723	0729	0807	1007	1207	1407	1607	1807	2014	2237
59	Livração d.	...	0742	0816	1016	1216	1416	1616	1816	2022	2251
64	Marco de Canaveses d.	...	0750	0824	1024	1224	1424	1624	1824	2030	2259
107	**Régua** a.	...	0846	0908	1108	1309	1508	1709	1908	2115	2354
	Pocinho (below) a.	...	...	1034	1241	...	1634	*1846*	2033	...	...

			IR 860	*IR* 864	*IR* 868	*IR* 870	*IR* 872	*IR* 878	*IR* 960	
	⚒						Ⓐ			
Pocinho (below) d.	...	...	...	*0718*	...	1119	1326	...	1722	1
Régua d.	0511	0611	0648	0848	1048	1248	1448	1648	1848	2
Marco de Canaveses d.	0608	0705	0735	0935	1135	1335	1535	1735	1935	2
Livração d.	0614	0710	0741	0941	1141	1341	1541	1741	1941	2
Caíde d.	0633	0731	0754	0954	1154	1354	1554	1754	1954	2
Ermesinde d.	*0714*	0809	0826	1026	1226	1426	1626	1826	2026	2
Porto Campanhã a.	*0725*	0821	0835	1035	1235	1435	1635	1835	2035	2
Porto São Bento a.	*0730*	...	0850	...	...	1450	...	1850	...	2

km		*IR* 861		*IR* 863		*IR* 867		*IR* 873		*IR* 871	
					△						△
	Porto Campanhã d.	0715	...	0915	...	1315	...	*1515*	...	1715	...
0	**Régua** d.	0909	...	1114	...	1509	...	1720	...	1909	...
23	Pinhão d.	0937	...	1142	...	1537	...	1746	...	1935	...
36	Tua a.	0951	...	1156	1205	1551	...	1801	...	1950	1955
90	Mirandela a.	|	...	|	1335	|	...	|	...	|	2115
68	**Pocinho** a.	1034	...	1241	...	1634	...	1846	...	2033	...

	IR 862		*IR* 870		*IR* 872	*IR* 876		*IR* 960		
		△			Ⓐ	Ⓒ			△	
Pocinho d.	0718	...	1119	...	1326	1508	...	1722	...	1
Mirandela d.	|	0955	|	...	|	|	...	|	1800	
Tua d.	0759	1142	1202	...	1407	1553	...	1804	1943	1
Pinhão d.	0814	...	1217	...	1422	1608	...	1819	...	2
Régua a.	0840	...	1243	...	1447	1635	...	1845	...	2
Porto Campanhã a.	*1035*	...	1435	...	1635	*1835*	...	2035	...	

△ – By Taxi Tua - Mirandela and v.v. (Auto Tuela ✆ 917 534 718).

steam-hauled tourist train Regua - Tua and v.v.: ⑥ June 4 - Oct. 22, 2016 (also ⑦ July 3 - Sept. 25 and ③ Aug. 3 - 31, also Aug. 15). Régua d. 1521 → Tua a. 1640 / d. 1724 → Régua a. 1839.

695 PORTO - BRAGA

km					*AP* 131				*IC* 721					*AP* 133				*AP* 135					*AP* 137		*IC* 723	
																	Ⓐ	Ⓑh						Ⓐ		
	Lisboa Sta Ap. **690** d.	...	...	...	0700	...	...	...	0930	...	...	...	...	1400	...	...	...	1600	...	...	...	...	1900	...	2000	
0	**Porto** São Bento △ d.	0645	0745	0845	|	0945	1045	1145	|	1245	1345	1445	1545	|	1645	1745	1815	|	1845	1915	1945	2045	|	2145	|	22
3	**Porto** Campanhã △ d.	0650	0750	0850	0946	0950	1050	1150	1246	1250	1350	1450	1550	1646	1650	1750	1820	1846	1850	1920	1950	2050	2146	2150	2246	22
12	Ermesinde △ d.	0702	0802	0902	|	1002	1102	1202	|	1302	1402	1502	1602	|	1702	1802	1832	|	1902	1932	2002	2102	|	2202	|	23
26	Trofa △ d.	0716	0816	0916	|	1016	1116	1216	|	1316	1416	1516	1616	|	1716	1816	1844	|	1916	1944	2016	2116	|	2216	|	23
35	Famalicão △ d.	0727	0827	0927	1009	1027	1127	1227	1309	1327	1427	1527	1627	1709	1727	1827	1852	1909	1927	1952	2027	2127	2209	2227	2309	23
42	Nine △ d.	0735	0835	0935	1015	1035	1135	1235	1315	1335	1435	1535	1635	1715	1735	1835	1857	1915	1935	1957	2035	2135	2215	2235	2315	23
57	**Braga** △ a.	0756	0856	0956	1025	1056	1156	1256	1325	1356	1456	1556	1656	1725	1756	1856	1909	1925	1956	2009	2056	2156	2225	2256	2325	23

		AP 130							*IC* 720				*AP* 132		*IC* 722						*AP* 134				*AP* 136	
	⚒			Ⓐ	Ⓒ														Ⓐ			Ⓐ			Ⓑh	
Braga ▽ d.	0534	0607	0634	0721	0734	0804	0834	0934	1005	1039	1134	1234	1307	1334	1405	1434	1534	1634	1721	1734	1807	1821	1834	1934	2007	20
Nine ▽ d.	0554	0618	0654	0733	0754	0824	0854	0954	1016	1059	1154	1254	1318	1354	1416	1454	1554	1654	1733	1754	1818	1833	1854	1954	2018	20
Famalicão ▽ d.	0602	0623	0702	0738	0802	0832	0902	1002	1021	1107	1202	1302	1323	1402	1421	1502	1602	1702	1738	1802	1823	1838	1902	2002	2023	2
Trofa ▽ d.	0613	|	0713	0746	0813	0843	0913	1013	|	1118	1213	1313	|	1413	|	1513	1613	1713	1746	1813	|	1846	1913	2013	|	2
Ermesinde ▽ d.	0629	|	0729	0759	0829	0859	0929	1029	|	1134	1229	1329	|	1429	|	1529	1629	1729	1759	1829	|	1859	1929	2029	|	2
Porto Campanhã ▽ a.	0641	0647	0741	0811	0841	0911	0941	1041	1052	1146	1241	1341	1347	1441	1752	1541	1641	1741	1811	1841	1847	1911	1941	2041	2047	2
Porto São Bento ▽ a.	0645	|	0745	0815	0845	0915	0945	1045	|	1150	1245	1345	|	1445	|	1545	1645	1745	1815	1845	|	1915	1945	2045	|	2
Lisboa Sta Ap. **690** a.	...	0930	...	...	...	...	...	...	1400	...	...	...	1630	...	1800	...	...	...	...	...	2130	...	...	...	2330	

d – Journey 55 minutes.
h – Not ⑦ if ① is a public holiday. Not ⑤ if it is a public holiday.

△ – Additional journeys: 0115, 0615Ⓐ**d**, 0715Ⓐ, 0815Ⓐ**d**, 1215Ⓐ**d**, 1615Ⓐ**d**, 1715Ⓐ**d**. For other trains Porto - Nine see Table 69
▽ – Additional journeys: 0434, 0621Ⓐ**d**, 0745Ⓐ, 1321Ⓐ**d**, 2134Ⓒ, 2234Ⓐ, 2332. For other trains Nine - Porto see Table **696**.

PORTO - GUIMARÃES 695a

m				AP141								IC621
					Ⓐ					Ⓐ		
ɔoa Sta Ap. 690 ..d.	...	...	...	0800	...	...	...	...	...	...	...	1730
São Bento .... ▷ d.	0720	0820	1020	|	1120	1220	1420	1620	1820	1855	2020	|
Campanhã.... ▷ d.	0725	0825	1025	1100	1125	1225	1425	1625	1825	1900	2025	2041
sinde .... ▷ d.	0737	0837	1037	|	1137	1237	1437	1637	1837	1910	2037	|
.... ▷ d.	0752	0852	1052	1121	1152	1252	1452	1652	1852	1921	2052	2100
arães ....a.	0836	0936	1133	1153	1236	1336	1533	1736	1937	1954	2133	2138

		IC620						AP140				
	Ⓐ								Ⓐ	Ⓐ	Ⓐ	
Guimarães ....d.	0706	0743	0848	0948	1159	1348	1548	1655	1712	1812	2012	2148
Trofa .... ▷ d.	0739	0824	0933	1033	1243	1433	1633	1727	1801	1901	2104	2233
Ermesinde............... ▷ d.	0751	|	0949	1049	1259	1449	1649	|	1819	1919	2119	2249
Porto Campanhã .... ▷ a.	0801	0852	1001	1101	1311	1501	1701	1744	1831	1931	2131	2301
Porto São Bento..... ▷ a.	0805	|	1005	1105	1315	1505	1705	|	1835	1935	2135	2305
Lisboa Sta Ap. **690** .. a.	...	1200	...	...	...	...	...	2040	...	...	...	...

See also Tables **695**, **696**.

onal trains: **Porto - Guimarães** 0620Ⓐ, 1720Ⓐ, 1920Ⓐ, 2120Ⓒ, 2220Ⓐ, 2320; **Guimarães - Porto** 0548Ⓐ, 0648Ⓒ, 0748Ⓐ, 1248Ⓐ, 1748Ⓒ, 1916Ⓐ, 1948Ⓒ, 2248.

PORTO - VIANA DO CASTELO - VALENÇA - VIGO 696

	IR851				421*						IR853				IR855			IR857		423*	IR859		
	Ⓐ	Ⓐ		⚒	2🅁			Ⓐ					Ⓐ							2🅁	Ⓐ		
Porto Campanhã .... ▷ d.	0610	0620	...	*0650*	0815	...	...	0820	...	*0950*	1310	1250	...	*1350*	1615	*1650*	...	1815	*1850*	1915	2015	2210	...
Ermesinde .... ▷ d.	0619	0632	...	*0702*	|	...	...	0832	...	*1002*	1321	1302	...	*1402*	1627	*1702*	...	1827	*1902*	|	2026	2221	...
Trofa .... ▷ d.	0630	0644	...	*0716*	|	...	...	0844	...	*1016*	1332	1316	...	*1416*	1638	*1716*	...	1838	*1916*	|	2038	2232	...
Famalicão....................... ▷ d.	0638	0652	...	*0727*	|	...	...	0852	...	*1027*	1340	1327	...	*1427*	1646	*1727*	...	1846	*1927*	|	2047	2241	...
Nine .... ▷ a.	0644	0656	...	*0735*	0842	...	...	0857	...	*1035*	1346	1335	...	*1435*	1652	*1735*	...	1852	*1935*	1942	2054	2247	...
Nine ....d.	0644	...	0706	0747	0843	...	...	...	0904	1104	1347	...	1400	1500	1656	1737	...	1856	2003	1943	2056	2248	...
Barcelos ....d.	0654	...	0720	0804	|	...	...	...	0917	1117	1357	...	1413	1513	1706	1750	...	1906	2016	|	2106	2302	...
Viana do Castelo................a.	0733	...	0802	0850	0916	...	...	...	1005	1200	1428	...	1456	1601	1738	1832	...	1936	2104	2016	2139	2343	...
Viana do Castelo................d.	0735	...	0824	...	0917	...	...	...	1016	...	1430	...	...	1615	1739	1838	...	1937	...	2017	2140	...	...
Vila Nova de Cerveira............d.	0804	...	0913	...	|	...	...	...	1059	...	1501	...	...	1657	1806	1920	....	2009	...	|	2207	...	...
Valença..................... 🏛 PT d.	0815	...	0932	...	0952	1000	...	...	1114	...	1512	...	...	1712	1817	1935	1944	2020	...	2052	2218	...	...
Tui.............................. 🏛 ES d.	...	...	...	...	|	1107	...	...	...	...	...	...	...	...	...	...	2051	...	...	|	...	...	...
Redondela **680** ....d.	...	...	...	...	|	1139	...	...	...	...	...	...	...	...	...	...	2124	...	...	|	...	...	...
Vigo Guixar ◐ **680** ....a.	...	...	...	...	1130	1150	...	...	...	...	...	...	...	...	...	...	2135	...	...	2230	...	...	...

					IR850	420*				IR852				IR854					IR856	422*				
		Ⓐ	Ⓐ	Ⓐ		2🅁						Ⓐ				Ⓐ				2🅁				
Guixar ◐ **680**................d.	...	...	...	...	...	0902	...	...	0920	...	...	...	...	...	...	...	...	...	...	2002	1812	...	...	...
ɔndela **680** ....d.	...	...	...	...	...	|	...	...	0931	...	...	...	...	...	...	...	...	...	...	|	1824	...	...	...
.... 🏛 ES d.	...	...	...	...	...	|	...	...	1003	...	...	...	...	...	...	...	...	...	...	|	1858	...	...	...
nça...................... 🏛 PT d.	...	...	0535	0617	0736	0840	...	...	0911	0921	1117	...	...	1430	1517	...	...	...	1752	1940	1806	1833	...	...
Nova de Cerveira.............d.	...	...	0548	0632	0747	|	...	...	...	0941	1132	...	...	1440	1532	...	...	...	1805	|	...	1848	...	...
a do Castelo.....................a.	...	...	0625	0715	0814	0912	...	...	...	1014	1215	...	...	1510	1614	...	...	...	1837	2013	...	1933	...	...
a do Castelo.....................d.	0511	...	0627	0716	0816	0916	...	0944	...	1015	1216	1350	...	1511	1621	...	...	1748	1840	2016	...	...	2024	...
elos ....d.	0554	...	0719	0803	0853	|	...	1028	...	1044	1259	1437	...	1540	1707	...	...	1834	1924	|	...	...	2105	...
....a.	0608	...	0735	0817	0903	0949	...	1043	...	1053	1313	1452	...	1549	1721	...	...	1848	1933	2049	...	...	2119	...
.... ▷ d.	...	0633	0732	*0824*	0904	0950	...	...	...	1054	*1354*	...	1454	1550	...	1733	...	*1854*	1935	2050	...	...	2119	...
alicão........................ ▷ d.	...	0638	0743	*0832*	0913	|	...	...	...	1102	*1402*	...	1502	1557	...	1738	...	*1902*	1942	|	...	...	2126	...
a..................................... ▷ d.	...	0646	0751	*0843*	0921	|	...	...	...	1109	*1413*	...	1513	1605	...	1746	...	*1913*	1949	|	...	...	2133	...
esinde .... ▷ d.	...	0659	0807	*0859*	0935	|	...	...	...	1121	*1429*	...	1529	1619	...	1759	...	*1929*	2001	|	...	...	2146	...
o Campanhã.................. ▷ a.	...	0710	0819	*0910*	0945	1018	...	...	...	1130	*1440*	...	1540	1630	...	1810	...	*1940*	2010	2118	...	...	2155	...

New terminus (1 km from Vigo Urzaiz).
See also Table **695**.

* – Trains **420 - 423** are branded *Celta*.

ES – Spain (Central European Time).
PT – Portugal (West European Time).

LISBOA - PINHAL NOVO - TUNES - FARO 697

1		AP180		IC570		IC572		IC574		AP186
	Porto Campanhã **690** ....d.	0547	...	...	...	...	...	...	...	1547
	Coimbra B **690**....................d.	0646	...	...	...	...	...	...	...	1646
0	**Lisboa** Oriente .... ⊙ d.	0823	...	1002	...	1402	...	1732	...	1823
7	Entrecampos .... ⊙ d.	0831	...	1010	...	1410	...	1740	...	1831
9	Sete Rios .... ⊙ d.	|	...	1014	...	1414	...	1744	...	|
3	Pragal................................ ⊙ d.	|	...	1026	...	1426	...	1756	...	|
7	Pinhal Novo .... ⊙ d.	0906	...	1048	...	1448	...	1818	...	1906
8	Grândola ....d.	|	...	1119	...	1516	...	1846	...	|
0	Funcheira ....d.	|	...	1155	...	1552	...	1929	...	|
4	**Tunes** .... ▷ d.	1054	...	1302	...	1704	...	2034	...	2055
9	Albufeira........................... ▷ d.	1101	...	1307	...	1710	...	2039	...	2102
6	Loulé .... ▷ d.	1113	...	1319	...	1722	...	2051	...	2114
2	**Faro** .... ▷ a.	1123	...	1330	...	1732	...	2102	...	2123

	AP182		IC670		IC672		AP184		IC674
Faro .... ▷ d.	0700	...	0824	...	1354	...	1505	...	1756
Loulé .... ▷ d.	0710	...	0835	...	1405	...	1516	...	1806
Albufeira .... ▷ d.	0723	...	0847	...	1417	...	1529	...	1818
Tunes............................. ▷ d.	0729	...	0853	...	1423	...	1535	...	1825
Funcheira..............................d.	0823	...	1000	...	1526	...	|	...	1929
Grândola...............................d.	0854	...	1037	...	1604	...	|	...	2008
Pinhal Novo .... ⊙ d.	0923	...	1107	...	1637	...	1723	...	2040
Pragal............................. ⊙ a.	|	...	1130	...	1704	...	|	...	2104
Sete Rios......................... ⊙ a.	|	...	1143	...	1714	...	|	...	2114
Entrecampos.................... ⊙ a.	0957	...	1146	...	1717	...	1757	...	2117
Lisboa Oriente .... ⊙ a.	1005	...	1156	...	1726	...	1805	...	2126
Coimbra B **690** ....a.	1145	...	...	...	...	...	1945	...	...
Porto Campanhã **690**......a.	1244	...	...	...	...	...	2044	...	...

LOCAL TRAINS LAGOS - TUNES - FARO

			⚒						Ⓐ		
0	**Lagos** ....d.	0616	0659	0748	1114	1310	1418	1705	1813	2001	...
8	Portimão.........................d.	0634	0718	0807	1133	1329	1437	1724	1832	2020	...
9	Silves ....d.	0650	0734	0824	1150	1350	1454	1745	1849	2037	...
2	Algoz ....d.	0705	0749	0840	1206	1409	1510	1801	1912	2054	...
6	**Tunes** .... ▷ d.	0711	0755	0853	1212	1423	1516	1807	1918	2107	...
2	Albufeira.................... ▷ d.	0722	0801	0859	1218	1429	1528	1818	1925	2114	...
9	Loulé .... ▷ d.	0743	0816	0919	1239	1444	1543	1834	1941	2130	...
5	**Faro** .... ▷ a.	0759	0837	0934	1254	1459	1559	1849	1956	2145	...

	⚒									
Faro .... ▷ d.	0711	0902	1023	1222	1619	1715	1812	1938	2018	...
Loulé .... ▷ d.	0728	0919	1039	1239	1636	1737	1834	2002	2035	...
Albufeira .... ▷ d.	0743	0935	1100	1307	1652	1755	1850	2021	2101	...
Tunes........................ ▷ d.	0755	0942	1106	1313	1706	1807	1857	2035	2107	...
Algoz ....d.	0801	0947	1112	1319	1712	1812	1902	2040	2112	...
Silves...............................d.	0824	1003	1130	1335	1729	1830	1918	2058	2128	...
Portimão ....d.	0837	1018	1150	1350	1745	1849	1932	2111	2143	...
Lagos...............................a.	0856	1036	1208	1408	1803	1907	1951	2128	2201	...

- See Table **698** for other fast trains, Table **699** for local services, including connections Barreiro - Pinhal Novo.

▷ – Also see other section of table above or below.

FARO - VILA REAL DE SANTO ANTÓNIO 697a

			Ⓐ			Ⓐ					Ⓐ	
0	**Faro** .... △ d.	0744	0857	0955	1134	1255	1355	1500	1624	1751	1828	1927
'0	Olhão .... △ d.	0759	0908	1006	1145	1306	1406	1511	1635	1802	1840	1938
32	Tavira.......... △ d.	0824	0938	1031	1210	1336	1436	1536	1705	1832	1905	2008
56	**Vila Real** §.........a.	0852	1006	1100	1238	1405	1505	1605	1733	1900	1938	2036

								Ⓐ			
Vila Real §.....d.	0548	0705	0722	0908	1113	1239	1333	1533	1635	1803	2042
Tavira .... △ d.	0613	0734	0751	0938	1139	1308	1407	1607	1705	1832	2110
Olhão........ △ d.	0634	0759	0821	1006	1206	1332	1432	1635	1729	1901	2139
Faro .... △ a.	0644	0810	0831	1017	1217	1343	1443	1646	1739	1912	2150

- Additional journeys : Faro - Villa Real at 2106, 2151; Villa Real - Faro at 0626Ⓐ, 1910Ⓐ.

§ – Vila Real de Santo António (± *1500m* from bus station/ferry terminal).

LISBOA - PINHAL NOVO - ÉVORA and BEJA 698

m		IC 590	IC 581	IC 592	IC 583	IC 594	IC 585	IC 596	IC 587	IC 598	IC 589
		Ⓐ	Ⓐ	Ⓐ	Ⓐ	Ⓒ	Ⓒ				
0	**Lisboa** Oriente ... ▷ d.	0702	...	0902	...	0952	...	1702	...	1902	...
7	Entrecampos....... ▷ d.	0710	...	0910	...	1000	...	1710	...	1910	...
9	Sete Rios........... ▷ d.	0714	...	0914	...	1004	...	1714	...	1914	...
'8	Pragal................ ▷ d.	0726	...	0926	...	1015	...	1726	...	1926	...
47	**Pinhal Novo** .... ▷ d.	0748	...	0948	...	1032	...	1748	...	1948	...
38	Vendas Novas .... d.	0818	...	1010	...	1102	...	1810	...	2010	...
22	Casa Branca........... a.	0831	...	1023	...	1115	...	1823	...	2023	...
22	Casa Branca........... d.	0832	0836	1024	1030	1116	1119	1824	1829	2024	2025
48	Évora .... a.	0842	|	1035	|	1126	|	1835	|	2035	|
35	**Beja**........................ a.	...	0926	...	1121	...	1210	...	1920	...	2115

	IC 580	IC 690		IC 582	IC 692		IC 584	IC 694		IC 586	IC 696
	Ⓐ	Ⓐ									
Beja .... d.	0623	...	...	0822	...	...	1611	...	...	1815	...
Évora .... d.	|	0706	...	|	0906	...	|	1657	...	|	1906
Casa Branca............ a.	0711	0716	...	0914	0916	...	1700	1707	...	1908	1916
Casa Branca............ d.	...	0717	...	...	0917	...	...	1708	...	...	1917
Vendas Novas .... d.	...	0731	...	...	0931	...	...	1722	...	...	1931
Pinhal Novo........ ▷ d.	...	0753	...	...	0953	...	...	1751	...	...	1953
Pragal................... ▷ a.	...	0814	...	...	1014	...	...	1814	...	...	2014
Sete Rios.............. ▷ a.	...	0824	...	...	1024	...	...	1824	...	...	2024
Entrecampos......... ▷ a.	...	0828	...	...	1028	...	...	1828	...	...	2028
Lisboa Oriente .... ▷ a.	...	0836	...	...	1036	...	...	1836	...	...	2036

- See Table **697** for other fast trains and Table **699** for local services, including connections Barreiro - Pinhal Novo.

699 OTHER LOCAL SERVICES

LISBOA - ESTORIL - CASCAIS

km																						
0	**Lisboa** Cais do Sodre d.	Ⓐ	0530	every	0700	every	1000	every	1700	every	2012	every	2132	2200	every	0130	Ⓒ	0530	every	0800	every	1900	every
24	Estoril d.		0606	30	0729	12	1036	20	1729	12	2048	20	2208	2236	30	0206		0606	30	0836	20	1936	30
26	**Cascais** a.		0610	mins	0733	mins	1040	mins	1733	mins	2052	mins	2212	2240	mins	0210		0610	mins	0840	mins	1940	mins

Cascais d.	Ⓐ	0530	0600	0630	0652	every	2104	2130	every	0130	...	Ⓒ	0530	every	0630	0704	every	1904	every	2104	2130	every
Estoril d.		0534	0604	0634	0656	12-20 ◧	2108	2134	30	0134	...		0534	30	0634	0708	20	1908	30	2108	2134	30
Lisboa Cais do Sodre a.		0610	0640	0710	0725	mins	2144	2210	mins	0210	...		0610	mins	0710	0744	mins	1944	mins	2144	2210	mins

◧ – Every 12 minutes 0704 - 1004 and 1704 - 2004; every 20 minutes 1004 - 1704.

LISBOA ORIENTE - SINTRA

		Ⓐ		Ⓐ		Ⓒ		Ⓒ
Lisboa Oriente d.	Ⓐ	0558		0108	Ⓒ	0608		0108
Roma Areeiro d.		0605	See	0115		0615	every	0115
Entrecampos d.		0607	note	0117		0617	30	0117
Sete Rios d.		0610	△	0120		0620	mins	0120
Monte Abraão d.		0625		0135		0635	until	0135
Agualva-Cacém d.		0631		0141		0641		0141
Sintra a.		0645		0155		0655		0155

		Ⓐ		Ⓐ		Ⓒ	
Sintra d.	Ⓐ	0506		0006	Ⓒ	0506	
Agualva-Cacém d.		0519	See	0019		0519	every
Monte Abraão d.		0524	note	0024		0524	30
Sete Rios d.		0539	▽	0039		0539	mins
Entrecampos d.		0542		0042		0542	until
Roma Areeiro d.		0544		0044		0544	
Lisboa Oriente a.		0552		0052		0552	

△ – 0558, 0618, every 10 mins 0638-0938, every 20 mins 0958-1638, every 10 mins 1648-1958, 2018, every 30 mins 2038-0108.

▽ – 0506, 0536, 0606, every 10 mins 0626-0936, every 20 mins 0956-1556, every 10 mins 1616-1936, 1956, 2016, every 30 mins 2036-0006.

LISBOA ROSSIO - SINTRA and MIRA SINTRA-MELEÇAS

	Ⓒ	Ⓐ			n		n
Lisboa Rossio d.	0601	0641		0101	0621	and	2021
Monte Abraão d.	0621	0701	See	0121	0641	hourly	2041
Agualva-Cacém d.	0627	0707	note	0127	0647	until	2047
Mira Sintra-Meleças a.	|	|	·△	|	0650	⊡	2050
Sintra a.	0641	0721		0141	...		...

Sintra d.	0520		0020	...		...
Mira Sintra-Meleças d.	|	See	|	0730	and	2030
Agualva-Cacém d.	0533	note	0033	0733	hourly	2033
Monte Abraão d.	0539	▽	0039	0739	until	2039
Lisboa Rossio a.	0559		0059	0759	⊡	2059

n – On Ⓒ runs 10 minutes later.

△ – Ⓐ: every 30 mins 0641-2011 (◧) and 2031-0101. Ⓒ: hourly 0601-2001, every 30 mins 2101-0101.

▽ – Ⓐ: every 30 mins 0520-0620, 0640-2010 (◐), 2050-0020. Ⓒ: 0520, hourly 0550-2050, every 30 mins 2120-0020.

⊡ – Additional services operate during peak hours on Ⓐ.

◧ – Between 0941Ⓐ and 1641Ⓐ runs at xx41, xx0

◐ – Between 0940Ⓐ and 1640Ⓐ runs at xx40, xx0

LISBOA - PINHAL NOVO - SETÚBAL

Operator: Fertagus. CP tickets not valid.

Roma Areeiro d.	Ⓐ	0043	0543		2243	2358	Ⓒ	0643		2343
Entrecampos d.		0045	0545	and	2245	0000		0645	and	2345
Sete Rios d.		0049	0549	every	2249	0004		0649	every	2349
Pragal d.		0100	0600	hour	2300	0015		0700	hour	0000
Pinhal Novo d.		0128	0628	until	2328	0043		0728	until	0028
Setúbal a.		0141	0641		2341	0056		0741		0041

Setúbal d.	Ⓐ	0548	0658		1858	1928	2018		0018	Ⓒ	0558		2
Pinhal Novo d.		0602	0712	and	1912	1942	2032	and	0032		0612	and	2
Pragal d.		0629	0739	every	1939	2009	2059	every	0059		0639	every	2
Sete Rios d.		0640	0750	hour	1950	2020	2110	hour	0110		0650	hour	2
Entrecampos d.		0644	0754	until	1954	2024	2114	until	0114		0654	until	2
Roma Areeiro a.		0646	0756		1956	2026	2116		0116		0656		2

Additional journeys on Ⓐ: from Roma Areeiro 1813, 1913, 2013, from Setúbal 0628, 0728, 0828. Trains run every 10 – 20 minutes (every 30 mins evenings and Ⓒ) Roma Areeiro - Pragal - Co

Catamaran LISBOA - BARREIRO

Soflusa / Transtejo

From Lisboa Terreiro do Paço: By ⛴ journey time 20 minutes. *10* km

Ⓐ: 0545, 0610, 0640, 0700 and every 10 minutes until 0920, 0940, 0955 and every 30 minutes until 1555, 1615, 1630, 1650 and every 10 minutes 2010, 2030, 2050, 2110, 2125, 2155, 2225, 2255, 2330, 0000, 0100, 0200.

Ⓒ: 0545, 0615, 0645, 0715, 0755, 0825⑥, 0855, 0925⑥, 0955, 1025⑥, 1055, 1155, 1255, 1355, 1455, 1525, 1625, 1655, 1725, 1755, 1825, 1855, 1925, 1955, 2055, 2125, 2155, 2225, 0000, 0100, 0200.

From Barreiro Barcos: By ⛴ journey time 20 minutes. *10* km

Ⓐ: 0515, 0545, 0615, 0635 and every 10 minutes until 0855, 0900, 0910, 0925, 0940, 0 and every 30 minutes until 1525, 1545, 1600, 1620 and every 10 minutes until 1940, 2 2020, 2040, 2100, 2125, 2155, 2225, 2300, 2330, 0030, 0130.

Ⓒ: 0515, 0545, 0620, 0650, 0725, 0755⑥, 0825, 0855⑥, 0925, 0955⑥, 1025, 1125, 1 1325, 1425, 1455, 1525, 1555, 1625, 1655, 1725, 1755, 1825, 1855, 1925, 2025, 2 2125, 2225, 2330, 0030, 0130.

BARREIRO - SETÚBAL

km		Ⓐ						
0	**Barreiro** d.	0555	0625	every 30 mins	2125	2232	2325	0029
15	Pinhal Novo d.	0614	0644	(hourly on Ⓒ)	2144	2251	2344	0048
28	**Setúbal** a.	0626	0656	until	2157	2303	2356	0100

	Ⓐ	Ⓒ	Ⓐ				Ⓐ			
Setúbal d.	0508	0548	0618	0648	every 30 mins	2048	2122	2151	2248	2
Pinhal Novo d.	0520	0600	0630	0700	(hourly on Ⓒ)	2100	2136	2202	2300	0
Barreiro a.	0538	0618	0648	0718	until	2118	2154	2223	2318	0

Most journeys continue to Praias do Sado A.

LISBOA - ENTRONCAMENTO - TOMAR

km			Ⓐ	⚒		Ⓐ		Ⓐ	Ⓐ		Ⓐ		Ⓐ			Ⓐ§		Ⓐ§				Ⓐ	
0	**Lisboa** Santa Apolónia ▷ d.	0015	0545	0645	0745	0845	0945	1045	1145	1245	1345	1445	1545	1615	1645	1715	1745	1815	1845	1945	2045	2145	2245
7	**Lisboa** Oriente ▷ d.	0025	0553	0653	0753	0853	0953	1053	1153	1253	1353	1453	1553	1623	1653	1723	1753	1823	1853	1953	2053	2153	2253
31	Vila Franca de Xira d.	0051	0611	0711	0811	0911	1011	1111	1211	1311	1411	1511	1611	1639	1711	1739	1811	1838	1911	2011	2111	2211	2311
75	Santarém d.	0135	0655	0755	0855	0949	1055	1148	1255	1348	1455	1549	1655	1706	1756	1806	1855	1907	1955	2055	2149	2259	2348
107	Entroncamento a.	0159	0719	0819	0919	1013	1119	1212	1319	1412	1519	1614	1719	1726	1820	1826	1919	1927	2019	2119	2214	2323	0012
130	**Tomar** a.	...	0751	0847	0947	...	1151	1247	...	1440	1551	1651	1751	...	1853	1900	1951	2000	2051	2147	2251	2351	0040

	①–⑥	Ⓐ	Ⓐ§		Ⓐ§		①–⑥		Ⓐ			Ⓐ		Ⓐ					Ⓐ	⑦d		Ⓐ	⑦d	
Tomar d.	...	0515	0605	0615r	0650	0711r	...	0802	...	1011	1111r	...	1315	...	1511	1611	1711	1811	1911	...	2011	...	...	22
Entroncamento d.	0415	0542	0626	0642	0711	0742	0808	0838	0942	1038	1142	1238	1342	1438	1542	1638	1742	1841	1944	2037	2042	2145	2226	22
Santarém d.	0439	0606	0645	0706	0731	0806	0827	0902	1006	1102	1206	1302	1406	1502	1606	1702	1806	1906	2008	2057	2106	2205	2245	23
Vila Franca de Xira d.	0518	0647	0717	0747	0802	0847	0856	0947	1047	1147	1247	1347	1447	1547	1647	1747	1847	1955	2047	2126	2147	2247	2326	23
Lisboa Oriente ▷ d.	0535	0705	0733	0805	0818	0905	0911	1005	1105	1205	1305	1405	1505	1605	1705	1805	1905	2012	2105	2142	2205	2305	2342	00
Lisboa Santa Apolónia ▷ a.	0543	0713	0741	0813	0828	0913	0920	1013	1113	1213	1313	1413	1513	1613	1713	1813	1913	2020	2113	2150	2213	2313	2350	00

▷ – Additional local trains are available. **d** – If ⑦ is a public holiday runs next day instead. **r** – ⚒ only. § – *IR* train.

ENTRONCAMENTO - COIMBRA

km		†	Ⓐ		Ⓐ						Ⓐ		Ⓑ
0	**Entroncamento** d.	...	0555	0655	0755	0905	1055	1255	1547	1740	1855	1955	2140
24	Fátima ⊙ d.	...	0616	0716	0816	0926	1116	1316	1608	1807	1916	2016	2201
64	Pombal d.	...	0648	0748	0848	0958	1148	1348	1640	1839	1948	2048	2233
91	Alfarelos d.	0710	0712	0812	0919	1031	1212	1412	1704	1903	2012	2119	2256
111	**Coimbra B** a.	0732	0732	0832	0941	1052	1232	1432	1725	1924	2032	2142	2317
111	**Coimbra B** d.	0737	0737	0837	0949	1059	1237	1437	1731	1935	2038	2153	...
113	**Coimbra** a.	0741	0741	0841	0953	1103	1241	1441	1735	1938	2041	2157	...

	⚒	Ⓐ					Ⓐ			(
Coimbra d.	0604	0714	0814	1014	1314	1614	1714	1814	1914	20
Coimbra B a.	0607	0717	0817	1017	1317	1617	1717	1817	1917	20
Coimbra B d.	0612	0722	0822	1022	1322	1622	1722	1822	1922	20
Alfarelos d.	0635	0745	0845	1045	1345	1645	1745	1845	1945	20
Pombal d.	0710	0818	0918	1118	1410	1718	1818	1918	2018	21
Fátima ⊙ d.	0744	0901	0950	1150	1450	1750	1901	1950	2050	21
Entroncamento a.	0804	0921	1011	1211	1511	1811	1921	2021	2111	22

r – Ⓐ only. ⊙ – Station is *20 km* from Fátima (full name of station is Chão de Maçãs - Fátima). *For fast trains Entroncamento - Coimbra B see Table* **690**.

AVEIRO - COIMBRA

km					Ⓐ		Ⓐ		Ⓐ				
0	**Aveiro** d.	0650	0750	0950	1050	1134	1224	1350	1450	1534	1750	1950	2150
41	Pampilhosa d.	0726	0826	1026	1126	1210	1300	1426	1526	1610	1826	2026	2226
55	**Coimbra B** a.	0740	0840	1040	1140	1224	1314	1440	1540	1626	1840	2040	2240
57	**Coimbra** a.	0753	0846	1046	1151	1231	1324	1446	1551	1633	1852	2052	2246

		⚒								
Coimbra d.	0630	0743	0846	1053	1343	1449	1643	1829	1943	22
Coimbra B d.	0634	0748	0851	1058	1348	1454	1648	1833	1949	22
Pampilhosa d.	0652	0805	0908	1115	1405	1512	1705	1856	2012	22
Aveiro a.	0729	0842	0945	1152	1442	1548	1742	1935	2048	23

Additional trains: **Aveiro - Coimbra**: 0550⚒, 0734Ⓐ, 0850Ⓐ, 1648Ⓐ, 1850Ⓐ, 2050Ⓐ. **Coimbra - Aveiro**: 0543Ⓐ, 1005Ⓐ, 1143Ⓐ, 1243Ⓐ, 1542Ⓐ, 1744Ⓐ, 2043Ⓐ.

Reservations are compulsory for travel by AP and IC trains (also Sud Expresso and Lusitania)

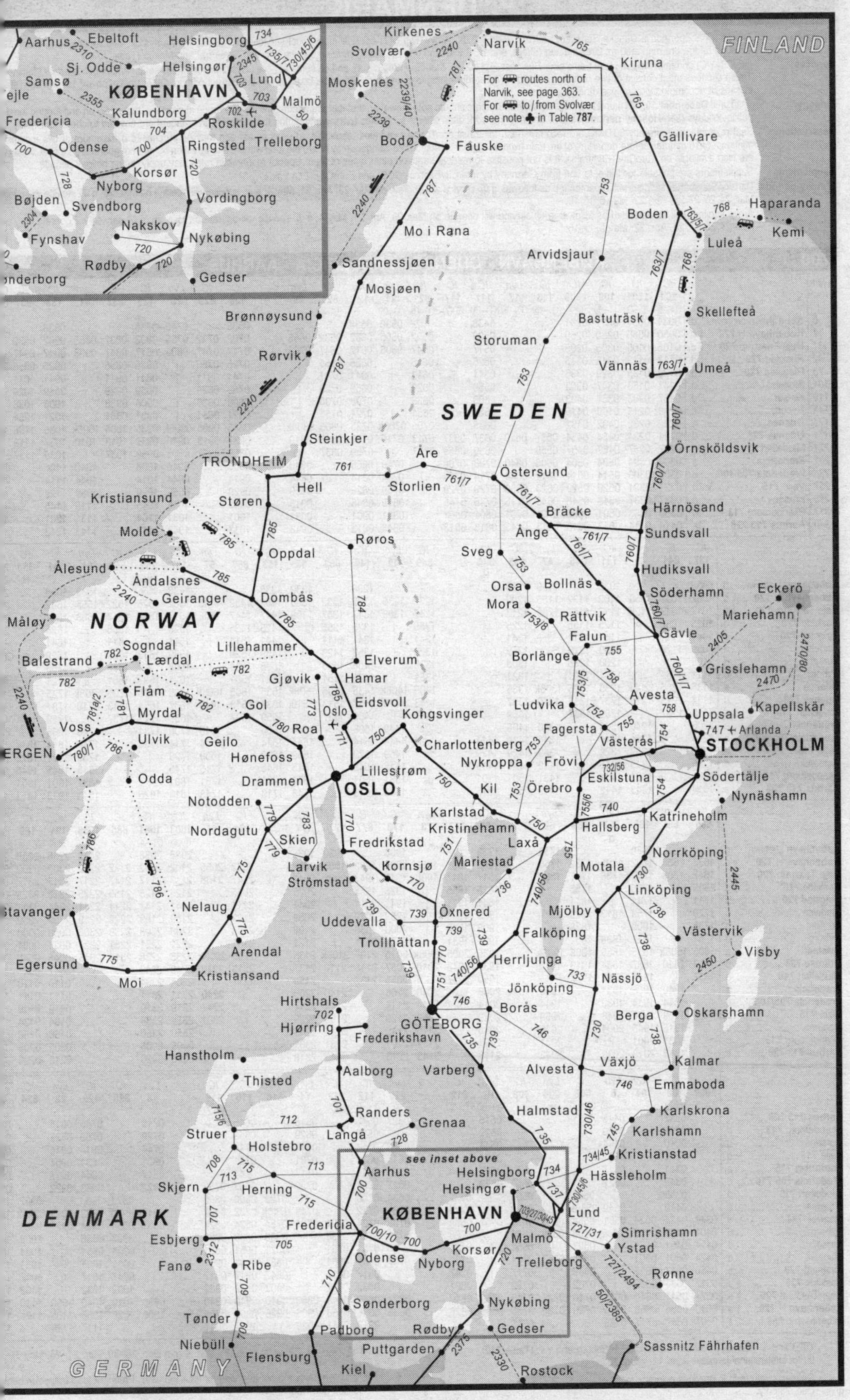

FINLAND
SWEDEN
NORWAY
DENMARK
GERMANY
KØBENHAVN
For routes north of Narvik, see page 363.
For to / from Svolvær see note ♣ in Table 787.
Kirkenes
Svolvær
Narvik
Kiruna
Moskenes
Bodø
Fauske
Gällivare
Mo i Rana
Boden
Haparanda
Kemi
Luleå
Sandnessjøen
Arvidsjaur
Mosjøen
Skellefteå
Brønnøysund
Bastuträsk
Storuman
Rørvik
Vännäs
Umeå
Örnsköldsvik
Steinkjer
TRONDHEIM
Hell
Åre
Storlien
Östersund
Kristiansund
Støren
Härnösand
Bräcke
Ånge
Sundsvall
Molde
Røros
Oppdal
Sveg
Hudiksvall
Ålesund
Åndalsnes
Geiranger
Dombås
Orsa
Mora
Bollnäs
Söderhamn
Eckerö
Mariehamn
Måløy
Rättvik
Falun
Gävle
Sogndal
Lillehammer
Balestrand
Lærdal
Elverum
Borlänge
Grisslehamn
Gjøvik
Hamar
Flåm
Eidsvoll
Avesta
Myrdal
Gol
Ludvika
Uppsala
Kapellskär
Voss
Kongsvinger
Fagersta
Arlanda
BERGEN
Ulvik
Geilo
Roa
Oslo
Charlottenberg
Västerås
STOCKHOLM
Hønefoss
Nykroppa
Frövi
Odda
Drammen
Lillestrøm
OSLO
Kil
Örebro
Eskilstuna
Södertälje
Nynäshamn
Notodden
Karlstad
Katrineholm
Nordagutu
Kristinehamn
Hallsberg
Skien
Fredrikstad
Laxå
Norrköping
Larvik
Kornsjø
Mariestad
Motala
Strömstad
Linköping
Stavanger
Nelaug
Mjölby
Uddevalla
Öxnered
Västervik
Falköping
Trollhättan
Arendal
Visby
Egersund
Herrljunga
Kristiansand
Moi
Jönköping
Nässjö
Hirtshals
Hjørring
Frederikshavn
GÖTEBORG
Borås
Berga
Oskarshamn
Hanstholm
Aalborg
Varberg
Alvesta
Växjö
Kalmar
Thisted
Emmaboda
Randers
Grenaa
Halmstad
Karlskrona
Struer
Langå
Karlshamn
Holstebro
Kristianstad
see inset above
Aarhus
Helsingborg
Helsingør
Hässleholm
Skjern
Herning
Lund
Fredericia
Malmö
Simrishamn
Esbjerg
Ystad
Odense
Korsør
Nyborg
Trelleborg
Fanø
Ribe
Rønne
Sønderborg
Nykøbing
Tønder
Padborg
Rødby
Gedser
Niebüll
Sassnitz Fährhafen
Flensburg
Puttgarden
Kiel
Rostock
Ebeltoft
Sj. Odde
Samsø
Vejle
Kalundborg
Roskilde
Ringsted
Bøjden
Svendborg
Vordingborg
Fynshav
Nakskov
Sønderborg

DENMARK

Operators: The principal operator is Danske Statsbaner (*DSB*): www.dsb.dk. Arriva Tog (*AT*) operate many local services in Jutland: www.arriva.dk. Additionally, local trains o Øresund bridge are marketed as Øresundståg (*Øtåg*), and DSB Øresund operate the *Kystbanen* service between Helsingør and Malmö (Table 703).

Services: InterCity (*IC*) and InterCityLyn (*Lyn*) trains offer *Business* (1st class), *Standard* (2nd class), and on some services *Hvilepladser* ('quiet' seats) and *Familiepladser* ('family' These services often consist of two or more portions for different destinations and care should be taken to join the correct portion. Other trains convey 1st and 2nd (sta classes of accommodation unless otherwise shown.

Timings: Valid until **December 10, 2016** unless otherwise stated. Readers should note, however, that minor amendments may be made at any time, especially on and around the d public holidays (see **Holiday periods** below). Engineering work often affects schedules (particularly during the summer) and readers are advised to check locally.

Reservations: Seat reservations (currently 30 DKK) are recommended for travel on *IC* and *Lyn* trains (especially at peak times) and may be purchased a maximum of two months minimum of 15 minutes before departure of the train from its *originating* station. Passengers may board the train without a reservation but are not guaranteed a seat. Reser are also available on EuroCity (*EC*) trains. It is not possible to reserve seats on other types of train. Special reservation rules may apply during holiday periods.

Supplements: Supplements are payable for travel to and from Germany by InterCityExpress (*ICE*) and EuroCity (*EC*) trains.

Holiday periods: Danske Statsbaner services will be amended as follows: a ⑤ service will operate on Mar. 23, Apr. 21, May 4; a ⑥ service will operate on Mar. 26; a ⑦ service will oper Mar. 24, 25, 27, 28, Apr. 22, May 5, 15, 16.
Arriva services will be amended as follows: a ⑤ service will operate on Mar. 23, Apr. 21, May 4; a ⑥ service will operate on Mar. 26; a ⑦ service will operate on Mar. 24, 25, 27, 28, Apr. 22, May 5, 15, 16.

700 KØBENHAVN - ODENSE - FREDERICIA - AARHUS

km		IC 101 ①–⑤	IC 1601 ⑥⑦	IC 109 ①–⑤	IC 1609 ⑥⑦	IC 113 ①–⑤	Lyn 17 ①–⑤	IC 117 ①–⑤	IC 117 ⑥⑦	IC 821 ①–⑤	Lyn 21 ①–⑤	IC 121	IC 821 ①–⑤	Lyn 25		IC 125	IC 829	Lyn 29	IC 129	IC 833	Lyn 41	IC 133	IC 837
0	**København** Lufthavn.....d.	0031	0031	0231	0231	...	...	0438	...	...	0530	0538	...	...	...	0638	...	0740	0738	...	...	0838	...
11	**København** H **720**....§ d.	0050	0050	0250	0250	...	...	0502	...	0532	0555	0602	0632	0655	...	0702	0732	0755	0802	0832	0855	0902	0932
31	Høje Taastrup **720**.....§ d.	0105	0105	0305	0305	...	...	0517	...	0547	0608	0617	0647	0708	...	0717	0747	0808	0817	0847	0908	0917	0947
42	Roskilde **720**............§ d.	0113	0113	0313	0313	...	...	0525	...	0555	|	0625	0655	|	...	0725	0755	|	0825	0855	|	0925	0955
75	Ringsted **720**...............d.	0129	0135	0329	0335	...	...	0541	...	0611	|	0641	0711	|	...	0741	0811	|	0841	0911	|	0941	1011
104	Slagelse.........................d.	0147	0153	0347	0353	...	...	0559	...	0629	|	0659	0729	|	...	0759	0829	|	0859	0929	|	0959	1029
119	Korsør............................d.	0157	0203	0357	0403	...	...	0608	...	0638	|	0708	0738	|	...	0808	0838	|	0908	0938	|	1008	1038
143	Nyborg...........................d.	0209	0215	0409	0415	...	...	0621	...	0651	|	0721	0751	|	...	0821	0851	|	0921	0951	|	1021	1051
171	**Odense**.........................a.	0232	0232	0432	0432	...	...	0635	...	0705	0708**k**	0735	0805	0808**k**	...	0835	0905	0908**k**	0935	1005	1008**k**	1035	1105
171	**Odense 728**..................d.	0234	0234	0434	0434	0537	0610	0637	0637	0713	0710	0737	0813	0810	...	0837	0913	0910	0937	1013	1010	1037	1113
221	Middelfart **710**...............d.	0257	0257	0457	0457	0559	|	0659	0659	0737	|	0759	0837	|	...	0859	0937	|	0959	1037	|	1059	1137
231	**Fredericia**......................a.	0304	0304	0504	0504	0606	0640	0706	0706	...	0740	0806	...	0840	...	0906	...	0940	1006	...	1040	1106	...
231	**Fredericia 705/10/5**.....d.	0306	0306	0514	0514	0614	0644	0714	0714	...	0744	0814	...	0844	...	0914	...	0944	1014	...	1044	1114	...
257	Vejle **715**.......................d.	0321	0321	0529	0529	0629	0659	0729	0729	...	0759	0829	...	0859	...	0929	...	0959	1029	...	1059	1129	...
288	Horsens..........................d.	0337	0337	0545	0545	0645	0715	0745	0745	...	0815	0845	...	0915	...	0945	...	1015	1045	...	1115	1145	...
317	Skanderborg **713**..........d.	0353	0353	0601	0600	0701	0731	0801	0801	...	0831	0901	...	0931	...	1001	...	1031	1101	...	1131	1201	...
340	**Aarhus 713 728**..........a.	0414	0414	0613	0613	0713	0743	0813	0813	...	0843	0913	...	0943	...	1013	...	1043	1113	...	1143	1213	...

	IC 137	IC 841	Lyn 45	IC 141	IC 845	Lyn 47	IC 145	IC 386 H		IC 849	Lyn 49	IC 149	IC 853	Lyn 53	IC 153	IC 857	Lyn 57	IC 157	Lyn 259 w	IC 861	Lyn 61	IC 161	IC 384 H
København Lufthavn..... d.	0938	...	...	1038	...	1130	1138	...	...	...	...	1238	...	1330	1338	...	...	1438	...	...	1530	1538	...
København H **720**......§ d.	1002	1032	1050	1102	1132	1155	1202	...	...	1232	1255	1302	1332	1355	1402	1432	1455	1502	1525	1532	1555	1602	...
Høje Taastrup **720**......§ d.	1017	1047	1108	1117	1147	1208	1217	...	...	1247	1308	1317	1347	1408	1417	1447	1508	1517	1538	1547	1608	1617	...
Roskilde **720**...............§ d.	1025	1055	|	1125	1155	|	1225	...	...	1255	|	1325	1355	|	1425	1455	|	1525	|	1555	|	1625	...
Ringsted **720**................ d.	1041	1111	|	1141	1211	|	1241	...	...	1311	|	1341	1411	|	1441	1511	|	1541	|	1611	|	1641	...
Slagelse.......................... d.	1059	1129	|	1159	1229	|	1259	...	...	1329	|	1359	1429	|	1459	1529	|	1559	1613	1629	|	1659	...
Korsør............................ d.	1108	1138	|	1208	1238	|	1308	...	...	1338	|	1408	1438	|	1508	1538	|	1608	|	1638	|	1708	...
Nyborg............................ d.	1121	1151	|	1221	1251	|	1321	...	...	1351	|	1421	1451	|	1521	1551	|	1621	1633	1651	|	1721	...
Odense......................... a.	1135	1205	1208**k**	1235	1305	1308**k**	1335	...	...	1405	1408**k**	1435	1505	1508**k**	1535	1605	1608**k**	1635	1650	1705	1708**k**	1735	...
Odense 728................... d.	1137	1213	1210	1237	1313	1310	1337	...	...	1413	1410	1437	1513	1510	1537	1613	1610	1637	1654	1713	1710	1737	...
Middelfart **710**............... d.	1159	1237	|	1259	1337	|	1359	...	...	1437	|	1459	1537	|	1559	1637	|	1659	1723	1737	|	1759	...
Fredericia..................... a.	1206	...	1240	1306	...	1340	1406	...	...	...	1440	1506	...	1540	1606	...	1640	1706	1731	...	1740	1806	...
Fredericia 705/10/5...... d.	1214	...	1244	1314	...	1344	1414	1414	...	...	1444	1514	...	1544	1614	...	1644	1714	1733	...	1744	1814	1814
Vejle **715**....................... d.	1229	...	1259	1329	...	1359	1429	1429	...	...	1459	1529	...	1559	1629	...	1659	1729	|	...	1759	1829	1829
Horsens........................... d.	1245	...	1315	1345	...	1415	1445	1445	...	...	1515	1545	...	1615	1645	...	1715	1745	|	...	1815	1845	1845
Skanderborg **713**.......... d.	1301	...	1331	1401	...	1431	1501	1501	...	...	1531	1601	...	1631	1701	...	1731	1801	|	...	1831	1901	1901
Aarhus 713 728.......... a.	1313	...	1343	1413	...	1443	1513	1513	...	...	1543	1613	...	1643	1713	...	1743	1813	1825	...	1843	1913	1913

	IC 865	Lyn 65	IC 165	Lyn 267 q	IC 869	Lyn 69		IC 169	IC 873	Lyn 73	IC 173	IC 877	Lyn 77	IC 177		IC 881	Lyn 81	IC 1683 ⑤⑥	IC 1681 ⑦–④	IC 885	IC 1685	IC 191 ⑤⑥	IC 189 ⑦–④
København Lufthavn..... d.	...	...	1638	...	...	1730	...	1738	...	...	1838	...	1930	1938	...	...	...	2038	2038	...	2138	2238	2238
København H **720**......§ d.	1632	1655	1702	1725	1732	1755	...	1802	1832	1855	1902	1932	1955	2002	...	2032	2055	2102	2102	2132	2202	2302	2302
Høje Taastrup **720**......§ d.	1647	1708	1717	1738	1747	1808	...	1817	1847	1908	1917	1947	2008	2017	...	2047	2108	2117	2117	2147	2217	2317	2317
Roskilde **720**...............§ d.	1655	|	1725	|	1755	|	...	1825	1855	|	1925	1955	|	2025	...	2055	|	2125	2125	2155	2225	2325	2325
Ringsted **720**................ d.	1711	|	1741	|	1811	|	...	1841	1911	|	1941	2011	|	2041	...	2111	|	2141	2141	2211	2241	2341	2341
Slagelse.......................... d.	1729	|	1759	1813	1829	|	...	1859	1929	|	1959	2029	|	2059	...	2129	|	2159	2159	2229	2259	2359	2359
Korsør............................ d.	1738	|	1808	|	1838	|	...	1908	1938	|	2008	2038	|	2108	...	2138	|	2208	2208	2238	2308	0008	0008
Nyborg............................ d.	1751	|	1821	1833	1851	|	...	1921	1951	|	2021	2051	|	2121	...	2151	|	2221	2221	2251	2321	0021	0021
Odense......................... a.	1805	1808**k**	1835	1850	1905	1908**k**	...	1935	2005	2008**k**	2035	2105	2108**k**	2135	...	2205	2208**k**	2238	2238	2315	2345	0045	0045
Odense 728................... d.	1813	1810	1837	1854	1913	1910	...	1937	2013	2010	2037	2113	2110	2137	...	2213	2210	2240	2240	...	...	0047	0047
Middelfart **710**............... d.	1837	|	1859	1923	1937	|	...	1959	2037	|	2059	2137	|	2159	...	2237	|	2304	2304	...	...	0110	0110
Fredericia..................... a.	...	1840	1906	1931	...	1940	...	2006	...	2040	2106	...	2140	2206	...	...	2240	2311	2311	...	...	0111	0111
Fredericia 705/10/5...... d.	...	1844	1914	1933	...	1944	...	2014	...	2044	2114	...	2144	2214	...	...	2247	2319	2319	...	...	0119	0119
Vejle **715**....................... d.	...	1859	1929	1948	...	1959	...	2029	...	2059	2129	...	2159	2229	...	...	2301	2334	2334	...	...	0134	0134
Horsens........................... d.	...	1915	1945	2004	...	2015	...	2045	...	2115	2145	...	2215	2245	...	...	...	2350	2350	...	...	0150	0150
Skanderborg **713**.......... d.	...	1931	2001	|	...	2031	...	2101	...	2131	2201	...	2231	2301	...	...	...	0005	0005	...	...	0205	0205
Aarhus 713 728.......... a.	...	1943	2013	2030	...	2043	...	2113	...	2143	2213	...	2243	2318	...	...	...	0018	0026	...	...	0218	0226

	1600 ①–⑤	IC 100 ⑥⑦	IC 104	Lyn 6 ①–⑤	IC 808 ①–⑤	Lyn 206 w	IC 108	Lyn 10 ①–⑤	IC 812 ①–⑤		Lyn 210 w	IC 112 ①–⑤	IC 112 ⑥⑦	Lyn 14	IC 816	IC 116 ①–⑤	IC 116 ⑥⑦		Lyn 18	IC 820	IC 120	Lyn 22	IC 824
Aarhus 713 728.......... d.	...	0242	...	0415	...	...	...	0515	...	...	0527	0545	...	0615	...	0645	...	...	0715	...	0745	0815	...
Skanderborg **713**.......... d.	...	0255	...	0429	...	...	...	0529	...	...	|	0559	...	0629	...	0659	...	...	0729	...	0759	0829	...
Horsens........................... d.	...	0310	...	0444	...	...	...	0544	...	...	0553	0614	...	0644	...	0714	...	...	0744	...	0814	0844	...
Vejle **715**....................... d.	...	0326	...	0501	...	...	...	0601	...	...	0611	0631	...	0701	...	0731	...	...	0801	...	0831	0901	...
Fredericia 715............. a.	...	0341	...	0517	...	...	...	0617	...	...	0625	0644	...	0717	...	0744	...	...	0817	...	0844	0917	...
Fredericia 705 710....... d.	...	0348	...	0522	...	...	0553	0622	...	...	0627	0653	...	0722	...	0753	0753	...	0822	...	0853	0922	...
Middelfart **710**............... d.	...	0355	...	|	0522	...	0600	|	0622	...	0634	0700	...	|	0722	0800	0800	...	|	0822	0900	|	0922
Odense......................... a.	...	0419	...	0549	0546**k**	...	0622	0649	0646**k**	...	0704	0722	...	0749	0746**k**	0822	0822	...	0849	0846**k**	0922	0949	0946**k**
Odense 728................... d.	0347	0424	0524	0551	0554	0609	0624	0651	0654	...	0709	0724	0724	0751	0754	0824	0824	...	0851	0854	0924	0951	0954
Nyborg............................ d.	0401	0438	0538	|	0608	0626	0638	|	0708	...	0726	0738	0738	|	0808	0838	0838	...	|	0908	0938	|	1008
Korsør............................ d.	0414	0451	0551	|	0621	|	0651	|	0721	...	|	0751	0751	|	0821	0851	0851	...	|	0921	0951	|	1021
Slagelse.......................... d.	0424	0501	0601	|	0631	0647	0701	|	0731	...	0747	0801	0801	|	0831	0901	0901	...	|	0931	1001	|	1031
Ringsted **720**................ a.	0450	0517	0617	|	0647	|	0717	|	0747	...	|	0817	0817	|	0847	0917	0917	...	|	0947	1017	|	1047
Roskilde **720**...............§ a.	0512	0533	0632	|	0702	|	0732	|	0802	...	|	0832	0832	|	0902	0932	0932	...	|	1002	1032	|	1102
Høje Taastrup **720**......§ a.	0524	0541	0640	0650	0710	0721	0740	0750	0810	...	0821	0840	0840	0850	0910	0940	0940	...	0950	1010	1040	1050	1110
København H **720**......§ a.	0540	0556	0656	0705	0726	0735	0756	0805	0826	...	0835	0856	0856	0905	0926	0956	0956	...	1005	1026	1056	1105	1126
København Lufthavn....... a.	0601	0617	0717	0729	...	...	0817	...	...	...	...	0917	0917	0929	...	1017	1017	...	...	...	1117	1129	...

H – 12 and 🍷 Aalborg / Aarhus / Fredericia - Hamburg and v.v. (Table **710**). Ⓡ for international journeys June 12 - Aug. 28.

k – Connects with train in previous column.

q – Dec. 23 only.

w – ①–⑤ Dec. 14 - June 24, Aug. 8 - Dec. 9 (not Dec. 28-30, Mar. 21-23, May 6).

§ – *IC* and *Lyn* trains are not available for local journeys. Frequent local trains run betv Roskilde and København.

AARHUS - FREDERICIA - ODENSE - KØBENHAVN 700

	Lyn 26	IC 828	IC 128	IC 383	Lyn 40	IC 832		IC 132	Lyn 42	IC 836	IC 136	Lyn 44	IC 840	IC 140	Lyn 46	IC 844		IC 144	IC 385	Lyn 48	IC 848	IC 148	Lyn 50	IC 852
				H															H					
us 713 728 .... d.	0915	...	0945	0945	1015	...	...	1045	1115	...	1145	1215	...	1245	1315	...	...	1345	1345	1415	...	1445	1515	...
derborg 713 .... d.	0929	...	0959	0959	1029	...	...	1059	1129	...	1159	1229	...	1259	1329	...	...	1359	1359	1429	...	1459	1529	...
ens .... d.	0944	...	1014	1014	1044	...	...	1114	1144	...	1214	1244	...	1314	1344	...	...	1414	1414	1444	...	1514	1544	...
715 .... d.	1001	...	1031	1031	1101	...	...	1131	1201	...	1231	1301	...	1331	1401	...	...	1431	1431	1501	...	1531	1601	...
ericia 715 .... a.	1017	...	1044	1044	1117	...	...	1144	1217	...	1244	1317	...	1344	1417	...	...	1444	1444	1517	...	1544	1617	...
ericia 705 710 .... d.	1022	...	1053	...	1122	...	...	1153	1222	...	1253	1322	...	1353	1422	...	...	1453	...	1522	...	1553	1622	...
elfart 710 .... d.	|	1022	1100	...	|	1122	...	1200	|	1222	1300	|	1322	1400	|	1422	...	1500	...	|	1522	1600	|	1622
se .... a.	1049	1046k	1122	...	1149	1146k	...	1222	1249	1246k	1322	1349	1346k	1422	1449	1446k	...	1522	...	1549	1546k	1622	1649	1646k
se 728 .... d.	1051	1054	1124	...	1151	1154	...	1224	1251	1254	1324	1351	1354	1424	1451	1454	...	1524	...	1551	1554	1624	1651	1654
rg .... d.	|	1108	1138	...	|	1208	...	1238	|	1308	1338	|	1408	1438	|	1508	...	1538	...	|	1608	1638	|	1708
ør .... d.	|	1121	1151	...	|	1221	...	1251	|	1321	1351	|	1421	1451	|	1521	...	1551	...	|	1621	1651	|	1721
else .... d.	|	1131	1201	...	|	1231	...	1301	|	1331	1401	|	1431	1501	|	1531	...	1601	...	|	1631	1701	|	1731
sted 720 .... a.	|	1147	1217	...	|	1247	...	1317	|	1347	1417	|	1447	1517	|	1547	...	1617	...	|	1647	1717	|	1747
lde 720 ....§ a.	|	1202	1232	...	|	1302	...	1332	|	1402	1432	|	1502	1532	|	1602	...	1632	...	|	1702	1732	|	1802
Taastrup 720 ......§ a.	1150	1210	1240	...	1250	1310	...	1340	1350	1410	1440	1450	1510	1540	1550	1610	...	1640	...	1650	1710	1740	1750	1810
enhavn H 720 ......§ a.	1205	1226	1256	...	1305	1326	...	1356	1405	1426	1456	1505	1526	1556	1605	1626	...	1656	...	1705	1726	1756	1805	1826
nhavn Lufthavn .... a.	...	...	1317	...	1329	...	...	1417	...	...	1517	1529	...	1617	...	...	...	1717	...	1729	...	1817	...	...

	IC 152	Lyn 54	IC 856	IC 156		Lyn 58	IC 860	IC 160	IC 387	Lyn 62	IC 864	IC 164	Lyn 66	IC 868		IC 168	IC 875	Lyn 70	IC 1672	IC 1676	IC 180	IC 184	IC 188	
									H															
us 713 728 .... d.	1545	1615	...	1645	...	1715	...	1745	1745	1815	...	1845	1915	...	...	1945	...	2015	2045	2145	2250	2350	0050	...
derborg 713 .... d.	1559	1629	...	1659	...	1729	...	1759	1759	1829	...	1859	1929	...	...	1959	...	2029	2059	2159	2304	0003	0104	...
ens .... d.	1614	1644	...	1714	...	1744	...	1814	1814	1844	...	1914	1944	...	...	2014	...	2044	2114	2214	2318	0018	0118	...
715 .... d.	1631	1701	...	1731	...	1801	...	1831	1831	1901	...	1931	2001	...	...	2031	...	2101	2131	2231	2335	0035	0135	...
ericia 715 .... a.	1644	1717	...	1744	...	1817	...	1844	1844	1917	...	1944	2017	...	...	2044	...	2117	2144	2244	2350	0050	0150	...
ericia 705 710 .... d.	1653	1722	...	1753	...	1822	...	1853	...	1922	...	1953	2022	...	...	2053	...	2122	2153	2253	2358	0058	0158	...
elfart 710 .... d.	1700	|	1722	1800	...	|	1822	1900	...	|	1922	2000	|	2022	...	2100	2122	|	2200	2300	0006	0105	0206	...
nse .... a.	1722	1749	1746k	1822	...	1849	1846k	1922	...	1949	1946k	2022	2049	2046k	...	2122	2146	2149	2222	2330	0035	0135	0235	...
nse 728 .... d.	1724	1751	1754	1824	...	1851	1854	1924	...	1951	1954	2024	2051	2054	...	2124	...	2151	2223	2337	0037	...	0237	...
org .... d.	1738	|	1808	1838	...	|	1908	1938	...	|	2008	2038	|	2108	...	2138	...	|	2239	2351	0051	...	0251	...
ør .... d.	1751	|	1821	1851	...	|	1921	1951	...	|	2021	2051	|	2121	...	2151	...	|	2251	0004	0104	...	0304	...
else .... d.	1801	|	1830	1901	...	|	1931	2001	...	|	2031	2101	|	2131	...	2201	...	|	2300	0014	0114	...	0314	...
sted 720 .... a.	1817	|	1847	1917	...	|	1947	2017	...	|	2047	2117	|	2147	...	2217	...	|	2317	0031	0131	...	0331	...
kilde 720 ....§ a.	1832	|	1902	1932	...	|	2002	2032	...	|	2102	2132	|	2202	...	2232	...	|	2332	0047	0147	...	0347	...
Taastrup 720 ......§ a.	1840	1850	1910	1940	...	1950	2010	2040	...	2050	2110	2140	2150	2210	...	2240	...	2250	2340	0055	0155	...	0355	...
enhavn H 720 ......§ a.	1856	1905	1926	1956	...	2005	2026	2056	...	2105	2126	2156	2205	2226	...	2256	...	2305	0005	0116	0216	...	0416	...
enhavn Lufthavn .... a.	1917	1929	...	2017	...	...	...	2117	...	2129	...	2217	...	...	...	2317	...	2329	0028	0136	0236	...	0436	...

(12) and ♀ Aalborg / Aarhus / Fredericia - Hamburg and v.v. (Table **710**).
Ⓡ for international journeys June 12 - Aug. 28.

Connects with train in previous column.
Dec. 23 only.
①–⑤ Dec. 14 - June 24, Aug. 8 - Dec. 9 (not Dec. 28-30, Mar. 21-23, May 6).

§ – *IC* and *Lyn* trains are not available for local journeys. Frequent local trains run between Roskilde and København.

AARHUS - AALBORG - FREDERIKSHAVN 701

d class only (*IC* & *Lyn* 1st & 2nd class)

			IC 101	IC 1601			IC 105		Lyn 9		IC 1609		Lyn 13	IC 113		Lyn 17		IC 117	Lyn 21	IC 121	Lyn 25	IC 125	Lyn 29	IC 129	Lyn 41	IC 133	Lyn 43
		①–⑤	①–⑤	⑥⑦	①–⑤	A	①–⑤	⑥⑦	①–⑤	A		⑥⑦	①–⑤		⑥⑦	①–⑤											
0	**Aarhus 712** .... d.	...	0421	0421	...	...	0521	...	0551	...	0621	...	0651	0721	...	0751	...	0821	0851	0921	0951	1021	1051	1121	1151	1221	1251
5	Langå **712** .... d.	...	0448	0448	...	...	0548	...	|	...	0648	...	|	0748	...	|	...	0848	|	0948	|	1048	|	1148	|	1248	|
9	Randers .... d.	...	0457	0457	...	...	0557	...	0622	...	0657	...	0722	0757	...	0822	...	0857	0922	0957	1022	1057	1122	1157	1222	1257	1322
1	Hobro .... d.	...	0513	0513	...	...	0613	...	0638	...	0713	...	0738	0813	...	0838	...	0913	0938	1013	1038	1113	1138	1213	1238	1313	1338
0	**Aalborg** .... a.	...	0551	0551	...	...	0651	...	0707	...	0751	...	0807	0850	...	0907	...	0950	1007	1050	1107	1150	1207	1250	1307	1350	1407
0	**Aalborg** .... d.	0512	...	...	0612	0642	...	0712	0712z	0742	...	0812	0812	...	0912	0912z	...	...	1012	...	1112	...	1212f	...	1312	...	1412f
8	Hjørring **702** .... d.	0601	...	...	0701	0735	...	0800	0804z	0838	...	0900	0900	...	1000	1000z	...	...	1100	...	1200	...	1309f	...	1400	...	1500f
5	**Frederikshavn** a.	0630	...	...	0730	0807	...	0829	0829z	0910	...	0924	0924	...	1029	1029z	...	...	1124	...	1229	...	1324f	...	1429	...	1529f

		IC 137	Lyn 45		IC 141	Lyn 47		IC 145	Lyn 49	IC 149	Lyn 53		IC 153	Lyn 57	IC 157	Lyn 61	IC 161	Lyn 65	IC 165	Lyn 69	IC 169		IC 173	IC 177		IC 1683	IC 191
	A			A			A																			⑤⑥	⑤⑥
hus 712 ......d.	...	1321	1351	...	1421	1451	...	1521	1551	1621	1651	...	1721	1751	1821	1851	1921	1951	2021	2051	2121	...	2221	2326	...	0025	0225
gå 712 ....d.	...	1348	|	...	1448	|	...	1548	|	1648	|	...	1748	|	1848	|	1948	|	2048	|	2148	...	2248	2352	...	0052	0252
ders ....d.	...	1357	1422	...	1457	1522	...	1557	1622	1657	1722	...	1757	1822	1857	1922	1957	2022	2057	2122	2157	...	2257	0001	...	0101	0301
ro ....d.	...	1413	1438	...	1513	1538	...	1613	1638	1713	1738	...	1813	1838	1913	1938	2013	2038	2113	2138	2213	...	2313	0017	...	0117	0317
borg ....a.	...	1450	1507	...	1550	1607	...	1650	1707	1750	1807	...	1850	1907	1950	2007	2050	2107	2150	2207	2250	...	2357	0101	...	0154	0354
borg ....d.	1442	...	1512	1542	...	1612r	1642	...	1712	...	1812	...	...	1912	...	2012	...	2112	...	2212	...	2312	...	...	...	...	...
ring 702 ......d.	1534	...	1604	1634	...	1700r	1734	...	1800	...	1900	...	...	2000	...	2100	...	2200	...	2300	...	0000	...	...	...	...	...
derikshavn .a.	1606	...	1629	1706	...	1724r	1806	...	1829	...	1924	...	...	2029	...	2124	...	2229	...	2324	...	0029	...	...	...	...	...

	Lyn 14	IC 116	Lyn 18	IC 120	Lyn 22	Lyn 22	IC 124		Lyn 26		Lyn 26	IC 128		Lyn 40	IC 132	Lyn 42	IC 136	Lyn 44	IC 140	Lyn 46	IC 144	Lyn 48	IC 148	Lyn 50	IC 152	Lyn 54	IC 156
	①–⑤	①–⑤	①–⑤		①–⑤	⑥⑦		A	⑥⑦y	A	A		A														
derikshavn .d.	...	...	0431	...	0535	...	...	0547	0631	0635	...	...	0647	0732	...	0831	...	0935	...	1031	...	1135	...	1231	...	1335	...
rring 702 ......d.	...	...	0504	...	0604	...	...	0634	0704	0704	...	...	0734	0804	...	0904	...	1004	...	1104	...	1204	...	1304	...	1404	...
borg ....a.	...	...	0544	...	0644	...	...	0714	0744	0744	...	...	0814	0844	...	0944	...	1044	...	1144	...	1244	...	1344	...	1444	...
borg ....d.	0451	0507	0551	0607	0651	0651	0707	...	0751	...	0751	0807	...	0851	0907	0921	1007	1051	1107	1151	1207	1251	1307	1351	1407	1451	1507
ro ....d.	0520	0545	0620	0645	0720	0720	0745	...	0820	...	0820	0845	...	0920	0945	1020	1045	1120	1145	1220	1245	1320	1345	1420	1445	1520	1545
ders ....d.	0536	0601	0636	0701	0736	0736	0801	...	0836	...	0836	0901	...	0936	1001	1036	1101	1136	1201	1236	1301	1336	1401	1436	1501	1536	1601
gå 712 ....d.	|	0609	|	0709	|	|	0809	...	|	...	|	0909	...	|	1009	|	1109	|	1209	|	1309	|	1409	|	1509	|	1609
hus 712 ......a.	0608	0638	0708	0738	0808	0808	0838	...	0908	...	0908	0938	...	1008	1038	1108	1138	1208	1238	1308	1338	1408	1438	1508	1538	1608	1638

		Lyn 58	Lyn 58	IC 160		Lyn 62	Lyn 62	IC 164		Lyn 66	Lyn 66	IC 168	Lyn 70	Lyn 70	IC 1672	Lyn 74	IC 1676		IC 180		IC 184		IC 188		IC 192	IC 102	
	A	⑥⑦y	A		A	①–⑤	⑥⑦		A	⑥⑦y	A		①–⑤	⑥⑦												⑥⑦	
derikshavn .d.	1347	1431	1435f	...	1451	1531	1535	...	1548	1631	1631f	...	1726	1735	...	1831	...	1935	...	2031	...	2135	...	2231	...	...	...
rring 702 ......d.	1434	1504	1504f	...	1534	1604	1604	...	1634	1704	1704f	...	1804	1804	...	1904	...	2004	...	2104	...	2204	...	2304	...	...	...
borg ....a.	1514	1544	1544f	...	1614	1644	1644	...	1714	1744	1744f	...	1844	1844	...	1944	...	2044	...	2144	...	2244	...	2344	...	...	...
borg ....d.	...	1551	1551	1607	...	1651	1651	1707	...	1751	1751	1807	1851	1851	1907	1951	2007	...	2107	...	2207	...	2307	...	0007	0207	...
ro ....d.	...	1620	1620	1645	...	1720	1720	1745	...	1820	1820	1845	1920	1920	1945	2020	2045	...	2147	...	2245	...	2347	...	0045	0245	...
nders ....d.	...	1636	1636	1701	...	1736	1736	1801	...	1836	1836	1901	1936	1936	2001	2036	2101	...	2202	...	2301	...	0002	...	0101	0301	...
gå 712 ....d.	...	|	|	1709	...	|	|	1809	...	|	|	1909	|	|	2009	|	2109	...	2211	...	2309	...	0011	...	0109	0309	...
hus 712 ......a.	...	1708	1708	1738	...	1808	1808	1838	...	1908	1908	1938	2008	2008	2038	2108	2138	...	2243	...	2343	...	0043	...	0143	0338	...

①–⑤ Dec. 14 - June 24, Aug. 8 - Dec. 9 (not Dec. 23-30, Mar. 21-23, May 6).

f – Connection on ⑤.
r – Connection on ①–⑤.

y – Also Dec. 23-30, Mar. 21-23, May 6, June 27 - Aug. 5.
z – Connection on Dec. 23, 28-30, Mar. 21-23, May 6; ①–⑤ June 27 - Aug. 5.

HJØRRING - HIRTSHALS 702

ordjyske Jernbaner A/S. 2nd class only

18 km Journey 22 minutes

m **Hjørring**:
-⑤: 0503, 0525, 0603, 0631, 0703, 0731, 0803, 0831, 0903, 1003, 1103, 1203, 1303, 1331, 1403, 1431, 1503, 1531, 1603, 1631, 1703, 1731, 1803, 1903, 2103, 2203, 2303.
⑦: 0703, 0803 and hourly until 1803, then 1903, 2103, 2203, 2303.

From **Hirtshals / Color Line**:
①–⑤: 0528, 0606, 0634, 0706, 0730, 0806, 0834, 0906, 0934, 1034, 1134, 1234, 1334, 1406, 1434, 1506, 1534, 1606, 1634, 1706, 1734, 1806, 1834, 2010, 2134, 2234, 2334.
⑥⑦: 0734, 0834 and hourly until 1734, then 1834, 2010, 2134, 2234, 2334.

703 HELSINGØR - KØBENHAVN - KØBENHAVN LUFTHAVN (KASTRUP) ✈ - MALMÖ

Subject to alteration owing to temporary cross-border arrangements between Denmark and Sweden (please check the latest situation before travelling)

km																												
0	**Helsingør** d.	...		...	0438	0458	0516	0543a	0603a	0623a	and	0823a	0843	0903	0923	and	1943	2005	...	2025	...	2045	...	and	2225	...	...	...
43	Østerport d.	0101	and	0501	0521	0541	0601	0621	0641	0701	every	0901	0921	0941	1001	every	2021	2050	2101	2110	2121	2130	2141	every	2310	2321	...	...
46	**København H** a.	0108	hourly	0508	0528	0548	0608	0628	0648	0708	20	0908	0928	0948	1008	20	2028	2057	2108	2117	2128	2137	2148	20	2317	2328	...	...
46	**København H** d.	0112	until	0512	0532	0552	0612	0632	0652	0712	mins	0912	0932	0952	1012	mins	2032	2100	2112	2120	2132	2140	2152	mins	2320	2332	...	0032
58	Lufthavn (Kastrup) a.	0124		0524	0544	0604	0624	0644	0704	0724	until	0924	0944	1004	1024	until	2044	2112	2124	2132	2144	2152	2204	until	2332	2344	...	0044
93	**Malmö C** a.	0146		0546	0606	0626	0646	0706	0726	0746		0946	1006	1026	1046		2106	...	2146	...	2206	...	2226		...	0006	...	0106

Malmö C d.	0033		0333	0413	0433	0453	and	0753	0833	0853	0913	and	1853	1913	...	1933	...	1953	...	and	2233	...	2253	...	2313	...	2333
Køb Lufthavn (Kastrup) ✈ d.	0054	and	0354	0434	0454	0514	every	0814	0854	0914	0934	every	1914	1934	1942	1954	2002	2014	2022	every	2254	2302	2314	2322	2334	2342	2354
København H a.	0108	hourly	0408	0448	0508	0528	20	0828	0908	0928	0948	20	1928	1948	1956	2008	2016	2028	2036	20	2308	2316	2328	2336	2348	2356	0008
København H d.	0112	until	0412	0452	0512	0532	mins	0832	0912	0932	0952	mins	1932	1952	2001	2012	2021	2032	2041	mins	2312	2321	...	2341	...	0001	...
Østerport a.	0119		0419	0459	0519	0539	until	0839	0919	0939	0959	until	1939	1959	2008	2019	2028	2039	2048	until	2319	2328	...	2348	...	0008	...
Helsingør a.	...		...	0536a	0556a	0616a		0916a	0956	1016	1036		2016	...	2054	...	2114	...	2134		...	0014	...	0034	...	0054	...

a – Ⓐ only.

704 KØBENHAVN - KALUNDBORG

km		①–⑤	①–⑤	①–⑤	①–⑤		①–⑤	①–⑤		①–⑤	①–⑤				①–⑤			①–⑤							
0	**København H** d.	0458	0528	0547	0558	0628	0647	0658	0728	0747	0758	0828	0847	and at	1658	1728	1747	1758	1828	1847	1928	1947	2028	2047	2
20	Høje Taastrup d.	0513	0543	0600	0613	0643	0700	0713	0743	0800	0813	0843	0900	the same	1713	1743	1800	1813	1843	1900	1943	2000	2043	2100	2
31	**Roskilde** d.	0524	0554	0609	0624	0654	0709	0724	0754	0809	0824	0854	0909	minutes	1724	1754	1809	1824	1854	1909	1954	2009	2054	2109	2
67	Holbæk a.	0555	0625	0629	0655	0725	0729	0755	0825	0829	0855	0925	0929	past	1755	1825	1829	1855	1925	1929	2025	2029	2125	2129	2
67	Holbæk d.	...	...	0630	...	0730c	0730	...	0830c	0830	...	...	0930	each hour	...	...	1830	...	...	1930	...	2030	...	2130	
111	**Kalundborg 2355** a.	...	...	0710	...	0810c	0810	...	0910c	0910	...	...	1010	until	...	...	1910	...	...	2010	...	2110	...	2210	

					⑥⑦					
København H d.	2147	2228	2328	0028	0228	...	EXTRA	1516	1616	1716
Høje Taastrup d.	2200	2243	2343	0043	0243	...	SERVICES	1529	1629	1729
Roskilde d.	2209	2254	2354	0054	0254	...	►►►	1537	1637	1737
Holbæk a.	2229	2325	0032	0132	0325	...	(see note z)	1558	1658	1758
Holbæk d.	2230	2330	0033	0133c	...	...		1559	1659	1759
Kalundborg 2355 a.	2310	0010	0112	0212c	...	...		1633	1733	1833

	①–⑤		①–⑤	①–⑤		①–⑤	①–⑤		①–⑤	①–⑤	
Kalundborg 2355 d.	...	0446	...	0546	0546c	...	0646	0646c	...	0746	07
Holbæk a.	...	0528	...	0628	0628c	...	0728	0728c	...	0828	08
Holbæk d.	0503	0533	0603	0629	0629	0703	0729	0733	0803	0829	0
Roskilde d.	0534	0604	0634	0649	0649	0734	0749	0804	0834	0849	0
Høje Taastrup d.	0544	0614	0644	0657	0657	0744	0757	0814	0834	0857	0
København H a.	0600	0630	0700	0712	0712	0800	0812	0830	0900	0912	0

	①–⑤				①–⑤													⑥⑦					
Kalundborg 2355 d.	...	0846	...	and at	...	1846	...	...	1946	...	2046	...	...	2146	...	2246	...	...	...	EXTRA	0523	0623	0723
Holbæk a.	...	0928	...	the same	...	1928	...	...	2028	...	2128	...	...	2228	...	2328	...	...	...	SERVICES	0555	0655	0755
Holbæk d.	0903	0929	0933	minutes	1903	1929	1933	...	2029	2033	2129	2133	...	2229	2233	2333	...	0333	...	►►►	0556	0656	0756
Roskilde d.	0934	0949	1004	past	1934	1949	2004	...	2049	2104	2149	2204	...	2249	2304	0004	...	0404	...	(see note z)	0619	0719	0819
Høje Taastrup d.	0944	0957	1014	each hour	1944	1957	2014	...	2057	2114	2157	2214	...	2257	2314	0014	...	0414	...		0627	0727	0827
København H a.	1000	1012	1030	until	2000	2012	2030	...	2112	2130	2212	2230	...	2312	2337	0037	...	0430	...		0642	0742	0842

c – ⑥⑦ only.

z – ①–⑤ Dec. 14 - June 24, Aug. 8 - Dec. 9 (not Dec. 23-30, Mar. 21-23, May 6).

705 FREDERICIA - ESBJERG

2nd class only (*IC* & *Lyn* 1st & 2nd cla

km		①–⑤		①–⑤		*IC* 821 ①–⑤		*IC* 825		*IC* 829		*IC* 833		*IC* 837		*IC* 841		*IC* 845		*IC* 849		*IC* 853		*IC* 857		8
	København H 700 d.	...	...	...	...	0532	...	0632a	...	0732	...	0832	...	0932	...	1032	...	1132	...	1232	...	1332	...	1432	...	1
	Odense 700 d.	...	...	0613	...	0713	...	0813	...	0913	...	1013	...	1113	...	1213	...	1313	...	1413	...	1513	...	1613	...	1
	Middelfart 700 d.	...	...	0637	...	0737	...	0837	...	0937	...	1037	...	1137	...	1237	...	1337	...	1437	...	1537	...	1637	...	1
	Aarhus 700 d.	...	...	|	0557a	|	0657	|	0757	|	0857	|	0957	|	1057	|	1157	|	1257	|	1357	|	1457	|	1557	
0	**Fredericia 700/10** d.	0511	0611	|	0711	|	0811	|	0911	|	1011	|	1111	|	1211	|	1311	|	1411	|	1511	|	1611	|	1711	
20	Kolding 710 d.	0525	0625	0651	0725	0751	0825	0851	0925	0951	1025	1051	1125	1151	1225	1251	1325	1351	1425	1451	1525	1551	1625	1651	1725	1
33	Lunderskov 710 d.	0533	0633	0659	0733	0759	0833	0859	0933	0959	1033	1059	1133	1159	1233	1259	1333	1359	1433	1459	1533	1559	1633	1659	1733	1
44	Vejen d.	0540	0640	0707	0740	0807	0840	0907	0940	1007	1040	1107	1140	1207	1240	1307	1340	1407	1440	1507	1540	1607	1640	1707	1740	1
72	Bramming 709 a.	0601	0701	0727	0801	0820	0901	0920	1001	1020	1101	1120	1201	1220	1301	1320	1401	1420	1501	1520	1601	1620	1701	1720	1801	1
88	**Esbjerg 709** a.	0612	0712	0739	0812	0832	0912	0932	1012	1032	1112	1132	1212	1232	1312	1332	1412	1432	1512	1532	1612	1632	1712	1732	1812	1

		IC 865		*IC* 869		*IC* 873		*IC* 877		
København H 700 d.	...	1632	...	1732	...	1832	...	1932	...	...
Odense 700 d.	...	1813	...	1913	...	2013	...	2113	...	...
Middelfart 700 d.	...	1837	...	1937	...	2037	...	2137	...	...
Aarhus 700 d.	1657	|	1757	|	1857	|	1957	|	...	...
Fredericia 700/10 d.	1811	|	1911	|	2011	|	2111	|	2212	2328
Kolding 710 d.	1825	1851	1925	1951	2025	2051	2125	2151	2225	2341
Lunderskov 710 d.	1833	1859	1933	1959	2033	2059	2133	2159	2233	2349
Vejen d.	1840	1907	1940	2007	2040	2107	2140	2207	2240	2357
Bramming 709 a.	1901	1920	2001	2020	2101	2120	2201	2220	2301	0017
Esbjerg 709 a.	1912	1932	2012	2032	2112	2132	2212	2232	2317	0034

	IC 808 ①–⑤	*IC* 812 ①–⑤	①–⑤	*IC* 816	⑥⑦	①–⑤	*IC* 820		*IC* 824	
Esbjerg 709 d.	...	0527	0547	0627a	0643	0647	0727	0747	0827	08
Bramming 709 d.	...	0538	0557	0638a	0653	0657	0738	0757	0838	08
Vejen d.	...	0552	0619	0652a	0715	0719	0752	0819	0852	09
Lunderskov 710 d.	...	0600	0626	0700a	0722	0726	0800	0826	0900	09
Kolding 710 d.	0508	0608	0634	0708	0730	0734	0808	0834	0908	09
Fredericia 700/10 a.	|	|	0648	|	0746	0748	|	0848	|	09
Aarhus 700 a.	|	|	0801	|	...	0901	|	1001	|	1
Middelfart 700 a.	0522	0622	...	0722	...	...	0822	...	0922	
Odense 700 a.	0546	0646	...	0746	...	...	0846	...	0946	
København H 700 a.	0726	0826	...	0926	...	...	1026	...	1126	

	IC 828		*IC* 832		*IC* 836		*IC* 840		*IC* 844		*IC* 848		*IC* 852		*IC* 856		*IC* 860		*IC* 864		*IC* 868					
Esbjerg 709 d.	0927	0947	1027	1047	1127	1147	1227	1247	1327	1347	1427	1447	1527	1547	1627	1647	1727	1747	1827	1847	1927	1947	2043	2143	2247	23
Bramming 709 d.	0938	0957	1038	1057	1138	1157	1238	1257	1338	1357	1438	1457	1538	1557	1638	1657	1738	1757	1838	1857	1938	1957	2053	2153	2257	23
Vejen d.	0952	1019	1052	1119	1152	1219	1252	1319	1352	1419	1452	1519	1552	1619	1652	1719	1752	1819	1852	1919	1952	2019	2114	2214	2319	00
Lunderskov 710 d.	1000	1026	1100	1126	1200	1226	1300	1326	1400	1426	1500	1526	1600	1626	1700	1726	1800	1826	1900	1926	2000	2026	2122	2222	2326	00
Kolding 710 d.	1008	1034	1108	1134	1208	1234	1308	1334	1408	1434	1508	1534	1608	1634	1708	1734	1808	1834	1908	1934	2008	2034	2130	2230	2334	00
Fredericia 700/10 a.	|	1048	|	1148	|	1248	|	1348	|	1448	|	1548	|	1648	|	1748	|	1848	|	1948	|	2048	2146	2246	2353	00
Aarhus 700 a.	|	1201	|	1301	|	1401	|	1501	|	1601	|	1701	|	1801	|	1901	|	2001	|	2101	|	2201	...	...	...	
Middelfart 700 a.	1022	...	1122	...	1222	...	1322	...	1422	...	1522	...	1622	...	1722	...	1822	...	1922	...	2022	...	...	...	...	
Odense 700 a.	1046	...	1146	...	1246	...	1346	...	1446	...	1546	...	1646	...	1746	...	1846	...	1946	...	2146	...	...	...	...	
København H 700 a.	1226	...	1326	...	1426	...	1526	...	1626	...	1726	...	1826	...	1926	...	2026	...	2126	...	2226	...	...	...	...	

a – ①–⑤ only.

707 ESBJERG - SKJERN

2nd class only. Operator: A

km															⑥	⑥		†					
0	**Esbjerg 705** ⊗ d.	Ⓐ	0457	0549	0648	0730	0830	0929	and	1729	...	1929	2129	...	Ⓒ	0443	0554	...	0643	0801	...	1001	and every	22
17	Varde ⊗ d.		0515	0617	0709	0801	0853	0954	hourly	1754	...	1952	2152	...		0503	0614	...	0703	0821	...	1021	two hours	22
60	**Skjern 708/13** a.		0552	0655	0748	0842	0931	1033	until	1833	...	2031	2231	...		0539	0650	...	0739	0857	...	1057	until	22

															⑥	⑥	†					
Skjern 708/13 d.	Ⓐ	*0503*	0609	0702	0814	0947	and	1747	...	1849	2049	2245	...	Ⓒ	0602	0703	0808	0903	...	1103	and every	2303
Varde ⊗ d.		0552	0651	0739	0854	1028	hourly	1828	...	1928	2128	2322	...		0640	0741	0849	0941	...	1141	two hours	2341
Esbjerg 705 ⊗ a.		0610	0709	0801	0916	1049	until	1849	...	1949	2149	2343	...		0658	0759	0911	0959	...	1159	until	2359

⊗ – Additional services operate Esbjerg - Varde and v.v.

SKJERN - STRUER 708

ator: *AT* 2nd class only

	Ⓐ													Ⓒ ⑥	⑥	†					
Skjern 707/13 d.	0435	0622	0716	0800	0845	0945	1045		1545	1645	1845	2045	2245	...	0541	0702	0742	...	0902		2102	2302
Ringkøbing a.	0453	0643	0735	0818	0903	1003	1103	and	1603	1703	1903	2103	2303	...	0603	0720	0803	...	0920	and every	2120	2320
Ringkøbing d.	0454	0644	0736	0819	0904	1004	1104	hourly	1604	1704	1904	2104	2304	...	0604	0721	0804	...	0921	two hours	2121	2321
Holstebro a.	0538	0723	0815	0901	0946	1046	1146	until	1646	1744	1944	2146	2346	...	0645	0800	0845	...	1000	until	2200	2400
Holstebro **715** d.	0544	0745	0816	0902	0947	1047	1147		1647	1745	1945	2147	2347	...	0647	0802	0847	...	1002		2202	0002
Struer 715 a.	0557	0757	0829	0915	1000	1100	1200		1700	1758	1958	2200	2400	...	0700	0815	0900	...	1015		2215	0015

	Ⓐ														Ⓒ ⑥	⑥	†					
r 715 d.	0453	0530	0628	0728	0901	1002	1102		1502	1602	1728	1928	2102	2302	...	0448	0548	0648	...	0748		1948	2148
bro 715 a.	0505	0542	0644	0744	0914	1014	1114	and	1514	1615	1744	1944	2114	2314	...	0500	0600	0700	...	0800	and every	2000	2200
bro d.	0505	0542	0650	0817	0915	1015	1115	hourly	1515	1615	1746	1946	2115	2315	...	0501	0602	0702	...	0802	two hours	2002	2202
øbing a.	0545	0622	0733	0857	1000	1059	1159	until	1559	1659	1825	2025	2155	2355	...	0541	0641	0741	...	0841	until	2041	2241
øbing d.	0545	0622	0736	0910	1010	1110	1210		1610	1710	1826	2026	2156	2356	...	0541	0642	0742	...	0842		2042	2242
n 707/13 a.	0604	0641	0755	0929	1029	1129	1229		1629	1729	1845	2045	2215	0015	...	0600	0701	0801	...	0901		2101	2301

ESBJERG - TØNDER - NIEBÜLL 709

ator: *AT* 2nd class only

	Ⓐ																Ⓒ ⑥					
Esbjerg 705 ⊗ d.	0500	0614	0758	0858	0958	1058	1158	1258	1358	1458	1558	1658	1758	1858	1958	2158	0519	0719	0919		1919	2019
Bramming **705** ⊗ d.	0513	0628	0811	0911	1011	1111	1211	1311	1411	1511	1611	1711	1811	1911	2011	2211	0533	0733	0933		1933	2033
Ribe ⊗ d.	0538	0647	0832	0932	1032	1132	1232	1332	1432	1532	1632	1732	1832	1932	2032	2232	0601	0801	1001	and every	2001	2053
Tønder a.	0629	0735	0920	1020	1120	1220	1320	1420	1520	1620	1720	1820	1920	2020	2120	2320	0649	0849	1049	two hours	2049	2145
	y																			until		
Tønder d.	0706	0832	...	1032	...	1232	1340	1432	1532	1632	...	1832	...	2032	...	...	...	0906e	1106		2106	2206t
Niebüll **821** a.	0725	0851	...	1051	...	1251	1359	1451	1551	1651	...	1851	...	2051	...	...	...	0925e	1125		2125	2225t

	Ⓐ	y															Ⓒ ⑥						
ll 821 d.	...	0639	0733	...	1006	...	1206	1320	1406	1506	1606	...	1806	...	2006	2206v	...	...	0839e	1039		2039	2139t
er a.	...	0656	0750	...	1023	...	1223	1337	1423	1523	1623	...	1823	...	2023	2223v	...	...	0856e	1056	and every two hours until	2056	2156t
er d.	0557	0638	0824	0924	1024	1124	1224	1324	1424	1524	1624	1724	1824	1924	2024	2224	0513	0713	0913	1113		2113	2213
⊗ d.	0649	0729	0914	1014	1114	1214	1314	1414	1514	1614	1714	1814	1914	2014	2114	2314	0607	0807	1007	1207		2207	2307
ming 705 ⊗ a.	0708	0748	0932	1032	1132	1232	1332	1432	1532	1632	1732	1832	1932	2032	2132	2332	0625	0826	1026	1226		2226	2326
rg 705 ⊗ a.	0721	0800	0945	1045	1145	1245	1345	1445	1545	1645	1745	1845	1945	2045	2145	2345	0639	0840	1040	1240		2240	2340

⑥ only.
Ⓒ Mar. 19 - Oct. 30.
v – Mar. 18 - Oct. 28.
y – Also Mar. 24, Apr. 22.
⊗ – Additional services operate Esbjerg - Ribe and v.v.

FREDERICIA - SØNDERBORG and FLENSBURG (- HAMBURG) 710

	IC 5744 ①–⑥	①–⑤	*IC* 5722	*IC* 821 ①–⑤	*Lyn* 921	*IC* 5720	*IC* 829	*Lyn* 929	*Lyn* 41	*IC* 383 H	*IC* 837	*Lyn* 943	*IC* 5736	*IC* 845	*Lyn* 947	*Lyn* 49	*IC* 385 H	*IC* 853	*Lyn* 953	*IC* 5752	*IC* 861	*Lyn* 961	*Lyn* 65	*IC* 387 H
København H **700** d.	...	...	...	0532	0555a	...	0732	0755	0855	...	0932	0955	...	1132	1155	1255	...	1332	1355	...	1532	1555	1655	...
Odense **700** d.	...	0510	...	0713	0710	...	0913	0910	1010	...	1113	1110	...	1313	1310	1410	...	1513	1510	...	1713	1710	1810	...
Aarhus **700** d.	...	|	0545a	|	|	0745	|	|	|	0945	|	|	1145	|	|	|	1345	|	|	1545	|	|	|	1745
Fredericia 700 d.	...	0549	0649a	|	0749	0849	|	0949	1040	1049	|	1149	1249	|	1349	1440	1449	|	1549	1649	|	1749	1840	1849
Middelfart **700** d.	...	|	|	0737	|	|	0937	|	...	|	1137	|	|	1337	|	...	|	1537	|	|	1737	|	...	|
Kolding **705** d.	...	0600	0700a	0751	0800	0900	0951	1000	...	1100	1151	1200	1300	1351	1400	...	1500	1551	1600	1700	1751	1800	...	1900
Lunderskov **705** d.	...	0608	0708a	0759	0808	0908	0959	1008	...	1108	1159	1208	1308	1359	1408	...	1508	1559	1608	1708	1759	1808	...	1908
Vojens d.	...	0624	0724a	...	0824	0924	...	1024	...	1124	...	1224	1324	...	1424	...	1524	...	1624	1724	...	1824	...	1924
Tinglev d.	0610	0644	0744	...	0844	0944	...	1044	...	1144	...	1244	1344	...	1444	...	1544	...	1644	1744	...	1844	...	1944
Sønderborg a.	|	0718	|	...	0918	|	...	1118	...	|	...	1318	|	...	1518	...	|	...	1718	|	...	1918	...	|
Padborg 🏛 a.	0620	...	0754	...	...	0954	...	...	...	1154	...	...	1354	...	...	...	1554	...	...	1754	...	...	...	1954
Flensburg 🏛 **823** a.	0635	...	0807	...	...	1007	...	...	...	1207	...	...	1407	...	...	...	1607	...	...	1807	...	...	...	2007
Hamburg Hbf **823** a.	...	...	...	...	...	...	...	...	...	1402v	...	...	...	...	...	...	1803t	...	...	...	...	...	...	2211h

	IC 869	*Lyn* 969	*IC* 5768	*IC* 877	*Lyn* 977	*IC* 5776	*IC* 1681 1683	*IC* 1681 1683		
benhavn H 700 d.	1732	1755	...	1932	1955	...	2102	2102	...	...
lense 700 d.	1913	1910	...	2113	2110	...	2240	2240	...	...
Aarhus 700 d.	|	|	...	|	|	...	|	|	...	...
ericia 700 d.	|	1949	2049	|	2149	2249	|	2328	2355	...
ddelfart 700 d.	1937	|	|	2137	|	|	2304	|	|	...
ng 705 d.	1951	2000	2100	2151	2200	2300	2341	2341	0006	...
lerskov 705 d.	1959	2008	2108	2159	2208	2308	2349	2349	0014	...
ns d.	...	2024	2124	...	2224	2324	...	...	0030	...
ev d.	...	2044	2144	...	2244	2348	...	...	0051	...
nderborg a.	...	2118	|	...	2318	...	...	...	0124	...
borg 🏛 a.	...	...	2154	...	...	...	...	...	...	...
sburg 🏛 823 a.	...	...	2207	...	...	...	...	...	...	...
mburg Hbf 823 a.	...	...	...	...	...	...	...	...	...	...

	IC 5717 ①–⑤	*Lyn* 914 ①–⑤	*IC* 816 ①–⑤	*IC* 5721	*Lyn* 922	*IC* 824	*IC* 5729	*Lyn* 940	*IC* 832	*IC* 5737
Hamburg Hbf **823** d.	...	...	...	...	...	...	...	...	...	...
Flensburg 🏛 **823** d.	...	...	...	0650d	...	...	0850	...	...	1050
Padborg 🏛 d.	...	...	...	0702d	...	...	0902	...	...	1102
Sønderborg d.	...	0538	...	|	0738	...	|	0938	...	|
Tinglev d.	0513	0613	...	0713	0813	...	0913	1013	...	1113
Vojens d.	0533	0633	...	0733	0833	...	0933	1033	...	1133
Lunderskov **705** d.	0548	0648	0700	0748	0848	0900	0948	1048	1100	1148
Kolding **705** d.	0556	0656	0708	0756	0856	0908	0956	1056	1108	1156
Middelfart **700** a.	|	|	0722	|	|	0922	|	|	1122	|
Fredericia 700 a.	0610	0708	|	0810	0908	|	1010	1108	|	1210
Aarhus **700** a.	...	|	|	0913	|	|	1113	|	|	1313
Odense **700** a.	...	0749	0746	...	0949	0946	...	1149	1146	...
København H **700** a.	...	0905	0926	...	1105	1126	...	1305	1326	...

	Lyn 944	*IC* 840	*IC* 386 H	*Lyn* 46	*Lyn* 948	*IC* 848		*IC* 5753	*Lyn* 954	*IC* 856	*IC* 384 H	*Lyn* 58	*Lyn* 962	*IC* 864	*IC* 5769	*Lyn* 970	*IC* 872	*IC* 382 H	*IC* 177	*IC* 1676	*IC* 1676		*IC* 5745		
mburg Hbf 823 d.	...	...	1052v	...	...	...	...	...	...	...	1452t	...	...	...	...	...	...	1901h	...	...	...	...	...	...	...
sburg 🏛 823 d.	...	...	1250	...	...	...	...	1450	...	...	1650	...	...	...	1850	...	...	2050	...	...	...	...	2250	...	...
borg 🏛 d.	...	...	1302	...	...	...	...	1502	...	...	1702	...	...	...	1902	...	...	2102	...	...	...	...	2302	...	...
nderborg d.	1138	...	|	...	1338	...	...	|	1538	...	|	...	1738	...	|	1938	...	|	...	...	...	2138	|	2338	...
lev d.	1213	...	1313	...	1413	...	...	1513	1613	...	1713	...	1813	...	1913	2013	...	2113	...	...	...	2213	2321	0012	...
ns d.	1233	...	1333	...	1433	...	...	1533	1633	...	1733	...	1833	...	1933	2033	...	2133	...	...	...	2233	2341	...	...
lerskov 705 d.	1248	1300	1348	...	1448	1500	...	1548	1648	1700	1748	...	1848	1900	1948	2048	2100	2148	...	2222	2222	2248	2356	...	...
ing 705 d.	1256	1308	1356	...	1456	1508	...	1556	1656	1708	1756	...	1856	1908	1956	2056	2108	2156	...	2230	2230	2256	0004	...	...
ddelfart 700 a.	|	1322	|	...	|	1522	...	|	|	1722	|	...	|	1922	|	|	2122	|	...	|	2300	|	|	...	...
ericia 700 a.	1308	|	1410	1422	1508	|	...	1610	1708	|	1810	1822	1908	|	2010	2108	|	2210	2214	2246	|	2314	0022	...	...
Aarhus 700 a.	|	|	1513	|	|	|	...	1713	|	|	1913	|	|	|	...	|	|	...	2318	|	|	|	...	...	...
lense 700 a.	1349	1346	...	1449	1549	1546	...	...	1749	1746	...	1849	1949	1946	...	2149	2146	...	...	2330	2330	2305	...	...	...
benhavn H 700 a.	1505	1526	...	1605	1705	1726	...	...	1905	1926	...	2005	2105	2126	...	2305	...	...	...	0116	0116	...	...	...	...

(12) and 🍷 Aalborg / Aarhus / Fredericia - Hamburg and v.v.
Ⓡ for international journeys June 12 - Aug. 28.

a – ①–⑤ only.
d – ①–⑥ only.
h – June 17 - Sept. 4.
t – Not Dec. 26.
v – Not Dec. 26, 27.

* – Middelfart - Kolding: *23 km.*

712 AARHUS - VIBORG - STRUER

2nd class only (*IC* & *Lyn* 1st & 2nd class). Operato

km		Ⓐ								♣								♣					Ⓒ	⑥	⑥	†
	København H **700** d.		...	...	...	...	...	...	...	...	...	...	...	...	...	...	...	...	...	...	...	...		...	...	...
0	**Aarhus 700** ⊗ d.		0442	0525	0625	0654	0754	0854	0954	1054	1154	1254	1354	1454	1554	1654	1754	1854	1954	2054	2154	2329		...	0554	...
46	Langå **701** ⊗ a.		0512	0550	0655	0724	0824	0924	1024	1122	1224	1324	1424	1524	1624	1724	1824	1922	2024	2124	2224	2359		...	0624	...
46	Langå ⊗ d.		0516	0559	0659	0728	0828	0928	1028	1128	1228	1328	1428	1528	1628	1728	1828	1928	2028	2128	2228	0003		...	0628	...
86	Viborg ⊗ d.		0547	0649	0729	0806	0906	1006	1106	1206	1306	1406	1506	1606	1706	1806	1906	2006	2106	2206	2306	0003		0559	0659	0659
116	Skive d.		0614	0715	0753	0828	0928	1028	1128	1228	1328	1428	1528	1628	1728	1828	1928	2028	2127	2228	2328	...		0621	0721	0721
148	**Struer 715 716** a.		0636	0740	0816	0855	0955	1055	1155	1255	1355	1455	1555	1655	1755	1855	1955	2055	...	2255	2351	...		0644	0744	0744

						♣	♣					♣				†	⑥	⑥		DSB *IC/Lyn* services ▶▶▶▶	629 ①–⑤	643 ⑥	645 ⑦	661 ⑥⑦	663 ①–⑤
København H **700** d.	...	...	...	...	...	...	...	...	...	...	...	...	...	...	...	...	...	...	...		0755	0955	1055	1555	1555
Aarhus 700 ⊗ d.	0754	0854	0954	1054	1154	1254	1354	1454	1554	1654	1754	1854	1954	2054	2154	2254	2254	2354	...		1054	1254	1354	1854	1854
Langå **701** ⊗ a.	0824	0924	1024	1124	1224	1324	1424	1524	1624	1724	1824	1922	2024	2124	2224	2324	2324	0024	...		1122	1324	1424	1922	1922
Langå ⊗ d.	0828	0928	1028	1128	1228	1328	1428	1528	1628	1728	1828	1928	2028	2128	2228	2328	2328	0028	...		1128	1328	1428	1928	1928
Viborg ⊗ d.	0859	0959	1059	1159	1259	1359	1459	1559	1659	1759	1859	1959	2059	2159	2259	2358	2359	0058	...		1206	1359	1459	1959	2006
Skive d.	0921	1021	1121	1221	1321	1421	1521	1621	1721	1821	1921	2021	2121	2222	2321	...	0021	...	...		1228	1421	1521	2021	2028
Struer 715 716 a.	0944	1044	1144r	1244	1344	1444	1544	1644	1744t	1844	1944	2044	2144	2245	2344	...	0044	...	...		1255	1444	1544	2044	2055

	Ⓐ					♣						♣										Ⓒ	⑥	⑥	⑥	†
Struer 715 716 d.		0447	0514	0549	0640	0720	0820	0920	1020	1120	1220	1320	1420	1520	1620	1720	1820	1920	2020	...	2220		...	0522	0622	...
Skive d.		0511	0538	0614	0703	0743	0843	0943	1043	1143	1243	1343	1443	1543	1643	1743	1843	1943	2043	2143	2243		...	0548	0648	...
Viborg ⊗ d.		0535	0608	0638	0738	0808	0908	1008	1108	1208	1308	1408	1508	1608	1708	1808	1908	2008	2108	2208	2308		0522	0622	0722	0722
Langå ⊗ a.		0612	0641	0711	0811	0841	0941	1041	1141	1241	1341	1441	1541	1641	1741	1841	1941	2041	2141	2241	2341		0553	0653	0753	0753
Langå **701** ⊗ d.		0616	0647	0718	0816	0847	0947	1047	1147	1247	1347	1447	1547	1647	1747	1847	1947	2047	2147	2247	2347		0557	0657	0757	0757
Aarhus 700 ⊗ a.		0648	0719	0750	0848	0919	1019	1119	1219	1319	1419	1519	1619	1719	1819	1919	2019	2119	2219	2319	0019		0629	0729	0829	0829
København H **700** a.		...	...	...	...	...	...	...	...	...	...	...	...	...	...	...	...	...	...	...	...		...	...	...	...

				⑥	†				♣	♣	⑥	†								DSB *IC/Lyn* services ▶▶▶▶	626 ①–⑤	628 ⑥⑦	652 ①–⑤	660 ⑥	664 ⑦
Struer 715 716 d.	0822	0922	1022	1122	...	1222	1322	1422	1522	1622	...	1722	1822	1922	2022	2122	2223	2322	...		0720	0722	1320	1522	1622
Skive d.	0848	0948	1048	1148	1148	1248	1348	1448	1548	1648	1748	1748	1848	1948	2048	2148	2248	2348	...		0743	0748	1343	1548	1648
Viborg ⊗ d.	0922	1022	1122	1222	1222	1322	1422	1522	1622	1722	1822	1822	1922	2022	2122	2222	2322	0021	...		0808	0822	1408	1622	1722
Langå ⊗ a.	0953	1053	1153	1253	1253	1353	1453	1553	1653	1753	1853	1853	1953	2053	2153	2253	2353	...	...		0841	0853	1441	1653	1753
Langå **701** ⊗ d.	0957	1057	1157	1257	1257	1357	1457	1557	1657	1757	1857	1857	1957	2057	2157	2257	2357	...	...		0847	0859	1447	1659	1757
Aarhus 700 ⊗ a.	1029	1129	1229	1329	1329	1429	1529	1629	1729	1829	1929	1929	2029	2129	2229	2329	0029	...	...		0919	0929	1519	1729	1829
København H **700** a.	...	...	...	...	...	...	...	...	...	...	...	...	...	...	...	...	...	...	...		1256	1256	1856	2056	2156

r – ⑥ only.
t – † only.

♣ – Runs as DSB *Lyn* service on some days / dates – see panel (and heading).
⊗ – Additional services operate Aarhus - Viborg and v.v.

See **Table 715** below for direct services Struer - Herr København and v.v.

713 AARHUS - HERNING - SKJERN

2nd class only. Operator

km		Ⓐ																	Ⓒ	⑥						
0	**Aarhus 700** ⊗ d.		0531	0636	0801	0831	0931	1001	and at	1631	1701	1731	1831	2019	2119	2219	2329	...		0619	0719	0819	and	1919	2019	2119
23	Skanderborg **700** ⊗ d.		0551	0659	0820	0851	0951	1020	the same	1651	1720	1751	1850	2038	2138	2238	2351	...		0639	0739	0839	every	1939	2039	2139
53	Silkeborg ⊗ d.		0616	0722	0849	0912	1012	1049	minutes	1712	1749	1812	1917	2108	2208	2304	0018	...		0709	0809	0909	two	2009	2109	2209
94	**Herning** ⊗ a.		0646	0754	0931	0946	1046	1131	past	1746	1831	1846	1953	2148	2248	2340	0054	...		0748	0848	0948	hours	2048	2148	2248
94	**Herning 715** d.		0705	0822	0938	...	1106	...	each hour	1806	...	...	2006	2206	2325	...	...	...		0806	...	1006	until	...	2206	2325
136	**Skjern 707 708** a.		0742	0857	1013	...	1141	...	until	1841	...	...	2041	2241	2400	...	...	...		0844	...	1041		...	2241	2400

	Ⓐ																Ⓒ	⑥								
Skjern 707 708 d.		0514	0605	0700	0810	...	0953	and at	...	1653	...	1753	1919	2119	2245	...		0519	...	0719	...	and	1919	...	2119	2245
Herning 715 a.		0553	0640	0735	0849	...	1034	the same	...	1734	...	1834	1954	2154	2320	...		0554	...	0754	...	every	1954	...	2154	2320
Herning ⊗ d.		0554	0647	0755	0854	1007	1054	minutes	1707	1754	1807	1914	2011	2211	2325	...		0611	0711	0811	0911	two	2011	2111	2211	2325
Silkeborg ⊗ d.		0629	0728	0828	0929	1051	1129	past	1751	1829	1851	1954	2050	2250	0003	...		0651	0751	0851	0951	hours	2051	2151	2251	0003
Skanderborg **700** ⊗ a.		0650	0749	0849	0950	1120	1150	each hour	1820	1850	1920	2020	2119	2319	0032	...		0720	0820	0920	1020	until	2120	2220	2320	0032
Aarhus 700 ⊗ a.		0709	0808	0908	1009	1139	1209	until	1839	1909	1939	2039	2138	2338	0051	...		0739	0839	0939	1039		2139	2239	2339	0051

⊗ – Additional services operate Aarhus - Herning an

715 FREDERICIA - STRUER - THISTED

2nd class only (*IC* & *Lyn* 1st & 2nd cla

km		*IC* 101 ①–⑤	①–⑤	*IC* 109 ①–⑤	①–⑤		*IC* 117 ①–⑤	*Lyn* 21 ①–⑤		*Lyn* 725	*IC* 125	*Lyn* 29		*Lyn* 741	*IC* 133	*Lyn* 43		*Lyn* 745	*Lyn* 47		*Lyn* 749	*Lyn* 53		*Lyn* 757	*Lyn* 761
	København H **700** d.	0050	...	0250	...	...	0502	0555	...	0655	0702	0755	...	0855	0902	0955	...	1055	1155	...	1255	1355	...	1455	1555
	Odense **700** d.	0234	...	0434	...	...	0637	0710	...	0810	0837	0910	...	1010	1037	1110	...	1210	1310	...	1410	1510	...	1610	1710
0	**Fredericia 700** d.	0306	0447	0514	0547	0647	0714	0744	0747	0847	0914	0944	0947	1047	1114	1144	1147	1247	1344	1347	1447	1544	1547	1647	1747
26	Vejle **700** d.	0319	0502	0528	0602	0702	0728	0758	0802	0902	0928	0958	1002	1102	1128	1158	1202	1302	1358	1402	1502	1558	1602	1702	1802
99	Herning a.	...	0558	...	0658	0758	...	...	0858	0958	...	...	1058	1158	...	...	1258	1358	...	1458	1558	...	1658	1758	1858
99	Herning **713** d.	...	0601	...	0701	0801	...	...	0901	1001	...	...	1101	1201	...	...	1301	1401	...	1501	1601	...	1701	1801	1901
140	Holstebro **708** d.	...	0632	...	0732	0832	...	...	0932	1032	...	...	1132	1232	...	...	1332	1432	...	1532	1632	...	1732	1832	1932
155	**Struer 708** a.	...	0643	...	0743	0843	...	...	0943	1043	...	...	1143	1243	...	...	1343	1443	...	1543	1643	...	1743	1843	1943
229	*Thisted* **716** a.	...	...	...	...	...	...	...	...	...	...	...	...	1405c	...	...	...	...	...	...	...	...	...	...	...

	Lyn 765 ①–⑤	*IC* 165	*Lyn* 69	*Lyn* 769 ⑥–④	*Lyn* 769 ⑤	*Lyn* 773	*Lyn* 77		*Lyn* 781
København H **700** d.	1655	1702	1755	...	1755	1855	1955	...	2055
Odense **700** d.	1810	1837	1910	...	1910	2010	2110	...	2210
Fredericia 700 d.	1847	1914	1940	1947	1947	2047	2144	2147	2247
Vejle **700** d.	1902	1928	...	2002	2002	2102	2158	2202	2302
Herning a.	1958	...	...	2058	2058	2158	...	2258	2358
Herning **713** d.	2001	...	...	2101	2101	2201	...	2301	0001
Holstebro **708** d.	2032	...	...	2132	2132	2232	...	2332	0032
Struer 708 a.	2043	...	...	2143	2143	2243	...	2343	0043
Thisted **716** a.	2217	...	...	...	...	...	...	...	...

	Lyn 710 ①–⑤	*Lyn* 714 ①–⑤	*Lyn* 718		*Lyn* 22	*IC* 124	*Lyn* 726			*Lyn* 40	*IC* 132	*Lyn* 742
Thisted **716** d.	...	...	...	...	...	...	0653	...	...	...	...	...
Struer 708 d.	0417	0517	0617	0717	...	...	0817	...	0917	...	...	1017
Holstebro **708** d.	0430	0530	0630	0730	...	...	0830	...	0930	...	...	1030
Herning **713** a.	0500	0600	0700	0800	...	...	0900	...	1000	...	...	1100
Herning d.	0502	0602	0702	0802	...	...	0902	...	1002	...	...	1102
Vejle **700** d.	0557	0657	0757	0857	0901	0931	0957	...	1057	1101	1131	1157
Fredericia 700 a.	0612	0712	0812	0912	0917	0944	1012	...	1112	1117	1144	1212
Odense **700** a.	0649	0749	0849	...	0949	1022	1049	...	...	1149	1222	1249
København H **700** a.	0805	0929	1005	...	1105	1156	1205	...	...	1305	1356	1405

	①–④	*Lyn* 44	*IC* 140	*Lyn* 746	*Lyn* 748 ①–⑤	⑥⑦	*Lyn* 48	*IC* 148	*Lyn* 750		*Lyn* 54	*IC* 156	*Lyn* 758		*Lyn* 62	*IC* 164	*Lyn* 766		*Lyn* 70	*IC* 1672		*IC* 1676		*IC* 180	
Thisted **716** d.	...	...	...	...	...	...	...	...	...	...	...	...	1453c	...	...	...	...	...	...	...	...	...	...	...	...
Struer 708 d.	1117	...	...	1217	1317	1317	...	...	1417	1517	...	...	1617	1717	...	...	1817	1917	...	...	2017	...	2117	...	2317
Holstebro **708** d.	1130	...	...	1230	1330	1330	...	...	1430	1530	...	...	1630	1730	...	...	1830	1930	...	...	2030	...	2130	...	2330
Herning **713** a.	1200	...	...	1300	1400	1400	...	...	1500	1600	...	...	1700	1800	...	...	1900	2000	...	...	2100	...	2200	...	2400
Herning d.	1202	...	...	1302	1402	1402	...	...	1502	1602	...	...	1702	1802	...	...	1902	2002	...	...	2102	...	2202	...	0001
Vejle **700** d.	1257	...	1331	1357	1457	1457	...	1531	1557	1657	1701	1731	1757	1857	1901	1931	1957	2057	2101	2131	2157	2231	2257	2335	0057
Fredericia 700 a.	1312	1322	1344	1412	1512	1512	1522	1544	1612	1712	1717	1744	1822	1912	1917	1944	2012	2112	2117	2144	2212	2244	2315	2350	0115
Odense **700** a.	...	1349	1422	1449	1549	...	1549	1622	1649	...	1749	1822	1849	...	1949	2022	2049	...	2149	2222	...	2330	...	0035	...
København H **700** a.	...	1505	1556	1605	1705	...	1705	1756	1805	...	1905	1956	2005	...	2105	2156	2205	...	2305	0005	...	0116	...	0216	...

c – ⑥⑦ only.

STRUER - THISTED 716

rator: AT (*Lyn* trains: *DSB*). 2nd class only (*Lyn* 1st & 2nd class)

	Ⓐ													Ⓒ										
																				741				
					‡							‡			⑥	⑥	⑦			K‡				‡
Struer 708/12/5 ....d.		0438	0536	0725	1004	1204	1305	1405	1505	1605	1705	1905	2100	2300	0523	0648	0723	0848	1048	1248	1448	1648	1848	2048	2248
Thisted ....a.		0600	0723	0914	1121	1322	1424	1524	1624	1724	1824	2022	2217	0017	0641	0805	0844	1005	1205	1405	1605	1805	2005	2205	0005

	Ⓐ														Ⓒ										
			726														726								
			K‡				‡						‡			⑥	K‡				‡				‡
ed ....d.		0606	0653	0753	0928	1130	1328	1428	1528	1628	1728	1828	2027	2227	...	0528	0653	0853	1053	1253	1453	1653	1853	2053	2253	...
r 708/12/5 ....a.		0722	0812	0912	1052	1252	1453	1552	1652	1752	1852	1952	2147	2347	...	0648	0812	1012	1212	1412	1612	1812	2012	2212	0012	...

12 København - Struer - Thisted and v.v. InterCityLyn (*Lyn*) service (see Table **715**). ‡ – Operated by *DSB*.

KØBENHAVN - RØDBY - PUTTGARDEN (- HAMBURG) 720

			EC						*ICE*						*ICE*					*ICE*				
	1213	1217		232					38					36				34				
	A	C	①–⑤	⊠S			①–⑤		⊠		①–⑤			⊠		①–⑤		⊠			①–⑤	
København H 700/4 ....d.	...	...	0510	0537	...	0610	0637	0710	0737	0810	0837	0910	...	0937	1010	1037	1110	1137	...	1210	1237	1310
Høje Taastrup **700/4** ....d.	...	...	0526	0551	...	0626	0651	0726	0751	0826	0851	0926	...	0951	1026	1051	1126	1151	...	1226	1251	1326
Roskilde **700/4** ....d.	...	...	0535	0600	...	0635	0700	0735	0800	0835	0900	0935	...	1000	1035	1100	1135	1200	...	1235	1300	1335
Ringsted **700** ....d.	...	...	0553	|	...	0652	|	0752	|	0852	|	0952	...	|	1052	|	1152	|	...	1252	|	1352
Næstved ....d.	...	...	0612	0631	...	0712	0731	0812	0831	0912	0931	1012	...	1031	1112	1131	1212	1231	...	1312	1331	1412
Vordingborg ....d.	...	...	0630	0646	...	0730	0746	0830	0846	0930	0946	1030	...	1046	1130	1146	1230	1246	...	1330	1346	1430
Nykøbing (Falster) ....⊙ d.	0544	0644	0658	0714	0744	0758	0810	0858	0910	0958	1010	1058	...	1110	1158	1210	1258	1310	...	1358	1410	1458
Rødby ....⛴▲a.	0606	0706	...	0735	0806	...	...	...	0935	...	...	...	...	1135	...	...	...	1335	...	...	...	...
Puttgarden ....⛴▲a.	...	...	...	0836	...	...	...	...	1036	...	...	...	...	1236	...	...	...	1436	...	...	...	...
Lübeck **825** ....a.	...	...	...	0937	...	...	...	...	1137	...	...	...	...	1337	...	...	...	1537	...	...	...	...
Hamburg Hbf **825** ....a.	...	...	...	1021	...	...	...	...	1221	...	...	...	...	1421	...	...	...	1622	...	...	...	...

	ICE					*ICE*							*ICE*										
	238	1253				32						2265	30						2277				
	⊠D			①–⑤		⊠	E		①–⑤	E			⊠F	x	E		①–⑤						
enhavn H § 700/4 ....d.	1337	1337	1410	1437	1510	1537	1540	1610	1637	1640	...	1710	1737	1737	1740	1810	1837	1910	2010	2110	2210	2310	0010
Taastrup § **700/4** ....d.	1351	1351	1426	1451	1526	1551	1556	1626	1651	1656	...	1726	1751	1751	1756	1826	1851	1926	2026	2126	2226	2326	0026
ilde § 700/4 ....d.	1400	1400	1435	1500	1535	1600	1605	1635	1700	1705	...	1735	1800	1800	1805	1835	1900	1935	2035	2135	2235	2335	0035
sted § 700 ....d.	|	|	1452	|	1552	|	1622	1652	|	1722	...	1752	|	|	1822	1852	|	1952	2052	2152	2252	2352	0059
tved § ....d.	1431	1431	1512	1531	1612	1631	1642	1712	1731	1742	...	1812	1831	1831	1842	1912	1931	2012	2112	2212	2312	0012	0117
ingborg ....d.	1446	1446	1530	1546	1630	1646	1709	1730	1746	1800	...	1830	1846	1846	1909	1930	1946	2030	2130	2230	2330	0037	0136
bing (Falster) ....⊙ d.	1510	1510	1558	1610	1658	1710	1738	1754	1810	1829	...	1903	1910	1910	1938	1954	2010	2058	2155	2258	2354	0100	0159
by ....⛴▲a.	1535	1535	...	...	...	1735	...	...	...	...	...	1925j	1935	...	...	...	...	...	2216	...	...	...	...
garden ....⛴▲a.	1636	...	...	...	...	1836	...	...	...	...	...	...	2036	...	...	...	...	...	...	...	...	...	...
beck **825** ....a.	1737	...	...	...	...	1937	...	...	...	...	...	...	2137	...	...	...	...	...	...	...	...	...	...
mburg Hbf **825** ....a.	1822	...	...	...	...	2021	...	...	...	...	...	...	2223	...	...	...	...	...	...	...	...	...	...

																			ICE			
								1212			1216				24020	24020				31			
	①–⑤		E	①–⑤		G	H	A	①–⑤		C	①–⑤			①–⑤	⑥⑦		①–⑤		⊠J	y		①–⑤
mburg Hbf **825** ....d.	...	...	...	...	...	...	...	...	...	...	...	...	...	...	...	...	...	...	...	0724	...	...	...
beck **825** ....d.	...	...	...	...	...	...	...	...	...	...	...	...	...	...	...	...	...	...	...	0806	...	...	...
garden ....⛴▲d.	...	...	...	...	...	...	...	...	...	...	...	...	...	...	...	...	...	...	...	0908	...	...	...
by ....⛴▲d.	...	...	...	...	...	...	...	0615	...	...	0715	...	...	...	0815	0815	...	...	...	1015	1015	...	...
bing (Falster) ....⊙ d.	0448	0503	0534	0548	0603	0617	0628	0648	0648	0659	0748	0748	0759	...	0848	0838	0859	0948	0959	1048	1048	1059	1148
lingborg ....d.	0509	0528	0558	0609	0628	0658	0658	0709	0709	0728	0809	0809	0828	...	0909	...	0928	1009	1028	1109	1109	1128	1209
stved ....d.	0527	0547	0617	0627	0647	0717	0717	0727	0727	0747	0827	0827	0847	...	0927	...	0947	1027	1047	1127	1127	1147	1227
sted 700 ....d.	|	0606	0637	|	0706	0737	0737	|	|	0806	|	|	0906	...	|	...	1006	|	1106	|	|	1206	|
ilde 700/4 ....a.	0557	0624	0654	0657	0724	0754	0754	0757	0757	0824	0857	0857	0924	...	0957	...	1024	1057	1124	1157	1157	1224	1257
Taastrup **700/4** ....a.	0606	0632	0702	0706	0739	0802	0802	0806	0806	0832	0906	0906	0932	...	1006	...	1032	1106	1132	1206	1206	1232	1306
enhavn H 700/4 ....a.	0622	0649	0719	0722	0749	0819	0819	0822	0822	0849	0922	0922	0949	...	1022	...	1049	1122	1149	1222	1222	1249	1322

		ICE				*ICE*						*ICE*			*ICE*			*ICE*			*EC*		
		33				233						35			37			39			239	4276	
		⊠		①–⑤		⊠K				①–⑤		⊠			⊠			⊠x			⊠S		
mburg Hbf **825** ....d.	...	0928	...	...	...	1128	...	...	...	...	...	1328	...	...	1528	...	...	1728	...	...	1925	...	...
beck **825** ....d.	...	1006	...	...	...	1206	...	...	...	...	...	1406	...	...	1606	...	...	1806	...	...	2006	...	...
garden ....⛴▲d.	...	1108	...	...	...	1308	...	...	...	...	...	1508	...	...	1708	...	...	1908	...	...	2108	...	...
by ....⛴▲d.	...	1215	...	...	...	1415	1415v	...	...	...	...	1615	...	...	1815	...	...	2015	...	...	2216	2239	...
bing (Falster) ....⊙ d.	1159	1248	1259	1348	1359	1448	1448	...	1459	1548	1559	1648	1659	1759	1848	1859	1959	2048	2103	2203	2248	2303	...
lingborg ....d.	1228	1309	1328	1409	1428	1509	1509	...	1528	1609	1628	1709	1728	1828	1909	1928	2028	2109	2128	2228	2309	2328	...
stved ....d.	1247	1327	1347	1427	1447	1527	1527	...	1547	1627	1647	1727	1747	1847	1927	1947	2047	2127	2147	2247	2327	2347	...
sted 700 ....d.	1306	|	1406	|	1505	|	|	...	1606	|	1706	|	1806	1906	|	2006	2106	|	2206	2306	|	0006	...
ilde 700/4 ....a.	1324	1357	1424	1457	1524	1557	1557	...	1624	1657	1724	1757	1824	1924	1957	2024	2124	2157	2224	2324	2357	0029	...
Taastrup **700/4** ....a.	1332	1406	1432	1506	1532	1606	1606	...	1632	1706	1732	1806	1832	1932	2006	2032	2132	2206	2232	2332	0006	0038	...
enhavn H 700/4 ....a.	1349	1422	1449	1522	1549	1622	1622	...	1649	1722	1749	1822	1849	1949	2022	2049	2149	2222	2249	2356	0029	0102	...

①–⑤ June 20 - Aug. 26.
①–⑤ Dec. 14 - June 17, Aug. 29 - Dec. 9.
Dec. 18 - Jan. 3, Mar. 18 - Apr. 3, June 18 - Sept. 4 (not Dec. 25, Jan. 1, Mar. 26, 27).
①–⑤ Dec. 14 - June 24, Aug. 8 - Dec. 9 (not Dec. 23 - 30, Mar. 21 - 23, May 6).
Dec. 18 - Jan. 3, Mar. 18 - Oct. 30 (not Dec. 24, 25, 31).
①–⑤ June 20 - 24, Aug. 8 - 26.
①–⑤ Dec. 14 - June 17, Aug. 29 - Dec. 9 (not Dec. 23 - 30, Mar. 21 - 23, May 6).
Dec. 18 - Jan. 3, Mar. 18 - Oct. 30 (not Dec. 25, Jan. 1).
Dec. 18 - Jan. 3, Mar. 18 - Apr. 3, June 18 - Sept. 4 (not Dec. 24, 25, 31, Mar. 26, 27).
June 18 - Sept. 4.

j – Dec. 13 - Mar. 17, Oct. 31 - Dec. 10 (not Dec. 18 - 23, 26 - 30, Jan. 1 - 3).
v – Not Dec. 24.
x – Not Dec. 24, 31.
y – Not Dec. 25, Jan. 1.
⊙ – Trains run approximately hourly (more frequent on ① – ⑤) Nykøbing (Falster) - Nakskov and v.v., journey 45 minutes. Operator: Lokaltog A/S.
▲ – Through trains are conveyed by ⛴ Rødby - Puttgarden and v.v. ✕ on board ship. Passengers to/from Rødby or Puttgarden may be required to leave or join the train on board the train-ferry. See **Table 2375** for other available sailings.
⊠ – Ⓡ for international journeys June 12 - Aug. 28.

KØBENHAVN - YSTAD - RØNNE 727

Rail service replaced by 🚌 until at least May 4. Replacement 🚌 service does not call at Kastrup in eastbound direction. Times may vary.

n		A		B	C		D	E		F	G
0	**København H** ....d.	0643	...	1043	1443	...	1644	1844	...	2044	2244
2	Kastrup ✈ ....d.	0657	...	1057	1457	...	1658	1858	...	2058	2258
4	**Ystad** ....a.	0749	...	1149	1549	...	1749	1949	...	2149	2349
	Ystad ⛴ ....d.	*0830*	...	*1230*	*1630*	...	*1830*	*2030*	...	*2230*	*0020*
	Rønne ⛴ ....a.	*0950*	...	*1350*	*1750*	...	*1950*	*2150*	...	*2350*	*0140*

	A		B	C		D	E		F	G
Rønne ⛴ ....d.	*0630*	...	*1030*	*1430*	...	*1630*	*1830*	...	*2030*	*2230*
Ystad ⛴ ....a.	*0750*	...	*1150*	*1550*	...	*1750*	*1950*	...	*2150*	*2350*
Ystad ....d.	0809	...	1209	1609	...	1809	2009	...	2209	0009
Kastrup ✈ ....a.	0905	...	1305	1705	...	1905	2105	...	2309	0105
København H ....a.	0920	...	1319	1720	...	1920	2120	...	2323	0116

Daily.
May 1, 2, 4, 5, 7 - 9, 12 - 16, 19 - 23, 26 - 30, June 2 - Sept. 5, Sept. 8 - 12, 15 - 19, 22 - 26, 29, 30, Oct. 1, 8, 14 - 18, 21 - 23, 29, Nov. 5, 12, 19, 26, Dec. 3, 10.
May 1, 4 - 8, 13, 15, 16, 20, 22, 27, 29, June 3 - 5, 10 - 12, 15 - 20, 24 - 27, 30, July 1 - 4, 7 - 11, 14 - 18, 21 - 25, 28 - 31, Aug. 1, 5 - 7, 12 - 14, 19 - 21, 26 - 28, Sept. 2 - 4, 9, 11, 16, 18, 23, 25, 30, Oct. 2, 7, 9, 14 - 16, 21 - 23, 28, 30, Nov. 4, 6, 11, 13, 18, 20, 25, 27, Dec. 2, 4, 9.
May 2, 3, 9 - 12, 17 - 19, 23 - 26, 30, 31, June 1, 2, 6 - 9, 13, 14, 21 - 23, 28, 29, July 5, 6, 12, 13, 19, 20, 26, 27, Aug. 2 - 4, 8 - 11, 15 - 18, 22 - 25, 29 - 31, Sept. 1, 5 - 8, 12 - 15, 19 - 22, 26 - 29, Oct. 3 - 6, 10 - 13, 17 - 20, 24 - 27, 31, Nov. 1 - 3, 7 - 10, 14 - 17, 21 - 24, 28 - 30, Dec. 1, 5 - 8.

E – May 1, 4 - 8, 13 - 16, 20 - 22, 27 - 29, June 3 - 5, 10 - 12, 15 - 20, 24 - 27, 30, July 1 - 4, 7 - 11, 14 - 18, 21 - 25, 28 - 31, Aug. 1, 5 - 7, 12 - 14, 19 - 21, 26 - 28, Sept. 2 - 4, 9 - 11, 16 - 18, 23 - 25, 30, Oct. 1, 2, 7 - 9, 14 - 16, 21 - 23, 28 - 30, Nov. 4 - 6, 11 - 13, 18 - 20, 25 - 27, Dec. 2 - 4, 9, 10.
F – May 2, 3, 9 - 12, 17 - 19, 23 - 26, 30, 31, June 1, 2, 6 - 9, 13, 14, 21 - 23, 28, 29, July 5, 6, 12, 13, 19, 20, 26, 27, Aug. 2 - 4, 8 - 11, 15 - 18, 22 - 25, 29 - 31, Sept. 1, 5 - 8, 12 - 15, 19 - 22, 26 - 29, Oct. 3 - 6, 10 - 13, 17 - 20, 24 - 27, 31, Nov. 1 - 3, 7 - 10, 14 - 17, 21 - 24, 28 - 30, Dec. 1, 5 - 8.
G – May 4, 8, 13, 16, 20, 22, 27, 29, June 3, 5, 10, 12, 15 - 20, 24, 26, 30, July 1 - 3, 7 - 10, 14 - 17, 21 - 24, 28 - 31, Aug. 5 - 7, 12 - 14, 19 - 21, 26 - 28, Oct. 14, 23,

728 BRANCH LINES in Denmark

2nd class

ÅRHUS - GRENAA: Valid until Aug. 26 — *69 km*

	①-⑤		①-⑤	and	①-⑤				
Århus .... d.	0507	...	0607	hourly	2007	...	...	...	...
Grenaa .... a.	0623	...	0723	until	2123	...	...	...	...

	①-⑤		①-⑤	and	①-⑤				
Grenaa .... d.	0529	...	0629	hourly	2129	...	...	...	...
Århus .... a.	0647	...	0747	until	2247	...	...	...	...

No services on ⑥⑦.

ODENSE - SVENDBORG:

	⑥⑦	①-⑤	⑥⑦	①-⑤			and		
Odense .... d.	0559	0613	0659	0713	...	0813	hourly	2313	...
Svendborg .... a.	0655	0655	0755	0755	...	0855	until	2355	...

	①-⑤	①-⑤	⑥⑦	①-⑤	⑥⑦		and		
Svendborg .... d.	0502	0602	0602	0702	0702	0802	hourly	2302	...
Odense .... a.	0545	0645	0658	0745	0758	0845	until	2345	...

Additional services operate.

ICELAND

There are no railways in Iceland but bus services serve most major settlements. Principal services enabling a circuit of the country (along road number 1) and some other important route shown below. Additional information may be obtained from the websites of the operators. For a complete listing of all routes, including local services and ferries, see www.publictransport.is. have scheduled stops in all settlements (often at N1 filling stations) but may also stop on demand at any point along the route (confirm with operator).

Winter timings: Only *STR* and a few shorter routes shown in 'Other Services' below operate. No long-distance services on Dec. 24, 25, 31, Jan. 1. Timings shown are from winter 2015/16; s services are expected in 2016/17.

Summer timings: In addition to *STR* services, many more routes are run by private operators, with bus passes available for the *STA/SBA* and *RE/SBA* networks, respectively.

Tourist excursions are also available all year. All schedules may change at short notice - contact operators for latest timings. Confirm timings, particularly in winter, as in adverse weather cond buses may be advanced, delayed or cancelled.

Public holidays in 2016: Jan. 1, Mar. 24, 25, 27, 28, Apr. 21, May 1, 5, 15, 16, June 17, Dec. 25, 26.

729 PRINCIPAL BUS SERVICES

KEFLAVÍK - REYKJAVÍK - AKUREYRI

km	operator		STR	STR	STR		STR	GL	STR	STR	STA
	route number	W	57	57	57	S	57	North	57	57	60
		I	VX	ⒶV	†V	U	N	T	ⒶN	©N	R
	Keflavík Airport .... d.	N	...	...	...	M	...	1700	...	...	...
0	Reykjavík (BSÍ terminal) ... ■ d.	T	0840**z**	*1657***d**	*1703***d**	M	0840**z**	1745**g**	*1658***d**	*1702***d**	2345**h**
7	Reykjavík (Mjódd) .... ■ d.	E	0900	1730	1730	E	0900	|	1730	1730	|
•426	Akureyri (Hof) .... a.	R	1529**y**	2359	2359	R	1529**y**	2300**r**	2359	2359	0550**r**

operator		STR	STR		STA	STR	STR
route number	W	57	57	S	60a	57	57
	I	ⒷV	V	U	R	N	N
Akureyri (Hof) .... d.	N	1015	1620	M	0730**r**	1015	1620
Reykjavík (Mjódd) .... ■ a.	T	1644	2249	M	|	1644	2249
Reykjavík (BSÍ terminal) ■ a.	E	*1703***e**	*2302***e**	E	1310**h**	*1703***e**	*2302***e**
Keflavík Airport .... a.	R	...	...	R	...	...	...

Additional local *STR* services operate Reykjavík (Mjódd) - Borgarnes (Hyrnan) (82 *km*, journey ±1h 23 mins.) and v.v. 3-8 services per day; no services on Dec. 25, Jan. 1, and on afternoo Dec. 24, 31.

Reykjavík - Keflavík Airport: 50 *km*, local services. From BSÍ terminal ■: *flybus*, operator *RE*, journey ±45 minutes. From Holtagardar terminal ■: *airportexpress*, operator *GL*, journey minutes. *GL* shuttle bus from Laekjartorg departs 30 minutes earlier. *RE* and *GL* both offer departures in connection with all flights. Optional hotel transfer available.
Additional stopping services operated by *STR* route 55 (Reykjavík BSÍ terminal (Umferdarmidstödin) during Ⓐ peak hours only) - Hafnarfjördur (Fjördur) - Keflavík Airport (FLE) and v.v. Durin peak hours and on © use *STR* city route 1 Hlemmur via city bus stop at BSÍ (direction Hfj. Vellir); change to route 55 in Hafnarfjördur (Fjördur). 7-13 services per day, total journey time 75 minutes.

AKUREYRI - EGILSSTADIR - HÖFN

km	operator		STR			STA	SBA	STA	STR	STR
	route number	W	56		S	70	62	78	56	56
		I	Y		U	S§	F§	S§	D	D
0	Akureyri (Hof) .... d.	N	1535**y**	...	M	0730**r**	0800**r**	...	1150	1535**y**
103	Reykjahlid (Mývatn) ...... (N1) d.	T	1705	...	M	0945	1000	...	1320	1705
266	Egilsstadir (Campsite) .... ❦ d.	E	1906	...	E	1400**s**	1300	1610	...	1906
533	Höfn í Hornafirdi .... (N1) ❦ a.	R	...	...	R	...	1730	2030**t**	...	...

operator		STR			STA	STR	STR	SBA
route number	W	56		S	70a	56	56	62a
	I	Y		U	S§	D	D	F§
Höfn í Hornafirdi ..... (N1) ❦ d.	N	...	...	M	...	...	...	0800
Egilsstadir (Campsite) .... ❦ d.	T	0909	...	M	0900	0909	...	1300
Reykjahlid (Mývatn) ... (N1) d.	E	1110	...	E	1400**s**	1110	1325	1525
Akureyri (Hof) .... a.	R	1240	...	R	1710**r**	1240	1455	1715**r**

❦ – No through service in winter. Additional local services run all year on separate routes Egilsstadir - Reydarfjördur (299 *km*) - *Breiddalsvík* (365 *km*) and v.v. (2-3 services per day), Djúpivogur (430 *km*) - Höfn and v.v. (5 services per week). Operator: *SVA*.

HÖFN - REYKJAVÍK

km	operator		STR	STR		STR	STA	RE	RE	STR	RE
	route number	W	51	51	S	51	12a	19	20a	51	21a
		I	©W	ⒶW	U	C	G§	L§	K§	C	P§
0	Höfn í Hornafirdi (N1) d.	N	1025**v**	1155**v**	M	0735**v**	0755**t**	0800	...	1605**v**	...
135	Skaftafell .... d.	T	1220	1350	M	0935	1125	1215	1230	1805	...
275	Vík í Mýrdal .... (N1) d.	E	1430**c**	1600**c**	E	1200**c**	1420	...	1530	2030**c**	2030
456	Reykjavík (Mjódd) . ■ a.	R	1715	1845	R	1445**f**	|	...	|	2315	|
461	Reykjavík (BSÍ) ..... ■ a.		*1733***e**	*1902***e**		*1503***e**	1815**h**	...	1935	*2332***e**	2345

operator		STR	STR		STA	RE	STR	RE	STR
route number	W	51	51	S	12	20	51	19	51
	I	©W	ⒶW	U	G§	L§	C	L§	C
Reykjavík (BSÍ) .... ■ d.	N	*1101***d**	*1231***d**	M	0730**h**	0800	*0840***z**	...	*1657***d**
Reykjavík (Mjódd) .... ■ d.	T	1130	1300	M	|	|	0900	...	1730
Vík í Mýrdal .... (N1) d.	E	1445**c**	1615**c**	E	1150	1400	1200**c**	...	2030**c**
Skaftafell .... d.	R	1650	1820	R	1420	1600	1410	1730	2240
Höfn í Hornafirdi ... (N1) a.		1835**v**	2005**v**		1700**t**	...	1555**v**	1930	0025**v**

Additional local *STR* services operate (Hvolsvöllur (N1) -) Selfoss (N1) - Reykjavík (Mjódd) and v.v. Hvolsvöllur - Selfoss - Mjódd (100 *km*), journey ±1h 40 mins., 3-8 services per day. Selfo Mjódd (52 *km*), journey 53 mins., 8-12 services per day. No services on Dec. 25, Jan. 1. On Dec. 24, 31 only first morning services operate.

OTHER SERVICES

Egilsstadir - Seydisfjördur: 27 *km*, journey ±35 minutes, operator *FAS*. Services connect with Smyril Line ferry (Table **2285**). Confirm departure point with operator.
Summer (June 16 - Aug. 31, 2015): From **Egilsstadir** (Campsite): 0900Ⓐ, 1015④, 1300⑥⑦, 1640Ⓐ. From **Seydisfjördur**: 0755Ⓐ **m**, 0930④ **n**, 1215⑥⑦ **m**, 1550Ⓐ **m**.
Winter (Sept. 1, 2015 - June 15, 2016): From **Egilsstadir** (Campsite): 0900Ⓐ, 1025⑥, 1100② **U**, 1640Ⓐ. From **Seydisfjördur**: 0750Ⓐ **m**, 0930⑥ **m**, 1015② **U n**, 1545Ⓐ **m**.

Reykjavík - Blue Lagoon: 48 *km*, journey ±45 minutes. From BSÍ terminal ■: operator *RE*. From Holtagardar terminal ■: operator *GL*. Departures several times per day, also infreq departures from Keflavík airport.

INTERIOR HIGHLAND ROUTE: Reykjavík - Akureyri via Selfoss - Geysir§ - Gulfoss§ - Kjölur§ (448 *km*).
Reykjavík BSÍ ■ d. 0800 → Akureyri (**r**) a. 1830. Akureyri (**r**) d. 0800 → Reykjavík BSÍ ■ a. 1830. Daily June 18 - Sept. 10, 2016, depending on road opening dates, §. Operator: *SBA* route 610a.

Reykjavík BSÍ - Thingvellir - Geysir - Gullfoss (Golden Circle): operator *RE* route 6/6a (with sightseeing stops). Departures June 13 - Sept. 14, 2016 from Reykjavík at 1000, arriving bac Reykjavík at 1845. Geysir / Gullfoss also served by *SBA* and *STA* Reykjavík - Kjölur - Akureyri services (see above). *Daily excursions also available from different operators, including during wi*

C – May 15 - Sept. 11, 2016.
D – May 29 - Aug. 28, 2016.
F – June 1 - Sept. 10, 2016.
G – June 1 - Sept. 9, 2016.
K – June 1 - Sept. 8, 2016.
L – June 1 - Sept. 7, 2016.
N – June 7 - Sept. 11, 2016.
P – June 1 - Aug. 31, 2016.
R – June 20 - Sept. 2, 2016.
S – June 22 - Sept. 4, 2016.
T – ②④⑦ Apr. 1 - May 31; daily June 1 - Sept. 13, 2016.
U – ② Sept. 1 - Oct. 25, 2015, Apr. 5 - June 15, 2016.
V – Sept. 13, 2015 - June 4, 2016 (not Dec. 24, 25, 31, Jan. 1).
W – Sept. 13, 2015 - May 4, 2016 (not Dec. 24, 25, 31, Jan. 1).
X – On Dec. 24, 31 only to Borgarnes (a. 1023).
Y – ①③⑤† Aug. 30 - May 28, 2016 (not Dec. 24, 25, 31, Jan. 1).

c – Change bus in Vík í Mýrdal.
d – *STR* city route 3 to Mjódd (direction Sel/Fell).
e – *STR* city route 3 from Mjódd (direction Hlemmur); departures at xx21 and xx51 minutes past each hour.
f – Change to route 52 at Selfoss N1 (a. 1348/d. 1352).
g – Reykjavík Holtagardar.
h – Reykjavík Harpa concert hall.
m – Seydisfjördur Herdubreid.
n – Seydisfjördur Smyril Line terminal.
r – Akureyri Hafnarstraeti 77/82 (500 metres south of *STR* bus stop at Hof concert hall).
s – Via Dettifoss§ (48 *km* detour). Change bus at Dettifoss (a. 1120, d. 1200).
t – Höfn campsite (opposite of N1).
v – Höfn STR bus stop at Víkurbraut/Heppuskóli (600 metres south of N1).
y – For connection between *STR* services 57 and 56 d. 1535 to Mývatn/Egilsstadir contact operator/bus driver.
z – † only; *STR* route 57 from BSÍ terminal; change bus in Mjódd. On other days connection with *STR* city route 3, d. *0831* from city bus stop near BSÍ.
§ – With sightseeing stops.
N1 – Bus stop is at N1 filling station.
• – *389 km* by *STA* services, *439 km* by *GL*.

■ Reykjavík terminals

Located around city centre: Harpa concert hall (*STA*); Laekjartorg (*GL*); bus terminal (*RE*, also some *STR* services on routes 52, 55, 57). Holtaga terminal (*GL*) is 5 *km* east of city centre; connections by *GL* shuttle bus f Laekjartorg. Mjódd bus terminal (*STR*) is 7 *km* southeast of city centre. *STR* city service 3 connects Hlemmur - Sel/Fell via Harpa, Laekjartorg, bus stop near BSÍ and Mjódd every 15 - 30 minutes. Journey time to Mj 28-32 minutes from Hlemmur, 18-23 minutes from BSÍ; no city services o mornings before 0950. Tickets valid on connecting *STR* services.

Operators:

FAS	Ferdathjónusta Austurlands +354 472 1515	www.visitseydisfjordur.
GL	Gray Line Iceland +354 540 1313	www.airportexpress.is
RE	Reykjavik Excursions +354 580 5400	www.re.is
SBA	SBA - Nordurleid +354 550 0700	www.sba.is
STA	Sterna +354 551 1166	www.sterna.is
STR	Straetó +354 540 2700	www.straeto.is
SVA	Straetisvagnar Austurlands +354 471 2320	www.svaust.is

SWEDEN

SEE MAP PAGE 341

tors: Most services are operated by **SJ AB** (*SJ*) - Swedish State Railways - formerly part of Statens Järnvägar: www.sj.se. There is, however, a number of other operators that run services shown within the European Rail Timetable; these are indicated by their initials in the relevant table heading, or at the top of each train column where more than one operator runs services on the same route.

AEX – Arlanda Express (A-Train AB) *IB* – Inlandsbanan AB *MTR* – MTR Nordic *NSB* – Norges Statsbaner
NT – Norrtåg *Øtåg* – Øresundståg *SKJB* – Skandinaviska Jernbanor *ST* – Svenska Tågkompaniet AB
Tågab – Tågåkeriet i Bergslagen AB *VEO* – Veolia Transport (Snälltåget)

The Regional Public Transport Authority is responsible for many local services, known collectively as Länstrafik (*LT*). Those shown within these pages are abbreviated as follows:
JLT – Jönköpings Länstrafik *KLT/ÖT* – Kalmar Läns Trafik / ÖstgötaTrafiken *Skåne* – Skånetrafiken
V – Västtrafik *VTAB* – Värmlandstrafik *XT* – X-Trafik

es: Trains convey first and second classes of accommodation, unless otherwise shown. The fastest trains are classified *Snabbtåg (Sn)* and *InterCity (IC)*. Sleeping cars (🛏) are of two basic types with a range of supplements: older cars (those without showers) have one berth in first class, two or three berths in second class. Newer cars either have compartments with shower and WC (one or two berth, first class only) or have shower and WC available in the car (one or two berths in first class, two berths in second class). Couchette cars (▬) have six berths and are second class only. Refreshment services (✕, 🍸, Bistro or Shop) may be available for part of the journey only.

gs: Valid **June 12 - August 14, 2016** except where shown otherwise. Alterations may be made on and around the dates of public holidays.

s: Through journeys between Länstrafik and SJ AB, Veolia Transport or Svenska Tågkompaniet are possible with a combined ticket known as 'Resplus'. Similarly, Arlanda Express may be combined with SJ AB journeys. However, Veolia Transport and Svenska Tågkompaniet have their own fare structures and tickets cannot be combined with those of SJ AB.

vations: Seat reservation is compulsory on all *Snabbtåg* and night trains, and for through journeys to København (excluding local and *Skåne* services). Reserved seats are not labelled and, if occupied, must be claimed by presenting the seat ticket on the train.

ements: Special supplements are payable for travel on *Snabbtåg* high-speed trains.

STOCKHOLM - MALMÖ - KØBENHAVN 730

	Sn	*Sn*	*Sn*	*Sn*	*VEO*		*Sn*			*Sn*	*VEO*	*VEO*	*Sn*			*Sn*			*Sn*	*Sn*	*Sn*	*Sn*		*Sn*
	519	**521**	**521**	**523**	**3931**		**525**			**527**	**3941**	**3941**	**529**			**531**			**533**	**535**	**537**	**537**		**539**
	[R] ✕	[R] ✕	[R] ✕	[R] ✕	✕		[R] ✕			[R] ✕	✕	✕	[R] ✕			[R] ✕			[R] ✕	[R] ✕	[R] ✕	[R] ✕		[R] ✕
	Ⓐ A	Ⓐ J	⚒ K p	Ⓐ	G	Ⓐ J		⚒ K			⚒	†		⚒ K	†	L	⚒			B	Ⓑ	⑥	Ⓐ	Ⓑ
Stockholm Central ‡ d.	0521	0621	0621	0721	0725	0759	0821	0851	...	0921	0914	0929	1021	1051	1055	1121	1140	...	1221	1321	1421	1421	1440	1521
Flemingsberg ‡ d.	|	|	|	0732	|	0810	|	|	...	0932	|	|	|	|	1106	1132	1151	...	|	1332	|	|	1451	|
Södertälje Syd ‡ d.	0539	0639	0639	|	0744	0821	0839	0908	...	|	0933	|	1039	1109	1119	|	1203	...	1239	|	1439	1439	1503	|
Katrineholm **740 754** d.	|	|	|	|	|	|	|	|	...	|	|	|	|	|	|	|	|	...	|	|	|	|	|	|
Nyköping d.	|	|	|	|	|	0901	|	|	...	|	|	|	|	|	1201	|	1244	...	|	|	|	|	1547	|
Norrköping d.	0635	0735	0735	0835	0850	0942	0935	1014	...	1035	1050	1051	1135	1212	1240	1235	1328	...	1335	1435	1535	1535	1627	1635
Linköping d.	0700	0800	0800	0900	0918	1008f	1000	1039	...	1100	1119	1119	1200	1238	1308	1300	...	...	1400	1500	1600	1600	...	1700
Mjölby 755 d.	|	0815	0815	|	|	...	1015	...	...	|	|	|	1215	...	...	|	...	...	1415	|	1615	1615	...	|
Tranås d.	|	|	|	0929	|	...	|	...	...	|	|	|	|	...	...	|	...	...	|	|	|	|	...	|
Nässjö 733 d.	0750	0853	0853	0953	1016	...	1053	...	...	1150	1218	1218	1253	...	...	1350	...	...	1453	1550	1653	1653	...	1750
Alvesta d.	0824	0927	0927	1027	1056	...	1127	...	...	1224	1259	1259	1327	...	...	1424	...	...	1527	1624	1727	1727	...	1824
Hässleholm **745/6** a.	0902	1002	1002	1102	1145s	...	1202	...	...	1302	1345s	1345s	1402	...	...	1502	...	...	1602	1702	1802	1802	...	1902
Lund **745/6** § a.	0935	1035s	1035	1135s	1225s	...	1235	...	...	1335s	1420s	1420s	1435	...	...	1535	...	...	1635	1735s	1835s	1835	...	1935
Malmö C **745/6** § a.	0947	1047	1047	1147	1240	...	1247	...	...	1347	1440	1440	1447	...	...	1547	...	...	1647	1747	1847	1847	...	1947
Malmö C **703** d.	1004	...	1050	...	...	...	1250	...	...	...	...	...	1450	...	...	...	...	...	1650	...	...	1850	...	1958
København (Kastrup) ✈ **703** a.	1025s	...	1108s	...	...	...	1308s	...	...	...	...	...	1508s	...	...	...	...	...	1709s	...	...	1908s	...	2017s
København H **703** a.	1042	...	1124	...	...	...	1324	...	...	...	...	...	1524	...	...	...	...	...	1724	...	...	1924	...	2032

	IC	*IC*			*Sn*	*VEO*	*VEO*		*VEO*	*VEO*	*Sn*		*Sn*	*Sn*	*Sn*	*Sn*		*Sn*	*Sn*		*Sn*				
	207	**209**			**541**	**3943**	**3943**		**3943**	**3943**	**513**		**505**	**543**	**543**	**515**		**555**	**545**		**547**				**1**
					[R] ✕	✕	✕		✕	✕	[R] ✕		[R] ✕	[R] ✕	[R] ✕	[R] ✕		[R] ✕	[R] ✕		[R] ✕				[R]
	④⑤	†	y	Ⓐ J		Ⓐ M	N		⑤ J	©	♦	Ⓐ	Z	C	Ⓑ Z	♦		D	E	Ⓑ J	F	Ⓑ J			♦
kholm Central ‡ d.	1514	1514	1540	1551	1621	1551	1555	...	1610	1627	1640	1655	1706	1721	1721	1729	1744	1821	1821	1840	1921	2051	2151	...	2314
ngsberg ‡ d.	|	|	1551	|	|	|	|	...	|	|	|	1706	|	|	|	|	1756	|	|	1851	|	2103	2202	...	|
rtälje Syd ‡ d.	1534	1546	1603	1609	1639	|	1625	...	1631	1647	1659	1717	|	1739	1739	1748	1809	|	1839	1903	1939	2115	2214	...	2338u
rineholm **740 754** d.	|	|	|	|	|	|	|	...	|	|	|	|	|	|	|	|	|	|	|	|	|	|	|	...	|
ping d.	|	|	1644	|	|	|	|	...	|	|	|	1802	|	|	|	|	1849	|	|	1944	|	2156	2254	...	|
köping d.	1655	1655	1729	1738	1735	1714	1751	...	1751	1751	1804	1842	|	1835	1835	1851	1927	1933	1935	2028	2035	2234	2334	...	0104
ping d.	1723	1723	1754	1805	1800	1739	1819	...	1819	1819	1840	1908r	|	1900	1900	1917	1954y	1958	2000	2053h	2100	2305	0007	...	0136
y 755 d.	|	|	...	...	1815	|	|	...	|	|	|	...	|	|	|	|	...	2015	2015	...	|	...	...	...	|
s d.	|	|	...	...	|	|	|	...	|	|	1911	...	|	|	|	1948	...	|	|	...	|	...	...	...	|
jö 733 d.	1822	1822	...	...	1853	1850	1920	...	1920	1920	1937	...	|	1950	1950	2017	...	2053	2053	...	2150	...	...	...	0338j
ta d.	1904	1904	...	...	1927	1934	2003	...	2003	2003	...	...	1956	2024	2024	...	...	2127	2127	...	2224	...	...	...	0439
eholm **745/6** a.	1945	1945	...	...	2002	2022s	2050s	...	2050s	2050s	...	...	2031	2101	2101	...	...	2202	2202	...	2302	...	...	...	0539s
745/6 § a.	2019s	2019s	...	...	2035s	2115s	2125s	...	2125s	2125s	...	...	2103s	2134s	2134	...	...	2235s	2235s	...	2335s	...	...	...	0631s
ö C 745/6 § a.	2031	2031	...	...	2047	2126	2140	...	2140	2140	...	...	2115	2146	2146	...	...	2247	2247	...	2347	...	...	...	0648
ö C 703 d.	...	...	...	...	...	...	...	...	...	...	...	...	...	...	2149	...	...	...	...	...	...	...	...	...	...
havn (Kastrup) ✈ **703** a.	...	...	...	...	...	...	...	...	...	...	...	...	...	...	2208s	...	...	...	...	...	...	...	...	...	...
nhavn H 703 a.	...	...	...	...	...	...	...	...	...	...	...	...	...	...	2223	...	...	...	...	...	...	...	...	...	...

				Sn	*Sn*	*Sn*		*Sn*	*Sn*	*Sn*		*Sn*	*Sn*		*VEO*		*Sn*		*Sn*	*Sn*	*Sn*		*VEO*	*Sn*	*Sn*
				514	**522**	**552**		**500**	**518**	**524**		**526**	**516**		**3932**		**528**		**530**	**10530**	**530**		**3940**	**532**	**534**
				[R] ✕	[R] ✕	[R] ✕		[R] ✕	[R] ✕	[R] ✕		[R] ✕	[R] ✕		✕		[R] ✕		[R] ✕	[R] ✕	[R] ✕		✕	[R] ✕	[R] ✕
	Ⓐ	Ⓐ	⑥	♦	Ⓐ J	Ⓐ M	⑥	Ⓐ A	♦	Ⓐ J	©	Ⓐ J	P	†	G		Q	©	⑥ S	R	Ⓑ L			B	
nhavn H **703** d.	...	...	...	...	...	...	...	...	...	...	...	...	...	...	...	...	...	...	...	0815	0824	...	...	...	...
nhavn Kastrup ✈ **703** d.	...	...	...	...	...	...	...	...	...	...	...	...	...	...	...	...	...	...	...	|	0838	...	...	...	...
ö C **703** a.	...	...	...	...	...	...	...	...	...	...	...	...	...	...	...	...	...	...	...	0900	0900	...	...	...	...
ö C **745/6** § d.	...	...	...	...	0511	0511	...	0536	...	0611	...	0711	0711	...	0720	...	0811	...	0911	0911	0911	...	0920	1011	1111
745/6 § d.	...	...	...	...	0523u	0523u	...	0548u	...	0623u	...	0723u	0723u	...	0731u	...	0823u	...	0923u	0923	0923	...	0930u	1023u	1123u
leholm **745/6** d.	...	...	...	...	0554	0554	...	0618	...	0654	...	0754	0754	...	0809u	...	0854	...	0954	0954	0954	...	1008u	1054	1154
sta **746** d.	...	...	...	...	0633	0633	...	|	...	0736	...	0833	0833	...	0853	...	0936	...	1033	1033	1033	...	1053	1136	1233
sjö 733 d.	...	...	...	0628	0707	0707	...	|	0751	0810	...	0907	0907	...	0934	...	1010	...	1107	1107	1107	...	1131	1210	1307
ås d.	...	...	...	0652	|	|	...	|	0815	|	...	|	|	...	|	...	|	...	|	|	|	...	|	|	|
by 755 d.	...	...	...	|	0742	0742	...	|	|	|	...	0942	0942	...	|	...	|	...	1142	1142	1142	...	|	|	1342
ping d.	0610	0640	0716	0726	0758	0758	0800	0809	0849	0858	0912	0958	0958	1004	1037	...	1058	1121	1158	1158	1158	1204h	1228	1258	1358
köping 754 d.	0640	0715	0743	|	0822	0822	0828	|	0916	0922	0945	1022	1022	1031	1105	...	1122	1148	1222	1222	1222	1232	1256	1322	1422
ping d.	0724	0756	|	0753	|	|	0909	|	|	|	|	|	|	1113	|	...	|	|	|	|	|	1314	|	|	|
trineholm **740 754** a.	|	|	|	|	|	|	|	|	|	|	|	|	|	|	|	...	|	|	|	|	|	|	|	|	|
rtälje Syd ‡ a.	0805	0840	0847	0900	|	0918	0950	|	|	1018	1048	|	1118	1153	1227	...	|	1249	1318	1318	1318	1355	1405	1418	1518
ingsberg ‡ a.	0816	0851	|	|	|	|	1001	|	1026	|	|	|	|	1204	|	...	1226	|	|	|	|	1406	|	|	|
kholm Central ‡ a.	0831	0905	0909	0922	0939	0939	1020	0946	1039	1039	1109	1139	1139	1220	1250	...	1239	1309	1339	1339	1339	1420	1431	1439	1539

NOTES (LISTED BY TRAIN NUMBER)

Ⓑ: 🛏, ▬, (2) and 🍸 Stockholm - Malmö.
\- Ⓐ June 13 - July 1: (12) and ✕ Stockholm - Nässjö - Jönköping.
\- Ⓐ June 13 - July 1: (12) and ✕ Jönköping - Nässjö - Stockholm.
\- † June 12 - 26 (also Aug. 14): (12) and ✕ Stockholm - Nässjö - Jönköping.
\- ⑥ June 18 - July 2: (12) and ✕ Jönköping - Nässjö - Stockholm.

June 13 - 23.
Ⓑ June 12 - July 1; daily July 3 - Aug. 14.
⑤† July 3 - Aug. 12.
© June 12 - July 2; ⑥ July 9 - Aug. 6; © from Aug. 13.
Ⓐ June 13 - 23; Ⓑ June 27 - Aug. 12.
①②③④† June 12 - 30 (also Aug. 14).
June 24 only.

J – Until July 1.
K – From July 2.
L – From July 3.
M – From July 4.
N – ①②③④ June 13 - 30.
P – © June 12 - July 2; daily July 3 - Aug. 14.
Q – Ⓐ June 13 - July 4; ①⑥ July 9 - Aug. 13.
R – Until July 2.
S – July 9 - Aug. 13.
Z – Not July 2 - Aug. 13.
f – ⑤ only.
h – † only.

j – Arrive 0254.
p – Also June 18.
r – July 4 - Aug. 12.
s – Stops to set down only.
u – Stops to pick up only.
y – July 2 - Aug. 13.
‡ – Most trains on this table may not be used for local journeys between Stockholm and Södertälje Syd or v.v. Local trains run every 30 mins Stockholm Central - Södertälje Hamn - Södertälje Centrum and v.v. (journey 42 mins). 🚌 Södertälje Syd - Södertälje Centrum runs every 30 mins.
§ – Frequent local trains run Lund - Malmö and v.v.
* – Södertälje Syd: *0 km* - Katrineholm: *95 km* - Norrköping: *143 km*.

730 KØBENHAVN - MALMÖ - STOCKHOLM

		Sn	Sn	Sn		Sn	Sn	Sn	Sn		Sn	Sn	Sn	Sn	IC	Sn	VEO	VEO	Sn	Sn	Sn	Sn	Sn	
		536	536	556		538	538	538	540		512	512	542*	542	204*	544	3942	3942	10546	546	558	550*	550	
		🅁✕	🅁✕	🅁✕		🅁✕	🅁✕	🅁✕	🅁✕		🅁✕	🅁✕	🅁✕	🅁✕		🅁✕	✕	✕	🅁✕	🅁✕	🅁✕	🅁✕	🅁✕	
		ⒶJ	Y	T		ⒶJ	K	ⒸU	Ⓑ		W	y	ⒷJ	ⒷV	④⑤†		†	X	R	L	†T	Ⓑ	ⒷV	
København H **703**	d.	...	1124	...	...	...	...	1228	1228	...	...	...	1424	...	1424	...	...	...	...	1556	1624	...	...	1824	...
København Kastrup ✈ **703**	d.	...	|	...	...	...	...	1241	|	...	...	...	1438	...	1438	...	...	...	...	|	1638	...	...	1838	...
Malmö C **703**	a.	...	1201	...	...	...	...	1302	1311	...	...	...	1459	...	1459	...	...	...	...	1700	1700	...	...	1858	...
Malmö C **745/6**	§ d.	...	1211	1211	1211	...	1311	1311	1311	1411	...	1511	1511	1511	1511	1505	1611	1620	1620	1711	1711	1835	1911	1911	...
Lund **745/6**	§ d.	...	1223	1223u	1223u	...	1323u	1323	1323	1423u	...	1523	1523	1523	1523	1517u	1623u	1630u	1630u	1723	1723	1847u	1923	1923	...
Hässleholm **745/6**	d.	...	1254	1254	1254	...	1354	1354	1354	1454	...	1554	1554	1554	1554	1601	1654	1709u	1709u	1754	1754	1918	1954	1954	...
Alvesta **746**	d.	...	1336	1336	1336	...	1433	1433	1433	1533	...	1633	1633	1633	1633	1645	1736	1752	1752	1833	1833	1959	2033	2033	...
Nässjö 733	d.	...	1410	1410	1410	...	1507	1507	1507	1607	...	1707	1707	1707	1707	1725	1810	1831	1831	1907	1907	2034	2107	2107	...
Tranås	d.	...	|	|	|	...	|	|	|	1630	...	|	|	|	|	|	|	|	|	|	|	|	2130	2130	...
Mjölby 755	d.	...	|	|	|	...	1542	1542	1542	|	...	1742	1742	1742	1742	|	|	|	|	1942	1942	|	|	|	...
Linköping	d.	1403h	1458	1458	1458	1520	1558	1558	1558	1658	1711	1758	1758	1758	1758	1821	1858	1928	1928	1958	1958	2124	2158	2158	...
Norrköping 754	d.	1432	1522	1522	1522	1548	1622	1622	1622	1722	1743	1822	1822	1822	1822	1850	1922	1956	1956	2022	2022	2150	2222	2222	...
Nyköping	d.	1514	|	|	|	|	|	|	|	|	|	|	|	|	|	|	|	|	|	|	|	|	|	|	...
Katrineholm **740 754**	a.	|	|	|	|	|	|	|	|	|	|	|	|	|	|	|	|	|	|	|	|	|	|	|	...
Södertälje Syd	‡ a.	1555	1618	1618	|	1650	1718	1718	1718	|	1849	1918	1918	|	|	2002	2018	|	2105	2118	2118	|	2318	2318	...
Flemingsberg	‡ a.	1607	|	|	|	|	|	|	|	1826	|	|	|	|	|	|	|	|	|	|	|	|	|	|	...
Stockholm Central	‡ a.	1620	1639	1639	1639	1709	1739	1739	1739	1839	1909	1939	1939	1946	1946	2024	2039	2122	2130	2139	2139	2309	2339	2339	...

♦ – **NOTES** (LISTED BY TRAIN NUMBER)

2 – Ⓑ: 🛏, 🛏, (2) and 🍸 Malmö - Stockholm.

J – Until July 1.
K – From July 2.
L – From July 3.
R – Until July 2.
T – June 12 - 26 (also Aug. 14).
U – June 12 - 26.

V – From Aug. 14.
W – June 18 only.
X – ①④⑤⑥ only.
Y – July 3 - Aug. 13.

h – † only.
s – Stops to set down only.
u – Stops to pick up only.
y – July 2 - Aug. 13.

* – Train number variations:
204 runs as 10204 from July 3; 542 runs as 10542 on Ⓐ; 550 runs as 10550

‡ – Most trains on this table may not be used for local journeys between Stockhol Södertälje Syd or v.v. Local trains run every 30 mins Stockholm Central - Söd Hamn - Södertälje Centrum and v.v. (journey 42 mins). 🚌 Södertälje Södertälje Centrum runs every 30 mins.

§ – Frequent local trains run Malmö - Lund.

731 MALMÖ - YSTAD - SIMRISHAMN

Operator: S

km			Ⓒ	Ⓐ	Ⓐ	⑥	Ⓐ		Ⓐ		⚒		❖	and at the		❖	⚒	†	⚒	⚒	†	⑤⑥	G	
0	**Malmö** C	d.	0108	...	0508	...	0538	0608	0638	0708	0726	0808	0838	same mins.	2108	2138	2208	2208	2238	2308	2308	2338	2344	0007
70	Ystad	◧ a.	0156	0458	0556	0558	0628	0656	0728	0756	0828	0856	0928	past each	2156	2228	2256	2256	2328	2356	2356	0028	0028	0056
116	Simrishamn	a.	...	0538	0638	0638	...	0738	...	0838	...	0938	...	hour until	2238	...	2338	...	...	0038	...	...	...	...

		②–⑤	Ⓒ	Ⓐ		Ⓐ		Ⓐ		Ⓐ			and at the				⚒		⚒		⚒		Ⓒ
Simrishamn	d.	0047	0047	...	...	...	0547a	...	0647d	...	0747	...	same mins.	1847	...	1947	...	2047	...	2147	...	2247	...
Ystad	◧ d.	0126	0130	0430	0530	0600	0630	0700	0730	0800	0830	0900	past each	1930	2000	2030	2100	2130	2200	2230	2300	2330	0000
Malmö C	a.	...	0221	0521	0621	0651	0721	0751	0821	0851	0921	0951	hour until	2021	2051	2121	2151	2221	2251	2321r	2351t	0021d	0051

G – ①②③④† only.

a – Ⓐ only.
d – ⚒ only.
f – ⑥⑦ only.

r – Arrive 2314 on ①②③④†.
t – Arrive 2344 on ①②③④.

❖ – 2038 and 2138 departures from Malmö run ⚒ only.

◧ – For direct services Ystad - København and v.v. see Table **727**.

732 STOCKHOLM - ESKILSTUNA - ARBOGA

Valid June 12 - Augu

km			2 Ⓐ	Ⓐ	2 ⑥	Ⓐ	⚒	2 †				j Ⓐ		m †	Ⓐ	Ⓐ		Ⓐ	Ⓐ	k †			Ⓐ	Ⓒ	①–④
0	**Stockholm** C	d.	...	0629	...	0755	0855	...	1044	...	1244	1344	1444	1544	1544	1629	1651	1729	1751	1751	...	1855	2040	2155	2255
36	Södertälje Syd	d.	...	0651	...	0817	0917	...	1106	...	1306	1406	1506	1606	1607	1652	1713	1752	1813	1813	...	1917	2102	2217	2317
67	Läggesta	● d.	...	0708	...	0834	0934	...	1123	...	1323	1422	1522	1622	1625	1710	1730	1810	1830	1830	...	1934	2119	2234	2334
83	Strängnäs	d.	0616j	0716	...	0843	0944	...	1132	...	1332	1432	1532	1632	1635	1723	1739	1819	1842	1842	...	1943	2128	2243	2343
115	Eskilstuna	a.	0639j	0739	...	0900	1001	...	1149	...	1349	1450	1550	1650	1654	1743	1756	1839	1900	1900	...	2000	2145	2300	2400
115	Eskilstuna	d.	0648	0741	0815	0902	1010	1010	1205	...	1405	...	1605	...	1700	1746	1800c	1842j	1902	1902	...	2002	2147	...	...
141	Kungsör	d.	0702	0757	0829	0916	1024	1024	1219	...	1419	...	1619	...	1714	1800	1814c	1856j	1916	1916	...	2016	2201	...	...
159	**Arboga 756**	a.	0713	0808	0840	0927	1035	1035	1230	...	1430	...	1630	...	1725	1811	1825c	1907j	1927	1927	...	2027	2212	...	...
	Örebro **756**	a.	...	0830	...	...	...	...	...	...	...	...	...	...	1749	1837	...	1931j	...	1949	...	...	2234j	...	...

		Ⓐ	j Ⓐ		⚒	j Ⓐ	Ⓐ		Ⓐ	⑥	†				j Ⓑ		Ⓐ	m †					⑥	Ⓑ
Örebro **756**	d.	...	...	...	0559a	...	0706	...	...	0813r	...	...	...	...	...	...	1608	...	...	...	...	...	...	...
Arboga 756	d.	...	0546	...	0622a	...	0729	...	0834	0834r	...	1120	...	1320	...	1520	1629	...	...	1725	1935	...	2125	2125
Kungsör	d.	...	0556	...	0632a	...	0739	...	0844	0844r	...	1130	...	1330	...	1530	1639	...	...	1735	1945	...	2135	2135
Eskilstuna	a.	...	0612	...	0648a	...	0756	...	0900	0900r	...	1146	...	1346	...	1546	1655	...	...	1751	2001	...	2151	2151
Eskilstuna	d.	0515	0615	...	0651	0714	0759	...	0904	0904	1011	1200	...	1400	1500	1600	1700	1700	...	1813	2004	...	...	2200
Strängnäs	d.	0531	0631	...	0709	0732	0817	...	0920	0920	1027	1216	...	1416	1516	1616	1716	1716	...	1832	2020	...	...	2216
Läggesta	● d.	0540	0640	...	0723	0742	0827	...	0929	0929	1036	1225	...	1425	1525	1625	1725	1725	...	1841	2029	...	...	2225
Södertälje Syd	d.	0557	0701	...	0741	0800	0845	...	0946	0946	1053	1242	...	1442	1542	1642	1742	1742	...	1858	2046	...	...	2242
Stockholm C	a.	0620	0724	...	0805	0824	0909	...	1009	1009	1116	1305	...	1505	1605	1705	1805	1805	...	1920	2109	...	...	2305

a – Ⓐ only.
c – Ⓒ only.
j – June 13 - July 1.

k – July 3 - Aug. 7.
m – June 12 - 26.
r – July 9 - Aug. 6.

● – Summer only narrow gauge service operates Mariefred - Läggesta (nedre) - Taxinge-Näsby and v.v. Operator: Östra Södermanlands Järnväg, Box 53, SE - 647 22 Mariefred. ✆ +46 (0)159 210 00, fax +46 (0)159 21

733 SKÖVDE - JÖNKÖPING - NÄSSJÖ

Operator: *V* (except *Sn* tra

2nd class only except where shown

km				*Sn* 514		*Sn* 518											B										B	C	D
			Ⓐ	♦	Ⓐ	♦		Ⓐ	†		⚒	⑥		Ⓐ		⑥	Ⓐ	Ⓐ	⑥			Ⓑ		†	Ⓐ		Ⓑ	Ⓐ	Ⓑ	Ⓐ
0	**Skövde 740**	d.	0445	...	0542j	...	0653g	0757	0836	...	0920	...	...	1133	...	1328	1333	...	...	...	1535	...	...	1738	1743	...	1918	...	...	...
	Göteborg	d.	|	...	|	...	|	|	|	...	|	...	...	|	...	|	|	1250	1255	...	|	1500	...	|	|	...	|	...	...	...
30	Falköping **740**	d.	0509	...	0617	...	0716	0820	0858	0916	0940	1015	1116	1154	1316	1349	1353	1415	1415	1516	1555	1616	1716	1818	1818	1917	1937	2015	2118	2218
100	Jönköping	a.	0552	...	0701	...	0758	0901	...	1000	...	1100	1200	...	1400	...	...	1500	1500	1603	...	1702	1800	1900	1900	2001	...	2100	2202	2302
100	Jönköping	d.	0558	0550	0706	0709	0806	0906	...	1004	...	1103	1205	...	1407	...	...	1502	1502	1605	...	1706	1806	1905	1905	2003	...	2106	2205	2307
143	**Nässjö 730**	a.	0634	0618	0739	0740	0842	0940	...	1041	...	1139	1242	...	1440	...	...	1541	1541	1640	...	1741	1842	1939	1939	2036	...	2140	2239	2340

											B				B									*Sn* 513	*Sn* 515		
		Ⓐ	Ⓐ	Ⓐ	⚒	⚒	Ⓐ		Ⓐ	Ⓐ		Ⓐ	⑥	⚒		Ⓐ	Ⓐ		†	Ⓐ	Ⓐ		Ⓑ			♦	♦	G	⑤⑥
Nässjö 730	d.	0446	0554	0715	0818	...	...	0919	1020	...	1118	1219	1219	...	1316	1416	...	1528	1620	1620	...	1717	1818	1916	...	1944	2036	2120	2120
Jönköping	a.	0519	0628	0749	0851	...	...	0953	1055	...	1153	1252	1258	...	1349	1450	...	1601	1659	1659	...	1753	1851	1951	...	2014	2102	2151	2151
Jönköping	d.	0521	0631	0758	0901	...	...	1000	1100	...	1200	1300	1300	...	1400	1500	...	1603	1702	1702	...	1800	1902	2002	...	...	...	2204	2204
Falköping **740**	a.	0606	0715	0845	0942	0950	1020	1046	1144	1202	1244	1344	1344	1421	1444	1543	1620	1651	1742	1742	1750	1844	1943	2045	2109	...	...	2246	2246
Göteborg	a.	|	|	...	1100	|	|	...	1305	|	...	...	1505	|	...	...	|	...	1900	1910	|	...	2105	...	|	...	...	|	|
Skövde 740	a.	0639	0737	...	...	1006	1036	...	...	1219	...	...	...	1438	...	...	1638	...	...	...	1808	...	...	...	2125	...	...	2304	2311

♦ – **NOTES** (LISTED BY TRAIN NUMBER)

513 – Ⓐ June 13 - July 1: (12) and ✕ Stockholm - Nässjö - Jönköping.
514 – Ⓐ June 13 - July 1: (12) and ✕ Jönköping - Nässjö - Stockholm.
515 – † June 12 - 26: (12) and ✕ Stockholm - Nässjö - Jönköping.
518 – ⑥ June 18 - July 2: (12) and ✕ Jönköping - Nässjö - Stockholm.

A – ⑥ July 9 - Aug. 6; ⚒ Aug. 13 - Dec. 10.
B – June 13 - 23.
C – June 12 - 26.
D – July 4 - Aug. 12.
E – July 2 - Aug. 14.
G – ①②③④† only.

g – ⑥ only.
j – Depart 0552 from July 11.

KRISTIANSTAD - HÄSSLEHOLM - HELSINGBORG 734

ator: Skåne 2nd class only

	Ⓐ	Ⓐ	Ⓐ		⚒	Ⓐ		Ⓐ		Ⓐ					Ⓐ			Ⓐ									Ⓒ
Kristianstad 745 ... d.	...	0502	0538	0602	...	0638	0702	0738	0802	0838	...	0902	and at	1402	1438	1502	and at	1738	1802	...	1902	2002	2102	2202	2302	...
Hässleholm 745 ... d.	...	0523	0557	0623	...	0657	0723	0757	0823	0857	...	0923	the same	1423	1457	1523	the same	1757	1823	...	1923	2023	2123	2223	2323	...
Hässleholm ... d.	0501	0531	0601	...	0631	0701	0731	0801	0831	0901	...	0931	minutes	1431	1501	1531	minutes	1801	1831	...	1931	2031	2131	2231	2331	0031
Åstorp ... d.	0540	0612	0640	...	0712	0740	0812	0840	0912	0940	...	1012	past each	1512	1540	1612	past each	1840	1912	...	2012	2112	2212	2312	0012	0112
Helsingborg ... a.	0603	0635	0703	...	0735	0803	0835	0903	0935	1003	...	1035	hour until	1535	1603	1635	hour until	1903	1935	...	2035	2135	2235	2335	0035	0135

	Ⓐ	Ⓐ	Ⓐ	⚒	Ⓐ	Ⓐ		Ⓐ		Ⓐ				Ⓐ			Ⓐ						⚒		Ⓒ
ıgborg ... d.	0417	...	0447	0517	...	0547	0617	0647	0717	0747	0817	and at	1317	1347	1417	and at	1647	1717	...	1817	and at	2217	2317	...	0017
ɔ ... d.	0440	...	0511	0540	...	0611	0640	0711	0740	0811	0840	the same	1340	1411	1440	the same	1711	1740	...	1840	the same	2240	2340	...	0040
eholm ... a.	0518	...	0548	0618	...	0648	0718	0748	0818	0848	0918	minutes	1418	1448	1518	minutes	1748	1818	...	1918	minutes	2318	0018	...	0118
eholm 745 ... d.	...	0531	0558	...	0631	0658	0731	0758	0831	0858	0931	past each	1432	1458	1531	past each	1758	1831	...	1931	past each	2331	...	0031	...
anstad 745 ... a.	...	0552	0619	...	0652	0719	0752	0819	0852	0919	0952	hour until	1452	1519	1552	hour until	1819	1852	...	1952	hour until	2352	...	0052	...

GÖTEBORG - MALMÖ - KØBENHAVN 735

rator: Øtåg (except Sn trains)

Subject to alteration owing to temporary cross-border arrangements between Denmark and Sweden (please check the latest situation before travelling)

	Ⓐ	Ⓐ	⚒	Sn 481 ⒶJ		Sn 483 ⚒R	Sn 10483 ⚒L				Sn 485 M		Sn 10477 N		Sn 487 M		Sn 10479 N		Sn 489 ⒷP		Sn 10499 N		Sn 491 ⒷP	
Göteborg C ... ▲ d.	...	...	0555a	0640	0655d	0740	0740	0755	0855	0955	1010	1055	1140	1155	1240	1255	1340	1355	1440	1455	1540	1555	1640	1655
Kungsbacka ... ▲ d.	...	...	0613a	|	0713d	|	|	0813	0913	1013	|	1113	|	1213	|	1313	|	1413	|	1513	|	1613	|	1713
Varberg ... ▲ d.	...	...	0634a	|	0734d	|	0812	0834	0934	1034	|	1134	1212	1234	|	1334	1411	1434	|	1534	1612	1634	|	1734
Falkenberg ... ▲ d.	...	...	0648a	|	0748d	|	|	0848	0948	1048	|	1148	|	1248	|	1348	|	1448	|	1548	|	1648	|	1748
Halmstad ... ▲ d.	0512	0612	0712	0741	0812	0840	0840	0912	1012	1112	1110	1212	1240	1312	1340	1412	1438	1512	1540	1612	1640	1712	1740	1812
Laholm ... d.	0522	0622	0722	|	0822	|	|	0922	1022	1126	|	1222	|	1322	|	1422	|	1522	|	1622	|	1722	|	1822
Båstad ... d.	0528	0628	0728	|	0828	|	|	0928	1028	1132	|	1228	|	1328	|	1428	|	1528	|	1628	|	1728	|	1828
Ängelholm ... d.	0541	0641	0741	|	0841	|	|	0941	1041	1143	|	1241	|	1341	|	1441	|	1541	|	1641	|	1741	|	1841
Helsingborg ... a.	0608	0708	0808	0818	0908	0919	0919	1008	1108	1208	1147	1308	1319	1408	1419	1508	1518	1608	1619	1708	1718	1808	1819	1908
Helsingborg 737 ... d.	0612	0712	0812	0820	0912	0921	0921	1012	1112	1212	1149	1312	1321	1412	1421	1512	1520	1612	1621	1712	1720	1812	1821	1912
Landskrona 737 ... d.	0623	0723	0823	|	0923	|	|	1023	1123	1223	|	1323	|	1423	|	1523	|	1623	|	1723	|	1823	|	1923
Lund 737 ... d.	0641	0741	0841	0847s	0941	0944s	0946	1041	1141	1241	1214s	1341	1345	1441	1444s	1541	1545	1641	1647s	1741	1745	1841	1844s	1941
Malmö C 737 ... a.	0651	0751	0851	0859	0951	0956	0956	1051	1151	1251	1226	1351	1355	1451	1456	1551	1555	1651	1659	1751	1756	1851	1856	1951
Malmö C 703 ... d.	0653	0753	0853	...	0953	...	1002	1053	1153	1253	...	1353	1400	1453	...	1553	1559	1653	...	1753	1759	1853	...	1953
København (Kastrup) ✈ 703 .. a.	0713	0813	0913	...	1013	...	1017s	1113	1213	1313	...	1413	1417s	1513	...	1613	1617s	1713	...	1813	1817s	1913	...	2013
København H 703 ... a.	0728	0828	0928	...	1028	...	1032	1128	1228	1328	...	1428	1432	1528	...	1628	1632	1728	...	1828	1832	1928	...	2028

	Sn 493 ⑥K	Sn 10493 N		Sn 439 ⒷP		Sn 497 †Q				
borg C ... ▲ d.	1740	1740	1755	1840	1855	1940	1955	2055	2155	2255
sbacka ... ▲ d.	|	|	1813	|	1913	|	2013	2113	2213	2313
erg ... ▲ d.	|	1812	1834	|	1934	|	2034	2134	2235	2335
nberg ... ▲ d.	|	|	1848	|	1948	|	2048	2148	2249	2349
stad ... ▲ d.	1840	1840	1912	1940	2012	2038	2112	2212	2312	0007
m ... d.	|	|	1922	|	2022	|	2122	2222	2322	...
ad ... d.	|	|	1928	|	2028	|	2128	2228	2328	...
lholm ... d.	|	|	1941	|	2041	|	2141	2241	2341	...
ngborg ... a.	1919	1919	2008	2019	2108	2118	2208	2308	0004	...
ngborg 737 ... d.	1921	1921	2012	2021	2112	2120	2212	2312	...	...
skrona 737 ... d.	|	|	2023	|	2123	|	2223	2323	...	...
737 ... a.	1944s	1946	2041	2044s	2141	2143s	2241	2341	...	...
ö C 737 ... a.	1956	1956	2051	2056	2151	2155	2251	2351	...	...
ö C 703 ... d.	...	2004	2053	...	2153	...	2253	...	...	...
havn (Kastrup) ✈ 703 ... a.	...	2024s	2113	...	2213	...	2313	...	...	...
enhavn H 703 ... a.	...	2039	2128	...	2228	...	2328	...	...	...

	Ⓐ	Ⓐ	⚒	Sn 426 ⒶJ	⚒	Sn 482 ⚒L	Sn 482 ⒶJ	Sn 418 ⑥K		
København H 703 ... d.	...	...	...	...	0532	0624	...	...	0632	0732
København (Kastrup) ✈ 703 . d.	...	...	...	...	0546	0638u	...	...	0646	0746
Malmö C 703 ... a.	...	...	...	...	0606	0658	...	...	0706	0806
Malmö C 737 ... d.	...	...	0508a	0605	0608	0659	0659	0702	0708	0808
Lund 737 ... d.	...	...	0520a	0617u	0620	0711	0711u	0714u	0720	0820
Landskrona 737 ... d.	...	...	0535a	|	0635	|	|	|	0735	0835
Helsingborg 737 ... a.	...	...	0548a	0640	0648	0740	0740	0740	0748	0848
Helsingborg ... d.	0453	...	0553a	0642	0653	0742	0742	0742	0753	0853
Ängelholm ... d.	0516	...	0616a	|	0716	|	|	|	0816	0916
Båstad ... d.	0526	...	0626a	|	0726	|	|	|	0826	0926
Laholm ... d.	0532	...	0632a	|	0732	|	|	|	0832	0932
Halmstad ... ▲ d.	0551	0621	0651	0718	0752	0818	0818	0818	0852	0952
Falkenberg ... ▲ d.	0607	0637	0707	|	0808	|	|	|	0908	1008
Varberg ... ▲ d.	0622	0652	0722	|	0824	|	|	|	0924	1024
Kungsbacka ... ▲ d.	0645	0715	0745	|	0845	|	|	|	0945	1045
Göteborg C ... ▲ a.	0705	0735	0805	0820	0905	0920	0920	0920	1005	1105

		Sn 484 M	Sn 10478 N		Sn 486 M			Sn 10488 N	Sn 488 ⒷP				Sn 492 ⒷP		Sn 10494 N	Sn 494 ⑥K		Sn 496 ⒷP			Sn 10498 P	Sn 498 †Q			
enhavn H 703 ... d.	0832	...	0924	0932	...	1032	1132	1223	...	1232	1332	1432	...	1532	1616	...	1632	...	1732	1832	1927	...	1932	2032	2232
nhavn (Kastrup) ✈ 703 ... d.	0846	...	0937u	0946	...	1046	1146	1237u	...	1246	1346	1446	...	1546	1630u	...	1646	...	1746	1846	1940u	...	1946	2046	2246
ö C 703 ... a.	0906	...	0957	1006	...	1106	1206	1257	...	1306	1406	1506	...	1606	1654	...	1706	...	1806	1906	1959	...	2006	2106	2306
ö C 737 ... d.	0908	0937	1005	1008	1105	1108	1208	1305	1305	1308	1408	1508	1600	1608	1700	1700	1708	1800	1808	1908	2005	2005	2008	2108	2308
737 ... d.	0920	0950u	1017	1020	1117u	1120	1220	1317	1317u	1320	1420	1520	1612u	1620	1712	1712u	1720	1812u	1820	1920	2017	2017u	2020	2120	2320
skrona 737 ... d.	0935	|	|	1035	|	1135	1235	|	|	1335	1435	1535	|	1635	|	|	1735	|	1835	1935	|	|	2035	2135	2335
ingborg 737 ... a.	0948	1013	1040	1048	1140	1148	1248	1340	1340	1348	1448	1548	1640	1648	1740	1740	1748	1840	1848	1948	2040	2040	2048	2148	2348
ingborg ... d.	0953	1015	1042	1053	1149	1153	1253	1342	1342	1353	1453	1553	1642	1653	1742	1742	1753	1842	1853	1953	2042	2042	2053	2153	2353
lholm ... d.	1016	|	|	1116	|	1216	1316	|	|	1416	1516	1616	|	1716	|	|	1816	|	1916	2016	|	|	2116	2216	0016
ad ... d.	1026	|	|	1126	|	1226	1326	|	|	1426	1526	1626	|	1726	|	|	1826	|	1926	2026	|	|	2126	2226	0026
lm ... d.	1032	|	|	1132	|	1232	1332	|	|	1432	1532	1632	|	1732	|	|	1832	|	1932	2032	|	|	2132	2232	0032
stad ... ▲ d.	1052	1051	1117	1152	1225	1252	1346	1416	1417	1452	1552	1652	1718	1752	1816	1818	1852	1918	1952	2052	2117	2118	2152	2252	0046
enberg ... ▲ d.	1111	|	|	1208	|	1308	1352	|	|	1508	1608	1708	|	1808	|	|	1908	|	2008	2108	|	|	2208	2308	...
erg ... ▲ d.	1126	|	1146	1224	|	1324	1424	1445	|	1524	1624	1724	|	1824	1847	|	1924	|	2024	2124	2146	|	2224	2324	...
sbacka ... ▲ d.	1145	|	|	1245	|	1345	1445	|	|	1545	1645	1745	|	1845	|	|	1945	|	2045	2145	|	|	2245	2345	...
borg C ... ▲ a.	1205	1150	1220	1305	1325	1405	1505	1520	1520	1605	1705	1805	1820	1905	1920	1920	2005	2020	2105	2205	2220	2220	2305	0005	...

June 13 - July 1. M – June 12 - July 2. Q – June 12 - 26. a – Ⓐ only. s – Stops to set down only. ▲ – Additional services operate on Ⓐ Göteborg - Halmstad and v.v.
June 18 - July 2. N – July 3 - Aug. 13. R – June 13 - July 2. d – ⚒ only. u – Stops to pick up only.
July 4 - Aug. 13. P – June 12 - July 1.

HALLSBERG - LIDKÖPING - HERRLJUNGA 736

erator: V 2nd class only

	Ⓐ	Ⓐ		Ⓒ	Ⓐ		Ⓐ	†		⑥	Ⓐ	Ⓐ		†	†		Ⓐ	†	⑥		Ⓐ		Ⓐ	†
Örebro C 755/6 ... d.	...	...	...	...	0757	...	...	...	...	...	...	...	...	...	...	...	...	...	...	...	1627	...	...	...
Hallsberg 740 ... d.	...	...	...	...	0817	...	...	...	...	...	...	...	...	1300	...	...	...	...	1555	...	1646	...	...	1847
Laxå 740 ... d.	...	...	...	...	0833	...	...	...	...	...	...	...	...	1316	...	...	...	...	1612	...	1703	...	...	1903
Mariestad ... d.	0530	0700	...	0835	0920	...	1008	...	...	1146	1221	1325	...	1403	1409	...	1546	1719	1725j	...	1752	...	...	2011t
Lidköping ... a.	0610	0748	...	0916	1008	...	1106	...	...	1234	1309	1419	...	...	1450	...	1642	1759	1813	...	1840	...	...	2101
Lidköping ... d.	0619	0759	...	0917	1010	...	1111	1155	...	1240	...	1441	...	...	1452	...	1705	1802	...	...	...	...	2013	...
Herrljunga 740 ... a.	0701	0846	...	0959	1057	...	1157	1246	...	1328	...	1526	...	...	1533	...	1750	1840	...	...	...	...	2057	...
Göteborg C 740 ... a.	0755	...	...	1055	1155	...	...	1355	...	1425	...	1625	...	...	1625	...	...	1935	...	...	...	...	...	...

	Ⓐ	Ⓐ	⑥	Ⓐ		Ⓐ	†	⑥	Ⓐ	⑥	⑥	Ⓐ	†	Ⓐ	Ⓐ		†	†	⑥	Ⓐ	Ⓐ	†	Ⓐ	Ⓐ	†
öteborg C 740 ... d.	...	...	...	...	...	...	...	...	0925	...	1105	...	1125	...	1255	...	1405	...	1455	...	1700	1750	...	...	2000
ljunga 740 ... d.	...	...	...	0702	...	...	...	1000	1020	...	1153	1205	1217	...	1356	...	1458	...	1543	1609	1759	1842	1918	2102	2103
öping ... a.	...	...	...	0751	...	...	...	1047	1103	...	1237	1248	1255	...	1439	...	1550	...	1628	1656	1842	1924	2003	2149	2143
öping ... d.	...	0614	...	0755	...	1009	1014	1048	1109	...	1239	...	1257	1321	1440	...	1555	...	1633	1658	1844	1926	...	...	...
estad ... d.	0550	0655	0840	0845	...	1101	1103	1138	1151	1305	1323	...	1339	1413	1529	...	1641	1703	1721	1745	1932	2008	...	...	...
å 740 ... d.	0635	...	0928	...	...	...	1151	...	...	1353	...	...	...	1508	...	...	...	1750	...	...	...	...	...	...	...
sberg 740 ... a.	0651	...	0944	...	...	...	1207	...	...	1409	...	...	...	1529	...	...	...	1807	...	...	...	...	...	...	...
rebro C 755/6 ... a.	0712	...	...	...	...	...	...	...	...	...	...	...	...	1559	...	...	...	...	...	...	...	...	...	...	...

Arrive 1659. t – Arrive 1950.

737 KØBENHAVN - LUFTHAVN (KASTRUP) ✈ - MALMÖ - HELSINGBORG

Operator: *Skåne* (Ø –

Subject to alteration owing to temporary cross-border arrangements between Denmark and Sweden (please check the latest situation before travelling)

km		ØⒶ	Ⓐ2	Ø	Ⓐ2	ØⒶ	2	Ⓐ2	Ø	2	ØⒶ	2	Ø	2	ØⒶ	2	Ø	Ⓐ2	2		Ø	2	Ø	2	Ø	2
	København H **703** d.	...	...	0532	...	...	...	...	0632	...	...	...	0732	...	...	...	0832	...	...	...	0932	...	1032	...	1132	...
	Lufthavn (Kastrup) **703** d.	...	...	0546	...	...	...	...	0646	...	...	...	0746	...	...	...	0846	...	...	...	0946	...	1046	...	1146	...
0	**Malmö** C **703 735** d.	0508	0514	0608	0614	0641	0644	0702	0708	0714	0741	0744	0808	0814	0841	0844	0908	0914	0944	...	1008	1044	1108	1144	1208	1244
16	Lund **735** d.	0520	0526	0620	0626	0653	0656	0714	0720	0726	0753	0756	0820	0826	0853	0856	0920	0926	0956	...	1020	1056	1120	1156	1220	1256
48	Landskrona **735** d.	0535	0550	0635	0650	0709	0720	0730	0735	0750	0808	0820	0835	0850	0908	0920	0935	0950	1020	...	1035	1120	1135	1220	1235	1320
69	**Helsingborg 735** a.	0548	0607	0648	0707	0723	0737	0745	0748	0807	0823	0837	0848	0907	0923	0937	0948	1007	1037	...	1048	1137	1148	1237	1248	1337

	2	Ø	Ⓐ2	2	Ø	Ⓐ2	ØⒶ	2	ØⒶ	Ø	Ⓐ2	ØⒶ	2		ØⒶ	Ø	Ⓐ2	ØⒶ	2	ØⒶ	Ø	Ⓐ2	2	Ø	Ⓐ2
København H **703** d.	...	1332	...	...	1432	...	1500	...	1520	1532	...	1600	...	...	1620	1632	...	1700	...	1720	1732	...	...	1832	...
Lufthavn (Kastrup) **703** d.	...	1346	...	...	1446	...	1514	...	1534	1546	...	1614	...	...	1634	1646	...	1714	...	1734	1746	...	...	1846	...
Malmö C **703 735** d.	1344	1408	1414	1444	1508	1514	1541	1544	1603	1608	1614	1641	1645	...	1703	1708	1714	1741	1745	1803	1808	1814	1844	1908	1914
Lund **735** d.	1356	1420	1426	1456	1520	1526	1553	1556	1615	1620	1626	1653	1657	...	1715	1720	1726	1753	1757	1815	1820	1826	1856	1920	1926
Landskrona **735** d.	1420	1435	1450	1520	1535	1550	1608	1620	1631	1635	1650	1708	1720	...	1732	1735	1750	1808	1820	1832	1835	1850	1920	1935	1935
Helsingborg 735 a.	1437	1448	1507	1537	1548	1607	1623	1637	1645	1648	1707	1723	1737	...	1745	1748	1807	1823	1837	1845	1848	1907	1937	1948	2007

	Ø	2	Ø	2	Ø	2	Ø	⚒2	Ø	2H
København H **703** d.	1932	...	2032	...	2132	...	2232	...	2332	...
Lufthavn (Kastrup) **703** d.	1946	...	2046	...	2146	...	2246	...	2346	...
Malmö C **703 735** d.	2008	2044	2108	2144	2208	2244	2308	2344	0008	0044
Lund **735** d.	2020	2056	2120	2156	2220	2256	2320	2356	0020	0056
Landskrona **735** d.	2035	2120	2135	2220	2235	2320	2335	0020	0035	0120
Helsingborg 735 a.	2048	2137	2148	2237	2248	2337	2348	0037	0048	0137

	ØⒶ	Ⓐ2	ØⒶ	2	Ø		Ⓐ2	ØⒶ	2
Helsingborg 735 d.	0508	0525	0540	0552	0612	...	0625	0640	0652
Landskrona **735** d.	0520	0542	0553	0609	0623	...	0642	0653	0709
Lund **735** d.	0541	0607	0610	0634	0641	...	0707	0710	0734
Malmö C **703 735** a.	0551	0617	0620	0644	0651	...	0717	0720	0744
Lufthavn (Kastrup) **703** a.	0613	...	...	...	0713	...	...	...	...
København H **703** a.	0628	...	...	...	0728	...	...	...	...

	Ⓐ2	2	Ø	Ⓐ2	Ⓐ2	Ⓐ2	2	Ø	Ⓐ2	2		Ø	2	Ø	2	Ø	2	Ø	2		Ø	2	Ø	ØⒶ	Ⓐ2
Helsingborg 735 d.	0725	0752	0812	0815	0825	0840	0852	0912	0925	0952	...	1012	1052	1112	1152	1212	1252	1312	1352	...	1412	1452	1512	1515	1525
Landskrona **735** d.	0742	0809	0823	0826	0842	0852	0909	0923	0942	1009	...	1023	1109	1123	1209	1223	1309	1323	1409	...	1423	1509	1523	1526	1542
Lund **735** d.	0807	0834	0841	0846	0907	0910	0934	0941	1007	1034	...	1041	1134	1141	1234	1241	1334	1341	1434	...	1441	1534	1541	1546	1607
Malmö C **703 735** a.	0817	0844	0851	0856	0917	0920	0944	0951	1017	1044	...	1051	1144	1151	1244	1251	1344	1351	1444	...	1451	1544	1551	1559	1617
Lufthavn (Kastrup) **703** a.	...	...	0913	...	...	...	...	1013	...	...	...	1113	...	1213	...	1313	...	1413	...	...	1513	...	1613	1621	...
København H **703** a.	...	...	0928	...	...	...	...	1028	...	...	...	1128	...	1228	...	1328	...	1428	...	...	1528	...	1628	1636	...

	2	Ø	ØⒶ	Ⓐ2	ØⒶ	2	Ø	ØⒶ	Ⓐ2	ØⒶ	2	Ø	Ⓐ2	2	Ø	2	Ø	2	Ø	2	Ø	2	Ø	⚒2	Ⓒ2
Helsingborg 735 d.	1552	1612	1615	1625	1640	1652	1712	1715	1725	1740	1752	1812	1825	1852	1912	1952	2012	2052	2112	2152	2212	2252	2312	2352	0048
Landskrona **735** d.	1609	1623	1627	1642	1653	1709	1723	1726	1742	1753	1809	1823	1842	1909	1923	2009	2023	2109	2123	2209	2223	2309	2323	0009	0105
Lund **735** d.	1634	1641	1646	1707	1710	1734	1741	1746	1807	1810	1834	1841	1907	1934	1941	2034	2041	2134	2141	2234	2241	2334	2341	0034	0130
Malmö C **703 735** a.	1644	1651	1656	1717	1720	1744	1751	1759	1817	1820	1844	1851	1917	1944	1951	2044	2051	2144	2151	2244	2251	2344	2351	0044	0144
Lufthavn (Kastrup) **703** a.	...	1713	1721	...	1741	...	1813	...	...	...	...	1913	...	...	2013	...	2113	...	2213	...	2313	...	...	...	...
København H **703** a.	...	1728	1736	...	1756	...	1828	...	...	...	...	1928	...	...	2028	...	2128	...	2228	...	2328	...	...	...	...

H – ②③④⑤⑥† only.

Ø – Operated by *Øtåg*.

738 South-eastern SECONDARY LINES

Operator: *KLT*

km		Ⓐ									Ⓑ
0	Västervik d.	0541	0737	...	1007	1203	...	1404	1605	1807	2005
77	Åtvidaberg d.	0648	0845	...	1115	1311	...	1511	1716	1916	2113
116	Linköping a.	0727	0921	...	1149	1349	...	1543	1749	1949	2149

	Ⓐ									
Linköping d.	0542	...	0808	1011	1210	...	1410	1610	1810	...
Åtvidaberg d.	0617	...	0844	1045	1243	...	1443	1647	1846	...
Västervik a.	0726	...	0950	1150	1348	...	1550	1752	1951	...

km		Ⓐ	Ⓐ	⑥						Ⓑ	Ⓑ
0	Linköping d.	...	0534	...	0827	1026	1224	1423	1624	1820	2024
41	Rimforsa d.	...	0611	...	0906	1106	1306	1506	1706	1906	2105
123	Hultsfred d.	0610	0711	0711	1008	1209	1409	1609	1809	2009	2203
159	Berga a.	0634	0736	0736	1032	1233	1433	1633	1833	2033	2227
159	Berga d.	0639	0741	0741	1037	1238	1438	1638	1838	2038	2228
188	Oskarshamn a.	|	|	|	|	|	|	|	|	|	2249
235	Kalmar **746** a.	0738	0840	0844	1138	1338	1538	1738	1938	2138	...

	Ⓐ	Ⓐ	⑥	Ⓐ	Ⓒ					Ⓑ
Kalmar **746** d.	...	0541	...	0637	0837	1036	1236	1436	1636	1836
Oskarshamn a.	0452	|	0625	|	|	|	|	|	|	|
Berga a.	0512	0638	0645	0734	0934	1133	1333	1533	1733	1933
Berga d.	0513	0646	0646	0739	0939	1138	1338	1538	1738	1938
Hultsfred d.	0538	0712	0712	0804	1004	1204	1404	1604	1804	2004
Rimforsa d.	0642	0812	0812	0906	1105	1304	1504	1704	1904	2103
Linköping a.	0720	0849	0849	0941	1139	1338	1539	1742	1940	2138

Additional services operate on Ⓐ **Berga - Oskarshamn and v.v.** (journey 20 minutes)
From **Berga**: 1038, 1238, 1438, 1638, 1838.
From **Oskarshamn**: 1112, 1312, 1512, 1712, 2010.

739 VARBERG - UDDEVALLA

2nd class only Operator: *V* (except *Sn* tra

km		Ⓐ	Ⓐ	Ⓐ	†	Ⓐ	Ⓐ	⑥	ⒶJ	Ⓒ	Ⓐ	Ⓐ	⑥	†	ⒶJ	ⒶJ	Ⓒ	ⒶJ	ⒶJ	Ⓐ	*Sn* 467 SⒶq	*Sn* 457 S†r		Ⓒ	Ⓐ	†	Ⓐ
0	**Varberg 735** d.	...	...	*0615*	...	0713	...	0844	0949	1044	...	...	...	...	1344	1444	1444	...	1544	1644	...	...	...	...	1844	1844	1945
84	Borås **746** a.	...	...	*0726*	...	0828	...	0956	1059	1154	...	...	...	...	1454	1557	1554	...	1659	1759	...	...	...	...	1957	1957	2059
84	Borås d.	0553	0655	0753	0756	...	0909	1001	1101	1217	1217	1342	1401	1401	1501	1615	1620	1646	...	1801	...	...	...	1801	2003	2008	...
127	Herrljunga **740** a.	0631	0737	0835	0831	...	0952	1036	1139	1255	1258	1420	1436	1436	1542	1654	1657	1721	...	1836	...	...	...	1836	2038	2043	...
127	Herrljunga d.	0646	0746	0853	0932	...	1036	1135	...	1329	1329	1527	1525	1534	1631	...	1737	1730	...	...	1913	1915	...	1934	2058	2058	...
191	Vänersborg d.	0731	0830	0941	1015	...	1122	1218	...	1419	1419	1621	1614	1617	1731	...	1821	1821	...	...	1955	1955	...	2018	2142	2142	...
195	Öxnered **750** d.	0737	0838	0947	1021	...	1128	1224	...	1425	1425	1631	1620	1623	1737	...	1827	1827	...	...	|	|	...	2024	2148	2148	...
217	**Uddevalla** C a.	0751	0854	1002	1037	...	1147	1240	...	1440	1440	1647	1636	1639	1754	...	1843	1843	...	...	2020	2020	...	2040	2203	2204	...

	ⒶJ	Ⓐ	Ⓒ	*Sn* 462 SⒶq	ⒶJ	*Sn* 460 S⑥p		Ⓐ	Ⓒ	Ⓐ	Ⓐ	Ⓐ	Ⓒ	Ⓐ	Ⓒ	ⒶJ	Ⓒ	Ⓐ	ⒶJ	⑥	Ⓐ	†	ⒶJ	Ⓒ	Ⓐ	†
Uddevalla C d.	...	0517	...	0525	0632	0655	...	0659	0725	...	0823	...	0920	1123	1142	...	1321	1321	...	1517	1517	1517	1616	1725	...	...
Öxnered **750** d.	...	0533	...	|	0648	|	...	0715	0741	...	0839	...	0935	1143	1158	...	1340	1340	...	1533	1533	1533	1632	1741	...	...
Vänersborg d.	...	0540	...	0551	0654	0718	...	0721	0747	...	0846	...	0941	1149	1207	...	1346	1346	...	1539	1539	1539	1638	1747	...	...
Herrljunga **746** a.	...	0628	...	0633	0739	0758	...	0815	0836	...	0941	...	1030	1237	1253	...	1432	1439	...	1626	1627	1628	1729	1833	...	...
Herrljunga d.	0540	0648	...	...	0745	...	...	0900	0923	...	1022	...	1125	1302	1302	1423	1525	1525	1602	1724	1724	1724	1840	1858g	1925	1930
Borås **746** a.	0621	0727	...	...	0824	...	...	0939	0958	...	1100	...	1203	1339	1340	1458	1601	1601	1643	1758	1758	1758	1917	1936g	2000	2005
Borås d.	0626	0730	0801	...	0832	...	...	...	...	0958	...	1204	1204	...	...	1500	1603	1603	1702	1802	1802	1802	...	...	2002	2007
Varberg 735 a.	0743	0846	0914	...	0944	...	...	...	...	1118	...	1318	1318	...	...	1614	1718	1718	1818	1918	1918	1918	...	...	2112	2117

GÖTEBORG - UDDEVALLA - STRÖMSTAD

km		⚒	w			m			w	Ⓑ	⑥
0	**Göteborg** C ▲ d.	0640	0840	1040	...	1240	...	1440	1640	1840	1840
89	Uddevalla C ▲ a.	0749	0949	1149	...	1349	...	1549	1749	1949	1949
89	Uddevalla C d.	0804	1007	1202	...	1400	...	1600	1800	2000	2010
173	Skee d.	0916	1126	1314	...	1520	...	1718	1928	2112	2122
180	**Strömstad** a.	0923	1132	1321	...	1530	...	1725	1935	2119	2129

	⚒	⚒y	†w				m		
Strömstad d.	0641	0820	0837	1034	...	1427	1626	...	1835
Skee d.	0649	0828	0845	1042	...	1435	1634	...	1843
Uddevalla C a.	0800	0956	0956	1152	...	1550	1751	...	1953
Uddevalla C ▲ d.	0805	1005	1005	1205	...	1605	1805	...	2005
Göteborg C ▲ a.	0915	1115	1115	1315	...	1715	1915	...	2115

J – June 13 - 23.
S – (12) and ✕ Stockholm - Herrljunga - Uddevalla and v.v. Ⓡ.
g – ⑥ only.
m – June 12 - July 2.

p – June 18 - July 2.
q – June 13 - July 1.
r – June 12 - 26.
w – From June 19.
y – From June 20.

▲ – Additional services **Göteborg - Uddevalla and v.v.**:
From **Göteborg** C: 0040Ⓒ, 0525Ⓐ, 0740Ⓐ, 0940⚒, 1340⚒, 1540⚒, 1710Ⓐ, 1740, 1 2040, 2140, 2240, 2340Ⓑ.
From **Uddevalla**: 0005Ⓒ, 0533Ⓐ, 0605Ⓐ, 0635Ⓐ, 0705⚒, 0805†, 0905⚒, 110 1305⚒, 1505⚒, 1705, 1905, 2105, 2205, 2305Ⓑ.
Operator: Västtrafik.

STOCKHOLM - HALLSBERG - GÖTEBORG 740

For additional services Stockholm - Hallsberg and v.v. see Table 750 (also Table 756 via Västerås). For long distance sleeper trains see Table 767

	Sn 401		Sn 421	MTR 2021	Sn 423	IC 10101	Sn 425	MTR 2061		Sn 427	Sn 463	Sn 419	Sn 10429	Sn 20429	MTR 2029	Sn 431	IC 103	Sn 433	MTR 2033	MTR 2071	SKJB 7075	Sn 435	Sn 10435
	🅁✕		🅁✕		🅁✕		🅁✕			🅁✕	🅁✕	🅁✕	🅁✕	🅁✕		🅁✕		🅁✕				🅁✕	🅁✕
	Ⓐ J	Ⓐ J	Ⓐ	Ⓐ	Ⓐ J	M		⑥		⚒ K	♦	Ⓒ y	Z	Ⓐ J	Ⓐ	Ⓑ x	†		Ⓐ	†	⑥	A	⑤ J
Stockholm C 730/50/6 d.	0606	...	0610	0636	0729	0814	0825	0836	...	0929	0951	1014	1014	1029	1036	1129	1140	1229	1236	1236	1255	1327	1327
Södertälje Syd 750 d.	|	...	0628u	0654u	|	0849u	0844u	0854u	...	|	1010u	1032u	1032u	|	1054u	|	1200u	|	1254u	1254u	|	|	|
Katrineholm 730/50 d.	|	...	0706	|	0822	|	0921	|	...	1021	|	1110	1110	1121	|	1221	|	1321	|	|	|	1421	1421
Hallsberg 750/55/6 a.	|	...	0730	|	|	0959	|	|	...	|	1118	|	|	|	|	|	1310	|	|	|	1423	|	|
Örebro C 755/6 d.	|	0622	|	|	|	|	|	|	...	|	|	|	|	|	|	|	|	|	|	|	|	|	|
Hallsberg 756 d.	|	0644	0732	|	|	1001	|	|	...	|	1120	|	|	|	|	|	1310	|	|	|	1425	|	|
Töreboda 756 d.	|	|	|	|	|	|	|	|	...	|	|	|	|	|	|	|	|	|	|	|	|	|	|
Skövde 756 d.	|	0730	0812	0841	0923	1058	1023	1041	...	1123	1204	1211	1212	|	1243	1323	1400	1423	1441	1441	1513	|	|
Falköping 756 d.	|	0754	|	|	|	|	|	|	...	|	1226	|	|	|	|	|	|	|	|	|	|	|	|
Herrljunga 736/9/56 d.	|	|	0844	0914	|	|	|	1114	...	|	1256	1244	|	1249	1315	|	|	|	1514	1514	|	1550	1550
Uddevalla C 739 a.	|	|	|	|	|	|	|	|	...	|	1355	|	|	|	|	|	|	|	|	|	|	|	|
Alingsås 756 a.	|	|	0900s	|	|	|	|	|	...	|	...	1300s	1255s	|	|	|	|	|	|	|	1601s	|	|
Göteborg C 756 a.	0856	0900	0930	0955	1030	1225	1130	1155	...	1230	...	1330	1325	1330	1355	1430	1525	1530	1555	1555	1630	1630	1630

	Sn 10415	Sn 437	SKJB 7071	Sn 439	MTR 2039	Sn 405	Sn 411	Sn 10441	Sn 10411	Sn 467		Sn 441	Sn 457	MTR 2075	MTR 2041	SKJB 7077		Sn 473	Sn 10407	Sn 443	MTR 2043	IC 109	IC 10109	Sn 455
	🅁✕	🅁✕		🅁✕		🅁✕	🅁✕	🅁✕	🅁✕	🅁✕		🅁✕	🅁✕					🅁✕	🅁✕	🅁✕				🅁✕
	† z		F	Ⓑ w	Ⓐ	A	⑥	Ⓐ L	†	♦		Ⓐ J	♦	†	D	†		⑥ K	A	Ⓑ	D	N	P	B
kholm C 730/50/6 d.	1327	1425	1506	1525	1536	1610	1614	1614	1614	1614	...	1625	1625	1636	1636	1640	...	1706	1710	1725	1736	1736	1736	1814
rtälje Syd 750 d.	|	1444u	|	|	1554u	|	1632u	1632u	1632u	|	...	1644u	|	1654u	1655u	|	...	1725u	|	1744u	|	1758u	1758u	1832u
neholm 730/50 d.	1421	1521	|	|	|	|	1710	1710	1710	|	...	1721	|	|	|	|	...	1806	|	1821	|	|	|	1910
berg 750/5/6 a.	|	|	1634	1639	|	|	|	|	|	|	...	|	|	|	|	1808	...	|	|	|	|	1909	1909	|
ebro C 755/6 d.	|	|	|	|	|	|	|	|	|	|	...	|	|	|	|	|	...	|	|	|	|	|	|	|
berg 756 d.	|	|	1635	1639	|	|	|	|	|	|	...	|	|	|	|	1810	...	|	|	|	|	1909	1909	|
boda 756 d.	|	|	|	|	|	|	|	|	|	1814	...	|	1816	|	|	|	...	|	|	|	|	|	|	|
vde 756 d.	1525	1623	1732	1719	1747	|	1812	1812	1813	1830	...	|	1831	1542	1842	1900	...	1914	|	1922	1940	1958	2018	2012
öping 756 d.	|	|	|	|	|	|	|	|	|	1850	...	|	1852	|	|	|	...	|	|	|	|	|	|	|
junga 736/9/56 d.	|	|	|	|	1820	|	1844	|	|	1913	...	|	1915	1915	1915	|	...	|	|	|	|	2036	2052	2044
devalla C 739 a.	|	|	|	|	|	|	|	|	|	2020	...	|	2020	|	|	|	...	|	|	|	|	|	|	|
sås 756 a.	|	|	1827s	|	|	|	|	1854s	1855s	...	...	1900s	...	|	|	2001s	...	|	|	|	|	|	|	|
borg C 756 a.	1630	1730	1855	1825	1900	1905	1925	1930	1925	...	...	1930	...	1955	1955	2035	...	2030	2005	2030	2055	2130	2135	2125

	Sn 445	Sn 10445	MTR 2079	SKJB 7091	Sn 447	SKJB 7079	SKJB 7081	Sn 10449	
	🅁✕	🅁✕			🅁✕			🅁✕	
	Ⓐ J	⑥	E	G	C	E	H	†	
kholm C 730/50/6 d.	1827	1829	1836	1914	1929	1936	1940	2029	...
ertälje Syd 750 d.	|	|	1854u	|	1948u	|	|	|	...
neholm 730/50 d.	1920	1920	|	|	|	|	|	2121	...
sberg 750/5/6 a.	|	|	|	2054	|	2103	2109	|	...
ebro C 755/6 d.	|	|	|	|	|	|	|	|	...
sberg 756 d.	|	|	|	2056	|	2105	2111	|	...
boda 756 d.	|	|	|	|	|	|	|	|	...
vde 756 d.	|	2023	2041	2151	2125	2153	2200	2223	...
öping 756 d.	|	|	|	|	|	|	|	2242s	...
junga 736/9/56 d.	2049	|	2114	|	|	|	|	|	...
devalla C 739 a.	|	|	|	|	|	|	|	|	...
sås 756 a.	|	2106s	|	2237s	|	2242s	2246s	|	...
eborg C 756 a.	2130	2135	2155	2335	2230	2325	2325	2330	...

	Sn 420	Sn 400	MTR 2020	Sn 462	Sn 422	Sn 452		MTR 2002	MTR 12002
	🅁✕	🅁✕		🅁✕	🅁✕	🅁✕			
	Ⓐ w	Ⓐ J	Ⓐ	♦	Ⓐ J	Q		Ⓐ k	Ⓐ m
Göteborg C 756 d.	0505	0600	0605	...	0630	0630	...	0635	0635
Alingsås 756 d.	0530u	|	|	...	|	|	...	|	|
Uddevalla C 739 d.	|	|	|	0525	|	|	...	|	|
Herrljunga 736/9/56 d.	0546	|	0649	0639	|	|	...	|	|
Falköping 756 d.	0601	|	|	0654	|	|	...	|	|
Skövde 756 d.	0617	|	0717	0710	0729	0729	...	0743	0743
Töreboda 756 d.	0637	|	|	|	|	|	...	|	|
Hallsberg 756 a.	0705	|	|	0759	|	|	...	|	|
Örebro C 755/6 a.	|	|	|	|	|	|	...	|	|
Hallsberg 750/5/6 d.	0708	|	|	0806	|	|	...	|	|
Katrineholm 730/50 d.	0733	|	|	|	0838	0838	...	|	|
Södertälje Syd 750 a.	0812s	|	|	|	|	0913s	...	0934s	0934s
Stockholm C 730/50/6 a.	0835	0854	0924	0931	0935	0935	...	0954	0954

	Sn 460	SKJB 7074	IC 10110	IC 10100	MTR 2024	MTR 2060		Sn 416	Sn 426	SKJB 7070	Sn 10428	Sn 418		Sn 430	IC 102	SKJB 7076	MTR 2030	Sn 10432	Sn 432		MTR 2070	Sn 434	Sn 414	MTR 2034
	🅁✕							🅁✕	🅁✕		🅁✕	🅁✕		🅁✕				🅁✕	🅁✕			🅁✕	🅁✕	
	♦	⑥	X	M	U	⑥		R	Ⓐ J	F	Ⓐ L	⑥			†	†	Ⓐ	† z	Ⓐ J		†	Ⓐ J	R	W
eborg C 756 d.	...	0745	0800	0800	0805	0805	...	0830	0835	0855	0930	0935	...	1030	1035	1055	1105	1130	1130	...	1205	1230	1235	1305
gsås 756 d.	...	0814u	|	|	|	|	...	0855u	|	0925u	|	|	...	|	|	1124u	|	|	|	...	|	|	|	|
ddevalla C 739 d.	0655	|	|	|	|	|	...	|	|	|	|	|	...	|	|	|	|	|	|	...	|	|	|	|
ljunga 736/9/56 d.	0807	|	|	|	0847	0847	...	0911	|	|	1008	|	...	|	|	|	1146	|	|	...	1248	1307	1311	1347
öping 756 d.	0822	|	|	|	|	|	...	|	|	|	|	|	...	|	|	|	|	|	|	...	|	|	|	|
vde 756 d.	0837	0906	0930	0930	0916	0916	...	0937	0934	1012	|	1034	...	1128	1142	1215	1215	1230	1230	...	1316	|	1340	1416
eboda 756 d.	|	|	|	|	|	|	...	|	|	|	|	|	...	|	|	|	|	|	|	...	|	|	|	|
sberg 756 a.	0925	0958	1021	1031	|	|	...	|	|	1103	|	|	...	|	1239	1308	|	|	|	...	|	|	|	|
rebro C 755/6 a.	|	|	|	|	|	|	...	|	|	|	|	|	...	|	|	|	|	|	|	...	|	|	|	|
sberg 750/5/6 d.	0927	1001	1023	1033	|	|	...	|	|	1105	|	|	...	|	1241	1310	|	|	|	...	|	|	|	|
ineholm 730/50 d.	|	|	|	|	|	|	...	1047	1042	|	|	|	...	1236	|	|	|	|	|	...	|	1436	1447	|
ertälje Syd 750 a.	1031s	|	1137s	1147s	1104s	1104s	...	1124s	|	|	1210s	|	...	|	1350s	|	1405s	1410s	1410s	...	1504s	|	1524s	1603s
ckholm C 730/50/6 a.	1052	1134	1201	1209	1124	1124	...	1146	1135	1248	1231	1233	...	1331	1416	1450	1424	1431	1433	...	1524	1531	1546	1624

	SKJB 7078	Sn 436	Sn 10436	SKJB 7078		MTR 2074	SKJB 7090	SKJB 7080	Sn 10438	MTR 2038		Sn 10470	Sn 10440	Sn 442	Sn 412	IC 10108	Sn 444		MTR 12078	Sn 10446	Sn 466	MTR 2048	Sn 450	
		🅁✕	🅁✕						🅁✕			🅁✕	🅁✕	🅁✕	🅁✕		🅁✕			🅁✕	🅁✕		🅁✕	
	† P	Ⓐ J	† z	E		E	G	H		Ⓐ		⑥ K	Ⓑ x	Ⓑ x	S	†	C		† P		♦	D	T	
eborg C 756 d.	1325	1330	1330	1335	...	1400	1400	1400	1430	1505	...	1525	1530	1630	1630	1700	1730	...	1805	1830	...	2005	2030	...
gsås 756 d.	1353u	|	|	1404u	...	|	1428u	1428u	|	|	...	|	|	|	1655u	|	1755u	...	|	|	...	|	|	...
ddevalla C 739 d.	|	|	|	|	...	|	|	|	|	|	...	|	|	|	|	|	|	...	|	|	1808	|	|	...
rljunga 736/9/56 d.	|	|	|	|	...	1445	|	|	|	1549	...	|	|	1706	1711	|	|	...	1848	|	1916	2048	|	...
köping 756 d.	|	|	|	|	...	|	|	|	|	|	...	|	|	|	|	|	|	...	|	|	1934	|	|	...
vde 756 d.	1451	1429	1434	1451	...	1513	1512	1512	1534	1617	...	1638	1634	1732	1738	1815	|	...	1919	1933	1954	2116	2129	...
eboda 756 d.	|	|	|	|	...	|	|	|	|	|	...	|	|	|	|	|	|	...	|	|	|	|	|	...
sberg 756 a.	1543	|	|	1543	...	|	1603	1603	|	|	...	|	|	|	|	1905	1914	...	|	|	2039	|	2215	...
rebro C 755/6 a.	|	|	|	|	...	|	|	|	|	|	...	|	|	|	|	|	|	...	|	|	|	|	|	...
sberg 750/5/6 d.	1545	|	|	1545	...	|	1605	1605	|	|	...	|	|	|	|	1907	1914	...	|	|	2041	|	2215	...
ineholm 730/50 d.	|	1536	1536	|	...	|	|	|	1637	|	...	|	1737	1842	1846	|	|	...	|	2037	|	|	|	...
ertälje Syd 750 a.	|	|	|	|	...	1703s	|	|	1714s	|	...	1828s	|	|	1924s	2028s	2014s	...	|	|	2147s	2304s	|	...
ckholm C 730/50/6 a.	1716	1633	1633	1716	...	1724	1752	1752	1735	1824	...	1850	1831	1939	1946	2050	2035	...	2124	2131	2209	2324	2331	...

NOTES (LISTED BY TRAIN NUMBER)

– † June 12-26 (also Aug. 14): [12] and ✕ Stockholm - Herrljunga - Uddevalla.
– ⑥ June 18 - July 2: [12] and ✕ Uddevalla - Herrljunga - Stockholm.
– Ⓐ June 13 - July 1: [12] and ✕ Uddevalla - Herrljunga - Stockholm.
– July 3 - Aug. 13: [12] and ✕ Stockholm - Herrljunga - Uddevalla.
– July 3 - Aug. 13: [12] and ✕ Uddevalla - Herrljunga - Stockholm.
– Ⓐ June 13 - July 1: [12] and ✕ Stockholm - Herrljunga - Uddevalla.

A – ①②③④ June 13-30.
B – † June 12-26; Ⓑ July 3 - Aug. 14.
C – Ⓑ June 12 - July 3; † Aug. 7-14.
D – Ⓐ June 13-17.
E – † June 12-19.
F – ①④⑤ only.
G – June 17 only.
H – ②③ June 28 - Aug. 10.
J – Until July 1.
K – Until July 2.
L – From July 4.
M – ①⑤ June 13 - July 1.
N – June 12 only.
P – June 19 - Aug. 14.
Q – ⑥ June 18 - July 2; Ⓐ July 4 - Aug. 12.
R – Ⓒ June 12-26; daily July 2 - Aug. 14.
S – ⑥ June 18-24; daily July 2 - Aug. 13.

T – Ⓑ June 12 - July 3; † July 10 - Aug. 14.
U – Ⓐ June 20 - Aug. 12.
W – ④⑤ June 12-17.
X – ①⑤ July 4 - Aug. 12.
Z – July 3 - Aug. 13.

k – Aug. 8-12.
m – July 4 - Aug. 5.
s – Stops to set down only.
w – Not July 9 - Aug. 7.
x – Not July 2 - Aug. 13.
y – Not July 3 - Aug. 13.
z – Not June 27 - Aug. 13.

‡ – Train renumbered: 435 runs as 10435 on ⑤.

Sn – High speed train. Special supplement payable.

745 KØBENHAVN - MALMÖ - KRISTIANSTAD - KARLSKRONA

Operator:

Subject to alteration owing to temporary cross-border arrangements between Denmark and Sweden (please check the latest situation before travelling)

km																										
		Ⓐ	Ⓐ	Ⓐ																						
0	**København** H **703/30** d.	...	...	0512	0552	0612	0652	0712	0752	0812	0852	0912	0952	1012	1052	1112	1152	1212	1252	1312	1352	1412	1452	1512	1552	1612
12	Kastrup ✈ **703/30** d.	...	...	0526	0606	0626	0706	0726	0806	0826	0906	0926	1006	1026	1106	1126	1206	1226	1306	1326	1406	1426	1506	1526	1606	1626
47	**Malmö** C **703** a.	...	...	0546	0626	0646	0726	0746	0826	0846	0926	0946	1026	1046	1126	1146	1226	1246	1326	1346	1426	1446	1526	1546	1626	1646
47	**Malmö** C **730/46** d.	...	0529	0548	0629	0648	0729	0748	0829	0848	0929	0948	1029	1048	1129	1148	1229	1248	1329	1348	1429	1448	1529	1548	1629	1648
63	Lund **730/46** d.	...	0541	0600	0641	0700	0741	0800	0841	0900	0941	1000	1041	1100	1141	1200	1241	1300	1341	1400	1441	1500	1541	1600	1641	1700
81	Eslöv **746** d.	...	|	0610	|	0710	|	0810	|	0910	|	1010	|	1110	|	1210	|	1310	|	1410	|	1510	|	1610	|	1710
130	Hässleholm **730/46** a.	...	0612	0637	0712	0737	0812	0837	0912	0937	1012	1037	1112	1137	1212	1237	1312	1337	1412	1437	1512	1537	1612	1637	1712	1737
130	Hässleholm **734** d.	0512	0612	...	0712	...	0812	...	0912	...	1012	...	1112	...	1212	...	1312	...	1412	...	1512	...	1612	...	1712	...
160	**Kristianstad 734** a.	0532	0632	...	0732	...	0832	...	0932	...	1032	...	1132	...	1232	...	1332	...	1432	...	1532	...	1632	...	1732	...
160	**Kristianstad** d.	0538	0638	...	0738d	...	0838	...	0938a	...	1038	...	1138d	...	1238	...	1338	...	1438	...	1538	...	1638	...	1738	...
191	Sölvesborg d.	0558	0658	...	0758d	...	0858	...	0958a	...	1058	...	1158d	...	1258	...	1358	...	1458	...	1558	...	1658	...	1758	...
222	**Karlshamn** d.	0619	0719	...	0819d	...	0919	...	1019a	...	1119	...	1219d	...	1319	...	1419	...	1519	...	1619	...	1719	...	1819	...
260	Ronneby d.	0646	0746	...	0846d	...	0946	...	1046a	...	1146	...	1246d	...	1346	...	1446	...	1546	...	1646	...	1746	...	1846	...
290	**Karlskrona** a.	0712	0812	...	0912d	...	1012	...	1112a	...	1212	...	1312d	...	1412	...	1512	...	1612	...	1712	...	1812	...	1912	...

København H **703/30** d.	1712	1752	1812	1852	1912	1952	2012	2052	2112	2152	2252
Kastrup ✈ **703/30** d.	1726	1806	1826	1906	1926	2006	2026	2106	2126	2206	2306
Malmö C **703** a.	1746	1826	1846	1926	1946	2026	2046	2126	2146	2226	2326
Malmö C **730/46** d.	1748	1829	1848	1929	1948	2029	2048	2129	2148	2229	2329
Lund **730/46** d.	1800	1841	1900	1941	2000	2041	2100	2141	2200	2241	2341
Eslöv **746** d.	1810	|	1910	|	2010	|	2110	|	2210	|	|
Hässleholm **730/46** a.	1837	1912	1937	2012	2037	2112	2137	2212	2237	2312	0012
Hässleholm **734** d.	...	1912	...	2012	...	2112	...	2212	...	2312	0012
Kristianstad 734 a.	...	1932	...	2032	...	2132	...	2232	...	2332	0032
Kristianstad d.	...	1938b	...	2038	...	2138b	...	2238	...	...	...
Sölvesborg d.	...	1958b	...	2058	...	2158b	...	2258	...	...	...
Karlshamn d.	...	2019b	...	2119	...	2219b	...	2319	...	...	...
Ronneby d.	...	2046b	...	2146	...	2246b	...	2346	...	...	...
Karlskrona a.	...	2112b	...	2212	...	2312b	...	0012	...	...	...

Karlskrona d.	...	...	0447a	...	0547d	...	0647a	...	0747
Ronneby d.	...	...	0508a	...	0608d	...	0708a	...	0808
Karlshamn d.	...	...	0535a	...	0635d	...	0735a	...	0835
Sölvesborg d.	...	...	0557a	...	0657d	...	0757a	...	0857
Kristianstad a.	...	...	0618a	...	0718d	...	0818a	...	0918
Kristianstad 734 d.	0524	...	0624	...	0724	...	0824	...	0924
Hässleholm **734** a.	0542	...	0642	...	0742	...	0842	...	0942
Hässleholm **730/46** d.	0544	0622	0644	0722	0744	0822	0844	0922	0944
Eslöv **746** d.	|	0647	|	0747	|	0847	|	0947	|
Lund **730/46** d.	0619	0701	0719	0801	0819	0901	0919	1001	1019
Malmö C **730/46** a.	0629	0711	0729	0811	0829	0911	0929	1011	1029
Malmö C **703** d.	0633	0713	0733	0813	0833	0913	0933	1013	1033
Kastrup ✈ **703/30** a.	0653	0733	0753	0833	0853	0933	0953	1033	1053
København H **703/30** a.	0708	0748	0808	0848	0908	0948	1008	1048	1108

Karlskrona d.	0847d	...	0947	...	1047d	...	1147	...	1247	...	1347	...	1447	...	1547	...	1647b	...	1747	...	1847b	...	1947	...	2047b
Ronneby d.	0908d	...	1008	...	1108d	...	1208	...	1308	...	1408	...	1508	...	1608	...	1708b	...	1808	...	1908b	...	2008	...	2108b
Karlshamn d.	0935d	...	1035	...	1135d	...	1235	...	1335	...	1435	...	1535	...	1635	...	1735b	...	1835	...	1935b	...	2035	...	2135b
Sölvesborg d.	0957d	...	1057	...	1157d	...	1257	...	1357	...	1457	...	1557	...	1657	...	1757b	...	1857	...	1957b	...	2057	...	2157b
Kristianstad a.	1018d	...	1118	...	1218d	...	1318	...	1418	...	1518	...	1618	...	1718	...	1818b	...	1918	...	2018b	...	2118	...	2218b
Kristianstad 734 d.	1024	...	1124	...	1224	...	1324	...	1424	...	1524	...	1624	...	1724	...	1824	...	1924	...	2024	...	2124	...	2224
Hässleholm **734** a.	1042	...	1142	...	1242	...	1342	...	1442	...	1542	...	1642	...	1742	...	1842	...	1942	...	2042	...	2142	...	2242
Hässleholm **730/46** d.	1044	1122	1144	1222	1244	1322	1344	1422	1444	1522	1544	1622	1644	1722	1744	1822	1844	1922	1944	2022	2044	2122	2144	2222	2244
Eslöv **746** d.	|	1147	|	1247	|	1347	|	1447	|	1547	|	1647	|	1747	|	1847	|	1947	|	2047	|	2147	|	2247	|
Lund **730/46** d.	1119	1201	1219	1301	1319	1401	1419	1501	1519	1601	1619	1701	1719	1801	1819	1901	1919	2001	2019	2101	2119	2201	2219	2301	2319
Malmö C **730/46** a.	1129	1211	1229	1311	1329	1411	1429	1511	1529	1611	1629	1711	1729	1811	1829	1911	1929	2011	2029	2111	2129	2211	2229	2311	2329
Malmö C **703** d.	1133	1213	1233	1313	1333	1413	1433	1513	1533	1613	1633	1713	1733	1813	1833	1913	1933	2013	2033	2113	2133	2213	2233	2313	2333
Kastrup ✈ **703/30** a.	1153	1233	1253	1333	1353	1433	1453	1533	1553	1633	1653	1733	1753	1833	1853	1933	1953	2033	2053	2133	2153	2233	2253	2333	2353
København H **703/30** a.	1208	1248	1308	1348	1408	1448	1508	1548	1608	1648	1708	1748	1808	1848	1908	1948	2008	2048	2108	2148	2208	2248	2308	2348	0008

a – Ⓐ only. b – Ⓑ only. d – ⚒ only.

746 KØBENHAVN, MALMÖ and GÖTEBORG - KALMAR

Subject to alteration owing to temporary cross-border arrangements between Denmark and Sweden (please check the latest situation before travelling)

km																									
		Øtåg Ⓐ	Øtåg Ⓐ	Øtåg Ⓐ	Ⓐ	Øtåg	Øtåg	Øtåg	Øtåg	⚒	Øtåg		Øtåg Ⓐ	†	Øtåg	Øtåg	⑥	Øtåg	Øtåg Ⓑ	Ⓑ	Øtåg	Øtåg Ⓐ	Ⓑ	Øtåg	Øtåg Ⓑ
0	**København** H **703** d.	...	0512	0612	...	0712	0812	0912	1012	...	1112	...	1212	...	1312	1412	...	1512	1612	...	1712	1812	...	1912	2012
12	Kastrup ✈ **703** d.	...	0526	0626	...	0726	0826	0926	1026	...	1126	...	1226	...	1326	1426	...	1526	1626	...	1726	1826	...	1926	2026
47	**Malmö** C **703** a.	...	0546	0646	...	0746	0846	0946	1046	...	1146	...	1246	...	1346	1446	...	1546	1646	...	1746	1846	...	1946	2046
47	**Malmö** C **730/45** d.	...	0548	0648	...	0748	0848	0948	1048	...	1148	...	1248	...	1348	1448	...	1548	1648	...	1748	1848	...	1948	2048
63	Lund **730/45** d.	...	0600	0700	...	0800	0900	1000	1100	...	1200	...	1300	...	1400	1500	...	1600	1700	...	1800	1900	...	2000	2100
80	Eslöv **745** d.	...	0610	0710	...	0810	0910	1010	1110	...	1210	...	1310	...	1410	1510	...	1610	1710	...	1810	1910	...	2010	2110
130	Hässleholm **730/45** d.	...	0640	0740	...	0840	0940	1040	1140	...	1240	...	1340	...	1440	1540	...	1640	1740	...	1840	1940	...	2040	2140
181	Älmhult d.	...	0703	0803	...	0903	1003	1103	1203a	...	1303	...	1403	...	1503	1603	...	1703	1803	...	1904	2003	...	2103	2203
	Göteborg C ▲ d.	...	|	|	0605	|	|	|	|	1005	|	...	|	1155	|	|	1405	|	|	1605	|	|	1805	|	|
	Borås ▲ d.	...	|	|	0659	|	|	|	|	1059	|	...	|	1257	|	|	1459	|	|	1705	|	|	1859	|	|
	Limmared d.	...	|	|	0727	|	|	|	|	1128	|	...	|	1325	|	|	1527	|	|	1733	|	|	1927	|	|
	Värnamo d.	...	|	|	0808	|	|	|	|	1210	|	...	|	1406	|	|	1609	|	|	1818	|	|	2013	|	|
228	Alvesta **730** a.	...	0725	0825	0835	0925	1025	1125	1225a	1235	1325	...	1425	1434	1525	1624	1636	1725	1826	1845	1925	2025	2039	2125	2227
228	Alvesta ▲ d.	0632	0726	0826	0838	0937	1037	1137	1226a	1236	1337	...	1437	1438	1537	1632t	1638	1737	1827v	1850	1937	2026	2042	2137	2232
245	**Växjö** ▲ d.	0648	0748	0838	0852	0948	1048	1148	1237a	1248	1348	...	1448	1451	1548	1643t	1651	1748	1838v	1902	1948	2037	2056	2148	2243
302	Emmaboda a.	0725	0825	...	0927	1025	1125	1225	...	1323	1425	...	1525	1527	1628	1727a	1726	1825	...	1936	2028	...	2130	2225	...
302	Emmaboda ▶ d.	0730	0830	...	0929	1030	1130	1230	...	1330	1430	...	1530	1530	1630	1730a	1730	1830	...	1937	2030	...	2132	2230	...
330	Nybro d.	0743	0843	...	0943	1043	1143	1243	...	1344	1443	...	1548	1544	1645	1743a	1744	1843	...	1951	2043	...	2146	2243	...
359	**Kalmar** a.	0759	0859	...	1001	1059	1159	1259	...	1405	1459	...	1604	1601	1701	1759a	1801	1859	...	2009	2059	...	2203	2259	...

km																									
		Øtåg Ⓐ	Ⓐ	Øtåg Ⓐ	Øtåg Ⓐ	Øtåg	⑥	Øtåg Ⓐ	Øtåg ⑥	Øtåg	Ⓑ	Øtåg Ⓐ	Øtåg	Ⓑ	Øtåg Ⓐ	Øtåg	Øtåg Ⓑ	Øtåg	⚒	Øtåg Ⓐ	Øtåg	†	Øtåg Ⓐ	Øtåg	Øtåg Ⓑ
	Kalmar d.	...	0500	...	0600	0700	0757	0800	...	0900	0955	...	1100	1151	...	1300	1400a	1500	1557	...	1655	1756	1800	1906	1951a
	Nybro d.	...	0517	...	0614	0714	0814	0814	...	0914	1012	...	1114	1211	...	1314	1414a	1514	1618	...	1714	1813	1814	1920	2006a
	Emmaboda ▶ a.	...	0531	...	0629	0729	0829	0829	...	0929	1027	...	1129	1225	...	1329	1429a	1529	1632	...	1729	1827	1829	1935	2021a
	Emmaboda d.	...	0533	...	0630	0730	0831	0830	...	0930	1030	...	1130	1227	...	1330	1430a	1530	1633	...	1732	1828	1830	1936	2030a
	Växjö ▲ d.	0518	0607	0618	0710	0810	0905	0909	0915	1010	1105	1119	1210	1302	1318	1410	1510	1610	1706	1718	1810	1902	1910	2010	2118
	Alvesta ▲ a.	0529	0620	0629	0721	0821	0918	0920	0928	1021	1118	1130	1221	1314	1329	1421	1521	1621	1719	1730	1821	1915	1921	2021	2129
0	Alvesta **730** d.	0531	0622	0631	0731	0831	0922	0931	0931	1031	1120	1131	1231	1316	1331	1431	1531	1631	1722	1731	1831	1922	1931	2031	2131
49	Värnamo d.	|	0647	|	|	|	0947	|	|	|	1145	|	|	1340	|	|	|	|	1749	|	|	1947	|	|	|
110	Limmared d.	|	0727	|	|	|	1028	|	|	|	1228	|	|	1420	|	|	|	|	1828	|	|	2030	|	|	|
149	Borås ▲ a.	|	0757	|	|	|	1058	|	|	|	1256	|	|	1449	|	|	|	|	1857	|	|	2058	|	|	|
222	**Göteborg** C ▲ a.	|	0855	|	|	|	1155	|	|	|	1350	|	|	1555	|	|	|	|	1955	|	|	2155	|	|	|
	Älmhult d.	0550	...	0650	0750	0850	...	0950	0950	1050	...	1150	1250	...	1350	1450	1550	1650	...	1750	1850	...	1950	2050	2150
	Hässleholm **730/45** d.	0622	...	0722	0822	0922	...	1022	1022	1122	...	1222	1322	...	1422	1522	1622	1722	...	1822	1922	...	2022	2122	2222
	Eslöv **745** a.	0647	...	0747	0847	0947	...	1047	1047	1147	...	1247	1347	...	1447	1547	1647	1747	...	1847	1947	...	2047	2147	2247
	Lund **730/45** d.	0701	...	0801	0901	1001	...	1101	1059	1201	...	1301	1401	...	1501	1601	1701	1801	...	1901	2001	...	2101	2201	2301
	Malmö C **730/45** a.	0711	...	0811	0911	1011	...	1111	1111	1211	...	1311	1411	...	1511	1611	1711	1811	...	1911	2011	...	2111	2211	2311
	Malmö C **703** d.	0713	...	0813	0913	1013	...	1113	1113	1213	...	1313	1413	...	1513	1613	1713	1813	...	1913	2013	...	2113	2213	2313
	Kastrup ✈ **703** a.	0734	...	0834	0934	1034	...	1134	1134	1234	...	1334	1434	...	1534	1634	1734	1834	...	1934	2034	...	2134	2234	2334
	København H **703** a.	0748	...	0848	0948	1048	...	1148	1148	1248	...	1348	1448	...	1548	1648	1748	1848	...	1948	2048	...	2148	2248	2348

▶ – CONNECTING SERVICES **Emmaboda - Karlskrona and v.v.** (2nd class only):

Operator:

km																									
		Ⓐ	⚒		⚒	⚒			⚒							Ⓑ			Ⓑ			Ⓑ			Ⓑ
0	Emmaboda d.	0634	0734	...	0834	0934	...	1034	1146	...	1234	...	1334	1434	...	1534	1636	...	1734	1834	...	1953	2034	...	2135
57	Karlskrona a.	0717	0817	...	0917	1017	...	1117	1229	...	1317	...	1417	1517	...	1617	1719	...	1817	1917	...	2036	2117	...	2218

	Ⓐ	⚒		⚒		⚒			⚒						Ⓑ			Ⓑ			Ⓑ		
Karlskrona a.	0542	0642	...	0742	...	0842	0942	...	1042	1135	...	1242	...	1342	1442	...	1542	1640	...	1742	1842	...	1942	...
Emmaboda d.	0624	0724	...	0824	...	0924	1024	...	1124	1217	...	1324	...	1424	1524	...	1624	1726	...	1824	1924	...	2024	...

a – Ⓐ only. t – 5 minutes later on Ⓐ. v – 10 minutes later on Ⓐ. ▲ – Additional trains run Göteborg - Borås and v.v., and Alvesta - Växjö and v.v.

STOCKHOLM - STOCKHOLM ARLANDA ✈ 747

...erator: A-Train AB (*AEX*) Arlanda Express

...ey time: 20 minutes. All services stop at Arlanda Södra (17 minutes from Stockholm, 2 minutes from Arlanda Norra). Södra serves terminals 2, 3 and 4; Norra serves terminal 5.

...**Stockholm** Central: 0435, 0505, 0520, 0535, 0550, 0605, 0620, 0635, 0650 and at the same minutes past each hour until 2205, then 2220, 2235, 2305, 2335, 0005, 0035.

From **Arlanda** Norra: 0505, 0535, 0550, 0605, 0620, 0635, 0650 and at the same minutes past each hour until 2205, then 2220, 2235, 2250, 2305, 2335, 0005, 0035, 0105.

Minor alterations to schedules are possible at peak times

STOCKHOLM - HALLSBERG - KARLSTAD - OSLO 750

	VTAB 2 Ⓐ	*NSB* 2 ⚒	*VTAB* 2 Ⓐ	*Sn* **619** R✕ ⒶJ	*ST* 2 Ⓒ	*VTAB* 2 Ⓐ	*Sn* **623** R✕ ⒶJ	*Sn* **625** R✕ K	*VTAB* 2 ⑥	*Sn* **631** R✕ A	*Sn* **633** R✕ ⑥L	*VTAB* 2 Ⓐ	*ST* †	*VTAB* 2 Ⓐ	*NSB* 2 Ⓑ	*IC* **57** ⒷM	*Tågab* Y	*VTAB* 2 Ⓐ	*Sn* **637** R✕ ⒷJ	*Sn* **635** R✕ ⑥L	*VTAB* 2 Ⓐ	*VTAB* 2 ⑥	*Sn* **639** R✕ ⒷJ	*Sn* **641** R✕ N	*VTAB* 2 ⒷJ
Stockholm C **730/40** ▲ d.	...	...	...	0555	...	...	0744	0814	...	1106	1106	...	...	...	...	1306	1336	...	1406	1414	...	...	1559	1606	...
Södertälje Syd **730/40** ▲ d.	...	...	...	|	...	...	0802u	0832u	...	1124u	|	...	...	...	...	1326u	|	...	1424u	1432u	...	...	|	1625u	...
Katrineholm **730/40** ▲ d.	...	...	...	|	...	...	0844	0910	...	1202	1204	...	...	...	...	1411	1439	...	1508	1510	...	...	|	1702	...
Hallsberg 740 ▲ d.	...	...	0610	0708	0712g	...	0914	0936	...	1228	1233	1321	...	...	...	1440	1516	...	1535	1536	...	...	|	1728	...
Degerfors d.	...	...	0642	|	0742g	...	0942	1003	...	1255	1301	1348	...	...	...	1515	1546	...	1605	1603	...	...	|	1754	...
Kristinehamn d.	...	...	0702	|	0802g	...	0958	1017	...	1308	1316	1402	...	1509	...	1531	1602	1611	1619	1617	1632	...	|	1807	...
Karlstad 751 a.	...	...	0726	0804	0829g	...	1017	1039	...	1328	1340	1429	...	1534	...	1554	1623	1635	1640	1638	1656	...	1807	1827	...
Karlstad d.	0541	...	0732	0806	0843	0848	▬	1041	1247	1330	...	1437	1529	1547	...	...	...	1635	...	1642	1709	1726	1809	1830	1842
Kil d.	0557	...	0749	|	0904	0905	...	|	1300	|	...	1450	1544	1602	...	...	...	1648	...	|	1724	1744	|	|	1854
Arvika d.	0631	...	0834	0850	0938	0937	*NSB*	1118	1339	1406	...	1526	1615	1635	...	...	...	1722	...	1720	1759	1820	1844	1904	1930
Charlottenberg 🏛 a.	0654	...	0859	|	1002	1000	2	|	1405	|	...	1553	1638	1658	...	...	...	1748	...	|	1826	1845	|	|	1953
Kongsvinger a.	0730	0736	...	0931	1036	1027	1036	1201	...	1448	...	...	1706	1727	1732	...	...	...	...	1801	...	...	1926	2001	...
Oslo Sentral a.	...	0856	...	1028	1210	...	1156	1310	...	1609	...	...	1844	...	1856	...	...	...	...	1908	...	...	2028	2104	...

	Sn **643** R✕ ⒷJ	*VTAB* 2 †	2 ⑤J	*Sn* **647** R✕ ⒷN	*Sn* **645** R✕ ⑥	*VTAB* 2 ⑥	*IC* **55** ⒷJ	*VTAB* 2 Ⓑ	*Tågab* †H	
Stockholm C **730/40** ▲ d.	1714	...	1740	1806	1814	...	1906	...	2143	...
Södertälje Syd **730/40** ▲ d.	1733u	...	1805	1825u	1833u	...	1926u	...	|	...
Katrineholm **730/40** ▲ d.	1811u	...	1854	1902	1910	...	2010	...	2242	...
Hallsberg 740 ▲ d.	1837	...	1927	1928	1936	...	2041	...	2311	...
Degerfors d.	1902	...	2003	1955	2003	...	2113	...	2354s	...
Kristinehamn d.	1916	...	2019	2014	2022	...	2133	...	0010	...
Karlstad 751 a.	1934	...	2044	2035	2042	...	2157	...	0035	...
Karlstad d.	...	2020	...	...	...	2135	...	2213j	...	...
Kil d.	...	2039	...	...	...	2150	...	2232	...	...
Arvika d.	...	2110	...	...	...	2223	...	2302	...	...
Charlottenberg 🏛 a.	...	2136	...	...	...	2246	...	2326	...	...
Kongsvinger a.	...	...	...	...	...	...	...	...	...	...
Oslo Sentral a.	...	...	...	...	...	...	...	...	...	...

	Sn **620** R✕ ⒶJ	*Sn* **622** R✕ ⒶP	*VTAB* 2 Ⓐ	*Sn* **626** R✕ ⒸK	*Sn* **624** R✕ ⒶJ	*VTAB* 2 Ⓐ	*Tågab* Y	*VTAB* 2 Ⓒ	*NSB* 2 Ⓐ	*VTAB* 2 Ⓐ	*VTAB* 2 ⑥
Oslo Sentral d.	...	...	...	...	0602	...	...	...	0604	...	...
Kongsvinger d.	...	...	...	...	0704	...	...	...	0722	0740	...
Charlottenberg 🏛 d.	...	...	0604	...	|	0707	...	0750	...	0809	0829
Arvika d.	...	...	0630	...	0743	0752	...	0815	...	0832	0855
Kil d.	...	...	0706	...	|	0826	...	0902	...	0906	0933
Karlstad 751 a.	...	...	0718	...	0822	0840	...	0915	...	0919	0946
Karlstad d.	0628	0726	0730	0805	0825	0842	0913	...	...	...	...
Kristinehamn d.	0646	0745	0758	0824	0842	0905	0940	...	...	...	...
Degerfors d.	0701	0758	...	0838	0857	...	0958	...	...	...	...
Hallsberg 740 ▲ d.	|	0834	...	0910	0926	...	1028	...	...	...	...
Katrineholm **730/40** ▲ a.	|	0859	...	0934	0950	...	1057	...	...	...	...
Södertälje Syd **730/40** ▲ a.	|	0938s	...	1012s	|	...	|	...	...	...	...
Stockholm C **730/40** ▲ a.	0839	1001	...	1035	1046	...	1201	...	...	...	...

	Sn **632** R✕ ⒶJ	*Sn* **630** R✕ †H	*Sn* **630** R✕ K	*NSB* 2	*VTAB* 2 Ⓐ	*Sn* **634** R✕ †H	*Sn* **636** R✕ ⒶJ	*Sn* **640** R✕ ⑥L	*Sn* **638** R✕ N	*IC* **58** ⑤†J	*IC* **54** B	*ST* 2 Ⓒ	*VTAB* 2 Ⓐ	*Sn* **642** R✕ ⑥L	*Sn* **644** R✕ ⒷJ	*VTAB* 2 Ⓐ	*Tågab* †H		*Sn* **648** R✕ N	*Sn* **646** R✕ ⒷJ	*NSB* 2	*VTAB* 2 Ⓐ	*VTAB* 2 ⑥	*VTAB* 2 Ⓐ	*VTAB* 2 Ⓐ	*ST* 2 †
Oslo Sentral d.	...	...	0856	1004	...	1056	1132	...	1146	...	...	1346	...	1456	...	...	...	...	1656	1656	1704	...	...	...	...	1936
Kongsvinger d.	...	...	1003	1122	1132	1203	1233	...	1258	...	...	1506	...	1603	...	...	...	...	1803	1803	1822	1833	...	...	...	2056
Charlottenberg 🏛 d.	...	...	|	...	1203	|	|	...	|	...	...	1533	1531	|	...	1608	...	...	|	|	...	1904	1930	2029	2137	2139
Arvika d.	...	...	1044	...	1229	1246	1313	...	1343	...	...	1554	1554	1644	...	1634	...	...	1846	1846	...	1930	1955	2051	2159	2201
Kil d.	...	...	|	...	1305	|	|	...	|	...	...	1630	1629	|	...	1719	...	...	|	|	...	2016	2035	2128	2234	2236
Karlstad 751 a.	...	...	1124	...	1318	1323	1351	...	1424	...	...	1642	1646	1726	...	1736	...	...	1927	1927	...	2028	2048	2139	2247	2249
Karlstad d.	1118	1127	1127	...	...	1331	1354	1415	1427	1505	1604	1645e	1655	1730	1733	1738	1809	...	1930	1932	...	...	...	...	...	...
Kristinehamn d.	1137	1147	1147	...	...	1349	1412	1434	1445	1526	1632	1710e	1718	1750	1757	1806	1831	...	1951	|	...	...	...	...	...	...
Degerfors d.	1152	1200	1200	...	...	1404	1425	1449	1500	1542	1647	1725e	1737	1803	1813	...	1846	...	2004	|	...	...	...	...	...	...
Hallsberg 740 ▲ d.	1227	1230	1230	...	...	1433	1452	1522	1528	1627	1721	1802e	1812	1832	1846	...	1927	...	2032	2030	...	...	...	...	...	...
Katrineholm **730/40** ▲ a.	1253	1254	1254	...	...	1457	|	1549	1554	1656	1751	...	...	1856	1912	...	1955	...	2056	2054	...	...	...	...	...	...
Södertälje Syd **730/40** ▲ a.	1334s	1331s	1331s	...	...	1536s	|	1631s	1632s	1739s	1838s	...	...	1932s	1954s	...	|	...	2132s	|	...	...	...	...	...	...
Stockholm C **730/40** ▲ a.	1354	1354	1354	...	...	1601	1609	1652	1654	1801	1905	...	...	1954	2016	...	2101	...	2154	2150	...	...	...	...	...	...

▲ – **Regional services STOCKHOLM - HALLSBERG and v.v.** (2nd class only):

	Ⓐ	Ⓐ	ⒶJ	†		⑥	Ⓐ	†	Ⓐ	Ⓑ	Ⓐ	Ⓐ
Stockholm C d.	0640	0836	1040	1040	1251	1329	1351	1436	1529	1740	1955	2219
Flemingsberg d.	0651	0847	1051	1051	1302	1340	1402	1447	1540	1752	2006	2229
Södertälje Syd d.	0703	0859	1102	1102	1314	1352	1414	1459	1557	1805	2017	2241
Flen d.	0739	0934	1137	1137	1349	1428	1448	1534	1634	1840	2050	2316
Katrineholm d.	0752	0949	1150	1150	1402	1441	1502	1549	1648	1853	2104	2328
Hallsberg a.	0823	1023	1221	1221	1435	1513	1552	1620	1730r	1925t	2134	2359

	Ⓐ	⑥	Ⓐ	†	Ⓐ	⑥	ⒶJ	†	⚒	Ⓐ	†	Ⓐ
Hallsberg d.	0527	0839	0940	1042	1126	1238	1338	1442	1539	1643	1747	1920
Katrineholm d.	0602	0913	1012	1113	1158	1311	1411	1513	1617	1714	1820	1952
Flen d.	0615	0925	1024	1125	1210	1323	1424	1525	1629	1725	1831	2004
Södertälje Syd d.	0651	1001	1108	1200	1250	1400	1500	1600	1705	1820	1907	2038
Flemingsberg d.	0702	1011	1119	1211	1302	1411	1511	1611	1717	1832	1918	2049
Stockholm C a.	0716	1024	1133	1224	1316	1424	1524	1624	1731	1846	1931	2105

Ⓑ June 13 - July 1; daily July 3 - Aug. 14.
①②③④ June 13 - 30.
June 12 - 26.
Until July 1.
From July 2.
June 18 - July 2.

M – July 3 - Aug. 12.
N – July 3 - Aug. 14.
P – July 4 - Aug. 5.
Y – ①③④⑤ until July 1.
e – † only.
g – ⑥ only.

j – Depart 2219 on †.
r – Arrive 1719 from July 4.
s – Stops to set down only.
t – Arrive 1942 from July 3.
u – Stops to pick up only.

Sn – High speed train. Special supplement payable.
▲ – For regional services Stockholm - Hallsberg and v.v. – see panel above.

KARLSTAD - GÖTEBORG 751

	Ⓐ		*Tågab* Ⓑ	⚒			Ⓑ	*Tågab* ⒷJ		*Tågab* K	H
Karlstad 750 d.	0613	0813	0945	1011	1214	1414	1612	1713	1817	1914	2209
Kil d.	0628	0829	1000	1026	1228	1428	1629	1728	1831	1932	2225
Säffle d.	0659	0859	1030	1059	1300	1458	1700	1757	1902	2001	2257
Åmål d.	0709	0909	1041	1109	1310	1509	1709	1808	1912	2012	2307
Mellerud d.	0741	0934	1106	1135	1335	1536	1735	|	1937	2043t	2333
Öxnered a.	0802	0954	1128	1155	1359	1556	1759	1854	1957	2100	2353
Trollhättan a.	0808	1000	1135	1205	1405	1602	1805	1901	2005	2106	2359
Göteborg C a.	0845	1035	1210	1240	1440	1645	1845	1945	2040	2140	0030

	Ⓐ	*Tågab* ⒶJ	Ⓐ	*Tågab* ⑥L		⚒		*Tågab* †	*Tågab* ⒶX		Ⓑ		*Tågab* †A
Göteborg C d.	0510	0615	0715	0840	0915	1115	1315	1345	1410	1515	1715	1915	2045
Trollhättan d.	0544	0651	0752	0914	0952	1152	1352	1418	1445	1552	1752	1952	2120
Öxnered d.	0550	0657	0800	0921	1000	1200	1400	1425	1451	1600	1800	2000	2127
Mellerud d.	0610	0716	0821	0944	1021	1220	1421	1447r	1510	1620	1819	2019	2148
Åmål d.	0633	0739	0845	1010	1044	1244	1444	1510	1536	1644	1847	2043	2210
Säffle d.	0644	0749	0859	1020	1059	1300	1500	1520	1546	1659	1900	2056	2220
Kil a.	0720	0821	0931	1052	1131	1331	1531	1550	1617	1729	1933	2131	2252
Karlstad 750 a.	0736	0836	0946	1107	1146	1346	1547	1605	1632	1749	1951	2146	2313

June 12 - 26 (also Aug. 14).
①②③④† only.
J – Until July 1.
K – From July 3.
L – Until July 2.
X – Not July 4 - Aug. 9.
r – Until July 3.
t – ⑥ only.

VÄSTERÅS - LUDVIKA 752

...perator: *ST* 2nd class only

	Ⓐ	Ⓐ	Ⓒ	Ⓐ	Ⓐr	Ⓐ	Ⓐr	Ⓒ		Ⓐr	Ⓐ	Ⓒ	Ⓐr	Ⓐ	Ⓒ	Ⓐ	Ⓒ	Ⓐ	Ⓐr	Ⓒ	Ⓐ	Ⓐr	Ⓐ	Ⓐ
Stockholm C **756** d.	...	...	...	...	...	...	...	1007z	...	...	...	1207z	...	...	1407z	...	1607z	...	...	1807z	...	...	...	...
Västerås 756 d.	0615	0715	0715	0815	0915	1015	1115	1115	...	1215	1315	1315	1415	1515	1515	1615	1715	1715	1815	1915	1915	2015	2127	2227
Fagersta C d.	0712	0810	0812	0912	1010	1125	1210	1212	...	1310	1412	1412	1510	1612	1612	1710	1812	1812	1910	2012	2012	2110	2230	2324
Ludvika a.	0754	...	0854	0954	...	1206	...	1255	...	...	1454	1454	...	1654	1654	...	1854	1854	...	2054	2054	...	2312	...

	Ⓐ	Ⓐ	Ⓐr	Ⓒ	Ⓐ	Ⓒ	Ⓐr	Ⓐ	Ⓒ	Ⓐr	Ⓐr		Ⓐ	Ⓒ	Ⓐ	Ⓐ	Ⓒ	Ⓐr			Ⓐr	Ⓐ	Ⓐ	Ⓐ	
Ludvika d.	...	0607	...	0707	0807	0907	...	1007	1107	...	...	...	1307	1307	...	1507	1507	...	...	1707	...	1907	...	2106	...
Fagersta C d.	0532	0650	0750	0750	0850	0950	0950	1050	1150	1150	1250	...	1350	1350	1450	1550	1550	1649	...	1750	1849	1950	2050	2150	...
Västerås 756 a.	0625	0745	0845	0845	0945	1045	1045	1145	1245	1245	1345	...	1445	1445	1545	1645	1645	1745	...	1845	1945	2045	2146	2243	...
Stockholm C **756** a.	...	...	...	0952z	...	1152z	...	...	1352z	...	...	...	...	1552z	...	...	1752z	...	...	...	...	...	...	...	...

Until July 1.
z – Aug. 13, 14.

753 KRISTINEHAMN - MORA - ÖSTERSUND - GÄLLIVARE

INLANDSBA

Temporarily relocated on page 358

754 NORRKÖPING - VÄSTERÅS - SALA

2nd class

km		Ⓐ	Ⓐ	⚒	⚒					B	
	Linköping 730 d.	...	...	0605a	0811g	1008	1208	1407	1607	1807	2008
0	**Norrköping 730** d.	...	...	0632a	0838	1036	1236	1436	1636	1836	2036
48	Katrineholm **730** d.	...	...	0658a	0904	1102	1302	1502	1702	1901	2102
71	Flen **730** d.	...	...	0711a	0917	1115	1315	1515	1715	1915	2115
112	Eskilstuna d.	0546	0652	0752	0952	1152	1352	1552	1752	1952	2152
160	**Västerås** a.	0619	0725	0825	1025	1225	1425	1625	1825	2025	2225
160	**Västerås** d.	0621	0727	0827	1027	1227	1427	1627	1827	2027b	...
199	Sala **758** a.	0648	0754	0854	1054	1254	1454	1654	1854	2054b	...

	Ⓐ		Ⓐ A						Ⓑ
Sala **758** d.	...	0703a	0803	0906d	1106	1306	1506	1706	1906
Västerås a.	...	0732a	0832	0932d	1132	1332	1532	1732	1932
Västerås d.	0529	0735	0835	0935	1135	1335	1535	1735	1935
Eskilstuna d.	0603	0809	0909	1009	1209	1409	1609	1809	2009
Flen **730** d.	0638	0843	0944	1044	1243	1443	1643	1843	2046
Katrineholm **730** d.	0652	0858	0958	1058	1258	1458	1658	1858	2104
Norrköping 730 a.	0717	0922	1022	1122	1322	1522	1722	1922	2128
Linköping 730 a.	0749	0950	1050	1151	1351	1550	1751	1951	2155

A – June 13 - July 1, Aug. 8 - 12.
B – Until July 10.
a – Ⓐ only.
b – Ⓑ only.
d – ⚒ only.
g – ⑥ only.

755 Valid until July 10 MJÖLBY - HALLSBERG - ÖREBRO - GÄVLE

Operator:

km		Ⓐ	Ⓐ	Ⓐ	⚒	Ⓐ y	Ⓐ	Ⓐ	Ⓐ	Ⓐ	Ⓐ y	⚒	Ⓐ y		Ⓐ y	⚒		Ⓐ y		Ⓐ y	Ⓑ		Ⓐ y	Ⓑ	⑤†	①-④
0	**Mjölby 730** d.	...	...	...	...	...	...	0600	...	...	...	0806	...	1006	...	...	1206	...	1406	...	...	1606	...	1806	...	...
27	Motala d.	...	...	...	...	...	...	0615	...	...	...	0821	...	1021	...	...	1221	...	1421	...	...	1621	...	1821	...	...
96	**Hallsberg** a.	...	...	...	...	...	...	0658	...	...	...	0906	...	1105	...	...	1306	...	1506	...	...	1706	...	1906	...	...
	Hallsberg 736/56 d.	...	...	...	0532a	0638	0659	0711	0734	0805	...	0919	...	1119	...	1250a	1319	...	1516	1638	1649a	1716	1837	1925	1940	1940
121	**Örebro C 736/56** a.	...	...	...	0550a	0656	0719	0729	0752	0823	...	0937	...	1137	...	1308a	1337	...	1534	1656	1708a	1734	1855	1943	1958	1958
	Örebro C d.	...	...	...	0554a	0700	0721	...	0800	0855	0900	1000	1100	1200	1300	1310	1359	1500	1559	1658	1710	1800	1900	1956	2001	2001
146	Frövi d.	...	...	...	0609a	0714	0735	...	0814	0909	0914	1015	1114	1214	1314	1324	1413	1514	1613	1712	1724	1814	1914	2010	2015	2015
204	Kopparberg d.	...	...	...	0659a	0758	|	...	0901	|	1001	1058	1159	1301	1359	|	1501	1601	1701	1800	|	1858	1958	2057	|	|
232	Grängesberg d.	...	...	...	0719a	0819	|	...	0922	|	1020	1122	1218	1320	1419	|	1521	1621	1721	1820	|	1919	2018	2120	|	|
247	Ludvika d.	...	...	0630	0729a	0834	|	...	0933	|	1031	1136	1231	1331	1429	|	1531	1631	1732	1831	|	1929	2031	2131	|	|
295	**Borlänge** a.	...	...	0657	0758a	0901	|	...	1000	|	1110	1203	1259	1358	1457	|	1559	1659	1759	1859	|	1957	2058	2203	|	|
	Borlänge 758 d.	0605	...	0708	0807	0909	|	...	1005	|	...	1207	...	1405	1502	|	1605	1702	1803	1912	|	2011	...	2219	|	|
317	Falun **758** d.	0630	...	0727	0828	0926	|	...	1023	|	...	1226	...	1423	1526	|	1624	1719	1823	1944	|	2027	...	2235	|	|
	Fagersta d.	|	0600	|	|	...	0816	...	|	0957	...	|	...	|	|	1406	|	|	|	...	1807	|	...	...	2113	2128
	Avesta Krylbo d.	|	0627	|	|	...	0840	...	|	1021	...	|	...	|	|	1429	|	|	|	...	1831	|	...	...	2140	2156
371	Storvik d.	0710	0715	0810	0912	...	0929	...	1105	1057	...	1305	...	1503	1604	1519	1704	1758	1904	...	1912	2107	...	...	2216	2232
385	Sandviken d.	0721	0735	0821	0923	...	0940	...	1117	1108	...	1317	...	1513	1615	1531	1714	1809	1915	...	1927	2119	...	...	2226	2242
408	**Gävle 760** a.	0741	0750	0847	0938	...	0955	...	1132	1123	...	1332	...	1534	1634	1546	1735	1824	1930	...	1942	2138	...	...	2242	2257

km		Ⓐ	Ⓐ	Ⓐ	⚒	Ⓐ y		Ⓐ	Ⓐ y	⚒		†	Ⓐ y		Ⓐ y	Ⓐ		Ⓐ y		Ⓐ y	Ⓑ		Ⓐ y	Ⓑ	†	Ⓐ
0	**Gävle 760** d.	...	0430	...	...	0518	0619d	0720	...	0826	0821d	1026	...	1020	...	1226	1221	1426	1420	...	1628	1621	1714	1820	1825	1856
23	Sandviken d.	...	0445	...	...	0534	0634d	0736	...	0842	0837d	1042	...	1036	...	1243	1237	1442	1436	...	1644	1637	1730	1835	1842	1913
37	Storvik d.	...	0456	...	...	0544	0646d	0747	...	0854	0847d	1052	...	1046	...	1254	1247	1453	1446	...	1655	1647	1741	1846	1852	1925
95	Avesta Krylbo d.	...	0533	...	...	|	|	|	...	0931	|	1131	...	|	...	1333	|	1533	|	...	1734	|	|	|	1933	2008
130	Fagersta d.	...	0559	...	...	|	|	|	...	0955	|	1156	...	|	...	1403	|	1558	|	...	1801	|	|	|	1958	2033
	Falun **758** d.	...	|	0455e	...	0629	0725d	0827	...	|	0926d	|	1029	1130	...	|	1329	|	1528	...	|	1728	1825	1931	...	...
	Borlänge 758 a.	...	|	0511e	...	0646	0742d	0843	...	|	0943d	|	1050	1147	...	|	1346	|	1545	...	|	1745	1843	1948	...	...
	Borlänge d.	...	|	0514	0554	0700	0800d	...	0903	|	1000	|	1114	1203	1259	|	1400	|	1600	1700	|	1800b	1900	2003	...	...
	Ludvika d.	...	|	0544	0628	0730	0830d	...	0931	|	1030	|	1150	1232	1329	|	1428	|	1630	1730	|	1828b	1928	2030	...	...
	Grängesberg d.	...	|	0554	0639	0740	0840d	...	0942	|	1040	|	1200	1242	1340	|	1439	|	1642	1741	|	1840b	1940	2041	...	...
	Kopparberg d.	...	|	0613	0659	0759	0901d	...	1001	|	1059	|	1223	1301	1359	|	1503	|	1701	1800	|	1859b	1959	2100	...	...
202	Frövi d.	...	0643	0705	0745	0843	0944d	...	1044	1039	1146	1240	1308	1350	1445	1448	1545	1641	1744	1843	1849	1942b	2043	2148	...	...
228	**Örebro** C a.	...	0657	0719	0759	0858	0958d	...	1058	1053	1207	1254	1322	1405	1459	1503	1559	1656	1758	1858	1903	1959b	2059	2202	...	...
	Örebro C **736/56** d.	0617	0700	0724	0815	0900	1014	...	...	1056a	1217	...	...	1414	...	1504	1610	1705	1808	...	1904	2012b	...	2204	...	...
252	**Hallsberg 736/56** a.	0635	0720	0744	0833	0918	1032	...	...	1114a	1235	...	...	1432	...	1522	1628	1724	1826	...	1922	2030b	...	2222	...	...
	Hallsberg d.	0647	...	...	0846	...	1043	...	...	...	1247	...	...	1447	...	...	1647	...	1847b	...	...	2043b	...	...	...	...
	Motala d.	0726	...	...	0925	...	1126	...	...	...	1326	...	...	1526	...	...	1726	...	1926b	...	...	2127b	...	...	...	...
	Mjölby 730 a.	0744	...	...	0943	...	1144	...	...	...	1344	...	...	1544	...	...	1744	...	1944b	...	...	2144b	...	...	...	...

a – Ⓐ only.
b – Ⓑ only.
d – ⚒ only.
e – ① only.
y – Until July 1.

756 Valid until Aug. 7 STOCKHOLM - VÄSTERÅS - ÖREBRO - HALLSBERG - GÖTEBORG

km		Ⓐ J	Ⓐ	Ⓐ	⚒	Ⓐ J		Ⓐ J		Ⓐ J			Ⓐ	A	† H	B	Ⓐ		Ⓐ J	† K	Ⓐ J		Ⓐ J
0	**Stockholm** C ⊡ d.	...	0520y	0629	0650y	0750y	0850y	0935y	1050y	1150y	1250y	...	1350y	1450y	1450y	1550y	1629	1650y	1729	1751	1750y	1850y	2040
72	Enköping ⊡ d.	...	0636	|	0806	0906	1006	1054	1206	1306	1406	...	1506	1606	1606	1709	|	1807	|	|	1906	2009	|
107	**Västerås 752** ⊡ d.	0517	0653	|	0825	0925	1025	1110	1225	1325	1425	...	1525	1625	1625	1730	|	1825	|	|	1927	2030	|
141	Köping d.	0533	0709	|	0841	0941	1041	1130	1241	1341	1441	...	1541	1641	1641	1748	|	1844	|	|	1945	2048	|
159	Arboga **757** d.	0545	0725	0809	0853	0953	1053	1142	1253	1353	1453	...	1553	1653	1653	1804	1812	1856	1908	1928	1957	2102	2213
205	**Örebro** C **736/40/55** ▲ d.	0622	0751	0835	0924	1018	1124	1206	1324	1418	1524	...	1617	1724	1724	1829	1841	1924	1931	1951	2021	2133	2236
230	**Hallsberg 736/40/55** ▲ d.	0644	0811	0855	0946	1038	1146	1226	1346	1438	1546	...	1637	1747	1751	1850	1901	1947	...	2011	2041	2153	2256
260	Laxå **736** d.	|	...	...	1000	...	1201	...	1401	...	1601	...	...	1800	1804	...	...	2000	...	...	...	...	...
305	Töreboda **740** d.	|	...	...	1019	...	1220	...	1420	...	1621	...	...	1820	1823	...	...	2019	...	...	...	...	...
344	**Skövde 740** d.	0730	...	...	1034	...	1235	...	1435	...	1637	...	...	1835	1845	...	...	2034	...	...	...	...	...
374	Falköping **740** a.	0752	...	...	1055	...	1256	...	1455	...	1658	...	...	1855	1905	...	...	2055	...	...	...	...	...
408	Herrljunga **736/9/40** a.	|	...	...	1116	...	1317	...	1517	...	1715	...	...	1917	1922	...	...	2116	...	...	...	...	...
443	Alingsås **740** a.	|	...	...	1135	...	1336	...	1536	...	1734	...	...	1937	1942	...	...	2135	...	...	...	...	...
488	**Göteborg** C **740** a.	0900	...	...	1205	...	1405	...	1605	...	1805	...	...	2005z	2010	...	...	2205	...	...	...	...	...

	Ⓐ	Ⓐ	Ⓐ J	Ⓐ	⑥	Ⓐ	Ⓐ	C	†	⑥ L	Ⓐ J		Ⓐ J		Ⓐ J		Ⓐ	Ⓐ				⚒	†
Göteborg C **740** d.	...	...	...	...	...	...	0545	0555	...	...	...	0755	...	0955	...	1155	...	...	...	1355	1555	1755	1800
Alingsås **740** d.	...	...	...	...	...	...	0613	0623	...	...	...	0823	...	1023	...	1223	...	...	...	1423	1623	1823	1827
Herrljunga **736/9/40** d.	...	...	...	...	...	...	0641	0642	...	...	...	0849	...	1042	...	1242	...	...	...	1447	1642	1842	1850
Falköping **740** d.	...	...	...	...	...	...	0706	0659	...	...	...	0906	...	1059	...	1259	...	...	...	1504	1659	1859	1907
Skövde 740 d.	...	...	...	...	...	...	0725	0725	...	...	...	0926	...	1121	...	1320	...	...	...	1525	1722	1922	1927
Töreboda **740** d.	...	...	...	...	...	...	0741	0741	...	...	...	0942	...	1138	...	1337	...	...	...	1541	1739	1939	1952
Laxå **736** d.	...	...	...	...	...	...	0800	0800	...	...	...	1001	...	1158	...	1359	...	...	...	1601	1802	2000	2011
Hallsberg 736/40/55 ▲ d.	0514	0537	0544	0609	0714	0725	0823	0823	0823	0912	0923	1020	1134	1223	1323	1423	1523	1545	...	1623	1820	2023	2027
Örebro C **736/40/55** ▲ d.	0536	0559	0607	0632	0737	0748	0846	0846	0846	0937	0946	1046	1156	1246	1346	1446	1546	1608	...	1646	1848	2046	2049
Arboga **757** d.	0559	0622	0630	0658	0800	0809	0907	0907	0907	1000	1007	1107	1218	1307	1407	1507	1607	1629	...	1707	1909	2107	2109
Köping d.	0609	|	0640	0709	0810	0819	0917	0917	0917	1010	1017	1117	1228	1317	1417	1517	1617	|	...	1717	1919	2117	2118
Västerås 752 ⊡ d.	0632	|	0703	0733	0833	0840	0940	0940	0940	1033	1040	1140	1253	1340	1440	1540	1640	|	...	1740	1940	2140	2140
Enköping ⊡ d.	0649	|	0720	0750	0850	0854	0954	0954	0954	1050	1054	1154	1307	1354	1454	1554	1654	|	...	1754	1954	2154	2154
Stockholm C ⊡ a.	0810y	0805	0840y	0910y	1010y	1010y	1110y	1110y	1110y	1210y	1210y	1310y	1425y	1510y	1610y	1710y	1810y	1805	...	1910y	2110y	2310y	2310y

A – ⚒ June 13 - July 2; daily July 3 - Aug. 7.
B – Daily June 12 - 26; ⚒ June 27 - Aug. 6.
C – ⑥ June 18 - 24; ⚒ July 2 - Aug. 6.
G – ①②③④† June 12 - 30.
H – June 12 - 26.
J – Until July 1.
K – July 3 - Aug. 7.
L – June 18 - July 2.
y – Connection by 🚌.
z – Arrive 2015 on ①②③④ June 13 - 30.
▲ – Svenska Tågkompaniet AB also operate services Hallsberg - Örebro and v
⊡ – Additional services operate **Stockholm - Västerås** and v.v.

STOCKHOLM - BORLÄNGE - FALUN and MORA 758

	Sn	Sn*	Sn*	IC	IC	Sn	Sn		Sn*	IC	IC		Sn*	IC		Sn*	Sn*	Sn		Sn*		IC	IC
	12	14	32	10016	42	16	28		18	36	38		20	46		22	24	10		48		26	26
	Ⓐy	⚒S	⚒M	†K	P	⚒M	Ⓐy		ⒸN	ⒷL	⑥R		⚒	†		P	ⒷL	Ⓐy				Ⓑy	†T
Stockholm C 760 ♠ d.	0615	0745	0745	0945	0945	0945	1108	...	1145	1145	1145	...	1345	1345	...	1545	1545	1646	...	1745	...	1945	1945
Arlanda C ✈ 760 ◧ ♠ d.	0636	0806	0806	1006	1006	1006	1133	...	1206	1206	1206	...	1406	1406	...	1606	1606	1705	...	1806	...	2006	2006
Uppsala 760 ◧ ♠ d.	0654	0824	0824	1024	1024	1024	1155	...	1224	1224	1224	...	1424	1424	...	1624	1624	1724	...	1824	...	2024	2024
Sala 754 d.	0739	0900	0900	1100	1100	1100	1231	...	1300	1300	1300	...	1500	1500	...	1700	1700	1805	...	1900	...	2100	2100
Avesta Krylbo d.	0759	0921	0921	1121	1121	1121	1258	...	1321	1321	1321	...	1521	1521	...	1721	1721	1823	...	1921	...	2121	2121
Borlänge 755 ▲ ● a.	0841	1010	1010	1202	1213	1210	1338	...	1410	1410	1410	...	1610	1610	...	1806	1810	1900	...	2002	...	2203	2203
Falun **755** ● a.	0900	1029	|	1224	|	1237	...	...	1429	|	|	...	1634	|	...	1825	1829	1920	...	|	...	2230	2230
Leksand ▲ d.	...	...	1051	...	1251	...	...	...	...	1440	1451	...	...	1650	...	...	...	...	...	2043	...	...	...
Rättvik ▲ d.	...	...	1109	...	1309	...	...	...	...	1458	1512	...	...	1709	...	...	...	...	...	2101	...	...	...
Mora 753 ▲ a.	...	...	1134	...	1334	...	...	...	...	1527	1537	...	...	1734	...	...	...	...	...	2126	...	...	...

	IC	Sn	IC	IC	IC	Sn*		Sn*	Sn	Sn*	IC	Sn*	Sn		Sn*	IC	Sn*	IC	IC		IC	IC	
	13	11	41	15	43	17		19	45	31	33	21	21		23	47	25	37	39		49	27	
	Ⓐy	Ⓐy	Ⓐ	⑥	⑥	Ⓑ		⚒	†A	⚒M	†K	ⒸN	Ⓐy		Q	P	P	⑥R	ⒷL		†	Ⓐy	
753 ▲ d.	...	...	0627	...	0831	...	...	...	1029	1222	1238	...	...	...	...	1432	...	1632	1642	...	1823	...	...
k ▲ d.	...	...	0651	...	0855	...	...	...	1053	1246	1302	...	...	...	...	1456	...	1656	1706	...	1847	...	...
nd ▲ d.	...	...	0709	...	0914	...	...	...	1112	1307	1321	...	...	...	...	1515	...	1715	1728	...	1907	...	...
un 755 ● d.	0531	0613	|	0739	|	0938	...	1138	|	|	|	1338	...	...	1538	|	1734	|	|	...	|	1927	...
nge 755 ▲ ● d.	0550	0633	0752	0758	0957	0957	...	1157	1157	1357	1357	1357	1357	...	1557	1557	1753	1757	1757	...	1948	1948	...
a Krylbo d.	0633	0708	0841	0841	1041	1041	...	1241	1241	1441	1441	1441	1441	...	1641	1641	1841	1841	1841	...	2041	2041	...
754 d.	0653	|	0900	0900	1100	1100	...	1300	1300	1500	1500	1500	1500	...	1700	1700	1900	1900	1900	...	2100	2100	...
ala 760 ◧ ♠ a.	0728	0802	0934	0934	1134	1134	...	1334	1334	1534	1534	1534	1534	...	1734	1734	1934	1934	1934	...	2134	2134	...
da C ✈ 760 ◧ ♠ a.	0752	0822	0952	0952	1152	1152	...	1352	1352	1552	1552	1552	1552	...	1752	1752	1952	1952	1952	...	2152	2152	...
kholm C 760 ♠ a.	0817	0844	1016	1016	1216	1216	...	1416	1416	1616	1616	1616	1616	...	1816	1816	2016	2016	2016	...	2216	2217	...

rator: *ST* (except *Tågab*)

▲ – Local services BORLÄNGE - MORA and v.v.

	Ⓐ	⚒	Y	⚒M	X	ⒷL	⚒		Ⓑ	
Borlänge d.	0640	0851	1020	1218	1421	1433	1619	1819	2213	...
Leksand d.	0712	0926	1052	1250	1455	1513	1651	1851	2245	...
Rättvik d.	0727	0942	1110	1305	1514	1530	1706	1907	2300	...
Mora 753 ♣ a.	0750	1005	1133	1328	1537	1553	1736	1930	2323	...
Morastrand ♣ a.	0754	1009	1137	1332	1541	1557	1740	1934	2327	...

	Ⓐ	⑥	Ⓑ	⚒	†K	†K	X	X	⚒	Ⓑ
Morastrand ♣ d.	0505	0628	0830	1022	1027	1212	1221	1620	1820	2032
Mora 753 ♣ d.	0510	0632	0834	1026	1031	1216	1225	1624	1824	2036
Rättvik d.	0533	0655	0857	1049	1054	1239	1248	1647	1848	2100
Leksand d.	0548	0710	0913	1106	1109	1257	1306	1705	1906	2116
Borlänge 755 a.	0620	0742	0947	1138	1141	1334	1338	1737	1938	2148

June 12 - 26 (also Aug. 14).
July 3 - Aug. 7.
July 3 - Aug. 12.
July 4 - Aug. 13.
June 12 - July 2.
June 12 - July 2 (also Aug. 14).
July 3 - Aug. 13.

R – July 9 - Aug. 13.
S – June 13 - July 2.
T – July 3 - Aug. 14.
X – Not July 3 - Aug. 13.
Y – Not July 4 - Aug. 13.
y – Until July 1.

* – Runs as *IC* train on some days / dates.
Sn – High speed train. Special supplement payable.
♠ – Frequent local services operate Stockholm - Uppsala and v.v.
● – Additional services operate Borlänge - Falun and v.v.
♣ – Local journeys are not permitted Mora - Morastrand and v.v.
▲ – For Borlänge - Mora and v.v. local services – see panel above.
◧ – Stops to pick up / set down only from / to Stockholm.

STOCKHOLM - SUNDSVALL - UMEÅ 760

For additional services Stockholm - Gävle and v.v. see Table 761. For sleeper services see Table 767.

	NT	Sn	Sn	Sn	NT	Sn	NT	NT	Sn	Sn	NT	Sn	Sn	NT	IC	NT	Sn	Sn	Sn	NT	Sn	Sn	Sn	Sn
		10560	10560	10564		10568			10572	10572		10576	10576		10060		10580	592	10582		10586	20584	10584	588
	2	R✕	R✕	R✕	2	R✕	2	2	R✕	R✕	2	R✕	R✕	2		2	R✕	R✕	R✕	2	R✕	R✕	R✕	R✕
	Ⓐ	ⒶB	Ⓐy			k		Ⓐy	ⒶA	k	J	§F	⑤y	Ⓒ	⑤	Ⓐ	G	Ⓐy	ⒶB		†C	†H	⚒	†C
Stockholm C d.	...	0622	0622	0822	...	1022	...	...	1222	1222	...	1422	1422	...	1445	...	1622	1722	1722	...	1822	1822	1822	2022
Arlanda C ✈ ‡ d.	...	0641	0641	0841	...	1041	...	...	1241	1241	...	1441	1441	...	1506	...	1641	1741	1741	...	1841	1841	1841	2041
Uppsala ‡ d.	...	0700	0700	0900	...	1100	...	...	1300	1300	...	1500	1500	...	1525	...	1700	1800	1800	...	1900	1900	1900	2100
Gävle C ▲ d.	...	0748	0748	0948	...	1148	...	...	1348	1348	...	1548	1548	...	1628	...	1748	1848	1848	...	1950	1950	1950	2148
Söderhamn ▲ d.	...	0834	0834	1033	...	1233	...	...	1433	1433	...	1633	1633	...	1716	...	1833	1927	1931	...	2029	2033	2033	2231
Hudiksvall ▲ d.	...	0901	0903	1102	...	1302	...	...	1500	1502	...	1702	1702	...	1801	...	1901	1954	2001	...	2055	2101	2104	2259
Sundsvall ▲ a.	...	...	1010	1210z	...	1410	...	...	...	1610	...	1810	1810	...	1902	...	2002	2050	2104	...	2152	2159	2202	2358
Sundsvall d.	0755	...	1015	...	1219	...	1407	1510	...	1615	1640	...	1815	1814	...	1912	2005	...	...	2100	...	...	...	...
Härnösand d.	0849	...	1113	...	1315	...	1458	1604	...	1714	1738	...	1911	1914	...	2013	2101	...	...	2152	...	...	...	...
Kramfors d.	0915	...	1137	...	1339	...	1522	1627	...	1740	1806	...	1937	1941	...	2037	2124	...	...	...	...	...	...	...
Örnsköldsvik C d.	0955	...	1213	...	1416	...	1614	1716	...	1814	1846	...	2010	2018	...	2116	2157	...	...	...	...	...	...	...
Umeå Östra ♠ a.	1051	...	1302	...	1511	...	1718	1814	...	1858	1944	...	2056	2115	...	2212	2243	...	...	...	...	...	...	...
Umeå C ♠ a.	1055	...	1306	...	1515	...	1722	1818	...	1902	1948	...	2100	2120	...	2215	2248	...	...	...	...	...	...	...

	Sn	Sn	NT	Sn	Sn	NT	NT	Sn	Sn	Sn	NT	Sn	NT	Sn	NT	Sn	IC	Sn	NT	Sn	Sn	NT	NT	NT	NT
	10561	10563		10567	10567			10571	30571	20571		10575		10579		10583	10061	10585		10587	20587				
	R✕	R✕	2	R✕	R✕	2	2	R✕	R✕	R✕	2	R✕	2	R✕	2	R✕		R✕	2	R✕	R✕	2	2	2	2
	ⒶZ	⚒A	Ⓐ	Ⓐy	Ⓒk	Ⓐ		Ⓐ	⑥k	†C	Ⓐy			§k		D	†	ⒶA	†	Ⓐ	Ⓒ	Ⓐy		E	†
å C ♠ d.	...	...	...	0517	...	0532	0645	...	...	...	0800	0907z	1051	...	1245	...	...	1354	1324	1507y	1507	1540	1625	2010	2135
å Östra ♠ d.	...	...	...	0520	...	0537	0649	...	...	...	0804	0910z	1055	...	1249	...	...	1357	1328	1510y	1510	1544	1629	2014	2140
sköldsvik C d.	...	...	0543	0603	...	0637	0749	...	...	...	0902	0953z	1152	...	1347	...	...	1447	1430	1553y	1553	1645	1730	2111	2238
nfors d.	...	...	0623	0639	...	0730	0829	...	...	...	0947	1034z	1234	...	1432	...	...	1529	1507	1635y	1635	1733	1816	...	...
ösand d.	...	...	0647	0702	...	0754	0853	...	...	...	1015	1056z	1258	...	1456	...	...	1551	1536	1657y	1657	1756	1839	...	...
dsvall a.	...	...	0735	0755	...	0848	0947	...	...	...	1117	1145z	1349	...	1548	...	...	1640	1640	1749y	1749	1854	1935	...	...
			Sn 593 R✕ Ⓐy			Sn 10567 R✕ ⒶB																			
dsvall ▲ d.	0458	0602	0614	0759	0759	...	...	0952y	0952	0955	...	1152z	...	1352	...	1552	1620	1653	...	1752	1752	...	...	...	...
ksvall ▲ d.	0559	0703	0708	0858	0858	0858	...	1057	1057	1057	...	1257	...	1457	...	1657	1728	1758	...	1857	1857	...	...	...	...
erhamn ▲ d.	0627	0731	0734	0929	0929	0929	...	1128	1128	1128	...	1329	...	1529	...	1728	1759	1828	...	1929	1929	...	...	...	...
e C ▲ d.	0710	0814	0814	1014	1014	1014	...	1214	1214	1214	...	1414	...	1614	...	1814	1900	1914	...	2014	2014	...	...	...	...
sala ‡ a.	0759	0859	0859	1059	1059	1059	...	1259	1259	1259	...	1459	...	1659	...	1859	1959	1959	...	2059	2059	...	...	...	...
nda C ✈ ‡ a.	0817	0917	0917	1117	1117	1117	...	1317	1317	1317	...	1517	...	1717	...	1917	2035	2017	...	2117	2117	...	...	...	...
ckholm C a.	0838	0938	0938	1138	1138	1138	...	1338	1338	1338	...	1538	...	1738	...	1938	2059	2038	...	2138	2138	...	...	...	...

erator: *XT*

▲ – Local services GÄVLE - SUNDSVALL and v.v. (2nd class only):

	Ⓐ	Ⓒ	Ⓐ	Ⓐ	Ⓒ	Ⓐ	⑥	Ⓐ	†	Ⓐ	†	Ⓐ
le C d.	0520	0836	0915	1205	1235	1405	1510	1610	1702	1702	1909	2119
erhamn d.	0601	0918	0957	1247	1317	1448	1557	1653	1756	1756	1955	2201
ksvall d.	0636	0948	1025	1318	1348	1518	1625	1725	1826	1826	2022	2230
dsvall a.	0738	1047z	1127y	1420y	1448z	1620y	1723k	1827	1923	1925	2120	2323

	Ⓐ	Ⓐ	⑥	Ⓐ	Ⓒ	Ⓐ	⑥	Ⓐ	†	⚒	Ⓐ	†
Sundsvall d.	0533	0831y	0850k	1218y	1258z	1435y	1610k	1646	1657	1925	2017	2026
Hudiksvall d.	0634	0934	0948	1319	1405	1536	1718	1744	1758	2028	2128	2131
Söderhamn d.	0702	1005	1016	1347	1433	1604	1746	1812	1830	2056	2200	2201
Gävle C a.	0744	1047	1104	1439	1514	1651	1829	1856	1921	2141	2247	2246

July 4 - Aug. 14.
Aug. 8 - 12.
June 12 - 26.
Ⓑ June 12 - July 3; † July 10 - Aug. 14.
①②③④† only.
①②③④⑥† June 12 - July 2; Ⓑ July 3 - Aug. 14.

G – Ⓑ June 12 - July 1; daily June 3 - Aug. 14.
H – July 3 - Aug. 14.
J – Ⓑ June 12 - July 8; Ⓐ July 11 - Aug. 12.
Z – Not July 2 - Aug. 7.

k – Until July 2.
y – Until July 1.
z – Until July 3.
§ – Train number variations: 10576 runs as 10574 on ⑥; 10579 runs as 20579 on Ⓒ.

Sn – High speed train. Special supplement payable.
‡ – From Stockholm stops to pick up only; to Stockholm stops to set down only.
♠ – Local journeys are not permitted Umeå C - Umeå Östra and v.v.
▲ – For Gävle - Sundsvall and v.v. local services – see panel above.

761 STOCKHOLM and SUNDSVALL - ÖSTERSUND - TRONDHEIM

For additional services Stockholm - Gävle and v.v. see Table 760. For sleeper services see Table 767

km		NT	NSB	NT	NT	NT		IC	IC		NT	NT		NT	NSB	NT		Sn	IC	NT		Sn		NT
								80	80									594	84			578		
		2	2	2	2	2					2	2		2	2	2				2		🅁✕		2
				Ⓐy	Ⓐ			j	⚒h		Ⓑ	⑥				Ⓐ		⑥D	⑤†y	Ⓑ		Ⓑ		⑥
0	**Stockholm** C .... ▲ d.	...	...	...	...	...	...	0813	0813	...	...	...	...	...	...	...	...	1422	1414	...	...	1652	...	...
39	Arlanda C ✈.......... ▲ d.	...	...	...	...	...	...	0835u	0835u	...	...	...	...	...	...	...	...	1441u	1435u	...	...	1711u	...	...
69	Uppsala.............. ▲ d.	...	...	...	...	...	...	0905u	0905u	...	...	...	...	...	...	...	...	1500u	1505u	...	...	1730u	...	...
182	**Gävle** C.............. ▲ d.	...	...	...	...	...	...	1003	1003	...	...	...	...	...	...	...	...	1548	1602	...	...	1826	...	...
281	Bollnäs ....d.	...	...	...	...	...	...	1059	1059	...	...	...	...	...	...	...	...	1645	1657	...	...	1917	...	...
344	Ljusdal.....................d.	...	...	...	...	...	...	1139	1139	...	...	...	...	...	...	...	...	1719	1745	...	...	1953	...	...
	Sundsvall...............d.	0510	...	0600	0745	1013	...	|	|	...	1216	1216	...	1408	...	1630	...	|	|	1818	...	|	...	2018
450	Ånge ....d.	0620	...	0726	0904	1133	...	1239	1239	...	1335	1336	...	1520	...	1753	...	1818	1841	1936	...	2051	...	2134
480	Bräcke.......................d.	0642	...	0745	0922	1151	...	1300	1300	...	1354	1353	...	1536	...	1809	...	1836	1900	1953	...	2109	...	...
551	**Östersund** C..............a.	0731	...	0846	1007	1241	...	1348	1348	...	1448	1439	...	1624	...	1856	...	1918	1944	2050	...	2155	...	...
551	**Östersund** C **753**.......d.	0733	...	...	1011y	1243	...	1351	...	...	...	1441	...	1626	...	...	...	...	...	2052	...	...	...	...
656	Åre ....d.	0841	...	...	1123y	1358	...	1510	...	...	...	1551	...	1745	...	...	...	...	...	2209	...	...	...	...
665	Duved.........................d.	0849	...	...	1130y	1405	...	...	...	...	...	1558	...	1754	...,	...	...	...	...	2216	...	...	...	...
713	Storlien 🏛 ....a.	0921	0940	...	...	...	...	...	...	...	...	...	...	1826	1840	...	...	...	...	...	...	...	...	...
819	**Trondheim 787**..........a.	...	1109	...	...	...	...	...	...	...	...	...	...	...	2012	...	...	...	...	...	...	...	...	...

km		NT	Sn	NT	NT		Sn	Sn		NT	NT	NT		NSB	NT		NT		NT	NT	IC	NT	NSB	NT
			565				569	20571													85			
		2	🅁✕	2	2		🅁✕	🅁✕		2	2	2		2	2		2		2	2		2	2	2
		Ⓐ	Ⓐy	†	⚒		B	†C		⚒h	⑥D	†					Ⓐ		Ⓑ			Ⓐy		
	Trondheim 787..........d.	...	...	...	...	...	...	...	...	...	...	...	...	0750	...	...	...	...	...	...	...	...	1650	...
	Storlien 🏛 ....d.	...	...	...	...	...	...	...	...	...	...	...	...	0925	0945	...	...	...	...	...	...	...	1825	1844
	Duved.........................d.	...	...	...	0600	...	...	...	...	...	...	0807	...	...	1018	...	1205y	...	...	1500	...	...	...	1919
	Åre ....d.	...	...	...	0609	...	...	...	...	...	...	0816	...	...	1027	...	1214y	...	...	1509	1554j	...	...	1928
	Östersund C..............a.	...	...	...	0716	...	...	...	...	...	...	0931	...	...	1139	...	1324y	...	...	1622	1713j	...	...	2038
	Östersund C **753**.......d.	0509	0546	...	0718	...	0745	0745	...	0925	0925	0933	...	...	1141	...	1326	...	1517	1624	1716	1924	...	2040
	Bräcke.......................d.	0600	0626	...	0811	...	0828	0824	...	1016	1016	1019	...	...	1225	...	1417	...	1607	1713	1759	2013	...	2130
0	Ånge ....d.	0618	0643	0829	0829	...	0845	0842	...	1034	1034	1037	...	...	1242	...	1435	...	1624	1731	1819	2031	...	2148
94	**Sundsvall**...............a.	0733	|	0945	0947	...	|	0952	...	1148	1148	1148	...	...	1349	...	1552	...	1740	1849	|	2146	...	2302
	Ljusdal.....................d.	...	0742	...	...	...	0942	|	...	...	...	...	...	...	...	...	...	...	...	...	1920	...	...	...
	Bollnäs ....a.	...	0817	...	...	...	1016	|	...	...	...	...	...	...	...	...	...	...	...	...	2006	...	...	...
	Gävle C.............. ▲ d.	...	0914	...	...	...	1114	1214	...	...	...	...	...	...	...	...	...	...	...	...	2108	...	...	...
	Uppsala.............. ▲ a.	...	0959s	...	...	...	1159s	1259s	...	...	...	...	...	...	...	...	...	...	...	...	2203s	...	...	...
	Arlanda C ✈.......... ▲ a.	...	1017s	...	...	...	1217s	1317s	...	...	...	...	...	...	...	...	...	...	...	...	2222s	...	...	...
	Stockholm C .... ▲ a.	...	1038	...	...	...	1238	1338	...	...	...	...	...	...	...	...	...	...	...	...	2246	...	...	...

▲ – Regional services STOCKHOLM - GÄVLE and v.v.

km		Ⓐy	Ⓐy	⑥	†A	Ⓒ	Ⓐy			Ⓑy	Ⓑ	
0	**Stockholm** C....... d.	0715	0800	0915	0915	1115	1115	1315	1515	1615	1715	1915
39	Arlanda C ✈......... d.	0734	0823	0934	0934	1134	1136	1334	1534	1635	1734	1934
69	Uppsala .... d.	0752	0846	0952	0952	1152	1200	1352	1552	1652	1752	1952
182	**Gävle** C............... a.	0846	0941	1042	1042	1246	1300	1442	1646	1742	1859	2042

	Ⓐy	⑥	Ⓐ	⑥			Ⓐy	Ⓒ		Ⓑy
Gävle C............ d.	0610	0714	0714	0918	1118	1318	1457	1510	1713	1918
Uppsala .... d.	0659	0806	0806	1006	1206	1406	1607	1601	1801	2006
Arlanda C ✈..... a.	0717	0824	0826	1024	1224	1424	1623	1617	1817	2024
Stockholm C.... a.	0738	0845	0846	1045	1245	1445	1645	1638	1838	2045

A – June 12 - 26 (also Aug. 14).
B – ⑥ June 12 - 24; daily July 2 - Aug. 14.
C – June 12 - 26.
D – July 9 - Aug. 13.
E – Ⓑ June 12 - July 3; † July 10 - Aug. 14.
h – Until July 2.
j – From July 3.
s – Stops to set down only.
u – Stops to pick up only.
y – Until July 1.
Sn – High speed train. Special supplement payable.

763 UMEÅ - LULEÅ

2nd class only. Operator

km		Ⓐ	Ⓐ	Ⓐ	Ⓐ	Ⓐ	⑥	Ⓐ	Ⓐ	Ⓐ	Ⓐ	†	Ⓐ
0	**Umeå** Östra **760** .. ♣ d.	0520	0635	0748	0900	1229	1250	1438	1616	1710	1728	1730	1830
2	**Umeå** C **760** .... ♣ d.	0523	0638	0750	0902	1231	1254	1440	1618	1715	1730	1734	1832
33	Vännäs .... ♣ d.	0546	0700	0812	0924	1254	1327	1502	1640	|	1752	1801	1854
142	Bastuträsk.................d.	...	...	...	...	...	1436	...	...	1837	...	1909	...
269	Älvsbyn.....................d.	...	...	...	...	...	1627	...	...	2024	...	2056	...
315	Boden **765** ....a.	...	...	...	...	...	1702	...	...	2110	...	2123	...
351	**Luleå 765** ....a.	...	...	...	...	...	1739	...	...	2145	...	2202	...

	Ⓐ	Ⓐ	Ⓐ	Ⓐ	Ⓒ	Ⓐ	Ⓐ	Ⓐ	Ⓐ	Ⓐ	Ⓐ
Luleå 765............. d.	...	...	...	0545	0730	...	...	...	...	...	...
Boden 765............. d.	...	...	...	0621	0802	...	...	...	...	...	...
Älvsbyn .... d.	...	...	...	0647	0828	...	...	...	...	...	...
Bastuträsk .... d.	...	...	...	0834	1006	...	...	...	...	...	...
Vännäs.............. ♣ d.	0555	0708	0828	|	1133	1145	1357	1532	1655	1759	1905
Umeå C **760**...... ♣ a.	0618	0730	0850	1011	1204	1207	1419	1553	1717	1820	1926
Umeå Östra **760** ♣ a.	0622	0734	0853	1015	1208	1210	1422	1556	1720	1823	1929

♣ – Additional services on Ⓒ Umeå - Vännäs and v.v., journey 22 minutes; all services commence from / continue to Umeå Östra (2 – 4 minutes earlier):

From **Umeå C**: 1035, 1542⑥, 1633†, 1734†, 1814⑥, 2133†.
From **Vännäs**: 0958⑥, 1133, 1431, 1726⑥, 2000⑥, 2016†.
All services continue to Umeå Östra (arrive 3 minutes after Umeå C).

765 LULEÅ - NARVIK

km					NT				IC	NT		NT
		3964	10094	94		13964	90		96			
		🅁	🅁	🅁	2	2	🅁		2	2		2
		◆	◆	◆	⚒	◆	◆		y	Ⓑ		
0	**Luleå 763** .... d.	0455	...	...	0627	0715	...	...	1107	1218	...	1635
36	Boden **763** .... d.	0528	0544	0544	0655	0750	0804	...	1137	1249	...	1704
204	Gällivare **753**........ d.	...	0815	0815	0859	...	1025	...	1356	1442	...	1902
304	**Kiruna** .... a.	...	0931	0931	1003	...	1140	...	1509	1556	...	2024
304	**Kiruna** .... d.	...	0949	0949	...	...	1158x	...	1527v	...	...	...
397	Abisko Östra .... d.	...	1052	1052	...	...	1301x	...	1641v	...	...	...
406	Björkliden............. d.	...	1108	1108	...	...	1318x	...	1656v	...	...	...
426	Vassijaure .... ◇ d.	...	|	|	...	...	|	...	1717v	...	...	...
433	Riksgränsen 🏛 .... d.	...	1152	1152	...	...	1349x	...	1729v	...	...	...
473	**Narvik 787**.......... a.	...	1236	1236	...	...	1438x	...	1822v	...	...	...

	NT		NT	IC		NT				
				95			10093	13963	93	3963
	2		2	2		2	🅁	🅁	🅁	🅁
			⚒	y		Ⓑ	◆	◆	◆	◆
Narvik 787........ d.	...	...	...	1038z	...	...	1303x	...	1512	...
Riksgränsen 🏛 . d.	...	...	...	1126z	...	...	1400x	...	1559	...
Vassijaure..... ◇ d.	...	...	...	1138z	...	...	|	...	|	...
Björkliden.......... d.	...	...	...	1200z	...	...	1434x	...	1626	...
Abisko Östra ..... d.	...	...	...	1218z	...	...	1451x	...	1643	...
Kiruna.............. a.	...	...	...	1336z	...	...	1632x	...	1800	...
Kiruna.............. d.	0551	...	1101	1354	...	1709	1649	...	1816	...
Gällivare **753**..... d.	0708	...	1208	1501	...	1818	1829	...	1924	...
Boden **763** .... a.	0923	...	1402	1709	...	2014	2052	2054	2137	2138
Luleå 763.......... a.	0948	...	1427	1741	...	2041	...	2116	...	2202

FOR NOTES – SEE TABLE 767

753 KRISTINEHAMN - MORA - ÖSTERSUND - GÄLLIVARE

INLANDSBANAN 2016 serv

km		W		♠	C
0	**Kristinehamn 750** ... d.	...	...	1037	...
40	Nykroppa .... d.	...	...	1111	...
131	Grängesberg .... d.	...	...	1218	...
146	Ludvika .... d.	...	...	1231	...
296	**Mora 758** .... d.	1345	...	1416t	1451
310	Orsa......................... d.	1356	...	...	1505
433	Sveg .... d.	1530	...	...	1656
617	**Östersund** C .... a.	1810	...	...	2103

	W		C	♠
Östersund C .... d.	0740	...	0825	...
Sveg .... d.	1010	...	1128	...
Orsa....................... d.	1145	...	1348	...
Mora 758 .... d.	1216	...	1402	1505j
Ludvika .... d.	...	...	...	1650
Grängesberg .... d.	...	...	...	1700
Nykroppa .... d.	...	...	...	1810
Kristinehamn 750 a.	...	...	...	1849

km		D	
0	**Östersund** C .... d.	0720	...
115	Ulriksfors .... d.	0907	...
244	Vilhelmina .... d.	1106	...
312	Storuman .... d.	1307	...
384	Sorsele .... d.	1425	...
473	Arvidsjaur................. d.	1555	...
646	Jokkmokk................. d.	1851	...
746	**Gällivare** .... a.	2102	...

	E
Gällivare................d.	0750
Jokkmokk ....d.	0915
Arvidsjaur ....d.	1243
Sorsele......................d.	1418
Storuman...................d.	1520
Vilhelmina.................d.	1709
Ulriksfors ....d.	1907
Östersund C.........a.	2049

All rail services operated by Railbus.

C – June 20 - Aug. 28.
D – June 20 - Aug. 27.
E – June 21 - Aug. 28.
W – Dec. 19 - Apr. 17 (not Dec. 24).

j – Depart 1447 on ⑥⑦.
t – Arrive 1427 on ⑥⑦.

♠ – July 4 - Aug. 13: 🚌 12 Göteborg - Mora and v.v. – see Tables **750/1/8**. Operated by *Tågab*.

🚂 – Steam train operates ⑤⑥ July 15 - 30, 2016 Arvidsjaur - Slagnäs and (*53 km*); depart 1745, arrive back 2200 (approximate timings). Contact: Arvidsjaur Järnvägsförening ✆ +46 (0)730 81 93 69.

Operator: Inlandsbanan AB, Box 561, 831 27, Östersund. ✆ +46 (0)771 53 53 fax +46 (0)63 19 44 06.

LONG DISTANCE SLEEPER TRAINS 767

	10094 Ⓡ ◆	94 Ⓡ ◆	3965 Ⓡ ◆		90 Ⓡ ◆	13965 Ⓡ ◆		13960 Ⓡ ◆	66 Ⓡ ◆	92 Ⓡ ◆
mö C 730 d.	...	...	...	...	...	...	...	...	...	...
org d.	...	...	...	...	...	...	...	...	...	1835j
unga d.	...	...	...	...	...	...	...	...	...	|
le d.	...	...	...	...	...	...	...	...	...	1957j
erg d.	...	...	...	...	...	...	...	...	...	2055j
kholm C a.	...	...	...	...	...	...	...	...	...	2233j
kholm C d.	1559	1628	...	...	1756	...	...	1828	2112	2240
da C ✈ d.	1624u	1653u	...	...	1823u	...	...	1851	2136u	2304
ala d.	1647u	1719u	...	...	1847u	...	...	1912	2200u	2325
e a.	1807	1836	...	...	1944	...	...	2024	|	0025
e d.	1819	1841	...	...	1951	...	...	2031	2307u	0030
hamn d.	1913	1928	...	...	2052	...	...	|	0007u	0113
svall d.	2009	2001	...	...	2127	...	...	|	0053u	0147
svall a.	2127	2100	...	...	2237	...	...	|	|	0258
svall d.	2136	2136	...	...	2242	...	...	|	|	0313
sand d.	2241	2241	...	...	2340	...	...	|	|	0423
fors d.	2311	2311	...	...	0016	...	...	|	|	0451
ge d.	|	|	...	...	|	...	...	|	0456s	|
cke d.	|	|	...	...	|	...	...	|	|	|
ersund C a.	|	|	...	...	|	...	...	|	0520s	|
ersund C d.	|	|	...	...	|	...	...	|	|	|
a.	|	|	...	...	|	...	...	|	0802s	|
ved a.	|	|	...	...	|	...	...	|	0826	|
orlien 🏛 a.	|	|	...	...	|	...	...	|	...	|
köldsvik d.	0004	0004	...	...	0104	...	...	|	...	0535
å C a.	0108	0108	...	...	0231	...	...	|	...	0703
å C d.	0111	0111	...	...	0332	...	...	|	...	0708
träsk d.	0251	0251	...	...	0509	...	...	0847	...	0847
yn d.	0454	0454	...	...	0714	...	...	1029	...	1029
en a.	0525	0525	0600	...	0745	0805	...	1104	...	1104
å a.	|	|	0631	...	|	0833	...	1209	...	1209
vik 765 a.	1236	1236	...	...	1438	...	...	...	...	...

	91 Ⓡ ◆	67 Ⓡ ◆		13961 Ⓡ ◆	13969 Ⓡ ◆	13962 Ⓡ ◆	10093 Ⓡ ◆		3962 Ⓡ ◆	93 Ⓡ ◆
Narvik **765** d.	...	...	...	...	...	...	1303	...	...	1512
Luleå d.	1647	...	...	1647	1933	2014	|	...	2108	|
Boden d.	1739	...	...	1739	2036	2052	2109	...	2131	2157
Älvsbyn d.	1811	...	...	1811	2103	...	2138	...	...	2227
Bastuträsk d.	2018	...	...	2018	2250	...	2332	...	...	0012
Umeå C a.	2155	...	...	|	0011	...	0057	...	...	0142
Umeå C d.	2200	...	...	|	0015	...	0101	...	...	0145
Örnsköldsvik d.	2307	...	...	|	0114	...	0157	...	...	0242
Storlien 🏛 d.	|	...	...	|	|	...	|	...	...	|
Duved d.	|	1935	...	|	|	...	|	...	...	|
Åre d.	|	2000u	...	|	|	...	|	...	...	|
Östersund C a.	|	|	...	|	|	...	|	...	...	|
Östersund C d.	|	2229u	...	|	|	...	|	...	...	|
Bräcke d.	|	2326u	...	|	|	...	|	...	...	|
Ånge d.	|	2348u	...	|	|	...	|	...	...	|
Kramfors d.	2354	|	...	|	0201	...	0320	...	...	0333
Härnösand d.	0023	|	...	|	0239	...	0402	...	...	0402
Sundsvall a.	0122	|	...	0540	0322	...	0510	...	...	0510
Sundsvall d.	0142	|	...	0545	0332	...	0546	...	...	0546
Hudiksvall d.	0254	0326s	...	0653	0653	...	0653	...	...	0653
Söderhamn d.	0328	0404s	...	0735	0735	...	0735	...	...	0735
Gävle a.	0426	0457s	...	0826	0826	...	0826	...	...	0826
Gävle d.	0430	|	...	0826	0829	...	0829	...	...	0829
Uppsala a.	0535	0626s	...	0927	0927s	...	0927s	...	...	0927s
Arlanda C ✈ a.	0604	0652s	...	0958	0958s	...	0958s	...	...	0958s
Stockholm C a.	0631	0716	...	1016	1023	...	1023	...	...	1023
Stockholm C d.	0641j	...	...	...	...	...	...	...	...	...
Hallsberg a.	0830j	...	...	...	...	...	...	...	...	...
Skövde a.	0948j	...	...	...	...	...	...	...	...	...
Herrljunga a.	|	...	...	...	...	...	...	...	...	...
Göteborg a.	1125j	...	...	...	...	...	...	...	...	...
Malmö C **730** a.	...	...	...	...	...	...	...	...	...	...

NOTES (LISTED BY TRAIN NUMBER)

July 3 - Aug. 19: 🛏 and ▬ Duved - Sundsvall (**91**) - Stockholm.
July 1 - Aug. 19: 🛏 and ▬ Stockholm (**92**) - Sundsvall - Duved.
July 24 - Aug. 14; not July 31 (from Stockholm, one day later from Boden): 🛏, ▬, [2] and ✕/🍷 Stockholm - Boden - Kiruna (- Narvik, not July 31).
Not July 28 - 30: 🛏, ▬, [2] and ✕ Luleå - Stockholm (- Göteborg, not July 7 - 10, 28 - 31). Conveys July 3 - Aug. 14: 🛏 and ▬ Duved (**67**) - Sundsvall - Stockholm.
Not July 28 - 30: 🛏, ▬, [2] and ✕ (Göteborg, not July 7 - 10, 28 - 31 -) Stockholm - Luleå. Conveys July 1 - Aug. 14: 🛏 and ▬ Stockholm - Sundsvall (**66**) - Duved.
June 12 - July 24 (not June 24, July 3, 4, 9, 16, 23): 🛏, ▬, [2] and ✕/🍷 Narvik - Boden - Stockholm.
Ⓒ June 12 - July 23; not June 24 (from Stockholm, one day later from Boden): 🛏, ▬, [2] and ✕/🍷 (Stockholm, not June 24, July 2, 3 -) Boden - Narvik.
– June 12 - July 24 (not June 24, July 3, 4, 9, 16, 23): 🛏, ▬, [2] and ✕/🍷 Luleå - Boden (**93**) - Stockholm.
– June 12 - July 24 (not June 24, July 3, 4, 9, 16, 23): [2] Narvik (**93**) - Boden - Luleå.
– June 12 - July 24 (not June 25, 26): [2] Luleå - Boden (**94/10094**) - Narvik.
– June 12 - July 23; not June 24, 25 (from Stockholm, one day later from Boden): 🛏, ▬, [2] and ✕/🍷 Stockholm (**94/10094**) - Boden - Luleå.
3 – July 25 - Aug. 14 (not Aug. 1): 🛏, ▬, [2] and ✕/🍷 (Narvik, not July 31 -) Kiruna - Boden - Stockholm.
4 – Ⓐ June 13 - July 22; not June 25 (from Stockholm, one day later from Boden): 🛏, ▬, [2] and ✕/🍷 Stockholm - Boden - Narvik.
0 – July 28 - 30: 🛏, ▬, [2] and ✕ Stockholm - Luleå; 🛏 and ▬ Stockholm - Sundsvall (**66**) - Duved.
1 – July 28 - 30: 🛏, ▬, [2] and ✕ Luleå - Stockholm; 🛏 and ▬ Duved (**67**) - Sundsvall - Stockholm.
2 – July 25 - Aug. 14 (not Aug. 1): 🛏, ▬, [2] and ✕ Luleå - Boden (**10093**) - Stockholm.
3 – July 25 - Aug. 14 (not Aug. 1): [2] (Narvik, not July 31 (**10093**) -) Kiruna - Boden - Luleå.

13964 – July 25 - Aug. 14: [2] Luleå - Boden (**90**) - Narvik.
13965 – July 24 - Aug. 14; not July 31 (from Stockholm, one day later from Boden): 🛏, ▬, [2] and ✕/🍷 Stockholm (**90**) - Boden - Luleå.
13969 – ⑥ July 9 - 23: 🛏, ▬, [2] and ✕ Luleå - Stockholm.

j – Not July 7 - 10, 28 - 31.
s – Stops to set down only.
u – Stops to pick up only.
v – Not July 3, 4, 30, 31, Aug. 1.
x – Not July 31.
y – Not July 3, 4, Aug. 1.
z – Not July 3, 4, 31, Aug. 1, 2.

◇ – Ticket point.

🚌 UMEÅ - LULEÅ - HAPARANDA - KEMI 768

UMEÅ - LULEÅ - HAPARANDA / TORNIO and v.v. Valid June 20 - Dec. 10, 2016 Länstrafiken Norrbotten, routes 20 / 100

	①-⑤		①-⑤	①-⑤	⑥⑦		⑥⑦	①-⑤		⑦	①-⑤		①-⑥		⑥⑦	⑦		①-⑤			①-⑤			
å d.	...	...	...	0515	0545	...	0730	0730	...	0900	0900	...	...	1315	1430	...	...	1525	1630	...	1725	1930	...	2100
eftea d.	...	0535	0635	0740	0800	...	0950	0955	...	1115	1125	...	...	1520	1635	...	...	1755	1835	...	1955	2135	...	2300
d.	...	0700	0805	0905	0925	...	1115	1120	...	1240	1250	...	...	1635	1750	...	...	1925	1950	...	2120	2250	...	...
å a.	...	0800	0905	1005	1025	...	1210	1215	...	1335	1345	...	...	1725	1840	...	...	2015	2040	...	2215	2340	...	...
å d.	0515	0820	0950	1050	1050	...	1230	1245	...	1350	1400	...	1510	1735	...	1855	...	...	2110	...	...	...	...	...
aranda / Tornio 🏛 § d.	0755	1035	1215	1320	1315	...	1500	1520	...	1635	1645	...	1745	1950	...	2110	...	...	2325	...	...	...	...	...

		①-⑤	⑥⑦		①-⑤	⑥		①-⑤		⑥⑦		⑦		①-⑤	⑥⑦		①-⑤	①-⑤	①-⑤		⑥⑦	①-⑤	⑦	①-⑤
aranda / Tornio 🏛 § d.	...	0530	...	...	0650	0725	0810	0955	...	1050	1230	...	...	1340	1345	...	1510	...	1610	...	1710	1720	1810	2015
å a.	...	0750	...	...	0945	0950	1030	1235	...	1310	1450	...	...	1605	1610	...	1750	...	1845	...	1940	1955	2040	2230
å d.	0540	0800	0800	...	1000	...	1040	1300	...	1320	1500	...	...	1635	1635	...	1810	...	1910	...	2005	2010	2055	...
d.	0635	0855	0855	...	1105	...	1135	1405	...	1415	1555	...	...	1750	1750	...	1915	...	2010	...	2105	2110	2150	...
eftea d.	0750	1015	1015	...	1230	...	1250	1535	...	1530	1715	1830	...	1925	1925	...	2025	2030	2130	...	2225	2230	2300	...
eå a.	0945	1210	1210	...	1435	...	1445	1740	...	1725	1910	2035	...	2130	2130	...	...	2235	2340	...	0035	...	...	...

HAPARANDA / TORNIO - KEMI and v.v. Valid until August 10, 2016 NET-Matkat, route 70

	①-⑤	①-⑤		①-⑤	①-⑤		①-⑥		①-⑤		①-⑥		①-⑤	①-⑤		①-⑥		①-⑤		①-⑥				
aranda / Tornio 🏛 § ⊡ d.	0605	0705	...	0805	0905	...	1005	...	1105	...	1205	...	1305	1405	...	1505	...	1605	...	1705	...	...	...	...
i ⊡ a.	0650	0750	...	0850	0950	...	1050	...	1150	...	1250	...	1350	1450	...	1550	...	1650	...	1750	...	...	...	...

	①-⑤	①-⑤		①-⑤	①-⑤	①-⑤		①-⑥		①-⑤		①-⑥		①-⑤	①-⑤		①-⑥		①-⑤		①-⑥			
i ⊡ d.	0605	0705	...	0805	0905	1005	...	1105	...	1205	...	1305	...	1405	1505	...	1605	...	1705	...	1805	...	...	...
aranda / Tornio 🏛 § ⊡ a.	0650	0750	...	0850	0950	1050	...	1150	...	1250	...	1350	...	1450	1550	...	1650	...	1750	...	1850	...	...	...

services on ⑦. From Kemi services call at Kemi railway station 1 minute later; from Haparanda / Tornio services continue to Kemi railway station upon request.
r services operated by NorthBus; www.northbus.fi

tops refer to bus stations except where shown otherwise.

Finnish time, one hour later than Swedish time.

Swedish name: Haparanda / Tornio;
Finnish name: Tornio / Haaparanta.

aranda / Tornio bus station is located approximately 200 metres on the Swedish side of the border.

Operators:
LN – Länstrafiken Norrbotten: www.ltnbd.se
NET – NET-Matkat: www.netmatkat.com
See also www.matkahuolto.fi

NORWAY

SEE MAP PAGE

Operator: Norges Statsbaner (NSB) www.nsb.no

Services: All trains convey second class seating accommodation. Many services, as identified in the notes, also convey *NSB Komfort* accommodation (see below). Sleeping-cars have one- and two-berth compartments; the sleeper supplement is 850 NOK per compartment (for two people travelling together, or sole use for single travellers). Mos distance express trains convey a bistro car (✗) serving hot and cold meals, drinks and snacks. 🍸 indicates that drinks and light refreshments are available from autor vending machines.

Timings: NSB services are valid **until December 10**, 2016 (unless otherwise stated).

Reservations: Seat reservation is highly recommended on long-distance routes Oslo - Kristiansand - Stavanger (Table **775**), Oslo - Bergen (Table **780**), Oslo - Trondheim / Åndalsnes (Table **785**) and Trondheim - Bodø (Table **787**).

NSB Komfort: *NSB Komfort* is a dedicated area provided on many trains with complimentary tea / coffee and newspapers; a supplement of 90 NOK is payable per single journey.

770 OSLO - HALDEN - GÖTEBORG

All trains convey *NSB Komfort* an

km	Norwegian train number	139		101	103	105	107	109	111	113	115	117	119	121	141	123	143	125	127	129	131	133	135
	Swedish train number					391						395			393				399				
				Ⓐ	Ⓐ	⚒		⚒b		⚒b				c	Ⓐn		Ⓐn	c		Ⓑn		Ⓑn	
0	**Oslo** Sentral d.	0001	...	0346	0601	0701	0802	0901	1001	1101	1201	1301	1401	1501	1528	1601	1628	1701	1802	1901	2001	2101	2201
60	Moss d.	0052	...	0446	0644	0745	0844	0944	1044	1144	1244	1344	1444	1546	1614	1645	1713	1745	1844	1944	2044	2144	2244
69	Rygge ✈ d.	0059	...	0453	0651	0752	0851	0951	1051	1151	1251	1351	1451	1553	1621	1652	1720	1752	1851	1951	2051	2151	2251
94	Fredrikstad d.	0119	...	...	0711	0812	0911	1016	1112	1211	1311	1411	1511	1616	1642	1713	1741	1812	1911	2011	2112	2211	2311
109	Sarpsborg d.	0133	...	...	0729	0825	0929	1033	1126	1225	1325	1425	1529	1633	1656	1727	1755	1826	1925	2028	2126	2225	2325
137	**Halden** ★ d.	0152	...	...	0748	0846	0948	1052	1145	1244	1344	1446	1548	1652	1722	1746	1820	1845	2002**z**	2047	2145	2244	2344
268	Öxnered **751** a.	...	...	...	...	1001	...	...	...	...	...	1601	...	...	1837	...	...	...	2116	...	...	...	...
278	Trollhättan **751** a.	...	...	...	...	1007	...	...	...	...	...	1608	...	...	1843	...	...	...	2122	...	...	...	...
350	**Göteborg 751** a.	...	...	...	...	1040	...	...	...	...	...	1650	...	...	1928	...	...	...	2200	...	...	...	...

Swedish train number							392			390						394					398		
Norwegian train number	102	154	104	142	156	106	144	108	110	112	114	116	118	120	122	124	126	128	130	132	134	136	
	Ⓐ	⑥	Ⓐ	Ⓐn	†	⚒	Ⓐn	⚒b		⚒		⚒b		c				c		Ⓑn		Ⓑn	
Göteborg 751 d.	...	...	...	...	...	...	0435	...	...	0655	...	...	...	...	...	1300	...	...	...	...	1755	...	...
Trollhättan **751** d.	...	...	...	...	...	...	0509	...	...	0735	...	...	...	...	...	1336	...	...	...	...	1834	...	...
Öxnered **751** d.	...	...	...	...	...	...	0515	...	...	0742	...	...	...	...	...	1342	...	...	...	...	1840	...	...
Halden ★ d.	0400	0500	0502	0533	0600	0602	0633	0700	0802	0910	1005	1103	1202	1302	1402	1510	1605	1703	1802	1902	2005	2102	...
Sarpsborg d.	0422	0520	0524	0553	0620	0624	0654	0721	0824	0930	1026	1125	1224	1324	1424	1530	1626	1725	1825	1924	2026	2124	...
Fredrikstad d.	0436	0534	0538	0608	0634	0638	0709	0736	0838	0944	1040	1139	1238	1338	1438	1544	1640	1739	1839	1938	2040	2138	...
Rygge ✈ d.	0454	0552	0556	0626	0652	0656	0727	0756	0856	1002	1058	1157	1256	1356	1456	1602	1658	1757	1857	1956	2058	2156	...
Moss d.	0503	0601	0608	0635	0701	0708	0736	0808	0908	1012	1108	1208	1308	1408	1508	1612	1711	1808	1908	2008	2108	2208	...
Oslo Sentral a.	0552	0651	0651	0722	0751	0751	0822	0851	0949	1052	1149	1249	1349	1449	1549	1652	1751	1849	1949	2049	2149	2249	...

b – Not ⑥ July 2 - Aug. 6.
c – Not ⑥⑦ July 2 - Aug. 7.
n – Not June 27 - Aug. 7.
z – Arrives 1944.
★ – 🏛 at Kornsjø (*km169*).
☛ Please note that Norwegian holiday dates apply to services between Oslo and Göteborg.

771 OSLO - OSLO GARDERMOEN ✈

*See also Tables **783** and*

Operated by Flytoget AS.
Special fares apply.
✆ +47 815 00 777.

Daily services (journey time: 22 minutes)
Trains call at Lillestrøm 10 minutes from Oslo
From Oslo Sentral every 20 minutes 0440 - 0000.
From Gardermoen every 20 minutes 0530 - 0050.

Additional services on Ⓑ (journey time: 19 minutes)
Non-stop services
From Oslo Sentral every 20 minutes: 0610 - 2230 on Ⓐ, 1210 - 2310 on ⑦.
From Gardermoen every 20 minutes: 0640 - 2300 on Ⓐ, 1240 - 2340 on ⑦.

773 OSLO - GJØVIK

All trains convey *NSB Komfort* anc

Subject to alteration August 1 – 7

km			c					Ⓐ				Ⓐh
0	**Oslo** S d.	0002	0702	0902	1102	1302	1502	1612	1702**e**	1902	2102	2302
56	Roa d.	0103	0800	0959	1158	1358	1600	1705	1803**e**	1959	2158	0003
70	Jaren d.	0119	0816	1015	1214	1414	1616	1722	1819	2015	2214	0019
99	Eina d.	0142**x**	0840	1039	1238	1437	1639	1750	1842	2039	2238	0042
110	Raufoss d.	0152	0850	1049	1248	1447	1649	1801	1852	2049	2248	0052
122	**Gjøvik** a.	0202	0900	1059	1258	1457	1659	1811	1902	2059	2258	0102

	Ⓐ	Ⓒc	Ⓐk	Ⓐm								
Gjøvik d.	0431	0528	0543	0631	0733	0932	1131	1327	1530	1729	1932	2
Raufoss d.	0442	0539	0554	0641	0744	0943	1142	1338	1541	1740	1943	2
Eina d.	0452**x**	0549	0604	0650	0754	0953	1152	1348	1551	1751	1953	2
Jaren d.	0515	0612	0627	0713	0817	1016	1215	1412	1615	1818	2016	2
Roa d.	0531	0628	0644	0730	0833	1032	1231	1429	1631	1834	2032	2
Oslo S a.	0628	0728	0744	0830	0930	1128	1330	1530	1730	1930	2130	2

c – Not ⑥⑦ July 2 - Aug. 7.
e – On ①–⑤ June 27 - Aug. 5 departs Oslo 1642, Roa 1751.
h – June 27 - Aug. 5 departs Oslo 2226, Roa d. 2334, Jaren 2350, Eina 0013, Raufoss 0023, arrives Gjøvik 0033.
k – June 27 - Aug. 5 departs Gjøvik 0547, Raufoss 0558, Eina 0608, Jaren 0639, Roa 0656, arrives Oslo 08
m – June 27 - Aug. 5 departs Gjøvik 0639, Raufoss 0649, Eina 0658, Jaren 0721, Roa 0738, arrives Oslo 08
x – Stops on request only.

775 OSLO - KRISTIANSAND - STAVANGER

km		701	709	715	719	719	723	729	733	733	737	745
		Ⓐ	Ⓐ**D**		Ⓐ	Ⓑ			Ⓑ		Ⓑ	Ⓑ
		✗⊡	✗⊡	✗⊡	✗⊡	✗⊡	✗⊡	✗⊡	✗⊡	✗⊡	✗⊡	♣✗
0	**Oslo** Sentral § d.	...	0419	0725	0925	...	1125	1425	1625	1625	1825	2225
41	Drammen § d.	...	0454**u**	0800**u**	1000**u**	...	1200**u**	1500**u**	1700**u**	1700**u**	1900**u**	2300**u**
87	Kongsberg § d.	...	0530	0836	1036	...	1236	1547	1747	1747	1946	2343
134	Nordagutu d.	...	0604	0911	1114	...	|	1622	1822	1822	2022	0020**x**
151	Bø d.	...	0619	0925	1128	...	1328	1636	1841	1841	2037	0037
209	Neslandsvatn d.	...	|	1010	1211	...	1412**x**	1719	1924	1924	2124	0126**x**
225	Gjerstad d.	...	0723**x**	1022**x**	1224**x**	...	|	1734	1937**x**	1937**x**	2137**x**	0140**x**
270	Nelaug d.	...	0755	1055	1256	...	1457	1807	2012	2012	2210	0216**x**
353	**Kristiansand** a.	...	0855	1153	1358	...	1600	1905	2108	2108	2313	0330
353	**Kristiansand** d.	0505	0909	1203	1408	1408	1615	1913	2115	...	...	0345
465	Moi d.	0632**x**	1036**x**	1333**x**	1533**x**	1533**x**	1749	2037**x**	2242**x**	...	...	0519**x**
514	Egersund ◇ d.	0706	1109	1406	1606	1606	1828	2110	2317	...	...	0558
573	Sandnes S ◇ a.	0752**z**	1152**z**	1452**z**	1705**z**	1705**z**	1922**z**	2151**z**	2400**z**	...	...	0649**z**
587	**Stavanger** ◇ a.	0805	1205	1505	1719	1719	1935	2204	0012	...	...	0705

	702	708	708	712	716	720	724	730	730	734	7
	Ⓐ	Ⓐ	⚒				Ⓑ	Ⓑ		Ⓑ	
	✗⊡	✗⊡	✗⊡	✗⊡	✗⊡	✗⊡	✗⊡	✗⊡	✗⊡	✗⊡	♣
Stavanger ◐ d.	...	0434	...	0648	0849	1017	1249	1533	1533	1749	2
Sandnes S ◐ d.	...	0448**v**	...	0702**v**	0903**v**	1031**v**	1303**v**	1550**v**	1550**v**	1803**v**	22
Egersund ◐ d.	...	0532	...	0746	0945	1120	1343	1646	1646	1846	2
Moi d.	...	0616	...	0823**x**	1021**x**	1201	1424	1723**x**	1723**x**	1923**x**	00
Kristiansand a.	...	0742	...	0946	1145	1333	1547	1846	1846	2048	0
Kristiansand d.	0445	0753	0753	0956	1155	1350	1602	1855	...	...	0
Nelaug d.	0545	0857	0857	1056	1256	1455	1702	1957	...	...	03
Gjerstad d.	0618**x**	0929**x**	0929**x**	1129**x**	1328**x**	|	1734	2029**x**	...	...	04
Neslandsvatn d.	0631	0942	0942	1143	1343	|	|	2043	...	...	04
Bø d.	0714	1027	1027	1227	1429	1622	1827	2127	...	...	0
Nordagutu d.	0728	1041	1041	1241	1444	1641	1842	2142	...	...	05
Kongsberg ‡ d.	0802	1117	1117	1317	1519	1717	1917	2217	...	...	0
Drammen ‡ a.	0851**s**	1151**s**	1151**s**	1350**s**	1551**s**	1751**s**	1951**s**	2251**s**	...	...	06
Oslo S ‡ a.	0925	1225	1225	1425	1625	1825	2025	2325	...	...	07

Nelaug - Arendal

km		Ⓐ		⚒							⑦	
0	Nelaug d.	0700	...	0905	1104	1304	1505	...	1815	2020	2218	...
36	Arendal a.	0737	...	0942	1141	1341	1542	...	1852	2057	2255	...

	Ⓐ		⚒				Ⓑ	⑥			
Arendal d.	0503	...	0811	1008	1209	1408	1615	1720	1911	...	2
Nelaug a.	0540	...	0848	1045	1246	1445	1652	1757	1948	...	2

D – Runs daily Kristiansand - Stavanager.
b – Not ⑥ July 2 - Aug. 6.
d – Not ⑦ July 3 - Aug. 7.
s – Stops to set down only.
u – Stops to pick up only.
v – Stops on request to pick up only.
x – Stops on request.
z – Stops on request to set down only.
♣ – Conveys 🛏 and ⟨2⟩. Reservation recommended.
⊡ – Reservation recommended. Conveys *NSB Komfort*.
★ – By 🚌 Klepp - Egersund and v.v. Klepp is located 50 km from Egersund. Journey time extended by approximately 30 minutes.

§ – Other local trains **Oslo** S - **Drammen** (35 minutes) - **Kongsberg** (75–81 minutes): 0009, 0609 Ⓐ, 0709, 0809 **d**, 0909, 1009 **d**, 1109, 1209 **d**, 1309, 1409, 1509, 1609, 1709, 1809, 1909 **b**, 2009, 2109 **b**, 2209 and 2309 **b**.

‡ – Other local trains **Kongsberg** - **Drammen** (43–44 minutes) - **Oslo** S (77–78 minutes): 0434 Ⓐ, 0534, 0634 **d**, 0734, 0834 **d**, 0934, 1034 **d**, 1134, 1234, 1334, 1434, 1534, 1633, 1734, 1834, 1933 **b**, 2034, 2134 **b** and 2234.

◇ – Other local trains **Egersund** - **Sandnes** S (51–57 minutes) - **Stavanger** (67–73 minutes): 0450 Ⓐ, 0520 Ⓐ, 0551 Ⓐ, 0621 ⚒, 0650 Ⓐ, 0720 ⚒, 0818 ⚒, 0920, 1019, 1118, 1223, 1317, 1419, 1450 Ⓐ, 1 1550 Ⓐ, 1620, 1650 Ⓐ, 1721, 1820, 1921, 2022, 2047 ⑥★, 2123 Ⓑ, 2147 ⑥★, 2223 Ⓑ and 2247★.

◐ – Other local trains **Stavanger** - **Sandnes** S (16 minutes) - **Egersund** (68–77 minutes): 0452 Ⓐ, 0524 Ⓐ, 0554 ⚒, 0654 ⚒, 0754 ⚒, 0854, 0954, 1054, 1154, 1254, 1324 Ⓐ, 1354, 1424 Ⓐ, 1454, 152 1554, 1624 Ⓐ, 1654, 1754, 1854, 1954, 2054 Ⓑ, 2054 ⑥★, 2154 Ⓑ, 2154 ⑥★, 2254 Ⓑ★ and 2324★.

PORSGRUNN - NOTODDEN 779

service on ©

	Ⓐ	Ⓐn	Ⓐ	Ⓐ	Ⓐn	Ⓐ	Ⓐn	Ⓐ
Porsgrunn . 783 d.		0633	0751	1151	1338	1442	1553	1754
Skien .... 783 d.	0530	0646	0800	1200	1349	1451	1603	1803
Nordagutu .... a.	0559	0721	0830	1230	1418	1525	1632	1832
Nordagutu .... d.	0606	0722	0832	1231	1419	1526	1634	1833
Notodden .... a.	0625	0740	0851	1250	1438	1545	1653	1852

	Ⓐ	Ⓐn	Ⓐ	Ⓐ	Ⓐn	Ⓐ	Ⓐn	Ⓐ
Notodden .... d.	0643	0809	0909	1302	1447	1611	1811	2010
Nordagutu .... a.	0701	0827	0928	1319	1505	1629	1829	2028
Nordagutu .... d.	0702	0831	0929	1320	1506	1632	1832	2029
Skien .... 783 a.	0732	0902	1000	1349	1536	1702	1902	2059
Porsgrunn .... 783 a.	0741	0911	1009	1358	1544	1711	1911	...

n – Not June 27 - Aug. 5.

OSLO - BERGEN 780

ect to alteration on June 4, 5

	609 B ✕⊡	61 ✕⊡	🚌 H	601 ✕⊡	607 ⑦C ✕⊡	63 ✕⊡		605 Ⓑ N✕	
Oslo Sentral .... 783 d.	0625	0825	...	1203	...	1543	...	2325	...
Drammen .... 783 d.	0700u	0900u	...	1238u	...	1618u	...	0003u	...
Hønefoss .... d.	0757	0954	...	1333	...	1712	...	0103	...
Nesbyen .... d.	0909	1103	...	1444	...	1822	...	0219	...
Gol .... d.	0924	1116	...	1500	...	1836	...	0234	...
Ål .... d.	0944	1136	...	1520	1541	1855	...	0300	...
Geilo .... d.	1009	1157	...	1541	1602	1921	...	0322	...
Ustaoset .... d.	1022	1208	...	1553	1615	1932	...	0334	...
Finse .... d.	1118	1235	...	1623	1648	2000	...	0407	...
Myrdal .... 781 a.	1148	1259	...	1648	1714	2024	...	0435	...
Voss .... 781 a.	1300	1342	1346	1736	1804	2111	...	0524	...
Dale .... 781 a.	...	1412k	1422	1812	|	2141	...	0556	...
Arna .... 781 a.	...	1446k	1457	1845	1904s	2218	...	0637s	...
Bergen .... 781 a.	...	1459k	1512	1858	1919	2232	...	0651	...

	62 ✕⊡	🚌 H	602 ✕⊡		64 ✕⊡	610 B ✕⊡	604 ⑤C ✕⊡		606 Ⓑ N✕
Bergen .... 781 d.	0757	1135	1159k	...	1559	...	1705	...	2259
Arna .... 781 d.	0809	1150	1211k	...	1611u	...	1717u	...	2311
Dale .... 781 d.	0841	1225	1242k	...	|	...	|	...	2348
Voss .... 781 d.	0910	1301	1313	...	1711	1745	1828	...	0021
Myrdal .... 781 d.	0952	...	1408	...	1754	1837	1911	...	0106
Finse .... d.	1018	...	1436	...	1820	1914	1941	...	0138
Ustaoset .... d.	1044	...	1505	...	1846	1952	2016	...	0210
Geilo .... d.	1056	...	1518	...	1858	2006	2030	...	0225
Ål .... d.	1116	...	1540	...	1918	2028	2049	...	0255
Gol .... d.	1140	...	1600	...	1939	2049	...	...	0318
Nesbyen .... d.	1152	...	1613	...	1954	2104	...	...	0332
Hønefoss .... d.	1304	...	1732	...	2107	2231	...	...	0454
Drammen .... 783 a.	1407s	...	1828s	...	2157s	2326s	...	...	0551s
Oslo Sentral .... 783 a.	1445	...	1907	...	2235	0005	...	...	0625

Until Sept. 23.
From Sept. 30.
①–⑤ Sept. 5–23.

N – Conveys 🛏 and 2 . Reservation recommended.
k – Not ①–⑤ Sept. 5–23.

s – Trains stop to set down only.
u – Trains stop to pick up only.

⊡ – Reservation recommended. Conveys *NSB Komfort*.

MYRDAL - VOSS - BERGEN and FLÅM 781

ect to alteration on June 4, 5

VALID UNTIL SEPTEMBER 23

	Ⓐ	605 ①–⑥ ✕◇	Ⓐ		▲	Ⓐ ▲	▲		Ⓐ ▲	▲	609 ✕◇	61 ✕◇	🚌 H		Ⓐ				601 ✕◇			63 ✕◇	⑥	⑤	Ⓑ
Oslo Sentral **780** .... d.	...	2325p	...	...	...	...	...	...	...	...	0625	0825	...	...	...	...	...	...	1203	...	...	1543	...	...	...
Myrdal .... d.	...	0436	...	...	...	...	...	0956	...	1112	1206	1301	...	1333	...	1437	...	1552	1650	1713	...	2026	...	2036	...
Mjølfjell .... d.	...	|	...	...	0747n	...	...	1014x	...	1130x	|	|	...	1351x	...	1454x	...	|	|	1737	...	|	...	2054x	...
Voss .... a.	...	0524	...	...	0821n	...	...	1051	...	1207	1300	1342	...	1428	...	1532	...	1633	1736	1815	...	2111	...	2131	...
Voss .... d.	0504	0529	0608	0721	0836	0922	1040	...	1127	1238	...	1346k	1346	...	1438	1539	1539	1637	1741	1840	1940	2114	2145	...	2239
Dale .... d.	0535	0600	0645	0752	0910	0959	1114	...	1202	1312	...	1414k	1422	...	1513	1614	1614	1714	1814	1914	2018	2143	2216	...	2314
Vaksdal .... d.	0554	|	0700	0807	0931	1014	1129	...	1227	1327	...	|	|	...	1529	1630	1630	1730	|	1929	2036	|	2235	...	2331
Arna .... ‡ d.	0613	0637s	0721	0832	0949	1034	1148	...	1245	1347	...	1446k	1457	...	1549	1648	1648	1748	1847	1947	2054	2221	2255	...	2350
Bergen .... ‡ a.	0623	0651	0731	0842	0959	1044	1158	...	1255	1357	...	1459k	1512	...	1559	1658	1658	1758	1858	1957	2104	2232	2305	...	2400

	①–⑥		Ⓐ		62 ✕◇		▲	Ⓐ ▲	🚌 H	602 ✕◇		▲	Ⓐ ▲			64 ✕◇	Ⓐ	610 ✕◇		⑤	Ⓐ		Ⓐ		606 Ⓑ ✕◇	⑥
en .... ‡ d.	0009	...	0533	0651	0757	0843	0959	1058	1135	1159k	...	1256	1358	...	1514	1559	1614	...	1658	...	1758	1858	2042	2149	2259	2320
.... ‡ d.	0019	...	0549	0701	0809	0853	1009	1108	1150	1211k	...	1306	1408	...	1525	1611u	1625	...	1708	...	1808	1908	2054	2159	2311	2330
dal .... d.	0036	...	0615	0719	|	0911	1030	1128	|	|	...	1326	1428	...	1545	|	1646	...	1729	...	1829	1929	2111	2217	|	2347
.... d.	0054	...	0630	0735	0841	0926	1044	1142	1225	1242k	...	1341	1443	...	1600	|	1701	...	1744	...	1844	1945	2125	2234	2348	0002
.... a.	0125	...	0703	0810	0908	0956	1115	1216	1301	1310k	...	1415	1514	...	1631	1709	1734	...	1818	...	1915	2016	2159	2311	0018	0033
.... d.	...	...	0705n	0831	0910	1001	1120	...	...	1313	1343	1441	...	1550	...	1711	...	1745	...	1823	...	...	...	...	0021	...
ell .... d.	...	...	0737n	0904x	|	1033x	|	...	...	|	|	1514	...	1621	...	|	...	|	...	1856x	...	...	...	...	|	...
al .... a.	...	...	...	0922	0950	1051	1206	...	...	1405	1424	1532	...	1639	...	1752	...	1826	...	1915	...	...	...	...	0103	...
lo Sentral **780** .... a.	...	...	...	...	1445	...	...	...	...	1907	...	...	...	...	...	2235	...	0005	...	...	...	...	...	...	0625	...

MYRDAL - FLÅM ⊠

	E									
Myrdal .... d.	0826	0940	1058	1213	1327	1443	1559	1715	1835	1948
Flåm .... a.	0920	1035	1155	1310	1425	1540	1655	1810	1930	2045

	E									
Flåm .... d.	0730	0835	0945	1105	1220	1335	1450	1605	1725	1840
Myrdal .... a.	0814	0928	1043	1201	1315	1431	1546	1703	1817	1936

①②③④⑥⑦ until Aug. 31.
①–⑤ Sept. 5–23.

Not ①–⑤ Sept. 5–23.
Ⓐ (not June 20 - Aug. 12).

p – Previous day.
s – Stops to set down only.
u – Stops to pick up only.
x – Stops on request.

◇ – Reservation recommended.
‡ – Additional local services operate.
▲ – Operated by 🚌 Voss - Bergen and v.v. on ①–⑤ Sept. 5–23 (please confirm timings locally).
⊠ – Operator: **Flåm Utvikling AS.** ✆ + 47 57 63 21 00. 30 % discount for rail pass holders.

⛴ FLÅM - GUDVANGEN and 🚌 GUDVANGEN - VOSS 781a

y 1 - Sept. 30

	⛴ A	⛴	⛴ B	⛴	⛴ C	⛴ A	⛴ B	⛴	⛴	⛴ B	⛴ C
.... d.	0800	0900	1000	1200	1300	1330	1400	1500	1700	1800	1900
angen .... a.	1000	1115	1130	1415	1515	1530	1530	1715	1915	1930	2115
angen .... d.	...	*1140**	*1140**	...	...	*1540**	*1540**	*1745**	...	...	...
.... a.	...	*1255**	*1255**	...	...	*1655**	*1655**	*1900**	...	...	...

	⛴ B	⛴	⛴ A	⛴ C	⛴ B	⛴ A	⛴	⛴ B	⛴ A	⛴ C	🚌 ①–⑤	⛴
Voss .... d.	...	...	...	...	*1010**	*1010**	...	*1440**	*1440**	...	1610	...
Gudvangen .... a.	...	...	...	...	*1120**	*1120**	...	*1540**	*1540**	...	1710	...
Gudvangen .... d.	0800	0930	1030	1030	1145	1145	1430	1600	1600	1630	...	1730
Flåm .... a.	0930	1145	1230	1245	1315	1400	1645	1730	1800	1845	...	1945

May 1–31.
B – June 1 - Sept. 30.
C – June 1 - Aug. 31.
* – Connection by 🚌.

⛴ / 🚌 LILLEHAMMER and GOL - FLÅM - BALESTRAND - BERGEN 782

y 1 - Sept. 30

	⛴ A	⛴ ⚒	🚌	⛴ ⑦t	⛴	🚌	🚌 h	🚌 s	🚌 Ⓑ	🚌	🚌 ⑤⑦	🚌 s
hammer skysst. d.	...	...	...	...	...	1030	...	...	...	...	...	...
gndal ⊕ .... d.	...	...	0755	...	...	|	1430	...	1715	...	...	...
upangersenteret. d.	...	...	0810	...	...	|	1445	...	1730	...	...	...
Øvre Årdal ◇ .... d.	...	*0535*e	*0740*	...	...	|	1430	...	*1705*	*1850*	*2030*	...
dnes .... d.	...	*0630*e	0835	...	...	|	1515	...	1755	1940	2120	...
Skysstasjon .... d.	...	|	|	...	...	|	|	1320	|	|	|	1900
al Rådhuset ...... d.	...	*0615*e	0845	...	...	|	1525	1525	1805	|	|	2105
angersenteret... d.	...	*0646*e	|	...	...	|	|	1600	|	2000	2140	2140
dal ⊕ .... d.	...	0705	|	1040	...	|	|	1620	|	2015	2155	2205
m .... d.	0600	|	0930	|	1530	1620	1620	|	1850	...	...	|
nger .... d.	0730	0730	|	1110	1630	|	|	1645	|	...	...	2230
strand .... d.	0800	0750	|	1130	1655	|	|	1735	|	...	...	2310
ss .... a.	...	|	1035	|	|	1730	1730	...	2000	...	...	...
en ⊡ .... a.	...	1150	1225	1520	2045	1915	1915	...	2145	...	...	...

	⛴ A	🚌 s	🚌 k	🚌	⛴	🚌 s	🚌	⛴ ⑥t	🚌	⛴ Ⓑ	🚌 Ⓑ
Bergen ⊡ .... d.	...	...	0845	0845	0800	...	...	1415	1530	1630	1715a
Voss .... d.	...	...	1035	1035	|	...	...	|	1725	|	1900c
Balestrand .... d.	0830	1000	|	|	1150f	1310	...	1820	|	2020f	|
Leikanger .... d.	0900	1045	|	|	1220	1350	...	1835	|	2045	|
Flåm .... a.	1030	|	1145	1145	1325	|	...	|	1835	|	2020
Sogndal ⊕ .... d.	...	1135	|	|	...	1430	1430	1900	|	2120	|
Kaupangersenteret ... d.	...	1145	|	|	...	1445	1445	...	|	...	|
Lærdal Rådhuset ...... a.	...	1225	1245	|	...	1525	|	...	1920	...	2105
Gol skysstasjon .... a.	...	1415	|	|	...	1715	|	...	|	...	|
Fodnes .... a.	...	...	1300	|	...	...	1515	...	1935	...	2115
Øvre Årdal ◇ .... a.	...	...	1345	|	...	...	*1600*	...	*2025*	...	*2200*
Kaupangersenteret .a.	...	...	1320	|	...	...	...	...	2000	...	2140
Sogndal ⊕ .... a.	...	...	1335	|	...	...	...	...	2015	...	2155
Lillehammer skysst .a.	...	...	...	1735	...	...	...	...	...	...	...

①–⑤ June 20 - Aug. 19.

①–⑤ only.
1910 on ⑦.
Ⓐ only. By 🚌 to Sogndal kai.
5 minutes later from June 19.

h – Change 🚌 at Håbakken (a. 1535, d. 1545).
k – Change 🚌 at Håbakken (a. 1225, d. 1235).
s – Change 🚌 at Sogndal.
t – Not June 25 - Aug. 14.

◇ – Øvre Årdal Farnes.

⊕ – 🚌: Sogndal skysstasjon. ⛴: Sogndal kai.
⊡ – 🚌: Bus station. ⛴: Strandkaiterminal.

🚌 operators: Nettbuss Sogn Billag ✆ +47 57 67 66 00.
NOR-WAY Bussekspress ✆ +47 815 44 444.
🚌 timings are subject to alteration from June 19.
⛴ operator: Norled AS ✆ +47 5186 8700.

783 EIDSVOLL - OSLO - SKIEN

All trains convey NSB Komfort ar

km		Ⓐ	⚒	Ⓒ	Ⓐ	⑥	Ⓐ	Ⓑ	⑥	⚒	Ⓑ	⑥		Ⓑ	⑥	Ⓒ	Ⓐ				Ⓑ	Ⓐ	Ⓒ	Ⓑ		
0	**Eidsvoll**....785 d.	0501	0601	0701	0701	0801	0801	0901	0901	1001	1101	1101	1201	1301	1301	1401	1401	1501	1601	1701	1801	1901	1901	2001	2101	2201
16	Oslo ✈ ●.785 d.	0513	0613	0713	0713	0813	0813	0913	0913	1013	1113	1113	1213	1313	1313	1413	1413	1513	1613	1713	1813	1913	1913	2013	2113	2213
47	Lillestrøm ..785 d.	0526	0626	0726	0726	0826	0826	0926	0926	1026	1126	1126	1226	1326	1326	1426	1426	1526	1626	1726	1826	1926	1926	2026	2126	2226
68	**Oslo** S......785 d.	0539	0639	0739	0739	0839	0839	0939	0939	1039	1139	1139	1239	1339	1339	1439	1439	1539	1639	1739	1839	1939	1939	2039	2139	2239
108	Drammen........ d.	0615	0715	0815	0815	0915	0915	1015	1015	1115	1215	1215	1315	1415	1415	1515	1515	1615	1715	1815	1915	2015	2015	2115	2215	2315
142	Holmestrand ... d.	0639	0739	0839	0839	0939	0939	1039	1039	1139	1239	1239	1339	1439	1439	1539	1539	1639	1739	1839	1939	2039	2039	2139	2239	2339
156	Skoppum .... d.	0649	0749	0849	0849	0949	0949	1049	1049	1149	1249	1249	1349	1449	1449	1549	1549	1649	1749	1849	1949	2049	2049	2149	2249	2349
172	Tønsberg .... d.	0701	0801	0901	0901	1001	1001	1101	1101	1201	1301	1301	1401	1501	1501	1601	1601	1701	1801	1901	2001	2101	2101	2201	2301	0001
191	Torp ✈ .... d.	0715	0815	0915	0915	1015	1015	1115	1115	1215	1315	1315	1415	1515	1515	1615	1615	1715	1815	1915	2015	2115	2115	2215	2315	0015
196	**Sandefjord** ..... d.	0722	0822	0922	0922	1022	1022	1122	1122	1222	1322	1322	1422	1522	1522	1622	1622	1722	1822	1922	2022	2122	2122	2222	2322	0022
215	Larvik............. a.	0736	0836	0936	0936	1036	1036	1136	1136	1236	1336	1336	1436	1536	1536	1636	1636	1736	1836	1936	2036	2136	2136	2236	2336	0036
215	Larvik............. d.	*0740**	*0840**	*0940**	0944	*1040**	1044	*1140**	1137	*1240**	*1340**	1344	*1440**	*1540**	1537	*1640**	1644	1744t	1844	1944	2044	*2140**	2144	2237	2337	0037
249	Porsgrunn .779 d.	*0805**	*0900**	*1000**	1021	*1100**	1118	*1200**	1212	*1300**	*1400**	1419	*1500**	*1600**	1611	*1700**	1721	1819t	1921	2021	2118	*2200**	2218	2311	0011	0111
258	**Skien**........779 a.	*0825**	*0918**	*1018**	1029	*1118**	1126	*1218**	1220	*1318**	*1418**	1427	*1518**	*1618**	1619	*1718**	1729	1827t	1929	2029	2126	*2218**	2226	2319	0019	0119

	Ⓐ	⚒		⚒	Ⓐ	Ⓒ	⚒	Ⓑ	⑥	Ⓐ	Ⓒ		Ⓑ	⑥	Ⓑ	⑥	Ⓑ	⑥	⚒	†	Ⓐ	Ⓒ		Ⓑ		Ⓑ
Skien ....779 d.	0341	0441	0538	0634	*0725**	0736	0825j	*0925**	0925	*1025**	1036	*1125**	1225	*1225**	1320	*1325**	1424	1436	*1520**	1525	*1620**	1625	*1725**	*1825**	*1925**	*2025**
Porsgrunn..779 d.	0350	0450	0547	0643	*0743**	0745	0834j	*0943**	0934	*1043**	1045	*1143**	1234	*1243**	1329	*1343**	1433	1445	*1543**	1534	*1643**	1634	*1743**	*1843**	*1943**	*2043**
Larvik ....a.	0423	0523	0621	0718	*0807**	0818	0907j	*1007**	1007	*1107**	1118	*1207**	1307	*1307**	1402	*1407**	1506	1518	*1607**	1607	*1707**	1707	*1807**	*1907**	*2007**	*2107**
Larvik ....d.	0424	0524	0622	0719	0819	0819	0919	1019	1019	1119	1119	1219	1319	1319	1419	1419	1519	1519	1619	1619	1719	1719	1819	1919	2019	2119
Sandefjord.......d.	0438	0538	0638	0738	0838	0838	0938	1038	1038	1138	1138	1238	1338	1338	1438	1438	1538	1538	1638	1638	1738	1738	1838	1938	2038	2138
Torp ✈.............d.	0442	0542	0642	0742	0842	0842	0942	1042	1042	1142	1142	1242	1342	1342	1442	1442	1542	1542	1642	1642	1742	1742	1842	1942	2042	2142
Tønsberg ....d.	0459	0559	0659	0759	0859	0859	0959	1059	1059	1159	1159	1259	1359	1359	1459	1459	1559	1559	1659	1659	1759	1759	1859	1959	2059	2159
Skoppum ....d.	0509	0609	0709	0809	0909	0909	1009	1109	1109	1209	1209	1309	1409	1409	1509	1509	1609	1609	1709	1709	1809	1809	1909	2009	2109	2209
Holmestrand .....d.	0519	0619	0719	0819	0919	0919	1019	1119	1119	1219	1219	1319	1419	1419	1519	1519	1619	1619	1719	1719	1819	1819	1919	2019	2119	2219
Drammen............d.	0547	0647	0747	0847	0947	0947	1047	1147	1147	1247	1247	1347	1447	1447	1547	1547	1647	1647	1747	1747	1847	1847	1947	2047	2147	2247
Oslo S.......785 d.	0624	0724	0824	0924	1024	1024	1124	1224	1224	1324	1324	1424	1524	1524	1624	1624	1724	1724	1824	1824	1924	1924	2024	2124	2224	2324
Lillestrøm....785 d.	0635	0735	0835	0935	1035	1035	1135	1235	1235	1335	1335	1435	1535	1535	1635	1635	1735	1735	1835	1835	1935	1935	2035	2135	2235	2335
Oslo ✈ ● .785 d.	0649	0749	0849	0949	1049	1049	1149	1249	1249	1349	1349	1449	1549	1549	1649	1649	1749	1749	1849	1849	1949	1949	2049	2149	2249	2349
Eidsvoll ... 785 a.	0659	0759	0859	0959	1059	1059	1159	1259	1259	1359	1359	1459	1559	1559	1659	1659	1759	1759	1859	1859	1959	1959	2059	2159	2259	2359

j – By 🚌 on ①–⑤ to June 10. t – By 🚌 on ⑦ (Larvik d. 1740, Porsgrunn d. 1800, Skien a. 1818). * – By 🚌 Larvik - Skien and v.v. ● – Oslo Lufthavn Garderm

784 HAMAR - RØROS - TRONDHEIM

km		Ⓐ	⑥	Ⓐ	⚒n	Ⓑ	Ⓐ	Ⓒ		Ⓑr	Ⓑ	
0	**Hamar**....................d.	...	...	0810	1011	1210	1210	...	1607	1811	2017	...
32	Elverum....................d.	...	...	0833	1036	1235	1235	...	1633	1834	2042	...
64	Rena ....d.	...	...	0855	1059	1257	1257	...	1656	1859	2104	...
120	Koppang....................d.	...	...	0937	1141	1339	1339	...	1739	1941	2146	...
273	**Røros**.......................d.	0505	0703	1130	1337	1531	1537	1630	1937	2133	2339	...
384	Støren ....785 d.	0640	0833	...	...	...	1710	1802	2108	...	...	...
435	**Trondheim** S ....785 a.	0735	0928	...	...	...	1802	1855	2200	...	...	...

	Ⓐ	⚒r	Ⓐ		Ⓑn	⑦		Ⓐ
Trondheim S....785 d.	...	...	0545	0945	...	1350	...	1615
Støren ....785 d.	...	...	0640	1039	...	1446	...	1712
Røros.......................d.	0419	0617	0818	1217	1410	1623	1623	1847
Koppang...................d.	0611	0809	1015	1416	1605	1817	1817	...
Rena ....d.	0653	0854	1059	1458	1656	1859	1859	...
Elverum.....................d.	0715	0916	1121	1520	1718	1921	1921	...
Hamar......................a.	0740	0941	1146	1545	1743	1946	1946	...

n – Not ①–⑤ June 20 - Aug. 12. r – Not ①–⑤ July 4 - Aug. 12.

785 OSLO - LILLEHAMMER - ÅNDALSNES and TRONDHEIM

Subject to alteration until June

km		407	41	2341	311	2343	45	2345	47	2347	329	405	
		Ⓐe	▲	2351		Ⓐ		2355	Ⓑ	Ⓑ	Ⓑ	Ⓑ	
			R	R		R	R	R	R	R		R	
			✕⊡	🍷	🍷⊡	🍷	✕⊡	🍷	✕⊡	🍷	🍷⊡	✕N	
0	**Oslo** Sentral........★ d.	...	0802	...	0934	...	1402	...	1602	...	1834	2246	...
21	Lillestrøm ....★ d.	...	0813u	...	0945	...	1414u	...	1613u	...	1845	2321u	...
52	Oslo ✈ ⊖...........★ d.	...	0828u	...	0959	...	1429u	...	1629u	...	1859	2340u	...
127	**Hamar**.................★ d.	...	0923	...	1059	...	1524	...	1724	...	2000	0037	...
185	**Lillehammer**.......★ d.	...	1010	...	1146	1202	1612	...	1817	...	2109	0125	...
243	Ringebu ....d.	...	1052	...	...	1251	1653	...	1858	...	2149	0212	...
267	Vinstra ....d.	...	1107	...	...	1307	1713	...	1919	...	2204	0233	...
298	Otta.........................d.	...	1130	...	...	1330	1734	...	1941	...	2225	0259	...
344	Dombås ....d.	...	1202	1204	...	1407	1807	1810	2013	2016	2257	0343	...
458	**Åndalsnes** ....a.	...	|	1328	...	1535	|	1937	|	2134	...	|	...
430	Oppdal......................d.	0645	1300	...	...	...	1905	...	2110	...	...	0449	...
502	Støren..............784 d.	0735	1348	...	...	...	1957	...	2204	...	...	0550	...
553	**Trondheim** S....784 a.	0830	1431	...	...	...	2045	...	2249	...	...	0654	...

	308	2340	316	2342	42	2344	44	2346	46
	⚒	Ⓐ		2352				2356	Ⓑ
		R		R	R	R	R	ⒷR	R
	🍷⊡	🍷	🍷⊡	🍷	✕⊡	🍷	✕⊡	🍷	✕⊡
Trondheim S .784 d.	...	...	...	...	0823	...	1328	...	1530
Støren ....784 d.	...	...	...	...	0907	...	1417	...	1615
Oppdal.................. d.	...	...	...	...	1003	...	1509	...	1706
Åndalsnes........ d.	...	0738	...	0929f	|	1434	|	1628f	|
Dombås................ d.	0513	0900	...	1056	1101	1554	1608	1754	1806
Otta .... d.	0545	0931	...	...	1132	...	1639	...	1836
Vinstra.................. d.	0609	0954	...	...	1154	...	1700	...	1857
Ringebu................ d.	0625	1010	...	...	1210	...	1717	...	1915
Lillehammer ....★ d.	0710	1056	1111	...	1253	...	1758	...	1956
Hamar..............★ d.	0803	...	1203	...	1339	...	1843	...	2041
Oslo ✈ ⊖.........★ a.	0901	...	1301	...	1432s	...	1933s	...	2133s
Lillestrøm..........★ a.	0915	...	1315	...	1449s	...	1949s	...	2149s
Oslo Sentral .....★ a.	0926	...	1326	...	1503	...	2004	...	2204

🚌					Ⓐ	⚒	Ⓑ			Ⓑ¶	⑦	Ⓐ
Åndalsnes..............d.	0620z	1000	1340	1345	1550	1550	1800	1945	1945	2135	2135	2200
Molde......................a.	0750	1125	|	1510	|	1715	1925	|	2110	|	2250	2325
Ålesund...................a.	...	...	1540	...	1750	...	...	2145	...	2345	...	...

🚌	Ⓐ			⚒			Ⓑ	Ⓑ	Ⓑ
Ålesund .... d.	...	0710	...	...	1200	...	1400	...	...
Molde.................. d.	0610	|	0755	1000	|	1300	|	1440	2015
Åndalsnes............ a.	0735	0915	0920	1120	1405	1420	1605	1605	2130

🚌	⚒		Ⓐ		Ⓑ		⑤⑦		Ⓑ			
Oppdal skysstasjon.............d.	0530	...	1050	...	1315	...	1810	...	2120	...	...	...
Kristiansund.....................a.	0915	...	1425	...	1635	...	2125	...	0030	...	...	...

🚌	Ⓐ		Ⓐ	⑥		Ⓑ		⑤⑦	
Kristiansund.......... d.	0630	...	1040	1120	...	1315	...	1635	...
Oppdal skysstasjon a.	0940	...	1445	1445	...	1645	...	2010	...

	Ⓐ	Ⓐ		⚒		⚒		⚒						Ⓑ		Ⓑ		Ⓑ	
Oslo Sentral 771 783 d.	...	0634	0734	0834	0934	1034	1134	1234	1334	1434	1534	1634	1734	1834	1934	2034	2134	2234	2334
Lillestrøm............783 d.	...	0645	0745	0845	0945	1045	1145	1245	1345	1445	1545	1645	1745	1845	1945	2045	2145	2245	2345
Oslo ✈ ⊖ ...771 783 d.	...	0659	0759	0859	0959	1059	1159	1259	1359	1459	1559	1659	1759	1859	1959	2059	2159	2259	2359
Eidsvoll...............783 d.	...	0709	0809	0909	1009	1109	1209	1309	1409	1509	1609	1709	1809	1909	2009	2109	2209	2309	0009
Hamar....................... a.	...	0755	0852	0952	1052	1153	1252	1354	1458	1552	1652	1754	1854	1954	2055	2153	2252	2346	0047
Hamar....................... d.	0657	0758	0857	1000	1059	1158	1258	1356	1501	1600	1659	1801	1900	2000	2100	2159	2254	2348	0049
Lillehammer .... a.	0743	0842	0943	1045	1146	1244	1350	1443	1546	1649	1747	1857	1947	2057	2145	2243	2338	0034	0133

	Ⓐ			⚒		⚒		⚒								Ⓑ		Ⓑ	
Lillehammer .... d.	0413	...	0525	0610	0710	0810	0910	1011	1111	1212	1306	1411	1512	1611	1713	1814	1913	2014	2110
Hamar....................... a.	0459	...	0610	0656	0757	0856	0959	1058	1157	1257	1351	1456	1559	1658	1800	1859	1959	2059	2158
Hamar....................... d.	0501	...	0612	0703	0803	0901	1003	1101	1203	1303	1401	1500	1603	1700	1803	1904	2001	2101	2200
Eidsvoll...............783 d.	0541	...	0652	0752	0852	0952	1052	1152	1252	1352	1452	1552	1652	1752	1852	1952	2052	2152	2252
Oslo ✈ ⊖ ...771 783 d.	0603	...	0703	0803	0903	1003	1103	1203	1303	1403	1503	1603	1703	1803	1903	2003	2103	2203	2303
Lillestrøm............783 d.	0616	...	0716	0816	0916	1016	1116	1216	1316	1416	1516	1616	1716	1816	1916	2016	2116	2216	2316
Oslo Sentral 771 783 a.	0626	...	0726	0826	0926	1026	1126	1226	1326	1426	1526	1626	1726	1826	1926	2026	2126	2226	2326

N – Conveys 🛏 and 🛌2.
R – Reservation recommended.
e – Not June 20 - Aug. 12.
f – 6 minutes later from Aug. 22.
s – Stops to set down only.
u – Stops to pick up only.
z – 0630 on ⑥⑦.
⊡ – Conveys *NSB Komfort*.
⊖ – Oslo Lufthavn Gardermoen.
¶ – Journey is by taxi and is only availa[ble] for passengers from train **2347** (plea[se] inform the on train staff).
★ – See also panel below main table.
▲ – On ①–⑥ until July 13 by 🚌 Oslo - Lillehammer (Oslo 0740, Lillestrøm (Oslo ✈ 0800, Hamar 0900).

786 SOUTHWEST NORWAY 🚌 LINKS

BERGEN - TRONDHEIM (Operator: NOR-WAY Bussekspress ✆ +47 815 44 444)
Bergen ⊡ d. 1630 → Oppdal a. 0440 → Trondheim a. 0642.
Trondheim d. 2230 → Oppdal d. 0032 → Bergen ⊡ a. 1220.

BERGEN - ÅLESUND (Operator: NOR-WAY Bussekspress ✆ +47 815 44 444)
From Bergen ⊡ at 0800 daily (Ålesund a. 1745) and 1230 Ⓑ (Ålesund a. 2215 ①–⑤ / 2245 ⑦).
From Ålesund at 0810 Ⓐ / 0815 ⑥ (Bergen a. 1820) and 1110 daily (Bergen a. 2025).

BERGEN - KRISTIANSAND (Operator: NOR-WAY Bussekspress ✆ +47 815 44 444)
Bergen ⊡ d. 0820 → Odda d. 1120 → Haukeli a. 1300, d. 1455 → Kristiansand ⊡ a. 1900.
Kristiansand ⊡ d. 0845 → Haukeli a. 1250, d. 1455 → Odda a. 1645 → Bergen ⊡ a. 2005.

BERGEN - STAVANGER (Operator: NOR-WAY Bussekspress ✆ +47 815 44 444)
Journey time: 4 hrs 30 m – 5 hrs 30 m. From Bergen ⊡ at 0900, 1040 ⑦, 1100 Ⓐ, 1130 ⑥, 1300, 1445 Ⓐ, 1500 ⑦, 1600 Ⓒ, 1615 Ⓐ, 1700 Ⓑ and 1900. From Stavanger ⊙ at 0715 Ⓐ, 0845 ⑥, 0915 Ⓑ, 1015 Ⓐ, 1045 Ⓒ, 1245 ⑥, 1315 Ⓑ, 1510 Ⓐ, 1515 Ⓒ, 1715 Ⓑ, 1835 Ⓑ and 1845 ⑥.

BERGEN - ODDA ★ 🚌/⛴ *Journey time: 2 hrs 45 m – 2 hrs 55 m.*
From Bergen ⊡ at 0820, 1150 Ⓑ and 2055 Ⓑ. From Odda ⊡ at 0530 ⚒, 1710 and 204

VOSS - ODDA ★ *Journey time: 1 hr 55 m – 2 hrs 10 m.*
From Voss at 0920, 1125 ⚒, 1250, 1550 ⚒, 1745 and 2205 Ⓑ.
From Odda ⊡ at 0620 Ⓐ, 0625 ⑥, 0720, 1225, 1410 ⚒‡, 1700, 2030 Ⓐ and 2035 ⑦.

VOSS - ULVIK ★ *Journey time: 55 – 65 minutes. A change of bus may be required.*
From Voss at 0755 Ⓐ, 0920 Ⓐ, 1005, 1120 ⚒, 1440 Ⓐ, 1550 ⚒, 1745, 1905 Ⓑ and 220
From Ulvik ⊡ at 0610 Ⓐ, 0725 Ⓐ, 0830, 1045, 1330 Ⓐ, 1515, 1740, 2130 ⑦ and 2135 Ⓐ

‡ – 1405 on schooldays.
⊡ – Bus station.
⊙ – Stavanger Byterminalen.
★ – Operator: Tide Buss AS / Skyss ✆ +47 55 55 90 70.

TRONDHEIM - BODØ and NARVIK — 787

	1781	1783	475		473	473	1785	471	1791		479	477
	Ⓐ	Ⓐ		🚌	⚒	Ⓐ	Ⓐk		Ⓐ	🚌	Ⓑk	Ⓑ
	🍷	🍷	N R	◇	🍷R	🍷R	🍷	✗R	🍷	◇	🍷R	🍷R
Trondheim S ...d.	...	...	2340	...	...	...	...	0738	...	...	...	1600
Værnes ✈ ‡ .....d.	...	...	0006	...	...	...	...	0811	...	...	...	1630u
Stjørdal............d.	...	...	0011	...	...	...	...	0817	...	...	...	1636u
Steinkjer ....d.	...	...	0129	...	...	...	...	0946	...	...	...	1801u
Grong ....d.	...	...	0240	...	...	...	...	1053	...	...	...	1909
Mosjøen ....d.	...	...	0458	...	0655	0655	...	1309	...	...	1655	2130
Mo i Rana.........d.	...	...	0608	...	0759	0800	...	1420	...	...	1757	2238
Rognan..............d.	0542	0642	0802	...	...	0953	1125	1615	1745	...	1941	...
Bodø ⊖........d.	|	|	|	0715	...	|	|	|	|	1645	|	...
Fauske ....a.	0601	0701	0825	0820	...	1013	1144	1637	1804	1750	1959	...
Fauske ....d.	0602	0702	0830	0850	...	1015	1145	1646	1811	1810	2000	...
Narvik ⊡ ♣..a.	|	|	|	1330	...	|	|	|	|	2300	|	...
Bodø................a.	0642	0742	0915	...	...	1055	1225	1728	1850	...	2040	...

	478	470	1784		472	1790	474		476	1792
		Ⓐk	Ⓐk	🚌		Ⓐ	Ⓑ	🚌		②–⑥
	🍷R	🍷R	🍷	◇	✗R	🍷	🍷R	◇	N R	🍷
Bodø.............d.	...	0747	1012	...	1227	1605	1730	...	2110	2345
Narvik ⊡ ♣d.	...	|	|	0700	|	|	|	1610	|	|
Fauske ....a.	...	0827	1058	1155	1308	1644	1808	2110	2154	0025
Fauske ....d.	...	0828	1059	1210	1311	1646	1809	2125	2158	0026
Bodø ⊖.....a.	...	|	|	1320	|	|	|	2230	|	|
Rognan..........d.	...	0847	1119	...	1332	1705	1832	...	2219	0045
Mo i Rana......d.	0815	1032	...	...	1531	...	2024	...	0020	...
Mosjøen.........d.	0926	1138	...	...	1641	...	2128	...	0140	...
Grong ....d.	1146	...	...	...	1907	...	...	...	0426	...
Steinkjer ....d.	1251	...	...	...	2016	...	...	...	0540	...
Stjørdal..........d.	1404	...	...	...	2133	...	...	...	0705	...
Værnes ✈ ‡ ..d.	1406	...	...	...	2135	...	...	...	0707	...
Trondheim....a.	1437	...	...	...	2205	...	...	...	0747	...

Local services Trondheim - Steinkjer and v.v.

▶	Ⓐ	⚒					Ⓐ		Ⓐ			Ⓑ
Trondheim S ...d.	0610	0710	0910	1110	1310	1510	1610	1710	1810	1910	2110	2310
Hell ● ....d.	0643	0743	0942	1141	1341	1541	1641	1741	1841	1941	2141	2341
Værnes ✈ ‡ ● ..d.	0645	0745	0944	1143	1343	1543	1643	1743	1843	1943	2143	2343
Stjørdal.............d.	0652	0752	0952	1152	1352	1552	1652	1752	1852	1952	2152	2347
Steinkjer..........a.	0819	0916	1116	1320	1516	1716	1816	1916	2016	2116	2313	0105

▶	Ⓐ								Ⓐk	
Steinkjer.......d.	0528	0728	0928	1128	1328	1528	1728	1925	2028	2128
Stjørdal..........d.	0652	0852	1052	1252	1452	1652	1852	2052	2152	2252
Værnes ✈ ‡ ● d.	0654	0854	1054	1254	1454	1654	1854	2054	2154	2254
Hell ● ....d.	0657	0857	1057	1257	1457	1657	1857	2057	2157	2257
Trondheim S.a.	0732	0932	1132	1332	1532	1732	1932	2132	2227	2332

Conveys 🛏, 2 and ✗.
Reservation recommended.

Not June 20 - Aug. 12.
Not July 4 - Aug. 12.
Stops to pick up only.

● – Trains stop on request.
⊡ – Bus station.
⊖ – Bodø Sentrumsterminalen.
‡ – Station for Trondheim Airport.
◇ – Operator: Saltens Bilruter Nordlandsbuss.

▶ – Additional services on Ⓐ Trondheim - Stjørdal - Steinkjer and v.v.:
From Trondheim at 0515 **k**, 0810, 1010 **k**, 1210, 1410 **k**, 1445 **k** and 1545 **n**.
From Steinkjer at 0500 **k**, 0600 **n**, 0628, 0828, 1028, 1228 **k**, 1428, 1628 **k** and 1828.

♣ – 🚌 **Narvik - Svolvær** (Lofoten). Operator: Veolia Transport. *253 km.* Journey time: 4 hrs 5 m - 4 hrs 30 m. **From Narvik** at 0920 ⑥, 0940 Ⓐ, 1145 ⑦ and 1530. **From Svolvær** sentrum at 0950, 1510 ⚒ and 1655 ⑦.

bject to alteration on and around the dates of public holidays

LAPLAND 🚌 LINKS — 789

rvik – Tromsø – Alta

Operator: Torghatten

	①–⑤	①–⑥			Ⓑ				⑦	
Narvik bus station ......d.	0520	...	...	1250	...	...	...	1520	1840	...
Narvik rail station ....d.	|	...	...	|	...	...	←	|	1845	...
Nordkjosbotn ....d.	0825	0825	...	1615	1620	...	1620	1845	2200	...
Tromsø Prostneset .d.	0930	0930	...	→	|	1600	1730	1950	2305	...
Lyngseidet...................d.	...	...	...	...	1731	1745	...	...	...	...
Alta..........................a.	...	...	...	...	...	2223	...	...	...	...

km		①–⑤			①–⑥	①–⑤		⑦	⑦	⑦
0	**Alta**...........................d.	...	...	...	1055	...	...	1410	...	...
224	Lyngseidet...............d.	...	...	...	1545	1545	...	1915	1915	...
293	**Tromsø** Prostneset .d.	0610	1000	...	1725	|	1600	2055	|	1920
	Nordkjosbotn ....d.	0725	1105	...	...	1653	1705	...	2023	2025
	Narvik rail station ....a.	|	|	...	...	...	|	...	...	|
	Narvik bus station ......a.	1030	1415	...	...	...	2010	...	...	2330

a – Hammerfest – Karasjok – Kirkenes

Operator: Snelandia

	①–⑤ N	Ⓑ	Ⓑ	⑦ N	①–⑤	①–⑤	Ⓑ		⑤⑦	Ⓑ	⑤⑦
Alta.........................d.	...	0900	...	...	...	1145	...	1430	1605	1950	...
Hammerfest ....d.	0720	|	...	1220	1225	|	1515	|	|	|	2040
Skaidi.......................d.	0820	1045	1145	1320	1325	1330	1615	1630	|	2120	2140
Hammerfest ....a.	|	|	1245	|	|	|	|	|	|	2220	|
Olderfjord ....d.	0845	1115	...	1345	1400	1400	1655	1655	|	...	2220
Honningsvåg ★ ....a.	|	1255	...	|	|	1545	|	1835	|	...	|
Nordkapp...............a.	|	1340**k**	...	|	|	...	|	...	|	...	|
Lakselv.....................d.	0955	...	...	1450	1515	...	1750	...	|	...	2320
Karasjok...................d.	|	...	...	|	1625	...	1900	...	1927	...	0030
Tanabru ....d.	1400	...	...	1845	...	...	...	...	|	...	...
Kirkenes ♠ ....a.	1630	...	...	2105	...	...	...	...	2335	...	...

	①–⑤	①–⑤	Ⓑ	Ⓑ	①–⑤ N		Ⓑ	Ⓑ	⑦ N	⑤⑦	⑤⑦
Kirkenes ♠ ....d.	...	...	...	...	0630	...	...	...	1120	1510	...
Tanabru ....d.	...	...	...	...	0855	...	...	...	1355	|	...
Karasjok.................d.	...	0615	...	...	|	...	1430	...	|	1928	2000
Lakselv ....d.	...	0730	...	...	1245	...	1545	...	1745	|	2115
Nordkapp...........d.	...	|	...	...	|	1440**k**	|	...	|	|	|
Honningsvåg ★ .d.	0655	|	...	0935	|	1520	|	...	|	|	|
Olderfjord..............d.	0845	0845	...	1115	1345	1655	1655	...	1845	|	2220
Hammerfest.......d.	|	|	1040	|	|	|	|	1640	|	|	|
Skaidi.....................d.	0910	0915	1140	1145	1405	1725	1725	1739	1905	|	2250
Hammerfest.......a.	|	1015	...	|	1505	|	1825	|	2005	|	2350
Alta.......................a.	1050	...	...	1320	...	1900	...	1900	...	2240	...

vaniemi – Muonio – Tromsø

Operator:	G	E	G
Rovaniemi bus station d.	0800	1130	1710
Rovaniemi rail station d.	0820	1100	1715
Kittilä ....d.	1040	1335	1925
Muonio ....d.	1300**z**	1505	2040
Karesuvanto ....d.	1435	1625**b**	...
Kilpisjärvi ⊡ .... FI d.	1625	1810**b**	...
Nordkjosbotn .... NO d.	...	1830**b**	...
Tromsø Prostneset .... a.	...	1930**b**	...

	G	E	G
Tromsø Prostneset .. d.	...	0730**e**	...
Nordkjosbotn...... NO d.	...	0830**e**	...
Kilpisjärvi ⊡ .... FI d.	...	1110**e**	1315
Karesuvanto.............d.	...	1240**e**	1515
Muonio.....................d.	0850	1405	1700**f**
Kittilä.......................d.	1015	1530	1835
Rovaniemi rail station a.	1213**x**	1725	2035**x**
Rovaniemi bus station a.	1215	1735	2040

vaniemi – Karasjok, Nordkapp, Tanabru, Kirkenes and Murmansk

Operator:	G	G	G	G	G	E	E		E	G/L
	①–⑤	①–⑤		①–⑤	⑥⑦		D			Ⓑ
Rovaniemi bus station d.	0530	...	0800	...	...	1145	1145	...	1720	2030
Rovaniemi rail station d.	|	...	0820	...	...	1100	1100	...	1725	2045
Sodankylä..................d.	0735	...	1020	...	...	1345	1345	...	1915	2235
Ivalo .... FI d.	1005	1100	1250	1300	1400	1625**f**	1625**f**	...	2125	0045
Inari...................... FI d.	...	1135	...	1340	1440	1655	1655	...	2200	...
Karasjok ⊖.......... NO a.	...	...	...	...	...	1740	1740	...	|	...
Lakselv, Statoil ....a.	...	...	...	...	...	...	1855	...	|	...
Honningsvåg...............a.	...	...	...	...	...	...	2135	...	|	...
Nordkapp ....a.	...	...	...	...	...	...	2215	...	|	...
Tanabru .... NO a.	...	...	...	...	...	...	...	...	2355**r**	...

Operator:	E		G	G/L		E	E		G	G	
			①–⑤	①–⑥		A					
anabru .... NO d.	0330**t**	...	...	...	...	...	...	...	...	...	...
dkapp....................d.	|	...	...	...	...	0100	...	...	...	...	...
ningsvåg................d.	|	...	...	...	...	0510**g**	...	...	...	...	...
selv, Statoil ....d.	|	...	...	...	...	0810	...	...	...	...	...
asjok ⊖............ NO d.	|	...	...	...	...	0915	0915	...	...	...	...
.... FI d.	0715	...	1105	...	...	1210	1210	...	1415	...	...
.... FI d.	0805	...	1140	1215	...	1315**f**	1315**f**	...	1450	1615	...
ankylä....................d.	1020	...	...	1500	...	1545	1545	...	...	1845	...
aniemi rail station . a.	1155	...	...	1715	...	1725	1725	...	...	2030	...
aniemi bus station a.	1205	...	...	1710	...	1730	1730	...	...	2035	...

rator codes

Eskelisen Lapin Linjat.
Gold Line.
L – Liikenne O. Niemelä.
M – Murmanskavtotrans.
P – Pikakuljetus Rovaniemi.

Nordkapp
Honningsvåg
Hammerfest
Tanabru
Skaidi
Ol.
Kirkenes
Alta
La.
Murmansk
Tromsø
Ly.
Karasjok
Nordkjosbotn
Inari
Ivalo
St Peterburg 1905
Svolvær 787
Narvik
Muonio
Boden, Stockholm 761 / 767
Sodankylä
Fauske 787
Rovaniemi
Trondheim, Oslo 787
Oulu, Helsinki 794

A – June 2 - Aug. 21.
B – May 1 - Sept. 30.
C – May 2 - Oct. 1.
D – June 1 - Aug. 20.
N – From May 1.

b – Runs Muonio - Tromsø June 1 - Sept. 17.
e – June 2 - Sept. 18.
f – Arrives 30 – 35 minutes earlier.
g – Arrives 0140.
k – May 1 - Sept. 30.
r – ③④⑤⑦ (Ⓑ June 15 - Aug. 15).
t – ①④⑤⑥ (①–⑥ June 16 - Aug. 16).
x – Stops on request.
z – Arrives 1200.

⊡ – Trekking centre (Retkeilykeskus).
⊖ – Karasjok Scandic Hotel
★ – **Honningsvåg - Nordkapp** and v.v. *34 km.* Journey time: 45 minutes. **From Honningsvåg** (Nordkapphuset) at 0745 **B**, 1130, 1550 **B**, 1840 **B** and 2130 **B** **From Nordkapp** at 0015 **C**, 0840 **B**, 1345, 1640 **B** and 1935 **B**.
♠ – **Kirkenes - Murmansk** (RU) and v.v. Journey time: 4 hours. Operated by Pasvikturist AS. www.pasvikturist.no Please check visa requirements. From Kirkenes at 1500 (1400 during winter time). From Murmansk at 0700.

FI – Finland (East European Time).
NO – Norway (Central European Time).
RU – Russia (Moskva Time).

FINLAND

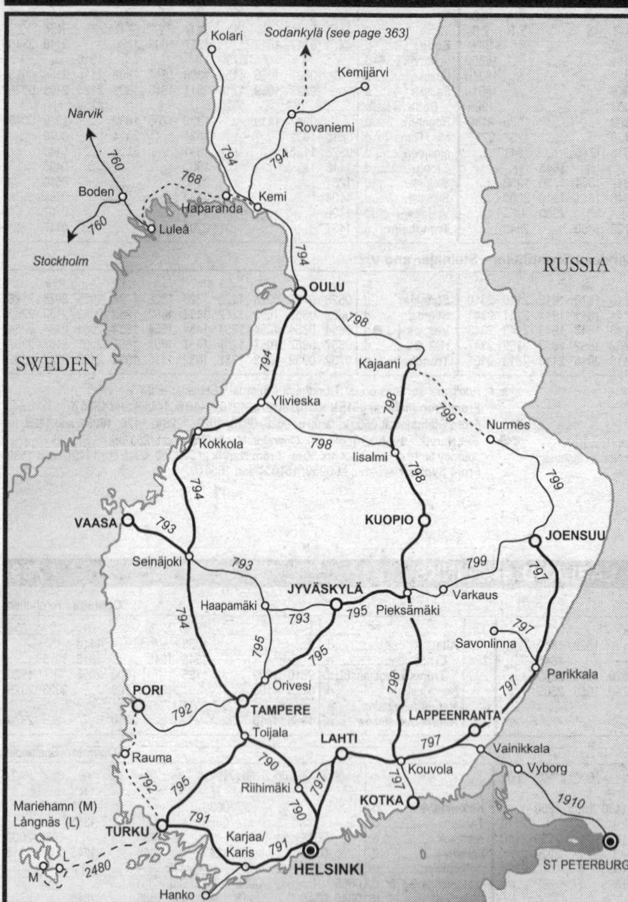

Operator: **VR** – VR-Yhtymä Oy www.vr.fi

Tickets and train types: For all except purely local journeys, tickets are always sold for travel by a specific train or combination of trains. Please note that travel classes in Finland are referred to as *Extra* (1st), *Eco* (2nd). There are four different pricing-scal corresponding to each of the following train ty (in descending order of cost):

- ▶ **S 220 Pendolino** (e.g. *S* **123**) – high-speed tilt trains (220 km/h), with *Extra* and *Eco* class se Reservation compulsory.
- ▶ **InterCity** (e.g. *IC* **124**) – quality fast trains betv major centres, with *Extra* and *Eco* class seats reservable.
- ▶ **Express**, *pikajunat* (train number only shown, **128**) – other fast trains, with *Eco* class seats, reservable. Night expresses convey sleeping-c and *Eco* class seats only (marked ★ in the tab
- ▶ **Regional**, *taajamajunat* (no train number show stopping-trains, normally with *Eco* class seats

S 220, InterCity and Express tickets include a reservation when purchased in advance.

Rail tickets are **not** valid on 🚌 services (exc Kemi - Tornio). However, special combined tra bus fares are available on certain routes.

Services: ✕ indicates a train with a restaurant car.

Trains marked 🍸 convey a *MiniBistro* trolley service.

A variable supplement is payable for travel in sleeping-cars (🛏) in addition to the appropria *Eco* class **Express** fare – the price to be paid depends on the date of travel and the type of accommodation required. A higher supplemen charged for occupancy of a single-berth cabin.

Timings: Timings are valid, unless otherwise indicated, **June 20 - August 14**, 2016.

In these tables Ⓐ = ①–⑤, ⚒ = ①–⑥.

Changes to the normal service pattern are li to occur on and around the dates of public holidays (see page 2).

790 HELSINKI - TAMPERE

For through journeys to / from **Oulu** and **Rovaniemi**, see Table **794**. For through journeys to / from **Jyväskylä** and **Pieksämäki**, see Table **795**.

km		IC 81		IC 21	IC 141	IC 41		IC 165	IC 167	IC 23	S 143	IC 43	S 169		IC 25	IC 173	IC 145		S 45	S 151		IC 27	IC 147	S 47	IC 177		S
		✕	2	✕	✕	✕	2	✕	✕	✕	[R]✕	✕	[R]✕	2	✕	🍸	✕	2	[R]✕	[R]✕	2	✕	✕	[R]✕	✕	2	[R]
		Ⓐ	Ⓐ	⚒		Ⓐ	Ⓐ	Ⓐ												Ⓑ			P		Ⓑ		
0	**Helsinki** d.	0527	0542	0627	0706	0727	0742	0827	0906	0927	1006	1027	1127	1142	1227	1306	1327	1342	1427	1506	1512	1527	1606	1627	1706	1712	1
3	Pasila d.	0533	0547	0633	0712	0733	0747	0833	0912	0933	1012	1033	1133	1147	1233	1312	1333	1347	1433	1512	1517	1533	1612	1633	1712	1717	1
16	Tikkurila ⊙ d.	0543	0556	0643	0722	0743	0756	0843	0922	0943	1022	1043	1143	1156	1243	1322	1343	1356	1443	1522	1526	1543	1622	1643	1722	1726	1
71	Riihimäki d.	|	0640	|	0752	|	0840	|	0952	|	1052	|	|	1240	|	1352	|	1440	|	1552	1613	|	1652	|	1752	1813	
108	Hämeenlinna d.	|	0702	|	0811	|	0902	|	1011	|	1111	|	|	1302	|	1411	|	1502	|	1611	1636	|	1711	|	1811	1836	
147	Toijala d.	|	0725	|	0831	|	0925	|	1031	|	1131	|	|	1325	|	1431	|	1525	|	1631	1659	|	1731	|	1831	1859	
187	**Tampere** a.	0656	0748	0756	0852	0856	0948	0956	1052	1056	1152	1156	1256	1348	1356	1452	1456	1548	1556	1652	1722	1656	1752	1756	1852	1922	1

	IC 179	IC 29	IC 149	263	IC 265		S 53	IC 187	S 91	IC 273	
	✕	✕	✕			2	[R]✕	✕	[R]✕		
				★	★	Ⓑ	N	⚒	⑦	★	
Helsinki d.	1806	1827	1906	1820	1852	1942	2027	2206	2206	2152	...
Pasila d.	1812	1833	1912	1827	1900	1947	2033	2212	2212	2200	...
Tikkurila ⊙ d.	1822	1843	1922	1910	1944	1956	2043	2222	2222	2244	...
Riihimäki d.	1852	|	1952	1959	2022	2043	|	2252	2252	2322	...
Hämeenlinna d.	1911	|	2011	2025	2048	2106	|	2311	2311	2348	...
Toijala d.	1931	|	2031	2050	|	2129	|	2331	2331	|	...
Tampere a.	1952	1956	2052	2118	2138	2152	2156	2352	2352	0040	...

	IC 266	IC 160	270	IC 162	IC 274	272	S 40	IC 164	S 42	IC 150	S 44	S 140	IC
		✕		✕			[R]✕	✕	[R]✕	✕	[R]✕	[R]✕	
	★	Ⓐ	★	Ⓐ	★	★	Ⓐ	P	⚒	⚒	⚒		
Tampere d.	0430	0520	0543	0604	0612	0622	0702	0707	0802	0807	0902	0907	1
Toijala d.	0457	0541	0610	0627	0640	0701	|	0728	|	0828	|	0928	
Hämeenlinna d.	0524	0601	0637	0648	0709	0753	|	0749	|	0849	|	0949	
Riihimäki d.	0548	0620	0702	0708	0736	0818	|	0809	|	0909	|	1009	
Tikkurila ⊙ a.	0625	0647	0746	0737	|	0856	0818	0837	0918	0937	1018	1037	1
Pasila a.	0658	0656	0824	0746	0852	0929	0827	0846	0927	0946	1027	1046	1
Helsinki a.	0706	0702	0832	0752	0900	0937	0833	0852	0933	0952	1033	1052	1

	S 54		IC 170	S 46	IC 142	IC 22	IC 174	S 172	S 178		IC 48	IC 144	IC 24		IC 86	S 84	IC 180		IC 50	S 146	IC 26	S 88	IC 184 / IC 186	S 56	IC 148	IC 28	S
	[R]✕	2	✕	[R]✕	✕	✕	✕	[R]✕	[R]✕	2	✕	✕	✕	2	✕	[R]✕	🍸	2	✕	[R]✕	✕	[R]✕	P✕	[R]✕	✕	✕	[R]
	⑦						L	⑤							Ⓑ	⑥	Ⓑ					⑤⑦		⑤⑦			
Tampere d.	1002	1006	1102	1202	1207	1302	1307	1307	1402	1411	1502	1507	1602	1611	1702	1702	1707	1737	1802	1807	1902	2002	2007	2102	2107	2202	23
Toijala d.	|	1029	|	|	1228	|	1328	1328	|	1434	|	1528	|	1634	|	|	1728	1800	|	1828	|	|	2028	|	2128	|	
Hämeenlinna d.	|	1052	|	|	1249	|	1349	1349	|	1457	|	1549	|	1657	|	|	1749	1823	|	1849	|	|	2049	|	2149	|	
Riihimäki d.	|	1114	|	|	1309	|	1409	1409	|	1519	|	1609	|	1719	|	|	1809	1845	|	1909	|	|	2109	|	2209	|	
Tikkurila ⊙ a.	1118	1203	1218	1318	1337	1418	1437	1437	1518	1603	1618	1637	1718	1803	1818	1818	1837	1933	1918	1937	2018	2118	2137	2218	2237	2318	0
Pasila a.	1127	1212	1227	1327	1346	1427	1446	1446	1527	1612	1627	1646	1727	1812	1827	1827	1846	1942	1927	1946	2027	2127	2146	2227	2246	2327	0
Helsinki a.	1133	1217	1233	1333	1352	1433	1452	1452	1533	1617	1633	1652	1733	1817	1833	1833	1852	1947	1933	1952	2033	2133	2152	2233	2252	2333	0

Regional trains (2nd class only) HELSINKI - RIIHIMÄKI and v.v. See also note ⊠.

km			Ⓐ								
0	**Helsinki** d.	0042	0512	0612	0712	0812	0912	1012	1042	and	2342
3	Pasila d.	0047	0517	0617	0717	0817	0917	1017	1047		2347
16	Tikkurila ⊙ d.	0056	0526	0626	0726	0826	0926	1026	1056	hourly	2356
37	Järvenpää d.	0111	0541	0641	0741	0841	0941	1041	1111		0011
59	Hyvinkää d.	0127	0557	0657	0757	0857	0957	1057	1127	until	0027
71	**Riihimäki** a.	0135	0605	0705	0805	0905	1005	1105	1135		0035

		⑥⑦	Ⓐ	Ⓐ							
Riihimäki d.	0411	0511	0525	0555	0625	and	2025	2055	2155	2255	2
Hyvinkää d.	0420	0520	0533	0603	0633		2033	2103	2203	2303	0
Järvenpää d.	0437	0537	0547	0617	0647	hourly	2047	2117	2217	2317	0
Tikkurila ⊙ d.	0502	0602	0603	0633	0703		2103	2133	2233	2333	0
Pasila a.	0517	0617	0612	0642	0712	until	2112	2142	2242	2342	0
Helsinki a.	0522	0622	0617	0647	0717		2117	2147	2247	2347	0

L – Not ⑤.
N – ①②③④⑦.
P – To / from Pori (Table **792**).

⊙ – For Helsinki ✈ Vantaa.
★ – Overnight train to / from northern Finland. Conveys 🛏, 💺 and ✕. For through cars and days of running see Table **794**.

⊠ – Additional journeys: **From Helsinki** at 0542 Ⓐ, 0642 Ⓐ, 0742 Ⓐ, 0842 0942 ⚒, 1112 and hourly until 2012. **From Riihimäki** at 0655 Ⓐ, 0755 0855 Ⓐ, 0955 ⚒, 1055 ⚒, 1155 and hourly until 1955.

HELSINKI - TURKU and HANKO 791

	IC 971		IC 943			IC 979	IC 981	IC 945	S 947		IC 951			IC 955	IC 957	IC 969	IC 959	IC 924	IC 961			IC 963	IC 965		S 967
	✕ Ⓐ		🍷 Ⓐ	2 Ⓐ	🚌 Ⓐ	🍷 Ⓐ	🍷 ⑥	✕	Ⓡ✕ ⚒		✕	2	🚌 Ⓐ	🍷	🍷 Ⓑ	🍷 Ⓐ	🍷 ⑥⑦		✕ Ⓑ	2	🚌 Ⓐ	✕	🍷 Ⓑ		Ⓡ✕
Helsinki d.	0517	...	0628	0635	...	0730	0737	0837	0937	...	1137	1243	...	1337	1437	1532	1537	...	1637	1643	...	1737	1837	...	2037
Pasila d.	0523	...	0634	0639	...	0736	0743	0843	0943	...	1143	1247	...	1343	1443	1538	1543	...	1643	1647	...	1743	1843	...	2043
Kirkkonummi d.	0548	...	|	0716	0730	|	|	|	|	...	|	1324	1330	|	|	|	|	...	|	1724	1730	|	|	...	|
Karjaa / Karis ★ d.	0615	...	0724	...	0820	0832	0832	0932	1032	...	1232	...	1420	1432	1532	1627	1632	...	1732	...	1820	1832	1932	...	2132
Salo d.	0652	...	0800	...	...	0900	0900	1000	1100	...	1300	...	...	1500	1600	1700	1700	...	1800	...	...	1900	2000	...	2200
Turku a.	0722	...	0830	...	...	0930	0930	1030	1130	...	1330	...	...	1530	1630	1730	1730	1812	1830	...	...	1930	2030	...	2230
Turku satama a.	0732	...	...	...	...	...	...	...	...	...	...	...	...	...	...	...	...	1819	...	...	...	1939	...	...	...

	IC 942			IC 944		S 978	IC 948	IC 950		IC 954			S 958	IC 960	IC 962			IC 964	IC 966	IC 988		IC 972				
	🍷 Ⓐ	🚌 Ⓐ	2 Ⓐ	✕ Ⓐ		Ⓡ✕ ⚒	✕	🍷 ⚒		🍷	🚌 Ⓐ	2	Ⓡ✕	✕ Ⓑ	✕	🚌 Ⓐ	2 Ⓐ	✕ Ⓑ	🍷	🍷 Ⓑ		✕				
satama d.	...	...	...	...	...	...	0810	...	...	...	...	...	...	...	...	...	...	...	...	...	...	2020	...	...	...	...
u d.	0532	...	...	0622	...	0730	0830	0930	...	1130	...	...	1330	1430	1530	...	...	1630	1730	1830	...	2030	...	...	...	...
d.	0603	...	...	0653	...	0801	0901	1001	...	1201	...	...	1401	1501	1601	...	...	1701	1801	1901	...	2101	...	...	...	...
a / Karis ★ d.	0630	0633	...	0720	...	0828	0928	1028	...	1228	1233	...	1428	1528	1628	1633	...	1728	1828	1928	...	2128	...	...	...	...
onummi d.	|	0723	0730	|	...	|	|	|	...	|	1323	1338	|	|	|	1723	1737	|	|	|	...	2155	...	...	...	...
a a.	0719	...	0806	0809	...	0917	1017	1117	...	1317	...	1414	1517	1617	1717	...	1814	1817	1917	2017	...	2220	...	...	...	...
nki a.	0725	...	0811	0815	...	0923	1023	1123	...	1323	...	1419	1523	1623	1723	...	1819	1823	1923	2023	...	2226	...	...	...	...

KARJAA / KARIS - HANKO and v.v. *50 km.* 2nd class only. Journey: 40 minutes.
From Karjaa at 0730 Ⓐ, 0939, 1239, 1439, 1639, 1839 and 2139.
From Hanko at 0632 Ⓐ, 0840, 1140, 1340, 1535, 1740 and 2040.

TAMPERE and TURKU - PORI 792

t trains convey ✕

	IC 461		IC 465	IC 467	IC 469	IC 471	IC 471	IC 473	IC 475	
	⚒						Ⓑ	Ⓑ		
Helsinki **790** d.	...	...	...	...	...	...	1606*	...	...	...
Tampere d.	0807	...	1215	1415	1615	1815	1815	2007	2207	...
Pori a.	0937	...	1345	1547	1747	1947	1947	2137	2337	...

	IC 164	IC 462	IC 466		IC 464		IC 468	IC 470	IC 472	IC 186
	⚒	⚒							⚒	⑦
Pori d.	0520	0615	0715	...	1015	...	1415	1615	1815	1815
Tampere a.	0650	0745	0850	...	1145	...	1545	1747	1945	1945
Helsinki **790** a.	0852	...	...	...	...	...	...	...	...	2152

🚌 TURKU - RAUMA - PORI ⊠

	🚌	🚌	🚌	🚌	🚌	🚌	🚌	🚌	🚌	🚌
	Ⓐ							Ⓑ	Ⓑ	
Turku bus station d.	0600	0815	1100	1500	...	1630	1800	...	1830	2030
Rauma bus station d.	|	0945	1230	|	1615	1805	|	1915	2010	|
Pori bus station a.	0815	1035	1320	1715	1715	...	2015	2015	...	2235

	🚌	🚌	🚌	🚌	🚌	🚌	🚌	🚌	🚌	🚌
		Ⓐ	Ⓐ	⚒						Ⓑ
Pori bus station d.	0530	0700	...	0830	0900	...	1200	1700	1900	2005
Rauma bus station d.	|	|	0850	0940	|	1040	1250	1800	|	2100
Turku bus station a.	0740	0915	1020	...	1115	1220	1415	1925	2115	...

Train number **147** Helsinki - Tampere.

⊠ – Selected journeys only (many additional services operate).

JYVÄSKYLÄ - SEINÄJOKI - VAASA 793

For full service Seinäjoki - Vaasa and v.v., see Table **794**.

		IC 41			S 47					
	2 ⚒	✕		2	Ⓡ✕					
Jyväskylä d.	0600	...	...	1625	...	...	...	...	...	...
Haapamäki d.	0707	...	...	1741	...	...	...	...	...	...
Alavus d.	0813	...	...	1842	...	...	...	...	...	...
Seinäjoki **794** d.	0845	1028	...	1913	1920	...	...	...	...	...
Vaasa **794** a.	...	1115	...	...	2007	...	...	...	...	...

	S 46			S 456						
	Ⓡ✕	2		Ⓡ✕ ⑤⑦	2 Ⓑ					
Vaasa **794** d.	0940	...	...	1830	...	...	...	...	...	...
Seinäjoki **794** d.	1027	1212	...	1917	1941	...	...	...	...	...
Alavus d.	...	1245	...	...	2014	...	...	...	...	...
Haapamäki d.	...	1352	...	...	2121	...	...	...	...	...
Jyväskylä a.	...	1457	...	...	2226	...	...	...	...	...

TAMPERE - VAASA, OULU, KOLARI and ROVANIEMI 794

	IC 273		IC 21	IC 711	IC 41	IC 41		IC 23	IC 413	IC 43		IC 25	IC 415	S 45	IC 27	S 47	S 51	S 51	S 49	IC 29	S 457		S 53	263	IC 265
	★⊕		✕ ⚒	2 K	✕ ⑥⑦	✕ Ⓐ		✕	2🍷	✕		✕	✕ Ⓑ	✕	✕	Ⓡ✕	Ⓡ✕ Ⓑ	Ⓡ✕ ④⑤	Ⓡ✕ Ⓑ	✕	Ⓡ✕		Ⓡ✕ B	★ A	★
Helsinki **790** d.	2152	...	0627	...	*0706*	0727	...	0927	...	1027	...	1227	...	1427	1527	1627	1627	1627	1727	1827	...	...	2027	1820	1852
Tampere d.	0115	...	0800	...	0900	0900	...	1100	...	1200	...	1400	...	1600	1700	1800	1800	1800	1900	2000	...	...	2200	2134	2211
Parkano d.	0211	...	|	...	0943	0943	...	|	...	1243	...	|	...	1635	|	1842	1842	1842	|	|	...	...	2234	|	2306
Seinäjoki a.	0302	...	0904	...	1016	1016	...	1204	...	1316	...	1504	...	1717	1804	1916	1916	1916	2004	2104	...	...	2308	2335	0008
Seinäjoki d.	0304	...	0908	...	1028	1028	...	1208	...	1328	...	1508	...	1720	1808	1920	1925	1925	2008	2108	2112	...	...	2338	0010
Vaasa a.	|	...	|	...	1115	1115	...	|	...	1415	...	|	...	1807	|	2007	|	|	2055	|	2159	...	...	|	|
Kokkola d.	0446	...	1023	...	...	...	...	1313	...	...	...	1623	...	...	1913	...	2045	2047	...	2213	...	...	...	0124	0139
Ylivieska d.	0546	...	1121	...	...	...	...	1409	...	...	...	1721	...	...	2009	...	...	2146	...	2310	...	...	...	0240	0315
Oulu a.	0727	...	1235	...	...	...	...	1515	...	...	...	1847	...	...	2115	...	...	2305	...	0025	...	...	...	0505	0441
Oulu d.	0752	...	...	1242	...	...	...	...	1522	...	...	...	1854	...	2120	...	...	...	...	...	...	...	...	0535	0450
Kemi d.	0908	...	...	1343	...	...	...	...	1631	...	...	...	1955	...	2228	...	...	...	...	...	...	...	...	0646	0602
Kolari a.	|	...	...	|	...	...	...	...	|	...	...	...	|	...	|	...	...	...	...	...	...	...	...	0946	|
Rovaniemi ⊡ a.	1035	...	...	1455	...	...	...	...	1747	...	...	...	2110	...	2348	...	...	...	...	...	...	...	...	...	0728
Kemijärvi ⊡ a.	...	...	...	...	...	...	...	...	...	...	...	...	...	...	...	...	...	...	...	...	...	...	...	...	0845

	S 40	S 52	S 42	S 44	IC 20	S 54	S 46	IC 22	IC 50	IC 48	IC 414	IC 24	IC 24	IC 50	IC 416	IC 26	S 456	S 56	IC 710	S 458	IC 28		IC 266	270	272	IC 274
	Ⓡ✕ Ⓐ	Ⓡ✕ ①–④	Ⓡ✕ ⚒	Ⓡ✕ ⚒	✕ ⚒	Ⓡ✕ ⑦	Ⓡ✕	✕ ⚒	✕	✕	✕ ⚒	✕ ⑦	✕	✕	2🍷	✕	Ⓡ✕ ⑤⑦	Ⓡ✕ ⑤⑦	2 K	Ⓡ✕ ①–④	✕		★⊕	★ ⑥	★ ④⑦	★
järvi ⊡ d.	...	...	...	...	...	...	...	...	...	...	...	...	...	...	...	...	...	...	...	...	...	...	...	...	...	1940
aniemi ⊡ d.	...	...	...	...	...	...	...	0553	...	...	0851	0851	...	...	1133	...	...	...	1520	...	...	...	1752	...	...	2110
lari d.	...	...	...	...	...	...	...	|	...	...	|	|	...	...	|	...	...	...	|	...	...	...	|	1820	1820	|
d.	...	...	...	...	...	...	...	0709	...	...	1011	1011	...	...	1251	...	...	...	1633	...	...	...	1918	2123	2123	2230
a.	...	...	...	...	...	...	...	0808	...	...	1117	1117	...	...	1355	...	...	...	1731	...	...	...	2033	2239	2239	2333
d.	...	...	...	...	0524	...	...	0813	0813	...	...	1135	1135	...	...	1402	...	1540	...	...	1738	...	2115	2312	2312	2343
eska d.	...	...	...	...	0644	...	...	0930	0930	...	...	1244	1244	...	...	1526	...	1659	...	...	1844	...	2309	0044	0044	0110
ola d.	...	0520	...	...	0741	...	...	1030	1030	...	...	1341	1341	...	...	1630	...	1805	...	...	1941	...	0017	0154	0154	0216
asa d.	...	|	0554	0650	|	0804	0940	|	|	1240	...	|	|	1548	...	|	1830	|	...	1934	|	...	|	|	|	|
äjoki a.	...	0637	0641	0737	0849	0851	1027	1149	1149	1327	...	1449	1449	1635	...	1749	1917	1930	...	2045	2049	...	0155	0351	0351	0359
äjoki d.	0545	0649	0649	0739	0853	0853	1037	1153	1153	1337	...	1453	1453	1638	...	1753	...	1934	...	...	2053	...	0157	0353	0353	0402
ano d.	0620	0724	0724	0814	|	|	1112	|	|	1412	...	|	|	1713	...	|	...	2014	...	...	|	...	0306	|	|	|
pere a.	0654	0758	0758	0855	0958	0958	1155	1258	1258	1455	...	1558	1558	1755	...	1858	...	2055	...	...	2158	...	0355	0535	0535	0546
lsinki **790** a.	0833	0933	0933	1033	1133	1133	1333	1433	1433	1633	...	1733	1733	1933	...	2033	...	2233	...	...	2333	...	0706	0832	0937	0900

③⑤⑥.
①②③④⑦.
From / to Kuopio (Table **798**).
From Aug. 10.

★ – Conveys 🛏, (2) and ✕.
⊕ – Conveys 🛏 Turku - Tampere - Rovaniemi and v.v. See Table **795**.
⊡ – Connecting 🚌 services Rovaniemi - Kemijärvi bus station and v.v. Journey time: 75 – 85 minutes.
From Rovaniemi rail station at 1135 Ⓐ **N**, 1535 Ⓐ, 1545 ⑥, 1725 Ⓑ and 2010 ⑦ **N**.
From Kemijärvi bus station at 0510 Ⓐ **N**, 0830 Ⓐ **N**, 1040 ⑥, 1045 Ⓐ, 1540 Ⓑ and 1845 ⑦ **N**.

795 TURKU - TAMPERE - PIEKSÄMÄKI

km		IC81	IC905	IC141	IC909	S143	IC917	IC145	S87	IC921	S151	IC923	IC147	S89	S89	IC927	IC149	IC931	IC933	S91
		✕	✕	✕	✕	🅁✕	✕	✕	🅁✕	✕	🅁✕	✕	✕	🅁✕	✕	✕	✕	✕	✕	✕
		Ⓐ	Ⓐ						⑤⑦	⑤⑦	Ⓑ				⑦K	⑤⑦			R	⑦
	Turku satama d.	...	...	...	*0810*	...	...	...	...	...	...	...	...	...	...	...	...	1945	...	...
0	**Turku** d.	...	0700	...	0905	...	1305	...	...	1505	...	1605	...	...	...	1805	...	2005	2125	...
66	Loimaa d.	...	0741	...	0944	...	1344	...	...	1544	...	1644	...	...	...	1844	...	2044	2212	...
86	Humppila d.	...	0754	...	0959	...	1359	...	...	1559	...	1659	...	...	...	1859	...	2059	2227	...
	Helsinki **790** d.	0527	|	0706	|	1006	|	1327	1427	|	1506	|	1606	1727	1727	|	1906	|	|	2206
128	Toijala **790** d.	|	0820	0831	1025	1131	1425	|	|	1625	1631	1725	1731	|	|	1925	2031	2125	2256	2331
168	**Tampere** **790** a.	0656	0842	0852	1047	1152	1447	1456	1556	1647	1652	1747	1752	1856	1856	1947	2052	2147	2322	2352
168	**Tampere** d.	0709	...	0905	...	1205	...	1505	1609	...	1705	...	1805	1913	1913	...	2105	...	...	2358
210	Orivesi d.	0734	...	0930	...	1230	...	1530	1634	...	1730	...	1830	1938	1938	...	|	...	...	|
266	Jämsä d.	0815	...	1005	...	1305	...	1610	1716	...	1805	...	1913	2020	2020	...	2200	...	...	0055
323	Jyväskylä d.	0845	...	1039	...	1339	...	1644	1746	...	1838	...	1943	2050	2052	...	2238	...	...	0130
403	**Pieksämäki** a.	...	...	1125	...	1425	...	1730	...	...	1925	...	...	...	2135	...	2332	...	...	...

	IC904	S80	IC150	S140	S140	IC910	IC142	IC916	IC144	IC922	IC924	IC86	S84	S146	IC928	IC930	S88	IC148	IC934	S152
	✕	🅁✕	✕	🅁✕	🅁✕	✕	✕	✕	✕	✕	✕	✕	🅁✕	🅁✕	✕	✕	🅁✕	✕	✕	🅁✕
	T	Ⓐ	⚒	⚒						⑤⑦		Ⓑ	⑥			⑦	⑤⑦		Ⓑ	⑦K
Pieksämäki d.	...	...	...	0630	...	...	0923	...	1223	...	...	...	...	1527	...	...	...	1818	...	2035
Jyväskylä d.	...	0525	0620	0720	0720	...	1013	...	1313	...	...	1515	1515	1617	...	...	1813	1920v	...	2126
Jämsä d.	...	0556	0651	0751	0751	...	1051	...	1351	...	...	1546	1546	1652	...	...	1849	1956	...	2159
Orivesi d.	...	|	0726	0826	0826	...	1126	...	1426	...	...	1626	1626	1727	...	...	|	2031	...	|
Tampere a.	...	0650	0750	0850	0850	...	1150	...	1450	...	...	1650	1650	1750	...	...	1944	2054	...	2254
Tampere ... **790** d.	0556	0702	0807	0907	0907	0911	1207	1211	1507	1511	1606	1702	1702	1807	1811	1911	2002	2107	2111	2302
Toijala **790** d.	0623	|	0828	0958	0958	0935	1228	1235	1528	1535	1635	|	|	1828	1835	1935	|	2128	2135	|
Helsinki **790** a.	|	0833	0952	1052	1052	|	1352	|	1652	|	|	1833	1833	1952	|	|	2133	2252	|	0033
Humppila d.	0652	...	...	...	...	1000	...	1300	...	1600	1700	...	...	...	1900	2000	...	...	2200	...
Loimaa d.	0706	...	...	...	...	1013	...	1313	...	1613	1713	...	...	...	1915	2013	...	...	2213	...
Turku a.	0750	...	...	...	...	1050	...	1355	...	1655	1750	...	...	...	1955	2055	...	...	2250	...
Turku satama a.	0809	...	...	...	...	...	...	...	...	...	1819	...	...	...	2007	...	...	...	...	...

TAMPERE - HAAPAMÄK

	⑥2	Ⓑ2
Tampere d.	1005	1617
Orivesi d.	1031	1643
Haapamäki a.	1124	1736

km		⑥2
0	**Haapamäki** d.	1224
72	Orivesi d.	1320
	Tampere a.	1345

G – ①②③④⑦.
K – To / from Kuopio (Table **798**).
R – [12] Turku - Tampere; convey
🛏 Turku - Tampere (**273**) - Rovaniemi.
T – [12] Tampere - Turku; convey
🛏 Rovaniemi (**266**) - Tampere
Turku.

v – Arrives 1909.

797 HELSINKI - KOUVOLA - JOENSUU

km		IC1	IC63	IC3	IC65		IC5	S67	S109	IC7	S9	S9	S69		IC111	IC11	S13	IC73	IC115	S113
		✕	✕	✕	✕	2	✕	🅁✕	🅁✕	✕	🅁✕	🅁✕	✕	2	✕	✕	🅁✕	✕	✕	🅁✕
			J		O			L	Ⓑ	Ⓑ		Ⓑ	ⒷJ	Ⓐ	Ⓑ	Ⓑ	⑥	K	Ⓑ	⑥
0	**Helsinki** d.	0717	0817	1017	1117	...	1317	1417	1417	1517	1617	1617	1617	1635	1717	1817	1817	1917	2017	2017
3	Pasila d.	0725	0823	1023	1123	...	1323	1423	1423	1523	1623	1623	1623	1641	1723	1823	1823	1923	2023	2023
16	Tikkurila ⊙ d.	0734	0833	1033	1133	...	1333	1433	1433	1533	1633	1633	1633	1650	1733	1833	1833	1933	2033	2033
104	**Lahti** d.	0808	0908	1108	1213	1241	1408	1508	1508	1608	1708	1708	1708	1745	1808	1908	1908	2008	2108	2108
166	**Kouvola** a.	0835	0935	1135	1242	1324	1435	1535	1535	1635	1735	1735	1735	1829	1835	1935	1935	2035	2135	2135
166	**Kouvola** d.	0837	...	1137	...	...	1437	...	1539	1637	1739	1739	...	...	...	1937	1937	...	2137	2137
252	Lappeenranta d.	0919	...	1219	...	...	1519	...	1616	1717	1820	1820	...	...	...	2017	2017	...	2217	2217
288	Imatra d.	0946	...	1246	...	...	1546	...	...	1740	1844	1846	...	...	...	2043	2043	...	2241	2241
352	Parikkala d.	1029	...	1329	...	...	1629	...	...	|	...	1931	...	...	...	2125	2125	...	...	...
482	**Joensuu** a.	1140	...	1440	...	...	1740	...	...	1923	...	2042	...	...	...	2236	2236	...	...	...

	2		2	2
Other	0635	and	1935	2112
local	0640	hourly	1940	2117
trains	0649	until	1949	2126
→	0736		2036	2213

		IC102	IC102		IC104	IC2	IC62	IC4	S100		S64	IC74	S6	S66	IC8	S114	IC68	IC10	IC70	IC12
	2	✕	✕	2	✕	✕	✕	✕	🅁✕	2	🅁✕	✕	🅁✕	🅁✕	✕	🅁✕	✕	✕	✕	✕
	Ⓐ	Ⓐ	⚒	Ⓐ	⚒	⚒	⚒K	⚒	⑦		⚒J	⑦K		M		Ⓑ	K		O	
Joensuu d.	...	...	...	...	...	0518	...	0617	...	...	...	...	0917	...	1217	...	...	1517	...	1817
Parikkala d.	...	...	...	...	...	0628	...	0731	...	...	...	...	1031	...	1331	...	...	1631	...	1933
Imatra d.	...	...	...	...	0615	0705	...	0812	0812	...	...	...	1112	...	1412	...	...	1712	...	2014
Lappeenranta d.	...	0542	...	...	0642	0728	...	0840	0840	...	...	...	1140	...	1440	1628	...	1742	...	2043
Kouvola a.	...	0620	...	...	0720	0806	...	0918	0918	...	...	...	1218	...	1518	1706	...	1820	...	2121
Kouvola d.	*0530*	0623	0623	0626	0723	0808	0823	0923	0923	1032	1123	1123	1223	1420	1523	1708	1723	1823	2016	2123
Lahti d.	0621	0652	0652	0712	0752	0837	0852	0952	0952	1115	1152	1152	1252	1449	1552	1737	1752	1852	2048	2152
Tikkurila ⊙ a.	0708	0726	0726	0808	0826	0911	0926	1026	1026	...	1226	1226	1326	1523	1626	1811	1826	1926	2126	2226
Pasila a.	0717	0735	0735	0818	0835	0920	0935	1035	1035	...	1235	1235	1335	1532	1635	1820	1835	1935	2135	2235
Helsinki a.	0722	0742	0742	0824	0842	0927	0942	1042	1042	...	1242	1242	1342	1539	1642	1827	1842	1942	2142	2242

	2	2	2	
Other	0802	0912	1021	and
local	0850	1008	1108	hourly
trains	0859	1017	1117	until
→	0904	1022	1122	

Branch lines **KOUVOLA - KOTKA** and **PARIKKALA - SAVONLINNA** (2nd class only).

km		⚒							⚒					
0	**Kouvola** d.	0609	0843	1253	1541	1752	...	**Kotka** satama d.	0704	1015	...	1425	1630	1920
51	**Kotka** a.	0653	0927	1337	1623	1836	...	**Kotka** d.	0707	1018	...	1428	1633	1923
52	**Kotka** satama a.	0656	0930	1340	1625	1839	...	**Kouvola** a.	0752	1103	...	1513	1715	2008

km					Ⓑ							Ⓑ		
0	**Parikkala** d.	1034	1334	1634	1936	...	...	**Savonlinna** d.	0930	1230	1530	1830	...	...
59	**Savonlinna** a.	1127	1427	1727	2029	...	...	**Parikkala** a.	1023	1323	1623	1923	...	...

Local trains **RIIHIMÄKI - LAHTI** and v.v. *59 km.* Journey time: 40–41 minutes. 2nd class only.
From Riihimäki at 0715⚒, 0915, 1115, 1315, 1515, 171 1915 and 2115.
From Lahti at 0546 Ⓐ◇, 0627⑥, 0806, 1006, 1206, 14 1606, 1806 and 2006.

J – To / from Kajaani (Table **798**).
K – To / from Kuopio (Table **798**).
L – [12] Helsinki - Kouvola - Kuopio (- Kajaani ⚒) (- Oulu Ⓐ). See Table **798**.
M – [12] (Oulu ②–⑥ -) (Kajaani ②–⑦ -) Kuopio - Kouvola - Helsinki.

O – To / from Oulu via Kuopio (Table **798**).

◇ – Departs 0555 June 27 - Aug. 7.

798 KOUVOLA - KUOPIO - OULU

km		IC811		IC711		IC63	IC713			IC65			S67	S67	S67	IC717	S69	S89	IC73
		2	🚌	2		✕	2	🚌		✕	🚌		🅁✕	🅁✕	🅁✕	2🍷	🅁✕	🅁✕	✕
		Z	Z	nR				Z			Z			⚒	Ⓐ	⑦	Ⓑ	⑦	
	Helsinki **797** d.	...	...	...	...	0817	...	...	...	1117	...	...	1417	1417	1417	...	1617	1727	1917
0	**Kouvola** d.	...	...	...	...	0949	...	...	...	1255	...	...	1549	1549	1549	...	1745	|	2049
113	Mikkeli d.	...	...	...	...	1056	...	...	...	1400	...	...	1656	1656	1656	...	1852	◇	2155
184	Pieksämäki d.	...	...	...	...	1139	...	...	...	1441	...	...	1738	1738	1738	...	1932	2137	2235
273	**Kuopio** a.	...	...	...	...	1239	...	...	...	1539	...	...	1832	1832	1832	...	2023	2225	2326
273	**Kuopio** d.	0740	...	0753	...	...	1245	...	...	1543	...	...	...	1838	1838	1838	2027	...	...
358	Iisalmi d.	0839	...	0857	...	...	1344	...	...	1643	...	...	...	1937	1937	1937	2131	...	...
441	**Kajaani** a.	0927	...	0953	...	...	1432	...	...	1731	...	...	...	2032	2032	2032	2220	...	...
441	**Kajaani** d.	...	0935	0957	...	...	1434n	1440	...	1748n	1740	...	...	...	2115	2115	...	...	...
484	Paltamo d.	...	1020	1028	...	...	1505n	1525	...	1819n	1825	...	...	...	2149	2149	...	...	...
633	**Oulu** a.	...	1220	1224	...	...	1656n	1725	...	2013n	2025	...	...	...	2335	2335	...	...	...

	IC62		S64	IC74		IC714	S66	S66	S66		IC716	IC68		IC70	S152		IC710		IC810
	✕		🅁✕	✕		2	🅁✕	🅁✕	🅁✕	🚌	2	✕	🚌	✕	🅁✕		2	🚌	2
	⚒		⚒	⑦		①	②–⑥	②–⑦		Z			Z		⑦		nV	Z	Z
Oulu d.	...	...	...	...	...	0700	0700	...	...	0910	0955n	...	1210	1243n	...	...	1749	1740	...
Paltamo d.	...	...	...	...	...	0850	0850	...	...	1110	1146n	...	1410	1435n	...	...	1934	1940	...
Kajaani a.	...	...	...	...	...	0920	0920	...	...	1155	1215n	...	1455	1514n	...	...	2004	2025	...
Kajaani d.	...	...	0633	...	...	0927	0927	0927	...	...	1217	...	...	1517	...	...	2006	...	2037
Iisalmi d.	...	...	0725	...	...	1019	1019	1019	...	...	1308	...	...	1611	...	...	2057	...	2128
Kuopio a.	...	...	0821	...	...	1115	1115	1115	...	...	1407	...	...	1708	...	...	2153	...	2224
Kuopio d.	0532	...	0826	0826	...	...	1123	1123	1123	...	...	1423	...	1712	1938	...	...	...	...
Pieksämäki d.	0626	...	0920	0920	...	...	1224	1224	1224	...	...	1520	...	1814	2035	...	...	...	...
Mikkeli d.	0706	...	1001	1001	...	...	1305	1305	1305	...	...	1601	...	1855	◇	...	...	...	...
Kouvola a.	0809	...	1107	1107	...	...	1409	1409	1409	...	...	1707	...	1959	|	...	...	...	...
Helsinki **797** a.	0942	...	1242	1242	...	...	1539	1539	1539	...	...	1842	...	2142	0033	...	...	...	...

IISALMI - YLIVIESKA

km		⚒2
0	**Iisalmi** d.	0737
99	Haapajärvi d.	0844
154	**Ylivieska** a.	0920

	2	
Ylivieska d.	1414	...
Haapajärvi d.	1450	...
Iisalmi a.	1600	...

R – To Rovaniemi (Table **794**).
V – From Rovaniemi (Table **794**) on ①③④⑤⑦ (also ⑥ from July 16 Train number **708** on ② (also ⑥ until July 9).
Z – ①–⑤ July 11 - Aug. 12.

n – Not ①–⑤ July 11 - Aug. 12.

◇ – Via Tampere (Table **795**).

class only

PIEKSÄMÄKI - JOENSUU - NURMES - KAJAANI 799

Service June 20 - August 14 (see May edition for service to June 19)

	🚌 Ⓐ		🚌							Ⓑ	
Pieksämäki .... d.	0705	...	1105	1142	...	1504	...	1743	...	1945	...
Varkaus .... d.	0750	...	1145	1217	...	1539	...	1818	...	2022	...
Joensuu ⊙ .... a.	0950	...	1325	...	...	...	...	...	...	2156	...

	🚌 Ⓐ	⚒		🚌			🚌			
Joensuu ⊙ .... d.	0515	0700	...	1120	...	...	1420	...	...	...
Varkaus .... d.	0700	0837	...	1315	1421	...	1610	1657	...	1830
Pieksämäki .... a.	0735	0912	...	...	1456	...	1645	1731	...	1905

	🚌 Ⓐ	🚌 ⚒			🚌 ⑦		🚌 ⚒	🚌 ⚒	🚌	Ⓑ	
Joensuu ⊙ .... d.	0710	0900	...	1147	1210	...	1410	1520	1630	1800	...
Lieksa ⊙ .... a.	0855	|	...	1306	|	...	|	1705	|	1919	...
Nurmes ⊙ .... a.	...	1055	...	1353	1350	...	1605	...	1825	2006	...
Kajaani bus station... a.	...	1300	...	...	1550	...	1800	...	2000	...	...

	⚒	🚌 ⚒		🚌				🚌		
Kajaani bus station d.	...	0640	...	1115	...	...	...	1710	...	...
Nurmes ⊙ .... d.	0640	0825	...	1250	...	1540	...	1905	...	...
Lieksa ⊙................ d.	0726	|	...	|	...	1626	...	1950	...	...
Joensuu ⊙ .... a.	0850	1000	...	1435	...	1745	...	2130	...	...

🚌 timings are at the bus station.

GERMANY

rator: Principal operator is Deutsche Bahn AG (DB) www.bahn.de
Many regional services are run by private operators – these are specified in the table heading (or by footnotes for individual trains).

ices: Trains convey first- and second-class seating accommodation unless otherwise shown (by '2' in the column heading, a footnote or a general note in the table heading). Overnight sleeping car (🛏) and couchette (▬) trains do not necessarily convey seating accommodation - refer to individual footnotes for details. Descriptions of sleeping and couchette cars appear on page 8.

There are various categories of trains in Germany. The type of train is indicated by the following letter codes above each column (or by a general note in the table heading):

ICE	**InterCity Express**	German high-speed (230 – 320 km/h) train.	*IRE*	**InterRegio Express**	Regional express train.
EC	**EuroCity**	International express train.	*RE*	**Regional Express**	Regional semi-fast train.
IC	**InterCity**	Internal express train.	*RB*	**Regional Bahn**	Regional stopping train.
TGV	**Train à Grande Vitesse**	French high-speed (320 km/h) train.	*S-Bahn*		Suburban stopping train.
RJ	**Railjet**	Austrian high-speed train.			

Overnight services:

CNL	**City Night Line**	Quality overnight express train. Most services convey *Deluxe* sleeping cars (1 / 2 / 3 berth) with en-suite shower and WC, *Economy* sleeping cars (1 / 2 / 3 berth), couchettes (6 berth) and seats. Please note that a maximum of five passengers will normally be booked in a couchette compartment. Reservation compulsory for travel in sleeping cars and couchettes. Seating cars are classified *IC*, have a different train number and, unless otherwise shown, can be used without prior reservation. See also page 8.
EN	**Euro Night**	International overnight express train. See also page 8.
D	**Durchgangszug**	Or **Schnellzug** – other express train (day or night).

Other long-distance service operators:

ALX	**alex**	Regional express train operated by *Vogtlandbahn* on the routes München - Oberstdorf / Lindau and München - Regensburg - Hof (also international services München - Regensburg - Schwandorf - Furth im Wald - Praha).
HKX	**Hamburg-Köln-Express**	Operates fast services on the Hamburg - Köln route (see Table **800a** below). Most national DB tickets are valid on these services (including Schönes-Wochenende-Ticket and Quer-durchs-Land-Ticket; local tickets and regional Länder tickets are **not** valid).

ngs: Valid **June 12 - December 10**, 2016 (except where shown otherwise).

Many long distance trains operate on selected days only for part of the journey. These are often indicated in the train composition footnote by showing the dated journey segment within brackets. For example '🚃12 Leipzig - Hannover (- Dortmund ⑦)' means that the train runs daily (or as shown in the column heading) between Leipzig and Hannover, but only continues to Dortmund on Sundays. Additional footnotes / symbols are often used to show more complex running dates, e.g. '🚃12 (München ⊡ -) Nürnberg - Hamburg' means that the train runs only on dates in note ⊡ between München and Nürnberg, but runs daily (or as shown in the column heading) between Nürnberg and Hamburg. Please note that international overnight trains that are not intended for internal German journeys are not usually shown in the German section (refer to the International section).

Engineering work may occasionally disrupt services at short notice (especially at weekends and during holiday periods), so it is advisable to check timings locally before travelling. Please see shaded panel below for information regarding major engineering work alterations affecting long-distance services until September 2016.

ets: There are three standard levels of fares, corresponding to travel by (in ascending order of price): ○ Regional trains. ○ *IC / EC* trains. ○ High-speed *ICE* (also *TGV / RJ*) trains. A variable supplement (*Aufpreis*) is payable for sleeping car and couchette accommodation on overnight *CNL* and *EN* trains, the cost of which depends on the type required. Unless shown otherwise, seats on overnight trains can be used without prior reservation.

ring: Two types of catering are indicated in the tables: 🍷 Bordbistro – hot and cold drinks, snacks and light meals; ✕ Bordrestaurant – full restaurant car service (bordbistro also available). First class passengers on *ICE* and *IC* trains benefit from an at-seat service. On overnight trains 🍷 indicates that drinks and light snacks are available, usually from the sleeping or couchette car attendant (the refreshment service may only be available to sleeping and couchette car passengers).

ervations: Reservation is only compulsory for travel in sleeping car and couchette accommodation on overnight *CNL* and *EN* trains (see above). Optional reservations are available on *ICE / EC / IC* trains (€ 4,50).

days: Jan. 1, Mar. 25, 28, May 5, 16, Oct. 3, Dec. 25, 26 are German national public holidays (trains marked ⚒ or Ⓐ do not run). In addition there are other regional holidays as follows: Jan. 6 – Heilige Drei Könige (Epiphany), May 26 – Fronleichnam (Corpus Christi), Aug. 15 – Mariä Himmelfahrt (Assumption), Oct. 31 – Reformationstag (Reformation Day), Nov. 1 – Allerheiligen (All Saints Day) and Nov. 16 – Buß und Bettag. On these days the regional service is usually that applicable on ⑦ (please refer to individual footnotes).

MAJOR ENGINEERING WORK ALTERATIONS AFFECTING SERVICES UNTIL SEPTEMBER 2016

□ **UNTIL JULY 20** timings of certain services between **München**, **Stuttgart** and **Mannheim** are subject to alteration due to signalling work taking place on the high-speed line between Stuttgart and Mannheim. During this period journey times may be extended by up to 20 minutes (earlier westbound departures from **München**, **Augsburg**, **Ulm**, **Stuttgart**, **Vaihingen** and other intermediate stations are possible). Please note that specific changes are **not** shown in our tables and travellers intending to use the following services until July 20 are strongly advised to confirm timings locally:
○ *ICE* services München - Stuttgart - Mannheim - Köln / Frankfurt / Berlin / Hamburg and v.v.
○ Northbound *IC* services Stuttgart - Heidelberg - Mannheim - Mainz - Köln.

□ **UNTIL SEPTEMBER 3** the line between **Lichtenfels** and **Bamberg** is closed. Services between **Berlin** and **München** run every two hours and are diverted between Leipzig and Nürnberg via Erfurt and Fulda. Alternative train/bus connections are available via the Saalfeld route, as shown in Table **851**. These diversions have knock-on effects to certain other services and, where this occurs, the service until September 3 is shown (details will be updated for the September edition).

□ **JULY 9 - AUGUST 21** services via **Solingen** and **Wuppertal** are subject to alteration. Services to / from **Berlin** via **Wuppertal** are either diverted between Köln and Wuppertal with journey times extended by up to 28 minutes (earlier departures / later arrivals at Köln Hbf) or cancelled altogether (as indicated in the relevant tables). *IC* services to / from **Hannover**, **Leipzig** and **Dresden** are diverted with journey times extended by up to 28 minutes (earlier departures / later arrivals at Köln Hbf), not calling at Solingen. *IC* services to / from **Hamburg** are diverted via Essen, not calling at **Solingen**, **Wuppertal** or **Hagen** (certain *ICE* services between München and Dortmund do not run north of Köln, in some cases replaced by the diverted Hamburg service). Please note that most of these alterations are included in the relevant tables in the German section.

□ **JULY 16 - AUGUST 28** engineering work between **Mannheim** and **Frankfurt** will result in some retimings on the routes **München** - **Stuttgart** - **Mannheim** - **Frankfurt** Flughafen / Hbf and v.v., also **Freiburg** - **Mannheim** - **Frankfurt** Flughafen / Hbf and v.v. During this period timings may vary by up to 10 minutes (earlier departures possible). Most *ICE* services Stuttgart - Hamburg and v.v. will not call at Frankfurt Flughafen. Most *ICE* services Basel - Hamburg and v.v. will not call at Frankfurt (Main) Hbf (but will call additionally at Frankfurt (Main) Süd). Please note that services from / to München are disrupted further from July 30 (see entry below). Timings of international *ICE / TGV* services between **Frankfurt** and **Paris** / **Marseille** via Mannheim and Strasbourg may vary by up to 35 minutes.

□ **JULY 16, 17, 23, 24, NOVEMBER 26, 27** certain *ICE* services do not run between **Basel** Badischer Bahnhof and Basel SBB.

□ **JULY 18 - SEPTEMBER 2** engineering work is taking place on the high-speed line between **Hannover** and **Göttingen**. During this period services are diverted, extending journey times by up to 47 minutes (earlier southbound departures **Berlin** - **Hildesheim** and **Hamburg** - **Hannover**; some northbound departure times may also be a few minutes earlier). In addition, many *IC* services do not run **Kassel** - **Hannover** - **Hamburg** and v.v., although most *ICE* services between München and Hamburg make additional calls at Celle, Uelzen and Lüneburg to compensate for the withdrawal of the *IC* stops at these stations. Most *ICE* services Oldenburg - Bremen - Hannover - München are replaced by *IC* trains and do not run south of Hannover. Therefore most journeys between Bremen and destinations south of Hannover will require a change of trains at Hannover (with earlier departures and later arrivals at Bremen).

□ **JULY 30 - SEPTEMBER 11** engineering work between **Augsburg** and **Ulm** will result in retimings at **München**, **Augsburg**, **Günzburg** and **Ulm**. During this period timings of domestic trains may vary by up to 33 minutes (earlier departures possible) and some trains will not run. Certain international trains to / from Austria do not run west of München, whilst others are retimed within Germany. We are unable to show all timing variations in our tables so please confirm timings locally and allow extra time for your journey. However, cancellations during this period are indicated in the relevant tables.

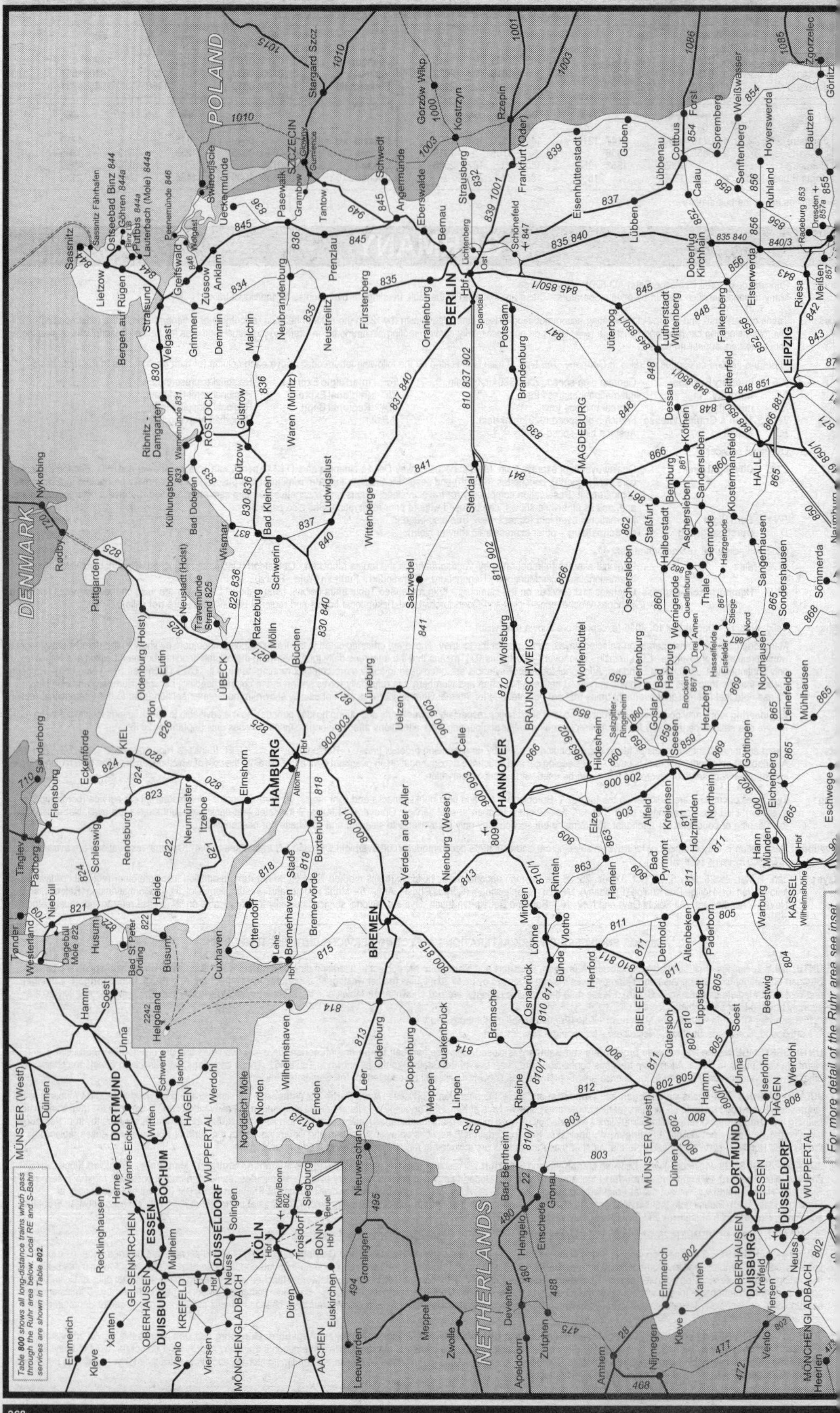
DENMARK
POLAND
NETHERLANDS
For more detail of the Ruhr area see inset
Table 800 shows all long-distance trains which pass through the Ruhr area below. Local RE and S-Bahn services are shown in Table 802.
BERLIN
HAMBURG
BREMEN
HANNOVER
LEIPZIG
MAGDEBURG
BRAUNSCHWEIG
ROSTOCK
KIEL
LÜBECK
HALLE
BIELEFELD
MÜNSTER (Westf)
DORTMUND
ESSEN
DÜSSELDORF
DUISBURG
KÖLN
BOCHUM
WUPPERTAL
HAGEN
KASSEL
SZCZECIN
Sassnitz
Stralsund
Greifswald
Schwerin
Wismar
Lüneburg
Uelzen
Celle
Wolfsburg
Stendal
Potsdam
Brandenburg
Dessau
Bitterfeld
Göttingen
Osnabrück
Oldenburg
Emden
Norddeich Mole
Wilhelmshaven
Cuxhaven
Flensburg
Puttgarden
Neumünster
Cottbus
Frankfurt (Oder)
Rheine
Hamm
Paderborn
Soest
Aachen
Bonn
Mönchengladbach

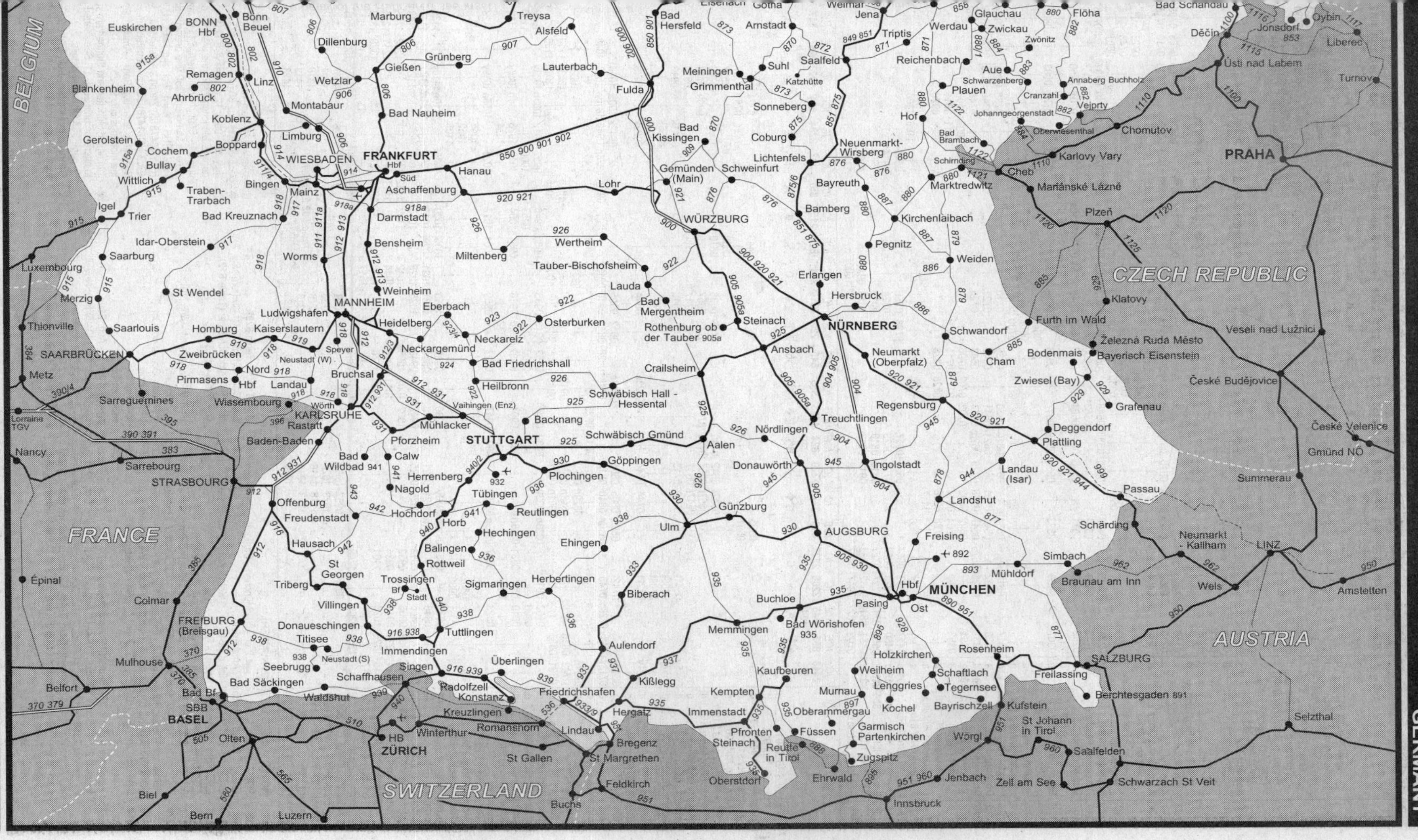
BELGIUM
CZECH REPUBLIC
AUSTRIA
SWITZERLAND
FRANCE
PRAHA
LINZ
SALZBURG
MÜNCHEN
NÜRNBERG
WÜRZBURG
FRANKFURT
MANNHEIM
KARLSRUHE
STUTTGART
AUGSBURG
STRASBOURG
BASEL
ZÜRICH
SAARBRÜCKEN
WIESBADEN
FREIBURG (Breisgau)
Ulm
Regensburg
Ingolstadt
Passau
Innsbruck
Luxembourg
Koblenz
Mainz
Heidelberg
Fulda
Hanau
Plzeň
Cheb
Karlovy Vary
České Budějovice
Konstanz
Lindau
Bregenz
Friedrichshafen
Kempten
Garmisch Partenkirchen
Berchtesgaden

800 KOBLENZ - KÖLN - DORTMUND - HAMBURG

km		*IC* 2020	*ICE* 1020	*IC* 2228	*IC* 2228	*ICE* 541	*IC* 2445	*IC* 2214	*IC* 2314	*IC* 2153	*ICE* 853	*ICE* 843	*IC* 2208	*IC* 2224	*IC* 1098	*CNL* 418	*CNL* 40478	*IC* 61478	*HKX* 1800	*ICE* 553	*ICE* 543	*ICE* 618	*ICE* 1018	*ICE* 1018
			Ⓐ 🍴	①g 🍷	Ⓐ 🍷	⚒ 🍴	⚒ D	Q 🍷	🍷♦	♦	⚒ 🍴	🍴	B N	K🍷	①–④ m🍷	⊗ 🍷♦	[R]⊗ ◇🍷	⊗ ◇2	①⑤ g★ 🍷	⚒ 🍴	🍴	⚒¶ 🍷	†n ‡🍷	⑦y ‡🍷
	Basel SBB 🏛 **912** d.	...	...	...	...	...	...	...	...	...	...	...	...	...	...	...	2313	2313		...	...	...	...	...
	Karlsruhe Hbf **912** d.	...	...	...	...	...	...	...	...	...	...	...	...	...	...	...	0129	0129	...	...	...	0349	0349	0349
	München Hbf **904 930** ⊠ d.	...	...	...	...	...	...	...	...	...	...	...	...	...	...	2250	|	|	...	...	...	0001	0001	0001
	Stuttgart Hbf **912** ⊠ d.	...	...	...	...	...	...	...	...	...	...	...	...	...	...	0135	|	|	...	...	...	0230	0230	0230
	Nürnberg Hbf **920** d.	...	...	...	...	...	...	...	...	...	...	...	...	...	...	|	|	|	...	...	...	|	|	|
	Frankfurt (Main) Hbf **910/1** d.	2324	...	...	...	...	...	...	...	...	...	...	...	...	...	|	|	0345	...	...	...	0544	0544	0544
	Frankfurt Flughafen ✈ § d.	2339	...	...	...	...	...	...	...	...	...	...	...	...	...	|	|	|	...	...	...	0601	0601	0601
	Mainz Hbf **911** d.	0001	...	...	...	...	...	...	...	...	...	...	...	...	...	|	|	|	...	...	...	|	|	|
0	**Koblenz** Hbf d.	0057	...	...	...	...	...	...	...	...	...	...	...	...	...	0511**s**	0511**s**	0513	...	0545**n**	...	|	|	|
18	Andernach d.	0109	...	...	...	...	...	...	...	...	...	...	...	...	...	|	|	|	...	0557**n**	...	|	|	|
39	Remagen d.	0121	...	...	...	...	...	...	...	...	...	...	...	...	...	|	|	|	...	|	...	|	|	|
59	**Bonn** Hbf d.	0135	...	...	...	...	...	...	...	...	...	...	...	...	...	0545**s**	0545**s**	0547	...	0621**n**	...	|	|	|
	Köln/Bonn Flughafen ✈ d.	|	...	...	...	...	...	...	...	...	...	...	...	...	...	|	|	|	...	|	...	|	|	|
93	**Köln** Hbf a.	0156	...	...	...	...	...	...	...	...	...	...	...	...	...	0615**s**	0615**s**	0615	...	0642**n**	...	0705	0705	0705
93	**Köln** Hbf d.	0210	...	0359	...	0429	0513**v**	0510	0510	0520	0544**v**	0528**n**	0541	0609	0616	|	|	0626	0701	0648**v**	...	0713	0710	0713
94	**Köln** Messe/Deutz d.	|	...	0404	...	|	|	|	|	|	|	|	|	|	|	|	|	|	|	|	...	|	|	|
	Solingen Hbf d.	|	...	|	...	|	0531**n**	|	|	|	0603**n**	|	|	|	|	|	|	|	|	|	...	|	0728	|
	Wuppertal Hbf d.	|	...	|	...	|	0543	|	|	|	0616	|	|	|	|	|	|	|	|	0716	...	|	0743	|
	Hagen Hbf d.	|	...	|	...	|	0601	|	|	|	0635	|	|	|	|	|	|	|	|	0735	...	|	0801	|
133	**Düsseldorf** Hbf d.	0234	...	0425	...	0453	|	0533	0533	0546	|	0552	0606	0633	0639	0651**s**	0651**s**	0656	0727	|	0649	0737	|	0738
140	Düsseldorf Flughafen ✈ d.	0242	...	0433	...	0501	|	|	|	0553	|	0600	0613	|	|	|	|	|	|	|	0657	|	|	|
157	**Duisburg** Hbf d.	0252	...	0443	...	0511	|	0546	0546	0604	|	0610	0626	0646	0651	0710**s**	0710**s**	0712	0742	|	0707	0750	|	0750
165	Oberhausen Hbf d.	|	...	|	...	|	|	|	|	|	|	|	0634	|	|	0719	0719	0719	|	|	|	|	|	|
176	**Essen** Hbf d.	0307	...	0459	...	0523	|	0559	0559	0617	|	0623	|	0659	0703	...	...	...	0755	|	0723	0803	|	0802
	Gelsenkirchen Hbf d.	|	...	|	...	|	|	|	|	|	|	|	0646	|	|	...	...	...	0805	|	|	|	|	|
	Wanne-Eickel Hbf d.	|	...	|	...	|	|	|	|	|	|	|	0652	|	|	...	...	...	|	|	|	|	|	|
	Recklinghausen Hbf d.	|	...	|	...	|	|	|	|	|	|	|	0700	|	|	...	...	...	|	|	|	|	|	|
192	Bochum Hbf d.	0317	...	0511	...	0534	|	0611	0610	0630	|	0635	|	0710	|	...	...	...	|	|	0735	0814**j**	|	0813
210	**Dortmund** Hbf a.	0328	...	0522	...	0545	0621	0621	0621	0641	|	0646	|	0721	|	...	...	...	|	|	0746	0825**j**	0821	0825
210	**Dortmund** Hbf **805** d.	0332	...	0525	0525	0547	0628	0625	0625	0643	|	0648	|	0725	|	...	...	...	|	|	0748	...	...	...
	Hamm (Westf) **805** a.	0351	...	|	|	0602	0642	|	|	0702	0702	0706	|	|	|	...	...	...	|	0802	0806	...	...	...
	Hamm (Westf) d.	0353	...	|	|	0604	0644	|	|	...	0711	0711	|	|	|	...	...	...	|	0811	0811	...	...	...
	Hannover Hbf **810** a.	|	...	|	|	0728	0818	|	|	...	0828	0828	|	|	|	...	...	...	|	0928	0928	...	...	...
	Leipzig Hbf **866** a.	|	...	|	|	|	1117	|	|	...	|	|	|	|	|	...	...	...	|	|	|	...	...	...
	Berlin Hbf **810** a.	|	...	|	|	0906	...	|	|	...	1009	1009	|	|	|	...	...	...	|	1106	1106	...	...	...
266	Münster (Westf) Hbf **801** d.	0417	...	0557	0557	...	...	0657	0657	...	...	...	0728	0758	|	...	...	...	0847	...	...	...	...	...
316	Osnabrück Hbf **801 815** d.	0450	...	0623	0623	...	...	0723	0723	...	...	...	...	0824	|	...	...	...	0914	...	...	...	...	...
438	**Bremen** Hbf **801 815** d.	0555	0717	0727	0727	...	...	0818	0818	...	...	...	...	0918	|	...	...	...	|	...	...	...	...	...
553	**Hamburg** Hbf **801** a.	0651	0812	0832	0832	...	...	0913	0913	...	...	...	...	1013	0945	...	...	...	1107	...	...	...	...	...
560	**Hamburg** Altona a.	0706	0827	0847	0847	...	...	0928	...	...	...	...	...	...	1000	...	...	...	1122	...	...	...	...	...

	IC 2443	*ICE* 855	*ICE* 845 1045	*IC* 2206	*IC* 2222	*ICE* 616	*IC* 2220	*IC* 2320	*ICE* 824	*ICE* 1223	*ICE* 555	*ICE* 545	*ICE* 220	*IC* 2310	*IC* 2441	*ICE* 822	*IC* 2155	*ICE* 857	*ICE* 847	*IC* 2204	*ICE* 614	*IC* 1028	*ICE* 557	*ICE* 547
	⚒ D	🍴	🍴	L N	Ⓐ C🍷	🍷	🍷♦	⊡ 🍷	Ⓐ H🍷	🍷♦	n 🍴	🍴	A🍷	🍷♦	D	⚒ 🍷	♦	🍴	🍴	E	🍷		n 🍴	🍴
Basel SBB 🏛 **912** d.	...	...	...	...	...	...	...	...	...	...	...	...	...	...	...	...	...	...	...	...	...	...	...	...
Karlsruhe Hbf **912** d.	...	...	...	...	...	...	...	...	...	...	...	...	...	...	...	...	...	...	...	...	...	...	...	...
München Hbf **904 930** ⊠ d.	...	...	...	...	...	0325	...	...	...	...	...	...	...	...	...	0449	...	...	...	...	0524	...	...	...
Stuttgart Hbf **912** ⊠ d.	...	...	...	...	...	0551	...	...	...	...	...	...	...	...	...	|	...	...	...	...	0751	...	...	...
Nürnberg Hbf **920** d.	...	...	...	...	...	|	...	...	...	...	...	...	...	...	...	0600	...	...	...	...	|	0527	...	...
Frankfurt (Main) Hbf **910/1** d.	...	...	...	...	...	|	0542**r**	0542	0710	...	...	...	0727	0638	...	0810	...	...	...	...	|	0742	...	...
Frankfurt Flughafen ✈ § d.	...	...	...	...	...	0709	0557**r**	0557	0725	0714	...	...	0743	0657	...	0825	...	...	...	...	0909	0758	...	...
Mainz Hbf **911** d.	...	...	...	...	...	|	0617**r**	0617	|	|	...	...	|	0717	...	|	...	...	...	...	|	0820	...	...
Koblenz Hbf d.	0545**y**	...	...	0641**t**	...	|	0713	0713	|	|	...	...	|	0813	...	|	...	...	...	0841**k**	|	0913	...	...
Andernach d.	0557**y**	...	...	0656**t**	...	|	|	|	|	|	...	...	|	|	...	|	...	...	...	0856**k**	|	|	...	...
Remagen d.	|	...	...	0708**t**	...	|	|	|	|	|	...	...	|	|	...	|	...	...	...	0908**k**	|	|	...	...
Bonn Hbf d.	0621**y**	...	...	0722**t**	...	|	0744	0744	|	|	0823**e**	...	|	0844	...	|	...	...	...	0922**k**	|	0945	...	...
Köln/Bonn Flughafen ✈ d.	|	...	0712**a**	|	...	|	|	|	|	|	|	...	|	|	...	|	...	...	...	|	|	|	...	...
Köln Hbf a.	0643**y**	...	|	0742**t**	...	0805	0805	0805	|	|	0843**e**	...	0832	0905	...	|	...	...	...	0942**k**	1005	1005	...	...
Köln Hbf d.	0713**v**	0748**v**	0728**z**	0746	...	0810**n**	0810	0810	|	|	0848	0828	0844	0910	0913**v**	|	...	0948**v**	0928**n**	0946	1010**n**	1010	1048	...
Köln Messe/Deutz d.	|	|	0730**a**	|	...	|	|	|	0817	0825	|	|	|	|	|	0917	...	|	|	|	|	|	|	...
Solingen Hbf d.	0731**n**	|	|	|	...	|	0829**n**	0829	|	|	|	|	|	|	0931**n**	|	...	|	|	|	|	1029**n**	|	...
Wuppertal Hbf d.	0743	0816	|	|	...	|	0843**n**	0843	|	|	0916	|	|	|	0943	|	...	1016	|	|	|	1043**n**	1116	...
Hagen Hbf d.	0801	0835	|	|	...	|	0901**n**	0901	|	|	0935	|	|	|	1001	|	...	1035	|	|	|	1102**n**	1135	...
Düsseldorf Hbf d.	|	|	0752	0812	...	0833**n**	0833**y**	|	0838	0846	|	0852	0913	0933	|	0938	0946	|	0952	1012	1033**n**	1033**y**	|	1052
Düsseldorf Flughafen ✈ d.	|	|	0800	|	...	|	|	|	|	|	|	0900	|	|	|	|	0953	|	1000	|	|	|	|	1100
Duisburg Hbf d.	|	|	0810	0826	0831	0846**n**	0846**y**	|	0851	0904	|	0910	0926	0946	|	0951	1004	|	1010	1026	1046**n**	1046**y**	|	1110
Oberhausen Hbf d.	|	|	|	0834	|	|	|	|	|	|	|	|	0932	|	|	|	|	|	|	1034	|	|	|	|
Essen Hbf d.	|	|	0823	|	0847	0859**n**	0859**y**	|	0902	0917	|	0923	...	0959	|	1004	1017	|	1023	|	1059**n**	1059**y**	|	1123
Gelsenkirchen Hbf d.	|	|	|	0846	|	|	|	|	...	|	|	|	...	|	|	|	|	|	|	1046	|	|	|	|
Wanne-Eickel Hbf d.	|	|	|	0852	|	|	|	|	...	|	|	|	...	|	|	|	|	|	|	1052	|	|	|	|
Recklinghausen Hbf d.	|	|	|	0900	|	|	|	|	...	|	|	|	...	|	|	|	|	|	|	1100	|	|	|	|
Bochum Hbf d.	|	|	0835	|	0857	0910**n**	0910**y**	|	...	0930	|	0935	...	1010	|	1015**j**	1030	|	1035	|	1110**n**	1110**y**	|	1135
Dortmund Hbf a.	0821	|	0846	|	0909	0921**n**	0921	0921	...	0940	|	0946	...	1021	1021	1029**j**	1041	|	1046	|	1121**n**	1123	|	1146
Dortmund Hbf **805** d.	0828	|	0848	|	0912	...	0925	0925	...	0942	|	0948	...	1025	1028	...	1043	|	1048	|	...	1126	|	1148
Hamm (Westf) **805** a.	0842	0902	0906	|	0932	...	|	|	...	1002	1002	1006	...	|	1042	...	1102	1102	1106	|	...	|	1202	1206
Hamm (Westf) d.	0844	0911	0911	|	0934	...	|	|	...	...	1011	1011	...	|	1044	...	...	1111	1111	|	...	|	1211	1211
Hannover Hbf **810** a.	1018	1028	1028	|	1101	...	|	|	...	...	1128	1128	...	|	1218	...	...	1228	1228	|	...	|	1328	1328
Leipzig Hbf **866** a.	1317	|	|	|	...	...	|	|	...	...	|	|	...	|	1517	...	...	|	|	|	...	|	|	|
Berlin Hbf **810** a.	...	1209	1209	|	1249	...	|	|	...	...	1307	1307	...	|	...	...	...	1409	1409	|	...	|	1506	1506
Münster (Westf) Hbf **801** d.	...	...	...	0928	...	...	0957	0957	...	...	...	...	...	1057	...	...	...	...	...	1128	...	1157	...	...
Osnabrück Hbf **801 815** d.	...	...	...	...	...	...	1023	1023	...	...	...	...	...	1123	...	...	...	...	...	...	...	1224	...	...
Bremen Hbf **801 815** d.	...	...	...	...	...	...	1118	1118	...	...	...	...	...	1218							...	1318	...	...
Hamburg Hbf **801** a.	...	...	...	...	...	...	1213	1213	...	...	...	...	...	1313							...	1413	...	...
Hamburg Altona a.	...	...	...	...	...	...	...	1228	...	...	...	...	...	...							...	1428	...	...

*See Table **802** for Rhein-Ruhr local RE and S-Bahn services*

♦ – **NOTES** (LISTED BY TRAIN NUMBER)

418 – POLLUX – 🛏 1, 2 cl. and 🛌 2 cl. ([R]) München - Stuttgart - Amsterdam; [2] (*IC* **60418**) München - Amsterdam.
1223 – [12] and 🍷 (Darmstadt Hbf, d. 0648 Ⓐ -) Köln - Kassel - München.
2153 – [12] Köln - Paderborn - Kassel - Erfurt - Jena.
2155 – [12] Düsseldorf - Paderborn - Kassel - Erfurt - Weimar.
2212 – RÜGEN – [12] and 🍷 Koblenz - Stralsund - Ostseebad Binz.
2220 – Daily to Oct. 30; ⑤⑦ from Nov. 4. FEHMARN – [12] and 🍷 Frankfurt - Köln - Hamburg - Lübeck Hbf (a. 1310) (- Fehmarn-Burg ♠).
2310 – NORDFRIESLAND – [12] and 🍷 Frankfurt - Köln - Westerland.
2314 – Until Oct. 30. DEICHGRAF – [12] and 🍷 Köln - Westerland.

A – To Amsterdam (Table **28**). Subject to alteration July 9–24.
B – ⑥ to June 25; ⑤⑥ July 1 - Aug. 13; ④–⑦ Aug. 19 - Oct. 23 (also Oct. 29). Train number **2358** on ⑦ Aug. 21 - Oct. 23 (timings may vary by 1–2 minutes).
C – From Aachen Hbf (d. 0708), Rheydt Hbf (d. 0748), Mönchengladbach Hbf (d. 0755), Viersen (d. 0804) and Krefeld Hbf (d. 0816). Also calls at Mülheim (Ruhr), d. 0839.
D – To Dresden (Table **842**).
E – To Emden (Table **812**).
H – From Würzburg (Table **920**) on ①–④.

K – To Kiel (Table **820**).
L – Daily to Nov. 5; ①–⑥ from Nov. 7.
N – To Norddeich Mole (Table **812**).
Q – From Oct. 31.

a – Ⓐ (not July 11 - Aug. 19).
e – ⚒ only.
g – Also Oct. 4; not Oct. 3.
j – ⑥ only.
k – Not ⑦.
m – Not Oct. 3.
n – Not July 9 - Aug. 21.
r – Daily to Oct. 30; ⑤ from Nov. 4.
s – Stops to set down only.
t – Ⓐ (not Nov. 1).
v – 11–27 minutes **earlier** July 9 - Aug. 21.
y – July 9 - Aug. 21 only.
z – © (not July 9 - Aug. 21).

⊡ – ①②③④⑥ from Oct. 31.
♠ – ①⑤⑥⑦ to Oct. 30 (daily June 10 - Au
¶ – July 30 - Sept. 12 runs as *ICE* **1218** ar departs München 2350 (the previous d
‡ – July 31 - Sept. 11 runs as *ICE* **1118** ar departs München 2350 (the previous d
◇ – PEGASUS – 🛏 1, 2 cl. and 🛌 2 cl. (*CNL* **40478** [R]) Zürich - Amsterdam; [2] (*IC* **61478**) Zürich - Amsterdam.
⊗ – Subject to alteration Bonn - Amsterdam the mornings July 9–25.
⊠ – Timings at München and Stuttgart are s to alteration until Sept. 11. See shaded on page 367 for further details.
★ – Operated by Hamburg-Köln-Express G www.hkx.de. Information on ticket valid can be found on page 367.
§ – Frankfurt Flughafen Fernbahnhof (Tables and **911**).

KOBLENZ - KÖLN - DORTMUND - HAMBURG 800

	ICE 916	IC 1959	IC 2010	IC 2010	IC 2018	HKX 1802	HKX 1802	IC 2216	ICE 202	IC 2049	ICE 728	ICE 859	ICE 849 1049	IC 2202	ICE 612	IC 2226	ICE 726	ICE 559	ICE 549	ICE 126	ICE 714	IC 2218	ICE 200	IC 2047	ICE 724
	Q	⑤⑦	Ⓐ	⑤	⑥	④⑥	†		①–④	⑤–⑦							⚒	n		U	⑥h		⑥n	Ⓑ	
	✕	♦	T🍷	🍷	♦	★🍷	★🍷	🍷♦	m🍷	c D	🍷	✕	✕	N	🍷	🍷♦	🍷	✕	✕	A🍷	✕	🍷	🍷	D	🍷
Basel SBB 🚌 912 d.	...	...	...	...	...	...	...	...	0713	...	...	...	...	...	...	...	...	...	...	...	...	...	0913	...	...
Karlsruhe Hbf 912 d.	...	...	...	...	...	...	...	...	0900	...	...	...	...	...	...	...	...	...	...	...	...	...	1100	...	...
inchen Hbf 904 930 ⊠ d.	...	...	...	...	...	...	...	...		...	0652	...	...	...	0727	...	0755	...	...	...	...	...		...	0855
ittgart Hbf 912 ⊠ d.	0836	...	0714	0714	0714	...	...	0737		...		...	...	...	0951	...		...	...	...	1041r	0937		...	
Nürnberg Hbf 920 d.		...				...	...			...	0800	...	...	...		0729e	0900	...	...	...				...	1000
ankfurt (Main) Hbf 910/1 d.		...				0830	...			...	1010	...	...	...		0942	1110	...	...	1129				...	1210
ankfurt Flughafen ✈ § d.	0955	...					...		1009	...	1025	...	...	...	1109	0958	1122	...	...	1143	1155		1209	...	1225
inz Hbf 911 d.		...	0848	0848	0848		...	0920		...		...	...	...		1020		...	...			1120		...	
enz Hbf d.		...	0943	0943	0943	0959	...	1013		...		...	...	...		1113		...	...			1213		...	
rnach d.		...	0956	0956	0956		...			...		...	...	...				...	...					...	
agen d.		...	1008	1008	1008		...			...		...	...	...				...	...					...	
n Hbf d.		...	1022	1022	1022	1031	...	1044		...		...	...	...		1144		1222e	...			1244		...	
ln/Bonn Flughafen ✈ d.		...					...			...		...	1112a	...					...					...	1314
Hbf a.		...	1042	1042	1042	1053	...	1105	1105	...		...		...	1205	1205		1242e	...	1232		1305	1305	...	
Hbf d.		...	1046	1046	1046	1059	1059	1110	1110	1113v		1148v	1128z	1146	1210n	1210		1248	1220y	1241		1310	1310	1313v	
Messe/Deutz d.	1046	...									1117		1130a				1228				1247				1327
lingen Hbf d.		...							1128	1131n						1229n							1328	1331n	
ippertal Hbf d.		...							1143	1143		1216				1243n		1316					1343	1343	
gen Hbf d.		...							1201	1201		1235				1301n		1335					1401	1401	
seldorf Hbf d.	1113	1113	1113	1118	1118	1127	1127	1133			1138		1152	1212	1233n	1233y	1250		1254	1309	1313	1333			1348
eldorf Flughafen ✈ d.			...										1200												
burg Hbf d.	1129	1129	...	1133		1142	1142	1146			1151		1210	1226	1246n	1246y	1304		1309	1326	1329	1346			1404
erhausen Hbf d.			...											1234						1332					
n Hbf d.	1141	1141	...	1147		1155	1155	1159			1204		1223		1259n	1259y	1317		1322	...	1341	1359			1417
lsenkirchen Hbf d.			...		1148	1205	1205							1246						...					
anne-Eickel Hbf d.			...											1252						...					
cklinghausen Hbf d.			...		1159									1300						...					
um Hbf d.	1152	1152	...	1158				1210			1216		1235		1310n	1310y	1329j		1334	...	1352	1410			1429k
mund Hbf a.	1203	1203	...	1209				1221	1221	1221	1230		1246		1321n	1321	1342j		1345	...	1403	1421	1421	1421	1442k
mund Hbf 805 d.	...	1207	...	1212				1225	...	1228	...		1248		...	1325	...		1347	...	...	1425	...	1428	...
amm (Westf) 805 a.	...	1228	...	1232					...	1242	...	1302	1306		...		...	1402	1406	...	...		...	1442	...
amm (Westf) d.	...	1233	...	1234					...	1244	...	1311	1311		...		...	1411	1411	...	...		...	1444	...
Hannover Hbf 810 a.	...		...	1401					...	1418	...	1428	1428		...		...	1528	1528	...	...		...	1618	...
Leipzig Hbf 866 a.	...		...						...	1717	...				...		...			...	...		...	1917	...
Berlin Hbf 810 a.	...	1836	...	1553					...	...	...	1609	1609		...		...	1706	1706	...	...		...	...	...
ster (Westf) Hbf 801 d.	...	...	...	...	1228	1249	1249	1257	...	...	...	...	...	1328	...	1357	...	...	...	...	...	1457	...	...	...
abrück Hbf 801 815 d.	...	...	...	...	...	1315	1315	1323	...	...	...	...	...	...	...	1423	...	...	...	...	...	1523	...	...	...
nen Hbf 801 815 d.	...	...	...	...	...			1417	...	...	...	...	...	...	...	1518	...	...	...	...	...	1618	...	...	...
burg Hbf 801 a.	...	...	...	...	...	1507	1507	1511	...	...	...	...	...	...	...	1613	...	...	...	...	...	1713	...	...	...
burg Altona a.	...	...	...	...	...	1521	1521	...	...	...	...	...	...	...	...	...	...	...	...	...	...	1728	...	...	...

	IC 2200	ICE 951	ICE 941	ICE 610	IC 2024	ICE 722	ICE 1122	ICE 651	ICE 641	ICE 124	IC 1920	IC 1920	IC 1216	IC 2312	ICE 108	IC 2045	ICE 720	IC 2157	ICE 953	ICE 943	IC 2006	IC 2014	IC 2004	ICE 518	ICE 1026
						Ⓐ	Ⓒ	n			①–④	⑦w	⑤		⑥k	Ⓑq		Ⓑq	Ⓑq		⑥	⑤			
	N	✕	✕	🍷	P🍷	🍷	🍷	✕	✕	A🍷	R	¶	S🍷	🍷	n🍷	D	🍷	◇	✕	✕	🍷♦	🍷♦	🍷♦	🍷	✕
Basel SBB 🚌 912 d.	...	...	...	...	...	...	...	...	...	...	...	...	...	...	1113	...	...	...	...	...	...	...	...	...	...
Karlsruhe Hbf 912 d.	...	...	...	...	...	...	...	...	...	...	...	...	...	...	1300	...	...	...	...	...	1221	...	1221w	...	...
inchen Hbf 904 930 ⊠ d.	...	...	...	0928	...	0955	0955	...	...	...	...	...	0848b	...		...	1055	...	...	...		...		1128	...
ittgart Hbf 912 ⊠ d.	...	...	...	1151	...			...	...	...	...	1004t	1114	1129		...		...	...	...		1209		1351	...
Nürnberg Hbf 920 d.	...	...	...		0929	1100	1100	...	...	...	...					...	1200	...	...	...					...
ankfurt (Main) Hbf 910/1 d.	...	...	...		1142	1310	1310	...	...	1329	...	1215d				...	1410	...	...	...					1344
ankfurt Flughafen ✈ § d.	...	...	...	1309	1158	1325	1322	...	...	1343	...	1228x			1409	...	1425	...	...	...				1509	1358
inz Hbf 911 d.	...	...	...		1220			...	...		...	1248x	1248	1320		...		...	...	...	1345	1345	1345w		1420
enz Hbf d.	...	...	...		1313			...	...		...	1343	1343	1413		...		...	...	...	1443	1443	1443		1513
rnach d.	...	...	...					...	...		...	1356	1356			...		...	...	...	1456	1456	1456		
agen d.	...	...	...					...	...		...	1408	1408			...		...	...	...	1508	1508	1508		
n Hbf d.	...	...	...		1344			1425	...		...	1422	1422	1444		...		...	...	...	1522	1522	1522		1545
ln/Bonn Flughafen ✈ d.	...	...	...						...		...					...		...	...	1512n					
Hbf a.	...	...	...	1405	1405			1445	...	1432	...	1442	1442	1505	1505	...		...	...		1542	1542	1542	1605	1605
Hbf d.	1346	1348v	...	1410n	1410			1448	1427y	1446	1445	1445	1445	1510	1510	1513v		1520	1548v		1546	1546	1546	1610n	1610
Messe/Deutz d.			...			1417	1427										1517			1527n					
lingen Hbf d.			...		1429n										1528	1531n									1629n
ippertal Hbf d.		1416	...		1444n			1516							1543	1543			1616						1643n
agen Hbf d.		1435	...		1502n			1535							1601	1601			1635						1702n
seldorf Hbf d.	1414		1352	1433n	1433y	1438	1448		1452	1513	1518	1518	1518	1533			1538	1546		1552	1611	1612	1612	1633n	1633y
seldorf Flughafen ✈ d.			1400						1500									1553		1600					
sburg Hbf d.	1428		1410	1446n	1446y	1454	1504		1510	1529	1533	1533	1533	1546			1551	1604		1610	1624	1626	1626	1646n	1646y
erhausen Hbf d.	1435									1534												1634	1634		
en Hbf d.			1423	1459n	1459y	1505	1517		1523	...	1545	1545	1545	1559			1604	1617		1623	1639			1659n	1659y
lsenkirchen Hbf d.	1446					...				...												1646	1646		
anne-Eickel Hbf d.	1452					...				...												1652	1652		
cklinghausen Hbf d.	1500					...				...												1700	1700		
um Hbf d.			1435	1510n	1510y	...	1529j		1535	...	1556	1556	1556	1609			1615k	1630		1635	1652			1710n	1710y
mund Hbf a.			1446	1521n	1521	...	1542j		1546	...	1608	1608	1608	1621	1621	1621	1629k	1641		1646	1703			1721n	1721
mund Hbf 805 d.			1448	...	1525	...	...		1548	...	1611	1611	1611	1625	...	1628	...	1643		1648	...			...	1725
amm (Westf) 805 a.		1502	1506	...		...	...	1602	1606	...	1632	1632	1632		...	1642	...	1702	1702	1706	...			...	
amm (Westf) d.		1511	1511	...		...	...	1611	1611	...	1634	1634	1634		...	1644	...	...	1711	1711	...			...	
Hannover Hbf 810 a.		1628	1628	...		...	...	1728	1728	...	1801	1801	1801		...	1818	...	...	1828	1828	...			...	
Leipzig Hbf 866 a.				...		...	...			...					...	2117	...	...			...			...	
Berlin Hbf 810 a.		1809	1809	...		...	...	1906	1906	...	1954	1954	1954		...	...	...	...	2009	2009	...			...	
ster (Westf) Hbf 801 d.	1529	...	...	...	1557	...	...	...	...	...	...	...	...	1658	...	...	...	...	...	...	...	1728	1728	...	1757
abrück Hbf 801 815 d.	...	...	...	...	1623	...	...	...	...	...	...	...	...	1724	...	...	...	...	...	...	...	...	...	...	1823
nen Hbf 801 815 d.	...	...	...	...	1718	...	...	...	...	...	...	...	...	1819	...	...	...							...	1917
burg Hbf 801 a.	...	...	...	...	1813	...	...	...	...	...	...	...	...	1914	...	...	...							...	2013
burg Altona a.	...	...	...	...	1828	...	...	...	...	...	...	...	...	1928	...	...	...							...	2028

See Table **802** for Rhein - Ruhr local RE and S-Bahn services

NOTES (LISTED BY TRAIN NUMBER)

– ⑤⑦ (also Oct. 3; not Oct. 2). [12] Düsseldorf - Kassel - Erfurt - Halle - Berlin.
– ①②③④⑦ (not Oct. 2). [12] and 🍷 (Konstanz - Karlsruhe ⑦**w** -) Koblenz - Emden.
– [12] and 🍷 Konstanz - Karlsruhe - Mannheim - Dortmund.
– [12] and 🍷 Stuttgart - Mannheim - Münster - Emden.
– ⑥ until Oct. 29. [12] Stuttgart - Münster - Emden - Norddeich Mole.
– [12] and 🍷 Stuttgart - Köln - Hamburg - Stralsund (- Greifswald Ⓐ).
– [12] and 🍷 (Passau ● -) (Regensburg - Nürnberg ⚒ -) Frankfurt - Köln - Kiel.

To Amsterdam (Table **28**). Subject to alteration July 9 – 24.
To Dresden (Table **842**).
To Norddeich Mole (Table **812**).
From Passau (Table **920**).
①②③④⑥ (not Oct. 3). Departs Stuttgart 0810 July 16 - Aug. 27.
①–④ (not Oct. 3).
⑤ (not July 29). From Salzburg (Table **890**).
Ⓐ (not Nov. 1). From Tübingen Hbf (d. 0611).
Daily to Oct. 30; ⑤ from Nov. 4.

a – Ⓐ (not July 11 - Aug. 19).
b – Not Aug. 5 - Sept. 9.
c – Also Oct. 3.
d – 1200 Sept. 4 - Oct. 30.
e – ⚒ only.
h – Not July 16.
j – ⑥ only.
k – ⑥ (also Oct. 2).
m – Not July 11 - Aug. 18, Oct. 3.
n – Not July 9 - Aug. 21.
q – Not Oct. 2.
r – 1010 July 21 - Aug. 27.
t – Sept. 4 - Oct. 30.
v – 20 – 25 minutes **earlier** July 9 - Aug. 21.
w – ⑦ (also Oct. 3; not Oct. 2).

x – Not Sept. 4 - Oct. 30.
y – July 9 - Aug. 21 only.
z – Ⓒ (not July 9 - Aug. 21).

◇ – [12] Köln - Kassel - Erfurt - Weimar - Halle.
● – ①⑤⑥ (also Oct. 4, Nov. 2; not Oct. 3, 31).
¶ – Train number **2412** Sept. 4 - Oct. 30.
⊠ – Timings at München and Stuttgart are subject to alteration until Sept. 11. See shaded panel on page 367 for further details.
★ – Operated by Hamburg-Köln-Express GmbH. www.hkx.de. Information on ticket validity will be found on page 367.
§ – Frankfurt Flughafen Fernbahnhof (Tables **910** and **911**).

800 KOBLENZ - KÖLN - DORTMUND - HAMBURG

	IC	*ICE*	*ICE*	*ICE*	*IC*	*EC*	*ICE*	*ICE*	*ICE*	*ICE*	*ICE*	*IC*	*ICE*	*IC*	*ICE*	*ICE*	*ICE*	*ICE*	*IC*	*EC*	*EC*	*IC*	*ICE*	*ICE*
	2196	**628**	**653**	**643**	**2012**	**8**	**106**	**626**	**122**	**955**	**945**	**2002**	**516**	**2022**	**624**	**1124**	**655**	**645**	**118**	**6**	**6**	**2041**	**606**	**104**
	Ⓑq		n								Ⓑq				Ⓐ	Ⓒ	n				Ⓑq	⑦	Ⓐn	
	🍷	🍷	✕	✕	🍷♦	✕♦	🍷	🍷	A🍷	✕	✕	E	🍷	🍷	🍷	🍷	✕	✕	♦	✕♦	✕♦	w		A🍷
Basel SBB 🏛 **912** d.	...	...	...	...	...	1220	1313	...	...	...	...	...	...	...	...	...	...	...	...	1427	1427	...	...	1513
Karlsruhe Hbf **912** d.	...	...	...	...	...	1412	1500	...	...	...	...	...	...	...	...	...	...	...	...	1612	1612	...	...	1700
München Hbf **904 930** ⊠ d.	...	1155	...	...	...	|	|	1255	...	...	...	...	1328	...	1355	1355	...	...	...	|	|	...	...	|
Stuttgart Hbf **912** ⊠ d.	...	|	...	...	1314	|	|	|	...	...	...	...	1551	...	|	|	...	...	1512	|	|	...	...	|
Nürnberg Hbf **920** d.	...	1300	...	...	|	|	|	1400	...	...	...	...	|	...	1500	1500	...	...	|	|	|	...	...	|
Frankfurt (Main) Hbf **910/1** d.	...	1510	...	...	|	|	|	1609	1629	...	...	...	|	1544	1710	1710	...	...	|	|	|	...	...	|
Frankfurt Flughafen ✈ § d.	...	1525	...	...	|	|	1609	1625	1643	...	...	...	1709	1558	1725	1722	...	...	|	|	|	...	...	1809
Mainz Hbf **911** d.	...	|	...	...	1448	1520	|	|	|	...	...	...	|	1620	|	|	...	...	1648	1720	1720	...	...	|
Koblenz Hbf d.	...	|	...	...	1543	1613	|	|	|	...	...	...	|	1713	|	|	...	...	1743	1813	1813	...	...	|
Andernach d.	...	|	...	...	1556	|	|	|	|	...	...	...	|	|	|	|	...	...	1756	|	|	...	...	|
Remagen d.	...	|	...	...	1608	|	|	|	|	...	...	...	|	|	|	|	...	...	1808	|	|	...	...	|
Bonn Hbf d.	...	|	...	...	1622	1644	|	|	|	...	...	...	|	1744	|	|	1825j	...	1822	1844	1844	...	...	|
Köln/Bonn Flughafen ✈ d.	...	|	...	1612a	|	|	|	|	|	...	...	...	|	|	|	|	|	1811n	|	|	|	...	...	|
Köln Hbf a.	...	|	...	|	1642	1705	1705	|	1732‡	...	...	...	1805	1805	|	|	1845j	|	1842	1905	1905	...	...	1905
Köln Hbf d.	1614	|	1648	1628y	1646	1710	1710n	|	1746	1748v	...	1745	1810n	1810	|	|	1848	1826y	1846	1910	1910	1913v	1913	1914
Köln Messe/Deutz d.	|	1619	|	1630a	|	|	|	1717	|	|	...	|	|	|	1816	1828¦	|	1824n	|	|	|	|	|	|
Solingen Hbf d.	|	|	|	|	|	|	1728n	|	|	|	...	|	|	1829n	|	|	|	|	|	|	|	1931n	1931	|
Wuppertal Hbf d.	|	|	1716	|	|	|	1743n	|	|	1816	...	|	|	1843n	|	|	1916	|	|	|	|	1943	1944	|
Hagen Hbf d.	|	|	1735	|	|	|	1801n	|	|	1835	...	|	|	1901n	|	|	1935	|	|	|	|	2001	2002	|
Düsseldorf Hbf d.	1637	1641	|	1652	1715	1733	|	1738	1814	|	1752	1817z	1833n	1833y	1837	1850¦	|	1846c	1911	1933	1933	|	|	1938
Düsseldorf Flughafen ✈ d.	|	|	|	1700	|	|	|	|	|	|	1800	|	|	|	|	|	|	1859	|	|	|	|	|	|
Duisburg Hbf d.	1650	1654	|	1710	1729x	1746	|	1751	1826	|	1810	1830	1846n	1847y	1850	1904¦	|	1910	1924	1946	1946	|	|	1951
Oberhausen Hbf d.	|	|	|	|	|	|	|	1801q	1832	|	|	1837	|	|	|	|	|	|	|	|	|	|	|	1956
Essen Hbf d.	1702	1717z	|	1723	1745	1759	|	1804k	...	|	1823	|	1859n	1859y	1904	1917¦	|	1923	1936	1959	1959	|	|	...
Gelsenkirchen Hbf d.	|	|	|	|	|	|	|	|	...	|	|	1849	|	|	|	|	|	|	1946	|	|	|	|	...
Wanne-Eickel Hbf d.	|	|	|	|	|	|	|	|	...	|	|	|	|	|	|	|	|	|	1952	|	|	|	|	...
Recklinghausen Hbf d.	|	|	|	|	|	|	|	|	...	|	|	1900	|	|	|	|	|	|	2000	|	|	|	|	...
Bochum Hbf d.	|	1729k	|	1735	1757	1811	|	1815k	...	|	1835	|	1910n	1911y	1916	1930¦	|	1935	|	2010	2010	|	|	...
Dortmund Hbf a.	|	1740k	|	1746	1809	1821	1821n	1829k	...	|	1846	|	1921n	1921	1930	1942¦	|	1946	|	2021	2021	2021	2021	...
Dortmund Hbf **805** d.	|	...	|	1748	1828	1825	...	...	...	|	1848	|	...	1925	...	...	|	1948	|	...	2025	2028	...	...
Hamm (Westf) **805** a.	|	...	1802	1806	1843	|	...	...	...	1902	1906	|	...	|	...	...	2002	2006	|	...	|	2042	...	...
Hamm (Westf) d.	|	...	1811	1811	1845	|	...	...	...	1911	1911	|	...	|	...	...	2011	2011	|	...	|	2044	...	...
Hannover Hbf **810** a.	|	...	1928	1928	2018	|	...	...	...	2028	2028	|	...	|	...	...	2128	2128	|	...	|	2218	...	...
Leipzig Hbf **866** a.	|	...	|	|	2321w	|	...	...	...	|	|	|	...	|	...	...	|	|	|	...	|	...	...	...
Berlin Hbf **810** a.	|	...	2106	2106	...	|	...	...	...	2219	2219	|	...	|	...	...	2306	2306	|	...	|	...	...	...
Münster (Westf) Hbf **801** d.	|	...	...	...	...	1857	...	...	...	...	...	1929	...	1957	...	...	...	...	2030	...	2057	...	...	...
Osnabrück Hbf **801 815** d.	|	...	...	...	...	1923	...	...	...	...	...	...	...	2023	...	...	...	...	...	...	2123	...	...	...
Bremen Hbf **801 815** d.	|	...	...	...	...	2018	...	...	...	...	...	...	...	2118	...	...	...	...	...	...	2219	...	...	...
Hamburg Hbf **801** a.	1946	...	...	...	...	2113	...	...	...	...	...	...	...	2213	...	...	...	...	...	...	2314	...	...	...
Hamburg Altona a.	2001	...	...	...	...	2128	...	...	...	...	...	...	...	2227	...	...	...	...	...	...	2329	...	...	...

	ICE	*ICE*	*EC*	*ICE*	*ICE*	*ICE*	*ICE*	*ICE*	*ICE*	*ICE*	*IC*	*IC*	*ICE*	*ICE*	*ICE*	*ICE*	*ICE*	*ICE*	*IC*	*IC*	*CNL*	*ICE*	*ICE*	*ICE*
	957	**947**	**114**	**26**	**514**	**620**	**120**	**710**	**657**	**657**	**2318**	**2318**	**1102**	**102**	**528**	**1522**	**512**	**526**	**1910**	**2210**	**40447**	**100**	**524**	**22**
	⑦w						Ⓑq	⑦d	⑦y	⑦w		Ⓑq	⑥k	Ⓑq				Ⓑq	⑦w	Ⓑq				
	✕	✕	🍷♦	B✕	🍷	G🍷	A¶🍷	🍷	✕	n✕	🍷	🍷	🍷	🍷	🍷	✕	🍷	🍷	🍷	🍷	♦	🍷	🍷	B✕
Basel SBB 🏛 **912** d.	...	...	...	...	...	...	...	...	...	...	...	...	1713	1713	...	...	...	...	...	...	...	1913	...	...
Karlsruhe Hbf **912** d.	...	...	...	...	...	...	...	...	...	...	...	...	1900	1900	...	...	...	...	...	...	...	2101	...	...
München Hbf **904 930** ⊠ d.	...	...	1346	...	1528	1555	...	...	...	...	...	...	|	|	1652	1618	1727	1755	1620	...	...	|	1855	...
Stuttgart Hbf **912** ⊠ d.	...	...	1609t	...	1751	|	...	1836	...	...	1737	1737	|	|	|	|	1951	|	1914	1918p	...	|	|	...
Nürnberg Hbf **920** d.	...	...	|	1529	|	1700	...	|	...	...	|	|	|	|	1800	1733	|	1901	|	|	...	|	2000	1929
Frankfurt (Main) Hbf **910/1** d.	...	...	|	1742	|	1910	1929	|	...	...	|	|	|	|	2010	1944	|	2110	|	|	...	|	2210	2146
Frankfurt Flughafen ✈ § d.	...	...	|	1758	1909	1922	1943	1955	...	...	|	|	2009	2009	2025	1958	2109	2125	|	|	...	2209	2225	2159
Mainz Hbf **911** d.	...	...	1745	1820	|	|	|	|	...	...	1920	1920	|	|	|	2020	|	|	2048	2120	...	|	|	2220
Koblenz Hbf d.	...	...	1843	1913	|	|	|	|	...	...	2013	2013	|	|	|	2113	|	|	2143	2213	...	|	|	2313
Andernach d.	...	...	1856	|	|	|	|	|	...	...	|	|	|	|	|	|	|	|	2156	|	...	|	|	|
Remagen d.	...	...	1908	|	|	|	|	|	...	...	|	|	|	|	|	|	|	|	2208	|	...	|	|	|
Bonn Hbf d.	...	...	1922	1944	|	|	|	|	...	2025	2044	2044	|	|	|	2145	|	|	2222	2244	...	|	|	2344
Köln/Bonn Flughafen ✈ d.	...	...	|	|	|	|	|	|	...	|	|	|	|	|	|	|	|	|	|	|	...	|	2330	|
Köln Hbf a.	...	...	1942	2005	2005	|	2032	|	...	2045	2105	2105	2105	2105n	|	2205	2205	|	2242	2305	...	2307	|	0005
Köln Hbf d.	1948v	1927e	1946	2010	2010r	|	2042	|	2020	2048	...	2110	2110	2110n	|	2210n	2210	|	2245	...	2313	2316	|	0011
Köln Messe/Deutz d.	|	|	|	|	|	2028	|	2047	|	|	...	|	|	2105y	2117	|	|	2217	|	...	|	|	2341	|
Solingen Hbf d.	|	|	|	2029n	|	|	|	|	|	|	...	|	|	2128n	|	2229n	|	|	|	...	|	|	|	|
Wuppertal Hbf d.	2016	|	|	2043n	|	|	|	|	|	2116	...	|	|	2143	|	2243n	|	|	|	...	|	|	|	|
Hagen Hbf d.	2035	|	|	2102n	|	|	|	|	|	2135	...	|	|	2201	|	2302n	|	|	|	...	|	|	|	|
Düsseldorf Hbf d.	|	1952	2011	2033y	2033r	2050	2109	2113	2045	|	...	2133	2133	|	2138	|	2233	2238	2309	...	2337	2342	0002	0034
Düsseldorf Flughafen ✈ d.	|	2000	|	|	|	|	|	|	2059	|	...	|	|	|	|	|	|	|	|	...	|	2350	|	|
Duisburg Hbf d.	|	2010	2024	2046y	2046r	2104	2126	2129	2110	|	...	2146	2146	|	2151	|	2246	2251	2322	...	2353	2359	0015	0047
Oberhausen Hbf d.	|	|	|	|	|	|	2132	|	|	|	...	|	|	|	|	|	|	|	|	...	|	|	|	|
Essen Hbf d.	|	2023	2039	2059y	2059r	2117	...	2141	2123	|	...	2159	2159	|	2204	|	2307z	2304	2338	...	0006	0011	0028	0059
Gelsenkirchen Hbf d.	|	|	|	|	|	|	...	|	|	|	...	|	|	|	|	|	|	|	|	...	|	|	|	|
Wanne-Eickel Hbf d.	|	|	|	|	|	|	...	|	|	|	...	|	|	|	|	|	|	|	|	...	|	|	|	|
Recklinghausen Hbf d.	|	|	|	|	|	|	...	|	|	|	...	|	|	|	|	|	2327	|	|	...	|	|	|	|
Bochum Hbf d.	|	2035	2049	2110y	2110n	2129	...	2151	2135	|	...	2210	2210	|	2216	|	|	2316	2349	...	0017	0022	0038	0110
Dortmund Hbf a.	|	2046	2100	2122	2121r	2142	...	2202	2146	|	...	2221	2221	2221	2230	2322n	|	2327	2359	...	0029	0033	0049	0121
Dortmund Hbf **805** d.	|	2048	...	2125	...	...	...	...	2148	|	...	2225w	2228	2228	...	...	|	...	...	...	0032	...	...	...
Hamm (Westf) **805** a.	2102	2106	...	|	...	...	...	...	2206	2202	...	|	2248	2248	...	...	|	...	...	...	0047	...	...	...
Hamm (Westf) d.	2111	2111	...	|	...	...	...	...	2211	2211	...	|	2250	2250	...	...	|	...	...	...	0049	...	...	...
Hannover Hbf **810** a.	2228	2228	...	|	...	...	...	...	2328	2328	...	|	0018	0018	...	...	|	...	...	...	0223	...	...	...
Leipzig Hbf **866** a.	|	|	...	|	...	...	...	...	|	|	...	|	...	...	...	...	|	...	...	...	|	...	...	...
Berlin Hbf **810** a.	0010	0010	...	|	...	...	...	...	0110	0110	...	|	...	...	...	...	|	...	...	...	0658f	...	...	...
Münster (Westf) Hbf **801** d.	...	...	...	2157	...	...	...	...	...	...	...	2254w	...	...	...	...	2356	...	...	...	...	...	...	...
Osnabrück Hbf **801 815** d.	...	...	...	2224	...	...	...	...	...	...	...	...	...	...	...	...	...	...	...	...	...	...	...	...
Bremen Hbf **801 815** d.	...	...	...	2319	...	...							...	...	...	...	...	...	...	...	...	...	...	...
Hamburg Hbf **801** a.	...	...	...	0014	...	...							...	...	...	...	...	...	...	...	...	...	...	...
Hamburg Altona a.	...	...	...	...	...	...							...	...	...	...	...	...	...	...	...	...	...	...

*See Table **802** for Rhein - Ruhr local RE and S-Bahn services*

♦ – **NOTES** (LISTED BY TRAIN NUMBER)

6 – [12] and ✕ Interlaken - Bern - Basel - Dortmund (- Hamburg Ⓑ**q**).
8 – [12] and ✕ Zürich - Basel - Hamburg.
114 – WÖRTHERSEE – [12] and 🍷 Klagenfurt - Salzburg - München - Dortmund.
118 – [12] Innsbruck - Bregenz - Lindau - Ulm - Münster.
2012 – ALLGÄU – [12] and 🍷 Oberstdorf - Stuttgart - Köln - Hannover (- Magdeburg ⊖) (- Leipzig ⑦**w**).
40447 – KOPERNIKUS – 🛏 1, 2 cl. and ▬ 2 cl. (Ⓡ) Köln - Berlin - Dresden - Praha; [2] (*IC* **61447**) Köln - Berlin - Dresden - Praha; 🛏 1, 2 cl., ▬ 2 cl. and [2] (*EN* **447** Ⓡ – JAN KIEPURA) Köln - Warszawa (see Table **24**).

A – To Amsterdam (Table **28**). Subject to alteration July 9 – 24.
B – From Wien (Tables **950/920**).
E – [12] Köln - Münster (- Emden ●).
G – From Garmisch on ⑥ (Table **895**).

a – Ⓐ (not July 11 - Aug. 19).
c – 1850 July 9 - Aug. 21.
d – Also Oct. 3; not July 17, Oct. 2. Departs Stuttgart 1812 July 24 - Aug. 28.
e – ⚒ (not July 9 - Aug. 20).

f – 0653 until Aug. 4.
j – ①–④ (not Oct. 3).
k – ⑥ (also Oct. 2).
n – Not July 9 - Aug. 21.
p – 1937 on ⑤⑦.
q – Ⓑ (not Oct. 2).
r – July 9 - Aug. 21 departs Köln 2013, Düsseldorf 2037, Duisburg 2050, Essen 2105, arrives Dortmund 2136.
t – Not July 30 - Sept. 11.

v – 21 – 28 minutes **earlier** July 9 - Aug. 21.
w – ⑦ (also Oct. 3; not Oct. 2).
x – 1733 on ⑤⑦ (also Oct. 3).
y – July 9 - Aug. 21 only.
z – Arrives 9 – 10 minutes earlier.

⊖ – ①④⑤⑦ (not Oct. 2).
● – Daily to Nov. 4, Ⓑ from Nov. 6.
‡ – 1739 on Ⓒ.
¦ – July 9 - Aug. 21 departs Köln Messe/Deutz 1831, Düsseldorf 1855, Duisburg 1917, Essen 1935, Bochum 1951, arrives Dortmund 2002.
¶ – Terminates at Köln July 8 – 24.
⊠ – Timings at München and Stuttgart are subject to alteration until Sept. 11. See shaded panel on page 367 for further details.
§ – Frankfurt Flughafen Fernbahnhof (Tables **910** and 9

HAMBURG - DORTMUND - KÖLN - KOBLENZ 800

	ICE	ICE	ICE	ICE	ICE	CNL	ICE	IC	ICE	IC	ICE	ICE	ICE	ICE	ICE	ICE	EC	ICE	ICE	EC	IC	ICE	ICE	ICE
	523	**511**	**23**	**1125**	**525**	**40458**	**101**	**2319**	**713**	**2003**	**813**	**1127**	**527**	**1521**	**513**	**815**	**115**	**529**	**103**	**7**	**119**	**121**	**646**	**656**
	⚒	① g		†	⚒	Ⓡ		⚒	⚒ r	Ⓐ	Ⓐ	⑥	Ⓐ			Ⓐ						①–⑥	Ⓐ	Ⓐ
	🍷	🍷	✕◆	🍷	🍷	🍷◆	🍷	🍷	🍷	p	🍷	G 🍷	🍷	✕	🍷	✕	🍷◆	🍷	🍷	✕◆	◆	A¶🍷	✕	✕
Hamburg Altona .... d.	...	...	...	...	...	...	...	...	...	...	...	...	...	...	...	...	...	...	...	0428e	...	...	...	...
Hamburg Hbf .... **801** d.	...	...	...	...	...	...	...	...	...	...	...	...	...	...	...	...	...	...	...	0442e	...	...	...	...
Bremen Hbf .... **801 815** d.	...	...	...	...	...	...	...	...	...	...	...	...	...	...	...	...	...	...	...	0540e	...	...	...	...
Osnabrück Hbf ...... **801 815** d.	...	...	...	...	...	...	...	...	...	...	...	...	...	...	...	...	...	...	...	0637e	...	...	...	...
Münster (Westf) Hbf ...... **801** d.	...	...	...	...	...	...	...	0503g	...	...	...	...	...	...	0601	...	0631	...	...	0703e	0727	...	...	...
Berlin Hbf **810** .... d.	...	...	...	...	...	2344x	...	|	...	...	...	...	...	...	|	...	|	...	...	|	|	...	0430	0430
Leipzig Hbf **866** .... d.	...	...	...	...	...	|	...	|	...	...	...	...	...	...	|	...	|	...	...	|	|	...	|	|
Hannover Hbf **810** .... d.	...	...	...	...	...	0340	...	|	...	...	...	...	...	...	|	...	|	...	0540	|	|	...	0621	0621
Hamm (Westf) .... a.	...	...	...	...	...	0510	...	|	...	...	...	...	...	...	|	...	|	...	0713	|	|	...	0748	0748
Hamm (Westf) .... **805** d.	...	...	...	...	...	0512	...	|	...	...	...	...	...	...	|	...	|	...	0715	|	|	...	0752	0754
Dortmund Hbf .... **805** a.	...	...	...	...	...	0531	...	0533g	...	...	...	...	...	...	0632	...	|	...	0732	0733e	|	...	0809	|
Dortmund Hbf .... d.	0406	0437n	0437	0514	0524	0535	0537t	0537	0552	0549	0600t	0614	0624	0636n	0637	0652	|	0724	0737	0737	|	...	0812	|
Bochum Hbf .... d.	0417	|	0449	0526	0538	|	|	0549	0605	|	|	0628	0638	|	0649	0704	|	0738	|	0749	|	...	0824	|
Recklinghausen Hbf .... d.	|	|	|	|	|	|	|	|	|	|	|	|	|	|	|	|	0700	|	|	|	0758	...	|	|
Wanne-Eickel Hbf .... d.	|	|	|	|	|	|	|	|	|	0606	|	|	|	|	|	|	0709	|	|	|	0806	...	|	|
Gelsenkirchen Hbf .... d.	|	|	|	|	|	|	|	|	|	0612	|	|	|	|	|	|	0715	|	|	|	0812	...	|	|
Essen Hbf .... d.	0428	|	0500	0538	0553	0604	|	0600	0615	|	|	0639	0653	|	0700	0715	|	0754	|	0800	0823	...	0836	|
Oberhausen Hbf .... d.	|	|	|	|	|	|	|	|	|	0626	|	|	|	|	|	|	0727	|	|	|	|	0826	|	|
Duisburg Hbf .... d.	0441	|	0512	0550	0607	0618	|	0613	0629	0633	|	0652	0707	|	0712	0729	0734	0808	|	0813	0838	0834	0849	|
Düsseldorf Flughafen ✈ .... d.	|	|	|	|	|	|	|	|	|	|	|	|	|	|	|	|	|	|	|	|	|	|	0859	|
Düsseldorf Hbf .... d.	0455	|	0527	0605	0621	0633	|	0627	0648	0652	|	0707	0721	|	0727	0747	0751	0822	|	0827	0852	0848	0908	|
Hagen Hbf .... d.	|	0457n	|	|	|	|	0557t	|	|	|	0621t	|	|	0657n	|	|	|	|	0757	|	|	|	|	0824
Wuppertal Hbf .... d.	|	0514n	|	|	|	|	0614t	|	|	|	0637t	|	|	0714n	|	|	|	|	0814	|	|	|	|	0841
Solingen Hbf .... d.	|	0527n	|	|	|	|	0627n	|	|	|	0650n	|	|	0727n	|	|	|	|	0827n	|	|	|	|	|
Köln Messe/Deutz .... a.	0515	|	|	0626	0642	|	|	|	0710	|	|	0728	0742	|	|	0809	|	0842	0854y	|	|	|	0928n	|
Köln Hbf .... a.	|	0546n	0550	|	|	0656	0646	0649	|	0715	0709	|	|	0746n	0749	|	0815	|	0846n	0850	0915	0912	|	0915v
Köln Hbf .... d.	|	0555	0553	|	|	...	0655	0653	|	0718	0720	|	|	0753	0755	|	0818	|	0855n	0853	0918	0927	|	...
Köln/Bonn Flughafen ✈ .... a.	0529	|	|	|	|	...	|	|	|	|	|	|	|	|	|	0820	|	|	|	|	|	|	0947n	...
Bonn Hbf .... d.	|	|	0614	|	|	...	|	0714	|	0737	|	|	|	0814	|	|	0837	|	|	0914	0937	|	...	...
Remagen .... d.	|	|	|	|	|	...	|	|	|	0751	|	|	|	|	|	|	0851	|	|	|	0951	|	...	...
Andernach .... d.	|	|	|	|	|	...	|	|	|	0803	|	|	|	|	|	|	0903	|	|	|	1003	|	...	...
Koblenz Hbf .... a.	|	|	0646	|	|	...	|	0746	|	0816	|	|	|	0846	|	|	0915	|	|	0946	1015	|	...	...
Mainz Hbf **911** .... a.	|	|	0738	|	|	...	|	0838	|	...	|	|	|	0938	|	|	1015	|	|	1038	1110	|	...	...
Frankfurt Flughafen ✈ § .... a.	0633	0649	0759	0733	0733	...	0749	|	0804	...	0826	0834	0833	0959	0849	0926	|	0933	0949	|	|	1016	...	...
Frankfurt (Main) Hbf **910/1** a.	0648	|	0813	0748	0748	...	|	|	|	...	0841	0848	0848	1013	|	0941	|	0948	|	|	|	1030	...	...
Nürnberg Hbf **920** .... a.	0859	|	1027	0959	0959	...	|	|	|	...	...	1059	1059	1224	|	...	|	1159	|	|	|	...	...	...
Stuttgart Hbf **912** .... ⊠ a.	|	0808	...	|	|	...	|	1024	0924	...	...	|	|	|	1008	...	1153j	|	|	|	1246	...	...	...
München Hbf **904 930** .. ⊠ a.	1004	1027	...	1104	1104	...	|	...	...	...	...	1204	1204	1338	1227	...	1411	1304	|	|	...	...	...	...
Karlsruhe Hbf **912** .... a.	...	...	...	...	...	...	0858	...	...	...	...	...	...	...	...	...	...	...	1058	1147	...	...	...	...
Basel SBB 🏛 **912** .... a.	...	...	...	...	...	...	1047	...	...	...	...	...	...	...	...	...	...	...	1247	1330	...	...	...	...

	ICE	IC	ICE	ICE	IC	IC	ICE	ICE	ICE	ICE	EC	IC	ICE	ICE	ICE	IC	ICE	IC	IC	ICE	ICE	IC	IC	ICE	IC
	621	**1099**	**515**	**27**	**2005**	**2005**	**623**	**946**	**956**	**105**	**9**	**2013**	**644**	**654**	**625**	**2023**	**517**	**1927**	**2009**	**944**	**954**	**2156**	**2156**	**627**	**2044**
		①–④			⚒	⑤⑥		⚒	⚒ n				⚒					Ⓐ			⚒ n	①–⑥	①–⑥		⚒
	🍷	m 🍷	🍷	✕◆	E	B 🍷	🍷	✕	✕	A 🍷	Z ✕	🍷◆	✕	✕	🍷	🍷	🍷		L	✕	✕	J H	K H	🍷	D
urg Altona .... d.	...	0558	...	...	...	...	...	...	...	...	0631	...	...	...	...	0731	...	...	...	...	...	...	...	...	...
urg Hbf .... **801** d.	...	0612	...	0546	...	...	...	...	...	...	0646	...	...	...	...	0746	...	...	...	...	...	...	...	...	...
en Hbf .... **801 815** d.	...	|	...	0644	...	...	...	...	...	...	0744	...	...	...	...	0844	...	...	...	...	...	...	...	...	...
orück Hbf .... **801 815** d.	...	|	...	0737	...	...	...	...	...	...	0837	...	...	...	...	0937	...	...	...	...	...	...	...	...	...
ter (Westf) Hbf .... **801** d.	...	|	...	0802	0832	0832	...	...	...	...	0903	...	...	...	...	1003	...	...	1032	...	...	...	...	...	...
erlin Hbf **810** .... d.	...	|	...	|	|	|	...	0538	0538	...	|	...	0652	0652	...	|	...	0701	|	0749	0749	...	...	...	...
Leipzig Hbf **866** .... d.	...	|	...	|	|	|	...	|	|	...	|	0430g	|	|	...	|	...	|	|	|	|	...	...	...	0643
annover Hbf **810** .... d.	...	|	...	|	|	|	...	0731	0731	...	|	0740	0831	0831	...	|	...	0856	|	0931	0931	...	...	...	0940
mm (Westf) .... a.	...	|	...	|	|	|	...	0848	0848	...	|	0913	0948	0948	...	|	...	1024	|	1048	1048	...	...	...	1114
mm (Westf) .... **805** d.	...	|	...	|	|	|	...	0852	0854	...	|	0915	0952	0954	...	|	...	1026	|	1052	1054	1056	1056	...	1116
nund Hbf .... **805** a.	...	|	...	0833	|	|	...	0909	|	...	0933	0932	1009	|	...	1033	...	1048	|	1109	|	1115	1115	...	1132
nund Hbf .... d.	0815c	|	0837n	0838	|	|	0916c	0912	|	...	0937	0952	1012	|	1016c	1036	1037n	1052	|	1112	|	1117	1117	1124c	1137
um Hbf .... d.	0829c	|	|	0849	|	|	0929c	0924	|	...	0949	1003	1024	|	1029c	1049y	1049n	1103	|	1124	|	1130	|	1138c	|
cklinghausen Hbf .... d.	|	|	|	|	0901	0901	|	|	|	...	|	|	|	|	|	|	|	|	1101	|	|	|	|	|	|
nne-Eickel Hbf .... d.	|	|	|	|	0909	0909	|	|	|	...	|	|	|	|	|	|	|	|	1109	|	|	|	|	|	|
lsenkirchen Hbf .... d.	|	|	|	|	0915	0915	|	|	|	...	|	|	|	|	|	|	|	|	1115	|	|	|	|	|	|
n Hbf .... d.	0840	0854	|	0900	|	|	0941	0936	|	...	1000	1014	1036	|	1040	1100y	1100n	1114	|	1136	|	1141	|	1153c	|
erhausen Hbf .... d.	|	|	|	|	0927	0927	|	|	|	1000	|	|	|	|	|	|	|	|	1127	|	|	|	|	1151a	|
urg Hbf .... d.	0855	0907	|	0912	0934	0934	0955	0949	|	1008	1013	1030	1049	|	1055	1113y	1112n	1130	1134	1149	|	1157	|	1207	|
eldorf Flughafen ✈ .... d.	|	|	|	|	|	|	|	0959	|	|	|	1040	1104	|	|	|	|	|	|	1159	|	1208	|	|	|
eldorf Hbf .... d.	0913	0921	|	0927	0949	0949	1012	1006	|	1022	1027	1051	1111	|	1108	1127y	1127n	1145	1150	1206	|	1216	|	1221	|
gen Hbf .... d.	|	|	0857n	|	|	|	|	|	0924	|	|	|	...	1024	|	1057n	|	|	|	|	1124	|	1147	|	1158
ppertal Hbf .... d.	|	|	0914n	|	|	|	|	|	0941	|	|	|	...	1041	|	1114n	|	|	|	|	1141	|	1209	|	1214
ingen Hbf .... d.	|	|	0927n	|	|	|	|	|	|	|	|	|	...	|	|	1127n	|	|	|	|	|	|	1221	|	1227n
Messe/Deutz .... a.	0933	|	|	|	|	|	1031	|	|	|	|	|	...	|	1128	|	|	|	|	1228y	|	|	|	1242	|
Hbf .... a.	|	0945	0946n	0950	1015	1015	|	1039y	1009	1046	1050	1115	...	1109v	|	1146	1149n	1212	1215	|	1209	1239	1239	|	1246v
Hbf .... d.	|	...	0955	0953	1018	1018	|	...	...	1055	1053	1118	...	1112d	|	1153	1155	...	...	|	...	...	...	|	...
n/Bonn Flughafen ✈ .... a.	|	...	|	|	|	|	1043	...	...	|	|	|	...	|	|	|	|	...	...	1240y	...	...	...	|	...
Hbf .... d.	|	...	|	1014	1037	1037	|	...	...	|	1114	1137	...	1132d	|	1214	|	...	...	...	...	...	...	|	...
agen .... d.	|	...	|	|	1051	1051	|	...	...	|	|	1151	...	...	|	|	|	...	...	...	...	...	...	|	...
rnach .... d.	|	...	|	|	1103	1103	|	...	...	|	|	1203	...	...	|	|	|	...	...	...	...	...	...	|	...
enz Hbf .... a.	|	...	|	1046	1115	1115	|	...	...	|	1146	1215	...	...	|	1246	|	...	...	...	...	...	...	|	...
inz Hbf **911** .... a.	|	...	|	1138	...	1215	|	...	...	|	1238	1310	...	...	|	1338	|	...	...	...	...	...	...	|	...
ankfurt Flughafen ✈ § .... a.	1034	...	1049	1159	...	|	1133	...	...	1149	|	|	...	...	1234	1359	1249	...	...	...	...	...	...	1330	...
ankfurt (Main) Hbf **910/1** a.	1048	...	|	1213	...	|	1148	...	...	|	|	|	...	...	1248	1412	|	...	...	...	...	...	...	1344	...
Nürnberg Hbf **920** .... a.	1259	...	|	1427	...	|	1403	...	...	|	|	|	...	...	1459	...	|	...	...	...	...	...	...	1559	...
ttgart Hbf **912** .... ⊠ a.	|	...	1208	...	...	|	|	...	...	|	|	1446	...	...	|	...	1408	...	...	...	...	...	...	|	...
nchen Hbf **904 930** .. ⊠ a.	1404	...	1427	...	...	|	1508	...	...	|	|	...	...	...	1606	...	1627	...	...	...	...	...	...	1704	...
Karlsruhe Hbf **912** .... a.	...	...	...	...	...	1334	...	...	...	1258	1347	...	...	...	...	...	...	...	...	...	...	...	...	...	...
Basel SBB 🏛 **912** .... a.	...	...	...	...	...	...	...	...	...	1447	1535	...	...	...	...	...	...	...	...	...	...	...	...	...	...

NOTES (LISTED BY TRAIN NUMBER)

[12] and ✕ (Hamburg ⚒ -) Dortmund - Basel - Bern - Interlaken.
[12] and ✕ Dortmund - Regensburg - Passau - Linz - Wien.
[12] and ✕ Hamburg - Dortmund - Regensburg - Passau - Linz - Wien.
\- WÖRTHERSEE – [12] and 🍷 Münster - München - Salzburg - Klagenfurt.
\- [12] Münster - Ulm - Lindau - Bregenz - Innsbruck.
– ALLGÄU – [12] and 🍷 (Leipzig ① g -) (Magdeburg ⚒ -) Hannover - Köln - Mannheim - Stuttgart - Ulm - Oberstdorf.
8 – KOPERNIKUS – 🛏 1, 2 cl. and ━ 2 cl. (Ⓡ) Praha - Dresden - Berlin - Köln; [2] (*IC* **61458**) Praha - Dresden - Berlin - Köln; 🛏 1, 2 cl., ━ 2 cl. and [2] (*EN* **446** Ⓡ – JAN KIEPURA) Warszawa - Köln (see Table **24**).

From Amsterdam (Table **28**). Subject to alteration July 9 – 24.
[12] and 🍷 Emden - Mannheim - Karlsruhe - Konstanz.
From Dresden (Table **842**).
From Emden (Table **812**).
⑥ (also Oct. 2). To Garmisch on ⑥ (Table **895**).
[12] Halle - Weimar - Erfurt - Kassel - Köln.

J – ①–⑥ to Sept. 3.
K – ①–⑥ from Sept. 5 (also Oct. 2; not Oct. 3).
L – [12] (Emden ★ -) Münster - Köln.
Z – To Zürich (Tables **510**).

a – Ⓐ only.
c – Ⓒ only.
d – ⚒ (not July 9 - Aug. 20).
e – ⚒ only.
g – ① (also Oct. 4; not Oct. 3).
j – Not July 30 - Sept. 11.
m – Not Oct. 3.
n – Not July 9 - Aug. 21.
p – Not Nov. 1.
r – Not July 16 – 20.
t – 22 – 25 minutes **earlier** July 9 - Aug. 21.

v – 17 – 32 minutes later July 9 - Aug. 21.
x – Not Aug. 1 – 3, Nov. 18 – 27 (see Table **810**). Departs 2316 from Aug. 5.
y – July 9 - Aug. 21 only.

¶ – Starts from Oberhausen July 9 – 25.
★ – Daily to Nov. 5; ①–⑥ from Nov. 7.
⊠ – Timings at München and Stuttgart are subject to alteration until Sept. 11. See shaded panel on page 367 for further details.
§ – Frankfurt Flughafen Fernbahnhof (Tables **910** and **911**).

800 HAMBURG - DORTMUND - KÖLN - KOBLENZ

	ICE	*IC*	*IC*	*ICE*	*ICE*	*ICE*	*ICE*	*ICE*	*IC*	*ICE*	*ICE*	*ICE*	*IC*	*ICE*	*IC*	*IC*	*IC*	*IC*	*ICE*	*ICE*	*ICE*	*ICE*	*ICE*	*IC*
	107	**2313**	**1911**	**123**	**642**	**652**	**1025**	**519**	**2201**	**942**	**952**	**721**	**2046**	**109**	**2217**	**2011**	**2011**	**2017**	**717**	**125**	**640**	**650**	**723**	**2027**
	†n		⑤⑦								n		⑥	Ⓑq		①–④	⑦w	⑤	⑦c				Ⓑq	
	🍸	🍸	♥🍸	A🍸	✕	✕	✕	🍸	N	✕	✕	🍸	D	n🍸	🍸◆	T🍸	🍸	F	🍸	A🍸	✕	✕	🍸	🍸◆
Hamburg Altona ... d.	...	0830	...	...	...	...	0931	...	...	...	...	...	...	...	...	...	...	...	...	...	...	...	...	1131
Hamburg Hbf ... 801 d.	...	0845	...	...	...	...	0946	...	...	...	...	...	...	...	1046	...	...	...	...	...	...	...	...	1146
Bremen Hbf ... 801 815 d.	...	0943	...	...	...	...	1044	...	...	...	...	...	...	...	1144	...	...	...	...	...	...	...	...	1244
Osnabrück Hbf ... 801 815 d.	...	1035	...	...	...	...	1137	...	...	...	...	...	...	...	1237	...	...	...	...	...	...	...	...	1337
Münster (Westf) Hbf ... 801 d.	...	1102	...	...	...	...	1202	...	1232	...	...	...	...	...	1303	...	...	...	...	...	...	...	...	1403
Berlin Hbf **810** ... d.	...	|	...	...	0852	0852	|	...	|	0949	0949	...	...	...	|	...	1002	...	...	...	1052	1052	...	|
Leipzig Hbf **866** ... d.	...	|	...	...	|	|	|	...	|	|	|	...	0843	...	|	...	|	...	...	...	|	|	...	|
Hannover Hbf **810** ... d.	...	|	...	...	1031	1031	|	...	|	1131	1131	...	1140	...	|	...	1156	1156	...	...	1231	1231	...	|
Hamm (Westf) ... a.	...	|	...	...	1148	1148	|	...	|	1248	1248	...	1314	...	|	...	1324	1324	...	...	1348	1348	...	|
Hamm (Westf) ... 805 d.	...	|	...	...	1152	1154	|	...	|	1252	1254	...	1316	...	|	...	1326	1326	...	...	1352	1354	...	|
Dortmund Hbf ... 805 a.	...	1133	...	...	1209	|	1233	...	|	1309	|	...	1332	...	1333	...	1347	1347	...	...	1409	|	...	1433
Dortmund Hbf ... d.	1137	1137	1152	...	1212	|	1236	1237n	|	1312	|	1324f	1337	1337	1337	...	1349	1352	1354	...	1412	|	1424g	1436
Bochum Hbf ... d.	|	1148	1203	...	1224	|	1249y	1249n	|	1324	|	1338f	|	|	1349	...	1401	1404	1406	...	1424	|	1438g	|
Recklinghausen Hbf ... d.	|	|	|	...	|	|	|	|	1301	|	|	|	|	|	|	...	|	|	|	...	|	|	|	|
Wanne-Eickel Hbf ... d.	|	|	|	...	|	|	|	|	1309	|	|	|	|	|	|	...	|	|	|	...	|	|	|	|
Gelsenkirchen Hbf ... d.	|	|	|	...	|	|	|	|	1315	|	|	|	|	|	|	...	|	|	|	...	|	|	|	|
Essen Hbf ... d.	|	1159	1214	...	1236	|	1300y	1300n	|	1336	|	1353	|	|	1400	...	1413	1414	1417	...	1436	|	1453	|
Oberhausen Hbf ... d.	|	|	|	1226	|	|	|	|	1327	|	|	|	|	|	|	...	|	|	|	1426	|	|	|	|
Duisburg Hbf ... d.	|	1212	1230	1234	1249	|	1312y	1312n	1334	1349	|	1407	|	|	1413	...	1427	1430	1432	1438	1449	|	1507	|
Düsseldorf Flughafen ✈ ... d.	|	|	|	|	1259	|	|	|	|	1359	|	|	|	|	|	...	|	|	|	|	1459	|	|	|
Düsseldorf Hbf ... d.	|	1226	1244	1248	1312	|	1327y	1327n	1348	1406	|	1421	|	|	1427	1446	1446	1446	1450	1454	1508	|	1521	|
Hagen Hbf ... d.	1157	|	|	|	|	1224	1257n	|	|	|	1324	|	1357	1357	|	|	|	|	|	|	|	1424	|	1457
Wuppertal Hbf ... d.	1214	|	|	|	|	1241	1314n	|	|	|	1341	|	1414	1414	|	|	|	|	|	|	|	1441	|	1515
Solingen Hbf ... d.	1227	|	|	|	|	|	1327n	|	|	|	|	|	1426n	1427	|	|	|	|	|	|	|	|	|	1527
Köln Messe/Deutz ... a.	|	|	|	|	1334n	|	|	|	|	|	|	1442	|	|	|	|	|	|	1512	|	1528a	|	1542	|
Köln Hbf ... a.	1246	1250	1312	1315	|	1309v	1346	1349n	1413	1439y	1409	|	1446v	1446	1450	1512	1512	1512	|	1518	|	1509v	|	1546
Köln Hbf ... d.	1255	1253	1318	1328	|	1312n	1353	1355	...	...	...	|	...	1455	1453	1518	1518	1518	|	1529	|	...	|	1553
Köln/Bonn Flughafen ✈ ... a.	|	|	|	|	1347n	|	|	|	...	...	...	|	...	|	|	|	|	|	|	|	1547a	...	|	|
Bonn Hbf ... d.	|	1314	1337	|	...	1332n	1414	|	...	...	...	|	...	|	1514	1537	1537	1537	|	|	...	...	|	1614
Remagen ... d.	|	|	1351	|	...	...	|	|	...	...	...	|	...	|	|	1551	1551	1551	|	|	...	...	|	|
Andernach ... d.	|	|	1403	|	...	...	|	|	...	...	...	|	...	|	|	1603	1603	1603	|	|	...	...	|	|
Koblenz Hbf ... a.	|	1346	1415	|	...	...	1446	|	...	...	...	|	...	|	1546	1615	1615	1615	|	|	...	...	|	1646
Mainz Hbf **911** ... a.	|	1438	1510	|	...	...	1538	|	...	...	...	|	...	|	1638	1710	1710	1710	|	|	...	...	|	1738
Frankfurt Flughafen ✈ § ... a.	1349	|	|	1416	...	...	1559	1449	...	...	...	1533	...	1549	|	|	|	|	1604	1616	...	...	1633	1759
Frankfurt (Main) Hbf **910/1** a.	|	|	|	1430	...	...	1613	|	...	...	...	1548	...	|	|	|	|	|	|	1630	...	...	1648	1813
Nürnberg Hbf **920** ... a.	|	|	|	...	...	...	...	|	...	...	...	1759	...	|	|	|	|	|	|	...	...	...	1859	2027
Stuttgart Hbf **912** ... ⊠ a.	|	1622	1646	...	...	...	...	1608	...	...	...	|	...	|	1825	1846	1846	1846	1718	...	...	...	|	...
München Hbf **904 930** .. ⊠ a.	|	...	...	...	...	...	...	1827	...	...	...	1907	...	|	...	...	...	2118‡	...	...	...	...	2004	...
Karlsruhe Hbf **912** ... a.	1456	...	...	...	...	...	...	...	...	...	...	...	...	1658	...	...	...	...	...	...	...	...	...	...
Basel SBB 🏛 **912** ... a.	1647	...	...	...	...	...	...	...	...	...	...	...	...	1847	...	...	...	...	...	...	...	...	...	...

	ICE	*IC*	*IC*	*ICE*	*ICE*	*ICE*	*IC*	*IC*	*HKX*	*IC*	*ICE*	*ICE*	*ICE*	*ICE*	*ICE*	*ICE*	*ICE*	*IC*	*ICE*	*IC*	*ICE*	*ICE*	*IC*	*ICE*
	611	**2019**	**2203**	**940**	**950**	**725**	**2048**	**2311**	**1805**	**1915**	**917**	**127**	**548**	**558**	**1228**	**1224**	**727**	**2229**	**613**	**2205**	**848**	**858**	**2152**	**729**
		⑥H	J		n				Q	⑤⑦	Ⓑq	G			Ⓐ	Ⓒ	Ⓑq					n		
	🍸	N	N	✕	✕	🍸	D	🍸◆	★🍸	U🍸	✕	A🍸	✕	✕	🍸◆	🍸◆	🍸	🍸◆	🍸	N	✕	✕	◆	🍸
Hamburg Altona ... d.	...	...	...	...	...	...	...	...	1236	...	...	...	...	...	...	...	...	...	...	...	...	...	...	...
Hamburg Hbf ... 801 d.	...	...	...	...	...	...	...	1246	1249	...	...	...	...	...	...	...	...	1346	...	...	...	...	...	...
Bremen Hbf ... 801 815 d.	...	...	...	...	...	...	...	1344	|	...	...	...	...	...	...	...	...	1444	...	...	...	...	...	...
Osnabrück Hbf ... 801 815 d.	...	...	...	...	...	...	...	1437	1444	...	...	...	...	...	...	...	...	1537	...	...	...	...	...	...
Münster (Westf) Hbf ... 801 d.	...	1432	1432	...	...	...	...	1503	1509	...	...	...	...	...	...	...	...	1603	...	1632	...	...	...	...
Berlin Hbf **810** ... d.	...	|	|	1149	1149	...	...	|	|	1202	...	...	1252	1252	...	...	...	|	...	|	1349	1349	...	...
Leipzig Hbf **866** ... d.	...	|	|	|	|	...	1043	|	|	|	...	...	|	|	...	...	...	|	...	|	|	|	...	...
Hannover Hbf **810** ... d.	...	|	|	1331	1331	...	1340	|	|	1356	...	...	1431	1431	...	...	...	|	...	|	1531	1531	...	...
Hamm (Westf) ... a.	...	|	|	1448	1448	...	1514	|	|	1524	...	...	1548	1548	...	...	...	|	...	|	1648	1648	...	...
Hamm (Westf) ... 805 d.	...	|	|	1452	1454	...	1516	|	|	1526	...	...	1552	1554	1556	1556	...	|	...	|	1652	1654	1656	...
Dortmund Hbf ... 805 a.	...	|	|	1509	|	...	1532	1533	|	1547	...	...	1609	|	1614	1614	...	1633	...	|	1709	|	1714	...
Dortmund Hbf ... d.	1437n	|	|	1512	|	1524k	1537	1537	|	1549	1556	...	1612	|	1616	1616	...	1636	1637n	|	1712	|	1716	1724k
Bochum Hbf ... d.	1449n	|	|	1524	|	1538k	|	1549	|	1601	1607	...	1624	|	1629	1629	...	1649y	1649n	|	1724	|	1729	1738k
Recklinghausen Hbf ... d.	|	1501	1501	|	|	|	|	|	|	|	|	...	|	|	|	|	...	|	|	1701	|	|	|	|
Wanne-Eickel Hbf ... d.	|	1509	1509	|	|	|	|	|	|	|	|	...	|	|	|	|	...	|	|	1709	|	|	|	|
Gelsenkirchen Hbf ... d.	|	1515	1515	|	|	|	|	|	1549	|	|	...	|	|	|	|	...	|	|	1715	|	|	|	|
Essen Hbf ... d.	1500n	|	|	1536	|	1554	|	1600	1604	|	1617	...	1636	|	1640	1640	1653	1700y	1700n	|	1736	|	1740	1754
Oberhausen Hbf ... d.	|	1527	1527	|	|	|	|	|	|	|	|	1626	|	|	|	|	|	|	|	1727	|	|	|	|
Duisburg Hbf ... d.	1512n	1534	1534	1549	|	1608	|	1613	1618	1628	1633	1638	1649	|	1655	1655	1707	1713y	1712n	1734	1749	|	1759	1808
Düsseldorf Flughafen ✈ ... d.	|	|	|	1559	|	|	|	|	|	|	|	|	1657s	|	|	|	|	|	|	|	1759	|	1817	|
Düsseldorf Hbf ... d.	1527n	1548	1548	1606	|	1622	|	1627	1633	1644	1648	1653	1712	|	1708	1708	1721	1727y	1727n	1749	1806	|	1824j	1822
Hagen Hbf ... d.	|	|	|	|	1524	|	1558	|	|	|	|	|	|	1624	|	|	|	1657n	|	|	|	1724	...	|
Wuppertal Hbf ... d.	|	|	|	|	1541	|	1614	|	|	|	|	|	|	1641	|	|	|	1714n	|	|	|	1741	...	|
Solingen Hbf ... d.	|	|	|	|	|	|	1626n	|	|	|	|	|	|	|	|	|	|	1727n	|	|	|	|	...	|
Köln Messe/Deutz ... a.	|	|	|	|	|	1642	|	|	|	|	1711	|	1734n	|	1728	|	1742	|	|	|	|	|	...	1842
Köln Hbf ... a.	1549n	1612	1613	1632y	1609	|	1645v	1650	1657	1712	|	1718	|	1709v	|	1732	|	1746	1749n	1813	1832y	1809	...	|
Köln Hbf ... d.	1555	1618	...	...	...	|	...	1653	1704	1718	|	1728	|	1714d	...	...	|	1753	1755	1818z	...	...	...	|
Köln/Bonn Flughafen ✈ ... a.	|	|	...	...	...	|	...	|	|	|	|	|	1747n	|	...	...	|	|	|	|	...	...	...	|
Bonn Hbf ... d.	|	1637	...	...	...	|	...	1714	1724	1737	|	|	...	1735d	...	...	|	1814	|	1837z	...	...	...	|
Remagen ... d.	|	1651	...	...	...	|	...	|	|	1751	|	|	...	...	...	...	|	|	|	1851z	...	...	...	|
Andernach ... d.	|	1703	...	...	...	|	...	|	|	1803	|	|	...	...	...	...	|	|	|	1903z	...	...	...	|
Koblenz Hbf ... a.	|	1715	...	...	...	|	...	1746	1759	1815	|	|	...	...	...	...	|	1846	|	1916z	...	...	...	|
Mainz Hbf **911** ... a.	|	1815	...	...	...	|	...	1838	|	1910	|	|	...	...	1854	...	|	1938	|	...	...	...	...	|
Frankfurt Flughafen ✈ § ... a.	1649	|	...	...	...	1734	...	|	|	|	1804	1816	...	...	1915	...	1834	1959	1849	...	...	...	...	1933
Frankfurt (Main) Hbf **910/1** a.	|	|	...	...	...	1748	...	|	1935	|	|	1830	...	...	1933	...	1848	2013	|	...	...	...	...	1948
Nürnberg Hbf **920** ... a.	|	|	...	...	...	1959	...	|	...	|	|	...	...	...	...	...	2059	2226q	|	...	...	...	...	2159
Stuttgart Hbf **912** ... ⊠ a.	1808	1958	...	...	...	|	...	2024	...	2046	1924t	...	...	...	...	...	|	...	2008	...	...	...	...	|
München Hbf **904 930** .. ⊠ a.	2027	...	...	...	...	2109p	...	...	...							...	2205	...	2226	...	...	...	...	2307
Karlsruhe Hbf **912** ... a.	...	...	...	...	...	...	...	...	...							...	...	...	...	...	...	...	...	...
Basel SBB 🏛 **912** ... a.	...	...	...	...	...	...	...	...	...							...	...	...	...	...	...	...	...	...

See Table ***802*** *for Rhein - Ruhr local RE and S-Bahn services*

◆ – **NOTES** (LISTED BY TRAIN NUMBER)

1224 – 🛏12 and 🍸 München - Kassel - Paderborn - Köln.
1228 – 🛏12 and 🍸 München - Kassel - Paderborn - Wiesbaden - Frankfurt.
2027 – ①–④ to June 30 / from Oct. 17 (also Dec. 2, 3, 4, 9, 10). 🛏12 and 🍸 Hamburg - Köln - Regensburg - Passau.
2152 – 🛏12 Jena - Weimar - Erfurt - Kassel - Paderborn - Düsseldorf.
2217 – 🛏12 and 🍸 (Greifswald Ⓐ -) Stralsund - Hamburg - Köln - Stuttgart.
2229 – 🛏12 and 🍸 Kiel - Köln - Frankfurt (- Nürnberg Ⓑ **q**) (- Passau ●).
2311 – NORDFRIESLAND – 🛏12 and 🍸 Westerland - Heidelberg - Stuttgart.
2327 – ⑤–⑦ to Nov. 27 (daily July 1 - Oct. 16). LÜBECKER BUCHT – 🛏12 and 🍸 Fehmarn-Burg - Lübeck - Hamburg - Köln - Frankfurt - Passau.

A – From Amsterdam (Table **28**). Subject to alteration July 9 – 24.
D – From Dresden (Table **841**).
F – From Wolfsburg (Table **810**).
G – Daily to Oct. 30; ⑤ from Nov. 4. On ⑥ (also Oct. 2) Duisburg d. 1634, Düsseldorf d. 1648, Köln a. 1712.
H – ⑥ until Oct. 29.
J – Ⓑ (daily from Oct. 30).
N – From Norddeich Mole (Table **812**).
Q – ①⑤ (also Oct. 4; not Oct. 3).
T – ①–④ (not Oct. 3, Nov. 1). To Tübingen Hbf (a. 1950).
U – ⑤⑦ (also Oct. 3; not Oct. 2). To Tübingen Hbf on ⑦ **w** (a. 2150).

a – ①–⑤ (not July 11 - Aug. 19).
b – Ⓑ July 8 - Aug. 21.
c – Also Oct. 3; not July 17, Oct. 2. Arrives Stuttgart 1750 July 24 - Aug. 28.
d – ①–④ (not July 11 - Aug. 18, Oct. 3).
e – Not July 8 - Aug. 21.
f – ⑤–⑦ (also Oct. 3).
g – Not ⑤.
h – 1909 July 8 - Aug. 21.
j – 1832 from Sept. 4.
k – ⑥ (also Oct. 2).
n – Not July 9 - Aug. 21.
p – 2105 from Sept. 4.
q – Ⓑ (not Oct. 2).
r – ①–⑤ July 8 - Aug. 19.
s – Stops to set down only.
t – 22 – 28 minutes later July 17 - Aug. 28.
v – 23 – 32 minutes later July 9 - Aug. 21.

w – ⑦ (also Oct. 3; not Oct. 2).
y – July 9 - Aug. 21 only.
z – Not ⑥.

● – ④⑤⑦ (also Oct. 3, Nov. 1; not Oct. 2,
♥ – ⑤⑦ (also Oct. 3; not Oct. 2). On ⑤ Sep Oct. 28 runs as *IC* **2415**, arrives Mainz Stuttgart 1725.
‡ – Not Aug. 5 - Sept. 9.
★ – Operated by Hamburg-Köln-Express Gr www.hkx.de. 🍸. Information on ticket va can be found on page 367.
⊠ – Timings at München and Stuttgart are su to alteration until Sept. 11. See shaded p on page 367 for further details.
§ – Frankfurt Flughafen ✈ Fernbahnhof (Ta **910** and **911**).

HAMBURG - DORTMUND - KÖLN - KOBLENZ 800

	IC 2213	*IC* 2223	*IC* 1917	*ICE* 129	*ICE* 821	*ICE* 546	*ICE* 556	*IC* 2195	*IC* 2197	*IC* 1029	*ICE* 615	*IC* 2207	*ICE* 846	*ICE* 1046	*ICE* 856	*IC* 2150	*ICE* 605	*IC* 2442	*IC* 2215	*IC* 2315	*HKX* 1807	*ICE* 221		*ICE* 544	*ICE* 554
		Ⓐ	⑦w		Ⓑq			Ⓐ	⑦w			E	Q	⑤B	n			Ⓑq	T		④⑥†				
	🍷♦	C 🍷		A🍷	🍷♦	✕	✕	🍷	L🍷		🍷		✕	✕	✕	♦	🍷	D	🍷	🍷♦	★🍷	A🍷		✕	✕
burg Altona d.	...		...	...	...	...	...	1556	1556	1531	...	...	...	...	...	...	...	...	1631	...	1636	...	...	...	...
burg Hbf **801** d.	1446	...	...	...	...	...	...	1610	1610	1546	...	...	...	...	...	...	...	...	1646	1646	1649	...	...	...	...
en Hbf **801 815** d.	1544	...	...	...	...	...	...	│	│	1644	...	...	...	...	...	...	...	...	1744	1744	│	...	...	...	...
brück Hbf **801 815** d.	1637	...	...	...	...	...	...	│	│	1737	...	...	...	...	...	...	...	...	1837	1837	1844	...	...	...	...
ter (Westf) Hbf **801** d.	1703	...	...	...	...	...	...	│	│	1802	...	1832	...	...	...	...	...	...	1903	1903	1909	...	...	...	...
Berlin Hbf **810** d.	│	1357	1357	...	...	1452	1452	│	│	│	...	│	1549	1549	1549	...	...	...	│	│	│	...	...	1652	1652
Leipzig Hbf **866** d.	│	│	│	...	...	│	│	│	│	│	...	│	│	│	│	...	...	1443	│	│	│	...	...	│	│
Hannover Hbf **810** d.	│	1556	1556	...	...	1631	1631	│	│	│	...	│	1731	1731	1731	...	...	1740	│	│	│	...	...	1831	1831
mm (Westf) a.	│	1724	1724	...	...	1748	1748	│	│	│	...	│	1848	1848	1848	...	...	1914	│	│	│	...	...	1948	1948
mm (Westf) **805** d.	│	1726	1726	...	...	1752	1754	│	│	│	...	│	1852	1852	1854	1856	...	1916	│	│	│	...	...	1952	1954
nund Hbf **805** a.	1733	1748	1748	...	...	1809	│	│	│	1833	...	│	1909	1909	│	1914	...	1932	1933	1933	│	...	...	2009	│
nund Hbf d.	1737	1752	1752	...	...	1812	│	│	│	1836	1837**n**	│	1912	1912	│	1916	1924**k**	1937	1937	1937	│	...	...	2012	│
um Hbf d.	1749	1803	1803	...	...	1824	│	│	│	1849**y**	1849**n**	│	1924	1924	│	1929	1938**k**	│	1949	1949	│	...	...	2024	│
cklinghausen Hbf d.	│	│	│	...	...	│	│	│	│	│	│	1901	│	│	│	│	│	│	│	│	│	...	...	│	│
anne-Eickel Hbf d.	│	│	│	...	...	│	│	│	│	│	│	1909	│	│	│	│	│	│	│	│	│	...	...	│	│
lsenkirchen Hbf d.	│	│	│	...	...	│	│	│	│	│	│	1915	│	│	│	│	│	│	│	│	1950	...	...	│	│
n Hbf d.	1800	1814	1814	...	...	1836	│	1854	1854	1900**y**	1900**n**	│	1936	1936	│	1940	1950	│	2000	2000	2004	...	...	2036	│
erhausen Hbf d.	│	│	│	1826	1847	│	│	│	│	│	│	1927	│	│	│	│	│	│	│	│	│	2026	...	│	│
burg Hbf d.	1812	1828	1830	1834	1855	1849	│	1907	1907	1912**y**	1912**n**	1934	1949	1949	│	1955	2004	│	2013	2013	2018	2034	...	2049	│
eldorf Flughafen ✈ d.	│	...	│	│	│	1903	│	│	│	│	│	│	1959	│	│	2006	│	│	│	│	│	│	...	2059	│
seldorf Hbf d.	1827	...	1852	1848	1908	1910	│	1921	1921	1927**y**	1927**n**	1949	2008	2016	│	2012	2018	│	2027	2027	2034	2048	...	2108	│
gen Hbf d.	│	...	│	│	│	...	1824	│	│	1857**n**	│	│	│	...	1924	...	│	1958	│	│	│	│	...	│	2024
ppertal Hbf d.	│	...	│	│	│	...	1841	│	│	1914**n**	│	│	│	...	1941	...	│	2014	│	│	│	│	...	│	2041
lingen Hbf d.	│	...	│	│	│	...	│	│	│	1927**n**	│	│	│	...	│	...	│	2027**n**	│	│	│	│	...	│	│
Messe/Deutz a.	│	...	│	│	1928	...	│	│	│	│	│	│	│	...	│	...	│	│	│	│	│	│	...	2128**n**	│
Hbf a.	1850	...	1915	1912	│	...	1909**x**	1945	1945	1946	1949**n**	2013	2039	...	2009	...	2041	2046**v**	2050	2050	2057	2112	...	2133**n**	2109**v**
Hbf d.	1853	...	1918	1921	│	...	1912**b**	...	...	1953	1957	...	...	...	2018**q**	...	2046	...	2053	2053	...	2128	...	▽	...
ln/Bonn Flughafen ✈ a.	│	...	│	│	│	...	│	...	...	│	│	...	...	...	│	...	│	...	│	│	...	│	...	...	...
n Hbf d.	1914	...	1937	│	│	...	1937**b**	...	...	2014	│	...	...	...	2038**q**	...	│	...	2114	2114	...	│	...	...	...
agen d.	│	...	1951	│	│	...	│	...	...	│	│	...	...	...	...	...	│	...	│	│	...	│	...	...	...
rnach d.	│	...	2003	│	│	...	2001**a**	...	...	│	│	...	...	...	...	...	│	...	│	│	...	│	...	...	...
enz Hbf a.	1946	...	2015	│	│	...	2011**a**	...	...	2046	│	...	...	...	...	...	│	...	2146	2146	...	│	...	...	...
ainz Hbf **911** a.	2038	...	2110	│	│	...	...	...	...	2141	│	...	...	...	...	...	│	...	2238	2238	...	│	...	...	...
ankfurt Flughafen ✈ § a.	│	...	│	2010	2034	...	...	...	...	2200	2049	...	...	...	...	...	2151	...	2259	2259	...	2216	...	...	...
ankfurt (Main) Hbf **910/1** a.	│	...	│	2025	2048	...	...	...	...	2213	│	...	...	...	...	...	│	...	2311	2311	...	2230	...	...	...
Nürnberg Hbf **920** a.	│	...	│	...	2259**h**	...	...	...	...	0037	│	...	...	...	...	...	│	...	...	...	...	...	...	...	...
uttgart Hbf **912** ⊠ a.	2224	...	│	...	│	...	...	...	...	...	2208	...	...	...	...	...	│	...	...	...	...	...	...	...	...
ünchen Hbf **904 930** ⊠ a.	...	...	│	...	0007**h**	...	...	...	...	...	0027	...	...	...	...	...	│	...	...	...	...	...	...	...	...
Karlsruhe Hbf **912** a.	...	...	2224	...	...	...	...	...	...	...	...	...	...	...	...	...	2300	...	...	...	...	...	...	...	...
Basel SBB 🏛 **912** a.	...	...	...	...	...	...	...	...	...	...	...	...	...	...	...	...	0056**r**	...	...	...	...	...	...	...	...

	IC 2321	*IC* 2221	*IC* 2209	*ICE* 619	*ICE* 844	*ICE* 854	*ICE* 854	*IC* 2307	*IC* 2444	*CNL* 419	*CNL* 40419	*IC* 61419	*IC* 1952	*ICE* 542	*ICE* 552	*IC* 2225	*IC* 1952	*ICE* 842	*ICE* 852	*IC* 2446	*IC* 2309	*IC* 2309		*ICE* 540	*IC* 2021
	H		R			Ⓑq	⑦‡		Ⓑq	A	[R] A	A	⑤⑦				⑦m		†	⑦w	J	⑤–⑦		⑤–⑦	
	🍷	🍷♦	N	🍷	✕	✕	✕	🍷	D	🍷♦	🍷◇	2◇	m♦	✕	✕	K🍷	♦	✕	✕	D	🍷	f🍷		t✕	
burg Altona d.	1731	...	...	...	...	...	...	1831	...	...	...	...	...	...	...	...	...	...	...	...	2031	2031	...	...	2231
burg Hbf **801** d.	1746	1746	...	...	...	...	...	1846	...	...	...	...	...	...	...	1946	...	...	...	...	2046	2046	...	...	2246
nen Hbf **801 815** d.	1844	1844	...	...	...	...	...	1944	...	...	...	...	...	...	...	2044	...	...	...	...	2144	2144	...	...	2344
abrück Hbf **801 815** d.	1937	1937	...	...	...	...	...	2037	...	...	...	...	...	...	...	2137	...	...	...	...	2238	2238	...	...	0037
ster (Westf) Hbf **801** d.	2003	2003	2032	...	...	...	...	2103	...	...	...	...	...	...	...	2203	...	...	...	...	2304	2304	...	...	0105
Berlin Hbf **810** d.	│	│	│	...	1749	1749	1749	│	...	...	...	...	1534	1852	1852	│	...	1949	1949	...	│	│	...	2107	│
Leipzig Hbf **866** d.	│	│	│	...	│	│	│	│	1643	...	...	...	│	│	│	│	...	│	│	1843	│	│	...	│	│
Hannover Hbf **810** d.	│	│	│	...	1931	1931	1931	│	1940	...	...	...	│	2031	2031	│	...	2131	2131	2140	│	│	...	2301	│
amm (Westf) a.	│	│	│	...	2048	2048	2048	│	2112	...	...	...	2135	2148	2148	│	...	2248	2248	2312	│	│	...	0028	0123
amm (Westf) **805** d.	│	│	│	...	2052	2054	2054	│	2113	...	...	...	2140	2152	2154	│	...	2252	2254	2313	│	│	...	0030	0125
tmund Hbf **805** a.	2033	2033	│	...	2109	│	│	2133	2132	...	...	...	2156	2209	│	2233	...	2309	│	2331	2333	2333	...	0048	0141
mund Hbf d.	2037	2037	│	2058	2112	│	│	2137	2137	...	...	...	2200	2212	│	2237	...	2312	│	2337	...	2337	...	0052	0144
um Hbf d.	2049	2049	│	2111	2124	│	│	2149	│	...	...	...	2211	2224	│	2249	...	2324	│	│	...	2349	...	0104	0155
ecklinghausen Hbf d.	│	│	2101	│	│	│	│	│	│	...	...	...	│	│	│	│	...	│	│	│	...	│	...	│	│
anne-Eickel Hbf d.	│	│	2109	│	│	│	│	│	│	...	...	...	│	│	│	│	...	│	│	│	...	│	...	│	│
elsenkirchen Hbf d.	│	│	2115	│	│	│	│	│	│	...	...	...	│	│	│	│	...	│	│	│	...	│	...	│	│
en Hbf d.	2100	2100	│	2125	2136	│	│	2200	│	...	...	...	2225	2236	│	2300	...	2336	│	│	...	0000	...	0115	0206
berhausen Hbf d.	│	│	2127	│	│	│	│	│	│	...	...	...	│	│	│	│	...	│	│	│	...	│	...	│	│
sburg Hbf d.	2113	2113	2134	2139	2149	│	│	2213	│	2234	2234	2234	2242	2249	│	2313	...	2349	│	│	...	0012	...	0129	0219
seldorf Flughafen ✈ d.	│	│	│	│	2159	│	│	│	│	│	│	│	│	2259	│	│	...	2359	│	│	...	│	...	0137**s**	0229
seldorf Hbf d.	2127	2127	2148	2155	2208	│	│	2227	│	2249**u**	2249**u**	2249	2300	2308	│	2327	...	0008	│	│	...	0027	...	0148	0239
agen Hbf d.	│	│	│	│	│	2124	2124	│	2158	│	│	│	│	│	2224	│	...	│	2324	2358	...	│	...	│	│
uppertal Hbf d.	│	│	│	│	│	2141	2141	│	2214	│	│	│	│	│	2241	│	...	│	2341	0014	...	│	...	│	│
olingen Hbf d.	│	│	│	│	│	│	│	│	2227**n**	│	│	│	│	│	2254**n**	│	...	│	│	0027**d**	...	│	...	│	│
Messe/Deutz a.	│	│	│	│	│	│	│	│	│	│	│	│	│	│	│	│	...	│	│	│	...	│	...	│	│
Hbf a.	2150	2150	2213	2219	2230**n**	2209**v**	2209	2250	2245**v**	│	│	2315	2325	2330**n**	2312**v**	2349	←	0030**g**	0011**v**	0046**e**	...	0050	...	0211	0301
Hbf d.	2153	2153	...	2230	...	...	2217	2253	...	2318**u**	2318**u**	2318	→	...	2322**p**	...	2353	...	...	...	...	...	...	0216**j**	0353
öln/Bonn Flughafen ✈ a.	│	│	...	2240	...	...	│	│	...	│	│	│	...	...	│	...	│	...	...	...	...	...	...	0228**j**	│
n Hbf d.	2214	2214	...	│	...	...	2237	2314	...	2339**u**	2339**u**	2339	...	...	2344**p**	...	0014	...	...	...	...	...	...	...	0416
agen d.	│	│	...	│	...	...	│	2328	...	│	│	│	...	...	...	...	│	...	...	...	...	...	...	...	0431
ernach d.	│	│	...	│	...	...	│	2341	...	│	│	│	...	...	...	...	│	...	...	...	...	...	...	...	0446
lenz Hbf a.	2246	2246	...	│	...	...	2313	2354	...	0017**u**	0017**u**	0015	...	...	...	...	0046	...	...	...	...	...	...	...	0459
ainz Hbf **911** a.	2338**z**	2338	...	│	...	...	...	...	...	│	│	│	...	...	...	...	0141	...	...	...	...	...	...	...	0626
ankfurt Flughafen ✈ § a.	2359**z**	2359	...	2347	...	...	...	...	...	│	│	│	...	...	...	...	0202	...	...	...	...	...	...	...	0646
ankfurt (Main) Hbf **910/1** a.	0013**z**	0013	...	2400	...	...	...	...	...	│	│	0142	...	...	...	...	0217	...	...	...	...	...	...	...	0702
Nürnberg Hbf **920** a.	...	...	...	│	...	...	...	...	...	│	│	│	...	...	...	...									
uttgart Hbf **912** ⊠ a.	...	...	...	0320	...	...	...	...	...	0421	│	│	...	...	...	...									
ünchen Hbf **904 930** ⊠ a.	...	...	...	0602	...	...	...	...	...	0710	│	│	...	...	...	...									
Karlsruhe Hbf **912** a.	...	...	...	0156	...	...	...	...	...	...	0400	0400	...	...	...	...									
Basel SBB 🏛 **912** a.	...	...	...	...	...	...	...	...	...	...	0619	0619	...	...	...	...									

- **NOTES** (LISTED BY TRAIN NUMBER)
- – POLLUX – 🛏 1, 2 cl. and 🛌 2 cl. ([R]) Amsterdam - München. [2] (**60419**) Amsterdam - München.
- – [12] Oberhausen - Frankfurt - Würzburg (- München ④⑤⑦ **h**).
-) – [12] Weimar - Erfurt - Kassel - Paderborn - Düsseldorf.
- 3 – RÜGEN – [12] and 🍷 Ostseebad Binz - Stralsund - Köln - Stuttgart.
- – Daily to Oct. 30; ⑤⑦ from Nov. 4. FEHMARN – [12] and 🍷 (Fehmarn-Burg ♠ -) Lübeck Hbf (d. 1635) - Hamburg - Frankfurt.
- 5 – Until Oct. 30. DEICHGRAF – [12] and 🍷 Westerland - Frankfurt.
- 2 – [12] Berlin - Erfurt - Kassel - Paderborn - Köln (- Frankfurt ⑦ **m**).

From Amsterdam (Table **28**). Subject to alteration July 9 – 24.
⑤ (not July 15 - Aug. 19). To Neuss Hbf (a. 2028) and Mönchengladbach Hbf (a. 2042).
To Krefeld Hbf (a. 1843), Viersen (a. 1855), Mönchengladbach Hbf (a. 1904), Rheydt Hbf (a. 1909) and Aachen Hbf (a. 1950).
From Dresden (Table **842**).
Daily to Nov. 4; Ⓑ from Nov. 6. From Emden (Table **812**).
①②③④⑥ from Oct. 31.
Daily to Nov. 4; Ⓑ from Nov. 6.
From Kiel (Table **820**).

L – From Flensburg (Table **823**).
N – From Norddeich Mole (Table **912**).
Q – ①②③④⑥⑦ (daily July 9 - Aug. 25).
R – ⑤–⑦ to June 26; ④–⑦ June 30 - Aug. 21; ③–⑦ Aug. 24 - Oct. 23 (also Oct. 3, 28, 29; not Oct. 2); ⑦ from Oct. 30.
T – From Oct. 31.

a – Ⓐ (not July 8 - Aug. 19).
b – Ⓑ (not July 8 - Aug. 21, Oct. 2).
d – Not mornings of June 13, 20, July 11 - Aug. 22.
e – 0058 on mornings July 11 - Aug. 22.
f – Also Oct. 3; not Nov. 5, 12, 19, 26, Dec. 3, 10.
g – Not mornings July 11 - Aug. 22.
h – Würzburg - Nürnberg - München on ④⑤⑦ (also Oct. 3; not Oct. 2).
j – Until Oct. 31.
k – ⑥ (also Oct. 2).
m – Also Oct. 3, Nov. 1; not Oct. 2, 30.
n – Not July 9 - Aug. 21.
p – Ⓑ (not July 10 - Aug. 21, Oct. 2).
q – Ⓑ (not Oct. 2).
r – Karlsruhe - Basel on ①②③④⑦ (not Oct. 2). Basel **Badischer Bf**.
s – Stops to set down only.
t – Also Oct. 3.
u – Stops to pick up only.
v – 14 – 24 minutes later July 9 - Aug. 21.
w – ⑦ (also Oct. 3; not Oct. 2).
x – 1926 on July 8. 1941 July 9 - Aug. 21.
y – July 9 - Aug. 21 only.
z – Koblenz - Frankfurt on ①–④.

♠ – ①⑤⑥⑦ to Oct. 30 (daily June 10 - Aug. 29).
▽ – On ⑦ (also Oct. 3; not July 10 - Aug. 21, Oct. 2) continues to Aachen Hbf (a. 2216).
‡ – Also Oct. 3; not July 10 - Aug. 21, Oct. 2.
◇ – PEGASUS – 🛏 1, 2 cl. and 🛌 2 cl. (*CNL* **40419** [R]) Amsterdam - Zürich; [2] (*IC* **61419**) Amsterdam - Zürich.
⊠ – Timings at München and Stuttgart are subject to alteration until Sept. 11. See shaded panel on page 367 for further details.
★ – Operated by Hamburg-Köln-Express GmbH. www.hkx.de. Information on ticket validity can be found on page 367.
§ – Frankfurt Flughafen Fernbf (Tables **910**/**911**).

801 Local services MÜNSTER - OSNABRÜCK and BREMEN - HAMBURG

See Table 800 for fast t

MÜNSTER - OSNABRÜCK and v.v. Operated by WestfalenBahn. Journey time: 36 minutes. Trains call at **Lengerich** (Westf), 21–22 minutes from Münster, 14 minutes from Osnabrü **From Münster** (Westf) Hbf at 0503 Ⓐ, 0603 ⚒, 0634 Ⓐ, 0703, 0734 Ⓐ, 0803, 0834 Ⓐ, 0903, 1003, 1103, 1203, 1303, 1334 Ⓐ, 1403, 1503, 1534 Ⓐ, 1603, 1634 Ⓐ, 1703, 1734 Ⓐ, 18 1834 Ⓐ, 1903, 2003, 2103, 2203 and 2303. **From Osnabrück** Hbf at 0519 Ⓐ, 0549 Ⓐ, 0619 ⚒, 0649 Ⓐ, 0719, 0749 Ⓐ, 0819, 0849 Ⓐ, 0919, 1019, 1119, 1219, 1319, 1419, 1447 Ⓐ, 1519, 1549 Ⓐ, 1619, 1649 Ⓐ, 1719, 1749 Ⓐ, 1819, 1919, 2019, 2119, 2219 and 2319.

BREMEN - HAMBURG and v.v. Operated by *metronom*. Journey time: 69–90 minutes. Trains call at **Rotenburg** (Wümme), 21–30 minutes from Bremen, 47–56 minutes from Hamb **From Bremen** Hbf at 0015 Ⓒ, 0115 Ⓒ, 0433 Ⓐ, 0459, 0528 Ⓐ, 0559, 0626 Ⓐ, 0633 Ⓒ, 0659, 0733, 0759, 0833, 0859 and at 33 and 59 minutes past each hour until 1633, 1659; then 1733, 1833, 1859, 1933, 1959, 2033, 2100, 2133 ⑤⑥ **b**, 2159 and 2315. **From Hamburg** Hbf at 0048 Ⓒ, 0315 Ⓒ, 0515 Ⓒ, 0538 ⚒ **h**, 0559 Ⓐ, 0615 Ⓒ, 0638, 0715, 0738, 0815, 0838 and at 15 a minutes past each hour until 2115, 2138; then 2238 and 2338.

b – Also Oct. 2.

h – Departs 0532 July 18 - Sept. 2.

802 RHEIN–RUHR LOCAL SERVICES

RE / *RB* serv

Services in this table (pages 376–378) are shown route by route. Sub-headings indicate the route number and principal stations served.

RE1 Aachen - Köln - Düsseldorf - Dortmund - Hamm (- Paderborn: Table 805) ⊡ *RE6* Düsseldorf - Dortmund - Bielefeld (- Minden) ⊡

km			m		Ⓐe	m		⚒r	m		m			m		m							⊖
0	**Aachen** Hbf 807 d.	...	...	...	...	...	0451e	...	...	0551	...		1751	...	1851	...	1951	...	2051	2151	...	2251	2351
31	Düren 807 d.	...	...	...	...	...	0517e	...	...	0617	...		1817	...	1917	...	2017	...	2117	2217	...	2317	0017
70	**Köln** Hbf 807 a.	...	...	...	...	...	0544e	...	...	0644	...		1844	...	1944	...	2044	...	2144	2244	...	2344	0044
70	**Köln** Hbf d.	...	...	...	...	...	0549	...	...	0649	...	and at	1849	...	1949	...	2049	...	2149	2249	...	2349	|
71	**Köln** Messe/Deutz d.	...	...	...	...	...	0552	...	...	0652	...		1852	...	1952	...	2052	...	2152	2252	...	2352	0051
83	Leverkusen Mitte d.	...	...	...	...	...	0604	...	...	0704	...	the same	1904	...	2004	...	2104	...	2204	2304	...	0004	▬
110	**Düsseldorf** Hbf d.	0421z	...	0521	...	0554e	0621	...	0654	0721	0754		1921	1954	2021	2054	2121	2154	2221	2321	...	0021	...
117	Düsseldorf Flughafen ✈ d.	0428z	...	0528	...	0602e	0628	...	0702	0728	0802	minutes	1928	2002	2028	2102	2128	2202	2228	2328	...	0028	...
134	**Duisburg** Hbf d.	0438	...	0538	...	0614e	0638	...	0714	0738	0814		1938	2014	2038	2114	2138	2214	2238	2338	...	0038	...
144	Mülheim (Ruhr) Hbf d.	0444	...	0544	...	0620e	0644	...	0720	0744	0820	past each	1944	2020	2044	2120	2144	2221	2244	2344	...	0044	...
153	**Essen** Hbf d.	0452	...	0552	...	0629e	0652	...	0729	0752	0829		1952	2029	2052	2129	2152	2229	2252	2352	...	0052	...
169	Bochum Hbf d.	0504	...	0604	...	0640e	0704	...	0740	0804	0840	hour until	2004	2040	2104	2140	2204	2240	2304	0004	...	0104	...
187	**Dortmund** Hbf d.	0517	0554	0617	...	0654	0717	...	0754	0817	0854		2017	2054	2117	2154	2217	2254	2317	0017	...	0117	Ⓒz
218	**Hamm** (Westf) 810 d.	0545	0615	0636t	0649	0715	0736	0749	0815	0836	0915		2036	2115	2145	2215	2245	2322k	2345	0045	0053	0145	0156
268	Gütersloh Hbf 810 d.	...	0649	...	0718	0749	...	0818	0849	*0918*	0949		*2118*	2149	...	2249	...	2355	...	...	0123	...	0225
285	**Bielefeld** Hbf 810 a.	...	0658	...	0732	0758	...	0832	0858	*0932*	0958		*2132*	2158	...	2258	...	0008	...	...	0137	...	0239

						m		m		m		m			m		m		m		m	⑤⑥v	⊖
Bielefeld Hbf 810 d.	0002	...	...	...	*0527*e	0558	*0627*e	0658	*0727*e	0758	*0827*r	0858	*0927*		1858	*1927*	1958	*2027*	2058	...	2158	...	...
Gütersloh Hbf 810 d.	0014	...	...	...	*0538*e	0608	*0638*e	0708	*0738*e	0808	*0838*r	0908	*0938*		1908	*1938*	2008	*2038*	2108	...	2208	...	...
Hamm (Westf) 810 d.	0044	0315	0415	0515	0615h	0644	0722j	0744	0822	0844	0922	0944	1022		1944	2022	2044	2116	2144	2215	2244	2315	2316
Dortmund Hbf d.	▬	0345	0445	0545	0645	0706	0745	0806	0845	0906	0945	1006	1045	and at	2006	2045	2106	2145	2206	2245	2304	2345	2345
Bochum Hbf d.	...	0355	0455	0555	0655	0718	0755	0818	0855	0918	0955	1018	1055		2018	2055	2118	2155	2218	2255	▬	2355	2355
Essen Hbf d.	...	0409	0509	0609	0709	0731	0809	0831	0909	0931	1009	1031	1109	the same	2031	2109	2131	2209	2231	2309	...	0009	0009
Mülheim (Ruhr) Hbf d.	...	0415	0515	0615	0715	0738	0815	0838	0915	0938	1015	1038	1115		2038	2115	2138	2215	2238	2315	...	0015	0015
Duisburg Hbf d.	...	0422	0522	0622	0722	0746	0822	0846	0922	0946	1022	1046	1122	minutes	2046	2122	2146	2222	2246	2322	...	0022	0020
Düsseldorf Flughafen ✈ d.	...	0432	0532	0632	0732	0756	0832	0856	0932	0956	1032	1056	1132		2056	2132	2156	2232	2256	2332	...	0032	...
Düsseldorf Hbf d.	...	0437	0539	0639	0739	0804	0839	0904	0939	1004	1039	1104	1139	past each	2104	2139	2204	2239	2304	2339	...	0039	...
Leverkusen Mitte d.	Ⓐe	...	0555	0655	0755	...	0855	...	0955	...	1055	...	1155		...	2155	...	2255	...	2355	...	0055	...
Köln Messe/Deutz d.	0508	...	0608	0708	0808	...	0908	...	1008	...	1108	...	1208	hour until	...	2208	...	2308	...	0008	0037	0108	...
Köln Hbf a.	0512	...	0612	0712	0812	...	0912	...	1012	...	1112	...	1212		...	2212	...	2312	...	0012	0039	0112	...
Köln Hbf 807 d.	0515	...	0615	0715	0815	...	0915	...	1015	...	1115	...	1215		...	2215	...	2315	...	0015	0040	0115	...
Düren 807 d.	0539	...	0639	0739	0839	...	0939	...	1039	...	1139	...	1239		...	2239	...	2339	...	0039	0118	0139	...
Aachen Hbf 807 a.	0607	...	0707	0807	0907	...	1007	...	1107	...	1207	...	1307		...	2307	...	0007	...	0107	0144	0207	...

RE2 Düsseldorf - Essen - Gelsenkirchen - Münster ⊡ *RB42* Essen - Münster

km		⚒r	Ⓐe	⚒r	⚒r	⚒r		⚒r					●										
0	**Düsseldorf** Hbf d.	...	...	0506	...	0606	...	...	0706	...	0806	...		1806	...	1906	...	2006	...	2106	...	2206	...
7	Düsseldorf Flughafen ✈ d.	...	...	0513	...	0613	...	...	0713	...	0813	...	and at	1813	...	1913	...	2013	...	2113	...	2213	...
24	**Duisburg** Hbf d.	...	...	0524	...	0624	...	...	0724	...	0824	...		1824	...	1927	...	2027	...	2124	...	2224	...
34	Mülheim (Ruhr) Hbf d.	...	...	0530	...	0630	...	...	0730	...	0830	...	the same	1830	...	1934	...	2036	...	2130	...	2230	...
43	**Essen** Hbf d.	0444	0518	0544	0618	0644	0644	0718	0744	0818	0844	0918		1844	1918	1944	2018	2044	2118	2144	2218	2244	2318
53	Gelsenkirchen Hbf d.	0453	0526	0553	0626	0653	0653	0726	0753	0826	0853	0926	minutes	1853	1926	1953	2026	2053	2126	2153	2226	2253	2326
58	Wanne-Eickel Hbf d.	0458	0531	0558	0631	0658	0658	0731	0758	0833	0858	0931		1858	1931	1958	2031	2058	2131	2158	2231	2258	2331
68	Recklinghausen Hbf d.	0506	0539	0605	0639	0705	0705	0739	0805	0841	0905	0939	past each	1905	1939	2005	2039	2105	2139	2205	2239	2305	2339
84	Haltern am See d.	0517	0550	0616	0650	0716	0716	0750	0816	0852	0916	0950	hour until	1916	1950	2016	2050	2116	2150	2216	2249	2316	2350
97	Dülmen d.	0526	0559	0625	0659	0725	0725	0759	0825	0901	0925	0959		1925	1959	2025	2059	2125	...	2225	...	2325	...
126	**Münster** (Westf) Hbf a.	0550	0622	0650	0722	0750	0750	0822	0852	0924	0950	1022		1950	2022	2052	2122	2150	...	2250	...	2350	...

		Ⓒz		⚒r	⚒r	⚒r	Ⓐe	⚒r		⚒r			⚒r				♥						
Münster (Westf) Hbf d.	0010	0010	0210	0410	...	0510	0536	...	0610	0636	...	0709	0736	...	0810	0836		2010	2036	2110	...	2212	2310
Dülmen d.	0033	0033	0233	0433	...	0533	0558	...	0633	0658	...	0732	0758	...	0833	0858	and at	2033	2058	2133	...	2234	2333
Haltern am See d.	0042	0043	0243	0443	0507	0543	0607	0607	0643	0707	0707	0742	0807	0807	0843	0907		2043	2107	2143	2207	2244	2343
Recklinghausen Hbf d.	...	0054	0254	0454	0518	0554	0618	0618	0654	0718	0718	0753	0818	0818	0854	0918	the same	2054	2118	2154	2218	2255	2354
Wanne-Eickel Hbf d.	...	0103	0303	0502	0527	0602	0627	0627	0702	0727	0727	0801	0827	0827	0902	0927		2102	2127	2202	2227	2304	0003
Gelsenkirchen Hbf d.	...	0108	0308	0508	0532	0608	0632	0632	0708	0732	0732	0807	0832	0832	0908	0932	minutes	2108	2132	2208	2232	2310	0008
Essen Hbf a.	...	0117	0317	0517	0542	0617	0642	0642	0717	0742	0742	0816	0842	0842	0917	0942	past each	2117	2142	2217	2242	2319	0017
Mülheim (Ruhr) Hbf a.	...	...	...	0526	...	0626	...	...	0726	...	...	0825	...	...	0926	...	hour until	2126	...	2226	...	2326	...
Duisburg Hbf a.	...	...	...	0533	...	0633	...	...	0733	...	...	0832	...	...	0933	...		2133	...	2233	...	2333	...
Düsseldorf Flughafen ✈ a.	...	...	...	0545	...	0645	...	...	0745	...	...	0845	...	...	0945	...		2145	...	2245	...	2345	...
Düsseldorf Hbf a.	...	...	...	0553	...	0653	...	...	0753	...	...	0853	...	...	0953	...		2153	...	2253	...	2353	...

RE3 Düsseldorf - Duisburg - Gelsenkirchen - Dortmund - Hamm ⊡ ◇

km		Ⓐe									
0	**Düsseldorf** Hbf d.	0445	0545	0645		1845	1945	2045	2145	2245	2345
7	Düsseldorf Flughafen ✈ d.	0453	0553	0653		1853	1953	2053	2153	2253	2353
24	**Duisburg** Hbf d.	0510	0610	0710	and	1910	2010	2110	2210	2310	0010
32	Oberhausen Hbf d.	0516	0616	0716		1916	2016	2116	2216	2316	0016
48	Gelsenkirchen Hbf d.	0529	0629	0729	hourly	1929	2029	2129	2229	2329	0029
53	Wanne-Eickel Hbf d.	0534	0634	0734	until	1934	2034	2134	2234	2334	0034
57	Herne d.	0538	0638	0738		1938	2038	2138	2238	2338	0038
78	**Dortmund** Hbf a.	0557	0657	0757		1957	2057	2157	2257	2357	0057
109	**Hamm** (Westf) a.	0629	0729r	0829		2029	*2145*	*2245*	*2345*	*0045*	*0145*

Hamm (Westf) d.	*0215*z	0530e	0630e	0730r	0830		2030	*2116*
Dortmund Hbf d.	0303	0603	0703	0803	0903		2103	2203
Herne d.	0320	0620	0720	0820	0920	and	2120	2220
Wanne-Eickel Hbf d.	0324	0624	0724	0824	0924	hourly	2124	2224
Gelsenkirchen Hbf d.	0329	0629	0729	0829	0929		2129	2229
Oberhausen Hbf d.	0343	0643	0743	0843	0943	until	2143	2243
Duisburg Hbf a.	0350	0650	0750	0850	0950		2150	2250
Düsseldorf Flughafen a.	0402	0702	0802	0902	1002		2202	2302
Düsseldorf Hbf a.	0412	0712	0812	0912	1012		2212	2312

RE11 Mönchengladbach - Duisburg - Dortmund ⊡ *RB33* Mönchengladbach - Duisburg

km		⚒r								
0	**Mönchengladbach** Hbf d.	0522	0622	0637	and at	2122	2137	2222	2237	2337
9	Viersen d.	0530	0630	0645		2130	2145	2230	2245	2345
24	Krefeld Hbf d.	0542	0642	0659	the same	2142	2159	2242	2259	2359
45	**Duisburg** Hbf a.	0558	0658	0724		2158	2224	2258	2324	0024
55	Mülheim (Ruhr) Hbf a.	0605	0705	...	minutes	2205	...	2305	...	...
64	**Essen** Hbf a.	0612	0712	...	past each	2212	...	2312	...	...
80	Bochum Hbf a.	0624	0724	...		2224	...	...	...	...
98	**Dortmund** Hbf a.	0637	0737	...	hour until	2237	...	...	...	...

	Ⓐe	⚒r					
Dortmund Hbf d.	...	0513	...	0621	...	and at	2221
Bochum Hbf d.	...	0525	...	0633	...		2233
Essen Hbf d.	...	0546	...	0646	...	the same	2246
Mülheim (Ruhr) Hbf d.	...	0552	...	0652	...		2252
Duisburg Hbf d.	0505	0600	0635	0700	0735	minutes	2300
Krefeld Hbf d.	0531	0618	0700	0718	0800	past each	2318
Viersen d.	0544	0633	0713	0733	0813		2333
Mönchengladbach Hbf a.	0551	0641	0720	0741	0820	hour until	2341

e – Ⓐ (not Nov. 1).
f – 4 minutes later on ✝ (also Nov. 1).
h – 0622 on Ⓐ (not Nov. 1).
j – 0718 on ✝ (also Nov. 1).
k – Arrives 2313.

m – To / from Minden (Table **811**).
r – ⚒ (not Nov. 1).
t – 0640 on ⑥ (also Nov. 1); 0645 on ✝.
v – Also Oct. 2, 31.
z – Ⓒ (also Nov. 1).

⊖ – ①②③④⑦ (not Oct. 2, 31).
⊡ – See note and shaded panel on page 377.
● – Trains may depart Duisburg / Mülheim 2–6 minutes later on certain days. Certain Münster arrivals are 2 minutes later.
♥ – Certain trains run 2 minutes later Münster - Essen.
◇ – Operated by **eurobahn** Keolis Deutschland GmbH & Co. KG.

Aachen - Mönchengladbach - Düsseldorf - Wuppertal - Dortmund ⊡ *RE13* Venlo - Mönchengladbach - Düsseldorf - Wuppertal - Hamm ⊡ ◇

		Ⓐe	⚒r	Ⓐe	⚒r	⚒r		⚒r															
Aachen Hbf ... 473 d.	0253	0413	0413	...	...	0513	0513	...	0613	...	0713	...		...	1813	...	1913	...	2013	...	2113	...	2237
Herzogenrath ... 473 d.	0307	0427	0427	...	...	0527	0527	...	0627	...	0727	...		...	1827	...	1927	...	2027	...	2127	...	2252
Rheydt Hbf ... d.	0341	0503	0503	...	...	0603	0603	...	0703	...	0803	...		...	1903	...	2003	...	2103	...	2203	...	2330
Venlo 🏛 ... d.	|	|	|	0505	0505	|	|	0605	|	0705	|	0805	and at	1805	|	1905	|	2005	|	2105	|	2205	|
Kaldenkirchen ... d.	|	|	|	0510	0510	|	|	0610	|	0710	|	0810		1810	|	1910	|	2010	|	2110	|	2210	|
Viersen ... d.	|	|	|	0527	0527	|	|	0627	|	0727	|	0827	the same	1827	|	1927	|	2027	|	2127	|	2227	|
Mönchengladbach Hbf d.	0349	0510	0510	0545j	0545j	0610	0610	0645j	0710	0745j	0810	0845j		1845j	1910	1945j	2010	2045j	2110	2145j	2210	2236	2336
Neuss Hbf ... d.	0403	0524	0524	0557	0557	0624	0624	0657	0724	0757	0824	0857	minutes	1857	1924	1957	2024	2057	2124	2157	2224	...	...
Düsseldorf Hbf ... a.	0413	0534	0534	0608	0608	0634	0634	0708	0734	0808	0834	0908		1908	1934	2008	2034	2108	2134	2208	2234	...	...
Düsseldorf Hbf ... d.	d	0540	...	0612	...	0640	...	0712	0740	0812	0840	0912	past each	1912	1940	2012	2040	...	2140	...	2240	...	...
Wuppertal Hbf ... d.	...	0602	...	0632	...	0702	...	0732	0802	0832	0902	0932		1932	2002	2032	2102	...	2202	...	2302	...	...
Hagen Hbf ... 804 d.	...	0630	...	0658	...	0730	...	0758	0830	0858	0930	0958	hour until	1958	2030	2055	2130	...	2230	...	2330	...	...
Witten ... d.	...	0641	...	|	...	0741	...	|	0841	|	0941	|		|	2041	|	2141	...	2241	...	2341	...	...
Dortmund Hbf ... d.	...	0651	...	|	...	0751	...	|	0851	|	0951	|		|	2051	|	2151	...	2251	...	2351	...	...
Schwerte (Ruhr) 804 d.	...	...	...	0708	...	...	...	0808e	...	0908r	...	1008		2008	...	*2133*	...	...	...	...	...	...	...
Unna ... d.	...	...	...	0720	...	...	...	0820e	...	0920r	...	1020		2020	...	*2144*	...	...	...	...	...	...	...
Hamm (Westf) ... d.	...	...	...	0734	...	...	...	0834e	...	0934r	...	1034		2034	...	*2157*	...	...	...	...	...	...	...

	⚒r	⚒r	⚒r		Ⓐe		⚒r		⚒r														
Hamm (Westf) ... d.	...	...	...	...	...	...	0625e	...	...	...	0725e	...	0825e	...	0925r	...	1025		1925	...	...	...	...
Unna ... d.	...	...	...	...	...	...	0637e	...	...	...	0737e	...	0837e	...	0937r	...	1037		1937	...	...	...	...
Schwerte (Ruhr) 804 d.	...	...	...	...	...	...	0649e	...	...	...	0749e	...	0849e	...	0949r	...	1049		1949	...	...	...	...
Dortmund Hbf ... d.	...	...	...	...	0609	...	|	...	0709	...	|	0809	|	0909	|	1009	|	and at	|	2009	...	2109	2209
Witten ... d.	...	...	...	...	0619	...	|	...	0719	...	|	0819	|	0919	|	1019	|		|	2019	...	2119	2219
Hagen Hbf ... 804 d.	...	...	0602e	...	0632	...	0702	...	0732	...	0802	0832	0902	0932	1002	1032	1102	the same	2002	2032	...	2132	2232
Wuppertal Hbf ... d.	...	...	0625e	...	0658	...	0725	...	0758	...	0825	0858	0925	0958	1025	1058	1125		2025	2058	...	2158	2258
Düsseldorf Hbf ... a.	...	...	0646e	...	0719	...	0746	...	0819	...	0846	0919	0946	1019	1046	1119	1146	minutes	2046	2119	...	2219	2319
Düsseldorf Hbf ... d.	0548	0622	0649	...	0722	0722	0749	0749	0822	0822	0849	0922	0949	1022	1049	1122	1149		2049	2122	2149	2222	2322
Neuss Hbf ... d.	0601	0636	0701	...	0736	0736	0801	0801	0836	0836	0901	0936	1001	1036	1101	1136	1201	past each	2101	2136	2201	2236	2336
Mönchengladbach Hbf d.	0625j	0649	0725j	0725	0749	0749	0825j	0825j	0849	0849	0925j	0949	1025j	1049	1125j	1149	1225j		2125j	2149	2225j	2249	2349
Viersen ... d.	0633	|	0733	0733	|	|	0833	0833	|	|	0933	|	1033	|	1133	|	1233	hour until	2133	|	2233	|	|
Kaldenkirchen ... a.	0650	|	0750	0750	|	|	0850	0850	|	|	0950	|	1050	|	1150	|	1250		2150	|	2250	|	|
Venlo 🏛 ... a.	0656	|	0756	0756	|	|	0856	0856	|	|	0956	|	1056	|	1156	|	1256		2156	|	2256	|	|
Rheydt Hbf ... d.	...	0654	...	...	0754	0754	...	...	0854	0854	...	0954	...	1054	...	1154	...		...	2154	...	2254	2354
Herzogenrath ... 473 d.	...	0729	...	...	0829	0829	...	...	0929	0929	...	1029	...	1129	...	1229	...		...	2229	...	2329	0029
Aachen Hbf ... 473 a.	...	0745	...	...	0845	0845	...	...	0945	0945	...	1045	...	1145	...	1245	...		...	2245	...	2345	0045

RE5 Koblenz - Bonn - Köln - Düsseldorf - Duisburg - Emmerich ⊡

	⚒r◐		Ⓐe	◐	⚒r															◐	◐		◐	◐
Koblenz Hbf ... d.	0426	...	0516	0526	0616	0716	0816	0916	1016	1116	1216	1316	1416	1516	1616	1716	1816	1916	2016	2026	2126	...	2226	2326
Andernach ... d.	0444	...	0528	0544	0628	0728	0828	0928	1028	1128	1228	1328	1428	1528	1628	1728	1828	1928	2028	2044	2144	...	2244	2344
Bad Breisig ... d.	0454	...	0535	0554	0635	0735	0835	0935	1035	1135	1235	1335	1435	1535	1635	1735	1835	1935	2035	2054	2154	...	2254	2354
Remagen ... d.	0511j	...	0543	0611j	0643	0743	0843	0943	1043	1143	1243	1343	1443	1543	1643	1743	1843	1943	2043	2111j	2211j	...	2311j	0011j
Bonn Hbf ... d.	0532	...	0601	0632	0701	0801	0901	1001	1101	1201	1301	1401	1501	1601	1701	1801	1901	2001	2101	2132	2232	...	2332	0032
Köln Hbf ... a.	0601	...	0628	0701	0728	0828	0928	1028	1128	1228	1328	1428	1528	1628	1728	1828	1928	2028	2128	2201	2301	...	0001	0101
Köln Hbf ... ♥ d.	▬	0631r	0631	▬	0731	0831	0931	1031	1131	1231	1331	1431	1531	1631	1731	1831	1931	2031	2131	...	▬	2349	▬	...
Leverkusen Mitte ... d.	...	0645r	0645	...	0745	0845	0945	1045	1145	1245	1345	1445	1545	1645	1745	1845	1945	2045	2145	...	...	0004	...	...
Düsseldorf Hbf ... d.	...	0703r	0703	...	0803	0903	1003	1103	1203	1303	1403	1503	1603	1703	1803	1903	2003	2103	2203	...	2323	0021	...	...
Düsseldorf Flughafen ✈ d.	...	0709r	0709	...	0809	0909	1009	1109	1209	1309	1409	1509	1609	1709	1809	1909	2009	2109	2209	...	2331	0028	...	...
Duisburg Hbf ... d.	0620	0720	0720	0820	0820	0920	1020	1120	1220	1320	1420	1520	1620	1720	1820	1920	2020	2120	2220	...	2344	0036	0044	...
Oberhausen Hbf ... d.	0627	0727	0727	0827	0827	0927	1027	1127	1227	1327	1427	1527	1627	1727	1827	1927	2027	2127	2227	...	2352	...	0051	...
Wesel ... d.	0655	0755	0755	0855	0855	0956	1055	1156	1255	1356	1455	1556	1655	1755	1856	1955	2055	2155	2255	...	0022	...	0119	...
Emmerich ... a.	0725	0821	0821	0925	0925	1021	1125	1221	1325	1421	1525	1621	1725	1821	1925	2021	2125	2228	2328	...	...	...	0152	...

	Ⓐe	◐	⚒r		⚒r														⚒r◐	†z◐		◐			
erich ... d.	...	...	0433e	0533	0533	0636	0740	0836	0940	1036	1140	1236	1340	1436	1540	1636	1740	1836	...	...	1940	...	2036	2140	2236
el ... d.	...	...	0506e	0606	0606	0706	0812j	0906	1006	1106	1212j	1306	1412j	1506	1612j	1706	1812j	1906	...	...	2012j	...	2106	2212j	2309
hausen Hbf ... d.	...	...	0533e	0633	0633	0733	0833	0933	1033	1133	1233	1333	1433	1533	1633	1733	1833	1933	...	...	2033	...	2133	2238	2337
burg Hbf ... d.	...	...	0542	0640	0642	0742	0842	0942	1042	1142	1242	1342	1442	1542	1642	1742	1842	1942	...	...	2042	...	2140	2244	2343
eldorf Flughafen ✈ d.	...	...	0550	▬	0650	0750	0850	0950	1050	1150	1250	1350	1450	1550	1650	1750	1850	1950	...	...	2050	...	*2204*	*2304*	*0004*
seldorf Hbf ... d.	...	...	0558	...	0658	0758	0858	0958	1058	1158	1258	1358	1458	1558	1658	1758	1858	1958	...	...	2058	...	*2212*	*2312*	*0012*
rkusen Mitte ... d.	...	...	0614	...	0714	0814	0914	1014	1114	1214	1314	1414	1514	1614	1714	1814	1914	2014	...	...	2114	...	▬	▬	...
Hbf ... ★ a.	...	...	0629	...	0729	0829	0929	1029	1129	1229	1329	1429	1529	1629	1729	1829	1929	2029	...	...	2129	...	◐	◐	...
Hbf ... d.	0532	0556	0632	0732	0732	0832	0932	1032	1132	1232	1332	1432	1532	1632	1732	1832	1932	2032	2056	2056	...	2156	2256	2356	...
n Hbf ... d.	0557	0627	0657	0757	0757	0857	0957	1057	1157	1257	1357	1457	1557	1657	1757	1857	1957	2057	2127	2131	...	2227	2327	0027	...
agen ... d.	0615	0654j	0715	0815	0815	0915	1015	1115	1215	1315	1415	1515	1615	1715	1815	1915	2015	2115	2157f	2157j	...	2254j	2354j	0054j	...
Breisig ... d.	0623	0702	0723	0823	0823	0923	1023	1123	1223	1323	1423	1523	1623	1723	1823	1923	2023	2123	2205	2205	...	2302	0002	0102	...
ernach ... d.	0630	0713	0730	0830	0830	0930	1030	1130	1230	1330	1430	1530	1630	1730	1830	1930	2030	2130	2216	2216	...	2313	0013	0113	...
enz Hbf ... a.	0642	0731	0742	0842	0842	0942	1042	1142	1242	1342	1442	1542	1642	1742	1842	1942	2042	2142	2234	2234	...	2331	0031	0131	...

RE7 Köln - Wuppertal - Hagen - Hamm - Münster (- Rheine: Table 812) ⊡ ⊠

SEE NOTE ⊠	Ⓐe									
Köln Hbf ... d.	...	0521e	0621r	0721		1921	2021	2121	2221	2352
Köln Messe/Deutz ... d.	...	0524e	0624r	0724	and	1924	2024	2124	2224	2355
Solingen Hbf ... d.	...	0543e	0643r	0743		1943	2043	2143	2243	0020
Wuppertal Hbf ... d.	...	0556e	0656r	0756	hourly	1956	2056	2156	2256	0036
Hagen Hbf ... d.	0522	0622	0722	0822		2022	2122	2222	2322	...
Schwerte (Ruhr) ... d.	0533	0633	0733	0833	until	2033	2133	2233	2333	...
Unna ... d.	0544	0644	0744	0844		2044	2144	2244	2344	...
Hamm (Westf) ... d.	0559	0659	0759	0859		2059	2159	2259	2357	...
Münster (Westf) Hbf ... a.	0622	0722	0822	0922		2122	2229	2329	*0040*	...

SEE NOTE ⊠	Ⓐe	⚒r	Ⓐe							
Münster (Westf) ... d.	...	...	0529	...	0634		2034	...	2134	2234
Hamm (Westf) ... d.	...	0500	0600	0600	0700	and	2100	...	2200	2300
Unna ... d.	...	0513	0613	0613	0713		2113	...	2213	2313
Schwerte (Ruhr) ... d.	...	0525	0626	0626	0725	hourly	2125	...	2225	2325
Hagen Hbf ... d.	0439	0539	0639	0639	0739		2139	...	2236	2339
Wuppertal Hbf ... d.	0504	0604	0704	0704	0804	until	2204	2320	...	0003t
Solingen Hbf ... d.	0515	0615	0715	0715	0815		2215	2337	...	...
Köln Messe/Deutz ... a.	0534	0634	0734	0734	0834		2234	0001	...	...
Köln Hbf ... a.	0538	0639	0738	0738	0839		2238	0005	...	...

Düsseldorf and Köln - Krefeld - Kleve ⊖

	⚒r	⚒r							
Düsseldorf Hbf ... d.	...	0609	...	0709		...	2209	...	2309
Köln Hbf ... d.	0542	|	0642	|	and at	2142	|	2242	|
Neuss Hbf ... d.	0607	|	0707	|	the same	2207	|	2307	|
Krefeld Hbf ... d.	0624	0636	0724	0736		2224	2236	2324	2336
Geldern ... d.	...	0702	...	0802	minutes	...	2302	...	0002
Kevelaer ... d.	...	0708	...	0808	past each	...	2308	...	0008
Weeze ... d.	...	0717	...	0817		...	2314	...	0014
Goch ... d.	...	0723	...	0823	hour until	...	2320	...	0020
Kleve ... a.	...	0735	...	0835		...	2332	...	0032

	⚒r								
Kleve ... d.	0526	...	0625	...	0721	...		2221	...
Goch ... d.	0539	...	0638	...	0738	...	and at	2238	...
Weeze ... d.	0545	...	0645	...	0745	...		2245	...
Kevelaer ... d.	0551	...	0651	...	0751	...	the same	2251	...
Geldern ... d.	0558	...	0658	...	0758	...	minutes	2258	...
Krefeld Hbf ... d.	0626	0635	0726	0735	0826	0835	past each	2326	2335
Neuss Hbf ... d.	|	0653	|	0753	|	0853		|	2353
Köln Hbf ... a.	|	0718	|	0818	|	0918	hour until	|	0018
Düsseldorf Hbf ... a.	0652	...	0752	...	0852	...		2352	...

To Düsseldorf Flughafen Terminal (a. 0425).
Ⓐ (not Nov. 1).
Arrives 2146.
Arrives 7 – 9 minutes earlier.
⚒ (not Nov. 1).
Hagen to Wuppertal on ⑤⑥ only.
Also Nov. 1.

Subject to alteration July 9 - Aug. 21.
Distances from Köln Hbf: Neuss *36 km*, Krefeld *54 km*.

◐ – Operated by Mittelrheinbahn.
◇ – *RE13* services operated by **eurobahn** Keolis Deutschland GmbH & Co. KG.
⊖ – Düsseldorf - Kleve is operated by Nord West Bahn GmbH.
♥ – Trains also call at Köln Messe/Deutz (3 minutes after Köln Hbf).
★ – Trains also call at Köln Messe/Deutz (3 – 4 minutes before Köln Hbf).
⊡ – See shaded panel for a summary of the principal Rhein – Ruhr *RE* routes.

	RE1	*RE2*	*RE3*	*RE4*	*RE5*	*RE6*	*RE7*	*RE11*	*RE13*
Aachen Hbf	●	...	...	●	...	...	...	...	...
Köln Hbf	●	...	...	|	●	...	●	...	...
Mönchengladbach Hbf	|	...	...	●	|	...	|	●	●
Düsseldorf Hbf	●	●	●	●	●	●	|	|	●
Duisburg Hbf	●	●	●	|	●	●	|	●	|
Essen Hbf	●	●	|	|	...	●	|	●	|
via Gelsenkirchen	|	●	●	|	...	|	|	|	|
via Wuppertal and Hagen	|	|	|	●	...	|	●	|	●
Dortmund Hbf	●	|	●	●	...	●	|	●	|
Hamm (Westf)	●	|	●	...	...	●	●	...	●
Münster (Westf) Hbf	...	●	...	...	...	...	●	...	...

802 RHEIN – RUHR LOCAL SERVICES *RE / RB serv*

RE8 / RB27 Mönchengladbach - Köln - Königswinter - Koblenz

km		Ⓐe	⚒r	⚒r		⚒r						▲								Ⓑ			
0	**Mönchengladbach** ⊖ d.	0440	0503e	0540	0603e	0640	0703e	0740	0803e	0840	...		1340	...	1440	1503e		1740	1803e	1840	1903e	*1940*	*2040*
3	Rheydt Hbf ⊖ d.	0444	0507e	0544	0607e	0644	0707e	0744	0807e	0844	...		1344	...	1444	1507e		1744	1807e	1844	1907e	*1944*	*2044*
22	Grevenbroich ⊖ d.	0502	0528e	0602	0628e	0702	0728e	0802	0828e	0902	...	and at	1402	...	1502	1528e	and at	1802	1828e	1902	1928e	*2002*	*2102*
56	**Köln** Hbf ⊖ a.	0535	0600e	0635	0700e	0735	0800e	0835	0900e	0935	...		1435	...	1535	1600e		1835	1900e	1935	2000e	*2035*	*2135*
56	**Köln** Hbf 807 d.	0538	0601t	0638	0701t	0738	0801t	0838	0901t	0938	1001t	the same	1438	1501t	1538	1601t	the same	1838	1901t	1938	2001t	2101	2201
57	**Köln** Messe/Deutz d.	0541	0604t	0641	0704t	0741	0804t	0841	0904t	0941	1004t		1441	1504t	1541	1604t		1841	1904t	1941	2004t	2104	2204
71	Köln/Bonn Flughafen ✈ d.	0551	|	0651	|	0751	|	0851	|	0951	|	minutes	1451	|	1551	|	minutes	1851	|	1951	|	|	|
83	Troisdorf 807 d.	0601	0623	0701	0723	0801	0823	0901	0923	1001	1023		1501	1523	1601	1623		1901	1923	2001	2023	2123	2223
92	**Bonn** Beuel d.	0611	0633	0711	0733	0811	0833	0911	0933	1011	1033	past each	1511	1533	1611	1633	past each	1911	1933	2011	2033	2133	2233
100	Königswinter d.	0620	0643	0720	0743	0820	0843	0920	0943	1020	1043		1520	1543	1620	1643		1920	1943	2020	2043	2143	2243
105	Bad Honnef d.	0626	0649	0726	0749	0826	0849	0926	0949	1026	1049	hour until	1526	1549	1626	1649	hour until	1926	1949	2026	2049	2149	2249
115	Linz (Rhein) d.	0637	0702	0735t	0802	0835	0902	0935	1002	1035	1102		1535	1602	1635	1702		1935	2002	2035	2102	2202	2302
122	Bad Hönningen d.	0642	0709	0740t	0809	0840	0909	0940	1009	1040	1109		1540	1609	1640	1709		1940	2009	2040	2109	2209	2309
138	Neuwied 914 d.	0655	0724	0751t	0824	0851	0924	0951	1024	1051	1124		1551	1624	1651	1724		1951	2024	2051	2124	2224	2324
◊153	**Koblenz** Hbf 914 a.	0715	0740	0813t	0840	0913	0940	1013	1040	1113	1140		1613	1640	1713	1740		2013	2040	2113	2140	2240	2340

	⚒r			Ⓐe		Ⓐe	⑥		⚒r													Ⓑ	
Koblenz Hbf 914 d.	...	...	0518r	0537	0618r	0637	0647	0718	0747	0818	0847		1147	1218	1246	1318	1347		1818	1847	1918	1947	2018
Neuwied 914 d.	...	...	0533r	0557	0633r	0657	0708	0733	0808	0833	0908		1208	1233	1306	1333	1408		1833	1908	1933	2008	2033
Bad Hönningen d.	...	...	0546r	0611	0646r	0711	0719	0746	0819	0846	0919	and at	1219	1246	1317	1346	1419	and at	1846	1919	1946	2019	2046
Linz (Rhein) d.	0453	...	0553	0618	0653	0718	0724	0753	0824	0853	0924		1224	1253	1322	1353	1424		1853	1924	1953	2024	2053
Bad Honnef d.	0503	...	0603	0629	0703	0729	0733	0803	0833	0903	0933	the same	1233	1303	1333	1403	1433	the same	1903	1933	2003	2033	2103
Königswinter d.	0509	...	0609	0635	0709	0735	0739	0809	0839	0909	0939		1239	1309	1339	1409	1439		1909	1939	2009	2039	2109
Bonn Beuel d.	0518	...	0618	0646	0718	0746	0749	0818	0849	0918	0949	minutes	1249	1318	1349	1418	1449	minutes	1918	1949	2018	2049	2118
Troisdorf 807 d.	0528	...	0628	0659	0728	0759	0759	0828	0859	0928	0959		1259	1328	1359	1428	1459		1928	1959	2028	2059	2128
Köln/Bonn Flughafen ✈ d.	|	...	|	0708	|	0808	0808	|	0908	|	1008	past each	1308	|	1408	|	1508	past each	|	2008	|	2108	
Köln Messe/Deutz d.	0550	0619	0650	0719	0750	0819	0819	0850	0919	0950	1019		1319	1350	1419	1450	1519		1950	2019	2050	2119	2150
Köln Hbf 807 a.	0553	0622	0653	0722	0753	0822	0822	0853	0922	0953	1022	hour until	1322	1353	1422	1453	1522	hour until	1953	2022	2053	2122	2153
Köln Hbf ⊖ d.	0559e	0625	0659e	0725	0759e	0825	0825	...	0925	...	1025		1325	...	1425	1459e	1525		1959e	2025	...	2125	*2225*
Grevenbroich ⊖ d.	0630e	0655	0730e	0755	0830e	0855	0855	...	0955	...	1055		1355	...	1455	1530e	1555		2030e	2055	...	2155	*2255*
Rheydt Hbf ⊖ d.	0651e	0715	0751e	0815	0851e	0915	0915	...	1015	...	1115		1415	...	1515	1551e	1615		2051e	2115	...	2215	*2315*
Mönchengladbach ⊖ a.	0656e	0720	0756e	0820	0856e	0920	0920	...	1020	...	1120		1420	...	1520	1556e	1620		2056e	2120	...	2220	*2320*

S-Bahn 13 Köln - Köln/Bonn Flughafen ✈ - Troisdorf

			Ⓒz	Ⓐe	Ⓒz	Ⓐe	Ⓐe		Ⓐe	Ⓒz	Ⓐe			Ⓐe	Ⓒz	Ⓐe						
Köln Hbf d.	0011	0041	0241	0245	0341	0345	0411	0441	0501	0511	0521	0541	and at the same	2001	2011	2021	2041	2111	2141	2211	2241	2311
Köln Messe/Deutz d.	0013	0043	0243	0247	0343	0347	0413	0443	0503	0513	0523	0543	minutes past	2003	2013	2023	2043	2113	2143	2213	2243	2313
Köln/Bonn Flughafen ✈ d.	0026	0056	0256	0259	0356	0359	0427	0456	0516	0526	0536	0556	each hour until	2016	2026	2036	2056	2126	2156	2226	2256	2326
Troisdorf a.	0036	0108	0308	...	0408	...	...	0508	0528	0536	0548	0608		2027	2036	2048	2108	2136	2208	2236	2308	2336

				Ⓒz		Ⓒz		Ⓐe		Ⓐe	Ⓒz	Ⓐe			Ⓐe	Ⓒz	Ⓐe					
Troisdorf d.	0013	0043	0113	0313	...	0413	...	...	0513	0533	0543	0553	and at the same	2013	2033	2043	2053	2113	2143	2213	2243	2313
Köln/Bonn Flughafen ✈ d.	0024	0054	0124	0324	0324	0424	0424	0444	0524	0544	0554	0604	minutes past	2024	2044	2054	2104	2124	2154	2224	2254	2324
Köln Messe/Deutz a.	0036	0106	0136	0336	0336	0436	0436	0456	0536	0556	0606	0616	each hour until	2036	2056	2106	2116	2136	2206	2236	2306	2336
Köln Hbf a.	0039	0109	0139	0339	0339	0439	0439	0459	0539	0559	0609	0619		2039	2059	2109	2119	2139	2209	2239	2309	2339

Dortmund - Unna - Soest ✣

km			Ⓒz	⚒r	⚒r	Ⓐe		Ⓐe		Ⓐe		Ⓐh			Ⓐh		Ⓐh		Ⓐh			
0	**Dortmund** Hbf 805 d.	0007	0107	0507	0607	0637	0707	0737	0807	0837	0907	0937	and at the same	1707	1737	1807	1837	1907	1937	2007	2107	2207
23	Unna d.	0032	0132	0532	0632	0702	0732	0802	0832	0902	0932	1002	minutes past	1732	1802	1832	1902	1932	2002	2032	2132	2232
53	**Soest** 805 a.	0054	0154	0554	0654	0724	0754	0824	0854	0924	0954	1024	each hour until	1754	1824	1854	1924	1954	2024	2054	2154	2254

		Ⓒz	Ⓒz	⚒r	Ⓐe	⚒r	Ⓐe		Ⓐe		Ⓐe		Ⓐh			Ⓐh		Ⓐh				
Soest 805 d.	0003	0103	...	0503	0533	0603	0633	0703	0733	0803	0833	0903	0933	and at the same	1703	1733	1803	1833	1903	2003	2103	2203
Unna d.	0027	0127	0237	0527	0557	0627	0657	0727	0757	0827	0857	0927	0957	minutes past	1727	1757	1827	1857	1927	2027	2127	2227
Dortmund Hbf 805 a.	0051	0151	0302	0551	0621	0651	0721	0751	0821	0851	0921	0951	1021	each hour until	1751	1821	1851	1921	1951	2051	2151	2251

RB 53 Dortmund - Schwerte - Iserlohn

km		Ⓐe	Ⓐe	Ⓐe		Ⓐe		Ⓐe			Ⓐe		Ⓐe		Ⓐe		Ⓐe		Ⓐe		Ⓐe		
0	**Dortmund** Hbf d.	0523	0553	0623	0653	0723	0753	0823	0853	and at the same	1523	1553	1623	1653	1723	1753	1823	1853	1923	1953	2023	2053	2153
18	Schwerte (Ruhr) d.	0545	0615	0645	0715	0745	0815	0842	0915	minutes past	1542	1615	1645	1715	1745	1815	1842	1915	1942	2015	2042	2115	2215
38	**Iserlohn** a.	0608	0638	0708	0738r	0808	0838	...	0938	each hour until	...	1638	1708	1738	1808	1838	...	1938	...	2038	...	2138	2238

	Ⓐe	Ⓐe	Ⓐe		Ⓐe		Ⓐe		Ⓐe			Ⓐe		Ⓐe		Ⓐe		Ⓐe		Ⓐe			
Iserlohn d.	...	0523	...	0617e	0647	0717r	0747	0817	...	0917	and at the same	...	1617	1647	1717	1747	1817	...	1917	...	2017	2117	2217
Schwerte (Ruhr) d.	0520	0550	0620	0650	0720	0750	0820	0850	0920	0950	minutes past	1620	1650	1720	1750	1820	1850	1920	1950	2020	2050	2150	2250
Dortmund Hbf a.	0539	0609	0639	0709	0739	0809	0839	0909	0939	1009	each hour until	1639	1709	1739	1809	1839	1909	1939	2009	2039	2109	2209	2309

BONN - REMAGEN (*20 km*) **- AHRBRÜCK** (*48 km*) and v.v.

From Bonn Hbf at 0749 ⚒r, 0849 and hourly until 2049; then 2149 ⑤⑥ **k**.
Trains depart Remagen 22 minutes later. Journey time from Bonn: 67 minutes.

From Ahrbrück at 0703 ⚒, 0803 and hourly until 2003 (also 2103 and 2203 to Remagen only). Journey time to Remagen 44 minutes, Bonn 66 minutes.

DUISBURG - MOERS - XANTEN and v.v. (45 km, journey time: 45 – 48 minutes) ⊠

From Duisburg Hbf at: 0556 ⚒r, 0656 ⚒r, 0810, 0910 and hourly until 2310.

From Xanten at: 0458 ⚒r, 0558 ⚒r, 0658, 0801, 0901 and hourly until 1601; then 1702, 1802, 1901, 2001, 2101 and 2201.

Trains call at Moers, 18 minutes from Duisburg, 27 – 29 minutes from Xanten.

OTHER USEFUL S-BAHN LINKS

Services operate every 20 minutes (every 30 minutes evenings and weekends)

Service	*Route (journey time in minutes)*
S 1	Solingen Hbf - Düsseldorf Hbf (22) - Düsseldorf Flughafen ✈ (35) - Duisburg Hbf (53) - Essen Hbf (72) - Bochum Hbf (90) - Dortmund Hbf (
S 3	Oberhausen Hbf - Mülheim Hbf (8) - Essen Hbf (17).
S 9	Essen Hbf - Wuppertal Hbf (46).
S 11	Düsseldorf Flughafen Terminal ✈ - Düsseldorf Hbf (12) - Neuss Hbf (3 Köln Hbf (82).

e – Ⓐ (not Nov. 1).
h – Also Nov. 26, Dec. 3, 10; not Nov. 1.
k – Also Oct. 2, 31.
r – ⚒ (not Nov. 1).
t – 2 – 4 minutes later on Ⓐ (not Nov. 1).
z – Also Nov. 1.

▲ – On Ⓐ (not Nov. 1) the 1040, 1140 and 1240 from Mönchengladbach run 2 – 6 minutes later Linz (Rhein) - Koblenz Hbf.
⊠ – Operated by Nord West Bahn GmbH.
✣ – Operated by **eurobahn** Keolis Deutschland GmbH & Co. KG (2nd class only).

◊ – Via Koblenz-Lützel (*159 km* via Ehrenbreitstein).
⊖ – Additional journeys Mönchengladbach Hbf - Köln Hbf and v.v.: **From Mönchengladbach** at 0040 Ⓒ **z**, 0440 ⑥, 0540 † **z**, 0627 Ⓐ **e**, 0640 † **z**, 1840 ⑥, 2240 and 2340. **From Köln** at 0025, 0125 Ⓒ **z**, 0525 ⚒ **r**, 0725 Ⓒ **z**, 0825 † **z**, 0925 † **z** and 2125 ⑥.

803 DORTMUND and MÜNSTER - ENSCHEDE *2nd class o*

km	△	Ⓐe	⚒r							
0	**Dortmund** Hbf d.	0552	0652	0752r	0852		1852	1952	2052	2152
44	Dülmen d.	0640	0740	0840r	0940	and	1940	2040	2140	2240
61	Coesfeld (Westf) d.	0705	0800	0900	1000	hourly	2000	2100	2153	2253
96	Gronau (Westf) d.	0739	0839	0939	1039	until	2039	2139q	...	...
103	**Enschede** a.	0750	0850	0950	1050		2050	2150q	...	...

△	Ⓐe	⚒r	⚒r	⚒r					
Enschede d.	...	...	0556e	0656	...	0756		1956	2
Gronau (Westf) d.	...	0524e	0620	0708j	...	0820	and	2020	2
Coesfeld (Westf) d.	0506	0603	0703	0803	0803	0903	hourly	2103	
Dülmen d.	0520	0617	0717	0817	0817	0917	until	2117	
Dortmund Hbf a.	0607	0707	0807	0907	0907	1007		2207	

km	△	Ⓐe	Ⓐe	⚒r						
0	**Münster** (Westf) Hbf d.	0508	0608	0708		0808	and	2108	2208	2308
56	Gronau (Westf) d.	0609	0709	0809	0809	0909	hourly	2209	2309	0004
63	**Enschede** a.	0620	0720	0820	0820	0920	until	2220	2320	...

△	⚒r	⚒r	①–⑥						⑤
Enschede d.	...	0626	0726	...	0826	and	2126	2226	2
Gronau (Westf) d.	0544	0644	0744	0744	0844	hourly	2144	2244	2
Münster (Westf) Hbf a.	0644	0744	0844	0844	0944	until	2244	2344	0

e – Ⓐ (not Nov. 1).
j – 0720 on ⑥.
q – Coesfeld - Enschede on † (also Nov. 1).
r – ⚒ (not Nov. 1).
s – Also Oct. 2, 31.
△ – German holiday dates apply.

 German national public holidays are on Jan. 1, Mar. 25, 28, May 5, 16, Oct. 3, Dec. 25, 26

HAGEN - KASSEL 804

ervices

SERVICE FROM JUNE 13

	Ⓐe	Ⓐe	⑥	Ⓐe	⑥			©z													©z			d
Hagen Hbf .... **802** d.	...	0505	...	0603	0613	0713	0813	...	0913	1013	1113	1213	1313	1413	1513	1613	1713	1813	1913	2013	2013	2113	2213	2322
Schwerte (Ruhr) .... **802** d.	...	0515	...	0613	0623	0723	0823	...	0923	1023	1123	1223	1323	1423	1523	1623	1723	1823	1923	2023	2023	2123	2223	2349
Arnsberg (Westf) .... d.	...	0545	...	0646	0656	0756	0856	...	0956	1056	1156	1256	1356	1456	1556	1656	1756	1856	1956	2056	2056	2156	2256	0020
Meschede .... d.	...	0603	...	0705	0715	0815	0915	...	1015	1115	1215	1315	1415	1515	1615	1715	1815	1915	2015	2115	2115	2215	2315	0038
Bestwig .... d.	...	0610	0623	0712	0723	0823	0923	...	1023	1123	1223	1323	1423	1523	1623	1723	1823	1923	2023	2122	2123	2224	2322	0045
Brilon Wald .... d.	...	0624	0638	0733	0738	0838	0938	...	1038	1138	1238	1338	1438	1538	1638	1738	1838	1938	2038	...	2138	2237	...	...
Marsberg .... d.	...	0650	0700	0800	0800	0900	1000	...	1100	1200	1300	1400	1500	1600	1700	1800	1900	2000	2100	...	2200	...	...	...
Warburg (Westf) .... a.	...	0709	0719	0819	0819	0919	1019	...	1119	1219	1319	1419	1519	1619	1719	1819	1919	2019	2119	...	2219	...	...	...
Warburg (Westf) .... **805** d.	0625	0721	0721	...	...	0921	...	1024	1129	...	1323	...	1523	...	1723	...	1923	*2024*	...	...	...	...	...	...
Hofgeismar .... d.	0640	0739	0739	...	...	0939	...	1039	1144	...	1339	...	1539	...	1739	...	1939	*2038*	...	...	...	...	...	...
Kassel Wilhelmshöhe .. **805** a.	0656	0757	0757	...	...	0957	...	1055	1209	...	1358	...	1557	...	1757	...	1956	*2055*	...	...	...	...	...	...

	⚒e	⚒e	Ⓐe	⑥		Ⓐe	⑥	Ⓐe	⚒e							©z									
sel Wilhelmshöhe ... **805** d.	...	...	...	...	...	...	...	0702	...	...	0800	...	1001	...	1200	1302	...	1354	...	1601	...	1802	2001	2102	...
eismar .... d.	...	...	...	...	...	...	...	0719	...	...	0819	...	1019	...	1219	1319	...	1422	...	1619	...	1820	2019	2119	...
urg (Westf) .... **805** a.	...	...	...	...	...	...	...	0733	...	...	0835	...	1035	...	1235	1333	...	1437	...	1636	...	1836	2035	2133	...
urg (Westf) .... d.	...	...	0530	0538	...	0630	0638	▬	0738	...	0838	0938	1038	1138	1238	...	1338	1438	1538	1638	1738	1838	2038	...	2138
berg .... d.	...	...	0552	0600	...	0649	0700	...	0800	...	0900	1000	1100	1200	1300	...	1400	1500	1600	1700	1800	1900	2100	...	2200
Wald .... d.	...	...	0620	0622	...	0715	0722	...	0822	...	0922	1022	1122	1222	1322	...	1423	1522	1622	1722	1822	1922	2122	...	2222
vig .... d.	0436	0536	0636	0636	0636	0736	0736	0736	0836	0836	0936	1036	1136	1236	1336	...	1437	1536	1636	1736	1836	1936	2136	...	2236
hede .... d.	0443	0543	0643	0643	0643	0743	0743	0743	0843	0843	0943	1043	1143	1243	1343	...	1444	1543	1643	1743	1843	1943	2143	...	2243
berg (Westf) .... d.	0501	0601	0701	0701	0701	0801	0801	0801	0901	0901	1001	1101	1201	1301	1401	...	1504	1601	1701	1801	1901	2001	2201	...	2301
erte (Ruhr) .... **802** d.	0535	0635	0735	0735	0735	0835	0835	0835	0935	0935	1035	1135	1235	1335	1435	...	1541	1635	1735	1835	1935	2035	2235	...	2335
n Hbf .... **802** a.	0545	0645	0745	0745	0745	0845	0845	0845	0945	0945	1045	1145	1245	1345	1445	...	1550	1645	1745	1845	1945	2045	2245	...	2345

From Dortmund Hbf (d. 2323).

e – Not Nov. 1.

z – Also Nov. 1.

DORTMUND and MÜNSTER - PADERBORN - KASSEL 805

SERVICE FROM JUNE 13

	◇ Ⓐe	◇ Ⓐe	◇ ⑥	RE 10101 ⚒r	◇ Ⓐe	◇ ©z		IC 2153 J	RE 10109	◇ Ⓐe	◇ ©z	◇ Ⓐe	◇ ©z	RE 10113	◇ Ⓐe	◇ ©z		ICE 1223 E🍷	◇ Ⓐe	◇ ©z	IC 2155 X	RE 10117	◇ Ⓐe	◇ ©z
Köln Hbf **800 802** .... d.	...	...	...	...	...	...	...	0520	0549	...	...	...	...	0749	...	...	...	0825**d**	...	...	...	0949	...	...
Düsseldorf Hbf **800 802** ... d.	...	...	...	0421**k**	...	...	...	0546	0621	...	...	...	...	0821	...	...	...	0846	...	...	0946	1021	...	...
Dortmund Hbf .... **802** d.	0450	...	...	0517	...	...	...	0643	0717	...	...	...	...	0917	...	...	...	0942	...	...	1043	1117	...	...
Münster (Westf) Hbf.. **802** d.	|	0510	0510	|	0610	0610	0634	|	|	0710	0710	0810	0810	|	0910	0910	0934	|	1010	1010	|	|	1110	1110
Hamm (Westf) .... **802** a.	0507	0537	0537	0545	0637	0637	0657	0702	0736	0737	0737	0837	0837	0936	0937	0937	0957	1002	1037	1037	1102	1136	1137	1137
Hamm (Westf) .... d.	0512	0546	0552	0604	0646	0652	...	0707	0741	0746	0752	0846	0852	0941	0946	0952	...	1007	1046	1052	1107	1141	1146	1152
Soest .... **802** d.	0525	0602	0608	0622	0702	0708	...	0722	0755	0802	0808	0902	0908	0955	1002	1008	...	1022	1102	1108	1122	1155	1202	1208
Lippstadt .... d.	0535	0614	0620	0635	0714	0720	...	0733	0806	0814	0820	0914	0920	1006	1014	1020	...	1033	1114	1120	1133	1206	1214	1220
Paderborn Hbf ..... **809 811** d.	0550	0642	0642	0701	0739	0744	...	0749	0825	0842	0842	0939	0942	1025	1042	1042	...	1049	1139	1140	1149	1225	1242	1242
Altenbeken .... **809 811** d.	0602	0654	0654	...	...	...	...	0804	...	0854	0854	...	0954	...	1054	1054	...	1103	...	...	1204	...	1254	1254
Warburg (Westf) .... **804** d.	0625	0716	0716	...	...	...	...	0826	...	0916	0916	...	1024**j**	...	1116	1116	...	1125	...	...	1226	...	1316	1316
Kassel Wilhelmshöhe .. **804** a.	0656	*0757*	*0757*	...	...	...	...	0857	...	*0957*	*0957*	...	1055	...	...	...	...	1156	...	...	1257	...	*1358*	*1358*

	IC 1959 ⑤⑦ B	◇ Ⓐe	◇ ©z	RE 10121	◇ Ⓐe	◇ ©z	◇ Ⓐe	◇ ©z	RE 10125	◇ Ⓐe	◇ ©z	◇ Ⓐe	◇ ©z		IC 2157 Ⓑ D	RE 10129	◇ Ⓐe	◇ ©z	◇ Ⓐe	◇ ©z	RE 10133	◇	◇	◇	◇
iln Hbf **800 802** .... d.	...	...	...	1149	...	...	...	...	1349	...	...	...	...	...	1520	1549	...	...	...	...	1749	...	...	...	...
isseldorf Hbf **800 802**.... d.	1113	...	...	1221	...	...	...	...	1421	...	...	...	...	...	1546	1621	...	...	...	...	1821	...	...	...	...
mund Hbf .... **802** d.	1207	...	...	1317	...	...	...	...	1517	...	...	...	...	...	1643	1717	...	...	...	...	1917	...	...	...	...
inster (Westf) Hbf .. **802** d.	|	1210	1210	|	1310	1310	1410	1410	|	1510	1510	1610	1610	1634	|	|	1710	1710	1810	1810	|	*1934*	*2034*	*2134***t**	*2234*
m (Westf) .... **802** a.	1228	1237	1237	1336	1337	1337	1437	1437	1536	1537	1537	1637	1637	1657	1702	1736	1737	1737	1837	1837	1936	*1957*	*2057*	*2157***t**	*2257*
m (Westf) .... d.	1233	1246	1252	1341	1346	1352	1446	1452	1541	1546	1552	1646	1652	...	1707	1741	1746	1752	1846	1852	1944	2007	2107	2207	2307
st .... **802** d.	1247	1302	1308	1355	1402	1408	1502	1508	1555	1602	1608	1702	1708	...	1722	1755	1802	1808	1902	1908	1958	2023	2123	2223	2323
stadt .... d.	1258	1314	1320	1406	1414	1420	1514	1520	1606	1614	1620	1714	1720	...	1733	1806	1814	1820	1914	1920	2009	2035	2135	2235	2335
erborn Hbf .... **809 811** d.	1317	1339	1340	1425	1442	1442	1539	1540	1625	1642	1642	1739	1740	...	1749	1825	1842	1842	1942	1942	2025	2100	2200	2300	2359
nbeken .... **809 811** d.	1330	...	...	...	1454	1454	...	...	...	1654	1654	...	...	...	1804	...	1854	1854	1954	1954	...	...	2211	...	...
burg (Westf) .... **804** d.	|	...	...	...	1516	1516	...	...	...	1716	1716	...	...	...	1826	...	1916	1916	2024**j**	2024**j**	...	...	2234	...	...
sel Wilhelmshöhe ... **804** a.	1417	...	...	...	*1557*	*1557*	...	...	...	*1757*	*1757*	...	...	...	1857	...	*1956*	*1956*	2055	2055	...	...	...	...	...

	◇ ⑥	◇ Ⓐe	◇	RE 10114 ⚒r	◇ Ⓐe		RE 10116	◇ ©z ¶	◇ Ⓐe	◇ ©z	◇ Ⓐe	RE 10120	IC 2156 ①-⑥ H		◇ ©z	◇ Ⓐe	◇ ©z	◇ Ⓐe	RE 10124	◇ ©z	◇ Ⓐe	◇ ©z	◇ Ⓐe	RE 10128	◇ ©z
sel Wilhelmshöhe ... **804** d.	...	...	...	...	...	...	...	...	0702	*0800*	*0800*	...	0859	...	...	...	*1001*	*1001*	...	...	...	*1200*	*1200*	...	1302
burg (Westf) .... **804** d.	...	...	...	...	0614	0639**r**	...	...	0739	0839	0839	...	0933	...	...	...	1039	1039	...	...	...	1239	1239	...	1339**j**
nbeken .... **809 811** d.	...	...	...	...	0638	0702**r**	...	...	0802	0902	0902	...	0956	...	...	...	1102	1102	...	...	...	1302	1302	...	1402
erborn Hbf .... **809 811** d.	0513	0544	0621	0638	0651	0721	0738	0816	0821**j**	0916	0921**j**	0938	1010	...	1016	1021	1116	1121**j**	1138	1216	1221	1316	1321**j**	1338	1416
stadt .... d.	0536	0607	0644	0653	0714	0744	0753	0836	0844	0936	0944	0953	1026	...	1036	1044	1136	1144	1153	1236	1244	1336	1344	1353	1436
st .... **802** d.	0548	0619	0656	0704	0726	0756	0804	0848	0856	0948	0956	1004	1037	...	1048	1056	1148	1156	1204	1248	1256	1348	1356	1404	1448
m (Westf) .... a.	0606	0637	0714	0718	0744	0814	0818	0906	0914	1006	1014	1018	1051	...	1106	1114	1206	1214	1218	1306	1314	1406	1414	1418	1506
m (Westf) .... **802** d.	0620	0650	0720	0722	0750	0820	0822	0920	0920	1020	1020	1022	1056	1059	1120	1120	1220	1220	1222	1320	1320	1420	1420	1422	1520
inster (Westf) Hbf .... **802** a.	0647	0717	0747	|	0817	0847	|	0947	0947	1047	1047	|	|	1122	1147	1147	1247	1247	|	1347	1347	1447	1447	|	1547
mund Hbf .... **802** a.	...	...	...	0743	...	...	0843	...	...	...	...	1043	1115	...	...	...	...	...	1243	...	...	...	...	1443	...
isseldorf Hbf **800 802**.... a.	...	...	...	0837	...	...	0937	...	...	...	...	1137	1214**v**	...	...	...	...	...	1337	...	...	...	...	1537	...
iln Hbf **800 802** .... a.	...	...	...	0912	...	...	1012	...	...	...	...	1212	1239	...	...	...	...	...	1412	...	...	...	...	1612	...

	◇ Ⓐe	ICE 1224 © M🍷	ICE 1228 Ⓐ A🍷		◇ ©z	◇ Ⓐe	RE 10132	IC 2152 K		◇ ©z	◇ Ⓐe	◇ ©z	◇ Ⓐe	RE 10136	IC 2150 X	◇ ©z	◇ Ⓐe	◇ ©z	◇ Ⓐe	RE 10140	◇	IC 1952 ⑤⑦ G	◇	◇	◇
sel Wilhelmshöhe ... **804** d.	...	1402	1402	...	...	...	...	1501	...	...	...	*1601*	*1601*	...	1700	...	...	*1802*	*1802*	...	...	1943	*2001*	2102	...
burg (Westf) .... **804** d.	...	1433	1433	...	1438	1438	...	1534	...	...	...	1639	1639	...	1734	...	...	1839	1839	...	...	2018	2039	2134	...
nbeken .... **809 811** d.	...	1456	1456	...	1502	1502	...	1556	...	...	...	1702	1702	...	1756	...	...	1902	1902	...	...	2040	2102	2157	...
erborn Hbf .... **809 811** d.	1421	1510	1510	...	1516	1521**j**	1538	1610	...	1616	1621	1716	1721**j**	1738	1810	1816	1821	1916	1921**j**	1938	2016	2054	2116	2210	2311
stadt .... d.	1444	1526	1526	...	1536	1544	1553	1626	...	1636	1644	1736	1744	1753	1826	1836	1844	1936	1944	1953	2039	2110	2139	2228	2334
st .... **802** d.	1456	1537	1537	...	1548	1556	1604	1637	...	1648	1656	1748	1756	1804	1837	1848	1856	1948	1956	2004	2051	2121	2151	2240	2346
m (Westf) .... a.	1514	1551	1551	...	1606	1614	1618	1651	...	1706	1714	1806	1814	1818	1851	1906	1914	2006	2014	2018	2111	2135	2211	2256	0004
m (Westf) .... **802** d.	1520	1556	1556	1559	1620	1620	1622	1656	1659	1720	1720	1820	1820	1822	1856	1920	1920	2020	2020	2022	2120	2140	2220	2304	0010
inster (Westf) Hbf .. **802** a.	1547	|	|	1622	1647	1647	|	|	1722	1747	1747	1847	1847	|	|	1947	1947	2047	2047	|	2147	|	2247	|	0040
tmund Hbf .... **802** a.	...	1614	1614	...	...	...	1643	1714	...	...	...	...	...	1843	1914	...	...	...	...	2043	...	2156	...	2321	...
isseldorf Hbf **800 802**.... a.	...	1706	1706	...	...	...	1737	1824**h**	...	...	...	...	...	1937	2012	...	...	...	...	2137	...	2256	...	...	...
iln Hbf **800 802** .... a.	...	1732	1728**d**	...	...	...	1812	...	...	...	...	...	...	2012	...	...	...	...	...	2212	...	2325	...	...	...

[12] and 🍷 München - Kassel - Düsseldorf - Wiesbaden - Frankfurt.
⑤⑦ (also Oct. 3; not Oct. 2). [12] Düsseldorf - Kassel - Erfurt - Halle - Berlin.
Ⓑ (not Oct. 2). [12] Köln - Kassel - Erfurt - Halle.
[12] and 🍷 (Darmstadt Ⓐ -) Köln - Kassel - Nürnberg - München.
⑤⑦ (also Oct. 3, Nov. 1; not Oct. 2, 30). [12] Berlin - Halle - Erfurt - Kassel - Köln (- Frankfurt ⑦**w**).
①-⑥ (also Oct. 2; not Oct. 3). [12] Halle - Erfurt - Kassel - Köln.
[12] Köln - Kassel - Erfurt - Jena.
[12] Jena - Erfurt - Kassel - Düsseldorf.

M – [12] and 🍷 München - Nürnberg - Kassel - Köln.
X – [12] Düsseldorf - Kassel - Erfurt - Weimar and v.v.

d – Köln **Messe/Deutz**.
e – Not Nov. 1.
h – 1832 from Sept. 4.
j – Arrives 6–7 minutes earlier.
k – ⑥ only.
r – ⚒ (not Nov. 1).

t – Not July 9 - Aug. 21.
v – Until Sept. 3.
w – Also Oct. 3, Nov. 1.
z – Also Nov. 1.

¶ – Change trains at Hamm on ⑥.
◇ – Operated by **eurobahn** Keolis Deutschland (2nd class only).

806 FRANKFURT - GIESSEN - KASSEL and SIEGEN

FRANKFURT - GIESSEN - KASSEL

km	SEE NOTES ⊖ AND ▲	RE 4170 †	RE 4150 ⚒	IC 2378 ⚒ 🍷	RE 4152	◇	IC 2376 🍷	RE 4154	◇	IC 2374 A 🍷	RE 4156	◇	IC 2372 🍷	RE 4158	IC 2370 ◧ 🍷	RE 4160	IC 2276 🍷	RE 4162	◇	IC 2274 🍷	RE 4164	◇	IC 2272 Ⓐ 🍷	IC 2172 ⑦w S 🍷	4
	Karlsruhe Hbf **912** d.	...	...	...	...	...	0702	...	...	0905	...	...	1110**p**	...	1310	...	1510	...	...	1710	...	...	1910	...	
	Heidelberg Hbf **912** d.	...	...	...	...	...	0746	...	...	0946	...	...	1146**p**	...	1346	...	1546	...	...	1746	...	...	1946	1946	
0	**Frankfurt (Main)** Hbf ¶ d.	0508	0522	0649	0718	0814**j**	0852	0922	1022	1052	1122	1222	1252	1322	1450	1522	1650	1720	1822	1849	1922	2021	2052	2052	2
34	Friedberg (Hess) ¶ d.	0530	0545	0715	0745	0845	0915	0945	1045	1115	1145	1245	1315	1345	1515	1545	1715	1745	1845	1915	1945	2045	2115	2115	2
66	**Gießen** ¶ d.	0604	0604	0735	0804	0905	0935	1004	1105	1136	1204	1305	1335	1404	1535	1604	1735	1804	1905	1935	2004	2105	2135	2135	2
96	Marburg (Lahn) ¶ d.	0620	0620	0750	0820	0920	0950	1020	1120	1151	1220	1320	1350	1420	1550	1620	1750	1820	1920	1950	2020	2120	2150	2150	2
118	Stadtallendorf d.	0634	0635	|	0834	0938	|	1034	1138	|	1235	1338	|	1434	|	1634	|	1835	1938	|	2034	2138	|	|	2
138	Treysa ¶ d.	0649	0649	0814	0849	0955	1014	1049	1155	1215	1249	1355	1414	1449	1614	1649	1814	1849	1955	2014	2049	2155	2214	2214	2
166	Wabern d.	0707	0707	0831	0907	1017	1031	1107	1217	1232	1307	1417	1431	1507	1631	1707	1831	1907	2017	2031	2107	2217	2231	2231	2
196	**Kassel** Wilhelmshöhe a.	0726	0726	0852	0926	1048	1053	1126	1248	1254	1326	1448	1452	1526	1652	1726	1852	1926	2048	2052	2126	2247	2255	2255	2
200	**Kassel** Hbf a.	0734	0734	|	0934	1055	|	1134	1255	|	1334	1455	|	1534	|	1734	|	1934	2055	|	2134	2253	...	...	2
	Hannover Hbf **900** ▲ a.	...	...	0956	...	...	1156	...	...	1356	...	...	1556	...	1756	...	1956	...	...	2156**v**	...	...	...	...	
	Hamburg Hbf **900** ▲ a.	...	...	1128	...	...	1328	...	...	1529	...	...	1732	...	1928	...	2128**p**	...	...	2328**w**	...	...	...	...	
	Stralsund Hbf **830** ▲ a.	...	...	...	...	...	1629	...	...	...	...	...	2028	...	2228**w**	...	...	...	...	...	...	...	...	...	

SEE NOTES ⊖ AND ▲	RE 4171 Ⓐ	RE 4151 ⑥	IC 2273 Ⓐ 🍷	RE 4173 Ⓐ	RE 4153 ©	IC 2271 ⚒ 🍷	RE 4155	IC 2277 ⚒ 🍷	◇	RE 4157	IC 2279 🍷	◇	RE 4159	IC 2371 🍷	RE 4161	IC 2373 🍷	RE 4163	IC 2375 B 🍷	◇	IC 1995 ⑦w D 🍷	RE 4165	IC 2377 🍷	RE 4167	IC 2379 ⑤⑦ v 🍷	4
Stralsund Hbf **830** ▲ d.	...	...	...	...	...	...	...	...	...	...	0525**r**	...	...	...	...	0927	...	...	...	...	...	1327	...	1527	
Hamburg Hbf **900** ▲ d.	...	...	...	...	...	...	...	0625	...	...	0828**r**	...	...	1028	...	1228	...	1428	...	...	...	1628	...	1828	
Hannover Hbf **900** ▲ d.	...	...	...	...	...	0601**a**	...	0801	...	...	1001**r**	...	...	1201	...	1401	...	1601	...	1703	...	1801	...	2001	
Kassel Hbf d.	0400	0423	...	0611	0615	|	0823	|	0903	1023	|	1103	1223	|	1423	|	1623	|	1703	|	1823	|	2023	|	2
Kassel Wilhelmshöhe d.	0405	0429	0459	0617	0621	0703	0829	0903	0908	1029	1103	1108	1229	1303	1429	1503	1629	1703	1708	1809	1829	1903	2029	2103	2
Wabern d.	0423	0448	0519	0639	0645	0722	0848	0922	0938	1048	1122	1138	1248	1322	1448	1522	1648	1722	1738	|	1848	1922	2048	2122	2
Treysa ¶ d.	0441	0506	0536	0700	0703	0739	0906	0939	1003	1106	1139	1203	1306	1339	1506	1539	1706	1739	1803	|	1906	1939	2106	2139	2
Stadtallendorf d.	0455	0519	0549	0716	0718	|	0919	|	1019	1119	|	1219	1319	|	1519	|	1719	|	1819	|	1919	|	2119	|	2
Marburg (Lahn) ¶ d.	0512	0535	0604	0734	0734	0804	0935	1004	1035	1135	1204	1235	1335	1404	1535	1604	1735	1804	1835	1906	1935	2004	2135	2204	2
Gießen ¶ d.	0536	0553	0623	0753	0753	0823	0953	1023	1054	1153	1223	1254	1353	1423	1553	1623	1753	1823	1854	1926	1953	2023	2153	2223	0
Friedberg (Hess) ¶ d.	0600	0612	0642	0812	0812	0842	1012	1042	1112	1212	1242	1312	1412	1442	1612	1642	1812	1842	1912	|	2012	2042	2212	2242	0
Frankfurt (Main) Hbf ¶ a.	0625	0634	0707	0837	0837	0907	1034*	1108	1135	1234*	1307	1335	1434*	1507	1637	1707	1837	1907	1935	2012	2034*	2105	2234	2304	0
Heidelberg Hbf **912** a.	...	...	0812	...	...	1012	...	1212**h**	...	...	1412	...	...	1612	...	1812	...	2012	...	2112	...	2247**f**	...	...	
Karlsruhe Hbf **912** a.	...	...	0852	...	...	1050	...	1250**k**	...	...	1452	...	...	1650	...	1852	...	2054	...	...	...	2327**f**	...	...	

FRANKFURT - GIESSEN - SIEGEN

km		†	◇ ⚒	Ⓐ	◇ Ⓐ	◇ Ⓐ	◇ ©	◇ ©	Ⓐ	◇ ⚒		◇ Ⓐ	◇ ©⊙		◇ ⚒		◇		◇		◇		◇		◇	
0	**Frankfurt** (Main) Hbf ‡ d.	0508	_0522_	0552	...	0615	0622	0622	0630**y**	_0718_	0749**y**	0814	0822	0831	_0922_	0952	1022	1031	_1122_	1152	1222	1231	_1322_	1352	1422**y**	14
34	Friedberg (Hess) ‡ d.	0530	_0545_	0615	...	0646	0645	0645	0657	_0745_	0815	0845	0845	0859	_0945_	1015	1045	1059	_1145_	1215	1245	1259	_1345_	1415	1445	1
38	Bad Nauheim ‡ d.	0535	|	0619	...	|	|	|	0701	|	0819	|	|	0903	|	1019	|	1103	|	1219	|	1303	|	1419	|	
66	**Gießen** ‡ a.	0602	_0602_	0635	...	0702	0702	0702	0724	_0802_	0835	0902	0902	0928	_1002_	1035	1102	1128	_1202_	1235	1302	1328	_1402_	1435	1502	1
66	**Gießen** **906** ‡ d.	0604	0612	0640	0652	0705	0705	0709	0740	0809	0839	0909	0909	0940	1009	1039	1109	1140	1209	1239	1309	1340	1409	1439	1505	1
	Marburg (Lahn) ‡ a.	0619	|	|	|	0719	0719	|	|	|	0904	|	|	|	|	1104	|	|	|	1304	|	|	|	1504	1519	
	Treysa ‡ a.	0649	|	|	|	0753	0753	|	|	|	...	|	|	|	|	...	|	|	|	...	|	|	|	...	1553	
79	Wetzlar **906** d.	...	0621	0650	0703	...	...	0718	0750	0818	...	0918	0918	0950	1018	...	1118	1150	1218	...	1318	1350	1418	...	...	1
101	Herborn d.	...	0634	0712	0730	...	...	0733	0812	0833	...	0933	0933	1012	1033	...	1133	1212	1233	...	1333	1412	1433	...	...	1
107	Dillenburg d.	...	0640	0722	0738	...	...	0738	0822	0838	...	0938	0938	1022	1038	...	1138	1222	1238	...	1338	1422	1438	...	...	1
139	**Siegen** a.	...	0705	...	0805	...	...	0805	...	0905	...	1005	1005	...	1105	...	1205	...	1305	...	1405	...	1505	...	...	1

		◇		◇ ©	◇	Ⓐ		Ⓐ	◇ ©	◇ Ⓐ		◇		◇		◇		◇			◇	◇			◇	
Frankfurt (Main) Hbf ‡ d.	1431	_1522_	1552	1622	1622	1631	1631	1701	_1720_	1730**x**	1752	1822	1831	_1922_	1952	2021	2031	_2122_	2152	2152	2222	2222	2231	2324	...	00
Friedberg (Hess) ‡ d.	1459	_1545_	1615	1645	1645	1659	1659	1725	_1745_	|	1815	1845	1859	_1945_	2015	2045	2059	_2145_	2215	2215	2245	2245	2259	2345	...	00
Bad Nauheim ‡ d.	1503	|	1619	|	|	1703	1703	1730	|	1758	1819	|	1903	|	2019	|	2103	|	2219	2219	|	|	2303	|	...	0
Gießen ‡ a.	1528	_1602_	1635	1702	1702	1728	1728	1748	_1802_	|	1835	1902	1928	_2002_	2035	2102	2128	_2202_	2235	2235	2302	2302	2328	0004	...	0
Gießen **906** ‡ d.	1540	1609	1639	1705	1709	1739	1740	1749**t**	1809	|	1839	1909	1940	2009	2039	2109	2139	2209	2240	2243	2305	2309	2333	0007	0011	0
Marburg (Lahn) ‡ a.	|	|	1704	1719	|	1804	|	1815**t**	|	|	1904	|	|	|	2104	|	2209	|	|	2309	2319	|	|	0031	|	0
Treysa ‡ a.	|	|	1742**a**	1753	|	1840	|	...	|	|	1939**r**	|	|	|	...	|	...	|	|	...	2355	|	|	0101	|	
Wetzlar **906** d.	1550	1618	...	...	1718	...	1750	...	1818	1821	...	1918	1950	2018	...	2118	...	2218	2250	...	...	2318	2343	...	0021	
Herborn d.	1612	1633	...	...	1733	...	1812	...	1833	1835	...	1933	2012	2033	...	2133	...	2233	2312	...	...	2333	0005	...	0043	
Dillenburg d.	1622	1638	...	...	1738	...	1822	...	1838	1839	...	1938	2022	2038	...	2138	...	2238	2322	...	...	2338	0015	...	0050	
Siegen a.	...	1705	...	...	1805	...	...	...	1905	1905	...	2005	...	2105	...	2205	...	2305	...	...	...	0005	...	...	0120	

		Ⓐ	⚒	◇ Ⓐ	Ⓐ	†	†	Ⓐt	◇ ⑥	◇ ⑥	◇ Ⓐ	Ⓐ	◇ ⚒	Ⓐ	⊗	⚒	◇	◇ ⚒		◇ ⚒		◇		◇ ⚒		
Siegen d.	...	...	...	0457	...	...	...	...	...	0554	0600	...	0654	...	...	...	0754	...	...	0854	...	0954	...	1054	...	1
Dillenburg d.	...	...	0503	0525	...	0552	...	...	...	0617	0626	...	0728	...	0733	...	0817	...	...	0917	0933	1017	...	1117	1133	1
Herborn d.	...	...	0511	0530	...	0600	...	...	...	0622	0631	...	0734	...	0740	...	0822	...	...	0922	0940	1022	...	1122	1140	1
Wetzlar **906** d.	...	...	0533	0547	...	0621	...	...	...	0637	0649	...	0751	...	0802	...	0837	...	...	0937	1002	1037	...	1137	1202	1
Treysa ‡ d.	...	...	|	|	...	|	...	0600	0559	|	|	...	|	...	|	0715**a**	|	0803**b**	0815**a**	|	|	|	...	|	|	
Marburg (Lahn) ‡ d.	0359	0440	|	|	0538	|	0608	0634	0635	|	|	0702	|	...	|	0748	|	0835	0848	|	|	|	1049	|	|	
Gießen **906** ‡ a.	0427	0510	0544	|	0604	0632	0637	0651	0651	0646	0658	0732	0801	...	0814	0818	0846	0851	0918	0946	1014	1046	1118	1146	1214	12
Gießen ‡ d.	0428	0514	...	|	0607	...	0639	0652	0654	0654	0705	0736	...	0809	0828	0828	0854	0854	0922	_0953_	1028	1054	1122	_1153_	1228	12
Bad Nauheim ‡ d.	0453	0538	...	0611	0624	...	0705	|	|	|	0724	0754	...	0826	0853	0853	|	|	0938	|	1053	|	1138	|	1253	
Friedberg (Hess) ‡ d.	0458	0542	...	|	0630	...	0710	0712	0712	0712	0728	0800	...	0830	0858	0858	0912	0912	0942	_1012_	1058	1112	1142	_1212_	1258	1
Frankfurt (Main) Hbf ‡ a.	0527	0607	...	0641**x**	0658	...	0737	0737	0735	0735	0753	0825**x**	...	0858	0927	0927	0935	0935	1007	_1034_*	1127	1135	1207	_1234_*	1327	1

		◇			◇	◇ T		◇		◇	◇ T		◇		◇		◇		◇		◇	◇	◇ ⑤⑥		◇	
Siegen d.	...	1254	...	...	1354	...	...	1454	...	1554	...	...	1654	...	1754	...	1854	...	1954	...	2054	2154	...	...	2311	
Dillenburg d.	...	1317	1333	...	1417	...	...	1517	1533	1617	...	...	1717	1733	1817	...	1917	1933	2017	...	2117	2217	...	...	2334	
Herborn d.	...	1322	1340	...	1422	...	...	1522	1540	1622	...	...	1722	1740	1822	...	1922	1940	2022	...	2122	2222	...	...	2339	
Wetzlar **906** d.	...	1337	1402	...	1437	...	...	1537	1602	1637	...	...	1737	1802	1837	...	1937	2002	2037	...	2137	2237	...	...	2352	
Treysa ‡ d.	...	|	|	1315**a**	|	1403	...	|	|	|	1603	...	|	|	|	...	|	|	|	...	|	|	2203	...	|	23
Marburg (Lahn) ‡ d.	1249	|	|	1348	|	1435	1449	|	|	|	1635	1649	|	|	|	1849	|	|	|	2048	|	|	2235	2243	|	23
Gießen **906** ‡ a.	1318	1346	1414	1418	1446	1451	1518	1546	1614	1646	1651	1718	1746	1814	1846	1918	1946	2014	2046	2118	2146	2246	2251	2312	0001	00
Gießen ‡ d.	1322	_1353_	1428	1428	1454	1454	1522	_1553_	1628	1654	1654	1722	_1753_	1828	1854	1922	_1953_	2028	2055	2122	_2153_	2255	2255	2315	...	00
Bad Nauheim ‡ d.	1338	|	1453	1453	|	|	1538	|	1653	|	|	1738	|	1853	|	1938	|	2053	|	2138	|	|	|	2338	...	00
Friedberg (Hess) ‡ d.	1342	_1412_	1458	1458	1512	1512	1542	_1612_	1658	1712	1712	1742	_1812_	1858	1912	1942	_2012_	2058	2113	2142	_2212_	2313	2313	2342	...	00
Frankfurt (Main) Hbf ‡ a.	1407	_1434_*	1527	1527	1535**x**	1535	1606	_1637_	1727	1735**x**	1735	1806**n**	_1837_	1927	1935	2007	_2034_*	2127	2135	2207	_2234_	2335	2335	0005	...	00

A – WATTENMEER – To Westerland daily to Oct. 30, ④–⑦ from Nov. 3 (Table **821**).
B – WATTENMEER – From Westerland daily to Oct. 31, ①⑤⑥⑦ from Nov. 4 (Table **821**).
D – (12) Berlin - Hannover - Frankfurt - Stuttgart. July 24 - Aug. 28 departs Hannover 1709, Kassel 1845, Marburg 1941, Gießen 1958, arrives Frankfurt 2041, Heidelberg 2143.
S – From Stuttgart (Table **912**).
T – ⑥⑦ to July 10; daily from July 16.
Y – ①–⑤ to July 15.

a – Ⓐ only.
b – 0800 on ⑥.
f – ⑤ (also Oct. 2).
h – ⑤⑥ only.
j – 0822 on ©.
k – ⑥ only.
n – 1811 on ①–⑤ to July 18.
p – ⑤–⑦ (also Oct. 3).
r – ⚒ only.
t – Not Sept. 12–23.
v – ⑤⑦ (also Oct. 3; not Oct. 2).
w – ⑦ (also Oct. 3; not Oct. 2).
x – Frankfurt (Main) **West** (not Hbf) on ①–⑤ to July 15.
y – 7–10 minutes **earlier** on ①–⑤ to July 15.

* – 3 minutes later until July 15.
⊕ – Change trains at Gießen on ①–⑤ to July 15.
⊗ – Change trains at Gießen on Oct. 1.
⊙ – Change trains at Gießen on †.
◧ – Not Oct. 2. Train number **2270** on †.
¶ – See also Frankfurt - Siegen panel.
‡ – See also Frankfurt - Kassel panel. Services to / from Treysa also call at Stadtallendorf.

◇ – Operated by Hessische Landesbahn.
▲ – July 18 - Sept. 2 most *IC* trains do no[t] run north of Kassel. Only the following trains continue to run beyond Kassel (with amended timings): **2374**; **2372** or **2370/2270** on ⑥⑦; **2274**; **2271** on ① **2371** on ⑤ (also on ⑥ from Hannove[r]) **2373** on ⑤; **2375**; **1995**.
⊖ – Additional journeys (◇) Frankfurt - Ka[ssel] and v.v.: **From Frankfurt** Hbf at 0615 0622 ©, 1415 **Y**, 1422 **T** and 1622 ©. **From Kassel** Hbf at 0703 ⚒, 1303 **T**, 1503 **T** and 2103 ⑤⑥.

RB services

AACHEN - KÖLN - SIEGEN 807

	Ⓒz	2		⚒r¶	Ⓒz2	Ⓐe2	Ⓐe¶	⚒r¶	⚒r														
Aachen Hbf .... 802 910 d.	...	...	...	...	...	...	...	...	0518e	0618e	0718e	0818r	0918		1418	1518	1618	1718	1818	1918	...	...	...
Düren .... 802 d.	...	...	...	...	0303	...	...	...	0545e	0645e	0745e	0845r	0945		1445	1545	1645	1745	1845	1945	...	...	...
Köln Hbf .... 802 910 a.	...	...	...	...	0340	...	...	...	0612e	0712e	0812e	0912r	1012		1512	1612	1712	1812	1912	2012	...	...	...
Köln Hbf .... 802 910 d.	0023	0031	...	...	0341	0431	...	...	0623	0723	0823	0923	1023	and	1523	1623	1723	1823	1924	2023	2123	2223	2323
Köln Messe/Deutz 802 910 d.	0026	0033	...	...	0343	0433	...	...	0626	0726	0826	0926	1026		1526	1626	1726	1826	1927	2026	2126	2226	2326
Troisdorf .... 802 d.	0041	0054	...	...	0409	0454	...	...	0641	0741	0841	0941	1041	hourly	1541	1641	1741	1841	1941	2041	2141	2241	2341
Siegburg/Bonn .... 910 d.	0046	0100	...	...	0414	0500	...	...	0646	0746	0846	0946	1046		1546	1646	1746	1846	1946	2046	2146	2246	2346
Hennef (Sieg) .... d.	0050	0106	...	...	0419	0506	...	...	0650	0750	0850	0950	1050	until	1550	1650	1750	1850	1950	2050	2150	2250	2350
Eitorf .... d.	0059	0118	...	...	0432	0518	...	...	0659	0759	0859	0959	1059		1559	1659	1759	1859	1959	2059	2159	2259	2359
Au (Sieg) .... d.	0116	0139	...	0448	0454	0541	0543	0613	0716	0816	0916	1016	1116		1616	1716	1816	1916	2016	2116	2216	2316	0016
Wissen (Sieg) .... d.	0124	...	...	0455	...	...	0550	0620	0721	0821	0921	1021	1121		1621	1721	1821	1921	2021	2122	2224	2324	0024
Betzdorf (Sieg) .... d.	0138	...	...	0509	...	...	0603	0634	0730	0830	0930	1030	1130		1630	1730	1830	1930	2030	2131	2238	2338	0038
Siegen .... a.	0200	...	...	0532	...	...	0629	0658	0750	0850	0950	1050	1150		1650	1750	1850	1950	2049	2150	2300	2400	0100

	Ⓐe	⚒r	Ⓐe							Ⓐe				2	2	⚒r¶
en .... d.	...	0454	0526	0610	0710	0810		1810	1910	...	2010	2110	2210	...	...	2308
lorf (Sieg) .... d.	...	0515	0546	0628	0728	0828		1828	1928	...	2028	2128	2228	...	...	2331
en (Sieg) .... d.	...	0528	0558	0637	0737	0837		1837	1937	...	2037	2137	2237	...	...	2343
ieg) .... d.	...	0537	0604	0643	0743	0843	and	1843	1943	...	2043	2143	2243	2320	...	2351
.... d.	...	0557	0624	0700	0800	0900		1900	2000	...	2100	2200	2300	2339	...	...
ef (Sieg) .... d.	...	0609	0637	0709	0809	0909	hourly	1909	2009	...	2109	2209	2309	2353	...	...
urg/Bonn .... 910 d.	...	0614	0641	0714	0814	0914		1914	2014	...	2114	2214	2314	2357	...	...
dorf .... 802 d.	...	0618	0647	0718	0818	0918	until	1918	2018	...	2118	2218	2318	0003	0013	...
Messe/Deutz ....802 910 d.	0533	0633	0709	0733	0833	0933		1933	2033	2041	2133	2234	2333	0027	0037	...
Hbf ....802 910 a.	0536	0636	0712	0736	0836	0936		1936	2036	2044	2136	2236	2336	0029	0039	...
Hbf ....802 910 d.	0548	0648e	...	0747e	0848r	0947		1947	...	2047	...	...	...	...	0040	...
n .... 802 d.	0614	0714e	...	0814e	0914r	1014		2014	...	2114	...	...	...	...	0118	...
en Hbf ....802 910 a.	0644	0744e	...	0844e	0944r	1044		2044	...	2145	...	...	...	...	0144	...

e – Ⓐ (not Nov. 1).
r – ⚒ (not Nov. 1).
z – Also Nov. 1.

¶ – Operated by Hessische Landesbahn.

ELLIO Rail NRW

ESSEN - HAGEN - SIEGEN 808

	Ⓒz	Ⓐe	Ⓐe	Ⓐe	Ⓐe	Ⓒz	Ⓐe		⚒r				⚒r		★	⚒r				⚒r				
Essen Hbf .... ⊡ d.	...	...	...	...	...	...	...	0634e	...	0734e	...	0834r	...	0934		...	1734	...	1834	...	1934	...	...	...
Bochum Hbf .. ⊡ d.	...	...	...	...	...	...	...	0647e	...	0747e	...	0847r	...	0947	and at	...	1747	...	1847	...	1947	...	...	...
Witten Hbf .... ⊡ d.	...	...	...	...	...	...	...	0657e	...	0757e	...	0857r	...	0957		...	1757	...	1857	...	1957	...	...	...
Hagen Hbf .... ⊡ a.	...	...	...	...	...	...	...	0709e	...	0809e	...	0909r	...	1009	the same	...	1809	...	1909	...	2009	...	...	...
Hagen Hbf .... d.	0024	...	...	0540	0610	0615	0640	0715	0740	0815	0840	0915	0940	1015		1740	1815	1840	1915	1940	2015	2115	2215	2315
Altena (Westf) ... d.	0050	...	...	0605	0636	0640	0705	0740	0805	0840	0905	0940	1005	1040	minutes	1805	1840	1905	1940	2005	2040	2140	2240	2340
Werdohl .... d.	0059	...	...	0614	0645	0649	0714	0749	0814	0849	0914	0949	1014	1049		1814	1849	1914	1949	2014	2049	2149	2249	2349
Finnentrop .... d.	0117	0502	0558	0631	0703	0707	0731	0807	0831	0907	0931	1007	1031	1107	past each	1831	1907	1931	2007	2031	2107	2207	2307	0007
Lennestadt ♥ ... d.	0129	0515	0610	0643	0715	0718	0743	0818	0843	0918	0943	1018	1043	1118		1843	1918	1943	2018	2043	2119	2219	2319	0019
Kreuztal .... d.	0152	0537	0633	0706	0738	0737	0806	0837	0906	0937	1006	1037	1106	1137	hour until	1906	1937	2006	2037	2106	2142	2242	2342	0042
Siegen .... a.	0204	0550	0644	0719	0750	0748	0819	0848	0919	0948	1019	1048	1119	1148		1919	1948	2020	2048	2121	2154	2254	2354	0054

	⚒r	Ⓐe	⚒r		Ⓐe		Ⓐe		⚒r		♣	⚒r					⚒r							
en .... d.	...	0402	0503	...	0543	0612	0635	0712	0743	0812		1543	1612	...	1643	1712	1744	1812	1844	1912	2011	2111	2211	2311
ztal .... d.	...	0413	0514	...	0554	0622	0647	0722	0754	0822	and at	1554	1622	...	1654	1722	1755	1822	1855	1922	2022	2122	2222	2323
estadt ♥ .... d.	...	0436	0537	...	0617	0641	0710	0741	0817	0841		1617	1641	...	1717	1741	1818	1841	1918	1941	2045	2145	2245	2347
entrop .... d.	0453	0453	0553	0553	0630	0653	0730	0754	0830	0853	the same	1630	1653	...	1730	1753	1831	1853	1931	1953	2058	2158	2258	2400
ohl .... d.	0510	0510	0610	0610	0647	0710	0747	0810	0847	0910		1647	1710	...	1747	1810	1848	1910	1948	2010	2115	2215	2315	...
a (Westf) .... d.	0518	0518	0618	0618	0655	0718	0755	0818	0855	0918	minutes	1655	1718	...	1755	1818	1856	1918	1956	2018	2123	2223	2323	...
n Hbf .... a.	0546	0546	0646	0646	0724	0746	0824	0846	0924	0946		1724	1746	...	1824	1846	1924	1946	2024	2046	2152	2252	2352	...
en Hbf ..... ⊡ d.	...	...	0651e	...	...	0751e	...	0851r	...	0951	past each	...	1751	...	...	1851	...	1951	...	...	...	...	...	...
n Hbf ..... ⊡ d.	...	...	0702e	...	...	0802e	...	0902r	...	1002		...	1802	...	...	1902	...	2002	...	...	...	...	...	...
um Hbf ... ⊡ d.	...	...	0714e	...	...	0814e	...	0914r	...	1014	hour until	...	1814	...	...	1914	...	2014	...	...	...	...	...	...
n Hbf ..... ⊡ a.	...	...	0729e	...	...	0829e	...	0929r	...	1029		...	1829	...	...	1929	...	2029	...	...	...	...	...	...

	⚒r									
en Hbf .... d.	0507	0607	0707	and	1907	2007	2107	2207	2307	...
um Hbf .... d.	0521	0621	0721	hourly	1921	2021	2121	2221	2321	...
n Hbf .... d.	0533	0633	0733	until	1933	2033	2133	2233	2333	...
en Hbf .... a.	0546	0646	0746		1946	2046	2146	2246	2346	...

	⚒r								
Hagen Hbf .... d.	0517	0617	0717	and	1917	2017	2117	2217	2317
Witten Hbf .... d.	0531	0631	0731	hourly	1931	2031	2131	2231	2331
Bochum Hbf .... d.	0542	0642	0742	until	1942	2042	2142	2242	2342
Essen Hbf .... a.	0556	0656	0756		1956	2056	2156	2256	2356

Ⓐ (not Nov. 1).
⚒ (not Nov. 1).
z – Also Nov. 1.
★ – The 1040, 1240, 1440 and 1640 from Hagen run daily.
♣ – The 0843, 1043, 1243 and 1443 from Siegen run daily.
⊡ – See also panel below main table.
♥ – Lennestadt - Altenhundem.

ahn 5

PADERBORN - HAMELN - HANNOVER - HANNOVER FLUGHAFEN ✈ 809

								Ⓐ	⑥			⚒	†				⚒	†						
Paderborn Hbf ..... 805 811 d.	...	...	...	...	...	...	...	0512	...	...	...	0615	...	...	0715	...	0815	...	...	0915	...	1015	...	1115
Altenbeken .... 805 811 d.	...	...	...	...	...	...	...	0524	...	...	...	0627	...	...	0727	...	0827	...	...	0927	...	1027	...	1127
Bad Pyrmont .... d.	...	...	...	...	...	0505r	...	0602	0605	...	0635e	0702	0705	0735e	0802	...	0902	0905	...	1002	...	1102	...	1202
Hameln .... a.	...	...	...	...	...	0519r	...	0616	0618	...	0649e	0716	0718	0749e	0816	...	0916	0918	...	1016	...	1116	...	1216
Hameln .... d.	...	...	...	0420e	0450r	0520	0550r	0620	0620	0620	0650r	0720	0720	0750r	0820	0850r	0920	0920	0950r	1020	1050r	1120	1150r	1220
Hannover Hbf .... a.	...	...	...	0503e	0533r	0603	0633r	0703	0703	0703	0733r	0803	0803	0833r	0903	0933r	1003	1003	1033r	1103	1133r	1203	1233r	1303
Hannover Hbf .... d.	0335	0410	0435	0505	0535	0605	0635	0705	0705	0705	0735	0805	0805	0835	0905	0935	1005	1005	1035	1105	1135	1205	1235	1305
Hannover Flughafen ✈ .... a.	0353	0428	0453	0523	0553	0623	0653	0723	0723	0723	0753	0823	0823	0853	0923	0953	1023	1023	1053	1123	1153	1223	1253	1323

																								⑤⑥f	A
rborn Hbf ......805 811 d.	...	1215	...	1313	...	1415	...	1515	...	1615	...	1715	...	1815	...	1915	...	2015	...	2115	...	2215	...	2310	...
beken ....805 811 d.	...	1227	...	1327	...	1427	...	1527	...	1627	...	1727	...	1827	...	1927	...	2027	...	2127	...	2227	...	2322	...
Pyrmont .... d.	...	1302	1335e	1402	...	1502	...	1602	1635e	1702	1735e	1802	1835e	1902	...	2002	...	2102	...	2202	...	2302	...	0002	0005
eln .... a.	...	1316	1349e	1416	...	1516	...	1616	1649e	1716	1749e	1816	1849e	1916	...	2016	...	2116	...	2216	...	2316	...	0016	0019
eln .... d.	1250r	1320	1350r	1420	1450r	1520	1550	1620	1650	1720	1750	1820	1850	1920	1950	2020	2050e	2120	...	2220	...	2320	...	0020	0020
nover Hbf .... a.	1333r	1403	1433r	1503	1533r	1603	1633	1703	1733	1803	1833	1903	1933	2003	2033	2103	2133e	2203	...	2303	...	0003	...	0103	0103
nover Hbf .... d.	1335	1405	1435	1505	1535	1605	1635	1705	1735	1805	1835	1905	1935	2005	2035	2105	2135	2205	2235	2305	2335	0005	0035	0105	0105
nover Flughafen ✈ .... a.	1353	1423	1453	1523	1553	1623	1653	1723	1753	1823	1853	1923	1953	2023	2053	2123	2153	2223	2253	2323	2353	0023	0053	0123	0123

								⚒		Ⓐ		⚒													
nover Flughafen ✈ .... d.	0006	0036	0106	0136	...	0406	...	0436	0436	0506	0506	0536	0536	0606	0636	0706	0736	0806	0836	0906	0936	1006	1036	1106	1136
nover Hbf .... a.	0024	0053	0123	0155	...	0424	...	0453	0453	0523	0523	0553	0553	0623	0653	0723	0753	0823	0853	0923	0953	1023	1053	1123	1153
nover Hbf .... d.	...	0100	...	...	...	...	...	0455	...	0525	...	0555	...	0625r	0655	0725r	0755	0825r	0855	0925r	0955	1025r	1055	1125r	1155
eln .... a.	...	0144	...	...	...	...	...	0540	...	0610	...	0640	...	0710r	0740	0810r	0840	0910r	0940	1010r	1040	1110r	1140	1210r	1240
eln .... d.	...	...	...	...	...	...	...	0544	...	0611	...	0644	...	0711e	0744	...	0844	...	0944	...	1044	...	1144	...	1244
Pyrmont .... d.	...	...	...	...	...	...	...	0600	...	0625	...	0700	...	0725e	0800	...	0900	...	1000	...	1100	...	1200	...	1300
beken ....805 811 d.	...	...	...	...	...	...	...	0633	...	...	...	0733	...	...	0833	...	0933	...	1033	...	1133	...	1233	...	1333
rborn Hbf ......805 811 a.	...	...	...	...	...	...	...	0646	...	...	...	0746	...	...	0846	...	0946	...	1046	...	1146	...	1246	...	1346

																						B	⑤⑥f		
nover Flughafen ✈ .... d.	1206	1236	1306	1336	1406	1436	1506	1536	1606	1636	1706	1736	1806	1836	1906	1936	2006	2036	2106	2136	2206	2236	2236	2306	2336
nover Hbf .... a.	1223	1253	1323	1353	1423	1453	1523	1553	1623	1653	1723	1753	1823	1853	1923	1953	2023	2053	2123	2153	2223	2253	2253	2323	2353
nover Hbf .... d.	1225r	1255	1325r	1355	1425r	1455	1525	1555	1625	1655	1725	1755	1825	1855	1925	1955	2025r	2055	2125e	2155	...	2255	2255	...	2355
eln .... a.	1310r	1340	1410r	1440	1510r	1540	1610	1640	1710	1740	1810	1840	1910	1940	2010	2040	2110r	2140	2210e	2240	...	2340	2340	...	0040
eln .... d.	1311e	1344	...	1444	...	1544	1611e	1644	1711e	1744	1811e	1844	...	1944	...	2044	...	2144	...	2244	...	2341	2344	...	...
Pyrmont .... d.	1325e	1400	...	1500	...	1600	1625e	1700	1725e	1800	1825e	1900	...	2000	...	2100	...	2200	...	2300	...	2355	0000	...	...
beken ....805 811 d.	...	1433	...	1533	...	1633	...	1733	...	1833	...	1933	...	2033	...	2133	...	2233	...	2333	...	...	0033	...	...
rborn Hbf ......805 811 a.	...	1446	...	1546	...	1646	...	1746	...	1846	...	1946	...	2046	...	2146	...	2246	...	2346	...	...	0046	...	...

Mornings of ①–⑤ (not Oct. 3, Nov. 1).
①②③④⑦ (not Oct. 2, 31).
e – Ⓐ only.
f – Also Oct. 2, 31.
r – ⚒ only.

810 HAMM and BAD BENTHEIM - HANNOVER - BERLIN

km		CNL	IC	CNL	IC		ICE	IC	ICE	IC	IC	ICE	ICE	IC	ICE	ICE	IC	IC	ICE	ICE	IC	ICE	ICE
		40447	**61447**	**40447**	**61447**		**649**	**2447**	**841**	**2179**	**2241**	**541**	**1041**	**2445**	**843**	**853**	**2343**	**245**	**543**	**553**	**2443**	**845**	**1045**
		★ Ⓡ	★	x Ⓡ	x ♥		Ⓐ	① g	⚒	Ⓐ	①–⑥	⚒	†	⚒		⚒	⑦	①–⑥		⚒	⚒	Ⓐ	Ⓒ
		B	B	B	B		✕	D	L ✕	H	M 🍷	✕	✕	D	✕	✕	N	🍷	✕	K ✕	D U	◐ ✕	✕
	Bonn Hbf **800** d.	...	...	...	...	...	...	...	...	...	...	...	...	...	...	...	...	...	...	0621r	0621y	...	...
	Köln Hbf **800** d.	2313	2313	2313	2313	...	...	...	...	...	...	0429	...	0513t	0528r	0544t	...	...	...	0648t	0713t	...	0728r
	Wuppertal Hbf **800** d.	│	│	│	│	...	...	...	...	...	...	│	...	0543	│	0616	...	...	...	0716	0743	...	│
	Düsseldorf Hbf **800** d.	2337	2337	2337	2337	...	...	...	...	...	...	0453	...	│	0552	│	...	...	0649	│	│	0752	0752
	Dortmund Hbf **800** d.	0032	0032	0032	0032	...	...	...	...	...	...	0547	...	0628	0648	│	...	...	0748	│	0828	0848	0848
0	**Hamm** (Westf) **802** d.	0049	0049	0049	0049	...	...	...	...	...	...	0604	...	0644	0711	0711	...	...	0811	0811	0844	0911	0911
50	Gütersloh Hbf **802** d.	0112	0112	0112	0112	...	...	...	...	...	...	0629	...	0707	│	│	...	...	│	│	0907	│	│
67	**Bielefeld** Hbf **802 811** d.	0124	0124	0124	0124	...	...	0516	...	...	...	0640	...	0719	0738	0738	...	...	0838	0838	0919	0938	0938
81	Herford **811** d.	│	│	│	│	...	...	0527	...	...	...	│	...	0728	│	│	...	...	│	│	0928	│	│
	Amsterdam C **22** d.	│	│	│	│	...	...	│	...	...	...	│	...	│	│	│	...	0502	│	│	│	│	│
	Bad Bentheim 🏛 **811** d.	│	│	│	│	...	...	│	...	...	...	│	...	│	│	│	...	0721	│	│	│	│	│
	Rheine **811** d.	│	│	│	│	...	...	│	...	...	...	│	...	│	│	│	...	0735	│	│	│	│	│
	Osnabrück Hbf **811** d.	│	│	│	│	...	...	│	...	...	0604	│	...	│	│	│	0804	0805	│	│	│	│	│
	Bünde (Westf) **811** d.	│	│	│	│	...	...	│	...	...	0626	│	...	│	│	│	0827	0826	│	│	│	│	│
97	Bad Oeynhausen **811** d.	│	│	│	│	...	...	0539	...	...	0639	│	...	│	│	│	0839	0839	│	│	0939	│	│
112	Minden (Westf) **811** d.	│	0153	│	0153	...	...	0549	...	...	0649	│	...	0749	│	│	0849	0849	│	│	0949	│	│
177	**Hannover** Hbf **811** a.	│	0223	│	0223	...	...	0618	...	...	0718	0728	...	0818	0828	0828	0918	0918	0928	0928	1018	1028	1028
177	**Hannover** Hbf d.	│	0226	│	0240	...	0527	0636	0631	0704	0721	0731	0731	0836	0831	0831	0921	0921	0931	0931	1036	1031	1031
	Magdeburg Hbf **866** a.	│	│	│	0402	...	▽	0756	│	│	│	│	│	0956	│	│	│	│	│	│	1156	│	│
	Leipzig Hbf **866** a.	│	│	│	│	...	│	0917	│	│	│	│	│	1117	│	│	│	│	│	│	1317	│	│
252	Wolfsburg **902** d.	│	│	│	│	...	0620	...	0704	0735	0755	│	0804	...	0905	0905	0955	0955	│	│	...	1105	1105
327	Stendal **838** d.	│	│	│	│	...	0648	...	0734	...	0827	│	0833	...	│	│	1027	1027	│	│	...	│	│
419	**Berlin** Spandau **838 902** a.	│	│	│	│	...	0721	...	0809	...	0904	0854	0906	...	0958	0958	1104	1104	1054	1054	...	1158	1158
435	**Berlin** Hbf **838 902** a.	0658f	0658f	0658f	0658f	...	0732	...	0824	...	0922	0906	0918	...	1009	1009	1122	1122	1106	1106	...	1209	1209
440	**Berlin** Ostbahnhof **838 902** a.	...	0429	...	...	...	...	...	...	...	0934	...	...	...	...	...	1134	1134	...	...	...	...	...

	IC	IC	ICE	ICE	IC	ICE	ICE	IC	ICE	ICE	IC	IC	ICE	ICE	ICE	IC	ICE	ICE	IC	ICE	ICE	IC	ICE
	2222	**141**	**545**	**555**	**2441**	**847**	**857**	**143**	**547**	**557**	**2010**	**2049**	**849**	**1049**	**859**	**145**	**549**	**559**	**2047**	**941**	**951**	**147**	**641**
	Ⓐ			r						r	⑤	⑤–⑦	Ⓐ	Ⓒ				r	Ⓑ				
	V 🍷	🍷	✕	✕	D	✕	✕	🍷	✕	✕	T 🍷	z D	◐ ✕	✕	✕	🍷	✕	✕	D	✕	✕	🍷	◐ ✕
Bonn Hbf **800** d.	...	...	...	0823e	...	...	...	...	...	...	1022	...	...	...	...	...	...	1222e	...	...	...	...	...
Köln Hbf **800** d.	...	...	0828	0848	0913t	0928r	0948t	...	...	1048	1046	1113t	...	1128r	1148t	...	1220y	1248	1313t	...	1348t	...	1427y
Wuppertal Hbf **800** d.	...	...	│	0916	0943	│	1016	...	...	1116	│	1143	...	│	1216	...	│	1316	1343	...	1416	...	│
Düsseldorf Hbf **800** d.	...	...	0852	│	│	0952	│	...	1052	│	1118	│	1152	1152	│	...	1254	│	│	1352	│	...	1452
Dortmund Hbf **800** d.	0912	...	0948	│	1028	1048	│	...	1148	│	1212	1228	1248	1248	│	...	1347	│	1428	1448	│	...	1548
Hamm (Westf) **802** d.	0934	...	1011	1011	1044	1111	1111	...	1211	1211	1234	1244	1311	1311	1311	...	1411	1411	1444	1511	1511	...	1611
Gütersloh Hbf **802** d.	0955	...	│	│	1107	│	│	...	│	│	1255	1307	│	│	│	...	│	│	1507	│	│	...	│
Bielefeld Hbf **802 811** d.	1006	...	1038	1038	1119	1138	1138	...	1238	1238	1306	1319	1338	1338	1338	...	1438	1438	1519	1538	1538	...	1638
Herford **811** d.	1015	...	│	│	1128	│	│	...	│	│	1315	1328	│	│	│	...	│	│	1528	│	│	...	│
Amsterdam C **22** d.	│	0701	│	│	│	│	│	0901	│	│	│	│	│	│	│	1101	│	│	│	│	│	1301	│
Bad Bentheim 🏛 **811** d.	│	0928	│	│	│	│	│	1128	│	│	│	│	│	│	│	1328	│	│	│	│	│	1528	│
Rheine **811** d.	│	0942	│	│	│	│	│	1142	│	│	│	│	│	│	│	1342	│	│	│	│	│	1542	│
Osnabrück Hbf **811** d.	│	1008	│	│	│	│	│	1208	│	│	│	│	│	│	│	1408	│	│	│	│	│	1608	│
Bünde (Westf) **811** d.	│	│	│	│	│	│	│	1229	│	│	│	│	│	│	│	│	│	│	│	│	1629	│
Bad Oeynhausen **811** d.	│	1039	│	│	1139	│	│	│	│	│	│	1339	│	│	│	1439	│	│	1539	│	│	│	│
Minden (Westf) **811** d.	│	1049	│	│	1149	│	│	1249	│	│	│	1349	│	│	│	1449	│	│	1549	│	│	1649	│
Hannover Hbf **811** a.	1101	1118	1128	1128	1218	1228	1228	1318	1328	1328	1401	1418	1428	1428	1428	1518	1528	1528	1618	1628	1628	1718	1728
Hannover Hbf d.	1104	1121	1131	1131	1236	1231	1231	1321	1331	1331	1404	1436	1431	1431	1431	1521	1531	1531	1636	1631	1631	1721	1731
Magdeburg Hbf **866** a.	│	│	│	│	1356	│	│	│	│	│	│	1556	│	│	│	│	│	│	1756	│	│	│	│
Leipzig Hbf **866** a.	│	│	│	│	1517	│	│	│	│	│	│	1717	│	│	│	│	│	│	1917	│	│	│	│
Wolfsburg **902** d.	1138	1155	│	│	...	1305	1305	1355	│	│	1438	...	1505	1505	1505	1555	│	│	...	1705	1705	1755	│
Stendal **838** d.	│	1227	│	│	...	│	│	1427	│	│	│	...	│	│	│	1627	│	│	...	│	│	1827	│
Berlin Spandau **838 902** a.	1239	1304	1254	1254	...	1358	1358	1504	1454	1454	1539	...	1558	1558	1558	1704	1654	1654	...	1758	1758	1904	1854
Berlin Hbf **838 902** a.	1249	1322	1307	1307	...	1409	1409	1522	1506	1506	1553	...	1609	1609	1609	1722	1706	1706	...	1809	1809	1922	1906
Berlin Ostbahnhof **838 902** a.	...	1334	...	...	...	...	...	1534	...	...	1606	...	...	...	...	1734	...	...	...	...	...	1934	...

	IC	IC	IC	ICE	ICE	IC	ICE	ICE	IC	ICE	ICE	IC	IC	ICE	ICE	IC	ICE	ICE		IC	ICE	ICE	ICE
	1216	**1920**	**2045**	**943**	**953**	**149**	**643**	**653**	**2012**	**945**	**955**	**241**	**241**	**645**	**655**	**2041**	**947**	**957**		**243**	**657**	**657**	**102**
	⑤	R	Ⓑ q		Ⓑ q			r		Ⓑ q		s	⑦ w		r	⑦ w		⑦ w		⑦	⑦ y	⑦ w	Ⓑ q
	J 🍷		D	◐ ✕	✕	🍷	◐ ✕	✕	A 🍷	✕	✕	🍷	🍷	◐ ✕	✕		✕	✕		🍷	✕	r ✕	Q 🍷
Bonn Hbf **800** d.	1422	1422w	...	...	...	...	...	...	1622	...	...	...	...	...	1825j	...	...	...	...	...	...	2025	...
Köln Hbf **800** d.	1445	1445	1513t	...	1548t	...	1628y	1648	1646	...	1748t	...	...	1826y	1848	1913t	1927d	1948t	...	...	2020	2048	2110c
Wuppertal Hbf **800** d.	│	│	1543	...	1616	...	│	1716	│	...	1816	...	...	│	1916	1943	│	2016	...	...	│	2116	2143
Düsseldorf Hbf **800** d.	1518	1518	│	1552	│	...	1652	│	1715	1752	│	...	...	1846b	│	│	1952	│	...	...	2045	│	│
Dortmund Hbf **800** d.	1611	1611	1628	1648	│	...	1748	│	1828	1848	│	...	...	1948	│	2028	2048	│	...	...	2148	│	2228
Hamm (Westf) **802** d.	1634	1634	1644	1711	1711	...	1811	1811	1845	1911	1911	...	...	2011	2011	2044	2111	2111	...	...	2211	2211	2250
Gütersloh Hbf **802** d.	1655	1655	1707	│	│	...	│	│	1905	│	│	...	...	│	│	2107	│	│	...	...	│	│	2310
Bielefeld Hbf **802 811** d.	1706	1706	1719	1738	1738	...	1838	1838	1916	1938	1938	...	...	2038	2038	2119	2138	2138	...	...	2238	2238	2320
Herford **811** d.	1715	1715	1728	│	│	...	│	│	1927	│	│	...	...	│	│	2128	│	│	...	...	│	│	2330
Amsterdam C **22** d.	│	│	│	│	│	1501	│	│	│	│	│	1701	1701	│	│	│	│	│	...	1901	│	│	│
Bad Bentheim 🏛 **811** d.	│	│	│	│	│	1728	│	│	│	│	│	1928	1928	│	│	│	│	│	...	2128	│	│	│
Rheine **811** d.	│	│	│	│	│	1742	│	│	│	│	│	1942	1942	│	│	│	│	│	...	2142	│	│	│
Osnabrück Hbf **811** d.	│	│	│	│	│	1808	│	│	│	│	│	2008	2008	│	│	│	│	│	...	2208	│	│	│
Bünde (Westf) **811** d.	│	│	│	│	│	│	│	│	│	│	2029	2029	│	│	│	│	│	...	│	│	│	│
Bad Oeynhausen **811** d.	│	│	1739	│	│	1839	│	│	1937	│	│	│	│	│	│	2139	│	│	...	2240	│	│	│
Minden (Westf) **811** d.	│	│	1749	│	│	1849	│	│	1949	│	│	2049	2049	│	│	2149	│	│	...	2252	│	│	2347
Hannover Hbf **811** a.	1801	1801	1818	1828	1828	1918	1928	1928	2018	2028	2028	2118	2118	2128	2128	2218	2228	2228	...	2326	2328	2328	0018
Hannover Hbf d.	1804	1804	1836	1831	1831	1921	1931	1931	2036p	2031	2031	...	2121	2131	2131	...	2231	2231	...	...	2331	2331	...
Magdeburg Hbf **866** a.	│	│	1956	│	│	│	│	│	2157p	│	│	...	│	│	│	...	│	│	...	...	│	│	...
Leipzig Hbf **866** a.	│	│	2117	│	│	│	│	│	2321w	│	│	...	│	│	│	...	│	│	...	...	│	│	...
Wolfsburg **902** d.	1838	1838	...	1905	1905	1955	│	│	...	2105	2105	...	2155	│	│	...	2305	2305	...	...	0004	0004	...
Stendal **838** d.	│	│	...	│	│	2027	│	│	...	2134	2134	...	2227	│	│	...	│	│	...	...	│	│	...
Berlin Spandau **838 902** a.	1939	1939	...	1958	1958	2104	2054	2054	...	2207	2207	...	2302	2254	2254	...	2358	2358	...	...	0058	0058	...
Berlin Hbf **838 902** a.	1954	1954	...	2009	2009	2122	2106	2106	...	2219	2219	...	2317	2306	2306	...	0010	0010	...	...	0110	0110	...
Berlin Ostbahnhof **838 902** a.	2008	2008	...	...	...	2134	...	...	...	...	...	...	2329	...	...	...	...	...	...	...	...	...	...

A – ALLGÄU – 🚃12 and 🍷 Oberstdorf - Ulm - Stuttgart - Mannheim - Koblenz - Köln - Hannover (- Magdeburg ①④⑤⑦ **p**) (- Leipzig ⑦ **w**).
B – KOPERNIKUS – 🛏 1, 2 cl. and 🛌 2 cl. (Ⓡ) Köln - Berlin - Dresden - Praha; 🚃2 (*IC* **61447**) Köln - Berlin - Dresden - Praha. Conveys 🛏 1, 2 cl., 🛌 2 cl. and 🚃2 (*EN* **447** Ⓡ – JAN KIEPURA) Köln - Warszawa (see Table **24**).
D – To Dresden (Table **842**).
H – From Hamburg (Table **900**).
J – ⑤ (not July 29). 🚃12 and 🍷 Salzburg - München - Stuttgart - Köln - Berlin.
K – 🚃12 and ✕ Koblenz Hbf (d. 0545) - Köln - Berlin. Starts from Köln July 9 - Aug. 20.
L – 🚃12 and ✕ (Oldenburg - Bremen Ⓐ ¶ -) Hannover - Berlin.
M – From Münster (Westf) Hbf (d. 0538).
N – From Münster (Westf) Hbf (d. 0738).
Q – 🚃12 and 🍷 Basel - Karlsruhe - Köln - Hannover.
R – ①②③④⑦ (not Oct. 2). From Frankfurt (Table **911**) on ⑦ **w**. Train number **2412** on ⑦ Sept. 4 - Oct. 30 (also Oct. 3).
T – From Tübingen via Stuttgart (Tables **911** and **912**).
U – From Koblenz July 9 - Aug. 20 (Table **800**).
V – From Aachen Hbf (d. 0708), Rheydt Hbf (d. 0748), Mönchengladbach Hbf (d. 0755), Viersen (d. 0804) and Krefeld Hbf (d. 0816).

b – 1850 July 9 - Aug. 21.
c – July 10 - Aug. 21 calls at Köln **Messe/Deutz** (d. 2105), not Köln Hbf.
d – ⚒ (not July 9 - Aug. 20).
e – ⚒ only.
f – 0653 until Aug. 4.
g – Also Oct. 4; not Oct. 3.
h – Also Oct. 2.
j – ①–④ (not Oct. 3).
p – ①④⑤⑦ (not Oct. 2).
q – Not Oct. 2.
r – Not July 9 - Aug. 21.
s – Not Oct. 2, Nov. 5, 12, 19, 26, Dec. 3, 10.
t – 11–28 minutes **earlier** July 9 - Aug. 21.
w – ⑦ (also Oct. 3; not Oct. 2).
x – Not Aug. 1–3, Nov. 18–27.
y – July 9 - Aug. 21 only.
z – Also Oct. 3.

¶ – Not July 19 - Sept. 2.
★ – Aug. 1–3, Nov. 18–27 only.
▽ – Via Braunschweig Hbf (d. 0601).
♥ – Also calls at Braunschweig Hbf (a. 0314), Brandenburg Hbf (a. 0 and Potsdam Hbf (a. 0505).
◐ – From Köln/Bonn Flughafen ✈ o dates in Table **800**.

BERLIN - HANNOVER - HAMM and BAD BENTHEIM 810

km		ICE 103	ICE 656	ICE 646	IC 242	ICE 956	ICE 946	IC 2013	ICE 654	ICE 644	IC 240	IC 240	IC 1927	ICE 954	ICE 944	IC 2044	ICE 652	ICE 642	IC 148	ICE 952	ICE 942	IC 2046	IC 2011	IC 2017
		L 🍷	Ⓐ ✕	Ⓐ ◐✕	①–⑥ 🍷	⚒r ✕	⚒ ✕	A 🍷	✕	⚒ ✕	①–⑥ 🍷	a 🍷	Ⓐ	⚒r ✕	✕	⚒ D	✕	◐✕	🍷	r ✕	✕	⑥ D	⑦w S 🍷	⑤ Y
0	**Berlin** Ostbahnhof . 838 902 d.	...	...	...	...	...	...	...	...	...	0623	...	0650	...	...	...	...	...	0823	...	...	...	0951	...
5	**Berlin** Hbf 838 902 d.	...	0430	0430	...	0538	0538	...	0652	0652	0634	...	0701	0749	0749	...	0852	0852	0834	0949	0949	...	1002	...
1	**Berlin** Spandau 838 902 d.	...	0442	0442	...	0550	0550	...	0703	0703	0652	...	0715	0801	0801	...	0903	0903	0852	1001	1001	...	1016	...
3	Stendal 838 d.	...	0516	0516	...	0626	0626	...	|	|	0734	...	|	|	|	...	|	|	0934	|	|	...	|	...
8	Wolfsburg 902 d.	...	0548	0548	...	0656	0656	...	0757	0757	0804	...	0820	0856	0856	...	|	|	1004	1056	1056	...	1121	1121
	Leipzig Hbf 866 d.	...	|	|	...	|	|	0430g	|	|	|	...	|	|	|	0643	|	|	|	|	|	0843	|	|
	Magdeburg Hbf 866 d.	...	|	|	...	|	|	0601e	|	|	|	...	|	|	|	0804	|	|	|	|	|	1004	|	|
3	**Hannover** Hbf a.	...	0618	0618	...	0728	0728	0723e	0828	0828	0837	...	0853	0928	0928	0923	1028	1028	1037	1128	1128	1123	1153	1153
3	**Hannover** Hbf 811 d.	0540	0621	0621	0640	0731	0731	0740	0831	0831	0840	0840	0856	0931	0931	0940	1031	1031	1040	1131	1131	1140	1156	1156
8	Minden (Westf) 811 d.	0612	0651	0651	0712	|	|	0812	|	|	0912	0912	|	|	|	1014	|	|	1112	|	|	1214	|	|
3	Bad Oeynhausen 811 d.	|	|	|	0722	|	|	0822	|	|	|	|	|	|	|	1023	|	|	1122	|	|	1223	|	|
9	Bünde (Westf) 811 d.	|	|	|	|	|	|	|	|	|	0932	0932	|	|	|	|	|	|	|	|	|	|	|	|
6	**Osnabrück** Hbf 811 d.	|	|	|	0753	|	|	|	|	|	0953	0953	|	|	|	|	|	|	1153	|	|	|	|	|
4	Rheine 811 d.	|	|	|	0821	|	|	|	|	|	1021	1021	|	|	|	|	|	|	1221	|	|	|	|	|
5	Bad Bentheim 🏛 811 a.	|	|	|	0834	|	|	|	|	|	1034	1034	|	|	|	|	|	|	1234	|	|	|	|	|
5	*Amsterdam C 22* a.	|	|	|	1100	|	|	|	|	|	1300	1300	|	|	|	|	|	|	1500	|	|	|	|	|
	Herford 811 d.	0632	0711	0711	...	|	|	0833	|	|	...	...	0944	|	|	1033	|	|	...	|	|	1233	1244	1244
	Bielefeld Hbf 802 811 d.	0641	0721	0721	...	0822	0822	0842	0922	0922	...	...	0953	1022	1022	1042	1122	1122	...	1222	1222	1242	1253	1253
	Gütersloh Hbf 802 d.	0651	|	|	...	|	|	0852	|	|	...	...	1003	|	|	1053	|	|	...	|	|	1253	1303	1303
	Hamm (Westf) 802 a.	0713	0748	0748	...	0848	0848	0913	0948	0948	...	...	1024	1048	1048	1114	1148	1148	...	1248	1248	1314	1324	1324
	Dortmund Hbf 800 a.	0732	|	0809	...	|	0909	0932	|	1009	...	...	1048	|	1109	1132	|	1209	...	|	1309	1332	1347	1347
	Düsseldorf Hbf 800 a.	|	|	0906	...	|	1006	1046	|	1111	...	...	1142	|	1206	|	|	1306	...	|	1406	|	1442	1442
	Wuppertal Hbf 800 a.	0812	0839	...	...	0939	|	|	1039	...	...	...	|	1139	...	1212	1239	...	...	1339	|	1412	|	|
	Köln Hbf 800 a.	0846f	0915t	...	...	1009	1039y	1115	1109t	...	...	...	1212	1209	...	1246t	1309t	...	...	1409	1439y	1446t	1512	1512
	Bonn Hbf 800 a.	...	...	...	...	...	...	1135	1132d	...	...	...	...	...	...	...	1332r	...	...	...	...	...	1535	1535

	ICE 650	ICE 640	IC 146	ICE 950	ICE 940	IC 2048	IC 1915	ICE 558	ICE 548	IC 144	ICE 858	ICE 848	IC 2440	IC 2223	IC 1917	ICE 556	ICE 546	IC 142	IC 1995		ICE 856	ICE 846	ICE 1046	IC 2442
	✕	◐✕	🍷	r ✕	✕	D	⑤⑦z S 🍷	✕	◐✕	🍷	r ✕	✕	D H	Ⓐ ⊡ 🍷	⑦w K	U ✕	✕	🍷	⑦w ♠ 🍷		r ✕	♣ ✕	⑤G ✕	Ⓑq D
lin Ostbahnhof .. 838 902 d.	...	...	1023	...	...	...	1151	...	...	1223	...	...	...	...	...	...	...	1423	1451	...	...	...	...	...
lin Hbf 838 902 d.	1052	1052	1034	1149	1149	...	1202	1252	1252	1234	1349	1349	...	1357	1357	1452	1452	1434	1502	...	1549	1549	1549	...
lin Spandau 838 902 d.	1103	1103	1052	1201	1201	...	1216	1303	1303	1252	1401	1401	...	1407	1407	1503	1503	1452	1516	...	1601	1601	1601	...
ndal 838 d.	|	|	1134	|	|	...	|	|	|	1334	|	|	...	1447	1449	|	|	1534	|	...	|	|	|	...
fsburg 902 d.	|	|	1204	1256	1256	...	1321	|	|	1404	1456	1456	...	1520	1520	|	|	1604	1621	...	1656	1656	1656	...
eipzig Hbf 866 d.	|	|	|	|	|	1043	|	|	|	|	|	|	1243	|	|	|	|	|	|	...	|	|	|	1443
agdeburg Hbf 866 d.	|	|	|	|	|	1204	|	|	|	|	|	|	1404	|	|	|	|	|	|	...	|	|	|	1604
nover Hbf a.	1228	1228	1237	1328	1328	1323	1353	1428	1428	1437	1528	1528	1523	1553	1553	1628	1628	1637	1652	...	1728	1728	1728	1723
nover Hbf 811 d.	1231	1231	1240	1331	1331	1340	1356	1431	1431	1440	1531	1531	1540	1556	1556	1631	1631	1640	...	...	1731	1731	1731	1740
den (Westf) 811 d.	|	|	1312	|	|	1414	|	|	|	1512	|	|	1614	|	|	|	|	1712	...	...	|	|	|	1814
Oeynhausen 811 d.	|	|	|	|	|	1423	|	|	|	1522	|	|	1623	|	|	|	|	|	...	...	|	|	|	|
ünde (Westf) 811 d.	|	|	1332	|	|	|	|	|	|	|	|	|	|	|	|	|	|	1732	...	...	|	|	|	|
snabrück Hbf 811 d.	|	|	1353	|	|	|	|	|	|	1553	|	|	|	|	|	|	|	1753	...	...	|	|	|	|
heine 811 d.	|	|	1421	|	|	|	|	|	|	1621	|	|	|	|	|	|	|	1821	...	...	|	|	|	|
ad Bentheim 🏛 811 a.	|	|	1434	|	|	|	|	|	|	1634	|	|	|	|	|	|	|	1834	...	...	|	|	|	|
Amsterdam C 22 a.	|	|	1700	|	|	|	|	|	|	1900	|	|	|	|	|	|	|	2100	...	...	|	|	|	|
ford 811 d.	|	|	...	|	|	1433	1444	|	|	...	|	|	1633	1644	1644	|	|	...	...	...	|	|	|	1833
lefeld Hbf 802 811 d.	1322	1322	...	1422	1422	1442	1453	1522	1522	...	1622	1622	1642	1653	1653	1722	1722	...	...	...	1822	1822	1822	1842
ersloh Hbf 802 d.	|	|	...	|	|	1453	1503	|	|	...	|	|	1653	1703	1703	|	|	...	...	...	|	|	|	1853
nm (Westf) 802 a.	1348	1348	...	1448	1448	1514	1524	1548	1548	...	1648	1648	1714	1724	1724	1748	1748	...	...	...	1848	1848	1848	1914
ortmund Hbf 800 a.	|	1409	...	|	1509	1532	1547	|	1609	...	|	1709	1732	1748	1748	|	1809	...	...	...	|	1909	1909	1932
üsseldorf Hbf 800 a.	|	1506	...	|	1606	|	1642	|	1710	...	|	1806	|	...	1842	|	1910	...	...	...	|	2006	2016	|
Wuppertal Hbf 800 a.	1439	...	...	1539	|	1612	|	1639	...	...	1739	|	1812	...	|	1839	...	...	...	...	1939	|	...	2012
öln Hbf 800 a.	1509t	...	...	1609	1632y	1645t	1712	1709t	...	...	1809	1832y	1846h	...	1915	1909j	...	...	...	...	2009	2039	...	2046t
onn Hbf 800 a.	...	...	...	...	...	...	1735	1735v	...	...	...	...	1933k	...	1935	1932b	...	...	...	...	2038q	...	...	...

	ICE 554	ICE 544	IC 140	ICE 854	ICE 844	IC 2444	ICE 552	ICE 542	IC 2242		IC 1932	ICE 852	ICE 842	ICE 832	IC 2446	IC 1932	IC 2240	ICE 540	ICE 540	ICE 850	CNL 40458	IC 61458	CNL 40458	IC 61458
	✕	✕	🍷	Ⓑq T✕	✕	Ⓑq D	✕	✕	M		⑦w R 🍷	† ✕	✕	⚒m O✕	⑦w D	⑦w R 🍷	⑦w N 🍷	✕	⑤–⑦ c✕	†m O✕	x Ⓡ B	x ♥ B	E Ⓡ B	E B
lin Ostbahnhof .. 838 902 d.	...	...	1623	...	...	...	...	...	1823	...	...	...	...	...	...	...	2023	...	...	...	2333◊	2333◊	0103	0103
lin Hbf 838 902 d.	1652	1652	1634	1749	1749	...	1852	1852	1834	...	...	1949	1949	1949	...	...	2034	2107	2107	2155	2344¦	2344¦	|	|
lin Spandau 838 902 d.	1703	1703	1652	1801	1801	...	1903	1903	1852	...	1950	2001	2001	2001	...	←	2052	2118	2118	2209	|	|	|	|
ndal 838 d.	|	|	1734	|	|	...	|	|	1934	...	2025	|	|	|	...	2031	2133	2154	2154	2245	|	|	|	|
fsburg 902 d.	|	|	1804	1856	1856	...	|	|	2005	...	→	2056	2056	2056	...	2104	2206	2223	2223	2313	|	|	|	|
eipzig Hbf 866 d.	|	|	|	|	|	1643	|	|	|	...	...	|	|	|	1843	|	|	|	|	|	|	|	|	|
agdeburg Hbf 866 d.	|	|	|	|	|	1804	|	|	|	...	...	|	|	|	2004	|	|	|	|	|	|	0109¦	|	|
nover Hbf a.	1828	1828	1837	1928	1928	1923	2028	2028	2037	...	...	2128	2128	2128	2123	2140	2237	2256	2256	2344	|	0244¦	|	0330
nover Hbf 811 d.	1831	1831	1840	1931	1931	1940	2031	2031	2040	...	...	2131	2131	...	2140	...	2240	...	2301	...	|	0340	|	0340
den (Westf) 811 d.	|	|	1912	|	|	2013	|	|	2112	...	...	|	|	...	2213	...	2312	...	|	...	|	0412	|	0412
Oeynhausen 811 d.	|	|	1922	|	|	2022	|	|	2122	...	...	|	|	...	2222	...	2322	...	|	...	|	|	|	|
ünde (Westf) 811 d.	|	|	|	|	|	|	|	|	2135	2146	...	|	|	...	|	...	2335	...	|	...	|	|	|	|
snabrück Hbf 811 d.	|	|	1953	|	|	|	|	|	2159	2214	...	|	|	...	|	...	2358	...	|	...	|	|	|	|
heine 811 d.	|	|	2021	|	|	|	|	|	...	2248	...	|	|	...	|	...	...	...	|	...	|	|	|	|
ad Bentheim 🏛 811 a.	|	|	2034	|	|	|	|	|	...	2303	...	|	|	...	|	...	...	...	|	...	|	|	|	|
Amsterdam C 22 a.	|	|	2300	|	|	|	|	|	...	...	...	|	|	...	|	...	...	...	|	...	|	|	|	|
ford 811 d.	|	|	...	|	|	2032	|	|	...	...	...	|	|	...	2232	...	...	...	2346	...	|	|	|	|
lefeld Hbf 802 811 d.	1922	1922	...	2022	2022	2041	2122	2122	...	...	...	2222	2222	...	2241	...	...	...	2357	...	0439	0439	0439	0439
ersloh Hbf 802 d.	|	|	...	|	|	2051	|	|	...	...	...	|	|	...	2251	...	...	...	0008	...	0450	0450	0450	0450
mm (Westf) 802 a.	1948	1948	...	2048	2048	2112	2148	2148	...	...	...	2248	2248	...	2312	...	...	...	0028	...	0510	0510	0510	0510
ortmund Hbf 800 a.	|	2009	...	|	2109	2132	|	2209	...	...	...	|	2309	...	2331	...	...	...	0048	...	0531	0531	0531	0531
üsseldorf Hbf 800 a.	|	2106	...	|	2206	|	|	2306	...	...	...	|	0006	...	|	...	...	...	0146	...	0631	0631	0631	0631
Wuppertal Hbf 800 a.	2039	|	...	2139	|	2212	2239	|	...	...	...	2339	|	...	0012	...	...	...	|	...	|	|	|	|
öln Hbf 800 a.	2109t	2133r	...	2209t	2230r	2245t	2312t	2330r	...	...	...	0011t	0030n	...	0046t	...	...	...	0211	...	0656	0656	0656	0656
onn Hbf 800 a.	...	...	...	2235‡	...	...	2344p	...	...	...	...	...	...	...	...	...	...	...	◐	...	...	...	...	...

- – ALLGÄU – [12] and 🍷 (Leipzig ① g -) (Magdeburg ⚒ -) Hannover - Köln - Stuttgart - Oberstdorf.
- – KOPERNIKUS – 🛏 1, 2 cl. and ▬ 2 cl. (Ⓡ) Praha - Dresden - Berlin - Köln; [2] (*IC* 61458) Praha - Dresden - Berlin - Köln. 🛏 1, 2 cl., ▬ 2 cl. and [2] (*EN* 446 Ⓡ – JAN KIEPURA) Warszawa - Köln (see Table **24**).
- – From Dresden (Table 842).
- – Mornings of Aug. 2–4 and Nov. 19–28 only.
- – ⑤ (not July 15 - Aug. 19). To Neuss Hbf (a. 2028) and Mönchengladbach Hbf (a. 2042).
- – To Koblenz on ①–⑤ July 8 - Aug. 19 (Table **800**).
- – To Karlsruhe (Tables **911** and **912**).
- – To Basel (Table **912**).
- – To Münster (Westf) Hbf (a. 2225). Conveys 🍷 on Ⓑ.
- – To Münster (Westf) Hbf (a. 0024). Does not run Hannover - Osnabrück - Münster on Oct. 3.
- – To Oldenburg via Bremen (Table **813**).
- – [12] and 🍷 Stralsund - Berlin - Bremen - Oldenburg.
- – To Stuttgart (Tables **911** and **912**).
- – To Koblenz Hbf (a. 2313) on ⑦‡.

- U – To Koblenz Hbf (a. 2011) on Ⓐ (not July 8 - Aug. 19).
- Y – [12] Wolfsburg - Köln - Stuttgart - München.
- a – Not Nov. 6, 13, 20, 27, Dec. 4.
- b – Ⓑ (not July 8 - Aug. 21, Oct. 2).
- c – Also Oct. 3.
- d – ⚒ (not July 9 - Aug. 20).
- e – ⚒ only.
- f – July 9 - Aug. 21 calls at Köln **Messe/Deutz** (a. 0854), not Köln Hbf.
- g – ① (also Oct. 4; not Oct. 3).
- h – 1909 July 8 - Aug. 21.
- j – 1926 on July 8. 1941 July 9 - Aug. 21.
- k – Ⓑ July 8 - Aug. 21.
- m – Not July 17 - Sept. 2.
- n – Not mornings July 11 - Aug. 22.
- p – Ⓑ (not July 10 - Aug. 21, Oct. 2).
- q – Ⓑ (not Oct. 2).
- r – Not July 9 - Aug. 21.
- t – 12–32 minutes later July 9 - Aug. 21.
- v – ①–④ (not July 11 - Aug. 18, Oct. 3).

- w – ⑦ (also Oct. 3; not Oct. 2).
- x – Not Aug. 1–3, Nov. 18–27.
- y – July 9 - Aug. 21 only.
- z – Also Oct. 3; not Oct. 2.
- ‡ – ⑦ (also Oct. 3; not July 10 - Aug. 21, Oct. 2).
- ♣ – ①②③④⑥⑦ (daily July 9 - Aug. 25).
- ◊ – Until Aug. 4.
- ¦ – From Aug. 5 departs Berlin Hbf 2316, Magdeburg 0130, arrives Hannover 0303
- ⊡ – To Krefeld Hbf (a. 1843), Viersen (a. 1855), Mönchengladbach Hbf (a. 1904), Rheydt Hbf (a. 1909) and Aachen Hbf (a. 1950).
- ♥ – Until Aug. 4 also calls at Potsdam Hbf (d. 0007), Brandenburg Hbf (d. 0027) and Braunschweig Hbf (d. 0209). From Aug. 5 also calls at Potsdam Hbf (d. 0029), Brandenburg Hbf (d. 0048) and Braunschweig Hbf (d. 0224).
- ♠ – [12] Berlin - Hannover - Frankfurt - Stuttgart.
- ◐ – Continues to Köln/Bonn Flughafen ✈ on dates in Table **800**.

811 Regional services BIELEFELD and BAD BENTHEIM - HANNOVER and PADERBORN

See Table **810** for faster *ICE*/*IC* services Bielefeld/ Bad Bentheim - Hannover and v.v.

km		⚒¶	⚒¶	⚒¶	⚒¶	¶	⚒n	¶	¶		¶	¶		¶	¶	A	A¶	B¶	A	A¶	B¶			
0	Bad Bentheim d.	...	...	...	...	...	...	0557e	...	...	0657r	...	...	0757r	...	...	0857	...	...	0957	...		...	1
21	**Rheine** d.	...	...	...	0514	...	...	0614e	0638	...	0714r	...	...	0814	0838	...	0914	...	...	1014	1038		...	1
43	Ibbenbüren d.	...	...	...	0528	...	...	0628e	0654	...	0728r	...	...	0828	0854	...	0928	...	...	1028	1054	and in	...	1
69	**Osnabrück** Hbf d.	...	0448	0516	0548	...	...	0648	0716	...	0748	...	...	0848	0916	...	0948	...	...	1048	1116	the same	...	1
106	Bünde (Westf) d.	...	0512	0538	0612	...	E	0712	0738	D	0812	...	D	0912	0938	D	1012	...	D	1112	1138	pattern	D	2
	Bielefeld Hbf d.	0424	|	|	|	0624	0659	|	|	0759	|	0824	0859	|	|	0959	|	1024	1059	|	|	every	1959	
120	Herford a.	0431	0526	|	0626	0631	0707	0726	|	0807	0826	0831	0907	0926	|	1007	1026	1031	1107	1126	|	two hours	2007	2
120	Herford d.	0433	0537	|	0637	0633	0708	0737	|	0808	0837	0833	0908	0937	|	1008	1037	1033	1108	1137	|	until	2008	2
134	**Bielefeld** Hbf a.	|	0548	|	0648	|	|	0748	|	|	0848	|	|	0948	|	|	1048	|	|	1148	|		|	2
	Löhne d.	0440	...	0551	...	0640	0714	...	0751	0814	...	0840	0914	...	0951	1014	...	1040	1114	...	1151		2014	
	Bad Oeynhausen d.	0445	...	0556	...	0645	0719	...	0756	0819	...	0845	0919	...	0956	1019	...	1045	1119	...	1156		2019	
	Minden (Westf) a.	0457	...	0607	...	0657	0730	...	0807	0830	...	0857	0930	...	1007	1030	...	1057	1130	...	1207		2030	
	Minden (Westf) d.	0507	...	0608	...	0707	*0735*	...	0808	*0835*	...	0907	*0935*	...	1008	*1035*	...	1107	*1135*	...	1208		*2035*	
	Hannover Hbf a.	0550	...	0651	...	0750	*0830*	...	0851	*0930*	...	0950	*1030*	...	1051	*1130*	...	1150	*1230*	...	1251		*2130*	
	Braunschweig Hbf **866** a.	0641	...	0741	...	0841	...	...	0941	...	...	1041	...	...	1141	...	...	1241	...	...	1341		...	

	¶		¶	¶	⚒n	¶	¶	Ⓑ	¶		¶
Bad Bentheim d.	...	...	1957	...	...	2057	...	...	2157	...	2312
Rheine d.	...	...	2014	2038	...	2114	...	...	2214	...	2329
Ibbenbüren d.	...	...	2028	2054	...	2128	...	...	2228	...	2344
Osnabrück Hbf d.	...	...	2048	2116	...	2148	...	...	2248	...	0002
Bünde (Westf) d.	...	D	2112	2138	D	2212	...	D	2312	...	...
Bielefeld Hbf d.	2024	2059	|	|	2159	|	2224	2259	|	2327	...
Herford a.	2031	2107	2126	|	2207	2226	2231	2307	2326	2335	...
Herford d.	2033	2108	2137	|	2208	*2237*	2233	2308	2337	2336	...
Bielefeld Hbf a.	|	|	2148	|	|	*2248*	|	|	2348	|	...
Löhne d.	2040	2114	...	2151	2214	▬	2240	2314	▬	2343	...
Bad Oeynhausen d.	2045	2119	...	2156	2219	...	2245	2319	...	2348	...
Minden (Westf) a.	2057	2130	...	2207	2230	...	2258	2330	...	2400	...
Minden (Westf) d.	2107	*2135*	...	2208	...	2235	...	...	2335	...	...
Hannover Hbf a.	2150	*2230*	...	2251	...	2330	...	...	0030	...	...
Braunschweig Hbf **866** a.	2241	...	...	2341	...	...	...	...	...	...	...

km			Ⓒz	Ⓐ¶	Ⓐt	⚒¶	⚒¶	⚒¶	
	Braunschweig Hbf **866** d.	...	...	...	...	...	0420	...	
0	**Hannover** Hbf d.	0028	...	...	...	...	0509	...	0
65	Minden (Westf) a.	0123	...	...	...	...	0554	...	0
65	Minden (Westf) d.	...	0127	...	0528	...	0555	...	0
80	Bad Oeynhausen d.	...	0138	...	0539	...	0606	...	0
86	Löhne d.	...	0143	...	0544	...	0611	...	0
	Bielefeld Hbf d.	...	|	...	|	0509	|	0609	
96	Herford a.	...	0149	...	0549	0520	|	0620	0
96	Herford d.	...	0150	...	0550	0533	|	0633	0
110	**Bielefeld** Hbf a.	...	0201	...	0557	|	|	|	0
	Bünde (Westf) d.	...	...	...	D	0546	0621	0646	
	Osnabrück Hbf d.	...	...	0514	...	0614	0645	0714	
	Ibbenbüren d.	...	...	0530	...	0630	0703	0730	
	Rheine d.	...	...	0548	...	0648	0721	0748	
	Bad Bentheim a.	...	...	0603	...	0703	...	0803	

	¶	¶	⚒n	B¶	A¶	A	B¶	A¶	A	♥	¶	¶		¶	¶		¶	¶	①–⑥	¶	¶	¶	⑤⑥¶	
Braunschweig Hbf **866** d.	0520	...	...	0620	...	...	0720	...	...		1820	...	...	1920	...	...	2020	...	...	2120	...	2222	2222	
Hannover Hbf d.	0609	...	*0628*	0709	...	*0728*	0809	...	*0828*		1909	...	*1928*	2009	...	*2028*	2109	...	*2128*	2209	...	2309	2309	2.
Minden (Westf) a.	0659	...	*0723*	0751	...	*0823*	0853	...	*0923*	and in	1951	...	*2023*	2053	...	*2123*	2151	...	*2223*	2253	...	2351	2351	0
Minden (Westf) d.	0702	...	0728	0752	...	0828	0902	...	0928		1952	...	2028	2102	...	2128	2152	...	2228	2302	...	...	2352	0
Bad Oeynhausen d.	0714	...	0739	0803	...	0839	0914	...	0939	the same	2003	...	2039	2114	...	2139	2203	...	2239	2314	...	...	0003	0
Löhne d.	0719	...	0744	0809	...	0844	0919	...	0944		2009	...	2044	2119	...	2144	2209	...	2244	2319	...	...	0009	0
Bielefeld Hbf d.	|	0709	|	|	0809	|	|	0909	|	pattern	|	2009	|	|	2109	|	|	2209	|	|	2309	...	|	
Herford a.	0725	0720	0749	|	0820	0849	0925	0920	0949	every	|	2020	2049	2125	2120	2149	|	2220	2249	2325	2320	...	|	0
Herford d.	0727	0733	0750	|	0833	0850	0927	0933	0950		|	2033	2050	2127	2133	2150	|	2233	2250	2327	2333	...	|	0
Bielefeld Hbf a.	0739j	|	0757	|	|	0857	0936	|	0957	two hours	|	|	2057	2136	|	2157	|	|	2257	2336	|	...	|	0
Bünde (Westf) d.	...	0746	D	0819	0846	D	...	0946	D	until	2019	2046	D	...	2146	E	2219	2246	E	...	2346	...	0019	
Osnabrück Hbf d.	...	0814	...	0845	0914	...	...	1014	...		2045	2114	...	...	2214	...	2245	2314	...	...	0012	...	0041	
Ibbenbüren d.	...	0830	...	0903	0930	...	...	1030	...		2103	2130	...	...	2230	...	2303k	2330	...	...	...	...	...	
Rheine d.	...	0848	...	0921	0948	...	...	1048	...		2120	2148	...	...	2248	...	2321k	2346	...	...	...	...	...	
Bad Bentheim a.	...	0903	...	...	1003	...	...	1103	...		...	2203	...	...	2303	...	...	...	...	...	...	...	...	

BIELEFELD - PADERBORN - HOLZMINDEN - KREIENSEN ⊖ and OTTBERGEN - GÖTTINGEN ★ ⊖

km			Ⓐt		⚒n	⚒n	⚒n																		
0	**Bielefeld** Hbf § d.	...	0434	...	0534	0634	0734	0834	0934	1034	1134	1234	1334	1434	1534	1634	1734	1834	...	1934	...	2034	2134	2234	23
44	**Paderborn** Hbf § a.	...	0527	...	0627	0727	0827	0927	1027	1127	1227	1327	1427	1527	1627	1727	1827	1927	...	2027	...	2127	2227	2327	0
	Change trains	Ⓐ	⚒	Ⓐ	d	⚒	d												†	Ⓐ	Ⓒ		⑤–⑦		
44	**Paderborn** Hbf **805 809** d.	0453	0553	...	0653	0753	0853	0953	1053	1153	1253	1353	1453	1553	1653	1753	1853	1953	...	2053	2106	2206	2315	...	
61	Altenbeken **805 809** d.	0507	0607	...	0707	0807	0907	1007	1107	1207	1307	1407	1507	1607	1707	1807	1907	2007	...	2107	2118	2219	2329	...	
92	Ottbergen ★ d.	0536	0636	...	0736	0836	0936	1036	1136	1236	1336	1436	1536	1636	1736	1836	1936	2036	...	2136	2143	2245	2355	...	
102	Höxter Rathaus d.	0545	0645	...	0745	0845	0945	1045	1145	1245	1345	1445	1545	1645	1745	1845	1945	2045	...	2145	2152	2253	0003	...	
110	Holzminden a.	0554	0654	...	0754	0854	0954	1054	1154	1254	1354	1454	1554	1654	1754	1854	1954	2054	...	2154	2200	2302	0012	...	
110	Holzminden d.	*0629*	...	0711	0758	...	0958	...	1158	...	1358	...	1558	1654e	1754f	...	1958	...	2158	...	...	...	...	...	
154	**Kreiensen** a.	*0703*	...	0745	0832	...	1032	...	1232	...	1432	...	1632	1728e	1828f	...	2032	...	2232	...	...	...	...	...	

		Ⓐ	⚒	⚒	Ⓐ	⑥											Ⓐ	Ⓒ		Ⓐ					
Kreiensen d.	...	...	...	0627e	0709	0723	...	0754e	0923	...	1123	...	1323	...	1523	...	1652	1723	...	1828	...	1923	...	2125	22
Holzminden a.	...	...	...	0700e	0742	0756	...	0827e	0956	...	1156	...	1356	...	1556	...	1725	1756	...	1900	...	1956	...	2158	23
Holzminden d.	...	0501	0601	0701	0801	0801	0801	0901	1001	1101	1201	1301	1401	1501	1601	1701	...	1801	1801	1901	1901	2001	2101	2201	23
Höxter Rathaus d.	...	0510	0610	0710	0810	0810	0810	0910	1010	1110	1210	1310	1410	1510	1610	1710	...	1810	1810	1910	1910	2010	2110	2210	23
Ottbergen ★ d.	...	0526	0626	0726	0826	0826	0826	0926	1026	1126	1226	1326	1426	1526	1626	1726	...	1826	1826	1926	1926	2026	2126	2226	23
Altenbeken **805 809** d.	...	0552	0652	0752	0852	0852	0852	0952	1052	1152	1252	1352	1452	1552	1652	1752	...	1852	1852	1952	1952	2052	2152	2252	00
Paderborn Hbf **805 809** a.	...	0605	0705	0805	0905	0905	0905	1005	1105	1205	1305	1405	1505	1605	1705	1805	...	1905	1905	2005	2005	2105	2205	2305	00
Change trains	⚒n	⚒n	⚒n																						
Paderborn Hbf § d.	0513	0613	0713	0813	...	...	0913	1013	1113	1213	1313	1413	1513	1613	1713	1813	...	...	1913	...	2013	2113	2213	2313	
Bielefeld Hbf § a.	0607	0707	0807	0907	...	...	1007	1107	1207	1307	1407	1507	1607	1707	1807	1907	...	...	2007	...	2107	2207	2307	0007	

MÜNSTER - BIELEFELD ⊡ ♠ and BIELEFELD - DETMOLD - ALTENBEKEN ⊡

km		⚒n		⚒n			⚒n				
0	**Bielefeld** Hbf ♠ d.	0749	0849	0949	1049	1249	1349	1449	1649	1849	2049
11	Oerlinghausen d.	0803	0903	1003	1103	1303	1403	1503	1703	1903	2103
22	Lage d.	0813	0913	1013	1113	1313	1413	1513	1713	1913	2113
31	Detmold a.	0820	0920	1020	1120	1320	1420	1520	1720	1920	2120
60	**Altenbeken** a.	...	0946v	1046	...	...	1446	1546v	...	1946v	2146n

	⚒n			⚒n			⚒n				⚒
Altenbeken d.	...	...	1013v	1113	...	...	1513	1613v	...	2013v	22
Detmold d.	0740	0840	1040	1140	1240	1440	1540	1640	1840	2040	22
Lage d.	0750	0850	1050	1150	1250	1450	1550	1650	1850	2050	22
Oerlinghausen d.	0800	0900	1100	1200	1300	1500	1600	1700	1900	2100	23
Bielefeld Hbf ♠ a.	0811	0911	1111	1211	1311	1511	1611	1711	1911	2111	23

HERFORD - PADERBORN ¶

km		Ⓐt		⚒n					N
0	**Herford** d.	0530	...	0633	0733	and	2133	2233	2233
8	Bad Salzuflen d.	0537	...	0640	0740		2140	2240	2240
19	Lage d.	0549	...	0652	0752	hourly	2152	2252	2252
28	Detmold d.	0559	...	0702	0802		2202	2258	2302
57	Altenbeken **805 809** a.	0624	...	0727	0827	until	2227	...	2327
74	**Paderborn** Hbf **805 809** a.	0638	...	0741	0841		2241	...	2341

	Ⓐt	⚒n			❖		L	
Paderborn Hbf **805 809** d.	...	0518	...	0621	and	2021	2121	...
Altenbeken **805 809** d.	...	0530	...	0633		2033	2133	...
Detmold d.	0458	0558	...	0701	hourly	2101	2201	...
Lage d.	0506	0606	...	0709		2109	2209	...
Bad Salzuflen d.	0517	0617	...	0720	until	2120	2220	...
Herford a.	0524	0624	...	0727		2127	2227	...

A – Train runs hourly.
B – Train runs every **two** hours.
D – From/ to Düsseldorf (Table **802**).
E – From/ to Dortmund (Table **802**).
L – To Bielefeld Hbf (a. 2248).
N – ⑤–⑦ (also Oct. 3, 31, Nov. 1).

d – Daily.
e – Ⓐ only.
f – 4 minutes later on Ⓒ.
j – 0736 on Ⓒ.
k – ⑤⑥ only.
n – ⚒ (not Nov. 1).
r – ⚒ only.
t – Ⓐ (not Nov. 1).
v – † (also Nov. 1).
z – Also Nov. 1.
* – Departs up to 5 minutes earlier July 18 - Aug. 26.
❖ – The 1221 from Paderborn runs 3–4 minutes later Detmold - Herford on Ⓐ (not Nov. 1).
♥ – Bielefeld d. 1413/1611 (not 1409/1609; arrives Herford 1423/1621).

§ – Additional trains run on Ⓐ (not Nov. 1).
¶ – Operated by Westfalen Bahn.
⊖ – Operated by NordWestBahn. 2nd class on
⊡ – Operated by **eurobahn** Keolis Deutschlan

★ – **OTTBERGEN - GÖTTINGEN** ⊖. *63 km.* Journey: 73–81 minutes (103 minutes for train marked
Most trains run from/to Paderborn, attached to Holzminden trains shown in the main table above
From Ottbergen at 0534 ⚒, 0634 ⚒, 0734, 0834 ⚒, 0934, 1034 ⚒, 1134, 1234 ⑥, 1234 Ⓐ ‡, 1334
1534, 1634 Ⓐ, 1734, 1834 Ⓐ, 1934 and 2034. **From Göttingen** at 0603 ⚒, 0711, 0803* ⚒, 09
1003* ⚒, 1111*, 1203* ⚒, 1311 Ⓒ, 1403* ⑥, 1511, 1603* Ⓐ, 1711, 1803* Ⓐ, 1911, 2003 Ⓐ and 2

♠ – **MÜNSTER - BIELEFELD** ⊡. *76 km.* Journey: 91–102 minutes. **From Münster (Westf)** at 0607
0717 ⚒n, 0817, 0917 ⚒n, 1017, 1117 ⚒n, 1217, 1317 ⑥, 1417, 1517 ⚒n, 1617, 1717 ⚒n, 181
1917 ⚒n, 2017, 2117 ⚒n and 2217 ⑥. **From Bielefeld Hbf** at 0608 ⑥, 0614 Ⓐ t, 0708 ⚒n, 08
0914 ⚒n, 1014, 1114 ⚒n, 1214, 1314 ⚒n, 1414, 1514 ⚒n, 1614, 1714 ⚒n, 1814, 1914 ⚒n, 20
and 2114.

 Ⓐ – Mondays to Fridays, except holidays Ⓑ – Daily except Saturdays Ⓒ – Saturdays, Sundays and holidays

MÜNSTER - EMDEN - NORDDEICH

	◇ Ⓐ	◇ ⚒	IC 2438 ⚒e	◇ ⚒	Ⓐt	◇	Ⓐt	IC 2208 A	◇		◇	Ⓐt	IC 2206 P	◇		◇	Ⓐt	IC 2204	IC 2432 e	◇ Ⓒ	◇ Ⓐ		IC 2018 ⑥ ♦		◇
Koblenz Hbf **800** .... d.	...	...	...	...	...	...	...	...	...	...	...	...	0641t	...	...	...	...	0841g	...	...	...	...	0943	...	...
Köln Hbf **800 802** ... d.	...	...	...	...	...	...	0521x	0541	...	0621n	...	0721x	0746	...	0821x	...	0921x	0946	...	...	...	1021x	1046	...	...
Düsseldorf Hbf **800** d.	...	...	...	...	...	...	|	0606	...	|	...	|	0812	...	|	...	|	1012	...	...	...	|	1118	...	...
Hagen Hbf **802** ... d.	...	...	...	...	0522	...	0622	|	...	0722	...	0822	|	...	0922	...	1022	|	...	...	...	1122	|	...	...
Münster (Westf) Hbf .. d.	0502	...	...	0602	0624	0702	0724	0731	0805	0824	0905	0924	0931	1005	1024	1105	1124	1131	...	1205	1205	1224	1231	...	1305
Greven .... d.	0513	...	...	0613	0637	0713	0733	|	0814	0833	0914	0933	|	1014	1033	1114	1133	|	...	1214	1214	1233	|	...	1314
Emsdetten .... d.	0522	...	...	0622	0646	0722	0740	|	0822	0840	0922	0940	|	1022	1040	1122	1140	|	...	1222	1222	1240	|	...	1322
Rheine .... d.	0534	0534	...	0634	0658	0734	0749	0756	0834	0851	0934	0949	0956	1034	1051	1134	1149	1156	...	1234	1234	1249	1256	...	1334
Lingen (Ems) .... d.	0555	0555	...	0655	▬	0755	...	0815	0855	▬	0955	...	1015	1055	▬	1155	...	1215	...	1255	1255	...	|	...	1355
Meppen .... d.	0609	0609	...	0709	...	0809	...	0829	0909	...	1009	...	1029	1109	...	1209	...	1229	...	1309	1328z	...	|	...	1409
Papenburg (Ems) ...... d.	0642	0642	...	0742	...	0842	...	0856	0942	...	1042	...	1056	1142	...	1242	...	1256	...	1342	1404	...	|	...	1442
Leer (Ostfriesl) ..... **813** d.	0653	0653	0715	0753	0824	0853	...	0909	0953	1024	1053	...	1109	1153	1224	1253	...	1309	1322	1353	1417	...	|	1424	1453
Emden Hbf ◧ ..... **813** a.	0709	0709	0731	0809	0840	0909	...	0925	1009	1040	1109	...	1125	1209	1240	1309	...	1325	1338	1409	1432	...	1416	1440	1509
Emden Hbf .... **813** d.	...	...	0742	...	0842	...	...	0942	...	1042	...	...	1142	...	1242	...	...	...	1342	...	...	...	1421	1442	...
Norden .... **813** d.	...	...	0808	...	0906	...	...	1005	...	1106	...	...	1205	...	1306	...	...	...	1408	...	...	...	1447	1506	...
Norddeich .... **813** a.	...	...	0814	...	0912	...	...	1011	...	1112	...	...	1211	...	1312	...	...	...	1414	...	...	...	1453	1512	...
Norddeich Mole ‡ **813** a.	...	...	0820	...	0916	...	...	1016	...	1116	...	...	1217	...	1316	...	...	...	1420	...	...	...	1500	1516	...

	Ⓐt	IC 2202	◇		◇	Ⓐt	IC 2200	◇		◇	Ⓐt	IC 2014 ⑤ 🍷♦	IC 2004 🍷♦	IC 2036 Ⓑe	◇		◇	Ⓐt	IC 2002 N	IC 2034 e	◇		◇	◇	◇	◇
blenz Hbf **800** ..... d.	...	...	...	...	...	...	...	...	...	...	...	1443	1443	...	...	...	...	...	...	...	...	...	...	...	...	...
ln Hbf **800 802** ... d.	1121x	1146	...	1221x	...	1321x	1346	...	1421x	...	1521x	1546	1546	...	...	1621x	...	1721x	1745	...	...	1821x	...	...	...	...
sseldorf Hbf **800**. d.	|	1212	...	|	...	|	1414	...	|	...	|	1612	1612	...	...	|	...	|	1817	...	...	|	...	...	...	...
Hagen Hbf **802** ... d.	1222	|	...	1322	...	1422	|	...	1522	...	1622	|	|	...	...	1722	...	1822	|	...	...	1922	...	...	...	...
ster (Westf) Hbf ... d.	1324	1331	1405	1424	1505	1524	1531	1605	1624	1705	1724	1731	1731	...	1805	1824	1905	1924	1931	...	2005	2024	2105	2211	2313	0013
en .... d.	1333	|	1414	1433	1514	1533	|	1614	1633	1714	1733	|	|	...	1814	1833	1914	1933	|	...	2014	2033	2114	2222	2326	0026
detten .... d.	1340	|	1422	1440	1522	1540	|	1622	1640	1722	1740	|	|	...	1822	1840	1922	1940	|	...	2022	2040	2122	2231	2335	0035
ne .... d.	1349	1356	1434	1451	1534	1549	1556	1634	1651	1734	1749	1756	1756	...	1834	1851	1934	1949	1956	...	2034	2051	2134	2252j	2346	0046
en (Ems) .... d.	...	1415	1455	▬	1555	...	1615	1655	▬	1755	...	1815	1815	...	1855	▬	1955	...	2015	...	2055	▬	2155	2313	...	...
pen .... d.	...	1429	1509	...	1609	...	1629	1709	...	1809	...	1829	1829	...	1909	...	2009	...	2029	...	2109	...	2209	2327	...	...
nburg (Ems) .... d.	...	1456	1542	...	1642	...	1656	1742	...	1842	...	1856	1856	...	1942	⑥	2042	...	2055	...	2142	...	2242	0000	...	...
(Ostfriesl) ..... **813** d.	...	1509	1553	1624	1653	...	1709	1753	1824	1853	...	1909	1909	1922	1953	2024	2053	...	2109	2122	2153	2224	2253	0012	...	...
en Hbf ◧ ...... **813** a.	...	1525	1609	1640	1709	...	1725	1809	1840	1909	...	1925	1925	1938	2009	2040	2109	...	2125	2138	2209	2240	2309	0028	...	...
en Hbf .... **813** d.	...	1542	...	1642	...	...	1728	...	1842	...	...	...	...	1942	...	2042	...	...	...	2142	...	2242	...	...	...	...
en .... **813** d.	...	1607	...	1706	...	...	1751	...	1906	...	...	...	...	2008	...	2106	...	...	...	2208	...	2306	...	...	...	...
deich .... **813** a.	...	1613	...	1712	...	...	1757	...	1912	...	...	...	...	2014	...	2112	...	...	...	2214	...	2312	...	...	...	...
deich Mole ‡ **813** a.	...	1618	...	1716	...	...	1805	...	1916	...	...	...	...	2019	...	2116	...	...	...	...	...	...	...	...	...	...

	⊙ ⚒d	Ⓐ	◇ ⚒		◇	IC 2035 ⚒e	IC 2005 ⚒ 🍷♦	Ⓐt	◇ Ⓐ	◇ Ⓒ		◇	IC 2037 ①–⑥ h	IC 2009 P	Ⓐt	◇		◇	IC 2201	Ⓐt	◇		◇ Ⓐ	◇ Ⓒ	◇ Ⓐ	IC 2019 ⑥ ♦
deich Mole ‡ **813** d.	...	...	...	...	...	...	...	...	...	...	...	...	0736	...	...	...	0839	...	0952	...	...	1039	...	...	...	1136
deich .... **813** d.	...	...	...	...	...	0536	...	...	...	...	0641	...	0739	...	...	...	0841	...	0955	...	...	1041	...	...	...	1139
en .... **813** d.	...	...	...	...	...	0543	...	...	...	...	0647	...	0746	...	...	...	0847	...	1004	...	...	1047	...	...	...	1146
en Hbf .... **813** a.	...	...	...	...	...	0607	...	...	...	...	0715	...	0814	...	...	...	0915	...	1026	...	...	1115	...	...	...	1214
en Hbf ◧ ...... **813** d.	...	...	0452	...	0552r	0609	0634	...	0642	0652	0717	0752	0816	0833	...	0852	0917	0952	1034	...	1052	1117	1152	1152	1224	1234
(Ostfriesland) **813** d.	...	...	0509	...	0609r	0626	0653	...	0659	0709	0733	0809	0833	0853	...	0909	0933	1009	1053	...	1109	1133	1209	1209	1241	1253
nburg (Ems) .... d.	...	...	0519	...	0619r	...	0704	...	0709	0719	▬	0819	...	0904	...	0919	▬	1019	1104	...	1119	▬	1219	1219	1251	1304
pen .... d.	...	...	0550	...	0650	...	0731	...	0750j	0750	...	0850	...	0931	...	0950	...	1050	1131	...	1150	...	1250	1250	1325	1331
en (Ems) .... d.	...	...	0604	...	0704	...	0744	...	0804	0804	...	0904	...	0944	...	1004	...	1104	1144	...	1204	...	1304	1304	→	1344
ne .... d.	0453	0608	0628	0708	0729	...	0804	0808	0829	0829	0908	0929	...	1004	1008	1029	1108	1129	1204	1208	1229	1308	1327	1329	...	1404
detten .... d.	0502	0616	0636	0716	0737	...	|	0817	0837	0837	0916	0937	...	|	1016	1037	1116	1137	|	1216	1237	1316	1337	1337	...	|
en .... d.	0511	0622	0644	0722	0745	...	|	0823	0845	0845	0923	0945	...	|	1023	1045	1123	1145	|	1223	1245	1323	1346	1345	...	|
ster (Westf) Hbf ... a.	0525	0633	0654	0733	0756	...	0829	0834	0856	0856	0933	0956	...	1029	1033	1056	1133	1156	1229	1233	1256	1333	1356	1356	...	1429
Hagen Hbf **802** ... a.	...	0736	...	0836	...	...	|	0936	...	...	1036	...	...	|	1136	...	1236	...	|	1336	...	1436	...	...	...	|
isseldorf Hbf **800**. a.	...	|	...	|	...	...	0947	|	...	...	|	...	...	1146	|	...	|	...	1346	|	...	|	...	...	...	1546
ln Hbf **800 802** ... a.	...	0839x	...	0938x	...	...	1015	1038x	...	...	1138x	...	...	1215	1238x	...	1338x	...	1413	1438x	...	1538x	...	...	...	1612
blenz Hbf **800** ..... a.	...	...	...	...	...	...	1115	...	...	...	...	...	...	...	...	...	...	...	...	...	...	...	...	...	...	1715

	IC 2203 E	Ⓐt	◇ Ⓐ	◇ Ⓒ		◇	IC 2205	Ⓐt	◇		◇	IC 2435 e	IC 2207 N	Ⓐt	◇		◇	IC 2209 B	Ⓐt	◇		◇	◇		◇ ⑤⑥	◇
deich Mole ‡ **813** d.	1136	...	...	...	1239	...	1351k	...	...	1439	...	1537	...	...	...	1639	...	1758	...	...	1839	...	...	2039	...	...
deich .... **813** d.	1139	...	...	...	1241	...	1357k	...	...	1441	...	1540	...	...	...	1641	...	1801	...	...	1841	...	...	2041	...	...
en .... **813** d.	1146	...	...	...	1247	...	1407k	...	...	1447	...	1547	...	...	...	1647	...	1808	...	...	1847	...	...	2047	...	...
en Hbf .... **813** a.	1214	...	...	...	1315	...	1429k	...	...	1515	...	1614	...	...	...	1715	...	1830	...	...	1915	...	...	2115	...	...
en Hbf ◧ ...... **813** d.	1234	...	...	1252	1317	1352	1434	...	1452	1517	1552	1616	1634	...	1652	1717	1752	1834	...	1852	1917	1952	2052	2117	2214	...
(Ostfriesland) **813** d.	1253	...	...	1309	1333	1409	1453	...	1509	1533	1609	1633	1653	...	1709	1733	1809	1853	...	1909	1933	2009	2109	2133	2231	...
nburg (Ems) .... d.	1304	...	←	1319	▬	1419	1504	...	1519	▬	1619	...	1704	...	1719	▬	1819	1904	...	1919	...	2019	2119	...	2240	...
pen .... d.	1331	...	1337	1350	...	1450	1531	...	1550	...	1650	...	1731	...	1750	...	1850	1931	...	1950	...	2050	2150	...	2313	...
en (Ems) .... d.	1344	...	1351	1404	...	1504	1544	...	1604	...	1704	...	1744	...	1804	...	1904	1944	...	2004	...	2104	2204	...	2327	...
ine .... d.	1404	1408	1429j	1429	1508	1529	1604	1608	1629	1708	1729	...	1804	1808	1829	1908	1929	2004	2008	2029	...	2129	2229	...	2349	2353
detten .... d.	|	1416	1437	1437	1516	1537	|	1616	1637	1716	1737	...	|	1816	1837	1916	1937	|	2016	2037	...	2137	2237	...	...	0002
ven .... d.	|	1423	1445	1445	1523	1545	|	1623	1645	1723	1745	...	|	1823	1845	1923	1945	|	2023	2046	...	2146	2245	...	...	0011
ster (Westf) Hbf ... a.	1429	1433	1456	1456	1533	1556	1629	1633	1656	1733	1756	...	1829	1833	1856	1933	1956	2029	2033	2056	...	2156	2256	...	...	0025
Hagen Hbf **802** ... a.	|	1536	...	...	1636	...	|	1736	...	1836	...	...	|	1936	...	2036	...	|	2136	...	...	...	...	...	...	...
isseldorf Hbf **800**. a.	1546	|	...	...	|	...	1746	|	...	|	...	...	1946	|	...	|	...	2146	|	...	...	...	...	...	...	...
ln Hbf **800 802** ... a.	1613	1638x	...	...	1738x	...	1813	1838x	...	1938x	...	...	2013	2038x	...	2138x	...	2213	2238x	...	...	...	...	...	...	...
blenz Hbf **800** ..... a.	...	...	...	...	...	...	1916b	...	...	...	...	...	...	...	...	...	...	...	...	...	...	...	...	...	...	...

NOTES (LISTED BY TRAIN NUMBER)

4 – ①②③④⑦ (not Oct. 2). [12] and 🍷 (Konstanz - Karlsruhe ⑦**w** -) Koblenz - Münster - Emden.
5 – [12] and 🍷 Emden - Münster - Koblenz (- Karlsruhe - Konstanz ⑤⑥).
4 – [12] and 🍷 Stuttgart - Mannheim - Münster - Emden.
3 – ⑥ until Oct. 29. [12] Stuttgart - Mannheim - Münster - Norddeich Mole.
9 – ⑥ until Oct. 29. [12] Norddeich Mole - Münster - Mannheim - Stuttgart.

⑥ to June 25; ⑤⑥ July 1 - Aug. 13; ④–⑦ Aug. 19 - Oct. 23 (also Oct. 29). Train number **2358** on ⑦ Aug. 21 - Oct. 23 (timings may vary by 1 – 2 minutes).
⑤–⑦ to June 26; ④–⑦ June 30 - Aug. 21; ③–⑦ Aug. 24 - Oct. 23 (also Oct. 3, 28, 29; not Oct. 2); ⑦ from Oct. 30.
Ⓑ (daily from Oct. 30).
Daily to Nov. 4; Ⓑ from Nov. 6.
Daily to Nov. 5; ①–⑥ from Nov. 7.

Not ⑥.
Not Nov. 1.
Not Nov. 12 – 28.
Not ⑦.

h – Also Oct. 2; not Oct. 3, Nov. 12 – 28.
j – Arrives 9 – 11 minutes earlier.
k – On ⑥ until Oct. 29 departs Norddeich Mole 1337, Norddeich 1340, Norden 1347, arrives Emden 1414.
n – ⚒ (not July 9 - Aug. 20, Nov. 1).
r – ⚒ only.
t – Ⓐ (not Nov. 1).
w – Also Oct. 3; not Oct. 2.
x – Not July 9 - Aug. 21.
z – Arrives 1307.

◇ – Operated by WestfalenBahn.
⊙ – Operated by WestfalenBahn on ⑥.
‡ – For ⛴ to / from Juist and Norderney.
◧ – For train / 🚌 / ⛴ connections to / from Borkum via Emden Außenhafen (certain Emden trains may be extended to / from Emden Außenhafen to connect with sailings).

813 NORDDEICH - EMDEN - BREMEN - HANNOVER

km	SEE NOTE ⊠	*RE* 4441	*ICE* 841	*RE* 4443	*IC* 2235	*IC* 2235	*RE* 4405	*RE* 4407	*ICE* 533	*RE* 4407	*IC* 2035	*IC* 2035	*RE* 4409	*ICE* 535	*ICE* 535	*RE* 4411	*IC* 2037	*RE* 4413	*ICE* 537	*ICE* 537	*RE* 4415	*IC* 2039	*RE* 4417	*ICE* 1139
			Ⓐ n		⚒				⚒ ⸙		⚒			Ⓒ ⸙	⸙				†					⸙ ▲
			✕				B		▲ ✕				B	▲ ✕	▲ ✕			B	▲ ✕	▲ ✕			B	✕
	Norddeich Mole ‡ 812 d.	...	...	...	...	...	...	...	...	...	...	...	...	...	...	...	0736t	...	...	...	0839	0936	...	...
0	**Norddeich** 812 d.	...	...	...	...	...	...	...	...	...	0536	...	...	...	...	0641	0739t	...	...	...	0841	0939	...	...
6	Norden 812 d.	...	...	...	...	...	...	...	...	...	0543	...	...	...	...	0647	0746t	...	...	...	0847	0946	...	...
35	**Emden** Hbf ◧ 812 d.	...	...	...	0416	...	...	0517	...	...	0609	...	...	...	...	0717	0816	...	...	...	0917	1016	...	...
62	Leer (Ostfriesland) 812 a.	...	...	...	0433	...	...	0533	...	...	0626	...	...	...	...	0733	0833	...	...	...	0933	1033	...	...
62	Leer (Ostfriesland) d.	...	...	...	0441	...	...	0541	...	...	0634	...	...	...	...	0741	0841	...	...	...	0941	1041	...	...
101	Bad Zwischenahn d.	...	...	...	0513	...	...	0612	...	...	0712	...	...	...	...	0812	0913	...	...	...	1012	1113	...	...
116	**Oldenburg** (Oldb) a.	...	...	...	0523	...	...	0623	...	...	0723	...	...	...	...	0823	0923	...	...	...	1023	1123	...	...
116	**Oldenburg** (Oldb) d.	...	0442	...	0535	...	...	0635	0641	...	0735	0735	...	0841	...	0835	0935	...	1041	...	1035	1135	...	...
147	Delmenhorst d.	...	0500	...	0554	...	...	0654	0659	...	0754	0754	...	0859	...	0854	0954	...	1059	...	1054	1154	...	...
161	**Bremen** Hbf a.	...	0510	...	0605	...	...	0705	0709	←	0805	0805	...	0909	...	0905*	1005	...	1109	...	1105*	1205	...	...
161	**Bremen** Hbf d.	0418	0512	0518	0609	0609	0618	→	0714	0718	0809	0809	0818	0914	0914	0918	1009	1018	1114	1114	1118	1209	1218	1314
196	Verden (Aller) d.	0442	0533	0542	0630	0630	0642	...	|	0742	0830	0830	0842	|	|	0942	1030	1042	|	|	1142	1230	1242	|
227	Nienburg (Weser) d.	0504	|	0604	0646	0646	0704	...	|	0804	0846	0846	0904	|	|	1004	1046	1104	|	|	1204	1246	1304	|
283	**Hannover** Hbf a.	0538	0614	0638	0713	0713	0738	...	0814	0838	0913	0913	0938	1014	1014	1038	1113	1138	1214	1214	1238	1313	1338	1414
	Magdeburg Hbf **866** a.	...	|	...	0857	0857	...	...	|	...	1057	...	...	|	|	...	1257	...	|	|	...	1457	...	|
	Berlin Hbf **810** a.	...	0824	...	|	|	...	...	|	...	|	...	...	|	|	...	|	...	|	|	...	|	...	|
	Leipzig Hbf **866** a.	...	...	...	1019	1019	...	...	|	...	1219	...	...	|	|	...	1419	...	|	|	...	1619	...	|
	Nürnberg Hbf **900** a.	...	...	...	...	...	...	...	|	...	...	...	...	|	|	...	...	...	|	|	...	...	...	|
	München Hbf **900** a.	...	...	...	...	...	...	...	1255	...	...	...	...	1507	1507	...	...	...	1700	1700	...	...	...	1857

SEE NOTE ⊠	*IC* 2431	*RE* 4421	*ICE* 631	*RE* 4423	*IC* 2433	*RE* 4425	*ICE* 633 1143	*RE* 4427	*IC* 2435	*RE* 4429	*ICE* 635	*ICE* 635	*ICE* 1135	*RE* 4431	*IC* 2437	*IC* 2437	*RE* 4433	*RE* 4435	*IC* 2439	*RE* 4437	♣	*RE* 4439		*RE* 4445
			⸙ ▲								⑧ q	⑤⑦ r	⑥ k			⑧ q								
	C	B	✕			B	⸙ ▲ ✕			B	⸙ ▲ ✕	⸙ ▲ ✕	✕				B			B				
Norddeich Mole ‡ 812 d.	...	...	...	1239	...	...		1439	1537	...			...	1639	...	...	...	1839	...	...	...	2039	...	...
Norddeich 812 d.	...	...	...	1241	...	...	...	1441	1540	...	...	...	...	1641	...	...	...	1841	...	...	...	2041	...	...
Norden 812 d.	...	...	...	1247	...	...	...	1447	1547	...	...	...	...	1647	...	...	...	1847	...	...	...	2047	...	...
Emden Hbf ◧ 812 d.	1218	...	...	1317	1416f	...	...	1517	1616	...	...	...	...	1717	1816	1816	...	1917	2016	...	...	2117	...	...
Leer (Ostfriesland) 812 a.	1235	...	...	1333	1433f	...	...	1533	1633	...	...	...	...	1733	1833	1833	...	1933	2033	...	...	2133	...	...
Leer (Ostfriesland) d.	1241	...	...	1341	1441	...	...	1541	1641	...	...	...	...	1741	1841	1841	...	1941	2041	...	...	2141	...	...
Bad Zwischenahn d.	1313	...	...	1412	1513	...	...	1612	1713	...	...	...	...	1812	1913	1913	...	2012	2113	...	2145	2212	...	...
Oldenburg (Oldb) a.	1323	...	...	1423	1523	...	...	1623	1723	...	...	...	...	1823	1923	1923	...	2023	2123	...	2157	2223	...	...
Oldenburg (Oldb) d.	1335	...	...	1435	1535	...	...	1635	1735	...	...	...	...	1835	1935	1935	...	2035	2135	...	2206	2235	...	...
Delmenhorst d.	1354	...	...	1454	1554	...	...	1654	1754	...	...	...	...	1854	1954	1954	...	2054	2154	...	2231	2254	...	...
Bremen Hbf a.	1405	...	...	1505*	1605	...	...	1705*	1805	...	...	...	...	1905*	2005	2005	...	2105*	2205	...	2244	2305	...	...
Bremen Hbf d.	1409	1418	1514	1518	1609	1618	1714	1718	1809	1818	1914	1914	1914	1918	...	2009	2018	2118	...	2218	...	2312	...	0013
Verden (Aller) d.	1430	1442	|	1542	1630	1642	|	1742	1830	1842	|	|	|	1942	...	2030	2042	2142	...	2242	...	2344	...	0044
Nienburg (Weser) d.	1446	1504	|	1604	1646	1704	|	1804	1846	1904	|	|	|	2004	...	2046	2104	2204	...	2304	...	0006	...	0106
Hannover Hbf a.	1513	1538	1614	1638	1713	1738	1814	1838	1913	1938	2014	2014	2014	2038	...	2113	2138	2238	...	2338	...	0039	...	0139
Magdeburg Hbf **866** a.	1657	...	|	...	1857	...	|	...	2057	...	|	|	...	...	...	2300	...	...	...	...	...	...	...	...
Berlin Hbf **810** a.	1822	...	|	...	|	...	|	...	|	...	|	|	...	...	...	...	...	...	...	...	...	...	...	...
Leipzig Hbf **866** a.	...	...	|	...	2019	...	|	...	2219	...	|	|	...	...	...	...	...	...	...	...	...	...	...	...
Nürnberg Hbf **900** a.	...	...	|	...	...	...	|	...	...	...	2350	2350	...	...	...	...	...	...	...	...	...	...	...	...
München Hbf **900** a.	...	...	2058	...	...	...	2300	...	...	...	...	0110	...	...	...	...	...	...	...	...	...	...	...	...

SEE NOTE ⊠	♣	*RE* 4438	*RE* 4440	*IC* 2438	*RE* 4402	*RE* 4404	*RE* 4404	*IC* 2436	*RE* 4406	*ICE* 636	*RE* 4408	*IC* 2434	*RE* 4410	*ICE* 634	*RE* 4412	*IC* 2432	*RE* 4414	*ICE* 1132	*RE* 4416	*IC* 2430	*RE* 4418	*ICE* 630	*RE* 4420	*IC* 2038
	Ⓐ	⚒		⚒		Ⓐ	Ⓒ			Ⓐ				⚒ ▲				⸙ ▲				▲		
			B			B	B			§ ✕	B			✕	B	C		✕	B			✕	B	
München Hbf **900** d.	...	...	...	...	...	...	...	...	...	...	...	...	...	0520a	...	...	...	0653	...	...	...	0905	...	...
Nürnberg Hbf **900** d.	...	...	...	...	...	...	...	...	...	...	...	...	...	0634	...	...	...	|	...	...	...	|	...	...
Leipzig Hbf **866** d.	...	...	...	...	...	...	...	...	...	...	...	0539e	...	|	...	...	...	|	...	0939	...	|	...	1139
Berlin Hbf **810** d.	...	...	...	...	...	...	...	...	...	...	...	|	...	|	...	0731	...	|	...	|	...	|	...	|
Magdeburg Hbf **866** d.	...	...	...	...	...	...	...	0501e	...	...	...	0700e	...	|	...	0902	...	|	...	1059	...	|	...	1259
Hannover Hbf d.	...	...	0421	...	0521	0618	0621	0645e	0721	0745	0821	0845	0921	0945	1021	1045	1121	1145	1221	1245	1321	1345	1421	1445
Nienburg (Weser) d.	...	...	0454	...	0554	0654	0654	0713e	0754	|	0854	0913	0954	|	1054	1113	1154	|	1254	1313	1354	|	1454	1513
Verden (Aller) d.	...	...	0516	...	0616	0716	0716	0730e	0816	|	0916	0930	1016	|	1116	1130	1216	|	1316	1330	1416	|	1516	1530
Bremen Hbf a.	...	...	0539	...	0639	0739	0739	0750e	0839	0844*	0939	0950	1039	1044*	1139	1150	1239	1244*	1339	1350	1439	1444*	1539	1550
Bremen Hbf d.	0415	...	...	0553	0653	...	...	0753	0853	...	...	0953	1053	...	...	1153	1253	...	...	1353	1453	...	...	1553
Delmenhorst d.	0428	...	...	0604	0703	...	...	0804	0903	...	...	1004	1103	...	...	1204	1303	...	...	1404	1503	...	...	1604
Oldenburg (Oldb) a.	0453	...	...	0623	0723	...	...	0823	0923	...	...	1023	1123	...	...	1223	1323	...	...	1423	1523	...	...	1623
Oldenburg (Oldb) d.	0458	0533	...	0626	0733	...	...	0833	0933	...	...	1033	1133	...	...	1233	1333	...	...	1433	1533	...	...	1633
Bad Zwischenahn d.	0510	0544	...	0637	0744	...	...	0844	0944	...	...	1044	1144	...	...	1244	1344	...	...	1444	1544	...	...	1644
Leer (Ostfriesland) a.	...	0613	...	0707	0813	...	...	0914	1013	...	...	1114	1213	...	...	1314	1413	...	...	1514	1613	...	...	1714
Leer (Ostfriesland) 812 d.	...	0624	...	0715	0824	...	...	0922	1024	...	...	1122	1224	...	...	1322	1424	...	...	1522	1624	...	...	1722
Emden Hbf ◧ 812 d.	...	0642	...	0742	0842	...	...	0938	1042	...	...	1138	1242	...	...	1342	1442	...	...	1538	1642	...	...	1738
Norden 812 d.	...	0706	...	0808	0906	...	...	...	1106	...	...	...	1306	...	...	1408	1506	...	...	...	1706	...	...	...
Norddeich 812 a.	...	0712	...	0814	0912	...	...	...	1112	...	...	...	1312	...	...	1414	1512	...	...	...	1712	...	...	...
Norddeich Mole ‡ 812 a.	...	0716	...	0820	0916	...	...	...	1116	...	...	...	1316	...	...	1420	1516	...	...	...	1716	...	...	...

SEE NOTE ⊠	*ICE* 1138	*RE* 4424	*IC* 2036	*RE* 4426	*RE* 4426	*ICE* 536	*RE* 4428	*IC* 2034	*IC* 1934	*RE* 4430	*ICE* 776	*RE* 4430	*RE* 4432	*IC* 2032	*IC* 2032	*RE* 4434	*ICE* 832	*IC* 1932	*RE* 4434	*RE* 4434	*RE* 4442	*ICE* 1032	*ICE* 732	*RE* 4444
	⸙ ▲				⑥	⸙ ▲			⑦ w		⑧ q			⑧ q			⚒ m	⑦ w		⑥		† △	⚒ ▲	
	H ✕	B				✕	B				F ✕		B				✕	S 🍷				✕	G ✕	
München Hbf **900** d.	1048	...	...	...	...	1254	...	...	...	...	...	...	...	...	...	...	...	...	...	...	...	1820	1820	...
Nürnberg Hbf **900** d.	|	...	...	...	...	|	...	...	...	...	...	...	...	...	...	...	...	...	...	...	...	1934	1934	...
Leipzig Hbf **866** d.	|	...	1339b	...	...	|	...	1539q	1558	...	...	...	...	1739	...	...	...	...	...	...	...	|	|	...
Berlin Hbf **810** d.	|	...	|	...	...	|	...	|	|	...	...	...	...	|	...	...	1949	1950z	...	...	...	|	|	...
Magdeburg Hbf **866** d.	|	...	1459b	...	...	|	...	1659q	1724	...	...	...	...	1859	...	...	|	|	...	...	...	|	|	...
Hannover Hbf d.	1545	1621	1645	1721	1721	1745	1821	1845	1901	1921	1950	...	2021	2045	2045	2121	2140	2143	...	...	2221	2245	2250	2321
Nienburg (Weser) d.	|	1654	1713	1754	1754	|	1854	1913	1929	1954	|	...	2054	2113	2113	2154	2209	2211	...	...	2254	2314	2319	2354
Verden (Aller) d.	|	1716	1730	1816	1816	|	1916	1930	1948	2016	|	...	2116	2130	2130	2216	2228	2229	...	...	2316	2332	2337	0016
Bremen Hbf a.	1644*	1739	1750	1839	1839	1844*	1939	1950	2009	2039	2047	←	2139	2150	2150	2239	2247	2247	←	←	2347	2351	2357	0047
Bremen Hbf d.	...	...	1753	1853	1853	...	...	1953	2013	→	2050	2054	...	2153	2153	→	2249	2249	2253	2253	...	2353	2359	...
Delmenhorst d.	...	...	1804	1903	1903	...	...	2004	2024		|	2104	...	2204	2204		2300	2300	2304	2304	...	0005	0011	...
Oldenburg (Oldb) a.	...	...	1823	1923	1923	...	...	2023	2040		2117	2123	...	2223	2223		2318	2318	2323	2323	...	0023	0029	...
Oldenburg (Oldb) d.	...	...	1833	1933	1933	...	...	2033	2042		...	2133	...	2233	...		...	...	...	2333	...	...	...	...
Bad Zwischenahn d.	...	...	1844	1944	1944	...	...	2044	2055		...	2144	...	2244	...		...	...	...	2344	...	...	...	...
Leer (Ostfriesland) a.	...	...	1914	2013	2013	...	...	2112	2128		...	2213	...	2313	...		...	...	...	0013	...	...	...	...
Leer (Ostfriesland) 812 d.	...	...	1922	2024	2024	...	...	2122	2136		...	2224	...	2322	...		...	...	...	0024	...	...	...	...
Emden Hbf ◧ 812 d.	...	...	1942	2040	2042	...	...	2142	2152		...	2242	...	2338	...		...	...	...	0040	...	...	...	...
Norden 812 d.	...	...	2008b	...	2106	...	...	2208	...		...	2306	...	...	...		...	...	...	...	...	...	...	...
Norddeich 812 a.	...	...	2014b	...	2112	...	...	2214	...		...	2312	...	...	...		...	...	...	...	...	...	...	...
Norddeich Mole ‡ 812 a.	...	...	2019b	...	2116	...	...	...	...		...	...	...	...	...		...	...	...	...	...	...	...	...

B – To / from Bremerhaven (Table 815).
C – To / from Cottbus on dates in Table **838**.
F – From Frankfurt (Table **900**). July 18 - Sept. 2 Hannover d. 2032, Bremen a. 2141, d. 2144, Oldenburg a. 2210.
G – From Garmisch (Table **895**) on ⑥ to Nov. 5.
H – From Garmisch (Table **895**) on ⑥ to Nov. 5 (also Oct. 2; not Oct. 1).
S – From Stralsund (Table **845**).

a – Ⓐ only.
b – Not ⑥.
e – ⚒ only.
f – 2 minutes later on ⑥ to Oct. 29.
k – Also Oct. 2. Runs as *IC* **2323** July 23 - Aug. 27.
q – Ⓑ (not Oct. 2).

r – Not Oct. 2.
m – Not July 17 - Sept. 2.
n – Not July 19 - Sept. 2.
t – ①-⑥ (also Oct. 2; not Oct. 3).
w – Also Oct. 3; not Oct. 2.
z – Berlin **Spandau**.

♣ – Operated by Nord West Bahn.
‡ – For sailings from / to Juist and Norderney.
◧ – For train / 🚌 / ⛴ connections from / to Borkum via Emden Außenhafen.

* – Connects with train in previous column.
▲ – July 18 - Sept. 2 runs with a different train number does not run München - Hannover and v.v.
△ – July 17 - Aug. 28 runs Hannover - Oldenburg only *IC* **2324**.
§ – Train number *IC* **2336** July 18 - Sept. 2.
⊠ – Nov. 12 – 28 *IC* trains do not run Oldenburg - Emd Norddeich Mole and v.v.
⸙ – München / Nürnberg timings are subject to alteratic from Sept. 4 (and a different train number may ap

OSNABRÜCK - OLDENBURG - WILHELMSHAVEN 814

d West Bahn

	⚒	Ⓐ					†	
Osnabrück Hbf .... d.	...	0457	0601		2201	2253	2253	...
Bramsche .... d.	...	0516	0618	and	2218	2315	2315	...
Quakenbrück .... d.	...	0538	0640		2240	2340	2340	...
Cloppenburg .... d.	...	0556	0656	hourly	2256	2356	2356	...
Oldenburg (Oldb) ..... a.	...	0629	0729		2329	0029	0029	...
Oldenburg (Oldb) ..... d.	0536	0636	0736	until	2336	...	0036	...
Varel (Oldb) .... d.	0559	0659	0759		2359	...	0059	...
Wilhelmshaven Hbf . a.	0619	0719	0819		0019	...	0119	...

	Ⓐ	⚒	⚒	Ⓐ		⊠				⑤⑥
Wilhelmshaven Hbf .... d.	...	0444	0544	0613	0644		2144	...	2313	2313
Varel (Oldb) .... d.	...	0501	0601	0630	0701	and	2201	...	2330	2330
Oldenburg (Oldb) .... a.	...	0525	0625	0653	0725		2225	...	2353	2353
Oldenburg (Oldb) .... d.	0406	0529	0629	0659	0729	hourly	2229	...	...	2359
Cloppenburg .... d.	0438	0606	0706	0736	0806		2306	...	...	0033
Quakenbrück .... d.	0453	0621	0721	0751	0821	until	2321	...	...	...
Bramsche .... d.	0516	0642	0741	0816	0841		2341	...	...	...
Osnabrück Hbf .... a.	0535	0658	0758	0835	0858		2358	...	...	...

On ⑥ depart Wilhelmshaven Hbf at *1329* (not 1344) and change trains at Sande (a. *1336*, d. 1350).

OSNABRÜCK - BREMEN - BREMERHAVEN - CUXHAVEN 815

services

	⚒¶	⚒	ⒶH	¶	⚒	H		H		H		H		H		H		H		H		¶	©	Ⓐ	¶
Osnabrück Hbf.. **800** d.	...	0417	...	...	0534	*0634r*	0734	*0834*	0934	*1034*	1134	*1234*	1334	*1434*	1534	*1634*	1734	*1834*	1934	*2034*	2134	...	2234	2252	...
Diepholz........ d.	...	0450	...	...	0604	*0704r*	0804	*0904*	1004	*1104*	1204	*1304*	1404	*1504*	1604	*1704*	1804	*1904*	2004	*2104*	2204	...	2304	2321	...
Bremen Hbf....... **800** a.	...	0546	...	...	0650	*0750r*	0850	*0950*	1050	*1150*	1250	*1350*	1450	*1550*	1650	*1750*	1850	*1950*	2050	*2150*	2250	...	2350	0007	...
Bremen Hbf........ d.	0540	...	0556	0640	0656	0756	0856	0956	1056	1156	1256	1356	1456	1556	1656	1756	1856	1956	2056	2156	...	2312	...	...	0012
Osterholz-Scharmbeck d.	0556	...	0610	0656	0710	0810	0910	1010	1110	1210	1310	1410	1510	1610	1710	1810	1910	2010	2110	2210	...	2328	...	...	0028
Bremerhaven Hbf..... a.	0625	...	0630	0725	0730	0830	0930	1030	1130	1230	1330	1430	1530	1630	1730	1830	1930	2030	2130	2230	...	2357	...	...	0057
Bremerhaven-Lehe .. a.	0630	...	0635	0730	0735	0835	0935	1035	1135	1235	1335	1435	1535	1635	1735	1835	1945j	2035	2135	2235	...	0002	...	...	0102

	©¶		⚒	⚒¶	ⒶH	⚒	⚒		H		H		H		H		H		H		H		H	¶		¶
(Brem)erhaven-Lehe ... d.	0008	...	...	0407	0523	...	0623	...	0723	0823	0923	1023	1123	1223	1323	1423	1523	1623	1723	1823	1923	2023	2123	2158	...	2258
(Brem)erhaven Hbf ..... d.	0012	...	...	0412	0528	...	0628	...	0728	0828	0928	1028	1128	1228	1328	1428	1528	1628	1728	1828	1928	2028	2128	2203	...	2303
(Oste)rholz-Scharmbeck. d.	0043	...	...	0444	0550	...	0650	...	0750	0850	0950	1050	1150	1250	1350	1450	1550	1650	1750	1850	1950	2050	2150	2233	...	2333
(Bre)men Hbf .... a.	0100	...	...	0504	0603	...	0703	...	0803	0903	1003	1103	1203	1303	1403	1503	1603	1703	1803	1903	2003	2103	2203	2250	...	2350
(Bre)men Hbf ....**800** d.	...	...	0507	...	...	0607	0707	0707	*0807*	0907	*1007*	1107	*1207*	1307	*1407*	1507	*1607*	1707	*1807*	1907	*2007*	2107	*2207*	...	2313	...
(Diep)holz .... d.	...	...	0549	...	...	0649	0749	0749	*0849*	0949	*1049*	1149	*1249*	1349	*1449*	1550	*1650*	1749	*1849*	1949	*2049*	2149	*2254*	...	0001	...
(Osn)abrück Hbf ...**800** a.	...	...	0621	...	...	0721	0821	0821	*0921*	1021	*1121*	1221	*1321*	1421	*1521*	1622	*1722*	1821	*1921*	2021	*2121*	2221	*2326*	...	0033	...

BREMERHAVEN - CUXHAVEN

⊡	Ⓐ	⚒					Ⓐ		
Bremerhaven Hbf..... d.	0506	0636	0736	0836	and	2036	2136	2236	...
Bremerhaven-Lehe..... d.	0511	0641	0741	0841	hourly	2041	2141	2241	...
Cuxhaven .... a.	0557	0727	0827	0927	until	2127	2227	2327	...

⊡	Ⓐ	⚒						Ⓐ	
Cuxhaven .... d.	0509	0639	0739	0839	and	1939	2039	2139	2239
Bremerhaven-Lehe........ d.	0549	0719	0819	0919	hourly	2019	2119	2219	2319
Bremerhaven Hbf........ a.	0553	0723	0823	0923	until	2023	2123	2223	2323

From/to Hannover (Table **813**).

1935 on ©.

⚒ only.

⊡ – Operated by Elbe-Weser.

¶ – Operated by Nord West Bahn (2nd class only).

☛ Additional stopping trains operate Bremen Hbf - Bremerhaven-Lehe (operated by Nord West Bahn): **From Bremen Hbf** at 0740, 0841, 0940, 1040 and hourly until 1840; then 1941, 2041 and 2141. **From Bremerhaven-Lehe** at 0453 Ⓐ, 0537 ⚒, 0556 Ⓐ, 0637, 0656 Ⓐ, 0737, 0837 and hourly until 2037.

HAMBURG - CUXHAVEN and BREMERHAVEN 818

(me)tronom; Elbe-Weser

❖	‡	Ⓐ‡	⚒◧	‡	Ⓐ	⚒	‡	⚒																	
Hamburg Hbf .... ⊖ d.	0028	0448	...	0528	*0602*	...	0628	0706	...	0806	0906	1006	1106	1206	1306	1406	1506j	1606	1706	1806	1906	2006	2106	2206	2306
Hamburg Harburg ⊖ d.	0041	0501	...	0541	0624	...	0641	0724	...	0824	0924	1024	1124	1224	1324	1424	1524	1624	1724	1824	1924	2024	2124	2224	2324
Buxtehude .... ⊖ d.	0106	0526	...	0606	0641	...	0706	0741	...	0841	0941	1041	1141	1241	1341	1441	1541	1641	1741	1841	1941	2041	2141	2241	2341
Stade .... ⊖ d.	0127	0547	0550	0627	0657	0657	0727	0757	0757	0857	0957	1057	1157	1257	1357	1457	1557	1657	1757	1857	1957	2057	2157	2257	2357
Otterndorf .... d.	...	...	0632	...	0737	0737	...	0837	0837	0937	1037	1137	1237	1337	1437	1537	1637	1737	1837	1937	2037	2137	2237	2337	0037
Cuxhaven .... a.	...	...	0645	...	0750	0750	...	0850	0850	0950	1050	1150	1250	1350	1450	1550	1650	1750	1850	1950	2050	2150	2250	2350	0050

❖	Ⓐ	⚒	Ⓐ		Ⓐ	©								†	⚒								‡	⑤⑥f	★	‡
(Cux)haven .... d.	0433	0510	0551	0610	0651	0710	0810	0910	1010	1110	1210	1310	1410	1510	1510	1610	1710	1810	1910	2010	2110	...	...	2210	2238	...
(Otte)rndorf .... d.	0444	0521	0602	0621	0702	0721	0821	0921	1021	1121	1221	1321	1421	1521	1521	1621	1721	1821	1921	2021	2121	...	...	2221	2250	...
(Sta)de .... ⊖ d.	0526	0603	0644	0703	0744	0803	0903	1003	1103	1203	1303	1403	1503	1603	1603	1703	1803	1903	2003	2103	2203	...	2235	2303	2332	2335
(Bux)tehude .... ⊖ d.	0544	0621	0702	0721	0802	0821	0921	1021	1121	1221	1321	1421	1521	1621	1621	1721	1821	1921	2021	2121	2221	...	2255	2321	...	2355
(Ham)**burg** Harburg . ⊖ a.	0559	0636	0717	0736	0817	0836	0936	1036	1136	1236	1336	1436	1536	1636	1636	1736	1836	1936	2036	2136	2236	...	2320	2336	...	0020
(Ham)**burg** Hbf .... ⊖ a.	*0620*	0658	0734	0756	0835	0854	0957	1058	1154	1256	1356	1453	1556	1657	1659	1755	1900	1956	2058	2157	2257	...	2334	2354	...	0034

△	⚒		Ⓐ	Ⓐ	Ⓐ	©	Ⓐ	©	Ⓐ	©	Ⓐ	Ⓐ	©	Ⓐ§	©	Ⓐ	Ⓐ	©	Ⓐ	Ⓐ	©	Ⓐ	Ⓐ	©	Ⓐ
Hamburg Hbf ..... ¶ d.	...	...	*0448*	*0548*	*0628*	*0648*	*0848*	*0858*	*1048*	*1058*	*1148*	*1248*	*1258*	*1408*	*1458*	*1508*	*1608*	*1658*	*1708*	*1808*	*1858*	*1908*	*2008*	*2058*	*2108*
Buxtehude .... d.	...	...	0537	0637	0717	0737c	0937	0945	1137	1145	1237	1337	1345	1452	1545	1552	1652	1745	1752	1852	1945	1952	2052	2145	2152
Bremervörde .... a.	...	...	0621	0722	0821	0821c	1021	1027	1221	1227	1321	1421	1427	1533	1627	1633	1733	1827	1833	1933	2027	2033	2133	2227	2233
Bremervörde .... d.	0538	0638	0638	0738	0838	0838	1038	1038	1238	1238	1338	1438	1438	1538	1638	1638	1738	1838	1838	1938	2038	...	...	...	...
Bremerhaven Hbf a.	0620	0720	0720	0820	0920	0920	1120	1120	1320	1320	1420	1520	1520	1620	1720	1720	1820	1920	1920	2020	2120	...	...	...	...

△	Ⓐ	⚒	†	⚒	Ⓐ	©	Ⓐ	©	Ⓐ	©	Ⓐ	©	Ⓐ	Ⓐ§	©	Ⓐ	Ⓐ	©	Ⓐ	Ⓐ	©		⚒	†	⑥	
(Brem)erhaven Hbf . d.	0536	...	...	0636	0736	0736	0836	0936	1036	1136	1236	1336	1336	1436	1536	1536	1636	1736	1736	1836	1936	1936	2036	2136	2236	2354
(Brem)ervörde .... a.	0620	...	...	0720	0820	0820	0920	1020	1120	1220	1320	1420	1420	1520	1620	1620	1720	1820	1820	1920	2020	2020	2120	2220	2320	0036
(Brem)ervörde .... d.	0625	0625	0632	0725	0825	0832	0925	1032	1125	1232	1325	1432	1440	1540	1632	1640	1740	1832	1840	1940	2032	...	...	...	...	...
(Bux)**tehude** .... a.	0709	0709	0716	0809	0909	0916	1009	1116	1209	1316	1409	1516	1526	1626	1716	1726	1826	1916	1926	2026	2116	...	...	...	...	...
(Ham)*burg Hbf* ...... ¶ a.	*0754*	*0754*	*0814*	*0854*	*0954*	*1004*	*1054*	*1204*	*1254*	*1404*	*1454*	*1604*	*1614*	*1714*	*1804*	*1814*	*1914*	*2004*	*2014*	*2114*	*2204*	...	...	...	...	...

On † Buxtehude d. 0745, Bremervörde a. 0827.

Also Oct. 2.

1507 July 18 - Sept. 2.

①②③④⑦ (not Oct. 2).

§ – Change trains at Bremervörde on ⑤.

◧ – Runs 6 minutes later on ⑥.

‡ – Hamburg S-Bahn (2nd class only).

⊖ – Additional S-Bahn trains operate.

❖ – Hamburg - Cuxhaven operated by *metronom*.

△ – Buxtehude - Bremerhaven operated by Elbe-Weser.

¶ – Connections shown are Hamburg S-Bahn services. Faster connections, operated by *metronom*, may be available (see Hamburg - Cuxhaven panel).

HAMBURG - KIEL 820

services except where shown

			⊖		Ⓐ	©	⚒ ❖	❖	❖		❖							*ICE* 1188 Ⓐn Y	*IC* 2224 N	*ICE* 674 K⊡	*ICE* 76 n Z	*IC* 2226 F	*ICE* 74 Z⊡	*EC* 378 L	*ICE* 1094 Ⓑq S⊡
Hamburg Hbf **823** d.	0045	0143	0430	0532	0617	0626	0717	0820	0921	and	2121	2146	2221	2322	2345	...	also	0900	1016	1138	1538	1616	1738	1913	2032
Elmshorn....... **823** d.	0115	0213	0500	0602	0647	0656	0747	0847	0947	hourly	2147	2216	2247	2348	0015	...		|	|	|	|	|	|	|	|
Neumünster .. **823** d.	0142	0240	0530	0630	0717	0733	0817	0917	1017	until	2217	2240	2317	0018	0040	...		0951	1104	1226	1627	1704	1826	2001	2123
Kiel Hbf .... a.	0209	0307	0557	0657	0738	0800	0838	0938	1038		2238	2307	2338	0039	0107	...		1009	1121	1244	1645	1721	1844	2018	2144

		Ⓐ	©	⚒	†	⚒ ❖	❖	❖		❖								*ICE* 973 ⚒ S⊙	*ICE* 73 ⚒ Z⊙	*EC* 379 L	*ICE* 1175 † Z⊙	*ICE* 77 Z⊙	*IC* 2229 F	*ICE* 883 M⊙	*ICE* 273 K⊙	*IC* 2225 N
(Kiel) Hbf........ d.	0002	0359	0402	0445	0459	0521	0621	0721	and	1921	2021	2102	2121	2202	2302	...	also	0613r	0713	0742	0911	1113t	1238r	1449r	1713r	1838r
(Neu)münster ... **823** d.	0028	0425	0428	0511	0525	0542	0642	0742	hourly	1942	2042	2129	2142	2232	2332	...		0632r	0732	0800	0930	1132t	1257r	1507r	1732r	1857r
(Elm)shorn .... **823** d.	0057	0454	0455	0536	0548	0611	0711	0811	until	2011	2111	2152	2211	2301	0001	...		|	|	|	|	|	|	|	|	|
(Ham)**burg** Hbf **823** a.	0127	0520	0524	0601	0617	0637	0737	0837		2037	2137	2221	2237	2331	0031	...		0719	0820	0848	1020	1220	1342	1558	1820	1942

(12) and 🍷 Nürnberg - Frankfurt - Köln - Kiel and v.v.

(12) and ✕ Kiel - Frankfurt - Karlsruhe and v.v.

(12) and ✕ Praha - Dresden - Berlin - Kiel and v.v.

(12) and ✕ Kiel - München.

(12) and 🍷 Köln - Kiel and v.v.

(12) and ✕ Kiel - Frankfurt - Stuttgart and v.v.

(12) and ✕ Frankfurt - Kiel.

Z – (12) and ✕ Kiel - Frankfurt - Basel - Zürich and v.v.

n – Not July 18 - Sept. 2.

q – Not Oct. 2.

r – Departs up to 14 minutes earlier June 1 – 16.

t – June 1 – 16 departs Kiel 1048, Neumünster 1111.

⊖ – Runs 10 – 13 minutes later on †.

❖ – July 25 - Sept. 4 diverted to run from/to Hamburg **Altona** (not serving Hamburg Hbf).

⊙ – 21 – 36 minutes **earlier** July 18 - Sept. 2.

⊡ – 18 – 33 minutes later July 18 - Sept. 2.

821 HAMBURG - WESTERLAND

Nord-Ostsee-Bahn (*IC* trains operated by

See Tables **820** and **823** for connecting *RE* services Hamburg Hbf - Elmshorn and v.v. Frequent S-Bahn services operate Hamburg Hbf - Altona and v.v.

km		◇	◇	◇ Ⓐ	◇	◇ ⑥z	◇	◇ Ⓐ	◇	◇	◇ ⑦	◇ ①–⑥	◇	◇	◇	*IC*• 2314 S 🍷	◇	*IC* 2314 S 🍷	◇	*IC*• 2072 D 🍷	◇	◇	*IC*• 2310 F 🍷	◇	
	Köln Hbf **800** d.	...	...	...	...	...	...	...	...	...	...	...	...	...	...	0510	...	...	...	...	...	...	0910	...	
	Berlin Hbf **840** d.	...	...	...	...	...	...	...	...	...	...	...	...	...	...	|	...	...	...	0906	...	...	|	...	
	Hamburg Hbf... **820** d.	...	...	...	...	...	...	...	...	...	...	...	...	...	...	0916	...	...	...	1116	...	...	1316	...	
0	**Hamburg** Altona d.	...	...	...	...	...	...	0529	...	...	0630	0640	...	0740	0840	|	0940	...	1040	|	1208	1240	|	1340	1
30	Elmshorn **820** d.	...	...	...	...	...	...	0549	...	...	0650	0701	...	0801	0901	|	1001	...	1101	|	1230	1301	|	1401	1
64	Itzehoe d.	...	...	0505	...	0538	...	0612	...	...	0715	0724	...	0824	0924	1014**t**	1024	...	1124	1214**t**	1253	1324	1414**t**	1424	1
123	Heide (Holst) a.	...	...	0548	...	0622	...	0656	...	...	0758	0758	...	0858	0958	1050	1058	...	1158	1250	1327	1358	1450	1459	1
123	Heide (Holst) d.	...	...	0549	...	0623	...	0702	...	...	...	0802	0802	0902	1002	1052	1102	...	1202	1252	1328	1402	1452	1502	1
157	Husum d.	0456**a**	0600	0615	0630	0649	0700	0730	0730	0800	...	0830	0830	0930	1030	1119	1130	...	1230	1319	1400	1430	1519	1540**t**	1
197	Niebüll a.	0528**a**	0628	...	0658	...	0728	0758	0758	0828	...	0858	0858	0958	1058	1150	1158	←	1258	1345	1428	1458	1545	1609	1
197	Niebüll d.	0531	0631	...	0701	...	0731	0801	0801	0831	...	0901	0901	1001	1101	→	1201	1231	1301	1401	1431	1501	1601	...	1
237	**Westerland** (Sylt) a.	0605	0705	...	0735	...	0805	0835	0835	0905	...	0937	0937	1035	1135	...	1235	1304	1337	1434	1505	1537	1634	...	1

	◇ Ⓒ S	◇	*IC*• 2374 Q K 🍷	◇	◇	◇	◇	◇	◇	◇ ⑤–⑦	◇	◇ ⑤⑥
Köln Hbf **800** d.	...	...	...	...	...	...	...	...	...	...	...	...
Berlin Hbf **840** d.	...	...	...	...	...	...	...	...	...	...	...	...
Hamburg Hbf.... **820** d.	1503	...	1548	...	...	...	...	...	...	...	...	...
Hamburg Altona d.	|	1540	|	1640	1740	1840	1938	2040	2140	2140	2240	2347
Elmshorn **820** d.	1530	1601	|	1701	1801	1901	1959	2101	2201	2201	2301	0006
Itzehoe d.	1553	1624	1644	1724	1824	1924	2024	2126	2226	2226	2326	0030
Heide (Holst) a.	1628	1658	1718	1758	1858	1958	2058	2209	2310	2310	0010	0112
Heide (Holst) d.	1629	1702	1720	1802	1902	2002	2102	2210	2312	2312	0011	0113
Husum d.	1700	1730	1742	1830	1930	2030	2130	2238	2338	2340	0037	0139
Niebüll a.	1727	1758	1807	1858	1958	2058	2158	2306	...	0008	...	...
Niebüll d.	1731	1801	1831	1901	2001	2101	2201	2307	...	0009	...	...
Westerland (Sylt) a.	1805	1835	1904	1935	2035	2135	2235	2344	...	0052	...	...

	◇ Ⓐ	◇ Ⓐ	◇	◇	◇	◇	◇	◇	2 H
Westerland (Sylt) d.	...	0420	...	0522	0622	0722	0822	0910	0
Niebüll a.	...	0451	...	0559	0659	0759	0859	0943	0
Niebüll d.	...	0452	...	0601	0701	0801	0901	0955	1
Husum d.	0423	0520	0523	0631	0731	0831	0931	1031	1
Heide (Holst) a.	0448	...	0548	0656	0756	0856	0956	1056	1
Heide (Holst) d.	0450	...	0550	0659	0802	0902	1002	1102	1
Itzehoe d.	0534	...	0634	0734	0837	0937	1037	1137	1
Elmshorn **820** d.	0600	...	0700	0800	0900	1000	1100	1200	
Hamburg Altona a.	0621	...	0721	0821	0921	1021	1121	1221	
Hamburg Hbf **820** a.	...	...	...	...	...	...	...	...	1
Berlin Hbf **840** a.	...	...	...	...	...	...	...	...	
Köln Hbf **800** a.	...	...	...	...	...	...	...	...	1

	◇	*IC*• 2375 R K 🍷	◇	◇ Ⓒ S	◇	◇	*IC*• 2315 S G 🍷	◇	◇	*IC*• 2073 D 🍷	◇ L	◇	◇	◇	◇	◇ ⑤	◇	◇	◇	◇	◇	◇ ⑥	△	◇	
Westerland (Sylt) d.	1022	1056	1122	1152	1222	1310	1326	1422	1452	1526	1552	1622	1652	1722	1752	1752	1822	1922	2022	2122	...	...	...	2222	2
Niebüll a.	1059	1129	1159	1229	1259	1343	1359	1459	1529	1559	1629	1659	1729	1759	1829	1829	1859	1959	2059	2159	...	...	...	2255	2
Niebüll d.	1101	1145	1201	1231	1301	1355	1413	1501	1555	1613	1631	1701	1731	1801	1831	1831	1901	2001	2101	2201	...	...	...	2256	2
Husum d.	1131	1212	1231	1256	1331	1431	1441	1531	1631	1642	1659	1731	1808	1831	1859	1901	1931	2031	2131	2229	2248	2248	...	2324	0
Heide (Holst) a.	1156	1233	1256	1316	1356	1456	1502	1556	1656	1706	...	1756	...	1856	...	1926	1956	2056	2156	...	2313	2313	...	—	
Heide (Holst) d.	1202	1235	1302	1317	1402	1458	1504	1602	1702	1708	...	1802	...	1902	...	1928	2002	2102	2202	...	2314	2314	...	...	
Itzehoe d.	1237	1312	1337	|	1437	1534	1554**r**	1637	1737	1755**t**	...	1837	...	1937	...	2003	2037	2145	2246	...	2357	2358	*0002*	...	
Elmshorn **820** d.	1300	|	1400	1415	1500	1600	|	1700	1800	|	...	1900	...	2000	...	2029	2100	2208	2309	...	...	0019	0033	0057	
Hamburg Altona a.	1321	|	1421	|	1521	1621	|	1721	1821	|	...	1921	...	2021	...	2050	2121	2229	2330	...	...	0042	0057	|	
Hamburg Hbf.... **820** a.	...	1410	...	1443	...	...	1642	...	...	1848	...	...	...	...	...	...	...	...	...	...	...	...	...	0127	
Berlin Hbf **840** a.	...	...	...	...	...	...	|	...	...	2055	...	...	...	...	...	...	...	...	...	...	...	...	...	...	
Köln Hbf **800** a.	...	...	...	...	...	...	2050	...	...	...	...	...	...	...	...	...	...	...	...	...	...	...	...	...	

D – UTHLANDE – From / to Dresden on dates in Table **840**.
F – NORDFRIESLAND – (12) and 🍷 Frankfurt - Köln - Westerland.
G – DEICHGRAF – (12) and 🍷 Westerland - Köln - Frankfurt.
H – NORDFRIESLAND – (12) and 🍷 Westerland - Köln - Stuttgart.
K – WATTENMEER – (12) and 🍷 Karlsruhe - Frankfurt - Hamburg - Westerland and v.v.
L – Daily to Oct. 29; ①–⑤ from Oct. 31.
Q – Daily to Oct. 30; ④–⑦ from Nov. 3.
R – Daily to Oct. 31; ①⑤⑥⑦ from Nov. 4.
S – Until Oct. 30.

a – Ⓐ only.
r – Arrives 1538.
t – Arrives 12 minutes earlier.
z – Also Oct. 3.

• – Conveys (2) to / from Dagebüll Mole on dates in Table **822**.
◇ – Operated by Nord-Ostsee-Bahn GmbH.
△ – Operated by Nordbahn Eisenbahngesellschaft.

822 SCHLESWIG-HOLSTEIN BRANCH LINES

NEUMÜNSTER - HEIDE - BÜSUM (Operated by *nordbahn*)

km		⚒		⚒	⑥		Ⓐ																		
0	Neumünster d.	...	...	...	0532	...	0532	...	0739	...	0939	...	1139	...	1339	...	1539	...	1739	...	1939	...	...	...	2
63	Heide a.	...	...	...	0643	...	0710	...	0847	...	1047	...	1247	...	1447	...	1647	...	1847	...	2047	...	...	...	2
63	Heide d.	0449	...	0558	0701	0701	...	0801	0901	1001	1101	1201	1301	1401	1501	1601	1701	1801	1901	2001	2101	...	2213	...	
87	Büsum a.	0515	...	0624	0727	0727	...	0827	0927	1027	1127	1227	1327	1427	1527	1627	1727	1827	1927	2027	2127	...	2239	...	

	⚒	⚒		⚒	⑥																			
Büsum d.	...	0519	...	0628	0628	...	0731	0831	0931	1031	1131	1231	1331	1431	1531	1631	1731	1831	1931	2031	2131	...	2243	...
Heide a.	...	0545	...	0654	0654	...	0757	0857	0957	1057	1157	1257	1357	1457	1557	1657	1757	1857	1957	2057	2157	...	2309	...
Heide d.	0514	...	...	...	0718	0718	...	0918	...	1118	...	1318	...	1518	...	1718	...	1918	...	2118	...	...	2318	...
Neumünster a.	0622	...	...	...	0828	0828	...	1028	...	1228	...	1428	...	1628	...	1828	...	2028	...	2228	...	...	0025	...

HUSUM - BAD ST PETER ORDING

km		Ⓐ								
0	Husum d.	0436	0536	0636	and	1836	1936	2036	2136	2242
21	Tönning d.	0501	0601	0701	hourly	1901	2001	2101	2201	2306
43	Bad St Peter Ording a.	0527	0627	0727	until	1927	2027	2127	2227	2332

	Ⓐ								
Bad St Peter Ording d.	0533	0633	0733	and	1933	2033	2133	2233	2
Tönning d.	0604	0704	0804	hourly	2004	2104	2204	2304	0
Husum a.	0625	0725	0825	until	2025	2125	2225	2325	0

NIEBÜLL - DAGEBÜLL MOLE *See note* ⊡

km	*Until Oct. 30*				⊗	★	n	★ C	★	★		★ ⊙
	Hamburg Hbf a.	...	...	...	...	0916	...	1116**j**	1116**n**	1316**k**	...	1548**k**
	Niebüll a.	...	...	...	...	1150	...	1345**j**	1345**n**	1545**k**	...	1807**k**
0	Niebüll neg d.	0735	0905	1010	1135	1205	1335	1410	1435	1605	1710	1825
14	Dagebüll Mole a.	0754	0924	1029	1154	1224	1354	1429	1454	1624	1729	1844

Until Oct. 30		★		★ ⑤–⑦		★	★ ⊖			⊕	
Dagebüll Mole d.	0815	0935	1035	1110	1200	1340	1505	1635	1735	1850	1
Niebüll neg a.	0834	0954	1054	1127	1227	1357	1524	1654	1754	1909	1
Niebüll d.	...	1013	...	1145	...	1413	1613	...	...	...	
Hamburg Hbf a.	...	1242	...	1410	...	1642	1848	...	...	...	

km	*From Oct. 31*	♥	Ⓐ		Ⓐ		Ⓐ					⑤–⑦
0	Niebüll neg d.	0635	0735	0905	1010	1125	1235	1335	1435	1603	1815	1910
14	Dagebüll Mole a.	0655	0754	0924	1029	1144	1254	1354	1454	1619	1832	1929

From Oct. 31	♥	Ⓐ		Ⓐ		Ⓐ					
Dagebüll Mole d.	0705	0815	0930	1035	1150	1305	1410	1505	1625	1835	1
Niebüll neg a.	0724	0834	0949	1054	1209	1324	1429	1524	1644	1854	1

C – ⑥⑦ June 25 - Sept. 4.
D – ⑤–⑦ June 25 - Sept. 4.
E – ⑤–⑦ (also Oct. 3; not June 25 - Sept. 4).
H – ⑤–⑦ (also Oct. 3). June 25 - Sept. 4 departs Dagebüll Mole 2000, arrives Niebüll neg 2019.

j – ⑥ only.
k – Not Oct. 30.
n – Not ⑥⑦ June 25 - Sept. 4.
t – Also ⑤ July 1 - Sept. 2; not Oct. 3.

♥ – Daily. By 🚌 on Ⓒ.
♣ – By 🚌 on ①–④.

★ – Conveys (2) (*IC*) from / to Hamburg and beyond (Table **821**).
◇ – On ⑥⑦ June 25 - Sept. 4 departs Niebüll neg 1410, Dagebüll Mole 1429.
⊗ – On ⑤ Niebüll d. 1105, Dagebüll Mole a. 1124.
⊖ – On ⑥⑦ June 25 - Sept. 4 departs Dagebüll Mole 1510, arrives Niebüll neg 1529.
⊙ – June 25 - Sept. 4 departs Niebüll neg 1830, arrives Dagebüll Mole 1849.
⊕ – Runs 10 minutes later June 25 - Sept. 4.
⊡ – **Operator**: Norddeutsche Eisenbahngesellschaft Niebüll GmbH. ✆ +49 (0) 4661 980 880. Niebüll neg station is situated a s distance from the Niebüll DB station forecourt. Dagebüll Mole is the station for ferries to / from the islands of Föhr and Amru
Additional journeys until Oct. 30:
Niebüll neg → Dagebüll Mole at 0635 Ⓐ, 0635 Ⓒ 🚌, 1025 ⑤–⑦, 1310, 1915 **E**, 1935 **D** and 2035 **C**.
Dagebüll Mole → Niebüll neg at 0705 Ⓐ, 0705 Ⓒ 🚌, 1245, 1400 **n**, 1440 **C** and 1935 ①–④ **t** 🚌 and 2100 **C**.

HAMBURG - NEUMÜNSTER - FLENSBURG — 823

RB services except where shown

									IC 386					*IC* 384						*IC* 1284				
	⚒		①–⑥ r		†	⚒			A					A						⑦w M◇	①–⑥ t	⑦w		
Hamburg Hbf .... **820** d.	*0430*	...	*0532*	*0617*q	0736	0740	0843	0943	1043	1053	1143	1243	1343	1443	1450	1543	1643	1747	1843	1943	2041	2043	2046	*2121*n	2243
Elmshorn .... **820** d.	*0500*	...	*0602*	*0647*q	0806	0810	0910	1010	1110	|	1210	1310	1410	1510	|	1610	1710	1814	1910	2010	|	2110	2113	*2147*	2313
Neumünster .... **820** d.	0530	...	0643	0733	0833	0833	0933	1033	1133	|	1233	1333	1433	1533	|	1633	1733	1842	1933	2033	2130	2133	2136	2242	2336
Rendsburg .... **824** d.	0559	...	0713	0802	0902	0902	1002	1102	1202	1213	1302	1402	1502	1602	1617	1702	1802	1913	2002	2102	2156	2202	2213	2310	0004
Schleswig .... **824** d.	0617	...	0731	0820	0920	0920	1017	1120	1217	|	1320	1417	1520	1617	|	1720	1817	1931	2017	2120	2211	2217	2231	2328	0022
Flensburg .... a.	0646	...	0800	0845	0949	0949	1043	1149	1243	1248	1349	1443	1549	1643	1648	1749	1843	1958	2043	2149	2233	2243	2257	2356	0053

											IC 1981	*IC* 383			*IC* 2197			*IC* 385								
	⑥z	⚒	①–⑥ r	①–⑥ r	⑦ s						⑤ M	A			⑦w K🍷			A								
sburg .... d.	0009	0411	0509	0609	0621	0709	0815	0909	1015	1109	1130	1209	1215	1309	1352	1415	1509	1609	1615	1709	1815	1909	2015	2109	2212	2309
swig ....**824** d.	0037	0438	0537	0637	0649	0737	0840	0937	1040	1137	1151	|	1240	1337	1415	1440	1537	|	1640	1737	1840	1937	2040	2137	2240	2337
sburg ....**824** d.	0058	0458	0558	0658	0710	0758	0858	0958	1058	1158	1207	1243	1258	1358	1433	1458	1558	1643	1658	1758	1858	1958	2058	2158	2301	2358
nünster ....**820** a.	0123	0523	0623	0723	0735	0823	0923	1023	1123	1223	1231	|	1323	1423	1457	1523	1623	|	1723	1823	1923	2023	2124	2224	2327	0023
horn ....**820** a.	*0154*	*0610*	0646	0746	|	0846	0946	1046	1146	1246	|	|	1346	1446	|	1546	1646	|	1746	1846	1946	2046	*2150*	*2300*	*2400*	*0056*
burg Hbf ......**820** a.	*0225*	*0637*p	0714	0814	0825	0914	1014	1114	1214	1314	1317	1402	1414	1516	1607	1614	1714	1803	1814	1916	2016	2116	*2221*	*2331*	*0031*	*0127*

[12] Aalborg - Aarhus - Fredericia - Padborg - Flensburg - Hamburg and v.v. 🅁 for international journeys June 12 - Sept. 4.
To Köln (Table **800**). Also calls at Hamburg Altona (a. 1540).
From / to München (Table **900**).

n – July 25 - Sept. 4 departs Hamburg **Altona** *2128* (not Hbf).
p – July 25 - Sept. 3 arrives Hamburg **Altona** *0632* (not Hbf).
q – 9 minutes later on Ⓒ.
r – Also June 19, 26.
s – Not June 19, 26.

t – Also Oct. 2; not Oct. 3.
w – Also Oct. 3; not Oct. 2.
z – Also Oct. 3.

◇ – Runs 29 – 31 minutes later July 24 - Aug. 28.

KIEL - HUSUM and FLENSBURG — 824

services

	L	⑦s	L							
Kiel Hbf ....d.	0503	*0535**	0603	0703	and hourly until	2003	2103	2203	2303	0003
Rendsburg . **823** d.	0535	0635	0635	0735		2035	2135	2235	2343	0043
Schleswig .. **823** d.	0553	0653	0653	0753		2053	2153	2253	0001	0101
Husum ....a.	0625	0725	0725	0825		2125	2225	2327	0033	0133

	⚒	L	⑦s						
Husum ....d.	0430	0535	0535	0635	and hourly until	2035	2135	2241	2335
Schleswig .... **823** d.	0502	0607	0607	0707		2107	2207	2312	0007
Rendsburg .... **823** d.	0521	0626	0625	0726		2126	2226	2331	0031
Kiel Hbf ....a.	0554	0657	*0725**	0757		2157	2257	0002	0113

	Ⓐ	⚒	Ⓐ	Ⓒ						
Kiel Hbf ....d.	0413	0518	0618	0640	0742	and hourly until	2042	2142	2247	2347
Eckernförde ......d.	0448	0548	0648	0710	0810		2110	2215	2320	0020
Süderbrarup......d.	0506	0607	0706	0730	0830		2130	2239	2340	0039
Flensburg ....a.	0536	0636	0736	0756	0856		2156	2305	0006	0106

	⚒								
Flensburg ....d.	0503	0603	0703	0803	and hourly until	2003	2103	2212	2312
Süderbrarup ....d.	0529	0629	0729	0829		2029	2129	2239	2339
Eckernförde ....d.	0549	0649	0749	0849		2049	2154	2259	2359
Kiel Hbf ....a.	0616	0716	0816	0916		2116	2224	2329	0029

①–⑥ (also June 19, 26).

s – Not June 19, 26.

* – By 🚌.

HAMBURG - LÜBECK - PUTTGARDEN and TRAVEMÜNDE — 825

/ *RE* services

HAMBURG - LÜBECK

			Ⓒ		⚒		Ⓐ			Ⓐ									J		ⒷG	
Hamburg Hbf ....d.	0025	0055	0255	...	0504	0604	0634	and at the same minutes past each hour until	2004	2034	...	2108	2208	...	2323	...	...	also	1100	...	2103	...
Bad Oldesloe ....d.	0051	0137	0337	...	0530	0630	0702		2030	2102	...	2132	2232	...	2348	...	...		|	...	|	...
Lübeck Hbf ....a.	0109	0155	0355	...	0548	0648	0720		2048	2120	...	2150	2250	...	0007	...	...		1138	...	2142	...

				⚒	Ⓐ		Ⓐ		Ⓐ			Ⓐ								H		E	
eck Hbf ....d.	0017	...	0414	0508	0541	0608	0641	0708	0743	and at the same minutes past each hour until	1908	1943	2008	...	2108	2208	2308	...	also	0816	...	1416	...
Oldesloe ....d.	0035	...	0432	0525	0558	0625	0658	0725	0800		1925	2000	2025	...	2125	2225	2325	...		|	...	|	...
burg Hbf ....a.	0109	...	0517	0551	0627	0653	0724	0751	0826		1951	2026	2051	...	2151	2251	2351	...		0856	...	1456	...

LÜBECK - TRAVEMÜNDE STRAND ⊠

	Ⓐ	⚒						
Lübeck Hbf ....d.	0503	0603	0703	0803r	and hourly until	2203r	2303	...
Travemünde Skandinavienkai ....a.	0519	0619	0719	0819		2219	2319	...
Travemünde Strand ....a.	0525	0625	0725	0825		2225	2325	...

	Ⓐ	⚒						
Travemünde Strand ....d.	0534	0634	0734	...	0834	and hourly until	2234	2334
Travemünde Skandinavienkai.......d.	0539	0639	0739	...	0839		2239	2339
Lübeck Hbf ....a.	0556	0656	0756	...	0858		2258	2356

HAMBURG - LÜBECK - PUTTGARDEN (- KØBENHAVN)

				ICE 31			*ICE* 33		*EC* 1233				*IC* 2220	*ICE* 35			*ICE* 37		*ICE* 39		*EC* 239			
	Ⓐ			YR	T	Ⓒ z	R🍷		L		z	N	F	R🍷	T	Ⓒ z	R🍷		🍷		W			
Hamburg Hbf ....d.	...	...	...	0724	...	0821	0928	...	1126j	...	...	...	1230	1328	...	1426k	1528	...	1728	...	1925t	...	...	...
Lübeck Hbf .... ⊡ d.	0512	...	0712	0806	0912	0915	1006	1112	1206	...	1308	1312	1314	1406	1512	1515	1606	1712	1806	1912	2006	2112	...	2312
Neustadt (Holst).. ⊡ a.	|	...	|	|	|	|	|	|	|	...	|	|	|	|	|	|	|	|	|	|	|	|	...	2345
Oldenburg (Holst) ....d.	0616	...	0816	0839	1016	1016	1039	1216	1239	...	1405	1416	1417	1439	1616	1616	1639	1816	1839	2016	2039	2216	...	0017
Fehmarn-Burg ....a.	0643	...	0840	|	1040	1042	|	1240	|	...	1428	1440	1443	|	1640	1642	|	1840	|	2040	|	2240	...	0040
Puttgarden ⛴ ....a.	0656	...	0855h	0905	1055p	1058	1105	1255z	1305	...	1440	...	...	1505	1655f	1658	1705	1855	1905	2055z	2105	2255	...	0055
København H **720** ...a.	...	...	...	1222	...	...	1422	...	1622	...	...	...	...	1822	...	...	2022	...	2222	...	0029	...	...	...

					EC 232	*IC* 2327			*ICE* 38			*ICE* 36			*ICE* 34	*IC* 2221		*EC* 1238			*ICE* 32			*ICE* 30	
		Ⓐ			W	A			R🍷	Ⓒ z	T	R🍷	z	N	R🍷	F		W🍷	Ⓒ z	T	R🍷			XR	
benhavn H **720** ....a.	...	...	...	...	0537	...	...	...	0737	...	...	0937	...	...	1137	...	...	1337	...	...	1537	...	...	1737	...
garden ⛴ ....d.	0519	0620	0720	...	0842	...	0915h	...	1042	1110	1115p	1242	1309	...	1442	...	1515z	1642	1710	1715f	1842	1915	...	2042	2115z
marn-Burg.................d.	0530	0631	0731	...	|	0908	0931	...	|	1125	1131	|	1320	1331	|	1508	1531	|	1725	1731	|	1931	...	|	2131
nburg (Holst) ....d.	0553	0654	0754	...	0907	0933	0954	...	1107	1151	1154	1307	1343	1354	1507	1534	1554	1707	1751	1754	1907	1954	...	2107	2154
ustadt (Holst)... ⊡ d.	0623	|	|	...	|	|	|	...	|	|	|	|	|	|	|	|	|	|	|	|	|	|	...	|	|
eck Hbf .... ⊡ a.	0654	0754	0854	...	0937	1034	1054	...	1137	1242	1254	1337	1454	1454	1537	1635	1654	1737	1842	1854	1937	2054	...	2137	2254
burg Hbf ....a.	...	...	...	...	1021	1121	...	...	1221v	1337	...	1421	...	...	1622	1731	...	1822	1938	....	2021	...	...	2223	...

⑤–⑦ to Nov. 27 (daily July 1 - Oct. 16). LÜBECKER BUCHT – [12] Fehmarn-Burg - Köln - Frankfurt - Passau. Arrives Hamburg 1131 July 25 - Sept. 2.
Daily to July 17 and Sept. 3 - Oct. 30; ⑤–⑦ from Nov. 4. *ICE* **1081**/**1141**. To München (Table **900**).
①⑤⑥⑦ to Oct. 30 (daily June 10 - Aug. 29). FEHMARN – [12] Frankfurt - Köln - Hamburg - Fehmarn-Burg and v.v. Also runs Frankfurt - Köln - Lübeck and v.v. on ②–④ Aug. 30 - Oct. 27 and ⑤⑦ from Nov. 4.
Ⓑ (not July 18 - Sept. 2, Oct. 2). *ICE* **584**/**1154**. From München (Table **900**).
①–⑥ (not July 18 - Sept. 2, Oct. 3). *ICE* **585**/**1155**. To München (Table **900**).
Daily to July 17 and Sept. 3 - Oct. 30; ⑤–⑦ from Nov. 4. *ICE* **784**/**1184**. From München (Table **900**).
June 17 - Sept. 4. 🅁 for international journeys.
From Oct. 31.
🅁 for international journeys June 12 - Sept. 4.
Ⓐ (daily from Oct. 31).
June 18 - Sept. 4. 🅁 for international journeys.
Until Oct. 30. Runs as *EC* **1130** June 18 - Sept. 4.
Until Oct. 30. Runs as *EC* **1131** June 18 - Sept. 4.

Ⓐ to Oct. 28.

h – Daily to Nov. 4; ①–⑤ from Nov. 7.
j – 1128 June 17 - July 24; 1124 on Sept. 3, 4.
k – 1418 July 30 - Sept. 4.
p – Ⓐ to Oct. 28; Ⓒ from Nov. 5.
r – 2 minutes **earlier** on Ⓒ to Oct. 30.
t – 1928 June 18 - July 24 and on Sept. 3; 1923 on Sept. 4.
v – 1226 July 25 - Sept. 4.
z – Until Oct. 30.

⊠ – Evening services (from approx. 1900) are subject to alteration July 22 – 31.
⊡ – Full service **Lübeck** - **Neustadt** (Holst) and v.v. (journey time 31 – 46 minutes):
From Lübeck Hbf at 0442 Ⓐ, 0512 Ⓐ, 0612, 0712, 0812, 0908 Ⓒ**z**, 0912 **T**, 1012, 1112, 1212, 1308 **z**, 1312 **N**, 1412, 1508 Ⓒ**z**, 1512 **T**, 1612, 1712, 1812, 1912, 2012, 2112, 2212 and 2312.
From Neustadt (Holst) at 0523 Ⓐ, 0623, 0653 Ⓐ, 0717 Ⓐ, 0723 Ⓒ, 0817, 0914 Ⓒ**z**, 0923 **T**, 1017, 1114 Ⓒ**z**, 1123 **T**, 1217 **T**, 1223 Ⓒ**z**, 1314 **z**, 1323 **N**, 1417, 1514 Ⓒ**z**, 1523 **T**, 1617, 1714 Ⓒ**z**, 1723 **T**, 1817 **T**, 1823 Ⓒ**z**, 1923, 2017, 2123, 2217 and 2317.

826 KIEL - LÜBECK

RE / RB serv

km		Ⓒ	Ⓐ	Ⓒ	Ⓐ							
0	**Kiel** Hbf d.	0543	0544	0643	0644	0744	and	1944	2044	2143	2243	2343
33	Plön d.	0615	0615	0713	0715	0815	hourly	2015	2115	2215	2315	0015
47	Eutin d.	0629	0629	0727	0729	0829	until	2029	2131	2229	2329	0029
80	**Lübeck** Hbf a.	0658	0652	0752	0752	0852		2052	2153	2258	2358	0058

	⑥	Ⓐ	Ⓒ	Ⓐ						
Lübeck Hbf d.	0501	0504	0601	0606	0704	0806	and	2006	2106	2201
Eutin d.	0529	0529	0629	0629	0729	0829	hourly	2029	2131	2229
Plön d.	0544	0544	0643	0645	0745	0845	until	2045	2145	2244
Kiel Hbf a.	0617	0615	0715	0715	0815	0915		2115	2215	2317

Other stopping trains Kiel - Lübeck and v.v. (journey 87–88 minutes): **From Kiel** Hbf at 0436 Ⓐ, 0444 Ⓒ, 0515 Ⓐ, 0604 Ⓐ, 0704 and hourly until 2004.
From Lübeck Hbf at 0017, 0356 Ⓐ, 0401 Ⓒ, 0528 Ⓐ, 0628 Ⓐ, 0728 and hourly until 2028.

827 LÜBECK - BÜCHEN - LÜNEBURG

RB serv

km		Ⓐ																				
0	**Lübeck** Hbf d.	0505	0605	0707	0809	0909	1009	1109	1209	1309	1409	1509	1609	1709	1809	1909	2009	2109	2219	...	2329
9	Lübeck Flughafen ✈ d.	0514	0614	0716	0819	0919	1019	1119	1219	1319	1419	1519	1619	1719	1819	1919	2019	2119	2229	...	2339
22	Ratzeburg d.	0527	0627	0730	0830	0930	1030	1130	1230	1330	1430	1530	1630	1730	1830	1930	2030	2130	2243	...	2352
31	Mölln (Lauenburg) d.	0534	0634	0737	0837	0937	1037	1137	1237	1337	1437	1537	1637	1737	1837	1937	2037	2137	2250	...	2359
50	Büchen a.	0546	0646	0748	0848	0948	1048	1148	1248	1348	1448	1548	1648	1748	1848	1948	2048	2148	2302	...	0011
50	Büchen d.	0555	0655	0750	0858	0950	1107	1150	1307	1350	1507	1550	1707	1750	1907	1950	2107	2201	2333	...	...
79	**Lüneburg** a.	0618	0718	0815	0921	1015	1130	1215	1330	1415	1530	1615	1730	1815	1930	2015	2130	2224	2356	...	...

	Ⓐ	Ⓐ	⑥	Ⓐ																⑥k	
Lüneburg d.	0431	0526	0545	0628	0631c	0745	0831	0945	1031	1145	1231	1345	1431	1545	1631	1745	1831	1945	2031	2138	2245
Büchen a.	0453	0547	0607	0650	0653c	0808	0853	1008	1053	1208	1253	1408	1453	1608	1653	1808	1853	2008	2053	2200	2308
Büchen d.	0455	0555	0608	0656	0709	0809	0909	1009	1109	1209	1309	1409	1509	1609	1709	1809	1909	2009	2109	2209	2333
Mölln (Lauenburg) d.	0509	0609	0620	0710	0722	0822	0922	1022	1122	1222	1322	1422	1522	1622	1722	1822	1922	2022	2122	2222	2345
Ratzeburg d.	0517	0617	0632	0717	0732	0832	0932	1032	1132	1232	1332	1432	1532	1632	1732	1832	1932	2032	2132	2232	2352
Lübeck Flughafen ✈ d.	0525	0625	0641	0726	0741	0841	0941	1041	1141	1241	1341	1441	1541	1641	1741	1841	1941	2041	2141	2241	0001
Lübeck Hbf a.	0536	0636	0652	0736	0752	0852	0952	1052	1152	1252	1352	1452	1552	1652	1752	1852	1952	2052	2154	2252	0011

c – Ⓒ only.
k – Also Oct. 2.

828 LÜBECK - BAD KLEINEN

RE / RB serv

km			ⒶS		S		S		S		S		S		P		N		G	A
0	**Lübeck** Hbf d.	0502	0602	0703	0802	0903	1002	1103	1202	1303	1402	1503	1602	1703	1802	1903	2002	2103	2206	2307
39	Grevesmühlen d.	0537	0637	0741	0837	0941	1037	1141	1237	1341	1437	1541	1637	1741	1837	1941	2037	2141	2242	2340
62	**Bad Kleinen** a.	0551	0655	0755	0855	0955	1055	1155	1255	1355	1455	1555	1655	1755	1855	1955	2055	2155	2300	2354

	ⒶA	ⒶT		N		S		S		S		S		S		S		S		
Bad Kleinen d.	0432	0518	0603	0703	0803	0903	1003	1103	1203	1303	1403	1503	1603	1703	1803	1903	2003	2103	...	2203
Grevesmühlen d.	0446	0539	0617	0721	0817	0921	1017	1121	1217	1321	1417	1521	1617	1721	1817	1921	2017	2121	...	2221
Lübeck Hbf a.	0525	0624	0656	0757	0856	0956	1056	1157	1256	1357	1456	1557	1656	1757	1856	1957	2056	2157	...	2301

A – From / to Schwerin (Table **830**
G – To Güstrow (Table **836**).
N – To / from Neubrandenburg (Table **836**).
P – To Pasewalk (Table **836**).
S – To / from Szczecin (Table **836**
T – From Szczecin (Table **836**) on (also Oct. 4).

830 HAMBURG - ROSTOCK - STRALSUND

km		*RE* 13001	*RE* 13003	*RE* 13190	*RE* 4301	*RE* 13005	*RE* 4331	*RE* 4374	*RE* 4305	*RE* 4305	*RE* 13007	*IC* 2184	*RE* 4307	*RE* 13009	*IC* 2182	*IC* 2238	*RE* 4309	*RE* 13011	*IC* 2212	*RE* 4311	*RE* 13013	*IC* 2376	*RE* 4313	*RE* 13015
			Ⓐn	Ⓐ			Ⓐ	Ⓐn	Ⓐ	Ⓒ														
		S	S	L		S					S	🍷◆		S	🍷◆	◆		S	🍷◆		S	🍷◆		S
0	**Hamburg** Hbf d.	...	...	...	...	...	0457	...	0613f	0618	...	0733	0818	...	0944	...	1017	...	1117	1221h	...	1344	1421h	...
47	Büchen d.	...	...	...	0459a	...	0533	...	0659t	0659t	...	|	0859t	...	|	...	1059t	...	|	1259t	...	|	1459t	...
123	**Schwerin** Hbf 836 837 d.	...	...	0413	0548	...	0638	0645	0748	0748	...	0837	0948	...	1037	1056	1148	...	1211	1348	...	1437	1548	...
140	Bad Kleinen 836 837 d.	...	...	0425	0603	...	...	0700	0803	0803	...	|	1003	...	|	1110	1203	...	|	1403	...	|	1603	...
181	Bützow 836 d.	...	...	...	0629	...	...	0724	0829	0829	...	0911	1029	...	1111	1132	1229	...	1245	1429	...	1511	1629	...
211	**Rostock** Hbf a.	...	...	...	0650	...	...	0750	0850	0850	...	0932	1050	...	1132	1152	1253	...	1306	1450	...	1532	1650	...
211	**Rostock** Hbf d.	0456	0554	...	...	0700	...	...	...	...	0901	0938	...	1101	1138	...	...	1301	1317	...	1501	1538	...	1701
240	Ribnitz-D'garten West d.	0516	0618	...	...	0723	...	...	...	...	0922	1000	...	1122	1200	...	...	1322	1339	...	1522	1600	...	1722
265	Velgast d.	0540	0640	...	...	0740	...	...	...	...	0940	1016	...	1140	1216	...	...	1340	1354	...	1540	1617	...	1740
283	**Stralsund** Hbf a.	0556	0656	...	...	0756	...	...	...	...	0956	1028	...	1159	1228	...	...	1356	1410	...	1556	1629	...	1756
	Ostseebad Binz 844 a.	...	...	...	...	...	...	...	...	...	...	1132v	...	...	...	...	...	...	1501	...	...	1720k	...	...

	RE 4315	*RE* 13017	*IC* 2372	*RE* 4317	*RE* 13019	*IC* 2188	*IC* 2270	*IC* 2404	*RE* 4319	*RE* 4321
						①–④	⑦w	⑤		
		S	🍷◆	‡	S	m🍷	🍷◆			
Hamburg Hbf d.	1611	...	1743	1811	...	1944	1944	1944	2021h	2258g
Büchen d.	1659p	...	|	1859p	...	|	|	|	2059t	2329
Schwerin Hbf 836 837 d.	1748	...	1837	1948	...	2037	2037	2037	2148	0017
Bad Kleinen 836 837 d.	1803	...	1850	2003	...	|	|	|	2203	0029
Bützow 836 d.	1829	...	1913	2029	...	2111	2111	2111	2229	0054
Rostock Hbf a.	1850	...	1933	2050	...	2132	2132	2130	2250	0114
Rostock Hbf d.	...	1901	1938	...	2101	...	2138	2138	...	...
Ribnitz-Damgarten West d.	...	1922	2000	...	2122	...	2200	2200	...	...
Velgast d.	...	1940	2016	...	2140	...	2216	2216	...	...
Stralsund Hbf a.	...	1956	2028	...	2156	...	2228	2228	...	...
Ostseebad Binz 844 a.	...	...	...	...	...	...	...	...	...	...

	RE 4300	*RE* 4338	*RE* 4330	*IC* 2189	*IC* 2189	*RE* 4302	*RE* 13000	*IC* 2279	*RE* 13002
	Ⓐ	Ⓒ	Ⓐ	①Y	Ⓐ		Ⓐn	⚒	
				🍷	🍷		S	🍷◆	S
Ostseebad Binz 844 d.	...	...	...	...	...	...	...	...	...
Stralsund Hbf d.	...	...	...	0405	...	...	0453	0525	0557
Velgast d.	...	...	...	0419	...	...	0508	0539	0614
Ribnitz-Damgarten West d.	...	...	...	0433	...	...	0526	0553	0632
Rostock Hbf a.	...	...	...	0452	...	...	0548	0615	0654
Rostock Hbf d.	...	...	...	0458	0458	0507	...	0625	...
Bützow 836 d.	...	...	...	0519	0519	0529	...	0646	...
Bad Kleinen 836 837 d.	...	...	...	0544	0544	0559	...	|	...
Schwerin Hbf 836 837 d.	0412	0444	0455	0558	0558	0612	...	0722	...
Büchen d.	0508	0540	0553	0634	0634	0707	...	|	...
Hamburg Hbf a.	0539	0611	0625	0702	0702	0738	...	0816	...

	IC 2217	*RE* 13004	*RE* 4306	*IC* 2373	*RE* 13006	*RE* 4308	*IC* 2213	*RE* 13008	*RE* 4310	*IC* 2239	*IC* 2377	*RE* 13010	*RE* 4312	*IC* 2379	*RE* 13012	*RE* 4314	*RE* 13038	*IC* 1989	*RE* 13014	*RE* 4316	*RE* 13016	*RE* 4318	*RE* 13018	*RE* 4320
																	①–④	⑦w						
	🍷◆	S		🍷◆	S		🍷◆	S		◆	🍷◆	S		🍷◆	S		m	🍷			S		S	
Ostseebad Binz 844 d.	...	...	...	...	...	...	1026	...	...	...	1215z	...	...	...	...	...	1604	...	1704	...	...	...	...	...
Stralsund Hbf d.	0727	0800	...	0927	1000	...	1127	1200	...	...	1327	1400	...	1527	1600	...	1700	1727	1800	...	2000	...	2200	...
Velgast d.	0741	0815	...	0941	1015	...	1141	1215	...	...	1341	1415	...	1541	1615	...	1712	1741	1815	...	2015	...	2215	...
Ribnitz-Damgarten West d.	0755	0833	...	0955	1033	...	1155	1233	...	...	1400	1433	...	1555	1633	...	1738	1801	1833	...	2033	...	2233	...
Rostock Hbf a.	0815	0855	...	1019	1055	...	1219	1255	...	...	1419	1455	...	1619	1655	...	1758	1820	1855	...	2055	...	2255	...
Rostock Hbf d.	0825	...	0907	1025	...	1107	1244	...	1307	1405	1425	...	1507	1625	...	1707	*1808*n	1825	...	1907	...	2107	...	2307
Bützow 836 d.	0846	...	0929	1046	...	1129	1304	...	1329	1426	1446	...	1529	1646	...	1729	*1830*n	1846	...	1929	...	2129	...	2329
Bad Kleinen 836 837 d.	|	...	0959	|	...	1159	|	...	1359	1449	|	...	1559	|	...	1759	*1904*n	|	...	1959	...	2159	...	2359
Schwerin Hbf 836 837 d.	0922	...	1012	1122	...	1212	1338	...	1412	1500	1522	...	1612	1722	...	1812	*1915*n	1922	...	2012	...	2210	...	0010
Büchen d.	|	...	1107	|	...	1312t	|	...	1512t	...	|	...	1712t	|	...	1912t	...	|	...	2112t	...	...	...	...
Hamburg Hbf a.	1016	...	1142	1215	...	1349	1433	...	1549	...	1616	...	1749	1815	...	1949	...	2016	...	2143	...	...	...	...

◆ – **NOTES** (LISTED BY TRAIN NUMBER)

2182 – Daily to Nov. 5; ①–⑥ from Nov. 7. [12] and 🍷 (Kassel Ⓐ -) (Hannover ⚒ -) Hamburg - Stralsund.
2184 – ⚒ to Oct. 29; ①–⑤ from Oct. 31. [12] and 🍷 (Hannover Ⓐ -) Hamburg - Stralsund (- Ostseebad Binz until Oct. 29). Departs Hamburg 0743 on ⑥.
2212 – RÜGEN – [12] and 🍷 Koblenz - Köln - Hamburg - Ostseebad Binz.
2213 – RÜGEN – [12] and 🍷 Ostseebad Binz - Hamburg - Köln - Koblenz - Stuttgart.
2216 – [12] and 🍷 Stuttgart - Koblenz - Köln - Hamburg - Stralsund (- Greifswald Ⓐ **n**).
2217 – [12] and 🍷 (Greifswald Ⓐ **n** -) Stralsund - Hamburg - Köln - Koblenz - Stuttgart.
2238/9 – Daily to Sept. 4; ⑤–⑦ Sept. 9 - Oct. 30 (also Oct. 3; not Oct. 2); ⑤ from Nov. 4. WARNOW – [12] Leipzig - Magdeburg - Rostock (- Warnemünde until Oct. 30 ●) and v.v.
2270 – [12] and 🍷 Karlsruhe - Frankfurt - Hannover - Hamburg - Stralsund.
2279 – [12] and 🍷 Stralsund - Hamburg - Hannover - Frankfurt - Karlsruhe. July 18 - Sept. 2 runs with train number **2087** and terminates at Hannover Hbf (a. 0938).
2372 – [12] and 🍷 (Karlsruhe ⑤⑥† -) Frankfurt - Hannover - Hamburg - Stralsund. On ①②③④⑥⑦ July 18 - Sept. 1 runs with train number **2088** and starts from Hannover Hbf (d. 1620).
2373 – [12] and 🍷 Stralsund - Hamburg - Hannover - Frankfurt - Karlsruhe. On ①②③④⑥⑦ July 18 - Sept. 1 runs with train number **2089** and terminates at Hannover Hbf (a. 1338).
2376 – [12] and 🍷 Karlsruhe - Frankfurt - Hannover - Hamburg - Stralsund (- Ostseebad Binz ⑥). July 18 - Sept. 2 runs with train number **2086** and starts from Hannover Hbf (d. 1217).
2377 – [12] and 🍷 Ostseebad Binz - Hamburg - Hannover - Frankfurt (- Karlsruhe ⑤). July 18 - Sept. 2 runs with train number **2285** departs Stralsund 1324 and terminates at Hannover Hbf (a. 173
2379 – Daily to Nov. 4; ⑧ from Nov. 6. [12] and 🍷 Stralsund - Hamb (- Hannover ⑧ **q**) (- Frankfurt ⑤⑦ **w**). July 18 - Sept. 2 runs train number **2289** and terminates at Hannover Hbf (a. 1938 ⑧)

L – To / from Lübeck (Table **828**).
S – To / from Sassnitz (Table **844**).
Y – ① to Oct. 31 (also Oct. 4; not Oct. 3).

a – Ⓐ only.
b – Not ⑥.
f – 0616 July 25 - Sept. 2, Oct. 4.
g – 2257 July 25 - Sept. 4.
h – 5–10 minutes **earlier** July 25 - Sept. 4.
k – ⑥ only.
m – Not Oct. 3.

n – Not Oct. 31.
p – Arrives 15–16 minutes ear
q – Not Oct. 2.
t – Arrives 7–11 minutes earli
v – Until Oct. 29.
w – Also Oct. 3; not Oct. 2.
z – Daily to Oct. 30; ⑦ from No
‡ – On Oct. 3 departs Hambur 1823, arrives Büchen 1853
● – **2238**: Warnemünde a. 121 **2239**: Warnemünde d. 134

ROSTOCK - WARNEMÜNDE 831

Bahn

STOCK - WARNEMÜNDE and v.v. *13 km*. Journey time: 21 minutes. Additional services run at peak times on Ⓐ.

m Rostock Hbf at 0433, 0448 Ⓐ, 0503, 0518 Ⓐ, 0533, 0548 Ⓐ, 0603, 0618 Ⓐ, 0633, 0648 Ⓐ, 0703, 0718 Ⓐ, 0733, 0748 Ⓐ, 0803, 0818, 0833, 0848, 0903, 0918, 0933, 0948 and at 18, 33 and 48 minutes past each hour until 2003, 2018, 2033, 2048; then 2103, 2133, 2203, 2233, 2303, 2333 and 0003.

m Warnemünde at 0403, 0430, 0448 Ⓐ, 0503, 0518 Ⓐ, 0533, 0548 Ⓐ, 0603, 0618 Ⓐ, 0633, 0648 Ⓐ, 0703, 0718 Ⓐ, 0733, 0748 Ⓐ, 0803, 0818 Ⓐ, 0833, 0848, 0903, 0918, 0933, 0948 at 03, 18, 33 and 48 minutes past each hour until 2003, 2018, 2033, 2048; then 2103, 2133, 2203, 2233, 2303, 2333 and 0003.

BERLIN - KOSTRZYN 832

ederbarnimer Eisenbahn (2nd class only)

m																								
			Ⓒ	Ⓐ							Ⓒ	Ⓐ				Ⓐ	Ⓒ							
0	**Berlin** Lichtenberg	d.	0537	0637	0637	0737	0837	0937	1037	1137	1237	1337	1437	1437	1537	1637	1737	1837	1837	1937	2037	2137	...	2337	...
3	Strausberg	d.	0555	0655	0655	0755	0855	0955	1055	1155	1255	1355	1455	1455	1555	1655	1755	1855	1855	1955	2055	2155	...	2355	...
7	Müncheberg (Mark) ¶	d.	0613	0713	0722	0813	0913	1013	1113	1213	1313	1413	1513	1517	1613	1717	1813	1913	1917	2013	2113	2213	...	0013	...
0	**Kostrzyn** 🏨	a.	0654	0744	0753	0854	0944	1054	1144	1254	1344	1454	1544	1548	1654	1748	1854	1944	1948	2054	2144	2254	...	0054	...

					Ⓐ	Ⓐ	Ⓒ								Ⓐ	Ⓒ				Ⓒ	Ⓐ				
strzyn 🏨	d.	0411	0508	0602	0617	0702	0711	0802	0911	1002	1111	1202	1311	1402	1505	1511	1602	1705	1802	1905	1911	2002	...	2202	...
cheberg (Mark) ¶	d.	0453	0549	0649	0700	0749	0749	0849	0949	1049	1149	1249	1349	1449	1549	1549	1649	1749	1849	1949	1949	2049	...	2249	...
usberg	d.	0510	0610	0710	0716	0810	0810	0910	1010	1110	1210	1310	1410	1510	1610	1610	1710	1810	1910	2010	2010	2110	...	2310	...
in Lichtenberg	a.	0528	0628	0728	0735	0827	0828	0928	1028	1128	1228	1328	1428	1528	1628	1628	1728	1828	1928	2028	2028	2128	...	2328	...

Station for the Buckower Kleinbahn (operates Ⓒ May - September).

WISMAR - ROSTOCK 833

services

m			⚒r	Ⓐr				
0	**Wismar**	d.	0442	0542	0642	and	2042	2142
22	Neubukow	d.	0511	0611	0711	hourly	2111	2211
1	Bad Doberan ▲	d.	0530	0630	0730	until	2130	2230
57	**Rostock** Hbf	a.	0551	0651	0751		2151	2251

		Ⓐr		⚒r				
Rostock Hbf	d.	0412	0506	0606	0706	and	2006	2106
Bad Doberan ▲	d.	0432	0532	0632	0732	hourly	2032	2132
Neubukow	d.	0451	0551	0651	0751	until	2051	2151
Wismar	a.	0515	0615	0715	0815		2115	2215

r – Not Oct. 31.

– **BAD DOBERAN - OSTSEEBAD KÜHLUNGSBORN WEST**. All services worked by steam locomotive. 2nd class only. Journey time: 39 – 47 minutes.
Operator: Mecklenburgische Bäderbahn Molli GmbH, Am Bahnhof, 18209 Bad Doberan. ✆ +49 (0) 38293 431331, Fax +49 (0) 38293 431332. **Service Mar. 24 - Oct. 31**, 2016.
From **Bad Doberan** at 0835 Ⓐ **r**, 0936, 1036 and hourly until 1636; then 1745 and 1845. From **Kühlungsborn West** at 0640 Ⓐ **r**, 0828, 0935, 1035 and hourly until 1735.

STRALSUND - NEUBRANDENBURG - NEUSTRELITZ 834

m																										
			Ⓐ	Ⓐd			Ⓐd									Ⓑ			Ⓑ			Ⓑ				
0	**Stralsund** Hbf	d.	...	0403	...	0501	0603	...	0700	0803r	0901	1003r	1101	1203r	1301	1403	...	1501	1603	...	1701	1803	...	1901	...	2101
23	Grimmen	d.	...	0424	...	0523	0624	...	0723	0824r	0923	1024r	1123	1224r	1323	1424	...	1523	1624	...	1723	1824	...	1923	...	2129
47	Demmin	d.	...	0446	...	0546	0646	...	0746	0846r	0946	1046r	1146	1246r	1346	1446	...	1546	1646	...	1746	1846	...	1946	...	2146
89	**Neubrandenburg**	a.	...	0529	...	0629	0729	...	0829	0929r	1029	1129r	1229	1329r	1429	1529	...	1629	1729	...	1829	1929	...	2029	...	2229
89	**Neubrandenburg**	d.	0429	0529	0529	0630	0730	0730	0830	0930	1030	1130	1230	1330	1430	1530	1530	1630	1730	1730	1830	1930	1930	2030	2130	2230
24	**Neustrelitz** Hbf	a.	0458	0557	0557	0659	0756	0756	0859	0956	1059	1156	1259	1356	1459	1556	1556	1659	1756	1756	1859	1956	1956	2059	2156	2259
	Berlin Hbf **835**	a.	0612	...	...	0812	...	...	1012	...	1213	...	1412	...	1612	...	...	1812	...	...	2012	...	...	2212	...	0013v

		Ⓐd	Ⓐ		Ⓐd									Ⓑ			Ⓑ			Ⓑ						
erlin Hbf **835**	d.	...	...	...	...	...	0545	...	0745	...	0945	...	1145	...	...	1346	...	...	1545	...	...	1745	...	1945	...	2145
ustrelitz Hbf	d.	...	0501	...	0603	0603	0701	0803	0901	1003	1101	1203	1301	1403	1403	1501	1603	1603	1701	1803	1803	1901	2003	2101	2203	2301
ubrandenburg	a.	...	0530	...	0630	0630	0730	0829	0930	1029	1130	1229	1330	1429	1429	1530	1629	1629	1730	1829	1829	1930	2029	2130	2229	2329
ubrandenburg	d.	0432	0532	0532	0632	...	0732	0832r	0932	1032r	1132	1232r	1332	1432	...	1532	1632	...	1732	1832	...	1932	...	2132	...	...
mmin	d.	0510	0610	0610	0710	...	0810	0910r	1010	1110r	1210	1310r	1410	1510	...	1610	1710	...	1810	1910	...	2010	...	2210	...	...
mmen	d.	0529	0629	0629	0729	...	0829	0929r	1029	1129r	1229	1329r	1429	1529	...	1629	1729	...	1829	1929	...	2029	...	2229	...	...
alsund Hbf	a.	0551	0651	0651	0751	...	0851	0951r	1051	1153r	1251	1351r	1451	1551	...	1651	1751	...	1851	1952	...	2051	...	2251	...	...

Not Oct. 31. r – ⚒ only. v – Neustrelitz - Berlin on ⑤⑥ (also Oct. 2).

ROSTOCK - BERLIN - ELSTERWERDA 835

m			*RE* 3503	*RE* 4353	*RE* 3505	*RE* 4355	*IC* ● 2383	*RE* 3507	*RE* 4357	*RE* 3509	*RE* 4359	*IC* ♥ 2387	*RE* 3511	*RE* 4361	*IC* ♠ 2185	*RE* 3513	*RE* 4363	*IC* 2389	*RE* 3515	*RE* 4365	*RE* 3517	*RE* 18491	*RE* 4367	*RE* 3519	*RE* 4369	*RE* 3521	*RE* 3525
							Ⓐ L🍷					⑥ L🍷			† L🍷			⑥N L🍷				Ⓒ D				⑤⑥ v	
	Warnemünde **831**	d.	...	...	...	...	...	...	...	...	...	1059r	...	...	1259r	...	...	1458	...	...	...	1759	...	...	...	...	...
0	**Rostock** Hbf **831**	d.	...	0434e	...	0634	0723	...	0834	...	1034	1123	...	1234	1323	...	1434	1523	...	1634	...	1822	1834	...	2034	...	2334
4	Güstrow	d.	...	0456e	...	0656	|	...	0856	...	1056	|	...	1256	|	...	1456	|	...	1656	...	|	1856	...	2056	...	2356
5*	Waren (Müritz)	d.	...	0535e	...	0735	0801	...	0935	...	1135	1201	...	1335	1401	...	1535	1601	...	1735	...	1909	1935	...	2135	...	0027
	Stralsund Hbf **834**	d.	...	|	0501	|	|	0700	|	0901	|	|	1101	|	|	1301	|	|	1501	|	1701	|	|	1901	|	2101	|
	Neubrandenburg **834**	d.	0429e	|	0630	|	|	0830	|	1030	|	|	1230	|	|	1430	|	|	1630	|	1830	|	|	2030	|	2230	|
20	**Neustrelitz** Hbf	a.	0458e	0556e	0659	0756	0818	0859	0956	1059	1157	1218	1259	1356	1418	1459	1557	1618	1659	1757	1859	1930	1957	2059	2156	2259	0048
20	**Neustrelitz** Hbf	d.	0500	0601	0700	0801	0820	0900	1001	1100	1201	1220	1300	1401	1420	1500	1601	1620	1700	1801	1900	1932	2001	2100	2201	2300	...
1	Fürstenberg (Havel)	d.	0511	0612	0711	0812	|	0911	1012	1111	1212	|	1311	1412	|	1511	1612	|	1711	1812	1911	1946	2012	2111	2212	2311	...
2	Gransee	d.	0525	0626	0724	0826	|	0924	1026	1124	1226	|	1324	1426	|	1524	1626	|	1724	1826	1924	|	2026	2124	2226	2324	...
1	Oranienburg	d.	0544	0643	0743	0843	|	0943	1043	1143	1243	|	1343	1443	|	1543	1643	|	1743	1843	1943	2016	2043	2143	2243	2343	...
3	**Berlin** Gesundbrunnen	d.	0608	0707	0808	0907	0918	1008	1107	1208	1307	1318	1408	1507	1518	1608	1707	1718	1808	1907	2008	2040	2107	2208	2307	0008	...
7	**Berlin** Hbf	a.	0612	0712	0812	0911	0923	1012	1111	1213	1311	1323	1412	1511	1523	1612	1711	1723	1812	1911	2012	2044	2111	2212	2312	0013	...
7	**Berlin** Hbf	d.	0616	0716	0816	0916	0930	1016	1116	1216	1316	1330	1416	1516	1530	1616	1716	1730	1815	1916	2016	...	2116	2216	...	...	...
3	**Berlin** Südkreuz	d.	0625	0725	0823	0925	0935	1023	1125	1223	1325	1335	1425	1525	1535	1625	1725	1735	1825	1925	2023	...	2125	2223	...	...	...
7	Doberlug-Kirchhain	a.	0757t	0906x	...	1106x	...	...	1306x	...	1506x	...	1557t	1706x	...	1757t	1906x	...	1957t	2106x	...	...	2306x	...	...	...	...
7	**Elsterwerda**	a.	0809t	0923x	...	1123x	...	...	1323x	...	1523x	...	1609t	1723x	...	1809t	1923x	...	2009t	2123x	...	...	2325x	...	...	...	...

		RE 4350	*RE* 3504	*RE* 4352	*RE* 3506	*RE* 18490	*RE* 4354	*RE* 3508	*IC* 2388	*RE* 4356	*RE* 3528	*RE* 3510	*RE* 4358	*RE* 3512	*IC* 2300	*RE* 4360	*RE* 3514	*IC* 2384	*RE* 4362	*RE* 3516	*IC* ❦ 2282	*RE* 4364	*RE* 3518	*RE* 4366	*RE* 3520	*RE* 4368	*RE* 3526
		Ⓐ				Ⓒ D			⑥N L🍷		Ⓐ	Ⓒ			⑥ M🍷			⑥N L🍷			Ⓑq L🍷						⑤⑥ v
terwerda	d.	...	...	0438x	0547t	...	0638x	0747t	...	0838x	...	...	1038x	...	...	1238x	...	...	1438x	1547t	...	1638x	1747t	1838x	1947t	2037x	...
berlug-Kirchhain	d.	...	...	0455x	0602t	...	0655x	0802t	...	0855x	...	...	1055x	...	...	1255x	...	...	1455x	1602t	...	1655x	1802t	1855x	2002t	2054x	...
lin Südkreuz	d.	...	0535e	0635	0735	...	0835	0935	1027	1035	...	1135	1235	1338	1424	1435	1536	1624	1635	1738	1824	1837	1935	2035	2135	2235	2335
lin Hbf	a.	...	0542e	0642	0742	...	0842	0942	1033	1042	...	1141	1242	1344	1430	1442	1542	1630	1642	1744	1830	1844	1942	2042	2142	2242	2342
lin Hbf	d.	0443	0545	0645	0745	0814	0845	0945	1038	1045	1145	1145	1245	1346	1438	1445	1545	1638	1645	1745	1838	1846	1945	2045	2145	2245	2346
lin Gesundbrunnen	d.	0449	0551	0651	0751	0820	0851	0951	1044	1051	1151	1151	1251	1352	1444	1451	1551	1644	1651	1751	1844	1851	1951	2051	2151	2251	2351
anienburg	d.	0512	0612	0712	0812	0842	0912	1012	|	1112	1212	1212	1312	1413	|	1512	1612	|	1712	1812	|	1912	2012	2112	2212	2312	0012
ansee	d.	0529	0632	0729	0832	|	0929	1032	|	1129	1232	1232	1329	1433	|	1529	1632	|	1729	1832	|	1929	2032	2129	2232	2329	0032
stenberg (Havel)	d.	0545	0645	0745	0845	0912	0945	1045	|	1145	1246	1246	1345	1446	|	1545	1645	|	1745	1845	|	1945	2045	2145	2245	2345	0048
ustrelitz Hbf	a.	0557	0658	0757	0858	0926	0957	1058	1138	1157	1258	1258	1357	1459	1538	1557	1658	1738	1757	1858	1938	1957	2058	2157	2258	2357	0101
ustrelitz Hbf	d.	0605	0701	0805	0901	0929	1005	1101	1140	1205	1301	1301	1405	1501	1540	1605	1701	1740	1805	1901	1940	2005	2101	2205	2301	0005	...
Neubrandenburg **834**	a.	|	0730	|	0930	|	|	1130	|	|	1330	1330	|	1530	|	|	1730	|	|	1930	|	|	2130	|	2329	|	...
Stralsund Hbf **834**	a.	|	0851	|	1051	|	|	1251	|	|	1451	1451	|	1651	|	|	1851	|	|	2051	|	|	2251	|	...	|	...
ren (Müritz)	d.	0630	...	0830	...	0951	1030	...	1159	1230	...	...	1430	...	1559	1630	...	1759	1830	...	1959	2030	...	2230	...	0028	...
strow	d.	0701	...	0901	...	|	1101	...	|	1301	...	...	1501	...	|	1701	...	|	1901	...	|	2101	...	2301	...	0059	...
stock Hbf **831**	a.	0723	...	0923	...	1038	1123	...	1237	1323	...	...	1523	...	1637	1723	...	1837	1923	...	2037	2123	...	2323	...	0121	...
rnemünde **831**	a.	...	...	...	...	1057	...	...	1258	...	...	...	...	...	1706r	...	...	...	...	...	...	...	...	...	...	...	...

- Until Oct. 30.
- To / from Leipzig (Table **850**).
- ⑥ from Sept. 10. From München via Leipzig (Table **851**).
- ⑥ until Sept. 3.

e – Ⓐ only.
q – Not Oct. 2.
r – Until Nov. 6.
t – Ⓐ to Aug. 4.
v – Also Oct. 2.
x – Until Aug. 4.

● – From Sept. 5 runs with train number **2355** and runs to München via Leipzig.
♥ – From Sept. 10 runs with train number **2301** and runs to München via Leipzig.
♠ – From Sept. 4 runs with train number **2303** and runs to München via Leipzig.
❦ – From Sept. 5 runs with train number **2356** and runs from München via Leipzig. On Sept. 4 starts from Berlin Gesundbrunnen.
* – Rostock to Waren direct is 78 km (not via Güstrow).

836 LÜBECK - PASEWALK - SZCZECIN and UECKERMÜNDE
DB (*RE* service

km		Ⓑ	Ⓐt			⚒v															B	⑤			
0	**Lübeck** Hbf .... **828** d.	...	...	...	...	...	0602a	...	0802	...	1002	...	1202	...	1402	...	1602	...	1802	...	...	...	2002	...	22
62	Bad Kleinen .. **828 830** d.	...	...	...	...	...	0705	...	0904	...	1104k	...	1304	...	1504	...	1705	...	1904	...	...	...	2104	...	23
103	Bützow .... **830** d.	...	...	0534	0634	0634	0734	0834	0934	1034	1134	1234	1334	1434	1534	1634	1734	1834	1934	2034	2034	2034	2134	2234	23
117	Güstrow .... a.	...	...	0543	0643	0643	0743	0843	0943	1043	1143	1243	1343	1443	1543	1643	1743	1843	1943	2043	2043	2043	2143	2243	23
117	Güstrow .... d.	...	...	0605	0705	0705	0805	0905	1005	1105	1205	1305	1405	1505	1605	1705	1805	1905	2005	2105	2105	2105	2205	2305	
146	Teterow .... d.	...	...	0634	0734	0734	0834	0934	1034	1134	1234	1334	1434	1534	1634	1734	1834	1934	2034	2134	2134	2134	2234	2329	...
160	Malchin .... d.	...	0529	0645	0745	0745	0845	0945	1045	1145	1245	1345	1445	1545	1645	1745	1845	1945	2045	2145	2145	2145	2245	2340	...
204	**Neubrandenburg** ... ⊠ a.	...	0601	0722	0822	0822	0922	1022	1122	1222	1322	1422	1522	1622	1722	1822	1922	2022	2122	2222	2222	2222	2319	0014	...
204	**Neubrandenburg** ... ⊠ d.	0513t	0604	0724	...	0824	0924	1024	1124	1224	1324	1424	1524	1624	1724	1824	1924	2024	2124	...	2224	2224	...	...	...
257	**Pasewalk** ⊙ .... ⊠ a.	0559t	0655	0813	...	0910	1010	1110	1210	1310	1410	1510	1613	1710	1813	1910	2010	2110	2210	...	2306	2306	...	...	...
257	**Pasewalk** ⊙ .... d.	0615	...	0815	...	...	1015	...	1215	...	1415	...	1615	...	1815	...	2015	...	...	...	...	2315	...	...	...
284	Grambow .... d.	0637	...	0837	...	...	1037	...	1237	...	1437	...	1637	...	1837	...	2037	...	...	...	...	2337	...	...	...
294	Szczecin Gumience 🏛 d.	0648	...	0848	...	...	1048	...	1248	...	1448	...	1648	...	1848	...	2048	...	...	...	...	2348	...	...	...
299	**Szczecin** Głowny .... a.	0654	...	0854	...	...	1054	...	1254	...	1454	...	1654	...	1854	...	2054	...	...	...	...	2354	...	...	...

	①m				Ⓐt		Ⓐt			⚒v											⑦w				
Szczecin Głowny .... d.	0226	...	...	...	0500	...	...	...	0700	...	...	0900	...	1100	...	1300	...	1500	...	1700r	1730	...	1900	...	21
Szczecin Gumience 🏛 .d.	0232	...	...	...	0506	...	...	...	0706	...	...	0906	...	1106	...	1306	...	1506	...	1706r	1736	...	1906	...	21
Grambow .... d.	|	...	...	...	0517	...	...	...	0717	...	...	0917	...	1117	...	1317	...	1517	...	1717r	1747	...	1917	...	21
Pasewalk ⊙ .... a.	0300	...	...	...	0539	...	...	...	0739	...	...	0939	...	1139	...	1339	...	1539	...	1739r	1809	...	1939	...	21
Pasewalk ⊙ .... ✣ d.	0301	...	...	...	0541	0541	0639	...	0752	0852	...	0952	1052	1152	1252	1352	1452	1552	1652	1752	1852	1852	1952	2052	21
Neubrandenburg ... ✣ a.	0338	...	...	...	0624	0624	0738	...	0838	0938	...	1038	1138	1238	1338	1438	1538	1638	1738	1838	1938	1938	2038	2138	22
Neubrandenburg ... ✣ d.	0340	...	0447	0543	0628	0628	0740	0740	0840	0940	0940	1040	1140	1240	1340	1440	1540	1640	1740	1840	1940	1940	2040	2140	
Malchin .... ✣ d.	0410	...	0530	0620	0708	0708	0817	0817	0917	1017	1017	1117	1217	1317	1417	1517	1617	1717	1817	1917	2017	2017	2117	2217	.
Teterow .... d.	0421	...	0540	0631	0731	0731	0831	0831	0931	1031	1031	1131	1231	1331	1431	1531	1631	1731	1831	1931	2031	2031	2131	2231	.
Güstrow .... a.	0439	...	0603	0653	0753	0753	0853	0853	0953	1053	1053	1153	1253	1353	1453	1553	1653	1753	1853	1953	2053	2053	2153	2253	.
Güstrow .... d.	0440	0505	0608	0708	0808	0808	0908	0908	1008	1108	1108	1208	1308	1408	1508	1608	1708	1808	1908	2008	2108	2108	2208	2308	.
Bützow .... **830** a.	0450	0515	0618	0718	0818	0818	0918	0918	1018	1118	1118	1218	1318	1418	1518	1618	1718	1818	1918	2018	2118	2118	2218	2318	.
Bad Kleinen ... **828 830** a.	0517	...	0648	...	0848	0848	...	...	1048	...	...	1248	...	1456	...	1648	...	1848	...	2048	...	...	2248	...	.
Lübeck Hbf .... **828** a.	0624	...	0757	...	0956	0956	...	...	1157	...	...	1357	...	1557	...	1757	...	1957	...	2157	...	...	...	...	.

B – ⑤–⑦ (also Oct. 3).

a – Ⓐ only.

k – 1056 on ⑤–⑦ to June 5, daily June 10 - Sept. 4, ⑤–⑦ Sept. 9 - Oct. 30 (also Oct. 3; not Oct. 2) and ⑤ from Nov. 4.

m – Also Oct. 4; not Oct. 3.

r – ①–⑥ (also Oct. 2; not Oct. 3).

t – Ⓐ (not Oct. 31).

v – Not Oct. 31.

w – Also Oct. 3; not Oct. 2.

z – Also Oct. 31.

⊠ – Until July 3 timings at Neubrandenburg and Pasewalk may vary by up to 8 minutes.

✣ – Until July 3 timings at Pasewalk, Neubrandenburg and Malchin may vary by up to 11 minu

⊙ – **PASEWALK - UECKERMÜNDE** (30 km, journey 32 – 36 minutes).
From Pasewalk at 0518 Ⓐ**t**, 0611 ⚒**v**, 0701 Ⓐ**t**, 0822, 1022, 1222, 1422, 1524 Ⓐ**t**, 1620 (change trains at Jatznick), 1822 and 2022.
From Ueckermünde Stadthafen at 0601 Ⓐ**t**, 0701 ⚒**v**, 0738 Ⓐ**t**, 0901, 1101, 1301, 1500 Ⓒ**z**, 1521 Ⓐ**t**, 1601 Ⓐ**t**, 1701, 1901 and 2101.

837 WISMAR - SCHWERIN - BERLIN - COTTBUS
DB (*RB* services); Ostdeutsche Eisenba

km		◇	◇	◇	◇	◇	◇	◇	◇	◇		◇	◇		◇	◇		◇	◇		◇	**2239**	◇		**2431**	◇
					Ⓐ			⚒														**L**			Ⓑq	
0	**Wismar** .... d.	...	...	...	0421	...	...	0521	...	...	0626	0734	...	0824	0924	...	1024	1124	...	1224	1324	...	...	1424	**E**	15
16	Bad Kleinen .... **830/6** d.	...	...	...	0437	...	...	0537	...	...	0642	0748	...	0840	0939	...	1040	1141	...	1240	1340	1449	...	1440	...	15
32	**Schwerin** Hbf . **830/6** a.	...	...	...	0449	...	...	0549	...	...	0654	0800	...	0852	0951	...	1052	1153	...	1252	1352	1500	...	1452	...	15
32	**Schwerin** Hbf .... d.	...	...	...	0500	0500	...	0601	...	...	0700	0802	...	0900	1000	...	1100	1200	...	1300	1400	1503	...	1501	...	16
72	Ludwigslust .... **840** d.	...	...	...	0534	0534	...	0635	...	...	0734	0835	...	0934	1034	...	1134	1234	...	1334	1434	1527	...	1535	...	16
116	Wittenberge .... **840** d.	0406	...	0506r	0606j	0606j	...	0704	0704	0806	▬	0904	1006	▬	1104	1206	▬	1304	1406	▬	1504	1548	1606	▬	...	17
207	Nauen .... d.	0501	...	0601r	0701	0701	...	0801	0801	0901	◇	1001	1101	◇	1201	1301	◇	1401	1501	◇	1601	|	1701	◇	...	18
	Stendal .... ⊡ d.	|	0444r	|	|	|	*0631*r	|	|	|	*0831*	|	|	*1031*	|	|	*1231*	|	|	*1431*	|	1622	|	*1631*	...	
	Rathenow .... ‡ d.	|	0503	|	|	|	0704	|	|	|	0909	|	|	1108	|	|	1309	|	|	1508	|	...	|	1708	...	
229	**Berlin** Spandau **840** ‡ d.	0517	0551	0617r	0721	0721	0751	0821	0821	0921	0951	1021	1121	1151	1221	1321	1351	1421	1521	1551	1621	...	1721	1751	...	18
241	**Berlin** Zoo .... d.	0526	|	0626	0730	0730	|	0830	0830	0930	|	1030	1130	|	1230	1330	|	1430	1530	|	1630	...	1730	|	...	18
245	**Berlin** Hbf .... **840** ‡ d.	0531	0601	0631	0735	0735	0801	0835	0835	0935	1001	1035	1135	1201	1235	1335	1401	1435	1535	1601	1635	...	1735	1801	1826	18
250	**Berlin** Ostbahnhof .... d.	0542	...	0642	0746	0746	...	0846	0846	0946	...	1046	1146	...	1246	1346	...	1446	1546	...	1646	...	1746	...	1839	18
283	Königs Wusterhausen d.	0608	...	0708	0811	0811	...	0911	0911	1011	...	1111	1211	...	1311	1411	...	1511	1611	...	1711	...	1811	...	1904	19
329	Lübben (Spreewald) ... d.	0632	...	0731	0834	0834	...	0934	0934	1034	...	1134	1234	...	1334	1434	...	1534	1634	...	1734	...	1834	...	1927	19
340	Lübbenau (Spreew) ... d.	0638	...	0737	0841	0841	...	0941	0941	1041	...	1141	1241	...	1341	1441	...	1541	1641	...	1741	...	1841	...	1935	19
370	**Cottbus** .... a.	0701	...	0759	0859	0859	...	0959	0959	1059	...	1159	1259	...	1359	1459	...	1559	1659	...	1759	...	1859	...	1951	19

	◇		◇	◇		◇	◇		◇	
Wismar .... d.	...	1624	1724	...	1824	1924	...	2024	2124	2224
Bad Kleinen ...... **830/6** d.	...	1640	1739	...	1840	1939	...	2040	2139	2240
Schwerin Hbf ... **830/6** a.	...	1652	1751	...	1852	1951	...	2052	2151	2252
Schwerin Hbf .... d.	...	1700	1800	...	1900	2000	...	2100	2200	...
Ludwigslust .... **840** d.	...	1734	1834	...	1934	2034	...	2134	2234	...
Wittenberge .... **840** d.	1806	▬	1904	2006	▬	2104	...	▬	2307j	...
Nauen .... d.	1901	◇	2001	2101	◇	2201	...	◇	0003	...
Stendal .... ⊡ d.	|	*1831*	|	|	*2031*	|	...	*2231*	|	...
Rathenow .... ‡ d.	|	1908	|	|	2108	|	...	2306	|	...
Berlin Spandau **840** ‡ d.	1921	1951	2021	2121	2151	2221	...	2349	0019	...
Berlin Zoo .... d.	1930	|	2030	2130	|	2230	...	|	0027	...
Berlin Hbf .... **840** ‡ d.	1935	2001	2035	2135	2201	2235	...	2400	0043j	...
Berlin Ostbahnhof ..... d.	1946	...	2046	2146	...	2246	2346	...	0055	...
Königs Wusterhausen d.	2011	...	2111	2211	...	2311	0012	...	0120	...
Lübben (Spreewald) ... d.	2034	...	2134	2234	...	2346	0047	...	0155	...
Lübbenau (Spreew) .... d.	2041	...	2141	2241	...	2353	0054	...	0202	...
Cottbus .... a.	2059	...	2159	2304	...	0016	0116	...	0225	...

		◇	◇	◇	◇	◇	◇	◇	**2432**	◇	◇
				⚒			⚒	†	⚒ **G**		
Cottbus .... d.	...	...	0357	0357	...	0456	0533	0557	0605	...	07
Lübbenau (Spreew) .... d.	...	...	0420	0420	...	0520	0556	0620	0621	...	07
Lübben (Spreewald) .... d.	...	...	0427	0427	...	0527	0602	0627	0629	...	07
Königs Wusterhausen ...... d.	...	...	0451	0451	...	0551	0628	0651	0652	...	07
Berlin Ostbahnhof .... d.	...	0409	0514	0514	...	0614	0654	0714	0720	...	08
Berlin Hbf .... **840** ‡ d.	...	0421	0526	0526	0558	0625	0705	0725	0727	0800	08
Berlin Zoo .... d.	...	0426	0530	0531	|	0631	0731e	0731	...	|	08
Berlin Spandau ...... **840** ‡ d.	...	0435	▬	0540	0610	0640	0741	0741	...	0812	08
Rathenow .... ‡ a.	...	|	...	|	0657	|	|	|	...	0856	|
Stendal .... ⊡ a.	...	|	...	|	*0725*r	|	|	|	...	*0925*	|
Nauen .... d.	...	0459	...	0559	▬	0659	0802	0802	...	▬	08
Wittenberge .... **840** d.	...	0604j	Ⓑ	0701	...	0757	0901	0901	...	...	09
Ludwigslust .... **840** d.	0506t	0630	0649t	0726	0826	...	0926	0926	...	1036	..
Schwerin Hbf .... a.	0538t	0659	0721t	0757	0858	...	0957	0957	...	1108	..
Schwerin Hbf .... **830/6** d.	0539	0700	0739	0806	0904	...	1006	1006	...	1109	..
Bad Kleinen .... **830/6** d.	0601j	0713	0801j	0819	0917	...	1019	1019	...	1122	..
Wismar .... a.	0616	0727	0816	0837	0937	...	1037	1037	...	1138	.

km		**2238**	◇	◇	◇	◇	◇	◇	◇	◇	◇	◇	◇	◇	◇	◇	◇	◇	◇	◇	◇	◇	◇	◇	◇	◇
		L																				Ⓑ				
	Cottbus .... d.	...	0801	...	0901	1001	...	1101	1201	...	1301	1401	...	1501	1601	...	1701	1801	...	1901	2001	2001	2101	...	2201	23
	Lübbenau (Spreew) ... d.	...	0820	...	0920	1020	...	1120	1220	...	1320	1420	...	1520	1620	...	1720	1820	...	1920	2020	2020	2120	...	2224	23
	Lübben (Spreewald) ... d.	...	0827	...	0927	1027	...	1127	1227	...	1327	1427	...	1527	1627	...	1727	1827	...	1927	2027	2027	2127	...	2230	23
	Königs Wusterhausen d.	...	0851	...	0951	1051	...	1151	1251	...	1351	1451	...	1551	1651	...	1751	1851	...	1951	2051	2051	2151	...	2255	00
	Berlin Ostbahnhof .... d.	...	0914	...	1014	1114	...	1214	1314	...	1414	1514	...	1614	1714	...	1814	1914	...	2014	2114	2114	2214	...	2319	00
0	**Berlin** Hbf .... **840** ‡ d.	...	0925	0958	1025	1125	1158	1225	1325	1400	1425	1525	1600	1625	1725	1800	1825	1925	1958	2025	2125	2125	2225	2308	...	00
	Berlin Zoo .... d.	...	0931	|	1031	1131	|	1231	1331	|	1431	1531	|	1631	1731	|	1831	1931	|	2031	2131	2131	2231	|	...	00
12	**Berlin** Spandau **840** ‡ d.	...	0940	1010	1040	1140	1210	1240	1340	1412	1440	1540	1612	1640	1740	1812	1840	1940	2010	2040	2140	2140	2240	2320	...	01
70	Rathenow .... ‡ a.	...	|	1051	|	|	1253	|	|	1450	|	|	1653	|	|	1856	|	|	2058	|	|	|	|	0001	...	01
104	**Stendal** .... ⊡ a.	0935	|	*1125*	|	|	*1325*	|	|	*1525*	|	|	*1725*	|	|	*1926*	|	|	*2125*	|	|	|	|	0020	...	
	Nauen .... d.	|	1002j	▬	1059	1202j	▬	1259	1402j	▬	1459	1602j	▬	1659	1802j	▬	1859	2002j	▬	2059	2202j	2202j	2256	...	...	
	Wittenberge .... **840** d.	1012	1101	...	1157	1301	...	1357	1501	...	1557	1701	...	1757	1901	...	1957	2101	...	2157	2301	2301	2357	...	...	
	Ludwigslust .... **840** d.	1031	1126	1226	...	1326	1426	...	1526	1626	...	1726	1826	...	1926	2026	...	2126	2256	...	2326	2326	...	...	...	
	Schwerin Hbf .... a.	1053	1157	1258	...	1357	1458	...	1557	1658	...	1757	1858	...	1957	2058	...	2157	2328	...	2357	2357	...	...	...	
	Schwerin Hbf . **830/6** d.	1056	1206	1304	...	1406	1504	...	1606	1704	...	1806	1904	...	2006	2104	...	2206	...	...	...	0006	...	...	...	
	Bad Kleinen .... **830/6** d.	1108	1219	1317	...	1419	1517	...	1619	1717	...	1819	1917	...	2019	2117	...	2219	...	...	...	0032	...	...	...	
	Wismar .... a.	...	1237	1337	...	1437	1537	...	1637	1737	...	1837	1937	...	2037	2137	...	2237	...	...	...	0046	...	...	...	

E – *IC* **2431**. 12 Emden - Bremen - Hannover - Magdeburg - Berlin - Cottbus.

G – *IC* **2432**. 12 Cottbus - Berlin - Magdeburg - Hannover - Bremen - Norddeich Mole.

L – Daily to Sept. 4; ⑤–⑦ Sept. 9 - Oct. 30 (also Oct. 3; not Oct. 2); ⑤ from Nov. 4. *IC* **2238/9**. WARNOW – 12 Leipzig - Magdeburg - Stendal - Rostock (- Warnemünde until Oct. 30) and v.v.

e – Arrives 0710.

j – Arrives 8 – 11 minutes earlier.

q – Not Oct. 2.

r – ⚒ only.

t – Ⓐ (not Oct. 31).

◇ – Operated by Ostdeutsche Eisenbahn.

⊡ – See Table **810** for fast *IC* / *ICE* trains Stendal - Berlin and v.v.

‡ – Additional journeys (◇) Rathenow - Berlin Hbf and v.v.
From Rathenow at 0402 Ⓐ, 0604, 0804, 1004, 1204, 1404, 1604, 18 2004 and 2204. **From Berlin Hbf** at 0458 Ⓐ, 0658, 0858, 1058, 125 1458, 1658, 1858, 2058 and 2200.

MAGDEBURG - BERLIN - FRANKFURT (ODER) - COTTBUS 839

ervices

													P				B	W♣		A			
Magdeburg Hbf d.	...	...	...	...	0524	0607	...	0708	...		1608	...	1659	1708	...	1808	...	1854	1908	2008	2108	2208	2323
Brandenburg Hbf d.	0423	0500	0525	0600	0625j	0700	0725j	0800	0825	and at	1700	1725	1739	1800	1825	1900	1925	|	2000	2100	2158	2258	0019
Potsdam Hbf d.	0451	0525	0555	0625	0655	0725	0755	0825	0855	the same	1725	1755	1800	1825	1855	1925	1955	2011	2025	2125	2225	2325	0048
Berlin Wannsee d.	0458	0532	0602	0632	0702	0732	0802	0832	0902	minutes	1732	1802	1808	1832	1902	1932	2002	2023	2032	2132	2232	2332	0055
Berlin Zoo d.	0511	0545	0615	0645	0715	0745	0815	0845	0915	past	1745	1815	|	1845	1915	1945	2015	2035	2045	2145	2245	2345	0107
Berlin Hbf **1001** d.	0517	0551	0621	0651	0721	0751	0821	0851	0921	each hour	1751	1821	1826	1851	1921	1951	2021	2040	2051	2151	2251	2351	...
Berlin Ostbahnhof **1001** d.	0530	0604	0634	0704	0734	0804	0834	0904	0934	until	1804	1834	1834	1904	1934	2004	2034	2051	2104	2204	2304	0004	...
Fürstenwalde (Spree) d.	0610	0643	0714	0743	0814	0843	0914	0943	1014		1843	1914	...	1943	2014	2043	2114	...	2145	2246	2347	0045	...
Frankfurt (Oder) 1001 a.	0627	0709	0732	0809	0832	0909	0932	1009	1032		1909	1932	...	2009	2032	2109	2132	...	2212	2313	0014	0112	...

		©					B		©♣	N		C										B		⑤⑥f
urt (Oder) **1001** d.	0028	0028	...	0350	...	0450	0534	0557	...	...	0634	0657	0734	0757		1834	1857	1934	1957	2034	2127	2230	2326	2326
nwalde (Spree) d.	0053	0053	...	0416	...	0517	0552	0624	...	...	0652	0724	0752	0824	and at	1852	1924	1952	2024	2052	2153	2255	2352	2352
Ostbahnhof **1001** d.	0129	0129	...	0459	0529	0559	0629	0659	0708	0720	0729	0759	0829	0859	the same	1929	1959	2029	2059	2129	2229	2336	0029	0029
Hbf **1001** d.	0141	0141	*0241*z	0511	0541	0611	0641	0711	0719	0731	0741	0811	0841	0911	minutes	1941	2011	2041	2111	2141	2241	2348	0041	0041
Zoo d.	0146	0147	*0247*z	0517	0547	0617	0647	0717	0725	|	0747	0817	0847	0917	past	1947	2017	2047	2116	2147	2247	2354	0047	0047
Nannsee d.	...	0200	*0300*z	0530	0600	0630	0700	0730	0738	0746	0800	0830	0900	0930	each hour	2000	2030	2100	...	2200	2300	0007	0100	0100
m Hbf d.	...	0209	*0309*z	0539	0609	0639	0709	0739	0746	0755	0809	0839	0909	0939	until	2009	2039	2109	...	2209	2309	0016	0109	0109
enburg Hbf d.	...	0235	0420	0600	0636	0700	0736	0800	|	0815	0836	0900	0936	1000		2036	2100	2138	...	2236	2338	0043	0135	0137
burg Hbf a.	...	...	0517	0649	...	0749	...	0849	0906	0858	...	0949	...	1049		...	2149	2234	...	...	0027	...	...	0225

FRANKFURT (ODER) - COTTBUS

	Ⓐ		Ⓐ					B	A
Frankfurt (Oder) d.	0411	0537	0604	0635	0737	and	2037	2134	2316
Eisenhüttenstadt d.	0431	0558	0619	0658	0758	hourly	2058	2154	2337
Guben d.	0453	0619	0636	0719	0819	until	2119	2214	2357
Cottbus a.	0529	0656	0700	0756	0856		2156	2249	0032

	⚒B		ⒶC					B		
Cottbus d.	0415	0506	0551	0606	and	1906	2006	2111	...	2306
Guben d.	0450	0544	0614	0644	hourly	1944	2043	2146	...	2343
Eisenhüttenstadt d.	0511	0604	0634	0704	until	2004	2104	2207	...	0004
Frankfurt (Oder) a.	0532	0626	0655	0726		2026	2124	2228	...	0024

n Ⓑ conveys [12] Magdeburg - Berlin - Frankfurt (Oder) - Cottbus.
[12] Brandenburg - Berlin - Frankfurt (Oder) - Cottbus and v.v.
[12] Cottbus - Frankfurt (Oder) - Berlin - Magdeburg.
:**2432**. [12] (Cottbus ⚒ -) Berlin - Hannover - Bremen - Norddeich Mole.
:**2431**. [12] Emden - Bremen - Hannover - Berlin (- Cottbus Ⓑ **q**).
)–⑦ (also Oct. 3).

f – Also Oct. 2.
j – 5 minutes later on Ⓐ.
q – Not Oct. 2.
z – © only.

♣ – *HARZ-BERLIN-EXPRESS.* [2] Berlin - Halberstadt - Thale (Table **862**) / Goslar (Table **860**) and v.v. Operated by Veolia Verkehr Sachsen-Anhalt. **DB tickets not valid**.

HAMBURG - BERLIN - DRESDEN 840

	EC	*ICE*	*ICE*	*EC*	*ICE*	*ICE*	*EC*	*ICE*	*IC*	*ICE*	*ICE*	*EC*	*ICE*	*ICE*	*EC*	*ICE*	*ICE*	*EC*	*ICE*	*ICE*	*IC*	*ICE*	*IC*	*IC*
	171	**701**	**1587**	**173**	**703**	**1589**	**379**	**1039**	**1109**	**1209**	**809**	**175**	**707**	**1683**	**177**	**709**	**1685**	**179**	**801**	**803**	**1918**	**1687**	**2071**	**2079**
	⊙	Ⓐ	e❦			❦		③⑦	R❦	❦	⑤❦			❦		❦	❦			⑤f	⑤	❦		T
	P✕	✕	M✕	H✕	✕	M✕	L✕	❦🍷		M✕	✕	P✕	✕	M✕	P✕	✕	M✕	P✕	✕	✕	🍷	M✕	✕	✕
Hamburg Altona d.	...	0512	0620	0636	0721	0819	...	0921	0921	1019	1037	...	1121	1221	1239	1321	1420	1437	1519	1553	...	1618	1639j	...
Hamburg Hbf **830** d.	...	0527	0634	0648	0738	0836	0851	0938	0938	1036	1051	...	1138	1236	1251	1338	1436	1451	1538	1605	...	1636	1651	...
Büchen **830** d.	...	|	|	0715	|	|	0915	|	|	|	1115	...	|	|	1315	|	|	1515	|	|	...	|	1715	...
Ludwigslust **837** d.	...	0613	|	0742	|	|	0942	|	|	|	1142	...	|	|	1342	|	|	1542	|	|	...	|	1742	...
Wittenberge **837** d.	...	0631	|	0802	|	|	1002	|	|	|	1202	...	|	|	1402	|	|	1602	|	|	...	|	1802	...
Berlin Spandau **837** d.	...	0712	0810	0846	0912	1010	1046	1113	1128	1210	1246	...	1312	1410	1446	1512	1610	1646	1712	1745	...	1810	1846	...
Berlin Hbf **837** a.	...	0721	0819	0855	0921	1019	1055	1122	1136	1219	1254	...	1321	1419	1455	1521	1619	1655	1721	1756	...	1819	1855	...
Berlin Hbf **835** d.	0658	|	0827	0900**y**	|	1027	1100**y**	|	|	1227	|	1300**y**	|	1428	1500**y**	|	1627	1700**y**	|	|	1803	1827	1900	1859
Berlin Südkreuz **835** d.	0704	0730	0834	0907**y**	0929	1034	1107**y**	1131	1145	1234	1303	1307**y**	1329	1434	1507**y**	1529	1634	1707**y**	1729	1811	1809	1834	1905	1906
Leipzig Hbf **851** a.	|	...	0943	|	...	1143	|	...	...	1343	...	|	...	1543	|	...	1743	|	...	...	|	1943	...	|
Elsterwerda **843 835** d.	|	...	...	|	...	...	|	...	...	...	...	1425**x**	...	...	|	...	...	1825**x**	...	...	|	...	...	|
Dresden Neustadt a.	|	...	...	|	...	...	|	...	...	...	...	|	...	...	|	...	...	|	...	...	2005**x**	...	...	|
Dresden Hbf **843** a.	0856	...	...	1056**y**	...	...	1256**y**	...	...	...	...	1458	...	...	1656**y**	...	...	1858	...	...	2014**h**	...	...	2058

	IC	*ICE*	*ICE*	*IC*	*IC*	*IC*	*ICE*	*ICE*	*ICE*	*ICE*
	2079	**1717**	**903**	**2073**	**2073**	**2077**	**805**	**1031**	**905**	**907**◊
	U		Ⓑq		⊡	③		Ⓑq		⑤⑦
	✕	E✕	✕	D🍷	D🍷	🍷	✕	❦🍷	✕	w✕
urg Altona d.	...	1720	1819	...	...	...	1921	2020	2137	2237
urg Hbf **830** d.	...	1735	1836	1851	1851	...	1938	2034	2151	2251
n **830** d.	...	|	|	1915	1915	...	|	|	2215	2315
gslust **837** d.	...	1819	|	1942	1942	...	|	2118	2242	2342
berge **837** d.	...	|	|	2002	2002	...	|	|	2303	0002
Spandau **837** d.	...	1913	2010	2046	2046	...	2112	2212	2343	0042
Hbf **837** a.	...	1922	2019	2055	2055	...	2121	2223	2354	0053
Hbf **835** d.	...	1927	2027	2100	2100	2100	2129	|	|	|
Südkreuz **835** d.	1909	1934	2034	2105	2107	2107	2136	2235	0002	0101
zig Hbf **851** a.	|	2043	2143	...	|	|	2248	...	...	...
verda **843 835** d.	2025	...	...	...	|	|	...	...	...	...
en Neustadt a.	2105	...	...	...	2254	2254	...	...	...	...
en Hbf **843** a.	2112	...	...	...	2301	2301	...	...	...	...

	IC	*IC*	*ICE*	*IC*	*ICE*	*IC*	*IC*	*ICE*	*IC*	*IC*
	1978	**1108**	**1618**	**2070**	**908**	**2078**	**2078**	**806**	**2076**	**2072**
	①g	①–⑥			⚒	①–⑥	⚒T		④⑦	⊖
		♥❦	✕	✕	✕	U✕	✕	✕	w🍷	D🍷
Dresden Hbf **843** d.	...	...	...	...	...	0554	0606	...	0654	0654
Dresden Neustadt d.	...	...	...	...	...	0602	0613	...	0701	0701
Elsterwerda **843 835** d.	...	...	...	...	...	0633	|	...	0733**x**	0733**x**
Leipzig Hbf **851** d.	...	...	0510**a**	...	0615	|	|	...	|	|
Berlin Südkreuz **835** d.	0458	0518	0624	0658	0729	0755	0811	0829	0850	0855
Berlin Hbf **835** a.	|	|	0630	|	0734	...	0820	|	0857	0900
Berlin Hbf **837** d.	0506	0526	0638	0706	0742	...	...	0839	...	0906
Berlin Spandau **837** d.	0516	0536	0648	0717	0752	...	...	0849	...	0917
Wittenberge **837** d.	0601	0621	|	0802	|	...	...	|	...	1002
Ludwigslust **837** d.	0621	0641	0741	0821	|	...	...	|	...	1021
Büchen **830** d.	0649	|	|	0849	|	...	...	|	...	1049
Hamburg Hbf **830** a.	0711	0724	0824	0910	0924	...	...	1021	...	1111
Hamburg Altona a.	0728	0739	0839	0922	0942	...	...	1036	...	...

	IC	*ICE*	*ICE*	*ICE*	*EC*	*ICE*	*ICE*	*EC*	*ICE*	*ICE*	*EC*	*ICE*	*IC*	*ICE*	*EC*	*ICE*	*ICE*	*EC*	*ICE*	*ICE*	*EC*	*ICE*	*ICE*	*ICE*	*IC*
	2072	**906**	**1616**	**1626**	**178**	**1684**	**1034**	**176**	**1682**	**800**	**174**	**1208**	**2015**	**802**	**378**	**1588**	**706**	**172**	**1586**	**704**	**170**	**1584**	**898**	**1694**	**61458**
			①–⑥	⑦s		❦	❦		❦			❦	⑦w	❦		❦	Ⓑc		❦	Ⓑ❦		❦	Q	⑤❦	
	D🍷	✕	v❦	E✕	P✕	M✕	🍷	P✕	M✕	✕	P✕	M✕	🍷	✕	L✕	M✕	✕	H✕	M✕	✕	P✕	M✕	✕	M✕	A
			✕																						
en Hbf **843** d.	...	...		...	0856	...	...	1056	...	...	1256	...	1339	...	1456	...	...	1656	...	...	1856	...	...	...	2107
en Neustadt d.	...	...	...	...	|	...	...	|	...	...	|	...	1345	...	|	...	...	|	...	...	|	...	...	...	2114
werda **843 835** d.	...	...	...	...	|	...	...	|	...	...	1333**x**	...	|	...	|	...	...	|	...	...	1933**x**	...	...	...	|
zig Hbf **851** d.	...	0815	...	0915	|	1015	...	|	1215	...	|	1415	|	...	|	1615	...	|	1815	...	|	2015	...	2127	|
Südkreuz **835** d.	0855	0928	1024	1024	1050	1128	1229	1252	1328	1424	1452	1528	1543	...	1652	1728	1829	1852	1928	2024**k**	2050	2128	2233	2236	2309**o**
Hbf **835** a.	0900	0933	|	1030	1058	1133	|	1258	1333	|	1458	1533	1548	...	1658	1733	|	1858	1933	|	2058	2133	|	2241	2340‡
Hbf **837** d.	0906	0942	1039	1039	...	1142	1238	1307	1342	1439	1506	1542	1556	1639	1706	1742	1839	1906	1942	2039	...	2142	2245	2245	...
Spandau **837** d.	0917	0952	1049	1049	...	1152	1248	1317	1352	1449	1517	1552	1605	1649	1717	1752	1849	1917	1952	2049	...	2152	2255	2255	...
berge **837** d.	1002	|	|	|	...	|	|	1402	|	|	1602	|	...	|	1802	|	|	2002	|	|	...	2232	2335	2335	...
gslust **837** d.	1021	|	|	|	...	|	|	1421	|	|	1621	|	...	|	1821	|	|	2021	|	|	...	2250	2353	2353	...
n **830** d.	1049	|	|	|	...	|	|	1449	|	|	1649	|	...	|	1849	|	|	2049	|	|	...	|	|	|	...
urg Hbf **830** a.	1111	1124	1221	1221	...	1324	1422	1511	1524	1621	1711	1724	...	1821	1911	1924	2021	2115	2124	2221	...	2333	0037	0036	...
urg Altona a.	...	1139	1237	1237	...	1339	1439	1525**j**	1540	1638	1724	1739	...	1838	...	1939	2039	2138	2148	2240	...	2349	...	...	...

[2] Praha - Berlin - Köln; conveys 🛏 1, 2 cl. and ▬ 2 cl.
CNL **456** Ⓡ – KOPERNIKUS) Praha - Köln.
JTHLANDE – To / from Westerland (Table **821**).
o / from Eisenach (Table **850**).
[12] and ✕ Budapest - Bratislava - Praha - Dresden - Hamburg and v.v.
[12] and ✕ Praha - Dresden - Hamburg - Kiel and v.v.
[12] and ✕ München - Nürnberg - Berlin - Hamburg and v.v.
o / from Praha (Tables **60/1100**).
lot ⑤.
)②④⑤⑥.
rom Aug. 5.
Jntil Aug. 4.

Ⓐ (not Oct. 31).

c – Also Oct. 1; not Oct. 2.
e – ①–⑥ only.
f – Not July 22 - Sept. 2.
g – Also Oct. 4; not Oct. 3.
h – 2026 from Aug. 5.
j – Not July 25 - Sept. 4.
k – ①–④ only.
o – Until Aug. 4 (also Nov. 18–27). Berlin **Ostbahnhof** (arrival time). Arrives 2343 Nov. 18–27.
q – Not Oct. 2.
s – Also Oct. 3, 31.
v – Not Oct. 3, 31.
w – Also Oct. 3; not Oct. 2.
x – Until Aug. 4.

y – 2–4 minutes later from Aug. 5.

‡ – Not Aug. 1–3, Nov. 18–27. Arrives 2310 from Aug. 5.
⊡ – ①②④⑤⑦ (not Oct. 2).
⊖ – ①②③⑤⑥ (not Oct. 3).
⊙ – Also conveys 🛏 1, 2 cl., ▬ 2 cl. and [2] (*CNL* **457** Ⓡ – KOPERNIKUS) Köln - Berlin - Praha. From Aug. 5 Berlin Hbf d. 0703, Berlin Südkreuz d. 0710, Dresden Hbf a. 0858.
♥ – On ③ (also Sept. 1–3) runs as *ICE* **1038** (departs Berlin stations 6–7 minutes later).
◊ – Train number **1703** on ⑤.
❦ – Service until Sept. 3. From Sept. 4 train number, running dates and timings may vary (details will be updated in the September edition).

841 MAGDEBURG - STENDAL - UELZEN and WITTENBERGE

RE / RB services except where s

km		⚒	Ⓐe		H		Ⓐe			A									Ⓐe	Ⓐe	Ⓒz			Ⓑq		
0	**Magdeburg** Hbf ... d.	0348	...	0508	0553	0608	0638	0708	0808	0858	0903	0908	1008	1103	1108	1208	1303	1308	1408	...	1408	1503	1508	1603	1608	1703
58	Stendal ... a.	0433	...	0555	0632	0656	0726	0756	0856	0933	0942	0956	1056	1142	1156	1256	1342	1356	1453	...	1455	1542	1556	1642	1656	1742
58	Stendal ... d.	0438	0500	0600	0634	0700e	0729	0800	0900r	0935	0944	1000	...	1144	1200	1300e	1343	1400	1456	1510	...	1544	1600	1644	1700e	1744
113	**Wittenberge** ... a.	|	0542	0642	|	0742e	|	0842	0942r	1010	|	1042	...	|	1242	1342e	|	1442	|	1553	...	|	1642	|	1742e	|
116	Salzwedel ... d.	0519	...	...	0714	...	0806	...	...	...	1015	...	...	1214	...	...	1414	...	1536	...	...	1614	...	1714	...	1814
167	**Uelzen** ... a.	0550	...	...	0746	...	...	...	...	...	1046	...	...	1246	...	...	1446	...	...	...	...	1646	...	1747	...	1847

Magdeburg Hbf ... d.	1808	1903	1908	2008	2108	2139	2214	2318
Stendal ... a.	1856	1942	1956	2056	2156	2218	2302	0005
Stendal ... d.	1900e	1944	2000	2107b	2200	2230b	...	*0032*v
Wittenberge ... a.	1942e	|	2042	2148b	2242	|	...	|
Salzwedel ... d.	...	2014	...	...	...	2311b	...	*0113*v
Uelzen ... a.	...	2046	...	...	...	...	...	...

					⚒					⚒r				
Uelzen ... d.	...	...	...	...	0619	...	...	...	0902	...	...	...	1102	...
Salzwedel ... d.	...	...	0554	...	0652	...	...	...	0934	...	1010	...	1136	...
Wittenberge ... d.	...	0510e	|	0610e	|	0710	0806e	0910	|	1010	|	1110	|	...
Stendal ... a.	...	0551e	0634	0651e	0721	0751	0847e	0951	1008	1051	1050	1151	1207	...
Stendal ... d.	0456	0556	0642	0657	0724e	0756	0858	0956	1010	...	1056	1156	1210	1256
Magdeburg Hbf ... a.	0543	0643	0725	0743	0813e	0843	0944	1043	1051	...	1143	1243	1251	1343

					A					Ⓑq			Ⓐe			H	Ⓑb	
Uelzen ... d.	1302	...	...	1502	...	...	...	1702	...	1802	...	1902	...	...	...	2103	...	...
Salzwedel ... d.	1335	...	...	1535	...	...	...	1735	...	1835	...	1935	...	2021	...	2135	...	...
Wittenberge ... d.	|	1410e	1510	|	1548	1610e	1710	|	1810e	|	1910	|	2010	|	2110	|	2210	2310
Stendal ... a.	1406	1451e	1551	1607	1622	1651e	1751	1807	1851e	1914	1951	2007	2051	2104	2151	2214	2251	2351
Stendal ... d.	1410	1456	1556	1610	1624	1656	1756	1810	1856	...	1956	2010	...	2107	2156	2215	...	2352
Magdeburg Hbf ... a.	1451	1543	1643	1651	1700	1743	1843	1851	1943	...	2043	2051	...	2156	2243	2255	...	0036

2nd class only	*IRE* **4276** E		*IRE* **4278** ⑦w
Berlin Hbf ... d.	0802‡	...	1320‡
Stendal ... d.	0903	...	1416
Salzwedel ... d.	0934	...	1455
Uelzen ... a.	1003s	...	1529s
Lüneburg ... a.	1029s	...	1548s
Hamburg Hbf ... a.	1104	...	1621

2nd class only	*IRE* **4273** D	*IRE* **4275** ⑦w	*IRE* **4277** F
Hamburg Hbf ... d.	0655	1241	1642
Lüneburg ... d.	0735u	1314u	1714u
Uelzen ... d.	0757u	1331u	1733u
Salzwedel ... d.	0821	1355	1812
Stendal ... a.	0853	1437	1841
Berlin Hbf ... a.	0942*	1542*	1942*

A – *IC* **2238/9**. Daily to Sept. 4; ⑤–⑦ Sept. 9 - Oct. 30 (also Oct. 3; not Oct. 2); ⑤ from Nov. 4. (12) Leipzig - Halle - Schwerin - Rostock (- Warnemünde until Oct. 30) and v.v.
D – ①–⑥ (also Oct. 2; not Oct. 3).
E – ④–⑥ to June 4; ①–⑥ from June 9 (also Oct. 2; not Oct. 3).
F – ④⑤ to June 3; Ⓐ from June 9.
H – From / to Halle (Table 866).

b – Ⓑ (not Oct. 2, 30).
e – Ⓐ (not Oct. 31).
h – 1924 July 23 - Aug. 28.

q – Not Oct. 2.
r – ⚒ (not Oct. 31).
s – Calls to set down only.
u – Calls to pick up only.
v – Mornings of ⑦ (also Oct. 3, 31).
w – Also Oct. 3; not Oct. 2.
z – Also Oct. 31.

* – Also calls at Berlin Spandau, Zoo and Ostbahnhof.
‡ – Also calls at Berlin Ostbahnhof, Zoo and Spandau.

842 LEIPZIG - DRESDEN

km		*ICE* **1659** ①g		*RE* **16501** ⚒r	*RE* **16503** ⚒r	*RE* **16503**		*CNL* **40470** 🅁 C🍷	*IC* **60470** C 2		*RE* **16505** ⚒r	*RE* **16507**	*IC* **2043** Ⓐ G	*RE* **16509**	*ICE* **1553** ①–⑥ e A ✕	*RE* **16511**	*IC* **2447** B	*RE* **16513**	*ICE* **1555** ✕	*RE* **16515**	*IC* **2445** ⚒ K	*RE* **16517**	*ICE* **1597** † ¶✕
	Frankfurt Flughafen § **850** .. d.	2102p	...	...	...	...	...	...	...	...	...	...	...	...		...	...	...	...	...	...	...	0902
	Frankfurt (Main) Hbf **850** .... d.	2119p	...	...	...	...	...	0054‡	0054‡	...	...	...	...	...	0458g	...	...	...	0718	...	...	...	0919
0	**Leipzig** Hbf ... d.	0031	...	...	0500	...	...	|	0555	...	0600	0700	0729	0800	0831	0900	0929	1000	1031	1100	1129	1200	1231
26	Wurzen ... d.	|	...	...	0518	...	...	|	|	...	0618	0718	|	0818	|	0918	|	1018	|	1118	|	1218	|
53	Oschatz ... d.	|	...	...	0536	...	...	|	|	...	0636	0736	|	0836	|	0936	|	1036	|	1136	|	1236	|
66	Riesa ... d.	0101	...	0445	0545	0545	...	0630s	0632	...	0645	0745	0801	0845	0901	0945	1001	1045	1101	1145	1201	1245	1301
102	Coswig ... **843 856 857** d.	|	...	0513	0613	0613	...	|	|	...	0713	0813	|	0913	|	1013	|	1113	|	1213	|	1313	|
110	Radebeul Ost ... **857** d.	|	...	0519	0619	0619	...	|	|	...	0719	0819	|	0919	|	1019	|	1119	|	1219	|	1319	|
116	**Dresden** Neustadt ... **856/7** a.	0130	...	0525	0625	0625	...	0659	0659	...	0725	0825	0830	0925	0930	1025	1030	1125	1130	1225	1230	1325	1330
120	**Dresden** Hbf ... **843 856 857** a.	0137	...	0532	0632	0632	...	0706	0706	...	0732	0832	0837	0932	0937	1032	1037	1132	1137	1232	1237	1332	1337

	RE **16519**	*IC* **2443** K	*RE* **16521**	*ICE* **1559** ¶✕	*RE* **16523**	*IC* **2441** K	*RE* **16525**	*ICE* **1651** ¶✕	*RE* **16527**	*IC* **2049** K	*RE* **16529**	*ICE* **1653** ¶✕	*RE* **16531**	*IC* **2047** Ⓑ K	*RE* **16533**	*ICE* **1655** ¶✕	*RE* **16535**	*IC* **2045** Ⓑq K		*IC* **2435** ⑥h S	*ICE* **1657** Ⓑq ¶✕	*RE* **16539**	
Frankfurt Flughafen § **850** ... d.	...	...	...	1102	...	...	...	1302	...	...	...	1502	...	...	...	1702	...	...	...	...	1902	...	...
Frankfurt (Main) Hbf **850** ... d.	...	...	...	1119	...	...	...	1319	...	...	...	1520	...	...	...	1720	...	...	...	...	1919	...	...
Leipzig Hbf ... d.	1300	1329	1400	1431	1500	1529	1600	1631	1700	1729	1800	1831	1900	1929	2000	2031	2100	2130	...	2231	2237	2300	...
Wurzen ... d.	1318	|	1418	|	1518	|	1618	|	1718	|	1818	|	1918	|	2018	|	2118	|	...	|	|	2318	...
Oschatz ... d.	1336	|	1436	|	1536	|	1636	|	1736	|	1836	|	1936	|	2036	|	2136	|	...	|	|	2336	...
Riesa ... d.	1345	1401	1445	1501	1545	1601	1645	1701	1745	1801	1845	1901	1945	2001	2045	2101	2145	2202	...	2301	2306	2345	...
Coswig ... **843 856 857** d.	1413	|	1513	|	1613	|	1713	|	1813	|	1913	|	2013	|	2113	|	2213	|	...	|	|	0013	...
Radebeul Ost ... **857** d.	1419	|	1519	|	1619	|	1719	|	1819	|	1919	|	2019	|	2119	|	2219	|	...	|	|	0019	...
Dresden Neustadt ... **856/7** a.	1425	1430	1525	1532	1625	1630	1725	1730	1825	1830	1925	1930	2025	2030	2125	2130	2225	2230	...	2332	2334	0025	...
Dresden Hbf ... **843 856 857** a.	1432	1437	1532	1539	1632	1637	1732	1737	1832	1837	1932	1937	2032	2037	2132	2137	2232	2237	...	2339	2341	0032	...

	RE **16500** ⚒r		*IC* **2044** Ⓐ K	*RE* **16502**		*ICE* **1654** ⚒ ¶✕	*RE* **16504** ⚒r		*IC* **2046** ⚒ K	*RE* **16506**	*ICE* **1652** ¶✕	*RE* **16508**	*IC* **2048** K	*RE* **16510**	*ICE* **1650** ¶✕	*RE* **16512**	*IC* **2440** K	*RE* **16514**	*ICE* **1558** ¶✕	*RE* **16516**	*IC* **2442** K	*RE* **16518**	*ICE* **1556** ¶✕
Dresden Hbf ... **843 856 857** d.	0415	...	0520	0515	...	0620	0615	...	0720	0715	0820	0815	0920	0915	1020	1015	1120	1115	1220	1215	1320	1315	1420
Dresden Neustadt ... **856/7** d.	0422	...	0527	0522	...	0627	0622	...	0727	0722	0827	0822	0927	0922	1027	1022	1127	1122	1227	1222	1327	1322	1427
Radebeul Ost ... **857** d.	0429	...	|	0529	...	|	0629	...	|	0729	|	0829	|	0929	|	1029	|	1129	|	1229	|	1329	|
Coswig ... **843 856 857** d.	0437	...	|	0537	...	|	0637	...	|	0737	|	0837	|	0937	|	1037	|	1137	|	1237	|	1337	|
Riesa ... d.	0505	...	0557	0605	...	0657	0705	...	0757	0805	0857	0905	0957	1005	1057	1105	1157	1205	1257	1305	1357	1405	1457
Oschatz ... d.	0514	...	|	0614	...	|	0714	...	|	0814	|	0914	|	1014	|	1114	|	1214	|	1314	|	1414	|
Wurzen ... d.	0531	...	|	0631	...	|	0731	...	|	0831	|	0931	|	1031	|	1131	|	1231	|	1331	|	1431	|
Leipzig Hbf ... a.	0550	...	0627	0650	...	0726	0750	...	0828	0850	0926	0950	1028	1050	1126	1150	1228	1250	1326	1350	1428	1450	1526
Frankfurt (Main) Hbf **850** ... a.	...	...	...	...	...	1037	...	...	...	...	1237	...	...	...	1437	...	...	...	1637	...	...	...	1837
Frankfurt Flughafen § **850** ... a.	...	...	...	...	...	1055	...	...	...	...	1255	...	...	...	1455	...	...	...	1655	...	...	...	1855

	IC **2444** K	*RE* **16522**	*ICE* **1594** ⑥h ✕	*ICE* **1554** Ⓑq R✕	*RE* **16524**	*IC* **2446** K	*RE* **16526**	*ICE* **1552** ✕	*RE* **16528**	*IC* **2030** Ⓑq H	*RE* **16530**	*ICE* **1550** ⑦w ✕	*RE* **16532**		*CNL* **458** 🅁 C🍷	*IC* **60458** C 2		*RE* **16536**		*RE* **16538**			
Dresden Hbf ... **843 856 857** d.	1520	1515	1620	1620	1615	1720	1715	1820	1815	1920	1915	2020	2015	...	2054	2054	...	2215	...	2315	...	...	...
Dresden Neustadt ... **856/7** d.	1527	1522	1627	1627	1622	1727	1722	1827	1822	1927	1922	2027	2022	...	2102	2102	...	2222	...	2322	...	...	...
Radebeul Ost ... **857** d.	|	1529	|	|	1629	|	1729	|	1829	|	1929	|	2029	...	|	|	...	2229	...	2329	...	...	...
Coswig ... **843 856 857** d.	|	1537	|	|	1637	|	1737	|	1837	|	1937	|	2037	...	|	|	...	2237	...	2337	...	...	...
Riesa ... d.	1557	1605	1657	1657	1705	1757	1805	1857	1905	1957	2005	2057	2105	...	2134u	2134	...	2305	...	0005	...	...	...
Oschatz ... d.	|	1614	|	|	1714	|	1814	|	1914	|	2014	|	2114	...	|	|	...	2314	...	...	...	...	...
Wurzen ... d.	|	1631	|	|	1731	|	1831	|	1931	|	2031	|	2131	...	|	|	...	2331	...	...	...	...	...
Leipzig Hbf ... a.	1628	1650	1726	1726	1750	1828	1850	1926	1950	2028	2050	2126	2150	...	|	2226	...	2350	...	...	...	...	...
Frankfurt (Main) Hbf **850** ... a.	...	...	2036	2036	...	...	...	2254	...	...	...	0037	...	...	0359‡	0359‡	...	...	...	...	...	...	...
Frankfurt Flughafen § **850** ... a.	...	...	2057	...	...	...	...	...	...	...	...	...	...	...	...	...	...	...	...	...	...	...	...

A – (12) and ✕ (Frankfurt ①g -) Eisenach - Leipzig - Dresden.
B – (12) (Bielefeld ①g -) (Hannover ⚒ -) Leipzig - Dresden.
C – CANOPUS – 🛏 1, 2 cl. and 🛏 2 cl. (*CNL* **458/40470** 🅁) Praha - Basel - Zürich and v.v.; (2) (*IC* **60458/60470**) Praha - Basel - Zürich and v.v.
G – From Magdeburg (Table **866**).
H – To Hannover (Table **866**).
K – (12) Köln - Dortmund - Hannover - Magdeburg - Dresden and v.v.
R – (12) and ✕ Saarbrücken - Mannheim - Frankfurt - Dresden and v.v.
S – (12) Emden - Bremen - Hannover - Magdeburg - Dresden.

g – ① (also Oct. 4; not Oct. 3).
h – Also Oct. 2.
p – Previous day.
q – Not Oct. 2.
r – Not Oct. 31, Nov. 16.
s – Stops to set down only.
u – Stops to pick up only.
w – Also Oct. 3; not Oct. 2.

‡ – Frankfurt (Main) **Süd**.
¶ – To / from Wiesbaden (Table **911**)
§ – Frankfurt Flughafen Fernbahnho

843 ELSTERWERDA - CHEMNITZ and DRESDEN; DÖBELN - LEIPZIG

RB services

⊡	Ⓐt	Ⓐf		Ⓐf		Ⓐf		Ⓐt		Ⓐt		Ⓐt		Ⓐf		Ⓐf			Ⓐf		†w	Ⓑ	⚒f	
Elsterwerda d.	...	0514	...	0614	...	0714	0814	...	1014	...	1214	...	1414	1514	1614	1714	...	1814	1914	2014	2114	...	2226	...
Riesa a.	...	0539	...	0639	...	0739	0839	...	1039	...	1239	...	1439	1539	1639	1739	...	1839	1939	2039	2139	...	2251	...
Riesa d.	0449	0549	0549	0649	0649	0749	0849	0949	1049	1149	1249	1349	1449	1549	1649	1749	1749	1849	1949	2049	2149	2149	2252	2252
Döbeln Hbf d.	0511	0611	0611	0711	0711	0811	0911	1011	1111	1211	1311	1411	1511	1611	1711	1811	1811	1911	2011	2111	2211	2211	2317	2317
Chemnitz Hbf a.	0551	0649	0649	0749	0749	0849	0949	1049	1149	1249	1349	1449	1549	1649	1749	1849	1849	1949	2049	2149	2253	2253	2358	2358

⊡	Ⓐf		Ⓐf		Ⓐt		Ⓐt		Ⓐt		Ⓐf			Ⓐf		Ⓐf		Ⓑ		⑥		Ⓐf			
nitz Hbf d.	0409	0509	0509	0609	0705	0809	0909	1009	1109	1209	1309	1409	1509	1509	1609	1709	1809	1909	2009	2009	...	2136	2236	...	...
n Hbf d.	0445	0545	0545	0645	0745	0845	0945	1045	1145	1245	1345	1445	1545	1545	1645	1745	1845	1945	2045	2045	...	2217	2317	...	...
a.	0509	0609	0609	0709	0809	0909	1009	1109	1209	1309	1409	1509	1609	1609	1709	1809	1909	2009	2109	2109	...	2240	2340	...	...
d.	0515	...	0615	0715	...	0915	...	1115	...	1315	1415	1515	...	1615	1715	1815	1915	2015	...	2115	...	2244	...	...	...
rwerda a.	0537	...	0637	0737	...	0937	...	1137	...	1337	1437	1537	...	1637	1737	1837	1937	2037	...	2137	...	2306	...	...	...

	Ⓐ		Ⓐf		⊠		
Elsterwerda-Biehla d.	0440	0540e	0640	0740	and every	2140	*2321*
Elsterwerda d.	0444	0544	0644	0744	**two** hours	2144	2344
Coswig ▷ d.	0523	0623	0723	0823	until	2223	0023
Dresden Hbf ▷ a.	0544	0644	0744	0844		2244	0044

		Ⓐf			⊠	⊠		Ⓐ				
Dresden Hbf ▷ d.	0508	0608	0708	0908	1108	1308	1508	1608	1708	1908	2108	2308
Coswig ▷ d.	0530	0630	0730	0930	1130	1330	1530	1630	1730	1930	2130	2330
Elsterwerda a.	0609	0709	0809	1009	1209	1409	1609	1709	1809	2009	2209	0009
Esterwerda-Biehla a.	0613	0713	0813	1013	1213	1413	1613	1713	1813	2013	...	...

	Ⓐt	Ⓐt					
Döbeln Hbf d.	0451	0551	0651	and hourly	2051	...	...
Leisnig d.	0503	0603	0703	on Ⓐt,	2103	...	...
Großbothen d.	0518	0618	0718	every **two**	2118	...	...
Grimma ob Bf d.	0525	0625	0725	hours on	2125	2306	...
Leipzig Hbf a.	0600	0700	0800	Ⓒ**w** until	2200	2339	...

	Ⓐt				
Leipzig Hbf d.	0506	0606	and hourly	2006	2206
Grimma ob Bf d.	0540	0640	on Ⓐt,	2040	2240
Großbothen d.	0546	0646	every **two**	2046	2246
Leisnig d.	0604	0704	hours on	2104	2300
Döbeln Hbf d.	0617	0717	Ⓒ**w** until	2117	2213

e – Ⓐ only.
w – Also Oct. 31.
f – Not Oct. 31.
t – Not Oct. 31, Nov. 16.
⊡ – Operator: Mitteldeutsche Regiobahn.
▷ – See also Tables **842, 856, 857**.

July 24 - Sept. 10 the following trains are replaced by 🚌 Coswig - Dresden and v.v.: 0940/1140 from Elsterwerda-Biehla, 1108/1308 from Dresden (🚌 departs Dresden 1040/1240).

844 STRALSUND - OSTSEEBAD BINZ / SASSNITZ

RB services except where shown

	Ⓐt		Ⓐt	Ⓐt	Ad	A			Ad	A			*IC* 2184 ⚒ 🍷♦	Ad	A			Ad	A			*IC* 2212 🍷♦	Ad	A
Rostock Hbf **830** d.	...	0456	...	0554	...	...	0700	...	...	...	0901	...	0938	...	...	1101	...	...	...	1301	...	1317	...	...
Stralsund Hbf d.	0501	0601	...	0702	0702	...	0801	...	0901	...	1001	...	1038	1101	...	1201	...	1301	...	1401	...	1413	1501	...
Bergen auf Rügen d.	0530	0630	...	0731	0731	...	0830	...	0930	...	1030	...	1106	1130	...	1230	...	1330	...	1430	...	1441	1530	...
Lietzow (Rügen) d.	0538	0638	0641	0739	0739	0742	0838	0841	0938	0941	1038	1041	|	1138	1141	1238	1241	1338	1341	1438	1441	|	1538	1541
Ostseebad Binz a.	|	|	0655	|	|	0756	|	0856	0953j	|	|	1056	1132	1153	|	|	1255	1355	|	|	1455	1501	1553	|
Sassnitz a.	0552	0652	...	0753	0753	...	0852	...	...	0955	1052	...	...	...	1155	1252	...	...	1355	1452	...	...	...	1555

	ICE 1535 Ⓒ ✕♦			*IC* 2376 ⑥ ♦	*ICE* 1735 ✕♦	*IC* 2255 ①–④ ♠B	Ad	A			*ICE* 208 Ⓑ ✕♦	*ICE* 1537 ⑥ ✕♦	*IC* 2257 ⒷD B	Ad	A			*IC* 2259 ⑦E B	*IC* 2426 ⑤F B	Ad	A	*IC* 1970 ⑤ B			Ⓑ
stock Hbf **830** d.	...	1501	...	1538	...	...	...	...	1701	...	...	...	...	...	...	1901	...	...	...	...	...	...	2101	...	...
sund Hbf d.	1556	1601	...	1632	1646	1646	1701	...	1801	...	1839	1839	1839	1901	...	2001	...	2010	2012	2101	...	2114	2202	...	2301
en auf Rügen d.	1620	1632	...	1657	1712	1712	1730	...	1830	...	1903	1904	1904	1930	...	2030	...	2040	2040	2130	...	2141	2231	...	2330
ow (Rügen) d.	|	1640	1643	|	|	|	1738	1741	1838	1841	|	|	|	1938	1941	2038	2041	|	|	2138	2141	|	2239	2242	...
tseebad Binz a.	1640	|	1657	1720	1733	1732	1755	|	|	1855	1934	1934	1934	1953	|	|	2055	2100	2102	2153	|	2200	|	2256	...
nitz a.	...	1654	...	...	...	...	...	1755	1852	...	...	...	...	...	1955	2052	...	...	...	...	2155	...	2253	...	...

	Ⓐt				Ⓐt	⚒t			A	Ad	*IC* 2250 ①–⑤ ★B	*ICE* 1630 ✕♦	*ICE* 1730 ①–④ ✕♦			A	Ad	*IC* 2213 🍷♦	*ICE* 1513 ✕♦	*IC* 2252 ❦B			A	Ad
Sassnitz d.	0400	...	0503	...	...	0601	...	0703	...	0803	...	...	...	...	0903	1000	...	...	...	...	...	1103	1200	...
Ostseebad Binz d.	|	...	|	...	0600	|	0702	|	0802	|	0844	0844	0844	0902	|	|	1004	1026	1044	1044	1102	|	|	1204
Lietzow (Rügen) d.	0414	...	0518	...	0613	0616	0715	0718	0815	0818	|	|	|	0915	0918	1014	1018	|	|	|	1115	1118	1214	1218
Bergen auf Rügen d.	0423	...	0527	...	...	0625	...	0727	...	0827	0908	0908	0908	...	0927	...	1027	1055	1106	1106	...	1127	...	1227
Stralsund Hbf a.	0451	...	0555	...	...	0653	...	0755	...	0855	0931	0931	0931	...	0955	...	1055	1119	1130	1130	...	1155	...	1255
Rostock Hbf **830** a.	0548	...	0654	...	...	...	...	0855	...	...	...	...	...	...	1055	...	...	1219	...	...	...	1255	...	...

	IC 2377 ♥ ♦	*ICE* 1536 ⑦ ✕♦			A	Ad			A	Ad			A	Ad			A	Ad			A	Ad			
nitz d.	...	...	...	1303	1400	...	...	1503	1600	...	1700	...	1800	...	...	1903	2000	...	...	2106	2200	...	...	...	...
tseebad Binz d.	1215	1254	1302	|	|	1404	1502	|	|	1604	|	1704	|	1804	1902	|	|	2004	2105	|	|	2204	...	...	...
ow (Rügen) d.	|	|	1315	1318	1414	1418	1515	1518	1614	1618	1714	1721	1814	1818	1915	1918	2014	2018	2118	2121	2214	2218	...	...	...
en auf Rügen d.	1242	1315	...	1327	...	1427	...	1527	...	1627	...	1730	...	1827	...	1927	...	2027	...	2130	...	2227	...	...	...
sund Hbf a.	1306	1338	...	1355	...	1455	...	1555	...	1655	...	1758	...	1855	...	1955	...	2055	...	2158	...	2255	...	...	...
stock Hbf **830** a.	1419	...	...	1455	...	...	...	1655	...	1758h	...	1855	...	...	...	2055	...	...	...	2255	...	...	...	...	...

NOTES (LISTED BY TRAIN NUMBER)

- Ⓑ from Sept. 4 (not Oct. 2). 🚃12 and ✕ Innsbruck - München - Leipzig - Berlin - Ostseebad Binz.
– From Sept. 5. 🚃12 and ✕ Ostseebad Binz - Berlin - Leipzig - München.
– Ⓒ (not Nov. 6, 13, 20, 27, Dec. 4). 🚃12 and ✕ Frankfurt - Erfurt - Berlin - Ostseebad Binz.
– 🚃12 and ✕ Ostseebad Binz - Berlin - Erfurt - Frankfurt.
– ⑥ (also Oct. 2). 🚃12 and ✕ Stuttgart - Frankfurt - Erfurt - Berlin - Ostseebad Binz.
– ⑥⑦ to Aug. 28; ⑤–⑦ from Sept. 3 (also Oct. 3). 🚃12 and ✕ Ostseebad Binz - Berlin - Erfurt - Frankfurt.
– ①–④ Sept. 5 - Oct. 31 (not Oct. 3). 🚃12 and ✕ Ostseebad Binz - Berlin - Erfurt.
– ⑤ (Ⓐ Sept. 2 - Oct. 31). 🚃12 and ✕ Erfurt - Berlin - Ostseebad Binz.
– ⚒ to Oct. 29. 🚃12 and 🍷 (Hannover Ⓐ -) Hamburg - Ostseebad Binz.
– RÜGEN – 🚃12 and 🍷 Koblenz - Köln - Hamburg - Ostseebad Binz.
– RÜGEN – 🚃12 and 🍷 Ostseebad Binz - Hamburg - Köln - Stuttgart.
– 🚃12 and 🍷 Karlsruhe - Frankfurt - Hannover - Hamburg - Ostseebad Binz. Train number **2086** July 23 - Aug. 27.
– 🚃12 and 🍷 Ostseebad Binz - Hamburg - Hannover - Frankfurt. Train number **2285** July 18 - Sept. 2.

A – Daily to Oct. 2; ①–⑤ from Oct. 4 (not Oct. 31).
B – From / to Berlin (Table **845**).
D – Ⓑ to Sept. 2.
E – ⑦ to Aug. 28.
F – ⑤ to Oct. 28.
d – Runs daily Stralsund - Bergen auf Rügen and v.v.
h – ①–④ (not Oct. 3, 31).
j – 0957 on ⑥ to Oct. 1.
t – Not Oct. 31.
❦ – Until Sept. 4.
★ – ①–⑤ to Sept. 2.
♠ – ①–④ to Sept. 1.
♥ – Daily to Oct. 30; ⑦ from Nov. 6.

844a BERGEN AUF RÜGEN - PUTBUS - LAUTERBACH and RÜGENSCHE BÄDERBAHN

ßnitztalbahn

SEE NOTE ★		r								r
Bergen auf Rügen d.	0740	0840	0940	1040	1140	1340	1540	1740	1940	2040
Putbus a.	0749	0849	0949	1049	1149	1349	1549	1749	1949	2049
Lauterbach Mole a.	0754	...	0954	1054	1154	1354	1554	1754	1954r	...

SEE NOTE ★	Ⓐt	Ⓒz		r						
Lauterbach Mole d.	0604	0704	0800	...	1000	1104	1304	1504	1704	1904
Putbus d.	0611	0711	0811	0854	1011	1111	1311	1511	1711	1911
Bergen auf Rügen a.	0620	0720	0820	0903	1020	1120	1320	1520	1720	1920

ENSCHE BÄDERBAHN — **SUMMER SERVICE VALID UNTIL OCTOBER 3.** Please note that Binz Lokalbahn station is situated 2½ km from Ostseebad Binz DB station.

										r
Lauterbach Mole d.	...	...	...	1122	1322	1522	...	1722	1922	...
Putbus a.	...	...	...	1129	1329	1529	...	1729	1929	...
Putbus d.	0808	...	1008	1208	1408	1608	...	1808	2008	...
Binz Lokalbahn ♥ d.	0840	0944	1040	1240	1440	1640	1744	1840	2040	2244
Sellin (Rügen) Ost ♥ d.	0909	1013	1109	1309	1509	1709	1813	1909	2109	2313
Göhren (Rügen) ♥ a.	0923	1027	1123	1323	1523	1723	1827	1923	2123	2327

										r
Göhren (Rügen) ♥ d.	0849	0953	1153	1353	1553	1649	1753	1849	1953	2149
Sellin (Rügen) Ost. ♥ d.	0907	1011	1211	1411	1611	1707	1811	1907	2011	2207
Binz Lokalbahn ♥ d.	0933	1040	1240	1440	1640	1733	1840	1936	2040	2233
Putbus a.	...	1106	1306	1506	1706	...	1906	2002	2106	...
Putbus d.	...	1111	1311	1511	1711	...	1911	...	...	...
Lauterbach Mole a.	...	1117	1317	1517	1717	...	1917	...	...	...

Until Sept. 4.
Not Oct. 31.
Also Oct. 31.

♥ – Additional journeys Binz Lokalbahn - Göhren:
From Binz at 1144, 1344 and 1544.
From Göhren at 1049, 1249 and 1449.

★ – Additional journeys **until Sept. 4** Bergen - Putbus - Lauterbach and v.v.:
From Bergen auf Rügen at 1240, 1440, 1640 and 1840.
From Lauterbach at 1200, 1400, 1600, 1800 and 2000.

845 LUTHERSTADT WITTENBERG - BERLIN - STRALSUND

RE services except where sh

km																								
					IC								*ICE*			*ICE*	*IC*		*ICE*			*ICE*	*IC*	
					2217								**1731**			**1524**	**2253**		**1535**			**1735**	**2255**	
		Ⓒ		⚒	Ⓐ								⑥Q			⑥B	⑥❦		Ⓒ	Ⓒ	Ⓐ	L	①–④	
					N				¶	S			✕			✕	🍷		G✕			✕	R‡🍷	S
0	**Lutherstadt Wittenberg 851** d.	0025	...	...	...	...	...	...	0613	...		0812	...	...	1012	1052	...	...	...	1212	1214	...	...	...
	Falkenberg (Elster) d.	|	...	...	...	...	...	0443	|	...	0643	|	...	0843	|	|	...	1043	...	|	|	...	...	...
32	Jüterbog d.	0053	...	...	...	...	0434	0536	0641	...	0733n	0842	...	0936	1041	|	...	1136	...	1241	1241	...	...	...
45	Luckenwalde d.	0100	...	...	...	...	0441	0544	0649	...	0740n	0850	...	0944	1049	|	...	1144	...	1249	1249	...	...	...
91	**Berlin** Südkreuz **851** d.	0148	...	...	...	...	0522	0621	0725	...	0821	0922	0856	1022	1121	1128	1133	1221	1256	1321	1321	1334	1331	...
97	**Berlin** Hbf **851** d.	0154	...	...	...	0421	0531	0632	0734	...	0830	0932	0942	1032	1132	1141	1141	1232	1304	1332	1332	1342	1342	...
101	**Berlin** Gesundbrunnen d.	...	...	...	...	0427	0537	0638	0740	0805	0838	0939	|	1038	1139	1147	1147	1238	|	1338	1338	1348	1348	1427
122	Bernau (b. Berlin) d.	...	...	...	...	0442	0551	0654	0755	0822	0854	0954	1001	1054	1154	1203	1203	1254	1323	1354	1354	1403	1403	1444
144	Eberswalde Hbf d.	...	...	...	...	0507	0607	0709	0810	0839	0909	1009	1020	1109	1209	1218	1218	1309	1339	1409	1409	1418	1419	1503
170	Angermünde a.	...	...	...	...	0526	0626	0728	0830	0854	0928	1028	1035	1128	1228	|	1233	1328	1354	1428	1428	1435	1436	1523
170	Angermünde d.	...	...	...	...	0533	0634	0733	0834	...	0933	1034	1037	1133	1234	|	1235	1333	1356	1434	1434	1437	1438	...
193	**Schwedt** (Oder) a.	...	...	...	...	|	0656	|	0856	...	|	1056	|	|	1258	|	|	|	|	1456	1456	|	|	...
	Prenzlau d.	...	...	...	...	0601	...	0801	...	...	1001	...	1100	1201	...	1257	1259	1401	1420	...	...	1500	1501	...
	Pasewalk d.	...	...	0419	...	0621	...	0819	...	...	1019	...	1116	1219	...	1314	1315	1419	1436	...	...	1517	1517	...
	Anklam d.	...	...	0450	...	0652	...	0851	...	...	1051	...	1142	1251	...	1343	1343	1451	1503	...	...	1543	1543	...
	Züssow **846** d.	...	...	0504	...	0706	...	0905	...	...	1105	...	1154	1305	...	1355	1355	1505	1517	...	...	1555	1555	...
	Greifswald **846** d.	...	...	0520	0703	0722	...	0920	...	...	1120	...	1207	1320	...	1408	1409	1520	1530	...	...	1608	1608	...
	Stralsund Hbf **846** a.	...	...	0541	0724	0744	...	0941	...	...	1141	...	1226	1341	...	1428	1429	1541	1549	...	...	1629	1629	...

		ICE	*ICE*	*IC*		*ICE*	*IC*	*IC*			*ICE*	*IC*											
		1537	**208**	**2257**		**1539**	**2259**	**2426**			**1739**	**1970**											
		⑥k	⑧J	⑧❦		†♥	⑦❦	⑤			①–④	⑤				⑤			①–④	⑥	⑤⑦	⑧	⑦	
		E✕	✕	‡🍷		T✕	🍷	🍷	S		D✕	‡⊗		⊖		S			t		w		w	
Lutherstadt Wittenberg 851 d.	1412	...	1452	...	...	...	...	...	...	1612	...	...	...	1812	...	...	2012	...	...	...	...	...	...	2225
Falkenberg (Elster) d.	|	...	|	...	1443	...	...	...	...	|	...	...	1643	|	1843	...	|	2043	2043	2043	...	...	...	|
Jüterbog d.	1441	...	|	...	1536	...	...	...	...	1641	...	...	1736	1841	1936	...	2041	2136	2136	2136	...	...	...	2252
Luckenwalde d.	1449	...	|	...	1544	...	...	...	...	1649	...	...	1744	1849	1944	...	2049	2144	2144	2144	...	...	...	2300
Berlin Südkreuz **851** d.	1521	1456	1528	1533	1621	1656	1647	...	...	1721	1734	...	1821	1921	2021	...	2121	2221	2221	2221	...	...	...	2348
Berlin Hbf **851** d.	1532	1542	1542	1542	1632	1704	1704	...	...	1732	1820	1823	1832	1933	2029	...	2132	2229	2233	2233	2235	...	...	2356
Berlin Gesundbrunnen d.	1539	|	|	|	1638	|	|	1707	1721	1739	1827	1829	1838	1939	2038	2105	2139	...	2239	2239	2240	...	...	0002
Bernau (b. Berlin) d.	1554	1601	1603	1603	1654	1723	1723	1724	1738	1754	|	|	1854	1954	2054	2123	2154	...	2254	2254	2256	...	...	0017
Eberswalde Hbf d.	1609	1619	1619	1619	1709	1740	1739	1739	1752	1809	1902	1902	1909	2009	2109	2137	2214	...	2313	2313	2316	...	...	0037
Angermünde a.	1628	1637	1637	1637	1728	1756	1755	1755	1807	1828	|	|	1928	2029	2128	2153	2233	...	2332	2332	2338	...	...	...
Angermünde d.	1634	1639	1639	1639	1733	1758	1757	1757	...	1834	|	|	1933	2034	2133	...	2234	...	2334q	2345	2340r	2345	2345	...
Schwedt (Oder) a.	1656	|	|	|	|	|	|	|	...	1856	|	|	|	2056	|	...	2256	...	2354q	|	0002r	|	|	...
Prenzlau d.	...	1702	1702	1702	1801	1821	1821	1820	...	...	1941	1941	2001	...	2201	...	...	...	...	0013	...	0013	0013	...
Pasewalk d.	...	1718	1718	1718	1819	1837	1837	1837	...	...	1957	1957	2019	...	2219	...	...	...	...	0029	...	0029	0030	...
Anklam d.	...	1744	1744	1744	1851	1903	1903	1903	...	...	2023	2022	2051	...	2251	...	...	...	...	...	...	...	0100	...
Züssow **846** d.	...	1758	1758	1758	1905	1916	1915	1925	...	...	|	|	2105	...	2305	...	...	...	...	...	...	...	0112	...
Greifswald **846** d.	...	1812	1812	1812	1920	1930	1930	1939	...	...	2046	2046	2120	...	2320	...	...	...	...	...	...	...	0127	...
Stralsund Hbf **846** a.	...	1832	1832	1832	1941	1949	1949	1958	...	...	2105	2108	2141	...	2341	...	...	...	...	...	...	...	0147	...

km																								
																ICE			*ICE*	*IC*	*ICE*			*ICE*
																1632			**1730**	**2250**	**1630**			**1513**
			Ⓒ		Ⓐ			①	Ⓐ	⚒						Ⓐ			①–④	①–⑤	♣			♠
			¶					g				S				T✕		S	M✕	❦‡🍷	H✕			C✕
0	**Stralsund** Hbf **846** d.	...	...	...	...	...	...	0406	...	0416	...	...	...	0616	...	0806	0816	...	0936	0936	0936	...	1016	1136
31	Greifswald **846** d.	...	...	...	...	...	...	0425	...	0437	...	...	...	0637	...	0826	0837	...	0956	0956	0956	...	1037	1156
49	Züssow **846** d.	...	...	...	...	...	...	0438	...	0453	...	...	...	0653	...	|	0853	...	1008	1008	1008	...	1053	1211
66	Anklam d.	...	...	...	...	...	...	0449	...	0505	...	...	...	0705	...	0848	0905	...	1020	1020	1020	...	1105	1222
109	**Pasewalk** d.	...	...	...	...	...	...	0520j	0520	0544j	0544	...	...	0744j	...	0913	0944j	...	1046	1046	1045	...	1144j	1247
133	Prenzlau d.	...	...	...	...	...	...	0537	0537	0602	0602	...	...	0802	...	0930	1002	...	1102	1103	1102	...	1202	1302
	Schwedt (Oder) d.	...	...	...	...	...	0508	|	|	|	|	...	0708	|	0908	|	|	...	|	|	|	1108	|	|
170	Angermünde a.	...	...	...	...	...	0530	0603	0603	0629	0629	...	0730	0829	0930	|	1029	...	|	1124	1123	1130	1229	1323
170	Angermünde d.	...	...	...	0427	...	0533	0606	0606	0633	0633	0707	0733	0833	0933	|	1033	1108	|	1126	1125	1133	1233	1325
196	Eberswalde Hbf d.	...	...	...	0448	0448	0554	0628	0628	0654	0654	0724	0754	0854	0954	1008	1054	1127	1138	1142	1142	1154	1254	1342
218	Bernau (b. Berlin) d.	...	...	...	0509	0509	0609	0644	0644	0709	0709	0741	0809	0909	1009	|	1109	1142	|	1157	1158	1209	1309	1357
239	**Berlin** Gesundbrunnen d.	...	...	...	0524	0524	0624	0700	0700	0724	0724	0756	0824	0925	1024	1037	1124	1157	|	1211	1214	1224	1325	1413
243	**Berlin** Hbf **851** d.	0032	0032	...	0531	0531	0631	0707	0707	0731	0731	...	0831	0931	1031	1042o	1131	...	1208o	1218	1219o	1231	1331	1418o
249	**Berlin** Südkreuz **851** d.	0041	0041	...	0540	0540	0640	0716	0716	0740	0740	...	0840	0940	1040	1108	1140	...	1219	...	1308	1240	1340	1432o
295	Luckenwalde d.	0120	0120	...	0614	0614	0711	...	...	0814	0814	...	0911	1014	1111	...	1214	...	...	...	...	1311	1414	|
308	Jüterbog d.	0128	0129	...	0625	0625	0719	...	...	0825	0825	...	0919	1025	1119	...	1225	...	...	...	...	1319	1425	|
357	**Falkenberg** (Elster) a.	...	|	...	0707	0707	|	...	...	0907	0907	...	|	1111	|	...	1307	...	...	...	...	|	1511	|
	Lutherstadt Wittenberg 851 a.	...	0144	...	...	...	0748	...	...	...	...	...	0948	...	1148	...	...	...	...	...	...	1348	...	1507

				ICE						*IC*		*IC*											
				1536						**1932**		**2216**											
				Ⓒb			⑤		Ⓒ		⑦w		Ⓐ	⑥⑦	①–⑤			●					①–⑥	⑤⑥
				H✕			S				A🍷		N			S							t	k
Stralsund Hbf **846** d.	...	1216	...	1345	1416	...	...	1616	1616	...	1704	...	1813	1816	1825	...	...	...	...	2016	...	...	2216	2216
Greifswald **846** d.	...	1237	...	1405	1437	...	...	1637	1637	...	1724	...	1833	1837	1846	...	...	...	...	2037	...	...	2237	2237
Züssow **846** d.	...	1253	...	1418	1453	...	...	1653	1653	...	|	...	...	1853	1902	...	...	...	...	2053	...	...	2253	2253
Anklam d.	...	1305	...	1430	1505	...	...	1705	1705	...	1746	...	...	1905	1915	...	...	...	...	2105	...	...	2305	2305
Pasewalk d.	...	1344j	...	1501	1544	...	...	1744j	1744j	...	1812	...	...	1946j	1946	...	...	...	...	2144j	...	...	2336	2344
Prenzlau d.	...	1402	...	1517	1602	...	...	1802	1802	...	1827	...	...	2003	2003	...	...	...	...	2202	...	...	...	0002
Schwedt (Oder) d.	1308	|	1508	|	|	1708	...	|	|	...	|	1908	...	|	|	...	2108	2108	...	|	2307	...	...	|
Angermünde a.	1330	1429	1530	1539	1629	1730		1829	1829	...	|	1930	...	2030	2030		2130	2130	...	2229	2328	...	...	0029
Angermünde d.	1333	1433	1533	1541	1633	1733	1740	1833	1833	...	|	1933	...	2033	2033	2046	2133	2133	...	2233	2333	...	...	0033
Eberswalde Hbf d.	1354	1454	1554	1559	1654	1754	1801	1854	1854	...	1903	1954	...	2054	2054	2104	2154	2154	...	2254	2354	...	...	0054
Bernau (b. Berlin) d.	1409	1509	1609	1614	1709	1809	1815	1908	1908	...	1919	2009	...	2109	2109	2120	2209	2209	...	2314	0009	...	...	0114
Berlin Gesundbrunnen d.	1424	1525	1624	1630	1725	1824	1830	1922	1922	...	1933	2024	...	2124	2124	2139	2224	2224	...	2328	0024	...	...	0128
Berlin Hbf **851** d.	1431	1531z	1631	1636o	1732	1831	...	1926	1935	1935	...	2031	...	2131	2131	...	2228	2236	2236	2333	0028	...	...	0136
Berlin Südkreuz **851** d.	1440	1540z	1640	1708	1740	1840	...	...	1944	1944	...	2040	...	2140	2140	...	...	2246	2246	...	...	...	...	...
Luckenwalde d.	1511	1614z	1711	...	1814	1911	...	...	2017	2017	...	2111	...	2217	2217	...	...	2324	2324	...	...	...	...	...
Jüterbog d.	1519	1625	1719	...	1825	1919	...	...	2025	2025	...	2119	...	2225	2225	...	...	2332	2332	...	...	...	...	...
Falkenberg (Elster) a.	|	1711	|	...	1911	|	...	...	2107	2107	...	|	...	2311	2311	...	...	|	|	...	...	...	...	...
Lutherstadt Wittenberg 851 a.	1548	...	1748	...	...	1948p	...	...	...	...	...	2142	...	...	...	...	...	2358	2358	...	...	...	...	...

A – [12] and 🍷 Stralsund - Berlin - Hannover - Bremen - Oldenburg.
B – ⑥ from Sept. 10. [12] ✕ München - Leipzig - Berlin - Stralsund.
C – [12] and ✕ Ostseebad Binz - Berlin - Leipzig - München.
D – ①–④ (not Oct. 3). [12] and ✕ Erfurt - Berlin - Stralsund.
E – [12] and ✕ Stuttgart - Frankfurt - Erfurt - Berlin - Ostseebad Binz.
G – [12] and ✕ Frankfurt - Erfurt - Berlin - Stralsund (- Ostseebad Binz Ⓒ **d**).
H – [12] and ✕ Ostseebad Binz - Berlin - Erfurt - Frankfurt.
J – ⑧ from Sept. 4 (not Oct. 2). [12] and ✕ Innsbruck - München - Leipzig - Berlin - Ostseebad Binz.
L – ⑤ to Aug. 26; Ⓐ from Sept. 2. [12] and ✕ Erfurt - Berlin - Stralsund (- Ostseebad Binz ◇).
M – ①–④ from Sept. 5 (not Oct. 3). [12] and ✕ (Ostseebad Binz ◐ -) Stralsund - Berlin - Erfurt.
N – Ⓐ (not Oct. 31). [12] and 🍷 Greifswald - Hamburg - Köln - Stuttgart and v.v.
Q – ⑥ to Oct. 29. [12] and ✕ Eisenach - Erfurt - Berlin - Stralsund.
R – ①–④ to Sept. 1.
S – To / from Szczecin (Table **949**).
T – To / from Frankfurt via Erfurt (Table **850**).

b – Not Nov. 5, 12, 19, 26, Dec. 3, 10.
d – Not Nov. 6, 13, 20, 27, Dec. 4.
g – Also Oct. 4; not Oct. 3.
j – Arrives 7 – 10 minutes earlier.
k – Also Oct. 2.
n – 3 – 4 minutes later until Aug. 4.
o – Arrival time.
p – 1942 on † (also ⑤ from Aug. 5).
q – Not Oct. 2.
r – Angermünde to Schwedt on ⑦ (also Oct. 3; not Oct. 2).
t – Also Oct. 2; not Oct. 3.
w – Also Oct. 3; not Oct. 2.
z – 3 – 4 minutes later on ⑤⑦ (also Oct. 3, Nov. 1).

● – ①②③④⑥ (also Oct. 2; not Oct. 3).
♣ – ⑥⑦ to Aug. 28; ⑤–⑦ from Sept. 3 (also Oc
♥ – From Sept. 4.
♠ – From Sept. 5.
❦ – Until Sept. 3.
✣ – Until Sept. 4.
◐ – Until Oct. 31.
◇ – ⑤ (Ⓐ Sept. 2 - Oct. 31).
⊗ – To Ostseebad Binz (Table **844**) until Oct. 2[illegible] July 22 - Sept. 2 departs Berlin Hbf 1827, B[illegible] Gesundbrunnen 1833, Pasewalk 1956, Ank[illegible] 2021 (other timings as shown).
⊖ – Change trains at Berlin on Ⓐ.
‡ – To / from Ostseebad Binz (Table **844**).
¶ – From / to Halle on Ⓒ (Tables **848**/**850**).

STRALSUND - ZÜSSOW - ŚWINOUJŚCIE — 846

omer Bäderbahn (2nd class only) — *Service until October 3*

Stralsund Hbf 845 d.	0521e	*0616*	0721	*0816*	0911	*1016*	1121	*1216*	1321	*1416*	1521	*1616*	1721	*1816*g	1921	*2016*	2122
Greifswald 845 d.	0545e	*0637*	0745	*0837*	0935	*1037*	1145	*1237*	1345	*1437*	1545	*1637*	1745	*1837*g	1945	*2037*	2146
Züssow 845 d.	0607e	0707	0807	0907	0955	1107	1205	1307	1407	1507	1607	1707	1807	1907	2007	2107	2207
Wolgast d.	0630	0730	0830	0930	1030k	1130	1230	1330	1430	1530	1630	1730	1830	1930	2030	2130	2230
Zinnowitz ▲ d.	0649	0749	0849	0952	1052	1152	1252	1352	1452	1552	1652	1752	1849	1949	2049	2149	2249
Seebad Heringsdorf d.	0730	0830	0942	1042	1142	1242	1342	1442	1542	1642	1742	1842	1930	2030	2130	2230	2324
Seebad Ahlbeck d.	0735	0835	0947	1047	1147	1247	1347	1447	1547	1647	1747	1847	1935	2035	2135	2235	...
Świnoujście Centrum a.	0740	0840	0952	1052	1152	1252	1352	1452	1552	1652	1752	1852	1940	2040	2140	2240	...

	Ⓐ		Ⓐ	Ⓒ														
ujście Centrum d.	0421	0518	0554	0618	0718	0818	0900	1000	1100	1200	1300	1400	1500	1600	1700	1800	1918	2118
d Ahlbeck d.	0426	0523	0600	0623	0723	0823	0906	1006	1106	1206	1306	1406	1506	1606	1706	1806	1923	2123
d Heringsdorf d.	0436	0533	0609	0633	0733	0833	0918	1018	1118	1218	1318	1418	1518	1618	1718	1818	1933	2133
witz ▲ d.	0511	0611	0648	0711	0811	0910	1009	1109	1209	1309	1409	1509	1609	1709	1809	1911	2011	2211
st d.	0528	0628	0728j	0728	0828	0928	1028	1128	1228	1328	1428	1528	1628	1728	1828	1928	2028	2228
w 845 a.	0546	0646	0746	0746	0846	0946	1046	1146	1246	1346	1446	1546	1646	1746	1846	1946	2046	2246
wald 845 a.	0619	*0721*	0819	0819	*0919*	1019	*1119*	1219	*1319*	1419	*1519*	1619	*1720*	1822	*1919*	2019	*2119*	*2319*
und Hbf 845 a.	0644	*0744*	0845	0845	*0941*	1044	*1141*	1244	*1341*	1444	*1541*	1644	*1742*	1847	*1941*	2044	*2141*	*2341*

e – Ⓐ only.
g – 9 minutes later on ①–⑤.
j – Arrives 0702.
k – Arrives 1014.
t – Not July 25 - Sept. 2.

▲ – **Zinnowitz - Peenemünde** and v.v. (*12 km*, journey 14 minutes).
From Zinnowitz at 0431 Ⓐ, 0513 Ⓐ, 0613, 0659 Ⓐ t, 0713 Ⓒ, 0813, 0913 and hourly until 2113.
From Peenemünde at 0452 Ⓐ, 0531 Ⓐ, 0631, 0717 Ⓐ t, 0731 Ⓒ, 0831, 0931 and hourly until 2131.

BERLIN SCHÖNEFELD ✈ - BERLIN - DESSAU — 847

ervices

		Ⓐ																	†		A				
Berlin Schönefeld ✈ d.	0444	0544	0644	0744	0844	0944	1044	1144	1244	1344	1444	1544	1644	1744	1844	1944	2044	2144	2144	2244	2244		0503		2303
Berlin Ostbahnhof d.	0503	0603	0703	0803	0903	1003	1103	1203	1303	1403	1503	1603	1703	1803	1903	2003	2103	2203	2203	2303	2303		0526	and	2325
Berlin Hbf d.	0515	0615	0715	0815	0915	1015	1115	1215	1315	1415	1515	1615	1715	1815	1915	2015	2115	2215	2215	2315	2315	also	0537	hourly	2337
Berlin Zoo d.	0521	0621	0721	0821	0921	1021	1121	1221	1321	1421	1521	1621	1721	1821	1921	2021	2121	2221	2221	2321	2321		0543	until	2343
Berlin Spandau a.	|	|	|	|	|	|	|	|	|	|	|	|	|	|	|	|	|	|	|	|	|		0554		2354
Berlin Wannsee d.	0534	0634	0734	0834	0934	1034	1134	1234	1334	1434	1534	1634	1734	1834	1934	2034	2134	2234	2234	2334	2334		...		...
Bad Belzig a.	0615	0715	0815	0915	1015	1115	1215	1315	1415	1515	1615	1715	1815	1915	2015	2115	2215	2315	2315	0015	0015		...		...
Roßlau (Elbe) 848 a.	0648	0749	0848	0949e	1048	1149e	1248	1349e	1448	1549e	1648	1749e	1848	1949e	2048	2149e	2248	...	2349	...	0048		...		...
Dessau Hbf 848 a.	0653	0754	0853	0954e	1053	1154e	1253	1354e	1453	1554e	1653	1754e	1853	1954e	2053	2154e	2253	...	2354	...	0053		...		...

			①–⑥																		Ⓐ	Ⓒ				
au Hbf 848 d.	...	0406e	0506	...	0606e	0706	0808e	0906	1008e	1106	1208e	1306	1408e	1506	1608e	1706	1808e	1906	2008e	2106	2217	2317		...		...
u (Elbe) 848 d.	...	0412e	0512	...	0612e	0712	0813e	0912	1013e	1112	1213e	1312	1413e	1512	1613e	1712	1813e	1912	2013e	2112	2222	2322		...		...
elzig d.	0343e	0443	0543	0543	0643	0743	0843	0943	1043	1143	1243	1343	1443	1543	1643	1743	1843	1943	2043	2143	2254	2354		...		...
Wannsee d.	0428e	0528	0628	0628	0728	0828	0928	1028	1128	1228	1328	1428	1528	1628	1728	1828	1928	2028	2128	2228	2340	0039		...	❖	...
lin Spandau d.	|	|	|	|	|	|	|	|	|	|	|	|	|	|	|	|	|	|	|	|	|	|		0454		2054
Zoo d.	0441	0541	0641	0641	0741	0841	0941	1041	1141	1241	1341	1441	1541	1641	1741	1841	1941	2041	2141	2241	2353	0052		0506	and	2106
Hbf d.	0447	0547	0647	0647	0747	0847	0947	1047	1147	1247	1347	1447	1547	1647	1747	1847	1947	2047	2147	2247	2359	0058	also	0513	hourly	2113
Ostbahnhof d.	0458	0558	0658	0658	0758	0858	0958	1058	1158	1258	1358	1458	1558	1658	1758	1858	1958	2058	2158	2256	0008	0108		0524	until	2124
Schönefeld ✈ a.	0520	0620	0720	0720	0820	0920	1020	1120	1220	1320	1420	1520	1620	1720	1820	1920	2020	2120	2220	...	...	...		0543		2143

①②③④⑦ (not Oct. 2). e – Ⓐ only. ❖ – Some departure times are up to 3 minutes later.

MAGDEBURG - DESSAU - LEIPZIG and HALLE (SAALE) — 848

RB / S-Bahn services

			ⒶeL					Ⓐ		Ⓐe															
Magdeburg Hbf d.	...	...	...	0434	...	...	0533r	...	...	0620	...	0703	...	...	0804	...	0904	and in	...	...	1604	...	1704	...
Roßlau (Elbe) 847 d.	0432e	...	...	0522	...	...	0623r	...	...	0708	...	0746	...	...	0857	...	0946	the same	...	...	1657	...	1746	...
Dessau Hbf 847 a.	0437e	...	...	0525	...	...	0626r	...	...	0712	...	0749	...	...	0900	...	0949		...	...	1700	...	1749	...
Dessau Hbf d.	0445	...	...	0527	0606	...	0628	...	0706	0716	...	0751	0806	...	0906	...	0951	pattern	1606	...	1706	...	1751	1806
Bitterfeld a.	0508	...	...	0551	0629	...	0647	...	0729	0733	...	0808	0829	...	0929	...	1008	every	1629	...	1729	...	1808	1829
Bitterfeld d.	0514	0512	0546	0553	0631	0634	0648	0657	0731	0734	0737	0809	0831	0837	0931	0937	1009		1631	1637	1731	1737	1809	1831
Halle (Saale) Hbf a.	|	0536	|	0615	|	0657	|	0719	|	0755	0801	|	|	0901	|	1001	|	**two** hours	|	1701	|	1801	|	|
Leipzig Hbf ★ a.	0543	...	0613	...	0658	...	0713	...	0758	...	...	0836	0858	...	0958	...	1036	until	1658	...	1758	...	1836	1858
Leipzig-Connewitz ★ a.	0554	...	0626	...	0709	...	...	...	0809	...	...	...	0909	...	1009	...	...		1709	...	1809	...	...	1909

									L				
eburg Hbf d.	...	1804	...	*1904*	...	2004	...	2104	...	...	2142	...	2314
u (Elbe) 847 d.	...	1857	...	*1946*	...	2057	...	2146	...	...	2232	...	0007
au Hbf 847 a.	...	1901	...	*1949*	...	2100	...	2149	...	...	2235	...	0010
au Hbf d.	...	1906	...	2006	...	2106	...	2150	...	2204	...	2257	▬
feld a.	...	1929	...	2029	...	2129	...	2212	...	2227	...	2317	...
feld d.	1837	1931	1937	2031	2037	2131	2134	2213	2219	2232	...	2319	2320
le (Saale) Hbf a.	1901	|	2001	|	2101	|	2157	|	|	2254	...	|	2343
ig Hbf ★ a.	...	1958	...	2058	...	2158	...	2236	2244	...	...	2344	...
ig-Connewitz ★ a.	...	2009	...	2111	...	2211	...	...	2255	...	...	2355v	...

	Ⓐ	ⒸL		Ⓐe	⚒r	Ⓐe	Ⓐe	
Leipzig-Connewitz ★ d.	0010t	0010	...	...	...	...	...	...
Leipzig Hbf ★ d.	0019	0020	...	...	...	...	...	0544
Halle (Saale) Hbf d.	|	|	...	0422	...	0511	0537	|
Bitterfeld a.	0046	0046	...	0445	...	0533	0559	0609
Bitterfeld d.	...	...	...	0446	...	0535	0600	0610
Dessau Hbf a.	...	...	...	0510	...	0558	0622	0629
Dessau Hbf 847 d.	...	...	0432	0519	0600	0600	0624	0630
Roßlau (Elbe) 847 d.	...	...	0437	0523	0603	0603	0628	0634
Magdeburg Hbf a.	...	...	0527	0613	0653	0653	...	0722

				Ⓐ																					
ig-Connewitz ★ d.	0553	...	0653	...	...	...	0753	...	0853	...	and in	...	1753	...	1853	...	...	1953	...	...	2108	...	2208	...	2308
ig Hbf ★ d.	0603	...	0703	...	0719	...	0803	...	0903	0919	the same	...	1803	...	1903	1919	...	2003	...	...	2118	...	2218	...	2318
le (Saale) Hbf d.	|	0701	|	0711	|	0801	|	0901	|	|		1801	|	1901	|	|	2001	|	...	2121	|	2221	|	2321	|
feld a.	0629	0725	0729	0736	0745	0825	0829	0925	0929	0945	pattern	1825	1829	1925	1929	1945	2025	2029	...	2144	2145	2244	2245	2344	2345
feld d.	0632	...	0732	...	0746	...	0832	...	0932	0946		...	1832	...	1932	1946	...	2032	...	...	2149	...	2249	...	2349
au Hbf a.	0655	...	0755	...	0803	...	0855	...	0955	1003	every	...	1855	...	1955	2003	...	2055	...	...	2212	...	2312	...	0012
au Hbf 847 d.	0700	...	...	...	0806	...	0900	...	...	1006	**two** hours	...	1900	...	...	2006	...	2057	2101	...	2214	...	2314	...	...
u (Elbe) 847 d.	0703	...	...	...	0810	...	0903	...	...	1010	until	...	1903	...	...	2010	...	2100	2105	...	2218	...	2317	...	...
eburg Hbf a.	0753	...	...	...	0853	...	0953	...	...	1053		...	1953	...	...	2053	...	...	2153	...	2300	...	0006	...	...

FALKENBERG - LUTHERSTADT WITTENBERG - DESSAU and HALLE (SAALE)

	ⒸH	Ⓐe		⚒r	Ⓐe	Ⓐe		Ⓐe						Ⓐe		Ⓐe		Ⓐe			Ⓐe			
Falkenberg (Elster) d.	...	...	...	...	0535	0620	...	...	...	...	...	...	...	...	...	...	...	1608	...	...	1813	...	...	2119
Lutherstadt Wittenberg d.	0145	0403	0439	0514	0623	0706	0723	0823	0923	1023	1223	1323	1423	1455	1523	1555	1623	1655	1723	1823	1858	1923	2023	2205
Roßlau (Elbe) d.	|	0432	0511	0544	0653	0733	0753	0853	0953	1053	1253	1353	1453	1522	1553	1623	1653	1722	1753	1853	...	1953	2053	2236
Dessau Hbf a.	0211	0437	0519	0548	0657	0737	0757	0857	0957	1057	1257	1357	1457	1526	1557	1627	1657	1726	1757	1857	...	1957	2057	2240

	Ⓐe		⚒r	Ⓐe		⚒r		⚒r					Ⓐe		Ⓐe		Ⓐe							Ⓐe	Ⓒd
au Hbf d.	0424	0527	0527	0624	0713	0803	0903	1003	1103	1203	1303	1403	1434	1503	1532	1603	1634	1703	1803	1903	2003	2057	...	2231	2321
au (Elbe) d.	0429	0532	0532	0629	0717	0807	0907	1007	1107	1207	1307	1407	1439	1507	1537	1607	1639	1707	1807	1907	2007	2101	...	2236	2326
erstadt Wittenberg d.	0459	0601	0602	0658	0751	0838	0938	1038	1138	1238	1338	1438	1506	1538	1602	1638	1706	1738	1838	1938	2038	2131	2136	2307	2357
nberg (Elster) a.	0545	...	0647	...	0835	...	...	...	...	...	...	...	1550	...	...	...	1750	...	...	...	...	...	2220	...	...

	ⒸH			ⒶeL	Ⓐ								Ⓐ	Ⓒ								L		
Falkenberg (Elster) d.	...	...	...	...	...	...	0706	...	0906	...	1106	...	...	1306	...	1506	...	1706	...	1906	...	...	...	...
Lutherstadt Wittenberg d.	0145	...	0441	0514	0626	0645	0753	0845	0953	1045	1153	1245	1353	1353	1445	1553	1645	1753	1845	1953	2052	2149	...	2245
Bitterfeld a.	0227	...	0510	0543	0654	0715	0821	0915	1021	1115	1221	1315	1421	1421	1515	1621	1715	1821	1915	2021	2120	2217	...	2314
Halle (Saale) Hbf a.	0244	...	0536	...	0719	0740a	...	0940a	...	1140a	...	1340a	1441	...	1540a	1642a	1740a	...	1940	...	2157	...	...	2343

	ⒸL	Ⓐ	ⒸS							Ⓒ	Ⓒ	Ⓐ			Ⓐe		Ⓒ	Ⓐ							
(Saale) Hbf d.	...	...	0502	0621	0711a	0821a	...	1021a	...	...	...	1229	...	1421a	...	...	...	1629	...	1821a	...	2021	2121	2221	2321
feld d.	0049	0538	0538	0645	0737	0845	0937	1045	1137	1137	1245	1253	1337	1445	1502	1537	1645	1653	1737	1845	1935	2045	2149	2249	2349
erstadt Wittenberg d.	0119	0608	0610	0717	0807	0917	1007	1117	1206	1207	1317	1325	1407	1517	1525	1607	1717	1722	1807	1917	2007	2136j	2219	2319	0019
nberg (Elster) a.	...	...	...	...	...	...	1049	...	...	1249	...	...	1449	...	...	1649	...	...	1849	...	2049	2220	...	...	...

12 Berlin - Lutherstadt - Dessau - Halle (Tables **845** and **850**).
12 Lutherstadt Wittenberg - Bitterfeld - Leipzig and v.v.
To Schwedt (Oder) via Berlin (Table **845**).
Ⓐ only.

d – Also Oct. 31.
e – Ⓐ (not Oct. 31).
j – Arrives 2117.
r – ⚒ (not Oct. 31).

t – Ⓐ to July 4; ① from July 11 (not Oct. 3).
v – Daily to July 3; ⑤–⑦ from July 8.
★ – Trains between Leipzig Hbf and Leipzig-Connewitz also call at Leipzig Markt, Wilhelm-Leuschner-Platz, Bayerischer Bahnhof and MDR stations.

849 Local services LEIPZIG and HALLE - EISENACH and SAALFELD

Operated by ABELLIO Rail Mitteldeutschland. See Tables **850** and **851** for faster *ICE* and *IC* trains.

km			Ⓐs		Ⓒd				Ⓐs					A				A						
0	**Halle** (Saale) Hbf .... d.	0425	0532	...	...	...	0625	...	0725	...	...	0825	...	0925	and in the same pattern every **two** hours until	...	1825	...	1925	...	2025	...	2125	2225
	Leipzig Hbf .... ★ d.	|	0455t	...	0552	...	|	0652	|	...	0752	|	0852	|		1752	|	1852	|	1952	|	2052	|	2210t
32	Weißenfels .... ★ d.	0454	0555	...	0629	...	0654	0729	0754	...	0829	0854	0929	0954		1829	1854	1929	1954	2029	2054	2129	2154	2257
46	Naumburg (Saale) Hbf d.	0505	0606	...	0638	...	0705	0738	0805	...	0844	0906	0938	1006		1844	1906	1938	2006	2044	2106	2138	2206	2307
72	Apolda .... d.	0526	0627	...	0656	0656	0726	0756	0826	...	0902	0927	0956	1027		1902	1927	1956	2027	2102	2127	2157	2227	2328
87	Weimar .... **858** d.	0538	0640	...	0707	0707	0740	0807	0840	0840	0913	0940	1007	1040		1913	1940	2007	2040	2113	2140	2208	2240	2340
108	**Erfurt** Hbf .... **858** a.	0553	0655	...	0721	0721	0755	0822	0855	0855	0926	0955	1022	1055		1926	1955	2022	2055	2126	2155	2222	2255	2355
108	**Erfurt** Hbf .... d.	0555	0700	0700	...	...	0800	...	0900	0900	...	1000	...	1100		...	2006	...	2100	...	2206	...	2301	0031
136	Gotha .... d.	0617	0722	0722	...	...	0825	...	0922	0922	...	1025	...	1122		...	2028	...	2127	...	2229	...	2323	0052
165	**Eisenach** .... a.	0639	0744	0744	...	...	0846	...	0944	0944	...	1046	...	1144		...	2049	...	2148	...	2250	...	2345	0115

			Ⓐs	Ⓐs				Ⓐs		Ⓐs			A					A				A		
Eisenach .... d.	...	...	0410	...	...	0502	...	0608	0647r	0711	...	...	0813	...	0911	and in the same pattern every **two** hours until	...	1813	...	1911	2013	2013	2113	...
Gotha .... d.	...	...	0433	...	...	0525	...	0631	0714	0733	...	...	0835	...	0933		...	1835	...	1933	2035	2035	2135	...
Erfurt Hbf .... a.	...	...	0455	...	...	0547	...	0652	0734	0756	...	...	0857	...	0955		...	1857	...	1955	2057	2057	2157	...
Erfurt Hbf .... **858** d.	...	...	0457	...	0531	0601	0621	0701	0736	0801	0801	0831	0901	0935	1001		1831	1901	1935	2001	▬	2101	2201	...
Weimar .... **858** d.	...	...	0513	...	0545	0618	0635	0718	0751	0818	0818	0846	0918	0951	1018		1846	1918	1951	2018	...	2118	2218	...
Apolda .... d.	...	...	0524	...	0555	0629	0648	0729	0801	0829	0829	0856	0929	1001	1029		1856	1929	2001	2029	...	2129	2229	...
Naumburg (Saale) Hbf . d.	0447	...	0545	...	0616	0651	0704	0751	0819	0851	0851	0914	0951	1019	1051		1914	1951	2019	2051	2121	2151	2254	...
Weißenfels .... d.	0458	0505	0555	0600	0626	0702	0732	0802	0828	0902	0902	0928	1002	1028	1102		1928	2002	2028	2102	2130	2202	2304	2308
Leipzig Hbf .... a.	|	0544	|	0638	|	|	0808	|	0904	|	|	1004	|	1104	|		2004	|	2104	|	2207	|	|	2347
Halle (Saale) Hbf .... a.	0527	...	0617	...	0654	0732	...	0832	...	0932	0932	...	1032	...	1132		...	2032	...	2132	...	2232	2335	...

km						⊡				⊡			⊡			⊕	
0	**Leipzig** Hbf .... d.	0552	...	...	0752	...	and in the same pattern every **two** hours until	...	1552	...	...	1752	...	...	1952	2052	2307t
	Halle (Saale) Hbf .... d.	|	0625	0747	|	0847		1547	|	1647n	1747	|	1847	1947	|	|	2325
40	Weißenfels .... d.	0629	0654	0810	0829	0910		1612	1629	1710	1810	1829	1910	2010	2029	2129	2354
56	Naumburg (Saale) Hbf d.	0638	0709	0820	0838	0924		1621	1638	1724	1820	1838	1924	2019	2038	2138	0010
95	**Jena** Paradies ... **875** d.	0717e	0742	...	0911	0956		...	1711	1756	...	1911	1956	...	2111	2221	0042
100	Jena-Göschwitz .. **875** d.	0721e	0751f	...	0916	1001		...	1716	1801	...	1916	2001	...	2116	2234	0047
132	Rudolstadt (Thür) **875** d.	0742e	0817f	...	0942	1027		...	1742	1827	...	1942	2027	...	2142	2300	...
142	**Saalfeld** (Saale) . **875** a.	0750e	0826f	...	0950	1036		...	1750	1836	...	1950	2036	...	2150	2308	...

	Ⓐs															A	⊙
Saalfeld (Saale) ... **875** d.	0402	0501	0611	...	0646	...	0807	...	0911	and in the same pattern every **two** hours until	1711	1807	...	1912	2000	...	2132j
Rudolstadt (Thür) . **875** d.	0411	0510	0620	...	0655	...	0816	...	0920		1720	1816	...	1921	2009	...	2141j
Jena-Göschwitz ... **875** d.	0434	0535	0647	...	0724	...	0842	...	0946		1746	1842	...	1947	2035	...	2211
Jena Paradies ..... **875** d.	0439	0540	0652	...	0730	...	0848	...	0952		1752	1848	...	1952	2041	...	2216
Naumburg (Saale) Hbf .. d.	0510	0611	0724	0738	0810	0838	0919	0938	1023		1823	1919	1938	2023	2121	2151	2254
Weißenfels .... d.	0520	0621	0732	0748	0828	0848	0928	0948	1048		1848	1928	1948	...	2130	2202	2304
Halle (Saale) Hbf ..... a.	0553	|	|	0810	|	0910	|	1010	1110		1910	|	2010	...	|	2232	2335
Leipzig Hbf .... a.	...	0706	0808	...	0904	...	1004	...	...		...	2004	...	...	2207	...	2347t

A – Ⓐ (also June 25, 26, Sept. 10, 11, Oc Nov. 26, Dec. 3, 10; not Oct. 31); run Weimar - Eisenach and v.v.
d – Runs daily from Sept. 4
e – Naumburg - Saalfeld on Ⓐ to Sept.
f – 7–8 minutes later from Sept. 4.
j – 7 minutes **earlier** from Sept. 4.
n – *1642* on ⑤⑦ (also Oct. 3, Nov. 1; n Oct. 2, 30).
r – 0650 on †.
s – Not Oct. 31.
t – Change trains at Weißenfels.
⊕ – Change trains at Großheringen (a. 2 d. 2156).
⊙ – Change trains at Großheringen (a. 22 d. 2243).
⊡ – Runs 7–8 minutes later Naumburg - Saalfeld from Sept. 4.

EISENACH - BEBRA Journey time: 34–47 minutes. Operated by CANTUS Verkehrsgesellschaft (2nd class only).

From Eisenach at 0440 Ⓐ, 0530 Ⓐ, 0613 ⚒, 0713 ⚒, 0813, 0903 ⚒, 1013, 1113 Ⓐ, 1213, 1303 Ⓐ, 1413, 1503 Ⓐ, 1613, 1703 Ⓐ, 1813, 1903 Ⓐ, 2013, 2113 Ⓐ and 2213 Ⓒ.
From Bebra at 0504 Ⓐ, 0559 ⑥, 0604 Ⓐ, 0659 Ⓐ, 0704 Ⓒ, 0723 Ⓐ, 0804 ⑥, 0904, 1004 Ⓐ, 1104, 1204 Ⓐ, 1304 Ⓒ, 1315 Ⓐ, 1404 Ⓐ, 1507, 1604 Ⓐ, 1704, 1804 Ⓐ, 1904, 2004 Ⓐ and

850 BERLIN and LEIPZIG - ERFURT - KASSEL and FRANKFURT

Other regional services: Table **845** Berlin - Lutherstadt Wittenberg. Table **848** Lutherstadt Wittenberg - Halle. Table **849** Leipzig / Halle - Weimar - Erfurt - Eisenach - Bebra.

km		*IC* 1950	*IC* 1950	*RE* 3363		*ICE* 1646	*ICE* 1656	*ICE* 1583	*IC* 2156	*ICE* 1644	*IC* 2156	*ICE* 1654	*ICE* 1585	*ICE* 1636	*ICE* 1642	*ICE* 1734	*ICE* 1652	*ICE* 1587	*ICE* 1634	*ICE* 1640	*ICE* 1650	*ICE* 1589	*ICE* 1632
		①	Ⓐ	Ⓒ		Ⓐ	⚒	①–⑥	①–⑥	⚒	①–⑥			Ⓐ		Ⓐ			Ⓒ				
		g				⊙		⊖	¶P		¶P		⊖					⊖				⊖	Q
						✖	✖	✖		✖		✖	✖	✖	✖	✖	✖	✖	✖	✖	✖	✖	✖
	Berlin Hbf .... **851 902** d.	0029	...	0032	...	...	...	0427	...	...	...	...	0627	0700t	...	0815	...	0827	0900t	...	...	1027	1100t
	Berlin Südkreuz .... **851** d.	0036	...	0041	...	...	...	0434	...	...	...	...	0634	0707t	...	0822	...	0834	0907t	...	...	1034	1107t
	Lutherstadt Wittenberg ... **851** d.	0113	...	0145	...	...	...	0509	...	...	...	...	0709	|	...	|	...	0909	|	...	...	1109	|
	Bitterfeld .... **851** d.	0129	...	0228	...	...	...	0526	...	...	...	...	0726	|	...	|	...	0926	|	...	...	1126	|
	Halle (Saale) Hbf .... **851** d.	0154	...	0244	...	...	...	|	0553	...	...	...	|	0814	...	0933	...	|	1014	...	...	|	1214
	Dresden Hbf **842** .... d.	|	...	...	...	...	...	|	|	...	...	0620r	|	|	...	|	0820	|	|	...	1020	|	|
0	**Leipzig** Hbf .... **851** d.	0238	...	...	...	0425	0533	0548	|	0631	...	0733	0748	|	0835	|	0933	0948	|	1035	1133	1148	|
	Naumburg (Saale) Hbf .... d.	|	...	...	...	|	|	|	0630	|	...	|	|	|	|	|	|	|	|	|	|	|	|
	Weimar .... d.	0338	...	...	...	|	|	|	0657	|	←	|	|	|	|	|	|	|	|	|	|	|	|
120	**Erfurt** Hbf .... d.	0355	...	...	...	0514	0618	0635	0710	0716	0725	0818	0834	0849	0920	1007	1018	1034	1049	1120	1218	1234	1249
147	Gotha .... d.	0411	...	...	...	0532	0635	|	→	0733	0743	0835	|	|	|	...	1035	|	|	|	1235	|	|
176	**Eisenach** .... d.	0426	...	...	...	0549	0651	|	...	0749	0758	0851	|	|	0949	...	1051	|	|	1149	1251	|	|
	Bebra .... **901** d.	0500	0500	...	...	|	|	|	...	|	0822	|	|	|	|	...	|	|	|	|	|	|	|
	Kassel Wilhelmshöhe. **901** a.	|	|	...	...	|	|	|	...	|	0857	|	|	|	|	...	|	|	|	|	|	|	|
233	Bad Hersfeld .... **901** d.	0511	0511	...	...	0618	|	|	...	0818	...	|	|	|	1018	...	|	|	|	1218	|	|	|
275	Fulda .... **900/1/2** d.	0541	0541	...	...	0645	0744	0800	...	0845	...	0944	0951	|	1045	...	1144	1154	|	1245	1344	1351	|
356	Hanau Hbf .... **900/1/2** d.	0624	0624	...	...	|	|	...	...	|	...	|	...	|	|	...	|	...	|	|	|	...	|
375	**Frankfurt** (Main) Süd .... a.	|	|	...	...	0737	|	...	...	0937	...	|	...	|	1137	...	|	...	|	1337	|	...	|
379	**Frankfurt** (Main) Hbf **900/1/2** a.	0642	0642	...	...	|	0837	...	...	|	...	1037	...	1056	|	...	1237	...	1256	|	1437	...	1456
	Frankfurt Flughafen ✈ § ... a.	...	...	...	...	0750	0855	...	...	0949	...	1055	...	...	1149	...	1255	...	...	1349	1455	...	...
	Wiesbaden Hbf **911** .... a.	...	...	...	...	...	0933	...	...	...	...	1133	...	...	...	...	1333	...	...	...	1533	...	...

	IC 2152	*IC* 2152	*ICE* 1730	*ICE* 1558	*ICE* 1209	*ICE* 1630	*ICE* 1546	*IC* 2150	*IC* 1956	*ICE* 1556	*ICE* 1683	*ICE* 1538	*IC* 1958	*ICE* 1544	*IC* 1952	*ICE* 1594	*ICE* 1554	*ICE* 1685	*ICE* 1536	*ICE* 1542	*ICE* 1552	*ICE* 1687	*ICE* 1534
			①–④			⑤–⑦			⑦			Ⓑq	⑦		⑤⑦		Ⓑq						⑤
	F	E	m		⊖	N		X	w		⊖		w		d		S	⊖	T			⊖	
			G✖	✖	✖	✖	✖		M	✖	✖	✖		✖	Y	🍷▮	✖	✖	✖	✖	✖	✖	✖
Berlin Hbf .... **851 902** d.	...	...	1214	...	1227	1300t	...	...	...	...	1428	1500t	...	...	1534	...	...	1627	1700t	...	...	1827	1903
Berlin Südkreuz .... **851** d.	...	...	1221	...	1234	1307t	...	...	...	...	1434	1507t	...	...	1541	...	...	1634	1707t	...	...	1834	1910
Lutherstadt Wittenberg .... **851** d.	...	...	|	...	1309	|	...	...	...	...	1509	|	...	...	1619	...	...	1709	|	...	...	1909	|
Bitterfeld .... **851** d.	...	...	|	...	1326	|	...	...	...	...	1526	|	...	...	|	...	...	1726	|	...	...	1926	|
Halle (Saale) Hbf .... **851** d.	...	...	1333	...	|	1414	...	...	...	...	|	1614	...	...	1648	...	...	|	1814	...	...	|	2017
Dresden Hbf **842** .... d.	...	...	|	1220	|	|	...	...	...	1420	|	|	...	...	|	1620h	1620	|	|	...	1820	|	|
Leipzig Hbf .... **851** d.	...	...	|	1333	1348	|	1435	...	1408	1533	1548	|	1538	1635	|	1733	1733	1748	|	1835	1941	1948	|
Naumburg (Saale) Hbf ..... d.	...	...	|	|	|	|	|	...	1451	|	|	|	1618	|	1717	|	|	|	|	|	|	|	|
Weimar .... d.	1306	1317	|	|	|	|	|	1508	1517	|	|	|	1651	|	1745	|	|	|	|	|	|	|	|
Erfurt Hbf .... d.	1327	1331	1407	1418	1434	1449	1520	1525	1531	1618	1634	1649	1710	1720	1801	1818	1818	1834	1849	1920	2026	2034	2052
Gotha .... d.	1343	|	...	1435	|	|	|	1541	1548	1635	|	|	1728	|	1817	1835	1835	|	|	|	2043	|	2108
Eisenach .... d.	1359	1359	...	1451	|	|	1549	1557	1604	1651	|	|	1744	1749	1834	1851	1851	|	|	1949	2059	|	2123
Bebra .... **901** d.	1423	1423	...	|	|	|	|	1622	|	|	|	|	|	|	1900	|	|	|	|	|	|	|	...
Kassel Wilhelmshöhe .. **901** a.	1459	1459	...	|	|	|	|	1658	|	|	|	|	|	|	1938	|	|	|	|	|	|	|	...
Bad Hersfeld .... **901** d.	...	...	...	|	|	|	1618	...	|	|	|	|	|	1818	...	|	|	|	|	2018	|	|	...
Fulda .... **900/1/2** d.	...	...	...	1544	1551	|	1645	...	1659	1744	1751	|	1837	1845	...	1944	1944	1951	|	2045	2158	2201	...
Hanau Hbf .... **900/1/2** d.	...	...	...	|	...	|	|	...	|	|	...	|	1915	|	...	|	|	...	|	2125	2239	...	...
Frankfurt (Main) Süd .... a.	...	...	...	|	...	|	1737	...	|	|	...	|	1929	|	...	|	|	...	|	2138	|	...	...
Frankfurt (Main) Hbf . **900/1/2** a.	...	...	...	1637	...	1656	|	...	1752	1837	...	1856	|	1940	...	2036	2036	...	2056	|	2254	...	...
Frankfurt Flughafen ✈ § .... a.	...	...	...	1655	...	...	1749	...	...	1855	...	...	1949	...	...	2057	...	...	...	2149	...	...	...
Wiesbaden Hbf **911** .... a.	...	...	...	1733	...	...	...	...	...	1933	...	...	...	...	...	2133	...	...	...	...	...	...	...

FOR NOTES SEE NEXT PAGE →

FRANKFURT and KASSEL - ERFURT - LEIPZIG and BERLIN 850

Other regional services: Table **845** Berlin - Lutherstadt Wittenberg. Table **848** Lutherstadt Wittenberg - Halle. Table **849** Leipzig / Halle - Erfurt - Eisenach - Bebra.

	ICE 1550		*CNL* 458	*IC* 60458	*CNL* 471	*IC* 60471		
	⑦w		Ⓡ		Ⓡ			
			A	A	B♠	B♠		
	✕		🍷	2	🍷	2		
n Hbf ..... **851 902** d.	...	...	...	...	2150	2150	...	...
n Südkreuz ..... **851** d.	...	...	...	...	2156	2156	...	...
rstadt Wittenberg .... **851** d.	...	...	...	...	2233**u**	2233	...	...
feld ..... **851** d.	...	...	...	...	2251**u**	2251	...	...
(Saale) Hbf ..... **851** d.	...	...	...	...	2310**u**	2310	...	...
esden Hbf **842** ..... d.	2020	...	2054	2054	|	|	...	...
ipzig Hbf ..... **851** d.	2133	...	2359**u**	2359	2359**u**	2359	...	...
Naumburg (Saale) Hbf ..... d.	|	...	0050**u**	0050	0050**u**	0050	...	...
Weimar ..... d.	|	...	|	0116	|	0116	...	...
t Hbf ..... d.	2218	...	|	0133	|	0133	...	...
a ..... d.	2235	...	|	|	|	|	...	...
nach ..... d.	2252	...	|	|	|	|	...	...
bra ..... **901** d.	|	...	|	|	|	|	...	...
ssel Wilhelmshöhe .. **901** a.	|	...	|	|	|	|	...	...
Hersfeld ..... **901** d.	|	...	|	|	|	|	...	...
..... **900/1/2** d.	2344	...	|	0300	|	0300	...	...
u Hbf ..... **900/1/2** d.	|	...	|	|	|	|	...	...
kfurt (Main) Süd ..... a.	|	...	0359	0359	0359	0359	...	...
kfurt (Main) Hbf . **900/1/2** a.	0037	...	...	...	...	...	...	...
ankfurt Flughafen ✈ § ..... a.	...	...	...	...	...	...	...	...
esbaden Hbf **911** ..... a.	...	...	...	...	...	...	...	...

km		*RE* 3342	*CNL* 470	*IC* 61470	*CNL* 40470	*IC* 60470	*ICE* 1716	*ICE* 1531	*ICE* 1731	*ICE* 1553	*ICE* 1553
		©	Ⓡ		Ⓡ		Ⓐ		⑥	①g	⚒
			B♥	B♥	A	A	a	V			
			🍷	2	🍷	2	✕	🍷	T✕	✕	✕
	Wiesbaden Hbf **911** ..... d.	...	...	...	...	...	...	...	...	...	...
0	**Frankfurt** Flughafen ✈ § .... d.	...	...	...	...	...	...	...	...	...	...
	Frankfurt (Main) Hbf **900/1/2** d.	...	...	...	...	...	...	...	...	0458	...
11	**Frankfurt** (Main) Süd ..... d.	...	0054	0054	0054	0054	...	...	...	|	...
	Hanau Hbf ..... **900/1/2** d.	...	|	|	|	|	...	...	...	|	...
—	Fulda ..... **900/1/2** d.	...	|	0209	|	0209	...	...	...	0554	...
	Bad Hersfeld ..... **901** d.	...	|	|	|	|	...	...	...	0621	...
0	**Kassel** Wilhelmshöhe. **901** d.	...	|	|	|	|	...	...	...	|	...
54	Bebra ..... **901** d.	...	|	|	|	|	...	...	...	|	...
99	**Eisenach** ..... d.	...	|	|	|	|	0551	...	0638	0651	0651
128	Gotha ..... d.	...	|	|	|	|	0609	...	0655	0708	0707
155	**Erfurt** Hbf ..... d.	...	|	0339	|	0339	0627	...	0712	0727	0727
	Weimar ..... a.	...	|	0353	|	0353	|	...	|	|	|
	Naumburg (Saale) Hbf .... a.	...	|	|	|	|	|	...	|	|	|
	Leipzig Hbf ..... **851** a.	...	0458**s**	0458	0458**s**	0458	0709	...	|	0810	0810
	Dresden Hbf **842** ..... a.	...	|	|	0706	0706	|	...	|	0937	0937
249	**Halle** (Saale) Hbf ..... **851** d.	0502	0558**s**	0600	...	...	|	0748	0748	...	...
279	Bitterfeld ..... **851** d.	0538	0618**s**	0622	...	...	|	|	|	...	...
316	Lutherstadt Wittenberg ... **851** d.	0613	0637**s**	0640	...	...	0748	|	|	...	...
406	**Berlin** Südkreuz ..... **851** a.	0723	0716	0716	...	...	0822	0854	0854	...	...
414	**Berlin** Hbf ..... **851 902** a.	0732	0723	0723	...	...	0830	0901	0901	...	...

	ICE 1626	*ICE* 1543	*ICE* 1533	*ICE* 1684	*ICE* 1555	*IC* 2153	*ICE* 1545	*ICE* 1535	*ICE* 1682	*ICE* 1557	*ICE* 1597	*ICE* 1735	*ICE* 1547	*ICE* 1537	*ICE* 1208	*ICE* 1559	*IC* 2155	*ICE* 1549	*ICE* 1539	*ICE* 1588	*ICE* 1651	*ICE* 1739	*IC* 1959	*ICE* 1641
	⑦	⚒	Ⓐ					©		⚒		Ⓐ							⑤–⑦			①–④	⑤⑦	
	b		♣	⊖		D		T	⊖	S		T		K	⊖		X		L	⊖		R	wX	✕
	H✕	✕	✕	✕	✕		✕	✕	✕	✕	🍷◐	✕	✕	✕	✕	✕		✕	✕	✕	✕	✕		
esbaden Hbf **911** ..... d.	...	...	...	...	...	...	...	...	...	...	0824**z**	...	...	...	...	1024	...	...	...	...	1224	...	...	...
ankfurt Flughafen ✈ § .... d.	...	...	...	...	...	...	0811	...	...	...	0902	...	1011	...	...	1102	...	1211	...	...	1302	...	...	1411
kfurt (Main) Hbf . **900/1/2** d.	...	0618	0702	...	0718	...	|	0902	...	0919	0919	...	|	1102	...	1119	...	|	1302	...	1319	...	...	|
kfurt (Main) Süd ..... d.	...	|	|	...	|	...	0822	|	...	|	|	...	1022	|	...	|	...	1222	|	...	|	...	...	1422
u Hbf ..... **900/1/2** d.	...	0634	|	...	|	...	|	|	...	|	|	...	|	|	...	|	...	|	|	...	|	...	...	|
..... **900/1/2** d.	...	0714	|	0807	0814	...	0914	|	1007	1014	1014	...	1114	|	1207	1214	...	1314	|	1407	1414	...	...	1514
Hersfeld ..... **901** d.	...	0740	|	|	|	...	0940	|	|	|	|	...	1140	|	|	|	...	1340	|	|	|	...	...	1540
ssel Wilhelmshöhe .. **901** d.	...	|	|	|	|	0859	|	|	|	|	|	...	|	|	|	|	1259	|	|	|	|	...	1419	|
bra ..... **901** d.	...	|	|	|	|	0935	|	|	|	|	|	...	|	|	|	|	1335	|	|	|	|	...	1503	|
nach ..... d.	0754	0809	|	|	0907	0958	1009	|	|	1107	1107	...	1209	|	|	1307	1359	1409	|	|	1507	...	1527	1609
a ..... d.	0810	|	|	|	0923	1013	|	|	|	1123	1123	...	|	|	|	1323	1415	|	|	|	1523	...	1542	|
rt Hbf ..... d.	0827	0839	0912	0927	0939	1032	1039	1112	1127	1139	1139	1144	1239	1312	1327	1339	1432	1439	1512	1527	1539	1544	1557	1639
Weimar ..... a.	|	|	|	|	|	1049	|	|	|	|	|	|	|	|	|	|	1449	|	|	|	|	|	1611	|
Naumburg (Saale) Hbf ..... a.	|	|	|	|	|	...	|	|	|	|	|	|	|	|	|	|	...	|	|	|	|	|	1641	|
ipzig Hbf ..... **851** a.	0910	0923	|	1010	1022	...	1123	|	1210	1222	1222	|	1323	|	1410	1422	...	1523	|	1610	1622	|	|	1723
esden Hbf **842** ..... a.	|	...	|	|	1137	...	...	|	|	1337	1337**j**	|	...	|	|	1539	...	...	|	|	1737	|	|	...
(Saale) Hbf ..... **851** d.	|	...	0948	|	...	...	...	1148	|	...	...	1222	...	1348	|	...	...	...	1548	|	...	1622	1716	...
feld ..... **851** d.	|	...	|	1034	...	...	...	|	1234	...	...	|	...	|	1434	...	...	...	|	1634	...	|	|	...
rstadt Wittenberg .... **851** d.	0948	...	|	1052	...	...	...	|	1252	...	...	|	...	|	1452	...	...	...	|	1652	...	|	1756	...
n Südkreuz ..... **851** a.	1022	...	1054	1126	...	...	...	1254	1326	...	...	1332	...	1454	1526	...	...	...	1654	1726	...	1732	1829	...
n Hbf ..... **851 902** a.	1030	...	1101	1133	...	...	...	1301	1333	...	...	1339	...	1501	1533	...	...	...	1701	1733	...	1739	1836	...

	IC 1955	*ICE* 1631	*ICE* 1586	*ICE* 1653	*IC* 1957	*ICE* 1643	*IC* 2398	*ICE* 1633	*ICE* 1584	*ICE* 1655	*IC* 2157	*ICE* 1694	*ICE* 1645	*IC* 2157	*ICE* 1635	*ICE* 1582	*ICE* 1657		*ICE* 1647	*ICE* 1659	*ICE* 1659	*ICE* 1659	*ICE* 1580	*ICE* 1580
	⑤				⑤		①–④	Ⓑq			Ⓑq		Ⓑq	Ⓑq	⑦J					Ⓑ	⑤⑦	⑦		⑤⑦
			⊖				m		⊖		P	⊖		P		⊖			◇	q	w	w	⊖	⊖
		✕	✕	✕		✕		✕	✕	✕		✕	✕		✕	✕	✕		✕	✕	✕	✕	✕	✕
esbaden Hbf **911** ..... d.	...	...	...	1424	...	...	...	...	...	1624	...	...	...	...	...	...	1824	...	...	2024	2024	2024	...	...
ankfurt Flughafen ✈ § .... d.	...	...	...	1502	...	1610	...	...	...	1702	...	...	1811	...	...	...	1902	...	...	2102	2102	2102	...	...
kfurt (Main) Hbf . **900/1/2** d.	1417	1502	...	1520	1546**f**	|	1617	1702	...	1720	...	...	|	...	1902	...	1919	...	2022	2119	2119	2119	...	...
kfurt (Main) Süd ..... d.	|	|	...	|	|	1622	|	|	...	|	...	...	1822	...	|	...	|	...	|	|	|	|	...	...
u Hbf ..... **900/1/2** d.	1438	|	...	|	|	|	1641	|	...	|	...	...	|	...	|	...	|	...	2038	|	|	|	...	...
..... **900/1/2** d.	1525	|	1607	1614	1658	1714	1724	|	1807	1814	...	1911**e**	1914	...	|	2007	2014	...	2118	2214	2214	2214	2232	2232
Hersfeld ..... **901** d.	|	|	|	|	1725	1740	1754	|	|	|	...	|	1940	...	|	|	|	...	2144	2239	2239	2239	|	|
ssel Wilhelmshöhe .. **901** d.	|	|	|	|	|	|	|	|	|	|	1859	|	|	...	|	|	|	...	|	|	|	|	|	|
bra ..... **901** d.	|	|	|	|	|	|	1804	|	|	|	1935	|	|	...	|	|	|	...	|	|	|	|	|	|
nach ..... d.	|	|	|	1707	1754	1809	...	|	|	1907	1959	|	2009	...	|	|	2107	...	2215	2309	2309	2309	|	|
a ..... d.	1633	|	|	1723	1809	|	...	|	|	1923	2015	|	2026	←	|	|	2123	...	2230	2325	2325	2325	|	|
rt Hbf ..... d.	1656	1712	1727	1739	1826	1841	...	1912	1927	1939	2030	2035	2042	2046	2114	2127	2139	...	2250	2341	2343	2343	0001	0001
Weimar ..... a.	1709	|	|	|	1838	|	...	|	|	|	→	|	|	2058	|	|	|	...	|	...	|	|	|	|
Naumburg (Saale) Hbf ..... a.	1739	|	|	|	1907	|	...	|	|	|	...	|	|	2125	|	|	|	...	|	...	|	|	|	|
ipzig Hbf ..... **851** a.	1822	|	1810	1823	1943	1925	...	|	2010	2022	...	2122	2126	|	|	2210	2222	...	2340	...	0026	0026	0043	0043
esden Hbf **842** ..... a.	...	|	|	1937	...	...	...	|	|	2137	...	|	...	|	|	|	2341**q**	...	...	...	...	0137	...	|
(Saale) Hbf ..... **851** d.	...	1748	|	...	...	...	...	1948	|	...	...	|	...	2209‡	2150	|	...	...	...	...	...	...	...	|
feld ..... **851** d.	...	|	1834	...	...	...	...	|	2034	...	...	|	...	|	|	2234	...	...	...	...	...	...	...	0108
rstadt Wittenberg .... **851** d.	...	|	1852	...	...	...	...	|	2052	...	...	2200	...	|	|	2252	...	...	...	...	...	...	...	0125
n Südkreuz ..... **851** a.	...	1854	1926	...	...	...	...	2054	2126	...	...	2234	...	2313**c**	2254	2326	...	...	...	...	...	...	...	0159
n Hbf ..... **851 902** a.	...	1901	1933	...	...	...	...	2101	2133	...	...	2241	...	2320**c**	2301	2333	...	...	...	...	...	...	...	0206

CANOPUS – 🛏 1, 2 cl. and 🛏 2 cl. (*CNL* **458/40470** Ⓡ) Praha - Basel - Zürich and v.v.;
(2) (*IC* **60458/60470**) Praha - Basel - Zürich and v.v.
SIRIUS – 🛏 1, 2 cl. and 🛏 2 cl. (*CNL* **470/471** Ⓡ) Zürich - Basel - Berlin and v.v.;
(2) (*IC* **61470/60471**) Zürich - Basel - Berlin and v.v.
(12) Köln - Hamm - Kassel - Weimar - Jena Paradies (a. 1125) - Jena Göschwitz (a. 1133).
Until Sept. 3. (12) Jena Göschwitz (d. 1233) - Jena Paradies (d. 1240) - Weimar - Kassel - Düsseldorf.
From Sept. 4. (12) Jena Göschwitz (d. 1221) - Jena Paradies (d. 1228) - Weimar - Kassel - Düsseldorf.
From Stralsund (Table **845**) from Sept. 5.
From / to Hamburg (Table **840**).
⑦ from Sept. 4 (also Oct. 3; not Oct. 2).
From Stuttgart (Table **912**) on ⑥. To Ostseebad Binz (Tables **844/845**) on ⑥ (also Oct. 2).
⑤–⑦ (also Oct. 3). To Stralsund (Table **845**) on ⑦ from Sept. 4 (also Oct. 3).
To Karlsruhe (Table **912**). Departs Leipzig 1403 on Sept. 4, 11, 18.
⑤–⑦ (also Oct. 3). From Ostseebad Binz (Tables **844/845**) on © (also ⑤ from Sept. 9).
(12) Halle - Kassel - Hamm - Köln and v.v.
From Stralsund (Table **845**) on Ⓐ.
①–④ (not Oct. 3). To Stralsund (Table **845**).
To / from Saarbrücken (Table **919**).
From / to Ostseebad Binz and Stralsund on dates in Tables **844** and **845**.
①–⑤ to Sept. 2; ②–⑤ from Sept. 6 (not Oct. 4).
To / from Düsseldorf (Tables **800/805**).
(12) Berlin - Kassel - Hamm - Köln.

Not Oct. 31.
Also Oct. 3, 31.
Runs Halle - Berlin on ④ only.

d – Also Oct. 3, Nov. 1; not Oct. 2, 30.
e – ①–⑥ only. 1914 on ⑥.
f – 1538 on July 22, 29, Aug. 5, 12, 19.

g – Also Oct. 4; not Oct. 3.
h – ⑥ (also Oct. 2).
j – † only.
m – Not Oct. 3.
q – Ⓑ (not Oct. 2).
r – ⚒ only.
s – Stops to set down only.
t – 3 minutes later until Aug. 4.
u – Stops to pick up only.
w – Also Oct. 3; not Oct. 2.
z – © only.

¶ – ①–⑥ (also Oct. 2; not Oct. 3). Departs Halle 0600 until Sept. 3.
‡ – Arrives 2157 until Sept. 2, 2207 from Sept. 4.
♣ – From Darmstadt Hbf (d. 0637).
◧ – Conveys ✕ on ⑥ (also Oct. 2).
◐ – Conveys ✕ on †.
⊙ – Also calls at Leipzig/Halle Flughafen (d. 0439).
◇ – Also calls at Leipzig/Halle Flughafen (a. 2327).
♠ – On ⑥⑦ June 25 - Aug. 28 (also June 4, 11, 18, Sept. 3, 10, 17, 24, Oct. 1) conveys through cars from Ostseebad Binz (d. 1738), Stralsund Hbf (d. 1828) and Rostock Hbf (d. 1934).
♥ – On the mornings of ⑥⑦ June 25 - Aug. 28 (also June 4, 11, 18, Sept. 3, 10, 17, 24, Oct. 1) continues to Rostock Hbf (a. 0931), Stralsund Hbf (a. 1048) and Ostseebad Binz (a. 1138).
⊖ – Until Sept. 3. To / from München (Table **900**).
§ – Frankfurt Flughafen Fernbahnhof.

For explanation of standard symbols see page 4

851 BERLIN - LEIPZIG - SAALFELD - NÜRNBERG

Other regional services: Table **845** Berlin - Lutherstadt Wittenberg. Table **848** Lutherstadt Wittenberg - Leipzig. Table **849** Leipzig / Halle - Saalfeld.

SERVICE UNTIL SEPTEMBER 3. Through *ICE* / *IC* services via Jena will be reinstated from September 4.

km		*ICE* 985	*ICE* 1581		*RE* 4981	🚌	*RE* 4801	*ICE* 1583	🚌 43292	*RE* 4983	🚌	*RE* 4803	*ICE* 1585	*IC* 2181	*RE* 4985	🚌	*RE* 4805	*ICE* 1587	*IC* 2383	*RE* 4987	🚌	*RE* 4807	*ICE* 1589	*IC* 2385
		Ⓐ r 🍴	Ⓐ r 🍴					①–⑥ 🍴	[R] ⊡				🍴	①–⑥ 🍷				🍴◇	R 🍷				🍴	🍷
	Hamburg Hbf **840** d.	...	...	...	...	...	...	...	...	...	...	...	...	...	...	...	...	0634e	...	...	...	...	0836	...
0	**Berlin** Hbf **850** d.	...	...	...	...	...	...	0427	...	...	...	...	0627	0730	...	...	...	0827	0930	...	...	...	1027	1130
6	**Berlin** Südkreuz **850** d.	...	...	...	...	...	...	0434	...	...	...	...	0634	0737	...	...	...	0834	0937	...	...	...	1034	1137
97	Lutherstadt Wittenberg **850** d.	...	...	...	...	...	...	0509	...	...	...	...	0709	0812	...	...	...	0909	1012	...	...	...	1109	1212
134	Bitterfeld **850** d.	...	...	...	...	...	...	0526	...	...	...	...	0726	|	...	...	...	0926	|	...	...	...	1126	|
167	**Leipzig** Hbf a.	...	...	...	...	...	...	0543	...	...	...	...	0743	0843	...	...	...	0943	1043	...	...	...	1143	1243
167	**Leipzig** Hbf **850** d.	...	...	...	...	...	...	0548	...	0709	...	...	0748	...	0909	...	...	0948	...	1109	...	...	1148	...
	Halle (Saale) Hbf **850** d.	...	...	...	0500	...	...	|	...	|	...	...	|	...	|	...	...	|	...	|	...	...	|	...
221	Naumburg (Saale) Hbf **850** d.	...	...	...	0539	...	...	|	...	0744	...	...	|	...	0944	...	...	|	...	1144	...	...	|	...
260	**Jena** Paradies d.	...	...	...	0607	...	...	|	0745	0809	...	...	|	...	1009	...	...	|	...	1209	...	...	|	...
307	**Saalfeld** (Saale) **875** d.	...	...	...	0641	...	...	●	|	0842	...	...	●	...	1042	...	...	●	...	1242	...	...	●	...
394	Lichtenfels **875** d.	...	...	...	0749	0758	...	|	|	0949	0959	...	|	...	1149	1158	...	|	...	1349	1359	...	|	...
426	**Bamberg** **875** d.	...	0647	...	...	0831	0836	|	|	...	1031	1036	|	...	...	1231	1236	|	...	...	1431	1436	|	...
464	Erlangen **875** d.	0607	0709	...	...	...	0900	|	|	...	...	1100	|	...	...	...	1300	|	...	...	...	1500	|	...
488	**Nürnberg** Hbf **875** a.	0625	0725	...	...	...	0919	0928	1015	...	...	1119	1128	...	...	...	1319	1328	...	...	...	1519	1525	...
	München Hbf **904 905** a.	0738	0841	...	...	...	...	1040	...	...	...	...	1241	...	...	...	...	1442	...	...	...	...	1639	...

	🚌	*RE* 4809	*ICE* 1209	🚌 43294	*IC* 2387	*RE* 4991	🚌	*RE* 4811	*ICE* 1683	*IC* 2185	*RE* 4993	🚌	*RE* 4813	*ICE* 1685	*IC* 2389	*RE* 4995	🚌	*RE* 4815	*ICE* 1687		*ICE* 1717		*ICE* 903	
			N 🍴	[R] ⊡	R 🍷				🍴	R 🍷				🍴◇	R 🍷				🍴		E 🍴		Ⓑ 🍴	
Hamburg Hbf **840** d.	...	...	1036	...	...	...	...	...	1236	...	...	...	...	1436	...	...	...	...	1636	...	1735	...	1836	...
Berlin Hbf **850** d.	...	...	1227	...	1330	...	...	...	1428	1530	...	...	...	1627	1730	...	...	...	1827	...	1927	...	2027	...
Berlin Südkreuz **850** d.	...	...	1234	...	1337	...	...	...	1434	1537	...	...	...	1634	1737	...	...	...	1834	...	1934	...	2034	...
Lutherstadt Wittenberg **850** d.	...	...	1309	...	1412	...	...	...	1509	1612	...	...	...	1709	1812	...	...	...	1909	...	2009	...	2109	...
Bitterfeld **850** d.	...	...	1326	...	|	...	...	...	1526	|	...	...	...	1726	|	...	...	...	1926	...	2026	...	2126	...
Leipzig Hbf a.	...	...	1343	...	1443	...	...	...	1543	1643	...	...	...	1743	1843	...	...	...	1943	...	2043	...	2143	...
Leipzig Hbf **850** d.	...	...	1348	...	...	1509	...	...	1548	...	1709	...	...	1748	...	1909	...	...	1948	...	...	...	...	...
Halle (Saale) Hbf **850** d.	...	...	|	...	...	|	...	...	|	...	|	...	...	|	...	|	...	...	|	...	...	...	...	...
Naumburg (Saale) Hbf **850** d.	...	...	|	...	...	1544	...	...	|	...	1744	...	...	|	...	1944	...	...	|	...	...	...	...	...
Jena Paradies d.	...	...	|	1545	...	1609	...	...	|	...	1809	...	...	|	...	2009	...	...	|	...	...	...	...	...
Saalfeld (Saale) **875** d.	...	...	●	|	...	1642	...	...	●	...	1842	...	...	●	...	2042	...	...	●	...	...	...	...	...
Lichtenfels **875** d.	1558	...	|	|	...	1749	1758	...	|	...	1949	2001	...	|	...	2149	2201	...	|	...	...	...	...	...
Bamberg **875** d.	1631	1636	|	|	...	...	1831	1838	|	...	...	2033	2038	|	...	...	2233	2238	|	...	...	...	...	...
Erlangen **875** d.	...	1700	|	|	...	...	...	1901	|	...	...	...	2101	|	...	...	...	2301	|	...	...	...	...	...
Nürnberg Hbf **875** a.	...	1719	1728	1815	...	...	...	1920	1949	...	...	...	2120	2128	...	...	...	2320	2327	...	...	...	...	...
München Hbf **904 905** a.	...	...	1841	...	...	...	...	...	2105	...	...	...	...	2241	...	...	...	...	0041	...	...	...	...	...

	ICE 1618		*ICE* 908	*ICE* 1716	*ICE* 906		🚌	*RE* 4980	*ICE* 1626	*IC* 2388	◧	*ICE* 1684	🚌	*RE* 29352	*IC* 2286	*ICE* 1682	*RE* 4844	🚌	*RE* 29354	*IC* 2186	*ICE* 1208	*RE* 4986	🚌	*RE* 29356
	①–⑤ 🍴		①–⑥ 🍴	①–⑥ E 🍴	🍴				⑦ E 🍴	①–⑥ R 🍷		🍴◇			🍷	🍴				🍷	N 🍴			
München Hbf **904 905** d.	...	...	...	...	...	...	...	...	...	...	...	0515	...	...	...	0720	...	...	...	...	0920	...	...	...
Nürnberg Hbf **875** d.	...	...	...	...	...	...	...	...	...	...	0549	0630	...	...	...	0833	0840	...	...	...	1033	1040	...	...
Erlangen **875** d.	...	...	...	...	...	...	...	...	...	...	0614	|	...	...	...	|	0900	...	...	...	|	1059	...	...
Bamberg **875** d.	...	...	...	...	...	...	0504	...	...	...	0646	|	0728	...	...	|	0923	0928	...	...	|	1123	1128	...
Lichtenfels **875** d.	...	...	...	...	...	...	0537	0542	...	...	...	|	0801	0810	...	|	...	1001	1010	...	|	...	1201	1210
Saalfeld (Saale) **875** d.	...	...	...	...	...	...	...	0701	...	...	...	●	...	0928	...	●	...	...	1128	...	●	...	...	1328
Jena Paradies d.	...	...	...	...	...	...	...	0736	...	...	...	|	...	1001	...	|	...	...	1201	...	|	...	...	1401
Naumburg (Saale) Hbf **850** d.	...	...	...	...	...	...	...	0814	...	...	...	|	...	1028	...	|	...	...	1228	...	|	...	...	1428
Halle (Saale) Hbf **850** a.	...	...	...	...	...	...	...	|	...	...	...	|	...	|	...	|	...	...	|	...	|	...	...	|
Leipzig Hbf **850** a.	...	...	...	...	...	...	...	0852	...	...	...	1010	...	1101	...	1210	...	...	1301	...	1410	...	...	1501
Leipzig Hbf d.	0510	...	0615	0715	0815	...	...	...	0915	0915	...	1015	...	...	1115	1215	...	...	...	1315	1415	...	...	...
Bitterfeld **850** d.	0532	...	0634	|	0834	...	...	...	|	|	...	1034	...	...	|	1234	...	...	...	|	1434	...	...	...
Lutherstadt Wittenberg **850** d.	0548	...	0652	0748	0852	...	...	...	0948	0948	...	1052	...	...	1148	1252	...	...	...	1348	1452	...	...	...
Berlin Südkreuz **850** a.	0622	...	0727	0822	0926	...	...	...	1022	1023	...	1126	...	...	1222	1326	...	...	...	1422	1526	...	...	...
Berlin Hbf **850** a.	0630	...	0734	0830	0933	...	...	...	1030	1033	...	1133	...	...	1230	1333	...	...	...	1430	1533	...	...	...
Hamburg Hbf **840** a.	0824	...	0924	...	1124	...	...	...	1221	...	...	1324	...	...	...	1524	...	...	...	...	1724	...	...	...

	🚌 43291	*ICE* 1588	*RE* 4988	🚌	*RE* 29358	*IC* 2282	*ICE* 1586	*RE* 4990	🚌	*RE* 29360	*IC* 2380	*ICE* 1584	*RE* 4992	🚌	*RE* 29362	*ICE* 1694	*ICE* 1582	*ICE* 1680	*RE* 4994	🚌	*RE* 29364	🚌 43293		*ICE* 1580
	[R] ⊡	🍴				R 🍷	🍴◇				🍷	🍴				🍴	🍴	①–④ 🍴				[R] ⊡		🍴
München Hbf **904 905** d.	...	1120	...	...	...	...	1320	...	...	...	...	1518	...	...	...	1618	1719	1719	...	...	...	...	...	1922
Nürnberg Hbf **875** d.	1145	1233	1240	...	...	...	1433	1441	...	...	...	1633	1641	...	...	1733	1833	1836	1840	...	...	1945	...	2033
Erlangen **875** d.	|	|	1259	...	...	...	|	1459	...	...	...	|	1659	...	...	|	|	1851	1859	...	...	|	...	|
Bamberg **875** d.	|	|	1323	1328	...	...	|	1523	1528	...	...	|	1723	1728	...	|	|	1912	1923	1928	...	|	...	|
Lichtenfels **875** d.	|	|	...	1401	1410	...	|	...	1601	1610	...	|	...	1801	1810	|	|	...	...	2001	2010	|	...	|
Saalfeld (Saale) **875** d.	|	●	...	...	1528	...	●	...	...	1728	...	●	...	...	1928	●	●	...	...	...	2128	|	...	●
Jena Paradies d.	1415	|	...	...	1601	...	|	...	...	1801	...	|	...	...	2001	|	|	...	...	...	2201	2215	...	|
Naumburg (Saale) Hbf **850** d.	...	|	...	...	1628	...	|	...	...	1828	...	|	...	...	2028	|	|	...	...	...	2226	...	...	|
Halle (Saale) Hbf **850** a.	...	|	...	...	|	...	|	...	...	|	...	|	...	...	|	|	|	...	...	...	2256	...	...	|
Leipzig Hbf **850** a.	...	1610	...	...	1701	...	1810	...	...	1901	...	2010	...	...	2101	2122	2210	...	...	...	...	...	...	0043
Leipzig Hbf d.	...	1615	...	...	...	1715	1815	...	...	...	1915	2015	...	...	...	2127	2215	...	...	...	...	...	...	...
Bitterfeld **850** d.	...	1634	...	...	...	|	1834	...	...	...	|	2034	...	...	...	|	2234	...	...	...	...	...	...	...
Lutherstadt Wittenberg **850** d.	...	1652	...	...	...	1748	1852	...	...	...	1948	2052	...	...	...	2200	2252	...	...	...	...	...	...	...
Berlin Südkreuz **850** a.	...	1726	...	...	...	1822	1926	...	...	...	2025	2126	...	...	...	2234	2326	...	...	...	...	...	...	...
Berlin Hbf **850** a.	...	1733	...	...	...	1830	1933	...	...	...	2033	2133	...	...	...	2241	2333	...	...	...	...	...	...	...
Hamburg Hbf **840** a.	...	1924	...	...	...	...	2124	...	...	...	...	2333	...	...	...	0036f	...	...	...	...	...	...	...	...

E – To / from Eisenach (Table **850**).
N – From / to Innsbruck via Kufstein (Table **951**).
R – From / to Rostock / Warnemünde on dates in Table **835**.

e – ①–⑥ only.
f – Berlin - Hamburg on ⑤ only.
r – Not Aug. 15.
s – Stops to set down only.
u – Stops to pick up only.

◧ – S-Bahn line 1.
⊡ – *IC Bus*. Normal *IC* fares apply. [R]. 🍷.
● – Via Würzburg, Fulda and Erfurt.
◇ – Connecting *IC* 🚌 available Erfurt - Bamberg - Erlangen and v.v. (see panel below).

ERFURT - BAMBERG - ERLANGEN *IC* 🚌 **connections**

	ICE 1587	🚌 43281	*ICE* 1685	🚌 43283
	🍴	[R] ⊡	🍴	[R] ⊡
Berlin Hbf d.	0827	...	1627	...
Leipzig Hbf d.	0948	...	1748	...
Erfurt Hbf a.	1032	...	1832	...
Erfurt Hbf d.	...	1045	...	1845
Bamberg a.	...	1245s	...	2045s
Erlangen a.	...	1330	...	2130

	🚌 43280	*ICE* 1684	🚌 43282
	[R] ⊡	🍴	[R] ⊡
Erlangen d.	0630	...	1430
Bamberg d.	0715u	...	1515u
Erfurt Hbf a.	0915	...	1715
Erfurt Hbf d.	...	0927	...
Leipzig Hbf a.	...	1010	...
Berlin Hbf a.	...	1133	...

COTTBUS - LEIPZIG 852

ᴾB services

…g timings are subject to alteration June 11 - Sept. 24 (arrivals may be up to 8 minutes later, departures up be 5 minutes **earlier**; a change of train at Leipzig-Thelka may be required).

	⚒									
Cottbus d.	0505	0705	0905	1105	1305	1505	1705	1905	2105	2309
Calau (Niederl) d.	0522	0722	0922	1122	1322	1522	1722	1922	2122	2327
Finsterwalde d.	0535	0735	0935	1135	1335	1535	1735	1935	2136	2342
Doberlug-Kirchhain d.	0543	0743	0943	1143	1343	1543	1743	1943	2144	2349
Falkenberg 856 d.	0600	0800	1000	1200	1400	1600	1800	2000	2212	0016
Torgau 856 d.	0612	0812	1012	1212	1412	1612	1812	2012	...	...
Eilenburg 856 d.	0634	0834	1034	1234	1434	1634	1834	2034	...	...
Leipzig Hbf 856 a.	0655	0855	1055	1255	1455	1655	1855	2056	...	...

			⚒							
Leipzig Hbf 856 d.	...	...	0703	0903	1103	1303	1503	1703	1903	2103
Eilenburg 856 d.	...	...	0728	0928	1128	1328	1528	1728	1928	2128
Torgau 856 d.	...	...	0750	0950	1150	1350	1550	1750	1950	2150
Falkenberg 856 d.	0451	0652	0804	1004	1204	1404	1604	1804	2004	2204
Doberlug-Kirchhain d.	0513	0714	0818	1018	1218	1418	1618	1818	2018	2218
Finsterwalde d.	0520	0722	0825	1025	1225	1425	1625	1825	2025	2225
Calau (Niederl) d.	0539	0736	0838	1038	1238	1438	1638	1838	2038	2238
Cottbus a.	0558	0755	0855	1055	1255	1455	1655	1855	2055	2255

…**stopping trains**: Cottbus → Falkenberg at 0605 Ⓐ, 0805, 1205, 1405, 1605, 1805, 2005. Falkenberg → Cottbus at 0352 Ⓐ, 0552 Ⓐ, 0852 ©, 0855 Ⓐ, 1255, 1455, 1652, 1852.

STEAM TRAINS IN SACHSEN 853

	Ⓐe							A	
Radebeul Ost 842 857 d.	0456	...	0826	1021	1256	1426	1726	1856	...
Moritzburg d.	0525	...	0853	1051	1323	1456	1754	1923	...
Radeburg a.	0546	...	...	1112	...	1517	...	...	...

	Ⓐe								A
Radeburg d.	0611	...	...	1136	...	1541	...	...	...
Moritzburg d.	0634	...	0903	1203	1333	1607	1803	...	1933
Radebeul Ost 842 857 a.	0701	...	0930	1230	1400	1633	1830	...	2000

		🍷		C	🍷		C d		🍷		C d		🍷		C d		C		🍷	🍷	🍷	🍷	🍷	🍷
Zittau d.	High season	0900	...	1008	1100	...	1208	...	1300	...	1408	...	1500	...	1608	...	...	Low season	0900	...	...	1300	...	...
Bertsdorf d.	until Oct. 31	0935	0935	1042	1135	1135	1240	1242	1335	1335	1440	1442	1535	1535	1640	1640	1738	♣	0931	1030	1131	1331	1430	1531
Kurort Oybin a.	→	0946	|	1053	1146	|	|	1253	1346	|	|	1453	1546	|	1651	|	1749	→	0942	|	1142	1342	|	1542
Kurort Jonsdorf a.		...	0947	*1055*z	...	1147	1253	...	...	1347	1453	...	...	1547	...	1653	...		...	1042	...	...	1442	...

			🍷		C d		🍷		C d		🍷		C d		🍷	C d	h	C		🍷	🍷	🍷	🍷	🍷	🍷
…Jonsdorf d.	High season	0957	...	...	1106	1157	...	...	1306	1357	...	...	1506	1557	...	...	1715	...	Low season	...	1055	...	...	1455	...
…rt Oybin d.	until Oct. 31	|	0958	1103	|	|	1158	1303	|	|	1358	1503	|	|	1558	1717	|	1758	♣	0954	|	1154	1354	|	1554
…orf d.	→	1008	1010	1114	1118	1208	1210	1314	1318	1408	1410	1514	1518	1608	1610	1728	1728	1810	→	1005	1105	1206	1405	1505	1606
… a.		...	1038	...	1149	...	1238	...	1349	...	1438	...	1549	...	1638	1758	1758	1838		...	...	1234	...	...	1634

…**tors**: Radebeul – SDG Sächsische Dampfeisenbahngesellschaft mbH, Lößnitzgrundbahn, Am Bahnhof 1, 01468 Moritzburg. ✆ +49 (0) 35207 89290. www.loessnitzgrundbahn.de
Zittau – SOEG - Sächisch Oberlausitzer Eisenbahngesellschaft mbH, Bahnhofstraße 41, 02763 Zittau. ✆ +49 (0) 3583 540540. www.soeg-zittau.de

…ntil Oct. 31.
…) (also Oct. 31).

d – Diesel train.
e – Not June 27 - Aug. 5, Oct. 3 – 14, 31, Nov. 16.

h – Change trains at Bertsdorf on © (also Oct. 31).
z – Change trains at Bertsdorf.

♣ – Low season: Nov. 26 - Dec. 10. **No service Nov. 1 – 25.**

SEUSSLITZ - DRESDEN - BAD SCHANDAU 853a

…24 - Nov. 1, 2016

Subject to alteration on May 1, 19, 20, Aug. 19, 20, 21. Contact the operator for service details on these dates.

	A			A	B	A	K			A	H
…tz d.	...	...	...	...	...	...	...	...	...	...	1330
…n d.	...	...	...	...	...	...	...	...	...	...	1500
…eul d.	...	...	...	...	...	...	...	...	...	...	1645
…**en** Terrassenufer d.	...	0930	1000	1015	...	...	1200	1400	...	1700	1815
… d.	...	1100	1150	|	1230	1245	1350	1550	...	1830	...
… d.	0930	1200	...	1240	1330	1345	...	...	...	1930	...
…stein d.	1130	1410	...	1445	1530	1545	...	...	...	...	...
…**chandau** a.	1230	...	...	1545	1615	1630	...	...	...	...	...

	H					K	A				A
Bad Schandau d.	...	...	0930	...	...	...	1300	...	...	...	1615
Königstein d.	...	...	1000	...	...	...	1330	...	1450	...	1645
Pirna d.	...	...	1120	...	...	...	1450	...	1610	...	1805
Pillnitz d.	...	...	1200	1210	...	1410	1530	1610	1650	...	1845
Dresden Terrassenufer d.	0945	...	...	1310	...	1510	1630	1710	1750	...	1945
Radebeul d.	1045	...	...	...	...	...	...	...	...	...	...
Meißen d.	1145	...	...	...	...	...	...	...	...	...	...
Seußlitz a.	1240	...	...	...	...	...	...	...	...	...	...

…lay 2 - Oct. 16.
…lar. 24 - Apr. 30 and Oct. 17 - Nov. 1.
…②–⑦ May 3 - Oct. 16 (also May 16, Oct. 3).

K – ⑤–⑦ Mar. 25 - Apr. 24 (also Mar. 28); daily Apr. 29 - Oct. 16; ⑤–⑦ Oct. 21 – 30.

Operator: Sächsische Dampfschiffahrts GmbH & Co. Conti Elbschiffahrts KG. Hertha-Lindner Straße 10, D-01067 Dresden. ✆ +49 (0) 351 866 090.

FORST - COTTBUS - GÖRLITZ - ZITTAU 854

…G ★ 2nd class only

	Ⓐt	Ⓐ	⚒							Ⓐt											Ⓐt				
Cottbus d.	...	0504	...	0604	0704	0804	0904	1004	1104	1104	1204	1304	1404	1504	1604	1704	1804	1904	2004	2104	2204	...	2309	...	...
Spremberg d.	...	0522	...	0622	0722	0822	0922	1022	1121	1122	1222	1322	1422	1522	1622	1722	1822	1922	2022	2122	2222	...	2326	...	...
Weißwasser d.	0436	0536	0536	0636	0736	0836	0936	1036	...	1136	1236	1336	1436	1536	1636	1736	1836	1936	2036	2136	2236	...	2344	...	...
Horka d.	0500	0600	0600	0700	0800	0900	1000	1100	...	1200	1300	1400	1500	1600	1700	1800	1900	2000	2100	2200	2300	...	0005	...	...
Görlitz a.	0516	0616	0616	0716	0816	0916	1016	1116	...	1216	1316	1416	1516	1616	1716	1816	1916	2016	2116	2216	2316	...	0020	...	...
Görlitz d.	0520	0620	0620	0720	0820	0920	1020	1120	...	1220	1320	1420	1520	1620	1720	1819	1920	2020	...	2220	...	...	...	...	...
Zittau a.	0555	0655	0655	0755	0855	0955	1055	1155	...	1255	1355	1455	1555	1655	1755	1857	1955	2055	...	2255	...	...	...	...	...

	Ⓐ	⚒	†						Ⓐd											Ⓐt
… d.	...	...	...	0501r	0601	0701	0801	0901	1003	1101	1201	1301	1401	1501	1601	1701	1803	1901	2101	2201
…z a.	...	...	...	0539r	0639	0739	0839	0939	1038	1139	1239	1339	1439	1539	1639	1739	1839	1939	2139	2239
…z d.	0344	0444	0445	0544	0644	0744	0844	0944	1045	1144	1244	1344	1444	1544	1644	1744	1844	1944	2144	2244
… d.	0358	0500	0500	0600	0700	0800	0900	1000	1101	1200	1300	1400	1500	1600	1700	1800	1900	2000	2200	2300
…vasser d.	0423	0521j	0521	0621	0721	0821	0921	1021	1121	1221	1321	1421	1521	1621	1721	1821	1921	2021	2221	2321
…nberg d.	0436	0538	0534	0638	0738	0838	0938	1038	1138	1238	1338	1438	1538	1638	1738	1838	1938	2038	2238	...
…**us** a.	0453	0555	0552	0655	0755	0855	0955	1055	1155	1255	1355	1455	1555	1655	1755	1855	1955	2055	2255	...

d – Ⓐ (not Oct. 31, Nov. 16); runs daily Spremberg - Cottbus.
j – 0524 on ⑥.
r – ⚒ only.
t – Not Oct. 31, Nov. 16.

★ – Ostdeutsche Eisenbahn. ✆ +49 (0) 30 514 88 88 88. www.odeg.de

…T (Lausitz) - **COTTBUS** and v.v. *22 km.* Journey time: 18 minutes.
Forst at 0431 Ⓐ, 0533, 0633 and hourly until 2133. **From Cottbus** at 0507 Ⓐ, 0607, 0707 and hourly until 2107; then 2312.

DRESDEN - GÖRLITZ and ZITTAU 855

…x (2nd class only)

	©z	©z	◇	⚒rw							w						w								
Dresden Hbf d.	0048	0533	0533j	0608	0635	0708	0808	0908	1008	1108	1208	1308	1408	1508	1608	1708	1808	1908	2008	2035	2134	2235	2235	2336	2336
Dresden Neustadt d.	0054	0540	0540j	0615	0642	0715	0815	0915	1015	1115	1215	1315	1415	1515	1615	1715	1815	1915	2015	2042	2142	2242	2242	2342	2342
Bischofswerda d.	0131	0618	0620	0646	0719	0745	0846	0945	1046	1145	1246	1345	1446	1545	1646	1745	1846	1945	2046	2119	2215	2321	2324	0021	0024
Ebersbach (Sachs) d.	|	|	0706	|	|	0816	|	1016	|	1216	|	1416	|	1616	|	1816	|	2016	|	|	2244	2357	|	0050	|
Neugersdorf d.	|	|	0710	|	|	0820	|	1020	|	1220	|	1420	|	1620	|	1820	|	2020	|	|	2248	0001	|	0054	|
Zittau a.	|	|	0736	|	|	0841	|	1041	|	1241	|	1441	|	1641	|	1841	|	2041	|	|	2309	0025	|	0115	|
Liberec **1117** a.	|	|	*0824*	|	|	0915	|	1120	|	*1355*	|	1524	|	1715	|	1920	|	*2116*	|	|	...	...	|	...	|
Bautzen d.	0146	0633	...	0658	0734	...	0858	...	1058	...	1258	...	1458	...	1658	...	1858	...	2058	2134	...	...	2339	...	0039
Löbau (Sachs) d.	0203	0653	...	0712	0754	...	0912	...	1112	...	1312	...	1512	...	1712	...	1912	...	2112	2154	...	...	2358	...	0058
Görlitz a.	0222	0714	...	0727	0815	...	0927	...	1127	...	1327	...	1527	...	1727	...	1927	...	2127	2215	...	...	0019	...	0119

	⚒r				⚒r			w									w					w			
Görlitz d.	...	0441	...	0544	0642	...	0744	0844	...	0944	1044	...	1244	...	1444	...	1644	...	1844	...	1944	2044	...	...	2244
Löbau (Sachs) d.	...	0502	...	0559	0657	...	0804	0859	...	1004	1059	...	1259	...	1459	...	1659	...	1859	...	2004	2059	...	...	2304
Bautzen d.	...	0521	...	0614	0714	...	0823	0914	...	1023	1114	...	1314	...	1514	...	1714	...	1914	...	2023	2114	...	...	2323
Liberec **1117** d.	...	|	...	|	|	*0602*	|	|	0838	|	|	1033	|	*1202*	|	1433	|	1633	|	1838	|	|	*2005*	...	|
Zittau d.	0351	|	0510	|	|	0720	|	|	0920	|	|	1120	|	1320	|	1520	|	1720	|	1920	|	|	2120	2212	|
Neugersdorf d.	0415	|	0531	|	|	0740	|	|	0940	|	|	1140	|	1340	|	1540	|	1740	|	1940	|	|	2140	2236	|
Ebersbach (Sachs) d.	0420	|	0535	|	|	0744	|	|	0944	|	|	1144	|	1344	|	1544	|	1744	|	1944	|	|	2144	2245	|
Bischofswerda d.	0500	0538	0604	0626	0726	0814	0839	0926	1014	1039	1126	1214	1326	1414	1526	1614	1726	1814	1926	2014	2039	2126	2214	2320	2339
Dresden Neustadt a.	0535	0612	0634	0653	0753	0842	0912	0953	1042	1112	1153	1242	1353	1442	1553	1642	1753	1842	1953	2042	2112	2153	2242	...	0012
Dresden Hbf a.	0542	0619	0641	0659	0759	0849	0919	0959	1049	1119	1159	1249	1359	1449	1559	1649	1759	1849	1959	2049	2119	2159	2249	...	0019

…2 minutes later on Ⓐ (not Oct. 31, Nov. 16).
…Not Oct. 31, Nov. 16.
…To / from Wrocław (Table **1085**).
…Also Oct. 31, Nov. 16.

◇ – From Oct. 30 Ebersbach d. 0701, Neugersdorf d. 0705, Zittau a. 0729.
¶ – 5 minutes later from Oct. 30

☛ **Other stopping trains**: Dresden Hbf → Görlitz at 0408 Ⓐ **r**, 0835, 1035, 1235, 1435, 1635 and 1835. Görlitz → Dresden Hbf at 0605, 1144, 1344, 1544 and 1744.
Dresden Hbf → Zittau at 0408 Ⓐ **r**, 0735, 0935, 1135, 1335, 1535, 1735 and 1935.
Zittau → Dresden Hbf at 0631, 0826 ¶, 1026 ¶, 1226 ¶, 1426 ¶, 1626 ¶, 1826 ¶ and 2026 ¶.

856 DRESDEN and LEIPZIG - RUHLAND - COTTBUS and HOYERSWERDA *RE / RB se*

See Tables **842**, **843** and **857** for other services Dresden - Coswig. See Table **852** for other direct services Leipzig - Falkenberg - Cottbus.

km			◐			◐		◐			
0	**Dresden** Hbf ..... d.	0550	0650	and in	1550	1650	1750	1850	1950	2050	2150
4	**Dresden** Neustadt ..... d.	0557	0657	the same	1557	1657	1757	1857	1957	2057	2157
18	Coswig ..... d.	0607	0707		1607	1707	1807	1907	2007	2107	2207
73	Ruhland ..... a.	0655	0757	pattern	1655	1757	1855	1957	2055	2157	2255
73	Ruhland ..... d.	0656	0800	every **two**	1656	1800	1856	2000	2056	2200	2256
	Hoyerswerda ..... a.	0718j	|		1718j	|	1918j	|	2119j	|	2319j
86	Senftenberg ..... d.	...	0810	hours until	...	1810	...	2010	...	2210	...
120	**Cottbus** ..... a.	...	0838		...	1838	...	2038	...	2238	...

		◐		◐					◐
Cottbus ..... d.	...	0515	...	0715	...	and in	...	1915
Senftenberg ..... d.	...	0544	...	0744	...	the same	...	1944
Hoyerswerda ..... d.	0439f	|	0639f	|	0840f		1840f	|
Ruhland ..... a.	0501	0554	0701	0754	0901	pattern	1901	1954
Ruhland ..... d.	0502	0602	0702	0802	0902	every **two**	1902	2002
Coswig ..... d.	0550	0655	0750	0850	0950		1950	2050
Dresden Neustadt ..... d.	0600	0704	0800	0901	1000	hours until	2000	2101
Dresden Hbf ..... a.	0606	0711	0806	0907	1006		2006	2107

km		Ⓐ◐		◐	Ⓐ◐			⚒◐			⚒◐		⊗	◐	⊗	◐	⊗	Ⓑ◐			Ⓑ◐			Ⓐ◐	
0	Leipzig-Stötteritz ★ ..... d.	...	...	...	...	...	0545	...	...	0745	...	...	0945	...	1145	...	1345	...	...	1545	...	...	1745	...	...
7	**Leipzig** Hbf ★ ..... d.	...	...	...	...	...	0558	...	...	0758	...	...	0958	...	1158	...	1358	...	...	1558	...	...	1758	...	...
32	Eilenburg ..... d.	...	...	...	...	...	0628	...	...	0828	...	...	1028	...	1228	...	1428	...	...	1628	...	...	1828	...	...
59	Torgau ..... d.	...	...	...	...	...	0650	...	...	0850	...	...	1050	...	1250	...	1450	...	...	1650	...	...	1850	...	...
77	Falkenberg (Elster) ..... a.	...	...	...	...	...	0704	...	...	0904	...	...	1104	...	1304	...	1504	...	...	1704	...	...	1904	...	...
77	Falkenberg (Elster) ..... d.	0412	...	E	0608	...	0712	0812	...	0912	1012	...	1105t	1208	1312	1412	1505	1608	...	1705	1808	...	1905	2008	...
101	Elsterwerda-Biehla ..... d.	0430	...	0522	0629	...	0733	0830	...	0933	1030	...	1126t	1230	1333	1430	1526	1629	...	1726	1829	...	1926	2029	...
127	Ruhland ..... a.	0452	...	0553	0652	...	0754	0852	...	0954	1052	...	1148t	1252	1354	1452	1547	1652	...	1747	1852	...	1947	2052	...
127	Ruhland ..... d.	0506	0506	0559	0706	0706	0802¦	0906	0906	1002¦	1106	1106	1202¦	1306	1402¦	1506	1602¦	1706	1706	1802¦	1906	1906	2002¦	2106	2106
152	**Hoyerswerda** ..... a.	|	|	|	|	|	0823¦	|	|	1023¦	|	|	1223¦	|	1423¦	|	1623¦	|	|	1823¦	|	|	2023¦	|	|
	Senftenberg ..... d.	0517	0517	0610	0717	0717	...	0917	0917	...	1117	1117	...	1317	...	1517	...	1717	1717	...	1917	1917	...	2117	2117
	Cottbus ..... a.	0548	0548	0641	0748	0748	...	0948	0948	...	1148	1148	...	1348	...	1548	...	1748	1748	...	1948	1948	...	2148	2148

	Ⓐ◐			Ⓐ◐	⊗		⚒◐	⊗		Ⓐ◐	⑥◐	⊗	◐		◐			Ⓑ◐			Ⓑ◐			Ⓐ◐	
Cottbus ..... d.	0415	...	0607	0607	...	0807	0807	...	1007	1007	1007	...	1207	...	1407	...	1607	1607	...	1807	1807	...	2007	2007	2207
Senftenberg ..... d.	0444	...	0638	0638	...	0838	0838	...	1038	1038	1038	...	1238	...	1438	...	1638	1638	...	1838	1838	...	2038	2038	2238
Hoyerswerda ..... d.	|	0534‡	|	|	0734‡	|	|	0934‡	|	|	|	1134‡	|	1334‡	|	1534‡	|	|	1734‡	|	|	1934‡	|	|	|
Ruhland ..... a.	0454	0556‡	0649	0649	0755‡	0849	0849	0955‡	1049	1049	1049	1155‡	1249	1355‡	1449	1555‡	1649	1649	1755‡	1849	1849	1955‡	2049	2049	2249
Ruhland ..... d.	0505	0602	...	0705	0802	...	0905	1002	...	1105	1105	1202	1305	1402	1505	1602	...	1705	1802	...	1905	2002	—	2105	2259
Elsterwerda-Biehla ..... d.	0527	0624	...	0727	0824	...	0927	1024	...	1127	1131	1224	1327	1424	1531	1624	...	1731	1824	...	1931	2024	...	2127	2321
Falkenberg (Elster) ..... a.	0546	0646	...	0746	0846	...	0946	1046	...	1148	1150	1246	1346	1446	1550	1646	...	1750	1846	...	1950	2046	...	2146	L
Falkenberg (Elster) ..... d.	...	0657	...	...	0857	...	...	1057	...	...	...	1257	...	1457	...	1657	...	...	1857	...	...	2057	...	...	...
Torgau ..... d.	...	0712	...	...	0912	...	...	1112	...	...	...	1312	...	1512	...	1712	...	...	1912	...	...	2112	2206	...	...
Eilenburg ..... d.	...	0735	...	...	0935	...	...	1135	...	...	...	1335	...	1535	...	1735	...	...	1935	...	...	2135	2232	...	...
Leipzig Hbf ★ ..... a.	...	0803	...	...	1003	...	...	1203	...	...	...	1403	...	1603	...	1803	...	...	2003	...	...	2203	2300	...	...
Leipzig-Stötteritz ★ ..... a.	...	0815	...	...	1015	...	...	1215	...	...	...	1415	...	1615	...	1815	...	...	2015	...	...	2215	2319	...	...

E – From Elsterwerda (d. 0519).
L – To Elsterwerda (a. 2325).

f – 19–20 minutes **earlier** until Sept. 24.
j – 20–21 minutes later until Sept. 24.
t – 6–7 minutes later on Ⓐ.

◐ – Change trains at Ruhland from Sept. 25.
¦ – By 🚌 until Sept. 24 (arrives Hoyerswerda 25 minutes later).
‡ – By 🚌 until Sept. 24 (departs Hoyerswerda 25 minutes **earlier**).
⊗ – Leipzig timings are subject to alteration on ①⑥⑦ June 11 - Aug. 1.
★ – Trains also call City Tunnel stations Leipzig MDR, Bayerischer Bahnhof, Wilhelm-Leuschner-Platz and

857 BAD SCHANDAU - DRESDEN - MEISSEN *S-*

km	S-Bahn					Ⓐ			⚒		❖										
0	**Bad Schandau** ⊡ ..... **1100** d.	0015	...	...	...	0445	...	0515	0545	...	0611	0645		2011	2045	2115	2145	2215	...	2315	...
23	Pirna ..... d.	0037	...	...	0437	0507	0507	0537	0607	0607	0637	0707	and at	2037	2107	2137	2207	2237	2307	2337	...
40	**Dresden** Hbf ..... **842/3 856 1100** d.	0058	...	0430	0500	0530	0530	0600	0630	0630	0700	0730	the same	2100	2130	2200	2230	2300	2330	0000	...
44	**Dresden** Neustadt ..... **842 856** d.	...	...	0437	0507	0537	0537	0607	0637	0637	0707	0737	minutes	2107	2137	2207	2237	2307	2337	0007	...
50	Radebeul Ost ..... d.	...	...	0446	0516	0546	0546	0616	0646	0646	0716	0746	past each	2116	2146	2216	2246	2316	2346	0016	...
58	Coswig ..... **842/3 856** d.	...	...	0456	0526	0556	0556	0626	0656	0656	0726	0756	hour until	2126	2156	2226	2256	2326	2356	0026	...
68	**Meißen** ..... a.	...	...	0504	0534	0604	0604	0634	0704	0704	0734	0804		2134	2204	2234	2304	2334	0004	0034	...

S-Bahn	Ⓐr			⚒r																		
Meißen ..... d.	...	0421	0451	0451	0521	0551		2021	2051	2121	2151	2221	2251	2321	...	...	...	...	...	...	...
Coswig ..... **842/3 856** d.	...	0430	0500	0500	0530	0600	and at	2030	2100	2130	2200	2230	2300	2330	...	...	...	...	...	...	...
Radebeul Ost ..... d.	...	0440	0510	0510	0540	0610	the same	2040	2110	2140	2210	2240	2310	2340	...	...	...	...	...	...	...
Dresden Neustadt ..... **842 856** d.	...	0450	0520	0520	0550	0620	minutes	2050	2120	2150	2220	2250	2320	2350	...	...	...	...	...	...	...
Dresden Hbf ..... **842/3 856 1100** d.	0429	0459	0529	0529	0559	0629	past each	2059	2129	2159	2229	2259	2329	0012f	...	...	...	...	...	...	...
Pirna ..... d.	0451	0521	0550	0551	0621	0651	hour until	2121	2151	2221	2250	2321	2350	0034	...	...	...	...	...	...	...
Bad Schandau ⊡ ..... **1100** a.	0513	0543	...	0613	0643	0713		2143	2213	2243	...	2143	...	0056	...	...	...	...	...	...	...

f – Arrives 2357.
r – Not Oct. 31, Nov. 16.

❖ – Subsequent trains depart Bad Schandau 0715, 0811, 0915, 1011, 1115, 1211, 1315, 1411, 1515, 1611, 1715, 1811 and 1915 (other timings follow the same pattern).

⊡ – A frequent ferry services links the railway station with Bad Schandau town centre. **Operator**: Oberelbische Verkehrsgesellschaft Pirna - Sebnitz mbH. ✆ +49 (0) 350

857a DRESDEN - DRESDEN FLUGHAFEN ✈ *S-*

km										
0	**Dresden** Hbf ..... d.	0418	0448	and every	2218	2248	2318	...	...	...
4	**Dresden** Neustadt ..... d.	0425	0455	30 minutes	2225	2255	2325	...	...	...
15	**Dresden** Flughafen ✈ ..... a.	0439	0509	until	2239	2309	2339	...	...	...

Dresden Flughafen ✈ ..... d.	0447	0517	and every	2247	2317	2347	...	...
Dresden Neustadt ..... a.	0500	0530	30 minutes	2300	2330	2400	...	...
Dresden Hbf ..... a.	0509	0539	until	2309	2339	0009	...	...

858 GLAUCHAU and ALTENBURG - GERA - ERFURT *RB / RE se*

SERVICE UNTIL SEPTEMBER 3. During this period the line between Jena Göschwitz and Weimar via Jena West is closed with trains calling at Jena Paradies instead of Jena We

km		Ⓐ‡	⚒		Ⓐ																	‡	‡
0	**Glauchau** (Sachs) ..... d.	...	0446	...	...	...	0706	...	0906	...	1106	...	1306	...	1506	...	1706	...	1906	...	2106	...	...
16	Gößnitz ..... a.	...	0459	...	...	...	0719	...	0919	...	1119	...	1319	...	1519	...	1719	...	1919	...	2119	...	...
16	Gößnitz ..... d.	...	0500	...	...	0616	0720	0816	0920	1016	1120	1216	1320	1416	1520	1616	1720	1816	1920	2016	2120	...	...
	Altenburg ⊡ ..... d.	...	|	...	...	|	|	|	|	|	|	|	|	|	|	|	|	|	|	|	|	...	...
51	**Gera** Hbf ..... a.	...	0531	...	...	0648	0749	0848	0949	1048	1149	1248	1349	1448	1549	1648	1749	1848	1949	2048	2150	...	...
	Gera Hbf ..... d.	0452	0542	0542	0605	0653	0754	0853	0954	1053	1154	1253	1354	1453	1554	1653	1754	1853	1954	2106	...	2211	2322
	Jena-Göschwitz ..... d.	0526	0610	0610	0633	0720	0821	0920	1021	1120	1221	1320	1421	1520	1621	1720	1821	1920	2021	2134	...	2245	2356
	Jena Paradies ..... d.	0531	0618	0618	0640	0726	0828	0926	1028	1126	1228	1326	1428	1526	1628	1726	1828	1926	2028	2139	...	2250	2400
	Weimar ..... **849 850** d.	0609	0652	0651	0717	0758	0859	0958	1059	1158	1259	1358	1459	1558	1659	1758	1859	1958	2059	2212	...	2328	...
	Erfurt Hbf ..... **849 850** a.	0625	0706	0706	0731	0810	0912	1010	1112	1210	1312	1410	1512	1610	1712	1810	1912	2010	2111	2224	...	2341	...
	Göttingen **865** ..... a.	...	...	...	...	0952	...	1152	...	1352	...	1552	...	1752	...	1952	...	2150	2256	...	...	...	...

km		‡	†	⚒	‡	Ⓐd															Ⓑ		
	Göttingen **865** ..... d.	...	...	...	...	...	...	0604	...	0808	...	1008	...	1208	...	1408	...	1608	...	1808	1808	...	2008
	Erfurt Hbf ..... **849 850** d.	0031	...	...	0427	0525	0644	0749	0844	0949	1044	1149	1244	1349	1444	1549	1644	1749	1845	1949	1949	2049	2149
	Weimar ..... **849 850** d.	0049	...	...	0442	0540	0659	0804	0859	1004	1059	1204	1259	1404	1459	1604	1659	1804	1859	2004	2004	2106	2204
	Jena Paradies ..... d.	0128	...	...	0518	0614	0731	0835	0931	1035	1133	1235	1331	1435	1531	1635	1731	1835	1931	2035	2035	2136	2235
	Jena-Göschwitz ..... d.	0134	...	...	0524	0621	0736	0840	0936	1040	1138	1240	1336	1440	1536	1640	1736	1840	1936	2040	2040	2142	2240
	Gera Hbf ..... a.	0204	...	...	0554	0648	0805	0907	1005	1107	1205	1307	1405	1507	1605	1707	1805	1907	2005	2107	2107	2209	2308
0	**Gera** Hbf ..... d.	...	0538	0539	...	0708	0807	0909	1007	1109	1207	1309	1407	1509	1607	1709	1807	1909	2007	...	2109	...	2319
50	**Altenburg** ⊡ ..... a.	...	|	|	...	|	|	|	|	|	|	|	|	|	|	|	|	|	|	...	|	...	2356
	Gößnitz ..... a.	...	0908	0609	...	0739	0836	0939	1036	1139	1236	1339	1436	1539	1636	1739	1836	1939	2036	...	2141	...	...
	Gößnitz ..... d.	...	0610	0610	...	...	0837	...	1037	...	1237	...	1437	...	1637	...	1837	...	2037	...	...	...	...
	Glauchau (Sachs) ..... a.	...	0626	0628	...	...	0851	...	1051	...	1251	...	1451	...	1651	...	1851	...	2051	...	...	...	...

d – Runs daily Gera - Gößnitz.

‡ – Operated by Erfurter Bahn.
* – By 🚌 to Weimar.

⊡ – Journeys between Altenburg and Gera are available via Gößnitz
Table **881** for connecting trains between Altenburg and Gößnitz)

BRAUNSCHWEIG - BAD HARZBURG, GOSLAR and HERZBERG — 859

RB services); erixx ⊠

	Ⓐ	Ⓐ	Ⓐ	⑥	⚒		Ⓐ	Ⓐ	Ⓒ				Ⓐ	Ⓐ	Ⓒ		Ⓒ	Ⓐ	Ⓐ		Ⓐ	⑥
Braunschweig Hbf d.	0524	...	0624	0624	...	0724	...	0824	0824	...	and in the same pattern every **two** hours until	1924	...	2024	2024	...	2124	*2124*	2124	...	2224	2224
Wolfenbüttel d.	0533	...	0633	0633	...	0733	...	0833	0833	...		1933	...	2033	2033	...	2133	*2133*	2133	...	2233	2233
Vienenburg 860 d.	0600	0602	0700	0702	0702	0800	0802	0900	0902	0902		2000	2002	2100	2102	2102	2201	2201	2202	...	2300	2302
Bad Harzburg 860 a.	|	0611	|	0711	0711	|	0811	|	0911	0911		|	2011	|	2111	2111	|	|	2211	...	|	2311
Goslar 860 a.	0612	...	0712	...	...	0812	...	0912	...	...		2012	...	2112	...	...	2213	2213	...	...	2312	...

	Ⓐ	Ⓐ	Ⓐ	Ⓐ	⚒		Ⓒ	Ⓐ	Ⓐ				Ⓒ	Ⓐ	Ⓐ				Ⓒ	Ⓐ		⑥
Goslar 860 d.	0447	...	0547	*0611*	0647	...	...	0747	...	0847	and in the same pattern every **two** hours until	...	...	1947	...	2047	...	...	...	2147	...	2247
Bad Harzburg 860 d.	|	0545	|	0626	|	0745	0745	|	0845	|		1945	1945	|	2045	|	...	2145	2145	|	...	|
Vienenburg 860 d.	0503	0553	0603	0635	0703	0753	0803	0803	0853	0903		1953	2003	2003	2053	2103	...	2153	2203	2203	...	2303
Wolfenbüttel d.	0526	...	0626	0659	0726	...	0826	0826	...	0926		...	2026	2026	...	2126	...	...	2226	2226	...	2326
Braunschweig Hbf a.	0535	...	0635	0708	0735	...	0835	0835	...	0935		...	2035	2035	...	2135	...	...	2235	2235	...	2335

	Ⓐ	Ⓐ		⚒d		⚒d		⚒d		⚒d		⚒d		⚒d		⚒d		⚒B					
Braunschweig Hbf d.	0503	0603	0703	0803	0903	1003	1103	1203	1303	1403	1503	1603	1703	1803	1903	2003	2103	2203	...	...	...	...	...
Salzgitter-Ringelheim d.	0528	0628	0728	0828	0928	1028	1128	1228	1328	1428	1528	1628	1728	1828	1928	2028	2128	2228	...	...	...	...	...
Seesen d.	0544	0644	0744	0844	0944	1044	1144	1244	1344	1444	1544	1644	1744	1844	1944	2044	2144	2244	...	...	...	...	...
Osterode (Harz) Mitte d.	0607	0707	0807	0907	1007	1107	1207	1307	1407	1507	1607	1707	1807	1907	2007	2107	2207	...	...	...	...	...	...
Herzberg (Harz) a.	0621	0721	0821	0921	1021	1121	1221	1321	1421	1521	1621	1721	1821	1921	2021	2121	2221	...	...	...	...	...	...

	ⒶB	Ⓐ	Ⓐ	⑥B	Ⓐ	Ⓒ	⚒d		⚒d		⚒d		⚒d		⚒d		⚒d		⚒d						
berg (Harz) d.	...	0534	0634	...	0730	0734	0834	0934	1034	1134	1234	1334	1434	1534	1634	1734	1834	1934	2034	2134	...	...	...	...	...
rode (Harz) Mitte d.	...	0547	0647	...	0745	0747	0847	0947	1047	1147	1247	1347	1447	1547	1647	1747	1847	1947	2047	2147	...	...	...	...	...
en d.	0513	0613	0713	0713	0813	0813	0913	1013	1113	1213	1313	1413	1513	1613	1713	1813	1913	2013	2113	2213	...	...	...	...	...
itter-Ringelheim d.	0529	0629	0729	0729	0829	0829	0929	1029	1129	1229	1329	1429	1529	1629	1729	1829	1929	2029	2129	2229	...	...	...	...	...
nschweig Hbf a.	0551	0651	0751	0751	0851	0851	0951	1051	1151	1251	1351	1451	1551	1651	1751	1851	1951	2051	2151	2251	...	...	...	...	...

	Ⓐ	Ⓒ	Ⓐ			Ⓒ															⚒B			
Bad Harzburg 860 d.	...	...	0630	0734	0748	0822	...	0934	1022	1134	1223	1334	1422	1534	1622	1734	1822	1934	2023	2134	...	...	...	...
Goslar 860 d.	0544	0636	0643	0758	0759	0836	0836	0958	1036	1158	1236	1358	1436	1556	1636	1758	1836	1958	2036	2158	...	...	...	...
Seesen d.	0603	0654	0702	0817	...	0854	0854	1017	1054	1217	1254	1417	1454	1615	1654	1817	1854	2017	2054	2217	2244	...	...	...
Bad Gandersheim d.	0613	0705	0713	0827	...	0905	0905	1027	1105	1227	1305	1427	1505	1625	1705	1827	1905	2027	2105	2227	2255	...	...	...
Kreiensen a.	0618	0711	0718	0832	...	0911	0911	1032	1111	1232	1311	1432	1511	1630	1711	1832	1911	2032	2111	2232	2301	...	...	...
Kreiensen 903 d.	*0623*	*0719*	*0723*	0839	...	*0919*	*0919*	1039	*1119*	1239	*1319*	1439	*1519*	1639	*1719*	1839	*1919*	2039	*2119*	2239	*2319*	...	...	...
Northeim (Han) 903 d.	*0636*	*0733*	*0736*	0856	...	*0935*	*0935*	1056	*1133*	1256	*1333*	1456	*1533*	1656	*1733*	1856	*1933*	2056	*2133*	2256	*2333*	...	...	...
Göttingen 903 a.	*0649*	*0747*	*0749*	0908	...	*0949*	*0949*	1108	*1147*	1308	*1347*	1508	*1547*	1708	*1747*	1908	*1947*	2108	*2147*	2308	*2347*	...	...	...

	ⒶB	Ⓐ	⚒	†		⑥B	Ⓒ	Ⓐ																	
ingen 903 d.	*0409*	*0504*	0607	0609	...	...	0649	0719	...	*0809*	0848	*1009*	1048	*1209*	1248	*1409*	1448	*1609*	1648	*1809*	1848	*2009*	2051h	...	...
eim (Han) 903 d.	*0422*	*0517*	0620	0622	...	...	0704	0733	...	*0822*	0902	*1022*	1102	*1222*	1302	*1422*	1502	*1622*	1702	*1822*	1902	*2022*	2104h	...	...
ensen 903 a.	*0436*	*0530*	0633	0636	...	...	0720	0748	...	*0836*	0917	*1036*	1117	*1236*	1317	*1436*	1517	*1636*	1717	*1836*	1917	*2036*	2120h	...	...
ensen d.	0456	0535	...	...	0642	0656	0724	0749	...	0842	0923	1042	1123	1242	1323	1442	1523	1642	1723	1842	1923	2042	2124	...	...
Gandersheim d.	0501	0540	...	...	0647	0701	0729	0755	...	0847	0929	1047	1129	1247	1329	1447	1529	1647	1729	1847	1929	2047	2129	...	...
en d.	0511	0551	...	...	0658	0711	0739	0805	...	0858	0939	1058	1139	1258	1339	1458	1539	1658	1739	1858	1939	2058	2140	...	...
ar 860 d.	...	0611	...	...	0717	...	0800	0825	0856	0917	1000	1117	1200	1317	1400	1517	1600	1717	1800	1917	2000	2117	2159	...	...
Harzburg 860 a.	...	0623	...	...	0729	...	0813	...	0906	0929	1013	1129	1213	1329	1413	1529	1613	1729	1814	1929	2014	2129	...	...	...

🚲12 Braunschweig - Seesen - Kreiensen and v.v. Runs daily Braunschweig - Seesen and v.v.

h – 2–3 minutes **earlier** July 18 - Aug. 26.

⊠ – Braunschweig - Goslar / Bad Harzburg operated by erixx GmbH. Service is subject to confirmation.

HANNOVER - BAD HARZBURG and GOSLAR - HALLE — 860

x; HEX ◇

HANNOVER - BAD HARZBURG ⊠

	Ⓐ								
Hannover Hbf d.	0548	0648	0748	and hourly until	1748	1845	1948	2048	2148	2248
Hildesheim Hbf d.	0614	0714	0814		1814	1914	2014	2114	2214	2314
Salzgitter-Ringelheim d.	0641	0741	0841		1841	1941	2041	2141	2241	2341
Goslar 859 d.	0656	0756	0856		1856	1956	2056	2156	2256	2356
Bad Harzburg 859 a.	0706	0806	0906		1906	2006	2106	2206	2306	0006

	Ⓐ								
Bad Harzburg 859 d.	...	0548e	0648	and hourly until	1748	1848	1948	2048	2148
Goslar 859 d.	0503	0603	0703		1803	1903	2003	2103	2203
Salzgitter-Ringelheim d.	0516	0616	0716		1816	1916	2016	2116	2216
Hildesheim Hbf d.	0544	0644	0744		1844	1943	2044	2144	2244
Hannover Hbf a.	0610	0710	0810		1910	2008	2110	2210	2310

GOSLAR - HALBERSTADT - HALLE ◇

	⚒		Ⓐ	Ⓐ	Ⓒ	Ⓐ		Ⓒ	Ⓐ	Ⓒ	Ⓐ														
Goslar 859 d.	...	...	...	...	...	...	...	...	...	...	0605	0704	...	0805	0904	...	1005	1104	...	1205	1304	...	1405	1504	...
Vienenburg 859 d.	...	...	...	...	...	...	...	...	...	...	0615	0715	...	0816	0915	...	1016	1115	...	1216	1315	...	1416	1515	...
Ilsenburg d.	...	...	0411	...	...	...	0529	...	...	0629	0629	0731	...	0831	0931	...	1031	1131	...	1231	1331	...	1431	1531	...
Wernigerode d.	...	...	0422	...	...	...	0540	...	...	0640	0640	0742	...	0840	0942	...	1040	1142	...	1240	1342	...	1440	1542	...
Halberstadt a.	...	...	0438	...	...	...	0556	...	...	0656	0656	0756	...	0856	0956	...	1056	1156	...	1256	1356	...	1456	1556	...
Halberstadt d.	0331	...	...	0446	0446	0528	...	0607	0607	0657	0701	...	0802	0901	...	1002	1101	...	1202	1301	...	1402	1501	...	1602
Aschersleben d.	0359	0359	...	0521	0521	0557	...	0641	0641	0726	0726	...	0824	0926	...	1024	1126	...	1224	1326	...	1424	1526	...	1624
Sandersleben (Anh) d.	0419	0419	...	0536	0536	0606	...	0656	0656	0737	0737	...	0836	0937	...	1036	1137	...	1236	1337	...	1436	1537	...	1636
Könnern d.	0432	0432	...	0551	0550	0618	...	0709	0709	0749	0749	...	0849	0949	...	1049	1149	...	1249	1349	...	1449	1549	...	1649
Halle (Saale) Hbf a.	0501	0501	...	0612	0622	0639	...	0738	0741	0812	0812	...	0912	1012	...	1112	1212	...	1312	1412	...	1512	1612	...	1712

									⑥		
lar 859 d.	1605	1704	...	1805	1904	...	2005	2104	2205	2304	...	...
enburg 859 d.	1616	1715	...	1816	1915	...	2016	2115	2216	2315	...	...
burg d.	1631	1731	...	1831	1931	...	2031	2131	2232	2331	2331	...
igerode d.	1640	1742	...	1840	1942	...	2040	2142	2243	2342	2342	...
erstadt a.	1656	1756	...	1856	1956	...	2056	2156	2258	2356	2356	...
erstadt d.	1701	A	1802	1901	...	2002	2101	...	2305	...	...	...
ersleben d.	1726	...	1824	1926	...	2024	2126	...	2333	...	...	...
dersleben (Anh) d.	1737	...	1836	1937	...	2036	2137	...	2347	...	...	...
ern d.	1749	...	1849	1949	...	2049	2149	...	0000	...	...	...
e (Saale) Hbf a.	1812	...	1912	2012	...	2112	2212	...	0029	...	...	...

	Ⓒ	Ⓐ	Ⓐ						
Halle (Saale) Hbf d.	...	0345	...	...	0526	0632	...	0747	0847
Könnern d.	...	0406	...	...	0551	0710	...	0810	0910
Sandersleben (Anh) d.	...	0418	0454	...	0610	0724	...	0822	0924
Aschersleben d.	...	0429	0507	...	0627	0737	...	0835	0937
Halberstadt a.	...	0458	0537	...	0656	0757	...	0859	0957
Halberstadt d.	0457	0459	...	0559	0704	...	0804	0904	...
Wernigerode d.	0514	0516	...	0616	0721	...	0818	0921	...
Ilsenburg d.	0525	0530	...	0630	0730	...	0830	0930	...
Vienenburg 859 d.	...	0542	...	0643	0742	...	0843	0942	...
Goslar 859 a.	...	0553	...	0654	0753	...	0854	0953	...

																		⑤⑥	⑥				⑤		
e (Saale) Hbf d.	...	0947	1047	...	1147	1247	...	1347	1447	...	1547	1647	...	1747	1847	...	1947	2047	2047	2047	...	...	2307	2307	...	2316
ern d.	...	1010	1110	...	1210	1310	...	1410	1510	...	1610	1710	...	1810	1910	...	2010	2110	2110	2110	...	...	2330	2330	...	2350
dersleben (Anh) d.	...	1022	1124	...	1222	1324	...	1422	1524	...	1622	1724	...	1822	1924	...	2022	2124	2124	2124	...	...	2346	2346	...	|
ersleben d.	...	1035	1137	...	1235	1337	...	1435	1537	...	1635	1737	...	1835	1937	...	2035	2137	2137	2137	...	...	0005	0005	...	0040
erstadt a.	B	1059	1157	...	1259	1357	...	1459	1557	...	1659	1757	...	1859	1957	...	2104	2159	2159	2159	...	...	0034	0034	...	0110
erstadt d.	1004	1104	...	1204	1304	...	1404	1504	...	1604	1704	...	1804	1904	...	2004	2105	...	2205	2205	2205	...	...	0038	0038	...
igerode d.	1018	1121	...	1218	1321	...	1418	1521	...	1618	1721	...	1818	1921	...	2018	2121	...	2219	2219	2219	...	...	0055	0055	...
burg d.	1030	1130	...	1230	1330	...	1430	1530	...	1630	1730	...	1830	1930	...	2030	2130	...	2230	2230	2230	...	...	0106	0106	...
enburg 859 d.	1043	1142	...	1243	1342	...	1443	1541	...	1643	1742	...	1843	1942	...	2043	2142	...	...	2243	...	...	...	...	...	...
lar 859 a.	1054	1153	...	1254	1353	...	1454	1552	...	1654	1753	...	1854	1953	...	2054	2153	...	...	2254	...	...	...	...	...	...

BERNBURG - HALLE ◇ ◧

	Ⓐ	⚒								
nburg d.	0448	0611	0722	0855	1055	1255	1455	1655	1855	2055
ern a.	0510	0635	0745	0918	1118	1318	1518	1718	1918	2118
e (Saale) Hbf a.	0545	0714	*0812*	0954	1154	1354	1554	1754	1954	2153

	⚒	⚒					Ⓐ					
Halle (Saale) Hbf d.	0506	0605c	0805	1005	1205	1405	1505	1605	1805	2005	2220	2316
Könnern d.	0539	0639	0841	1041	1241	1441	1553	1641	1841	2041	2256	2350
Bernburg a.	0605	0704	0905	1105	1305	1505	1617	1705	1905	2105	2320	0014

To Berlin via Magdeburg on ⑤–⑦ (also Oct. 3). See Tables **862**/**839**.
From Berlin via Magdeburg on Ⓒ. See Tables **839**/**862**.

c – 0559 on ⑥.
e – Ⓐ only.

⊠ – Operated by erixx GmbH.
◇ – *Harz Elbe Express*. Operated by Veolia Verkehr.
◧ – Bernburg to Könnern is *16 km*.

861 MAGDEBURG - SANGERHAUSEN - ERFURT and DESSAU - ASCHERSLEBEN *RE / RB ser*

Magdeburg - Erfurt and Aschersleben

km																									
		Ⓐt		Ⓐt	Ⓐt										Ⓐt	Ⓒz	Ⓐt			Ⓐt					
0	**Magdeburg** Hbf .... d.	...	...	0437	0512	0609	0712	0826	0912	1026	1112	1226	1312	1426	1457	1512	1533	1626	1712	1712	...	1826	1912	2026	2112
17	Schönebeck (Elbe) .... d.	...	...	0450	0528	0622	0726	0838	0926	1038	1126	1238	1325	1438	1508	1526	1545	1638	1726	1726	...	1838	1926	2038	2126
37	Staßfurt .... d.	...	...	0509	0551	0648	0751	0852	0951	1052	1151	1252	1351	1452	1534	1551	1608	1652	1751	1751	...	1852	1951	2052	2151
44	Güsten .... d.	...	...	0515	0558	0658	0758	0858	0958	1058	1158	1258	1358	1458	1541	1558	1615	1658	1759	1803	...	1858	1958	2058	2158
	Aschersleben .... a.	...	...	|	0610	|	0810	|	1010	|	1210	|	1410	|	|	1610	1627	|	1811	|	...	|	2010	|	2210
60	Sandersleben .... d.	...	...	0546	—	0711	—	0911	—	1111	—	1311	—	1511	1554	—	...	1711	...	1816	...	1911	—	2111	...
66	Hettstedt .... d.	...	...	0554	...	0718	...	0918	...	1118	...	1318	...	1518	1601	...	...	1718	...	1823	...	1918	...	2118	...
75	Klostermansfeld .... d.	...	...	0603	...	0728	...	0928	...	1128	...	1328	...	1528	1610	...	...	1728	...	1832	...	1928	...	2128	...
97	**Sangerhausen** .... d.	0348	0546	0623	0642	0748	0852	0948	1052	1148	1252	1348	1452	1548	1629	1652	...	1748	...	1856	1911	1947	2052	2158j	...
142	Sömmerda .... d.	0431	0632	0702	0731	0829	0931	1029	1131	1229	1331	1429	1531	1629	...	1731	...	1829	...	...	1957	2029	2137	2242	...
167	**Erfurt** Hbf .... a.	0451	0654	0724	0751	0850	0951	1050	1151	1250	1351	1451	1551	1650	...	1751	...	1850	...	...	2018	2050	2157	2303	...

	Ⓐt	Ⓐt	Ⓒz	Ⓐt	Ⓐt		Ⓒz	Ⓐt	Ⓐt															
Erfurt Hbf .... d.	...	...	...	...	...	0506	...	...	0613	0705	0809	0910	1009	1110	1209	1310	1409	1509	1609	1710	1809	1910	...	2031	2114
Sömmerda .... d.	...	...	...	...	...	0524	...	...	0634	0730	0829	0932	1029	1132	1229	1332	1429	1532	1629	1732	1829	1932	...	2051	2138
Sangerhausen .... d.	...	...	...	0510	...	0615	...	...	0721	0818	0909	1018	1109	1218	1309	1418	1509	1618	1709	1818	1909	2018	...	2136	2225
Klostermansfeld .... d.	...	...	...	0529	...	0635	...	...	...	0837	—	1037	—	1237	—	1437	—	1637	—	1837	—	2037		...	...
Hettstedt .... d.	...	...	...	0538	...	0645	...	...	...	0846	...	1046	...	1246	...	1446	...	1646	...	1846	...	2046	...	...	...
Sandersleben .... d.	...	...	...	0545	...	0653	...	...	...	0853	...	1053	...	1253	...	1453	...	1653	...	1853	...	2053	...	...	...
Aschersleben .... d.	0449	0530	0544	|	0620	|	0745	0747	...	|	0947	|	1147	|	1347	|	1547	|	1747	|	1947	|	2145	...	...
Güsten .... d.	0501	0542	0556	0559	0632	0707	0759	0759	...	0907	0959	1107	1159	1307	1359	1507	1559	1707	1759	1907	1959	2107	2159	...	...
Staßfurt .... d.	0510	0552	0604	0609	0641	0714	0808	0808	...	0914	1008	1114	1208	1314	1408	1514	1608	1714	1808	1914	2008	2114	2208	...	...
Schönebeck (Elbe) ..... d.	0531	0613	0626	0626	0703	0729	0829	0829	...	0929	1029	1129	1229	1329	1429	1529	1629	1729	1829	1929	2029	2129	2230	...	...
Magdeburg Hbf .... a.	0542	0625	0637	0639	0715	0740	0840	0840	...	0940	1040	1140	1240	1340	1440	1540	1640	1740	1840	1940	2040	2140	2247	...	...

Dessau - Aschersleben

km																									
		Ⓐt	Ⓒz	Ⓐt	Ⓐt	Ⓒz	Ⓐt	Ⓒz	Ⓐt								Ⓐt	Ⓒz							
0	**Dessau** Hbf .... d.	0424	0453	0516	0553	0600	0643	0712	0731	0802	0902	1002	1102	1202	1302	1402	1502	1502	1602	1702	1802	1902	2002	2112	2147
21	Köthen .... a.	0447	0516	0537	0620	0622	0712	0734	0753	0825	0923	1025	1123	1225	1323	1425	1523	1523	1625	1723	1825	1923	2025	2134	2214
21	Köthen .... d.	0448	0517	0538	0633	0630	0722	0735	0753	0827	0924	1027	1124	1227	1324	1427	1524	1524	1627	1724	1827	1924	2027	2135	...
42	Bernburg .... d.	0509	0539	0558	0653	0653	0743	0756	0813	0853	0943	1053	1143	1253	1343	1453	1543	1543	1653	1743	1853	1943	2053	2156	...
54	Güsten .... d.	0519	0550	0610	0703	0703	0754	0810	0823	0903	0954	1103	1154	1303	1354	1503	1554	1554	1703	1754	1903	1954	2103	2210	...
66	**Aschersleben** .... a.	0531	0601	0621	0714	0714	*0810*	0822	0831	0914	*1010*	1114	*1210*	1314	*1410*	1514	1605	*1610*	1714	*1811*	1914	*2010*	2114	2222	...

	Ⓒz	Ⓐt	Ⓐt			Ⓒz	Ⓐt								Ⓐt	Ⓒz								
Aschersleben .... d.	0432	0432	0516	0557	0649	0745	*0747*	0849	*0947*	1049	*1147*	1249	*1347*	1449	1537	*1547*	1649	*1747*	1849	*1947*	2046	...	...	...
Güsten .... d.	0443	0443	0527	0608	0702	0802	0802	0902	1002	1102	1202	1302	1402	1502	1549	1602	1701	1802	1902	2002	2057	2110	...	
Bernburg .... d.	0454	0454	0538	0618	0713	0813	0813	0913	1013	1113	1213	1313	1413	1513	1600	1613	1713	1813	1913	2013		2121	...	...
Köthen .... a.	0516	0516	0600	0638	0735	0834	0834	0935	1034	1135	1234	1335	1434	1535	1622	1634	1735	1834	1935	2034	...	2142	...	...
Köthen .... d.	0517	0517	0601	0639	0736	0835	0835	0936	1035	1136	1235	1336	1435	1536	1635	1635	1736	1835	1936	2035	...	2143	...	2220
Dessau Hbf .... a.	0540	0545	0623	0701	0758	0855	0855	0958	1055	1158	1255	1358	1455	1558	1655	1655	1758	1855	1958	2055	...	2205	...	2242

j – Arrives 2146. t – Not Oct. 31. z – Also Oct. 31.

862 MAGDEBURG - HALBERSTADT - THALE *HE*

km																								
		Ⓐ t							Ⓒ ▲		⊕													
	Berlin Ostbf **839** ...... d.	...	...	...	...	...	...	...	0708	...	...	...	...	...	...	...	...	...	...	...	...	...	...	...
0	**Magdeburg** Hbf .... d.	0429	...	...	0544	0709	0809	0909	0909	1009	1109	1209	1309	1409	1509	1609	1709	1809	1844	1909	2007	2107	2207	2317
39	Oschersleben (Bode) ... d.	0507	...	...	0625	0742	0842	0942	0942	1042	1142	1242	1342	1442	1542	1642	1742	1842	1925	1942	2045	2145	2247	2354
59	**Halberstadt** .... a.	0524	...	...	0642	0758	0858	0958	0958	1058	1158	1258	1358	1458	1558	1658	1758	1858	1942	1958	2101	2201	2302	0010
59	**Halberstadt** .... d.	0537	0537	0606	0706	0806	0906	1006	1006	1106	1206	1306	1406	1506	1606	1706	1806	1906	...	2006	2106	2203	...	...
77	Quedlinburg .... a.	0553	0553	0623	0723	0823	0923	1023	1023	1123	1223	1323	1423	1523	1623	1723	1823	1923	...	2023	2123	2220		
77	Quedlinburg .... d.	0554	0554	0630	0730	0830	0930	1030	1030	1130	1230	1330	1430	1530	1630	1730	1830	1930	...	2030	2130	2221	...	...
87	**Thale** Hbf .... a.	0606	0606	0642	0742	0842	0942	1042	1042	1142	1242	1342	1442	1542	1642	1742	1842	1942	...	2042	2142	2232	...	...

	Ⓐ t				Ⓐ t						⊕							⑤–⑦ b▲						
Thale Hbf .... d.	...	...	...	0522	...	0617	0717	0817	0917	1017	1117	1217	1317	1417	1517	1617	1717	1717	1817	1917	2017	2117	...	2233
Quedlinburg .... a.	...	...	...	0532	...	0628	0728	0828	0928	1028	1128	1228	1328	1428	1528	1628	1728	1728	1828	1928	2028	2128	...	2243
Quedlinburg .... d.	...	...	...	0533	...	0633	0733	0833	0933	1033	1133	1233	1333	1433	1533	1633	1733	1733	1833	1933	2033	2133	...	2244
Halberstadt .... a.	...	...	...	0549	...	0649	0749	0849	0949	1049	1149	1249	1349	1449	1549	1649	1749	1749	1849	1949	2049	2149	...	2300
Halberstadt .... d.	0330	0443	0540	0601	0618	0701	0801	0901	1001	1101	1201	1301	1401	1501	1601	1701	1801	1801	1901	2001	2103	...	2203	...
Oschersleben (Bode) .... d.	0346	0459	0556	0617	0635	0717	0817	0917	1017	1117	1217	1317	1417	1517	1617	1717	1817	1817	1917	2017	2119	...	2219	...
Magdeburg Hbf .... a.	0423	0537	0637	0644	0715	0744	0844	0944	1044	1144	1244	1344	1444	1544	1644	1744	1844	1844	1944	2056	2148	...	2258	...
Berlin Ostbf **839** .... a.	...	...	...	...	...	...	...	...	...	...	...	...	...	...	...	...	...	2051	...	...	...	...	...	...

b – Also Oct. 3.
t – Not Oct. 31.
⊕ – Change trains at Halberstadt on Ⓒ.
◇ – *Harz Elbe Express.* Operated by Veolia Verkehr Sachsen-Anhalt GmbH.
▲ – *HARZ-BERLIN-EXPRESS.* **DB tickets not valid for journeys from / to Be** Conveys 2nd class Berlin - Halberstadt - Goslar and v.v. (Table **860**).

863 BRAUNSCHWEIG - HILDESHEIM - HAMELN - BÜNDE *Nord West Bah*

km																									
		Ⓐ	⚒	⑥	Ⓐ			Ⓐ			Ⓐ			Ⓐ			Ⓐ			Ⓐ			Ⓐ		
0	**Hildesheim** Hbf .... d.	...	0537	0634	0637	0737	0834	0834	0937	1034	1034	1137	1234	1234	1337	1434	1434	1537	1634	1634	1737	1834	1834	1937	2034
18	Elze .... a.	...	0553	0650	0653	0753	0850	0850	0953	1050	1050	1153	1250	1250	1353	1450	1450	1553	1650	1650	1753	1850	1850	1953	2050
18	Elze .... d.	...	0602	0702	0702	0802	0902	0902	1002	1102	1102	1202	1302	1302	1402	1502	1502	1602	1702	1702	1802	1902	1902	2002	2102
47	**Hameln** .... d.	0529	0629	0727	0729	0829	0927	0929	1029	1127	1129	1229	1327	1329	1429	1527	1529	1629	1727	1729	1829	1927	1929	2029	2127
71	Rinteln .... d.	0546	0646	...	0746	0846	...	0946	1046	...	1146	1246	...	1346	1446	...	1546	1646	...	1746	1846	...	1946	2046	...
88	Vlotho .... d.	0601	0701	...	0801	0901	...	1001	1101	...	1201	1301	...	1401	1501	...	1601	1701	...	1801	1901	...	2001	2101	...
100	Löhne (Westf) ..... **811** a.	0614	0714	...	0814	0914	...	1014	1114	...	1214	1314	...	1414	1514	...	1614	1714	...	1814	1914	...	2014	2114	...
110	**Bünde** (Westf) .... **811** a.	0625	0725e	...	0825	...	...	1025	...	...	1225	1325e	...	1425	...	...	1625	1725e	...	1825	...	...	...	...	...

	⚒	Ⓐ	⚒	⚒		Ⓐ			Ⓐ			Ⓐ			Ⓐ			Ⓐ			Ⓐ			Ⓐ	
Bünde (Westf) ..... **811** d.	...	...	...	0632e	...	0732	...	0832e	...	...	1032e	...	...	1232e	1332	...	1432e	...	...	1632e	1732	...	1832e	...	...
Löhne (Westf) ...... **811** d.	...	0545	...	0645	...	0745	...	0845	0945	...	1045	1145	...	1245	1345	...	1445	1545	...	1645	1745	...	1845	1945	...
Vlotho .... d.	...	0559	...	0659	...	0759	...	0859	0959	...	1059	1159	...	1259	1359	...	1459	1559	...	1659	1759	...	1859	1959	...
Rinteln .... d.	...	0610	...	0710	...	0810	...	0910	1010	...	1110	1210	...	1310	1410	...	1510	1610	...	1710	1810	...	1910	2010	...
Hameln .... d.	0528	0628	0628	0728	0728	0828	0828	0928	1028	1028	1128	1228	1228	1328r	1428	1428	1528	1628	1628	1728	1828	1828	1928	2028	2028
Elze .... a.	0553	0652	0652	0753	0753	0852	0852	0953	1052	1052	1153	1252	1252	1353r	1452	1452	1553	1652	1652	1753	1852	1852	1953	2052	2052
Elze .... d.	0602	0702	0702	0802	0802	0907	0907	1002	1107	1107	1202	1307	1307	1402	1507	1507	1602	1707	1707	1802	1907	1907	2002	2107	2107
Hildesheim Hbf .... a.	0620	0720	0720	0820	0820	0925	0925	1020	1125	1125	1220	1325	1325	1420	1525	1525	1620	1725	1725	1820	1925	1925	2020	2125	2125

Regional trains WOLFSBURG - BRAUNSCHWEIG - HILDESHEIM ⊠

km		Ⓐ	⚒					A	
0	**Wolfsburg** Hbf .... d.	0514	0614	0714	0814	and	2214	2314	...
32	**Braunschweig** Hbf ... d.	0535	0635	0735	0835	hourly	2235	2335	...
75	**Hildesheim** Hbf .... a.	0602	0702	0802	0902	until	2302	0002	...

	Ⓐ	⚒	⚒							
Hildesheim Hbf ...... d.	0455	...	0555	...	0655	0755	and	1955	2109	2155
Braunschweig Hbf. d.	0526	0526	0626	0626	0726	0826	hourly	2026	2136	2226
Wolfsburg Hbf .... a.	0545	0545	0645	0645	0745	0845	until	2045	2200	2245

A – ⑤–⑦ (also Oct. 3).
e – Ⓐ only.
r – On Ⓐ (not June 23 - Aug. 3, Oct. 4 – 14) Hameln d. 1335, Elze a. 1401.
★ – Bünde - Hildesheim operated by Nord West Bahn.
⊠ – Operated by *enno*. See Table **902** for faster *ICE* trains operated by DB.

TUS Verkehrsgesellschaft (2nd class only) — GÖTTINGEN - KASSEL local services — 864

	Ⓐ	⑥	⑥	Ⓐ	Ⓒ	Ⓐ	⚒		⚒			Ⓒ	Ⓐ				Ⓑ	Ⓐ	Ⓒ	Ⓑ	⚒	Ⓑ	Ⓐ	⑥	Ⓒ
Göttingen 908 d.	0442	0444	0543	0600	0703	0714	0814	0914	1018	1114	1218	1314	1335	1418	1514	1614	1714	1814	1818	1914	2014	2118	2214	2219	2359
Eichenberg 908 a.	0456	0458	0557	0613	0717	0728	0828	0928	1032	1128	1232	1328	1350	1432	1528	1628	1728	1828	1832	1928	2028	2132	2228	2233	0013
Eichenberg 865 d.	0508	0502	0603	0623	0723	0733	0833	0933	1033	1133	1233	1333	1356	1433	1533	1633	1733	1833	1833	1933	2033	2133	2234	2239	0014
Hann Münden 865 d.	0528	0523	0623	0644	0743	0753	0853	0953	1053	1153	1253	1353	1416	1453	1553	1653	1753	1853	1853	1953	2053	2153	2254	2301	0033
Kassel Hbf ⊡ 865 a.	0549	0543	0643	0703	0803	0813	0913	1013	1113	1213	1313	1413	1437	1513	1613	1713	1813	1913	1913	2013	2113	2213	2319	2324	0054

	Ⓐ		Ⓐ	⑥	Ⓐ	Ⓒ		⚒	†	⚒	⚒						Ⓑ				Ⓑ	⚒			Ⓐ	Ⓒ
l Hbf ⊡ 865 d.	0416	...	0535	0546	0625	0636	...	0746	0846	0846	0946	1046	1146	1246	1346	1446	1546	1646	1746	1846	1946	2046	2146	...	2314	2346
Münden 865 d.	0436	...	0555	0606	0645	0656	...	0806	0906	0906	1006	1106	1206	1306	1406	1506	1606	1706	1806	1906	2006	2106	2206	...	2334	0006
ıberg 865 a.	0456	...	0615	0626	0705	0715	...	0826	0926	0926	1026	1126	1226	1326	1426	1526	1626	1726	1825	1926	2026	2126	2226	...	2355	0026
ıberg 908 d.	0502	...	0624	0627	0707	0722	...	0832	0927	0932	1032	1127	1232	1327	1432	1527	1632	1727	1832	1927	2032	2127	2227	...	0003	0027
gen 908 a.	0515	...	0637	0640	0721	0735	...	0845	0940	0945	1045	1140	1245	1340	1445	1540	1645	1740	1845	1940	2045	2140	2240	...	0018	0040

ꞩee Tables **804**, **806** and **901** for connecting trains to / from Kassel Wilhelmshöhe.

RE / RB services); Abellio — ERFURT and HALLE - LEINEFELDE - KASSEL and GÖTTINGEN — 865

	Ⓐt‡	Ⓐ	Ⓐt‡	Ⓐ		Ⓐt	‡	‡		Ⓐt‡			‡	A	⚒z‡			‡	A	⊕‡			‡	A
Erfurt Hbf 849 850 d.	...	...	...	...	0430	0502	...	...	0612	...	0623	0709	...	0812	...	0828	0917	...	1012	...	1028	1117	...	1212
Gotha 849 850 d.	...	...	...	...	0500	◇	...	...	0637	...	|	◇	...	0839	...	|	◇	...	1039	...	|	◇	...	1239
Bad Langensalza d.	...	...	...	0450	0512	0555	...	...	0648	...	0710	0800	...	0850	...	0914	1000	...	1050	...	1114	1200	...	1250
Mühlhausen (Thür) d.	...	...	...	0506	0526	0611	...	...	0700	...	0726	0815	...	0900	...	0926	1015	...	1100	...	1126	1215	...	1300
Bitterfeld 848 ◧ d.	...	...	...	|	|	|	...	...	|	...	|	|	...	|	0737	|	|	0837	|	0937	|	|	1037	|
Halle (Saale) Hbf 848 ◧ d.	...	...	...	|	|	|	0502	...	|	0534	|	|	0704	|	0804	|	|	0904	|	1004	|	|	1104	|
Lutherstadt Eisleben ◧ d.	...	...	...	|	|	|	0530	...	|	0614	|	|	0733	|	0833	|	|	0933	|	1033	|	|	1133	|
Sangerhausen ◧ d.	...	...	0415	|	|	|	0549	...	|	0633	|	|	0752	|	0855	|	|	0952	|	1055	|	|	1152	|
Nordhausen ◧ d.	...	...	0448	|	|	|	0622	0632	|	0706	|	|	0825	|	0921	|	|	1025	|	1121	|	|	1225	|
Leinefelde a.	...	...	0528	0531	0545	0634	0651	0712	0717	0746	0750	0839	0855	0917	0952	0950	1039	1055	1117	1152	1150	1239	1255	1317
Leinefelde d.	0425	0502	...	0532	0548	...	0652	...	0720	...	0751	...	0856	0919	...	0955	...	1056	1119	...	1155	...	1256	1319
Heilbad Heiligenstadt d.	0439	0513	...	0547	0559	...	0703	...	0731	...	0801	...	0907	0930	...	1005	...	1107	1130	...	1205	...	1307	1330
Göttingen a.	|	0539	...	|	0625	...	|	...	0752	...	|	...	|	0952	...	|	...	|	1152	...	|	...	|	1352
Eichenberg 864 d.	0452	...	...	0602	...	...	0718	...	...	...	0816	...	0918	...	...	1019	...	1118	...	...	1219	...	1318	...
Hann Münden 864 d.	*0528*	...	...	0622	...	...	0736	...	...	...	0833	...	0936	...	...	1036	...	1136	...	...	1236	...	1336	...
Kassel Hbf 864 a.	*0549*	...	...	0643	...	...	|	...	...	...	|	...	|	...	...	|	...	|	...	...	|	...	|	...
Kassel Wilhelmshöhe 864 a.	...	...	...	0656	...	...	0753	...	...	...	0852	...	0953	...	...	1053	...	1153	...	...	1253	...	1355	...

	⊕‡			‡	A	⊕‡			‡	A	⊕‡			‡	A	‡			‡	A		⊕‡	⑥	L	
t Hbf 849 850 d.	...	1228	1317	...	1412	...	1428	1517	...	1612	...	1628	1717	...	1812	...	1828	1917	...	2012	2031	...	...	2113	2244
ha 849 850 d.	...	|	◇	...	1439	...	|	◇	...	1639	...	|	◇	...	1839	...	|	◇	...	2039	|	...	...	2139	◇
angensalza d.	...	1314	1400	...	1450	...	1514	1600	...	1650	...	1714	1800	...	1850	...	1914	2000	...	2050	2112	...	...	2151	2332
ausen (Thür) d.	...	1326	1415	...	1500	...	1526	1615	...	1700	...	1726	1815	...	1900	...	1926	2015	...	2100	2125	...	...	2204	2348
terfeld 848 ◧ d.	1137	|	|	1237	|	1337	|	|	1437c	|	1537	|	|	1637c	|	1737	|	...	1837	|	|	1937	...	|	...
le (Saale) Hbf 848 ◧ d.	1204	|	|	1304	|	1404	|	|	1504	|	1604	|	|	1704	|	1804	|	...	1904	|	|	2004	...	|	...
ıerstadt Eisleben ◧ d.	1233	|	|	1333	|	1433	|	|	1533	|	1633	|	|	1733	|	1833	|	...	1933	|	|	2033	...	|	...
ıgerhausen ◧ d.	1255	|	|	1352	|	1455	|	|	1552	|	1655	|	|	1752	|	1855	|	...	1952	|	|	2055	...	|	...
rdhausen ◧ d.	1321	|	|	1425	|	1521	|	|	1625	|	1721	|	|	1825	|	1921	|	...	2025	|	|	2123	...	|	...
felde a.	1352	1349	1439	1455	1517	1552	1550	1639	1655	1717	1752	1750	1839	1855	1917	1952	1950	...	2055	2117	2144	2203	...	2222	...
felde d.	...	1355	...	1456	1519	...	1555	...	1656	1719	...	1755	...	1856	1919	...	1955	...	2056	2119	2150	▬	...	2224	...
ıd Heiligenstadt d.	...	1405	...	1507	1530	...	1605	...	1707	1730	...	1805	...	1907	1930	...	2005	...	2107	2130	2201		...	2234	...
ttingen a.	...	|	...	|	1552	...	|	...	|	1752	...	|	...	|	1952	...	|	...	|	2150	|	Ⓐ	...	2256	...
ıberg 864 d.	...	1419	...	1519	...	...	1619	...	1718	...	...	1819	...	1918	...	...	2019	...	2118	...	2212	2234	2239	...	...
Münden 864 d.	...	1436	...	1536	...	...	1636	...	1736	...	...	1836	...	1936	...	...	2036	...	2136	...	...	2254	2301	...	...
el Hbf 864 a.	...	|	...	|	...	...	|	...	|	...	...	|	...	|	...	...	|	...	2154	...	...	2319	2324	...	...
el Wilhelmshöhe 864 a.	...	1453	...	1553	...	...	1656	...	1753	...	...	1855	...	1954	...	...	2053	...	...	...	...	...	...	...	...

		Ⓐt‡	Ⓐt	A	Ⓐ‡	Ⓒ‡		Ⓐ		Ⓐt‡	A	‡			⚒z‡	A	‡			⊕‡	A	‡		
Kassel Wilhelmshöhe 864 d.	...	...	...	...	...	...	...	0704	...	...	...	0806	...	0906	...	...	1006	...	1106	...	...	1206	...	1306
Kassel Hbf 864 d.	...	*0416*	...	...	0559	0606	...	|	...	...	...	|	...	|	...	...	|	...	|	...	...	|	...	|
Hann Münden 864 d.	...	*0436*	...	...	0615	0622	...	0724	...	...	...	0822	...	0922	...	...	1022	...	1122	...	...	1222	...	1322
Eichenberg 864 d.	...	0501	...	...	0633	0640	...	0744	...	...	...	0840	...	0941	...	...	1040	...	1141	...	...	1240	...	1341
Göttingen d.	...	|	...	0604	|	|	...	|	...	...	0808	|	...	|	...	1008	|	...	|	...	1208	|	...	|
Heilbad Heiligenstadt d.	0444t	0514	...	0628	0647	0652	...	0758	...	...	0831	0852	...	0955	...	1031	1052	...	1155	...	1231	1252	...	1355
Leinefelde a.	0459t	0525	...	0639	0701	0702	...	0807	...	...	0841	0902	...	1005	...	1041	1102	...	1205	...	1241	1302	...	1405
Leinefelde d.	0501	0526	0547	0640	0702	0703	0719t	0808	0808	*0811*	0843	0903	0919	1007	1010	1043	1103	1119	1207	1209	1243	1303	1319	1407
Nordhausen ◧ d.	|	0559	|	|	0734	0734	|	|	|	*0841*	|	0934	|	|	1040	|	1134	|	|	1240	|	1334	|	|
Sangerhausen ◧ d.	|	0629	|	|	0809	0809	|	|	|	0912	|	1009	|	|	1112	|	1209	|	|	1312	|	1409	|	|
Lutherstadt Eisleben ◧ d.	|	0647	|	|	0828	0828	|	|	|	0929	|	1028	|	|	1129	|	1228	|	|	1329	|	1428	|	|
Halle (Saale) Hbf 848 ◧ a.	|	0728	|	|	0858	0858	|	|	|	0958	|	1058	|	|	1158	|	1258	|	|	1358	|	1458	|	|
Bitterfeld 848 ◧ a.	|	...	|	|	0925	0925	|	|	|	1025	|	1125	|	|	1225	|	1325	|	|	1425	|	1525c	|	|
Mühlhausen (Thür) d.	0524	...	0613	0659	...	...	0742	0832	0832	...	0901	...	0942	1032	...	1101	...	1142	1232	...	1301	...	1342	1432
Bad Langensalza d.	0536	...	0629	0709	...	...	0759	0844	0844	...	0911	...	0959	1044	...	1111	...	1159	1244	...	1311	...	1359	1444
Gotha 849 850 a.	0549	...	⊙	0721	...	...	⊙	|	|	...	0923	...	⊙	|	...	1123	...	⊙	|	...	1323	...	⊙	|
Erfurt Hbf 849 850 a.	0617	...	0723	0745	...	...	0842	0930	0930	...	0945	...	1042	1130	...	1145	...	1242	1330	...	1345	...	1442	1530

	⊕‡	A	Ⓒc‡	Ⓐt‡			⊕‡	A	‡			⊕‡	A	‡			‡	‡	L	‡	G				
el Wilhelmshöhe 864 d.	...	...	1406	1406	...	1506	...	...	1606	...	1706	...	...	1805	...	1906	...	...	...	2006	...	2106	...	...	...
el Hbf 864 d.	...	...	|	|	...	|	...	...	|	...	|	...	...	|	...	|	...	...	...	|	...	|	2146	...	...
Münden 864 d.	...	...	1422	1422	...	1522	...	...	1622	...	1722	...	...	1822	...	1922	...	...	...	2022	...	2122	2206	...	...
ıberg 864 d.	...	...	1440	1440	...	1541	...	...	1640	...	1741	...	...	1840	...	1941	...	...	...	2040	...	2141	2226	2241	...
ttingen d.	...	1408	|	|	...	|	...	1608	|	...	|	...	1808	|	...	|	...	...	2008	|	2108	|	▬	|	2308
ıd Heiligenstadt d.	...	1431	1452	1452	...	1555	...	1631	1652	...	1755	...	1831	1852	...	1955	...	...	2031	2052	2132	2155	...	2253	2332
efelde a.	...	1441	1502	1502	...	1605	...	1641	1702	...	1805	...	1841	1902	...	2005	...	...	2041	2102	2142	2205	‡	2303	2343
efelde d.	1410	1443	1503	1503	1519	1607	1609	1643	1703	1719	1807	1810	1843	1903	1919	2007	2010	...	2043	2103	2145	2223	2226	...	...
rdhausen ◧ d.	1440	|	1534	1536	|	|	1640	|	1734	|	|	1840	|	1934	|	|	2040	2057	|	2136	|	|	2305	...	...
ıgerhausen ◧ d.	1512	|	1609	1610	|	|	1712	|	1809	|	|	1912	|	2009	|	|	...	2130	|	2211	|	|	2336	...	...
ıerstadt Eisleben ◧ d.	1529	|	1628	1628	|	|	1729	|	1828	|	|	1929	|	2028	|	|	...	2149	|	2230	|	|	2355	...	...
lle (Saale) Hbf 848 ◧ a.	1558	|	1658	1658	|	|	1758	|	1858	|	|	1958	|	2058	|	|	...	2228	|	2301	|	|	0033	...	...
terfeld 848 ◧ a.	1625	|	1725	...	|	|	1825	|	1925	|	|	2025	|	...	|	|	...	...	|	...	|	|	...	...	...
ıausen (Thür) d.	...	1501	...	...	1542	1632	...	1701	...	1742	1832	...	1901	...	1942	2027	...	...	2101	...	2203	2242	...	...	...
.angensalza d.	...	1511	...	...	1559	1644	...	1711	...	1759	1844	...	1911	...	1959	2039	...	...	2111	...	2213	2258	...	...	...
tha 849 850 a.	...	1523	...	...	⊙	|	...	1723	...	⊙	|	...	1923	...	⊙	|	...	...	2122	...	2224	|	...	...	...
t Hbf 849 850 a.	...	1545	...	...	1642	1730	...	1745	...	1842	1930	...	1945	...	2045	2123	...	...	2145	...	2252	2338	...	...	...

Other services **BITTERFELD - HALLE - NORDHAUSEN - LEINEFELDE** (operated by Abellio Rail Mitteldeutschland)

			Ⓐt	Ⓐt	Ⓐt			Ⓐt		
rfeld d.	...	...	...	...	...	...	2037	...	...	...
(Saale) Hbf d.	0011	...	...	0629	1231	2035	2104	2144	2234	2313
ɾstadt Eisleben d.	0054	...	...	0704	1308	2118	2133	2224	2318	2342
erhausen d.	0114	...	0524	0725	1327	2138	2152	2244	2338	0001
hausen a.	...	...	0556	0757	1359	...	2224	...	...	0033
efelde a.	...	...	0636	0839	1443	...	...	...	...	...

	Ⓐt		⚒r		⚒r			Ⓐt	Ⓐt	Ⓐt
Leinefelde d.	...	...	...	*0445*t	0549h	...	...	...	...	...
Nordhausen d.	...	...	0427	0534	0631	...	...	1257	1457	...
Sangerhausen d.	0354	0427	0501	0611	0711	0912	1112	1330	1530	1627
Lutherstadt Eisleben d.	0414	0447	0520	0630	0729	0929	1129	1349	1549	1647
Halle (Saale) Hbf a.	0454	0528	0549	0659	0758	0958	1158	1428	1628	1728
Bitterfeld a.	...	...	...	0725	0825	1025	1225	...	...	...

From / to Glauchau (Table **858**).
To Gera (Table **858**).
From / to Altenburg (Table **858**).

Ⓒ (also Oct. 31).
0600 on ⑥.

r – Not Oct. 31.
t – Ⓐ (not Oct. 31).
z – ⚒ (not Oct. 31). Change trains at Sangerhausen on Ⓐ.

⊕ – Change trains at Sangerhausen on Ⓐ**r**.

◇ – Connecting trains Gotha - Bad Langensalza (journey time: 18 minutes). **From Gotha** at 0531 Ⓐ**t**, 0737, 0937, 1137, 1337, 1537, 1737, 1937 and 2245.
⊙ – Connecting trains Bad Langensalza - Gotha (journey time: 19 minutes). **From Bad Langensalza** at 0650, 0801, 1001, 1201, 1401, 1601, 1801 and 2001.
◧ – See panel below main table for other services Bitterfeld - Halle - Nordhausen - Leinefelde.
‡ – Operated by Abellio Rail Mitteldeutschland.

866 HANNOVER - MAGDEBURG - LEIPZIG

See panels below main table for regional / S-Bahn trains. See Table **848** for other regional trains between Magdeburg and Leipzig via Dessau.

km		IC	IC	IC	IC	IC	IC	IC	IC	IC	IC	IC	IC	IC	IC	IC	IC	IC	IC	IC	IC	IC	RE	IC
		2043	**2233**	**2447**	**2235**	**2445**	**2035**	**2443**	**2037**	**2441**	**2039**	**2049**	**2049**	**1949**	**2431**	**2239**	**2047**	**2433**	**2045**	**2435**	**2012**	**2012**	**17639**	**2437**
		Ⓐ	Ⓐ	⚒		⚒	⚒						⑤–⑦ d	⑤	C	A	Ⓑ		Ⓑ q		T D 🍷	⑦ w D 🍷		Ⓑ q
	Köln Hbf **800** d.	...	...	...	...	0513v	...	0713b	...	0913v	...	...	1113v	...	...	...	1313v	...	1513v	...	1646	1646	...	...
	Dortmund Hbf **800** d.	...	...	...	...	0628	...	0828e	...	1028	...	...	1228	...	...	...	1428	...	1628	...	1828	1828	...	...
	Bielefeld Hbf **810** d.	...	...	0516g	...	0719	...	0919e	...	1119	...	...	1319	...	...	...	1519	...	1719	...	1916	1916	...	...
	Norddeich **813** ⊠ d.	...	...	|	...	|	0536	|	0739j	|	0939	...	|	...	...	...	|	...	|	1540	|	|	...	...
	Emden Hbf **813** ⊠ d.	...	...	|	0416e	|	0609	|	0816	|	1016	...	|	...	1218	...	|	1416f	|	1616	|	|	...	1816
	Oldenburg (Oldb) **813** d.	...	...	|	0535e	|	0735	|	0935	|	1135	...	|	...	1335	...	|	1535	|	1735	|	|	...	1935
	Bremen Hbf **813** d.	...	...	|	0609	|	0809	|	1009	|	1209	...	|	...	1409	...	|	1609	|	1809	|	|	...	2009
0	**Hannover** Hbf d.	...	0531	0636	0736	0836	0936	1036	1136	1236	1335	1436	1436	1511	1536	...	1636	1736	1836	1936	2036	2036	...	2136
35	Peine d.	...	0552	|	|	|	|	|	|	|	|	|	|	1533	|	...	|	|	|	|	|	|	...	2156
61	**Braunschweig** Hbf d.	...	0610	0711	0810	0911	1010	1111	1210	1311	1410	1511	1511	1550	1610	...	1711	1810	1911	2010	2111	2111	...	2212
97	Helmstedt d.	...	0632	|	0832	|	1032	|	1232	|	1432	|	|	1612	1632	...	|	1832	|	2032	|	|	...	2235
145	**Magdeburg** Hbf a.	...	0657	0756	0857	0956	1057	1156	1257	1356	1457	1556	1556	1637	1657	...	1756	1857	1956	2057	2157	2157	...	2300
145	**Magdeburg** Hbf d.	0559	0702	0801	0902	1001	1102	1201	1302	1401	1502	1601	1601	1639	1659	1703	1801	1902	2001	2102	...	2201	2207	...
	Berlin Hbf **839** a.	|	|	|	|	|	|	|	|	|	|	|	|	|	1822	|	|	|	|	|		|	|	...
195	Köthen d.	0628	|	0830	|	1030	|	1230	|	1430	|	1630	1630	|	...	|	1830	|	2030	2130	...	|	2248	...
231	**Halle** (Saale) Hbf a.	0651	0750	0852	0950	1052	1150	1252	1350	1452	1550	1652	1652	◐	...	1750	1852	1950	2052	2150	...	⊖	2317	...
231	**Halle** (Saale) Hbf d.	0654	0752	0854	0952	1054	1152	1254	1352	1454	1552	1654	1654	|	...	1752	1854	1952	2054	2152	...	|	*2346*	...
249	Leipzig/Halle Flughafen ✈ a.	|	|	|	|	|	|	|	|	|	|	|	|	|	...	|	|	|	|	|	...	|	*2356*	...
268	**Leipzig** Hbf a.	0717	0819	0917	1019	1117	1219	1317	1419	1517	1619	1717	1717	1815	...	1819	1917	2019	2117	2219	...	2321	*0016*	...
	Dresden Hbf **842** a.	0837	...	1037	...	1237	...	1437	...	1637	...	1837	1837	...	...	...	2037	...	2237	2339h	...	...	...	...

	IC	IC	IC	IC	IC	IC	IC	IC	IC	IC	IC	IC	IC	IC	IC	IC	IC	IC	IC	IC	IC	IC	IC	IC
	2436	**2013**	**2013**	**2013**	**2434**	**2044**	**2238**	**2432**	**2046**	**2046**	**2430**	**2048**	**2038**	**2440**	**2036**	**2442**	**2442**	**2034**	**1934**	**2444**	**2444**	**2032**	**2446**	**2446**
	⚒	① g E 🍷	⚒ E 🍷	⑦ s E 🍷	⚒	⚒	A	C	⚒	⑥					Ⓑ		Ⓑ q	Ⓑ q	⑦ w		Ⓑ q	Ⓑ q		⑦ w
Dresden Hbf **842** d.	...	...	...	...	...	0520a	...	...	0720	0720	...	0920	...	1120	...	1320	1320	...	...	1520	1520	...	1720	1720
Leipzig Hbf d.	...	0430	...	...	0539	0643	0739	...	0843	0843	0939	1043	1139	1243	1339	1443	1443	1539	1558	1643	1643	1739	1843	1843
Leipzig/Halle Flughafen ✈ d.	...	|	...	...	|	|	|	...	|	|	|	|	|	|	|	|	|	|	|	|	|	|	|	|
Halle (Saale) Hbf a.	...	|	...	...	0605	0705	0805	...	0905	0905	1005	1105	1205	1305	1405	1505	1505	1605	|	1705	1705	1805	1905	1905
Halle (Saale) Hbf d.	...	⊕	...	...	0607	0707	0807	...	0907	0907	1007	1107	1207	1307	1407	1507	1507	1607	◧	1707	1707	1807	1907	1907
Köthen d.	...	|	...	...	0627	0728	|	...	0928	0928	|	1128	|	1328	|	1528	1528	|	|	1728	1728	|	1928	1928
Berlin Hbf **839** d.	...	|	...	...	|	|	|	0731	|	|	|	|	|	|	|	|	|	|	|	|	|	|	|	|
Magdeburg Hbf a.	...	0554	...	...	0655	0757	0854	0858	0957	0957	1054	1157	1254	1357	1454	1557	1557	1654	1719	1757	1757	1854	1957	1957
Magdeburg Hbf d.	0501	0601	0601	...	0700	0804	...	0902	1004	1004	1059	1204	1259	1404	1459	1604	1604	1659	1724	1804	1804	1859	2004	2004
Helmstedt d.	0528	0628	0628	...	0727	|	...	0927	|	|	1127	|	1327	|	1527	|	|	1727	|	|	|	1927	|	|
Braunschweig Hbf d.	0551	0651	0651	0705	0751	0851	...	0951	1051	1051	1151	1251	1351	1451	1551	1651	1651	1751	1816	1851	1851	1951	2051	2051
Peine d.	0606	|	|	|	|	|	...	|	|	|	|	|	|	|	|	|	|	|	|	|	|	|	|	|
Hannover Hbf a.	0626	0723	0723	0737	0823	0923	...	1023	1123	1123	1223	1323	1423	1523	1623	1723	1723	1823	1851	1923	1923	2023	2123	2123
Bremen Hbf **813** a.	0750	|	|	|	0950	|	...	1150	...	|	1350	|	1550	|	1750	...	|	1950	2009	...	|	2150	...	|
Oldenburg (Oldb) **813** a.	0823	|	|	|	1023	|	...	1223	...	|	1423	|	1623	|	1823	...	|	2023	2040	...	|	2223	...	|
Emden Hbf **813** ⊠ a.	0938	|	|	|	1138	|	...	1338	...	|	1538	|	1738	|	1938	...	|	2138	2152	...	|	2338	...	|
Norddeich **813** ⊠ a.	...	|	|	|	...	|	...	1414	...	|	...	|	...	|	2014	...	|	2214	...	...	|	...	...	|
Bielefeld Hbf **810** a.	...	0840	0840	0840	...	1040	...	...	...	1240	...	1440	...	1640	...	...	1840	...	...	...	2039	...	...	2239
Dortmund Hbf **800** a.	...	0932	0932	0932	...	1132	...	...	...	1332	...	1532	...	1732	...	...	1932	...	...	...	2132	...	...	2331
Köln Hbf **800** a.	...	1115	1115	1115	...	1246‡	...	...	...	1446‡	...	1645‡	...	1846r	...	...	2046‡	...	...	...	2245‡	...	...	0046‡

Other regional trains **HANNOVER - BRAUNSCHWEIG** (operated by WestfalenBahn; most trains start from / continue to Bielefeld or Rheine – see Table **811**)

			⚒						
Hannover Hbf d.	0013	...	0455	0555	0655	and	2155	2255	...
Peine d.	0039	...	0524	0624	0724	hourly	2224	2323	...
Braunschweig Hbf a.	0056	...	0540	0641	0741	until	2241	2341	...

	⚒							
Braunschweig Hbf d.	0420	...	0520	and	2120	...	2222	2320
Peine d.	0438	...	0538	hourly	2138	...	2240	2338
Hannover Hbf a.	0505	...	0605	until	2205	...	2307	0005

Other regional trains **BRAUNSCHWEIG - MAGDEBURG** (calling at all stations)

	†		Ⓐ	Ⓒ		Ⓐ		Ⓐ		Ⓐ		Ⓐ	Ⓒ	Ⓐ	Ⓐ		Ⓐ		Ⓐ			Ⓑ q	⑥ h	Ⓑ q
Braunschweig Hbf d.	0107	...	0529	0541	...	0617	0717	0817	0917	1017	1117	1217	1318	1320	1417	1517	1617	1717	1817	1917	2017	2117	2147	2217
Helmstedt d.	0136	...	0602	0610	0610	0646	0746	0846	0946	1046	1146	1246	1346	1348	1446	1546	1646	1746	1846	1946	2046	2146	2216	2246
Magdeburg Hbf a.	0218	...	...	0652	0652	0728	0828	0928	1028	1128	1228	1328	1428	1428	1528	1628	1728	1828	1928	2028	2128	2228	2258	2328

	⑥	Ⓐ					Ⓐ			Ⓐ		Ⓐ			Ⓐ			Ⓐ			Ⓐ			
Magdeburg Hbf d.	0253	0433	0533	0633	0733	...	0833	0933	...	1033	1133	1233	1333	...	1433	1533	...	1633	1733	...	1833	1933	2033	2203
Helmstedt d.	0333	0513	0613	0713	0813	0913	0913	1013	1113	1113	1213	1313	1413	1513	1513	1613	1713	1713	1813	1913	1913	2013	2113	2243
Braunschweig Hbf a.	0403	0542	0642	0742	0842	0942	0942	1042	1142	1142	1242	1342	1442	1542	1542	1642	1742	1742	1842	1942	1942	2042	2142	2312

Other regional / S-Bahn trains **MAGDEBURG - HALLE - LEIPZIG**

				Ⓐ t																			U	
Magdeburg Hbf d.	...	0424	...	0500	...	...	...	0537	...	...	and at	1937	...	...	...	2037	...	...	...	2207	...	2307	...
Schönebeck (Elbe) d.	...	0435	...	0513	...	...	...	0550	...	...	the same	1950	...	...	...	2050	...	...	...	2220	...	2320	...
Köthen d.	...	0500	...	0536	...	...	...	0618	...	...	minutes	2018	...	...	...	2118	...	...	...	2248	...	2348	...
Halle (Saale) Hbf a.	...	0527	...	0600	...	...	...	0645	...	...	past each	2045	...	...	...	2145	...	...	...	2317	...	0015	...
Halle (Saale) Hbf ■ d.	0413	...	0536	...	0616	0636	...	...	0716	0736	hour until	...	2116	2136	...	...	2216	2246	...	...	2346	...	0022
Leipzig/Halle Flughafen ✈ ■ a.	0424	...	0546	...	|	0646	...	...	|	0746		...	|	2146	...	...	|	2257	...	...	2356	...	|
Leipzig Hbf ■ a.	0438	...	0608	...	0653	0708	...	...	0753	0808		...	2153	2208	...	...	2253	2316	...	...	0016	...	0100

		U	Ⓐ t	Ⓒ z	Ⓐ t		Ⓐ t																	
Leipzig Hbf ■ d.	0406	...	0438	...	...	0523	...	0553	0608	...	0653	0708	...	and at	1853	1908	...	2038	2053	...	2153	...	2327
Leipzig/Halle Flughafen ✈ ■ d.	0420	...	|	...	...	0540	...	0610	|	...	0710	|	...	the same	1910	|	...	|	2110	...	2210	...	2344
Halle (Saale) Hbf ■ a.	0434	...	0513	...	...	0554	...	0624	0643	...	0724	0743	...	minutes	1924	1943	...	2113	2124	...	2224	...	2359
Halle (Saale) Hb d.	...	0441t	...	0543	0543	...	0613	...	...	0715	...	...	0813	past each	...	...	2013	...	...	2129	...	2243	...
Köthen d.	...	0510	...	0612	0612	...	0643	...	...	0744	...	...	0842	hour until	...	...	2042	...	...	2158	...	2312	...
Schönebeck (Elbe) d.	...	0537	...	0638	0640	...	0709	...	...	0810	...	...	0908		...	...	2108	...	...	2224	...	2338	...
Magdeburg Hbf a.	...	0550	...	0651	0652	...	0723	...	...	0823	...	...	0921		...	...	2121	...	...	2237	...	2351	...

A – WARNOW – 🚃12 Leipzig - Magdeburg (- Schwerin - Rostock ♣) (- Warnemünde ♥) and v.v.
C – To / from Cottbus on dates in Table **838**.
D – ALLGÄU – 🚃12 and 🍷 Oberstdorf - Stuttgart - Köln - Hannover - Magdeburg (- Leipzig ⑦ **w**).
E – ALLGÄU – 🚃12 and 🍷 (Leipzig ① **g** -) (Magdeburg ⚒ -) Braunschweig - Hannover - Köln - Stuttgart - Oberstdorf.
T – ①④⑤⑦ (not Oct. 2).
U – From / to Uelzen (Table **841**).

a – Ⓐ only.
b – ⚒ only. 0647 July 9 - Aug. 20.
d – Also Oct. 3.
e – ⚒ only.
f – 1418 on ⑥ to Oct. 29.
g – ① (also Oct. 4; not Oct. 3).
h – ⑥ (also Oct. 2).
j – ①–⑥ (also Oct. 2; not Oct. 3).
q – Not Oct. 2.
r – 1909 July 8 - Aug. 21.

s – Not Oct. 2.
t – Ⓐ (not Oct. 31).
v – 11–27 minutes earlier July 9 - Aug. 21.
w – Also Oct. 3; not Oct. 2.
z – Also Oct. 31.

‡ – 12–24 minutes later July 9 - Aug. 21.
◐ – Via Dessau Hbf (d. 1731) and Bitterfeld (d. 1748).
◧ – Via Bitterfeld (d. 1621) and Dessau Hbf (d. 1641).
⊖ – Via Dessau Hbf (d. 2246).
⊕ – Via Dessau Hbf (d. 0515).
♣ – Daily to Sept. 4; ⑤–⑦ Sept. 9 - Oct. 30 (also Oct. 3; not Oct. 2); ⑤ from Nov. 4.
♥ – Daily to Sept. 4; ⑤–⑦ Sept. 9 - Oct. 30 (also Oct. 3; not Oct. 2).
⊠ – Nov. 12–28 *IC* trains do not run Norddeich - Emden - Oldenburg and v.v.
■ – See also Table **881**.

class only

HARZER SCHMALSPURBAHNEN 867

Nordhausen - Wernigerode: *Die Harzquerbahn*; Eisfelder Talmühle - Stiege - Alexisbad - Quedlinburg: *Die Selketalbahn*; Drei Annen Hohne - Brocken: *Die Brockenbahn*

Summer service valid until Nov. 6, 2016

		🚂	🚂	🚂	🚂	🚂 B	🚂	🚂	🚂 B	🚂	
Wernigerode § d.	0725	0855	0940	1025	1155	...	1325	1455	...	1625	1625
Drei Annen Hohne a.	0802	0932	1017	1102	1232	...	1402	1532	...	1702	1702
Drei Annen Hohne ◇ d.	0810	0945	1030	1115	1240	1245	1415	1546	1540	1716	1718
Schierke ◇ a.	|	0957	1042	1127	|	1257	1427	1558	|	1728	|
Schierke ◇ d.	|	1005	1050	1135	|	1313	1440	1621	|	1748	|
Brocken ◇ a.	|	1036	1121	1206	|	1344	1530	1652	|	1819	|
Elend d.	0822	▬	...	...	1252	▬	...	...	1552	...	1730
Sorge d.	0841	...	...	...	1311	...	...	...	1611	...	1749
Benneckenstein d.	0850	...	...	...	1320	...	...	...	1620	...	1758
Eisfelder Talmühle a.	0919	⊕	...	...	1349	...	...	...	1650	...	1827
Eisfelder Talmühle d.	...	0943	...	...	...	1402	...	...	1702	...	*1833*
Ilfeld d.	...	0959	...	...	...	1417	...	...	1717	...	*1850*
Nordhausen Nord § a.	...	1023*	...	...	...	1439**e**	...	...	1739	...	*1913*

	⊕	🚂 B	🚂	🚂		🚂	🚂	🚂	🚂		
Nordhausen Nord § d.	*0854**	1024	...	...	1325	...	...	...	...	*1754**	...
Ilfeld d.	*0917*	1047	...	...	1346	...	...	...	...	1817	...
Eisfelder Talmühle a.	*0931*	1101	...	...	1400	...	...	...	...	1831	...
Eisfelder Talmühle d.	0938	1108	...	...	▬	1408	...	...	...	▬	1838
Benneckenstein d.	1008	1138	...	...	...	1438	...	...	...	...	1908
Sorge d.	1016	1146	...	...	...	1446	...	...	...	...	1916
Elend d.	1035	1205	...	...	🚂 B	1505	...	...	...	🚂	1935
Brocken ◇ d.	|	|	1136	1314	1451	|	1622	1707	1749	1831	|
Schierke a.	|	|	1216	1354	1521	|	1702	1746	1829	1901	|
Schierke ◇ d.	|	|	1224	1355	1522	|	1703	1747	1830	1902	|
Drei Annen Hohne ◇ a.	1046	1216	1236	1406	1533	1516	1714	1759	1841	1913	1946
Drei Annen Hohne d.	1108	...	1253	1423	...	1553	1723	1808	1853	1923	1954
Wernigerode § a.	1145	...	1333	1503	...	1633	1800	1845	1930	2000	2030

	🚂	◧	🚂	◧	🚂	◧				◧	🚂
Quedlinburg § d.	...	0830	1030	1340	...	...	...	1530	...	1753	1943
Gernrode a.	...	0845	1045	1355	...	...	...	1545	...	1808	1958
Gernrode d.	0734	0846	1046	▬	1357	1502	...	1546	...	1809	▬
Mägdesprung d.	0805	0918	1117	...	1429	1533	...	1618	...	1843	...
Harzgerode d.	|	|	|	1212	|	|	1620	|	...	|	1841
Alexisbad a.	0819	0932	1131	1222	1443	1547	1630	1632	...	1857	1851
Alexisbad d.	0826	0939	*1133*	1230	1456	▬	▬	1633	1634	1904	1859
Harzgerode a.	0835	|	*1143*	|	|	...	...	|	1643	1913	|
Silberhütte d.	▬	0950	▬	1241	1507	...	...	1644	▬	▬	1910
Straßberg (Harz) d.	...	1001	...	1252	1521	...	...	1655	...	...	1921
Güntersberge d.	...	1010	...	1301	1530	🚂	...	1704	...	...	1930
Hasselfelde d.	1012	|	...	|	|	1610	...	|	1757	...	|
Stiege a.	1025	1026	...	1317	1546	1623	...	1720	1810	...	1946
Stiege d.	...	1027	...	1327	1547	1624	...	1735	1811	...	1947
Hasselfelde a.	...	|	...	|	1600	|	🚂 B	1748	|	...	|
Eisfelder Talmühle d.	...	1050	1103	1402**r**	...	1644	1702	...	1833	1915	2015
Ilfeld d.	...	...	1118	1417	...	...	1717	...	1850	1929	2029
Nordhausen Nord § a.	...	...	1139	1439**e**	...	...	1739	...	1913	1952	2053*

		⊕		🚂 B	◧					🚂	
Nordhausen Nord § d.	0825	0854*	...	1024	...	1225	1325	...	1625	...	...
Ilfeld d.	0849	0917	...	1047	...	1246	1346	...	1646	...	...
Eisfelder Talmühle d.	0903	0932	...	1101	1106	1301	1401	...	1700	1702	...
Hasselfelde d.	▬	|	1012	▬	|	|	|	1440	▬	|	...
Stiege a.	...	0953	1025	...	1126	1321	1422	1453	...	1723	...
Stiege d.	...	0954	1031	...	1127	1322	1423	1454	...	1733	1735
Hasselfelde a.	...	1007	|	...	|	|	1436	|	...	|	1748
Güntersberge d.	...	▬	1047	...	1145	1341	...	1510	...	1749	▬
Straßberg (Harz) d.	...	...	1057	...	1155	1350	...	1520	...	1758	...
Silberhütte d.	...	🚂	1108	...	1206	1402	...	1531	...	1810	◧
Harzgerode d.	...	0845	|	...	|	|	...	|	...	⊙	1923
Alexisbad a.	...	0855	1119	🚂	1217	1412	...	1542	◧	1820	1933
Alexisbad d.	...	0902	1133	1146	1224	1413	...	1549	1602	1827	1940
Harzgerode a.	...	|	1143	|	|	|	...	1559	|	⊙	|
Mägdesprung d.	...	0919	...	1201	1238	1430	...	...	1619	1842	1955
Gernrode a.	◧	0949	...	1231	1308	1500	...	...	1649	1912	2025
Gernrode d.	0759	0959	...	...	1309	1501	...	...	1659	1913	...
Quedlinburg § a.	0815	1015	...	...	1325	1516	...	...	1715	1928	...

(2) Brocken - Nordhausen and v.v.

Nordhausen **Bahnhofsplatz**. Arrives *1523* on Ⓐ (not June 27 - Aug. 10, Oct. 10–21, 31). Arrives 1349.

-Steam train.

* – Nordhausen **Bahnhofsplatz**.
§ – Adjacent to DB station.
◧ – Steam train on ④⑤⑥.
⊙ – Connecting trains: Harzgerode d. 1812 → Alexisbad a. 1822. Alexisbad d. 1826 → Harzgerode a. 1836.
⊕ – Change trains at Ilfeld on Ⓐ (through train on Ⓒ).

◇ – Additional journeys (🚂) Drei Annen Hohne - Brocken and v.v.: From Drei Annen Hohne at 1200, 1339, 1506 and 1647. From Brocken at 1051, 1221, 1359 and 1540.

Operator: Harzer Schmalspurbahnen GmbH.
Friedrichstraße 151, 38855 Wernigerode.
✆ + 49 (0) 3943 558 0.
Fax + 49 (0) 3943 558 148.

RB services

ERFURT - NORDHAUSEN 868

		Ⓐt																	
0	**Erfurt** Hbf d.	0450	0602	0702	0802	0902	1002	1102	1202	1302	1402	1502	1602	1702	1802	1902	2002	...	2214
7	Straußfurt d.	0516	0625	0730	0825	0930	1025	1130	1225	1330	1425	1530	1625	1730	1825	1930	2025	...	2242
0	Sondershausen d.	0553	0658	0804	0858	0958	1058	1158	1258	1358	1458	1558	1658	1758	1858	1958	2058	...	2313
0	**Nordhausen** a.	0615	0715	0825	0920	1015	1120	1215	1320	1415	1520	1615	1720	1815	1920	2015	2120	...	2335

	Ⓐt	Ⓐt																	
…dhausen d.	0422	0530	...	0639	0725	0831	0935	1031	1135	1231	1335	1431	1535	1631	1735	1831	1935	...	2136
…dershausen d.	0445	0552	...	0658	0747	0858	0958	1058	1158	1258	1358	1458	1558	1658	1758	1858	1958	...	2157
…ußfurt d.	0516	0625	...	0730	0825	0930	1024	1130	1224	1330	1424	1530	1624	1730	1824	1930	2024	...	2227
…rt Hbf a.	0542	0651	...	0751	0855	0951	1055	1151	1255	1351	1455	1551	1655	1751	1855	1951	2056	...	2257

t – Not Oct. 31.

services

NORDHAUSEN - GÖTTINGEN 869

		Ⓐ	⚒																
0	**Nordhausen** d.	...	0539	0639	0739	0839	0939	1039	1139	1239	1339	1439	1539	1639	1739	1839	1939	2039	2139
0	Walkenried d.	...	0603	0703	0803	0903	1003	1103	1203	1303	1403	1503	1603	1703	1803	1903	2003	2103	2203
3	Bad Sachsa d.	...	0608	0708	0808	0908	1008	1108	1208	1308	1408	1508	1608	1708	1808	1908	2008	2108	2208
7	Bad Lauterberg ⊡ d.	...	0619	0719	0819	0919	1019	1119	1219	1319	1419	1519	1619	1719	1819	1919	2019	2119	2219
3	Herzberg (Harz) d.	0523	0626	0726	0826	0926	1026	1126	1226	1329	1426	1526	1626	1726	1826	1926	2026	2126	2226
0	Northeim (Han) 903 a.	0546	0650	0750	0850	0950	1050	1150	1250	1353	1450	1550	1650	1750	1850	1950	2050	2151	2250
0	**Göttingen** 903 a.	0605	0710	0808j	*0908*	1008	*1108*	1208	*1308*	1410	*1508*	1608	*1708*	1808	*1908*	2008	*2108*	2207	*2308*

	Ⓐ	⚒	Ⓐ	Ⓒ															⑤⑥f
…tingen 903 d.	*0409*	0549	0638	*0649*	0749	*0848*	0949	*1048*	1149	*1248*	1349	*1448*	1549	*1648*	1749	*1848*	1949	*2051*r	2149
…heim (Han) 903 d.	0506	0606	0702	0706	0806	0906	1006	1106	1206	1306	1406	1506	1606	1706	1806	1906	2006	2108	2206
…berg (Harz) d.	0530	0630	0730	0730	0830	0930	1030	1130	1230	1330	1430	1530	1630	1730	1830	1930	2030	2132	2230
Lauterberg ⊡ d.	0536	0636	0736	0736	0836	0936	1036	1136	1236	1336	1436	1536	1636	1736	1836	1936	2036	2137	2236
Sachsa d.	0547	0647	0747	0747	0847	0947	1047	1147	1247	1347	1447	1547	1647	1747	1847	1947	2047	2148	2247
…kenried d.	0552	0652	0752	0752	0852	0952	1052	1152	1252	1352	1452	1552	1652	1752	1852	1952	2052	2152	2252
…dhausen a.	0615	0715	0815	0815	0915	1015	1115	1215	1315	1414	1515	1615	1715	1815	1915	2015	2115	2215	2315

f – Runs daily Göttingen - Herzberg.
j – 0810 on ① (also Oct. 4).
r – *2048* July 18 - Aug. 26.

⊡ – Bad Lauterberg im Harz Barbis.

(*RE* services); *STB*; *EB*

ERFURT - MEININGEN - SCHWEINFURT - WÜRZBURG 870

		▽			▽ Ⓐt		▽ Ⓐt		▽		▽		▽		▽		▽		▽			▽		▽	
0	**Erfurt** Hbf 872 d.	0010	...	...	0400	0500	...	...	0646	0734	0846	0934	1046	1134	1246	1334	1446	1534	1646	1734	1830	1846	1934	2046	2213
3	Arnstadt Hbf 872 d.	0031	...	...	0416	0516	...	...	0706	0751	0906	0951	1106	1151	1306	1351	1506	1551	1706	1751	1847	1906	1951	2106	2230
1	Plaue (Thür) d.	0042	...	...	0424	0523	...	...	0724v	0758	0919j	0958	1119j	1158	1319j	1358	1519j	1558	1719j	1758	1853	1919j	1958	2119j	2241
7	Gräfenroda d.	0047	...	...	0428	0528	...	...	0729	0803	0924	1003	1124	1203	1324	1403	1524	1603	1724	1803	1858	1924	2003	2124	2246
3	Oberhof (Thür) d.	0101	...	...	0443	0540	...	...	0744	0815	0943	1015	1143	1215	1343	1415	1543	1615	1743	1815	1910	1943	2015	2145j	2257
8	Zella-Mehlis d.	0107	...	...	0450	0545	...	...	0751	0819	0950	1019	1150	1219	1350	1419	1550	1619	1750	1819	1915	1950	2019	2151	2302
4	Suhl d.	0113	...	...	0511v	0551	...	...	0757	0825	0957	1025	1157	1225	1357	1425	1557	1625	1757	1825	1920	1957	2025	2158	2307
4	Grimmenthal 873 a.	0129	...	...	0532	0603	0625	...	0813	0836	1013	1036	1213	1236	1413	1436	1613	1636	1813	1836	1938	2013	2036	2214	2318
2	**Meiningen** 873 a.	0136	...	...	0541	|	0631	...	0821	*0848*	1021	*1048*	1221	*1248*	1421	*1448*	1621	*1648*	1821	*1848*	1948	2021	*2048*	2221	2325
					▬	|			▬	|	▬	|	▬	|	▬	|	▬	|	▬	|	▬		|	▬	▬
			◇ Ⓐe	◇	▽ Ⓐt	|	◇ Ⓐe	◇ ⚒e	◇	|	◇	|	◇	|	◇	|	◇	|	◇	|	◇		|	◇	◇
	Meiningen 873 d.	...	0414	0524	0544	|	0642	...	0720k	*0822*	0924	*1022*	1124	*1222*	1324	*1422*	1541	*1622*	1724	*1822*	1924	...	*2022*	2124	...
4	Grimmenthal 873 d.	...	|	|	0550	0605	|	...	|	0836	|	1036	|	1236	|	1436	|	1636	|	1836	|	...	2036	|	...
0	Mellrichstadt d.	...	0438	0548	...	0623	0709	0709	0748	0849	0948	1049	1148	1249	1348	1449	1608	1649	1748	1849	1948	...	2049	2148	...
4	Bad Neustadt (Saale) d.	...	0447	0601	...	0637	0718	0718	0800	0857	0959	1057	1159	1257	1359	1457	1620	1657	1759	1857	1959	...	2057	2159	2259
4	Münnerstadt d.	...	0455	0609	...	0645	0728	0728	0808	0904	1007	1104	1207	1305	1407	1505	1628	1704	1807	1904	2007	...	2104	2207	2307
9	Ebenhausen (Unterfr) d.	...	0506	0625	...	0659	0739	0739	0825j	0916	1025j	1116	1225j	1316	1425j	1516	1639	1716	1825j	1916	2025j	...	2116	2229v	2325j
3	**Schweinfurt** Hbf 876 a.	...	*0521*	0637	...	0714	0751	0751	0841	0926	1041	1125	1241	1325	1440	1526	1651	1726	1840	1926	2040	...	2126	2240	2336
6	**Würzburg** Hbf 876 a.	...	...	*0722*	...	0744	*0820*	*0820*	*0922*	0955	*1122*	1155	*1319*	1355	*1521*	1555	*1722*	1755	*1921*	1955	*2122*	...	2157	...	*0016*

Not Aug. 15, Nov. 1.
Arrives 6–8 minutes earlier.
0724 on Ⓒ (also Aug. 15, Nov. 1).

t – Not Oct. 31.
v – Arrives 11–16 minutes earlier.

▽ – Operated by Süd Thüringen Bahn (2nd class only).
◇ – Operated by Erfurter Bahn (2nd class only).

870 WÜRZBURG - SCHWEINFURT - MEININGEN - ERFURT

DB (RE services); STB

				▽ Ⓐt	◇ ⚒r	◇ Ⓐe	◇ Ⓐe	◇ †z	◇ ⑥		◇		◇		◇ Ⓐe	◇ Ⓒz		◇		◇		◇		◇
Würzburg Hbf ...... 876 d.	...	...	0454r	...	...	...	0635	0604	0604	0801	0835	1001	1035	1201	1207	1235	1401	1435	1601	1636	1801	1836	2001	2139
Schweinfurt Hbf ...... 876 d.	...	...	0530	...	0611	0611	0703	0716	0716	0830	0911	1030	1111	1230	1242	1311	1430	1511	1630	1711	1830	1911	2030	2214
Ebenhausen (Unterf) ...... d.	...	...	0541	...	0629	0629	0717	0732	0740v	0840	0932	1040	1132	1240	1253	1332	1441	1532	1640	1732	1840	1932	2040	2231
Münnerstadt ...... d.	...	...	0550	...	0646	0646	0728	0744	0751	0849	0944	1049	1144	1249	1305	1344	1450	1545	1649	1744	1849	1944	2049	2242
Bad Neustadt (Saale) ...... d.	...	...	0557	...	0654	0654	0737	0758	0800	0857	0958	1057	1158	1257	1319	1358	1457	1558	1657	1758	1857	1958	2057	2251
Mellrichstadt ...... d.	...	...	0606	...	0703	0707	0746	0807	0809	0906	1007	1106	1207	1306	1328	1407	1506	1607	1706	1807	1906	2007	2106	2259
Grimmenthal ...... 873 a.	...	...	0621	0625		|	|	|	|	0919	|	1119	|	1319	|	|	1519	|	1719	|	1919	|	2120	|
Meiningen ...... 873 a.	...	...	|	0631	...	0734	0810	0831	0833	0932	1031	1132	1231	1332	1358	1431	1532	1631	1732	1831	1932	2031	2132	2322

		▽			▽	◇ Ⓐe					▽		▽		▽			▽		▽		▽		▽
Meiningen ...... 873 d.	0506	0525	0611	0711	0733	0805	...	...	...	0906	0933	1106	1133	1306	1333	...	1506	1533	1706	1733	1906	1933	2106	2133
Grimmenthal ...... 873 d.	0512	0533	0621	0718	0740	|	...	...	...	0919	0940	1119	1140	1319	1340	...	1519	1540	1719	1740	1919	1940	2121	2140
Suhl ...... d.	0524	0550	0633	0731	0758	0838	...	...	...	0931	0958	1131	1158	1331	1358	...	1531	1558	1731	1758	1931	1958	2133	2158
Zella-Mehlis ...... d.	0532	0559	0639	0737	0808	0846	...	...	...	0937	1008	1137	1208	1337	1408	...	1537	1608	1737	1808	1937	2008	2139	2208
Oberhof (Thür) ...... d.	0537	0604	0644	0742	0815	|	...	...	...	0942	1015	1142	1215	1342	1415	...	1542	1615	1742	1815	1942	2015	2144	2215
Gräfenroda ...... d.	0549	0619	0654	0752	0829	|	...	...	...	0952	1029	1152	1229	1352	1429	...	1552	1629	1752	1829	1952	2029	2154	2229
Plaue (Thür) ...... d.	0553	0631j	0659	0757	0842j	|	...	...	...	0957	1042j	1157	1242j	1357	1442j	...	1557	1642j	1757	1842j	1957	2042j	2159	2242j
Arnstadt Hbf ...... 872 d.	0602	0639	0706	0806	0850	0913	...	...	...	1006	1050	1206	1250	1406	1450	...	1606	1650	1806	1850	2006	2050	2206	2250
Erfurt Hbf ...... 872 a.	0617	0655	0720	0820	0905	0928	...	...	...	1022	1105	1222	1305	1422	1505	...	1622	1705	1822	1905	2022	2105	2223	2309

e – Not Aug. 15, Nov. 1.
j – Arrives 7–8 minutes earlier.
r – ⚒ (not Aug. 15, Nov. 1).
t – Not Oct. 31.
v – Arrives 0728.
z – Also Aug. 15, Nov. 1.
▽ – Operated by Süd Thüringen Bahn (2nd class only
◇ – Operated by Erfurter Bahn (2nd class only).

871 LEIPZIG - GERA - SAALFELD

Erfurter Bahn; 2nd class

km				Ⓐt	Ⓐt	Ⓒz	Ⓐt		Ⓐt◧		◧		◧		◧		◧		◧					
0	**Leipzig** Hbf ...... d.	0009	...	...	...	...	0508	0609	0656	0756	0856	0956	1056	1156	1256	1356	1456	1556	1656	1756	1856	1956	2056	2156
45	Zeitz ...... d.	0048	...	...	0437	...	0548	0655	0735	0836	0935	1035	1135	1235	1335	1435	1535	1635	1735	1835	1935	2035	2135	2235
72	**Gera** Hbf ...... a.	0112	...	...	0501	...	0617	0725	0759	0858	0958	1058	1158	1258	1358	1458	1558	1658	1758	1858	1958	2059	2206	2259
72	**Gera** Hbf ...... d.	...	...	0454	0526	0615	0620	0728	0801	0901	1001	1101	1201	1301	1401	1501	1601	1701	1801	1901	2001	2110	2208	2301
84	Weida ...... d.	...	...	0507	0538	0627	0631	0745	0812	0913	1014	1113	1214	1313	1414	1513	1614	1713	1814	1913	2014	2122	2220	2313
99	Triptis ...... d.	...	...	0520	0553	0640	0645	0759	...	0927	1030	1127	1230	1327	1430	1527	1630	1727	1830	1927	2030	2140	...	2331
108	Neustadt (Orla) ...... d.	...	...	0527	0600	0647	0652	0806	...	0934	1037	1134	1237	1334	1437	1534	1637	1734	1837	1934	2037	2147	...	2338
139	**Saalfeld** (Saale) ...... a.	...	...	0558	0627	0714	0718	0836	...	1002	1058	1202	1258	1402	1458	1602	1700	1802	1858	2002	2058	2215	...	0005

	Ⓐt		Ⓐt	⚒t		Ⓐt		Ⓐt			◧		◧		◧		◧		◧		◧		◧	⑤⑥
Saalfeld (Saale) ...... d.	...	...	...	0517	...	0553	...	0620	0652z	0755	0857	0955	1057	1155	1257	1355	1457	1555	1657	1755	1857	1955	2050	...
Neustadt (Orla) ...... d.	...	...	...	0544	...	0624	...	0654	0723z	0822	0919	1022	1119	1222	1319	1422	1519	1622	1719	1822	1919	2022	2118	...
Triptis ...... d.	...	...	...	0553	...	0631	...	0702	0730z	0830	0927	1030	1127	1230	1327	1430	1527	1630	1727	1830	1927	2030	2125	...
Weida ...... d.	...	...	...	0609	...	0645	...	0715	0746	0843	0946	1043	1146	1243	1346	1443	1546	1643	1746	1843	1946	2043	2141	...
Gera Hbf ...... a.	...	...	...	0621	...	0656	...	0727	0757	0855	0957	1055	1157	1255	1357	1455	1557	1655	1757	1855	1957	2056	2151	...
Gera Hbf ...... d.	0350	0500	0540	0630	0630	0701	0701	...	0801	0901	1001	1101	1201	1301	1401	1501	1601	1701	1801	1901	2001	...	2153	2244
Zeitz ...... d.	0415	0526	0606	0655	0655	0726	0726	...	0826	0925	1025	1125	1225	1325	1425	1525	1625	1725	1825	1925	2025	...	2217	2313
Leipzig Hbf ...... a.	0453	0603	0644	0732	0732	0803	0803	...	0906	1006	1106	1206	1306	1406	1506	1606	1706	1806	1906	2006	2106	...	2253	2350

km			Ⓐt						
	Leipzig Hbf .... d.	...	0656	...	0856	1056	1256	1456	1656
0	**Gera** Hbf ...... d.	0556	0801	0801	1001	1201	1401	1601	1801
12	Weida ...... d.	0609	0815	0815	1016	1216	1416	1616	1816
84	**Hof** Hbf ...... a.	0724	0925	0925	1125	1325	1525	1725	1925

Hof Hbf ...... d.	0832	1032	1232	1432	1632	1832	2035
Weida ...... a.	0942	1142	1342	1542	1742	1942	2140
Gera Hbf ...... a.	0957	1157	1357	1557	1757	1957	2151
Leipzig Hbf a.	1106	1306	1506	1706	1906	2106	2253

t – Not Oct. 31.
z – Ⓒ (also Oct. 31).
◧ – Conveys [12] Leipzig - Weida - and v.v. (see panel below main ta

872 ERFURT - SAALFELD and ROTTENBACH - KATZHÜTTE

DB; Erfurter Bahn★; 2nd class

km											
0	**Erfurt** Hbf ...... 870 d.	0630	*0734*	0841	and in the same pattern every **two** hours until	*1734*	1841	*1934*	2041	*2213*	*2315*
23	Arnstadt Hbf ...... 870 d.	0646	0801	0902		1801	1902	2000	2102	2235	2339
38	Stadtilm ...... d.	0658	0814	0915		1814	1915	2013	2115	2248	2352
54	Rottenbach ...... d.	0711	0829	0929		1829	1929	2027	2129	2302	0004
62	Bad Blankenburg ...... d.	0718	0837	0937		1837	1937	2034	2137	2309	0011
70	**Saalfeld** (Saale) ...... a.	0725	0845	0945		1845	1945	2042	2144	2318	0019

								△
Saalfeld (Saale) ...... d.	0604	0656	0814	0914	and in the same pattern every **two** hours until	1814	1914	2011
Bad Blankenburg ...... d.	0611	0703	0821	0921		1821	1921	2018
Rottenbach ...... d.	0619	0713	0829	0929		1829	1929	2028
Stadtilm ...... d.	0631	0726	0842	0942		1842	1942	2041
Arnstadt Hbf ...... 870 a.	0644	0740	0855	0955		1855	1955	2054
Erfurt Hbf ...... 870 a.	0706	*0810*	0916	*1022*		1916	*2022*	2116

km		Ⓐt									⑤⑦j
0	Rottenbach ...... d.	0541	0631	0721	0841	and hourly until	1641	1741	1841	1941	2041
15	Obstfelderschmiede ...... a.	0604	0655	0744	0905		1705	1805	1905	2005	2105
25	Katzhütte ...... a.	0620	0712	0802	0922		1722	1822	1922	2022	2122

	Ⓐt							
Katzhütte ...... d.	0535	0626	...	0736	0836	0936	and hourly until	1936
Obstfelderschmiede d.	0552	0643	...	0754	0853	0953		1953
Rottenbach ...... a.	0614	0705	...	0817	0917	1017		2017

j – Also Oct. 3, 31; not Oct. 2, 30.
t – Not Oct. 31.
△ – Runs 30–34 minutes later from Sept. 4.
★ – Erfurt - Saalfeld operated by Erfurter Bahn. Rottenbach - Katzhütte operated by DB.

☛ **Oberweißbacher Bergbahn**. Obstfelderschmiede - Lichtenhain - Cursdorf. Journey: 26–44 minut **From Obstfelderschmiede** at 0625, 0700, 0730 and every 30 minutes until 1730; then 1808, 183 1908, 1930. **From Cursdorf** at 0614, 0640, 0706, 0734, 0814, 0844 and every 30 minutes until 1

873 EISENACH - MEININGEN - SONNEBERG

Süd Thüringen Bahn (2nd class o

km		Ⓐt	Ⓐt	Ⓐt	Ⓐt										Ⓒz	Ⓐt		Ⓒz	Ⓐt						
0	**Eisenach** ...... d.	...	0358	...	0450	...	0604	0714	0814	0914	1014	1114	1214	1314	1414	1414	1514	1614	1614	1714	1814	1914	2014	2114	2220
27	Bad Salzungen ...... d.	...	0423	...	0522	...	0636	0741	0841	0941	1041	1141	1241	1341	1441	1441	1541	1641	1641	1741	1841	1941	2041	2141	2250
41	Wernshausen ...... d.	...	0438	...	0537	...	0651	0758	0858	0958	1058	1158	1258	1358	1458	1458	1558	1658	1658	1758	1858	1958	2058	2158	2306
61	**Meiningen** ...... a.	...	0501	...	0601	...	0707	0814	0914	1014	1114	1214	1314	1414	1514	1514	1614	1714	1714	1814	1914	2014	2115	2215	2323
61	**Meiningen** ...... 870 d.	0406	...	0544	0611	0611	0719	0822	0919	1022	1119	1222	1319	1422	1519	1519	1622	1719	1719	1822	1919	2022	...	2235	...
68	Grimmenthal ...... 870 d.	0412	...	0551	0631k	0631k	0731	0831	0931	1031	1131	1231	1331	1431	1531	1542k	1631	1731	1742k	1831	1942k	2031	...	2242	...
82	Themar ...... d.	0430	...	0605	0643	0643	0743	0843	0943	1043	1143	1243	1343	1443	1543	1554	1643	1743	1754	1843	1954	2043	...	2254	...
94	Hildburghausen ...... d.	0443	...	0617	0701	0701	0801	0901	1001	1101	1201	1301	1401	1501	1601	1605	1701	1801	1805	1901	2005	2101	...	2305	...
109	**Eisfeld** ...... d.	0511k	...	0643	0716	0716	0815	0916	1015	1116	1215	1316	1415	1516	1615	1620	1716	1815	1820	1916	2020	2115	...	2320	...
141	**Sonneberg** (Thür) Hbf a.	0555	...	0727	0759	0759	...	0959	...	1159	...	1359	...	1559	...	...	1759	...	...	1959	...	...	...	...	...

	Ⓐt	Ⓒz	Ⓐt	Ⓐt																
Sonneberg (Thür) Hbf d.	...	...	...	...	...	0558	...	0802	...	1002	...	1202	...	1402	...	1602	...	1802	...	2002
Eisfeld ...... d.	0401	...	...	0535	...	0645	0745	0845	0945	1045	1145	1245	1345	1445	1545	1645	1745	1845	1945	2045
Hildburghausen ...... d.	0416	...	...	0550	...	0659	0759	0859	0959	1059	1159	1259	1359	1459	1559j	1659	1759j	1859	2006	2059
Themar ...... d.	0428	...	...	0605	...	0711	0811	0911	1011	1111	1211	1311	1411	1511	1611j	1711	1811j	1911	2017	2111
Grimmenthal ...... 870 d.	0440	...	...	0625	...	0726	0829	0926	1029	1126	1229	1326	1429	1526	1629	1726	1829	1926	2029	2126
Meiningen ...... 870 a.	0447	...	...	0631	...	0732	0835	0932	1035	1132	1235	1332	1435	1532	1635	1732	1835	1932	2035	2132
Meiningen ...... d.	0448	0526	0545	0632	0632	0739	0839	0939	1039	1139	1239	1339	1439	1539	1639	1739	1839	1939	2039	2139
Wernshausen ...... d.	0506	0544	0604	0652	0652	0757	0857	0957	1057	1157	1257	1357	1457	1557	1657	1757	1857	1957	2057	2157
Bad Salzungen ...... d.	0520	0558	0618	0710	0710	0810	0910	1010	1110	1210	1310	1410	1510	1610	1710	1810	1910	2010	2110	2210
Eisenach ...... a.	0544	0629	0643	0740	0740	0840	0940	1040	1140	1240	1340	1440	1540	1640	1740	1840	1940	2040	2140	2235

j – 6–7 minutes later on Ⓐ (not Oct. 31).
k – Arrives 14–17 minutes ea
t – Not Oct. 31.
z – Also Oct. 31.

874 LEIPZIG - CHEMNITZ

km			⚒r				
0	**Leipzig** Hbf ...... 856 d.	0518	0620	0720	and hourly until	2120	2326
33	Bad Lausick ...... d.	0547	0647	0747		2147	2353
44	Geithain ...... 856 d.	0556	0656	0756		2156	0002
66	Burgstädt ...... d.	0613	0713	0813		2213	0020
81	**Chemnitz** Hbf ...... a.	0625	0725	0825		2225	0031

		⚒r				
Chemnitz Hbf ...... d.	0421	0531	0631	and hourly until	2031	2244
Burgstädt ...... d.	0433	0543	0643		2043	2256
Geithain ...... 856 d.	0451	0600	0700		2100	2313
Bad Lausick ...... d.	0500	0609	0709		2109	2322
Leipzig Hbf ...... 856 a.	0525	0630	0730		2130	2348

r – Not Oct. 31, Nov. 16.

Operator: Mitteldeutsche Regiob

German national public holidays are on Jan. 1, Mar. 25, 28, May 5, 16, Oct. 3, Dec. 25, 26

RB services — Regional services NÜRNBERG - LICHTENFELS - SONNEBERG and JENA — 875

SERVICE UNTIL SEPTEMBER 3. All services Bamberg - Lichtenfels and v.v. are replaced by 🚌 until September 3.

	Ⓐ *				W	W	W	W	W	W	W	W		W		W		W	W	W	W			
Nürnberg Hbf .... **921** d.	0449	...	0540	0549	0642	0740	0840	0940	1040	1140	1240	1340	1405	1441	1505	1540	1605	1641	1740	1840	1940	2040	2140	2247	2346
Fürth (Bay) Hbf ... **921** d.	0457	...	0547	0557	0650	0746	0847	0947	1047	1147	1247	1347	|	1448	|	1547	|	1648	1747	1847	1947	2047	2147	2253	2352
Erlangen .... d.	0514	...	0558	0614	0701	0759	0900	0959	1059	1159	1259	1359	|	1459	|	1559	|	1659	1759	1859	1959	2059	2159	2304	0003
Forchheim (Oberfr) .... d.	0527	...	0608	0627	0709	0808	0908	1008	1108	1208	1308	1408	⊕	1508	⊕	1608	⊕	1708	1808	1908	2008	2108	2208	2314	0012
Bamberg .... a.	0546	...	0623	0646	0727	0823	0923	1023	1123	1223	1323	1423	|	1523	|	1623	|	1723	1823	1923	2023	2123	2227	2331	0028
Bamberg .... **876** ▲ d.	...	0617	0628	0659	0735	0828	0928	1028	1128	1228	1328	1428	|	1528	|	1628	|	1728	1828	1928	2028	2128	2238	2336	0037
Lichtenfels ...... **876** ▲ a.	...	0650	0721	0801	0820	0901	1001	1101	1201	1301	1401	1501	1552	1601	1655	1701	1752	1801	1901	2001	2101	2201	2315	0013	0132
Lichtenfels .... d.	...	0659	...	0810	...	0910	1010	1110	1210	1310	1410	1510	1603	1626e	1703	1722e	1803	1823e	1910	2010	2110	2210	2321	0018	...
Coburg .... d.	...	0721	...	0831	...	0931	1031	1131	1231	1331	1431	1531	1620	1645e	1721	1743e	1821	1838e	1931	2031	2131	2231	2342	0038	...
Sonneberg (Thür) Hbf a.	...	0744	...	0852	...	0952	1052	1152	1252	1352	1452	1552	1642	1706e	1743	1805e	1843	...	1952	2052	2152	2252	0002	0059v	...

	Ⓒ	Ⓐ	Ⓒ	Ⓐ		Ⓐ W	Ⓒ	Ⓐ	W		W	W	W	W	W	W	W	W	W	W		W	W	W		
neberg (Thür) Hbf d.	...	0410	...	...	0509	...	0611	0605	...	0712	0807	0907	1007	1107	1207	1308	1407	1507	1611	1652e	1711	1811	1907	2007	2107	2207
urg .... d.	...	0431	0413h	0508	0530	0612	0632	0632	0712e	0740	0830	0930	1030	1130	1230	1330	1430	1530	1638	1720e	1740	1839	1930	2030	2133	2230
enfels .... a.	...	0451	0429h	0529	0551	0635	0649	0650	0739e	0757	0852	0952	1052	1152	1252	1349	1452	1552	1656	1738e	1758	1856	1952	2049	2152	2252
enfels ...... **876** ▲ d.	0429	0457	0536	0553	0605	0651	0658	0658	0758	0806	0858	0959	1058	1158	1258	1359	1458	1558	1701	1758	...	1901	2001	2101	2201	2328
berg .... **876** ▲ a.	0530	0530	0621	0626	0638	0731	0730	0738	0831	|	0931	1031	1131	1231	1331	1431	1531	1631	1733	1831	...	1933	2033	2133	2233	0026
berg .... d.	0536	0536	0631	0631	0702e	0736	0736	0758	0836	|	0936	1036	1136	1236	1336	1436	1536	1636	1736	1838	...	1938	2038	2138	2238	0031
heim (Oberfr) ..... d.	0550	0554	0647	0647	0720e	0750	0750	0815	0850	⊕	0950	1050	1150	1250	1351	1450	1550	1650	1750	1851	...	1951	2051	2151	2251	0049
gen .... d.	0600	0603	0657	0657	0730e	0800	0800	0825	0900	|	1000	1100	1200	1300	1401	1500	1600	1700	1800	1901	...	2000	2101	2201	2301	0102
(Bay) Hbf ..... **921** d.	0611	0615	0709	0709	0746e	0811	0811	0840	0911	|	1011	1111	1211	1311	1413	1511	1611	1711	1811	1912	...	2011	2112	2213	2312	0119
berg Hbf ...... **921** a.	0619	0623	0716	0716	0752e	0819	0819	0847	0919	0955	1019	1119	1219	1319	1419	1519	1619	1719	1819	1920	...	2019	2120	2220	2320	0129

BAMBERG - SAALFELD - JENA ⊠

	L		L		L		L	Ⓒd	Ⓐt	L	Ⓒ	Ⓐ	L		L		H				⑤⑥			
Nürnberg Hbf (see above) d.	...	...	...	...	...	...	...	...	...	...	...	...	...	...	...	...	...	...	...	...	...	...	...	...
Bamberg .... d.	0504*	...	0728*	0735*	0928*	0935*	1128*	1135*	1135*	1328*	1335*	1335*	1528*	1535*	1728*	1735*	1928*	1938*	...	2128*	2128*	...	...	...
Lichtenfels .... d.	0542	0640	0810	0829	1010	1029	1210	1229	1240	1410	1429	1429	1610	1629	1810	1841	2010	2041	...	2214	2214	...	...	...
Kronach .... d.	0603	0702	0822	0850	1022	1050	1222	1250	1307	1422	1450	1459	1622	1650	1822	1901	2022	2101	...	2234	2235	...	...	...
Saalfeld (Saale) .... **849** d.	0701	0801	0928	0951	1128	1150	1328	1350	1405	1528	1550	1558	1728	1749	1928	1959	2128	2200	...	...	2332	...	...	...
Rüdolstadt (Thür) .... **849** d.	0709	...	0935	...	1135	...	1335	...	...	1535	...	...	1735	...	1935	...	2135	...	...	...	...	...	...	...
Jena-Göschwitz .... **849** d.	0730	...	0956	...	1156	...	1356	...	...	1556	...	...	1756	...	1956	...	2156	...	...	...	...	...	...	...
Jena Paradies .... **849** a.	0735	...	1000	...	1200	...	1400	...	...	1600	...	...	1800	...	2000	...	2200	...	...	...	...	...	...	...

	Ⓐ	Ⓐ	Ⓐ	Ⓒ	Ⓐ	H		L		L		L		L		L		L		L					
Paradies .... **849** d.	...	...	...	...	...	0607	...	0809	...	1009	...	1209	...	1409	...	1609	...	1809	...	2009	...	...	...	...	...
-Göschwitz .... **849** d.	...	...	...	...	...	0612	...	0813	...	1013	...	1213	...	1413	...	1613	...	1813	...	2013	...	...	...	...	...
olstadt (Thür) .... **849** d.	...	...	...	...	...	0633	...	0834	...	1034	...	1234	...	1434	...	1634	...	1834	...	2034	...	...	...	...	...
feld (Saale) .... **849** d.	...	...	...	0535	0603	0641	0811	0842	1011	1042	1211	1242	1411	1442	1611	1642	1811	1842	2005	2042	...	2206	...	...	...
ach .... d.	0525	0611	0633	0633	0702	0736	0910	0936	1110	1136	1310	1336	1510	1536	1710	1736	1910	1936	2103	2136	...	2304	...	...	...
enfels .... a.	0545	0633	0653	0653	0719	0749	0930	0949	1130	1149	1330	1349	1530	1549	1730	1749	1930	1949	2123	2149	...	2324	...	...	...
berg .... a.	0626*	0730*	0738*	0730*	0821*	0831*	1021*	1031*	1221*	1231*	1421*	1431*	1621*	1631*	1821*	1831*	2021*	2033*	...	2233*	...	0026*	...	...	...
irnberg Hbf (see above) . a.	...	...	...	...	...	...	...	...	...	...	...	...	...	...	...	...	...	...	...	...	...	...	...	...	...

To/ from Halle (Table **851**).
To/ from Leipzig (Table **851**).
Conveys 🚃12 Nürnberg - Bamberg - Würzburg and v.v. See Table **876**.

d – Runs daily from July 30.
e – Ⓐ only.
h – ⑥ only.
t – Until July 29.
v – Mornings of ⑦ only.

* – By 🚌.
▲ – All services Bamberg - Lichtenfels and v.v. are operated by 🚌 (shaded timings).
⊕ – Via Bayreuth.
⊠ – **Service until September 3**. Rail services between Bamberg and Lichtenfels are expected to restart from September 4.

RB services — WÜRZBURG - BAMBERG - HOF — *Service until September 3* ⊠ — 876

	‡Ⓐ																							
Bamberg ..... **851 875** d.	...	0504*	0504*	0617*	...	0728*	0728*	0735*	...	0928*	0928*	0935*	...	1128*	1128*	1135*	...	1328*	1328*	1335*	1335*	1528*	1528*	1535*	...
Lichtenfels .... **851 875** d.	0512	0548	0548	0656	...	0806	0806	0859	...	1006	1006	1059	...	1206	1206	1259	...	1406	1406	1459	1459	1606	1606	1659	...
Kulmbach .... d.	0536	0611	0611	0717	...	0826	0826	0916	...	1026	1026	1118	...	1226	1226	1316	...	1426	1426	1518	1518	1626	1626	1716	...
Neuenmarkt-Wirsberg a.	0547	0623	0623	0725	...	0833	0833	0924	...	1033	1033	1126	...	1233	1233	1324	...	1433	1433	1526	1526	1633	1633	1724	...
Neuenmarkt-Wirsberg d.	0547	0626	0634	0732	0728	0835	0838	0932	0928	1035	1038	1128	1132	1235	1238	1332	1327	1435	1438	1528	1532	1635	1638	1732	1728
Bayreuth Hbf .... a.	0608	|	0657	0757	|	|	0856	0956	|	|	1056	|	1156	|	1256	1356	|	|	1456	|	1556	|	1656	1756	|
Münchberg .... **880** d.	...	0652	...	...	0755	0900	...	...	0955	1100	...	1155	...	1300	...	...	1355	1500	...	1555	...	1700	...	...	1755
Schwarzenbach .... d.	...	0704	...	...	0806	0909	...	...	|	1109	...	|	...	1309	...	...	|	1509	...	|	...	1709	...	...	|
Hof Hbf .... **880** a.	...	0716	...	...	0818	0920	...	...	1018	1120	...	1218	...	1320	...	...	1418	1520	...	1618	...	1720	...	...	1818

									‡	‡		T
berg ...... **851 875** d.	1728*	1728*	1735*	...	1928*	1928*	1938*	...	2128*	...	2238*	2238*
tenfels .... **851 875** d.	1806	1806	1859	...	2006	2006	2059	...	2209	...	2321	2321
bach .... d.	1826	1826	1916	...	2026	2026	2119	...	2231	...	2346	2346
enmarkt-Wirsberg a.	1833	1833	1924	...	2033	2033	2128	...	2243	...	2358	2358
enmarkt-Wirsberg d.	1835	1838	1932	1928	2035	2038	2130	2132	2243	2247	2359	2359
ayreuth Hbf .... a.	|	1856	1956	|	|	2058	2157	|	2303	|	0026	|
chberg .... **880** d.	1900	...	...	1955	2100	...	...	2159	...	2314	...	0036
warzenbach .... d.	1909	...	...	|	2109	...	...	2210	...	2327	...	0045
Hbf .... **880** a.	1920	...	...	2019	2119	...	...	2223	...	2340	...	0057

		Ⓐ	Ⓒ						
Hof Hbf .... **880** d.	...	0527	0535	0636	...	0736j	...	...	0836
Schwarzenbach .... d.	...	0537	0543	0645	...	|	...	...	0845
Münchberg .... **880** d.	...	0546	0553	0656	...	0754j	...	...	0856
Bayreuth Hbf .... d.	0545	|	|	|	0700	|	0801	0901	|
Neuenmarkt-Wirsberg .... a.	0608	0615	0615	0725	0719	0822	0826	0920	0925
Neuenmarkt-Wirsberg .... d.	...	0616	0616	...	0728	0829	0829	0927	0927
Kulmbach .... d.	...	0626	0626	...	0736	0837	0837	0936	0936
Lichtenfels .... **851 875** a.	...	0646	0646	...	0752	0853	0853	0954	0954
Bamberg .... **851 875** a.	...	0731*	0753*	...	0831*	0931*	0931*	1031*	1031*

																								R	
Hbf .... **880** d.	0936	...	1036	...	1136	...	...	1236	1336	...	1436	...	1536	...	1636	...	1736	...	...	1835	1936	...	...	2036	2136	...
warzenbach .... d.	|	...	1045	...	|	...	...	1245	|	...	1445	...	|	...	1645	...	|	...	...	1844	|	...	...	2045	|	...
chberg .... **880** d.	0954	...	1056	...	1154	...	...	1256	1354	...	1456	...	1554	...	1656	...	1754	...	...	1855	1954	...	...	2056	2153	...
ayreuth Hbf .... d.	|	1001	|	1101	|	1201	1259	|	|	1401	|	1501	|	1602	|	1701	|	1801	1901	|	|	2001	2103	|	|	2204
enmarkt-Wirsberg a.	1021	1026	1125	1120	1221	1226	1320	1325	1421	1426	1525	1520	1621	1626	1725	1720	1821	1826	1920	1925	2021	2026	2121	2125	2230	2230
enmarkt-Wirsberg d.	1029	1029	...	1128	1229	1229	1327	1327	1429	1429	...	1528	1629	1629	...	1728	1829	1829	1927	1927	2029	2029	...	2127	2233	2233
nbach .... d.	1037	1037	...	1136	1237	1237	1336	1336	1437	1437	...	1536	1637	1637	...	1736	1837	1837	1936	1936	2037	2037	...	2136	2246	2246
tenfels .... **851 875** a.	1053	1053	...	1152	1255	1255	1354	1354	1453	1453	...	1552	1655	1655	...	1752	1853	1853	1954	1954	2055	2055	...	2156	2306	2306
berg ...... **851 875** a.	1131*	1131*	...	1231*	1331*	1331*	1431*	1431*	1531*	1531*	...	1631*	1733*	1733*	...	1831*	1933*	1933*	2033*	2033*	2133*	2133*	...	2233*	0026*	0026*

WÜRZBURG - BAMBERG

		Ⓒz		Ⓐe	⚒e		Ⓐe																	Ⓒz
Würzburg Hbf ... **870** d.	0036	0036	...	...	0454	0604	0635	0738	0835	0935	1035	1135	1235	1338	1435	1538	1636	1738	1836	1938	2035	2139	2236	2336	2336
Schweinfurt Hbf.. **870** d.	0106	0107	...	0436	0544f	0636	0700	0802	0900	1000	1059	1200	1259	1402	1459	1602	1659	1802	1859	2002	2059	2202	2301	0009	0010
Haßfurt .... d.	...	0126	...	0455	0601	0653	0713	0816	0913	1014	1112	1214	1312	1416	1512	1616	1712	1816	1912	2016	2112	2216	2319	...	0029
Bamberg .... a.	...	0147	...	0520	0621	0717	0733	0832	0930	1032	1130	1232	1330	1432	1530	1632	1730	1832	1930	2032	2129	2232	2343	...	0054
Nürnberg Hbf 875 .. a.	...	...	...	...	...	...	0819	0919	1019	1119	1219	1319	1419	1519	1619	1719	1819	1920	2019	2120	2220	...	...	...	...

	Ⓐe	Ⓒz		Ⓐe	Ⓒz	Ⓐe																			
ürnberg Hbf 875 ... d.	...	...	...	...	...	...	...	0642a	0740	...	0840	0940	1040	1140	1240	1340	1441	1540	1641	1740	1840	1940	...	...	...	...
nberg .... d.	0034	0104	...	0446	0446	0552	0629	0729	0826	0838	0925	1026	1125	1226	1325	1426	1525	1626	1725	1826	1925	2026	2038	2138	...	2304
furt .... d.	0055	0126	...	0507	0507	0615	0644	0745	0843	0900	0942	1043	1142	1242	1342	1443	1542	1643	1742	1843	1942	2043	2100	2200	...	2326
weinfurt Hbf ... **870** d.	0113	0144	...	0525	0525	0641	0658	0758	0857	0918	0956	1057	1156	1256	1356	1457	1556	1657	1756	1857	1956	2057	2118	2218	...	2345
zburg Hbf ..... **870** a.	...	0215	...	0548	0600	0718	0722	0820	0922	0951	1020	1122	1220	1319	1420	1521	1620	1722	1820	1921	2020	2122	2150	2251	...	0016

Change trains at Trebgast (a. 2215, d. 2225).
Change trains at Trebgast (a. 0004, d. 0011).
Ⓐ only.

e – Not Aug. 15.
f – Arrives 0525.
j – On † departs Hof 0744, Münchberg 0801.
z – Also Aug. 15.

* – By 🚌.
‡ – Operated by *agilis* (2nd class only).
⊠ – Rail services between Bamberg and Lichtenfels are expected to restart from September 4.

877 LANDSHUT - MÜHLDORF - SALZBURG

RB serv…

km		Ⓐe	⑥								
0	**Landshut** (Bay) Hbf .... d.	...	...	*0609*r	0836	1036	1237	1436	1636	1836	2036
55	Mühldorf (Oberbay) ..... a.	...	...	*0712*r	0928	1128	1328	1528	1729	1928	2128
55	Mühldorf (Oberbay) ..... d.	0556	0617	0741	0943	1143	1343	1544	1743	1943	2146
120	Freilassing .... **890/1** a.	0704	0711	0839	1043	1243	1445	1643	1845	2043	2239
126	**Salzburg** Hbf.... **890/1** a.	*0719*	*0728*	0852	1055	*1319*	1453	1655	1854	*2119*	2256

	Ⓐe	⚒r							
Salzburg Hbf. **890/1** d.	*0513*v	...	*0703*q	0909	1109	*1313*	1509	1709	1909
Freilassing ..... **890/1** d.	0535	...	0718	0924	1123	1326	1523	1726	1923
Mühldorf (Oberbay)... a.	0628	...	0814	1018	1217	1417	1617	1817	2017
Mühldorf (Oberbay)... d.	...	0633	0830	1030	1230	1430	1630	1830	2032
Landshut (Bay) Hbf.. a.	...	0723	0921	1121	1321	1521	1721	1921	2121

e – Not Aug. 15, Nov. 1.
f – ⑤ only.
q – *0650* on ⑥; *0642* on ⑦ (also Aug. 15, Oct. 3, Nov. 1).
r – ⚒ (not Aug. 15, Nov. 1).
v – *0515* from Aug. 6.

878 MÜNCHEN - REGENSBURG

DB (*RE* services);

km		*ALX* ⚒rP	N	*ALX*	N	*ALX*	*ALX* P	N	*ALX*	N	*ALX* P	*ALX* ⑤	N	*ALX*	N	*ALX*	*ALX* P	N	*ALX*	N	*ALX*	*ALX* ⑦w		*ALX*
0	**München** Hbf ...... **944** d.	0455	0544	0644	0744	0844	0901	0944	1044	1144	1244	1244	1343	1444	1544	1604	1702	1744	1844	1944	2044	2044	2144	2244
42	Freising .... **944** d.	0518	0608	0709	0808	0909	|	1008	1109	1208	1309	1309	1408	1509	1608	1629	1728	1808	1909	2008	2109	2109	2208	2309
76	Landshut (Bay) Hbf **944** d.	0538	0632	0731	0832	0931	0944	1032	1132	1232	1332	1332	1432	1531	1632	1650	1749	1832	1932	2032	2132	2132	2232	2335
99	Neufahrn (Niederbay) .. d.	|	0649	0748	0849	0948	|	1049	1148	1249	1348	1348	1449	1548	1649	|	|	1849	1948	2049	2148	2148	2249	2351
138	**Regensburg** Hbf .... a.	0614	0717	0811	0914	1011	1020	1115	1211	1314	1411	1411	1514	1611	1715	1726	1825	1916	2012	2116	2211	2211	2320	0017
	Schwandorf **879 885** a.	0649	...	0846	...	1050	1059	...	1247	...	1447	1447	...	1647	...	1802	1902	...	2102	...	2252	2252	...	...
	Hof Hbf **879** .... a.	...	...	1019	...	1220	...	...	1420	...	...	1619	...	1819	...	1933	...	...	2235	...	...	0026	...	...

	ALX ⚒r	*ALX*	Ⓐe	*ALX* ©z	*ALX* Ⓐe	ⒶeN	*ALX*	N	*ALX* P	*ALX*	N	*ALX*	N	*ALX* P	*ALX*	N	*ALX*	N	*ALX* P	N	*ALX*	*ALX*	N	*ALX* P
Hof Hbf **879** .... d.	...	...	...	...	...	...	0531	...	...	0740	...	0940	...	...	1140	...	1340	...	...	...	1740	1841w	...	...
Schwandorf **879 885**. d.	...	0501r	...	...	...	...	0703	...	0902	0909	...	1109	...	1302	1309	...	1510	...	1708	...	1909	2009w	...	2104
Regensburg Hbf .... d.	0442	0546	0622	0646	0653	0702	0747	0844	0951	0951	1044	1146	1244	1342	1346	1444	1546	1644	1746	1844	1946	2046	2050	2141
Neufahrn (Niederbay) .. d.	0508	0610	0647	0711	|	0728	0811	0911	1014	1014	1111	1211	1311	|	1411	1511	1611	1711	1811	1911	2011	2111	2120	|
Landshut (Bay) Hbf **944** d.	0527	0628	0706	0729	0732	0747	0827	0929	1030	1030	1129	1227	1329	1419	1428	1529	1627	1729	1827	1929	2027	2127	2139	2220
Freising .... **944** d.	0548	0649	0730	0751	|	0810	0848	0951	1050	1050	1149	1248	1349	|	1449	1549	1648	1749	1849	1951	2048	2147	*2210*	2241
München Hbf .... **944** a.	0615	0715	0757	0819	0819	0835	0917	1018	1118	1118	1217	1317	1417	1505	1516	1617	1716	1817	1915	2017	2116	2217	*2235*	2305

N – To / from Nürnberg (Table **921**).
P – (12) München - Schwandorf - Furth im Wald 🏛 - Praha and v.v. See also Tables **57** and **885**.
e – Not Aug. 15, Nov. 1.
r – ⚒ (not Aug. 15, Nov. 1).
w – ⑦ (also Oct. 3, Nov. 1; not Oct. 2, 30).
z – Also Aug. 15, Nov. 1.
ALX – Operated by Vogtlandbahn. 🍸.

879 REGENSBURG - HOF

DB (*RE* services); *ALX*; Oberpfalzb…

km		2 Ⓐe		2	*ALX*	2	*ALX*	2	*ALX*	2	2	*ALX* ⑤	H	2	*ALX*	2	*ALX*		2	2	*ALX*	2	*ALX*	*ALX* ⑦w	2
	München Hbf **878** .. d.	...	...	...	0644	...	0844	...	1044	...	...	1244	...	...	1444	...	1604	...	...	...	1844	...	2044	2044	...
0	**Regensburg** Hbf **885** d.	*0512*	0628	0703	0821	0857	1021	1057	1221	1257	1357	1419	1431	1457	1621	1657	1734	1828	1857	1957	2031	2138	2221	2221	...
42	Schwandorf......... **885** a.	*0541*	0654	0732	0846	0926	1050	1126	1247	1326	1426	1447	1458	1526	1647	1726	1802	1855	1926	2026	2102	2207	2252	2252	...
42	Schwandorf................ d.	0552	0656	0733	0847	0927	1051	1127	1247	1327	1427	1451	1459	1527	1647	1727	1803	1905	1927	2028	2103	2209	...	2256	2307
86	Weiden (Oberpf) .... d.	0630	0721	0809	0914	1003	1117	1203	1314	1403	1502	1517	1521	1603	1714	1803	1831	1928	2003	2103	2130	2248	...	2322	2342
137	Marktredwitz ...... **880** a.	0711	0753	0850c	0951	1044	1152	1244	1351	1444	1543	1552	1552	1644	1751	1844	1906	2001	2044	2144	2208	2327	...	2357	...
179	**Hof** Hbf............... **880** a.	*0754*	0819	*0924*c	1019	*1124*	1220	*1324*	1420	*1524*	...	1619	1619	*1724*	1819	*1924*	1933	2024	*2125*	...	2235	...	...	0026	...

	ALX ⚒r	Ⓐe	2 ©z	*ALX*	2	*ALX*	2	*ALX*	2	*ALX*	2	*ALX*	2	*ALX* ⑤	2		2	2 ⑦w	2	*ALX*	2	*ALX* ⑦w		2	2
Hof Hbf ....**880** d.	...	0420	...	0531	*0629*	0740	*0840*	0940	*1040*	1140	*1240*	1340	...	1447	*1440*	1540	...	*1640*	*1640*h	1740	...	1841	1940	*2001*	*2040*
Marktredwitz ....**880** d.	...	0447	...	0557	0704	0806	0915	1006	1115	1206	1315	1406	1415	1513	1516	1604	1615	1705	1715h	1806	1815	1910	2003	2040	2132
Weiden (Oberpf)......... d.	*0413*e	0524	0519	0636	0741	0842	0955	1042	1155	1242	1355	1442	1455	1545	1556	1638	1655	1741	1755	1842	1855	1944	2035	2123	2222j
Schwandorf................. a.	*0451*e	0545	0556	0701	0806	0908	1031	1108	1231	1308	1431	1509	1531	1612	1632	1700	1731	1807	1831	1908	1931	2008	2057	2159	2259
Schwandorf...........**885** d.	0501	0548	0604	0703	0807	0909	1032	1109	1232	1309	1432	1510	1532	1613	1633	1702	1732	1808	1832	1909	1932	2009	2058	2207	*2302*
Regensburg Hbf .**885** a.	0536	0615	0635	0737	0837	0938	1104	1137	1304	1338	1504	1537	1604	1638	1704	1731	1804	1837	1904	1937	2003	2038	2126	2238	*2330*
München Hbf **878**... a.	0715	...	...	0917	...	1118	...	1317	...	1516	...	1716	...	...	...	...	...	...	...	2116	...	2217	...	...	...

H – Daily except ⑤.
c – © (also Nov. 1).
e – Ⓐ (not Aug. 15, Nov. 1).
h – ①–⑥ (also Oct. 2, 30; not Oct. 3, Nov. 1).
j – Arrives 2211.
r – Not Aug. 15, Nov. 1.
w – Also Oct. 3, Nov. 1; not Oct. 2, 30.
z – Also Aug. 15, Nov. 1.
ALX – Operated by Vogtlandbahn.

880 NÜRNBERG - HOF - DRESDEN

IRE / *RE* / *RB* servi…

NÜRNBERG - HOF

km				©z	©z	Ⓐe	Ⓐe				Ⓐe					A						A		
0	**Nürnberg** Hbf................... ● d.	0540	0540	0631	0631	0637	0637	0656	0738	0738	0758	0837	0905	0938	0938	1005	1037	1037	1105	1138	1138	1205	1237	1237
28	Hersbruck (r Pegnitz)....... ● d.	0558	0558	0652	0652	|	|	0715	0754	0754	0815	|	0920	|	|	1019	|	|	1120	|	|	1219	|	|
67	Pegnitz .... ● a.	0622	0622	0713	0713	0714	0714	0738	0822	0822	0839	0914	0942	1015	1015	1042	1114	1114	1142	1215	1215	1242	1314	1314
67	Pegnitz .... d.	0628	0624	0715	0722	0715	0722	0739	0824	0828	0841	0916	0943	1017	1022	1043	1116	1122	1143	1217	1222	1243	1316	1322
	Bayreuth Hbf .... d.	|	0647	0732	|	0732	|	0758	0847	|	0855	0932	1000	1042	|	1058	1132	|	1200	1242	|	1258	1332	|
	Münchberg .... **876** d.	|	▬	0805	|	0805	|	...	...	|	▬	1005	...	...	|	▬	1205	|	...	...	|	▬	1405	|
94	Kirchenlaibach .... **887** d.	0643	⊖	|	0744t	|	0744t	...	...	0845	⊖	|	...	...	1044t	⊖	|	1144t	...	...	1244t	⊖	|	1344t
125	Marktredwitz .... **879 1121** d.	0700	0712	|	0802	|	0802	...	...	0901	0908	|	...	...	1101	1108	|	1202	...	...	1301	1308	|	1402
	Cheb..................... **1121** a.	|	0737	|	0822	|	0822	...	...	|	0933	|	...	...	|	1133	|	1222	...	...	|	1333	|	1422
167	**Hof** Hbf.......... **876 879 887** a.	0723	...	0823	...	0823	...	...	...	0924	...	1023	...	...	1124	...	1223	...	...	...	1324	...	1423	...

			A						A						A									
Nürnberg Hbf.................. ● d.	1338	1338	1405	1437	1437	1505	1538	1538	1605	1637	1637	1705	1738	1738	1805	1837	1837	1905	1938	1938	2055	2055	2155	2155
Hersbruck (r Pegnitz)......... ● d.	|	|	1420	|	|	1520	|	|	1620	|	|	1720	|	|	1820	|	|	1920	1954	1954	2112	2112	2212	2212
Pegnitz .... ● a.	1415	1415	1442	1514	1514	1542	1615	1615	1642	1714	1714	1742	1815	1815	1842	1914	1914	1942	2021	2021	2137	2137	2237	2237
Pegnitz .... d.	1417	1422	1443	1516	1522	1543	1617	1622	1643	1716	1722	1743	1817	1822	1843	1916	1920	1943	2023	2028	2139	2144	2239	2244
Bayreuth Hbf.................. d.	1442	|	1458	1532	|	1601	1642	|	1658	1732	|	1801	1842	|	1858	1932	|	2000	2049	|	2158	|	2259	|
Münchberg .... **876** d.	...	|	▬	1605	|	...	...	|	▬	1805	|	...	...	|	▬	2005	|	...	...	|	...	|	▬	|
Kirchenlaibach .... **887** d.	...	1444	⊖	|	1544t	...	...	1644t	⊖	|	1744t	...	...	1844t	⊖	|	1935	...	...	2044	...	2158	⊖	2258
Marktredwitz ....**879 1121** d.	...	1501	1508	|	1602	...	...	1701	1708	|	1802	...	...	1901	1911	|	2000	...	...	2100	...	2216	2218	2321
Cheb...................... **1121** a.	...	|	1533	|	1622	...	...	|	1733	|	1822	...	...	|	1936	|	...	...	...	|	...	|	2243	|
Hof Hbf ....**876 879 887** a.	...	1524	...	1623	...	...	...	1724	...	1823	...	...	...	1924	...	2024	...	...	...	2125	...	2242	...	2349

HOF - DRESDEN ⊠

km		©w																					
0	**Hof** Hbf........................ **881** d.	...	...	...	...	0427	...	0527	...		1727	...	1827	...	1936	...	2030	...	...	...	...	...	...
48	Plauen (Vogtl) ob Bf ..... **881** d.	...	...	...	...	0459	...	0559	...	and at	1759	...	1859	...	2008	...	2102	...	...	...	...	...	...
73	Reichenbach (Vogtl) ob Bf **881** d.	...	...	...	...	0515	...	0615	...	the same	1815	...	1915	...	2024	...	2118	...	...	...	...	...	...
96	**Zwickau** (Sachs) Hbf........... d.	0343	...	...	0439	0532	0539	0631	0639		1831	1839	1931	1939	2040	2045	2134	2143	...	2243	...	2343	...
112	Glauchau (Sachs) .... **858** d.	0359	...	...	0455	0542	0555	0641	0655	minutes	1841	1855	1941	1955	2050	2101	2144	2158	...	2258	...	2358	...
144	**Chemnitz** Hbf .... **858** d.	0430	0430	0503	0530	0603	0630	0703	0730		1903	1930	2003	2030	2112	2132	2205	2230	...	2330	...	0029	...
157	Flöha .... d.	0443	0443	0513	0543	0613	0643	0713	0743	past each	1913	1943	2013	2043	2122	2144	...	2243	...	2343	...	...	...
183	Freiberg (Sachs).................... d.	0508	0508	0531	0608	0631	0708	0731	0808	hour until	1931	2008	2031	2108	2139	2208	...	2308	...	0008	...	...	...
223	**Dresden** Hbf......................... a.	0551	0551	0603	0651	0703	0751	0803	0851		2003	2051	2103	2151	2212	2251	...	2351	...	0051	...	...	...

A – Daily to Oct. 14; Ⓐ from Oct. 17 (not Nov. 1).
e – Ⓐ (not Nov. 1).
t – Arrives 7–8 minutes earlier.
w – Also Oct. 31, Nov. 16.
z – Also Nov. 1.

⊖ – Operated by Oberpfalzbahn.
◇ – Operated by Vogtlandbahn.
⊠ – Operated by Mitteldeutsche Regiobahn (2nd class only).
● – Certain trains between Nürnberg and Pegnitz convey portions for two separate destinati… Passengers should take care to join the correct portion for their destination.

DRESDEN - HOF - NÜRNBERG 880

RE services

DRESDEN - HOF ⊠

	Ⓐj◇	Ⓒw																				◇			
den Hbf d.	...	...	...	...	0453	0507	0553	0607	0653	and at	1607	1653	1707	1753	1807	1853	1907	1953	2007	2053	...	2107	2207	2307
erg (Sachs) d.	...	...	...	...	0525	0550	0625	0650	0725	the same	1650	1725	1750	1825	1850	1925	1950	2025	2050	2125	...	2150	2250	2350
d.	...	...	...	...	0544	0613	0644	0713	0744	minutes	1713	1744	1813	1844	1913	1944	2013	2044	2113	2144	...	2213	2313	0013
nnitz Hbf 858 d.	...	0250	0410	...	0555	0631	0655	0731	0755	past each	1731	1755	1831	1855	1931	1955	2031	2055	2131	2155	...	2231	2331	0025
chau (Sachs) 858 d.	...	0321	0441	...	0617	0702	0717	0802	0817	hour until	1802	1817	1902	1917	2002	2017	2102	2117	2202	2217	...	2302	0002	...
kau (Sachs) Hbf d.	0359	0337	0457	0510	0628	0718	0728	0818	0828		1818	1828	1918	1928	2018	2028	2118	2128	2218	2228	2239	2319	0018	...
henbach (Vogtl) ob Bf 881 d.	0418	...	...	0527	0643	...	0743	...	0843		...	1843	...	1943	...	2043	...	2143	...	...	2307	...	...	...
en (Vogtl) ob Bf 881 d.	0442	...	...	0546	0700	...	0800	...	0900		...	1900	...	2000	...	2100	...	2200	...	...	2331	...	...	...
Hbf 881 a.	0521	...	...	0618	0732	...	0832	...	0932		...	1932	...	2032	...	2132	...	2232	...	...	...	...	...	...

HOF - NÜRNBERG

		Ⓐe	Ⓐe	Ⓐe	Ⓒz	Ⓒz	Ⓐe	⊖				⚒e	A	⊖					A	⊖				⊖
Hof Hbf 876 879 887 d.	...	0420	...	...	...	*0531*	0527	...	0629	...	...	0736	...	...	0840	...	...	0936	...	...	1040	...	1136	...
Cheb 1121 d.	...	|	...	...	...	|	|	0629	|	...	...	|	...	0829	|	...	0938	|	...	1027	|	...	|	1227
Marktredwitz 879 1121 d.	...	0442	0547	...	...	0600	|	0654	0657	...	...	|	...	0854	0902	...	1001	|	...	1052	1102	...	|	1252
Kirchenlaibach 887 d.	...	0506	0608	...	...	0616	|	━━	0713	...	...	|	...	━━	0919	...	1023	|	...	━━	1119	...	|	━━
Münchberg 876 d.	...	|	|	...	...	|	0546	Ⓐe	|	...	...	0754	...	...	|	...	|	0954	...	...	|	...	1154	A
Bayreuth Hbf d.	0500	|	|	0605	0605	|	0627	0703	|	0712	0800	0830	0903	0915	|	1001	|	1029	1103	1115	|	1201	1229	1303
Pegnitz a.	0521	0527	0622	0626	0626	0630	0642	0717	0731	0735	0817	0844	0918	0941	0935	1018	1038	1044	1118	1141	1135	1219	1243	1318
Pegnitz d.	0529	0529	0630	0630	0633	0633	0642	0718	0738	0738	0818	0845	0919	0944	0944	1019	1046	1046	1119	1144	1144	1219	1246	1319
Hersbruck (r Pegnitz) d.	0552	0552	0654	0654	0656	0656	|	0742	0802	0802	0839	|	0939	|	|	1039	|	|	1139	|	|	1241	|	|
Nürnberg Hbf a.	0607	0607	0710	0710	0712	0712	0718	0758	0819	0819	0857	0922	0955	1020	1020	1055	1122	1122	1155	1220	1220	1256	1322	1355

						A	⊖					A	⊖					⊖					⊖		
Hbf 876 879 887 d.	1240	...	...	...	1336	...	...	1440	...	...	1536	...	...	1640	...	...	1736	...	1839	...	...	1936	...	2040	2136
heb 1121 d.	|	...	...	1338	|	...	1427	|	...	1538	|	...	1627	|	...	1738	|	1827	|	...	1945	|	2027	|	|
ktredwitz 879 1121 d.	1302	...	...	1401	|	...	1452	1502	...	1601	|	...	1652	1702	...	1801	|	1852	1901	...	2009	|	2052	2102	|
henlaibach 887 d.	1319	...	...	1423	|	...	━━	1519	...	1623	|	...	━━	1719	...	1823	|	━━	1918	...	2025	|	━━	2122	|
ünchberg 876 d.	|	...	...	|	1354	...	...	|	...	|	1554	...	...	|	...	|	1754	...	|	...	|	1954	...	|	2153
ayreuth Hbf d.	|	1315	1401	|	1429	1503	1515	|	1601	|	1629	1703	1715	|	1801	|	1829	1915	|	2001	|	2029	2113	|	2227
nitz a.	1335	1341	1419	1438	1444	1518	1541	1535	1619	1638	1644	1718	1741	1735	1819	1838	1844	1941	1935	2019	2039	2044	2133	2138	2246
nitz d.	1344	1344	1419	1446	1446	1519	1544	1544	1619	1646	1646	1719	1744	1744	1819	1846	1846	1944	1944	2019	2047	2047	2141	2141	2247
bruck (r Pegnitz) d.	1405	1405	1440	|	|	1539	|	|	1640	|	|	1739	|	|	1840	|	|	2007	2007	2040	2112	2112	2207	2207	2314
nberg Hbf a.	1420	1420	1456	1522	1522	1555	1620	1620	1656	1722	1722	1755	1820	1820	1856	1922	1922	2022	2022	2056	2128	2128	2222	2222	2329

Daily to Oct. 14; Ⓐ from Oct. 17 (not Nov. 1).

Not Nov. 1.

j – Not Oct. 31, Nov. 16.
w – Also Oct. 31, Nov. 16.
z – Also Nov. 1.

⊖ – Operated by Oberpfalzbahn.
◇ – Operated by Vogtlandbahn.
⊠ – Operated by Mitteldeutsche Regiobahn (2nd class only).

ZWICKAU - LEIPZIG - HALLE 881

Bahn 5

Zwickau (Sachs) Hbf 858 d.	...	0341	...	0504e	0514	0604	...	0704e	0713	0804	...	0904	and in	1904	1913	2004	...	2104e	2113	...	2213	...
Werdau 858 d.	...	0351	...	0512e	0526	0612	...	0712e	0726	0812	...	0912	the same	1912	1926	2012	...	2112e	2126	...	2226	...
Gößnitz 858 d.	...	0408	...	0526e	0542	0626	...	0726e	0743	0826	...	0926	pattern	1926	1943	2026	...	2126e	2142	...	2242	...
Altenburg d.	...	0434	0504	0539	0604	0639	0704	0739	0804	0839	0904	0939	every	1939	2004	2039	2104	2139	2157	...	2257	...
Leipzig-Connewitz ★ d.	0356	0512	0542	0612	0642	0712	0742	0812	0842	0912	0942	1012	two hours	2012	2042	2112	2142	2212	2246	2317	2346	0017
Leipzig Hbf ★ 866 d.	0406	0523	0553	0623	0653	0723	0753	0823	0853	0923	0953	1023	until	2023	2053	2123	2153	2223	2308k	2327	0008k	0027
Leipzig/Halle Flughafen ✈ 866 d.	0420	0540	0610	0637	0710	0737	0810	0837	0910	0937	1010	1037		2037	2110	2137	2210	2240	|	2344	|	0044
Halle (Saale) Hbf 866 a.	0434	0554	0624	...	0724	...	0824	...	0924	...	1024	...		...	2124	...	2224	2256	2343	2359	0043	0059

e (Saale) Hbf 866 d.	0413	...	...	0536f	...	0636	...	0736	...	and in	1836	...	1936	...	2036	...	2136	...	2216	2246	2316	2346	0048
zig/Halle Flughafen ✈ 866 d.	0424	0449	0524	0549	0624	0649	0724	0749	0824	the same	1849	1924	1949	2024	2049	2124	2149	2222	|	2301	|	0001	0101
zig Hbf ★ 866 d.	0439	0509	0539	0609	0639	0709	0739	0809	0839	pattern	1909	1939	2009	2039	2109	2139	2209	2240	2303	2317	0003	0016	0117
zig-Connewitz ★ d.	0449	0519	0549	0619	0649	0719	0749	0819	0849	every	1919	1949	2019	2049	2119	2149	2219	2250	2313	2328	0013	0027	0127
nburg d.	0520e	0559j	0620	0656	0720	0759j	0820	0856	0920	two hours	1959j	2020	2056	2120	2156	2220	2256	...	0008	...	0102	...	...
nitz 858 d.	0533e	0616	0633e	...	0733	0816	0833	...	0933	until	2016	2033	...	2133	...	2233	...	...	0021	...	...	...	...
dau 858 d.	0547e	0634	0647e	...	0747	0834	0847	...	0947		2034	2047	...	2147	...	2250	...	...	0039	...	...	...	...
ckau (Sachs) Hbf 858 a.	0557e	0645	0657e	...	0757	0845	0857	...	0957		2045	2057	...	2157	...	2301	...	...	0050	...	...	...	...

PLAUEN - WERDAU ◇

	Ⓐt								Ⓐt
Cheb **1122** d.	...	...	...	1005	1205	...	1605	1805	...
Plauen (Vogt) ob Bf d.	0529	0729	0929	1129	1329	1529	1729	1929	2030
Reichenbach (Vogt) ob Bf d.	0552	0752	0952	1152	1352	1552	1752	1952	2052
Werdau a.	0605	0805	1005	1205	1405	1605	1805	2005	2105
Zwickau (Sachs) Hbf a.	0622	0822	1022	1222	1422	1622	1822	2022	2125

									H	
Zwickau (Sachs) Hbf d.	0536	0736	0936	1136	1336	1536	1736	1936	2046	2239
Werdau d.	0552	0752	0952	1152	1352	1552	1752	1952	2102	2254
Reichenbach (Vogt) ob Bf a.	0605	0805	1005	1205	1405	1605	1805	2005	2114	2307
Plauen (Vogt) ob Bf a.	0629	0829	1029	1229	1429	1629	1829	2029	2138	2331
Cheb **1122** a.	...	0954	1154	...	1554	1754	...	...	...	...

To Hof Hbf (a. 2218).
Ⓐ (not Oct. 31).
0535 from Oct. 2.

j – 3 minutes later from Sept. 4.
k – Arrives 13 minutes earlier.
t – Not Oct. 31, Nov. 16.

★ – All trains also call at Leipzig MDR, Leipzig Bayerischer Bahnhof, Leipzig Wilhelm-Leuschner-Platz and Leipzig Markt.
◇ – Operated by Vogtlandbahn (2nd class only).

CHEMNITZ - CRANZAHL - VEJPRTY - CHOMUTOV 882

(RB services); ČD

									C		
Chemnitz Hbf 880 d.	0636	0836	0936	1136	1236	1336	1436	1636	...	1836	2036
Flöha 880 d.	0647	0847	0947	1147	1247	1347	1447	1647	...	1847	2047
Zschopau d.	0708	0908	1008	1208	1308	1410	1508	1708	...	1910	2108
Annaberg-Buchholz ¶ d.	0743	0943	1048	1243	1348	1445	1543	1743	...	1945	2143
Cranzahl ⊖ d.	...	0955	1102	1255	1400	1501	1555v	1755	1804r	...	...
Bärenstein ⊗ d.	...	...	1114z	━━	...	...	...	...	1816r	...	...
Vejprty 🏛 a.	...	...	1116z	C	...	...	...	...	1818r	...	...
Vejprty 🏛 d.	...	...	...	1150	...	...	...	...	1820	...	...
Chomutov a.	...	...	...	1310	...	...	...	...	1942	...	...

		C						C		
Chomutov d.	...	0952	...	...	...	...	...	1609	...	...
Vejprty 🏛 a.	...	1123	...	...	...	...	...	1740	...	...
Vejprty 🏛 d.	...	━━	1139z	...	...	...	...	1742r	...	...
Bärenstein ⊗ d.	...	...	1141z	...	...	...	...	1746r	...	...
Cranzahl ⊖ d.	...	1001	1155	1301	1445	1557	1655v	1758r	1801	...
Annaberg-Buchholz ¶ d.	0807	1013	1207	1313	1507	1609	1707	...	1813	2007
Zschopau d.	0844	1047	1244	1347	1544	1644	1744	...	1847	2044
Flöha 880 a.	0908	1108	1308	1408	1608	1708	1808	...	1908	2108
Chemnitz Hbf 880 a.	0920	1120	1320	1420	1620	1720	1820	...	1920	2120

Cranzahl - Kurort Oberwiesenthal *Fichtelbergbahn* (17 km, narrow gauge steam). Journey: 57 – 64 minutes. **No service Nov. 1 – 24.**
Operator: SDG Sächsische Dampfeisenbahngesellschaft GmbH, Bahnhofstraße 7, 09484 Kurort Oberwiesenthal. ✆ + 49 (0) 37348 151 0.
From **Cranzahl** at 0959, 1137, 1315, 1504, 1640 ⊡ and 1813. From **Kurort Oberwiesenthal** at 0835, 1014, 1152, 1330, 1519 ⊡ and 1655.

⑥⑦ to Sept. 25 (also July 5, 6, Sept. 28).

r – Not July 5, 6, Sept. 28.
v – Ⓒ (also Oct. 31, Nov. 16).
z – ⑥⑦ to Sept. 25.

⊡ – ⑥⑦ (also Oct. 31; runs daily June 25 - Oct. 16).
⊗ – Trains stop on request only.
¶ – Annaberg-Buchholz unterer Bf.

CHEMNITZ - AUE 883

services

Chemnitz Hbf d.	0605	0810	0910	1110	1310	1510	1710	1910	2116	2245
Thalheim d.	0658	0857	0958	1157	1357	1557	1757	1957	2157	2325
Zwönitz d.	0709	0908	1009	1208	1408	1608	1808	2008	2208	2336
Lößnitz unt Bf. ⊗ d.	0719	0918	1019	1218	1418	1618	1818	2018	2218	2347
Aue (Sachs) a.	0724	0923	1024	1223	1423	1623	1823	2023	2223	2352

		Ⓐe								Ⓒz	Ⓐe	Ⓒz	
Aue (Sachs) d.	0410	0526	0629	0828	0929	1128	1328	1528	1728	1829	1928	2035	2125
Lößnitz unt Bf ⊗ d.	0415	0531	0634	0833	0934	1133	1333	1533	1733	1834	1933	2040	2130
Zwönitz d.	0427	0543	0646	0845	0946	1145	1345	1545	1745	1846	1945	2052	2142
Thalheim d.	0438	0558	0658	0858	0958	1158	1358	1558	1758	1858	1958	2104	2158
Chemnitz Hbf a.	0516	0636	0741	0941	1041	1241	1441	1641	1841	1941	2041	2147	2237

Not Oct. 31, Nov. 16.

z – Also Oct. 31, Nov. 16.

⊗ – Trains stop on request only.

884 ZWICKAU - JOHANNGEORGENSTADT - KARLOVY VARY

DB; ČD (2nd class or

km		Ⓐt								⑤⑥f
0	**Zwickau** (Sachs) Hbf . d.	0507	...	0607	and	1907	2007	2107	2207	2307
27	Aue (Sachs) .... d.	0540	0540	0640	hourly	1940	2040	2140	2239	2340
37	Schwarzenberg (Erzg) . d.	0555	0555	0655	until	1955	2055	2153	...	2353
56	**Johanngeorgenstadt**. a.	0620	0620	0720		2020	2120	...	...	...

	Ⓐt								
Johanngeorgenstadt ...... d.	0429	...	0529	0629	and	1829	1929	2029	
Schwarzenberg (Erzg) ...... d.	0455	0455	0555	0655	hourly	1855	1955	2055	2
Aue (Sachs) .... d.	0509	0509	0609	0709	until	1909	2009	2109	2
Zwickau (Sachs) Hbf .... a.	0541	0541	0641	0741		1941	2041	2141	2

km	See note ▶	Ⓐ	⊗	Ⓐ	Ⓒ					Ⓒ	
0	**Johanngeorgenstadt**. d.	...	0725	0925	1025	1235	1445	1623	2040	2040	...
1	Potučky 🏛 .... d.	0600	0728	0928	1029	1239	1450	1626	2050	2050	...
28	Nejdek .... d.	0700	0814	1014	1115	1328	1542	1714	2135	2138	2224
44	**Karlovy Vary**............ a.	0726	0840	1040	1142	1354	1608	1742	...	2204	2250
47	**Karlovy Vary** dolní ... a.	*0734*	0848	1048	1148	1400	1616	1750	...	2210	...

See note ▶					Ⓐ	Ⓒ	Ⓐ	Ⓒ		
Karlovy Vary dolní .... d.	0540e	0741	0940	1255	1405	1432	1705	1806	2103	
Karlovy Vary.................... d.	0546	0747	0946	1301	1411	1447	1715	1813	2111	
Nejdek .... d.	0618	0814	1016	1328	1440	1515	1742	1839	2137	2
Potučky 🏛 .... d.	0708	0901	1103	1415	1524	1602	1824	1924	...	2
Johanngeorgenstadt...... a.	0710	0903	1105	1417	1526	1604	1826	1926	...	

e – Ⓐ only. f – Also Oct. 2, 30. t – Not Oct. 31, Nov. 16. ⊗ – Change trains at Nejdek on Ⓐ. ▶ – Czech holiday dates apply (see page 2).

885 REGENSBURG - SCHWANDORF - FURTH IM WALD - PLZEŇ

km			◇ Ⓐe	◇	351 ‡	◇		◇	◇	353 ‡	◇	◇	◇	◇	355 ‡🍷	◇	◇		◇	A¶	◇	357 ‡🍷	◇	¶	
	München Hbf **878**....d.	...	...	...	0455r	...	...	*0644*	...	0901	...	...	*1044*	...	1244	...	...	...	*1444*	...	*1604*	1702	...	*1844*	
0	**Regensburg** Hbf . **879** d.	...	*0512*	...	0623r	*0732*a	...	*0821*	*0932*	1031	...	*1132*	*1221*	*1332*	1419	...	*1532*	...	*1621*	*1657*	*1734*	1835	*1932*	*2031*	2
42	**Schwandorf**........ **879** d.	...	0550	0630	0705	0802	...	0904	1004	1107	1114	1202	1304	1404	1507	1514	1602	...	1704	1735	1805	1909	2007	2108	2
90	Cham (Oberpf) ....d.	...	0628	0715	0736	0846	...	0942	1039	1135	1152	1245	1342	1439	1535	1552	1645	...	1740	1821	1840	1938	2047	2143	2
109	**Furth im Wald** 🏛.......d.	...	0644	0732	0750	0906	...	0959	1055	1150	1209	1301	1358z	1456	1550	1609	1705	...	1756	1833	1856	1952	2104	2159	2
131	Domažlice...............⊠ d.	0532	...	...	0810	0927	0939	...	...	1210	...	...	...	...	1610	...	1727	1739	...	...	...	2012	...	...	
190	**Plzeň** Hlavni ....⊠ a.	0642	...	...	0857	...	1048	...	...	1257	...	...	...	...	1657	...	...	1848	...	...	...	2059	...	...	
	Praha Hlavní **1120** ..a.	...	...	...	1041	...	...	...	...	1441	...	...	...	...	1841	...	...	...	...	...	...	2241	...	...	

	Ⓐa¶	¶	‡🍷	◇	◇	356 ‡🍷	◇		◇	◇	354 ‡🍷	◇ Ⓒz	◇	◇	◇	352 ‡	◇	Ⓐ	◇		◇	350 ‡	◇		
Praha Hlavní **1120**....d.	...	...	...	...	...	0512	...	...	...	...	0912	...	...	...	...	1312	...	...	...	...	...	1712	...	...	
Plzeň Hlavni ....⊠ d.	...	...	...	...	...	0700	...	0810	...	...	1100	...	...	...	...	1500	...	1610	...	1710	...	1900	...	2110	2
Domažlice.................⊠ d.	...	...	...	...	...	0746	...	0925	0937	...	1146	...	...	...	...	1546	...	1728	1737t	1820	1837c	1946	...	2220	2
Furth im Wald 🏛........d.	0446	0606	...	0657	0755	0812	0905	...	1002	1100	1212	1302	...	1402	1501	1612	1704	...	1804	...	1901	2014	2106	...	
Cham (Oberpf) ....d.	0502	0624	...	0715	0812	0826	0922	...	1018	1117	1226	1322	1322	1418	1517	1626	1721	...	1821	...	1918	2028	2124	...	
Schwandorf......... **879** a.	0535	0655	0703	0755	0844	0854	0955	...	1055	1154	1254	1356	1356	1455	1555	1655	1755	...	1857	...	1956	2056	2158	...	
Regensburg Hbf .. **879** a.	*0615*e	...	0737	*0837*	...	0929	*1030*	...	*1137*	*1230*	1330	*1430*	*1430*	*1537*	*1630*	1736	*1832*	...	*1937*	...	*2030*	2133	*2238*	...	
München Hbf **878**.....a.	...	...	0917	...	...	1118	...	...	*1317*	...	1505	...	...	*1716*	...	1915	...	...	*2116*	...	...	2305	...	...	

A – ①–④ (not Oct. 3, Nov. 1).
B – ⑤–⑦ (also Aug. 15, Oct. 3, Nov. 1).
a – Ⓐ (not Nov. 1).
c – ⑥⑦ (also July 5, 6, Sept. 28, Oct. 28, Nov. 17).
e – Ⓐ (not Aug. 15, Nov. 1).
r – ⚒ (not Aug. 15, Nov. 1).
t – ①–⑤ (not July 5, 6, Sept. 28, Oct. 28, Nov. 17).
z – Ⓒ (also Aug. 15, Nov. 1).
¶ – From / to Nürnberg (Table **886**).
◇ – Operated by Oberpfalzbahn (2nd class).
‡ – Train category *ALX* in Germany (operated by Vogtlandbahn).
⊠ – Other local trains Domažlice - Plzeň and v.v. (journey 68 – 80 minu
From Domažlice at 0345, 0429 Ⓐ, 0614 Ⓐ, 0731, 1131, 1339, 1429 Ⓐ, 1531, 1629 Ⓐ and 1931. **From Plzeň Hlavni** at 0505 Ⓐ 0605, 0710, 1110, 1310, 1410 Ⓐ, 1506, 1810 Ⓐ and 1910.

886 NÜRNBERG - SCHWANDORF and WEIDEN

RE servic

km				Ⓐt		Ⓐt	Ⓒz										Ⓐtf		⊡		⊡		f			
0	**Nürnberg** Hbf........ ◧d.	0017	...	0434	0536	0624	0631	0738	0843	0943	1043	1143	1243	1343	1443	1543	1605	1643	1705	1743	1805	1843	1938	2055	2155	2
28	Hersbruck (r Pegnitz) ◧d.	0033	...	0449	0551	0652‡	0648	0757	0858	0958	1058	1158	1258	1358	1458	1558	1625	1658	1725	1758	1825	1858	1958	2117	2216	2
56	Sulzbach-Rosenberg . d.	0059	...	0515	0619	0728	0728	0826	0925	1026	1126	1226	1326	1426	1526	1626	1649	1726	1749	1826	1852	1926	2026	2142	2240	2
68	Amberg.................... d.	0106	...	0526	0627	0736	0736	0833	0935	1033	1133	1233	1333	1433	1533	1633	1701	1736	1801	1833	1901	1933	2036	2150	2248	2
94	**Schwandorf** .... a.	...	...	0543	0643	0757	0757	0848	0949	1048	1148	1248	1350	1448	1548	1650	1722	1751	1824	1848	1926	1947	2051	2204	2301	0

	Ⓐt	⚒t	†z	Ⓐt	Ⓐtf	Ⓒz	Ⓐt	f	Ⓐt																
Schwandorf......................... d.	0407	0509	0516	0544	0558	0609	0644	0707	0740	0806	0906	1006	1106	1206	1306	1406	1504	1605	1705	1807	1908	2006	2107	2212	0
Amberg.................................. d.	0423	0526	0532	0559	0615	0626	0700	0725	0756	0822	0921	1021	1121	1221	1321	1421	1521	1621	1721	1821	1922	2021	2121	2226	0
Sulzbach-Rosenberg............. d.	0432	0535	0541	0607	0627	0634	0707	0732	0807	0829	0929	1029	1129	1229	1329	1429	1529	1629	1729	1829	1929	2029	2129	2234	
Hersbruck (r pegnitz)............ d.	0503	0607	0607	|	0649	0707	|	0757	0841	0900	0959	1100	1159	1300	1359	1500	1559	1700	1759	1900	1959	2112‡	2207‡	2314‡	
Nürnberg Hbf........................ a.	0518	0621	0621	0651	0706	0722	0751	0814	0857	0915	1014	1115	1214	1316	1414	1515	1614	1715	1814	1916	2014	2128	2222	2329	

km			Ⓐt	Ⓒz								
0	**Nürnberg** Hbf........ ◧d.	0536	0624	0631	0738	0843	and	1843	1938	2055	2155	2257
28	Hersbruck (r Pegnitz) ◧d.	0551	0645	0648	0757	0858	hourly	1858	1958	2117	2216	2316
97	**Weiden** (Oberpf)........ a.	0645	0734	0748	0852	0950	until	1950	2051	2214	2314	0008

	Ⓒz	Ⓐt			❖					
Weiden (Oberpf)..... d.	0610	0610	0658	0806	and	1703	1803	1906	2003	2
Hersbruck (r Pegnitz) a.	0706	0707	0756	0859	hourly	1758	1859	1958	2059	2
Nürnberg Hbf .... a.	0722	0724	0814	0915	until	1814	1916	2014	2128	2

f – To / from Furth im Wald (Table **885**).
t – Not Nov. 1.
z – Also Nov. 1.
⊡ – ①–④ (not Oct. 3, Nov. 1).
‡ – Arrives 8 – 13 minutes earlier.
❖ – Weiden d. 1403 / 1603 (not 1406 / 1606).
◧ – Certain trains from Nürnberg and Hersbruck convey portions for two separate destinati
Passengers should take care to join the correct portion for their destination.

887 BAYREUTH - WEIDEN

Operated by *agilis* (2nd class on

km		Ⓐt												Ⓒz	Ⓐt												
0	**Bayreuth** Hbf.. d.	0507	0624	0718	0805	0859	0919	0959	1059	1119	1159	1259	1319	1359	1401	1459	1519	1601	1659	1719	1759	1824	1859	1959	2023	2201	0
19	Kirchenlaibach a.	0528	0639	0740	0826	0915	0941	1016	1115	1141	1215	1315	1341	1415	1417	1515	1541	1619	1715	1741	1816	1840	1915	2016	2039	2216	0
19	Kirchenlaibach d.	0528	0652	...	0826	0920	...	1020	1120	...	1220	1320	...	1420	1420	1520	...	1620	1720	...	1820	...	1920	2020	...	2217	
59	**Weiden**........... a.	0557	0726	...	0855	0950	...	1050	1150	...	1249	1353	...	1449	1449	1549	...	1649	1749	...	1849	...	1949	2049	...	2245	

	Ⓐt	Ⓐt		Ⓐt									Ⓒz	Ⓐt													
Weiden ....d.	...	0525	...	0638	...	*0734*	...	...	0907	1007	1107	1207	1307	1323	...	1407	1507	...	1607	1707	...	1807	1907	2007	...	2107	
Kirchenlaibach ..a.	...	0600	...	0707	...	*0803*	...	...	0941	1041	1141	1241	1341	1354	...	1441	1541	...	1641	1741	...	1841	1940	2041	...	2137	
Kirchenlaibach ..d.	0509	0606	0657	0720	0720	0807	0840	0921	0941	1042	1142	1242	1342	1355	1418	1442	1543	1619	1642	1742	1817	1842	1941	2044	2120	2137	23
Bayreuth Hbf ...a.	0524	0622	0716	0735	0735	0823	0856	0937	0957	1058	1158	1258	1358	1415	1437	1458	1559	1638	1658	1758	1837	1857	1957	2100	2136	2153	23

t – Not Nov. 1. z – Also Nov. 1.

888 KEMPTEN - REUTTE IN TIROL - GARMISCH-PARTENKIRCHEN

RE / RB servic

km											
0	**Kempten** (Allgäu) Hbf d.	0540	0734	0934	1134	1334	1534	1634	1734	1951	2253
18	Oy-Mittelberg .... d.	0607	0801	1001	1201	1401	1601	1701	1801	2018	2323
24	Nesselwang .... d.	0620	0812	1012	1212	1412	1612	1712	1812	2029	2334
31	Pfronten-Ried............. d.	0629	0822	1022	1222	1422	1622	1722	1822	2038	2344
33	**Pfronten-Steinach** 🏛 d.	0634	0828	1031	1227	1427	1627	1731	1831	2042	2347
38	Vils in Tirol 🏛 .... d.	0643h	0837	1040	1236	1436	1636	1740	1840	2051	...
48	**Reutte in Tirol** .... a.	0657h	0851	1054	1250	1450	1650	1754	1854	2105	...

Reutte in Tirol .... d.	0709a	0804c	0907	1109	1309	1509	1707	1807	1903	2
Vils in Tirol 🏛 .... d.	0723a	0818c	0921	1123	1323	1523	1721	1821	1917	2
Pfronten-Steinach 🏛...... d.	0734	0834	0934	1134	1334	1534	1734	1834	1927	2
Pfronten-Ried...................... d.	0738	0838	0938	1138	1338	1538	1738	1838	1931	2
Nesselwang .... d.	0748	0848	0948	1148	1348	1548	1748	1848	1940	2
Oy-Mittelberg .... d.	0801	0901	1001	1201	1401	1601	1801	1901	1950	2
Kempten (Allgäu) Hbf .... a.	0828	0928	1028	1228	1428	1628	1828	1928	2018	2

km		h		h			a			a	d		a	d		
0	**Reutte in Tirol** ....d.	0526	0701	0801	0901	1101	1158	1301	1501	1601	1626	1701	1801	1826	1901	2107
20	Lermoos...............................d.	0550	0725	0825	0925	1125	1225	1325	1525	1625	1652	1725	1825	1852	1925	2131
23	Ehrwald Zugspitzbahn 🏛 ....d.	0556	0731	0831	0931	1131	1231	1331	1531	1631	1658	1731	1831	1858	1931	2137
45	**Garmisch**-Partenkirchen.....a.	0623	0757	0901	0957	1157	1257	1357	1557	1657	1729	1757	1857	1929	1957	2203
	München Hbf **895** ....a.	...	0926z	1026e	1126	1326	1426	1525	1726z	1826	1847	1926	2026e	2047	2126	...

	h	c	a		a				a		d		r		Ⓑb	
München Hbf **895** .... d.	...	0532r	...	0632z	0732	0832	...	1032	1132	1232	...	1432z	1532	1632	1732	1832
Garmisch-Partenkirchen...... d.	0637	0704	0722	0804	0904	1004	...	1204	1304	1404	1504	1604	1657v	1804	1904k	2004
Ehrwald Zugspitzbahn 🏛 ..... d.	0702	0731	0752	0831	0931	1031	...	1231	1400j	1431	1531	1631	1731	1831	1931	2031
Lermoos .... d.	0706	0735	0756	0835	0935	1035	...	1235	1404	1435	1535	1635	1735	1835	1935	2035
Reutte in Tirol .... a.	0736	0800	0833	0900	1000	1100	...	1300	1431	1500	1600	1700	1800	1900	2000	2100

a – ①–⑤ (not Aug. 15, Oct. 26, Nov. 1, Dec. 8).
b – Not Aug. 14, Oct. 25, 31, Dec. 7.
c – ⑥⑦ (also Aug. 15, Oct. 26, Nov. 1, Dec. 8).
d – ⑥⑦ (also Aug. 15, Nov. 1).
e – ①–⑤ (not Aug. 15, Oct. 3, 26, Nov. 1, Dec. 8
h – ①–⑥ (not Aug. 15, Oct. 26, Nov. 1, Dec. 8).
j – Arrives 1329.
k – 1856 on ⑦ (also Aug. 15, Oct. 26, Nov. 1, Dec
r – Not Oct. 26, Dec. 8.
v – 1704 on ①–⑤ (not Aug. 15, Nov. 1).
z – ⑥⑦ (also Aug. 15, Oct. 3, Nov. 1).

German national public holidays are on Jan. 1, Mar. 25, 28, May 5, 16, Oct. 3, Dec. 25, 26

erische Oberlandbahn; DB

MÜNCHEN - SALZBURG 890

SERVICE UNTIL AUGUST 5. *Services from / to Frankfurt and Stuttgart are subject to alteration from July 30 (see Table **930**, also shaded panel on page 367).*

	◇ Ⓐ		◇ Ⓒ	◇ Ⓐ	RJ 265 ①–⑥ ✕	◇	RJ 61 B✕	◇	EC 111 ✕♦	◇	RJ 63 ⑥⑦ B✕	RJ 63 ①–⑤ B✕	◇	EC 217 🍷♦	◇	RJ 65 B✕	◇	EC 113 ✕♦	◇	RJ 67 B✕	◇	IC 2083 🍷♦	EC 115 🍷♦
Frankfurt (Main) Hbf **912** d.	...	...	...	...	...	...	...	...	...	...	0517	...	...	...	...	...	...	0822f	...	...	...	...	...
Stuttgart Hbf **930** d.	...	...	...	...	...	...	...	...	...	...	0658	...	...	0758f	...	...	...	0958f	...	...	...	...	1158c
München Hbf **951** d.	...	...	0549	0553	0620	0655	0715	0755	0818	0854	0924z	0924	0955	1018	1055	1124	1155	1218	1255	1324	1355	...	1418
München Ost **951** d.	...	...	0557	0601	0629	0704	|	0804	|	0904	|	|	1004	|	1104	|	1204	|	1304	|	1404	1412	|
Rosenheim **951** d.	0532	...	0634	0640	0658	0734	0754	0834	0853	0934	|	|	1034	1053	1134	|	1234	1253	1334	|	1434	1441	1453
Bad Endorf d.	0543	...	0645	0652	|	0745	|	0845	|	0945	|	|	1045	|	1145	|	1245	|	1345	|	1445	1454	|
Prien am Chiemsee d.	0549	...	0651	0658	|	0751	|	0851	0910	0951	|	|	1052	1110	1151	|	1251	1310	1351	|	1451	1502	1510
Traunstein d.	0613	...	0716	0722	|	0816	|	0916	0933	1016	|	|	1116	1133	1216	|	1316	1333	1416	|	1516	1525	1533
Freilassing **891** d.	0633	...	0734	0743	|	0834	|	0934	0951	1034	|	|	1134	1151	1234	|	1334	1351	1434	|	1534	1547	1551
Salzburg Hbf 🏨 **891** a.	0640	...	0741	0752	0758	0841	0902	0941	0959	1041	1102	1102	1141	1159	1241	1302	1341	1359	1441	1502	1541	...	1559
Wien Hbf **950** a.	...	...	...	...	1030	...	1130	...	...	...	1330	1330	...	...	...	1530	...	...	...	1730	...	...	...

	◇	RJ 69 ✕	◇ Ⓐ	◇	EC 219 🍷♦	◇ Ⓐ	◇	RJ 261 ✕	◇ Ⓐ	◇	EC 117 Ⓑ 🍷♦	EC 1217 ⑥ 🍷♦	◇	IC 1269 Ⓑ K🍷	◇	EC 391 L🍷	◇		◇		◇	EN 463 Ⓡ 🍷♦	EN 499 Ⓡ 🍷♦	◇
ankfurt (Main) Hbf **912** d.	...	...	...	...	1220c	...	...	...	...	...	1420c	...	...	...	...	1620c	...	...	...	...	...	...	...	...
ttgart Hbf **930** d.	...	...	...	...	1358c	...	...	...	...	...	1558c	1558	...	1653f	...	1758f	...	...	...	...	...	...	...	...
chen Hbf **951** d.	1455	1518	1529	1555	1617	1635	1655	1717	1730	1755	1818	1818	1855	1917	1955	2018	2044	...	2144	...	2244	2331j	2331j	2350
hen Ost **951** d.	1504	|	1537	1604	|	1643	1704	|	1738	1804	|	|	1904	|	2004	|	2052	...	2152	...	2252	2343j	2343j	2359
nheim **951** d.	1534	|	1611	1634	1652	1714	1734	|	1812	1834	1853	1853	1935	1954	2034	2054	2131	...	2231	...	2331	|	|	0035
Endorf d.	1545	|	1624	1645	|	1725	1745	|	1824	1845	|	|	1946	|	2046	2106	2142	...	2242	...	2342	|	|	0046
am Chiemsee d.	1551	|	1631	1651	1710	1732	1751	|	1830	1851	1910	1910	1952	2010	2052	2114	2148	...	2248	...	2348	|	|	0052
nstein d.	1616	|	...	1716	1733	...	1816	|	...	1916	1933	1933	2016	2033	2116	2136	2214	...	2316	...	0013	|	|	0116
assing **891** d.	1634	|	...	1734	1751	...	1834	|	...	1934	1951	1951	2034	2051	2134	2155	2233	...	2336	...	0032	|	|	0135
burg Hbf 🏨 **891** a.	1641	1702	...	1741	1759	...	1841	1902	...	1941	1959	1959	2041	2059	2141	2203	2240	...	2343	...	0039	0119	0119	0142
en Hbf **950** a.	...	1930	...	...	...	...	...	2130	...	...	...	...	...	...	...	...	...	...	...	...	...	0635	...	...

	◇ Ⓐ	EN 462 Ⓡ 🍷♦	EN 498 Ⓡ 🍷♦		◇ Ⓐ	◇	◇ Ⓐ	IC 1296 ①–⑥ 🍷	◇ Ⓐ	◇	IC 1268 ⊡ K🍷	IC 1216 ⑤ 🍷♦	◇ Ⓐ	◇ Ⓐ	◇ Ⓒ	EC 390 L🍷	◇	◇ Ⓐ	RJ 260 ✕	◇	IC 2082 🍷♦	EC 218 🍷♦	◇	RJ 262 ✕
en Hbf **950** d.	...	2325	...	...	...	...	...	...	...	...	...	...	...	...	...	...	...	...	0630	...	...	...	...	0830
burg Hbf 🏨 **891** d.	0356	0428	0428	...	...	0513	...	0545	...	0615	0643	0643	...	*0703*	0715	0800	0815	...	0856	0915	...	1000	1015	1056
assing **891** d.	0405	|	|	...	...	0522	...	0553	...	0624	0651	0651	...	*0723*	0723	0808	0824	...	|	0924	0941	1008	1024	|
nstein d.	0424	|	|	...	0513	0542	...	0610	...	0644	0708	0708	...	*0743*	0743	0826	0844	0903	|	0944	0959	1026	1044	|
am Chiemsee d.	0447	|	|	...	0538	0606	0622	0629	0650	0707	0731	0731	0744	*0806*	0806	0846	0908	0927	|	1008	1023	1049	1110	|
Endorf d.	0454	|	|	...	0544	0612	0629	0637	0656	0714	0739	0739	0751	*0813*	0813	|	0915	0933	|	1015	1033	|	1117	|
nheim **951** d.	0508	|	|	...	0559	0629	0644	0652	0712	0729	0753	0753	0806	*0829*	0829	0906	0929	0951	|	1029	1047	1107	1129	|
chen Ost **951** a.	0535	0558h	0558h	...	0627	0658	0711	|	0739	0756	|	|	0841	*0856*	0856	|	0956	1019	|	1056	1115	|	1156	|
chen Hbf **951** a.	0545	0611h	0611h	...	0640	0707	0721	0730	0749	0806	0829	0829	0850	*0906*	0906	0941	1006	1029	1034	1105	...	1141	1206	1234
ttgart Hbf **930** a.	...	...	...	...	...	...	...	1000c	...	...	1107f	1107	...	...	...	1200c	...	...	...	...	...	1400c	...	...
ankfurt (Main) Hbf **912** a.	...	...	...	...	...	...	...	1140c	...	...	...	...	...	...	...	1340c	...	...	...	...	...	1540c	...	...

	◇	EC 114 🍷♦	◇	RJ 60 B✕	◇	EC 112 ✕♦	◇	RJ 62 B✕	◇	EC 216 🍷♦	◇	RJ 64 B✕	◇		◇	RJ 66 N B✕	RJ 66 ⑤⑥ B✕	◇	EC 110 ✕♦	◇	RJ 68 B✕	◇		◇
en Hbf **950** d.	...	...	...	1030	...	...	...	1230	...	...	...	1430	...	...	...	1630	1630	...	...	...	1830	...	...	...
burg Hbf 🏨 **891** d.	1115	1200	1215	1256	1313	1400	1415	1456	1515	1600	1615	1656	1715	...	1815	1856	1856	1915	2000	2015	2056	2113	...	2300
assing **891** d.	1124	1208	1224	|	1324	1408	1424	|	1524	1608	1624	|	1724	...	1824	|	|	1925	2008	2026	|	2122	...	2310
nstein d.	1144	1226	1244	|	1344	1426	1444	|	1544	1625	1644	|	1744	...	1844	|	|	1944	2026	2046	|	2141	...	2329
am Chiemsee d.	1208	1249	1308	|	1408	1450	1508	|	1608	1648	1708	|	1808	...	1908	|	|	2011	2048	2111	|	2206	...	2353
Endorf d.	1215	|	1315	|	1415	|	1515	|	1615	|	1715	|	1815	...	1915	|	|	2018	|	2118	|	2213	...	2359
nheim **951** d.	1229	1306	1329	|	1429	1507	1529	|	1629	1707	1729	|	1829	...	1929	|	|	2032	2107	2132	2203	2232t	...	0012
chen Ost **951** a.	1256	|	1356	|	1456	|	1556	|	1656	|	1756	|	1856	...	1956	|	|	2105	|	2205	|	2305	...	0046
chen Hbf **951** a.	1306	1341	1406	1434	1506	1541	1606	1633	1706	1741	1806	1837	1906	...	2006	2026	2026x	2115	2143	2215	2241	2315	...	0057
ttgart Hbf **930** a.	...	1600c	...	...	...	1759	...	...	...	2000	...	...	...	...	...	...	2259	...	...	...	...	...	...	...
ankfurt (Main) Hbf **912** a.	...	...	...	...	...	1940	...	...	...	...	...	...	...	...	...	...	0042	...	...	...	...	...	...	...

NOTES (LISTED BY TRAIN NUMBER)

- – 12 and ✕ Klagenfurt - Villach - München and v.v.
- 3 – 12 and ✕ Klagenfurt - Villach - München - Frankfurt and v.v.; 12 Zagreb (**212/3**) - Ljubljana - Jesenice 🏨 - Villach - München - Frankfurt and v.v.
- – WÖRTHERSEE – 12 and 🍷 Klagenfurt - München - Mannheim - Dortmund.
- – WÖRTHERSEE – 12 and 🍷 Münster - Köln - Mannheim - München - Klagenfurt.
- – Ⓑ (also July 30). 12 and 🍷 Frankfurt - Salzburg - Villach - Klagenfurt.
- 7 – 12 and 🍷 Graz - Bischofshofen - Salzburg - Mannheim - Saarbrücken and v.v.
- 9 – 12 and 🍷 Graz - Bischofshofen - Salzburg - Frankfurt and v.v.
- 3 – KÁLMÁN IMRE – 🛏 1, 2 cl., 🛏 2 cl., 2 and 🍷 Budapest - München and v.v.
- 9 – LISINSKI – 🛏 1, 2 cl., 🛏 2 cl. and 2 Zagreb - Ljubljana - Jesenice 🏨 - Villach - München and v.v.
- – ⑤ (not Aug. 5). 12 and 🍷 Salzburg - Mannheim - Mainz - Köln - Dortmund - Berlin.
- – ⑥ (not July 30). 12 and 🍷 Karlsruhe - Salzburg - Villach - Klagenfurt.
- 2/3 – KÖNIGSSEE – 12 and 🍷 Berchtesgaden - Augsburg - Hamburg and v.v.

- **B** – To / from Budapest (Table **1250**).
- **K** – To / from Karlsruhe (Table **931**).
- **L** – From / to Linz on dates in Table **950**.
- **N** – ①②③④⑦.
- **c** – Until July 29.
- **f** – Subject to alteration from July 30.
- **h** – On the mornings of ⑦ June 5 - July 17 arrives München Ost 0709, Hbf 0721.
- **j** – 17 minutes earlier on ⑥⑦ June 4 - July 17.
- **t** – Arrives 2225.
- **x** – Not July 29, 30 (calls at München Ost, a. 2018).
- **z** – Not July 30, 31 (calls at München Ost, d. 0930).
- ⊡ – ①②③④⑥ (also Aug. 5).
- ◇ – *Meridian* regional service (operated by Bayerische Oberlandbahn). German holiday dates apply.

chtesgadener Land Bahn *

SALZBURG - FREILASSING - BERCHTESGADEN 891

WARNING! Subject to alteration September 12 - November 9

	Ⓐ t	‡	Ⓐ t	Ⓒ z					⊡					A										
Salzburg Hbf **890** d.	0451	*0615*	*0703*	*0715*	*0815*	0842	*0915*	0942	and at	1342	*1415*	*1442*	1525	*1542*	*1615*	1642	*1715*	1742	*1815*	*1842*	*1915*	*2042*	*2142*	2229
Freilassing **890** a.	0503	*0622*	*0712*	*0722*	*0822*	0854	*0922*	0954	the same	1354	*1422*	*1454*	1537	*1554*	*1622*	1654	*1722*	1754	*1822*	*1854*	*1922*	*2054*	*2154*	2241
Freilassing d.	0505	0634	0718	0739	0839	0858	0942	1004	minutes	1404	1442	1504	1542	1604	1642	1704	1742	1804	1842	1904	1942	2059	2200	2246
Bad Reichenhall d.	0522	0655	0741	0759	0902	0920	1002	1022	past each	1422	1502	1522	1558	1624	1702	1722	1802	1822	1902	1922	2002	2121	2217	2305
Berchtesgaden Hbf a.	...	0726	0810	0827	0930	...	1030	...	hour until	...	1530	...	...	1655	1730	...	1830	...	1930	...	2030	2149	2245	2333

	Ⓐ t	① g	Ⓐ t		Ⓒ z		Ⓐ t	①–⑥ r		A			♥						‡						
htesgaden Hbf d.	...	0531	...	0621	...	0706	...		...	0828	...	0931	and at	...	1531	...	1618	...	1731	...	1831	...	1931	2031	2208
Reichenhall d.	0528	0601	0601	0654	...	0740	0801	...	0834	0901	0937	1001	the same	1537	1601	1637	1701	1737	1801	1837	1901	1937	2001	2101	2242
assing a.	0545	0618	0618	0711	...	0757	0820	...	0856	0918	1000	1020	minutes	1600	1621	1659	1720	1800	1821	1859	1920	2001	2017	2117	2304
assing **890** d.	0547	0620	0620	*0717*r	0734	*0807*	...	0826	*0907*	*0934*	1007	*1034*	past each	1607	*1634*	1707	*1734*	1807	*1834*	*1907*	*1934*	2007	*2023*	*2134*	*2307*
burg Hbf **890** a.	0558	0631	0631	*0728*r	0741	*0819*	...	0837	*0919*	*0941*	1019	*1041*	hour until	1619	*1641*	1719	*1741*	1819	*1841*	*1919*	*1941*	2019	*2037*	*2141*	*2319*

IC **2082/3**: KÖNIGSSEE – 12 and 🍷 Berchtesgaden - München Ost - Hamburg and v.v. Train category *RE* Berchtesgaden - Freilassing and v.v. Operated by DB.

Also Aug. 16; not Aug. 15.
①–⑥ (not Aug. 15, Oct. 26, Nov. 1, Dec. 8).
Not Aug. 15
Also Aug. 15.

- ⊡ – The 1042 and 1242 from Salzburg require a change of trains at Freilassing. Connection departs Salzburg *1313* (not *1315*).
- ♥ – The 1037, 1237 and 1437 from Bad Reichenhall require a change of trains at Freilassing.
- * – Services to / from Bad Reichenhall or Berchtesgaden are operated by Berchtesgadener Land Bahn GmbH (Salzburg AG / Arriva). 2nd class only. Other trains are operated by either DB or ÖBB. German holiday dates apply.
- ‡ – Operated by DB. Conveys 🍷.

892 FLUGHAFEN MÜNCHEN ✈ (S-Bahn services S1, S8) 2nd class

km		S8	S8	S8	S8		S8	S1	S8	S1	S8	S1	S8		S1	S8	S1	S8	S1	S8
0	**München** Pasing .... d.	0005	0045	0125	0305	and every	0445	...	0505	...	0525	...	0545	and at the	...	2245	...	2305	...	2325
7	**München** Hbf (low level) .... d.	0015	0055	0135	0315	20 minutes	0455	0503	0515	0523	0535	0543	0555	same minutes	2243	2255	2303	2315	2323	2335
11	**München** Ost .... d.	0024	0104	0144	0324	until	0504	|	0524	|	0544	|	0604	past each	|	2304	|	2324	|	2344
44	**München Flughafen** Terminal ✈ .a.	0055	0135	0215	0355		0535	0546	0555	0606	0615	0626	0635	hour until	2326	2335	2346	2355	0006	0015

km *		S8	S8	S8	S8		S8	S1	S8	S1	S8	S1	S8		S1	S8	S1	S8	S1	S8
0	**München Flughafen** Terminal ✈ .d.	0004	0044	0124	0404	and every	0544	0551	0604	0611	0624	0631	0644	and at the	2251	2304	2311	2324	2331	2344
	München Ost .... a.	0035	0115	0155	0435	20 minutes	0615	|	0635	|	0655	|	0715	same minutes	|	2335	|	2355	|	0015
41	**München** Hbf (low level) .... a.	0045	0125	0205	0445	until	0625	0637	0645	0657	0705	0717	0725	past each	2337	2345	2357	0005	0017	*0027*
	München Pasing .... a.	0055	0135	0215	0455		0635	...	0655	...	0715	...	0735	hour until	...	2355	...	0015	...	*0037*

* – Via Neufahrn (b Freising).

☛ Many **S1** trains from München Hbf are combined with a Freising service - travel in the rear portion for the Airport.

893 MÜNCHEN - MÜHLDORF - SIMBACH

km				⚒e			⊡						Ⓐe	Ⓒz	Ⓐe	Ⓒz	Ⓐe	Ⓐe		Ⓐe		Ⓐe		⊙	⊡
0	**München** Hbf .... d.	...	0606	0706	0807z	0907	1007	1107	1207	1307	1407	1506	1522	1607	1626	1707	1707	1725	1806	1830	1907	1948	2027	2129	2228
10	**München** Ost .... d.	...	0616	0716	0816	0917	1017	1117	1217	1317	1417	1515	1532	1617	1638	1717	1718	1739	1817	1840	1917	1957	2038	2139	2238
85	**Mühldorf** (Oberbay) .. a.	...	0722	0818	0919	1016	1116	1216	1316	1417	1517	1619	1630	1717	1731	1816	1820	1829	1919	1931	2021	2100	2140	2236	2336
			|	◇	¶	¶	|	¶	¶	¶	¶	¶	|		◇	¶		|		◇	¶		¶	|	|
		⚒e										Ⓒz				Ⓒz									
85	**Mühldorf** (Oberbay) .. d.	0637	0737	0830	0937	1037	1137	1227	1337	1437	1538	1637	1634	...	1737	1836	...	1833	...	1937	2037	...	2146	2247	2343
124	**Simbach** (Inn) .... **962** a.	0713	0813	0858	1013	1113	1213	1258	1413	1513	1614	1713	1709	...	1813	1914	...	1907	...	2013	2113	...	2217	2318	0015

			Ⓐe	Ⓒz	Ⓐe	Ⓐe	Ⓒz					⊡							Ⓐe	Ⓒz		Ⓐe	Ⓒz		
Simbach (Inn) ...... **962** d.	...	...	0507	0543k	0554	0648	0648	...	0749	0900	0949	1049	1149	1259	1349	1449	1550	...	1639	1649	1749	1839	1849	1949	2049
Mühldorf (Oberbay) ... a.	...	...	0540	0614k	0628	0722	0722	...	0822	0932	1021	1123	1220	1332	1421	1525	1622	...	1718	1722	1822	1917	1922	2022	2122
			¶	|	|	|	¶		¶	¶	¶	|	¶	¶	¶	¶	¶			◇	¶		¶	¶	|
	⚒e	⚒e	Ⓐe				Ⓒz	Ⓐe									Ⓒz	Ⓐe					Ⓒz		
Mühldorf (Oberbay) ... d.	0429	0522	0546	0623	0637	0732	0731	0739	0830	0937	1030	1138	1228	1340	1429	1538	1630	1633	...	1737	1842	...	1940	2032r	2146
München Ost .... a.	0523	0625	0640	0724	0722	0822	0826	0844	0926	1045	1127	1246	1327	1443	1525	1645	1725	1745	...	1845	1945	...	2043	2142	2247
München Hbf .... a.	0533	0636	0652	0736	0734	0833	0837	0855	0935	1055	1137	1256	1337	1454	1536	1655	1736	1754	...	1856	1955	...	2055	2154	2257

e – Not Aug. 15, Nov. 1.
k – ⑥ only.
r – 2034 on Ⓒ (also Aug. 15, Nov. 1).
z – Ⓒ (also Aug. 15, Nov. 1).
⊡ – Change trains at Mühldorf on Ⓒ (also Aug. 15, Nov. 1).
⊙ – Change trains at Mühldorf on † (also Aug. 15, Nov. 1).
◇ – Change trains. Daily from Mühld
¶ – Change trains.

895 MÜNCHEN - GARMISCH - INNSBRUCK

DB; ÖBB (2nd class only in Aus

km		Ⓐe		◧ Ⓒz	◧	◧	◧		◧	◧	*ICE* 1127 ⑥D	◧	*ICE* 1153 ⑥L		◧	*ICE* 1207 Q K	◧	◧	◧	◧					
0	**München** Hbf .... d.	0453	...	0532	0632	0732	0832	0932	1032	1132	1211	1232	1308	1332	1432	1455	1532	1632	1732	1832	1932	2032	2132	2232	2332
7	München Pasing .... d.	0500	...	0539	0639	0739	0839	0939	1039	1139	|	1239	|	1339	1439	|	1539	1639	1739	1839	1939	2039	2139	2240	2339
40	Tutzing .... d.	0528	...	0601	0701	0801	0901	1001	1101	1201	1242	1301	1353	1401	1501	1522	1601	1700	1801	1901	2001	2101	2201	2301	0001
54	Weilheim (Oberbay) ... d.	0545	...	0612	0712	0812	0912	1011	1112	1212	|	1312	|	1412	1512	|	1612	1712	1812	1912	2012	2112	2212	2312	0012
75	Murnau .... d.	0605	...	0628	0728	0828	0928	1028	1128	1228	1310	1328	1422	1428f	1528	1558	1628	1728	1828	1928	2028	2128	2228	2328	0028
101	**Garmisch**-Partenk. ... a.	0630	...	0654	0754	0854	0954	1054	1155	1254	1337	1354	1451	1454f	1554	1622	1655	1755	1854	1954	2054	2154	2254	2354	0054
101	**Garmisch**-Partenk. ... d.	0632	0632	...	*0802*	0906	1002	1102	*1202*	1302	...	1402	...	1502	*1602*	1625	1702	1802	1902	*2002*	2102	2202	2302	0002	...
118	**Mittenwald** .... a.	0653	0653	...	*0823*	0927	1023	1123	*1223*	1323	...	1423	...	1523	*1623*	1653	1723	1823	1923	*2023*	2123	2223	2323	0023	...
118	**Mittenwald** 🛃 .... d.	0655	0655	...	*0826*	0936	1026	1136c	*1226*	1336c	...	1426	...	1536	*1626*	...	1736c	1826	1936	*2026*	...	...	...	...	...
125	Scharnitz 🛃 .... ⊡ d.	0703	0703	...	*0834*	0944	1034	1144c	*1234*	1344c	...	1434	...	1544	*1634*	...	1744c	1834	1944	*2034*	...	...	...	...	...
135	Seefeld in Tirol ...... ⊡ d.	0716	0716	...	*0846*	0956	1046	1156c	*1246*	1356c	...	1446	...	1556	*1646*	...	1756c	1846	1956	*2046*	...	...	...	...	...
160	**Innsbruck** Hbf ...... ⊡ a.	0753	0753	...	*0923*	1053t	1123	...	*1323*	...	...	1523	...	1653t	*1723*	...	...	1923	2053t	*2123*	...	...	...	...	...

	⚒e	Ⓐe	Ⓒz	Ⓐe	Ⓒz	◧	*ICE* 1138 ⑥P	Ⓒz	◧ Ⓐe	◧		*ICE* 1206 R K	◧	◧	◧	*ICE* 620 ⑥D	⊕	◧	*ICE* 732 ⑥B	◧	◧	◧ ⊕	◧		
Innsbruck Hbf ...... ⊡ d.	...	...	...	...	...	*0638*	...	...	...	0838	*0908*t	...	*1038*	...	1238	...	...	*1438*	...	*1508*t	1638	...	*1838*	*1908*t	2038
Seefeld in Tirol ...... ⊡ d.	...	...	...	...	...	*0715*	...	...	...	0915	1004	...	*1115*	1204c	1315	...	1404c	*1515*	...	1604	1715	1804c	*1915*	2004	2115
Scharnitz 🛃 .... ⊡ d.	...	...	...	...	...	*0728*	...	...	...	0928	1016	...	*1128*	1216c	1328	...	1416c	*1528*	...	1616	1728	1816c	*1928*	2016	2128
Mittenwald 🛃 .... a.	...	...	...	...	...	*0735*	...	...	...	0935	1024	...	*1135*	1224c	1335	...	1424c	*1535*	...	1624	1735	1824c	*1935*	2024	2135
Mittenwald .... d.	...	0530	0536	0634	0634	*0736*	...	0836	0836	0936	1036	1054	*1136*	1236	1336	...	1436	*1536*	...	1636	1736	1836	*1936*	2036	2136
Garmisch-Partenk. ..... a.	...	0551	0557	0700	0700	*0757*	...	0857	0900	1000	1057	1119	*1157*	1300	1400	...	1500	*1557*	...	1700	1800	1900	*1957*	2057	2157
Garmisch-Partenk. ..... d.	0500	0559	0607	0702	0707	0807	0837	0905	0907	1007	1107	1121	1207	1307	1407	1413	1507	1607	1624	1705	1805	1905v	2005	2107	2207
Murnau .... d.	0524	0626	0632	0728	0732	0832	0904	0932	0932	1032	1132	1151	1232	1332	1432	1447	1532	1632	1652	1732	1832	1932	2031	2132	2232
Weilheim (Oberbay) .... d.	0541	0646	0649	0746	0749	0849	|	0949	0949	1049	1149	|	1249	1349	1449	|	1549	1649	|	1750	1850	1950	2049	2149	2249
Tutzing .... d.	0555	0700	0700	0800	0800	0900	|	1000	1000	1100	1200	|	1300	1400	1500	1516	1600	1700	1721	1800	1900	2000	2100	2200	2300
München Pasing .... a.	0614	0719	0719	0819	0819	0919	|	1019	1019	1119	1219	1248	1319	1419	1519	|	1619	1719	|	1819	1919	2019	2119	2219	2319
München Hbf .... a.	0621	0726	0726	0826	0826	0926	1035	1026	1026	1126	1226	1257	1326	1426	1525	1544	1626	1726	1756	1826	1926	2026	2126	2226	2326

MÜNCHEN - TUTZING - KOCHEL

km		Ⓐe	⚒e	Ⓐe						Ⓒz	Ⓐe				Ⓐe	Ⓒz	Ⓐe	Ⓒz	Ⓐe	Ⓒz	Ⓐe	Ⓒz		◇		
0	**München** Hbf . d.	0532	0559	0632	0659	0759	0900	0959	1132	1159	*1232*	1259	1359	1459	1556	1559	1656	1659	1756	1759	1856	1859	1959	2032	*2132*	*2232*
7	München Pasing d.	0539	0605	0639	0705	0805	0906	1005	1139	1205	*1239*	1305	1405	1506	1604	1605	1704	1705	1804	1805	1904	1905	2005	2039	*2139*	*2240*
40	Tutzing .... d.	0601	0628	0703	0731	0828y	0933	1033	1203	1233	1310	1333	1433	1533	1630	1633	1731	1733	1830	1833	1930	1933	2031v	2103	2203	2303
75	**Kochel** .... a.	0637	0707	0738	0808	0908	1008	1108	1239	1308	1346	1412	1508	1608	1708	1708	1808	1808	1908	1908	2008	2008	2108	2138	2238	2338

	Ⓐe		⚒e	Ⓐe	Ⓐe	Ⓒz	Ⓐe	Ⓒz	Ⓐe					Ⓒz	Ⓐe	Ⓒz	Ⓐe			Ⓐe						
Kochel .... d.	0435	0510	0545	0615	0645	0645	0715	0745	0745	0845	0945	1045	1145	1245	1259	1345	1352	1445	1545	1615	1645	1745	1845	1945	2116	2216
Tutzing .... a.	0510	0547	0625	0652	0724	0724	0754	0825	0827	0924	1024	1124	1225	1324	1334	1424	1425	1524	1625	1653	1725	1825	1925	2025	2153	2253
München Pasing a.	*0535*	0614	0657	0719	0753	0800	0819	0902	0902	0952	1052	1152	1252	1352	1401	1452	1452	1552	1652	*1719*	1752	1852	1952	2052	*2219*	*2319*
München Hbf ... a.	*0544*	0621	0705	0726	0800	0808	0826	0909	0909	1000	1100	1200	1300	1400	1409	1500	1500	1600	1700	*1726*	1800	1900	2000	2100	*2226*	*2326*

B – ⑥ to Nov. 5. ZUGSPITZE – [12] and ✕ Garmisch - Nürnberg - Bremen.
D – [12] and 🍸 Dortmund - Frankfurt - Nürnberg - Garmisch and v.v.
K – [12] and ✕ Berlin - Nürnberg - München - Innsbruck and v.v.
L – ⑥ to Nov. 5. [12] and ✕ Hamburg - Nürnberg - Garmisch. Train number **583** and runs 18–29 minutes **earlier** from Sept. 10.
P – ⑥ to Nov. 5 (also Oct. 2; not Oct. 1). [12] and ✕ Garmisch - Hannover - Bremen. Train number **538** and runs 19–39 minutes later from Sept. 10.

Q – ⑥ Sept. 10 - Oct. 29 (also Oct. 2).
R – Ⓒ Sept. 10 - Oct. 30.
c – ⑥⑦ (also Aug. 15, Oct. 26, Nov. 1, Dec. 8).
e – Not Aug. 15, Nov. 1.
f – 4–5 minutes later on ⑥ to Sept. 3.
t – ①–⑤ (not Aug. 15, Oct. 26, Nov. 1, Dec. 8).
v – 2 minutes later on Ⓒ (also Aug. 15, Nov. 1).
y – 0833 on Ⓒ (also Aug. 15, Nov. 1).
z – Also Aug. 15, Nov. 1.

◇ – Change trains at Tutzing on Ⓐ (not Aug. 15, Nov.
⊕ – Change trains at Mittenwald on Oct. 26, Dec. 8.
◧ – Conveys [12] München - Garmisch - Reutte in Tir and v.v. on dates in Table **888**.
⊡ – Other journeys Scharnitz - Seefeld - Innsbruck and **From Scharnitz** at 0003, 0633, 0733 ⚒, 0803 ⚒, 0 1303, 1403 Ⓐ, 1503, 1703, 1803 Ⓐ, 1903 and 213 **From Innsbruck** Hbf at 0708 ⚒, 0808, 1208, 1308 1408, 1608, 1708 Ⓐ, 1808, 2008 and 2308.

A rack railway operates between Garmisch-Partenkirchen and the Zugspitz mountain: departures at 0815 and hourly to 1415, returning from Bf Zugspitzplatt at 0930 and hourly to 1630. All trains call at Eibsee (30 minutes from Garmisch, 45 minutes from Zugspitzplatt). Service may be suspended in bad weather conditions – please check locally before travelling. Cable cars between Eibsee and Zugspitzgipfel (Eibsee-Seilbahn) and between Zugspitzplatt and Zugspitzgipfel summit (Gletscherbahn). **Operator**: Bayerische Zugspitzbahn AG ✆ + 49 (0) 88 217

897 MURNAU - OBERAMMERGAU

RB servi

km		Ⓐe	⑥	Ⓐe													
0	**Murnau** .... d.	0512	0553	0600	0648	0742	0842	0942	1042	1142	1234	1334	1442	and	2242	...	2334
12	Bad Kohlgrub .... d.	0530	0611	0619	0706	0801	0901	1001	1101	1201	1253	1353	1501	hourly	2301	...	2353
24	**Oberammergau** .... ♥ a.	0550	0631	0638	0726	0821	0921	1021	1121	1221	1312	1412	1521	until	2321	...	0012

	Ⓐe	⑥	Ⓐe													
Oberammergau .... ♥ d.	0507	0548	0556	0643	0738	0838	0938	1038	1138	1229	1329	1438	and	2238	...	2329
Bad Kohlgrub .... d.	0529	0610	0618	0705	0800	0900	1000	1100	1200	1252	1352	1500	hourly	2300	...	2352
Murnau .... a.	0547	0628	0636	0723	0819	0919	1019	1119	1219	1310	1410	1519	until	2319	...	0010

e – Not Aug. 15, Nov. 1.

♥ – All trains call at Unterammergau (km 4–6 minutes from Oberammergau.

 German national public holidays are on Jan. 1, Mar. 25, 28, May 5, 16, Oct. 3, Dec. 25, 26

NÜRNBERG and FRANKFURT - HAMBURG 900

km	SEE NOTE ✣	ICE 990	IC 2178	IC 2184	EN 490	IC 2176	CNL 478	IC 60478	CNL 40418	IC 61418	ICE 988	ICE 1188	IC 2182	ICE 672	ICE 888	ICE 774	ICE 1684	ICE 784	ICE 634	IC 2378	IC 2378	ICE 674	ICE 886
		① g	Ⓐ	Ⓐ		Ⓐ	🅁 ⊗	⊗	🅁 ⊗	⊗	⑥ ‡	Ⓐ n	⚒		Ⓐ	⚒	⊖	1184	⚒ n	⚒ n	n q		
				🍷♦	♦	🍷	A 🍷	A 2	E 🍷	E 2	✕	K ✕	T 🍷	Q ✕	✕	✕	✕	◇ ✕	✕	🍷	🍷	K ✕	✕
	Basel SBB 912 d.	...	...	...	...	...	2313	2313	...	...	...	...	...	...	...	...	...	...	...	...	...	0511b	...
	Karlsruhe Hbf 912 ⊠ d.	...	...	...	...	...	0129	0129	...	...	...	...	...	...	...	...	...	...	...	...	...	0651	...
	Stuttgart Hbf 912 ⊠ d.	2305p	...	...	...	...	|	|	...	...	...	...	...	...	...	0502	...	...	...	...	...	|	...
	Mannheim Hbf 912 ⊠ d.	2351p	...	...	...	...	|	0215	...	...	...	...	...	...	...	0605	...	...	...	...	...	0716	...
	Frankfurt Flughafen Fernbf ✈ *912* d.	0031	...	...	...	...	|	|	...	...	...	...	...	0539	...	0642r	...	...	...	...	...	|	...
	Frankfurt (Main) Hbf ... **850 901 902** d.	0055	...	...	...	...	|	0349	...	...	0506	0506	...	0555	...	0658	...	...	...	0649	...	0758y	...
	Hanau Hbf **850 901 902** d.	0113	...	...	...	...	|	|	...	...	0522	0522	...	0611	...	|	...	...	...	|	...	|	...
	München Hbf 904 905 d.	|	...	...	...	...	|	|	2250	2250	|	|	...	|	0415	|	0515	0520t	0520a	|	...	|	0617
	Augsburg Hbf 905 d.	|	...	...	...	...	|	|	2320	2320	|	|	...	|	|	|	|	|	|	◧	...	|	|
0	**Nürnberg** Hbf **920 921** d.	|	...	...	0130	...	|	|	|	|	|	|	...	|	0532	|	0630	0634	0634	|	...	|	0734
2	**Würzburg** Hbf **920 921** d.	|	...	...	0226	...	|	|	|	|	|	|	...	|	0630	|	0725	0729	0729	|	...	|	0830
5	Fulda **850 901 902** d.	0158	...	...	|	...	|	|	|	|	0604	0604	...	0653n	0707	|	0805	0803	0803	|	...	|	0904
5	**Kassel** Wilhelmshöhe **901 902** d.	|	...	...	|	...	0552s	0554	0552s	0554	0636	0636	0623a	0724	0739	0821	...	0836	0836	0854	...	0921	0936
0	Göttingen **902 903** d.	0325	...	...	0509	0545	0615s	0617	0615s	0617	0656	0656	0645a	0744	0759	0840n	...	0856	0856	0917	...	0940n	0956
0	**Hannover** Hbf **903** a.	0421	...	...	0613	0655	0658s	0658	0658s	0658	0732	0732	0756a	0817	0833	0917	...	0932	0932	0956	...	1017	1032
0	**Hannover** Hbf **903** d.	0424	0511	0555	0616	0700	|	0706	|	0706	0736	0736	0759	0820	0836	0920	...	0936	0945	1000	1000	1020	1036
	Bremen Hbf 813 a.	|	|	|	|	|	|	|	|	|	|	|	|	|	|	|	...	|	1044	|	|	|	|
1	Celle **903** d.	|	0532	0619	|	0720	|	|	|	|	|	|	0819n	|	|	|	...	|	...	1020	1020	|	|
3	Uelzen **903** d.	|	0556	0642	|	0742	|	|	|	|	|	|	0842n	|	|	|	...	|	...	1042	1042	|	|
9	Lüneburg **903** d.	0515	0613	0658	|	0758	0800s	0802	0800s	0802	|	|	0902n	|	|	|	...	|	...	1058	1058	|	1128
8	**Hamburg** Hbf **903** a.	0550	0643	0728	0751	0828	0836	0836	0836	0836	0856	0856	0933	0935	0953	1035	...	1055	...	1128	1128	1135	1156
5	**Hamburg** Altona a.	...	0659	...	0806	0845	0853	0853	0853	0853	0913	...	...	0950	1008	1050	...	...	...	1144	1144	...	1212

SEE NOTE ✣	ICE 772	ICE 1682	ICE 1162	ICE 1132	IC 2376	IC 2086	ICE 78	ICE 882	ICE 770	ICE 1208	ICE 680	ICE 630	IC 2374	ICE 76	ICE 880	IC 1972	ICE 1224	ICE 578	ICE 1588	ICE 1158	ICE 1138	IC 2372	IC 2088
		⊖		n	n	V	♥			⊖		n	D			⑤	1228		⊖		d G	§	Y
	✕	✕	❦✕	❦✕	🍷♦	T 🍷	Z ✕	✕	✕	✕	✕	✕	🍷	✕♦	✕		H 🍷	✕	✕	❦✕	❦✕	T 🍷	T 🍷
asel SBB 912 d.	...	...	...	...	...	...	0706	...	...	...	...	...	...	0906	...	...	...	...	...	...	...	...	...
arlsruhe Hbf 912 ⊠ d.	...	...	...	...	0702	...	0851	...	...	...	...	...	0905	1051	...	...	...	...	...	...	...	1110c	...
Stuttgart Hbf 912 ⊠ d.	0726	...	...	...	|	...	|	...	0925x	...	...	...	|	|	...	...	...	1125	...	...	...	|	...
annheim Hbf 912 ⊠ d.	0806	...	...	...	|	...	0916	...	1006	...	...	...	|	1116	...	...	...	1206	...	...	...	|	...
rankfurt Flughafen Fernbf ✈ *912* d.	0842r	...	...	...	|	...	|	...	1042r	...	...	...	|	|	...	...	...	1242r	...	...	...	|	...
nkfurt (Main) Hbf ... **850 901 902** d.	0858r	...	...	...	0852	...	0958y	...	1058	...	...	...	1052	1158y	...	1217	...	1258	...	...	...	1252	...
au Hbf **850 901 902** d.	|	...	...	...	|	...	|	...	|	...	...	...	|	|	...	1238	...	|	...	...	...	|	...
ünchen Hbf 904 905 d.	|	0720	0653	0653	|	...	|	0822	|	0920	0905	0905	|	|	1022	|	1055	|	1120	1048	1048	|	...
Augsburg Hbf 905 d.	|	|	0732	0732	◧	...	|	|	|	|	0938	0938	◧	|	|	|	|	|	|	1119	1119	◧	...
ürnberg Hbf **920 921** d.	|	0833	|	|	|	...	|	0933	|	1033	|	|	|	|	1133	|	1200	|	1233	|	|	|	...
ürzburg Hbf **920 921** d.	|	0925	0929	0929	|	...	|	1030	|	1125	1129	1129	|	|	1230	|	1301j	|	1325	1329	1329	|	...
da **850 901 902** d.	|	1005	1003	1003	|	...	|	1104	|	1205	1203	1203	|	|	1304	1320	1332	|	1405	1403	1403	|	...
ssel Wilhelmshöhe **901 902** d.	1021	...	1036	1036	1055	...	1121	1136	1221	...	1236	1236	1256	1320	1336	1359	1400	1421	...	1436	1436	1454	...
tingen **902 903** d.	1040n	...	1056	1056	1117	...	1140n	1156	1240n	...	1256	1256	1318	1340n	1356	1420	...	1440n	...	1456	1456	1517	...
nnover Hbf **903** a.	1117	...	1132	1132	1156	...	1217	1232	1317	...	1332	1332	1356	1417	1432	1459	...	1517	...	1532	1532	1556	...
nnover Hbf **903** d.	1120	...	1136	1145	1159	1217	1220	1236	1320	...	1336	1345	1359	1420	1436	1502	...	1520	...	1536	1545	1559	1620
remen Hbf 813 a.	|	...	|	1244	|	|	|	|	|	...	|	1444	|	|	|	|	...	|	...	|	1644	|	|
le **903** d.	|	...	|	...	1219	|	|	|	|	...	|	...	1419n	|	|	1522n	...	|	...	|	...	1619n	|
zen **903** d.	|	...	|	...	1242	|	|	|	|	...	|	...	1442n	|	|	1544n	...	|	...	|	...	1642n	|
eburg **903** d.	|	...	|	...	1259	|	|	|	|	...	|	...	1501n	|	|	1600n	...	|	...	|	...	1703n	|
nburg Hbf **903** a.	1235	...	1253	...	1328	1337	1335	1354	1435	...	1454	...	1529	1535	1554	1628	...	1635	...	1653	...	1732	1737
nburg Altona a.	1250	...	1306	...	...	...	1350n	1410	1450	...	1508	...	...	...	1609	1646	...	1650	...	1709	...	...	...

SEE NOTE ✣	ICE 74	ICE 788	IC 2082	ICE 576	ICE 1586	ICE 1156	ICE 536	IC 2370	ICE 72	ICE 1166	IC 1284	ICE 1094	ICE 574	ICE 1584	ICE 1154	ICE 1134	ICE 776	IC 2276	IC 2276	IC 2386	ICE 70	ICE 1522	ICE 90
					⊖		n				⑦ w	Ⓑ q	⑥ k	⊖	Ⓑ q	⑥ h	Ⓑ q	n	⑤–⑦	①–④			
	✕♦	✕	🍷♦	✕	✕	❦✕	❦✕	🍷♦	✕♦	❦✕	F	K ✕	✕	✕	n ❦ L ✕	❦✕	N ✕	🍷	c n 🍷	m	✕♦	⊡ ✕	✕♦
asel SBB 912 d.	1106	...	...	...	...	...	...	...	1306	...	...	...	...	...		...	...	...		...	1506	...	...
arlsruhe Hbf 912 ⊠ d.	1251	...	...	...	...	...	...	1310	1451	...	...	...	...	...	...	...	...	1510	1510	...	1651	...	...
Stuttgart Hbf 912 ⊠ d.	|	...	...	1325	...	...	...	|	|	...	...	1525	1525	...	...	...	...	|	|	...	|	...	...
annheim Hbf 912 ⊠ d.	1316	...	...	1406	...	...	...	|	1516	...	...	1606	1606	...	...	...	...	|	|	...	1716	...	...
rankfurt Flughafen Fernbf ✈ *912* d.	|	...	...	1442r	...	...	...	|	|	...	...	1642r	1642r	...	...	...	...	|	|	...	|	...	...
nkfurt (Main) Hbf ... **850 901 902** d.	1358y	...	...	1458	...	...	...	1450	1558y	...	...	1658	1658	...	...	...	1716	1650	1650	...	1758y	...	...
au Hbf **850 901 902** d.	|	...	...	|	...	...	...	|	|	...	...	|	|	...	...	...	|	|	|	...	|	...	...
ünchen Hbf 904 905 d.	|	1222	1117o	|	1320	1254	1254	|	|	1422	1355	|	|	1518	1449	1449	|	|	|	...	|	1618	...
Augsburg Hbf 905 d.	|	|	1230	|	|	|	|	◧	|	|	1425	|	|	|	1518	1518	|	◧	◧	...	|	|	...
ürnberg Hbf **920 921** d.	|	1333	|	|	1433	|	|	|	|	1534	|	|	|	1633	|	|	|	|	|	...	|	1733	1729
ürzburg Hbf **920 921** d.	|	1430	1439	|	1525	1529	1529	|	|	1630	1638	|	|	1725	1729	1729	|	|	|	...	|	1825	1832j
da **850 901 902** d.	|	1504	1518	|	1605	1603	1603	|	|	1704	1717	|	|	1805	1803	1803	1818	|	|	...	|	...	1907
ssel Wilhelmshöhe **901 902** d.	1521	1536	1554	1621	...	1636	1636	1654	1721	1736	1758	|	1821	...	1836	1836	1851	1857	1857	...	1921	...	1940
tingen **902 903** d.	1540n	1556	1615	1640n	...	1656	1656	1717	1740n	1756	1820	|	1841n	...	1856	1856	1912	1918	1918	...	1943n	...	|
nnover Hbf **903** a.	1617	1632	1654	1717	...	1732	1732	1756	1817	1832	1859	1906	1917	...	1932	1932	1947	1956	1956	...	2017	...	2032
nnover Hbf **903** d.	1620	1636	1657	1720	...	1736	1745	1759	1820	1836	1905	1909	1920	...	1936	1936	1950	...	1959	2000	2020	...	2036
remen Hbf 813 a.	|	|	|	|	...	|	1844	|	|	|	|	|	|	...	|	|	2047	...	|	|	|	...	|
le **903** d.	|	|	1718n	|	...	|	...	1819n	|	|	1931	|	|	...	|	|	...	...	2019	2020n	|	...	|
zen **903** d.	|	|	1742n	|	...	|	...	1842n	|	|	1955	|	|	...	|	|	...	...	2042	2042n	|	...	|
eburg **903** d.	|	|	1758n	|	...	|	...	1858n	|	|	2011	|	2012	...	2028	2028	...	...	2058	2058n	|	...	|
nburg Hbf **903** a.	1735	1753	1829	1835	...	1853	...	1928	1935	1953	2038	2024	2038	...	2058	2058	...	...	2128	2128	2138	...	2153
nburg Altona a.	...	1807	1844	1850	...	1908	...	1946e	1950	2009	...	...	2059	...	...	2113	...	...	2143	2143	2153	...	2209

– **NOTES** (LISTED BY TRAIN NUMBER)

2 – 🚃12 and ✕ Chur - Zürich - Basel - Hamburg.

6 – 🚃12 and ✕ Zürich - Basel - Hamburg - Kiel.

– 🚃12 and ✕ Wien - Linz - Passau - Regensburg - Hamburg.

) – 🛏 1, 2 cl., 🛌 2 cl. and 🚃2 Wien - Passau - Nürnberg - Hamburg; 🚃2 (*IC* **60490**) Nürnberg - Hamburg.

32 – KÖNIGSSEE – 🚃12 and 🍷 Berchtesgaden - München - Hamburg; conveys 🚃12 Oberstdorf (**2084**) - Augsburg (**2082**) - Hamburg.

34 – 🚃12 and 🍷 Hannover - Hamburg - Stralsund (- Ostseebad Binz until Oct. 28).

70 – Not ①–⑤ July 18 - Sept. 2, Oct. 2. 🚃12 and 🍷 Karlsruhe - Frankfurt - Hamburg (- Stralsund ⑦ **w**). Train number **2270** on ⑦ **w**.

76 – 🚃12 and 🍷 Karlsruhe - Frankfurt - Hamburg - Stralsund (- Ostseebad Binz ⑥).

- KOMET – 🛏 1, 2 cl. and 🛌 2 cl. (*CNL* **478** 🅁) Zürich - Hamburg; 🚃2 (*IC* **60478**) Zürich - Hamburg.
- WATTENMEER – To Westerland daily to Oct. 30, ④–⑦ from Nov. 3 (Table **821**).
- PYXIS – 🛏 1, 2 cl. and 🛌 2 cl. (*CNL* **40418** 🅁) München - Stuttgart Hbf (d. 0135) - Hamburg; 🚃2 (*IC* **61418**) München - Stuttgart - Hamburg. July 30 - Sept. 11 departs München 2228, Augsburg 2301.
- To Flensburg (Table **823**). From Schwarzach July 3 - Sept. 4 (Table **960**).
- From Garmisch on dates in Table **895**.
- 🚃12 and 🍷 München - Kassel - Paderborn - Hamm - Düsseldorf.
- To Kiel (Table **820**).
- To Lübeck (Table **825**).
- To Oldenburg (Table **813**).
- From Wiesbaden (Table **911**).
- To Stralsund (Table **830**).
- July 18 - Sept. 2 only.

Y – ①②③④⑥⑦ July 18 - Sept. 1.
Z – From Zürich (Table **510**).
a – Ⓐ only.
b – Ⓒ only. Basel **Badischer Bahnhof**.
c – ⑤–⑦ (also Oct. 3).
d – Runs to July 17 / from Sept. 3 (also on ⑥ July 23 - Aug. 27 from Garmisch to Hannover only).
e – ①–⑥ (also Oct. 2; not Oct. 3).
g – Also Oct. 4; not Oct. 3.
h – ⑥ (also Oct. 2; daily July 18 - Sept. 3).
j – Arrives 8 – 10 minutes earlier.
k – Also Oct. 2.
m – Not Oct. 3. July 18 - Sept. 1 departs Hannover 2028, arrives Hamburg Hbf 2138, Hamburg Altona 2153.
n – Not July 18 - Sept. 2.
o – München **Ost**.
p – Previous day.
q – Not Oct. 2.
r – Not July 16 - Aug. 28.
s – Stops to set down only.
t – Ⓐ (not Aug. 15. Nov. 1).
w – Also Oct. 3; not Oct. 2.
x – Not ①–⑤ until July 20.
y – Not July 16 - Aug. 28 (during this period calls additionally at Frankfurt **Süd**).
‡ – Also ①–⑤ July 18 - Sept. 2.
§ – Not ①②③④⑥⑦ July 18 - Sept. 1.
◧ – Via Gießen (Table **806**).

◇ – To Lübeck on dates in Table **825**. Train number **684** on ①–⑤ July 18 - Sept. 2 (not Aug. 15) and ①–④ from Oct. 31 (not Nov. 1), **1004** on ⑥⑦ July 23 - Aug. 28 (also Aug. 15).
⊖ – Until Sept. 3. To Berlin via Erfurt (Table **850**).
⊡ – Until Sept. 3 conveys 🚃12 (**1694**) München - Würzburg - Erfurt - Berlin.
⊗ – Later timings at Hannover, Lüneburg and Hamburg July 18 - Sept. 2.
♥ – July 18 - Sept. 2 continues to Kiel Hbf (a. 1510).
✣ – **July 18 - Sept. 2** services Kassel - Hannover - Hamburg are subject to alteration. Many *IC* services do not run north of Kassel (as indicated), although most München - Hamburg *ICE* services call additionally at Celle, Uelzen and Lüneburg to replace the *IC* stops at those stations. *ICE* services, also those *IC* services that do run, are diverted between Göttingen and Hannover with journey times extended by up to 47 minutes. Most journeys to Bremen require a change of train at Hannover (later arrivals).
⊠ – Timings at Stuttgart are subject to alteration until Aug. 28. Timings at Karlsruhe and Mannheim are subject to alteration July 16 - Aug. 28. See shaded panel on page 367.
❦ – Service until Sept. 3. From Sept. 4 may operate with a different train number and amended timings south of Würzburg. Details will be updated in the September edition.

900 NÜRNBERG and FRANKFURT - HAMBURG

SEE NOTE ✣	*IC* 1980	*ICE* 572	*ICE* 1582	*ICE* 1152	*IC* 2274	*IC* 2274	*ICE* 376	*ICE* 782	*ICE* 732	*ICE* 592	*ICE* 782	*ICE* 732	*ICE* 570	*ICE* 580	*ICE* 580	*ICE* 292	*ICE* 580	*ICE* 1172	*ICE* 272	*ICE* 1580	*ICE* 780	*ICE* 992	*I*… 6…
	⑦w	✕	⊖ ✕	⚘✕	⑤⑦ w🍷	⑦w 🍷	⑤⑦ ✕♦	♥ ✕	★ G✕	✕	♥ ✕	★ G✕	⑦w ✕	Ⓑq ✕	⑦w ✕	⑦w ✕♦	⑦w ✕	⑥k Z✕	Ⓐ Z✕	⊖ ✕	⑦w ✕	⑦w ✕	
Basel SBB **912** ▦ d.	...	...	...	...	...	...	1706	...	...	...	...	...	...	...	...	1813	...	1813	1813	...	...	...	
Karlsruhe Hbf **912** ⊠ d.	...	...	...	...	1710	1710	1851	...	...	...	...	...	...	...	...	2000	...	2000	2000	...	...	...	
Stuttgart Hbf **912** ⊠ d.	...	1725x	...	...	|	|	|	...	...	1851	...	...	1925	...	...	|	...	|	|	...	...	2051	2
Mannheim Hbf **912** ⊠ d.	...	1806x	...	...	|	|	1916	...	...	1932	...	...	2006	...	...	2032	...	2032	2032	...	...	2132	2
Frankfurt Flughafen Fernbf ✈ **912** d.	...	1842r	...	...	|	|	|	...	...	|	...	...	2042r	...	...	|	...	|	|	...	...	|	
Frankfurt (Main) Hbf ... **850 901 902** d.	...	1858	...	...	1849	1849	1958y	...	...	2013	...	...	2058	...	...	2113	...	2113	2113	...	...	2222	22
Hanau Hbf **850 901 902** d.	...	1914	...	...	|	|	|	...	...	2029	...	...	2114	...	...	2129	...	2129	2129	...	...	2238	22
München Hbf **904 905** d.	1552	|	1719	1705	|	|	|	1820	1820	|	...	...	|	1854	1854	|	...	|	|	1922	2022	|	
Augsburg Hbf **905** d.	1625	|	|	1734	◧	◧	|	|	|	|	...	...	|	1932	1932	|	...	|	|	|	|	|	
Nürnberg Hbf **920 921** d.	|	|	1833	|	|	|	|	1934	1934	|	...	...	|	|	|	|	...	|	|	2033	2135	|	
Würzburg Hbf **920 921** d.	1833	|	1925	1929	|	|	|	2030	2030	|	...	...	|	2131	2131	|	...	|	|	2158	2230	|	
Fulda **850 901 902** d.	1914	|	2005	2003	|	|	|	2104	2104	|	...	...	|	2204	2204	2211	...	2211	2211	2230	2304	2322	23
Kassel Wilhelmshöhe **901 902** d.	1951	2025	...	2036	2055	2055	2121	2136	2136	2140	←	←	2225	2234	2236	2243	←	2243	2243	...	2338	2356	00
Göttingen **902 903** d.	2012	2046n	...	2056	2117	2117	2140n	2155	2155	2159	2205	2205	2245n	...	2255	2301	2306	2306	2305	...	...	0047	
Hannover Hbf **903** a.	2051	2119	...	2132	2156	2156	2217	→	→	...	2240	2240	2318	...	→	...	2341	2341	0002	...	...	0146	
Hannover Hbf **903** d.	2055	2122	...	2136	...	2159	2220	...	...	...	2244	2250	2321	...	...	...	2345	2344	0005	...	...	0149	
Bremen Hbf **813** a.	|	|	...	|	...	|	|	...	...	...	|	2357	|	...	...	...	|	|	|	...	...	|	
Celle **903** d.	2119	|	...	|	...	2219	2240	...	...	...	|	...	|	...	...	...	0005	|	0027	...	...	|	
Uelzen **903** d.	2142	|	...	|	...	2242	2303	...	...	...	2322	...	|	...	...	...	0027	0023	0050	...	...	|	
Lüneburg **903** d.	2158	2214n	...	|	...	2258	2319	...	...	...	2339	...	0015	...	...	...	0044	0041	0106	...	...	|	
Hamburg Hbf **903** a.	2227	2244	...	2254	...	2328	2351	...	...	...	0009	...	0044	...	...	...	0113	0111	0138	...	...	0308	
Hamburg Altona a.	2245	2302	...	2310	...	2344	0006r	...	...	...	0024	...	0102	...	...	...	0129	0126	0159	...	...	0324	

SEE NOTE ✣	*ICE* 271	*ICE* 591	*ICE* 591	*ICE* 781	*ICE* 781	*IC* 2271	*ICE* 1151	*ICE* 1583	*ICE* 571	*IC* 2179	*ICE* 1097	*ICE* 783	*ICE* 71	*ICE* 71	*IC* 2277	*ICE* 533	*ICE* 1153	*ICE* 1585	*ICE* 973	*ICE* 573	*IC* 2083	*ICE* 91	*IC* 15…
	①g ♦	Ⓐ ✕	⚒ ✕	①g B✕	⚒ ✕	Ⓐd 🍷	⚘✕	①–⑥ ⊖✕	⚒ ✕	Ⓐ H	Ⓐ D✕	①–⑥ ✕	Ⓒ ✕♦	Ⓐ ✕♦	⚒¶ 🍷	⚒n N⚘	⚘ G✕	⊖ ✕	⚒ K✕	† ✕	🍷♦	✕♦	
Hamburg Altona d.	0029r	0306	...	...	...	...	0441	...	0500	0505	0553	0539	0557	0603	0610	✕	0646	...	...	0707	0713	0747	
Hamburg Hbf **903** d.	0044	0321	...	...	...	...	0456	...	0516	0525	0608	0555	0611	0618	0625	...	0701	...	0722	0722	0729	0803	
Lüneburg **903** d.	|	0354	...	...	...	...	0526	...	0547	0555	|	|	0642	0648	0655	...	|	...	|	|	0801	|	
Uelzen **903** d.	|	0410	...	...	...	...	0543	...	|	0615	|	|	0659	|	0715	...	|	...	|	|	0817	|	
Celle **903** d.	|	0435	...	...	...	...	|	...	|	0638	|	|	0721	|	0739	...	|	...	|	|	0840	|	
Bremen Hbf **813** d.	|	|	...	...	...	...	|	...	|	|	|	|	|	|	|	0714	|	...	|	|	|	|	
Hannover Hbf **903** a.	0207	0454	...	...	...	...	0621	...	0638	0657	0719	0723	0739	0738	0758	0814	0821	...	0838	0838	0859	0921	
Hannover Hbf **903** d.	0210	0514	0514	...	...	0601	0626	...	0641	...	0722	0726	0741	0741	0801	0826	0826	...	0841	0841	0903	0926	
Göttingen **902 903** d.	0307	0555	0555	0602	...	0640	0702	...	0716n	...	|	0802	0816n	0816n	0840	0902	0902	...	0916n	0916n	0944	1003	
Kassel Wilhelmshöhe **901 902** d.	|	0616	0616	0623	0623	0703	0723	...	0737	...	|	0823	0837	0837	0903	0923	0923	...	0937	0937	1006	1025	
Fulda **850 901 902** d.	0434	0648	0648	0656	0656	|	0756	0802	|	...	|	0856	|	|	|	0956	0956	0957	|	|	1043	1057	
Würzburg Hbf **920 921** d.	|	|	|	0729	0729	|	0830	0834	|	...	|	0929	|	|	|	1030	1030	1033	|	|	1122	1128	11
Nürnberg Hbf **920 921** a.	|	|	|	0824	0824	◧	|	0928	|	...	|	1024	|	|	◧	|	|	1128	|	|	|	→	12
Augsburg Hbf **905** a.	|	|	|	|	|	|	1029	|	|	...	|	|	|	|	|	1223	1223	|	|	|	1331	...	
München Hbf **904 905** a.	|	|	|	0938	0938	|	1104	1040	|	...	|	1138	|	|	|	1255	1255	1241	|	|	1410o	...	13
Hanau Hbf **850 901 902** d.	0522	0730	0730	...	...	|	...	...	|	...	|	...	|	|	|	...	...	...	|	|	...	...	
Frankfurt (Main) Hbf ... **850 901 902** a.	0537	0745	0745	...	...	0907	...	...	0900	...	0928	...	1000y	1000y	1108	...	...	...	1100	1100	...	...	
Frankfurt Flughafen Fernbf ✈ **912** a.	|	|	|	...	...	|	...	...	0916r	...	...	...	|	|	|	...	...	...	1116r	1116r	...	...	
Mannheim Hbf **912** ⊠ a.	0625	0827	0827	...	...	|	...	...	0954	...	...	...	1043	1043	|	...	...	...	1154	1154	...	...	
Stuttgart Hbf **912** ⊠ a.	|	0908	0908	...	...	|	...	...	1035	...	...	...	|	|	|	...	...	...	1235	1235	...	...	
Karlsruhe Hbf **912** ⊠ a.	0656	...	...	...	...	1050	...	...	...	...	...	...	1108	1108	1250h	...	...	...	...	...	...	...	
Basel SBB **912** a.	0847	...	...	...	...	...	...	...	...	...	...	...	1254	1254	...	...	...	...	...	...	...	...	

SEE NOTE ✣	*ICE* 91	*ICE* 73	*ICE* 1173	*IC* 2087	*IC* 2279	*ICE* 535	*ICE* 1145	*ICE* 1155	*ICE* 1587	*ICE* 575	*ICE* 1223	*ICE* 787	*ICE* 75	*ICE* 1175	*IC* 2371	*ICE* 537	*ICE* 587	*ICE* 1589	*ICE* 577	*ICE* 789	*ICE* 77	*IC* 2089	*I*… 23…
	✕♦	⚒ ✕♦	† Z✕	①–⑥ V T	⚒n T🍷	n⚘ N✕	†t ⚘✕	⚒n L⚘	⊖ ✕	✕	🍷♦	✕	⚒ ✕♦	† ✕♦	△ 🍷	n N✕	✕	⊖ ✕	✕	✕	✕♦	Y T🍷	▽ T
Hamburg Altona d.	...	...	0807r	🍷	...	...	0846	✕	...	0906	...	0946	1009	...	1014	...	1046	...	1109	1146	...	...	
Hamburg Hbf **903** d.	...	0824	0824	0824	0828	...	0901	0901	...	0924	...	1001	1024	1024	1028	...	1101	...	1124	1201	1224	1224	12
Lüneburg **903** d.	...	|	|	|	0859	...	|	|	...	|	...	|	|	|	1059n	...	|	...	|	|	|	|	12
Uelzen **903** d.	...	|	|	|	0916	...	|	|	...	|	...	|	|	|	1115n	...	|	...	|	|	|	|	13
Celle **903** d.	...	|	|	|	0939	...	|	|	...	|	...	|	|	|	1139n	...	|	...	|	|	|	|	13
Bremen Hbf **813** d.	...	|	|	|	|	0914	|	|	...	|	...	|	|	|	|	1114	|	...	|	|	|	|	
Hannover Hbf **903** a.	...	0938	0938	0938	0958	1014	1021	1021	...	1038	...	1121	1138	1138	1158	1214	1223	...	1238	1321	1338	1338	13
Hannover Hbf **903** d.	...	0941	0941	...	1001	1026	1026	1026	...	1041	...	1126	1141	1141	1201	1226	1226	...	1241	1326	1341	...	14
Göttingen **902 903** d.	...	1016n	1016n	...	1040	1102	1102	1102	...	1116n	...	1202	1216n	1216n	1240	1302	1302	...	1316n	1402	1416n	...	14
Kassel Wilhelmshöhe **901 902** d.	...	1037	1037	...	1103	1123	1123	1123	...	1137	1158	1223	1237	1237	1303	1323	1323	...	1337	1424	1437	...	15
Fulda **850 901 902** d.	←	|	|	...	|	1156	1156	1156	1157	|	1228	1256	|	|	|	1356	1356	1357	|	1456	|	...	
Würzburg Hbf **920 921** d.	1135	|	|	...	|	1230	1230	1230	1233	|	1310	1329	|	|	|	1430	1430	1433	|	1529	|	...	
Nürnberg Hbf **920 921** a.	1227	|	|	...	◧	|	|	|	1328	|	1403	1424	|	|	◧	|	|	1525	|	1624	|	...	
Augsburg Hbf **905** a.	...	|	|	...	|	1433	1433	1433	|	|	|	|	|	|	|	1626	1626	|	|	|	|	...	
München Hbf **904 905** a.	...	|	|	...	|	1507	1507	1507	1442	|	1508	1541	|	|	|	1700	1700	1639	|	1738	|	...	
Hanau Hbf **850 901 902** d.	...	|	|	...	|	...	...	...	...	|	...	...	|	|	|	...	...	...	|	...	|	...	
Frankfurt (Main) Hbf ... **850 901 902** a.	...	1200y	1200y	...	1307	...	...	...	...	1300	...	...	1400y	1400y	1507	...	...	...	1500	...	1600y	...	17
Frankfurt Flughafen Fernbf ✈ **912** a.	...	|	|	...	|	...	...	...	...	1316r	...	...	|	|	|	...	...	...	1516r	...	|	...	
Mannheim Hbf **912** ⊠ a.	...	1243	1243	...	|	...	...	...	...	1354	...	...	1443	1443	|	...	...	...	1554x	...	1643	...	
Stuttgart Hbf **912** ⊠ a.	...	|	|	...	|	...	...	...	...	1435	...	...	|	|	|	...	...	...	1635x	...	|	...	
Karlsruhe Hbf **912** ⊠ a.	...	1308	1308	...	1452	...	...	...	...	...	...	...	1508	1508	1650	...	...	...	...	...	1708	...	18
Basel SBB **912** a.	...	1454	1454	...	...	...	...	...	...	...	...	...	1654	1654	...	...	...	...	...	...	1854	...	

♦ – **NOTES** (LISTED BY TRAIN NUMBER)

71/5 – 🚃12 and ✕ Hamburg - Basel - Zürich - Chur.
73/7 – 🚃12 and ✕ Kiel - Hamburg - Basel - Zürich.
91 – 🚃12 and ✕ Hamburg - Regensburg - Passau - Linz - Wien.
271 – 🚃12 Hamburg - Basel - Zürich - Chur. ✕ Frankfurt - Chur.
292 – 🚃12 and ✕ Zürich - Basel - Berlin.
376 – ⑤⑦ (also Oct. 3; not Oct. 2). 🚃12 and ✕ Interlaken - Bern - Basel - Hamburg.
1175 – 🚃12 and ✕ Kiel - Hamburg - Basel - Zürich. Continues to Chur on Oct. 3.
1223 – 🚃12 and 🍷 Köln - Paderborn - Kassel - München.
2083 – KÖNIGSSEE – 🚃12 and 🍷 Hamburg - München Ost - Berchtesgaden; conveys 🚃12 Hamburg - Augsburg (**2085**) - Oberstdorf.

- **B** – From Berlin (Table **902**).
- **D** – To Darmstadt Hbf (a. 0953).
- **G** – From / to Garmisch on dates in Table **895**.
- **H** – To Wolfsburg (Table **810**). Departures at Hamburg, Lüneburg and Uelzen are 3–9 minutes earlier July 18 - Sept. 2.
- **K** – From Kiel (Table **820**).
- **L** – From Lübeck (Table **825**).
- **N** – From Oldenburg on dates in Table **813**.
- **T** – From Stralsund (Table **830**).
- **V** – July 18 - Sept. 2 only.
- **Y** – ①②③④⑥⑦ July 18 - Sept. 1.
- **Z** – From / to Zürich (Table **510**).

- **d** – Not ②–⑤ July 19 - Sept. 2.
- **g** – Also Oct. 4; not Oct. 3.
- **h** – ⑥ only.
- **k** – Also Oct. 2.
- **n** – Not July 18 - Sept. 2.
- **o** – München **Ost**.
- **q** – Not Oct. 2.
- **r** – Not July 16 - Aug. 28.
- **t** – Runs daily July 17 - Sept. 2.
- **w** – Also Oct. 3; not Oct. 2.
- **x** – Not July 16–20.
- **y** – Not July 16 - Aug. 28 (during this period calls additionally at Frankfurt **Süd**).

- ♥ – Runs 6–8 minutes **earlier** Göttingen - Hamburg on ⑦ (connection at Göttingen w… train **592** not available). Train number **1182** on ⑥ to Nov. 5.
- ★ – Runs to July 16 / from Sept. 3 (also ⑥ July 23 - Aug. 27 Garmisch - Hannover on… To Oldenburg (Table **813**). Runs 5–8 minutes **earlier** Göttingen - Bremen on ⑦ (connection at Göttingen with train **592** not available). On Oct. 3 Hannover d. 224… Bremen a. 2351. Train number **1032** on ⑦ (also Oct. 3). Terminates at Hannover ⑥ July 23 - Aug. 27.
- ⊖ – Until Sept. 3. To / from Berlin via Erfurt (Table **850**).
- ¶ – July 18 - Sept. 2 runs Hamburg - Hannover only as *IC* **2081**.
- △ – Not ①②③④⑦ July 18 - Sept. 1. Starts from Hannover on ⑥ July 23 - Aug. 27.
- ▽ – Not ①②③④⑥⑦ July 18 - Sept. 1.
- ✣ – **July 18 - Sept. 2** services Hamburg - Hannover - Kassel and v.v. are subject to alteration. Many *IC* services do not run north of Kassel (as indicated), although m… *ICE* services Hamburg - München and v.v. call additionally at Lüneburg, Uelzen a… Celle to replace the *IC* stops at those stations. *ICE* services, also those *IC* servic… that do run, are diverted between Hannover and Göttingen with journey times extended by up to 47 minutes (earlier southbound departures Hamburg - Hannov… Most journeys from / to Bremen require a change of trains at Hannover (earlier departures / later arrivals).
- ⊠ – Timings at Stuttgart are subject to alteration until Aug. 28. Timings at Karlsruhe a… Mannheim are subject to alteration July 16 - Aug. 28. See shaded panel on page 3… for further details.
- ⚘ – Service until Sept. 3. From Sept. 4 may operate with a different train number and amended timings south of Würzburg (please confirm locally). Details will be upda… in the September edition.
- ◧ – Via Gießen (Table **806**).

HAMBURG - FRANKFURT and NÜRNBERG 900

SEE NOTE ✣	ICE 1139 n ❦✗	ICE 1159 ❦✗	ICE 1209 ⊖ ✗	ICE 579 ✗	IC 1981 ⑤⑦ w♣	ICE 881 ✗	ICE 79 Z✗	IC 2375 L🍷	ICE 631 n ❦✗	ICE 1141 1161 ❦✗	ICE 1683 ⊖ ✗	ICE 771 ✗	IC 1995 ⑦w B🍷	IC 2171 ⑤⑦ w🍷	IC 2281 ①–④ m🍷	ICE 883 K✗	ICE 1171 ✗	IC 2285 V O🍷	IC 2377 n O🍷	ICE 1143 b ❦✗	ICE 1163 Ⓑq ❦✗	ICE 1685 ⊖ ✗	ICE 773 ✗
urg Altona ... d.	...	1246	...	1310	...	1346	1409	...	...	◇	...	1509	...	1514	1514	...	1609	...	...	...	1646	...	1709
urg Hbf ... 903 d.	...	1301	...	1324	1328	1401	1424	1428	...	1501	...	1524	...	1528	1528	1601	1624	1624	1628	...	1701	...	1724
urg ... 903 d.	...	|	...	|	1359n	1429	|	1459n	...	|	...	|	...	1558n	1558n	|	|	|	1659	...	|	...	|
n ... 903 d.	...	|	...	|	1414n	|	|	1515n	...	|	...	|	...	1619n	1619n	|	|	|	1715	...	|	...	|
... 903 d.	...	|	...	|	|	|	|	1539n	...	|	...	|	...	1641n	1641n	|	|	|	1739	...	|	...	|
men Hbf 813 ... d.	1314	|	...	|	|	|	|	|	1514	|	...	|	...	|	|	|	|	|	|	1714	|	...	|
over Hbf ... 903 a.	1414	1421	...	1438	1451	1522	1538	1558	1614	1621	...	1638	...	1700	1700	1721	1738	1738	1757	1814	1821	...	1838
over Hbf ... 903 d.	1426	1426	...	1441	1454	1526	1541	1601	1626	1626	...	1641	1703	1707	1703	1726	1741	...	1801	1826	1826	...	1841
gen ... 902 903 d.	1503	1503	...	1516n	1534	1602	1616n	1641	1702	1702	...	1716n	1744	1748	1814	1802	1816n	...	1840	1902	1902	...	1917n
el Wilhelmshöhe ... 901 902 d.	1525	1525	...	1537	1558	1623	1637	1703	1723	1723	...	1737	1809	1810	...	1823	1837	...	1903	1923	1923	...	1938
... 850 901 902 d.	1557	1557	1557	|	1632	1656	|	|	1756	1756	1757	|	|	1852	...	1856	|	...	|	1956	1956	1957	|
rzburg Hbf ... 920 921 d.	1631	1631	1634	|	1713	1729	|	|	1830	1830	1834	|	|	|	...	1929	|	...	|	2030	2030	2033	|
rnberg Hbf ... 920 921 a.	|	|	1728	|	|	1824	|	◧	|	|	1949	|	◧	|	...	2024	|	...	◧	|	|	2128	|
ugsburg Hbf 905 ... a.	1825	1825	|	|	1929	|	|	|	2026	2026	|	|	|	|	...	|	|	...	|	2226	2226	|	|
nchen Hbf 904 905 ... a.	1857	1857	1841	|	2002	1940	|	|	2058	2058	2105	|	|	|	...	2141	|	...	|	2300	2300	2241	|
u Hbf ... 850 901 902 d.	...	...	...	|	...	...	|	|	...	...	...	|	|	1935	...	...	|	...	|	...	...	...	|
kfurt (Main) Hbf ... 850 901 902 a.	...	...	...	1700	...	...	1800y	1907	...	...	...	1900	2012	1950	...	...	2000y	...	2105	...	...	...	2100
nkfurt Flughafen Fernbf ✈ 912 a.	...	...	...	1716r	...	...	|	|	...	...	...	1916r	|	|	...	...	|	...	|	...	...	...	2116r
nnheim Hbf 912 ... ⊠ a.	...	...	...	1754	...	...	1843	|	...	...	...	1954	|	|	...	...	2043	...	|	...	...	...	2154
Stuttgart Hbf 912 ... ⊠ a.	...	...	...	1835	...	...	|	|	...	...	...	2035	2156	2155f	...	...	|	...	|	...	...	...	2250
rlsruhe Hbf 912 ... ⊠ a.	...	...	...	...	...	...	1908	2054	...	...	...	...	...	...	...	...	2108	...	2327d	...	...	...	...
sel SBB 912 ... a.	...	...	...	...	...	...	2054	...	...	...	...	...	...	...	...	...	2300c	...	...	...	...	...	...

SEE NOTE ✣	IC 2173 Ⓑq 🍷	IC 2173 ⑦w 🍷	ICE 885 ❦✗	ICE 273 K✗	ICE 273 ⑤⑥ sK ✗	IC 2289 ⒷV T🍷	IC 2379 Ⓑn qT 🍷	IC 2379 ⑤⑦ nw T🍷	ICE 635 Ⓑj ❦✗	ICE 685 ❦✗	ICE 635 ⑤⑦j ❦✗	ICE 685 ⑤–⑦ t❦✗	ICE 1687 ⊖ ✗	ICE 775 ⑤⑦ w✗	ICE 887 Ⓑq N✗	ICE 1087 ⑥s N✗	CNL 479 Ⓡ⊗ D🍷	IC 60479 ⊗ D2	CNL 40479 Ⓡ⊗ E🍷	IC 61479 ⊗ E2	EN 491 H		IC 1985 ⑦w 🍷
burg Altona ... d.	1713	1713	1746	...		...			...	1846	...	1846	...	1909	1946	1946	2014	2014	2014	2014	2035	...	2114
burg Hbf ... 903 d.	1728	1728	1801	1824	1824	1824	1828	1828	...	1901	...	1901	...	1924	2001	2001	2029	2029	2029	2029	2052	...	2128
burg ... 903 d.	1757n	1757n	|	|	|	|	1859	1859	...	|	...	|	...	|	2028	2028	2059u	2059	2059u	2059	|	...	2200
en ... 903 d.	1819n	1819n	|	|	|	|	1914	1914	...	|	...	|	...	|	2044	2044	|	|	|	|	|	...	2216
... 903 d.	1841n	1841n	|	|	|	|	1938	1938	...	|	...	|	...	|	|	|	|	|	|	|	|	...	2239
emen Hbf 813 ... d.	|	|	|	|	|	|	|	|	1914	|	1914	|	...	|	|	|	|	|	|	|	|	...	|
over Hbf ... 903 a.	1905	1905	1921	1938	1938	1938	1958	1958	2014	2023	2014	2023	...	2038	2123	2123	|	2155	|	2155	2222	...	2258
over Hbf ... 903 d.	...	1909	1926	1941	1941	...	...	2001	2026	2026	2026	2026	...	2041	2126	2137	2201u	2201	2201u	2201	2227	...	2301
gen ... 902 903 d.	...	2022	2002	2016n	2016n	...	...	2040	2102	2102	2102	2102	...	2116n	2202	2213	2243u	2243	2243u	2243	2327	...	2339
el Wilhelmshöhe ... 901 902 d.	...	2048	2027	2037	2037	...	...	2103	2123	2123	2123	2123	...	2137	2223	2234	2306u	2306	2306u	2306	|	...	...
... 850 901 902 d.	...	...	2100	|	|	...	...	|	2156	2156	2156	2156	2203	|	2256	2306	|	|	|	|	|	...	...
rzburg Hbf ... 920 921 d.	...	...	2134	|	|	...	...	|	2229	2229	2229	2229	2236	|	|	|	|	|	|	|	0201	...	...
rnberg Hbf ... 920 921 a.	...	...	2228	|	|	...	...	◧	2350	2350	2350	2350	2327	|	|	|	|	|	|	|	0257	...	...
Augsburg Hbf 905 ... a.	...	...	|	|	|	...	...	|	...	...	|	|	|	|	|	|	|	|	0633	0633	...	...	...
nchen Hbf 904 905 ... a.	...	...	2340	|	|	...	...	|	...	...	0110	0110	0041	|	|	|	|	|	0710	0710	...	...	...
u Hbf ... 850 901 902 d.	...	...	...	|	|	...	...	|	...	...	...	...	...	|	2340	2352	|	|	...	...	...	...	...
kfurt (Main) Hbf ... 850 901 902 a.	...	...	...	2200y	2200y	...	...	2304	...	...	...	...	...	2300	2355	0008	|	0113	...	...	...	...	...
nkfurt Flughafen Fernbf ✈ 912 a.	...	...	...	|	|	...	...	...	...	...	...	...	...	...	0024	0024	|	|	...	...	...	...	...
nnheim Hbf 912 ... ⊠ a.	...	...	...	2243	2243	...	...	...	...	...	...	...	...	...	...	...	|	0329	...	...	...	...	...
Stuttgart Hbf 912 ... ⊠ a.	...	...	...	|	|	...	...	...	...	...	...	...	...	...	...	...	|	|	...	...	...	...	...
rlsruhe Hbf 912 ... ⊠ a.	...	...	...	2308	2308	...	...	...	...	...	...	...	...	...	...	...	0400	0400	...	...	...	...	...
sel SBB 912 ... a.	...	...	...	...	0100	...	...	...	...	...	...	...	...	...	...	...	0619	0619	...	...	...	...	...

From Berlin (Table **810**). July 24 - Aug. 28 departs Hannover 1709, Göttingen 1823, Kassel 1845, arrives Frankfurt 2041, Stuttgart 2235.
KOMET – 🛏 1, 2 cl. and 🛌 2 cl. (*CNL* **479** Ⓡ) Hamburg - Zürich; (2) (*IC* **60479**) Hamburg - Zürich.
PYXIS – 🛏 1, 2 cl. and 🛌 2 cl. (*CNL* **40479** Ⓡ) Hamburg - Stuttgart Hbf (a. 0421) - München; (2) (*IC* **61479**) Hamburg - Stuttgart - München. Later Augsburg / München arrivals July 30 - Sept. 11.
🛏 1, 2 cl., 🛌 2 cl. and (2) Hamburg - Passau - Wien; (2) (*IC* **60491**) Hamburg - Nürnberg. Ⓡ for journeys beyond Nürnberg.
From Kiel (Table **820**).
WATTENMEER – From Westerland daily to Oct. 31, ①⑤⑥⑦ from Nov. 4 (Table **821**).
To Wiesbaden (Table **911**).
From Stralsund (Table **830**), also Ostseebad Binz on dates in Table **845**.
From Stralsund (Table **830**).
July 18 - Sept. 2 only.
To Zürich (Table **510**).

Runs to July 17 / from Sept. 3 (also on ⑥ July 23 - Aug. 27 from Hannover to München only).
Ⓒ only.
⑤ (also Oct. 2).
⑤ only.
Not July 18 - Sept. 2, Oct. 2.
Not Oct. 3.

n – Not July 18 - Sept. 2.
q – Not Oct. 2.
r – Not July 16 - Aug. 28.
s – Also Oct. 2.
t – Also Oct. 3.
u – Stops to pick up only.
w – Also Oct. 3; not Oct. 2.

y – Not July 16 - Aug. 28 (during this period calls additionally at Frankfurt **Süd**).
◇ – From Lübeck on dates in Table **825**.
♣ – From Flensburg (Table **823**) on ⑤.
⊗ – July 18 - Sept. 2 Hamburg Altona d. 1946, Hamburg Hbf d. 2001, Lüneburg d. 2029, Hannover a. 2126, d. 2129.
⊖ – Until Sept. 3. From Berlin via Erfurt (Table **850**).
✣ – **July 18 - Sept. 2** services Hamburg - Hannover - Kassel are subject to alteration. Many *IC* services do not run north of Kassel (as indicated), although most Hamburg - München *ICE* services call additionally at Lüneburg, Uelzen and Celle to replace the *IC* stops at those stations. *ICE* services, also those *IC* services that do run, are diverted between Hannover and Göttingen with journey times extended by up to 47 minutes (earlier departures Hamburg - Hannover). Most journeys from Bremen require a change of trains at Hannover (earlier departures).
⊠ – Timings at Stuttgart are subject to alteration until Aug. 28. Timings at Mannheim and Karlsruhe are subject to alteration July 16 - Aug. 28. See shaded panel on page 367 for further details.
❦ – Service until Sept. 3. From Sept. 4 may operate with a different train number and amended timings south of Würzburg (please confirm locally). Details will be updated in the September edition.
◧ – Via Gießen (Table **806**).

/ RB services — Local services FRANKFURT - FULDA - KASSEL 901

r *ICE* / *IC* services: Table **850** for Bebra - Kassel Wilhelmshöhe and v.v., also Frankfurt - Fulda - Bad Hersfeld and v.v. Tables **900** / **902** for Frankfurt - Fulda - Kassel Wilhelmshöhe and v.v.

					A	
Frankfurt (Main) Hbf ..... **921** d.	0524	0626	and hourly until	2126	2226	2326
Frankfurt (Main) Süd ... **921** d.	0530	0633		2133	2233	2333
Offenbach (Main) Hbf .... **921** d.	0535	0638		2138	2238	2338
Hanau Hbf ... **921** d.	0545	0648		2148	2248	2348
Fulda ... a.	0646	0749		2250	2349	0049

		ⒶB	†	⚒	ⒶB						
Fulda ... d.	0401	0438	0508	0515	0600	0608	0708	0808	0908	and hourly until	2309
Hanau Hbf ... **921** d.	0500	0539	0609	0616	0656	0709	0809	0909	1009		0009
Offenbach (Main) Hbf . **921** d.	0509	0548	0617	0624	|	0717	0817	0921t	1017		0017
Frankfurt Main) Süd .. **921** d.	0515	0553	0623	0630	0711	0723	0823	0927t	1023		0023
Frankfurt (Main) Hbf .. **921** a.	0520	0558	0628	0636	0716	0728	0828	0932t	1028		0028

FULDA - KASSEL. Operated by CANTUS Verkehrsgesellschaft (except trains marked with note **B**). 2nd class only.

	Ⓐ	Ⓐ		Ⓐ	Ⓒg												G	⑤⑦f				g		ⒶB
Fulda ... d.	...	0548	0616	0644	0655	0719	0819	0919	1019	1121	1219	1319	1419	1519	1619	1721	1819	1819	1919	2019	2122e	2221	2301	2357
Bad Hersfeld ... d.	0511	0616	0644	0714	0721	0747	0847	0947	1047	1149	1247	1347	1447	1547	1647	1749	1847	1847	1947	2047	2149	2250	2329	0027
Bebra ... d.	0525	0627	0657	0727	0731	0758	0857	0958	1057	1159	1257	1358	1457	1558	1657	1759	1857	1904	1958	2058	2200	2301	2340	0041
Rotenburg (Fulda) ... d.	0531	0633	0703	0733	...	0804	0903	1004	1103	1206	1303	1404	1503	1604	1703	1806	1903	1910	2004	2104	2206	...	...	...
Melsungen ... d.	0550	0653	0723	0753	...	0824	0923	1024	1123	1225	1323	1424	1523	1624	1723	1825	1923	1929	2024	2124	2225	...	...	...
Kassel Wilhelmshöhe **804/6** a.	0609	0711	0741	0811	...	0841	0941	1041	1141	1242	1341	1441	1541	1641	1741	1842	1941	1948	2041	2142	2251	...	...	...
Kassel Hbf ... **804/6** a.	0616	0718	0748	0818	...	0849	0948	1048	1148	1248	1348	1448	1548	1648	1748	1848	1948	1954	2048	2150	2257	...	...	...

		ⒶB	ⒶB	⚒	Ⓒ	Ⓐ		g													Ⓐ	Ⓒ		Ⓑ	
sel Hbf ... **804/6** d.	...	...	...	0506	0605	0626	0709	...	0810j	0910	1010	1110	1210	1310	1409	1510	1610	1710	1810	1910	2010	2010	2110	2210	2310
sel Wilhelmshöhe **804/6** d.	...	...	...	0510	0614	0630	0714k	...	0814	0914	1014	1115	1214	1314	1413	1514	1614	1715	1814	1914	2014	2014	2115	2214	2316
sungen ... d.	...	...	...	0529	0634	0648	0733	...	0833	0932	1033	1132	1233	1332	1433	1532	1633	1733	1833	1933	2033	2033	2132	2233	2336
nburg (Fulda) ... d.	...	...	...	0549	0653	0708	0752	...	0852	0951	1052	1151	1252	1351	1452	1551	1652	1751	1852	1951	2052	2052	2151	2252	2355
ra ... d.	0315	0359	0522	0558	0700	0716	0800	0815	0859	0958	1059	1158	1259	1358	1459	1558	1659	1758	1859	1958	2059	2059	2159	2304	0002
Hersfeld ... d.	0325	0409	0531	0608	0709	0725	0810	0824	0908	1008	1108	1208	1308	1408	1508	1608	1708	1808	1908	2008	2108	2111	2209	2315	0012
da ... a.	0354	0436	0558	0637	0737	0753	...	0852	0937	1037	1137	1237	1337	1437	1537	1637	1737	1840	1937	2037	2137	2140	2237	...	...

To Bebra on Ⓐ.
(12) Bebra - Fulda - Frankfurt and v.v.
①②③④⑥ (not Oct. 3, Nov. 1).

e – Ⓐ only.
f – Also Oct. 3, Nov. 1.
g – To / from Göttingen (Table **908**).

j – 0806 on †.
k – 0713 on ① (also Oct. 4).
t – 4 minutes earlier on Ⓒ.

902 FRANKFURT - BRAUNSCHWEIG - BERLIN

See Table **850** for other fast services Frankfurt - Berlin via Erfurt. Subject to alteration July 18 - September 2 – SEE NOTE ▼.

km		*ICE* **649**	*ICE* **1188**	*ICE* **876**	*ICE* **1092**	*ICE* **1092**	*ICE* **696**	*ICE* **874**	*ICE* **694**	*ICE* **374**	*ICE* **692**	*ICE* **372**	*ICE* **690**	*ICE* **370**	*ICE* **598**	*ICE* **278**	*ICE* **596**	*ICE* **276**	*ICE* **1090**	*ICE* **594**	*IC* **1076**	*IC* **1998**	*ICE* **274**	*ICE* **592**
		Ⓐ ✕	⚒ ‡✕	⚒ ✕	①g ✕	①–④ m✕	①g ✕	✕	✕	✕	✕	✕	✕	✕	✕	✕	✕	✕	Ⓑq ◧✕	⑥k ✕	⑤⑦ w§ 🍷	④	✕	s ✕
	Interlaken Ost **560** d.	...	...	...	...	...	...	...	...	...	...	0600	...	...	...	1000	...	...	...	...	...	...	...	...
	Bern **560** d.	...	...	...	...	...	...	...	...	...	...	0704	...	...	...	1104	...	...	...	...	...	...	...	...
	Basel SBB **912** d.	...	...	...	...	...	...	0412b	...	0608	...	0813	...	1013	...	1213	...	1413	...	...	...	...	1613	...
	Karlsruhe Hbf **912** ⊠ d.	...	...	...	0500	...	...	0558	...	0800	...	1000	...	1200	...	1400	...	1601	...	...	...	...	1801	...
	Ulm Hbf **930** ⊠ d.	...	...	...	|	...	...	|	...	|	0751a	|	0951	|	1151	|	1351	|	1551	1551	...	...	|	1751
	Stuttgart Hbf **912** ⊠ d.	...	...	...	|	...	...	|	0651	|	0851	|	1051	|	1251	|	1451	|	1651	1651	...	...	|	1851
	Mannheim Hbf **912** ⊠ d.	...	...	...	0528	...	...	0632	0732	0832	0932	1032	1132	1232	1332	1432	1532	1632	1732	1732	...	...	1832	1932
0	**Frankfurt** (Main) Hbf **850 900** d.	...	0506	0513g	0614	0614	...	0713	0813	0913	1013	1113	1213	1313	1413	1513	1613	1713	1814	1813	1822	1822	1913	2013
23	Hanau Hbf **850 900** d.	...	0522	0529g	|	|	...	0729	0829	0929	1029	1129	1229	1329	1429	1529	1629	1729	|	1829	1838	1840	1929	2029
104	Fulda **850 900** d.	...	0604	0611g	|	|	...	0811	0911	1011	1111	1211	1311	1411	1511	1611	1711	1811	|	1911	1920	1931	2011	|
194	**Kassel** Wilhelmshöhe **900** d.	...	0636	0643	|	|	0743	0843	0943	1043	1143	1243	1343	1443	1543	1643	1743	1843	|	1944	1959	2008	2043	2140
239	Göttingen **900** d.	...	0654	0702	|	|	0804	0902	1002	1102	1202	1302	1403	1502	1602	1702	1802	1902	|	2004	2021	2029	2102	2201
317	Hildesheim Hbf **863** d.	...	...	0734	|	|	0834	0934j	1034	1134	1234	1334	1434	1534	1634	1734	1834	1934	|	2034	2059	2105	2134	2234
360	**Braunschweig** Hbf **863** d.	0601	...	0759	|	|	0859	0959	1059	1159	1259	1359	1459	1559	1659	1759	1859	1959	|	2059	2124	2128	2159	2259
392	Wolfsburg **810 863** d.	0620	...	0817	|	|	0917	1017	|	1217	|	1417	|	1617	|	1817	|	2017	|	2117	2143	2148	2217	2317
559	**Berlin** Spandau **810** a.	0721	...	0912	0940	0940	1011	1111	1207	1311	1407	1511	1607	1711	1807	1911	2007	2111	2151	2212	2244	2249	2311	0020
575	**Berlin** Hbf **850 810** a.	0732	...	0926	0955	0955	1025	1128	1225	1328	1425	1528	1625	1728	1825	1928	2026	2128	2203	2227	2259	2303	2326	0035
580	**Berlin** Ostbahnhof **810** a.	...	...	0937	1006	1006	1037	1139	1237	1339	1437	1539	1637	1739	1837	1939	2037	2139	...	2238	2310	2315	2338	0046

	ICE **781**		*ICE* **275**		*ICE* **593**	*ICE* **1091**	*ICE* **277**	*ICE* **595**	*ICE* **279**	*ICE* **597**	*ICE* **371**	*ICE* **599**	*ICE* **373**	*ICE* **691**	*ICE* **375**	*IC* **1995**	*ICE* **693**	*ICE* **377**	*ICE* **695**	*ICE* **1093**	*ICE* **877**	*ICE* **697**	*ICE* **997**	*ICE* **887**
	①g M		Ⓐ ✕		Ⓒ ✕	Ⓐ ✕	✕	✕	✕	✕	✕	✕	✕	✕	✕	⑦w 🍷◇	✕	✕	⑥k ✕	Ⓑq ✕	✕	⑤⑦ w✕	①–④ m✕	Ⓑq ✕
Berlin Ostbahnhof **810** d.	0232	...	0421	...	0520	0553	0620	0723	0820	0923	...	1123	1220	1323	1420	1451	1523	1620	1723	1752	1820	1920	...	...
Berlin Hbf **850 810** d.	0244	...	0432	...	0531	0604	0631	0734	0831	0934	1035	1134	1231	1334	1431	1502	1534	1631	1734	1803	1831	1931	1935	...
Berlin Spandau **810** d.	|	...	0446	...	0545	0618	0645	0748	0845	0948	1046	1148	1245	1348	1445	1516	1548	1645	1748	1817	1845	1945	1945	...
Wolfsburg **810 863** d.	|	...	0540	...	0641	|	0740	|	0940	|	1140	|	1340	|	1540	1621	|	1740	|	|	1940	|	|	...
Braunschweig Hbf **863** d.	0454	...	0558	...	0700	|	0758	0858	0958	1058	1158	1258	1358	1458	1558	|	1658	1758	1858	|	1958	2058	2058	...
Hildesheim Hbf **863** d.	0518	...	0625	...	0725	|	0825	0925	1025	1125	1225	1325	1425	1525	1625	|	1725	1825	1925	|	2025	2125	2125	...
Göttingen **900** d.	0602	...	0655	...	0755	|	0855	0955	1055	1155	1255	1355	1455	1555	1655	1744	1755	1855	1955	|	2055	2155	2155	2202
Kassel Wilhelmshöhe **900** d.	0623	...	0716	...	0816	|	0916	1016	1116	1216	1316	1416	1516	1616	1716	1809	1816	1916	2016	|	2116	2216	2215	2223
Fulda **850 900** d.	0654	...	0748	...	0848	|	0948	1048	1148	1248	1348	1448	1548	1648	1748	|	1848	1948	2048	|	2148	2248	...	2256
Hanau Hbf **850 900** d.	...	...	0829	...	0929	|	1029	1129	1229	1329	1429	1529	1629	1729	1829	|	1929	2029	|	|	2229	2329	...	2340
Frankfurt (Main) Hbf **850 900** a.	...	...	0844	...	0944	0944	1044	1144	1244	1344	1444	1544	1644	1744	1844	2012	1944	2044	2142	2142	2248	2344	...	2355
Mannheim Hbf **912** ⊠ a.	...	...	0927	...	1027	1027	1127	1227	1327	1427	1527	1627	1727	1827	1927	|	2027	2127	2228	2228	2353	...	...	...
Stuttgart Hbf **912** ⊠ a.	...	...	|	...	1108	1108	|	1308	|	1508	|	1708	|	1908	|	2156	2108	|	2308	2310	|	...	...	...
Ulm Hbf **930** ⊠ a.	...	...	|	...	1207	1207	|	1407f	|	1607	|	1807	|	2007n	|	...	2207r	|	...	0011t	|	...	...	...
Karlsruhe Hbf **912** ⊠ a.	...	...	0958	...	...	...	1158	...	1358	...	1558	...	1758	...	1958	...	...	2158	...	...	0022	...	...	...
Basel SBB **912** a.	...	...	1147	...	...	...	1347	...	1547	...	1747	...	1947	...	2147	...	...	2354	...	...	...	...	...	...
Bern **560** a.	...	...	1256	...	...	...	...	...	...	...	1856	...	2056	...	...	...	...	...	...	...	...	...	...	...
Interlaken Ost **560** a.	...	...	1357	...	...	...	...	...	...	...	1957	...	2157	...	...	...	...	...	...	...	...	...	...	...

M – To München (Table **900**). Also calls at Potsdam Hbf (d. 0306), Brandenburg Hbf (d. 0325) and Magdeburg Hbf (d. 0406). Conveys ✕ Braunschweig - München.
Z – From Zürich HB (d. 1700).

a – Ⓐ only.
b – ① (also Oct. 4; not Oct. 3). Basel **Badischer Bahnhof**.
f – Not July 30 - Sept. 11.
g – ① (also Oct. 4; not Oct. 3).
j – 0932 on ① (also Oct. 4; not Oct. 3).
k – Also Oct. 2.

m – Not Oct. 3.
n – Ⓑ to July 1; daily from July 3.
q – Not Oct. 2.
r – Daily to July 8; Ⓑ from July 10 (not Oct. 2).
s – Also calls at Stendal (d. 2346).
t – Stuttgart - Ulm on ⑦ (also Oct. 3; not Oct. 2).
w – Also Oct. 3; not Oct. 2.

§ – Train number **1992** on ⑤ from Sept. 9.
‡ – Train number **988** on ⑥ (daily July 18 - Sept. 3).
◧ – Also calls at Hannover Hbf (a. 2021).

◇ – Via Hannover and Gießen (Tables **806/810/900** July 24 - Aug. 21 departs Göttingen 1823, Kass 1845, arrives Frankfurt 2041, Stuttgart 2235.
⊠ – Timings at Ulm and Stuttgart are subject to alte until Aug. 28. Timings at Karlsruhe and Mannhe may also vary by up to 5 minutes July 16 - Aug See shaded panel on page 367 for further detai
▼ – **July 18 - Sept. 2** all services are diverted betw Göttingen and Hildesheim extending journey tim During this period services run up to 47 minutes **earlier** Berlin - Göttingen and up to 40 minutes Göttingen - Berlin.

903 Local services GÖTTINGEN - HANNOVER - UELZEN - HAMBURG

metror

Services below are operated by ***metronom*** (except trains **A**, **B**, **D** and **E**). For faster *ICE* and *IC* services see Table **900**.

km																											
				⚒		Ⓐ A🍷	hz	Ⓐ B🍷																			
0	**Göttingen** d.	...	...	0409	0504	0545	0607	0645	...	0707	0809	0907	1009	1107	1209	...	1305	1409	1507	1609	1707	1809	1907	2009	...	2107	2
20	Northeim (Han) d.	...	...	0422	0517	0559	0620	0658	...	0720	0822	0920	1022	1120	1222	...	1318	1422	1520	1622	1720	1822	1920	2022	...	2120	2
39	Kreiensen d.	...	...	0437	0533	0612	0633	0712	...	0733	0837	0933	1037	1133	1237	...	1334	1437	1533	1637	1733	1837	1936	2037	...	2133	2
58	Alfeld (Leine) d.	...	...	0450	0546	0625	0646	0725	...	0746	0850	0946	1050	1146	1250	...	1347	1450	1546	1650	1746	1850	1949	2050	...	2146	2
75	Elze (Han) d.	...	...	0503	0558	0636	0658	0736	...	0758	0903	0958	1103	1158	1303	...	1358	1503	1558	1703	1758	1903	2000	2103	...	2158	2
108	**Hannover** Hbf. a.	...	...	0526	0624	0655	0723	0756	...	0823	0926	1023	1126	1223	1326	...	1423	1526	1623	1726	1823	1926	2025	2126	...	2223	2
108	**Hannover** Hbf. d.	...	...	0540	0640	0700	0740	0759	...	0840	0940	1040	1140	1240	1340	...	1440	1540	1640	1740	1840	1940	2040	2140	...	2248	2
149	Celle d.	...	...	0606	0706	0720	0806	0819e	...	0906	1006	1106	1206	1306	1406	...	1506	1606	1706	1806	1906	2006	2106	2206	...	2315	0
201	Uelzen a.	...	...	0638	0738	0740	0838	0840e	...	0938	1038	1138	1238	1338	1438	...	1538	1638	1738	1838	1938	2038	2138	2238	...	2346	0
				Ⓐ																				N	⑦w	Ⓒ	
201	Uelzen d.	0501	0605	0647	0704	0742	0802	0842e	0902	1002	1101	1201	1301	1401	1445f	1501	1601	1701	1801	1903	2001	2102	2201	2306	2306	0005	
214	Bad Bevensen d.	0509	0614	0655	0713	|	0810	0850e	0910	1010	1109	1209	1309	1409	1455f	1509	1609	1709	1809	1911	2009	2110	2209	2314	2315	0013	
237	Lüneburg d.	0524	0629	0709	0728	0758	0828	0902e	0928	1028	1131j	1228	1328	1428	1512f	1528	1628	1728	1828	1929	2031	2128	2228	2328	2336	0032	
256	Winsen (Luhe) d.	0535	0640	0720	0740	|	0839	|	0939	1039	1142	1239	1339	1439	1523f	1539	1639	1739	1839	1940	2042	2139	2239	2344	2351	0047	
286	**Hamburg** Hbf a.	0556	0702	0741	0802	0828	0901	0933	1001	1101	1204	1301	1401	1502	1545f	1601	1701	1801	1902	2001	2102	2201	2301	0018	0024	0120	

					①–⑤	⑥⑦ r									①–④ D🍷			⑦ E🍷									
Hamburg Hbf d.	...	...	...	...	0543	0601	0652	0757	0857	0957	1057	1157	1257	1357	1528	1457	1557	1728	1657	1757	1857	1957	2057	2158	2234	2334	0
Winsen (Luhe) d.	...	...	...	...	0604t	0622	0713	0819	0919	1019	1119	1219	1319	1419	|	1519	1619	|	1719	1819	1919	2019	2119	2220	2307	0008	0
Lüneburg d.	...	...	...	...	0615t	0633	0724	0834	0933	1033	1133	1233	1333	1433	1558e	1533	1633	1757e	1733	1833	1933	2033	2130	2231	2323	0023	0
Bad Bevensen d.	...	...	...	...	0630t	0647	0742	0848	0948	1048	1148	1248	1348	1448b	1610e	1548	1648	1809e	1748	1848	1948	2048	2145	2246	2337	0037	0
Uelzen a.	...	...	...	...	0638t	0655	0750	0856	0956	1056	1156	1256	1356	1456b	1617e	1556	1656	1817e	1756	1856	1956	2056	2153	2253	2348	0045	0
	⚒	Ⓒ	Ⓐ	h	Ⓐ	Ⓒ																					
Uelzen d.	0413	0513	0513	0609	0651	0709	0809	0909	1009	1109	1209	1309	1409	1509	1619e	1609	1709	1819e	1809	1909	2009	2109	2209	2309	...	...	
Celle d.	0447	0547	0547	0647	0747v	0747	0847	0947	1047	1147	1247	1347	1447	1547	1641e	1647	1747	1841e	1847	1947	2047	2147	2247	2347	...	...	
Hannover Hbf a.	0514	0614	0614	0714	0814	0814	0914	1014	1114	1214	1314	1414	1514	1614	1700	1714	1814	1905	1914	2014	2114	2216	2316	0012	...	...	
Hannover Hbf d.	0536	0633	0636	0736	0833	0833	0936	1033	1136	1233	1336	1433r	1536	1633	1703	1736r	1833	1909	1936	2033	2133k	2233	2333	...	...	...	
Elze (Han) d.	0558	0655	0658	0758	0855	0855	0958	1055	1158	1255	1358	1455	1558	1655	1722	1758	1855	1929	1958	2055	2158	2255	2355	...	...	...	
Alfeld (Leine) d.	0610	0706	0710	0810	0906	0906	1010	1106	1210	1306	1410	1506	1610	1706	1733	1810	1906	1940	2010	2106	2210	2306	0011	...	...	...	
Kreiensen d.	0623	0719	0723	0823	0919	0919	1023	1119	1223	1319	1423	1519	1623	1719	1746	1823	1919	1953	2023	2119	2223	2319	0025	...	...	...	
Northeim (Han) d.	0636	0733	0736	0836	0935	0935	1036	1133	1236	1333	1436	1533	1636	1733	1759	1836	1933	2007	2036	2133	2236	2333	0038	...	...	...	
Göttingen a.	0649	0747	0749	0849	0949	0949	1049	1147	1249	1347	1449	1547	1649	1747	1814	1849	1947	2020	2049	2147	2249	2347	0050	...	...	...	

A – *IC* **2176**. Operated by DB.
B – *IC* **2182**. Operated by DB. From Kassel Wilhelmshöhe (d. 0623). July 18 - Sept. 2 Elze d. 0739, Hannover a. 0759, d. 0819, Hamburg a. 0936.
D – ①–④ (not Oct. 3). *IC* **2281**. Operated by DB. July 18 - Sept. 1 Hamburg d. 1524, Hannover a. 1638, d. 1653, Elze 1721 and then as shown.
E – ⑦ (also Oct. 3; not Oct. 2). *IC* **2173**. Operated by DB. To Kassel Wilhelmshöhe (a. 2048). July 24 - Aug. 28 Hamburg d. 1724, Hannover a. 1840, d. 1908.
L – On Ⓒ Hannover Hbf d. 2348, Celle d. 0015, Uelzen a. 0046.

N – ①–⑥ (not July 22, 29, Aug. 5, 12, 19, 26, Sept. 2).

b – On ⑤ (not July 22, 29, Aug. 5, 12, 19, 26, Sept. 2) Bad Bevensen d. 1452, Uelzen a. 1459.
e – Not July 18 - Sept. 2.
f – ⑤ only.
h – Change trains at Hannover on Ⓐ.
j – Arrives 1124.

k – 2136 on Ⓐ.
r – 2–3 minutes earlier July 18 - Sep
t – 3 minutes later July 18 - Sept. 2.
v – Arrives 0728.
w – Also July 22, 29, Aug. 5, 12, 19, 2 Sept. 2.
z – Runs 2–5 minutes later Götting Hannover on †.

MÜNCHEN - INGOLSTADT - NÜRNBERG 904

	ICE 888	ICE 822	ICE 1684	ICE 784‡ 1184	ICE 634	ICE 820	ICE 886	ICE 728	ICE 1682	ICE 726	ICE 882	ICE 724	ICE 1208	ICE 722 1122	ICE 880	ICE 720	ICE 1588	ICE 628	ICE 788	ICE 626	ICE 1586	ICE 624 1124	ICE 1166
	Ⓐ	⚒			Ⓐ	⚒				⚒													
		K	≋	Ⓐt	♣	K		K	≋	K		K	B≋	K		K♠	≋	K		K	≋	K	≋
	✕	🍷	✕	✕	✕	🍷	✕	🍷	✕	🍷	✕	🍷	✕	🍷	✕	🍷	✕	🍷	✕	🍷	✕	🍷	✕
München Hbf d.	0415	0449	0515	0520	0520	0552	0617	0652	0720	0755	0822	0855	0920	0955	1022	1055	1120	1155	1222	1255	1320	1355	1422
Ingolstadt Hbf d.	0453	0528	0552	0558	0558	0630	0655	0730	0758	|	0901	|	0958	|	1101	|	1158	|	1301	|	1358	|	1501
Nürnberg Hbf a.	0523	0555	0625	0629	0629	0657	0725	0757	0830	0857	0930	0957	1030	1057	1130	1157	1230	1257	1330	1357	1430	1457	1530
Würzburg Hbf **900 920** a.	0627	0653	0723	0727	0727	0753	0828	0853	0923	0953	1028	1053	1123	1153	1227	1253	1323	1353	1428	1453	1523	1553	1628
Frankfurt (Main) Hbf **920** a.	|	0804	|	|	...	0904	|	1004	|	1104	|	1204	|	1304	|	1404	|	1504	|	1604	|	1704	|
Leipzig Hbf **851** a.	|	...	1010	|	...	...	|	...	1210	...	|	...	1410	...	|	...	1610	...	|	...	1810	...	|
Berlin Hbf **851** a.	|	...	1133	|	...	...	|	...	1333	...	|	...	1533	...	|	...	1733	...	|	...	1933	...	|
Hamburg Hbf **900** ● a.	0953	...	...	1055	...	...	1156	...	...	...	1354	...	...	...	1554	...	...	...	1753	...	...	...	1953

	ICE 622	ICE 1584	ICE 620	ICE 1522	ICE 1694	ICE 528	ICE 1582	ICE 526	ICE 782 1182	ICE 524	ICE 1580	ICE 1580	ICE 522	ICE 780	ICE 520	ICE 1620	ICE 922		ICE 920					
								Ⓑq				⑤⑦		⑦w	①–④	⑥	⑤⑦							
	K	≋	G K	K	≋	K	≋	K	☆	K	≋	≋	K	A	m	h	w							
	🍷	✕	🍷	✕	✕	🍷	✕	🍷	✕	🍷	✕	✕	🍷	✕	🍷	✕	✕		✕					
chen Hbf d.	1455	1518	1555	1618	1618	1652	1719	1755	1820	1855	1922	1922	1952	2022	2055	2055	2055	...	2255	...	...	...	...	...
lstadt Hbf d.	|	1558	|	1657	1657	1730	1757	|	1901	|	1959	1959	2030	2101	2133	|	2133	...	2333	...	...	...	...	...
berg Hbf a.	1557	1630	1657	1729	1729	1757	1829	1857	1931	1957	2030	2030	2057	2132	2201	2201	2202	...	0005	...	...	...	...	...
ürzburg Hbf **900 920** a.	1653	1723	1753	1825	1825	1853	1923	1953	2028	2053	2156	2156	2153	2228	2255	2255	2255	...	...	...	...	...	...	...
ankfurt (Main) Hbf **920** a.	1804	|	1904	1936	|	2004	|	2104	|	2204	|	|	2305	...	0004	0004	0004	...	...	...	...	...	...	...
Leipzig Hbf **851** a.	...	2010	...	...	2122	...	2210	...	|	...	0043	0043	...	...	...	...	...	...	...	...	...	...	...	...
Berlin Hbf **851** a.	...	2133	...	...	2241	...	2333	...	|	...	...	0206	...	...	...	...	...	...	...	...	...	...	...	...
amburg Hbf **900** ● a.	...	...	...	...	...	...	...	...	0009	...	...	...	...	...	...	...	...	...	...	...	...	...	...	...

	ICE 823	ICE 985	ICE 827	ICE 1581	ICE 521	ICE 781	ICE 523	ICE 1583	ICE 525 1125	ICE 783	ICE 527	ICE 1127	ICE 1585	ICE 529	ICE 1521	ICE 621	ICE 1587	ICE 623	ICE 787	ICE 625	ICE 1589	ICE 627	ICE 789	ICE 629
	Ⓐt	Ⓐa	Ⓐ	Ⓐa		⚒	⚒	①–⑥		①–⑥	Ⓐ	⑥h												
		M	K	E≋	K	N	K	≋	K		K	K G	≋	K	K	K	≋	K♠		K	≋	K		K
	🍷	✕	🍷	✕	🍷	✕	🍷	✕	🍷	✕	🍷	🍷	✕	🍷	✕	🍷	✕	🍷	✕	🍷	✕	🍷	✕	🍷
amburg Hbf **900** ● d.	...	...	...	...	...	...	...	...	...	0555	...	...	...	...	...	...	...	...	1001	...	...	...	1201	...
Berlin Hbf **851** d.	...	...	...	...	...	...	...	0427	...	|	...	...	0627	...	...	...	0827	...	|	...	1027	...	|	...
Leipzig Hbf **851** d.	...	...	...	...	...	...	...	0548	...	|	...	...	0748	...	...	...	0948	...	|	...	1148	...	|	...
ankfurt (Main) Hbf **920** d.	...	...	0454	...	0551	...	0654	|	0754	|	0854	0854	|	0954	1018	1054	|	1154	|	1254	|	1354	|	1454
ürzburg Hbf **900 920** d.	...	...	0604	...	0704	0729	0804	0834	0904	0929	1004	1004	1033	1104	1132	1204	1233	1310	1329	1404	1433	1504	1529	1604
nberg Hbf d.	0558	0628	0702	0728	0802	0827	0902	0931	1002	1027	1102	1102	1131	1202	1227	1302	1331	1406	1427	1502	1528	1602	1627	1702
lstadt Hbf d.	0627	0701	0731	0803	|	0901	|	1004	|	1101	|	|	1205	|	1301	|	1405	|	1501	|	1601	|	1701	|
chen Hbf a.	0703	0738	0807	0841	0904	0938	1004	1040	1104	1138	1204	1204	1241	1304	1338	1404	1442	1508	1541	1606	1639	1704	1738	1804

	ICE 1209	ICE 721	ICE 881	ICE 723	ICE 681 1081	ICE 1683	ICE 725	ICE 883	ICE 727	ICE 1685	ICE 729	ICE 885	ICE 821	ICE 1687	ICE 685	ICE 635								
				Ⓑq					Ⓑq				Q		⑤–⑦	⑤⑦r								
	≋B	K		K	⊖T	≋	K	L	K	≋	K	≋	K	≋	u≋	¶≋								
	✕	🍷	✕	🍷	✕	✕	🍷	✕	🍷	✕	🍷	✕	🍷	✕	✕	✕								
amburg Hbf **900** ● d.	...	...	1401	...	1501	...	...	1601	...	...	...	1801	...	...	1901	...	...	...	...	...	...	...	...	...
Berlin Hbf **851** d.	1227	...	|	...	|	1428	...	|	...	1627	...	|	...	1827	|	...	...	...	...	...	...	...	...	...
Leipzig Hbf **851** d.	1348	...	|	...	|	1548	...	|	...	1748	...	|	...	1948	|	...	...	...	...	...	...	...	...	...
ankfurt (Main) Hbf **920** d.	|	1554	|	1654	|	|	1754	|	1854	|	1954	|	2054	|	|	...	...	...	...	...	...	...	...	...
ürzburg Hbf **900 920** d.	1634	1704	1729	1804	1830	1834	1904	1929	2004	2033	2104	2134	2205	2236	2229	2229	...	...	...	...	...	...	...	...
nberg Hbf d.	1731	1802	1827	1902	1928	1952	2002	2027	2103	2131	2202	2231	2302	2331	2357	2357	...	...	...	...	...	...	...	...
lstadt Hbf d.	1805	1831	1901	|	2001	2029	|	2101	|	2205	2231	2303	2331	0005	0030	0030	...	...	...	...	...	...	...	...
chen Hbf a.	1841	1907	1940	2004	2038	2105	2109g	2141	2205	2241	2307	2340	0007	0041	0110	0110	...	...	...	...	...	...	...	...

RE services via the high-speed line (SEE NOTE ✣).

n																									
		Ⓐt	⑥	†b	⚒t	Ⓐt	Ⓒz	⑥		Ⓒz	Ⓐt	⑤	Ⓒs	Ⓒz	Ⓐt	Ⓒz	Ⓐt		Ⓐt	Ⓐt	Ⓒz	Ⓒz	Ⓐt	Y	X
0	**München** Hbf d.	0455	0522	0605	0705	0901	0906	1006	1105	1300	1305	1400	1402	1500	1504	1600	1600	1658	1712	1800	1806	1900	1909	2109	2129
0	Pfaffenhofen (Ilm) d.	0521	0549	0631	0731	0930	0932	1028	1131	1329	1331	1429	1428	1529	1530	1626	1629	1729	1745	1829	1828	1929	1935	2135	2205
1	**Ingolstadt** Hbf a.	0539	0607	0650	0751	0952	0952	1048	1151	1351	1351	1450	1447	1550	1550	1645	1650	1752	1805	1850	1848	1950	1955	2154	2228
1	**Ingolstadt** Hbf d.	0541	0609	0705	0805	*1005*	1005	1105	1205	*1407*	1407	*1505*	1505	*1605*	1605	1707	*1707*f	*1807*z	1807	...	1905	*2005*	2005	2156	*2236*
1	**Nürnberg Hbf** a.	0635	0652	0748	0848	*1048*	1048	1148	1248	*1450*	1450	*1548*	1548	*1648*	1648	1751	*1751*f	*1851*z	1851	...	1948	*2048*	2048	2239	*2319*

	Ⓐt	Ⓐt	Ⓒz	Ⓐt	⑥	Ⓒz	Ⓐt		⑥	Ⓐt	Ⓒz	⑤	Ⓐt	Ⓒz	Ⓒz	Ⓐt	Ⓐt	Ⓒz	Ⓒz	Ⓐt	Ⓐt	Ⓒz	Y	X	⑤⑥y
nberg Hbf d.	0510	*0607*	0632	0732	0810	0910	*0910*	1110	1210	1310	*1310*	*1411*	1510	*1510*	1610	*1610*f	1710	*1710*	1810	...	1910	*1910*	2110	*2140*	2340
olstadt Hbf a.	0554	*0655*	0717	0817	0855	0955	*0955*	1155	1255	1355	*1355*	*1456*	1555	*1555*	1655	*1656*f	1755	*1755*	1855	...	1955	*1955*	2155	*2225*	0025
olstadt Hbf d.	0600	0705	0719	0819	0905	1008p	1008	1209	1305	1409	1411	1505	1605	1605	1705	1705	1809	1810	1905	1905	2009	2009	2208p	2235	0034
ffenhofen (Ilm) d.	0618	0727	0738	0838	0926	1029p	1030	1230	1326	1430	1433	1527	1626	1627	1726	1727	1830	1832	1926	1927	2030	2031	2229p	2259	0055
nchen Hbf a.	0645	0757	0804	0900	0954	1055	1100	1257c	1353	1453	1500	1601	1657p	1658	1754	1757	1858	1902	1953	1957	2057	2101	2256	2336	0122

RE services via EICHSTÄTT and TREUCHTLINGEN.

n																									
		◧	Ⓐt		◧		◧		◧		◧		◐		◐		◐		Ⓐ	Ⓒ			⑥		
0	**München** Hbf d.	...	0526	...	0626	0728	0829	0929	1029	1129	1229	1329	1429	1529	1625	1729	1829	1927	2021	2029	2129	2228	2228	2329	0032
0	Pfaffenhofen (Ilm) d.	...	0602	...	0702	0805	0905	1006	1105	1205	1305	1405	1505	1605	1702	1806	1905	2003	2102	2105	2205	2305	2305	0005	0108
1	**Ingolstadt** Hbf d.	0528	0629	0629	0730	0830	0930	1030	1130	1230	1330	1430	1530	1630	1730	1830	1930	2030	2130	2130	2232	2329	2330	0028	0130
8	Eichstätt Bahnhof ♥ d.	0556	0656	0656	0756	0856	0956	1057	1156	1256	1356	1456	1556	1656	1756	1857	1956	2056	2156	2156	2258	...	2357	...	...
7	Treuchtlingen a.	0620	0719	0719	0820	0919	1020	1120	1220	1319	1420	1519	1620	1719	1820	1920	2020	2119	2220	2220	2321	...	0021	...	...
7	Treuchtlingen **905** d.	0624	0725	0725	0825¦	0925	1025¦	1125	1225¦	1325	1425¦	1525	1625	1725	1825	1925	2025	2125	*2225*	2225	2325	...	...	...	...
6	Weißenburg (Bay) **905** d.	0631	0732	0732	0832¦	0932	1032¦	1131	1232¦	1332	1432¦	1532	1632	1732	1832	1931	2032	2132	*2232*	2232	2332	...	...	...	...
9	**Nürnberg** Hbf **905** a.	0716	0817	0817	0917¦	1017	1117¦	1217	1320	1417	1517¦	1617	1717	1817	1917	2017	2117	2217	*2317*	2317	0017	...	...	...	...

	Ⓒz	Ⓐt	⚒t	†b	Ⓐt	Ⓒz	⚒t	†b		◧		◧	Ⓒz	Ⓐt	◧		◐		◐		◐		◐		
nberg Hbf **905** d.	...	...	*0435*	0439	0521	0538	*0629*	0639	0738	0839	0938	1039	1138	1138	1239	1337	1439	1538	1639	1738	1839	1938	2039	2139	2342
ßenburg (Bay) **905** d.	...	...	*0518*	0523	0605	0622	*0716*	0723	0822	0923	1022	1123	1222	1222	1323	1422	1523	1622	1723	1822	1923	2022	2123	2223	0027
uchtlingen **905** a.	...	...	*0525*	0530	0613	0629	*0723*	0730	0829	0930	1029	1130	1229	1229	1330	1429	1530	1630	1730	1830	1930	2030	2130	2230	0034
uchtlingen d.	...	0450	0532	0532	0629	0634	0735	0735	0835	0935	1035	1135	1235	1240	1336	1435	1535	1635	1735	1835	1935	2035	2135	2235	...
nstätt Bahnhof ♥ d.	...	0514	0556	0556	0654	0657	0759	0759	0900	0959	1059	1159	1259	1303	1400	1459	1559	1659	1759	1859	1959	2059	2159	2259	...
olstadt Hbf d.	0531	0533	0631j	0631j	0734j	0734j	0833	0833	0933	1031	1131	1231	1331	1335	1435j	1531	1631	1731	1834	1931	2036p	2132	2235j	2334	...
ffenhofen (Ilm) d.	0556	0556	0655	0655	0759	0759	0857	0857	0957	1055	1155	1255	1355	1359	1459	1556	1655	1755	1858	1955	2100p	2156	2259	2358	...
nchen Hbf a.	0634	0634	0734	0734	0837	0837	0934	0934	1034	1134	1235	1335	1435	1437	1537	1634	1735	1835	1936	2035	2138p	2236	2336	0036	...

To Kassel (Table **900**).
From / to Innsbruck via Kufstein (Table **951**).
From Bamberg (Table **851**).
From / to Garmisch on dates in Table **895**.
To / from Köln, Essen or Dortmund (Table **910**).
From Kiel (Table **820**).
From Erlangen (Table **851**).
From Kassel (also Berlin on ①). Tables **900/2**.
④⑤⑦ (also Oct. 3; not Oct. 2).
From Sept. 4.
①–④ (not Aug. 15, Oct. 3, Nov. 1).
⑤–⑦ (also Aug. 15, Oct. 3, Nov. 1).

Not Aug. 15, Oct. 31, Nov. 1.
Also Aug. 15, Nov. 1.
1301 on Ⓒ (also Aug. 15, Nov. 1).
⑤ only.
2105 from Sept. 4.

h – Also Oct. 2.
j – Arrives 10 – 14 minutes earlier.
m – Not Oct. 3.
p – 3 – 5 minutes **earlier** from Sept. 4.
q – Not Oct. 2.
r – Not July 18 - Sept. 2, Oct. 2.
s – Also Nov. 1.
t – Not Aug. 15, Nov. 1.
u – Also Oct. 3.
w – Also Oct. 3; not Oct. 2.
y – Also Oct. 2, 31.
z – Ⓒ (also Aug. 15, Nov. 1).

‡ – Train number **684** on ①–⑤ July 18 - Sept. 2 (not Aug. 15) and ①–④ from Oct. 31 (not Nov. 1).
¶ – From Bremen (Table **900**).
¦ – 3 – 4 minutes later on ⚒ (not Aug. 15, Nov. 1).
◧ – Change at Treuchtlingen on ⚒ (not Aug. 15, Nov. 1).

◐ – Change at Treuchtlingen on Ⓐ (not Aug. 15, Nov. 1).
☆ – Conveys on dates in Table **900**: 🛏12 (**732/1032**) Garmisch - München - Hannover - Bremen.
♣ – Ⓐ (not July 18 - Sept. 2). 🛏12 München - Hannover - Bremen.
⊖ – Conveys 🛏12 München - Hannover - Bremen and v.v. (see Table **900**).
♠ – Conveys 🛏12 Köln - Paderborn - Kassel - Würzburg - München and v.v. See Tables **805/900**.
♥ – Connecting trains (operated by Bayerische Regiobahn) run Eichstätt Bahnhof - Eichstätt Stadt (*5 km*).
≋ – Service until Sept. 3. From Sept. 4 may operate with a different train number and amended timings (please confirm locally). Details will be updated in the September edition.
● – Hamburg timings may vary by up to 47 minutes July 18 - Sept. 2 (earlier departures possible).
✣ – *RE* services via the high-speed line call at Kinding and Allersberg (located 112 and 146 km from München respectively).

905 MÜNCHEN - AUGSBURG - NÜRNBERG and WÜRZBURG

See Table **904** for services via Ingolstadt. See Table **905a** for local trains Treuchtlingen - Würzburg.

ICE and *IC* services

	IC 2162 Ⓐu ❦		*ICE* 1162 ❦⊖ ✕	*IC* 2160 Ⓐu ❦		*ICE* 680 ⊖ ✕	*IC* 2068 ❦	*ICE* 1158 ❦⊖ ✕	*IC* 2066 ❦	*IC* 2082 A 🍷	*ICE* 1156 ❦⊖ ✕	*IC* 2064 ❦	*IC* 1284 ⑦w F	*ICE* 1134 1154 ❦ L✕	*IC* 2062 ❦	*IC* 1980 ⑦w G		*ICE* 1152 ❦ ✕	*IC* 2060 2168 Ⓑ❦		*ICE* 580 Ⓑq Q ✕	*ICE* 580 ⑦w ✕		
München Ost ... d.		...	...	...	...	...	...	...	...	1117	...	...	...	...	...	...	...	...	...	...	...	...	...	...
München Hbf ... **930** d.	0538	...	0653	0739	...	0905	0952	1048	1139	|	1254	1340	1355	1449	1540	1552	...	1705	1739	...	1854	1854	...	...
München Pasing ... **930** d.	0547	...	0702	0748	...	0913	|	|	1148	1130	|	|	|	|	1548	1600	...	|	1748	...	1902	1902	...	...
Augsburg Hbf ... **930** d.	0612	...	0732	0814	...	0938	1022	1119	1214	1230**h**	|	1413	1425	1518	1613	1625	...	1734	1813	...	1932	1932	...	...
Donauwörth ... d.	0630	...	0752	0838	...	|	|	|	|	1249	|	|	1444	|	1633	1645	...	1753	1833	...	1952	1952	...	...
Treuchtlingen ... d.	0651	...	|	|	...	|	|	|	|	1310	|	|	1506	|	1654	1707	...	|	1855	...	2012	2012	...	...
Nürnberg Hbf ... **900 920** a.	0726	...	|	0929	...	|	1129	|	1327	|	|	1527	|	|	1728	|	...	|	1929	...	|	|	...	...
Leipzig Hbf **851** ... a.	...	...	|	...	...	|	...	|	...	|	|	...	|	|	...	|	...	|	...	...	|	|	...	...
Berlin Hbf **851** ... a.	...	...	|	...	...	|	...	|	...	|	|	...	|	|	...	|	...	|	...	...	|	|	...	...
Würzburg Hbf ... **900 920** a.	...	...	0927	...	...	1127	...	1327	...	1437	1527	...	1636	1727	...	1829	...	1927	...	...	2129	2129	...	...
Hamburg Hbf **900** ... ● a.	...	...	1253	...	...	1454	...	1653	...	1829	1853	...	2038	2058	...	2227	...	2254	...	...	...	0113	...	...

	ICE 981 Ⓐt ✕	*IC* 2287 Ⓐa	*ICE* 989 Ⓐt ✕		*IC* 2061 Ⓐu ❦	*ICE* 1151 ❦ ✕	*IC* 2063 ❦	*ICE* 1153 ❦⊖ P✕		*IC* 2083 A 🍷	*IC* 2065 ❦	*ICE* 1145 1155 ❦⊖ L✕		*IC* 2067 ❦	*ICE* 587 ⊖ ✕		*IC* 2069 ❦	*ICE* 1159 ❦⊖ ✕		*IC* 1981 ⑤⑦ wN	*IC* 2161 Ⓑ ❦	*ICE* 1141 1161 ❦⊖ L✕		*ICE* 1143 E❦ ✕
Hamburg Hbf **900** ... ● d.	...	...	...	...	...	0456	...	0701	...	0729	...	0901	...	...	1101	...	...	1301	...	1328	...	1501	...	...
Würzburg Hbf ... **900 920** d.	...	...	...	...	...	0830	...	1030	...	1122	...	1230	...	...	1430	...	...	1631	...	1713	...	1830	...	2030
Berlin Hbf **851** ... d.	...	...	...	...	...	|	...	|	...	|	...	|	...	...	|	...	...	|	...	|	...	|	...	|
Leipzig Hbf **851** ... d.	...	...	...	...	...	|	...	|	...	|	...	|	...	...	|	...	...	|	...	|	...	|	...	|
Nürnberg Hbf ... **900 920** d.	...	0547	0615	...	0828	|	1028	|	...	|	1228	|	...	1428	|	...	1629	|	...	|	1830	|	...	|
Treuchtlingen ... d.	...	0622	0651	...	|	0951	|	|	...	1250	|	|	...	|	|	...	|	|	...	1844	|	|	...	|
Donauwörth ... d.	0600	0644	0711	...	|	1011	|	|	...	1312	|	|	...	|	1608	...	1725	|	...	1907	1925	|	...	2208
Augsburg Hbf ... **930** a.	0620	0705	0731	...	0935	1029	1134	1223	...	1331	1334	1433	...	1534	1626	...	1744	1825	...	1929	1944	2026	...	2226
München Pasing ... **930** a.	0645	0733	0758	...	|	1055	|	|	...	1357	|	|	...	|	1650	...	|	|	...	1953	|	|	...	2250
München Hbf ... **930** a.	0655	0742	0808	...	1010	1104	1204	1255	...	|	1416	1507	...	1606	1700	...	1814	1857	...	2002	2016	2058	...	2300
München Ost ... a.	...	...	...	...	...	...	...	...	...	1410	...	...	...	...	...	...	...	...	...	...	...	...	...	...

RE services. See Table **930** for other connecting trains München - Augsburg and v.v.

km		Ⓒz	⚒s		⚒s		⚒s H	⚒s		⚒s		⚒s		Ⓐt		Ⓐt	⑥ H		Ⓐt H	Ⓐt		Ⓒz H	Ⓐt		
0	**München** Hbf ... **930** d.	*0200*	...	0532	...	0735	...	...	0936	...	1135*	...	1336	...	1536	...	...	1735	...	...	1936	...	...	2101	2201
7	München Pasing **930** d.	*0206*	...	0538	...	0742	...	...	0943	...	1142	...	1343	...	1542	...	...	1742	...	...	1943	...	...	2107	2209
62	**Augsburg** Hbf ... **930** a.	*0246*	...	0619	...	0819	...	...	1019	...	1218	...	1419	...	1619	...	...	1819	...	...	2019	...	...	2148	2244
62	**Augsburg** Hbf ... d.	0315	0516	0628	0717**f**	0828	0840	0923	1028	1126	1224	1327	1429	1526	1628	1719**f**	1738**c**	1828	1918	1921	2028	2118	2126	2154	2254
103	Donauwörth ... d.	0358	0558**k**	0659	0758	0858	0905	1000	1059	1158	1300	1358	1459	1558	1659	1758	1759**c**	1859	1940	1958	2059	2139	2158	2233	2332
137	Treuchtlingen ... a.	0417	0620	0720	0820	0920	|	1020	1120	1220	1320	1420	1520	1620	1720	1820	1816	1920	|	2020	2120	2159	2220	2253	...
137	Treuchtlingen ... **904** d.	0418	0624	*0725*	0829	*0925*	|	1029	*1125*	1229	*1325*	1429	*1525*	1625	*1725*	1825	1817	*1925*	|	2025	*2125*	2200	2225	*2325*	...
146	Weißenburg (Bay) **904** d.	0424	0631	*0732*	0836	*0932*	|	1036	*1131*	1236	*1332*	1436	*1532*	1632	*1732*	1832	|	*1931*	|	2032	*2132*	|	2232	*2332*	...
199	**Nürnberg** Hbf ... **904** a.	0507	0716	*0817*	0920	*1017*	0953	1120	*1217*	1320	*1417*	1520	*1617*	1717	*1817*	1917	1848	*2017*	2028	2117	*2217*	2232	2317	*0017*	...

	Ⓒz	Ⓐt	Ⓒz	Ⓐt	⚒s		⚒s	H	⊗	⚒s		⚒s		⚒s		Ⓐt		Ⓐt	H		Ⓐt		Ⓐt		Ⓒz
Nürnberg Hbf ... **904** d.	0053	...	...	...	0435	*0521***b**	0629	0717	*0738*	0839	*0938*	1039	*1138*	1239	*1337*	1439	*1538*	1639	1732	*1738*	1839	*1938*	2039	2139	...
Weißenburg (Bay) **904** d.	0135	...	...	...	0518	*0605***b**	0716	|	*0822*	0923	*1022*	1123	*1222*	1323	*1422*	1523	*1622*	1723	|	*1822*	1923	*2022*	2123	2223	...
Treuchtlingen ... **904** a.	0141	...	...	...	0525	*0613***b**	0723	0748	*0829*	0930	*1029*	1130	*1229*	1330	*1429*	1530	*1630*	1730	|	*1830*	1930	*2030*	2130	2230	...
Treuchtlingen ... d.	0142	...	...	...	0526	0634	0731**y**	0749	0834	0935	1034	1135	1234	1335	1434	1535	1634	1735	|	1834	1935	2035**e**	2135	*2235***t**	2235
Donauwörth ... d.	0205	0414	0520	0527	0604**j**	0658	0754	0807	0858	1000⁝	1058	1158	1258	1358	1458	1558	1658	1758	1818	1858	1958	2058**e**	2158	*2256***t**	2258
Augsburg Hbf ... a.	0228	0453	0558	0612	0639	0728	0826	0828	0928	1041⁝	1128	1237**g**	1328	1432	1528	1636	1728	1836**c**	1839	1928	2036**c**	2128	2236**c**	...	2328
Augsburg Hbf ... **930** d.	...	0502	0606	0615	*0649***t**	0739	...	...	0939	...	1139	...	1339	...	1539	...	1739	...	...	1939	...	2139	...	...	*2339*
München Pasing ... **930** a.	...	0541	0645	0653	*0728***t**	0813	...	...	1013	...	1213	...	1413	...	1613	...	1813	...	...	2013	...	2222	...	...	*0022*
München Hbf ... **930** a.	...	0549	0652	0702	*0738***t**	0821	...	...	1021	...	1221	...	1421	...	1621	...	1821	...	...	2021	...	2230	...	...	*0030*

A – KÖNIGSSEE – [12] and 🍷 Berchtesgaden - Freilassing - Augsburg - Hamburg and v.v.; [12] Oberstdorf (**2084/5**) - Augsburg - Hamburg and v.v.
E – Daily to July 17; ⑥ July 23 - Aug. 27; daily from Sept. 3. From Bremen to July 17 / from Sept. 23. From Hannover on ⑥ July 23 - Aug. 27. See Table **900**.
F – To Flensburg (Table **823**). From Schwarzach (Tables **960/951**) July 3 - Sept. 4. Also calls at Gunzenhausen (d. 1519) and Ansbach (d. 1536).
G – Also calls at Gunzenhausen (d. 1720) and Ansbach (d. 1736).
H – From / to Lindau and Oberstdorf (Table **935**).
L – From Lübeck on dates in Table **825**.
N – Also calls at Ansbach (d. 1814) and Gunzenhausen (d. 1830). From Flensburg on ⑤ (Table **823**).
P – To Garmisch (Table **895**) on ⑥ until Nov. 5 (also Oct. 31).
Q – To Kassel (Table **900**).

a – Not Aug. 15, Oct. 31, Nov. 1.
b – 16–17 minutes later on Ⓒ (also Aug. 15, Nov. 1).
c – 2–5 minutes earlier from Sept. 5.
e – On ⑥⑦ to Sept. 3 (also Aug. 15) departs Treuchtlingen 2038, Donauwörth 2059.
f – 3–7 minutes later from Sept. 5.
g – 1229 from Sept. 5.
h – Arrives 1200.

j – Arrives 0550.
k – Arrives 0549.
q – Not Oct. 2.
s – Not Aug. 15, Nov. 1.
t – Ⓐ (not Aug. 15, Nov. 1).
u – Not Aug. 15.
w – Also Oct. 3; not Oct. 2.
y – 0725 on ⑥.
z – Also Aug. 15, Nov. 1.

***** – 1134 July 30 - Sept. 11.
⁝ – From Sept. 5 departs Donauwörth 0958, arrives Augsburg 1031.
⊗ – Change trains at Donauwörth on Ⓒ (also Aug. 15, Nov. 1).
⊖ – Conveys [12] München - Hannover - Bremen and v.v. (see Table 90
● – Hamburg timings may vary by up to 41 minutes July 18 - Sept. 2 (ear departures possible).
❦ – Service until Sept. 3. May run with a different train number, together w amended running dates and timings from Sept. 4 (please confirm loca Details will be updated in the September edition.

905a TREUCHTLINGEN - WÜRZBURG

RB services (except train

km		⚒r	Ⓒz	Ⓐt	Ⓐt	Ⓐt	Ⓒz		⑥						Ⓐt	A🍷									
0	**Treuchtlingen** ... d.	...	0502	0512	0535	0614	0626	*0705***t**	0725	0825	0925	1025	1125	1225	1306	1310	1325**z**	1425	1525	1625	1725	1825	1925	2025	2125
24	Gunzenhausen ... d.	...	0515	0527	0550	0626	0639	*0719***t**	0739	0839	0939	1039	1139	1239	1318	1324	1339**z**	1439	1539	1639	1739	1839	1939	2039	2139
51	Ansbach ... a.	...	0535	0547	0611	0645	0659	*0739***t**	0759	0859	0959	1059	1159	1259	1339	1341	1359**z**	1459	1559	1659	1759	1859	1959	2059	2159
51	Ansbach ... d.	0440	0536	0606	0627	0701	0710	0810	0810	0910	1010	1110	1210	1311	...	1343	1410	1510	1610	1710	1810	1910	2010	2112	...
83	Steinach (b Rothenb) ◐ d.	0503	0559	0628	0650	0723	0732	0832	0832	0932	1032	1132	1232	1332	...	1404	1432	1532	1632	1732	1832	1932	2032	2134	...
140	**Würzburg** Hbf ... a.	0547	0642	0713	0738	0810	0816	0918	0918	1016	1118	1216	1318	1416	...	1437	1518	1616	1718	1816	1918	2018	2118	2218	...

	⚒r	Ⓐt	Ⓒz	Ⓐt	Ⓐt	Ⓒz					A🍷	Ⓒz	Ⓐt											†w
Würzburg Hbf ... d.	0430	...	0531	0541	0632	0641	0739	0841	0941	1041	1122	1141	1141	1241	1341	1441	1541	1641	1741	1841	1941	2041	2142	2241
Steinach (b Rothenb) ◐ ... d.	0512	...	0614	0624	0716	0724	0824	0924	1024	1124	1156	1224	1224	1326	1424	1524	1624	1724	1824	1924	2024	2124	2224	2324
Ansbach ... a.	0535	...	0636	0646	0737	0746	0846	0946	1046	1146	1215	1246	1247	1347	1446	1546	1646	1746	1846	1946	2046	2146	2246	2347
Ansbach ... d.	0537	0610	0654	0711	0754	0754	0854	0954	1054	1154	1217	1254	1317	1354	1454	1554	1654	1754	1854	1954	2054	2154	2247	...
Gunzenhausen ... d.	0556	0629	0715	0730	0815	0815	0915	1015	1115	1215	1234	1315	1336	1415	1515	1615	1715	1815	1915	2015	2115	2215	2306	...
Treuchtlingen ... a.	0609	0643	0730	0744	0830	0830	0930	1030	1130	1230	1248	1330	1350	1430	1530	1630	1729	1830	1930	2030	2129	2230	2321	...

◐ – Local trains **STEINACH** (b Rothenb) - **ROTHENBURG OB DER TAUBER** and v.v. 2nd class only *12 km* Journey time: 14 minutes
From Steinach at 0517 ⚒**r**, 0617 Ⓒ**z**, 0631 Ⓐ**t**, 0726 Ⓐ**t**, 0735 Ⓒ**z**, 0835, 0935, 1035, 1135, 1235, 1335, 1435, 1535, 1635, 1735, 1835 Ⓒ**z**, 1845 Ⓐ**t**, 1935, 2035 and 2235.
From Rothenburg ob der Tauber at 0445 ⚒**r**, 0541 Ⓒ**z**, 0606 Ⓐ**t**, 0657 Ⓐ**t**, 0706 Ⓒ**z**, 0806, 0906, 1006, 1106, 1206, 1309, 1406, 1506, 1606, 1706, 1806, 1906, 2006 and 2206.

A – *IC* **2082**/**3**. KÖNIGSSEE – [12] and 🍷 Berchtesgaden - Augsburg - Hamburg and v.v.; [12] Oberstdorf (**2084/5**) - Augsburg - Hamburg and v.v.
r – Not Nov. 1.
t – Ⓐ (not Nov. 1).
w – Also Nov. 1.
z – Ⓒ (also Nov. 1).

GIESSEN - KOBLENZ; LIMBURG - FRANKFURT and WIESBADEN 906

RE services); HLB ★

⊠		⚒	⚒									Ⓒz
Gießen .... **807** d.	...	0618	0716	0916	1116	1316	1516	1716	1916	2021	2116	2221
Wetzlar .... **807** d.	...	0630	0726	0926	1126	1326	1526	1726	1926	2033	2126	2233
Weilburg .... d.	...	0656	0742	0942	1142	1342	1542	1742	1942	2058	2142	2258
Limburg (Lahn) .. a.	...	0733	0807	1007	1207	1407	1607	1807	2007	2136	2207	2336
		◧ d	|	|	|	|	|	|	|	▬	|	▬
Limburg (Lahn) .. d.	0645	0745	0808	1008	1208	1408	1608	1808	2008	2045	2208	2245
Diez .... d.	0649	0749	0812	1012	1212	1412	1612	1812	2012	2049	2212	2249
Nassau (Lahn) .... d.	0715	0815	0832	1032	1232	1432	1632	1832	2032	2115	2232	2315
Bad Ems .... d.	0725	0825	0839	1039	1239	1439	1639	1839	2039	2125	2239	2325
Niederlahnstein ... d.	0743	0843	0852	1052	1252	1452	1652	1852	2052	2143	2252	2343
Koblenz Hbf ...... a.	0750	0852	0859	1059	1259	1459	1659	1859	2059	2150	2259	2352

⊠	Ⓐ										
Koblenz Hbf .... d.	0509	0658	0858	1058	1258	1458	1658	1858	1909	2109	2209
Niederlahnstein .... d.	0516	0704	0904	1104	1304	1504	1704	1904	1916	2116	2216
Bad Ems .... d.	0533	0718	0918	1118	1318	1518	1718	1918	1933	2133	2233
Nassau (Lahn) ...... d.	0543	0726	0926	1126	1326	1526	1726	1926	1943	2143	2243
Diez .... d.	0609	0746	0946	1146	1346	1546	1746	1946	2009	2209	2309
Limburg (Lahn) .... a.	0613	0749	0949	1149	1349	1549	1749	1949	2013	2213	2313
	◧	|	|	|	|	|	|	|	◧	▬	▬
	Ⓐ									Ⓐ	Ⓒ
Limburg (Lahn) .... d.	0618	0750	0950	1150	1350	1550	1750	1950	2023	2123	2223
Weilburg .... d.	0655	0816	1016	1216	1416	1616	1816	2016	2100	2200	2300
Wetzlar .... **807** d.	0720	0833	1033	1233	1433	1633	1833	2033	2126	2226	2326
Gießen .... **807** a.	0731	0842	1042	1242	1442	1642	1842	2043	2138	2238	2338

Limburg - Niedernhausen - Frankfurt and Wiesbaden

	⚒	Ⓐ	Ⓐ	⑥	Ⓐ	Ⓒ	Ⓐ	Ⓐ	Ⓐ	⚒	†	Ⓐ		⚒	†		⚒	†		⚒	†	Ⓐ		⚒	†
Limburg (Lahn) .... d.	0418	0448	0518	0518	0555	0618	0625	0638	0655	0718	0718	0755	0818	0918	0918	1018	1118	1118	1218	1318	1318	1355	1418	1518	1518
Bad Camberg .... d.	0442	0512	0542	0542	0614	0642	0644	0703	0714	0742	0742	0814	0842	0942	0942	1042	1142	1142	1242	1342	1342	1414	1442	1542	1542
Idstein .... d.	0451	0521	0551	0551	0621	0651	0651	0713	0721	0751	0751	0821	0851	0951	0951	1051	1151	1151	1251	1351	1351	1421	1451	1551	1551
Niedernhausen .... ‡ a.	0457	0527	0557	0559	0627	0657	0657	0722	0727	0757	0759	0827	0857	0957	0959	1057	1157	1159	1257	1357	1359	1427	1457	1557	1559
Wiesbaden Hbf ..... a.	|	*0555*	*0625*	0625	*0655*	*0725*k	|	0744	|	*0827*	0825	*0857*	*0925*	*1025*	1025	*1125*	*1225*	1225	*1325*	*1427*	1425	*1457*	*1527*	*1627*	1625
Frankfurt (Main) Hbf ‡ a.	0528	0557	0628	...	0658	0728	0729	...	0758	0828	...	0858	0928	1028	...	1128	1228	...	1328	1428	...	1458	1528	1632	...

	Ⓐ		Ⓐ	⚒	†	Ⓐ		⚒	†			
urg (Lahn) .... d.	1555	1618	1655	1718	1718	1755	1818	1918	1918	2018	2118	2218
amberg .... d.	1614	1642	1714	1742	1742	1814	1842	1942	1942	2042	2142	2242
n .... d.	1621	1651	1721	1751	1751	1821	1851	1951	1951	2051	2152	2252
rnhausen .... ‡ a.	1627	1657	1727	1757	1759	1827	1857	1957	1959	2057	2158	2258
esbaden Hbf ...... a.	*1657*	*1727*	*1757*	*1827*	1825	*1857*	*1927*	*2027*	2025	*2125*	2225	*2325*
kfurt (Main) Hbf ‡ a.	1658	1728	1758	1828	...	1858	1928	2028	...	2128	...	2333

		Ⓐ	Ⓒ	Ⓐ	Ⓐ	Ⓒ	Ⓐ		⚒	†
Frankfurt (M) Hbf . ‡ d.	...	0601	0631	0643	0731	...	...	0834	0931	...
Wiesbaden Hbf .. d.	0531v	*0601*	*0636*k	*0650*	*0720*	0736k	0806	*0836*	*0936*	0936
Niedernhausen ..... ‡ d.	0601	0631	0701	0718	0801	0801	0831	0903	1001	1001
Idstein .... d.	0608	0638	0708	0725	0808	0808	0838	0910	1008	1008
Bad Camberg .... d.	0617	0647	0717	0734	0817	0817	0847	0919	1017	1017
Limburg (Lahn) ...... a.	0641	0711	0741	0801	0841	0841	0910	0942	1041	1041

		⚒	†		⚒	†		Ⓐ		Ⓐ	Ⓒ	Ⓐ	Ⓐ	⚒	†	Ⓐ		Ⓐ	⚒	†		Ⓐ	Ⓒ			
kfurt (Main) Hbf ‡ d.	1031	1131	...	1234	1331	...	1431	1501	1530k	1601	1634	...	1701	1731	...	1801	1831	1901	1930	...	2031	2131	...	2231	...	0028
esbaden Hbf ...... d.	*1036*	*1136*	1136	*1236*	*1336*	1336	*1436*	*1506*	1536b	*1606*	*1636*	1636	*1706*	*1736*	1736	*1806*	*1836*	*1906*	*1936*	1936	*2036*	*2136*	2136	*2236*	2336	|
rnhausen .... ‡ d.	1101	1201	1201	1303	1401	1401	1501	1531	1601	1631	1703	1701	1731	1801	1801	1831	1901	1931	2001	2001	2101	2201	2201	2301	0001	0101
n .... d.	1108	1208	1208	1310	1408	1408	1508	1538	1608	1638	1710	1708	1738	1808	1808	1838	1908	1938	2008	2008	2108	2208	2208	2308	0008	0108
Camberg .... d.	1117	1217	1217	1319	1417	1417	1517	1545	1617	1645	1719	1717	1745	1817	1817	1845	1917	1945	2017	2017	2117	2217	2217	2317	0017	0117
urg (Lahn) .... a.	1141	1241	1241	1342	1441	1441	1541	1604	1641	1704	1742	1741	1804	1841	1841	1904	1941	2004	2041	2041	2141	2241	2241	2341	0041	0141

Change trains at Niedernhausen on ⑥.
Daily.
⑥ only.
⚒ only. 0536 on ⑥.

◧ – Change trains at Limburg.
★ – Hessische Landesbahn.
⊠ – Additional stopping trains operate.

‡ – **Additional S-Bahn** *S2* **services** Frankfurt - Niedernhausen and v.v. Journey: 35 minutes. Subject to alteration July 16 - Aug. 25.
From Frankfurt (Main) Hbf: On ⚒ every 30 minutes 0452 – 2352; on † at 0452, 0521, 0552, 0621, 0652, 0721, 0752, 0822, 0852 and every 30 minutes 2352.
From Niedernhausen: On ⚒ every 30 minutes 0433 – 2333; on † at 0433, 0533, 0603, 0633 and every 30 minutes until 2333.

GIESSEN - FULDA 907

sische Landesbahn

	Ⓐ	Ⓐ	⑥	Ⓐ	⚒	⑥	Ⓐ		D		D		Ⓐ	C		Ⓐ	Ⓒ		Ⓐ	Ⓒ		†	Ⓐ		
Gießen .... d.	...	0524	...	0617	...	0744	0747	0844	0947	1044	1147	1241	1346	1347	1444	1544	1547	1644	1744	1747	1844	1947	1947	2047	2209
Grünberg (Oberhess). d.	...	0549	...	0709	...	0811	0817	0911	1013	1111	1213	1311	1411	1413	1511	1611	1613	1711	1811	1813	1911	2013	2016	2114n	2237
Alsfeld (Oberhess) ..... d.	0515	0633	0649	0749	0749	0849	0849	0949	1049	1149	1249	1349	1449	1449	1549	1649	1649	1749	1849	1849	1949	2049	2053	2149n	2311
Lauterbach (Hess) ..... d.	0529	0649	0703	0803	0803	0903	0903	1003	1103	1203	1303	1403	1503	1503	1603	1703	1703	1803	1903	1903	2003	...	...	...	...
Fulda .... a.	0602	0719	0729	0829	0829	0929	0929	1029	1129	1229	1329	1429	1529	1529	1629	1729	1729	1829	1929	1929	2029	...	...	...	...

	Ⓐ	Ⓐ	⑥	Ⓐ	⑥	Ⓐ	Ⓐ	⑥		D		C	Ⓐ		C	Ⓐ		Ⓒ	Ⓐ		Ⓒ	Ⓐ		Ⓐ		
a .... d.	...	...	...	0535	...	0610	0653	0735	0835	0935	1035	1135	1135	1235	1335	1335	1435	1535	1535	1635	1735	1735	1835	1935	2035	2135
erbach (Hess) ...... d.	...	...	...	0612j	...	0654j	0723	0805	0905	1005	1105	1205	1205	1305	1405	1405	1505	1605	1605	1705	1805	1805	1905	2005	2100	2200
ld (Oberhess) ...... d.	0415	0532	0616	0631	0712	0719j	0757j	0819	0919	1019	1119	1219	1219	1319	1419	1419	1519	1619	1619	1719	1819	1819	1919	2019	2113	2213
berg (Oberhess) .. d.	0456	0614	0651	0705	0747	0753	0838	0850	0953	1050	1153	1250	1253	1353	1450	1453	1553	1650	1653	1753	1850	1853	1953	2058	...	...
en .... a.	0521	0640	0716	0729	0816	0818	0906	0915	1018	1115	1218	1315	1315	1418	1515	1515	1618	1715	1715	1818	1915	1915	2018	2120	...	...

Ⓒ to Nov. 5; ⑥ from Nov. 12.
D – Daily to Nov. 5; ①–⑥ from Nov. 7.
j – Arrives 10 – 12 minutes earlier.
n – On Ⓐ Grünberg d. 2117, Alsfeld a. 2202.

GÖTTINGEN - BEBRA 908

NTUS Verkehrsgesellschaft (2nd class only)

	Ⓐ	⑥	Ⓐ	ⒶF	ⒸF	Ⓒ	⚒		Ⓐ						Ⓐ	Ⓒ	Ⓐ	Ⓒ	Ⓐ	Ⓐ	Ⓒ		Ⓑ	⑥
Göttingen .... **864** d.	0442	0543	0600	0703	0703	...	0814	0914	1040	1114	1240	1314	1440	1514	1614	1640	1714	1714	1814	1914	1914	2014	2214	2219
Eichenberg .... **864** d.	0458	0558	0618	0718	0719	...	0830	0930	1054	1130	1254	1330	1454	1530	1630	1654	1730	1730	1830	1930	1930	2030	2229	2235
Bad Sooden Allendorf . d.	0509	0608	0628	0728	0729	...	0840	0940	1105	1140	1305	1340	1505	1540	1640	1705	1740	1740	1840	1940	1940	2040	2239	2244
Eschwege .... a.	0520	0619	0639	0739	0741	...	0852	0952	1116	1152	1316	1352	1516	1552	1651	1716	1751	1751	1851	1952	1952	2051	2250	2255
Eschwege .... d.	0525	0624	0644	0746	0746	0821	0921	1018	1121	1218	1321	1418	1521	1618	1656	1721	1756	1818	1856	1957	2018	2056	2256	2300
Bebra .... a.	0553	0652	0711	0814	0814	0849	0949	1047	1149	1247	1349	1447	1549	1647	1724	1751	1824	1847	1924	2027	2047	2124	2324	2328

	Ⓐ	Ⓐ	⑥	Ⓐ	G	⚒	Ⓐ	Ⓒ	Ⓐ							Ⓐ	Ⓒ		Ⓐ					ⒸF	ⒶF
ra .... d.	0404	0523	0622	0633	0731	0832	0905	0932	1003	1105	1203	1305	1403	1505	1603	1705	1705	...	1803	1905	2003	2103	...	2303	2303
wege .... a.	0433	0553	0650	0700	0800	0900	0934	1000	1031	1134	1231	1334	1431	1534	1631	1734	1734	...	1831	1934	2031	2131	...	2331	2331
wege .... d.	0438	0558	0655	0705	0805	0905	1005	1005	1036	1205	1236	1405	1436	1605	1636	1739	1805	1805	1836	2005	2036	2136	...	2336	2336
Sooden Allendorf . d.	0450	0609	0707	0716	0816	0916	1016	1016	1047	1216	1247	1416	1447	1616	1647	1750	1816	1816	1847	2016	2047	2147	...	2347	2347
enberg .... **864** d.	0502	0624	0722	0732	0832	0932	1032	1032	1100	1232	1301	1432	1500	1632	1700	1806	1832	1832	1900	2032	2100	2200	...	0003	0003
ingen .... **864** a.	0515	0637	0735	0745	0845	0945	1045	1045	1113	1245	1314	1445	1513	1645	1713	1820	1845	1845	1913	2045	2113	2215	...	0016	0018

To / from Fulda (Table **901**).
G – From Fulda (Table **901**) on Ⓒ.

WÜRZBURG - BAD KISSINGEN - GEMÜNDEN 909

(*RB* services); EB ★

	⚒r						Ⓒz	Ⓐe																
Würzburg Hbf .... **870 876** ‡ d.	...	*0454*r	*0738*	0801	*0835*	*0935*	1001	*1135*	*1135*	1201	*1338*	1401	*1435*	*1538*	1601	*1636*	*1738*	1801	*1836*	*1938*	2001	*2035*	*2139*	*2236*
Schweinfurt Hbf. **870 876** ‡ d.	0450e	0611	0811	0830	0911	1011	1030	1205	1205	1230	1411	1430	1511	1612	1630	1711	1811	1830	1911	2012	2030	2111	2214	2347
Ebenhausen (Unterf) ... **870** ‡ d.	0511e	0625	0825	0843	0930	1025	1043	1224	1224	1243	1425	1443	1530	1625	1643	1730	1825	1843	1930	2025	2043	2130	2228	0003
Bad Kissingen .... a.	0520e	0634	0834	0853	0939	1034	1053	1233	1233	1253	1434	1453	1539	1634	1653	1739	1834	1853	1939	2034	2053	2139	2237	0012
Bad Kissingen .... d.	0540	0640	0839	...	...	1039	...	1239	1239	*1327*e	1439	...	1544e	1639	...	1744e	1839	...	1944	2047	...	2144	...	...
Hammelburg .... d.	0607	0707	0908	...	...	1106	...	1308	1313	*1400*e	1506	...	1608e	1706	...	1808e	1906	...	2007	2114	...	2212	...	...
Gemünden (Main) .... a.	0639	0741	0942	...	...	1141	...	1341	1350	*1441*e	1541	...	1641e	1741	...	1841e	1941	...	2039	2151	...	...	...	...

	Ⓐe		Ⓒz	Ⓐe	Ⓐe							Ⓒz	Ⓐe												
ünden (Main) .... d.	...	...	...	0607	...	0707r	...	0812	...	1012	...	1212	1212	*1320*e	1412	1507e	...	1609	1707e	...	1809	1907e	...	2115	2210
melburg .... d.	0546	*0616*e	0645	0645	0715	0746r	...	0844	...	1044	...	1244	1244	*1358*e	1444	1543e	...	1644	1743e	...	1844	1943e	...	2151	2247
Kissingen .... a.	0609	*0638*e	0708	0708	0738	0808r	...	0907	...	1107	...	1307	1307	*1420*e	1507	1610e	...	1707	1809e	...	1907	2009e	...	2213	2309
Kissingen .... d.	0614	0644	0720	...	0746	0814	0901	0919	1101	1119	1301	1319	1334	1501	1519	1615	1701	1719	1814	1901	1919	2014	2101	2218	*2314*
hausen (Unterf) ..... **870** a.	0623	0653	0729	...	0755	0823	0910	0928	1110	1128	1310	1328	1343	1510	1528	1624	1710	1728	1823	1910	1928	2023	2110	2227	*2323*
weinfurt Hbf .... **870 876** a.	0637	0714	0743	...	0809	0841	0926	0943	1125	1144	1325	1343	1357	1526	1543	1640	1726	1743	1840	1926	1943	2040	2126	2240	*2336*
zburg Hbf .... **870 876** a.	*0718*	0744	*0820*	...	*0851*	*0922*	0955	*1020*	1155	*1220*	1355	*1420*	*1451*	1555	*1620*	*1722*	1755	*1820*	*1921*	1955	*2020*	*2122*	2157	...	*0016*v

Ⓐ (not Aug. 15, Nov. 1).
⚒ (not Aug. 15, Nov. 1).
Not Nov. 1.
Change trains at Schweinfurt.
Ⓒ (also Aug. 15, Nov. 1).

★ – Erfurter Bahn (2nd class only).
‡ – Trains between Würzburg, Schweinfurt and Ebenhausen are often combined with a service to Meiningen or Erfurt. Passengers should take care to join the correct portion for their destination.

☛ **Additional journeys** Schweinfurt - Bad Kissingen and v.v.:
From Schweinfurt at 0530, 0703 Ⓐ**e**, 0716 Ⓒ**z**, 0737 Ⓐ**e**, 1111, 1303 Ⓐ**e**, 1311 Ⓒ**z**, 1330 Ⓐ**e**, 1545 Ⓐ**e** and 1745 Ⓐ**e**.
From Bad Kissingen at 0459 Ⓐ**t**, 0528 Ⓐ**e**, 0703 Ⓐ**e**, 1014, 1214, 1414, 1548 Ⓐ**e** and 1747 Ⓐ**e**.

910 AACHEN - KÖLN - FRANKFURT via high-speed line

See Tables **800**/**911** for services via Bonn and Koblenz. See Table **20** for *Thalys* services Paris - Brussels - Aachen - Köln.
Services from Amsterdam are subject to alteration July 9–24.

km		*ICE* 827	*ICE* 827 Ⓐ		*ICE* 521 🍷	*ICE* 523 ⚒ 🍷	*ICE* 511 ①g 🍷	*ICE* 511 🍷	*ICE* 711 Ⓐ ✕	*ICE* 811 Ⓐ 🍷	*ICE* 1125 † 🍷	*ICE* 525 ⚒ 🍷	*ICE* 101 🍷	*ICE* 713 ⚒d 🍷	*ICE* 813 Ⓐ 🍷	*ICE* 1127 ⑥ G🍷	*ICE* 527 Ⓐ 🍷	*ICE* 513 M🍷	*ICE* 11 ⚒ 🍷	*ICE* 11 † 🍷	*ICE* 815 Ⓐ ✕	*ICE* 529 🍷	*ICE* 103 H🍷
	Dortmund Hbf **800** d.	...	...	...	...	0406	0437	...	...	...	0514	0524	0537v	0552	0600t	0614	0624	0637	...	...	0652	0724	0737
	Essen Hbf **800** d.	...	...	...	...	0428	│	...	...	...	0538	0553	│	0615	│	0639	0653	0700	...	...	0715	0754	│
	Amsterdam Centraal **28** d.	...	...	...	...	│	│	...	...	...	│	│	│	│	│	│	│	│	...	...	│	│	│
	Düsseldorf Hbf **800** d.	...	...	...	...	0455	◐	...	...	...	0605	0621	◐	0648	◐	0707	0721	0727	...	...	0747	0822	◐
	Brussels Midi/Zuid **21** d.	...	...	...	...	│	│	...	...	...	│	│	│	│	│	│	│	│	0625	0625	│	│	│
	Aachen Hbf **802 807** d.	...	...	...	...	│	│	...	...	...	│	│	│	│	│	│	│	│	0740	0740	│	│	│
	Köln Hbf **800 802 807** a.	...	...	...	...	│	0546	...	...	...	│	│	0646	│	0709	│	│	0749	0815	0815	│	│	0846n
0	**Köln** Hbf **802 807** d.	0317	0317	...	0418	│	0555	0555	0611	0620	│	│	0655	│	0720	│	│	0755	0827	0820	│	│	0855n
1	**Köln** Messe/Deutz **802** d.	│	│	...	│	0518	│	│	│	│	0628	0644	│	0713	│	0730	0744	│	│	│	0811	0844	0856z
	Köln/Bonn Flughafen ✈ **802** d.	0329	0329	...	│	0531	│	│	│	│	│	│	│	│	│	│	│	│	│	│	0822	│	│
25	Siegburg/Bonn 🚋 **807** d.	0340	0340	...	0433	0542	0610	0610	0626	0636	0642	│	0710	│	0736	0744	│	0810	│	0836	0832	│	0910
88	Montabaur d.	0402	0402	...	0453	0602	│	│	0646	0656	0702	│	│	│	0756	0804	│	│	│	0856	0857	│	│
110	Limburg Süd d.	0414	0414	...	0504	0613	│	│	0657	0707	0713	│	│	│	0807	0815	│	│	│	0907	0908	│	│
	Wiesbaden Hbf a.	│	│	...	│	│	│	│	0719	│	│	│	│	│	│	│	│	│	│	│	│	│	│
	Mainz Hbf a.	│	│	...	│	│	│	│	0744	│	│	│	│	│	│	│	│	│	│	│	│	│	│
169	**Frankfurt** Flughafen Fernbf ✈ a.	0435	0435	...	0527	0633	0649	0649	│	0726	0733	0733	0749	0804	0826	0834	0833	0849	0916	0926	0926	0933	0949
180	**Frankfurt** (Main) Hbf a.	0448	0448	...	0544	0648	│	│	│	0741	0748	0748	│	│	0841	0848	0848	│	0930	0941	0941	0948	│
	Nürnberg Hbf **920** a.	...	0659	...	0759	0859	│	│	│	...	0959	0959	│	│	...	1059	1059	│	...	...	...	1159	│
	Mannheim Hbf **912** ⊖ a.	...	│	...	│	│	0723	0723	0824	...	│	│	0823	0840	...	│	│	0923	...	...	...	│	1023
	Karlsruhe Hbf **912** ⊖ a.	...	│	...	│	│	│	│	│	...	│	│	0858	│	...	│	│	│	...	...	...	│	1058
	Basel SBB **912** a.	...	│	...	│	│	│	│	│	...	│	│	1047	│	...	│	│	│	...	...	...	│	1247
	Stuttgart Hbf **912** ⊠ a.	...	│	...	│	│	0808	0808	0928	...	│	│	...	0924	...	│	│	1008	...	...	...	│	...
	München Hbf **904 930** ⊠ a.	...	0807	...	0904	1004	1027	1027	...	...	1104	1104	...	...	...	1204	1204	1227	...	...	...	1304	...

	ICE 621 🍷	*ICE* 515 🍷	*ICE* 623 🍷	*ICE* 105 🍷	*ICE* 505 🍷	*ICE* 625 🍷	*ICE* 517 🍷	*ICE* 15 🍷	*ICE* 627 🍷	*ICE* 107 †n 🍷	*ICE* 107 🍷	*ICE* 123 🍷	*ICE* 629 🍷	*ICE* 519 🍷	*ICE* 721 🍷	*ICE* 109 Ⓑn 🍷	*ICE* 109 🍷	*ICE* 717 ⑦w d🍷	*ICE* 717 Ⓑq d🍷	*ICE* 817 Ⓒj 🍷	*ICE* 817 Ⓐf 🍷	*ICE* 125 🍷	*ICE* 723 Ⓑq 🍷
Dortmund Hbf **800** d.	0815c	0837n	0916c	...	...	1016c	1037n	...	1124c	1137	...	...	...	1237n	1324y	1337	...	1354	...	...	...	...	1424r
Essen Hbf **800** d.	0840	│	0941	...	...	1040	1100n	...	1153c	│	...	...	...	1300n	1353	│	...	1417	...	...	...	...	1453
Amsterdam Centraal **28** d.	│	│	│	0805	...	│	│	...	│	│	...	1035	...	│	│	│	...	│	...	...	...	1235	│
Düsseldorf Hbf **800** d.	0913	◐	1012	1022	...	1108	1127n	...	1221	◐	...	1248	1308	1327n	1421	◐	...	1450	1450	...	...	1454	1521
Brussels Midi/Zuid **21** d.	│	│	│	│	...	│	│	1025	│	│	...	│	│	│	│	│	...	│	│	...	...	│	│
Aachen Hbf **802 807** d.	│	│	│	│	...	│	│	1139	│	│	...	│	│	│	│	│	...	│	│	...	...	│	│
Köln Hbf **800 802 807** a.	│	0946n	│	1046	...	│	1149n	1215	│	1246	...	1315	│	1349n	│	1446	...	│	│	...	...	1518	│
Köln Hbf **802 807** d.	│	0955	│	1055	1055	│	1155	1218	│	1255	1255	1328	│	1355	│	1455	1455	│	│	1458	1501	1529	│
Köln Messe/Deutz **802** d.	0936	│	1033	│	│	1130	│	│	1244	│	│	│	1333	│	1444	│	│	1514	1514	│	│	│	1544
Köln/Bonn Flughafen ✈ **802** d.	│	│	1045	│	│	│	│	1231	│	│	│	│	│	│	│	│	│	│	│	│	│	│	│
Siegburg/Bonn 🚋 **807** d.	│	1010	│	1110	1110	1145	1210	│	│	1310	1310	│	1347	1410	│	1510	1510	│	│	1517	1517	│	│
Montabaur d.	1005	│	│	│	│	1205	│	│	│	│	│	│	1407	│	│	│	│	│	│	1542	1542	│	│
Limburg Süd d.	1015	│	│	│	│	1216	│	│	│	│	│	│	1418	│	│	│	│	│	│	1553	1553	│	│
Wiesbaden Hbf a.	│	│	│	│	│	│	│	│	│	│	│	│	│	│	│	│	│	│	│	│	│	│	│
Mainz Hbf a.	│	│	│	│	│	│	│	│	│	│	│	│	│	│	│	│	│	│	│	│	│	│	│
Frankfurt Flughafen Fernbf ✈ a.	1034	1049	1133	1149	1149	1234	1249	1316	1330	1349	1349	1416	1436	1449	1533	1549	1549	1604	1604	1612	1612	1616	1633
Frankfurt (Main) Hbf a.	1048	│	1148	│	│	1248	│	1330	1344	│	│	1430	1449	│	1548	│	│	│	│	1625	1625	1630	1648
Nürnberg Hbf **920** a.	1259	│	1403	│	│	1459	│		1559	│	│	...	1659	│	1759	│	│	│	│	...	...	...	1859
Mannheim Hbf **912** ⊖ a.	│	1123	│	1223	1223	│	1323	...	│	1423	1423	...	│	1523	│	1623	1623	1638‡	1638‡	...	...	...	│
Karlsruhe Hbf **912** ⊖ a.	│	│	│	1258	1258	│	│	...	│	1456	1456	...	│	│	│	1658	1658	│	│	...	...	...	│
Basel SBB **912** a.	│	│	│	1447	1447	│	│	...	│	1647	1647	...	│	│	│	1847	1847	│	│	...	...	...	│
Stuttgart Hbf **912** ⊠ a.	│	1208	│	...	...	│	1408	...	│	...	...	...	│	1608	│	...	...	1718‡	1718‡	...	...	...	│
München Hbf **904 930** ⊠ a.	1404	1427	1508	...	...	1606	1627	...	1704	...	...	...	1804	1827	1907	...	...	...	...	...	...	...	2004

	ICE 17 Ⓐ 🍷	*ICE* 17 Ⓒ 🍷	*ICE* 725 🍷	*ICE* 913 Ⓐ ✕	*ICE* 201 🍷	*ICE* 917 Ⓑq ✕	*ICE* 127 T 🍷	*ICE* 1228 Ⓐ L🍷	*ICE* 727 Ⓑq 🍷	*ICE* 613 🍷	*ICE* 819 🍷	*ICE* 729 🍷	*ICE* 1103 † 🍷	*ICE* 203 ⚒ 🍷	*ICE* 129 🍷	*ICE* 821 Ⓑq N🍷	*ICE* 821 Q 🍷	*ICE* 615 🍷	*ICE* 19 🍷	*ICE* 605 🍷	*ICE* 605 R 🍷	*ICE* 221 🍷	
Dortmund Hbf **800** d.	...	...	1524k	...	...	1556	...	1616	...	1637n	...	1724k	...	...	...	...	...	1837n	...	1924k	...	...	...
Essen Hbf **800** d.	...	...	1554	...	...	1617	...	1640	1653	1700n	...	1754	...	...	...	...	...	1900n	...	1950	1950	...	...
Amsterdam Centraal **28** d.	...	...	│	...	...	│	1435	│	│	│	...	│	...	...	1635	...	...	│	...	│	│	1835	...
Düsseldorf Hbf **800** d.	...	...	1622	...	...	1648	1653	1708	1721	1727n	...	1822	...	...	1848	1908	1908	1927n	...	2018	2018	2048	...
Brussels Midi/Zuid **21** d.	1425	1425	│	...	...	│	│	│	│	│	...	│	...	...	│	│	│	│	1825	│	│	│	...
Aachen Hbf **802 807** d.	1539	1539	│	...	...	│	│	│	│	│	...	│	...	...	│	│	│	│	1939	│	│	│	...
Köln Hbf **800 802 807** a.	1615	1615	│	...	...	│	1718	│	│	1749n	...	│	...	...	1912	│	│	1949n	2015	2041	2041	2112	...
Köln Hbf **802 807** d.	1620	1620	│	1628	1655	│	1728	│	│	1755	1819	│	1855	1855	1921	│	│	1957	2028	2046	2046	2128	...
Köln Messe/Deutz **802** d.	│	│	1644	│	│	1713	│	1733	1744	│	│	1844	│	│	│	1930	1930	│	│	│	│	│	...
Köln/Bonn Flughafen ✈ **802** d.	│	│	│	│	│	│	│	│	│	│	│	│	│	│	│	│	│	│	│	│	│	│	...
Siegburg/Bonn 🚋 **807** d.	│	1636	│	1644	1710	│	│	1747	│	1810	1836	│	1910	1910	│	1944	1944	2012	│	2101	2101	│	...
Montabaur d.	│	1656	│	1704	│	│	│	1807	│	│	1856	│	│	│	│	2004	2004	│	│	2121	2121	│	...
Limburg Süd d.	│	1707	│	1719	│	│	│	1820	│	│	1907	│	│	│	│	2015	2015	│	│	2132	2132	│	...
Wiesbaden Hbf a.	│	│	│	│	│	│	│	1841	│	│	│	│	│	│	│	│	│	│	│	│	│	│	...
Mainz Hbf a.	│	│	│	│	│	│	│	1854	│	│	│	│	│	│	│	│	│	│	│	│	│	│	...
Frankfurt Flughafen Fernbf ✈ a.	1709	1726	1734	1740	1749	1804	1816	1915	1834	1849	1926	1933	1949	1949	2010	2034	2034	2049	2116	2151	2151	2216	...
Frankfurt (Main) Hbf a.	1730	1741	1748	1756	│	│	1830	1933	1848	│	1941	1948	│	│	2025	2048	2048	│	2130	│	│	2230	...
Nürnberg Hbf **920** a.	...	...	1959	...	│	│	...	...	2059	│	...	2159	│	│	...	...	2259	│	...	│	│	...	...
Mannheim Hbf **912** ⊖ a.	...	...	│	...	1823	1838⁝	...	...	│	1923	...	│	2023	2023	...	...	│	2123	...	2224	2224	...	...
Karlsruhe Hbf **912** ⊖ a.	...	...	│	...	1858	│	...	...	│	│	...	│	2100	2100	...	...	│	│	...	2300	2300	...	...
Basel SBB **912** a.	...	...	│	...	2047	│	...	...	│	│	...	│	2250	2300a	...	...	│	│	...	...	0056b	...	...
Stuttgart Hbf **912** ⊠ a.	...	...	│	...	...	1924⁝	...	...	│	2008	...	│	...	...	...	...	│	2208	...	...	...	...	...
München Hbf **904 930** ⊠ a.	...	...	2109p	...	...	...	...	...	2205	2226	...	2307	...	...	...	...	0007	0027	...	...	...	...	...

G – ⑥ (also Oct. 2). To Garmisch on ⑥ (Table **895**).
H – From Hannover (Table **810**).
L – 🚲12 and 🍷 Kassel - Paderborn - Dortmund - Mainz - Frankfurt.
M – From Münster (Table **800**).
N – 🚲12 and 🍷 Oberhausen (Table **800**) - Würzburg (Table **920**).
Q – ④⑤⑦ (also Oct. 3; not Oct. 2). From Oberhausen (Table **800**).
R – ①②③④⑦ (not Oct. 2).
T – Daily to Oct. 30; ⑤ from Nov. 4. On ⑥ (also Oct. 2) Düsseldorf d. 1648, Köln a. 1712.

a – Ⓐ only.
b – Basel **Badischer Bahnhof**.
c – Ⓒ only.
d – Not July 16–20.
f – Not Nov. 1.
g – Also Oct. 4; not July 11 - Aug. 15, Oct. 3.
j – Also Nov. 1.
k – ⑥ (also Oct. 2).
n – Not July 9 - Aug. 21.
p – 2105 from Sept. 4.

q – Not Oct. 2.
r – Not ⑤.
t – 0535 July 11 - Aug. 19.
v – 0514 July 9 - Aug. 21.
w – Also Oct. 3; not Oct. 2.
y – ⑤–⑦ (also Oct. 3).
z – July 9 - Aug. 21 only.

‡ – July 21 - Aug. 28 arrives Mannheim 1704, Stuttgart 1750.
⁝ – 22–28 minutes later July 17 - Aug. 28.
❖ – Starts from Oberhausen July 9–25.
◐ – Via Wuppertal (Table **800**).
⊠ – Timings at Stuttgart are subject to alteration until Aug. 28. Timings at München (services via Stuttgart) are subject to alterat[ion] until Sept. 11. See shaded panel on page 367 for further details.
⊖ – Timings at Mannheim and Karlsruhe may vary by up to 10 minute[s] July 16 - Aug. 28. See shaded panel on page 367 for further det[ails].

🚋 – Frequent light-rail services operate from / to Bonn Hbf.

FRANKFURT - KÖLN - AACHEN via high-speed line **910**

See Tables **800**/**911** for services via Koblenz and Bonn. See Table **20** for *Thalys* services Köln - Aachen - Brussels - Paris.
Services to Amsterdam are subject to alteration July 9 – 24.

	ICE 1018	ICE 618	ICE 716	ICE 18	ICE 616	ICE 1223	ICE 824	ICE 1223	ICE 220	ICE 604	ICE 822	ICE 818	ICE 614	ICE 820	ICE 128	ICE 916	ICE 202	ICE 202	ICE 728	ICE 16	ICE 16	ICE 612	ICE 726
	†❦	⚒◇	Ⓐ			Ⓐ	Ⓐ	Ⓐ			⚒			⚒		⚒		①–④		†	⚒		⚒
	🍷	🍷		🍷	🍷	D🍷	E🍷	D🍷	🍷	🍷	🍷	🍷	🍷	🍷	🍷	✕	🍷	m🍷	🍷	🍷	🍷	🍷	🍷
München Hbf **904 930** ⊠ d.	0001	0001	...	...	0323	...	...	...	...	...	0449	...	0524	0552	...	...	...	...	0652	...	...	0727	0755
Stuttgart Hbf **912** ⊠ d.	0230	0230	...	...	0551	...	...	...	...	...	|	...	0751	|	...	0836c	...	...	|	...	...	0951	|
Basel SBB **912** d.	|	|	...	...	|	...	...	...	...	0515b	|	...	|	|	...	|	0713e	0713	|	...	...	|	|
Karlsruhe Hbf **912** ⊖ d.	0349	0349	...	...	|	...	...	...	...	0700	|	...	|	|	...	|	0900	0900	|	...	...	|	|
Mannheim Hbf **912** ⊖ d.	0440	0440	...	...	0636	...	...	...	...	0736	|	...	0836	|	...	0921c	0936	0936	|	...	...	1036	|
Nürnberg Hbf **920** d.	|	|	...	...	|	...	...	...	...	|	0600	...	|	0700	...	|	|	|	0800	...	...	|	0900
Frankfurt (Main) Hbf d.	0544	0544	...	0629	|	...	0710	...	0727	|	0810	0816	|	0909	0929	|	|	|	1010	1016	1029	|	1110
Frankfurt Flughafen Fernbf ✈ d.	0601	0601	...	0643	0709	0714	0725	...	0743	0809	0825	0831	0909	0922	0943	0955	1009	1009	1025	1031	1043	1109	1122
Mainz Hbf d.	|	|	0607	|	|	|	|	...	|	|	|	|	|	|	|	|	|	|	|	|	|	|	|
Wiesbaden Hbf d.	|	|	0623	|	|	|	|	...	|	|	|	|	|	|	|	|	|	|	|	|	|	|	|
Limburg Süd d.	0620	0620	0644	|	|	0733	|	←	|	|	|	0850	|	0941	|	|	|	|	|	1050	|	|	1141
Montabaur d.	0631	0631	0656	|	|	0742	|	0749	|	|	|	0901	|	0952	|	|	|	|	|	1101	|	|	1152
Siegburg/Bonn 🚋 **807** d.	0651	0651	|	|	0749	→	|	0811	|	0849	|	0923	0949	1012	|	|	1049	1049	|	|	|	1149	1212
Köln/Bonn Flughafen ✈ **802** a.	|	|	|	0726	|	...	|	|	|	|	|	|	|	|	|	|	|	|	|	|	|	|	|
Köln Messe/Deutz **802** a.	|	|	|	|	|	...	0814	0823	|	|	0914	|	|	1025	|	1042	|	|	1114	|	|	|	1225
Köln Hbf **802 807** a.	0705	0705	0728	0739	0805	...	|	|	0832	0905	|	0939	1005	|	1032	|	1105	1105	|	1132	1132	1205	|
Köln Hbf **800 802 807** d.	0710	0713	...	0743	0810n	...	|	|	0844	...	|	0943w	1010n	|	1041	|	...	1110	|	1143	1143	1210n	|
Aachen Hbf **802 807** a.	|	|	...	0816	|	...	|	|	|	...	|	|	|	|	|	|	...	|	|	1216	1216	|	|
Brussels Midi/Zuid **21** a.	|	|	...	0935	|	...	|	|	|	...	|	|	|	|	|	|	...	|	|	1335	1335	|	|
Düsseldorf Hbf **800** a.	◐	0735	...	...	0831n	...	0836	0844	0911	...	0936	1005w	1031n	1048	1105	1109	...	◐	1136	...	...	1231n	1248
Amsterdam Centraal **28** a.	|	|	...	...	|	...	|	|	1127	...	|	...	|	...	1327	|	...	|	|	...	...	|	|
Essen Hbf **800** a.	|	0801	...	...	0857n	...	0902	0915	...	...	1002	...	1057n	...	...	1139v	...	|	1202	...	...	1257n	1315
Dortmund Hbf **800** a.	0821	0825k	...	...	0921n	...	...	0940	...	...	1029k	...	1121n	...	...	1203v	...	1221	1230	...	...	1321n	1342k

	ICE 126	ICE 714	ICE 200	ICE 200	ICE 724	ICE 610	ICE 722	ICE 1122	ICE 124	ICE 912	ICE 108	ICE 108	ICE 720	ICE 14	ICE 518	ICE 628	ICE 816	ICE 106	ICE 626	ICE 826	ICE 122	ICE 826	ICE 712	ICE 516
	T	⚒		⑥n			Ⓐ	Ⓒ		Ⓐ		⑥h								Ⓐ		Ⓐ	Ⓐ	
	🍷	♠🍷	🍷	🍷	🍷	🍷	🍷	🍷	🍷	✕	🍷	n🍷	🍷	🍷	🍷	🍷	🍷	🍷	🍷	🍷	🍷	🍷	✕	🍷
ünchen Hbf **904 930** ⊠ d.	...	...	...	...	0855	0928	0955	0955	...	...	...	...	1055	...	1128	1155	...	...	1255	1255	...	...		1328
Stuttgart Hbf **912** ⊠ d.	...	1041	...	...	|	1151	|	|	...	...	...	...	|	...	1351	|	...	...	|	|	...	...	1433	1551
Basel SBB **912** d.	...	|	0913	0913	|	|	|	|	...	...	1113	1113	|	...	|	|	...	1313	|	|	...	...	|	|
Karlsruhe Hbf **912** ⊖ d.	...	|	1100	1100	|	|	|	|	...	...	1300	1300	|	...	|	|	...	1500	|	|	...	...	|	|
Mannheim Hbf **912** ⊖ d.	...	1121	1136	1136	|	1236	|	|	...	...	1336	1336	|	...	1436	|	...	1536	|	|	...	...	1533	1636
ürnberg Hbf **920** d.	...	|	|	|	1000	|	1100	1100	...	...	|	|	1200	...	|	1300	...	|	1400	1400	...	...	|	|
nkfurt (Main) Hbf d.	1129	|	|	|	1210	|	1310	1310	1329	1335	|	|	1410	1429	|	1510	1517	|	1609	1609	1629	...	|	|
nkfurt Flughafen Fernbf ✈ d.	1143	1155	1209	1209	1225	1309	1325	1322	1343	1349	1409	1409	1425	1443	1509	1525	1531	1609	1625	1630	1643	...	|	1709
ainz Hbf d.	|	|	|	|	|	|	|	|	|	|	|	|	|	|	|	|	|	|	|	|	|	...	1622	|
iesbaden Hbf d.	|	|	|	|	|	|	|	|	|	|	|	|	|	|	|	|	|	|	|	|	|	...	1645	|
burg Süd d.	|	|	|	|	|	|	|	1341	|	1408	|	|	|	|	|	|	1550	|	|	1649	|	←	1707	|
ntabaur d.	|	|	|	|	|	|	|	1352	|	1419	|	|	|	|	|	|	1601	|	|	1658	|	1707	1718	|
gburg/Bonn 🚋 **807** d.	|	|	1249	1249	1303	1349	|	1412	|	1440	1449	1449	|	|	1549	|	1623	1649	|	→	|	1728	1738	1749
öln/Bonn Flughafen ✈ **802** a.	|	|	|	|	1312	|	|	|	|	|	|	|	|	|	|	|	|	|	|	...	|	|	1747	|
n Messe/Deutz **802** a.	|	1242	|	|	1324	|	1414	1425	|	|	|	|	1514	|	|	1614	|	|	1714	...	|	|	|	|
n Hbf **802 807** a.	1232	|	1305	1305	|	1405	|	|	1432	1456	1505	1505	|	1533	1605	|	1639	1705	|	...	1732y	1742f	1801	1805
n Hbf **800 802 807** d.	1241	|	...	1310	|	1410n	|	|	1446	...	...	1510	|	1542	1610n	|	...	1710n	|	...	1746	...	...	1810n
achen Hbf **802 807** a.	|	|	...	|	|	|	|	|	|	...	...	|	|	1616	|	|	...	|	|	...	|	...	...	|
russels Midi/Zuid **21** a.	|	|	...	|	|	|	|	|	|	...	...	|	|	1735	|	|	...	|	|	...	|	...	...	|
sseldorf Hbf **800** a.	1305	1309	...	◐	1346	1431n	1436	1446	1511	...	...	◐	1536	...	1631n	1639	...	◐	1736	...	1812	...	...	1831n
Amsterdam Centraal **28** a.	1527	|	...	|	|	|	|	|	1727	...	...	|	|	...	|	|	...	|	|	...	2027	...	...	|
ssen Hbf **800** a.	...	1339k	...	|	1415	1457n	1505	1515	...	...	...	|	1602	...	1657n	1707	...	|	1802h	...	...	...	...	1857n
ortmund Hbf **800** a.	...	1403k	...	1421	1442h	1521n	...	1542k	...	...	...	1621	1629h	...	1721n	1740h	...	1821n	1829h	...	...	...	...	1921n

	ICE 624	ICE 1124	ICE 814	ICE 504	ICE 104	ICE 622	ICE 812	ICE 10	ICE 812	ICE 514	ICE 620	ICE 120	ICE 710	ICE 710	ICE 102	ICE 1102	ICE 528	ICE 810	ICE 512	ICE 526	ICE 100	ICE 524	ICE 1110	ICE 522
	Ⓐ	Ⓒ	Ⓐ				Ⓑq		Ⓑq			Ⓑq	Ⓑq	⑦w	Ⓑq	⑥h				Ⓑq			⑦w	
	🍷	🍷	🍷	🍷	🍷	🍷	¶	🍷	¶	🍷	G🍷	🍷✣	♠🍷	♠🍷	H🍷	H🍷	🍷	🍷	M🍷	🍷	🍷	🍷	🍷	🍷
ünchen Hbf **904 930** ⊠ d.	1355	1355	...	...	...	1455	...	...	...	1528	1555	...	...	...	...	...	1652	...	1727	1755	...	1855	1928	1952
Stuttgart Hbf **912** ⊠ d.	|	|	...	...	...	|	...	...	...	1751	|	...	1836	1836	...	...	|	...	1951	|	...	|	2151	|
Basel SBB **912** d.	|	|	...	1513	1513	|	...	...	...	|	|	...	|	|	1713	1713	|	...	|	|	1913	|	|	|
Karlsruhe Hbf **912** ⊖ d.	|	|	...	1700	1700	|	...	...	...	|	|	...	|	|	1900	1900	|	...	|	|	2101	|	|	|
Mannheim Hbf **912** ⊖ d.	|	|	...	1736	1736	|	...	...	...	1836	|	...	1921	1921	1936	1936	|	...	2036	|	2136	|	2237	|
ürnberg Hbf **920** d.	1500	1500	...	|	|	1600	...	...	...	|	1700	...	|	|	|	|	1800	...	|	1901	|	2000	|	2100
nkfurt (Main) Hbf d.	1710	1710	1717	|	|	1810	1816	1829	...	|	1910	1929	|	|	|	|	2010	2029	|	2110	|	2210	|	2310
nkfurt Flughafen Fernbf ✈ d.	1725	1722	1731	1809	1809	1825	1831	1843	...	1909	1922	1943	1955	1955	2009	2009	2025	2042	2109	2125	2209	2225	2311	2325
ainz Hbf d.	|	|	|	|	|	|	|	|	...	|	|	|	|	|	|	|	|	|	|	|	|	|	|	|
iesbaden Hbf d.	|	|	|	|	|	|	|	|	...	|	|	|	|	|	|	|	|	|	|	|	|	|	|	|
burg Süd d.	|	1741	1750	|	|	|	1850	|	←	|	1941	|	|	|	|	|	|	2101	|	|	|	2244	|	2344
ntabaur d.	|	1752	1801	|	|	|	1859	|	1907	|	1952	|	|	|	|	|	|	2112	|	|	|	2255	|	2355
gburg/Bonn 🚋 **807** d.	|	1812	1823	1849	1849	|	→	1922	1929	1949	2012	|	|	|	2049	2049	|	2133	2149	|	2253	2320	2351	0020
öln/Bonn Flughafen ✈ **802** a.	|	|	|	|	|	|	...	|	1937	|	|	|	|	|	|	|	|	2141	|	|	|	2328	|	|
n Messe/Deutz **802** a.	1813	1826	|	|	|	1914	...	|	|	|	2025	|	2043	2043	2102z	|	2114	|	|	2214	|	2339	|	|
n Hbf **802 807** a.	|	|	1839	1905	1905	|	...	1939	1956	2005	|	2032	|	|	2105n	2105	|	2156	2205	|	2307	|	0007	0042
n Hbf **800 802 807** d.	|	|	...	...	1914	|	...	1943	...	2010r	|	2042	|	|	2110n	2110	|	...	2210	|	2316	|	...	0045
achen Hbf **802 807** a.	|	|	...	...	|	|	...	2016	...	|	|	|	|	|	|	|	|	...	|	|	|	|	...	|
russels Midi/Zuid **21** a.	|	|	...	...	|	|	...	2135	...	|	|	|	|	|	|	|	|	...	|	|	|	|	...	|
sseldorf Hbf **800** a.	1835	1848t	...	...	1936	1944	...	...	...	2031r	2048	2105	2109	2109	◐	2131	2136	...	2231	2236	2339	2400	...	0106
Amsterdam Centraal **28** a.	|	|	...	...	2156	|	...	...	...	|	|	2327	...	|	|	|	|	...	|	|	|	|	...	|
ssen Hbf **800** a.	1901	1915t	...	...	...	2015	...	...	...	2057r	2115	...	...	2139	|	2157	2202	...	2257	2302	0009	0026	...	0135
ortmund Hbf **800** a.	1930	1942t	...	...	...	2042	...	...	...	2121r	2142	...	...	2202	2221	2221	2230	...	...	2327	0033	0049	...	0158

- 12 and 🍷 Darmstadt Hbf (d. 0648) - Dortmund - Paderborn - Kassel.
- From Würzburg (Table **920**) on ①–④.
- From Garmisch on ⑥ (Table **895**).
- To Hannover (Table **810**).
- To Münster (Table **800**).
- Daily to Oct. 30; ⑤ from Nov. 4.
- Ⓐ only. Basel **Badischer Bahnhof**.
- July 16 - Aug. 27 departs Stuttgart 0810, Mannheim 0859.
- ⚒ only.
- 1745 July 11 - Aug. 19.
- ⑥ (also Oct. 2).
- ⑥ only.
- Not July 11 - Aug. 18, Oct. 3.
- Not July 9 - Aug. 21.
- Not Oct. 2.
- July 9 - Aug. 21 departs Köln 2013, arrives Düsseldorf 2035, Essen 2103, Dortmund 2136.
- July 9 - Aug. 21 arrives Düsseldorf 1852, Essen 1931, Dortmund 2002.

v – Not ⑤.
w – ⑦ (also Oct. 3; not Oct. 2).
y – 1739 on Ⓒ.
z – July 9 - Aug. 21 only.

¶ – ✕ on Ⓐ; 🍷 on ⑦.
✣ – Terminates at Köln July 8 – 24.
◐ – Via Wuppertal (Table **800**).
◇ – July 30 - Sept. 12 runs as *ICE* **1218** and departs München 2350 (the previous day).
❦ – July 31 - Sept. 11 runs as *ICE* **1118** and departs München 2350 (the previous day). July 10 - Aug. 21 departs Köln Hbf 0713, arrives Dortmund 0825 (not running via Wuppertal and calling additionally at Düsseldorf, a. 0736 and Essen, a. 0800).
♠ – Not July 16 – 20. July 21 - Aug. 28 departs Stuttgart and Mannheim 24 – 31 minutes **earlier**.
⊠ – Timings at Stuttgart are subject to alteration until Aug. 28. Timings at München (services via Stuttgart) are subject to alteration until Sept. 11. See shaded panel on page 367 for further details.
⊖ – Timings at Mannheim and Karlsruhe may vary by up to 10 minutes July 16 - Aug. 28. See shaded panel on page 367 for further details.

🚋 – Frequent light-rail services operate from / to Bonn Hbf.

Engineering work may affect services – see shaded panel on page 3

911 KOBLENZ - MAINZ - MANNHEIM and FRANKFURT

km		ICE 672	ICE 991	IC 2021	ICE 23	IC 2317	ICE 711	IC 2319	ICE 1597	ICE 1521	EC 115	EC 7	ICE 1559	IC 119	ICE 27	IC 2005	EC 9	ICE 1651	IC 2013	IC 2023	IC 2313	ICE 1653	IC 1911
		H ✕	Ⓐ ✕	◇	✕♦	⑥	Ⓐ ✕	⚒ 🍷	D🍷	✕	🍷♦	✕♦	D✕	♦	✕♦	⑤⑥ 🍷♦	Z✕	D✕	🍷♦	🍷	🍷	D✕	⑤⑦ m🍷
	Hamburg Hbf **800** d.	...	...	2246	...	...	...	...	...	...	...	0442e	...	...	0546	...	0646	...	...	0746	0845	...	...
	Dortmund Hbf **800** d.	...	...	0144	0437	...	...	0537	...	0636n	...	0737	...	...	0838	...	0937	...	0952	1036	1137	...	1152
	Köln Hbf **800** d.	...	...	0353	0553	...	0611	0653	...	0753	0818	0853	...	0918	0953	1018	1053	...	1118	1153	1253	...	1318
	Bonn Hbf **800** d.	...	...	0416	0614	...	|	0714	...	0814	0837	0914	...	0937	1014	1037	1114	...	1137	1214	1314	...	1337
0	**Koblenz** Hbf **914** d.	...	...	0531	0648	...	|	0748	...	0848	0917	0948	...	1017	1048	1117	1148	...	1217	1248	1348	...	1417
61	Bingen (Rhein) Hbf **914** d.	...	...	0609	|	...	|	|	...	|	0952	|	...	1052	|	1152	|	...	1252	|	|	...	1452
	Wiesbaden Hbf **917a** d.	0501	0524	|	|	...	0732	|	0824c	|	|	|	1024	|	|	|	|	1224	|	|	|	1424	|
91	**Mainz** Hbf **914 917a** a.	0510	0535	0626	0738	...	0744	0838	0835c	0938	1015	1038	1035	1110	1138	1215	1238	1235	1310	1338	1438	1435	1510
91	**Mainz** Hbf **911a 917a** d.	0512	0540	0628	0740	0743	0746	0840	0843	0940	1017	1040	1043	1112	1140	1217	1240	1243	1312	1340	1440	1443	1512
117	**Frankfurt** Flughafen ✈ ◧ **917a** a.	0530	|	0646	0759	|	|	|	0900	0959	|	|	1100	|	1159	|	|	1300	|	1359	|	1500	|
128	**Frankfurt** (Main) Hbf **917a** a.	0550	|	0702	0813	|	|	|	0912	1013	|	|	1113	|	1213	|	|	1313	|	1412	|	1515	|
	Nürnberg Hbf **920** a.	...	|	...	1027	|	|	|	...	1224	|	|	...	|	1427	|	|	...	|	...	|	...	|
	Worms Hbf **911a** d.	...	0608	...	...	|	|	|	...	|	1045	|	...	|	...	1245	|	...	|	...	|	...	|
	Mannheim Hbf **911a** a.	...	0623	...	...	0824	0824	0921	...	|	1100	1121	...	1152	...	1307	1321	...	1352	...	1521	...	1552
	Stuttgart Hbf **912** ⊠ a.	...	0708	...	...	0928	0928	1024	...	|	1153t	|	...	1246	...	|	|	...	1446	...	1622	...	1646
	München Hbf **930** ⊠ a.	...	0927	...	...	...	...	...	...	1338	1411	|	...	...	...	|	|	...	...	...	...	...	...
	Karlsruhe Hbf **912** a.	...	...	...	...	...	...	...	...	...	...	1147	...	...	...	1334	1347	...	...	...	...	...	...
	Basel SBB **912** a.	...	...	...	...	...	...	...	...	...	...	1330	...	...	...	...	1535	...	...	...	...	...	...

	ICE 1025	IC 2217	ICE 1655	IC 2011	IC 2017	IC 2027	IC 2019	IC 2311	ICE 1657	ICE 1228	IC 1915	IC 2229	IC 2213	ICE 1659	ICE 1625	IC 1917	IC 1029	IC 2215	IC 2315	IC 2221	IC 2321	IC 60419	IC 61419
	✕	🍷♦	D✕	🍷♦	⑤ N	🍷♦	⑥ ♦	G🍷	✕♦	Ⓐ 🍷	⑤⑦ 🍷♦	🍷♦	🍷♦	Ⓑq ✕♦	⑥k ✕	⑦w B		T 🍷	S G🍷	🍷♦	①–④ T🍷	2⊡	2⊡
Hamburg Hbf **800** d.	0946	1046	...	...	...	1146	...	1246	...	...	...	1346	1446	...	...	...	1546	1646	1646	1746	1746	...	...
Dortmund Hbf **800** d.	1236	1337	...	1349w	1352	1436	...	1537	...	1616	1549	1636	1737	...	...	1752	1836	1937	1937	2037	2037	...	...
Köln Hbf **800** d.	1353	1453	...	1518	1518	1553	1618	1653	...	|	1718	1753	1853	...	...	1918	1953	2053	2053	2153	2153	2318h	2318h
Bonn Hbf **800** d.	1414	1514	...	1537	1537	1614	1637	1714	...	|	1737	1814	1914	...	...	1937	2014	2114	2114	2214	2214	2339h	2339h
Koblenz Hbf **914** d.	1448	1548	...	1617	1617	1648	1717	1748	...	|	1817	1848	1948	...	...	2017	2048	2148	2148	2248	2248	0017	0017
Bingen (Rhein) Hbf **914** d.	|	|	...	1652	1652	|	1752	|	...	|	1852	|	|	...	...	2052	2123	|	|	|	|	|	|
Wiesbaden Hbf **917a** d.	|	|	1624	|	|	|	|	|	1824	1846	|	|	|	2024	2024	|	|	|	|	|	|	|	|
Mainz Hbf **914 917a** a.	1538	1638	1635	1710	1710	1738	1815	1838	1835	1854	1910	1938	2038	2035	2035	2110	2141	2238	2238	2338	2338	|	|
Mainz Hbf **911a 917a** d.	1540	1640	1643	1712	1712	1740	1817	1840	1843	1856	1912	1940	2040	2043	2043	2112	2143	2240	2240	2340	2340	|	|
Frankfurt Flughafen ✈ ◧ **917a** a.	1559	|	1700	|	|	1759	|	|	1900	1915	|	1959	|	2100	2100	|	2200	2259	2259	2359	2359	|	|
Frankfurt (Main) Hbf **917a** a.	1613	|	1715	|	|	1813	|	|	1913	1933	|	2013	|	2113	2113	|	2213	2311	2311	0013	0013	0142	0142
Nürnberg Hbf **920** a.	...	|	...	|	|	2027	|	|	...	...	|	2226q	|	...	2326	|	0037	...	...	...	...	|	|
Worms Hbf **911a** d.	...	|	...	|	|	...	1845	|	...	...	|	...	|	...	...	|	...	...	...	...	...	|	|
Mannheim Hbf **911a** a.	...	1721	...	1752	1752	...	1901	1921	...	...	1952	...	2121	...	...	2152	...	...	...	...	...	|	0329
Stuttgart Hbf **912** ⊠ a.	...	1825	...	1846	1846	...	1958	2024	...	...	2046	...	2224	...	...	|	...	...	...	...	...	0421	|
München Hbf **930** ⊠ a.	...	...	...	...	2118‡	...	...	...	...	...	...	...	...	...	...	|	...	...	...	...	...	0710	|
Karlsruhe Hbf **912** a.	...	...	...	...	...	...	...	...	...	...	...	...	...	...	...	2224	...	...	...	...	...	...	0400
Basel SBB **912** a.	...	...	...	...	...	...	...	...	...	...	...	...	...	...	...	...	...	...	...	...	...	...	0619

km		ICE 887 1087	IC 61478	IC 60418	IC 2220	IC 2320	IC 2310	IC 1114	IC 1028	IC 2018	IC 2010	ICE 1656	IC 2216	IC 2226	ICE 1654	IC 2218	IC 2024	IC 2412	IC 1920	IC 1216	ICE 1652	IC 2312	IC 2006
		H	2⊡	2⊡	🍷♦	★ 🍷	⊖ G🍷	Ⓐ		⑥ ♦	Ⓐ 🍷♦	✕♦	🍷♦	🍷♦	✕♦	🍷	P🍷	⑦Q B	⑦g B	⑤ 🍷♦	D✕	🍷	⑥ 🍷♦
	Basel SBB **912** d.	...	2313	...	...	...	...	...	...	...	...	...	...	...	...	...	...	...	...	...	...	...	...
	Karlsruhe Hbf **912** d.	...	0129	...	...	...	...	...	...	...	...	...	...	...	...	...	...	...	...	...	...	...	1221
	München Hbf **930** ⊠ d.	...	|	2250	...	...	...	...	...	...	...	...	...	...	...	...	...	...	...	0848	...	...	|
	Stuttgart Hbf **912** ⊠ d.	...	|	0135	...	...	...	0630	...	0714	0714	...	0737	...	...	0937	...	1004	...	1114	...	1129	|
0	**Mannheim** Hbf **911a** d.	...	0215	|	...	...	...	0734	...	0808	0808	...	0839	...	...	1039	...	|	...	1208	...	1236	1258
24	Worms Hbf **911a** d.	...	|	|	...	...	...	|	...	|	|	...	|	...	...	|	...	|	...	|	...	|	1315
	Nürnberg Hbf **920** d.	...	|	|	...	...	...	|	0527	|	|	...	|	0729e	...	|	0929	|	...	|	...	|	|
	Frankfurt (Main) Hbf **917a** d.	0013	0345	0345	0542	0542	0638	|	0742	|	|	0842	|	0942	1042	|	1142	1200	1215	|	1242	|	|
	Frankfurt Flughafen ✈ ◧ **917a** d.	0027	|	|	0557	0557	0657	|	0758	|	|	0858	|	0958	1058	|	1158	|	1228	|	1258	|	|
70	**Mainz** Hbf **911a 917a** a.	0044	|	|	0615	0615	0715	0815	0818	0846	0846	0915	0918	1018	1115	1118	1218	|	1246	1246	1315	1318	1343
70	**Mainz** Hbf **914 917a** d.	0046	|	|	0617	0617	0717	...	0820	0848	0848	0922	0920	1020	1122	1120	1220	|	1248	1248	1322	1320	1345
80	**Wiesbaden** Hbf **917a** a.	0057	|	|	|	|	|	...	|	|	|	0933	|	|	1133	|	|	|	|	|	1333	|	|
	Bingen (Rhein) Hbf **914 917a** d.	...	|	|	0635	0635	|	...	|	0906	0906	...	|	|	...	|	|	|	1306	1306	...	|	1406
	Koblenz Hbf **914 917a** a.	...	0511	0511	0711	0711	0811	...	0911	0941	0941	...	1011	1111	...	1211	1311	1341	1341	1341	...	1411	1441
	Bonn Hbf **800** a.	...	0545j	0545j	0742	0742	0842	...	0943	1020	1020	...	1042	1142	...	1242	1342	1420	1420	1420	...	1442	1520
	Köln Hbf **800** a.	...	0615	0615	0805	0805	0905	...	1005	1042	1042	...	1105	1205	...	1305	1405	1442	1442	1442	...	1505	1542
	Dortmund Hbf **800** a.	...	...	...	0921	0921	1021	...	1123	...	1209f	...	1221	1321	...	1421	1521	1608	1608	1608	...	1621	1703
	Hamburg Hbf **800** a.	...	...	...	1213	1213	1313	...	1413	...	...	...	1511	1613	...	1713	1813	...	...	...	...	1914	...

♦ – **NOTES** (LISTED BY TRAIN NUMBER)

6 – [12] and ✕ Interlaken - Bern - Basel - Dortmund (- Hamburg Ⓑ **q**).
7 – [12] and ✕ (Hamburg ⚒ -) Dortmund - Basel - Bern - Interlaken.
22/3 – [12] and ✕ Wien - Linz - Passau - Regensburg - Dortmund and v.v.
26/7 – [12] and ✕ Wien - Linz - Passau - Regensburg - Dortmund - Hamburg and v.v.
114 – WÖRTHERSEE – [12] and 🍷 Klagenfurt - Villach - Salzburg - München - Dortmund. Departs Mannheim 1655 July 16 - Aug. 28.
115 – WÖRTHERSEE – [12] and 🍷 Münster - München - Salzburg - Villach - Klagenfurt.
118/9 – [12] Innsbruck - Bregenz - Lindau - Stuttgart - Münster and v.v.
1216 – Not July 29. [12] and 🍷 Salzburg - München - Stuttgart - Dortmund - Berlin. Does not run Salzburg - München - Stuttgart Aug. 5 - Sept. 9.
1654 – [12] and ✕ (Dresden ⚒ -) Leipzig - Frankfurt - Wiesbaden.
1656 – [12] and ✕ (Leipzig ⚒ -) Frankfurt - Wiesbaden.
1657 – [12] and ✕ Wiesbaden - Frankfurt - Leipzig (- Dresden Ⓑ **q**).
1659 – [12] and ✕ Wiesbaden - Frankfurt - Erfurt (- Leipzig ⑤⑦ **w**) (- Dresden ⑦ **w**).
1915 – ⑤⑦ (also Oct. 3; not Oct. 2). [12] and 🍷 Berlin - Köln - Mannheim - Stuttgart (- Tübingen ⑦ **w**).
1952 – ⑦ (also Oct. 3, Nov. 1; not Oct. 2, 30). [12] Berlin - Erfurt - Kassel - Hamm - Frankfurt.
2004 – [12] and 🍷 Konstanz - Karlsruhe - Münster - Emden.
2005 – [12] and 🍷 Emden - Münster - Karlsruhe - Konstanz.
2006 – [12] and 🍷 Konstanz - Karlsruhe - Dortmund.
2010 – Ⓐ (not Nov. 1). [12] and 🍷 Tübingen - Stuttgart - Köln - Düsseldorf (- Berlin ⑤).
2011 – ①②③④⑦ (not Oct. 2, Nov. 1). [12] (Berlin ⑦ **w** -) Düsseldorf - Koblenz - Stuttgart. On ①–④ (not Oct. 3, Nov. 1) continues to Tübingen Hbf (a. 1950).
2012/3 – ALLGÄU – [12] and 🍷 Oberstdorf - Kempten - Ulm - Stuttgart - Köln - Dortmund - Hannover (- Magdeburg - Leipzig ♣) and v.v.
2014 – [12] and 🍷 Stuttgart - Münster - Emden.
2018/9 – ⑥ until Oct. 29. [12] Stuttgart - Münster - Norddeich Mole and v.v.
2027 – [12] and 🍷 Hamburg - Köln - Nürnberg - Regensburg - Passau. Runs with train number **2327** and starts from Fehmarn-Burg (Table **825**) on ⑤–⑦ to Nov. 27 (daily July 1 - Oct. 16).
2213 – RÜGEN – [12] and 🍷 Ostseebad Binz - Stralsund - Rostock - Hamburg - Stuttgart.
2216/7 – [12] and 🍷 Stuttgart - Hamburg - Rostock - Stralsund (- Greifswald Ⓐ) and v.v.
2220 – Daily to Oct. 30; ⑤ from Nov. 4. FEHMARN – [12] Frankfurt - Köln - Lübeck (- Fehmarn-Burg ♠).
2221 – Daily to Oct. 30; ⑤⑦ from Nov. 4. FEHMARN – [12] (Fehmarn-Burg ♠ -) Lübeck - Köln - Frankfurt.
2226 – [12] and 🍷 (Passau ● -) (Regensburg ⚒ -) Frankfurt - Köln - Kiel.
2229 – [12] and 🍷 Kiel - Köln - Frankfurt (- Nürnberg Ⓑ **q**) (- Passau ●).
2318 – [12] and 🍷 Stuttgart - Köln (- Dortmund Ⓑ **q**) (- Münster ⑦ **w**).

B – From / to Berlin (Table **810**).
D – To / from Dresden via Leipzig (Table **850**).
G – From / to Westerland (Table **821**).
H – To / from Hamburg (Table **900**).
N – From Wolfsburg (Table **810**).
P – From Passau (Table **920**).
Q – ⑦ Sept. 4 - Oct. 30 (also Oct. 3; not Oct. 2). Via Rüdesheim (d. 12
R – ⑤ Sept. 2 - Oct. 28. Via Rüdesheim (d. 1512).
S – Until Oct. 30.
T – From Oct. 31.
Z – To / from Zürich (Tables **510**).

c – Ⓒ only.
e – ⚒ only.
f – ⑤ only.
g – Not Sept. 4 - Oct. 30.
h – July 9 – 24 departs Köln Hbf 2245, Bonn-Beuel 2323 (not Bonn Hb
j – Calls at Bonn-**Beuel** July 9 – 25 (not Bonn Hbf).
k – Also Oct. 2.
m – Also Oct. 3; not Oct. 2; not ⑤ Sept. 2 - Oct. 28.
n – Not July 9 - Aug. 21.
q – Ⓑ (not Oct. 2).
r – 1937 on ⑤⑦.
t – Not July 30 - Sept. 11.
w – ⑦ (also Oct. 3; not Oct. 2).

♠ – ①⑤⑥⑦ to Oct. 30 (daily June 10 - Aug. 29).
★ – ①②③④⑥ from Oct. 31.
‡ – Not Aug. 5 - Sept. 9.
● – See Table **920** for days of running from / to Passau.
⊕ – Train number **1010** on ⑤⑥ (also Oct. 2), **1190** on ⑦ (also Oct. 3; not Oct. 2). Also conveys ✕ on ①–④ (not Oct. 3).
◇ – Also calls at Boppard Hbf (d. 0544).
⊖ – Also calls at Boppard Hbf (d. 0758).
⊙ – Also calls at Boppard Hbf (d. 0043).
♣ – See Table **866** for running dates to / from Magdeburg and Leipzig.
⊠ – Timings are subject to alteration at Stuttgart until Aug. 28 and at München until Sept. 11. See shaded panel on page 367 for further details.
⊡ – To / from Amsterdam. For *City Night Line* cars and other timings se international Tables **28** and **73**.
◧ – Frankfurt Flughafen Fernbahnhof.

See Table 910 for Köln - Frankfurt ICE services via the high-speed line

MANNHEIM and FRANKFURT - MAINZ - KOBLENZ 911

	IC 2014	ICE 1026	IC 2012	ICE 1650	EC 8	IC 2022	ICE 712	IC 118	ICE 1558	EC 6	EC 114	IC 2316	ICE 26	ICE 1556	IC 2318	ICE 1522	IC 1910	ICE 1594	IC 2210		ICE 22		ICE 510	IC 2020
	⑤						Ⓐ					Ⓑq					⑦w		Ⓑq				⊕	
	🍷◆	✕	🍷◆	D✕	Z✕	🍷	✕	◆	D✕	✕◆	🍷◆		✕◆	D✕	🍷◆	✕	🍷	D🍷	🍷		✕◆		🍷	⊙
asel SBB 912 d.	...	...	...	...	1220	...	...	...	...	1427	...	...	...	...	...	...	...	...	...	...	...	...	...	...
Karlsruhe Hbf 912 d.	...	...	...	...	1412	...	...	...	...	1612	...	...	...	...	...	...	...	...	...	...	...	...	...	...
nchen Hbf 930 ⊠ d.	...	...	...	...	|	...	...	...	...	|	1346	...	...	...	...	1618	1620	...	...	...	...	...	1928	...
ttgart Hbf 912 ⊠ d.	1209	...	1314	...	|	...	1433	1512	...	|	1609t	1636	...	...	1737	|	1914	...	1918r	...	...	...	2151	...
nheim Hbf 911a d.	1258	...	1408	...	1439	...	1533	1608	...	1639	1658	1738	...	...	1839	|	2008	...	2039	...	...	...	2237	...
ns Hbf 911a d.	1315	...	|	...	|	...	|	|	...	|	1714	|	...	...	|	|	|	...	|	...	...	...	|	...
Nürnberg Hbf 920 d.	|	...	|	...	|	...	|	|	...	|	|	|	1529	...	|	1733	|	...	|	...	1929	...	|	...
nkfurt (Main) Hbf 917a d.	|	1344	|	1442	|	1544	|	|	1642	|	|	|	1742	1842	|	1944	|	2042	|	...	2146	...	|	2324
nkfurt Flughafen ✈ ◧.. 917a d.	|	1358	|	1458	|	1558	|	|	1658	|	|	|	1758	1858	|	1958	|	2059	|	...	2159	...	2313	2339
z Hbf 911a 917a a.	1343	1418	1446	1515	1518	1618	1615	1646	1715	1718	1740	1815	1818	1915	1918	2018	2046	2115	2118	...	2218	...	2329	2359
z Hbf 914 917a d.	1345	1420	1448	1522	1520	1620	1622	1648	1722	1720	1745	...	1820	1922	1920	2020	2048	2122	2120	...	2220	...	2331	0001
esbaden Hbf 917a a.	|	|	|	1533	|	|	1633	|	1733	|	|	...	|	1933	|	|	|	2133	|	...	|	...	2344	|
en (Rhein) Hbf 914 917a d.	1406	|	1506	...	|	|	|	1706	...	|	1806	...	|	...	|	|	2106	...	|	...	|	...	...	0018
enz Hbf 914 917a a.	1441	1511	1541	...	1611	1711	|	1741	...	1811	1841	...	1911	...	2011	2111	2141	...	2211	...	2311	...	...	0055
nn Hbf 800 a.	1520	1543	1620	...	1642	1742	|	1820	...	1842	1920	...	1942	...	2042	2143	2220	...	2242	...	2342	...	...	0133
ln Hbf 800 a.	1542	1605	1642	...	1705	1805	1801	1842	...	1905	1942	...	2005	...	2105	2205	2242	...	2305	...	0005	...	...	0156
rtmund Hbf 800 a.	...	1721	1809	...	1821	1921	...	...	...	2021	2100	...	2122	...	2221q	2322n	2359	...	...	...	0121	...	...	0328
mburg Hbf 800 a.	...	2013	...	...	2113	2213	...	...	...	2314q	...	...	0014	...	...	...	...	...	...	...	...	...	...	0651

OR NOTES SEE PREVIOUS PAGE

Local services MAINZ - MANNHEIM and MAINZ - SPEYER - KARLSUHE 911a

RB services

		Ⓐe	⚒r	Ⓐe		⚒r	Ⓐe																		
Mainz Hbf 911 d.	0008	0456	0515	0545	0552b	0622	0652	0656	0722r	0752	0813	0822e	0913	0952	1013	1117	1152	1213	1317	1352	1413	1517	1553	1613	1625r
Worms Hbf 911 a.	0051	0540	0556	0614	0634b	0706	0719	0739	0806r	0836	0839	0903e	0940	1036	1039	1144	1236	1239	1344	1436	1439	1544	1636	1639	1718r
Worms Hbf 911 d.	...	0541	0556	0615	0635	0712	0720	0746	0816	0848	0840	0916	0941	1048	1040	1145	1249	1240	1345	1448	1440	1545	1648	1640	1718
Ludwigshafen Hbf 918 d.	...	0558	0616	0638	0653	0731	0736	0804	0837	0909	0857	0937	0958t	1111	1057	1204t	1309	1257	1404t	1508	1457	1604t	1709	1656	1737
Speyer Hbf 918 d.	...	|	|	0700	|	|	|	|	|	|	0914	|	|	|	1114	|	|	1314	|	|	1514	|	|	1714	|
Germersheim 918 a.	...	|	|	0714	|	|	|	|	|	|	0922	|	|	|	1122	|	|	1322	|	|	1522	|	|	1722	|
Karlsruhe Hbf a.	...	|	|	0752	|	|	|	|	|	|	0952	|	|	|	1152	|	|	1352	|	|	1552	|	|	1753	|
Mannheim Hbf 911 a.	...	0603	0621	...	0658	0736	0742	0811	0842	0915	...	0942	1001	1116	...	1207	1314	...	1407	1514	...	1606	1714	...	1742

		Ⓐe	Ⓒz				Ⓐe					
z Hbf 911 d.	1652	1718	1717	1752	1813	1917	1925	1952	2013	2052	2208	2308
ns Hbf 911 a.	1736	1744	1744	1836	1839	1944	2008	2036	2039	2136	2251	2351
ns Hbf 911 d.	1749	1745	1745	1848	1840	1945	2018	2048	2040	2148	2251	2351
igshafen Hbf 918 d.	1809	1800	1806t	1909	1857	2004t	2038	2111	2057	2209	2309	0008
eyer Hbf 918 d.	|	1819	|	|	1914	|	|	|	2114	|	|	|
rmersheim 918 a.	|	1828	|	|	1922	|	|	|	2122	|	|	|
rlsruhe Hbf a.	|	...	|	|	1952	|	|	|	2152	|	|	|
nheim Hbf 911 a.	1814	...	1810	1914	...	2007	2043	2115	...	2214	2314	0013

		⚒r	Ⓐ	⚒r		⚒r	Ⓐe		Ⓐe
Mannheim Hbf 911 d.	0012	0430	0500	0530	0550e	0618	...	0650	...
Karlsruhe Hbf d.	|	|	|	|	|	|	...	|	...
Germersheim 918 d.	|	|	|	|	|	|	0620	|	0718
Speyer Hbf 918 d.	|	|	|	|	|	|	0632	|	0728
Ludwigshafen Hbf 918 d.	0017	0436	0505	0535	0558e	0624	0654	0659	0750
Worms Hbf 911 a.	0039	0454	0524	0552	0615e	0644	0712	0718	0804
Worms Hbf 911 d.	...	0455	0525	0555	0622	0655	0713	0725	0805
Mainz Hbf 911 a.	...	0537	0607	0637	0706	0737	0747	0807	0836

	Ⓐe	Ⓒz																								
nheim Hbf 911 d.	0748	0752	0844	...	0916	0944	0958	1044	...	1149	1244	...	1349	1444	...	1549	1644	...	1752	1844	...	1951	2044	...	2144	2248
rlsruhe Hbf d.	|	|	|	0808	|	|	|	|	1008	|	|	1208	|	|	1408	|	|	1608	|	|	1808	|	|	2008	|	|
rmersheim 918 d.	|	|	|	0838	|	|	|	|	1038	|	|	1238	|	|	1438	|	|	1638	|	|	1838	|	|	2038	|	|
eyer Hbf 918 d.	|	|	|	0847	|	|	|	|	1047	|	|	1247	|	|	1447	|	|	1647	|	|	1847	|	|	2047	|	|
igshafen Hbf 918 d.	0755	0755t	0850	0904	0921	0950	1000t	1050	1104	1152t	1250	1303	1352t	1450	1504	1552t	1650	1704	1754t	1850	1904	1954t	2050	2104	2150	2253
ns Hbf 911 a.	0814	0816	0914	0919	0938	1014	1019	1111	1119	1216	1311	1319	1416	1514	1519	1616	1714	1719	1816	1913	1919	2016	2114	2119	2213	2312
ns Hbf 911 d.	0825	0817	0925	0920	0955e	1025	1020	1125	1120	1217	1325	1320	1417	1525	1520	1617	1725	1720	1817	1925	1920	2017	2125	2120	2218	2315
z Hbf 911 a.	0907	0843	1007	0947	1036e	1107	1046	1207	1147	1243	1407	1347	1443	1607	1547	1652	1807	1747	1843	2007	1947	2043	2207	2147	2300	2358

Not ⑥. e – Ⓐ (not Nov. 1). r – ⚒ (not Nov. 1). t – Ludwigshafen (Rhein) **Mitte**. z – Also Nov. 1.

FRANKFURT - BASEL and STUTTGART 912

km	SEE NOTE ⊠	ICE 619	ICE 879	CNL 479	IC 60479	CNL 40419	IC 61419	CNL 419	IC 60419	CNL 40479	CNL 471	IC 60458 60471	ICE 3		RJ 63	IC 2099	ICE 991	ICE 271	ICE 271		TGV 9578	EC 217	ICE 511	ICE 5
			①m	Ⓡ		Ⓡ		Ⓡ			Ⓡ		Ⓐ		Ⓒ	Ⓐ	Ⓐ	①m	⚒		①–⑥			
		◆		C🍷	C2	D🍷	D2	E🍷	E2	F🍷	B🍷	B2	✕	◐2	✕◆		G✕	H	H✕	◐2	Ⓡ◆	🍷◆	🍷	✕
	Berlin Hbf **810 902** d.	...	2031p	...	...	...	...	...	...	...	2150	2150	...	...	...	...	...	...	...	...	...	...	...	...
	Hamburg Hbf **800 900** d.	...	|	2029t	2029t	...	...	...	...	2029t	|	|	...	...	...	...	...	0044	...	...	...	...	...	...
	Hannover Hbf **810 900** d.	...	|	2201t	2201t	...	...	...	...	2201t	|	|	...	...	...	...	...	0210	...	...	...	...	...	...
	Dortmund Hbf **800** d.	2058	|	|	|	...	...	...	...	|	|	|	...	...	...	...	...	|	...	...	...	...	0437g	...
	Köln Hbf **800 910** d.	2230	|	|	|	2318	2318	2318r	2318r	|	|	|	...	...	...	...	...	|	...	...	...	...	0555	...
	Koblenz Hbf **911** d.	|	|	|	|	0017	0017	0017	0017	|	|	|	...	...	...	...	...	|	...	...	...	...	|	...
	Mainz Hbf **911** d.	|	|	|	|	|	|	|	|	|	|	|	...	...	...	...	0540	|	...	...	...	...	|	...
0	**Frankfurt** (Main) Hbf 913 d.	0009	0109	|	0248	|	0248	|	0213	|	|	0402x	...	...	0517	0520	|	0550	0550	...	...	...	|	0650
	Frankfurt Flughafen ✈ ◧ d.	0028	|	|	|	|	|	|	|	|	|	|	...	...	0539	|	|	|	|	...	...	...	0653	|
	Mannheim Hbf 913 a.	0104	0148	|	0329	|	0329	|	|	|	0440s	0440	...	...	0610	|	0623	0625	0625	...	...	...	0723	0727
	Mannheim Hbf 913 d.	0106	0151	|	0331	|	0331	|	|	|	|	0442	...	...	0612	|	0629	0633	0633	...	...	0712	0731	0736
28	Darmstadt Hbf 913 d.	|	|	|	|	|	|	|	|	|	|	|	...	...	|	0537	|	|	|	...	...	|	|	|
50	Bensheim 913 d.	|	|	|	|	|	|	|	|	|	|	|	...	...	|	0550	|	|	|	...	...	|	|	|
64	Weinheim 913 d.	|	|	|	|	|	|	|	|	|	|	|	...	...	|	0600	|	|	|	...	...	|	|	|
87	**Heidelberg** Hbf 913 931 d.	0119	|	|	|	|	|	|	|	|	|	|	...	...	|	0615	|	|	|	...	...	|	|	|
120	Bruchsal 913 931 d.	0139	|	|	|	|	|	|	|	|	|	|	...	...	|	|	|	|	|	...	...	|	|	|
	Vaihingen (Enz) 931 d.	0248	|	|	|	|	|	|	|	|	|	|	...	...	|	|	|	|	|	...	...	|	|	|
	Stuttgart Hbf 931 a.	0320	|	|	|	|	|	0421	0421	0421	|	|	...	...	0652	0700	0708	|	|	...	0649	0754	0808	|
	München Hbf **930** a.	0602	|	|	|	|	|	0710	0710	0710	|	|	...	...	0910j	...	0927	|	|	...	|	1011	1027	|
141	**Karlsruhe** Hbf 913 916 d.	0156a	0215	0400s	0402	0400s	0402	...	...	...	0507s	0509	0556	...	...	...	...	0658	0658	...	0732	...	...	0800
172	Baden-Baden 916 d.	...	...	|	|	|	|	...	...	...	0527s	0529	0613	...	...	...	...	0715	0715	...	|	...	...	|
	Offenburg 916 ☆ ▶ d.	...	...	0449s	0451	0449s	0451	...	...	...	0545s	0547	0629	0632	...	...	...	0732	0732	0734	|	...	...	0829
217	Kehl 🏛 ▶ d.	...	...	|	|	|	|	...	...	...	|	|	|	0653	...	...	...	|	|	0754	|	...	...	|
225	**Strasbourg** ▶ a.	...	...	|	|	|	|	...	...	...	|	|	|	0704	...	...	...	|	|	0807	0813	...	...	|
	Freiburg (Brsg) Hbf ☆ d.	...	...	0529s	0531	0529s	0531	...	...	...	0620s	0622	0702	...	...	...	...	0802	0802	...	...	...	...	0901
	Basel Bad Bf 🏛 ☆ a.	...	...	0609	0609	0609	0609	...	...	...	0706	0706	0735	...	...	...	...	0834	0834	...	...	...	...	0934
	Basel SBB ☆ a.	...	...	0619	0619	0619	0619	...	...	...	0720	0720	0747	...	...	...	...	0847	0847	...	...	...	...	0947
	Zürich HB **510** a.	...	...	0805	0805	0805	0805	...	...	...	0905	0905	0900	...	...	...	...	1000	1000	...	...	...	...	...

NOTES (LISTED BY TRAIN NUMBER)

(12) and ✕ Frankfurt - Salzburg - Wien - Budapest.

– (12) and 🍷 Saarbrücken - Salzburg - Bischofshofen - Graz. July 30 - Sept. 11 departs Mannheim 0649, arrives Stuttgart 0733.

– (12) Dortmund - Frankfurt - Mannheim - Karlsruhe - Stuttgart - München.

– To Paris (Table **32**). Timings vary by up to 5 minutes to July 2 / from Aug. 29.

SIRIUS – 🛏 1, 2 cl. and 🛌 2 cl. (*CNL* **471** Ⓡ) Berlin - Leipzig - Zürich; (2) (*IC* **60471**) Berlin - Zürich. Conveys 🛏 1, 2 cl. and 🛌 2 cl. (*CNL* **458** – CANOPUS Ⓡ) Praha - Dresden - Leipzig - Zürich; (2) (*IC* **60458**) Praha - Zürich. Berlin portion starts from Ostseebad Binz on dates in Table **850** (note ♠ page 399).

KOMET – 🛏 1, 2 cl. and 🛌 2 cl. (*CNL* **479** Ⓡ) Hamburg - Zürich; (2) (*IC* **60479**) Hamburg - Zürich.

PEGASUS – 🛏 1, 2 cl. and 🛌 2 cl. (*CNL* **40419** Ⓡ) Amsterdam - Zürich; (2) (*IC* **61419**) Amsterdam - Zürich.

POLLUX – 🛏 1, 2 cl. and 🛌 2 cl. (*CNL* **419** Ⓡ) Amsterdam - München; (2) (*IC* **60419**) Amsterdam - München.

F – PYXIS – 🛏 1, 2 cl. and 🛌 2 cl. (*CNL* **40479** Ⓡ) Hamburg - Stuttgart - München; (2) (*IC* **61479**) Hamburg - Stuttgart - München.

G – From Wiesbaden Hbf (d. 0524).

H – To Chur (Table **520**).

L – ①–⑤ (not Nov. 1).

a – Arrival time (calls before Vaihingen).

g – ① (also Oct. 4; not July 11 - Aug. 15, Oct. 3).

j – Not July 30, 31.

m – Also Oct. 4; not Oct. 3.

p – Previous day from Berlin (1959 July 24 - Aug. 28).

r – 2245 July 9 – 24.

s – Stops to set down only.

t – July 18 - Sept. 2 Hamburg 2001, Hannover 2129.

x – Frankfurt (Main) **Süd**.

⊠ – Timings at Vaihingen, Stuttgart and München are subject to alteration until Sept. 11. Timings of services via Mannheim may vary by up to 10 minutes July 16 - Aug. 28. See shaded panel on page 367 for further details.

▶ – Additional journeys Offenburg - Strasbourg (◐): 0704 **L**, 0804 **L**.

◐ – Operated by Südwestdeutsche Verkehrs.

* – Distance via Katzenberg Tunnel (3 km further via the original route).

☆ – See also panel on page 426.

◧ – Frankfurt Flughafen Fernbahnhof.

912 FRANKFURT - BASEL and STUTTGART

SEE NOTE ⊠	ICE 9568			IC 2273	IC 2317	ICE 711	ICE 591	ICE 999	ICE 101	TGV 9576		ICE 713	EC 113	IC 2319	ICE 513	ICE 275	ICE 9566		ICE 571	IC 2271	ICE 1091	ICE 593	ICE 103	ICE 71
	Ⓑ		①–⑤	Ⓐ	⑥	Ⓐ	⚒	†			⑥⑦	⚒x		⚒			⑥	①–⑤	⚒	⚒	Ⓐ	Ⓒ		
	🅁♦	◐2	◐2	L🍷		✕	✕	✕	🍷	🅁♦	◐2	🍷	✕♦	🍷	M✕	N✕	🅁♦	◐2	✕	🍷♦	✕	✕	🍷	C✕
Berlin Hbf 810 902 ♣ d.	...	...	...	...	...	...	...	...	...	...	...	...	...	...	...	0432t	...	...	...	...	0604	0531	...	...
Hamburg Hbf 800 900 ♣ d.	...	...	...	...	...	...	0321t	...	...	...	...	...	...	...	...	|	...	...	0516	...	|	|	...	0618h
Hannover Hbf 810 900 ♣ d.	...	...	...	...	...	...	0514	...	...	...	...	...	...	...	...	|	...	...	0641	0601t	|	|	0540	0741
Dortmund Hbf 800 d.	...	...	...	...	...	...	|	...	0537u	...	...	0552	...	0537	0637	|	...	...	|	|	|	|	0737	|
Köln Hbf 800 910 d.	...	...	...	...	...	0611	|	...	0655	...	...	0713d	...	0653	0755	|	...	...	|	|	|	|	0855g	|
Koblenz Hbf 911 d.	...	...	...	...	...	|	|	...	|	...	...	|	...	0748	|	|	...	...	|	|	|	|	|	|
Mainz Hbf 911 d.	...	...	...	...	0743	0746	|	...	|	...	...	|	...	0840	|	|	...	...	|	|	|	|	|	|
Frankfurt (Main) Hbf 913 d.	0658	...	...	0714	|	|	0750	0750	|	...	...	|	0822	|	|	0850	0856	...	0905	0920	0950	0950	|	1005z
Frankfurt Flughafen ✈ d.	|	...	...	|	|	|	|	|	0753	...	...	0809	|	|	0853	|	|	...	0920z	|	|	|	0951	|
Mannheim Hbf 913 a.	0737	...	...	|	0824	0824	0827	0827	0823	...	...	0840	|	0921	0923	0927	0937	...	0954	|	1027	1027	1023	1043
Mannheim Hbf 913 d.	0739	...	...	|	0826	0826	0830	0830	0836	...	...	0842	|	0923	0931	0936	0940	...	0956	|	1030	1030	1036	1045
Darmstadt Hbf 913 d.	|	...	...	0731	|	|	|	|	|	...	...	|	0838	|	|	|	|	...	|	0937	|	|	|	|
Bensheim 913 d.	|	...	...	0746	|	|	|	|	|	...	...	|	0850	|	|	|	|	...	|	0950	|	|	|	|
Weinheim 913 d.	|	...	...	0758	|	|	|	|	|	...	...	|	0900	|	|	|	|	...	|	1000	|	|	|	|
Heidelberg Hbf 913 931 d.	|	...	...	0814	0838	0838	|	|	|	...	...	|	0914	0936	|	|	|	...	|	1014	|	|	|	|
Bruchsal 913 931 d.	|	...	...	0838	|	|	|	|	|	...	...	|	|	|	|	|	|	...	|	1036	|	|	|	|
Vaihingen (Enz) 931 d.	|	...	...	|	0909	0909	|	|	|	...	...	|	|	1006	|	|	|	...	|	|	|	|	|	|
Stuttgart Hbf 931 a.	|	...	...	|	0928	0928	0908	0908	|	0849	...	0924	0954	1024	1008	|	|	...	1035	|	1108	1108	|	|
München Hbf 930 a.	|	...	...	|	...	...	1127	1127	|	|	...	...	1210	...	1227	|	|	...	...	|	1327	1327	|	|
Karlsruhe Hbf 913 916 d.	0807	...	...	0852	...	...	...	...	0900	0932	...	...	...	...	...	1000	1006	...	...	1050	...	...	1100	1110
Baden-Baden 916 d.	|	...	...	...	...	...	...	...	0917	|	...	...	...	...	...	|	|	...	...	...	...	...	|	1127
Offenburg 916 ☆ d.	|	0843	0904	...	...	...	...	...	0936	|	1004	...	...	...	...	1029	|	1034	...	...	...	...	1129	|
Kehl 🏛 d.	|	0900	0922	...	...	...	...	...	|	|	1022	...	...	...	...	|	|	1052	...	...	...	...	|	|
Strasbourg a.	0847	0910	0934	...	...	...	...	...	|	1012	1034	...	...	...	...	|	1047	1104	...	...	...	...	|	|
Freiburg (Brsg) Hbf ☆ d.	...	...	...	...	...	...	...	...	1007	...	...	...	...	...	...	1101	...	...	...	...	...	...	1201	1212
Basel Bad Bf 🏛 ☆ a.	...	...	...	...	...	...	...	...	1038	...	...	...	...	...	...	1134	...	...	...	...	...	...	1234	1245
Basel SBB ☆ a.	...	...	...	...	...	...	...	...	1047	...	...	...	...	...	...	1147	...	...	...	...	...	...	1247	1254
Zürich HB 510 a.	...	...	...	...	...	...	...	...	...	...	...	...	...	...	...	...	...	...	...	...	...	...	...	1400

SEE NOTE ⊠		IC 2293	EC 115	EC 7	ICE 515		ICE 277	IC 119	ICE 973	IC 2277	IC 2277	ICE 595	ICE 505		ICE 73	TGV 9574		EC 219	IC 2005	EC 9	ICE 517	ICE 279		IC 2013
	⑥⑦								⊖	⑤	Ⓒq			①–⑤	□	QP	⑥⑦		⑤⑥					
	◐2	🍷	🍷♦	N✕	🍷	◐2	✕	♦	K✕	🍷	🍷	✕	🍷♦	◐2	K✕	🅁🍷	◐2	🍷♦	🍷♦	✕	🍷	✕	◐2	🍷♦
Berlin Hbf 810 902 ♣ d.	...	...	...	...	...	...	0631	...	...	...	...	0734	...	...	...	...	...	...	...	...	...	0831	...	...
Hamburg Hbf 800 900 ♣ d.	...	...	...	0442e	...	...	|	...	0722	0625	0625◊	|	...	...	0824	...	...	...	...	0646	...	|	...	...
Hannover Hbf 810 900 ♣ d.	...	...	...	|	...	...	|	...	0841	0801	0801◊	|	...	...	0941	...	...	...	...	|	...	|	...	0740
Dortmund Hbf 800 d.	...	...	...	0737	0837n	...	|	...	|	|	|	|	...	...	|	...	...	...	...	0937	1037n	|	...	0952
Köln Hbf 800 910 d.	...	...	0818	0853	0955	...	|	0918	|	|	|	|	1055	...	|	...	...	...	1018	1053	1155	|	...	1118
Koblenz Hbf 911 d.	...	...	0917	0948	|	...	|	1017	|	|	|	|	|	...	|	...	...	...	1117	1148	|	|	...	1217
Mainz Hbf 911 d.	...	...	1017	1040	|	...	|	1112	|	|	|	|	|	...	|	...	...	...	1217	1240	|	|	...	1312
Frankfurt (Main) Hbf 913 d.	...	1020	|	|	|	...	1050	|	1105	1120	1120	1150	|	...	1205z	...	...	1220	|	|	|	1250	...	|
Frankfurt Flughafen ✈ d.	...	|	|	|	1053	...	|	|	1120z	|	|	|	1153	...	|	...	...	|	|	|	1253	|	...	|
Mannheim Hbf 913 a.	...	|	1100	1121	1123	...	1127	1152	1154	|	|	1227	1223	...	1243	...	...	|	1307	1321	1323	1327	...	1352
Mannheim Hbf 913 d.	...	|	1102	1123	1131	...	1136	1154	1156	|	|	1230	1236	...	1245	...	...	|	1309	1323	1331	1336	...	1354
Darmstadt Hbf 913 d.	...	1037	|	|	|	...	|	|	|	1137	1137	|	|	...	|	...	...	1237	|	|	|	|	...	|
Bensheim 913 d.	...	|	|	|	|	...	|	|	|	1150	1150	|	|	...	|	...	...	1250	|	|	|	|	...	|
Weinheim 913 d.	...	1056	|	|	|	...	|	|	|	1200	1200	|	|	...	|	...	...	1300	|	|	|	|	...	|
Heidelberg Hbf 913 931 d.	...	1110	|	|	|	...	|	1206	|	1212	1214	|	|	...	|	...	...	1314	|	|	|	|	...	1406
Bruchsal 913 931 d.	...	|	|	|	|	...	|	|	|	...	1236	|	|	...	|	...	...	|	|	|	|	|	...	|
Vaihingen (Enz) 931 d.	...	|	1137•	|	|	...	|	|	|	...	|	|	|	...	|	...	...	|	|	|	|	|	...	|
Stuttgart Hbf 931 a.	...	1150	1153•	|	1208	...	|	1246	1235	...	|	1308	|	...	|	1250	...	1354	|	|	1408	|	...	1446
München Hbf 930 a.	...	...	1411	|	1427	...	|	▬	...	...	|	1528•	|	...	|	...	...	1611•	|	|	1627	|	...	▬
Karlsruhe Hbf 913 916 d.	...	...	...	1149	...	...	1200	①–⑤	...	...	1250	...	1300	...	1310	1333	...	...	1336	1349	...	1400	...	①–⑤
Baden-Baden 916 d.	...	...	...	|	...	...	1218	◐2	...	...	|	...	|	...	1327	|	...	...	1356	1407	...	|	...	◐2
Offenburg 916 ☆ d.	1204	...	...	|	...	1234	1234	1304	...	...	...	...	1329	1336	|	|	1404	...	1415	|	...	1429	1434	1504
Kehl 🏛 d.	1222	...	...	|	...	1252	|	1322	...	...	...	...	|	1354	|	|	1422	...	...	|	...	|	1452	1522
Strasbourg a.	1234	...	...	|	...	1304	|	1334	...	...	...	...	|	1404	|	1411	1434	...	...	|	...	|	1504	1534
Freiburg (Brsg) Hbf ☆ d.	...	...	...	1251	...	...	1306	...	...	...	...	...	1401	...	1412	...	...	...	...	1455	...	1501	...	...
Basel Bad Bf 🏛 ☆ a.	...	...	...	1322	...	...	1338	...	...	...	...	...	1434	...	1445	...	...	...	...	1527	...	1534	...	...
Basel SBB ☆ a.	...	...	...	1330	...	...	1347	...	...	...	...	...	1447	...	1454	...	...	...	...	1535	...	1547	...	...
Zürich HB 510 a.	...	...	...	...	...	...	...	...	...	...	...	...	...	...	1600	...	...	...	...	1700	...	...	...	...

SEE NOTE ⊠	IC 2279	ICE 597	ICE 107	TGV 9580	ICE 75	TGV 9580	ICE 9572	IC 2299	EC 117	IC 2313	ICE 519	ICE 371	ICE 577	IC 1911	IC 2415	IC 2371	ICE 599	ICE 109	ICE 717	ICE 77	TGV 9572		EC 391	IC 2217
				🅁		🅁	GP	⑥p	Ⓑ				x	⑤⑦	⑤D				Ⓑq		HP	①–⑤		
	🍷♦	✕	🍷	🍷♦	✕♦	🍷♦	🅁	🍷	🍷♦	🍷	🍷	N✕	✕	y🍷	🍷	🍷	✕	🍷	♥🍷	K✕	🅁🍷	◐2	🍷♦	🍷♦
Berlin Hbf 810 902 ♣ d.	...	0934	...	...	...	...	...	...	...	...	...	1035	...	...	...	...	1134	...	...	...	...	...	...	...
Hamburg Hbf 800 900 ♣ d.	0828e	|	...	...	1024	...	...	...	...	0845	...	|	1124	...	...	1028	|	...	...	1224	...	...	...	1046
Hannover Hbf 810 900 ♣ d.	1001e	|	...	...	1141	...	...	...	...	|	...	|	1241	...	...	1201	|	...	...	1341	...	...	...	|
Dortmund Hbf 800 d.	|	|	1137v	...	|	...	...	...	...	1137	1237n	|	|	1152	1152	|	|	1337b	1354w	|	...	...	...	1337
Köln Hbf 800 910 d.	|	|	1255	...	|	...	...	...	...	1253	1355	|	|	1318	1318	|	|	1455	1514d	|	...	...	...	1453
Koblenz Hbf 911 d.	|	|	|	...	|	...	...	...	...	1348	|	|	|	1417	1420	|	|	|	|	|	...	...	...	1548
Mainz Hbf 911 d.	|	|	|	...	|	...	...	...	...	1440	|	|	|	1512	1544	|	|	|	|	|	...	...	...	1640
Frankfurt (Main) Hbf 913 d.	1320	1350	|	1359	1405z	...	...	1420	1420	|	|	1450	1505	|	|	1520	1550	|	|	1605z	...	...	1620	|
Frankfurt Flughafen ✈ d.	|	|	1353	|	|	...	...	|	|	|	1453	|	1520z	|	|	|	|	1553	1607	|	...	...	|	|
Mannheim Hbf 913 a.	|	1427	1423	1437z	1443	...	...	|	|	1521	1523	1527	1554	1552	1624	|	1627	1623	1638	1643	...	...	|	1721
Mannheim Hbf 913 d.	|	1430	1434	1439z	1445	...	...	|	|	1523	1531	1536	1556	1554	1626	|	1630	1636	1640	1645	...	...	|	1723
Darmstadt Hbf 913 d.	1337	|	|	|	|	...	...	1437	1437	|	|	|	|	|	|	1537	|	|	|	|	...	...	1637	|
Bensheim 913 d.	1350	|	|	|	|	...	...	|	1450	|	|	|	|	|	|	1550	|	|	|	|	...	...	1650	|
Weinheim 913 d.	1400	|	|	|	|	...	...	1456	1500	|	|	|	|	|	|	1600	|	|	|	|	...	...	1700	|
Heidelberg Hbf 913 931 d.	1414	|	|	|	|	...	...	1510	1514	|	|	|	|	1606	1644	1614	|	|	|	|	...	...	1714	1736
Bruchsal 913 931 d.	1438	|	|	|	|	...	...	|	|	|	|	|	|	|	|	1636	|	|	|	|	...	...	|	|
Vaihingen (Enz) 931 d.	|	|	|	|	|	...	...	|	|	1605	|	|	|	|	|	|	|	|	|	|	...	...	|	1808
Stuttgart Hbf 931 a.	|	1508	|	|	|	...	1449	1550	1554	1622	1608	|	1635	1646	1725	|	1708	|	1718	|	1650	...	1754	1825
München Hbf 930 a.	|	1727	|	|	|	←	|	▬	1811	...	1827	|	▬	▬	...	|	1927	|	▬	|	|	...	2011	...
Karlsruhe Hbf 913 916 d.	1452	...	1458	1504	1510	1512	1532	...	...	...	...	1600	①–⑤	...	...	1650	...	1700	①–⑤	1710	1733	...	...	...
Baden-Baden 916 d.	...	...	|	→	1527	1534	|	◐2	...	...	...	|	◐2	◐2	...	...	...	|	◐2	1727	|	...	...	...
Offenburg 916 ☆ d.	...	...	1529	...	|	|	|	1604	...	...	...	1629	1634	1704	...	...	...	1729	1734	|	|	1804	...	...
Kehl 🏛 d.	...	...	|	...	|	|	|	1622	...	...	...	|	1652	1722	...	...	...	|	1753	|	|	1822	...	...
Strasbourg a.	...	...	|	...	|	1600	1612	1634	...	...	...	|	1704	1734	...	...	...	|	1804	|	1810	1834	...	...
Freiburg (Brsg) Hbf ☆ d.	...	...	1601	...	1612	...	...	...	...	...	...	1701	...	...	...	...	...	1801	...	1812	...	...	...	...
Basel Bad Bf 🏛 ☆ a.	...	...	1634	...	1645	...	...	...	...	...	...	1734	...	...	...	...	...	1834	...	1845	...	...	...	...
Basel SBB ☆ a.	...	...	1647	...	1654	...	...	...	...	...	...	1747	...	...	...	...	...	1847	...	1854	...	...	...	...
Zürich HB 510 a.	...	...	...	...	1800	...	...	...	...	...	...	...	...	...	...	...	...	...	...	2000	...	...	...	...

Regional trains **OFFENBURG - BASEL** (German holiday dates apply). On Nov. 1 regional services between Offenburg and Basel Bad Bf run as on ⑦.

	†	Ⓐ	Ⓐ		①–⑥	⚒	Ⓐ		⚒																
Offenburg d.	0049	0425	0522	...	...	0551	0632	...	0706	...	0807	0907	1007	1107	1204	1307	1404	1507	1607	1707	1807	1907	2007	...	2107
Freiburg (Brsg) Hbf a.	0131	0525	0626	...	...	0649	0727	...	0756	...	0855	0955	1055	1155	1253	1355	1450	1555	1656	1756	1856	1955	2055	...	2202
Freiburg (Brsg) Hbf d.	0132	0526	0628	0628	...	0710	0732	...	0815	0815	0915	1011	1115	1215o	1315	1415o	1515	1615o	1715	1815o	1915	2015o	...	2145	▬
Müllheim (Baden) d.	0152	0547	0655	0655	...	0731	0749	...	0835	0835	0935	1035	1135	1235	1337	1435	1535	1635	1735	1835	1935	2035	...	2212	...
Basel Bad Bf 🏛 a.	0220	0625	0732	0732	0745	0806	0811	0819	0911	0911	1011	1111	1211	1311	1412	1511	1611	1711	1811	1911	2011	2111	...	2249	2319
Basel SBB a.	...	0650	...	...	0750	...	0820⁝	0825	0925	0925	1025	1125	1225	1325	1425	1525	1620§	1720§	1820§	1925	2025	2125	...	...	2325

FOR NOTES SEE NEXT PAGE →

FRANKFURT - BASEL and STUTTGART 912

SEE NOTE ⊠	*ICE* 373		*TGV* 9560	*ICE* 579	*IC* 2011	*IC* 2017	*IC* 2373	*ICE* 691	*ICE* 201	*ICE* 917	*ICE* 79	*TGV* 9570		*IC* 1956	*IC* 2295	*IC* 2019	*IC* 2311	*ICE* 613	*IC* 2264	*ICE* 375	*IC* 2264	*IC* 1915	*ICE* 771	*IC* 2375	*ICE* 693
			R E			⑤				Ⓑq		X P		⑦w	Ⓑq	⑥			Ⓑq		Ⓑq	⑤⑦			
	N✕	◐2	🅁🍷	✕	F🍷		A🍷	✕	🍷	✕	✕	🅁🍷	◐2	♦	🍷	♦	J🍷	🍷	🍷♦	✕	🍷♦	T🍷	✕	B🍷	✕
Berlin Hbf **810 902** ....♣ d.	1231	...	...	...	1002w	...	...	1334	...	...	...	...	...	...	...	...	...	...	...	1431	...	1202	...	...	1534
mburg Hbf **800 900** ..♣ d.	|	...	...	1324	|	...	1228	|	...	...	1424	...	...	...	...	...	1246	...	...	|	...	|	1524	1428	|
nnover Hbf **810 900** .♣ d.	|	...	...	1441	1156w	1156	1401	|	...	...	1541	...	...	...	...	...	|	...	...	|	...	1356	1641	1601	|
rtmund Hbf **800** .... d.	|	...	...	|	1349w	1352	|	|	...	1556	|	...	...	...	...	...	1537	1637n	...	|	...	1549	|	|	|
ln Hbf **800 910** .... d.	|	...	...	|	1518	1518	|	|	1655	1713d	|	...	...	...	...	1618	1653	1755	...	|	...	1718	|	|	|
blenz Hbf **911**............... d.	|	...	...	|	1617	1617	|	|	|	|	|	...	...	...	...	1717	1748	|	...	|	...	1817	|	|	|
inz Hbf **911**.................. d.	|	...	...	|	1712	1712	|	|	|	|	|	...	...	...	...	1817	1840	|	...	|	...	1912	|	|	|
kfurt (Main) Hbf ..... **913** d.	1650	...	1657	1705	|	|	1720	1750	|	|	1805z	...	...	1759	1820	|	|	|	...	1850	...	|	1905	1920	1950
ankfurt Flughafen ✈ ◧. d.	|	...	|	1720z	|	|	|	|	1753	1807	|	...	...	|	|	|	|	1853	...	|	...	|	1920	|	|
nheim Hbf .... **913** a.	1727	...	1737	1754	1752	1752	|	1827	1823	1838‡	1843	...	...	|	|	1901	1921	1923	...	1927	...	1952	1954	|	2027
nheim Hbf .... **913** d.	1736	...	1740	1756	1754	1754	|	1830	1836	1840‡	1845	...	...	|	|	1903	1923	1931	...	1936	...	1954	1956	|	2030
rmstadt Hbf .... **913** d.	|	...	|	|	|	|	1737	|	|	|	|	...	...	1821	1837	|	|	|	...	|	...	|	|	1937	|
nsheim .... **913** d.	|	...	|	|	|	|	1750	|	|	|	|	...	...	1835	1850	|	|	|	...	|	...	|	|	1950	|
einheim .... **913** d.	|	...	|	|	|	|	1800	|	|	|	|	...	...	1848	1900	|	|	|	...	|	...	|	|	2000	|
idelberg Hbf ...**913 931** d.	|	...	|	|	1806	1806	1814	|	|	|	|	...	...	1902	1914	1916	1936	|	...	|	...	2006	|	2014	|
Bruchsal ....**913 931** d.	|	...	|	|	|	|	1836	|	|	|	|	...	...	|	|	|	|	|	...	|	...	|	|	2038	|
ihingen (Enz) .... **931** d.	|	...	|	|	|	|	|	|	|	|	|	...	...	|	|	|	2005	|	...	|	...	|	|	|	|
uttgart Hbf .... **931** a.	|	...	|	1835	1846	1846	|	1908	|	1924‡	|	1849	...	|	1954	1958	2024	2008	...	|	...	2046	2035	|	2108
München Hbf **930** .... a.	|	...	|	▬	...	2118•	|	2127j	|	...	|	|	...	|	2214•	...	...	2226	...	|	...	▬	2319f	|	2329r
sruhe Hbf ....**913 916** d.	1800	...	1807	①–⑤	...	...	1852	...	1900	...	1910	1932	...	1940	...	...	...	...	1955	2000	...	...	...	2054	...
en-Baden............... **916** d.	|	...	|	◐2	...	...	...	...	|	...	1927	|	...	...	...	...	...	...	|	2018	...	◐2	...	...	...
nburg ....**916** ☆ d.	1829	1834	|	1904	...	...	...	...	1929	...	|	|	2004	...	...	...	...	...	2026	2034	...	2104	...	...	...
hl 🏛 .... d.	|	1852	|	1922	...	...	...	...	|	...	|	|	2022	...	...	...	...	...	|	|	...	2122	...	...	...
rasbourg .... a.	|	1904	1911*	1934	...	...	...	...	|	...	|	2013	2034	...	...	...	...	...	|	|	←	2134	...	...	...
burg (Brsg) Hbf ....☆ d.	1901	...	...	...	...	...	...	...	2001	...	2012	...	...	...	...	...	...	...	2100	2106	2112	...	...	...	...
el Bad Bf 🏛 ....☆ a.	1934	...	...	...	...	...	...	...	2034	...	2045	...	...	...	...	...	...	...	→	2138	2154	...	...	...	...
el SBB ....☆ a.	1947	...	...	...	...	...	...	...	2047	...	2054	...	...	...	...	...	...	...	...	2147	...	...	...	...	...
irich HB **510** .... a.	...	...	...	...	...	...	...	...	...	...	2200	...	...	...	...	...	...	...	...	...	...	...	...	...	...

SEE NOTE ⊠	*ICE* 203	*ICE* 1103	*ICE* 1171	*ICE* 1171	*ICE* 203	*IC* 2171	*IC* 1995	*IC* 2297 2397	*IC* 2213	*ICE* 615	*ICE* 377		*IC* 1917	*ICE* 773	*ICE* 695	*ICE* 1093	*ICE* 1093	*ICE* 605	*IC* 2377	*IC* 1973	*ICE* 273	*ICE* 273	*ICE* 605	*ICE* 877	*ICE* 1593
	⚒	†		Ⓒ	Ⓐ	⑤	⑦w					▲	⑦w		⑥k	Ⓑq	⑦w		⑤p	⑦w		⑤⑥	⊙		⊕
	🍷	🍷	✕	✕	🍷	🍷	S🍷	Y🍷	🍷♦	🍷	✕	◐2		✕	✕	✕	✕	🍷♦	A🍷	¶✕	K✕	p K ✕	🍷♦	✕	🍷
Berlin Hbf **810 902** ....♣ d.	...	...	...	...	...	...	1502	...	...	...	1631	...	1357	...	1734	1803	1803	...	...	...	...		...	1831	...
mburg Hbf **800 900** ..♣ d.	...	...	1624	1624	...	1528	|	...	1446	...	|	...	|	1724	|	|	|	...	1628	...	1824	1824	...	|	...
nnover Hbf **810 900** .♣ d.	...	...	1741	1741	...	1707	1703	...	|	...	|	...	1556	1841	|	|	|	...	1801	...	1941	1941	...	|	...
rtmund Hbf **800** .... d.	...	...	|	|	...	|	|	...	1737	1837n	|	...	1752	|	|	|	|	1924k	|	...	|	|	...	|	...
ln Hbf **800 910** .... d.	1855	1855	|	|	...	|	|	...	1853	1957	|	...	1918	|	|	|	|	2046	|	...	|	|	...	|	...
blenz Hbf **911**............... d.	|	|	|	|	...	|	|	...	1948	|	|	...	2017	|	|	|	|	|	|	...	|	|	...	|	...
inz Hbf **911**.................. d.	|	|	|	|	...	|	|	...	2040	|	|	...	2112	|	|	|	|	|	|	...	|	|	...	|	...
kfurt (Main) Hbf ..... **913** d.	|	|	2005z	2005z	...	2015	2020	2020	|	|	2050	...	|	2105	2151	2151	2151	|	2155	2155	2205z	2205z	...	2300	2308
ankfurt Flughafen ✈ ◧. d.	1953	1953	|	|	...	|	|	|	|	2053	|	...	|	2120z	|	|	|	2154	|	|	|	|	...	2317	|
nheim Hbf .... **913** a.	2023	2023	2043	2043	...	|	|	|	2121	2123	2127	...	2152	2154	2228	2228	2228	2224	|	|	2243	2243	...	2353	|
nheim Hbf .... **913** d.	2036	2036	2045	2045	...	|	|	|	2123	2131	2136	...	2158	2156	2231	2231	2231	2236	|	|	2245	2245	...	2358	|
rmstadt Hbf .... **913** d.	|	|	|	|	...	2037	2037	2037	|	|	|	...	|	|	|	|	|	|	2212	2212	|	|	...	|	2327
nsheim .... **913** d.	|	|	|	|	...	2050	2050	2050	|	|	|	...	|	|	|	|	|	|	2224	2224	|	|	...	|	2341
einheim .... **913** d.	|	|	|	|	...	2100	2100	2100	|	|	|	...	|	|	|	|	|	|	2234	2234	|	|	...	|	|
idelberg Hbf ...**913 931** d.	|	|	|	|	...	2114	2114	2114	2136	|	|	...	|	2210	|	|	|	|	2249	2249	|	|	...	|	0004
Bruchsal ....**913 931** d.	|	|	|	|	...	|	|	|	|	|	|	...	|	|	|	|	|	|	2311	|	|	|	...	|	|
ihingen (Enz) .... **931** d.	|	|	|	|	...	|	|	|	2205	|	|	...	|	|	|	|	|	|	|	2321	|	|	...	|	0032
uttgart Hbf .... **931** a.	|	|	|	|	...	2155	2156	2155	2224	2208	|	...	|	2250	2308	2310	2310	|	|	2338	|	|	...	|	0103
München Hbf **930** .... a.	|	|	|	|	←	▬	...	...	...	0027	|	...	|	...	...	...	0133	|	|	...	|	|	←	|	...
sruhe Hbf ....**913 916** d.	2100	2102	2108	2112	2112	▲	...	...	...	...	2200	...	2224	...	...	...	...	2300	2327	...	2308	2312	2312	0022	...
en-Baden............... **916** d.	→	2119	...	2129	2129	◐2	...	...	...	...	2218	...	...	...	...	...	...	→	...	...	...	2329	2331	...	...
nburg ....**916** ☆ d.	...	2135	...	2145	2145	2204	...	...	...	...	2237	2325	...	...	...	...	...	...	...	...	...	2345	2350	...	...
hl 🏛 .... d.	...	|	...	|	|	2222	...	...	...	...	|	2348	...	...	...	...	...	...	...	...	...	|	|	...	...
rasbourg .... a.	...	|	...	|	|	2234	...	...	...	...	|	2400	...	...	...	...	...	...	...	...	...	|	|	...	...
burg (Brsg) Hbf ....☆ d.	...	2208	...	2217	2217	...	...	...	...	...	2311	...	...	...	...	...	...	...	...	...	...	0017	0022	...	...
el Bad Bf 🏛 ....☆ a.	...	2242	...	2251	2251	...	...	...	...	...	2346	...	...	...	...	...	...	...	...	...	...	0050	0056	...	...
el SBB ....☆ a.	...	2250	...	2300	2300	...	...	...	...	...	2354	...	...	...	...	...	...	...	...	...	...	0100	...	...	...
irich HB **510** .... a.	...	...	...	...	...	...	...	...	...	...	...	...	...	...	...	...	...	...	...	...	...	...	...	...	...

NOTES (LISTED BY TRAIN NUMBER) for pages 426 and 427

– [12] and ✕ Hamburg - Zürich (- Chur ①–⑥). On † runs with train number **1175** and starts from Kiel (Table **820**).

– [12] and ✕ Frankfurt - Salzburg - Villach - Klagenfurt; [12] Frankfurt - Villach (**213**) - Ljubljana - Zagreb.

– WÖRTHERSEE – [12] and 🍷 Münster - München - Salzburg - Villach - Klagenfurt.

– Ⓑ (not Oct. 2). [12] and 🍷 Frankfurt - München - Salzburg - Klagenfurt. On ①–⑤ Aug. 1 - Sept. 9 runs Frankfurt - Stuttgart only (as *IC* **2097**). On ⑦ July 31 - Sept. 11 runs as *IC* **1269** Frankfurt - München Hbf (a. 1911) - Salzburg Hbf (a. 2059).

– [12] Münster - Ulm - Lindau - Bregenz - Innsbruck.

– [12] and 🍷 Frankfurt - München - Salzburg - Bischofshofen - Selzthal - Graz. Runs Frankfurt - Stuttgart only July 30 - Sept. 11 (as *IC* **2199**).

– [12] and 🍷 Frankfurt - München - Salzburg (- Linz Ⓑ). Runs Frankfurt - Stuttgart only July 30 - Sept. 11 (as *IC* **2191**).

– [12] and 🍷 Köln - Basel; conveys [12] and 🍷 (*ICE* **105**) Amsterdam - Köln - Basel.

– [12] and 🍷 (Dortmund ⑥**k** -) Essen - Karlsuhe (- Basel Bad Bf ⊙).

6 – [12] Leipzig - Erfurt - Frankurt - Karlsruhe.

5 – [12] and 🍷 Emden - Münster - Konstanz.

3 – ALLGÄU – [12] and 🍷 Hannover - Dortmund - Stuttgart - Ulm - Oberstdorf.

9 – ⑥ until Oct. 29. [12] Norddeich Mole - Münster - Stuttgart.

3 – RÜGEN – [12] and 🍷 Ostseebad Binz - Stralsund - Rostock - Hamburg - Stuttgart.

7 – [12] and 🍷 (Greifswald Ⓐ -) Stralsund - Rostock - Hamburg - Köln - Stuttgart.

4 – [12] and 🍷 München - Stuttgart - Basel.

1 – [12] and 🍷 (Hannover Ⓐ -) Kassel - Karlsruhe.

9 – [12] and 🍷 (Stralsund - Hamburg ⚒ -) Kassel - Frankfurt - Karlsruhe.

6 – ⑥ from July 9. [12] and ✕ Frankfurt - Strasbourg - Paris.

3 – Ⓑ from July 3. [12] and ✕ Frankfurt - Strasbourg - Paris.

6 – [12] and 🍷 München - Stuttgart - Paris. Timings vary by up to 5 minutes to July 2 and from Aug. 29.

0 – [12] and 🍷 Frankfurt - Strasbourg - Mulhouse - Lyon - Marseille.

From Stralsund (Table **830**).
WATTENMEER – From Westerland daily to Oct. 31, ①⑤⑥⑦ from Nov. 4 (Table **821**).
To Chur (Table **520**).
⑤ Sept. 2 - Oct. 28.
[12] and 🍷 Frankfurt - Strasbourg - Paris.
①②③④⑦ (not Oct. 2, Nov. 1).
On ①–④ (not Oct. 3, Nov. 1) continues to Tübingen Hbf (a. 1950).
From July 3. Runs as *TGV* **9592** on ⑥.
ICE conveys ✕, *TGV* conveys 🍷.

H – ⑥⑦ to July 2.
J – From Westerland (Table **821**).
K – From Kiel (Table **820**).
L – From Kassel (Table **806**).
M – From Münster (Table **800**).
N – To Interlaken via Bern (Table **560**).
P – [12] Stuttgart - Paris (Table **32**). Timings may vary by up to 5 minutes to July 2 and from Aug. 29.
Q – Until July 2.
R – From July 3.

S – July 24 - Aug. 28 Hannover d. 1709, Frankfurt d. 2046, Darmstadt d. 2103, Bensheim d. 2116, Weinheim d. 2126, Heidelberg d. 2145, Stuttgart a. 2235.
T – ⑤⑦ (also Oct. 3; not Oct. 2). To Tübingen (a. 2150) on ⑦**w**.
X – ①–⑤ (daily from July 3).
Y – ①②③④⑥ (not Oct. 3).

b – Ⓑ (not July 10 - Aug. 21, Oct. 2).
d – Köln **Messe/Deutz**.
e – ⚒ only.
f – ⑤ only.
g – July 9 - Aug. 21 calls at Köln **Messe/ Deutz** (not Köln Hbf).
h – 0611 on Ⓒ.
j – Ⓑ to July 1; daily from July 3.
k – ⑥ (also Oct. 2).
n – Not July 9 - Aug. 21.
o – 4 minutes earlier July 16 - Aug. 28.

p – Also Oct. 2.
q – Not Oct. 2.
r – Daily to July 8; Ⓑ from July 10 (not Oct. 2).
t – Ⓐ only.
u – 0514 July 9 - Aug. 21.
v – † (not July 10 - Aug. 21).
w – ⑦ (also Oct. 3; not Oct. 2).
x – Not July 16 – 20.
y – Also Oct. 3; not Oct. 2; not ⑤ Sept. 2 - Oct. 28.
z – Not July 16 - Aug. 28.
‡ – 22 – 28 minutes later July 17 - Aug. 28.
* – 1847 from Aug. 29.
• – Not July 30 - Sept. 11.
⁝ – Not Aug. 1.
◊ – ⑥ only.
⊙ – ①②③④⑦ (not Oct. 2).

⊖ – Train number **573** on †.
□ – Train number **1173** on †.
¶ – Train number **1977** July 31 - Sept. 4 (conveys 🍷, not ✕).
⊕ – Not Oct. 2. Runs as *IC* **2395** on ⑥, *ICE* **1572** on †.
♥ – Not July 17 – 20. July 21 - Aug. 28 Mannheim a. 1704, d. 1706, Stuttgart a. 1750.
▲ – Not Sept. 19 – 23, Oct. 3 – 7, 10 – 14, 17, 18.
❦ – Timings Frankfurt - Stuttgart are 23 – 44 minutes **earlier** July 30 - Sept. 11.
⊠ – Timings at Vaihingen, Stuttgart and München are subject to alteration until Sept. 11. Timings of services via Mannheim may vary by up to 10 minutes July 16 - Aug. 28 (timings of international *ICE* / *TGV* services between Frankfurt and Paris / Marseille may vary by up to 31 minutes). See shaded panel on page 367 for further details.
♣ – **July 18 - Sept. 2** Berlin, Hamburg and Hannover departures may be up to 47 minutes **earlier**. During this period many *IC* trains do not run north of Kassel (see Table 900). See shaded panel on page 367 for further details.
§ – On ⑥⑦ (also Aug. 1) change trains at Basel Badischer Bf (arrives Basel SBB 5 minutes later).
☆ – See panel on page 426 for other local services.
◐ – Operated by Südwestdeutsche Verkehrs. On Nov. 1 local services between Offenburg and Strasbourg run as on ⑦.
◧ – Frankfurt Flughafen Fernbahnhof.

912 BASEL and STUTTGART - FRANKFURT

km	km	SEE NOTE ⊠	ICE 618	ICE 1092	ICE 774	ICE 874	ICE 616	IC 2278	ICE 674	ICE 674	IC 2396	ICE 604	ICE 604	ICE 694	IC 1114	IC 2376		ICE 676	ICE 772	IC 2018	IC 2010	IC 2392	IC 2265	ICE 374
				①g	⚒			Ⓐ	Ⓒ		Ⓐ	Ⓐ			Ⓐ			Ⓐ		⑥	Ⓐ	①m	⚒	
			⊖	✕	✕	✕	🍷		K✕	K✕	⊕✕	🍷	🍷	✕		A🍷	◐2	✕	✕	♦	🍷♦		🍷♦	✕
		Zürich HB 510 d.	...	...	...	...	...	...	...	...	...	...	...	...	...	...	...	...	...	...	...	...	...	...
		Basel SBB ☆ d.	...	...	...	...	...	...	...	...	...	...	...	...	...	...	...	...	...	...	...	...	...	0608
		Basel Bad Bf ☆ d.	...	...	...	0412g	...	...	0511	...	...	0515	...	...	...	...	...	0545	...	...	...	...	0552	0618
		Freiburg (Brsg) Hbf ☆ d.	...	...	...	0447g	...	...	0546	...	...	0552	...	...	...	...	...	0622	...	...	...	...	0643	0652
0		**Strasbourg** ▶ d.	...	...	...		...	...		...	...		...	...	...	...	0622		...	...	...	...		
8		Kehl ▶ d.	...	...	...		...	...		...	...		...	...	...	...	0634		...	...	...	...		
29		Offenburg 916 ☆ ▶ d.	...	...	...	0520g	...	...	0618	...	...	0626	...	...	...	...	0652	0657	...	...	...	...	0731	0724
—		Baden-Baden 916 d.	...	...	...	0536g	...	...	0634	...	...	0641	...	...	...	...	...	0714	...	...	...	...	0749	0741
		Karlsruhe Hbf 913 916 d.	0349	0500	...	0558	...	0615	0651	0651	...	0700	0700	...	...	0702	...	0736	...	...	...	...	0806	0800
		München Hbf 930 d.	0001		...		0323				...			...	...		...		...	...	...	...		
0	0	**Stuttgart** Hbf 931 d.	0230		0502		0551				0602			0651	0630		...		0726	0714	0714	0717	0849	
29	29	Vaihingen (Enz) 931 d.	0259		0519						0620				0648		...						...	
		Bruchsal 913 931 d.	0405					0633								0724	...						...	
	92	**Heidelberg** Hbf 913 931 d.	0428		0547			0654			0658				0720	0746	...			0755	0755	0800	...	
		Weinheim 913 d.									0714					0800	...					0817	...	
		Bensheim 913 d.									0728					0809	...					0828	...	
		Darmstadt Hbf 913 d.									0742					0824	...					0841	...	
107	109	**Mannheim** Hbf 913 a.	0438	0526	0559	0623	0628	0709z	0714	0714		0723	0723	0729	0732		...	0800	0804	0806	0806		...	0823
107		**Mannheim** Hbf 913 d.	0440	0528	0605	0632	0636	0711z	0716	0716		0736	0736	0732	0734		...	...	0806	0808	0808		...	0832
179		**Frankfurt** Flughafen ✈ a.	0512		0638z		0706					0806	0806				...	...	0838z				...	
		Frankfurt (Main) Hbf 913 a.	0533	0608	0652	0708		0752	0752z	0752z	0802			0808		0840	...	...	0852z			0902	...	0908
		Mainz Hbf 911 a.						...			...				0815		...	...		0846	0846	...	...	
		Koblenz Hbf 911 a.						...			...				...		...	...		0941	0941	...	...	
		Köln Hbf 800 910 a.	0705				0805	...			...	0905	0905		...		...	...		1042	1042	...	...	
		Dortmund Hbf 800 a.	0825x				0921n	...			...	...	...		...		...	...		...	1209f	...	...	
		Hannover Hbf 810 900 ♣ a.	...		0917		...	...	1017	1017	...	...	...		...	1156	...	...	1117	...	1401f	...	...	
		Hamburg Hbf 800 900 ♣ a.	...		1035		...	...	1135	1135	...	...	...		...	1328	...	...	1235	...		...	...	
		Berlin Hbf 810 902 ♣ a.	...	0955	...	1128	...	...	...	...	...	...	...	1225	...	...	...	...	...	...	1553f	...	...	1328

SEE NOTE ⊠	IC 2216	IC 2294	ICE 78	ICE 916		ICE 202	ICE 202	ICE 692	IC 2374	ICE 770	ICE 1537		ICE 9571		TGV 9561	ICE 372	ICE 612	IC 2218	IC 1296		TGV 9571	ICE 76	ICE 714	ICE 200
				⚒		⚒				△	⑥	①–⑤	R P	①–⑤	①–⑥				⊡		Q P		⚒	
	🍷♦	🍷	✕	♥✕	◐2	🍷	🍷	✕	B🍷	✕	✕♦	◐2	Ⓡ✕	◐2	ⓇF 🍷	N✕	🍷	🍷	G🍷	◐2	Ⓡ🍷	K✕	♠🍷	🍷
Zürich HB 510 d.	...	...	0600	...	...	...	...	...	...	...	...	...	...	...		...	...	...	...	...	...	0800	...	...
Basel SBB ☆ d.	...	...	0706	...	...	0713	...	...	...	...	...	...	...	...	...	0813	...	...	...	...	...	0906	...	0913
Basel Bad Bf ☆ d.	...	...	0715	...	...	0722	...	...	...	...	...	...	...	...	...	0823	...	...	...	...	...	0915	...	0923
Freiburg (Brsg) Hbf ☆ d.	...	...	0749	...	...	0755	...	...	...	...	...	...	...	...	...	0857	...	...	...	...	...	0949	...	0957
Strasbourg ▶ d.	...	...		...	0750		...	...	...	...	...	0820	0831	0852	0913		...	...	...	0922	0947		...	
Kehl ▶ d.	...	...		...	0804		...	...	...	...	...	0831		0904			...	...	...	0934			...	
Offenburg 916 ☆ ▶ d.	...	...		...	0822	0827	...	...	...	...	...	0849		0922		0930	...	...	...	0952			...	1030
Baden-Baden 916 d.	...	...	0834	...	...	0843	...	...	...	...	...	...		...			...	...	...	...		1034	...	
Karlsruhe Hbf 913 916 d.	...	...	0851	...	...	0900	0900	...	0905	...	...	...	0910	...	0955	1000	...	...	...	...	1028	1051	...	1100
München Hbf 930 d.	...	0536s		...	...			0630a		...	...	...		...			0727	...	0746r	...			...	
Stuttgart Hbf 931 d.	0737	0805		0836	...			0851		0925	0904	...	0952	...			0951	0937	1004	...	1104		1041	
Vaihingen (Enz) 931 d.	0755				...						0928	...	...	...				0955		...	...			
Bruchsal 913 931 d.					...				0923			...	...	...						...	...			
Heidelberg Hbf 913 931 d.	0825	0846			...				0946		0956	...	...	...				1025	1046	...	...			
Weinheim 913 d.		0900			...				1000			...	...	...					1100	...	...			
Bensheim 913 d.		0909			...				1009		1022	...	...	...					1109	...	...			
Darmstadt Hbf 913 d.		0924			...				1024		1040	...	...	...					1124	...	...			
Mannheim Hbf 913 a.	0837		0914	0919	...	0924	0924	0929		1004		...	...	...	1018	1024	1028	1037		...	...	1114	1119	1124
Mannheim Hbf 913 d.	0839		0916	0921	...	0936	0936	0932		1006		...	...	...	1021	1032	1036	1039		...	...	1116	1121	1136
Frankfurt Flughafen ✈ a.				0953	...	1006	1006			1038z		...	...	...			1106			...	...		1153	1206
Frankfurt (Main) Hbf 913 a.		0940	0953z		...			1008	1040	1052	1057	...	...	...	1058	1108			1140	...	...	1153z		
Mainz Hbf 911 a.	0918	...			...							...	...	...	...			1118	...	...	...			
Koblenz Hbf 911 a.	1011	...			...							...	...	...	...			1211	...	...	...			
Köln Hbf 800 910 a.	1105	...		1042d	...	1105	1105					...	...	...	...		1205	1305	...	...	...		1242d	1305
Dortmund Hbf 800 a.	1221	...		1203t	...	1221e	...					...	...	...	...		1321n	1421	...	...	...		1403◊	1421y
Hannover Hbf 810 900 ♣ a.		...	1217	...	...	...	...		1356	1317		...	...	...	...		...		...	...	...	1417	...	...
Hamburg Hbf 800 900 ♣ a.	1511	...	1335	...	...	...	...		1529	1435		...	...	...	...		...	1713	...	...	...	1535	...	...
Berlin Hbf 810 902 ♣ a.	...	...	...	...	...	...	...	1425	...	...	1501	...	...	...	...	1528	...	...	...	...	...	...	...	...

SEE NOTE ⊠	IC 2372	IC 1216	ICE 578		ICE 370	ICE 610	IC 2312	EC 390	IC 2006	IC 2004	IC 2014	ICE 74	ICE 108	ICE 598	IC 2370	IC 2012	ICE 576	ICE 9573		ICE 278	ICE 518	EC 8	EC 218	
	⑤–⑦	⑤u							⑥	⑦w	⑤							T P						
	vA 🍷	G🍷	✕	◐2	✕	🍷	🍷	🍷♦	🍷♦	🍷♦	🍷♦	K✕	🍷	✕	🍷♦	🍷♦	✕	Ⓡ	◐2	N✕	🍷	✕	🍷♦	◐2
Zürich HB 510 d.		...	...	...	...	...	...	...	...	...	...	1000	...	...	...	...	...	...	...	...	...	1100	...	...
Basel SBB ☆ d.	...	...	...	...	1013	...	...	...	...	...	...	1106	1113	...	...	...	...	...	...	1213	...	1220	...	...
Basel Bad Bf ☆ d.	...	...	...	...	1023	...	...	...	...	...	...	1115	1123	...	...	...	...	...	...	1223	...	1230	...	...
Freiburg (Brsg) Hbf ☆ d.	...	...	...	...	1057	...	...	...	...	...	...	1149	1157	...	...	...	...	...	...	1257	...	1304	...	...
Strasbourg ▶ d.	...	...	...	1052		...	...	...	...	...	...			...	...	...	...	1246	1252		...		...	1322
Kehl ▶ d.	...	...	...	1104		...	...	...			...			...	...	...	...		1304		...		...	1335
Offenburg 916 ☆ ▶ d.	...	...	...	1122	1130	...	...	...	1139	1139	...		1230	...	...	...	...		1322	1330	...		...	1353
Baden-Baden 916 d.	...	...	...	...		...	...	...	1202	1202	...	1234		...	...	...	...		...		...	1352	...	...
Karlsruhe Hbf 913 916 d.	1110	...	...	...	1200	...	...	...	1221	1221	...	1251	1300	...	1310	...	...	1328	...	1400	...	1412	...	...
München Hbf 930 d.		0848●	...	...		0928	...	0946			...			1028		...	...	...	...		1128		1146	...
Stuttgart Hbf 931 d.		1114	1125	...		1151	1129	1204			1209			1251		1314	1325	1409	...		1351		1404	...
Vaihingen (Enz) 931 d.				...			1148				1226							...	...					...
Bruchsal 913 931 d.	1124			...											1324			...	...					...
Heidelberg Hbf 913 931 d.	1146	1155		...				1246							1346	1355		...	...				1446	...
Weinheim 913 d.	1200			...				1300							1400			...	...				1500	...
Bensheim 913 d.	1209			...				1309							1409			...	...				1509	...
Darmstadt Hbf 913 d.	1224			...				1324							1424			...	...				1524	...
Mannheim Hbf 913 a.		1206	1204	...	1223	1228	1228		1250	1250	1256	1314	1323	1329		1406	1404	...	...	1423	1428	1437		...
Mannheim Hbf 913 d.		1208	1206	...	1232	1236	1236		1258	1258	1258	1316	1336	1332		1408	1406	...	...	1432	1436	1439		...
Frankfurt Flughafen ✈ a.			1238z	...		1306							1406				1438z	...	...		1506			...
Frankfurt (Main) Hbf 913 a.	1240		1252	...	1308			1340				1353z		1408	1440		1452	...	...	1508			1540	...
Mainz Hbf 911 a.		1246		...			1318	...	1343	1343	1343					1446		...	...			1518	...	...
Koblenz Hbf 911 a.		1341		...			1411	...	1441	1441	1441					1541		...	...			1611	...	...
Köln Hbf 800 910 a.		1442		...		1405	1505	...	1542	1542	1542		1505			1642		...	...		1605	1705	...	...
Dortmund Hbf 800 a.		1608		...		1521n	1621	...	1703	...	...		1621j			1809		...	...		1721n	1821	...	...
Hannover Hbf 810 900 ♣ a.	1556	1801	1517	...		...		...	...	...	...	1617	...		1756	2018	1717	...	...		...		...	...
Hamburg Hbf 800 900 ♣ a.	1732		1635	...		...	1914	...	...	...	...	1735	...		1928	...	1835	...	...		...	2113	...	...
Berlin Hbf 810 902 ♣ a.	...	1954	...	...	1728	...	...	...	...	...	...	...	...	1825	...	...	...	...	...	1928	...	...	...	...

Regional trains **BASEL - OFFENBURG** (German holiday dates apply). On Nov. 1 regional services between Basel Bad Bf and Offenburg run as on ⑦.

km		①–⑥		Ⓐ													Ⓐ	Ⓒ		⑥				①–⑥	
0	**Basel** SBB d.	0532	...	*0603*	...	0736§	0836§	*0934*	*1034*	*1134*	*1234*	*1334*	*1434*	*1534*	1636§	1736§	*1804*	*1834*	1836§	*1904*	...	*1934*	...	2104	...
5	**Basel** Bad Bf d.	0538	0549	0625	0634	0748	0848	0948	1048	1148	1248	1348	1448	1548	1648	1748	1826	1848	1848	1926	...	1948	...	2110	2126
37	Müllheim (Baden) d.	▬	0620	0649	0707	0823	0923	1023	1123	1223	1323	1423	1523	1623	1723	1823	1855	1923	1923	1955	...	2023	2054	...	2158
66	**Freiburg** (Brsg) Hbf a.	...	0646	0718	0736	0847	0944	1044	1144	1244	1344	1444	1544	1644	1744	1844	1923	1944	1944	2021	...	2044	2122	...	2219
66	**Freiburg** (Brsg) Hbf d.	0555	0656	0722	0803	0903	1003	1103	1203	1307	1403	1500	1603	1705	1803	1903	1925	2003	...	...	2025	...	2125	...	2225
129	**Offenburg** a.	0645	0745	0814	0851	0953	1053	1153	1253	1353	1450	1553	1650	1753	1850	1949	2021	2050	...	...	2121	...	2221	...	2318

FOR NOTES SEE NEXT PAGE →

BASEL and STUTTGART - FRANKFURT 912

SEE NOTE ⊠		TGV 9583 [R] 🍷♦	ICE 72 H🍴	TGV 9583 [R] 🍷♦	ICE 106 🍷	ICE 596 🍴	ICE 712 Ⓐ 🍴	IC 2276 🍷	IC 118 ♦	ICE 1094 Ⓑq K🍴	ICE 574 ⑥h 🍴	◐2
h HB 510	d.	...	1200	...	...	...	...	...	...	...	...	...
SBB ☆	d.	...	1306	...	1313	...	...	...	...	...	...	...
ad Bf 🏛 ☆	d.	...	1315	...	1323	...	...	...	...	...	...	...
g (Brsg) Hbf ☆	d.	...	1349	...	1357	...	...	...	...	...	...	...
bourg ▶	d.	1355	|	...	|	...	...	...	...	...	...	1452
🏛 ▶	d.	|	|	...	|	...	...	...	...	...	...	1504
rg 916 ☆ ▶	d.	|	|	...	1430	...	...	...	...	...	...	1522
Baden 916	d.	1425	1434	←	|	...	...	...	...	...	...	...
he Hbf 913 916	d.	1446	1451	1454	1500	...	...	1510	...	...	...	...
nchen Hbf 930	d.	→	|	|	|	1228	...	|	...	...	...	...
gart Hbf 931	d.	...	|	|	|	1451	1433	|	1512	1525	1525	...
ngen (Enz) 931	d.	...	|	|	|	|	1454	|	|	|	|	...
chsal 913 931	d.	...	|	|	|	|	|	1524	|	|	|	...
elberg Hbf 913 931	d.	...	|	|	|	|	1520	1546	1555	|	|	...
heim 913	d.	...	|	|	|	|	|	1600	|	|	|	...
heim 913	d.	...	|	|	|	|	|	1609	|	|	|	...
stadt Hbf 913	d.	...	|	|	|	|	|	1624	|	|	|	...
eim Hbf 913	a.	...	1514	1518z	1523	1529	1531	|	1606	1604	1604	...
eim Hbf 913	d.	...	1516	1521z	1536	1532	1533	|	1608	1606	1606	...
kfurt Flughafen ✈ ◧	a.	...	|	|	1606	|	|	|	|	1638z	1638z	...
urt (Main) Hbf 913	a.	...	1553z	1558	|	1608	|	1640	|	1652	1652	...
z Hbf 911	a.	...	|	...	|	|	1615	|	1646	|	|	...
enz Hbf 911	a.	...	|	...	|	|	|	|	1741	|	|	...
Hbf 800 910	a.	...	|	...	1705	|	1801	|	1842	|	|	...
mund Hbf 800	a.	...	|	...	1821n	|	...	|	...	|	|	...
over Hbf 810 900 ♣	a.	...	1817	...	...	|	...	1956	...	1906	1917	...
burg Hbf 800 900 ♣	a.	...	1935	...	...	|	...	2128v	...	2024	2038	...
rlin Hbf 810 902 ♣	a.	...	...	...	...	2026	...	...	...	...	...	...

SEE NOTE ⊠		ICE 276 🍴	ICE 516 🍷	EC 6 N🍴	IC 2292 🍷	EC 114 🍷♦	①–⑤ ◐2	TGV 9575 RP [R]🍷	ICE 70 H🍴	ICE 504 🍷♦	ICE 1090 Ⓑq 🍴	ICE 594 ⑥h 🍴	IC 2316 Ⓑq	IC 2274 🍷♦	ICE 572 c 🍴
h HB 510	d.	...	...	...	...	...	...	...	1400	...	...	...	...	...	...
SBB ☆	d.	1413	...	1427	...	...	...	...	1506	1513	...	...	...	...	...
ad Bf 🏛 ☆	d.	1423	...	1435	...	...	...	...	1515	1523	...	...	...	...	...
g (Brsg) Hbf ☆	d.	1455	...	1507	...	...	...	...	1549	1557	...	...	...	...	...
bourg ▶	d.	|	...	|	...	...	1522	1546	|	|	...	...	...	...	...
🏛 ▶	d.	|	...	|	...	...	1534	|	|	|	...	...	...	...	...
rg 916 ☆ ▶	d.	1527	...	|	...	...	1552	|	|	1630	...	...	...	...	...
Baden 916	d.	1543	...	|	...	...	...	|	1634	|	...	...	...	...	...
he Hbf 913 916	d.	1601	...	1612	...	...	...	1628	1651	1700	...	...	...	1710	...
nchen Hbf 930	d.	|	1328	|	...	1346	...	|	|	|	1428	1428	...	|	...
gart Hbf 931	d.	|	1551	|	1604	1609•	...	1709	|	|	1651	1651	1636	|	1725
ngen (Enz) 931	d.	|	|	|	|	1626	...	...	|	|	|	|	|	|	|
chsal 913 931	d.	|	|	|	|	|	...	...	|	|	|	|	|	1724	|
elberg Hbf 913 931	d.	|	|	|	1646	|	...	...	|	|	|	|	1720	1746	|
heim 913	d.	|	|	|	1700	|	...	...	|	|	|	|	|	1800	|
heim 913	d.	|	|	|	1709	|	...	...	|	|	|	|	|	1809	|
stadt Hbf 913	d.	|	|	|	1724	|	...	...	|	|	|	|	|	1824	|
eim Hbf 913	a.	1624	1628	1637	|	1656	...	...	1714	1723	1729	1729	1736	|	1804
eim Hbf 913	d.	1632	1636	1639	|	1658	...	...	1716	1736	1732	1732	1738	|	1806
kfurt Flughafen ✈ ◧	a.	|	1706	|	|	|	...	...	|	1806	|	|	|	|	1838z
urt (Main) Hbf 913	a.	1708	|	|	1740	|	...	...	1753z	|	1808	1808	|	1840	1852
z Hbf 911	a.	|	|	1718	...	1740	...	...	|	|	|	|	1815	|	|
enz Hbf 911	a.	|	|	1811	...	1841	...	...	|	|	|	|	...	|	|
Hbf 800 910	a.	|	1805	1905	...	1942	...	...	|	1905	|	|	...	|	|
mund Hbf 800	a.	|	1921n	2021	...	2100	...	...	|	...	|	|	...	|	|
over Hbf 810 900 ♣	a.	|	...	|	...	...	...	...	2017	...	2021	|	...	2156k	2119
burg Hbf 800 900 ♣	a.	|	...	2314q	...	...	...	...	2138	...	|	|	...	2328w	2244
rlin Hbf 810 902 ♣	a.	2128	...	...	...	...	...	...	...	...	2203	2227	...	...	...

SEE NOTE ⊠		◐2	①–⑤ ◐2	ICE 9563 E [R]🍴	ICE 274 🍴	ICE 514 🍷	IC 2318 🍷♦	EC 112 🍴♦	ICE 710 Ⓑq ♠🍷	◐2	TGV 9577 Y [R]🍷	ICE 376 N🍴
h HB 510	d.	...	...	...	...	...	...	...	...	...	...	...
SBB ☆	d.	...	...	...	1613	...	...	...	...	...	...	1706
Bad Bf 🏛 ☆	d.	...	...	...	1623	...	...	...	...	...	...	1715
rg (Brsg) Hbf ☆	d.	...	...	...	1655	...	...	...	...	...	...	1749
sbourg ▶	d.	1622	1652	1713	|	...	...	...	...	1722	1747	|
🏛 ▶	d.	1634	1704	|	|	...	...	...	...	1734	|	|
urg 916 ☆ ▶	d.	1652	1722	|	1727	...	...	...	...	1752	|	|
Baden 916	d.	...	...	|	1743	...	...	...	...	...	|	1834
uhe Hbf 913 916	d.	...	...	1755	1801	...	...	...	...	...	1828	1851
ünchen Hbf 930	d.	...	...	|	|	1528	...	1547	...	...	|	|
tgart Hbf 931	d.	...	...	|	|	1751	1737	1805	1836	...	1909	|
ngen (Enz) 931	d.	...	...	|	|	|	1755	|	|	...	...	|
uchsal 913 931	d.	...	...	|	|	|	|	|	|	...	...	|
elberg Hbf 913 931	d.	...	...	|	|	|	1825	1846	|	...	...	|
heim 913	d.	...	...	|	|	|	|	1900	|	...	...	|
heim 913	d.	...	...	|	|	|	|	1909	|	...	...	|
nstadt Hbf 913	d.	...	...	|	|	|	|	1924	|	...	...	|
eim Hbf 913	a.	...	...	1818	1824	1828	1837	|	1919	...	...	1914
eim Hbf 913	d.	...	...	1821	1832	1836	1839	|	1921	...	...	1916
kfurt Flughafen ✈ ◧	a.	...	...	|	|	1906	|	|	1953	...	...	|
urt (Main) Hbf 913	a.	...	...	1858	1908	|	|	1940	|	...	...	1953¦
z Hbf 911	a.	...	...	...	|	|	1918	...	|	...	...	|
enz Hbf 911	a.	...	...	...	|	|	2011	...	|	...	...	|
Hbf 800 910	a.	...	...	...	|	2005	2105	...	2043d	...	...	|
mund Hbf 800	a.	...	...	...	|	2121b	2221q	...	2202w	...	...	|
over Hbf 810 900 ♣	a.	...	...	...	|	...	...	...	...	...	...	2217k
burg Hbf 800 900 ♣	a.	...	...	...	|	...	...	...	...	...	...	2351k
rlin Hbf 810 902 ♣	a.	...	...	...	2326	...	...	...	...	...	...	...

SEE NOTE ⊠		◐2	ICE 102 ¶ 🍷	ICE 592 🍴	IC 2172 ⑦w L🍷	IC 2272 Ⓐ L🍷	ICE 570 ⑦w 🍴	IC 1910 ⑦w 🍷	①–⑤ ◐2	ICE 1172 ⑥h 🍴	ICE 272 Ⓐ 🍴	ICE 292 ⑦w 🍴	ICE 512 M🍷	IC 2210 ①–④ 🍷	IC 2210 ⑤⑦ o🍷
h HB 510	d.	...	...	...	...	...	...	...	...	1700	1700	1700	...	...	...
SBB ☆	d.	...	1713	...	...	...	...	...	...	1813	1813	1813	...	...	...
Bad Bf 🏛 ☆	d.	...	1723	...	...	...	...	...	...	1823	1823	1823	...	...	...
rg (Brsg) Hbf ☆	d.	...	1756	...	...	...	...	...	...	1857	1857	1857	...	...	...
sbourg ▶	d.	1752	|	...	...	...	...	...	1852	|	|	|	...	...	...
🏛 ▶	d.	1804	|	...	...	...	...	...	1904	|	|	|	...	...	...
urg 916 ☆ ▶	d.	1822	1827	...	...	...	...	...	1920	1930	1930	1930	...	...	...
Baden 916	d.	...	1843	...	...	...	...	...	...	|	|	|	...	...	...
uhe Hbf 913 916	d.	...	1900	...	...	1910	...	...	...	2000	2000	2000	...	...	...
ünchen Hbf 930	d.	...	|	1628	...	|	...	1620	...	|	|	|	1727	...	...
tgart Hbf 931	d.	...	|	1851	1903	|	1925	1914	...	|	|	|	1951	1918	1937
ngen (Enz) 931	d.	...	|	|	|	|	|	|	...	|	|	|	|	|	1955
uchsal 913 931	d.	...	|	|	|	1924	|	|	...	|	|	|	|	|	|
elberg Hbf 913 931	d.	...	|	|	1946	1946	|	1955	...	|	|	|	|	2025*	2025
heim 913	d.	...	|	|	2000	2000	|	|	...	|	|	|	|	|	|
heim 913	d.	...	|	|	2009	2009	|	|	...	|	|	|	|	|	|
nstadt Hbf 913	d.	...	|	|	2024	2024	|	|	...	|	|	|	|	|	|
eim Hbf 913	a.	...	1924	1929	|	|	2004	2006	...	2024	2024	2024	2028	2037	2037
eim Hbf 913	d.	...	1936	1932	|	|	2006	2008	...	2032	2032	2032	2036	2039	2039
kfurt Flughafen ✈ ◧	a.	...	2006	|	|	|	2038z	|	...	|	|	|	2106	|	|
urt (Main) Hbf 913	a.	...	|	2008	2040	2040	2052	|	...	2108	2108	2108	|	|	|
z Hbf 911	a.	...	|	|	...	...	|	2046	...	|	|	|	|	2118	2118
enz Hbf 911	a.	...	|	|	...	...	|	2141	...	|	|	|	|	2211	2211
Hbf 800 910	a.	...	2105‡	|	...	...	|	2242	...	|	|	|	2205	2305	2305
mund Hbf 800	a.	...	2221	|	...	...	|	2359	...	|	|	|	...	...	...
over Hbf 810 900 ♣	a.	...	0018	|	...	...	2318	...	...	2341	0002	|	...	...	...
burg Hbf 800 900 ♣	a.	...	...	|	...	...	0044	...	...	0111	0138	|	...	...	...
rlin Hbf 810 902 ♣	a.	...	...	0035	...	...	...	...	...	...	...	0126	...	...	...

NOTES (LISTED BY TRAIN NUMBER)

[12] and 🍴 Klagenfurt - Villach - Salzburg - Frankfurt; [12] Zagreb (**212**) - Ljubljana - Villach (**112**) - Frankfurt.
WÖRTHERSEE – [12] and 🍷 Klagenfurt - Villach - Salzburg - München - Dortmund.
July 16 - Aug. 28 does not call at Vaihingen, Mannheim a. 1653, d. 1655.
[12] Innsbruck - Bregenz - Lindau - Ulm - Stuttgart - Münster.
[12] and 🍷 Graz - Selzthal - Bischofshofen - Salzburg - Frankfurt.
July 30 - Sept. 11 runs Stuttgart - Frankfurt only (as *IC* **2198**).
[12] and 🍷 (Linz ①–⑥ -) Salzburg - München - Frankfurt. Runs as *IC* **1268** July 30 - Sept. 11. On ①–⑥ July 30 - Sept. 10 runs Salzburg - München Hbf (d. 0910) - Frankfurt.
[12] and 🍷 Basel - Köln; conveys [12] and 🍷 (*ICE* **104**) Basel - Köln - Amsterdam.
[12] and 🍴 Stuttgart - Frankfurt - Erfurt - Berlin - Stralsund - Ostseebad Binz.
[12] and 🍷 Konstanz - Karlsruhe - Münster - Emden.
[12] and 🍷 Konstanz - Karlsruhe - Dortmund.
Ⓐ (not Nov. 1). [12] and 🍷 Tübingen Hbf (d. 0611) - Stuttgart - Düsseldorf (- Berlin ⑤).
ALLGÄU – [12] and 🍷 Oberstdorf - Ulm - Stuttgart - Dortmund - Hannover.
[12] and 🍷 Stuttgart - Münster - Emden.
⑥ until Oct. 29. [12] Stuttgart - Münster - Emden - Norddeich Mole.
[12] and 🍷 Stuttgart - Hamburg - Rostock - Stralsund (- Greifswald Ⓐ).
[12] and 🍷 Basel - Stuttgart - München.
[12] and 🍷 Karlsruhe - Frankfurt - Kassel (- Hannover ⑤⑦**k**) (- Hamburg ⑦**w**).
[12] and 🍷 Stuttgart - Köln (- Dortmund Ⓑ**q**) (- Münster ⑦**w**).
Not Oct. 2. [12] and 🍷 Karlsruhe - Frankfurt - Hamburg. On ⑦ (also Oct. 3; not Oct. 2) runs with train number **2270** and continues to Stralsund (Table **830**).
[12] and 🍷 Marseille - Lyon - Mulhouse - Strasbourg - Frankfurt.

o Stralsund (Table **830**).
ATTENMEER – To Westerland daily to Oct. 30, ④–⑦ from Nov. 3 (Table **821**).
om July 3. [12] and 🍴 Paris - Strasbourg - Frankfurt.
–⑥ from July 4. [12] and 🍷 Paris - Strasbourg - Frankfurt.
om Salzburg (Table **890**).
rom Chur (Table **520**).
o Kiel (Table **820**).
o Kassel (Table **806**).
o Münster (Table **800**).
om Interlaken via Bern (Table **560**).
[12] Paris - Strasbourg - Stuttgart (Table **32**). Stuttgart timings may vary by up to 5 minutes
om Aug. 29.
ntil July 2.
om July 3.
om July 3. Runs as *TGV* **9593** on ⑥. *ICE* conveys 🍴, *TGV* conveys 🍷.
aily to July 8; Ⓑ from July 10. Train number **9575** until July 2. [12] and 🍷 Paris - trasbourg - München. From Aug. 29 departs Strasbourg 1746, arrives Stuttgart 1904.

a – Ⓐ only.
b – 2136 July 9 - Aug. 21.
c – Not July 16 – 20.
d – Köln **Messe/Deutz**.
e – ①–④ (not Oct. 3).
f – ⑤ only.
g – ① (also Oct. 4; not Oct. 3).
h – Also Oct. 2.
j – ⑥ (also Oct. 2; not July 9 - Aug. 20).
k – ⑤⑦ (also Oct. 3; not Oct. 2).
m – Also Oct. 4, Nov. 2; not Oct. 3, 31.
n – Not July 9 - Aug. 21.
o – Not Oct. 2.
q – Ⓑ (not Oct. 2).
r – ⚒ (not July 30 - Sept. 10).
s – Ⓐ (not Aug. 1 - Sept. 9).
t – Not ⑤.
u – Not July 29.
v – ⑤–⑦ (also Oct. 3).
w – ⑦ (also Oct. 3; not Oct. 2).
x – Ⓒ only. 0821 on † to July 3/ from Aug. 28.
y – ⑥ (not July 9 - Aug. 20).
z – Not July 16 - Aug. 28.
* – Arrives 2002.
¦ – Not ⑤⑦ July 17 - Aug. 28.
• – Not July 30 - Sept. 11.
◊ – ⑥ only.

‡ – On Ⓑ July 10 - Aug. 21 calls at Köln **Messe/Deutz** (a. 2102), not Köln Hbf.
¶ – Train number **1102** on ⑥ (also Oct. 2).
⊕ – Train number **2296** Aug. 1 - Sept. 9 (and conveys 🍷, not 🍴).
⊖ – Train number **1018** on † to July 24 / from Sept. 18, **1118** on ⑦ July 31 - Sept. 11, **1218** on ①–⑥ July 30 - Sept. 12. [12] München - Stuttgart - Karlsruhe - Frankfurt - Essen / Dortmund. July 30 - Sept. 12 departs München 2350 (the previous day).
⊡ – Not Oct. 2. Runs as *IC* **2096** July 30 - Sept. 10 (not Sept. 4). On ⑦ Sept. 4 - Oct. 30 (also Oct. 3) runs as *IC* **2412** and continues to Rüdesheim, Koblenz, Köln and Dortmund (see Tables **911** and **800**).
♥ – July 16 - Aug. 27 Stuttgart d. 0810, Mannheim a. 0857, d. 0859.
♠ – Not July 16 – 20. July 21 - Aug. 27 timings at Stuttgart and Mannheim are 24 – 31 minutes earlier.
△ – On ①–⑤ until July 20 does not run Stuttgart - Mannheim.
⊠ – Timings at München, Stuttgart and Vaihingen are subject to alteration until Sept. 11. Timings of services via Mannheim may vary by up to 10 minutes July 16 - Aug. 28 (timings of international *ICE* / *TGV* services between Paris / Marseille and Frankfurt may vary by up to 35 minutes). See shaded panel on page 367 for further details.
♣ – July 18 - Sept. 2 Hannover, Hamburg and Berlin arrivals may be up to 40 minutes later. During this period many *IC* trains do not run north of Kassel (see Table **900**). See shaded panel on page 367 for further details.
§ – On ⑥⑦ (also Aug. 1) depart Basel SBB 2 minutes earlier and change trains at Basel Bad Bf.
☆ – See panel on page 428 for other local services.
▶ – Additional journeys Strasbourg - Offenburg (◐): 0722 ①–⑤, 1422 ①–⑤, 1822 ①–⑤.
◐ – Operated by Südwestdeutsche Verkehrs. On Nov. 1 local services between Strasbourg and Offenburg run as on ⑦.
◧ – Frankfurt Flughafen Fernbahnhof.

912 BASEL and STUTTGART - FRANKFURT

	EC	*IC*		*TGV*	*TGV*	*ICE*	*ICE*		*ICE*	*ICE*	*ICE*	*ICE*	*RJ*		*CNL*	*IC*			*CNL*	*IC*	*CNL*	*IC*	*CNL*	*IC*
SEE NOTE ⊠	**216**	**1976**		**9579**	**9579**	**100**	**590**		**4**	**1110**	**510**	**990**	**66**		**470**	**60470**			**478**	**60478**	**40478**	**61478**	**418**	**6041**
		①–⑥		**H**	**L**					⑦**w**		**A**	⑤⑥		[R]	**61470**	▲	△	[R]		[R]		[R]	
	🍷♦	**h**	◐2	[R]🍷	[R]🍷	🍷	🍴♦	◐2	🍴	🍷	🍷♦	🍴	🍴♦	◐2	**B**🍷	**B**2	◐2	◐2	**C**🍷	2**C**	**D**🍷	**D**2	**E**🍷	**E**2
Zürich HB **510** d.	...	...	...	...	...	...	...	...	1900	...	...	...	...	...	1942	1942	...	...	2142	2142	2142	2142	...	...
Basel SBB ☆ d.	...	...	...	...	...	1913	...	...	2013	...	...	...	...	...	2113	2113	...	...	2313	2313	2313	2313	...	...
Basel Bad Bf 🏛 ☆ d.	...	...	...	...	...	1923	...	...	2023	...	...	...	...	...	2122**u**	2122	...	...	2323**u**	2323	2323**u**	2323	...	...
Freiburg (Brsg) Hbf ☆ d.	...	...	...	...	...	1956	...	...	2055	...	...	...	...	...	2158**u**	2158	...	...	0005**u**	0005	0005**u**	0005	...	...
Strasbourg d.	...	...	1922	1946	2007	|	...	2022	|	...	...	...	...	2152	|	|	2252	0005	|	|	|	|	...	...
Kehl 🏛 d.	...	...	1934	|	|	|	...	2034	|	...	...	...	...	2204	|	|	2304	0016	|	|	|	|	...	...
Offenburg **916** ☆ d.	...	...	1952	|	|	2028	...	2052	2127	...	...	...	...	2222	2230**u**	2230	2321	0034	0044**u**	0044	0044**u**	0044	...	...
Baden-Baden **916** d.	...	...	...	|	|	2044	...	...	2143	...	...	...	...	...	|	|	...	...	0108**u**	0108	0108**u**	0108	...	...
Karlsruhe Hbf **913 916** d.	...	...	...	2028	2055	2101	...	...	2201	...	...	...	...	...	2304**u**	2304	...	...	0129**u**	0129	0129**u**	0129	...	...
München Hbf **930** d.	1746	...	...	|	|	|	1828	...	|	1928	1928	2045	2045	...	|	|	...	...	|	|	|	|	2250	2250
Stuttgart Hbf **931** d.	2004	2009	...	2104	2149	|	2051	...	|	2151	2151	2305	2305	...	|	|	...	...	|	|	|	|	0135	0135
Vaihingen (Enz) **931** d.	|	|	...	...	...	|	|	...	|	|	|	|	|	...	|	|	...	...	|	|	|	|	|	|
Bruchsal **913 931** d.	|	|	...	...	...	|	|	...	|	|	|	|	|	...	|	|	...	...	|	|	|	|	|	|
Heidelberg Hbf **913 931** d.	|	2054	...	...	...	|	|	...	|	|	|	|	|	...	2333**u**	2333	...	...	|	|	|	|	|	|
Weinheim **913** d.	|	2109	...	...	...	|	|	...	|	|	|	|	|	...	|	|	...	...	|	|	|	|	|	|
Bensheim **913** d.	|	2119	...	...	...	|	|	...	|	|	|	|	|	...	|	|	...	...	|	|	|	|	|	|
Darmstadt Hbf **913** d.	|	2133	...	...	...	|	|	...	|	|	|	|	|	...	|	|	...	...	|	|	|	|	|	|
Mannheim Hbf **913** a.	2048	|	...	...	...	2124	2129	...	2224	2229	2229	2345	2345	...	|	2346	...	...	|	0213	|	0213	|	|
Mannheim Hbf **913** d.	...	|	...	...	...	2136	2132	...	2233	2237	2237	2351	2351	...	2359**u**	2359	...	...	|	0215	|	0215	|	|
Frankfurt Flughafen ✈ ◧ a.	...	|	...	...	...	2206	|	...	|	2308	2308	0023	0023	...	|	|	...	...	|	|	|	|	|	|
Frankfurt (Main) Hbf **913** a.	...	2152	...	...	...	|	2208	...	2313	|	|	0042	0042	...	|	0051**x**	...	...	|	0259	|	0259	|	0312
Mainz Hbf **911** a.	...	...	...	...	...	|	|	...	...	|	2329	|	...	...	|	|	...	...	|	|	|	|	|	|
Koblenz Hbf **911** a.	...	...	...	...	...	|	|	...	...	|	...	|	...	...	|	|	...	...	|	|	0511	0511	0511	0511
Köln Hbf **800 910** a.	...	...	...	...	...	2307	|	...	...	0007	...	|	...	...	|	|	...	...	|	|	0615	0615	0615	0615
Dortmund Hbf **800** a.	...	...	...	...	...	0033	|	...	...	...	...	|	...	...	|	|	...	...	|	|	...	...	...	...
Hannover Hbf **810 900** a.	...	...	...	...	...	...	0146	...	...	...	...	0421**g**	...	...	|	|	...	...	0658**t**	0658**t**	...	...	...	...
Hamburg Hbf **800 900** a.	...	...	...	...	...	...	0308	...	...	...	...	0550**g**	...	...	|	|	...	...	0836**t**	0836**t**	...	...	...	...
Berlin Hbf **810 902** a.	...	...	...	...	...	...	...	...	...	...	...	...	...	...	0723	0723	...	...	...	...	...	...	...	...

♦ – NOTES (LISTED BY TRAIN NUMBER)

66 – ⑤⑥ (also Oct. 2). [12] and 🍴 Budapest - Wien - Salzburg - Frankfurt. On July 29, 30 does not call at München Hbf (calls at München Ost 2020 / München Pasing 2033).

216 – [12] and 🍷 Graz - Selzthal - Bischofshofen - Salzburg - Saarbrücken.

510 – [12] and 🍷 München - Wiesbaden Hbf (a. 2344). Train number **1010** on ⑤⑥ (also Oct. 2), **1190** on ⑦ (also Oct. 3; not Oct. 2). Also conveys 🍴 on ①–④ (not Oct. 3)

590 – [12] and 🍴 München - Frankfurt (- Kassel ⑤⑦**w**) (- Hannover - Hamburg ⑦**w**). Train number **698** on ⑤, **992** on ⑦ (also Oct. 3; not Oct. 2).

A – ①②③④⑦ (not Oct. 2). Train number **1590** on ④.

B – SIRIUS – 🛏 1, 2 cl. and 🛌 2 cl. (*CNL* **470** [R]) Zürich - Leipzig - Berlin; [2] (*IC* **61470**) Zürich - Berlin. Conveys 🛏 1, 2 cl. and 🛌 2 cl. (*CNL* **459** – CANOPUS [R]) Zürich - Leipzig - Dresden - Praha; [2] (*IC* **60470**) Zürich - Leipzig - Praha. Berlin portion is extended to Ostseebad Binz on dates in Table **850** (note ♥ page 399).

C – KOMET – 🛏 1, 2 cl. and 🛌 2 cl. (*CNL* **478** [R]) Zürich - Hamburg; [2] (*IC* **60478**) Zürich - Hamburg.

D – PEGASUS – 🛏 1, 2 cl. and 🛌 2 cl. (*CNL* **40478** [R]) Zürich - Amsterdam; [2] (*IC* **61478**) Zürich - Amsterdam.

E – POLLUX – 🛏 1, 2 cl. and 🛌 2 cl. (*CNL* **418** [R]) München - Amsterdam; [2] (*IC* **60418**) München - Amsterdam.

F – PYXIS – 🛏 1, 2 cl. and 🛌 2 cl. (*CNL* **40418** [R]) München - Stuttgart - Hamburg; [2] (*IC* **61418**) München - Stuttgart - Hamburg.

H – From Aug. 29. [12] and 🍷 Paris - Strasbourg - Stuttgart (- München ⑥).

L – ⑧ to July 1; daily July 3 - Aug. 28. [12] and 🍷 Paris - Strasbourg - Stuttgart. Train number **9577** until July 1.

g – Mornings of ① (also Oct. 4; not Oct. 3).

h – Also Oct. 2; not Oct. 3. Conveys 🍷 on ⑥.

t – July 18 - Sept. 2 Hannover a. 0731, Hamburg a. 0905

u – Stops to pick up only.

w – Also Oct. 3; not Oct. 2.

x – Frankfurt (Main) **Süd**.

▲ – Not Sept. 19 – 23, Oct. 3 – 7, 10 – 14, 17, 18.

△ – Not Sept. 20 – 24, Oct. 4 – 8, 11 – 15, 18, 19.

⊠ – Timings at München, Stuttgart and Vaihingen are subject to alteration until Sept. 11. Timings of services via Ma may vary by up to 10 minutes July 16 - Aug. 28. See panel on page 367 for further details.

☆ – See panel on page 428 for other local services.

◐ – Operated by Südwestdeutsche Verkehrs-AG.

◧ – Frankfurt Flughafen Fernbahnhof.

913 Local trains FRANKFURT - HEIDELBERG - KARLSRUHE

RE / RB / S-Bahn se

Certain timings may vary by up to 4 minutes July 16 - Aug. 28. See Table **912** for *ICE / IC* services.

FRANKFURT - DARMSTADT - HEIDELBERG and MANNHEIM

	Ⓐ	Ⓐ		Ⓒ	Ⓐ	⑦	①–⑥		Ⓐ	⑦	①–⑥				Ⓐ		Ⓐ		Ⓒ	Ⓐ			
Frankfurt (Main) Hbf d.	...	0506	0606	...	0633	0706	0706	0806	0834	0906	0906	1006		1706	1734	1806	1833	1906	2006	2034	2106	2206	2312
Darmstadt Hbf d.	0426	0530	0630	...	0653	0730	0734	0830	0853	0930	0930	1030	and	1730	1757	1830	1853	1930	2030	2054	2130	2230	2331
Bensheim d.	0452	0557	0655	...	0709	0755	0757	0859	0909	0955	0959	1059	hourly	1759	1825	1859**j**	1909	1958	2059	2109	2155	2255	2356
Weinheim (Bergstr) d.	0508	0612	0710	...	0722	0811	0811	0914	0922	1010	1014	1114		1814	1842	1914	1922	2017	2117	2122	2210	2310	0010
Mannheim Friedrichsfeld a.	0521	0624	0723	0732	0732	0824	0824	0927	|	1023	1027	1127	until	1827	1856	1927	|	2029	2130	2131	2223	2323	0023
Mannheim Hbf a.	*0545***t**	*0644***r**	|	0743	0745	*0842*	*0842*	*0942*	0940	*1042*	*1042*	*1142*		*1842*	1910	*1942*	1940	*2042*	*2143*	*2143*	*2242*	*2343*	|
Heidelberg Hbf a.	0532	0634	0736	...	...	0835	0834	0939	...	1037	1039	1139		1838	...	1939	...	2041	2141	2142	2237	2334	0035

	Ⓐ		Ⓐ		Ⓐ	Ⓒ	Ⓐ		Ⓐ						Ⓐ			Ⓐ					
Heidelberg Hbf d.	0422	0524	...	0625	...	...	...	0724	...	0821	0921		1421	1525	...	1621	1724	...	1821	1921	2021	2124	2221
Mannheim Hbf d.	|	*0515*	0607	*0612*	0652	0716	0720	|	0820	*0816*	*0916*	and	*1416*	*1516*	1620	*1616*	*1716*	1820	*1816*	*1916*	*2016*	*2116*	*2216*
Mannheim Friedrichsfeld d.	0434	0533	|	0635	0706	0726	0731	0733	|	0831	0932		1432	1535	|	1632	1734	|	1832	1932	2032	2135	2232
Weinheim (Bergstr) d.	0448	0548	0626	0648	0719	...	...	0746	0839	0845	0945	hourly	1446	1545	1639	1645	1745	1839	1845	1945	2045	2149	2245
Bensheim d.	0503	0603	0642	0703	0733	...	...	0800	0851	0900	1000	until	1500	1600	1652	1700	1800	1852	1900	2000	2100	2204	2259
Darmstadt Hbf d.	0530	0630	0658	0730	0758	...	...	0830	0906	0930	1030		1530	1630	1706	1730	1830	1906	1930	2030	2130	2230	2330
Frankfurt (Main) Hbf a.	0548	0648	0716	0748	0816	...	...	0848	0924	0948	1048		1548	1648	1724	1748	1848	1924	1948	2048	2148	2248	2348

FRANKFURT - BIBLIS - WORMS and MANNHEIM

	⚒	⚒			⚒					⚒				Ⓐ				Ⓐ				Ⓐ	
Frankfurt (Main) Hbf d.	0608	...	0710	...	0810	...	0913	...	and in the same	1610	...	1713	...	1810	...	1913	...	2010	...	2113	...	2210	...
Biblis d.	0657	0658	0758	0804	0858	0904	0958	1004	pattern every	1658	1704	1758	1804	1858	1904	1958	2004	2058	2104	2158	2204	2258	2304
Worms Hbf a.	|	0708	|	0814	|	0914	|	1014	**two** hours until	|	1714	|	1814	|	1913	|	2014	|	2114	|	2214	|	2314
Mannheim Hbf a.	0719	...	0819	...	0919	...	1019	...		1719	...	1819	...	1919	...	2019	...	2119	...	2219	...	2319	...

km				Ⓐ		⚒	⚒	⊖			⚒					Ⓐ				Ⓐ				
	Mannheim Hbf d.	0013	...	...	0532	...	0639	...	0739	...	0839	...	0939	and in the same	...	1839	...	1939	...	2039	...	2139	...
0	**Worms** Hbf d.	|	...	0540	|	0640	|	0743	|	0843	|	0943	|	pattern every	1843	|	1943	|	2043	|	2143	|	2243
10	Biblis d.	0038	...	0550	0559	0650	0659	0753	0759	0853	0859	0953	0959	**two** hours until	1853	1859	1953	1959	2053	2059	2153	2159	2253
63	**Frankfurt** (Main) Hbf a.	0134	...	...	0645	...	0747	...	0845	...	0947	...	1045		...	1947	...	2045	...	2147	...	2245	...

MANNHEIM - HEIDELBERG - KARLSRUHE

S-Bahn				†z	⑥	Ⓐt	Ⓒz	Ⓐt										Ⓒz	Ⓐt						
Mannheim Hbf ⊡ d.	0007	...	0457	0535	*0535*	0544	*0637*	0647	0729**k**	0830	0930	1030	1130	1230	1330	1430	1530	1630	1630	1730	1830	1930	2030	2137	2237
Heidelberg Hbf ⊡ d.	0024	...	0517	0558	0558	0603	0706	0706	0748	0848	0948	1048	1148	1248	1348	1448	1548	1648	1648	1748	1848	1948	2048	2155	2255
Bruchsal d.	0053	...	0544	0625	0625	0630	0732	0733	0817	0915	1016	1115	1216	1315	1415	1515	1615	1715	1716	1816	1916	2016	2116	2222	2321
Karlsruhe Hbf a.	0112	...	0601	0646	0646	0648	0750	0750	0833	0936	1033	1133	1233	1336	1433	1536	1632	1732	1736	1833	1933	2033	2133	2236	2335

S-Bahn			Ⓐt	Ⓐt	⑥	†z	Ⓐt	Ⓒz	Ⓐt	Ⓐt															
Karlsruhe Hbf d.	0012	0327	0420	0534	0611	0614	0620	0725	0727	0754	0827	0927	1027	1128	1227	1327	1427	1527	1627	1727	1827	1927	2027	2127	2228
Bruchsal d.	0026	0344	0438	0558	0633	0632	0638	0744	0743	0814	0843	0943	1044	1144	1244	1342	1443	1543	1643	1743	1843	1943	2043	2143	2244
Heidelberg Hbf ⊡ d.	0054	0413	0505	0634	0709**f**	0659	0709	0813	0813	0843	0913	1013	1113	1213	1313	1413	1513	1613	1713	1813	1913	2013	2114	2214	2314
Mannheim Hbf ⊡ a.	0114	0429	0522	0651	0725	*0718*	0725	0829	0829	0901	0929	1029	1129	1229	1329	1429	1529	1629	1729	1829	1929	2029	2132	2232	2332

f – Arrives 0700.

j – 1855 on ⑥.

k – 0728 until June 18.

r – *0648* on Nov. 1.

t – Not Nov. 1.

z – Also Nov. 1.

⊖ – 2 minutes later on Ⓐ.

⊡ – See also Tables **918**, **919**, **923** and **924**.

Local trains KOBLENZ - WIESBADEN - FRANKFURT and KOBLENZ - MAINZ - FRANKFURT 914

Neuwied - Koblenz - St Goarshausen - Wiesbaden - Frankfurt *(Rechte Rheinstrecke)* ✣

	Ⓐ	⚒	Ⓐ								Ⓐ		Ⓐ								Ⓒ	Ⓐ	Ⓒ	Ⓐ	
Neuwied .... **802** d.	0437	...	0537	...	0637**z**	0737	0837	0937	1037	1137	...	1237	...	1337	1437	1537	1637	1737	1837	1937	2037	2037	2137	2137	2237
Koblenz Hbf **.802 906** d.	0453	...	0553	...	0653	0753	0853	0953	1053	1153	1223	1253	1323	1353	1453	1553	1653	1753	1853	1953	2053	2053	2153	2153	2253
Niederlahnstein .. **906** d.	0459	...	0559	...	0659	0759	0859	0959	1059	1159	1229	1259	1329	1359	1459	1559	1659	1759	1859	1959	2059	2059	2159	2159	2259
Braubach .... d.	0506	...	0606	...	0706	0806	0906	1006	1106	1206	1236	1306	1336	1406	1506	1606	1706	1806	1906	2006	2106	2106	2206	2206	2306
Kamp-Bornhofen .... d.	0516	...	0616	...	0716	0816	0916	1016	1116	1216	1246	1316	1346	1416	1516	1616	1716	1816	1916	2016	2116	2116	2216	2216	2316
St Goarshausen .... d.	0526	...	0626	...	0726	0826	0926	1026	1126	1226	1256	1326	1356	1426	1526	1626	1726	1826	1926	2026	2126	2126	2226	2226	2326
Kaub .... d.	0536	...	0636	0636	0736	0836	0936	1036	1136	1236	1306	1336	1406	1436	1536	1636	1736	1836	1936	2036	2136	2136	2236	2236	2335
Lorch (Rhein) .... d.	0542	...	0642	0642	0742	0842	0942	1042	1142	1242	1312	1342	1412	1442	1542	1642	1742	1842	1942	2042	2142	2142	2242	2242	...
Rüdesheim (Rhein) .... d.	0553	0553	0653	0653	0753	0853	0953	1053	1153	1253	1323	1353	1423	1453	1553	1653	1753	1853	1953	2053	2153	2153	2253	2253	...
Wiesbaden Hbf .... a.	0625	0625	0725	0725	0825	0925	1025	1125	1225	1325	1355	1425	1455	1525	1625	1725	1825	1925	2025	2125	2225	2225	2325	2325	...
Wiesbaden Hbf .... d.	0632	0632	0732	0732	0832	0932	1032	1132	1232	1332	...	1432	...	1532	1632	1732	1832	1932	2032	2132	2232	*2235*¦	2332	*2335*¦	...
Frankfurt (Main) Hbf.. a.	0705	0705	0805	0805	0905	1005	1105	1205	1305	1405	...	1505	...	1605	1705	1805	1905	2005	2105	2205	2305	*2318*¦	0005	*0018*¦	...

	Ⓐ	Ⓐ		⚒										Ⓐ		Ⓐ		Ⓐ		Ⓐ					Ⓐ	Ⓒ
kfurt (Main) Hbf .. d.	...	...	...	0553**e**	0653	0753	0853	0953	1053	1153	1253	1353	1453	1523	1553	1622	1653	1723	1753	1823	1853	1953	2053	2153	...	2253
baden Hbf .... a.	...	...	...	0628**e**	0728	0828	0928	1028	1128	1228	1328	1428	1528	1558	1628	1658	1728	1758	1828	1858	1928	2028	2128	2228	...	2328
sbaden Hbf .... d.	...	...	0533**e**	0633	0733	0833	0933	1033	1133	1233	1333	1433	1533	1603	1633	1703	1733	1803	1833	1903	1933	2033	2133	2233	2333	2333
esheim (Rhein) ..... d.	...	0532	0606**e**	0706	0806	0906	1006	1106	1206	1306	1406	1506	1606	1636	1706	1736	1806	1836	1906	1936	2006	2106	2206	2306	0004	0004
h (Rhein) .... d.	...	0541	0615**e**	0715	0815	0915	1015	1115	1215	1315	1415	1515	1615	1645	1715	1745	1815	1845	1915	1945	2015	2115	2215	2315	...	...
.... d.	0450	0550	0623	0723	0823	0923	1023	1123	1223	1323	1423	1523	1623	1653	1724	1753	1823	1854	1924	1954	2023	2123	2223	2323	...	...
oarshausen .... d.	0459	0559	0632	0732	0832	0932	1032	1132	1232	1332	1432	1532	1632	1702	1732	1802	1832	1902	1932	2002	2032	2132	2232	...	...	...
o-Bornhofen .... d.	0510	0610	0643	0743	0843	0943	1043	1143	1243	1343	1443	1543	1643	1713	1743	1813	1843	1913	1943	2013	2043	2143	2243	...	...	...
oach .... d.	0521	0621	0654	0754	0854	0954	1054	1154	1254	1354	1454	1554	1654	1724	1754	1824	1854	1924	1954	2024	2054	2154	2254	...	...	...
erlahnstein .... **906** d.	0527	0627	0700	0800	0900	1000	1100	1200	1300	1400	1500	1600	1700	1730	1800	1830	1900	1930	2000	2030	2100	2200	2300	...	...	...
enz Hbf **.802 906** a.	0533	0633	0706	0806	0906	1006	1106	1206	1306	1406	1506	1606	1706	1736	1806	1836	1906	1937	2006	2037	2106	2206	2306	...	...	...
wied .... **802** a.	0556	...	0726	0826	0926	1026	1126	1226	1326	1426	1526	1626	1726	...	1826	...	1926	...	2026	...	2126	2226	2326	...	...	...

Koblenz - Bingen - Mainz - Frankfurt *(Linke Rheinstrecke)* ⊠

		Ⓐ	Ⓐ										Ⓐt		⚒t								
Koblenz Hbf .... d.	0507	0606	0617	0707	0902	1102	1302	1502	1702	1902	2102		0452	...	0552	...	...	0652		2052	...	2152	2252
Boppard Hbf .... d.	0519	0620	0632	0719	0915	1115	1315	1515	1715	1915	2115		0507	...	0607	...	...	0707		2107	...	2207	2307
Boppard-Bad Salzig .. d.	|	|	0636	|	|	|	|	|	|	|	|	Other	0511	...	0611	...	...	0711		2111	...	2211	2311
St Goar .... d.	|	|	0645	|	|	|	|	|	|	|	|		0519	...	0619	...	...	0719	and	2119	...	2219	2319
Oberwesel .... d.	0533	0635	0651	0733	0930	1130	1330	1530	1730	1930	2130	Stopping	0525	...	0625	...	...	0725		2125	...	2225	2325
Bacharach .... d.	0537	|	0656	0737	0936	1136	1336	1536	1736	1936	2136		0530	...	0630	...	...	0730	hourly	2130	...	2230	2330
Bingen (Rhein) Hbf ..... a.	0546	0647	0709	0746	0946	1146	1346	1546	1746	1946	2146	services	0543	...	0643	...	...	0743		2143	...	2242	2345
Bingen (Rhein) Hbf ..... d.	0547	0648	0713	0747	0947	1147	1347	1547	1747	1947	2147		0552	0552	0654	0654	...	0754	until	2154	...	2254	...
Bingen (Rhein) Stadt .. d.	|	|	0716	|	|	|	|	|	|	|	|	→	0555	0555	0657	0657	...	0757		2157	...	2257	...
Ingelheim .... d.	0556	0656	0722	0755	0955	1155	1355	1555	1755	1955	2155		0605	0605	0707	0707	...	0807		2207	...	2307	...
Mainz Hbf .... a.	0608	0708	0736	0808	1008	1208	1408	1608	1808	2008	2208	⊡	0624	0624	0725	0725	...	0825		2226	...	2325	...
Frankfurt Flughafen ◧ a.	0634	0734	0805	0834	1034	1234	1434	1634	1834	2034	2235		...	...	...	...	...	...		...	...	...	...
Frankfurt (Main) Hbf.. a.	0647	0751	0823	0849	1049	1249	1449	1649	1851	2051	2249		...	...	...	...	...	...		...	...	...	...

	Ⓐt						Ⓐ		Ⓐ					⚒t			▲	▲						
kfurt (Main) Hbf .. d.	0508	0706	0908	1108	1308	1508	1608	1708	1808	1908	2108	2308		...	...	...	...		...	...	...	...	...	...
kfurt Flughafen ◧ d.	0521	0721	0924	1124	1324	1524	1623	1724	1823	1924	2124	2324		...	...	...	...		...	...	...	...	...	...
z Hbf .... ¶ d.	0544	0751	0951	1151	1351	1551	1651	1751	1850	1951	2151	2351	Other	0532**e**	0632	0721	0832		1632	1732**j**	1832	1932	2003	2103
heim .... ¶ d.	0556	0802	1002	1202	1402	1602	|	1802	1903	2002	2202	0002		0550**e**	0650	0739	0850	and	1650	1750**j**	1850	1950	2021	2121
en (Rhein) Stadt ¶ d.	|	|	|	|	|	|	|	|	|	|	|	|	Stopping	0600**e**	0700	0749	0900		1700	1805	1905	2003	2031	2131
en (Rhein) Hbf ..... a.	0606	0811	1011	1211	1411	1611	1709	1811	1911	2011	2211	0011		0604**e**	0704	0753	0902	hourly	1702	1809	1909	2005	2034	2134
en (Rhein) Hbf ..... d.	0607	0813	1013	1213	1413	1613	1710	1813	1912	2013	2216	0022	services	0610	0710	0816	0916		1713	1816	1916	2016	2046	2146
arach .... d.	0615	0821	1021	1221	1421	1621	1718	1821	1921	2021	2228	0034		0622	0722	0828	0928	until	1728	1828	1928	2028	2058	2158
wesel .... d.	0620	0826	1026	1226	1426	1626	1723	1826	1926	2026	2232	0038	→	0626	0726	0832	0932		1733	1832	1932	2032	2102	2202
oar .... d.	|	|	|	|	|	|	|	|	|	|	2238	0044		0632	0732	0838	0938		1739	1838	1938	2038	2108	2208
ard-Bad Salzig ... d.	|	|	|	|	|	|	|	|	|	|	2247	0053	⊡	0640	0740	0846	0946		1747	1846	1946	2046	2116	2216
ard Hbf .... d.	0635	0840	1040	1240	1440	1640	1737	1840	1941	2040	2251	0057		0645	0745	0851	0951		1752	1851	1951	2051	2121	2221
enz Hbf .... a.	0651	0854	1054	1254	1454	1654	1751	1854	1957	2054	2309	0115		0702	0802	0908	1008		1808	1908	2008	2108	2138	2238

Ⓐ only.
On Ⓐ (not Nov. 1) Mainz Hbf d. 1736, Ingelheim d. 1751.
Not Nov. 1.
Ⓒ only.

¦ – Not July 16 - Aug. 25.
◧ – Frankfurt Flughafen Regionalbahnhof ✈.
▲ – The 1032 and 1432 from Mainz Hbf run 6 minutes **earlier** Bingen (Rhein) Hbf - Koblenz. Certain other services may run a few minutes later Bingen (Rhein) Stadt - Bingen (Rhein) Hbf.

✣ – Operated by VIAS GmbH.
¶ – Additional journeys Mainz Hbf - Bingen (Rhein) Hbf: 0008, 2203 and 2303.
⊠ – See Table **911** for long-distance *ICE / IC* services. See Table **917a** for S-Bahn service Mainz - Frankfurt Flughafen ✈ - Frankfurt (M) Hbf and v.v.
⊡ – Stopping services are operated by Mittelrheinbahn.

n Düsseldorfer Deutsche Rheinschiffahrt — KÖLN - KOBLENZ - MAINZ — *2016 service* 914a

	A	A ⛴	K ◇	D	C	E ⊠	F ⊠	Q	R	H
Köln (Rheingarten) ..... d.	...	...	...	...	...	...	...	0930	0930	...
Bonn .... d.	...	...	...	...	...	0730	0730	1230	1230	...
Bad Godesberg .... d.	...	...	...	...	...	0800	0800	1300	1300	...
Königswinter Fähre ..... d.	...	...	...	...	...	0815	0815	1330	1330	...
Bad Honnef (Rhein) ..... d.	...	...	...	...	...	0835	0835	1350	1350	...
Remagen .... d.	...	...	...	...	...	0910	0910	1420	1420	...
Linz am Rhein .... d.	...	...	...	...	...	0930	0930	1450	1450	...
Bad Breisig .... d.	...	...	...	...	...	1000	1000	▬	1520	...
Bad Hönningen .... d.	...	...	...	...	...	1005	1005	...	1525	...
Andernach .... d.	...	...	...	...	...	1050	1050	A	...	...
Koblenz ⊙ .... d.	...	0900	0945	...	...	1300	1300	1400	...	1810
Winningen (Mosel) ... a.	...	|	1055	...	...	1430	|	|	...	|
Cochem (Mosel) ...... a.	...	|	1500	...	...	...	|	|	...	|
Oberlahnstein .... d.	...	0940	...	...	...	...	|	1440	...	1845
Braubach .... d.	...	1005	...	...	...	...	1345	1505	...	1910
Boppard .... d.	0900	1100	...	1300	1400	...	1430	1600	...	2000
Kamp-Bornhofen .... d.	0910	1110	...	1310	1410	...	...	1610	...	...
Bad Salzig .... d.	0925	1125	...	1325	1425	...	...	1625	...	...
St Goarshausen ... ★ d.	1010	1210	...	1410	1510	...	...	1710	...	...
St Goar .... ★ d.	1020	1220	...	1420	1520	...	...	1720	...	...
Oberwesel .... d.	1050	1250	...	1450	1550	...	...	1750	...	...
Kaub .... d.	1105	1305	...	1505	1605	...	...	1805	...	...
Bacharach .... d.	1130	1330	...	1530	1630	...	...	1830	...	...
Assmannshausen .... d.	1230	1430	...	1630	1730	...	...	1930	...	...
Bingen (Rhein) ...... ♥ d.	1300	1500	...	1700	1800	...	...	2000	...	...
Rüdesheim (Rhein) ♥ d.	1315	1515	...	1715	1815	...	...	2015	...	...
Wiesbaden-Biebrich .... d.	...	...	...	1900	2000**t**	...	...	...	...	...
Mainz .... a.	...	...	...	1930	2030**t**	...	...	...	...	...

	L	R	A	D	C	F ⊠	A	H	K ◇	A ⛴
Mainz .... d.	...	...	...	0830	0930**v**	...	...	...	...	...
Wiesbaden-Biebrich . d.	...	...	...	0845	0945**v**	...	...	...	...	...
Rüdesheim .... ♥ d.	...	...	0915	1015	1115	...	1415	1415	...	1615
Bingen (Rhein) ... ♥ d.	...	...	0930	1030	1130	...	1430	1430	...	1630
Assmannshausen ..... d.	...	...	0945	1045	1145	...	1445	1445	...	1645
Bacharach .... d.	...	...	1015	1115	1215	...	1515	1515	...	1715
Kaub .... d.	...	...	1025	1125	1225	...	1525	1525	...	1725
Oberwesel .... d.	...	...	1035	1135	1235	...	1535	1535	...	1735
St Goar .... ★ d.	...	...	1055	1155	1255	...	1555	1555	...	1755
St Goarshausen ★ d.	...	...	1105	1205	1305	...	1605	1605	...	1805
Bad Salzig .... d.	...	...	1130	|	|	...	1630	1630	...	1830
Kamp-Bornhofen ...... d.	...	...	1140	1240	1340	...	1640	1640	...	1840
Boppard .... d.	...	...	1150	1250	1350	1600	1650	1650	...	1850
Braubach .... d.	...	...	1220	...	...	1630	▬	1720	...	1920
Oberlahnstein .... d.	...	...	1240	...	...	|	...	1740	...	1940
Cochem (Mosel) .... d.	...	...	|	...	...	|	E ⊠	|	1540	|
Winningen (Mosel) d.	...	...	|	...	...	|	1540	|	1845	|
Koblenz ⊙ .... d.	...	...	1310	...	...	1700	1700	1810	2000	2010
Andernach .... d.	...	...	...	...	...	1805**s**	1805**s**	...	...	...
Bad Hönningen .... d.	...	1615	...	...	...	1830**s**	1830**s**	...	...	...
Bad Breisig .... d.	...	1620	...	...	...	1840**s**	1840**s**	...	...	...
Linz am Rhein .... d.	1450	1650	...	...	...	1905**s**	1905**s**	...	...	...
Remagen .... d.	1500	1700	...	...	...	1915**s**	1915**s**	...	...	...
Bad Honnef (Rhein) .. d.	1525	1725	...	...	...	1940**s**	1940**s**	...	...	...
Königswinter Fähre .. d.	1540	1740	...	...	...	2000	2000	...	...	...
Bad Godesberg .... d.	1545	1745	...	...	...	2010	2010	...	...	...
Bonn .... d.	1615	1815	...	...	...	2030	2030	...	...	...
Köln (Rheingarten) ... a.	1800	2000	...	...	...	...	...	...	...	...

Mar. 25 - Oct. 23.
Apr. 23 - Oct. 23.
Apr. 23 - Oct. 3.
① July 4 - Aug. 29.
③ July 6 - Aug. 31.
①⑤⑥⑦ Mar. 25 - Apr. 18; daily Apr. 22 - Oct. 3; ①⑤⑥⑦ Oct. 7 - 23.
⑤-⑦ June 10 - Oct. 2.
⑤⑥ Apr. 23 - Oct. 1; ⑤-⑦ Oct. 7 - 23.
Daily Apr. 23 - Oct. 3; ⑤-⑦ Oct. 7 - 23.

R – ①②③④⑦ Apr. 24 - Oct. 3.

s – Sets down only.
t – Daily July 1 - Sept. 4; ④-⑦ Sept. 8 - Oct. 23.
v – Daily July 1 - Aug. 31; ①⑤⑥⑦ Sept. 2 - Oct. 23.

⛴ – Operated by paddlesteamer *Goethe* Apr. 23 - Oct. 3.
⊠ – Operated by Personenschifffahrt Siebengebirge.
◇ – Operated by Personenschifffahrt Gilles.
⊙ – Koblenz (Konrad-Adenauer-Ufer).

◐ – Distance in metres from rail station to river landing stage.
★ – A frequent ferry service operates St Goar - St Goarshausen and v.v. Operator: Rheinschifffahrt Goar. ✆ + 49 (0) 6771 26 20.
♥ – Passenger ferry Bingen - Rüdesheim and v.v. Operator: Bingen-Rüdesheimer Fahrgastschiffahrt. ✆ + 49 (0) 6721 30808 10. Service **May 1 - Oct. 31**: From Bingen at 0700 and hourly until 2100. From Rüdesheim at 0730 and hourly until 2130.

Operator: Köln Düsseldorfer Deutsche Rheinschiffahrt, Frankenwerft 35, D-50667 Köln. ✆ +49 (0) 221 20 88 318, Fax +49 (0) 221 20 88 345. A special service operates on "Rhein in Flammen" days.

915 KOBLENZ - TRIER - LUXEMBOURG and SAARBRÜCKEN

RE services except where sh

Many Saarbrücken services continue to / start from Mannheim (see Table **919**).

km			Ⓐ	†	①–⑤ e	Ⓒ z	①–⑤ a		①–⑤ e		①–⑤ a		①–⑤ e	①–⑤ e		①–⑤ e		⑥					
0	**Koblenz** Hbf d.	...	...	...	...	...	...	...	...	...	...	...	0603	0603	...	...	0706	0706	...	0806	0806	and at	1806
47	Cochem (Mosel) d.	...	...	...	...	...	...	...	...	...	...	...	0638	0638	...	...	0741	0741	...	0841	0841		1841
59	Bullay d.	...	...	...	...	...	...	...	...	...	...	...	0647	0647	...	...	0751	0751	...	0851	0851		1851
76	Wittlich Hbf d.	...	...	...	...	...	...	...	0550	...	...	...	0700	0700	...	0705	0803	0803	...	0903	0903	the same	1903
112	**Trier** Hbf a.	...	...	...	...	...	...	...	0627	...	...	...	0730	0730	...	0745	0830	0830	...	0930	0930		1930
112	**Trier** Hbf d.	...	0456	0532	0536	0551	0607	0632	0636	0636	0713	0732	0732	0736	0736	0750	0832	0836	0836	0932	0936	minutes	1932
163	**Luxembourg** a.	...	|	|	0629	|	0709	|	0729	0729	0809	|	|	0829	0829	0850	|	0929	0929	|	1029		|
135	Saarburg d.	...	0514	0550	...	0618	...	0650	...	...	...	0750	0750	...	...	...	0850	...	...	0950	...	past each	1950
161	Merzig (Saar) d.	0435	0534	0610	...	0645	...	0710	...	...	...	0810	0810	...	...	...	0910	...	...	1010	...		2010
173	Dillingen (Saar) d.	0446	0543	0619	...	0656	...	0720	...	...	...	0820	0820	...	...	...	0920	...	...	1020	...	hour until	2020
177	Saarlouis Hbf d.	0450	0547	0623	...	0659	...	0724	...	...	...	0824	0824	...	...	...	0924	...	...	1024	...		2024
190	Völklingen d.	0500	0556	0632	...	0710	...	0732	...	...	...	0832	0832	...	...	...	0932	...	...	1032	...		2032
200	**Saarbrücken** Hbf a.	0513	0605	0641	...	0724	...	0741	...	...	...	0841	0841	...	...	...	0941	...	...	1041	...		2041

							①–⑤	⑥⑦		
Koblenz Hbf d.	1906	1906	2006	2006	2106	2106	2206	2206	2206	2318
Cochem (Mosel) d.	1941	1941	2041	2041	2141	2141	2241	2241	2241	2353
Bullay d.	1951	1951	2051	2051	2151	2151	2251	2251	2251	0003
Wittlich Hbf d.	2003	2003	2103	2103	2203	2203	2303	2303	2303	0016
Trier Hbf a.	2030	2030	2130	2130	2230	2230	2330	2330	2330	0042
Trier Hbf d.	2032	2036	2132	2136	2232	2236	2332	2332	2336	...
Luxembourg a.	|	2129	|	2229	|	2329	|	|	0031	...
Saarburg d.	2050	...	2201	...	2250	...	2356	2356	...	...
Merzig (Saar) d.	2110	...	2226	...	2310	...	0020	0022	...	...
Dillingen (Saar) d.	2120	...	2235	...	2319	...	0028	0034	...	...
Saarlouis Hbf d.	2124	...	2239	...	2323	...	0032	0038	...	...
Völklingen d.	2132	...	2248	...	2332	...	0041	0050	...	...
Saarbrücken Hbf a.	2141	...	2256	...	2341	...	0050	0101	...	...

	Ⓐ e	Ⓐ e	Ⓒ z	①–⑤ e	Ⓐ e	⚒ e			
Saarbrücken Hbf d.	...	...	...	...	0459	...	0520	...	0619
Völklingen d.	...	...	...	...	0507	...	0531	...	0627
Saarlouis Hbf d.	...	...	...	...	0515	...	0541	...	0635
Dillingen (Saar) d.	...	...	...	...	0519	...	0545	...	0638
Merzig (Saar) d.	...	...	...	...	0528	...	0555	...	0647
Saarburg d.	...	...	...	...	0548	...	0622h	...	0707
Luxembourg d.	...	...	...	0518	|	...	|	0612	|
Trier Hbf a.	...	...	...	0605	0608	...	0652h	0709	0728
Trier Hbf d.	0412	0512	0527	0612	0612	0627	...	0712	0732
Wittlich Hbf d.	0436	0536	0554	0636	0636	0702	...	0736	0756
Bullay d.	0450	0550	0607	0650	0650	0718	...	0750	0810
Cochem (Mosel) d.	0459	0559	0628j	0659	0659	0728	...	0759	0819
Koblenz Hbf a.	0535	0635	0721	0735	0735	0822	...	0835	0855

			✣									①–⑤ a								⑤	⑥ k		
Saarbrücken Hbf d.	...	0719		...	1519	...	1619	...	1719	...	1819	...	...	1920	...	2019	...	2119	...	...	2222	2222	...
Völklingen d.	...	0727	and at	...	1527	...	1627	...	1727	...	1827	...	...	1928	...	2027	...	2127	...	...	2231	2231	...
Saarlouis Hbf d.	...	0735		...	1535	...	1635	...	1735	...	1835	...	...	1936	...	2035	...	2135	...	...	2239	2239	...
Dillingen (Saar) d.	...	0738	the same	...	1538	...	1638	...	1738	...	1838	...	...	1939	...	2038	...	2138	...	...	2242	2242	...
Merzig (Saar) d.	...	0747		...	1547	...	1647	...	1747	...	1847	...	...	1948	...	2047	...	2147	...	...	2250	2250	...
Saarburg d.	...	0807	minutes	...	1607	...	1707	...	1807	...	1907	...	...	2008	...	2107	...	2207	...	...	2309	2309	...
Luxembourg ▷ d.	0731	|		1531	|	1631	|	1731	|	1831	|	1859	1931	|	2031	|	2131	|	2231	2231	|	|	2331
Trier Hbf ▷ a.	0825	0828	past each	1625	1628	1725	1728	1825	1828	1925	1928	2004	2025	2028	2125	2128	2225	2228	2325	2325	2328	2328	0025
Trier Hbf d.	0832	0832		1632	1632	...	1732	1832	1832	1932	1932	...	2032	2032	2132	2132	...	2232	...	2332	2332	...	...
Wittlich Hbf d.	0856	0856	hour until	1656	1656	...	1756	1856	1856	1956	1956	...	2056	2056	2156	2156	...	2256	...	2356	2356	...	...
Bullay d.	0910	0910		1710	1710	...	1810	1910	1910	2010	2010	...	2110	2110	2210	2210	...	2310	...	0010	0010	...	...
Cochem (Mosel) d.	0919	0919		1719	1719	...	1819	1919	1919	2019	2019	...	2119	2119	2219	2219	...	2319	...	0019	0019	...	...
Koblenz Hbf a.	0955	0955		1755	1755	...	1855	1955	1955	2055	2055	...	2155	2155	2255	2255	...	2355	...	0055	0055	...	...

E – ⑥⑦ (also Nov. 1).
G – ⑥⑦ (also Oct. 3, Nov. 1).

a – Not June 23, Nov. 1.
e – Not Nov. 1.
h – On Ⓒ (also Nov. 1) departs Saarburg 0631, arrives Trier 0658.
j – Arrives 0615.
k – Also Oct. 2.
r – 1742 on Oct. 3.
t – Not July 3, 10, 17.
z – Also Nov. 1.

✣ – The 0931 from Luxembourg requires a change of trains at Trier on Ⓒ.
▷ – Additional journeys Luxembourg - Trier: 1659 ①–⑤ **a**, 1759 ①–⑤ **a**.

BULLAY - TRABEN-TRARBACH

13 km Journey time: 18 mi

Operated by Rhenus Veniro

From Bullay at 0558 ⚒, 0700, 0822, 0922 and hourly until 2122.

From Traben-Trarbach at 0621 ⚒, 0745, 0845 and hourly until 2145.

TRIER - PERL - METZ

km		E		G	
0	**Trier** Hbf d.	1041	...	1941	...
49	Perl 🏛 d.	1115	...	2015	...
70	Thionville a.	1152	...	2053	...
100	**Metz** a.	1213	...	2118	...

	E		G
Metz d.	0844t	...	1744r
Thionville d.	0908t	...	1808
Perl 🏛 d.	0946	...	1846
Trier Hbf a.	1020	...	1920

Other local *RB* services **Trier** - **Perl** and v.v. Journey time: 49 – 56 minutes.

From Trier Hbf at 0506 Ⓐ **e**, 0623 Ⓐ **e**, 0704 ⚒ **e**, 0746, 0846, 0946, 1046, 1146, 1246, 1323 Ⓐ **e**, 1346 Ⓒ **z**, 1446, 1605, 1646, 1746, 1846, 1946, 2046 and 2217.

From Perl at 0505 Ⓐ **e**, 0625 ⚒ **e**, 0649 Ⓐ **e**, 0725 ⚒ **e**, 0825, 0925, 1025, 1125, 1225, 1325, 1425 Ⓒ **z**, 1525, 1625, 1725, 1825, 1925, 2025 and 2125.

915a KÖLN - GEROLSTEIN - TRIER

RE / *RB* serv

km		Ⓐ e		Ⓐ e	⑥	† z	† z	⚒ e	† z	⚒ e	† z	⚒ e	⚒ e	⚒ e	† z	† z	† z	⚒ e			⚒ e		† z	
0	**Köln** Messe/Deutz d.	...	...	...	...	...	0605	0605	0705	0715	0805	0815	0858	0915	0915	0955	1015	1015	1115	1215	1256	1315	1355	1415
1	**Köln** Hbf d.	...	...	...	...	...	0611	0611	0711	0721	0811	0821	0905	0921	0921	1005	1021	1021	1121	1221	1305	1321	1405	1421
41	Euskirchen d.	...	...	...	...	...	0656	0656	0756	0800	0900	0900	0943	1000	1000	1043	1100	1100	1200	1300	1343	1400	1443	1500
56	Mechernich d.	...	...	...	...	...	0707	0707	0807	0809	0909	0909	0952	1009	1009	1052	1109	1109	1209	1309	1352	1409	1452	1509
65	Kall d.	...	...	...	...	...	0717	0717	0817	0817	0917	0917	1000	1017	1017	1100	1117	1117	1217	1317	1400	1417	1500	1517
81	Blankenheim d.	...	...	...	...	...	0732	0732	0832	0832	0932	0932	|	1032	1032	|	1132	1132	1232	1332	|	1432	|	1532
94	Jünkerath d.	0514	0538k	0654	...	...	0746	0746	0846	0846	0946	0946	1022	1046	1046	1122	1146	1146	1246	1346	1422	1446	1522	1546
113	**Gerolstein** d.	0531	0559	0712	0719	0725	0802	0803	0903	0903	1003	1003	1035	1102	1103	1135	1202	1203	1303	1403	1435	1503	1535	1603
143	Bitburg-Erdorf d.	0604	0633	0758	0758	0758	0834	0841	0941	0941	1041	1041	1100	1133	1141	1200	1233	1241	1341	1441	1500	1541	1600	1641
182	**Trier** Hbf a.	0652	0717	0839	0839	0839	0927	0927	1027	1027	1127	1127	1140	1227	1227	1240	1327	1327	1427	1527	1540	1627	1640	1727

	Ⓒ z	Ⓐ e					† z	⚒ e		
Köln Messe/Deutz d.	1615	1615	1713	1815	1915	1956	2005	2015	2105	2205
Köln Hbf d.	1621	1621	1721	1821	1921	2005	2011	2027	2111	2211
Euskirchen d.	1700	1700	1800	1900	2000	2043	2056	2110	2200	2300
Mechernich d.	1709	1709	1809	1909	2009	2052	2107	2121	2211	2311
Kall d.	1717	1717	1817	1917	2017	2100	2117	2132	2220	2320
Blankenheim d.	1732	1732	1832	1932	2032	|	2132	2149	2236	2336
Jünkerath d.	1746	1746	1846	1946	2046	2122	2146	2203	2250	2350
Gerolstein d.	1802	1803	1903	2003	2103	2135	2203	2227	2307	0007
Bitburg-Erdorf d.	1833	1841	1941	2041	2141	2200	2241	2259	...	...
Trier Hbf a.	1927	1927	2027	2127	2227	2240	2327	2347	...	...

	⚒ e	Ⓐ e	Ⓐ e	⑥	⚒ e	Ⓐ e	⑥	† z	Ⓐ e	⑥
Trier Hbf d.	...	...	...	...	...	...	0543	0543	0615	0622
Bitburg-Erdorf d.	...	...	...	...	...	...	0617	0617	0658	0710
Gerolstein d.	0441	0524	0544	0548	0618	0651	0656	0656	0736	0756j
Jünkerath d.	0500	0543	0601	0605	0635	0713	0713	0713	0813	0813
Blankenheim d.	0514	0557	0615	0619	0649	0727	0727	0727	0827	0827
Kall d.	0531	0613	0632	0635	0706	0742	0742	0742	0842	0842
Mechernich d.	0540	0622	0641	0644	0715	0749	0749	0749	0849	0849
Euskirchen d.	0556	0639	0656	0656	0729	0803	0803	0807	0903	0903
Köln Hbf a.	0639	0716	0739	0739	0812	0839	0839	0852	0939	0939
Köln Messe/Deutz a.	0644	0721	0745	0745	0817	0845	0845	0857	0945	0945

	⚒ e	⚒ e	† z	† z				⚒ e		† z						Ⓑ	⑥	Ⓒ z	Ⓐ e					
Trier Hbf d.	0725	0735	0735	0825	0835	0935	1035	1125	1135	1225	1235	1335	1435	1535	1635	1735	1735	1825	...	1835	1935	2035	2135	2235
Bitburg-Erdorf d.	0758	0819	0819	0858	0919	1019	1119	1158	1219	1258	1319	1419	1519	1619	1719	1819	1819	1858	...	1919	2019	2119	2219	2321
Gerolstein d.	0823	0856	0900	0923	0956	1056	1156	1223	1256	1323	1356	1456	1556	1656	1756	1856	1856	1923	1920	1956	2053	2156	2253	2355
Jünkerath d.	0836	0913	0913	0936	1013	1113	1213	1236	1313	1336	1413	1513	1613	1713	1813	1913	1913	1936	1943	2009	...	2217	...	...
Blankenheim d.	|	0927	0927	|	1027	1127	1227	|	1327	|	1427	1527	1627	1727	1827	1927	1927	|	1957	2023	...	2231	...	...
Kall d.	0859	0942	0942	0959	1042	1142	1242	1259	1342	1359	1442	1542	1642	1742	1842	1942	1942	1959	2012	2039	...	2247	...	...
Mechernich d.	0906	0949	0949	1006	1049	1149	1249	1306	1349	1406	1449	1549	1649	1749	1849	1949	1949	2006	2019	2047	...	2256	...	...
Euskirchen d.	0917	1003	1003	1017	1103	1203	1302	1317	1402	1417	1503	1603	1703	1803	1903	2003	2002	2017	2030	2107	...	2307	...	...
Köln Hbf a.	0952	1039	1039	1052	1139	1239	1339	1352	1439	1452	1539	1639	1739	1839	1939	2039	2044	2052	2112	2151	...	2351	...	...
Köln Messe/Deutz a.	0957	1044	1044	1057	1144	1244	1344	1357	1444	1457	1544	1644	1744	1845	1944	2044	2049	2057	2117	2157	...	2357	...	...

e – Not Nov. 1. **j** – Arrives 0746. **k** – ⑥ only. **z** – Also Nov. 1.

KARLSRUHE - OFFENBURG - KONSTANZ 916

ervices except where shown

Warning! Services between Singen and Konstanz are subject to alteration until July 17

												IC 2005 ⑤⑥ E🍷				⊡	IC 2364 Ⓐ S				⑤	† t	A	⑤† z d
	Ⓐ e	⑥	Ⓒ z																					
Karlsruhe Hbf ...... **912 943** d.	...	0500	...	0607	0704	0809**h**	0909	1009	1109**k**	1209	1309**k**	1336	1409	1509**k**	1609	1709	1733	1809	1909**k**	2009	2116	2116	2116	2209
Rastatt .... **943** d.	...	0513	...	0619	0718	0823	0923	1023	1123**k**	1223	1323**k**	|	1423	1523**k**	1623	1723	1746	1823	1923**k**	2023	2129	2129	2129	2228
Baden-Baden .... **912** d.	...	0519	...	0625	0726	0830	0930	1030	1130	1230	1330	1356	1430	1530	1630	1730	1754	1830	1930	2030	2136	2136	2136	2235
Offenburg .... **912 942** d.	0523	0554**j**	...	0658	0759	0859	0959	1059	1159	1259	1359	1418	1459	1559	1659	1759	1813	1859	1959	2059	2205	2205	2205	2323**c**
Hausach .... **942** d.	0548	0619	...	0721	0821	0921	1021	1121	1221	1321	1421	1439	1521	1621	1721	1821	...	1921	2021	2124	2229	2229	2229	2348
Hornberg (Schwarzw) .... d.	0556	0627	...	0729	0829	0929	1029	1129	1229	1329	1429	1448	1529	1629	1729	1829	...	1929	2029	2132	2237	2237	2237	2356
Triberg .... d.	0609	0640	...	0743	0843	0943	1043	1143	1243	1343	1443	1503	1543	1643	1743	1843	...	1943	2043	2146	2250	2250	2250	0009
St Georgen (Schwarzw) .... d.	0625	0655	...	0757	0857	0957	1057	1157	1257	1357	1457	1520	1557	1657	1757	1857	...	1957	2057	2201	2304	2305	2304	0023
Villingen (Schwarzw) ..... **938** d.	0636	0705	0705	0806	0906	1006	1106	1206	1306	1406	1506	1531	1606	1706	1806	1906	...	2006	2106	2210	2313	2313	2313	0032
Donaueschingen .... **938** d.	0654**j**	0714	0714	0817	0917	1017	1117	1217	1317	1417	1517	1542	1617	1717	1817	1917	...	2017	2117	2219	2323	2323	*2343*	...
Immendingen .... **938** d.	0706	0726	0726	0828	0928	1028	1128	1228	1328	1428	1528	1554	1628	1728	1828	1928	...	2028	2128	2235	2333	2335	...	...
Engen .... **940** d.	0719	0738	0738	0840	0940	1040	1140	1240	1340	1440	1540	|	1640	1740	1840	1940	...	2040	2140	2248	2347	|	...	...
Singen .... **939 940** d.	0735	0752	0752	0852	0952	1052	1152	1252	1352	1452	1552	1618	1652	1752	1852	1952	...	2052	2152	2302	2355	2356	...	...
Radolfzell .... **939** d.	0746	0800	0800	0900	1000	1100	1200	1300	1400	1500	1600	1628	1700	1800	1900	2000	...	2100	2200	2311	...	0003	...	...
Konstanz .... a.	0810	0816	0816	0916	1016	1116	1216	1316	1416	1516	1616	1645	1716	1816	1916	2016	...	2116	2216	2330	...	0018	...	...

	IC 2365 Ⓐ S	⚒ r	⚒ r	Ⓐ e	Ⓒ z	† t	⚒ r			IC 2004 ⑦w E🍷	IC 2006 ⑥ D🍷	⊕									⑤† z			
tanz .... d.	...	...	0502**e**	0524	0549	0640	0640	0735	0840	0909	0909	0940	1040	1140	1240	1340	1440	1540	1640	1740	1840	1940	2040	2159	2322
lfzell .... **939** d.	...	...	0516**e**	0539	0606	0656	0656	0753	0857	0923	0923	0957	1057	1157	1257	1357	1457	1557	1657	1757	1857	1957	2058	2223	2346
en .... **939 940** d.	...	...	0530**j**	0556**j**	0614	0706	0706	0806	0906	0932	0932	1006	1106	1206	1306	1406	1506	1606	1706	1806	1906	2006	2106	2234	0000
n .... **940** d.	...	...	0539	|	|	0715	0715	0815	0915	|	|	1015	1115	1215	1315	1415	1515	1615	1715	1815	1915	2015	2115	2250	0013
ndingen .... **938** d.	...	...	0552	0617	0635	0728	0728	0829	0929	0953	0953	1030	1129	1230	1329	1430	1529	1630	1729	1830	1929	2030	2128	2307	...
ueschingen .... **938** d.	...	*0510*	0603	0629	0645	0740	0740	0840	0940	1005	1005	1040	1140	1240	1340	1440	1540	1640	1740	1840	1940	2040	2140	2319	...
jen (Schwarzw) ..... **938** d.	...	0535	0612	0640	0655	0750	0750	0850	0950	1016	1016	1050	1150	1250	1350	1450	1550	1650	1750	1850	1950	2050	2150	2328	...
eorgen (Schwarzw) .... d.	...	0544	0621	0649	0703	0759	0759	0859	0959	1026	1026	1059	1159	1259	1359	1459	1559	1659	1759	1859	1959	2059	2159	...	...
rg .... d.	...	0558	0635	0704	0718	0814	0814	0914	1014	1042	1042	1114	1214	1314	1414	1514	1614	1714	1814	1914	2014	2114	2213	...	...
berg (Schwarzw) .... d.	...	0612	0649	0717	0726	0826	0828	0926	1026	1057	1057	1126	1226	1326	1426	1526	1626	1726	1826	1926	2026	2128	2227	...	...
ach .... **942** d.	...	0621	0657	0726	0739	0837	0837	0937	1037	1105	1105	1137	1237	1337	1437	1537	1637	1737	1837	1937	2037	2137	2235	...	...
burg .... **912 942** a.	0558	0647	0719	0746	0759	0859	0859	0959	1059	1125	1125	1159	1259	1359	1459	1559	1659	1759	1859	1958	2059	2159	2300	...	...
n-Baden .... **912** a.	0616	0724	0800**e**	0819	0827	0927	*0930*	1027	1127	1200	1200	1227	1327	1427	1527	1627	1727	1827	1927	2027	2127	2227**t**	2347	...	...
tt .... **943** a.	0624	0731	0806**e**	0825	0833	0934	*0937*	1033	1133	|	|	1233	1333	1433	1533	1633	1733	1833	1933	2033	2133	2233**t**	2353	...	...
ruhe Hbf .... **912 943** a.	0635	0750	0821**e**	0839	0849	0949	*0952*	1049	1149	1219	1219	1249	1349	1449	1549	1649	1749	1849	1949	2049	2149	2249**t**	0007	...	...

①②③④⑥ (not Oct. 3, Nov. 1). Change trains at Offenburg on ①–④.
[12] and 🍷 Konstanz - Mannheim - Köln - Dortmund.
[12] and 🍷 Konstanz - Mannheim - Köln - Emden and v.v.
Ⓐ (not Oct. 31, Nov. 1). From / to Stuttgart (Table **931**).

Arrives 2301.
Runs daily Karlsruhe - Hausach.

e – Ⓐ (not Nov. 1).
h – 0811 on † (also Nov. 1).
j – Arrives 8–11 minutes earlier.
k – 3 minutes earlier July 16 - Aug. 28.
r – Not Nov. 1.
t – † (also Nov. 1).
w – Also Oct. 3; not Oct. 2.

z – Also Nov. 1.

⊕ – Change trains at Offenburg on † (also Nov. 1).
⊡ – On ①②③④⑦ change trains at Offenburg (departs Offenburg 1801). On ①②③④⑦ July 17 - Aug. 28 departs Karlsruhe 1706, Rastatt 1720.

FRANKFURT - MAINZ - IDAR OBERSTEIN - SAARBRÜCKEN 917

xx

	⚒r¶	⚒v¶	¶	Ⓐr	¶	⚒r																		⑤⑥f
Frankfurt (Main) Hbf .... ‡ d.	...	...	...	...	...	...	...	0725	0825	*0908*	1025	*1108*	1225	*1308*	1425	1524**e**	1625	1724**e**	1825	*1908*	2025	*2108*	2225	...
Frankfurt Flughafen ✈ § .... ‡ d.	...	...	...	...	...	...	...	0737	0837	*0924*	1037	*1124*	1237	*1324*	1437	1538**e**	1637	1738**e**	1837	*1924*	2037	*2124*	2237	...
Mainz Hbf .... ‡ d.	...	...	...	...	...	0556	0655	0800	0900	0956	1100	1156	1300	1356	1500	1600	1700	1800	1900	1956	2100	2156	2300	2338
Bad Kreuznach .... d.	...	...	...	0514	...	0624	0724	0826	0926	1024	1126	1224	1326	1424	1526	1626	1726	1826	1926	2024	2126	2224	2326	0018
Bad Sobernheim .... d.	...	...	...	0536	...	0644	0744	0846	0946	1044	1146	1244	1346	1444	1546	1646	1746	1846	1946	2044	2146	2244	2346	0041
Kirn .... d.	...	...	...	0551	...	0654	0754	0856	0956	1054	1156	1254	1356	1454	1556	1656	1756	1856	1956	2054	2156	2254	2356	0056
Idar-Oberstein .... d.	...	...	...	0606	...	0705	0805	0907	1007	1105	1207	1305	1407	1505	1607	1707	1807	1907	2007	2105	2207	2305	0007	0110
Türkismühle .... d.	0409	0440	0541	0632	0642	0725	0826	0926	1026	1126	1226	1326	1426	1526	1626	1726	1826	1926	2026	2126	2226	2326	0026	...
St Wendel .... d.	0425	0457	0557	0651	0659	0738	0837	0937	1037	1137	1237	1337	1437	1537	1637	1737	1837	1937	2037	2137	2237	2337	0037	...
Ottweiler (Saar) .... d.	0434	0506	0606	0658	0708	0745	0844	0944	1044	1144	1244	1344	1444	1544	1644	1744	1844	1944	2044	2144	2244	2344	0044	...
Neunkirchen (Saar) .... d.	0445	0513	0613	0705	0717	0753	0852	0952	1052	1152	1252	1352	1452	1552	1652	1752	1852	1952	2052	2152	2252	2352	0052	...
Saarbrücken Hbf .... a.	0510	0540	0638	0723	0743	0813	0912	1012	1112	1212	1312	1412	1512	1612	1712	1812	1911	2011	2112	2212	2312	0012	0112	...

	¶									Ⓐr	Ⓒz		Ⓐ	Ⓒ							¶		¶	¶	¶
brücken Hbf .... d.	0122	0346	0446	0546	0651	0751	0851	0951	1051	1151	1151	1249	1351	1351	1451	1549	1651	1751	1851	1951	2035	2112	2135	2235	2335
kirchen (Saar) .... d.	0148	0404	0504	0604	0710	0810	0910	1010	1110	1210	1210	1310	1410	1410	1510	1608	1710	1810	1910	2010	2100	2130	2214	2313**j**	0000
eiler (Saar) .... d.	0155	0410	0510	0610	0715	0815	0915	1015	1115	1215	1215	1315	1415	1415	1515	1613	1715	1815	1915	2015	2107	2135	2221	2320	0007
endel .... d.	0204	0417	0517	0617	0722	0822	0922	1022	1122	1222	1222	1322	1422	1422	1522	1620	1722	1822	1922	2022	2127	2143	2231	2330	0017
smühle .... d.	...	0428	0528	0628	0732	0832	0932	1032	1132	1232	1232	1332	1432	1432	1532	1632	1732	1832	1932	2032	2142	2154	2247	2345	...
Oberstein .... d.	...	0449	0549	0649	0752	0852	0952	1052	1152	1252	1252	1352	1452	1452	1552	1652	1752	1852	1952	2052	...	2214	...	...	...
.... d.	...	0500	0600	0700	0803	0903	1003	1103	1203	1303	1303	1403	1503	1503	1603	1703	1803	1903	2003	2103	...	2225	...	...	...
Sobernheim .... d.	...	0509	0610	0710	0812	0912	1012	1112	1212	1312	1312	1412	1512	1512	1612	1712	1812	1912	2012	2112	...	2234	...	...	...
Kreuznach .... d.	...	0530	0631	0731	0832	0932	1032	1132	1232	1330	1332	1432	1530	1532	1632	1732	1832	1932	2032	2132	...	2300	...	...	...
z Hbf .... ‡ a.	...	0558	0658	0758	0858	0959	1058	1159	1258	1359	1359	1458	1558	1559	1658	1759	1858	1959	2058	2159	...	2328	...	...	...
kfurt Flughafen ✈ § .... ‡ a.	...	0620	0720	0820**e**	0920	*1034*	1120	*1234*	1320	*1434*	*1434*	1520	1620	*1634*	1720	*1834*	1920	*2034*	2120	*2235*	...	...	...	...	...
kfurt (Main) Hbf .... ‡ a.	...	0636	0736	0836**e**	0936	*1049*	1136	*1249*	1336	*1449*	*1449*	1536	1636	*1649*	1736	*1851*	1936	*2051*	2136	*2249*	...	...	...	...	...

Ⓐ only.
Also Oct. 31.
Arrives 2300.

r – Not Nov. 1.
v – Not Aug. 15, Nov. 1.
z – Also Nov. 1.

‡ – See also Tables **911** / **914** / **917a**.
§ – Frankfurt Flughafen Regionalbahnhof.
¶ – Operated by DB.

Operator: Vlexx GmbH (except trains marked ¶ which are operated by DB).

FRANKFURT - FRANKFURT FLUGHAFEN ✈ - MAINZ - WIESBADEN 917a

ahn 8/9

Warning! Subject to alteration July 16 - Aug. 25

			①	②–⑦									⚒					⚒						
kfurt (Main) Hbf ▽ d.	0002	0017	0043*	0047	0216*	0315*	0346*	0415*	0447	0502	0517	0532	0532	and at	1202	1217	1232	1232	1247	1302	1317	1332	1347	and at
kfurt Flughafen.. ¶ d.	0014	0029	0059	0059	0229	0329	0357	0429	0459	0514	0529	0542	0544	the same	1214	1229	1242	1244	1259	1314	1329	1344	1359	the same
z Hbf .... d.	|	0057	0127	0127	0257	0357	|	0457	0527	|	0557	...	|	minutes	|	1257	...	|	1327	|	1357	|	1427	minutes
ainz-Kastel .... d.	0039	|	|	|	|	|	0424	|	|	0539	|	...	0609	past each	1239	|	...	1309	|	1339	|	1409	|	past each
baden Hbf .... a.	0048	0110	0140	0140	0310	0410	0433	0510	0540	0548	0610	...	0618	hour until	1248	1310	...	1318	1340	1348	1410	1418	1440	hour until

kfurt (Main) Hbf ▽ d.	2102	2117	2132	2147	2202	2217	2232	2247	2302	2317	2347
kfurt Flughafen.. ¶ d.	2114	2129	2144	2159	2214	2229	2242	2259	2314	2329	2359
z Hbf .... d.	|	2157	|	2227	|	2257	...	2327	|	2357	0027
ainz-Kastel .... d.	2139	|	2209	|	2239	|	...	|	2339	|	|
baden Hbf .... a.	2148	2210	2218	2240	2248	2310	...	2340	2348	0010	0040

								⚒		
Wiesbaden Hbf ..... d.	0019	0049	0149	0249	0349	0411	0419	0441	...	and at
Mainz-Kastel .... d.	|	|	|	|	|	0419	|	0449	...	the same
Mainz Hbf .... d.	0033	0103	0203	0303	0403	|	0433	|	...	minutes
Frankfurt Flughafen ¶ d.	0102	0132	0232	0335	0432	0447	0502	0517	0517	past each
Frankfurt (Main) Hbf a.	0116	0146	0244	0349	0443	0458	0513	0528	0528	hour until

				⚒																					
baden Hbf .... d.	1049	1111	1119	1141	...	1149	1211	1219	1241	and at	1949	2011	2019	2041	2049	2111	2119	...	2149	2211	2219	2249	2311	2319	2349
ainz-Kastel .... d.	|	1119	|	1149	...	|	1219	|	1249	the same	|	2019	|	2049	|	2119	|	...	|	2219	|	|	2319	|	|
z Hbf .... d.	1103	|	1133	|	...	1203	|	1233	|	minutes	2003	|	2033	|	2103	|	2133	...	2203	|	2233	2303	|	2333	0003
kfurt Flughafen.. ¶ d.	1132	1147	1202	1217	1217	1232	1247	1302	1317	past each	2032	2047	2102	2117	2132	2147	2202	2217	2232	2247	2302	2332	2347	0002	0032
kfurt (Main) Hbf .. a.	1143	1158	1213	1228	1228	1243	1258	1313	1328	hour until	2043	2058	2113	2128	2143	2158	2213	2228	2243	2258	2313	2343	2358	0013	0047

From the underground platforms.

¶ – Frankfurt Flughafen Regionalbahnhof ✈.

* – Departs from the main station (not underground platforms).

918 RHEINLAND-PFALZ LOCAL SERVICES

RB / S-Bahn serv

PIRMASENS - SAARBRÜCKEN

km		Ⓐe	⚒r	Ⓐe	⚒r	†w				
0	**Pirmasens** Hbf........d.	0515	0552	*0622*	*0732*	0732	0832	and	1932	2032
7	Pirmasens Nord........d.	0522	0559	0641	0743	0743	0843	hourly	1943	2043
31	Zweibrücken Hbf........d.	0552	0640	0713	0813	0813	0913	until	2013	2113
67	**Saarbrücken** Hbf.......a.	0631	0723	0751	0851	0851	0951		2051	2151

	Ⓒz	⚒r	Ⓐe					
Saarbrücken Hbf.....d.	0045	0602	0633	0705	0807	and	1907	2007
Zweibrücken Hbf......d.	0128	0643	0712	0745	0845	hourly	1945	2045
Pirmasens Nord.......a.	0157	0715	0741	0815	0915	until	2015	2115
Pirmasens Hbf........a.	0205	*0728*j	0753	0826	0926		2026	2126

PIRMASENS - LANDAU (Pfalz)

km		Ⓐe	⑥	Ⓐe	Ⓐe					
0	**Pirmasens** Hbf..........d.	0440	0542	0544	0622	0702	and	1902	2002	...
7	Pirmasens Nord..........d.	0452	0555	0609	0634	0718	hourly	1918	2018	...
55	**Landau** (Pfalz) Hbf......a.	0547	0658	0708	0734	0818	until	2018	2118	...

	Ⓐe	Ⓐe	⑥					
Landau (Pfalz) Hbf...d.	0528	0608	0641	...	0741	and	1841	1941
Pirmasens Nord.......a.	0632	0715	0740	...	0840	hourly	1940	2040
Pirmasens Hbf........a.	0657	0728	0757	...	0857	until	1957	2057

BINGEN - KAISERSLAUTERN - PIRMASENS

km		Ⓐe	Ⓐe	⚒r	⚒r												Ⓐe	Ⓒz		Ⓐe				†w
0	**Bingen** (Rhein) Hbf.....d.	...	...	...	0549	...	0649	...	0755	...	0855	...		1655	...	1728	1755	...	1755	1855	...	1955	2102
16	Bad Kreuznach..........d.	...	0508	...	0610	...	0710	...	0816	...	0916	...	and at	1716	...	1752	1816	...	1832b	1916	...	2016	2132
43	Rockenhausen...........d.	...	0536	...	0639	...	0740	...	0855v	...	0955	...	the same	1755	...	1821	1855	...	1901	1955	...	2055	2159
79	**Kaiserslautern** Hbf....a.	...	0611	...	0717	...	0812	...	0926v	...	1026	...	minutes	1826	...	1857	1928	...	1943	2026	...	2130	2239
79	**Kaiserslautern** Hbf....d.	0516	...	0626	...	0735	...	0835	...	0935	...	1035	past each	...	1835	...	...	1935	...	...	2035	...	...
108	Pirmasens Nord..........a.	0553	...	0707	...	0806	...	0906	...	1006	...	1106	hour until	...	1906	...	...	2006	...	...	2107	...	...
115	**Pirmasens** Hbf..........a.	0608	...	0719	...	0818	...	0918	...	1018	...	1118		...	1918	...	...	2018	...	...	2118	...	...

	⚒r	Ⓐe	Ⓐe	B																			
Pirmasens Hbf............d.	...	0531	...	0640	...	0732t	...	0841	...		1441	...	1541	...	1641	...	1741	...	1841	...	1941	...	2041
Pirmasens Nord............d.	...	0538	...	0648	...	0750	...	0850	...	and at	1450	...	1550	...	1650	...	1750	...	1850	...	1950	...	2050
Kaiserslautern Hbf.....a.	...	0609	...	0720	...	0826	...	0926	...	the same	1526	...	1626	...	1726	...	1826	...	1926	...	2026	...	2126
Kaiserslautern Hbf.....d.	0517	*0624*	0640	...	0735	...	0832	...	0932	minutes	...	1532	...	1636	...	1738	...	1838	...	1932	...	2032	...
Rockenhausen.............d.	0551	*0656*	0713	...	0810	...	0901	...	1001	past each	...	1601	...	1709	...	1808	...	1908	...	2001	...	2101	...
Bad Kreuznach............d.	0643	*0724*	0743	...	0841	...	0941	...	1041	hour until	...	1641	...	1741	...	1841	...	1941	...	2041	...	2137	...
Bingen (Rhein) Hbf......a.	0702	...	0803	...	0901	...	1001	...	1101		...	1701	...	1801	...	1901	...	2001	...	2101	...	2157	...

NEUSTADT (Weinstr) - KARLSRUHE and WISSEMBOURG

km		Ⓐe	Ⓐe	Ⓐe	⚒r	⚒r	⚒r	Ⓐe	†w	⑥							D	†E		D	†E			Ⓐe
0	**Neustadt** (Weinstr) Hbf.d.	0422	...	*0506**	0529	0610	0636e	0659	0700	0709	0736	0809	0836	0909	0936	1009	1036	1045	1109	1136	1144	1209	1236	1305
18	Landau (Pfalz) Hbf......d.	0449	...	*0535*	0555	0634	0658e	0713	0722	0722	0758	0822	0858	0922	0958	1022	1058	1058	1122	1158	1158	1222	1258	1319
31	Winden (Pfalz)............d.	0503	0505	0555	0603	0650	0708	0722	0731	0731	0809	0831	0909	0931	1009	1031	1109	1109	1131	1209	1209	1231	1309	1331
47	**Wissembourg** ▦ ◐ a.	|	0521	0615	|	|	0726	|	|	|	0827	|	0927	|	1028	|	1127	1127	|	1227	1227	|	1327	|
44	Wörth (Rhein).............d.	0520	...	...	0617	0709	...	0735	0744	0744	...	0844	...	0944	...	1044	...	...	1144	...	...	1244	...	1344
58	**Karlsruhe** Hbf...........a.	0534	...	...	0636	0726	...	0753	0754	0754	...	0854	...	0954	...	1054	...	...	1154	...	...	1254	...	1354

			❖								⑥
Neustadt (Weinstr) Hbf..d.	1336	1409	and at	1909	1936	2009	2104	*2136*	2226	2335	2335
Landau (Pfalz) Hbf.......d.	1358	1422	the same	1922	1958	2022	2122	*2158*	2248	2356	2357
Winden (Pfalz).............d.	1409	1431	minutes	1931	2009	2031	2131	2229	2304	...	0006
Wissembourg ▦ ◐ .a.	1427	|	past each	|	2027	|	|	|	|	...	|
Wörth (Rhein).............d.	...	1444	hour until	1944	...	2044	2144	2244	2320	...	0019
Karlsruhe Hbf............a.	...	1454		1954	...	2054	2154	2256	2337	...	0029

	Ⓐe	Ⓐe	⚒r		Ⓒz	Ⓐe	
Karlsruhe Hbf..................d.	0430	...	0600	...	0705	0716	...
Wörth (Rhein).....................d.	0447	...	0617	...	0715	0736	...
Wissembourg ▦ ◐ ....d.	|	0526	|	0626e	|	|	0733r
Winden (Pfalz)....................d.	0502	0553	0631	0647e	0727	0748	0757r
Landau (Pfalz) Hbf...............d.	0518	0607	0645	0701	0736	0757	0807
Neustadt (Weinstr) Hbf.......a.	0540	0628	0705	0722	0750	0811	0826

	Ⓒz						Ⓐe	Ⓒz	†E	D	Ⓐe	Ⓒz	†E	D							⑥		
Karlsruhe Hbf.............d.	0806	...	0906	and at	1506	...	1601	1606	...	...	1705	1706	...	...	1806	...	1906	...	2006	...	...	2106	2206
Wörth (Rhein)...............d.	0816	...	0916	the same	1516	...	1616	1616	...	...	1716	1716	...	...	1816	...	1916	...	2016	...	...	2116	2216
Wissembourg ▦ ◐ .d.	|	0833	|	minutes	|	1533	|	|	1633	1633	|	|	1733	1733	|	1833	|	1933	|	2033	2103	|	|
Winden (Pfalz).............d.	0829	0853	0929	past each	1529	1553	1629	1629	1653	1653	1729	1729	1753	1753	1829	1853	1929	1953	2029	2053	2123	2131	2229
Landau (Pfalz) Hbf.......d.	0838	0903	0938	hour until	1538	1603	1638	1638	1702	1703	1738	1738	1802	1803	1838	1903	1938	2003	2038	2103	2131	2140	2238
Neustadt (Weinstr) Hbf.a.	0851	0924	0950		1551	1624	1651	1651	1713	1724	1751	1751	1816	1824	1851	1924	1951	2024	2051	2124	...	2202	2256

GERMERSHEIM - SPEYER - MANNHEIM - HEIDELBERG

km			Ⓐe	Ⓐe	Ⓐe	⑥	Ⓐe	Ⓐe	Ⓒz¶	Ⓐe													
0	**Germersheim** ....‡ d.	0409e	0517	0555	0620	0622	0643	0703	0700	0725	0749z	0812	0849	0912	0949	1012	and at	1549	1612	1649	1712	1749	1812
14	Speyer Hbf..............‡ d.	0423	0533	0609	0632	0635	0659	0713	0713	0738	0802	0825	0902	0925	1002	1025	the same	1602	1625	1702	1725	1802	1825
23	Schifferstadt ....‡ d.	0434	0548	0627	0640	0647	0711	|	0729	0801h	0811	0835	0911	0935	1011	1035	minutes	1611	1635	1711	1735	1811	1835
34	Ludwigshafen Hbf....‡ d.	0451	0604	0640	0649	0700	0725	|	0742	0814	0821	0848	0921	0948	1021	1048	past each	1621	1648	1720	1749	1821	1848
37	**Mannheim** Hbf.......⊡ a.	0456	*0617*	0645	*0705*	0705	...	0732	0747	0818	0825	0853	0926	0953	1026	1053	hour until	1626	1653	1726	1753	1826	1853
54	**Heidelberg** Hbf......⊡ a.	0514	*0630*	0704	*0723*	0723	...	0748	*0823*	0845	0845	0918r	0944	1016r	1044	1116r		1645	1716r	1744	1816e	1845	1916e

						⊖				
Germersheim...........‡ d.	1912	1949	2012	...	2049	2120	2157	2256	2322	...
Speyer Hbf..................‡ d.	1925	2002	2025	...	2102	2135	2212	2309	2335	...
Schifferstadt...............‡ d.	1935	2011	2034	2045	2119	2149	2229	2318	2347	2350
Ludwigshafen Hbf.....‡ d.	1948	2021	...	2057	2130	2200	2241	...	...	0001
Mannheim Hbf........⊡ a.	1953	2026	...	2103	2135	2206	2251	...	...	0006
Heidelberg Hbf.......⊡ a.	2016e	2045	...	2123	2153	2223	2313	...	...	0023

	Ⓐe			Ⓐe	Ⓒz	Ⓐs	Ⓐe	⑥		
Heidelberg Hbf....⊡ d.	*0505*	0534r	...	*0602*	0634	0644	0709	0709	0733	0742e
Mannheim Hbf.....⊡ d.	0526	0554	...	*0622*	0656	0705	0728	0730	0756	0804
Ludwigshafen Hbf .‡ d.	0532	0600	0612	0638	0703	0712	0734	0737	0803	0810
Schifferstadt..........‡ d.	0550	0611	0627	0650	0718	0730	0755	0755	0814	0824
Speyer Hbf.............‡ d.	0559	...	0637	0700	0727	0740	0805	0804	...	0833
Germersheim.......‡ a.	0612	...	0652	0714	0741	0754	0819	0818	...	0845

																				m		
Heidelberg Hbf ....⊡ d.	0843e	0913	0943r	1013	1043r	and at	1513	1543r	1613	1643r	1713	1743	1813	1843r	1913	1943e	2013	2037	...	2114	2144	2214	...
Mannheim Hbf.........⊡ d.	0904	0931	1004	1031	1104	the same	1531	1605	1631	1704	1731	1804	1831	1904	1931	2004	2031	2056	...	2137	2208	2242	...
Ludwigshafen Hbf.....‡ d.	0910	0936	1009	1036	1110	minutes	1536	1610	1636	1710	1736	1810	1836	1910	1936	2010	2036	2103	...	2142	2215	2250k	...
Schifferstadt..............‡ d.	0924	0947	1024	1047	1124	past each	1546	1624	1647	1724	1747	1823	1847	1924	1947	2024	2047	2114	2124	2158	2233	2305	...
Speyer Hbf.................‡ d.	0932	0956	1033	1056	1132	hour until	1557	1633	1657	1733	1757	1833	1857	1933	1957	2033	2057	...	2133	2207	2243	2314	...
Germersheim...........‡ a.	0945	1009	1045	1109	1145		1609	1645	1709	1745	1809	1845	1909	1945	2009	2045	2109	...	2145	2223	2255	2328	...

WÖRTH (Rhein) - GERMERSHEIM

km			Ⓒz	Ⓐe	Ⓐe	Ⓐe	Ⓐe	Ⓒz	Ⓐe	Ⓒz	Ⓐe	Ⓒz	Ⓐe	Ⓒz	Ⓐe	Ⓒz	Ⓐe	Ⓐe	Ⓒz	Ⓐe		Ⓐe
0	**Wörth** (Rhein).............d.	0030	0130	0536	0610	0627	0712	0725	0731	0825	0835	0925	0935	1025	1035	1125	1135	1218	1225	1233	and at the same minutes past	1918
27	**Germersheim** ....a.	0102	0202	0603	0639	0659	0745	0757	0803	0857	0907	0957	1007	1057	1107	1157	1207	1244	1257	1307	each hour until	1944

	Ⓐe	Ⓒz	Ⓐe				
Wörth (Rhein)..............d.	1933	2025	2035	2119	2219	2329	...
Germersheim..............a.	2007	2057	2107	2152	2252	0004	...

	Ⓒz	⚒r	⑥	Ⓐe	⑥	Ⓐe	Ⓐe	Ⓒz	Ⓐe	Ⓐe	Ⓒz	Ⓐe	Ⓒz
Germersheim .... d.	0027	0437	0519	0550	0601	0616	0655	0701	0725	0756	0801	0850	0901
Wörth (Rhein) .... a.	0058	0508	0551	0623	0634	0650	0729	0734	0758	0827	0834	0922	0934

	Ⓒz	Ⓐe	Ⓒz	Ⓐe	Ⓒz	Ⓐe	Ⓐe		Ⓒz	Ⓐe	Ⓐe	Ⓒz	Ⓐe	Ⓐe	Ⓒz	Ⓐe	Ⓐe	Ⓒz				
Germersheim.............d.	1001	1050	1101	1150	1201	1214	1250	and at the same minutes past	1601	1614	1650	1701	1714	1741	1801	1814	1850	1901	1950	2050	2150	2225
Wörth (Rhein)..............a.	1034	1122	1134	1222	1234	1240	1322	each hour until	1634	1640	1722	1734	1740	1815	1834	1840	1922	1934	2022	2122	2222	2256

B – On † (also Nov. 1) Pirmasens Hbf d. 0641, Pirmasens Nord d. 0652, Kaiserslautern a. 0724.
D – ⚒ (daily from Oct. 24).
E – † to Oct. 23.

b – Arrives 1815.
e – Ⓐ (not Nov. 1).
h – Arrives 13 minutes earlier.
j – *0757* on ⑥.
k – 2247 until June 18.
m – Change trains at Mannheim on Ⓑ.
r – ⚒ (not Nov. 1).
s – Ⓐ (not Nov. 1). Change trains at Schifferstadt from Sept. 26.

t – 0741 on † (also Nov. 1).
v – On † to Oct. 23 Rockenhausen d. 0857, Kaiserslautern a. 09
w – Also Nov. 1.
z – Ⓒ (also Nov. 1).

❖ – Neustadt d. 1505 (not 1509) and 1705 (not 1709).
⊖ – On Ⓒ (also Nov. 1) passengers travelling from Germershein or Speyer to Heidelberg should change trains at Schifferstad
* – Change trains at Landau and Winden.
◐ – For Strasbourg connections see Table **396**.
⊡ – See also Tables **913**, **919**, **923** and **924**.
‡ – See also Table **911a**.

 Ⓐ – Mondays to Fridays, except holidays   Ⓑ – Daily except Saturdays   Ⓒ – Saturdays, Sundays and holidays

WIESBADEN - MAINZ - DARMSTADT - ASCHAFFENBURG — 918a

services

	⚒r	⚒r	Ⓐt		Ⓐt										Ⓐt		Ⓐt		Ⓐt						
Wiesbaden Hbf .... d.	...	0538	0608	0638	0702	0738	0838	0938	1038	1138	1238	1338	1438	1538	1602	1638	1702	1738	1802	1838	1938	2038	2138	2238	2338
Mainz Hbf .... d.	...	0549	0619	0649	0715	0749	0849	0949	1049	1149	1249	1349	1449	1549	1615	1649	1715	1749	1815	1849	1949	2049	2149	2249	2349
Darmstadt Hbf .... a.	...	0621	0656	0723	0750	0821	0921	1021	1121	1221	1321	1421	1521	1621	1650	1721	1750	1821	1850	1921	2021	2121	2222	2321	0021
Darmstadt Hbf .... d.	0452	0632	0703	0732	0800	0832r	0932	1032r	1132	1232r	1332	1432r	1532	1632r	1700	1732	1800	1832t	1900	1932	2032t	2132	...	...	...
Aschaffenburg Hbf .. a.	0535	0713	0745	0813	0843	0913r	1013	1113r	1213	1313r	1413	1513r	1613	1713r	1742	1813	1842	1913t	1942	2013	2113t	2213	...	...	...

	Ⓐt	Ⓐt		Ⓐt		Ⓐt									Ⓐt		Ⓐt		Ⓐt		Ⓐt					
affenburg Hbf ... d.	...	0510	0542r	0606	0640r	0716	0746	0846r	0946	1046r	1146	1246r	1346	1446r	1516	1546	1616	1646r	1716	1746	1816	1846t	1946	2046t	2146	...
nstadt Hbf .... a.	...	0552	0623r	0651	0727r	0759	0827	0927r	1027	1127r	1227	1327r	1427	1527r	1559	1627	1659	1727r	1759	1827	1859	1927t	2027	2127t	2227	...
nstadt Hbf .... d.	0440	0610	0640	0706	0740	0810	0840	0940	1040	1140	1240	1340	1440	1540	1610	1640	1710	1740	1810	1840	1910	1940	2040	2140	2240	2337
z Hbf .... d.	0513	0645	0713	0745	0813	0845	0913	1013	1113	1213	1313	1413	1513	1613	1645	1713	1745	1813	1845	1913	1945	2013	2113	2213	2313	0013
sbaden Hbf .... a.	0525	0655	0725	0755	0825	0855	0925	1025	1125	1225	1325	1425	1525	1625	1655	1725	1755	1825	1855	1925	1955	2025	2125	2225	2325	0025

⚒ only.   t – Ⓐ only.

SAARBRÜCKEN - MANNHEIM - FRANKFURT and STUTTGART — 919

services except where shown

SERVICE JUNE 19 - SEPTEMBER 24 ✣

		EC 217		ICE 1557					IC 2059			TGV 9551				ICE 9553					ICE 9555			ICE 9557	
	Ⓐ	⊠	Ⓐ	①–⑥	⑦	Ⓑ	⑥		①–⑥												Ⓑ			⊡	
		G🍷		L✕					S			R🍷				R✕					R✕			R✕	
Trier Hbf **915** .... d.	...	...	0456	...	0532	0632	0632	0732	...	0832	0932	...	1032	1132	1232	...	...	1432	1532	1632	...	...	1832	...	2032
Saarbrücken Hbf .... d.	0446	0531	0608	0642	0645	0747	0747	0847	0851	0947	1047	1057	1147	1249	1347	1459	1503	1547	1646	1747	1859	1903	1947	2059	2147
Homburg (Saar) Hbf .... d.	0507	0552	0632	0702	0706	0809	0809	0909	0917	1009	1109	|	1209	1311	1409	|	1527	1609	1708	1809	|	1927	2009	|	2209
Kaiserslautern Hbf .... d.	0530	0617	0654	0726	0730	0830	0833	0929	0937	1033	1129	1135	1230	1333	1433	1537	1554	1629	1729	1830	1937	1954	2033	2137	2232
Neustadt (Weinstr) Hbf .... d.	0552	0641	0717	0749	0756	0853	0854	...	1001	1055	...	|	1253	1401	1455	|	...	1651	1751	1852	|	...	2055	|	2306j
Ludwigshafen Hbf .... d.	0610	0705	0734	|	|	|	|	...	|	|	...	|	|	|	|	|	...	|	|	|	|	...	|	|	|
Ludwigshafen Mitte .... d.	|	|	|	|	0813	0910	0911	...	|	1111	...	|	1310	1420	1514	|	...	1710	1815	1908	|	...	2111	|	2332
Mannheim Hbf .... **918** a.	0616	0709	0742	0811	0816	0913	0915	...	1021	1114	...	1215	1313	1424	1516	1617	...	1713	1818	1912	2017	...	2114	2217	2335
Mannheim Hbf **912 918** ▽ d.	...	0712	0746	0813	...	...	...	...	1023	...	...	1218	...	...	...	1619	...	...	...	...	2019	...	...	2219	...
Heidelberg Hbf **912 918** d.	...	|	0801	|	...	...	...	...	|	...	...	|	...	...	...	|	...	...	...	...	|	...	...	|	...
Stuttgart Hbf .... **912** a.	...	0754	...	|	...	...	...	...	1118	...	...	|	...	...	...	|	...	...	...	...	|	...	...	|	...
Darmstadt Hbf .... ▽ a.	...	...	...	0846	...	...	...	...	...	...	...	|	...	...	...	|	...	...	...	...	|	...	...	|	...
Frankfurt (Main) Hbf ...... ▽ a.	...	...	...	0904	...	...	...	...	...	...	...	1258h	...	...	...	1658h	...	...	...	...	2058h	...	...	2258h	...

		ICE 9558				ICE 9586				ICE 9556			ICE 9554		TGV 9552					IC 2058		ICE 9550	EC 216		ICE 1554	
		①–⑤		⑥	Ⓑ	⑥			⑥⑦	①–⑤		①–⑤	⑥⑦							Ⓑ		Ⓑ			Ⓑ	
		R✕				R✕			n	R✕			R✕		R🍷					S		R✕	G🍷		L✕	
kfurt (Main) Hbf ...... ▽ d.	...	0558e	...	...	...	0658e	...	...	...	0856e	...	...	1058e	...▲	1258e	...	...	...	...	...	...	1858e	...	...	2054	...
nstadt Hbf .... ▽ d.	...	|	...	...	...	|	...	...	...	|	...	...	|	...	|	...	...	...	...	...	...	|	...	...	2111	...
uttgart Hbf .... **912** d.	...	|	...	...	...	|	...	...	...	|	...	...	|	...	|	...	...	...	...	1655	...	|	2004	...	|	...
eidelberg Hbf . **912 918** d.	...	|	...	...	...	|	...	...	...	|	...	...	|	...	|	...	...	...	...	|	...	|	|	...	|	...
nheim Hbf . **912 918** ▽ a.	...	0638	...	...	...	0737	...	...	...	0939	...	...	1141	...	1338	...	...	...	...	1745	...	1938	2048	...	2146	...
nheim Hbf .... **918** d.	...	0639	...	0718	0736	0738	0839	...	0939	0940	1039	1136	1142	1239	1340	1439	1543	1636	1739	1747	1835	1939	2050	...	2148	2239
wigshafen Mitte .... d.	...	|	...	0721	0739	|	0842	...	0942	|	1042	1139	|	1242	|	1442	|	|	1742	|	1839	|	|	...	|	2242
wigshafen Hbf .... **918** d.	...	|	...	|	|	|	|	...	|	|	|	|	|	|	|	|	1548	1641	|	|	|	|	|	...	|	|
stadt (Weinstr) Hbf .... d.	...	|	...	0740	0801v	|	0906	...	1000	|	1107	1200	|	1305	|	1508	1609	1705	1803	1811	1905	|	2112	...	2210	2306
erslautern Hbf .... d.	0626	0721	0732	0804	0831	0822	0935	1003	1023	1022	1133	1231j	1228	1331	1422	1535	1631	1731	1830	1835	1935j	2022	2135	2210	2233	2329
burg (Saar) Hbf .... d.	0652	|	0752	0831	0852	|	0956	1030	1052	|	1153	1252	|	1352	|	1555	1652	1752	1851	1856	1956	|	2157	2238	2255	2356
rbrücken Hbf .... a.	0715	0759	0816	0857	0915	0901	1015	1056	1115	1100	1215	1315	1306	1415	1500	1615	1715	1815	1913	1918	2016	2100	2218	2304	2316	0019
ier Hbf **915** .... a.	0828	...	0928	1028	1028	...	1128	...	1228	...	1328	1428	...	1528	...	1728	1828	1928	2028	...	2128	...	...	...	...	...

OTHER S-BAHN SERVICES

		Ⓐ		Ⓒ	Ⓐ			¶										◇					¶			
erslautern Hbf .... d.	0415	0456	0609	0704	0707	0732	0758	0832p	0858	0928	0958	1035	1058	1129	1158	1232	1258	1324	1358	1438	1458	1530	1558	1633	1658	1733
stadt (Weinstr) Hbf .... d.	0443	0526	0643j	0730	0738	0805	0831	0906	0931	1005j	1031	1105	1131	1201j	1230	1305	1331	1405k	1431	1507	1531	1605j	1632j	1706	1729	1811j
fferstadt .... d.	0458	0542	0700	0752	0753	0819	0846	0920	0946	1019	1045	1119	1146	1219	1244	1319	1345	1419	1445	1521	1545	1620	1646	1720	1747	|
wigshafen Hbf .... d.	0510	0554	0718	0801	0801	0829	0857	0929	0957	1029	1057	1128	1157	1228	1257	1329	1357	1429	1457	1529	1557	1628	1657	1729	1759	1830
nheim Hbf .... a.	0515	0559	0722	0806	0806	0834	0903	0934	1003	1034	1102	1134	1203	1234	1303	1334	1403	1434	1503	1535	1603	1634	1703	1734	1804	1835
nheim Hbf .... d.	*0535**	0607	0729	0807	0807	0838	0907	0938	1007	1038	1107	1138	1207	1238	1307	1338	1407	1438	1507	1538	1607	1638	1707	1738	1807	1838
delberg Hbf .... a.	*0553**	0625	0744	0823	0823	0854	0923	0954	1023	1054	1123	1154	1223	1254	1323	1354	1423	1454	1523	1554	1623	1654	1723	1753	1823	1854

							Ⓒ		
erslautern Hbf .... d.	1759	1858	1931	1958	2042	...	2058	2141	2302
stadt (Weinstr) Hbf .... d.	1831	1931	2005j	2031	2111	...	2130	2210	2330
fferstadt .... d.	1845	1945	2019	2045	2126	2149	2149	2229	2350
wigshafen Hbf .... d.	1857	1957	2029	2057	2141	2200	2200	2241	0001
nheim Hbf .... a.	1903	2003	2034	2103	2149	2206	2206	2251	0006
nheim Hbf .... d.	1907	2007	2038	2107	...	2207	2207	2257	0007
delberg Hbf .... a.	1923	2023	2054	2123	...	2223	2223	2313	0023

	⚒	Ⓐ		Ⓒ	Ⓐ	Ⓐ	Ⓒ					
Heidelberg Hbf .... d.	0413	0505	0534r	0602	0616	0644	*0634*	0733	0804	0833	0903	0933
Mannheim Hbf .... a.	0429	0522	0551r	0619	0631	0702	*0651*	0751	0818	0851	0920	0951
Mannheim Hbf .... d.	0431	0526	0554	0634	0635	0705	0705	0756	0819	0856	0926	0954
Ludwigshafen Hbf .... d.	0438	0532	0600	0640	0646	0712	0712	0803	0824	0903	0931	1003
Schifferstadt .... d.	0448	0547	0613	0652	0655	0727	0729	0815	0833	0915	|	1015
Neustadt (Weinstr) Hbf .... d.	0506	0612j	0632	0709	0712	0744	0814b	0832	0858j	0932	1004j	1032
Kaiserslautern Hbf .... a.	0535	0640	0659	0737	0739	0811	0842	0859	0926	0959	1029	1059

													◐													
delberg Hbf .... d.	1003	1033	1103	1133	1203	1233	1303	1333	1403	1433	1503	1536	1603	1636	1703	1733	1803	1833	1903	1933	2003	2037	2114	2144	2214	2244
nheim Hbf .... a.	1017	1051	1119	1151	1218	1251	1318	1351	1417	1451	1520	1552	1619	1653	1719	1751	1817	1851	1920	1951	2020	2055	2132	2202	2232	2302
nheim Hbf .... d.	1021	1056	1120	1156	1219	1256	1322	1356	1421	1456	1526	1556	1621	1656	1721	1756	1821	1856	1926	1956	2021	2056	2137	2208	2242	2326
wigshafen Hbf .... d.	1026	1103	1126	1203	1224	1303	1327	1403	1426	1503	1531	1603	1627	1704	1726	1804	1827	1903	1931	2003	2027	2103	2142	2215	2250	2331
fferstadt .... d.	|	1115	1134	1216	1233	1315	|	1415	|	1515	1541	1616	1635	1715	|	1816	|	1915	1940	2015	2036	2115	2206k	2230	2303	2343
stadt (Weinstr) Hbf .... d.	1058j	1132	1212c	1234	1255	1332	1404k	1432	1458j	1532	1613k	1632	1652	1732	1806k	1832	1909k	1931	2004j	2032	2057	2131	2223	2247	2322	0002
erslautern Hbf .... a.	1126	1159	1239	1301	1323	1359	1429	1459	1526	1559	1639	1659	1721	1759	1832	1859	1938	1959	2028	2059	2125	2159	2251	2314	2350	...

[12] and 🍷 Graz - Salzburg - München - Stuttgart - Saarbrücken and v.v.
[12] and ✕ Saarbrücken - Frankfurt - Erfurt - Leipzig - Dresden and v.v.
From July 3. From / to Paris (Table **390**). Ⓡ for international journeys.
See May edition for international journeys until July 2.
From July 3.

Arrives 0745.
Arrives 1148.
13–21 minutes **earlier** July 16 - Aug. 28.
18–21 minutes later July 16 - Aug. 28.
Arrives 7–10 minutes earlier.
Arrives 13–19 minutes earlier.

n – Not June 25, 26.
p – 3 minutes later on Ⓒ.
r – ⚒ only.
v – 0758 on †.
* – 8–9 minutes later on Ⓐ.

⊡ – On ⑥ runs as *TGV* **9559** (conveys 🍷, not ✕).
¶ – On ①–⑤ passengers travelling from Kaiserslautern to Heidelberg should move to the front portion of the train at Mannheim.
◇ – On ①–④ passengers travelling from Kaiserslautern to Heidelberg should move to the front portion of the train at Mannheim.
◐ – On ⑥⑦ Mannheim d. 1619, Ludwigshafen d. 1625, Schifferstadt d. 1633, Neustadt a. 1648, d. 1709, Kaiserslautern a. 1736.
✣ – International services from / to Paris are valid from July 3.
⊠ – Retimed July 30 - Sept. 11 as follows: Saarbrücken d. 0449, Homburg d. 0512, Kaiserslautern d. 0536, Neustadt d. 0604, Ludwigshafen d. 0627, Mannheim a. 0642, d. 0649, Stuttgart a. 0733.
▽ – See also Table **912** (*ICE* trains) and Table **913** (local trains).
▲ – *209 km* for trains running non-stop Mannheim - Frankfurt.

920 FRANKFURT - NÜRNBERG - PASSAU (- WIEN)

See Table 921 for other regional tr…

km								RE	RE	ICE	ICE	ICE	ICE	ICE	ICE	ICE	ICE	ICE	ICE	ICE	ICE	ICE	ICE
								59493	59275	827	521	21	523	1125	525	23	1127	527	529	91	1521	91	621
		⚒t	Ⓐs	Ⓐt		⚒s	Ⓒz	Ⓐs	ⒸP	Ⓐ			⚒	†	⚒		⑥k	Ⓐ					
		◐		◐			◐			🍷	🍷	✕	🍷	🍷	🍷	✕	G🍷	🍷	🍷	✕	✕	✕	🍷
	Hamburg Hbf **800 900** d.	...	...	...	...	...	...	...	...	...	...	...	...	...	...	...	...	...	...	0803y	...	...	...
	Dortmund Hbf **800** d.	...	...	...	...	...	...	...	...	...	...	...	0406	0514	0524	0437	0614	0624	0724	|	0636b	...	0815c
	Essen Hbf **800** d.	...	...	...	...	...	...	...	...	...	...	...	0428	0538	0553	0500	0639	0653	0754	|	|	...	0840
	Düsseldorf Hbf **800** d.	...	...	...	...	...	...	...	...	...	...	...	0455	0605	0621	0527	0707	0721	0822	|	|	...	0913
	Köln Hbf **800 910** d.	...	...	...	...	...	...	...	...	0317	0418	...	|	|	|	0553	|	|	|	|	0753	...	|
	Köln Messe/Deutz **910** d.	...	...	...	...	...	...	...	...	|	|	...	0518	0628	0644	|	0730	0744	0844	|	|	...	0936
	Bonn Hbf **800** d.	...	...	...	...	...	...	...	...	|	|	...	|	|	|	0614	|	|	|	|	0814	...	|
	Koblenz Hbf **911** d.	...	...	...	...	...	...	...	...	|	|	...	|	|	|	0648	|	|	|	|	0848	...	|
	Mainz Hbf **911** d.	...	...	...	...	...	...	...	...	|	|	...	|	|	|	0740	|	|	|	|	0940	...	|
0	**Frankfurt** Flughafen ✈ § d.	...	...	...	...	...	...	...	...	0437	0534	...	0635	0735	0735	0802	0836	0835	0935	|	1002	...	1036
11	**Frankfurt** (Main) Hbf d.	...	...	...	...	...	...	...	...	0454	0551	0622	0654	0754	0754	0819*	0854	0854	0954	|	1018	...	1054
35	Hanau Hbf d.	...	...	...	...	...	...	...	...	|	0608	0638	|	|	|	0836*	|	|	|	|	1035	...	|
57	Aschaffenburg Hbf d.	...	...	...	...	...	...	...	...	0524	0624	0653	0724	0824	0824	|	0924	0924	1024	|	|	←	1124
136	**Würzburg** Hbf **900** d.	...	...	...	...	...	...	...	...	0604	0704	0733	0804	0904	0904	0933	1004	1004	1104	1128	1132f	1135	1204
238	**Nürnberg** Hbf **900** a.	...	...	...	...	...	...	...	...	0659	0759	0827	0859	0959	0959	1027	1059	1059	1159	→	1224	1227	1259
238	**Nürnberg** Hbf d.	...	0501	...	0521	0541	...	0615	0705	0702	0802	0830	0902	1002	1002	1030	1102	1102	1202	...	1227	1230	1302
	München Hbf **904** a.	...	|	...	|	|	...	|	|	0807	0904	|	1004	1104	1104	|	1204	1204	1304	...	1338	|	1404
271	Neumarkt (Oberpf) d.	...	0534	0555	0554	0614	0620	0638	0726	...	...	|	...	...	...	|	...	...	...	...	...	|	...
335	**Regensburg** Hbf d.	0540	...	0657	...	...	0716	0725	0811	...	...	0927	...	...	...	1127	...	...	...	...	...	1327	...
375	Straubing d.	0607	...	0722	...	...	0741	...	0838	...	...	|	...	...	...	|	...	...	...	...	...	|	...
400	Plattling **944** d.	0623	...	0738	...	...	0756	...	0853	...	...	1000	...	...	...	1200	...	...	...	...	...	1400	...
452	**Passau** Hbf 🏛 **944** a.	*0718*	...	*0833*	...	...	*0836*	...	0930	...	...	1034	...	...	...	1234	...	...	...	...	...	1434	...
	Linz Hbf **950** a.	...	...	...	...	...	...	...	...	...	...	1142	...	...	...	1342	...	...	...	...	...	1542	...
	Wien Hbf **950** a.	...	...	...	...	...	...	...	...	...	...	1309	...	...	...	1509	...	...	...	...	...	1709	...

	ICE	ICE	ICE	ICE	RE	ICE	ICE	ICE	ICE	ICE	IC	ICE	ICE	IC	IC	RE		ICE	ICE	ICE	IC		EN
	27	625	627	29	59495	629	721	229	723	725	2027	727	729	2229	2229	59499		821	821	1625	1029		491
					Ⓐs				Ⓑq		2327	Ⓑq		Ⓑq	V			Ⓑq	T	⑥k			Ⓡ
	✕	🍷	🍷	✕		🍷	🍷	✕	🍷	🍷	🍷	🍷	🍷	🍷	🍷		◐	O🍷	O🍷	D✕			N🍷
Hamburg Hbf **800 900** d.	0546	...	...	...	...	...	...	...	...	...	1146	...	...	1346	1346	...	...	...	...	...	1546	...	2052
Dortmund Hbf **800** d.	0838	1016c	1124c	...	...	...	1324n	...	1424g	1524k	1436	...	1724k	1636	1636	...	...	...	...	...	1836	...	|
Essen Hbf **800** d.	0900	1040	1153c	...	...	...	1353	...	1453	1554	|	1653	1754	|	|	...	...	...	...	...	|	...	|
Düsseldorf Hbf **800** d.	0927	1108	1221	...	...	1308	1421	...	1521	1622	|	1721	1822	|	|	...	...	1908	1908	...	|	...	|
Köln Hbf **800 910** d.	0953	|	|	...	...	|	|	...	|	|	1553	|	|	1753	1753	...	...	|	|	...	1953	...	|
Köln Messe/Deutz **910** d.	|	1130	1244	...	...	1333	1444	...	1544	1644	|	1744	1844	|	|	...	...	1930	1930	...	|	...	|
Bonn Hbf **800** d.	1014	|	|	...	...	|	|	...	|	|	1614	|	|	1814	1814	...	...	|	|	...	2014	...	|
Koblenz Hbf **911** d.	1048	|	|	...	...	|	|	...	|	|	1648	|	|	1848	1848	...	...	|	|	...	2048	...	|
Mainz Hbf **911** d.	1140	|	|	...	...	|	|	...	|	|	1740	|	|	1940	1940	...	...	|	|	2043	2143	...	|
Frankfurt Flughafen ✈ § d.	1202	1236	1332	...	...	1438	1535	...	1635	1736	1802	1836	1935	2002	2002	...	...	2036	2036	2102	2202	...	|
Frankfurt (Main) Hbf d.	1221	1254	1354	1421	...	1454	1554	1621	1654	1754	1818	1854	1954	2018	2018	...	...	2054	2054	2119	2218	...	|
Hanau Hbf d.	1238	|	|	1438	...	|	|	1638	|	|	1835	|	|	2035	2035	...	...	|	|	2135	2235	...	|
Aschaffenburg Hbf d.	|	1324	1424	|	...	1524	1624	1652	1724	1824	1849	1924	2024	2049	2049	...	...	2124	2124	2150	2249	...	|
Würzburg Hbf **900** d.	1333	1404	1504	1533	...	1604	1704	1733	1804	1904	1933	2004	2104	2131	2131	...	...	2203	2205	2233	2343	...	0201
Nürnberg Hbf **900** a.	1427	1459	1559	1627	...	1659	1759	1827	1859	1959	2027	2059	2159	2226	2226	...	...	...	2259	2326	0037	...	0257
Nürnberg Hbf d.	1431	1502	1602	1630	1636	1702	1802	1830	1902	2002	2031	2103	2202	...	2237	2257	...	...	2302	...	...	...	0300
München Hbf **904** a.	|	1606	1704	|	|	1804	1907	|	2004	2109j	|	2205	2307	...	|	|	...	...	0007	...	...	...	|
Neumarkt (Oberpf) d.	|	...	...	|	1657	...	...	|	...	...	|	...	...	...	|	2319	...	...	...	...	...	...	|
Regensburg Hbf d.	1527	...	...	1727	1747	...	...	1927	...	...	2133	...	...	...	2340	0005	0009	...	...	...	...	...	|
Straubing d.	|	...	...	|	...	...	...	|	...	...	2155	...	...	...	0003	...	0036	...	...	...	...	...	|
Plattling **944** d.	1600	...	...	1800	...	...	...	2000	...	...	2209	...	...	...	0018	...	0050	...	...	...	...	...	|
Passau Hbf 🏛 **944** a.	1634	...	...	1834	...	...	...	2034	...	...	2241	...	...	...	0049	...	*0130*	...	...	...	...	...	0510
Linz Hbf **950** a.	1742	...	...	1942	...	...	...	2142	...	...	...	...	...	...	...	...	...	...	...	...	...	...	0623
Wien Hbf **950** a.	1909	...	...	2109	...	...	...	2309	...	...	...	...	...	...	...	...	...	...	...	...	...	...	0816

D – From Wiesbaden Hbf (d. 2024).
G – To Garmisch on ⑥ (Table **895**).
N – Conveys 🛏 1, 2 cl., 🛏 2 cl. and (2).
O – From Oberhausen (Table **800**).
P – Ⓒ to Oct. 9 (also Aug. 15). Departs Nürnberg 0659 on Aug. 15.
T – ④⑤⑦ (also Oct. 3; not Oct. 2).
V – ④⑤⑦ (also Oct. 3, Nov. 1; not Oct. 2, 30).

b – Not July 9 - Aug. 21.

c – Ⓒ only.
f – Arrives 7 – 9 minutes earlier.
g – Not ⑤.
j – 2105 from Sept. 4.
k – ⑥ (also Oct. 2).
n – ⑤–⑦ (also Oct. 3).
q – Not Oct. 2.
r – Frankfurt Flughafen **Regionalbahnhof**.
s – Not Nov. 1.

t – Not Aug. 15, Nov. 1.
x – Frankfurt (Main) **Süd**.
y – 0729 July 18 - Sept. 2.
z – Also Aug. 15, Nov. 1.
* – On ⑦ (also July 16, 23, 30, Aug. 6, 13, … Frankfurt d. 0821, Hanau d. 0837.
◐ – Operated by *agilis*.
§ – Frankfurt Flughafen Fernbahnhof.

921 Local trains FRANKFURT - WÜRZBURG - NÜRNBERG - REGENSBURG - PASSAU

RE / RB servi…

For faster *ICE / IC* trains see Table **920** above. Neumarkt - Regensburg - Plattling trains are operated by *agilis*.

km					Ⓐ										Ⓒ	Ⓐ		Ⓒ	Ⓐ						
0	**Frankfurt** (Main) Hbf d.	...	0502	...	0520	0634	0730	0834	0930	1034	1130	1234	1330	1434	1530	1534	1634	1730	1734	1834	1930	2034	2130	2230	2330
4	**Frankfurt** (Main) Süd d.	...	0507	...	0526	0640	0736	0840	0936	1040	1136	1240	1336	1440	1536	1540	1640	1736	1740	1840	1936	2040	2136	2236	2336
10	Offenbach (Main) Hbf d.	...	|	...	|	0645	|	0845	|	1045	|	1245	|	1445	|	1545	1645	|	1745	1845	|	2045	|	|	|
24	Hanau Hbf d.	...	0529	...	0550	0659	0759	0859	0959	1059	1159	1259	1359	1459	1559	1559	1659	1759	1759	1859	1959	2059	2159	2259	2359
46	Aschaffenburg Hbf d.	0503	0552	0613	0613	0717	0817	0917	1017	1117	1217	1317	1417	1517	1617	1617	1717	1817	1817	1917	2017	2117	2219	2322	0022
84	Lohr Bahnhof d.	0533	...	0643	0643	0743	0843	0943	1043	1143	1243	1343	1443	1543	1643	1643	1743	1843	1843	1943	2043	2143	2249	2353	0052g
96	Gemünden (Main) d.	0545	...	0657	0657	0757	0857	0957	1057	1157	1257	1357	1457	1557	1656	1656	1757	1857	1857	1957	2057	2157	2300	0004	0103g
109	Karlstadt (Main) d.	0555	...	0705	0705	0805	0905	1005	1105	1205	1305	1405	1505	1605	1704	1704	1805	1905	1905	2005	2105	2205	2310	0012	...
136	**Würzburg** Hbf a.	0617	...	0721	0721	0821	0921	1021	1121	1221	1321	1421	1521	1621	1720	1720	1821	1921	1921	2021	2121	2221	2332	0028	...

km				⚒r		⚒r	Ⓐr																		
0	**Würzburg** Hbf d.	0038	...	0438	...	0536	0607	...	0637	0742	0842	0942	1042	1142	1242	1342	1442	1542	1642	1742	1842	1942	2042	2148	...
23	Kitzingen d.	0059	...	0456	...	0554	0623	...	0655	0801	0901	1001	1101	1201	1301	1401	1501	1601	1701	1801	1901	2001	2101	2208	...
61	Neustadt (Aisch) Bf d.	...	...	0519	0546	0616	0648	0648	0717	0826	0926	1026	1126	1226	1324	1426	1526	1626	1726	1826	1926	2026	2126	2239	...
94	Fürth (Bay) Hbf d.	...	...	0546	0614	0644	0711	0711	0740	0847	0947	1047	1147	1247	1347	1447	1547	1647	1747	1847	1947	2047	2147	2309	...
102	**Nürnberg** Hbf a.	...	...	0553	0621	0652	0719	0719	0749	0854	0954	1054	1154	1254	1353	1454	1554	1654	1754	1854	1954	2054	2154	2316	...

	Ⓐt					Ⓒz															L			
Nürnberg Hbf d.	0551	*0621*	0735	...	*0817*	...	0934	...	*1017*	1136	...	*1217*c	1336	...	*1417*	1536	...	*1617*n	1736	...	*1817*	1936	...	*2021*	2136
Neumarkt (Oberpf) d.	0619	0706	0759	0806	0906	...	0959	1006	1106	1159	1206	1306c	1359	1406	1506	1559	1606	1706	1759	1807	1906	1959	2006	2106	2159
Regensburg Hbf a.	0659	0758	0838	0858	0957	...	1038	1058	1159	1238	1258	1357c	1438	1458	1558	1638	1658	1758	1838	1858	1958	2038	2058	2158	2238
Regensburg Hbf d.	0702	0801	0844	0901	1001t	1001	1044	1101	1201	1244	1301	1401	1444	1501	1601	1644	1701	1801	1844	1901	2001	...	2101	2201	2245
München Hbf **878** a.	0835	|	1018	|	|	|	1217	|	|	1417	|	|	1617	|	|	1817	|	|	2017	|	|	...	|	|	0023
Straubing d.	...	0827	...	0927	1027t	1027	▬	1127	1227	...	1327	1427	...	1527	1627	...	1727	1827	...	1927	2027	...	2128	2228	...
Plattling a.	...	0844	...	0943	1044t	1042	...	1144	1244	...	1344	1444	...	1544	1644	...	1744	1844	...	1944	2044	...	2144	2244	...
Plattling **944** d.	...	*0901*	...	*1004*	...	1046p	1102	*1204*	*1302*	...	*1404*	*1502*	...	*1604*	*1702*	...	*1804*	*1902*	...	*2004*	*2102*	...	*2157*	*2306*	...
Passau Hbf **944** a.	...	*0934*	...	*1038*	...	1130p	1136	*1239*	*1336*	...	*1439*	*1536*	...	*1639*	*1736*	...	*1839*	*1937*	...	*2039*	*2139*	...	*2232*	*2340*	...

L – To Landshut (Table **878**).

c – Ⓒ (daily July 30 - Sept. 12 and Oct. 29 - Nov. 6).
g – Aschaffenburg - Gemünden on the mornings of ①⑦ (also Aug. 16, Oct. 4, Nov. 2).
n – *1636* on Ⓐ (not Nov. 1).

p – Until Oct. 16.
r – Not Nov. 1.
t – Ⓐ (not Aug. 15, Nov. 1).
z – Also Aug. 15, Nov. 1.

(WIEN -) PASSAU - NÜRNBERG - FRANKFURT 920

able 921 for other regional trains

	ICE 824 ①–④ m🍷	IC 1028	ICE 822 ⚒ 🍷	RE 59496 Ⓒz	RE 59492 Ⓐs	ICE 820 ⚒ 🍷	IC 2226 A 🍷	IC 2226 ⚒ 🍷	ICE 728 🍷	RE 4053	◐	Ⓐt ◐	RE 4850	ICE 726 ⚒ 🍷	IC 2024 🍷	ICE 724 🍷	ICE 722 Ⓐ 🍷	ICE 1122 Ⓒ 🍷	ICE 228 ✕	ICE 720 🍷	ICE 628 🍷	ICE 28 ✕	ICE 626 🍷	ICE 826 Ⓐ 🍷
Hbf **950** d.	...	...	...	...	...	...	...	...	...	...	...	...	...	...	...	...	...	...	0650	...	...	0850	...	...
Hbf **950** d.	...	...	...	...	...	...	...	...	...	...	...	...	...	...	...	...	...	...	0814	...	...	1014	...	...
Hbf 🏛 **944** d.	...	...	...	...	...	...	0511	...	...	0523	...	...	...	...	0717	...	...	...	0924	...	...	1124	...	...
944 d.	...	...	...	...	...	...	0544	...	...	0558	0609	0629	...	...	0751	...	...	...	0958	...	...	1158	...	...
g d.	...	...	...	...	...	...	0558	...	...	...	0625	0645	...	...	0806	...	...	...	|	...	...	|	...	...
burg Hbf d.	...	...	...	0530	0530	...	0622	0622	...	...	0656	0710	0719	...	0827	...	...	...	1029	...	...	1229	...	...
kt (Oberpf) d.	...	...	...	0618	0620	...	0700	0700	...	...	0750	...	0800	...	|	...	...	...	|	...	...	|	...	...
hen Hbf **904** d.	...	...	0449	|	|	0552	|	|	0652	...	...	...	|	0755	|	0855	0955	0955	|	1055	1155	|	1255	1255
rg Hbf a.	...	...	0555	0640	0642	0657	0721	0721	0757	...	...	...	0823	0857	0925	0957	1057	1057	1126	1157	1257	1326	1357	1357
rg Hbf **900** d.	...	0527	0600	...	...	0700	0729	0729	0800	...	...	...	...	0900	0929	1000	1100	1100	1129	1200	1300	1329	1400	1400
rg Hbf **900** d.	0555	0626	0655	...	...	0755	0826	0826	0855	...	...	...	...	0955	1026	1055	1155	1155	1227	1257	1355	1427	1455	1455
enburg Hbf d.	0636	0708	0736	...	...	0836	|	|	0936	...	...	...	...	1036	|	1136	1236	1236	|	1336	1436	|	1536	1536
Hbf d.	|	|	|	...	...	|	0920	0920	|	...	...	...	...	|	1120	|	|	|	1320	|	|	1520	|	|
rt (Main) Hbf a.	0704	0736	0804	...	...	0904	0936	0936	1004	...	...	...	...	1104	1136	1204	1304	1304	1336	1404	1504	1536	1604	1604
rt Flughafen ✈ § a.	0722	0755	0822	...	...	0920	0955	0955	1022	...	...	...	...	1120	1155	1222	1322	1320	...	1422	1522	...	1622	1622
inz Hbf **911** a.	|	0818	|	...	...	|	1018	1018	|	...	...	...	...	|	1218	|	|	|	...	|	|	...	|	|
blenz Hbf **911** a.	|	0911	|	...	...	|	1111	1111	|	...	...	...	...	|	1311	|	|	|	...	|	|	...	|	|
nn Hbf **800** a.	|	0943	|	...	...	|	1142	1142	|	...	...	...	...	|	1342	|	|	|	...	|	|	...	|	|
Messe/Deutz **910** a.	0814	|	0914	...	...	1025	|	|	1114	...	...	...	...	1225	|	1324	1414	1425	...	1514	1614	...	1714	|
Hbf **800 910** a.	|	1005	|	...	...	|	1205	1205	|	...	...	...	...	|	1405	|	|	|	...	|	|	...	|	1742f
eldorf Hbf **800** a.	0836	|	0936	...	...	1048	|	|	1136	...	...	...	...	1248	|	1346	1436	1446	...	1536	1639	...	1736	...
n Hbf **800** a.	0902	|	1002	...	...	...	|	|	1202	...	...	...	...	1315	|	1415	1505	1515	...	1602	1707	...	1802k	...
nund Hbf **800** a.	...	1123	1029h	...	...	...	1321	1321	1230	...	...	...	...	1342h	1521	1442k	...	1542h	...	1629k	1740k	...	1829k	...
burg Hbf **800 900** a.	...	1413	...	...	...	...	1613	1613	...	...	...	...	...	...	1813	...	...	...	...	...	...	...	...	...

	ICE 624 Ⓐ 🍷	ICE 1124 Ⓒ 🍷	ICE 26 ✕	ICE 622 🍷	ICE 620 G🍷	ICE 90 ✕	ICE 1522 ✕	ICE 90 ✕	ICE 528 🍷	ICE 526 Ⓑq 🍷	ICE 22 ✕	ICE 524 🍷	RE 59272 ⒸP	ICE 522 🍷	ICE 20 ✕	ICE 520 ①–④ m🍷	ICE 1620 ⑥k ✕	ICE 922 ⑤⑦ w✕	RE 4089	◐	RB 59494	◐	EN 490 Ⓡ N🍷	EN 420 Ⓡ N🍷
Hbf **950** d.	...	...	1050	...	...	1250	...	...	...	...	1450	...	...	...	1650	...	...	...	...	...	...	...	2039	2139
Hbf **950** d.	...	...	1214	...	...	1414	...	...	...	...	1614	...	...	...	1814	...	...	...	...	...	...	...	2219	2319
Hbf 🏛 **944** d.	...	...	1324	...	...	1524	...	...	...	...	1724	...	1831	...	1924	...	...	...	2128	...	...	...	2328	0030
944 d.	...	...	1358	...	...	1558	...	...	...	...	1758	...	1903	...	1958	...	...	...	2200	2210	...	2311	|	|
ng d.	...	...	|	...	...	|	...	...	...	...	|	...	1916	...	|	...	...	...	...	2226	...	2327	|	|
sburg Hbf d.	...	...	1429	...	...	1629	...	...	...	...	1830	...	1944	...	2029	...	...	...	...	2253	2324	2355	|	|
kt (Oberpf) d.	...	...	|	...	...	|	...	...	...	...	|	...	2032	...	|	...	...	...	...	...	0021	...	|	|
hen Hbf **904** d.	1355	1355	|	1455	1555	|	1618	...	1652	1755	|	1855	|	1952	|	2055	2055	2055	...	...	|	...	|	|
erg Hbf a.	1457	1457	1526	1557	1657	1726	1729	...	1757	1857	1926	1957	2053	2057	2126	2201	2201	2202	...	...	0044	...	0127	|
erg Hbf **900** d.	1500	1500	1529	1600	1700	1729	1733	←	1800	1901	1929	2000	...	2100	2129	2205	2205	2205	...	...	...	...	0130	|
urg Hbf **900** d.	1555	1555	1627	1655	1755	1822	1829	1832	1855	1955	2027	2055	...	2155	2227	2257	2257	2257	...	...	...	...	0226	|
fenburg Hbf d.	1636	1636	|	1736	1836	→	|	|	1936	2036	|	2136	...	2236	2308	2336	2336	2336	...	...	...	...	|	|
Hbf d.	|	|	1720	|	|	...	1920	|	|	|	2120	|	...	2250	2322	|	|	|	...	...	...	...	|	|
urt (Main) Hbf a.	1704	1704	1736	1804	1904	...	1936	|	2004	2104	2136	2204	...	2305	2340	0004	0004	0004	...	...	...	...	|	0523x
urt Flughafen ✈ § a.	1722	1720	1755	1822	1920	...	1956	|	2022	2122	2157	2222	...	2322	...	...	...	...	...	...	...	...	|	0536r
inz Hbf **911** a.	|	|	1818	|	|	...	2018	|	|	|	2218	|	...	|	...	...	...	...	...	...	...	...	|	0602
blenz Hbf **911** a.	|	|	1911	|	|	...	2111	|	|	|	2311	|	...	|	...	...	...	...	...	...	...	...	|	0705
nn Hbf **800** a.	|	|	1942	|	|	...	2143	|	|	|	2342	|	...	|	...	...	...	...	...	...	...	...	|	|
Messe/Deutz **910** a.	1813	1826	|	1914	2025	...	|	|	2114	2214	|	2339	...	|	...	...	...	...	...	...	...	...	|	|
Hbf **800 910** a.	|	|	2005	|	|	...	2205	|	|	|	0005	|	...	0042	...	...	...	...	...	...	...	...	|	0815
eldorf Hbf **800** a.	1835	1848y	|	1944	2048	...	|	|	2136	2236	0032	2400	...	0106	...	...	...	...	...	...	...	...	|	0841
n Hbf **800** a.	1901	1915y	|	2015	2115	...	|	|	2202	2302	0057	0026	...	0135	...	...	...	...	...	...	...	...	|	...
nund Hbf **800** a.	1930	1942y	2122	2042	2142	...	2322b	|	2230	2327	0121	0049	...	0158	...	...	...	...	...	...	...	...	|	...
burg Hbf **800 900** a.	...	...	0014	...	...	...	...	2153e	...	...	...	...	...	...	...	...	...	...	...	...	...	...	0751	...

⑤⑥ (also Oct. 4, Nov. 2; not Oct. 3, 31).
rom Garmisch on ⑥ (Table **895**).
onveys 🛏 1, 2 cl., ▬ 2 cl. and [2].
) to Oct. 9 (also Aug. 15).

ot July 9 - Aug. 21.
227 July 18 - Sept. 2.
745 July 11 - Aug. 19.
only.
(also Oct. 2).
ot Oct. 3.

q – Not Oct. 2.
r – Frankfurt Flughafen **Regionalbahnhof**.
s – Not Nov. 1.
t – Not Aug. 15, Nov. 1.
w – Also Oct. 3; not Oct. 2.
x – Frankfurt (Main) **Süd**.
y – July 9 - Aug. 21 arrives Düsseldorf 1852, Essen 1931, Dortmund 2002.
z – Also Nov. 1.

§ – Frankfurt Flughafen Fernbahnhof ✈.
◐ – Operated by *agilis*.

Local trains PASSAU - REGENSBURG - NÜRNBERG - WÜRZBURG - FRANKFURT 921

RB services

For faster *ICE* / *IC* trains see Table **920** above. Plattling - Regensburg - Neumarkt trains are operated by *agilis*.

		Ⓐt																Ⓐt	Ⓒz							
u Hbf **944** d.	...	0604	*0627***z**	*0725*	...	*0825*	*0916*	...	*1025*	*1116*	...	*1225*	*1316*	...	*1425*	*1516*	1625	...	1632**p**	*1715*	...	*1822*	*1916*	...	*2025*	...
g **944** a.	...	0640	*0701***z**	*0759*	...	*0900*	*0950*	...	*1100*	*1150*	...	*1259*	*1349*	...	*1459*	*1550*	1659	...	1703**p**	*1751*	...	*1857*	*1949*	...	*2058*	...
g d.	...	...	0710	0810	...	0910	1010	...	1110	1210	...	1310	1410	...	1510	1610	▬	1710	1710	1810	...	1910	2010	...	2110	...
ng d.	...	...	0728	0826	...	0926	1026	...	1126	1226	...	1326	1426	...	1526	1626	...	1726	1726	1826	...	1926	2026	...	2126	...
chen Hbf **878** d.	0544	...	|	|	0744	|	|	0944	|	|	1144	|	|	1343	|	|	1544	|	|	|	1744	|	|	1944	|	...
sburg Hbf a.	0717	...	0753	0853	0914	0950	1052	1115	1151	1253	1314	1352	1452	1514	1553	1653	1715	1752	1752	1852	1916	1951	2052	2116	2152	...
sburg Hbf d.	0719	...	0756	0856	0918	0956	1056	1118	1156	1256	1318	1356	1456	1518	1556	1656	1718	1756	...	1856	1918	1956	2056	2118	...	2156
rkt (Oberpf) d.	0800	...	0852	0950	1000	1053	1150	1200	1253	1350	1400	1451	1550	1600	1652	1750	1800	1852	...	1950	2000	2050	2150	2200	...	2250
erg Hbf a.	0823	...	*0942*	...	1023	*1142*	...	1223	*1342*	...	1423	*1542*	...	1623	*1742*	...	1823	*1942*	...	...	2023	*2142*	...	2223	...	*2338*

				⚒r													Ⓐr									
erg Hbf d.	0101	...	...	0443	...	0605	0705	0805	0905	1005	1105	1205	1305	1405	1505	1605	1624	1705	1805	1905	2005	2105	2206	2239	...	2335
Bay) Hbf d.	0109	...	...	0451	...	0611	0711	0811	0911	1011	1111	1211	1311	1411	1511	1611	1632	1711	1811	1911	2011	2111	2212	2247	...	2344
dt (Aisch) Bf d.	0138	...	...	0521	...	0634	0734	0834	0934	1034	1134	1234	1334	1434	1534	1634	1701	1734	1834	1934	2034	2134	2235	2316	...	0013
en d.	...	...	...	0543	...	0657	0757	0857	0957	1057	1157	1257	1357	1457	1557	1657	1725	1757	1857	1957	2057	2157	2258	...	...	0034
urg Hbf a.	...	...	...	0603	...	0716	0817	0916	1016	1116	1216	1316	1416	1516	1616	1716	1747	1816	1916	2016	2116	2220	2316	...	...	0053

		Ⓐt			Ⓐ	Ⓒ								⑤	A		⚒	†		D	⑦w					
urg Hbf d.	...	0420	...	0515	0637	0637	0737	0837	0937	1037	1137	1237	1337	1437	1437	1537	1637	1637	1737	1837	1837	1937	2037	2133	2235	2340
dt (Main) d.	...	0443	...	0538	0652	0652	0752	0852	0952	1052	1152	1252	1352	1452	1452	1552	1652	1652	1752	1852	1852	1952	2052	2154	2256	0002
den (Main) d.	...	0454	...	0549	0704	0704	0804	0904	1004	1104	1204	1304	1404	1504	1504	1604	1704	1704	1804	1904	1904	2004	2104	2205	2307	0012
ahnhof d.	...	0504	...	0600	0715	0715	0815	0915	1015	1115	1215	1315	1415	1515	1515	1615	1715	1715	1815	1915	1915	2015	2115	2215	2317	0023
fenburg Hbf d.	0428	0540	0540	0640j	0743	0743	0843	0943	1043	1143	1243	1343	1443	1543	1543	1643	1743	1743	1843	1943	1943	2043	2143	2243	2348	0056
Hbf d.	0455	0602	0602	0702	0802	0803	0902	1003	1102	1203	1302	1403	1502	1601	1603	1702	1803	1803	1902	2003	2003	2102	2208	2308	0015	...
ach (Main) Hbf d.	|	0612	0612	0712	0812	|	0912	|	1112	|	1312	|	1512	|	|	1712	|	|	1912	|	|	2112	|	|	|	...
urt (Main) Süd a.	0517	0616	0616	0716	0816	0825	0916	1025	1116	1225	1316	1425	1516	|	1625	1716	1825	1825	1916	2025	2025	2116	2231	2330	0037	...
urt (Main) Hbf a.	0524	0624	0624	0724	0824	0832	0924	1032	1124	1232	1324	1432	1524	1619	1632	1724	1832	1840	1924	2032	2040	2124	2237	2336	0044	...

aily except ⑤.
–⑥ (also Oct. 2; not Oct. 3).

j – Arrives 0631.
p – Until Oct. 16.
r – Not Nov. 1.

t – Not Aug. 15, Nov. 1.
w – Also Oct. 3; not Oct. 2.
z – Ⓒ (also Aug. 15, Nov. 1).

922 WÜRZBURG - HEILBRONN - STUTTGART

RE se

km		Ⓒz	Ⓐe	Ⓐe				Ⓐe				⑤†f						
0	**Würzburg** Hbf d.	...	...	...	0637	...	0837	0937	1037	1237	1437	1537	1637	1737	1837	1937	2037	2137
43	Lauda d.	...	...	*0532*	0710	0718e	0910	1008	1110	1310	1510	1608	1710	1807	1910	2007	2110	2207
78	Osterburken d.	...	0502	0616	0733	0802e	0933	1032	1133	1333	1533	1631	1733	1830	1933	2030	2133	2230
94	Möckmühl d.	...	0519	0632	0745	0819e	0945	1043	1145	1345	1545	1643	1745	1841	1945	2042	2145	2242
116	Bad Friedrichshall Hbf d.	...	0544	0658	0801	0845e	1001	1101	1201	1401	1601	1700	1801	1858	2001	2058	2202	2258
127	**Heilbronn** Hbf ★ d.	0554	0559	0712	0812	0856	1012	1111	1212	1412	1612	1713	1812	1909	2012	2108	2211	2309
140	Lauffen (Neckar) ★ d.	0604	0610	|	|	0904	|	|	|	|	|	|	|	|	|	2117	2219	2318
180	**Stuttgart** Hbf ★ a.	0643	0651	0747	0853	0943	1053	1146	1253	1453	1653	1758	1853	1949	2053	2158	2254	2356

	Ⓐe	Ⓒz	Ⓐe					⑤†f				Ⓒz	Ⓐe					⑥⊠
Stuttgart Hbf ★ d.	0450	0456	0558	0659h	0907	1107	1307	1409	1504	1555	1704	1805	1809	1907	1942	2103	2315	...
Lauffen (Neckar) ★ d.	0525	0532	|	0739	|	|	|	|	|	|	|	|	|	|	2017	2136	2351	...
Heilbronn Hbf ★ d.	0536	0544	0641	0749	0945	1145	1345	1446	1545	1645	1745	1845	1844	1945	2027	2151	0005	0005
Bad Friedrichshall Hbf d.	0549	0554	0650	0800	0955	1155	1355	1456	1555	1655	1755	1855	1854	1955	2036	2201	0026b	0026
Möckmühl d.	0605	0611	0713	0817	1012	1213	1413	1513	1612	1713	1812	1913	1918	2012	2059	2218	0051b	0051
Osterburken d.	0616	0622	0727	0828	1027	1227	1427	1527	1627	1727	1827	1927	1930	2027	2127v	2229	0108b	0108
Lauda d.	0643	0650	0750	0851	1050	1250	1450	1550	1650	1750	1850	1953	1953	2050	2156p	2253	...	...
Würzburg Hbf a.	0724	0720	0820	0921	1121	1321	1521	1621	1721	1821	1921	2024	2024	2121	...	2325	...	...

b – Mornings of ①⑦ (also Oct. 4, Nov.
e – Ⓐ (not Nov. 1).
f – Also Nov. 1.
h – 0702 on Ⓐ (not Nov. 1).
m – To / from Mannheim (Table **924**) on (also Nov. 1).
p – ①②③④⑦ (not Oct. 2, 31).
v – Arrives 2115.
z – Ⓒ (also Nov. 1).

⊠ – Mornings of ⑥.
❖ – Timings may vary by up to 3 minute
‡ – To / from Mannheim (Table **924**).
★ – See also panel below main table.

	Ⓐe	Ⓒz	Ⓐe		Ⓐe				Ⓐe	Ⓒz	Ⓐe	m		Ⓐe		m	❖		Ⓐe‡		m		
Neckarsulm d.	...	...	0620	0642e	0717	0750e	0818	0920	...	1020	1023	1050z	1120	...	1220	1250z	and in the same	1720	1744	1820	1850z	1921	2020
Heilbronn Hbf d.	0435	0446	0627	0653	0725	0758	0826	0926	0956	1026	1029	1056	1126	1156	1227	1256	pattern every	1726	1754	1826	1856	1926	2026
Lauffen (Neckar) d.	0445	0456	0637	0704	0736	0806	0837	0937	1004	1037	1039	1104	1137	1204	1237	1304	**two** hours until	1737	1802	1837	1904	1937	2037
Stuttgart Hbf a.	0523	0535	0718	0743	0815	0843	0915	1015	1043	1115	1115	1146	1215	1243	1315	1343		1815	1839	1915	1943	2015	2115

			Ⓒz	Ⓐe	Ⓐe		m		Ⓐe		m			Ⓐe		m		Ⓐe‡		m		Ⓐe	m
Stuttgart Hbf d.	0015	...	0545	0545	0634	0745	0815	0845	0915	0945	1015	1045	and in the same	1515	1545	1613	1645	1715	1745	1815	1845	1914	2015
Lauffen (Neckar) d.	0051	...	0621	0623	0712	0820	0850	0920	0953	1020	1050	1120	pattern every	1553	1620	1650	1720	1753	1820	1850	1920	1953	2051
Heilbronn Hbf a.	0101	...	0630	0633	0722	0830	0901	0929	1001	1029	1101	1129	**two** hours until	1601	1629	1701	1729	1801	1829	1901	1929	2001	2101
Neckarsulm a.	...	...	0635	0639	0730	0835	0908z	0935	...	1035	1108z	1135		...	1635	1708z	1735	1810	1835	1908z	1935	...	2108

923 MANNHEIM - EBERBACH - OSTERBURKEN

S

Warning! Subject to alteration July 9 - September 11

km		Ⓐe	†w	Ⓐe	⑥	Ⓐe	Ⓐe	Ⓐe	Ⓒz							⑥t	
0	**Mannheim** Hbf ¶ **924** d.	0416	0457	*0457*	0535	...	0601	*0623*	0637	0729j	0838		2038	*2142*	2257	2257	0007
17	**Heidelberg** Hbf ¶ **924** d.	0434	0520	0555	0555	...	0631	0655	0655	0755	0855		2055	2201	2316	2316	0026
28	Neckargemünd **924** d.	0448	0534	0608	0608	...	0645	0709	0709	0809	0909	and	2109	2215	2336	2336	0039
34	Neckarsteinach d.	0454	0540	0614	0614	...	0651	0715	0715	0815	0915		2115	2221	2342	2342	0045
41	Hirschhorn (Neckar) d.	0501	0547	0621	0621	...	0658	0722	0722	0822	0922	hourly	2122	2228	2349	2349	0052
50	Eberbach **924** d.	0510	0553	0628	0628	...	0712f	0729	0729	0829	0929		2129	2235	2356	2356	0059
69	Mosbach-Neckarelz **924** d.	0535	0616	0646	0646	0709	0733	0748	0748	0848	0948	until	2148	2258	0014	0014	0118
72	Mosbach (Baden) d.	0539	0620	0651	0651	0714	0738	0752	0752	0852	0952		2152	2302	0018	0018	0123
101	**Osterburken** a.	0612	...	0721	0721	0751	...	0823	0823	0923	1023		2223	2333	...	0049	...

	⚒r	Ⓐe	Ⓐe	⑥	Ⓑ	Ⓐe		Ⓐe		⚒r						⑥	
Osterburken d.	...	...	0513	0529	...	0604	0632z	0643	...	0706e	0736		1836	1936	2036	2139	2239
Mosbach (Baden) d.	0434	0510	0543	0558	0605	0633	0705	0718	...	0735	0805		1905	2005	2105	2208	2308
Mosbach-Neckarelz **924** d.	0439	0522g	0548	0603	0610	0638	0710	0724	0729	0740	0810	and	1910	2010	2110	2213	2313
Eberbach **924** d.	0458	0541	0607	0622	0629	0657	0729	...	0743	0759	0829		1929	2029	2129	2232	2332
Hirschhorn (Neckar) d.	0505	0548	0614	0629	0636	0704	0736	...	|	0806	0836	hourly	1936	2036	2136	2239	2339
Neckarsteinach d.	0511	0555	0620	0635	0642	0710	0742	...	|	0812	0842		1942	2042	2142	2245	2345
Neckargemünd **924** d.	0518	0601	0627	0642	0649	0718	0749	...	|	0819	0849	until	1949	2049	2149	2252	2352
Heidelberg Hbf ¶ **924** a.	0533	0615	0640	0655	0702	0732	0802	...	0809	0832	0902		2002	2103	2203	2306	0006
Mannheim Hbf ¶ **924** a.	0551	0631	0702	0712	0718	0751	0818	...	0824	0851	0920		2020	2132	2232	2332	0030

e – Ⓐ (not Nov. 1).
f – Arrives 0705.
g – Arrives 0514.
j – 0728 until June 18. Change t at Heidelberg on † (also Nov.
r – Not Nov. 1.
t – Also Oct. 2, 31.
w – Also Nov. 1.
z – Ⓒ (also Nov. 1).

¶ – See also Tables **913**, **918**, **91**

924 MANNHEIM - HEILBRONN

RE / RB / S-Bahn se

VIA EBERBACH *Subject to altertation July 9 - Sept. 11 – see note ⊠*

km		2	Ⓐe	Ⓒz2	Ⓐe	Ⓒz2	Ⓐe	Ⓐe	Ⓐe	Ⓒz	Ⓐe	Ⓒz	Ⓐe	Ⓒz	Ⓐe	Ⓒz	Ⓐe	Ⓒz	Ⓐe	Ⓒz			2	
0	**Mannheim** Hbf ¶ **923** d.	...	...	...	...	...	...	0736	0935	0935	1135	1135	1335	1335	1535	1535	1735	1735	1935	1935	2142		...	
17	**Heidelberg** Hbf ¶ **923** d.	...	...	...	...	...	...	0749	0949	0949	1149	1149	1349	1349	1549	1549	1749	1749	1949	1949	2158		...	
50	Eberbach **923** d.	...	...	...	...	...	...	0814	1014	1018	1214	1218	1414	1418	1614	1618	1814	1818	2014	2018	2223	A	...	
69	Mosbach-Neckarelz **923** d.	0510	0616	0650	0652	0750	0752	0829	1029	1032	1229	1232	1429	1432	1629	1632	1829	1832	2029	2032	2237	L	0850	and
87	Bad Friedrichshall Hbf **922** d.	0528	0636	0708	0712	0808	0811	0842	1042	1045	1242	1245	1442	1445	1642	1645	1842	1845	2042	2045	2250	S	0908	hourly
92	Neckarsulm **922** d.	0538	0642	0718	0717	0816	0818	0847	1047	1050	1247	1250	1447	1450	1647	1650	1847	1850	2047	2050	2255	O	0918	until
98	**Heilbronn** Hbf **922** a.	0557	0649	0737	0723	*0824*	0824	0851	1051	1054	1251	1254	1451	1454	1651	1654	1851	1854	2052	2054	2259		0937	
	Stuttgart Hbf **922** a.	...	0743	...	0815	*0915*	0915	...	...	1146	...	1343	...	1543	...	1743	...	1943	...	...	...		...	

	Ⓐe	Ⓐe	Ⓒz2		Ⓒz	Ⓐe	Ⓒz	Ⓐe	Ⓒz	Ⓐe	Ⓒz	Ⓐe	Ⓒz	Ⓐe	Ⓒz	Ⓐe	Ⓒz			2		2	2	2
Stuttgart Hbf **922** d.	...	0545	*0545*	...	0815	...	1015	...	1215	...	1415	...	1613	...	1815	...	2015	...		...		...	...	...
Heilbronn Hbf **922** d.	0456	0634	*0631*	0700	0904	0906	1104	1106	1304	1306	1504	1505	1704	1705	1904	1906	2105	2105		0718		1918	2118	2218
Neckarsulm **922** d.	0500	0640	0639	0705	0909	0911	1109	1111	1309	1311	1509	1511	1709	1711	1909	1911	2109	2109	A	0739	and	1939	2139	2239
Bad Friedrichshall Hbf **922** d.	0504	0645	0648	0710	0914	0916	1114	1116	1314	1316	1514	1516	1714	1716	1914	1916	2113	2113	L	0748	hourly	1948	2148	2248
Mosbach-Neckarelz **923** d.	0518	0702	0707	0729	0927	0929	1127	1129	1327	1329	1527	1529	1727	1729	1927	1929	2131	2131	S	0807	until	2007	2207	2307
Eberbach **923** d.	0532	...	...	0743	0941	0943	1141	1143	1341	1343	1541	1543	1741	1743	1941	1943	2144	2144	O	...		...	...	...
Heidelberg Hbf ¶ **923** a.	0556	...	...	0809	1009	1009	1209	1209	1409	1409	1609	1609	1809	1809	2009	2009	2208	2208		...		...	...	...
Mannheim Hbf ¶ **923** a.	0612	...	...	0824	1024	1024	1224	1224	1424	1424	1624	1624	1824	1824	2024	2024	2224	2224		...		...	...	...

VIA SINSHEIM

km		Ⓐe2	Ⓒz2	Ⓒz	Ⓐe	Ⓒz	Ⓐe2	Ⓒz2		2		2		2		2	S	2		2		2		
0	**Mannheim** Hbf ★ ¶ **923** d.	...	...	*0535*	0618	...	*0701*	*0707*k	0835	*0907*	1035	*1107*	1235	*1307*	1435	*1507*	1635	*1707*	1835	*1907*	2044	*2107*	2207‡	2257
17	**Heidelberg** Hbf ¶ **923** d.	...	...	0631	0641	...	*0714*	*0734*j	0849	*0934*j	1049	*1134*j	1249	*1334*j	1449	*1534*j	1649	*1734*j	1849	*1934*j	2059	*2131*	2231	2316
29	Neckargemünd **923** d.	...	...	0645	0652	...	*0726*	*0745*	|	*0945*	|	*1145*	|	*1345*	|	*1545*	|	*1745*	|	*1945*	|	*2145*	2245	2332
49	Sinsheim (Elsenz) Hbf d.	0511	0611	0708	0710	0711	0806	0811	0913	1011	1113	1211	1313	1411	1513	1611	1713	1811	1913	2011	2125	2211	2307	2355
66	Bad Rappenau d.	0530	0630	...	0727	0727	0829	0830	0927	1030	1127	1230	1327	1430	1527	1630	1727	1830	1927	2030	2142	2230	...	0012
72	Bad Wimpfen d.	0542	0638	...	0732	0732	0842	0838	0932	1042	1132	1242	1332	1442	1532	1642	1732	1842	1932	2042	2147	2238	...	0018
75	Bad Friedrichshall Hbf **922** d.	0548	0648	...	0741	0743	0848	0848	0938	1048	1138	1248	1338	1448	1538	1648	1738	1848	1938	2048	2151	2243	...	0023
80	Neckarsulm **922** a.	0557	0656	...	0745	0749	0856	0856	0943	1056	1143	1257	1343	1457	1543	1657	1743	1857	1943	2057	2156	2252	...	0031
86	**Heilbronn** Hbf **922** a.	0617	0717	...	0751	0755	0917	0917	0951	1117	1151	1317	1351	1517	1551	1717	1751	1917	1951	2117	2201	2312	...	0036

	⑥	Ⓑ	Ⓐe	Ⓒz	Ⓐe	Ⓒz2	Ⓐe2	Ⓐe	Ⓒz	2		2		2		2		2	S	2		2		2
Heilbronn Hbf **922** d.	...	...	0542	...	...	0636	0638	0806	0806	0840	1006	1040	1206	1240	1406	1440	1605	1640	1805	1840	2006	2018	2207	*2301*
Neckarsulm **922** d.	...	...	0547	...	...	0656	0657	0811	0811	0859	1011	1059	1211	1259	1411	1459	1611	1659	1811	1859	2011	2039	2211	2313
Bad Friedrichshall Hbf **922** d.	...	...	0553	...	...	0710	0710	0818	0818	0910	1018	1110	1218	1310	1418	1510	1618	1710	1820	1910	2018	2051	2218	2322
Bad Wimpfen d.	...	...	0556	...	...	0718	0718	0822	0822	0918	1022	1118	1222	1318	1422	1518	1622	1718	1824	1918	2022	2056	2222	2327
Bad Rappenau d.	...	...	0604	...	...	0727	0726	0827	0830	0927	1030	1127	1230	1327	1430	1527	1630	1727	1830	1927	2030	2107	2230	2335
Sinsheim (Elsenz) Hbf d.	0545	0549	0620	0649	0649	0745	0745	0840	0844	0945	1044	1145	1244	1345	1444	1545	1644	1745	1844	1945	2044	2130	2245	2354
Neckargemünd **923** a.	0610	0610	|	0710	0715	*0810*	*0811*	|	|	*1010*	|	*1210*	|	*1410*	|	*1610*	|	*1810*	|	*2010*	|	*2210*	*2310*	...
Heidelberg Hbf ¶ **923** a.	0624	0624	0648	0726	0728	*0826*	*0825*	0909	0909	*1026*	1109	*1226*	1309	*1426*	1509	*1626*	1709	*1826*	1909	*2026*	2109	*2226*	*2326*	...
Mannheim Hbf ★ ¶ **923** a.	*0651*	*0651*	0706	0751	0746	*0851*	*0851*	0924	0924	*1051*	1124	*1251*	1324	*1451*	1524	*1653*	1724	*1851*	1924	*2055*	2124	*2302*	*0001*	...

S – To / from Stuttgart (Table **922**) on Ⓐ (not Nov. 1).

e – Not Nov. 1.
j – 3 minutes earlier on † (also Nov. 1).

k – ⑥ only.
z – Also Nov. 1.

‡ – Change trains at Heidelberg on Ⓐ (not Nov. 1).

★ – Connecting times at Mannheim (shown in italics) may requ additional change of trains at Heidelberg.
⊠ – July 9 - Sept. 11 most services from / to Mannheim are div via Sinsheim and do not call at Eberbach or Mosbach-Nec
¶ – See also Tables **913**, **918**, **919**.

services except where shown — STUTTGART - BACKNANG / AALEN - NÜRNBERG — 925

			IC 2061				IC 2063			IC 2065			IC 2067			IC 2069			IC 2161				IC 2163		
		Ⓐt	Ⓐt	⚒v															Ⓑq		Ⓒz	Ⓐt			
	2				2																				
Karlsruhe Hbf **931** d.	...	...	...	...	...	...	0706e	...	...	0906	...	...	1106	...	...	1306	...	...	1506	...	...	...	1706	...	...
Stuttgart Hbf ‡ d.	0032	0543	0605	0620t	...	0643	0807	0822	0841f	1007	1022	1041f	1207	1222	1241f	1407	1422	1441f	1607	1619k	1641	1658	1807	1819k	1841f
Backnang d.	|	0607	|	|	...	0708	|	|	0906f	|	|	1106f	|	|	1306f	|	|	1506f	|	|	1706	1725	|	|	1906f
Schwäbisch H-H ⊡ a.	|	0653	|	|	...	0747f	|	|	0947f	|	|	1147f	|	|	1347f	|	|	1547f	|	|	1747	1758	|	|	1947f
Schwäbisch H-H ⊡ d.	|	0654	|	|	...	0759	|	|	0959	|	|	1159	|	|	1359	|	|	1559	|	|	1759	1759	|	|	1959
Schwäbisch Gmünd ‡ d.	0118	|	0642	0705	...	|	0842	0905	|	1040	1105	|	1240	1305	|	1440	1505	|	1640	1705	|	|	1840	1905	|
Aalen ‡ a.	0139	|	0657	0725	...	|	0857	0925	|	1055	1125	|	1255	1325	|	1455	1525	|	1655	1725	|	|	1855	1925	|
Aalen d.	—	|	0659	—	0728	|	0859	*0928*	|	1057	*1128*	|	1257	*1328*	|	1457	*1528*	|	1657	*1728*	|	|	1857	*1928*	|
Ellwangen d.	...	|	0710	...	0748	|	0910	*0948*	|	1108	*1149*	|	1308	*1349*	|	1508	*1549*	|	1708	*1748*	|	|	1908	*1948*	|
Crailsheim d.	0606	0714	0726	⚒v	0812	0818	0926	*1012*	1018	1125	*1212*	1218	1325	*1412*	1418	1525	*1612*	1618	1725	*1812*	1818	1818	1925	*2012*	2018
Ansbach d.	0641	0745	0750	0754	...	0850	0950	...	1050	1150	...	1250	1350	...	1450	1550	...	1650	1750	...	1850	1850	1950	...	2050
Nürnberg Hbf a.	0717	...	0818	0835	...	0925	1018	...	1125	1218	...	1325	1418	...	1525	1618	...	1725	1818	...	1925	1925	2018	...	2125

				IC 2165								
	Ⓒz	Ⓒz	Ⓐt	A		Ⓒz	Ⓐt		⑥p	Ⓑq		
		2									k	
rlsruhe Hbf **931** d.	...	...	...	1906	...	...	...	...	...	...	...	...
gart Hbf ‡ d.	*1945**	...	1958	2007	2022	2057	2058	2232	*2245**	2258	2332	2358
cknang d.	2022	...	2025	|	|	2123	2125	|	2325	2325	|	0026
hwäbisch H-H ⊡ a.	2054	...	2102	|	|	2202	2202	|	0001	0001	|	0102
hwäbisch H-H ⊡ d.	...	2059	2103	|	|	2203	2203	|	0002	0002	|	0103
väbisch Gmünd ‡ d.	...	|	|	2040	2105	|	|	2316	|	|	0016	|
n ‡ a.	...	|	|	2055	2125	|	|	2338	|	|	0038	|
n d.	...	|	|	2057	*2128*	|	|	*2344*	|	|	...	|
ngen d.	...	|	|	2108	*2148*	|	|	*0004*	|	|		|
sheim d.	...	2121	2121	2125	*2209*	2222	2222	*0020*	0020	0020	...	0121
ach d.	...	...	...	2150	...	...	...	...	...	...	...	...
berg Hbf a.	...	...	...	2218	...	...	...	...	...	...	...	...

km							IC 2164			
		Ⓐt	Ⓐt	Ⓐt	Ⓒz	Ⓐt	Ⓐt	Ⓐt	Ⓒz	Ⓐt
0	**Nürnberg** Hbf d.	...	...	...	...	...	0538	...	...	...
44	Ansbach d.	...	...	...	...	...	0603	...	...	...
90	Crailsheim d.	0452	*0514*	0533	0552	*0549*	0632	0634	0635	*0646*
111	Ellwangen d.	|	*0530*	|	|	|	0648	|	|	*0710*
127	**Aalen** a.	|	*0550*	|	|	|	0658	|	|	*0727*
127	**Aalen** ‡ d.	|	0600	|	|	|	0701	|	|	0733
152	Schwäbisch Gmünd ‡ d.	|	0621	|	|	|	0718	|	|	0752
	Schwäbisch H-H ⊡ a.	0510	|	0551	0610	*0608*	|	0652	0653	|
	Schwäbisch H-H ⊡ d.	0511	|	0552	0611	0612	|	0653	0701	|
	Backnang d.	0551	|	0635	0651	0652	|	0736	0737	|
203	**Stuttgart** Hbf ‡ a.	0618	0714	0703	0718	0719	0753	0803	*0815**	0843
	Karlsruhe Hbf **931** a.	...	...	...	...	...	0853	...	...	...

				IC 2162			IC 2160			IC 2068				IC 2066			IC 2064			IC 2062			IC 2060		
	Ⓒz			⚒							Ⓒz	Ⓐt											A		
																									2
berg Hbf d.	...	0636	...	0739	0833k	...	0935r	1036	...	1135r	1236	1236	...	1334r	1436	...	1535r	1636	...	1735r	1836	...	1935r	...	2037	...
ach d.	...	0707	...	0807	0907	...	1007	1107	...	1207	1307	1310	...	1407	1507	...	1607	1707	...	1807	1907	...	2007	...	2109	...
sheim d.	*0651*	0742	*0752*	0835	0942	*0952*	1035	1142	*1152*	1235	1342	1343	*1352*	1435	1542	*1552*	1635	1742	*1752*	1835	1942	*1952*	2035	*2042z*	2142	2149
ngen d.	*0712*	|	*0812*	0851	|	*1012*	1051	|	*1212*	1251	|	|	*1412*	1451	|	*1612*	1651	|	*1812*	1851	|	*2012*	2051	*2112*	|	2207
n a.	*0732*	|	*0832*	0901	|	*1032*	1101	|	*1232*	1301	|	|	*1432*	1501	|	*1632*	1701	|	*1832*	1901	|	*2032*	2101	*2129*	|	2221
n ‡ d.	0735	|	0835	0903	|	1035	1103	|	1235	1303	|	|	1435	1503	|	1635	1703	|	1835	1903	|	2035	2103	2135	|	2222
väbisch Gmünd ‡ d.	0754	|	0854	0919	|	1054	1119	|	1254	1319	|	|	1454	1519	|	1654	1719	|	1854	1919	|	2054	2119	2154	|	2240
hwäbisch H-H ⊡ a.	|	0759	|	|	0959	|	|	1159	|	|	1359	1401	|	|	1559	|	|	1759	|	|	1959	|	|	|	2159	|
hwäbisch H-H ⊡ d.	|	0812f	|	|	1012f	|	|	1212	|	|	1412	1414	|	|	1612f	|	|	1812f	|	|	2003h	|	|	|	2203	|
cknang d.	|	0851	|	|	1051	|	|	1251	|	|	1451	1451	|	|	1651	|	|	1851	|	|	2051	|	|	|	2251	|
gart Hbf ‡ a.	0843	0918	0937	0953	1118	1137	1153	1318	1337	1353	1518	1518	1537	1553	1718	1743c	1753	1918	1943c	1953	2118	2137	2153	2237	2318	2329
rlsruhe Hbf **931** a.	...	...	...	1053	...	...	1253	...	...	1448	...	...	...	1653	...	...	1853	...	...	2048	...	...	2259	...	...	...

④⑤⑦ (also Oct. 3, Nov. 1; not Oct. 2, 30).
6 minutes earlier on Ⓒ (also Nov. 1).
⚒ only.
2–5 minutes later on Ⓐ (not Nov. 1).
2012 on Ⓒ (also Nov. 1).
2–3 minutes later on Ⓒ (also Nov. 1).
Also Oct. 2.

q – Not Oct. 2.
r – 4–5 minutes later from Sept. 4.
t – Ⓐ (not Nov. 1).
v – Not Nov. 1.
z – Ⓒ (also Nov. 1).
⊡ – Schwäbisch Hall-Hessental.
* – S-Bahn (underground) platforms.

‡ – Other *RE* trains Stuttgart - Schwäbisch Gmünd - Aalen and v.v.
From Stuttgart Hbf at 0453 Ⓐ t, 0532 Ⓐ t, 0650 Ⓐ t, 0719 Ⓐ t, 0722 Ⓒ z, 0922, 1122, 1322, 1449 Ⓐ t, 1519 Ⓐ t, 1522 Ⓒ z, 1549 Ⓐ t, 1636 Ⓐ t, 1649 Ⓐ t, 1719 Ⓐ t, 1722 Ⓒ z, 1748 Ⓐ t, 1846 Ⓐ t, 1919 Ⓐ t, 1922 Ⓒ z and 2122.
From Aalen at 0426 Ⓐ t, 0503 Ⓐ t, 0518 Ⓐ t, 0533 Ⓐ t, 0535 Ⓒ z, 0625 Ⓐ t, 0635 Ⓒ z, 0704 Ⓐ t, 0805 Ⓐ t, 0935, 1135, 1335, 1535, 1605 Ⓐ t, 1708 Ⓐ t, 1735, 1805 Ⓐ t and 1935.

/RB services — HEILBRONN / ASCHAFFENBURG - CRAILSHEIM and AALEN - DONAUWÖRTH / ULM — 926

ASCHAFFENBURG - LAUDA - CRAILSHEIM ⊠

	Ⓐt	Ⓒz							
Aschaffenburg Hbf d.	...	...	0639f	0922	1123	1323	1523	1723	1923g
Miltenberg d.	...	...	0750	0959	1159	1359	1559	1759	1959
Wertheim d.	...	*0626*	0828j	1035	1235	1435	1635	1835	2035
Tauberbischofsheim d.	0545	*0653*	0900	1100	1300	1500	1700	1900	2101
Lauda a.	0555	*0702*	0906	1106	1306	1506	1706	1906	2106
Lauda d.	0608	0713	0913	1113	1313	1513	1713	1913	2113
Bad Mergentheim d.	0620	0725	0925	1125	1325	1525	1725	1925	2124
Crailsheim a.	0726	0830	1028	1228	1428	1628	1828	2028	...

	Ⓐt	Ⓒz	Ⓐt								
Crailsheim d.	...	...	*0520*	0731	0931	1131	1328s	1531	1731	1931	
Bad Mergentheim d.	...	...	*0636*	0833f	1033	1233	1433	1633	1833	2033	2053t
Lauda a.	...	...	*0647*	0843f	1043	1243	1443	1643	1843	2043	2104t
Lauda d.	...	0614	0702	0853	1053	1253	1453	1653	1853	—	2110
Tauberbischofsheim d.	...	0624	0712	0900	1059	1259	1459	1659	1859	...	2120
Wertheim d.	0600	0700	0800p	0921	1121	1321	1521	1721	1921	...	2147
Miltenberg d.	0636	0740	0840	0959	1159	1359	1559	1759	1959	2037	2222
Aschaffenburg Hbf a.	0712	0830	0930	1037	1237	1437	1637	1837	2034z	2121	2307

HEILBRONN - CRAILSHEIM ⊠

	Ⓐt		Ⓒz	Ⓐt		Ⓒz	Ⓐt	Ⓒz	Ⓐt
Heilbronn Hbf d.	*0546*	0803	1003	1005	and every	1803	1805	2003	2005
Öhringen d.	0618	0825	1025	1027	**two** hours	1825	1827	2025	2027
Schwäbisch Hall d.	0642	0851	1051	1051	until	1851	1851	2051	2051
Schwäbisch Hall-H ⊡ a.	0649	0858	1058	1058		1858	1858	2058	2058
Crailsheim a.	*0713*	0921	1121	1121		1921	1921	2121	*2121*

	Ⓐt	Ⓒz	Ⓐt	Ⓒz		Ⓐt	Ⓒz	Ⓒz	Ⓐt
Crailsheim d.	*0634*	*0635*	0838	0838	and every	1838	1838	2038	2038
Schwäbisch Hall-H ⊡ d.	0658	0658	0858	0900	**two** hours	1858	1900	2103	2106
Schwäbisch Hall d.	0705	0704	0905	0906	until	1905	1906	2110	2112
Öhringen a.	0729	0729	0928	0930		1928	1930	2136	2136
Heilbronn Hbf a.	0752	0752	0951	0952		1951	1952	*2221*	*2221*

AALEN - DONAUWÖRTH

	Ⓐt	Ⓐt	Ⓒz	Ⓐt	Ⓐt	Ⓐt			Ⓐt		Ⓐt	Ⓒz	Ⓐt	Ⓐt		Ⓐt		Ⓐt		Ⓐt				
Aalen d.	...	...	0531	...	0603	0625	...	0735	0835	0935	1035	1135	1135	1235	1335	1435	1535	1635	1735	1835	1935	2035	...	...
Nördlingen a.	...	...	0613	...	0638	0706	...	0813	0913	1013	1113	1213	1219	1313	1413	1513	1613	1713	1813	1913	2013	2113	...	...
Nördlingen d.	0518	0600	0614	0624	0639	0707	...	0814	0914	1014	1114	1214	1221	1314	1414	1514	1614	1714	1814	1914	2014	2114	...	...
Donauwörth a.	0546	0632	0644	0652	0706	0734	...	0845	0945	1045	1145	1244	1248	1345	1445	1545	1646	1745	1846	1945	2045	2145	...	...

	Ⓐt				Ⓒz	Ⓐt	Ⓐt		Ⓐt				Ⓐt		Ⓐt		Ⓐt	Ⓐt			Ⓐt			Ⓐt	Ⓒz
uwörth d.	...	...	0608	...	0703	0708	0803	0903	1004	1103	1203	1303	1403	1503	1603	1703	1744	1803	1845	1903	2003	2103	...	2211	2242
lingen a.	...	...	0638	...	0739	0739	0831	0931	1031	1131	1236	1331	1431	1531	1631	1731	1811	1831	1912	1931	2031	2131	...	2238	2309
lingen d.	0532	...	0641	0641	0744	0744	0844	0944	1044	1144	1244	1344	1444	1544	1644	1744	...	1844	...	1944	...	2134	...	...	...
n a.	0614	...	0721	0721	0826	0826	0926	1026	1126	1226	1326	1426	1526	1626	1726	1826	...	1926	...	2026	...	2215	...	...	...

AALEN - ULM ⊠

	Ⓐt	⑥	Ⓐt	Ⓐt	Ⓒz	Ⓐt			Ⓐt			⚒r													
Aalen d.	0442	0529	0554	0625	0633	0702	0733	0833	0907	0933	1033	1107	1133	1307	1333	1507	1533	1633	1706	1733	1833	1907	1933	2039b	2130
Heidenheim d.	0506	0552	0617	0647	0659	0725	0756h	0859	0923	0955	1059	1123	1154	1323	1354	1523	1554	1659	1722	1754	1859	1923	1953	2107	2152
Ulm Hbf a.	0554	0642	0709	0743	0744	0756	0844	0944	0954	1044	1144	1154	1244	1354	1444	1554	1644	1744	1754	1844	1944	1954	2044	2151	2238

	Ⓐt	Ⓐt	Ⓐt	Ⓒz	Ⓐt	Ⓒz	Ⓐt			⚒r																
Hbf d.	0430	0542	0603	0609	0648	0711	0803	0813	0913	1000	1013	1113	1200	1213	1313	1400	1413	1513	1600	1613	1713	1800	1813	1913	2013	2223
enheim d.	0520	0630	0656	0658	0800	0800	0835	0859	1005	1032	1059	1205	1232	1259	1403	1432	1459	1605	1634	1659	1805	1832	1859	2003	2059	2312
n a.	0545	0651	0721	0721	0823	0823	0851	0924	1027	1050	1124	1227	1250	1324	1426	1450	1525	1627	1650	1724	1827	1850	1924	2026	2124	2335

2035 on † (also Nov. 1).
3 minutes later on Ⓐ (not Nov. 1).
1928 on Ⓒ (also Nov. 1).
0800 on Ⓒ (also Nov. 1).
0835 on Ⓐ (not Nov. 1).

p – Arrives 0738.
r – Not Nov. 1.
s – 1331 on Ⓒ (also Nov. 1). 1334 on ①–⑤ July 28 - Sept. 9, Oct. 31, Nov. 2–4.
t – Ⓐ (not Nov. 1).
z – Ⓒ (also Nov. 1).

⊠ – 2nd class only.
⊡ – Schwäbisch Hall-Hessental.

928 MÜNCHEN - BAYRISCHZELL, LENGGRIES and TEGERNSEE

Bayerische Oberlandbahn G

On Aug. 15, Nov. 1 services run as on ⑦

km																										
				©		Ⓐ	©		©						Ⓐ				Ⓐ							
0	**München** Hbf . d.	0005	...	0605	...	0703	0705	0805	0828	0905	0925	1005	1105	1205	1230	1305	1405	1505	1528	1605	1705	1805	1905	2005	2105	2205
37	Holzkirchen ..... d.	0032	...	0632	...	0732	0732	0832	0855	0932	0956	1032	1132	1232	1302	1332	1432	1532	1555	1632	1732	1832	1932	2032	2132	2232
61	Schliersee .... d.	0101	...	0701	...	0801	0801	0901	0921	1001	1022	1101	1201	1301	1331	1401	1501	1601	1621	1701	1801	1901	2001	2101	2201	2301
78	**Bayrischzell** ... a.	0124	...	0724	...	0824	0824	0925	...	1024	...	1124	1224	1324	1354	1424	1524	1624	...	1724	1824	1924	2024	2124	2224	2324

km																										
					Ⓐ	Ⓐ	©		©						Ⓐ				Ⓐ							
0	**München** Hbf . d.	0005	...	0605	0630	0703	0705	0805	0828	0905	0925	1005	1105	1205	1230	1305	1405	1505	1528	1605	1705	1805	1905	2005	2105	2205
37	Holzkirchen ..... d.	0035	...	0635	0705	0735	0735	0835	0858	0935	0958	1035	1135	1235	1305	1335	1435	1535	1558	1635	1735	1835	1935	2035	2135	2235
47	Schaftlach .... d.	0048	...	0648	0717	0748	0748	0848	0915	0948	1015	1048	1148	1248	1318	1348	1448	1548	1615	1648	1748	1848	1948	2048	2148	2248
57	Bad Tölz .... d.	0100	...	0700	0730	0800	0800	0900	0927	1000	1027	1100	1200	1300	1330	1400	1500	1600	1627	1700	1800	1900	2000	2100	2200	2300
67	**Lenggries** ...... a.	0111	...	0711	0741	0811	0811	0911	0938	1011	1038	1111	1211	1311	1341	1411	1511	1611	1638	1711	1811	1911	2011	2111	2211	2311

km																										
					Ⓐ	Ⓐ	©		©						Ⓐ				Ⓐ						⊡	
0	**München** Hbf . d.	0005	...	0605	0630	0703	0705	0805	0828	0905	0925	1005	1105	1205	*1230*	1305	1405	1505	1528	1605	1705	1805	1905	2005	2105	*2205*
37	Holzkirchen ..... d.	0035	0035r	0635	0705	0735	0735	0835	0858	0935	0958	1035	1135	1235	*1305*	1335	1435	1535	1558	1635	1735	1835	1935	2035	2135	*2235*
47	Schaftlach .... d.	0045	0048	0648	0717	0748	0748	0848	0915	0948	1015	1048	1148	1248	1317	1348	1448	1548	1615	1648	1748	1848	1948	2048	2148	2248
59	**Tegernsee** ...... a.	...	0109	0709	0739	0809	0809	0909	0936	1009	1036	1109	1209	1309	1338	1409	1509	1609	1636	1709	1809	1909	2009	2109	2209	2309

	Ⓐ	⑥	Ⓐ		Ⓐ	©	Ⓐ	Ⓐ	⑥						©	Ⓐ										
Bayrischzell ..... d.	...	...	0449	0532	0607	0632	0634	0705	...	0732	0832	0932	1032	1132	1232	1232	1332z	1432	1532	1632	...	1732	1832	1932	2032	2132
Schliersee .... d.	0444	0459	0516	0559	0635	0659	0702	0734	0734	0759	0859	0959	1059	1159	1259	1303	1359	1459	1559	1659	...	1759	1859	1959	2059	2159
Holzkirchen .... d.	0510	0528	0544	0628	0705	0728	0732	0804	0804	0828	0928	1028	1128	1228	1328	1332	1428	1528	1628	1728	...	1828	1928	2028	2128	2228
München Hbf ... a.	0535	0553	0612	0653	0735	0753	0758	0831	0832	0856j	0956j	1054	1153	1254	1353	1357	1453	1556j	1656j	1756j	...	1854	1953	2054	2153	2253

	Ⓐ	⑥	Ⓐ		Ⓐ	©	Ⓐ	Ⓐ	⑥						©	Ⓐ					©				⊖	
Lenggries .... d.	0431	0447	0506	0547	0622	0647	0647	0718	0717	0747	0847	0947	1047	1147	1247	1247	1347	1447	1547	1647	1717	1747	1847	1947	2047	2147
Bad Tölz .... d.	0443	0500	0518	0600	0634	0700	0700	0731	0730	0800	0900	1000	1100	1200	1300	1305	1400	1500	1600	1700	1730	1800	1900	2000	2100	2200
Schaftlach .... d.	0454	0516	0531	0616	0647	0716	0716	0747	0747	0816	0916	1016	1116	1216	1316	1318	1416	1516	1616	1716	1747	1816	1916	2016	2116	2216
Holzkirchen .... d.	0510	0528	0544	0628	0701	0728	0732	0804	0804	0828	0928	1028	1128	1228	1328	1332	1428	1528	1628	1728	1804	1828	1928	2028	2128	2228
München Hbf ... a.	0535	0553	0612	0653	0731	0753	0758	0831	0832	0856j	0956j	1054	1153	1254	1353	1357	1453	1556j	1656j	1756j	1831	1854	1953	2054	2153	2253

		⑥	Ⓐ		Ⓐ	©	Ⓐ	Ⓐ	⑥						©	Ⓐ					©				⊡	
Tegernsee .... d.	...	0452	0505	0552	0621	0652	0652	0722	0722	0752	0852	0952	1052	1152	1252	1252	1352	1452	1552	1652	1722	1752	1852	1952	2052	2152
Schaftlach .... a.	...	0513	0525	0613	0641	0713	0713	0743	0743	0813	0913	1013	1113	1213	1313	1313	1413	1513	1613	1713	1743	1813	1913	2013	2113	2213
Holzkirchen .... a.	...	0526	0541	0626	0656	0726	0726	0756	0756	0826	0926	1026	1126	1227	1326	1327	1426	1526	1626	1726	1757	1826	1926	2026	2126	*2226*
München Hbf ... a.	...	0553	0612	0653	0731	0753	0758	0831	0832	0856j	0956j	1054	1153	1254	1353	1357	1453	1556j	1656j	1756j	1831	1854	1953	2054	2153	*2253*

j – 3 minutes earlier on ©.
r – ①–⑥ only.
z – © only.

⊖ – On ①②③④⑦ passengers travelling from Lenggries or Bad Tölz to München should change trains at Schaftl
♥ – Change trains at Schliersee on ①②③④⑦ (not Aug. 14, Oct. 2, 31).
⊕ – Change trains at Schaftlach on ⑤–⑦ (also Aug. 15, Oct. 3, Nov. 1).
⊡ – Change trains at Schaftlach on ⑥.

929 PLATTLING - BAYERISCH EISENSTEIN - PLZEŇ

Waldbahn ⊠; ČD; 2nd class

km																								
			7511			773						775						777						
			◇§		Ⓐ	◇		Ⓐ	Ⓐe	Ⓐe		◇			k			◇						
0	**Plattling** .... d.	0101	...	...	...	...	...	...	0520	0629	0659	...	0806	0906	...	1006	1106	...	1206	1306	...	1406	...	1506
9	Deggendorf Hbf.................. d.	0110	...	...	...	...	...	...	0531	0638	0709	...	0816	0916	...	1016	1116	...	1216	1316	...	1416	...	1516
33	Gotteszell............................ d.	0129	...	...	...	...	...	...	0554	0657	0733	...	0835	0935	...	1035	1135	...	1235	1335	...	1435	...	1535
48	Regen................................. d.	0143	...	...	...	...	...	...	0609	0712	0748	...	0849	0949	...	1049	1149	...	1249	1349	...	1449	...	1549
58	Zwiesel (Bay)...................... d.	0153	...	...	...	...	...	...	0623	0725	0800	...	0900	1000	...	1100	1200	...	1300	1400	...	1500	...	1600
72	**Bayerisch Eisenstein** ☆ 🏛 a.	...	...	...	...	...	...	...	0636	0738	0813	...	0913	1013	...	1113	1213	...	1313	1413	...	1513	...	1613
72	**Železná Ruda-Alžbětín** ☆ 🏛 d.	...	...	0408	...	...	...	0608	▬	▬	...	0845	...	...	1045	▬	...	1245	▬	...	1445	...	1532j	...
76	Železná Ruda Město .... d.	...	...	0416	...	...	...	0616	...	...	...	0853	...	...	1053	...	...	1253	...	...	1453	...	1541j	...
79	Špičák................................. d.	...	...	0421	...	...	...	0621	...	...	...	0859	...	...	1059	...	...	1259	...	...	1459	...	1547j	...
131	**Klatovy** .... a.	...	...	0516	...	...	...	0716	Ⓐ	...	...	0953	...	...	1153	...	...	1353	...	...	1554	...	1639j	...
131	**Klatovy** .... d.	...	0400	...	0530	0606	0646	...	0806	0846	...	1006	...	...	1206	1246	...	1406	1446	...	1606	...	1646	...
141	Švihov u Klatov.................... d.	...	0412	...	0541	0615	0658	...	0815	0858	...	1015	...	...	1215	1258	...	1415	1458	...	1615	...	1658	...
170	**Plzeň** Hlavni .... a.	...	0459	...	0630	0656	0746	...	0856	0946	...	1056	...	...	1256	1346	...	1456	1546	...	1656	...	1746	...
	Praha Hlavní **1120** .... a.	...	0641	...	...	0841	...	...	...	...	...	1241	...	...	...	...	...	1641	...	...	...	...	...	...

Plattling .... d.	1606	...	1706	1806	...	1906	2006	2102	2213	2307
Deggendorf Hbf .... d.	1616	...	1716	1816	...	1916	2016	2111	2223	2318
Gotteszell .... d.	1635	...	1735	1835	...	1935	2035	2135	2241	2337
Regen.................................. d.	1649	...	1749	1849	...	1949	2049	2149	2255	2351
Zwiesel (Bay) .... d.	1700	...	1800	1900	...	2000	2100	2158	2304	0001
Bayerisch Eisenstein ☆ 🏛 . a.	1713	...	1813	1913	...	2013	2113	...	...	...
Železná Ruda-Alžbětín ☆ 🏛 . d.	...	1732	...	...	1932	...	...	...	...	...
Železná Ruda Město........... d.	...	1741	...	...	1939	...	...	...	...	...
Špičák .... d.	...	1747	...	...	1944	...	...	...	...	...
Klatovy .... a.	...	1839	...	...	2039	...	...	...	...	...
Klatovy .... d.	...	1846	...	...	2046	...	...	...	...	...
Švihov u Klatov.................... d.	...	1858	...	...	2058	...	...	...	...	...
Plzeň Hlavni .... a.	...	1946	...	...	2146	...	...	...	...	...
Praha Hlavní **1120** .... a.	...	...	...	...	...	...	...	...	...	...

	Ⓐe	Ⓐe	©z	Ⓐe	©z		Ⓐe	
Praha Hlavní **1120** .... d.	...	...	...	...	...	...	...	...
Plzeň Hlavni .... d.	...	...	...	...	...	...	...	...
Švihov u Klatov....................... d.	...	...	...	...	...	...	...	...
Klatovy .... a.	...	...	...	...	...	...	...	...
Klatovy .... d.	...	...	...	...	...	...	...	...
Špičák .... d.	...	...	...	...	...	...	...	...
Železná Ruda Město .... d.	...	...	...	...	...	...	...	...
Železná Ruda-Alžbětín ☆ 🏛 ..... a.	...	...	...	...	...	...	...	...
Bayerisch Eisenstein ☆ 🏛 ...... d.	...	...	...	...	...	...	0705	0744e
Zwiesel (Bay) .... d.	0416	0529	0559	0621	0655	...	0722	0759
Regen...................................... d.	0426	0539	0608	0630	0705	...	0732	0808
Gotteszell................................ d.	0440	0555	0622	0644	0721	...	0751	0822
Deggendorf Hbf........................ d.	0501	0614	0645	0709	0739	0739	0815	0845
Plattling .... a.	0510	0623	0654	0718	0748	0748	0825	0854

						778						776							774					772
	Ⓐ	k				◇		Ⓐ				◇		Ⓐ				Ⓑq	◇					◇
Praha Hlavní **1120** .... d.	...	...	...	...	...	0712	...	...	...	...	...	1112	...	...	...	...	...	...	1512	...	...	...	...	1912
Plzeň Hlavni .... d.	0607	0702	...	0811	...	0902	...	1011	1102	1211	...	1302	...	*1411*	...	1502	...	1611	1702	...	...	1811	*1911*	2102
Švihov u Klatov.................... d.	0658	0743	...	0858	...	0943	...	1058	1143	1258	...	1343	...	*1458*	...	1544	...	1658	1743	...	...	1858	*1958*	2143
Klatovy .... a.	0711	0752	...	0911	...	0952	...	1111	1152	1311	...	1352	...	*1511*	...	1553	...	1711	1752	...	...	1911	*2011*	2152
Klatovy .... d.	▬	0804	...	0919j	...	1004	...	▬	1204	▬	...	1404	...	1514	...	1604	...	▬	...	1804	...	▬	2018	▬
Špičák .... d.	...	0859	...	1016j	...	1059	...	...	1259	...	...	1459	...	1613	...	1659	...	...	...	1859	...	...	2115	...
Železná Ruda Město........... d.	...	0905	...	1022j	...	1105	...	...	1305	...	...	1505	...	1618	...	1705	...	...	...	1905	...	...	2120	...
Železná Ruda-Alžbětín ☆ 🏛 . a.	...	0912	...	1028j	...	1112	...	...	1312	w	...	1512	...	1624	...	1712	...	...	...	1912	...	...	2126	...
Bayerisch Eisenstein ☆ 🏛 . d.	0841	...	0944	...	1041	...	1141	1241	...	1341	1444	...	1541	...	1641	...	1741	1841	...	...	1941	2041	...	2141
Zwiesel (Bay) .... d.	0859	...	0959	...	1059	...	1159	1259	...	1359	1459	...	1559	...	1659	...	1759	1859	...	...	1959	2059	...	2204r
Regen.................................. d.	0908	...	1008	...	1108	...	1208	1308	...	1408	1508	...	1608	...	1708	...	1808	1908	...	...	2008	2108	...	2214
Gotteszell .... d.	0922	...	1022	...	1122	...	1222	1322	...	1422	1522	...	1622	...	1722	...	1822	1922	...	...	2022	2122	...	2228
Deggendorf Hbf .... d.	0945	...	1045	...	1145	...	1245	1345	...	1445	1545	...	1645	...	1745	...	1845	1945	...	...	2045	2141	...	2251
Plattling .... a.	0954	...	1054	...	1154	...	1254	1354	...	1454	1554	...	1654	...	1754	...	1854	1954	...	...	2054	2150	...	2300

ZWIESEL - GRAFENAU and BODENMAIS ⊠

ZWIESEL - GRAFENAU *32 km.* Journey time: 47–49 minutes.
From Zwiesel (Bay) at 0702 © **z**, 0713 Ⓐ **e**, 0902, 1102, 1304, 1502, 1702 and 1902. **From Grafenau** at 0805, 1000, 1200, 1400, 1600, 1800 and 2000.

ZWIESEL - BODENMAIS *15 km.* Journey time: 20 minutes.
From Zwiesel at 0624 Ⓐ **e**, 0802 Ⓐ **e**, 0902, 1002 and hourly until 2002; then 2202. **From Bodenmais** at 0558 Ⓐ **e**, 0649 Ⓐ **e**, 0829, 0929 and hourly until 2029.

e – Ⓐ (not Aug. 15, Nov. 1).
j – June 11 - Sept. 18.
k – Change trains at Klatovy on Ⓐ.
r – Arrives 2154.

q – Not July 5, Oct. 28.
w – Change trains at Zwiesel on Ⓐ (not Aug. 15, Nov. 1).
z – Also Aug. 15, Nov. 1.

◇ – Also conveys 🚃 Praha - Klatovy and v.v.
§ – Train number **771** Plzeň - Praha.
⊠ – Operated by *Regentalbahn - Die Länderbahn* (under contract from *DB Regio*).
☆ – Bayerisch Eisenstein (German) / Železná Ruda-Alžbětín (Czech) is the same stati

STUTTGART - MÜNCHEN 930

SEE NOTE ⊠	*ICE*	*CNL*	*IC*	*IC*	*IC*	*RE*	*RB*	*IC*	*RB*	*RE*	*ICE*	*RJ*	*IRE*	*IRE*	*ICE*	*RB*	*RE*	*EC*	*IRE*	*ICE*	*IC*	*ICE*	*ICE*
	619	**419**	**60419**	**2095**	**2095**	**19201**	**19297**	**2291**	**19301**	**19203**	**699**	**63**	**4241**	**4221**	**991**	**19307**	**19205**	**217**	**4223**	**511**	**2265**	**999**	**591**
		Ⓡ	**61479**	①m	Ⓐd	Ⓐt	Ⓒz	Ⓐk	Ⓐt	Ⓒz	Ⓐ	Ⓒ	Ⓐt	Ⓒz	Ⓐ	Ⓒz	Ⓐt					†	⚒
		♣🍷	♥2					🍷			🍴	🍴♦	L	L	🍴♦			🍷♦	L	🍷	🍷♦	🍴	🍴♦
Dortmund Hbf **800** d.	2058	...	...	...	...	...	...	...	...	...	...	...	...	...	...	...	...	...	...	0437**g**	...	...	...
Köln Hbf **800 910** d.	2230	2318**r**	2318**r**	...	...	...	...	...	...	...	...	...	...	...	...	...	...	...	...	0555	...	...	...
Frankfurt (Main) Hbf **912** d.	0009	|	0213	...	...	...	...	...	...	...	...	0517	...	...	...	...	...	...	...	|	...	0750	0750
Frankfurt Flughafen ✈ **912** d.	0028	|	|	...	...	...	...	...	...	...	...	0539	...	...	...	...	...	...	...	0653	...	|	|
Mannheim Hbf **912** d.	0106	|	|	...	...	...	...	...	...	...	...	0612	...	...	0629	...	...	0712	...	0731	...	0830	0830
Heidelberg Hbf **912** d.	0119	|	|	...	...	...	...	...	...	...	...	|	...	...	|	...	...	|	...	|	...	|	|
Karlsruhe Hbf **931** d.	0211	|	|	...	...	...	...	0455	...	...	...	|	...	...	|	...	...	|	...	|	0806	|	|
Stuttgart Hbf **936** ◇ d.	0336	|	0435	0459	...	0529	0531	0553	0608	0631	0656	0658	0659	0700	0713	0717	0732	0758	0802	0813	0853	0913	0913
Plochingen **936** ◇ d.	0353	0449**s**	0451	0518	...	0548	0549	0609	0630	0649	|	|	0713	0714	|	0736	0751	|	0816	|	0909	|	|
Göppingen ◇ d.	|	0502**s**	0504	0531	...	0602	0607	0621	0649	0707	|	|	0725	0725	|	0754	0807	|	0827	|	0921	|	|
Geislingen (Steige) ◇ d.	|	|	|	0544	...	0622	0629	|	0711	0724	|	|	0736	0736	|	0815	0823	|	0840	|	|	|	|
Ulm Hbf **945** ◇ d.	0442	0540**s**	0542	0609	0609	0649	0700	0656	0740	0749	0756	0756	0758	0758	0809	0847	0848	0856	0902	0909	0956	1009	1009
Günzburg **945** d.	0458	0557**s**	0559	0627	0627	...	...	0710	...	...	0811	|	...	...	|	...	...	0910	...	|	|	|	|
Augsburg Hbf **905** d.	0532	0633**s**	0636	0659	0659	...	...	0742	...	...	0842	0839	...	...	0855	...	...	0942	...	0955	1039	1056	1056
München Pasing **905** a.	0553	|	|	0721	0721	...	...	0804	...	...	0903	0901	...	...	0918	...	...	|	...	1018**k**	1101	1118	1118
München Hbf **905** a.	0602	0710	0710	0731	0731	...	...	0814	...	...	0913	0910	...	...	0927	...	...	1011	...	1027	1111	1127	1127
Salzburg Hbf **890** a.	...	...	...	...	...	...	...	...	...	...	...	1102	...	...	...	...	...	1159	...	...	...	...	...

SEE NOTE ⊠	*EC*	*IRE*	*ICE*	*IC*	*ICE*	*ICE*	*EC*	*IRE*	*ICE*	*IC*	*IC*	*ICE*	*EC*	*IRE*	*ICE*	*IC*	*ICE*	*EC*	*EC*	*IRE*	*ICE*	*IC*	*IRE*	*ICE*
	113	**4225**	**513**	**2093**	**1091**	**593**	**115**	**4227**	**515**	**2261**	**119**	**595**	**219**	**4229**	**517**	**2013**	**597**	**117**	**1217**	**4231**	**519**	**1269**	**4233**	**599**
				⑤k	Ⓐ	Ⓒ		**4247**		k		k	k					Ⓑ	⑥k			Ⓑq	Ⓐt	
	🍴♦	L	M🍴	🍷	B🍴	B🍴	🍷♦	L	🍷	🍷	♦	B🍴	🍷♦	L	🍷	🍷♦	B🍴	🍷♦	🍷♦	L	🍷	●🍷	L	B🍴
rtmund Hbf **800** d.	...	...	0637	...	...	...	...	...	0837**n**	...	...	...	...	...	1037**n**	0952	...	...	...	...	1237**n**	...	...	...
ln Hbf **800 910** d.	...	...	0755	...	...	...	0818	...	0955	...	0918	...	...	...	1155	1118	...	...	...	...	1355	...	...	...
ankfurt (Main) Hbf **912** d.	0822	...	|	...	0950	0950	|	...	|	...	|	1150	1220	...	|	|	1350	1420	...	...	|	...	...	1550
ankfurt Flughafen ✈ **912** d.	|	...	0853	...	|	|	|	...	1053	...	|	|	|	...	1253	|	|	|	...	...	1453	...	...	|
nnheim Hbf **912** d.	|	...	0931	...	1030	1030	1102	...	1131	...	1154	1230	|	...	1331	1354	1430	|	...	...	1531	...	...	1630
idelberg Hbf **912** d.	0914	...	|	...	|	|	|	...	|	...	1206	|	1314	...	|	1406	|	1514	...	...	|	...	...	|
Karlsruhe Hbf **931** d.	|	...	|	...	|	|	|	...	|	1205	|	|	|	...	|	|	|	|	1505	...	|	1605	...	|
gart Hbf **936** ◇ d.	0958	1002	1013	1053	1113	1113	1158**k**	1202	1213	1253	1257	1313	1358	1402	1413	1454	1513	1558	1558	1602	1613	1653	1702	1712
ingen **936** ◇ d.	|	1016	|	1109	|	|	|	1216	|	1309	|	|	|	1416	|	1510	|	|	|	1616	|	1709	1716	|
ingen ◇ d.	|	1027	|	1121	|	|	|	1227	|	1321	1325	|	|	1427	|	1524	|	|	|	1627	|	1721	1727	|
ingen (Steige) ◇ d.	|	1040	|	|	|	|	|	1240	|	|	|	|	|	1440	|	|	|	|	|	1640	|	|	1740	|
Hbf **945** ◇ d.	1057	1102	1109	1156	1209	1209	1256**j**	1302	1309	1356	1401	1409	1456	1502	1509	1602	1609	1656	1656	1702	1709	1756	1802	1809
burg **945** d.	1110	...	|	|	|	|	1310**j**	...	|	|	...	|	1510	...	|	...	|	1710	1710	...	|	|	...	|
sburg Hbf **905** d.	1142	...	1155	1239	1255	1255	1342	...	1355	1440	...	1455	1542	...	1555	...	1655	1742	1742	...	1755	1839	...	1855
chen Pasing **905** a.	|	...	1218**k**	1301	1318**k**	1318**k**	|	...	1418	1502	...	1518	|	...	1618**k**	...	1718	|	|	...	1818	1901**k**	...	1918
chen Hbf **905** a.	1210	...	1227	1311	1327	1327	1411	...	1427	1512	...	1528	1611	...	1627	...	1727	1811	1811	...	1827	1911	...	1927
lzburg Hbf **890** a.	1359	...	...	...	...	...	1559	...	...	...	...	...	1759	...	...	...	...	1959	1959	...	...	2059	...	...

SEE NOTE ⊠	*EC*	*IRE*	*ICE*	*IC*	*IC*	*IC*	*ICE*	*TGV*	*TGV*	*IC*	*IRE*	*ICE*	*RE*	*IC*	*ICE*	*IC*	*IC*	*TGV*	*ICE*	*RB*	*ICE*	*RB*	*ICE*	*RB*
	391	**4235**	**611**	**2267**	**2011**	**2017**	**691**	**9575**	**9577**	**2295**	**4237**	**613**	**19245**	**1915**	**771**	**2269**	**2269**	**9579**	**693**	**19347**	**615**	**19349**	**1093**	**19351**
	k			k	①–④	⑤k	X	⑥Q	ⒷN	Ⓑq				⑦w	⑤	Y	⑦c	⑥R	U				⑦w	
	🍷♦	L	🍷	🍷	🍷♦		B🍴	A🍷	A🍷	🍷	F	🍷		T🍷	H🍴			A🍷	B🍴		🍷		B🍴	
rtmund Hbf **800** d.	...	...	1437**n**	...	...	1352	...	...	...	...	...	1637**n**	...	1549	...	...	...	...	...	...	1837**n**	...	...	...
ln Hbf **800 910** d.	...	...	1555	...	1518	1518	...	...	...	...	...	1755	...	1718	...	...	...	...	...	...	1957	...	...	...
ankfurt (Main) Hbf **912** d.	1620	...	|	...	|	|	1750	...	...	1820	...	|	...	|	1905	...	...	...	1950	...	|	...	2151	...
ankfurt Flughafen ✈ **912** d.	|	...	1653	...	|	|	|	...	...	|	...	1853	...	|	1920	...	...	...	|	...	2053	...	|	...
nnheim Hbf **912** d.	|	...	1731	...	1754	1754	1830	...	...	|	...	1931	...	1954	1956	...	...	...	2030	...	2131	...	2231	...
idelberg Hbf **912** d.	1714	...	|	...	1806	1806	|	...	...	1914	...	|	...	2006	|	...	...	...	|	...	|	...	|	...
Karlsruhe Hbf **931** d.	|	...	|	1805	|	|	|	1828	1828	|	...	|	...	|	|	2005	2005	2028	|	...	|	...	|	...
gart Hbf **936** ◇ d.	1758	1802	1813	1853	1850	1856	1913	1913	1922**f**	1958	2002	2013	2028	2050	2054	2053	2053	2112	2113	2131	2213	2231	2315	2335
ingen **936** ◇ d.	|	1816	|	1909	1904	1915	|	|	|	|	2016	|	2046	2106	|	2109	2109	|	|	2151	|	2252	|	2356
ingen ◇ d.	|	1827	|	1921	...	|	|	|	|	|	2027	|	2104	...	|	2121	2121	|	|	2209	|	2312	|	0016
ingen (Steige) ◇ d.	|	1840	|	|	...	1938	|	|	|	|	2040	|	2125	...	|	2134	2134	|	|	2232	|	2336	|	0040
Hbf **945** ◇ d.	1856	1902	1909	1956	...	2002	2009	2010	2020	2056	2102	2109	2151	...	2158	2155	2158	2210	2209	2302	2309	0007	0014	0112
burg **945** d.	1910	...	|	|	...	|	|	|	|	2110**k**	...	|	...	...	2215**k**	...	2215	|	|	...	|	...	0030	...
sburg Hbf **905** d.	1942	...	1955	2039	...	2045	2055	2058	2103	2142**k**	...	2155	...	...	2247	...	2247	2258	2255	...	2355	...	0101	...
chen Pasing **905** a.	|	...	2018	2101	...	2108	2118	|	|	2205**k**	...	2216	...	...	2309	...	2310	|	2320	...	0017	...	0123	...
chen Hbf **905** a.	2011	...	2027	2111	...	2118	2127	2129	2136	2214**k**	...	2226	...	...	2319	...	2319	2329	2329	...	0027	...	0133	...
lzburg Hbf **890** a.	2203	...	...	...	...	...	...	...	...	...	...	...	...	...	...	...	...	...	...	...	...	...	...	...

Regional trains ULM - MÜNCHEN *Subject to alteration July 30 - Sept. 11 – see note* ❖

		Ⓐy		Ⓐy		Ⓐy																		
Hbf d.	...	0446	0523	0549	0621	0643**e**	0723	0823	0923**e**	1023	1123	1223	1324	1423	1523	1623	1723	1824	1923	2023	2123	2221	...	2323
burg d.	...	0504	0542	0608	0640	0702	0742	0842	0942	1042	1142	1242	1342	1442	1542	1642	1742	1842	1942	2042	2142	2240	...	2341
sburg Hbf a.	...	0559	0633	0659	0733	0802	0833	0933	1033	1133	1233	1333	1433	1533	1633	1733	1833	1933	2033	2133	2233	2333	...	...
sburg Hbf d.	0539	0605	0639	0705	0739	0806	0839	0939	1039	1139	1239	1339	1439	1539	1639	1739	1839	1939	2039	2139	2239	2339	...	...
chen Pasing a.	0613	0641	0714	0745	0813	0843	0913	1013	1113	1213	1313	1413	1514	1613	1713	1813	1913	2013	2114	2222	2315	0022	...	...
chen Hbf a.	0621	0649	0721	0753	0821	0850	0921	1021	1121	1221	1321	1421	1524	1621	1722	1821	1921	2021	2121	2230	2323	0030	...	...

NOTES (LISTED BY TRAIN NUMBER)

12 and 🍴 Frankfurt - Wien - Budapest. On July 30, 31 does not call at München Hbf.
– 12 and 🍴 Frankfurt - Salzburg - Villach - Klagenfurt; conveys 12 Frankfurt - Villach (**213**) - Ljubljana - Zagreb. Timings Frankfurt - Günzburg are 23–44 minutes **earlier** July 30 - Sept. 11.
– WÖRTHERSEE – 12 and 🍷 Münster - Köln - Koblenz - Salzburg - Villach - Klagenfurt.
– Ⓑ (not ①–⑤ Aug. 1 - Sept. 9, Oct. 2). 12 and 🍷 Frankfurt - Salzburg - Villach - Klagenfurt. On ⑦ July 31 - Sept. 11 runs as *IC* **1269** Frankfurt - München Hbf (a. 1911) - Salzburg (a. 2059).
– 12 Münster - Köln - Koblenz - Ulm - Lindau - Bregenz - Innsbruck.
– 12 and 🍷 Saarbrücken - Salzburg - Bischofshofen - Selzthal - Graz. July 30 - Sept. 11 departs Mannheim 0649, Stuttgart 0738, Ulm 0834, Günzburg 0848.
– 12 and 🍷 Frankfurt - Salzburg - Bischofshofen - Selzthal - Graz.
– 12 and 🍷 Frankfurt - Salzburg (- Linz Ⓑ).
– 12 and 🍴 (Hamburg Ⓐ -) Hannover - Frankfurt - München.
– 12 and 🍴 Wiesbaden - Mainz - München.
– ⑥ (also Oct. 2). 12 and 🍷 Karlsruhe - Stuttgart - Salzburg - Villach - Klagenfurt.
– ①–④ (not Oct. 3, Nov. 1). 12 and 🍷 Düsseldorf - Stuttgart - Plochingen - Nürtingen (a. 1917) - Reutlingen Hbf (a. 1937) - Tübingen Hbf (a. 1950).
– ALLGÄU – 12 and 🍷 Hannover - Dortmund - Köln - Koblenz - Ulm - Kempten - Oberstdorf.
– 12 and 🍷 (Basel ⚒ -) Karlsruhe - München.

12 and 🍷 Paris - Strasbourg - München. Ⓡ for international journeys.
From Berlin (Table **902**).
To Friedrichshafen (Table **933**).
From Hamburg (Table **900**).
To Lindau (Table **933**).
From Münster (Table **800**).
Train number **9575** until July 1. July 31 - Sept. 11 Augsburg d. 2133, München a. 2200.
⑥ to July 2.
⑥ from Sept. 3. On Sept. 3, 10 Augsburg d. 2312, München a. 2341.
To Nürtingen (a. 2118), Reutlingen Hbf (a. 2137) and Tübingen Hbf (a. 2150).
Daily to July 8; Ⓑ from July 10 (not Oct. 2).
Ⓑ to July 1; daily from July 3.

Y – ①②③④⑦ (not Oct. 2).
c – Also Oct. 3, Nov. 1; not July 31 - Sept. 4, Oct. 2, 31.
d – Not Aug. 1 - Sept. 9, Oct. 31, Nov. 1.
e – 1–2 minutes earlier July 16–29.
f – 1919 on ⑦ to June 26.
g – ① (also Oct. 4; not July 11 - Aug. 15, Oct. 3).
j – 16 minutes earlier July 30 - Sept. 11.
k – Not July 30 - Sept. 11.
m – Also Oct. 4, Nov. 2; not Aug. 1 - Sept. 5, Oct. 3, 31.

n – Not July 9 - Aug. 21.
q – Not Oct. 2.
r – 2245 July 9–24.
s – Arrival time. Stops to set down only.
t – Not Nov. 1.
w – Also Oct. 3; not Oct. 2.
y – Not Aug. 15, Nov. 1.
z – Also Nov. 1.

♣ – POLLUX – 🛏 1, 2 cl. and 🛌 2 cl. (*CNL* **419** Ⓡ) Amsterdam - München; conveys 🛏 1, 2 cl. and 🛌 2 cl. (*CNL* **40479** Ⓡ – PYXIS) Hamburg - München.
♥ – 2 (*IC* **60419**) Amsterdam - Köln - München; conveys from Frankfurt 2 (*IC* **61479**) Hamburg - München.
● – July 31 - Sept. 11 runs as *EC* **391** (running 60–64 minutes later from Augsburg).
⊠ – Long-distance services are subject to amended timings until Sept. 11. See shaded panel on page 367 for further details.
❖ – July 30 - Sept. 11 timings may vary by up to 30 minutes (earlier departures possible).
◇ – See panel below for other regional trains Stuttgart - Ulm.

		Ⓒz	Ⓐt			Ⓒz	Ⓐt
Stuttgart Hbf d.	0831	0917	0931	and in	1831	1917	1930
Plochingen d.	0849	0936	0949	the same	1849	1938	1948
Göppingen d.	0907	0954	1007	pattern	1907	1957	2006
Geislingen (Steige) d.	0924	1015	1024	every **two**	1924	2017	2023
Ulm Hbf a.	0949	1047	1049	hours until	1949	2047	2049

930 MÜNCHEN - STUTTGART

SEE NOTE ⊠	ICE 618 ‡	RB 19296	ICE 616	RB 19300	IC 2268 ①g 🍷	IC 2268 Ⓐ 🍷	IC 2010 Ⓐt 🍷♦	RE 19202 Ⓒz	RB 19310 Ⓐt	ICE 614 🍷	IRE 4240 Ⓐt F	IRE 4220 Ⓒz F	IC 2294 Ⓐ 🍷	RE 19206 Ⓐt	RB 19316 Ⓒz	TGV 9576 ①–⑤ N♦	TGV 9576 R ♦	TGV 9576 ①–⑤ k♦	TGV 9576 ⑥⑦ m♦	ICE 692 Ⓐ B✕	IC 2266 ①–⑥ k🍷	ICE 612 🍷	IRE 4222 4224 L
Salzburg Hbf **890** d.	...	...	...	...	...	...	...	...	...	...	...	...	...	...	...	...	...	...	...	...	...	...	...
München Hbf **905** d.	0001	...	0323	...	0443	...	...	...	...	0524	...	...	0536k	...	...	0546	0620	0624	0628	0630	0646	0727	...
München Pasing **905** d.	0009	...	0333	...	0451	...	...	...	...	0533	...	...	|	...	...	|	|	|	|	0638	0655	0736	...
Augsburg Hbf **905** d.	0031	...	0357	...	0516	...	...	...	...	0601	...	...	0611k	...	...	0615	0648	0656	0705	0706	0721	0803	...
Günzburg **945** d.	0101	...	|	...	0546	...	...	...	...	|	...	...	0641k	...	...	|	|	|	|	|	|	|	...
Ulm Hbf **945** ◇ d.	0116	0411	0440x	0455	0602	0602	...	0601	0612	0651	0654	0654	0659	0705	0709	0742	0746	0742	0750	0751	0804	0851	0854
Geislingen (Steige) ◇ d.	|	0435	|	0525	0625	0625	...	0625	0643	|	0717	0717	0722	0732	0737	|	|	|	|	|	|	|	0917
Göppingen ◇ d.	|	0457	|	0548	0639	0639	...	0644	0706	|	0729	0729	|	0751	0757	|	|	|	|	|	0838	|	0929
Plochingen **936** ◇ d.	0200	0518	|	0607	0651	0651	0655	0705	0722	|	|	0740	0746	0805	0815	|	|	|	|	|	0850	|	0940
Stuttgart Hbf **936** ◇ a.	0216	0538	0537	0626	0707	0707	0710	0724	0738	0746	0756	0756	0800	0824	0832	0839	0847	0839	0842	0846	0907	0946	0956
Karlsruhe Hbf **931** a.	0335	...	|	...	0753	0753	|	...	...	|	...	...	|	...	...	0930	0930	0930	0930	|	0953	|	...
Heidelberg Hbf **912** a.	0426	...	|	...	...	...	0753	...	...	|	...	...	0844	...	...	...	...	...	...	|	...	|	...
Mannheim Hbf **912** a.	0438	...	0628	...	...	...	0806	...	...	0828	...	...	|	...	...	...	...	...	...	0929	...	1028	...
Frankfurt Flughafen ✈ **912** a.	0512	...	0706	...	...	...	|	...	...	0906	...	...	|	...	...	...	...	...	...	|	...	1106	...
Frankfurt (Main) Hbf **912** a.	0533	...	|	...	...	...	|	...	...	|	...	...	0940	...	...	...	...	...	...	1008	...	|	...
Köln Hbf **800 910** a.	0705	...	0805	...	...	...	1042	...	...	1005	...	...	...	...	...	...	...	...	...	...	...	1205	...
Dortmund Hbf **800** a.	0825c	...	0921n	...	...	...	1209f	...	...	1121n	...	...	...	...	...	...	...	...	...	...	...	1321n	...

SEE NOTE ⊠	ICE 690 B✕	IC 1268 Y 🍷	IC 1216 ⑤k ⊗🍷	ICE 610 🍷	IRE 4226 4232 L	EC 390 🍷♦	ICE 598 B✕	IC 2012 🍷♦	ICE 518 🍷	IRE 4228 L	EC 218 k 🍷♦	ICE 596 B✕	IC 118 ♦	IC 2260 k 🍷	ICE 516 🍷	IRE 4230 L	EC 114 🍷♦	ICE 1090 Ⓑq B✕	ICE 594 ⑥j B✕	IRE 4244 Ⓐt L	IC 2362 ⑤k 🍷	ICE 514 🍷	IRE 4234 4246 L
Salzburg Hbf **890** d.	...	0643h	0643	...	...	0800	...	...	...	...	1000	...	...	...	...	...	1200	...	...	...	...	...	...
München Hbf **905** d.	0828	0848	0848	0928	...	0946	1028	...	1128	...	1146	1228	...	1248	1328	...	1346	1428	1428	...	1441s	1528	...
München Pasing **905** d.	0837	0856	0856	0937	...	|	1037	...	1137	...	|	1237	...	1256	1337	...	|	1437	1437	...	1449s	1537	...
Augsburg Hbf **905** d.	0903	0921	0921	1003	...	1017	1103	...	1203	...	1217	1303	...	1321	1403	...	1417	1503	1503	...	1521	1603	...
Günzburg **945** d.	|	|	|	|	...	1048	|	...	|	...	1247	|	...	|	|	...	1448	|	|	...	|	|	...
Ulm Hbf **945** ◇ d.	0951	1004	1004	1051	1054	1104	1151	1157	1251	1254	1304	1351	1356	1404	1451	1454	1504	1551	1551	1554	1604	1651	1654
Geislingen (Steige) ◇ d.	|	|	|	|	1117	|	|	|	|	1317	|	|	|	|	|	1517	|	|	|	1617	|	|	1717
Göppingen ◇ d.	|	1038	1038	|	1129	|	|	1235	|	1329	|	|	1433	|	|	1529	|	|	|	1629	|	|	1729
Plochingen **936** ◇ d.	|	1050	1050	|	1140	|	|	1249	|	1340	|	|	|	1449	|	1540	|	|	|	1640	1650	|	1740
Stuttgart Hbf **936** ◇ a.	1046	1107	1107	1146	1156	1200	1246	1305	1346	1356	1400	1446	1458	1504	1546	1556	1600k	1646	1646	1656	1704	1746	1756
Karlsruhe Hbf **931** a.	|	1153	|	|	...	|	|	|	|	...	|	|	|	1550	|	...	|	|	|	...	1753	|	...
Heidelberg Hbf **912** a.	|	...	1153	|	...	1244	|	1353	|	...	1444	|	1553	...	|	...	|	|	|	...	...	|	...
Mannheim Hbf **912** a.	1129	...	1206	1228	...	|	1329	1406	1428	...	|	1529	1606	...	1628	...	1656	1729	1729	...	...	1828	...
Frankfurt Flughafen ✈ **912** a.	|	...	|	1306	...	|	|	|	1506	...	|	|	|	...	1706	...	|	|	|	...	...	1906	...
Frankfurt (Main) Hbf **912** a.	1208	...	|	|	...	1340	1408	|	|	...	1540	1608	|	...	|	...	|	1808	1808	...	...	|	...
Köln Hbf **800 910** a.	...	...	1442	1405	...	...	...	1642	1605	...	...	...	1842	...	1805	...	1942	...	...	...	...	2005	...
Dortmund Hbf **800** a.	...	...	1608	1521n	...	...	...	1809	1721n	...	...	...	...	...	1921n	...	2100	...	...	...	...	2121e	...

SEE NOTE ⊠	IC 1910 ⑦w 🍷	ICE 592 B✕	IC 1910 ⑦w 🍷	IC 2264 🍷♦	IC 2094 Ⓐd	ICE 512 M🍷	IRE 4236 L	EC 216 🍷♦	ICE 590 ⊡ ✕	IRE 4214 †Q L	IC 2092 Ⓑk q🍷	RE 19246	ICE 1110 ⑦w 🍷	ICE 510 ★ E🍷	IRE 4238 Ⓒz L	RB 19354 Ⓐt	RB 19356 Ⓒz	ICE 990 P ✕	RJ 66 ⑤⑥ ✕♦	RB 19360 Ⓒz	RE 19248	IC 2090 ⑦v	IC 60418 ♥2
Salzburg Hbf **890** d.	...	...	...	...	...	...	...	1600	...	...	...	...	...	...	...	...	...	...	1856	...	...	...	...
München Hbf **905** d.	1620	1628	...	1648	1711	1727	...	1746	1828	...	1845	...	1928	1928	...	...	...	2045	2045	...	...	2151	2250
München Pasing **905** d.	1628k	1637	...	1656	1719	1736	...	|	1837	...	1853	...	1937	1937	...	...	...	2053	2053k	...	...	2159	|
Augsburg Hbf **905** d.	1653	1703	...	1721	1745	1802	...	1817	1904	...	1918	...	2003	2003	...	...	...	2117	2117	...	...	2224	2320
Günzburg **945** d.	1728	|	...	|	1816	|	...	1847	|	...	1948	...	|	|	...	...	...	2147	2147	...	...	2253	2353
Ulm Hbf **945** ◇ d.	1744	1751	←	1804	1835	1851	1854	1904	1951	1954	2004	2009	2051	2051	2054	2104	2109	2204	2204	2209	2245	2310	0010
Geislingen (Steige) ◇ d.	1808	|	1816	|	...	|	1917	|	|	|	|	2033	|	|	2117	2133	2137	|	|	2239	2311	|	|
Göppingen ◇ d.	→	|	1830	1838	...	|	1929	|	|	2028	2038	2050	|	|	2129	2155	2157	|	|	2301	2326	2344	0048
Plochingen **936** ◇ d.	...	|	|	1850	...	|	1940	|	|	2039	2050	2109	|	|	2140	2213	2215	|	|	2321	2340	2356	0102
Stuttgart Hbf **936** ◇ a.	...	1846	1858	1907	...	1946	1956	2000	2046	2054	2106	2128	2146	2146	2156	2231	2232	2259	2259	2340	0001	0011	0116
Karlsruhe Hbf **931** a.	...	|	|	1953	...	|	...	|	|	...	2153	...	|	|	...	...	...	|	|	...	...	...	|
Heidelberg Hbf **912** a.	...	|	1953	...	...	|	...	|	|	...	...	...	|	|	...	...	...	|	|	...	...	...	|
Mannheim Hbf **912** a.	...	1929	2006	...	...	2028	...	2048	2129	...	...	...	2229	2229	...	...	...	2345	2345	...	...	...	|
Frankfurt Flughafen ✈ **912** a.	...	|	|	...	...	2106	...	...	|	...	...	...	2308	2308	...	...	...	0023	0023	...	...	...	|
Frankfurt (Main) Hbf **912** a.	...	2008	|	...	...	|	...	...	2208	...	...	...	|	...	...	...	...	0042	0042	...	...	...	0312
Köln Hbf **800 910** a.	...	...	2242	...	...	2205	...	...	...	...	...	...	0007	...	...	...	...	...	...	...	...	...	0615
Dortmund Hbf **800** a.	...	...	2359	...	...	...	...	...	...	...	...	...	...	...	...	...	...	...	...	...	...	...	...

Regional trains MÜNCHEN - ULM *Subject to alteration July 30 - Sept. 11 – see note* ✣

		Ⓒr		⚒y																			
München Hbf d.	0008	0008	...	...	...	0532	0637	0735	0836	0936	1036	1135	1236	1336	1436	1536	1636	1735	1836	1936	2036	2101	2201
München Pasing d.	0015	0015	...	...	...	0538	0644	0742	0843	0943	1043	1142	1243	1343	1443	1542	1643	1742	1843	1943	2043	2107	2209
Augsburg Hbf a.	0050	0050	...	...	...	0619	0720	0819	0919	1019	1119	1218	1319	1419	1519	1619	1719	1819	1919	2019	2119	2148	2244
Augsburg Hbf d.	...	0054	...	...	0524	0625	0725	0825	0925	1025	1125	1222	1325	1425	1525	1625	1725	1825	1925	2025	2125	2151	2251
Günzburg d.	...	0147	...	0529	0616	0716	0819¦	0927o	1016	1116	1216	1321	1416	1516	1616	1716	1821	1916	2017	2116	2216	2242	2342
Ulm Hbf a.	...	0205	...	0547	0635	0735	0840¦	0946¦	1034	1134	1235	1339	1434	1535	1635	1735	1839	1934	2036	2135	2235	2302	0002

♦ – **NOTES** (LISTED BY TRAIN NUMBER)

66 – ⑤⑥ (also Oct. 2). [12] and ✕ Budapest - Wien - Frankfurt. On July 29, 30 does not call at München Hbf (calls at München Ost 2020 / München Pasing 2033).
112 – [12] and ✕ Klagenfurt - Villach - Salzburg - Frankfurt; conveys [12] Zagreb (**212**) - Ljubljana - Frankfurt.
114 – WÖRTHERSEE – [12] and 🍷 Klagenfurt - Villach - Salzburg - Koblenz - Köln - Dortmund.
118 – [12] Innsbruck - Bregenz - Lindau - Ulm - Koblenz - Köln - Münster.
216 – [12] and 🍷 Graz - Selzthal - Bischofshofen - Salzburg - Saarbrücken.
218 – [12] and 🍷 Graz - Selzthal - Bischofshofen - Salzburg - Frankfurt.
390 – Not ⑦ July 31 - Sept. 11. [12] and 🍷 (Linz ①–⑥ -) Salzburg - Frankfurt. On ①–⑥ July 30 - Sept. 10 runs as *IC* **1268** Salzburg (d. 0643) - München Hbf (d. 0910) - Augsburg (d. 0945) - Frankfurt.
2010 – [12] and 🍷 Tübingen Hbf (d. 0611) - Reutlingen (d. 0623) - Nürtingen (d. 0642) - Stuttgart - Düsseldorf (- Berlin ⑤).
2012 – ALLGÄU – [12] and 🍷 Oberstdorf - Kempten - Ulm - Köln - Dortmund - Hannover.
2264 – [12] and 🍷 München - Karlsruhe (- Basel Ⓑ**q**).
9576 – [12] and 🍷 München - Strasbourg - Paris. Ⓡ for international journeys. Timings at Augsburg, Ulm and Stuttgart may vary by up to 7 minutes on ⑥⑦.

B – To Berlin (Table **902**).
E – To Wiesbaden (Table **911**).
F – From Friedrichshafen (Table **933**).
L – From Lindau (Table **933**).
M – To Münster (Table **800**).
N – Aug. 1 - Sept. 9.
P – ①②③④⑦ (not Oct. 2). Train number **1590** on ④.
Q – † to Oct. 16.
R – ⑥ July 30 - Sept. 10 (also Sept. 4, 11).
Y – ①②③④⑥⑦ (not July 30 - Sept. 11).

c – Ⓒ only. Arrives 0821 on † to July 3 / from Aug. 28.
d – Not Aug. 1 - Sept. 9, Oct. 31, Nov. 1.
e – 2136 July 9 - Aug. 21.
f – ⑤ only.
g – Also Oct. 4, Nov. 2; not Aug. 1 - Sept. 5, Oct. 3, 31.
h – ①②③④⑥.
j – Also Oct. 2.
k – Not July 30 - Sept. 11.
m – Not July 10, 17, 24, 30, 31, Aug. 6 - Sept. 11.
n – Not July 9 - Aug. 21.
o – Arrives 0916. Departs 0925 July 16 - Aug. 28.
q – Not Oct. 2.
r – Also Aug. 15, Nov. 1.
s – 7 minutes later from Sept. 16.
t – Not Nov. 1.
u – Stops to pick up only.
v – Also Oct. 3, Nov. 1; not July 31 - Sept. 11, Oct. 2.
w – Also Oct. 3; not Oct. 2
x – Not July 2, 3, 9, 10, 16,
y – Not Aug. 15, Nov. 1.
z – Also Nov. 1.

♣ – POLLUX – 🛏 1, 2 cl. and ▬ 2 cl. (*CNL* **418** Ⓡ) München - Köln - Amsterd conveys 🛏 1, 2 cl. and ▬ 2 cl. (*CNL* **40418** Ⓡ – PYXIS) München - Hamb
♥ – [2] (*IC* **60418**) München - Köln - Amsterdam); conveys to Frankfurt [2] (*IC* **61418**) München - Hamburg.
★ – Train number **1010** on ⑤⑥ (also Oct. 2), **1190** on ⑦ (also Oct. 3; not Oct. Also conveys ✕ on ①–④ (not Oct. 3).
‡ – Train number **1018** on † to July 24 / from Sept. 18, **1118** on ⑦ July 31 - Sep **1218** on ①–⑥ July 30 - Sept. 12. Runs up to 11 minutes earlier July 30 - Se (departing München stations the previous day).
⊡ – On ⑤ runs with train number **698** and continues to Kassel (Table **900**). On ⑦ (also Oct. 3; not Oct. 2) runs with train number **992** and continues to Hamburg (Table **900**).
¦ – 2–4 minutes earlier July 16 - Aug. 28.
⊗ – On July 29 runs Salzburg - München - Stuttgart only.
⊠ – Long-distance services are subject to amended timings until Sept. 11. See shaded panel on page 367 for further details.
✣ – July 30 - Sept. 11 timings may vary by up to 15 minutes (earlier departures possible).
¥ – Timings may vary by 1–2 minutes.
◇ – See panel below for other regional trains Ulm - Stuttgart.

		Ⓐt	Ⓒz	¥		Ⓐt
Ulm Hbf d.	0809	0909	0909	and in	1809	1909
Geislingen (Steige) d.	0832	0933	0937	the same	1832	1932
Göppingen d.	0850	0951	0957	pattern	1850	1954
Plochingen d.	0909	1009	1015	every **two**	1908	2013
Stuttgart Hbf a.	0928	1028	1032	hours until	1926	2032

KARLSRUHE - STUTTGART (also local trains HEIDELBERG - STUTTGART) 931

See Table **32** for full details of international *TGV* services from / to Paris. See Table **912** for fast trains Heidelberg - Stuttgart and v.v.

km	km		*ICE* 619		*IC* 2291	*IRE* 19011	*IC* 2363	*IRE* 4901	*RE* 19503	*IC* 2365	*IC* 2367	*IC* 2063	*RE* 19525	*IC* 2369	*IC* 2265	*IRE* 4903	*RE* 19505	*IC* 2065	*RE* 19527 19529	*IRE* 4905	*RE* 19507	*IC* 2067	*RE* 19531 19533	*IC* 2261	*IRE* 4907
					Ⓐk	Ⓐt	⚒	Ⓐt	Ⓒz	Ⓐd	Ⓐt	⚒	Ⓒz	Ⓐd											
			R				🍷			O🍷	🍷	N			B🍷			N				N		🍷	
0		**Karlsruhe** Hbf ....d.	0211	...	0455	...	0559	0601	...	0637	0658	0706	0719	0741	0806	0805	...	0906	0919	1005	...	1106	1119	1205	1205
26		Pforzheim ....d.	|	...	|	0546	|	0624	...	|	|	0727	0743	|	|	0826	...	0927	0943	1026	...	1127	1143	|	1226
	0	**Heidelberg** Hbf **912** d.	|	...	|	|	|	|	0610	|	|	|	|	|	|	|	0810	|	|	|	1010	|	|	|	|
	33	Bruchsal........... **912** d.	|	...	0513	|	0617	|	0632	0654	0719	|	|	0758	0819	|	0833	|	|	|	1033	|	|	1219	|
39	65	Mühlacker...................d.	|	...	|	0555	|	0632	0656	|	|	0737	0755	|	|	0834	0859	0937	0955	1034	1059	1137	1155	|	1234
47	73	Vaihingen (Enz).... **912** d.	0248	...	0532	0602	|	0639	0705	|	|	0746	0804	|	|	0841	0907	0946	1007	1041	1107	1146	1204	|	1241
86	112	**Stuttgart** Hbf....... **912** a.	0320	...	0549	0619	0648	0657	0740	0725	0750	0803	0839	0829	0849	0858	0939	1003	1039	1058	1139	1203	1239	1249	1258
		München Hbf **930** ● a.	0602	...	0814	...	...	...	...	...	...	...	...	...	1111	...	...	...	...	...	...	...	...	1512**k**	...

	RE 19509	*IC* 2069	*IC* 2263	*IRE* 4909	*RE* 19511	*EC* 1217	*IC* 2161	*IC* 2361	*IC*◧ 1269	*IRE* 4911	*RE* 19513	*IC* 2163	*IC* 2267	*IRE* 4913	*TGV* 9577	*RE* 19515	*IC* 2165	*RE* 19547 19549	*IC* 2269	*IRE* 4915	*TGV* 9579	*RE* 19517	*IC* 2167	*RE* 19551	*RE* 19553
			⑤			⑥	Ⓑq	⑤	Ⓑq				k		T				Ⓑq		⑥Y		Ⓑr		
		N	🍷			A🍷	N		S🍷			N	🍷		P🍷		L		G🍷		P🍷				
rlsruhe Hbf ....d.	...	1306	1405	1405	...	1505	1506	1544	1605	1605	...	1706	1805	1805	1828	...	1906	1919	2005	2005	2028	...	2106	2208	2321
rzheim ....d.	...	1327	|	1426	...	|	1527	|	|	1626	...	1727	|	1826	|	...	1927	1943	|	2026	|	...	2127	2231	2343
leidelberg Hbf. **912** d.	1210	|	|	|	1410	|	|	|	|	|	1610	|	|	|	|	1810	|	|	|	|	|	2010	|	|	|
Bruchsal........... **912** d.	1233	|	1419	|	1433	1518	|	1558	1619	|	1633	|	1819	|	|	1833	|	|	2019	|	|	2030	|	|	|
hlacker....................d.	1259	1337	|	1434	1459	|	1537	|	|	1634	1659	1737	|	1834	|	1859	1937	1955	|	2034	|	2055	2137	2243	2356
hingen (Enz)..... **912** d.	1307	|	|	1441	1507	|	1546	|	|	1641	1707	1746	|	1841	|	1907	1946	2007	|	2041	|	2103	2146	2252	0005
ttgart Hbf........ **912** a.	1339	1359	1449	1458	1539	1554	1603	1629	1649	1658	1739	1803	1849	1858	1909◊	1939	2003	2039	2049	2058	2104	2137	2203	2325	0040
München Hbf **930**. ● a.	...	...	...	...	...	1811**k**	...	...	1911	...	...	...	2111	...	2136**y**	...	...	...	2319**h**	...	2329	...	...	...	...

km		*RE* 19518 19556	*ICE* 618 1018		*IC* 2376	*RE* 19500	*RE* 19522	*IC* 2268	*RE* 19524	*RE* 19526	*IC* 2164	*IC* 2164	*RE* 19502	*TGV* 9576	*IRE* 4902	*IC* 2266	*RE* 19528	*RE* 19530	*IC* 2162	*RE* 19504	*IRE* 4904	*IC* 1268	*IC* 2160	*RE* 19506	*IRE* 4906
					Ⓐe		Ⓐt	Ⓐ	Ⓒz	Ⓐt	⑥z	Ⓐt		⊗		①–⑥	Ⓒz	Ⓐt	⚒			§			
			R❦		¶			H🍷				N		P🍷		k🍷			N			S🍷	N		
	München Hbf **930** ● d.	...	0001	...	...	...	...	0443**g**	...	...	...	...	...	0624	...	0646	...	...	...	...	...	0848**v**	...	...	...
0	**Stuttgart** Hbf....... **912** d.	0019	0230	...	0546	0614	0626	0711	0717	0722	0758	0758	0819	0849	0900	0911	0917	0919	0959	1019	1059	1111	1159	1219	1259
29	Vaihingen (Enz).... **912** d.	0052	0259	...	0603	0645	0704	|	0750	0753	0816	0816	0850	|	0916	|	0950	0952	1016	1050	1115	|	1216	1250	1315
	Mühlacker...................d.	0101	|	...	0611	0700	0714	|	0759	0801	|	|	0900	|	0922	|	0959	1000	1023	1100	1121	|	1223	1300	1321
66	Bruchsal........... **912** d.	|	|	...	|	0728	|	0740	|	|	|	|	0929	|	|	0940	|	|	|	1129	|	1140	|	1329	|
	Heidelberg Hbf **912** a.	|	|	...	|	0748	|	|	|	|	|	|	0949	|	|	|	|	|	|	1149	|	|	|	1349	|
	Pforzheim ....d.	0114	|	...	0622	...	0729	|	0813	0814	|	|	...	|	0930	|	1013	1013	1034	...	1130	|	1234	...	1330
87	**Karlsruhe** Hbf ....a.	0144⁝	0335	...	0645	...	0753	0753	0838	0838	0848	0853	...	0930	0953	0953	1038	1038	1053	...	1153	1153	1253	...	1353

	IC 2262	*IC* 2068	*RE* 19508	*IRE* 4908	*IC* 2260	*IC* 2066	*RE* 19510	*IC* 2364	*IRE* 4910	*IC* 2362	*IC* 2362	*IC* 2360	*IC* 2064	*RE* 19514	*IRE* 4912	*IC* 2264	*RE* 19548	*RE* 19550	*IC* 2062	*RE* 19516	*IRE* 4914	*IC* 2092	*IC* 2060	*RE* 19552 19554	*IC* 1966
	⑤							Ⓐd		⑤k		Ⓐe					Ⓒz	Ⓐt				U	Ⓑr		⑦w
	🍷	N			🍷	N		O🍷		🍷	‡	🍷	N			B🍷			N			🍷	L		🍷
München Hbf **930**. ● d.	...	...	...	...	1248**k**	...	...	...	...	1441**b**	...	...	...	...	...	1648	...	...	...	...	...	1845**k**	...	...	...
ttgart Hbf........ **912** d.	1303	1358	1419	1459	1508	1559	1617	1641	1659	1708	1708	1734	1759	1819	1859	1911	1918	1922	1958	2019	2059	2111	2159	2219	2309
hingen (Enz)..... **912** d.	|	1416	1450	1515	|	1616	1650	|	1715	|	|	|	1816	1850	1915	|	1950	1953	2016	2051	2115	|	2216	2254	2326
hlacker....................d.	|	|	1500	1521	|	1623	1700	|	1721	|	|	|	1823	1900	1921	|	1959	2001	|	2100	2121	|	2224	2303	2334
ruchsal............ **912** d.	1339	|	1529	|	1537	|	1729	1712	|	1737	1737	1804	|	1929	|	1940	|	|	|	2129	|	2140	|	|	|
leidelberg Hbf. **912** a.	|	|	1549	|	|	|	1749	|	|	|	|	|	|	1949	|	|	|	|	|	2156	|	|	|	|	|
rzheim ....d.	|	|	...	1530	|	1634	...	|	1730	|	|	|	1834	...	1930	|	2013	2014	|	...	2130	|	2234	2317	2344
rlsruhe Hbf ....a.	1352	1448	...	1553	1550	1653	...	1731	1753	1753	1753	1821	1853	...	1953	1953	2038	2038	2048	...	2153	2153	2259	2340	0008

- ⑥ (also Oct. 2). [12] and 🍷 Karlsruhe - Stuttgart - Salzburg - Villach - Klagenfurt. Terminates at Stuttgart July 30 - Sept. 10.
- From / to Basel on dates in Table **912**.
- [12] Karlsruhe - Stuttgart (- Ulm ♣) (- München ⑦**c**).
- [12] (München ①**g** -) Ulm - Stuttgart - Karlsruhe.
- [12] Karlsruhe - Stuttgart (- Nürnberg ♥) and v.v.
- [12] Karlsruhe - Stuttgart - Nürnberg and v.v.
- To / from Offenburg (Table **916**).
- [12] and 🍷 München - Stuttgart - Paris and v.v.
  Ⓡ for international journeys.
- From / to Dortmund or Essen via Frankfurt (Tables **800/912**).
- From / to Salzburg (Table **890**).
  Daily to July 8; Ⓑ from July 10. Train number **9575** until July 2.
- Ⓑ to July 29; ⑤ Aug. 5 - Sept. 9; Ⓑ from Sept. 12 (not Oct. 2).
  ⑥ from Sept. 3. Arrives München 2341 on Sept. 3, 10.

b – 1448 from Sept. 16.
d – Not Oct. 31, Nov. 1.
e – Not Oct. 31.
g – ① (also Oct. 4, Nov. 2; not Aug. 1 - Sept. 5, Oct. 3, 31).
h – ⑦ (also Oct. 3, Nov. 1; not July 31 - Sept. 4, Oct. 2, 31).
k – Not July 30 - Sept. 11.
q – Not Oct. 2.
r – Not Oct. 2, 30, 31.
t – Not Nov. 1.
v – ①②③④⑥⑦ (not July 30 - Sept. 11).
w – ⑦ (also Oct. 3; not Oct. 2).
y – 2129 on ⑥. 2200 July 31 - Sept. 11.
z – Also Nov. 1.

♣ – ①②③④⑦ (not Oct. 2).
♥ – ④⑤⑦ (also Oct. 3, Nov. 1; not Oct. 2, 30).
⊗ – Not ⑦ July 10 - Aug. 28. Timings may vary by up to 5 minutes to July 2 / from Aug. 29. Departs München 0628 on ⑥⑦ (July 30 - Sept. 11 departs München 0546①–⑤, 0620⑥⑦).
● – München timings are subject to alteration July 30 - Sept. 11. See shaded panel on page 367 for further details.
⁝ – 0137 on Ⓐ (not Nov. 1).
◊ – 1904 from Aug. 29.
◧ – July 31 - Sept. 11 runs as *EC* **391** (arrives München 2011).
❦ – July 30 - Sept. 12 runs with train number **1118/1218** and departs München 2350 (the previous day).
§ – Train number **1968** July 30 - Sept. 11.
¶ – Train number **2368** on ①⑤ (also Oct. 4, Nov. 2).
‡ – Not June 12, Oct. 2. Train number **2366** on ⑦ (also Oct. 3, Nov. 1; not Oct. 2). Train number **2166** on ⑥.

Bahn 2/3 STUTTGART - STUTTGART FLUGHAFEN / MESSE ✈ 932

20 km. Journey time: 27 minutes. On Nov. 1 services run as on ⑦. **An amended service operates July 13 - Aug. 14.**

m **Stuttgart Hbf**: 0025, 0055, 0455 Ⓐ, 0515 Ⓐ, 0525, 0545 Ⓑ, 0555 ⚒, 0615 Ⓐ, 0625, 0645 Ⓑ, 0655 ⚒, 0715 Ⓐ, 0725, 0745, 0755, 0815, 0825, 0845, 0855 and at 15, 25, 45 and 55 minutes t each hour until 1815, 1825, 1845, 1855, 1915 Ⓐ, 1925, 1945 Ⓐ, 1955, 2015 Ⓐ, 2025, 2045 Ⓐ, 2055, 2115 Ⓐ, 2125, 2145 Ⓐ, 2155, 2215 Ⓐ, 2225, 2245 Ⓐ, 2255, 2315 Ⓐ, 2325, 2355.

m **Stuttgart Flughafen** ✈: 0008, 0038, 0508, 0518 Ⓐ, 0538 ⚒, 0548 Ⓑ, 0608, 0618 Ⓐ, 0638 ⚒, 0648 Ⓑ, 0708, 0718 Ⓐ, 0738 ⚒, 0748 Ⓑ, 0808, 0818, 0838, 0848 and at 08, 18, 38 and 48 utes past each hour until 1808, 1818, 1838, 1848, 1908, 1918, 1938, 1948 Ⓐ, 2008, 2018 Ⓐ, 2038, 2048 Ⓐ, 2108, 2118 Ⓐ, 2138, 2148 Ⓐ, 2208, 2218 Ⓐ, 2238, 2248 Ⓐ, 2308, 2318 Ⓐ, 8, 2348 Ⓐ.

E / *RE* services (except trains **C** and **D**) ULM - FRIEDRICHSHAFEN - LINDAU 933

m		Ⓒz	Ⓐe	⊕	B			B			B			B	C		B			B					S2
	Stuttgart Hbf **930** ....d.	...	...	...	...	0659**f**	0802	...	...	1002	...	...	1202	...	1257	1402	...	...	1602	...	1702**e**	1802	...	2002	...
0	**Ulm** Hbf..............................d.	0550	0552	0707**h**	0805	0812	0912	1004	1012	1112	1205	1212	1312	1405	1411	1512	1605	1612	1712	1805	1812	1914	2012	2112	2217
7	Biberach (Riß) ....d.	0618	0621	0733**h**	0825	0835	0935	1025	1035	1135	1225	1235	1335	1425	1433	1535	1626	1635	1735	1825	1835	1940	2035	2138	2242
2	Aulendorf ....d.	0638	0640	0753	|	0855	0955	|	1054	1155	|	1254	1355	1442**z**	1451	1554	|	1654	1754	|	1855	2002	2055	2157	2300
4	Ravensburg ....d.	0651	0653	0806	0852	0908	1008	1052	1107	1208	1252	1307	1408	1456	1505	1607	1652	1707	1807	1852	1908	2015	2108	2210	2313
5	Meckenbeuren ....d.	0658	0701	0814	|	0916	1016	|	1114	1216	|	1314	1416	|	1513	1614	|	1714	1815	|	1916	2022	2116	2219	2320
9	Friedrichshafen Flughafen ✈ d.	0702	0706	|	0901	|	|	1101	|	|	1301	|	|	1505	|	|	1701	|	|	1900	|	|	|	2224	2324
3	Friedrichshafen Stadt ▲......a.	0707	0715	0822	0906	0924	1023	1106	1123	1224	1306	1323	1424	1510	1521	1624	1706	1723	1824	1905	1924	2030	2124	2229	2330
3	Friedrichshafen Stadt ... **939** d.	*0728*	0728	0828	...	0928	1029	...	1128	1229	...	1328	1429	...	1535	1629	...	1728	1829	...	1929	2037	2132	*2234*	*2344*
7	**Lindau** Hbf 🏨.............. **939** a.	*0750*	0750	0857	...	0952	1055	...	1153	1255	...	1351	1455	...	1554	1655	...	1751	1855	...	1951	2100	2156	*2256*	*0016*

	◇	Ⓐe			⊕	B			B		D	Ⓒz B	Ⓐe B			B			B			B		B	2
dau Hbf 🏨 .... **939** d.	...	...	0559	0701**k**	0804**k**	...	0906	1006	...	1102	1202	...	...	1302	1406	...	1500	1606	...	1702	1806	...	1902	*2012*	*2134*
drichshafen Stadt.... **939** a.	...	...	0622	0727	0827	...	0927	1027	...	1127	1220	...	...	1327	1427	...	1527	1627	...	1727	1828	...	1927	*2035*	*2209*
drichshafen Stadt ▲ ...... d.	0521	0549	0628	0732	0832	0850	0931	1032	1049	1131	1233	1245	1250	1331	1432	1450	1531	1632	1650	1731	1832	1847	1932	2050	2231
drichshafen Flughafen ✈ d.	|	|	0632	|	|	0855	|	|	1054	|	|	1250	1255	|	|	1455	|	|	1655**z**	|	|	1852	|	|	2236
ckenbeuren ....d.	0529	|	0637	0739	0839	|	0938	1039	|	1138	1241	|	|	1338	1439	|	1538	1639	|	1738	1839	|	1939	2056	2241
ensburg ....d.	0537	0601	0645	0747	0846	0905	0945	1046	1104	1145	1250	1259	1305	1345	1446	1505	1545	1646	1705	1745	1846	1901	1946	2103	2250
endorf..............................d.	0552	|	0700**k**	0803	0901	|	1001	1101	|	1201	1306	1314	|	1401	1501	|	1601	1701	|	1801	1901	1915	2001	2117	2305
erach (Riß)......................d.	0610	0627	0720	0820	0920	0930	1020	1120	1129	1220	1322	1330	1330	1420	1520	1530	1620	1720	1730	1820	1920	1930	2020	2133	2325
Hbf...................................a.	0641	0650	0745	0844	0945	0953	1045	1145	1153	1244	1345	1352	1353	1444	1545	1553	1645	1745	1753	1844	1945	1952	2044	2158	2359
tuttgart Hbf **930** ....a.	0756**z**	0756	...	0956	...	...	1156	...	...	1356	1458	...	...	1556	1656**e**	...	1756	...	...	1956	2054**r**	...	2156**z**	...	...

To / from Basel (Table **939**).
IC **119**: [12] Münster - Lindau - Bregenz - Innsbruck.
IC **118**: [12] Innsbruck - Bregenz - Lindau - Münster.
To Singen (Table **939**).

e – Ⓐ (not Nov. 1).
f – 0700 on Ⓒ (also Nov. 1).
h – On Ⓐ (not Nov. 1) Ulm d. 0712, Biberach d. 0736.
k – 2–3 minutes later on Ⓒ (also Nov. 1).
r – ✝ to Oct. 16.

z – Ⓒ (also Nov. 1).
◇ – Runs up to 3 minutes **earlier** on Ⓐ (not Nov. 1).
⊕ – Change trains at Friedrichshafen Stadt on Ⓐ (not Nov. 1).
▲ – Regular services operate to / from Friedrichshafen Hafen.

935 MÜNCHEN, AUGSBURG and ULM - OBERSTDORF and LINDAU *RE / RB services except where show*

SERVICE UNTIL OCTOBER 20. For services to / from Bad Wörishofen see panel at foot of page (also on page 445). For regional services Memmingen - Lindau (via Kißlegg) see Table 9

km		Ⓐe	ALX ⚒r‡		Ⓐe	Ⓐe	Ⓐ	Ⓐe	ALX Ⓐe	ALX Ⓒz	Ⓒz	★	⊠ Ⓐe	⊠ Ⓒz	Ⓒ			Ⓐ	Ⓒ	EC 196 ♥	ALX					
0	**München** Hbf ⊡ d.	...	0448	...	...	...	...	...	0553	0553	...	...	...	...	...	0653	...	...	...	0703	0720	...	...	0753	...	08
7	München Pasing d.	...	0455	...	...	...	...	...	0600	0600	...	...	...	...	...	0700	...	...	...	|	0727	...	...	0800	...	08
42	Geltendorf d.	...	0517	...	...	...	...	...	0622	0622	...	...	...	...	...	0722	...	...	...	|	|	...	...	0822	...	08
56	Kaufering d.	...	0526	...	...	...	...	...	0631	0631	...	...	...	...	...	0731	...	...	...	|	0757	...	...	0832	...	09
	Nürnberg Hbf **905** d.	...	|	...	...	...	...	...	|	|	...	...	...	...	...	|	...	...	...	|	|	...	...	|	0717	|
	Augsburg Hbf d.	0500	|	...	...	...	...	0548	|	|	...	0618	...	...	...	|	0703	...	...	|	|	0730	0815	|	0830	|
68	Buchloe a.	0533	0534	...	...	...	...	0621	0640	0639	...	0649	...	...	...	0738	0735c	...	...	0747	0806	0759c	0843	0841	0851	09
68	Buchloe d.	▬	0536	...	0615	...	...	0631	0641	0652	0642	0650	...	...	...	0739	0749	...	...	0748	0807	0818	▬	0846	0854	09
88	Kaufbeuren d.	...	0549	0554	0628	...	...	|	|	|	0655	0700	...	...	...	0752	0801	...	...	|	0821	|	...	0859	0906	|
94	Biessenhofen d.	...	0554	0600	0634	...	...	|	|	|	0701	0705	...	...	...	0757v	0806	...	...	|	|	|	...	0905	|	|
100	Marktoberdorf d.	...	|	0610	0646	...	...	|	|	|	0712	|	...	...	...	|	0817	...	...	|	|	|	...	0915	|	|
131	**Füssen** a.	...	|	0649	0726	...	...	|	|	|	0752	|	...	...	...	|	0855	...	...	|	|	|	...	0956	|	|
	Türkheim (Bay) d.	...	|	▬	▬	...	...	0638	0700t	0659	...	|	...	...	...	|	...	...	...	|	|	0825	...	...	|	09
	Mindelheim d.	Ⓒ	|	...	...	...	...	0648	0713	0709	...	|	...	...	...	|	...	...	...	|	|	0835	...	...	|	09
	Ulm Hbf d.	0511	|	...	...	...	0549	|	|	|	...	|	...	...	0618	|	...	0659	0717	|	|	|	0819	...	|	|
	Memmingen a.	0555	|	...	...	...	0644	0709	0733	0729	...	|	...	...	0721	|	...	0759	0800	0816	|	0855	0855	...	|	09
	Memmingen **937** d.	0556	|	...	...	*0559*	0646	0723	0738	0738	...	|	...	...	0728	|	...	0802	0802	0820	|	▬	0904	...	|	▬
131	**Kempten** Hbf a.	0620	0621	...	...	*0633*	0717	0757	|	|	...	0726	...	...	0757	0819v	...	0826	0827	|	0848	...	0925	...	0928	..
131	**Kempten** Hbf d.	...	0625	⊠	⊠	0651	...	0800	|	|	...	0729	...	...	0800	...	...	0828	0828	|	0852	...	...	...	0931	..
152	Immenstadt a.	...	0641	Ⓒ	Ⓐe	0708	...	0814	|	|	...	0743	...	...	0814	...	...	0842	0842	|	0907	⊠	...	...	0945	⊠
152	Immenstadt d.	...	0656	0646	0646	0719	...	0820	|	|	...	0751	0748	0748	0820	...	...	0850	0850	|	0914	0912	...	...	0951	09
	Sonthofen d.	...	0706	|	|	0730	...	0829	|	|	...	0801	|	|	0829	...	...	0900	0900	|	0922	|	...	...	1001	|
	Oberstdorf a.	...	0729	|	|	0748	...	0851	|	|	...	0819	|	|	0851	...	...	0918	0918	|	0939	|	...	...	1023	|
197	Hergatz **937** d.	...	...	0732	0737	...	...	...	0836	0836	...	...	0839t	0833	...	...	...	...	...	|	...	0959	...	...	...	10
203	Wangen (Allgäu) **937** a.	...	...	|	0741	...	...	...	|	|	...	...	0844	|	...	...	...	...	...	|	...	|	...	...	...	|
220	**Lindau** Hbf **937** a.	...	...	0746	*0754*h	...	...	...	0853	0853	...	...	*0853*h	*0853*	...	...	...	...	...	0944	...	1014	...	...	...	10

	Ⓒz	†z			ALX	◐				⊠				ALX	◐					EC 194 ♥			ALX	◐	IC 2085 H	
München Hbf ⊡ d.	0820	0840	0853	...	0919	...	...	0953	...	...	1020	1053	...	1119	...	...	1153	...	1220	1233	1253	...	1319	...	...	..
München Pasing d.	0827	0847	0900	...	0927	...	...	1000	...	...	1027	1100	...	1127	...	...	1200	...	1227	|	1300	...	1327	...	...	..
Geltendorf d.	0849	|	0922	...	|	...	...	1022	...	...	1049	1122	...	|	...	...	1222	...	1249	|	1322	...	|	...	...	..
Kaufering d.	0900	|	0931	...	0955	...	...	1032	...	...	1059	1131	...	1155	...	...	1232	...	1259	|	1331	...	1355	...	...	..
Nürnberg Hbf **905** d.	|	|	|	...	|	...	...	|	...	...	|	|	...	|	...	...	|	...	|	|	|	...	|	...	...	..
Augsburg Hbf d.	|	|	|	0903	|	0930	1015	|	1030	...	|	|	1103	|	1130	1215	|	1230	|	|	|	1303	|	1330	1356	14
Buchloe a.	0908	|	0939k	0935c	1003	0959c	1043	1041	1051	...	1108	1138	1135c	1203	1159c	1243	1241	1251	1308	1315	1338	1335c	1403	1401c	1421	14
Buchloe d.	0911	|	0941k	0947	1005	1006	...	1046	1054	...	1111	1139	1147	1205	1206	...	1246	1254	1309	1317	1339	1347	1405	1406	1422	..
Kaufbeuren d.	|	|	0954k	1000	1018	|	...	1059	1106	...	|	1153	1200	1218	|	...	1259	1306	|	|	1353	1400	1418	|	1438	..
Biessenhofen d.	|	|	1000	1006	|	|	...	1105	|	...	|	1159	1206	|	|	...	1305	|	|	|	1359v	1406	|	|	|	..
Marktoberdorf d.	|	0950	|	1016	|	|	...	1115	|	...	|	|	1216	|	|	...	1315v	|	|	|	|	1416	|	|	|	..
Füssen a.	|	1027	|	1055	|	|	...	1155	|	...	|	|	1255	|	|	...	1355v	|	|	|	|	1455	|	|	|	..
Türkheim (Bay) d.	0918	...	|	▬	|	1014	...	▬	|	...	1118	|	▬	|	1214	...	▬	|	1316	|	|	▬	|	1414	|	..
Mindelheim d.	0930	...	|	...	|	1032t	...	...	|	...	1130	|	...	|	1232t	...	...	|	1335t	|	|	...	|	1430	|	..
Ulm Hbf d.	|	...	|	0919	|	|	...	1019	|	...	|	|	1119	|	|	...	1219	|	|	|	|	1317	|	|	|	..
Memmingen a.	0951	...	|	0954	|	1053	...	1055	|	...	1151	|	1200	|	1253	...	1255	|	1355	1345	|	1355	|	1451	|	..
Memmingen **937** d.	0954	...	|	1002	|	▬	...	1104	|	...	1154	|	1202	|	▬	...	1304	|	▬	1346	|	1402	|	▬	|	..
Kempten Hbf a.	|	...	1025k	1026	1046	...	...	1126	1128	...	|	1221	1226	1246	...	...	1326	1328	...	|	1421v	1426	1446	...	1509	..
Kempten Hbf d.	|	...	...	1031	1047	...	...	...	1131	...	|	...	1231	1247	...	...	...	1331	...	|	...	1431	1447	...	1511	..
Immenstadt a.	|	...	...	1045	1102	⊠	...	...	1145	...	|	...	1245	1302	⊠	...	...	1345	⊠	|	...	1445	1502	⊠	1527	..
Immenstadt d.	|	...	...	1052	1115	1107	...	...	1151	1150	|	...	1251	1319	1307	...	...	1351	1350	|	...	1451	1514	1507	1542	..
Sonthofen d.	|	...	...	1102	1123	|	...	...	1201	|	|	...	1301	1330	|	...	...	1401	|	|	...	1501	1522	|	1552	..
Oberstdorf a.	|	...	...	1120	1140	|	...	...	1219	|	|	...	1319	1348	|	...	...	1419	|	|	...	1519	1539	|	1611	..
Hergatz **937** d.	1059	...	...	...	...	1154	...	...	...	1236	1259	...	...	...	1353	...	...	...	1445	|	...	...	...	1559	...	..
Wangen (Allgäu) **937** a.	|	...	...	...	...	|	...	...	...	|	|	...	...	...	|	...	...	...	|	|	...	...	...	|	...	..
Lindau Hbf **937** a.	1116	...	...	...	...	1209	...	...	...	1251	1316	...	...	...	1408	...	...	...	1500	1447	...	...	...	1614	...	..

			⊠	ALX			ALX	⊠	RE 2013 A 🍷	◐				⊠		EC 192 ♥	Ⓐe	Ⓒz	Ⓐe	Ⓒz	ALX Ⓐe	◐	ALX Ⓒz			
München Hbf ⊡ d.	1353	...	...	1420	1452	...	1519	...	...	...	...	1552	...	...	1620	1633	...	1652	1652	...	1713	...	1719	...	1752	18
München Pasing d.	1400	...	...	1427	1459	...	1527	...	...	...	...	1559	...	...	1627	|	...	1659	1659	...	1720	...	1727	...	1759	18
Geltendorf d.	1422	...	...	1449	1522	...	|	...	...	...	...	1622	...	...	1649	|	...	1722	1722	...	|	...	|	...	1822	18
Kaufering d.	1432	...	...	1459	1531	...	1555	...	...	...	...	1632	...	...	1659	|	...	1731	1732	...	1750	...	1755	...	1832	18
Nürnberg Hbf **905** d.	|	...	...	|	|	...	|	...	...	...	...	|	...	...	|	|	...	|	|	...	|	...	|	...	|	|
Augsburg Hbf d.	|	1430	...	|	|	1503	|	...	...	1530	1615	|	1630	...	|	|	1703	|	|	1703	|	1729	|	1815	|	|
Buchloe a.	1441	1451	...	1508	1538	1535c	1603	...	...	1559c	1643	1641	1651	...	1708	1715	1735	1738	1741	1735c	1759	1759c	1803	1843	1841	19
Buchloe d.	1446	1454	...	1511	1539	1547	1605	...	...	1606	...	1646	1654	...	1709	1717	1736	1739	1742	1747	1802	1806	1805	▬	1846	19
Kaufbeuren d.	1459	1506	...	|	1553	1600	1618	...	...	|	...	1659	1706	...	|	|	1749	1753	1756	1800	1816	|	1818	...	1859	|
Biessenhofen d.	1505	|	...	|	1600	1606	|	...	...	|	...	1705	|	...	|	|	1806t	1801	1801	1806	|	|	|	...	1905	|
Marktoberdorf d.	1515	|	...	|	|	1616	|	...	...	|	...	1715	|	...	|	|	1816	|	|	1818	|	|	|	...	1915	|
Füssen a.	1557	|	...	|	|	1655	|	...	...	|	...	1756	|	...	|	|	1855	|	|	1856	|	|	|	...	1955	|
Türkheim (Bay) d.	▬	|	...	1518	|	▬	|	...	...	1614	...	...	|	...	1716	|	...	|	|	▬	|	1814	|	...	▬	19
Mindelheim d.	...	|	...	1530	|	...	|	...	...	1635t	...	...	|	...	1735t	|	...	|	|	...	|	1830	|	...	...	19
Ulm Hbf d.	1419	|	...	|	|	1519	|	...	1615	|	...	...	|	...	|	|	...	|	|	1717	|	|	|	...	1819	|
Memmingen a.	1455	|	...	1551	|	1555	|	...	1643	1655	...	...	|	...	1755	1745	...	|	|	1757	|	1851	|	...	1855	19
Memmingen **937** d.	1504	|	...	1554	|	1602	|	...	1645	...	...	...	|	...	...	1746	...	|	|	1801	|	...	|	...	1902	20
Kempten Hbf a.	1526	1528	...	|	1622	1626	1646	...	1707	...	...	...	1728	...	...	|	...	1823	1829	1825	1846	...	1846	...	1927	|
Kempten Hbf d.	...	1531	...	|	...	1631	1647	...	1709	...	...	...	1731	...	...	|	...	...	...	1832	1847	...	1847	...	1931	|
Immenstadt a.	...	1545	...	|	...	1645	1702	...	1724	...	...	...	1745	...	...	|	...	...	...	1846	1902	...	1902	⊠	1945	◇
Immenstadt d.	...	1551	1550	|	...	1651	1714	1707	1740	...	...	...	1751	1750	...	|	...	...	...	1852	1915	...	1915	1907	1951	|
Sonthofen d.	...	1601	|	|	...	1701	1722	|	1752	...	...	...	1801	|	...	|	...	...	...	1902	1923	...	1923	|	2001	|
Oberstdorf a.	...	1619	|	|	...	1719	1739	|	1813	...	...	...	1819	|	...	|	...	...	...	1920	1940	...	1940	|	2019	|
Hergatz **937** d.	...	...	1636	1659	...	...	...	1753	...	...	...	...	...	1845	...	|	...	...	...	...	...	...	...	1953	...	21
Wangen (Allgäu) **937** a.	...	...	|	|	...	...	...	|	...	...	...	...	...	|	...	|	...	...	...	...	...	...	...	|	...	21
Lindau Hbf **937** a.	...	...	1651	1716	...	...	...	1808	...	...	...	...	...	1901	...	1847	...	...	...	...	...	...	...	2009	...	21

A – ALLGÄU – 🚃12 (*IC* **2013**) Hannover - Dortmund - Köln - Stuttgart - Ulm (*RE* **2013**) - Oberstdorf.
H – NEBELHORN – 🚃12 Hamburg (**2083**) - Augsburg (**2085**) - Oberstdorf.
R – ⑤–⑦ (also Aug. 15, Oct. 3).

c – Connects with train in preceding column.
e – Ⓐ (not Aug. 15).
h – Change trains at Hergatz.
k – On Ⓒ (also Aug. 15) Buchloe a. 0938, d. 0939, Kaufbeuren d. 0953, Kempten a. 1022.
r – Not Aug. 15.

t – Arrives 7 – 12 minutes earlier.
v – 2 – 3 minutes later on Ⓐ (not Aug. 15).
z – Also Aug. 15.

★ – Change trains at Immenstadt on Ⓐ (not Aug. 15).
‡ – Runs daily from Kempten.
⊠ – By 🚌 Immenstadt - Oberstaufen (20 minutes from Immenstadt), then train.
♥ – 🚃12 and ✕ München - Bregenz - St Gallen - Zürich (Table **75**).

◐ – Conveys 🚃12 Augsburg - Türkheim - Bad Wörisho (see panel below).
◇ – Via Kißlegg (Table **937**).
♣ – Additional journeys Türkheim - Bad Wörishofen: 0525 Ⓐ **e**, 0559 Ⓐ **e**, 0627 Ⓐ **e**, 0726 Ⓐ **e** and 2247
⊡ – Most trains in Table **935** use platforms 27 – 36 at München Hbf (minimum connecting time from other services is 10 minutes).

ALX – Operated by Vogtlandbahn. 🍷.

AUGSBURG - TÜRKHEIM - BAD WÖRISHOFEN

km		Ⓐe	Ⓒz																					R		
0	**Augsburg** Hbf d.	...	...	...	...	...	0930	...	...	1130	...	...	1330	...	...	1530	...	...	1729	...	...	1930	...	...	2131	...	23
40	Buchloe d.	...	...	...	...	...	1006	...	...	1206	...	...	1406	...	...	1606	...	...	1806	...	...	2006	...	...	2209	...	00
48	Türkheim (Bay) ♣ d.	0658	0702	0816	0847	0920	1017	1047	1120	1217	1247	1320	1417	1447	1520	1617	1647	1719	1817	1847	1920	2017	2047	2121	2219	2321	00
53	**Bad Wörishofen** ♣ a.	0704	0708	0822	0853	0926	1023	1053	1126	1223	1253	1326	1423	1453	1526	1623	1653	1725	1823	1853	1926	2023	2053	2128	2226	2328	00

RB services except where shown MÜNCHEN, AUGSBURG and ULM - OBERSTDORF and LINDAU 935

ICE UNTIL OCTOBER 20. For services to / from Bad Wörishofen see panel at foot of page (also on page 444). For regional services Memmingen - Lindau (via Kißlegg) see Table **937**.

				EC			*ALX*									*ALX*								*ALX*		
		⊠	⊠	**190**									⊠				⊠			⑤–⑦	⑤–⑦					
		R	S	♥				◐							◐					R	R				◐	
hen Hbf ⊡ d.	...	...	...	1833	1852	...	1919	...	...	1952	2020	...	...	...	...	2119	...	...	...	...	...	2220	...	2319	...	0001
hen Pasing d.	...	...	...	│	1859	...	1927	...	...	1959	2027	...	...	...	...	2127	...	...	...	...	...	2227	...	2327	...	0008
ndorf d.	...	...	...	│	1922	...	│	...	...	2022	2050	...	...	...	...	2148	...	...	...	...	...	2249	...	2348	...	0030
ring d.	...	...	...	│	1931	...	1955	...	...	2032	2101	...	...	...	...	2158	...	...	...	...	...	2259	...	2358	...	0040
nberg Hbf **905** d.	1732	...	...	│	│	...	│	...	...	│	│	...	...	...	...	│	...	...	...	...	...	│	...	│	...	│
gsburg Hbf d.	1844	...	...	│	│	1903	│	1930	2015	│	│	2050	...	...	2131	│	...	...	2233	2233	...	│	...	│	2331	│
oe a.	1904	...	...	1915	1939	1935**c**	2003	1959**c**	2043	2041	2110	2109	...	...	2203	2206**c**	...	...	2305	2305	...	2307**c**	...	0006	0003**c**	0049
oe d.	1911	...	...	1917	1941	1947	2005	2006	▬	2050	2112	2114	...	...	2209	2207	...	...	2310	2310	...	2312	...	0007	0009	...
ufbeuren d.	1923	...	...	│	1954	2000	2018	│	...	2103	│	2125	...	...	│	2221	...	2227	2321	2321	2329	│	...	0020	│	...
ssenhofen d.	│	...	...	│	2000	2006	│	│	...	2109	│	2130	...	...	│	│	...	2236	2325	2325	2334	│	...	0025	│	...
arktoberdorf d.	│	...	...	│	│	2016	│	│	...	2120	│	│	...	...	│	│	...	2246	│	│	2346	│	...	│	│	...
üssen a.	│	...	...	│	│	2055	│	│	...	2200	│	│	...	...	│	│	...	2326	│	│	0026	│	...	│	│	...
eim (Bay) d.	│	...	...	│	│	▬	│	2014	...	▬	2119	│	...	...	2217	│	...	▬	│	│	▬	2319	...	│	0017	...
elheim d.	│	...	...	│	│	...	│	2030	...	...	2130	│	...	...	2230	│	...	...	│	│	...	2330	...	│	0027	...
n Hbf d.	│	...	...	│	│	1919	│	│	...	2019	│	│	...	2119	│	│	...	2221	│	│	...	│	2323	│	│	...
mingen a.	│	...	...	1945	│	1955	│	2051	...	2056	2151	│	...	2159	2251	│	...	2254	│	│	...	2352	0003	│	0047	...
mingen **937** d.	│	...	...	1946	│	2003	│	▬	...	2105	...	│	...	2200	...	│	...	2256	│	│	...	...	0004	│	...	...
mpten Hbf a.	1946	...	...	│	2025	2028	2046	...	...	2129	...	2152	...	2230	...	2250	...	2320	2347	2347	...	...	0029	0052	...	...
mpten Hbf d.	1949	...	...	│	...	...	2048	⊠	⊠	...	...	2154	...	...	...	2254	...	2324	...	2349	⊠	...	...	...	...	...
nenstadt a.	2003	...	...	│	...	...	2103	**R**	**S**	...	...	2208	...	...	...	2309	...	2340	...	0003	**T**	...	...	...	...	...
nenstadt d.	2015	2008	2008	│	...	...	*2111*	2108	2108	...	...	2214	2213	...	...	...	2315	2346	...	...	0008	...	...	...	...	...
onthofen d.	2025	│	│	│	...	...	*2121*	│	│	...	...	2224	│	...	...	...	│	2356	...	...	│	...	...	...	...	...
berstdorf a.	2049	│	│	│	...	...	*2139*	│	│	...	...	2242	│	...	...	...	│	0014	...	...	│	...	...	...	...	...
atz **937** d.	...	2056	2055	│	...	...	...	2154	2153	...	...	...	2312	...	...	...	0006	...	...	...	0054	...	...	...	...	...
ngen (Allgäu) **937** a.	...	│	│	│	...	...	...	│	│	...	...	...	│	...	...	...	│	...	...	...	│	...	...	...	...	...
au Hbf **937** a.	...	2111	*2121*	2047	...	...	...	2209	*2226*	...	...	...	2327	...	...	...	0021	...	...	...	0109	...	...	...	...	...

km																									
			ALX											*ALX*											
												❖			❖								❖		
		Ⓐe	⚒r	Ⓐe		Ⓐe		Ⓐe	Ⓐ	Ⓐe						t	⚒r	⚒r	†z	†z		†z			
	Lindau Hbf **937** d.	...	...	...	...	...	...	...	...	...	...	...	0505	...	...	0556	...	...	...	...	...	...	0707	0658	...
	Wangen (Allgäu) **937** d.	...	...	...	...	...	...	...	...	...	...	...	│	...	...	│	...	...	...	...	...	...	0730	│	...
	Hergatz **937** d.	...	...	...	...	...	...	...	...	...	...	...	0519	...	...	0611	...	...	...	...	...	...	0724	0715	...
0	**Oberstdorf** d.	...	...	...	...	...	...	...	0501	...	...	...	│	...	0542	│	0622	...	...	0631	...	...	│	│	0734**f**
13	Sonthofen d.	...	...	...	...	...	...	...	0520	...	...	...	│	...	0601	│	0641	...	...	0654	...	...	│	│	0801
21	Immenstadt a.	...	...	...	...	...	...	...	0529	...	...	...	0618	...	0610**c**	0658	0650	...	...	0706	...	...	◇	0811	0810
21	Immenstadt d.	...	...	...	...	...	...	...	0536	...	...	...	▬	0623	0629		0703	...	...	0717	...	...	│	...	0816
42	**Kempten** Hbf a.	...	...	...	...	...	...	...	0552	...	...	...	...	0638	0646	...	0717	...	...	0731	...	...	│	...	0829
42	**Kempten** Hbf d.	...	0446	...	0529	0521	0548	...	0556	0601	...	...	...	0641	0648	...	0722	...	...	0732	0732**k**	0734	│	...	0832
77	Memmingen **937** a.	...	│	...	0554	│	│	...	0620	│	...	...	Ⓐe	0708	│	...	│	...	...	0801	0801	│	0813	...	│
77	Memmingen d.	0451	│	0525	0556	│	│	0552	0622	│	0626	...	0647	0710	│	...	│	0739	0739	0804	0804	│	0817	...	│
129	**Ulm** Hbf a.	│	│	│	0643	│	│	│	0719	│	│	...	│	0743	│	...	│	│	│	0839	0839	│	│	...	│
	Mindelheim d.	0513	│	0548	▬	│	│	0613	▬	│	0648	...	0713	...	│	...	│	0800	0800	▬	▬	│	0836	...	│
	Türkheim (Bay) d.	0521	│	0557	Ⓐe	│	│	0622	...	│	0656**d**	...	0722	...	│	...	│	0810	0809	Ⓒz	Ⓐe	│	0844	...	│
	Füssen d.	│	│	│	0452	│	│	│	...	│	│	0600	│	...	│	...	│	│	│	0702	0704	│	│	...	│
	Marktoberdorf d.	│	│	│	0534	│	│	│	...	│	│	0644	│	...	│	...	│	│	│	0746	0749	│	│	...	│
	Biessenhofen d.	│	0513	│	0542	0548	0614	│	...	0627	│	0652	│	...	│	...	0745	│	│	0754	0757	0801	│	...	│
	Kaufbeuren d.	│	0519	│	0547	0553	0619	│	...	0634	│	0657	│	...	0717	...	0751	│	│	0759	0802	0807	│	...	0856
	Buchloe a.	0528	0530**c**	0604	...	0605**c**	0632	0629**c**	...	0647	0704**d**	0709**c**	0729	...	0730**c**	...	0802	0817	0817	0812**c**	0815**c**	0818**c**	0851	...	0907
	Buchloe d.	0535	0532	0609	...	0607	0633	0640	0648	0648	0712	0712	0739	...	0732	...	0805	0820	0824	0824	0824	0819	0853	...	0909
	Augsburg Hbf a.	0607	│	│	...	0640	│	0712	0716	0718	│	0744	0811	...	│	...	0829	│	0856	0856	0856	│	│	...	0930
	Nürnberg Hbf **905** a.	...	│	│	...	...	│	...	...	...	│	...	...	...	│	...	0953	│	...	...	...	│	│	...	...
	Kaufering d.	...	0541	0617	...	...	0641	...	...	...	0720	...	...	...	0741	...	...	0829	...	...	...	0828	0901	...	...
	Geltendorf d.	...	│	0628	...	...	0650	...	...	...	0730	...	...	...	│	...	...	0838	...	...	...	0837	0910	...	...
	München Pasing a.	...	0610	0650	...	...	0711	...	...	...	0756	...	...	...	0809	...	...	0857	...	...	...	0856	0933	...	...
	München Hbf ⊡ a.	...	0618	0658	...	...	0718	...	...	...	0804	...	...	...	0819	...	...	0904	...	...	...	0905	0941	...	...

				ALX			*EC*						*IC*	*IC*		*ALX*			*ALX*	*EC*						*ALX*
		❖	❖				**191**		❖				**2084**	**2012**	❖					**193**	❖				❖	
		Ⓐe	Ⓒz				♥						**H**	**A** 🍷						♥						
au Hbf **937** d.	...	*0741*h	0752	...	...	...	0912	...	0902	...	...	...	...	...	0954	...	...	...	1040	1112	1105	...	...	...	1152	...
ngen (Allgäu) **937** d.	...	0751	│	...	...	...	│	...	│	...	...	...	...	...	│	...	...	...	│	│	│	...	...	...	│	...
atz **937** d.	...	0801	0807	...	...	...	│	...	0917	...	...	...	...	...	1008	...	...	...	1059	│	1119	...	...	...	1207	...
berstdorf d.	...	│	│	0822	0837	...	│	0904	│	...	...	...	0940	0948	│	1024	1039**g**	...	│	│	│	1142	...	...	│	1222
onthofen d.	...	│	│	0839	0901	...	│	0931	│	...	...	...	1001	1012	│	1041	1102	...	│	│	│	1201	...	...	│	1239
nenstadt a.	...	0855	0855	0847	0910	...	│	0940	1011	...	...	...	1009**c**	1021	1055	1049	1111	...	│	│	1211	1210	...	...	1255	1247
nenstadt d.	...	▬	▬	0900	0917	...	│	▬	...	1016	...	...	1027	1036	▬	1100	1117	...	│	│	▬	1216	...	...	▬	1300
mpten Hbf a.	...	...	...	0914	0931	...	│	...	...	1029	...	...	1043	1052	...	1114	1131	...	│	│	...	1229	...	...	...	1314
mpten Hbf d.	0835	...	...	0916	0934	0941	│	...	...	1032	...	...	1045	1055	...	1116	1134	1141	│	│	...	1232	1235	...	...	1316
mingen **937** a.	0857	...	◧	│	0958	│	1013	...	...	│	...	...	│	1123	◧	│	1158	│	1153	1213	*ALX*	│	1257	...	◧	│
mingen d.	0904	...	0907	│	1002	│	1015	1005	...	│	...	...	│	1127	1107	│	1204	│	1205	1215		│	1304	...	1307	│
n Hbf a.	0939	...	│	│	1039	│	│	│	...	│	...	...	│	1155	│	│	1239	│	│	│	←	│	1339	...	│	│
elheim d.	▬	...	0932	│	▬	│	│	1037**j**	...	│	...	...	│	...	1132	│	▬	│	1226	│	1237	│	▬	...	1332	│
eim (Bay) d.	...	...	0946	│	...	│	│	1045	...	│	...	...	│	...	1146	│	...	│	→	│	1245	│	...	...	1346	│
üssen d.	0806	...	│	│	0905	│	│	│	...	│	1006	...	│	...	│	│	1105	│	...	│	│	│	1206	...	│	│
arktoberdorf d.	0849	...	│	│	0949	│	│	│	...	│	1049	...	│	...	│	│	1147	│	...	│	│	│	1249	...	│	│
ssenhofen d.	0858	...	│	│	0957	1005	│	│	...	│	1058	...	│	...	│	│	1156	1205	...	│	│	│	1258	...	│	│
ufbeuren d.	0903	...	│	0943	1002	1010	│	│	...	1056	1103	...	1115	...	│	1143	1201	1210	...	│	│	1256	1303	...	│	1343
oe a.	0915	...	0952	0954**c**	1016	1021**c**	1041	1052	...	1107	1115	...	1129	...	1152	1154**c**	1213	1221**c**	...	1241	1252	1307	1315	...	1352	1354**c**
oe d.	0918	0918	1000	0955	1024	1022	1043	1053	...	1109	1118	1118	1131	...	1200	1155	1224	1222	...	1243	1253	1309	1318	1318	1400	1355
gsburg Hbf a.	│	0945	1029	│	1056	│	│	│	...	1130	│	1145	1156	...	1229	│	1256	│	...	│	│	1330	│	1345	1429	│
nberg Hbf **905** a.	│	...	...	│	...	│	│	│	...	...	│	...	...	...	...	│	...	│	...	│	│	...	│	...	...	│
ering d.	0928	...	...	1003	..	1029	│	1101	...	...	1128	...	...	...	...	1203	...	1230	...	│	1301	...	1328	...	...	1403
ndorf d.	0937	...	...	│	...	1038	│	1110	...	...	1137	...	...	...	...	│	...	1238	...	│	1310	...	1337	...	...	│
hen Pasing a.	0958	...	...	1033	...	1058	│	1133	...	...	1158	...	...	...	...	1233	...	1258	...	│	1333	...	1357	...	...	1433
chen Hbf ⊡ a.	1005	...	...	1041	...	1105	1128	1141	...	...	1205	...	...	...	...	1241	...	1305	...	1328	1341	...	1404	...	...	1441

ALLGÄU – [12] Oberstdorf - Stuttgart - Köln - Hannover.
NEBELHORN – [12] Oberstdorf - Augsburg (**2082**) - Hamburg.
⑤–⑦ (also Aug. 15, Oct. 3).
①–④ (not Aug. 15, Oct. 3).
①⑥⑦ (also Aug. 16, Oct. 4).
Change trains at Buchloe on ⑥.
Connects with train in preceding column.
2–3 minutes later on Ⓒ (also Aug. 15).

e – Ⓐ (not Aug. 15).
f – 0739 on Ⓒ (also Aug. 15).
g – 1044 on Ⓐ (not Aug. 15).
h – Change trains at Hergatz.
j – Arrives 1026.
k – 0734 on Ⓐ.
r – Not Aug. 15.
t – 7–9 minutes **earlier** on Ⓒ**z**.
z – Also Aug. 15.
◇ – Via Kißlegg (Table **937**).

⊠ – By 🚌 Immenstadt - Oberstaufen (20 minutes from Immenstadt), then train.
❖ – By train to Oberstaufen, then 🚌 to Immenstadt (🚌 departs Oberstaufen 20 minutes before Immenstadt).
◐ – Conveys [12] Augsburg - Türkheim - Bad Wörishofen (see panel on page 444).
◧ – Conveys [12] Bad Wörishofen - Türkheim - Augsburg (see panel below).
♥ – [12] and ✕ München - Bregenz - St Gallen - Zürich and v.v. (Table **75**).
♣ – Additional journeys Bad Wörishofen - Türkheim: 0611 Ⓐ**e**, 0709 Ⓐ**e**, 0758 Ⓐ**e** and 2308 **R**.
⊡ – Most trains in Table **935** use platforms 27–36 at München Hbf (minimum connecting time from / to other services is 10 minutes).
ALX – Operated by Vogtlandbahn. 🍷.

BAD WÖRISHOFEN - TÜRKHEIM - AUGSBURG

	Ⓐe	Ⓐe		Ⓒz																						R	
Wörishofen ♣ d.	0510	0544	0645	0739	0833	0907	0932	1034	1107	1132	1234	1302	1332	1428	1507	1532	1634	1705	1731	1828	1905	1932	2028	2108	2133	2231	2343
eim (Bay) ♣ a.	0517	0551	0652	0746	0840	0914	0939	1041	1114	1139	1241	1309	1339	1435	1514	1539	1641	1712	1737	1835	1912	1939	2035	2115	2139	2238	2349
oe a.	...	...	...	0753	...	...	0952	...	...	1152	...	...	1352	...	...	1552	...	...	1752	...	...	1952	...	...	2152	...	0002
burg Hbf a.	...	...	...	0829**b**	...	...	1029	...	...	1229	...	...	1429	...	...	1629	...	...	1829	...	...	2029	...	...	2245	...	0049

935 LINDAU and OBERSTDORF - ULM, AUGSBURG and MÜNCHEN

RE / RB services except where sh

SERVICE UNTIL OCTOBER 20. For services from / to Bad Wörishofen see pages 444 and 445. For regional services Lindau - Memmingen (via Kißlegg) see Table **937**.

	©z			©z	❖				❖	*ALX*				*EC* 195 ♥	❖				❖	*ALX*	◧		©z		Ⓐe
Lindau Hbf **937** d.	...	...	...	1240	1309	...	...	...	1353	...	...	...	1440e	1512	1505	...	...	...	1549	...	...	...	...	...	...
Wangen (Allgäu) **937** d.	...	...	...	|	|	...	...	...	|	...	...	...	...	|	|	...	...	...	|	...	...	...	...	...	...
Hergatz **937** d.	...	...	...	1259	1324	...	...	...	1407	...	...	...	1459e	|	1520	...	...	...	1603	...	...	...	...	...	...
Oberstdorf d.	...	1237f	...	|	|	1334	...	...	|	1422	1442	...	|	|	|	1540	...	...	|	1622	...	1637	...	...	1704
Sonthofen d.	...	1301	...	|	|	1401	...	...	|	1439	1501	...	|	|	|	1601	...	...	|	1639	...	1701	...	...	1730
Immenstadt a.	...	1310	...	|	1411	1410	...	...	1455	1447	1510	...	|	|	1611	1610	...	...	1655	1647	...	1710	...	...	1739
Immenstadt d.	...	1317	...	|	▬	1416	...	...	▬	1500	1517	...	|	|	▬	1616	...	...	▬	1700	...	1717	...	...	1749
Kempten Hbf a.	...	1331	...	|	...	1429	...	...	...	1514	1531	...	|	|	...	1629	...	...	...	1714	...	1731	...	...	1803
Kempten Hbf d.	...	1334	1341	|	...	1432	1435	...	...	1516	1534	1541	|	|	...	1632	1635	...	...	1716	...	1734	1736	...	1809
Memmingen **937** a.	...	1359	|	1345	...	|	1456	...	◧	|	1558	|	1545e	1613	...	|	1704	...	...	|	...	1759	|	...	|
Memmingen d.	...	1404	|	1408	1408	|	1504	...	1507	|	1602	|	1605	1615	...	|	1705	...	...	|	1707	1804	|	...	|
Ulm Hbf a.	...	1439	|	|	|	|	1539	...	|	|	1641	|	|	|	←	|	1739	...	...	|	|	1840	|	...	|
Mindelheim d.	...	▬	|	1430	1430	|	▬	...	1532	|	▬	|	1626	|	1637	|	▬	...	...	|	1731	▬	|	...	|
Türkheim (Bay) d.	...	Ⓐe	|	1439	1439	|	...	...	1546	|	...	|	→	|	1645	|	...	...	†w	|	1746	...	|	...	|
Füssen d.	1305	1305	|	|	|	|	1406	...	|	|	1505	|	...	|	|	|	1606	...	1634	|	|	1705	|	...	|
Marktoberdorf d.	1347	1351	|	|	|	|	1449	...	|	|	1548t	|	...	|	|	|	1649	...	1718	|	|	1749	|	...	|
Biessenhofen d.	1356	1359	1405	|	|	|	1458	...	|	|	1557t	1605	...	|	|	|	1658	...	|	|	|	1757	1804	...	1831
Kaufbeuren d.	1401	1404	1410	|	|	1456	1503	...	|	1543	1602t	1610	...	|	|	1656	1703	...	|	1743	|	1803	1809	...	1836
Buchloe a.	1413	1417	1421c	1445	1445	1507	1515	...	1552	1554c	1614t	1621c	...	1641	1652	1707	1715	...	|	1754	1752c	1815	1820c	...	1848
Buchloe d.	1424	1424	1422	1453	1453	1509	1518	1518	1600	1555	1624	1622	...	1643	1653	1709	1718	1719	|	1755	1800	1824	1821	1821	1849
Augsburg Hbf a.	1456	1456	|	|	|	1530	|	1545	1629	|	1656	|	...	|	|	1730	|	1746	|	|	1829	1856	|	|	1914
Nürnberg Hbf **905** a.	...	...	|	|	|	...	|	...	...	|	...	|	...	|	|	1848k	|	...	|	|	...	...	|	|	2028
Kaufering d.	...	...	1430	1501	1501	...	1528	...	...	1603	...	1629	...	|	1701	...	1728	...	|	1803	...	...	1830	1830	...
Geltendorf d.	...	...	1438	1510	1510	...	1537	...	...	|	...	1638	...	|	1710	...	1737	...	|	|	...	...	1840	1840	...
München Pasing a.	...	...	1458	1533	1533	...	1558	...	...	1633	...	1658	...	|	1733	...	1758	...	1811	1833	...	...	1910	1910	...
München Hbf ⊡ a.	...	...	1508	1541	1541	...	1605	...	...	1641	...	1705	...	1728	1741	...	1805	...	1820	1841	...	...	1917	1917	...

	❖	†w	⑥		Ⓐe	❖	*ALX*		*ALX*	❖			❖	*ALX*	◧	*EC* 197 ♥			⑤–⑦ R❖		◧	⑤–⑦ R❖	*ALX*		❖
Lindau Hbf **937** d.	1659	...	...	...	...	1753	...	...	1840	1849	...	...	1947	...	...	2015	...	...	2049	...	...	2158	...	...	2250
Wangen (Allgäu) **937** d.	|	...	...	...	...	|	...	...	|	|	...	...	|	...	...	|	...	...	|	...	...	|	...	...	|
Hergatz **937** d.	1713	...	...	...	...	1807	...	...	1858	1903	...	...	2001	...	...	|	...	...	2106	...	...	2212	...	...	2304
Oberstdorf d.	|	1725	1740	...	1740	|	1823	1838	|	|	1906	1942	|	2020	...	|	...	2102	|	...	...	|	*2228*	...	|
Sonthofen d.	|	1750	1801	...	1801	|	1840	1902	|	|	1933	2001	|	2037	...	|	...	2121	|	...	...	|	*2252*	...	|
Immenstadt a.	1802	1801	1810	...	1810	1855	1848	1911	|	1951	1942	2010	2050	2045	...	|	...	2130	2152	...	...	2301	*2301*	...	2358
Immenstadt d.	▬	1807	1817	...	1817	▬	1900	1917	|	...	1956	2017	▬	2055	...	|	...	2136	▬	2157R	...	▬	2306	...	...
Kempten Hbf a.	...	1821	1831	...	1831	...	1914	1931	|	...	2010	2031	...	2109	...	|	...	2150	...	2211R	...	...	2323	...	...
Kempten Hbf d.	...	1829	1836	1834	1834	...	1916	1934	|	...	2012	2034	...	2113	...	|	...	2155	...	2212	...	...	2325	2334	...
Memmingen **937** a.	...	|	|	1856	1856	◧	|	1959	1945	...	|	2058	...	|	...	2120	...	2221	...	|	...	...	|	2400	...
Memmingen d.	1807	|	|	1904	1904	1907	|	2004	2008	...	|	2105	...	|	2108	2126	2208	2227	...	|	2317	...	|	0004	...
Ulm Hbf a.	|	|	|	1939	1939	|	|	2039	|	...	|	2155b	...	|	|	|	|	2315	...	|	|	...	|	0045	...
Mindelheim d.	1830	|	|	▬	▬	1932	|	▬	2030	...	...	...	...	...	2132	|	2233	...	⑤–⑦	|	2343	...	|	▬	...
Türkheim (Bay) d.	1838	|	|	...	...	1946	|	...	2039	...	...	...	...	...	2146	|	2241	...	R	|	2356	...	|	...	...
Füssen d.	|	|	|	1806	...	|	|	1905	|	...	|	...	2033	|	|	|	|	...	2111	|	|	2238	|	...	...
Marktoberdorf d.	|	|	|	1849	...	|	|	1948	|	...	|	...	2118	|	|	|	|	...	2153	|	|	2320	|	...	...
Biessenhofen d.	|	|	|	1858	...	|	|	1956	|	...	|	...	2126	|	|	|	|	...	2201	2233	|	2329	2351	...	...
Kaufbeuren d.	|	1852	1858	1903	...	|	1943	2010j	|	...	2038	...	2132	2141	|	|	|	...	2206	2238	|	2334	2356	...	...
Buchloe a.	1845c	1902	1909	1915	...	1952	1954c	2022	2045	...	2048c	...	...	2153	2152c	2203c	2248	...	...	2248c	0002	...	0008	←	...
Buchloe d.	1851	1903	1910	1918	1918	2000	1955	2024	2052	...	2052	...	...	2155	2215	2205	2251	...	...	2253	→	...	0009	0016	...
Augsburg Hbf a.	|	1922	1930	|	1945	2029	|	2056	|	...	2121h	...	...	|	2245	|	|	...	...	2321	...	...	|	0049	...
Nürnberg Hbf **905** a.	|	...	...	|	...	...	|	...	...	...	2232z	...	...	|	...	|	|	...	...	...	...	...	...	...	...
Kaufering d.	1900	...	...	1928	...	...	2003	...	2101	...	...	...	...	2203	...	|	2301	...	...	...	...	...	0017	...	...
Geltendorf d.	1910	...	...	1937	...	...	|	...	2110	...	...	...	...	|	...	|	2310	...	...	...	...	...	0027	...	...
München Pasing a.	1933	...	...	1958	...	...	2033	...	2133	...	...	...	...	2233	...	|	2333	...	...	...	...	...	0049	...	...
München Hbf ⊡ a.	1941	...	...	2005	...	...	2041	...	2141	...	...	...	...	2241	...	2245	2341	...	...	...	...	...	0057	...	...

R – ⑤–⑦ (also Aug. 15, Oct. 3).

b – 2139 on ©.
c – Connects with train in preceding column.
e – Ⓐ (not Aug. 15).
f – 1242 on ©.
h – 2116 on © (also Aug. 15).
j – Arrives 2000.

k – ⑥ only.
t – 2 minutes later on Ⓐ (not Aug. 15).
w – Also Aug. 15.
z – © (also Aug. 15).

♥ – (12) and ✕ Zürich - St Gallen - Bregenz - München (Table **75**).

◧ – Conveys (12) Bad Wörishofen - Türkheim - Augsburg (see panel on page 445).
❖ – By train to Oberstaufen, then 🚌 to Immenstadt (🚌 departs Oberstaufen 20 m before Immenstadt).
⊡ – Most trains in Table **935** use platforms 27 – 36 at München Hbf (minimum connec time to other services is 10 minutes).

ALX – Operated by Vogtlandbahn. 🍸.

936 STUTTGART - TÜBINGEN - AULENDORF

DB (*IRE / RB* services); Hz

km		Ⓐe2		2	Ⓐe2	Ⓐe	©z2		2		2		2		2		2		2		2		2	2	2
0	**Stuttgart** Hbf ☆ d.	...	...	...	...	...	...	...	...	0816	...	1016	...	1216	...	1416	...	1616	...	1816	...	2016	...	...	...
57	Reutlingen ☆ d.	...	...	...	...	...	...	0644e	...	0849	...	1049	...	1249	...	1449	...	1649	...	1849	...	2049	...	...	...
71	**Tübingen** Hbf ☆ d.	...	...	...	0546	...	0607	0658	0727	0900	0928	1100	1128	1300	1328	1500	1528	1700	1728	1900	1928	2100	2136	2236	2339
96	Hechingen d.	...	...	...	0615	...	0631	0719	0753	0920	0952	1120	1152	1320	1352	1520	1552	1720	1752	1920	1952	2120	2204	2300	0003
113	Balingen (Württ) d.	...	...	...	0637	...	0647	0733	0808	0935	1007	1135	1207	1335	1407	1535	1607r	1735	1807	1935	2007	2132	2219	2315	...
131	Albstadt-Ebingen d.	...	...	...	0655	0703	0704	0747	0832	0947	1032	1147	1232	1347	1432	1547	1632	1747	1832	1948	2032	2149	2238	2333	...
158	**Sigmaringen** a.	...	...	...	...	0725	...	0811	0856	1011	1056	1211	1256	1411	1456	1611	1656	1811	1856	2011	2056	2210	...	...	...
158	**Sigmaringen** **938** d.	0538	...	0652	...	0727	...	0812	*0903*	1012	*1103*	1212	*1303*	1412	*1503*	1612	*1703*	1812	*1903*	2013	*2105*	2215	...	...	...
175	Herbertingen **938** d.	0554	...	0708	...	0741	...	0824	*0917*	1024	*1117*	1224	*1317*	1424	*1517*	1624	*1717*	1824	*1917*	2025	*2121*	2230	...	...	...
184	Bad Saulgau d.	0608	...	0724j	...	...	...	0833	*0929*	1033	*1129*	1233	*1329*	1433	*1529*	1633	*1729*	1833	*1929*	2034	*2137*	2239	...	...	...
203	**Aulendorf** d.	0624	...	0740	...	...	...	0850	*0944*	1050	*1144*	1250	*1344*	1448	*1544*	1650	*1744*	1850	*1944*	2050	*2153*	2254	...	...	...

	2	Ⓐe	⑥2	Ⓐe2	Ⓐe2	Ⓐe2	©z2	Ⓐe2		2		2		2		2		2		2		2	A2	2	2
Aulendorf d.	...	...	...	...	0551	...	...	0632	0705	*0812*	0912	*1012*	1112	*1212*	1312	*1412*	1512	*1612*	1712	*1812*	1912	*2012*	...	2119	2203
Bad Saulgau d.	...	...	...	...	0607	...	...	0647	0721	*0833*	0928	*1033*	1128	*1233*	1328	*1433*	1528	*1633*	1728	*1833*	1928	*2033*	...	2136	2219
Herbertingen **938** d.	...	...	...	...	0616	...	...	0656	0730	*0844*	0937	*1044*	1137	*1244*	1337	*1444*	1537	*1644*	1737	*1844*	1937	*2046*	...	2145	2231
Sigmaringen **938** a.	...	...	...	...	0630	...	...	0715	0746	*0859*	0949	*1059*	1149	*1259*	1349	*1459*	1549	*1659*	1749	*1859*	1949	*2100*	...	2201	2247
Sigmaringen d.	...	0542	...	...	0633	...	...	...	0750	0903	0950	1103	1150	1305	1350	1503	1550	1703	1750	1905	1950	2105	...	...	...
Albstadt-Ebingen d.	0503	0605	0626	0633	0657	0703	0726	...	0812	0928	1011	1128	1211	1329	1411	1528	1611	1728	1811	1929	2011	2129	2254	...	...
Balingen (Württ) d.	0521	0619	0646	0700	...	0734	0751	...	0827	0952	1027	1152	1227	1352	1427	1552	1627	1752	1827	1952	2027	2148	2315	...	...
Hechingen d.	0536	0634	0701	0718	...	0752	0807	...	0839	1007	1039	1207	1239	1407	1439	1607	1639	1807	1840	2007	2039	2204	2330	...	...
Tübingen Hbf ☆ a.	0601	0652	0726	0744	...	0818	0830	...	0857	1030	1057	1230	1257	1430	1457	1630	1657	1830	1857	2030	2057	2229	2356	...	...
Reutlingen ☆ a.	...	0707	...	...	...	...	...	...	0908	...	1108	...	1308	...	1508	...	1708	...	1908	...	2108f	...	...	...	...
Stuttgart Hbf ☆ a.	...	0743h	...	...	...	...	...	...	0943h	...	1143	...	1343h	...	1543	...	1743h	...	1943	...	2143f	...	...	...	...

Other services Stuttgart - Tübingen

km		⊖	Ⓐe	©z	Ⓐe				
0	**Stuttgart** Hbf **930** d.	0048	0522	*0531*	0616	0722	0822		2322
22	Plochingen **930** d.	0107	0541	0611	0637	0742	0844	and	2344
35	Nürtingen d.	0120	0552	0622	0649	0755	0855	hourly	2355
57	Reutlingen Hbf d.	0137	0608	0641	0706	0812	0912	until	0012
71	**Tübingen** Hbf a.	0150	0619	0654	0720	0823	0923		0023

		©z	Ⓐe	©z	Ⓐe		©z	Ⓐe				
Tübingen Hbf d.	0537	0622	0625	0732	0737	0837	0932	0937	1037		2037	2136
Reutlingen Hbf d.	0547	0632	0636	0743	0748	0848	0943	0948	1048	and	2048	2150
Nürtingen d.	0604	0649	0652	0759	0804	0904	0959	1004	1104	hourly	2104	2206
Plochingen **930** d.	0618	0700	0704	0818	0818	0918	1018	1018	1118	until	2118	2218
Stuttgart Hbf **930** a.	0638	0718	0723	0838	0838	0938	1038	1038	1138		2138	2238

A – ⑤⑥ (also Oct. 2, 31).

e – Ⓐ (not Nov. 1).

f – ⑤–⑦ (also Oct. 3, 31, Nov. 1).
h – 3 minutes later July 16 - Aug. 28.
j – Arrives 0717.

r – 1611 on Ⓐ (not Nov. 1).
z – Also Nov. 1.

⊖ – Runs 9 minutes later on ①.
☆ – See panel below main table for other ser
◇ – Hohenzollerische Landesbahn.

MEMMINGEN - FRIEDRICHSHAFEN and AULENDORF 937

/ RB services; 2nd class only

	q	Ⓐe	©z							M	
Memmingen ..... **935** d.	...	0625	...	...	...	...	...	...	...	2005	2102
Leutkirch ....d.	...	0704	0725	...	...	...	...	...	...	2038	2144
Kißlegg...................d.	0541	0715	0742	0946	1145	1337	1546	1738	1943	2047	2153
Wangen (Allgäu) **935** d.	0552	0731	0754	1001	1202	1401	1601	1801	2001	2101	2204
Hergatz .... **935** d.	0557	0737	0800	1006	1207r	1406	1606	1806	2006	2106	2209
Lindau Hbf .... **935** a.	...	0754	0817	1022	1223r	1422	1623	1822	2022	2121	2226
Friedrichshafen ⊖ ..a.	...	0827	0907	1106	1306	1507	1707	1907	*2125*	*2209*	2323

	Ⓐe	⑥	M								
Friedrichshafen ⊖ d.	...	...	*0622*	0700e	*0847*	1050	1239v	1450	1650	1850	...
Lindau Hbf .... **935** d.	...	0602	0707	0741	0936	1136	1336	1538	1736	1936	*2250*‡
Hergatz .... **935** d.	0615	0618	0724	0759	0954	1155	1355	1555	1755	1955	2328
Wangen .... **935** d.	0620	0623	0730	0804	1007	1207	1402	1607	1802	2002	2333
Kißlegg ....d.	0631	0633	0741	0816	1018	1218	1413	1618	1813	2013	2346
Leutkirch ....d.	0640	0642	0750	...	...	...	...	...	...	...	2355
Memmingen .. **935** a.	0707	0707	0813	...	...	...	...	...	...	...	...

	Ⓐe	⑥	©z	Ⓐe	r									Ⓐe		
Memmingen .. d.	...	...	...	...	...	0900	1100	...	1300	...	1500	...	1700	...	1900	...
Leutkirch .... d.	0540	0622	K	L	...	0924	1124	...	1324	...	1524	...	1724	1815	1924	...
Kißlegg........... d.	0550	0636	0712	0717	0822	0934	1134	1226	1334	1426	1534	1626	1734	1827	1934	2050
Bad Waldsee.. d.	0615	0652	0731	0733	0840	0950	1150	1242	1350	1444	1550	1642	1750	1843	1950	2106
Aulendorf ...... a.	0623	0700	0739	0741	0848	0958	1158	1250	1358	1452	1558	1650	1758	1851	1958	2114

	ⒶeJ	©z				©z	©D	Ⓐt							Ⓐe		H
endorf .... d.	0554	0708	0759e	0906	1002	1108	1202	1202	1308	1402	1508	1602	1708	1802	1906	2004	2201
Waldsee ... d.	0609	0716	0807e	0914	1009	1116	1209	1209	1316	1409	1516	1609	1716	1809	1914	2012	2209
egg .... d.	0627	0736	0825	0931	1026	1131	1226	1226	1331	1426	1531	1626	1731	1826	1931	2028	2227
kirch.......... d.	...	...	0833	...	1035	...	1235	1246	...	1435	...	1635	...	1835	...	2037	...
mmingen.... a.	...	...	0859	...	1059	...	1259	1316	...	1459	...	1659	...	1859	...	2101	...

D – Daily July 28 - Sept. 11 and Oct. 29 - Nov. 6.
H – To Wangen (a. 2242) and Hergatz (a. 2247).
J – To Wangen (a. 0643) and Hergatz (a. 0648).
K – From Hergatz (d. 0650) and Wangen (d. 0655).
L – From Hergatz (d. 0656) and Wangen (d. 0701).
M – 12 München - Lindau and v.v. (Table 935).

e – Ⓐ (not Nov. 1).
q – 12 minutes later on Ⓐe.
r – 3–4 minutes later on Ⓐe.
t – Not July 28 - Sept. 9, Oct. 31 - Nov. 4.
v – 1250 on ©D.

z – © (also Nov. 1).
‡ – *2310* from Oct. 21.
⊖ – **Friedrichshafen Stadt**. See also Tables **933/9**.

ULM and ROTTWEIL - NEUSTADT (Schwarzw) - FREIBURG 938

(RE / RB services); HzL ◇

	©z	Ⓐe2	Ⓐe2		2	Ⓐe	©z													†v2	2		2	2
Ulm Hbf ....d.	...	...	...	...	...	0600	0604	...	0817k	0915	1016	1116	1216	1316	1416	1516	1616	1716	1817	1917	1917	2017	2117	2217
Blaubeuren ....d.	...	...	...	...	...	0613	0616	...	0829k	0926	1028	1128	1228	1328	1428	1528	1628	1727	1829	1928	1928	2029	2133	2233
Ehingen (Donau) ....d.	...	...	...	...	...	0630	0630	...	0842	0938	1044	1140	1244	1340	1444	1540	1644	1741	1844	1940	1940	2045	2149	2248
Herbertingen .... **937** d.	...	...	...	...	...	0709	0709	...	0917	1007	1117	1208	1317	1408	1517	1608	1717	1808	1918	2009	2009	2122	2218	2320
Sigmaringen .... **937** a.	...	...	...	...	...	0724	0724	...	0931	1027	1131	1227	1331	1427	1531	1627	1731	1827	1931	2028	2028	2135	2233	2335
Sigmaringen ....d.	...	...	...	...	...	0730	0728	...	0933	▬	1133	▬	1333	▬	1533	▬	1733	▬	1933	2032	▬	▬	▬	▬
Tuttlingen...............................d.	...	...	...	...	...	0813	0813	...	1013	...	1213	...	1413	...	1613	...	1813	...	2013	2116j	...	...	...	...
Immendingen .... **916** d.	...	...	...	...	...	0821	0821	...	1021	...	1221	...	1421	...	1621	...	1821	◧	2021	2124	2	...	Ⓐe2	©z2
Rottweil ....d.	...	...	0643	0702z	0747	|	|	0909	|	1109	|	1309	|	1509	|	1710	|	1909	|	...	2055	...	2203	2253
Trossingen Bahnhof ▲ ....d.	...	...	0654	0713z	0759	|	|	0918	|	1118	|	1318	|	1518	|	1719	|	1918	|	...	2107	...	2214	2304
Villingen (Schwarzw) . **916** d.	0604	0620	0721j	0737	0821	|	|	0937	|	1137	|	1337	|	1537	|	1737	|	1937	|	...	2124	2210	2236	2325
Donaueschingen .... **916** a.	0614	0640	0739	0748	0839	0834	0834	0948	1034	1148	1234	1348	1434	1548	1634	1748	1834	1948	2034	...	...	2218	2254	2343
Donaueschingen ....d.	0615	0642	...	0749	...	0848	0848	0949	1048	1149	1247	1349	1448	1549	1648	1749	1848	1949	2048	...	...	...	...	...
Neustadt (Schwarzw).........a.	0652	0726	...	0825	...	0925	0925	1025	1125	1225	1324	1425	1525	1625	1725	1825	1925	2025	2125	...	...	...	...	...

	©z2	Ⓐe2	⚒r2	Ⓐe	Ⓐe2	2	Ⓐe	©z														2	©z2	
Neustadt (Schwarzw).........d.	...	...	...	...	0626	...	...	...	0732	0832	0932	1032	1132	1231	1330n	1432	1532	1632	1732	1832	1932	2032	...	2202
Donaueschingen ....a.	...	...	...	...	0707	...	...	...	0808	0909	1008	1109	1208	1309	1408	1509	1608	1709	1808	1909	2008	2109	...	2240
Donaueschingen .... **916** d.	...	...	0510	0515	0708	0714z	0717	0721	0809	0922	1010	1122	1209	1322	1409	1522	1609	1722	1809	1922	2009	2110	2115	2241
Villingen (Schwarzw) . **916** d.	...	...	0533	|	0724	0734f	|	|	0826j	|	1026	|	1226j	|	1426j	|	1623	|	1826j	|	2026j	2129j	2139	2259
Trossingen Bahnhof ▲ ....d.	...	...	0551	|	▬	0800	|	|	0839	|	1039	|	1239	|	1439	|	1636	|	1839	|	2039	2146e	2157	...
Rottweil ....a.	...	...	0603	|	...	0810	|	|	0848	|	1048	|	1248	|	1448	|	1645	|	1848	|	2048	2158e	2208	...
Immendingen .... **916** d.	...	...	▬	0530	...	...	0733	0735	▬	0935	▬	1135	▬	1335	▬	1535	▬	1735	▬	1935	...	...	...	...
Tuttlingen...............................d.	...	...	...	0538	...	...	0750j	0747	...	0946	...	1146	...	1346	...	1546	...	1746	...	1946	...	...	...	...
Sigmaringen ....a.	...	...	©z2	0620	...	...	0828	0823	...	1027	...	1227	...	1427	...	1628	...	1827	...	2027	...	...	...	...
Sigmaringen .... **937** d.	0525	0521	0626	0631	0727	...	0830	0830	0933	1030	1134	1230	1332	1430	1534	1630	1734	1830	1934	2032	...	...	...	...
Herbertingen .... **937** d.	0539	0535	0641	0644	0742	...	0844	0844	0948	1044	1148	1244	1348	1444	1548	1644	1748	1845	1948	2046	...	...	...	...
Ehingen (Donau) ....d.	0607	0612	0716	0716	0815	...	0912	0912	1019	1112	1219	1312	1419	1512	1619	1713	1819	1913	2020	2115	...	...	...	...
Blaubeuren ....d.	0627	0627	0732	0732	0830	...	0928	0928	1031	1128	1231	1328	1431	1528	1631	1728	1831	1929	2032	2134	...	...	...	...
Ulm Hbf ....a.	0644	0639	0744	0744	0842	...	0940	0940	1042	1140	1242	1340	1442	1540	1642	1740	1843	1940	2044	2146	...	...	...	...

	e 🚌	Ⓐe	⚒r	e 🚌	Ⓐe	Ⓐe	©z	Ⓐe	©z	Ⓐe	Ⓑ											🚌	
Neustadt (Schwarzw) d.	...	0529	0558	...	0631	0642	0656	...	0708	...	0731	0801	...	0831	...	and at the same	1931	...	2031	...	2131	...	2223
Seebrugg ⊠ .... d.	0459	|	|	0601	|	|	|	0641	|	0705	|	|	...	|	0839	minutes past	|	1939	|	2021	|	2132	|
Titisee...................... d.	0531	0536	0605	0633	0638	0649	0703	0708	0715	0731	0738	0808	...	0838	0908	each hour until	1938	2008	2038	2048	2138	2204	2230
Freiburg (Brsg) Hbf .. a.	...	0615	0643	...	0718	0738	0741	0748	...	...	0818	0848	...	0918	0948		2018	2048	2118	...	2218	...	2313

	Ⓐe	Ⓐe	Ⓐe	Ⓐe	©z	©z	Ⓐe	Ⓐe											🚌	⊙			
Freiburg (Brsg) Hbf ... d.	...	0538	...	0640	0638	...	0710	...	0742	...	0810	0840	and at the same	1810	1840	1910	1940	2010	...	...	2110	2225	2325
Titisee...................... d.	0608	0615	0630	0719	0722	0724	0749	0752	0819	...	0849	0919	minutes past	1849	1919	1949	2019	2049	2055	2058	2149	2301	0001
Seebrugg ⊠ .... a.	0633	|	0658	|	0749	|	|	0818	|	...	0916	|	each hour until	1916	|	2015	|	|	2129	|	|	|	|
Neustadt (Schwarzw) a.	...	0621	...	0725	...	0730	0755	...	0825	...	...	0925		...	1925	...	2025	2055	...	2104	2155	2307	0007

Ⓐ (not Nov. 1).
0739 on © (also Nov. 1).
Arrives 8 – 10 minutes earlier.
On © (also Nov. 1) Ulm d. 0812, Blaubeuren d. 0825.

n – 1332 on © (also Nov. 1).
r – Not Nov. 1.
v – Also Nov. 1.
z – © (also Nov. 1).

◧ – Change trains at Villingen on Ⓐ (not Nov. 1).
◇ – Hohenzollerische Landesbahn.
▲ – Connecting services run to / from Trossingen Stadt (operated by HzL). Journey time: 5 minutes.

⊙ – From July 2.
⊠ – Journeys to / from Seebrugg are subject to alteration until July 1.

LINDAU - SCHAFFHAUSEN - BASEL 939

E / RB services

	①–⑤		Ⓐe	©z	Ⓐe	©z	2	U	2	U	2	U	2	U	2	U	2	U	2		2	2	2	U2
Lindau Hbf .... **933** d.	...	...	*0508*	*0559*	0634	0654	*0701*b	*0834*	*0906*	*1037*	*1102*	*1237*	*1302*	*1427*k	*1500*f	*1637*	*1702*	*1837*	*1902*	...	2012	*2103*	*2134*	*2244*
Friedrichshafen Stadt . **933** d.	0440	...	0547	0633	0702	0713	0739	0913	0938	1113	1138	1313	1338	1513	1538	1713	1738	1913	1933	...	2036	2129	2236	2333
Überlingen ....d.	0514	...	0625	0708	0730	0733	0813	0933	1012	1133	1212	1333	1412	1533	1612	1735	1812	1933	2011	...	2113	2158	2316	0010
Radolfzell..................... **916** d.	0543	...	0648	0733	0751	0752	0842	0952	1042	1153	1242	1353	1442	1553	1642	1753	1842	1953	2042	...	2140	2217	2341	0034
Singen .... **916** a.	0555	...	*0703*	*0747*	0758	0759	*0856*	0959	*1056*	1200	*1256*	1400	*1456*	1600	*1656*	1800	*1856*	2000	*2056*	...	2150	*2232*	2350	0042
	|				|	|	①–⑤	|	①–⑤	|	①–⑤	|	①–⑤	|	B	|	Ⓑ	|		⑥s2				
Singen 🏛 .... **940** d.	0600	0651	...	...	0802	0802	0902	1002	1102	1202	1302	1402	1502	1602	1702	1802	1902	2002	2101	...	2206	2236	0006	...
Schaffhausen 🏛 .... **940** d.	0613	0716	...	...	0816	0816	0916	1016	1116	1216	1316	1416	1516	1616	1716	1816	1916	2016	2116	...	2224	2254	0024	...
Erzingen (Baden) 🏛 ....d.	0625	0729	...	...	0829	0829	0929	1029	1129	1229	1329	1429	1529	1629	1729	1829	1929	2029	2130	...	*2308*	*2338*	...	...
Waldshut...............................d.	0641	0742	...	...	0842	0842	0942	1042	1142	1242	1342	1442	1542	1642	1742	1842	1942	2042	2150	2258	...	...	...	...
Bad Säckingen......................d.	0654	0756	...	...	0856	0856	0956	1056	1156	1256	1356	1456	1556	1656	1756	1856	1956	2056	2214	2320	...	...	...	...
Rheinfelden (Baden)............d.	0704	0806	...	...	0906	0906	1006	1106	1206	1306	1406	1506	1606	1706	1806	1906	2006	2106	2232	2335	...	...	...	...
Basel Bad Bf......................a.	0715	0816	...	...	0916	0916	1016	1116	1216	1316	1416	1516	1616	1716	1816	1916	2016	2116	2249	2350	...	...	...	...

				Ⓐe2	Ⓐe	©z	©zU	ⒶeU	①–⑤	U	E	U	①–⑤	U	①–⑤	U		①–⑤	U	Ⓑ	U	Ⓑ			2
el Bad Bf........................ d.	...	...	...	...	0459	...	0612	0635	0742	0842	0942	1042	1142	1242	1342	1442	...	1542	1642	1742	1842	1942	2042	...	2147
infelden (Baden)............. d.	...	...	...	...	0516	...	0631	0645	0751	0851	0951	1051	1151	1251	1351	1451	...	1551	1651	1751	1851	1951	2051	...	2203
Säckingen .... d.	...	...	...	...	0533	...	0647	0655	0801	0901	1001	1101	1201	1301	1401	1501	...	1601	1701	1801	1901	2001	2101	...	2221
dshut .... d.	...	...	...	...	0604	0604	0711	0711	0814	0914	1014	1114	1214	1314	1414	1514	...	1614	1714	1814	1914	2014	2114	...	2252
ngen (Baden) 🏛 .... d.	...	...	...	*0518*	0629	0629	0729	0729	0829	0929	1029	1129	1229	1329	1429	1529	...	1629	1729	1829	1929	2029	2129	*2148*	2311
affhausen 🏛.......... **940** d.	...	...	0528	0551	0643	0643	0743	0743	0843	0943	1043	1143	1243	1343	1443	1543	...	1643	1743	1843	1943	2043	2143	2230	*2339*
jen 🏛...................... **940** a.	...	...	0547	0610	0700	0656	0756	0756	0856	0956	1056	1156	1256	1356	1456	1556	...	1656	1756	1856	1956	2056	2156	2249	...
	Ⓐe2	Ⓐe	©z2	|		|	|	|	2d	|	2d	|	2d	|	2d	|	2	2d	|	2d	|	2d	|	2	
jen .... **916** d.	0423	0538	0610	0615	...	0658	0757	0757	*0902*	0957	*1102*	1157	*1302*	1357	*1502*	1557	*1602*	*1702*	1757	*1902*	1957	*2102*	2217	*2302*	...
olfzell...................... **916** d.	0432	0546	0620	0623	...	0709	0805	0805	0914	1005	1114	1205	1314	1405	1514	1605	1618	1714	1806	1928	2005	2118	2227	2315	...
rlingen .... d.	0456	0610	0642	0655	...	0740	0823	0823	0942	1023	1142	1223	1342	1423	1542	1623	1645	1742	1823	1954	2026	2141	2250	2343	...
drichshafen Stadt.. **933** a.	0541	0648	0723	0738	...	0822	0842	0842	1021	1041	1221	1242	1421	1442	1621	1642	1722	1821	1842	2027	2045	2220	2323	0020	...
dau Hbf.................. **933** a.	*0621*	*0736*	*0750*	0825	...	*0857*	*0907*	*0907*	*1055*	*1122*	*1255*	*1351*j	*1455*	*1522*	*1655*	*1723*	*1751*	*1855*	*1923*	*2100*	*2127*	2256	*0016*	...	...

Daily to Sept. 30; Ⓑ from Oct. 2.
Daily to Sept. 30; ①–⑤ from Oct. 3.
From / to Ulm (Table **933**).

b – *0703* on © (also Nov. 1).
d – Daily.
e – Not Nov. 1.

f – *1502* on © (daily July 28 - Sept. 11 and Oct. 29 - Nov. 6).
j – *1322* on © (daily July 28 - Sept. 11 and Oct. 29 - Nov. 6).
k – *1437* on © (daily July 28 - Sept. 11 and Oct. 29 - Nov. 6).

s – Also Oct. 2.
z – Also Nov. 1.

940 STUTTGART - SINGEN - SCHAFFHAUSEN - ZÜRICH

SUBJECT TO ALTERATION JULY 13 - AUGUST 14

km			◇				IC181		IC183		IC185		IC187		IC281		IC283		IC285				◇		
		Ⓐe	Ⓐe	Ⓐe	Ⓐe														Ⓑb			⚒r	†w		
0	**Stuttgart** Hbf .... **942** d.	0516	...	0548	...	0718	0829	0918	1029	1118	1229	1318	1429	1518	1624t	1718	1829	1918	2029	2018	2118	2118	...	2225	2
26	Böblingen .... **942** d.	0537	...	0609	...	0738	0850	0938	1050	1138	1250	1338	1450	1538	1650	1738	1850	1938	2050	2038	2138	2138	...	2246	2
42	Herrenberg .... **942** d.	0547	...	0620	...	0750	|	0950	|	1150	|	1350	|	1550	|	1750	|	1950	|	2050	2150	2150	...	2256	2
57	Eutingen im Gäu.. **942** d.	0600	...	0637	...	0806	|	1006	|	1206	|	1406	|	1606	|	1806	|	2006	|	2111	2206	2206	...	2313	2
67	Horb ....d.	0607	...	0645	...	0814	0915	1014	1115	1214	1315	1414	1515	1614	1715	1814	1915	2014	2115	2121	2214	2214	...	2321	2
110	Rottweil ....d.	0638	0641	0720	0733	0851	0944	1051	1144	1251	1344	1451	1544	1651	1744	1851	1944	2051	2144	2154r	2245	2246	2253	2354	2
138	Tuttlingen ....d.	...	0722	...	0759	0914	1000	1115	1200	1314	1400	1514	1600	1714	1800	1914	2000	2114	2200	...	...	2308	2318	...	0
157	Engen.................. **916** d.	...	0737	...	|	0930	|	1130	|	1330	|	1530	|	1730	|	1930	|	2130	|	...	...	2324	...	...	0
172	**Singen** .... **916** a.	...	0747	...	0824	0942	1025	1142	1225	1342	1425	1542	1625	1742	1825	1942	2025	2142	2225	...	...	2333	...	...	0
172	**Singen** .... **939** d.	...	*0802*	...	*0829*	*1002*	1032	*1202*	1232	*1402*	1432	*1602*	1632	*1802*	1832	*2002*	2032	*2206*	2232	...	...	*2336*	...	...	
191	**Schaffhausen** ▦ . **939** a.	...	*0814*	...	*0843*	*1014*	1045	*1214*	1245	*1414*	1445	*1614*	1645	*1814*	1845	*2014*	2045	*2224*	2245	...	...	*2354*	...	...	
239	**Zürich** HB ....a.	...	...	...	...	...	1125	...	1325	...	1525	...	1725	...	1925	...	2125	...	2325	...	...	...	...	...	

									IC284			IC282		IC280			IC186		IC184		IC182		IC180	
	Ⓐe	Ⓐe		Ⓐe	Ⓐe	Ⓐe	Ⓒw		★						Ⓒw	Ⓐe							n	
Zürich HB ....d.	...	...	...	...	...	...	...	...	0635	...	...	0835	...	1035	...	...	1235	...	1435	...	1635	...	1835	
Schaffhausen ▦........... **939** d.	...	...	...	*0528*	*0551*	...	*0551*	...	0716	0743	0755e	0916	*0943*	1116	*1143*	*1143*	1316	*1343*	1516	*1543*	1716	*1743*	1916	1
Singen .... **939** a.	...	...	...	*0547*	*0610*	...	*0610*	...	0730	0756	0811e	0930	*0956*	1130	*1156*	*1156*	1330	*1356*	1530	*1556*	1730	*1756*	1930	1
Singen .... **916** d.	...	...	...	0551	0617	...	0618	...	0737	▬	0818	0937	1018	1137	1218	1218	1337	1418	1537	1618	1737	1818	1937	2
Engen......................... **916** d.	...	...	...	0600	0626	...	0627	...	|	...	0827	|	1027	|	1227	1227	|	1427	|	1627	|	1827	|	2
Tuttlingen..................................d.	...	...	...	0615	0641	...	0643	...	0800	...	0843	1000	1043	1200	1243	1243	1400	1443	1600	1644	1800	1843	2000	2
Rottweil ....d.	0508	0538	0612	0639	0702	0705	0704	0803	0817	...	0907	1017	1107	1217	1307	1309	1417	1507	1617	1707	1817	1907	2017	2
Horb ....d.	0546	0616	0646	0710	...	0745	0743	0837	0846	←	0946	1046	1146	1246	1346	1346	1446	1546	1646	1746	1846	1946	2046	2
Eutingen im Gäu............. **942** d.	0555	0625	0655	|	...	0757	0755	0847	|	0857	0955	|	1155	|	1355	1355	|	1555	|	1755	|	1955	|	2
Herrenberg .... **942** d.	0612	0642	0712	0727	...	0811	0811	→	|	0912	1012	|	1212	|	1412	1412	|	1612	|	1812	|	2012	|	2
Böblingen .... **942** d.	0623	0652	0722	0736	...	0822	0822	...	0911	0922	1022	1111	1222	1311	1422	1422	1511	1622	1711	1822	1911	2022	2111	2
Stuttgart Hbf.................. **942** a.	0642	0712	0742	0757	...	0842	0842	...	0933	0942	1042	1133	1242	1333	1442	1442	1536	1642	1736	1842	1933	2042	2133	2

SCHAFFHAUSEN - ZÜRICH (operated by SBB)

km								
0	**Schaffhausen** ....d.	0547	0616	and at the same	2116	2147	2247	2327
28	Bülach ....d.	|	0638	minutes past	2138	|	|	2358
48	**Zürich** HB ....a.	0625	0655	each hour until	2155	2225	2325	0023

Zürich HB ....d.	0005	...	0605	0635	and at the same	2035	2105	2205	2
Bülach ....d.	0023	...	0623	|	minutes past	|	2123	2223	2
Schaffhausen ....a.	0043	...	0643	0713	each hour until	2113	2143	2243	2

b – Also Nov. 26, Dec. 3, 10.
e – Ⓐ (not Nov. 1).
r – ⚒ (not Nov. 1).
t – 1629 on Ⓒ.
w – Also Nov. 1.
★ – ①–⑥ (also Nov. 27, Dec. 4).
◇ – Operated by Hohenzollerische Landesbahn. 2nd class only.

941 TÜBINGEN - HORB - PFORZHEIM - BAD WILDBAD

RB services (2nd class o

km		Ⓐe	⑥	Ⓐe		Ⓐe	Ⓒz													
	Tübingen ....⊡ d.	...	...	...	...	...	0727	...	0927	...	1127	...	1327	...	1527	...	1727	...	1927	2127
0	**Horb**......................⊡ d.	0440	0600	0611	0651	0758	0758	0851	0958	1051	1158	1251	1358	1451	1558	1651	1758	1851	1959	2200
15	Hochdorf (b. Horb) ..... d.	0451	0610	0622	0702	0809	0809	0902	1009	1102	1208	1302	1408	1502	1608	1702	1808	1902	2009	2220
25	Nagold .... d.	0506	0622	0632	0719	0820	0820	0913	1020	1113	1220	1313	1420	1513	1620	1713	1820	1913	2021	2231
34	Wildberg (Württ) .... d.	0514	0629	0646	0729	0832	0832	0920	1028	1121	1228	1321	1428	1521	1628	1721	1828	1921	2029	2239
45	Calw .... d.	0524	0639	0656	0739	0842	0842	0934	1038	1134	1238	1334	1438	1534	1638	1734	1838	1934	2039	2249
52	Bad Liebenzell .... d.	0532	0646	0704	0750	0849	0849	0945	1046	1145	1245	1345	1445	1545	1645	1745	1845	1942	2047	2300
71	**Pforzheim** Hbf.......... a.	0552	0708	0724	0810	0910	0910	1006	1107	1207	1307	1407	1507	1607	1707	1807	1907	2005	2111	2320

	Ⓐe	Ⓐe	Ⓒz	⚒r										Ⓐe		Ⓐe				
Pforzheim Hbf........... d.	0446	0637	0651	0753	0853	0950	1050	1149	1250	1350	1450	1550	1650	1720	1750	1823	1851	1950	2043	2238
Bad Liebenzell .... d.	0506	0708	0712	0816	0915	1011	1113	1211	1313	1411	1513	1611	1713	1743	1811	1848	1913	2011	2103	2258
Calw .... d.	0513	0715	0719	0823	0922	1018	1120	1218	1320	1418	1520	1618	1720	1750	1818	1855	1920	2018	2110	2305
Wildberg (Württ) .... d.	0526	0728	0729	0832	0932	1029	1132	1229	1332	1429	1533	1629	1732	1803	1829	1905	1932	2031	2120	2315
Nagold......................... d.	0534	0739	0739	0840	0940	1039	1140	1239	1339	1439	1540	1639	1739	1821	1839	1914	1940	2039	2128	2323
Hochdorf (b. Horb) ...... d.	0544	0751	0751	0852	0951	1051	1151	1251	1351	1450	1551	1650	1751	1832	1850	1925	1952	2050	2148	2340
Horb...................... ⊡ a.	...	0802	0802	0903	1002	1102	1203	1302	1402	1502	1602	1702	1802	1843	1902	1937	2003	2102	2159	2351
Tübingen .... ⊡ a.	...	...	0833	...	1033	...	1233	...	1433	...	1633z	1759e	1833z	...	...	...	2033	...	2232	...

e – Ⓐ (not Nov. 1).
r – Not Nov. 1.
z – Ⓒ (also Nov. 1).
⊡ – See panel below main tab for full service Tübingen - and v.v.
⊠ – The 1235 from Bad Wildb Kurpark runs only on Ⓒ z (see also note ▶ below).
▶ – S-Bahn route **S6**. Addition journeys on Ⓐ (not Nov. **From Pforzheim** Hbf at 0 0705, 1227, 1317, 1617, 1 1817 and 1917. **From Bad Wildbad** Kurp at 0505, 0601, 0805, 090 1215, 1305, 1605, 1705 a 1805.

km		Ⓐe	Ⓐe	Ⓐe	Ⓐe	Ⓒz						Ⓐe					Ⓐe								
0	**Tübingen** Hbf........... d.	0535	0558	0630	0724	0727	0835	0927	1035	1127	1235	1304	1327	1435	1527	1636	1704	1727	1836	1927	2036	2127	2236	...	...
32	**Horb**........................ a.	0603	0637	0706	0754	0754	0911	0954	1111	1154	1311	1336	1354	1511	1554	1711	1736	1754	1911	1955	2111	2156	2309	...	...

			Ⓐe	Ⓐe	Ⓒz	Ⓐe								Ⓐe		Ⓐe	Ⓒz		Ⓐe	Ⓐe	Ⓒz	Ⓐe				
Horb........................ d.	0455	...	0617	0648	0652	0725	0806	0853	1006	1053	1206	1253	1406	1424	1453	1605	1606	1653	1717	1805	1806	1824	1853	2006	2053	2
Tübingen Hbf........... a.	0526	...	0651	0723	0723	0801	0833	0924	1033	1124	1233	1324	1433	1455	1524	1632	1633	1724	1759	1832	1833	1855	1924	2033	2124	2

km	*SEE NOTE* ▶	Ⓐe	Ⓐe	⑥						
0	**Pforzheim** Hbf ....d.	0514	0647	0647	0747	and	2147	2217	2321	0017
23	**Bad Wildbad** Bf ....d.	0545	0714	0719	0819	hourly	2219	2249	2351	0049
25	**Bad Wildbad** Kurpark a.	0547	0716	0722	0822	until	2222	2252	2353	0052

SEE NOTE ▶	Ⓐe	⚒e	Ⓐe		⊠			
Bad Wildbad Kurpark........d.	0532	0635	0659	0735	and	2135	2245	2
Bad Wildbad Bf ....d.	0536	0639	0703	0739	hourly	2139	2249	2
Pforzheim Hbf...................a.	0609	0710	0731	0810	until	2210	2320	0

942 STUTTGART - FREUDENSTADT - OFFENBURG

Services from / to Stuttgart are subject to alteration July 13 - August 14

km		Ⓐe2		2		2		2		2		2		2		2		2		Ⓐe			Ⓒz2
0	**Stuttgart** Hbf................ **940** d.	...	...	...	0818	...	1018	...	1218	...	1418	...	1618	...	1818	...	2018	...	...	...	...	2235u	...
26	Böblingen .... **940** d.	...	...	...	0838	...	1038	...	1238	...	1438	...	1638	...	1838	...	2038	...	...	...	...	2259	...
42	Herrenberg .... **940** d.	...	...	...	0850	...	1050	...	1250	...	1450	...	1650	...	1850	...	2050	...	...	...	...	2313	2317
57	Eutingen im Gäu............ **940** d.	0639	0709	0810	0909	1010	1109	1210	1309	1410	1509	1610	1709	1810	1909	2010	2109	2211	...	2316	...	...	2333
62	Hochdorf (b. Horb) ....d.	0644	0713	0814	0913	1014	1113	1214	1313	1414	1513	1614	1713	1814	1913	2014	2113	2215	...	2320	...	...	2337
87	**Freudenstadt** Hbf ....a.	0711	0741	0841	0941	1041	1141	1241	1341	1441	1541	1641	1741	1841	1941	2041	2141	2241	...	2345	...	...	0001

	Ⓐe2	Ⓐe	Ⓒz	2		2		2		2		2		2		2		Ⓒz	2	Ⓐe	Ⓒz2	2	
Freudenstadt Hbf ....d.	0519	0615	0619	0719	0819	0919	1019	1119	1219	1319	1419	1519	1619	1719	1819	1919	2019	2019	2119	2219	2219	...	...
Hochdorf (b. Horb)...................d.	0544	0644	0646	0744	0846	0944	1046	1144	1246	1344	1446	1544	1646	1744	1846	1944	2045	2045	2144	2246	2244	...	...
Eutingen im Gäu............. **940** a.	0549	0649	0650	0749	0850	0949	1050	1149	1250	1349	1450	1549	1650	1749	1850	1949	2050	2050	2149	2250	2255	...	...
Herrenberg .... **940** a.	...	...	...	...	0911	...	1111	...	1311	...	1511	...	1711	...	1911	...	...	2110	...	2307	2310	2316	...
Böblingen .... **940** a.	...	...	...	...	0922	...	1122	...	1322	...	1522	...	1722	...	1922	...	...	...	...	...	...	2330	...
Stuttgart Hbf.................... **940** a.	...	...	...	...	0942	...	1142	...	1342	...	1542	...	1742	...	1942	...	...	...	...	...	...	2355	...

FREUDENSTADT - OFFENBURG (operated by Südwestdeutsche Verkehrs-AG; 2nd class only)

km		Ⓐe	⚒e				❖		Ⓐe	
0	**Freudenstadt** Hbf ......d.	0533	0643	0743	0843	0943	and	2043	2143	...
16	Alpirsbach...................d.	0552	0659	0758	0858	0959		2059	2159	...
25	Schiltach.....................d.	0603	0710	0810	0910	1010	hourly	2110	2210	...
35	Wolfach ....d.	0613	0720	0820	0920	1020	until	2120	2221	...
39	Hausach.............. **916** a.	0618	0725	0825	0925	1025		2125	2225	2235
72	**Offenburg**........... **916** a.	0711	0755	0855	0955	1055		2155	...	2300

	Ⓐe	⑥	Ⓐe						
Offenburg .... **916** d.	0458	*0554*	0558	0702	0804	and	2004	...	2
Hausach .... **916** d.	0525	0627	0627	0732	0832		2032	...	2
Wolfach ....d.	0530	0632	0632	0737	0837	hourly	2037	...	2
Schiltach.......................d.	0540	0642	0642	0747	0847	until	2047	...	2
Alpirsbach....................d.	0551	0701	0701	0801	0901		2101	...	2
Freudenstadt Hbf....a.	0607	0717	0717	0817	0917		2117	...	2

e – Not Nov. 1.
u – Underground platforms.
z – Also Nov. 1.
❖ – The 1243 from Freudenstadt runs on Ⓒ (daily July 28 - Sept. 11 and Oct. 29 - Nov. 6). On other dates service is retimed to run as follows: Freudenstadt d. 1220, Alpirsbach d. 1236 Schiltach d. 1254, Wolfach d. 1305, Hausach a. 1309, Offenburg a. 1345.

KARLSRUHE - FREUDENSTADT 943

ahn (2nd class only)

	Ⓐe	Ⓐe	⑥	Ⓐe	Ⓒz		†w															
Karlsruhe Bahnhofsvorplatz d.	0431	0509	0511	...	0611	0711z	...	0805j	0911	1011	1111		2011	2111	2211	2311		...	...	...	...	...
Karlsruhe Hbf .... 916 d.	|	|	|	0611	|	0707e	0806	|	|	|	|		|	|	|	|		1010	1210	1410	1610	1810
Rastatt .... 916 d.	0503	0534	0538	0634	0638	0738	0829	0838	0938	1038	1138	and	2038	2138	2238	2338	also	1029	1229	1429	1629	1829
Gernsbach Bf .... d.	0525	0556	0600	0656	0700	0800	0844	0900	1000	1100	1200		2100	2200	2300	0000	faster	1044	1244	1444	1644	1844
Forbach (Schwarzw) .... d.	0544	0613	0618	0718	0718	0818	0900	0918	1018	1118	1218	hourly	2118	2218	2318	0018		1100	1300	1500	1700	1900
Schönmünzach .... d.	0556	0624	0631	0729	0729	0829	0911	0929	1029	1129	1229		2129	2229	2329	0034	trains	1111	1311	1511	1711	1911
Baiersbronn Bf .... d.	0612	0642	0649	0750	0749	0849	0922	0949	1049	1149	1249	until	2149	2249	2346	0050	at	1122	1322	1522	1722	1922
Freudenstadt Stadt .... a.	0620	0650	0657	0758	0757	0857	0930	0957	1057	1157	1257		2157	2257	2354	0058		1130	1329	1530	1730	1930
Freudenstadt Hbf .... a.	0625	0705	0707	0807	0807	0907	0937	1007	1112	1215	1307		2207	2307	2400	0104		1137	1337	1537	1737	1937

	†	Ⓐe	Ⓐe	Ⓒz	Ⓐe	Ⓐe	Ⓒz	Ⓐe	Ⓐe	Ⓒz	⚒r													Ⓒz
denstadt Hbf .... d.	0004	0443	0524	0601	0614	0648	0653	0720	0745	0753	0823	0853		1953	2053	2153	2253		1023	1223	1423	1623	1823
denstadt Stadt .... d.	0010	0449	0530	0607	0620	0654	0703	0730	0803	0803	0830	0903		2003	2103	2203	2306	also	1030	1230	1430	1630	1830
sbronn Bf .... d.	0018	0458	0539	0616	0628	0702	0711	0738	0811	0811	0838	0911	and	2011	2111	2211	2314	faster	1038	1238	1438	1638	1838
nmünzach .... d.	0034	0513	0555	0631	0645	0710	0729	0749	0829	0829	0849	0929		2029	2129	2229	2330		1049	1249	1449	1649	1849
ach (Schwarzw) .... d.	0045	0525	0612	0643	0701	0742	0742	0801	0842	0842	0901	0942	hourly	2042	2153t	2300v	2341	trains	1101	1259	1501	1701	1901
sbach Bf .... d.	0101	0541	0631	0659	0728	0800	0800	0815	0900	0900	0915	1000		2100	2211	2316	0000	at	1115	1313	1515	1715	1915
att .... 916 d.	0122	0557	0706t	0722	0754	0822	0822	0830	0922	0922	0931	1022	until	2122	2232	2338	0022		1131	1330	1530	1730	1931
rlsruhe Hbf .... 916 a.	0146	0614	0728	|	0816	|	|	0849	|	|	0949	|		|	|	|	|		1149	1349	1549	1749	1949
ruhe Bahnhofsvorplatz a.	...	...	...	0746	...	0846	0846	...	0946	0946	...	1046		2146	2256	0002	0046		...	...	...	...	...

Ⓐ (not Nov. 1). j – 0811 on Ⓒ (also Nov. 1). r – Not Nov. 1. t – Arrives 13 minutes earlier. v – Arrives 2240. w – Also Nov. 1. z – Ⓒ (also Nov. 1).

MÜNCHEN - PASSAU 944

services

	Ⓐe	⚒e	Ⓐe	Ⓐe	Ⓒz											Ⓐe	Ⓐe						
München Hbf .... 878 d.	...	0455	0524	0604	0624	0724	0824	0924	1024	1124	1224	1324	1424	1524	1622	1642	...	1723	1824	1924	2024	2124	2325
Freising .... 878 d.	...	0518	0549	0628	0651	0748	0848	0948	1048	1148	1248	1348	1448	1548	1648	1708	1713	1749	1848	1948	2048	2148	2349
Landshut (Bay) Hbf .... 878 d.	...	0543	0613	0650	0714	0809	0909	1014	1109	1212	1314	1414	1510	1613	1709	1730	1744	1815	1910	2013	2111	2211	0014
Landau (Isar) .... d.	...	0625	0701v	0737n	0743	0845	0944	1048	1144	1244	1343	1449	1544	1648	1744	...	1823	1848	1941	2045	2143	2248	0044
Plattling .... a.	...	0640	0714	0750	0755	0857	0953	1100	1153	1256	1354	1500	1554	1700	1755	...	1835	1900	1953	2056	2155	2301	0055
Plattling .... 920 d.	0600	0642	0725	0800	0802	0901	1004	1102	1204	1302	1404	1502	1604	1702	1804	...	...	1902	2004	2102	2157	2306	0057
Passau Hbf .... 920 a.	0633	0718	0800	0833	0836	0934	1038	1136	1239	1336	1439	1536	1639	1736	1839	...	...	1937	2039	2139	2232	2340	0130

	⚒e		Ⓐe	Ⓒz	Ⓐe																			
au Hbf .... 920 d.	0442	0523	0604	0627	0646	...	0725	0825	0916	1025	1116	1225	1316	1425	1516	1625	1715	1822	1916	2025	...	2128	...	2313
ing .... 920 a.	0514	0558	0640	0701	0720	...	0759	0900	0950	1100	1150	1259	1349	1459	1550	1659	1751	1857	1949	2058	...	2200	...	2347
ing .... d.	0521	0600	0642	0702	0723	...	0802	0901	1002	1102	1202	1301	1402	1502	1602	1702	1801	1902	2002	2100	...	2202	...	2350
au (Isar) .... d.	0533	0613	0656	0714	0735	...	0814	0913	1012	1114	1212	1313	1413	1515	1612	1714	1811	1915	2013	2112	...	2216	...	0003
shut (Bay) Hbf .... 878 d.	0608	0647	0727	0749	0807	...	0849	0947	1048	1148	1248	1349	1448	1548	1648	1748	1848	1949	2049	2149	...	2248	...	0038
ing .... 878 d.	0629	0709	0748	0810	0830	...	0910	1009	1110	1210	1310	1410	1510	1610	1710	1810	1910	2011	2110	2210	...	2310	...	...
chen Hbf .... 878 a.	0655	0736	0815	0835	0855	...	0937	1035	1135	1235	1335	1435	1535	1636	1735	1835	1935	2035	2135	2235	...	2336	...	...

Not Aug. 15, Nov. 1. n – Arrives 0729. v – Arrives 0649. z – Also Aug. 15, Nov. 1.

REGENSBURG - INGOLSTADT - DONAUWÖRTH - ULM 945

is

On Aug. 15, Nov. 1 services run as on ⑦

		Ⓐ		Ⓐ	Ⓐ	Ⓐ	Ⓐ	Ⓐ	Ⓐ	Ⓐ	Ⓐ	Ⓐ	Ⓐ	Ⓐ	Ⓐ	Ⓐ	Ⓐ	Ⓐ	Ⓐ	Ⓐ	Ⓐ	Ⓐ	Ⓐ	Ⓐ	Ⓐ
Regensburg Hbf ...... d.	Ⓐ	...	...	0405	0452	0509	0534	0609	...	0713	0745	0845	0945	1045	1145	1245	1345	1445	1545	1614	1645	1728	1745	1845	...
Neustadt (Donau) ...... d.		...	...	0442	0534	0556	0622	0656	...	0802	0830	0931	1027	1131	1230	1323	1427	1527	1630	1702	1731	1812	1832	1929	...
Ingolstadt Hbf .... a.		...	...	0502	0554	0622	0652	0719	...	0826	0851	0954	1051	1153	1251	1349	1452	1547	1652	1733	1755	1835	1854	1950	...
Ingolstadt Hbf .... d.		...	...	0507	0607	0633	0702	...	0807	...	0908	1003	1109	1209	1309	1407	1508	1607	1708	1740	1810	1841	1909	...	2044
Neuburg (Donau) .... d.		...	...	0528	0626	0647	0729	...	0828	...	0926	1029	1129	1228	1328	1428	1528	1628	1723	1802	1828	1855	1928	...	2108
Donauwörth .... a.		...	...	0553	0653	0725	0753	...	0852	...	0950	1053	1153	1253	1353	1453	1553	1653	1748	1834	1853	1920	1953	...	2136
Donauwörth .... d.		0500	...	0603	0703	...	0803	...	0901	...	1002	1101	1202	1302	1400	1503	1602	1703	1801	...	1901	...	2016	...	2139
Dillingen (Donau) .... d.		0524	...	0639	0730	...	0823	...	0925	...	1032	1121	1223	1331	1428	1525	1624	1725	1824	...	1922	...	2040	...	2204
Günzburg .... 930 a.		0541	...	0655	0746	...	0840	...	0940	...	1050	1140	1240	1347	1444	1540	1640	1740	1840	...	1940	...	2056	...	2221
Ulm Hbf .... 930 a.		0610	...	0716	0810	...	0858j	...	0958	...	1110	1158	1310	1410	1510k	1558	1658	1758	1858	...	1958	...	2115	...	2302b

	Ⓐ	Ⓐ	Ⓐ	Ⓐ			Ⓒ		Ⓒ	Ⓒ	Ⓒ	Ⓒ	Ⓒ	Ⓒ	Ⓒ	Ⓒ	Ⓒ	Ⓒ	Ⓒ	Ⓒ	Ⓒ	Ⓒ	Ⓒ	⑥	Ⓒ	Ⓒ
ensburg Hbf .... d.	1945	2012	2111	2222	...	Ⓒ	...	...	...	0557	0651	0759	0845	1000	1045	1200	1245	1358	1445	1600	1645	1800	1845	1946	2046	2222
stadt (Donau) .... d.	2027	2101	2207	2302	...		...	...	...	0638	0732	0838	0932	1038	1132	1238	1332	1438	1532	1638	1732	1838	1932	2029	2132	2302
lstadt Hbf .... a.	2053	2121	2228	2322	...		...	...	...	0654	0753	0854	0955	1054	1154	1254	1354	1454	1552	1654	1755	1854	1952	2050	2152	2322
lstadt Hbf .... d.	...	2143	2240	2336	...		...	...	0608	0707	0809	0907	1008	1107	1209	1307	1409	1507	1609	1707	1808	1907	2038	...	2240	2336
burg (Donau) .... d.	...	2203	2258	2351	...		...	...	0627	0722	0824	0922	1024	1122	1224	1322	1424	1522	1624	1722	1824	1922	2059	...	2258	2351
auwörth .... a.	...	2228	2323	0021	...		...	...	0653	0747	0853	0947	1053	1147	1253	1347	1453	1546	1653	1746	1853	1946	2123	...	2323	0021
auwörth .... d.	...	2237	2337	...	...		0503	...	0703	0750	0901	0950	1101	1150	1303	1350	1503	1550	1703	1750	1901	1950	2138	...	2337	...
gen (Donau) .... d.	...	2302	2358	...	...		0524	...	0723	0807	0925	1007	1122	1207	1324	1407	1525	1607	1725	1807	1922	2007	2159	...	2358	...
zburg .... 930 a.	...	2319	0014	...	...		0541	...	0740	0823	0940	1022	1140	1222	1340	1422	1540	1622	1740	1825	1940	2023	2221	...	0014	...
Hbf .... 930 a.	...	2337	0033	...	...		0610	...	0758	0845t	0958	1040j	1158	1240	1358	1440	1558	1640	1758	1844n	1958	2040	2302b	...	0033	...

		Ⓐ	Ⓐ	Ⓐ	Ⓐ	Ⓐ	Ⓐ	Ⓐ	Ⓐ	Ⓐ	Ⓐ	Ⓐ	Ⓐ	Ⓐ	Ⓐ	Ⓐ	Ⓐ	Ⓐ	Ⓐ	Ⓐ	Ⓐ	Ⓐ	Ⓐ	Ⓐ	Ⓐ	Ⓐ
Hbf .... 930 d.	Ⓐ	...	...	...	0450	0533	...	0630	...	0745	0848	0948	1048	1148	1248	1348	...	1448	1548	1648	1744v	1831	...	1944v	...	2048
zburg .... 930 d.		...	...	...	0509	0551	...	0650	...	0804	0913	1012	1115	1212	1314	1412	...	1514	1612	1714	1804	1851	...	2005	...	2115
gen (Donau) .... d.		...	...	...	0524	0607	...	0707	...	0829	0933	1028	1132	1231	1331	1428	...	1533	1632	1733	1829	1907	...	2021	...	2132
auwörth .... a.		...	...	...	0545	0629	...	0730	...	0850	0953	1049	1153	1251	1353	1450	...	1553	1652	1753	1851	1932	...	2042	...	2153
auwörth .... d.		...	0502	...	0554	0631	0701	0731	0801	0859	1004	1102	1202	1302	1402	1501	...	1602	1702	1801	1901	1940	2005	2043	2138	...
burg (Donau) .... d.		...	0527	...	0627	0704	0728	0804	0829	0928	1029	1129	1229	1328	1429	1533	...	1630	1734	1829	1928	2008	2030	2108	2205	...
lstadt Hbf .... a.		...	0546	...	0648	0723	0747	0833	0846	0949	1046	1146	1245	1354	1445	1552	...	1648	1750	1848	1946	2022	2047	2125	2222	...
lstadt Hbf .... d.		0521	0600	0628	0705	0730	0805	...	0905	1006	1106	1206	1318	1405	1505	1605	1622	1705	1805	1905	2006	2030	2108	2138	2236	...
stadt (Donau) .... d.		0545	0622	0656	0729	0752	0827	...	0928	1027	1127	1227	1339	1427	1527	1627	1650	1727	1827	1927	2027	2047	2133	2202	2302	...
ensburg Hbf .... a.		0628	0707	0739	0811	0836	0910	...	1010	1110	1210	1310	1422	1510	1611	1711	1734	1810	1910	2010	2110	2129	2210	2251	2343	...

	Ⓐ	Ⓐ	Ⓐ			Ⓒ	Ⓒ	Ⓒ	Ⓒ	Ⓒ	Ⓒ	Ⓒ	Ⓒ	Ⓒ	Ⓒ	Ⓒ	Ⓒ	Ⓒ	Ⓒ	Ⓒ	Ⓒ	Ⓒ	Ⓒ		Ⓒ	Ⓒ
Hbf .... 930 d.	...	2221	2255	...	Ⓒ	...	0555	0718	0745	0918	0948	1118	1148	1318	1348	1518	1550	1718	1744v	1918	...	1944v	...	...	2221	2255
zburg .... 930 d.	...	2243	2318	...		...	0614	0736	0804	0936	1012	1136	1212	1336	1412	1536	1612	1736	1812	1936	...	2004	...	...	2243	2318
gen (Donau) .... d.	...	2301	2334	...		...	0631	0752	0829	0952	1032	1152	1232	1352	1432	1552	1632	1752	1832	1952	...	2029	...	...	2301	2334
auwörth .... a.	...	2323	2400	...		...	0653	0812	0850	1013	1052	1212	1252	1412	1452	1612	1652	1812	1852	2012	...	2051	...	...	2323	2400
auwörth .... d.	2238	2338	...	...		0504	0701	0814	0904	1014	1101	1214	1302	1414	1502	1615	1702	1814	1902	2014	...	2138	...	...	2338	...
burg (Donau) .... d.	2309	0004	...	...		0528	0732	0837	0932	1037	1133	1237	1332	1437	1533	1637	1733	1837	1933	2037	...	2205	...	...	0004	...
lstadt Hbf .... a.	2326	0021	...	...		0547	0749	0851	0949	1051	1148	1251	1349	1451	1549	1651	1749	1851	1948	2056	...	2222	...	...	0021	...
lstadt Hbf .... d.	2338	...	...	...		0605	0805	0905	1005	1105	1205	1305	1405	1505	1605	1705	1805	1905	2005	2105	2206	...	2338	...	...	...
stadt (Donau) .... d.	2359	...	...	...		0627	0827	0921	1027	1121	1227	1321	1427	1521	1627	1721	1827	1921	2029	2121	2227	...	2359	...	...	...
ensburg Hbf .... a.	0043	...	...	...		0708	0910	0953	1110	1155	1310	1355	1510	1555	1710	1754	1910	1955	2111	2156	2312	...	0043	...	...	...

2317 July 30 - Sept. 11.
2–3 minutes later July 30 - Sept. 11.
k – 1503 Aug. 1 - Sept. 9.
n – 1851 July 16–24.
t – 0840 July 16 - Aug. 28.
v – 1–2 minutes earlier July 16 - Aug. 28.

ANGERMÜNDE - SZCZECIN 949

	⚒							E	⑤	
Berlin Gesund. 845 ..d.		0805	...	...	1427	1721	...	...	2105	...
Angermünde .... d.	0640	0856	1040	1331	1531	1808	1931	2131	2155	...
Tantow .... d.	0719	0929	1119	1410	1610	1848	2013	2210	2234	...
Szczecin Gumience ⊞ d.	0733	0942	1133	1424	1623	1907	2027	2224	2248	...
Szczecin Glowny .... a.	0738	0948	1138	1429	1629	1913	2033	2229	2254	...

		⚒				E	⑤		
Szczecin Glowny .... d.	0605	0825	1007	1221	1431	1631	1637	1825	1951
Szczecin Gumience ⊞ .... d.	0611	0831	1013	1227	1437	1637	1643	1831	1957
Tantow .... d.	0625	0845	1027	1241	1451	1651	1657	1847	2011
Angermünde .... a.	0705	0925	1106	1321	1530	1730	1736	1925	2044
Berlin Gesund. 845 .... a.	0756	...	1157	...	...	...	1830	...	2139

Daily except ⑤.

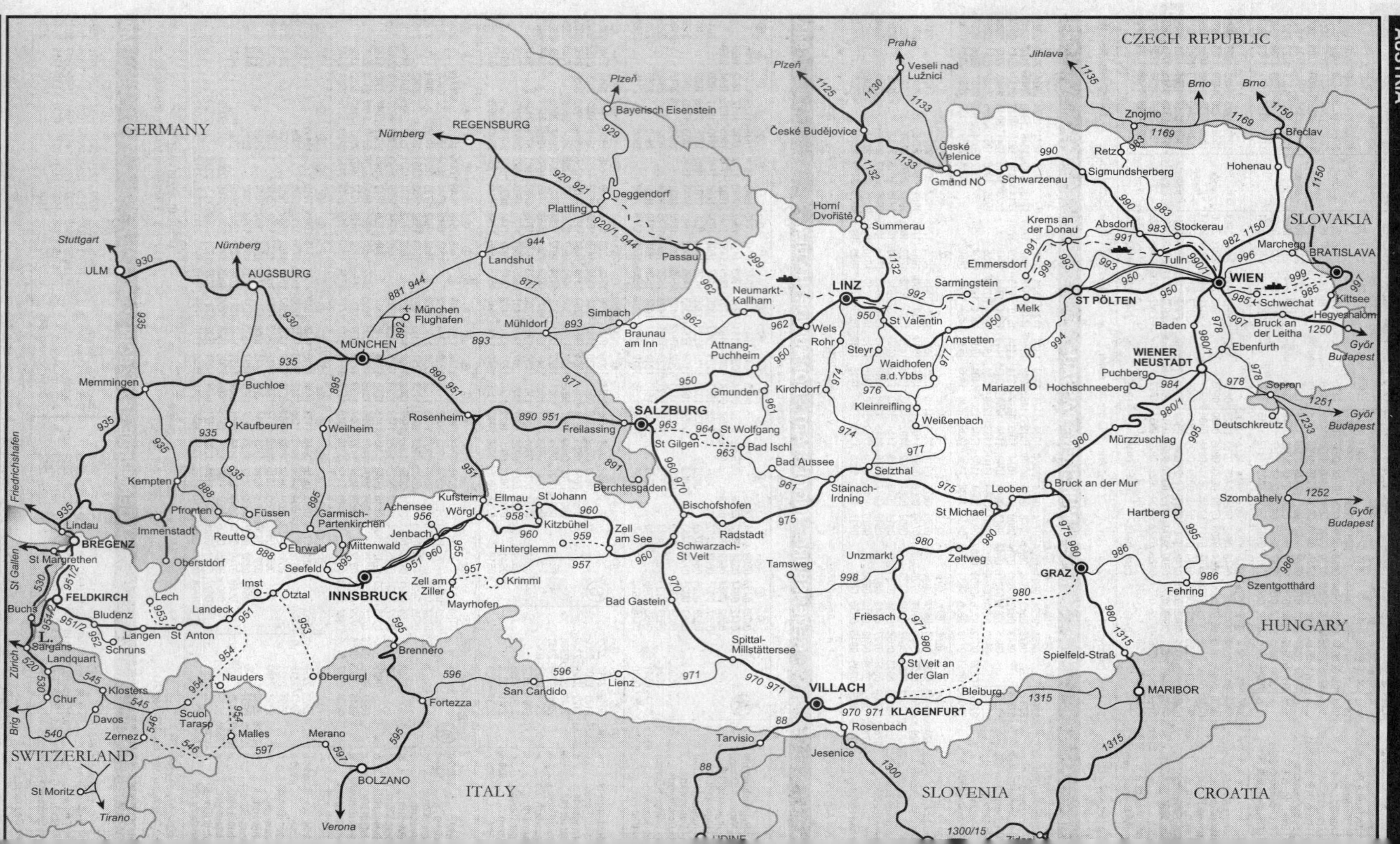

A list of Scenic Rail Routes appears elsewhere in the timetable – see Contents page

AUSTRIA

erator: Except where otherwise stated, rail services are operated by Österreichische Bundesbahnen (**ÖBB**) www.oebb.at

nings: **Valid until December 10**, 2016. unless stated otherwise in individual tables. See page 2 for public holiday dates.

rvices: Trains convey both first- and second-class seating unless footnotes show otherwise or there is a '2' in the train column. Overnight sleeping car (🛏) or couchette (🛏) trains do not necessarily convey seating accommodation - refer to individual footnotes for details. Descriptions of sleeping and couchette cars appear on page 8.

ain categories:

RJ	**Railjet**	Austrian high-speed train. Conveys first and economy (2nd) class. *Business class* also available to first class ticket holders (supplement payable).
ICE	**InterCity Express**	German high-speed train.
EC	**EuroCity**	International express train.
IC	**InterCity**	Internal or international express train.
D	**Schnellzug**	Ordinary fast train.
EN	**EuroNight**	(also *CNL*) Overnight express train. Special fares payable.
WB	**Westbahn**	Wien - Linz - Salzburg private operator (special fares – ÖBB tickets are not valid).
REX	**Regional Express**	Semi-fast regional train.
	Regional / S-Bahn	Local stopping trains – no category or train number shown.

servations: Seats may be reserved on all express trains (*RJ, ICE, EC, IC, CNL, EN, D*).

tering: Three types of catering are indicated in the tables: ✕ – Restaurant car; ⊗ – Bordbistro; 🍷 – At seat trolley service.

FLUGHAFEN WIEN - WIEN - LINZ - SALZBURG 950

km	SEE NOTE ⊠	*REX* 5885		*EC* 390	*RJ* 362	*IC* 540	*RJ* 660	*RJ* 260	*ICE* 228	*IC* 542	*RJ* 160	*RJ* 560	*IC* 662	*RJ* 262	*ICE* 28	*IC* 690	*RJ* 162	*RJ* 562	*IC* 548	*IC* 720	*RJ* 60	*RJ* 860	*ICE* 26	*IC* 640	*RJ* 564	*IC* 642
		⚒ F2		①–⑥ mJ ⊗	①–⑥ d✕	🍷	✕	✕	Q✕		✕	✕		✕	Q✕	V🍷	B✕	✕	🍷	Ⓒ △🍷	B✕	✕	R✕	🍷	✕	🍷
0	**Flughafen Wien** ✈ ¶ d.	...	...		...	...	...	...	...	0633	...	0703	0733	0803	...	0833	...	0903	0933	...	...	1003	...	1033	1103	1133
17	**Wien** Hbf d.	...	...	...	0530	0555	0630	0630	0650	0655	0730	0730	0755	0830	0850	0855	0930	0930	0955	1015	1030	1030	1050	1055	1130	1155
21	**Wien** Meidling d.	...	...	...	0537	0602	0637	0637	0657	0702	0737	0737	0802	0837	0857	0902	0937	0937	1002	1022	1037	1037	1057	1102	1137	1202
52	Tullnerfeld **993** d.	...	...	...	|	0617	|	|	|	0717	|	|	0817	|	|	0917	|	|	1017	|	|	|	|	1117	|	1217
82	**St Pölten** Hbf **993** d.	...	...	...	0600	0632	0700	0700	0722	0732	0800	0800	0832	0900	0922	0932	1000	1000	1032	1047	1100	1100	1122	1132	1200	1232
42	Amstetten d.	...	...	...	|	0700	|	|	|	0800	|	|	0900	|	|	1000	|	|	1100	|	|	|	|	1200	|	1300
79	St Valentin **976** d.	...	...	...	|	0716	|	|	|	0816	|	|	0916	|	|	1016	|	|	1116	|	|	|	|	1216	|	1316
04	**Linz** Hbf **976** a.	...	...	...	0646	0730	0746	0746	0812	0830	0846	0846	0930	0946	1012	1030	1046	1046	1130	1135	1146	1146	1212	1230	1246	1330
04	**Linz** Hbf **962** d.	0504	...	0632	0648	0732	0748	0748	0814	0832	0848	0848	0932	0948	1014	1032	1048	1048	1132	1137	1148	1148	1214	1232	1248	1332
29	**Wels** Hbf **962** d.	0520	...	0645	|	0745	|	|	0831	0845	|	|	0945	|	1031	1045	|	|	1145	1150	|	|	1231	1245	|	1345
	Passau Hbf **962** 🏛 a.	|	...	|	|	|	|	|	0918	|	|	|	|	|	1118	|	|	|	|	|	|	|	1318	|	|	|
59	Attnang-Puchheim d.	0544	...	0700	|	0800	|	|	...	0900	|	|	1000	|	...	1100	|	|	1200	1203	|	|	...	1300	|	1400
64	Vöcklabruck d.	0549	...	0706	|	0806	|	|	...	0906	|	|	1006	|	...	1106	|	|	1206	...	|	|	...	1306	|	1406
29	**Salzburg** Hbf a.	0648	...	0748	0752	0848	0852	0852	...	0948	0952	0952	1048	1052	...	1148	1152	1152	1248	...	1252	1252	...	1348	1352	1448
	München Hbf **890** a.	...	...	0941	|	...	|	1025‡	...	|	|	|	|	1225‡	...	...	|	|	...	...	1425‡	|	...	...	|	...
	Innsbruck Hbf **951** a.	...	...	...	0938	...	1054	...	...	1336z	1138	1138	1254	...	...	...	1340	1340	...	...	...	1454	...	...	1539	...
	Zürich HB **520** a.	...	...	...	1320	...	...	...	...	...	1520	|	|	...	...	...	1720	|	...	...	...	...	...	...	...	...
	Bregenz **951** a.	...	...	...	...	...	...	...	...	...	...	1417	1547	...	...	...	...	1617	...	...	...	...	...	...	...	...

SEE NOTE ⊠	*RJ* 62	*RJ* 862	*ICE* 90	*IC* 644	*RJ* 166	*RJ* 566	*IC* 646	*RJ* 64	*RJ* 864	*ICE* 22	*IC* 692	*RJ* 168	*RJ* 568	*IC* 722	*IC* 740	*RJ* 66	*RJ* 866	*ICE* 20	*IC* 742	*RJ* 760	*RJ* 960	*IC* 744	*RJ* 68	*RJ* 868	*IC* 746	*RJ* 762
	B✕	✕	E✕		✕	✕	🍷	B✕	✕	R✕	K🍷	✕	✕	Ⓐ 🍷	🍷	N✕	✕	Q✕		✕	✕	🍷	B✕	✕	◇ 🍷	✕
ughafen Wien ✈ ¶ d.	...	1203	...	1233	...	1303	1333	...	1403	...	1433	...	1503	...	1533	...	1603	...	*1633*	...	1703	*1733*	...	1803	1833	1903
ien Hbf d.	1230	1230	1250	1255	1330	1330	1355	1430	1430	1450	1455	1530	1530	1550	1555	1630	1630	1650	1655	1730	1730	1755	1830	1830	1855	1930
ien Meidling d.	1237	1237	1257	1302	1337	1337	1402	1437	1437	1457	1502	1537	1537	1557	1602	1637	1637	1657	1702	1737	1737	1802	1837	1837	1902	1937
llnerfeld **993** d.	|	|	|	1317	|	|	1417	|	|	|	1517	|	|	|	1617	|	|	|	1717	|	|	1817	|	|	1917	|
Pölten Hbf **993** d.	1300	1300	1322	1332	1400	1400	1432	1500	1500	1522	1532	1600	1600	1623	1632	1700	1700	1722	1732	1800	1800	1832	1900	1900	1932	2000
nstetten d.	|	|	|	1400	|	|	1500	|	|	|	1600	|	|	1649	1700	|	|	|	1800	|	|	1900	|	|	2000	|
Valentin **976** d.	|	|	|	1416	|	|	1516	|	|	|	1616	|	|	|	1716	|	|	|	1816	|	|	1916	|	|	2016	|
nz Hbf **976** a.	1346	1346	1412	1430	1446	1446	1530	1546	1546	1612	1630	1646	1646	1715	1730	1746	1746	1812	1830	1846	1846	1930	1946	1946	2030	2046
nz Hbf **962** d.	1348	1348	1414	1432	1448	1448	1532	1548	1548	1614	1632	1648	1648	...	1732	1748	1748	1814	1832	1848	1848	1932	1948	1948	2032	2048
els Hbf **962** d.	|	|	1431	1445	|	|	1545	|	|	1631	1645	|	|	...	1745	|	|	1831	1845	|	|	1945	|	|	2045	|
Passau Hbf **962** 🏛 a.	|	|	1518	|	|	|	|	|	|	1718	|	|	|	...	|	|	|	1918	|	|	|	|	|	|	|	|
tnang-Puchheim d.	|	|	...	1500	|	|	1600	|	|	...	1700	|	|	...	1800	|	|	...	1900	|	|	2000	|	|	2100	|
ɔcklabruck d.	|	|	...	1506	|	|	1606	|	|	...	1706	|	|	...	1806	|	|	...	1906	|	|	2006	|	|	2106	|
alzburg Hbf a.	1452	1452	...	1548	1552	1552	1648	1652	1652	...	1748	1752	1752	...	1848	1852	1852	...	1948	1952	1952	2048	2052	2052	2148	2152
München Hbf **890** a.	1631‡	|	...	...	|	|	...	1825‡	|	...	...	|	|	...	...	2025‡	|	...	...	|	|	...	2226‡	|	...	|
Innsbruck Hbf **951** a.	...	1654	...	...	1738	1738	...	...	1854	...	...	1940	1940	...	...	...	2055	...	...	2138	2138h	...	...	2254b	...	2348
Zürich HB **520** a.	...	|	...	...	2120	|	...	...	...	...	...	2320	|	...	...	...	...	...	...	|	...	...	...	...	...	...
Bregenz **951** a.	...	1922	...	...	...	2017	...	...	...	...	...	...	2217	...	...	...	...	...	...	0010	...	...	...	...	...	...

SEE NOTE ⊠	*IC* 748	*RJ* 42	*RJ* 664	*EN* 490	*IC* 840	*EN* 466	*EN* 420	*IC* 820	*EN* 246	*EN* 462	*EN* 60466
	🍷	B✕	✕	H♣	🍷	W	Y♣		♥	D♣	⊙
ughafen Wien ✈ ¶ d.	1933	...	2003	...	2033	...	...	2133j	*2233*	...	...
ien Hbf d.	1955	2030	2030	2039	2055	2125	2139	2155	2255	2325	2325
ien Meidling d.	2002	2037	2037	2047	2102	2133	2147	2202	2303	2333	2332
llnerfeld **993** d.	2017	|	|	|	2117	|	|	2217	2320	|	|
Pölten Hbf **993** d.	2032	2100	2100	2116	2132	2202	2216	2232	2339	0002	0002
nstetten d.	2100	|	|	2146	2200	2232	2246	2300	0013	|	|
Valentin **976** d.	2116	|	|	|	2216	|	|	2316	0035	|	|
nz Hbf **976** a.	2130	2146	2146	2217	2230	2303	2317	2330	0051	0100	0100
nz Hbf **962** d.	2132	2148	2148	2219	2232	2305	2319	...	0106	0102	0102
els Hbf **962** d.	2145	|	|	2236	2245	2322	2336	...	0123	|	|
Passau Hbf **962** 🏛 a.	|	|	|	2326	|	|	0026	...	|	|	|
tnang-Puchheim d.	2200	|	|	...	2300	2340	...	...	0142	|	|
ɔcklabruck d.	2206	|	|	...	2306	|	...	...	|	|	|
alzburg Hbf a.	2248	2252	2252	...	2348	0028	...	...	0230	0210	0210
München Hbf **890** a.	...	...	...	...	...	|	...	...	|	0611g	|
Innsbruck Hbf **951** a.	...	...	...	...	...	0423	...	...	0519	...	0423
Zürich HB **520** a.	...	...	...	...	...	0820	...	...	|	...	0820
Bregenz **951** a.	...	...	...	...	...	...	...	...	0823	...	...

	EN 463	*EN* 60467	*EN* 247	*IC* 821	*IC* 823	*EN* 467	*IC* 541	*EN* 491	*EN* 421	*RJ* 761
	D♣	⊖	♥		Ⓐ 🍷	X	🍷	H♣	Y♣	✕
Bregenz **951** d.	...	...	2146	...	...	...	...	...	...	...
Zürich HB **520** d.	...	2140	|	...	...	2140	...	...	...	...
Innsbruck Hbf **951** d.	...	0128	0044	...	...	0128	...	...	...	...
München Hbf **890** d.	2336¦	|	|	...	...	|	...	...	...	...
Salzburg Hbf d.	0350	0350	0332	...	...	0438	0512	...	...	0605
Vöcklabruck d.	|	|	|	...	...	|	0554	...	...	|
Attnang-Puchheim d.	|	|	0420	...	...	0527	0600	...	...	0650
Passau Hbf **962** 🏛 d.	|	|	|	...	...	|	|	0512	0522	|
Wels Hbf **962** d.	|	|	0438	...	...	0545	0616	0609	0619	|
Linz Hbf **962** a.	0501	0501	0453	...	...	0601	0628	0623	0635	0712
Linz Hbf **976** d.	0503	0503	0516	0530	0605	0610	0630	0634	0638	0714
St Valentin **976** d.	|	|	0534	0545	|	|	0645	|	|	|
Amstetten d.	|	|	0556	0602	0634	0644	0702	0707	0711	|
St Pölten Hbf **993** d.	0600	0600	0640	0630	0700	0715	0730	0738	0742	0802
Tullnerfeld **993** a.	|	|	|	0642	|	|	0742	|	|	|
Wien Meidling a.	0627	0627	0712	0658	0723	0746	0758	0808	0812	0823
Wien Hbf a.	0635	0635	0720	0705	0730	0755	0805	0816	0820	0830
Flughafen Wien ✈ ¶ a.	*0657*	*0657*	...	0727	*0757*	...	0827	...	...	0857

	IC 543		*RJ* 49	*RJ* 949	*IC* 545	*RJ* 763	*RJ* 265	*IC* 547	*RJ* 861	*RJ* 61	*IC* 549	*RJ* 765	*IC* 693	*ICE* 21	*RJ* 863	*RJ* 63	*IC* 643	*RJ* 161	*IC* 645	*ICE* 23	*RJ* 665	*RJ* 65	*IC* 865	*RJ* 563	*IC* 649	*ICE* 91
	🍷		①–⑥ dB✕	✕	🍷	✕	①–⑥ u✕	◇ 🍷	✕	B✕		✕	K🍷	Q✕	✕	M✕	🍷	✕	🍷	R✕	⑥v ✕	B✕		✕	🍷	E✕
Bregenz **951** d.	...	...	...	...	...	...	...	...	...	...	...	0547	...	...	0639	...	...	...	...	...	...	...	0810	...	...	...
Zürich HB **520** d.	...	...	...	...	...	...	...	...	...	...	...	|	...	...	|	...	...	0640	...	...	...	...	|	...	...	...
Innsbruck Hbf **951** d.	...	...	0505	0505y	...	0609	...	...	0705	...	...	0820	...	...	0905	...	...	1022	...	...	...	...	1105	1220	...	...
München Hbf **890** d.	...	...	|	|	...	|	0624§	...	|	0731§	...	|	...	...	|	0934§	...	|	...	...	...	1134§	|	|	...	...
alzburg Hbf d.	0612	...	0708	0708	0712	0808	0808	0812	0908	0908	0912	1008	1012	...	1108	1108	1112	1208	1212	...	1308	1308	1312	1408	1412	...
ɔcklabruck d.	0654	...	|	|	0754	|	|	0854	|	|	0954	|	1054	...	|	|	1154	|	1254	...	|	|	1354	|	1454	...
tnang-Puchheim d.	0700	...	|	|	0800	|	|	0900	|	|	1000	|	1100	...	|	|	1200	|	1300	...	|	|	1400	|	1500	...
Passau Hbf **962** 🏛 d.	|	...	|	|	|	|	|	|	|	|	|	|	|	1038	|	|	|	|	|	1238	|	|	|	|	|	1438
els Hbf **962** d.	0716	...	|	|	0816	|	|	0916	|	|	1016	|	1116	1128	|	|	1216	|	1316	1328	|	|	1416	|	1516	1528
nz Hbf **962** a.	0728	...	0812	0812	0828	0912	0912	0928	1012	1012	1028	1112	1128	1142	1212	1212	1228	1312	1328	1342	1412	1412	1428	1512	1528	1542
nz Hbf **976** d.	0730	...	0814	0814	0830	0914	0914	0930	1014	1014	1030	1114	1130	1147	1214	1214	1230	1314	1330	1347	1414	1414	1430	1514	1530	1547
Valentin **976** d.	0745	...	|	|	0845	|	|	0945	|	|	1045	|	1145	|	|	|	1245	|	1345	|	|	|	1445	|	1545	|
mstetten d.	0802	...	|	|	0902	|	|	1002	|	|	1102	|	1202	|	|	|	1302	|	1402	|	|	|	1502	|	1602	|
Pölten Hbf **993** d.	0830	...	0902	0902	0930	1002	1002	1030	1102	1102	1130	1202	1230	1237	1302	1302	1330	1402	1430	1437	1502	1502	1530	1602	1630	1637
llnerfeld **993** a.	0842	...	|	|	0942	|	|	1042	|	|	1142	|	1242	|	|	|	1342	|	1442	|	|	|	1542	|	1642	|
ien Meidling a.	0858	...	0923	0923	0958	1023	1023	1058	1123	1123	1158	1223	1258	1302	1323	1323	1358	1423	1458	1502	1523	1523	1558	1623	1658	1702
ien Hbf a.	0905	...	0930	0930	1005	1030	1030	1105	1130	1130	1205	1230	1305	1309	1330	1330	1405	1430	1505	1509	1530	1530	1605	1630	1705	1709
ughafen Wien ✈ ¶ a.	0927	...	...	0957	1027	1057	...	1127	1157	...	1227	1257	1327	...	1357	...	1427	*1457*	1527	...	1557	*1557*	*1627*	1657	*1727*	...

☛ See page 452 for regional trains Wien Westbf - St Pölten - Melk - Amstetten - Linz, also services Wien - Linz - Salzburg operated by *Westbahn*.

FOR NOTES SEE PAGE 452 →

950 SALZBURG - LINZ - WIEN

	RJ 867	RJ 67	IC 741	RJ 565	RJ 165	IC 691	ICE 27	RJ 869	RJ 69	IC 721 Ⓒ	IC 745	RJ 167	RJ 567	IC 747	ICE 29	RJ 661	RJ 261	IC 749	RJ 169	RJ 569	IC 841	ICE 229	RJ 663	IC 843	RJ 361	E 39 Ⓑ
	✕	B✕	🍷	✕	B✕	K🍷	R✕	✕	✕	△🍷	🍷	✕	✕		Q✕	✕	✕	🍷	✕	✕	🍷	Q✕	✕	🍷	✕	⊗
Bregenz **951** d.	...	...	...	1140	...	...	...	...	...	...	...	...	1340	...	...	1410	...	...	...	1540	...	...	...	...	...	..
Zürich HB **520** d.	...	...	...	|	1040	...	...	...	...	...	...	1240	|	...	...	|	...	...	1440	|	...	...	...	...	1640	..
Innsbruck Hbf **951** d.	1305	...	...	1420	1420	...	...	1505	...	...	...	1622	1622	1424z	...	1705	...	...	1822	1822	...	...	1905	...	2022	..
München Hbf **890** d.	|	1334§	...	|	|	...	...	|	1534§	...	...	|	|	|	...	|	1734§	...	|	|	...	...	|	...	|	20
Salzburg Hbf d.	1508	1508	1512	1608	1608	1612	...	1708	1708	...	1712	1808	1808	1812	...	1908	1908	1912	2008	2008	2012	...	2108	2112	2208	22
Vöcklabruck d.	|	|	1554	|	|	1654	...	|	|	...	1754	|	|	1854	...	|	|	1954	|	|	2054	...	|	2154	|	22
Attnang-Puchheim d.	|	|	1600	|	|	1700	...	|	|	1755	1800	|	|	1900	...	|	|	2000	|	|	2100	...	|	2200	|	23
Passau Hbf **962** ▦ d.	|	|	|	|	|	|	1638	|	|	|	|	|	|	|	1838	|	|	|	|	|	|	2038	|	|	|	|
Wels Hbf **962** d.	|	|	1616	|	|	1716	1728	|	|	1811	1816	|	|	1916	1928	|	|	2016	|	|	2116	2128	|	2216	|	23
Linz Hbf **962** a.	1612	1612	1628	1712	1712	1728	1742	1812	1812	1823	1828	1912	1912	1928	1942	2012	2012	2028	2112	2112	2128	2142	2212	2228	2312	23
Linz Hbf **976** d.	1614	1614	1630	1714	1714	1730	1747	1814	1814	1826	1830	1914	1914	1930	1947	2014	2014	2030	2114	2114	2130	2147	2214	...	2314	...
St Valentin **976** d.	|	|	1645	|	|	1745	|	|	|	|	1845	|	|	1945	|	|	|	2045	|	|	2145	|	|	...	|	...
Amstetten d.	|	|	1702	|	|	1802	|	|	|	|	1902	|	|	2002	|	|	|	2102	|	|	2202	|	|	...	|	...
St Pölten Hbf **993** d.	1702	1702	1730	1802	1802	1830	1837	1902	1902	1915	1930	2002	2002	2030	2037	2102	2102	2130	2202	2202	2230	2237	2302	...	0002	...
Tullnerfeld **993** a.	|	|	1742	|	|	1842	|	|	|	|	1942	|	|	2042	|	|	|	2142	|	|	2242	|	|	...	|	...
Wien Meidling a.	1723	1723	1758	1823	1823	1858	1902	1923	1923	1939	1958	2023	2023	2058	2102	2123	2123	2158	2223	2223	2258	2302	2323	...	0023	...
Wien Hbf a.	1730	1730	1805	1830	1830	1905	1909	1930	1930	1946	2005	2030	2030	2105	2109	2130	2130	2205	2230	2230	2305	2309	2330	...	0030	...
Flughafen Wien ✈ ¶ a.	1757	...	1827	1857	...	1927	...	1957	...	...	2027	...	2057	2127j	...	2157	...	2227	...	...	...	...	...	...	...	...

Regional ÖBB trains **WIEN - MELK - AMSTETTEN - ST VALENTIN - LINZ** (2nd class only)

km		⚒	ⒶT	⚒	Ⓐt		¶t	P	Ⓐt			t	t	t	t	Ⓒ	Ⓐt	Ⓒ	Ⓐt	Ⓒ	Ⓐt	Ⓒ	Ⓐt	⚒		
0	**Wien** Westbahnhof ◧ d.	...	0417	...	0620	0554c	0720	...	0820	*0854*	*1054*	1220e	1320e	1420e	1520e	*1554*	1620	*1654*	1720	1754	1820	1854	1920	*1954*	...	235
6	**Wien** Hütteldorf ◧ d.	...	0423	...	0628	0600c	0728	...	0828	*0900*	*1100*	1228e	1328e	1428e	1528e	*1600*	1628	*1700*	1728	1800	1828	1900	1928	*2000*	...	000
	Tullnerfeld d.	...	|	...	0640	|	0740	0812	0840	|	|	1240e	1340e	1440e	1540e	|	1640	|	1740	|	1840	|	1940	|	...	|
61	**St Pölten** Hbf ◧ a.	...	0518	...	0653	0655c	0753	0850	0853	*0955*	*1155*	1253e	1353e	1453e	1553e	*1655*	1653	*1755*	1753	1855	1853	1955	1953	*2055*	...	005
61	**St Pölten** Hbf d.	0435	0520	0550	...	0703	0805	0855	0905	1005	1205	1305	1405	1505	1605	1705	1705	1805	1805	1905	1905	2005	2005	2105	2235	010
85	Melk d.	0457	0537	0612	...	0722	0822	0911	0922	1022	1222	1322	1422	1522	1622	1722	1722	1822	1822	1922	1922	2022	2022	2122	2257	012
94	Pöchlarn d.	0507	0544	0619	...	0729	0829	0920	0929	1029	1229	1329	1429	1529	1629	1729	1729	1829	1829	1929	1929	2029	2029	2129	2304	012
107	Ybbs an der Donau d.	0519	0552	0631	...	0739	0840	0931	0940	1040	1240	1340	1440	1540	1640	1740	1740	1840	1840	1940	1940	2040	2040	2140	2316	013
124	Amstetten a.	0533	0607	0647	...	0755	0855	0942	0955	1055	1255	1355	1455	1555	1655	1755	1755	1855	1855	1955	1955	2055	2055	2155	2330	015
163	**St Valentin** a.	0607	*0631*	...	...	...	...	1008	...	...	...	...	...	...	...	...	1839	...	1939	...	2039	...	...	...	...	...
188	**Linz** Hbf a.	*0636*	*0651*	...	...	...	...	1035	...	...	...	...	...	...	...	...	*1908*	...	*2008*	...	*2108*	...	...	...	...	...

	t	⚒	Ⓐt	Ⓐt	Ⓐt		Ⓐt	⚒T		Ⓐ						t	t					Ⓒ⊕	P		Ⓒ	⊗
Linz Hbf d.	...	...	...	...	*0430*	...	...	...	...	...	...	...	...	...	...	...	...	...	...	*1652*	*1752*	...	1925	...	...	...
St Valentin d.	...	*0353*e	...	0432	0501	...	0521	...	...	...	...	...	...	1121e	...	...	...	...	...	1721	1821	...	1948	...	...	...
Amstetten d.	0412	0431	0442	0507	0537	0553	0607	0616	0705	0805	0905	...	1105	1205	1305	1405	1505	1605	1705	1805	1905	2005	2015	...	2105	220
Ybbs an der Donau d.	0426	0445	0456	0521	0551	0608	0621	0630	0719	0819	0919	...	1119	1219	1319	1419	1519	1619	1719	1819	1919	2019	2028	...	2119	221
Pöchlarn d.	0435	0458	0505	0530	0600	0621	0630	0643	0729	0829	0930	1023	1130	1230	1330	1430	1530	1630	1730	1830	1930	2030	2039	2054	2130	223
Melk d.	0441	0504	0511	0536	0606	0628	0636	0650	0736	0836	0936	1029	1136	1236	1336	1436	1536	1636	1736	1836	1936	2036	2048	2101	2136	223
St Pölten Hbf a.	0500	0527	0530	0555	0625	0652	0655	0716	0755	0855	0955	1053	1155	1255	1355	1455	1555	1655	1755	1855	1955	2055	2106	2124	2155	225
St Pölten Hbf ◧ d.	0503	0535	0533	0607	0637	*0705*	0707	*0735*	*0807*e	*0907*e	*1005*	*1105*	*1205*	*1305*	*1405*	1507e	1607e	1707e	1807e	1905	2005	2105	...	...	*2205*	230
Tullnerfeld a.	0515	|	0545	0619	0649	|	0719	|	*0819*e	*0919*e	|	|	|	|	|	1519e	1619e	1719e	1819e	|	|	|	...	...	|	|
Wien Hütteldorf ◧ a.	0527	0628	0557	0631	0701	*0758*	0731	*0828*	*0831*e	*0931*e	*1058*	*1158*	*1259*	*1358*	*1459*	1531e	1631e	1731e	1831e	1958	2059	2158	...	...	*2323*	002
Wien Westbahnhof ◧ a.	0536	0636	0606	0640	0710	*0806*	0740	*0836*	*0840*e	*0940*e	*1106*	*1206*	*1307*	*1406*	*1507*	1540e	1640e	1740e	1840e	2006	2107	2206	...	...	*2332*	003

SERVICES OPERATED BY *WESTBAHN* **WIEN - LINZ - SALZBURG**. Special fares payable (ÖBB tickets not valid). All trains convey 🍷.

km		WB 900 ⚒	WB 940 ⚒		WB 902 ⚒	WB 902	WB 904	WB 906	WB 908	WB 910	WB 912	WB 914	WB 970 ⑤	WB 916	WB 918	WB 920	WB 944	WB 922	WB 968	WB 926	WB 976 †s		WB 928	WB 928 ⊡		WB 930 ♠
0	**Wien** Westbahnhof d.	...	0546	...	0642	...	0740	0840	0940	1040	1140	1240	1316	1340	1440	1540	1616	1640	1740	1840	1916	...	1940	1940	...	204
6	**Wien** Hütteldorf d.	...	|	...	0648	...	0746	0846	0946	1046	1146	1246	1322	1346	1446	1546	1622	1646	1746	1846	1922	...	1946	1946	...	204
30	Tullnerfeld d.	...	|	...	|	...	0757	0857	0957	1057	1157	1257	|	1357	1457	1557	|	1657	1757	1857	|	...	1957	1957	...	205
60	**St Pölten** Hbf d.	...	0611	...	0710	...	0810	0910	1010	1110	1210	1310	1343	1410	1510	1610	1643	1710	1810	1910	1943	...	2010	2010	...	211
120	Amstetten d.	...	|	...	0733	...	0833	0933	1033	1133	1233	1333	1409	1433	1533	1633	1709	1733	1833	1933	2009	...	2033	2033	...	213
182	**Linz** Hbf **962** d.	0653	0700	...	0800	0800	0900	1000	1100	1200	1300	1400	1438	1500	1600	1700	1735	1800	1900	2000	2035	...	2059	2100	...	215
207	**Wels** Hbf **962** d.	0705	|	...	0812	0812	0912	1012	1112	1212	1312	1412	...	1512	1612	1712	...	1812	1912	2012	...	...	...	2112	...	...
237	Attnang-Puchheim d.	0717	|	...	0825	0825	0925	1025	1125	1225	1325	1425	...	1525	1625	1725	...	1825	1925	2025	...	...	...	2125	...	...
307	**Salzburg** Hbf a.	...	0805	...	0908	0908	1008	1108	1208	1308	1408	1508	...	1608	1708	1808	...	1908	2008	2108	...	...	...	2208	...	...

	WB 903 ⚒	WB 905 ⚒	WB 941 ⚒	WB 907 †	WB 907	WB 961	WB 911	WB 913	WB 915	WB 917	WB 919	WB 979 ⑤	WB 921	WB 923	WB 925	WB 981 †s	WB 927	WB 929	WB 931	WB 933 ⊡						
Salzburg Hbf d.	...	0552	0700	0700	...	0752	0852	0952	1052	1152	1252	...	1352	1452	1552	...	1652	1752	1852	1952	...	...	...	...	...	...
Attnang-Puchheim d.	...	0635	|	0744	0744	0835	0935	1035	1135	1235	1335	...	1435	1535	1635	...	1735	1835	1935	2035	...	...	...	...	...	...
Wels Hbf **962** d.	...	0648	|	0757	0757	0848	0948	1048	1148	1248	1348	...	1448	1548	1648	...	1748	1848	1948	2048	...	...	...	...	...	...
Linz Hbf **962** d.	0601	0701	0804	0809	0809	0901	1001	1101	1201	1301	1401	1444	1501	1601	1701	1744	1801	1901	2001	2101	...	...	...	...	...	...
Amstetten d.	0627	0727	|	0835	0835	0927	1027	1127	1227	1327	1427	1512	1527	1627	1727	1816	1827	1927	2027	2127	...	...	...	...	...	...
St Pölten Hbf d.	0651	0751	|	0858	0858	0951	1051	1151	1251	1351	1451	1539	1551	1651	1751	1842	1851	1951	2051	2151	...	...	...	...	...	...
Tullnerfeld d.	0703	0803	|	|	|	1003	1103	1203	1303	1403	1503	|	1603	1703	1803	|	1903	2003	2103	2203	...	...	...	...	...	...
Wien Hütteldorf a.	0714	0814	0910	0919	0919	1014	1114	1214	1314	1414	1514	1604	1614	1714	1814	1904	1914	2014	2114	2214	...	...	...	...	...	...
Wien Westbahnhof a.	0720	0820	0916	0925	0925	1020	1120	1220	1320	1420	1520	1610	1620	1720	1820	1910	1920	2020	2120	2220	...	...	...	...	...	...

B – From / to Budapest (Table **1250**).
D – KÁLMÁN IMRE – 🛏 1, 2 cl., ▬ 2 cl. and [2] Budapest - Wien - München and v.v.
E – [12] and ✕ Hamburg - Hannover - Nürnberg - Regensburg - Passau - Wien and v.v.
F – To Freilassing (a. 0702).
H – 🛏 1, 2 cl., ▬ 2 cl. and [2] Wien - Hannover - Hamburg and v.v.
J – [12] and ⊗ Linz - München - Stuttgart - Frankfurt and v.v.
K – To / from Klagenfurt (Table **970**).
M – [12] and ✕ (Frankfurt ⑥⑦ **k** -) München - Wien - Budapest.
N – [12] and ✕ Budapest - Wien - München (- Frankfurt ⑤⑥ **f**).
P – May 1 - Oct. 26. [2] Wien Franz-Josefs-Bf - Passau and v.v.
Q – [12] and ✕ Frankfurt - Nürnberg - Regensburg - Passau ▦ - Wien and v.v.
R – [12] and ✕ Dortmund - Frankfurt - Nürnberg - Regensburg - Passau ▦ - Wien and v.v.
T – To / from Kleinreifling (Table **977**).
V – To Villach (Table **970**).
W – 🛏 1, 2 cl., ▬ 2 cl. and [2] Wien - Zürich; conveys 🛏 1, 2 cl., ▬ 2 cl. and [2] (*EN* **237**) Wien - Salzburg - Villach - Tarvisio ▦ - Venezia.
X – 🛏 1, 2 cl., ▬ 2 cl. and [2] Zürich - Wien; conveys 🛏 1, 2 cl., ▬ 2 cl. and [2] (*EN* **236**) Venezia - Tarvisio ▦ - Villach - Salzburg - Wien.
Y – 🛏 1, 2 cl., ▬ 2 cl. and [2] Wien - Köln - Düsseldorf and v.v.
b – Ⓑ (not Mar. 27, May 15, Aug. 14).
c – Ⓒ only.
d – Not Mar. 28, May 16, Aug. 15.
e – Ⓐ only.
f – ⑤⑥ to Feb. 20; ⑤⑥ from May 13 (also May 15, Oct. 2).
g – 0721 on the mornings of ⑦ June 5 - July 17.
h – ⑦ (also Mar. 28, May 16, Aug. 15; not Mar. 27, May 15, Aug. 14).
j – Change trains at Wien Hbf on †.
k – ⑥⑦ to Feb. 21; ⑥⑦ from May 14 (also May 16, Oct. 3).
m – Not Mar. 26, 28, May 16.
q – Not Mar. 25, 27, May 15.
s – Also ⑤⑥ from Sept. 30.

t – Classified *REX 200* (via high-speed line).
u – Not Jan. 6, Mar. 28, May 16, Dec. 8.
v – Also May 5, 26.
y – ① (also Mar. 29, May 17, Aug. 16; not Mar. 28, May 16, Aug. 15).
z – Ⓒ only. Via Zell am See (Table **960**).
⊡ – ④–⑦ (also Jan. 6, Mar. 28, May 16, Aug. 15, Oct. 26, Nov. 1).
♠ – ④⑤⑦ (also Jan. 6, Mar. 28, May 16, Aug. 15, Oct. 26, Nov. 1).
‡ – Arrives up to 16 minutes later Feb. 26 - Aug. 5.
§ – Departs up to 19 minutes **earlier** from Feb. 26 - Aug. 5.
⁝ – 2331 daily Feb. 25 - June 3, ①–⑤ June 6 - July 15 and daily July 18 - Aug. 5. 2314 on ⑥⑦ June 4 - July 17. 2223 on Jan. 16.
¶ – Change trains at St Pölten on Ⓐ.
⊗ – Change trains at St Pölten on Ⓒ.
⊕ – Change trains at St Pölten on ⑥.
⊙ – 🛏 1, 2 cl., ▬ 2 cl. and [2] Budapest (**462**) - Salzburg (**466**) - Zürich. Booking number **60466**.
⊖ – 🛏 1, 2 cl., ▬ 2 cl. and [2] Zürich (**467**) - Salzburg (**463**) - Budapest. Booking number **60467**.
♥ – Conveys 🛏 1, 2 cl., ▬ 2 cl. and [2].
◇ – Conveys [2] Wien - Salzburg - Saalfelden and v.v. (Table **960**).
△ – [12] Wien - Attnang-Puchheim and v.v.; [2] Wien - Attnang-Puchheim - Stainach-Irdning and v.v. (Table **961**).
♣ – 🅁 for journeys to / from Germany.
⊠ – Passengers travelling on *RJ* services from Austria to Germany may have to change trains at Salzburg (in the same timings). Germany to Austria journeys are unaffected
◧ – Other stopping services Wien - St Pölten and v.v.:
From Wien Westbahnhof at 0054 Ⓒ, 0454, 0524 ⚒, 0554, 0624 ⚒, 0654, 0724 Ⓐ, 0754, 0954, 1124 Ⓐ, 1154 and at 24 Ⓐ and 54 minutes past each hour until 1824 Ⓐ, 1854; then 1954, 2054, 2128 and 2228. **From St Pölten** at 0439 Ⓐ, 0509, 0605, 0635 ⚒, 0805, 0835 Ⓐ, 0905, 1205, 1235 Ⓐ and at 05 and 35 Ⓐ minutes past each hour until 2005, 2035 Ⓐ; then 2105 and 2205.

SALZBURG and MÜNCHEN - INNSBRUCK - BREGENZ - LINDAU 951

	EN 466	*EN* 60466		*EN* 464	*EN* 246	*RJ* 666	*IC* 1285			*RJ* 360	*RJ* 962	*IC* 118	*EC* 81	*RJ* 362		*RJ* 660		*EC* 85	*RJ* 160	*RJ* 560	*IC* 662	*EC* 87	*RJ* 162	*RJ* 562	*RJ* 860
							⑥	⚒					¶				⚒								
	N	⊙	2	◆	N	✕	◆	2	2	✕	✕	🍷◆	A✕	✕	2	✕	2	A✕	✕	F✕	F	A✕	♥✕	F✕	F✕
Wien Hbf **950** d.	2125	2325	...	...	2255	...	...	...	...	...	...	...	...	0530t	...	0630	...	...	0730	0730	0755	...	0930	0930	1030
Linz Hbf **950** d.	2305	0102	...	...	0106	...	...	...	...	...	...	...	...	0648t	...	0748	...	...	0848	0848	0932	...	1048	1048	1148
Salzburg Hbf d.	0230	0230	...	...	0306	...	...	...	...	...	0700	...	...	0756	...	0900	...	...	0956	0956	1100	...	1156	1156	1300
München Hbf **890** ‡ d.	|	|	...	...	|	...	0455x	...	...	...	|	...	0738x	|	...	|	...	0938x	|	|	|	1138x	|	|	|
München Ost **890** ‡ d.	|	|	...	...	|	...	0505x	...	...	...	|	...	0747x	|	...	|	...	0947x	|	|	|	1147x	|	|	|
Rosenheim .. **890** ‡ d.	|	|	...	...	|	...	0537	...	...	...	|	...	0819	|	...	|	...	1019	|	|	|	1219	|	|	|
Kufstein 🏛 ‡ d.	|	|	...	...	|	...	0559	0613	0619b	...	0814	...	0841	|	0848e	1014	...	1041	|	|	1214	1241	|	|	1414
Wörgl Hbf **960** d.	|	|	...	...	|	*0530*	0611	0630	0636	...	0824	...	0851	|	0900e	1024	...	1051	|	|	1224	1251	|	|	1424
Jenbach **960** d.	|	|	...	...	|	*0550*	▬	0651	0658	...	0838	...	0906	|	0920e	1038	...	1106	|	|	1238	1306	|	|	1438
Innsbruck Hbf **960** a.	0423	0423	...	...	0519	*0619*	...	0721	0732	...	0854	...	0923	0938	0947e	1054	...	1123	1138	1138	1254	1323	1340	1340	1454
Innsbruck Hbf d.	0431	0431	...	0453	0523	0630	...	...	...	0740	▬	0902	...	0944	0957	...	1057	...	1144	1144	1301	...	1344	1344	...
Ötztal d.	|	|	...	|	0551	0701	...	...	...	0804	...	0931	...	1008	1039	...	1131	...	1208	1208	1329	...	1408	1408	...
Imst-Pitztal d.	|	|	...	|	0602	0712	...	...	...	0814	...	0941	...	1018	1049	...	1143	...	1218	1218	1341	...	1418	1418	...
Landeck-Zams d.	|	|	...	0545	0622	0727	...	...	...	0828	...	0954	...	1034	1104	...	1158	...	1232	1232	1355	...	1432	1432	...
St Anton am Arlberg d.	|	|	...	0610	0648	0751	...	...	...	0852	...	1019	...	1058	▬	...	...	...	1256	1256	1419	...	1456	1456	...
Langen am Arlberg d.	|	|	...	0620	0659	0800	...	...	...	0902	...	1030	...	1108	...	...	...	...	1306	1306	1429	...	1506	1506	...
Bludenz **952** d.	0623	0623	0633	0706	0735	0830	①–⑤	...	...	0930	...	1102	...	1135	...	...	...	...	1333	1333	1500	...	1533	1533	...
Feldkirch **952** a.	0637	0637	0653	0721	0749	0842	a 2	...	...	0941	2	1113	...	1146	2	...	...	...	1344	1344	1512	...	1544	1544	...
Feldkirch **952** d.	0640	0640	0656	0738	0755	0847	0849	...	...	0943	0947	1115	...	1148	1150	...	...	...	1348	1353	1517	...	1548	1553	...
Buchs 🏛 **952** a.	0656	0656	|	0753	|	|	0911	...	...	0958	|	|	...	1205	|	...	...	...	1406	|	|	...	1606	|	...
Zürich HB **520** a.	0820	0820	|	0920	|	|	...	...	...	1120	|	|	...	1320	|	...	...	...	1520	|	|	...	1720	|	...
Dornbirn **952** d.	...	...	0713	...	0815	0906	...	...	...	...	1009	1132	...	...	1211	...	...	...	...	1407	1536	...	...	1607	...
Bregenz 🏛 **952** a.	...	...	0722	...	0823	0917	...	...	...	...	1018	1140	...	...	1220	...	...	...	...	1417	1547	...	...	1617	...
Lindau Hbf 🏛 **952** a.	...	...	0736	...	*0901*	*0932*	...	...	...	...	1031	1153	...	...	1233	...	...	...	...	*1432*	...	...	...	*1632*	...

		EC 89	*RJ* 564	*EC* 164		*IC* 1287	*RJ* 862		*IC* 1281	*EC* 83	*RJ* 166	*RJ* 566	*RJ* 864		*EC* 189	*RJ* 168	*RJ* 568	*ICE* 209 1209	*RJ* 866		*RJ* 760		*CNL* 485	*RJ* 868	*RJ* 762	
	⚒				Ⓐ	⑥C			⑥					Ⓐ									🅁	Ⓑw		
	2	A✕	F✕	✕◆	2	🍷	F✕	2	◆	A✕	✕	F✕	F✕	2	✕	✕	F✕	●✕	F✕	2	✕	2	🍷◆	F✕	F✕	2
en Hbf **950** d.	...	...	1130	...	...	...	1230	...	...	...	1330	1330	1430	...	...	1530	1530	...	1630	...	1730	...	...	1830	1930	...
z Hbf **950** d.	...	...	1248	...	...	...	1348	...	...	...	1448	1448	1548	...	...	1648	1648	...	1748	...	1848	...	...	1948	2048	...
ourg Hbf d.	...	...	1356	...	...	...	1500	...	...	...	1556	1556	1700	...	...	1756	1756	...	1900	...	1956	...	...	2100	2156	...
inchen Hbf **890** ‡ d.	...	1338x	|	...	...	1439	|	...	1521	1538x	|	|	|	...	1738x	|	|	1901x	|	...	|	...	2108	|	|	...
inchen Ost **890** ‡ d.	...	1347x	|	...	...	|	|	...	|	1547x	|	|	|	...	1747x	|	|	1910x	|	...	|	...	|	|	|	...
senheim.... **890** ‡ d.	...	1419	|	...	...	1521	|	...	1600	1619	|	|	|	...	1819	|	|	1941	|	...	|	...	2145	|	|	...
ein 🏛 ‡ d.	...	1441	|	...	*1453*	1546	1614	...	1624	1641	|	|	1814	...	1841	|	|	2004	2014	2019	|	2119	2207	2214	2308	...
l Hbf **960** d.	...	1451	|	1500	*1504*	1559	1624	...	1635	1651	|	|	1824	...	1851	|	|	2015	2024	2036	|	2136	2217	2224	2318	...
ach **960** d.	...	1506	|	1516	*1524*	1618	1638	...	...	1706	|	|	1838	...	1906	|	|	2033	2038	2058	|	2158	2233	2238	2332	...
oruck Hbf **960** a.	...	1523	1539	1535	*1549*	1640	1654	...	...	1723	1738	1738	1854	...	1923	1940	1940	2051	2055	2132	2138	2232	2258	2254	2348	...
oruck Hbf d.	1457	...	...	1543	1623	...	1657	1701	...	...	1744	1744	...	1857	...	1944	1944	...	...	...	2144	2237r	...	...	...	0006
al d.	1531	...	...	1607	1702	...	|	1731	...	...	1808	1808	...	1931	...	2008	2008	...	...	...	2208	2316r	...	...	...	0057
Pitztal d.	1541	...	...	1617	1713	...	|	1741	...	...	1818	1818	...	1941	...	2018	2018	...	...	...	2218	2326r	...	...	...	0108
eck-Zams d.	1556	...	...	1630	1728	...	1741	1757	...	...	1832	1832	...	1956	...	2032	2032	...	...	...	2232	2341r	...	...	...	0124
nton am Arlberg d.	...	...	...	1654	▬	...	1806	...	...	...	1856	1856	...	...	...	2056	2056	...	...	...	2256	...	...	...	...	...
en am Arlberg d.	...	...	...	1704	...	...	|	...	...	...	1906	1906	...	...	...	2106	2106	...	...	...	2306	...	...	...	...	...
enz **952** d.	...	...	...	1731	...	...	1845	...	...	...	1933	1933	...	...	...	2133	2133	...	...	...	2333	...	...	...	...	...
kirch **952** a.	...	...	...	1742	2	...	1856	...	...	...	1944	1944	...	...	...	2144	2144	...	...	...	2344	...	...	...	...	...
kirch **952** d.	...	...	...	1744	1747	...	1858	...	...	...	1948	1953	...	...	...	2148	2153	...	...	...	2347	...	...	...	...	...
uchs 🏛 **952** a.	...	...	...	1758	|	...	|	...	...	...	2006	|	...	...	...	2203	|	...	...	...	|	...	...	...	...	...
rich HB **520** a.	...	...	...	1920	|	...	|	...	...	...	2120	|	...	...	...	2320	|	...	...	...	|	...	...	...	...	...
birn **952** d.	...	...	...	...	1809	...	1912	...	...	...	...	2007	...	...	...	...	2207	...	...	...	0002	...	...	...	...	...
genz 🏛 **952** a.	...	...	...	...	1818	...	1922	...	...	...	...	2017	...	...	...	...	2217	...	...	...	0010	...	...	...	...	...
au Hbf 🏛 **952** a.	...	...	...	...	1832	...	*2005*	...	...	...	...	*2032*	...	...	...	...	2232	...	...	...	...	...	...	...	...	...

	CNL 484	*RJ* 49			*RJ* 763				*RJ* 861	*ICE* 208 1208		*RJ* 765		*RJ* 863		*RJ* 161	*EC* 82		*IC* 865	*IC* 1284		*EC* 163	*RJ* 563	*EC* 88	*RJ* 867
	🅁	①–⑥				⚒	⑥	Ⓐ					①–⑤					①–⑤		⑦					
	🍷◆	t♥ ✕	2	2	F✕	2	2	2	F✕	●✕	2	F✕	a 2	F✕	2	✕	✕	a 2		◆	2	✕◆	F✕	A✕	F✕
Lindau Hbf 🏛 **952** d.	...	...	...	...	...	...	...	...	...	...	...	...	...	*0624*	0727	...	...	...	*0754*	...	0927	...	...	...	...
Bregenz 🏛 **952** d.	...	...	...	...	...	...	...	...	...	...	...	0547	...	0639	0740	...	...	...	0810	...	0940	...	...	...	...
Dornbirn **952** d.	...	...	...	...	...	...	...	...	...	...	...	0556	...	0653	0751	...	...	...	0822	...	0951	...	...	...	...
Zürich HB **520** d.	...	...	...	...	...	...	...	...	...	...	...	|	...	|	|	0640	...	...	|	...	|	0840	...	...	...
Buchs 🏛 **952** d.	...	...	...	...	...	...	...	...	...	...	...	|	0617	|	|	0754	...	0819	|	...	|	0959	...	...	...
Feldkirch **952** a.	...	...	...	...	...	...	...	...	...	...	...	0610	0639	0709	0812	0809	...	0841	0846	...	1012	1014	...	...	...
Feldkirch **952** d.	...	...	...	...	...	...	...	...	...	...	...	0615	▬	0711	▬	0815	...	▬	0851	...	▬	1016	...	...	...
Bludenz **952** d.	...	...	...	...	...	...	...	...	...	...	...	0628	...	0726	...	0828	...	...	0912	...	...	1029	...	...	...
Langen am Arlberg d.	...	...	...	...	...	...	...	...	...	...	...	0654	...	|	...	0854	...	...	0943	...	...	1055	...	...	...
St Anton am Arlberg d.	...	...	...	...	...	...	...	...	...	...	...	0705	...	|	...	0905	...	2	|	...	2	1105	...	...	...
Landeck-Zams d.	...	...	0409r	0434	...	0535e	0604	0605	...	...	0647	0729	...	0821	...	0929	...	0950	1017	...	*1102*r	1129	...	...	...
Imst-Pitztal d.	...	...	0425r	0451	...	0550e	0619	0620	...	...	0711	0742	*IC*	|	...	0942	...	1005	|	...	*1117*r	1142	...	...	...
Ötztal d.	...	...	0437r	0504	...	0604	0631	0631	...	...	0722	0753	**515**	|	*IC*	0953	...	1018	|	...	*1128*r	1153	...	...	...
Innsbruck Hbf a.	...	...	0526r	0553	...	0653	0702	0702	...	...	0801	0816		0902	**1280**	1016	...	1058	1102	...	*1202*r	1216	...	...	...
Innsbruck Hbf **960** d.	0436	0505	0528	...	0609	0658	...	...	0705	0709	*0813*e	0820	0824	0905	⑥	1022	1036	...	1105	...	1210	1224	1220	1236	1305
Jenbach **960** d.	0500	0522	0602	...	0626	0732	...	...	0722	0730	*0839*e	|	0846	0922	◆	|	1055	...	1122	...	1236	1245	|	1255	1322
Wörgl Hbf **960** d.	0518	0537	0628	...	0641	...	...	...	0737	0747	*0857*e	|	0900	0937	1024	|	1110	...	1137	1222	1257	1300	|	1310	1337
Kufstein 🏛 ‡ d.	0529	0546	0641	...	0651	...	...	...	0746	0758	*0907*e	|	...	0946	1037	|	1119	...	1146	1233	1310	...	|	1319	1346
Rosenheim ... **890** ‡ a.	0550	|	...	...	|	...	...	...	|	0817	...	|	...	|	1057	|	1139	...	|	1255	...	...	|	1339	|
München Ost **890** ‡ a.	|	|	...	...	|	...	...	...	|	0848	...	|	...	|	|	|	1210x	...	|	1328	...	...	|	1410x	|
München Hbf **890** ‡ a.	0633	|	...	...	|	...	...	...	|	0859	...	|	...	|	1133x	|	1221x	...	|	1345	...	...	|	1421x	|
Salzburg Hbf a.	...	0658	...	...	0802	...	...	...	0858	...	...	1003	...	1058	...	1203	...	...	1258	...	...	...	1403	...	1458
Linz Hbf **950** a.	...	0812	...	...	0912	...	...	...	1012	...	...	1112	...	1212	...	1312	...	...	1428	...	...	...	1512	...	1612
Wien Hbf **950** a.	...	0930	...	...	1030	...	...	...	1130	...	...	1230	...	1330	...	1430	...	...	1605	...	...	...	1630	...	1730

NOTES (LISTED BY TRAIN NUMBER)

– [12] Innsbruck - Lindau - Ulm - Stuttgart - Köln - Münster.
4 – TRANSALPIN – [12] and ✕ Zürich - Kitzbühel - Schwarzach - Selzthal - Graz and v.v.
– 🛏 1,2 cl., ▬ 2 cl. and [2] Graz - Schwarzach - Zürich; 🛏 1,2 cl.*, ▬ 2 cl.* and [2] Beograd (**414**) - Zagreb - Ljubljana - Villach - Schwarzach (**464**) - Zürich.
5 – LUPUS – 🛏 1,2 cl., ▬ 2 cl. and [2] Roma - Brennero 🏛 - München and v.v. 🅁. For overnight journeys from/to Italy only.
) – ⑥ Dec. 26 - Apr. 2; ⑥ July 9 - Sept. 3. [12] Zell am See - Wörgl - München.
– ⑥ Dec. 19 - Apr. 2; ⑥ July 2 - Sept. 3. [12] München - Wörgl - Schwarzach.
– ⑦ Dec. 27 - Apr. 3 (also Mar. 28; not Mar. 27); ⑦ July 3 - Sept. 4. [12] Schwarzach - Wörgl - München - Hamburg - Flensburg.
5 ⑥ Jan. 2 - Apr. 2. [12] München - Wörgl - Zell am See.

To/from Verona, Bologna or Venezia via Brennero (Table **70**).
⑥ Dec. 19 - Apr. 2; ⑥ July 9 - Aug. 27.
From/to Wien Flughafen ✈ (Table **950**).
Conveys 🛏 1,2 cl., ▬ 2 cl. and [2].

Not Mar. 28, May 5, 16, 26, Nov. 1, Dec. 8.
Not ⑥.
Ⓐ only.

r – ⚒ only.
t – ①–⑥ (not Mar. 28, May 16, Aug. 15).
w – Not Mar. 27, May 15, Aug. 14.
x – Timings may vary by a few minutes Aug. 6 - Oct. 30.

♥ – From/to Budapest (Table **1250**).
● – To/from Berlin via Nürnberg (Table **851**).
¶ – Train number **1289** on ⑥⑦.

⊙ – 🛏 1,2 cl., ▬ 2 cl. and [2] Budapest (**462**) - Salzburg (**466**) - Zürich. Booking number **60466**.
* – 🛏 1,2 cl. and ▬ 2 cl. from Zagreb.
‡ – See panel below for *Meridian* regional services (operated by Bayerische Oberlandbahn GmbH) München - Kufstein and v.v.
⊕ – Change trains at Rosenheim on ①–⑥ (not May 16, 26).

SERVICE UNTIL AUGUST 5

									⊕	
München Hbf d.	0642	0744	0844	and	1844	1944	2044	2144	*2244*
München Ost d.	0651	0752	0852	hourly	1852	1952	2052	2152	*2252*
Rosenheim d.	0728	0830	0931	until	1931	2035	2135	2235	2335
Kufstein a.	0756	0857	0958		1958	2102	2202	2303	0003
Kufstein d.	0602	0700	0802	and	1902	1959	2058	2158	2342
Rosenheim d.	0632	0732	0832	hourly	1932	2026	2125	2225	0008
München Ost a.	0705	0805	0905	until	2005	*2105*	*2205*	*2305*	*0046*
München Hbf a.	0717	0815	0915		2016	*2115*	*2215*	*2315*	*0057*

951 LINDAU - BREGENZ - INNSBRUCK - MÜNCHEN and SALZBURG

	RJ 565	RJ 165	EC 80	RJ 869	RJ 567	RJ 167	EC 84	RJ 661	RJ 569	RJ 169	EC 86	IC 119	RJ 663		RJ 361	EC 188 ◧		RJ 669 ⑦w		RJ 363		EN 247	EN 465		EN 60467
	F✕	✕♦	A✕	F✕	F✕	✕	A✕	F✕	✕	✕	A✕	🍸♦	✕	2	✕	A✕	2	✕	2	✕	2	N	♦	2	◇
Lindau Hbf 🏛 ..... 952 d.	*1125*	...	...	...	*1325*	...	...	...	*1525*	...	...	1601	...	1727	...	...	...	...	1927	...	...	*2104*	...	2227	...
Bregenz 🏛 ..... 952 d.	1140	...	...	...	1340	...	...	1410	1540	...	...	1611	...	1740	...	...	...	1840	1940	...	...	2146	...	2240	...
Dornbirn ..... 952 d.	1150	...	...	...	1350	...	...	1420	1550	...	...	1621	...	1750	...	...	...	1850	1951	...	...	2156	...	2251	...
Zürich HB **520** ..... d.	|	1040	...	...	|	1240	...	|	|	1440	...	|	...	|	1640	...	...	|	|	1840	...	|	2040	|	2140
Buchs 🏛 ..... 952 d.	|	1154	...	...	|	1354	...	|	|	1554	...	|	...	|	1759	...	...	|	|	1954	...	|	2205	|	2305
Feldkirch ..... 952 a.	1205	1209	...	...	1405	1409	...	1445	1605	1609	...	1638	...	1809	1814	...	...	1915	2012	2009	...	2212	2220	2312	2321
Feldkirch ..... 952 d.	1215	1215	...	...	1415	1415	...	1447	1615	1615	...	1640	...	▬	1816	...	...	1917	▬	2015	...	2227	2242	...	2324
Bludenz ..... 952 d.	1228	1228	...	...	1428	1428	...	1500	1628	1628	...	1656	...	...	1829	...	...	1932	...	2028	...	2242	2258	...	2340
Langen am Arlberg ..... d.	1254	1254	...	...	1454	1454	...	|	|	|	...	1728	...	⚒	|	...	...	1958	...	2054	...	2310	2331	...	|
St Anton am Arlberg .. d.	1305	1305	...	...	1505	1505	...	1537	1701	1701	...	1738	...	2	1905	...	...	2009	2	2105	...	2320	2341	...	|
Landeck-Zams ..... d.	1329	1329	...	...	1529	1529	...	1602	1725	1725	...	1805	...	1902	1929	...	...	2033	2045	2129	...	2348	0009	...	|
Imst-Pitztal ..... d.	1342	1342	...	...	1542	1542	...	1616	1742	1742	...	1822	...	1917	1942	...	...	2047	2100	2142	...	0002	|	...	|
Ötztal ..... d.	1353	1353	...	...	1553	1553	...	1626	1753	1753	...	1832	...	1928	1953	...	...	2058	2111	2153	...	0013	|	...	|
Innsbruck Hbf ..... a.	1416	1416	...	...	1616	1616	...	1657	1816	1816	...	1901	...	2002	2016	...	...	2127	2200	2216	...	0039	0054	...	0120
Innsbruck Hbf ..... 960 d.	1420	1420	1436	1505	1622	1622	1636	1705	1822	1822	1836	...	1905	2013**e**	2022	2036	2128	...	...	...	2228	0044	0056	...	0128
Jenbach ..... 960 d.	|	|	1455	1522	|	|	1655	1722	|	|	1855	...	1922	2039**e**	|	2055	2202	...	...	...	2302	|	0119	...	|
Wörgl Hbf ..... 960 d.	|	|	1510	1537	|	|	1710	1737	|	|	1910	...	1937	2100**e**	|	2110	2228	...	...	...	2325	|	0136	...	|
Kufstein 🏛 ..... ‡ d.	|	|	1519	1546	|	|	1720	1746	|	|	1920	...	1946	2110**e**	|	2120	2241	...	...	...	2338	|	...	...	|
Rosenheim ..... 890 ‡ a.	|	|	1539	|	|	|	1739	|	|	|	1939	...	|	...	|	2139	...	...	...	...	...	|	...	...	|
München Ost 890 ‡ a.	|	|	1610**x**	|	|	|	1810**x**	|	|	|	2010**x**	...	|	...	|	2210**x**	...	...	...	...	...	|	...	...	|
München Hbf 890 ‡ a.	|	|	1624**x**	|	|	|	1821**x**	|	|	|	2021**x**	...	|	...	|	2221**x**	...	...	...	...	...	|	...	...	|
Salzburg Hbf ..... a.	1603	1603	...	1658	1803	1803	...	1858	2003	2003	...	...	2103	...	2206	...	...	...	...	...	...	0258	...	...	0323
Linz Hbf **950** ..... a.	1712	1712	...	1812	1912	1912	...	2012	2112	2112	...	...	2212	...	2312	...	...	...	...	...	...	0453	...	...	0501
Wien Hbf **950** ..... a.	1830	1830	...	1930	2030	2030	...	2130	2230	2230	...	...	2330	...	0030	...	...	...	...	...	...	0720	...	...	0635

♦ – **NOTES** (LISTED BY TRAIN NUMBER)

119 – [12] Münster - Köln - Stuttgart - Ulm - Lindau - Innsbruck.

165 – [12] and ✕ Zürich - Wien - Budapest.

465 – ZÜRICHSEE – 🛏 1,2 cl., ▬ 2 cl. and [2] Zürich - Schwarzach - Graz; 🛏 1,2 cl.*, ▬ 2 cl.* and [2] Zürich - Schwarzach (**415**) - Villach - Ljubljana - Zagreb - Beograd.

A – From Verona, Bologna or Venezia via Brennero (Table **70**).

F – From / to Wien Flughafen ✈ (Table **950**).

N – Conveys 🛏 1,2 cl., ▬ 2 cl. and [2].

e – Ⓐ only.

w – Also Jan. 6, Mar. 28, May 16, Nov. 1; not Mar. 27, May 15, July 10 - Sept. 4, Oct. 30.

x – Timings may vary by a few minutes Aug. 6 - Oct. 30.

* – 🛏 1,2 cl. and ▬ 2 cl. to Zagreb.

◇ – 🛏 1,2 cl., ▬ 2 cl. and [2] Zürich (**467**) - Salzburg (**463**) - Budapest. Booking number 60

◧ – Train number **1288** on ⑥⑦.

‡ – See panel on page 453 for other regional services Kufstein - München.

952 VORARLBERG LOCAL SERVICES

2nd class only (except where sho

BLUDENZ - BREGENZ - LINDAU ⊖ △

		Ⓐ																								
Bludenz ..... d.	0439	0509	0600	0656	0730	0800	0839	0939	1009	1139	1209	1300	1339	1430	1539	1600	1630	1700	1800	1809	1900	1909	1939	2039	2209	2239
Feldkirch ..... d.	0500	0530	0617	0715	0747	0817	0900	1000	1030	1200	1230	1317	1400	1447	1600	1617	1647	1717	1817	1830	1917	1930	2000	2100	2230	2300
Dornbirn ..... d.	0529	0559	0639	0739	0809	0839	0929	1029	1059	1229	1259	1339	1429	1509	1629	1639	1709	1739	1839	1859	1939	1959	2029	2129	2259	2329
Bregenz 🏛 ..... d.	0545	0615	0649	0748	0819	0849	0945	1045	1115	1245	1315	1349	1445	1519	1645	1648	1719	1749	1849	1915	1948	2020	2045	2145	2315	2344
Lindau Hbf 🏛 ..... a.	0556	0629	0658	...	0831	0901	0957	1057	1127	1257	1327	1401	1457	1531	1657	...	1732	1801	1901	1927	...	2032	2057	2157	2327	...

											Ⓐd			Ⓐd						Ⓐd						
Lindau Hbf 🏛 ..... d.	...	...	0624	0657	0831	0901	1001	1031	1101	1157	1227	1301	1401	1427	...	1459	1627	1701	1757	1827	1901	1957	2031	2104	2201	2301
Bregenz 🏛 ..... d.	0514	0610	0644	0710	0844	0914	1014	1044	1114	1210	1240	1314	1414	1440	1510	1514	1640	1714	1810	1840	1914	2010	2044	2114	2214	2314
Dornbirn ..... d.	0530	0621	0700	0721	0900	0930	1030	1100	1130	1221	1251	1330	1430	1451	1521	1530	1651	1730	1821	1851	1930	2021	2100	2130	2230	2330
Feldkirch ..... d.	0601	0644	0731	0744	0931	1001	1101	1131	1201	1244	1314	1401	1501	1514	1544	1601	1714	1801	1844	1914	2001	2044	2131	2201	2301	0001
Bludenz ..... a.	0621	0659	0751	0759	0951	1021	1121	1151	1221	1259	1329	1421	1521	1529	1559	1621	1729	1821	1859	1929	2021	2059	2151	2221	2321	0021

ST MARGRETHEN - BREGENZ - LINDAU △

km							EC 191			EC 193					EC 195						EC 197				
		Ⓒ	Ⓐ		Ⓐ		♥			♥					♥						♥				
0	St Margrethen 🏛 ..... d.	0625	0625	0655	0725	0755	0842	0855	0955	1042	1055	1155	1255	1355	1442	1455	1555	1655	1755	1855	1942	1955	2055	2155	2255
12	**Bregenz** 🏛 ..... a.	0640	0640	0710	0740	0810	0853	0910	1010	1053	1110	1210	1310	1410	1453	1510	1610	1710	1810	1910	1953	2010	2110	2210	2310
22	**Lindau** Hbf 🏛 ..... a.	0650	*0658*	*0736*	*0759*	*0831*	0905	*0932*	*1031*	1105	*1127*	*1233*	*1327*	*1432*	1505	*1531*	*1632*	*1732*	*1832*	*1927*	2005	*2032*	*2127*	*2232*	*2327*

							EC 196						EC 194							EC 192			EC 190	
				Ⓐ			♥						♥		Ⓐ		Ⓐ			♥			♥	
Lindau Hbf 🏛 ..... d.	...	...	*0624*	*0657*	*0727*	*0831*	*0927*	0954	*1031*	*1125*	*1227*	*1325*	*1427*	1454	*1525*	1605	*1627*	*1701*	*1727*	*1827*	1854	*1927*	*2031*	2054	*2131*
Bregenz 🏛 ..... d.	0542	0617	0647	0717	0747	0849	0947	1006	1049	1147	1247	1347	1449	1506	1547	1617	1647	1717	1747	1847	1906	1949	2047	2106	2147
St Margrethen 🏛 ..... a.	0558	0634	0704	0734	0804	0904	1004	1018	1104	1204	1304	1404	1504	1518	1604	1634	1704	1734	1804	1904	1918	2004	2104	2118	2204

FELDKIRCH - BUCHS ⊖

km		A	A	A¶	A	A		A	A	A	A	
0	**Feldkirch** ..... d.	0533	0649	0714	0745	0849	...	1612	1645	1715	1815	...
16	Schaan-Vaduz d.	0552	0708	0733	0806	0908	...	1634	1704	1734	1834	...
19	**Buchs** 🏛 ..... a.	0555	0711	0736	0809	0911	...	1637	1707	1737	1837	...

	A	A	A		A		A	A	A	A
Buchs 🏛 ..... d.	0617	0716	0819	...	1234	...	1619	1649	1719	1819
Schaan-Vaduz ..... d.	0620	0719	0822	...	1237	...	1622	1652	1722	1822
Feldkirch ..... a.	0639	0737	0841	...	1256	...	1641	1711	1741	1841

BLUDENZ - SCHRUNS

Operated by Montafonerbahn. *12 km.* Journey time: 19 minu

From Bludenz at 0535 Ⓐ, 0632 ⚒, 0702, 0737, 0805, 0837, 0937, 1037, 1137, 1205 ⚒, 1237, 1305 ⚒, 1337, 1437, 1537, 1605, 1634, 1705, 1737, 1805, 1837, 1937, 2037, 2137, 2245, 2

From Schruns at 0504 Ⓐ, 0534 ⚒, 0631, 0701, 0736, 0804, 0904, 1004, 1104, 1136 ⚒, 1204, 1236 ⚒, 1304, 1404, 1504, 1536, 1604, 1633, 1704, 1736, 1804, 1904, 2004, 2110, 2210, 2

A – ①–⑤ (not Mar. 28, May 5, 16, 26, Nov. 1, Dec. 8).

d – Runs daily Lindau - Bregenz.

♥ – [12] and ✕ Zürich - München and v.v. See Table **75**.

⊖ – Local trains. See Table **951** for long distance trains.

¶ – From Bludenz (d. 0647).

△ – Austrian holiday dates apply.

953 🚌 IMST - ÖTZTAL - OBERGURGL, ST ANTON - LECH

ÖBB-Post

km	🚌 Route **4194/8352**									Ⓒ	Ⓐ	Ⓐ	Ⓒ	Ⓒ	Ⓐ	Ⓒ	Ⓐ	Ⓒ	Ⓐ	Ⓐ		
0	**Imst** (Terminal Post) ..... d.	0605	0632	...	0805	0855	1000	1115	1155	1230	1235	1340	1400	1450	1510	1530	1600	1630	1645	...	1800	...
13	**Ötztal** (Bahnhof) ..... a.	0622	0649	...	0822	0909	1017	1132	1212	1247	1252	1357	1417	1507	1527	1544	1617	1647	1702	...	1817	...
13	**Ötztal** (Bahnhof) ..... d.	0623	0700	0800	0825	0910	1020	1135	1215	1248	1300	1400	1420	1510	1535	1545	1618	1648	1705	1745	1818	...
21	Oetz (Posthotel Kassel) ..... d.	0637	0714	0813	0839	0924	1034	1149	1229	1302	1314	1414	1434	1524	1549	1559	1632	1702	1719	1759	1832	...
54	Sölden (Postamt) ..... d.	0725	0802	0902	0927	1012	1122	1237	1317	1350	1402	1502	1522	1612	1637	1647	1720	1750	1807	1842	1920	...
58	Zwieselstein (Gh Neue Post) ..... d.	0733	0810	0910	0935	1020	1130	1245	1325	1358	1410	1510	1530	1620	1645	1655	1728	1758	1815	1850	1928	...
68	**Obergurgl** (Zentrum) ..... a.	0748	0825	0925	0950	1035	1145	1300	1340	1413	1425	1525	1545	1635	1700	1710	1743	1813	1830	...	1943	...

🚌 Route **4194/8352**	Ⓐ									Ⓐ	Ⓒ	Ⓐ	Ⓒ									
Obergurgl (Zentrum) ..... d.	...	...	...	0650	0750	0845	...	1015	1115	1205	1215	1305	1315	1345	...	1515	1545	1615	1645	1715	1745	1815
Zwieselstein (Gh Neue Post) ..... d.	...	0548	...	0705	0805	0900	...	1030	1130	1220	1230	1320	1330	1400	...	1530	1600	1630	1700	1730	1800	1830
Sölden (Postamt) ..... d.	0525	0558	...	0715	0815	0910	...	1040	1140	1230	1240	1330	1340	1410	...	1540	1610	1640	1710	1740	1810	1840
Oetz (Posthotel Kassel) ..... d.	0612	0645	...	0807	0907	1002	...	1132	1232	1322	1332	1424	1432	1502	...	1632	1702	1732	1802	1832	1902	1932
Ötztal (Bahnhof) ..... a.	0622	0655	...	0817	0917	1012	...	1142	1242	1332	1342	1432	1442	1512	...	1642	1712	1742	1812	1842	1912	1942
Ötztal (Bahnhof) ..... d.	...	0700	...	0820	0920	1015	...	1145	1245	1335	1345	1435	1445	1515	...	1645	...	1745	...	1845	...	1945
Imst (Terminal Post) ..... a.	...	0715	...	0835	0935	1030	...	1200	1300	1350	1400	1450	1500	1530	...	1700	...	1800	...	1900	...	2000

🚌 Route **92**: **ST ANTON AM ARLBERG - LECH** *20 km* Journey time: 31 – 32 minutes Service **June 4 - September 25**.

From St Anton Bahnhof at 0731, 0910, 1110, 1310, 1510 and 1710.

From Lech Schlosskopf at 0810, 1010, 1210, 1410, 1610 and 1810.

☛ All services call at St Christoph a. Arlberg and Zürs (Posth

🚌 LANDECK - NAUDERS - SCUOL and MALLES 954

Landeck - Nauders and Martina

Routes **4218/4220**												Ⓐ												
deck-Zams Bahnhof.......d.	0650	0800	0855	1000	1055	1212	1255	1400	1455	1600	1647	1702	1805	1905	...	...	...	...	...	...	...	...	...	...
l im Oberinntal.................d.	0718	0828	0923	1028	1123	1240	1323	1428	1523	1628	1715	1730	1833	1933	...	...	...	...	...	...	...	...	...	...
artina cunfin 🏛..................a.	|	|	0956	|	1156	|	1356	|	1556	|	1756	|	|	|	...	...	...	...	...	...	...	...	...	...
ders Mühle ....a.	0800	0910	...	1110	...	1322	...	1510	...	1710	...	1812	1915	2015	...	...	...	...	...	...	...	...	...	...
ders Mühle ....d.	0607	0647	...	0847	...	1047	...	1247	...	1447	...	1647	...	1847	...	...	...	...	...	...	...	...	...	...
artina cunfin 🏛..................d.	|	|	...	|	1000	|	1200	|	1400	|	1600	|	1800	|	...	...	...	...	...	...	...	...	...	...
l im Oberinntal.................d.	0647	0727	...	0927	1032	1127	1232	1327	1432	1527	1632	1727	1832	1927	...	...	...	...	...	...	...	...	...	...
deck-Zams Bahnhof.......a.	0712	0752	...	0952	1057	1152	1257	1352	1457	1552	1657	1752	1857	1952	...	...	...	...	...	...	...	...	...	...

Scuol Tarasp - Nauders - Malles

	⚒	⚒										
ol Tarasp Staziun ....d.	0630	...	0730	...	and at	1730	...	1830	...	1930	...	...
tina cunfin 🏛...............................d.	0655	0705	0755	0805	the same	1755	1805	1855	1910	2003	2010	...
ders Mühle 🏛..............................d.	...	0716	...	0816	minutes	...	1816	...	1921	...	2021	...
chenpass/Passo di Resia 🏛......d.	...	0720	...	0820	past each	...	1820	...	1925	...	2025	...
ia..d.	...	0723	...	0823	hour until	...	1823	...	1928	...	2028	...
les Stazione **597**.........................a.	...	0753	...	0853		...	1853	...	1958	...	2058	...
	⚒	⚒								⚒		
les Stazione **597**.........................d.	0601	...	0701	...	and at	1801	...	1901	...	2001	...	...
ia..d.	0631	...	0731	...	the same	1831	...	1931	...	2031	...	...
so di Resia/Reschenpass 🏛......d.	0634	...	0734	...	minutes	1834	...	1934	...	2034	...	...
ders Mühle 🏛..............................d.	0638	...	0738	...	past each	1838	...	1938	...	...	...	...
tina cunfin 🏛...............................d.	0649	0701	0749	0801	hour until	1849	1901	1949	1952	...	...	...
ol Tarasp Staziun ....a.	...	0728	...	0828		...	1928	...	2028	...	...	...

Operators

Landeck - Nauders: ÖBB-Postbus GmbH, Landeck. ✆ +43 (0) 5442 64 422.

Scuol Tarasp - Martina: Auto Da Posta, Svizra. CH-7550 Scuol. ✆ +41 (0) 58 453 28 28.

Martina - Nauders - Malles: Servizi Autobus Dolomiti (SAD). Corso Italia 13N, I-39100 Bolzano. ✆ +39 0471 450 111.

JENBACH - MAYRHOFEN 955

d class only Narrow gauge Zillertalbahn *

m																🚂 A
0	**Jenbach** Zillertalbahnhof § ...d.	0628	0652	0737	0810	0844	and at	1610	1644	1710	1744	1815	1848	1948		0947
1	Fügen-Hart ....d.	0646	0709	0754	0829	0859	the same	1629	1659	1729	1759	1832	1904	2004		1017
7	Kaltenbach-Stumm ....d.	0656	0720	0807	0840	0910	minutes	1640	1710	1740	1810	1843	1915	2015	also	1034
21	Aschau im Zillertal ....d.	0703	0727	0813	0846	0916	past each	1646	1716	1746	1816	1849	1920	2020		1049
25	**Zell am Ziller** ....d.	0710	0735	0820	0853	0923	hour until	1653	1723	1753	1822	1855	1927	2027		1100
2	**Mayrhofen** ....a.	0722	0747	0833	0904	0934		1704	1734	1804	1833	1906	1938	2038		1119

	Ⓒ	Ⓐ														🚂 A
yrhofen ....d.	0543	0601	0609	0638	0731	0822	0852	and at	1622	1652	1722	1752	1852	1952		1207
am Ziller ....d.	0554	0610x	0620	0650	0741	0834	0904	the same	1634	1704	1734	1804	1904	2004		1224
hau im Zillertal ....d.	0600	0616x	0626	0656	0747	0840	0910	minutes	1640	1710	1740	1810	1910	2010	also	1233
enbach-Stumm......................d.	0607	0621x	0633	0702	0754	0846	0916	past each	1646	1716	1746	1816	1916	2016		1249
en-Hart ....d.	0617	0630x	0645	0716	0804	0858	0927	hour until	1658	1727	1758	1829	1928	2028		1310
bach Zillertalbahnhof § ....a.	0634	0646	0703	0733	0821	0916	0943		1716	1743	1814	1845	1943	2043		1332

A – Daily Dec. 25 - Jan. 6 (not Dec. 31); ⑥⑦ Apr. 30 - May 22; ③–⑦ May 25 - Oct. 9.

x – Stops on request only.

🚂 – Steam train. Special fares apply.

§ – Adjacent to ÖBB station.

* – Zillertaler Vehrkehrsbetriebe, Austraße 1, A-6200 Jenbach. ✆ +43 (0) 5244 606 0.

JENBACH - ACHENSEE 956

d class only *Achenseebahn*

row gauge rack railway operated by steam locomotives (special fares apply). *7 km.* Journey time 42–50 minutes. **Service May 1 - Oct. 30, 2016.**

erator: Achenseebahn AG, A-6200 Jenbach: ✆ +43 (0) 5244 62243, Fax +43 (0) 5244 622435. Jenbach Achensee Bf is adjacent to the ÖBB station.

y 1–27 and **Oct. 10–30**: **From Jenbach Achensee Bf** at 1100, 1300 and 1500. **From Achensee Seespitz Bahnstation** at 1200, 1400 and 1600.

y 28 - Oct. 9: **From Jenbach Achensee Bf** at 0815, 1000, 1045, 1200, 1345, 1500 and 1645. **From Achensee Seespitz Bahnstation** at 0915, 1105, 1220, 1405, 1520, 1600 and 1740.

ZELL AM SEE - KRIMML and 🚌 KRIMML - MAYRHOFEN 957

d class only

ZELL AM SEE - KRIMML ⊡

					🚂 S		🚂 S				Ⓐ				Ⓐ	Ⓒ
0	**Zell am See** Lokalbahn........d.	0630	0800	0900	0918	1000	←	1100	and	1600	1650	1700	1800	1900	2000	2050
9	Mittersill ....d.	0723	0848	0948	1038	1048	1108	1148	hourly	1648	1729	1748	1848	1948	2048	2138
9	Bramberg..................................d.	0737	0904	1004	→	1104	1131	1204	until	1704	1740	1804	1904	2004	2104	2154
3	**Krimml** ....a.	0756	0923	1023	...	1123	1203	1223		1723	1755	1823	1923	2023	2123	2213

		Ⓐ	Ⓐ					🚂 S		🚂 S					
mml..d.	0533	0603	0628	0640	0733	and	1433	1453	1533	...	1633	1733	1833	...	...
mberg...d.	0552	0621	0644	0658	0751	hourly	1451	1523	1551	←	1651	1751	1851	...	...
ersill...d.	0608	0638	0656	0720	0808	until	1508	1545	1608	1615	1708	1808	1908	...	...
l **am See** Lokalbahn....................a.	0655	0725	0737	0805	0855		1555	→	1655	1728	1755	1855	1955	...	...

🚌 Krimml Bahnhof - Krimml Wasserfälle and v.v. Route **670**. *3 km.* Journey time: 5–8 minutes.

From Krimml Bahnhof at 0757, 0929, 1029 and hourly until 1729; then 1829 **B**, 1844 and 1934.

From Krimml Wasserfälle at 0823, 1023, 1123 and hourly until 1723; then 1823 **B**.

🚌 routes **673** and **4094**: KRIMML - KÖNIGSLEITEN - MAYRHOFEN *Summer service valid June 4 - October 2*

m			A			A			A	
0	**Krimml** Bahnhof...................d.	...	*0834*t	...	...	*1429*	...	...	*1629*	...
3	Krimml Wasserfälle...............d.	...	0845	...	...	1435	...	...	1635	...
16	Königsleiten Dorfbahn...........d.	...	0907	1000	1100	1453a	1502a	1600	1657	1715
25	**Gerlos** Gasthaus Oberwirt....d.	0821	...	1013	1113	...	1513	1613	...	1728
45	Zell am Ziller Bf .... **955** a.	0856	...	1053	1153	...	1553	1653	...	1801
53	**Mayrhofen** Bahnhof ...... **955** a.	0909	...	...	1206	...	...	1706	...	1809

		A				A		A		
Mayrhofen Bahnhof.... **955** d.	0830	...	0920	...	...	1440	...	...	1840
Zell am Ziller Bahnhof. **955** d.	0845	...	0935	1327	...	1455	...	1616	1855
Gerlos Gasthaus Oberwirt .d.	0927	...	1017	1402	...	1534	...	1654	1928
Königsleiten Dorfbahn ....d.	0940	0948	1030	1415	1458	1547	1658	1707	...
Krimml Wasserfälle ....a.	...	1012	...	...	1522	...	1722	...	...
Krimml Bahnhof ....a.	...	*1028*	...	...	*1528*	...	*1728*	...	...

July 9 - Sept. 11.

June 1 - Sept. 30.

S – ④ May 26 - Sept. 29 (also ②③ July 12 - Aug. 31; also Sept. 10). Steam train with special fares.

a – Königsleiten Almdorf.

t – *0839* on Ⓒ.

⊡ – Narrow gauge railway. **Operator**: Pinzgauer Lokalbahn. Trains call at Mittersill and Bramberg on request only.

🚌 WÖRGL - ELLMAU - KITZBÜHEL and ST JOHANN 958

BB-Postbus routes **4006**, **4060**, **4902**

	⚒	Ⓐ¶	⑥	⚒	Ⓐ	⑥	⚒	†	⚒		⚒		Ⓐ	⑥	†	⚒	⚒	†		⚒	Ⓐ	⚒	Ⓐ	†
rgl Hauptbahnhof ....d.	...	0545	...	0640	0743	0743	...	...	0905	...	1120	...	1210	1210	...	...	1405	...	...	1610	...	1740	1835	...
l (Dorf)................................ ♥ d.	...	0605	0612	0659	0805	0810	...	0917	0937	...	1140	...	1240	1240	1240	...	1437	1545	...	1640	...	1810	1905	1905
heffau am Wilden Kaiser ★ ....d.	...	0612	0621	...	0812	0817	...	0927	0947	...	1150	...	1250	1250	1250	...	1447	1555	...	1650	...	1820	1913	1913
nau (Dorf) ....d.	0622	0621	0633	...	0821	0826	0900	0942	1002	...	1205	...	1305	1305	1305	1315	1502	1610	...	1705	1715	1835	1924	1924
Kitzbühel Bahnhof.......................a.	0650	|	|	...	|	|	0924	|	|	...	|	...	|	...	|	1345	|	|	...	|	1745	|	|	|
Johann in Tirol Bahnhof ....a.	...	0641	0654	...	0841	0847	...	1004	1024	...	1227	...	1327	...	1327	...	1524	1632	...	1727	...	1857	1940	1940

	Ⓐ	⑥	Ⓐ	⚒	⚒	†	⚒	⚒	†	⚒	⚒	Ⓐ	⑥	†	⚒	⚒	Ⓐ	†	Ⓐ	⑥	⑥	Ⓐ	Ⓐ	Ⓐ
Johann in Tirol Bahnhof ....d.	...	0535	0535	...	0725	0750	...	0855	1055	1055	...	1235	...	1340	1340	1555	...	1655	1655	...	1755	1755	...	1857
Kitzbühel Bahnhof.......................d.	...	|	|	...	|	|	0803	|	|	|	1215	|	...	|	|	|	1620	|	|	...	|	|	1815	|
nau (Dorf) ....d.	...	0552	0552	...	0747	0812	0833	0917	1117	1117	1245	1302	1305	1402	1402	1617	1650	1717	1717	...	1817	1817	1843	1919
heffau am Wilden Kaiser ★ ....d.	...	0559	0559	...	0753	0818	...	0923	1123	1123	...	1308	1311	1408	1408	1623	...	1723	1723	...	1823	1823	...	1925
l (Dorf)................................ ♥ d.	0550	0612	0615	0715	0810	0832	...	0940	1137	1140	...	1325	1325	1422	1425	1645e	...	1737	1745e	1745	1837	1840	...	1942
rgl Hauptbahnhof ....a.	0620	...	0645	0750	0840	...	...	1010	...	1210	...	1355	1352	...	1455	1715	...	...	1808	1808	...	1903	...	2005

Arrives 8 minutes earlier.

– Scheffau am Wilden Kaiser Am Trattenbach. Runs 5–11 minutes later during school holiday periods.

♥ – 🚌 **KUFSTEIN** Bahnhof → **SÖLL** Dorf (journey time: 27–29 minutes): 0540 ⚒, 0639 Ⓐ, 0735 Ⓐ, 0740 ⑥, 0840 Ⓐ, 0845 Ⓒ, 1010, 1110, 1210 Ⓐ, 1300 Ⓒ, 1310 Ⓐ, 1410 Ⓐ, 1510 Ⓒ, 1524 Ⓐ, 1610 ⚒, 1710 Ⓐ, 1740 Ⓒ, 1810 Ⓐ and 1907 Ⓐ.
🚌 **SÖLL** Dorf → **KUFSTEIN** Bahnhof (journey time: 25–29 minutes): 0610 ⚒, 0706 Ⓐ, 0812 ⚒, 0915 Ⓒ, 0940 Ⓐ, 1040, 1140, 1240 Ⓐ, 1330 Ⓒ, 1337 Ⓐ, 1440 Ⓐ, 1540 Ⓒ, 1551 Ⓐ, 1640 ⑥, 1642 Ⓐ, 1742 Ⓐ, 1810 †, 1840 ⚒ and 1934 Ⓐ.

959 ZELL AM SEE - HINTERGLEMM

ÖBB-Postbus Route

km		⚒	E	E		E		E		A		A		A	
0	**Zell am See** Bahnhof .... d.	0610p	0656	0820	0920	1020	1120	1220	1320	1420	1520	1620	1720	1820	1920
20	Saalbach Schattberg .... a.	0637	0725	0852	0952	1052	1152	1252	1352	1452	1552	1652	1752	1852	1952
23	**Hinterglemm** Ellmauweg ...... a.	0643	0730	0857	0957	1057	1157	1257	1357	1457	1557	1657	1757	1857	1957

	⚒	E			E		E		E		A		A		A
Hinterglemm Ellmauweg .... d.	0611	0657	0750	...	0920	1020	1120	1220	1320	1420	1520	1620	1720	1820	1916
Saalbach Schattberg .... d.	0618	0703	0800	...	0930	1030	1130	1230	1330	1430	1530	1630	1730	1830	1922
Zell am See Bahnhof .... a.	0646	0732	0830	...	1000	1100	1200	1300	1400	1500	1600	1700	1800	1900	1950

A – Ⓐ (daily to Apr. 1, June 13 - Sept. 30 and from Nov. 28).
E – ⚒ (daily to Apr. 2, June 13 - Oct. 1 and from Nov. 28).
p – Zell am See Postplatz (not Bahnhof).

Information: ✆ +43 (0) 6542 5444-18

960 SALZBURG - SCHWARZACH - INNSBRUCK

km		EN	EN							IC			IC			IC		IC		EC		IC		
		237	464							590			1280			592		1284		111		542		
					⚒	⚒	©	Ⓐ	Ⓐ		⚒		⑥N		⚒		⚒	⑦M			Ⓐ	©		
		2⊖	A	2	2	2	2	2	2	✕⊖	2	2		2	2	🍷⊖	2		2	✕⊖	2		2	2
	Wien Hbf **950** .... d.	2125	...	...	...	...	...	...	...	...	...	...	...	...	...	...	...	...	...	...	...	0655	...	...
0	**Salzburg** Hbf **951 970 975** ‡ d.	0134	...	...	...	...	0425	0441	...	0612	...	...	...	0708	...	0812	...	...	0908	1012	...	1015	...	...
29	Golling-Abtenau .... **970** ‡ d.	|	...	...	...	...	0505	0505	...	0633	...	...	...	0734	...	0833	...	...	0934	1033	...	1038	...	...
53	**Bischofshofen** .... **970 975** ‡ d.	|	0158	...	...	...	0529	0529	...	0654	...	...	...	0756	...	0854	...	...	0956	1054	...	1102	...	...
61	St Johann im Pongau. **970** ‡ d.	|	|	...	...	...	0539	0539	...	0703	...	...	...	0804	...	0903	...	...	1004	1103	...	1111	...	...
67	**Schwarzach - St Veit**. **970** ‡ a.	0223	0211	...	...	...	0545	0545	...	0709	...	...	...	0810	...	0909	...	...	1010	1109	...	1117	...	...
67	**Schwarzach - St Veit** .... d.	...	0232	...	...	...	0547	0547	...	...	0712	...	...	0812	...	...	0912	1005	1012	▬	1112	1119	...	...
99	**Zell am See** .... d.	...	|	...	...	...	0623	0623	...	...	0745	...	0839	0845	...	...	0945	1035	1045	...	1145	1148	...	...
113	Saalfelden .... d.	...	|	0410	0530	0554	0636	0636	...	...	0756	...	0850	0856	...	...	0954	1046	1056	...	1156	1158	...	...
131	Hochfilzen .... d.	...	|	0427	0547	0614	0653	0653	...	...	0814	...	0906	0914	1014	...	...	1102	1114	*IC*	1214	|	...	...
148	St Johann in Tirol .... d.	...	|	0443	0603	0632	0710	0710	0757	...	0832	0918	0923	0932	1032	...	...	1118	1132	**662**	1232	1228	...	1318
157	**Kitzbühel** .... d.	...	|	0451	0611	0641	0718	0718	0806	...	0841	0926	0931	0941	1041	...	...	1127	1141		1241	1236	...	1326
166	Kirchberg in Tirol .... d.	...	|	0500	0622	0652	0727	0727	0817	...	0852	0934	0943	0952	1052	...	...	1139	1152	**B**	1252	1244	...	1334
192	Wörgl Hbf .... **951** a.	...	|	0527	0647	0721	0752	0752	0846	...	0921	0959	1011	1019	1121	...	...	1207	1219	1224	1321	1305	1336	1359
217	Jenbach .... **951** a.	...	|	0549	*0708*r	*0749*e	0812	0812	*0904*	...	*0957*	1019	...	*1036*	*1157*	...	...	...	...	1236	...	|	1357	1419
251	**Innsbruck** Hbf .... **951** a.	...	0449	0619	*0737*r	*0817*e	0840	0837	*0923*	...	*1032*	1047	...	*1054*	*1232*	...	...	...	...	1254	...	1336	1432	1447

	IC	EC				EC				EC	IC						IC					EC		
	690	164				113				115	518						692					117		
			⚒	Ⓐ			⚒	Ⓐ				Ⓐ			Ⓐ	Ⓐ			Ⓑ	Ⓐ		1217		
	🍷⊖	Z✕	2	2	2	✕⊖	2	2	2	⊗⊖	G🍷	2	2	2	2	2	🍷⊖	2	2	2	2	⊗⊖	2	2W
Wien Hbf **950** .... d.	0855	...	...	...	...	...	...	...	...	...	...	...	...	...	...	...	1455	...	...	...	...	...	...	1855
Salzburg Hbf. **951 970 975** ‡ d.	1212	...	...	...	1308	1412	...	...	1508	1612	...	...	...	1708	...	1741	1812	...	...	...	1908	2012	...	2211
Golling-Abtenau .... **970** ‡ d.	1233	...	...	...	1334	1433	...	...	1534	1633	...	...	...	1734	...	1810	1833	...	...	...	1934	2033	...	2237
Bischofshofen ..... **970 975** ‡ d.	1254	1250	...	...	1356	1454	...	...	1556	1654	1650	...	...	1756	...	1835	1854	...	...	...	1956	2054	...	2259
St Johann im Pongau .. **970** ‡ d.	1303	1259	...	...	1404	1503	...	...	1604	1703	1659	...	...	1804	...	1845	1903	...	...	...	2004	2103	...	2307
Schwarzach - St Veit ... **970** ‡ a.	1309	1305	...	...	1410	1509	...	...	1610	1709	1705	...	...	1810	...	1850	1909	...	...	...	2010	2109	...	2313
Schwarzach - St Veit .... d.	...	1312	...	...	1412	▬	1512	...	1612	...	1712	...	...	1813	...	1853	...	1912	1912	...	2012	▬	2112	2315
Zell am See .... d.	...	1343	...	...	1445	...	1545	...	1645	...	1743	...	...	1846	...	1927	...	1948	1948	...	2045	...	2148	2350
Saalfelden .... d.	...	1352	1356e	...	1456	...	1556	...	1656	...	1752	1756	...	1856	...	1938	...	2000	2001	...	2056	...	2200	0001
Hochfilzen .... d.	...	|	1414	...	1514	*RJ*	1614	1702	1714	...	|	1814	1902	1914	1946	...	...	...	2017	2102	2114	...	...	...
St Johann in Tirol .... d.	...	1420	1432	1518	1532	**862**	1632	1718	1732	...	1820	1832	1918	1932	2004	...	...	...	2035	2118	2132	...	...	...
Kitzbühel .... d.	...	1428	1441	1526	1541		1641	1726	1741	...	1828	1841	1926	1941	2013	...	...	...	2044	2126	2141	...	...	...
Kirchberg in Tirol .... d.	...	1436	1452	1534	1552	**B**	1652	1734	1752	...	1836	1852	1934	1952	2024	...	...	...	2053	2134	2152	2	...	...
Wörgl Hbf .... **951** a.	...	1458	1521	1559	1619	1624	1721	1759	1819	...	1858	1921	1959	2019	2053	...	...	...	2121	2159	2219	2236	...	...
Jenbach .... **951** a.	...	1514	*1557*	1619	...	1636	*1757*	1819	*1836*	...	1914	*1957*	2019	*2036*	...	...	...	...	*2157*	2219	*2236*b	2257	...	...
Innsbruck Hbf .... **951** a.	...	1535	*1632*	1647	...	1654	*1832*	1847	*1854*	...	1936	*2032*	2047	*2055*	...	...	...	...	*2232*	2247	*2254*b	2332	...	...

	EN	EN									IC	IC					IC	EC			IC			
	465	236									693	1285					515	114			865			
			⚒			⚒	Ⓐ		⚒	Ⓐ		⑥Q	Ⓐ			Ⓐ				⚒				⚒
	A	2⊖	2	2X	2	2	2	2	2	2	🍷⊖		2	2	2	2	G🍷	⊗⊖	2	2	B	2	2	2
Innsbruck Hbf .... **951** d.	0056	...	...	...	...	*0505*	*0511*	...	*0528*	*0528*	...	...	*0613*	*0705*	0713	*0728*	0824	...	0849	*0928*	1105	...	1113	*1128*
Jenbach .... **951** d.	0119	...	...	...	...	*0522*	*0537*	...	*0602*	*0602*	...	...	*0640*	*0722*	0741	*0802*	0846	...	0915	*1002*	1122	...	1139	*1202*
Wörgl Hbf .... **951** d.	0138	...	...	...	...	0538	0601	...	0631	0631	...	0636	0707	0738	0802	0838	0902	...	0938	1038	1135	1138	1200	1238
Kirchberg in Tirol .... d.	|	...	...	...	...	0608	0631	...	0701	0701	...	0712	0733	0808	0828	0908	0924	...	1008	1108	▬	1208	1226	1308
Kitzbühel .... d.	|	...	...	...	...	0619	0642	...	0712	0712	...	0723	0744	0819	0838	0919	0932	...	1019	1119	...	1219	1234	1319
St Johann in Tirol .... d.	|	...	...	...	...	0628	0652	...	0721	0721	...	0731	0751	0828	0845	0928	0940	...	1028	1128	...	1228	1241	1328
Hochfilzen .... d.	|	...	...	...	...	0646	0710	...	0739	0741	...	0752	...	0846	...	0946	|	...	1046	1146	...	1246	...	1346
Saalfelden .... d.	|	...	0458	0555	0705	0705	0727	0735	...	0800	...	0808	...	0905	...	...	1008	...	1105	1205	*EC*	1305	...	1402e
Zell am See .... d.	|	...	0508	0605	0715	0715	...	0748	...	0813	...	0819	...	0915	...	...	1019	...	1115	1215	**112**	1315	...	...
Schwarzach - St Veit .... a.	0317	...	0541	0638	0747	0747	...	0823	...	0847	...	...	...	0947	...	...	1048	...	1147	1247	✕⊖	1347	...	...
Schwarzach - St Veit ... **970** ‡ d.	0324	0320	0542	0640	0749	0749	...	0824	...	...	0850	...	...	0949	...	...	1056	1050	1149	...	1250	1349	...	...
St Johann im Pongau .. **970** ‡ d.	|	|	0548	0647	0755	0755	...	0829	...	...	0856	...	...	0955	...	...	1102	1056	1155	...	1256	1355	...	...
Bischofshofen ..... **970 975** ‡ d.	0336	|	0558	0656	0804	0804	...	0840	...	...	0905	...	...	1004	...	...	1110	1105	1204	...	1305	1404	...	...
Golling-Abtenau .... **970** ‡ d.	...	|	0620	0718	0825	0825	...	0904	...	...	0925	...	...	1025	...	...	...	1125	1225	...	1325	1425	...	...
Salzburg Hbf. **951 970 975** ‡ a.	...	0409	0645	0744	0851	0851	...	0940	...	...	0948	...	...	1051	...	...	...	1148	1251	...	1348	1451	...	...
Wien Hbf **950** .... a.	...	0755	...	1105	...	...	...	...	...	...	1305	...	...	...	...	...	...	...	...	...	...	...	...	...

	IC				IC	IC					EC	IC		RJ					IC					
	691				747	591					110	1281		661					593					
			Ⓐ	Ⓐ	©			Ⓐ	Ⓐ			⑥P	Ⓐ			©	Ⓐ			⚒	Ⓐ	©	Ⓐ	
	🍷⊖	2	2	2		🍷⊖	2	2	2	2	✕⊖		2	B	2	2	2	2	✕⊖	2	2	2	2	2
Innsbruck Hbf .... **951** d.	...	*1305*	1313	*1328*	1424	...	*1505*	1513	*1528*	...	...	...	*1636*	1705	...	1713	1724	*1728*t	...	*1905*	1913	*1928*	*1952*	*2128*
Jenbach .... **951** d.	...	*1322*	1339	*1402*	|	...	*1522*	1539	*1602*	...	...	...	*1655*	1722	...	1741	1745	*1802*t	...	*1922*	1939	*2002*	*2017*	*2202*
Wörgl Hbf .... **951** d.	...	1338	1400	1438	1455	...	1538	1600	1638	...	...	1647	1715	1735	1738	1802	1806	1838	...	1938	2000	2038	2044	2238
Kirchberg in Tirol .... d.	...	1408	1426	1508	1517	...	1608	1626	1708	...	...	1719	1741	...	1807	1828	1832	1908	...	2008	2026	2108	2110	2308
Kitzbühel .... d.	...	1419	1434	1519	1525	...	1619	1634	1719	...	...	1729	1750		1818	1836	1840	1919	...	2019	2034	2119	2119	2319
St Johann in Tirol .... d.	...	1428	1441	1528	1533	...	1628	1642	1728	...	...	1737	1759	...	1827	1844	1848	1928	...	2028	2042	2128	2127	2328
Hochfilzen .... d.	...	1446	...	1546	|	...	1646	1656	1746	...	...	1758	1815	...	1844	1858	1902	1946	...	2046	2100	2146	2143	2346
Saalfelden .... d.	...	1505	...	1605	1603	...	1705	...	1805	1805	...	1813	...	...	1903	...	...	2005	...	2103k	2117	2203	2202	0003
Zell am See .... d.	...	1515	...	1615	1613	...	1715	...	1815	1815	...	1825	...	...	1914	...	...	2015	...	...	...	...	2214	...
Schwarzach - St Veit .... a.	...	1547	...	1647	1642	...	1747	...	1847	1847	...	1854	...	...	1947	...	...	2047	...	...	...	...	2247	...
Schwarzach - St Veit ... **970** ‡ d.	1450	1549	...	...	1644	1650	1749	...	...	...	1850	...	...	...	1949	...	...	...	2050	...	...	...	...	...
St Johann im Pongau .. **970** ‡ d.	1456	1555	...	...	1650	1656	1755	...	...	...	1856	...	...	...	1955	...	...	...	2056	...	...	...	...	...
Bischofshofen ..... **970 975** ‡ d.	1505	1604	...	...	1659	1705	1804	...	...	...	1905	...	...	...	2004	...	...	...	2105	...	...	...	...	...
Golling-Abtenau .... **970** ‡ d.	1525	1625	...	...	1721	1725	1825	...	...	...	1925	...	...	...	2025	...	...	...	2125	...	...	...	...	...
Salzburg Hbf. **951 970 975** ‡ a.	1548	1651	...	...	1744	1748	1851	...	...	...	1948	...	...	...	2051	...	...	...	2148	...	...	...	...	...
Wien Hbf **950** .... a.	1905	...	...	...	2105	...	...	...	...	...	...	...	...	...	...	...	...	...	...	...	...	...	...	...

A – ZÜRICHSEE – 🛏 1, 2 cl., ▬ 2 cl. and (2) Graz - Feldkirch - Buchs 🏛 - Zürich and v.v. Conveys from / to Schwarzach 🛏 1, 2 cl.*, ▬ 2 cl.* and (2) Beograd - Zagreb - Ljubljana - Villach - Zürich and v.v.
B – To / from Bregenz (Table **951**).
G – From / to Graz (Table **975**).
M – ⑦ Dec. 27 - Apr. 3 (also Mar. 28; not Mar. 27); ⑥ July 3 - Sept. 4. (12) Schwarzach - München - Hamburg - Flensburg.
N – ⑥ Dec. 26 - Apr. 2; ⑥ July 9 - Sept. 3. (12) Zell am See - München.
P – ⑥ Dec. 19 - Apr. 2; ⑥ July 2 - Sept. 3. (12) München - Schwarzach.
Q – ⑥ Jan. 2 - Apr. 2. (12) München - Zell am See.
W – (2) Wien Flughafen (*IC* **746**) - Salzburg (*REX* **1516**) - Saalfelden.
X – (2) Saalfelden (*REX* **1501**) - Salzburg (*IC* **547**) - Wien Flughafen.
Z – TRANSALPIN – (12) ✕ Graz - Selzthal - Bischofshofen - Innsbruck - Buchs 🏛 - Zürich and v.v.

b – Ⓑ (not Mar. 27, May 15, Aug. 14).
c – Mornings of © only.
e – Ⓐ only.
f – Also Jan. 5, Mar. 27, May 4, 15, 25, Aug. 14, Oct. 25, 31, Dec. 7.
k – ⑥ only.
r – On ⑥ Jenbach a. *0719*, Innsbruck a. *0747*.
t – On Ⓐ Innsbruck d. *1743*, Jenbach d. *1809*.

* – 🛏 1, 2 cl., ▬ 2 cl. from / to Zagreb.
⊖ – See Table **970** for further details.
▲ – Please ensure you join the correct portion of the train at Innsbruck and Jenbach.
‡ – See panel below main table for other local stopping trains.

Freilassing .... **890** d.	0607		2207	2307
Salzburg Hbf...... **890** d.	0621	and	2221	2321
Golling-Abtenau .... d.	0659	hourly	2259	2359
Bischofshofen .... d.	0724	until	2324	0024
St Johann im Pongau d.	0734		2334	0034c
Schwarzach - St Veit. a.	0739		2339	0039c

Schwarzach - St Veit. d.	0524	0554	0624	
St Johann im Pongau d.	0529	0559	0629	and
Bischofshofen .... d.	0540	0610	0640	hourly
Golling-Abtenau .... d.	0604	0634	0704	until
Salzburg Hbf...... **890** a.	0640	0710	0740	
Freilassing .... **890** a.	0657	0726	0754	

lass only

ATTNANG-PUCHHEIM - STAINACH-IRDNING 961

	⚒		Ⓐ									©A											
Wien Hbf 950 d.	...	...	...	...	...	...	...	...	...	...	...	1015	...	...	...	...	...	...	...	...	...	...	...
Attnang-Puchheim d.	...	...	0447	...	0603	0715	0811	0911	1011	1111	1211	1211	1311	1411	1511	1611	1711	1811	1911	2005	2105	...	...
Gmunden d.	...	...	0503	...	0621	0732	0826	0932	1026	1132	1226	1226	1332	1426	1532	1626	1732	1826	1932	2023	2123	...	...
Altmünster am Traunsee d.	...	...	0510	...	0626	0738	0832	0938	1032	1138	1232	1232	1338	1432	1538	1632	1738	1832	1938	2029	2130	...	...
Traunkirchen d.	...	...	0517	...	0633	0744	0838	0944	1038	1144	1238	1238	1344	1438	1544	1638	1744	1838	1944	2035	2135	...	...
Ebensee Landungsplatz d.	...	...	0523	...	0640	0752	0844	0952	1044	1152	1244	1244	1352	1444	1552	1644	1752	1844	1952	2042	2143	...	...
Ebensee d.	...	...	0527	...	0643	0758	0847	0958	1047	1158	1247	1247	1358	1447	1558	1647	1758	1847	1958	2045	2146	...	...
Bad Ischl d.	...	...	0548	...	0705	0820	0903	1020	1103	1220	1303	1303	1420	1503	1620	1703	1820	1903	2020	2103	2207	...	...
Bad Goisern d.	...	...	...	...	0719	0833	0913	1033	1113	1233	1313	1313	1433	1513	1633	1713	1833	1913	2033	2116	...	...	...
Hallstatt ⊡ d.	...	...	...	...	0731	0848	0925	1048	1125	1248	1325	1325	1448	1525	1648	1725	1848	|	|	|	...	...	...
Obertraun-Dachsteinhöhlen d.	...	...	...	...	0735	0851	0928	1051	1128	1251	1328	1328	1451	1528	1651	1728	1851	1928	2051	2131	...	...	...
Bad Aussee d.	0503	0632	...	...	0749	...	0942	...	1142	...	1342	1342	...	1542	...	1742	...	1942	2104	2143	...	...	...
Bad Mitterndorf d.	0521	0650	...	...	0804	...	0959	...	1159	...	1359	1359	...	1559	...	1759	...	1959	...	...	...	...	...
Stainach-Irdning a.	0538	0707	...	...	0818	...	1015	...	1215	...	1415	1415	...	1615	...	1815	...	2015	...	...	...	...	...

			Ⓐ	⚒	⚒											©B	©	Ⓐ				©	Ⓐ	
ch-Irdning d.	...	...	...	...	0611	...	0713	...	0940	...	1140	...	1340	...	1540	1540	...	...	1740	...	...	1940	1940	2047
tterndorf d.	...	...	...	...	0629	...	0730	...	0959	...	1159	...	1359	...	1559	1559	...	...	1759	...	...	1959	1959	2104
ussee d.	...	0457	...	0604	0650	0650	0811r	...	1016	...	1216	...	1416	...	1616	1616	...	...	1816	...	...	2016	2016	2121
aun-Dachsteinhöhlen d.	...	0509	...	0616	0702	0702	0824	0904	1028	1104	1228	1304	1428	1504	1628	1628	1704	1704	1828	1905	...	2028	...	...
tt ⊡ d.	...	|	...	|	0706	0706	0828	0907	1032	1107	1232	1307	1432	1507	1632	1632	1707	1707	1832	|	...	|	...	...
oisern d.	...	0525	...	0631	0720	0720	0842	0922	1043	1122	1243	1322	1443	1522	1643	1643	1722	1722	1843	1922	...	2043	...	...
chl d.	0433	0538	0600	0644	0733	0733	0853	0935	1053	1135	1253	1335	1453	1535	1653	1653	1735	1740	1853	1935	...	2053	...	...
ee d.	0453	0559	0621	0707	0758	0758	0911	0958	1111	1158	1311	1358	1511	1558	1711	1711	1758	1758	1911	1958	...	2112	...	...
ee Landungsplatz d.	0456	0602	0624	0710	0800	0800	0913	1001	1113	1201	1313	1401	1513	1601	1713	1713	1801	1801	1913	2001	...	2114	...	...
irchen d.	0503	0609	0633	0718	0808	0808	0919	1009	1119	1209	1319	1409	1519	1609	1719	1719	1809	1809	1919	2009	...	2120	...	...
ster am Traunsee d.	0509	0615	0639	0724	0814	0814	0925	1016	1125	1216	1325	1416	1525	1616	1725	1725	1816	1816	1925	2016	...	2131	...	...
den d.	0516	0621	0645	0732	0826	0826	0931	1026	1131	1226	1331	1426	1531	1626	1731	1731	1826	1826	1931	2023	...	2137	...	...
g-Puchheim a.	0531	0638	0703	0748	0842	0842	0947	1044	1147	1244	1347	1444	1547	1644	1747	1747	1844	1844	1947	2041	...	2155	...	...
Hbf 950 a.	...	...	...	...	...	...	...	...	...	...	...	...	...	...	...	1946	...	...	...	...	...	...	...	...

– Wien (720) - Attnang-Puchheim - Stainach-Irdning.
– Stainach-Irdning - Attnang-Puchheim (721) - Wien.

uns daily May - October.
rrives 0748.

⊡ – services operate Hallstatt Bahnhof - Hallstatt Markt. Journey: 8 minutes. **Operator**: Hallstättersee-Schifffahrt Hemetsberger KG ✆ +43 (0)6134 8228.
From Hallstatt Bahnhof at 0707⚒, 0735⚒**d**, 0830, 0900, 0930, 1035, 1100, 1130, 1235, 1300, 1330, 1435, 1500, 1530, 1635, 1700, 1730 and 1850.
From Hallstatt Markt at 0650⚒, 0715⚒, 0810⚒**d**, 0845, 0915, 1015, 1045, 1215, 1245, 1315, 1415, 1445, 1515, 1615, 1645, 1715 and 1815.

LINZ - PASSAU and SIMBACH 962

									ICE 228					*ICE* 28	5914					*ICE* 26				
	Ⓐ 2	⚒ 2	G2	2	Ⓐ 2	Ⓐ 2	© 2	© 2	✕	2	2	2	Ⓐ 2	✕	⊖2	2	2	2	⚒ 2	D✕	2	2	⚒ 2	⚒ 2
Wien Hbf 950 d.	...	...	...	...	...	...	...	...	0650	...	...	...	...	0850	0723f	...	...	...	...	1050	...	...	...	...
Linz Hbf 950 d.	...	0452	0543	0600	0700	...	0736	...	0814	0852	...	0952	...	1014	1038	1052	...	1152	...	1214	1252	...	1352	...
Wels Hbf 950 d.	0445	0516	0612	0620	0731	...	0754	...	0831	0909	...	1009	...	1031	1054	1109	...	1209	...	1231	1309	...	1409	...
Neumarkt-Kallham d.	0509	0543	0642	0645	0757	0811	0823	0832	|	0936	0940	1033	1040	|	1116	1140	1140	1233	1240	|	1336	1340	1433	1440
Ried im Innkreis d.	0529	|	|	0710	|	0831	|	0855	|	|	1001	|	1101	|	|	1201	|	|	1301	|	|	1401	|	1501
Braunau am Inn a.	0603	|	|	0740	|	0907	|	0940	|	|	1040	|	1140	|	|	1240	|	|	1340	|	|	1440	|	1540
Simbach (Inn) 893 a.	*0644*	|	|	0744	|	*0945*	|	0945	|	|	1045	|	1145	|	|	1245	|	|	1345	|	|	1445	|	1545
Schärding d.	...	0615	0714	...	0827	...	0853	...	|	1009	...	1059	...	|	1141	...	1213	1259	...	|	1409	...	1459	...
Passau Hbf a.	...	0630	0729	...	0842	...	0908	...	0918	1023	...	1113	...	1118	1155	...	1227	1313	...	1318	1423	...	1513	...
Nürnberg Hbf 920 a.	...	...	...	...	...	...	...	...	1126	...	...	...	...	1326	...	...	...	...	...	1526	...	...	...	...
Frankfurt (Main) Hbf 920 a.	...	...	...	...	...	...	...	...	1336	...	...	...	...	1536	...	...	...	...	...	1736	...	...	...	...

	ICE 90					*ICE* 22								*ICE* 20						*IC* 748		*EN* 490	*IC* 840		*EN* 420
	H✕	2	2	2	⚒ 2	D✕	Ⓐ 2	Ⓐ 2	2	2	Ⓐ 2	Ⓐ 2	2	✕	2	Ⓐ 2	2	2	2	🍷	2	⊡♣	🍷	2	◇♣
n Hbf 950 d.	1250	...	...	...	...	1450	...	...	...	...	...	...	...	1650	...	...	...	...	...	1955	...	2039	2055	...	2139
bf 950 d.	1414	1452	...	1552	...	1614	1625	1636	1652	...	1725	1752	1752	1814	1852	...	1952	...	2052	2132	...	2219	2232	...	2319
Hbf 950 d.	1431	1509	...	1609	...	1631	1642	1653	1709	...	1742	1809	1814k	1831	1909	...	2009	...	2109	2143	2148	2236	2243	2248	2336
arkt-Kallham d.	|	1540	1540	1633	1640	|	1704	1720	1736	1740	1809	1833	1840	|	1936	1940	2036	2040	2136	...	2216	|	...	2315	|
im Innkreis d.	|	1601	|	|	1701	|	|	1737	|	1801	|	|	1901	|	|	2001	|	2105	|	...	2237	|	...	|	|
unau am Inn a.	|	1640	|	|	1740	|	|	1809	|	1840	|	|	1940	|	|	2040	|	2141	|	...	2311	|	...	|	|
bach (Inn) 893 a.	|	1645	|	|	1745	|	|	...	|	1845c	|	|	1945	|	|	2045	|	2145	|	...	...	|	...	|	|
ding d.	|	...	1613	1659	...	|	1730	...	1809	...	1842	1859	...	|	2009	...	2109	...	2209	...	...	|	...	2347	|
u Hbf a.	1518	...	1627	1713	...	1718	...	...	1823	...	1858	1913	...	1918	2023	...	2123	...	2223	...	...	2326	...	...	0026
nberg Hbf 920 a.	1726	...	...	...	...	1926	...	...	...	...	...	...	...	2126	...	...	...	...	...	...	...	0127	...	...	|
kfurt (Main) Hbf 920 a.	...	...	...	...	...	2136	...	...	...	...	...	...	...	2340	...	...	...	...	...	...	...	...	...	...	0523j

				EN 491	*EN* 421															*ICE* 21				
	⚒ 2	Ⓐ 2	2	⊡♣	◇♣	⚒ 2	† 2	2	⚒ 2	Ⓐ 2	Ⓐ 2	2	⚒ 2	Ⓐ 2	2	2	© 2	2	2	✕	Ⓐ 2	2	2	2
Frankfurt (Main) Hbf 920 d.	...	...	...	...	0007j	...	...	...	...	...	...	...	...	...	...	...	...	...	...	0622	...	...	...	...
Nürnberg Hbf 920 d.	...	...	...	0300	|	...	...	...	...	...	...	...	...	...	...	...	...	...	...	0830	...	...	...	...
Passau Hbf d.	...	0408	0420c	0512	0522	...	...	0536	0606	...	0622	...	0647	...	...	0804	...	0933	...	1038	...	1042	...	1136
Schärding d.	0359	0423	0435	|	|	...	...	0551	0621	...	0637	...	0702	...	...	0819	...	0948	...	|	...	1056	...	1151
Simbach (Inn) 893 d.	|	|	|	|	|	...	...	|	|	...	|	...	|	0717	...	|	0817	|	0919	|	1019	|	1119	|
Braunau am Inn d.	|	|	|	|	|	0513	0525	|	|	0610	|	0628	|	0723	0751	|	0821	|	0923	|	1023	|	1123	|
Ried im Innkreis d.	|	|	|	|	|	0552	0601	|	|	0643	|	0710	|	0755	0831	|	0855	|	1001	|	1101	|	1201	|
Neumarkt-Kallham d.	0430	0451	0507	|	|	0613	0619	0623	0648	0702	0706	0730	0736	0812	0850	0854	0912	1019	1024	|	1119	1125	1219	1224
Wels Hbf 950 d.	0457	0515	0534	0609	0619	0636	...	0651	0718	...	0728	0758z	0807	0835	...	0923	0935	...	1051	1128	...	1151	...	1251
Linz Hbf 950 a.	0520	0532	0557	0623	0635	0652e	...	0708	0743	...	0747	...	0824	0855	...	0940	0955	...	1108	1142	...	1208	...	1308
Wien Hbf 950 a.	...	...	...	0816	0820	...	...	...	...	...	...	...	...	...	...	...	...	...	...	1309	...	...	...	...

	ICE 23					*ICE* 91					*ICE* 27				5927	*ICE* 29			*IC* 749		*IC* 841	*ICE* 229			*IC* 843
	D✕	⚒ 2	2	2	2	H✕	⚒ 2	⚒ 2	2	2	D✕	⚒ 2	2	2	⊖2	✕	2	2	🍷	2	🍷	✕	Ⓐ 2	2	
kfurt (Main) Hbf 920 d.	0819v	...	...	...	...	...	...	...	...	...	1221	...	...	...	...	1421	...	...	...	...	...	1621	...	...	...
nberg Hbf 920 d.	1030	...	...	...	...	1230	...	...	...	...	1431	...	...	...	...	1630	...	...	...	...	...	1830	...	...	...
u Hbf d.	1238	...	1242	1333	...	1438	...	1442	...	1536	1638	...	1642	...	1745	1838	...	1851	...	...	...	2038	...	2051	...
ding d.	|	...	1256	1348	...	|	...	1456	...	1551	|	...	1656	...	1800	|	...	1905	...	...	...	|	...	2105	...
bach (Inn) 893 d.	|	1219e	|	|	1319	|	1419	|	1519	|	|	1619	|	1719	|	|	1819	|	...	1919	...	|	*2017*	|	...
unau am Inn d.	|	1223	|	|	1323	|	1423	|	1523	|	|	1623	|	1723	|	|	1823	|	...	1923	...	|	2023	|	...
im Innkreis d.	|	1301	|	|	1401	|	1501	|	1601	|	|	1701	|	1801	|	|	1901	|	...	2001	...	|	2101	|	...
arkt-Kallham d.	|	1319	1325	1419	1424	|	1519	1525	1619	1624	|	1719	1725	1824	1835	|	1924	1937	...	2024	...	|	2119	2137	...
Hbf 950 d.	1328	...	1351	...	1451	1528	...	1551	...	1651	1728	...	1751	1851	1905	1928	1951	2006	2016	2051	2116	2128	...	2204	2216
bf 950 a.	1342	...	1408	...	1508	1542	...	1608	...	1708	1742	...	1808	1908	1922	1942	2008	2023c	2028	...	2128	2142	...	...	2228
n Hbf 950 a.	1509	...	...	...	...	1709	...	...	...	...	1909	...	...	...	2235f	2109	...	...	2205	...	2305	2309	...	...	...

o / from Dortmund (Table **800**).
rom Garsten (Table **976**).
o / from Hamburg (Table **900**).
) only.
Ⓐ only.

f – Wien **Franz-Josefs-Bahnhof**.
j – Frankfurt (Main) **Süd**.
k – 1817 on Ⓐ.
v – 0821 on ⑦ (also July 16, 23, 30, Aug. 6, 13, 20).
z – † only.

⊖ – May 1 - Oct. 26. [2] Wien Franz-Josefs-Bf - Tulln - St Pölten - Passau and v.v.
◇ – 1, 2 cl., 2 cl. and [2] Wien - Frankfurt - Köln - Düsseldorf and v.v.
⊡ – 1, 2 cl., 2 cl. and [2] Wien - Nürnberg - Hamburg and v.v.
♣ – 🅁 for journeys to Germany.

963 SALZBURG and ST WOLFGANG - STROBL - BAD ISCHL

Routes 150

km	Route 150	⚒	†	Ⓐ	⑥		⚒		k	Ⓐm	©	Ⓐ	⚒	©	Ⓐ	⚒	©	Ⓐ	Ⓐ	©	Ⓐ		†	Ⓐ
0	**Salzburg** Hbf △ d.	0555	...	*0625*	0645	0815	0915	1015	1115	1115	1215	1220	1320r	1415	1420	1520r	1615	1625	1725	1815	1820	1915	2015	2015
32	St Gilgen (Busbahnhof) d.	0645	0650	0730	0735	0910	1010	1110	1210	1220	1310	1315	1410	1510	1510	1610	1710	1710	1810	1910	1910	2005	2058	2105
45	Strobl (Busbahnhof) d.	0703	0706	0748	0751	0928	1028	1128	1228	1235	1328	1333	1428	1528	1528	1628	1728	1728	1828	1928	1928	2021	2113	2121
57	**Bad Ischl** Bahnhof a.	0725	0725	0810	0810	0950	1050	1150	1250	1257	1350	1355	1450	1550	1550	1650	1750	1750	1850	1947	1950	2040	2130	2140

	Route 150	⚒	Ⓐ	Ⓐ		⚒		†	⚒		k	Ⓐm	©	Ⓐ	⑥	Ⓐ		⚒		⚒		Ⓐ		⑥
	Bad Ischl Bahnhof d.	0504	...	...	0611	0646	0746	0824	0924	1024	1124	*1124*	1224	1224	1324	1336	1424	1524	1624	1724	1824	1924	2024	...
	Strobl (Busbahnhof) d.	0520	0550	0615	0631	0707	0807	0845	0945	1045	1145	*1145*	1245	1245	1345	1357	1445	1545	1645	1745	1845	1945	2040	...
	St Gilgen (Busbahnhof) d.	0535	0605	0629	0645	0727	0827	0905	1005	1105	1205	1220	1305	1315	1405	1415	1505	1605	1705	1805	1905	2005	2054	2105
	Salzburg Hbf △ a.	0619	0649	0715	0731	0819	0919	0953	1057	1157	1257	1307	1357	1407	1457	1507	1557	1657	1757	1857	1953	2053	...	2153

km	Route 546	Ⓐ	⚒	⚒	©	†	Ⓐ	Ⓐ	Ⓐ		Ⓐ	©	Ⓐ		Ⓐ		Ⓐ			Ⓐ	©	Ⓐ	©	
0	**St Wolfgang** ⊡ ‡... ♥ d.	0500	0600	0648	0735	0735	0740	0753	0900	0913	1013	1013	1100	1213	1318	1413	1513	1613	1713	1713	1813	1813	1828	1913
7	Strobl (Busbahnhof) ♥ d.	0512	0612	0703	0746	0747	|	0804	|	0926	|	1028	|	1228	1333	1428	1528	1628	1726	1728	|	1828	1841	1926
19	**Bad Ischl** Bahnhof a.	0531	0639	0729	...	0806	0811	...	0931	...	1044	1050	1131	1250	1359	1450	1554	1650	...	1754	1844	1850	...	...

	Route 546	Ⓐ	⚒	⚒		Ⓐ	Ⓐ	©	Ⓐ			⚒			Ⓐ		Ⓐ			Ⓐ				
	Bad Ischl Bahnhof d.	0605	0642	...	0823	0913	...	0913	1023	...	1113	1223	...	1330	1423	...	1513	1623	...	1713	1823	...	1913	...
	Strobl (Busbahnhof) d.	0630	0706	0806	|	|	0930	0935	1045	1045	1135	1245	1245	1355	1445	1445	1535	1645	1645	1735	1845	1845	|	1930
	St Wolfgang ⊡ ‡ a.	0645	0721	0820	0853	0943	0945	0950	1100	1100	1150	1300	1300	1410	1500	1500	1550	1700	1700	1750	1900	1900	1943	1945

k – ⑥ (also May 17, 27, Nov. 2; runs on ⚒ Dec. 24 - Jan. 5, Feb. 6 – 13, Mar. 19 – 29 and July 9 - Sept. 10).
m – Not Dec. 24 - Jan. 6, Feb. 8 – 12, Mar. 21 – 29, May 17, 27, July 11 - Sept. 9, Nov. 2.
r – 5 minutes **earlier** on ⑥.

△ – All services also call at Mirabellplatz.
⊡ – St Wolfgang Schafbergbahnhof. All services also call at St Wolfgang Markt.
♥ – Additional services St Wolfgang - Strobl: 1028 Ⓐ, *1113 ©, 1313 © and 1513 ©.
‡ – The **Schafbergbahn** narrow-gauge steam rack railway operates St Wolfgang - Schafbergspitze (6 Services operate subject to demand and weather conditions **Apr. 30 - Oct. 26**, 2016. 2nd class on Special fares payable. Journey time: 35 minutes each way. ✆ +43 (0) 6138 2232 0.

964 STROBL - ST GILGEN (WOLFGANGSEE)

Service June 18 - Se

			⛴			⛴			⛴			⛴					
Strobl Schiffstation ⊡ d.	...	0845	...	0925	1025	...	1125	1225	...	1325	1425	...	1525	1625	1725	1820	1920
St Wolfgang Markt d.	...	|	0935	|	|	1125	1200	1300	1325	1400	1500	1525	1600	1700	1800	1835	1933
St Wolfgang Schafbergbahnhof ‡ d.	0830	0910	0945	0955	1055	1133	1208	1308	1333	1408	1508	1533	1608	1708	1808	1845	1941
St Wolfgang Markt d.	|	0918	|	1005	1105	|	|	|	|	|	|	|	|	|	|	...	...
St Gilgen Schiffstation ● a.	0855	0955	1015	1045	1145	1215	1245	1345	1415	1445	1545	1615	1645	1745	1845	...	...

					⛴			⛴			⛴			⛴			
St Gilgen Schiffstation ● d.	...	...	0900	1000	1030	1100	1200	1230	1300	1400	1430	1500	1600	1630	1700	1800	1850
St Wolfgang Markt d.	...	...	|	|	|	|	|	|	|	|	|	|	|	|	|	|	1925
St Wolfgang Schafbergbahnhof ‡ d.	0825	0855	0937	1037	1109	1137	1237	1309	1337	1437	1509	1537	1637	1709	1737	1837	1935
St Wolfgang Markt d.	|	0905	0950	1050	1117	1150	1250	1317	1350	1450	1517	1550	1650	1717	1750	1850	...
Strobl Schiffstation ⊡ a.	0840	0920	1015	1115	...	1215	1315	...	1415	1515	...	1615	1715	...	1815	1915	...

‡ – See note under Table **963**.
⊡ – Approximately 400 metres fr Strobl Busbahnhof.
● – Approximately 500 metres fr St Gilgen Busbahnhof.
⛴ – July 9 - Aug. 28 (subject to w conditions). Operated by pad steamer *Kaiser Franz Josef* Supplement payable (€ 1).

969 TAUERN TUNNEL CAR-CARRYING TRAINS

BÖCKSTEIN - MALLNITZ-OBERVELLACH *11 km.* Transit time: 11 minutes. Passengers without cars are also conveyed. ✆ 05-1717. E-mail: autoschleuse.tauernbahn@pv.o
From Böckstein at 0620, 0720 and hourly until 2320. **From Mallnitz-Obervellach** at 0550, 0650 and hourly until 2250.

970 SALZBURG - VILLACH - KLAGENFURT

km		*EN* 499 R ♦	*EN* 237 R ♦	⚒ 2		*EN* 415 R ♦	2		⚒ 2	2	*IC* 590 ✕	*IC* 592 🍷	*EC* 111 ✕	*IC* 690 🍷	*IC* 790 ✕	*EC* 113 ✕♦	*EC* 115 ⊗♦	Ⓐ 2		*IC* 692 🍷		*EC* 117 ⊗♦
	Wien Hbf **950** d.	...	2125	...	...	...	...	...	...	...	...	...	...	0855	...	...	...	...	...	1455	...	...
	München Hbf **890** d.	2336j	|	...	...	...	...	...	...	...	...	...	0818	|	...	1218	1418	...	...	|	...	1818
0	**Salzburg** Hbf **960 975** d.	0134	0134	...	...	...	...	...	...	...	0612	0812	1012	1212	...	1412	1612	...	...	1812	...	2012
29	Golling-Abtenau **960** d.	|	|	...	...	...	...	...	...	...	0633	0833	1033	1233	...	1433	1633	...	...	1833	...	2033
53	**Bischofshofen** **960 975** d.	|	|	...	...	...	...	...	...	...	0654	0854	1054	1254	...	1454	1654	...	...	1854	...	2054
61	St Johann im Pongau **960** d.	|	|	...	...	...	...	...	...	...	0703	0903	1103	1303	...	1503	1703	...	...	1903	...	2103
67	**Schwarzach - St Veit** **960** d.	0226	0226	...	...	0427	...	...	...	...	0711	0911	1111	1311	...	1511	1711	...	...	1911	...	2111
86	Bad Hofgastein d.	|	|	...	...	0444	...	...	...	...	0729	0929	1129	1329	...	1529	1729	...	...	1929	...	2129
97	Bad Gastein d.	|	|	...	...	0501	...	...	...	...	0742	0942	1142	1342	...	1542	1742	...	...	1942	...	2142
113	Mallnitz-Obervellach d.	|	|	...	...	0516	...	...	0647	...	0756	0956	1156	1356	...	1556	1756	1800	...	1956	...	2156
146	Spittal-Millstättersee **971** d.	0327	0327	...	...	0542	...	...	0717	0729	0820	1020	1220	1420	...	1620	1820	1830	...	2020	...	2220
182	**Villach** Hbf **971** a.	0351	0351	...	...	0605	...	...	...	0753	0843	1043	1243	1443	...	1643	1843	...	...	2043	...	2243
182	**Villach** Hbf **971** d.	...	...	0450	...	...	0620	...	...	0755	0846	1046	1246	...	1446	1649	1846	...	...	2046	...	2248
198	Velden am Wörthersee **971** d.	...	...	0505	...	...	0634	...	...	0806	0857	1057	1257	...	1457	1700	1857	...	...	2057	...	2259
207	Pörtschach am Wörthersee **971** d.	...	...	0513	...	...	0642	...	...	|	0904	1104	1304	...	1504	1707	1904	...	...	2104	...	2306
220	**Klagenfurt** Hbf **971** a.	...	...	0528	...	...	0656	...	...	0822	0912	1112	1315	...	1513	1718	1915	...	...	2115	...	2317

	EN 236 R ♦	*EN* 498 R ♦		Ⓐ F 2	⚒ 2		*IC* 693 🍷		*EC* 114 ⊗♦	*EC* 112 ✕♦		*IC* 691 🍷		*IC* 791 ✕	*IC* 591 🍷	Ⓐ 2	Ⓐ 2	*EC* 110 ✕		*IC* 593 ✕		2
Klagenfurt Hbf **971** d.	...	...	...	...	...	...	0645	...	0842	1027	...	1245	...	1445	...	1532	...	1642	...	1845	...	2232
Pörtschach am Wörthersee **971** d.	...	...	...	...	...	...	0655	...	0855	1040	...	1255	...	1455	...	1547	...	1655	...	1855	...	2247
Velden am Wörthersee **971** d.	...	...	...	...	...	...	0702	...	0902	1047	...	1302	...	1502	...	1554	...	1702	...	1902	...	2254
Villach Hbf **971** a.	...	...	...	...	...	...	0713	...	0913	1058	...	1313	...	1513	...	1609	...	1713	...	1913	...	2309
Villach Hbf **971** d.	0146	0146	...	...	0529	...	0716	...	0916	1116	...	1316	...	...	1516	1610	...	1716	...	1916	...	...
Spittal-Millstättersee **971** d.	0209	0209	...	...	0604	...	0740	...	0940	1140	...	1340	...	...	1540	1634	1644	1740	...	1940	...	...
Mallnitz-Obervellach d.	|	|	...	...	0633	...	0804	...	1004	1204	...	1404	...	...	1604	...	1714	1804	...	2004	...	...
Bad Gastein d.	|	|	...	0625	...	...	0817	...	1017	1217	...	1417	...	...	1617	...	...	1817	...	2017	...	...
Bad Hofgastein d.	|	|	...	0636	...	...	0830	...	1030	1230	...	1430	...	...	1630	...	...	1830	...	2030	...	...
Schwarzach - St Veit **960** d.	0320	0320	...	0655	...	...	0850	...	1050	1250	...	1450	...	...	1650	...	...	1850	...	2050	...	...
St Johann im Pongau **960** a.	|	|	...	0700	...	...	0855	...	1055	1255	...	1455	...	...	1655	...	...	1855	...	2055	...	...
Bischofshofen **960 975** a.	|	|	...	0709	...	...	0903	...	1103	1303	...	1503	...	...	1703	...	...	1903	...	2103	...	...
Golling-Abtenau **960** a.	|	|	...	|	...	...	0924	...	1124	1324	...	1524	...	...	1724	...	...	1924	...	2124	...	...
Salzburg Hbf **960 975** a.	0409	0409	...	0748	...	...	0948	...	1148	1348	...	1548	...	...	1748	...	...	1948	...	2148	...	...
München Hbf **890** a.	|	0611**k**	...	...	...	...	|	...	1341	1541	...	|	...	...	...	...	...	2143	...	...	...	...
Wien Hbf **950** a.	0755	...	...	...	...	...	1305	...	...	...	...	1905	...	...	...	...	...	...	...	...	...	...

♦ – **NOTES** (LISTED BY TRAIN NUMBER)

112 – 🚃12 and ✕ Klagenfurt - München - Stuttgart - Frankfurt; 🚃12 Zagreb (**212**) - Villach (**112**) - Frankfurt.
113 – 🚃12 and ✕ Frankfurt - Stuttgart - München - Klagenfurt; 🚃12 Frankfurt - Villach (**213**) - Zagreb.
114 – WÖRTHERSEE – 🚃12 and ⊗ Klagenfurt - München - Stuttgart - Köln - Dortmund.
115 – WÖRTHERSEE – 🚃12 and ⊗ Münster - Köln - Stuttgart - München - Klagenfurt.
117 – 🚃12 and ⊗ (Frankfurt ⑧ / Karlsruhe ⑥ -) Stuttgart - München - Salzburg - Klagenfurt. Train number **1217** on ⑥ (also Mar. 25, Oct. 2; not July 30 - Sept. 10).
236/7 – 🛌 1, 2 cl., 🛏 2 cl. and 🚃2 Venezia - Tarvisio ▦ - Villach - Salzburg - Wien Hbf and v.v.
414 – 🚃2 Beograd - Zagreb - Ljubljana - Villach - Schwarzach (**464**) - Innsbruck - Feldkirch - Zürich; 🛌 1, 2 cl. and 🛏 2 cl. Zagreb - Ljubljana - Villach - Schwarzach (**464**) - Innsbruck - Feldkirch - Zürich.
415 – 🚃2 Zürich (**465**) - Feldkirch - Innsbruck - Schwarzach (**415**) - Villach - Ljubljana - Zagreb - Beograd; 🛌 1, 2 cl. and 🛏 2 cl. Zürich (**465**) - Feldkirch - Innsbruck - Schwarzach (**415**) - Villach - Ljubljana - Zagreb.
498/9 – LISINSKI – 🛌 1, 2 cl., 🛏 2 cl. and 🚃2 Zagreb - Dobova ▦ - Ljubljana - Jesenice ▦ - Villach - München and v.v.

F – To Freilassing (a. 0759).
R – Ⓡ for international journeys.

j – 2331 daily Feb. 25 - June 3, ①–⑤ June 6 - Ju and daily July 18 - Aug. 5; 2314 on ⑥⑦ June July 17.
k – 0721 on ⑦ June 5 - July 17.

LIENZ - VILLACH - KLAGENFURT - FRIESACH (- WIEN) 971

	⚒ 2	EN 234 ★ 2	RJ 530 ✕	U 2	2	2	2	D 734 Ⓐ 2	RJ 532 ✕	2	2	⚒ 2	IC 590 ◐ ✕	RJ 534 ✕	2	⚒ 2	IC 592 ◐ 🍷	2	D 736 ⑥ 2	RJ 536 ✕	2	Ⓐ 2	⚒ 2	EC 111 ◐ ✕	RJ 538 ✕
d.	...	...	...	...	...	...	0524	0548	...	...	0629	...	...	...	0719	*0824*e	...	0924	0953	...	...	...	1024e	...	...
l-Millstättersee a.	...	...	...	...	...	...	0627	0632	...	...	0727	...	...	...	0822	*0922*e	...	1022	1042	...	...	...	1122e	...	...
l-Millstättersee 970 d.	...	...	...	0448r	0530e	...	0630	0637	...	0642e	0729	0732	0820	...	0832	0932	1020	1032	1046	...	...	...	1132	1220	...
ch Hbf 970 a.	...	...	...	0520r	0558e	...	0656	0701	...	0715e	0753	0804	0843	...	0904p	1004	1043	1104	1109	...	←	...	1204	1243	...
ch Hbf 970 d.	0450	0511	0526	0529	0604	0620	0659e	...	0714	0720	0755	0820	0846	0914	0920	1020	1046	1120	...	1114	1120	1150	1220	1246	1314
n am Wörthersee 970 d.	0505	|	|	0543	|	0634	0711e	...	0725	0734	0806	0834	0857	|	0934	1034	1057	→	...	1125	1134	1204	1234	1257	|
chach am W'see ⊡ 970 d.	0513	|	|	0551	|	0642	|	...	|	0742	|	0842	0904	0929	0942	1042	1104	...	...	|	1142	1212	1242	1304	1329
pendorf d.	0519	|	|	0557	|	0648	|	...	|	0748	|	0848	|	|	0948	1048	|	...	...	|	1148	1218	1248	1309	|
enfurt Hbf 970 a.	0528	0532	0547	0605	0625	0656	0728e	...	0737	0756	0822	0856	0912	0937	0956	1056	1112	...	...	1137	1156	1226	1256	1315	1337
enfurt Hbf 980 d.	...	0533	0549	0607	0627	0704	...	...	0739	0804	0823	0904	...	0939	1004	1104	...	...	...	1139	1204	1228	1304	...	1339
it an der Glan 980 d.	...	|	0602	0627	0640	0724	...	...	0753	0824	0838	0924	...	0953	1024	1124	...	...	...	1153	1224	1247	1324	...	1353
ach 980 a.	...	|	|	0659	0703	0756	...	...	|	0856	...	0956	...	1015	1056	1156	...	...	...	|	1256	...	1356	...	1415
en Hbf 980 a.	...	0948	0935	...	...	...	...	...	1135	...	...	...	...	1335	...	...	...	...	...	1535	...	...	...	...	1735

	2	Ⓐ 2	⚒ 2	Ⓐ 2	RJ 630 ✕	2	Ⓐ 2	⚒ 2	EC 113 ◐ ✕	2	RJ 632 ✕	2	Ⓐ 2	RJ 732 ⑦w ✕	⚒ 2	EC 115 ◐ ⊗	EC 30 V✕	2	⚒ 2	⚒ 2	IC 692 ◐ 🍷	◇ 2	⚒ 2	EC 117 1217 ◐⊗	2
d.	1124	...	1224e	...	...	1324	...	1424e	...	1524	1553	...	...	...	1624e	...	...	1724	1824e	...	...	1924	2024e	...	...
al-Millstättersee a.	1222	...	1322e	...	...	1422	...	1522e	...	1622	1642	...	...	...	1722e	...	...	1822	1922e	...	...	2022	2122e	...	...
al-Millstättersee 970 d.	1232	...	1332	...	...	1432	...	1532	1620	1632	1646	...	...	...	1732	1820	...	1832	1932	...	2020	2032	2132	2220	...
ch Hbf 970 a.	1304p	...	1404	...	...	1504p	...	1604	1643	1704	1709	←	...	...	1804	1843	...	1904p	2004	...	2043	2104	2204	2243	...
ch Hbf 970 d.	1320	1350	1420	1450	1514	1520	1550	1620	1649	1720	1714	1720	1750	1814	1820	1846	1914	1920	...	2020	2046	2120	2220	2248	2350
en am Wörthersee 970 d.	1334	1404	1434	1504	1525	1534	1604	1634	1700	→	|	1734	1804	|	1834	1857	1925	1934	...	2034	2057	2134	2234	2259	0004
chach am W'see ⊡ 970 d.	1342	1412	1442	1512	|	1542	1612	1642	1707	...	1729	1742	1812	1829	1842	1904	|	1942	...	2042	2104	2142	2242	2306	0012
pendorf d.	1348	1418	1448	1518	|	1548	1618	1648	1712	...	|	1748	1818	|	1848	1909	|	1948	...	2048	2109	2148	2248	2311	0018
enfurt Hbf 970 a.	1356	1426	1456	1526	1537	1556	1626	1656	1718	...	1737	1756	1826	1837	1856	1915	1937	1956	...	2056	2115	2156	2256	2317	0026
enfurt Hbf 980 d.	1404	1428	1504	1528	1539	1604	1628	1704	...	...	1739	1804	1828	1839	1904	...	1939	2004	...	2104	...	2204	2304	...	0028
eit an der Glan 980 d.	1424	1447	1524	1547	1553	1624	1647	1724	...	...	1753	1824	1847	1853	1924	...	1953	2024	...	2124	...	2224	2324	...	0047
ach 980 a.	1456	...	1556	...	|	1656	...	1756	...	...	1815	1856	...	1918	1956	...	|	2056	...	2156	...	2256	2356	...	...
en Hbf 980 a.	...	...	...	...	1935	...	...	...	...	...	2135	...	...	2235	...	...	2335	...	...	...	...	...	...	...	...

	⚒ 2	⚒ 2	2	⚒ 2	IC 693 ◐ 🍷	⚒ 2	⚒⊖ U 2	◇ 2	EC 114 ◐ ⊗	⚒ 2	2	EC 31 V✕	EC 112 ◐ ✕	⚒ 2	2	RJ 533 ✕	2	Ⓐ 2	IC 691 ◐ 🍷	⚒ 2	Ⓐ 2	2	RJ 535 ✕	Ⓐ 2
Wien Hbf 980 d.	...	...	...	...	...	...	...	...	...	...	...	0625	...	...	...	0825	...	...	...	...	...	...	1025	...
Friesach 980 d.	...	...	0508	0545	...	0608	0643	0708	...	0808	0908	|	...	1008	1108	1144	...	...	...	1208	...	1308	|	...
St Veit an der Glan 980 d.	...	0512	0542	0616	...	0642	0718	0742	...	0842	0942	1008	...	1042	1142	1208	...	1212	...	1242	1312	1342	1408	1412
Klagenfurt Hbf 980 a.	...	0530	0600	0631	...	0700	0738	0800	...	0900	1000	1020	...	1100	1200	1220	...	1230	...	1300	1330	1400	1420	1430
Klagenfurt Hbf 970 d.	...	0532	0602	0633	0645	0702	0744	0802	0842	0902	1002	1022	1027	1102	1202	1222	...	1232	1245	1302	1332	1402	1422	1432
Krumpendorf d.	...	0541	0611	0643	|	0711	0752	0811	0849	0911	1011	|	1034	1111	1211	|	...	1241	|	1311	1341	1411	|	1441
Pörtschach am W ⊡ 970 d.	...	0547	0617	0648	0655	0717	0757	0817	0855	0917	1017	|	1040	1117	1217	1232	...	1247	1255	1317	1347	1417	|	1447
Velden am Wörthersee 970 d.	...	0554	0624	0654	0702	0724	0804	0824	0902	0924	1024	1036	1047	1124	1224	|	...	1254	1302	1324	1354	1424	1436	1454
Villach Hbf 970 a.	...	0609	0639	0710	0713	0739	0820	0839	0913	0939	1039	1046p	1058	1139	1239	1246	←	1309	1313	1339	1409	1439	1446p	1509
Villach Hbf 970 d.	*0529*	0617e	0654	...	0716	0754	...	0854	0916	0954	1054	...	1116	1154	1254	1250	1254	...	1316	1354	...	1454	...	...
Spittal-Millstättersee 970 a.	*0602*	0650e	0726	...	0738	0826	...	0926	0938	1026	1126	...	1138	1226	→	1314	1326	...	1338	1426	...	1526	...	...
Spittal-Millstättersee d.	0632	...	0737	...	...	0837e	...	0937	...	1037e	1137	...	...	1237e	...	1316	1337	...	...	1437e	...	1537	...	...
Lienz a.	0732	...	0837	...	...	0937e	...	1037	...	1137e	1237	...	...	1337e	...	1406	1437	...	...	1537e	...	1637	...	...

	⚒ 2	Ⓐ 2	2	RJ 537 ✕	D 735 Ⓑb 2	2	Ⓐ 2	EC 110 ◐ ✕	⚒ 2	Ⓐ 2	2	RJ 539 ✕	Ⓐ 2	IC 593 ◐ ✕	⚒ 2	Ⓐ 2	2	RJ 631 ✕	⚒ 2	2	RJ 633 ✕	Ⓑ 2	2	EN 235 ★ 2	2
en Hbf 980 d.	...	...	...	1225	...	...	...	...	...	...	...	1425	...	...	...	...	...	1625	...	...	1825	...	...	1923	...
sach 980 d.	1408	...	1508	1544	...	...	...	...	1608	...	1708	|	...	...	1808	...	1908	1944	2008	2108	|	...	...	2259	...
eit an der Glan 980 d.	1442	1512	1542	1608	...	...	1612	...	1642	1712	1742	1808	1812	...	1842	1912	1942	2008	2042	2142	2200	...	...	|	...
enfurt Hbf 980 a.	1500	1530	1600	1620	...	...	1630	...	1700	1730	1800	1820	1830	...	1900	1930	2000	2020	2100	2200	2212	...	...	2333	...
enfurt Hbf 970 d.	1502	1532	1602	1622	...	...	1632	1642	1702	1732	1802	1822	1832	1845	1902	1932	2002	2022	2102	...	2214	...	2232	2335	2341
pendorf d.	1511	1541	1611	|	...	...	1641	1649	1711	1741	1811	|	1841	|	1911	1941	2011	|	2111	...	|	...	2241	|	2350
chach am W'see ⊡ 970 d.	1517	1547	1617	1632	...	...	1647	1655	1717	1747	1817	|	1847	1855	1917	1947	2017	2032	2117	...	|	...	2247	|	2357
en am Wörthersee 970 d.	1524	1554	1624	|	...	...	1654	1702	1724	1754	1824	1836	1854	1902	1924	1954	2024	|	2124	...	|	...	2254	|	0004
ch Hbf 970 a.	1539	1609	1639	1646	...	←	1709	1713	1739	1809	1839	1846p	1909	1913	1939	2009	2039	2046p	2139	...	2236	...	2309	2358	0019
ch Hbf 970 d.	1554	1610	1654	...	1650	1654	1710	1716	1754	1810	1854	...	...	1916	1954	...	2054	...	2154	...	...	2254	*2316*	...	...
al-Millstättersee 970 a.	1626	1634	→	...	1714	1726	1734	1738	1826	1834	1926	...	...	1938	2026	...	2126	...	2226	...	...	2326	*2339*	...	...
al-Millstättersee d.	...	1637	...	...	1716	1737	...	...	1837e	...	1937	...	...	...	*2037*e	...	2137	...	...	...	...	...	...	...	...
z a.	...	1737	...	...	1806	1837	...	...	1937e	...	2037	...	...	...	*2136*e	...	2235	...	...	...	...	...	...	...	...

To / from Unzmarkt (Table **980**).
12 Venezia - Tarvisio 🏛 - Villach - Wien and v.v.

Not Jan. 6, Mar. 27, May 5, 15, 26, Aug. 14, Oct. 26, Nov. 1, Dec. 8.

e – Ⓐ only.
p – Connects with train in previous column.
r – ⚒ only.
w – Also Jan. 6, Mar. 28, May 16, Aug. 15, Nov. 1; not Mar. 27, May 15, Aug. 14, Oct. 30.

⊖ – Change trains at Klagenfurt on Ⓐ to July 8 / from Sept. 12.
★ – See Table **980** for through cars to / from Roma and Milano.
◐ – See Table **970** for further details.
◇ – Change trains at Spittal-Millstättersee on Ⓐ.
⊡ – Pörtschach am Wörthersee.

class only LINZ - SELZTHAL 974

SERVICE JUNE 20 - AUGUST 28 AND FROM SEPTEMBER 12

	⚒	Ⓐ					*IC* 15503				Ⓒ	Ⓐ		⚒	Ⓐ		*IC* 15601		Ⓐ			Ⓐ		
Linz Hbf d.	0506	0536	0635	0703	0736	0836	0914	1058	1136	1258	1336	1404	1458	1536	1607	1636	1714	1736	1810	1858	1936	2036	2136	2336
Rohr - Bad Hall d.	0540	0609	0709	0728	0810	0910	0935	1121	1209	1321	1409	1429	1521	1609	1631	1709	1735	1809	1834	1921	2009	2109	2209	0009
Kremsmünster d.	0546	0616	0715	|	0815	0915	|	1125	1214	1325	1414	1435	1525	1614	1636	1714	|	1814	1838	1925	2014	2114	2214	0014
Kirchdorf a. d. Krems d.	0604	0633	0733	0743	0835	0934	0948	1140	1232	1340	1435	1451	1540	1632	1653	1732	1749	1833	1853	1939	2033	2132	2232	0032
Hinterstoder ★ d.	0625	...	...	0801	0856	...	|	1201	...	1401	1457	1513	1601	...	1714	...	|	...	1914	2001	2103	...	...	...
Windischgarsten d.	0639	...	...	0814	0910	...	|	1215	...	1415	1511	1527	1615	...	1728	...	|	...	1928	2015	2118	...	...	...
Spital am Pyhrn d.	0645	...	...	0820	0915	...	|	1220	...	1420	1516	1532	1620	...	1733	...	|	...	1934	2020	2123	...	...	...
Selzthal a.	*0708*¦	...	...	*0843*¦	...	...	*1041*¦	*1243*¦	...	*1443*¦	...	...	*1643*¦	...	*1756*¦	...	*1842*¦	...	...	*2043*¦	*2146*¦	...	...	...
Liezen 975 a.	...	...	...	*0856*‡	...	...	...	*1253*‡	...	*1453*‡	...	...	*1653*‡	...	...	...	...	...	...	...	...	...	...	...
Graz Hbf 975 a.	...	...	...	...	...	...	...	...	...	...	...	...	...	...	...	...	...	...	...	...	...	...	...	...

	⚒	Ⓐ		⚒		⚒	Ⓐ	Ⓒ		*IC* 15502								Ⓐ		*IC* 15600				Ⓐ	
az Hbf 975 d.	...	...	...	...	...	...	...	...	...	...	...	...	...	...	...	...	...	...	...	...	...	...	...	...	...
ezen 975 d.	...	...	...	...	...	...	...	...	...	...	...	...	...	...	*1305*‡	...	*1505*‡	...	...	...	...	...	...	...	...
thal d.	...	*0422*¦	...	...	...	*0539*¦	*0608*¦	*0608*¦	*0718*¦	*0918*¦	...	...	*1116*¦	...	*1318*¦	...	*1518*¦	...	...	*1718*¦	...	...	*1918*¦	...	...
l am Pyhrn d.	...	0445	...	...	...	0604	0632	0632	0740	|	...	1044	1140	...	1340	...	1540	...	1643	|	...	...	1940	2043	...
ischgarsten d.	...	0452	...	...	...	0610	0640	0640	0746	|	...	1050	1146	...	1346	...	1546	...	1649	|	...	...	1947	2049	...
rstoder ★ d.	...	0505	...	...	...	0625	0654	0654	0801	|	...	1105	1200	...	1400	...	1600	...	1703	|	...	...	2000	2103	...
dorf a. d. Krems d.	0428	0526	0526	0556	0627	0646	0717	0725	0821	1011	1026	1126	1221	1326	1421	1526	1621	1655	1726	1811	1826	1926	2021	2126	2126
ismünster d.	0445	0546	0546	0616	0645	0703	0732	0746	0836	|	1045	1145	1236	1345	1436	1545	1636	1715	1745	|	1846	1945	2036	2145	2145
- Bad Hall d.	0449	0550	0550	0620	0650	0708	0737	0750	0840	1025	1049	1149	1240	1349	1440	1549	1640	1719	1750	1825	1850	1949	2040	2149	2149
Hbf a.	0524	0624	0624	0654	0728j	0735	0803	0824	0903	1047	1124	1224	1303	1424	1503	1624	1703	1754	1824	1847	1924	2024	2103	2224	2224

0724 on Ⓒ.
By 🚌.
Ⓐ only. By 🚌.

★ – 🚌 services operate Hinterstoder rail station - Hinterstoder town centre and v.v. Journey time: 18 minutes.
Operated by Riedler Reisen & Touristik GmbH.
From Hinterstoder rail station at 0655 ⑥, 0810, 0900, 1203, 1403, 1515 Ⓐ, 1603 and 1715.
From Hinterstoder Gemeindehaus at 0600 Ⓐ, 0630 ⚒, 0735 Ⓐ, 0739 Ⓒ, 1138, 1338, 1538 and 1638.

975 SALZBURG - BISCHOFSHOFEN - SELZTHAL - GRAZ

See Table **980** for connecting *RJ* services Leoben - Bruck a. d. Mur - Wien and v.v.

km			*EN* 465						*IC* 719			*IC* 513	*IC* 503		*EC* 111	*IC* 515			*EC* 217			*EC* 113	*EC* 163
		⚒ 2	A	⚒ 2	⚒ 2	Ⓐ 2	Ⓐ 2	2	⊗	Ⓐw 2	2	🍷	△ 🍷	2	✕	🍷	Ⓐw 2L	2	S⊗	Ⓐw 2L	Ⓑ 2	✕	Z✕
0	**Salzburg** Hbf 960 970 d.	...	...	...	...	...	...	...	0615	...	...	0815	...	...	1012	...	...	...	1215	...	...	1412	...
	Innsbruck Hbf **960** d.	...	0056	...	...	...	...	...	|	...	...	|	...	...	|	0824	...	...	|	...	...	|	1224
53	**Bischofshofen** 960 970 a.	...	0336	...	...	...	...	...	0702	...	...	0902	...	...	1052	1110	...	...	1302	...	...	1452	1510
53	**Bischofshofen** d.	...	0338	...	...	...	...	...	0713	...	0741v	0913	...	...	...	1113	...	...	1313	...	...	...	1513
77	Radstadt d.	...	|	...	...	...	...	0610	0736	...	0809	0936	...	...	...	1136	...	...	1336	...	...	...	1536
94	Schladming d.	...	0416	0500	...	...	...	0629	0752	...	0831	0952	...	1031	...	1152	...	1231	1352	...	1431	...	1552
133	**Stainach-Irdning** d.	0415	0447	0541	...	...	...	0710	0821	...	0912	1021	...	1112	...	1221	...	1312	1421	...	1512	...	1621
145	Liezen d.	0427	|	0553	...	...	...	0726	0832	0857	0926	1032	...	1126	...	1232	1305	1326	1432	1505	1526	...	1632
	Linz Hbf **974** d.	|	|	|	...	...	...	|	|	|	|	|	0914	|	...	|	|	|	|	|	|	...	|
152	**Selzthal** a.	0433	0504	0559	...	...	...	0733	0839	0904	0933	1039	1041	1133	...	1239	1312	1333	1439	1512	1533	...	1639
152	**Selzthal** d.	0440	0513	0606	...	0716	...	0739	0846	...	0939	1048	1048	1139	...	1248	...	1339	1446	...	1539	...	1648
158	Stadt Rottenmann d.	0447	|	0613	...	0722	...	0745	0853	...	0945	|	|	1145	...	|	...	1345	1453	...	1545	...	|
169	Trieben d.	0455	|	0621	...	0729	...	0753	|	...	0953	|	|	1153	...	|	...	1353	|	...	1553	...	|
215	St Michael a.	0530	0550	0655	...	0802	...	0828	0921	...	1028	1121	1121	1228	...	1321	...	1428	1521	...	1628	...	1721
215	St Michael **980** d.	0531	0551	0701	0706	0803	...	*0833*	0922	...	*1033*	1122	1122	*1233*	...	1322	...	*1433*	1522	...	*1633*	...	1722
225	Leoben Hbf **980** d.	0540	0601	0709	0715	0811	0818	*0841*	0930	...	*1041*	1130	1130	*1241*	...	1330	...	*1441*	1530	...	*1641*	...	1730
	Bruck a. d. Mur **980** a.	|	0612	|	0728	0824	|	*0853*	|	...	*1053*	|	|	*1253*	...	|	...	*1453*	|	...	*1653*	...	|
293	**Graz** Hbf **980** a.	0633	0700	0801	...	...	0903	...	1014	...	...	1214	1214	...	...	1414	...	...	1614	...	...	...	1814

		IC 611	*IC* 601			*EC* 219	*EC* 117 1217		
	2	🍷	△ 🍷	2	Ⓐ 2	F⊗	⊗	2	Ⓑ 2
Salzburg Hbf 960 970 d.	...	1615	...	...	*1641*	1815	2012	...	...
Innsbruck Hbf **960** d.	...	|	...	...	|	|	|	...	...
Bischofshofen 960 970 a.	...	1702	...	...	*1733*	1902	2052	...	...
Bischofshofen d.	...	1713	...	...	1741	1913	...	2100	...
Radstadt d.	...	1736	...	...	1810	1936	...	2130	...
Schladming d.	1631	1752	...	1831	...	1952	...	2149	2155
Stainach-Irdning d.	1712	1821	...	1912	...	2021	...	...	2234
Liezen d.	1726	1832	...	1926	...	2032	...	...	...
Linz Hbf **974** d.	|	|	1714	|	...	|	...	...	...
Selzthal a.	1733	1839	1841	1933	...	2039	...	...	...
Selzthal d.	1739	1848	1848	1939	...	2046	...	...	...
Stadt Rottenmann d.	1745	|	|	1945	...	2053	...	...	...
Trieben d.	1753	|	|	1953	...	|	...	...	...
St Michael a.	1828	1921	1921	2028	...	2121	...	...	...
St Michael **980** d.	*1833*	1922	1922	*2033*	...	2122	...	...	...
Leoben Hbf **980** d.	*1841*	1930	1930	*2041*	...	2130	...	...	...
Bruck a. d. Mur **980** a.	*1853*	|	|	*2053*	...	|	...	...	...
Graz Hbf **980** a.	...	2014	2014	...	...	2214	...	...	...

						EC 218			*IC* 502
	⚒ 2	⚒ 2	2	Ⓐ 2	⚒ 2	F⊗	2	Ⓐw 2L	△ 🍷
Graz Hbf **980** d.	...	...	...	...	...	0545	...	...	0745
Bruck a. d. Mur **980** d.	...	...	...	*0536*	0613	|	*0708*	...	|
Leoben Hbf **980** d.	...	...	...	*0549*	0625	0631	*0721*	...	0831
St Michael **980** a.	...	...	...	*0556*	...	0637	*0728*	...	0837
St Michael d.	...	...	...	0600	...	0638	0731	...	0838
Trieben d.	...	...	...	0636	...	|	0805	...	|
Stadt Rottenmann d.	...	...	...	0644	...	0708	0812	...	|
Selzthal a.	...	...	...	0650	...	0713	0818	...	0911
Selzthal d.	...	0544	...	...	...	0719	0823	0844	0918
Linz Hbf **974** a.	...	|	...	...	...	|	|	|	1047
Liezen d.	...	0552	...	...	...	0727	0832	0851	...
Stainach-Irdning d.	...	0604	...	...	...	0737	0845	...	...
Schladming d.	0506	0648	0648	...	...	0810	0928	...	...
Radstadt d.	0525	0706	0706	...	...	0826	...	...	...
Bischofshofen a.	0554	0735	0735	...	...	0848	...	...	...
Bischofshofen 960 970 d.	*0558*	*0740*	*0740*	...	...	0857	...	...	...
Innsbruck Hbf **960** a.	|	|	|	...	...	|	...	...	...
Salzburg Hbf 960 970 a.	*0645*	*0840*	*0840*	...	...	0944	...	...	...

		EC 164	*EC* 112			*EC* 216			*IC* 518	*IC* 591				*IC* 600	*IC* 610					*IC* 718			
	2	Z✕	✕	Ⓑ 2	Ⓐw 2L	S⊗	2	Ⓐw 2L	🍷	🍷	2	Ⓐw 2L	⚒ 2	△ 🍷	🍷	Ⓐ 2	Ⓑ 2	⚒ 2	⚒ 2	⊗	Ⓐ 2	† 2	⑥ 2
Graz Hbf **980** d.	...	0945	...	...	...	1145	...	...	1345	...	...	...	1501	1545	1545	...	...	1701	...	1745	...	...	...
Bruck a. d. Mur **980** d.	*0908*	|	...	*1108*	...	|	*1308*	...	|	...	*1508*	...	|	|	|	...	*1708*	|	...	|	*1908*	1908	1908
Leoben Hbf **980** d.	*0921*	1031	...	*1121*	...	1231	*1321*	...	1431	...	*1521*	...	1557	1631	1631	...	*1721*	1755	1801	1831	*1921*	1921	1921
St Michael **980** a.	*0928*	1037	...	*1128*	...	1237	*1328*	...	1437	...	*1528*	...	1605	1637	1637	...	*1728*	...	1809	1837	*1928*	1928	1928
St Michael d.	0931	1038	...	1131	...	1238	1331	...	1438	...	1531	...	1608	1638	1638	...	1731	...	1810	1838	1931	1931	1931
Trieben d.	1005	|	...	1205	...	|	1405	...	|	...	1605	...	1644	|	|	...	1805	...	1846	|	2005	2005	2005
Stadt Rottenmann d.	1012	|	...	1212	...	1308	1412	...	|	...	1612	...	1652	|	|	...	1812	...	1854	1908	2012	2012	2012
Selzthal a.	1018	1111	...	1218	...	1313	1418	...	1511	...	1618	...	1658	1711	1711	...	1818	...	1900	1913	2018	2018	2018
Selzthal d.	1023	1119	...	1223	1244	1319	1423	1444	1519	...	1623	1641	...	1718	1719	...	1823	...	...	1919	2023	2023	2023
Linz Hbf **974** a.	|	|	...	|	|	|	|	|	|	...	|	|	...	1847	|	...	|	...	...	|	|	|	|
Liezen d.	1032	1127	...	1232	1251	1327	1432	1451	1527	...	1632	1648	...	...	1727	...	1832	...	...	1927	2032	2032	2032
Stainach-Irdning d.	1045	1137	...	1245	...	1337	1445	...	1537	...	1645	...	...	...	1737	...	1845	...	...	1937	2045	2045	2045
Schladming d.	1128	1210	...	1328	...	1410	1528	...	1610	...	1728	...	...	...	1810	...	1929	...	...	2010	2126	2126	2127
Radstadt d.	...	1226	...	...	...	1426	...	...	1626	...	...	...	...	...	1826	1920	1952	...	...	2026	...	...	2147
Bischofshofen a.	...	1248	...	...	...	1448	...	...	1648	...	...	...	...	...	1848	1950	...	...	...	2048	...	...	...
Bischofshofen 960 970 d.	...	1250	1305	...	...	1457	...	...	1650	1705	...	...	...	...	1857	*2004*	...	...	...	2057	...	...	...
Innsbruck Hbf **960** a.	...	1535	|	...	...	|	...	...	1936	|	...	...	...	...	|	|	...	...	...	|	...	...	...
Salzburg Hbf 960 970 a.	...	...	1348	...	...	1544	...	...	...	1748	...	...	...	...	1944	*2051*	...	...	...	2144	...	...	...

A – ZÜRICHSEE – 🛏 1, 2 cl., 🛏 2 cl. and (2) Graz - Innsbruck - Buchs 🏛 - Zürich and v.v.
F – (12) and ⊗ Graz - München - Stuttgart - Frankfurt and v.v.
L – To/ from Linz (Table **974**). See Table **974** for amended timings from June 20.
S – (12) and ⊗ Graz - München - Stuttgart - Saarbrücken and v.v.
Z – TRANSALPIN – (12) and ✕ Zürich - Buchs 🏛 - Innsbruck - Graz and v.v.

v – ⚒ only.
w – Until June 17.

△ – Operated by 🚌 Kirchdorf - Selzthal and v.v. from June 20. See Table

976 LINZ - STEYR - KLEINREIFLING - WEISSENBACH

2nd class

km		⚒	⚒		Ⓐ	Ⓒ		Ⓒ	Ⓐ	⚒		Ⓒ	Ⓐ	Ⓐ		Ⓒ	Ⓐ	⚒	Ⓐ		Ⓒ	Ⓐ	⚒	Ⓐ	
0	**Linz** Hbf 950 992 d.	0430	0512	0610	0649	0649	0752	0752	*0830*	0852	0952	0952	*1030*	*1130*	1152	1152	1222	1252	1252	1352	1352	1422	1452	*1530*	1552
17	Enns 992 d.	0448	0530	0633	0707	0707	0810	0810	|	0910	1010	1010	|	|	1210	1210	1240	1310	1310	1410	1410	1440	1510	|	1610
25	St Valentin 950 d.	0509	0540	0649	0721	0721	0821	0821	0851	0921	1021	1021	1051	1151	1221	1221	1251	1321	1321	1421	1421	1451	1521	1551	1621
45	**Steyr** d.	0532	0605	0714	0754t	0754t	0846	0846	0912	0946	1046	1046	1112	1212	1246	1246	1312	1346	1346	1446	1446	1512	1546	1612	1646
47	Garsten d.	0536	0608	0717	0758	0758	0849	0850	0916	0949	1049	1050	1116	1215	1249	1250	1316	1349	1350	1449	1450	1516	1549	1616	1649
67	Losenstein d.	0601	...	...	0822	0822	...	0917	0937	...	...	1117	1137	▬	...	1317	1337	...	1423	...	1517	1537	...	1640	...
89	Kastenreith 977 a.	0628	...	...	0848	0852	...	0941	1004	...	...	1141	1204	Ⓐ	...	1341	1404	...	1447	...	1541	1603	...	1704	...
92	**Kleinreifling** 977 a.	0633	...	...	0852	0856	...	0946	1008	...	...	1146	1208	1300	...	1346	1408	...	1451	...	1546	1607	...	1708	...
106	Weißenbach ⊡ 977 a.	0648e	...	...	0907	*0917*	...	...	...	...	...	*1215*	...	1314	...	*1415*	...	...	...	...	...	1622	...	1723	...

	Ⓐ	⚒	Ⓐ		Ⓒ	Ⓐ				
Linz Hbf 950 992 d.	1622	1652	*1730*	1752	1752	1822	*1852*	1952	2152	2252
Enns 992 d.	1640	1710	|	1810	1810	1840	*1910*	2010	2210	2310
St Valentin 950 d.	1651	1721	1751	1821	1821	1851	1921	2021	2221	2321
Steyr d.	1712	1746	1812	1846	1846	1912	1946	2046	2246	2346
Garsten d.	1716	1749	1816	1849	1850	1916	1949	2049	2249	2349
Losenstein d.	1737	...	1841	...	1917	1937	...	2112	...	...
Kastenreith 977 a.	1803	...	1905	...	1941	2002	...	2135	...	...
Kleinreifling 977 a.	1807	...	1910	...	1946	2006	...	2139	...	...
Weißenbach ⊡ 977 a.	1822	...	1924	...	...	...	...	...	...	...

	P	Ⓐ	⚒		⚒			Ⓐ	Ⓐ	Ⓒ	
Weißenbach ⊡ 977 d.	...	...	...	...	...	0603e	...	0706	...	...	...
Kleinreifling 977 d.	...	0437	0513	...	...	0618	...	0721	0754	0812	...
Kastenreith 977 d.	...	0441	0517	...	...	0622	...	0724	0758	0816	...
Losenstein d.	...	0505	0540	...	...	0647	...	...	0822	0843	...
Garsten d.	0442	0527	0601	0610	0637	0709	0809	...	0843	0909	0909
Steyr d.	0446	0532	0606	0614	0642	0714	0814	...	0847	0914	0914
St Valentin 950 a.	0508	0555	0622	0639	0705	0737	0837	...	0907	0937	0937
Enns 992 a.	0520	0602	0628	0645	0719	0749	0849	...	|	0949	0949
Linz Hbf 950 992 a.	0538	0618	0641	0702	0738	0808	0908	...	*0930*	1008	1008

	Ⓒ		⚒	Ⓐ	Ⓒ		⚒	Ⓐ	Ⓒ		⚒	Ⓐ	Ⓒ		Ⓐ	⑥	Ⓐ	Ⓒ			
Weißenbach ⊡ 977 d.	...	...	...	...	...	...	...	1338	*1341*	...	...	...	*1541*	...	1641	...	1738	*1747*	...	...	*1939*
Kleinreifling 977 d.	1015	...	...	1154	1215	...	...	1354	1415	...	...	1554	1615	...	1708	...	1753	1815	...	...	2021
Kastenreith 977 d.	1019	...	...	1158	1219	...	...	1358	1419	...	...	1558	1619	...	1712	...	1757	1819	...	...	2025
Losenstein d.	1044	...	...	1222	1244	...	...	1422	1444	...	...	1621	1644	...	1744	...	1821	1844	...	...	2050
Garsten d.	1109	1109	1209	1243	1309	1309	1409	1443	1509	1509	1609	1643	1709	1709	1809	1809	1843	1909	1909	2009	2114
Steyr d.	1114	1114	1214	1247	1314	1314	1414	1447	1514	1514	1614	1647	1714	1714	1814	1814	1847	1914	1914	2014	2118
St Valentin 950 a.	1137	1137	1237	1307	1337	1337	1437	1507	1537	1537	1637	1707	1737	1737	1837	1837	1907	1937	1937	2037	2140
Enns 992 a.	1149	1149	1249	|	1349	1349	1449	|	1549	1549	1649	|	1749	1749	1849	|	|	1949	1949	2049	2149
Linz Hbf 950 992 a.	1208	1208	1308	*1330*	1408	1408	1508	*1530*	1608	1608	1708	*1730*	1808	1808	1908	*1930*	*1930*	2008	2008	2108	2208

P – To Passau (Table

e – Ⓐ only.
k – ⑥ only.
t – Arrives 0745.

⊡ – Weißenbach-St Ga

ass only

AMSTETTEN - KLEINREIFLING - SELZTHAL 977

	⑥	Ⓐ	⚒W	†◇	©	©	Ⓐ	Ⓐ	©	Ⓐ	Ⓐ	©	Ⓐ	Ⓐ	©	Ⓐ	Ⓐ	©	Ⓐ	†	Ⓐ	©	Ⓐ	Ⓑt	
Amstetten d.	0515	0515	0621	0705	0805	0905	0905	1005	1105	1105	1205	1305	1305	1405	1505	1505	1605	1705	1705	1805	1805	1905	1905	2005	2105
Waidhofen a. d. Ybbs. d.	0541	0550	0703j	0731	0831	0931	0931	1030	1131	1131	1231	1331	1331	1431	1531	1531	1631	1731	1731	1831	1831	1931	1933	2030	2132
Weyer d.	0604	0608	0729	0749	0850	0949	0949	...	1149	1149	1249	1349	1349	1449	1549	1553	1649	1749	1749	1849	1849	1949	2008r	...	...
Kastenreith 976 d.	0608	0612	0733	0753	0856	0953	0952	...	1153	1152	1253	1353	1352	1453	1553	1556	1653	1753	1752	1853	1853	1953	2012	...	...
Kleinreifling 976 a.	0611	0615	0737	0757	0859	0957	1008	...	1157	1208	1257	1357	1408	1457	1557	1607	1657	1757	1807	1857	1857	1957	2015	...	...
Weißenbach ⊡ .. 976 a.	...	0648	...	...	0917	...	...	...	1215	...	1314	1415	...	...	...	1622	1723	1815k	1822	1912	1924	...	...	...	...
Selzthal a.	...	...	...	...	1019	...	...	...	...	...	...	...	...	...	...	...	...	...	...	...	...	...	...	...	...

	⚒		ⒶP	©		Ⓐ	Ⓐ		⚒	Ⓐ	©	Ⓐ	Ⓐ	©	Ⓐ	Ⓐ	©	Ⓐ	Ⓐ	©	Ⓐ	Ⓐ	©	†	Ⓐ	©
l d.	...	...	...	...	...	...	...	...	...	...	...	...	...	...	...	...	...	...	...	...	...	...	1644	...	...	...
bach ⊡ 976 d.	...	...	...	...	...	0603	0706	...	...	0940	...	...	...	...	...	1338	1341	...	...	1541	1641	1738	1747	...	1939	1939
ifling 976 d.	...	...	0519	0556	...	0622	0721	0802	...	0954	1002	...	1154	1202	1302	1354	1402	1502	1554	1602	1658	1753	1802	1902	1956	2002
eith 976 d.	...	...	0523	0600	...	0630	0725	0806	...	1006	1006	...	1206	1206	1306	1406	1406	1506	1606	1606	1706	1806	1806	1906	2004	2006
d.	...	...	0527	0608	...	0634	0728	0810	...	1010	1010	...	1210	1210	1310	1410	1410	1510	1610	1610	1710	1810	1810	1910	2010	2010
fen a. d. Ybbs. d.	0430	0518	0547	0629	0629	0653	...	0830	0930	1030	1030	1130	1230	1230	1330	1430	1430	1530	1630	1630	1730	1830	1830	1930	2031	2031
ten a.	0455	0546	0614	0655	0655	0719	...	0857	0955	1055	1055	1155	1255	1255	1355	1455	1455	1555	1655	1655	1755	1855	1855	1955	2055	2055

om Wien (Table **950**).
St Pölten (Table **950**).

j – Arrives 0652.
k – ⑥ only.

r – Arrives 1951.
t – Not Jan. 5, Mar. 27, May 4, 15, 25, Aug. 14, Oct. 25, 31, Dec. 7.

◇ – Runs daily Amstetten - Waidhofen.
⊡ – Weißenbach-St Gallen.

ass only

WIEN and WIENER NEUSTADT - SOPRON - DEUTSCHKREUTZ 978

WIEN - EBENFURTH - SOPRON - DEUTSCHKREUTZ *Operated by GySEV Györ-Sopron-Ebenfurti Vasút (in German Raab-Oedenburg-Ebenfurter Eisenbahn – ROeEE)*

	Ⓐ	Ⓐ		Ⓐ		Ⓐ		Ⓐ		Ⓐ		Ⓐ		Ⓐ				Ⓑw
Bratislava-P ⊖ **997** d.	...	...	0615	0715	0815	0915	1015	1115	1215	1315	1415	1515	1615z	...	1815z	1915e	...	...
Wien Hbf d.	0520	0619	0719	0819	0919	1019	1119	1219	1319	1419	1519	1619	1719	1819	1919	2019	...	...
Wien Meidling d.	0525	0625	0725	0825	0925	1025	1125	1225	1325	1425	1525	1625	1725	1825	1925	2025	...	...
Ebenfurth d.	0600	0701	0801	0902	1002	1102	1202	1302	1402	1502	1602	1702	1802	1902	2002	2102	...	2243
Sopron 🏛 a.	0637	0737	0837	0937	1037	1137	1237	1337	1437	1537	1637	1737	1837	1937	2037	2137	...	2318
Deutschkreutz a.	0657	0754	0847	0947	1047	1147	1247	1347	1447	1547	1647	1747	1847	1947	2047	2147	...	2331

	Ⓐ	Ⓐ	Ⓐ		Ⓐ		Ⓐ	Ⓐ		Ⓐ		Ⓐ		Ⓐ		Ⓐ		Ⓐ	
hkreutz d.	0413	0513	0535	0613	0635	0712	0735	0813	0913	1013	1113	1213	1313	1413	1513	1613	1713	1813	1913
🏛 d.	0423	0523	0545	0623	0646	0722	0746	0823	0923	1023	1123	1223	1323	1423	1523	1623	1723	1823	1923
th d.	0504	0604	0626	0704	0726	0804	0826	0904	1004	1104	1204	1304	1404	1504	1604	1704	1804	1904	2004
eidling a.	0535	0635	0700	0735	0800	0835	0900	0935	1035	1135	1235	1335	1435	1535	1635	1735	1835	1935	2035
bf a.	0542	0642	0707	0742	0824	0842	0907	0942	1042	1142	1242	1342	1442	1542	1642	1742	1842	1942	2042
slava-P ⊖ **997** a.	0644	0744	...	0844e	...	0944	...	1044	1144	1244	1344z	1444	1544	...	1744z	1844	1944	...	2144

e – Ⓐ only.
h – Continues to Wien Hbf (arrives 8 minutes later).
w – From Wiener Neustadt Hbf (d. 2233).
z – © only.

⊖ – Bratislava - Petržalka.
⊠ – **Additional journeys** from Wiener Neustadt to Sopron at 1301 Ⓐ, 1337 ©, 1401 Ⓐ, 1501 Ⓐ, 1537 ©, 1601 Ⓐ, 1701 Ⓐ, 1801 Ⓐ and 1901 Ⓐ.

WIENER NEUSTADT - SOPRON - DEUTSCHKREUTZ ⊠ *Operated by ÖBB*

	Ⓐ						Ⓐ			Ⓐ	Ⓐ	©	Ⓐ	Ⓐ	©	Ⓐ	©	Ⓐ	©	Ⓐ		Ⓐ		Ⓑ	
Wien Meidling **980/1** d.	...	...	...	...	...	...	...	...	...	...	...	...	...	1600	...	1700	...	1800	...	...	...	...	...	...	...
Wiener Neustadt Hbf. d.	0503	0603	0703	0739	0837	0937	1037	1137	1237	1331	1431	1437	1531	1631	1637	1731	1737	1831	1837	1931	1937	2037	2137	2233	2237
Mattersburg d.	0527	0626	0726	0803	0902	1002	1102	1202	1302	1344	1444	1502	1544	1644	1702	1744	1802	1844	1902	1944	2002	2102	2202	|	2302
Sopron 🏛 a.	0542	0641	0741	0818	0917	1017	1117	1217	1317	1400	1500	1717	1600	1700	1717	1800	1817	1900	1917	2000	2018	2117	2217	2318	2317
Deutschkreutz a.	...	...	...	...	...	...	...	...	...	1410	1510	...	1610	1710	...	1810	...	1910	...	2010	...	...	2227e	2331	...

	Ⓐ	Ⓐ	Ⓐ		Ⓐ	⑥	Ⓑ	Ⓐ				Ⓐ										Ⓐ			Ⓐ	
hkreutz d.	...	...	0459	...	0559	0635	...	0659	...	...	...	...	...	...	...	...	...	...	...	...	...	...	...	...	2234	...
🏛 d.	0418	0447	0509	0547	0609	0645	0647	0709	0747	0844	0944	1044	1144	1244	1344	1444	1544	1644	1744	1844	1944	2044	2144	...	2244	2244
burg d.	0434	0503	0527	0603	0627	0702	0703	0727	0803	0902	1002	1102	1202	1302	1402	1502	1602	1702	1802	1902	2002	2102	2202	...	2302	2302
Neustadt Hbf a.	0453	0525	0539	0625	0639	0725	0725	0739	0825	0925	1025	1125	1225	1325	1425	1525	1625	1725	1825	1925	2025	2125	2225	...	2325	2325
Meidling **980/1** a.	...	...	0615h	...	0715h	...	...	0815	...	...	...	...	...	...	...	...	...	...	...	...	...	...	...	...	...	...

WIEN and GRAZ - KLAGENFURT (- VILLACH) 980

				RJ 72			🚌 851	RJ 551	RJ 554	EC 31	🚌 853	RJ 553		EC 151	RJ 558	RJ 533	RJ 557		🚌 855	RJ 559	EC 158	RJ 535	RJ 71	
	⚒ 2	⚒ 2	⚒ 2	✕	2	2	☆	✕	✕	V✕	☆	✕	2	E✕	✕	L✕	✕	2	☆	✕	✕	✕	P✕	2
Wien Hbf 981 d.	...	...	...	...	...	...	...	0558	...	0625	...	0658	...	0758	...	0825	0858	...	...	0958	...	1025	1058	...
Wien Meidling 981 d.	...	...	...	...	...	...	...	0605	...	0632	...	0705	...	0805	...	0832	0905	...	...	1005	...	1032	1105	...
Wiener Neustadt Hbf 981 a.	...	...	...	...	...	...	...	0628	...	0655	...	0728	...	0828	...	0855	0928	...	...	1028	...	1055	1128	...
Wiener Neustadt Hbf 981 d.	...	...	...	...	...	...	...	0632	...	0657	...	0732	...	0832	...	0857	0932	...	...	1032	...	1057	1132	...
Semmering 981 d.	...	...	...	...	...	...	...	|	...	|	...	|	...	0915	...	|	1015	...	...	1115	...	|	|	...
Mürzzuschlag 981 d.	...	0526	...	...	0621r	0621h	...	0730	...	|	...	0830	...	0930	...	|	1030	...	...	1130	...	|	1230	...
Graz Hbf 975 d.	...	|	...	0625	|	|	0630	|	0725	|	0800	|	0825	|	0925	|	|	1025	1030	|	1125	|	|	1225
Bruck an der Mur a.	...	0607	...	0701	0702r	0702h	|	0756	0801	0813	|	0856	0901	0956	1001	1013	1056	1101	|	1156	1201	1213	1256	1301
Bruck an der Mur 975 ‡ d.	0439	0608	0613	...	0708	0708	|	0758	...	0815	|	0858	0908	0958	...	1015	1058	1108	|	1158	...	1215	1258	1308
Graz Hbf ‡ a.	|	0655	|	...	|	0755	|	0833	...	|	|	0933	|	1033	...	|	1133	|	|	1233	...	|	1333	|
Leoben Hbf 975 d.	0453	▬	0626	...	0721	...	|	...	...	0827	|	...	0921	...	...	1027	...	1121	|	...	...	1227	...	1321
St Michael 975 a.	0501	...	|	...	0728	...	|	...	...	|	|	...	0928	...	...	|	...	1128	|	...	...	|	...	1328
St Michael d.	0508	...	|	...	0734	...	|	...	...	|	|	...	0934	...	...	|	...	1134	|	...	...	|	...	1334
Knittelfeld d.	0528	...	0648	...	0752	...	|	...	...	0847	|	...	0952	...	...	1047	...	1152	|	...	...	1247	...	1352
Zeltweg d.	0535	⚒	0654	...	0758	...	|	...	...	|	|	...	0958	...	...	|	...	1158	|	...	...	|	...	1358
Judenburg d.	0543	2	0702	...	0806	...	|	...	...	0859	|	...	1006	...	...	1059	...	1206	|	...	...	1259	...	1406
Unzmarkt d.	0559	0608	0718	...	0822	...	|	...	...	0913	|	...	1022	...	...	1113	...	1222	|	...	...	1313	...	1422
Friesach 971 a.	...	0642	...	...	0855e	...	|	...	...	|	|	...	1055e	...	...	1143	...	1255e	|	...	...	|	...	1455e
St Veit an der Glan 971 a.	...	0716	...	...	...	...	|	...	...	1006	...	...	...	...	...	1206	...	...	|	...	...	1406	...	...
Klagenfurt Hbf 971 a.	...	0738	...	...	...	...	0830	...	...	1020	1000	...	...	...	...	1220	...	...	1230	...	...	1420	...	...
Villach Hbf **970 971** a.	...	0820t	...	...	...	...	...	...	...	1046	...	...	...	...	...	1246	...	...	...	...	...	1446	...	...

	🚌 857	RJ 653	RJ 656	RJ 537	RJ 73		🚌 859	RJ 657	RJ 750	RJ 539	RJ 75		🚌 951		EC 159	RJ 754	RJ 631	RJ 77		🚌 953		D 459	RJ 755 1255		RJ 633
	☆	✕	✕	✕	P✕	2	☆	✕	✕	✕	P✕	2	☆	⚒ 2	F✕	✕	✕	P✕	2	☆	Ⓐ 2	Ⓐ 2	H✕	2	✕
bf 981 d.	...	1158	...	1225	1258	...	...	1358	...	1425	1458	...	...	...	1558	...	1625	1658	...	...	...	1725	1758	...	1825
eidling 981 d.	...	1205	...	1232	1305	...	...	1405	...	1432	1505	...	...	...	1605	...	1632	1705	...	...	...	1732	1805	...	1832
Neustadt Hbf 981 a.	...	1228	...	1255	1330	...	...	1428	...	1455	1530	...	...	...	1630	...	1655	1730	...	...	...	1755	1830	...	1855
Neustadt Hbf 981 d.	...	1232	...	1257	1332	...	...	1432	...	1457	1532	...	...	...	1632	...	1657	1732	...	...	...	1757	1832	...	1857
ering 981 d.	...	1315	...	|	|	...	...	|	...	|	1615	...	...	...	|	...	|	1815	...	...	...	1849	|	...	|
schlag 981 d.	...	1330	...	|	1430	...	...	1530	...	|	1630	...	...	...	1730	...	|	1830	...	...	...	1902	1930	...	|
Hbf 975 d.	1230	|	1325	|	|	1425	1430	|	1525	|	|	1625	1630	1701	|	1725	|	|	1825	1845	1901	...	|	1925	|
an der Mur a.	|	1356	1401	1413	1456	1501	|	1556	1601	1613	1656	1701	|	|	1756	1801	1813	1856	1901	|	|	...	1956	2001	2013
an der Mur 975 ‡ d.	|	1358	...	1415	1458	1508	|	1558	...	1615	1658	1708	|	|	1758	...	1815	1858	1908	|	|	...	1958	2008	2015
Hbf ‡ a.	|	1433	...	|	1533	|	|	1633	...	|	1733	|	|	|	1833	...	|	1933	|	|	|	...	2033	|	|
Hbf 975 d.	|	...	...	1427	...	1521	|	...	...	1627	...	1721	|	1758	...	...	1827	...	1921	|	1956	...	...	2021	2027
chael 975 a.	|	...	...	|	...	1528	|	...	...	|	...	1728	|	|	...	...	|	...	1928	|	2003	...	...	2028	|
chael d.	|	...	...	|	...	1534	|	...	...	|	...	1734	|	|	...	...	|	...	1934	|	2009	...	...	2034	|
eld d.	|	...	...	1447	...	1552	|	...	...	1647	...	1752	|	1821	...	...	1847	...	1952	|	2027	...	...	→	2047
d.	|	...	...	|	...	1558	|	...	...	|	...	1758	|	1827	...	...	|	...	1958	|	2034	...	...	...	|
urg d.	|	...	...	1459	...	1606	|	...	...	1659	...	1806	|	1835	...	...	1859	...	2006	|	2042	...	...	...	|
kt d.	|	...	...	1513	...	1622	|	...	...	1713	...	1822	|	1851	...	...	1913	...	2021	|	2057	...	...	...	|
h 971 a.	|	...	...	1543	...	1655e	|	...	...	|	...	1855b	|	...	...	...	1943	...	...	|	...	...	...	...	|
an der Glan 971 a.	|	...	...	1606	...	...	|	...	...	1806	...	...	|	...	...	...	2006	...	...	|	...	...	...	...	2158
furt Hbf 971 a.	1430	...	...	1620	...	...	1630	...	...	1820	...	...	1830	...	...	...	2020	...	...	2045	...	...	...	...	2212
h Hbf **970 971** a.	...	...	...	1646	...	...	...	...	...	1846	...	...	...	...	...	...	2046	...	...	...	...	...	...	...	2236

OTES SEE NEXT PAGE →

980 WIEN and GRAZ - KLAGENFURT (- VILLACH)

		RJ		*EN*	*RJ*	*EN*	*RJ*		*REX*
		79		**235**	**759**	**1237**	**371**		**1975**
						D		⑤–⑦	
	2	P✕	2	AR	✕	R	P✕	2	2
Wien Hbf ... 981 d.	...	1858	...	1923	1958	2023	2058	...	2259
Wien Meidling ... 981 d.	...	1905	...	1931	2005	2031	2105	...	2305
Wiener Neustadt Hbf ... 981 a.	...	1928	...	1956	2028	2056	2128	...	2330
Wiener Neustadt Hbf ... 981 d.	...	1932	...	1958	2032	2058	2132	...	2332
Semmering ... 981 d.	...	|	...	|	|	|	|	...	0029
Mürzzuschlag ... 981 d.	...	2030	...	|	2130	|	2230	...	0043
Graz Hbf ... 975 d.	...	|	*2025*	|	|	|	|	*2224*	...
Bruck an der Mur ... a.	...	2056	*2101*	2123	2156	2220	2256	*2301*	...
Bruck an der Mur ... 975 ‡ d.	...	2058	2108	2125	2158	2222	2258	2308	...
Graz Hbf ... ‡ a.	...	2133	|	|	2233	|	2333	|	...
Leoben Hbf ... 975 d.	...	...	2121	2140	...	2236	...	2321	...
St Michael ... 975 a.	←	...	2128	|	...	|	...	|	...
St Michael ... d.	2034	...	2134	|	...	|	...	|	...
Knittelfeld ... d.	2052	...	2152	2203	...	|	...	2344	...
Zeltweg ... d.	2058	...	2158	|	...	|	...	2350	...
Judenburg ... d.	2106	...	2206	|	...	|	...	2358	...
Unzmarkt ... d.	2121	...	2221	|	...	|	...	0014	...
Friesach ... 971 a.	...	...	...	2258	...	|	...	...	...
St Veit an der Glan ... 971 a.	...	...	...	|	...	|	...	...	...
Klagenfurt Hbf ... 971 a.	...	...	...	2333	...	0019	...	...	...
Villach Hbf 970 971 ... a.	...	...	...	2358	...	0043	...	...	...

	REX	*D*			*RJ*	*EN*			*RJ*	
	1956	**458**			**550**	**1236**			**72**	
	Ⓒ	Ⓐ	⚒	⚒		**B**	⚒	⚒		⚒
	2	2	2	2	✕	R	2	2	P✕	2
Villach Hbf 970 971 ... d.	...	...	...	...	...	0344	...	...	...	...
Klagenfurt Hbf ... 971 d.	...	...	...	...	...	0409	...	...	...	...
St Veit an der Glan ... 971 d.	...	...	...	...	...	|	...	...	...	*050*
Friesach ... 971 d.	...	...	...	...	...	|	...	...	...	*052*
Unzmarkt ... d.	...	...	0440	...	...	|	0527	0549	...	0608
Judenburg ... d.	...	...	0456	...	...	|	0543	0605	...	0624
Zeltweg ... d.	...	...	0504	...	...	|	0552	0613	...	063
Knittelfeld ... d.	...	...	0510	...	...	|	0558	0619	...	0638
St Michael ... a.	...	...	0528	...	...	|	|	|	...	0657
St Michael ... 975 d.	...	...	0535	0531	...	|	|	|	...	0706
Leoben Hbf ... 975 d.	...	...	0543	0540	...	0608	0623	0643	...	0715
Graz Hbf ... ‡ d.	...	...	|	|	0527	|	|	|	0625	|
Bruck an der Mur ... 975 ‡ a.	...	...	0557	|	0603	0621	|	0655	0701	0728
Bruck an der Mur ... d.	...	...	...	|	0605	0624	|	*0708*	0703	...
Graz Hbf ... 975 a.	...	...	...	0633	|	|	0714	*0755*	|	...
Mürzzuschlag ... 981 d.	0521	0524	...	...	0634	|	...	...	0732	...
Semmering ... 981 d.	0537	0538	...	...	|	|	...	...	0746	...
Wiener Neustadt Hbf ... 981 a.	0626	0626	...	...	0728	0751	...	...	0828	...
Wiener Neustadt Hbf ... 981 d.	0630	0630	...	...	0730	0754	...	...	0832	...
Wien Meidling ... 981 a.	0655	0655	...	...	0755	0855y	...	...	0855	...
Wien Hbf ... 981 a.	0702	0702	...	...	0802	0903y	...	...	0902	...

	EN	*RJ*	*RJ*				*RJ*	🚌	*RJ*	*EC*	*RJ*	🚌		*RJ*	*RJ*	*RJ*	*EC*	🚌		*RJ*	*RJ*	*RJ*	*RJ*	
	234	**530**	**551**				**74**	**852**	**532**	**151**	**558**	**854**		**76**	**534**	**559**	**158**	**856**		**78**	**536**	**653**	**656**	
	AR	✕	✕	2	2	2	P✕	☆	✕	✕	✕	☆	2	P✕	✕	✕	F✕	☆	2	P✕	✕	✕	G✕	2
Villach Hbf 970 971 ... d.	0511	0526	...	...	0529	...	...	...	0714	...	...	...	...	...	0914	...	...	...	...	...	1114	...	...	...
Klagenfurt Hbf ... 971 d.	0533	0549	...	...	0607	...	...	0720	0739	...	...	0920	...	...	0939	...	...	1120	...	...	1139	...	...	...
St Veit an der Glan ... 971 d.	|	0602	...	...	0627	...	...	|	0753	...	...	|	...	...	0953	...	...	|	...	...	1153	...	...	...
Friesach ... 971 d.	|	|	...	...	0700	...	...	|	|	...	...	|	0903e	...	1016	...	...	|	1103e	...	|	...	...	1303
Unzmarkt ... d.	|	|	...	0656	0733	0737	...	|	0847	...	...	|	0937	...	1047	...	...	|	1137	...	1247	...	...	1337
Judenburg ... d.	|	|	...	0712	▬	0753	...	|	0901	...	...	|	0953	...	1101	...	...	|	1153	...	1301	...	...	1353
Zeltweg ... d.	|	|	...	0720	...	0801	...	|	|	...	...	|	1001	...	|	...	...	|	1201	...	|	...	...	1401
Knittelfeld ... d.	|	|	...	0726	*RJ*	0807	...	|	0914	...	...	|	1007	...	1114	...	...	|	1207	...	1314	...	...	1407
St Michael ... a.	|	|	...	|	**554**	0826	...	|	|	...	...	|	1026	...	|	...	...	|	1226	...	|	...	...	1426
St Michael ... 975 d.	|	|	...	|		0833	...	|	|	...	...	|	1033	...	|	...	...	|	1233	...	|	...	...	1433
Leoben Hbf ... 975 d.	0720	0734	...	0747	✕	0841	...	|	0934	...	...	|	1041	...	1134	...	...	|	1241	...	1334	...	...	1441
Graz Hbf ... ‡ d.	|	|	...	|	0725	|	0825	|	|	...	0925	|	|	1025	|	...	1125	|	|	1225	|	...	1325	|
Bruck an der Mur ... 975 ‡ a.	0731	0744	...	0758	0801	0853	0901	|	0944	...	1001	|	1053	1101	1144	...	1201	|	1253	1301	1344	...	1401	1453
Bruck an der Mur ... d.	0733	0746	0758	*0808*	0803	*0858*	0903	|	0946	0958	1003	|	*1058*	1103	1146	1158	1203	|	*1258*	1303	1346	1358	1403	*1458*
Graz Hbf ... 975 a.	|	|	0833	*0855*	|	*0933*	|	0920	|	1033	|	1120	*1133*	|	|	1233	|	1320	*1333*	|	|	1433	|	*1533*
Mürzzuschlag ... 981 d.	|	|	...	...	0832	...	0932	...	|	...	1032	...	...	1132	|	...	1232	...	...	1332	|	...	1432	...
Semmering ... 981 d.	|	|	...	...	0846	...	0946	...	|	...	|	...	...	1146	|	...	|	...	...	1346	|	...	|	...
Wiener Neustadt Hbf ... 981 a.	0858	0903	...	...	0928	...	1028	...	1103	...	1128	...	...	1228	1303	...	1328	...	...	1428	1503	...	1528	...
Wiener Neustadt Hbf ... 981 d.	0900	0905	...	...	0932	...	1032	...	1105	...	1132	...	...	1232	1305	...	1332	...	...	1432	1505	...	1532	...
Wien Meidling ... 981 a.	0940	0928	...	...	0955	...	1055	...	1128	...	1155	...	...	1255	1328	...	1355	...	...	1455	1528	...	1555	...
Wien Hbf ... 981 a.	0948	0935	...	...	1002	...	1102	...	1135	...	1202	...	...	1302	1335	...	1402	...	...	1502	1535	...	1602	...

	🚌	*RJ*	*RJ*	*RJ*		*RJ*	🚌	*RJ*	*EC*	*RJ*		*RJ*	🚌	*RJ*	*D*	*RJ*	*EC*		*RJ*		*RJ*	🚌	*EC*	*RJ*
	858	**538**	**657**	**750**		**372**	**950**	**630**	**159**	**754**		**756**	**952**	**632**	**15030**	**755**	**150**		**732**		**758**	**954**	**30**	**759**
															⑦z	**1255**			⑦z					
	☆	✕	✕	✕	2	P✕	☆	✕	✕	✕	2	✕	☆	L✕	2	✕	E✕	2	✕	2	✕	☆	V✕	✕
Villach Hbf 970 971 ... d.	...	1314	...	...	...	...	...	1514	...	...	...	...	...	1714	...	...	...	...	1814	...	...	...	1914	...
Klagenfurt Hbf ... 971 d.	1345	1339	...	...	...	...	1545	1539	...	...	...	...	1745	1739	...	...	...	...	1839	...	...	1945	1939	...
St Veit an der Glan ... 971 d.	|	1353	...	...	...	...	|	1553	...	...	...	...	|	1753	...	...	...	...	1853	...	...	|	1953	...
Friesach ... 971 d.	|	1416	...	...	1503e	...	|	|	...	...	1703e	...	|	1816	...	...	...	1903b	1919	...	...	|	|	...
Unzmarkt ... d.	|	1447	...	...	1537	...	|	1647	...	...	1737	...	|	1847	1856	...	...	1937	|	...	...	|	2047	...
Judenburg ... d.	|	1501	...	...	1553	...	|	1701	...	...	1753	...	|	1901	1910	...	...	1953	2001	...	...	|	2101	...
Zeltweg ... d.	|	|	...	...	1601	...	|	|	...	...	1801	...	|	|	1918	...	...	2001	|	...	...	|	|	...
Knittelfeld ... d.	|	1514	...	...	1607	...	|	1714	...	...	1807	...	|	1914	1924	...	...	2007	2014	...	...	|	2114	...
St Michael ... a.	|	|	...	...	1626	...	|	|	...	...	1826	...	|	|	|	...	...	2026	|	←	...	|	|	...
St Michael ... 975 d.	|	|	...	...	1633	...	|	|	...	...	1833	...	|	|	|	...	...	2033	|	2033	...	|	|	...
Leoben Hbf ... 975 d.	|	1534	...	...	1641	...	|	1734	...	...	1841	...	|	1934	1945	...	...	→	2034	2041	...	|	2134	...
Graz Hbf ... ‡ d.	|	|	...	1525	|	1625	|	|	...	1725	|	1825	|	|	|	...	1925	...	|	|	2025	|	|	...
Bruck an der Mur ... 975 ‡ a.	|	1544	...	1601	1653	1701	|	1744	...	1801	1853	1901	|	1944	|	...	2001	...	2044	2053	2101	|	2144	...
Bruck an der Mur ... d.	|	1546	1558	1603	*1658*	1703	|	1746	1758	1803	*1858*	1903	|	1946	|	1958	2003	...	2046	*2058*	2103	|	2146	2158
Graz Hbf ... 975 a.	1545	|	1633	|	*1733*	|	1745	|	1833	|	*1933*	|	1945	|	2030	2033	|	...	|	*2133*	|	2145	|	2233
Mürzzuschlag ... 981 d.	...	|	...	1632	...	1732	...	|	...	1832	...	1932	...	|	...	...	2032	...	|	...	2132	...	|	...
Semmering ... 981 d.	...	|	...	1646	...	1746	...	|	...	1846	...	|	...	|	...	...	|	...	|	...	|	...	|	...
Wiener Neustadt Hbf ... 981 a.	...	1703	...	1728	...	1828	...	1903	...	1928	...	2028	...	2103	...	...	2128	...	2203	...	2228	...	2303	...
Wiener Neustadt Hbf ... 981 d.	...	1705	...	1732	...	1832	...	1905	...	1932	...	2032	...	2105	...	...	2132	...	2205	...	2232	...	2305	...
Wien Meidling ... 981 a.	...	1728	...	1755	...	1855	...	1928	...	1955	...	2055	...	2128	...	...	2155	...	2228	...	2255	...	2328	...
Wien Hbf ... 981 a.	...	1735	...	1802	...	1902	...	1935	...	2002	...	2102	...	2135	...	...	2202	...	2235	...	2302	...	2335	...

Local stopping trains **BRUCK AN DER MUR - GRAZ - SPIELFELD-STRASS** (for international services Graz - Spielfeld Straß - Maribor - Ljubljana / Zagreb see Table **1315**).

km				Ⓐ	⊙	⊙		◇		⊙	⊙		⊙		⊙		◇	⊖	⊙	⚒			⚒	⚒
	Bruck a. d. Mur ... d.	0457	0608	0650	0708	0808	*0908*	0958	1008	1108	1208	*1308*	1408	*1508*	1608	*1708*	1758	1808	1908	*2008*	*2108*	2208	2208	2308
	Graz Hbf ... a.	0544	0655	0729	0755	0855	*0955*	1033	1055	1155	1255	*1355*	1455	*1555*	1655	*1755*	1833	1855	1955	*2055*	*2155*	2255	2255	2355
0	**Graz** Hbf ... 1315 d.	0558	0708	0738	0808	0908	1008	1038	1108	1208	1308	1408	1508	1608	1708	1808	1838	1908	2008	2108	2208	...	2308	...
9	Flughafen Graz ✈ ... d.	0610	0720	0750	0820	0920	1020	|	1120	1220	1320	1420	1520	1620	1720	1820	|	1920	2020	2120	2220	...	2320	...
35	Leibnitz ... d.	0636	0750	0820	0850	0950	1047	1059	1150	1250	1350	1450	1550	1650	1749	1847	1859	1950	2047	2147	2247	...	2347	...
47	**Spielfeld-Straß** ... 1315 a.	0648	0800	0830	0900	1000	1100	1108	1200	1300	1400	1500	1600	1700	1759	1900	1908	2000	2057	2157	2257	...	2357	...

	Ⓐ				Ⓐ		⊙	⊙	⊙	⊙	◇		⊙		⊙		⊙		⊙	◇		⚒	⊕	⚒
Spielfeld-Straß ... 1315 d.	0352	0431	0504	...	0549	0609	0709	0809	0909	1009	1048	1109	1209	1309	1409	1509	1609	1709	1809	1848	1909	2009	2109	2209
Leibnitz ... d.	0403	0442	0515	...	0600	0620	0720	0820	0920	1020	1058	1120	1220	1320	1420	1520	1620	1720	1820	1858	1920	2020	2120	2220
Flughafen Graz ✈ ... d.	0431	0510	0542	...	0628	0649	0748	0848	0948	1048	|	1148	1248	1348	1448	1548	1648	1748	1848	|	1948	2048	2148	2248
Graz Hbf ... 1315 a.	0442	0521	0554	...	0639	0701	0759	0859	0959	1059	1120	1159	1259	1359	1459	1559	1659	1759	1859	1920	1959	2059	2159	2259
Graz Hbf ... d.	0449	...	0559e	0611	0642	*0708*	0805	0905	1005	1105	1125	*1205*	1305	*1405*	1505	*1605*	1705	*1805*	1905	1925	*2005*	*2105*	2205	2305
Bruck a. d. Mur ... a.	0535	...	0641e	0657	0728	*0754*	0851	0951	1051	1151	1201	*1251*	1351	*1451*	1551	*1651*	1751	*1851*	1951	2001	*2051*	*2151*	2251	2351

A – 🛏 1,2 cl., ▬ 2 cl. and (2) Roma - Bologna - Venezia - Wien and v.v.; 🛏 1,2 cl. and ▬ 2 cl. Milano - Venezia - Wien and v.v.

B – Fom Villach on ⑤⑦ Mar. 20 - Oct. 16 (also Mar. 29, May 17, Aug. 16). Previous night from Livorno. 🛏 1,2 cl., ▬ 2 cl. and (2) Livorno - Pisa - Firenze - Bologna - Wien. Train number **1238** on ⑤ (also Mar. 29, May 17, Aug. 16).

D – ③⑤ Mar. 18 - Oct. 14 (also Mar. 27, May 15, Aug. 14). 🛏 1,2 cl., ▬ 2 cl. and (2) Wien - Bologna - Firenze - Pisa - Livorno.

E – EMONA – (12) and ✕ Ljubljana - Maribor - Spielfeld-Straß 🛃 - Graz - Wien and v.v.

F – CROATIA – (12) and ✕ Zagreb - Maribor - Spielfeld-Straß 🛃 - Graz - Wien and v.v.

G – To Flughafen Wien ✈ (a. 1627).

H – From Flughafen Wien ✈ (d. 1733).

L – To / from Lienz (Table **971**).

P – (12) and ✕ Graz - Wien - Břeclav 🛃 - Praha and v.v.

R – 🅁 for journeys from / to Italy.

V – (12) and ✕ Wien - Villach - Tarvisio 🛃 - Udine - Venezia and v.v.

b – Not ⑥.

e – Ⓐ only.

h – † only.

r – ⚒ only.

t – Change trains at Klagenfurt on Ⓐ to July 8 / from S

y – On ⑦ arrives Wien Meidling 0826, Wien Hbf 0832.

z – Also Jan. 6, Mar. 28, May 16, Aug. 15, Nov. 1; not Mar. 27, May 15, Aug. 14, Oct. 30.

◇ – *EC* train (see main panel, also Table **1315**).

‡ – For other local journeys see panel below main table.

⊙ – Change trains at Graz Hbf on Ⓐ.

⊖ – Change trains at Graz Hbf on Ⓒ.

⊕ – Change trains at Graz Hbf on Ⓑ.

◧ – Leoben - St Michael is *10 km*. St Michael - Knittelfeld is *22 km*.

☆ – **ÖBB** *Intercitybus*. Rail tickets valid. 1st and 2nd class. 🍸 in 1st class. Number of seats limited so reservation is recommended.

Local trains WIEN - WIENER NEUSTADT - MÜRZZUSCHLAG 981

WIEN - WIENER NEUSTADT ⊡

		⚒P						P
Wien Praterstern	d.	0418	0518	0548		2218	2248	2348
Wien Mitte-Landstraße	d.	0422	0522	0552	and at	2222	2252	2352
Wien Hbf	d.	0429	0529	0559	the same	2229	2259	2359
Wien Meidling ●	d.	0437	0537	0607	minutes	2237	2307	0007
Mödling	d.	0449	0549	0619	past each	2249	2319	|
Baden	d.	0457	0557	0627	hour until	2257	2327	0021
Wiener Neustadt Hbf	a.	0521	0621	0649		2321	2349	0034

		P	P	P	P	P						P
Wiener Neustadt Hbf	d.	0533	0603	0633	0703	0733	0811	0838		2111	2138	2238
Baden	d.	0553	0623	0653	0723	0753	0832	0902	and at	2132	2202	2302
Mödling	d.	0600	0630	0700	0730	0800	0839	0909	the same	2139	2209	2309
Wien Meidling ●	a.	0612	0642	0712	0742	0812	0853	0923	minutes	2153	2223	2323
Wien Hbf	a.	0620	0650	0720	0750	0820	0859	0929	past each	2159	2229	2329
Wien Mitte–Landstraße	a.	0628	0658	0728	0758	0828	0907	0937	hour until	2207	2237	2337
Wien Praterstern	a.	0632	0702	0732	0802	0832	0911	0941		2211	2241	2341

WIENER NEUSTADT - PAYERBACH-REICHENAU - MÜRZZUSCHLAG ⊡

		⚒P							Q	P			⚒	†	⚒		Ⓒ	Ⓐ	Ⓐ	Ⓒ	Ⓐ	Ⓒ	ⒶY	Ⓐ	Ⓒ
Wiener Neustadt Hbf	d.	0535	0635	0735	and	2035	2135	2235	2332	0035	...		...	...	...	...	...	...	...	...	...	...	1757	...	...
Neunkirchen NÖ	d.	0546	0646	0746	hourly	2046	2146	2246	2343	0046	...	A	...	...	...	...	...	...	...	...	...	...	|	...	...
Gloggnitz	d.	0559	0659	0759	until	2059	2159	2259	2355	0059	...	L	...	...	...	...	...	...	...	...	...	...	1813	...	...
Payerbach-Reichenau	d.	0608	0708	0808		2108	2208	2308	0004	0108	...	S	0710	0811	0838	1011	1211	1238	1538	1611	1738	1811	1823	1938	2022
Semmering	a.	...	...	...		...	...	...	0028	...	...	O	0734	0840	0907	1040	1240	1307	1607	1640	1807	1840	1848	2007	2051
Mürzzuschlag	a.	...	...	...		...	...	...	0043	...	...		...	0856	...	1056z	1256	1323	...	1656	...	1856	1902	2023	2107

		ⒶD	ⒶP	ⒶG	ⒸP	⚒P	ⒸR	ⒶW	ⒸP	ⒶH	P				P		⚒		Ⓒ	Ⓐ	Ⓒ	Ⓐ	Ⓐ	Ⓒ	Ⓐ	Ⓒ
zuschlag	d.	0345	...	...	...	...	0521	0524	...	...	*0603*	...		...	...		...	0907t	1107	...	1307	1337	...	1707	...	1907
mering	d.	0400	...	...	...	...	0537	0538	...	...	*0618*	...		...	...	A	0752	0922	1122	1152	1322	1352	1652	1722	1852	1922
rbach-Reichenau	d.	0427	0455	0527	0527	0552	0604	0604	0627	0627	0655	0755	and	1955	2158	L	0822	0952	1152	1222	1352	1422	1722	1752	1922	1952
gnitz	d.	0436	0504	0536	0536	0601	0612	0612	0636	0636	0704	0804	hourly	2004	2217	S	...	...	...	...	...	...	...	...	...	...
kirchen NÖ	d.	0447	0515	0547	0547	0612	|	|	0647	0647	0715	0815	until	2015	2228	O	...	...	...	...	...	...	...	...	...	...
er Neustadt Hbf	a.	0458	0525	0558	0558	0622	0626	0626	0658	0658	0725	0825		2025	2238		...	...	...	...	...	...	...	...	...	...

To Wien Meidling (a. 0529) and Wien Hbf (a. 0536).
To Wien Meidling (a. 0629) and Wien Hbf (a. 0638).
To Wien Meidling (a. 0729).
2 Wien - Wiener Neustadt - Payerbach-Reichenau and v.v.
REX **1975**. From Wien (Table **980**).

R – *REX* **1956**. To Wien (Table **980**).
W – *D* **458**. To Wien (Table **980**).
Y – *D* **459**. From Wien (Table **980**).

t – † only.

z – Ⓒ only.

⊡ – Only selected services are shown Wien - Wiener Neustadt - Payerbach-Reichenau and v.v. Additional trains run at peak times. See Table **980** for long-distance services.

WIEN - BŘECLAV 982

strian Holiday dates apply

		2	*RJ* 70 ✗	*EC* 104 ✗♠	2	*RJ* 72 ✗	2	2 Ⓐ	*RJ* 74 ✗	2	*RJ* 76 ✗	*EC* 102 ✗♠	2	*RJ* 78 ✗	2 Ⓐ	2	*RJ* 370 ✗	2 Ⓐ	*D* 100 B	2	*RJ* 372 ✗	2	2	2	*EN* 40406 2★
Graz Hbf **980**	d.	...	...	...	...	0625	...	...	0825	...	1025	...	...	1225	...	...	1425	...	...	...	1625	...	...	...	...
Wiener Neustadt Hbf **980/1**	d.	0516e	...	...	0716e	0832	0911	1011	1032	1111	1232	...	1311	1432	1438	1511	1632	1638	...	1711	1832	1911	2011	2138	...
Wien Meidling **980/1**	d.	0557	...	...	0800	0858	0954	1054	1058	1154	1258	...	1354	1458	1524	1554	1658	1724	...	1754	1858	1954	2054	2224	...
Wien Hbf **980/1**	d.	0603	0709	0809	0806	0909	1000	1100	1109	1200	1309	1409	1400	1509	1530	1600	1709	1730	1809	1800	1909	2000	2100	2230	2250
Wien Mitte-Landstraße **981**	d.	0611	|	|	0814	|	1008	1108	|	1208	|	|	1408	|	1538	1608	|	1738	|	1808	|	2008	2108	2238	|
Wien Praterstern **981**	d.	0615	|	|	0818	|	1012	1112	|	1212	|	|	1412	|	1542	1612	|	1742	|	1812	|	2012	2112	2242	|
Wien Floridsdorf	d.	0623	|	|	0826	|	1020	1120	|	1220	|	|	1420	|	1550	1620	|	1750	|	1820	|	2020	2120	2250	|
Gänserndorf	d.	0645	|	|	0848	|	1042	1142	|	1242	|	|	1442	|	1612	1642	|	1813	|	1842	|	2042	2142	2323	|
Hohenau 🏛	a.	0717	|	|	0920	|	1114	1214	|	1314	|	|	1514	|	1644	1714	|	1837	|	1914	|	2114	2214	2355	|
Břeclav 🏛	a.	...	0804	0904	0935	1004	1129	...	1204	...	1404	1504	1529c	1604	1658	1729c	1804	1852	1904	1929c	2004	...	...	...	2350
Praha hlavní **1150**	a.	...	1108	...	...	1308	...	...	1508	...	1708	...	...	1908	...	...	2108	...	...	...	2308	...	...	...	0408

		EN 40477 2★	2 Ⓐ	2	*D* 101 B	2	*RJ* 71 ✗	2	*RJ* 73 ✗	2	*EC* 103 ♠✗	2 Ⓐ	*RJ* 75 ✗	2	2 Ⓐ	*RJ* 77 ✗	2	2 Ⓐ	*RJ* 79 ✗	2	*EC* 105 ♠✗	2 Ⓐ	*RJ* 371 ✗	2	*RJ* 373 ✗	2
aha hlavní **1150**	d.	2358	...	...	...	...	0652	...	0852	...	...	...	1052	...	...	1252	...	...	1452	...	...	...	1652	...	1852	...
clav 🏛	d.	0549	0557	0627k	0856	...	0956	1027	1156	1227	1256	...	1356	...	...	1556	1627c	1727	1756	1827c	1856	1927	1956	2027c	2156	...
enau 🏛	d.	|	0612	0642	|	0842	|	1042	|	1242	|	1342	|	1442	1542	|	1642	1742	|	1842	|	1942	|	2042	|	2242
serndorf	d.	|	0645	0715	|	0915	|	1115	|	1315	|	1415	|	1515	1615	|	1715	1815	|	1915	|	2015	|	2115	|	2315
Floridsdorf	a.	|	0708	0738	|	0938	|	1138	|	1338	|	1438	|	1538	1638	|	1738	1838	|	1938	|	2038	|	2138	|	2338
Praterstern **981**	a.	|	0717	0747	|	0947	|	1147	|	1347	|	1447	|	1547	1647	|	1747	1847	|	1947	|	2047	|	2147	|	2347
Mitte-Landstraße **981**	a.	|	0721	0751	|	0951	|	1151	|	1351	|	1451	|	1551	1651	|	1751	1851	|	1951	|	2051	|	2151	|	2351
Hbf **980/1**	a.	0702	0728	0758	0951	0958	1051	1158	1251	1358	1351	1458	1451	1558	1658	1651	1758	1858	1851	1958	1951	2058	2051	2158	2251	2358
Meidling **980/1**	a.	...	0734	0804	...	1004	1102	1204	1302	1404	...	1504	1502	1604	1704	1702	1804	1904	1902	2004	...	2104	2102	2204	...	0004
er Neustadt Hbf **980/1**	a.	...	0821	0849	...	1049	1128	1249	1330	1449	...	1549	1530	1649	1749	1730	1849	1949	1928	2049	...	2149	2128	2249	...	0034
az Hbf **980**	a.	...	...	...	...	...	1333	...	1533	...	...	...	1733	...	...	1933	...	...	2133	...	...	...	2333	...	...	...

To / from Bohumín (Table **1155**).
Ⓒ only.

e – Ⓐ only.
k – ⑥ only.

♠ – International service to / from Poland (see Table **99**).
★ – See Tables **60** and **99** for details of through cars.

WIEN - RETZ - ZNOJMO 983

class only; Austrian holiday dates apply

		H	⚒		G	⑥		Ⓐ		Ⓐ		Ⓐ		Ⓐ	Ⓐ	Ⓐ		Ⓐ	Ⓐ	Ⓐ		Ⓐ			
Wien Meidling	d.	...	0545	0645	0745	0745	0845	0945	1045	1145	1245	1345	1445	1515	1545	1615	1645	1715	1745	1815	1845	1945	2045	2151	2315
Wien Hbf	d.	...	0551	0651	0751	0751	0851	0951	1051	1151	1251	1351	1451	1521	1551	1621	1651	1721	1751	1821	1851	1951	2051	2157	2321
Wien Mitte-Landstraße	d.	...	0559	0659	0759	0759	0859	0959	1059	1159	1259	1359	1459	1529	1559	1629	1659	1729	1759	1829	1859	1959	2059	2205	2329
Wien Praterstern	d.	...	0603	0703	0803	0803	0903	1003	1103	1203	1303	1403	1503	1533	1603	1633	1703	1733	1803	1833	1903	2003	2103	2209	2333
Wien Floridsdorf	d.	...	0611	0711	0811	0811	0911	1011	1111	1211	1311	1411	1511	1541	1611	1641	1711	1741	1811	1841	1911	2011	2111	2217	2341
Stockerau	d.	...	0628	0728	0828	0828	0928	1028	1128	1228	1328	1428	1528	1601	1628	1701	1728	1801	1828	1901	1928	2028	2128	2243	2358
Hollabrunn	d.	...	0645	0745	0845	0845	0945	1045	1145	1245	1345	1445	1545	1623	1645	1723	1745	1823	1845	1923	1945	2045	2154	...	0024
Retz 🏛	d.	0617	0712	0815	0912	0915	1012	1112	1215	1312	1415	1512	1615	1652	1712	1752	1815	1852	1912	1952	2012	2112	2220	...	0050
Šatov 🏛	d.	0625	...	0823	...	0923	...	...	1223	...	1423	...	1623	...	...	...	1823	...	...	...	...	...	...	...	...
Znojmo	a.	0636	...	0834	...	0934	...	...	1234	...	1434	...	1634	...	...	...	1834	...	...	...	...	...	...	...	...

		Ⓐ	Ⓐ	Ⓐ	⑥	Ⓒ	Ⓐ	Ⓐ	⚒	Ⓐ	H		⚒		⑥	⚒		Ⓐ		Ⓐ		Ⓐ		Ⓐ		
jmo	d.	...	...	...	...	...	...	...	...	...	0653	...	...	0855	0955	...	...	...	1255	...	1455	...	1655	...	1855	...
v 🏛	d.	...	...	...	...	...	...	...	...	...	0704	...	...	0906	1006	...	...	...	1306	...	1506	...	1706	...	1906	...
🏛	d.	0359	0434	0510	0510	0514r	0530	0552	0617	0636	0715	0715	0817	0917	1017	1017	1117	1217	1317	1417	1517	1617	1717	1817	1917	2017
brunn	d.	0427	0502	0539	0539	0543	0558	0620	0645	0706	0745	0745	0845	0945	1045	1045	1145	1245	1345	1445	1545	1645	1745	1845	1945	2045
kerau	d.	0444	0527	0556	0556	0615	0625	0640	0702	0728	0802	0802	0902	1002	1102	1102	1202	1302	1402	1502	1602	1702	1802	1902	2002	2102
Floridsdorf	a.	0459	0547	0617	0617	0641	0647	0659	0717	0747	0817	0817	0917	1017	1117	1117	1217	1317	1417	1517	1617	1717	1817	1917	2017	2117
Praterstern	a.	0511	0556	0626	*0638*	0650	0656	0708	0726	0756	0826	0826	0926	1026	1126	1126	1226	1326	1426	1526	1626	1726	1826	1926	2026	2126
Mitte-Landstraße	a.	0515	0600	0630	*0642*	0654	0700	0712	0730	0800	0830	0830	0930	1030	1130	1130	1230	1330	1430	1530	1630	1730	1830	1930	2030	2130
Hbf	a.	0522	0607	0637	*0649*	0701	0707	0719	0737	0807	0837	0837	0937	1037	1137	1137	1237	1337	1437	1537	1637	1737	1837	1937	2037	2137
Meidling	a.	0528	0613	0643	*0655*	0707	0713	0725	0743	0813	0843	0843	0943	1043	1143	1143	1243	1343	1443	1543	1643	1743	1843	1943	2043	2143

WIEN - STOCKERAU - ABSDORF-HIPPERSDORF

										Ⓐ	
Wien Meidling	d.	0533	0751	0951	1151	1351	1521	...	1751	1851	1951
Wien Hbf	d.	0539	0757	0957	1157	1357	1527	...	1757	1857	1957
Wien Mitte-Landstraße	d.	0547	0805	1005	1205	1405	1535	...	1805	1905	2005
Wien Praterstern	d.	0551	0809	1009	1209	1409	1539	...	1809	1909	2009
Wien Floridsdorf	d.	0559	0817	1017	1217	1417	1547	...	1817	1917	2017
Stockerau ❖	d.	0631j	0845	1045	1245	1445	1613	1631	1845	1945	2045
Absdorf-Hippersdorf ❖	a.	0646	0900	1100	1300	1500	...	1646	1900	2000	2100

										Ⓐ
Absdorf-Hippersdorf ❖	d.	0626	*0811*	0928	1128	1328	1528	*1811*	1928	2028
Stockerau ❖	d.	0645	0845	0945	1145	1345	1545	1845	1945	2045
Wien Floridsdorf	a.	0711	0911	1011	1211	1411	1611	1911	2011	2111
Wien Praterstern	a.	0720	0920	1020	1220	1420	1620	1920	2020	2120
Wien Mitte-Landstraße	a.	0724	0924	1024	1224	1424	1624	1924	2024	2124
Wien Hbf	a.	0731	0931	1031	1231	1431	1631	1931	2031	2131
Wien Meidling	a.	0737	0937	1037	1237	1437	1637	1937	2037	2137

⚒ (daily Apr. 25 - Oct. 29).
①–⑥ (not Mar. 28).

j – Arrives 0618.
r – † only.

❖ – **Additional journeys** on Ⓐ Stockerau - Absdorf-Hippersdorf and v.v.
From Stockerau at 0435, 0501, 0531, 0731, 1345, 1545 and 1731.
From Absdorf-Hippersdorf at 0458, 0528, 0711, 1428, 1628, 1711 and 1911.

984 WIENER NEUSTADT - PUCHBERG am Schneeberg - HOCHSCHNEEBERG
2nd class

WIENER NEUSTADT - PUCHBERG am Schneeberg *28 km.* Journey time: ± 45 minutes.

From Wiener Neustadt at 0043 †, 0611 Ⓐ, 0737, 0837 **A**, 0937, 1037 **E**, 1137, 1237 **E**, 1337, 1437 **E**, 1537, 1637, 1737, 1837 Ⓑ **r**, 1937, 2037 Ⓑ **r** and 2137.

From Puchberg at 0455 Ⓐ, 0525 Ⓐ, 0555 ⚒, 0624 Ⓐ, 0638 Ⓒ, 0647 Ⓐ, 0738, 0838, 0938 **C**, 1038, 1138 **E**, 1238, 1338 **E**, 1438, 1538 **E**, 1638, 1738, 1838, 1938 Ⓑ **r** and 2038 ⑤⑥ **t**.

PUCHBERG am Schneeberg - **HOCHSCHNEEBERG** *Schneebergbahn* (narrow-gauge rack railway). *9 km.* Journey time: ± 40 minutes.
Services run **Apr. 23 - Oct. 26, 2016** subject to demand and weather conditions. **Operator**: NÖ Schneebergbahn GmbH, Bahnhofplatz 1, A-2734 Puchberg. ✆ +43 (0) 2636 3661
From Puchberg at 0900, 1030, 1200, 1400, 1530. **From Hochschneeberg** at 0945, 1115, 1315, 1445, 1615. Additional trains operate during July and August, also at other times when th
sufficient demand. A steam service operates on ⑦ July 3 - Sept. 4 (also Aug. 15): Departs Puchberg 1120, departs Hochschneeberg 1517 (journey time ± 80 minutes – special fares ap

A – Ⓐ (daily Apr. 18 - Oct. 31).
C – Ⓒ Apr. 23 - Oct. 30.
E – ⚒ (daily Apr. 18 - Oct. 31).
r – Not Mar. 27, May 15, Aug. 14.
t – Also Jan. 5, Mar. 27, May 4, 15, 25, Aug. 14, Oct. 25, 31, Dec. 7.

985 FLUGHAFEN WIEN ✈ Schwechat
CAT ★; S-Bahn (2nd class o

km		Ⓐ			★		★		★			★		★		★					
0	**Wien** Praterstern d.	0415	0445	0515	...	0545	...	0615	...	0645	and at the same	...	2215	...	2245	...	...	2345	...	...	...
2	**Wien** Mitte-Landstraße d.	0419	0449	0519	0536	0549	0606	0619	0636	0649	minutes past	2206	2219	2236	2249	2306	...	2349	...	...	...
21	**Flughafen Wien** ✈ a.	0442	0512	0542	0552	0612	0622	0642	0652	0712	each hour until	2222	2242	2252	2312	2322	...	0012	...	...	...

					★		★		★		★		★		★			★		★	
Flughafen Wien ✈ d.	0018	...	0518	0548	0609	0618	0639	0645	0709	0718	0739	0745	0809	0818	0839	0848	and at the same	2239	2248	2309	2318
Wien Mitte-Landstraße a.	0043	...	0543	0613	0625	0643	0655	0710	0725	0743	0755	0810	0825	0843	0855	0913	minutes past	2255	2313	2325	2343
Wien Praterstern a.	0047	...	0547	0617	...	0647	...	0714	...	0747	...	0814	...	0847	...	0917	each hour until	...	2317	...	2347

★ – *City Airport Train (CAT).* Non-stop service with special fares.

RJ and *IC* trains **Wien Hbf - Flughafen Wien** ✈ and v.v. Journey time: 15 – 18 minutes. Most trains run from / to Salzburg, Linz and St Pölten (see Table **950**).
From Wien Hbf at 0539, 0611, 0639 and at 11 and 39 minutes past each hour until 2111, 2139 and 2211.
From Flughafen Wien ✈ at 0633, 0703, 0733 and at 03 and 33 minutes past each hour until until 2203, 2233 and 2303.

🚌 *Vienna Airport Lines*: Wien Westbahnhof (Europaplatz) – Flughafen Wien ✈ and v.v. Journey time: 45 minutes Westbahnhof - Flughafen / 35 minutes Flughafen - Westbahnhof.
🚌 From **Wien Westbahnhof**: 0515, 0545 and every 30 minutes until 2315, 2345. 🚌 From **Flughafen Wien** ✈: 0005, 0605, 0635 and every 30 minutes until 2305, 2335.

🚌 ÖBB-Postbus / Slovak Lines: **Bratislava**, AS Mlynské nivy (bus station) – **Flughafen Wien** ✈ and v.v. Journey time: 60 minutes.
Reservation recommended ✆ +43 (0) 810 222333-6 or +421 2 55422734. Please note that a much reduced service operates on Dec. 24, 25, 26, 31, Jan. 1.
🚌 From **Bratislava** AS Mlynské nivy at 0440, 0530, 0600, 0700, 0730 ①–⑤, 0800, 0830, 0900, 0930 ①–⑤, 1000, 1100, 1200, 1300, 1400, 1500, 1600, 1700, 1800, 1900, 2000 and 2
🚌 From **Flughafen Wien** ✈ at 0630, 0815, 0830, 0940, 1000 ①–⑥, 1030, 1130, 1230, 1300 ①–⑤, 1330, 1430, 1500 ①–⑤, 1530, 1630, 1730, 1800, 1830, 1930, 2030, 2130, 2230 and 2

986 GRAZ - SZENTGOTTHÁRD - SZOMBATHELY
ÖBB, GySEV •; 2nd class o

km		A ⁄	W		W				Ⓒ W	Ⓐ		Ⓐ ◇		Ⓐ		Ⓐ	P	Ⓐ ⊡		⚒		Ⓐ			⚒
0	**Graz** Hbf d.	0608	0708	0808	0908	1008	1108	1208	1308	1308	1408	1438	1508	1538	1608	1638	1708	1738	1808	1838	1908	1938	2008	2108	2213
29	Gleisdorf d.	0650	0750	0850	0950	1050	1150	1250	1350	1350	1450	1513	1550	1613	1650	1713	1750	1813	1850	1913	1950	2013	2050	2150	2253
53	Feldbach d.	0715	0814	0914	1014	1114	1214	1314	1414	1414	1514	1529	1614	1629	1714	1729	1814	1829	1914	1929	2014	2029	2114	2217	2316
62	Fehring d.	0727	0824	0925	1024	1125	1233t	1325	1424	1430	1525	1542	1624	1638	1725	1738	1824	1842	1925	1941	2024	2040	2125	2227	2326
82	**Szentgotthárd** 🛃 a.	0748	...	0947	...	1147	1255	1347	...	1451	1547c	1603	...	*1702*	1747c	*1802*	...	1903	1947c	2002e	...	2101	2146	...	...

	Ⓐ		Ⓐ		Ⓐ	Ⓐ	⑥	†	Ⓐ	⚒	Ⓐ H			P		P								N	Ⓐ
Szentgotthárd 🛃 d.	...	...	*0445*	0516k	*0532*	...	...	0616	*0619*	0640k	...	...	0816	...	1016	...	1210	1303	1408	*1509*e	1616	1716e	1813	...	...
Fehring d.	0409	0440	0511	0540	0557	0615	0615	0640	0644	0703	0730	0740	0840	0940	1040	1140	1240t	1327	1430	1540	1640	1740	1840	1940	2040
Feldbach d.	0420	0450	0522	0550	0606	0627	0627	0650	0654	0715	0742	0750	0850	0950	1050	1150	1250	1350z	1450z	1550	1650	1750	1850	1950	2050
Gleisdorf d.	0443	0513	0540	0613	0626	0650	0655	0713	0713	0738	0802	0813	0913	1013	1113	1213	1313	1413	1513	1613	1713	1813	1913	2013	2113
Graz Hbf a.	0519	0553	0615	0652	0703	0724	0734	0753	0748	0816	0837	0853	0953	1053	1153	1253	1353	1453	1553	1653	1753	1853	1953	2053	2153

SZENTGOTTHÁRD - SZOMBATHELY •

km		S	Ⓐ ⊖	S			A ⁄	S					Ⓐ S			S	S		S ‡		S		S	Ⓐ	
0	**Szentgotthárd** 🛃 d.	0406	0506	0606	0636	0706	0822	0836	...	1006	...	1206	1236	1306	1406	1436	1536	1636	1706	1806	1836	...	2006	2106	...
28	Körmend d.	0430	0530	0630	0700	0730	0841	0900	...	1030	...	1230	1300	1330	1430	1500	1600	1700	1730	1830	1900	...	2030	2130	...
64	**Szombathely** a.	0453	0553	0653	0723	0753	0900	0923	...	1053	...	1253	1323	1353	1453	1523	1623	1723	1753	1853	1923	...	2053	2153	...

	S	S			S							Ⓐ		Ⓐ	S	S	S	S		Ⓐ ⊖			B ⁄		
Szombathely d.	0436	0506	0606	0636	0706	...	0906	...	1106	...	1236	1306	1336	1406	1436	1536	1636	1736	1836	1906	...	2036	2058	2136	...
Körmend d.	0500	0530	0630	0700	0730	...	0930	...	1130	...	1300	1330	1400	1430	1500	1600	1700	1800	1900	1930	...	2100	2118	2200	...
Szentgotthárd 🛃 a.	0524	0554	0654	0724	0754	...	0954	...	1154	...	1324	1354	1424	1459	1524	1624	1724	1824	1924	1954	...	2124	2135	2224	...

A – [12] Graz (**317**) - Szentgotthárd (*IC* **317**) - Budapest.
B – [12] Budapest (*IC* **318**) - Szentgotthárd (**318**) - Graz.
H – From Hartberg (Table **995**).
N – From Wiener Neustadt on Ⓒ (Table **995**).
P – To / from Wiener Neustadt on Ⓐ (Table **995**).
S – From / to Sopron (Table **1233**).
W – To / from Wiener Neustadt (Table **995**).

c – Ⓒ only.
e – Ⓐ only.
k – ⑥ only.
t – Arrives 8 – 9 minutes earlier.
z – Arrives 11 – 13 minutes earlier.

◇ – On ⑤ change trains at Fehring (Fehring d. *1546*, Szentgotthárd a. *16*
‡ – Runs 30 minutes later until Apr. 3.
⊡ – Change trains at Fehring on ①–④.
⊖ – *IC* train to / from Budapest (Table **1250**). [R] and supplement payable
⁄ – [R] and supplement payable in Hungary.
• – Szentgotthárd - Szombathely operated by Györ-Sopron-Ebenfurti Va

990 WIEN - GMÜND - ČESKÉ VELENICE
2nd class o

km				⚒		⚒					⑤			Ⓐ	Ⓐ		Ⓐ		B		A		
0	**Wien** Franz-Josefs-Bf. **991/3** d.	0628	...	0732	0828	0932	1028	1132	1228	1332	1359	1428	1528	1558	1617	1628	1658	1728	1758	1828	1858	1928	2028
1	Wien Spittelau ● **991/3** d.	0631	...	0735	0831	0935	1031	1135	1231	1335	1402	1431	1531	1601	1620	1631	1701	1731	1801	1831	1901	1931	2031
3	Wien Heiligenstadt △ **991/3** d.	0634	...	0738	0834	0938	1034	1138	1234	1338	1405	1434	1534	1604	1623	1634	1704	1734	1804	1834	1904	1934	2034
33	Tulln a. d. Donau **991/3** d.	0656	...	0800	0856	1000	1056	1200	1256	1400	|	1456	1556	1625	|	1656	1728	1756	1828	1856	1928	1956	2056
44	Absdorf-Hippersdorf **991** d.	0705	...	0809	0905	1009	1105	1209	1305	1409	|	1505	1605	1634	|	1705	|	1805	1837	1905	|	2005	2105
79	Eggenburg d.	0734	...	0839	0934	1039	1134	1239	1334	1439	1453	1534	1638	1705	1715	1734	1804	1838	1905	1934	2004	2038	2134
89	Sigmundsherberg d.	0742	...	0847	0942	1047	1142	1247	1342	1447	1502	1542	1646	1713	1723	1742	1814	1846	1914	1942	2013	2046	2142
121	Göpfritz an der Wild d.	0806	...	...	1006	...	1206	...	1406	...	1522	1606	...	...	1747	1806	1839	...	1936	2006	2037	...	2206
138	Schwarzenau im Waldviertel d.	0820	...	...	1020	...	1220	...	1420	...	1535	1620	...	...	1801	1820	1851	...	1951	2020	2051	...	2220
162	**Gmünd** NÖ a.	0841	...	...	1041	...	1241	...	1441	...	1552	1641	...	...	1822	1841	1914	...	2014	2041	2112	...	2241
162	**Gmünd** NÖ 🛃 d.	0844	...	...	1044	...	1244	...	1444	...	...	1646	...	...	...	1846	...	...	...	2044	...	...	...
164	**České Velenice** 🛃 **1133** a.	0848	...	...	1048	...	1248	...	1448	...	...	1650	...	...	...	1850	...	...	...	2048	...	...	...

	Ⓐ	⚒	⚒	Ⓑ	Ⓐ	Ⓐ		Ⓐ		Ⓐ			⚒						Ⓐ	Ⓒ		†	
České Velenice 🛃 **1133** d.	...	...	...	...	...	...	...	...	0602	0707	...	0907	...	1107	...	1307	...	1507	...	...	1705	...	1907
Gmünd NÖ 🛃 a.	...	...	...	...	...	...	...	...	0606	0711	...	0911	...	1111	...	1311	...	1511	...	...	1709	...	1911
Gmünd NÖ d.	...	0350	...	...	...	0453	0510	...	0611	0714	...	0914	...	1114	...	1314	...	1514	...	...	1712	...	1914
Schwarzenau im Waldviertel d.	...	0412	...	...	...	0517	0533	...	0632	0735	...	0935	...	1135	...	1335	...	1535	...	...	1733	...	1935
Göpfritz an der Wild d.	...	0425	...	...	...	0532	0547	...	0646	0749	...	0949	...	1149	...	1349	...	1549	...	...	1749	...	1949
Sigmundsherberg d.	0409	0449	0455	0509	0539	0557	0612	0639	0709	0814	0909	1014	1109	1214	1309	1414	1509	1614	1656	1709	1814	1909	2014
Eggenburg d.	0418	0458	0503	0518	0548	0606	0620	0648	0718	0822	0918	1022	1118	1222	1318	1422	1518	1622	1718	1718	1822	1918	2022
Absdorf-Hippersdorf **991** d.	0448	|	0533	0548	0618	|	0650	0718	0748	0852	0948	1052	1148	1252	1348	1455	1548	1652	1748	1748	1852	1948	2052
Tulln a. d. Donau **991/3** d.	0457	|	0542	0557	0627	|	0659	0726	0757	0901	0957	1101	1157	1301	1457	1504	1557	1701	1757	1757	1901	1957	2101
Wien Heiligenstadt △ **991/3** a.	0520	0547	0603	0619	0648	0656	0721	0749	0818	0922	1019	1122	1219	1322	1419	1525	1619	1722	1819	1819	1922	2019	2122
Wien Spittelau ● **991/3** a.	0523	0551	0607	0622	0652	0700	0725	0752	0822	0925	1022	1125	1222	1325	1422	1529	1622	1725	1822	1822	1925	2022	2125
Wien Franz-Josefs-Bf. **991/3** a.	0526	0554	0610	0625	0655	0703	0728	0755	0825	0928	1025	1128	1225	1328	1425	1532	1625	1728	1825	1825	1928	2025	2128

A – ①–④ (not Jan. 5, 6, Mar. 28, May 4, 5, 16, 25, 26, Aug. 15, Oct. 25, 26, 31, Nov. 1, Dec. 7, 8).
B – ①–④ (not Jan. 6, Mar. 28, May 5, 16, 26, Aug. 15, Oct. 26, Nov. 1, Dec. 8).

w – Also Mar. 28, May 16, Aug. 15; not Mar. 27, May 15, Aug. 14.

△ – S-Bahn trains run every 10 – 15 minutes from / to Wien Hüttel (journey: 21 – 23 minutes).
● – Direct U-Bahn links: Line **U4** – Wien Mitte - Spittelau.
Line **U6** – Wien Meidling - Westbahnhof - Spittelau - Floridsd

WIEN - KREMS an der Donau - EMMERSDORF — 991

ass only

	Ⓐ						Ⓐ	Ⓐ	Ⓒ	Ⓐ		Ⓐ		Ⓐ		Ⓐ					
Wien Franz-Josefs-Bf .... 990/3 d.	0505	0605	0705		1405	1505	1533	1602	1605	1633	1705	1733	1805	1833	1905	1933	2005	2105	2205	2305	0009
Wien Spittelau .... ● 990/3 d.	0508	0608	0708	and	1408	1508	1536	1605	1608	1636	1708	1736	1808	1836	1908	1936	2008	2108	2208	2308	0011
Wien Heiligenstadt .... △ 990/3 d.	0511	0611	0711	hourly	1411	1511	1539	1608	1611	1639	1711	1739	1811	1839	1911	1939	2011	2111	2211	2311	0015
Tulln a. d. Donau .... 990/3 d.	0533	0633	0733	until	1433	1533	1601	1633	1633	1701	1733	1801	1833	1901	1933	2001	2033	2133	2233	2333	0051
Absdorf-Hippersdorf .... 990 d.	0542	0642	0742		1442	1542	1610	1642	1642	1710	1742	1810	1842	1910	1942	2010	2042	2142	2242	2342	...
Krems a. d. Donau .... a.	0614	0716	0814		1514	1614	1636	1714	1714	1736	1814	1836	1914	1936	2014	2036	2114	2214	2314	0014	...

	Ⓐ	⚒	Ⓐ		Ⓐ	Ⓐ		Ⓐ														
a. d. Donau .... d.	0429	0451	0529	0551	0617	0629	0651	0729	0751		1251	1343	1451	1551	1651	1750	1851	1951	2051	2151	...	...
-Hippersdorf .... 990 d.	0454	0522	0554	0622	0644	0654	0722	0754	0822	and	1322	1422	1522	1622	1722	1822	1922	2022	2122	2222	...	...
d. Donau .... 990/3 d.	0503	0531	0603	0631	0653	0703	0731	0803	0831	hourly	1331	1431	1531	1631	1731	1831	1931	2031	2131	2231	...	...
eiligenstadt .... △ 990/3 a.	0525	0551	0625	0652	0718	0725	0752	0825	0851	until	1351	1451	1551	1651	1751	1851	1951	2051	2151	2251	...	...
pittelau .... ● 990/3 a.	0528	0555	0628	0656	0722	0728	0756	0828	0855		1355	1455	1555	1655	1755	1855	1955	2055	2155	2255	...	...
ranz-Josefs-Bf .... 990/3 a.	0531	0558	0631	0659	0725	0731	0759	0831	0858		1358	1458	1558	1658	1758	1858	1958	2058	2158	2258	...	...

KREMS - EMMERSDORF ⊠

	R		R		R			
Krems an der Donau .... d.	1020	...	1320	...	1620	...	...	...
Spitz an der Donau .... d.	1053	...	1353	...	1653	...	...	...
Emmersdorf an der Donau .... a.	1125	...	1425	...	1725	...	...	...

	R		R		R			
Emmersdorf an der Donau .... d.	1140	...	1440	...	1740	...	...	...
Spitz an der Donau .... d.	1213	...	1513	...	1813	...	...	...
Krems an der Donau .... a.	1245	...	1545	...	1845	...	...	...

Apr. 16 - Oct. 26 (daily July 2 - Sept. 25). pecial fares apply.

● – Direct U-bahn links: Line **U4** – Wien Mitte - Spittelau. Line **U6** – Wien Meidling - Westbahnhof - Spittelau - Floridsdorf.

△ – S-Bahn trains run every 10 – 15 minutes from / to Wien Hütteldorf (journey: 21 – 23 minutes).

⊠ – Operated by NÖVOG. ✆ +43 (0) 2742 360 990-99. A connecting 🚌 service operates Emmersdorf - Melk and v.v. Journey time: 10 minutes. From Emmersdorf at 1135 and 1735. From Melk at 1120 and 1720.

LINZ and ST VALENTIN - GREIN - SARMINGSTEIN — 992

lass only

	Ⓐ	Ⓐ	⚒						Ⓐ		⚒		Ⓐ	⚒	Ⓐ	Ⓐ		Ⓐ	Ⓐ		Ⓒ	Ⓐ	Ⓐ	
Linz Hbf .... 976 d.	0430	0525	0630	0649	...	0834	...	1034	1130	1230	1330	1434	1452	1530	1530	1606	1634	1706	1730	1752	1830	1834	1934	2030
Enns .... 976 d.	0448	0539	|	0707	...	0848	...	1048	|	|	|	1448	1510	|	|	1620	1648	1720	|	1810	|	1848	1948	|
St Valentin .... d.	0502	|	0649	0719	...	|	...	|	1150	1250	1350	|	1521	1550	1550	|	|	|	1750	1821	1850	|	|	2050
Perg .... d.	0526	0609	0713	0744	...	0914	...	1114	1214	1314	1414	1514	1545	1614	1614	1644	1714	1745	1814	1845	1914	1914	2014	2113
Grein-Bad Kreuzen ..... d.	0601	0644	0744	0816	...	0945	...	1145	1245	1345	1445	1545	1613	1644	1645	1714	1745	1816	1845	1915	1945	1945	2043	2142
Grein Stadt .... d.	0604	0648	0747	0819	...	0948	...	1148	1248	1348	1448	1548	...	...	1648	...	1748	1819	1847	1918	1948	1948	2046	...
St Nikola-Struden .... a.	0610	0655	0753	0825	...	0954	...	1154	1254	1354	1454	1554	...	...	1654	...	1754	1825	...	1924	1954	1954	2052	...
Sarmingstein .... a.	0615	...	...	...	...	...	...	...	...	...	...	...	...	...	...	...	...	1830	...	...	1959	1959	2057	...

	Ⓐ	Ⓐ		Ⓐ	⚒		Ⓐ			Ⓐ	Ⓐ	Ⓒ	⚒		Ⓐ	Ⓐ	Ⓒ	Ⓐ	Ⓐ	Ⓐ	Ⓒ	Ⓐ	Ⓑ	
Sarmingstein .... d.	...	0511	0525	...	...	0627	...	...	...	...	...	...	...	...	...	...	...	...	...	...	...	1858	...	...
St Nikola-Struden .... d.	...	0516	0530	...	...	0632	0703	0803	1003	...	1203	1203	1303	1403	1503	1603	1603	...	1703	1803	1803	1903	...	1933
Grein Stadt .... d.	0401	0523	0537	...	...	0639	0710	0810	1010	1110	1210	1210	1310	1410	1510	1610	1610	...	1710	1810	1810	1910	1910	1940
Grein-Bad Kreuzen ..... d.	0405	0526	0540	0601	0612	0644	0714	0815	1015	1115	1215	1215	1315	1415	1515	1615	1615	1644	1715	1815	1815	1915	1915	1945
Perg .... d.	0432	0554	0610	0630	0641	0713	0744	0844	1044	1144	1244	1244	1344	1444	1544	1644	1644	1714	1744	1844	1844	1944	1944	2014
St Valentin .... a.	0454	|	0632	|	0706	|	0807	|	|	1207	|	1307	1407	|	|	|	1707	1738	1807	|	1907	2007	2007	2036
Enns .... 976 a.	0520	0613	0645	0652	|	0736	|	0907	1107	|	1307	|	|	1507	1607	1707	|	1749	|	1907	|	|	|	2049
Linz Hbf .... 976 a.	0538	0628	0702	0708	0730	0752	0830	0922	1122	1230	1322	1330	1430	1522	1622	1722	1730	1808	1830	1922	1930	2030	2030	2108

ST PÖLTEN - KREMS and TULLN — 993

lass only

ST PÖLTEN - KREMS

	⚒	Ⓐ		Ⓐ					Ⓐ					Ⓐ		Ⓐ		Ⓐ			Ⓐ		T
St Pölten Hbf .... d.	0505	0539	0605	0639	0705	0805	0905	1005	1105	1205	1305	1405	1505	1539	1605	1639	1705	1739	1805	1905	2005	2105	2205
Herzogenburg .... d.	0514	0548	0614	0648	0714	0814	0914	1014	1114	1214	1314	1414	1514	1548	1614	1648	1714	1748	1814	1914	2014	2114	2214
Krems a. d. Donau .... a.	0541	0626	0641	0726	0741	0841	0941	1041	1141	1241	1341	1441	1541	1612	1641	1712	1741	1812	1841	1941	2041	2141	2241

	⚒	⚒		Ⓐ	⚒	Ⓐ			Ⓐ				Ⓒ	Ⓐ						Ⓐ			T
s a. d. Donau .... d.	0519	0546	0617	0646	0718	0746	0819	0919	1019	1119	1219	1319	1419	1421	1519	1619	1719	1819	1919	2019	2119	...	2219
jenburg .... d.	0547	0613	0646	0715	0746	0813	0847	0947	1047	1147	1246	1347	1447	1446	1547	1646	1747	1846	1947	2047	2147	...	2247
ten Hbf .... a.	0555	0622	0655	0724	0755	0822	0855	0955	1055	1155	1255	1355	1455	1455	1555	1655	1755	1855	1955	2055	2155	...	2255

ST PÖLTEN - TULLN - WIEN

	⚒		⚒	Ⓐ			Ⓐ		Ⓐ		Ⓐ		Ⓐ		Ⓐ		Ⓐ		Ⓐ	P			
St Pölten Hbf .... 950 d.	0401	...	0512	0545	0612	0715	0812	0912	...	1112	1212	1312	1412	1512	1612	1712	1812	1912	2012	2118	...	...	...
Herzogenburg .... d.	0415	...	0532	0603	0632	0732	0835	0930	...	1132	1232	1332	1432	1532	1632	1732	1832	1932	2032	2127	...	...	...
Tullnerfeld .... 950 a.	0449	...	0611	0637	0711	0811	0911	1011	...	1211	1311	1411	1511	1611	1711	1811	1911	2011	2111	|	...	...	...
Tullnerfeld .... d.	0450	...	0624	0654	0724	0824	0924	1024	1124	1224	1324	1424	1524	1624	1724	1824	1924	2024	2124	|	...	...	...
Tulln Stadt .... d.	0456	...	0630	0700	0730	0830	0930	1030	1130	1230	1330	1430	1530	1630	1730	1830	1930	2030	2130	2200	...	2235	2335
Tulln a. d. Donau .... 990/1 a.	0459	...	0632	0702	0732	0832	0932	1032	1132	1232	1332	1432	1532	1632	1732	1832	1932	2032	2132	2202	...	2237	2337
Wien Heiligenstadt ...... 990/1 a.	0544	...	0714	0744	0814	0914	1014	1114	1214	1314	1414	1514	1614	1714	1814	1914	2014	2114	2214	2228	...	2314	0014
Wien Spittelau .... 990/1 a.	0548	...	0718	0748	0818	0918	1018	1118	1218	1318	1418	1518	1618	1718	1818	1918	2018	2118	2218	2231	...	2318	0018
Wien Franz-Josefs-Bf . 990/1 a.	0550	...	0720	0750	0820	0920	1020	1120	1220	1320	1420	1520	1620	1720	1820	1920	2020	2120	2220	2235	...	2320	0020

	Ⓐ	⚒	⚒		⚒		P	Ⓐ		Ⓐ		Ⓐ		Ⓐ		Ⓐ		Ⓐ		Ⓐ			
Franz-Josefs-Bf .... 990/1 d.	...	...	0509	0539	0609	0639	0723	0739	0839	0939	1039	1139	1239	1339	1439	1539	1639	1739	1839	1939	2039	2139	2239
Spittelau .... 990/1 d.	...	...	0511	0541	0611	0641	|	0741	0841	0941	1041	1141	1241	1341	1441	1541	1641	1741	1841	1941	2041	2141	2241
Heiligenstadt .... 990/1 d.	...	...	0515	0545	0615	0645	0730	0745	0845	0945	1045	1145	1245	1345	1445	1545	1645	1745	1845	1945	2045	2145	2245
a. d. Donau .... 990/1 d.	0442	0527	0559	0627	0658	0727	0757	0827	0927	1027	1127	1227	1327	1427	1527	1627	1727	1827	1927	2027	2127	2223	2323
Stadt .... d.	0445	0529	0601	0629	0700	0729	0803	0829	0929	1029	1129	1229	1329	1429	1529	1629	1729	1829	1929	2029	2129	2225	2325
rfeld .... a.	0450	0534	0606	0634	0705	0734	0808	0834	0934	1034	1134	1234	1334	1434	1534	1634	1734	1834	1934	2034	2134	...	...
rfeld .... 950 d.	0451	0548	0619	0648	0718	0748	0812	0848	0948	...	1148	1248	1348	1448	1548	1648	1748	1848	1948	2048	...	...	...
genburg .... d.	0525	0630	0658	0730	0753	0830	0841	0930	1030	...	1230	1330	1430	1530	1630	1732	1830	1930	2030	2130	...	...	...
lten Hbf .... 950 a.	0538	0648	0714	0744	0805	0844	0850	0944	1044	...	1248	1348	1444	1548	1648	1748	1844	1944	2044	2144	...	...	...

May 1 - Oct. 26. 🚃2 Wien Franz-Josefs-Bf - St Pölten - Linz - Passau and v.v.

T – ④–⑥ (not May 5, 26, Dec. 8).

ST PÖLTEN - MARIAZELL — 994

ow gauge 2nd class only

			★	C	S Ⓡ					
St Pölten Hbf .... d.	0635	0737	0837	0907	0907	1037	1237	1437	1637	1837
Ober Grafendorf .... d.	0654	0754	0854	0925	0925	1054	1254	1454	1654	1854
Kirchberg a. d. Pielach . d.	0723	0823	0923	1000	1005	1123	1323	1523	1723	1923
Frankenfels .... ⊗ d.	0741	0841	0941	1021	1031	1141	1341	1541	1741	1941
Laubenbachmühle .... d.	0750	0850	0950	1040	1050	1150	1350	1550	1750	1949
Gösing .... ⊗ d.	0820	0919‡	1020	1115	1138	1220	1420	1619	1820	...
Mitterbach .... ⊗ d.	0845	0945‡	1045	1140	1205	1245	1445	1645	1845	...
Mariazell .... a.	0852	0952‡	1052	1147	1212	1252	1452	1652	1852	...

						C	S Ⓡ	★		
Mariazell .... d.	...	0907	1107	1307	1507	1527	1522	1607‡	1707	1907
Mitterbach .... ⊗ d.	...	0913	1113	1313	1513	1533	1529	1613‡	1713	1913
Gösing .... ⊗ d.	...	0938	1138	1338	1538	1600	1600	1638‡	1738	1938
Laubenbachmühle .... d.	0654	1009	1209	1409	1609	1634	1649	1709	1809	2009
Frankenfels .... ⊗ d.	0702	1017	1217	1417	1617	1643	1658	1717	1817	2017
Kirchberg a. d. Pielach d.	0726	1036	1236	1436	1636	1702	1722	1736	1836	2036
Ober Grafendorf .... d.	0754	1104	1304	1504	1704	1735	1754	1804	1904	2104
St Pölten Hbf .... a.	0812	1122	1322	1522	1722	1802	1817	1822	1922	2122

Runs on ⑥ May 7 - Oct. 22 (also Nov. 26, Dec. 3, 10). ÖTSCHERBÄR – Traditional loco-hauled electric train. Conveys 🚃12 and ✕.

Runs on May 8, June 12, July 10, Aug. 14, Sept. 11, Oct. 9 and Dec. 8 only. Steam train with special fares. Conveys 🚃12 and ✕.

★ – Runs daily. On Ⓒ May 1 - Oct. 26 and Ⓒ from Nov. 26 also conveys first class panorama cars with special fares (Ⓡ).

‡ – May 1 - Oct. 26 and from Nov. 26.

⊗ – Trains call on request only.

Operator: NÖVOG. ✆ +43 (0) 2742 360 990 99. www.noevog.at/mariazellerbahn

995 (WIEN -) WIENER NEUSTADT - FEHRING
2nd clas

km		⚒	Ⓐ			Ⓐ			†	Ⓐ		Ⓐ	Ⓐ		Ⓑ	Ⓑ	
0	**Wien** Meidling .... **980/1** d.	...	...	...	...	...	...	...	1435r	1600	...	1735	1800	...	...	...	...
44	**Wiener Neustadt** Hbf. **980/1** d.	...	0640	0903	1103	...	1303	1503	1503	1633	1703	1801	1833	1903	2003	2103	2139
99	Friedberg .... d.	...	0802	1002	1202	...	1402	1602	1602	1734	1802	1857	1931	2002	2100	2200	2247
126	Hartberg .... d.	0621	0835	1035	1234	1326	1435	1634	1635	1812	1835	1929	...	2035	2132e	2232	...
157	Fürstenfeld .... d.	0653	0910	1110	...	1359	1510	...	1710	...	1910	...	...	2110	...	...	...
177	**Fehring** .... a.	0723	0937	1137	...	1426	1537	...	1737	...	1937	...	...	2137	...	...	...
	Graz Hbf **986** .... a.	0837e	1053	1253e	...	...	...	...	...	...	2053z	...	...	...	...	...	...

	Ⓐ	Ⓐ	Ⓐ	⚒	Ⓐ	Ⓑ	Ⓐ				Ⓐ			†			†r
Graz Hbf **986** .... d.	...	...	...	...	...	...	...	...	0708	0908	...	...	1308z	...	...	1708e	...
Fehring .... d.	...	...	...	...	...	...	0457	0622	0827	1027	1227	...	1427	1627	...	1827	1827
Fürstenfeld .... d.	...	...	...	...	...	...	0526	0653	0855	1055	1255	...	1455	1655	...	1855	1855
Hartberg .... d.	...	...	0435	0533	0533	...	0559	0724	0927	1127	1327	1327	1527	1727	1727	1929	1929
Friedberg .... d.	0343	0425	0509	0608	0608	0633	0633	0758	1002	1202	1402	1402	1602	1802	1802	2002	2002
Wiener Neustadt Hbf .. **980/1** a.	0451	0527	0610	0711	0711	0728	0728	0851	1057	1257	1457	1457	1657	1857	1857	2057	2057
Wien Meidling .... **980/1** a.	...	0559	0645	...	0745	...	...	...	...	...	...	...	...	...	...	...	2131
Wien Hbf .... **980/1** a.	...	0606	0652	...	...	...	...	...	...	...	...	...	...	...	...	...	2141

e – Ⓐ only.
r – † (not Mar. 27, May 15, Aug. 1
z – Ⓒ only.

996 WIEN - BRATISLAVA via Marchegg
2nd class only; Austrian holiday dates

km						Ⓐ				
0	**Wien** Hbf .... d.	0516	0616		1816	1916	2016	2133	2216	...
4	**Wien** Simmering ⊖ .... d.	0522	0622	and	1822	1922	2022	2139	2222	...
47	Marchegg ▦ .... d.	0602	0702	hourly	1902	2002	2102	2230	2302	...
53	Devínska Nová Ves ▦ .... d.	0610	0710	until	1910	2010	2110	...	2310	...
66	**Bratislava** hlavná .... a.	0622	0722		1922	2022	2122	...	2322	...

		Ⓐ				
Bratislava hlavná .... d.	0538	0606	0638		1838	2038
Devínska Nová Ves ▦ .... d.	0551	0619	0651	and	1851	2051
Marchegg ▦ .... d.	0601	0629	0701	hourly	1901	2101
Wien Simmering ⊖ .... a.	0637	0718	0737	until	1937	2137
Wien Hbf .... a.	0643	0724	0743		1943	2143

⊖ – For U-Bahn connections (line U3) from / to Wien Mitte and Wien Westbahnhof.

997 WIEN - BRATISLAVA via Bruck an der Leitha
2nd class only; Austrian holiday dates

km					Ⓐ	Ⓐ	Ⓒ	Ⓐ		Ⓐ		Ⓐ	Ⓒ	Ⓐ	Ⓐ		Ⓐ	Ⓒ	Ⓐ	Ⓐ		Ⓐ	Ⓐ	Ⓒ
0	**Wien** Meidling .... d.	...	...	...	0537	0637	...	0737	0837	0937	1037	1137	1237	...	1337	1437	...	1637	...	1737	1837	...	2036	2037
4	**Wien** Hbf .... d.	0050	...	0444	0545	0645	0645	0745	0844	0945	1045	1145	1244	1244	1344	1444	1544	1644	1644	1744	1844	1945	2045	2045
45	Bruck an der Leitha .... d.	0129	...	0513	0613	0713	0713	0813	0913	1013	1113	1213	1313	1313	1413	1513	1613	1713	1713	1813	1913	2013	2113	2113
73	Kittsee ▦ .... a.	0154	...	0538	0638	0738	0738	0838	0938	1038	1138	1238	1338	1338	1438	1538	1638	1738	1738	1838	1938	2038	2138	2138
78	**Bratislava** - Petržalka ▦ ☆ . a.	0200	...	0544	0644	0744	0744	0844	0944	1044	1144	1244	1344	1344	1444	1544	1644	1744	1744	1844	1944	2044	2144	2144

		Ⓐ	Ⓐ		Ⓐ	Ⓐ		Ⓐ		Ⓐ		Ⓐ		Ⓐ	Ⓒ	Ⓐ	Ⓐ	Ⓒ	Ⓐ	Ⓐ		Ⓐ	
Bratislava - Petržalka ▦ ☆ .... d.	0427	0515	0546	0615	0646	0715	0815	0915	1015	1115	1215	1315	1415	1515	1615	1615	1715	1815	1815	1915	2015	2115	...
Kittsee ▦ .... d.	0433	0521	0552	0621	0652	0721	0821	0921	1021	1121	1221	1321	1421	1521	1621	1621	1721	1821	1821	1921	2021	2121	...
Bruck an der Leitha .... d.	0458	0547	0617	0647	0717	0747	0846	0946	1046	1146	1246	1346	1446	1546	1646	1646	1746	1846	1846	1946	2046	2146	...
Wien Hbf .... a.	0539	0616	0646	0716	0746	0815	0914	1014	1114	1214	1314	1414	1514	1614	1714	1714	1815	1914	1914	2014	2114	2214	...
Wien Meidling .... a.	...	...	...	0724	...	0824	0924	1024	1124	1224	1324	1424	1524	1624	1724	...	...	1924	...	2024	...	...	...

☆ – Bus 93 links Petržalka station with Bratislava hlavná every 5–10 minutes (journey time ±12 minutes). ☛ Many services run as through trains from / to Deutschkreutz (Table

998 UNZMARKT - TAMSWEG
2nd class only; Narrow g

km		Ⓐ		④B 🚂	Ⓒ 🚌	Ⓐ	②A 🚂		Ⓒ 🚌		Ⓐ	Ⓒ 🚌	Ⓐ		Ⓐ 🚌	Ⓒ		🚌
0	**Unzmarkt** .... d.	0719	0922	...	1118	1122	...	1322	1518	...	1522	1718	1722	1922	...	1922	...	2125
27	Murau-Stolzalpe .... d.	0800	1000	1015	1200	1200	1250	1400	1558	1600	1600	1800	1810	1957	2000	2000	...	2205
34	St Lorenzen .... d.	0811	1011	1035	1212	1211	1310	1411	...	1611	1611	1812	1821	...	2008s	2011	...	2213s
44	Stadl an der Mur .... d.	0825	1025	1105	1225	1225	1343	1425	...	1625	1625	1825	1835	...	2019s	2025	...	2224s
65	**Tamsweg** .... a.	0855	1055	1153	1252	1255	1431	1455	...	1655	1655	1852	1905	...	2040	2055	...	2245

	Ⓐ		Ⓐ	Ⓒ		Ⓐ	Ⓒ 🚌		Ⓒ 🚌	Ⓐ	④B 🚂		Ⓐ	②A 🚂		Ⓐ 🚌	🚌	Ⓒ 🚌
Tamsweg .... d.	...	...	0655	0705	...	0905	0910	1105	1310	1305	1335	1505	1505	1615	1710	1820	...	1910
Stadl an der Mur .... d.	...	...	0722	0732	...	0932	0930	1132	1330	1332	1425	1532	1532	1710	1738	1840	...	1930
St Lorenzen .... d.	...	...	0736	0746	...	0946	0945	1146	1345	1346	1446	1546	1546	1732	1752	1853	...	1945
Murau-Stolzalpe .... d.	0615	...	0800	0800	...	1000	1000	1200	1400	1400	1500	1558	1600	1745	1806	1905	2000	2000
Unzmarkt .... a.	0653	...	0837	0837	...	1037	1040	1237	1440	1437	...	...	1637	...	1840	...	2040	2040

A – June 28 - Sept. 6.
B – June 16 - Sept. 22.

s – Stops to set down only.

🚂 – Steam train. Special fares payable.

Operator: Steiermärkische Landesbahnen

999 Danube shipping: BUDAPEST - BRATISLAVA - WIEN - LINZ - PASSAU
2016 se

Hydrofoil services. 🍸	W [R]♠	E [R]♠	B [R]◇	Q ⊙	W [R]♠	P ⊙	W [R]♠	Y ⊙	T [R]♠
Wien Reichsbrücke ▲ .... d.	...	...	0900	0945	...	1600	...	1730	...
Wien Schwedenplatz ▲ .. d.	0830	0900	|	|	1230	|	1630	|	1800
Bratislava .... d.	0945	1015	|	1115	1345	1730	1745	1900	1915
Budapest § .... a.	...	...	1430	...	...	...	...	...	...

Hydrofoil services. 🍸	Z ⊙	W [R]♠	A [R]◇	W [R]♠	E [R]♠	R ⊙	S ⊙	W [R]♠
Budapest § .... d.	...	...	0900	...	...	...	...	...
Bratislava .... d.	0900	1030	|	1430	1600	1600	1730	1830
Wien Schwedenplatz .... a.	|	1200	|	1600	1730	|	|	2000
Wien Reichsbrücke ▲ .... a.	1045	...	1530	...	...	1745	1915	...

All sailings convey ✕	J ⊡	U ⊡	C ◐	⑦N ⊖	K ◐	⑦D ◐[R]	F ⊡	K ◐	K ◐
Wien Reichsbrücke ▲ .... d.	...	...	...	...	...	0830	...	...	...
Tulln .... d.	...	...	...	0900n	...	1120	...	...	...
Krems an der Donau ...... d.	0900	1010	1015	1150	1310	1400	1540	1545	...
Dürnstein .... d.	0930	1040	1050	1220	1340	1430	1610	1620	...
Spitz an der Donau .... d.	...	1140	1145	1315	1445r	...	1700	1720	1730
Melk .... a.	...	1300	1320	1450	1605	...	*1730**	...	1850
Grein .... d.	...	...	...	1820	...	...	...	...	...
Linz Lentos .... a.	...	...	...	2220	...	...	...	...	...

All sailings convey ✕	J ⊡	K ◐	U ⊡	C ◐	⑥N ⊖	⑦D ◐[R]	F ⊡	K ◐
Linz Lentos .... d.	...	...	...	...	0900	...	...	...
Grein .... d.	...	...	...	...	1200	...	...	...
Melk .... d.	...	1100	1345	1350	1440	...	...	1625
Spitz an der Donau .... d.	...	1200t	1435	1440	1520	...	1705	1710
Dürnstein .... d.	0930	1230	1505	1510	1600	1640	1730	...
Krems an der Donau .... d.	0950	1250	1530	1530	1620	1700	1755	...
Tulln .... d.	...	...	...	...	1820q	1900	...	...
Wien Reichsbrücke ▲ .... a.	...	...	...	...	2030q	2100	...	...

All sailings convey ✕	⊖H	⊖N		⊖M
Linz Lentos .... d.	...	...	...	1420
Schlögen .... d.	...	1425	...	1800
Obernzell .... d.	...	1615	...	1935
Passau Liegestelle 11 ▦ d.	1515	1715	...	2050
Deggendorf .... a.	2030	...	...	...

All sailings convey ✕	⊖L		⊖N	⊖G
Deggendorf .... d.	...	...	...	1000
Passau Liegestelle 11 ▦ d.	0900	...	1200	1400
Obernzell .... d.	0945	...	1245	...
Schlögen .... a.	1110	...	1410	...
Linz Lentos .... a.	1410	...	...	...

A – ②④⑥ May 10 - Sept. 29.
B – ③⑤⑦ May 11 - Sept. 30.
C – Apr. 16 - Oct. 26.
D – ⑦ May 22 - Sept. 11 (not June 12, 19, July 24).
E – Mar. 25 - Oct. 30.
F – May 1 - Oct. 4.
G – ④⑥ May 14 - Sept. 8 (not June 18, Aug. 13, 27).
H – ④ May 19 - Sept. 8 (not June 16, July 7).
J – July 1 - Aug. 31.
K – May 1 - Oct. 2.
L – ②–⑦ Apr. 29 - Oct. 2 (also Oct. 8, 15, 22).

M – ②③④⑥⑦ Apr. 30 - Oct. 2 (also Oct. 8, 15, 22; not May 26, June 15, 16, Aug. 11).
N – Apr. 30 - Oct. 3.
P – ⑤–⑦ Sept. 16 - Oct. 23.
Q – ③–⑦ Apr. 20 - June 19; daily June 22 - Aug. 28; ③–⑦ Aug. 31 - Sept. 25; ⑤–⑦ Sept. 30 - Oct. 23.
R – ③–⑦ Sept. 14 – 25; ⑤–⑦ Sept. 30 - Oct. 23.
S – ③–⑦ Apr. 20 - June 19; daily June 22 - Aug. 28; ③–⑦ Aug. 31 - Sept. 11.
T – ⑤⑥ May 6 - Sept. 3.
U – Apr. 18 - Oct. 26.
W – ⑤–⑦ Mar. 25 - Apr. 24 (also Mar. 28); daily Apr. 29 - Oct. 2; ⑤–⑦ Oct. 7 – 30 (also Oct. 26).
Y – ③–⑦ Apr. 20 - June 26; daily June 29 - Sept. 4 (also Sept. 9, 10, 11).
Z – ③–⑦ Apr. 20 - June 26; daily June 29 - Sept. 4; ⑤–⑦ Sept. 9 - Oct. 23.

n – Not June 19, Sept. 4.
q – Not June 18, Sept. 3.
r – Arrives 1435.
t – Arrives 1140.

* – By 🚌 from Spitz.
§ – Nemzetközi Hajóállomás (International shipping terminal).

▲ – DDSG operates Wien sightseeing cruises Schwedenplatz - Reichsbrücke and v.v. Daily Mar. 25 - Nov. 1.
From Schwedenplatz (duration 1 h 55 m via Schleuse Freud
at 1030, 1400 (also 1130, 1500 Mar. 25 – 28 and Apr. 16 - O
From Reichsbrücke (duration 1 h 20 m via Schleuse Nussd
at 1230, 1600 (also 1330, 1700 Mar. 25 – 28 and Apr. 16 - O

Operators:
⊡ – Brandner Schiffahrt GmbH, Ufer 50, A-3313 Wallsee. ✆ +43 (0) 7433 25 90 21, Fax +43 (0) 7433 25 90 25.
◐ – DDSG Blue Danube Schiffahrt GmbH, Handelskai 265, A-1020 Wien. ✆ +43 (0)1 588 80, Fax +43 (0)1 588 80 44
⊖ – Wurm und Köck, Höllgasse 26, D-94032 Passau. ✆ +49 (0) 851 92 92 92, Fax +49 (0) 851 355 18.
⊙ – SPaP - LOD – Slovenská Plavba a Prístavy - Lodná Osobná Doprava a.s., Fajnorovo nábrežie 2, 811 02 Bratislava. Reservation recommended. Check-in 15 minutes before depa Bratislava: ✆ +421 2 529 32 226, Fax +421 2 529 32 231
◇ – MAHART PassNave, H-1056 Budapest, Belgrád rakpart. Check-in 60 minutes before departure. Budapest: ✆ +36 1 484 4013, Fax +36 1 266 4201.
♠ – *Twin City Liner.* DDSG Blue Danube GmbH, Handelskai 265 A-1020 Wien. Check-in 30 minutes before departure. ✆ +43 (0)1 588 80. Internet booking: www.twincityliner.com

POLAND

…ators: Express services are operated by PKP Intercity www.intercity.pl. Most local trains are operated by Przewozy Regionalne (PR) www.przewozyregionalne.pl. Certain local services are operated by regional companies owned by local government: e.g. Koleje Dolnośląskie, Koleje Mazowieckie, Koleje Śląskie and Koleje Wielkopolskie.

…ces: **PKP InterCity**: Note reservation is compulsory (Ⓡ) on all services operated by PKP InterCity (*EC, EIC, EIP, EN, IC, MP, TLK*):

EC, EIC and *EIP* trains are fast premium-rate trains on long-distance routes (*EC* or *EuroCity* trains run on international routes) - first and second class seats, higher rate of fares apply and a supplement is payable for pass holders. *EC, EIC* and *EIP* trains normally convey ✕ or 🍸 for at least part of the route.

IC and *TLK* trains are lower-cost long distance trains with first and second class seats (also sleepers and couchettes on nights routes as shown in the tables). *TLK* is short for *Twoje Linie Kolejowe* (Your Railway Lines). Certain trains convey 🍸 but it is not possible to identify these in the tables.

MP is the classification (within Poland) for other international trains; *TLK* fares apply within Poland. Note that Russian/Ukrainian sleeping car services cannot be used for journeys in or between Poland and Germany unless seating cars are also conveyed. *EN* trains are *EuroNight* services with 'global' fares which include the sleeping accommodation. Descriptions of sleeping (🛏) and couchette (▬) cars appear on page 8.

Przewozy Regionalne and other local operators:

IR (InterRegio) and *RE* (*Regional Express*) trains are semi-fast trains operated by Przewozy Regionalne on longer distance routes, with second class seats. Fares are cheaper than *TLK* services but slightly higher than local *Regio* trains.

All other trains are local *R* (*Regio*) trains, second class only, calling at all or most stations en route. No train category is shown in our tables for these trains. They are operated by Przewozy Regionalne unless otherwise shown in the table heading or by a footnote. Fares on *Regio* trains are the cheapest available.

…ngs: Valid until **June 11, 2016** except where shown otherwise. However, alterations are possible at any time (particularly on and around public holidays) and readers are advised to check locally before travelling. Engineering work can often affect schedules; major changes are shown in the tables where possible but other changes may occur at short notice. A number of long-distance trains running only in high summer (particularly to coastal resorts) are not shown owing to lack of space. Note that train numbers often change en route by one or two digits. In station names, Gł. is short for Główny or Główna, meaning main station.

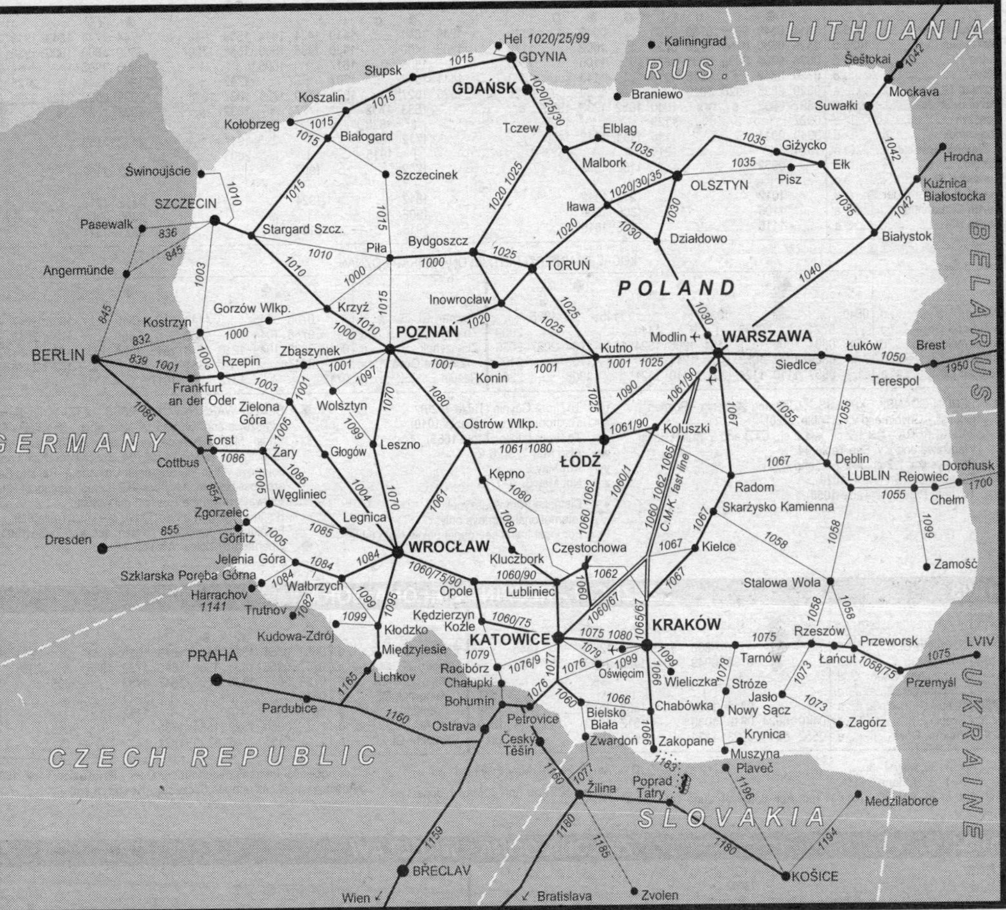

KOSTRZYN - KRZYŻ - POZNAŃ and BYDGOSZCZ 1000

…n		*TLK* 83104 Ry			z	*IC* 83100 Vy	*TLK* 81108 Sy									*TLK* 81102 W								*TLK* 80202 m	*TLK* 80202 Y
0	**Kostrzyn** d.	...	...	...	0531	...	...	0658	...	...	0900	1059	...	...	1352	...	...	1524	1604	...	...	1753	2110	...	...
3	Gorzów Wlkp. d.	...	...	...	0612	0700	...	0736	...	...	0941	1138	...	...	1435	1515	...	1604	1643	...	...	1834	2150	2210	2322
3	Krzyż **1010** d.	...	0504	...	0706	0809j	0812	0831	0839	1046	1059	1241	1334	...	1527	1613	...	1659	1736	1741	...	1926	2242	2258	0010
6	**Poznań** **1010** a.	...	|	...	0818	0913	|	...	|	|	1203	...	|	...	...	|	...	1802	...	|	...	...	...	...	...
3	Piła Gł. d.	0434	0554	0559	...	...	0911	...	0933	1142	...	...	1424	1455	...	1721	1809	...	...	1829	1937	...	...	...	...
8	**Bydgoszcz** a.	0544	...	0724	...	...	1022	...	...	*1319*	...	...	...	1620	...	1831	1936	...	...	...	2102	...	...	...	...

	TLK 88203 p	*TLK* 88203 Z						z	*TLK* 18103 W									*TLK* 18109 Sx	*TLK* 38101 Vx						*TLK* 38105 Rx
…goszcz d.	...	...	...	...	...	...	*0735*	...	1005	...	*1140*	...	...	...	...	...	1557	1747	...	...	1805	...	1947	...	2225
… Gł. d.	...	...	...	...	0740	...	0904	...	1145	...	1325	...	...	1543	1703	...	1721	1907	...	...	1929	1938	2112	2255	2334
…oznań **1010** d.	...	...	...	...	|	...	|	0855	|	1215	|	...	...	|	|	...	...	|	1855	1900	...	|	...	|	...
…ź **1010** d.	0416	0437	0511	0625	0833	0839	0957	1007	1232	1323	1417	1451	1606	1635	1756	1819	...	1955	2028t	2012	...	2031	...	2347	...
…zów Wlkp. d.	0509	0530	0610	0724	...	0940	...	1110	1331	1427	...	1551	1704	...	...	1920	...	...	2122	2122	...	...	...	...	...
…trzyn a.	...	...	0648	0802	...	1018	...	1147	...	1504	...	1629	1742	...	...	1957	...	...	...	2158	...	...	...	...	...

… To/from Rzeszów (Table **1058**).
… To/from Szczecin (Table **1010**).
… To/from Kraków (Table **1080**).

W – To/from Warszawa (Table **1001**/**1025**).
Y – Ⓑ (not May 1, 2, 3, 26, 27, 29).
Z – ①–⑥ (not Apr. 30, May 2, 3, 26-28).

j – Arrive 0750.
m – May 1, 3, 26, 27, 29.
p – Apr. 30, May 2, 26-28.
t – Arrive 2000.

x – Ⓑ (not May 2).
y – ①–⑥ (not May 3).
z – Not May 3, 26.

POLAND

1001 BERLIN - POZNAŃ - WARSZAWA

km		TLK	TLK	EIC	EIC	EIC	EN	EC	TLK	TLK	EIC	MP	EC	TLK	TLK		EC	EIC	TLK	TLK	EC	EIC	EC
		61201	71102	8106	7100	8102	447	41	83106	75102	8104	453	43	75106	81106		45	7102	77102	82100	55	8100	47
		61200	71103	8107	7101	8103	71010	71000	83107		8105		71002		81107		71004	7103		82101	75000	8101	71006
			①–⑥	z	①–⑥			①–⑥				⊗						Ⓑy					Ⓑ
		N	z		z		J▽	≋	P	g			≋	O			≋			u	G		≋
0	**Berlin** Hbf ⊖ d.	...	...	...	...	...	0637	0637	...	...	...	0713	0937	...	...	...	1237	...	...	...	1437	...	1637
5	**Berlin** Ostbahnhof ⊖ d.	...	...	...	...	...	0650	0650	...	...	...	|	0950	...	...	...	1250	...	...	...	1450	...	1650
87	Frankfurt an der Oder ▦ ⊖ d.	...	...	...	...	...	0745	0745	...	...	...	0855	1045	...	...	...	1345	...	...	...	1545	...	1745
98	Kunowice ▦ ⊖ d.	...	...	...	...	...	|	|	...	...	...	|	|	...	...	...	|	...	...	...	|	...	|
110	Rzepin ▷ d.	...	...	...	...	...	0808	0808	...	...	...	0919	1108	...	...	...	1408	...	...	...	1608	...	1808
•58	**Zielona Góra** ▷ d.	...	...	...	0557	...	|	|	...	0852	...	|	|	1239	...	...	|	...	1528	...	|	...	|
185	Zbąszynek ▷ d.	...	...	...	0648	...	0846	0846	...	0936	...	|	1146	1323	...	...	1446	...	1619	...	1646	...	1846
191	Zbąszyń ▷ d.	...	...	...	|	...	|	|	...	0942	...	|	|	1329	...	...	|	...	1625	...	|	...	|
266	**Poznań** Gł. ▷ a.	...	...	s	0730	s	0924	0924	s	1025	s	1040	1224	1419	s	...	1524	...	1714	s	1724	s	1924
266	**Poznań** Gł. d.	0332	0512	0640	0740	0842	0940	0940	0928	...	1042	1047	1240	...	1428	...	1541	1640	1732	1732	...	1844	1931
366	Konin d.	0443	0617	|	0828	|	1029	1029	1053	...	|	|	1329	...	1533	...	1629	1729	1836	1836	...	|	2021
445	Kutno **1025** d.	0534	0705	0810	|	|	1110	1110	1143	...	1211	|	1410	...	1619	...	1710	|	1924	1924	...	2013	2101
572	**Warszawa** Cent **1025** a.	0704	0815	0921	1017	1118	1215	1215	1327	...	1316	1335	1516	...	1729	...	1815	1915	2035	2035	...	2119	2210
577	**Warszawa** Wsch **1025** a.	0747	0831	0936	1031	1131	1236	1236	1351	...	1336	1346	1530	...	1740	...	1831	1930	2056	2056	...	2130	2224

	TLK	EC	EIC	TLK	TLK	EC	EC	TLK	TLK		EIC	EC	TLK	TLK	MP	EIC	EIC	EIC		EC	EN	EIC	TLK
	17100	46	1800	28100	70103	54	44	57107	18106		1702	42	57103	38106	452	1804	1700	1802		40	446	1806	17102
	17101	17000	1801	28101		57001	17002		18107		1703	17004		38107		1805	1701	1803		17006	17010	1807	17103
		①–⑥									Ⓑy				⊗		Ⓑy			Ⓑ		y	Ⓑy
		≋		u		G	≋	O				≋	g	P						≋	J▽		
Warszawa Wsch **1025** d.	0514	0549	0649	0709	0709	...	0949	...	1119	...	1249	1344	...	1419	1424	1444	1539	1649	...	1744	1744	1849	1919
Warszawa Cent **1025** d.	0525	0600	0700	0725	0725	...	1000	...	1130	...	1300	1400	...	1430	1435	1500	1558	1700	...	1800	1800	1900	1930
Kutno **1025** d.	0636	0704	0805	0835	0835	...	1106	...	1240	...	|	1505	...	1617	|	1605	|	|	...	1906	1906	|	2041
Konin d.	0720	0742	|	0918	0918	...	1145	...	1323	...	1441	1543	...	1707	|	|	1742	|	...	1944	1944	|	2125
Poznań Gł. a.	0820	0826	0926	1016	1016	...	1229	...	1425	...	1525	1627	...	1822	1720	1726	1827	1928	...	2029	2029	2125	2225
Poznań Gł. ▷ d.	0837	0832	s	s	1040	1032	1233	1335	s	...	...	1633	1732	s	1727	s	1832	s	...	2033	2033	s	...
Zbąszyń ▷ d.	0927	|	...	...	1129	|	|	1425	...	...	...	|	1820	...	|	...	|	...	...	|	|	...	...
Zbąszynek ▷ d.	0940	0911	...	...	1136	1111	1312	1436	...	...	...	1712	1828	...	|	...	1917	...	...	2112	2112	...	...
Zielona Góra ▷ a.	1024	|	...	...	1219	|	|	1523	...	...	...	|	1915	...	|	...	2003	...	...	|	|	...	...
Rzepin ▷ d.	...	0952	...	...	...	1152	1352	...	...	...	...	1752	...	...	1902	...	...	...	...	2152	2152	...	...
Kunowice ▦ ⊖ d.	...	|	...	...	...	|	|	...	...	...	...	|	...	...	|	...	...	...	...	|	|	...	...
Frankfurt an der Oder ▦ ⊖ d.	...	1012	...	...	...	1212	1412	...	...	...	...	1812	...	...	1924	...	...	...	...	2212	2212	...	...
Berlin Ostbahnhof ⊖ a.	...	1106	...	...	...	1306	1506	...	...	...	...	1906	...	...	|	...	...	...	...	2306	2306	...	...
Berlin Hbf ⊖ a.	...	1115	...	...	...	1315	1515	...	...	...	...	1915	...	...	2104	...	...	...	...	2321	2321	...	...

LOCAL TRAINS RZEPIN / ZIELONA GORA - POZNAŃ

			♣			♣			♣	⑥⑦ w	
Rzepin d.	0540	...	...	...	1039	...	...	1445	...	1925	...
Zielona Góra d.	|	0721	...	0938	|	...	1440	|	...	|	2009
Zbąszynek d.	0643	0804	1006	1027	1151	1206	1524	1548	1704	2027	2055
Zbąszyń d.	...	0809	1011	1033	...	1211	1530	...	1709	...	2100
Poznań Gł. a.	...	0857	1110	1124	...	1310	1621	...	1808	...	2201

			♣				♣			
Poznań Gł. d.	...	0706	0945	...	1149	...	1510	...	1638	1947
Zbąszyń d.	...	0758	1044	...	1239	...	1559	...	1738	2046
Zbąszynek d.	0610	0805	1049	1210	1246	1515	1604	1658	1744	2054
Zielona Góra a.	|	0847	...	|	1351	|	...	|	1827	2136
Rzepin a.	0712	...	...	1312	...	1617	...	1813	...	...

G – BERLIN GDANSK EXPRESS – (12) and ✕ Berlin - Poznań - Gdansk - Gdynia and v.v. (Table **1020**).
J – JAN KIEPURA – 🛏 1, 2 cl., 🛏 2 cl., (2) and 🍸 Köln - Berlin - Warszawa and v.v. See Table **54**.
N – Conveys 🛏 1, 2 cl., 🛏 2 cl. and (12).
O – To/from Olsztyn (Table **1020**).
P – To/from Przemyśl (Table **1058**).

g – To/from Gdynia (Table **1020**).
s – To/from Szczecin (Table **1010**).
u – To/from Lublin (Table **1055**).
w – Also May 2, 3, 26, 27.
y – Not May 2.
z – Not May 3.

• – Distance from Zbąszynek.
▽ – International journeys only.
▷ – For local trains see panel below main table.

≋ – BERLIN WARSZAWA EXPRESS – (12) ✕ Ⓡ, Berlin - Warszawa and v.v. Special fares apply. See Table 56
⊗ – Paris - Moskva service; for composition and days of running see Tables **24/56/94**. Special conditions apply. Journeys within the European Union (e.g. Paris to Berlin) are possible, but only bookable through agents of Russian Railways or via the Russian rail website.
⊖ – Berlin - Frankfurt an der Oder: see also Table **839**. Frankfurt an der Oder - Rzepin: see also Table **1003**.
♣ – Operated by Koleje Wielkopolskie.

1003 SZCZECIN - RZEPIN - ZIELONA GÓRA

km							C	D			
0	**Szczecin** Gł. d.	...	...	...	0806	...	1245	1257j	...	1545	...
104	Kostrzyn d.	...	...	0738	0949	...	1426	1439	...	1747	...
	Frankfurt/Oder d.	...	...	|	|	...	|	|	...	|	1820
	Kunowice ▦ d.	...	...	|	|	...	|	|	...	|	1831
136	Rzepin a.	...	...	0818	1029	...	1505	1518	...	1827	1839
136	Rzepin d.	0449	0634	0819	1030	...	1512	1519	...	...	1840
207	**Zielona Góra** a.	0552	0744	0923	1134	...	1623	1623	...	...	1945

			A	B					
Zielona Góra d.	0652	0754	1328	1405	1543	1628	1841	...	2231
Rzepin a.	0757	0856	1435	1508	1646	1732	1944	...	2336
Rzepin d.	0758	0857	1436	1509	1647	1733	...	2005	...
Kunowice ▦ d.	0806	|	|	|	|	1741	...	|	...
Frankfurt/Oder a.	0817	|	|	|	|	1752	...	|	...
Kostrzyn d.	...	0950	1529	1554	1736	...	...	2048	...
Szczecin Gł. a.	...	1133	1715	1729	1921	...	...	...	...

A – Apr. 3-30, May 4-30.
B – May 1-3, 31, June 2-11.
C – Apr. 3-24, Apr. 30 - June 11 (not Apr. 6, May 4, June 1).
D – Apr. 6, 25-29, May 4, June 1.
j – Depart 1239 on Apr. 6, May 4, June 1.

For additional trains Frankfurt an der Oder - Rzepin see Table 100
Additional services operate **Szczecin - Kostrzyn** and v.v.

1004 ZIELONA GÓRA - WROCŁAW

km				IC 73102 P							
0	**Zielona Góra** d.	0513	0645	0722	0829	1102	...	1557	1715	1936	...
23	Nowa Sól d.	0532	0704	0739	0848	1121	...	1616	1734	1955	...
54	Glogów d.	0613	0745	0813	0937	1210	...	1658	1815	2036	...
154	**Wrocław** Gł. a.	0809	0941	0958	1143	1408	...	1858	2017	2232	...
	Katowice **1075** a.	...	...	|	...	...	...	...	...	...	...
	Kraków **1075** a.	...	...	1349	...	...	...	...	...	...	...

	①–⑤ w	①–⑤ x	⑥⑦ m						IC 37103 P
Kraków **1075** d.	...	...	...	...	...	...	...	...	1442
Katowice **1075** d.	...	...	...	...	...	...	...	...	|
Wrocław Gł. d.	0527	0527	0709	0842	...	1255	1435	1700	1826
Glogów d.	0743	0809	0931	1101	...	1514	1700	1928	2034
Nowa Sól d.	0825	0850	1013	1143	...	1556	1742	2009	2110
Zielona Góra a.	0846	0911	1034	1204	...	1617	1803	2030	2128

P – To/from Przemyśl (Table **1075**).
k – Also May 1, 2, 25, 26.
m – Also May 2, 3, 26, 27.
w – Apr. 3-14, Apr. 30 - June 10.
x – Apr. 15 - May 25 (not May 2, 3).

1005 ZIELONA GÓRA - WEGLINIEC - JELENIA GÓRA

km		⊖	⊖		⊖	①–⑤ z	⊖ ①–⑤ z	⊖	⊖	①–⑤ z	⑥⑦ y
0	**Zielona Góra** d.	...	...	0735	...	1234	...	1533	...	1847	2147
54	Zary **1086** d.	...	...	0839	...	1332	...	1642	...	1946	2246
67	Żagań **1086** a.	...	...	|	...	1344	...	|	...	1958	2258
94	Wegliniec **1085** d.	0516	...	0944	...	...	1601	1739	...	...	...
118	Zgorzelec Miasto d.	0537	...	1000	...	...	1622	1800	...	...	...
	Görlitz **1085** d.	|	0740	|	1358	...	|	1807	1824	...	...
120	Zgorzelec **1085** d.	|	0744	|	1402	...	|	...	1828	...	...
144	Lubań Śląski d.	0609	0816	1029	1435	...	1700	...	1900	...	...
196	**Jelenia Góra** a.	0719	0919	1130	1537	...	1803	...	2003	...	...

		⊖	①–⑤ z	⊖ ①–⑤ z	⊖ ⑥⑦ y	⊖	⊖ ①–⑤ z	①–⑤ z	⑥⑦ y
Jelenia Góra d.	...	0552	...	0753	0753	1141	...	1331	1602
Lubań Śląski d.	...	0655	...	0902	0902	1244	...	1440	1704
Zgorzelec **1085** d.	...	0728	...	|	|	1318	...	|	|
Görlitz **1085** a.	...	0731	...	|	|	1321	...	|	|
Zgorzelec Miasto d.	...	...	...	0934	0934	...	...	1514	1736
Wegliniec **1085** d.	...	...	...	0955	1002	...	1324	1549	1805
Żagań **1086** d.	0506	...	0911	...	|	...	|	|	|
Zary **1086** d.	0518	...	0928	...	1054	...	1418	1640	1856
Zielona Góra a.	0616	...	1029	...	1152	...	1517	1737	1953

y – Also May 2, 3, 26, 27.
z – Not May 2, 3, 26, 27.
⊖ – Operated by Koleje Dolnośląskie.
☛ Local 🚌 service 'P' links Görlitz Bahnhof with Zgorzelec Miasto station every 30 mins (journey 22 mins).

SZCZECIN - POZNAŃ 1010

	EIC 8106	IC 84102	EIC 8102	TLK 81108	TLK 83106	EIC 8105 8104	EIC 8104	IC 8312	IC 8402		TLK 81106	IC 8310	IC 8400	TLK 82100		EIC 8100	IC 8120	IC 86102			IC 83200	TLK 83260	TLK 87201 87200
	①–⑥ y			①–⑥ y	P	C	D	A						U		Ⓑ	L	Ⓑ			NP	EZ	N
Świnoujście ... d.	...	...	...	...	...	0637	...	...	...	0815	...	...	...	...	1310d	...	...	...	...	...	...	...	2045
Szczecin Gł. ... 1015 d.	0404	0543	0606	0620	0648	0810	0810	0906	0950	1006	1135	1302	1351	1435	1509	1608	1702	1800	1810	...	1948	1958	2228
Szczecin Dąbie ... 1015 d.	0418	0557	0620	0635	0702	0824	0824	0920	1004	1020	1151	1316	1405	1451	1526	1622	1715	1814	1824	...	2005	2012	2243
Stargard Szczeciński ... 1015 d.	0438	0623	0637	0658	0719	0841	0841	0937	1023	1041	1211	1333	1423	1509	1548	1641	1732	1833	1845	...	2025	2032	2304
Krzyż ... 1000 d.	|	0723	0732	0812	0816	0933	0933	1027	1122	1152	1311	1424	1519	1609	1703	1732	1827	1932	2008	...	2133	2142	0041
Poznań Gł. ... 1000 a.	0628	0825	0832	|	0919	1032	1032	1124	1221	1300	1417	1522	1620	1713	1811	1830	1925	2033	2120	...	2239	2253	0154
Wrocław Gł. 1070 ... a.	|	1058	|	|	|	|	|	|	1440	...	|	|	1837	|	...	|	...	2315	...	...	|	|	...
Warszawa Cent. 1001 ... a.	0921	|	1118	1415	1327	1316	1316	|	|	...	1729	|	|	2035	...	2119	...	...	...	...	|	|	...
Katowice 1075 1080 ... a.	...	1345	...	...	...	...	...	|	1704	...	...	|	2121	...	...	...	...	...	...	...	0312	|	...
Kraków Gł 1075 1080 ... a.	...	...	...	...	...	...	...	1700	...	...	...	2056	...	...	...	...	...	...	...	...	0531	0422	...

	TLK 78201	IC 38261	IC 38201		IC 68103	IC 1821	EIC 1801	TLK 28101		IC 4803	IC 3811		TLK 18107	IC 4801	IC 3813		EIC 1805 1804	EIC 1805 1804	TLK 38107	TLK 18109	EIC 1803	IC 48103	EIC 1807	
	N	FZ	NP		①–⑥	L	①–⑥	U							A		A	B	P	Ⓑ x			Ⓑ x	
ów Gł. 1075 1080 ... d.	...	2224	2224	...	...	...	...	...	...	...	0702	...	...	...	1103	...	...	...	0821	...	...	...	...	...
wice 1075 1080 ... d.	...	0047	0047	...	...	...	...	...	...	0715	|	...	...	1101	|	...	...	...	|	...	...	1439j	...	...
zawa Cent. 1001 ... d.	...	|	|	...	...	...	0700	0725	...	|	|	...	1130	|	|	...	1500	1500	1430	1415	1700	|	1900	...
law Gł. 1070 ... d.	...	|	|	...	0532	...	|	|	...	0931	|	...	|	1321	|	...	|	|	|	|	|	1716	|	...
Gł. ... 1000 d.	0248	0601	0601	0652	0802	0845	0936	1040	...	1147	1243	1352	1441	1544	1637	1705	1736	1736	1832	|	1938	1959	2137	...
... 1000 d.	0413	0708	0708	0813	0905	0943	1034	1141	...	1249	1341	1502	1553	1649	1739	1814	1835	1835	1937	2011	2037	2104	|	...
d Szczeciński ... 1015 d.	0526	0807	0804	0924	1001	1033	1125	1236	...	1346	1432	1615	1655	1746	1829	1931	1927	1927	2040	2113	2136	2210	2329	...
n Dąbie ... 1015 d.	0545	0827	0824	0948	1019	1053	1143	1254	...	1404	1450	1640	1717	1804	1847	1956	1946	1951	2102	2132	2157	2231	2349	...
in Gł. ... 1015 a.	0601	0843	0841	1004	1035	1107	1159	1310	...	1419	1502	1657	1733	1819	1901	2010	1959	2006	2116	2146	2213	2247	0004	...
ujście ... a.	0757	1033	...	1153	...	...	...	...	...	...	...	1854b	...	...	...	2158	2131	...	...	...	...	...	...	...

	h	g	h	h			d			Ⓑ
Świnoujście ... d.	0444	0550	0605	0815	1000	...	1310	1540	1732	2012
Szczecin Dąbie ... a.	0612	0715	0735	0941	1126	...	1436	1706	1901	2138
Szczecin Gł. ... a.	0628	0730	0750	0956	1141	...	1452	1722	1916	2153

	h		h			d		Ⓑ		
Szczecin Gł. ... d.	0400	0538	0730	1010	...	1315	1535	1709	...	2015
Szczecin Dąbie ... d.	0414	0552	0746	1024	...	1329	1550	1725	...	2029
Świnoujście ... a.	0546	0719	0912	1155	...	1457	1720	1854	...	2200

									Ⓑ	
Szczecin Gł. ... d.	...	...	0818	...	1128	...	1500	...	1849	...
Szczecin Dąbie ... d.	...	...	0834	...	1144	...	1516	...	1904	...
Stargard Szczeciński .. d.	0458	...	0853	...	1204	...	1538	...	1933	...
Kalisz Pomorski ... d.	0601	...	0953	...	1307	...	1651	...	2057	...
Wałcz ... d.	0645	...	1035	...	1352	...	1735	...	2141	...
Piła Główna ... a.	0714	...	1103	...	1421	...	1804	...	...	...

	①–⑥								⑦z	
Piła Główna ... d.	...	...	0754	...	1319	...	1453	...	1904	...
Wałcz ... d.	0357	...	0822	...	1355	...	1522	...	1932	...
Kalisz Pomorski ... d.	0440	...	0905	...	1439	...	1604	...	2013	...
Stargard Szczeciński . d.	0555	...	1015	...	1545	...	1708	...	2119	...
Szczecin Dąbie ... d.	0618	...	1037	...	1610	...	1730	...	2143	...
Szczecin Gł. ... d.	0633	...	1053	...	1625	...	1745	...	2159	...

om Apr. 30.
r. 3 - 29.
om May 1.
r. 3 - 30.
⑥ Apr. 29 - June 4 (also May 1, 2, 25, 26).
⑦ Apr. 30 - June 5 (also May 2, 3, 26, 27).
/from Łódź (Tables **1025**).

N – Conveys 🛏 1, 2 cl., 🛏 2 cl. and (12).
P – To/from Przemyśl (Table **1075**).
U – To/from Lublin (Table **1055**).
Z – To/from Zakopane (Table **1066**).

b – Ⓑ only.
d – ①–⑥ (not May 3, 26).

g – ⑥⑦ (also May 3, 26).
h – ①–⑤ (not May 3, 26).
j – Depart 1345 until Apr. 12.
x – Not May 2.
y – Not May 3.
z – Runs 10 - 21 minutes earlier Apr. 10, May 8, 15.

SZCZECIN - KOSZALIN - GDYNIA - GDAŃSK 1015

	EIP 8300	TLK 81100	TLK 85102				TLK 81104	IC 48101 48100	TLK 80103		TLK 85100			IC 38103				TLK 85104	TLK 83202			IC 68107 68106		TLK 81200
	B t ①–⑥		G‡				E	V	⑥k		G			v ①–⑤	J				D	Ⓑ		W		y EN
Szczecin Gł. ... § d.	...	...	0639	0735	...	...	1045	...	...	1250	1412	...	...	1450	...	...	1635	1732	...	...	...	...	2030	2145
Szczecin Dąbie ... § d.	...	...	0654	0751	...	...	1059	...	...	1305	1426	...	...	1504	...	...	1650	1746	...	...	...	...	2044	2200
Stargard Szczeciński ... § d.	...	...	0711	0813	...	...	1118	...	...	1326	1445	...	...	1528	...	...	1713	1805	...	...	...	...	2118	2217
Poznań Gł. ... d.	...	...	|	|	0632	...	|	0953	...	|	|	...	1234	|	1413	1435	|	|	...	1630	...	1757	|	|
Piła Gł. ... d.	...	...	|	|	0832	...	|	1138	1201	|	|	...	1443	|	1551	1630	|	|	...	1833	...	1935	|	|
Szczecinek ... d.	...	...	|	|	0938	...	|	1231	1308	|	|	...	1552	|	1651	1745	|	|	...	1935	...	2029	|	|
Białogard ... a.	...	...	0828	0953	1038	...	1246	1328	1359	1452	1611	...	1652	1706	1753	1846	1841	1924	...	2037	...	2119	2238	2330
Białogard ... d.	...	...	0834	0954	1040	...	1249	1330	1402	1458	1615	...	1700	1707	1755	1847	1851	1928	...	2039	...	2120	2239	2331
Kołobrzeg ... a.	...	...	|	|	1116	...	|	|	1441	|	|	...	1735	|	1823	1922	|	|	...	|	...	|	|	|
Kołobrzeg ... d.	0547	0720	|	|	...	...	|	|	...	|	|	...	...	|	...	...	|	|	1937	|	...	|	|	|
Koszalin ... d.	0627	0801	0854	1014	...	...	1306	1345	...	1525	1635	...	...	1728	...	...	1913	1945	2025	2058	...	2137	2255	0002
Słupsk ... d.	0707	0845	0940	1110	...	...	1357	...	...	1612	1720	...	...	1816	...	...	2000	2029	2118	...	...	2221	...	0042
Lębork ... d.	0742	0928	1023	...	...	...	1429	...	...	...	1754	...	...	...	...	...	...	2120	2159	...	...	...	...	0115
Gdynia Gł. ... a.	0818	1021	1111	...	...	...	1515	...	...	...	1846	...	...	...	...	...	...	2208	2244	...	...	...	...	0155
Gdynia Gł. ... ▷ d.	0824	1039	1130	...	...	...	1533	...	...	...	1856	...	...	...	...	...	...	2210	2259	...	...	...	...	0218
Sopot ... ▷ a.	0833	1050	1140	...	...	...	1544	...	...	...	1905	...	...	...	...	...	...	2221	2310	...	...	...	...	0227
Gdańsk Gł. ... ▷ a.	0850	1106	1159	...	...	...	1601	...	...	...	1921	...	...	...	...	...	...	2237	2327	...	...	...	...	0241
Warszawa C. 1025/30 . a.	1150	1515	...	...	...	...	...	...	...	...	...	...	...	...	...	...	...	...	...	...	...	...	...	...

		TLK 18201		IC 86107 86106		TLK 58105		IC 83102	TLK 38203		TLK 58101		IC 84101 84100	TLK 88104	TLK 18105		TLK 18105			TLK 58103		TLK 18101		EIP 3801	
	①–⑥	z EN		W				J	D		G‡		V	⑦m	E		E			G				A Ⓑr	
szawa C. 1025/30 . d.	...	...	...	...	...	...	...	...	...	...	...	...	...	...	...	...	...	...	...	...	...	1300	...	1620	...
k Gł. ... ▷ d.	...	0218	...	...	...	0601	...	...	0629	...	0844	...	...	...	1158	...	...	...	...	1603	...	1700	...	1911	...
... ▷ d.	...	0236	...	...	...	0619	...	...	0645	...	0900	...	...	...	1214	...	...	...	...	1620	...	1717	...	1926	...
a Gł. ... ▷ a.	...	0245	...	...	...	0630	...	...	0655	...	0910	...	...	...	1223	...	...	...	...	1630	...	1726	...	1935	...
a Gł. ... d.	...	0316	...	...	...	0634	...	...	0724	...	0917	...	...	...	1242	...	...	...	...	1643	...	1739	...	1943	...
... d.	...	0358	...	...	...	0719	...	...	0824	...	1005	...	...	...	1332	...	...	...	...	1735	...	1829	...	2023	...
... d.	...	0438	0508	0542	...	0807	...	...	0904	...	1042	1226	...	...	1418	...	...	...	...	1820	1842	1903	2032	2055	...
lin ... d.	0500	0536	0559	0630	...	0853	...	...	0946	...	1127	1324	1423	...	1504	...	...	1552	...	1912	1944	2003	2139	2137	...
brzeg ... a.	|	|	|	|	...	|	...	...	1027	...	|	|	|	...	|	...	...	|	...	|	|	2049	|	2215	...
brzeg ... d.	|	|	|	|	0827	|	...	1007	...	...	|	|	|	1416	|	1445	...	|	...	|	|	...	|	...	...
ard ... a.	0515	0552	0618	0647	0904	0907	←	1038	...	...	1143	1346	1439	1446	1520	1521	←	1612	...	1926	2003	...	2158	...	...
ard ... d.	0521	0553	0629	0651	→	0909	0912	1040	...	...	1145	1404	1440	1457	→	1525	1528	1614	...	1928	2006	...	...	...	...
zecinek ... d.	0624	|	|	0743	...	|	1026	1134	...	...	|	|	1535	1552	...	1634	|	|	...	|	|	...	...	...	...
Gł. ... d.	0739	|	|	0840	...	|	1136	1243	...	...	|	|	1630	1658	...	1741	|	|	...	|	|	...	...	...	...
nań Gł. ... a.	0934	|	|	1021	...	|	1333	1425	...	...	|	|	1818	...	...	1927	|	|	...	|	|	...	...	...	...
rd Szczeciński ... § d.	...	0712	0810	...	...	1026	...	...	...	...	1308	1535	...	...	...	...	1648	1749	...	2050	2127	...	...	...	...
cin Dąbie ... § a.	...	0731	0832	...	...	1046	...	...	...	...	1327	1558	...	...	...	...	1710	1816	...	2110	2151	...	...	...	...
cin Gł. ... § a.	...	0745	0846	...	...	1102	...	...	...	...	1341	1613	...	...	...	...	1727	1832	...	2124	2205	...	...	...	...

rom Apr. 29.
rom Apr. 30.
🛏 1, 2 cl., 🛏 2 cl., (12) Kołobrzeg - Gdańsk - Kraków and v.v. (Table **1067**).
(12) Szczecin - Gdańsk - Białystok and v.v. (Table **1035**).
(12) Szczecin - Gdańsk - Olsztyn and v.v. (Table **1035**).
(12) Kraków - Katowice - Poznań - Kołobrzeg and v.v. (Table **1075**).
onveys 🛏 1, 2 cl., 🛏 2 cl. and (12).
o/from Katowice (Table **1075**).
o/from Wrocław (Table **1070**).

k – Also Apr. 29, May 1, 2, 25 - 27.
m – Also Apr. 30, May 2, 3, 26 - 28.
r – Not May 2.
t – Not May 3.
v – Not May 3, 26.
y – Apr. 28 - May 3, May 25 - 29.
z – Apr. 30 - May 5, May 27 - 31.

‡ – Subject to retiming ①–⑤ May 16 - 25, May 30 - June 7.

* – Distance from Białogard.
** – Distance from Koszalin.
§ – See also Table **1010**.
▷ – Frequent local trains runs between Gdynia and Gdansk.

1020 GDYNIA - GDAŃSK - BYDGOSZCZ - POZNAŃ

km		IC 5324 5325			TLK 57100 57101	TLK 5600 5601	EC 54 57000	TLK 5602 5603			TLK 57106 57107	TLK 5704 5705		IC 5606 5607			TLK 16114 16115	TLK 57102 57103		IC 5608 5609	TLK 57104 57105	IC 5700 5701	
			①–⑤		①–⑥																		
		R	v				B				Z						Y	Z					
	Hel d.	...	...	...	...	...	...	...	...	...	...	...	...	...	...	...	...	...	...	...	...	...	...
0	**Gdynia** Gł. ▷ d.	...	...	...	...	0552	0710	0753	...	...	...	0955	...	1152	...	...	...	1351	...	1538	...	1749	...
9	Sopot ▷ d.	...	...	...	...	0601	0719	0802	...	...	...	1004	...	1204	...	...	...	1402	...	1550	...	1758	...
21	**Gdańsk** Gł. ▷ d.	...	...	...	...	0624	0736	0821	...	...	...	1024	...	1224	...	...	...	1422	...	1609	...	1820	...
53	Tczew ▷ d.	...	...	...	...	0642	0753	0839	...	...	...	1042	...	1242	...	...	...	1440	...	1629	...	1838	...
181	**Bydgoszcz** Gł. ▷ a.	...	...	...	...	0750	0900	0951	...	...	...	1156	...	1351	...	...	...	1553	...	1737	...	1948	...
181	**Bydgoszcz** Gł. d.	0547	0553	...	...	0752	0903	0953	...	1042	...	1158	...	1354	1437	...	...	1555	...	1746	...	1950	...
•198	**Olsztyn** Gł. d.	|	|	...	0515	|	|	|	...	|	0924	|	...	|	|	...	1251	|	...	|	1721	|	...
•129	Iława d.	|	|	...	0608	|	|	|	...	|	1021	|	...	|	|	...	1347	|	...	|	1815	|	...
•35	**Toruń** Gł. d.	|	|	0643	0734	|	|	|	...	|	1142	|	1250	|	|	...	1513	|	1647	|	1939	|	...
227	Inowrocław d.	0614	0634	0722	0800	0820	0929	1021	...	1129	1206	1225	1325	1421	1518	...	1538	1622	1723	1814	2003	2018	...
283	Gniezno d.	0649	0723	0814	0839	0853	1000	1052	...	1216	1242	1259	1413	1453	1622	...	1616	1654	1811	1847	2043	2052	...
334	**Poznań** Gł. a.	0723	0814	0905	0910	0931	1027	1125	...	1309	1325	1330	1516	1534	1716	...	1652	1727	1912	1922	2120	2130	...
	Wrocław **1070** a.	...	...	...	...	1155	...	1346	...	...	...	...	...	1802	...	...	1928	...	...	2158	...	...	...

	TLK 65251 65250	IC 7500 7501	TLK 75104 75105		IC 6508 6509		TLK 75102 75103	TLK 61115 61114			IC 6507 6506		TLK 6505 6504	TLK 75106 75107	TLK 7503 7502	TLK 7503 7502	EC 55 75000		TLK 6501 6500	TLK 75100 75101		
	§								①–⑤													
	N						Z	Y	v					Z	D	E	B					
Wrocław **1070** d.	0005	...	...	...	0625	...	...	0812	...	...	1020	...	1225	...	...	...	...	...	1625	...	...	...
Poznań Gł. d.	0358	0633	0645	0750	0847	0951	1044	1053	1149	...	1245	1347	1449	1435	1635	1635	1730	1751	1843	1902	...	1951
Gniezno d.	0435	0702	0717	0838	0919	1047	1114	1124	1238	...	1313	1439	1517	1506	1703	1721	1758	1840	1911	1934	...	2042
Inowrocław d.	0509	0733	0753	0936	0949	1136	1145	1202	1332	...	1345	1528	1551	1557	1734	1752	1828	1932	1942	2010	...	2131
Toruń Gł. d.	|	|	0822	|	|	1210	|	1227	|	...	|	1602	|	1625	|	|	|	|	|	2034	...	2205
Iława d.	|	|	0943	|	|	...	|	1354	|	...	|	...	|	1748	|	|	|	|	|	2151	...	...
Olsztyn Gł. a.	|	|	1039	|	|	...	|	1452	|	...	|	...	|	1858	|	|	|	|	|	2253	...	...
Bydgoszcz Gł. a.	0537	0803	...	1030	1015	...	1210	...	1428	...	1414	...	1620	...	1800	1818	1853	2027	2011	...	...	...
Bydgoszcz Gł. ▷ d.	0544	0803	...	...	1018	...	1213	...	...	...	1414	...	1621	...	1803	1821	1856	...	2011	...	...	...
Tczew ▷ d.	0706	0914	...	...	1128	...	1323	...	...	...	1527	...	1733	...	1913	1931	2002	...	2122	...	...	...
Gdańsk Gł. ▷ a.	0726	0934	...	...	1144	...	1340	...	...	...	1544	...	1752	...	1930	1948	2018	...	2139	...	...	...
Sopot ▷ a.	0749	0953	...	...	1203	...	1401	...	...	...	1608	...	1812	...	1954	2006	2036	...	2157	...	...	...
Gdynia Gł. ▷ a.	0758	1002	...	...	1213	...	1415	...	...	...	1619	...	1820	...	2002	2014	2044	...	2206	...	...	...
Hel a.	...	...	...	...	...	...	...	...	...	...	...	...	...	...	...	...	...	...	...	...	...	...

B – (12) and ✕ Gdynia - Poznań - Berlin and v.v. (Table **1001**).
D – Apr. 3 - 21.
E – Apr. 22 - June 11.
N – Conveys 🛏 1, 2 cl., 🛏 2 cl. and (2).
R – To / from Kraków (Tables **1025/62**).

Y – To / from Białystok (Table **1035**).
Z – To / from Zielona Góra (Table **1001**).
v – Not May 3, 26.
z – Not May 3.

§ – Train number varies on some days / dates: 5625(as 57200/1; 65251/0 runs as 75200/1.
• – Distance from Inowrocław.
▷ – See also Table **1025**. Frequent local services ru between Gdynia and Gdansk (see Table **1035**).

1025 GDYNIA - GDAŃSK - BYDGOSZCZ - WARSZAWA / ŁODŹ

km		IC 5110 5111	IC 5325 5324	TLK 83104 83105	IC 54102 54103	TLK 51112	IC 5112 5113		TLK 81108 81109	IC 8312 8313	IC 54106 54107	IC 5114 5115		TLK 53106 53107	IC 54108 54109	IC 8310 8311	IC 5116 5117		TLK 81102 81103	IC 8120 8121	IC 51116	
						①–⑥																
				R		y			S	S				P		S			G	S	m	
	Hel d.	...	...	...	...	...	...	...	...	...	...	...	...	...	...	...	...	...	...	...	...	...
0	**Gdynia** Gł. ▷ d.	...	...	...	0505	...	...	...	...	...	0850	...	...	...	1301	...	...	...	...	...	1652	...
9	Sopot ▷ d.	...	...	...	0514	...	...	...	...	...	0901	...	...	...	1310	...	...	...	...	...	1702	...
21	**Gdańsk** Gł. ▷ d.	...	...	...	0531	...	...	...	...	...	0918	...	...	...	1329	...	...	...	...	...	1723	...
53	Tczew ▷ d.	...	...	...	0552	...	...	...	...	...	0938	...	...	...	1349	...	...	...	...	...	1746	...
181	**Bydgoszcz** Gł. ▷ a.	...	...	...	0701	...	...	...	...	...	1049	...	...	...	1500	...	...	...	...	...	1910	...
181	**Bydgoszcz** Gł. d.	0518	0547	0612	0713	0725	0840	...	1037	...	1105	1232	...	1408	1512	...	1634	...	1834	...	1923	...
	Inowrocław d.	|	0614	|	|	0755	|	...	|	...	|	|	...	|	|	...	|	...	|	...	|	...
232	**Toruń** Gł. d.	0558	|	0655	0754	|	0920	...	1128	...	1146	1315	...	1452	1553	...	1715	...	1917	...	2005	...
287	Włocławek d.	0636	|	0736	0833	|	1000	...	1213	...	1227	1354	...	1537	1632	...	1754	...	1959	...	2043	...
	Poznan Gł d.	|	0733	|	|	|	|	...	|	1134	|	|	...	|	|	1535	|	...	|	1937	|	...
	Konin d.	|	0834	|	|	|	|	...	|	1222	|	|	...	|	|	1624	|	...	|	2036	|	...
342	Kutno d.	0714	0916	0819	0919	0924	1039	...	1253	1314	1317	1432	...	1622	1722	1716	1831	...	2038	2119	2122	...
469	**Warszawa** Centralna a.	0823	|	0938	|	1045	1149	...	1415	|	|	1540	...	1730	|	|	1939	...	2200	|	2245	...
474	**Warszawa** Wschodnia a.	0836	|	0956	|	1101	1206	...	1435	|	|	1550	...	1800	|	|	1951	...	2211	|	2256	...
410	**Łódź** Kaliska a.	...	|	...	1033	...	...	...	...	|	1439	...	...	...	1837	|	...	...	...	2246	...	...
	Częstochowa **1060/62** a.	...	|	...	|	...	...	...	...	|	|	...	...	...	|	|	...	...	...	...	...	...
	Katowice **1060** a.	...	|	...	1333	...	...	...	...	|	1740	...	...	...	2143	|	...	...	...	...	...	...
	Kraków **1062/65** a.	...	1256	...	...	...	...	...	...	1700	...	...	...	...	...	2056	...	...	...	...	...	...
	Zakopane **1066** a.	...	...	...	...	...	...	...	...	...	...	...	...	...	...	...	...	...	...	...	...	...

	TLK 45203		IC 1820 1821	IC 15117	TLK 18102 18103	IC 1516 1517	IC 3810 3811	IC 45108 45109	TLK 35106 35107		IC 1514 1515	IC 45106 45107	IC 3812 3813	TLK 18108 18109	IC 1512 1513	TLK 15112 15113		IC 3524 3525	IC 45102 45103	TLK 38104 38105		IC 1510 1511
																Ⓑ x						
	B		S	n	G		S		P				S n	S						R		
Zakopane **1066** d.	...	...	...	...	...	...	...	...	...	...	...	...	...	...	...	...	...	...	...	...	...	...
Kraków **1062/65** d.	...	...	...	...	...	...	0702	...	...	...	...	...	1103	...	...	...	...	1504	...	...	...	...
Katowice **1060** d.	2304	...	...	...	...	...	|	0639	...	...	...	1033	|	...	...	...	...	|	1443	...	...	...
Częstochowa **1060/62** d.	|	...	...	...	...	...	|	|	...	...	...	|	|	...	...	...	...	|	|	...	...	...
Łódź Kaliska d.	0237	...	0529	...	...	...	|	0939	...	...	...	1328	|	...	...	...	...	|	1739	...	...	...
Warszawa Wschodnia d.	|	...	|	0519	0619	0814	|	|	1009	...	1214	|	|	1404	1614	1714	...	|	|	1819	...	2014
Warszawa Centralna d.	|	...	|	0530	0630	0825	|	|	1025	...	1225	|	|	1415	1625	1725	...	|	|	1830	...	2030
Kutno d.	0343	...	0656	0707	0757	0933	1100	1103	1149	...	1332	1443	1459	1537	1734	1846	...	1901	1849	1957	...	2138
Konin d.	|	...	0736	|	|	|	1139	|	|	...	|	|	1538	|	|	|	...	1939	|	|	...	|
Poznan Gł a.	|	...	0833	|	|	|	1224	|	|	...	|	|	1622	|	|	|	...	2045	|	|	...	|
Włocławek d.	0424	...	...	0745	0837	1012	...	1142	1231	...	1411	1523	...	1618	1814	|	...	|	1927	2036	...	2217
Toruń Gł. d.	0510	...	...	0827	0920	1053	...	1223	1315	...	1452	1609	...	1704	1858	|	...	|	2012	2119	...	2301
Inowrocław d.	|	...	...	|	|	|	...	|	|	...	|	|	...	|	|	2014	...	2147	|	|	...	|
Bydgoszcz Gł a.	0546	...	...	0907	1011	1132	...	1300	1358	...	1531	1648	...	1744	1937	2043	...	2212	2051	2159	...	2342
Bydgoszcz Gł. ▷ d.	0601	...	...	0928	...	...	...	1312	...	...	...	1700	...	...	...	...	...	...	2107	...	...	...
Tczew ▷ d.	0722	...	...	1052	...	...	...	1424	...	...	...	1821	...	...	...	...	...	...	2219	...	...	...
Gdańsk Gł. ▷ a.	0742	...	...	1112	...	...	...	1444	...	...	...	1841	...	...	...	...	...	...	2238	...	...	...
Sopot ▷ a.	0801	...	...	1133	...	...	...	1502	...	...	...	1901	...	...	...	...	...	...	2256	...	...	...
Gdynia Gł. ▷ a.	0811	...	...	1141	...	...	...	1512	...	...	...	1909	...	...	...	...	...	...	2304	...	...	...
Hel a.	...	...	...	...	...	...	...	...	...	...	...	...	...	...	...	...	...	...	...	...	...	...

B – 🛏 1, 2 cl., 🛏 2 cl., (2) Szczecin - Gdynia - Katowice - Bielsko Biała and v.v.
G – To / from Gorzów Wlkp (Table **1000**).
P – To / from Przemyśl (Table **1058**).
R – (12) Rzeszów (Table **1058**) - Warszawa (- Piła) and v.v. (Table **1000**).

S – To / from Szczecin (Table **1010**).
m – From Apr. 29.
n – From Apr. 30.
x – Not May 2.
y – Not May 3.

▷ – See also Table **1020**. Frequent local se run between Gdynia and Gdansk.
△ – Operated by Arriva.

GDYNIA - GDAŃSK - (OLSZTYN -) WARSZAWA 1030

Subject to alteration from May 27; many trains are retimed and use Warszawa Gdańska station instead of Warszawa Centralna and Wschodnia

	EIP	IC	TLK	EIP	TLK	EIP	EIC	EIP	IC	EC	IC	EIP	TLK	EIP		EIP	EIP	IC	EIP	EIP	EIP	TLK	EIP	EIP	IC	IC	TLK
	5300	5326	51108	5400	5420	5302	5322	8300	5328	105	5330	5306	81100	5402		5308	5404	5210	5310	5106	5312	51106	5102	5100	5120	51100	83202
	5301	5327	51109	5401	5421	5303	5323	8301	5329	54000	5331	5307	81101	5403		5309	5405	5211	5311		5313	51107	5103	5101	5121	51101	83203
	①–⑥	①–⑥	①–⑥					§										§			§						
		y	y	B						S				B													D
Kołobrzeg **1015** d.	...	...	...	...	...	...	...	0547b	...	...	...	...	0720	...	...	...	...	...	...	...	...	...	...	...	...	...	1937
Gdynia Gł. ▶ d.	0428	...	0434	0533	...	0624	0720	0824	...	0924	...	1025	1031	1124	...	1225	1325	...	1425	1523	1625	1636	1733	1825	...	1925	2259
Sopot ▶ d.	0438	...	0444	0542	...	0633	0728	0833	...	0933	...	1034	1041	1133	...	1234	1335	...	1436	1534	1635	1646	1742	1834	...	1934	2310
Gdańsk Gł. ▶ d.	0456	...	0502	0600	...	0651	0746	0853	...	0951	...	1054	1108	1153	...	1254	1355	...	1455	1553	1654	1707	1802	1854	...	1951	2332
Tczew ▶ d.	0513	...	0527	|	...	0708	0804	|	...	1007	...	1111	1130	|	...	1311	1412	...	1512	|	|	1728	1819	1911	...	2009	2355
Malbork ▶ d.	0525	...	0542	|	...	0721	0816	0920	...	1019	...	1123	1148	1220	...	1323	1424	...	1524	1620	|	1742	|	1923	...	2021	0010
Olsztyn ▶ d.	|	0541	|	|	0731	|	|	|	0943	|	1341	|	|	|	...	|	|	1742	|	|	|	|	|	|	1929	|	|
Iława Gł. ▶ d.	0558	|	0633	0657	|	0755	|	0954	|	1054	|	1156	1237	|	...	1356	1457	|	1557	1652	1753	1829	1902	1956	2022	2058	0054
Działdowo d.	|	0645	0709	|	0843	|	0922	|	1045	|	1444	|	1328	1322	...	|	|	1845	|	1724	|	1906	|	|	2053	2131	|
Ciechanów d.	|	0710	0758	|	0914	|	|	1047	1110	|	1509	|	1401	1345	...	|	|	1911	|	|	|	1941	1954	|	2116	2155	0202
Modlin ✈ d.	|	0739	0834	|	0947	|	|	|	1139	|	1538	|	1435	|	...	|	|	1939	|	|	|	2030	|	|	|	|	|
Warszawa Wschodnia a.	0736	0802	0906	0832	1016	0932	1032	1132	1202	1232	1601	1332	1507	1432	...	1532	1632	2002	1732	1832	1928	2102	2039	2132	2202	2246	0300
Warszawa Centralna a.	0745	0810	0915	0840	1040	0940	1045	1140	1210	1240	1610	1340	1515	1440	...	1540	1640	2010	1740	1840	1935	2110	2046	2140	2210	2255	|
Katowice **1060** a.	|	|	...	1116	1327	|	|	|	|	1521	|	|	...	1712	...	|	1913	...	|	...	|	...	...	...	...	...	|
Kraków Gł. **1065** a.	1014	1231	...	...	...	1211	1328	1414	1631	...	2027	1611	...	...	...	1807	...	...	2010	...	2215	...	...	...	...	...	0804
Zakopane **1066** a.	...	...	...	...	...	...	...	...	...	...	...	...	...	...	...	...	...	...	...	...	...	...	...	...	...	...	...

	TLK	IC	IC	EIP	TLK	EIP	IC	EIP	EIP	EIP	EIP	IC	EIP	TLK	EIP	EIP	EC	IC	EIP	EIC	TLK		EIP	TLK	EIP	IC	EIP
	38202	15100	1520	1500	15106	1502	2510	3500	4502	3502	4500	3530	3504	18100	4504	3506	104	3528	3800	3522	4520		3510	15108	4506	3526	3512
	38203	15101	1521	1501	15107	1503	2511	3501	4503	3503	4501	3531	3505	18101	4505	3507	45001	3529	3801	3523	4521		3511	15109	4507	3527	3513
							§	①–⑥		§									§					Ⓑ		Ⓑ	Ⓑ
	D								B		B						S							x	B	x	
Zakopane **1066** d.	...	...	...	...	...	...	...	...	...	...	...	...	...	...	...	...	...	...	...	...	...	...	...	...	...	...	...
Kraków Gł. **1065** d.	2124	...	...	...	...	...	...	0541	...	0747	...	0721	0940	...	...	1135	...	1125	1338	1433	...	...	1539	...	...	1515	1745
Katowice **1060** d.	|	...	...	...	...	...	...	|	0648	|	0843	|	|	...	1043	|	1242	|	|	|	1413	...	|	...	1637	|	|
Warszawa Centralna d.	|	0520	0550	0620	0655	0720	0755	0820	0920	1020	1120	1155	1220	1300	1320	1420	1520	1555	1620	1720	1725	...	1820	1855	1920	1955	2020
Warszawa Wschodnia d.	0244	0528	0558	0628	0705	0728	0805	0828	0928	1028	1128	1205	1228	1308	1328	1428	1528	1603	1630	1728	1744	...	1828	1908	1928	2005	2028
Modlin ✈ d.	|	|	|	|	0738	|	0830	|	|	|	|	1230	|	1341	|	|	|	1630	|	|	1812	...	|	1940	|	2030	|
Ciechanów d.	0344	0616	0644	|	0827	0814	0859	|	|	|	|	1257	|	1426	1413	|	|	1658	1715	|	1844	...	|	2024	|	2057	|
Działdowo d.	|	0641	0708	|	0902	|	0925	|	1034	|	|	1323	|	1459	1437	|	|	1724	|	1836	1917	...	|	2058	|	2123	|
Iława Gł. ▶ d.	0450	0715	0741	0803	0939	0906	|	1006	1106	1203	1303	|	1403	1536	|	1606	1706	|	1808	|	|	...	2003	2135	2103	|	2203
Olsztyn ▶ a.	|	|	0836	|	|	|	1031	|	|	|	|	1430	|	|	|	|	|	1830	|	|	2022	...	|	|	|	2225	|
Malbork ▶ d.	0530	0750	...	0837	1025	|	...	|	1140	1237	1337	...	1437	1623	1541	1640	1740	...	1842	1941	...	...	2037	2222	|	...	2237
Tczew ▶ d.	0552	0804	...	0850	1040	0950	...	|	|	1250	1350	...	1450	1637	|	1652	1752	...	|	1954	...	...	2050	2237	|	...	2249
Gdańsk Gł. ▶ a.	0619	0822	...	0907	1100	1006	...	1104	1207	1306	1406	...	1506	1657	1607	1709	1808	...	1908	2010	...	...	2106	2300	2201	...	2306
Sopot ▶ a.	0645	0840	...	0927	1120	1026	...	1126	1227	1326	1426	...	1526	1717	1627	1729	1826	...	1927	2027	...	...	2125	2319	2220	...	2325
Gdynia Gł. ▶ a.	0655	0848	...	0936	1129	1038	...	1138	1237	1337	1436	...	1536	1726	1637	1738	1834	...	1935	2035	...	...	2133	2328	2228	...	2335
Kołobrzeg **1015** a.	1027	...	...	...	...	...	...	...	...	...	...	...	...	2049	...	...	...	...	2215a	...	...	...	...	...	...	...	...

To / from Bielsko Biała (Table **1060**).
1, 2 cl., 2 cl., (2) Kołobrzeg - Gdańsk - Kraków and v.v. (Table **1015**).
SOBIESKI – (12) and ✕ Gdynia - Warszawa - Wien and v.v.

a – Ⓑ (not May 2).
b – ①–⑥ (not May 3).
x – Not May 2.
y – Not May 3.
§ – Train number varies on some days / dates: 2510/1 runs as 1518/9; 3502/3 runs as 3550/1; 3800/1 runs as 3508/9; 5210/1 runs as 5118/9; 5312/3 runs as 5350/1; 8300/1 runs as 5304/5.

▶ – For additional trains Gdynia - Gdansk - Iława (- Olsztyn) see Table **1035**. Frequent local trains run between Gdynia and Gdańsk operated by *SKM* (every 10 - 30 minutes).

• – Olsztyn - Działdowo: *84 km*.

GDYNIA - GDAŃSK - EŁBLAG - OLSZTYN - BIAŁYSTOK 1035

km		TLK		TLK	TLK	TLK	TLK		TLK		TLK	
		81200		51104	85102	61115	85102		81104		85100	
		81201		51105	85103	61114	85103		81105		85101	
		y			p	W	q					
	Szczecin Gł. **1015** d.	2145	...	...	0639	...	0639	...	1045	...	1412	...
0	**Gdynia** Gł. ▶ d.	0218	0542	0759	1126	...	1205	1415	1533	1742	1856	2047
9	Sopot ▶ d.	0227	0551	0808	1138	...	1214	1427	1544	1751	1905	2057
21	**Gdańsk** Gł. ▶ d.	0246	0605	0827	1204	...	1232	1443	1612	1807	1927	2114
53	Tczew ▶ d.	0307	0637	0850	1230	...	1255	1519	1633	1844	1948	2148
72	Malbork ▶ d.	0321	0656	0904	1245	...	1309	1545	1647	1903	2003	2207
01	**Ełblag** d.	0344	0721	0926	1309	...	1330	1614	1707	1930	2025	2233
	Iława Gł. ▶ a.	|	...	|	|	...	|	...	|	...	|	...
	Iława Gł. d.	|	...	|	|	...	|	...	|	...	|	...
00	**Olsztyn** a.	0508	...	1053	1444	...	1508	...	1841	...	2204	...
00	**Olsztyn** d.	0559	...	1114	...	1459	...	...	1903	...	...	...
19	Giżycko d.	0801	...	1248	...	1641	...	...	2042	...	...	...
66	Ełk a.	0840	...	1326	...	1720	...	...	2121	...	...	...
66	Ełk d.	0841	...	1338	...	1722	...	...	2123	...	...	...
70	**Białystok** a.	1006	...	1452	...	1838	...	...	2236	...	...	...

		TLK	TLK		TLK	TLK		TLK		TLK
		58101	18104		16115	58103		15104		18200
		58100	18105		16114	58102		15105		18201
					W					z
Białystok d.	...	...	0542	...	0855	...	...	1305	...	1957
Ełk a.	...	...	0700	...	1012	...	...	1429	...	2119
Ełk d.	...	...	0701	...	1016	...	...	1441	...	2123
Giżycko d.	...	...	0741	...	1057	...	...	1525	...	2203
Olsztyn a.	...	...	0913	...	1231	...	...	1700	...	2338
Olsztyn d.	...	0611	0931	...	...	1324	...	1727	...	2353
Iława Gł. a.	...	|	|	...	...	|	...	|	...	|
Iława Gł. ▶ d.	...	|	|	...	...	|	...	|	...	|
Ełblag d.	0624	0741	1056	1143	...	1455	1545	1853	1937	0116
Malbork ▶ d.	0652	0807	1119	1210	...	1518	1612	1916	2004	0137
Tczew ▶ d.	0712	0821	1133	1229	...	1534	1641	1930	2024	0152
Gdańsk Gł. ▶ a.	0737	0841	1153	1301	...	1553	1712	1959	2058	0212
Sopot ▶ a.	0755	0900	1214	1318	...	1620	1730	2019	2127	0236
Gdynia Gł. ▶ a.	0805	0910	1223	1328	...	1630	1740	2027	2140	0245
Szczecin Gł. **1015** a.	...	1341j	1727	...	...	2124	...	...	...	0747

LOCAL SERVICES OLSZTYN - EŁK - BIAŁYSTOK

km									Ⓑ	Ⓑ		
0	**Olsztyn** d.	...	0828	0856	...	1333	...	1608	...	1732	...	2036
45	Szczytno d.	...	0908	|	...	|	...	|	...	1818	...	|
02	Pisz d.	...	1024	|	...	|	...	|	...	1934	...	|
	Giżycko d.	...	|	1058	...	1524	...	1809	...	|	...	2234
57	Ełk d.	0540	1203	1141	1450	1607	...	1853	1910	2114	...	2316
61	**Białystok** a.	0724	...	...	1629	...	...	...	2052	...	...	...

					Ⓑ					Ⓑ
Białystok d.	...	...	...	...	...	1045	...	1502	...	1718
Ełk d.	0335	0457	0717	...	1205	1219	1231	1638	1644	1858
Giżycko d.	|	0541	0800	...	|	...	1322	...	1736	...
Pisz d.	0517	|	|	...	1346	...	|	...	|	...
Szczytno d.	0633	|	|	...	1503	...	|	...	|	...
Olsztyn a.	0712	0738	0951	...	1543	...	1511	...	1924	...

Conveys 1, 2 cl., 2 cl. and (12).
To / from Wrocław (Table **1020**).
Arrive 1435 on ①–⑤ May 16 - June 7 (not May 26, 27).
Not on dates in note **q**.

q – ①–⑤ May 16 - 25, May 30 - June 7.
y – Apr. 28 - May 3, May 25 - 29.
z – Apr. 29 - May 4, May 26 - 30.

▶ – For additional trains Gdynia - Gdansk - Iława (- Warszawa) see Table **1030**. Frequent local trains run between Gdynia and Gdańsk operated by *SKM* (every 10 - 30 minutes).

* – *210 km* via Iława.

WARSZAWA - BIAŁYSTOK 1040

Subject to alteration from May 27; trains use Warszawa Gdańska station instead of Warszawa Centralna and Wschodnia (services may be retimed)

km		IC	TLK	IC	TLK	IC	TLK	IC	IC	IC
		10100	31010	10106	41108	10104	10108	61104	31112	61102
		10101		10107	41109	10105	10109	61105	31113	61103
		x	H		B		S	R	K	J
0	**Warszawa** Cent. d.	0605	0736	1005	1205	1402	1505	1610	1804	2015
5	**Warszawa** Wsch. d.	0614	0744	1014	1214	1414	1514	1618	1814	2023
95	Małkinia d.	0738	0912	1131	1333	1531	1639	1739	1932	2142
84	**Białystok** a.	0835	1010	1228	1430	1629	1739	1837	2030	2240

	IC	TLK	IC	IC	IC	IC	IC	TLK	IC
	16102	10118	13112	16104	10114	14108	10116	13010	10110
	16103	10119	13113	16105	10115	14109	10117		10111
	J	U	K	R		B		H	y
Białystok d.	0516	0654	0758	0932	1134	1331	1525	1750	2000
Małkinia d.	0615	0755	0856	1031	1233	1429	1625	1851	2100
Warszawa Wsch. a.	0731	0912	1011	1147	1347	1545	1747	2008	2215
Warszawa Cent. a.	0740	0920	1020	1155	1355	1553	1755	2016	2225

To / from Bielsko Biała (Table **1060**).
HAŃCZA – (12) Kraków - Warszawa - Białystok - Suwałki and v.v. (Table **1042**).
To / from Jelenia Góra (Table **1084**).
To / from Kraków (Table **1065**).

R – To / from Wrocław (Table **1061**).
S – Ⓑ (not May 2): (12) Warszawa - Suwałki (Table **1042**).
U – ①–⑥ (not May 3): (12) Suwałki - Warszawa (Table **1042**).

x – ①–⑥ (not May 3).
y – Ⓑ (not May 2).

1042 (WARSZAWA) - BIAŁYSTOK - VILNIUS and HRODNA

PKP, BCh

km			IR 192	TLK 31010				TLK 10108	IR 194	
		①-⑤	W•	H	Ⓑ			S	•	Ⓑ
0	*Warszawa Cent.* **1040** d.	...	0635	0736	...	...	...	1505	1700	...
5	*Warszawa Wsch.* **1040** d.	...	0653	0744	...	...	...	1514	1712	...
184	**Białystok** d.	0638	0956	1022	1400	1506	1638	1754	2005	2038
225	Sokółka d.	0725	1040	1100	1443	1546	1727	1832	2042	2118
324	**Suwałki** a.	0853	|	1215	|	1725	|	1954	|	2248
	Mockava 🏛 ◐ § a.	...	|	...	|	...	|	...	|	...
377	Šeštokai § a.	...	|	...	|	...	|	...	|	...
471	**Kaunas** 1811 § a.	...	|	...	|	...	|	...	|	...
575	**Vilnius** 1811 § a.	...	|	...	|	...	|	...	|	...
241	Kuźnica Białostocka 🏛 a.	...	1056	...	1500	...	1744	...	2058	...
241	Kuźnica Białostocka 🏛 d.	...	1156	...	...	...	...	...	2213	...
268	**Hrodna** 🏛 ‡ a.	...	1439	...	...	...	...	...	0056	...

		TLK 10119		IR 191			TLK 13010	IR 193
		U	①-⑥	W•	①-⑤	Ⓑ	H	•
Hrodna 🏛 ‡ d.	...	...	...	0706	...	...	...	1700
Kuźnica Białostocka 🏛 a.	...	...	...	0549	...	...	...	1543
Kuźnica Białostocka 🏛 d.	0515	...	...	0709	...	1511	...	1711
Vilnius 1811 § d.	|	...	...	|	...	|	...	|
Kaunas 1811 § d.	|	...	...	|	...	|	...	|
Šeštokai § d.	|	...	...	|	...	|	...	|
Mockava 🏛 ◐ d.	|	...	...	|	...	|	...	|
Suwałki d.	|	0438	0514	|	0914	|	1528	|
Sokółka d.	0533	0556	0645	0725	1043	1528	1646	1726
Białystok a.	0615	0633	0723	0802	1129	1619	1724	1820
Warszawa Wsch. **1040** a.	...	0912	..	1117	...	...	2008	2111
Warszawa Cent. **1040** a.	...	0920	...	1125	...	...	2016	2120

H – HAŃCZA – (12) Kraków - Warszawa - Białystok - Suwałki and v.v. (Tables **1040/65**).
S – Ⓑ (not May 2): (12) Warszawa - Suwałki.
U – ①-⑥ (not May 3): (12) Suwałki - Warszawa.
W – (2) Warszawa - Hrodna and v.v.

• – *To commence at a date to be announced.*
§ – Lithuanian time (Polish time +1 hour).
‡ – Belarus time (Polish time +1 hour in summer; +2 hours in winter).
◐ – 🏛 = Trakiszki (Poland) / Mockava (Lithuania); ticketing point is Mock

1050 WARSZAWA - TERESPOL - BREST

km		TLK 11101		IC 31115			TLK 11105	MP 453	TLK 11103		MP 11010 10
				K				⊠	Ⓑ x		⊡M
0	**Warszawa** Centralna d.	0610	...	0925	...	...	1325	1340	1600	...	1840
5	**Warszawa** Wschodnia d.	0619	...	0933	...	...	1334	1417	1618	...	1928
93	Siedlce a.	0721	...	1020	...	...	1432	|	1713	...	2029
93	Siedlce d.	0722	...	1022	...	...	1434	|	1715	...	2031
121	Łuków d.	0740	...	1038	...	...	1453	|	1734	...	2053
173	Biała Podlaska d.	0814	...	1108	...	...	1526	|	1808	...	2131
210	Terespol 🏛 a.	0843	1125	1136	1512	...	1558	1617	1840	2015	2158
217	**Brest** Tsentralny 🏛 ‡ a.	...	1346	...	1733	...	...	1950	...	2236	0139

	TLK 11112	MP 9 11016		TLK 11114		MP 452		IC 13114	
	①-⑥ y	⊡M				⊠		K	
Brest Tsentralny 🏛 ‡ d.	...	0654	0945	...	...	1303	1515	...	1902
Terespol 🏛 d.	0515	0601	0803	0913	...	1201	1333	1550	1722
Biała Podlaska d.	0548	0634	...	0946	...	|	...	1620	...
Łuków d.	0621	0714	...	1019	...	|	...	1651	...
Siedlce a.	0639	0735	...	1036	...	|	...	1706	...
Siedlce d.	0641	0736	...	1038	...	|	...	1708	...
Warszawa Wschodnia a.	0737	0831	...	1137	...	1353	...	1756	...
Warszawa Centralna a.	0750	0900	...	1145	...	1430	...	1810	...

K – To/from Kraków (Table **1065**).
M – To/from Minsk/Moskva (Table **94**).
x – Not May 2.
y – Not May 3.

‡ – Belarus time (Polish time +1 hour in summer; +2 hours in winter).
⊡ – For composition and days of running see Tables **56/94**.
⊠ – Paris - Moskva service; for composition and days of running see Tables **24/56/94**. Special conditions appl Journeys within the European Union (e.g. Paris to Berlin) are possible, but only bookable through agents of Ru Railways or via the Russian rail website.

1055 WARSZAWA - LUBLIN - CHEŁM - DOROHUSK

km			TLK 13108 13109			TLK 32101	IC 42104 42105		TLK 83104 83105		IC 62106 62107		TLK 83106 83107		TLK 62105		TLK 42106 42107	IC 12102 12103	TLK 62103		TLK 53106 53107		MP 68 12010	TLK 32103	
			①-⑥ Zy	①-⑤ q	①-⑤ q	R			PZ		W		A		W		Ⓑ x		‡ Ⓑ Wx		E		K	R	
0	**Warszawa** Cent d.	...	0545	...	...	...	0751	...	0950	...	1210	...	1345	...	...	...	1550	1650	...	...	1754	...	1950	...	...
5	**Warszawa** Wsch d.	...	0554	...	...	...	0759	...	0959	...	1218	...	1359	...	...	...	1559	1659	...	...	1802	...	1958	...	...
•62	Łuków d.	...	|	0633	...	...	|	0824	|	...	|	...	|	1510	...	...	|	|	...	...	|	1915	|	...	...
104	Dęblin d.	...	0726	0730	0740	...	0923	0930	1116	...	1334	...	1514	1604	...	1618	1714	1817	...	...	1915	2023	2115	...	...
125	Puławy Miasto d.	...	0743	...	0803	0928	0941	0954	1131	...	1349	...	1529	...	1627	1640	1729	1831	1907	...	1931	2046	2131	2202	...
175	**Lublin** a.	...	0816	...	0855	1007	1020	1046	1204	...	1424	...	1603	...	1704	1728	1803	1905	1944	...	2007	2138	2208	2235	...
175	**Lublin** d.	0621	...	...	...	...	...	...	...	1209	...	1435	...	...	...	1729	...	...	...	1949	...	...	2213	...	2242
228	Rejowiec d.	0717	...	...	...	...	...	...	...	1305	...	1531	...	...	...	1820	...	...	...	2045	...	...	2253	...	2338
249	Chełm a.	0733	...	...	...	...	...	...	...	1322	...	1547	...	...	...	1835	...	...	...	2101	...	...	2310	...	2354
270	**Dorohusk** 🏛 a.	...	...	...	...	...	...	...	...	...	...	...	...	...	...	...	...	...	...	...	...	...	2330	...	...

	TLK 28100 28101			IC 21102 21103	TLK 23102	MP 67 21010		TLK 26102	TLK 35106 35107	TLK 26102		IC 24106 24107	TLK 38106 38107	TLK 26104		IC 26106 26107		TLK 38104 38105	TLK 24100			IC 24104 24105	TLK 23100		TLK 31108 31109
	S	①-⑤ q			R	K		①-⑥ Wg	E	①-⑥ Why		①-⑥ y	A	W		W		PZ			①-⑤ q		R		Ⓑ Zx
Dorohusk 🏛 a.	...	...	...	...	...	0526	...	...	...	...	...	...	...	...	...	...	...	...	...	...	...	...	...	...	...
Chełm d.	...	...	0448	...	...	0548	...	...	...	...	0808	...	...	...	1152	...	...	...	...	1523	...	...	...	1819	...
Rejowiec d.	...	...	0505	...	...	0607	...	...	...	...	0823	...	...	...	1209	...	...	...	...	1540	...	...	...	1836	...
Lublin a.	...	...	0555	...	...	0645	...	...	...	...	0915	...	...	...	1304	...	...	...	...	1634	...	...	...	1930	...
Lublin d.	0454	0522	...	0601	0639	0650	0717j	0740	0752	0825	...	0944	1209	1220	...	1349	...	1604	1617	...	1640	1804	1819	...	1944
Puławy Miasto d.	0533	0615	...	0636	0717	0730	0809j	0822	0832	0903	...	1020	1247	1256	...	1424	...	1641	1654	...	1732	1839	1856	...	2021
Dęblin d.	0548	0639	...	0650	...	0746	0842	...	0848	...	...	1036	1303	...	...	1439	1645	1657	...	...	1806	1855	...	...	2036
Łuków a.	|	0736	...	|	...	|	0943	...	|	...	...	|	|	...	...	|	1742	|	...	...	1904	|	...	...	|
Warszawa Wsch a.	0705	...	...	0802	...	0901	...	...	1003	...	...	1153	1416	...	...	1552	...	1817	...	...	...	2017	...	...	2203
Warszawa Cent a.	0715	...	...	0815	...	0910	...	...	1015	...	...	1200	1425	...	...	1601	...	1825	...	...	...	2025	...	...	2215

A – (12) Przemyśl/Rzeszów (Table **1058**) - Warszawa - Szczecin and v.v. (Table **1010**).
E – (12) Przemyśl/Rzeszów/Lublin (Table **1058**) - Warszawa - Bydgoszcz and v.v. (Table **1025**).
K – KYÏV EKSPRES / KIEV EXPRESS – 🛏 1,2 cl. Warszawa - Kyïv and v.v. (Table **1730**). International journeys only.
P – To/from Piła (Table **1000**).

R – To/from Kraków (Table **1067**).
S – To/from Szczecin (Table **1010**).
W – To/from Wrocław (Table **1067**).
Z – To/from Przemyśl/Rzeszów (Table **1058**).

g – Until Apr. 21.
h – From Apr. 22.
j – 10 minutes later from Apr. 22 (not May 31 - June 3).

q – Not May 3, 26.
x – Not May 2.
y – Not May 3.
‡ – Runs 34 minutes later until Apr.
• – Distance from Dęblin.

1058 LUBLIN - STALOWA WOLA - RZESZÓW - PRZEMYŚL

km				TLK 13109		TLK 83105		TLK 83107		TLK 53107
				①-⑥ y	①-⑤ q	P		A		Ⓑ Ex
	Warszawa Cent. **1055** d.	...	...	0536	...	0950	...	1345	...	1754
	Warszawa Wsch. **1055** d.	...	...	0554	...	0959	...	1359	...	1802
0	**Lublin** d.	0552	...	0836	...	1224	...	1623	...	2027
103	Stalowa Wola Rozwadów d.	0758	...	|	...	|	...	|	...	|
132	Tanobrzeg a.	0828	...	1009	...	1401	...	1805	...	2206
204	**Rzeszów** a.	0945	...	1104	...	1507	...	1905	...	2259
	Rzeszów 1075 d.	...	0952	...	1124	...	1544	1919	2237	2313
178	Przeworsk 1075 d.	...	1026	...	1159	...	1620	1946	2315	2342
193	Jarosław 1075 d.	...	1046	...	1221	...	1640	2007	2336	0001
228	**Przemyśl** 1075 a.	...	1125	...	1300	...	1721	2039	0019	0034

	TLK 35106	TLK 38106		TLK 38104			TLK 31108	
	①-⑥ Ey	A		P		①-⑤ q	Ⓑ x	
Przemyśl 1075 d.	0315	0746	1038	...	1348	1457	...	...
Jarosław 1075 d.	0347	0818	1117	...	1437	1542	...	...
Przeworsk 1075 d.	0407	0838	1137	...	1457	1601	...	...
Rzeszów 1075 a.	0433	0904	1211	...	1535	1636	...	...
Rzeszów d.	0447	0918	...	1300	...	...	1650	1730
Tanobrzeg d.	0548	1013	...	1406	...	...	1742	1839
Stalowa Wola Rozwadów d.	|	|	...	|	...	...	|	1914
Lublin a.	0724	1150	...	1545	...	...	1925	2103
Warszawa Wsch. **1055** a.	1003	1416	...	1817	...	...	2203	...
Warszawa Cent. **1055** a.	1015	1425	...	1825	...	...	2215	...

A – (12) Przemyśl/Rzeszów (Table **1058**) - Warszawa - Szczecin and v.v. (Table **1010**).
E – (12) Przemyśl/Rzeszów - Warszawa - Bydgoszcz and v.v. (Table **1025**).
P – (12) Rzeszów - Warszawa - Bydgoszcz/Piła and v.v. (Tables **1000/25**).

q – Not May 3, 26.
x – Not May 2.
y – Not May 3.

Reservation is compulsory for travel by all EC, EIC, EIP, EN, IC, MP and TLK trains

WARSAWA/ŁÓDŹ - KATOWICE - BIELSKO BIAŁA and WROCŁAW 1060

For other trains Warszawa - Wrocław see Table **1061**

	TLK	EC	IC	TLK	EIC	EC	IC	EIP	EC	IC	TLK	IC	IC	EC	EC	EIP	IC	EIP	IC	TLK	EIP	EC	IC	IC	TLK	EIP	MP
	54203	116	14111	14100	1650	103	14102	5400	131	54103	5420	16110	24106	105	112	5402	54107	1400	74102	14108	5404	110	54109	16106	14112	1402	407
		14004		14101	1651	14000	14103	5401	14002		5421	16111	24107	54000	14006	5403		1401	74103	14109	5405	14008		16107	14113	1403	14010
				§	§								①-⑥											Ⓑ		Ⓑ	
	GN	Y			E	P		G	V	G	O		Uy	S	M	Gx	G		Za	B	G	Q	G	x	R	x	C
Gdańsk Gł. **1025/30** d.	2131	...	...	...	...	...	...	0600	...	0531	...	...	...	0951	...	1151	0918	...	...	...	1355	...	1329	...	...	...	...
Warszawa Wschodnia d.	|	0524	...	0624	0724	0644	0824	0834	0944	|	1034	1124	1154	1234	1339	1434	|	1551	...	1547	1634	1739	|	1824	1844	1949	2114
Warszawa Centralna .. d.	|	0535	...	0640	0745	0655	0835	0855	0955	|	1050	1145	1235	1255	1356	1450	|	1602	...	1635	1650	1755	|	1840	1855	2000	2125
Łódź Kaliska .... d.	0313	|	0629	|	|	|	|	|	|	1036	|	|	|	|	|	|	1443	|	...	|	|	|	1843	|	|	|	|
Koluszki .... d.	|	|	|	0754	|	|	0947	|	|	|	|	|	1348	|	|	|	|	|	...	1756	|	|	|	|	|	|	|
Piotrków Trybunalski ... d.	0407	|	0721	0818	|	|	1011	|	|	1128	|	1305	1411	|	|	|	1539	|	...	1820	|	|	1936	1959	|	|	|
Częstochowa .... d.	0537	|	0814	0910	0950	|	1108	|	|	1226	|	1400	1508	|	|	|	1632	|	...	1912	|	|	2035	2053	|	|	|
Zawiercie .... d.	0613	0732	0845	0942	|	0852	1140	|	1151	1258	1252	|	1540	1450	1557	|	1703	1754	...	1943	|	1952	2107	|	2101	|	2328
Sosnowiec Gł. .... d.	0641	0755	0924	1009	|	0914	1207	1107	1213	1325	1318	|	1607	1513	1620	1703	1730	1817	...	2009	1904	2014	2134	|	2128	2213	2352
Katowice .... a.	0651	0804	0933	1018	|	0923	1216	1116	1222	1333	1327	|	1616	1521	1628	1712	1740	1826	...	2017	1913	2023	2143	|	2137	2222	0001
Katowice .... **1075** d.	0658j	0818	...	1021v	|	0926	1230z	1119	1225	...	...	|	...	1524	1631	1715	...	1829	1905	2020	1917	2032	...	|	2147	2226	...
Rybnik .... ▷ a.	|	0905	...	|	|	|	|	|	|	...	...	|	...	|	1714	|	...	|	|	|	|	2115	...	|	|	|	...
Tychy .... ▷ d.	0716j	...	...	1038v	|	0943	1252z	1135	1243	...	...	|	...	1542	...	|	...	1844	1922	2037	|	...	...	|	|	2244	...
Bielsko Biała ...... ▷ a.	0801j	...	...	...	|	...	1338z	1217	...	...	...	|	...	....	...	|	...	1927	2005	2149	|	...	...	|	|	2325	...
Gliwice .... **1075** d.	...	...	...	...	|	...	...	...	...	...	...	|	...	...	...	1739	...	...	...	...	1941	...	...	|	2211	...	...
Opole Gł. .... **1075** d.	...	...	...	...	1050	...	...	...	...	...	...	1503	...	...	...	...	...	...	...	...	...	...	...	2154	...	...	...
Wrocław Gł. ...... **1075** a.	...	...	...	...	1136	...	...	...	...	...	...	1554	...	...	...	...	...	...	...	...	...	...	...	2247	...	...	...

	MP	EIP	IC	IC	EIP	EC	TLK	EIP	IC	TLK	EIP	IC	EC	IC	EC	IC	TLK	IC	EC	EIP	IC	EIC	TLK	EC	IC	EC	TLK
	406	4100	61106	45108	4502	111	41108	4500	47102	41112	4504	45106	113	42106	104	61110	4520	45102	130	4506	41102	6150	41150	102	41110	117	45202
	41010	4101	61107		4503	14009	41109	4501	47103	41113	4505		14007	42107	45000	61111	4521		41002	4507	41103	6151	41151	41000		14005	
		①–⑥	①-⑥				‡	①–⑥						Ⓑ								§	§				
	C	y	y	G	G	Q	B	Gy	Z	R	G	G	M	x	S		O	G	V			E		P		Y	GN
Wrocław Gł. ...... **1075** d.	...	...	0431	...	...	...	...	...	...	...	...	...	...	...	...	1213	...	...	...	...	...	1718	...	...	...	...	...
Opole Gł. .... **1075** d.	...	...	0531	...	...	...	...	...	...	...	...	...	...	...	...	1310	...	...	...	...	...	1806	...	...	...	...	...
Gliwice .... **1075** d.	...	0503	|	...	...	...	...	...	...	0900	1014	...	...	...	...	|	...	...	...	...	...	|	...	...	...	...	...
Bielsko Biała ...... ▷ d.	...	|	|	...	0545	...	0656	0740	0828	|	|	...	...	...	...	|	...	...	...	1536	1447z	|	...	...	...	...	2200
Tychy .... ▷ d.	...	|	|	...	0628	...	0737	0823	0911	|	|	...	...	...	1220	|	...	...	1520	1617	1530z	|	1721v	1820	...	...	2243
Rybnik .... ▷ d.	...	|	|	...	|	0639	|	|	|	|	|	...	1044	...	|	|	...	...	|	|	|	|	|	|	...	1845	|
Katowice .... **1075** a.	...	0528	|	...	0644	0724	0807	0839	0934	0927	1039	...	1129	...	1239	|	...	...	1538	1634	1545z	|	1745v	1838	...	1932	2258
Katowice .... d.	0419	0532	|	0639	0648	0727	0810	0843	...	0943	1043	1033	1135	1143	1242	|	1411	1443	1541	1637	1600	|	1748	1841	1847	1942	2304
Sosnowiec Gł. .... d.	0428	0542	|	0649	0658	0736	0821	0853	...	0953	1053	1043	1144	1153	1251	|	1422	1453	1550	1647	1609	|	1758	1850	1857	1952	2314
Zawiercie .... d.	0451	0605	|	0716	|	0759	0852	|	...	1022	|	1110	1207	1220	1314	|	1450	1521	1613	|	1636	|	1825	1913	1924	2015	2339
Częstochowa .... d.	|	|	0639	0750	|	|	0925	|	...	|	|	1144	|	1254	|	1415	|	1555	|	|	1720	1916	1857	|	1958	|	0031
Piotrków Trybunalski ... d.	|	|	0731	0841	|	|	1017	|	...	|	|	1236	|	1345	|	1508	|	1647	|	|	1812	|	1949	|	2049	|	0137
Koluszki .... d.	|	|	|	|	|	|	1041	|	...	|	|	|	|	1408	|	|	|	|	|	|	1836	|	2013	|	|	|	|
Łódź Kaliska .... a.	|	|	|	0936	|	|	|	|	...	|	|	1325	|	|	|	|	|	1737	|	|	|	|	|	|	2140	|	0235
Warszawa Centralna .. a.	0649	0758	0855	|	0908	0959	1155	1103	...	1236	1303	|	1405	1521	1508	1631	1649	|	1811	1858	1950	2124	2132	2107	...	2214	|
Warszawa Wschodnia a.	0711	0816	0906	|	0926	1016	1211	1126	...	1246	1326	|	1416	1556	1526	1642	1731	|	1822	1926	2005	2136	2145	2141	...	2234	|
Gdańsk Gł. **1025/30** a.	...	...	...	1444	1207	...	...	1406	...	...	1607	1841	...	...	1808	...	...	2238	...	...	...	...	...	...	...	...	0742

To/from Białystok (Table **1040**).
CHOPIN – Warszawa - Budapest/Praha/Wien and v.v. For days of running and composition see Table **99**.
To/from Jelenia Góra on some days/dates (Table **1084**).
To/from Gdynia (Tables **1025/30**).
PORTA MORAVICA – 🛏 and ✕ Warszawa - Praha and v.v.
Conveys 🛏 1, 2 cl., 🛏 2 cl. and 🛏.
To/from Olsztyn (Table **1030**).
POLONIA – 🛏 and ✕ Warszawa - Wien and v.v.
COMENIUS – 🛏 and ✕ Warszawa - Ostrava and v.v.
To/from Racibórz (Table **1076**).
SOBIESKI – 🛏 and ✕ Gdynia - Warszawa - Wien and v.v.
To/from Lublin (Table **1055**).
VARSOVIA – 🛏 and ✕ Warszawa - Budapest and v.v.
PRAHA – 🛏 and ✕ Warszawa - Praha and v.v.
To/from Poznań (Table **1080**).

a – Runs 18-30 minutes later until Apr. 29.
j – From Apr. 30.
v – ⑥⑦ (also May 3, 26).
x – Not May 2.
y – Not May 3.
z – ⑥⑦ from Apr. 30 (also May 2, 3, 26, 27).

‡ – Subject to alteration from May 27; trains use Warszawa Gdańska station instead of Warszawa Centralna and Wschodnia (retimings possible).

§ – Train number varies on some days/dates: 1650/1 runs as 1620/1; 6150/1 runs as 6120/1; 14100/1 runs as 14150/1; 41150/1 runs as 41100/1.

▷ – For local trains Katowice - Bielsko Biała and Rybnik see Tables **1077/79**.

• – Częstochowa - Opole Gł: *91 km*.

WARSZAWA - ŁÓDŹ - WROCŁAW 1061

km		EIP	IC	EIP	IC	EIP	EIC	IC	EIP	EIC	IC
		1600	16102	1602	16104	1604	1622	26106	1656	1624	17104
		1601	16103	1603	16105	1605	1623	26107	1657	1625	17105
			‡		‡				§	Ⓑ	
			BJ		B			U	E	v	
0	**Warszawa** Wsch .... d.	0529	0734	0924	1149	1319	1518	1555	1719	1909	2029
4	**Warszawa** Cent .... d.	0540	0805	0935	1205	1335	1530	1605	1730	1925	2045
•	Częstochowa .... d.	|	|	1137	|	1537	1742	|	1933	2133	|
30	**Łódź** Widzew .... ▷ d.	|	0935	|	1334	|	|	1733	|	|	2215
57	Kalisz .... ▷ d.	|	1125	|	1535	|	|	1932	|	|	0005
81	Ostrów Wlkp .... ▷ d.	|	1146	|	1556	|	|	1954	|	|	0024
	Opole Gł. .... d.	0835	|	1234	|	1634	1841	|	2029	2231	...
*32**	**Wrocław** Gł. .... ▷ a.	0921	1318	1317	1726	1717	1926	2128	2112	2315	...

	IC	EIC	EIP	IC	EIC	EIP	IC	EIP	IC	EIP
	71104	6124	6156	62106	6122	6104	61104	6102	16102	6100
	71105	6125	6157	62107	6123	6105	61105	6103	16103	6101
		①–⑥	§				‡		‡	
		w	E	U			B		BJ	
Wrocław Gł. .... ▷ d.	...	0540	0647	0635	0841	1045	1030	1445	1431	1827
Opole Gł. .... d.	...	0623	0731	|	0926	1128	|	1528	|	1911
Ostrów Wlkp .... ▷ d.	0501	|	|	0816	|	|	1221	|	1619	|
Kalisz .... ▷ d.	0521	|	|	0836	|	|	1241	|	1639	|
Łódź Widzew ...... ▷ d.	0721	|	|	1040	|	|	1440	|	1840	|
Częstochowa .... d.	|	0724	0827	|	1024	1224	|	1624	|	|
Warszawa Cent .... a.	0851	0925	1030	1206	1226	1428	1605	1828	2010	2206
Warszawa Wsch ..... a.	0902	0946	1041	1216	1241	1439	1616	1842	2031	2220

To/from Białystok (Table **1040**).
To/from Jelenia Góra on some days/dates (Table **1084**).
To/from Jelenia Góra/Szklarska Poreba Górna (Table **1084**).
To/from Lublin (Table **1055**).

Not May 1, 2, 26, 27.
Not May 2, 3, 27, 28.

‡ – Subject to alteration from May 27; trains use Warszawa Gdańska station instead of Warszawa Centralna and Wschodnia (retimings possible).

§ – Train number varies on some days/dates: 1656/7 runs as 1606/7; 6156/7 runs as 6106/7.

▷ – For local trains see Table **1080**.
* – *406 km* via CMK.
• – *232 km* via CMK.

ŁÓDŹ - KRAKÓW 1062

km		IC		IC		IC		IC	
		13117		5325		8312		8311	
						8362			
		①–⑥							
		y		B		Sm		S	
0	**Łódź** Kaliska .... **1060** d.	0549	...	...	...	...	...	...	...
5	**Łódź** Widzew .... d.	0606	...	1036	...	1436	...	1836	...
7	Piotrków Trybunalski .... **1060** d.	0639	...	|	...	|	...	|	...
53	**Częstochowa** .... **1060** d.	0741	...	|	...	|	...	|	...
*9**	**Kraków** Gł. .... a.	0923	...	1256	...	1700	...	2056	...

	IC		IC		IC		IC	
	3810		3812		3524		31116	
			3862				Ⓑ	
	S		Sm		B		x	
Kraków Gł. .... d.	0702	...	1103	...	1504	...	1916	...
Częstochowa .... **1060** d.	|	...	|	...	|	...	2049	...
Piotrków Trybunalski ..... **1060** d.	|	...	|	...	|	...	2139	...
Łódź Widzew .... a.	0922	...	1323	...	1725	...	2212	...
Łódź Kaliska .... **1060** a.	...	...	...	...	...	...	2229	...

To/from Bydgoszcz (Tables **1020/5**).
To/from Szczecin (Table **1010**).

m – From Apr. 30.
x – Not May 2.
y – Not May 3.

* – *274 km* via CMK.

1065 WARSZAWA - KRAKÓW

Via CMK high-speed line (ticketing route is via Idziko

km	For trains via Kielce see Table 1067	TLK	EIP	EIP	IC	EIC	EIP	IC	EIC	EIC	EIP	EIP	IC	EIP	EIP	TLK	EIP	IC	EIC	EIP	IC	EIC	EIP	EIP
		13100	1300	5300	5326	1352	5302	13112	5322	5322	8300	5304	5328	1302	5306	13110	5308	5330	1324	5310	13114	1326	5350	5312
		13101	1301	5301	5327	1353	5303	13113	5323	5323	8301	5305	5329	1303	5307	13111	5309	5331	1325	5311	13115	1327	5351	5313
											①-⑥	⑦							Ⓑ				⑥	Ⓑ
		§			‡			‡	g	h	y	p	‡					‡	a	n	T	L	q	x
0	**Warszawa** Wschodnia ....d.	0534	0634	0739	0804	0849	0934	1014	1039	1100	1134	1134	1204	1239	1334	1434	1534	1604	1644	1734	1804	1839	1929	1929
5	**Warszawa** Centralna ....d.	0545	0650	0755	0820	0900	0950	1030	1055	1110	1155	1155	1220	1250	1350	1455	1547	1615	1655	1750	1845	1850	1955	1955
297	**Kraków** Gł. ....a.	0829	0909	1014	1231	1128	1211	1355	1328	1340	1414	1414	1631	1509	1611	1750	1807	2027	1923	2010	2207	2121	2215	2215

	TLK	EIP	EIC	IC	IC	EIP	EIP	EIC	EIP	TLK	IC	EIP	EIP	EIP	IC	EIC	EIP	IC	EIP	EIP	EIC	EIC	EIP
	31010	3500	3124	31114	3530	3502	3550	3126	3504	31110	3528	3506	3800	3508	31112	3522	3510	3526	3102	3512	3152	3122	3100
	141	3501	3125	31115	3531	3503	3551	3127	3505	31111	3529	3507	3801	3509	31113	3523	3511	3527	3103	3513	3153	3123	3101
		①-⑥				①-⑥	⑦	①-⑥					Ⓑ	⑥							⑥⑦	①-⑤	
	‡H		L	T	‡	y	p	b			‡		x	q	‡			‡				c	
Kraków Gł. ....d.	0452	0541	0631	0547	0721	0747	0747	0823	0940	1011	1125	1135	1338	1338	1414	1433	1539	1515	1642	1745	1907	1907	2000
Warszawa Centralna ....a.	0732	0802	0900	0917	1135	1006	1006	1058	1200	1256	1535	1355	1557	1557	1745	1702	1758	1935	1903	2005	2136	2136	2219
Warszawa Wschodnia ....a.	0742	0826	0911	0931	1201	1026	1026	1111	1226	1311	1601	1426	1626	1626	1810	1726	1826	2001	1916	2026	2149	2149	2242

H – HAŃCZA – (12) Kraków - Warszawa - Suwałki and v.v. (Table **1042**).
L – Conveys Warszawa - Kraków (**6300/3601**) - Przemyśl - Lviv and v.v. See Table **1075**.
T – To/from Terespol (Table **1050**).

a – Not May 1, 2, 26, 27, 29.
b – Not Apr. 30, May 2, 3, 26 - 28.
c – Not May 2, 3, 26, 27.
g – Until May 26.
h – From May 27.

n – Also Apr. 30.
p – Also May 3.
q – Also May 2.
x – Not May 2.
y – Not May 3.

‡ – Subject to alteration from May 27; trains use Wars Gdańska station instead of Warszawa Centralna Wschodnia (retimings possible).
§ – Train number varies on some days/dates: 13100/1 runs as 13106/7; 31100/1 runs as 3110

1066 KRAKÓW - ZAKOPANE

km		TLK	TLK	TLK		TLK	TLK		EIC	
		13201	13251	83261		43201	33171		1353	
		p	g	Sq		n	n		q	
	Warszawa C. **1065/67** ....d.	2110	2210	...	...	...	...	...	0900	...
0	**Kraków** Gł. ....d.	0221	0305	0433	...	0714	...	...	1133	...
5	Kraków Płaszów ....d.	0328	0347	0454	...	0735	0912	...	1154	...
68	Sucha Beskidzka ....d.	0458	0513	0635	...	0857	1036	...	1313	...
103	Chabówka ....a.	0536	0551	0713	...	0934	1114	...	1347	...
105	Rabka Zdroj ....d.	|	|	|	...	|	|	...	|	...
103	Chabówka ....d.	0550	0606	0727	...	0948	1128	...	1401	...
126	Nowy Targ ....d.	0618	0634	0755	...	1016	1156	...	1428	...
147	**Zakopane** ....a.	0643	0658	0820	...	1040	1219	...	1448	...

	EIC	TLK		TLK		TLK		TLK
	3152	33172		34200		38260		31250
	q	n		n		Sq		h
Zakopane ....d.	1550	1630	...	1834	...	2045	...	2109
Nowy Targ ....d.	1609	1653	...	1857	...	2109	...	2132
Chabówka ....a.	1635	1719	...	1925	...	2137	...	2158
Rabka Zdroj ....d.	|	|	...	|	...	|	...	|
Chabówka ....d.	1649	1733	...	1939	...	2151	...	2212
Sucha Beskidzka ....d.	1738	1824	...	2031	...	2244	...	2305
Kraków Płaszów ....a.	1844	1934	...	2141	...	2356	...	0009
Kraków Gł. ....a.	1903	...	...	2203	...	0036	...	0047
Warszawa Cent. **1065/67** a.	2136	...	...	...	...	...	...	0525

S – To/from Szczecin (Table **1010**).
g – Apr. 29, May 2, 25, 28.
h – Apr. 30, May 3, 26, 29.
n – ⑥⑦ from Apr. 30 (also Apr. 2, 3, May 2, 3, 26, 27).
p – ⑤⑥ from Apr. 29 (also Apr. 1, 2, May 1, 2, 25, 26).
q – ⑥⑦ from Apr. 30 (also May 2, 3, 26, 27).

1067 WARSZAWA and LUBLIN - KIELCE - KRAKÓW

km	For fast trains to Kraków see Table 1065		TLK	TLK			TLK	TLK	TLK	IC	IC	TLK	TLK	IC	IC		TLK		TLK	IC	IC	TLK	TLK	TLK
			83202	83202			26101	23103	26103	5326	5326	26103	26105	5328	5328		13105		24101	5330	5330	12100	23101	13201
			83203	83203						5327	5327			5329	5329					5331	5331	12101		
							①-⑥		①-⑥			①-⑥					⑤		Ⓑ			Ⓑ		
			Kg	Kh			y		m	Og	Oh	ny		Og	Oh		v		kx	Og	Oh	x		⊙
0	**Warszawa** Centralna ....d.	...	...	...	...	...	...	...	...	0820	...	...	...	1220	...	...	1425	...	...	1615	...	1630	...	2110
4	**Warszawa** Wschodnia ....d.	...	0320	0335	...	...	...	...	...	0804j	...	...	...	1204j	...	...	1433	...	...	1604j	...	1639	...	2119
	Dęblin ....d.	...	0441	0452	...	...	...	...	...	|	...	...	...	|	...	...	1609	...	...	|	...	1802	...	2240
•	**Lublin** ....d.	...	|	|	...	...	...	0639	0740	|	...	0825	1220	|	...	...	|	...	1617	|	...	|	1819	|
107*	Radom ....d.	...	0523	0535	...	...	...	0806	0915	|	...	0950	1344	|	...	...	1651	...	1742	|	...	1844	1945	2329
148	Skarżysko Kamienna **1058**..d.	...	0552	0607	0617	0818	...	0833	0942	|	...	1016	1412	|	...	*1425*	1718	1725	1809	|	...	1914	2011	2358
192	Kielce ....d.	0557	0628	0642	0703	0902	...	0913	1031	1104	1104	1105	1501	1505	1505	1533	...	1812	1859	1901	1901	1950	2054	0039
	Zawiercie ....d.	|	|	|	|	...	0934	|	1201	|	|	1225	1623	|	|	|	...	|	2020	|	|	...	|	|
	Sosnowiec Gł. ....d.	|	|	|	|	...	1002	|	1228	|	|	1252	1650	|	|	|	...	|	2047	|	|	...	|	|
	Katowice ....a.	|	|	|	|	...	1011	|	1238	|	|	1301	1659	|	|	|	...	|	2058	|	|	...	|	|
	Wrocław Gł **1075** ....a.	|	|	|	|	...	1040	|	1516	|	|	1521	1922	|	|	|	...	|	...	|	|	...	|	|
324	**Kraków** Gł. ....a.	0755	0804	0817	0903	...	...	1041	...	1231	1231	...	...	1631	1631	1729	...	2005	...	2027	2027	...	2228	0211
	Zakopane **1066** ....a.	...	...	...	...	...	...	...	...	...	...	...	...	...	...	...	...	...	...	...	...	...	...	0643

km		TLK	TLK	TLK	TLK		IC	IC	IC	IC	TLK	IC	IC	TLK	TLK			TLK		TLK	TLK			TLK
		31250	31200	21100	32100		3530	3530	3528	3528	62104	3526	3526	62102	62102			31104		62100	32102			38202
		31251	31201	21101			3531	3531	3529	3529		3527	3527					31105						38203
				①										Ⓑ	Ⓑ			⑦		Ⓑ				
		⊙	⊙	w			Oh	Og	Oh	Og		Oh	Og	qx	p			u		x				K
	Zakopane **1066** ....d.	2109	2147	...	...	...	...	...	...	...	...	...	...	...	...	...	...	...	...	...	...	...	...	...
	Kraków Gł. ....d.	0052	0205	...	0602	0637	0721	0721	1125	1125	...	1515	1515	...	...	1545	...	...	1703	...	1835	1929	...	2124
	Wrocław Gł **1075** ....d.	|	|	...	|	|	|	|	|	|	0922	|	|	1229	1310	|	...	...	|	1548	|	|	...	|
0	**Katowice** ....d.	|	|	...	|	|	|	|	|	|	1212	|	|	1449	1524	|	...	...	|	1824	|	|	...	|
9	Sosnowiec Gł. ....d.	|	|	...	|	|	|	|	|	|	1222	|	|	1459	1534	|	...	...	|	1834	|	|	...	|
44	Zawiercie ....d.	|	|	...	|	|	|	|	|	|	1250	|	|	1527	1601	|	...	...	|	1900	|	|	...	|
161	Kielce ....d.	0219	0346	0655	0736	0833	0850	0855	1254	1257	1433	1648	1654	1711	1744	1742	1752	...	1908	...	2010	2125	2230	2303
	Skarżysko Kamienna **1058**..d.	0255	0428	0734	0815	...	...	|	...	|	1513	...	|	1752	1822	...	1836	1901	1952	...	2048	...	2315	2342
	Radom ....d.	0323	0457	0800	0842	...	...	|	...	|	1540	...	|	1819	1849	...	...	1927	...	...	2115	...	...	0011
	Lublin ....a.	|	|	|	1007	...	...	|	...	|	1704	...	|	1944	2017	...	...	|	...	...	2235	...	...	|
	Dęblin ....d.	0400	0538	0838	...	...	...	|	...	|	...	...	|	...	...	...	...	2006	...	...	...	...	...	0054
	Warszawa Wschodnia ....a.	0516	0711	0958	...	...	...	1201j	...	1601j	...	...	2001j	...	...	...	...	2143	...	...	...	...	...	0218
	Warszawa Centralna ....a.	0525	0720	1009	...	...	...	1135	...	1535	...	...	1935	...	...	...	...	2155	...	...	...	...	...	...

K – 1,2 cl., 2 cl., (2) Kołobrzeg - Gdynia - Gdańsk - Kraków and v.v. (Table **1015**).
O – To/from Olsztyn (Table **1030**).
g – Until May 26.

h – From May 27.
j – Via Warszawa Centralna.
k – From May 1.
m – Until Apr. 21.

n – From Apr. 22.
p – Until Apr. 12.
q – From Apr. 13.
u – Also May 3; not May 1.

v – Also May 25; not May 27.
w – Also May 4, 27, 28.
x – Not May 2.
y – Not May 3.

⊙ – For days of running see Table **1066**.
• – Lublin - Radom: *121 km*
* – *161 km* via Dęblin

1070 POZNAŃ - WROCŁAW

km				IC		TLK		IC		TLK		IC		IC		IC	IC	IC		TLK	IC			IC
				84102		5601		86106		5603		8402		83102		5607	5607	8400		16115	84100			5608
						5600				5602						5606	5606			16114				5609
		n	m	KS		G				G		KS		M		Gm	Gn	KS		B	K			G
0	**Poznań** Gł. ....d.	0643	0730	0840	0850	0950	...	1041	1051	1137	...	1236	1253	1437	...	1540	1555	1629	1639	1655	1841	1850	...	1932
69	Leszno ....d.	0803	0856	0942	1015	1052	...	1141	1208	1239	...	1343	1412	1550	...	1651	1657	1731	1802	1820	1943	2018	...	2040
165	**Wrocław** Gł. ....a.	0916	1024	1058	1143j	1155	...	1242	1338	1353	...	1447	1541	1700	...	1754	1802	1837	1923	1928	2050	2141	...	2158

	IC	IC			IC	TLK		IC		IC		IC		TLK		IC			IC	IC	IC		
	68103	6509			48101	61115		4803		6507		38103		6505		4801			68107	6501	48103		
		6508			48153	61114				6506				6504						6500			
	S	G			K	B		KS		G	m	M		G	n	KS				G	KS		
Wrocław Gł ....d.	0532	0625	0642	...	0732	0812	0855	0931	...	1020	1047	1134	...	1225	1234	1321	1436	...	1529	1625	1716	...	1842
Leszno ....d.	0646	0732	0814	...	0842	0931	1045	1032	...	1128	1220	1251	...	1325	1408	1432	1603	...	1645	1734	1835	...	2027
Poznań Gł ....a.	0759	0838	0935	...	0948	1039	1218	1135	...	1241	1342	1405	...	1443	1553	1538	1738	...	1751	1839	1950	...	2151

B – To/from Białystok (Table **1035**).
G – (12) Gdynia - Poznań - Wrocław and v.v. (Tables **1015/20**).
K – To/from Katowice (Table **1075**).

M – (12) Kraków - Katowice - Wrocław - Poznań - Kołobrzeg and v.v. (Tables **1015/75**).
S – To/from Szczecin (Table **1010**).

j – Arrive 1214 May 30 - June 4.
m – Until Apr. 10.
n – From Apr. 11.

RZESZÓW - JASŁO - ZAGÓRZ 1073

km			TLK				TLK			
		①–⑤	30203	⑦	①–⑤	⑦	33113	①–⑤	⑤	⑥⑦
		p	A	q	p	h	A	z	g	n
0	**Rzeszów** Gł. d.	...	...	...	...	1435	1521	1520	1550	1950
9	Boguchwała d.	...	...	...	...	1448	1531	1533	1603	2003
52	Przybówka d.	...	...	...	...	1540	|	1625	1656	2055
71	**Jasło** d.	0458	0645	0730	1509	1558	1643	1643	1722	2113
94	Krosno d.	0530	0715	0802	1541	...	1714	...	1754	...
33	Sanok d.	...	0821	0859	...	...	1814	...	1851	...
39	Nowy Zagórz a.	...	|	0906	...	...	|	...	1858	...
40	**Zagórz** a.	...	0832	0908	...	...	1826	...	1901	...

					TLK				TLK
	①–⑤		①–⑤	⑥	30112	①–⑤	⑥	⑦	33202
	p		p	f	A	p	n	q	A
Zagórz d.	...	...	...	0651	0940	...	...	1603	2015
Nowy Zagórz d.	...	...	...	0653	|	...	...	1606	|
Sanok d.	...	...	...	0700	0952	...	...	1613	2027
Krosno d.	...	...	0610	0756	1052	1608	...	1718	2127
Jasło d.	0504	0553	0642	0828	1133	1640	1716	1758	2155
Przybówka d.	0522	0611	...	...	|	...	1734	1816	...
Boguchwała d.	0614	0702	...	...	1233	...	1825	1908	...
Rzeszów Gł. a.	0627	0715	...	...	1243	...	1838	1921	...

- ⑥⑦ (also May 2, 3, 26, 27).

f – Also May 26; not May 28.
g – Also May 25; not May 27.
h – Also May 3; not May 1.
n – Not Apr. 30.
p – Not May 3, 26.
q – Not May 1.
z – Not May 27.

WROCŁAW - KATOWICE - KRAKÓW - PRZEMYŚL 1075

For other trains Poznań - Katowice / Kraków see Tables **1080** (via Ostrów Wlkp) and **1025** (via Łódź)

km		IC	EIC	IC	EIP	IC	EIC	TLK	IC	EIP	IC	IC	TLK	TLK	IC	TLK	EIP	IC	IC	TLK	TLK	IC	IC
		61106	6124	6308	6156	64106	6122	62104	73102	6104	84102	61110	62102	83107	6306	62102	6102	6302	8402	13105	62100	6304	6304
		61107	6125	6309	6157		6123		73103	6105		61111			6307		6103	6303				6305	6305
		①–⑥	①–⑥		§	①–⑥							Ⓑ			Ⓑ				⑤	Ⓑ		
		Wy	Wk		W	y	W	U	Z	W		W	Uqx			Up	W			Wv	x	q	p
	Świnoujście **1010** d.	...	...	...	...	...	...	...	...	...	...	...	...	...	...	...	...	...	...	...	...	...	...
	Szczecin Gł. **1010** d.	...	...	...	...	...	...	...	...	...	0543	...	...	...	...	...	...	...	0950	...	...	...	...
	Poznań Gł. **1070** d.	...	...	...	...	...	...	...	...	...	0840	...	...	...	...	...	...	...	1236	...	...	...	...
0	**Wrocław** Gł. **1060** d.	0431	0540	0610	0647	0723	0841	0922	1028	1045	1122	1213	1229	...	1305	1310	1445	1450	1455	...	1548	1627	1705
42	Brzeg d.	0456	|	0633	|	0751	|	0951	1050	|	1150	1238	1255	...	1328	1337	|	1517	1521	...	1615	1649	1729
82	Opole Gł. **1060** d.	0526	0622	0704	0730	0819	0924	1018	1117	1127	1219	1315	1321	...	1353	1402	1527	1549	1548	...	1641	1713	1752
62	Gliwice **1060** d.	...	...	|	...	0913	...	1110	|	...	1312	...	1413	...	|	1455	...	|	1640	...	1756	|	|
90	**Katowice** **1060** a.	...	...	|	...	0941r	...	1204	|	...	1345	...	1441	...	|	1519	...	|	1704	...	1821	|	|
90	**Katowice** d.	...	...	|	...	...	...	...	|	...	...	...	...	...	|	...	...	|	...	...	...	|	|
68	**Kraków** Gł. a.	...	...	0930	...	...	...	...	1349	...	...	...	...	...	1622	...	...	1823	...	...	...	1943	2034
68	**Kraków** Gł. **1078** d.	...	...	0947	...	...	...	...	1414	...	...	...	...	...	1703	...	...	1844	...	...	...	...	...
73	Kraków Płaszów **1078** d.	...	...	0955	...	...	...	...	1422	...	...	...	...	...	1710	...	...	1851	...	...	...	...	...
46	Tarnów **1078** d.	...	...	1055	...	...	...	...	1518	...	...	...	...	...	1808	...	...	1950	...	...	...	...	...
79	Dębica d.	...	...	1126	...	...	...	...	1550	...	...	...	...	...	1838	...	...	2017	...	...	...	...	...
26	**Rzeszów** **1058** d.	...	...	1219	...	...	...	...	1636	...	...	...	...	1919	1923	...	...	2058	...	...	...	...	...
63	Przeworsk **1058** d.	...	...	1247	...	...	...	...	1705	...	...	...	...	1946	1950	...	...	2125	...	2130	...	...	...
78	Jarosław **1058** d.	...	...	1307	...	...	...	...	1726	...	...	...	...	2007	2011	...	...	2145	...	2150	...	...	...
13	**Przemyśl** **1058** a.	...	...	1340	...	...	...	...	1759	...	...	...	...	2039	2043	...	...	2218	...	2224	...	...	...

	EIC	IC	TLK	EIP	IC	EIP	IC	IC	IC
	6121	83102	64102	6100	6300	5312	8400	84100	63200
	6151		64103	6101	6301	5313			63201
						Ⓑ			⑤⑥
	W	K		W	LN	Gx			f
Świnoujście **1010** d.	...	...	...	...	...	...	...	...	...
Szczecin Gł. **1010** d.	...	...	...	...	...	...	1351	...	...
Poznań Gł. **1070** d.	...	1445	...	...	...	...	1629	1841	...
rocław Gł. **1060** d.	1718	1710	1801	1827	1832	...	1910	2057	2135
zeg d.	|	1746	1832	|	1856	...	1937	2126	2204
pole Gł. **1060** d.	1804	1815	1900	1910	1922	...	2003	2153	2232
iwice **1060** d.	...	1911	...	...	|	...	2057	2245	2349
atowice **1060** a.	...	1937	...	...	|	...	2121	2310	0014
atowice d.	...	1943	...	...	|	...	...	...	0019
raków Gł. a.	...	2157	...	...	2146	...	...	...	|
raków Gł. **1078** d.	...	...	...	...	2205	2218	...	...	|
aków Płaszów **1078** d.	...	...	...	...	2213	2226	...	...	0300
rnów **1078** d.	...	...	...	...	2308	2314	...	...	0356
ębica d.	...	...	...	...	2335	2341	...	...	0428
zeszów **1058** d.	...	...	...	...	0022	0017	...	...	0526
zeworsk **1058** d.	...	...	...	...	0051	...	...	...	0556
rosław **1058** d.	...	...	...	...	0112	...	...	...	0616
zemyśl **1058** a.	...	...	...	...	0145	...	...	...	0650

	IC	IC	EIP	IC	IC	TLK	IC	EIP	IC
	36200	48101	1600	4803	3600	46102	38103	3502	3604
	36201		1601		3601	46103		3503	3605
	⑥⑦					①–⑥		①–⑥	
	e				MN	g	K	Gy	
Przemyśl **1058** d.	2122	...	...	...	0153	...	...	...	...
Jarosław **1058** d.	2157	...	...	...	0228	...	...	...	...
Przeworsk **1058** d.	2217	...	...	...	0248	...	...	...	...
Rzeszów **1058** d.	2304	...	...	...	0318	...	...	0544	...
Dębica d.	2344	...	...	...	0400	...	...	0622	...
Tarnów **1078** d.	0017	...	...	...	0444	...	...	0649	...
Kraków Płaszów **1078** d.	0120	...	...	...	0548	...	...	0737	...
Kraków Gł. **1078** a.	|	...	...	...	0555	...	...	0744	...
Kraków Gł. d.	|	...	...	...	0618	...	0652	...	0813
Katowice a.	0336	...	...	...	|	...	0856	...	|
Katowice **1060** d.	0339	0508	...	0715	|	...	0901	...	|
Gliwice **1060** d.	0405	0540	...	0745	|	...	0928	...	|
Opole Gł. **1060** d.	0522	0634	0835	0840	0846	0946	1026	...	1041
Brzeg d.	0550	0659	|	0904	0909	1012	1053	...	1104
Wrocław Gł. **1060** a.	0620	0726	0921	0928	0942	1004	1126	...	1131
Poznań Gł. **1070** a.	...	0948	...	1135	...	...	1405	...	...
Szczecin Gł. **1010** a.	...	...	...	1419	...	...	...	...	...
Świnoujście **1010** a.	...	...	...	...	...	...	...	...	...

	EIC	TLK	IC	EIP	IC	TLK	IC	IC	TLK	TLK	IC	IC	EIP	IC	EIC	TLK	IC	EIP	IC	TLK	IC	TLK	EIC
	1620	26101	4801	1602	3602	38106	3606	16110	26103	26103	48103	48103	1604	37102	1622	26105	46107	1656	3608	46116	16106	31104	1624
	1650			1603	3603		3607	16111					1605	37103	1623			1657	3609	46117	16107		1625
		①–⑥							①–⑥	①–⑥							Ⓑ	§		⑦	Ⓑ	⑦	Ⓑ
	W	y		W				W	Um	Uny	p	q	W	Z	W	U	x	W		h	Wx	Wh	Wz
zemyśl **1058** d.	...	...	...	...	0614	0746	0822	...	...	...	...	...	...	1030	...	...	...	...	1358	...	...	1423	...
rosław **1058** d.	...	...	...	...	0647	0818	0854	...	...	...	...	...	...	1103	...	...	...	...	1430	...	...	1457	...
zeworsk **1058** d.	...	...	...	...	0706	0838	0914	...	...	...	...	...	...	1123	...	...	...	...	1449	...	...	1516	...
zeszów **1058** d.	...	...	...	...	0741	0904	0941	...	...	...	...	...	...	1151	...	...	...	...	1526	...	...	...	...
ębica d.	...	...	...	...	0823	...	1022	...	...	...	...	...	...	1233	...	...	...	...	1612	...	...	...	...
rnów **1078** d.	...	...	...	...	0902	...	1054	...	...	...	...	...	...	1306	...	...	...	...	1651	...	...	...	...
aków Płaszów **1078** d.	...	...	...	...	0956	...	1148	...	...	...	...	...	...	1400	...	...	...	...	1750	...	...	...	...
raków Gł. **1078** a.	...	...	...	...	1003	...	1155	...	...	...	...	...	...	1407	...	...	...	...	1757	...	...	...	...
raków Gł. d.	...	...	...	...	1045	...	1217	...	...	...	...	...	...	1442	...	...	...	...	1821	...	...	...	...
atowice a.	...	...	...	...	|	...	|	...	...	...	...	...	...	|	...	...	...	...	|	...	...	...	...
atowice **1060** d.	...	1017	1101	...	|	...	|	...	1246	1308	1345	1439	...	|	...	1704	1837	...	|	...	...	...	...
iwice **1060** d.	...	1043	1128	...	|	...	|	...	1313	1334	1456	1505	...	|	...	1730	1910	...	|	...	...	...	...
pole Gł. **1060** d.	1050	1202	1221	1234	1310	...	1455	1503	1408	1429	1552	1601	1634	1715	1841	1826	2008	2029	2052	2130	2154	...	2231
zeg d.	|	1226	1245	|	1334	...	1519	1526	1432	1454	1619	1631	|	1743	|	1852	2035	|	2116	2158	2218	...	|
rocław Gł. **1060** a.	1136	1305	1309	1317	1402	...	1546	1554	1516	1521	1651	1702	1717	1808	1926	1922	2107	2112	2150	2239	2247	...	2315
Poznań Gł. **1070** a.	...	...	1538	...	...	...	...	...	...	...	1950	1950	...	...	...	...	...	...	...	...	...	...	...
Szczecin Gł. **1010** a.	...	...	1819	...	...	...	...	...	...	...	2247	2253	...	...	...	...	...	...	...	...	...	...	...
Świnoujście **1010** a.	...	...	...	...	...	...	...	...	...	...	...	...	...	...	...	...	...	...	...	...	...	...	...

– Runs on uneven dates in Jan., Mar., June; even dates in Feb., Apr., May.
– Runs on even dates in Jan., Mar., June; uneven dates in Feb., Apr., May.
– To / from Gdynia (Table **1030**).
– To / from Kołobrzeg (Table **1015**).
– LVIV EXPRESS / CHEŁMONSKI – 🛏 2 cl. Kraków (**6301**) - Przemyśl (**35**) - Lviv. Conveys 🛏 Warszawa (**1326/7**) - Kraków - Lviv.
– LVIV EXPRESS / BARBAKAN – 🛏 2 cl. Lviv (**36/52**) - Przemyśl (**3600**) - Kraków. Conveys 🛏 Lviv - Kraków (**3124/5**) - Warszawa.
– Conveys 🛏 2 cl. Kraków - Przemyśl - Lviv and v.v. (see panel on right).
– To / from Lublin (Table **1067**).
– To / from Warszawa.
– To / from Zielona Góra (Table **1004**).

– Also May 2, 3, 26, 27.
– Also May 1, 2, 25, 26.
– Also May 1; not May 3.
– Also May 3; not May 1.

j – Not Apr. 29 - May 2, May 25 - 28.
k – Not May 2, 3, 27, 28.
m – Until Apr. 21.
n – From Apr. 22.

p – Until Apr. 12.
q – From Apr. 13.
r – Arrive 1008 May 10 - 14, 16.
v – Also May 25; not May 27.
x – Not May 2.
y – Not May 3.
z – Not May 1, 2, 26, 27.

§ – Train number varies on some days / dates: 1656/7 runs as 1606/7; 6156/7 runs as 6106/7.

– Via Ostrów Wlkp. (Table **1080**).
‡ – Ukrainian (East European) time.

PRZEMYŚL - LVIV

km		33011 35 AL	33015 51 BL
	Kraków Gł. (see above) d.	2205	2205
0	**Przemyśl** d.	0252	0356
13	Medyka 🛃 d.	|	|
20	Mostiska II 🛃 ‡ d.	0451	0600
98	**Lviv** ‡ a.	0603	0715

	52 33016 BM	36 33012 AM
Lviv ‡ d.	2259	2359
Mostiska II 🛃 ‡ d.	2345	0045
Medyka 🛃 d.	|	|
Przemyśl a.	0020	0117
Kraków Gł. (see above) a.	0555	0555

1076 KATOWICE and KRAKÓW - BOHUMÍN - OSTRAVA

km		*EC* 116 ✕⁄ Y	*EC* 103 ✕⁄	*EC* 105 ✕⁄ S	*EC* 112 ✕⁄ M	*EC* 110 ✕⁄ N	*MP* 402 444 [R] W	*MP* 402 407 K	*MP* 407 444 P	*MP* 407 C
	Warszawa Cent. **1060** d.	0535	0655	1255	1356	1755	...	...	2125	2125
0	**Katowice** d.	0818	0926	1524	1631	2032	...	...	0007	0007
•116	**Kraków** Gł. ▷ d.	|	|	|	|	|	2158	2158	|	|
•51	Oświecim ▷ d.	|	|	|	|	|	2336	2336	|	|
74	Zebrzydowice d.	|	1023	1623	|	|	0054	0054	0103	0103
45	Rybnik ▷ d.	0906	|	|	1715	2116	|	|	|	|
82	Racibórz ▷ d.	|	|	|	|	|	|	|	|	|
102	Chałupki ▷ d.	0935	|	|	1744	2145	|	|	|	|
Δ94	Bohumín a.	0941	1042	1640	1750	|	0111	0111	0120	0120
94	Bohumín **1160** d.	1007	1052	1652	1807	|	0210	0220	0210	0220
102	**Ostrava** hlavní **1160** a.	1013	1100	1700	1813	2156	0217	0227	0217	0227
	Praha hlavní **1160** a.	1339	|	|	2139	...	0638	|	0638	|
	Wien Hbf **1150** a.	...	1351	1951	...	...	...	0702	...	0702

	MP 406 C	*MP* 406 403 K	*MP* 445 406 P	*MP* 445 403 [R] W	*EC* 111 ✕⁄ N	*EC* 113 ✕⁄ M	*EC* 104 ✕⁄ S	*EC* 102 ✕⁄	*E*… 11… ✕ Y
Wien Hbf **1150** d.	2250	2250	...	...	...	...	0809	1409	..
Praha hlavní **1160** d.	|	|	2200	2200	...	0624	|	|	14…
Ostrava hlavní **1160** d.	0156	0156	0217	0217	0556	0948	1059	1659	17…
Bohumín **1160** a.	0203	0203	0225	0225	|	0955	1105	1705	17…
Bohumín d.	0300	0404	0300	0404	|	1007	1120	1720	18…
Chałupki ▷ d.	|	|	|	|	0608	1013	|	|	18…
Racibórz ▷ d.	|	|	|	|	|	|	|	|	|
Rybnik ▷ d.	|	|	|	|	0639	1044	|	|	18…
Zebrzydowice d.	0319	0424	0319	0424	|	|	1138	1739	|
Oświecim ▷ a.	|	0535	|	0535	|	|	|	|	|
Kraków Gł. ▷ a.	|	0705	|	0705	|	|	|	|	|
Katowice a.	0407	...	0407	...	0724	1129	1239	1838	19…
Warszawa Cent. **1060** a.	0649	...	0649	...	0959	1405	1508	2107	22…

C – CHOPIN – 🛏 1,2 cl., ▬ 2 cl. and [2] Warszawa - Wien and v.v.; 🛏 1,2 cl., ▬ 2 cl. and [2] Warszawa - Bratislava - Budapest and v.v.
K – 🛏 1,2 cl. Kraków - Wien and v.v.; 🛏 1,2 cl. and ▬ 2 cl. Kraków - Bratislava - Budapest and v.v.
M – PORTA MORAVICA – [12] and ✕ Warszawa - Praha and v.v.
N – COMENIUS – [12] and ✕ Warszawa - Ostrava and v.v.
P – 🛏 1,2 cl. and [2] Warszawa - Praha and v.v. Also conveys ▬ 2 cl. on dates in Table **99**.
S – SOBIESKI – [12] and ✕ Gdynia - Warszawa - Wien and v.v.
W – SILESIA – 🛏 1,2 cl., ▬ 2 cl. and [2] Kraków - Praha and v.v.
Y – PRAHA – [12] and ✕ Warszawa - Praha and v.v.
• – Distance from Zebrzydowic…
⁄ – Supplement payable.
▷ – For local trains see Tables **1079/99**.
Δ – *106 km* via Chałupki.

1077 KATOWICE - BIELSKO BIAŁA - ZWARDOŃ - ŽILINA

Koleje Śląskie, 2nd clas…

km			c			a				a					
0	**Katowice** **1060** d.	0459	0705	0931	1129	1239	1330	1412	1529	1636	1719	1834	1931	2123	2305
17	Tychy d.	0530	0725	0952	1150	1259	1351	1431	1547	1657	1740	1855	1951	2146	2328
44	Czechowice Dziedzice d.	0609	0758	1030	1224	1333	1424	1512	1621	1730	1821	1924	2033	2218	0002
55	**Bielsko Biała** **1060** d.	0653	0818	1103	1253	1354	1447	1539	1650	1754	1855	2000	2054	2239	0033
76	Zywiec a.	0723	0900	1135	1344	1442	1518	1621	1724	1825	1941	2031	2135	2320	...
113	**Zwardoń** a.	0828	1003	1248	1450	...	1633	1723	1834	1927	2054	...	2239	0024	...

		a					a								
Zwardoń d.	0325	0427	...	0623	0711	...	0903	1108	1312	...	1505	1648	1759	1930	...
Zywiec d.	0426	0531	0637	0725	0822	0929	1027	1218	1421	1530	1629	1800	1920	2042	...
Bielsko Biała **1060** d.	0501	0607	0712	0800	0912	1009	1101	1259	1459	1619	1709	1842	1955	2117	2223
Czechowice Dziedzice d.	0524	0630	0734	0820	0932	1030	1120	1321	1524	1645	1733	1913	2014	2139	2244
Tychy d.	0555	0658	0814	0858	1006	1101	1148	1352	1553	1716	1805	1946	2044	2210	2318
Katowice **1060** a.	0617	0731	0834	0928	1029	1124	1234	1423	1628	1752	1833	2013	2121	2235	0001

	a	a	c	a		a	
Katowice d.	...	...	...	...	...	...	...
Czech. Dziedzice d.	0435	0602	0613	0848	1439	1633	184…
Zebrzydowice d.	0524	0652	0703	0936	1527	1723	193…
Cieszyn ★ a.	0558	0726	0737	1011	1601	1757	201…

		a		a	a	c	a
Cieszyn ★ d.	0345	0610	0834	1428	1628	1708	184…
Zebrzydowice d.	0432	0654	0918	1512	1713	1752	192…
Czech. Dziedzice a.	0518	0739	1002	1556	1759	1838	201…
Katowice a.	...	...	...	...	...	...	...

ZWARDÓN - ŽILINA

km					①–⑤	
0	**Zwardoń** d.	0642	...	1541	1642	1952
22	Čadca **1160** a.	0726	...	1626	1732	2026
52	**Žilina** **1160** a.	0813	...	1713	1813	2113

			①–⑤		
Žilina **1160** d.	0448	1348	1448	...	1748
Čadca **1160** d.	0544	1437	1537	...	1837
Zwardoń a.	0617	1510	1610	...	1910

a – ①–⑤ (not May 2, 3, 26, 27).
c – ⑥⑦ (also May 2, 3, 26, 27).
★ – Cieszyn station (Poland) is situated ± 1500 metres from Český Těšín station (Czech Republic).

Katowice - Zwardoń and v.v. is subject to alteration.

1078 KRAKÓW - NOWY SĄCZ - KRYNICA

km		*TLK* 33201 A	①–⑤ w		‡	*TLK* 13101 A	①–⑤ ‡			⑧
	Warszawa C. **1065/75** d.	...	...	...	...	0545	...	...	...	...
0	**Kraków** Gł. **1075** d.	0300	...	...	0619	0836	...	1431	1644	2001
5	Kraków Płaszów **1075** d.	0308	...	...	0626	0855	...	1437	1650	2007
78	Tarnów **1075** a.	0400	...	...	0737	0947	...	1551	1800	2125
78	Tarnów d.	0403	0422	0530	0740	0949	1338	1554	1803	2128
136	Stróze d.	0521	0550	0653	0859	1056	1459	1714	1922	2246
167	**Nowy Sącz** d.	0604	0629	0733	0938	1134	1540	1753	2001	2326
217	Muszyna d.	0722	...	...	1052	1252	1703	...	...	...
228	**Krynica** a.	0741	...	...	1121	1311	1721	...	...	...

			①–⑥ ‡z		*TLK* 31100 A	⑧ ‡	①–⑤ ‡w	*TLK* 30200 A	
Krynica d.	...	...	0430	...	1505	1600	1741	2105	...
Muszyna d.	...	...	0455	...	1537	1619	1800	2137	...
Nowy Sącz d.	0319	0440	0603	...	1643	1737	1918	2242	...
Stróze d.	0357	0518	0642	...	1719	1816	1956	2332	...
Tarnów a.	0517	0639	0821	...	1837	1935	2118	0039	...
Tarnów **1075** d.	0518	0642	...	...	1838	1938	...	0040	...
Kraków Płaszów **1075** a.	0632	0747	...	...	1929	2047	...	0129	...
Kraków Gł. **1075** a.	0639	0802	...	...	1955	2054	...	0137	...
Warszawa C. **1065/75** a.	...	...	...	...	2301	...	...	...	...

A – ⑥⑦ (also May 2, 3, 26, 27).
w – Not May 2, 3, 26, 27.
z – Not May 2, 3.
‡ – Subject to partial 🚌 substitution.

1079 LOCAL SERVICES IN SILESIA

2nd class

KATOWICE - OSWIECIM

Operator: Koleje Śląskie

km		a						a				
0	Katowice d.	0636	0838	...	1223	1432	...	1538	1641	...	1842	...
33	Oswiecim d.	0743	0951	...	1341	1545	...	1645	1745	...	1943	...
54	Czech. Dziedzice a.	...	...	...	...	...	...	...	...	...	...	...

	a						a	c	a		
Czech. Dziedzice d.	...	...	...	...	...	...	...	...	...	...	...
Oswiecim d.	0526	0631	...	0834	...	1223	1429	1536	1600	1733	...
Katowice a.	0625	0732	...	0934	...	1328	1534	1634	1658	1833	...

KATOWICE - RYBNIK - RACIBÓRZ

Operator: Koleje Śląskie

km		w						a		a	
0	**Katowice** d.	0423	0522	0842	1124	...	1325	1518	1648	1749	1940	2139
45	Rybnik d.	0521	0637	0943	1226	...	1425	1615	1751	1847	2039	2237
81	**Racibórz** a.	0613	0729	1034	1318	...	1517	1707	1843	1938	2131	2329

						c	a	a			
Racibórz d.	0438	0550	0754	1038	1241	1431	1531	1657	1801	1953	215…
Rybnik d.	0530	0647	0852	1129	1333	1524	1630	1753	1853	2045	224…
Katowice a.	0628	0743	0949	1229	1434	1640	1730	1857	1957	2154	234…

RACIBÓRZ - CHAŁUPKI

Operator: Koleje Śląskie

km		a							a			
0	Racibórz d.	0540	0753	...	1340	...	1522	...	1625	...	1955	...
22	Chałupki △ a.	0612	0825	...	1412	...	1554	...	1657	...	2027	...

	a							a			
Chałupki △ d.	0431	...	0642	...	0914	...	1436	1604	...	1907	...
Racibórz a.	0457	...	0708	...	0940	...	1501	1630	...	1932	...

(WROCŁAW -) OPOLE - KEDZIERZYN-KOŹLE - RACIBÓRZ

Operator: Przewozy Regionalne

km												
	Wrocław Gł d.	0728	...	0930	1130	...	...	1343	1459	...	1914	...
0	Opole Gł. d.	0905	...	1105	1305	...	...	1505	1615	...	2034	...
42	Kedzierzyn-Koźle d.	1001	...	1201	1355	1401	...	1602	1708	...	2124	...
74	Racibórz a.	1049	...	1249	...	1449	...	...	1756	...	2212	...

	a	a									
Racibórz d.	0558	...	0713	...	1002	...	1311	1506	...	1713	...
Kedzierzyn-Koźle a.	0646	0650	0804	...	1051	...	1400	1554	1607	1805	...
Opole Gł. a.	...	0742	0905	...	1143	...	1514	...	1700	1856	...
Wrocław Gł a.	...	0903	1023	...	1305	...	1647	...	1827	2033	...

a – ①–⑤ (not May 2, 3, 26, 27).
c – ⑥⑦ (also May 2, 3, 26, 27).
w – ①–⑥ (not May 3, 26).

△ – Chałupki station is situated ± 1600 metres from Stary Bohumín, where a 🚌 service runs approximately every 30 minutes from the main square (náměsti Svobody) to Bohumín (journey 15 mins) and Ostrava (journey 45 mins).

POZNAŃ - OSTRÓW - KATOWICE - KRAKÓW 1080

For other trains Poznań - Katowice - Kraków (via Wrocław) see Table **1075**; for Poznań - Kraków via Łódź see Table **1025**

		TLK 74104			*IC* 83100		*IC* 74102	*IC* 73106	*IC* 83200	*TLK* 83260
		①–⑥ y			①–⑥ y		D		NP	CE
Szczecin Gł. **1010** d.	...	...	...	...	...	...	...	...	1948	1958
Poznań Gł. d.	...	0726	...	...	0938	...	1435	1735	2246	2302
Jarocin d.	...	0817	...	...	1035	...	1532	1831	2340	2358
Ostrów Wlkp. d.	...	0851	...	...	1111	...	1606	1905	0020	0037
Kępno d.	...	0922	...	...	1142	...	1636	1935	0052	|
Częstochowa ✥ d.	...	|	...	...	|	...	|	|	|	|
Kluczbork d.	...	0948	...	...	1208	...	1703	2001	0119	0133
Lubliniec d.	0657	1023	...	1154	1248	1557	1739	2035	0154	0207
Gliwice d.	|	1128	...	|	|	|	1825	|	|	|
Bytom d.	0759	|	...	1257	|	1655	|	|	|	|
Katowice a.	0824	1155	...	1322	|	1720	1850	|	0312	|
Kraków Gł. a.	...	...	...	...	1452	...	...	2236	0545	0422

	TLK 38261	*IC* 38201	*IC* 37107		*IC* 47103		*TLK* 38101		*TLK* 47105	
	CF	NP			D		Ⓑ x		Ⓑ x	
Kraków Gł. d.	0028	2224	0517	...	...	...	1315	...	...	...
Katowice d.	|	0047	|	0741	0949	1332	|	1537	1727	2042
Bytom d.	|	|	|	0812	|	1402	|	1608	|	2112
Gliwice d.	|	|	|	|	1014	|	|	|	1756	|
Lubliniec d.	0234	0240	0724	0924	1057	1515	1524	1717	1840	2220
Kluczbork d.	0307	0316	0759	...	1131	...	1600	...	1915	...
Częstochowa ✥ d.	|	|	|	...	|	...	|	...	|	...
Kępno d.	|	0346	0825	...	1156	...	1626	...	1940	...
Ostrów Wlkp. d.	0406	0422	0856	...	1230	...	1704	...	2011	...
Jarocin d.	0442	0455	0930	...	1305	...	1739	...	2045	...
Poznań Gł. a.	0528	0545	1026	...	1355	...	1836	...	2132	...
Szczecin Gł. **1010** a.	0817	0841	...	...	...	...	...	...	...	...

class

LOCAL TRAINS POZNAŃ / WROCŁAW - OSTRÓW WLKP - ŁÓDŹ

		a			a				
ań Gł. d.	...	0550	...	...	1045	1242	1448	...	...
cin d.	...	0651	...	...	1149	1343	1549	...	...
ocław Gł. **1061** d.	...	|	0740	...	|	|	|	1607	1937
w Wlkp. **1061** d.	0510	0742	1026	...	1240	1434	1637	1832	2145
z **1061** d.	0535	0807	1052	...	1306	1459	1702	1857	...
Kaliska **1061** a.	0732	1005	1300	...	1504	1658	1859	2102	...

								a		
Łódź Kaliska **1061** d.	...	0458	0710	1009	1210	1407	...	1610	1810	...
Kalisz **1061** d.	...	0657	0901	1201	1400	1600	...	1802	2001	...
Ostrów Wlkp. **1061** d.	0529	0735	0950	1237	1448	1634	1637	1841	2026	2037
Wrocław Gł. **1061** a.	0735	0937	|	|	|	1824	|	|	...	|
Jarocin d.	...	...	1029	1316	1527	...	1717	1920	...	2120
Poznań Gł. a.	...	...	1129	1416	1626	...	1820	2046	...	2225

1, 2 cl., 2 cl. and Świnoujście / Szczecin - Poznań - Kraków - Zakopane and v.v. (Table **1066**).
To / from Bielsko Biała (Table **1060**).
⑤⑥ Apr. 29 - June 4 (also May 1, 2, 25, 26).
⑥⑦ Apr. 30 - June 5 (also May 2, 3, 26, 27).

N – Conveys 1, 2 cl., 2 cl. and .
P – To / from Przemyśl (Table **1075**).
a – ①–⑤ (not May 3, 26).
x – Not May 2.
y – Not May 3.

✥ – Częstochowa **Stradom**.
* – *331 km* via Gliwice.

JELENIA GÓRA - TRUTNOV 1082

winter service

		S		S		S			
Jelenia Góra d.	...	...	...	1158	...	1628	...	...	...
Sędzisław d.	...	0809	...	1234	...	1703	...	...	...
Lubawka 🏛 d.	...	0833	...	1259	...	1728	...	...	...
Královec 🏛 d.	...	0842	...	1308	...	1737	...	...	...
Trutnov hlavní a.	...	0911	...	1337	...	1806	...	...	...

		S		S		S			
Trutnov hlavní d.	...	0929	...	1425	...	1909	...	...	...
Královec 🏛 d.	...	1000	...	1501	...	1943	...	...	...
Lubawka 🏛 d.	...	1010	...	1511	...	1945	...	...	...
Sędzisław d.	...	1039	...	1540	...	2008	...	...	...
Jelenia Góra a.	...	1111	...	1610	...	...	...	...	...

⑥⑦ Apr. 23 - Aug. 28 (also May 3, 26, 27, Aug. 15).

Operated by Koleje Dolnośląskie (in Czech Republic by GW Train Regio).

SZKLARSKA POREBA GÓRNA - JELENIA GÓRA - WAŁBRZYCH - WROCŁAW 1084

	EIP 6156	*IC* 60100	⊖	*IC* 61102		*EIC* 6150	*IC* 61100	⊖	⊖	*TLK* 66152
	L			BY	P	J	Y			
Jelenia Góra d.	0451	0758	1016	1224	1402	1437	1615	1745	2014	2114
Sedzisław d.	|	0830	1048	1249	1437	|	1641	1814	2043	2149
Wałbrzych Gł. d.	|	0849	1112	1308	1500	1525	1704	1841	2112	2212
Jaworzyna Śląska d.	|	0930	1157	1347	1541	1603	1745	1923	2154	2254
Wrocław Gł. a.	0635	1005	1248	1421	1624	1637	1820	2007	2244	2328
Warszawa C. △ a.	1030	...	...	2010r	...	2124	...	...	...	...

	TLK 66151	⊖		*IC* 16101	*EIC* 1651	⊖	*IC* 16103	*IC* 66101		*EIP* 1657
			P	Y	J		BY		P	K
Warszawa C. △ d.	...	...	...	...	0745	...	0805r	...	...	1730
Wrocław Gł. d.	0548	0715	0932	1004	1154	1250	1336	1844	1945	2118
Jaworzyna Śląska d.	0625	0800	1015	1037	1229	1334	1410	1919	2037	|
Wałbrzych Gł. d.	0704	0842	1050	1112	1304	1417	1454	1957	2128	|
Sedzisław d.	0724	0904	1110	1136	|	1439	1513	2016	2153	|
Jelenia Góra a.	0758	0936	1142	1202	1355	1512	1540	2054	2229	2303

		H	⊖		⊖	⊖	⊖	⊖	⊖Ⓑ
Jelenia Góra d.	0727	0813	0937	...	1307	1518	1518	1734	1913
Szklarska Poreba Górna a.	0816	0901	1026	...	1416	1613	1613	1823	2002

	⊖d	⊖		P	⊖	⊖		⊖	H
Szklarska Poreba Górna d.	0636	1037	...	1312	1445	1643	...	1912	2005
Jelenia Góra a.	0725	1126	...	1400	1557	1732	...	2005	2054

Białystok - Warszawa - Jelenia Góra and v.v. (Table **1040**).
⑥⑦ (also May 2, 3, 26, 27).
⑥⑦ from Apr. 16 (also May 2, 3, 26, 27).
⑧ from Apr. 29 (not May 2).
①–⑥ from Apr. 30 (not May 3).

P – To / from Poznań (Table **1070**).
Y – From Apr. 30.
d – ①–⑥ only.
r – Until May 26 only.

⊖ – Operated by Koleje Dolnośląskie.
△ – **1060** via Katowice; **1070** via Poznań; **1090** via Łódź.

GÖRLITZ - WROCŁAW 1085

erator: Koleje Dolnośląskie

Dresden **855** d.	0608	...	...	...	...	...	1208	...	1808	...
Görlitz 🏛 d.	0733	...	1034	...	1241	...	1333	...	1933	2100
Zgorzelec 🏛 **1005** d.	0737	...	1038	...	1245	...	1337	...	1937	2104
Zgorzelec Miasto d.	0741	...	1041	...	1248	...	1341	...	1941	2107
Węgliniec **1005** d.	0804	1000	1103	1108	1310	1315	1400	1543	2004	2130
Bolesławiec d.	0824	1018	...	1126	...	1333	1416	1601	2024	*2202*
Legnica **1086** d.	0902	1052	...	1201	...	1408	1447	1635	2102	*2236*
Wrocław Gł. **1086** a.	1010	1149	...	1259	...	1506	1547	1734	2207	*2334*

									Z	
Wrocław Gł. **1086** d.	0453	0606	0938	...	1125	...	1425	1539	...	1805
Legnica **1086** d.	0555	0711	1042	...	1227	...	1524	1643	...	1910
Bolesławiec d.	0627	0749	1116	...	1301	...	1554	1717	...	1949
Węgliniec **1005** d.	0642	0809	1133	1142	1318	1333	1612	1734	1739	2009
Zgorzelec Miasto d.	*0719*	0829	...	1203	...	1354	1629	...	1800	2029
Zgorzelec 🏛 **1005** d.	*0723*	0833	...	1207	...	1405	1633	...	1804	2033
Görlitz 🏛 a.	...	0837	...	1210	...	1408	1637	...	1807	2037
Dresden **855** a.	...	0959	...	...	...	...	1759	...	...	2159

From Zielona Góra (Table **1005**).

COTTBUS - FORST - WROCŁAW 1086

		①-⑤	⊖	⑥⑦	⊖ ⑥⑦	⑥⑦	①-⑤	⊖	①-⑤	⑥⑦		⊖
		z		y	wh	q	p		z	y		
Berlin Licht d.	...	...	...	...	0831	...	...	...	...	...	...	...
Cottbus **854** d.	...	*0607*	...	*0907*	0953u	...	...	...	*1607*	*1707*	...	...
Forst 🏛 **854** a.	...	*0626*	...	*0926*	1006u	...	...	...	*1626*	*1726*	...	...
Forst d.	...	0635	...	0940	1008u	...	...	...	1644	1735	...	...
Tuplice d.	...	0650	...	0955	|	...	...	...	1659	1750	...	...
Záry **1005** d.	0513	0711	0807	1016	1041	1220	1332	1637	1720	1811	1832	2057
Zagań **1005** d.	0526	0723	0819	1028	1058	1232	1344	1650	1732	1823	1844	2109
Legnica **1085** d.	0657	...	0954	...	1219	1356	1511	1815	...	...	2015	2233
Wrocław Gł. **1085** a.	...	...	1053	...	1305	...	...	1915	...	...	...	...

	①-⑤	⊖	⑥⑦	①-⑤	⑥⑦	①-⑤	⊖	⑥⑦		⊖ ⑦	⊖	⊖ ⑥	
	z		y	p	q	z		y		xh		w	
Wrocław Gł. **1085** d.	...	...	...	...	...	...	1302	...	...	1629	1715	1921	...
Legnica **1085** d.	...	0600	...	0748	0853	...	1411	...	1544	1713	1815	2006	2135
Zagań **1005** d.	0537	0724	0825	0911	1020	1519	1541	1630	1713	1846	1937	2133	2302
Záry **1005** d.	0549	0736	0838	0923	1033	1558	1553	1642	1726	1858	1949	2148	2315
Tuplice d.	0611	...	0859	...	...	1619	...	1704	...	|	...	|	...
Forst a.	0626	...	0914	...	...	1634	...	1719	...	1930s	...	2220s	...
Forst 🏛 **854** d.	*0633*	...	*0933*	...	...	...	...	*1733*	...	1942s	...	2222s	...
Cottbus **854** a.	*0651*	...	*0951*	...	...	...	...	*1751*	...	2005s	...	2239	...
Berlin Licht a.	...	...	...	...	...	...	...	...	...	2135	...	2354	...

Also May 5, 16.
Not May 2, 3, 26, 27.
Also May 2, 3, 26, 27.

s – Stops to set down only.
u – Stops to pick up only.
w – Apr. 30 - June 11.

x – May 1 - June 5.
y – Also May 3, 26.
z – Not May 3, 26.

⊖ – Operated by Koleje Dolnośląskie.
▽ – Via Table **1085**.

1090 WARSZAWA - ŁÓDŹ

km		IR	TLK	IC	TLK	IR	IC	♣	IR	TLK	TLK	IR	TLK	IC	IC	TLK	IR		TLK	TLK	TLK	IR	♣	IC
		10120	19108	16102	19100	10122	16104		10124	19102	19158	10126	19160	26106	1910	19164	10128		19166	19104	19168	10130		17104
		10121	19109	16103	19101	10123	16105		10125	19103	19159	10127	19161	26107	1911	19165	10129		19167	19105	19169	10131		17105
								⑥⑦	①–⑤		①–⑤		①–⑤		①–⑤	①–⑤			①–⑤		①–⑤	①–⑤	⑥⑦	
				J			W	h	m		m		m	W	m	m			m		m	m	h	O
0	**Warszawa** Wschodnia .. d.	0406	0554	0734r	0954	1024	1149r	1254	1254	1400	1454	1504	1522	1555	1624	1653	1659	...	1726	1754	1853	1933	1934	2029
4	**Warszawa** Centralna .. d.	0417	0605	0805r	1005	1035	1205r	1315	1305	1410	1504	1514	1534	1606	1645	1704	1714	...	1740	1805	1904	1941	1945	2045
70	Skierniewice .... d.	0503	0655	0853	1057	1122	1254	1348	1353	1456	1551	1600	1624	1652	|	1749	1814	...	1828	1855	1950	2028	2016	2134
109	Koluszki .... d.	0527	0719	0919	1122	1148	1318	1415	1419	1523	1618	1627	1652	1719	|	1818	1839	...	1858	1925	2019	2055	2037	2159
137	**Łódź** Chojny .... a.	0548	0742	0945	1146	1212	1344	1443	1444	1550	1643	1653	1717	1744	1802	1844	1905	...	1924	1949	2043	2118	2116	2225
144	**Łódź** Kaliska .... a.	0557	0749	...	1153	1220	...	1451	1452	1557	1650	1702	1724	...	1809	1851	1913	...	1931	1956	2050	2126	2124	...

	TLK	TLK	TLK	IC	TLK	IR	IC	IR	♣	TLK	TLK	TLK	IC	IR	TLK	IR	IC	IR	♣	TLK	TLK	IC	IR
	91151	91153	91155	9111	91157	10133	71105	10135		91103	91103	91159	62107	10137	91105	10139	61105	10141		91107	91167	61103	10143
	91150	91152	91154	9110	91156	10132	71104	10134		91102	91102	91158	62106	10136	91104	10138	61104	10140		91106	91166	61102	10142
	①–⑤		①–⑤	①–⑤	①–⑤			①–⑤	⑥⑦			①–⑤						①–⑤	⑥⑦		①–⑤		
	m		m	m	m		O	m	h	B	A	m	W				W	m	h		m	J	
Łódź Kaliska .... d.	0432	0503	0537	0623	0640	0649	...	0803	0803	0813	0813	0913	...	1156	1212	1344	...	1541	1543	1613	1716	...	1905
Łódź Chojny .... d.	0441	0511	0545	0630	0648	0657	0708	0813	0811	0821	0821	0921	1021	1205	1220	1353	1421	1550	1551	1621	1724	1819	1914
Koluszki .... d.	0507	0538	0611	|	0712	0724	0735	0840	0840	0846	0846	0951	|	1229	1244	1417	|	1613	1613	1648	1751	1854	1936
Skierniewice .... d.	0534	0605	0638	|	0741	0753	0804	0902	0903	0910	0923	1018	1120	1256	1309	1442	1518	1637	1634	1714	1817	1920	2006
Warszawa Centralna .... a.	0625	0700	0728	0751	0832	0839	0851	0948	0946	0955	1013	1109	1206	1344	1401	1528	1605r	1733	1710	1803	1908	2010r	2052
Warszawa Wschodnia .... a.	0636	0711	0738	0806	0845	0850	0902	1001	1001	1006	1035	1135	1216	1400	1412	1541	1616r	1746	1717	1814	1934	2021r	2101

A – Until May 20.
B – From May 21.
J – To / from Jelenia Góra / Szklarska Poreba Górna (Tables **1061/84**).
O – To / from Ostrów Wlkp (Table **1061**).
W – To / from Wrocław (Table **1061**).

h – Also May 3.
m – Not May 3, 26.
r – Until May 26 only.
♣ – Operator: Łódźka Kolej Aglomeracyjna (ŁKA).

1095 WROCŁAW - KŁODZKO

Certain trains continue beyond Kłodzko – see Table **1165**

km													
									①-⑥				
		a		c		z	y					b	
0	**Wrocław** Gł. .... d.	0535	0634	0721	0830	0957	1040	1307	1405	1454	1645	1758	2255
72	Kamieniec Ząbkowicki ..... d.	0659	0755	0838	0945	1113	1156	1412	1517	1601	1753	1909	0014
94	**Kłodzko** Gł. **1165** .... a.	0726	0822	0901	1013	1140	1223	1436	1544	1630	1822	1937	0042

								c	
Kłodzko Gł. **1165** .... d.	0531	0632	0734	0850	1038	1226	1455	1614	1850
Kamieniec Ząbkowicki ... d.	0558	0700	0801	0917	1102	1253	1522	1637	1916
Wrocław Gł. .... a.	0707	0807	0910	1028	1205	1402	1634	1747	2022

a – ①–⑤ (not May 2, 3, 26, 27). **b** – ⑧ (not May 1, 2, 26). **c** – ⑥⑦ (also May 2, 3, 26, 27). **y** – Not Apr. 15 - May 16. **z** – Apr. 15 - May 16.

1099 OTHER LOCAL SERVICES

Subject to alteration on and around holidays 2nd class o

GDYNIA - HEL *77 km, journey 1 hr 50 mins - 2 hrs*

Gdynia Główna depart: 0548, 0704, 0900, 1036, 1228, 1403, 1532, 1706, 1909, 2118.
Hel depart: 0450, 0625, 0920, 1212, 1302, 1428, 1548, 1713, 1915.

KŁODZKO - KUDOWA-ZDRÓJ *44 km, journey 1 hr 10 mins*

Kłodzko Główne depart: 0735, 0905, 1214, 1440, 1758, 1945⑧.
Kudowa-Zdrój depart: 0603①–⑥, 0921, 1106, 1330, 1559, 1919.
Operator: Koleje Dolnośląskie.

KRAKÓW - KRAKÓW BALICE AIRPORT ✈ *12 km, journey 18 mins*

Kraków Główny depart: 0405, 0505, 0535, 0605, 0635 and every 30 minutes until 2035, then 2118, 2135, 2205, 2235, 2305, 2335.
Kraków Balice ✈ depart: 0516, 0546, 0616, 0646 and every 30 minutes until 2046, then 2111, 2146, 2211, 2241, 2311, 2341, 0015.

KRAKÓW - OŚWIĘCIM (for Auschwitz-Birkenau Memorial and Museum)

VIA TRZEBINIA 65 km *Journey 1 hr 45 mins - 1 hr 50 mins*
Kraków Główny depart: 0644, 1040, 1138, 1340, 1437, 1545, 1640, 1758, 1940, 2207.
Oświęcim depart: 0336, 0401, 0511, 0609, 0709, 0915, 1236, 1345, 1551, 1747, 1946.

KRAKÓW - WADOWICE *62 km, journey 1 hr 45 mins*

Currently subject to partial 🚌 replacement; timings vary.
Kraków Płaszów depart:
Wadowice depart:
Wadowice is the birthplace of Pope John Paul II.

KRAKÓW - WIELICZKA (for Salt Mine) *15 km, journey 25–30 mins*

Kraków Główny depart: 0508, 0539, 0609, 0637, 0709, 0739, 0809, 0839 and every 30 minutes until 2039, then 2108, 2209.
Wieliczka Rynek depart: 0538, 0608, 0638, 0708, 0738 and every 30 minutes until 2038, then 2108, 2136, 2238.

Subject to confirmation

LESZNO - WOLSZTYN - ZBĄSZYNEK Operator: *Koleje Wielkopolsk*

	B	L	M			A			
Leszno .... d.	0525	0754	0843	1051	...	1350	1438	...	1630
Wolsztyn .... d.	0622	0859	0941	1148	...	1448	1536	...	1734
Zbąszyń .... d.	0649	...	...	1215	...	...	1604	...	...
Zbąszynek .... a.	0656	...	...	...	...	...	1610	...	...

		B		L	M		A		
Zbąszynek .... d.	...	0710	...	...	...	...	...	1627	...
Zbąszyń .... d.	...	0716	...	...	...	1224	...	1633	...
Wolsztyn .... d.	0625	0743	...	0939	0951	1251	1500	1700	...
Leszno .... a.	0723	0841	...	1037	1049	1348	1604	1757	...

POZNAN - WOLSZTYN *81 km, journey 1 hr 25 mins - 2 h*

Poznan Główny depart: 0617 **y**, 0734 **D**, 0754 **C**, 0959 **A**, 1148 **z**, 1338 **y**, 1453 **A**, 1602, 1701⑧, 1800 **C**, 1819 **D**, 1952 **C**, 2006 **D**.
Wolsztyn depart: 0449①–⑥, 0546, 0800 **y**, 0948, 1151 **A**, 1344 **z**, 1541 **z**, 1654 **A**, 1753,
Operator: Koleje Wielkopolskie.

REJOWIEC - ZAMOŚĆ *63 km, journey 1 hr 10 mi*

Rejowiec depart: 0956 **E**, 1419 **G**, 1432 **H**, 1742, 2132⑧.
Zamość depart: 0525 ①–⑥, 0826, 1210, 1552 **E**.

WAŁBRZYCH - KŁODZKO *51 km, journey 1 hr 25 mi*

Wałbrzych Główny depart: 0605 **A**, 0855, 1318, 1640, 1936.
Kłodzko Główne depart: 0435 **A**, 0717, 1041, 1443, 1728.
Operator: Koleje Dolnośląskie.

WARSZAWA - WARSZAWA MODLIN AIRPORT ✈ *40 km, journey 36 mi*

Warszawa Centralna depart: 0315, 0420, 0515, 0615, 0715, 0815, 0915, 1015, 1115, 1
1315, 1415, 1515, 1615, 1715, 1815, 1915, 2015, 2115, 2215, 2315.
Modlin ✈ depart: 0423, 0522, 0620, 0722, 0822, 0922, 1022, 1120, 1222, 1322, 1420, 1
1621, 1722, 1822, 1920, 2020, 2120, 2228, 2323.

Subject to alteration from May 27

A 🚌 connects the rail station with the terminal. Additional slower trains run Modlin ✈ to Warszawa Gdánska, with metro connection to city centre.
Operator: Koleje Mazowieckie.

A – ①–⑤ (not May 2, 3, 26, 27).
B – ①–⑥ (not May 2, 3, 27, 28).
C – Until Apr. 10.
D – From Apr. 11.
E – Not Apr. 30 - May 3.
G – From Apr. 15.
H – Until Apr. 14.
L – Not May 16 - 23, 26, 28.
M – May 16 - 23.
y – Not May 26, 28.
z – Not Apr. 30.

CZECH REPUBLIC

ices:	Operator: České Dráhy (ČD), www.cd.cz. Railway infrastructure and timetables are the responsibility of Správa železniční dopravní cesty (SŽDC), www.szdc.cz. All daytime trains convey first and second classes of travel unless otherwise shown by '2' at the top of the column or by a note (which may be in the table heading).
ngs:	Valid **June 12 - December 10, 2016**. Certain trains are cancelled during the Christmas / New Year period, particularly the evening of Dec. 24, 31 and the morning of Dec. 25, 26, Jan. 1; passengers travelling during this period are advised to confirm train times before travel.
ervations:	It is possible to reserve seats on most Express trains.
olements:	SuperCity (*SC*) tilting trains have a compulsory reservation fee of 250 CZK. *Business* class on Railjet (RJ) trains requires a first class ticket and a supplement of 250 CZK.
on names:	hlavní = main; západ = west; východ = east; horní = upper; dolní = lower; střed = centre, starý = old; město = town; předměstí = suburban; nádraží = station.

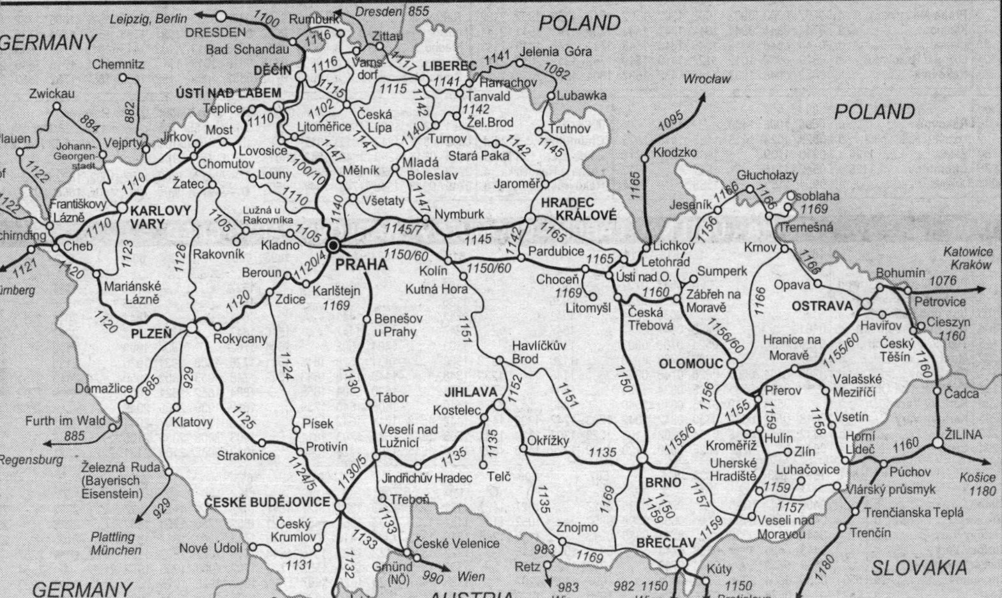

PRAHA - ÚSTÍ NAD LABEM - DĚČÍN - DRESDEN — 1100

m	*Praha - Ústí : see also* **1110**	*EN* 476 M	616 C	*EC* 178 B	692	*EC* 176 H	690	*EC* 174 H	688	*EC* 378 K	686	*EC* 172 J	684	682 Ⓐ	1171 2	*EC* 170 B	680	678 Ⓐ	*EN** 458 LN	676	674 Ⓐ	672		670
0	**Praha** hlavní ▷ d.	0427	0517	0627	...	0827	...	1027	...	1227	...	1427	...	...	...	1627	...	...	1827	...	...	...	...	2331
	Praha Masarykovo d.	|	|	|	0653	|	0853	|	1053	|	1253	|	1453	1553	...	|	1653	1753	|	1853	1953	2053	2141	|
3	**Praha** Holešovice ▷ d.	0436	0526	0636	|	0836	|	1036	|	1236	|	1436	|	|	...	1636	|	|	1836	|	|	|	|	2340
7	Kralupy nad Vltavou d.	|	0548	|	0718	|	0918	|	1118	|	1318	|	1518	1618	...	|	1718	1818	|	1918	2018	2118	2215	0001
6	Roudnice nad Labem d.	|	0609	|	0743	|	0943	|	1143	|	1343	|	1543	1643	...	|	1743	1843	|	1943	2043	2143	2250	0026
4	Lovosice d.	|	0622	|	0759	|	0959	|	1159	|	1359	|	1559	1659	1708a	|	1759	1859	|	1959	2059	2159	2306	0042
6	**Ústí nad Labem** hlavní ▷ a.	0541	0639	0741	0815	0941	1015	1141	1215	1341	1415	1541	1615	1716	1724a	1741	1815	1915	1941	2015	2116	2215	2326	0058
6	**Ústí nad Labem** hlavní ▶ d.	0543	*0658*	0743	0817	0943	1017	1143	1217	1343	1417	1543	1617	...	1726	1743	1817	1917	1943	2017	*2120*	2217	2327	0100
9	**Děčín** ▶ a.	0558	*0724*	0758	0832	0958	1032	1158	1232	1358	1432	1558	1632	...	1743	1758	1832	1932	1958	2032	*2136*	2232	2346	0115
9	**Děčín** 🏛 ⊖ d.	0600	...	0800	...	1000	...	1200	...	1400	...	1600	...	...	...	1800	...	...	2000	...	...	...	...	...
1	Bad Schandau 🏛 ⊖ **857** d.	|	...	0817	...	1017	...	1217	...	1417	...	1617	...	...	...	1817	...	...	2017	...	...	...	...	...
1	**Dresden** Hbf **857** a.	0644	...	0844	...	1044	...	1244	...	1444	...	1644	...	...	...	1844	...	...	2045	...	...	...	...	...

	671	673	675 Ⓐ	677	*EN** 459 L	1172 2	679 Ⓐ	681	*EC* 171 BN	683	*EC* 173 J	2Ⓐ	685	*EC* 379 K	687	*EC* 175 B	689	*EC* 177 H	691	*EC* 179 H		617 C	*EN* 477 M	2
sden Hbf **857** d.	...	...	...	...	0708	...	...	...	0908	...	1108	...	...	1308	...	1508	...	1708	...	1908	...	...	2108	...
Schandau 🏛 ⊖ **857** d.	...	...	...	...	0738	...	...	...	0938	...	1138	...	...	1338	...	1538	...	1738	...	1938	...	...	|	...
čín 🏛 ⊖ a.	...	...	...	...	0753	...	...	...	0953	...	1153	...	...	1353	...	1553	...	1753	...	1953	...	...	2153	...
čín ▶ d.	0424	0524	0624	0724	0756	0816	...	0924	0956	1124	1156	...	1324	1356	1524	1556	1724	1756	1924	1956	2042	...	2156	2228
í nad Labem hlavní ▶ a.	0439	0539	0639	0739	0811	0832	...	0939	1011	1139	1211	...	1339	1411	1539	1611	1739	1811	1939	2011	2108	...	2211	2257
í nad Labem hlavní ▷ d.	0441	0541	0641	0741	0813	...	0841	0941	1013	1141	1213	1242	1341	1413	1541	1613	1741	1813	1941	2013	...	2113	2213	2300
osice d.	0458	0558	0658	0758	|	...	0858	0958	|	1158	|	1259	1358	|	1558	|	1758	|	1958	|	...	2131	|	2322
ıdnice nad Labem d.	0513	0613	0713	0813	|	...	0913	1013	|	1213	|	1314	1413	|	1613	|	1813	|	2013	|	...	2145	|	2337
upy nad Vltavou d.	0538	0638	0738	0838	|	...	0938	1038	|	1238	|	...	1438	|	1638	|	1838	|	2038	|	...	2210	|	...
ha Holešovice ▷ a.	|	|	|	|	0918	...	|	|	1118	|	1318	...	|	1518	|	1718	|	1918	2058	2118	...	2229	2318	...
raha Masarykovo a.	0602	0702	0802	0902	|	...	1002	1102	|	1302	|	...	1502	|	1702	|	1902	|	|	|	...	|	|	...
ha hlavní ▷ a.	...	...	...	...	0928	...	...	...	1128	...	1328	...	...	1528	...	1728	...	1928	2108	2128	...	2239	2328	...

ADDITIONAL LOCAL TRAINS DĚČÍN - DRESDEN AND V.V.

			W					S			
merice město d.	...	...	...	...	...	...	...	1617	...	...	...
í n.L. hlavní d.	...	...	0918	...	...	...	...	1652	...	...	...
čín 🏛 ⊖ **1116** d.	0640	0840	0936	1040	1240	1440	1640	1710	1840	2040	2240
Schandau **1116** a.	*0708*	0908	0951	1108	1308	1508	1708	1727	1908	2108	2308
Schandau **857** d.	*0715*	*0915*	0952	*1115*	*1315*	*1515*	*1715*	1729	*1915*	*2115*	*2315*
sden Hbf ◇ **857** a.	*0758*	*0958*	1021	*1158*	*1358*	*1558*	*1758*	1806	*1958*	*2158*	*2358*

		S					W				
Dresden Hbf ◇ **857** d.	*0559*	0750	*0759*	*0959*	*1159*	*1359*	1605	*1559*	*1759*	*1959*	*2259*
Bad Schandau . **857** a.	*0643*	0825	*0843*	*1043*	*1243*	*1443*	1633	*1643*	*1843*	*2043*	*2343*
Bad Schandau **1116** d.	0650	0826	0850	1050	1250	1450	1635	1650	1850	2050	2350
Děčín 🏛 ⊖ **1116** a.	0717	0844	0917	1117	1317	1517	1652	1717	1917	2117	0012
Ústí n.L. hlavní a.	...	0904	...	...	...	...	1710	...	...	...	...
Litomerice město a.	...	0940	...	...	...	...	...	...	...	...	...

- [12] Praha - Dresden - Berlin and v.v.
- [12] Praha - Ústí nad Labem - Karlovy Vary - Cheb and v.v.
- [12] ✕ Praha - Dresden - Berlin - Hamburg and v.v.
- HUNGARIA – [12] ✕ Budapest - Bratislava - Brno - Praha - Dresden - Berlin - Hamburg and v.v.
- [12] ✕ Praha - Dresden - Berlin - Hamburg - Kiel and v.v.
- KOPERNIKUS – [2] Praha - Dresden - Leipzig and v.v.; 🛏 1, 2 cl., ▬ 2 cl., [2] (🅁) Praha - Leipzig - Erfurt - Frankfurt Süd - Basel - Zürich and v.v. (Table **54**).
- METROPOL – 🛏 1, 2 cl., ▬ 2 cl., [2] (⊡) Budapest - Bratislava - Brno - Praha - Dresden - Berlin and v.v.; 🛏 1, 2 cl., ▬ 2 cl., [2] (⊡) Wien - Brno - Praha - Dresden - Berlin and v.v. (Table **60**).
- Conveys 🛏 1, 2 cl., ▬ 2 cl., [2] (🅁) Praha - Dresden - Berlin - Köln and v.v. (Table **54**).
- ⑥⑦ Apr. 2 - Oct. 30, also Mar. 25 - 28, Oct. 31.
- Dec. 13, 19, 20; ⑥⑦ Nov. 26 - Dec. 10.
- Ⓐ only.

▶ – Ústí nad Labem - Děčín: see also Table **1115** and foot of Table **1110**.
▷ – For other non-stop trains Praha - Ústí nad Labem and v.v. see Table **1110**.
◇ – Local trains continue to / from Meissen.
⊖ – Routeing point for international tickets: Schöna.
⊡ – 🅁 for international journeys.
* – Classified *CNL* in Germany.

FOR OTHER TRAIN NAMES SEE TABLE **60**.

For additional non-stop trains Praha - Ústí nad Labem see Table **1110**.

1102 LOVOSICE - LITOMĚŘICE - ČESKÁ LIPA

2nd cl

km										
0	**Lovosice 1100** d.	0601	0801	1001	1201	1401	1601	1801	2001	2214
8	Litoměřice horní d.	0616	0816	1016	1216	1416	1616	1816	2016	2227
50	**Česká Lípa** a.	0723	0923	1123	1323	1523	1723	1923	2123	...

		Ⓐ									
Česká Lípa d.	...	0443	0633	0833	1033	1233	1433	1633	1833	2033	
Litoměřice horní d.	0021	0559	0740	0940	1140	1340	1540	1740	1940	2141	2
Lovosice 1100 a.	0034	0614	0752	0952	1152	1352	1552	1752	1952	2153	2

Also: Lovosice - Litoměřice horní: 0055, 0500, 0638Ⓐ, 0736, 0836, 0936, 1036, 1136, 1236, 1336, 1436, 1501Ⓐ, 1536, 1636, 1701Ⓐ, 1736, 1836, 1901Ⓐ, 1936, 2036, 2138, 2238Ⓐ, 2
Litoměřice horní - Lovosice: 0502, 0531Ⓐ, 0640Ⓐ, 0659Ⓐ, 0759, 0840Ⓐ, 0903, 0959, 1103, 1159, 1303, 1359, 1439Ⓐ, 1459, 1559, 1639Ⓐ, 1659, 1759, 1839Ⓐ, 1859, 1959, 2114, 2

1105 PRAHA - RAKOVNIK - CHOMUTOV - JIRKOV

km			2◧		2◧			2Ⓐ			R
0	**Praha** Masarykovo d.	0702	0802	0902	1002	1302	1502	1618	1702	1902	2102
31	Kladno a.	0741	0841	0941	1041	1341	1541	1708	1741	1941	2141
31	Kladno d.	0743	*0846*	0943	*1046*	1343	1543	1711	1743	1943	2143
64	Lužná u Rakovnika a.	0819	*0927*	1019	*1127*	1419	1619	1752	1819	2019	2219
73	**Rakovník** a.	0832	*0948*	1032	*1140*	1432	1632	1804	1832	2032	2232

	⚒n	2			2◐			2◐		(
Rakovník d.	0516	0618	0722	0922	*1006*	1322	1522	*1606*	1722	1
Lužná u Rakovnika d.	0527	0632	0735	0935	*1021*	1335	1535	*1621*	1735	1
Kladno a.	0604	0711	0813	1013	*1103*	1413	1613	*1703*	1813	2
Kladno d.	0608	0715	0815	1015	1115	1415	1615	1715	1815	2
Praha Masarykovo a.	0646	0752	0852	1052	1152	1452	1652	1752	1852	2

km	*2nd class*	Ⓒ					
0	**Rakovnik** d.	*0806*	*1006*	1406	...	1806	...
9	Lužná u Rakovnika d.	0823	1023	1418	1423	1818	1823
50	Žatec **1126** d.	0910	1109	...	1509	...	1911
75	**Chomutov 1126** a.	0942	1135	...	1541	...	1942
81	Jirkov a.	0954	1153	...	1553	...	1954

	Ⓐ	Ⓒ			⑦e	⑤⑥
Jirkov d.	0551	0800	1200	1600	1800	...
Chomutov 1126 d.	0602	0812	1212	1612	1812	*1928*
Žatec **1126** d.	0643	0843	1243	1643	1843	2001
Lužná u Rakovnika a.	0729	0929	1329	1729	1929	2043
Rakovník a.	0749	*0948*	*1348*	*1748*	*1944*	2059

R – Ⓑ to Kladno; ⑦**e** to Rakovnik.
e – Also Mar. 28, July 6; not Dec. 27, Mar. 27, Ju
n – ①–⑥ (not Dec. 25, 26, Jan. 1, 2, Mar. 28, 6, Oct. 29).
◧ – Also at 1202, 1402, 1602, 1802, 2002.
◐ – Also at *0806*, *1207*, *1406*, *1806*, *2033*.

1110 PRAHA - ÚSTI NAD LABEM - CHOMUTOV - KARLOVY VARY - CHEB

km		1690				616	614		612			610		1694	608		1696	606			604		602		
			2	Ⓐ			K	Ⓐ	m		Ⓐ			Ⓐ			2Ⓐ		2Ⓒ	Ⓐ		2			
0	**Praha** hlavní ▶ d.	...	...	...	...	0517	0727	...	0927	...	...	1127	...	...	1327	...	...	1527	...	...	1727	...	1927	...	
3	**Praha** Holešovice ▶ d.	...	...	...	...	0526	0736	...	0936	...	...	1136	...	...	1336	...	...	1536	...	...	1736	...	1936	...	
106	**Ústí nad Labem** hl ▶ a.	...	...	...	...	0639	0841	...	1041	...	...	1241	...	...	1441	...	...	1641	...	...	1841	...	2041	...	
106	**Ústí nad Labem** hl d.	0101	...	...	0458	0647	0847	...	1047	...	...	1247	...	1346	1447	...	1546	1647	...	*1746*	1847	...	2047	...	2
123	Teplice v Čechách d.	0120	...	...	0521	0703	0903	...	1103	...	...	1303	...	1404	1503	...	1604	1703	...	*1804*	1903	...	2103	...	2
152	**Most** d.	0147	...	...	0600	0728	0928	...	1128	...	*1213*	1328	...	1431	1528	1613	1631	1728	1808	*1831*	1930	...	2130	...	2
177	**Chomutov** d.	0205	0404	0508	0625	0748	0948	...	1148	...	*1233*	1348	...	1449	1548	1633	1649	1748	1833	1853	1950	...	2148	2151	2
196	Klášterec nad Ohři d.	▬	0439	0531	0643	0804	1004	...	1204	...	*1252*	1404	...	1520	1604	1655	...	1804	1852	1921	2006	...	▬	2209	
236	**Karlovy Vary** ⊙ a.	...	0524	0619	0726	0840	1040	...	1240	...	*1336*	1440	...	1606	1640	1739	...	1840	1939	2005	2042	...	2	2252	
236	**Karlovy Vary** ⊙ d.	0418	*0530*	0622	0730	0842	1042	1203	1242	1308	1412	1442	1518	1611	1642	1744	...	1842	1940	2007	2044	2122	2222	...	
262	Sokolov d.	0442	*0554*	0648	0754	0903	1103	1229	1303	1334	1437	1503	1544	1636	1703	1811	...	1903	2008	2035	2105	2148	2248	...	
291	**Cheb** a.	0513	*0625*	0722	0825	0929	1129	1300	1329	1405	1509	1529	1615	1707	1729	1842	...	1929	2042	2106	2131	2221	2321	...	

	601	1691	603		1695	605		607		609			611			613		615			617				
	Ⓐ	2Ⓐ		2	2Ⓐ		2Ⓒ				Ⓒ	Ⓐ		Ⓐ	Ⓒ	m		K	Ⓒ	Ⓐ			2	2	
Cheb d.	...	0400	...	0425	...	0625	0735	0827	...	1027	1121	1121	1227	*1243*	1321	1427	1547	1627	*1705*	1722	1827	...	2003	...	2
Sokolov d.	...	0425	...	0456	...	0650	0809	0852	...	1052	1151	1151	1252	*1315*	1351	1452	1621	1652	*1736*	1753	1852	...	2036	...	2
Karlovy Vary ⊙ a.	...	0447	...	0520	...	0711	0835	0913	...	1113	1216	1216	1313	*1340*	1416	1513	1645	1713	*1801*	1817	1913	...	2103	...	2
Karlovy Vary ⊙ d.	...	0448	*0448*	▬	0558	0713	...	0915	1022	1115	...	1222	1315	1422	1422	1515	1648	1715	1822	1822	1915	2022	▬	2257	
Klášterec nad Ohři d.	...	0539	*0539*	Ⓐ	0643	0750	...	0952	1106	1152	...	1306	1352	1506	1506	1552	1733	1752	1906	1906	1952	2126*	Ⓐ	2354	
Chomutov d.	0504	0556	0604	0626	0702	0805	...	1007	1125	1207	...	1325	1407	1525	1525	1607	1750r	1807	1925	1925	2007	2143	2300	0023	
Most d.	0523	...	0623	0649	0721	0824	...	1026	1144	1226	...	1349	1426	1544	1544	1626	...	1826	1944	1944	2026	2202	2318	...	
Teplice v Čechách d.	0551	...	0651	0716	0749	0851	...	1051	...	1251	...	...	1451	...	...	1651	...	1851	...	...	2051	2235	...	...	
Ústí nad Labem hl a.	0607	...	0707	0733	0808	0907	...	1107	...	1307	...	...	1507	...	...	1707	...	1907	...	...	2107	2257	...	...	
Ústí nad Labem hl. ▶ d.	0613	...	0713	...	...	0913	...	1113	...	1313	...	...	1513	...	...	1713	...	1913	...	...	2113	...	...	...	
Praha Holešovice ▶ a.	0718	...	0818	...	...	1018	...	1218	...	1418	...	...	1618	...	...	1818	...	2018	...	...	2229	...	...	...	
Praha hlavní ▶ a.	0728s	...	0828	...	...	1028	...	1228	...	1428	...	...	1628	...	...	1828	...	2028	...	...	2239	...	...	...	

km	*via Louny (2 cl.)*	Ⓒ§	Ⓐ§
0	**Praha** Masarykovo d.	0726	1623
47	Slaný d.	0825	1730
90	Louny d.	0911	1825
115	**Most** a.	0940	...

via Louny (2 cl.)	Ⓐ§	Ⓒ§
Most d.	...	1647
Louny d.	0529	1715
Slaný d.	0625	1801
Praha Masarykovo a.	0732	1856

Local trains (2 cl.)				⊡
Děčín ▶ d.	0530	and	1930	2042
Ústí n. L. hlavní ▶ d.	0558	hourly	1958	2120
Teplice v Čechách d.	0621	⊡	2021	2140
Most a.	0654	until	2054	2209

Local trains (2 cl.)				
Most d.	0502	and	2002	2
Teplice v Čechách d.	0535	hourly	2035	2
Ústí n. L. hlavní ▶ d.	0558	⊖	2058	2
Děčín ▶ a.	0624	until	2124	

K – Also conveys 🛏 1, 2 cl. Cheb - Karlovy Vary - Praha (**445/4**) - Žilina - Košice and v.v. (not Dec. 24. 31).
m – Conveys on ③⑤ from Moskva, ④⑥ from Cheb: 🛏 1, 2 cl. Moskva - Praha - Cheb and v.v. (Table **95**).
r – Ⓐ only (on Ⓒ terminates at Klášterec nad Ohři).
s – Praha **Masarykovo**.
▶ – For other non-stop trains see Table **1100**.
⊙ – Known locally as Karlovy Vary horní (upper).
⊖ – Also Ústí - Děčín at 0456, 0527, 1432Ⓐ, 2227.
⊡ – Also Děčín - Ústí at 0016, 0600Ⓐ, 0658Ⓐ, 2120, 222
§ – For other journeys Praha - Louny change at Kralupy n.
* – Arrives 2105.

1115 ÚSTÍ NAD LABEM - DĚČÍN - ČESKÁ LIPA - LIBEREC

2nd cla

km		1997	1999	1161	1163	1165	1167	1169	1171	1173	1175
		Ⓐ									Ⓑh
0	**Ústí nad Labem** hl. § d.	...	...	0727	0927	1127	1327	1527	1726	1927	2120
23	**Děčín** § d.	0427	0526	0745	0945	1145	1345	1545	1745	1945	2137
54	Česká Lipa d.	0512	0610	0826	1026	1226	1426	1626	1826	2022	2213
113	**Liberec** a.	0624	0729	0943	1143	1343	1543	1743	1943	2131	...

	1174	1172	1170	1168	1166	1164	1162	1160		
	⚒n									
Liberec d.	...	0628	0828	1028	1228	1428	1628	1828	2040	
Česká Lipa d.	0609	0738	0938	1138	1338	1538	1738	1938	2208	22
Děčín § d.	0647	0816	1016	1216	1416	1616	1816	2016	...	23
Ústí nad Labem hl. § a.	0704	0832	1032	1232	1432	1632	1832	2032	...	

h – Not Dec. 24, 25, 31, Jan. 1, Mar. 27, July 5, Oct. 28.
n – ①–⑥ (not Dec. 25, 26, Jan. 1, 2, Mar. 28, July 6, Oct. 29).
§ – See also Table **1100** and foot of Table **111**

1116 DĚČÍN - RYBNIŠTĚ - RUMBURK / DĚČÍN - SEBNITZ - RUMBURK

km	🚌							Ⓐc			
0	**Děčín** d.	0615	0815	1015	1215	1415	1615	1713	1815	2015	2236
25	Česká Kamenice d.	0649	0849	1049	1249	1449	1649	1745	1849	2049	2307
50	Rybniště a.	0725	0923	1125	1325	1525	1725	1825	1918	2118	2332
61	**Rumburk** a.	0741	0936	1141	1341	1541	1741	1840	1931	2131	2345

🚌	Ⓐ							Ⓐc		
Rumburk d.	0359	0617	0817	1014	1214	1422	1622	1714	1814	20
Rybniště d.	0414	0630	0830	1030	1230	1435	1635	1728	1827	20
Česká Kamenice d.	0443	0710	0910	1110	1310	1510	1710	1810	1910	21
Děčín a.	0512	0744	0944	1144	1344	1544	1744	1849	1944	21

km		Ⓒ	Ⓐ								
0	**Děčín** ▷ d.	...	...	0640	0840	1040	1240	1440	1640	1840	2040
22	Bad Schandau 🏛 ▷ d.	...	...	0718	0918	1118	1318	1518	1718	1918	2118
37	Sebnitz d.	0627	0639	0741	0941	1141	1341	1541	1741	1941	2141
38	Dolní Poustevna 🏛 d.	0631	0643	0745	0945	1145	1345	1545	1745	1945	2145
65	**Rumburk** a.	0711	0724	0835	1026	1226	1427	1626	1826	2025	2225

	Ⓐ									
Rumburk d.	0430	0525	0728	0920	1120	1320	1519	1720	1920	20
Dolní Poustevna 🏛 d.	0512	0612	0812	1012	1212	1412	1612	1812	2012	21
Sebnitz d.	0518	0618	0818	1018	1218	1418	1618	1818	2018	21
Bad Schandau 🏛 ▷ a.	0539	0639	0839	1039	1239	1439	1639	1839	2039	
Děčín ▷ a.	0617	0717	0917	1117	1317	1517	1717	1917	2117	

c – Change at Jedlová (*41 km* from Děčín).
u – Runs 5 mins later on Ⓒ (Děčín a. 2147).
▷ – See also Table **1100**.
🚌 – Partly by 🚌 Apr. 25 - June 13 in revised tim

1117 RYBNIŠTĚ - VARNSDORF - ZITTAU - LIBEREC

2nd cla

km		Ⓐr				d			d				①–⑤	d			d			d				
0	**Rybniště** d.	0413	...	0632	...	...	0832	...	...	1032	...	1232	...	...	...	1532	...	...	1732	...	1832	...	2049	...
11	Varnsdorf 🏛 d.	0430	0552	0652	0728	...	0852	1006	...	1052	1152	1252	1352	...	1452	1552	...	1652	1806	...	1852	2005	2106	2133
29	**Zittau** 🏛 d.	0450	0616	0716	0749	0844	0916	1024	1044	1116	1216	1316	1416	1444	1516	1615	1644	1716	1824	1847	1916	2044	...	2153
56	**Liberec** a.	0523	0655	0755	0824	0915	0955	...	1120	1155	1255	1355	1455	1524	1555	...	1715	1755	...	1920	1955	2116	...	2229

					d			d			①–⑤		d			d	E	E	F		d				
Liberec d.	0500	0602	0702	0802	0838	0854r	1002	1033	...	1202	1302	1402	1433	1502	1602	1633	...	...	...	1802	1838	...	...	2005	22
Zittau 🏛 d.	0545	0645	0749	0845	0910	0945	1045	1110	1145	1245	1345	1445	1510	1545	1645	1710	1713	...	1745	1845	1914	1938	...	2045	23
Varnsdorf 🏛 d.	0604	0704	0808	0904	...	1004	1104	...	1204	1304	1404	1504	...	1604	1704	...	1731	1804	1804	1904	...	1957	2004	2104	23
Rybniště a.	0622	...	0826	...	...	1022	...	...	1222	...	...	1522	...	...	1722	...	...	1822	1822	...	...	...	2022	...	

E – Dec. 13 - Apr. 30, Oct. 30 - Dec. 10.
F – May 1 - Oct. 29.
d – From/to Dresden (Table **855**).
r – ①–⑤ (not Dec. 24 - Jan. 1, Mar. 28, July 5, 6, Sept. 28, Oct. 28, Nov. 17).

Operator: Vogtlandbahn *Trilex*.

PRAHA - PLZEŇ - MARIÁNSKÉ LÁZNĚ - CHEB 1120

	768	*EC* 356	1980	766	778	1982	764	*EC* 354	762	*SC•* 512	776	760	*Ex* 352	1988	758	774	1990	756	*SC•* 506	*Ex* 350	754	772	752	770	750
	⚒	🍷	2			2		🍷		🅁				2			2		🅁				Ⓑ		Ⓑ
	n	M	a		z	E		M		b	z		M			z	Ⓑh			M		k	h		h
Ostrava hl. **1160** .... d.	...	...	...	...	...	...	...	...	...	0714	...	...	...	...	...	...	...	...	1314	...	...	...	...	...	...
Praha hlavní .... **1124** d.	...	0512	...	0612	0712	...	0812	0912	1012	1037	1112	1212	1312	...	1412	1512	...	1612	1637	1712	1812	1912	2012	2112	2337
Praha Smíchov .... **1124** d.	...	0520	...	0620	0720	...	0820	0920	1020	1045	1120	1220	1320	...	1420	1520	...	1620	1645	1720	1820	1920	2020	2120	2345
Beroun .... **1124** d.	...	0550	...	0650	0750	...	0850	0950	1050	|	1150	1250	1350	...	1450	1550	...	1650	|	1750	1850	1950	2050	2150	0014
Zdice .... **1124** d.	...	|	...	0659	|	...	0859	|	1059	|	|	1259	|	...	1459	|	...	1659	|	|	1859	|	2059	|	0023
Rokycany .... d.	...	0628	...	0728	0828	...	0928	1028	1128	|	1228	1328	1428	...	1528	1628	...	1728	|	1828	1928	2028	2128	2228	0050
Plzeň hlavní .... a.	...	0648	...	0748	0848	...	0948	1048	1148	1159	1248	1348	1448	...	1548	1648	...	1748	1759	1848	1948	2048	2148	2248	0110
Plzeň hlavní .... d.	0605	...	0700	0805	...	0859	1005	...	...	1206	...	1405	...	1500	1605	...	1659	—	1806	...	2005	...	...	—	—
Stříbro .... d.	0631	...	0731	0831	...	0927	1031	...	...	1229	...	1431	...	1531	1631	...	1728	...	1829	...	2031	...	...	...	...
Planá u Marián. Lázni .. d.	0653	...	0758	0853	...	0957	1053	...	...	1247	...	1453	...	1602	1653	...	1758	Ⓑh	1847	...	2053	...	...	Ⓐ	Ⓐ
Mariánské Lázně .... d.	0704	...	0811	0907	...	1007	1107	...	...	1256	...	1504	...	1631	1707	...	1809	1840	1856	...	2104	...	...	0554	0650
Cheb .... **1122** a.	0724	...	0841a	0926	...	...	1126	...	...	1314	...	1523	...	1702	1726	...	...	1910	1914	...	2125	...	...	0623	0720
Františkovy Lázně **1122** a.	...	...	...	...	...	...	...	...	...	1323	...	...	...	...	...	...	...	...	...	...	...	...	...	...	...

	771	753	1981	773	*SC•* 505	755	1983	*Ex* 351	757	775	759	*Ex* 353	761	1987	777	*SC•* 515	763	763	1989	*EC* 355	765	1991	779	767	*EC* 357	
		⚒	2		🅁		2									🅁			2	🍷		2			🍷	☆
	★	n	⚒n	k				M‡		z		M		Ⓐ	z	b		⑦e		M		E	z		M	
iškovy Lázně.. **1122** d.	...	...	...	...	...	...	...	...	...	...	...	...	...	...	...	1437	...	...	...	...	...	...	...	...	...	...
.... **1122** d.	...	0433	0504	...	0644	...	*0646*	...	0834	...	1034	...	1234	*1318*	...	1446	...	...	1519	...	1634	...	...	1834	...	2003
ánské Lázně ....d.	...	0455	0549	...	0704	...	0746	...	0855	...	1055	...	1255	*1350*	...	1504	...	1507	1551	...	1655	1747	...	1855	...	2034
u Marián. Lázni ....d.	...	0504	0600	...	0712	...	0802	...	0904	...	1104	...	1304	1403	...	1512	...	1516	1602	...	1704	1759	...	1904	...	...
o ....d.	...	0527	0631	...	0732	...	0831	...	0927	...	1127	...	1327	1431	...	1532	...	1539	1631	...	1727	1829	...	1927	...	...
ň hlavní ....a.	...	0554	0659	...	0755	...	0859	...	0954	...	1154	...	1354	1459	...	1555	...	1605	1700	...	1754	1858	...	1954	...	...
ň hlavní ....d.	0507	0607	...	0707	0759	0807	...	0907	1007	1107	1207	1307	1407	...	1507	1557	1607	1607	...	1707	1807	...	1907	2007	2109	...
cany.......................d.	0528	0628	...	0728	|	0828	...	0928	1028	1128	1228	1328	1428	...	1528	|	1628	1628	...	1728	1828	...	1928	2028	2129	...
.... **1124** d.	0554	0654	...	|	|	0854	...	|	1054	|	1254	|	1454	...	|	|	1654	1654	...	|	1854	...	|	2054	|	...
un...................... **1124** d.	0604	0704	...	0804	|	0904	...	1004	1104	1204	1304	1404	1504	...	1604	|	1704	1704	...	1804	1904	...	2004	2104	2204	...
a Smíchov ...... **1124** a.	0633	0733	...	0833	0908	0933	...	1033	1133	1233	1333	1433	1533	...	1633	1706	1733	1733	...	1833	1933	...	2033	2133	2233	...
a hlavní.......... **1124** a.	0641	0741	...	0841	0916	0941	...	1041	1141	1241	1341	1441	1541	...	1641	1716	1741	1741	...	1841	1941	...	2041	2141	2241	...
strava hl. **1160**..........a.	...	...	...	...	1244	...	...	...	...	...	...	...	...	...	...	2044	...	...	...	...	...	...	...	...	...	...

Ⓒ May 1 - Sept. 28 (daily July 1 - Aug. 31).
[12] Praha - Regensburg - München and v.v. (Table **76**, **885**).
Daily to Mariánské Lázně, Ⓐ to Cheb.
From/to Bohumín (Table **1160**).
Also Mar. 28, July 6; not Dec. 27, Mar. 27, July 3.
Not Dec. 24, 25, 31, Jan. 1, Mar. 27, July 5, Oct. 28.

k – To/from Klatovy (Table **929**).
n – ①–⑥ (not Dec. 25, 26, Jan. 1, 2, Mar. 28, July 6, Oct. 29).
z – To/from Klatovy and Železná Ruda (Table **929**).
• – *SUPERCITY PENDOLINO* tilting train, 🅁, 🍷, reservation fee CZK 250. On section Plzeň - Cheb - F. Lázně 🅁 is only required in 1st class.

☆ – Additional journey: 2248 Ⓐ.
★ – Additional journey: 0407 ⚒ **n**.
‡ – Starts from Schwandorf on ⑦ (Table **885**).
TRAIN NAMES:
350/3 ALBERT EINSTEIN, **351/2** JAN HUS, **354/7** FRANZ KAFKA, **355/6** KAREL ČAPEK

CHEB - MARKTREDWITZ 1121

*27 km**													
..............d.	0629	0829	0938	1027	1227	1338	1427	1538	1627	1738	1827	1945	2027
nding 🛃..d.	0642	0842	|	1040	1240	|	1440	|	1640	|	1840	|	2040
tredwitz..a.	0654	0854	0958	1052	1252	1358	1452	1558	1652	1758	1852	2004	2052
irnberg § ..a.	*0819*	*1020*	1122	*1220*	*1420*	1522	*1620*	1722	*1820*	1922	*2022*	2128	*2222*

Nürnberg § . d.	*0540*	0637	*0738*	*0938*	1037	*1138*	1237	*1338*	1437	*1538*	1637	*1738*	*2055*
Marktredwitz d.	0712	0802	0908	1108	1202	1308	1402	1508	1602	1708	1802	1911	2218
Schirnding 🛃 d.	0724	|	0920	1120	|	1320	|	1520	|	1720	|	1923	2230
Cheb............. a.	0737	0822	0933	1133	1222	1333	1422	1533	1622	1733	1822	1936	2243

Cheb - Schirnding = 13 km, Cheb - Marktredwitz = 27 km. Local trains Cheb - Marktredwitz are operated by Vogtlandbahn (2nd class only).

§ – See Table **880**.

CHEB - FRANTIŠKOVY LÁZNĚ - HOF / PLAUEN 1122

d class

	△	△	⊖	△	⊖	△	△	⊖	△	⊖	△
Cheb.................. ▶ d.	0738	0937	1005	1137	1205	1337	1537	1605	1737	1805	1937
Františkovy Lázně ▶ d.	0745	0945	1012	1145	1212	1345	1545	1612	1745	1812	1945
Aš 🛃 .... d.	0808	1008	|	1208	|	1408	1608	|	1808	|	2008
Hof .... a.	0843	1048	|	1243	|	1443	1643	|	1848	|	2043
Bad Brambach 🛃.... a.	...	...	1035	...	1235	...	...	1635	...	1835	...
Plauen .... a.	...	...	1128	...	1328	...	...	1728	...	1928	...

	△	⊖	△	⊖	△	△	⊖	△	⊖	△	△
Plauen .... d.	...	0830	...	1030	...	...	1430	...	1630	...	...
Bad Brambach 🛃 .... d.	...	0923	...	1123	...	...	1523	...	1723	...	...
Hof .... d.	0709	|	0907	|	1107	1307	|	1507	|	1707	1907
Aš .... d.	0747	|	0947	|	1147	1347	|	1547	|	1747	1947
Františkovy Lázně ▶ d.	0812	0947	1012	1147	1212	1412	1547	1612	1747	1812	2012
Cheb .... ▶ a.	0819	0954	1019	1154	1219	1419	1554	1619	1754	1819	2019

Operator: Vogtlandbahn. Trains continue beyond Plauen to/from Zwickau. Marktredwitz (Table **1121**) - Cheb - Hof and v.v.

▶ – For *SC* trains see Table **1120**. Additional trains: From Cheb: 0458Ⓐ, 0518⑥, 0600Ⓐ, 0637, 1445Ⓐ, 2250. From Františkovy Lázně: 0609Ⓐ, 0614⑥, 0714Ⓐ, 2119.

KARLOVY VARY - MARIÁNSKÉ LÁZNĚ 1123

erator: GW TrainRegio. 2nd class

n										
0	**Karlovy Vary** dolní (lower) ... d.	...	0617	0900	1055	1300	1500	1705	1927	2127
3	Bečov nad Teplou .... d.	0448	0649	0933	1127	1333	1533	1738	1959	2159
3	**Mariánské Lázně** .... a.	0535	0736	1020	1214	1420	1620	1825	2046	2246

Mariánské Lázně .... d.	0559	0827	1037	1227	1427	1632	1909	2109	2250
Bečov nad Teplou .... d.	0650	0916	1128	1316	1516	1721	2000	2200	2338
Karlovy Vary dolní (lower). a.	0722	0950	1200	1350	1550	1755	2032	2232	...

PRAHA - BEROUN - PŘÍBRAM - PISEK - ČESKÉ BUDĚJOVICE 1124

d class

n		1254	1252	1250		1248	1246	1244	1242	1240
		Ⓐ	①d		◧	Ⓒ	Ⓐ	⑤f		
0	**Praha** hlavní .... **1120** d.	...	0542	0742	*0812*	0942	1142	1342	1542	1742
4	Praha Smichov .... **1120** d.	...	0550	0750	*0820*	0950	1150	1350	1550	1750
3	Beroun .... **1120** d.	...	0619	0819	0858	1019	1219	1419	1619	1819
2	Zdice .... **1120** d.	...	0626	0826	0908	1026	1226	1426	1626	1826
2	Přibram .... d.	...	0657	0857	0950	1057	1257	1457	1657	1857
0	Březnice .... d.	...	0715	0915	1016	1115	1315	1515	1715	1915
2	Pisek .... d.	0558	0758	0958	1109	1158	1358	1558	1758	1958
5	Protivín .... **1125** d.	0613	0813	1013	1124	1213	1413	1613	1813	2013
2	**České Budějovice** ...... **1125** a.	0643	0843	1043	...	1243	1443	1643	1843	2043r

	1241	1243		1245	1247	1249	1251	1253	
			◐	⑤f			⑦e		
České Budějovice ... **1125** d.	0510z	0710	...	1110	1310	1510	1710	1910	...
Protivín .... **1125** d.	0543	0743	1035	1143	1343	1543	1743	1943	2213
Pisek .... d.	0557	0757	1050	1157	1357	1557	1757	1956	2228
Březnice .... d.	0637	0837	1143	1237	1437	1637	1837	...	2315
Přibram .... d.	0657	0857	1208	1257	1457	1657	1857	...	...
Zdice .... **1120** d.	0726	0926	1245	1326	1526	1726	1926	...	...
Beroun .... **1120** a.	0733	0933	1255	1333	1533	1733	1933	...	...
Praha Smichov .... **1120** a.	0803	1003	*1333*	1403	1603	1803	2003	...	...
Praha hlavní .... **1120** a.	0811	1011	*1341*	1411	1611	1811	2011	...	...

Also Mar. 29, July 7; not Dec. 28, Mar. 28, July 4.
Also Mar. 28, July 6; not Dec. 27, Mar. 27, July 3.
Also Dec. 23, Oct. 27, Nov. 16; not Dec. 25, Jan. 1, Oct. 28, Nov. 18.
⑤–⑦ (also Dec. 23, Mar. 28, July 4-6, Sept. 27, 28, Oct. 27, Nov. 16, 17).

z – ① (also Mar. 29, July 7, Sept. 29, Nov. 18; not Mar. 28).
◧ – Also at 1012, 1212Ⓐ, 1412Ⓑ, 1612 (change at Beroun).
◐ – Also at 0835, 1235, 1435Ⓐ, 1635Ⓑ, 1835 (change at Beroun).

For direct trains Praha - České Budějovice see Table **1130**

PLZEŇ - ČESKÉ BUDĚJOVICE 1125

n		623	661	663	665	667	669	625	627	629
		⚒n						h		Ⓑr
0	**Plzeň** hlavní .... d.	...	0602	0802	1002	1202	1402	1602	1802	2002
4	Nepomuk .... d.	...	0631	0831	1031	1231	1431	1631	1831	2031
9	Horaždovice předměstí .... d.	...	0652	0852	1052	1252	1452	1652	1852	2052
6	Strakonice .... d.	0501	0708	0908	1108	1308	1508	1708	1908	2108
9	Protivín .... **1124** d.	0521	0727	0927	1127	1327	1527	1727	1927	2127
6	**České Budějovice** ...... **1124** a.	0555	0755	0955	1155	1355	1555	1755	1955	2155
	Jihlava **1135** .... a.	0833	1033	1233z	1433	1633	1833	2031r	...	...
	Brno **1135** .... a.	1036	1236	1436z	1636	1836	2036	...	...	...

	628	626	624	668	666	664	662	660	
			h					Ⓑr	Ⓑr
Brno **1135** .... d.	...	...	...	0720	0920z	1120	1320	1520	...
Jihlava **1135** .... d.	...	0525a	0725	0925	1125z	1325	1525	1725	...
České Budějovice ... **1124** d.	0605	0805	1005	1205	1405	1605	1805	2005	2243
Protivín .... **1124** d.	0633	0833	1033	1233	1433	1633	1833	2033	2327
Strakonice .... d.	0653	0853	1053	1253	1453	1653	1853	2053	2350
Horaždovice předměstí .... d.	0709	0909	1109	1309	1509	1709	1909	2109	...
Nepomuk .... d.	0729	0929	1129	1329	1529	1729	1929	2129	...
Plzeň hlavní .... a.	0757	0957	1157	1357	1557	1757	1957	2157	...

①–⑤ (also Nov. 19; not Dec. 24, 25, Jan. 1, Mar. 28, July 6, Oct. 28, Nov. 17).
To/from Havlíčkův Brod on dates in Table **1152**.
①–⑥ (not Dec. 25, 26, Jan. 1, 2, Mar. 28, July 6, Oct. 29).

r – Ⓑ (not Dec. 24, 25, 31, Jan. 1, Mar. 27, July 5, Oct. 28).
z – ⑤⑥⑦ (daily May 27 - Sept. 11), also Dec. 23, 24, Sept. 28, Oct. 27, 28, Nov. 16, 17; not Nov. 18.

1126 PLZEŇ - CHOMUTOV - MOST

km		1798	1192	1190	1188	1186	1184	1182	1180	
		2Ⓐ						Ⓑh	⑦e	
0	**Plzeň** hlavní d.	...	0605	1005	1205	1405	1605	1805	2005	...
59	Blatno u Jesenice d.	0454	0710	1110	1310	1510	1710	1909	2110	...
107	Žatec **1105** d.	0551	0802	1202	1402	1602	1802	2002	2202	...
130	Chomutov **1110** d.	0617	0829	1229	1429	1629	1829	2029	2229	...
155	**Most** **1110** a.	...	0850	1250	1450	1650	1850	2050	2250	...

	1181	1183	1185		1187	1189	1191	1193
	⚒n							⑦e
Most **1110** d.	0505	0705	0905	...	1305	1505	1705	1905
Chomutov **1110** d.	0528	0728	0928	...	1328	1528	1728	1928
Žatec **1105** d.	0553	0753	0953	...	1353	1553	1753	1953
Blatno u Jesenice d.	0645	0845	1045	...	1445	1645	1845	2045
Plzeň hlavní a.	0754	0954	1154	...	1554	1754	1954	2151

e – Also Mar. 28, July 6; not Dec. 27, Mar. 27, July 3. **h** – Not Dec. 24, 25, 31, Jan. 1, Mar. 27, July 5, Oct. 28. **n** – ①–⑥ (not Dec. 25, 26, Jan. 1, 2, Mar. 28, July 6, Oct.

1130 PRAHA - TÁBOR - ČESKÉ BUDĚJOVICE

km		1839	1541	633	635	637	1543		641	643	1545	645	647		649	651	653	655	657		659	659	
		2Ⓐ		⚒n		⚒n				Ⓐz							Ⓑh						⚒n
	Praha Holešovice d.	...	...	...	0716n	0816	0916	...	1116	1216	1316	...	1516	...	1616	1716	1816	1916	2016	...	...	...	...
0	**Praha** hlavní d.	...	0534	0634	0734	0834	0934	...	1134	1234	1334	1434	1534	...	1634	1734	1834	1934	2034	...	2234	2234	...
49	Benešov u Prahy d.	...	0616	0716	0816	0916	1016	...	1216	1316	1416	1516	1616	...	1716	1816	1916	2016	2116	...	2316	2316	...
103	**Tábor** d.	0613	0702	0802	0902	1002	1102	...	1302	1402	1502	1602	1702	...	1802	1902	2002	2102	2202	...	0001	0002	...
130	Veselí nad Lužnicí ▷ d.	0644	0725	0825	0925	1025	1125	...	1325	1425	1525	1625	1725	...	1825	1925	2025	2125	2225	...	...	0025	0033
169	**České Budějovice** ▷ a.	0722	0757	0857	0957	1057	1157	...	1357	1457	1557	1657	1757	...	1857	1957	2057	2157	2257	...	...	0057r	0120
	Linz Hbf **1132** a.	...	1024	...	...	...	1424	...	...	...	1824	...	...	...	...	...	...	...	...	...	...	...	...

	658	656	654	652		650	648	646		644	642	1540		640	638	636	1542		632	630			
	⚒n	⚒n		⚒n			Ⓐz														2⊡		
Linz Hbf **1132** d.	...	...	...	...	...	...	...	*0721*	...	...	...	1135	...	...	...	...	1535	...	...	...	...	...	...
České Budějovice ▷ d.	...	0503	0603	0703	...	0803	0903	1003	...	1203	1303	1403	...	1503	1603	1703	1803	...	1903	2003	2234	...	...
Veselí nad Lužnicí ▷ d.	...	0536	0636	0736	...	0836	0936	1036	...	1236	1336	1436	...	1536	1636	1736	1836	...	1936	2036	2334	...	...
Tábor d.	0459	0559	0659	0759	...	0859	0959	1059	...	1259	1359	1459	...	1559	1659	1759	1859	...	1959	2059	0010	...	...
Benešov u Prahy d.	0545	0645	0745	0845	...	0945	1045	1145	...	1345	1445	1545	...	1645	1745	1845	1945	...	2045	2145	...	...	...
Praha hlavní a.	0626	0726	0826	0926	...	1026	1126	1226	...	1426	1526	1626	...	1726	1826	1926	2026	...	2126	2226	...	...	...
Praha Holešovice a.	0638	0738	0838	...	...	1038	1138	1238	...	1438	1538	1638	...	1738h	1838	1938	...	...	...	...	...	...	...

h – Ⓑ (not Dec. 24, 25, 31, Jan. 1, Mar. 27, July 5, Oct. 28).
n – ①–⑥ (not Dec. 25, 26, Jan. 1, 2, Mar. 28, July 6, Oct. 29).
r – ⑦ (also Jan. 2, Mar. 28, July 6, Oct. 29).
z – Not Dec. 28 - 31.
▷ – See also Table **1135**.
⊡ – Change at Veselí nad Lužnicí on ⑦.

1131 ČESKÉ BUDĚJOVICE - ČESKÝ KRUMLOV - NOVÉ ÚDOLÍ

km		T			R		B		Ⓐ		
0	**České Budějovice** d.	0607	0808	1019	1219	1419	1513	1608	1821	2007	2245
31	Český Krumlov d.	0657	0900	1105	1305	1505	1603	1700	1907	2052	2329
68	Horní Planá a.	0802	0957	1157	1357	1557	...	1757	1958	...	...
96	**Nové Údolí** a.	...	1041	1241c	1441	1641	...	1841r	...	...	...

	Ⓐ	⚒n	⑦u	P	N		R			
Nové Údolí d.	...	...	...	...	...	0915z	1115	1315c	1515	1715
Horní Planá d.	...	...	...	0717	0803	0958	1158	1358	1558	1758
Český Krumlov d.	0436	0614	0714	0810	0859	1049	1249	1449	1655	1852
České Budějovice a.	0519	0657	0757	0854	0943	1133	1333	1533	1739	1939

B – Ⓐ (not Dec. 23 - 31, Jan. 29, Mar. 24, 25, July 1 - Aug. 31, Oct. 26, 27).
N – Ⓒ (daily Dec. 23 - 31, July 1 - Aug. 31).
P – Ⓐ (not Dec. 23 - 31, July 1 - Aug. 31).
R – Ⓐ (daily Apr. 25 - Nov. 4).
T – Ⓐ (daily Dec. 13 - Apr. 1, Apr. 25 - Oct. 7).
V – Ⓐ (daily Apr. 25 - Oct. 7).
c – Ⓒ Apr. 2 - Dec. 10 (daily Apr. 30 - Oct. 2).
n – ①–⑥ (not Dec. 25, 26, Jan. 1, 2, Mar. 28, July 6, Oct. 29).
r – Apr. 30 - Oct. 2 (also Ⓒ Oct. 8 - 30).
u – Also Dec. 26, Jan. 2, Mar. 28, July 6, Oct. 29.
z – Ⓒ (daily Apr. 30 - Oct. 2).

1132 ČESKÉ BUDĚJOVICE - LINZ

km				1541	3801	1543	3803	1545		3805	
		2	2		2		2		2	2	2
	Praha hlavní **1130** d.	...	...	0534	...	0934	...	1334	...	...	...
0	**České Budějovice** d.	0602	...	0813	1002	1213	1355	1613	...	1802	2012
50	Rybnik ⊡ d.	0657	...	0858	1059	1258	1454	1658	...	1857	2113
64	Summerau ⊞ a.	0713	...	0912	1114	1312	1510	1712	...	1912	...
64	Summerau d.	...	0716	0914	1117	1314	1512	1714	1810	1914	...
73	Freistadt d.	...	0724	0922	1125	1322	1520	1723	1819	1922	...
126	**Linz** Hbf a.	...	0825	1024	1224	1424	1624	1824	1924	2025	...

			3800	3802	1540	3804	1542		
	2	2	2	2		2		2Ⓐ	2Ⓐ
Linz Hbf d.	...	...	0721	0915	1135	1315	1535	1652	...
Freistadt d.	...	...	0821	1018	1235	1420	1634	1744	...
Summerau a.	...	...	0830	1027	1243	1429	1642	1753	...
Summerau ⊞ d.	...	0725	0841	1042	1245	1436	1644	...	1840
Rybnik ⊡ d.	0620	0741	0900	1100	1300	1455	1700	...	1858
České Budějovice a.	0720	0842	0953	1158	1345	1555	1745	...	1957
Praha hlavní **1130** a.	...	...	*1226*	...	1626	...	2026	...	...

NAMES: **1540/1** F. A. GERSTNER, **1542/3** ANTON BRUCKNER. ⊡ – Rybnik - Lipno nad Vltavou (*22 km*, 40 mins): every 2 hrs 0702 - 1902, returning every 2 hrs 0810 - 1810, 2030

1133 ČESKÉ BUDĚJOVICE - ČESKÉ VELENICE - (WIEN)

km		Ⓐ	2Ⓐ			N		Ⓑh		Ⓑh	
0	České Budějovice d.	0511	0609	0809	1009	1209	1409	1609	1809	2009	2246
50	České Velenice ⊞ a.	0559	0704	0857	1057	1257	1457	1657	1857	2057	2333
	České Velenice **990** d.	*0602*	*0707*r	*0907*	*1107*	*1307*	*1507*	*1705*	*1907*	...	...
	Gmünd NÖ **990** a.	*0606*	*0711*r	*0911*	*1111*	*1311*	*1511*	*1709*	*1911*	...	...
	Wien FJB **990** a.	*0825*	*0928*r	*1128*	*1328*	*1532*	*1728*	*1928*	*2128*	...	...

	Ⓐ		Ⓐ		Ⓐz		Ⓑh		F
Wien FJB **990** d.	...	...	...	*0628*	*0828*	*1028*	*1228*	*1428*	*1628*
Gmünd NÖ **990** d.	...	...	...	*0844*	*1044*	*1244*	*1444*	*1646*	*1846*
České Velenice **990** a.	...	...	...	*0848*	*1048*	*1248*	*1448*	*1650*	*1850*
České Velenice ⊞ d.	0400	0500	0640	0903	1103	1303	1503	1703	1903
České Budějovice a.	0449	0555	0729	0952	1152	1352	1552	1752	1952

VESELÍ NAD LUŽNICÍ - ČESKÉ VELENICE *For connections Praha - Veselí nad Lužnicí see Table* **1130**. *For connections České Velenice - Wien see Table* **990**.

km			Ⓐ	Ⓒ			E				Ⓒ	Ⓐ
0	Veselí nad Lužnicí d.	0455	0555	0751	0944	1144	1344	1549	1744	1944	2152	2229
21	Třeboň d.	0521	0620	0816	1009	1209	1409	1612	1809	2009	2215	2254
55	České Velenice a.	0559	0701	0855	1048	1248	1448	1650	1848	2048	2253	2333

	Ⓐ	⚒	Ⓒ		E				
České Velenice d.	0420	0609	0715	0910	1110	1310	1510	1710	1910
Třeboň d.	0500	0649	0756	0949	1149	1349	1549	1749	1949
Veselí nad Lužnicí a.	0523	0712	0819	1012	1212	1412	1615	1812	2012

E – Ⓐ (daily Apr. 25 - Oct. 7).
F – Ⓑ (daily July 6 - Sept. 2), also July 2; not Dec. 24 - 26, 31, Jan. 1, Mar. 27, Oct. 28.
N – Ⓐ (also ⑥ July 2 - Aug. 27; not Dec. 23 - 31).
h – Not Dec. 24, 25, 31, Jan. 1, Mar. 27, July 5, Oct. 28.
r – ①–⑤ (not Dec. 25, Jan. 1, 6, Mar. 28, May 16, 26, Aug. 15, Oct. 26, Nov. 1, Dec. 8
z – Not Dec. 23 - 31.

1135 ČESKÉ BUDĚJOVICE - JIHLAVA - BRNO

km		1869	621	623	661	663	665	667	669	2	625
		2Ⓐ	⚒n			H					Ⓑh
	Plzeň **1125** d.	...	...	...	0602	0802	1002	1202	1402	...	1602
0	**České Budějovice** d.	...	0412z	0612	0812	1012	1212	1412	1612	...	1812
39	Veselí nad Lužnicí ▷ d.	...	0445z	0645	0845	1045	1245	1445	1645	...	1845
65	Jindřichův Hradec ▷ d.	...	0516z	0716	0916	1116	1316	1516	1716	...	1916
117	Kostelec u Jihlavy ▲ d.	...	0615z	0815	1015	1215	1415	1615	1815	...	2013
132	**Jihlava** a.	...	0633z	0833	1033	1233	1433	1633	1833	...	2031
132	**Jihlava** d.	0530	0640	0840	1040	1240	1440	1640	1840	1930	▽
161	Okříšky d.	0603	0707	0907	1107	1307	1507	1707	1907	2018	...
173	Trebič d.	0620	0724	0924	1124	1324	1524	1724	1924	2046	...
236	**Brno** hlavní a.	0737	0836	1036	1236	1436	1636	1836	2036	2211	...

	626	624	668	666	664	662	660	622
	Ⓐt			H				
Brno hlavní d.	...	...	0720	0920	1120	1320	1520	1720
Trebič d.	...	...	0833	1033	1233	1433	1633	1833
Okříšky d.	...	...	0847	1047	1247	1447	1647	1847
Jihlava a.	...	▽	0918	1118	1318	1518	1718	1918
Jihlava d.	0525	0725	0925	1125	1325	1525	1725	1934s
Kostelec u Jihlavy ▲ d.	0543	0743	0943	1143	1343	1543	1743	1953s
Jindřichův Hradec ▷ d.	0643	0843	1043	1243	1443	1643	1843	2055s
Veselí nad Lužnicí ▷ d.	0716	0916	1116	1316	1516	1716	1916	2130s
České Budějovice a.	0748	0948	1148	1348	1548	1748	1948	2202s
Plzeň **1125** a.	0957	1157	1357	1557	1757	1957	2157h	...

km		Ⓐ	Ⓐx	J				Ⓑv			
0	Okříšky d.	0443	0610	0710	0917	1117	1317	1517	1717	1920	...
32	Moravské Budějovice a.	0518	0645	0744	0952	1152	1352	1552	1752	2000	...
70	Znojmo a.	0631	0730	0848	1048	1248	1448	1648	1848	2048f	...

	Ⓐx	Ⓐ	J			⑦d	Ⓐ		
Znojmo d.	0421	0529x	0659n	0902	1102	1302	*1302*	1502	1702
Moravské Budějovice d.	0522	0623	0803	1003	1203	1403	1427	1603	1803
Okříšky a.	0557	0703	0839	1039	1239	1439	1503	1639	1839

H – ⑤⑥⑦ (daily May 27 - Sept. 11), also Dec. 23, 24, Mar. 28, Sept. 28, Oct. 27, Nov. 16, 17; not Nov. 18.
J – ⚒ (daily Feb. 15 - Dec. 10), not Dec. 26, Jan. 2.
d – Also Mar. 28, July 6, Sept. 28, Nov. 17; not Dec. 27, Mar. 27.
e – Also Mar. 28, July 6; not Dec. 27, Mar. 27, July 3.
f – ⑤ (also July 4, Sept. 27; not Dec. 25, Jan. 1, Oct. 28).
h – Ⓑ (not Dec. 24, 25, 31, Jan. 1, Mar. 27, July 5, Oct. 28).
n – ①–⑥ (not Dec. 25, 26, Jan. 1, 2, Mar. 28, July 6, Oct. 29).
s – ⑤⑦ (also Dec. 23, Mar. 28, July 6, Oct. 27, Nov. 16; not Dec. 25, 27, Jan. 1, Mar. 27, July 3, Oct. 28, Nov. 18).
t – Also July 5, Sept. 28, Nov. 19.
u – Not Dec. 23 - 31.
v – Not Dec. 24, 25, Jan. 1, Mar. 27, July 5, Oct. 28.
x – Ⓐ (not Dec. 28 - 31).
z – ① (also Mar. 29, July 7; not Dec. 28, Mar. 28, July 4).
▷ – Additional trains: from Veselí nad Lužnicí 0742, 0942, 1142Ⓐ, 1342, 1547Ⓑ**h**, 1742, 1942Ⓐ, 2142, 2332; from Jindřichův Hradec 0552Ⓐ, 0642Ⓒ, 0730, 0940, 1140, 1340Ⓐ, 1540Ⓑ**h**, 1740, 1940, 2222Ⓐ. Journey 36 minutes.
▽ – To / from Havlíčkův Brod on dates in Table **1152**.
⊡ – To Jihlava, arrive 2105.
▲ – Connections Kostelec - Telč (36 mins, *23* km): From Kostelec: 0637Ⓐ, 0820, 1018, 1111Ⓐ, 1316 1421Ⓐ, 1512Ⓒ, 1522Ⓐ, 1710, 1818⑦**e**, 1907⚒, 2019⑦**e**, 2128Ⓐ**u**. From Telč: 0404⚒**n**, 0516Ⓐ, 0719Ⓑ, 0803Ⓐ, 0901Ⓒ, 0935Ⓐ, 1204, 1327Ⓐ, 1404Ⓒ, 1441Ⓐ, 1 1655⑦**e**, 1823⚒, 1910⑦**e**, 2028Ⓐ**u**.

PRAHA - MLADÁ BOLESLAV - TURNOV - (LIBEREC) 1140

d class

m			1148 T	1146 T		1144 T	1142 T	1942 Ⓐ	1140	1940	
0	**Praha** hlavní	d.	0548	0724	0924	1148	1324	1524	1624	1724	1924	2106
34	Neratovice	d.	0632	0800	1000	1232	1400	1600	1703	1800	2000	2149
40	Všetaty	d.	0643	0807	1007	1243	1407	1607	1712	1807	2007	2157
72	**Mladá Boleslav**	a.	0718	0833	1033	1321	1433	1633	1745	1833	2033	2232
72	**Mladá Boleslav**	d.	...	0834	1034	*1347*	1434	1634	*1747*	1834	2034	2241
88	Mnichovo Hradiště	d.	...	0858	1058	*1409*	1458	1658	*1809*	1858	2058	2259
02	**Turnov**	a.	...	0912	1112	*1428*	1512	1712	*1828*	1912	2116	2315
	Turnov **1142**	d.	...	*0921*	*1121*	*1440**	*1521*	*1721*	*1840**	*1921*	*2121*	*2319*
	Liberec **1142**	a.	...	*0956*	*1156*	*1524**	*1556*	*1756*	*1924**	*1956*	*2156*	*2356*

		1941 Ⓐ	1141	1143 T		1145	1147 T	1149 T	1151 T		Ⓒ
Liberec **1142**	d.	*0400*	*0602*	*0802*	*0830**	*1202*	*1402*	*1602*	*1802*	...	*2030*
Turnov **1142**	a.	*0438*	*0639*	*0839*	*0915**	*1239*	*1439*	*1639*	*1839*	...	*2114*
Turnov	d.	0441	0644	0844	*0922*	1244	1444	1644	1844	*1922*	2122
Mnichovo Hradiště	d.	0459	0658	0858	*0940*	1258	1458	1658	1858	*1939*	2140
Mladá Boleslav	a.	0519	0715	0915	*1000*	1315	1515	1715	1915	*2000*	2200
Mladá Boleslav	d.	0521	0724	0924	1037	1324	1524	1724	1924	2037	2207
Všetaty	d.	0550	0751	0951	1120	1351	1551	1751	1951	2121	2248
Neratovice	d.	0558	0800	1000	1130	1400	1600	1800	2000	2130	2257
Praha hlavní	a.	0634	0838	1038	1212	1438	1639	1838	2038	2212	2335

- To/from Tanvald on dates in Table **1142**. * – Change at Turnov.

LIBEREC - TANVALD - HARRACHOV - SZKLARSKA POŖEBA GÓRNA 1141

nd class

km				Ⓐ																			
0	**Liberec**	▷ d.	0035	0435	0535	0635	0735	0835	0935	1035	1135	1235	1335	1435	1535	1635	1735	1835	1935	2035	2135	2235	...
12	Jablonec nad Nisou	▷ d.	0054	0456	0556	0656	0756	0856	0956	1056	1156	1256	1356	1456	1556	1656	1756	1856	1956	2056	2156	2256	...
27	**Tanvald**	▷ a.	0119	0525	0625	0725	0825	0925	1025	1125	1225	1325	1425	1525	1625	1725	1825	1925	2025	2125	2225	2325	...
27	**Tanvald**	d.	...	0527	...	0730	0830s	0933	1030	1130s	1227	1330	1430	1530	1630	1730	1830	1930x	...	...	...	...	...
34	Kořenov	a.	...	0543	...	0745	0845s	0948	1045	1145s	1243	1345	1445	1545	1645	1745	1845	1945x	...	...	...	...	...
39	Harrachov	a.	...	...	...	0753s	0853s	0955	1053	1153s	1251s	1355	1453s	1553	1653s	1753	1853	1953x	...	...	...	...	...
55	**Szklarska Poręba Górna**	◇ a.	...	...	...	0821s	0921r	1021	1121r	1221s	...	1421	...	1621s	...	1821	...	2021x	...	...	...	...	...

klarska Poręba Górna	◇ d.	...	...	...	...		0829s	0929r	1029	1129r	1229s	...	1429	...	1629s	...	1829	...	2029x	...	...	...	...
rrachov	d.	...	...	...	...	0757c	0857s	0957s	1057	1157	1257s	1357s	1457	1557s	1657	1757s	1857	...	2057x	...	...	...	...
řenov	d.	...	...	...	...	0804c	0904	1004s	1104	1204	1304	1404	1504	1604	1704	1804	1904	...	2104x	...	...	...	...
nvald	d.	...	...	...	...	0823c	0923	1023s	1123	1223	1323	1423	1523	1623	1723	1823	1923	...	2123x	...	...	...	...
nvald	▷ d.	0429	0529	0629	0729	0829	0929	1029	1129	1229	1329	1429	1529	1629	1729	1829	1929	2029	2129	2229	...	...	...
blonec nad Nisou	▷ d.	0457	0557	0657	0759	0857	0957	1057	1157	1257	1357	1457	1557	1657	1757	1857	1957	2057	2157	2257	...	...	...
berec	▷ a.	0518	0618	0718	0820	0918	1018	1118	1218	1318	1418	1518	1618	1718	1818	1918	2018	2118	2218	2318	...	...	...

- Ⓒ (also Dec. 28-31).
- ⑥⑦ Dec. 26 - Jan. 24 (also Dec. 28 - Jan. 1); daily Jan. 30 - Mar. 20; ⑥⑦ Apr. 30 - June 19 (also May 2, 3, 26, 27); daily June 25 - Sept. 4; ⑥⑦ Sept. 10 - Oct. 30 (also Sept. 28, Oct. 28).
- Daily Dec. 26 - Mar. 20; ⑥⑦ Mar. 26 - June 19 (also Mar. 28, May 2, 3, 26, 27); daily June 25 - Sept. 4; ⑥⑦ Sept. 10 - Oct. 30 (also Sept. 28, Oct. 28).

x – June 25 - Sept. 4.
◇ – 🏛 Czech Republic/Poland = Jakuszyce.
▷ – Additional journeys Liberec - Tanvald and v.v. on Ⓐ (not Dec. 28-31):
From Liberec: 0505, 0605, 0705, 1305, 1405, 1505, 1605, 1705, 1805.
From Tanvald: 0346, 0459, 0559, 0659, 0759, 1259, 1359, 1459, 1559, 1659.

LIBEREC - HRADEC KRÁLOVÉ - PARDUBICE 1142

nd class

km			1261	1263	1265		1275	1277
0	**Liberec**	d.	0400	0602	0802		1802	2002
38	Turnov	d.	0439	0642	0842		1842	2042
52	Železný Brod ★	d.	0455	0659	0859	and	1859	2059
76	Stará Paka	d.	0525	0727	0927	every	1927	2127
107	Dvůr Králové n. L.	d.	0600	0800	1000	**two**	2000	2201
122	Jaroměř	d.	0616	0819	1019	hours	2020	2222
139	**Hradec Králové**	a.	0631	0834	1034	until	2035	2239
139	**Hradec Králové** ▶	d.	0634	0839	1038		2038	2242
161	**Pardubice** ▶	a.	0652	0900	1056		2056	2305

		1276		1262	1260
Pardubice ▶	d.	0502		1902	2102
Hradec Králové ▶	a.	0521		1921	2121
Hradec Králové	d.	0525	and	1925	2125
Jaroměř	d.	0542	every	1942	2144
Dvůr Králové n. L.	d.	0559	**two**	1959	2200
Stará Paka	d.	0631	hours	2031	2235
Železný Brod ★	d.	0700	until	2100	2301
Turnov	d.	0721		2121	2319
Liberec	a.	0756		2156	2356

		△		d		Ⓑh	Ⓑh
Praha hl **1140**	d.	...	0724	0924	1324	1524	*1724*
Turnov	d.	...	0919	1119	1519	1719	1926
Železný Brod	a.	0701	0937	1137	1537	1737	1945
Tanvald	a.	0727	1004	1210	1604	1804	2009
		⚒	▽	⑥u	d	d	
Tanvald	d.	0427	0627	0752	1340	1551	1752
Železný Brod	a.	0453	0653	0818	1415	1618	1818
Turnov	a.	...	...	0836	1436	1636	1836
Praha hl **1140**	a.	...	...	1038	1639	1838	2038

- – Change at Turnov on Ⓐ.
- – Not Dec. 24, 25, 31, Jan. 1, Mar. 27, July 5, Oct. 28.
- – ⑥ (also ①–⑤ July 1 - Aug. 31), also Dec. 23, 24, 28-31, Sept. 28, Oct. 28, Nov. 17; not Dec. 26, Jan. 2, July 6, Oct. 29.
- – Also 0901, 1101Ⓒ, 1301, 1414Ⓐ, 1501, 1701, 1901, 2101, 2302Ⓐ.
- – Also 0510Ⓐ, 0827, 1027, 1227, 1427, 1627, 1827, 2027.
- – For Pardubice - Tanvald change at Železný Brod (see right hand panel).

▶ – Additional trains **Hradec Kralové - Pardubice** and v.v. (journey 20-30 minutes):
From Hradec Kralové: 0038, 0433, 0505Ⓐ, 0530Ⓐ, 0544, 0605, 0704, 0730, 0805, 0905, 0935Ⓐ, 1005, 1105, 1135, 1205, 1305, 1335, 1405, 1505, 1535, 1605, 1705, 1735, 1805, 1905, 1935Ⓒ, 2005, 2104, 2204.
From Pardubice: 0111, 0432Ⓐ, 0532, 0605Ⓐ, 0628Ⓐ, 0633Ⓒ, 0716Ⓐ, 0739, 0805, 0840, 0932, 1032, 1132, 1205, 1234, 1332, 1406, 1435, 1532, 1605, 1635, 1732, 1805, 1835, 1929, 2001Ⓒ, 2032, 2132, 2257.

Apr. 18 - Aug. 2: by 🚌 Jaroměř - Hradec Králové/Pardubice and v.v. (🚌 runs 12-15 mins earlier).

PRAHA - HRADEC KRÁLOVÉ - TRUTNOV 1145

km			1780	941 Ⓐ	1782 ⑥t	921	943	1784 2	923	945	1786 2Ⓐ	925	1788 2	927	947 Ⓐ	1790 2	929	935 L	1792 2	931	949	951	1796	953	955	957
0	**Praha** hlavní	d.	...	0511	...	0611	0711	...	0811	0911	...	1011	...	1211	1311	...	1411	1511	...	1611	1711	1811	...	1911	2011	2211
35	Lysá nad Labem ▷	d.	...	0542	...	0642	0742	...	0842	0942	...	1042	...	1242	1342	...	1442	1542	...	1642	1742	1842	...	1942	2042	2242
50	Nymburk ▷	d.	...	0555	...	0655	0755	...	0855	0955	...	1055	...	1255	1355	...	1455	1555	...	1655	1755	1855	...	1955	2055	2255
57	Poděbrady ▷	d.	...	0601	...	0701	0801	...	0901	1001	...	1101	...	1301	1401	...	1501	1601	...	1701	1801	1901	...	2001	2101	2301
116	**Hradec Králové**	a.	...	0651	...	0751	0851	...	0951	1051	...	1151	...	1351	1451	...	1551	1651	...	1751	1851	1951	...	2051	2151	2348
116	**Hradec Králové**	d.	0600	...	0700	0804	...	0901	1004	...	1101	1204	1301	1404	...	1501	1604	...	1701	1804	...	...	2001	...	...	...
137	Jaroměř	d.	0617	...	0718	0820	...	0917	1020	...	1117	1220	1317	1420	...	1517	1620	...	1717	1820	...	...	2020	...	...	...
189	**Trutnov** hlavní	a.	0720	...	0820	0920	...	1020	1120	...	1220	1320	1420	1520	...	1620	1720	...	1820	1920	...	...	2120	...	...	...

		952 Ⓐ	1781 ⚒n	950	1783 2	934 L	932	1785 2	948	930	1787 2Ⓐ	928	1789 2	946 Ⓐ	926	1791 2	944	924	1793 2	942	922	1795 2Ⓒ	940	920	2	2
rutnov hlavní	d.	...	0439	...	0541	...	0641	0743	...	0841	0941	1041	1141	...	1241	1341	...	1441	1541	...	1641	1741	...	1841	...	...
aroměř	d.	...	0541	...	0641	...	0741	0844	...	0941	1044	1141	1244	...	1341	1444	...	1541	1644	...	1741	1844	...	1941	...	...
radec Králové	a.	...	0558	...	0658	...	0755	0858	...	0955	1058	1155	1258	...	1355	1459	...	1555	1659	...	1755	1858	...	1955	...	...
radec Králové	d.	0509	...	0609	...	0709	0809	...	0909	1009	...	1209	...	1309	1409	...	1509	1609	...	1709	1809	...	1909	2009	...	...
oděbrady ▷	d.	0553	...	0653	...	0753	0853	...	0953	1053	...	1253	...	1353	1453	...	1553	1653	...	1753	1853	...	1953	2053	2153	...
ymburk ▷	d.	0602	...	0702	...	0802	0902	...	1002	1102	...	1302	...	1402	1502	...	1602	1702	...	1802	1902	...	2002	2102	2206	2306
ysá nad Labem ▷	d.	0613	...	0713	...	0813	0913	...	1013	1113	...	1313	...	1413	1513	...	1613	1713	...	1813	1913	...	2013	2113	2225	2325
raha hlavní	a.	0643	...	0743	...	0843	0943	...	1043	1143	...	1343	...	1443	1543	...	1643	1743	...	1843	1943	...	2043	2143	2302	0002

- – To/from Letohrad (Table **1165**).
- – ①–⑥ (not July 6, Oct. 29).

t – Not Oct. 29.
▷ – See also Table **1147**.

Apr. 18 - Aug. 2: by 🚌 Hradec Králové - Jaroměř and v.v. (🚌 runs 15-20 mins earlier).

DĚČÍN - ÚSTÍ NAD LABEM - MĚLNÍK - KOLÍN and RUMBURK - KOLÍN 1147

km			781 ⚒n	783		793	795 Ⓑh
0	**Ústí n. L** západ	d.	0447	0647		1647	1847
2	**Ústí n. L** Střekov	d.	0452	0652		1652	1852
27	Litoměřice město	d.	0512	0712	and	1712	1912
63	**Mělník**	d.	0539	0739	every	1739	1939
73	Všetaty	d.	0547	0747	**two**	1747	1947
85	Stará Boleslav	d.	0556	0756	hours	1756	1956
96	Lysá nad Labem. ▷	d.	0606	0806	until	1806	2006
112	Nymburk ▷	d.	0618	0818		1818	2018
118	Poděbrady ▷	d.	0624	0824		1824	2024
134	**Kolín**	a.	0640	0840		1840	2040
			⊖				
0	**Děčín** hlavní	d.	0603	0802	1202	1402	1602	1802
28	**Ústí n. L** Střekov	a.	0644	0844	1244	1444	1644	1844

		794 ⚒n	792		782	780 Ⓑh
Kolín	d.	0715	0915		1915	2115
Poděbrady ▷	d.	0730	0930		1930	2130
Nymburk ▷	d.	0740	0940	and	1940	2140
Lysá nad Labem ▷	d.	0752	0952	every	1952	2152
Stará Boleslav	d.	0759	0959	**two**	1959	2159
Všetaty	d.	0809	1009	hours	2009	2209
Mělník	d.	0818	1018	until	2018	2218
Litoměřice město	d.	0845	1045		2045	2245
Ústí n. L Střekov	a.	0903	1103		2103	2303
Ústí n. L západ	a.	0908	1108		2108	2308
		⊖				
Ústí n. L Střekov	d.	0655	0912	1312	1512	1712	1912
Děčín hlavní	a.	0734	0954	1354	1554	1754	1954

RUMBURK - ČESKA LIPÁ - KOLÍN

							E
Rumburk	d.	0503a	0714	1114c	1314	1514	1714
Česka Lipá	d.	0624	0824	1224	1424	1624	1824
Mladá Boleslav	d.	0722	0922	1322	1522	1722	1922
Nymburk ▷	d.	0748	0948	1348	1548	1748	1948
Poděbrady ▷	d.	0756	0956	1356	1556	1756	1956
Kolín	a.	0811	1011	1411	1611	1811	2011
							E
Kolín	d.	0744	0944	1344	1544	1744	1944
Poděbrady ▷	d.	0759	0959	1359	1559	1759	1959
Nymburk ▷	d.	0808	1008	1408	1608	1808	2008
Mladá Boleslav	a.	0835	1035	1435	1635	1835	2035
Česka Lipá	a.	0936	1136	1536	1736	1936	2136
Rumburk	a.	1039	1239c	1635	1840	2039	

- – ⑤⑥⑦ (daily May 27 - Sept. 18), also Dec. 23, Mar. 28, Sept. 28, Nov. 17; not Dec. 25, Nov. 18.
- – Ⓐ only.

c – Ⓒ only.
h – Not Dec. 24, 25, 31, Jan. 1, Mar. 27, July 5, Oct. 28.
n – ①–⑥ (not Dec. 25, 26, Jan. 1, 2, Mar. 28, July 6, Oct. 29).

▷ – See also Table **1145**.
⊖ – 2nd class only. For Dečín - Ústí nad Labem hlavní see Table **1100**.

1150 PRAHA - PARDUBICE - BRNO - BŘECLAV - WIEN / BRATISLAVA

km	FAST TRAINS	EC 271	Ex 571	EC 273	RJ 71	EC 275	RJ 73	EC 277	RJ 75	EC 279	RJ 77	EC 131	EC 173	RJ 79	Ex 573	EC 281	RJ 371	IC 575	EC 283	Ex 577	RJ 373	RJ 581	EN 477	477 407
		✕		✕	✕	✕	✕	✕	✕	✕	✕	✕	✕	✕		✕	✕	✕	✕		✕	✕		
			Ⓐ		G		G	S	G		G	V	H	G	Ⓐ		G			⑦e		§	M	W
0	**Praha** hlavní .... **1160** d.	...	0452	0552	0652	0752	0852	0952	1052	1152	1252	...	1352	1452	1521	1552	1652	1721	1752	1821	1852	1952	2358	2358
62	Kolín .... **1160** d.	...	0528	0628	|	0828	|	1028	|	1228	|	...	1428	|	|	1628	|	|	1828	|	|	2028	|	|
104	**Pardubice** .... **1160** d.	...	0549	0649	0749	0849	0949	1049	1149	1249	1349	...	1449	1549	1619	1649	1749	1819	1849	1919	1949	2049	0108	0108
164	Česká Třebová ..... **1160** d.	...	0623	0723	0823	|	1023	|	1223	|	1423	...	|	1623	|	|	1823	|	|	|	2023	2123	|	|
255	**Brno** hlavní .... a.	...	0722	0822	0922	1022	1122	1222	1322	1422	1522	...	1622	1722	1751	1822	1922	1951	2022	2051	2122	2222	0243	0243
255	**Brno** hlavní .... **1159** d.	0622	...	0824	0924	1024	1124	1224	1324	1424	1524	...	1624	1724	...	1824	1924	1954	2024	...	2124	...	0315	0315
314	**Břeclav** .... **1159** a.	0652	...	0853	0953	1053	1153	1253	1353	1453	1553	...	1653	1753	...	1853	1953	2024	2053	...	2153	...	0349	0349
314	**Břeclav** .... d.	0659	...	0859	0956	1059	1156	1259	1356	1459	1556	1559	1659	1756	...	1859	1956	...	2059	...	2156	...	0440	0549
	Wien Hbf **982** .... a.	|	...	*0951**	1051	|	1251	*1351**	1451	|	1651	|	|	1851	...	*1951**	2051	...	|	...	...	...	|	0702
332	Kúty 🏛 .... d.	0713	...	0913	...	1113	...	1313	...	1513	...	1613	1713	...	...	1913	...	...	2113	...	...	...	0455	...
396	**Bratislava** hlavná .... a.	0750	...	0950	...	1150	...	1350	...	1550	...	1650	1750	...	...	1950	...	...	2150	...	...	...	0536	...
	Budapest Keleti **1175** . a.	1035	...	1235	...	1435	...	1635	...	1835	...	1935	2035	...	...	2235	...	...	...	...	...	...	0837	...

	RJ 580	IC 578	Ex 576	IC 574	Ex 572	EC 282	RJ 70	EC 280	RJ 72	EC 172	EC 130	RJ 74	EC 278	RJ 76	Ex 570	EC 276	RJ 78	EC 274	RJ 370	EC 272	RJ 372	EC 270	406 476	EN 476	47 87
	✕	✕		✕		✕	✕	✕	✕	✕	✕	✕	✕	✕		✕	✕	✕	✕	✕	✕	✕			
	⚒n		Ⓐ		Ⓐ				G	H	V	G		G	⑦e	S	G		G		G		W	M	P
Budapest Keleti **1175** .. d.	...	...	...	...	...	...	...	0525	...	0725	0822	...	0925	...	...	1125	...	1325	...	1525	...	1725	...	2005	200
Bratislava hlavná .... d.	...	...	...	...	...	0610	...	0810	...	1010	1110	...	1210	...	...	1410	...	1610	...	1810	...	2010	...	2301	230
Kúty 🏛 .... d.	...	...	...	...	...	0649	...	0849	...	1049	1149	...	1249	...	...	1449	...	1649	...	1849	...	2049	...	2343	234
Wien Hbf **982** .... d.	...	...	...	...	...	|	0709	*0807**	0909	|	|	1109	|	1309	...	*1409**	1509	|	1709	*1809**	1909	|	2250	|	|
Břeclav .... a.	...	...	...	...	...	0701	0804	0901	1004	1101	1201	1204	1301	1404	...	1501	1604	1701	1804	1901	2004	2101	2350	2356	235
Břeclav .... **1159** d.	...	...	...	0607	...	0707	0807	0907	1007	1107	...	1207	1307	1407	...	1507	1607	1707	1807	1907	2007	2107	0020	0020	002
Brno hlavní .... **1159** a.	...	...	...	0636	...	0736	0836	0936	1036	1136	...	1236	1336	1436	...	1536	1636	1736	1836	1936	2036	2136	0054	0054	005
Brno hlavní .... d.	0431	0538	0608	0638	0708	0738	0838	0938	1038	1138	...	1238	1338	1438	1508	1538	1638	1738	1838	1938	2038	...	0127	0127	012
Česká Třebová ..... **1160** d.	0538	0638	|	0738	|	|	0938	|	1138	|	...	1338	|	1538	|	|	1738	|	1938	2038	2138	...	|	|	|
Pardubice .... **1160** d.	0612	0712	0743	0812	0843	0912	1012	1112	1212	1312	...	1412	1512	1612	1641	1712	1812	1912	2012	2112	2212	...	0259	0259	053
Kolín .... **1160** d.	|	0732	|	|	|	0932	|	1132	|	1332	...	|	1532	|	|	1732	|	1932	|	2132	2232	...	|	|	060
Praha hlavní .... **1160** a.	0708	0808	0842	0908	0942	1010	1108	1208	1308	1410	...	1508	1608	1708	1737	1808	1908	2008	2108	2208	2308	...	0408	0408	064

km	STOPPING TRAINS	883	861	885	863	865	889	867	891	869	893	871	851	873	853	875	877	877	899	879	IC 553
		◇	T	◇			◇		◇		⊖		▽		▽	Ⓑh		Ⓑh			⚒n
0	**Praha** hlavní .... d.	...	0555	0655	0755	0955	1055	1155	1255	1355	1455	1555	1655	1755	1855	2003	2055	2055	2202	0001	0001
62	Kolín .... d.	⊡	0635	0735	0835	1035	1135	1235	1335	1435	1535	1635	1735	1835	1935	2044	2134	2134	2242	0039	0039
104	**Pardubice** .... d.	0604	0704	0804	0904	1104	1204	1304	1404	1504	1604	1704	1804	1904	2004	2111	2159	2159	2307	0103	0111
139	Choceň .... d.	0625	0725	0825	0925	1125	1225	1325	1423	1525	1625	1725	1825	1925	2025	2130	2217	2217	...	...	0128
154	Ústí nad Orlicí .... d.	0638	0738	0838	0938	1138	1238	1338	1436	1538	1638	1738	1838	1938	2038	2143	2230	2230	...	...	0141
164	**Česká Třebová** .... d.	0648	0747	0848	0947	1147	1248	1347	1448	1547	1648	1747	1848	1947	2048	2152	2238	2239	...	...	0151
	Brno hlavní .... a.	|	0902	|	1102	1302	|	1502	|	1702	|	1902	|	2102	|	...	...	2347	...	...	|
204	Zábřeh na Moravé .... d.	0711	...	0911	...	...	1311	...	1511	...	1711	...	1911	...	2111	...	...	...	...	...	|
250	**Olomouc** .... a.	0740	...	0940	...	...	1340	...	1540	...	1740	...	1940	...	2140	...	...	...	...	...	0232

PRAHA - OLOMOUC For fast trains see Table **1160**

	898	878	876	IC 552	892	852	874	850	872	870	888	868	886	866	884	864	882	862	862	EC 120	
			⚒n	⚒n	⊖	▽		▽			◇		◇		◇		◇		Ⓒc	z	
Olomouc .... d.	...	...	...	0508	0521	0621	...	0821	...	...	1221	...	1421	...	1621	...	1821	...	...	2018	...
Zábřeh na Moravé .... d.	...	...	...	|	0551	0651	...	0851	...	...	1251	...	1451	...	1651	...	1851	...	...	2047	...
Brno hlavní .... d.	...	...	...	|	|	|	0655	|	0857	1057	|	1257	|	1457	|	1655	|	1857	1857	|	...
Česká Třebová .... d.	...	...	0514	|	0614	0714	0814	0914	1014	1214	1314	1414	1514	1614	1714	1814	1914	2014	2014	2109	...
Ústí nad Orlicí .... d.	...	...	0523	0555	0623	0723	0823	0923	1023	1223	1323	1423	1523	1623	1723	1823	1923	2023	2023	2118	...
Choceň .... d.	...	...	0535	|	0635	0735	0835	0935	1035	1235	1335	1435	1535	1635	1735	1835	1935	2035	2035	2130	...
Pardubice .... d.	0501	0534	0556	0621	0656	0756	0856	0956	1056	1256	1356	1456	1556	1656	1756	1856	1956	2054	2056	2148	...
Kolín .... d.	0527	0601	0624	|	0724	0824	0924	1024	1124	1324	1424	1524	1624	1724	1824	1924	2024	...	2124	2212	...
Praha hlavní .... a.	0606	0643	0704	0715	0804	0904	1004	1104	1204	1404	1504	1604	1704	1804	1904	2004	2104	...	2204	2252	...

ČESKA TŘEBOVA - BRNO: Fast trains - see above. Stopping trains - see below.

km	STOPPING TRAINS	1973	1975	861	863	865	867	1977	869	871	873	877
		⚒n	2Ⓐ	T				2Ⓐ				Ⓑh
	Praha hlavní .... d.	...	...	0555	0755	0955	1155	...	1355	1555	1755	2055
0	**Česká Třebová** .... d.	0543	0643	0748	0948	1148	1348	1448	1548	1748	1948	2239
17	Svitavy .... d.	0559	0700	0759	0959	1159	1359	1504	1559	1759	1959	2249
44	Letovice .... d.	0627	0732	0819	1019	1219	1419	1532	1619	1819	2019	2308
69	Blansko .... d.	0649	0752	0841	1041	1241	1441	1554	1641	1841	2041	2327
91	**Brno** hlavní .... a.	0714	0816	0902	1102	1302	1502	1614	1702	1902	2102	2347

	580 •	874	872	870	868	866	864	862	860	858
	⚒n								⑦e	Ⓐ
Brno hlavní .... d.	0431	0655	0857	1057	1257	1457	1655	1857	2046	205
Blansko .... d.	0451	0718	0918	1118	1318	1518	1718	1918	2107	211
Letovice .... d.	0509	0738	0938	1138	1338	1538	1738	1938	2127	213
Svitavy .... d.	0527	0800	1000	1200	1400	1600	1800	2000	2147	220
Česká Třebová .... a.	0537	0811	1011	1211	1411	1611	1811	2011	2158	221
Praha hlavní .... a.	0708	1004	1204	1404	1604	1804	2004	2204c	...	...

G – [12] ✕ Praha - Brno - Wien - Graz and v.v. (Table **60**).
H – HUNGARIA – [12] ✕ Hamburg - Berlin - Dresden - Praha - Bratislava - Budapest and v.v. Conveys on ②⑤ June 17 - Sept. 2 🛏 1, 2 cl. Praha - Budapest - Beograd - Bar, returning from Bar on ④⑦ June 19 - Sept. 4.
M – METROPOL – 🛏 1, 2 cl., ▬ 2 cl., [2] Berlin - Dresden - Praha - Bratislava - Budapest and v.v. For other cars Břeclav - Budapest and v.v. see Tables **95** / **99**.
P – 🛏 1, 2 cl., ▬ 2 cl., [2] Budapest (**476**) - Bratislava - Pardubice (**878**) - Praha.
S – SLOVAN – [12] ✕ Praha - Budapest and v.v. On ②⑤ June 17 - Aug. 26 conveys 🛏 1, 2 cl. Praha - Budapest (**1204/5**) - Zagreb - Split, returning next day.
T – From Praha on ① **g**; from Pardubice on ①–⑥ **n**; runs daily Česká Třebová - Brno.
V – VARSOVIA – [12] ✕ Warszawa - Katowice - Ostrava - Břeclav - Budapest and v.v.
W – 🛏 1, 2 cl., ▬ 2 cl., [2] Berlin - Dresden - Praha - Břeclav (**407/6**) - Wien Hbf and v.v.
c – ⑥⑦ (also Dec. 25, Jan. 1, Mar. 28, July 5, 6, Oct. 28; not Dec. 27, July 3).

e – Also Mar. 28, July 6; not Dec. 27, Mar. 27, July 3.
g – Also Mar. 29, July 7; not Dec. 28, Mar. 28, July 4.
h – Ⓑ (not Dec. 24, 25, 31, Jan. 1, Mar. 27, July 5, Oct. 28).
n – ①–⑥ (not Dec. 25, 26, Jan. 1, 2, Mar. 28, July 6, Oct. 29).
u – ①–⑤ (also Dec. 27, July 3; not Dec. 24, 25, 31, Jan. 1, July 5, 6, Oct. 28).
z – From Žilina (Table **1160**).
§ – *IC* (not Railjet) on ⑥, also Mar. 27, July 5, Oct. 28.
⊖ – To / from Staré Město u Uherské Hradiště (Table **1159**).
▽ – To / from Vsetin (Table **1158**).
◇ – To / from Luhačovice (Table **1159**).
⊡ – From Hradec Králové (depart 0544).
• – Railjet train.

* – Change at Břeclav.
RJ – Railjet train.

OTHER TRAIN NAMES SEE TABLE **60**.

1151 PRAHA - HAVLIČKŮV BROD - BRNO

See also Table 115

km		975	977	979	981	983	985	987	961	989	991	963
		⚒n					Ⓐ		Ⓑh		G	
0	**Praha** hlavní ...... ▷ d.	0606	0806	1006	1206	1406	1506	1606	1706	1806	1906	2006
62	Kolín .... ▷ d.	0646	0846	1046	1246	1446	1546	1646	1746	1846	1946	2046
73	Kutná Hora .... d.	0656	0856	1056	1256	1456	1556	1656	1756	1856	1956	2056
82	Čáslav .... d.	0704	0904	1104	1304	1504	1604	1704	1804	1904	2004	2104
136	**Havličkův Brod** ..... d.	0804	1004	1204	1404	1604	1704	1804	1902	2004	2104	2203
	Jihlava **1152** .... a.	|	|	|	|	|	|	|	1923	|	|	...
169	Ždár nad Sázavou .. d.	0830	1030	1230	1430	1630	1730	1830	...	2030	2130	...
257	**Brno** hlavní .... a.	0941	1141	1341	1541	1741	1841	1941	...	2144	2236	...

	962	960	990	988	986	984	982	980	978	976	972
	⚒n		E						Ⓑh		
Brno hlavní .... d.	...	...	0520	0620	0820	1020	1220	1420	1520	1620	182
Ždár nad Sázavou. d.	...	...	0630	0730	0930	1130	1330	1530	1630	1730	193
Jihlava **1152** ...... d.	...	0532n	|	|	|	|	|	|	|	|	|
Havličkův Brod .... d.	0455	0555	0655	0755	0955	1155	1355	1555	1655	1755	195
Čáslav .... d.	0552	0652	0752	0852	1052	1252	1452	1652	1752	1852	205
Kutná Hora .... d.	0601	0701	0801	0901	1101	1301	1501	1701	1801	1901	210
Kolín .... ▷ d.	0612	0712	0812	0912	1112	1312	1512	1712	1812	1912	211
Praha hlavní ..... ▷ a.	0651	0751	0851	0951	1151	1351	1551	1751	1851	1951	215

E – ① (also Mar. 29, July 7; not Mar. 28) from Brno, Ⓐ from Ždár nad Sázavou, ⚒ **n** from Havličkův Brod.
G – Ⓑ **h** to Havličkův Brod, ⑤ **z** to Brno.
h – Not Dec. 24, 25, 31, Jan. 1, Mar. 27, July 5, Oct. 28.

n – ①–⑥ (not Dec. 25, 26, Jan. 1, 2, Mar. 28, July 6, Oct. 29).
z – Also Dec. 23, 30, July 4, Sept. 27, Oct. 27, Nov. 16; not Dec. 25, Jan. 1, Oct. 28.
▷ – See also Tables **1150** / **60**.

ADDITIONAL JOURNEYS:
0502Ⓐ, 0604, 0804 Havličkův Brod - Brno.
1720Ⓐ Brno - Havličkův Brod.
2206 Praha - Čáslav (to Havličkův Brod night of ⑤⑥)

1152 HAVLÍČKŮV BROD - JIHLAVA

2nd clas

27 km		Ⓐ		R§					Ⓐ		Ⓐ		Ⓐ		P	Ⓐz		
Havlíčkův Brod ..... d.	0448	0603	0647	0700	0807	1007	1207	1313	1407	1513	1607	1712	1807	1902	2007	2108	2211
Jihlava .... a.	0516	0632	0717	0722	0835	1035	1236	1343	1437	1542	1637	1742	1836	1923	2035	2137	2240

		P		Ⓐ				Ⓐ		Ⓐ		Ⓐ		Ⓐz		S§	
Jihlava .... d.	0519	0532	0605	0655	0727	0922	1122	1237	1322	1438	1521	1616	1721	1815	1924	2036	2138
Havlíčkův Brod ..... a.	0548	0553	0643	0734	0751	0950	1150	1305	1351	1506	1550	1644	1750	1843	1952	2058	2207

P – To / from Praha. For days of running see Table **1151**.
R – ①⑥ (also Dec. 24, Mar. 29, July 7, Sept. 28, Nov. 17 not Dec. 26 - Jan. 2, Mar. 28, July 4, Oct. 29, Nov. 19)
S – ⑤⑦ (also Dec. 23, Mar. 28, July 6, Oct. 27, Nov. 16; n Dec. 24 - Jan. 1, Mar. 27, July 3, Oct. 28, Nov. 18).
z – Not Dec. 23 - 31. § – To / from Plzeň (Table **1135**).

BRNO - PŘEROV - OSTRAVA - BOHUMÍN 1155

	EN 406 C	821 ⚒n	823 ⚒n	Ex 530	825	EC 104 S	827	829	EC 130 V	831	833	835	EC 102 P	837	839	841	843 Ⓑh	Ex* 100 M	845	847 ⑦e	849	
Brno hlavní ... **1156** d.	...	0502	0602	...	0702	...	0902	1102	...	1202	1302	1402	...	1502	1602	1702	1802	...	1902	2002	2102	...
Vyškov na Moravě ... **1156** d.	...	0545	0645	...	0745	...	0945	1145	...	1245	1345	1445	...	1545	1645	1745	1845	...	1945	2045	2142	...
Kojetin ... d.	...	0610	0710	...	0810	...	1010	1210	...	1310	1410	1510	...	1610	1710	1810	1910	...	2010	2110	2210	...
Wien Hbf **982** ... d.	2250	|	|	...	|	0809	|	|	...	|	|	|	1409	|	|	|	|	1809	|	|	|	...
Břeclav **1159** ... d.	0013	|	|	0713	|	0913	|	|	1213	|	|	|	1513	|	|	|	|	1913	|	|	|	...
Přerov ... **1160** d.	0105	0627	0727	0809	0827	1009	1027	1227	1309	1327	1427	1527	1609	1627	1727	1827	1927	2009	2027	2127	2227	...
Hranice na Moravě ... **1160** d.	|	0645	0745	0826	0845	1026	1045	1245	1326	1345	1445	1545	1626	1645	1745	1845	1945	2026	2045	2145	2245	...
Ostrava Svinov ... **1160** a.	0145	0718	0818	0849	0918	1049	1118	1318	1349	1418	1518	1618	1649	1718	1818	1918	2018	2049	2118	2218	2318	...
Ostrava hlavní ... **1160** a.	0154	0727	0827	0857	0927	1057	1127	1327	1357	1427	1527	1627	1657	1727	1827	1927	2027	2057	2127	2227	2327	...
Bohumín ... **1160** a.	0203	0734	0834	...	0934	1105	1134	1334	1405	1434	1534	1634	1705	1734	1834	1934	2034	2105	2134	2234	2334	...

	EN 407 C	848 ⚒n	846 ⚒n	844	Ex* 101 M	842	840		838	EC 103 P	836	834	EC 131 V	832	830	828	EC 105 S	826 Ⓑh	824	Ex 531	822 ⑦e	820	
mín ... **1160** d.	0220	0435	0535	0635	0652	0735	0835	...	1035	1052	1235	1335	1352	1435	1535	1635	1652	1735	1835	...	1935	2035	...
ava hlavní ... **1160** d.	0229	0442	0542	0642	0700	0742	0842	...	1042	1100	1242	1342	1400	1442	1542	1642	1700	1742	1842	1900	1942	2042	...
va Svinov ... **1160** d.	0238	0451	0551	0651	0708	0751	0851	...	1051	1108	1251	1351	1408	1451	1551	1651	1708	1751	1851	1908	1951	2051	...
ce na Moravě ... **1160** d.	|	0522	0622	0722	0733	0822	0922	...	1122	1133	1322	1422	1433	1522	1622	1722	1733	1822	1922	1933	2022	2122	...
v ... **1160** d.	0320	0541	0641	0741	0752	0841	0941	...	1141	1152	1341	1441	1452	1541	1641	1741	1752	1841	1941	1952	2041	2141	...
eclav **1159** ... a.	0414	|	|	|	0848	|	|	...	|	1248	|	|	1548	|	|	|	1848	|	|	2048	|	|	...
en Hbf **982** ... a.	0702	|	|	|	0951	|	|	...	|	1351	|	|	...	|	|	|	1951	|	|	...	|	|	...
in ... d.	...	0557	0657	0757	...	0857	0957	...	1157	...	1357	1457	...	1557	1657	1757	...	1857	1957	...	2057	2157	...
ov na Moravě ... **1156** d.	...	0620	0720	0820	...	0920	1020	...	1220	...	1420	1520	...	1620	1720	1820	...	1920	2020	...	2120	2220	...
hlavní ... **1156** d.	...	0659	0757	0857	...	0957	1057	...	1257	...	1459	1559	...	1659	1759	1859	...	1957	2056	...	2156	2256	...

CHOPIN – 🛏 1, 2 cl., ▬ 2 cl., [2] Wien - Bohumín - Katowice - Warszawa and v.v.; 🛏 1, 2 cl. Wien - Bohumín (**403/2**) - Kraków and v.v. (also ▬ 2 cl. on dates in Table **99**); 🛏 1, 2 cl., ▬ 2 cl., [2] Budapest (**476/7**) - Bratislava - Břeclav (**406/7**) - Warszawa and v.v.; 🛏 1, 2 cl., ▬ 2 cl. Budapest (**476/7**) - Bratislava - Břeclav (**406/7**) - Bohumín (**403/2**) - Kraków and v.v.

MORAVIA – [12] Wien - Břeclav - Bohumín and v.v. Conveys on dates in Table **95** 🛏 1, 2 cl. Wien - Bohumín (**405/4**) - Minsk - Moskva / St Peterburg and v.v.

POLONIA – [12] ✕ Wien - Břeclav - Ostrava - Katowice - Warszawa and v.v.

SOBIESKI – [12] ✕ Wien - Břeclav - Ostrava - Katowice - Warszawa - Gdansk - Gdynia and v.v.

V – VARSOVIA – [12] ✕ Budapest - Bratislava - Břeclav - Ostrava - Katowice - Warszawa and v.v. Conveys on dates in Table **95** 🛏 1, 2 cl. Budapest - Warszawa - Moskva and v.v. (also Burgas / Varna - Budapest - Moskva and v.v. on summer dates in Table **95**).

e – Also Mar. 28, July 6; not Dec. 27, Mar. 27, July 3.
h – Not Dec. 24, 25, 31, Jan. 1, Mar. 27, July 5, Oct. 28.
n – ①–⑥ (not Dec. 25, 26, Jan. 1, 2, Mar. 28, July 6, Oct. 29).
* – Classified *R* in Austria.

BRNO - OLOMOUC - ŠUMPERK and JESENÍK 1156

	901 Ⓐb	903 Ⓒ	905	907	909 Ⓐ	909 Ⓒ	911	913	1629 2	915	917 E
Brno hlavní ... ▷ d.	0523	0628	0718	0918	1118	1118	1318	1518	...	1718	1918
Vyškov na Moravé ▷ d.	0602	0704	0802	1002	1202	1202	1402	1602	...	1802	2002
Nezamyslice ... d.	0620	0720	0820	1020	1220	1220	1420	1620	...	1820	2020
Prostějov ... d.	0635	0735	0835	1035	1235	1235	1435	1635	...	1835	2035
Olomouc ... a.	0651	0751	0851	1051	1251	1251	1452	1651	...	1851	2051
Olomouc ... ▽ d.	0656	0756	0856	1056	1256	▬	1456	1656	1800	1856	2056
Zábřeh na Moravé. ▽ a.	0722	0825	0922	1122	1322	Ⓒ	1522	1722	|	1924	2124
Zábřeh na Moravé ... d.	0731	0834	0931	1131	1325	1331	1531	1731	u	1926	2126
Šumperk ... a.	0740r	0842r	0939r	1139r	1339r	|	1539r	1739r	1908	1942	2140
Hanušovice ... a.	0800	0901	1000	1200	1400	1400	1600	1800	2000	...	...
Lipová Lázně ... a.	0859	1002	1059	1259	1459	1459	1659	1859	2052	...	...
Jeseník ... a.	0910	1009	1110	1310	1511	1511	1710	1910	2101	...	...

	1638 Ⓐ	914 F	912	910	908 Ⓐ	1708 Ⓒ	906	904	902	900 Ⓒ
Jeseník ... d.	...	...	0654	0854	1054	1054	1254	1454	1654	*1845*z
Lipová Lázně ... d.	...	...	0703	0903	1103	1103	1303	1503	1703	*1854*z
Hanušovice ... d.	...	...	0801	1001	1201	1201	1401	1601	1801	*1953*z
Šumperk ... d.	0453	0609	0809s	1009s	1209s	|	1409s	1609s	1809s	2015
Zábřeh na Moravé ... a.	0510	0629	0826	1026	1222	1226	1426	1626	1826	2033
Zábřeh na Moravé ▽ d.	0514	0632	0836	1036	1236	▬	1436	1636	1836	2036
Olomouc ... ▽ a.	0550	0702	0903	1103	1303	Ⓒ	1503	1705	1905	2103
Olomouc ... d.	0558	0707	0907	1107	1307	1307	1507	1707	1907	2107
Prostějov ... d.	0615	0725	0925	1125	1325	1325	1525	1725	1925	2125
Nezamyslice ... d.	0637	0740	0940	1140	1340	1340	1540	1740	1940	2140
Vyškov na Moravé ▷ d.	0700	0802	1002	1202	1402	1402	1602	1802	2002	2202
Brno hlavní ... ▷ a.	0746	0842	1042	1242	1443	1443	1643	1842	2039	2239

Daily Brno - Olomouc, Ⓑ **h** to Šumperk.
①–⑥ **n** from Šumperk, daily Olomouc - Brno.
Also runs Olomouc - Jeseník on Ⓒ (no Šumperk portion).
Not Dec. 24, 25, 31, Jan. 1, Mar. 27, July 5, Oct. 28.
Not Dec. 25, 26, Jan. 1, 2, Mar. 28, July 6, Oct. 29.

r – Šumperk portion detatches at Zabreh (dep. xx25).
s – Šumperk portion attaches at Zabreh (arr. xx22).
u – Via Uničov.
z – Change at Bludov (a. 2017 / d. 2022).
▷ – See also Table **1155**. ▽ – See also Table **1160**.

Different train numbers apply between Zabreh and Jeseník.

Apr. 14 - Oct. 3: by 🚌 Zábřeh na Moravé - Jeseník and v.v. in similar timings.

BRNO - UHERSKÉ HRADIŠTĚ - LUHAČOVICE / TRENČIANSKA TEPLÁ 1157

class

❦				⑤f					
Brno hlavní ... d.	0735	0928	1128	1249	1328	1528	1728	1928	2128
Kyjov ... d.	0837	1032	1232	1351	1432	1632	1832	2032	2232
Veselí nad Moravou ... d.	0901	1101	1301	1413	1501	1701	1901	2101	2258
Kunovice ... a.	|	|	|	1430	|	|	1919	2119	...
Uherské Hradiště ... ▷ a.	0919	1119	1319	...	1519	1719	*1931*	*2125*	...
Staré Město u Uh. H .. ▷ a.	0927	1127	1327	...	1527	1727	*1939*	*2132*	...

❦										
Staré Město u Uh. H . ▷ d.	...	...	0835	1035	1235	1435	1635	1835	2024	...
Uherské Hradiště ... ▷ d.	...	0634	0841	1041	1241	1441	1641	1841	2031	...
Kunovice ... d.	...	|	|	|	|	|	|	|	|	...
Veselí nad Moravou ... d.	0601	0701	0901	1101	1301	1501	1701	1901	2051	2101
Kyjov ... d.	0628	0728	0928	1128	1328	1528	1728	1928	...	2128
Brno hlavní ... a.	0733	0834	1033	1233	1433	1633	1833	2033	...	2233

			A♣		Ⓐ	⑤f			
Praha hlavní **1160** ... d.	...	...	0840	...	...	...	...	...	...
Brno hlavní ... ▷ d.	...	...	|	...	...	1249	...	1728	1928
Staré Město u Uh. H .. ▷ d.	0825	1005	1205	1225	1333	|	1605	*1850*r	|
Uherské Hradiště ... ▷ a.	0831	1011	1212	1231	1339	|	1611	*1856*r	|
Uherské Hradiště ... ▷ d.	0832	1032	1212	1232	1341	|	1632	*1918*r	*2114*r
Kunovice ... d.	0835	1035	|	1235	1344	1436	1635	1925	2125
Uherský Brod ... ▷ d.	0855	1055	1228	1255	1415	1455	1655	1945	2146
Újezdec u Luhačovic ... a.	0858	1058	|	1258	1419	1458	1658	1949	2150
Luhačovice ... ▷ a.	*0916*	*1116*	|	*1316*	*1516*	*1516*	*1716*	*2018*x	*2206*
Bojkovice ... a.	0913	1113	1242n	1313	1434	1513	1713	2003	2206
Bylnice ... a.	0950	1152	1312	1351	1517	1552	1752	2042	2242
Vlárský průsmyk 🏛 ... a.	*0959*	...	|	...	1524	1603	...	...	...
Trenčianska Teplá **1180** a.	...	...	1331	...	...	*1624*	...	...	...
Trenčin ... **1180** a.	...	...	1342	...	...	...	...	...	...

	Ⓒ					B♣	⑤f		⑦t	
Trenčin ... **1180** d.	...	...	...	...	...	1419	...	...	...	...
Trenčianska Teplá . **1180** d.	...	...	...	...	...	1426	*1445*	...	*1737*	...
Vlárský průsmyk 🏛 ... d.	...	*0751*	*1001*	...	...	|	1541	...	1756	...
Bylnice ... d.	...	0800	1010	1200	1400	1448	1548	1600	1803	1805
Bojkovice ... d.	0707	0845	1047	1245	1445	1517n	...	1645	...	1845
Luhačovice ... ▷ d.	*0700*	*0842*	*1042*	*1242*	*1442*	|	...	*1642*	...	*1842*v
Újezdec u Luhačovic ... d.	0719	0859	1100	1259	1459	|	...	1659	...	1859
Uherský Brod ... ▷ d.	0724	0904	1105	1304	1504	1532	...	1704	...	1904
Kunovice ... a.	0742	0923	1123	1324	1523	|	...	1723	...	1923
Uherské Hradiště ... ▷ a.	0745	0927	1127	1327	1527	1547	...	1727	...	*1931*r
Uherské Hradiště ... ▷ d.	0746	0933	1145	1345	1533	1547	...	1745	...	*1933*r
Staré Město u Uh. H .. ▷ a.	0751	0939	1151	1351	1539	1554	...	1751	...	*1939*r
Brno hlavní ... ▷ a.	...	...	...	...	...	|	...	...	...	...
Praha hlavní **1160** ... a.	...	...	...	...	...	1924	...	...	...	...

⑥ (also Mar. 25, Oct. 28; not Mar. 26, Oct. 29). Train *Ex* **1093**.
⑦ (also Mar. 28, July 6; not Mar. 27, July 3). Train *Ex* **1094**.
Also Oct. 27, Nov. 16; not Mar. 25, July 1 - Sept. 2, Oct. 28, Nov. 18.
Bojkovice **město**.
Change at Kunovice.

t – Also Mar. 28; not Mar. 27, July 3 - Aug. 28.
v – Ⓑ (not Mar. 27, July 5, Oct. 28).
x – ⑥ (also Mar. 27, July 5, Oct. 28).
♣ – Operated by Arriva. Separate fare tariff applies.

▷ – See also Table **1159**.
❦ – Certain journeys are replaced by 🚌 Brno - Slavkou and v.v. (27 *km*) in revised timings until May 21.

(PRAHA) - OLOMOUC - VSETÍN - HORNÍ LIDEČ - ŽILINA 1158

For the complete service Praha - Olomouc - Žilina (including trains via Ostrava) see Table **1160**

	2	EC* 121 ✕	EC* 123 ✕	EC* 125 ✕	EC* 127 ✕	EC* 221 ✕	EC* 129 ✕	851	853
Praha hl. **1160** ... d.	...	0524	0724	0924	1124	1324	1524	1655r	1855r
Olomouc ... d.	...	0745	0945	1145	1345	1545	1745	1954	2154
Hranice na Moravě ... d.	0636	0814	1014	1214	1414	1617	1814	2031	2226
Valašské Meziříčí ... d.	0709	0839	1039	1239	1439	1641	1839	2056	2251
Vsetín ... d.	0727	0857	1057	1257	1457	1658	1857	2112	2307
Horní Lideč 🏛 ... d.	...	0917	1117	1317	1517	1717	1917	...	...
Púchov ... a.	...	0940	1140	1340	1540	1740	1940	...	...
Púchov ... d.	...	1001	1201	1401	1601	1801	2001	...	...
Považská Bystrica ... d.	...	1013	1213	1413	1613	1813	2013	...	...
Žilina ... a.	...	1048	1248	1448	1648	1848	2048	...	...

	852	850	EC* 220	EC* 128	EC* 126	EC* 124	EC* 122	EC* 120	2
Žilina ... d.	...	...	0712	0912	1112	1312	1512	1712	...
Považská Bystrica ... d.	...	...	0747	0947	1147	1347	1547	1747	...
Púchov ... a.	...	...	0759	0959	1159	1359	1559	1759	...
Púchov ... d.	...	...	0820	1020	1220	1420	1620	1820	...
Horní Lideč 🏛 ... d.	...	...	0846	1046	1246	1446	1646	1846	...
Vsetín ... d.	0453s	0650	0904	1104	1304	1504	1704	1904	1950
Valašské Meziříčí ... d.	0510s	0707	0922	1122	1322	1522	1722	1922	2010
Hranice na Moravě ... d.	0533	0733	0945	1145	1345	1545	1745	1945	2040
Olomouc 1160 ... a.	0604	0804	1016	1216	1416	1616	1816	2016	...
Praha hl. **1160** ... a.	0904r	1104r	1239	1439	1639	1839	2039	2252	...

Stopping train (Table **1150**). Faster journey possible by changing at Olomouc (Table **1160**).

s – 7 mins earlier to July 19.
* – Classified *Ex* in Slovakia.

*Change at Púchov for Poprad Tatry and Košice (Table **1180**)*

1159 OLOMOUC - UHERSKÉ HRADIŠTĚ - BŘECLAV - BRNO

For direct services Olomouc - Brno see Table **1156**. For night train **406/7** Warszawa - Wien see Tables **99** and **1155** (also calls at Otrokovice: **406** at 0048, **407** at 0337)

km				Ex					LE♠	EC				EC				EC		♥		LE♠	Ex	IC	
		881	**814**	**101**	**883**	**812**	**885**	**810**	**1355**	**103**	**887**	**808**	**889**	**131**	**806**	**891**	**804**	**105**	**893**	**1015**	**802**	**1365**	**531**	**561**	**800**
		Ⓐ		**M**	⊡				[R] 🍷	**P**§				**V**§				**S**§				[R] 🍷		✕	Ⓑ h
	Praha hl. **1160** d.	...	...	...	...	...	0655r	...	0911	...	...	...	1055r	...	...	1255r	...	...	1455r	1646	...	1711	...	1724	...
0	**Olomouc** ▽ d.	0557	0710	...	0754	0910	0954	1110	1126	...	1154	1310	1354	...	1510	1554	1710	...	1754	1904	1910	1926	...	1945	2110
	Ostrava hl. **1155** d.	|	|	0700	|	|	|	|	|	1100	|	|	|	1400	|	|	|	1700	|	|	|	|	1900	|	|
22	Přerov ▽ d.	0612	0725	0752	0811	0925	1011	1126	1139	1152	1211	1325	1411	1452	1525	1611	1725	1752	1811	1919	1925	1939	1952	2001	2125
37	Hulín d.	0625	0736	|	0824	0936	1024	1136	1149	|	1224	1336	1424	|	1536	1624	1736	|	1824	1930	1936	1949	|	2012	2136
50	Otrokovice d.	0635	0745	0809	0834	0945	1034	1145	1158	1209	1234	1345	1434	1509	1545	1634	1745	1809	1834	1940	1945	1958	2009	2022	2145
61	**Zlín** střed ▷ a.	|	|	|	|	|	|	|	|	|	|	|	|	|	|	|	|	|	|	|	|	|	|	|	|
68	Staré Město U.H. ⊖ a.	0646	0754	0818	0845	0945	1045	1154	1208	1218	1245	1354	1445	1518	1554	1645	1754	1818	1845	1951	1954	2008	2018	2033	2154
68	Staré Město U.H. ⊖ d.	0655	0756	0819	0853	0956	1053	1156	...	1219	1253	1356	1453	1519	1556	1653	1756	1819	*1850*	...	1956	...	2019	2045	2156
73	Uherské Hradiště a.	0701	|	|	0859	|	1059	|	...	|	1259	|	1459	|	|	1659	|	|	*1856*	...	|	...	|	2051	|
90	Uherský Brod a.	0726	|	|	0918	|	1118	|	...	|	1318	|	1518	|	|	1718	|	|	...	...	|	...	|	u	|
104	**Luhačovice** a.	0745	|	|	0937	|	1137	|	...	|	1337	|	1537	|	|	1737	|	|	...	...	|	...	|	...	|
102	Hodonín d.	...	0817	0836	...	1017	...	1217	...	1236	...	1417	...	1536	1617	...	1817	1836	...	...	2017	...	2036	...	2217
122	**Břeclav** a.	...	0830	0848	...	1030	...	1230	...	1248	...	1430	...	1548	1630	...	1830	1848	...	...	2030	...	2048	...	2230
122	**Břeclav** **1150** d.	...	0840	*0907*	...	1040	...	1240	...	*1307*	...	1440	...	*1607*	1640	...	1840	*1907*	...	...	2040	...	*2107*	...	...
181	**Brno** hlavní **1150** a.	...	0924	*0936*	...	1124	...	1324	...	*1336*	...	1524	...	*1636*	1724	...	1924	*1936*	...	...	2124	...	*2136*	...	...

		IC	♥		LE♠	IC	Ex			EC				LE♠	EC				EC					Ex	
	892	**550**	**1002**	**801**	**1354**	**560**	**530**	**803**	**890**	**104**	**805**	**888**	**807**	**1360**	**130**	**886**	**809**	**884**	**102**	**811**	**882**	**813**	**880**	**100**	**815**
		✕		⚒ n	[R] 🍷	✕			Ⓐ	**S**§				[R] 🍷	**V**§				**P**§					**M**	
Brno hlavní **1150** d.	...	...	...	...	...	...	*0622*	0636	...	*0824*	0836	...	1036	...	*1124*	...	1236	...	*1424*	1436	...	1636	...	*1824*	1836
Břeclav **1150** a.	...	...	...	...	...	...	*0652*	0720	...	*0853*	0920	...	1120	...	*1153*	...	1320	...	*1453*	1520	...	1720	...	*1853*	1920
Břeclav d.	...	...	...	0528	...	...	0713	0728	...	0913	0928	...	1128	...	1213	...	1328	...	1513	1528	...	1728	...	1913	1928
Hodonín d.	...	...	...	0542	...	...	0726	0742	...	0926	0942	...	1142	...	1226	...	1342	...	1526	1542	...	1742	...	1926	1942
Luhačovice d.	...	...	...	|	...	...	|	|	0820	|	|	1020	|	...	|	1220	|	1420	|	|	1620	|	1820	|	|
Uherský Brod d.	...	...	...	|	...	u	|	|	0839	|	|	1039	|	...	|	1239	|	1439	|	|	1639	|	1839	|	|
Uherské Hradiště d.	...	...	...	|	...	0709	|	|	0900	|	|	1100	|	...	|	1300	|	1500	|	|	1700	|	1900	|	|
Staré Město U.H. ⊖ a.	...	...	...	0600	...	0716	0742	0800	0906	0942	1000	1106	1200	...	1242	1306	1400	1506	1542	1600	1706	1800	1906	1942	2000
Staré Město U.H. ⊖ d.	0418	...	0550	0602	0628	0728	0743	0802	0918	0943	1002	1118	1202	1231	1243	1318	1402	1518	1543	1602	1718	1802	1918	1943	2002
Zlín střed ▷ d.	|	0515	|	|	|	|	|	|	|	|	|	|	|	|	|	|	|	|	|	|	|	|	|	|	|
Otrokovice d.	0429	0540	0601	0614	0639	0740	0753	0814	0929	0953	1014	1129	1214	1242	1253	1329	1414	1529	1553	1614	1729	1814	1929	1953	2014
Hulín d.	0439	0551	0611	0623	0648	0751	|	0823	0939	|	1023	1139	1223	1250	|	1339	1423	1539	|	1623	1739	1823	1939	|	2023
Přerov ▽ a.	0449	0601	0621	0632	0657	0801	0807	0832	0949	1007	1032	1149	1232	1259	1307	1349	1432	1549	1607	1632	1749	1832	1949	2007	2032
Ostrava hl. **1155** a.	|	|	|	|	|	|	0857	|	|	1057	|	|	|	|	1357	|	|	|	1657	|	|	|	|	2057	|
Olomouc ▽ a.	0517	0616	0635	0646	0712	0816	...	0846	1004	...	1046	1204	1246	1312	...	1404	1446	1604	...	1646	1804	1846	2004	...	2046
Praha hl. **1160** a.	0804s	0839	0858	...	0922	1039	...	...	...	...	...	1504r	...	1522	...	1704r	...	1904r	...	...	2104r	...	...	...	...

M – MORAVIA – (12) Bohumín - Ostrava - Břeclav - Wien and v.v. Conveys on dates in Table **95** 🛏 1, 2 cl. Moskva / St Peterburg - Bohumín - Břeclav - Wien and v.v.
P – POLONIA – (12) ✕ Warszawa - Katowice - Ostrava - Břeclav - Wien and v.v. (Table **99**).
S – SOBIESKI – (12) ✕ Gdynia - Gdansk - Warszawa - Katowice - Ostrava - Břeclav - Wien and v.v. (Table **99**).
V – VARSOVIA – (12) Warszawa - Katowice - Ostrava - Břeclav - Bratislava - Budapest and v.v. (Table **99**). For 🛏 1, 2 cl. Varna / Sofia / Budapest - Moskva and v.v. see Table **95**.
h – Ⓑ (not Dec. 24, 25, 31, Jan. 1, Mar. 27, July 5, Oct. 28).
n – ①–⑥ (not Dec. 25, 26, Jan. 1, 2, Mar. 28, July 6, Oct. 29).
r – Stopping train (Table **1150**). Faster journey possible by changing at Olomouc (Table **1160**).
s – Stopping train (Table **1150**). Faster journey possible by changing at Přerov (Table **1160**).
u – To / from Veseli nad Moravou (a. 2111 / d. 0654).

♥ – Operated by REGIOJET. Only Regiojet tickets are valid.
♠ – Operated by LEO Express. Only Leo Express tickets are valid.
⊖ – Full name: Staré Město u Uherské Hradiště.
⊡ – From Hradec Králové via Pardubice (Table **1160**).
▽ – See also Table **1160**.
▷ – Local trains Otrokovice - Zlín: 1-2 per hour (or trolleybus every 10 minutes).
§ – [R] for international journeys to / from Poland.

ADDITIONAL TRAINS operated by LEO Express (with connections from / to Praha) [R]
1348: Staré Mesto u U.H. 0526 - Otrokovice 0537 - Hulín 0545 - Přerov 0554.
1369: Přerov 2145 - Hulín 2155 - Otrokovice 2203 - Staré Mesto u U.H. 2213.

1160 PRAHA - OLOMOUC - OSTRAVA - ŽILINA - (KOŠICE)

FAST TRAINS. For semi-fast trains Praha - Česká Třebová - Olomouc see Table **1150**. For additional trains Přerov - Ostrava - Bohumín see Table **1155**.

km		IC	Ex	Ex	Ex	EC*	♥	EC	SC•	Ex	EC*	IC	♥	LE♠	Ex	Ex♣	LE♠	EC*	SC•	♥	LE♠	Ex	LE♠
		553	**141**	**143**	**143**	**121**	**1001**	**113**	**241**	**145**	**123**	**503**	**1003**	**1353**	**147**	**1093**	**1355**	**125**	**505**	**1005**	**1357**	**149**	**1359**
		✕	🍷	🍷	🍷	✕	🍷	🍷	[R] 🍷	🍷	✕	[R] 🍷	🍷	[R] 🍷	🍷		[R] 🍷	✕	[R] 🍷	🍷	[R] 🍷	✕	[R] 🍷
		⚒ n		① g			⚒	♦						T		⑥ b			⊕				
0	**Praha** hlavní **1150** d.	0001	...	0424	...	0524	0546	0624	0643	...	0724	0743	0746	0811	0824	0840	0911	0924	0943	0946	1011	1024	1111
62	Kolín **1150** d.	0039	...	0503	...	0603	|	0703	0719	...	0803	|	|	0849	0903	|	0949	1003	|	|	1049	1103	1149
104	**Pardubice** **1150** d.	0111	...	0525	...	0625	0642	0725	0739	...	0825	0837	0842	0908	0925	0941	1008	1025	1037	1042	1108	1125	1208
164	Česká Třebová **1150** d.	0151	...	0559	...	0659	0717	0759	0812	...	0859	|	|	|	0959	|	|	1059	|	1117	|	1159	|
206	Zábřeh na Moravé d.	|	...	0621	...	0721	0739	0821	|	...	0921	|	0936	1001	1021	|	1101	1121	|	1139	1201	1221	1301
252	**Olomouc** d.	0234	...	0645	...	0745	0804	0845	0853	...	0945	0950	1001	1026	1045	1113	1126	1145	1150	1204	1226	1245	1326
	Přerov **1159** **1155** d.	0247	...	|	...	|	|	|	|	...	|	|	|	1042	|	1128	1138	|	|	|	1242	|	1342
303	Hranice na Moravě **1155** d.	...	...	0713	...	0814	0833	0913	|	...	1014	|	1030	1100	1113	♡	△	1214	|	1233	1300	1313	1400
353	Ostrava Svinov **1155** d.	...	0545	0745	0745	|	0901	0939	0944	...	|	1036	1057	1130	1139	...	...	|	1236	1301	1330	1339	1430
381	Opava východ a.	...	|	|	|	|	|	|	|	...	|	|	|	|	|	...	...	|	|	|	|	|	|
358	**Ostrava** hlavní **1155** d.	...	0553	0754	0754	|	0909	0946	0953	0956	|	1044	1105	1139	1148	...	...	|	1244	1309	1339	1348	1439
366	Bohumín **1155** d.	...	0602	0802	0802	|	|	...	|	1003	|	...	|	1148	1202	...	...	|	...	|	1348	1402	1448
381	Karviná hlavní d.	...	0616	0816	0816	⇊	|	...	|	1016	⇊	...	|	1204	1216	...	...	⇊	...	|	1404	1416	1505
376	Havířov d.	...	|	|	|	|	0929	...	|	|	|	...	1125	...	|	...	...	|	...	1329	...	|	|
397	**Český Těšín** d.	...	0637	0837	0837	|	...	...	1029	1037	|	...	1144	...	1237	...	...	|	...	...	...	1437	1526
405	Trinec centrum d.	...	0645	0845	0845	|	...	...	|	1045	|	...	1152	...	1245	...	...	|	...	...	...	1445	1537
417	Návsi d.	...	0653	0853	0853	|	...	...	|	1053	|	...	|	...	1253	...	...	|	...	...	...	1453	...
435	Čadca 🏛 d.	...	0711	0911	0911	|	...	...	|	1111	|	...	1215	...	1311	...	...	|	...	...	...	1511	...
△466	**Žilina** a.	...	0738	0938	0938	1048	...	...	1118	1138	1248	...	1237	...	1338	...	...	1448	...	...	...	1538	...
	Poprad Tatry **1180** a.	...	...	...	...	*1235*r	...	...	1259	...	*1435*r	...	1422	...	...	...	...	*1635*r	...	...	...	...	...
	Košice **1180** a.	...	...	...	...	*1352*r	...	...	1405	...	*1552*r	...	1544	...	...	...	...	*1752*r	...	...	...	...	...

	EC*	SC•	♥	Ex	IC	EC	EC*	IC	♥	LE♠	EC	Ex	♥	EC*	SC•	♥	LE♠	EC*	IC	♥	LE♠	IC	SC•
	127	**507**	**1007**	**151**	**543**	**243**	**221**	**509**	**1009**	**1361**	**117**	**153**	**1011**	**129**	**511**	**1013**	**1363**	**155**	**513**	**1015**	**1365**	**561**	**515**
	✕	[R] 🍷	🍷	🍷	🍷	🍷	✕	[R] 🍷	🍷	[R] 🍷	✕	🍷	🍷	✕	[R] 🍷	🍷	[R] 🍷	✕	[R] 🍷	🍷	[R] 🍷	✕	[R] 🍷
					⑤ f	⑤ f				**P**	♦					**m**			Ⓑ h			**V**	⊗
Praha hlavní **1150** d.	1124	1143	1146	1224	1306	1306	1324	1343	1346	1411	1424	...	1446	1524	1543	1546	1611	1624	1643	1646	1711	1724	1743
Kolín **1150** d.	1203	|	|	1303	|	|	1403	|	|	1449	1503	...	|	1603	|	|	1649	1703	|	|	1749	1803	|
Pardubice **1150** d.	1225	1237	1242	1325	1400u	1400u	1425	1437	1442	1508	1525	...	1542	1625	1637	1642	1708	1725	1737	1742	1808	1825	1837
Česká Třebová **1150** d.	1259	|	1317	1359	|	|	1459	|	1517	|	1559	...	1617	1659	|	1717	|	1759	|	1817	|	1859	|
Zábřeh na Moravé d.	1321	|	1339	1421	|	|	1521	|	1539	1601	1621	...	1639	1721	|	1739	1801	1821	|	1839	1901	1921	|
Olomouc d.	1345	1350	1404	1445	1515	1515	1545	1550	1604	1626	1645	...	1704	1745	1750	1804	1826	1845	1851	1904	1926	1945	1950
Přerov **1159** **1155** d.	|	|	|	|	|	|	|	|	|	1642	|	...	|	|	|	|	1842	|	|	1917	1938	1957	|
Hranice na Moravě **1155** d.	1414	|	1433	1513	|	|	1617	|	1633	1700	1713	...	1733	1814	|	1833	1900	1913	|	△	△	...	|
Ostrava Svinov **1155** d.	|	1436	1501	1539	1611	1618	|	1636	1701	1730	1739	...	1801	|	1836	1901	1928	1939	1946	...	...	...	2036
Opava východ a.	|	|	|	|	1633	|	|	|	|	|	|	...	|	|	|	|	|	|	2008	...	...	...	|
Ostrava hlavní **1155** d.	|	1444	1509	1548	...	1626	|	1644	1709	1739	1748	...	1809	|	1844	1909	1937	1948	...	...	...	...	2044
Bohumín **1155** d.	|	...	|	1602	...	|	|	...	|	1748	1755	1802	|	|	1852	|	...	2002	...	...	...	...	2052
Karviná hlavní d.	⇊	...	|	1616	...	|	⇊	...	|	1805	...	1816	|	⇊	...	|	...	2016	...	...	...	...	...
Havířov d.	|	...	1529	|	...	|	|	...	1729	|	...	|	1830	|	...	1930	...	|	...	...	...	...	...
Český Těšín d.	|	...	...	1637	...	1701	|	...	...	1826	...	1837	1849	|	...	1949	...	2037	...	...	...	...	...
Trinec centrum d.	|	...	...	1645	...	|	|	...	...	1837	...	1845	1857	|	...	1957	...	2045	...	...	...	...	...
Návsi d.	|	...	...	1653	...	1713	|	...	...	|	...	1853	|	|	...	2008	...	2053	...	...	...	...	...
Čadca 🏛 d.	|	...	...	1711	...	1730	|	...	...	1902	...	1911e	1921	|	...	...	...	2111h	...	...	...	...	...
Žilina a.	1648	...	...	1738	...	1752	1848	...	...	1924	...	1938e	1943	2048	...	...	...	2138h	...	...	...	...	...
Poprad Tatry **1180** a.	*1835*r	...	...	...	...	1935	*2035*r	...	...	2113	...	...	▽	...	...	...	...	...	...	...	...	...	...
Košice **1180** a.	*1952*r	...	...	...	...	2045	*2152*r	...	...	2255	...	...	...	...	...	...	...	...	...	...	...	...	...

 SC and IC trains are not available for local travel Ostrava Svinov - Ostrava hlavní - Bohumín or v.v.

(KOŠICE) - ŽILINA - OSTRAVA - OLOMOUC - PRAHA 1160

	Ex	EN	LE♠	IC	SC•	♥	♥	EN	EN
	541	**405**	**1367**	**551**	**517**	**1019**	**1021**	**445**	**443**
	🍷	⊠	[R]🍷	🍴	[R]🍷	🍷	🍷	⊖	⊖
	E	◆	P	Z			◆	◆	◆K
Praha hlavní ..... 1150 d.	1824	1846	1911	1924	1943	1946	2146	2200	2309
Kolín ..... 1150 d.	1903	|	1949	2003	|	|	|	2251	2359
Pardubice ..... 1150 d.	1925	1941	2008	2025	2037	2042	2242	2316	0023
Česká Třebová ..... 1150 d.	1959	|	|	2059	|	2117	|	|	0102
Zábřeh na Moravé ..... d.	2021	|	2101	2121	|	2139	2339	|	0127
Olomouc ..... d.	2045	2101	2126	2145	2150	2204	0006	0041	0155
Přerov **1159** ..... 1155 d.	|	|	2142	2157	|	|	|	0126v	|
Hranice na Moravě ..... 1155 d.	2113	|	2200	...	|	2233	0036	|	|
Ostrava Svinov ..... 1155 d.	2147	|	2230	...	2236	2301	0104	|	0251
Opava východ ..... a.	|	|	|	...	|	|	|	|	|
Ostrava hlavní ..... 1155 d.	2156	2202	2239	...	2244	2309	0112	0217	0300
Bohumín ..... 1155 d.	2207	2209	2248	...	2252	|	|	0249	0337
Karviná hlavní ..... d.	2221	...	2305	...	...	|	|	|	0352
Havířov ..... d.	|	...	|	...	...	2330	0133	|	|
Český Těšín ..... d.	2241	...	2326	...	...	2349	0153	|	0413
Třinec centrum ..... d.	2248	...	2337	...	...	2357	0201	|	0420t
Návsí ..... d.	2256	...	|	...	...	0008	|	|	|
Čadca 🏨 ..... d.	...	...	0002	...	...	...	0225	|	0446
Žilina ..... a.	...	...	0024	...	...	...	0250	0414	0514
Poprad Tatry **1180** ..... a.	...	...	0211	...	...	...	0451	0622	0705
Košice **1180** ..... a.	...	...	0403	...	...	...	0614	0741	0839

	EN	♥	IC	EN	♥	EN	LE♠	SC•	
	444	**1020**	**552**	**442**	**1000**	**404**	**1352**	**516**	
	⊖	🍷	🍴	⊖	🍷	⊠	[R]🍷	[R]🍷	
	◆L	◆	⚒n	◆	⚒	◆	P		
Košice **1180** ..... d.	2020	2122	...	2208	...	...	2323	...	...
Poprad Tatry **1180** ..... d.	2153	2238	...	2325	...	...	0115	...	...
Žilina ..... d.	0005	0042	...	0134	...	...	0324	...	...
Čadca 🏨 ..... d.	|	0107	...	0201	...	...	0347	...	...
Návsí ..... d.	|	|	...	|	0332	...	|	...	...
Trinec centrum ..... d.	|	0132	...	0223t	0342	...	0409	...	...
Český Těšín ..... d.	|	0142	...	0230	0350	...	0419	...	...
Havířov ..... d.	|	0203	...	|	0411	...	|	...	...
Karviná hlavní ..... d.	|	|	...	0249	|	...	0439	...	...
Bohumín ..... 1155 d.	0210	|	...	0338	|	0450	0455	0506	...
Ostrava hlavní ..... 1155 d.	0220	0223	...	0347	0431	0459	0503	0514	...
Opava východ ..... d.	|	|	...	|	|	|	|	|	...
Ostrava Svinov ..... 1155 d.	|	0232	...	0357	0440	|	0511	0522	...
Hranice na Moravě ..... 1155 d.	|	0259	...	0435	0507	|	0540	|	...
Přerov **1159** ..... d.	0340z	|	0455	|	|	|	0600	|	...
Olomouc ..... d.	0359	0331	0508	0513	0537	0557	0614	0610	...
Zábřeh na Moravé ..... d.	|	0357	|	0538	0601	|	0637	|	...
Česká Třebová ..... 1150 d.	0449	|	|	0605	0623	|	|	|	...
Pardubice ..... 1150 d.	0525	0458	0621	0642	0658	0723	0728	0721	...
Kolín ..... 1150 d.	0551	|	|	|	|	|	0747	|	...
Praha hlavní ..... 1150 a.	0638	0558	0715	0739	0758	0828	0822	0815	...

	IC	♥	IC	LE♠	Ex	♥	SC•	LE♠	IC	♥	EC*	♥	SC•	EC*	LE♠	Ex	EC	♥	IC	EC*	LE♠	Ex	♥	LE♠
	550	**1002**	**514**	**1354**	**540**	**1004**	**512**	**1356**	**560**	**1006**	**154**	**1008**	**510**	**220**	**1358**	**152**	**116**	**1010**	**508**	**128**	**1360**	**150**	**1012**	**1362**
	🍴	🍷	[R]🍷	[R]🍷	🍷	🍷	[R]🍷	[R]🍷	🍴	🍷	🍴	🍷	[R]🍷	🍴	[R]🍷	🍷	🍴	🍷	[R]🍷	🍴	[R]🍷	🍷	🍷	[R]🍷
	Z		⚒n		F		⊗		V	k					P		◆							T
Košice **1180** ..... d.	...	...	...	...	...	...	...	...	...	...	...	...	...	...	0445	...	...	...	...	*0608*r	...	...	0744	...
Poprad Tatry **1180** ..... d.	...	...	...	...	...	...	...	...	...	...	...	▽	...	...	0633	...	...	...	...	*0725*r	...	...	0855	...
Žilina ..... d.	...	...	...	...	...	...	...	...	...	...	0622n	0642	...	0712	0817	0822	...	...	...	0912	...	1022	1042	...
Čadca 🏨 ..... d.	...	...	...	...	...	...	...	...	...	...	0651n	0708	...	|	0845	0851	...	...	...	|	...	1051	1108	...
Návsí ..... d.	...	...	...	...	0506	0532	...	...	...	0632	0706	0726	...	|	|	0906	...	0932x	...	|	...	1106	|	...
Třinec centrum ..... d.	...	...	...	...	0514	0542	...	...	...	0642	0714	0736	...	|	0907	0914	...	0942x	...	|	...	1114	1136	...
Český Těšín ..... d.	...	...	...	...	0522	0550	...	...	...	0650	0722	0750	...	|	0917	0922	...	0950x	...	|	...	1122	1150	...
Havířov ..... d.	...	...	...	...	|	0611	...	...	...	0711	|	0811	...	|	|	|	...	1011	...	|	...	|	1211	...
Karviná hlavní ..... d.	...	...	...	...	0541	|	...	0639	...	|	0741	|	...	⋙	0937	0941	...	|	...	⋙	...	1141	|	1239
Bohumín ..... 1155 d.	...	...	...	...	0558	|	0706	0655	...	|	0807	|	0906	|	0955	0959	1007	|	...	|	...	1207	|	1255
Ostrava hlavní ..... 1155 d.	...	...	...	...	0606	0631	0714	0704	...	0731	0815	0831	0914	|	1004	...	1015	1031	1111	|	...	1215	1231	1304
Opava východ ..... d.	...	...	0551	...	|	|	|	|	...	|	|	|	|	|	|	...	|	|	|	|	...	|	|	|
Ostrava Svinov ..... 1155 d.	...	...	0619	...	0614	0640	0722	0711	...	0740	0824	0840	0922	|	1011	...	1024	1040	1119	|	...	1224	1240	1311
Hranice na Moravě ..... 1155 d.	...	△	|	△	0649	0707	|	0740	...	0807	0849	0907	|	0945	1040	...	1049	1107	|	1145	△	1249	1307	1340
Přerov **1159** ..... d.	0603	0622	|	0700	|	|	|	0800	0803	|	|	|	|	|	1100	...	|	|	|	|	1300	|	|	1400
Olomouc ..... d.	0618	0637	0710	0714	0718	0737	0810	0814	0818	0837	0918	0937	1010	1018	1114	...	1118	1137	1210	1218	1314	1318	1337	1414
Zábřeh na Moravé ..... d.	0641	0701	|	0737	0741	0801	|	0837	0841	0901	0941	1001	|	1041	1137	...	1141	1201	|	1241	1337	1341	1401	1437
Česká Třebová ..... 1150 d.	0703	0723	|	|	0803	0823	|	|	0903	0923	1003	1023	|	1103	|	...	1203	1223	|	1303	|	1403	1423	|
Pardubice ..... 1150 d.	0739	0758	0821	0828	0839	0858	0921	0928	0937	0958	1037	1058	1121	1137	1228	...	1237	1258	1321	1337	1428	1437	1458	1528
Kolín ..... 1150 d.	0802	|	|	0847	0902	|	|	0947	0958	|	1058	|	|	1158	1247	...	1258	|	|	1358	1447	1458	|	1547
Praha hlavní ..... 1150 a.	0839	0858	0915	0922	0939	0958	1015	1022	1039	1058	1139	1158	1215	1239	1322	...	1339	1358	1415	1439	1522	1539	1558	1622

	SC•	EC*	Ex	♥	LE♠	SC•	EC*	EC	IC	Ex♣	Ex	♥	LE♠	IC	EC*	Ex	EC	♥	SC•	EC*	Ex	Ex	Ex	
	506	**126**	**148**	**1014**	**1364**	**504**	**124**	**242**	**542**	**1094**	**146**	**1016**	**1366**	**502**	**122**	**144**	**112**	**1018**	**240**	**120**	**142**	**142**	**140**	
	[R]🍷	🍴	🍷	🍷	[R]🍷	[R]🍷	🍴	🍷	🍷		🍷	🍷	[R]🍷	[R]🍷	🍴	🍷	🍷	🍷	[R]🍷	🍴	🍷	🍷	🍷	
	⊕							⑦e	⑦e	⑦d							◆					⑦e		
Košice **1180** ..... d.	...	*0808*r	...	...	...	...	*1008*r	1144	...	...	...	...	...	...	*1208*r	...	...	...	1447	*1408*r	...	...	...	...
Poprad Tatry **1180** ..... d.	...	*0925*r	...	...	...	...	*1125*r	1253	...	...	...	...	...	...	*1325*r	...	...	...	1555	*1525*r	...	...	...	...
Žilina ..... d.	...	1112	1222	...	...	...	1312	1432	...	...	1422	...	...	...	1512	1622	...	...	1741	1712	1822	1822	2022e	...
Čadca 🏨 ..... d.	...	|	1251	...	...	...	|	1456	...	...	1451	...	...	...	|	1651	...	...	|	|	1851	1851	2051e	...
Návsí ..... d.	...	|	1306	...	...	...	|	1511	...	...	1506	...	...	...	|	1706	...	...	|	|	1906	1906	2106	...
Třinec centrum ..... d.	...	|	1314	...	...	...	|	|	...	...	1514	...	1609	...	|	1714	...	...	|	|	1914	1914	2114	...
Český Těšín ..... d.	...	|	1322	...	...	...	|	1524	...	...	1522	...	1619	...	|	1722	...	...	1832	|	1922	1922	2122	...
Havířov ..... d.	...	|	|	1411	...	...	|	|	...	...	|	1611	|	...	|	|	...	1811	|	|	|	|	|	...
Karviná hlavní ..... d.	...	⋙	1341	|	1439	...	⋙	|	...	...	1541	|	1639	...	⋙	1741	...	|	|	⋙	1941	1941	2141	...
Bohumín ..... 1155 d.	...	|	1407	|	1455	...	|	|	...	...	1607	|	1655	...	|	1757	...	|	|	|	1958	1958	2158	...
Ostrava hlavní ..... 1155 d.	1314	|	1415	1431	1504	1514	|	1601	...	...	1615	1631	1704	1711	|	1804	1815	1831	1914	|	2006	2006	2206	...
Opava východ ..... d.	|	|	|	|	|	|	|	|	1550	...	|	|	|	|	|	...	|	|	|	|	|	|	|	...
Ostrava Svinov ..... 1155 d.	1322	|	1424	1440	1511	1522	|	1619	1619	...	1624	1640	1711	1719	|	...	1824	1840	1922	|	2013	2024	2213	...
Hranice na Moravě ..... 1155 d.	|	1345	1449	1507	1540	|	1545	|	|	♡	1649	1707	1740	|	1745	...	1849	1907	|	1945	...	2049	...	...
Přerov **1159** ..... d.	|	|	|	|	1600	|	|	|	|	1625	|	|	1800	|	|	...	|	|	|	|	...	|	...	...
Olomouc ..... d.	1410	1418	1518	1537	1614	1610	1618	1710	1710	1643	1718	1737	1814	1810	1818	...	1918	1937	2010	2018	...	2118	...	...
Zábřeh na Moravé ..... d.	|	1441	1541	1601	1637	|	1641	|	|	|	1741	1801	1837	|	1841	...	1941	2001	|	2047	...	2141	...	...
Česká Třebová ..... 1150 d.	|	1503	1603	1623	|	|	1703	|	|	|	1803	1823	|	|	1903	...	2003	2023	2050	2109	...	2203	...	...
Pardubice ..... 1150 d.	1521	1537	1637	1658	1728	1721	1737	1821	1821	1817	1837	1858	1928	1921	1937	...	2037	2058	2122	2148	...	2237	...	...
Kolín ..... 1150 d.	|	1558	1658	|	1747	|	1758	|	|	|	1858	|	1947	|	1958	...	2058	|	2142	2212	...	2258	...	...
Praha hlavní ..... 1150 a.	1615	1639	1739	1758	1822	1815	1839	1915	1915	1924	1939	1958	2022	2015	2039	...	2139	2158	2219	2252	...	2338	...	...

NOTES (LISTED BY TRAIN NUMBER)

/3 – PORTA MORAVICA – [12] 🍷 Praha - Ostrava - Katowice - Warszawa and v.v.

/7 – PRAHA – [12] 🍴 Praha - Ostrava - Bohumín - Katowice - Warszawa and v.v.

/5 – VLTAVA – for days of running see Table **95**. 🛏 1,2 cl. Praha - Katowice - Minsk - Moskva and v.v.; 🛏 1,2 cl. Praha - St Peterburg and v.v., 🛏 1,2 cl. Cheb (**613/2**) - Karlovy Vary - Praha - Moskva and v.v.

/3 – BOHEMIA – [12] 🍷 Praha - Bohumín and v.v.; 🛏 1,2 cl., ▬ 2 cl., [2] Praha - Bohumín - Košice - Humenné and v.v.; 🛏 1,2 cl. Praha - Košice (**8807/20**) - Čierna nad Tisou (**8862/3**) - Čop (**81/771**) - Kyïv and v.v.

/5 – SLOVAKIA – not Dec. 24, 31. 🛏 1,2 cl., ▬ 2 cl., [2] Praha - Bohumín - Košice and v.v.; 🍷 Praha - Ostrava and v.v.; 🛏 1,2 cl. Praha - Žilina - (**1841/54**) - Banská Bystrica and v.v.; 🛏 1,2 cl., [2] [R] Praha - Bohumín (**406/7**) - Katowice - Warszawa and v.v. (also ▬ 2 cl. Mar. 12 - Nov. 2 from Praha, Mar. 11 - Nov. 1 from Warszawa); 🛏 1,2 cl. Cheb (**615/4**) - Karlovy Vary - Praha (**445/4**) - Košicé and v.v.

0/1 – 🛏 (1,2,3 berth), ▬ (6 berth), [12] Praha - Košice and v.v.

Daily to Bohumín; Ⓑ **h** to Návsi.

①–⑥ **n** from Návsi, daily from Bohumín.

Conveys 🛏 1,2 cl., [2] Praha (**443**) - Bohumín (**403**) - Kraków (also ▬ 2 cl. Mar. 11 - Nov. 1).

Conveys 🛏 1,2 cl., [2] Kraków (**402**) - Bohumín (**444**) - Praha (also ▬ 2 cl. Mar. 12 - Nov. 2 from Kraków).

[12] Praha - Prešov - Košice and v.v. (Table **1180**).

Daily except ②.

To/from Veseli nad Moravou (Table **1159**).

To/from Zlín střed (Table **1159**).

Also Mar. 25, Oct. 28; not Mar. 26, Oct. 29.

Also Mar. 28, July 6; not Mar. 27, July 3.

⑦ (also Mar. 28, July 6; not Mar. 27, July 3).

Also Oct. 27, Nov. 16; not Oct. 28, Nov. 18.

g – Also Mar. 29, July 7; not Mar. 28, July 4.
h – Ⓑ (not Mar. 27, July 5, Oct. 28),
k – Not Mar. 28, May 1, 8, July 5, 6, Sept. 28, Oct. 28, Nov. 17.
m – Not Mar. 27, Apr. 30, May 7, July 4, 5, Sept. 27, Oct. 27, Nov. 16.
n – ①–⑥ (not Mar. 28, July 6, Oct. 29).
r – Change at Púchov (Tables **1158**/**1180**).
t – Trinec (not Trinec centrum).
u – Calls to pick up only.
v – Train **445** arrives Přerov 0056.
x – ⑦ (also Mar. 28, July 5, 6, Sept. 28, Oct. 28, Nov. 17).
z – Train **444** arrives Přerov 0308.
♥ – Operated by REGIOJET. Separate fare tariff applies.
♠ – Operated by LEO Express. Separate fare tariff.
♣ – Operated by ARRIVA. Separate fare tariff applies.
⋙ – Via Vsetín and Horní Lideč (Table **1158**).
• – *SUPERCITY PENDOLINO* train, [R] (fee CZK 250).
⊕ – From/to Cheb via Plzeň (Table **1120**).
⊗ – From/to Františkovy Lázně via Cheb and Plzeň (Table **1120**).
△ – To/from Staré Město u Uherské Hradiště (Table **1159**).
▽ – To/from Zvolen (Table **1185**).
♡ – To/from Trenčin (Table **1157**). Also calls at Otrokovice (**1093** at 1153, **1094** at 1607).
⊖ – [R] for international journeys.
⊠ – International journeys only.
∆ – *439 km* via Vsetin.
* – Classified *Ex* in Slovakia.

Český Těšín - Havířov - Ostrava:
From Český Těšín every two hours 0609Ⓐ - 1809Ⓐ, from Ostrava hlavní every two hours 0648Ⓐ - 1848Ⓐ, journey 40 - 44 minutes. Local trains run hourly Český Těšín - Havířov - Ostrava Svinov (journey 50 mins).

Český Těšín - Cieszyn (Poland):
From Český Těšín every two hours 0815 - 1815, from Cieszyn every two hours 0831 - 1831. Journey 5 minutes. Trains continue beyond Český Těšín to/from Frýdek-Mistek.

1165 ÚSTI NAD ORLICI - LETOHRAD - LICHKOV - KLODZKO

Most trains 2nd c

km	⊡		Ⓒ	Ⓐ								Ⓒ
	Praha hlavní ... **1150** d.	...	...	*0655*	*0755*	*1055*	*1255*	...	*1455*	*1655*	*1755*	*1855*
	Pardubice .... **1150** d.	*0604*	0731	*0804*	*0904*	*1204*	*1404*	...	*1604*	*1804*	*1904*	*2004*
	Ústi nad Orlici . **1150** a.	*0637*	0823	*0837*	*0937*	*1237*	*1435*	...	*1637*	*1837*	*1937*	*2037*
0	**Ústi nad Orlici** ...... ⊡ d.	0649	0825	0846	0946	1246	1446	...	1643	1846	1946	2050
14	Letohrad .... ⊡ a.	0711	0845	0906	1007	1306	1507	...	1704	1906	2009	2114
14	Letohrad .... d.	0714	0848	0908	1008	1307	1508	...	1706	1910	...	2115
35	Lichkov 🏛 .... d.	0742	0915	0934	1036	1336	1537	1542	1735	1940	...	2143
44	Międzylesie .... d.	0754	...	...	...	1347	...	1551	...	2001	...	...
80	**Klodzko** Gl. .... a.	0849	...	...	...	1431	...	1636	...	2046	...	...
	Wroclaw **1095** .... a.	1023	...	...	...	*1634*	...	1830	...	2237	...	...

⊡	Ⓐ							
Wroclaw **1095** .... d.	...	0634	...	...	1040	...	*1307*	...
Klodzko Gl. .... d.	...	0823	...	...	1226	...	1445	...
Międzylesie 🏛 .... d.	...	0907	...	...	1313	...	1531	...
Lichkov .... d.	0803	0915	1217	1300	1322	1505	1604r	1703
Letohrad .... a.	0829	0945	1243	1331	...	1531	1630	1730
Letohrad .... ⊡ d.	0846	0946	1246	1346	...	1546	1643	1746
Ústi nad Orlici ...... ⊡ a.	0909	1009	1309	1409	...	1609	1708	1809
Ústi nad Orlici **1150** d.	*0923*	*1023*	*1323*	*1423*	...	*1623*	*1723*	*1823*
Pardubice .... **1150** a.	*0954*	*1054*	*1354*	*1454*	...	*1654*	*1754*	*1854*
Praha hlavní ... **1150** a.	*1104*	*1204*	*1504*	*1604*	...	*1804*	*1904*	*2004*

km		Ⓐ	Ⓒ						935		
	Praha hlavní **1145** ..... d.	...	...	...	...	...	...	...	1511	...	...
0	**Hradec Králové** .... d.	0705	0705	0905	1105	...	1305	1505	1705	1905	...
21	Týniště nad Orlicí .... d.	0733	0733	0931	1131	...	1331	1531	1731	1931	...
36	Doudleby nad Orlici .... d.	0752	0753	0951	1151	...	1351	1551	1751	1951	...
62	**Letohrad** .... a.	...	0829	1027	1231	...	1431	1631	1831	2030	...

	934	Ⓐ	Ⓒ						
Letohrad .... d.	0534	...	0729	0833	1133	1333	1533	1733	2011
Doudleby nad Orlici ...... d.	0610	0810	0810	0910	1210	1410	1610	1810	2057
Týniště nad Orlicí .... d.	0631	0831	0831	0931	1231	1431	1631	1831	...
Hradec Králové .... a.	0653	0853	0853	0953	1253	1453	1653	1853	...
Praha hlavní **1145** ..... a.	0843	...	...	...	...	...	...	...	...

c – ⑥⑦ (also July 5, 6, Oct. 28; not July 3).
d – Change at Častolovice (a. 2115 / d. 2118).
r – Arrive 1540.
⊡ – Ústi - Letohrad: by 🚌 Apr. 18 - June 26. Some dep's 6 mins earlier.

Timings may vary from June 12.

1166 OLOMOUC - KRNOV - OPAVA - OSTRAVA

2nd cl

km									Ⓐ	Ⓐ	Ⓐ
0	**Olomouc** .... d.	...	0707r	*0859*	1107	1307	1507	1707	1907	...	...	...
64	Bruntál .... d.	...	0829r	*1030*	1229	1429	1629	1829	2029	...	...	...
87	Krnov .... a.	...	0855r	*1055*	1255	1455	1655	1855	2055	...	...	...
87	Krnov .... d.	0703	0903	1103	1303	1503	1703	1903	*2109*	...	...	...
116	**Opava** východ ... ▷ d.	0737	0937	1137	1337	1537	1737	1937	*2142*	0608	every	1808
144	Ostrava Svinov .. ▷ a.	0757	0957	1157	1357	1557	1757	1958	...	0633	**two**	1833
149	**Ostrava** hlavní ...... a.	0810	...	1210	1410	1610	...	...	...	0647	hours	1847

									Ⓐ	Ⓐ
Ostrava hlavní ...... d.	...	...	...	...	1349	1549	1749	...	0656	every
Ostrava Svinov .. ▷ d.	0602	0802	1002	1202	1402	1602	1802	...	0713	**two**
Opava východ ... ▷ d.	0626	0826	1026	1226	1426	1626	1826	2032	0736	hours
Krnov .... a.	0658	0857	1057	1257	1457	1657	1857	2108	...	...
Krnov .... d.	0705	0905	*1105*	1305	1505	1705	...	*2112*	...	...
Bruntál .... d.	0734	0934	*1134*	1334	1534	1734	...	*2138*	...	...
Olomouc .... a.	0852	1052	*1254*	1452	1652	1852	...	*2303*	...	...

km								
0	Jesenik .... d.	0530	0930	...	1325	...	1725	...
22	Glucholazy (Poland) . d.	0611	1011	...	1406	...	1806	...
43	Tremešná ve Slezsku . d.	0640	1040	1240	1440	1640	1840	2042
60	Krnov .... a.	0658	1058	1259	1458	1659	1858	2101

Krnov .... d.	0705	0908	1105	1308	1505	1708	1905
Tremešná ve Slezsku d.	0725	0928	1125	1328	1525	1728	1925
Glucholazy (Poland). d.	0800	...	1200	...	1600	...	2000
Jesenik .... a.	0837	...	1237	...	1637	...	2037

r – ①–⑥ (not July 6, Oct. 29).
▷ – Local trains approx hourly (jny 35 m

Bruntál / Krnov - Opava is by 🚌 to Dec in revised times - please enquire.

1169 OTHER LOCAL SERVICES

2nd class. May vary on holida

BRNO - ZNOJMO *89 km* Journey 2 hours Change at Miroslav and Hrušovany

From Brno: 0649⑥**t**, 0849Ⓒ, 1254Ⓒ, 1454 **R**, 1654Ⓒ.
From Znojmo: 0903Ⓒ, 1303Ⓒ, 1503 **R**, 1703Ⓒ.

CHOCEŇ - LITOMYŠL *24 km* Journey 55 minutes

From Choceň: 0503Ⓐ, 0627, 0839Ⓒ, 1039, 1239Ⓒ, 1429Ⓐ, 1539Ⓒ, 1639Ⓐ, 1839Ⓒ.
From Litomyšl: 0439Ⓐ, 0603Ⓐ, 0719, 0931Ⓒ, 1231, 1532, 1731, 1932Ⓒ.
Change at Vysoké Myto město on certain journeys.

JINDŘICHŮV HRADEC - NOVÁ BYSTŘICE *33 km* Narrow gauge, 80 mins

Nov. to Apr.: from Jindřichův Hradec 0925Ⓒ, 1524; from Nová Bystřice 1120Ⓒ, 1720.
May / June / Sept / Oct: 2 - 3 journeys. July / Aug: 5 journeys. Operator: JHMD www.jhmd.cz
Steam train: daily July 1 - Aug. 31: from Jindřichův Hradec 1044, returning 1515.
⑥ May 7 - June 25, ⑥ Sept. 3 - 24, also Oct. 29: from Jindřichův Hradec 1044, returning 1411.

KOJETIN / HULIN - KROMĚŘÍŽ *8 km* Journey 8 minutes

Kojetin - Kroměříž: approx hourly. *9 km*, journey 12 minutes.
Hulin - Kroměříž: 1 - 2 trains per hour connecting with trains in Table **1159**.

PRAHA - KARLŠTEJN *33 km* Journey 42 minutes

From Praha hlavní: hourly 0417 - 2317 (every 30 minutes 1217 - 1917). From Karlštejn: h
0453 - 2253 (every 30 mins 1253 - 1953). Most trains continue to / from Beroun (8 mins).

TŘEMEŠNÁ VE SLEZSKU - OSOBLAHA *20 km* Narrow gauge, 45 minu

From Třemešná: 0450Ⓐ **n**, 0650Ⓐ **n**, 0730⑥ **u**, 1045 **s**, 1130, 1525, 1930.
From Osoblaha: 0350 Ⓐ **n**, 0550 ⚒, 0950, 1350, 1508 **s**, 1750.

ZNOJMO - BŘECLAV *69 km* Journey 90 minutes

From Znojmo: 0658, 0903, 1103, every 2 hours 1255 - 1655 (hourly 1155-1755 on Ⓐ), 1
From Břeclav: approx every 2 hours 0731 - 1931 (also 1233Ⓐ, 1433Ⓐ, 1633Ⓐ, 2139Ⓐ

R – Ⓒ Mar. 26 - Sept. 28.
n – Not Dec. 23 - 31, July 1 - Aug. 31.
s – Ⓒ July 2 - Sept. 17 (also Dec. 27, May 8, June 4, 18, 25, Nov. 5, Dec. 3; not Sept. 4, 11). Steam journey; special fares.
t – Also July 5, Sept. 28, Oct. 28; not Dec. 26, Jan. 2, Oct.
u – Also Ⓐ July 1 - Aug. 31.

SLOVAKIA

Operator: National railway operator is Železničná spoločnosť Slovensko (ŽSSK), www.slovakrail.sk, which runs on the network of Železnice Slovenskej Republiky (ŽSR), www.zsr.

Services: All trains convey first and second class seating, **except** where shown otherwise in footnotes or by '2' in the train column, or where the footnote shows sleeping and/or couch cars only. Descriptions of sleeping (🛏) and couchette (▬) cars appear on page 8.

Timings: Valid **December 13, 2015 - December 10, 2016**. Amendments from June 12 were not available in time for this edition. Holiday cancellation dates of mainline trains are show the tables, but certain local trains may also be cancelled during the period Dec. 24 - Jan. 1 and these cancellations may not be shown in the tables.

Supplements: A higher level of fares applies to travel by *EC* and *IC* trains. It is possible to reserve seats on most Express trains.

1170 BRATISLAVA - LEVICE - ZVOLEN - BANSKÁ BYSTRICA

km		831	833	835	837	839	851	841	843	845	847	801
							Ⓐ 2z		Ⓐ z			Ⓑ P
0	**Bratislava** hlavná ▷ d.	0601	0801	1001	1201	1401	1431	1601	1657	1801	2001	2349
49	Galanta .... ▷ d.	0637	0837	1037	1237	1437	1513	1637	1731	1837	2037	0027
60	Šal'a .... ▷ d.	0647	0847	1047	1247	1447	1522	1647	1740	1847	2047	0037
89	Šurany .... d.	0709	0909	1109	1309	1509	1546	1709	1804	1909	2109	0101
132	Levice .... d.	0750	0950	1150	1350	1550	...	1750	1850	1950	2150	0148
187	Žiar nad Hronom ..... d.	0840	1040	1240	1440	1640	...	1840	1940	2040	2240	0238
209	**Zvolen** osob. .... a.	0858	1058	1258	1458	1658	...	1858	1958	2058	2258	0257
209	**Zvolen** osob. .... d.	0901	1101	1301	1501	1701	...	1901	2001	2101	2301	...
230	**Banská Bystrica** ..... a.	0925	1125	1325	1525	1725	...	1925	2025	2125	2325	...

	830	*Ex* 530	832	834	836	838	840	1530	842	844
	△	Ⓐ ✕z						⑦ e§		
Banská Bystrica ..... d.	0435	0535	0635	0835	1035	1235	1435	1511	1635	1835
Zvolen osob. .... a.	0459	0553	0659	0859	1059	1259	1459	1540	1659	1859
Zvolen osob. .... d.	0502	0554	0702	0902	1102	1302	1502	1552	1702	1902
Žiar nad Hronom ...... d.	0521	0613	0721	0921	1121	1321	1521	1613	1721	1921
Levice .... d.	0613	0659	0813	1013	1213	1413	1613	1709	1813	2013
Šurany .... d.	0651	0740	0851	1051	1251	1451	1651	1756	1851	2051
Šal'a .... ▷ d.	0714	|	0914	1114	1314	1514	1714	1817	1914	2114
Galanta .... ▷ d.	0725	|	0925	1125	1325	1525	1725	1826	1925	2125
Bratislava hlavná ▷ a.	0759	0836	0959	1159	1359	1559	1759	1901	1959	2159

LOCAL TRAINS ZVOLEN - BANSKÁ BYSTRICA

		▶		Ⓐ	Ⓐz		Ⓐz						Ⓐz		⚒	⑦e	Ⓐz		⊡			Ⓐz		
Zvolen .... d.	0439	0503	0522	0557	0639	0700	0732	0801	1001	1110	1201	1310	1339	1401	1510	1520	1538	1601	1710	1814	1910	2019	2134	2221
Banská Bystrica .... a.	0512	0527	0554	0629	0711	0729	0802	0831	1031	1141	1231	1340	1410	1431	1541	1559	1612	1631	1741	1848	1941	2051	2206	2252

			Ⓐz	Ⓐz		Ⓐz							Ⓐz			Ⓐz						▶		
Banská Bystrica .... d.	0447	0542	0606	0646	0716	0749	0818	0928	...	1129	1218	1327	1346	1418	1528	1546	1618	...	1728	1818	1928	2029	2140	2228
Zvolen .... a.	0521	0614	0635	0718	0750	0821	0850	0959	...	1159	1250	1359	1419	1450	1559	1619	1650	...	1759	1850	1959	2053	2211	2258

P – POL'ANA – 🛏 1, 2 cl. (2) Bratislava - Zvolen - Košice - Prešov and v.v. For days of running see Table **1190**.
e – Also Jan. 6, Mar. 28, Aug. 29, Nov. 1; not Dec. 27, Mar. 27, Aug. 28.
z – Not Dec. 24 - Jan. 10.
▶ – (2) Zvolen - Žilina and v.v. (Table **1185**).
▷ – For additional trains see Table **1175**.
⊡ – 11 mins later on ⑦**e** (daily July 3 - Aug. 28).
△ – Additional train on Ⓐ **z**: Šurany d. 0605, Šal'a d. 0632, Gala d. 0641, Bratislava a. 0716 (train **850**).
§ – Additional train **1532** runs two hours later, runs ⑦ (also Jan Mar. 28, Nov. 1; not Dec. 27, Mar. 27, July 3 - Aug. 28).

1171 BRATISLAVA - KOMÁRNO

Operator: RegioJet. 2nd cla

km		Ⓒ	Ⓐ					Ⓐ		Ⓐ		
0	**Bratislava** hlavná .... d.	0605	0705	0805	1005	1205	1405	1513	1605r	1713	1805	2005
42	Dunajská Streda ...... d.	0711	0821	0911	1111	1311	1511	1606	1711	1805	1911	2111
94	**Komárno** .... a.	0813	0922	1013	1213	1413	1613	1703	1813	1903	2013	2213

	Ⓐ§		x			Ⓐ	Ⓒ	Ⓐ	Ⓒ	Ⓐ
Komárno .... d.	0643	0743	0943	1143	1343	1433	1543	1635	1743	1835
Dunajská Streda .... d.	0750	0850	1050	1250	1450	1550	1650	1750	1850	1950
Bratislava hlavná .... a.	0841	0950	1150	1350	1550	1650	1750	1850	1950	2050

r – Depart 1613 on Ⓐ.

Subject to alteration Dec. 24 - Jan. 6.

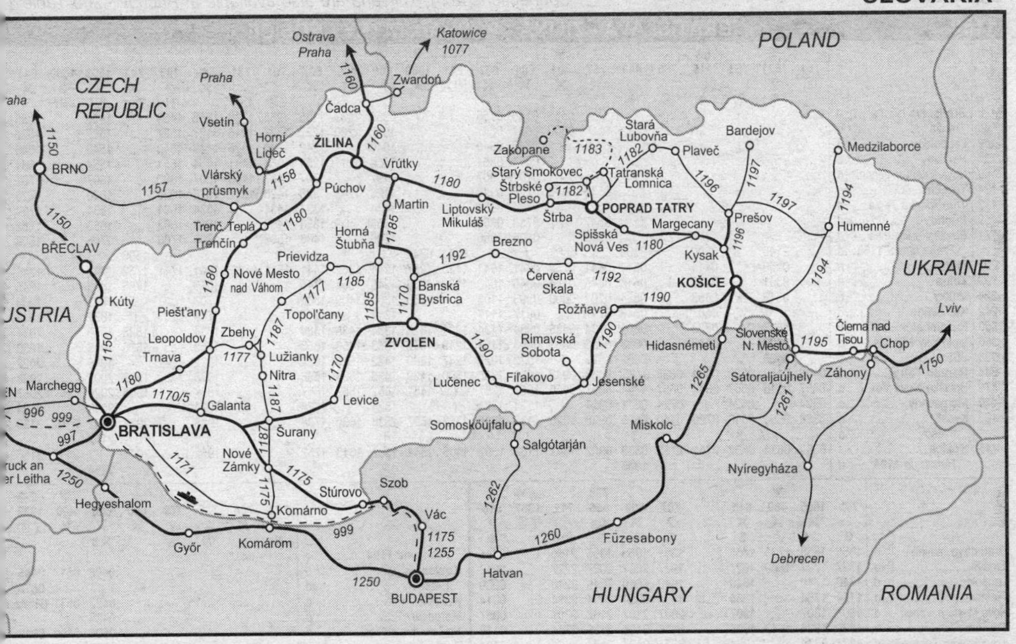

BRATISLAVA - ŠTÚROVO - BUDAPEST 1175

	EN 477	EC 271	EC 273	EC 275	EC 277	EC 279	EC 131	EC 173	EC 281
		✕	✕	✕	✕	✕	✕	✕	✕
	M				S		V	H	
Praha hlavní **1150** ....d.	2358	...	0549	0749	0949	1149	...	1349	1549
Brno hlavní **1150** ....d.	0315	0622	0824	1024	1224	1424	...	1624	1824
Břeclav **1150** ....d.	0440	0659	0859	1059	1259	1459	1559	1659	1859
Bratislava hlavná ....d.	0548	0753	0953	1153	1353	1553	1653	1753	1953
Nové Zámky ....d.	0644	0846	1046	1246	1446	1646	1746	1846	2046
Štúrovo 🏛 ....d.	0713	0914	1114	1314	1514	1714	1814	1914	2114
Szob 🏛 ....▷ d.	0723	0925	1125	1325	1525	1725	1825	1925	2125
Nagymaros-Visegrád .....▷ d.	|	0935	1135	1335	1535	1735	1835	1935	2135
Vác..............................▷ d.	0750	0950	1150	1350	1550	1750	1850	1950	2150
Budapest Keleti ....▷ a.	0837	1035	1235	1435	1635	1835	1935	2035	2235

	EC 280	EC 172	EC 130	EC 278	EC 276	EC 274	EC 272	EC 270	EN 476	476 878
	✕	✕	✕	✕	✕	✕	✕	✕		
		H	V		S				M	P
Budapest Keleti.........▷ d.	0525	0725	0822	0925	1125	1325	1525	1725	2005	2005
Vác...........................▷ d.	0610	0810	0910	1010	1210	1410	1610	1810	2048	2048
Nagymaros-Visegrád ..▷ d.	0624	0824	0924	1024	1224	1424	1624	1824	|	|
Szob 🏛 ....▷ d.	0636	0836	0936	1036	1236	1436	1636	1838	2110	2110
Štúrovo 🏛 ....d.	0649	0849	0949	1049	1249	1449	1649	1850	2124	2124
Nové Zámky ....d.	0716	0916	1016	1116	1316	1516	1716	1916	2152	2152
Bratislava hlavná ....a.	0807	1007	1107	1207	1407	1607	1807	2007	2246	2246
Břeclav **1150** ....a.	0901	1101	1201	1301	1501	1701	1901	2101	2356	2356
Brno hlavní **1150** ....a.	0936	1136	...	1336	1536	1736	1936	2136	0054	0054
Praha hlavní **1150** .....a.	1208	1408	...	1608	1808	2008	2208	...	0408	0643

class

LOCAL TRAINS BRATISLAVA - NOVÉ ZAMKY

△		Ⓐz	Ⓒx		Ⓐz		Ⓐz			Ⓐz		
slava hl....§ d.	0707	0807	0907	1107	1207	1307	1501	1507	1707	1831	1907	2107
nta...........§ d.	0757	0857	0957	1157	1257	1357	1537	1557	1757	1913	1957	2157
...............§ d.	0807	0907	1007	1207	1307	1407	1547	1607	1807	1922	2007	2207
Zámky ..... a.	0836	0936	1036	1236	1336	1436	1606	1636	1836	1943	2036	2236

▽		Ⓐ	Ⓐz					Ⓐz		Ⓐz	
Nové Zámky ... d.	0518	0618	0722	0922	1122	1322	1522	1622	1722	1822	1922
Šaľa ....§ d.	0539	0639	0752	0952	1152	1352	1552	1652	1753	1852	1952
Galanta.........§ d.	0549	0649	0809	1004	1204	1404	1604	1704	1804	1904	2004
Bratislava hl..§ a.	0630	0730	0857	1052	1252	1452	1652	1752	1852	1952	2052

HUNGARIA – 🚃12 ✕ Hamburg - Berlin - Dresden - Praha - Budapest and v.v. Conveys ②⑤ June 17 - Sept. 2 🛏 1, 2 cl. Praha - Budapest (**341/0**) - Beograd - Bar, returning from Bar ④⑦ June 19 - Sept. 4.
METROPOL – 🛏 1, 2 cl., 🛌 2 cl., 🚃2 Berlin - Dresden - Praha - Bratislava - Budapest and v.v.; 🛏 1, 2 cl., 🛌 2 cl., 🚃2 Warszawa (**407/6**) - Břeclav (**477/6**) - Budapest and v.v.; 🛏 1, 2 cl., 🛌 2 cl., 🚃2 Kraków (**402/3**) - Bohumin (**407/6**) - Břeclav (**477/6**) - Budapest and v.v. 🛏 1, 2 cl., 🛌 2 cl., 🚃2 Budapest (**476**) - Bratislava - Pardubice (**878**) - Praha.
SLOVAN – 🚃12 ✕ Praha - Bratislava - Budapest and v.v. On ②⑤ June 17 - Aug. 26 conveys 🛏 1, 2 cl. Praha - Budapest (**1204/5**) - Zagreb - Split, returning next day.
VARSOVIA – 🚃12 and ✕ Warszawa - Katowice - Ostrava - Břeclav - Bratislava - Budapest and v.v.; 🛏 1, 2 cl. Moskva - Warszawa - Budapest and v.v. See Table **95** for 🛏 1, 2 cl. Moskva / Minsk - Budapest - Sofija - Varna / Burgas and v.v. and Moskva / Minsk - Budapest - Beograd - Bar and v.v.

Ⓒ (daily Dec. 24 - Jan. 10).

z – Not Dec. 24 - Jan. 10.
▷ – For local trains Szob - Budapest Nyugati see Table **1255**.
△ – Also at: 0444, 1407Ⓐ **z**, 1607Ⓐ **z**, 1807Ⓐ, 2307.
▽ – Also at: 0326, 0430, 0454Ⓐ **z**, 0530, 0554Ⓐ **z**, 1422Ⓐ **z**.
§ – See also Table **1170**.

OTHER TRAIN NAMES: **270/1** PETROV, **272/3** CSÁRDÁS, **274/5** JAROSLAV HAŠEK, **278/9** DANUBIUS, **280/1** JÁN JESENIUS.

Nové Zámky - Komárno (*29 km*, journey 30 minutes):
From Nové Zámky every 2 hours 0452 - 2052 (also 0552Ⓐ **z**, 0735Ⓐ **z**, 1352Ⓐ **z**, 1552Ⓐ **z**, 1752Ⓐ **z**). From Komárno every 2 hours 0442 - 2042 (also 0542Ⓐ **z**, 0737Ⓐ **z**, 1342Ⓐ **z**, 1542Ⓐ **z**, 1742Ⓐ **z**).

class

BRATISLAVA - NITRA and PRIEVIDZA 1177

			721				723					725						727						
	Ⓐ														Ⓐ	Ⓒ		Ⓑh	Ⓑh	①–⑥	⑦		Ⓐn	
Bratislava hl. .... **1180** d.	*0411*	*0555*	0639	...	*0755*	*0955*	1039	...	*1155*	...	*1355*	1439	...	*1555*	*1655*	...	*1755*	1839	...	*1955*	*1955*	2100	2200	2300
Trnava.............. **1180** d.	*0501*	*0627*	0716	...	*0827*	*1027*	1116	...	*1227*	...	*1427*	1516	...	*1627*	*1727*	...	*1827*	1916	...	*2027*	*2027*	2150	2248	2348
Leopoldov.......... **1180** a.	*0515*	*0638*	0728	...	*0838*	*1038*	1128	...	*1238*	...	*1438*	1528	...	*1638*	*1738*	...	*1838*	1928	...	*2038*	*2038*	2204	...	...
Leopoldov.....................d.	0536	0642	0743	...	0842	1042	1143	...	1242	...	1442	1543	...	1642	1750	...	1842	1943	...	2042	2125	...	...	...
Zbehy............................d.	0609	0713	0807	0819	0909	1113	1207	1219	1313	1419	1513	1607	1619	1713	1823	1823	1913	2007	2019	2113	2152	...	...	...
Lužianky.......................a.	0615	0719	|	0825	0915	1120	|	1225	1320	1425	1520	|	1625	1720	1829	1829	1920	|	2025	2120	2159	...	...	...
Nitra ....a.	0626	0730	|	*0841*	0926	1139	|	1249	1339	1448	1539	|	1649	1739	1849	1849	1939	|	2049	2131	2210	...	...	...
Topoľčany ....▷ a.	...	◇	0832	...	...	◇	1232	◇	◇	◇	◇	1632	◇	◇	◇	...	...	2032	...	...	...	...	...	...
Partizánske.............▷ a.	...	...	0901	...	...	...	1301	...	...	...	...	1701	...	...	...	...	...	2101	...	...	...	...	...	...
Prievidza ....▷ a.	...	...	0935	...	...	...	1335	...	...	...	...	1735	...	...	...	...	...	2135	...	...	...	...	...	...

			720					722					724							726			1520		
		⚒b	⚒b	Ⓐ		Ⓐ									Ⓐ	Ⓐ						Ⓑh	⑦e		
vidza...............▽ d.	...	...	0443	...	...	...	...	0833	...	...	...	...	1233	...	...	...	...	...	...	1633	...	...	1840	...	...
zánske.............▽ d.	...	...	0516	...	...	...	...	0916	...	...	...	...	1316	...	...	...	...	...	...	1716	...	...	1914	...	...
ol'čany.............▽ d.	...	...	0541	...	◇	...	...	0941	...	...	...	...	1341	...	◇	...	...	...	◇	1741	...	◇	1939	...	...
tra ....d.	*0423*	0537	|	0630	0744	...	0944	|	1026	1144	1226	1344	|	1426	1515	...	1544	1626	1744	|	1826	1944	|	2026	...
anky ....d.	0439	0549	|	0641	0754	...	0954	|	1041	1154	1241	1354	|	1441	1525	1534	1554	1641	1754	|	1837	1954	|	2041	...
ny ....d.	0446	0555	0607	0648	0809	...	1001	1007	1048	1201	1248	1401	1407	1448	t	1541	1601	1648	1801	1807	1848	2000	2010	2048	...
oldov..................a.	0513	...	0629	0715	0836	...	...	1029	1116	...	1316	...	1429	1515	...	1615	...	1716	...	1829	1916	...	2035	2116	...
oldov.......... **1180** d.	...	...	0643	*0720*	...	0856	...	1043	*1120*	...	*1320*	...	1443	*1520*	...	*1620*	...	*1720*	...	1843	*1920*	...	2040	*2120*	*2156*
va................ **1180** d.	...	...	0657	*0734*	...	0912	...	1057	*1134*	...	*1334*	...	1457	*1534*	...	*1634*	...	*1734*	...	1857	*1934*	...	2056	*2134*	2235
islava hl....... **1180** a.	...	...	0733	*0805*	...	0959	...	1133	*1205*	...	*1405*	...	1533	*1605*	...	*1705*	...	*1805*	...	1933	*2005*	...	2136	*2205*	2322

①–⑥ (not Dec. 25 - Jan. 6, Mar. 26, 28, Aug. 29).
Also Jan. 6, Mar. 28, Nov. 1; not Dec. 27, Mar. 27, July 3 - Aug. 28.
Not Dec. 24 - Jan. 5, Mar. 25, 27, Aug. 28.
Not Dec. 24 - Jan. 10.

t – To Topoľcany (Table **1187**). Through portion for next col.
◇ – To / from Nové Zámky (Table **1187**).
▷ – Local trains Topoľčany - Prievidza (journey 60 - 80 mins) §: 0354Ⓐ, 0445, 0550Ⓐ, 0651, 0917, 1115, 1318, 1404Ⓐ **n**, 1527, 1718, 1839 (not ⑦ **e**), 1942⑦ **e**, 2223Ⓐ.

▽ – Local trains Prievidza - Topoľčany (journey 60 - 80 mins) §: 0414Ⓐ, 0520, 0623, 0717Ⓐ, 0928, 1115, 1328, 1425Ⓐ, 1525, 1728Ⓐ, 1810⑦ **e**, 1840, 2231Ⓐ.
§ – Certain journeys run from / to Nitra (see Table **1187**).

1180 BRATISLAVA - ŽILINA - POPRAD TATRY - KOŠICE

km		761	1021	763	445	765	443	767	401	601	603	241	1003	605	405	607	701	731	609	703	243	1603	1609	611
			♥		*EN*				♥			*SC* •	♥		♥						*EC*			
		Ⓐ	🍸		⊖		⊖	✕	✕	✕	✕	🅁✕	✕	✕	✕	✕			✕	2	✕	✕	2	✕
			♦	Ⓐ	♦	Ⓐ	♦										2Ⓐ	2Ⓐ		H	⑤n	⑤f	⑤f	
0	**Bratislava** hlavná ... ▷ d.	...	...	...	...	...	...	...	0533	0555	0755	...	...	0955	1133	1155	1255	1339	1355	1455	...	1455	...	1555
46	Trnava ▷ d.	...	...	...	...	...	...	...	0600	0627	0827	...	...	1027	1200	1227	1327	1416	1427	1527	...	1527	...	1627
63	Leopoldov ▷ d.	...	...	...	...	...	...	...	|	0640	0840	...	...	1040	|	1240	1340	1428	1440	1540	...	1540	...	1640
81	Piešťany d.	...	...	...	...	...	...	...	|	0654	0854	...	...	1054	|	1254	1354	1441	1454	1554	...	1554	...	1654
99	Nové Mesto n. Váhom d.	...	...	...	...	...	...	...	|	0707	0907	...	...	1107	|	1307	1407	1455	1507	1607	...	1607	...	1707
124	**Trenčín** d.	...	...	...	...	...	...	0515	0643	0726	0926	...	...	1126	1243	1326	1426	1517	1526	1626	...	1626	...	1726
132	Trenčianska Teplá d.	...	...	...	...	...	...	0523	|	0734	0934	...	...	1134	|	1334	1434	...	1534	1634	...	1634	...	1734
159	**Púchov** ▷ d.	...	...	...	...	...	...	0547	|	0753	0953	...	...	1153	|	1353	1453	...	1553	1653	...	1653	...	1753
171	Považská Bystrica ▷ d.	...	...	...	...	...	...	0559	|	0806	1006	...	...	1206	|	1406	1506	...	1606	1706	...	1706	...	1806
	Praha hlavní **1160** d.	...	2146	...	2200	...	2309	|	|	|	|	0643	0746	|	|	|	|	...	|	|	1306	|	...	|
203	**Žilina** ▷ a.	...	0250	...	0414	...	0514	0641	0752	0841	1041	1118	1237	1241	1352	1441	1541	...	1641	1741	1752	1741	...	1841
203	**Žilina** ▷ d.	...	0301	...	0435	...	0516	0645	0754	0845	1045	1120	1239	1245	1354	1445	...	...	1645	...	1756	1803	...	1845
224	Vrútky ▷ d.	...	0319	...	0453	...	0534	0703	0809	0903	1103	|	1256	1303	1409	1503	...	...	1703	...	|	1821	...	1903
242	Kraľovany d.	...	|	...	0507	...	0548	0717	|	0917	1117	|	|	1317	|	1517	...	...	1717	...	|	1837	...	1917
260	Ružomberok d.	...	0347	...	0523	...	0604	0734	0835	0934	1134	1201	1323	1334	1435	1534	...	...	1734	...	1838	1856	...	1934
286	Liptovský Mikuláš d.	...	0409	...	0542	...	0623	0753	0853	0953	1153	1219	1342	1353	1453	1553	...	...	1753	...	1856	1916	...	1953
325	Štrba d.	...	0438	...	|	...	0652	0822	|	1022	1222	1247	1409	1422	1520	1622	...	...	1822	...	|	1946	...	2022
344	**Poprad-Tatry** d.	0438	0456	0538	0624	0638	0725*	0838	0932	1038	1238	1300	1429	1438	1534	1638	...	...	1838	...	1937	2002	...	2038
370	Spišská Nová Ves d.	0457	0516	0557	0642	0657	0744	0857	0950	1057	1257	|	1451	1457	1552	1657	...	...	1857	...	1955	2020	...	2057
410	Margecany d.	0524	|	0624	|	0724	0811	0924	|	1124	1324	|	|	1524	|	1724	...	...	1924	...	|	2048	...	2124
429	Kysak ▷ a.	0538	0554	0640	0720	0740	0825	0938	1028	1138	1338	1352	1527	1538	1630	1738	...	...	1938	...	2032	2102	2107	2138
	Prešov a.	|	|	|	|	|	|	|	|	|	|	|	|	|	|	|	...	...	|	...	|	2142	|	|
445	**Košice** ▷ a.	0552	0614	0652	0741	0752	0839	0952	1041	1152	1352	1405	1544	1552	1643	1752	...	...	1952	...	2045	|	2119	2152
	Humenné **1194** a.	...	...	...	...	...	1033	...	...	...	...	...	...	...	...	...	...	...	...	...	...	2254	...	...

	705	1605	409	613		707	709	709/445	711	1367	615
			♥							*LE* ♠	
	2	✕	✕	✕	2	2	✕	🛏		🍸🅁	2
	G	⑤f		E		F		R	Ⓑh		♦
Bratislava hlavná ▷ d.	1655	1655	1733	1755	...	1855	1955	1955	2155	...	2345
Trnava ▷ d.	1727	1727	1800	1827	...	1927	2027	2027	2227	...	0017
Leopoldov ▷ d.	1740	1740	|	1840	...	1940	2040	2040	2240	...	0030
Piešťany d.	1754	1754	|	1854	...	1954	2054	2054	2254	...	0044
Nové Mesto n. Váhom d.	1807	1807	|	1907	...	2007	2107	2107	2307	...	0057
Trenčín d.	1826	1826	1843	1926	...	2026	2126	2126	2324	...	0116
Trenčianska Teplá d.	1834	1834	|	1934	...	2034	2134	2134	...	...	0124
Púchov ▷ d.	1853	1853	|	1953	...	2053	2153	2153	...	...	0143
Považská Bystrica ▷ d.	1906	1906	|	2006	...	2106	2206	2206	...	...	0156
Praha hlavní **1160** d.	|	|	|	|	...	|	|	|	...	1911	|
Žilina ▷ a.	1941	1941	1948	2041	...	2141	2241	2241	...	0024	0231
Žilina ▷ d.	...	2000	1954	2045	2124	...	...	0435	...	0026	0243
Vrútky ▷ d.	...	2017	2009	2103	2144	...	...	0453	...	0044	0301
Kraľovany d.	...	2031	|	2117	2206	...	...	0507	...	|	0315
Ružomberok d.	...	2047	2035	2134	2230	...	...	0523	...	0111	0332
Liptovský Mikuláš d.	...	2105	2053	2153	2255	...	...	0542	...	0130	0351
Štrba d.	...	2133	2120	2222	—	...	...	|	...	0158	|
Poprad-Tatry d.	...	2148	2134	2238	2242	...	...	0624	...	0213	0432
Spišská Nová Ves d.	...	2206	2152	2257	2310	...	...	0642	...	0232	0451
Margecany d.	...	2232	|	2324	2353	...	...	|	...	|	0518
Kysak ▷ a.	...	2246	2230	2338	...	...	...	0720	...	0348z	0532
Prešov a.	...	|	|	|	...	...	...	|	...	0324	|
Košice ▷ a.	...	2300	2243	2352	...	...	...	0741	...	0403	0546
Humenné **1194** a.	...	...	...	...	...	...	...	...	...	...	0750

	702	704	736	706	600	600	400	1358
							♥	*LE* ♠
	2	✕	2	2	✕	✕	✕	🍸🅁
	N		Ⓐ	Ⓐ		⚒b		
Humenné **1194** d.	...	...	...	...	...	...	...	...
Košice ▷ d.	...	...	...	...	...	0408	0517	0445
Prešov d.	...	...	...	...	...	|	|	0525
Kysak ▷ d.	...	...	...	...	...	0422	0531	0458z
Margecany d.	...	...	...	...	...	0438	|	|
Spišska Nová Ves d.	...	...	...	...	...	0505	0609	0616
Poprad-Tatry d.	...	...	...	...	...	0525	0628	0633
Štrba d.	...	...	...	...	...	0541	0642	0647
Liptovský Mikuláš d.	...	...	...	...	...	0611	0709	0716
Ružomberok d.	...	...	...	...	...	0628	0726	|
Kraľovany d.	...	...	...	...	...	0645	|	|
Vrútky ▷ d.	...	...	...	...	...	0659	0751	0759
Žilina ▷ a.	...	...	...	...	...	0715	0807	0815
Žilina ▷ d.	0419	0519	...	0611	0719	0719	0809	0817
Praha hlavní **1160** a.	|	|	...	|	|	|	|	1322
Považská Bystrica ▷ d.	0455	0555	...	0655	0755	0755	|	...
Púchov ▷ d.	0509	0609	...	0709	0809	0809	|	...
Trenčianska Teplá d.	0526	0626	...	0726	0826	0826	|	...
Trenčín d.	0534	0634	0647	0734	0834	0834	0918	...
Nové Mesto n. Váhom d.	0554	0654	0714	0754	0854	0854	|	...
Piešťany d.	0607	0707	0729	0807	0907	0907	|	...
Leopoldov ▷ d.	0620	0720	0743	0820	0920	0920	|	...
Trnava ▷ d.	0634	0734	0757	0834	0934	0934	1001	...
Bratislava hlavná ▷ a.	0705	0805	0833	0905	1005	1005	1027	...

	1012	604	606	404	708	242	608	1710	610	240	1604	760	1602	612	408	762		444	1020	442	442/704		614	1352
	♥			♥		*EC*				*SC* •					♥			*EN*	♥					*LE* ♠
	✕	✕	✕	✕		✕	✕	2	✕	🅁✕	✕	2	✕	✕	✕	✕		⊖	🍸	⊖	🛏			🍸🅁
					Ⓑh	⑦e		⑦r			⑦g	Ⓐ	⑦g				2	♦	♦	♦	S		♦‡	P
Humenné **1194** d.	...	...	...	...	...	...	...	...	...	...	...	...	1344	...	...	...	...	...	...	1946	...	...	2137	...
Košice ▷ d.	0744	0808	1008	1109	...	1144	1208	...	1408	1447	1457	1512	|	1608	1717	1808	1927	2020	2122	2208	2208	...	2334	2323
Prešov d.	|	|	|	|	...	|	|	...	|	|	|	|	1518	|	|	|	|	|	|	|	|	...	|	2358
Kysak ▷ d.	0757	0822	1022	1122	...	1157	1222	...	1422	1501	1510	1525	|	1622	1731	1822	1945	2034	2136	2222	2222	...	2348	2336z
Margecany d.	|	0838	1038	|	...	|	1238	...	1438	|	|	1540	1549	1638	|	1838	2006	|	|	2238	2238	...	0005	|
Spišska Nová Ves d.	0835	0905	1105	1200	...	1235	1305	...	1505	|	1549	1607	1621	1705	1809	1905	2050	2114	2216	2305	2305	...	0033	0053
Poprad-Tatry d.	0855	0925	1125	1218	...	1253	1325	...	1525	1555	1610	1625	1642	1725	1828	1925	2118	2153	2238	2325	2325	...	0057	0115
Štrba d.	0910	0942	1142	|	...	|	1342	...	1542	1608	|	...	1658	1742	1842	1942	...	|	2255	2342	2342	...	|	0129
Liptovský Mikuláš d.	0938	1010	1210	1258	...	1332	1410	...	1610	1635	1652	...	1729	1810	1909	2010	...	2236	2325	0010	0010	...	0142	0158
Ružomberok d.	0957	1028	1228	1315	...	1349	1428	...	1628	1653	1710	...	1750	1828	1926	2028	...	2255	2345	0028	0028	...	0203	0219
Kraľovany d.	|	1045	1245	|	...	|	1445	...	1645	|	|	...	1807	1845	|	2045	...	2311	|	0045	0045	...	0219	|
Vrútky ▷ d.	1024	1059	1259	1340	...	|	1459	...	1659	|	1735	...	1822	1859	1951	2059	...	2327	0016	0059	0059	...	0233	0246
Žilina ▷ a.	1040	1115	1315	1356	...	1430	1515	...	1715	1734	1751	...	1838	1915	2007	2115	...	2343	0032	0115	0115	...	0249	0303
Žilina ▷ d.	1042	1119	1319	1358	1403	1432	1519	1611	1719	1741	1754	...	1841	1919	2009	2119	...	0005	0042	0134	0519	...	0301	0324
Praha hlavní **1160** a.	1558	|	|	|	|	1915	|	|	|	2219	|	...	|	|	|	|	...	0638	0558	0739	|	...	|	0822
Považská Bystrica ▷ d.	...	1155	1355	|	1455	...	1555	1655	1755	...	1830	...	|	1955	|	2201	...	...	...	...	0555	...	0337	...
Púchov ▷ d.	...	1209	1409	|	1509	...	1609	1709	1809	...	1844	...	|	2009	|	2215	...	...	...	...	0609	...	0401	...
Trenčianska Teplá d.	...	1226	1426	|	1526	...	1626	1734	1826	...	|	...	|	2026	|	2241	...	...	...	...	0626	...	0418	...
Trenčín d.	...	1234	1434	1458	1534	...	1634	1742	1834	...	1907	...	1953	2034	2118	2248	...	...	...	...	0634	...	0426	...
Nové Mesto n. Váhom d.	...	1254	1454	|	1554	...	1654	1803	1854	...	|	...	|	2054	|	...	...	...	...	...	0654	...	0446	...
Piešťany d.	...	1307	1507	|	1607	...	1707	1816	1907	...	|	...	|	2107	|	...	...	...	...	...	0707	...	0459	...
Leopoldov ▷ d.	...	1320	1520	|	1620	...	1720	1829	1920	...	1947	...	|	2120	|	...	...	...	...	...	0720	...	0512	...
Trnava ▷ d.	...	1334	1534	1547	1634	...	1734	1844	1934	...	2001	...	2041	2134	2201	...	...	...	...	...	0734	...	0527	...
Bratislava hlavná ▷ a.	...	1405	1605	1612	1705	...	1805	1918	2005	...	2033	...	2113	2205	2227	...	...	...	...	...	0805	...	0611	...

♦ – **NOTES** (LISTED BY TRAIN NUMBERS)

442/3 – BOHEMIA – 🛏 1, 2 cl., ▬ 2 cl., 🚃2 Praha - Žilina - Košice - Humenné and v.v.; 🛏 1, 2 cl. Praha - Košice (**8807/20**) - Čierna nad Tisou (**8862/3**) - Čop (**83/143**) - Kyïv and v.v.

444/5 – SLOVAKIA – 🛏 1, 2 cl., ▬ 2 cl., 🚃2 Praha - Bohumín - Žilina - Poprad Tatry - Košice and v.v.; 🛏 1, 2 cl. Cheb (**615/4**) - Karlovy Vary - Praha (**445/4**) - Košice and v.v.

614/5 – ZEMPLÍN – 🛏 1, 2 cl., ▬ 2 cl., 🚃2 Bratislava - Humenné and v.v.

1020/1 – 🛏 (1,2,3 berth), ▬ (6 berth), 🚃12 Praha - Košice and v.v.

E – Daily to Žilina, Ⓑ **u** to Poprad Tatry, ⑤ **f** to Košice. Numbered **1613** on ⑤, **1615** on ⑥.

F – Daily to Trenčín, ⑤ to Žilina (also Mar. 24, July 4, Aug. 31, Sept. 14, Oct. 31, Nov. 16; not Mar. 25).

G – ①②③④⑦ (not Mar. 27, Aug. 28).

H – ①–④ (not Mar. 24, 28, July 5, Aug. 29, 31, Sept. 1, 14, 15, Oct. 31, Nov. 1, 16, 17).

N – Ⓐ from Žilina; ①–⑥ from Trenčín (not Mar. 26, 28, Aug. 29).

P – 🚃12 Praha (**1361/52**) - Prešov (**1363/50**) - Košice and v.v.

R – 🛏 1, 2 cl. Bratislava (**709**) - Žilina (**445**) - Košice.

S – 🛏 1, 2 cl. Košice (**442**) - Žilina (**704**) - Bratislava.

b – ①–⑥ (not Mar. 26, 28, July 5, Aug. 29).

e – Also Mar. 28, July 6; not Mar. 27, July 3. Train number *IC* **542** Ostrava - Praha.

f – Also Mar. 24, Aug. 31, Sept. 14, Oct. 31, Nov. 16; not Mar. 25.

g – Also Mar. 28, Aug. 29, Sept. 1, 15, Nov. 1, 17; not Mar. 27, Aug. 28.

h – Not Mar. 25, 27, Aug. 28.

n – Also Oct. 27, Nov. 16; not Oct. 28, Nov. 18. Train number *IC* **543** Praha Ostrava.

r – Also Mar. 28, July 5, Aug. 29, Sept. 1, 15, Nov. 1, 17; not Mar. 27, Aug.

u – Not Mar. 25, 27, July 4, Aug. 28.

x – Arrive 1555.

z – Calls after Prešov (before Prešov in the Košice - Praha direction).

▷ – For other trains see Table **1177** Bratislava - Leopoldov, **1160** Puchov - Ž **1185** Žilina - Vrútky, **1196** Kysak - Košice.

⊖ – 🅁 for international journeys.

• – *SUPERCITY PENDOLINO*, 🅁, supplement payable.

♥ – Operated by REGIOJET. Separate fare tariff applies.

♠ – Operated by LEO Express. Separate fare tariff applies.

‡ – Train number **1614** on ⑤⑥ (Bratislava arrive 0605).

* – Arrive 0705.

LOCAL LINES IN POPRAD TATRY AREA 1182

class

													Ⓐz			⑦e	Ⓐz	Ⓐz			Ⓐz			
Poprad Tatry .... d.	0402	...	0546	...	0646	...	0846	...	1046	...	1246	...	1346	1446	...	...	1546	...	1646	...	1746	1846	...	2200
Studený Potok .... a.	0414	0423	0558	0602	0658	0702	0858	0904	1058	1104	1258	1304	1358	1458	1504	...	1558	1604	1658	1704	1758	1858	1904	2212
Tatranská Lomnica .. a.	|	0434	|	0613	|	0713	|	0915	|	1115	|	1315	|	|	1515	...	|	1615	|	1715	|	|	1915	|
Kežmarok .... a.	0448	...	0618	...	0712	...	0914	...	1114	...	1314	...	1412	1514	...	...	1612	...	1714	...	1812	1914	...	2224
Stará Lubovňa .... a.	0533	...	0703a	...	...	...	0957	...	1157z	...	1357	...	...	1600	...	1705	...	...	1757	...	...	1957r	...	2307
Plaveč .... a.	...	...	...	...	...	...	...	...	...	...	...	...	...	1619f	...	1724	...	...	...	...	...	...	...	...

												Ⓐz			Ⓐz	⑦e	Ⓐz			Ⓐz	⑤f				
eč .... d.	...	...	...	...	...	...	...	...	...	...	...	...	...	...	...	...	...	...	...	...	1635	...	1741e	...	...
á **Lubovňa** .... d.	...	...	0458	...	0558a	...	0803	...	1003	...	1203z	...	...	1403	...	1453	...	...	1603	...	1653	...	1803	...	2203r
narok .... d.	...	0450	0550	...	0650	...	0850	...	1050	...	1250	1350	...	1450	...	1550	1550	...	1650	1750	...	...	1850	...	2254
transká Lomnica ... d.	0439	|	|	0643	|	0843	|	1043	|	1243	|	|	1443	|	1543	|	|	1643	|	|	...	1843	|	2158	|
ený Potok .... d.	0452	0501	0601	0656	0701	0856	0901	1056	1101	1256	1301	1401	1456	1501	1556	1601	1601	1656	1701	1801	...	1856	1901	2214	2305
rad Tatry .... a.	...	0514	0614	...	0714	...	0914	...	1114	...	1314	1414	...	1514	...	1614	1614	...	1714	1814	...	...	1914	2227	2318

rad Tatry - Starý Smokovec (24 mins, *13* km, narrow gauge): 0504, 0604, 0629Ⓐ, k, 0829, 0929, 1004 **N**, 1029, 1129 **N**, 1229, 1329, 1429, 1504, 1529, 1629, 1729, 1829, , 2029 **S**, 2129, 2240. Most continue to Štrbské Pleso (see below).

ý Smokovec - Štrbské Pleso (41 mins, *16* km, narrow gauge): 0531, 0631, 0701Ⓐ, **d**, 0901, 1001, 1031 **N**, 1101, 1201 **N**, 1301, 1401, 1501, 1531, 1601, 1701, 1801, 1901, , 2101 **S**, 2201, 2308. Most start from Poprad Tatry (see above).

ý Smokovec - Tatranská Lomnica (14 mins, *6* km, narrow gauge): 0416, 0556, 0656, **k**, 0902, 1002, 1102, 1202 **N**, 1302 and hourly to 2202 (1902 is **d**).

ské Pleso - Štrba (18 mins, *5* km, rack): 0520, 0620, 0720, 0814, 0914, 1014, 1114, 1214, , 1354, 1444, 1544, 1644, 1744, 1844, 1944, 2244.

Starý Smokovec - Poprad Tatry (23 mins, *13* km, narrow gauge): 0437, 0555, 0655, 0735Ⓐ, 0755, 0855, 0955, 1055, 1155 **N**, 1255, 1355, 1455, 1555, 1635 **N**, 1655, 1755, 1855 **k**, 1955, 2055, 2155, 2306. Most start from Štrbské Pleso (see below).

Štrbské Pleso - Starý Smokovec (39 mins, *16* km, narrow gauge): 0513, 0613, 0643Ⓐ, 0715, 0813, 0913, 1013, 1113 **N**, 1213, 1313, 1413, 1513, 1543 **N**, 1613, 1713, 1813 **d**, 1913, 2013, 2113, 2213. Most continue to Poprad Tatry (see above).

Tatranská Lomnica - Starý Smokovec (14 mins, *6* km, narrow gauge): 0514, 0614, 0714 **b**, 0834, 0934, 1034, 1134 **N**, 1234, 1334, 1434, 1534, 1634, 1734, 1824 **k**, 1934, 2034, 2134, 2234.

Štrba - Štrbské Pleso (15 mins, *5* km, rack): 0456, 0556, 0659, 0746, 0836, 0946, 1036, 1146, 1251, 1336, 1426, 1516, 1626, 1716, 1826, 1916, 2026.

Dec. 13 - Mar. 29, May 16 - Sept. 25.
May 16 - Sept. 25.
Ⓐ only.
0734 on Ⓒ (daily Dec. 24 - Jan. 10, July 1 - Sept. 4).
Štrbské Pleso - Starý Smokovec - Tatranská Lomnica and v.v.

e – ⑦ (also Jan. 7, Feb. 1, Mar. 29, Sept. 15, Nov. 1, 17; not Dec. 27, Jan. 3, 31, Feb. 14, Mar. 27, July 3 - Aug. 28, Oct. 30).
f – ⑤ (also Dec. 22, Mar. 23, June 30, Sept. 14, Oct. 27, Nov. 16; not Dec. 25, Jan. 1, Feb. 19, Mar. 25, July 1 - Sept. 2, Oct. 28).
k – Tatranská Lomnica - Starý Smokovec - Poprad Tatry and v.v.

r – Ⓑ (not holidays).
z – Ⓐ (not Dec. 24 - Jan. 10).

POPRAD TATRY - ZAKOPANE 1183

RAMA

		S	S	S	S		V	V	
rad Tatry (Bus Stn stand 4) d.	...	0850	1150	1650	1750	...	1150	1650	...
ý Smokovec (Bus Station) ... d.	...	0910	1210	1710	1810	...	1210	1710	...
anská Lomnica (Bus Stn)..... d.	...	0924	1224	1724	1824	...	1224	1724	...
pane (Bus Station)............ a.	...	1033	1333	1833	1933	...	1333	1833	...
pane (ul Balzera Nosal)...... a.	...	...	1339	1839	1939	...	1339	1839	...

		S	S	S	S		V	V	
Zakopane (ul Balzera Nosal).... d.	...	0600	0900	...	1600	...	0900	1500	...
Zakopane (Bus Stn stand 3).... d.	...	0615	0915	1115	1615	...	0915	1515	...
Tatranská Lomnica (Bus Stn) ... d.	...	0727	1027	1227	1727	...	1027	1627	...
Starý Smokovec (Bus Station).. d.	...	0737	1037	1237	1737	...	1037	1637	...
Poprad Tatry (Bus Station) ..... a.	...	0753	1053	1253	1753	...	1053	1653	...

June 17 - Sept. 30. **V** – Oct. 1 - 16. Rail tickets not valid. ▦ = Lysa Polana. Dates are 2016. Bus stations at Poprad Tatry and Zakopane are adjacent to railway station.

ŽILINA - VRÚTKY - MARTIN - BANSKÁ BYSTRICA and ZVOLEN 1185

d class

			1841		**1843**		**1845**		**1847**		**1849**		**1851**				**1853**			**1855**			**1857**		**1011**	
		Ⓐ	**Ps**		Ⓐu	Ⓐu					**k**				Ⓐ	Ⓐz			Ⓐz			⚒		**R**	♥	**n**
	Praha hl. **1160** .... d.	...	2200	...	...	...	...	...	...	...	...	...	...	...	...	...	...	...	...	...	...	...	...	...	1446	
0	**Žilina** .... **1180** d.	...	0454	...	0554	*0624*	0654	...	0854	...	1054	...	1254	...	*1327*	*1428*	1454	...	*1557*	1654	...	*1805*r	1854	...	1945	...
1	Vrútky .... **1180** a.	...	0511	...	0611	*0643*	0711	...	0911	...	1111	...	1311	...	*1346*	*1447*	1511	...	*1616*	1711	...	*1820*r	1911	...	2001	...
1	Vrútky .... d.	0450	0513	0520	0613	0650	0713	0720	0913	0920	1113	1120	1313	1320	1420	1450	1513	1520	1620	1713	1720	1827	1913	1920	2003	2120
8	**Martin** .... d.	0458	0520	0528	0620	0658	0720	0728	0920	0928	1120	1128	1320	1328	1428	1458	1520	1528	1628	1720	1728	1835	1920	1928	2021	2128
1	Turčianske Teplice .... d.	0527	0538	0557	0638	0727	0738	0757	0938	0957	1138	1157	1338	1357	1457	1527	1538	1557	1657	1738	1757	1904	1938	1957	2039	2157
7	**Banská Bystrica** ... a.	|	0626	|	0726	|	0826	|	1026	|	1226	|	1426	|	|	|	1626	|	|	1826	|	|	2026	|	2124	|
0	Horná Štubňa .... d.	0538	...	0609	...	0738	...	0808	...	1008	...	1209	...	1408	1508	1538	...	1609	1708	...	1808	1915	|	2015	|	2208
0	Kremnica .... d.	...	...	0636	...	...	...	...	...	...	...	1235	...	◇	...	...	...	1635	...	...	...	...	|	2042	|	...
6	Hronská Dúbrava ...... d.	...	...	0708	...	...	...	...	...	...	...	1308	...	...	...	...	...	1708	...	...	...	...	|	2115	|	...
7	**Zvolen** osob. .... a.	...	...	0718	...	...	...	...	...	...	...	1318	...	...	...	...	...	1718	...	...	...	...	2053	2125	2152	...

		1008			**1856**			**1840**		**1842**		**1844**				**1846**		**1848**		**1850**			**1852**	**1854**	
		♥	Ⓐ	Ⓒ		Ⓐz		**k**					Ⓐ	Ⓐu		**k**	Ⓐ	Ⓐu			Ⓐz			**P**	
len osob. .... d.	...	0408	0424	...	0503	...	0619	...	...	...	...	...	...	...	...	...	...	...	1425	...	1525	...	...	...	1904
ská Dúbrava .... d.	...	|	0434	...	|	...	0629	...	...	...	...	...	...	...	...	...	...	...	1435	...	1535	...	...	...	1914
nnica .... d.	...	|	0515	...	|	...	0707	...	◇	...	...	...	...	...	...	...	...	...	1510	...	1610	...	...	...	1947
á Štubňa .... d.	0452	|	0552	0552	|	0652	0752	...	0952	...	1152	...	1246	...	1352	...	1452	...	1552	...	1652	1752	...	...	2020
anská Bystrica ..... d.	|	0457	|	|	0534	|	|	0734	|	0934	|	1134	|	...	|	1334	|	1434	|	1534	|	|	1734	1934	|
ianske Teplice .... d.	0502	0544	0602	0602	0621	0702	0802	0821	1002	1021	1202	1221	1256	...	1402	1421	1502	1521	1602	1621	1702	1802	1821	2021	2030
tin .... d.	0532	0616	0632	0632	0640	0732	0832	0840	1032	1040	1232	1240	1326	...	1432	1440	1532	1540	1632	1640	1732	1832	1840	2040	2100
ky .... a.	0540	0623	0640	0640	0647	0740	0840	0847	1040	1047	1240	1247	1334	...	1440	1447	1540	1547	1640	1647	1740	1840	1847	2047	2108
ky .... **1180** d.	*0545*a	0624	...	...	0649	*0805*	...	0849	...	1049	...	1249	...	1340	...	1449	...	1558	...	1649	*1805*	...	1849	2049	*2113*
a .... **1180** a.	*0605*a	0640	...	...	0706	*0825*	...	0906	...	1106	...	1306	...	1400	...	1506	...	1615	...	1706	*1825*	...	1906	2106	*2132*
raha hl. **1160** .... a.	...	1158	...	...	...	...	...	...	...	...	...	...	...	...	...	...	...	...	...	...	...	...	...	0638	...

							◇				
0	Horná Štubňa .... d.	0417	0617	0817	1017	1217	1417	1617	1817	2017	...
8	Handlová .... d.	0440	0640	0840	1040	1240	1440	1640	1840	2040	...
7	Prievidza .... a.	0511	0711	0911	1111	1311	1511	1711	1911	2111	...

			◇							
Prievidza .... d.	0438	0641	0841	1041	1241	1441	1641	1841	2145	...
Handlová .... d.	0521	0717	0917	1117	1317	1517	1717	1917	2221	...
Horná Štubňa .... a.	0544	0741	0941	1141	1341	1541	1741	1941	2244	...

2 Žilina - Banská Bystrica and v.v.; 1, 2 cl. Praha (**445/4**) - Žilina - Banská Bystrica and v.v.
Daily to Horná Štubňa, ⑤⑦ to Zvolen.
Ⓐ only.

k – Not Dec. 25, 26, Jan. 1.
n – Runs one hour later on ⚒.
r – Ⓑ (not Dec. 24, 25).
s – Not Dec. 25, 26, Jan. 1 (previous day from Praha).

u – Not Dec. 24 - Jan. 10, July 1 - Sept. 4.
z – Not Dec. 24 - Jan. 10.
◇ – 2 Vrutky - Horná Štubňa - Prievidza and v.v.
♥ – Operated by RegioJet, Ⓡ, 🍷.

NOVÉ ZAMKY - NITRA - TOPOL'ČANY 1187

d class

										Ⓐ				Ⓐ					Ⓐ	Ⓒ				
0	**Nové Zamky** .... d.	...	0427	0520	0627	0724	0920	1120	1250	1320	1423	1450	...	1520	1615	1650	1720	1815	1852	1920	1920	2120	...	2242	...
0	Šurany .... a.	...	0440	0531	0638	0735	0932	1132	1305	1334	1436	1505	...	1531	1626	1705	1734	1826	1904	1934	1934	2131	...	2253	...
0	Šurany .... d.	...	0443	0537	0641	0741	0935	1135	...	1335	1437	...	...	1535	1635	...	1735	1835	...	1935	1935	2133	...	2254	...
6	**Nitra** .... a.	...	0516	0616	0720	0813	1007	1207	...	1407	1512	...	...	1607	1716	...	1807	1916	...	2007	2007	2215	...	2331	...
6	**Nitra** .... d.	0423	0547	0638	0744	0818	1018	1218	...	1418	1515	...	...	1618	1744	...	1818	...	...	2018	...	...	2240	...	...
0	Lužianky .... d.	0436	0601	0648	0754	0829	1029	1229	...	1429	1529	...	...	1629	1754	...	1831	...	...	2029	...	...	2253	...	...
9	**Topol'čany** .... a.	0512	0647	0730	◇	0905	1105	1305	...	1505	1613	...	...	1705	...	...	1905	...	...	2107	...	...	2329	...	...
	Prievidza **1177** .... a.	...	0806	...	...	1036	1216	1432	...	1625	...	...	...	1835	...	...	...	...	...	...	...	...	...	...	...

			Ⓐ							Ⓐ				Ⓐ			Ⓐ	Ⓐ							
ievidza **1177** .... d.	...	0414a	0520	...	0623	0717a	0928	...	...	...	...	...	...	...	1328	...	1425	...	1525	...	...	...	1728a	...	...
ol'čany .... d.	0425	0523	0626	◇	0737	0845	1045	◇	...	...	1245	◇	...	...	1445	◇	1526	...	1645	◇	...	◇	1845	2045	...
anky .... d.	0514	0600	0704	0720	0831	0929	1129	1129	...	1239	1329	1329	...	1438	1529	1529	1602	1639	1729	1729	...	1839	1929	2132	...
a .... a.	0524	0610	0715	0730	0841	0939	1139	1139	...	1249	1339	1339	...	1448	1539	1539	1613	1649	1739	1739	...	1849	1939	2144	...
a .... d.	0526	0631	▬	0750	▬	0945	...	1145	...	1253	...	1345	...	1450	...	1545	▬	1653	...	1745	...	1853	...	2150	2243
any .... a.	0558	0701	Ⓐ	0828	...	1023	...	1223	...	1323	...	1423	...	1528	...	1623	...	1723	...	1823	...	1923	...	2224	2315
any .... d.	0559	0711	0745	0828	0855	1024	...	1224	1255	1324	...	1426	1455	1533	...	1628	1655	1724	...	1828	1855	1924	...	2225	2316
vé Zamky .... a.	0611	0723	0757	0840	0907	1036	...	1236	1307	1337	...|	1440	1507	1545	...	1640	1707	1736	...	1840	1909	1936	...	2238	2328

Ⓐ only.

◇ – To / from Leopoldov (Table **1177**).

1190 ZVOLEN - LUČENEC - KOŠICE

2nd cl

km		931 ⚒d			933		935	1933 ⑦e		937		801 ⒷP
	Bratislava hl. **1170** d.	...	...	...	...	...	...	...	...	...	...	2349
0	**Zvolen** osob. d.	0713	0723	0923	1113	1323	1513	1713	1723	1913	2223	0316
54	Lučenec d.	0801	0835	1035	1201	1435	1601	1801	1835	2001	2335	0407
69	Fil'akovo d.	0814	0853	1053	1214	1453	1614	1814	1853	2014	2353	0421
98	Jesenské d.	0841	...	...	1241	...	1641	1841	...	2041	...	0449
162	Rožňava d.	0940	...	...	1339	...	1737	1940	...	2140	...	0546
202	Moldava nad Bodvou d.	1012	...	...	1412	...	1810	2012	...	2212	...	0621
233	**Košice** a.	1037	...	...	1437	...	1837	2037	...	2237	...	0648
	Prešov **1196** a.	...	...	...	...	...	...	...	...	...	...	0739

		930		932		934		936		
Prešov **1196** d.	...	...	...	...	...	...	...	...	...	...
Košice d.	...	0523	...	0923	...	1323	...	1523	...	...
Moldava nad Bodvou d.	...	0550	...	0948	...	1348	...	1548	...	...
Rožňava d.	...	0623	...	1021	...	1421	...	1619	...	...
Jesenské d.	...	0720	...	1120	...	1520	...	1720	...	...
Fil'akovo d.	0700	0746	0910	1146	1310	1546	1710	1746	2016	...
Lučenec d.	0729	0801	0929	1201	1329	1601	1729	1801	2033	2235
Zvolen osob a.	0840	0849	1040	1249	1440	1649	1840	1849	...	2346
Bratislava hl. **1170** a.	...	...	...	...	...	...	...	...	...	...

CONNECTIONS TO RIMAVSKÁ SOBOTA *Connections from/to Zvolen are made at Jesenské on certain journeys*

km												
0	Fil'akovo d.	0600	...	...	0855	1055	...	1455	...	1655	1855	...
29	Jesenské d.	0644	0725	0844	0944	1144	1244	1544	1644	1744	1940	2044
40	Rimavská Sobota a.	0658	0739	0858	0958	1158	1258	1558	1658	1758	1954	2058

				Ⓐz						
Rimavská Sobota d.	0600	0700	0817	1017	1101	1217	1417	1501	1617	1701
Jesenské a.	0614	0714	0831	1031	1115	1231	1431	1515	1631	1715
Fil'akovo a.	0649	...	0908	1108	...	1308	1508	...	1708	...

P – POL'ANA – 🛏 1, 2 cl., (2) from Bratislava and Prešov on Ⓑ (not Dec. 24, 25, 31, Jan. 1, Mar. 25, 27, Aug. 28). Conveys on dates in Table **96** 🛏 1, 2 cl. Bratislava - Košice - Kyïv and v.v.
d – ①–⑥ (also Dec. 27, Mar. 27, July 3 - Aug. 28; not Jan. 6, Mar. 28, Nov. 1).
e – Also Jan. 6, Mar. 28, Nov. 1; not Dec. 27, Mar. 27, July 3 - Aug. 28.
z – Not Dec. 24 - Jan. 10.

1192 BANSKÁ BYSTRICA - BREZNO - MARGECANY - (KOŠICE)

2nd cl

km		781 Ⓐ	785 Ⓒ				783				
0	**Banská Bystrica** ▷ d.	0536	0739	0836	1036	1236	1330	1436	1635	1746	...
43	Brezno ▷ d.	0624	0834	0935	1136	1336	1419	1541	1739	1849	...
86	Červená Skala d.	0721	0938	▬	▬	▬	1514	...	▬	...	...
106	Dobšinká L'adová Jas. d.	0744	1000	...	...	...	1536	...	...	...	1935
114	Dedinky d.	0754	1010	...	...	...	1546	...	...	...	1945
139	Nálepkovo d.	0831	1036	1039	1239	1424	1620	...	1837	...	2018
171	Gelnica d.	0905	1108	1141	1340	1521	1654	...	1930	...	2109
179	**Margecany** a.	0914	1117	1152	1352	1532	1703	...	1941	...	2120
	Margecany **1185** d.	*0924*	*1124*	...	...	...	*1724*	...	...	...	...
	Košice **1185** a.	*0952*	*1152*	...	...	...	*1752*	...	...	...	...

	Ⓐ	780	Ⓒ				782		
Košice **1185** d.	...	*0608*	...	...	...	...	*1408*	...	...
Margecany **1185** a.	...	*0636*	...	...	...	...	*1436*	...	...
Margecany d.	...	0646	0808	1008	1208	1408	1446	1608	1808
Gelnica d.	...	0656	0820	1020	1220	1420	1456	1620	1820
Nálepkovo d.	...	0729	0903	1115	1334	1513	1529	1716	1903
Dedinky d.	...	0806	▬	▬	▬	▬	1603	1753	▬
Dobšinká L'adová Jas. d.	...	0816	...	...	...	...	1614	1803	...
Červená Skala d.	...	0836	...	...	...	...	1637	...	...
Brezno ▽ d.	0820	0937	1020	1220	1421	1514	1741	...	2023
Banská Bystrica ▽ a.	0924	1024	1124	1324	1524	1614	1830	...	2123

z – Not Dec. 24 - Jan. 10.
▷ – Also at 0618, 1544Ⓐ**z**, 1855, 1946Ⓐ**z**, 2033, 2230.
▽ – Also at 0557, 0726, 0804Ⓒ, 1626Ⓐ, 1821, 2215.

1194 KOŠICE - HUMENNÉ - MEDZILABORCE

2nd cl

km		615 Y	443 B	901	903 Ⓐ	905	907 Ⓐ	909	911	913	915 △
	Bratislava hl **1180** d.	2345	...	...	...	...	...	...	...	...	...
0	**Košice** d.	0611	0901	1101	1301	1501	1538	1701	1901	2110	2253
68	Trebišov d.	0657	0947	1150	1350	1550	1630	1750	1950	2159	2342
88	Michalovce d.	0718	1011	1211	1411	1611	1651	1811	2011	2220	0003
112	**Humenné** a.	0750	1033	1233	1433	1633	1713	1833	2033	2242	0025

	902 b	904	906 Ⓐ	908	1910 ⑦	910 ①–⑥	912	914	442 B
Humenné d.	0528	0728	0928	1128	1312	1328	1528	1728	1946
Michalovce d.	0550	0750	0950	1150	1334	1350	1550	1750	2012
Trebišov d.	0623	0813	1013	1213	1357	1413	1613	1813	2041
Košice a.	0659	0859	1059	1259	1443	1459	1659	1859	2128
Bratislava hl **1180** a.	...	...	...	...	...	...	...	...	...

km					Ⓐ	Ⓐ				Ⓐ	
0	Humenné d.	0636	0836	1036	1236	1329	1436	1636	1836	2036	2247
41	Medzilaborce a.	0741	0941	1141	1341	1423	1541	1741	1941	2141	2344
43	Medzilaborce mesto a.	0750a	0950	1150	1350	...	1550	1750	1950	...	...

		Ⓐ				◇			
Medzilaborce mesto d.	0418	...	0618	0818a	1018	1206	1417	1617	1818
Medzilaborce d.	0427	0500	0627	0827	1027	1210	1427	1627	1827
Humenné a.	0524	0556	0724	0924	1124	1307	1524	1724	1924

B – BOHEMIA – 🛏 1, 2 cl., ▬ 2 cl., (2) Praha - Košice - Humenné and v.v.
Y – ZEMPLÍN – 🛏 1, 2 cl., ▬ 2 cl., (2) Bratislava - Košice - Humenné and v.v. Train number **1614** on ⑤⑥.
a – Ⓐ only.
b – Also at 0337Ⓐ (train **900**).
◇ – 17 minutes later on ①–⑥.
△ – 11 minutes later on ⑤ (also Mar. Aug. 31, Sept. 14, Oct. 31, Nov. not Mar. 25).

1195 KOŠICE - ČIERNA NAD TISOU - CHOP

2nd cl

km				Ⓐ	8807 K			Ⓐ	965	Ⓐ		△
0	**Košice** d.	0506	0706	0806	1006	1206	1416	1516	1631	1716	1906	2016
62	Slovenské N. Mesto d.	0614	0814	0914	1114	1314	1520	1622	1723	1821	2014	2123
95	**Čierna nad Tisou** a.	0651	0851	0951	1151	1351	1559	1659	1802	1859	2051	2159

	▽	964		Ⓐ				Ⓐ		8820 K
Čierna nad Tisou d.	0504	0557	0704	0804	1004	1204	1404	1504	1604	1804
Slovenské N. Mesto d.	0543	0637	0743	0843	1043	1243	1443	1544	1643	1843
Košice a.	0654	0728	0854	0954	1154	1354	1554	1654	1754	1954

km			K
0	Čierna nad Tisou 🏛 d.	0700	1215
10	Chop 🏛 ⊕ a.	0840	1410

		K
Chop 🏛 ⊕ d.	0943	1735
Čierna nad Tisou 🏛 a.	0947	1740

K – Conveys 🛏 1, 2 cl. Praha (**443/2**) - Košice - Čierna nad Tisou - Chop - Lviv - Kyïv and v.v. (Table **96**). Conveys on dates in Table **96** 🛏 1, 2 cl. Bratislava (**801/0**) - Košice - Čierna nad Tisou - Chop - Lviv - Kyïv and v.v.
⊕ – East European time (o hour ahead).
△ – Additional journey: 230
▽ – Also at 0304, 0404.

1196 KOŠICE - PREŠOV - PLAVEČ

2nd cl

km					801 Pb			①–⑥	⑦	Ⓐ	⑦	①–⑥					Ⓐ			Ⓒ	Ⓐ	Ⓑ		n	1350 ♠🅁
0	**Košice** 1180 d.	0358	0536	0636	0700	0735	0836	*0927*	0936	1036	*1121*	1136	1236	1336	1436	1536	1636	1736	1836	*1927*	1936	...	*2127*	2213	2323
16	Kysak 1180 d.	0433	0553	0653	0723	0753	0853	0953	0953	1053	1153	1153	1253	1355	1453	1553	1653	1753	1853	1953	1953	2045	2153	2230	2341
33	**Prešov** a.	0455	0615	0716	0739	0815	0916	1015	1015	1116	1215	1215	1315	1417	1515	1615	1715	1815	1915	2015	2015	2101	2217	2252	2352
33	**Prešov** d.	0519	0636a	0726a	...	0819	...	1019	1019	...	1219	1219	1319a	1419	1519	1619	1719	1819	1919	...	2019	...	...	2254	...
65	Lipany a.	0556	0713a	0803a	...	0856	...	1056	1056	...	1256	1256	1356a	1456	1556	1656	1756	1856	1956	...	2056	...	...	2331	...
88	**Plaveč** a.	...	...	...	...	...	...	...	...	...	...	...	...	...	1629x	...	...	...	...	...	...	...	...	...	...

	①–⑥			Ⓐ		①–⑥		⑦					Ⓑ			Ⓐ	⑥	⑦				800 Rb		1363 ♠🅁	⑦
Plaveč d.	...	...	...	...	...	...	...	...	...	...	...	...	...	...	...	...	...	...	1730x	...	...	...	...	...	...
Lipany d.	...	0422	0503	0557	0646	...	0903	...	1103a	1203a	1303	...	1403	1503	1603a	1703	...	1703	1803	...	2029	...	...	...	...
Prešov a.	...	0459	0540	0634	0724	...	0940	...	1140a	1240a	1340	...	1440	1540	1640a	1740	...	1740	1840	...	2107	...	←	...	...
Prešov d.	0351	0501	0542	0642	0742	0842	0942	1122	1142	1242	1344	1421	1442	1542	1642	1742	1742	1742	1842	1941	→	2127	2142	2225	2330
Kysak 1180 a.	0413	0523	0606	0706	0806	0906	1006	1144	1206	1306	1408	1443	1506	1606	1706	1806	1806	1806	1906	2006	...	2142	2206	2242	2344
Košice 1180 a.	*0441*	0541	0624	0724	0823	...	1024	...	1224	1324	1425	1503	1524	1624	1724	1824	*1832*	*1832*	1924	*2032*	...	2158	2224	2255	...

P – ①–⑥ (not Mar. 26, 28, Aug. 29). From Bratislava previous day. 🛏 1, 2 cl. and (2).
R – Ⓑ (not Mar. 25, 27, Aug. 28). 🛏 1, 2 cl. and (2).
a – Ⓐ only.
b – From/to Bratislava (Table **1190**).
n – Runs 20 minutes later on ⑤ (also Mar. 24, Aug. 31, Sept. 14, Nov. 16; not Mar. 25, Sept. 2, 16, Nov. 18).
x – ⑤⑦ (also Feb. 1, Mar. 23, 29, June 30, Sept. 14, 15, Oct. 27, Nov. 1, 16, 17; not Feb. 14, 19, Mar. 25, 27, July 1 - Sept. 2, Oct. 28, 30).
♠ – Operated by LEO Express, 🅁, 🍷. (12) Praha (**1361/52**) - Prešov (**1363/50**) - Košice and v.v. See Table **1180**.

1197 PREŠOV - BARDEJOV and HUMENNÉ

2nd cl

km		§	Ⓐ	Ⓒ		Ⓐ					§	
0	Prešov d.	0416	0603	0626	0824	1024	1224	1424	1624	1824	2044	...
45	Bardejov a.	0532	0710	0733	0931	1131	1331	1531	1731	1931	2155	...

		Ⓐ	Ⓒ		Ⓐ		⚒			§
Bardejov d.	0430	0608	0631	0829	1029	1229	1429	1629	1829	1958
Prešov a.	0535	0713	0736	0934	1134	1334	1534	1734	1934	2109

km						Ⓐ	Ⓐ					⑤b
0	Prešov d.	0416	0610	0844	1044	1244	1344	1444r	1644	1844	2044	2144
70	Humenné a.	0602	0802	1020	1220	1420	1520	1620	1820	2020	2214	2254

		Ⓐ		△			⚒	⑦b		
Humenné d.	0352	0440	0540	0728	0940	1140	1340	1344	1540	1740
Prešov a.	0527	0633	0723	0908	1108	1308	1508	1457	1708	1908

b – Train **1603/2**, (12) Bratislava - Prešov - Humenné and v.v. For days of running see Table **1180**.
r – 1434 on ⑦ (also Mar. 28, Aug. 29, Sept. 1, 15, Nov. 1, 17; not Mar. 27, Aug. 28).
z – Runs 17-21 minutes later on ⑤ (also Mar. 24, Aug. 31, Sept. 14, Oct. 31, Nov. 16; not Mar. 25).
△ – Change at Strážske (a. 0737 / d. 0750).
§ – Change at Kapušany pri Prešove.

HUNGARY

ator: MÁV-START (www.mav-start.hu) running on the network of MÁV (www.mav.hu). Certain services in the west are operated by Györ-Sopron-Ebenfurthi Vasút (GySEV).

ces: All trains convey first and second class seating, **except** where shown otherwise in footnotes or by '2' in the train column, or where the footnote shows sleeping- and/or couchette cars only. Descriptions of sleeping- (🛏) and couchette (🛏) cars appear on page 8. Certain international services, as indicated in the tables, cannot be used for internal journeys in Hungary, whilst others generally convey dedicated carriages for internal journeys, which may be made without reservation.

gs: Valid **December 13, 2015 - December 10, 2016**. Summer timings June 18 - Aug. 28 for the Balaton area were not available by press date. Engineering work alterations may affect travel - it is not always possible to show short-term changes in our tables. Many trains are cancelled on the evening of Dec. 24, 31 and on the morning of Dec. 25 and Jan. 1.

rvations: Most InterCity (*IC*) and Express (*Ex*) trains have **compulsory** reservation, as shown by 🅁 in the tables. *IC* trains also require a supplement; the amount depends on distance of the journey. Passengers having passes which include the supplement (e.g. Eurail) have to pay the reservation fee only. Higher supplements and reservation fees apply at peak times (Friday and Sunday afternoons), and if purchased on day of travel. For **domestic** journeys on **international** *EC/IC/RJ/EN* trains, a supplement is required (and seat reservation is compulsory where shown as 🅁 in tables). For **international** journeys on these trains the supplement does not apply but seat reservation is possible (and is **compulsory** where shown in the tables). If a seat reservation or supplement is not paid in advance, an additional supplement of 500 HUF must be paid on the train.

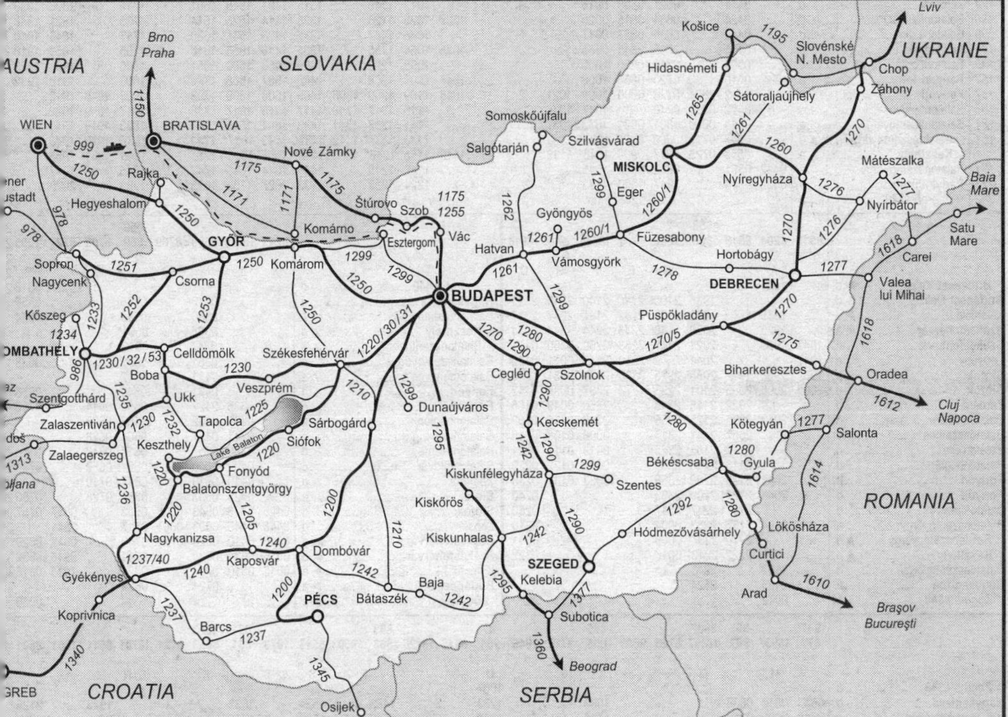

BUDAPEST - DOMBÓVÁR - PÉCS 1200

	IC 800 🅁	2 ◇	IC 802 🅁	IC 812 🅁	IC 804 🅁	2 ◇	IC 814 🅁	IC 204 ⊖ R	2 ◇	IC 806 🅁	IC 816 🅁	IC 828 2🅁 n	2 ◇	IC 808 🅁	IC 818 🅁
Budapest Keleti ..... d.	0545	...	0745	0945	1145	...	1345	1445	...	1545	1645	1645	...	1745	1945
Budapest Déli .... d.	|	0655	|	|	|	1255	|	|	1455	|	|	|	1655	|	|
Kelenföld .... d.	0559	0702	0759	0959	1159	1302	1359	1459	1502	1559	1659	1659	1702	1759	1959
Sárbogárd .... d.	0659	0826	0859	1059	1259	1426	1459	|	1626	1659	|	|	1826	1859	2059
Dombóvár .... a.	0749	0942	0949	1149	1349	1542	1549	1655	1742	1749	1855	1855	1944	1949	2149
Dombóvár .... d.	0753	*1005*	0953	1153	1353	*1605*	1553	...	*1805*	1753	1909	...	*2005*	1953	2153
Szentlörinc .... d.	0826	*1046*	1026	1226	1426	*1646*	1626	...	*1846*	1826	1942	...	*2046*	2026	2226
Pécs .... a.	0840	*1102*	1040	1240	1440	*1702*	1640	...	*1902*	1840	1956	...	*2102*	2040	2240

	IC 809 🅁	IC 819 🅁	IC 829 2🅁 n	IC 807 🅁	2 ◇	IC 817 🅁	2 ◇	IC 805 🅁	IC 815 🅁	IC 803 🅁	IC 801 🅁	2 ◇	IC 205 ⊖ R	IC 811 🅁	2 ◇	2
.... d.	0514	0602	...	0714	*0646*	0914	*0847*	1114	1314	1514	1714	*1647*	...	1914	*1847*	2047
tlörinc .... d.	0528	0619	...	0728	*0707*	0928	*0907*	1128	1328	1528	1728	*1707*	...	1928	*1907*	2107
bóvár .... a.	0601	0648	...	0801	*0750*	1001	*0950*	1201	1401	1601	1801	*1750*	...	2001	*1954*	2153
bóvár .... d.	0605	0658	0658	0805	0810	1005	1010	1205	1405	1605	1805	1810	1858	2005	2010	...
ogárd .... d.	0659	|	|	0859	0927	1059	1127	1259	1459	1659	1859	1927	|	2059	2127	...
föld .... a.	0758	0858	0858	0958	1054	1158	1254	1358	1558	1758	1958	2054	2058	2158	2254	...
pest Déli .... a.	|	|	|	|	1104	|	1304	|	|	|	|	2104	|	|	2304	...
pest Keleti ...... a.	0814	0914	0914	1014	...	1214	...	1414	1614	1814	2014	...	2114	2214	...	...

RIPPL-RÓNAI – 🚃12 and ✕ Budapest - Zagreb and v.v.
To/from Nagykanizsa (Table **1240**).
Budapest Déli - Kelenföld: *4 km.*

⊖ – 🅁 for domestic journeys within Hungary.
◇ – Local trains run in similar pattern every 2 hours.

FONYÓD - PÉCS 1205

km	*2nd class*	8807 c	8873 K	8803 P	
	Tapolca **1232** ..... d.	0830	1718	1718	...
	Keszthely **1220** ... d.	0914	1757	1757	...
0	**Fonyód** .... ▶ d.	1013	1850	1850	2128
53	Kaposvár .... ▶ a.	1132	2008	2008	2252
82	Dombóvár alsó ...... d.	...	...	2053	...
129	Szentlörinc .... d.	...	...	2127	...
148	**Pécs** .... a.	...	...	2141	...

	8872 K	8802 P		8806 c	
Pécs .... d.	...	0719	...	...	...
Szentlörinc .... d.	...	0733	...	...	...
Dombóvár alsó .... d.	...	0814	...	...	...
Kaposvár .... ▶ d.	0857	0857	1320	1708	1852
Fonyód .... ▶ a.	1012	1012	1443	1840	2022
Keszthely **1220** .... a.	1116	1116	...	1931	...
Tapolca **1232** ...... a.	1148	1148	...	2005	...

K – Ⓐ to Apr. 29/from Sept. 19.
N – Ⓐ (daily June 18 - Aug. 28).
P – Ⓒ (daily Apr. 30 - Sept. 18).
c – From/to Celldömölk or Szombathely (Table **1232**).
▶ – **Additional trains** Journey 80-90 minutes, *53* km. Fonyód-Kaposvár: 0330⚒, 0526, 0723, 1150, 1306 **N**, 1511, 1703. Kaposvár-Fonyód: 0336, 0545, 0738, 1016 **N**, 1515, 2255Ⓑ.

BUDAPEST - SÁRBOGÁRD - SZEKSZÁRD - BAJA 1210

class (except *Ex* trains)

	8320	IR 8300 ⚒	IR 8302	IR 8304 ⚒	Ⓐ	IR 8306	Ex 1836 🅁F	IR 18396 ⑤⑦	Ex 838 🅁	IR 8308	8318
Budapest Keleti ▷ d.	...	...	...	...	...	...	1515	...	1715	...	...
Kelenföld .... ▷ d.	...	...	...	...	...	...	1529	...	1729	...	...
Sárbogárd .... ▷ d.	0544	0702	0902	1102	...	1502	|	1702	|	1902	2102
Szekszárd .... a.	0658	0757	0957	1157	1422	1557	1715	1757	1915	1957	2205
Bátaszék .... **1242** a.	0724	0818	1018	1218	1441	1618	1732	1818	1932	2018	2249
Baja .... **1242** a.	*0753*	0838	1038	1239	1503	1639**r**	1751	1837	1951	2037	2311

	8319 ⚒	Ex 839 🅁	IR 8307	IR 8397 ⚒	IR 8305	IR 18393 ⑤⑦	8313 P	Ex 1833 🅁N	IR 8303	IR 8301
Baja .... **1242** d.	0425	0604	0712	0913	1312	1511	1508	1601	1712	1912
Bátaszék .... **1242** d.	0445	0620	0734	0934	1334	1534	1533	1620	1734	1934
Szekszárd .... d.	0545	0637	0759	0959	1357	1559	1620	1637	1759	1959
Sárbogárd .... ▷ a.	0649	|	0854	1054	1454	1654	1733	|	1854	2054
Kelenföld .... ▷ a.	...	0828	...	...	...	...	...	1833	...	...
Budapest Keleti ▷ a.	...	0844	...	...	...	...	...	1849	...	...

⑤ (not Dec. 18, 25, Jan. 1, June 17 - Aug. 26).
⑦ (not Dec. 20, 27, June 19 - Aug. 28).
①-④ except holidays.

r – 1652 on dates in note **N**.
▷ – For connections see Table **1200**.

Sárbogárd - Székesfehérvár *39 km* Journey 54 mins.
From Sárbogárd 0903, 1503. From Székesfehérvár 0800, 1400.
Operated by 🚌 *until further notice.*

1220 BUDAPEST - SIÓFOK - FONYÓD - KESZTHELY / NAGYKANIZSA

2nd class (*IC* also

Service Apr. 29 - June 10 (by 🚌 Siófok - Balatonszemes and v.v.)

km						*IC*	850	8872					852		854		844			856	8806		
		8540	8530	8612	8510	200	860	8802	8722	18502	1862	18502	862	8624	864	8514	874	8524	8724	866	18806	8506	18706
						⊖																	
		Ⓐ	b			C		K	Y	Z	©T	Z		Ⓐ				J	Ⓐ		Q		⑤R
•	**Budapest** Keleti ▶ d.	...	...	...	...	...	...	...	...	...	...	...	...	...	...	...	...	...	...	...	...	...	...
0	**Budapest** Déli ▶ d.	...	...	...	0405	0605	0735	...	...	0800	0835	...	0935	...	1135	...	1335	...	...	1535	...	1600	1645
4	Kelenföld ⊡ ▶ d.	...	...	...	0412	0612	0742	...	*0742*	0807	0842	...	0942	...	1142	*1142*	1342	...	*1442*	1542	...	1607	1652
67	**Székesfehérvár** ▶ a.	...	...	...	0509	0703	0820	...	*0840*	0845	0955	...	1020	...	1220	*1240*	1420	...	*1540*	1620	...	1645	1733
67	**Székesfehérvár** d.	...	...	...	0511	0704	0821	...	0850	0850	0957	...	1021	...	1221	1247	1421	1447	1547	1621	...	1647	1745
95	Lepsény d.	...	...	...	0533	|	0841	...	0917	0917	|	←	1041	...	1241	1317	1441	1517	1612	1641	...	1717	|
115	**Siófok** a.	...	...	...	0557	0745	0855	...	0937	0936	|	0936	1055	...	1255	1337	1455	1537	1632	1655	...	1737	1818
115	**Siófok** d.	...	0354	...	0604	0751	0901	...	...	0955	|	0955	1101	...	1301	1344	1501	1544	...	1701	...	1751	1824
124	Zamárdi d.	...	0411	...	0621	0805	0915	...	...	→	|	1012	1115	...	1315	1401	1515	1601	...	1715	...	1808	1838
130	Balatonföldvár d.	...	0424	...	0634	0815	0925	...	...	...	1009	1025	1125	...	1325	1414	1525	1614	...	1725	...	1821	1848
139	Balatonszemes d.	...	0446	...	0656	0837	0947	...	...	...	|	1046	1147	...	1347	1436	1547	1636	...	1747	...	1843	1910
146	Balatonlelle d.	...	0455	...	0705	0845	0955	...	...	...	1035	1054	1155	...	1355	1446	1555	1646	...	1755	...	1853	1918
149	Balatonboglár d.	...	0500	...	0710	0850	1000	...	...	...	|	1059	1200	...	1400	1458	1600	1651	...	1800	...	1901	1923
157	**Fonyód** a.	...	0510	...	0720	0858	1008	...	...	...	1047	1108	1208	...	1408	1507	1608	1700	...	1808	...	1910	1932
157	**Fonyód** d.	...	0512	0621	0728	0900	1009	1021	...	...	1048	1109	1209	1308	1409	1508	1609	1708	...	1809	1848	1912	...
165	Balatonfenyves d.	...	0522	0631	0740	|	1017	1036	...	...	|	1119	1217	1318	1417	1518	1617	1718	...	1817	1859	1922	...
181	Balatonszentgyörgy a.	...	0543	0659	0801	0921	1033	1057	...	...	|	1141	1233	1341	1433	1541	1633	1741	...	1833	1919	1941	...
181	Balatonszentgyörgy ▲ d.	...	*0547*	0713	*0805*	*0926*	1037*	1104	...	...	|	*1143*	1237*	1342	1437*	*1543*	1637*	*1743*	...	1837*	1920	*1943*	...
	Keszthely ▲ a.	...	*0559*	0725	*0817*	*0938*	1048*	1116	...	...	1119	*1155*	1248*	1353	1448*	*1555*	1648*	*1755*	...	1848*	1931	*1955*	...
181	Balatonszentgyörgy d.	0442	0551	...	0802	0924	1045	...	...	...	...	1142	1245	...	1445	1544	1645	1742	...	1845	...	1942	...
221	**Nagykanizsa** a.	0525	0648	...	0847	1000	1133	...	...	...	...	1224	1333	...	1533	1627	1733	1825	...	1923	...	2028	...
352	*Zagreb* **1340** a.	...	...	...	...	1248	...	...	...	...	...	...	...	...	...	...	...	...	...	...	...	...	...

				858					
	8518	1204	8518	868	1868		18748	18718	18618
		A			G	E	F	U	U
Budapest Keleti ▶ d.	...	1823	...	...	...	...	...	...	...
Budapest Déli ▶ d.	...	|	...	1935	2100	*2140*	2140	2240	2340
Kelenföld ⊡ ▶ d.	...	1839	...	1942	2107	*2147*	2147	2247	2347
Székesfehérvár ▶ a.	...	1923	...	2020	2146	*2245*	2244	2344	0044
Székesfehérvár d.	1847	1925	...	2021	2147	2253	2250	2350	0101
Lepsény d.	1917	|	←	2041	|	2319	2315	0011	0120
Siófok a.	1937	1958	1937	2055	2225	2339	2335	0031	0140
Siófok d.	2005	2000	2005	2101	2231	...	2337	0036	0142
Zamárdi d.	→	|	2022	2115	2245	...	2350	0049	0155
Balatonföldvár d.	...	2012	2035	2125	2255	...	2358	0056	0202
Balatonszemes d.	...	|	2057	2147	2317	...	0008	0108	0215
Balatonlelle d.	...	|	2111	2155	2325	...	0018	0117	0224
Balatonboglár d.	...	|	2116	2200	2330	...	0023	0122	0229
Fonyód a.	...	2041	2125	2208	2338	...	0033	0131	0238
Fonyód d.	...	2043	2127	2209	2339	...	...	...	0240
Balatonfenyves d.	...	|	2137	2217	2347	...	...	...	0250
Balatonszentgyörgy a.	...	2104	2157	2233	0004	...	...	...	0310
Balatonszentgyörgy ▲ d.	...	|	*2210*	2237*	0005	...	...	...	0311
Keszthely ▲ a.	...	|	*2222*	2248*	0016	...	...	...	0322
Balatonszentgyörgy d.	...	2109	...	2245	...	...	...	...	...
Nagykanizsa a.	...	2153	...	2324	...	...	...	...	...
Zagreb **1340** a.	...	0012	...	...	...	...	...	...	...

					859			
	8749	18729	8509	8769	869	8759	8727	1205
	X	L		Ⓐ		Ⓐ		B
Zagreb **1340** d.	...	...	...	...	...	...	...	0318
Nagykanizsa d.	...	...	0310	...	0433	...	...	0556
Balatonszentgyörgy a.	...	...	0350	...	0510	...	...	0634
Keszthely ▲ d.	...	...	*0335*	...	0501*	...	...	|
Balatonszentgyörgy ▲ a.	...	...	*0347*	...	0512*	...	...	|
Balatonszentgyörgy d.	...	...	0351	...	0522	...	...	0638
Balatonfenyves d.	...	...	0411	...	0542	...	...	|
Fonyód a.	...	...	0421	...	0549	...	...	0658
Fonyód d.	...	0326	0422	...	0550	0614	...	0700
Balatonboglár d.	...	0336	0432	...	0559	0623	...	|
Balatonlelle d.	...	0341	0437	...	0604	0628	...	|
Balatonszemes d.	...	0350	0451	...	0617	0642	...	|
Balatonföldvár d.	...	0402	0506	...	0631	0657	...	0744
Zamárdi d.	...	0410	0519	...	0641	0710	...	|
Siófok a.	...	0423	0537	...	0657	0728	...	0756
Siófok d.	0425	0425	0543	0628	0703	...	0817	0757
Lepsény d.	0445	0445	0603	0651	0717	...	0841	|
Székesfehérvár a.	0510	0510	0629	0721	0740	...	0912	0829
Székesfehérvár ▶ d.	0516	0524	0630	...	0741	...	*0916*	0832
Kelenföld ⊡ ▶ a.	0615	0610	0714	...	0821	...	*1015*	0916
Budapest Déli ▶ a.	...	...	0724	...	0829	...	...	|
Budapest Keleti ▶ a.	...	...	...	...	...	...	...	0936

	847		857	8807			855			*IC*			853				851	8873					
	877	18537	867	18807	8725	9657	865	8715	9645	201	8615	18725	863	18503	8513	1873	861	8803	8721	18701	8511	1861	8531
										⊖													
		H		Q				Ⓐ		D				Z	S	©T		K		⑦R		G	
Zagreb **1340** d.	...	...	...	...	...	...	...	...	...	1007	...	...	...	...	...	...	...	...	...	...	...	...	...
Nagykanizsa d.	0633	0812	0833	...	...	...	1033	...	...	1233	...	...	1433	1514	1524	...	1633	...	...	...	1925	...	2126
Balatonszentgyörgy a.	0710	0900	0910	...	...	...	1110	...	...	1310	...	...	1510	1607	1607	...	1710	...	...	...	2008	...	2207
Keszthely ▲ d.	0701*	...	0901*	0914	...	0957	1052*	...	1157	1301*	1357	...	1501*	*1557*	*1557*	1658	1701*	1757	...	...	*1957*	2025	*2155*
Balatonszentgyörgy ▲ a.	0712*	...	0912*	0925	...	1009	1103*	...	1209	1312*	1409	...	1512*	*1609*	*1609*	1709	1712*	1808	...	...	*2009*	2036	*2207*
Balatonszentgyörgy d.	0722	...	0922	0926	...	...	1122	...	...	1322	1412	...	1522	1614	1627	1710	1722	1812	...	...	2014	2037	2213
Balatonfenyves d.	0740	...	0940	0950	...	...	1140	...	...	1340	1437	...	1540	1636	1646	|	1740	1836	...	...	2036	2056	2236
Fonyód a.	0747	...	0947	1001	...	...	1147	...	...	1347	1447	...	1547	1647	1657	1737	1747	1847	...	...	2047	2103	2245
Fonyód d.	0748	...	0948	...	...	...	1148	...	...	1348	1448	...	1548	1701	1701	1741	1748	...	...	1853	2048	2105	2246
Balatonboglár d.	0759	...	0959	...	...	...	1159	...	...	1359	1458	...	1559	1711	1711	1750	1759	...	...	1902	2058	2116	2255
Balatonlelle d.	0804	...	1004	...	...	...	1204	...	...	1404	1503	...	1604	1716	1716	1755	1804	...	...	1907	2103	2121	2300
Balatonszemes d.	0817	...	1017	...	...	...	1217	...	...	1417	1519	...	1617	1736	1731	|	1817	...	...	1924	2119	2134	2314
Balatonföldvár d.	0831	...	1031	...	...	...	1231	...	...	1431	1534	...	1631	1751	1743	1812	1831	...	...	1939	2134	2148	2329
Zamárdi d.	0841	...	1041	...	...	...	1241	...	...	1441	1547	...	1641	1804	1750	|	1841	...	...	1952	2147	2158	2342
Siófok a.	0857	...	1057	...	...	...	1257	...	...	1457	1605	...	1657	1822	1802	1829	1857	...	...	2010	2205	2214	2400
Siófok d.	0903	...	1103	...	1217	...	1303	1417	...	1503	...	1617	1703	1828	...	1833	1903	...	2017	2017	2211	2235	...
Lepsény d.	0917	...	1117	...	1241	...	1317	1441	...	1517	...	1641	1717	1853	...	|	1917	...	2040	2041	2231	|	...
Székesfehérvár a.	0940	...	1140	...	1312	...	1340	1512	...	1540	...	1712	1740	1921	...	1907	1940	...	2105	2108	2252	2319	...
Székesfehérvár ▶ d.	0941	...	1141	...	*1316*	...	1341	*1516*	...	1541	...	*1716*	1741	1923	...	1915	1941	...	...	2116	2253	2320	...
Kelenföld ⊡ ▶ a.	1021	...	1221	...	*1415*	...	1421	*1615*	...	1621	...	*1815*	1821	2006	...	1956	2021	...	...	2201	2351	2400	...
Budapest Déli ▶ a.	1029	...	1229	...	...	...	1429	...	...	1629	...	...	1829	2014	...	2009	2029	...	...	2209	2359	0009	...
Budapest Keleti ▶ a.	...	...	...	...	...	...	...	...	...	...	...	...	...	...	...	...	...	...	...	...	...	...	...

A – ADRIA – ②⑤⑦ June 17 - Aug. 26. 🛏 1, 2 cl., ▬ 2 cl., 🚃2 Budapest - Zagreb - Split; 🚃2 Budapest - Zagreb. Conveys on ②⑤ June 17 - Aug. 26 🛏 1, 2 cl. Praha (*EC* **277**) - Budapest - Zagreb - Split.

B – ADRIA – ①③⑥ June 18 - Aug. 27 from Split (next day from Zagreb). 🛏 1, 2 cl., ▬ 2 cl., 🚃2 Split - Zagreb - Budapest; 🚃2 Zagreb - Budapest. Conveys on ③⑥ June 18 - Aug. 27 (from Split) 🛏 1, 2 cl. Split - Budapest (*EC* **276**) - Praha.

C – AGRAM – 🚃12 ✕ Budapest - Gyekenyes - Zagreb.

D – AGRAM – 🚃12 ✕ Zagreb - Gyekenyes - Budapest; 🚃12 Keszthely - Budapest.

E – Dec. 13 - June 16, Aug. 29 - Dec. 10.

F – June 17 - Aug. 28.

G – ⑤⑥⑦ Apr. 29 - June 17 (also May 16; not May 15).

H – ⑥⑦ Apr. 30 - June 17 (also May 16; not May 15).

J – Ⓑ to Apr. 29; daily Apr. 30 - June 17; Ⓑ from Aug. 29.

K – Kaposvár - Fonyód - Keszthely - Tapolca and v.v. (Table **1205**). From / to Pécs on © and daily Apr. 30 - Sept. 18.

L – June 18 - Aug. 29.

Q – 🚃2 Kaposvár - Fonyód - Keszthely - Tapolca - Celldömölk (- Szombathely Apr. 30 - Aug. 28) and v.v. (Table **1205**).

R – Apr. 29 - June 17, Aug. 29 - Sept. 18.

S – Ⓐ to Apr. 29; Ⓐ from Aug. 29.

T – Aug. 29 - Sept. 18.

U – ④⑤⑥ June 17 - Aug. 28.

X – Dec. 13 - June 17, Aug. 30 - Dec. 10.

Y – Not dates in note **Z**.

Z – ⑥⑦ Apr. 2 - 24; daily Apr. 30 - June 17; ⑥⑦ Sept. 3 - Oct. 29 (also Nov. 1; not Oct

b – Starts from Fonyód Dec. 21 - Jan. 3.

d – Terminates at Fonyód Dec. 20 - Jan. 2.

⊖ – Ⓡ for domestic journeys within Hungary.

⊡ – Connection with metro line 4 (see city plan page 29).

▶ – See also Tables **1225** and **1230**.

▲ – See also Table **1232**. *Italic* times: change at Balatonszentgyörgy.

• – Keleti - Kelenföld: *13 km.*

* – Portion is detached / attached at Balatonszentgyörgy.

Engineering work Apr. 29 - June 10

Service is by 🚌 Siófok - Balatonszemes and v.v. in the timings shown above. Timings are subject to alteration.

Summer timings June 18 - Aug. 28 were not available by press date and will be shown in the July edition

BUDAPEST - SZÉKESFEHÉRVÁR - BALATONFÜRED - TAPOLCA 1225

class

	9740 Ⓐ	9710	8510	9720	900	9712	972 ◇	246	9722	1974 D◇	904	9714	974 H◇	9004	9724	9006	9716	1976 ⑤F	906	9726	978 ◇	908	9718	9738
Budapest Déli ▶ d.	...	...	0405	...	0630	...	0745	0830	...	0945	1030	...	1145	1230	...	1430	...	1545	1630	...	1745	1830	...	*2140*
Kelenföld ▶ d.	...	...	0412	...	0637	...	0751	0837	...	0951	1037	...	1151	1237	...	1437	...	1551	1637	...	1751	1837	...	*2147*
Székesfehérvár ▶ a.	...	...	0509	...	0715	...	|	0915	...	|	1115	...	|	1315	...	1515	...	|	1715	...	|	1915	...	*2244*
Székesfehérvár d.	...	0430r	...	0532	...	0722	|	...	0922	|	...	1122	|	...	1322	...	1522	|	...	1722	|	...	1922	2250
Balatonkenese d.	...	0513r	...	0621	...	0810	0929	...	1010	1129	...	1210	1329	...	1410	...	1610	1729	...	1810	1929	...	2010	2335
Balalatonalmádi d.	...	0527r	...	0635	...	0827	0943	...	1027	1143	...	1227	1343	...	1427	...	1627	1743	...	1827	1943	...	2027	2348
Alsóörs d.	...	0534r	...	0642	...	0834	0949	...	1034	1149	...	1234	1349	...	1434	...	1634	1749	...	1834	1949	...	2034	2355
Balatonfüred d.	0400	0546	...	0654	...	0848	1000	...	1048	1200	...	1248	1400	...	1448	...	1648	1800	...	1848	2000	...	2048	0006
Révfülöp d.	0437	0627	...	0730	...	0930	1027	...	1130	1227	...	1330	1427	...	1530	...	1730	1827	...	1930	2027	...	2125	...
Badacsonytomaj d.	0455	0642	...	0745	...	0945	1038	...	1145	1238	...	1345	1438	...	1545	...	1745	1838	...	1945	2038	...	2140	...
Badacsony d.	0458	0645	...	0748	...	0948	1041	...	1148	1241	...	1348	1441	...	1548	...	1748	1841	...	1948	2041	...	2143	...
Tapolca a.	0516	0703	...	0810	...	1010	1057	...	1210	1255	...	1410	1457	...	1610	...	1810	1855	...	2005	2057	...	2200	...

	9739	9719	9729	979 ◇	9729	909	9717	907	9727	905	9715	9005	975 H	9725	247	1973 ⑦G	9713	903	971	9723	901	1971 E	9711 Ⓑ	9711 ⑥	8511
ca d.	...	0435	0530	0558	...	...	0750	...	0950	...	1150	...	1301	1350	...	1503	1550	...	1701	1750	...	1903	2015	2015	...
sony d.	...	0452	0547	0613	...	...	0807	...	1007	...	1207	...	1316	1407	...	1516	1607	...	1716	1807	...	1916	2032	2032	...
sonytomaj d.	...	0455	0550	0616	...	...	0810	...	1010	...	1210	...	1319	1410	...	1519	1610	...	1719	1810	...	1919	2038	2038	...
öp d.	...	0510	0605	0627	...	...	0827	...	1027	...	1227	...	1330	1427	...	1530	1627	...	1730	1827	...	1930	2052	2052	...
onfüred d.	0345	0550	0641	0655	←	...	0908	...	1108	...	1308	...	1359	1508	...	1559	1708	...	1759	1908	...	1959	2129	2125	...
s d.	0356	0601	→	0703	0708	...	0919	...	1119	...	1319	...	1407	1519	...	1607	1719	...	1807	1919	...	2007	2139	...	...
tonalmádi d.	0403	0608	...	0709	0727	...	0927	...	1127	...	1327	...	1413	1527	...	1613	1727	...	1813	1927	...	2013	2147	...	...
nkenese d.	0416	0621	...	0723	0743	...	0943	...	1143	...	1343	...	1427	1543	...	1627	1743	...	1827	1943	...	2027	2200	...	...
sfehérvár a.	0506	0708	...	|	0834	...	1034	...	1234	...	1434	...	|	1634	...	|	1834	...	|	2034	...	|	2244	...	...
sfehérvár ▶ d.	*0518*	*0718*	...	|	...	0842	...	1042	...	1242	...	1442	|	...	1642	|	...	1842	|	...	2042	|	...	...	2248
öld ▶ a.	*0615*	*0815*	...	0906	...	0921	...	1121	...	1321	...	1521	1605	...	1721	1804	...	1921	2020	...	2121	2205	...	...	2345
pest Déli ▶ a.	...	...	...	0914	...	0929	...	1129	...	1329	...	1529	1614	...	1729	1814	...	1929	2044	...	2129	2214	...	...	2354

⑥ Apr. 30 - June 11; ⑥ Sept. 3-24.
⑦ May 1 - June 12; ⑦ Sept. 4-25.
⑤ (not Dec. 18-Jan. 1, June 24 - Aug. 26).
⑦ (not Dec. 20, 27, June 19 - Aug. 28).

H – Mar. 25 - Nov. 1.
r – ⚒ only.
▶ – See also Tables **1220** and **1230**.
◇ – Subject to alteration from May 10.

Timings may vary due to engineering work. Summer timings June 18 - Aug. 28 were not available by press date and will be shown in the July edition

BUDAPEST - SZÉKESFEHÉRVÁR - ZALAEGERSZEG and SZOMBATHELY 1230

class (*IC* also 1st)

For faster trains Budapest - Szombathely (via Györ) see Table **1250**. The section of line between Szombathely and Porpác (17 km) is operated by GySEV.

	9510	900	900 9590	246 C	246 902	962	904	904 9594	9524	9004	9004 9504	9516	964 Ⓑ	9006	9006 9596	9526	966 Ⓑ	906	906 956	*IC* 958 🅁	9518	908	968	9008
Budapest Déli ▶ d.	...	0630	0630	0830	0830	0930	1030	1030	...	1230	1230	...	1330	1430	1430	...	1530	1630	1630	1730	...	1830	1930	2030
Kelenföld ▶ d.	...	0637	0637	0837	0837	0937	1037	1037	...	1237	1237	...	1337	1437	1437	...	1537	1637	1637	1737	...	1837	1937	2037
Székesfehérvár ▶ d.	...	0716	0716	0916	0916	1016	1116	1116	...	1316	1316	...	1416	1516	1516	...	1616	1716	1716	1816	...	1916	2016	2116
Várpalota d.	...	0733	0733	0933	0933	1036	1133	1133	...	1333	1333	...	1436	1533	1533	...	1636	1733	1733	|	...	1933	2036	2133
Veszprém d.	...	0802	0802	1002	1002	1057	1202	1202	...	1402	1402	...	1510	1602	1602	...	1700	1802	1802	1855	...	2002	2057	2157
Ajka d.	...	0833	0833	1033	1033	▬	1233	1233	...	1433	1433	...	...	1633	1633	...	...	1833	1833	1925	...	2033	▬	2231
Celldömölk d.	0606	|	|	|	|	1206	|	|	1401	|	|	1606	...	|	|	1801	...	|	|	|	2006	|	2206	|
Boba a.	0614	0900	0900	1100	1100	1214	1300	1300	1409	1500	1500	1614	...	1700	1700	1809	...	1900	1900	|	2014	2106	2214	2302
Boba d.	0615	0905	0909	1109	1105	1215	1305	1309	1410	1505	1509	1615	...	1705	1709	1810	...	1905	1909	|	2015	2108	2215	2306
Ukk d.	0635	|	0929	1124	|	1235	|	1329	1435	|	1524	1635	...	|	1729r	1835	...	|	1924	2001	2035	|	2235	|
Zalaszentiván a.	0705	|	0959	1145	|	1305	|	1359	1505	|	1545	1705	...	|	1759r	1905	...	|	1945	2023	2105	|	2305	|
Zalaegerszeg a.	0714	|	1012	1155	|	1314	|	1412	1514	|	1555	1714	...	|	1812	1914	...	|	1955	2032	2114	|	2314	|
Celldömölk ▷ d.	...	0914	...	...	1114	...	1314	...	...	1514	...	...	...	1714	...	...	...	1914	...	...	...	2120	...	2315
Szombathely ▷ a.	...	0947	...	...	1147	...	1347	...	...	1547	...	...	...	1747	...	...	...	1947	...	...	...	2159	...	...

	9009	*IC* 959 🅁	909	9517	907	957 907	905	9597 905	9005	9505 9005	9517	247 C	9003 247	9063 Ⓑ	9513	903	953 903	9523	*IC* 1951 🅁N	961 Ⓑ	901	9591 901	9511	9021	9521
bathely ▷ d.	...	...	0605	...	0805	...	1005	...	1205	...	...	...	1403	...	...	1605	...	...	...	...	1805	...	...	2003	...
ömölk ▷ d.	0440	...	0645	...	0843	...	1043	...	1243	...	...	...	1444	...	...	1643	...	...	...	...	1843	...	...	2046	...
aegerszeg d.	|	0527	|	0646	|	0804	|	0945	|	1204	1246	1345	|	...	1446	|	1604	1646	1716	...	|	1745	1846	|	2046
aszentiván d.	|	0535	|	0654	|	0812	|	1002	|	1212	1254	1402	|	...	1454	|	1612	1654	|	...	|	1802	1854	|	2054
(d.	|	0601	|	0723	|	0835	|	1032	|	1235	1328	1432	|	...	1523	|	1635	1728	|	...	|	1832	1923	|	2123
a.	0448	|	0653	0740	0851	0851	1051	1051	1251	1251	1345	1451	1452	...	1540	1651	1651	1745	|	...	1851	1851	1940	2055	2140
d.	0449	|	0655	0741	0901	0901	1101	1101	1301	1301	1346	1501	1501	...	1541	1701	1701	1746	|	...	1901	1901	1941	2056	2141
ldömölk a.	|	|	|	0752	|	|	|	|	|	|	1357	|	|	...	1552	|	|	1757	|	...	|	|	1952	|	2152
d.	0524	0635	0726	▬	0926	0926	1126	1126	1326	1326	▬	1526	1526	...	...	1726	1726	...	1818	...	1926	1926	...	2143	...
prém d.	0602	0705	0802	0900	1002	1002	1202	1202	1402	1402	1500	1602	1602	1700	...	1802	1802	...	1856	1900	2002	2002	...	2224	...
lota d.	0624	|	0824	0921	1024	1024	1224	1224	1424	1424	1521	1624	1624	1721	...	1824	1824	...	|	1921	2024	2024	...	...	...
esfehérvár ▶ d.	0642	0742	0842	0942	1042	1042	1242	1242	1442	1442	1542	1642	1642	1742	...	1842	1842	...	1932	1942	2042	2042	...	...	...
föld ▶ a.	0722	0822	0922	1022	1122	1122	1322	1322	1522	1522	1622	1722	1722	1822	...	1922	1922	...	2012	2022	2122	2122	...	...	...
pest Déli ▶ a.	0729	0829	0929	1029	1129	1129	1329	1329	1529	1529	1629	1729	1729	1829	...	1929	1929	...	2019	2029	2129	2129	...	...	...

CITTADELLA – 🚃12 ✕ Budapest - Zalaegerszeg - Hodoš - Ljubljana and v.v.; 🚃2 Budapest - Ljubljana - Koper and v.v.
⑦ (not Dec. 20, 27, June 19 - Aug. 28).

r – On ⑦**N** Ukk d. 1724, Zalaszentiván a. 1746.
▶ – See also Tables **1220** and **1225**.
▷ – See also Tables **1232** and **1250**.

Most arrivals at Budapest are 5 minutes later until May 9.

SZOMBATHELY - CELLDÖMÖLK - UKK - TAPOLCA - KESZTHELY 1232

class

Service Apr. 29 - June 10

	9639	9619		9637	9629	8807 k		9617	865	19807 E		9625		9615	9613	9603		9623	8803 n	9611		9621	
Szombathely 1230 d.	...	...	...	...	...	0643r	...	...	...	0925	...	...	...	...	...	...	...	...	...	...	...	...	...
Celldömölk 1230 d.	...	*0453*	...	...	*0606*	0730	...	...	...	1000	...	...	...	...	*1401*	1450	...	*1606*	...	*1801*	...	*2006*	...
Boba 1230 d.	...	*0502*	...	...	*0615*	0741	...	*0909*	...	|	...	...	...	*1309*	*1410*	1514	...	*1615*	...	*1810*	...	*2015*	...
Ukk 1230 d.	...	0522	...	...	0636	0800	...	0936	...	|	...	...	...	1336	1436	1538	...	1636	...	1836	...	2036	...
Sümeg d.	...	0533	...	...	0647	0810	...	0947	...	1030	...	...	...	1347	1447	1549	...	1647	...	1847	...	2048	...
Tapolca a.	...	0555	...	...	0709	0828	...	1009	...	1048	...	...	...	1409	1509	1609	...	1709	...	1909	...	2109	...
Tapolca d.	0428	0556	...	0645	...	0830	...	1018	...	1050	...	1213	...	1428	1518	1613	...	...	1718	1919	...	2123	...
Keszthely a.	0459	0626	...	0716	...	0859	...	1049	...	1115	...	1246	...	1459	1549	1645	...	...	1749	1953	...	2154	...
Keszthely 1220 d.	*0501*	0627	...	...	...	0914	...	...	1052	...	...	*1301*	...	*1501*	1557	...	...	...	1757	1957	...	2155	...
B'tonszentgyörgy 1220 a.	*0512*	0639	...	...	...	0925	...	...	1103	...	...	*1312*	...	*1512*	1609	...	...	...	1808	2009	...	2207	...

	9610	9519	9630 Ⓐ	9630 Ⓒ	9620	9632	9612	8802 n	9604	9634	8624 Ⓐ	9624	864	9616	9656	9636	19804 E	9646		8806 k	9618	9618	9658	9658
szentgyörgy 1220 d.	...	...	...	...	0547	...	0839	1104	...	...	1342	...	1437	...	1543	...	...	1743	...	1920	1943	*2037*	2210	*2237*
thely 1220 a.	...	...	...	...	0559	...	0851	1116	...	...	1353	...	1448	...	1555	...	...	1755	...	1931	1955	*2048*	2222	*2248*
thely d.	...	...	0523	...	0605	0655	0905	1117	...	1227	...	1355	...	1506	...	1627	1647	1805	...	1935	...	2050	...	2250
lca a.	...	...	0553	...	0639	0727	0936	1148	...	1258	...	1426	...	1539	...	1658	1712	1836	...	2005	...	2121	...	2321
lca d.	0440	...	0600	0600	0640	...	0940	...	1200	...	...	1440	...	1540	...	...	1713	1840	...	2007	...	...	...	...
eg d.	0500	...	0621	0621	0708	...	1008	...	1221	...	...	1508	...	1608	...	...	1731	1908	...	2025	...	...	...	...
1230 a.	0512	0523	0633	0633	0720	...	1020	...	1233	...	...	1520	...	1620	...	...	|	1920	...	2033	...	...	...	...
1230 a.	...	0540	0652	0652	*0740*	...	*1051*	...	1259	...	...	*1540*	...	*1651*	...	...	|	*1940*	...	2051	...	...	...	...
ömölk 1230 a.	...	0552	0704	0704	*0752*	...	...	...	1319	...	...	*1552*	...	...	...	...	1801	*1952*	...	2107	...	...	...	...
bathely 1230 a.	...	...	...	...	...	...	...	...	...	...	...	...	...	...	...	...	1854	...	...	2143r	...	...	...	...

Ⓒ Apr. 30 - Sept. 25 (daily June 18 - Aug. 28).
To / from Kaposvár (Table **1205**).

n – To / from Kaposvár (train **8872/3**) or Pécs (train **8802/3**), Table **1205**.

r – Apr. 30 - Aug. 28 (train **18807/6**).
▷ – See also Table **1230**.

1233 SOPRON - SZOMBATHELY

Operated by GySEV. 2nd

km																							
		◇	◇	◇			P						◇	◇	Ⓐ◇	◇			Ⓐ				
0	**Sopron** d.	0407	0455	0549	0644	...	0810	0933	...	1109	1208	...	1343	1443	1543	1643	1757	...	1909	2011	...	2230	...
38	Bük d.	0440	0528	0630	0717	...	0836	1006	...	1141	1240	...	1416	1516	1616	1716	1830	...	1946	2043	...	2307	...
62	**Szombathely** a.	0500	0549	0654	0737	...	0851	1024	...	1200	1259	...	1434	1534	1634	1734	1851	...	2004	2103	...	2325	...

		◇		◇		◇						Ⓐ◇		◇		◇		Q	Ⓐ◇		◇		
Szombathely d.	0422	0508	0632	0714	...	0926	...	1139	1237	1331	1436	1536	...	1636	1710	1830	...	1910	1941	...	2108	2226	...
Bük d.	0441	0527	0652	0734	...	0944	...	1157	1255	1354	1454	1554	...	1654	1732	1848	...	1925	2000	...	2127	2244	...
Sopron a.	0517	0601	0728	0806	...	1017	...	1231	1328	1428	1528	1628	...	1728	1813	1928	...	1952	2035	...	2200	2317	...

P – To Pécs (Table **1237**). Runs 18 mins earlier May 17 - Aug. 15. **Q** – From Pécs (Table **1237**). Runs 8 - 12 mins later May 17 - Aug. 15. ◇ – To / from Szentgotthárd (Table

1234 SZOMBATHELY - KOSZEG

Operated by GySEV. 2nd

From **Szombathely**: 0506, 0606, 0706Ⓐ, 0806, 0906, 1006Ⓐ, 1106, 1206Ⓐ, 1335, 1430, 1522, 1614Ⓐ, 1706, 1806Ⓐ, 1906, 2106, 2236.

From **Köszeg**: 0432, 0532, 0632, 0732Ⓐ, 0832, 0932Ⓐ, 1032, 1132Ⓐ, 1232, 1401, 1456, 1548Ⓐ, 1640, 1732Ⓐ, 1832, 2032, 2208.

18 km, journey time 20 - 25 m

1235 SZOMBATHELY - ZALASZENTIVÁN - ZALAEGERSZEG

MÁV-START / GySEV. 2nd

km		8900						8902				8904								8906				
		△						△				△		Ⓐ					Ⓐ	△				
	Sopron **1233** d.	...	...	...	...	...	...	0810	...	...	...	...	...	...	...	...	...	...	...	...	...	...	...	...
0	**Szombathely** d.	0509	...	0612	...	0708	...	0908	...	1108	...	1308	...	1402	...	1432	...	1602	1638	1708	...	1800	1908	2230
24	Vasvár d.	0529	...	0638	...	0734	...	0929	...	1134	...	1329	...	1428	...	1458	...	1628	1704	1729	...	1829	1934	2256
49	Zalaszentiván a.	0552	...	0701	...	0757	...	0951	...	1157	...	1351	...	1451	...	1521	...	1651	1727	1751	...	1852	1957	2319
49	Zalaszentiván ▶ d.	...	0554	...	0706	...	0812	...	1004	...	1212	...	1404	...	1506	...	1546	1700	...	...	1804	1859	2004	2324
58	**Zalaegerszeg** ▶ a.	...	0603	...	0714	...	0821	...	1012	...	1221	...	1412	...	1514	...	1555	1708	...	...	1812	1908	2013	2333

								8907				8905								8903				8901
								△				△		Ⓐ						△				△
Zalaegerszeg ▶ d.	0348	0446	...	0541	0730	...	0945	...	1135	...	1345	...	1446	...	1535	...	...	1722	1745	...	...	1935	2135	...
Zalaszentiván ▶ a.	0357	0453	...	0550	0739	...	0954	...	1144	...	1354	...	1453	...	1544	...	...	1730	1754	...	...	1944	2144	...
Zalaszentiván d.	0402	...	0455	0602	...	0802	...	1002	...	1202	...	1402	...	1502	...	1602	...	1733	...	1802	...	2002	...	2202
Vasvár d.	0426	...	0519	0626	...	0826	...	1025	...	1226	...	1427	...	1530	...	1627	...	1800	...	1828	...	2026	...	2225
Szombathely a.	0451	...	0545	0653	...	0851	...	1045	...	1251	...	1452	...	1555	...	1700	...	1825	...	1848	...	2051	...	2250
Sopron **1233** a.	...	...	...	...	...	...	...	...	...	...	...	...	...	...	...	...	...	...	...	1952	...	...	...	...

△ – To / from Pécs (Tables **1236/7**).
▶ – See also Tables **1230** and **1236**.

May 17 - Aug. 15: *by 🚌 Szombathely - Zalaszentiván and v.v. in revised timings*

1236 ZALAEGERSZEG - ZALASZENTIVÁN - NAGYKANIZSA

2nd c

km			8900		8902		8904			8906	
					△						
	Szombathely **1235** d.	...	0509	...	0908	...	1308	...	...	1708	...
0	**Zalaegerszeg** ▶ d.	0541	|	0945	|	1345	|	1652	1745	|	...
9	Zalaszentiván ▶ a.	0550	0552	0954	0951	1354	1351	1700	1754	1751	...
9	Zalaszentiván d.	...	0600	...	1000	...	1400	1712	...	1800	...
61	**Nagykanizsa** a.	...	0651	...	1049	...	1449	1818	...	1849	...
	Pécs **1237** a.	...	0936	...	1336	...	1736	...	...	2147	...

		8907		8905		8903		8901
						▽		
Pécs **1237** d.	...	0615	...	1015	...	1415	...	1815
Nagykanizsa d.	0610	0908	...	1308	...	1708	...	2108
Zalaszentiván a.	0712	0957	...	1357	...	1757	...	2159
Zalaszentiván ▶ d.	0713	1002	1004	1402	1404	1802	1804	2202
Zalaegerszeg ▶ a.	0722	|	1012	|	1412	|	1812	|
Szombathely **1235** a.	...	1045	...	1452	...	1848	...	2250

△ – From Sopron (depart 0810). ▽ – To Sopron (arrive 1952). ▶ – See also Tables **1232** and **1235**. ***Subject to alteration May 17 - Aug. 15***

1237 NAGYKANIZSA - PÉCS

2nd c

km		8910	8900	8954	8902	8914	8904	18958	8906	
				Ⓐ	△			⑦		
	Szombathely **1235** d.	...	0509r	...	0908r	...	1308r	...	1708r	...
0	**Nagykanizsa** **1240** d.	0353	0653	...	1052	...	1452	...	1852	...
29	Gyékényes **1240** d.	0437	0720	...	1120	1255	1520	...	1920	...
84	Barcs d.	0611	0826	1012	1226	1412	1626	1812	2026	...
114	Szigetvár d.	0658	0857	1056	1257	1455	1657	1855	2110	...
129	Szentlörinc d.	0734	0913	1115	1313	1529	1713	1914	2130	...
148	**Pécs** a.	0754	0936	1138	1336	1549	1736	1938	2147	...

	8907	8905	8955	8903	8953	8913	8901	8961
				▽				
Pécs d.	0615	1015	1212	1415	1453	1612	1815	2012
Szentlörinc d.	0638	1038	1237	1438	1518	1637	1838	2050
Szigetvár d.	0654	1054	1258	1454	1536	1658	1854	2109
Barcs d.	0725	1125	1337	1525	1615	1738	1925	2148
Gyékényes **1240** a.	0838	1238	...	1638	...	1843	2038	...
Nagykanizsa **1240** a.	0906	1306	...	1706	...	1936	2106	...
Szombathely **1235** a.	1045r	1452r	...	1848r	...	...	2250r	...

r – Subject to alteration May 17 - Aug. 15 (by 🚌 Szombathely - Zalaszentiván and v.v.). ⊡ – Runs earlier on ⑦ June 18 - Aug. 28 (Pécs 2207, Barcs 2335).

1240 (BUDAPEST) - DOMBÓVAR - KAPOSVÁR - NAGYKANIZSA

2nd c

For Budapest - Nagykanizsa trains see Table **1220**

km		8919	8250	8250	8212	8202	*IC* 201	8214	8905	8254	8216	8256	8903	8256	8226	8236	*IC* 204	8913	8206	8901	*IC* 828	8561	8218	8208
			⚒	†			G⊖				Ⓐb				Ⓐ		R⊖				[R]Z			Ⓑ
	Budapest Keleti **1200** d.	...	...	...	...	...	...	...	...	...	...	...	...	...	...	...	1445	...	...	...	1645	...	...	...
0	**Dombóvár** d.	...	0415	...	0618	0807	...	1007	...	*1207*	...	1407	...	...	...	1607	1700	...	1807	...	1900	...	2007	2207
31	**Kaposvár** a.	...	0456	...	0702	0838	...	1048	...	*1248*	...	1448	...	...	...	1648	1731	...	1844	...	1931	...	2052	2238
31	**Kaposvár** d.	...	0458	0458	0705	0905	...	1105	...	1305	1404	1505	...	...	1554	1705	1736	...	1904	...	1933	...	2110	2241
71	Somogyszob d.	...	0610	0610	0800	1000	...	1200	...	1400	1459	1600	...	...	1650	1800	1824	...	2000	...	2019	...	2214	2331
101	Gyékényes a.	...	0640	0640	0830	1030	...	1230	...	1430	1528	1630	...	←	1720	1830	1851	...	2030	...	2046	...	2244	0001
101	Gyékényes **1237** d.	0615	0720	0720	*0839*	...	1215	...	1239	1431	...	→	1639	1656	...	...	...	1900	...	2039	...	2053	...	...
130	**Nagykanizsa** **1237** a.	0649	0752	0752	*0906*	...	1244	...	1306	1508	...	...	1706	1732	...	...	...	1936	...	2106	...	2124	...	...

	8219	8219	8229	8910	*IC* 829	8259	8207	8900	8217	*IC* 200	8902	8225	8205	8215	8253	8904	8253	*IC* 205	8263	8906	8201	8568	8251	18251
	⚒	†	Ⓐ		[R]Z					G⊖								R⊖				Ⓑ	Ⓑ	⑥
Nagykanizsa **1237** d.	...	...	...	0353	...	0455	0630	0653	...	0929	1052	...	...	...	1428	1452	...	...	1633	1852	...	1918	2108	2108
Gyékényes **1237** a.	...	...	...	0427	...	0527	0707	0719	...	0954	1119	...	...	...	1513	1519	←	...	1719	1919	...	1955	2142	2142
Gyékényes d.	0334	...	0417	...	0502	0529	0722	...	0929	...	...	1129	...	1329	→	...	1529	1654	1721	...	1925	...	2143	2143
Somogyszob d.	0405	...	0448	...	0530	0605	0801	...	1001	...	...	1201	...	1401	...	...	1559	1729	1800	...	1956	...	2214	2214
Kaposvár a.	0455	...	0541	...	0614	0700	0850	...	1050	...	...	1250	...	1450	...	...	1650	1815	1854	...	2045	...	2306	2302
Kaposvár d.	0508	0508	...	...	0616	0708	0918	...	1108	...	...	...	1318	1508	...	...	1700	1816	1900	...	2109	...	2307	...
Dombóvár a.	0549	0549	...	...	0647	0749	0949	...	1149	...	...	...	1349	1549	...	...	1744	1847	1944	...	2140	...	2348	...
Budapest Keleti **1200** a.	...	...	...	...	0914	...	...	...	...	...	...	...	...	...	...	...	...	2114	...	...	...	...	...	...

G – AGRAM – [12] ✕ Budapest - Fonyód - Zagreb and v.v. (Table **1220**).
R – RIPPL-RÓNAI – [12] ✕ Budapest - Zagreb and v.v.
Z – Conveys 🛏 1, 2 cl., 🛌 2 cl., [2] Budapest - Zagreb - Split on ②⑤ May 27 - June 14, ②⑤ Aug. 30 - Sept. 30, returning next day from Split.
b – Not Dec. 19 - Jan. 2, June 16 - Aug. 31.
⊖ – [R] for domestic journeys within Hungary.

1242 DOMBÓVAR - BAJA - KISKUNFÉLEGYHÁZA - KECSKEMÉT

2nd class (*Ex* also

km							u			d	
0	**Dombóvár** d.	...	0611	...	1411	...	1611	...	1811	...	...
60	Bátaszék **1210** d.	0520	0732	...	1529	...	1732	...	1920	1933	...
80	**Baja** **1210** a.	0540	0753	...	1550	...	1753	...	...	1951	...

	⚒	Ⓐ		Ⓐ					
Baja **1210** d.	0425	...	...	0616	...	...	1416	1555x	...
Bátaszék **1210** d.	0444	0448	...	0635	0638	...	1438	1638	...
Dombóvár a.	...	0554	...	...	0745	...	1545	1745	...

km			Ⓐ						Ⓐr		
0	**Baja** d.	0413	0517	0609	0809	1009	1209	1409	1511	1609	1809
76	Kiskunhalas a.	0520	0630	0720	0920	1120	1320	1520	1630	1720	1920
76	Kiskunhalas d.	0532	0639	0732	0932	1132	1332	1532	...	1732	1932
122	Kiskunfélegyháza **1290** d.	0615	0721	0815	1015	1215	1415	1615	...	1815	2014
147	**Kecskemét** **1290** a.	0636	...	0836	1036	1236	1436	1636	...	1836	...

	Ⓐ						Ⓐ		
Kecskemét **1290** d.	...	0510	0722	0922	1122	1322	...	1522	1722
Kiskunfélegyháza **1290** d.	...	0545	0745	0945	1145	1345	1438	1545	1745
Kiskunhalas a.	...	0625	0825	1025	1225	1425	1518	1625	1825
Kiskunhalas d.	0528	0637	0837	1037	1237	1437	1528r	1637	1837
Baja a.	0638	0742	0942	1142	1342	1542	1638r	1742	1942

d – Train *Ex* **838**, [R].
r – Not Dec. 19 - Jan. 2, June 16 - Aug. 31.
u – On ⑤ (not Dec. 18 - Jan. 1, June 17 - Aug. 26) change at Bátaszék to *Ex* **1836** [R].
x – 1609 on ⑦ (not Dec. 20, 27, June 19 - Aug. 28).

BUDAPEST - GYÖR - WIEN 1250

	9400	EN* 346	IC 910	RJ 162	IC 930	RJ 60	IC 912	EC 140	IC 932	RJ 62	IC 922	IC 942	RJ 64	IC 914	IC 934	RJ 66	IC 924	9204	IC 936	RJ 68	9304	IC 916	EC 344	9306
	2	D§	R	✕⊖ Z	R	✕⊖ M	R	✕⊖ H	R	✕⊖ M	R	R	✕⊖ M	R	R	✕⊖ Mf	R	2	R	✕⊖ M	2 Ⓐ	R	✕⊖ A	2 Ⓐ
Budapest Keleti d.	...	0540	0610	0640	0705	0740	0810	0840	0905	0940	1010	1105	1140	1210	1305	1340	1410	1440	1505	1540	1553	1610	1640	1653
Ferencváros d.	...	0549	|	|	|	|	|	|	|	|	|	|	|	|	|	|	|	1449	|	|	1601	|	|	1701
Kelenföld ☆ d.	...	0555	0624	0655	0719	0755	0824	0855	0919	0955	1024	1119	1155	1224	1319	1355	1424	1455	1519	1555	1610	1624	1655	1710
Tatabánya d.	...	0626	0655	0726	0750	0826	0855	0926	0950	1026	1055	1150	1226	1255	1350	1426	1455	1533	1550	1626	1647	1655	1726	1747
Tata d.	...	|	0703	|	0758	|	0903	|	0958	|	1103	1158	|	1303	1358	|	1503	1541	1558	|	1655	1703	|	1755
Komárom d.	...	|	0716	|	0812	|	0916	|	1012	|	1116	1212	|	1316	1412	|	1516	1556	1612	|	1708	1716	|	1808
Györ a.	...	0700	0735	0800	0835	0900	0935	1000	1035	1100	1135	1235	1300	1335	1435	1500	1535	1625	1635	1700	1730	1735	1800	1830
Györ d.	*0548*	0702	△	0802	▽	0902	△	1002	▽	1102	△	▽	1302	△	▽	1502	△	...	▽	1702	...	△	1802	...
Mosonmagyaróvár d.	*0614*	0720	...	0820	...	0920	...	1020	...	1120	...	...	1320	...	...	1520	...	...	...	1720	...	...	1820	...
Hegyeshalom 🏛 d.	0629	0732	...	0832	...	0932	...	1032	...	1132	...	...	1332	...	...	1532	...	...	...	1732	...	...	1832	...
Wien Hbf a.	0724	0818	...	0918	...	1018	...	1118	...	1218	...	...	1418	...	...	1618	...	...	...	1818	...	...	1918	...

	IC 946	RJ 42	9308	IC 318	EC 148	IC 938	Ex 1948	IC 948	EN 462	
	R	✕⊖ S	2 Ⓐ	R G	🍷⊖	R	2R ⑦	R	R K	2 ⊡
Budapest Keleti d.	1710	1740	1753	1810	1840	1905	1940	2010	2040	2120d
Ferencváros d.	|	|	1801	|	|	|	1949	|	|	|
Kelenföld ☆ d.	1724	1755	1810	1824	1855	1919	1956	2024	2055	2128
Tatabánya d.	1755	1826	1847	1855	1926	1950	2034	2055	2126	2215
Tata d.	1803	|	1855	1903	|	1958	2042	2103	|	2226
Komárom d.	1816	|	1908	1916	|	2012	2055	2117	|	2249
Györ a.	1835	1900	1930	1935	2000	2035	2120	2140	2200	2316
Györ d.	▽	1902	...	△	2002	▽	...	...	2202	...
Mosonmagyaróvár d.	...	1920	...	...	2020	...	...	...	2220	...
Hegyeshalom 🏛 d.	...	1932	...	...	2032	...	...	...	2232	...
Wien Hbf a.	...	2018	...	...	2118	...	...	...	2318	...

	9409	IC 949		9407	IC 919	9209	EN 463	IC 917	RJ 41	IC 937
	2 Ⓐ	R	2 c	2 Ⓐ	R	2	R K	R	✕⊖	R
Wien Hbf d.	...	...	0444	...	...	...	0642	...	0742	...
Hegyeshalom 🏛 d.	0506	...	0545	0606	...	...	0728	...	0828	...
Mosonmagyaróvár d.	0514	...	...	0614	...	...	0736	...	0836	...
Györ a.	0540	...	...	0640	△▽	...	0753	△	0853	▽
Györ d.	0547	0616	...	0647	0721	0726	0756	0821	0856	0921
Komárom d.	0609	0638	...	0709	0743	0751	|	0839	|	0943
Tata d.	0623	0652	...	0723	0757	0807	|	0852	|	0957
Tatabánya d.	0632	0700	...	0732	0805	0816	0829	0900	0929	1005
Kelenföld ☆ a.	0707	0732	...	0807	0838	0901	0906	0932	1002	1038
Ferencváros a.	0714	|	...	0814	|	0910	|	|	|	|
Budapest Keleti a.	0722	0749	...	0822	0854	0919	0924	0949	1019	1054

	EC 345	IC 317	RJ 49	IC 947	IC 927	RJ 61	IC 945	IC 915	RJ 63	IC 933	EC 145	IC 925	RJ 65	IC 943	Ex 1943	EC 147	IC 913	RJ 67	IC 931	RJ 165	IC 911	EN* 347			
	✕⊖ A	R G	✕⊖ v	R	R	✕⊖ M	R	R	✕⊖ Mf	R	🍷⊖	R	✕⊖ M	R	2R ⑦	✕⊖ H	R	✕⊖ M	R	✕⊖ Z	R	D§	2	2b	2
Wien Hbf d.	0842	...	0942	...	...	1142	...	...	1342	...	1442	...	1542	...	...	1642	...	1742	...	1842	...	1942	...	2045	...
Hegyeshalom 🏛 d.	0928	...	1028	...	...	1228	...	...	1428	...	1528	...	1628	...	...	1728	...	1828	...	1928	...	2028	...	2146	...
Mosonmagyaróvár d.	0936	...	1036	...	...	1236	...	...	1436	...	1536	...	1636	...	...	1736	...	1836	...	1936	...	2036	...	2154	...
Györ a.	0953	△	1053	▽	△	1253	▽	△	1453	▽	1553	△	1653	▽	...	1753	△	1853	▽	1953	△	2053	...	2220	...
Györ d.	0956	1021	1056	1121	1221	1256	1321	1421	1456	1521	1556	1621	1656	1721	1735	1756	1821	1856	1921	1956	2021	2056	2139	...	2239
Komárom d.	|	1039	|	1143	1239	|	1343	1439	|	1543	|	1639	|	1743	1800	|	1839	|	1943	|	2039	|	2204	...	2304
Tata d.	|	1052	|	1157	1252	|	1357	1452	|	1557	|	1652	|	1757	1815	|	1852	|	1957	|	2052	|	2227	...	2322
Tatabánya d.	1029	1100	1129	1205	1300	1329	1405	1500	1529	1605	1629	1700	1729	1805	1824	1829	1900	1929	2005	2029	2100	2129	2240	...	2332
Kelenföld ☆ a.	1102	1132	1202	1238	1332	1402	1438	1532	1602	1638	1702	1732	1802	1838	1857	1902	1932	2004	2038	2102	2132	2202	2327	...	...
Ferencváros a.	|	|	|	|	|	|	|	|	|	|	|	|	|	|	1905	|	|	|	|	|	|	2211	|	...	...
Budapest Keleti a.	1119	1149	1219	1254	1349	1419	1454	1549	1619	1654	1719	1749	1819	1854	1914	1919	1949	2019	2054	2119	2149	2220	2339d	...	...

AVALA – 🚃 ✕ Beograd - Budapest - Wien and v.v.
DACIA – 🛏 1, 2 cl., 🛌 2 cl., 🚃 Wien - Budapest - Bucureşti and v.v.
RÁBA – 🚃 Budapest - Szombathely - Graz and v.v.
HORTOBÁGY – 🚃 ✕ Nyiregyháza - Debrecen - Budapest - Wien and v.v.
KÁLMÁN IMRE / WIENER WALZER – 🛏 1, 2 cl., 🛌 2 cl., 🚃 Budapest - Wien - München and v.v.; 🛏 1, 2 cl., 🛌 2 cl., 🚃 Budapest - Wien - Salzburg (**466/7**) - Zürich and v.v.
🚃 and ✕ Budapest - Wien - Salzburg - München and v.v. (Table **65**).
🚃 and ✕ Budapest - Wien - Salzburg and v.v. (Table **65**).
🚃 ✕ Budapest - Wien - Salzburg - Innsbruck - Zürich and v.v. (Table **86**).
Change at Bruck an der Leitha (a. 2112 / d. 2118).
Change at Bruck an der Leitha (a. 0512 / d. 0520).
Budapest **Déli**.
Extended to / from Frankfurt on dates in Tables **912** / **930**.
From Innsbruck and Salzburg on dates in Table **86**.
Reservation compulsory for domestic journeys within Hungary.
To / from Szombathely (Table **1252**).

▽ – To / from Sopron (Table **1251**).
⊡ – Additional trains run Budapest Déli - Komárom at 2220, 2320.
☆ – See also Tables **1200**, **1220**, **1225**, **1230**. Kelenföld is also served by metro line 4 from Budapest Keleti.
§ – Reservation compulsory for international journeys.
* – *EN* classification applies only in Austria.
RJ – *Railjet* service, first and economy (2nd) class. *Business class* also available to first class ticket holders (supplement payable).

Györ - Hegyeshalom - Bruck an der Leitha *79 km* Journey 1h 15m - 1h 22m
From Györ 0448, 0748, 0948, 1148, 1348, 1548, 1748, 1948.
From Bruck an der Leitha 0748, 0948, 1048, 1248, 1448, 1748, 1848, 2118.

Komárom - Székesfehérvár *82 km* Journey 1h 25m
From Komárom 0845, 1610 (1630 until May 9). From Székesfehérvár 0558, 1425.

GYÖR - SOPRON 1251

erator: GySEV

	9910	9920	9912	9922	9932	IC 930	9942	IC 932	9914	IC 942	9924	9934	IC 934	9916	9926	IC 936	9936	9946	IC 946	9918	9948	IC 938	9928	9938
		Ⓐ			Ⓐ	R		R		R		Ⓐ	R			R			R		⑦e	R		
Budapest Kel. **1250** d.	...	...	...	...	...	0705	...	0905	...	1105	...	...	1305	...	...	1505	...	...	1710	...	...	1905	...	...
Györ d.	0408	0519	0603	0649	0751	0838	0851	1038	1051	1238	1251	1351	1438	1451	1551	1638	1651	1751	1838	1851	1951	2038	2051	2251
Csorna d.	0435	0546	0631	0723	0821	0859	0921	1059	1121	1259	1323	1421	1459	1520	1621	1659	1720	1821	1859	1920	2020	2059	2117	2317
Sopron a.	0523	0647	0723	0813	0908	0938	1006	1138	1205	1338	1414	1513	1538	1613	1713	1738	1814	1913	1938	2013	2106	2138	2201	0001

	9919	9929	9939	IC 939	9917	9927		IC 937	9937	IC 947	9915	IC 945	9925	IC 933		9913	9923	IC 943	9933	9943	IC 931	9911	9921	9931	
				R	Ⓐ			R		R		R		R		Ⓐ		R	Ⓐ		R				
ron d.	0350	0446	0548	0608	0617	0745	...	0821	0944	1021	1144	1221	1345	1421	...	1446	1545	1621	1646	1746	1821	1846	1944	2229	...
na d.	0435	0530	0639	0659	0706	0834	...	0859	1034	1059	1233	1259	1434	1459	...	1535	1634	1659	1735	1834	1859	1935	2034	2317	...
r a.	0501	0601	0708	0719	0733	0906	...	0919	1106	1119	1307	1319	1506	1519	...	1606	1706	1719	1806	1906	1919	2006	2106	2343	...
dapest Kel. **1250** a.	...	...	...	0854	...	...	...	1054	...	1254	...	1454	...	1654	...	...	...	1854	...	...	2054	...	...	...	...

Not Dec. 20, 27, June 19 - Aug. 28.

GYÖR - CSORNA - SZOMBATHELY 1252

For alternative services Budapest - Szombathely via Székesfehérvár see Table **1230**

	IC 910	IC 912	IC 922	IC 914	IC 924	IC 916	IC 318	IC 938	
	R	R	R	R	R	R	R	R	2
Budapest Keleti **1250** d.	0610	0810	1010	1210	1410	1610	1810	1905	...
Györ d.	0738	0938	1138	1338	1538	1738	1938	2038	...
Csorna d.	0759	0959	1159	1359	1559	1759	1959	2058	2107
Szombathely a.	0849	1049	1249	1449	1649	1849	2049	...	2218
Graz **986** a.	...	...	...	...	...	...	2300	...	...

	IC 919	IC 917	IC 317	IC 927	IC 915	IC 925	IC 913	IC 911	
	R	R	R	R	R	R	R	R	2
Graz **986** d.	...	...	0608	...	...	...	...	...	...
Szombathely d.	0600	0710	0910	1110	1310	1510	1710	1910	2230
Csorna d.	0659	0759	0959	1159	1359	1559	1759	1959	2340
Györ a.	0719	0819	1019	1219	1419	1619	1819	2019	...
Budapest Keleti **1250** a.	0854	0949	1149	1349	1549	1749	1949	2149	...

GYÖR - CELLDÖMÖLK - SZOMBATHELY 1253

Györ d.	0741	0840	0933	1040	1237	1456	1640	1750	1840	1948	2040
Pápa d.	0848	0927	1032	1127	1333	1600	1727	1848	1927	2046	2127
Celldömölk a.	0919	0953	1103	1153	1404	1634	1753	1919	1953	2117	2153
Celldömölk d.	...	1006	...	1206	...	...	1806	...	2006	...	2205
Szombathely a.	...	1044	...	1244	...	...	1844	...	2044	...	2242

Szombathely d.	0523	0704	...	...	1304	...	1504	...	1704	...	...
Celldömölk a.	0555	0751	...	...	1351	...	1551	...	1751	...	...
Celldömölk d.	0606	0806	0926	1126	1406	1449	1606	1649	1806	1926	2126
Pápa d.	0631	0831	1000	1200	1431	1523	1631	1735	1831	2000	2200
Györ a.	0716	0916	1054	1254	1516	1619	1716	1831	1916	2056	2301

tional trains: Györ - Celldömölk 0506, 0636, 1350Ⓐ, 1602; Celldömölk - Györ 0440, 0650, 1249Ⓑ.

1255 BUDAPEST - VÁC - SZOB

Local trains, 2nd c

km										
0	**Budapest** Nyugati d.	0048	0441	0541	0707	then	2107	2148	2248	2348
34	Vác d.	0134	0534	0630	0734	hourly	2134	2234	2334	0034
51	Nagymaros-Visegrád ¶ d.	0149	0549	0645	0749	until	2149	2249	2349	0049
64	**Szob** a.	0205	0605	0700	0805		2205	2305	0005	0105

Szob d.	0456	0556	0656	then	1856	2001	2101	2201
Nagymaros-Visegrád ¶ d.	0511	0611	0711	hourly	1911	2016	2116	2216
Vác d.	0528	0628	0728	until	1928	2034	2134	2234
Budapest Nyugati a.	0554	0654	0754		1954	2117	2217	2317

¶ – A ferry operates across the river to Visegrád.

For *EC* trains see Table **1175**.

1260 BUDAPEST - MISKOLC - NYÍREGYHÁZA

Fast t

For slower trains Budapest - Miskolc see Table **1261**. Most *IC* trains continue beyond Debrecen to / from Budapest Nyugati. For trains Budapest - Debrecen - Nyiregyháza see Table 1

km	*FAST TRAINS*	*IC* 580 🅁	510 2	*IC* 182 ⊖ R	*IC* 560 🅁	*IC* 502 🅁	*IC* 562 🅁	*IC* 512 🅁	2	*IC* 564 🅁	*IC* 504 🅁	2	*IC* 566 🅁	*IC* 514 🅁	2	*IC* 568 🅁	*IC* 506 🅁	2	*IC* 586 🅁	*IC* 186 ⊖ H	2	*IC* 508 🅁	2	2 Ⓑ
0	**Budapest** Keleti ▶ d.	...	...	0630	0730	0830	0930	1030	...	1130	1230	...	1330	1430	...	1530	1630	...	1730	1830	...	1930	...	...
126	Füzesabony ▶ d.	...	...	0751	0851	0951	1051	1151	...	1251	1351	...	1451	1551	...	1651	1751	...	1851	1951	...	2051	...	...
183	**Miskolc** ▶ a.	...	...	0827	0927	1027	1127	1227	...	1327	1427	...	1527	1627	...	1727	1827	...	1927	2027	...	2127	...	...
183	**Miskolc** d.	0626	0730	...	0930	...	1130	...	*1235*	1330	...	*1435*	1530	...	*1635*	1730	...	*1835*	1930	...	*2035*	...	2135	2310
221	Szerencs d.	0651	0755	...	0955	...	1155	...	1316	1355	...	1516	1555	...	1716	1755	...	1916	1955	...	2116	...	2216	2348
239	Tokaj d.	0704	0808	...	1008	...	1208	...	1334	1408	...	1534	1608	...	1734	1808	...	1934	2008	...	2134	...	2234	0006
271	**Nyíregyháza** a.	0733	0833	...	1033	...	1233	...	1415	1433	...	1615	1633	...	1815	1833	...	2015	2033	...	2215	...	2315	0040
	Debrecen **1270** a.	0805	...	...	1105	...	1305	...	...	1505	...	...	1705	...	...	1905	...	...	2105	...	...	...	...	...

FAST TRAINS	2	529 2	*IC* 519 🅁	2	*IC* 187 ⊖ H	*IC* 682 🅁	*IC* 517 🅁	*IC* 650 🅁	*IC* 515 🅁	*IC* 652 🅁	2	*IC* 505 🅁	*IC* 654 🅁	2	*IC* 513 🅁	*IC* 656 🅁	2	*IC* 503 🅁	*IC* 658 🅁	2	*IC* 181 ⊖ R	511 2	2	2
Debrecen **1270** d.	...	...	...	...	...	0651	...	0851	...	1051	...	...	1251	...	...	1451	...	...	1651	...	...	...	...	...
Nyíregyháza d.	0343	...	0523	0539	...	0723	...	0923	...	1123	1139	...	1323	1339	...	1523	1539	...	1723	1739	...	1923	1939	2039
Tokaj d.	0418	...	0548	0620	...	0748	...	0948	...	1148	1220	...	1348	1420	...	1548	1620	...	1748	1820	...	1948	2020	2120
Szerencs d.	0435	0445	0602	0640	...	0802	...	1002	...	1202	1239	...	1402	1439	...	1602	1639	...	1802	1839	...	2002	2039	2220r
Miskolc a.	...	0522	0627	0713	...	0827	...	1027	...	1227	*1322*	...	1427	*1522*	...	1627	*1722*	...	1827	*1922*	...	2027	*2122*	2257
Miskolc ▶ d.	...	0535	0630	...	0730	0830	0930	1030	1130	1230	...	1330	1430	...	1530	1630	...	1730	1830	...	1930	...	...	...
Füzesabony ▶ d.	...	0623	0707	...	0807	0907	1007	1107	1207	1307	...	1407	1507	...	1607	1707	...	1807	1907	...	2007	...	...	...
Budapest Keleti ▶ a.	...	0800	0830	...	0930	1030	1130	1230	1330	1430	...	1530	1630	...	1730	1830	...	1930	2030	...	2130	...	...	...

H – HERNÁD / HORNÁD – (12) Budapest - Miskolc - Košice and v.v.
R – RÁKÓCZI – (12) Budapest - Miskolc - Košice and v.v.
r – Arrive 2139.

▶ – For slower services see Table **1261**.
⊖ – Compulsory reservation for domestic journeys within Hungary.

Timings are subject to alterat Mar. 29 - Apr. 9

1261 BUDAPEST - MISKOLC - SÁTORALJAÚJHELY

Slower trains. 2nd c

For fast trains Budapest - Miskolc - Szerencs see Table **1260**. For faster journeys use *IC* train (Table **1260**) and change at Füzesabony (for Eger) or Szerencs (for Sátoraljaújhely).

km	*SLOWER TRAINS*	5520	5330	5010	5312	5500	5200	542	520	552	5224	544	524	554	526 ⑤⑦	5236 ④⑥	546	528	556	1528 E 🅁	5208	5508	5008	5108
0	**Budapest** Keleti ▶ d.	...	...	...	...	0500	0600	0700	0800	0900	...	1100	1200	1300	1400	...	1500	1600	1700	1755	1800	1900	2000	2200
67	Hatvan d.	0405	...	0505	...	0555	0653	0753	0853	0953	...	1153	1253	1353	1453	...	1553	1653	1753	|	1853	1955	2053	2254
87	Vámosgyörk ⊡ d.	0421	...	0520	...	0610	0705	0805	0905	1005	...	1205	1305	1405	1505	...	1605	1705	1805	|	1905	2010	2105	2307
126	Füzesabony ▶ a.	0457	...	0555	...	0647	0729	0829	0929	1029	...	1229	1329	1429	1529	...	1629	1729	1829	1916	1929	2046	2129	2331
126	Füzesabony ▶ d.	0504	0502	*0604*	0602	0650	0732	0831	0932	1031	...	1231	1332	1431	1532	...	1631	1732	1831	1926	1932	2108	2132	2334
143	**Eger** ⊙ a.	0521	|	*0621*	|	0710	|	0850	|	1050	...	1250	|	1450	|	...	1650	|	1850	|	|	2125	|	|
139	Mezőkövesd d.	▬	0513	▬	0613	▬	0743	...	0943	▬	...	▬	1343	▬	1543	...	▬	1743	▬	|	1943	▬	2143	2344
183	**Miskolc** ▶ a.	...	0552	...	0652	...	0817	...	1017	...	...	...	1417	...	1617	...	...	1817	...	2003	2017	...	2217	0018
183	**Miskolc** ▶ d.	*0535*	...	*0635*	...	*0735*	0835	...	1035	*1135*	1235	*1335*	1435	*1535*	1635	1635	*1735*	1835	*1935*	2016	2035	*2135*	...	...
221	Szerencs ▶ d.	0614	...	0714	...	0814	0914	...	1114	1214	1314	1414	1514	1614	1714	1714	1814	1914	2014	2047	2114	2226	...	...
257	Sárospatak a.	0702	...	0802	...	0902	1002	...	1202	1302	1402	1502	1602	1702	1802	1802	1902	2002	2102	2134	2202	2306	...	...
267	**Sátoraljaújhely** a.	0712	...	0812	...	0912	1012	...	1212	1312	1412	1512	1612	1712	1812	1812	1912	2012	2112	2143	2212	2316	...	...

SLOWER TRAINS		5009	5509	529		5209		527	545			5205		523 ⑤⑦	④⑥		521	1521 G 🅁		5201				
Sátoraljaújhely d.	...	...	...	0353	0448	0548	0648	0748	...	0948	1048	1148	1248	1348	1348	1448	1548	1620	1648	1748	1848	1948	2048	...
Sárospatak d.	...	...	...	0404	0504	0604	0704	0804	...	1004	1104	1204	1304	1404	1404	1504	1604	1630	1704	1804	1904	2004	2104	...
Szerencs ▶ d.	...	...	...	0445	0543	0645	0743	0845	...	1045	1143	1245	1343	1445	1445	1543	1645	1713	1743	1845	1943	2045	2143	2220
Miskolc ▶ a.	...	...	...	0522	*0622*	0722	*0822*	0922	...	1122	*1222*	1322	*1422*	1522	1522	*1622*	1722	1739	*1822*	1922	*2022*	2122	...	2257
Miskolc ▶ d.	...	0328	...	0535	▬	0735	▬	0935	...	...	▬	1335	▬	1535	...	▬	1735	1748	▬	1935	...	...	...	*2300*
Mezőkövesd d.	...	0406	...	0610	...	0810	...	1010	...	...	...	1410	...	1610	...	...	1810	|	...	2010	...	...	...	*2338*
Eger ⊙ d.	...	|	0438	|	0704	|	0904	|	1104	...	1304	|	1504	|	...	1704	|	|	1904	|	...	...	...	|
Füzesabony ▶ a.	...	0417	0455	0619	0722	0819	0922	1019	1122	...	1322	1419	1522	1619	...	1722	1819	1826	1921	2019	...	...	...	*2350*
Füzesabony ▶ d.	0343	0419	0504	0623	0723	0823	0923	1023	1123	...	1323	1423	1523	1623	...	1723	1823	1831	1922	2023	...	...	...	...
Vámosgyörk ⊡ d.	0418	0454	0540	0651	0751	0851	0951	1051	1151	...	1351	1451	1551	1651	...	1751	1851	|	1955	2051	...	...	...	...
Hatvan d.	0436	0511	0558	0706	0806	0906	1006	1106	1206	...	1406	1506	1606	1706	...	1806	1906	|	2010	2106	...	...	...	...
Budapest Keleti ▶ a.	0550	0620	0720	0800	0900	1000	1100	1200	1300	...	1500	1600	1700	1800	...	1900	2000	2005	2106	2200	...	...	...	...

E – ⑤ (not Dec. 18 - Jan. 1, June 17 - Aug. 26).
G – ⑦ (not Dec. 20, 27, June 19 - Aug. 28).
▶ – For faster trains see Table **1260**.
⊡ – Connecting trains **Vámosgyörk - Gyöngyös** and v.v. (journey 16 mins):
From Vámosgyörk: 0522, 0610, 0708, 0908, 1108, 1308, 1408Ⓐ, 1508, 1608, 1708, 1908.
From Gyöngyös: 0546, 0633, 0732, 0932, 1132, 1332, 1432Ⓐ, 1532, 1632, 1732, 1932.

⊙ – Additional local trains **Füzesabony - Eger** and v.v. (journey 17 minutes):
From Füzesabony: 0420, 0704Ⓐ, 0808Ⓐ, 0908, 1008Ⓐ, 1108, 1208Ⓐ, 1308 1408Ⓐ, 1508, 1608Ⓐ, 1708, 1808Ⓐ, 2008Ⓐ, 2208Ⓐ, 2255.
From Eger: 0322, 0531Ⓐ, 0631, 0731Ⓐ, 0831, 0931Ⓐ, 1031, 1131Ⓐ, 1231, 1331Ⓐ, 1431, 1531Ⓐ, 1631, 1731Ⓐ, 1831, 1931Ⓐ, 2031, 2131Ⓐ, 2231.

1262 HATVAN - SALGÓTARJÁN - SOMOSKÖÚJFALU

2nd cl

km										n	
0	Hatvan d.	0410	0610	0810	1013	1213	1410	1610	1813	2013	2213
59	Salgótarján a.	0540	0740	0940	1140	1340	1540	1740	1940	2140	2340
65	Somosköújfalu 🏛 a.	0551	0751	0951	1151	1351	1551	1751	1951	2151	2351

						⑦b			
Somosköújfalu 🏛 d.	0617	0817	1017	1217	1417	1600	1617	1817	2017
Salgótarján d.	0629	0829	1029	1229	1429	1612	1629	1829	2029
Hatvan a.	0750	0950	1150	1350	1550	1728	1750	1950	2150

b – ⑦ (not Dec. 20, 27, June 19 - Aug. 28). To Budapest Keleti, arrive 1840.
n – On ⑦ (not Dec. 20, 27, June 19 - Aug. 28) starts from Budapest Keleti, depart 1905.

Additional journeys: Hatvan to Somosköújfalu: 0510Ⓐ, 1310Ⓐ, 1510Ⓐ, 1910Ⓐ.
Somosköújfalu to Hatvan: 0317, 0417, 0517Ⓐ, 1317Ⓐ, 1517Ⓐ.

1265 MISKOLC - KOŠICE

2nd class (also 1st class in

km			*IC** 182 R ⊖						*IC** 186 H ⊖	
	Budapest Keleti **1260/1** d.	...	0630	...	...	...	...	...	1830	...
	Füzesabony **1260/1** d.	0602	0751	0802	1002	1202	1402	1602	1951	...
0	**Miskolc** d.	0706	0830	0906	1106	1306	1506	1706	2030	2106
61	Hidasnémeti a.	0813	0926	1013	1213	1413	1613	1813	2126	2213
61	Hidasnémeti 🏛 d.	...	0937	...	...	...	...	...	2137	...
87	**Košice** a.	...	0959	...	...	...	...	...	2159	...

		*IC** 187 H ⊖						*IC** 183 R ⊖
Košice d.	...	0602	...	...	...	...	...	1802
Hidasnémeti 🏛 a.	...	0623	...	...	...	...	...	1823
Hidasnémeti d.	0547	0633	0947	1147	1347	1547	1647	1833
Miskolc a.	0653	0728	1053	1253	1453	1653	1753	1928
Füzesabony **1260/1** a.	0750	0806	...	1350	1550	1750	1850	2006
Budapest Keleti **1260/1** a.	...	0930	...	...	...	...	...	2130

H – HERNÁD – (12) Budapest - Miskolc - Košice and v.v.
R – RÁKÓCZI – (12) Budapest - Miskolc - Košice and v.v.

⊖ – Compulsory reservation for domestic journeys within Hungary.

* – Classified *EC* in Slovakia.

Other local trains run Miskolc - Hidasnéme

BUDAPEST - DEBRECEN - NYÍREGYHÁZA - ZÁHONY - CHOP 1270

For trains to / from Romania see Table **1275**.

	IC	IC	IC	IC	IC	IC	IC	IC	IC	IC	IC	IC	IC	IC	IC	IC	EC								
	682	**650**	**34**	**652**	**612**	**654**	**614**	**656**	**624**	**658**	**626**	**628**	**616**	**616**	**608**	**618**	**147**					**6202**		**6208**	
	[R]	[R]	[R]	[R]	[R]	[R]	[R]	[R]	[R]	[R]	[R]	[R]	[R]	[R]	[R]	[R]	⊖		2	2	2	2		2	2
	◇	◇	L	◇		◇		◇		◇				⑤			H								d
Budapest Nyugati .. ◧ d.	...	0623	0723	0823	0923	1023	1123	1223	1323	1423	1523	1623	1723	1723	1823	1923	1940k	S	...	...	0503	0628	E	1828	2028
Kőbánya Kispest ... ◧ d.	...	0637	0737	0837	0937	1037	1137	1237	1337	1437	1537	1637	1737	1737	1837	1937	|	L	...	...	0518	0642	V	1842	2042
Ferihegy ✈ .... ◧ d.	...	0643	0743	0843	0943	1043	1143	1243	1343	1443	1543	1643	1743	1743	1843	1943	|	O	...	...	0527	0648	E	1848	2048
Cegléd .... ◧ d.	...	0718	0818	0918	1018	1118	1218	1318	1418	1518	1618	1718	1818	1818	1918	2018	|	W	...	...	0624	0724	R	1924	2124
Szolnok .... ◧ d.	...	0738	0838	0938	1038	1138	1238	1338	1438	1538	1638	1738	1838	1838	1938	2038	2105		...	0555	0650	0750	Y	1950	2150
Püspökladány .... d.	...	0821	0921	1021	1121	1221	1321	1421	1521	1621	1721	1821	1921	1921	2021	2121	2204	T	0455	0700	0755	0855		2055	2255
Hajdúszoboszló .... d.	...	0836	0936	1036	1136	1236	1336	1436	1536	1636	1736	1836	1936	1936	2036	2136	2219	R	0514	0719	0814	0914	2	2114	2314
Debrecen .... a.	...	0849	0949	1049	1149	1249	1349	1449	1549	1649	1749	1849	1949	1949	2049	2149	2233	A	0529	0734	0829	0929		2129	2329
Debrecen .... d.	0651	0851	0951	1051	1151	1251	1351	1451	1551	1651	1757	1851	1951	1951	2051	2151	2235	I	0534	0741	0834	0934	H	2134	...
Nyíregyháza .... a.	0721	0921	1021	1121	1221	1321	1421	1521	1621	1721	1827	1921	2021	2021	2121	2221	2305	N	0616	0823	0916	1016	O	2216	...
Nyíregyháza .... d.	...	...	1031	...	...	...	...	...	1631	...	1831	1931	...	2031	...	...	...	S	0648	0848	0948	1048	U	2248	...
Kisvárda .... d.	...	...	1102	...	...	...	...	...	1702	...	1902	2002	...	2102	...	...	...		0732	0932	1032	1132	R	2332	...
Záhony ▦ .... ▶ a.	...	...	1121	...	...	...	...	...	1721	...	1921	2021	...	2121	...	...	...		0757	0957	1057	1157	S	2357	...
Chop ▦ .... ⊙ ▶ a.	...	...	1340	...	...	...	...	...	...	...	...	...	...	...	...	...	...		...	...	...	...		...	...

	EC	IC	IC	IC	IC	IC	IC	IC	IC	IC	IC	IC	IC	IC	IC	IC	IC									
	140	**619**	**629**	**580**	**627**	**617**	**560**	**605**	**562**	**615**	**564**	**33**	**566**	**613**	**613**	**568**	**586**			**6109**	**6207**	**6297**		**6293**		
	⊖	[R]	[R]	[R]	[R]	[R]	[R]	[R]	[R]	[R]	[R]	[R]	[R]	[R]	[R]	[R]	[R]		2	2	2	2		2	2	2
	H			◇			◇		◇		◇	L	◇	⑦		◇	◇									h
p ▦ .... ⊙ ▶ d.	...	...	...	...	...	...	...	...	...	...	...	1420	...	...	...	...	...	S	...	...	...	...		...	...	...
ɔny ▦ .... ▶ d.	...	...	0528	...	0735	...	...	...	...	...	...	1440	...	1629	...	...	...	L	0358	...	0553	0803	E	1603	1703	1803
árda .... d.	...	...	0547	...	0754	...	...	...	...	...	...	1459	...	1648	...	...	...	O	0423	...	0618	0828	V	1628	1728	1828
egyháza .... a.	...	...	0618	...	0825	...	...	...	...	...	...	1530	...	1719	...	...	...	W	0507	...	0702	0912	E	1712	1812	1912
egyháza .... d.	0455	0535	0623	0735	0835	0935	1035	1135	1235	1335	1435	1535	1635	1735	1735	1835	2035		▬	0544	0744	0944	R	1744	1844	1944
ecen .... a.	0525	0605	0656	0805	0905	1005	1105	1205	1305	1405	1505	1605	1705	1805	1805	1905	2105	T	2	0626	0828	1026	Y	1826	1926	2026
ecen .... d.	0527	0607	0707	0807	0907	1007	1107	1207	1307	1407	1507	1607	1707	1807	1807	1907	...	R	0414	0631	0826	1031		1831	1931	▬
úszoboszló .... d.	0541	0621	0721	0821	0921	1021	1121	1221	1321	1421	1521	1621	1721	1821	1821	1921	...	A	0430	0647	0847	1047	2	1847	1947	...
ökladány .... d.	0557	0637	0737	0837	0937	1037	1137	1237	1337	1437	1537	1637	1737	1837	1837	1937	...	I	0453	0708	0908	1108		1908	2008	2
nok .... ◧ d.	0657	0722	0822	0922	1022	1122	1222	1322	1422	1522	1622	1722	1822	1922	1922	2022	...	N	0605	0815	1015	1215	H	2015	2115	2225
éd .... ◧ d.	|	0743	0843	0943	1043	1143	1243	1343	1443	1543	1643	1743	1843	1943	1943	2043	...	S	0628	0838	1038	1238	O	2038	2148	2250
egy ✈ .... ◧ d.	|	0815	0915	1015	1115	1215	1315	1415	1515	1615	1715	1815	1915	2015	2015	2115	...		0715	0910	1110	1310	U	2110	2240	2348
ánya Kispest ..... ◧ a.	|	0820	0920	1020	1120	1220	1320	1420	1520	1620	1720	1820	1920	2020	2020	2120	...		0720	0915	1115	1315	R	2115	2248	2357
apest Nyugati .. ◧ a.	0820k	0837	0937	1037	1137	1237	1337	1437	1537	1637	1737	1837	1937	2037	2037	2137	...		0737	0932	1132	1332	S	2132	2305	0014

HORTOBÁGY – (12) ✕ Wien - Budapest - Debrecen and v.v.
LATORCA – (12) Budapest - Záhony and v.v.; (2) Záhony - Chop and v.v.; 🛏 1, 2 cl. Budapest - Chop - Kyïv and v.v.; 🛏 1, 2 cl. Budapest - Chop - Lviv and v.v.
An additional journey runs 2 hours later.
Additional journeys run at 1929, 2003.
Budapest **Keleti**.
Ukrainian (East European) time, one hour ahead of Hungarian time.
Compulsory reservation for domestic journeys within Hungary.

◧ – Also **1290** Budapest - Cegléd; **1280** Budapest - Szolnok. Ferihegy ✈ is served by 5 - 6 trains per hour.
◇ – To / from Miskolc, Table **1260** (most trains continue beyond Miskolc to / from Budapest Keleti).

▶ – Full service Záhony - Chop, 2nd class (minimum 15 minutes connection time):

				L								L			
Záhony .. d.	0342	0634	0835	1223	1422	1802	2015	Chop ⊙ d.	0530	0822	1025	1420	1615	1957	2220
Chop . ⊙ a.	0500	0752	0953	1340	1540	1920	2133	Záhony .. a.	0448	0740	0943	1337	1533	1915	2138

BUDAPEST - BIHARKERESZTES - ORADEA 1275

		IC*				IC*	IC*	
	6120	**369**	**367**	**6204**	**365**		**407**	**363**	
	2		H [R]	2	2	2	C [R]	A [R]	2
Budapest Keleti .... **1270** d.	...	...	0555	1028n	...	...	1440	1740	...
Szolnok .... **1270** d.	0530	...	0718	1150	...	...	1603	1903	...
Püspökladány .... **1270** d.	0632	0637	0825	1252	1310	1526	1710	2010	2125
Biharkeresztes ....a.	...	0729	0917	...	1410	1636	1810	2102	2217
Biharkeresztes ▦ ....d.	...	0754	0950	...	1435	...	1839	2130	...
Episcopia Bihor ▦ .... ⊙ a.	...	0909	1105	...	1550	...	1954	2245	...
Episcopia Bihor .... ⊙ d.	...	0924	1120	...	1607	...	2010	2300	...
Oradea .... ⊙ a.	...	0933	1128	...	1615	...	2018	2308	...
Cluj Napoca **1612** .... ⊙ a.	...	...	1406	...	...	...	2312r	...	...

	IC*		IC*				IC	IC*	
	406		**362**	**364**	**6205**	**368**	**33**	**366**	
	C [R]	2	A [R]	2	2	2	[R]	H [R]	2
Cluj Napoca **1612** .... ⊙ d.	0224	...	0654	...	...	...	...	1509	...
Oradea .... ⊙ d.	0504	...	0941	1147	...	1440	...	1752	...
Episcopia Bihor .... ⊙ a.	0512	...	0949	1155	...	1448	...	1800	...
Episcopia Bihor ▦ .... ⊙ d.	0535	...	1004	1210	...	1503	...	1815	...
Biharkeresztes ▦ ....a.	0450	...	0919	1125	...	1418	...	1730	...
Biharkeresztes ....d.	0530	0653	0949	1151	...	1508	...	1751	1955
Püspökladány .... **1270** a.	0632	0748	1050	1249	1308	1606	1637	1849	2048
Szolnok .... **1270** a.	0756	...	1156	...	1410	...	1720	1956	...
Budapest Keleti .... **1270** a.	0920	...	1320	...	1532n	...	1837n	2120	...

ADY ENDRE – (12) 🍷 Budapest - Oradea; (12) 🍷 Cluj Napoca - Budapest.
CORONA – 🛏 1, 2 cl., ▬ 2 cl., (12) 🍷 Budapest - Cluj Napoca - Deda - Brasov and v.v.
HARGITA – (12) 🍷 Budapest - Cluj Napoca - Deda - Braşov and v.v.; (2) Budapest - Cluj Napoca - Târgu Mures and v.v.

n – Budapest **Nyugati**.
r – Subject to alteration from June 18.
⊙ – Romanian (East European) time, one hour ahead of Hungary.
* – Classified *IR* in Romania.

d class — DEBRECEN and NYÍREGYHÁZA - MÁTÉSZALKA 1276

								△			Ⓑ
Debrecen ....d.	0508	0715	0915	1115	1315	1515	1715	1807	1920	2115	2246
Nyírbátor ....d.	0632	0832	1032	1232	1432	1632	1832	1913	2039	2236	0000
Mátészalka ....a.	0656	0856	1056	1256	1456	1656	1856	1932	2102	2300	0024

			▽								
Mátészalka.....d.	0413	0458	0530	0703	0903	1103	1303	1503	1703	1900	2107
Nyírbátor.........d.	0437	0522	0551	0727	0927	1127	1327	1527	1727	1934	2131
Debrecen ....a.	0553	0635	0652	0840	1040	1240	1442	1642	1849	2050	2244

	⚒				⚒	⑦					
Nyíregyháza ....d.	0530	...	0837	...	1435	1435	...	1635	...	...	...
Nyírbátor ....d.	0704	...	0959	...	1559	1559	...	1759	...	...	...
Mátészalka ....a.	0728	...	1021	...	1621	1636	...	1821	...	...	...

		▽								
Mátészalka.....d.	...	0530	∴	...	0734	...	1534	...	1725	...	...
Nyírbátor.........d.	...	0550	0553	...	0758	...	1558	...	1758	...	...
Nyíregyháza..a.	...	...	0711	...	0922	...	1722	...	1916	...	...

- (2) [R] Budapest Nyugati (*IC* **626** d. 1523) - Debrecen (*IC* **638**) - Mátészalka.
▽ – (2) [R] Mátészalka (*IC* **639**) - Debrecen (*IC* **629**) - Budapest Nyugati (a. 0937).

d class — DEBRECEN - ORADEA and BAIA MARE and other cross-border services 1277

	6812	**6822**	**6826**
			b
Debrecen .... d.	0712	0912	1512
Nyírábrány ▦ .... a.	0751	0951	1551
Valea lui Mihai ▦ . ⊙ a.	0923	1123	1728
Valea lui Mihai ...... ⊙ d.	0943	1138	1757
Oradea .... ⊙ a.	1118	|	|
Carei .... **1618** ⊙ a.	...	1213	1833
Satu Mare.... **1618** ⊙ a.	...	1256	1925
Baia Mare ... **1616** ⊙ a.	...	...	2203

	6827	**6823**	**6811**
	d		
Baia Mare ... **1616** ⊙ d.	0414	...	...
Satu Mare.... **1618** ⊙ d.	0620	1500	...
Carei............ **1618** ⊙ d.	0708	1543	...
Oradea............. ⊙ d.	|	|	1635
Valea lui Mihai ...... ⊙ a.	0747	1617	1819
Valea lui Mihai ▦.. ⊙ d.	0837	1637	1837
Nyírábrány ▦............ d.	0809	1609	1809
Debrecen .... a.	0848	1648	1848

km								
0	**Békéscsaba** .. **1280** d.	0638	1550	...	**Salonta** ▦ .... ⊙ d.	0940	1830	...
16	Gyula .... **1280** d.	0659	1609	...	Kötegyán ▦ .... d.	0915	1815	...
36	Kötegyán ▦ .... a.	0727	1645	...	Gyula .... **1280** d.	0950	1854	...
50	**Salonta** ▦ .... ⊙ a.	0900	1805	...	**Békéscsaba** .. **1280** a.	1010	1910	...
km								
0	**Mátészalka** .... d.	0535	1410	...	**Carei** .... ⊙ d.	0927	1738	...
18	Tiborszállás ▦ .... a.	0605	1440	...	Tiborszállás ▦........ a.	0853	1704	...
18	Tiborszállás ▦ .... d.	0620	1455	...	Tiborszállás ▦........ d.	0908	1719	...
33	**Carei**.................. ⊙ a.	0746	1621	...	**Mátészalka** .... a.	0952	1803	...

To Jibou (arrive 2358). **d** – From Jibou (depart 0301). ⊙ – Romanian (East European) time, one hour ahead of Hungary.

d class — DEBRECEN - FÜZESABONY 1278

									Ⓑ	
Debrecen ....d.	0450	0645	0845	1045	1245	1445	1645	1850	2000	2245
Hortobágy ....d.	0536	0736	0936	1136	1336	1536	1736	1936	2050	2331
Tiszafüred.....................d.	0613	0813	1013	1213	1413	1613	1813	2013	2126	0007
Füzesabony ....a.	0647	0847	1047	1247	1447	1647	1847	2047	...	...

									Ⓑ	
Füzesabony ....d.	0458	0658	0858	1058	1258	1458	1658	1858	2102	2158
Tiszafüred.....................d.	0534	0734	0934	1134	1334	1534	1734	1934	2137	2233
Hortobágy ....d.	0616	0816	1016	1216	1416	1616	1816	2016	...	...
Debrecen ....a.	0700	0900	1100	1300	1500	1700	1904	2100	...	...

1280 BUDAPEST - BÉKÉSCSABA - LÖKÖSHÁZA - ARAD (- BUCURESTI)

km					7400	IC* 73	481	7402	IC* 75	7404	IC 752	1471	7504	IC 754	7506	IC* 79	1696	7406	IC 756	IC 748	EN* 473	17408		3
			2	2	2	[R]	[R]	2	[R]	2	[R]		2	[R]	2	[R]	[R]	2	[R]	[R]	[R]	2	2	
						T	S		R			N				K	Y				B	⑤		
0	**Budapest** Keleti **1270**	d.	...	...	0610	0710	0710	0810	0910	1010	1110	1110	1210	1310	1410	1510	...	1610	1710	1810	1910	2010	...	2
100	Szolnok **1270**	d.	0445a	0545	0734	0834	0834	0934	1034	1134	1234	1234	1334	1434	1534	1634	...	1734	1834	1934	2034	2134	...	0
141	Mezőtúr	d.	0525	0625	0800	0900	0900	1000	1100	1200	1300	1300	1400	1500	1600	1700	...	1800	1900	2000	2100	2200	...	
159	Gyoma	d.	0547	0647	0813	0913	0913	1013	1113	1213	1313	1313	1413	1513	1613	1713	...	1813	1913	2013	2113	2213	...	
196	**Békéscsaba**	a.	0619	0719	0839	0939	0939	1039	1139	1239	1339	1339	1439	1539	1639	1739	...	1839	1939	2039	2139	2239	...	0
196	**Békéscsaba**	d.	0635	...	...	0943	0943	...	1143	...	1343	1343	1443	1543	1643	1743	...	...	1943	...	2143	...	2245	0
225	Lökösháza	a.	0713	...	...	1010	1010	...	1210	...	1410	1410	1513	1613	1713	1813	...	...	2010	...	2210	...	2312	0
225	Lökösháza 🛃	d.	...	...	...	1035	1035	...	1235	...	...	1435	...	...	...	1838	...	...	...	...	2240	...	...	0
236	Curtici 🛃	⊙ d.	...	...	...	1210	1210	...	1407	...	...	1615	...	...	...	2016	...	...	...	...	0015	...	...	0
253	**Arad**	⊙ a.	...	...	...	1224	1224	...	1421	...	...	1629	...	...	...	2030	...	...	...	...	0029	...	...	0
	Timisoara **1614**	⊙ a.	...	...	...	1314	1314	...	|	...	...	...	...	...	...	2125	2220	...	...	...	|	...	...	
	Brasov **1600**	⊙ a.	...	...	...	|	...	...	2245	...	...	...	...	...	...	...	|	...	...	...	0920	...	...	1
	Bucuresti Nord **1600**	⊙ a.	...	...	...	2256	...	...	...	...	...	...	...	...	...	...	0820	...	...	...	1200	...	...	1

		346	7509	EN* 472	IC 759	7507	1695	IC* 78	7407	IC 757	7405	IC 755	7403	1470	IC* 74		IC* 72	480	IC 753	7501	IC 751	17411	
		⊡	2	[R]	[R]	2	[R]	[R]	2	[R]	2	[R]	2		[R]		[R]	[R]	[R]	2	[R]	2	2
		D		B			Y	K						N	R		T	S				④⑦	
Bucuresti Nord **1600**	⊙ d.	1400	...	1745	...	...	2145	...	...	...	...	...	...	...	...	...	0545	...	...	...	...	...	...
Brasov **1600**	⊙ d.	1631	...	2022	...	...	|	...	...	...	...	...	...	...	0600	...	|	...	...	...	...	...	...
Timisoara **1614**	⊙ d.	|	...	|	...	...	0707	0750	...	...	...	...	...	...	|	...	1448	1448	...	...	...	...	...
Arad	⊙ d.	0127	...	0522	...	...	...	0840	...	...	...	...	...	1234	1428	...	1539	1539	...	...	...	...	...
Curtici 🛃	⊙ d.	0205	...	0605	...	...	...	0914	...	...	...	...	...	1320	1514	...	1614	1614	...	...	...	...	...
Lökösháza 🛃	a.	0115	...	0515	...	...	...	0824	...	...	...	...	...	1230	1424	...	1524	1524	...	...	...	...	...
Lökösháza	d.	0150	0450	0549	0649	0749	...	0849	...	1049	...	1249	...	1310	1449	...	1549	1549	1649	1749	1849	...	...
Békéscsaba	a.	0215	0517	0616	0716	0816	...	0916	...	1116	...	1316	...	1335	1516	...	1616	1616	1716	1816	1916	...	...
Békéscsaba	d.	0220	0530	0620	0720	0820	...	0920	1020	1120	1220	1320	1420	1420	1520	...	1620	1620	1720	1820	1920	2040	...
Gyoma	d.	|	0601	0647	0747	0847	...	0947	1047	1147	1247	1347	1447	1447	1547	...	1647	1647	1747	1847	1947	2113	...
Mezőtúr	d.	|	0616	0701	0801	0901	...	1001	1101	1201	1301	1401	1501	1501	1601	...	1701	1701	1801	1901	2001	2136	...
Szolnok **1270**	d.	0318	0649	0727	0827	0927	...	1027	1127	1227	1327	1427	1527	1527	1627	...	1727	1727	1827	1927	2027	2215	2219
Budapest Keleti **1270**	a.	0455	0815	0850	0950	1050	...	1150	1250	1350	1450	1550	1650	1650	1750	...	1850	1850	1950	2050	2150	...	0015

B – ISTER – 🛏 1, 2 cl., 🛌 2 cl., (2) 🍸 Budapest - Arad - Sibiu - Brasov - Bucuresti and v.v.
D – DACIA – 🛏 1, 2 cl., 🛌 2 cl., (12) Wien - Budapest - Arad - Sigisoara - Brasov - Bucuresti and v.v.
K – KÖRÖS / CRIS – (12) Budapest - Arad - Timisoara and v.v.
N – NESEBAR – ②⑤ June 17 - Sept. 2 from Budapest; ③⑥ June 18 - Sept. 3 from Burgas (next day from Arad). 🛏 1, 2 cl., 🛌 2 cl., (2) 🍸 Budapest - Craiova - Ruse - Burgas and v.v.; (2) Budapest - Lökösháza and v.v.
R – TRANSSYLVANIA – (12) Budapest - Arad - Simeria - Sibiu - Brasov and v.v.
S – BONONIA – (2) 🛌 2 cl. Budapest - Timisoara - Craiova - Vidin - Sofia and v.v. (also 🛏 1, 2 cl. from Budapest to June 13 / from Sept. 6; from Sofia to June 14 / from Sept. 7).
T – TRAIANUS – (12) Budapest - Timisoara - Craiova - Bucuresti and v.v.
Y – 🛏 1, 2 cl., 🛌 2 cl. and (12) Bucuresti - Timisoara and v.v.

a – Ⓐ only.
b – Not ⑤.
s – Not Dec. 20, 27, June 19 - Aug. 28. To / from Szeged (Table **1292**).
⊙ – Romanian (East European) time, one hour ahead of Hungary.
⊡ – [R] in Romania.
* – Classified *IR* in Romania.

Note: *IC* trains on this line have designated carriages for the use of passengers without seat reservations.

BÉKÉSCSABA - GYULA

16 km 2nd class. Journey 17 - 20 m

From **Békéscsaba**: 0523, 0638, 07 0950, 1150, 1250, 1350, 1427 Ⓐ, 1450, 1550, 1617⑦ **s**, 1650, 1750, 1950, 2050, 2230 **b**, 2243⑤.

From **Gyula**: 0459, 0548, 0617Ⓐ, 0659, 0750, 0854, 0950, 1054, 125 1450, 1550, 1650, 1728⑦ **s**, 1750, 1854, 1950, 2050.

1290 BUDAPEST - KECSKEMÉT - SZEGED

km			7020	IC 700	IC 702	IC 712		IC 708	IC 718	IC 728	
			2	[R]	[R]	[R]		[R]	[R]	[R]	
										⑤⑦	
0	**Budapest** Nyugati	▷ d.	0400	0553	0653	0753		1853	1953	2053	...
11	Kőbánya Kispest	▷ d.	0415	0607	0707	0807	and	1907	2007	2107	...
18	Ferihegy ✈	▷ d.	0424	0613	0713	0813	hourly	1913	2013	2113	...
73	Cegléd	▷ d.	0531	0648	0748	0848	until	1948	2048	2148	...
106	**Kecskemét**	d.	0605	0711	0811	0911		2011	2111	2211	...
131	Kiskunfélegyháza	d.	0630	0730	0830	0930		2030	2130	2228	...
191	**Szeged**	a.	0715	0815	0915	1015		2115	2215	2317	...

		7029	7009	IC 709	IC 707	IC 717		IC 701	IC 711	IC
		2	2	[R]	[R]	[R]		[R]	[R]	
Szeged	d.	...	0436	0547	0645	0745		1845	1945	2
Kiskunfélegyháza	d.	...	0523	0631	0731	0831	and	1931	2031	2
Kecskemét	d.	0435	0539	0648	0748	0848	hourly	1948	2048	2
Cegléd	▷ d.	0508	0608	0713	0813	0913	until	2013	2113	2
Ferihegy ✈	▷ a.	0554	0654	0744	0844	0944		2044	2144	2
Kőbánya Kispest	▷ a.	0600	0700	0750	0850	0950		2050	2150	2
Budapest Nyugati	▷ a.	0617	0717	0807	0907	1007		2107	2207	2

▷ – For additional trains see Table **1270**.

Note: *IC* trains on this line have designated carriages for the use of passengers without seat reservations.

1292 SZEGED - BÉKÉSCSABA

2nd cla

km					d	d		Ⓐ				
0	**Szeged**	d.	0521	0621	0721	0921	1121	1221	1321	and	1921	2021
31	Hódmezővásárhely	d.	0601	0705	0801	1001	1201	1305	1401	hourly	2001	2105
62	Orosháza	d.	0631	0731	0831	1031	1231	1331	1431	until	2031	2133
97	**Békéscsaba**	a.	0712	0810	0910	1110	1310	1410	1510		2110	...

					h	h	Ⓐ			
Békéscsaba	d.	0547	0647	0747	0947	1147	1247	1345	and	1
Orosháza	d.	0632	0732	0832	1032	1232	1332	1432	hourly	2
Hódmezővásárhely	d.	0702	0802	0902	1102	1302	1402	1502	until	2
Szeged	a.	0740	0840	0940	1140	1340	1440	1540		2

d – Additional journeys run at 0821©, 1021©.
h – Additional journeys run at 0847©, 1047©.

1295 BUDAPEST - KISKUNHALAS - KELEBIA - (BEOGRAD)

km			7920	7912	343	EC 345	7916	7926	7918	7928	341
			2	2	D	L	2	2	2	2	B
0	**Budapest Keleti**	d.	...	0605	0805	1205	1405	1605	1805	1932r	2225
7	Ferencváros	d.	...	0614	0814	1214	1414	1614	1814	1941	2234
61	Kunszentmiklós-Tass	d.	0510	0709	0909	1309	1509	1709	1909	2050	2320
107	Kiskőrös	d.	0601	0801	1001	1401	1601	1801	2001	2138	0006
134	Kiskunhalas	a.	0632	0832	1032	1432	1632	1832	2032	2208	0034
163	**Kelebia** 🛃	a.	0711	0911	1111	1511	1711	1911	2111	...	0105
	Subotica **1360**	a.	...	...	1155	1555	...	...	...	...	0154
	Beograd **1360**	a.	...	...	1632	2013	...	...	...	...	0621

		340	7929	7927	7937	EC 344	7923	342	7911
		B	2	2	2	L n	2	D	2
Beograd **1360**	d.	2150	...	...	...	0720	...	1135	...
Subotica **1360**	d.	0216	...	...	...	1159	...	1600	...
Kelebia 🛃	d.	0300	0448	0646	0846	1246	1446	1646	1846
Kiskunhalas	d.	0328	0525	0725	0925	1325	1525	1725	1925
Kiskőrös	d.	0358	0600	0800	1000	1400	1600	1800	2000
Kunszentmiklós-Tass	d.	0442	0649	0850	1050	1450	1650	1850	2050
Ferencváros	a.	0537	0749	0945	1145	1545	1745	1945	2145
Budapest Keleti	a.	0546	0758	0954	1154	1554	1754	1954	2154

B – BEOGRAD – 🛌 2 cl., (12) Budapest - Beograd and v.v.; 🛏 1, 2 cl. Moskva - Budapest - Beograd - Sofia and v.v. (extended to / from Varna / Burgas on summer dates in Table **95**). Conveys on ②⑤ June 17 - Sept. 2 🛏 1, 2 cl. Praha (**173/2**) - Budapest - Beograd - Bar, returning from Bar on ④⑦ June 19 - Sept. 4.
D – IVO ANDRIĆ – (12) Budapest - Beograd and v.v.
L – AVALA – (12) ✕ Wien - Györ - Budapest - Beograd and v.v. Conveys on ②⑤ June 17 - Sept. 2 🛏 1, 2 cl., 🛌 2 cl., (2) Budapest - Subotica - Bar, returning from Bar on ③⑥ June 18 - Sept. 3 (next day from Subotica).
n – [R] from Beograd.
r – Kőbánya Kispest.

1299 OTHER LOCAL SERVICES

2nd cla

BUDAPEST - DUNAÚJVÁROS *80* km, journey 85 - 90 minutes
From **Budapest** Déli: 0555, 0655, 0855, 1055, 1255, 1355, 1455, 1555, 1655, 1855, 2055.
From **Dunaújváros**: 0629, 0729, 0829, 1034, 1229, 1434, 1534, 1634, 1729, 1834, 2029.

BUDAPEST - ESZTERGOM *53 km*, journey 86-88 minutes
From **Budapest** Nyugati: 0436, 0536, 0610, 0720 and hourly until 2320. Additional journeys on Ⓐ (journey 73-77 mins) run hourly 0754Ⓐ - 1954Ⓐ.
From **Esztergom**: 0332, 0415, 0502, 0542Ⓐ, 0607, 0645, 0712 and hourly until 2212. Additional journeys on Ⓐ (journey 79-83 mins) run hourly 0747Ⓐ - 1247Ⓐ, 1351Ⓐ - 1851Ⓐ.
© Mar. 26 - Nov. 6: 1020, 1120, 1320 call at **Vasútmúzeum**, returning 1430, 1530, 1630.

BUDAPEST - SZENTENDRE *21 km*, journey time 41 minutes
HÉV suburban trains from Budapest Batthyány tér, every 20 - 30 minutes.

ESZTERGOM - KOMÁROM *53 km*, journey time 1h 30m – 1h 45m
From **Esztergom**: 0653, 1623. From **Komárom**: 0513, 1410.

EGER - SZILVÁSVÁRAD *34 km*, journey time 65 min
From **Eger**: 0445 Ⓐ, 0900 **G**, 1400 Ⓐ, 1455 © **H**, 1750 Ⓐ.
From **Szilvásvárad**: 0555 Ⓐ, 1135 **K**, 1340 © **H**, 1555Ⓐ, 1755©**N**, 1900Ⓐ.
Via Szilvásvárad-Szalajkavölgy (for the forest railway), 5 minutes before Szilvásvárad.

HATVAN - SZOLNOK *68 km*, journey 71 - 73 min
From **Hatvan**: 0613, 0813, 1013, 1213, 1413, 1513Ⓐ, 1613, 1713Ⓐ, 1813, 1913Ⓐ, 20
From **Szolnok**: 0631, 0831, 1031, 1231, 1431, 1531Ⓐ, 1631, 1731Ⓐ, 1831, 1931Ⓐ, 20

KISKUNFÉLEGYHÁZA - CSONGRÁD - SZENTES *39 km*, journey time 53 min
From **Kiskunfélegyháza**: 0534Ⓐ, 0734, 0934, 1334, 1534, 1734, 1934, 2134.
From **Szentes**: 0428Ⓐ, 0634, 0834, 1234, 1434, 1634, 1834 (calls Csongrád 18 mins la

G – ⑤⑥⑦ (daily Apr. 15 - Oct. 23).
H – © Apr. 16 - Oct. 23.
K – ⑤ (runs Ⓐ Apr. 18 - Oct. 23).
N – © Mar. 28 - Nov. 4.

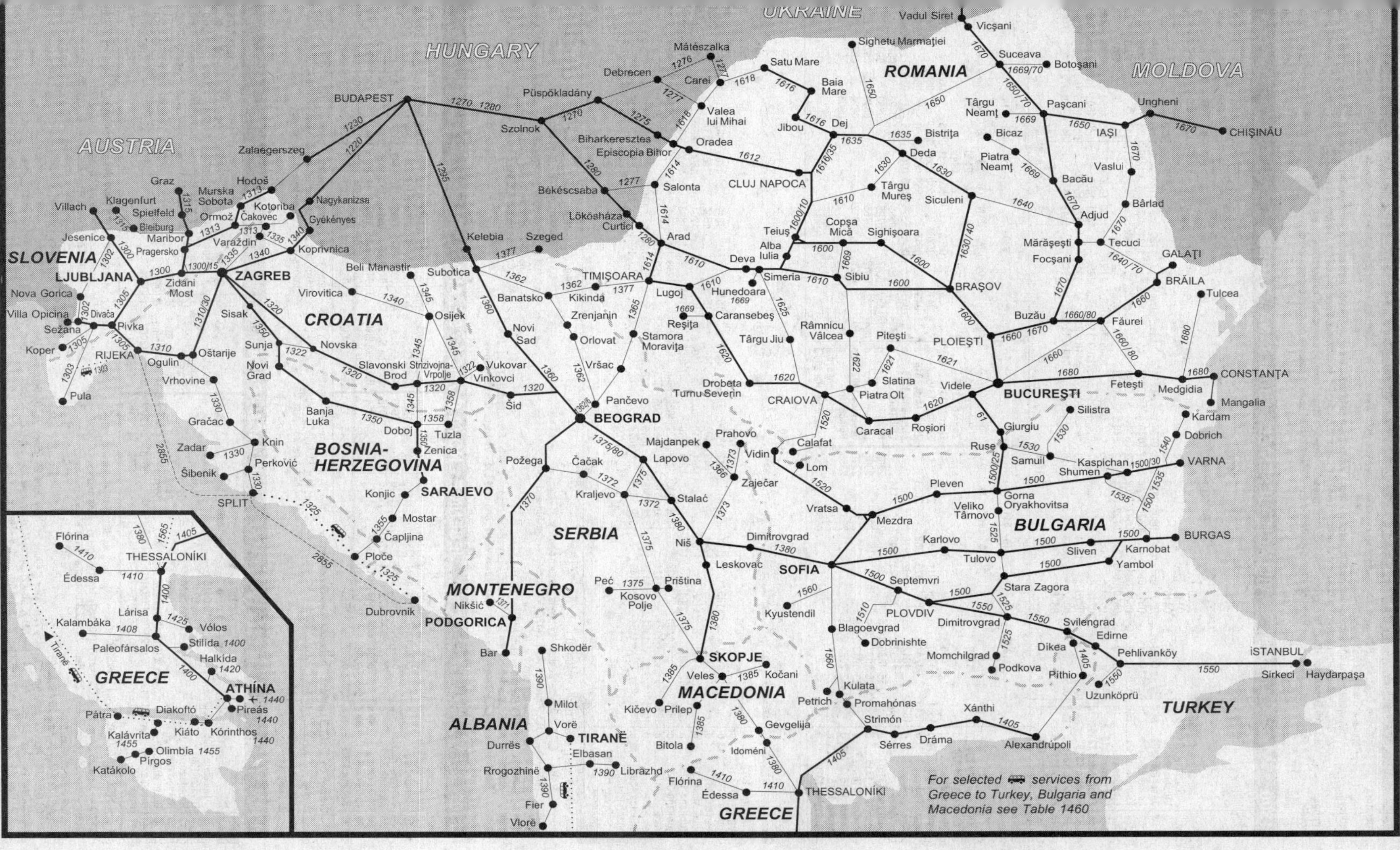
UKRAINE
HUNGARY
AUSTRIA
ROMANIA
MOLDOVA
SLOVENIA
CROATIA
BOSNIA-HERZEGOVINA
SERBIA
MONTENEGRO
ALBANIA
MACEDONIA
BULGARIA
GREECE
TURKEY
BUDAPEST
CHIŞINĂU
BUCUREŞTI
LJUBLJANA
ZAGREB
SARAJEVO
BEOGRAD
PODGORICA
TIRANË
SKOPJE
SOFIA
İSTANBUL
THESSALONÍKI
ATHÍNA
CLUJ NAPOCA
TIMIŞOARA
BRAŞOV
PLOIEŞTI
CRAIOVA
CONSTANŢA
GALAŢI
BRĂILA
IAŞI
VARNA
BURGAS
PLOVDIV
SPLIT
RIJEKA
For selected services from Greece to Turkey, Bulgaria and Macedonia see Table 1460

SLOVENIA, CROATIA and BOSNIA-HERZEGOVINA

Operators: Slovenske Železnice (SŽ): www.slo-zeleznice.si; Hrvatske Železnice (HŽ): www.hzpp.hr; Željeznice Federacije Bosne i Hercegovine (ŽFBH): www.zfbh.ba; and Želj Republike Srpske (ŽRS): www.zrs-rs.com.

Services: All trains convey first and second class seating, **except** where shown otherwise in footnotes or by '2' in the train column, or where the footnote shows sleeping and / or cou cars only. Descriptions of sleeping (🛏) and couchette (▬) cars appear on page 8. In Slovenia, travel by *ICS* train requires reservation and payment of a special fare

Timings: Valid until **December 10, 2016** except where indicated otherwise. Readers should note, however, that further changes are possible.

Tickets: A supplement is payable for travel by internal express trains. Reservation of seats is possible on most express trains.

1300 VILLACH - JESENICE - LJUBLJANA - ZAGREB

SŽ, HŽ,

km					499					415												211		631		
		2	2	2		2	2	2	2		2	2	2	2	2	2	2	2	2	2	2		2	2	2	2
			Ⓐ		♦			Ⓐ	Ⓐ	♦	Ⓐ	Ⓐ	Ⓒ	Ⓐ		Ⓐ	Ⓐ			Ⓐ	Ⓐ	♦	Ⓐ	Ⓐ		
	München Hbf **890** d.	...	...	...	2336	...	...	...	...	...	...	...	...	...	...	...	...	...	...	...	...	...	...	...	...	...
	Salzburg Hbf **970** d.	...	...	...	0134	...	...	...	...	...	...	...	...	...	...	...	...	...	...	...	...	...	...	...	...	...
0	**Villach** Hbf d.	...	...	...	0415	...	...	...	...	0625	...	...	...	...	...	...	...	...	...	...	...	1253	...	...	...	...
38	**Jesenice 1302** 🛃 d.	...	0430	...	0505	0532	...	0605	0625	0715	0732	...	0754	...	...	0946	...	1120	...	...	1235	1340	...	...	1418	...
51	Lesce-Bled d.	...	0444	...	0517	0547	...	0620	0640	0731	0746	...	0813	...	...	1003	...	1134	...	...	1249	1351	...	...	1435	...
74	Kranj d.	...	0508	...	0539	0611	...	0647	0708	0752	0814	...	0838	...	...	1028	...	1158	...	...	1321	1411	...	...	1500	...
102	**Ljubljana** a.	...	0539	...	0559	0645	...	0722	0744	0812	0846	...	0908	...	...	1059	...	1228	...	...	1352	1431	...	...	1531	...
102	**Ljubljana 1315** d.	0450a	...	0550	0620	...	0650	...	...	0825	...	0852	...	0955	*1050*	...	1150	...	*1250*	*1350*	...	1445	1450	1535	...	1545
166	Zidani Most **1315** d.	0604	...	0657	0712	...	0755	...	...	0917	...	1001	...	1100	1155	...	1255	...	1401	1455	...	1540	1601	1635	...	1700
182	Sevnica **1315** d.	0623	...	0715	0728	...	0814	...	...	0933	...	1020	...	1118	1213	...	1313	...	1420	1514	...	1556	1620	1651	...	1719
215	Dobova **1315** 🛃 d.	0653	...	0744	0807	...	0843	...	...	1015	...	1050	...	1147	1242	...	1342	...	1449	1543	...	1641	1649	1721	...	1749
245	**Zagreb 1315** a.	...	...	...	0838	...	...	...	...	1046	...	...	...	...	...	...	...	...	...	...	...	1712	...	...	...	...
	Beograd **1320** a.	...	...	...	...	...	...	...	...	1733	...	...	...	...	...	...	...	...	...	...	...	...	...	...	...	...

			EC 213				315	411		
	2	2		2	2	2			2	2
	Ⓐ		♦				♦	♦	N	Ⓐ
München Hbf **890** d.	...	...	1218	...	...	...	...	...	...	...
Salzburg Hbf **970** d.	...	...	1412	...	...	...	...	...	...	...
Villach Hbf. d.	...	...	1653	...	...	...	1853	...	...	...
Jesenice 1302 🛃 d.	1531	...	1740	...	1806	1911	1947	...	2022	...
Lesce-Bled d.	1545	...	1751	...	1820	1925	1958	...	2036	...
Kranj d.	1623	...	1812	...	1846	1952	2018	...	2101	...
Ljubljana a.	1652	...	1832	...	1920	2023	2040	...	2134	...
Ljubljana 1315 d.	...	1755	1835	1855	...	...	...	2105	...	2205
Zidani Most **1315** d.	...	1905	1927	2000	...	...	...	2202	...	2308
Sevnica **1315** d.	...	1923	1943	2019	...	...	...	2218	...	2326
Dobova **1315** 🛃 d.	...	1952	2023	2048	...	...	...	2257	...	2355
Zagreb 1315 a.	...	...	2054	...	...	...	...	2328	...	...
Beograd **1320** a.	...	...	...	...	...	...	...	0554	...	...

				630			410	632	314			
	2	2	2	2	2	2		2		2	2	2
	Ⓐ		Ⓐ	Ⓐ	ⒸN	Ⓐ	♦	Ⓐ	♦		Ⓐ	
Beograd **1320** d.	...	...	...	...	...	...	2130	...	...	...	...	...
Zagreb 1315 d.	...	...	...	...	...	...	0445	...	...	...	...	...
Dobova **1315** 🛃 d.	...	...	...	0453	...	*0505*	0531	0546	...	0600	...	0705
Sevnica **1315** d.	...	0413	...	0526	...	*0535*	0556	0613	...	0630	...	0735
Zidani Most **1315** d.	...	0431	...	0547	...	0555	0612	0630	...	0658	...	0755
Ljubljana 1315 a.	...	0534	...	0643	...	0659	0708	0725	...	0800	...	0901
Ljubljana d.	0434	...	0611	...	0655	...	...	...	0728	...	0826	...
Kranj d.	0508	...	0647	...	0725	...	...	...	0752	...	0900	...
Lesce-Bled d.	0547	...	0712	...	0755	...	...	...	0813	...	0924	...
Jesenice 1302 🛃 a.	0601	...	0725	...	0812	...	...	...	0824	...	0937	...
Villach Hbf. a.	...	...	...	...	...	...	...	...	0908	...	...	...
Salzburg Hbf **970** a.	...	...	...	...	...	...	...	...	...	...	...	...
München Hbf **890** a.	...	...	...	...	...	...	...	...	...	...	...	...

											210													414		
	2	2	2	2	2	2	2	2	2	2		2	2	2	2	2	2	2	2	2	2	2	2		2	2
			Ⓐ			Ⓐ	Ⓐ	A			♦		Ⓐ	Ⓐ	Ⓐ		Ⓐ			Ⓑ	Ⓐ			♦	Ⓑ	Ⓑ
Beograd **1320** d.	...	...	...	...	...	...	...	...	...	...	...	...	...	...	...	...	...	...	...	...	...	...	...	1100	...	...
Zagreb 1315 d.	...	...	...	...	...	...	...	...	...	...	1237	...	...	...	...	...	...	...	...	...	...	...	...	1838	...	...
Dobova **1315** 🛃 d.	...	0911	1011	...	1105	...	1211	...	...	1312	1338	...	...	1410	...	1513	...	...	1612	...	1706	1807	...	1925	1910	2010
Sevnica **1315** d.	...	0941	1041	...	1135	...	1241	...	...	1342	1402	...	...	1440	...	1543	...	...	1642	...	1737	1837	...	1949	1940	2040
Zidani Most **1315** d.	...	1000	1100	...	1155	...	1300	...	...	1401	1418	...	...	1500	...	1602	...	...	1701	...	1800	1858	...	2005	2009	2100
Ljubljana 1315 a.	...	1102	1202	...	1301	...	1402	...	...	1503	1510	...	...	1602	...	1704	...	...	1803	...	1902	2004	...	2056	2111	2202
Ljubljana d.	0955	...	...	1250	...	1332	...	1425	1445	...	1527	1532	1548	...	1621	...	1718	1753	...	1857	...	...	2024	2110	...	...
Kranj d.	1028	...	...	1321	...	1411	...	1500	1518	...	1552	1603	1623	...	1655	...	1750	1826	...	1932	...	...	2101	2131	...	...
Lesce-Bled d.	1052	...	...	1351	...	1435	...	1522	1545	...	1613	1627	1648	...	1719	...	1820	1849	...	1958	...	...	2125	2151	...	...
Jesenice 1302 🛃 a.	1105	...	...	1404	...	1448	...	1539	1559	...	1624	1640	1702	...	1732	...	1833	1901	...	2012	...	...	2138	2202	...	...
Villach Hbf. a.	...	...	...	...	...	...	...	...	...	...	1709	...	...	...	...	...	...	...	...	...	...	...	...	2243	...	...
Salzburg Hbf **970** a.	...	...	...	...	...	...	...	...	...	...	...	...	...	...	...	...	...	...	...	...	...	...	...	...	...	...
München Hbf **890** a.	...	...	...	...	...	...	...	...	...	...	...	...	...	...	...	...	...	...	...	...	...	...	...	...	...	...

♦ – **NOTES** (LISTED BY TRAIN NUMBER)

210/1 – SAVA – [12] Vinkovci - Zagreb - Ljubljana - Villach and v.v.
212/3 – MIMARA – [12] Zagreb - Villach (**112/3**) - München - Frankfurt and v.v.
314/5 – [12] Villach - Ljubljana and v.v.
410/1 – ▬ 2 cl. and [12] Beograd - Ljubljana and v.v.
414/5 – ALPINE PEARLS – 🛏 1, 2 cl., ▬ 2 cl. and [2] Zagreb - Ljubljana - Villach - Schwarzach-St Veit (**464/5**) - Zürich and v.v.; [2] Beograd - Zagreb - Ljubljana - Villach and v.v.; [12] Vinkovci - Zagreb and v.v.
498/9 – LISINSKI – 🛏 1, 2 cl., ▬ 2 cl. and [2] Zagreb - Salzburg (**462/3**) - München and v.v.

A – ⑤ Dec. 18 - June 17, Sept. 2 - Dec. 9 (also Dec. 24, Apr. 2 not Dec. 25, Jan. 1, Apr. 29).
N – Conveys on Ⓒ: [2] Ljubljana - Jesenice - Nova Gorica and
a – Ⓐ only.

1302 JESENICE - NOVA GORICA - SEŽANA

2nd class only

km		Ⓐ	q	t	Ⓐ	N		Ⓐ	Ⓐ		Ⓑ	
0	**Jesenice 1300** d.	...	0414	0414	0606	0820	1114	...	1434	1653	...	1904
10	Bled Jezero d.	...	0430	0430	0622	0837	1130	...	1450	1708	...	1920
28	Bohinjska Bistrica d.	...	0451	0451	0650	0858	1150	...	1510	1727	...	1940
56	Most na Soči d.	...	0527	0527	0725	0934	1226	...	1605	1803	...	2016
89	Nova Gorica ♣ a.	...	0604	0604	0814	1012	1306	...	1643	1840	...	2054
89	Nova Gorica ♣ d.	0455	0608	...	0912	...	...	1530	...	...	1847	...
130	**Sežana 1305** a.	0552	0708	...	1010	...	...	1628	...	...	1945	...

	Ⓐ				w			ⒸN	Ⓑy	Ⓑy
Sežana 1305 d.	...	...	0625a	1018a	...	1432a	1640	...	...	2050
Nova Gorica ♣ a.	...	...	0720a	1111a	...	1524a	1732	...	...	2142
Nova Gorica ♣ d.	0331	0526	0735	1116	1447	1527	...	1801	1933	...
Most na Soči d.	0406	0609	0814	1157	1526	1604	...	1847	2019	...
Bohinjska Bistrica d.	0453	0648	0859	1244	1605	1642	...	1943	2057	...
Bled Jezero d.	0513	0708	0919	1304	1625	1709	...	2001	2116	...
Jesenice 1300 a.	0529	0724	0936	1321	1642	1726	...	2015	2132	...

N – Conveys on Ⓒ: [2] Ljubljana - Jesenice - Nova Gorica and v.v.
a – Ⓐ only.
h – June 25 - Aug. 28.
q – Ⓐ (daily June 25 - Aug. 28).
t – ⑥ (not June 25 - Aug. 28).
w – Not Ⓒ June 27 - Aug. 31.
y – Not June 25 - Aug. 28.
♣ – Line **1** 🚌 service operates between Nova Gorica (bus 100 metres from station on Italian side) and Gorizia Centrale (stations. Total journey time ± 20 minutes.

1303 DIVAČA - PULA

2nd class only HŽ,

km					1272	1274							
		Ⓐ		w	♦	♦		z	Ⓐ				
	Ljubljana **1305** d.	...	...	...	0610	0610	...	...	...	...	...	...	...
0	**Divača 1305** d.	...	...	...	0745	0745	...	...	...	1501	...	...	...
12	Hrpelje-Kozina d.	...	...	...	0800	0800	...	...	...	1518	...	...	...
30	Rakitovec 🛃 d.	...	...	...	0835	0835	...	...	...	1543	...	...	...
36	Buzet 🛃 d.	...	0513z	0705	0902	0902	1117	1300	...	1551	1556	...	1954r
43	Lupoglav ▲ d.	0440	0535	0727	0921	0921	1139	1322	1513	...	1618	...	2016
117	**Pula** a.	0615	0721	0903	1042	1042	1311	1459	1649	...	1752	...	2152

										1273	1275
	Ⓐ	w	z					Ⓐ	v	♦	♦
Pula d.	...	0500	0650	0915	1320	...	1427	1534	1720	1810	1810
Lupoglav ▲ a.	...	0635	0827	1049	1507	...	1610	1716	1900	1930	1930
Buzet 🛃 d.	...	0658	0847	1109	1531	1600	1638	1736	1920r	2000	2000
Rakitovec 🛃 d.	0528	...	...	...	...	1610	...	...	...	2021	2021
Hrpelje-Kozina d.	0552	...	...	...	...	1634	...	...	...	2050	2050
Divača 1305 a.	0604	...	...	...	...	1646	...	...	...	2102	2102
Ljubljana **1305** a.	...	...	...	...	...	...	...	...	...	2238	2238

♦ – **NOTES** (LISTED BY TRAIN NUMBER)

1272/3 – June 25 - Aug. 28: [2] Maribor (**1604/5**) - Hrpelje-Kozina - Pula and v.v.
1274/5 – Apr. 23 - May 2, Aug. 29 - Sept. 25: [2] Ljubljana - Pula and v.v.

h – Not June 25, Aug. 15.
r – Apr. 23 - May 2, June 25 - Sept. 25.
v – Ⓐ Dec. 14 - Apr. 22; daily Apr. 23 - May 2; Ⓐ May 3 - June 24; daily June 25 - Sept. 25; Ⓐ Sept. 26 - Dec. 10.
w – ⚒ Dec. 14 - Apr. 23; daily Apr. 24 - May 1; ⚒ May 2 - June 24; daily June 25 - Sept. 25; ⚒ Sept. 26 - Dec. 10.
z – Ⓐ Dec. 14 - 23, Jan. 11 - Mar. 18, Mar. 29 - June 10, Sept. 5 - Dec. 9.

▲ – 🚌 service **Lupoglav - Rijeka and v.v.**: Journey 40 minu
From Lupoglav: 0639⚒ **h**, 1110, 1618, 2120.
From Rijeka: 0555⚒ **h**, 1025, 1425Ⓐ, 1535Ⓒ, 1930.

Ž 2nd class only except where shown — LJUBLJANA - RIJEKA, KOPER, SEŽANA and VILLA OPICINA — 1305

								ICS			*IC*	*ICS*											*IC*				
				1274	1605		481	29			505	35							483				509				
	Ⓐ	Ⓒ		♦	♦		♦	Ⓡ h			z	Ⓡ y		Ⓐ	Ⓐ				♦		Ⓑ	Ⓐ			Ⓐ	A	
Maribor **1315** d.	...	...	...	...	0340	...	...	0548	...	...	0655	0748	...	...	...	...	...	...	...	...	...	...	...	...	...	...	...
Ljubljana d.	0432	...	0550	0610	0610	...	0635	0742	0810	...	0935	0942	...	1040	1210	1312	...	1433	1510	1542	1610	1657	1745	1854	1950	...	2100
Postojna d.	0536	...	0655	0709	0709	...	0732	0830	0915	...	1034	1035	...	1144	1316	1419	...	1539	1610	1648	1710	1802	1846	1959	2055	...	2204
Pivka ▲ d.	0550	...	0709	0722	0722	...	0745	0841	0929	...	1047	1046	...	1158	1330	1434	...	1553	1623	1701	1722	1816	1857	2012	2109	...	2218
Ilirska Bistrica 🏨 ▲ d.	|	...	|	|	|	...	0814	|	|	...	|	|	...	|	|	|	...	|	1650	|	|	|	|	|	|	...	|
Šapjane 🏨 d.	|	...	|	|	|	...	0843	|	|	...	|	|	...	|	|	|	...	|	1718	|	|	|	|	|	|	...	|
Rijeka 1310 a.	|	...	|	|	|	...	0920	|	|	...	|	|	...	|	|	|	...	|	1755	|	|	|	|	|	|	...	|
Divača **1303** a.	0611	...	0730	0743	0743	...	...	0900	0950	...	1107	1104	...	1219	1351	1454	...	1614	...	1722	1741	1837	1917	2033	2130	...	2239
Divača d.	0613	...	0732	0745	0745	0757	...	0902	0951	...	1109	1106	1111	1221	1352	1455	1538	1615	...	1724	1742	1838	1918	2034	2131	2131	2240
Hrpelje-Kozina ⊡ d.	|	...	|	0757	0805	0809	...	0914	|	...	1120	1117	|	|	|	|	|	|	...	1737	|	|	1931	|	|	|	|
Koper ⊡ a.	|	...	|	...	0840	0845	...	0945	|	...	1155	1148	|	|	|	|	|	|	...	1813	|	|	2004	|	|	|	|
Sežana 🏨 a.	0622	...	0741	...	...	...	...	...	1000	...	...	...	1121	1230	1401	1505	1548	1624	...	...	1751	1848	...	2044	2140	2140	2249
Sežana 🏨 d.	0623	0623	...	...	...	...	...	...	1001	...	...	...	...	1231	...	...	...	1625	...	...	...	...	...	2045	2141	2141	...
Villa Opicina **601** a.	0633	0633	...	...	...	...	...	...	1011	...	...	...	...	1241	...	...	...	1635	...	...	...	...	...	2055	2151	2151	...

					IC										*IC*	*ICS*			*ICS*								
					508						482				504	34			28				1275	1604	480		
		Ⓐ	Ⓐ	Ⓐ		Ⓐ		Ⓐ			♦	Ⓐ	Ⓐ		z	Ⓡ y	Ⓐ		Ⓡ h	Ⓑ			♦	♦	♦		B
Villa Opicina **601** d.	...	...	...	...	...	...	0700	...	1030	...	...	1324	...	...	...	...	...	1724	...	...	...	...	...	...	...	2119	2236
Sežana 🏨 a.	...	...	...	...	...	...	0710	...	1040	...	...	1334	...	...	...	...	...	1734	...	...	...	...	...	...	...	2129	2246
Sežana 🏨 d.	...	0430	0510	0558	...	...	0711	0923	1041	...	...	1335	1433	1516	...	...	1649	1735	...	1820	1954	...	...	...	...	...	...
Koper ⊡ d.	...	|	|	|	0525	...	|	|	|	1003	...	|	|	|	1444	1447	|	|	1639	|	|	1915	...	2015	...	...	...
Hrpelje-Kozina ⊡ d.	...	|	|	|	0558	...	|	|	|	1036	...	|	|	|	1518	1518	|	|	1709	|	|	1952	2050	2050	...	...	...
Divača **1303** a.	...	0439	0521	0608	0610	...	0720	0932	1051	1048	...	1344	1442	1526	1529	1528	1658	1744	1718	1828	2004	2005	2102	2102	...	...	...
Divača d.	...	0440	0522	...	0612	...	0721	0933	...	1100	...	1345	1443	...	1531	1530	1700	1745	1719	1829	...	2016	2107	2107	...	...	...
Rijeka 1310 d.	...	|	|	...	|	...	|	|	...	|	1155	|	|	...	|	|	|	|	|	|	...	|	|	|	2050	...	...
Šapjane 🏨 d.	...	|	|	...	|	...	|	|	...	|	1250	|	|	...	|	|	|	|	|	|	...	|	|	|	2143	...	...
Ilirska Bistrica 🏨 ▲ d.	...	|	|	...	|	0632	|	|	...	|	1323	|	|	...	|	|	|	|	|	|	...	|	|	|	2212	...	...
Pivka ▲ d.	0410	0502	0544	...	0636	0650	0742	0956	...	1123	1339	1408	1506	...	1552	1549	1723	1808	1738	1850	...	2038	2129	2129	2228	...	...
Postojna d.	0423	0515	0557	...	0648	0703	0756	1009	...	1136	1353	1421	1519	...	1604	1600	1738	1822	1749	1902	...	2052	2141	2141	2241	...	...
Ljubljana a.	0526	0621	0703	...	0748	0807	0900	1114	...	1240	1450	1527	1624	...	1704	1656	1841	1925	1836	2000	...	2155	2238	2238	2336	...	...
Maribor **1315** a.	...	...	...	...	...	...	...	...	...	...	...	...	...	...	1950	1902	...	...	2040	...	...	...	...	0113	...	...	...

NOTES (LISTED BY TRAIN NUMBER)

– OPATIJA – 12 Rijeka - Ljubljana and v.v.
– LJUBLJANA – 12 Rijeka - Ljubljana and v.v.
5 – Apr. 23 - May 2, Aug. 29 - Sept. 25: 2 Pula - Ljubljana and v.v.
– ISTRA – June 25 - Aug. 28: 2 Koper - Ljubljana - Maribor. Conveys on ②⑤: 🛏 1, 2 cl., 🛏 2 cl., 2 and 🍷 Koper - Maribor (**1247**) - Hodoš - Zalaegerszeg (**959**) - Budapest.
– ISTRA – June 25 - Aug. 28: 2 Maribor - Ljubljana - Koper. Conveys on ①④ (from Budapest): 🛏 1, 2 cl., 🛏 2 cl., 2 and 🍷 Budapest (**1246**) - Hodoš - Maribor - Koper.

Ⓒ Apr. 23 - May 2, June 25 - Sept. 25.
Ⓐ (also Ⓒ Apr. 23 - May 2, June 25 - Sept. 25).
Ⓒ June 25 - Sept. 25. **y** – Not Apr. 23 - Sept. 25. **z** – Apr. 23 - Sept. 25.

▲ – Local services **Pivka - Ilirska Bistrica and v.v.**: Journey 16 minutes.
From Pivka: 0555Ⓐ, 0935Ⓐ, 1206Ⓐ, 1339Ⓐ, 1508Ⓐ, 1725Ⓑ, 1820Ⓑ.
From Ilirska Bistrica: 0523Ⓐ, 0632Ⓐ, 1100Ⓐ, 1306Ⓐ, 1415Ⓐ, 1529Ⓐ, 1747Ⓑ, 1952Ⓑ.

⊡ – 🚌 service **Koper - Trieste and v.v.**: Journey 45 minutes.
From **Koper**: 0600⚒, 0642Ⓐ, 0700Ⓐ, 0730⚒, 1030⚒, 1200Ⓐ, 1400⚒, 1730⚒.
From **Trieste**: 0700⚒, 0900Ⓐ, 1115Ⓐ, 1230⚒, 1300⚒, 1400Ⓐ, 1530⚒, 1900⚒.
Service subject to alteration. No service on ⑦, Slovenian and Italian holidays.
Operator: Veolia Transport Slovenija.
An irregular 🚌 service also operates Trieste - Hrpelje-Kozina and v.v.

2nd class only except where shown — RIJEKA - ZAGREB — 1310

			703						701				16001
		⚒	♦			⚒		Ⓐ	♦				♦
Rijeka 1305 d.	...	...	0540	0725	...	...	1330	1525	1735	...	1935	...	2310
Delnice d.	...	...	0645	0836	...	...	1444	1635	1836	...	2052	...	|
Moravice d.	...	0608	0717	0915	...	...	1519	1714	1906	1950	2127	...	|
Ogulin **1330** d.	0413	0640	0747	0945	1027	1218	1613	1744	1939	2021	2157	...	0120
Oštarije **1330** d.	0420	0647	0754	...	1035	1225	1620	...	1946	2029	...	...	|
Karlovac **1330** d.	0522	0754	0850	...	1137	1327	1728	...	2035	2128	...	...	|
Zagreb 1330/40 a.	0615	0850	0931	...	1232	1423	1824	...	2115	2218	...	...	0252
Osijek **1340** a.	...	...	1435	...	...	...	...	...	...	...	...	...	...

	16000			700							702		
	♦		Ⓐ	♦		⚒			Ⓐ		♦	Ⓐ	
Osijek **1340** d.	...	...	...	...	...	...	...	...	...	...	1200	...	...
Zagreb 1330/40 d.	0025	...	...	0630	0812	0952	1315	...	1439	1545	1705	1714	2140
Karlovac **1330** d.	|	...	...	0710	0907	1048	1410	...	1536	1640	1746	1808	2235
Oštarije **1330** d.	|	...	...	0759	1010	1152	1513	...	1637	1744	1834	1909	2336
Ogulin **1330** d.	0330	0407	0605	0808	1017	1158	1519	1604	1643	1751	1842	1915	2342
Moravice d.	|	0438	0637	0838	1048	...	...	1635	...	1821	1910	...	...
Delnice d.	|	0512	0716	0908	1123	...	...	1708	...	...	1940	...	...
Rijeka 1305 a.	0524	0626	0832	1008	1233	...	...	1822	...	...	2041	...	...

NOTES (LISTED BY TRAIN NUMBER)

– 12 Zagreb - Rijeka and v.v.
– 12 Osijek - Zagreb - Rijeka and v.v.

16000/1 – ADRIA – ②⑤⑦ June 17 - Aug. 26 (from Budapest, one day later from Zagreb); ①③⑥ June 18 - Aug. 27 (from Rijeka): 🛏 1, 2 cl., 🛏 2 cl. and ✕ Budapest (**1204/5**) Gyékényes (**15800/1**) - Ogulin - Rijeka and v.v.

MÁV 2nd class only except where shown — MARIBOR - ČAKOVEC, MURSKA SOBOTA and ZALAEGERSZEG — 1313

	1247								640	247										1642	518					642	
	♦	Ⓐ	Ⓐ	Ⓐ	Ⓐ	Ⓐ	Ⓐ	Ⓒ		♦	Ⓐ	⚒	g	Ⓐ	Ⓐ		Ⓐ			j	♦	y			Ⓐ	♦	Ⓐ
Ljubljana **1315** d.	2250	...	...	...	...	...	...	...	...	0845	...	...	...	...	...	...	...	...	...	...	1515	...	...	...	...	...	...
Maribor 1315 d.	0200	...	...	...	...	0702	...	0702	...	|	1040	1225	1225	1332	...	1432	...	1530	...	...	|	...	...	...	1830	...	2205
Pragersko **1315** d.	|	...	...	...	0616	|	...	0733	1010	1100	1110	1301	1301	|	...	1503	...	|	...	1602	1725	1725	...	...	1900	1942	2235
Ptuj d.	0227	...	...	...	0640	0746	...	0755	1025	1115	1132	1330	1330	1417	...	1525	...	1615	...	1628	1740	1740	...	...	1922	1956	2257
Ormož d.	|	...	0447	0532	0703	0811	0815	0820	1042	1131	1156	1401	1401	1440	...	1552	1552	1639	1643	1653	1757	1757	1758	...	1945	2013	2320
Središče 🏨 a.	|	...	0458	|	▬	|	0828	|	|	|	...	|	|	1451	...	|	1603	|	1654	|	|	|	1809	...	...	|	...
Čakovec 1335 a.	|	...	...	|	...	|	0841	|	|	|	...	|	|	...	...	|	▬	|	...	|	|	|	1824	...	...	|	...
Murska Sobota d.	0309	0320	...	0618	...	0855	...	0904	1116	1208	...	1445	1446	...	1520	1636	...	1723	...	1737	1832	1832	...	...	...	2058	...
Hodoš a.	0331	0349	...	...	...	...	...	...	...	1229	...	...	1514	...	1548	...	...	...	...	...	1859	1859	...	...	...	2125	...
Hodoš 🏨 d.	0353	...	...	...	0620	...	...	...	...	1252	...	...	...	...	...	...	1610	...	...	...	...	...	...	1930	...	...	...
Zalaegerszeg a.	0431	...	...	...	0710	...	...	...	...	1330	...	...	...	...	...	...	1706	...	...	...	...	...	...	2020	...	...	...
Budapest D **1230** a.	0829	...	...	...	...	...	...	...	...	1729	...	...	...	...	...	...	...	...	...	...	...	...	...	...	...	...	...

		519		643							246									1641			1643				1246
		♦	Ⓐ	♦	Ⓐ		Ⓐ	Ⓐ	Ⓐ	Ⓐ	♦		Ⓐ	⚒	g	Ⓐ	Ⓐ		Ⓐ	g			g		Ⓐ		♦
Budapest D **1230** d.	...	...	...	...	...	...	...	...	...	...	0830	...	...	...	...	...	...	...	...	...	...	...	...		...	...	2030
Zalaegerszeg d.	...	...	...	...	...	0520	...	...	...	...	1212	...	...	...	...	...	...	1450	...	...	...	1645	...	1820	...	...	0010
Hodoš 🏨 a.	...	...	...	...	...	0610	...	...	...	...	1250	...	...	...	...	...	...	1539	...	...	...	1734	...	1910	...	...	0048
Hodoš d.	...	0426	...	0510	0600	▬	...	...	...	...	1303	...	...	...	...	...	...	▬	1556	1613	...	...	...	...	1915	...	0110
Murska Sobota d.	...	0455	...	0539	0628	...	0943	...	...	1220	1327	...	...	1453	1453	...	...	...	1624	1643	...	...	1825	...	1943	1948	0134
Čakovec 1335 d.	...	|	...	|	|	...	|	1010	...	|	|	...	...	|	|	...	...	...	...	|	1832	...	|	...	...	|	|
Središče 🏨 d.	0434	|	0540	|	|	Ⓐ	|	1025	...	|	|	...	1505	|	|	1611	...	1713	...	|	1847	...	|	...	...	|	|
Ormož d.	0446	0526	0557	0624	0710	0721	1026	1035	1209	1303	1402	...	1516	1536	1536	1622	1701	1725	...	1729	1857	...	1900	...	...	2035	|
Ptuj d.	0510	0542	0620	0640	...	0746	1053	...	1233	1327	1417	...	...	1559	1559	...	1724	...	...	1753	...	...	1916	...	...	2100	0220
Pragersko **1315** d.	0540	0608	0651	0654	...	0816	1136	...	1302	1357	1442	...	...	1629	1629	...	1747	...	...	1823	...	...	1933	...	...	|	|
Maribor 1315 a.	0602	|	0714	...	...	0839	1159	...	1325	1420	|	...	...	1652	1652	...	...	...	...	|	...	...	|	...	...	2144	0244
Ljubljana **1315** a.	...	0810	...	...	...	...	...	...	...	...	1643	...	...	...	...	...	...	...	...	2024	...	...	2130	...	...	...	0606

NOTES (LISTED BY TRAIN NUMBER)

7 – CITADELLA – 12 Budapest - Ljubljana and v.v.
9 – PTUJ – Ⓐ (not June 25 - Aug. 28): 2 Ljubljana - Hodoš and v.v.
3 – MURA – 12 Pragersko - Hodoš and v.v.
– ISTRA – ①④ June 27 - Aug. 25: 🛏 1, 2 cl., 🛏 2 cl., 2 and 🍷 Budapest - Hodoš - Maribor (**1605**) - Koper.

1247 – ISTRA – ②⑤ June 28 - Aug. 27: 🛏 1, 2 cl., 🛏 2 cl., 2 and 🍷 Koper (**1604**) - Maribor - Hodoš - Zalaegerszeg (**959**) - Budapest.

g – ⑦ Dec. 13 - June 19, Sept. 4 - Dec. 4 (also Feb. 8, Mar. 28, May 2, Nov. 1; not Dec. 27, Feb. 7, Mar. 27, May 1, Oct. 30).
j – ⑤ Dec. 18 - June 17, Sept. 2 - Dec. 9 (also Dec. 24, Apr. 26; not Dec. 25, Jan. 1, Apr. 29).
y – Ⓐ June 25 - Aug. 28.

SLOVENIA and CROATIA

1315 LJUBLJANA and ZAGREB - MARIBOR - GRAZ

SŽ, HŽ,

km		2 h	2 Ⓐ	ICS 12 R	2	ICS 14 R	EC 158 ✕ ♦	247 ♦	2	ICS 18 R	2	IC 506 Ⓐ	2 ⚒	2 Ⓐ	ICS 20 R	2	IC 518 2 ♦	EC 150 ✕ ♦	ICS 22 R z	ICS 34 R ♦	2 y	IC 502 ♦	IC 504 ♦	ICS 28 R ♦	ICS 26 R	2	1604 ♦
	Koper **1305** d.	...	...	...	...	...	...	...	...	...	...	...	...	...	...	...	...	...	...	1447	...	...	1444	1639	...	...	2015
0	**Ljubljana 1300** d.	0050	...	0545	...	0805	...	0845	...	1312	1250	1345	1350	...	1512	...	1515	1600	1712	1712	...	1725	1725	1850	2012	2050	2250
*	**Zagreb 1300** d.	|	...	|	...	|	0725	|	...	|	|	|	|	...	|	...	|	|	|	|	...	|	|	|	|	|	|
	Dobova **1300** 🏛 d.	|	...	|	...	|	0813	|	...	|	|	|	|	...	|	...	|	|	|	|	...	|	|	|	|	|	|
	Sevnica **1300** d.	|	...	|	...	|	0840	|	...	|	|	|	|	...	|	...	|	|	|	|	...	|	|	|	|	|	|
64	Zidani Most **1300** d.	0148	...	0630	0700	0850	|	0941	1200	1357	1402	1443	1500	...	1557	1604	1609	1657	1757	1757	...	1825	1825	1935	2057	2154	2351
89	Celje d.	0213	...	0650	0725	0910	0919	1007	1225	1417	1427	1510	1525	...	1617	1629	1638	1723	1817	1817	...	1851	1851	1955	2117	2219	0017
137	Pragersko **1313** d.	0251	...	0722	0810	0942	1000	1046	1311	1449	1511	1551	1611	...	1649	1715	1720	1800	1849	1849	...	1934	1934	2027	2149	2304	0100
156	**Maribor 1313** ▲ a.	0306	...	0735	0828	0955	1014	...	1329	1502	1529	1607	1629	...	1702	1733	...	1816	1902	1902	...	1950	1950	2040	2202	2322	0113
156	**Maribor** d.	...	0502	...	0833	...	1019	...	1334	...	...	...	...	1635	...	1735	...	1819	...	...	1940	...	...	...	...	...	...
172	Spielfeld-Straß 🏛 a.	...	0525	...	0852	...	1036	...	1353	...	...	...	...	1658	...	1755	...	1836	...	...	2002	...	...	...	...	...	...
172	Spielfeld-Straß **980** 🏛 d.	...	...	...	...	...	1048	...	...	...	...	...	...	...	...	...	...	1848	...	...	...	...	...	...	...	...	...
219	**Graz** Hbf **980** a.	...	...	...	...	...	1120	...	...	...	...	...	...	...	...	...	...	1920	...	...	...	...	...	...	...	...	...
	Wien Meidling **980** a.	...	...	...	...	...	1402	...	...	...	...	...	...	...	...	...	...	2202	...	...	...	...	...	...	...	...	...

	2 h	605 2 w	1605 ♦	2	ICS 11 R v	ICS 29 R ♦	IC 519 2 ♦	2 Ⓐ	IC 503 ♦	IC 505 ♦	ICS 13 R t	ICS 35 R ♦	2	EC 151 ✕ ♦	ICS 17 R	2	246 ♦	ICS 19 R	1611 2 g	2 Ⓐ	ICS 21 R x	1615 2 g	1641 2 ♦	2	1643 2 ♦	ICS 23 R	EC 159 ✕ ♦
Wien Hbf **980** d.	...	...	...	...	...	...	...	...	...	...	...	...	...	0758	...	...	...	...	...	...	...	...	...	...	...	...	1558
Graz Hbf **980** d.	...	...	...	...	...	...	...	...	...	...	...	...	...	1038	...	...	...	...	...	...	...	...	...	...	...	...	1838
Spielfeld-Straß **980** 🏛 a.	...	...	...	...	...	...	...	...	...	...	...	...	...	1108	...	...	...	...	...	...	...	...	...	...	...	...	1908
Spielfeld-Straß 🏛 d.	...	...	...	...	...	...	...	0545	...	...	...	...	0903	1120	...	1405	...	...	...	1710	...	...	...	1802	...	...	1920
Maribor a.	...	...	...	...	...	...	...	0608	...	...	...	...	0923	1137	...	1423	...	...	...	1731	...	...	...	1818	...	...	1937
Maribor 1313 ▲ d.	0115	0340	0340	0425	0548	0548	...	...	0655	0655	0748	0748	0926a	1150	1248	1427	...	1548	1620	...	1748	1800	...	1825a	...	1948	1955
Pragersko **1313** d.	0133	0356	0356	0444	0602	0602	0608	...	0715	0715	0802	0802	0945a	1206	1302	1448	1442	1602	1639	...	1802	1817	1823	1844a	1933	2002	2012
Celje d.	0214	0440	0440	0529	0634	0634	0652	...	0757	0757	0834	0834	1030a	1245	1334	1535	1520	1634	1724	...	1834	1858	1905	1928a	2013	2034	2051
Zidani Most **1300** d.	0237	0507	0507	0555	0653	0653	0719	...	0828	0828	0853	0853	1054a	1312	1353	1558	1547	1653	1750	...	1853	1924	1930	1951a	2038	2053	|
Sevnica **1300** d.	|	|	|	|	|	|	|	...	|	|	|	|	...	|	|	...	|	|	|	...	|	|	|	...	|	|	2131
Dobova **1300** 🏛 d.	|	|	|	|	|	|	|	...	|	|	|	|	...	|	|	...	|	|	|	...	|	|	|	...	|	|	2211
Zagreb 1300 a.	|	|	|	|	|	|	|	...	|	|	|	|	...	|	|	...	|	|	|	...	|	|	|	...	|	|	2242
Ljubljana 1300 a.	0332	0606	0606	0659	0738	0738	0810	...	0925	0925	0938	0938	...	1406	1438	...	1643	1738	1841	...	1938	2018	2024	...	2130	2138	...
Koper **1305** a.	...	...	0840	...	...	0945	...	...	...	1155	...	1148	...	...	...	...	...	...	...	...	...	...	...	...	...	...	...

ADDITIONAL SERVICES MARIBOR - ZIDANI MOST and v.v.: 2nd class only

		Ⓐ	Ⓐ	Ⓐ		Ⓐ	Ⓐ	Ⓐ		Ⓐ		Ⓐ		Ⓑ
Maribor ▲ d.	0520	0620	0720	0820	1020	1120	1220	1320	1522	1620	1720	1920	2020	2100
Pragersko d.	0539	0639	0739	0839	1039	1139	1239	1339	1541	1639	1739	1939	2041	2119
Celje d.	0624	0725	0825	0924	1124	1225	1324	1424	1626	1724	1824	2024	2125	2204
Zidani Most d.	0648	0749	0849	0948	1148	1249	1348	1448	1650	1748	1848	2048	2148	2228

		Ⓐ	Ⓐ	Ⓐ	Ⓐ	Ⓐ	Ⓐ			Ⓐ		
Zidani Most d.	0500	0600	0800	0922	1001	1104	1305	1702	1801	1900	2005
Celje d.	0525	0625	0825	0947	1026	1129	1330	1727	1826	1925	2032
Pragersko d.	0610	0710	0910	1032	1111	1214	1414	1813	1912	2010	2117
Maribor ▲ a.	0628	0728	0928	1050	1129	1232	1432	1831	1930	2028	2135

♦ – **NOTES** (LISTED BY TRAIN NUMBER)

28/9 – Ⓒ June 25 - Sept. 25: (12) and 🍷 Maribor - Ljubljana / Koper and v.v.
34/5 – Not Apr. 23 - Sept. 25: (12) and 🍷 Maribor - Ljubljana / Koper and v.v.
150/1 – EMONA – (12) and ✕ Ljubljana - Wien and v.v.
158/9 – CROATIA – (12) and ✕ Zagreb - Wien and v.v.
246/7 – CITADELLA – (12) Budapest - Ljubljana and v.v.
502/3 – POHORJE – Not Apr. 23 - Sept. 25: (12) Ljubljana - Maribor and v.v.
504/5 – POHORJE – Apr. 23 - Sept. 25: (12) Maribor - Ljubljana - Koper and v.v.
518/9 – PTUJ – Ⓐ (not June 25 - Aug. 28): (2) Ljubljana - Hodoš and v.v.
1604 – ISTRA – June 25 - Aug. 28: (2) Koper - Ljubljana - Maribor. Conveys on ②⑤: 🛏 1, 2 cl., ▬ 2 cl., (2) and 🍷 Koper - Maribor (**1247**) - Hodoš - Zalaegerszeg (**959**) - Budapest.
1605 – ISTRA – June 25 - Aug. 28: (2) Maribor - Ljubljana - Koper. Conveys on ①④ (from Budapest): 🛏 1, 2 cl., ▬ 2 cl., (2) and 🍷 Budapest (**1246**) - Hodoš - Maribor - Koper.
1641 – ⑦ Dec. 13 - June 19, Sept. 4 - Dec. 4 (also Feb. 8, Mar. 28, May 2, Nov. 1; not Dec. 27, Feb. 7, Mar. 27, May 1, Oct. 30): (2) Hodoš - Ljubljana.
1643 – ⑦ Dec. 13 - June 19, Sept. 4 - Dec. 4 (also Feb. 8, Mar. 28, May 2, Nov. 1; not Dec. 27, Feb. 7, Mar. 27, May 1, Oct. 30): (2) Murska Sobota - Ljubljana.

a – Ⓐ only.
g – ⑦ Dec. 13 - June 19, Sept. 4 - Dec. 4 (also Feb. 8, Mar. 28, May 2, Nov. 1; not Dec. 27, Feb. 7, Mar. 27, May 1, Oct. 30).

h – Dec. 13 - Jan. 1, June 12 - Sept. 25.
t – Apr. 23 - Sept. 25.
v – Not Ⓒ June 25 - Sept. 25.
w – Not June 25 - Aug. 28.
x – Not Ⓒ Apr. 23 - Sept. 25.
y – June 25 - Aug. 28 runs 13 minutes later.
z – Ⓐ Apr. 23 - Sept. 25.

▲ – For Maribor - Bleiburg (- Klagenfurt) services see panel be

MARIBOR - BLEIBURG (- KLAGENFURT) and v.v.:

km		Ⓐ	Ⓐ
0	Maribor d.	0520	1445
87	Bleiburg 🏛 a.	0736	1705
126	*Klagenfurt* a.	*0837*	*1750*

	Ⓐ
Klagenfurt d.	*0806*
Bleiburg 🏛 d.	0854
Maribor a.	1101

Other services are available Bleiburg - Klagenfurt and v.v.

* – Zagreb - Celje: *104 km*.

1320 ZAGREB - VINKOVCI - BEOGRAD

SŽ, H

km		741	2	415 ♦	743 ⚒	745	211 ♦	2 ⚒	747	411 ♦
	Ljubljana **1300** d.	...	...	0825	...	...	1445	...	...	2105
0	**Zagreb** d.	0615	0746	1106	1308	1520	1742	1905	2137	2348
105	Novska d.	0809	1009	1303	1505	1719	1934	2123	2329	0140
191	Slavonski Brod d.	0910	1127	1404	1606	1819	2033	2243	0032	0238
224	Strizivojna-Vrpolje **1345** d.	0928	1157	1422	1624	1837	2051	2313	0053	0256
	Osijek **1345** a.	|	|	|	|	|	|	|	|	|
256	**Vinkovci** d.	0944	1222	1450	1640	1853	2107	2337	0115	0320
288	Šid 🏛 a.	...	...	1515	...	...	...	...	...	0345
407	**Beograd** a.	...	...	1733	...	...	...	...	...	0554

	740	742	744 ⚒	210 ♦	746	414 ♦	748	2 Ⓐ
Beograd d.	...	...	...	...	...	1100	...	...
Šid 🏛 d.	...	...	...	...	...	1356	...	...
Vinkovci d.	0255	0554	0731	0900	1200	1442	1720	1940
Osijek **1345** d.	|	|	|	|	|	|	|	|
Strizivojna-Vrpolje **1345** d.	0319	0611	0748	0917	1217	1500	1742	2005
Slavonski Brod d.	0342	0629	0807	0936	1236	1519	1806	2034
Novska d.	0450	0731	0905	1034	1335	1622	1909	2152
Zagreb a.	0645	0928	1054	1224	1526	1812	2106	0004
Ljubljana **1300** a.	...	...	...	1510	...	2056	...	...

♦ – **NOTES** (LISTED BY TRAIN NUMBER)

210/1 – SAVA – (12) Vinkovci - Zagreb - Ljubljana - Villach and v.v.
410/1 – ▬ 2 cl. and (12) Beograd - Ljubljana and v.v.
414/5 – ALPINE PEARLS – 🛏 1, 2 cl., ▬ 2 cl. and (2) Zagreb - Ljubljana - Vil Schwarzach-St Veit (**464/5**) - Zürich and v.v.; (2) Beograd - Zagreb - Ljubl Villach and v.v.; (12) Vinkovci - Zagreb and v.v.

1322 LOCAL SERVICES in Croatia

2nd class only

ZAGREB - SISAK CAPRAG and v.v.: Journey 60–75 minutes. All services call at Sisak (6 minutes from Sisak Caprag).
From Zagreb: 0544Ⓐ, 0633, 0751Ⓐ, 1101, 1159Ⓐ, 1353, 1454Ⓐ, 1547, 1649Ⓐ, 1746Ⓐ, 1854, 1958, 2051Ⓐ, 2251.
From Sisak Caprag: 0416⚒, 0520, 0613, 0702Ⓐ, 0812Ⓐ, 1037⚒, 1214, 1414Ⓐ, 1513, 1608Ⓐ, 1655, 1807Ⓐ, 2000, 2112.

SISAK CAPRAG - SUNJA and v.v.: Journey 25 minutes.
From Sisak Caprag: 0350⚒, 0704Ⓐ, 0744, 1215, 1456, 1656, 1853Ⓐ, 1959, 2350.
From Sunja: 0454⚒, 0547, 0636Ⓐ, 1148, 1253Ⓐ, 1629, 1930, 2046, 2140Ⓐ.

SUNJA - NOVSKA and v.v.: Journey 70 minutes.
From Sunja: 0810, 1241, 2035Ⓑ.
From Novska: 0436, 0525Ⓐ, 1037, 1758Ⓑ.

VINKOVCI - VUKOVAR and v.v.: Journey 40 minut
From Vinkovci: 0400Ⓐ, 1000Ⓐ, 1520, 1933Ⓐ.
From Vukovar: 0452Ⓐ, 1111Ⓐ, 1633, 2022Ⓐ.

1325 🚌 SPLIT - PLOČE - DUBROVNIK

🚌 SPLIT - DUBROVNIK: Up to 18 departures per day. Journey 4 hrs - 5 hrs 10 mins.
🚌 SPLIT - PLOČE: Up to 22 departures per day. Journey 2 hrs - 2 hrs 50 mins.
🚌 PLOČE - DUBROVNIK: Up to 17 departures per day. Journey 2 hrs - 2 hrs 20 mins.

Note: various operators run on these routes; tickets are not interchangeable.
Split and Ploče bus stations are situated adjacent to the railway stations.
Buses pass through Bosnia between Ploče and Dubrovnik (passports required

ZAGREB - ZADAR, ŠIBENIK and SPLIT — 1330

2nd class only except where shown

km		15800						ICN 521							ICN 523						821	15802		
							🚌	R		🚌				🚌	R									🚌
		♦	⚒	Ⓐ		Ⓐq	Ⓐ	♀	Ⓐ	Ⓒ	Ⓐ				♀	Ⓐ	Ⓐ	p			♦	♦		h
	Zagreb 1310 d.	0025	...	...	...	...	...	0735	...	...	...	...	...	...	1521	...	...	...	...	...	2305	2305	...	...
	Karlovac **1310** d.	|	...	...	...	...	...	0812	...	...	...	...	...	...	1556	...	...	...	...	...	2344	2344	...	...
	Oštarije **1310** d.	|	...	...	...	...	...	0903	...	...	...	...	...	...	1642	...	...	...	...	...	|	|	...	...
	Ogulin 1310 d.	0205	...	...	...	...	...	|	...	...	...	...	...	...	|	...	...	...	...	...	0052	0052	...	...
	Gospić d.	|	...	...	...	...	...	1031	...	...	...	...	...	...	1812	...	...	...	...	...	0309	0309	...	...
	Gračac d.	|	...	...	...	...	...	1104	...	...	...	...	...	...	1846	...	...	...	...	...	0347	0347	...	...
	Knin a.	0546	...	...	...	...	...	1153	...	...	...	...	...	...	1935	...	...	...	...	...	0452	0452	...	...
0	Knin d.	0549	...	0737	...	...	1110	1154	...	1200	...	1521	...	1715	1936	1947	...	...	0414	...	0453	0453	...	0505
95	**Zadar** ⊡ a.	|	...	|	...	...	1328	|	...	1418	...	|	...	1933	|	|	...	...	|	...	|	|	...	0724
—	Perković a.	0706	...	0839	...	...	...	1241	...	...	...	1627	...	...	2022	2049	...	...	0516	...	0552	0552	←	...
0	Perković d.	0707	0713	0844	0855	1220	...	1252	1255	...	1456	1634	1646	...	2033	2054	2122	2247	→	0525	0553	0553	0555	...
22	**Šibenik** ⊡ a.	|	0743	0914	|	|	...	|	1325	...	1526	1704	|	...	|	2124	|	2312	...	|	|	|	0625	...
	Split ⊡ a.	0809	...	...	1005	1325	...	1338	...	...	...	...	1751	...	2120	...	2231	...	...	0630	0654	0654	...	...

						ICN 520						ICN 522					15801							820	
			🚌			R						R	🚌									🚌			
	Ⓐ	⚒	h			♀		Ⓐ	Ⓐq		Ⓐ	♀			Ⓐ		♦			Ⓐ			p	♦	
⊡ d.	...	...	...	0738	...	0827	...	...	1032	...	...	1435	...	1526	...	...	1912	...	...	1942	...	...	...	2143	...
enik ⊡ d.	0451	0634	...	|	0812	|	...	1105	|	...	1410	|	...	|	1600	...	|	...	2022	|	...	...	2210	|	...
vić a.	0520	0704	...	0843	0842	0914	...	1135	1137	...	1440	1522	...	1631	1630	...	2012	...	2052	2053	←	...	2238	2245	...
vić d.	0522	...	...	...	0845	0915	...	...	...	...	...	1523	...	...	1633	...	2023	...	→	...	2055	...	...	2246	...
Zadar ⊡ d.	|	...	0735	...	|	|	...	...	...	...	...	|	1440	...	|	...	|	...	...	...	|	2030	...	|	...
a.	0630	...	0956	...	0949	1002	...	...	...	...	...	1608	1701	...	1737	...	2117	...	...	...	2159	2251	...	2345	...
d.	...	...	...	...	...	1003	...	...	...	...	...	1609	...	...	...	...	2119	...	...	...	...	...	...	2346	...
ac d.	...	...	...	...	...	1105	...	...	...	...	...	1701	...	...	...	...	|	...	...	...	...	...	...	0058	...
ić d.	...	...	...	...	...	1137	...	...	...	...	...	1735	...	...	...	...	|	...	...	...	...	...	...	0137	...
in 1310 d.	...	...	...	...	...	|	...	...	...	...	...	|	...	...	...	...	0120j	...	...	...	...	...	...	0400	...
ije 1310 d.	...	...	...	...	...	1307	...	...	...	...	...	1926	...	...	...	...	|	...	...	...	...	...	...	|	...
vac 1310 d.	...	...	...	...	...	1354	...	...	...	...	...	2014	...	...	...	...	|	...	...	...	...	...	...	0500	...
eb 1310 a.	...	...	...	...	...	1430	...	...	...	...	...	2050	...	...	...	...	0252	...	...	...	...	...	...	0540	...

NOTES (LISTED BY TRAIN NUMBER)

0 – ADRIA – ②⑤⑦ June 17 - Aug. 26 (from Budapest, one day later from Zagreb): 🛏 1, 2 cl., ▬ 2 cl. and [12] Budapest (**1204**) - Gyékényes - Zagreb - Split; 🛏 1, 2 cl. Praha (**277**) - Budapest - Split; 🛏 1, 2 cl., ▬ 2 cl. and ✕ Budapest - Ogulin (**16000**) - Rijeka.

1 – ADRIA – ③⑥ May 28 - June 15; ①③⑥ June 18 - Aug. 27; ③⑥ Aug. 31 - Oct. 1 (from Split, one day later from Zagreb): 🛏 1, 2 cl., ▬ 2 cl. and [12] Split - Zagreb - Gyékényes (**1205/9**) - Budapest; 🛏 1, 2 cl. Split - Budapest (**276**) - Praha; 🛏 1, 2 cl., ▬ 2 cl. and ✕ Rijeka (**16001**) - Ogulin - Budapest.

2 – ②⑤ May 27 - June 14, Aug. 30 - Sept. 30 (from Budapest, one day later from Zagreb): 🛏 1, 2 cl., ▬ 2 cl. and [12] Budapest (**1208**) - Gyékényes - Zagreb (**821**) - Split.

\- ②④⑦ (daily Apr. 30 - Oct. 30): 🛏 1, 2 cl., ▬ 2 cl. and [2] Split - Zagreb.

821 – ①③⑤ (daily Apr. 29 - Oct. 29): ▬ 2 cl. and [2] Zagreb - Split. Conveys ②⑤ May 27 - June 14, Aug. 30 - Sept. 30 (from Budapest): 🛏 1, 2 cl., ▬ 2 cl. and [12] Budapest (**1208**) - Gyékényes (**15802**) - Zagreb - Split.

h – ⚒ (daily May 1 - Oct. 30).
j – Arrive 0049.
p – ②④⑦ (daily Apr. 30 - Oct. 30).
q – Not June 13 - Sept. 2.

⊡ – Frequent 🚌 services operate Zadar - Šibenik - Split and v.v.; some continue to Ploče and Dubrovnik (see Table **1325**). Bus station locations: Zadar, Split and Ploče are adjacent to rail station, Šibenik approximately 10 minutes walk.

ZAGREB - VARAŽDIN - NAGYKANIZSA — 1335

MÁV 2nd class only except where shown

There is currently no service Kotoriba - Murakeresztúr and v.v.

					990								992		790	770											
	⚒			Ⓐ		⚒	⚒		⚒	⚒	Ⓐ	Ⓐ			Ⓐ	♦	Ⓐ			Ⓐ	ⒶV	⚒	V				
Zagreb d.	...	...	...	0541	0715	...	0902	...	1115	...	...	1308	1401	...	1512	1536	...	1524	...	1633	...	1823	...	1931	...	2110	2226
Zabok d.	...	...	...	0657	0809	...	1002	...	1222	...	...	1416	1508	...	1603	k	...	1629	...	1739	...	1935	...	2038	...	2224	2325
Varaždin ▲ d.	0526	0653	...	0831	0942	0954	1140	1305	1355	1425	1515	1600	1637	1642	1723	1732	1735	1802	1916	1944	2015	2113	2116	2212	2218	2357	0055
Čakovec **1313** d.	0538	0710	...	...	0952a	1005	▬	1326	...	1437	1527	...	▬	1654	...	...	1746	...	1936	▬	2027	...	2128	...	2229	0007	...
Kotoriba 🏛 d.	0615	0742	...	...	...	1037	...	1359	...	1516	1602	...	...	1731	...	...	1815	...	2011	...	2100	...	2205a	...	2306	...	...
Murakeresztúr 🏛 d.	...	...	0854	...	...	...	1254	...	...	...	...	...	1654	...	...	...	...	...	...	2054	...	...	...	...	...	...	...
Nagykanizsa a.	...	...	0906	...	...	...	1306	...	...	...	...	...	1706	...	...	...	...	...	...	2106	...	...	...	...	...	...	...

					991	771																995					
		⚒	⚒	⚒	⚒	♦		⚒			⚒		Ⓐ	Ⓐ	Ⓐ	⚒	⚒			Q				Ⓐ		Ⓐ	
kanizsa d.	...	...	...	...	...	...	...	...	0653	...	...	1052	...	...	...	...	...	...	1452	...	...	...	...	...	1852	...	...
keresztúr 🏛 d.	...	...	...	...	...	...	...	...	0704	...	...	1104	...	...	...	...	...	...	1504	...	...	...	...	...	1904	...	...
iba 🏛 d.	...	...	...	0422	...	...	0546	0634	...	0803	...	...	1109	...	1156	1246	...	1448d	...	1611	1703	...	1828	1918	...	2117	2219
vec 1313 d.	...	...	...	0458	...	...	0623	0709	...	0844	1007a	...	1143	...	1234	1320	...	1529d	...	1655	1748	...	1903	2002	...	2151	2252
ždin ▲ d.	0246	0336	0425	0508	0524	0533	0644	0719	...	0854	1041	...	1153	1213	1244	1330	1417	1544	...	1705	1758	1805	1925	2012	...	2201	2302
k d.	0423	0510	0625	...	0654	k	0842	...	...	...	1221	...	...	1351	...	...	1604	1738	...	...	...	1934	2113	...	...	...	...
eb a.	0521	0611	0729	...	0749	0724	0943	...	...	...	1322	...	...	1452	...	...	1708	1837	...	...	...	2032	2214	...	...	...	...

VARAŽDIN - KOPRIVNICA and v.v. 2nd class only except where shown:

		771								
	⚒	♦		⚒	⚒		⚒	Q		Ⓐ
Varaždin d.	0430	0533	0652	1020	1308	1426	1605	1707	1917	2215
Koprivnica a.	0515	0609	0736	1105	1353	1510	1650	1752	2002	2259

								770			
	Ⓐ			⚒	⚒	Ⓐ		♦	⑦q	ⒶV	V
Koprivnica d.	0431	0545	0833	1125	1307	1443	1538	1657	1802	1916	2022
Varaždin a.	0518	0638	0918	1210	1358	1535	1631	1732	1847	2014	2106

NOTES (LISTED BY TRAIN NUMBER)

1 – Ⓐ: [2] Zagreb - Koprivnica - Varaždin and v.v.

Q – ⑦ (also Mar. 28, Aug. 15; not Mar. 27, Aug. 15): [2] Kotoriba - Varaždin - Koprivnica.
V – [2] Koprivnica - Varaždin - Kotoriba and v.v.

a – Ⓐ only.
d – ⚒ only.
k – Via Koprivnica.
q – Not Mar. 27, Aug. 14.

ZAGREB - KOPRIVNICA - NAGYKANIZSA and OSIJEK — 1340

MÁV

		15801	783	703	201	981	205	770	IC 581	971	
	2	♦		♦	♦	2	♦	♦	R	2	2
Rijeka **1310** d.	...	...	...	0540	...	...	...	...	...	...	...
Zagreb d.	...	0318	0652	1007	1007	1257	1434	1536	1640	1841	2029
Križevci d.	...	0359	0737	1051	1051	1353	1536	1626	1721	1931	2130
Koprivnica ● **1335** d.	...	0421	0807	1120	1121	1444	1615	1644	1755	2005	2159
Gyékényes ● 🏛 d.	...	0535	|	|	1215	|	1654	...	|	...	...
Nagykanizsa a.	...	0556	|	|	1244	|	|	...	|	...	...
Budapest Déli **1220** a.	...	0936k	|	|	1624	|	2114k	...	|	...	...
Virovitica d.	0418	...	0923	1225	...	1601	...	...	1909	...	...
Našice d.	0538	...	1036	1348	...	1732	...	...	2019	...	...
Osijek 1345 a.	0640	...	1122	1435	...	1826	...	...	2102	...	...

	980	771	IC 580	200	702		204	782	15802	15800	
	2	♦	R	♦		2	♦	♦	♦	♦	2
Osijek 1345 d.	0115a	...	0530	...	1200	...	...	1620	...	...	1950
Našice d.	0201a	...	0614	...	1245	...	...	1705	...	...	2056
Virovitica d.	0320a	...	0727	...	1402	...	...	1821	...	...	2215
Budapest Déli **1220** d.	|	...	|	0600	|	...	1445k	|	1823k	1823k	...
Nagykanizsa d.	|	...	|	0929	|	...	|	|	2154	2154	...
Gyékényes ● 🏛 d.	|	...	|	1045	|	...	1916	|	2125	2253	...
Koprivnica ● **1335** d.	0443	0621	0839	1117	1515	1717	1940	1940	2141	2311	...
Križevci d.	0522	0642	0859	1149	1535	1750	2002	2002	2201	2332	...
Zagreb a.	0620	0724	0937	1248	1616	1848	2046	2046	2241	0012	...
Rijeka **1310** a.	...	...	...	...	2041	...	...	...	...	...	...

NOTES (LISTED BY TRAIN NUMBER)

\- AGRAM – [12] (also ✕ May 13 - Sept. 25) Budapest - Koprivnica (**2204**) - Zagreb.
\- AGRAM – [12] (also ✕ May 13 - Sept. 25) Zagreb (**703**) - Koprivnica - Budapest.
\- [12] and ✕ Budapest - Koprivnica (**782**) - Zagreb.
\- [12] and ✕ Zagreb (**2207**) - Koprivnica - Budapest.
\- [12] Rijeka - Zagreb - Osijek; [12] (also ✕ May 13 - Sept. 25) Zagreb - Koprivnica (**201**) - Budapest.
1 – Ⓐ: [2] Zagreb - Koprivnica - Varaždin and v.v.

782 – [12] Osijek - Zagreb; [12] and ✕ Budapest (**204**) - Koprivnica - Zagreb.

15800 – ADRIA – ②⑤⑦ June 17 - Aug. 26 (from Budapest): 🛏 1, 2 cl., ▬ 2 cl. and [12] Budapest (**1204**) - Gyékényes - Zagreb - Split; 🛏 1, 2 cl. Praha (**277**) - Budapest - Split; 🛏 1, 2 cl., ▬ 2 cl. and ✕ Budapest - Ogulin (**16000**) - Rijeka.

15801 – ADRIA – ③⑥ May 28 - June 15; ①③⑥ June 18 - Aug. 27; ③⑥ Aug. 31 - Oct. 1 (from Split, one day later from Zagreb): 🛏 1, 2 cl., ▬ 2 cl. and [12] Split - Zagreb - Gyékényes (**1205/9**) - Budapest; 🛏 1, 2 cl. Split - Budapest (**276**) - Praha; 🛏 1, 2 cl., ▬ 2 cl. and ✕ Rijeka (**16001**) - Ogulin - Budapest.

15802 – ②⑤ May 27 - June 14, Aug. 30 - Sept. 30 (from Budapest): 🛏 1, 2 cl., ▬ 2 cl. and [12] Budapest (**1208**) - Gyékényes - Zagreb (**821**) - Split.

a – Ⓐ only.
k – Budapest **Keleti**.

● – Koprivnica - Gyékényes and v.v. is reported as currently suspended (services replaced by 🚌).

1345 PÉCS - OSIJEK - DOBOJ

2nd class only except where shown HŽ, MÁV,

There is currently no service Slavonski Šamac - Šamac - Doboj and v.v.

km																											
		⚒	🚌 Ⓐ	Ⓐ			⚒	Ⓐ	⚒	⚒	⚒		⚒	Ⓐ				🚌	⚒							Ⓐ	Ⓑ
	Budapest Déli **1200** d.	...	...	...	...	...	...	...	...	...	...	...	...	...	...	...	...	...	...	...	...	...	...	...	...	...	...
0	**Pécs** d.	...	...	...	*0512*	...	...	...	...	...	...	...	...	...	...	...	...	...	...	...	...	*1710*	...	...	...	...	...
36	Villány d.	...	...	...	0558	...	...	...	...	...	...	...	...	...	...	...	...	...	...	...	...	1755	...	...	...	...	...
43	Magyarbóly ● 🛃 d.	...	...	...	0630	...	...	...	...	...	...	...	...	...	...	...	...	...	...	...	...	1820	...	...	...	...	...
54	Beli Manastir ● 🛃 d.	...	...	0542	0641	0701	...	...	0820	...	...	1051	1224	...	...	1410	...	...	...	1615	...	1831	1846	...	...	2005	...
82	**Osijek 1340** a.	...	...	0611	...	0730	...	...	0849	...	...	1120	1253	...	...	1439	...	...	...	1644	...	...	1915	...	...	2034	...
82	**Osijek 1340** d.	0427	...	...	...	...	0747	0812	...	0900	1048	...	...	1350	1353	...	1540	...	1623	...	1815	...	...	2002	2025	...	2225
	Vinkovci a.	|	...	...	...	...	0829	|	...	|	1130	...	...	|	1435	...	|	...	1705	...	1857	...	...	|	2107	...	2307
130	Strizivojna-Vrpolje **1320** d.	0525	0507	...	...	...	...	0911	...	1000	...	...	...	1448	...	...	1640	1650	...	...	...	...	...	2101	...	...	...
150	Slavonski Šamac 🛃 d.	...	0530	...	...	...	...	...	...	...	...	...	...	...	...	...	...	1713	...	...	...	...	...	...	...	...	...
154	Šamac 🛃 d.	...	...	...	...	...	...	...	...	...	...	...	...	...	...	...	...	...	...	...	...	...	...	...	...	...	...
226	**Doboj 1350** a.	...	...	...	...	...	...	...	...	...	...	...	...	...	...	...	...	...	...	...	...	...	...	...	...	...	...

km																											
		Ⓐ	⚒		Ⓐ	🚌 Ⓐ	⚒	⚒	⚒	⚒		Ⓐ	⚒	⚒				⚒	Ⓐ			Ⓐ		🚌		Ⓑ	
	Doboj 1350 d.	...	...	...	...	...	...	...	...	...	...	...	...	...	...	...	...	...	...	...	...	...	...	...	...	...	...
	Šamac 🛃 d.	...	...	...	...	...	...	...	...	...	...	...	...	...	...	...	...	...	...	...	...	...	...	...	...	...	...
	Slavonski Šamac 🛃 d.	...	...	...	...	0537	...	...	...	...	...	...	...	...	...	...	...	...	...	...	...	...	...	1717	...	...	...
	Strizivojna-Vrpolje **1320** d.	...	...	...	0535	0600	0617	...	...	...	...	1012	...	1130	...	...	...	...	1651	...	...	...	...	1740	1858	...	2111
0	Vinkovci d.	...	0536	...	|	━	|	0640	...	0836	...	|	...	|	1201	...	...	1522	|	1723	...	...	1905	...	|	2112	|
35	**Osijek 1340** a.	...	0618	...	0634	...	0718	0722	...	0918	...	1111	...	1230	1243	...	...	1604	1750	1805	...	...	1947	...	1956	2154	2210
	Osijek 1340 d.	0502	...	0621	...	...	...	...	0740	...	1010	...	1141	...	...	1325	1527	...	...	*1808*	...	1926	...	...	...	...	...
	Beli Manastir ● 🛃 d.	0532	...	0651	...	0705	...	...	0810	...	1040	...	1211	...	...	1355	1557	...	...	*1838*	1905	1956	...	...	...	...	...
	Magyarbóly ● 🛃 d.	...	...	...	...	0736	...	...	...	...	...	...	...	...	...	...	...	...	...	...	1939	...	...	...	...	...	...
	Villány a.	...	...	...	...	0743	...	...	...	...	...	...	...	...	...	...	...	...	...	...	1946	...	...	...	...	...	...
	Pécs a.	...	...	...	...	*0842*	...	...	...	...	...	...	...	...	...	...	...	...	...	...	*2042*	...	...	...	...	...	...
	Budapest Déli **1200** a.	...	...	...	...	...	...	...	...	...	...	...	...	...	...	...	...	...	...	...	...	...	...	...	...	...	...

● – Magyarbóly - Beli Manastir and v.v. is reported as currently suspended.

1350 ZAGREB - DOBOJ - SARAJEVO

2nd class only except where shown HŽ, ŽFBH, Ž

km																							
			715													**397**							
0	**Zagreb 1322** d.	...	...	...	...	...	...	...	...	...	...	...	...	...	...	0859	...	...	...	...	...	...	...
72	Sunja **1322** d.	...	...	...	...	...	...	...	...	...	...	...	...	...	...	1015	...	...	...	...	...	...	...
92	Volinja 🛃 d.	...	...	...	...	...	...	...	...	...	...	...	...	...	...	1112	...	...	...	...	...	...	...
98	Dobrljin 🛃 d.	...	...	...	...	...	...	...	...	...	...	...	0630	...	...	1145	...	...	...	...	...	...	...
112	Novi Grad d.	...	...	...	...	...	...	...	0432	...	...	...	0705	...	...	1201	...	...	...	...	...	...	...
214	Banja Luka d.	...	...	...	...	0435	...	...	0629	0723	...	...	0903	...	...	1337	...	...	1535	...	...	...	1924
324	**Doboj 1345** a.	...	...	...	...	0637	...	...	...	0926	...	...	...	...	...	1512	...	...	1747	...	...	...	2127
324	**Doboj 1345** d.	...	0349	...	...	...	...	...	...	...	...	...	...	...	...	1523	...	...	...	...	...	...	...
347	Maglaj d.	...	0415	...	0515	...	...	...	...	...	0930	...	...	...	...	1549	...	...	...	1708	...	...	...
370	Zavidovici d.	...	0438	...	0543	...	...	...	...	...	0958	...	...	...	...	1611	...	...	...	1736	...	...	...
419	Zenica d.	0457	0530	...	0643	...	0748	...	...	...	1058	1114	...	1527	...	1700	...	...	...	1836	1917	...	...
447	Kakanj d.	0531	0557	...	...	...	0830	...	...	...	...	1153	...	1601	...	1727	...	1745	...	...	1951	...	...
465	Visoko d.	0553	0614	...	...	...	0852	...	...	...	...	1215	...	1630	...	1744	...	1813	...	...	2013	...	...
472	Podlugovi d.	0602	0622	...	...	...	0901	...	...	...	...	1224	...	1638	...	1752	...	1822	...	...	2022	...	...
496	**Sarajevo 1355** a.	0639	0653	...	...	...	0938	...	...	...	...	1301	...	...	...	1823	...	1859	...	...	2059	...	...

										396									**714**				
Sarajevo 1355 d.	...	...	...	0439	...	...	...	0717	...	1021	...	...	1101	...	...	...	1540	...	1628	...	...	...	...
Podlugovi d.	...	...	...	0517	...	...	...	0755	...	1053	...	...	1139	...	...	...	1618	...	1700	...	1732	...	...
Visoko d.	...	...	...	0526	...	...	...	0804	...	1101	...	...	1148	...	...	...	1627	...	1708	...	1746	...	...
Kakanj d.	...	...	...	0559	...	...	...	0826	...	1118	...	...	1216	...	...	...	1648	...	1729	...	1808	...	...
Zenica d.	...	...	...	0632	...	0723	...	0859	...	1146	...	...	1249	...	1531	...	...	...	1757	...	1841	1923	...
Zavidovici d.	...	...	...	...	...	0824	...	...	...	1234	...	...	...	...	1632	...	...	...	1848	...	...	2024	...
Maglaj d.	...	...	...	...	...	0851	...	...	...	1255	...	...	...	...	1659	...	...	...	1910	...	...	2051	...
Doboj 1345 a.	...	...	...	...	...	...	...	...	...	1320	...	...	...	...	...	...	...	...	1935	...	...	...	...
Doboj 1345 d.	...	0418	...	...	0731	...	...	...	...	1330	...	...	...	1525	...	...	...	...	...	1932	...	...	...
Banja Luka d.	...	0624	0730	...	0941	...	...	...	...	1509	...	1525	...	1728	...	...	...	1923	...	2142	...	...	...
Novi Grad d.	0600	...	0938	...	...	...	...	...	...	1645	...	1730	...	...	...	...	...	2124	...	...	...	...	...
Dobrljin 🛃 d.	0619	...	...	...	...	...	...	...	...	1721	...	1749	...	...	...	...	...	...	...	...	...	...	...
Volinja 🛃 d.	...	...	...	...	...	...	...	...	...	1759	...	...	...	...	...	...	...	...	...	...	...	...	...
Sunja **1322** d.	...	...	...	...	...	...	...	...	...	1827	...	...	...	...	...	...	...	...	...	...	...	...	...
Zagreb 1322 a.	...	...	...	...	...	...	...	...	...	1942	...	...	...	...	...	...	...	...	...	...	...	...	...

1355 SARAJEVO - PLOČE

Most services 2nd class only HŽ, ŽF

Sarajevo - Čapljina is currently closed. There is no rail service Čapljina - Metković and v.v. (see note below).

km		🚌 ⚒	🚌 ⚒	**723** ⊗		🚌 Ⓐ	⊗	🚌 ⚒		**721** ⊗	⊗
	Zagreb **1350** d.	...	...	...	...	...	...	...	...	...	...
0	**Sarajevo 1350** d.	...	...	0715	...	...	1530	...	...	1857	1921
67	Konjic d.	...	...	0855	...	...	1709	...	...	2024	2105
129	Mostar d.	...	...	0959	...	...	...	...	...	2128	...
149	Žitomislići d.	...	...	1016	...	...	...	...	...	2145	...
163	Čapljina 🛃 d.	...	...	1032	...	...	...	...	...	2201	...
173	Metković d.	0510	0630	...	...	1325	...	1705	...	...	...
194	**Ploče** a.	0545	0705	...	...	1400	...	1740	...	...	...

	⊗	**720** ⊗	🚌 ⚒		🚌 Ⓐ		🚌 ⚒	⊗	
Ploče d.	...	...	0550	...	1245	...	1420	...	...
Metković d.	...	...	0625	...	1320	...	1455	...	...
Čapljina 🛃 d.	...	0637	...	...	...	...	...	...	...
Žitomislići d.	...	0654	...	...	...	...	...	...	...
Mostar d.	...	0712	...	...	...	...	...	...	...
Konjic d.	0503	0815	...	...	...	...	...	1716	...
Sarajevo 1350 a.	0642	0948	...	...	...	...	...	1855	...
Zagreb **1350** a.	...	...	...	...	...	...	...	...	...

⊗ – Service temporarily suspended owing to engineering work.

Alternative 🚌 services are available Sarajevo - Mostar - Metković - Dubrovnik and
Connections are possible at Metković to / from Ploče.

1358 LOCAL SERVICES in Bosnia

2nd class only HŽ, ŽFBH, Ž

VINKOVCI - TUZLA and v.v. :

There is currently no service Gunja - Brčko - Tuzla and v.v.

km		Ⓐ						Ⓐ
0	Vinkovci d.	0328	...	0950	...	1500	...	1934
49	Gunja d.	0425	...	1049	...	1559	...	2033
53	Brčko 🛃 d.	...	...	...	...	...	...	...
127	Tuzla a.	...	...	...	...	...	...	...

	Ⓐ						Ⓐ
Tuzla d.	...	...	...	...	...	...	...
Brčko 🛃 d.	...	...	...	...	...	...	...
Gunja d.	0433	...	1056	...	1609	...	2042
Vinkovci a.	0532	...	1156	...	1709	...	2142

TUZLA - DOBOJ and v.v. :

km				Ⓐ				
0	Tuzla d.	...	1020	...	...	1709	...	...
32	Petrovo Novo d.	0540	1104	1410	...	1753	2035	...
60	Doboj a.	0628	1152	1458	...	1841	2123	...

				Ⓐ			
Doboj d.	0442	0728	...	1315	1528	1930	...
Petrovo Novo d.	0530	0817	...	1403	1617	2018	...
Tuzla a.	...	0900	...	...	1700	...	...

SERBIA, MONTENEGRO and FYRO MACEDONIA

MAP PAGE 501

tors: Železnice Srbije (ŽS): www.zeleznicesrbije.com; Železnice Crne Gore (ŽCG): www.zcg-prevoz.me; Makedonski Železnici (MŽ): www.mztransportad.com.mk; Trainkos (KŽ/HK): www.trainkos.com.

ces: All trains convey first- and second-class seating, except where shown otherwise in footnotes, by a '2' in the train column, or where the footnote shows that the train conveys sleeping- (🛏) and / or couchette (▬) cars only. Descriptions of sleeping- and couchette cars are given on page 8.

gs: Valid until **December 10, 2016** except where indicated otherwise. Readers should note, however, that further changes are possible. *Services may be amended or cancelled at short notice and passengers are strongly advised to check locally before travelling.*

ts: A supplement is payable for travel by internal express trains. Reservation of seats is possible on most express trains.

: Most nationals do not require a visa to enter Serbia and Montenegro, but must obtain an entry stamp in their passport, sight of which will be required by officials on leaving the country. These must be obtained at a border crossing recognised by the authorities - this excludes Kosovo's external borders with Montenegro, Former Yugoslav Republic Of Macedonia (FYROM) and Albania. Note also that Serbia should not be entered from Kosovo unless initial travel into Kosovo was via Serbia. Visas are not required for entry into FYROM for most nationals.

ency: Visitors must declare large amounts of foreign currency upon arrival; currently €2000 in Montenegro, and €10000 in Serbia and FYROM. It is reported, however, that FYROM may now be operating on a threshold of €2000. A certificate issued by the customs officer must be presented on departure, otherwise any funds held may be confiscated.

rity: Following the declaration of independence by Kosovo (which has not been recognised by Serbia) caution should be exercised when travelling in southern Serbia and northern Kosovo. Caution is also advised in the northern and western border regions of the Former Yugoslav Republic Of Macedonia.

(BUDAPEST -) KELEBIA - SUBOTICA - BEOGRAD 1360

					IC									IC						EC					
	341	741	743	841		541	745		747	749	843		641	343	751		753		845	345	755	757	1137		
	◐				2	R 2		2				2		◐		2		2		⚡				2	2
	B					◧								C						V			P		
Budapest Keleti **1295** d.	2225	...	...	...	...	...	...	...	...	...	...	...	...	0805	...	...	...	...	...	1205	...	...	...	...	...
Kelebia 🏛 d.	0140	...	...	...	...	...	...	...	...	...	...	...	...	1141	...	...	...	...	...	1541	...	...	...	...	...
Subotica 1362 🏛 a.	0154	...	...	...	...	...	...	...	...	...	...	...	...	1155	...	...	...	...	...	1555	...	...	...	...	...
Subotica d.	0224	...	...	0345	...	0545	...	0713	...	...	1011	...	...	1226	...	1320	...	...	1531	1623	...	...	1830	1907	...
Novi Sad **1362** a.	0448	...	...	0628	...	0803	...	0951	...	...	1252	...	...	1455	...	1551	...	...	1808	1840	...	...	2102	2142	...
Novi Sad d.	0451	0540	0617	...	0711	0807	0910	...	1008	1105	...	1321	1445	1505	1524	...	1700	1756	...	1845	1928	2030	2132	...	2245
Novi Beograd d.	0609	0706	0752	...	0851	0921	1037	...	1129	1239	...	1456	1608	1621	1651	...	1821	1936	...	2001	2053	2207	2249	...	0013
Beograd a.	0621	0717	0803	...	0902	0932	1049c	...	1140	1250c	...	1507	1619	1632	1702	...	1832	1947	...	2013	2104	2218	...	...	0025

						EC						IC								IC					
		740	1136		840	742	344		744	746	842		342		640	748		750		752	540	754	844		340	756
	2			2			⚡	2				2	◐				2		2		R 2			2	◐	
			P				V						C								◧				B	
rad d.	...	0340	...	0458	...	0557	0720	...	0835	1005	...	1044	1135	...	1232c	1318	...	1428c	1530	1635	1705	1835	...	2020	2150	2305
Beograd d.	...	0352	0435	0509	...	0608	|	...	0846	1016	...	1055	|	...	1238	1330	...	1444	1542	1646	1716	1846	...	2031	|	2316
Sad **1362** a.	...	0520	0602	0639	...	0733	0855	...	1007	1139	...	1220	1301	...	1352	1504	...	1607	1719	1815	1828	2010	...	2201	2317	0039
Sad d.	0355	...	0633	...	0708	...	0900	0958	...	...	1204	...	1304	...	...	...	1546	...	...	...	1838	...	2028	...	2320	...
otica 1362 a.	0625	...	0909	...	0945	...	1122	1223	...	...	1434	...	1522	...	...	...	1819	...	...	...	2102	...	2310	...	0141	...
otica 🏛 d.	...	...	...	...	...	...	1159	...	...	...	...	...	1600	...	...	...	...	...	...	...	...	...	...	...	0216	...
bia 🏛 a.	...	...	...	...	...	...	1213	...	...	...	...	...	1614	...	...	...	...	...	...	...	...	...	...	...	0230	...
dapest Keleti **1295** a.	...	...	...	...	...	...	1554	...	...	...	...	...	1954	...	...	...	...	...	...	...	...	...	...	...	0546	...

BEOGRAD – 🛏 1, 2 cl., ▬ 2 cl. and 12 Budapest - Beograd and v.v. Conveys Dec. 13 - June 6, Sept. 16 - Dec. 8 (from Moskva, two days later from Beograd); Dec. 16 - June 9, Sept. 19 - Dec. 10 (from Sofia and Beograd): 🛏 1, 2 cl. Moskva (**9/10**) - Warszawa (**130/1**) - Budapest (**340/1**) - Beograd (**490/1**) - Sofia and v.v. Conveys June 6 - Sept. 14 (from Moskva, two days later from Beograd); June 9 - Sept. 17 (from Varna, one day later from Sofia and Beograd): 🛏 1, 2 cl. Moskva - Beograd - Sofia (**3636/7**) - Varna and v.v. Conveys June 7 - Sept. 15 (from Moskva, two days later from Beograd); June 10 - Sept. 18 (from Burgas, one day later from Sofia and Beograd): 🛏 1, 2 cl. Moskva - Beograd - Sofia - Karnobat (**8686/7**) - Burgas and v.v. Conveys ④⑥ June 9 - Sept. 15 (from Minsk, one day later from Beograd); ①⑥ June 11 - Sept. 17 (from Varna, one day later from Sofia and Beograd): 🛏 1, 2 cl. Minsk (**9/10**) - Warszawa (**130/1**) - Budapest (**340/1**) - Beograd (**490/1**) - Sofia (**3636/7**) - Varna and v.v. Conveys ①③ June 6 - Sept. 14 (from Moskva); ④⑥ June 9 - Sept. 17 (from Bar): 🛏 1, 2 cl. Moskva - Beograd (**430/1**) - Bar and v.v. Conveys ① June 13 - Sept. 12 (from Minsk); ③ June 15 - Sept. 14 (from Bar): 🛏 1, 2 cl. Minsk - Beograd - Bar and v.v. Conveys ②⑤ June 17 - Sept. 2 (from Praha); ④⑦ June 19 - Sept. 4 (from Bar): 🛏 1, 2 cl. and ▬ 2 cl. Praha (**172/3**) - Beograd (**430/1**) - Bar and v.v.

C – IVO ANDRIĆ – 12 Beograd - Budapest and v.v. Conveys ②⑤ June 17 - Sept. 2 (from Budapest); ③⑥ June 18 - Sept. 3 (from Thessaloníki): 🛏 1, 2 cl. and 2 Budapest - Beograd (**334/5**) - Thessaloníki and v.v.

P – PANONIJA – June 3 - Sept. 4 (from Subotica); June 4 - Sept. 5 (from Bar): 🛏 1, 2 cl., ▬ 2 cl. and 2 Subotica - Bar and v.v. Conveys ②⑤ June 17 - Sept. 2 (from Budapest); ③⑥ June 18 - Sept. 3 (from Bar): 🛏 1, 2 cl., ▬ 2 cl. and 2 Budapest (**344/5**) - Subotica - Bar and v.v.

V – AVALA – 12 and ✕ Wien - Budapest - Beograd and v.v. Conveys ②⑤ June 17 - Sept. 2 (from Budapest); ③⑥ June 18 - Sept. 3 (from Bar): 🛏 1, 2 cl., ▬ 2 cl. and 2 Budapest - Subotica (**1136/7**) - Bar and v.v.

c – Beograd **Centar**.

◧ – Train with 'global' price.

◐ – Supplement payable for travel in Serbia.

⚡ – Supplement payable for travel in Hungary and Serbia.

SUBOTICA and KIKINDA - ZRENJANIN - PANČEVO - BEOGRAD 1362

2nd class only

Subotica 1360 ⊖ d.	...	...	...	...	0730	...	...	...	...	...
Senta ⊖ d.	...	...	...	...	0853	...	...	...	...	...
Banatsko Miloševo ⊖ d.	...	...	...	...	0943	...	...	...	...	...
Kikinda 1377 ⊖ d.	...	...	0435	...	1000	1131	...	...	1635	...
Banatsko Miloševo d.	...	...	0453	...	...	1149	...	...	1653	...
Zrenjanin d.	0400	...	0641	0740	...	1337	1415	...	1841	2020
Orlovat stajalište d.	0455	...	...	0835	...	...	1510	...	...	2115
Pančevo glavna **1365/6** d.	...	...	...	0951	...	...	1626	...	...	2232
Pančevački most **1365/6** d.	...	...	...	1018	...	...	1654	...	...	...
Beograd Dunav **1365** a.	...	...	...	1021	...	...	1657	...	...	...

Beograd Dunav **1365** d.	...	...	...	...	1040	...	1725	...	...	...
Pančevački most **1365/6** d.	...	...	...	...	1044	...	1729	...	...	...
Pančevo glavna **1365/6** d.	...	...	...	...	1108	...	1753	...	...	2250
Orlovat stajalište d.	0623	...	...	...	1224	...	1911	...	...	0008
Zrenjanin d.	0717	...	0915	...	1318	1420	2005	2015	...	0102
Banatsko Miloševo a.	...	...	1103	...	...	1608	...	2203	...	...
Kikinda 1377 ⊖ a.	...	1010	1121	...	...	1626	...	2221	...	...
Banatsko Miloševo ⊖ d.	...	1035	...	...	...	...	...	...	...	...
Senta ⊖ d.	...	1125	...	...	...	...	...	...	...	...
Subotica 1360 ⊖ a.	...	1240	...	...	...	...	...	...	...	...

For alternative 🚌 services Subotica - Kikinda and v.v. see www.polazak.com.

BEOGRAD - VRŠAC - TIMISOARA 1365

CFR

	2			2		2			2
Beograd Dunav **1362** d.	0725	...	...	1150	...	1615	...	...	2020
Pančevački most **1362/6** d.	0729	...	...	1154	...	1619	...	...	2024
Pančevo glavna **1362/6** d.	0753	...	...	1218	...	1643	...	...	2048
Vršac a.	0903	...	...	1328	...	1753	...	...	2200
Vršac 🏛 d.	...	1018	...	...	...	...	1840	...	...
Stamora Moravita 🏛 § a.	...	1140	...	...	...	...	2002	...	...
Stamora Moravita § d.	...	1217	...	...	...	...	2032	...	...
Timisoara Nord § a.	...	1322	...	...	...	...	2134	...	...

	2			2		2			2
Timisoara Nord § d.	...	...	0750	...	...	...	...	1638	...
Stamora Moravita § a.	...	...	0900	...	...	...	...	1753	...
Stamora Moravita 🏛 § d.	...	...	0930	...	...	...	...	1823	...
Vršac 🏛 a.	...	...	0852	...	...	...	...	1745	...
Vršac d.	0520	...	...	0940	...	1410	...	...	1825
Pančevo glavna **1362/6** d.	0634	...	...	1052	...	1522	...	...	1937
Pančevački most **1362/6** d.	0702	...	...	1120	...	1550	...	...	2005
Beograd Dunav **1362** d.	0705	...	...	1123	...	1553	...	...	2008

§ – Romanian (East European) time.

NOVI BEOGRAD - PANČEVO 1366

2nd class only

Beograd d.	0617	and	2117	...	2147	2232	...
rad centar d.	0623	hourly	2123	...	2153	2238	...
čevački most **1362/5** d.	0632	until	2132	...	2202	2247	...

Pančevački most **1362/5** d.	0604	and	1504	1602	and	2002	2104	2149	2219	2304
Beograd centar d.	0614	hourly	1514	1613	hourly	2013	2114	2159	2229	2314
Novi Beograd a.	0619	until	1519	1618	until	2018	2119	2204	2234	2319

čevački most **1362/5** d.	0500	0640	0820	0955	1145	1320	1500	1810	1945	2150
čevo glavna **1362/5** a.	0518	0658	0838	1014	1203	1338	1518	1828	2003	2208

Pančevo glavna **1362/5** d.	0601	0739	0916	1104	1240	1421	1725	1906	2106	2301
Pančevački most **1362/5** a.	0622	0800	0937	1138	1301	1442	1746	1927	2127	2322

SERBIA and MONTENEGRO

1370 BEOGRAD - PODGORICA - BAR ŽCG

km																IC	IC							
										431			713		581	513				433		1343		
		2	2	2	2	2	2	2	2		2	2		2	[R]	[R]	2		2		2		2	2
										T					K ⊗					L		A		
0	**Beograd** d.	...	...	0250	...	0704	...	...	...	0910	...	1030	1245	1454	1655	1655	...	...	1905	2010	...	2110	...	...
93	Valjevo d.	...	...	0507	...	0924	...	...	...	1103	...	1243	1434	1709	1844	1844	...	...	2122	2205	...	|	...	...
159	Požega **1372** d.	...	...	0648	...	1059	...	...	...	1230	...	1432	1559	1854	2007	2022	...	...	2303	2332	...	0038	...	...
185	Užice d.	...	...	0727	...	1135	...	...	...	1301	...	1508	1632	1934	...	2042	...	...	2333	0003	...	0117	...	0236
292	Prijepolje teretna d.	...	...	0959	...	1403	...	...	...	1526	...	1747	...	2203	...	2249	...	...	...	0304	...	0431	...	0513
328	Vrbnica 🛃 a.	...	...	...	...	...	...	...	...	1606	...	1830	...	...	...	...	...	...	...	|	...	|	...	0557
338	Bijelo Polje 🛃 d.	...	0903	...	...	...	...	...	...	1721	1833	...	...	...	...	...	...	...	...	0420	...	0549	0630	...
468	**Podgorica 1371** d.	1030	1130	...	1250	...	1520	1650	1801	1930	2115	...	...	...	...	...	0535	...	...	0633	0750	0827	0855	...
524	**Bar** a.	1128	1234	...	1348	...	1618	1756	1858	2031	2213	...	...	...	...	...	0629	...	...	0738	0848	0938	...	...

		IC	IC																			
		580	512						430			714						1136			432		
	2	[R]	[R]	2	2	2	2	2		2	2		2	2	2	2	2			2		2	2
		K ⊗							T									P			L		
Bar d.	...	...	...	...	...	0515	0640	...	0900	0913	1140	...	1405	...	1440	1635	...	1700	...	1825	1900	1930	...
Podgorica 1371 d.	...	...	...	...	...	0625	0739	...	1000	1017	1238	...	1503	...	1550	1736	...	1800	...	1929	2005	2035	...
Bijelo Polje 🛃 d.	...	...	...	...	...	0843	...	...	1230	...	...	...	...	...	1814	...	...	2040	...	...	2240	...	...
Vrbnica 🛃 d.	...	...	...	...	0655	...	...	...	1306	...	...	...	...	...	...	...	1905	|	...	...	|	...	...
Prijepolje teretna d.	...	...	0305	0330	0740	...	...	1115	1351	...	...	...	...	1530	...	...	1949	2204	...	...	0004	...	...
Užice d.	0235	...	0521	0612	1026	...	...	1403	1614	...	...	1757	...	1813	...	...	2245	0039	...	...	0224	...	0235
Požega **1372** d.	0305	0437	0542	0649	1100	...	...	1431	1636	...	...	1821	...	1855	...	...	...	0102	...	...	0246	...	0305
Valjevo d.	0442	0605	0711	0841	1244	...	...	1612	1802	...	...	1955	...	2049	...	...	...	0235	...	...	0412	...	0442
Beograd a.	0644	0751	0852	1055	1449	...	...	1840	1953	...	...	2155	...	2301	...	...	...	0433n	...	...	0602	...	0644

A – AUTO-VOZ – June 3 - Sept. 4 (from Beograd); June 4 - Sept. 5 (from Bar): 🛏 1, 2 cl. and ▬ 2 cl. Beograd - Bar and v.v.
K – [12] Beograd - Požega - Kraljevo and v.v.
L – LOVĆEN – 🛏 1, 2 cl., ▬ 2 cl. and [2] Beograd - Bar and v.v.
P – PANONIJA – June 3 - Sept. 4 (from Subotica); June 4 - Sept. 5 (from Bar): 🛏 1, 2 cl., ▬ 2 cl. and [2] Subotica - Bar and v.v. Conveys ②⑤ June 17 - Sept. 2 (from Budapest); ③⑥ June 18 - Sept. 3 (from Bar): 🛏 1, 2 cl., ▬ 2 cl. and [2] Budapest (**344/5**) - Subotica - Bar and v.v.
T – TARA – [12] Beograd - Bar and v.v. Also conveys cars from / to Moskva / Minsk / Praha. See Table **1360** for composition and dates.

n – Novi Beograd.
⊗ – Service currently suspended.

1371 PODGORICA - NIKŠIĆ ŽCG

km											
0	**Podgorica 1370** d.	0630	0740	0930	1105	1245	1400	1510	1614	1900	2040
25	Danilovgrad d.	0701	0807	0957	1136	1316	1427	1537	1645	1927	2111
61	**Nikšić** a.	0740	0846	1036	1215	1355	1506	1616	1728	2005	2150

Nikšić d.	0620	0805	0910	1055	1235	1425	1535	1650	1740
Danilovgrad d.	0700	0850	0958	1135	1315	1510	1620	1730	1820
Podgorica 1370 a.	0726	0926	1024	1202	1341	1541	1646	1756	1846

1372 POŽEGA - KRALJEVO - STALAĆ 2nd class only

tariff km										581 K ⊗
0	**Požega 1370** d.	...	...	0830	...	1250	...	1650	...	2025
45	Čačak d.	...	0525	0905	...	1325	...	1725	...	2052
83	**Kraljevo 1375** a.	0434	0603	0942	...	1402	1425	1802	...	2116
155	Stalać **1380** a.	0657	...	...	...	...	1648	...	...	...

	580 K ⊗							
Stalać **1380** d.	...	...	...	...	...	0915	...	...
Kraljevo 1375 d.	0342	0410	0630	...	1050	1138	1440	1830
Čačak d.	0410	0445	0705	...	1129	...	1519	1909
Požega 1370 a.	0435	...	0737	...	1204	...	1554	1944

K – [12] Beograd - Požega - Kraljevo and v.v.

⊗ – Service currently suspended.

1373 MAJDANPEK and PRAHOVO - ZAJEČAR - NIŠ 2nd class only except where shown

tariff km										
0	Majdanpek d.	0345	...	...	...	0855	...	1705	...	...
★	Prahovo pristanište d.	|	0425		0845	|		|	1750	...
97	**Zaječar** d.	0558	0611	0625	1031	1109	1150	1919	1936	1956
144	Knjaževac d.	...	...	0729	...	...	1304	...	...	2102
221	**Niš 1380** a.	...	...	0936	...	...	1509	...	...	2307

Niš 1380 d.	0225	...	...	1053	...	...	1540	...
Knjaževac d.	0434	...	...	1259	...	...	1751	...
Zaječar d.	0540	0620	0635	1402	1430	1530	1857	2225
Prahovo pristanište a.	...	|	0820	...	|	1716	...	|
Majdanpek d.	...	0831	...	...	1641	...	...	0036

★ – Prahovo - Zaječar: *81 km*.

1375 LAPOVO and PRIŠTINA - KOSOVO POLJE - SKOPJE 2nd class only ŽS,

km										
	Beograd **1380** d.	...	...	...	...	...	...	...	...	...
0	**Lapovo 1380** d.	...	...	0338	...	1110	...	...	1853	...
28	**Kragujevac** d.	...	...	0432	...	1204	...	...	1947	...
82	Kraljevo **1372** d.	...	0240	0623	0640	1355	...	1455	2138	...
163	Raška d.	...	0418	...	0821	...	...	1636	...	...
180	Lešak / Leshak d.	...	...	...	0853	...	...	1708	...	...
210	Zvečan / Zveçan ♣ d.	...	...	...	1002	...	...	1817	...	...
		891	—		—		761	—		
		⊠ h	⊠		⊠		⊠	⊠		
214	Mitrovica / Mitrovicë ♣ d.	...	...	...	...	...	...	...	...	...
	Priština / Prishtinë d.	0710	0750	...	...	...	1630	...	...	...
247	**Kosovo Polje / Fushë Kosovë** ♣ d.	0722	0801	...	1605	...	1641	1848	...	...
*	Peć / Pejë a.	|	0950	...	|	...	1826	|	...	...
276	Uroševac / Ferizaj d.	0802	...	...	1649	...	...	1935	...	...
304	Deneral Janković / Hani I Elezit 🛃 a.	0900	...	...	1730	...	...	2016	...	...
331	**Skopje 1380/5** a.	0951	...	...	...	...	...	...	...	...

			760					892
		⊠	⊠		⊠	⊠		⊠ h
Skopje 1380/5 d.	...	...	...	...	...	...	...	1610
Deneral Janković / Hani I Elezit 🛃 d.	...	0548	...	...	1050	...	...	1745
Uroševac / Ferizaj d.	...	0632	...	...	1135	...	...	1829
Peć / Pejë d.	...	|	0532	...	|	1210	...	|
Kosovo Polje / Fushë Kosovë ♣ d.	...	0714	0721	...	1219	1359	...	1910
Priština / Prishtinë a.	...	...	0732	...	...	1410	...	1920
Mitrovica / **Mitrovicë** ♣ d.	...	...	...	...	...	...	...	...
		—			—			—
Zvečan / Zveçan ♣ d.	...	...	...	1028	...	...	1843	...
Lešak / Leshak d.	...	...	...	1135	...	...	1950	...
Raška d.	0435	...	...	1210	...	...	2025	...
Kraljevo **1372** d.	0611	0644	...	1346	1449	...	2201	2225
Kragujevac d.	...	0836	...	...	1641	...	...	0017
Lapovo 1380 a.	...	0929	...	...	1734	...	...	0112
Beograd **1380** a.	...	...	...	...	...	...	...	...

h – A change of train may be necessary at Deneral Janković / Hani I Elezit (connection between trains is guaranteed).

⊠ – Service operated by KŽ (see country heading).
♣ – Currently no service Zvečan - Mitrovica - Kosovo Polje and v.v.
* – Kosovo Polje - Peć: *82 km*.

1377 MINOR BORDER CROSSINGS 2nd class only ŽS, MÁV, C

SUBOTICA - SZEGED and v.v. :

km			⊗	
0	Subotica d.	0726	1103	*1427*
24	Horgoš 🛃 d.	0835	1210	1533
31	Röszke 🛃 a.	0852	1227	1550
43	Szeged ● a.	*0930*	*1300*	1620

		⊗	
Szeged ● d.	*0822*	*1153*	1430
Röszke 🛃 d.	0907	1242	1500
Horgoš 🛃 d.	0939	1314	1517
Subotica a.	1034	1409	*1825*

KIKINDA - JIMBOLIA - TIMISOARA and v.v. :

km							
0	Kikinda **1362** d.	...	...	...	...	...	...
19	Jimbolia 🛃 § d.	0515	0610	0840	1230	1430	1740
58	Timisoara § a.	0607	0702	0932	1322	1521	1832

Timisoara § d.	0705	0808	1330	1624	1930
Jimbolia 🛃 § d.	0755	0921	1420	1714	2020
Kikinda **1362** a.	...	...	...	...	...

⊗ – Service currently suspended.
● – Röszke - Szeged and v.v. is reported as currently suspended.

§ – East European time, one hour ahead of Central European time.

BEOGRAD - NIŠ - SOFIA, SKOPJE and THESSALONÍKI — 1380

ŽS, MŽ, BDŽ

Gevgelija - Thessaloníki and v.v. is subject to 🚌 replacement; times may vary.

								791			337	491							795				335		293
	2	2	2	2	2	2	2⚒		2	2	S⊗	B	2	2	2x	2	2	2		2	2		H⊗	2	N
Beograd 1375 d.	...	...	...	...	...	0335	...	0610	...	0714	0735	0735	←	...	...	1110	...	...	1515	...	1527	...	1850	1920	2205
Lapovo **1375** d.	...	...	0350	...	...	0610	...	0819	...	0952	0933	0933	1003	...	...	1342	1551	...	1714	...	1806	...	2048	2153	0003
Jagodina d.	...	...	0418	...	...	0638	...	0844	...	→	0957	0957	1031	...	...	1410	1619	...	1739	...	1834	...	2112	...	0027
Paraćin d.	...	...	0433	...	...	0653	...	0900	...	...	1014	1014	1046	...	...	1424	1634	...	1755	...	1849	...	2129	...	0038
Stalać **1372** d.	...	...	0458	...	...	0717	...	0923	...	...	1039	1039	1111	...	...	...	1659	...	1818	...	1914	...	2154	...	0103
Niš 1373 a.	...	...	0631	...	...	0855	...	1032	...	...	1144	1144	1249	...	...	...	1831	...	1927	...	2045	...	2259	...	0214
Niš d.	...	0335	...	...	0711	...	...	...	...	...	1200	1210	▬	1526	1550	...	▬	...	...	1932	...	...	2315	...	0240
Dimitrovgrad ▦ d.	...	|	...	...	|	...	...	...	...	...	|	1515	...	|	|	...	...	...	...	|	...	...	|	...	0540
Dragoman ▦ § d.	...	|	...	...	|	...	...	...	...	...	|	1736	...	|	|	...	...	...	...	|	...	...	|	...	0740
Sofia § a.	...	|	...	...	|	...	...	...	...	...	|	1815	...	|	|	...	...	...	...	|	...	...	|	...	0845
Leskovac d.	...	0437	...	...	0824	...	...	...	...	...	1254	...	...	1630	1655	...	...	...	...	2032	...	...	0000	...	...
Preševo ▦ d.	...	0712x	...	...	...	...	...	...	...	...	1552	...	2	...	1925	...	2	...	...	2257x	...	...	0255	...	...
Tabanovci ▦ d.	0516	...	...	0747	...	...	...	...	...	...	1635	...	1750	...	...	...	2016	...	...	...	...	...	0340	...	...
Skopje a.	0610	...	...	0845	...	...	...	...	...	...	1715	...	1844	...	...	...	2110	...	...	...	...	...	0420	...	...
Skopje 1375/85 d.	0620	...	...	0900	...	...	1320	...	1655	...	...	...	...	...	...	...	...	2240	...	...	...	...	0445	...	...
Veles **1385** d.	0722	...	...	0951	...	...	1411	...	1746	...	...	...	...	...	...	...	...	2330	...	...	...	...	0526	...	...
Gevgelija a.	0908	...	...	...	...	...	...	...	1938	...	...	...	...	...	...	...	...	...	...	...	...	...	0651	...	...
Gevgelija ▦ d.	...	...	...	...	...	...	...	...	...	...	...	...	...	...	...	...	...	...	...	...	...	...	0723	...	...
Idoméni ▦ a.	...	...	...	...	...	...	...	...	...	...	...	...	...	...	...	...	...	...	...	...	...	...	0828	...	...
Idoméni d.	...	...	...	...	...	...	...	...	...	...	...	...	...	...	...	...	...	...	...	...	...	...	0900	...	...
Thessaloníki 1400 § a.	...	...	...	...	...	...	...	...	...	...	...	...	...	...	...	...	...	...	...	...	...	...	1007	...	...

					790							336		490							292			334
	2	2	2	2		2	2	2⚒	2	2	2	S⊗		B		2	2	2	2⚒	2	2x	N	2	2	H⊗
Thessaloníki 1400 § d.	...	...	...	...	...	...	...	...	...	...	...	...	...	...	...	...	...	...	...	...	...	...	...	...	1830
Idoméni a.	...	...	...	...	...	...	...	...	...	...	...	...	...	...	...	...	...	...	...	...	...	...	...	...	1937
Idoméni ▦ d.	...	...	...	...	...	...	...	...	...	...	...	...	...	...	...	...	...	...	...	...	...	...	...	...	2011
Gevgelija ▦ a.	...	...	...	...	...	...	...	...	...	...	...	...	...	...	...	...	...	...	...	...	...	...	...	...	1916
Gevgelija d.	...	...	...	...	...	...	...	...	0443	...	...	...	...	...	...	...	...	...	...	...	...	...	...	1655	1946
Veles **1385** d.	...	...	...	...	...	0503	...	0610	0635	...	...	...	...	...	...	1148	...	...	1423	...	...	...	...	1840	2113
Skopje 1375/85 a.	...	...	...	...	...	0558	...	0705	0734	...	...	...	...	...	...	1239	...	...	1519	...	...	...	...	1931	2154
Skopje d.	...	...	...	...	...	0630	...	▬	...	...	...	0820	...	...	...	▬	...	...	...	1634	...	...	1900	...	2219
Tabanovci ▦ a.	...	...	...	...	...	0724	...	...	...	...	...	0926	...	...	...	...	...	...	...	1732	...	...	1955	...	2329
Preševo ▦ d.	...	...	...	0250x	...	...	...	...	...	0815x	...	1007	...	...	...	...	...	...	...	...	2005	...	...	...	0020
Leskovac d.	...	...	...	0520	...	...	...	...	...	1048	...	1235	1250	...	...	...	1715	...	...	...	2233	...	...	...	0233
Sofia § d.	...	...	...	|	...	...	...	...	...	|	...	|	|	1130	...	...	|	...	...	...	|	2025	...	...	|
Dragoman ▦ § d.	...	...	...	|	...	...	...	...	...	|	...	|	|	1213	...	...	|	...	...	...	|	2152	...	...	|
Dimitrovgrad ▦ d.	...	...	...	|	...	...	...	...	...	|	...	|	|	1240	...	...	|	...	...	...	|	2120	...	...	|
Niš 1373 a.	...	...	...	0623	...	...	...	2	...	1152	...	1322	1400	1504	...	2	1819	...	...	...	2339	2345	...	...	0317
Niš d.	...	0310	...	...	0632	...	0730	1105	...	...	...	1335	...	1530	...	1545	...	1924	...	...	...	0016	...	...	0330
Stalać **1372** d.	...	0450	0657	...	0745	...	0901	1239	...	...	...	1441	...	1636	...	1727	...	2059	...	...	...	0122	...	...	0436
Paraćin d.	...	0513	0726	...	0805	...	0924	1301	...	...	1444	1503	...	1658	...	1749	...	2121	...	...	...	0144	...	...	0458
Jagodina d.	...	0528	0741	...	0821	...	0939	1323	...	...	1459	1520	...	1709	...	1812	...	2147	...	...	...	0155	...	...	0515
Lapovo **1375** d.	0346	0606	...	...	0845	...	1016	1351	...	...	1532	1542	...	1731	...	1850	...	2214	...	...	...	0217	...	...	0537
Beograd 1375 a.	0613	0838	...	...	1118	...	1242	...	...	...	1752	1808	...	1935	...	2126	...	...	...	...	...	0436	...	...	0742

B – BALKAN – [2] Beograd - Sofia and v.v. Also conveys 🛏 1, 2 cl. Moskva / Minsk - Beograd - Sofia - Burgas / Varna and v.v. See Table **1360** for dates of running.
H – HELLAS – 🛏 2 cl. and [2] Beograd - Skopje - Thessaloníki and v.v. Conveys ②⑤ June 17 - Sept. 2 (from Budapest); ③⑥ June 18 - Sept. 3 (from Thessaloníki): 🛏 1, 2 cl. and [2] Budapest (**342/3**) - Beograd - Thessaloníki and v.v.
N – NUŠIĆ – 🛏 2 cl. and [2] Beograd - Sofia and v.v.
S – [2] Beograd - Skopje and v.v.

x – Service temporarily suspended.
⊗ – Service suspended until June 11.
§ – East European time.

BRANCH LINES in FYRO Macedonia — 1385

2nd class only

SKOPJE - KOČANI and BITOLA and v.v. :

			R §			
Skopje **1380** d.	0642	1430	1522	1710	2012	...
Veles **1380** d.	0748	1524	1621	1752	2113	...
Kočani a.	|	|	1814	|	|	...
Prilep d.	0934	1710	...	1917	2258	...
Bitola a.	1016	1752	...	1951	2340	...

		R §				
Bitola d.	0310	0518	...	1250	1825	...
Prilep d.	0350	0553	...	1334	1922	...
Kočani d.	|	|	0550	|	|	...
Veles **1380** d.	0540	0721	0751	1522	2117	...
Skopje **1380** a.	0635	0802	0841	1614	2205	...

SKOPJE - KIČEVO and v.v. :

km		⊗		
0	Skopje d.	0805	1650	...
86	Tetovo d.	0911	1753	...
163	Kičevo a.	1012	1854	...

	⊗		
Kičevo d.	0533	1218	...
Tetovo d.	0633	1319	...
Skopje a.	0735	1422	...

R – Also conveys [1].
⊗ – Service reported as temporarily suspended.
★ – Veles - Kočani : *110 km.*

ALBANIA

SEE MAP PAGE 501

Operator: Hekurudha Shqiptarë (HSH).
Services: Trains convey one class of accommodation only. Tickets are not sold in advance, only for the next available departure.
Timings: Timings have been compiled from the latest information received, but readers should be aware that timetable amendments usually come into effect at short notice, and are advised to check information locally before travelling.
Security: Most visits to Albania are reported to be trouble free, but travellers are advised to avoid the north-east of the country.

ALBANIAN RAILWAYS — 1390

One class only

Kashar - central Tiranë and v.v. is operated by 🚌 *(approximately 7.5 km)*

km										
0	**Shkodër** d.	...	...	...	...	0545	...	...	...	...
82	Vorë d.	...	...	...	...	0905*	...	...	...	...
98	**Tiranë** 🚌 d.	...	...	...	...	|	...	...	...	...
—	Kashar 🚌 d.	0635	...	0830	...	|	...	...	...	...
	Durrës a.	0718	...	0912	...	0935	...	...	...	...
0	**Durrës** d.	0735	...	...	...	...	...	1240	...	...
36	Rrogozhinë d.	0846	...	...	...	...	...	1350*	...	...
77	Elbasan a.	|	...	...	...	...	...	1528	...	...
98	**Librazhd** a.	|	...	...	...	...	...	1618	...	...
	Lushnjë a.	x	...	...	...	...	...	...	...	...
	Fier a.	x	...	...	...	...	...	...	...	...
	Vlorë a.	x	...	...	...	...	...	...	...	...

Vlorë d.	...	...	...	...	...	...	x	...	...
Fier d.	...	...	...	...	...	...	x	...	...
Lushnjë d.	...	...	...	...	...	...	x	...	...
Librazhd d.	...	...	...	...	...	...	|	1630	...
Elbasan d.	...	0745	...	...	...	...	|	1718	...
Rrogozhinë d.	...	0925*	...	...	...	...	1410	...	...
Durrës a.	...	1036	...	...	...	...	1521	...	...
Durrës d.	0620	...	...	1300	1445	...	...	...	...
Kashar 🚌 a.	0702	...	...	|	1527	...	...	...	...
Tiranë 🚌 a.	...	...	...	|	...	...	...	...	...
Vorë d.	...	...	...	1320*	...	...	...	...	...
Shkodër a.	...	...	...	1645	...	...	...	...	...

x – Times not available.
* – Estimated time.

GREECE

SEE MAP PAGE

Operator: TRAINOSE S.A., ΤΡΑΙΝΟΣΕ Α.Ε.: www.trainose.gr.

Services: All trains convey first and second class seating except where shown otherwise in footnotes or by '2' in the train column, or where the footnote shows sleeping and/or cou cars only. Descriptions of sleeping (🛏) and couchette (▬) cars appear on page 8. Services that convey catering may vary from day to day.

Timings: Timings have been compiled from the latest information received. Readers should be aware that timetable amendments may come into effect at short notice, and are adv check information locally before travelling.

Tickets: Reservation of seats is possible (and recommended) on most express trains. *IC* trains carry a supplement which varies depending upon distance travelled. Break of jou only permitted when tickets are so endorsed before travel with the station quoted.

1400 ATHÍNA - LÁRISA - THESSALONÍKI

km				590		*IC* 50		884		2590	*IC* 52		3520		*IC* 56			*IC* 58		*IC* 60		1510	
		2	2		2	✕⁄	2	🍷	2	2	✕⁄	2		2	✕⁄	2	2	🍷⁄	2	✕⁄	2		2
													⑤⑦										
0	**Athína** Lárisa **1420** d.	...	...	...	...	0718	...	0827	...	...	1018	...	1118	...	1418	...	...	1616	...	1818	...	1917	...
7	SKA (Acharnon) **1420/40** d.	...	...	...	...	0728	...	0836	...	...	1028	...	1127	...	1427	...	...	1625	...	1827	...	1926	...
61	Inói **1420** d.	...	...	...	...	0808	...	0916	...	...	1108	...	1206	...	1508	...	...	1706	...	1908	...	2005	...
89	Thíva d.	...	...	...	...	0824	...	0931	...	...	1124	...	1222	...	1524	...	...	1721	...	1924	...	2021	...
129	Levadiá d.	...	...	...	...	0843	...	0953	...	...	1143	...	1247	...	1543	...	...	1741	...	1943	...	2046	...
154	Tithoréa d.	...	...	...	...	|	...	1006	...	...	|	...	1308	...	|	...	...	|	...	1955	...	2107	...
169	Amfíklia d.	...	...	...	...	|	...	1019	...	...	|	...	1320	...	|	...	...	1804	...	2006	...	2119	...
210	Lianokládi d.	0515	0645	...	0815	0941	1015	1102	1115	...	1241	1315	1402	1515	1641	1650	1810	1839	1958	2041	2110	2202	2215
	Lamia d.	0525	0655	...	0825	|	1024	|	1125	...	|	1325	...	1525	|	1659	1820	|	2007	|	2119	...	2225
	Stilída a.	0548	0718	...	0848	|	...	|	1148	...	|	1348	...	1548	|	...	1843	|	...	|	...	...	2248
291	Paleofársalos **1408** d.	...	...	0917	...	1100	...	1222	...	1232	1400	...	...	...	1805	...	...	1958	...	2200	...	...	...
	Kalambáka **1408** a.	...	...	0819**p**	...	|	...	1318	...	|	|	...	...	...	|	...	...	|	...	|	...	...	...
333	**Lárisa 1425** ▲ d.	...	...	0941	...	1120	...	...	...	1252	1420	...	...	...	1824	...	...	2017	...	2219	...	...	...
417	Kateríni ▲ d.	...	...	1031	...	1157	...	...	...	1338	1457	...	...	...	1902	...	...	2055	...	2257	...	...	...
465	Platí **1410** ▲ d.	...	...	1057	...	1218	...	...	...	1402	1518	...	...	...	1923	...	...	2117	...	2318	...	...	...
502	**Thessaloníki 1410** ▲ a.	...	...	1124	...	1241	...	...	...	1428	1541	...	...	...	1946	...	...	2139	...	2341	...	...	...

km			1511		*IC* 51		*IC* 53			*IC* 55				3521		*IC* 59	591		885		*IC* 61		
		2		2	🍷⁄	2	✕⁄	2	2	✕⁄	2		2		2	✕⁄		2	🍷	2	✕⁄	2	2
			①											⑤⑦									
	Thessaloníki 1410 ▲ d.	...	...	...	0513	...	0704	...	...	1004	...	...	...	...	...	1504	1617	...	...	...	1804	...	...
	Platí **1410** ▲ d.	...	...	...	0536	...	0728	...	...	1028	...	...	...	...	...	1528	1645	...	...	...	1828	...	...
	Kateríni ▲ d.	...	...	...	0556	...	0749	...	...	1049	...	...	...	...	...	1549	1712	...	...	...	1849	...	...
	Lárisa 1425 ▲ d.	...	...	...	0633	...	0826	...	...	1126	...	...	...	...	...	1626	1801	...	...	...	1926	...	...
	Kalambáka **1408** d.	...	...	...	|	...	|	...	...	|	...	...	...	...	...	|	1925**p**	...	1722	...	|	...	...
	Paleofársalos **1408** d.	...	...	...	0652	...	0845	...	...	1145	...	...	...	...	...	1645	1824	...	1830	...	1945	...	...
0	Stilída d.	0607	...	0723	|	0857	|	...	1157	|	1357	...	1557	...	...	|	...	1857	|	...	|	...	2254
17	Lamia d.	0630	...	0746	|	0920	|	1045	1220	|	1420	...	1620	...	1741	|	...	1920	|	2021	|	2145	2317
23	Lianokládi d.	0639	0649	0755	0810	0929	1006	1054	1229	1306	1429	...	1629	1642	1750	1803	...	1929	1945	2030	2105	2154	2326
	Amfíklia d.	...	0729	...	0844	...	|	...	...	|	...	...	...	1722	...	1840	...	...	2025	...	|	...	...
	Tithoréa d.	...	0740	...	0854	...	1050	...	...	1350	...	...	...	1733	...	1850	...	...	2036	...	|	...	...
	Levadiá d.	...	0800	...	0904	...	1101	...	...	1401	...	...	...	1753	...	1901	...	...	2048	...	2201	...	...
	Thíva d.	...	0825	...	0921	...	1121	...	...	1421	...	...	...	1818	...	1921	...	...	2110	...	2221	...	...
	Inói **1420** d.	...	0841	...	0936	...	1137	...	...	1437	...	...	...	1837	...	1937	...	...	2125	...	2236	...	...
	SKA (Acharnon) **1420/40** d.	...	0919	...	1015	...	1216	...	...	1516	...	...	...	1912	...	2016	...	...	2204	...	2315	...	...
	Athína Lárisa **1420** a.	...	0928	...	1023	...	1224	...	...	1524	...	...	...	1922	...	2024	...	...	2212	...	2324	...	...

▲ – Local service Thessaloníki - Litóhoro - Lárisa and v.v.:

Thessaloníki d.	0537	0640	0800	...	1258	1425	1714	1837	2147
Platí d.	0604	0707	0827	...	1325	1452	1741	1904	2214
Kateríni d.	0628	0731	0851	...	1349	1516	1805	1928	2238
Litóhoro ⛰ d.	0638	0741	0901	...	1359	1526	1815	1938	2248
Lárisa a.	0712	0815	0935	...	1433	1600	1849	2012	2322

Lárisa d.	0600	0723	0830	1043	...	1450	1645	1900
Litóhoro ⛰ d.	0637	0800	0907	1120	...	1527	1722	1937
Kateríni d.	0646	0809	0916	1129	...	1536	1731	1946
Platí d.	0711	0834	0941	1154	...	1601	1756	2011
Thessaloníki a.	0736	0859	1006	1214	...	1626	1821	2036

FOR NOTES SEE TABLE 1405

1405 THESSALONÍKI - ALEXANDRÚPOLI - DÍKEA

OSE, B

There are currently no cross-border services from/to Turkey

km		1682		600		1684		*IC* 90		
		2				2		⁄		
0	**Thessaloníki** d.	...	...	0655	...	...	...	1601	...	...
42	Kilkis d.	...	...	0735	...	...	...	1637	...	...
97	Rodópoli d.	...	...	|	...	...	...	|	...	...
130	Strimón d.	...	...	|	...	...	...	|	...	...
162	Sérres d.	...	...	0930	...	...	...	1806	...	...
232	Dráma d.	...	...	1021	...	...	...	1853	...	...
327	Xánthi d.	...	...	1222	...	...	...	2054	...	...
374	Komotiní d.	...	...	1255	...	...	...	2124	...	...
443	**Alexandrúpoli** a.	...	...	1354	...	...	...	2220	...	...
443	**Alexandrúpoli** d.	0745	...	...	...	1441	...	2252	...	...
556	Píthio d.	0915	...	...	...	1611	...	0018	...	...
*	*İstanbul Sirkeci* **1550** a.	|	...	...	...	|	...	|	...	...
574	Néa Orestiáda d.	0933	...	...	...	1629	...	0031	...	...
611	Díkea a.	1004	...	...	...	1700	...	0101	...	...

	IC 91		1683		601		1685	
	⁄		2				2	
Díkea d.	0411	...	1208	...	...	...	1905	...
Néa Orestiáda d.	0442	...	1239	...	...	...	1936	...
İstanbul Sirkeci **1550** d.	|	...	|	...	...	...	|	...
Píthio d.	0455	...	1257	...	...	...	1954	...
Alexandrúpoli a.	0619	...	1426	...	...	...	2124	...
Alexandrúpoli d.	0652	...	...	...	1519	...	...	...
Komotiní d.	0751	...	...	...	1618	...	...	...
Xánthi d.	0821	...	...	...	1652	...	...	...
Dráma d.	1020	...	...	...	1854	...	...	...
Sérres d.	1108	...	...	...	1944	...	...	...
Strimón d.	|	...	...	...	|	...	...	...
Rodópoli d.	|	...	...	...	|	...	...	...
Kilkís d.	1237	...	...	...	2145	...	...	...
Thessaloníki a.	1312	...	...	...	2222	...	...	...

p – Via Paleofársalos.

⁄ – Ⓡ with supplement payable. *Icity* train.

⛰ – Station for Mount Ólimbos.

* – Píthio - İstanbul: *268 km*.

1408 LÁRISA - PALEOFÁRSALOS - KALAMBÁKA

km		880		882		884		886	888
		♦				🍷		♦	
	Thessaloníki **1400** d.	...	...	...	...	...	...	1617	...
	Athína **1400** d.	...	...	...	...	0827	...	|	...
	Lárisa 1400 d.	0411	...	...	...	|	...	1801	...
0	Paleofársalos **1400** d.	0438	...	0658	...	1222	...	1831	2029
31	Kardítsa d.	0458	...	0718	...	1242	...	1851	2049
60	Tríkala d.	0517	...	0737	...	1303	...	1910	2108
82	**Kalambáka 1400** ⊡ a.	0532	...	0752	...	1318	...	1925	2123

	881	883		885		887	
		♦		🍷			
Kalambáka 1400 ⊡ d.	0542	0819	...	1732	...	1930	...
Tríkala d.	0558	0835	...	1742	...	1946	...
Kardítsa d.	0617	0854	...	1809	...	2005	...
Paleofársalos **1400** a.	0636	0913	...	1828	...	2024	...
Lárisa 1400 a.	...	0940	...	|	...	...	...
Athína **1400** a.	...	|	...	2212	...	...	...
Thessaloníki **1400** a.	...	1124	...	...	...	...	...

♦ – **NOTES** (LISTED BY TRAIN NUMBER)

880 – 🚌12 Lárisa (**561**) - Paleofársalos - Kalambáka.
883 – 🚌12 Kalambáka - Paleofársalos (**590**) - Thessaloníki.
886 – 🚌12 Thessaloníki (**591**) - Paleofársalos - Kalambáka.
889 – 🚌12 Kalambáka - Paleofársalos (**562**) - Lárisa.

⁄ – Ⓡ with supplement payable. *Icity* train.

⊡ – An infrequent bus service operates Kalambáka - Igumenítsa and v.v. (approximately *250 km*).

THESSALONÍKI - ÉDESSA - FLÓRINA 1410

	IC81		IC83				IC85			
Thessaloníki 1400/05 d.	0714	...	1223	...	1547	...	1930	...	2132	...
Platí **1400** d.	0741	...	1250	...	1616	...	1957	...	2203	...
Véria d.	0803	...	1311	...	1645	...	2018	...	2232	...
Skídra d.	0822	...	1330	...	1708	...	2037	...	2255	...
Édessa a.	0837	...	1345	...	1722	...	2052	...	2309	...
Amíndeo d.	0921	...	1429	...	...	...	2136	...	...	...
Flórina a.	0947	...	1455	...	...	...	2202	...	...	...

			IC82		IC84		IC86			
Flórina d.	...	...	0615	...	0959	...	1612	...	...	...
Amíndeo d.	...	...	0644	...	1027	...	1639	...	...	...
Édessa d.	0450	...	0727	...	1111	...	1723	...	2056	...
Skídra d.	0504	...	0742	...	1126	...	1738	...	2110	...
Véria d.	0528	...	0802	...	1145	...	1757	...	2133	...
Platí **1400** d.	0556	...	0822	...	1205	...	1818	...	2202	...
Thessaloníki 1400/05 a.	0624	...	0848	...	1231	...	1845	...	2230	...

PIREÁS - ATHÍNA - HALKÍDA 1420

			Ⓐ											Ⓐ									
Pireás d.	...	...	0525	...	0625	...	0825	...	1025	...	1225	...	1425	1525	...	1625	...	1825	...	2025	...	2225	...
Athína Lárisa **1400** d.	...	0427	0544	...	0644	...	0844	...	1044	...	1244	...	1444	1544	...	1644	...	1844	...	2044	...	2244	...
SKA (Acharnon) **1400/40** d.	...	0439	0556	...	0656	...	0856	...	1056	...	1256	...	1456	1556	...	1656	...	1856	...	2056	...	2256	...
Afidnai d.	...	0458	0621	...	0721	...	0921	...	1121	...	1321	...	1521	1621	...	1721	...	1921	...	2121	...	2321	...
Inói **1400** d.	0500	0525	0650	...	0750	...	0950	...	1150	...	1350	...	1550	1650	...	1750	...	1950	...	2150	...	2350	...
Halkída a.	0520	...	0712	...	0812	...	1012	...	1212	...	1412	...	1612	1712	...	1812	...	2012	...	2212	...	0012	...

				Ⓐ												Ⓐ								
da d.	...	0627	...	0727	...	0827	...	1027	...	1227	...	1427	...	1627	...	1727	1827	...	2027	...	2227	...	0020	...
400 d.	0529	0651	...	0751	...	0851	...	1051	...	1251	...	1451	...	1651	...	1751	1851	...	2051	...	2251	...	0040	...
ai d.	0557	0722	...	0822	...	0922	...	1122	...	1322	...	1522	...	1722	...	1822	1922	...	2122	...	2322	...	...	...
(Acharnon) **1400/40** d.	0617	0742	...	0842	...	0942	...	1142	...	1342	...	1542	...	1742	...	1842	1942	...	2142	...	2342	...	...	...
a Lárisa **1400** a.	0628	0753	...	0853	...	0953	...	1153	...	1353	...	1553	...	1753	...	1853	1953	...	2153	...	2353	...	...	...
s a.	0651	0814	...	0914	...	1014	...	1214	...	1414	...	1614	...	1814	...	1914	2014	...	2214	...	0014	...	...	...

ange of train is necessary at Afidnai.

LÁRISA - VÓLOS 1425

				🚌		🚌		🚌				
Lárisa **1425** d.	0437	0637	0837	0950	1130	1230	1430	1510	1630	1830	2018	2230
Vólos a.	0525	0725	0925	1035	1218	1330	1518	1610	1718	1918	2106	2318

			🚌		🚌		🚌					
Vólos d.	0530	0730	0830	1025	1120	1225	1340	1525	1725	1925	2125	2335
Lárisa **1425** a.	0618	0818	0930	1113	1220	1313	1440	1613	1813	2013	2213	0023

class. *Subject to confirmation* ATHÍNA AIRPORT ✈ and ATHÍNA - KÓRINTHOS - KIÁTO 1440

km										
	Athína Airport ✈ ▲ d.	0526	...	0544	0611	and	2111	2126	...	2144
	Neratziótissa ▲ d.	0549	...	0607	0634	at the	2134	2149	...	2207
0	**Athína** Lárisa d.	|	0550	|	|	same	|	|	2150	|
7	SKA (Acharnon) **1400/20** d.	0555	0600	0613	0640	minutes	2140	2155	2200	2213
	Ano Liosia d.	0558	...	0617	0643	past each	2143	2158	...	2217
	Kórinthos d.	...	...	0706	...	hour	...	...	...	2306
	Kiáto 1450 a.	...	...	0719	...	until	...	...	...	2319

Kiáto 1450 d.	...	0525	...	...	and	...	...	2125	...
Kórinthos d.	...	0539	...	...	at the	...	...	2139	...
Ano Liosia d.	0602	0628	...	0647	same	2147	2202	2228	...
SKA (Acharnon) **1400/20** d.	0605	0632	0641	0650	minutes	2150	2205	2232	2241
Athína Lárisa a.	|	|	0650	|	past each	|	|	|	2250
Neratziótissa ▲ d.	0612	0638	...	0657	hour	2157	2212	2238	...
Athína Airport ✈ ▲ a.	0635	0701	...	0720	until	2220	2235	2301	...

Frequent Metro services operate as follows:
Line 1 (green): Pireás - Monastiraki - Omónia - Attiki - Neratziótissa - Kifissia.
Line 2 (red): Aghios Dimitrios - Syntagma - Omónia - Athína Lárisa (for **Athína** mainline station) - Attiki - Aghios Antonios.
Line 3 (blue): Egaleo - Monastiraki - Syntagma - Athína Airport ✈.
Operators: ISAP Line 1; Attiko Metro Lines 2 and 3.

Additional trains operate on Ⓐ Athína Airport - Neratziótissa and v.v.

bject to confirmation KIÁTO - PÁTRA 🚌 services (including Pireás, Athína and Athína Airport connections) 1450

s d.	0530	...	0730	...	1030	...	1330	...	1530	...	1730	...
a Lárisa d.	0550	...	0750	...	1150	...	1350	...	1550	...	1750	...
ína Airport ✈ d.	|	0544	|	0744	|	1144	|	1344	|	1544	|	1744
ziótissa d.	|	0607	|	0807	|	1207	|	1407	|	1607	|	1807
(Acharnon) d.	0600	0613	0800	0813	1200	1213	1400	1413	1600	1613	1800	1813
thos d.	...	0706	...	0906	...	1306	...	1506	...	1706	...	1906
) a.	...	0719	...	0919	...	1319	...	1519	...	1719	...	1919
change to bus												
		🚌		🚌		🚌		🚌		🚌	🚌	🚌
1440 d.	...	0730	...	0930	...	1330	...	1530	...	1730	1830	1930
astro d.	...	|	...	|	...	|	...	|	...	|	1850	|
ftó 1455 d.	...	|	...	|	...	1415	...	|	...	|	1930	|
a a.	...	0900	...	1100	...	1510	...	1700	...	1900	2030	2100

	🚌		🚌	🚌	🚌		🚌		🚌		🚌	
Pátra d.	0730	...	0830	0945	1130	...	1415	...	1630	...	1830	...
Diakoftó **1455** d.	|	...	|	1045	|	...	1500	...	|	...	|	...
Xilókastro d.	|	...	|	1135	|	...	|	...	|	...	|	...
Kiáto 1440 a.	0915	...	1015	1210	1315	...	1615	...	1815	...	2015	...
change to train												
Kiáto d.	0925	...	1025	...	1325	...	1625	...	1825	...	2025	...
Kórinthos d.	0939	...	1039	...	1339	...	1639	...	1839	...	2039	...
SKA (Acharnon) d.	1032	1041	1132	1141	1432	1541	1732	1741	1932	1941	2132	2141
Neratziótissa d.	1038	|	1138	|	1438	|	1738	|	1938	|	2138	|
Athína Airport ✈ a.	1101	|	1201	|	1501	|	1801	|	2001	|	2201	|
Athína Lárisa d.	...	1050	...	1150	...	1550	...	1750	...	1950	...	2150
Pireás a.	...	1108	...	1208	...	1608	...	1808	...	2008	...	2208

bject to confirmation PELOPÓNNISOS narrow-gauge branches 1455

akoftó – Kalávrita

2nd class only, rack railway

			Ⓒ		Ⓒ
Diakoftó **1450** d.	0845	1115	1233	1432	1550
Kalávrita a.	0952	1222	1343	1542	1700

			Ⓒ		Ⓒ
Kalávrita d.	0957	1227	1430	1550	1650
Diakoftó **1450** a.	1104	1337	1540	1700	1757

Service currently suspended.

Katákolo – Pírgos – Olimbía

2nd class only

km					⊗	⊗			⊗	⊗	⊗
0	Katákolo d.	...	0840	...	1030	1211	...	...	1405	1550	1730
12	Pírgos a.	0700	0904	...	1050	1233	1235	...	1425	1610	1752
33	Olimbía a.	0728	0932	...	1112	...	1303	...	1447	1632	...

		⊗		⊗			⊗	⊗	⊗	
Olimbía d.	0733	...	0937	1120	...	1308	...	1500	1637	...
Pírgos d.	0804	1000	1005	1144	...	1336	1338	1524	1701	...
Katákolo a.	0826	1018	...	1202	...	...	1400	1542	1719	...

INTERNATIONAL BUS SERVICES 1460

mber of operators run long-distance 🚌 services to and from Greece, and selected services are listed below. Details should be checked with the relevant operator before travel. tickets and passes are not valid. Further details about travelling to Greece by bus can be found on www.europebyrail.eu

ÍNA - ISTANBUL: Depart Athína 1700. Depart Istanbul 1800. Journey 16 hours. Operator: Metro www.metroturizm.com.tr

SSALONIKI - ISTANBUL: Depart Thessaloniki 2100. Depart Istanbul 2100. Journey 10 - 11 hours. Operator: Simeonidis Tours www.simeonidistours.gr
Depart Thessaloniki 1000, 2200, 2330. Depart Istanbul 1000, 1800, 2200. Journey 10 - 11 hours. Operator: Metro www.metroturizm.com.tr

SSALONIKI - SKOPJE: Depart Thessaloniki 1730 ①–⑥. Depart Skopje 0600 ①–⑥. Journey 4 - 5 hours. Operator: Simeonidis Tours www.simeonidistours.gr

SSALONIKI - SOFIA: Coach services are operated by Union Ivkoni (www.union-ivkoni.com) as follows:
Pireás (0730) → Athína (0830) → Thessaloniki (1530) → Sofia (2030) → Varna (0500).
Varna (2345) → Sofia (0800) → Thessaloniki (1300) → Athína (2000) → Pireás (2100).
Kórinthos → Pireás → Athína (1900) → Thessaloniki (0130) → Sofia (0645) → Plovdiv → Burgas.
Burgas → Plovdiv → Sofia (2000) → Thessaloniki (0100) → Athína (0800) → Pireás → Kórinthos.

BULGARIA and TURKEY IN EUROPE

SEE MAP PAGE

Operators: Bâlgarski Dârzhavni Zheleznitsi (BDZh) www.bdz.bg
Türkiye Cumhuryeti Devlet Demiryolları (TCDD) www.tcdd.gov.tr

Services: Trains convey first- and second-class seating, except where shown otherwise in footnotes or by '2' in the train column, or where the footnote shows sleeping and / or cou cars only. Descriptions of sleeping (🛏) and couchette (▬) cars appear on page 8. Seat reservation is possible on most long-distance trains (compulsory on express t

Timings: BDŽ schedules valid **until December 10**, 2016. **Timetable amendments are possible at short notice so it is advisable to confirm timings locally before travellir** Please refer to Tables **61**, **98** and **99** for international through cars to / from Burgas and Varna (summer only). TCDD schedules are the latest available. For services in Asian Turkey see pages 514 – 516.

1500 SOFIA - RUSE, BURGAS and VARNA

km	km						8631	8611	2601	3621	460	2611			8601	2613	3623	8613	4612	3601	8641	2641	9647	8637	3637	8627
									⚡R		R								⚡R	⚡R		⚡R				
			2	2	2	2					A		2	2						⑤f			L	Z	ZD	Z
0	0	**Sofia** .... **1520** d.	...	...	...	...	...	0630	0700	0700	0800	1030	...	...	1035	1300	1305	1335	1530	1630	1700	1740	2025	...	2230	2240
	103	Septemvri .... d.	...	...	...	...	...	0806	|	|	|	|	...	...	1224	|	|	1526	|	|	1851	|	|	...	|	0035
	119	Pazardzhik .... d.	...	...	...	...	...	0825	|	|	|	|	...	...	1243	|	|	1547	|	|	1910	|	|	...	|	0055
	156	**Plovdiv** .... a.	...	...	...	...	...	0904	|	|	|	|	...	...	1325	|	|	1629	|	|	1957	|	|	...	|	0138
	156	**Plovdiv** .... d.	...	...	...	...	0725	0907	|	|	|	|	...	...	1331	|	|	1637	|	|	2007	|	|	2330	|	0150
	262	Stara Zagora .... d.	...	...	...	...	0910	1051	|	|	|	|	...	...	1525	|	|	1833	|	|	2205	|	|	0123	|	0343
	340	Yambol .... d.	...	0605	...	...	1008	1148	|	|	|	|	...	...	1628	|	|	1931	|	|	2300	|	|	0219	|	0442
		Karlovo .... d.	...	|	0525	...	|	|	|	0930	|	|	...	*1120*	|	|	1527	|	|	1848	...	|	|	|	0053	|
		Kazanlak .... d.	...	|	0720j	...	|	|	|	1032	|	|	...	1340	|	|	1630	|	|	1948	...	|	|	|	0151	|
		Tulovo .... d.	...	|	0753j	...	|	|	|	1047	|	|	...	1356	|	|	1647	|	|	2002	...	|	|	|	0205	|
		Sliven .... d.	0515	|	0915	0930	|	|	|	1204	|	|	1420	1516	|	|	1818	|	|	2108	...	|	|	|	0319	|
		Zimnitsa .... d.	0539	0621	▬	0954	1021	|	|	1221	|	|	1444	1538	1640	|	1835	1944	|	2125	...	|	|	|	|	|
	389	Karnobat ..... **1535** d.	0613	0656	...	1120t	1050	1226	|	1252	|	|	1518	...	1711	|	1906	2015	|	2153	...	|	|	0303	0410	0525
	450	**Burgas** .... **1535** a.	0730	0813	**2655**	1235	|	1312	|	1340	|	|	1635	...	*1833**	|	1955	2105	|	2242	...	|	|	-	|	0615
88		Mezdra .... **1520** d.	▬	▬		...	|	...	0825	▬	0929	1159	...	...	|	1429	...	...	1657	▬	...	1907	2201	|	|	...
194		Pleven .... d.	...	...	0712	...	|	...	0936	...	1041	1316	...	...	|	1546	...	...	1812	**4640**	...	2026	2320	|	|	...
239		Levski .... d.	...	...	0745	...	|	...	1006	...	1110	1347	...	...	|	1616	...	...	1842	**4680**	...	2057	2349	|	|	...
294		Gorna Oryakhovitsa . a.	...	...	0825	...	|	...	1045	...	1148	1427	...	...	|	1657	...	...	1922	**p**	...	2138	0027	|	|	...
294		Gorna Oryakhovitsa . d.	...	...	0830	...	|	...	1050	...	1203	1437	...	...	|	1707	...	...	1932	1934	...	...	0037	|	|	...
405		**Ruse** 🏛 .... a.	2	2u	|	...	|	...	|	Ⓐ2	1400	|	...	...	|	|	...	...	2131	|	...	...	0234	|	|	...
435		Shumen .... **1530/5** d.	0530	0717	1022	...	|	...	1239	1420	...	1628	...	...	|	1859	...	...	...	2136	...	...	...	|	|	...
459		Kaspichan .... **1530/5** d.	0556	0744	1040	...	|	...	|	1448	...	1648	...	...	|	1917	...	...	...	2154r	...	...	...	|	|	...
518		Povelyanovo **1530/5** d.	0707	0852	1133	...	1251	...	|	1556	...	1739	...	...	1914	2009	...	...	...	2249r	...	...	...	0508	0624	...
543	546	**Varna** .... **1530/5** a.	0737	0922	1157	...	1315	...	1409	1626	...	1803	...	...	1938	2033	...	...	...	2313r	...	...	...	0532	0648	...

km		2640	8640	4641	4611		2602	3622	8602		2612	4613	2614	3624	8612		461		8632		2654		8626	2626	9646	3636
		⚡R		4681	⚡R		⚡R										R									
			V	p		2				2						2	A	Ⓐ2		2		2	Z	Z	S	ZK
	Varna .... **1530/5** d.	...	...	0440q	...	0600	0725	...	0850	...	1108	...	1325	...	...	...	...	1415	1600	1655	1740	1935	...	2155	...	2205
	Povelyanovo. **1530/5** d.	...	...	0505q	...	0632	0747	...	0915	...	1133	...	1350	...	...	...	...	1447	1625	1727	|	2007	...	2220	...	2244
	Kaspichan .... **1530/5** d.	...	...	0558q	...	0745	0836	...	|	...	1225	...	1441	...	...	...	...	1556	|	1835	1857	2115	...	2313	...	|
	Shumen .... **1530/5** d.	...	...	0617	...	0810	0855	...	|	...	1243	...	1501	...	...	...	...	1622	|	1900	1915	2140	...	2335	...	|
	Ruse 🏛 .... d.	...	...	|	0628	▬	|	...	|	...	|	1315	|	...	...	...	1630	|	|	▬	|	▬	...	|	2338	|
	Gorna Oryakhovitsa..a.	...	...	0820	0825	...	1046	...	|	...	1432	1516	1654	...	...	...	1828	*1910*	|	...	2110	...	...	0133	0136	|
	Gorna Oryakhovitsa..d.	0500	...	▬	0832	...	1053	...	|	...	1442	1526	1706	...	...	...	1833	▬	|	...	2115	...	...	0153	0153	|
	Levski .... d.	0540	...	**3602**	0912	...	1135	...	|	...	1521	1605	1747	...	...	...	1911	...	|	...	2154	...	...	0236	0236	|
	Pleven .... d.	0608	...	⚡R	0942	**8610**	1206	...	|	...	1552	1635	1818	...	...	...	1940	...	|	...	2222	...	...	0311	0311	|
	Mezdra .... **1520** d.	0724	...	⑥h	1058		1321	...	|	...	1707	1755	1940	...	...	...	2054	2	|	2	...	2	...	0437	0437	|
0	**Burgas** .... **1535** d.	|	...	0530	|	0635	|	0905	*0930**	1150	|	|	|	1420	1500	...	|	1552	*1655**	1655	...	1930	2230	|	|	|
61	Karnobat...... **1535** d.	|	...	0618	|	0726	|	0957	1117	1306	|	|	|	1511	1546	...	|	1715	1820	1843v	...	2045	2323	|	|	0053
95	Zimnitsa .... d.	|	...	|	|	0756	|	1027	|	1341	|	|	|	1541	1614	1650	|	1750	1848	1925	...	2120	|	|	|	|
119	Sliven .... d.	|	...	0700	|	|	|	1043	|	1402	|	|	|	1558	|	1712	|	|	|	1945	...	|	|	|	|	0138
195	Tulovo .... d.	|	...	0805	|	|	|	1151	|	...	|	|	|	1725c	|	1839	|	|	|	...	...	|	|	|	|	0244
210	Kazanlak .... d.	|	...	0819	|	|	|	1205	|	...	|	|	|	1740	|	1856	|	|	|	...	...	|	|	|	|	0259
269	Karlovo .... d.	|	...	0918	|	|	|	1306	|	...	|	|	|	1850	|	2027	|	|	|	...	...	|	|	|	|	0358
	Yambol .... d.	|	0500	|	|	0811	|	|	1204	...	|	|	|	|	1627	...	|	1805	1900	...	...	2135	0006	|	|	|
	Stara Zagora .... d.	|	0610	|	|	0920	|	|	1314	...	|	|	|	|	1736	...	|	...	2010	...	...	...	0115	|	|	|
	Plovdiv .... a.	|	0748	|	|	1110	|	|	1455	...	|	|	|	|	1912	...	|	...	2147	...	...	...	0255	|	|	|
	Plovdiv .... d.	|	0800	|	|	1122	|	|	1502	...	|	|	|	|	1916	...	|	...	...	...	...	...	0305	|	|	|
	Pazardzhik .... d.	|	0849	|	|	1206	|	|	1546	...	|	|	|	|	1957	...	|	...	...	...	...	...	0348	|	|	|
	Septemvri .... d.	|	0908	|	|	1225	|	|	1604	...	|	|	|	|	2015	...	|	...	...	...	...	...	0407	|	|	|
418	**Sofia** .... **1520** a.	0849	1105	1130	1223	1422	1446	1530	1801	...	1833	1925	2107	2110	2157	...	2220	...	...	...	...	...	0605	0610	0610	0618

Other trains **SOFIA - PLOVDIV**

		1621	1623		1625	1627	491
	Ⓐ2		d	2	d		T
Sofia .... d.	0540	0830	1230	1430	1530	1820	1915
Septemvri .... d.	0825v	1019	1419	1634	1720	2015	2101
Pazardzhik .... d.	0850	1038	1438	1659	1739	2034	2119
Plovdiv .... a.	0940	1120	1520	1747	1821	2116	2200

	1620	1622		1624			1626
			Ⓐ2		2	2	d
Plovdiv .... d.	0605	0700	1145	1315	1405	1735	1823
Pazardzhik .. d.	0649	0743	1244	1400	1502	1828	1911
Septemvri .... d.	0708	0802	1308	1419	1525	1850	1930
Sofia .... a.	0902	0950	1523	1614	1745	2056	2126

Other local trains **GORNA ORYAKHOVITSA - RUSE**

	2	2	2	2
Gorna Oryakhovitsa .... d.	0430	0730	1057	1445
Ruse .... a.	0654	0956	1314	1719

	2	2	2	
Ruse .... d.	0755	1146	1413	...
Gorna Oryakhovitsa .... a.	1018	1415	1645	...

A – ROMANIA – [2] Sofia - Bucuresti and v.v. See Table **61**.
D – Conveys 🛏 1, 2 cl. and [2] Sofia - Povelyanovo - Dobrich. See Table **1540**.
K – Conveys 🛏 1, 2 cl. and [2] Kardam - Povelyanovo - Sofia. See Table **1540**.
L – 🛏 1, 2 cl. and [2] Sofia - Ruse - Silistra (Table **1530**).
S – 🛏 1, 2 cl. and [2] Silistra - Ruse - Gorna (**2626**) - Sofia.
T – BALKAN EXPRESS – [2] Sofia - Svilengrad; ▬ 2 cl. Sofia - Çerkezköy (Table **1550**).
V – Conveys from Plovdiv [2] Svilengrad - Sofia, ▬ 2 cl. Çerkezköy - Sofia (Table **1550**).
Z – Conveys 🛏 1, 2 cl. and [12].

c – Arrives 1706.
d – To / from Dimitrovgrad (Table **1550**).
f – Also Mar. 2, Apr. 28, May 5, Sept. 21; not Mar. 4, Apr. 29, May 6.
h – Also Mar. 3, Apr. 29, May 6, Sept. 22; not Mar. 5, Apr. 30, May 7.
j – Arrives Kazanlak 0640, Tulovo 0736.
p – From / to Plovdiv via Tulovo (Table **1525**).

q – Apr. 1 - Nov. 1.
r – Mar. 31 - Oct. 31.
t – Arrives 1027.
u – 18 minutes later June 18 - Sept
v – Arrives 28 – 32 minutes earlier.
* – Change trains at Karnobat.
⚡ – Express train. Higher fare payal

1510 SEPTEMVRI - DOBRINISHTE

Narrow gauge; 2nd class

km									
0	**Septemvri** .... d.	0205	...	0825	...	1320	...	1650	...	...
39	Velingrad .... d.	0353	...	1000	...	1455	...	1830	...	...
119	Bansko .... d.	0708	...	1308	...	1805	...	2143	...	...
125	**Dobrinishte** .... a.	0720	...	1320	...	1817	...	2155	...	...

Dobrinishte .... d.	...	...	0520	...	0854	...	1355	...	1850
Bansko .... d.	...	...	0535	...	0911	...	1413	...	1905
Velingrad .... d.	0440	...	0832	...	1220	...	1709	...	2200
Septemvri .... a.	0609	...	1005	...	1348	...	1835	...	2325

1520 SOFIA - VIDIN - CRAIOVA

km					7620		7622		7624		7630	7626
		2	2	Ⓐ2		2		2		2		★
0	**Sofia** ..... **1500** d.	...	...	...	0715	...	1200	...	1645	...	1925	2300
88	Mezdra .. **1500** d.	0545	...	0654	|	...	1339	...	1827	...	2115	0120
106	Vratsa .... d.	0605	...	0714	0859	...	1356	...	1844	...	2132	0137
182	Brusartsi ..... ⊖ d.	0734	0740	0903	1015	1020	1517	1528	2001	2013	2252	0253
204	Lom .... ⊖ a.	|	0808	0930	|	1048	|	1556	|	2041	2320	|
269	**Vidin** ★ .... a.	0920	...	...	1150	...	1647	...	2140	...	...	0420

	7627	2660	7631		7621					7623		
	★			2		Ⓐ2	2	2	2		Ⓐ2	2
Vidin ★ ...... d.	0005	...	...	...	0555	...	...	0945	...	1225	...	...
Lom ..... ⊖ d.	|	...	0535	0655	|	0825	1102	|	1325	|	1640	1802
Brusartsi .. ⊖ d.	0137	...	0608	0722	0732	0905	1128	1133	1350	1357	1708	1828
Vratsa .... d.	0253	0550	0743	...	0848	1035	...	1258	...	1511	1839	...
Mezdra **1500** a.	0308	0604	0758	...	|	1053	...	1316	...	1525	1857	...
Sofia .. **1500** a.	0540	0742	0943	...	1025	...	...	...	...	1706	...	...

km			480		
		①–⑥	★		
	Vidin 🏛 ...... d.	...	0505	...	...
0	**Calafat** .... d.	0340	|	0522	1250
107	**Craiova** .... a.	0638	0832	0832	1606

km					481
					★
0	**Craiova** .... d.	0810	1655	1955	1955
	Calafat .... a.	1130	1955	2328	|
119	Vidin 🏛 ..... a.	...	...	...	2320

★ – Conveys 🛏 1, 2 cl., ▬ 2 cl., [2] (*EN* **480/1** – SERDICA) Sofia - Budapest and v.v. See also Table **61**.
⊖ – Other services Brusartsi - Lom and v.v.: From Brusartsi at 0613, 1200, 1405, 1720 and 1843. From Lom at 0942, 1445 and 1930.

For explanation of standard symbols see page 4

RUSE - STARA ZAGORA - DIMITROVGRAD - MOMCHILGRAD - PODKOVA 1525

	2	2J	4641‡ V	2C	2	2	2L	461/5 Ⓡ B	2
Ruse 1500 d.	...	...	*0628*	...	*0755*	*1146*	...	1630	*1800*
Gorna Oryakhovitsa 1500 d.	0505	...	0838	...	1125	1443	...	1845	2125
Veliko Târnovo d.	0523	...	0855	...	1145	1503	...	1906	2144
Tulovo d.	0809j	0928	1056	...	1401	1730r	2006	|	...
Stara Zagora 1500 d.	0851	1007	1140	1328	1440	1809	2046	2138	...
Plovdiv 1500 a.	...	...	1327	|	...	...	...	|	...
Dimitrovgrad Sever d.	...	...	...	1445	...	...	...	2244	...
Dimitrovgrad a.	...	...	...	1450	...	...	...	2250	...

	2	2	464/0 Ⓡ B	2	2C	2K	2	4640§ V	2
Dimitrovgrad d.	...	...	0650	...	1035	...	...	...	...
Dimitrovgrad Sever d.	...	...	0657	...	1042	...	...	...	...
Plovdiv 1500 d.	...	...	|	...	|	...	...	1435	...
Stara Zagora 1500 d.	...	0700	0810	1055	1205	1356	1500	1625	...
Tulovo d.	...	0741	0848	1135	...	1440	1541	1702	...
Veliko Târnovo d.	0649	1016	1051	1402	...	...	1800	1905	2028
Gorna Oryakhovitsa 1500 a.	0708	1035	1107	1420	...	...	1820	1920	2045
Ruse 1500 a.	*0956*	*1314*	1400	*1719*	...	...	...	*2131*	...

	2	2	2C
Dimitrovgrad d.	0505	...	1522
Haskovo d.	0536	...	1552
Kârdzhali d.	0722	1320	1736
Momchilgrad a.	0742	1340	1756
Podkova a.	0806	1404	1821

	2C	2	2	2
Podkova d.	0620	0815	1410	...
Momchilgrad d.	0645	0840	1433	1710
Kârdzhali d.	0805f	0859	...	1740t
Haskovo d.	0949	...	...	1923
Dimitrovgrad a.	1017	...	...	1950

B – BOSPHOR – 🚃 Bucuresti - Dimitrovgrad and v.v.; 🛏 1, 2 cl. and ▬ 2 cl. Bucuresti - Çerkezköy and v.v.
C – 🚃 Stara Zagora - Dimitrovgrad - Podkova and v.v.
J – From Karlovo (d. 0735) and Kazanlak (d. 0855).
K – To Kazanlak (a. 1515) and Karlovo (a. 1642).
L – From Karlovo (d. 1755) and Kazanlak (d. 1919).
V – From / to Shumen or Varna (Table **1500**).

f – Arrives 0704.
j – Arrives 0737.
r – Arrives 1719.
t – Arrives 1729.

‡ – **4681** Apr. 1 - Nov. 1.
§ – **4680** Mar. 31 - Oct. 31.

RUSE - SILISTRA and VARNA 1530

	9647 H	s2	9621	2	2655	2	Ⓐ◊2	9623	2	2
Ruse d.	0238	...	0600	0705	...	...	1418	1610	*1722*	...
Ruse Razpr d.	0255	...	0609	0718	...	...	1427	1619	1825	...
Razgrad d.	0404	...	0716	0835	...	...	1544	1726	1949	...
Samuil d.	0443f	0540	0738	0858	...	1005	1605	1747	2010	2030
Silistra a.	0703	|	|	|	...	1240	...	|	...	2307
Kaspichan 1500 a.	...	0637	0828	1003	1040	...	...	1837	...	...
Povelyanovo 1500 a.	...	...	0929	...	1132	...	...	1931	...	...
Varna 1500 a.	...	...	0952	...	1157	...	...	1956	...	...

km		2	2	2602 ⚡	t2	9620	2	9622	2654	2	9646 D
	Varna 1500 d.	...	...	0725	...	0900	...	1530	1740	...	...
	Povelyanovo 1500 d.	...	...	0747	...	0925	...	1555	|	...	...
	Kaspichan 1500 d.	...	...	0835	0845	1044j	...	1652	1856	1925	...
0	**Silistra** d.	...	0445	...	|	|	1455	|	...	|	1915
113	Samuil d.	0525	0730	...	0954	1135	1732	1748	...	2026	2157
	Razgrad d.	0547	...	...	1015	1155	...	1808	...	2047	2217
	Ruse Razpr a.	0716	...	...	1130	1300	...	1915	...	2204	2322
	Ruse a.	*0753*	...	...	*1143*	1309	...	1924	...	2214	2335

🛏 1, 2 cl. and 🚃 Sofia - Ruse - Silistra.
🛏 1, 2 cl. and 🚃 Silistra - Gorna Oryakhovitsa (**2626**) - Sofia.

f – Arrives 0423.
j – Arrives 1018.

s – To Shumen (a. 0715).
t – From Shumen (d. 0800).

◊ – Not July 1 - Sept. 14.
⚡ – Express train. Higher fare payable.

VARNA and SHUMEN - BURGAS 1535

	2	8602	2	3660 A	2	2	G2	2	8632	3623	Ⓑt2
Varna 1500 d.	0620	0850	...	...	1045	...	...	1345	1600	...	1800
Povelyanovo 1500 d.	0653	0915	...	...	1118	...	...	1417	1625	...	1831
Kaspichan 1500 d.	|	|	...	1023	|	...	...	|	|	...	|
Shumen 1500 d.	|	|	...	1046	|	...	1355	|	|	...	|
Komunari d.	0748	0959	...	1137	1214	...	1455	1512	1706	...	1925
Karnobat 1500 d.	0953j	1115	1120	1313r	1359	1415	...	1716j	1819	1906	2112
Burgas 1500 a.	1105	...	1235	1401	...	1530	...	1833	...	1955	...

	★2	2	2	2	8631	2	3661 A	2	8601	2
Burgas 1500 d.	...	...	0735	0930	...	1347	1525	1552	...	...
Karnobat 1500 d.	0345	...	0905r	1044	1050	1525j	1627r	1706	1711	1730
Komunari d.	0555	0610	1051	...	1208	1715	1753	...	|	1924
Shumen 1500 a.	|	0712	|	...	|	|	1843	...	|	|
Kaspichan 1500 a.	|	0743h	|	...	|	|	1903	...	|	|
Povelyanovo 1500 d.	0650	...	1147	...	1251	1811	...	...	1914	2023
Varna 1500 a.	0720	...	1217	...	1315	1845	...	...	1938	2053

June 1 - Sept. 15 only.
From Gorna Oryakhovitsa (d. 1105).

h – 0801 June 18 - Sept. 3.
j – Arrives 23–25 minutes earlier.
r – Arrives 12–15 minutes earlier.

t – Also Mar. 12, May 14, 21, Sept. 10, 17; not Mar. 3, 4, Apr. 29, May 1, 6, Sept. 22, 23.

★ – ①–⑥ (also Mar. 13, May 15, 22, Sept. 11, 18; not Mar. 4, 5, Apr. 30, May 2, 7, Sept. 23, 24).

VARNA - DOBRICH - KARDAM 1540

	2	D				
Varna 1500 d.	0600	...	1235	1545	1900	...
Sofia 1500 d.	|	2230	|	|	|	...
Povelyanovo 1500 d.	0630	0635	1307	1622	1938	...
Dobrich a.	...	0754	1422	1745	2052	...
Kardam a.	...	...	...	1855	2159	...

					E	A
Kardam d.	0455	...	...	...	1935	...
Dobrich d.	0603	0925	1430	...	2055	...
Povelyanovo 1500 a.	0729	1048	1545	...	2215	2249
Sofia 1500 a.	|	|	|	...	0618	|
Varna 1500 a.	0800	1119	1616	...	...	2313

A – Mar. 31 - Oct. 31.
D – 🛏 1, 2 cl. and 🚃 Sofia (**3637**) - Povelyanovo (**2637**) - Dobrich.
E – 🛏 1, 2 cl. and 🚃 Kardam (**2636**) - Povelyanovo (**3636**) - Sofia.

(SOFIA -) PLOVDIV - SVILENGRAD - İSTANBUL 1550

Ž; TCDD

Bulgarian train number					1623			1625		461/5	491
Turkish train number				Ⓐ			Ⓑ			81031	81031
	2	2	2	2		2	E2		2	Ⓡ B	Ⓡ A
Bucureşti 61 d.	...	...	...	...	...	...	...	...	...	1250	...
Sofia 1500 d.	...	...	...	...	1230	...	...	1530	...	|	1915
Plovdiv ⊡ d.	0605	0916	1310	1410	1525	1610	1710	1824	2010	|	2212
Parvomaj ⊡ d.	0651	1000	1352	1451	1602	1655	1758	1859	2057	|	2244
Dimitrovgrad ⊡ a.	0722	1025	1419	1516	1623	1725	1824	1920	2129	2250	2305
Dimitrovgrad d.	0734	*1037*	...	...	...	*1732*	...	*2000*	...	2330	2330
Svilengrad a.	0850	*1155*	...	...	...	*1850*	...	*2118*	...	0040	0040
Svilengrad 🛃 d.	...	...	...	...	...	...	...	...	...	0130	0130
Kapıkule 🛃 a.	...	...	...	...	...	...	...	...	...	0148	0148
Kapıkule d.	...	...	...	...	...	...	...	...	...	0256	0256
Edirne d.	...	...	...	...	...	...	...	...	...	0320	0320
Uzunköprü d.	...	...	...	...	...	...	...	...	...	|	|
Pehlivanköy d.	...	...	...	...	...	...	...	...	...	|	|
Alpullu d.	...	...	...	...	...	...	...	...	...	0427	0427
Çerkezköy a.	...	...	...	...	...	...	...	...	...	0544	0544
Halkalı ¶ a.	...	...	...	...	...	...	...	...	...	0706*	0706*
İstanbul Sirkeci ¶ a.	...	...	...	...	...	...	...	...	...	0750*	0750*

km	Turkish train number		81032	81032							
	Bulgarian train number		492	464/2		①–⑥			1626		
			Ⓡ A	Ⓡ B	2	D2	2	2		2	2
0	**İstanbul** Sirkeci ¶ d.	...	2200*	2200*	...	...	...	...	...	...	...
28	Halkalı ¶ d.	...	2238*	2238*	...	...	...	...	...	...	...
115	Çerkezköy d.	...	0002	0002	...	...	...	...	...	...	...
215	Alpullu d.	...	0124	0124	...	...	...	...	...	...	...
237	Pehlivanköy d.	...	|	|	...	...	...	...	...	...	...
258	Uzunköprü a.	...	|	|	...	...	...	...	...	...	...
	Edirne d.	...	0230	0230	...	...	...	...	...	...	...
	Kapıkule a.	...	0250	0250	...	...	...	...	...	...	...
	Kapıkule 🛃 d.	...	0405	0405	...	...	...	...	...	...	...
	Svilengrad 🛃 a.	...	0425	0425	...	...	...	...	...	...	...
	Svilengrad d.	...	0515	0515	0600	...	*0900*	...	*1540*	...	1940
	Dimitrovgrad a.	...	0627	0627	0716	...	*1017*	...	*1657*	...	2100
	Dimitrovgrad ⊡ d.	0530	0642	0650	0728	0930	1030	1600	1705	1830	2105
	Parvomaj ⊡ d.	0600	0706	|	0758	1001	1057	1632	1728	1900	2136
	Plovdiv ⊡ a.	0641	0740	|	0843	1043	1139	1714	1807	1942	2221
	Sofia 1500 a.	...	1105	|	...	...	...	...	2126	...	...
	Bucureşti 61 a.	...	...	1724	...	...	...	...	...	...	...

BALKAN EXPRESS – ▬ 2 cl. Sofia - Çerkezköy and v.v.; 🚃 Sofia - Svilengrad and v.v.
BOSPHOR – Conveys 🛏 1, 2 cl. and ▬ 2 cl.
①–⑥ (not Mar. 4, 5, Apr. 30, May 2, 7, Sept. 23, 24).
Ⓑ (also Mar. 12, May 14, 21, Sept. 10, 17; not Mar. 3, 4, Apr. 29, May 1, 6, Sept. 22, 23).

* – By 🚌 from / to Çerkezköy. During certain periods the bus connection may operate from / to Kapıkule (in similar timings).
¶ – For İstanbul suburban services via the Marmaray tunnel see Table **1570**.
⊡ – Additional journeys Plovdiv - Dimitrovgrad and v.v.: **From Plovdiv** at 0515 Ⓐ, 0710, 0810 **D**, 1924. **From Dimitrovgrad** at 0700 Ⓐ, 0830, 1431 Ⓐ, 1730 Ⓑ **E**, 1955.

SOFIA - KYUSTENDIL, PETRICH, KULATA and THESSALONÍKI 1560

st trains 2nd class only

								361 Ⓡ				
Sofia d.	...	0530	0705	0755	1020	1145	*1225*	1520	...	1700	*1840*	2008
Pernik d.	...	0622	0747	0841	1109	1228	1340	1559	...	1746	1945	2055
Radomir d.	...	0648	0811	0902	1135	1251	1406	1619	1623	1808	2011	2116
Kyustendil a.	...	|	|	1028	|	|	1543	|	1753	|	2142	|
Dupnitsa d.	0600	0757	0853	▬	1235	1331	▬	1659	▬	1850	▬	2202
Blagoevgrad a.	0647	0836	0925	...	1312	1359	...	1727	...	1928	...	2230
Blagoevgrad d.	0701	▬	*0931*	...	...	*1410*	...	1728	...	1929	...	...
Sandanski d.	0811	...	*1050*	...	...	*1528*	...	1824	...	2031	...	...
General Todorov. a.	0823	...	*1102*	...	...	*1540*	...	1833	...	2043	...	...
General Todorov. d.	0824	0830	*1112*	1115	...	*1550*	1555	1834	1840	2051	2053	...
Petrich a.	|	0843	*1125*	|	...	*1603*	|	|	1853	|	2106	...
Kulata 🛃 a.	0838	...	...	1129	...	...	1609	1845	...	2105	...	...
Promahónas 🛃 a.	...	...	...	...	...	...	...	1921	...	...	...	...
Thessaloníki a.	...	...	...	...	...	...	...	2222	...	...	...	...

						360 Ⓡ					
Thessaloníki d.	...	...	...	...	...	0655	...	...	...	...	...
Promahónas 🛃 d.	...	...	...	...	...	0950	...	...	...	...	...
Kulata 🛃 d.	...	0530	0645	...	...	1027	1405	...	1700	...	1930
Petrich d.	0510	|	|	0640	1015	|	|	*1405*	|	*1700*	*1925*t
General Todorov a.	0523	0543	0659	0653	1028	1037	1419	*1418*	1714	*1714*	1946
General Todorov d.	▬	0545	▬	0708	▬	1038	▬	*1430*	▬	*1726*	1947
Sandanski d.	...	0557	...	0721	...	1048	...	*1443*	...	*1739*	2001
Blagoevgrad a.	...	0659	...	0838	...	1140	...	*1553*	...	*1856*	2120
Blagoevgrad d.	0600	0700	...	0839	0940	1141	1405	1558	...	1905	2121
Dupnitsa d.	0634	0730	...	0923	1021	1210	1441	1635	...	1940	2159
Kyustendil d.	|	|	0718	...	|	|	|	|	1800	|	...
Radomir d.	0715	0810	0844	...	1118	1250	1537	1719	1927	2027	...
Pernik d.	0734	0831	0910	...	1141	1305	1600	1736	1949	2044	...
Sofia a.	0824	0916	0958	...	1235	1345	1646	1818	2037	2125	...

Additional journeys Radomir - Kyustendil and v.v.: **From Radomir** at 0725, 1143 and 1812. **From Kyustendil** at 0415, 0936, 1135, 1400 and 1608. Journey: 89–97 minutes.

Change trains at General Todorov.

TURKEY IN ASIA

Operator: Türkiye Cumhuryeti Devlet Demiryolları (TCDD).

Services: *YHT* (high-speed) trains convey first and second class seating. Long distance trains convey a single class of seating known locally as 'Pullman' (shown as [1] in footnote may also convey sleeping and/or couchette cars. Local trains convey 2nd class seating, shown as '2' in the train column. Descriptions of sleeping (🛏) and couchette (appear on page 8. Reservation of seats (free of charge) is required for *YHT* and express trains.

Timings: Schedules are the latest available. Timetable amendments are possible at short notice so please confirm timings locally before travelling.

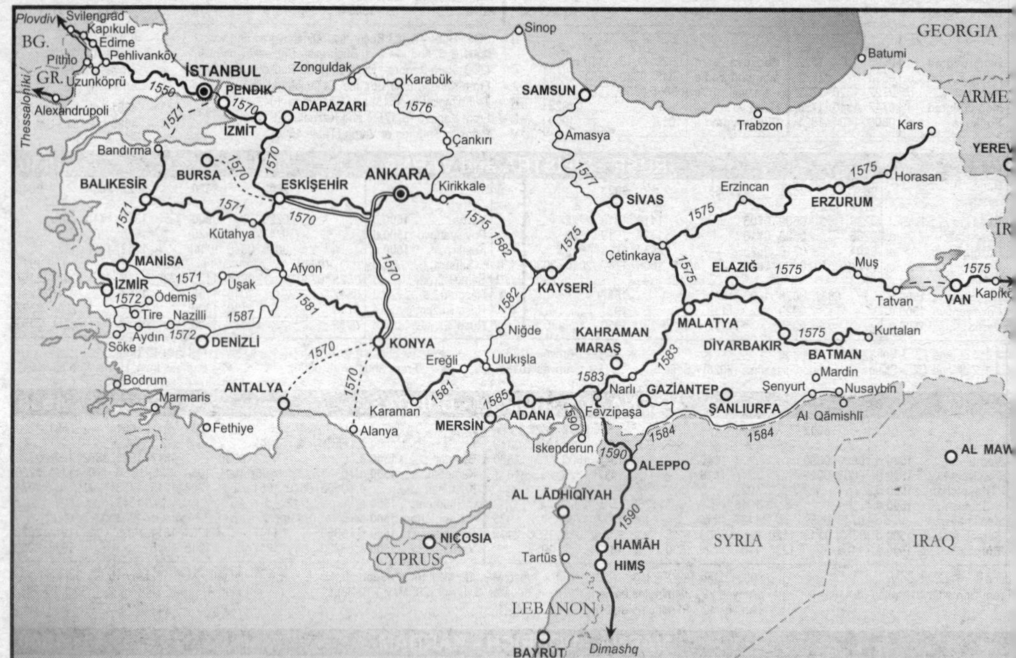

1570 İSTANBUL - ESKIŞEHIR - KONYA and ANKARA

km		YHT 91052 [R]	YHT 91202 [R]	31129 B	YHT 91054 [R]	YHT 91002 [R]	YHT 91204 [R]	YHT 91302 [R]	11604 A	YHT 91004	YHT 91206 [R]	YHT 91056 [R]	YHT 91006 [R]	YHT 91208 [R]	11606 A	YHT 91210 [R]	YHT 91008 [R]	YHT 91058 [R]	YHT 91212 [R]	YHT 91010 [R]	11612 A	YHT 91304 [R]	YHT 91060 [R]	YHT 91214 [R]	YHT 91012 [R]
	İstanbul (Pendik) d.	...	...	...	...	0630	...	0730	0800	0830	...	...	1045	...	1015	...	1400	...	...	1730	1730	1810	...	...	1920
	Izmit d.	...	...	...	...	0720	...	0820	0847	0920	...	...	1135	...	1102	...	|	...	...	1820	1817	1900	...	...	2010
	Arifiye d.	...	...	...	...	0741	...	0841	0917	|	...	...	1156	...	1132	...	|	...	...	1841	1847	1921	...	...	|
	Adapazarı a.	...	...	...	...	|	...	|	*0940*	|	...	...	|	...	*1205*	...	|	...	...	|	*1915*	|	...	...	|
	Bilecik d.	...	...	...	...	0824	...	0924	...	|	...	...	|	...	...	...	1551	...	...	1924	...	2004	...	...	|
	Bozüyük d.	...	...	...	...	0847	...	0947	...	|	...	...	|	...	...	...	|	...	...	1947	...	2027	...	...	|
0	**Eskişehir** d.	0630	...	0549	0830	0908	...	1008	...	1101	...	1245	1317	...	...	...	1631	1815	...	2008	...	2047	2100	...	2151
355	**Konya** a.	|	...	|	|	|	...	1151	...	|	...	|	|	...	...	...	|	|	...	|	...	2231	|	...	|
	Konya d.	|	0630	|	|	|	0910	...	...	|	1110	|	|	1350	...	1545	|	|	1830	|	...	...	|	2115	|
156	Polatli YHT d.	0719	0735	0819**p**	0919	0956	1015	...	...	|	|	1334	1405	1455	...	1650	|	1904	1935	2056	...	...	2149	2220	|
220	Sincan d.	0739	0755	0929	0939	1016	1035	...	...	1206	1230	1354	1425	1515	...	|	1737	1924	1955	2117	...	...	2209	2240	2256
245	**Ankara** a.	0756	0812	0953	0956	1033	1052	...	...	1223	1247	1411	1442	1532	...	1724	1754	1941	2012	2134	...	...	2226	2257	2313

km		11601 A	11603 A	YHT 91001 [R]	YHT 91051 [R]	YHT 91301 [R]	YHT 91201 [R]	YHT 91203 [R]	YHT 91003 [R]	YHT 91053 [R]	YHT 91205 [R]	11609 A	YHT 91005 [R]	YHT 91207 [R]	YHT 91007 [R]	YHT 91055 [R]	YHT 91209 [R]	YHT 91009 [R]	YHT 91057 [R]	YHT 91303 [R]	YHT 91211 [R]	YHT 91011 [R]	YHT 91059 [R]	11611 A	YHT 91213 [R]
0	**Ankara** d.	...	...	0600	0630	...	0645	0850	0915	1045	1120	...	1145	1330	1455	1530	1615	1720	1750	...	1825	1900	2045	...	2130
25	Sincan d.	...	...	0618	0648	...	0703	0908	0933	1103	1138	...	1203	1348	1513	1548	1633	1738	1808	...	1843	1918	2103	...	2148
89	Polatllı YHT d.	...	...	0637	0708	...	0723	0927	|	1123	|	...	1222	1408	|	1608	1653	1757	1828	...	1903	|	2123	...	2208
309	**Konya** a.	...	...	|	|	...	0830	1035	|	|	1302	...	|	1515	|	|	1800	|	|	...	2010	|	|	...	2315
	Konya d.	...	...	|	|	0705	...	...	|	|	...	...	|	...	|	|	...	|	|	1745	...	|	|	...	...
245	**Eskişehir** d.	...	...	0730	0756	0849	...	...	1042	1211	...	...	1315	...	1622	1656	...	1850	1916	1930	...	2027	2211	...	...
	Bozüyük d.	...	...	0747	...	0906	...	...	|	...	...	...	|	...	|	...	...	1907	...	1947	...	|	...	...	...
	Bilecik d.	...	...	0807	...	0927	...	...	|	..	...	...	|	...	|	..	..	1927	...	2007	...	|	...	...	...
	Adapazarı d.	*0545*	*0720*	|	...	|	...	...	|	...	...	*1335*	|	...	|	...	...	|	...	|	...	|	...	*1835*	...
	Arifiye d.	0610	0745	0848	...	1009	...	...	|	...	...	1400	1427	...	|	...	...	2008	...	2048	...	|	...	1900	...
	Izmit d.	0641	0816	0911	...	1032	...	...	1216	...	...	1431	1450	...	1756	...	...	2031	...	2111	...	2201	...	1931	...
506	**İstanbul** (Pendik) a.	0727	0902	1000	...	1121	...	...	1304	...	...	1517	1538	...	1845	...	...	2120	...	2200	...	2250	...	2017	...

🚌 CONNECTIONS

km											
0	Eskişehir d.	0815	0905	1045	1405	1505	1655	1735	1945	2030	...
	Bursa a.	1030	1120	1255	1620	1720	1910	1950	2200	2245	...

Bursa d.	0415	0705	0750	0925	1201	1315	1525	1545	1755
Eskişehir a.	0630	0920	1005	1140	1416	1530	1740	1800	2010

km											
0	Konya d.	0850	0915	1130	1440	...	1730	2305	...	...	...
	Alanya a.	1330	|	|	|	...	2215	|	...	...	...
	Antalya a.	...	1415	1615	1920	...	...	0420	...	...	...

Antalya d.	...	...	1000	1230	1430	...	...	...	...
Alanya d.	0730	1000	|	|	|	1600	...	...	...
Konya a.	1205	1445	1500	1750	2040	2040	...	...	...

A – ADA EKSPRES TRENİ – [1] İstanbul (Pendik) - Arifiye and v.v.
B – IZMIR MAVI TRENI – 🛏, [1] and ✕ Izmir - Eskişehir and v.v.

p – Polatllı (Not YHT station).

* – The Marmaray tunnel (13.6km from near Kazlıçeşme station to near Ayrılıkçeşmesi station) includes the world's deepest immersed tube tunnel at 60.46 metres below sea level (1.4km in length, between Sirkeci and Üsküdar).

'MARMARAY*' SUBURBAN SERVICES

Kazlıçeşme d.	0600	and at	2400
Yenikapı d.	0605	least	0005
Sirkeci d.	0609	every 10	0009
Üsküdar d.	0613	minutes	0013
Ayrılıkçeşmesi a.	0618	until	0018

Ayrılıkçeşmesi d.	0600	and at
Üsküdar d.	0605	least
Sirkeci d.	0609	every 10
Yenikapı d.	0613	minutes
Kazlıçeşme a.	0618	until

ESKIŞEHIR, BANDIRMA and AFYON - IZMIR — 1571

	71136	21316	32526	21130	31622	32420	32528	31002	31004	31620
	A			B				C	D	
Ankara **1570** d.	...	...	...	1805	...	...	...	...	...	...
Eskişehir ♧ d.	...	...	...	2142	...	...	...	...	...	...
Kütahya ♧ d.	...	...	...	2319	...	...	...	...	...	...
Tavşanllı d.	...	...	...	|	...	...	...	...	...	...
Bandirma Şehir d.	...	...	...	|	...	0700	...	...	...	...
Bandirma Gar d.	...	...	...	|	...	0703	...	...	...	...
Afyon Ali Çetinkaya d.	0001	...	...	0105	...	|	...	...	...	...
Usak d.	0231	...	...	0351	0615	|	...	...	...	1620a
Alaşehir d.	0449	...	0520	0614	0847	|	1500	...	...	1900a
Ballıkesir d.	|	0400b	|	|	|	0847	|	...	...	|
Soma d.	|	0533	|	|	|	...	|	1530	1830	|
Akhisar d.	|	0616	|	|	|	...	|	1616	1913	|
Manisa d.	0623	0708	0723	0751	1050	...	1700	1713	2008	2107
Izmir Alsancak a.	0748	0830	0859	0919	1222		...	1839	2127	2236

	31001	31619	32525	31003	32421	31621	32527	31315	31129	31135
	C			D					B	A
Izmir Alsancak d.	0650	0730	1100	1400	...	1525	...	1755	1835	2110
Manisa d.	0818	0907	1229	1525	...	1701	1840	1931	2005	2236
Akhisar d.	0914	|	|	1615	...	|	|	2026	|	|
Soma d.	0958	|	|	1656	...	|	|	2110	|	|
Ballıkesir d.	...	|	|	...	1800	|	|	2241b	|	|
Alaşehir d.	...	1106a	1425	...	|	1901	2038	...	2145	1104
Usak d.	...	1335a	...	...	|	2136	...	...	0027	0229
Afyon Ali Çetinkaya a.	...	...	...	...	|	...	...	...	0312	0500
Bandirma Gar a.	...	...	...	...	1945	...	...	...	|	...
Bandirma Şehir a.		...	...	...	1947	...	...	...	|	...
Tavşanllı d.	...	...	...	...	...	...	...	...	|	...
Kütahya ♧ d.	...	...	...	...	...	...	...	...	0520	...
Eskişehir ♧ a.	...	...	...	...	...	...	...	...	0645	...
Ankara **1570** a.	...	...	...	...	...	...	...	...	1014	...

Istanbul - Bandirma

İstanbul Deniz Otobüsleri *

İstanbul Yenikapi d.	0700	...	...	...	...	...	1830	...	...	...
Bandirma Şehir a.	0910	...	...	...	...	...	2040	...	...	...

	①-⑤	⑥								
Bandirma Şehir d.	0730	0930	...	...	...	...	1830	...	...	...
İstanbul Yenikapi a.	0940	1140	...	...	...	...	2040	...	...	...

KONYA MAVI TRENI – [couchette], [sleeper], [1] and ✕ Konya - Izmir Basmane and v.v.
IZMIR MAVI TRENI – [couchette], [1] and ✕ Izmir - Eskişehir and v.v.
6 EYLÜL EKSPRESI – [1] Bandirma - Soma - Izmir and v.v. ♠
17 EYLÜL EKSPRESI – [1] Bandirma - Soma - Izmir and v.v. ♠
Service between Alaşehir and Usak currently suspended.
Non confirmed connection by bus.

♠ – All services currently only operate to/from Soma.
♧ – For local services see Table **1581**.
‡ – Bandirma Sehir - Bandirma Gar: *1 km*. Bandirma Sehir - Ballıkesir *101 km*.
◇ – Afyon - Manisa: *355 km*. Usak - Manisa: *220 km*. Alaşehir - Manisa: *122 km*.
* – İstanbul Deniz Otobüsleri ✆ +90 (212) 455 6900. www.ido.com.tr

IZMIR - TIRE, ÖDEMIŞ, SÖKE and DENIZLI — 1572

2nd class

	32333	32321	32251	32253	32323	32393	32415	32255	32341	32395	32263	32417	32397	32325	32257	32413	32259	32327	32335	32261	32419	32352	32329	32343
																								⑤–⑦
Izmir Basmane ⊡ d.	...	0620	0745	0900	0923	...	1010	1125	1220	...	1330	1355	...	1510	1540	1610	1630	1710	...	1815	1830	1910	1957	2130
Adnan Menderes ⊡ d.	...	0639	0806	0921	0943	...	1030	1145	1242	...	1351	1417	...	1529	1602	1631	1654	1730	...	1837	1853	1930	2018	2154
Torballı d.	...	0709	0833	0950	1018	...	1058	1212	1312	...	1418	1446	...	1603	1638	1708	1729	1800	...	1907	1927	2006	2053	2222
Çatal d.	0600	0756	|	|	1104	...	1137	|	1348	...	|	1525	...	1652	|	1748	|	1843	1843	|	2008	|	2132	2300
Tire a.	0610	|	|	|	|	...	1150	|	|	...	|	1538	...	|	|	1801	|	|	1854	|	2021	|	|	|
Ödemiş Gar a.	▬	0825	|	|	1129	...	...	|	1413	...	|	...	...	1724	|	...	|	1909	...	|	...	|	2158	2325
Ödemiş Şehir a.	**32391**	0828	|	|	1132	...	...	|	1416	...	|	...	...	1727	|	...	|	1912	...	|	...	|	2201	2328
Selçuk d.		...	0901	1018	...	...	...	1239	...	...	1443	...	...	...	1705	...	1757	...	...	1933	...	2043	...	...
Söke d.	0630	...	|	|	...	1035	...	|	...	1400	|	...	1520	...	|	...	|	...	...	|	...	2132	...	...
Ortaklar d.	0658	...	0925	1042	...	1107	...	1305	...	1424	1507	...	1548	...	1729	...	1822	...	...	1957	...	...	...	...
Aydin d.	0729	...	0955	1111	...	1144	...	1342	...	1456	1538	...	1619	...	1759	...	1856	...	...	2027	...	...	...	...
Nazilli d.	0824	...	1043	1158	...	1236	...	1431	...	1547	1631	...	1718	...	1849	...	1945	...	...	2114	...	...	...	...
Goncali **1587** d.	0937	...	1150	1304	...	...	...	1538	...	...	...	...	1832	...	1954	...	2051	...	...	2221	...	...	...	...
Denizli **1587** a.	0948	...	1201	1315	...	...	...	1549	...	...	...	...	1843	...	2005	...	2102	...	...	2232	...	...	...	...

	32334	32322	32412	32352	32252	32324	32416	32254	32326	32392	32256	32394	32328	32396	32342	32258	32420	32260	32398	32330	32266		32344	32262
																						⑤–⑦	⑤–⑦	
Denizli **1587** d.	...	...	...	...	0420	...	...	0545	...	0655	0820	1005	...	...	...	1250	...	1450	...	...	...	...	...	1715
Goncali **1587** d.	...	...	...	...	0433	...	...	0557	...	0708	0832	1018	...	...	...	1303	...	1503	...	...	...	...	...	1727
Nazilli d.	...	...	...	...	0540	...	...	0704	...	0822	0945	1133	...	1250	...	1409	...	1611	1645	...	1734	...	...	1847
Aydin d.	...	...	...	...	0626	...	...	0755	...	0914	1032	1228	...	1344	...	1457	...	1700	1740	...	1830	...	...	1940
Ortaklar d.	...	...	...	0619‡	0654	...	...	0824	...	0945	1100	1302	...	1423	...	1525	...	1728	1820	...	1859	...	...	2014
Söke a.	...	...	...	0555‡	|	...	...	|	...	1007	|	1324	...	1445	...	|	...	|	1842	...	|	...	...	|
Selçuk d.	...	...	...	0649	0722	...	...	0900	...	...	1128	▬	...	...	...	1553	...	1758	▬	...	1932	...	...	2044
Ödemiş Şehir d.	...	0520	...	|	|	0658	...	|	0844	...	|	**32418**	1205	...	1457	|	...	|	...	1743	|	...	1920	|
Ödemiş Gar d.	...	0524	...	|	|	0703	...	|	0849	...	|	...	1210	...	1502	|	...	|	...	1747	|	...	1925	|
Tire d.	0535	|	0617	|	|	|	0740	|	|	...	|	1157	|	...	|	|	1610	|	1804	|	|	1939	|	|
Çatal d.	0545	0556	0631	|	|	0728	0755	|	0914	...	|	1211	1234	...	1526	|	1625	|	1815	1818	|	1949	1949	|
Torballı d.	...	0644	0710	0722	0747	0810	0838	0927	0955	...	1152	1249	1313	...	1606	1618	1707	1822	...	1906	2003	...	2028	2112
Adnan Menderes ⊡ a.	...	0714	0736	0758	0816	0837	0909	0959	1025	...	1219	1321	1346	...	1635	1646	1733	1849	...	1934	2031	...	2058	2141
Izmir Basmane ⊡ a.	...	0731	0754	0820	0839	0857	0930	1022	1043	...	1239	1342	1407	...	1655	1708	1754	1909	...	1954	2053	...	2119	2203

‡ – Calls at Söke then Ortaklar.

⊡ – Frequent local trains operate 0600 - 2300.

ANKARA - KARS, KURTALAN, TATVAN and TEHRAN — 1575

	42102	42104	11512	11532	11542	42822	22576	11410	21124	51516
			③	②⑦	△					②
	2	2	A ❦	B	C	2	2	D	E	F ❦
Ankara **1582** d.	...	...	1025	1115	1115	...	1737	1800	1900	...
Irmak **1582** d.	...	...	1200	1249	1249	...	1910	1928	2022	...
Kirikkale **1582** d.	...	...	|	1315	1315	...	1933	1953	2046	...
Boğazköprü **1582** d.	...	...	1654	1756	1756	...	...	0020	0104	...
Kayseri d.	...	...	1730	1827	1827	...	...	0048	0136	...
Sivas a.	...	...	2055	2158	2158	...	...	0406	0500	...
Sivas d.	0900	1940	2136	2210	2210	...	...	0412	0512	...
Çetinkaya d.	1021	2108	|	0007	0007	...	...	0549	0702	...
Divriği d.	1127	2220	|	|	|	0502	...	0709	|	...
Erzincan d.	▬	...	|	|	|	0828	...	1007	|	...
Erzurum d.	...	...	|	|	|	▬	▬	1357	|	...
Horasan d.	...	...	|	|	|	...	...	1527	|	...
Sarkamis d.	...	...	|	|	|	...	...	1716	|	...
Kars a.	...	...	|	|	|	...	...	1829	|	...
Malatya d.	**52538**	...	0302	0247	0247	...	**52546**	...	0925	...
Yolçatı d.	2	...	|	0500	0450	...	2	...	...	...
Diyarbakir d.	0730	...	|	|	0849	**52862**	1758	...	...	...
Batman d.	0950	...	|	|	1106	②⑤⑦	2017	...	...	...
Kurtalan a.	...	...	|	|	1249	2 a	...	...	...	...
Elăzig d.	...	...	0631	0520	...	0705	...	...	...	...
Mus d.	...	...	1223	1219	...	1408	...	...	...	...
Tatvan Gar a.	...	...	1440	1437	...	1650	...	...	...	...
Tatvan Iskele ♡ a.	...	...	1453	...	...	...	...	...	...	...
Van Iskele ♡ d.	...	...	2130	...	...	...	...	...	...	...
Van Gar d.	...	...	2154	...	...	...	...	...	...	2000
Kapiköy 🏛 d.	...	...	0130	...	...	...	...	...	...	2315
Razi d.	...	...	0235	...	...	...	...	...	...	0110
Tabriz a.	...	...	0635	...	...	...	...	...	...	0625
Tabriz d.	...	...	0823	...	...	...	...	...	...	...
Tehran a.	...	...	2020	...	...	...	...	...	...	...

	42103	51123	52545	41409	51511	52861	51515	51541	51531	52537
					③	①③⑥	①	▽	②④	
	2	E	2	D	A ❦	2 a	F ❦	C	B	2
Tehran d.	...	...	...	...	2125	...	...	...	...	...
Tabriz a.	...	...	...	...	0926	...	...	...	...	...
Tabriz d.	...	...	...	...	1056	...	2230	...	...	...
Razi d.	...	...	...	...	1540	...	0400	...	...	...
Kapiköy 🏛 d.	...	...	...	...	1740	...	0415	...	...	...
Van Gar a.	...	...	...	...	1933	...	0606	...	...	...
Van Iskele ♡ a.	...	...	...	...	1956	...	...	...	...	...
Tatvan Iskele ♡ d.	...	...	...	...	0457	...	...	...	...	...
Tatvan Gar d.	...	...	...	...	0715	0715	...	...	0720	...
Mus d.	...	...	...	...	0944	0946	...	...	0943	...
Elăzig d.	...	...	...	...	1545	1621	...	...	1604	...
Kurtalan d.	...	...	...	...	|	...	...	0930	|	...
Batman d.	...	...	0504	...	|	...	...	1110	|	1500
Diyarbakir d.	...	...	0721	...	|	...	...	1314	|	1715
Yolçatı d.	...	...	▬	...	|	...	...	1637	1637	▬
Malatya d.	...	1530	...	...	1820	...	...	1849	1849	...
Kars d.	...	|	...	0745	|	...	...	|	|	...
Sarkamis d.	...	|	...	0901	|	...	...	|	|	...
Horasan d.	...	|	**42821**	1044	|	...	...	|	|	...
Erzurum d.	...	|	2	1226	|	...	...	|	|	**42101**
Erzincan d.	...	|	1400	1616	|	...	...	|	|	2
Divriği d.	1600	|	1723	1912	|	...	...	|	|	0600
Çetinkaya d.	1738	1757	▬	2029	|	...	...	2137	2137	0714
Sivas a.	1855	1937	...	2202	2238	...	...	2320	2320	0833
Sivas d.	...	1947	**22571**	2207	2255	...	...	2335	2335	...
Kayseri d.	...	2318	...	0126	0241	...	...	0330	0330	...
Boğazköprü **1582** d.	...	2346	2	0153	|	...	...	0354	0354	...
Kirikkale **1582** d.	...	0415	0600	0616	|	...	...	0837	0837	...
Irmak **1582** d.	...	0439	0624	0639	|	...	...	0902	0902	...
Ankara **1582** a.	...	0610	0802	0805	0922	...	...	1035	1035	...

TRANSASYA EKSPRESI – [sleeper] and ✕ Ankara(**11512/51511**) - Tatvan and v.v.;
[sleeper] and ✕ Van (**11512/51511**) - Razi (**59/60**) - Tehrān and v.v.
VAN GÖLÜ EKSPRESI – [couchette] [sleeper] and [2] Ankara - Tatvan and v.v.
GÜNEY KURTALAN EKSPRESI – [couchette] [sleeper] and [2] Ankara - Kurtalan and v.v.
DOĞU EKSPRESI – [couchette] [sleeper] [12] Ankara - Kars and v.v.
4 EYLÜL MAVI – [12] [sleeper] and ✕ Ankara - Malatya and v.v.
[2] and 🍷 Tabriz(**494/495**) - Kapiköy(**51515/51516**) - Van and v.v.

a – Subject to confirmation.

△ – ①③④⑤⑥.
▽ – ①③⑤⑥⑦.
❦ – Service currently suspended.
♡ – By [ferry] Tatvan - Van and v.v. Passengers must leave the train at Tatvan and rejoin it at Van. Note that different sets of coaching stock are used either side of the ferry.

1576 ANKARA - ZONGULDAK TCDD

km		22302				22301	
0	**Ankara** d.	...	...	**Zonguldak** ♡ d.		1330	...
70	Irmak d.	...	...	Karabük d.		1704	...
172	Çankiri d.	...	...	Çankiri d.		...	...
364	Karabük d.	0830	...	Irmak d.		...	...
486	**Zonguldak** ♡ a.	1203	...	**Ankara** a.		...	...

Note: Services Çankiri - Zonguldak and v.v. are suspended for engineering work with no reopening date given. Please check with operator before travelling.

♡ – Local service Zonguldak - Filyos and v.v. (journey 36 minutes). From Zonguldak at 0640, 0945, 1550, 1730, 1835. From Filyos at 0633, 0731, 1323, 1458, 1928.

1577 SIVAS - AMASYA - SAMSUN T

Services are suspended for engineering works until December 2

km								
0	**Sivas** d.	...	...	...	**Samsun** d.	...	...
111	Yenice d.	...	...	...	Havza d.	...	...
181	Turhal d.	...	...	...	Suluova d.	...	...
245	**Amasya** d.	...	...	...	**Amasya** d.	...	...
272	Suluova d.	...	...	...	Turhal d.	...	...
292	Havza d.	...	...	...	Yenice d.	...	...
378	**Samsun** a.	...	...	...	**Sivas** a.	...	...

1581 ESKIŞEHIR - KONYA - ADANA T

For YHT (high-speed) services between Eskisehir and Konya, see Table 1570.

km		72406	72206	21130	31135	72442	72444	71322	72202	71306	72204
			2	C	F	2 ❦	2 ❦	H	2	G	2
0	**Eskişehir** 1571 d.	1810	1940	2142	...	...	...	1000	1040	...	1455
79	Kütahya 1571 d.	1939	2056	2319	...	...	...	1135	1157	...	1611
163	Afyon Ali Çetinkaya d.	2126	...	0105	0500	...	...	1321	...	...	...
261	Akşehir d.	...	...	...	0627	0630	1220	...	...	...	...
435	Konya ♡ d.	...	...	...	0858	0902	1452	...	...	...	...
537	Karaman ♡ d.	...	...	...	...	...	...	...	...	1530	...
	Ereğli d.	...	...	...	...	...	...	...	...	1640	...
672	Ulukışla 1582 d.	...	...	...	...	...	...	...	...	1724	...
781	Yenice 1582 d.	...	...	...	...	...	...	...	...	1922	...
804	**Adana** 1582 d.	...	...	...	...	...	...	...	...	1945	...

	72203	72441	71321	61305	72205	72443	71136	31129	72201
	2	2 ❦	H	G	2	2 ❦	F	C	2
Adana 1582 d.	...	...	...	0745	...	...	...	...	...
Yenice 1582 d.	...	...	...	0815	...	...	...	...	...
Ulukışla 1582 d.	...	...	...	1017	...	...	...	...	...
Ereğli d.	...	...	...	1105	...	...	...	...	...
Karaman ♡ d.	...	...	...	1215	...	...	...	...	...
Konya ♡ d.	...	0920	...	...	...	1730	2000	...	...
Akşehir d.	...	1150	...	...	...	2000	2235	...	...
Afyon Ali Çetinkaya d.	...	...	1233	...	...	...	0001	0312	...
Kütahya 1571 d.	1240	...	1438	...	1635	...	...	0509	0752
Eskişehir 1571 a.	1354	...	1606	...	1745	...	...	0635	0907

km		🚌	🚌	🚌	🚌	🚌	🚌				
0	Konya ♡ d.	0850	1130	1230	1445	1700	2030	...	...	...	...
102	Karaman ♡ d.	1020	1300	1400	1615	1830	2200	...	...	...	...

	🚌	🚌	🚌	🚌	🚌	🚌			
Karaman ♡ d.	0750	1030	1300	1530	1610	1900	...	...	...
Konya ♡ d.	0920	1200	1430	1700	1740	2030	...	...	...

C – IZMIR MAVI TRENI – 🛏, 1 and ✕ Izmir - Eskişehir and v.v.
F – KONYA MAVI TRENI – 🛏, 🛏, 1 and ✕ Konya - Izmir Basmane and v.v.
G – TOROS EKSPRESİ – 1 Adana - Karaman and v.v.
H – PAMUKKALE EKSPRESİ – 1 and ✕ Eskişehir - Denizli and v.v.
♡ – Rail services Konya - Karaman and v.v. are suspended until suspended until Dec.
❦ – Service suspended.

1582 ANKARA - ADANA TC

km		11512	21532	22576	11410	21124	21206	21302	71306	
		A ③❦	B △	2	D	E	F	G ❦	J	
0	**Ankara** 1575 d.	1025	1115	1737	1800	1900	2005	...	...	...
70	Irmak 1575 d.	1200	1249	1910	1928	2022	2125	...	...	...
92	Kirikkale 1575 d.	|	1315	1933	1953	2046	2148	...	...	...
365	Boğazköprü 1575 d.	1654	1756	...	0020	0104	0217a	...	...	...
381	Kayseri 1575 d.	1713	1815	...	0040	0124	|	0700	...	...
479	Niğde d.	...	...	...	...	...	0352	0856	...	...
542	Ulukışla 1581 d.	...	...	...	...	...	0502	1004	1724	...
651	Yenice 1581 d.	...	...	...	...	...	0709	1212	1922	...
674	**Adana** 1581 d.	...	...	...	...	...	0728	1234	1945	...

	61301	51123	61205	22571	41409	51511	51531	61305
	G ❦	E	F	2	D	A ⑥❦	B ▽	J
Adana 1581 d.	1645	...	1930	...	...	...	...	0745
Yenice 1581 d.	1710	...	1951	...	...	...	...	0815
Ulukışla 1581 d.	1936	...	2219	...	...	...	...	1017
Niğde d.	2041	...	2319	...	...	...	...	...
Kayseri 1575 d.	2233	2318	|	...	0126	0241	0330	...
Boğazköprü 1575 d.	...	2346	0057b	...	0153	|	0354	...
Kirikkale 1575 d.	...	0415	0539	0600	0616	|	0837	...
Irmak 1575 d.	...	0439	0605	0624	0639	|	0902	...
Ankara 1575 a.	...	0610	0734	0802	0805	0922	1035	...

A – TRANSASYA EKSPRESI – 🛏 and ✕ Ankara(**11512/51511**) - Tatvan and v.v.; 🛏 and ✕ Van(**11512/51511**) - Razi(**59/60**) - Tehrān and v.v.
B – VAN GÖLÜ EKSPRESI – 🛏 🛏 and 2 Haydarpaşa - Tatvan and v.v.
C – GÜNEY EKSPRESI – 🛏 🛏 and 2 Ankara - Kurtalan and v.v.
D – DOĞU EKSPRESI – 🛏 🛏 12 Ankara - Kars and v.v.
E – 4 EYLÜL MAVI – 12 🛏 and ✕ Ankara - Malatya and v.v.
F – CUKUROVA MAVI TREN – 🛏 and 1 Ankara - Adana and v.v.
G – ERCIYES EKSPRESI – 1 Kayseri - Adana and v.v.
J – TOROS EKSPRESİ – 1 Adana - Konya and v.v.
a – Boğazköprü Muselles. A connecting 🚌 departs Kayseri at 0145.
b – Boğazköprü Muselles. A connecting 🚌 departs Kayseri at 0040.
△ – Runs as **21542** on ①③④⑤⑥ (see note **C**).
▽ – Runs as **51541** on ①②④⑥⑦ (see note **C**).
❦ – Service suspended.

1583 ADANA - ELAZIG TCDD

km		61502			51501	51501
		L			L	LA
0	**Adana** d.	0740	...	**Elāzig** d.	0735	0645
79	Toprakkale d.	0858	...	Yolçatı d.	0801	0711
142	Fevzipaşa d.	1042	...	Malatya d.	1016	0926
211	Narlı d.	1205	...	Doğansehir d.	1131	1041
336	Doğansehir d.	1459	...	Narlı d.	1418	1330
392	Malatya d.	1638	...	Fevzipaşa d.	1559	1511
487	Yolçatı d.	1844	...	Toprakkale d.	1716	1628
511	**Elāzig** a.	1904	...	**Adana** a.	1823	1735

L – FIRAT EKSPRESI – 1 Elazig - Adana and v.v.
A – Service retimed between April 17 2016 and July 1 2016.

1584 GAZIANTEP - ALEPPO & NUSAYBIN TC

km					
0	**Gaziantep** d.	...	...	**Nusaybin** d.	...
	Nizip d.	...	...	Şenyurt d.	...
88	Karkamiş d.	...	...	**Aleppo** d.	...
143	Çobanbey 🏛 d.	...	...	Çobanbey 🏛 d.	...
218	**Aleppo** a.	...	...	Karkamiş d.	...
356	Şenyurt a.	...	...	Nizip d.	...
381	**Nusaybin** a.	...	...	**Gaziantep** a.	...

SERVICE SUSPENDED.

1585 MERSIN - ADANA TC

km																	J	K							
0	**Mersin** d.	0600	0637	0730	0800	0900	0930	1030	1100	1200	1230	1330	1420	1500	1610	1630	1705	1720	1750	1810	1840	1910	2005	2050	2133	2
26	Tarsus d.	0618	0707	0748	0823	0918	0953	1048	1129	1218	1254	1348	1449	1518	1628	1659	1723	1749	1819	1839	1858	1939	2023	2113	2159	2
43	Yenice d.	0629	0722	0759	0836	0929	1006	1059	1143	1229	1308	1359	1502	1529	1639	1712	1734	1804	1834	1852	1909	1955	2035	2126	2213	2
67	**Adana** a.	0645	0746	0815	0856	0945	1026	1115	1206	1245	1328	1415	1526	1545	1655	1734	1750	1829	1857	1916	1925	2018	2051	2146	2236	2

								K	J																
Adana d.	...	0600	0646	0738	0805	0820	0901	0932	1003	1100	1115	1200	1330	1420	1510	1600	1630	1710	1736	1813	1853	1910	2015	2115	2215	2
Yenice d.	...	0617	0713	0755	0828	0844	0918	0957	1030	1117	1140	1217	1347	1445	1527	1618	1656	1728	1803	1839	1910	1936	2032	2137	2239	2
Tarsus d.	...	0628	0727	0806	0842	0858	0929	1011	1044	1128	1153	1228	1358	1458	1538	1629	1709	1739	1818	1852	1921	1950	2043	2150	2253	2
Mersin a.	...	0645	0754	0825	0904	0924	0946	1040	1113	1145	1218	1245	1415	1525	1555	1646	1734	1758	1846	1919	1938	2017	2100	2211	2319	0

J – 1 Islahiye - Adana - Mersin and v.v.
K – 1 Iskenderun - Adana - Mersin and v.v.

1587 AFYON - BURDUR, ISPARTA & DENIZLI TCDD

km		71322						71321
		H	🚌	🚌		🚌	🚌	H
	Eskişehir ◇ d.	1000	...	...	**Denizli** 1572 d.	...	...	0800
0	**Afyon** AC ♡ d.	1326	...	...	Goncali 1572 d.	...	...	0812e
114	Karakuyu d.	1525	...	...	Isparta d.	0830	...	|
129	Dinar d.	1544	1640	1640	Burdur d.	|	0830	|
	Burdur a.	|	1740	|	Dinar d.	0930	0930	1009
	Isparta a.	|	...	1740	Karakuyu d.	...	...	1028
254	Goncali d.	1743	...	...	**Afyon** AC ♡ a.	...	...	1222
263	**Denizli** a.	1755	...	...	*Eskişehir* ◇ a.	...	...	1606

H – PAMUKKALE EKSPRESİ – 1 and ✕ Eskişehir - Denizli and v.v.
e – Goncali Muselles.
◇ – See Table **1581**.
♡ – Afyon Ali Çetinkaya.

1590 ADANA - ALEPPO - DIMASHQ CFS, TC

All trains in Syria are believed to have been withdrawn.

km		2J	2K		2K	
0	**Adana** d.	1832	1900	**Dimashq** Kadem d.	...	
79	Toprakkale d.	1942	2008	Himş II d.	...	
138	Iskenderun a.	|	2115	Hamah d.	...	
142	Fevzipaşa d.	2057	...	**Aleppo** d.	...	
	Islahiye d.	2109	...	Meydan Ekbez 🏛 d.	...	
174	Meydan Ekbez 🏛 a.	...	...	Islahiye d.	...	0
274	**Aleppo** a.	...	...	Fevzipaşa d.	...	0
418	Hamah d.	...	...	Iskenderun a.	0715	
479	Himş II d.	...	...	Toprakkale d.	0822	0
623	**Dimashq** Kadem a.	...	...	**Adana** a.	0932	1

J – 1 Islahiye - Adana - Mersin and v.v.
K – 1 Iskenderun - Adana - Mersin and v.v.

Route 32: The Semmering railway

Cities: ★★★ Culture: ★★ History: ★★ Scenery: ★★★
Countries covered: Austria (AT), Italy (IT)
Journey time: 7 hrs | Distance: 620 km

This is a tremendous journey over one of **Europe's first mountain rail routes** and links two very fine cities: Vienna and Venice. The railway between the two was fostered by imperial ambition, with the Austrian authorities keen to see a rail link between the capital and the country's only major port at Trieste. (For more on Trieste as an important Adriatic outpost of Austrian life and culture see p211). But the notion of building a main-line railway over the rugged Alpine terrain south-west of Vienna was daunting. In 1844 **Carlo Ghega** stepped up to the challenge. Ghega was born in Venice of Albanian parents; as a young engineer he has worked on several early railway projects in Moravia.

The **Semmering Railway** opened in 1854. In 1998, it was inscribed on UNESCO's World Heritage List. The citation commends the route as "one of the greatest feats of civil engineering during the pioneering phase of railway building. Set against a spectacular mountain landscape, the railway line remains in use today thanks to the quality of its tunnels, viaducts, and other works, and has led to the
along its tracks."

A number of other **Alpine**
36) follow routes whi
is different: it was de
heavy passenger trai
book for capturing t
comfortable long-dist

Fifty years ago,
Moscow to Rome ser
over the Semmering,
25). Today, the Semm
from Vienna to Graz
of Styria and Carinth
cities in Italy. And it's

Itinerary hints

This is a journey you'll de
which leaves Vienna ever
train in each direction bet
windows – perfect for sig

There's talk of a **se**
likely that Railjets will be
daytime train leaves Vien

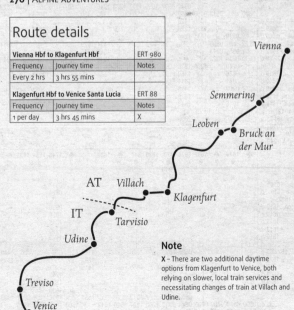

Route details

Vienna Hbf to Klagenfurt Hbf		ERT 980
Frequency	Journey time	Notes
Every 2 hrs	3 hrs 55 mins	
Klagenfurt Hbf to Venice Santa Lucia		**ERT 88**
Frequency	Journey time	Notes
1 per day	3 hrs 45 mins	X

Vienna
Semmering
Leoben
Bruck an der Mur
AT
Villach
Klagenfurt
IT
Tarvisio
Udine
Treviso
Venice

Note

X – There are two additional daytime options from Klagenfurt to Venice, both relying on slower, local train services and necessitating changes of train at Villach and Udine.

ROMANIA

SEE MAP PAGE

Operator: Societatea Naţională de Transport Feroviar de Călători (CFR Călători): www.cfrcalatori.ro. Additionally, Regiotrans, Trans-Feroviar and Softrans operate some services and are identified in the relevant tables where applicable.

Services: Trains convey 1st- and 2nd-class seating accommodation unless otherwise indicated. Sleeping- (🛏) and couchette (▬) cars are described on page 8. Russian-type sleeping as used in trains to and from destinations in Belarus, Moldova, Russia and Ukraine, are described on page 530; these cars are not accessible to passengers making journeys within Romania or between Romania and Bulgaria.

Timings: Valid from **June 12, 2016** unless stated otherwise. Alterations to schedules are possible at any time.

Tickets: Reservation is obligatory for travel by all CFR Călători services for which a train number is shown in the tables, and passengers boarding without a prior reservation are surcha Supplements are payable for travel by **Intercity** (*IC*) and most other fast trains. Trains shown without numbers are slow stopping-services calling at all, or most, stations.

♦ – **NOTES for all tables in Romania section** (LISTED BY TRAIN NUMBER)

- **72/3** – TRAIANUS – [12] and ✕ Bucureşti - Arad - Budapest and v.v.; ▬ 2 cl. and [2] Sofia (**480/1**) - Craiova - Budapest and v.v.
- **74/5** – TRANSILVANIA – [12] Braşov - Budapest and v.v.
- **78/9** – CRIŞ – [12] Budapest - Arad - Timişoara and v.v.; [2] Budapest - Timişoara (**1695/6**) - Bucureşti and v.v.
- **346/7** – DACIA – 🛏 1, 2 cl., ▬ 2 cl., [12] and ✕ Bucureşti - Budapest - Wien and v.v.
- **362/3** – ADY ENDRE – [12] Budapest - Oradea / Cluj Napoca and v.v.
- **366/7** – HARGHITA – [12] and ✕ Braşov - Cluj Napoca - Budapest and v.v.; [2] Târgu Mureş (**4536/7**) - Cluj Napoca - Budapest and v.v.
- **380/1** – [12] Bucureşti - Suceava and v.v.; [2] Bucureşti - Suceava - Vadul Siret and v.v. Conveys 🛏 1, 2 cl. Bucureşti - Suceava - Vadul Siret - Chernivtsi - Kyïv and v.v. on ⑦ from Bucureşti, ⑤ from Kyïv (see Table **1700**).
- **401/2** – PRIETENIA – 🛏 1, 2 cl. and [2] Bucureşti - Ungheni (**106/5**) - Chişinău and v.v.
- **406/7** – CORONA – 🛏 1, 2 cl., ▬ 2 cl. and [12] Budapest - Cluj Napoca - Braşov and v.v.
- **472/3** – ISTER – 🛏 1, 2 cl., ▬ 2 cl., [12] and ✕ Bucureşti - Budapest and v.v.
- **480/1** – SERDICA – ▬ 2 cl. and [2] Budapest (**72/3**) - Craiova - Sofia and v.v.
- **1540/1** – [12] Braşov - Siculeni - Iaşi and v.v.
- **1621/2** – [12] Bucureşti - Sibiu - Timişoara and v.v.
- **1638/9** – 🛏, ▬ and [2] Cluj Napoca - Dej (**1641/2**) - Bucureşti and v.v.
- **1641** – 🛏, ▬ and [12] Bucureşti - Baia Mare; 🛏 and [2] Bucureşti - Sărăţel (**1648**) - Bistriţa; 🛏, ▬ and [2] Bucureşti - Dej (**1639**) - Cluj Napoca; [2] Bucureşti - Baia Mare (**4090**) - Satu Mare; [2] Bucureşti - Deda (**4541**) - Târgu Mureş.
- **1642** – 🛏, ▬ and [12] Baia Mare - Bucureşti; 🛏 and [2] Bistriţa (**1649**) - Sărăţel - Bucureşti; 🛏, ▬ and [2] Cluj Napoca (**1638**) - Dej - Bucureşti; [2] Satu Mare (**4091**) - Baia Mare - Bucureşti.
- **1643** – 🛏, ▬ and [2] Bucureşti - Beclean pe Someş; 🛏, ▬ and [2] Bucureşti - Beclean pe Someş (**4133**) - Sighetu Marmaţiei.
- **1644** – 🛏, ▬ and [2] Beclean pe Someş - Bucureşti; 🛏, ▬ and [2] Sighetu Marmaţiei (**4136**) - Beclean pe Someş - Bucureşti; [2] Târgu Mureş (**4550**) - Deda - Bucureşti.
- **1645** – [12] Bucureşti - Târgu Mureş; [12] Bucureşti - (**1539**) - Cluj Napoca.
- **1646** – [12] Târgu Mureş - Bucureşti.
- **1648/9** – 🛏 and [2] Bucureşti (**1641/2**) - Sărăţel - Bistriţa and v.v.
- **1651** – [12] Bucureşti - Suceava; [2] Bucureşti - Bacău (**5481**) - Bicaz.
- **1652** – [12] Suceava - Bucureşti; [2] Piatra Neamţ (**1858**) - Bacău - Bucureşti.
- **1653/4** – 🛏, ▬ and [12] Bucureşti - Suceava - Vatra Dornei Băi and v.v.
- **1659** – [12] Bucureşti - Suceava; [2] Bucureşti - Bacău (**1859**) - Piatra Neamţ.
- **1695/6** – 🛏, ▬ and [12] Bucureşti - Timişoara and v.v.; [2] Bucureşti - Timişoara (- Budapest and v.v.; [2] Bucureşti - Caransebeş (**9161/70**) - Reşiţa Sud and
- **1736/7** – [12] Râmnicu Vâlcea - Sibiu - Cluj Napoca and v.v.
- **1741** – 🛏, ▬, [12] and 🍸 Bucureşti - Cluj Napoca - Oradea - Satu Mare.
- **1742** – Not June 24 - Sept. 10: 🛏, ▬, [12] and 🍸 Satu Mare - Oradea - Cluj Nap Bucureşti.
- **1743/4** – [12] Timişoara - Arad - Oradea - Baia Mare and v.v.
- **1754** – 🛏, ▬ and [12] Suceava - Bucureşti; [2] Bicaz (**5482**) - Bacău - Bucure
- **1765** – ▬ and [12] Iaşi - Cluj Napoca - Timişoara; [2] Sighetu Marmaţiei (**41** Timişoara.
- **1766** - ▬ and [12] Timişoara - Cluj Napoca - Iaşi.
- **1824** – [12] Deva - Târgu Jiu - Craiova - Bucureşti.
- **1829** – [12] Bucureşti (**1835**) - Simeria - Deva.
- **1831/2** – [12] Galaţi - Iaşi - Cluj Napoca and v.v.
- **1833/4** – [12] Iaşi - Cluj Napoca - Oradea - Timişoara and v.v.
- **1835** – [12] Bucureşti - Târgu Jiu - Cluj Napoca; [12] Bucureşti - Simeria (**1829**) - D
- **1836** – [12] Cluj Napoca - Târgu Jiu - Bucureşti.
- **1837/8** – 🛏, ▬ and [12] Iaşi - Cluj Napoca - Timişoara and v.v.
- **1843** – [12] Timişoara - Beclean pe Someş; [2] Timişoara - Beclean pe Someş (**41** Sighetu Marmaţiei.
- **1856/7** – Not June 17 - Sept. 9 (from Suceava); not June 18 - Sept. 10 (from Consta [2] Suceava Nord - Mărăşeşti (**1861/2**) - Constanţa and v.v.
- **4090/1** – [2] Bucureşti (**1641/2**) - Baia Mare - Satu Mare and v.v.
- **4133** – 🛏, ▬ and [2] Bucureşti (**1643**) - Beclean pe Someş - Sighetu Marmaţiei
- **4135** – [2] Timişoara (**1843**) - Beclean pe Someş - Sighetu Marmaţiei.
- **4136** – 🛏, ▬ and [2] Sighetu Marmaţiei - Beclean pe Someş (**1644**) - Bucureşti; Sighetu Marmaţiei (**1765**) - Timişoara.
- **4541/50** – [2] Bucureşti (**1641/4**) - Deda - Târgu Mureş and v.v.
- **9161/70** – [2] Bucureşti (**1695/6**) - Caransebeş - Reşiţa Sud and v.v.

For trains **1593/4**, **1632/3**, **1821/2**, **1861/2**, **1921/2**, **1931/2**, **1944/5**, **1946/7**, **1948/9**, **19** **1961/2**, **1970/1**, **1991/2**, **1995/6** and **1998/9** – see Table **1680**.

♣ – Operated by Regiotrans. § – Operated by Transferoviar Grup SA.
□ – Operated by Softrans S.R.L. • – Subject to cancellation for scheduled maintena

1600 BUCUREŞTI - BRAŞOV - SIBIU and CLUJ NAPOCA

km		74 ♦	1737 ♦	2•	♣⑥ 2T	1745	1631	1636	1732 g	♣ 2	1621 ♦	2	♣ 2	1645 ♦	1539 🍸	1937 y	346 ♦	1527 🍸	1633 ♦	♣ 2	472 ♦	1643 ♦		1741 ♦	1945 ♦	1931 ♦	1641 ♦
	Constanţa **1680** ... d.	...	...	...	...	...	...	0530	...	...	...	...	...	...	...	1030	...	...	1400y	...	...	...	...	...	1715	1745	...
0	**Bucureşti** Nord ...... d.	...	...	...	...	0600	0700	0815	...	0850	1000	...	1145	1215	...	1315	1400	1545	1645	1723	1745	1800	...	1845	1940b	2045	2100
59	Ploieşti Vest .... d.	...	...	...	...	0644	0743	0857	0919p	0957	1048	...	1236	1258	...	1358	1439	1628	1735	1829	1825	1846	...	1929	2028	2132	2144
92	Câmpina .... d.	...	...	...	...	0709	0808	0920	0948	1036	1114	...	1311	1322	...	|	|	1655	1759	1903	|	1913	...	1954	2055	2157	2212
121	Sinaia .... d.	...	...	...	...	0739	0833	0946	1014	1117	1141	...	1359	1348	...	1445	1525	1721	1827	1954	1910	1942	...	2020	2122	2225	2238
140	Predeal .... d.	...	...	...	...	0805	0900	1013	1040	1144	1208	...	1428	1416	...	1509	1546	1748	1854	2022	1934	2008	...	2047	2148	2252	2306
166	**Braşov** .... a.	...	...	...	...	0842	0937	1050	1117	1223	1245	...	1507	1455	...	1545	1623	1826	1930	2102	2010	2045	...	2124	2226	2329	2343
166	**Braşov** .... d.	0600	...	0612	0730	0852	...	...	...	...	1300	1430	...	...	1503	...	1645	1842	...	...	2022	...	...	2134	2238	2343	2356
294	Sighişoara ..... **1669** d.	|	...	|	1006	1128	...	...	...	...	|	|	...	...	1735	...	|	|	...	...	|	...	...	0007	|	0216	|
332	Mediaş .... **1669** d.	|	...	|	1120	1226	...	...	...	...	|	|	...	...	1837	...	|	|	...	...	|	...	...	0105	|	0312	|
343	Copşa Mică ... **1669** d.	|	0719	|	1141	1244	...	...	...	...	|	|	...	...	1901	...	|	|	...	...	|	...	...	0123	|	0328	|
	Făgăraş .... d.	0712	|	0805	|	|	...	...	...	...	1414	1628	...	...	|	...	1814	2023	...	...	2135	...	...	|	|	|	|
	Podu Olt..... **1622** d.	|	0551	0943	|	|	...	...	...	...	1515	1745	...	...	|	...	|	2210	...	...	|	...	...	|	|	|	|
	Sibiu......**1622/69** a.	0830	0616	1022	|	|	...	...	...	...	1538	1830	...	...	|	...	1943	2240	...	...	2252	...	...	|	|	|	|
373	Blaj .... d.	|	0759	...	1238	1326	...	...	...	...	...	...	...	...	1946	...	|	...	...	...	|	...	...	0206	◐	0411	◐
394	Teiuş .... **1610** d.	|	0830	...	...	1359	...	...	...	...	...	...	...	...	2018	...	|	...	...	...	|	...	...	0238	|	0442	|
407	Aiud............... **1610** d.	|	0841	...	...	1411	...	...	...	...	...	...	...	...	2030	...	|	...	...	...	|	...	...	0250	|	0454	|
427	Războieni ...... **1610** d.	|	0902	...	...	1433	...	...	...	...	...	...	...	...	2053	...	|	...	...	...	|	...	...	0310	|	0513	|
444	Câmpia Turzii **1610** d.	|	0918	...	...	1449	...	...	...	...	...	...	...	...	2110	...	|	...	...	...	|	...	...	0327	|	0529	|
496	**Cluj Napoca** . **1610** a.	|	1016	...	...	1543	...	...	...	...	...	...	...	...	2210	...	|	...	...	...	|	...	...	0424	|	0624	|
	Oradea **1612** .... a.	|	...	...	...	|	...	...	...	...	...	...	...	...	...	...	|	...	...	...	|	...	...	0728	|	0930	|
	Baia Mare **1616**... a.	|	...	...	...	2008	...	...	...	...	...	...	...	...	...	...	|	...	...	...	|	...	...	|	|	...	0927
	Satu Mare **1616** .. a.	|	...	...	...	2157	...	...	...	...	...	...	...	...	...	...	|	...	...	...	|	...	...	0941	1014	...	1120
	Arad **1610** .... a.	1418	...	...	...	...	...	...	...	...	...	...	...	...	...	...	0117	...	...	...	0510	...	...	...	...	...	...
	Budapest K **1280** a.	1750	...	...	...	...	...	...	...	...	...	...	...	...	...	...	0455	...	...	...	0850	...	...	...	...	...	...

km		♣ 2	1644 ♦	♣ 2	1632 ♦	1526	473 ♦	1936 y	347 ♦	♣ 2	1630		♣ 2	1746	1731 g	1635	①–⑤ 2	1622 ♦	1646 ♦	⑥⑦ 2	1538 🍸	♣⑦ 2T	1736 ♦	75 ♦	1944 ♦	1642 ♦	1932 ♦
	Budapest K **1280** d.	...	...	...	...	...	1910	...	2250	...	...	...	...	...	...	...	...	...	...	...	...	...	...	0910	...	...	...
	Arad **1610** .... d.	...	...	...	...	...	0015	...	0421	...	...	...	...	...	...	...	...	...	...	...	...	...	...	1426	...	...	...
	Satu Mare **1616** .. d.	...	...	...	...	...	|	...	|	...	...	...	...	0347	...	...	...	...	...	...	...	...	...	|	1330	1610	...
	Baia Mare **1616**... d.	...	...	...	...	...	|	...	|	...	...	...	...	0524	...	...	...	...	...	...	...	...	...	|	|	1820	...
	Oradea **1612** .... d.	...	...	...	...	...	|	...	|	...	...	...	...	|	...	...	...	...	...	...	...	...	...	|	|	|	1839
	Cluj Napoca . **1610** d.	...	...	...	...	...	|	...	|	...	...	...	...	0930	...	...	...	...	...	...	1330	...	1602	|	|	|	2140
	Câmpia Turzii **1610** d.	...	...	...	...	...	|	...	|	...	...	...	...	1026	...	...	...	...	...	...	1420	...	1657	|	|	|	2234
	Războieni ...... **1610** d.	...	...	...	...	...	|	...	|	...	...	...	...	1045	...	...	...	...	...	...	1439	...	1716	|	|	|	2253
	Aiud............... **1610** d.	...	...	...	...	...	|	...	|	...	...	...	...	1105	...	...	...	...	...	...	1459	...	1736	|	|	|	2312
	Teiuş .... **1610** d.	...	...	...	...	...	|	...	|	...	...	...	...	1123	...	...	...	...	...	...	1518	...	1752	|	|	|	2331
	Blaj .... d.	...	...	...	...	...	|	...	|	...	...	...	...	1156	...	...	...	...	...	...	1550	1612	1821	|	◐	◐	0003
0	**Sibiu**......**1622/69** d.	...	...	...	...	0525	0629	...	1020	...	...	1154	...	|	...	...	1440	1459	...	1540	|	|	2014	2008	|	|	|
22	Podu Olt..... **1622** d.	...	...	...	...	0554	|	...	|	...	...	1232	...	|	...	...	1530	1524	...	1615	|	|	2041	|	|	|	|
84	Făgăraş .... d.	...	...	...	...	0710	0804	...	1155	...	...	1415	...	|	...	...	1702	1630	...	1829	|	|	|	2134	|	|	|
	Copşa Mică ... **1669** d.	...	...	...	...	|	|	...	|	...	...	|	...	1243	...	...	|	|	...	|	1641	1709	1900	|	|	|	0045
	Mediaş .... **1669** d.	...	...	...	...	|	|	...	|	...	...	|	...	1301	...	...	|	|	...	|	1658	1730	...	|	|	|	0104
	Sighişoara ..... **1669** d.	...	...	...	...	|	|	...	|	...	...	|	...	1400	...	...	|	|	...	|	1809	1843	...	|	|	|	0203
149	**Braşov** .... a.	...	...	...	...	0832	0920	...	1312	...	...	1551	...	1637	...	...	1838	1744	...	2002	2036	2110	...	2245	0100	0338	0437
	Braşov .... d.	0500	0540	0700	0735	0844	0932	1200	1327	1340	1412	...	1600	1650	1710	1725	...	1800	1850	...	2042	...	...	...	0115	0352	0450
	Predeal .... d.	0540	0622	0740	0812	0918	1006	1234	1401	1418	1447	...	1639	1729	1744	1759	...	1834	1925	...	2115	...	...	...	0200	0433	0530
	Sinaia .... d.	0607	0650	0807	0838	0944	1029	1255	1422	1444	1513	...	1706	1754	1809	1825	...	1902	1953	...	2140	...	...	...	0228	0455	0558
	Câmpina .... d.	0648	0723	0846	0909	1013	|	|	|	1522	1545	...	1748	1823	1837	1853	...	1933	2022	...	2207	...	...	...	0256	0523	0627
	Ploieşti Vest .... d.	0727	0749	0926	0935	1038	1119	1344	1509	1600	1614	...	1824	1848	1905p	1919	...	2000	2048	...	2230	...	...	...	0323	0552	0653
	Bucureşti Nord ...... a.	0817	0832	1029	1021	1120	1200	1425	1550	1649	1658	...	1922	1930	...	2003	...	2047	2130	...	2310	...	...	...	0418b	0634	0735
	Constanţa **1680** ... a.	...	...	...	1259y	...	...	1740	...	...	...	...	...	...	...	2300	...	...	...	...	...	...	...	...	0654	...	1104

T – From / to Timişoara (Table **1610**).
b – Bucureşti **Băneasa**.
g – From / to Galaţi via Ploieşti Sud (Table **1660**).
p – Ploieşti Sud.
y – June 11 - Sept. 11.
◐ – Via Miercurea Ciuc (Table **1630**).

For notes ♦, ♣, §, □ and • see headi

CLUJ NAPOCA and SIBIU - DEVA - ARAD and TIMIŞOARA 1610

	1765		1811	1821	1837				1836	74			♣			1621			1736	1819	346						472
	♦	2		♦	♦	2	2	2	♦	♦	2	2	2⑥	2	2	♦	2	2	♦		♦	2		2	2	2	♦
Cluj Napoca .... **1600** d.	0045	...	...	...	0429	0530	...	...	0700	...	...	...	...	...	1207	...	...	1445	1602	...	...	...	...	...	1945	...	...
Câmpia Turzii .... **1600** d.	0139	...	...	...	0525	0640	...	...	0756	...	...	...	...	...	1317	...	...	1600	1657	...	...	...	...	...	2055	...	...
Târgu Mureş .... d.	|	...	...	...	|	|	...	0303	|	...	0710	...	...	...	|	...	1438	|	|	1615	...	1735	...	1920	|	2220	...
Luduş .... d.	|	...	...	...	|	|	...	0417	|	...	0816	...	...	...	|	...	1545	|	|	1709	...	1846	...	2036	|	2330	...
Războieni .... **1600** d.	0158	...	...	...	0544	0703	...	0448	0817	...	0843	...	...	...	1340	...	1610	1624	1715	1736	...	1912	...	2105	2118	2358	...
Aiud .... **1600** d.	0219	...	...	...	0605	0728	...	0516	0839	...	...	...	...	...	1407	...	...	...	...	1758	...	1935	...	...	2149	...	...
Teiuş .... **1600** d.	0236	...	...	...	0621	0745	...	0534	0857	...	...	...	...	...	1421	...	...	...	...	1818	...	1949	...	...	2204	...	...
Bucureşti Nord **1600** .... d.	|	...	...	2345	|	|	...	|	|	...	...	...	...	...	...	1000	...	...	...	|	1400	...	...	...	...	...	1745
Braşov **1600** .... d.	|	...	...	|	|	|	...	|	|	0600	...	...	0730	...	...	1300	...	...	...	|	1645	...	...	...	...	...	2022
Sibiu .... d.	|	...	0330	|	|	|	...	0948	|	0838	...	...	|	...	...	1546	...	...	...	|	1948	...	...	...	...	...	2255
Sebeş Alba .... d.	|	...	0506	▽	|	|	...	...	|	1004	...	...	|	...	...	1718	...	...	...	|	|	...	...	...	...	...	0023
Alba Iulia .... d.	0306	...	|	|	0652	0828	...	...	0935	|	...	...	1342	...	...	|	...	...	...	1851	|	...	...	...	...	...	|
Vinţu de Jos .... d.	0322	...	0517	|	0707	0846	...	...	0952	1016	...	...	1400	...	...	1730	...	...	...	1906	|	...	...	...	...	...	0036
Simeria .... **1625** d.	0435	0620	0633	0751	0835	1007	1014	...	1107	1139	...	1240	1518	1543	...	1904	...	...	...	2021	2256	...	...	...	...	...	0220
Deva .... **1625** d.	0448	0632	0644	0804	0848	1019	1027	...	...	1153	...	1254	1528	1557	...	1917	...	...	...	2035	2308	...	...	...	...	...	0235
Ilia .... d.	0514	0715	0712	0831	0915	...	1100	...	...	1220	...	1328	1552	1631	...	1944	...	...	...	2103	|	...	...	...	...	...	|
Radna .... d.	0630	0913	|	0947	|	...	1245	...	...	1341	...	1518	1700	1816	...	2101	...	...	...	|	|	...	...	...	...	...	|
Arad .... a.	0714n	0955	|	1022	|	...	1325	...	...	1417	...	1559	1730	1856	...	2146n	...	...	...	|	0117	...	...	...	...	...	0510
Budapest Keleti **1280** ... a.	|	...	|	...	|	...	...	...	...	1750	...	...	|	...	...	|	...	...	...	|	0455	...	...	...	...	...	0850
Lugoj .... **1620** a.	|	...	0840	...	1046	...	...	...	...	...	...	...	|	...	...	|	...	...	...	2240	...	...	...	...	...	...	...
Timişoara Nord ..... **1620** a.	0803	...	0951	...	1154	...	...	...	...	...	...	...	1845	...	...	2238	...	...	...	2348	...	...	...	...	...	...	...

		1737		347			1820		1622		♣			75	1766			1812		1838	1822			1835	1843	473	
	2	♦	2Ⓐ	♦	2•	2		2	♦		2⑦	2	2	♦	♦	2	2		2	♦	♦	2	2	♦	♦	♦	
şoara Nord .... **1620** d.	...	...	...	...	...	...	0738	...	0811	...	0954	...	...	...	1340	1351	...	1602	...	1755	...	...	...	...	2145	...	...
j .... **1620** d.	...	...	...	...	...	...	0848	...	|	...	|	...	...	...	|	|	...	1709	...	1903	...	...	...	...	|	...	...
dapest Keleti **1280** .... d.	...	...	...	2250	...	...	|	...	|	...	|	...	...	0910	|	|	...	|	...	|	...	...	...	...	|	1910	...
rad .... d.	...	...	...	0421	...	0748	|	...	0858n	...	1104	...	...	1429	1429n	1521	...	|	1638	|	1920	1814	1956	...	2232n	0039	...
adna .... d.	...	...	...	|	...	0829	|	...	0939	...	1136	...	...	1501	1511	1602	...	|	1719	|	1953	1900	2037	...	2312	|	...
.... d.	...	...	...	|	...	1015	1034	...	1056	...	1249	...	...	1619	1631	1755	...	1840	1914	2036	2110	2128	2252	...	0026	|	...
a .... **1625** d.	...	...	...	0626	...	1049	1103	...	1122	...	1313	1415	...	1646	1657	1833	...	1906	1947	2102	2136	2204	2326	...	0051	0247	...
eria .... **1625** d.	...	...	...	0655	...	1102	1124	...	1147	...	1326	1429	...	1710	1718	1846	...	1920	2000	2126	2152	2217	2339	0042	0103	0312	...
u de Jos .... d.	...	...	...	|	...	...	1231	...	1309	...	1441	1545	...	1821	1832	...	...	2057	...	2241	|	...	...	0155	0224	0436	...
a Iulia .... d.	...	...	...	|	...	...	1245	...	|	...	1458	1602	...	|	1852	...	...	|	...	2256	|	...	...	0212	0243	|	...
ebeş Alba .... d.	...	...	...	|	...	...	|	...	1321	...	|	|	...	1833	|	...	...	2110	...	|	▽	...	...	|	|	0449	...
biu .... a.	...	...	...	1012	...	...	|	...	1459	...	|	|	1553	2002	|	...	...	2243	...	|	|	...	...	|	|	0629	...
aşov **1600** .... a.	...	...	...	1312	...	...	|	...	1744	...	2110	|	|	2245	|	...	...	...	...	|	|	...	...	|	|	0920	...
ucureşti Nord **1600** .... a.	...	...	...	1550	...	...	|	...	2047	...	...	|	|	...	|	...	...	...	...	|	0559	...	...	|	|	1200	...
ş .... **1600** d.	0630	...	1050	...	...	...	1320	1423	...	...	...	1640	1914	...	1928	...	1950	...	...	2330	...	...	...	0251	0326	...	...
.... **1600** d.	0642	...	1101	...	...	...	1332	1434	...	...	...	1651	1925	...	1940	...	2002	...	...	2342	...	...	...	0303	0337	...	...
oieni .... **1600** d.	0707	0902	1129	...	1146	...	1353	1500	...	1638	...	1714	2005	...	2003	...	2029	...	...	0003	...	...	...	0322	0356	...	...
uduş .... d.	0735	|	|	...	1214	...	1420	|	...	1708	...	|	2035	...	|	...	|	...	...	|	...	...	...	|	|	...	...
ârgu Mureş .... a.	0847	|	|	...	1328	...	1510	|	...	1815	...	|	2139	...	|	...	|	...	...	|	...	...	...	|	|	...	...
pia Turzii .... **1600** d.	...	0918	1150	...	...	...	...	1519	...	...	...	1733	...	...	2019	...	2048	...	...	0019	...	...	...	0338	0412	...	...
Napoca .... **1600** a.	...	1016	1309	...	...	...	...	1633	...	...	...	1849	...	...	2114	...	2158	...	...	0114	...	...	...	0434	0505	...	...

Aradu **Nou**. ▽ – Via Craiova and Târgu Jiu (Table **1625**). ∆ – Distance from Vinţu de Jos. For notes ♦, ♣, §, □ and • see page 518.

CLUJ NAPOCA - ORADEA 1612

	406	1741	1531	1931	362			1533	366	1833		1535
	♦	♦	T	♦	♦	§	⚒§	•	♦	♦	§	
Bucureşti N **1600** .... d.	...	1845	...	2045	...	...	...	...	...	...	...	...
Braşov **1600/35** ...... d.	1843	2134	...	2343	...	...	...	...	0758	...	...	...
Cluj Napoca .... d.	0224	0439	0545	0640	0654	0731	0912	1340	1509	1549	1621	2007
Huedin .... d.	0316	0535	0637	0737	0749	0832	1010	1432	1606	1651	1718	2100
Oradea .... a.	0456	0728	0825	0930	0938	1045	1228	1625	1750	1843	1943	2301
Budapest K **1275** .... a.	0920	...	...	...	1320	...	...	...	2120	...	...	...

		1532	1834	367			1534	1742	1932	1536	407
	⚒§		♦	♦	§•	§	Ⓑ	♦	♦	•T	♦
Budapest K **1275** . d.	...	...	...	0555	...	...	...	...	...	...	1440
Oradea .... d.	0500	0600	0957	1130	1137	1521	1705	1839	1839	2014	2022
Huedin .... d.	0706	0746	1149	1315	1331	1745	1856	2031	2031	2212	2220
Cluj Napoca .... a.	0802	0835	1242	1406	1424	1842	1952	2140	2124	2300	2312
Braşov **1600/35** ... a.	...	...	...	2157	...	...	...	0437	0437	...	0714
Bucureşti N **1600** . a.	...	...	...	...	...	...	...	0735	0735	...	...

From / to Timişoara (Table **1614**). For notes ♦, ♣, §, □ and • see page 518.

Additional services **Cluj Napoca - Oradea and v.v.**:
From Cluj Napoca: 0213, 0740, 1640Ⓑ. From Oradea: 0247, 0730, 1530Ⓑ.

ORADEA - ARAD - TIMIŞOARA 1614

	1744			1531	369	73	481			79	1833	
	m	2	2⚒	Ⓑ•	P2	♦	♦	2	2	♦	♦	2
Cluj Napoca **1612** ... d.	...	...	...	0545	...	...	...	...	...	...	1549	...
Oradea .... d.	0307	0505	0740	0829	0954	...	...	...	1600	...	1847	1954
Salonta .... d.	0350	0553	0835	0910	1037	...	...	...	1648	...	1934	2103
Arad .... a.	0507	0738	1020	1034	...	...	...	...	1849	...	2056	2253
Arad .... **1669** d.	0513	0751	...	1036	...	1227	1227	1625	1902	2036	2110	2330j
Timişoara Nord **1669** a.	0606	0921	...	1126	...	1314	1314	1747	2017	2125	2211	0049j

		1834	78	368		72	480	1743	1536		
	2	♦	♦	P2	2	♦	♦	m	•	2	2
Timişoara N .. **1669** d.	0518	0636	0750	...	1303	1448	1448	1550	1715	1735	2019
Arad .... **1669** a.	0644	0734	0838	...	1411	1537	1537	1645	1807	1851	2137
Arad .... d.	0656	0746	...	...	1425	...	...	1655	1811	1906	...
Salonta .... d.	0834	0911	...	1340	1607	...	...	1819	1932	2102	...
Oradea .... a.	0927	0953	...	1425	1702	...	...	1905	2012	2149	...
Cluj Napoca **1612** a.	...	1242	...	...	...	...	...	...	2300	...	...

From / to Püspökladány (Table **1275**).
12 Timişoara - Arad - Budapest and v.v. (Table **1280**).

j – Not nights of ⑤/⑥ and ⑥/⑦.
m – From / to Baia Mare (Table **1618**).

For Cluj - Timişoara via Teiuş see Table **1610**.
For notes ♦, ♣, §, □ and • see page 518.

CLUJ NAPOCA - BAIA MARE - SATU MARE 1616

		1741	1945	1641 4090				1546	1745	1544	1744
	D2	♦	♦	♦	2	2	2			Ⓐ	♦
Bucureşti N **1600** ... d.	...	1845	1940b	2100	...	...	...	...	0600	...	...
Braşov **1600** .... d.	...	2134	2238	2356	...	...	...	...	0852	...	...
Cluj Napoca .... d.	...	0439	▽	▽	0535	...	1410	1410	1555	1820	...
Dej Călători .... d.	...	|	0546	0649	0720	...	1528	1528	1724	1943	...
Jibou .... d.	0301	△	0726	0820	0857	...	1708	1715	1844	2123	...
Baia Mare .... a.	0400	|	0835	0927	...	...	1818	|	2008	2225	...
Baia Mare .... **1669** d.	0414	|	0850	0945	...	1545	...	|	2022	...	2326
Satu Mare .... **1669** a.	0605	0941	1014	1120	...	1724	...	1946	2157	...	0047

	1746			1545		1944	1543	4091 1642	1742		1743
		2Ⓐ	2		2	♦	⑦	♦	♦	D2	♦
Satu Mare .... **1669** d.	0347	0512	...	0733	0743	1330	...	1610	1615	1953	2120
Baia Mare .... **1669** a.	0510	0707	...	|	0934	1452	...	1804	|	2203	2240
Baia Mare .... d.	0524	...	0845	|	...	1507	1702	1820	|	2247	...
Jibou .... d.	0639	...	1019	1019	...	1618	1824	1933	△	2358	...
Dej Călători .... d.	0811	...	1149	1149	...	1745	2003	2110	|	...	...
Cluj Napoca .... a.	0918	...	1253	1253	...	▽	2108	▽	2140	...	...
Braşov **1600** .... a.	1637	...	...	...	...	0100	...	0338	0437	...	...
Bucureşti N **1600** ... a.	1930	...	...	...	...	0418b	...	0634	0735	...	...

From / to Debrecen (Table **1277**).
Bucureşti **Băneasa**.

△ – Via Oradea (Tables **1612** / **1618**).
▽ – Via Miercurea Ciuc (Table **1630**).

For notes ♦, ♣, §, □ and • see page 518.

ORADEA - CAREI - SATU MARE 1618

	①–⑥	1741			1546				1743	
	2	♦	2	D2		2	D	D2	♦	2
Oradea .... d.	0310	0738	0750	...	...	1536	...	1635	1913	1937
Valea lui Mihai .... d.	0441	0844	0919	1138	...	1719	1757	1837	2018	2127
Carei .... d.	0518	0910	...	1214	1917	1756	1840	...	2043	2200
Satu Mare .... a.	0602	0941	...	1256	1946	1838	1925	...	2112	2239
Baia Mare **1616** .... a.	...	...	...	...	...	...	2203	...	2240	...

	1744	⚒		1545					1742	
	♦	2	D2		2	D2	D2	2	♦	2
Baia Mare **1616** .... d.	2326	...	0414	...	...	...	...	...	...	...
Satu Mare .... d.	0057	0327	0620	0733	0740	...	1500	1543	1615	2000
Carei .... d.	0129	0359	0708	0802	0837	...	1543	1625	1650	2045
Valea lui Mihai .... d.	0154	0432	0837	...	0928	0943	1637	1731	1717	2123
Oradea .... a.	0259	0555	...	...	...	1118	...	1855	1825	2247

From / to Debrecen (Table **1277**).

For notes ♦, ♣, §, □ and • see page 518.

1620 BUCUREŞTI - CRAIOVA - TIMISOARA

km		1821	1991	1999		1698		1827	72	480	1591		1823		1521	1691	1599	1595		1825	1693	1835	1593	1597	1695
		♦	♦	♦	2	2Ⓐ	2	T	♦	♦		2	2T	2		2			2⚒	T		♦	♦	2	♦
0	**Bucureşti** Nord d.	2345	0010b	0010b	...	...	...	...	0545	...	0645	0748	0850	...	0935	1040	1215	1340	...	1445	1545	1625	1745	1945	2145
51	Videle d.	0037	0105	0105	...	...	...	...	0637	...	0737	0900	0944	...	1027	1132	1309	1435	...	1538	1637	1717	1837	2037	2237
100	Roşiori Nord d.	0120	0148	0148	...	...	...	...	0722	...	0820	1002	1036	...	1110	1215	1401	1520	...	1622	1720	1800	1920	2120	2320
155	Caracal d.	0212	0237	0237	...	...	...	0718	0810	...	0909	1106	1137	...	1159	1307	1502	1610	...	1714	1809	1853	2011	2211	0010
209	**Craiova** a.	0252	0318	0318	...	...	...	0758	0849	...	0949	1210	1222	...	...	1347	1548	1650	...	1754	1849	1934	2051	2251	0050
209	**Craiova** 1625 d.	0300	0330	0330	...	...	...	0800	0900	0900	0952	▬	1224	1232	...	1355	...	▬	...	1758	1855	1942	...	...	0100
245	Filiaşi 1625 d.	0328	|	|	...	...	...	0828	0929	0929	1020	...	1255	1320	...	1423	...	2⑦	...	1825	1923	2010	...	...	0129
323	Drobeta Turnu Severin d.	...	0530	0530	...	...	...	...	1057	1057	1159	...	...	1516	...	1600	...	1819	1819	...	2052	...	...	...	0258
347	Orşova d.	...	0600	0600	...	...	...	...	1127	1127	...	...	...	1543	...	1632	...	1847	1847	...	2122	...	...	...	0330
364	Băile Herculane d.	...	0624	0624	...	...	...	...	1151	1151	...	2	...	...	...	1703	...	1914	1914	...	2147	...	...	...	0356
435	Caransebeş d.	...	0802	0815	0445	0642	0740	...	1311	1311	...	1314	...	...	...	1824	...	2114	2139	...	2308	...	...	...	0530
	Reşiţa Sud 1669 a.	...	|	0910	|	0524r	|	...	|	|	...	|	...	...	...	|	...	|	|	...	|	...	...	...	|
474	Lugoj 1610 d.	...	0834	...	0536	0710	0838	...	1341	1341	...	1400	...	...	...	1855	...	2158	2226	...	2340	...	...	...	0602
533	**Timişoara** Nord 1610 a.	...	0940	...	0653	0806	0953	...	1440	1440	...	1530	...	...	...	1953	...	2315	2344	...	0038	...	...	...	0707

		1826	1692	1824	1596	1828	1522	1590	1836			73	481			1699			1998	1992	1822	1592	1594	1696	9170 1696
	2	T		♦	2	T	R		♦	2	2	♦	♦	2	2	2Ⓐ	2	2	♦	♦	♦	2	♦	♦	♦
Timişoara Nord 1610 d.	...	...	0530	...	...	...	...	...	...	...	1251	1349	1349	...	1425	1622	1627	1918	...	1902	...	...	...	2220	...
Lugoj 1610 d.	...	...	0628	...	...	...	...	...	...	...	1416	1453	1453	...	1542	1723	1758	2050	...	2009	...	...	...	2318	...
Reşiţa Sud 1669 d.	...	...	|	...	...	...	...	...	...	...	|	|	|	...	|	1911r	|	|	1921	|	...	...	...	|	2230
Caransebeş d.	...	...	0700	...	...	...	...	...	...	...	1458	1523	1523	←	1626	1812	1843	2134	2053	2053	...	...	...	0012	0012
Băile Herculane d.	...	...	0822	...	...	...	...	...	...	...	1704	1644	1644	1704	...	...	...	...	2229	2229	...	...	...	0136	0136
Orşova d.	...	...	0846	...	...	...	...	...	...	1602	→	1709	1709	1732	...	...	...	...	2253	2253	...	...	...	0201	0201
Drobeta Turnu Severin d.	0420	...	0917	...	...	...	...	1425	...	1642	...	1740	1740	1759	...	...	...	...	2332	2332	...	...	...	0232	0232
Filiaşi 1625 d.	0617	0644	1048	1152	...	1505	...	1551	1615	1847	...	1902	1902	...	...	...	...	...	|	|	0212	...	...	0405	0405
Craiova 1625 a.	0706	0712	1117	1222	...	1535	...	1619	1649	1945	...	1930	1930	...	...	...	...	...	0133	0133	0240	...	...	0436	0436
Craiova d.	...	0715	1125	1230	1420	1540	...	1625	1705	...	...	1950	...	...	...	...	...	...	0145	0145	0250	0302	0425	0450	0450
Caracal d.	...	0754	1204	1310	1500	1618	1630	1706	1800	...	...	2030	...	...	...	...	...	...	0223	0223	0329	0346	0504	0530	0530
Roşiori Nord d.	...	0848	1255	1400	1555	...	1719	1759	1900	...	...	2119	...	...	...	...	...	...	0310	0310	0420	0448	0555	0625	0625
Videle d.	...	0936	1343	1448	1645	...	1813	1850	1955	...	...	2206	...	...	...	...	...	...	0357	0357	0509	0546	0647	0716	0716
Bucureşti Nord a.	...	1033	1439	1544	1740	...	1904	1940	2048	...	...	2256	...	...	...	...	...	...	0456b	0456b	0559	0644	0743	0820	0820

R – From/to Râmnicu Vâlcea (Table **1622**).
T – From/to Târgu Jiu (Table **1625**).
b – Bucureşti **Băneasa**.
r – Via Caransebeş.
For notes ♦, ♣, §, □ and • see page 518.

1621 BUCUREŞTI - PITESTI - CRAIOVA

km		1891	1781	1783	1893	1785	1895	1787	1897	1789	1791	1793	1922
		•											♦
0	**Bucureşti** Nord d.	0606	0730	0930	1330	1430	1530	1630	1730	1830	1930	2030	2312
108	Piteşti d.	0815	0928	1132	1538	1625	1735	1830	1938	2025	2125	2225	0140
189	Slatina d.	0938	...	...	1652	...	1858	...	2050	...	...	...	0255
206	Piatra Olt 1622 d.	0959	...	...	1713	...	1920	...	2112	...	...	...	0314
250	**Craiova** 1622 a.	1042	...	...	1825	...	2005	...	2155	...	...	...	...

	1780	1782	1890	1892	1784	1786	1788	1894	1790	1792	1896
								•			
Craiova 1622 d.	...	...	0430	0730	...	...	...	1230	...	...	1610
Piatra Olt 1622 d.	...	...	0514	0813	...	...	...	1314	...	...	1714
Slatina d.	...	...	0536	0835	...	...	...	1336	...	...	1736
Piteşti d.	0500	0600	0700	1000	1100	1300	1400	1500	1600	1700	1900
Bucureşti Nord a.	0641	0741	0842	1141	1235	1441	1540	1635	1736	1841	2035

For notes ♦, ♣, §, □ and • see page 518.

1622 SIBIU - RÂMNICU VÂLCEA - CRAIOVA

km		1722		1720			1522			1725	1921	1736
			2⚒		2⚒			2⚒	2		♦	♦
0	**Sibiu** 1600 d.	0255	0328	0650	0740	...	...	...	1610	1720	1842	2014
	Braşov 1600 d.	|	|	|	|	...	...	...	|	|	|	|
22	Podu Olt 1600 d.	|	0400	0718	0820	...	...	1310	1647	1749	|	2041
83	Călimănesti d.	0447	0539	0845	1008	...	1425	1453	1849	1914	2043	2212
99	**Râmnicu Vâlcea** d.	0515	0605	0905	1035	...	1445	1520	1945	1935	2102	2230
186	Piatra Olt 1621 d.	0630	0809	1023	...	...	1555	1732	2204	2041	2245	...
*	Caracal a.	0705	...	|	...	...	1630	...	|	|	|	...
	Bucureşti N 1620 a.	...	...	|	...	...	1904	...	|	|	0228	...
230	**Craiova** 1621 a.	...	...	1115	...	...	...	...	2312	2123	...	...

		1737	1922			1724	1521		1721	1723
	2⚒	♦	♦	2⚒	2			2Ⓑ		
Craiova 1621 d.	...	...	...	...	0510	0805	...	...	1450	...
Bucureşti N 1620 d.	...	...	2312	...	|	|	0935	...	|	...
Caracal d.	...	...	|	...	|	|	1200	...	|	1812
Piatra Olt 1621 d.	...	...	0332	0352	0632	0910	1234	...	1557	1856
Râmnicu Vâlcea d.	0250	0400	0450	0630	0910	1020	1345	1608	1705	2011
Călimănesti d.	0315	0419	0515	0654	0935	1037	1403	1634	1723	2027
Podu Olt 1600 a.	0527	0549	0656	0855	1117	1159	...	1821	|	2203
Braşov 1600 a.	|	|	|	...	|	|	...	|	|	|
Sibiu 1600 a.	0605	0616	0725	...	1152	1223	...	1857	1928	2228

* – 32 km from Piatra Olt.
For notes ♦, ♣, §, □ and • see page 518.

1625 CRAIOVA - TÂRGU JIU - DEVA

Local trains 2nd class o

km			1821			1995	1827	1823		1825	1829	1835	
		2	♦	2	2	♦	C•		2		♦	♦	2
	Bucureşti N 1620 d.	...	2345	...	...	0010b	...	0850	...	1445	1625	1625	...
0	**Craiova** 1620 d.	...	0300	0305	...	0342	0800	1224	1612	1758	1942	1942	...
36	Filiaşi 1620 d.	...	0329	0407	...	0411	0829	1256	1712	1826	2011	2011	...
107	**Târgu Jiu** d.	...	0445	0552	...	0540	0950	1418	1855	1951	2130	2130	2302
157	Petroşani a.	...	0553	0730	...	0655	1106e	▬	2028	...	2239	2239	0025
157	Petroşani d.	0320	0557	...	0735	0657	...	1850	...	...	2242	2242	0026
237	Simeria 1610 d.	0552	0751	...	1014	0850	...	2117	...	...	0043	0042	0212
246	**Deva** 1610 a.	0604	0802	...	1027	0902	...	2127	...	...	0054	|	...
	Cluj Napoca 1610 a.	...	|	...	|	...	...	...	...	...	...	0434	...
	Arad 1610 a.	...	1022	...	1325	...	...	...	...	...	...	...	...

	1826			1824	1836					1996
		2	2	♦	♦	2	2	2Ⓐ	2	♦
Arad 1610 d.	...	...	...	...	...	...	...	...	...	...
Cluj Napoca 1610 d.	...	...	...	...	0700	...	...	...	...	...
Deva 1610 d.	...	...	...	0710	|	...	1550	...	...	2003
Simeria 1610 d.	...	...	*0445*	0725	1127	...	1605	...	1906	2023
Petroşani a.	...	...	*0715*	0927	1320	...	1830	...	2124	2210
Petroşani d.	...	0440	0805	0930	1325	1430a	...	1905	2150	2212
Târgu Jiu d.	0520	0628	0951	1040	1455	1616	...	2044	2320	2335
Filiaşi 1620 a.	0643	0808	1129	1151	1614	1755	...	2226	...	0053
Craiova 1620 a.	0712	0920	1218	1222	1649	1845	...	2315	...	0123
Bucureşti N 1620 a.	1033	...	...	1544	2048	...	...	...	...	0456b

C – From/to Caracal (Table **1620**).
a – Ⓐ only.
b – Bucureşti **Băneasa**.
e – ⑤⑥† only.
For notes ♦, ♣, §, □ and • see page

1630 BRAŞOV - MIERCUREA CIUC - DEDA - TÂRGU MURES

km			366		1540	1645		406	1643	1945	1641	4541
		2	♦•	2	♦	♦	2	♦	♦	♦	♦	♦
	Bucureşti N 1600 d.	...	...	...	...	1215	...	...	1800	1940b	2100	2100
0	**Braşov** 1640 d.	0355	0758	...	1415	1517	1617	1843	2057	2238	2356	2356
32	Sfântu Gheorghe 1640 d.	0459	0827	...	1446	1549	1657	1913	2128	2309	0030	0030
95	**Miercurea Ciuc** 1640 d.	0742	0929	1540	1603	1658	1923	2014	2236	0024	0136	0136
	Galaţi 1640 d.	|	|	|	|	|	|	|	|	|	|	|
103	Siculeni 1640 d.	0755	0938	1554	1612	1710	1931	2025	2250	0038	0152	0152
150	Gheorghieni d.	0909	1027	1710	...	1801	2045	2115	2342	0138	0244	0244
184	Topliţa d.	...	1101	1753	...	1851	2126	2149	0007	0222	0319	0319
228	**Deda** a.	...	1200	1910	...	1952	...	2249	0116	0322	0418	0418
228	**Deda** d.	...	...	1923	...	2012	...	...	...	0401t	...	0440
250	Reghin d.	...	...	2004	...	2045	...	...	...	0432t	...	0510
282	**Târgu Mureş** a.	...	...	2057	...	2120	...	...	...	0507t	...	0551

	407		1541		1646		367	1944	1642	4550
	♦	2	♦	2		2	♦	♦	♦	♦
Târgu Mureş d.	...	...	...	1055	1255	1423	...	1830j	...	2255
Reghin d.	...	...	...	1144	1337	1509	...	1915j	...	2343
Deda a.	...	...	...	1225	1400	1542	...	1941j	...	0016
Deda d.	0237	...	...	1239	1413	1555	1729	2022	2316	0046
Topliţa d.	0351	0419	...	1350	1513	1705	1829	2128	0018	0203
Gheorghieni d.	0429	0504	...	1437	1551	1802	1907	2213	0056	0245
Siculeni 1640 d.	0519	0625	1129	1553	1648	1913	1959	2314	0153	0342
Galaţi 1640 a.	|	|	|	|	|	|	|	|	|	|
Miercurea Ciuc 1640 d.	0530	0706	1139	1617	1701	1936	2015	2325	0204	0353
Sfântu Gheorghe 1640 d.	0630	0828	1254	1750	1806	2105	2127	0031	0309	0458
Braşov 1640 a.	0714	0908	1323	1827	1835	2151	2157	0100	0338	0527
Bucureşti N 1600 a.	...	...	...	...	2130	...	...	0418b	0634	0832

b – Bucureşti **Băneasa**.
j – Train number **1948**.
t – Train number **1949**.
For notes ♦, ♣, §, □ and • see page 518.

DEDA and BISTRIŢA - DEJ - CLUJ NAPOCA 1635

		1945	1641	1639	366				1649	406	1643
	2	♦	♦	♦	♦	2	2	2	♦	♦	♦
Bucureşti Nord **1600** ... d.	...	1940**b**	2100	2100	...	...	...	...	...	...	1800
Braşov **1630** ... d.	...	2238	2356	2356	0758	...	...	...	...	1843	2057
)eda ... d.	...	0335	0428	0428	1201	...	...	...	...	2250	0119
Bistriţa Nord ... d.	0345	|	|	|	|	0730	1533	1920	2145	|	|
Sărăţel ... d.	0407	0433	0541	0541	1251	0747	1551	1936	2159	2355	0209
Beclean pe Someş **1650** d.	0441	0504	0606	0606	1315	0821	1633	2019	...	0020	0233
)ej Călători ... **1616/50** d.	0524	0546	0649	0659	1348	0903	1716	2102	...	0057	...
Baia Mare **1616** ... a.	|	0835	0927	|	|	|	|	...	...	|	...
Cluj Napoca ... **1616/50** a.	0649	...	...	0804	1453	1030	1843	...	...	0202	...
Budapest Keleti **1275** .. a.	...	...	...	...	2120	...	...	...	...	0920	...

	1648			367	1944		1638	1642		1644	407
	♦	2	2	♦	♦		♦	♦	2	♦	♦
Budapest Keleti **1275** ... d.	...	...	...	0555	...	...	...	...	...	...	1440
Cluj Napoca ... **1616/50** d.	...	...	1127	1422	...	...	1925	...	1935	...	2330
Baia Mare **1616** ... d.	...	...	|	|	1507	...	|	1822	|	...	|
Dej Călători ... **1616/50** d.	...	0502	1306	1544	1758	...	2110	2110	2124	...	0051
Beclean pe Someş .. **1650** d.	...	0544	1342	1612	1843	...	2140	2140	2202	2240	0117
Sărăţel ... d.	0550	0623	1415	1638	1910	...	2224	2224	2235	2307	0140
Bistriţa Nord ... a.	0604	0642	1432	|	|	...	|	|	2253	|	|
Deda ... a.	...	...	...	1727	2000	...	2313	2313	...	0011	0235
Braşov **1630** ... a.	...	...	...	2157	0100	...	0338	0338	...	0527	0714
Bucureşti Nord **1600** ... a.	...	...	...	...	0418**b**	...	0634	0634	...	0832	...

ucureşti **Băneasa**.

Δ – Distance from Sărăţel.

For notes ♦, ♣, §, □ and • see page 518.

BRAŞOV - MIERCUREA CIUC - ADJUD - GALAŢI 1640

								1540		
	2	2	2	2	2	2•	2		2	2
Braşov ... **1630** d.	...	0355	...	0606	...	1224	...	1415	...	...
Sfântu Gheorghe ... **1630** d.	...	0459	...	0650	...	1311	...	1446	...	...
Miercurea Ciuc ... **1630** a.	...	0631	...	0817	...	1440	...	1558	...	...
Miercurea Ciuc ... **1630** d.	...	▬	0712	▬	1152	1446	...	1603	1615	1945
Târgu Mureş **1630** ... d.	...	2	|	...	|	|	...	|	|	|
Siculeni ... **1630** d.	...	0420	0725	...	1205	1454	...	1616	1626	2003
Ghimeş ... d.	...	0532	0828	2	1313	▬	...	1711	1733	2114
Comăneşti ... d.	0425	0620	0917	1000	1408	...	...	1756	1825	2205
Oneşti ... d.	0525	0740	▬	1101	1507	...	1540	1839	1938	2323
Adjud ... **1670** d.	0630	0839	...	1202	...	...	1636	1950	2031	0017
Mărăşeşti ... **1670** a.	0704	0913	2	1239	...	2	1714	|	2107	0053
Mărăşeşti ... d.	...	...	1105	...	...	1608	...	|	...	...
Iaşi **1670** ... a.	...	...	|	...	...	|	...	2249	...	...
Tecuci ... **1670** d.	...	...	1131	...	...	1633	...	...	...	...
Galaţi ... **1670** a.	...	...	1344	...	...	1836	...	...	...	...

			1541							
	2	2		2	2	2	2	2	2	2
Galaţi ... **1670** d.	...	...	...	...	0740	...	...	1540	...	1945
Tecuci ... **1670** d.	...	...	...	...	0946	...	...	1745	...	2150
Iaşi **1670** ... d.	...	...	0505	...	|	...	...	|	...	|
Mărăşeşti ... a.	...	...	|	...	1011	...	...	1810	...	2217
Mărăşeşti ... **1670** d.	...	0420	|	0840	▬	...	1420	...	1852	...
Adjud ... **1670** d.	...	0515	0821	0918	...	1259	1510	...	1932	...
Oneşti ... d.	...	0605	0901	1012	...	1347	1558	...	2026	...
Comăneşti ... d.	0410	0704	0947	1116	...	1458	1659	...	2124	...
Ghimeş ... d.	0501	0754	1027	...	2	1547	1751	...	...	...
Siculeni ... **1630** a.	0618	0915	1129	...	1332	...	1906	...	...	...
Târgu Mureş **1630** ... a.	|	|	|	...	|	...	|	...	...	...
Miercurea Ciuc . **1630** a.	0627	0924	1137	...	1340	...	1915	...	...	...
Miercurea Ciuc . **1630** d.	...	...	1139	...	1343	...	...	...	...	...
Sfântu Gheorghe **1630** d.	...	...	1254	...	1511	...	...	...	...	...
Braşov ... **1630** a.	...	...	1323	...	1557	...	...	...	...	...

For notes ♦, ♣, §, □ and • see page 518.

IAŞI - SUCEAVA - DEJ - CLUJ NAPOCA 1650

		1653	1833	1947	1831		4136	1765	1837
	2⚒	♦		♦	♦	2	♦	♦	♦
Iaşi ... d.	...	...	0603	...	1057	...	...	1503	1925
Paşcani ... **1670** d.	...	0332	0713	...	1206	...	...	1612	2034
Vereşti ... **1670** d.	...	0406	0749	...	1240	...	...	1646	2108
Suceava ... **1670** a.	...	0422	0805	...	1256	...	...	1702	2124
Suceava ... d.	...	0437	0820	...	1311	...	...	1718	2136
Gura Humorului Oraş ... d.	...	0525	0909	...	1359	...	...	1806	2224
Câmpulung Moldovenesc d.	...	0607	0951	...	1448	...	...	1852	2306
Vatra Dornei Băi ... d.	...	0713	1056	...	1552	...	...	1958	0011
Năsăud ... d.	...	...	1304	...	1803	...	...	2200	0206
Sighetu Marmaţiei ... d.	0100	...	|	1419	|	1550	1742	|	|
Vişeu de Jos ... d.	0317	...	|	1610	|	1754	2012	|	|
Salva ... d.	0512	...	1312	1741	1811	1938	2148	2208	0214
Beclean pe Someş. **1635** d.	0543	...	1340	1811	1837	2013	2222	2256	0238
Dej Călători ... **1635** d.	0625	...	1414	...	1916	2051	...	2329	0312
Cluj Napoca ... **1635** a.	0748	...	1526	...	2022	2204	...	0033	0417
Oradea **1612** ... a.	...	...	1843	...	...	...	...	|	|
Timişoara N **1610 / 14** .. a.	...	...	2211	...	...	...	...	0803	1154

	4133	1838	1946	1843	4135	1832	1834		1654	1766
	♦	♦	♦	♦	♦	♦•		2⚒	♦	♦
Timişoara N **1610 / 14** ... d.	...	1755	...	2145	...	...	0636	...	...	1340
Oradea **1612** ... d.	...	|	...	|	...	...	0957	...	...	|
Cluj Napoca ... **1635** d.	...	0126	...	0519	...	0920	1256	1435	...	2129
Dej Călători ... **1635** d.	...	0242	...	0641	...	1039	1415	1615	...	2253
Beclean pe Someş ... **1635** d.	0250	0310	0515	0712	0722	1108	1443	1650	...	2321
Salva ... d.	0337	0334	0548	...	0804	1131	1509	1739	...	2344
Vişeu de Jos ... d.	0513	|	0716	...	0948	|	|	1927	...	|
Sighetu Marmaţiei ... a.	0715	|	0906	...	1150	|	|	2122	...	|
Năsăud ... d.	...	0343	...	...	...	1140	1520	...	...	2352
Vatra Dornei Băi ... d.	...	0544	...	...	...	1341	1732	...	2110	0158
Câmpulung Moldovenesc .. d.	...	0650	...	...	...	1446	1837	...	2218	0303
Gura Humorului Oraş ... d.	...	0733	...	...	...	1529	1923	...	2309	0347
Suceava ... a.	...	0819	...	...	...	1613	2008	...	2356	0432
Suceava ... **1670** d.	...	0831	...	...	...	1623	2022	...	0016	0444
Vereşti ... **1670** d.	...	0845	...	...	...	1636	2035	...	0029	0457
Paşcani ... **1670** d.	...	0927	...	...	...	1716	2117	...	0108	0539
Iaşi ... a.	...	1037	...	...	...	1824	2227	...	...	0649

Δ – Distance from Salva.

For notes ♦, ♣, §, □ and • see page 518.

BUCUREŞTI - GALAŢI 1660

	1961	1771	1571		1773		§		1971		1775	1731
	♦			2		2Ⓑ		2	♦	2Ⓑ		V
Bucureşti Nord ... **1670** d.	...	0640	0830	...	1337	...	1520	1540	...	...	1808	...
Ploieşti Sud ... **1670** d.	...	|	0916	...	|	...	|	|	...	...	|	1907
Buzău ... **1670** d.	...	|	1030	1341	|	1520	|	|	...	1852	|	2020
Urziceni ... d.	...	0809	|	|	1452	|	1634	1726	...	|	1924	|
Feteşti ... d.	...	|	|	|	|	|	|	|	1740	|	|	|
Făurei ... d.	0114	0938	1113	1447	1602	1625	1746	1847	|	2014	2047	2104
Brăila ... d.	0202	1027	1202	1612	1650	1719	1836	1946	1959	2116	2136	2154
Galaţi ... a.	...	1105	1241	1633	1726	1800	1917	2030	2038	2203	2214	2233

	1962	1772	1732		§	1970	1774		1572		1776	
	♦		V	2	•	♦	•	2		2		2
Galaţi ... d.	...	0450	0550	0608	0650	0730	0900	1110	1425	1530	1730	1950
Brăila ... d.	0316	0530	0629	0652	0735	0812	0939	1158	1505	1620	1809	2038
Făurei ... d.	0406	0619	0721	0752	0823	|	1028	1259	1555	1724	1858	2138
Feteşti ... a.	...	|	|	|	|	1013	|	|	|	|	|	|
Urziceni ... d.	...	0729	|	0912	0938	...	1137	|	|	|	2020	|
Buzău ... **1670** d.	...	|	0805	|	|	...	|	1359	1641	1827	|	2235
Ploieşti Sud ... **1670** d.	...	|	0917	|	|	...	|	...	1800	...	|	...
Bucureşti Nord .. **1670** a.	...	0850	...	1037	1052	...	1300	...	1847	...	2140	...

From / to Braşov (Table **1600**).

** – Buzău - Făurei: *40 km.*
Δ – Feteşti - Făurei: *89 km.*

For notes ♦, ♣, §, □ and • see page 518.

LOCAL SERVICES 1669

l trains, 2nd class only

ĂU - PIATRA NEAMŢ - BICAZ:

						B	B
Bacău ... d.	0414	0525	0715	1430	1635	1902	2213
Piatra Neamţ . d.	0543	0657	0857	1608	1817	2033	2325
Bicaz ... a.	0627	...	...	...	1901**b**	2118	...

			B			Ⓑ	B
... d.	...	0700	...	...	...	1949**b**	2212
Neamţ ... d.	0455	0738	0919	1622	1731	2036	2244
ı ... a.	0642	0907	1029	1751	1900	2205	0007

'RIŢA - DEDA:

		Ⓐ				
Bistriţa Nord ... d.	0345	0446	0730	1220	1543	1938
Sărăţel ... d.	0401	0501	0746	1236	1615	2012
Deda ... a.	...	...	...	...	1721	2114

... d.	0457	...	...	...	1658	...
el ... d.	0617	0901	...	1415	1831	2235
a Nord ... a.	0633	0917	...	1432	1846	2253

ng-distance trains see Table **1635**.

SIGHIŞOARA - SIBIU:

km								
		⚒						•
0	**Sighişoara** ... d.	...	...	0620	...	1500	...	...
39	Mediaş ... d.	0429	0540	0742	1213	1612	...	2035
50	Copşa Mică ... d.	0450	0610	0804	1247	1656	...	2110
95	**Sibiu** ... a.	0557	0720	0913	1355	1805	...	2217

			•	•		•	Ⓑ
Sibiu ... d.	0730	...	1204	1543	...	1935	2323
Copşa Mică ... d.	0841	...	1322	1657	...	2055	0034
Mediaş ... d.	0900	...	1341	1715	...	2134	0052
Sighişoara ... a.	...	...	1450	...	...	2248	...

TÂRGU MUREŞ - RÂZBOIENI:

km								
				•				
0	**Târgu Mureş** . d.	0303	0710	1154	1438	1735	1920	2220
40	Luduş ... d.	0417	0816	1255	1545	1846	2036	2330
59	**Războieni** ... a.	0446	0843	1322	1610	1911	2105	2358

				•			
Războieni ... d.	0345	0520	0707	1146	...	1638	2005
Luduş ... d.	0416	0546	0735	1214	...	1708	2035
Târgu Mureş ... a.	0525	0651	0847	1328	...	1815	2139

For long-distance trains see Table **1610**.

ARAD - TIMISOARA *57 km*, ± 75 minutes

From Arad: 0440, 0554, 0751, 1340, 1625, 1751, 1902**y**.
From Timişoara: 0418Ⓐ, 0518, 1303, 1351, 1627, 1735, 2019, 2354.
For long-distance trains see Table **1614**.

BAIA MARE - SATU MARE *59 km*, ± 110 minutes

From Baia Mare: 0414, 0740, 0945•, 1221⚒•, 1545, 1928Ⓑ.
From Satu Mare: 0512Ⓐ, 0743, 1122⚒•, 1610, 1953.
For long-distance trains see Table **1616**.

PAŞCANI - TÂRGU NEAMT *31 km*, ± 45 minutes

From Paşcani: 0440, 0700, 1000•, 1425•, 1634, 1918.
From Târgu Neamt: 0555, 0802, 1102•, 1527•, 1736, 2020.

REŞIŢA - CARANSEBEŞ *43 km*, ± 80 minutes

From Reşiţa Sud: 0550, 0848, 1320, 1510, 1755, 2230.
From Caransebeş: 0345, 0551, 0730, 1333, 1631, 1932.
For long-distance trains see Table **1620**.

SIMERIA - HUNEDOARA *16 km*, ± 30 minutes

From Simeria: 0450, 1335, 1720.
From Hunedoara: 0545, 1430, 1820.

VEREŞTI - BOTOŞANI *44 km*, ± 65 minutes

From Vereşti: 0528, 0636, 0813, 1335•, 1748, 1850.
From Botoşani: 0508, 0804, 1122, 1511, 1917, 2100.
For long-distance trains see Table **1670**.

S for all routes

Conveys [2] from / to Bucureşti (see Table **1670**).
Ⓑ only.
①②③④⑦ only.
otes ♦, ♣, §, □ and • see page 518.

1670 BUCUREŞTI - BUZĂU - BACĂU - IASI and SUCEAVA

km		1961	1857	1861	1953	1831	1661	380	1655	♣	§	1753	1663	§	1651	1657	♣	1540	1665	1659	§	402	1559	§	1653	1667
☆		♦	♦	♦	♦	♦		♦		J2•					♦		B2•	V		♦		⊠♦		⑦	♦	⊙
0	**Bucureşti** Nord .... **1660** d.	...	...	...	...	...	0550	0615	0715	...	1015	1100	1200	1208	1345	1500	...	...	1600	1700	1737	1915	2010	2115	2130	2300
59	Ploieşti Sud .... **1660** d.	...	...	...	...	...	0635	0701	0800	0936	1111	1147	1245	1309	1433	1545	1613	...	1646	1746	1837	2006	2056	2205	2215	2345
128	**Buzău** .... **1660/80** d.	...	...	0147	0309	...	0749	0815	0914	1046	1221	1301	1359	1422	1549	1659	1728	...	1800	1856	1950	2129	2207	2315	2329	0059
161	Râmnicu Sărat .... d.	...	...	0220	0343	...	0822	0848	0947	1118	...	1333	1431	▬	1622	1731	1801	...	1833	1928	...	|	▬	...	0003	0132
199	Focşani .... d.	...	...	0300	0423	...	0902	0928	1027	1157	...	1413	1511	...	1702	1811	1841	...	1913	2008	...	2244	...	...	0044	0212
219	Mărăşeşti .... **1640** d.	...	0330	0336	0449	...	|	0951	1050	1225	...	1435	|	...	1724	1834	1913	...	|	2031	...	2312	...	...	0109	|
244	Adjud .... **1640** d.	...	0357	|	0518	...	|	1019	1118	|	...	1503	|	...	1752	1901	|	1950	|	2058	...	2342	...	...	0137	|
303	**Bacău** .... d.	...	0437	|	0559	...	|	1108	1157	|	...	1551	|	**1866**	1845	1940	|	2038	|	2151	...	0029	...	...	0228	|
346	Roman .... d.	...	0509	|	0631	...	|	1141	▬	|	...	1623	|	2	1916	...	|	2111	|	2223	...	0105	...	...	0301	|
	Galaţi .... **1640** d.	...	|	|	|	0600	|	|	...	|	...	|	|	1642	|	...	|	|	|	|	...	|	...	...	|	|
238	Tecuci .... **1640** d.	0400	|	0401n	|	0747	0955	|	...	|	...	|	1604	1826	|	...	|	|	2007	|	...	|	...	...	|	0305
288	Bârlad .... d.	0445	|	0445	|	0836	1040	|	...	1330	...	|	1655	1918	|	...	2029	|	2100	|	...	|	...	...	|	0350
340	Vaslui .... d.	0530	|	0530	|	0918	1123	|	...	1412	...	|	1738	2003	|	...	2117	|	2143	|	...	|	...	...	|	0433
408	**Iaşi** .... a.	0638	|	0638	|	1025	1231	|	2	1520	...	|	1846	2110	|	...	2232	2249	2251	|	...	0249	2	...	|	0541
408	**Iaşi** .... RO d.	...	|	...	|	...	...	|	1312	...	...	|	...	...	|	...	...	...	...	|	...	0309	0451	...	|	...
431	Ungheni **1720** 🏛 MD a.	...	|	...	|	...	...	|	1505	...	...	|	...	...	|	...	...	...	...	|	...	0502	0655	...	|	...
538	**Chişinău 1720** .... a.	...	|	...	|	...	...	|	...	...	...	|	...	...	|	...	...	...	...	|	...	0906	...	...	|	...
387	Paşcani .... **1650** d.	...	0540	...	0702	...	...	1212	...	...	...	1654	...	...	1947	...	...	...	...	2254	...	...	...	...	0332	...
432	Vereşti .... **1650** a.	...	0615	...	0738	...	...	1247	...	...	...	1736	...	...	2021	...	...	...	...	2330	...	...	...	...	0406	...
476	Botoşani **1669** .... a.	...	|	...	|	...	...	|	...	...	...	1854x	...	...	|	...	...	...	...	|	...	...	...	...	|	...
448	**Suceava** .... **1650** a.	...	0627	...	0750	...	...	1301	...	...	...	1753	...	...	2032	...	...	...	...	2349	...	...	...	...	0422	...
450	**Suceava** Nord .... ▲ RO a.	...	0638	...	0801	...	...	1330	...	...	...	...	...	...	2043	...	...	...	...	...	...	...	...	...	...	...
499	Vadul Siret .... 🏛 UA a.	...	...	...	...	...	...	1540	...	...	...	...	...	...	...	...	...	...	...	...	...	...	...	...	...	...
539	Chernivtsi .... UA a.	...	...	...	...	...	...	1910r	...	...	...	...	...	...	...	...	...	...	...	...	...	...	...	...	...	...

	1654	1558	§	1658	1650	1541	1662	1652	§	1863	1752	§	1656	1664	♣	381	1666	1832		1952	1962	1856	1862	1754	401	1668
	♦				🍷	V		♦		2•		⑦			K2•	♦		♦	2	♦	♦	♦	♦	♦	⊠♦	⊙
Chernivtsi .... UA d.	...	...	...	...	...	...	...	...	...	...	...	...	...	...	...	0925t	...	...	...	...	...	...	...	...	...	...
Vadul Siret .... 🏛 UA d.	...	...	...	...	...	...	...	...	...	...	...	...	...	...	...	1340	...	...	...	...	...	...	...	...	...	...
Suceava Nord .... ▲ RO d.	...	...	...	...	...	...	...	0850	...	...	...	...	...	...	...	1543	...	...	...	2025	...	2210	...	...	...	...
Suceava .... **1650** d.	0016	...	...	...	0500	...	...	0857	...	...	1230	...	...	...	...	1601	...	1623	...	2032	...	2217	...	2210	...	...
Botoşani **1669** .... d.	|	...	...	...	|	...	...	|	...	...	1122x	...	...	...	...	|	...	|	...	|	...	|	...	2100x	...	...
Vereşti .... **1650** d.	0029	...	...	...	|	...	...	0911	...	...	1257	...	...	...	...	1615	...	1636	...	2048	...	2232	...	2238	...	...
Paşcani .... **1650** d.	0112	...	...	...	0549	...	...	0951	...	...	1340	...	...	...	...	1657	...	1716	...	2128	...	2313	...	2321	...	...
Chişinău 1720 .... d.	|	...	...	...	|	...	...	|	...	...	|	...	...	...	...	|	...	|	...	|	...	|	...	|	1645	...
Ungheni **1720**. 🏛 MD d.	|	...	...	...	|	...	...	|	...	...	|	...	...	...	...	|	...	|	1700	|	...	|	...	|	2039	...
Iaşi .... RO a.	|	...	...	...	|	...	...	|	...	...	|	...	...	...	...	|	...	1824	1829	|	...	|	...	|	2218	...
Iaşi .... d.	|	...	...	...	|	0505	0610	|	...	0750	|	...	...	1430	1531	|	1642	1835	...	|	2235	|	2235	|	2238	2316
Vaslui .... d.	|	...	...	...	|	|	0722	|	...	0901	|	...	...	1541	1649	|	1802	1944	...	|	2348	|	2348	|	|	0034
Bârlad .... d.	|	...	...	...	|	|	0807	|	...	0949	|	...	...	1625	1732	|	1847	2028	...	|	0033	|	0033	|	|	0119
Tecuci .... **1640** d.	|	...	...	...	|	|	0904	|	...	1041	|	...	...	1707n	1814n	|	1943	2114	...	|	0117	|	0118n	|	|	0217
Galaţi .... **1640** a.	|	...	...	...	|	|	|	|	...	1218	|	...	...	|	|	|	|	2254	...	|	...	|	|	|	|	|
Roman .... d.	0140	...	...	...	0616	0638	|	1020	...	...	1408	...	...	|	|	1725	|	...	...	2155	...	2342	|	2350	0020	|
Bacău .... d.	0225	...	...	0433	0650	0719	|	1107	...	...	1449	...	1624	|	|	1800	|	...	...	2228	...	0016	|	0037	0100	|
Adjud .... **1640** d.	0312	...	...	0517	0733	0801	|	1151	...	...	1533	...	1707	|	|	1844	|	...	...	2312	...	0103	|	0120	0148	|
Mărăşeşti .... **1640** d.	0341	...	...	0547	0802	...	|	1220	...	...	1601	...	1746	1746	1850	1912	|	...	...	2341	...	0130	0200	0148	0216	|
Focşani .... d.	0407	...	...	0613	0828	...	0951	1246	...	...	1627	...	1812	1812	1917	1937	2029	...	...	0009	...	...	0225	0214	0242	0305
Râmnicu Sărat .... d.	0445	...	...	0652	0907	...	1029	1325	...	...	1705	...	1850	1850	1955	2015	2107	...	...	0050	...	...	0304	0252	|	0344
Buzău .... **1660/80** d.	0519	0650	0715	0725	0947	...	1102	1359	1455	...	1738	1900	1923	1923	2028	2048	2140	...	...	0123	...	...	0335	0331	0358	0417
Ploieşti Sud .... **1660** d.	0634	0805	0827	0839	1101	...	1217	1515	1605	...	1853	2013	2035	2035	2140	2202	2253	...	...	...	...	...	...	0446	0509	0532
Bucureşti Nord .... **1660** a.	0720	0857	0917	0925	1148	...	1303	1600	1704	...	1940	2100	2120	2120	...	2250	2337	...	...	...	...	...	...	0532	0604	0618

B – [2] Braşov - Ploieşti Vest (d. 1606) - Iaşi.
J – ①⑥⑦: [2] Braşov - Ploieşti Vest (d. 0930) - Iaşi.
K – ⑤⑥⑦: [2] Iaşi - Ploieşti Vest (a. 2148) - Braşov.
V – From / to Braşov (Table **1640**).

n – Tecuci **Nord**.
r – [2] Vadul Siret - Chernivtsi - Kyïv. On ⑦ also conveys 🛏 1, 2 cl. Bucureşti - Suceava - Vadul Siret - Chernivtsi - Kyïv.
t – [2] Kyïv - Chernivtsi - Vadul Siret. On ⑥ (⑤ from Kyïv) also conveys 🛏 1, 2 cl. Kyïv - Chernivtsi - Vadul Siret - Suceava - Bucureşti.
x – Portion attached to / detached from main train at Vereşti.

⊙ – Also conveys 🛏 1, 2 cl.
⊠ – For international journeys only.
▲ – 🏛 is Vicşani (RO).
☆ – Tecuci - Galaţi *85 km*; Iaşi - Roman 1
MD Moldova. RO Romania. UA Ukraine.
For notes ♦, ♣, §, □ and • see page 518.

1680 BUCURESTI - CONSTANŢA - MANGALIA — Summer service

km		1952	1921	1944		1962	1862	1992	1822	1989	1981	1594	1932	♣	1983	1970	1583	15983	1632		1585			1936	1587		1589	
		♦	♦	♦	2y	♦	♦	♦	♦	2y	y	♦y	♦	z	y	♦	x	□p	♦y	2w		2	2w	Ry		2t		2y
0	**Bucureşti** Nord ..... d.	...	0255	0418b	...	...	...	0456b	0617	0642	0725	0805	0820	0845	0900	...	0930	0955	1040	...	1400	...	...	1510	1600	...	1700	...
	Buzău .... d.	0144	|	|	...	...	0355	|	|	|	|	|	|	|	|	...	|	|	|	...	|	...	...	|	|	...	|	...
	Făurei .... d.	0235	|	|	...	0426	0439	|	|	|	|	|	|	|	|	...	|	|	|	...	|	...	...	|	|	...	|	...
146	Feteşti .... d.	0350	0429	0535	...	0551	0605	0619	0740	0817	0844	0921	0943	|	|	1016	1050	1108	1156	...	1520	...	...	1630	|	...	1819	...
190	Medgidia .... d.	0438	0516	0622	0629	0637	0651	|	0825	0910	0926	|	1029	|	|	1102	1135	|	|	...	1605	1619	...	1716	|	...	1905	...
334	**Tulcea** Oraş ...... a.	|	|	|	1005	|	|	|	|	1200	|	|	|	|	|	|	|	|	|	...	|	1945	...	|	|	...	|	...
225	**Constanţa** .... a.	0502	0605	0654	...	0701	0718	0732	0856	...	0949	1026	1104	1143	1100	1125	1158	1210	1259	...	1628	...	...	1740	1800	...	1928	...
225	**Constanţa** .... d.	0526	0630	0717	...	...	...	0747	0922v	...	1005	1047	1131	...	...	...	...	...	...	1411	...	...	1701	...	...	1901	...	1952
239	Eforie Nord .... d.	0551	0702	0744	...	...	...	0822	0950v	...	1031	1114	1157	...	...	...	...	...	...	1437	...	...	1727	...	...	1935	...	2021
268	**Mangalia** .... a.	0651	0809	0847	...	...	...	0920	1055v	...	1129	1222	1314	...	...	...	...	...	...	1544	...	...	1826	...	...	2047	...	2130

km		1636				1580		1937	1582		1633	1593	15984	1988	1971	1586	1945	1931		♣	1588	1982	1922		1821	1991	1861	1961
		R	2y	2	2y		2w	Ry		2y	♦y	♦y	□p	2y	♦		♦	♦	2n	z		y	♦	2	♦	♦	♦	♦
	Mangalia .... d.	...	0500	...	0700	...	0900	...	...	1109	...	1255	...	...	...	...	1523	1556	1606	...	...	1720	1805	...	1848v	1935	...	...
	Eforie Nord .... d.	...	0607	...	0802	...	1008	...	...	1215	...	1400	...	...	...	...	1626	1659	1707	...	...	1829	1916	...	1956v	2042	...	...
	Constanţa .... a.	...	0654	...	0830	...	1037	...	...	1242	...	1436	...	...	...	...	1652	1729	1735	...	...	1859	1942	...	2025v	2109	...	...
0	**Constanţa** .... d.	0530	...	...	...	0840	...	1030	1300	...	1400	1500	1603	...	1630	1700	1715	1745	...	1808	1850	1924	2000	...	2045	2135	2200	2210
	Tulcea Oraş ...... d.	|	...	0525	...	|	...	|	|	...	|	|	|	1335	|	|	|	|	...	|	|	|	|	1615	|	|	|	|
35	Medgidia .... d.	0553	...	0848	...	0904	...	1054	|	...	1424	1524	|	1632	1654	1725	1740	1810	...	|	|	1948	2026	1942	2109	2201	2225	2235
79	Feteşti .... d.	0638	...	...	...	0949	...	1139	|	...	1509	1608	1707	1720	1740	1810	1825	1857	...	|	|	2029	2112	...	2156	2248	2312	2330
168	Făurei .... d.	|	...	...	...	|	...	|	|	...	|	|	|	|	...	|	|	|	...	|	|	|	|	...	|	|	0046	0056
208	Buzău .... a.	|	...	...	...	|	...	|	|	...	|	|	|	|	...	|	|	|	...	|	|	|	|	...	|	|	0127	...
	Bucureşti Nord ..... a.	0757	...	...	...	1107	...	1257	1500	...	1627	1726	1820	1856	...	1927	1940b	2022	...	2055	2050	2147	2245	...	2320	0010b	...	...

♦ – NOTES (LISTED BY TRAIN NUMBER)

1593/4 – [12] Craiova - Bucureşti (- Mangalia, June 11 - Sept. 11) and v.v.

1632/3 – [12] Braşov - Bucureşti (- Constanţa, June 11 - Sept. 11) and v.v.

1821/2 – 🛏, 🛌 and [12] Arad - Craiova - Bucureşti - Constanţa and v.v. Train extended Constanţa - Mangalia and v.v. June 10 - Sept. 9 (from Arad), June 11 - Sept. 10 (from Mangalia).

1861/2 – Not June 17 - Sept. 9 (from Iaşi and Suceava); not June 18 - Sept. 10 (from Constanţa): [12] Iaşi - Constanţa and v.v.; [2] Suceava Nord - Mărăşeşti (**1856/7**) and v.v.

1921/2 – June 10 - Sept. 10 (from Sibiu); June 9 - Sept. 9 (from Mangalia): [12] Sibiu - Bucureşti - Mangalia and v.v.

1931/2 – June 24 - Sept. 10 (from Oradea); June 25 - Sept. 11 (from Mangalia): 🛏, 🛌 and [12] Oradea - Bucureşti - Constanţa - Mangalia and v.v.

1944/5 – June 17 - Sept. 11 (from Satu Mare / Sighetu Marmaţiei / Târgu Mureş); June 18 - Sept. 12 (from Mangalia): 🛏, 🛌 and [12] Satu Mare - Mangalia and v.v.; [12] Sighetu Marmaţiei (**1946/7**) - Beclean pe Someş - Mangalia and v.v.; [2] Târgu Mureş (**1948/9**) - Deda - Mangalia and v.v.

1946/7 – June 17 - Sept. 11 (from Sighetu Marmaţiei); June 18 - Sept. 12 (from Mangalia): [12] Sighetu Marmaţiei - Beclean pe Someş (**1944/5**) - Mangalia and v.v.

1948/9 – June 17 - Sept. 11 (from Târgu Mureş); June 18 - Sept. 12 (from Mangalia): [2] Târgu M Deda (**1944/5**) - Mangalia and v.v.

1952/3 – June 17 - Sept. 9 (from Suceava); June 18 - Sept. 10 (from Mangalia): 🛌 and [12] Suc Constanţa - Mangalia and v.v.

1961/2 – June 17 - Sept. 9 (from Iaşi); June 18 - Sept. 10 (from Constanţa): [12] Iaşi - Constar and v.v.

1970/1 – June 18 - Sept. 11: [12] Galaţi - Constanţa and v.v.

1991/2 – June 10 - Sept. 10 (from Timişoara / Reşiţa / Deva); June 11 - Sept. 11 (from Mangalia): 🛏 and [12] Timişoara - Mangalia and v.v.; [12] Reşiţa Sud (**1998/9**) - Caransebeş - Ma and v.v.; [12] Deva (**1995/6**) - Craiova - Mangalia and v.v.

1995/6 – June 10 - Sept. 10 (from Deva); June 11 - Sept. 11 (from Mangalia): [12] Deva - C (**1991/2**) - Mangalia and v.v.

1998/9 – June 10 - Sept. 10 (from Reşiţa); June 11 - Sept. 11 (from Mangalia): [12] Reşiţa Caransebeş (**1991/2**) - Mangalia and v.v.

R – From / to Braşov.
b – Bucureşti **Băneasa**.
n – Not June 25 - Sept. 11.
p – May 15 - Sept. 15.
t – June 9 - Sept. 11.

v – June 11 - Sept. 10.
w – June 11 - Sept. 12.
x – June 25 - Sept. 11.
y – June 11 - Sept. 11.
z – June 17 - Sept. 4.

For notes ♦, ♣, §, □ and • see page 518.

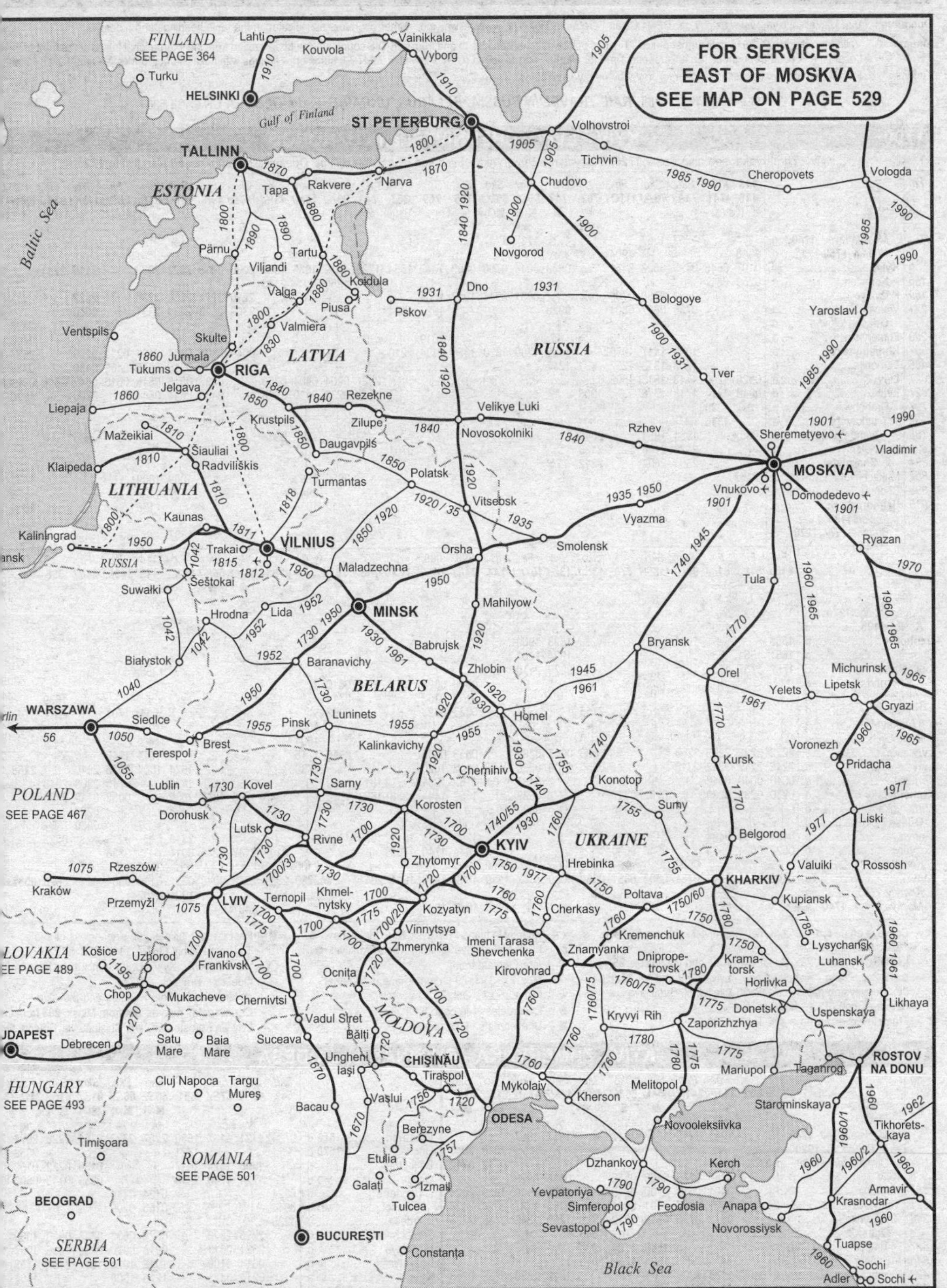

FOR SERVICES EAST OF MOSKVA SEE MAP ON PAGE 529
FINLAND
SEE PAGE 364
Lahti
Kouvola
Vainikkala
Vyborg
Turku
HELSINKI
Gulf of Finland
ST PETERBURG
Volhovstroi
Tichvin
Cheropovets
Vologda
TALLINN
ESTONIA
Tapa
Rakvere
Narva
Chudovo
Novgorod
Baltic Sea
Pärnu
Viljandi
Tartu
Koidula
Valga
Piusa
Pskov
Dno
Bologoye
Yaroslavl
Ventspils
Skulte
Valmiera
LATVIA
RUSSIA
Jurmala
Tukums
RIGA
Jelgava
Tver
Liepaja
Rezekne
Krustpils
Zilupe
Velikye Luki
Novosokolniki
Rzhev
Sheremetyevo
Vladimir
Mažeikiai
Šiauliai
Radviliškis
Daugavpils
Klaipeda
LITHUANIA
Turmantas
Polatsk
MOSKVA
Vnukovo
Domodedevo
Vitsebsk
Vyazma
Kaunas
Kaliningrad
Trakai
VILNIUS
Smolensk
Ryazan
RUSSIA
Orsha
Šeštokai
Suwałki
Maladzechna
Tula
Hrodna
Lida
MINSK
Mahilyow
Białystok
Babrujsk
Bryansk
Baranavichy
BELARUS
Zhlobin
Orel
Michurinsk
Lipetsk
Yelets
WARSZAWA
Siedlce
Pinsk
Luninets
Homel
Gryazi
Terespol
Brest
Kalinkavichy
Chernihiv
Kursk
Voronezh
Pridacha
POLAND
SEE PAGE 467
Lublin
Kovel
Sarny
Konotop
Dorohusk
Korosten
Sumy
Liski
Lutsk
Rivne
KYIV
UKRAINE
Belgorod
Zhytomyr
Hrebinka
Valuiki
Rossosh
Kraków
Rzeszów
KHARKIV
Przemyžl
LVIV
Ternopil
Khmelnytsky
Kozyatyn
Poltava
Kupiansk
Cherkasy
Vinnytsya
Zhmerynka
Imeni Tarasa Shevchenka
Kremenchuk
Znamyanka
Lysychansk
SLOVAKIA
SEE PAGE 489
Košice
Uzhorod
Ivano Frankivsk
Ocniţa
Kirovohrad
Dnipropetrovsk
Kramatorsk
Luhansk
Horlivka
Chop
Mukacheve
Chernivtsi
Donetsk
Likhaya
Vadul Siret
MOLDOVA
Krivyi Rih
Zaporizhzhya
Uspenskaya
BUDAPEST
Debrecen
Satu Mare
Baia Mare
Suceava
Bălţi
Ungheni
Iaşi
CHIŞINĂU
Tiraspol
Mariupol
Taganrog
ROSTOV NA DONU
HUNGARY
SEE PAGE 493
Cluj Napoca
Targu Mureş
Vaslui
Mykolaiv
Kherson
Melitopol
Bacau
ODESA
Starominskaya
Novooleksiivka
Berezyne
Tikhoretskaya
Timişoara
Etulia
Dzhankoy
Kerch
ROMANIA
SEE PAGE 501
Galaţi
Izmail
Yevpatoriya
Simferopol
Feodosia
Anapa
Armavir
Krasnodar
BEOGRAD
Tulcea
Sevastopol
Novorossiysk
Tuapse
BUCUREŞTI
SERBIA
SEE PAGE 501
Constanţa
Black Sea
Sochi
Adler

UKRAINE and MOLDOVA

SEE MAP PAGE

Operators: **UZ**: Ukrzaliznytsya, www.uz.gov.ua **CFM**: Calea Ferată din Moldova, www.railway.md Other operators as indicated in the table headings and notes.

Timings: Valid from **March 27, 2016** until further notice.. Timings of international services to and from non-CIS countries should be verified from the international tables at the front of this Local time is used throughout: East European Time for Ukraine and Moldova (GMT+2 winter, GMT+3 summer) – timings within Russia are in Moskva time (GMT+3 all y

Tickets: Prior reservation is necessary except for travel by purely local trains.

SEE ALSO THE PANEL ***RAIL TRAVEL IN RUSSIA, BELARUS, UKRAINE, and MOLDOVA*** ON PAGE 530

1700 KYÏV - LVIV - CHERNIVTSI and UZHOROD — UZ,

Kyïv - Zhmerynka: see also Table **1720**. Kozyatyn - Zhmerynka - Lviv: see also Table **1775**. Odesa - Zhmerynka: see also Table **1720**.

km		113 115	IC 741 ≋	Sko 73AJ ★	Sko 73AJ ☆	Fir 111OJ	702 ♥ ④–②	IC 747 ≋	Sko 55MJ ■(3) ★	Sko 55MJ ■(3) ☆	755	769	357	IC 743 ≋	Sko 99KJ	Sko 13KJ	Sko 43KJ	Sko 117LJ B	Fir 49KJ	Sko 81DJ L	Sko 81DJ	Fir 26SH	Sko 143KJ	Fir 91KJ	Fir 108SH
	Moskva Kiyev. **1740** d.	...	...	1557	1557	...	...	...	1737	1737	...	...	...	...	...	...	...	...	...	...	...	...	...	...	...
	Kharkiv **1750** d.	1848	...	|	|	1904	...	...	|	|	...	...	...	...	...	...	...	...	...	...	...	...	...	...	...
0	**Kyïv** d.	0107	0645	0423	0523	0451	...	0653	0544	0700	0803	1642	1654	1720	1739	1835	1850	2005	2015	2022	2022	...	2110	2241	...
156	Korosten d.	0256	0817	|	|	|	...	|	|	|	|	|	|	1852	1950	|	2113	|	|	|	|	...	|	|	...
159	Kozyatyn d.	|	|	0633	0758	0700	...	|	0831	0946	1017	1832	|	|	|	|	|	2210	2221	2236	2236	...	2322	|	...
221	Vinnytsya d.	|	|	0736	0857	0804	...	0926	|	|	|	1923	1954	|	|	|	|	2303	2315	2331	2331	...	0020	|	...
	Odesa Holovna d.	|	|	|	|	|	...	|	|	|	|	|	|	|	|	⊙	|	|	|	|	|	1826	|	|	2126
268	Zhmerynka d.	|	|	|	|	0913	...	|	|	|	|	2019	|	|	|	|	|	|	|	|	|	0041	|	|	0403
367	**Khmelnytsky** d.	|	|	1003	1117	1050	...	1109	1200	1320	1350	2134	2210	|	|	|	|	0049	0101	0124	0124	0211	0226	|	0537
486	Ternopil d.	|	|	1203	1313	1257	...	1242	...	...	...	...	2359	|	|	|	|	|	0245	0315	0315	0406	0430	|	0738
*627	**Lviv** a.	0825	1200	1413	1515	1502	...	...	...	...	...	...	|	2221	0204	0404	0253	|	0432	0516	0516	0615	0642	0606	0944
*627	**Lviv** d.	0848	1214	1718	1718	...	1908	...	...	...	...	...	|	...	0232	0430	0313	|	0455	0544	0544	...	0708	...	1010
727	Drohobych a.	|	1325	|	|	...	|	...	...	...	...	...	|	...	|	|	|	|	0730	|	|	...	|	...	|
739	**Truskavets** a.	|	1346	|	|	...	|	...	...	...	...	...	|	...	|	|	|	|	0759	|	|	...	|	...	|
768	Ivano-Frankivsk a.	1058x	...	1954	1954	...	2048	...	...	...	...	...	|	...	|	|	0544	|	...	|	|	...	0935	...	|
823	Kolomyya a.	|	...	2126	2126	...	2138	...	...	...	...	...	0701	...	|	|	...	|	...	|	|	...	...	...	|
894	**Chernivtsi** a.	|	...	2304	2304	...	2242	...	...	...	...	...	⊡	...	|	|	...	0710	...	|	|	...	...	...	|
852	Mukacheve d.	1246x	...	...	...	...	...	...	...	...	...	...	...	...	0650	0853	...	...	...	1009	1009	...	...	...	1433
893	Chop § a.	...	...	...	...	...	...	...	...	...	...	...	...	...	|	0947	...	...	...	1107	1107	...	...	...	1523
915	**Uzhhorod** a.	...	...	...	...	...	...	...	...	...	...	...	...	...	0812	1035	...	...	...	|	1158	...	...	...	1616
	Košice **1195** a.	...	...	...	...	...	...	...	...	...	...	...	...	...	...	...	...	...	...	|	...	...	...	...	...
	Budapest Ny. **1270** a.	...	...	...	...	...	...	...	...	...	...	...	...	...	...	...	...	...	...	1837	...	...	...	...	...

	Fir 81LJ	Fir 81LJ L	Fir 81LJ P	Sko 99LJ	Sko 118SH B	770	Sko 43CJ	Sko 13LJ	Fir 107LJ	IC 744 ≋	608 74LJ ★	608 74LJ ☆	772	IC 748 ≋	702 ♥ ⑤–③	IC 742 ≋	755	Sko 55KJ ● ★	Sko 55KJ ● ☆	Fir 112LJ	114 115	Sko 143LJ	Fir 26LJ	358	Fir 92LJ
Budapest Ny. **1270** d.	...	0723	...	...	...	...	...	...	...	...	...	...	...	...	...	...	...	...	...	...	...	...	...	...	...
Košice **1195** d.	...	|	1006	...	...	...	...	...	...	...	...	...	...	...	...	...	...	...	...	...	...	...	...	...	...
Uzhhorod d.	1550	|	|	1644	...	...	...	1828	1900	...	...	...	...	...	...	...	...	...	...	...	...	...	...	...	...
Chop § d.	1651	1651	1651	|	...	...	...	1924	2002	...	...	...	...	...	...	...	...	...	...	...	...	...	...	...	...
Mukacheve d.	1757	1757	1757	1817	...	...	...	2029	2110	...	...	...	...	...	...	...	...	...	...	...	1355z	...	...	...	...
Chernivtsi d.	|	|	|	|	1955	...	...	|	|	...	0028	0028	...	...	0610	...	...	...	...	...	|	...	...	⊡	...
Kolomyya d.	|	|	|	|	|	...	...	|	|	...	0152	0152	...	...	0711	...	...	...	...	...	|	...	...	1639	...
Ivano-Frankivsk d.	|	|	|	|	|	...	2155	|	|	...	0323	0323	...	...	0802	...	...	...	...	...	1534z	1701	...	|	...
Truskavets d.	|	|	|	|	|	...	|	|	|	...	|	|	...	...	|	1543	...	...	...	...	|	|	...	|	...
Drohobych d.	|	|	|	|	|	...	|	|	|	...	|	|	...	...	|	1604	...	...	...	...	|	|	...	|	...
Lviv a.	2222	2222	2222	2258	|	...	0030	0045	0205	...	0655	0655	...	...	0945	1715	...	...	...	...	1744	1945	...	|	...
Lviv d.	2242	2242	2242	2318	|	...	0050	0108	0228	0620	0942	1020	...	...	...	1730	...	...	...	1624	1804	2005	2040	|	2258
Ternopil d.	0040	0040	0040	|	|	...	|	|	0437	|	1152	1231	...	1514	...	|	...	...	...	1838	|	2215	2308	2343	|
Khmelnytsky d.	0230	0230	0230	|	0252	0317	|	|	0639	|	1352	1444	1358	1653	...	|	1648	1748	1848	2036	|	0032	0110	0136	|
Zhmerynka d.	|	|	|	|	|	0456	|	|	0830	|	|	|	1533	|	...	|	|	|	|	2228	|	|	0258	|	|
Odesa Holovna a.	|	|	|	|	|	|	|	⊙	1441	|	|	|	|	|	...	|	|	|	|	|	|	|	0850	|	|
Vinnytsya d.	0434	0434	0434	|	0450	0538	|	|	...	|	1550	1646	1617	1833	...	|	|	|	|	2318	|	0233	...	0323	|
Kozyatyn d.	0524	0524	0524	|	0546	0630	|	|	...	|	1644	1740	1709	|	...	|	2109	2147	2246	0014	|	0326	...	|	|
Korosten d.	|	|	|	0502	|	|	0642	|	...	0950	|	|	|	|	...	2100	|	|	|	|	2338	|	...	|	|
Kyïv a.	0743	0743	0743	0731	0803	0831	0850	1000	...	1119	1852	1946	1911	2051	...	2230	2311	2348	0048	0221	0119	0551	...	0626	0637
Kharkiv **1750** a.	...	...	...	...	...	...	...	...	...	...	|	|	...	...	...	...	...	|	|	1221	0802	...	...	...	...
Moskva Kiyev. **1740** a.	...	...	...	...	...	...	...	...	...	...	1037	1037	...	...	...	...	...	1437	1437	...	...	...	...	...	...

B – Conveys on ⑤ 🛏 1, 2 cl. Kyïv - Chernivtsi - Bucuresti (Table **1670**), returning on ⑦.

L – LATORCA – 🛏 1, 2 cl. Budapest - Kyïv and v.v. (Table **96**).

P – 🛏 1, 2 cl. Praha - Košice - Chop - Lviv - Kyïv and v.v. (Table **96**). Conveys on dates in Table **96** 🛏 1, 2 cl. Bratislava - Košice - Chop - Lviv - Kyïv and v.v.

R – From/to Kovel; for days see Table **1730**.

x – Kharkiv to Ivano-Frankivsk ■, to Mukacheve ●.

z – From Mukacheve ■, from Ivano-Frankivsk ●.

≋ – *InterCity* fast train.

☆ – Mar. 27 - Oct. 29 (summer time in Ukraine).

★ – Not Mar. 27 - Oct. 29.

● – Even dates (see page 530).

■ – Uneven dates (see page 530).

♥ – Fast diesel multiple unit; single class of seats.

⊡ – To/from Rakhiv (**357** a. 1112/**358** d. 1230).

⊙ – Via Berdychiv (Kyïv - Lviv via this route is *566 km*).

⊖ – Odessa - Tiraspol: *120 km*.

§ – 🏛 for trains to/from Hungary and Slovakia.

‡ – Certain dates runs as **284** from Minsk, **283** from O

* – Lviv via Korosten *572 km*, Chişinău via Tiraspol *69*

1720 KYÏV - ZHMERYNKA - CHIŞINĂU and ODESA — UZ, C

km		802	Pas 341FJ ★	Pas 341FJ ☆	Sko 65MJ ● ★	Sko 65MJ ● ☆	Sko 642 ⑤–⑦	Sko 47MZ ★	Sko 47MZ ☆	Sko 61MZ ■(3) ★	Sko 61MZ ■(3) ☆
	Moskva Kiyev. **1740** d.	...	1243	1243	1617	1617	...	1957	1957	...	...
	St P'burg Vit. **1920** d.	...	|	|	|	|	...	|	|	2040	2040
	Orsha Tsent. **1920** d.	...	|	|	|	|	...	|	|	0712	0712
0	**Kyïv** ▷ d.	...	0140	0245	0456	0556	...	0835	0929	|	|
157	Kozyatyn ▷ d.	...	0401	0513	0700	0815	...	1052	1140	1929	2024
221	Vinnytsya ▷ d.	...	0505	0625	0801	0914	...	1153	1237	2029	2126
268	Zhmerynka UA d.	...	0611	0735	0912	1022	...	1259	1343	2133	2234
⊖	**Odesa** d.	...	|	|	|	|	1648	|	|	|	|
627	Tiraspol MD d.	...	|	|	1548	1704	1930	|	|	|	|
640	Bender 2 d.	...	|	|	1634	1750	2013	|	|	|	|
422	Ocniţa MD d.	0407	1135	1306	|	|	|	1812	1830	0135	0248
520	Bălţi Oraş d.	0644	1433	1553	|	|	|	2015	2033	0344	0457
598	Ungheni **1670** a.	0830	1626	1739	|	|	|	|	|	|	|
*705	**Chişinău** **1670** a.	1048	1934	2039	1825	1933	2154	2355	0013	0717	0831

	Sko 642 ⑤–⑦	Sko 47SZ ★	Sko 47SZ ☆	801	Sko 66SZ ■(3) ★	Sko 66SZ ■(3) ☆	Sko 61SZ ■(1) ★	Sko 61SZ ■(1) ☆	Pas 341MZ ★
Chişinău **1670** d.	0734	1121	1137	1550	2257	2323	2151	2226	2037
Ungheni **1670** d.	|	|	|	1821	|	|	|	|	2359
Bălţi Oraş d.	|	1508	1524	2017	|	|	0136	0222	0150
Ocniţa MD d.	|	1724	1740	2249	|	|	0355	0443	0503
Bender 2 d.	0924	|	|	...	0134	0144	|	|	|
Tiraspol MD d.	0944	|	|	...	0158	0209	|	|	|
Odesa a.	1225	|	|	...	|	|	|	|	|
Zhmerynka UA d.	...	2235	2320	...	0827	0835	0846	0930	1009
Vinnytsya ▷ d.	...	2321	0015	...	0918	0926	0935	1036	1057
Kozyatyn ▷ d.	...	0014	0109	...	1012	1023	1047	1151	1152
Kyïv ▷ a.	...	0214	0311	...	1216	1308	|	|	1404
Orsha Tsent. **1920** a.	...	|	|	...	|	|	0028	0028	|
St P'burg Vit. **1920** a.	...	|	|	...	|	|	1143	1143	|
Moskva Kiyev. **1740** a.	...	1659	1659	...	0432	0432	...	...	0518

km		84 R	Sko 94BJ ● ★‡	Sko 94BJ ● ☆‡	Sko 89KJ ■(3) ★	Sko 89KJ ■(3) ☆	Fir 23MJ ★	Fir 23MJ ☆		IC 763 ≋	Fir 105KJ
	Moskva Kiyev. **1740** d.	...	...	...	1737	1737	2121	2121	...	...	...
	Minsk **1930** d.	...	1348	1348	|	|	|	|	...	...	...
0	**Kyïv** ▷ d.	...	0115	0206	0544	0700	0858	1008	...	1636	2103
159	Kozyatyn ▷ d.	0156	0319	0410	0806	0921	1106	1217	...	|	2314
221	Vinnytsya ▷ d.	0305	0422	0509	0908	1029	1210	1321	...	1852	0010
268	Zhmerynka **1700** d.	0411	0528	0614	0958	1118	1310	1422	...	1927	0107
387	**Odesa** Holovna **1700** a.	1005	1109	1205	...	...	1901	2009	...	2331	0618

	IC 764 ≋	Sko 90KJ ● ★	Sko 90KJ ● ☆		Sko 94SH ■(3) ★‡	Sko 94SH ■(3) ☆‡	Fir 24SH ★	Fir 24SH ☆	84 R
Odesa Holovna **1700** d.	0542	...	...	...	1433	1549	1513	1540	1816
Zhmerynka **1700** d.	0953	1908	2008	...	2057	2206	2110	2153	0033
Vinnytsya ▷ d.	1028	2002	2102	...	2146	2253	2159	2242	0127
Kozyatyn ▷ d.	|	2147	2246	...	2241	2349	2253	2340	0238
Kyïv ▷ a.	1241	2348	0048	...	0047	0153	0054	0142	...
Minsk **1930** a.	...	|	|	...	1339	1339	|	|	...
Moskva Kiyev. **1740** a.	...	1437	1437	...	...	...	1516	1516	...

FOR OTHER NOTES SEE TABLE 1700

▷ – See also Table **1700**.

MD – Moldova (GMT+2 in winter, GMT+3 in summer).

UA – Ukraine (GMT+2 in winter, GMT+3 in summer).

Note that Tiraspol and Bender (formerly Tighina) are locat in the partly-recognised autonomous region of Transnistria

KYÏV - KOVEL - DOROHUSK - (WARSZAWA) 1730

PKP

	84	77	77	141	767	67	97	371	371
	R	M	M			K		■(1)	■(1)
		★	☆					★	☆
Moskva Kiyevskaya **1740** . d.	...	1557	1557	...	...	...	...	...	...
Kyïv d.	...	0443	0538	1544	1648	1648	2146	...	...
Korosten d.	...	0655	0744	1825	|	|	2352	...	...
Minsk d.	...	|	|	|	|	|	|	1942	1942
Baranavichy Polesskiye d.	...	|	|	|	|	|	|	2234	2234
Luninets BY d.	...	|	|	|	|	|	|	0035	0035
Sarny ‡UA d.	▽	|	|	2142	|	|	|	0303	0417
Rivne d.	0648	1149	1225	|	2202	2202	0352	0433	0602
Lutsk d.	0830	1327	1401	|	2339	2339	0534	|	|
Kovel d.	1046	1512	1546	0022	0120	0145	0735	|	|
Lviv a.	...	...	...	0440	...	|	...	0800	0923
Yahodyn UA d.	...	...	...	...	...	0457	...	...	...
Dorohusk PL a.	...	...	...	...	...	0411	...	...	...
Lublin **1055** a.	...	...	...	...	...	0645	...	...	...
Warszawa Cent. **1055** a.	...	...	...	...	...	0910	...	...	...

	1201 68	768	78	78	84	372	372	98	142
	K		M	M	S	●	●		
			★	☆		★	☆		
Warszawa Cent. **1055** d.	1950	...	...	...	...	...	...	...	...
Lublin **1055** d.	2213	...	...	...	...	...	...	...	...
Dorohusk PL d.	0010	...	...	...	...	...	...	...	...
Yahodyn UA d.	0320	...	...	...	...	...	...	...	...
Lviv d.	|	...	...	...	...	1752	1830	...	2146
Kovel d.	0440	0440	0917	1013	1755	|	|	2016	0213
Lutsk d.	0635	0635	1127	1233	2012	|	|	2226	|
Rivne d.	0752	0752	1249	1354	2136	2152	2244	2355	|
Sarny ‡UA d.	|	|	|	|	▽	2325	0018	|	0440
Luninets BY d.	|	|	|	|	...	0427	0427	|	|
Baranavichy Polesskiye d.	|	|	|	|	...	0704	0704	|	|
Minsk a.	|	|	|	|	...	0910	0910	|	|
Korosten d.	|	|	1700	1752	...	...	...	0355	0810
Kyïv a.	1258	1258	1921	2012	...	...	...	0557	1020
Moskva Kiyevskaya **1740** a.	...	...	1037	1037	...	...	...	...	...

KYÏV EKSPRES / KIEV EXPRESS – 1, 2 cl. Kyïv - Warszawa and v.v.
Moskva (**73/4**) - Kyïv (**77/8**) - Kovel and v.v.
From Odesa ● (daily June 3 - Sept. 19).

S – ■(1) (daily June 2 - Sept. 18).
☆ – Mar. 27 - Oct. 29 (summer time in Ukraine).
★ – Not Mar. 27 - Oct. 29.
▽ – To / from Odesa (Table **1720**).

● – Even dates (see page 530).
■ – Uneven dates (see page 530).
‡ – : Horyn (BY) / Udrytsk (UA).
* – Distance from Lviv.

BY – Belarus (GMT + 3 all year).
PL – Poland (Central European Time).
UA – Ukraine (East European Time).

MOSKVA - BRYANSK - KONOTOP - KYÏV 1740

D, UZ

	Pas 341*FJ*	*Pas* 341*FJ*	*Sko* 103*MJ*	*Sko* 61*KH*	*Sko* 61*KH*	*Sko* 73*AJ*	*Sko* 73*AJ*	*Sko* 65*MJ*	*Sko* 65*MJ*		*Sko* 55*MJ*	*Sko* 55*MJ*	*Fir* 5*JA*	*Fir* 5*JA*	*Fir* 5*JA*	*Fir* 5*JA*	*Sko* 105*MJ*	*Sko* 47*MZ*	*Sko* 47*MZ*	*Fir* 23*MJ*	*Fir* 23*MJ*	*Fir* 99*CH*
				●	●	L	L	●	●		■(3)	■(3)										
	★	☆		★	☆	★	☆	★	☆		★	☆	★	★	☆	☆		★	☆	★	☆	
Moskva Kiyevskaya d.	1243	1243	1330	1533	1533	1557	1557	1617	1617	...	1737	1737	1855	1855	1855	1855	1920	1957	1957	2121	2121	2355
Bryansk Orlovski d.	|	|	1745	|	|	2203	2203	2312	2312	...	|	|	|	|	|	|	2335	|	|	0302x	0302x	0655
Suzemka RU d.	|	|	...	2350	2350	|	|	|	|	...	|	|	|	|	|	|	...	|	|	0443	0443	...
Zernove UA d.	|	|	...	2345	0045	|	|	|	|	...	|	|	|	|	|	|	...	|	|	|	|	...
Konotop d.	2234	2334	...	0136	0233	0120	0220	0215	0315	...	0255	0355	0352	0410	0452	0510	...	0527	0622	0558	0658	...
Chernihiv a.	|	|	...	△	△	|	|	|	|	...	|	|	|	0730	|	0835	...	|	|	|	|	...
Kyïv a.	0120	0220	...	...	...	0403	0503	0441	0541	...	0533	0631	0623	...	0726	...	...	0816	0906	0840	0936	...
Odesa Holovna **1720** a.	|	|	...	...	...	|	|	|	|	...	▽	▽	...	...	...	...	...	|	|	1901	2009	...
Chişinău **1720** a.	1934	2039	...	...	...	|	|	1825	1933	...	...	...	...	...	...	...	...	2355	0013	...	...	...
Lviv **1700** a.	...	...	...	...	...	1413	1515	...	...	...	...	...	...	...	...	...	...	...	...	...	...	...
Chernivtsi **1700** a.	...	...	...	...	...	2304	2304	...	...	...	...	...	...	...	...	...	...	...	...	...	...	...

	Sko 55*KJ*	*Sko* 55*KJ*	*Fir* 24*SH*	*Fir* 24*SH*	*Sko* 47*SZ*	*Sko* 47*SZ*	*Sko* 104*MJ*	*Sko* 106*MJ*	*Sko* 66*SZ*	*Sko* 66*SZ*	*Pas* 341*MZ*	*Pas* 341*MZ*	*Fir* 100*CH*		*Fir* 6*OJ*	*Fir* 6*OJ*	*Fir* 6*OJ*	*Fir* 6*OJ*		*Sko* 74*LJ*	*Sko* 74*LJ*	*Sko* 61*SH*	*Sko* 61*SH*
	●	●‡							■(3)	■(3)						⊙		⊙		L	L	■(1)	■(1)
	★	☆	★	☆	★	☆			★	☆	★	☆			★	★	☆	☆		★	☆	★	☆
ernivtsi **1700** d.	...	...	...	...	...	...	...	...	...	...	...	...	...	...	...	...	...	...	...	0028	0028	...	...
v **1700** d.	...	...	...	...	...	...	...	...	...	...	...	...	...	...	...	...	...	...	...	0942	1020	...	...
işinău **1720** d.	...	...	...	...	1121	1137	...	...	2257	2323	2037	2132	...	...	...	...	...	...	...	|	|	...	...
esa Holovna **1720** d.	▽	▽	1513	1540	|	|	...	...	|	|	|	|	...	...	...	...	...	...	...	|	|	...	...
d.	2358	0058	0109	0202	0229	0328	...	...	1236	1328	1424	1524	...	...	1938	...	2035	...	...	1952	2042	...	...
ernihiv d.	|	|	|	|	|	|	...	...	|	|	|	|	...	...	|	1903	|	1957	...	|	|	△	△
top d.	0257	0357	0355	0455	0523	0623	...	...	1552	1652	1725	1825	...	...	2238	2238	2338	2338	...	2249	2346	2344	0044
ove UA d.	|	|	|	|	|	|	...	...	|	|	|	|	...	...	|	|	|	|	...	|	|	0208	0308
mka RU d.	0640	0640	0730	0730	0944	0944	...	...	2026	2026	2204	2204	...	...	|	|	|	|	...	|	|	|	|
nsk Orlovski d.	|	|	0910	0910	|	|	1330	1855	2215	2215	|	|	2345	...	|	|	|	|	...	0451	0451	|	|
kva Kiyevskaya a.	1437	1437	1516	1516	1659	1659	1745	2315	0432	0432	0518	0518	0644	...	0948	0948	0948	0948	...	1037	1037	1111	1111

Also conveys Moskva - Kyïv - Kovel and v.v. (Table **1730**).
Bryansk **Lgovski**.
To / from Mykolaiv and Kherson (Table **1760**).
To / from Khmelnytsky (Table **1700**) and Zhmerynka (Table **1720**).

☆ – Mar. 27 - Oct. 29 (summer time in Ukraine).
★ – Not Mar. 27 - Oct. 29.
● – Even dates (see page 530).
■ – Uneven dates (see page 530).

⊙ – Train number **658***KJ* Chernihiv - Konotop.
‡ – Next day from Kyïv.
RU – Russia (Moskva Time GMT + 3).
UA – Ukraine (GMT + 2 in winter, GMT + 3 in summer).

KYÏV - POLTAVA - KHARKIV 1750

	114 115	112	*IC* 712	*IC* 722	*IC* 724	92	*IC* 726	126	124	64
Lviv **1700** d.	1804	1624	...	...	...	...	...	...	...	...
Kyïv d.	0139	0241	0624	0648	1335	...	1803	1926	2118	2222
Hrebinka d.	|	0438	|	|	|	...	|	2148	|	0024
Poltava Kyïvska d.	0525	0803	0926	0951	1636	1745	2106	0135	▽	0342
Kharkiv a.	0802	1221	|	1123	1811	2029	2240	|	0644	0627
Slovyansk a.	...	...	1213	...	...	...	...	0641	1058	...
Kramatorsk a.	...	...	1224	...	...	...	...	0703	1144	...
Kostiantynivka a.	...	...	1246	...	...	...	...	0737	1217	...
Donetsk ◇ a.	...	...	...	...	...	...	...	...	...	...

	IC 725	91	*IC* 723	*IC* 712	*IC* 721	113 115	111	63	124	126
Donetsk ◇ d.	...	...	...	...	...	...	...	...	...	...
Kostiantynivka d.	...	...	...	1629	...	...	...	...	1846	2046
Kramatorsk d.	...	...	...	1653	...	...	...	...	1923	2112
Slovyansk d.	...	...	...	1704	...	...	...	...	2009	2132
Kharkiv d.	0723	1040	1316	|	1839	1848	1904	2207	0023	|
Poltava Kyïvska d.	0900	1310	1453	1951	2016	2106	2250	0104	▽	0306
Hrebinka d.	|	...	|	|	|	|	0231	0413	|	0700
Kyïv a.	1202	...	1754	2258	2319	0047	0431	0623	0929	0913
Lviv **1700** a.	...	...	...	...	...	0825	1502	...	...	...

InterCity fast train.
▽ – Via Sumy (Table **1755**).
◇ – Service suspended.

KYÏV - SUMY - KHARKIV 1755

	776	798	*Sko* 143	*Sko* 143		100	100	780	124	134
			●	●		■(1)	■(1)			
		M	★	☆		★	☆			
St Peterburg **1930** d.	...	...	1531	1531	...	...	...	...	...	...
Minsk **1930** d.	...	...	|	|	...	0744	0744	...	...	...
Homel **1930** d.	...	...	0759	0759	...	1246	1246	...	...	...
Kyïv d.	0020	...	|	|	...	|	|	1709	2118	2324
Konotop d.	0310	...	1345	1445	...	1740	1845	1927	0016	0221
Sumy d.	0536	1645	1657	1748	...	2034	2138	2119	0308	0543
Kharkiv a.	0825	2008	2051	2120	...	2354	0058	...	0644	0926
Lysychansk **1785** a.	...	...	...	...	...	⊡	⊡	...	△	1524

	124	779	100	100	*Sko* 143*PC*	*Sko* 143*PC*	797		775	134
			■(3)	■(3)	■(1)	■(1)				
			★	☆	★	☆	M			
Lysychansk **1785** d.	△	...	⊡	⊡	...	...	...	...	...	1640
Kharkiv d.	0023	...	0540	0620	0600	0642	1021	...	2130	2242
Sumy d.	0358	0539	0914	1004	0954	1044	1345	...	0027	0234
Konotop d.	0633	0736	1159	1249	1241	1333	...	...	0247	0528
Kyïv a.	0929	0949	|	|	|	|	...	...	0535	0818
Homel **1930** a.	...	...	1832	1832	2014	2014	...	...	...	...
Minsk **1930** a.	...	...	0008	0008	|	|	...	...	...	...
St Peterburg **1930** a.	...	...	...	...	1220	1220	...	...	...	...

Sumy - Kharkiv - Moskva (Table **1770**) and v.v.
Mar. 27 - Oct. 29 (summer time in Ukraine).
Not Mar. 27 - Oct. 29.

● – Even dates (see page 530).
■ – Uneven dates (see page 530).

△ – To / from Kostiantynivka (Table **1750**).
⊡ – To / from Zaporizhzhya (Table **1780**) extended to Novooleksiivka in summer.

CHIŞINĂU - BASARABEASCA 1756

M

n		821	6820
		E	¶
0	**Chişinău** **1720** d.	0643	1855
	Ungheni **1720** a.	0855	|
	Socola (Romania) a.	1059	|
5	Basarabeasca a.	...	2334
1	Etulia ◇ a.	...	...

	6819	822
	¶	E
Etulia ◇ d.	...	...
Basarabeasca d.	0202	...
Socola (Romania) d.	|	1708
Ungheni **1720** d.	|	1917
Chişinău **1720** a.	0625	2113

①⑤⑥⑦. ◇ – Service suspended. ¶ – only.

ODESA - BEREZYNE and IZMAÏL 1757

UZ

km		686*PC*	686*OJ*
		P	P
0	**Odesa** Holovna d.	1620	1620
85	Bilhorod-Dnistrovsky d.	1847	1847
175	Artsyz d.	2041	2057
210	Berezyne a.	|	2252
282	**Izmaïl** a.	2254	...

	686*SH*	686*KJ*
	P	P
Izmaïl d.	...	2359
Berezyne d.	2312	|
Artsyz d.	0239	0239
Bilhorod-Dnistrovsky d.	0431	0431
Odesa Holovna a.	0648	0648

P – ②⑤⑦ (also ③⑥ June 1 - Sept. 30).

1760 KYÏV and KHARKIV - MYKOLAIV - KHERSON

km		61KH	61KH	318	793	63	59	102	76	121	375
		● ★	● ☆	●		E					
	Moskva Kiyev. **1740** d.	1533	1533	...	...	...	...	...	...	...	...
	Konotop d.	0136	0233	...	...	...	...	...	...	...	...
	Cherkasy d.	0708	0821	...	...	...	...	...	...	...	...
0	**Kyïv** d.	|	|	...	...	...	...	2048	2125	2139	...
216	Im. T. Shevchenka d.	0809	0933	...	...	...	...	0022	0046	0149	...
*353	**Kharkiv** d.	|	|	...	1550	...	1747	|	|	|	1940
*213	Poltava d.	|	|	...	1800	...	2106	|	|	|	2302
*94	Kremenchuk d.	|	|	...	2006	...	2320	|	|	|	0148
*224	**Dnipropetrovsk** d.	|	|	|	|	1910	|	|	|	|	|
308	Znamyanka d.	0959	1124	...	2135	2350	0119	|	0345	|	0400
362	Kirovohrad d.	|	|	...	...	0043	0218	|	0435	|	|
720	**Odesa** Holovna d.	|	|	1442	...	0627	0759	|	...	|	|
448	Kryvyi Rih d.	|	|	|	...	...	...	0455	...	|	0804
651	**Mykolaiv** a.	1403	1525	1958	...	...	...	|	...	0700	1247
706	Kherson a.	1543	1659	2113	...	...	...	0859	...	...	1352
1062	Zaporizhzhya I a.	...	...	0540	...	...	...	...	...	...	...
	Simferopol ◇ a.	...	...	...	...	...	...	...	...	...	...

	957 61SH	957 61SH	962	60	375	794	122	102	64
	■(1) ★	■(1) ☆							F
Simferopol ◇ d.	...	...	...	...	...	...	...	...	...
Zaporizhzhya I d.	...	...	...	...	...	...	...	...	...
Kherson d.	0852	0915	...	...	1548	...	...	1848	...
Mykolaiv d.	1052	1120	...	...	1713	...	1944	|	...
Kryvyi Rih d.	|	|	...	...	2202	...	|	2310	...
Odesa Holovna d.	|	|	...	1844	|	...	|	|	2157
Kirovohrad d.	|	|	2315	0030	|	...	|	|	0327
Znamyanka d.	1524	1608	0108	0145	0153	0238	|	|	0437
Dnipropetrovsk d.	|	|	|	|	|	|	|	|	0850
Kremenchuk d.	|	|	|	0346	0435	0427	|	|	...
Poltava d.	|	|	|	0557	0743	0634	|	|	...
Kharkiv d.	|	|	|	0919	1051	0832	|	|	...
Im. T. Shevchenka d.	1712	1757	0227	...	...	...	0123	0405	...
Kyïv a.	|	|	0517	...	...	...	0545	0711	...
Cherkasy d.	1756	1838	...	...	...	...	...	...	...
Konotop a.	2341	0041	...	...	...	...	...	...	...
Moskva Kiyev. **1740** a.	1111	1111	...	...	...	...	...	...	...

E – Uneven dates (daily May 26 - Sept. 29).
F – Even dates (daily May 27 - Sept. 30).
◇ – Service suspended.
☆ – Mar. 27 - Oct. 29 (summer time in Ukraine).
★ – Not Mar. 27 - Oct. 29.
* – Distance from Znamyanka.
● – Even dates (see page 530).
■ – Uneven dates (see page 530).

1770 MOSKVA - OREL - KHARKIV

RZhD

km		1	723	5	73JA	73JA	3	735	19	19	105
			≋		d ★	d ☆		≋	s ★	s ☆	
0	**Moskva** Kurskaya d.	0625	0830	1200	1458	1458	1600	1755	2145	2145	2330
194	Tula I d.	0829	1034	1404	1835	1835	1804	1955	0014	0014	0201
383	Orel d.	1029	1222	1605	2125	2125	2005	2148	0235	0235	0514
537	Kursk d.	1210	...	1745	2343	2343	2145	2325	0421	0421	0745
697	Belgorod § RU d.	1410	...	1945	0253	0253	2345	...	0727	0727	...
781	**Kharkiv** § UA a.	...	...	...	0311	0411	...	...	0751	0851	...
	Kryvyi Rih **1780** a.	...	...	...	1326	1428	...	...	...	...	...

	726	4	6	736	2	106	20	20	74
	≋			≋			s ★	s ☆	d ★
Kryvyi Rih **1780** d.	...	...	...	...	...	...	...	...	1052
Kharkiv § UA d.	...	...	...	...	...	...	2116r	2216r	2244
Belgorod § RU d.	...	0645	1200	...	1600	...	0028	0028	0158
Kursk d.	0620	0844	1359	...	1759	2110	0255	0255	0422
Orel d.	0802	1023	1538	1810	1938	0026	0449	0449	0619
Tula I d.	0955	1224	1739	2003	2139	0321	0702	0702	0852
Moskva Kurskaya a.	1200	1430	1945	2208	2345	0630	0950	0950	1125

d – Conveys portion to / from Dnipropetrovsk (Table **1780**).
r – Passengers must board by 2045 ★ 2145 ☆.
s – Conveys portion to / from Sumy (Table **1755**).
☆ – Mar. 27 - Oct. 29 (summer time in Ukraine).
★ – Not Mar. 27 - Oct. 29.
≋ – *Lastochka* (Swallow) fast day train.
§ – 🛃 : Krasny Khutor (RU) / Kozacha Lopan (UA).
RU – Russia (Moskva Time GMT + 3).
UA – Ukraine (GMT + 2 winter, GMT + 3 summer).

1775 LVIV and KYÏV - DNIPROPETROVSK - MARIUPOL and MELITOPOL

km		IC 732	70	84	IC 734	12	86	72	42	76	80
		≋			≋		■(1)		△		
0	**Lviv** ▷ d.	...	0029	...	...	...	1123	...	1220	...	...
141	Ternopil ▷ d.	...	0253	...	...	...	1332	...	1425	...	...
260	Khmelnytsky ▷ d.	...	0503	...	...	...	1531	...	1621	...	...
359	Zhmerynka ▷ d.	...	0655	...	...	...	1716	...	1804	...	...
406	Vinnytsya ▷ d.	...	0803	...	...	...	1806	...	1855	...	...
468	Kozyatyn ▷ d.	...	0902	...	...	...	1921	...	2007	...	...
*216	**Kyïv** d.	0715	|	1639	1735	1948	|	2022	|	2125	2258
772	Im. T. Shevchenka d.	0924	1349	2010	1944	2222	2340	0004	0036	0046	0141
864	Znamyanka d.	1024	1515	2128	2044	2334	0100	0122	0204	0224	0302
909	Oleksandria d.	1053	1600	2207	2113	|	0146	0201	0244	0303	0344
1046	**Kryvyi Rih** a.	|	|	|	|	|	|	|	|	0605	|
1052	Dniprodzerzhynsk d.	1225	1851	0032	2245	0225	0415	0426	0533	...	0610
1088	**Dnipropetrovsk** d.	1301	1948	0124	2324	0316	0512	0522	0610	...	0650
1291	Krasnoarmiisk a.	|	|	|	0143	|	|	|	...	...	...
1357	Donetsk ◇ a.	|	|	|	...	|	|	|	...	...	...
1214	Zaporizhzhya I d.	1422	2200	0321	...	0507	0724	0730	...	...	...
1589	Mariupol a.	...	0630	1059	...	|	|	...	...	...	...
1326	**Melitopol** a.	...	...	...	...	0650	0910	...	...	...	...
1417	Novooleksiivka a.	...	...	...	...	0825	1105	...	...	...	...
1570	Simferopol ◇ a.	...	...	...	...	...	...	...	...	...	...
1648	Sevastopol ◇ a.	...	...	...	...	...	...	...	...	...	...

	IC 733	41	IC 732	86	76	72	79	70	12
	≋	▽	≋	●					
Sevastopol ◇ d.	...	...	...	...	...	...	...	...	...
Simferopol ◇ d.	...	...	...	...	...	...	...	...	...
Novooleksiivka d.	...	...	...	1207	...	...	...	...	1955
Melitopol d.	...	...	...	1358	...	...	...	...	2135
Mariupol d.	...	...	...	|	...	...	...	1300	|
Zaporizhzhya I d.	...	...	1537	1551	...	1905	...	2036	2322
Donetsk ◇ d.	...	...	|	|	...	|	...	|	|
Krasnoarmiisk d.	0441	...	|	|	...	|	...	|	|
Dnipropetrovsk d.	0710	1125	1710	1800	...	2142	2225	2241	0133
Dniprodzerzhynsk d.	0739	1202	1739	1847	...	2220	2302	2318	0210
Kryvyi Rih d.	|	|	|	|	2101	|	|	|	|
Oleksandria d.	0912	1444	1911	2136	0014	0055	0134	0152	|
Znamyanka d.	0941	1534	1940	2221	0108	0136	0215	0231	0512
Im. T. Shevchenka a.	1042	1712	2041	0001	0227	0303	0342	0424	0626
Kyïv a.	1250	|	2249	|	0517	0558	0657	|	0919
Kozyatyn ▷ d.	...	2151	...	0438	...	...	...	0909	...
Vinnytsya ▷ d.	...	2250	...	0540	...	...	...	1010	...
Zhmerynka ▷ d.	...	0009	...	0653	...	...	...	1116	...
Khmelnytsky ▷ d.	...	0150	...	0826	...	...	...	1257	...
Ternopil ▷ d.	...	0351	...	1021	...	...	...	1506	...
Lviv ▷ a.	...	0558	...	1235	...	...	...	1719	...

≋ – *InterCity* fast train.
◇ – Service suspended.
● – Even dates (see page 530).
■ – Uneven dates (see page 530).
△ – From Truskavets (d. 0941).
▽ – To Truskavets (a. 0836).
▷ – See also Table **1700**.
* – Distance from Im. T. Shevchenka

1780 KHARKIV - DNIPROPETROVSK, KRYVYI RIH and MELITOPOL

km		100	100	73JA	73JA 106	73JA	73JA 106	120	795	81
		■(1) ★	■(1) ☆	★	★	☆	☆			
	Moskva Kurs. **1770** d.	...	...	1458	1458	1458	1458	...	...	...
	Minsk **1930** d.	0744	0744	|	|	|	|	...	...	...
0	**Kharkiv** d.	0021	0120	0401	0401	0501	0501	...	1805	2325
303	**Dnipropetrovsk** a.	|	|	|	0951	|	1025	...	2208	|
327	Zaporizhzhya I d.	0443	0559	0935	...	1026	...	1220	...	0405
512	Kryvyi Rih a.	...	|	1326	...	1428	...	1654	...	|
439	**Melitopol** a.	...	0758r	...	...	...	...	...	...	0550
530	Novooleksiivka a.	...	0925r	...	...	...	...	...	...	0715
683	Simferopol ◇ a.	...	...	...	...	...	...	...	...	...
761	Sevastopol ◇ a.	...	...	...	...	...	...	...	...	...

	796	120	106 74	74	106 74	74	82	100
			★	★	☆	☆		■(3) ★
Sevastopol ◇ d.	...	...	...	...	...	...	...	...
Simferopol ◇ d.	...	...	...	...	...	...	...	...
Novooleksiivka d.	...	...	...	...	...	...	2150	...
Melitopol d.	...	...	...	...	...	...	2331	...
Kryvyi Rih d.	...	1040	...	1052	...	1140	|	...
Zaporizhzhya I d.	...	1516	...	1613	...	1650	0112	0048
Dnipropetrovsk d.	0633	...	1550	|	1703	|	|	|
Kharkiv a.	1047	...	2145	2145	2245	2245	0553	0519
Minsk **1930** a.	...	...	|	|	|	|	...	0008
Moskva Kurs. **1770** a.	...	...	1125	1125	1125	1125	...	...

r – June 1 - Sept. 21 (from Minsk).
s – Even dates June 2 - Sept. 22.
☆ – Mar. 27 - Oct. 29 (summer time in Ukraine).
★ – Not Mar. 27 - Oct. 29.
● – Even dates (see page 530).
■ – Uneven dates (see page 530).
◇ – Service suspended.

1785 KHARKIV - LYSYCHANSK

km				134 K		609		409			
0	**Kharkiv** d.	...	...	0955	...	1449	...	2200	...	...	...
129	Kupiansk-Vuslov d.	...	...	1250	...	1748	...	0308	...	...	...
254	Lysychansk a.	...	...	1524	...	2023	...	0554	...	...	...
382	**Luhansk** ◇ a.	...	...	...	...	...	...	...	...	...	...
280	Horlivka ◇ a.	...	...	...	...	...	...	...	...	...	...
333	**Donetsk** ◇ a.	...	...	...	...	...	...	...	...	...	...

			410		134 K		610		
Donetsk ◇ d.	...	...	...	...	...	...	...	...	...
Horlivka ◇ d.	...	...	...	...	...	...	...	...	...
Luhansk ◇ d.	...	...	...	...	...	...	...	...	...
Lysychansk d.	...	...	0633	...	1640	...	2140	...	...
Kupiansk-Vuslov d.	...	...	0935	...	1940	...	0040	...	...
Kharkiv a.	...	...	1204	...	2214	...	0533	...	...

K – Kyïv (Table **1755**) - Kharkiv - Lysychansk and v.v.
◇ – Service suspended.

CRIMEAN PENINSULA

Although recognised by most countries as part of Ukraine, the region is *de facto* controlled by Russia. There are currently no rail services between Ukraine and Crimea; access to the region is from mainland Russia by way of the ferry across the Kerch Strait. A road and rail bridge is under construction across the strait. For local services see Table **1790**.

CRIMEAN PENINSULA — 1790

ean Railway

See note re Crimea at the foot of the previous page. Timings are in Moskva time (GMT+3).

	K									
Solone Ozero d.	...	...	...	0525	...	0940	1355	...	...	1905
Dzhankoy d.	0247	...	0455	0610	...	1035	1445	...	...	2010
Simferopol a.	0440	...	0730	0855	...	1310	1720	...	...	2245
Simferopol d.	0455	0515	*0830*	...	0915	*1440*	...	1750	1755	...
Yevpatoriya a.	0715	|	*1040*	...	|	*1650*	...	2010	|	...
Sevastopol a.	0650	0730	...	...	1130	...	...	...	2010	...

										L
Sevastopol d.	...	...	0505	...	0820	...	...	1725	...	2130
Yevpatoriya d.	...	0505	|	...	|	*1130*	...	|	*1750*	2120
Simferopol a.	...	0720	0725	...	1040	*1340*	...	1940	*2015*	2330
Simferopol d.	0510	...	...	0845	...	1425	1830	...	2035	2350
Dzhankoy d.	0810	...	...	1145	...	1710	2110	...	2310	0134
Solone Ozero a.	0845	...	...	1215	...	1745	2145	...	...	...

	L									
Armyansk d.	...	...	...	...	...	0715	...	...	1450	...
Dzhankoy d.	0155	0135	...	0615	...	0948	1435	...	1720	...
Vladyslavivka d.	0400	0425	0613	0906	0920	1214	1705	1715	1955	2155
Feodosia a.	|	|	0703	|	1008	1255	|	1800	2037	2230
Kerch a.	0600	0705	...	1135	...	...	1940	...	...	...

										K
Kerch d.	...	...	0820	...	1425	...	...	...	2045	2210
Feodosia d.	0610	0805	|	1540	|	1810	2015	2305	|	|
Vladyslavivka d.	0703	0846	1131	1625	1705	1900	2115	2340	0020	0009
Dzhankoy d.	0950	...	1400	...	1935	2130	...	...	0245	0226
Armyansk a.	1145	...	...	...	...	...	...	...	...	...

rain **615** Kerch - Dzhankoy - Simferopol - Sevastopol / Yevpatoriya and v.v.

L – Train **616** Sevastopol / Yevpatoriya - Simferopol - Dzhankoy - Kerch.

LITHUANIA, LATVIA and ESTONIA

SEE MAP PAGE 523

ators: Lithuania: **LG** (Lietuvos Geležinkeliai), www.litrail.lt Latvia: **LDz** (Latvijas Dzelzcelš), www.ldz.lv Estonia: **Elron** www.edel.ee

ces: Trains convey first- and second-class seating unless indicated otherwise. International trains to and from CIS countries (Belarus, Russia, Ukraine) are composed of Russian-style sleeping-cars (for details of train types and classes of travel in the CIS, see the panel on page **530**).

gs: Valid from **December 13, 2015**. Amendments are incorporated as they are received. Timings are expressed in local time at the station concerned (time comparison chart: page 2).

vations: Reservation is compulsory for travel by international services to / from Russia.

RIGA - TALLINN, ST PETERBURG, VILNIUS and KALININGRAD — 1800

IGA - TALLINN ⊡
ey time: 4 hours 25 mins.
Riga: 0305, 0700, 0900, 1000, 1115, 1445, 1600, 1700, 1830, 2035.
Tallinn: 0600, 0700, 0830, 1000, 1115, 1445, 1600, 1700, 1830, 2230.

RIGA - ST PETERBURG ⊡
Journey time: 10h 20m - 11h 30m.
From Riga: 0855, 1845, 2245, 2355.
From St Peterburg Baltiski: 0015, 1155, 2000, 2140.

RIGA - VILNIUS ⊡
Journey time: 4h 10m - 4h 30m
From Riga: 0255, 0700, 0900, 1035, 1230, 1445, 1530, 1700, 1815, 2250.
From Vilnius: 0630, 0800, 1000, 1115, 1230, 1415, 1610, 1830, 2300.

RIGA - KALININGRAD ⊙
Journey time: 7 hours 40 mins.
From Riga: 2330.
From Kaliningrad: 2230◇.

⊡ – Operator: Lux Express (www.luxexpress.eu).
⊙ – Operator: Ecolines (ecolines.net).

◇ – One hour earlier when Latvia is on summer time (Mar. 27 - Oct. 29).

Riga and Vilnius coach stations are adjacent to the railway stations. Tallinn coach station is 3 km from the railway station (by tram).

VILNIUS - ŠIAULIAI - KLAIPEDA — 1810

2nd class §

		781		17		23		36 ⑤⑦	783	19	
Vilnius 1811 d.	...	0647	...	1000	...	1415	...	...	1637	1744	...
Kaišiadorys 1811 d.	...	|	...	1047	...	1500	...	...	|	1831	...
Kaunas d.	...	|	...	|	...	|	...	1530	|	|	...
Radviliškis d.	0555	|	...	1217	1320	1628	1638	1723	|	2001	...
Šiauliai d.	0624	0859	0910	1239	1353	1647	1714	1744	1849	2023	2035
Mažeikiai a.	|	|	1025	|	1506	...	|	...	|	|	2150
Klaipeda a.	0911	1032	...	1434	...	...	1956	...	2022	2216	...

		18			780		24		782	38 ⑤⑦	20
Klaipeda d.	...	0640	0825	...	1040	...	...	1450	1635	...	1700
Mažeikiai d.	0710	|	|	1045	|	1550	...	|	|	...	|
Šiauliai d.	0823	0843	1114	1156	1222	1703	1726	1734	1815	1848	1907
Radviliškis d.	...	0902	1145	1231	|	...	1745	1810	|	1910	1925
Kaunas a.	...	|	...	...	|	...	|	...	|	2103	|
Kaišiadorys 1811 d.	...	1039	...	...	|	...	1918	...	|	...	2054
Vilnius 1811 a.	...	1125	...	...	1427	...	2004	...	2023	...	2155

Trains where no train number is shown are 3rd class.

** – *138 km* Kaunas - Radviliškis.

VILNIUS - KAUNAS — 1811

1,2 class

	Ⓐ																			Ⓑ		
Vilnius 1810 d.	0440	0445	0620	0730	0848	0935	1025	1115	1140	1225	1405	1445	1557	1630	1650	1730	1752	1829	1952	2057	...	...
Kaišiadorys 1810 d.	0523	0546	0710	0820	0946	1016	1111	1202	1236	1306	1453	1542	1640	1711	1749	1815	1844	1929	2042	2151	...	...
Kaunas a.	0550	0621	0737	0849	1021	1040	1137	1231	1311	1330	1520	1617	1704	1735	1825	1839	1915	2005	2109	2228	...	...

	⚒		Ⓐ																				
as d.	0502	0528	0623	0707	0809	0914	1100	1208	1352	1440	1540	1632	1705	1719	1755	1841	1922	1948	2019	2145	...	...	...
adorys 1810 d.	0529	0600	0652	0737	0836	0942	1132	1234	1421	1505	1611	1657	1730	1751	1821	1906	1952	2014	2054	2212	...	...	...
us 1810 a.	0631	0707	0738	0838	0923	1040	1239	1320	1521	1549	1714	1738	1816	1858	1910	1950	2055	2101	2145	2301	...	...	...

VILNIUS - VILNIUS AIRPORT — 1812

3rd class

Vilnius d.	0545	0800	0845	0935	...	1050	1145	1248	1330	1406	1450	...	1600	1657	1745	1920	2010	2136	...	...	...	...
Vilnius Airport ⊡ a.	0552	0807	0852	0942	...	1057	1152	1255	1337	1413	1457	...	1607	1704	1752	1927	2017	2143	...	...	...	...

us Airport ⊡ d.	0557	0812	0857	0947	...	1102	1157	1300	1342	1418	1505	...	1612	1709	1757	1932	2037	2152	...	...	...	...	...
us a.	0605	0820	0905	0955	...	1110	1205	1308	1350	1426	1513	...	1620	1717	1805	1940	2045	2200	...	...	...	...	...

Oro uostas in Lithuanian.

VILNIUS - TRAKAI — 1815

3rd class

Vilnius d.	0500	0610	0740	1230	1330	1534	1815	2031	...
Trakai a.	0535	0646	0816	1306	1405	1610	1851	2107	...

Trakai d.	0545	0712	0837	1321	1427	1646	1937	2130	...
Vilnius a.	0624	0751	0916	1400	1506	1725	2016	2209	...

VILNIUS - TURMANTAS — 1818

3rd class

					Ⓐ				
Vilnius d.	0534	0804	1144	1510	1642	1753	1925	2111	...
Ignalina d.	0718	0952	1332	1653	1808	1917	2113	2242	...
Turmantas a.	0801	1035	1415	1736	...	1955	...	2319	...

								Ⓐ	
Turmantas d.	...	0429	0526	0826	1206	1610	1753	...	...
Ignalina d.	0424	0506	0602	0909	1249	1653	1836	2030	...
Vilnius a.	0605	0625	0723	1053	1433	1834	2017	2153	...

RIGA - VALMIERA - VALGA — 1830

Riga d.	0621	0754	1038	1230	1400	1542	1728	1808	1837	1938	2130
Sigulda d.	0747	0910	1151	1346	1516	1658	1844	1901	1954	2054	2245
Cesis d.	0829	...	1233	...	...	...	...	1933	2036	...	...
Valmiera d.	0900	...	1304	...	...	...	...	2001	2108	...	...
Lugaži 🏛 LV a.	...	...	1348	...	...	...	...	2044	...	...	...
Valga 🏛 EE a.	...	...	1354	...	...	...	...	2050	...	...	...

Valga 🏛 EE d.	...	0517	...	...	...	...	...	1442	...	...	...
Lugaži 🏛 LV d.	...	0524	...	...	...	...	...	1449	...	...	...
Valmiera d.	0500	0607	...	...	0949	...	...	1532	...	...	...
Cesis d.	0534	0633	...	...	1023	...	...	1604	...	...	...
Sigulda d.	0615	0705	0804	0924	1104	1407	1535	1645	1712	1914	2135
Riga a.	0726	0758	0917	1037	1215	1520	1648	1738	1825	2027	2248

Estonia. LV – Latvia.

☛ For trains Valga - Tallinn see Table **1880**.

1840 RIGA - REZEKNE - ST PETERBURG and MOSKVA

LDz, R

km			808	*Pas* 662*AJ*	702 Ⓒ	*Fir* 2*RJ* L ★	*Fir* 38*RJ* B ★	816	*Fir* 2*RJ* L ☆	*Fir* 38*RJ* B ☆
0	**Riga**	**1850** d.	0947	...	1138	1650	1650	1700	1730	1730
51	Lielvarde	**1850** d.	1041	...	|	|	|	1750	|	|
129	Krustpils (Jekabpils)	**1850** d.	1151	...	1319	1837	1837	1857	1920	1920
224	**Rezekne II**	d.	1324	...	1426	2000	2000	2031	2055	2055
279	Zilupe	🏛 LV d.	1427	...	...	2140	2140	2134	2240	2240
306	Sebezh	🏛 RU d.	...	...	...	2358	2358	...	2358	2358
417	Novosokolniki	d.	...	...	...	0210	0329	...	0210	0329
593	Dno	d.	...	...	...	|	0603	...	|	0603
838	**St Peterburg** Vitebski	a.	...	...	...	|	0933	...	|	0933
446	**Velikiye Luki**	d.	...	2115	...	0257	...	...	0257	...
687	Rzhev	d.	...	0227	...	0600	...	...	0600	...
922	**Moskva** Rizhskaya	a.	...	0658	...	1017	...	...	1017	...

		815	*Fir* 1*RJ* L ★	*Fir* 37*RJ* B ★	*Fir* 1*RJ* L ☆	*Fir* 37*RJ* B ☆	*Pas* 661*AJ*	701 Ⓒ
Moskva Rizhskaya	d.	...	1704	...	1706	...	1956	...
Rzhev	d.	...	2110	...	2110	...	0013	...
Velikiye Luki	d.	...	0035	...	0035	...	0600	...
St Peterburg Vitebski	d.	...	|	1720	|	1720	...	...
Dno	d.	...	|	2112	|	2112	...	...
Novosokolniki	d.	...	0121	0135	0121	0135	...	...
Sebezh	🏛 RU d.	...	0410	0410	0410	0410	...	...
Zilupe	🏛 LV d.	0327	0422	0422	0522	0522	...	...
Rezekne II	d.	0432	0522	0522	0622	0622	...	1505
Krustpils (Jekabpils)	**1850** d.	0605	0633	0633	0733	0733	...	1613
Lielvarde	**1850** d.	0726	|	|	|	|	...	|
Riga	**1850** a.	0820	0828	0828	0924	0924	...	1758

B – BALTIJA – 🛏 1, 2 cl. Ⓡ
L – LATVIJAS EKSPRESIS – 🛏 1, 2 cl. Ⓡ
☆ – Mar. 27 - Oct. 29 (summer time in Latvia).
★ – Not Mar. 27 - Oct. 29.
LV – Latvia (GMT+2 winter, GMT+3 summer).
RU – Russia (Moskva Time GMT+3).

1850 RIGA - DAUGAVPILS - MINSK

LDz,

km			802	Ⓒ		810 ⑤–⑦		704	818	*Sko* 88*BJ* ●(4) ★	*Sko* 88*BJ* ●(4) ☆	
0	**Riga**	▷ d.	0740	0830	0947	1301	1525	1612	1738	1920	2020	2110
51	Lielvarde	▷ d.	0828	0928	1041	1350	1619	|	1826	|	|	2213
129	Krustpils ⊡	▷ d.	0944	1047	1151	1500	1738	1753	1940	2104	2204	2329
218	**Daugavpils**	LV d.	1104	...	...	1629	...	1858	2100	2229	2327	...
379	Polatsk	§ BY d.	...	...	...	...	...	...	...	0346	0350	...
578	Maladzechna	d.	...	...	...	...	...	...	...	0656	0659	...
655	**Minsk**	a.	...	...	...	...	...	...	...	0819	0819	...

			703	*Sko* 87*BJ* ■(3) ★	*Sko* 87*BJ* ■(3) ☆	817	Ⓒ	801 ⑤–⑦		
Minsk	d.	...	...	2225	2225	...	...	...	...	...
Maladzechna	d.	...	...	0002	0002	...	...	...	...	...
Polatsk	§ BY d.	...	...	0310	0310	...	...	...	...	...
Daugavpils	LV d.	...	0615	0607	0707	0717	...	1255	...	...
Krustpils ⊡	▷ d.	0454	0721	0710	0810	0844	1153	1422	...	...
Lielvarde	▷ d.	0620	|	|	|	1004	1319	1542	1652	1747
Riga	▷ a.	0729	0907	0900	1000	1052	1416	1630	1751	1846

⊡ – Station for Jekabpils.
☆ – Mar. 27 - Oct. 29 (summer time in Latvia).
★ – Not Mar. 27 - Oct. 29.
● – Even dates (see page 530).
■ – Uneven dates (see page 530).
▷ – See also Table **1840**. Local trains run Riga - Lielvarde.
§ – 🏛 : Indra (LV) / Bihosava (BY).
LV – Latvia (GMT+2 winter, +3 summer).
BY – Belarus (GMT+3).

1860 RIGA - LIEPAJA, TUKUMS and SAULKRASTI

			⑤
0	**Riga**	▷ d.	1825
43	Jelgava	▷ d.	1911
125	Saldus	d.	2027
223	**Liepaja**	a.	2146

		⑦
Liepaja	d.	1730
Saldus	d.	1850
Jelgava	▷ d.	2005
Riga	▷ a.	2043

RIGA - JURMALA ◧ - TUKUMS *65 km* Journey 1h 25m

From **Riga**: 0551, 0736, 0920, 1300, 1417, 1556, 1706, 1856, 2140, 2240, 2336. From **Tukums** II: 0451, 0547, 0627, 0813, 0925, 1117, 1451, 1633, 1745, 1933, 2100.

Riga - Jurmala (Sloka) ◧ 1-2 trains per hour, journey ± 50 mins.

RIGA - SAULKRASTI *48 km* Journey 1 hour

From **Riga**: 0615, 0720, 0814, 1018, 1220, 1440, 1557Ⓐ, 1743, 1830, 1929, 2033, 2154. From **Saulkrasti**: 0506, 06 0746, 0847, 0947, 1149, 1349, 1621, 1708Ⓐ, 1803, 1915,

Certain trains continue to / from Skulte, *56 km* ± 70 minutes

▷ – Riga - Jelgava: 1-2 trains per hour.
◧ – Jurmala's 33 km coastline has several stations; principal stations are Majori (*22 km*) and Sloka (*32 km*). There is no station called Jurr

1870 TALLINN - ST PETERBURG - MOSKVA

Elron, GoRail, R

km			220		34*KH* A§ ★	34*KH* A ☆		222	224	226	
0	**Tallinn**	**1880** d.	0851	...	1609	1709	...	1530	1832	2125	...
77	Tapa	**1880** d.	0952	...	1701	1801	...	1631	1933	2226	...
104	Rakvere	d.	1010	...	|	|	...	1650	1953	2244	...
165	Jõhvi	d.	1057	...	1758	1858	...	1737	2042	...	...
209	Narva	🏛 EE d.	1135	...	1913	2013	...	1812	2115	...	...
380	**St Peterburg** Ladozhski	RU a.	...	...	2352	2352	...	...	...	...	...
633	Bologoye	**1900** a.	...	...	0435	0435	...	...	...	...	...
797	Tver	**1900** a.	...	...	0718	0718	...	...	...	...	...
964	**Moskva** Oktyabrskaya	**1900** a.	...	...	0940	0940	...	...	...	...	...

		221	223		34*AJ* A§ ★	34*AJ* A ☆		225	227
Moskva Oktyabrskaya	**1900** d.	...	...	...	2310	2310	...	...	...
Tver	**1900** d.	...	...	...	0111	0111	...	...	...
Bologoye	**1900** d.	...	...	...	|	|	...	...	...
St Peterburg Glavni	RU d.	...	...	...	0629	0629	...	...	...
Narva	🏛 EE d.	...	0705	...	1022	1102	...	1305	1827
Jõhvi	d.	...	0740	...	1102	1141	...	1340	1903
Rakvere	d.	0615	0829	...	|	|	...	1429	1954
Tapa	**1880** d.	0635	0849	...	1210	1246	...	1449	2014
Tallinn	**1880** a.	0735	0951	...	1305	1338	...	1549	2114

Lux Express (www.luxexpress.eu) 🚌 TALLINN - ST PETERBURG Reservation compuls

🚌		Ⓑ				Ⓒ				
Tallinn coach station ◇	d.	0600	0700	0800	1015	1135	1430	1545	2300	2359
St Peterburg coach station ¶	a.	1325*	1525*	1550*	1915*	1925*	2220*	2310*	0700*	0850*

🚌						Ⓑ		Ⓒ	
St Peterburg coach station ¶	d.	0645	0815	1030	1315	1700	1810	2200	2230
Tallinn coach station ◇	a.	1300r	1415r	1810r	1955r	2320r	0015r	0500r	0600r

A – 🛏 1, 2 cl. Ⓡ. Operated by Go Rail.
☆ – Mar. 27 - Oct. 29 (summer time in Estonia).
★ – Not Mar. 27 - Oct. 29.
r – One hour later Mar. 27 - Oct. 29.
¶ – Also calls at Baltiski station.
◇ – 3 km by tram from railway station.
§ – Timings may vary.
* – One hour earlier Mar. 27 - Oct. 29.
EE – Estonia (GMT+2 winter, GMT+ summer).
RU – Russia (Moskva Time GMT+3).

1880 TALLINN - TARTU - VALGA

E

km			210	10 ◇	12 ◇	14 ◇	212	16 ◇	214	18 ◇	216
0	**Tallinn**	**1870** d.	0610	0813	1006	1250	1412	1510	1650	1739	1955
77	Tapa	**1870** d.	0711	0905	1058	1342	1514	1602	1751	1832	2056
142	Jõgeva	d.	0800	0952	1138	1422	1603	1645	1846	1917	2144
190	**Tartu**	a.	0836	1021	1207	1450	1641	1714	1922	1946	2223
190	**Tartu**	d.	...	1024	...	1453	...	1718	...	...	...
215	Elva	d.	...	1051	...	1521	...	1746	...	...	...
273	**Valga**	a.	...	1136	...	1606	...	1831	...	...	...
	Riga **1830**	a.	...	...	...	...	...	...	...	...	...

		211	11 ◇	13 ◇	15 ◇	213	17 ◇	215	19 ◇
Riga **1830**	d.	...	...	...	...	...	*1038*	...	...
Valga	d.	...	0617**a**	0730**c**	...	...	1403	...	1701
Elva	d.	...	0659**a**	0812**c**	...	...	1446	...	1745
Tartu	a.	...	0726**a**	0839**c**	...	...	1513	...	1812
Tartu	d.	0619	0729	0842	0938	1402	1516	1718	1816
Jõgeva	d.	0658	0759	0912	1012	1442	1545	1755	1846
Tapa	**1870** d.	0749	0840	0958	1058	1538	1628	1848	1931
Tallinn	**1870** a.	0849	0929	1047	1147	1638	1718	1948	2020

a – Ⓐ only. c – Ⓒ only. s – May 1 - Sept. 25.

◇ – Classified *Ekspress* between Tallinn and Tartu (higher fares apply). Different train numbers apply between Tartu and Valga but trains normally run through.

☛ Fast 🚌 services operate between Tallinn and Tartu approx 18 times daily (journey: 2½ hrs); operator Lux Express (www.luxexpress.eu). Tallinn coach station is located 3 km south of Tallinn railway station (by tram).

0	Tartu	d.	1026	1719
43	Pölva	d.	1108	1801
72	Orava	d.	1133	1826
85	Koidula	a.	1143	1836
92	Piusa	a.	1202**s**	...

		Ⓐ	Ⓒ
Piusa	d.	...	...
Koidula	d.	0602	0811
Orava	d.	0612	0821
Pölva	d.	0635	0844
Tartu	a.	0719	0928

1890 TALLINN - VILJANDI and PÄRNU

E

km													
0	**Tallinn**	d.	0745	0745	0936	1111	1417	1629	1732	1801	1827	1925	2210
54	Rapla	d.	0841	0841	1038	1213	1519	1733	1827	1858	1936	2034	2313
72	Lelle	d.	0857	0858	1054	...	1535	1749	1841	1917	1952	2050	2329
98	Türi	a.	0922	|	1115	...	1557	1810	1903	|	2013	2112	2350
151	**Viljandi**	a.	1003	|	...	...	1638	...	1944	|	...	2153	...
136	**Pärnu**	a.	...	1000	...	...	...	...	...	2019	...	...	...

					Ⓒ	Ⓐ	Ⓒ					
Pärnu	d.	...	...	0721	...	...	...	...	...	...	...	1814
Viljandi	d.	...	0630	|	0837	0846	...	...	1317	...	1737	|
Türi	d.	0558	0712	|	0922	0922	1032	1250	1359	...	1819	|
Lelle	d.	0620	0734	0824	0944	0944	1054	1312	1421	...	1842	1918
Rapla	d.	0636	0748	0840	0958	0958	1110	1328	1437	1650	1856	1936
Tallinn	a.	0738	0843	0934	1053	1053	1215	1432	1544	1758	1953	2030

☛ Pärnu railway station is situated approx 4 km from the centre. 🚌 services operate between Tallinn coach station and Pärnu 7 times daily (journey 1h 50m); operator Lux Express (www.luxexpress.eu). Tallinn coach station is located 3 km south of Tallinn railway station (by tram).

Subject to alteration May 28 - June 22

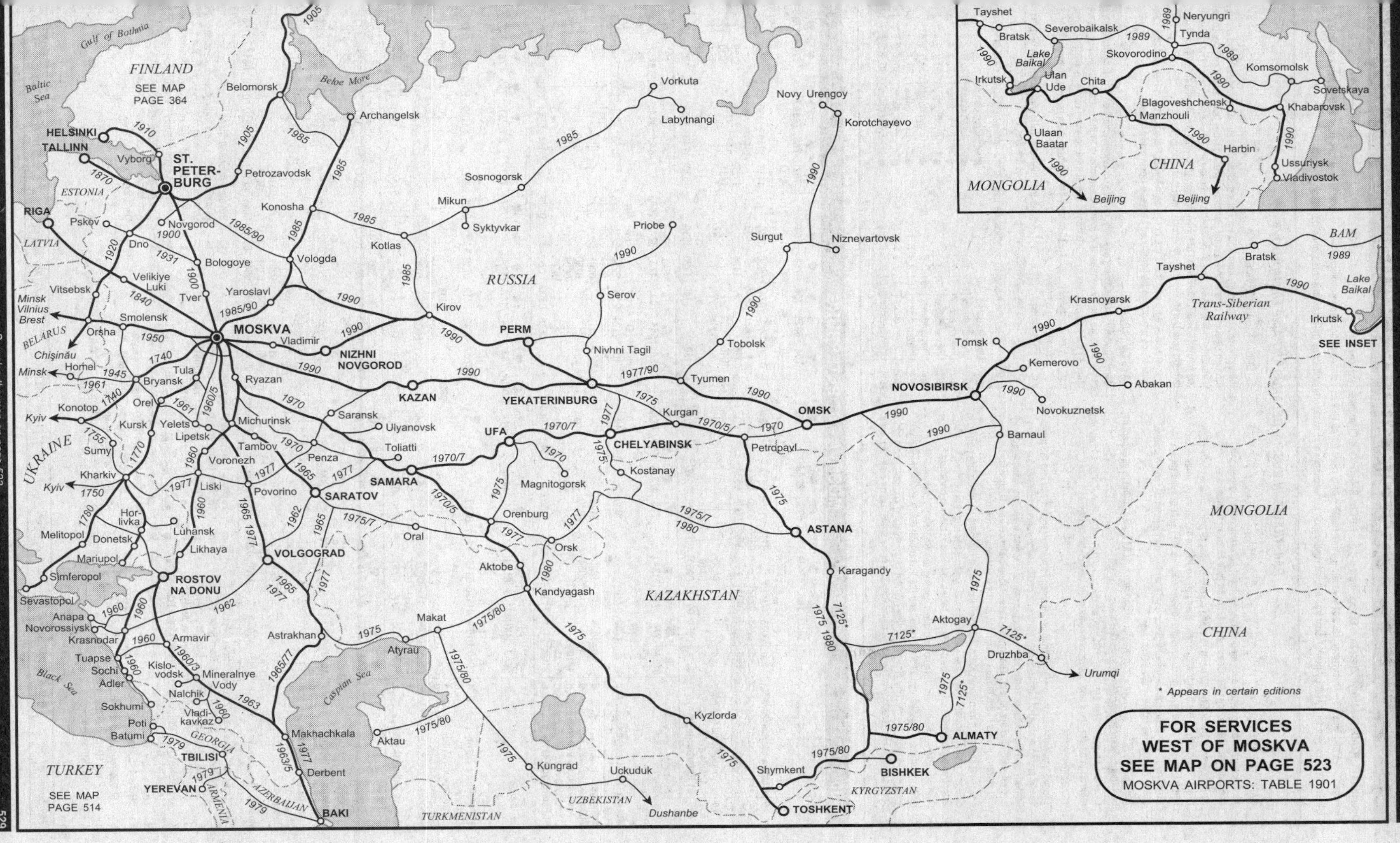

See also the map on page 523

RUSSIA and BELARUS

SEE MAPS PAGES 523/

Operators: **RZhD**: Rossiskiye Zheleznye Dorogi, www.rzd.ru **BCh**: Belaruskaya Chyhunka, www.rw.by

Timings: Valid **May 28 - December 10, 2016**. Moskva Time (GMT+3) is used for all Russian stations (including Kaliningrad, where local time is one hour behind Moskva Time).

Tickets: Except for travel by purely local trains, prior reservation is necessary and passports and visas must be presented when purchasing tickets.

RAIL TRAVEL IN RUSSIA, BELARUS, UKRAINE and MOLDOVA

CARRIAGE TYPES

As trains generally operate over long distances, most accommodation is designed for overnight as well as day use. Carriage types (with their Russian names) are:

Spálny vagón SV or СВ – 2-berth sleeping compartments (9 per carriage) with wash basin, found only in the best trains. Sometimes referred to as 1st class. A small number of named trains also have *de luxe* carriages (also known as *VIP*) with ensuite facilities.

Kupéiny К – 4-berth compartments (9 per carriage) found in almost all long-distance trains. Sometimes referred to as 2nd class.

Platskártny ПЛ – open-plan dormitory-style carriage with 54 bunks, found in all except the best trains. Sometimes referred to as 3rd class.

Óbshchi О – open-plan carriages with hard seating, found in some slow trains. Sometimes referred to as 4th class and not recommended for long-distance travel.

TRAIN TYPES

The top grade of fast long-distance train is classified *Firménny* (shown as *Fir* in the tables). These are composed of higher-quality carriages dedicated to a particular service (often named) and higher fares apply. Normal long-distance express trains are classified *Skóry* (shown as *Sko* in the tables). The lowest class of long-distance train is classified *Passazhírsky* (*Pas* in the tables) which call at many stations en-route.

The most important trains on a route are given the lowest numbers (numbers are reused in different areas). Specific trains are identified by a cyrillic letter after the number, or a two-letter transliteration which is shown in some tables to assist in making bookings.

High-speed train types with 1st and 2nd class seating are *Sapsan* (Peregrine Falcon) running between Moskva and St Peterburg, and the Talgo-built *Strizh* (Swift) running between Moskva and Nizhny Novgorod (also with 1st class sleeping compartments for daytime use). Fast *Lastochka* (Swallow) trains with 2nd class seats run on several routes.

INTERNATIONAL SERVICES

International services to, from and via Poland, Slovakia, Hungary and Romania convey through sleeping cars of the normal European ('RIC') types, with single and double co partments in first class, and 3- or 4-berth compartments in second class. The railways the former Soviet Union being of broad gauge (1520mm), the bogies (trucks) of these through cars are changed at the frontier with these countries.

High-speed *Allegro* day trains are in use between St Peterburg and Helsinki, and Talgo hotel trains are due to be introduced between Berlin and Moskva.

DAYS OF RUNNING

Many trains run on alternate days only, on even or uneven numbered dates. The exampl below illustrate the system used to indicate exceptions to the pattern of even or uneve dates at the end of a month with 31 days and at the beginning of the month following:

e.g. "Uneven dates [... *29, 1* ...]" means that the train does not run on the 31st of a month with 31 days.

e.g. "Even dates [... *30, 1, 4* ...]" means that the train, **following a month with 31 days**, runs exceptionally on the 1st, but not the 2nd, of the month.

In these cases, the following symbols are used in the tables to indicate days of running

■ – Uneven dates.	● – Even dates.
■(1) – Uneven dates [.. *29, 1* ..]	●(3) – Even dates [.. *30, 1, 3, 8* ..]
■(2) – Uneven dates [.. *31, 2, 3* ..]	●(4) – Even dates [.. *30, 1, 4* ..]
■(3) – Uneven dates [.. *31, 3* ..]	●(5) – Even dates [.. *30, 1, 3, 4* ..]
■(5) – Uneven dates [.. *31, 2, 5* ..]	●(6) – Even dates [.. *30, 1, 3, 6* ..]
■(7) – Uneven dates [.. *31, 2, 4, 7* ..]	●(7) – Even dates [.. *30, 1, 6* ..]
■(8) – Uneven dates [.. *31, 2, 4, 6, 8, 10, 11* ..]	●(8) – Even dates [.. *30, 1, 3, 5, 8* ..]
■(9) – Uneven dates [.. *31, 2, 4, 6, 9* ..]	●(9) – Even dates [.. *30, 1, 3, 5, 7, 10*

1900 MOSKVA - ST PETERBURG

km		20UJ	16AJ	874JA	30AJ	59GJ	62AJ		752		754	6925	756	758	760		762	768	748AJ		770	772
		⊡	*Fir*	≋	*Sko*	*Fir*	*Sko*		♥		♥		♥	♥	♥		♥	♥	♡		♥	♥
																	⑥⑦		①–⑥			
		◐	m			n	F															
0	**Moskva** Oktyabrskaya § ... d.	0028	0041	...	0115	0135**k**	0153	...	0540	...	0730	...	0740	0930	0940	...	1130	1340	1350	...	1530	1540
167	Tver ... d.	0218	0232	...	0305	0330	0344	...	|	...	|	...	0845	|	1043	...	|	1445	|	...	|	1643
331	Bologoye ... d.	|	0431	...	0452	0508	0534	...	|	...	0926	...	|	1126	|	...	1327	|	|	...	1729	|
532	Chudovo ... d.	|	|	...	|	|	|	...	|	...	1040	1050	|	|	|	...	1431	|	|	...	1830	|
*74	Novgorod na Volkhove ... d.	|	|	0620	|	|	|	...	|	...	|	1214	|	|	|	...	|	|	|	...	|	|
532	Chudovo ... d.	|	|	0746	|	|	|	...	|	...	|	...	|	|	|	...	|	|	|	...	|	|
650	**St Peterburg** Glavny ‡ ... a.	0859	0912**c**	0950	1028	1016	1057	...	0920	...	1130	...	1140	1320	1330	...	1520	1740	1755	...	1920	1930

	872JA	774	776	712AJ		778	873JA	780	32AJ		18AJ	56AJ	8AJ	42AJ	92AJ	26AJ		6AJ	34AJ	4AJ	54CH	2AJ
	≋	♥	♥	≋		♥	≋	♥	*Fir*		*Fir*	*Sko*	*Fir*	*Sko*	*Sko*	*Fir*		*Fir*	*Fir*	*Fir*	⊡	*Fir*
									▽						△					Ⓑ	⊠	K
		N							h		p	D	⊙		m	R		⊙	t	◧		◧
Moskva Oktyabrskaya § ... d.	...	1730	1740	...	...	1930	...	1940	1953	...	2102	2124	2150	2205	2215	2228	...	2250	2310	2330	2340	2355
Tver ... d.	...	|	1843	...	...	|	...	2045	2144	...	2254	2329	2357	0011	0029	0046	...	|	0111	|	|	|
Bologoye ... d.	...	1926	|	1840	...	2126	...	|	|	...	0052	0117	|	0203	0221	0227	...	|	|	|	|	|
Chudovo ... d.	...	|	|	2054	...	2240	2249	|	|	...	...	|	|	0450	...	|	...	|	|	|	|	|
Novgorod na Volkhove ... d.	1810	|	|	|	...	|	2359	|	|	...	...	|	|	0605	...	|	...	|	|	|	|	|
Chudovo ... d.	1932	|	|	|	...	|	...	|	|	...	...	|	|	...	...	|	...	|	|	|	|	|
St Peterburg Glavny ‡ ... a.	2102	2121	2130	2211	...	2330	...	2340	0206**c**	...	...	0519	0606	...	...	0620	...	0634	0544	0830	0836	0756

	55AJ	34KH	31AJ	61AJ		751	17AJ		91AJ	874JA	753	755	711AJ	711AJ		757	759		761	765	767	747AJ
	Sko	*Fir*	*Fir*	*Sko*		♥	*Fir*		*Sko*	≋	♥	♥	≋	≋		♥	♥		♥	♥	♥	♡
			▽						△										⑥⑦			Ⓑ
	E	t	h	G			p		m		N											
St Peterburg Glavny ‡ ... d.	0050	0109**c**	0153**c**	0145	...	0530	...	...	...	...	0700	0710	0719	0719	...	0900	0910	...	1100	1300	1310	1320
Chudovo ... d.	|	|	|	|	...	|	...	...	...	...	|	|	0857	|	...	|	|	...	|	|	|	|
Novgorod na Volkhove ... d.	|	|	|	|	...	|	...	...	...	0620	|	|	1008	|	...	|	|	...	|	|	|	|
Chudovo ... d.	|	|	|	|	...	|	...	...	...	0734	|	0801	...	0855	...	|	|	...	|	|	1401	|
Bologoye ... d.	0501	0549	|	0607	...	|	0511	...	0643	...	|	0909	...	1030	...	1044	|	...	|	1453	|	|
Tver ... d.	0839	0733	0651	0922	...	|	0720	...	0913	...	0955	|	...	...	...	1141	|	...	|	1551	|	|
Moskva Oktyabrskaya § ... a.	1036	1006	0919	1210	...	0910	0957	...	1138	...	1100	1110	...	...	...	1250	1300	...	1450	1700	1710	1725

	769	771		775	59AJ		777	872JA	779		42CH	873JA	7AJ	29AJ	19UJ	5AJ	15AJ		3AJ	25AJ	53CH	1AJ
	♥	♥		♥	*Fir*		♥	≋	♥		*Sko*	≋	*Fir*	*Sko*	⊡	*Fir*	*Fir*		*Fir*	*Fir*	⊡	*Fir*
																			Ⓑ		⊠	K
					n								⊙		◐	⊙	m		◧	R		◧
St Peterburg Glavny ‡ ... d.	1500	1510	...	1710	1803	...	1900	...	1910	...	...	2035	2152	2211	2229	2250	2241**c**	...	2330	2336	2342	2355
Chudovo ... d.	|	|	...	|	|	...	|	...	|	...	...	2249	|	|	|	|	|	...	|	|	|	|
Novgorod na Volkhove ... d.	|	|	...	|	|	...	|	1810	|	...	2120	2359	|	|	|	|	|	...	|	|	|	|
Chudovo ... d.	|	|	...	|	|	...	|	1922	2001	...	2239	...	|	|	|	|	|	...	|	|	|	|
Bologoye ... d.	1645	|	...	1900	2232	...	2053	...	|	...	0131	...	|	0201	|	|	0302	...	|	|	|	|
Tver ... d.	1743	|	...	|	0017	...	2151	...	|	...	0330	...	0344	0351	0358	0426	0446	...	|	0501	|	|
Moskva Oktyabrskaya § ... a.	1850	1900	...	2100	0208**k**	...	2300	...	2310	...	0515	...	0606	0549	0557	0646	0654	...	0830	0719	0814	0756

D – Daily Apr. 28 - Sept. 25; ②–⑦ from Sept. 27.
E – Daily Apr. 28 - Sept. 27; ④–② from Sept. 28.
F – June 25 - Aug. 28 (also certain dates in June).
G – June 28 - Aug. 30 (also certain dates in June).
K – KRASNAYA STRELA (RED ARROW) - 🛏 1 cl. (ensuite), 🛏 1, 2 cl., ✕.
N – ①–⑤ May 30 - Sept. 5.
R – Runs 4-5 times per week.

c – St Peterburg **Ladozhski**.
h – To/from Helsinki (Table **1910**).
k – Moskva **Kurskaya**.

m – To/from Murmansk (Table **1905**).
n – To/from Nizhni Novgorod (Table **1990**).
p – To/from Petrozavodsk (Table **1905**).
t – To/from Tallinn (Table **1870**).

♥ – *Sapsan* high-speed train, special fares payable. ✕ Ⓡ.
≋ – *Lastochka* (Swallow) fast day train.
♡ – NEVSKIY EKSPRESS – first class seats only.
△ – For days of running see Table **1905**.
▽ – For days of running see Table **1910**.
⊙ – Modern low-cost double deck train, 🛏 2 cl. only, food and drink included in fare.

⊡ – Privately operated train.
⊠ – *Grand Express* luxury train: 🛏 1 cl. (ensuite), sh sofa, air conditioning, TV, DVD, wi-fi, 🛏 1, 2 cl.
◧ – Offers increased level of service, VIP cabins, wi
◐ – *Megapolis* - operated by Tverskoy Express.
§ – Also known as *Leningradski vokzal*.
‡ – Also known as *Moskovski vokzal*.
* – Distance from Chudovo.

Named trains: **3/4** EKSPRESS **7/8** NEVA **17/18** KAREIIYA **25/26** SMENA **31/32** LEV TOLSTOI

MOSKVA AIRPORTS ✈ 1901

·KVA DOMODEDOVO AIRPORT ✈
:xpress rail service Moskva Paveletskaya - Moskva odedovo ✈. *35 km* Journey time 40 - 47 minutes.
Moskva Paveletskaya: 0600, 0630, 0700 and every inutes (not 1230) until 2330, 0000, 0030.
Domodedovo ✈: 0600, 0630, 0700 and every 30 :es (not 1230) until 2330, 0000.

MOSKVA SHEREMETYEVO AIRPORT ✈
Aeroexpress rail service Moskva Belorusskaya - Moskva Sheremetyevo ✈. *35 km* Journey time 35 minutes.
From **Moskva Belorusskaya**: 0530, 0600, 0630 and every 30 minutes (not 1300) until 2330, 0000, 0030.
From **Sheremetyevo** ✈: 0500, 0600, 0630 and every 30 minutes (not 1200) until 2330, 0000, 0030.

MOSKVA VNUKOVO AIRPORT ✈
Aeroexpress rail service Moskva Kiyevskaya - Moskva Vnukovo ✈. *28 km* Journey time 34 - 42 minutes.
From **Moskva Kiyevskaya**: 0600 and every 60 minutes (also 1030, 1530, 1730, 1930; not 1200) until 2300, 0000.
From **Vnukovo** ✈: 0600 and every 60 minutes (also 0937, 1630, 1830) until 2300, 0000.

(MOSKVA) - ST PETERBURG - PETROZAVODSK - MURMANSK 1905

:D

ı		Fir 18AJ K	Sko 92AJ E n	Fir 16AJ		Pas 806CH	Sko 22CH	Sko 12AJ Ⓑ n	
	Moskva Oktyabrskaya **1900** . d.	2102	2215	0041	...	...	...	...	...
0	**St Peterburg** Ladozhski .... d.	|	|	0950	...	1800	1948	2320	...
4	Volkhovstroi I .... d.	0425v	0605v	1153	...	|	2148	0121	...
4	**Petrozavodsk** .... d.	0855	1148	1714	...	2255	0255	0700	...
3	Belomorsk .... d.	...	2124	2358	...	...	1003	...	...
1	Kandalaksha .... d.	...	0452	0655	...	...	1708	...	...
8	**Murmansk** .... a.	...	1032	1155	...	...	2215	...	...

	Sko 21CH		Fir 15AJ	Pas 805CH	Fir 17AJ K	Sko 91AJ F n		Sko 11AJ Ⓑ n
Murmansk .... d.	0911	...	1920	...	...	2045	...	...
Kandalaksha .... d.	1448	...	0050	...	...	0316	...	...
Belomorsk .... d.	2151	...	0733	...	...	1048	...	...
Petrozavodsk .... d.	0451	...	1508	1800	2020	2052	...	2240
Volkhovstroi I .... d.	1034	...	2015	|	0100v	0154v	...	0434
St Peterburg Ladozhski .... a.	1226	...	2216	2255	|	|	...	0624
Moskva Oktyabrskaya **1900**. a.	...	...	0654	...	0957	1138	...	...

②③④⑤⑦ (daily Apr. 26 - Aug. 29).
②④⑤⑥⑦ (daily Apr. 28 - Aug. 31).
K – KARELIYA.
n – Days of running may vary.
v – Volkhovstroi II.
* – Moskva - Vokhovstroi : *641 km.*

MOSKVA - ST PETERBURG - HELSINKI 1910

ıD, VR

ı		WINTER					SUMMER				
		151 AE30 A ★	Fir 32AJ Ln ★	153 AE34 A ★	155 AE36 A ★	157 AE38 A ★	151 AE30 A ☆	Fir 32AJ Lb ☆	153 AE34 A ☆	155 AE36 A ☆	157 AE38 A ☆
	Moskva Okt. § .... d.	...	1953	...	...	...	...	1953	...	...	...
	Tver .... d.	...	2144	...	...	...	...	2144	...	...	...
*	**St Peterburg** Lad. ‡ ..... d.	...	0221	...	...	...	...	0221	...	...	...
0	**St Peterburg** Fin. ‡ ...... d.	0640	|	1125	1525	2025	0641	|	1031	1531	2031
9	Vyborg .... a.	0735	0358	1220	1620	2120	0735	0358	1125	1625	2125
9	Vyborg .... 🏛 RU d.	0745	0448	1230	1630	2130	0745	0448	1135	1635	2135
9	Vainikkala .... 🏛 FIN a.	0714	0429	1159	1559	2059	0808	0529	1158	1658	2158
9	Vainikkala .... d.	0721	0544	1206	1606	2106	0815	0644	1205	1705	2205
0	**Kouvola** .... 797 a.	0800	0648	1245	1645	2145	0854	0739	1244	1744	2244
2	Lahti .... 797 a.	0826	0821	1311	1711	2211	0920	0822	1310	1810	2310
0	Tikkurila .... 797 a.	0901	0943	1346	1746	2246	0954	0943	1344	1844	2344
3	Pasila .... 797 a.	0910	1018	1355	1755	2255	|	1018	|	|	|
6	**Helsinki** .... 797 a.	0916	1026	1401	1801	2301	1008	1026	1358	1858	2358

	WINTER					SUMMER				
	AE33 152 A ★	AE35 154 A ★	AE37 156 A ★	Fir 31AJ Ln ★	AE39 158 A ★	AE33 152 A ☆	AE35 154 A ☆	AE37 156 A ☆	Fir 31AJ Lb ☆	AE39 158 A ☆
Helsinki .... 797 d.	0612	1000	1500	1723	1900	0620	1100	1600	1822	2000
Pasila .... 797 d.	0618	1006	1506	1729	1906	|	|	|	1828	|
Tikkurila .... 797 d.	0628	1016	1516	1740	1916	0633	1113	1613	1838	2013
Lahti .... 797 d.	0702	1050	1550	1836	1950	0707	1147	1647	1934	2047
Kouvola .... 797 d.	0728	1116	1616	1917	2016	0733	1213	1713	2015	2113
Vainikkala .... a.	0807	1155	1655	2012	2055	0813	1253	1753	2112	2153
Vainikkala .... 🏛 FIN d.	0814	1202	1702	2112	2102	0820	1300	1800	2212	2200
Vyborg .... 🏛 RU a.	0939	1327	1827	2253	2227	0842	1322	1822	2253	2222
Vyborg .... d.	0944	1332	1832	2343	2232	0847	1327	1827	2343	2227
St Peterburg Fin. ‡ ...... a.	1048	1436	1936	|	2336	0947	1427	1927	|	2327
St Peterburg Lad. ‡ ...... a.	...	...	...	0118	...	...	...	...	0118	...
Tver .... a.	...	...	...	0650	...	...	...	...	0650	...
Moskva Okt. § .... a.	...	...	...	0919	...	...	...	...	0919	...

Allegro (12) ✕ Ⓡ St Peterburg - Helsinki and v.v.
LEV TOLSTOI – 🛏 1 cl. (ensuite), 🛏 1, 2 cl., ✕ Moskva - Helsinki and v.v.
Ⓑ (daily Apr. 28 - May 10, June 2 - Aug. 31).
n – Not on ⑥ Jan. 16 - Mar. 19.
☆ – Mar. 27 - Oct. 29 (summer time in Finland).
★ – Not Mar. 27 - Oct. 29.
§ – Moskva Oktyabrskaya, also known as Leningradski.
‡ – Lad. = Ladozhski; Fin. = Finlyandski.
** – *143 km* St Peterburg Ladozhski - Vyborg.
FIN – Finland (GMT + 2 in winter, GMT + 3 in summer).
RU – Russia (Moskva Time GMT + 3).

ST PETERBURG - HOMEL and KOZYATYN ○ 1920

hD, BCh, UZ

n		Sko 49BJ A	Fir 53AJ ●	Sko 79CH K	Fir 55BJ	Sko 83AJ	Fir 51BJ	Sko 61MZ ■(3) ★	Sko 61MZ ■(3) ☆	Sko 57MJ ④ H
0	**St Peterburg** Vitebski .... d.	1405	1531	1613	...	1720	1820	2040	2040	2147
5	Dno .... d.	1750	1908	1955	...	2112	2208	0012	0012	0142
1	Novosokolniki .... RU d.	2036	2204	2249	...	0012	0050	0313	0313	0517
8	Vitsebsk .... § BY d.	2324	0040	0119	...	0249	0314	0529	0529	0757
0	Polatsk .... d.	|	|	0310	...	|	|	|	|	|
8	Maladzechnia .... a.	|	|	0549	...	|	|	|	|	|
	Moskva Bel. **1950** .... d.	|	|	▽	2023	|	|	|	|	|
2	**Orsha** Tsentralnaya .... a.	0040	0154	...	0337	0417	0426	0650	0650	0909
2	**Orsha** Tsentralnaya .... d.	0113	0216	...	0409	0439	0448	0712	0712	...
	Minsk **1950** .... a.	0344	|	...	|	|	0715	|	|	...
	Brest Tsent. **1950** .... a.	0825	|	...	|	|	1403x	|	|	...
6	Mahilyow I .... d.	...	0340	...	0600	0651	...	0841	0841	...
3	Zhlobin .... **1930** d.	...	0602	...	0812	0902	...	1100	1100	...
	Homel .... **1930** a.	...	0736	...	0935	1027	...	|	|	...
	Kyïv **1930** .... a.	...	1303r	...	...	...	...	|	|	...
4	Kalinkavichy .... BY d.	...	...	...	...	...	...	1237	1237	...
9	Korosten .... ‡ UA d.	...	...	...	...	...	...	1546	1646	...
1	Zhytomyr .... d.	...	...	...	...	...	...	1724	1833	...
7	**Kozyatyn** .... a.	...	...	...	...	...	...	1900	2004	...
	Chişinău **1720** .... a.	...	...	...	...	...	...	0717	0831	...

	Fir 52BJ J	Sko 50BJ B	Sko 83BJ	Sko 80CH K		Fir 55MZ	Sko 61SZ ■(1) ★	Sko 61SZ ■(1) ☆	Sko 54KJ ■(1)
Chişinău **1720** .... d.	...	...	...	...	...	...	2151	2226	...
Kozyatyn .... d.	...	...	...	...	...	...	1047	1151	...
Zhytomyr .... d.	...	...	...	...	...	...	1218	1322	...
Korosten .... UA d.	...	...	...	...	...	...	1404	1506	...
Kalinkavichy .... ‡ BY d.	...	...	...	...	...	...	1856	1856	...
Kyïv **1930** .... d.	...	...	...	...	...	...	|	|	1245s
Homel .... **1930** d.	...	...	1716	...	...	1808	|	|	2039
Zhlobin .... **1930** d.	...	...	1831	...	...	1952	2104	2104	2156
Mahilyow I .... d.	...	...	2140	...	...	2220	2306	2306	0035
Brest Tsent. **1950** .... d.	1157z	1405	|	...	...	|	|	|	|
Minsk **1950** .... d.	1800	1845	|	...	...	|	|	|	|
Orsha Tsentralnaya .... a.	2030	2116	2245	...	...	2337	0028	0028	0146
Orsha Tsentralnaya .... d.	2053	2142	2307	...	...	0001	0050	0050	0208
Moskva Bel. **1950** .... a.	|	|	|	▽	...	0657	|	|	|
Maladzechnia .... d.	|	|	|	2036	...	...	|	|	|
Polatsk .... d.	|	|	|	2356	...	...	|	|	|
Vitsebsk .... BY d.	2213	2311	0036	0155	...	...	0221	0221	0338
Novosokolniki .... § RU d.	0114	0249	0329	0444	...	...	0528	0528	0633
Dno .... d.	0345	0533	0603	0729	...	...	0809	0809	0853
St Peterburg Vitebski .... a.	0723	0917	0933	1109	...	...	1143	1143	1220

Mar. 21 - Apr. 5, June 1 - Sept. 16, Oct. 25 - Nov. 10.
Mar. 21 - Apr. 4, June 1 - Sept. 15, Oct. 24 - Nov. 9.
④: 🛏 1, 2 cl. St Peterburg - Orsha (**21**JA) - Brest - Praha and Wien (Table **95**). See Table **1950** for Orsha - Brest times.
Conveys once weekly (⑥ from Praha): 🛏 1, 2 cl. Praha and Wien - Warszawa - Brest (**22**JA) - Orsha (**52**BJ) - St Peterburg (Table **95**). See Table **1950** for Brest - Orsha times.
For days of running see Table **1950**.
r – Arrive 1403 Mar. 27 - Oct. 29.
s – Depart 1355 Mar. 27 - Oct. 29.
x – Train **681**BJ (conveys through portion St Peterburg - Brest except dates in note **A**).
z – Train **652**BJ (through portion except dates in note **B**).
☆ – Mar. 27 - Oct. 29 (summer time in Ukraine).
★ – Not Mar. 27 - Oct. 29.
▽ – To / from Vilnius and Kaliningrad (Table **1950**).
● – Even dates (see page 530).
■ – Uneven dates (see page 530).
BY – Belarus (GMT + 3)
RU – Russia (Moskva Time GMT + 3).
UA – Ukraine (GMT + 2 winter, GMT + 3 summer).
§ – 🏛 : Yezyaryshcha (BY) / Zaverezhye (RU).
‡ – 🏛 : Slovechno (BY) / Berezhest (UA).

MINSK - HOMEL - KYÏV 1930

:h, UZ

n		WINTER					SUMMER				
		Sko 100BJ ■(1) ★	Sko 94BJ ● ★‡	Fir 86BJ ★	Fir 53AJ ● ★	Sko 143 ● ★	Sko 100BJ ■(1) ☆	Sko 94BJ ● ☆‡	Fir 86BJ ☆	Fir 53AJ ● ☆	Sko 143 ● ☆
	St P'burg Vit. **1920** . d.	...	...	...	1531	1531	...	...	...	1531	1531
0	**Minsk** .... d.	0744	1348	2242	|	|	0744	1348	2242	|	|
4	Zhlobin .... **1920** d.	1100	1712	0139	0602	0602	1100	1712	0139	0602	0602
4	**Homel** .... **1920** a.	1223	1850	0253	0736	0736	1223	1850	0253	0736	0736
4	**Homel** .... BY d.	1246	1926	0317	0759	0759	1246	1926	0317	0759	0759
5	Chernihiv .... § UA d.	|	2216	|	1017	1017	|	2316	|	1117	1117
4	**Kyïv** .... a.	|	0055	0751	1303	|	|	0146	0852	1403	|
	Kharkiv **1755** .... a.	2354	|	...	...	2051	0058	|	...	...	2120
	Odesa **1720** .... a.	▽	1109	...	...	...	▽	1205	...	...	...

	WINTER					SUMMER				
	Sko 100PC ■(3) ★	Fir 54KJ ■(1) ★	Sko 143PC ■(1) ★	Fir 86KJ ★	Sko 94SH ■(3) ★‡	Sko 100PC ■(3) ☆	Fir 54KJ ■(1) ☆	Sko 143PC ■(1) ☆	Fir 86KJ ☆	Sko 94SH ■(3) ☆‡
Odesa **1720** .... d.	▽	...	...	...	1433	▽	...	...	...	1549
Kharkiv **1755** .... d.	0540	...	0600	...	|	0620	...	0642	...	|
Kyïv .... d.	|	1245	|	2119	0115	|	1355	|	2228	0213
Chernihiv .... § UA d.	|	1637	1637	|	0417	|	1736	1736	|	0517
Homel .... BY a.	1832	2014	2014	0406	0829	1832	2014	2014	0406	0829
Homel .... **1920** d.	1914	2039	2039	0437	0854	1914	2039	2039	0437	0854
Zhlobin .... **1920** d.	2100	2224	2224	0627	1017	2100	2224	2224	0546	1017
Minsk .... a.	0008	|	|	0917	1339	0008	|	|	0838	1339
St P'burg Vit. **1920** .. a.	...	1220	1220	...	...	...	1220	1220	...	...

- To / from Zaporizhzhya or Novooleksiivka (Table **1780**).
- Mar. 27 - Oct. 29 (summer time in Ukraine).
- Not Mar. 27 - Oct. 29.
● – Even dates (see page 530).
■ – Uneven dates (see page 530).
§ – 🏛 : Teryukha (BY) / Hornostayivka (UA).
‡ – On certain dates numbered **284** / **283**.
BY – Belarus (GMT + 3).
UA – Ukraine (GMT + 2 winter, GMT + 3 summer).

1931 MOSKVA - PSKOV

km		Fir 10AJ		Fir 10CH
0	**Moskva** Okt. ▷ d.	2023	**Pskov** d.	1930
167	Tver ▷ d.	2236	Dno d.	2112
331	Bologoye ▷ d.	0054	Bologoye ▷ d.	0219
588	Dno d.	0620	Tver ▷ d.	0405
687	**Pskov** a.	0805	**Moskva** Okt. ▷ a.	0614

▷ – See also Table **1900**.

1935 MOSKVA - POLATSK

km		Fir 39SZ		Fir 39BJ
0	**Moskva** Bel. d.	1958	**Polatsk** BY d.	1830
419	Smolensk a.	0137	Vitsebsk ‡ RU d.	2045
419	Smolensk d.	0226	Smolensk a.	2257
560	Vitsebsk ‡ RU d.	0535	Smolensk d.	2337
662	**Polatsk** BY a.	0710	**Moskva** Bel. a.	0519

‡ – ⊞ : Rudnya (RU) / Zavolsha (BY)
BY Belarus (GMT+3). RU Russia (GMT+3).

1945 MOSKVA - HOMEL

km		Sko 75BJ ▽		
0	**Moskva** Bel. d.	1518	**Homel** d.	
485	Bryansk Orlov. d.	0004	Dobrush BY d.	
713	Zlynka RU d.	0408	Zlynka RU d.	
739	Dobrush BY d.	0433	Bryansk Orlov. d.	
764	**Homel** a.	0500	**Moskva** Bel. a.	

▽ – Conveys portion to / from Brest (Table **1955**).
BY Belarus (GMT+3). RU Russia (GMT+3).

1950 MOSKVA - MINSK - VILNIUS, KALININGRAD and BREST

RZhD, BCh.

km		Pas 805BJ	Pas 803BJ	Pas 607BJ	🚄 741	Sko 57MJ ④ J	Sko 21JA ☆ V	Sko 21JA ★ V	Pas 651BJ	Pas 807BJ	Sko 25BJ	Sko 17BJ ☆ N	Sko 17BJ ★ N	Fir 27BJ	Sko 9JA ☆ P	Sko 9JA ★ P	Fir 29CH	🚄 751	Sko 49BJ A	Sko 95BJ	Sko 79CH K	Fir 39SZ
0	**Moskva** Belorusskaya d.	...	...	...	0650	...	0644	0746	...	...	0945	1018	1118	1512	1506	1627	1720	1830	...	1935	...	1958
243	Vyazma d.	...	...	...	0913	...	0926	1032	...	...	1313	1333	1447	1823	1800	1921	2034	2055	...	2306	...	2339
419	**Smolensk** RU d.	...	...	...	1100	...	1116	1224	...	...	1518	1526	1638	2026	1949	2110	2239	2240	...	0205	...	0226
	St Peterburg Vitebski ◐ d.	...	...	...	...	2147	|	|	...	...	|	|	|	|	|	|	|	...	1405	|	1613	▽
538	Orsha Tsentralnaya BY a.	...	...	...	...	0909	1225	1334	...	...	1658	1649	1749	2142	2059	2220	0012	...	0040	0327	|	...
538	Orsha Tsentralnaya d.	...	...	...	...	...	1242	1349	...	...	1712	1703	1803	2158	2113	2234	0030	...	0113	0341	⊡	...
750	**Minsk** a.	...	...	...	...	...	1503	1610	...	...	2007	1920	2020	0031	2326	0046	0251	...	0344	0609	|	...
750	**Minsk** d.	0800	1110	1330	...	...	1517	1625	1727	1952	...	1933	2035	0105	2356	0116	0314	...	0402	0625	|	...
827	Maladzechna BY d.	0900	1210	|	...	...	|	|	|	2054	...	|	|	|	|	|	0423	...	|	|	0603	...
943	**Vilnius** LT a.	0930r	1257r	|	...	...	|	|	|	2122r	...	|	|	|	|	|	0633r	...	|	|	0823r	...
943	**Vilnius** LT d.	...	...	|	...	...	|	|	|	...	...	|	|	|	|	|	0708r	...	|	|	0840r	...
1285	**Kaliningrad** Ka a.	...	...	|	...	...	|	|	|	...	...	|	|	|	|	|	1400	...	|	|	1550	...
892	Baranavichy Tsentralnye d.	...	...	1522	...	...	1703	1803	1912	...	...	|	|	0308	0140	0253	...	...	0553	0921p	...	...
1094	**Brest** Tsentralny a.	...	...	1801	...	...	1856	1952	2142	...	...	2310	0010	0544	0554	0654	...	...	0825	1211	...	...
	Warszawa Wschodnia **1050** a.	...	...	...	...	...	2319	2319	...	...	...	0319	0319	...	0832	0832	...	...	...	...	...	...

	Sko 23JI ☆ T	Sko 23JI ★ T	Sko 3BJ ●	Sko 7MJ ■	Fir 51BJ	51BJ 681BJ C	Fir 1BJ	Sko 147CH F	Fir 33ZH
Moskva Belorusskaya d.	2111	2215	2203	2203	...	...	2140	2238	2354
Vyazma d.	2356	0100	0047	0047	...	...	0120	0155	0353
Smolensk RU d.	0151	0255	|	|	...	...	0319	0400	0630
St Peterburg Vitebski ◐ d.	|	|	|	|	1820	1820	|	|	...
Orsha Tsentralnaya BY a.	0301	0405	0355	0355	0426	0426	0440	0516	...
Orsha Tsentralnaya d.	0317	0417	0407	0407	0448	0448	0456	0536	...
Minsk a.	0542	0643	0618	0618	0715	0715	0725	0807	...
Minsk d.	0556	0657	0636	0636	...	0928	...	0833	...
Maladzechna BY d.	|	|	|	|	...	|	...	0941	...
Vilnius LT a.	|	|	|	|	...	|	...	1152	...
Vilnius LT d.	|	|	|	|	...	|	...	1209	...
Kaliningrad Ka a.	|	|	|	|	...	|	...	1914	...
Baranavichy Tsentralnye d.	0752	0856	0838	0838	...	1126	...	...	...
Brest Tsentralny a.	0950	1052	1041	1041	...	1403	...	...	...
Warszawa Wschodnia **1050** a.	1353	1353	...	...	...	...	...	...	...

	Pas 804TJ	Pas 668BJ	Sko 18BJ ☆ M	Sko 18BJ ★ M	🚄 752	Sko 22AJ ☆ V	Sko 22AJ ★ V
Warszawa Wschodnia **1050** d.	...	...	0155	0155	...	0344	0344
Brest Tsentralny d.	...	0630	0840	0940	...	1012	1120
Baranavichy Tsentralnye d.	...	0905	|	|	...	1220	1315
Kaliningrad Ka d.	...	|	|	|	...	|	|
Vilnius LT a.	...	|	|	|	...	|	|
Vilnius LT d.	0620r	|	|	|	...	|	|
Maladzechna d.	0850	|	|	|	...	|	|
Minsk a.	0950	1057	1221	1315	...	1406	1501
Minsk d.	...	...	1234	1330	...	1420	1518
Orsha Tsentralnaya a.	...	...	1500	1558	...	1638	1730
Orsha Tsentralnaya BY d.	...	...	1514	1614	...	1652	1744
St Peterburg Vitebski ◐ a.	...	...	|	|	...	|	|
Smolensk RU d.	...	...	1637	1735	1830	1809	1901
Vyazma d.	...	...	1856	1954	2021	2015	2105
Moskva Belorusskaya a.	...	...	2130	2230	2240	2243	2335

	Pas 652BJ ♡	Fir 52BJ	Sko 50BJ B	Pas 808TJ	Sko 26BJ	Fir 39BJ	Fir 34ZH	Sko 80CH L	Fir 55MZ	Sko 4BJ ■(1)	Sko 8BJ ●	Pas 806TJ	Fir 2BJ	Sko 28BJ	Fir 30CH	Pas 802TJ ⑥⑦	Sko 24JI ☆ U	Sko 24JI ★ U	🚄 744	Sko 148CH F	Sko 96BJ	Sko 10ZH ☆ P
Warszawa Wschodnia **1050** d.	...	...	...	...	...	...	...	...	...	...	...	...	...	...	...	...	1417	1417	...	...	...	1927
Brest Tsentralny d.	1157	...	1405	...	...	...	...	...	...	1740	1740	...	...	1750	...	...	2107	2200	...	...	2324	0252
Baranavichy Tsentralnye d.	1448	...	1638	...	...	...	...	...	...	1941	1941	...	...	2020	...	...	2307	0003	...	...	0242p	0450
Kaliningrad Ka d.	|	...	|	...	...	...	...	1029	...	|	|	...	...	|	1347	...	|	|	...	1729	|	|
Vilnius LT a.	|	...	|	...	...	...	...	1530r	...	|	|	...	...	|	1845r	...	|	|	...	2330	|	|
Vilnius LT d.	|	...	|	1458r	...	...	...	1547r	...	|	|	1812r	...	|	1910r	2005r	|	|	...	2347	|	|
Maladzechna d.	|	...	|	1748	...	...	...	2036	...	|	|	2042	...	|	2321	2350	|	|	...	0302	|	|
Minsk a.	1636	...	1829	1845	...	...	...	|	...	2125	2125	2142	...	2204	0025	0049	0050	0139	...	0407	0444	0633
Minsk d.	...	1800	1845	...	1900	...	...	|	△	2144	2144	...	2208	2223	0048	...	0104	0153	...	0430	0500	0703
Orsha Tsentralnaya a.	...	2030	2116	...	2145	...	...	⊡	2337	2358	2358	...	0026	0050	0305	...	0318	0406	...	0706	0734	0935
Orsha Tsentralnaya BY d.	...	2053	2142	...	2159	...	...	|	0001	0009	0009	...	0040	0105	0319	...	0333	0421	...	0721	0748	0949
St Peterburg Vitebski ◐ a.	...	0723	0917	...	|	▽	...	1109	|	|	|	...	|	|	|	...	|	|	...	|	|	|
Smolensk RU d.	...	...	...	...	2326	2337	2354	...	0138	|	|	...	0228	0239	0439	...	0451	0540	0740	0903	0932	1111
Vyazma d.	...	...	...	...	0207	0218	0250	...	0405	0352	0352	...	0449	0516	0633	...	0654	0743	0931	1153	1229	1312
Moskva Belorusskaya a.	...	...	...	...	0510	0519	0630	...	0657	0647	0647	...	0805	0840	0916	...	0921	1010	1150	1457	1608	1539

A – Mar. 21 - Apr. 5, June 1 - Sept. 16, Oct. 25 - Nov. 10.
B – Mar. 21 - Apr. 4, June 1 - Sept. 15, Oct. 24 - Nov. 9.
C – Not dates in note **A**.
F – Runs four times per week May 28 - Aug. 31.
J – Conveys once weekly on dates in Table **95** 🛏 1, 2 cl. St Peterburg - Orsha - Warszawa - Praha and Wien for or from train **V**.
K – ③⑤⑦ (also ① May 30 - Sept. 5).
L – ②④⑥ (also ⑦ May 29 - Sept. 4).
M – ⑥ (from Nice): 🛏 1 cl (lux), 🛏 1, 2 cl. Nice - Warszawa - Moskva (Table **25**, journey two nights); ✕ (RZD) Brest - Moskva.
N – ④: 🛏 1 cl (lux), 🛏 1, 2 cl. Moskva - Warszawa - Nice (Table **25**, journey two nights); ✕ (RZD) Moskva - Brest.
P – POLONEZ – 🛏 1, 2 cl., 🍸 Moskva - Warszawa and v.v. ✕ Moskva - Brest and v.v. Conveys 🛏 1, 2 cl. Moskva - Budapest - Beograd - Sofia and v.v. (Table **95**).
T – TRANSEUROPEAN EXPRESS – ①④⑤: 🛏 1, 2 cl. Moskva (**23JI**) - Brest (**452**) - Berlin - Paris (Table **24**); ✕ Moskva - Brest.
U – TRANSEUROPEAN EXPRESS – ③⑥⑦ (from Paris): 🛏 1, 2 cl. Paris (**453**) - Berlin - Brest (**24JI**) - Moskva (Table **24**); ✕ Brest - Moskva.
V – VLTAVA – conveys on dates in Table **95** 🛏 1, 2 cl. Moskva - Warszawa - Praha, Cheb and Wien and v.v.; ✕ Moskva - Brest and v.v.

p – Baranavichy Polesskiye.
r – One hour later Mar. 27 - Oct. 29 (summer time in Lithuania).
☆ – Mar. 27 - Oct. 29 (summer time in Lithuania / Poland).
★ – Not Mar. 27 - Oct. 29.
△ – To / from Homel (Table **1920**).
▽ – To / from Polatsk (Table **1935**).
⊡ – Via Vitsebsk (Table **1920**).
♡ – Conveys through portion for train in next column except when train **B** runs.
🚄 – *Lastochka* (Swallow) fast day train.
◐ – See Table **1920**.
● – Even dates (see page 530).
■ – Uneven dates (see page 530).
■(1) – Uneven dates [.. 29, 1 ..]
BY – Belarus (GMT+3).
Ka – Kaliningrad region of Russia (train times are Moskva time GMT+3, local time is GMT+2).
LT – Lithuania (GMT+2 in winter, GMT+3 in summer).

RU – Russia (Moskva Time GMT+3).

BORDER CROSSINGS

Between Smolensk and Orsha:
Krasnoye (RU) / Osinovka (BY).
Between Maladzechna and Vilnius:
Hudahai (BY) / Kena (LT).
Between Vilnius and Kaliningrad:
Kybartai (LT) / Nesterov (Ka).

OTHER NAMED TRAINS

1/2	BELORUSSIYA / BELARUS
3/4	MINSK
7/8	SLAVYANSKI EKSPRESS
29/30	YANTAR

1952 MINSK - HRODNA

BCh

km		Pas 673BJ	Pas 627BJ	Pas 629BJ		Pas 630BJ	Pas 674BJ	Pas 628BJ
0	**Minsk** d.	0701	1531	1650	**Hrodna** d.	0625	1515	2341
77	Maladzechna d.	0805	△	1801	Lida d.	0817	1706	|
205	Lida d.	0956	|	2013	Maladzechna d.	1028	1900	▽
337	**Hrodna** a.	1142	2256	2203	**Minsk** a.	1129	2002	0725

△ – Via Baranavichy Polesskiye (d. 1800). ▽ – Via Baranavichy Polesskiye (d. 0520).

1955 HOMEL - BREST

km		Pas 675FJ ⊡	Pas 603BJ		Pas 676FJ ⊡
0	**Homel** d.	0539	2012	**Brest** Tsentralny d.	1025
129	Kalinkavichy d.	0754	2241	Luninets d.	1430
306	Luninets d.	1118	0154	Kalinkavichy d.	1733
534	**Brest** Tsentralny a.	1510	0606	**Homel** a.	1935

⊡ – Conveys portion from / to Moskva (Table **1945**).

MOSKVA - VORONEZH - ROSTOV NA DONU - SOCHI - ADLER 1960

	49AJ Sko L	43SJ Fir ■(5)	87GJ Fir E	126EI Sko N	35AJ Fir ◇ Q	302BJ Pas n	70GJ Fir	4SJ Fir ☆	104VJ Fir ◇	12MJ Fir	102MJ Fir ☆ C	30SJ Fir ☆	46VJ Fir ◇ w	20SJ Fir	139NJ Sko U	306MJ Pas S	34SJ Sko	62CH Fir	156MJ Sko A	25JA Fir ☆	77CH Sko ◧	29MJ Fir	202MJ Sko G
St Peterburg Glavny ... d.	1330	1354	...	...	2006	...	...	...	...	...	...	...	...	...	...	...	...	...	...	...	...	...	...
Bologoye ... d.	1721	1825	...	...	0003	...	...	...	...	...	...	...	...	...	...	...	...	...	...	...	...	...	...
Tver ... d.	1903	2054	g	...	0148	...	...	...	...	...	...	...	...	...	...	...	...	...	...	...	...	...	...
Moskva Kazanskaya ... d.	2151r	|	|	0025	|	...	0810	0820	1052	1020	1408	1418	1652	1838	...	1950	2150	2218	2328	...	...	...	2316
Moskva Paveletskaya ... d.	|	|	|	|	|	...	|	|	|	|	|	|	|	|	...	|	|	|	|	2114	2104	2142	|
Ryazan II ... d.	|	0251	0422	0346	0656	...	1039	1057	1310	1303	1652	1702	1910	2143	...	2254	0110	0123	0241	|	|	|	0206
Michurinsk Uralski ... d.	|	0645	0733	0750	|	...	|	|	|	|	|	|	|	|	...	|	0420	|	0635	|	0518	|	|
Michurinsk Voronezhski ... d.	|	|	|	|	0955	⊡	1253	1328	1540	1533	1916	1933	2120	0015	...	0141	|	0412	|	0452	|	|	0444
Yelets ... d.	0615	|	|	|	|	0806	|	|	|	|	|	|	|	|	...	|	|	|	|	|	|	0545	|
Lipetsk ... d.	0739	|	|	|	|	0930	|	|	|	|	|	|	|	|	...	|	|	|	|	|	|	0700	|
Gryazi Voronezhski ... d.	|	0750	0838	0905	1056	|	1333	|	|	|	|	|	2200	0059	...	0227	0520	0500	0738	0542	0623	...	0529
Voronezh I ... d.	|	|	|	|	1300	1230	1455	|	|	|	|	|	2322	|	...	0522	|	0908	|	0758	|	...	0800
Voronezh Pridacha ... d.	1108	1017	1040	1121	|	|	...	1547	1755	1755	2133	2146	...	0246	d	|	0755	|	1006	...	0844	...	|
Liski ... d.	1240	1135	1207	1231	1445	1415	...	1658	1906	1912	2246	2258	...	0347	0449	0711	0918	1049	1118	...	0955	...	0947
Rossosh ... d.	1504	1401	1419	1445	1722	1637	...	1843	2042	2057	0025	0038	...	0535	0706	0928	1136	1252	1303	...	1335	...	1149
Likhaya ... d.	1949	1958	|	1926	2153	2134	...	|	|	|	|	|	...	0938	1157	1415	1637	1701	1744	...	1851	...	1606
Rostov na Donu ... a.	2300	2320	2220	2251	0034	0043	...	0023	0207	0219	0546	0558	...	1212	1440	1730	1942	2023	2051	...	2229	...	1915
Rostov na Donu ... d.	2318	2340	2240	2310	0050	0101	...	0040	0222	0234	0610	0620	...	...	1520	1815	2014	2103	2111	...	2251	...	1942
Tikhoretskaya ... d.	0217	|	|	|	|	|	...	|	|	|	|	|	...	...	1820	|	2304	2359	|	...	0120	...	2231
Starominskaya Tim. ... d.	|	0108	0008	0051	|	0227	...	|	|	|	|	|	...	...	|	1943	|	|	2251	...	u	...	|
Krasnodar I ... d.	|	0403	0309	|	0438	0514	...	|	0539	|	|	0940	...	...	|	2230	|	|	|	...	...	...	|
Novorossiysk ... a.	|	0720	|	0630	|	|	...	|	|	|	|	1255	...	...	|	|	|	|	|	...	...	...	|
Anapa ... a.	|	...	|	...	|	|	...	|	|	0948	|	...	...	...	|	|	|	|	0500	...	...	...	|
Armavir Rostovski ... d.	0428	...	|	...	|	|	...	0452	|	...	|	...	...	...	2118t	|	0134	0222	...	...	...	...	0113t
Mineralnye Vody ... d.	0830	...	|	...	|	|	...	0732	|	...	|	...	...	...	|	|	0443	0516	...	...	...	...	|
Pyatigorsk ... d.	0914	...	|	...	|	|	...	0809	|	...	|	...	...	...	|	|	v	m	...	...	...	...	|
Kislovodsk ... a.	1011	...	|	...	|	|	...	0905	|	...	|	...	...	...	|	|	...	...	...	...	...	...	|
Tuapse ... d.	...	...	0711	...	0751	0937	...	...	0828	...	1144	...	...	...	0233	0220	...	...	...	...	...	...	0559
Sochi ... a.	...	...	0915	...	1003	1143	...	...	1012	...	1330	...	...	...	0434	0417	...	...	...	...	...	...	0843
Adler ▦ ◐ ... a.	...	...	0958	...	1043	1231	...	...	1051	...	1406	...	...	...	0515	0454	...	...	...	...	...	...	0921
Gagra ... a.	...	...	...	...	...	...	...	...	...	...	...	...	...	...	...	0812	...	...	...	...	...	...	...
Sukhumi ... a.	...	...	...	...	...	...	...	...	...	...	...	...	...	...	...	1024	...	...	...	...	...	...	...

	49CH Sko M	104ZH Fir ◇	30JI Fir ☆	44SJ Fir ■(3)	88SJ Fir F	36AJ Fir ◇ R	302SJ Pas ■(3)	102SJ Fir ☆ D	3SJ Fir ☆	69VJ Fir	77SJ Sko ◧	140NJ Sko V	306SJ Pas T	61SJ Fir	33SJ Sko	202SJ Sko H	29VJ Fir	25VJ Fir ☆	19SJ Fir	155SJ Sko B	11EI Fir	45VJ Fir ◇ w	126SJ Sko P	
khumi ... d.	...	...	...	...	...	...	...	...	...	...	...	...	1400	...	...	...	...	...	...	...	...	...	...	...
gra ... d.	...	...	...	...	...	...	...	...	...	...	...	...	1621	...	...	...	...	...	...	...	...	...	...	...
r ▦ ◐ ... d.	...	1825	...	...	1505	1632	1657	2016	...	...	...	1351	1937	...	...	2054	...	...	...	...	...	...	...	...
i ... d.	...	1910	...	...	1552	1715	1743	2054	...	...	...	1431	2015	...	...	2139	...	...	...	...	...	...	...	...
se ... d.	...	2105	...	...	1805	1953	2026	2243	...	...	...	1638	2252	...	...	2345	...	...	...	...	...	...	...	...
slovodsk ... d.	1336	|	...	...	|	|	|	|	1949	...	...	|	|	...	...	|	...	...	...	...	...	...	...	...
atigorsk ... d.	1432	|	...	...	|	|	|	|	2046	...	...	|	|	m	v	|	...	...	...	...	...	...	...	...
neralnye Vody ... d.	1547	|	...	...	|	|	|	|	2137	...	...	|	|	2309	2225	|	...	...	...	...	...	...	...	...
navir Rostovski ... d.	1832	|	...	...	|	|	|	|	0002	...	...	2241t	|	0137	0106	0542t	...	...	...	...	...	...	...	...
Anapa ... d.	|	|	...	...	|	|	|	|	|	...	...	|	|	|	|	|	...	...	...	0910	1340	...	...	...
Novorossiysk ... d.	|	|	2020	1700	|	|	|	|	|	...	...	|	|	|	|	|	...	...	...	|	|	...	1335	...
nodar I ... d.	|	2324	2310	1949	2146	2300	2340	|	|	...	...	|	0133	|	|	|	...	...	...	|	|	...	|	...
arominskaya Tim. ... d.	|	|	|	2338	0058	|	0236	|	|	...	u	|	0434	|	|	|	...	...	...	1532	|	...	1952	...
retskaya ... d.	2038	|	|	|	|	|	|	|	0203	...	0149	0128	|	0357	0325	0755	...	...	...	|	|	...	|	...
ov na Donu ... a.	2325	0244	0254	0111	0340	0229	0408	0423	0431	...	0450	0440	0604	0627	0636	1026	...	...	...	1651	2039	...	2117	...
ov na Donu ... d.	2343	0259	0309	0128	0400	0244	0426	0438	0448	...	0515	0505	0627	0712	0703	1053	...	...	1415	1709	2059	...	2135	...
ya ... d.	0253	|	|	0445	|	0622	0815	|	|	...	0838	0828	1043	1100	1114	1359	...	...	1659	2038	|	...	0058	...
osh ... d.	0735	0824	0835	0939	1126	1100	1336	1014	1024	...	1308	1326	1519	1535	1558	1740	...	...	2058	0044	0241	...	0517	...
... d.	0920	1011	1024	1130	1309	1247	1527	1155	1205	...	1518	1549	1700	1720	1805	1912	...	...	2236	0230	0424	...	0711	...
nezh Pridacha ... d.	1205	1113	1127	1237	1424	|	|	1303	1318	...	1625	b	|	|	1925	|	...	...	2339	|	0527	...	0822	...
nezh I ... d.	|	|	|	|	|	1457	1802	|	|	1610	|	...	1937	2005	|	2115	...	2130	|	0433	|	0725	|	...
zi Voronezhski ... d.	|	|	|	1557	1633	1646	|	|	|	1730	1828	...	2125	2235	2140	2300	...	2320	0125	0710	0657	0845	1103	...
etsk ... d.	1512	|	|	|	|	|	2108	|	|	|	|	...	|	|	|	|	2035	|	|	|	|	|	|	...
lets ... d.	1704	|	|	|	|	|	2310	|	|	|	|	...	|	|	|	|	2227	|	|	|	|	|	|	...
urinsk Voronezhski ... d.	|	1331	1348	|	|	1747	⊡	1524	1544	1815	|	...	2230	2338	|	2356	|	0039	0214	0813	0757	0928	|	...
urinsk Uralski ... d.	|	|	|	1755	1824	|	...	|	|	|	2009	...	|	|	0004	|	|	|	|	|	|	|	1259	...
an II ... d.	|	1556	1606	2153	2143	2050	...	1751	1801	2033	|	...	0129	0210	0316	0245	|	|	0444	1125	1028	1140	1643	...
kva Paveletskaya ... a.	|	|	|	|	|	|	...	|	|	|	0500	...	|	|	|	|	0615	0750	|	|	|	|	|	...
kva Kazanskaya ... a.	0202r	1823	1833	|	|	|	...	2015	2055	2255	...	...	0452	0523	0628	0555	...	...	0735	1435	1338	1355	1937	...
er ... d.	0420	...	...	0337	h	0225	...	...	...	...	...	...	...	...	...	...	...	...	...	...	...	...	...	...
logoye ... d.	0609	...	...	0515	...	0413	...	...	...	...	...	...	...	...	...	...	...	...	...	...	...	...	...	...
Peterburg Glavny ... a.	1223	...	...	1022	...	0745	...	...	...	...	...	...	...	...	...	...	...	...	...	...	...	...	...	...

May 25 - Sept. 18.
May 27 - Sept. 20.
Even dates ●(4) (daily May 26 - Sept. 30).
Even dates ● (daily May 24 - Sept. 28).
Uneven dates ■(3) (daily May 25 - Oct. 11).
Uneven dates ■(5) (daily May 27 - Oct. 13).
Uneven dates ■(3) May 25 - Sept. 27.
Uneven dates ■(5) May 27.- Sept. 29.
②④⑤⑦ (daily Dec. 24 - Jan. 8, Apr. 21 - Sept. 23).
②④⑥⑦ (daily Dec. 26 - Jan. 10, Apr. 23 - Sept. 25).
Uneven dates ■(3) (daily Dec. 27 - Jan. 13, June 1 - Oct. 3).
Uneven dates ■(1) (daily Dec. 25 - Jan. 11, May 29 - Oct. 1).
Even dates ● (also certain uneven dates June 3 - Sept. 29).
Even dates ●(4) (also certain uneven dates June 5 - Oct. 1).
Daily Apr. 23 - Sept. 30; uneven dates Oct. 1 - 31; every 4 days Nov. 1 - 29, Dec. 3 - 7. Journey 2 nights.
Daily Apr. 25 - Oct. 3; uneven dates Oct. 5 - 31 (also Nov. 2); every 4 days Nov. 3 - 27, Dec. 1 - 9. Journey 2 nights.
From Novosibirsk on even dates (daily June 20 - Aug. 30). Departs Liski on 4th day, arrive Adler on 5th day.

V – Even dates ●(6) (daily June 24 - Sept. 3). Arrive Novosibirsk 5th day.
Y – From Rostov every four days Apr. 22 - 30, May 4 - 28, June 1 - 29, July 3 - 31, Aug. 4 - 28, Sept. 1 - 29, Oct. 3 - 15, returning from Baki two days later.

b – To Novosibirsk (Table **1990**). Via Penza (0305 3rd day), Saransk (0613 3rd day).
d – From Novosibirsk (Table **1990**). Via Saransk (1434 3rd day), Penza (1811 3rd day).
g – From Nizhni Novgorod (d. 1907) via Vladimir (d. 2250).
h – To Nizhni Novgorod (a. 0719) via Vladimir (a. 0344).
m – To / from Nalchik (arrive 0816; depart 1920).
n – ■(1) from Minsk, next day from Yelets (Table **1961**).
r – Moska **Kurskaya**.
t – Armavir **Tuapsinkii**.
u – To / from Stavropol (arrive 0605; depart 2116).
v – To / from Vladikavkaz (arrive 0920; depart 1746).
w – Will not run on ⑥ Apr. 23 - Sept. 17.

◐ – ▦ = Veseloe (Russia) / Tsandryphsh (Abkhazia Autonomous Region).
☆ – Includes Lux sleeping car with ensuite shower/toilet.

⊡ – From / to Minsk (Table **1961**).
◧ – Runs 2 - 3 times per week.
◇ – Train consists of new double-deck sleeping cars.

● – Even dates. See page 530.
●(4) – Even dates [.. *30, 1, 4* ..]
●(6) – Even dates [.. *30, 1, 3, 6* ..]

■ – Uneven dates. See page 530.
■(1) – Uneven dates [.. *29, 1* ..]
■(3) – Uneven dates [.. *31, 3* ..]
■(5) – Uneven dates [.. *31, 2, 5* ..]

AZ – Azerbaijan (GMT + 4).
▦ = Yalama.
BY – Belarus (GMT + 3).
RU – Russia (Moskva time GMT + 3).

MINSK - ADLER 1961

n		302BJ Pas ■(1)		302SJ Pas ■(3)
0	**Minsk** ..... **1930** d.	1159	**Adler** ... d.	1657
6	Homel ... BY d.	1740	Sochi ... d.	1743
7	Bryansk O... RU d.	2350	**Rostov na D.** ... d.	0426
8	Yelets ... d.	0806	Yelets ... d.	2310
7	**Rostov na D.** ... d.	0101	Bryansk O. ... RU d.	0710
8	Sochi ... a.	1143	Homel ... BY a.	1217
1	**Adler** ... a.	1231	**Minsk** ...... **1930** a.	1802

further stations between Yelets and Adler see Table **1960**.

SARATOV - ADLER 1962

km		14ZH Sko △		14SJ Sko ▽
0	**Saratov** I ... d.	0947	**Adler** ... d.	1834
429	Volgograd I ... d.	1654	Sochi ... d.	1918
964	Tikhoretskaya .. d.	0237	Tuapse ... d.	2121
1100	**Krasnodar** I ... d.	0523	**Krasnodar** I ... d.	0045
1248	Tuapse ... d.	1026	Tikhoretskaya .. d.	0326
1328	Sochi ... a.	1223	Volgograd I ... d.	1414
1351	**Adler** ... a.	1310	**Saratov** I ... a.	2045

△ – Uneven dates ■(3) (daily May 25 - Sept. 30).
▽ – Even dates ●(4) (daily May 26 - Oct. 2).

ROSTOV - BAKI 1963

km		392SJ Pas Y		391SZ Pas Y
0	**Rostov na D.** .. d.	1807	**Baki** ... AZ d.	2230
307	Armavir Rost. ... d.	2326	Derbent ... d.	0725
495	Mineralnye Vody d.	0225	Makhachkala ... d.	1017
773	Gudermes ... d.	0952	Gudermes ... d.	1520
896	Makhachkala ... d.	1412	Mineralnye Vody d.	0015
1025	Derbent ... d.	1642	Armavir Rost. ... d.	0254
1286	**Baki** ... AZ a.	0315	**Rostov na D.** ... a.	0811

FOR NOTES SEE TABLE **1960**.

1965 MOSKVA - SARATOV, VOLGOGRAD and BAKI

km		79AJ	1IJ	9GJ	17MJ	15JI	55CH	86VJ	7CJ	31CH	5GJ
		Sko	Fir	Fir	Fir	Sko	Sko	Sko	Sko	Fir	Fir
		B					⑥t		●(4)		
	St Peterburg Glavny . d.	2027	...	...	...	...	...	...	...	...	...
	Tver . d.	0158	...	...	...	...	...	...	...	...	...
0	**Moskva** Paveletskaya . d.	0410r	1342	1813	2000	2009	2240r	2112k	2133	2200	2359
198	Ryazan II . d.	|	|	|	|	|	△	0042	|	|	|
408	Michurinsk Uralski . d.	|	|	0118	0331	|	|	0402	0547	0612	0906
	Michurinsk Voronezhski . d.	|	2016	|	|	0340	|	|	|	|	|
426	Yelets . d.	1336	|	|	|	|	0635	|	|	|	|
504	Lipetsk . d.	1501	|	|	|	|	0807	|	|	|	|
541	Gryazi Voronezhski . d.	1625	2140	|	|	0510	0933	|	|	|	|
481	Tambov I . d.	|	|	0230	0443	|	|	0526	0659	0730	1027
861	**Saratov** I . a.	|	|	0850	1141	|	|	1203	1322	...	1735
778	Povorino . d.	2230	0206	...	...	1010	1405	|	a	...	|
1145	**Volgograd** I . a.	0458	0825	...	...	1653	2030	|	...	...	|
1595	Astrakhan I . a.	...	...	...	...	...	0458	2342	...	...	0602
⊡	Makhachkala . a.	...	...	...	...	...	1607	1235	...	...	...
2212	Derbent . a.	...	...	...	...	...	1905	...	...	...	...
2473	**Baki** AZ a.	...	...	...	...	...	0525*	...	...	...	...

	9ZH	1ZH	17ZH	7RJ	15ZH	5ZH	79ZH	55SZ	85SJ
	Fir	Fir	Fir	Sko	Sko	Fir	Sko	Sko	Sko
				E			C	④t	
Baki AZ d.	...	...	...	...	...	...	...	0115*	...
Derbent . d.	...	...	...	...	...	...	...	0835	...
Makhachkala . d.	...	...	...	...	...	...	...	1113	1445
Astrakhan I . d.	...	...	...	...	...	1455	...	2054	0142
Volgograd I . d.	...	1514	...	...	1713	|	0107	0517	|
Povorino . d.	...	2152	...	a	0013	|	0830	1255	|
Saratov I . d.	1630	|	1903	1935	|	0321	|	|	1349
Tambov I . d.	2253	|	0154	0214	|	1017	|	|	2034
Gryazi Voronezhski . d.	|	0227	|	|	0530	|	1445	1755	|
Lipetsk . d.	|	|	|	|	|	|	1544	1841	|
Yelets . d.	|	|	|	|	|	|	1800	2023	|
Michurinsk Voronezhski d.	|	0325	|	|	0624	|	|	|	|
Michurinsk Uralski . d.	0032	|	0336	0353	|	1155	|	|	2242
Ryazan II . d.	|	|	|	|	|	|	|	▽	0220
Moskva Paveletskaya . a.	0720	0958	1029	1038	1400	1910	0259r	0330r	0530k
Tver . d.	...	...	...	...	...	...	0527	...	...
St Peterburg Glavny a.	...	...	...	...	...	...	1240	...	...

B – Even dates (daily Mar. 24 - Sept. 7).
C – Uneven dates (daily Mar. 23 - Sept. 7).
E – ■(1) from Almaty, from Saratov 3rd day.

a – To/from Almaty (Table **1975**).
k – Moskva **Kazanskaya**.
r – Moska **Kurskaya**.
t – Journey 3 nights.

● – Even dates. See page 530.
■ – Uneven dates. See page 530.
△ – Via Tula I (d. 0149).
▽ – Via Tula I (d. 0100).

⊡ – *1537 km* (*2083 km* via Volgograd).
* – One hour later during daylight saving tir Mar. 27 - Oct. 29.
AZ – Azerbaijan (GMT + 4 winter, + 5 summe

1970 MOSKVA - SAMARA - UFA - CHELYABINSK

km		66JI	68JI	40JI	32UJ	50MJ	10JI	14EJ	6FJ	18SZ	72/84
		Sko	Sko	Fir	Fir	Sko	Fir	Fir	Sko	Sko	Sko
			●	■(3)	F				T	B	A
0	**Moskva** Kaz. . d.	1520	1708	1708	1716	1810	2008	2122	2240	2240	2248
197	Ryazan I . d.	1832	2025	2025	2035	2102	2259	0037	0152	0152	0214
601	Ruzayevka ⊡ . d.	0109	0224	0224	0238	0259	0350	0556	0757	0757	0845
712	Inza . d.	0250	0405	0405	|	0434	|	|	0941	0941	|
908	Syzran I . d.	0622	0644	0644	0724	0711	0740	0959	|	|	1324
1044	**Samara** . a.	t	0900	0900	0931	0909	0918	1204	1522	1522	1542
1044	**Samara** . d.	...	...	0943	1018	...	...	1245	1602	1602	1627
1216	Buzuluk' . d.	...	...	|	1357	...	...	|	1914	1914	|
1462	Orenburg . a.	...	...	|	1808	...	...	|	2301	2301	|
1567	**Ufa** . a.	...	...	1825	...	...	...	2116	...	...	0046
1933	Magnitogorsk . a.	...	...	...	...	...	...	0729e	...	...	|
2048	**Chelyabinsk** . a.	...	...	...	...	...	...	0640	...	...	1015

	67JI	39JI	13UJ	49JI	9JI	66EI	31UJ	17SZ	5FJ
	Sko	Fir	Fir	Sko	Fir	Sko	Fir	Sko	Sko
	■(1)	●					G	B	T
Chelyabinsk . d.	...	...	1940	...	...	...	...	...	...
Magnitogorsk . d.	...	...	1808e	...	...	...	...	...	...
Ufa . d.	...	0504	0454	...	...	...	...	...	...
Orenburg . d.	...	|	|	...	...	...	0923	1055	1055
Buzuluk' . d.	...	|	|	...	...	...	1354	1507	1507
Samara . a.	...	1311	1323	...	...	...	1703	1816	1816
Samara . d.	1359	1359	1409	1702	1840	t	1803	1904	1904
Syzran I . d.	1643	1643	1653	1909	2022	2031	2044	|	|
Inza . d.	|	|	|	2155	|	2318	|	0028	0028
Ruzayevka ⊡ . d.	2115	2115	2201	2346	0025	0114	0126	0218	0218
Ryazan I . d.	0238	0238	0307	0539	0456	0643	0653	0810	0810
Moskva Kaz. . a.	0546	0546	0620	0908	0755	1024	1029	1115	1115

MOSKVA - PENZA, SARANSK, ULYANOVSK

km		22JI	132UJ	52JI	42JI
		Fir	Sko	Fir	Fir
0	**Moskva** Kaz . d.	1908	1510	2040	2132
197	Ryazan I . d.	2236	1833r	0005r	0047
313	Ryazhsk I . d.	|	2033	0143	|
710	**Penza** I . d.	|	0526	0755	|
601	Ruzayevka ⊡ . d.	0435	n	...	0634
627	**Saransk** I . a.	|	...	...	0705
712	Inza . d.	0641	...	...	...
873	**Ulyanovsk** . a.	0920	...	...	...

	41JI	131UJ	51JI	21JI
	Fir	Sko	Fir	Fir
Ulyanovsk . d.	...	...	...	1940
Inza . d.	...	...	...	2256
Saransk . d.	2040	...	...	|
Ruzayevka ⊡ d.	2128	o	...	0049
Penza I . d.	|	1919	2103	|
Ryazhsk I . d.	|	0405	0315	|
Ryazan I . d.	0257	0556r	0505r	0550
Moskva Kaz . a.	0603	0938	0823	0930

PENZA - SAMARA - CHELYABINSK - OMSK

km		124VJ	12UJ
		Sko	Sko
		v	△
0	**Penza** I . d.	0558	...
253	Syzran I . d.	0929	...
389	**Samara** . d.	1235	...
912	Ufa . d.	2208	...
1393	**Chelyabinsk** . d.	0822	2100
1651	Kurgan . d.	1216	0049
1918	Petropavl § d.	1649	0526
2191	**Omsk** . a.	2101	0948

	123NJ	11UJ
	Sko	Sko
	w	▽
Omsk . d.	1945	0050
Petropavl § d.	0056	0548
Kurgan . d.	0510	1011
Chelyabinsk . d.	0925	1346
Ufa . d.	1917	...
Samara . d.	0448	...
Syzran I . d.	0731	...
Penza I . a.	1142	...

A – To/from Astana (for days of running see Table **1975**).
B – To/from Bishkek (for days of running see Table **1975**).
F – Uneven dates ■(3) (daily Dec. 23 - Jan. 15, May 27 - Sept. 7).
G – Even dates (daily Dec. 22 - Jan. 14, May 26 - Sept. 6).
T – To/from Toshkent (for days of running see Table **1975**).
e – Portion detached/attached at Ufa. From Moskva and Magnitogorsk on unven dates in Jan., Mar., June, July, Sept. Oct., even dates in Feb., Apr., May, Aug., Nov., Dec.

n – To Samara (a. 1246), Orenburg (a. 2121), Orsk (a. 0350).
o – From Orsk (d. 2040), Orenburg (d. 0317), Samara (d. 1141).
r – Ryazan II.
t – To/from Toliatti (a. 0920/d. 1700).
v – From Belgorod (0758), Voronezh I (1750), Tambov (2316). To Novosibirsk (a. 0617).
w – From Novosibirsk (d. 1052). To Tambov (1827), Voronezh I (0028), Belgorod (0950).

△ – From Chelyabinsk ■(1). To Chita (Table 1
▽ – From Chita ■(5) (Table **1990**). Depart Om 4th day.
⊡ – Also known as Saransk Gorod or Sarans
§ – Petropavl (Kazakhstan). Moskva time.
● – Even dates. See page 530.
■ – Uneven dates. See page 530.

1975 TRAINS TO KAZAKHSTAN AND BEYOND

km	TOSHKENT	6FJ	18SZ	381EI
		Sko	Sko	Pas
		E	G	②⑥
0	*Moskva Kaz* ‡ . d.	2240	2240	...
1044	**Samara** . d.	1602	1602	...
	Ufa . d.	|	|	1052
1462	Orenburg . d.	2346	2346	2013
1734	Aktobe KA d.	1108	1108	0806
1828	Kandyagash KA d.	1243	1243	0945
2767	Kyzlorda KA d.	0453	0453	0440
3315	**Toshkent** UZ a.	1650	|	1827
3240	Shymkent KA d.	...	1347	...
3720	**Bishkek** II KY a.	...	2306	...

	5FJ	17SZ	381MZ
	Sko	Sko	Pas
	F	H	④⑦
Bishkek II KY d.	...	0939	...
Shymkent KA d.	...	0059	...
Toshkent UZ d.	1850	|	0145
Kyzlorda KA d.	0956	0956	1756
Kandyagash KA d.	0247	0247	1220
Aktobe KA d.	0429	0429	1406
Orenburg . d.	1055	1055	2131
Ufa . a.	|	|	0601
Samara . a.	1816	1816	...
Moskva Kaz ‡ . a.	1115	1115	...

km	ALMATY	7CJ	34TJ	310KH
		Sko	Sko	Pas
		●(4)		
0	*Moskva Pav* § . d.	2133	...	...
856	**Saratov** I . d.	1400	...	...
1291	Oral/Uralsk KA d.	0402	...	...
1750	**Aktobe** KA d.	1446	2152	0101
1844	Kandyagash KA d.	1633	2329	0310
2940	**Aktau** ⊙ KA a.	|	|	0610*
2783	Kyzlorda KA d.	0807	1636	...
3256	Shymkent KA d.	1659	0216	...
4008	**Almaty** I KA a.	0600	1533	...
4017	**Almaty** II KA a.	0627	...	...

	309KH	7RJ
	Pas	Sko
		■(1)
Almaty II KA d.	...	0734
Almaty I KA d.	...	0800
Shymkent KA d.	...	2150
Kyzlorda KA d.	...	0714
Aktau ⊙ KA d.	1300	|
Kandyagash KA d.	1601*	2302
Aktobe KA d.	1745	0051
Oral/Uralsk KA d.	...	1120
Saratov I . a.	...	1856
Moskva Pav § . a.	...	1038

km	ASTANA	90UJ	84CJ	72CJ	304CJ	306SZ	316FJ
		Sko	Sko	Sko	Pas	Pas	Pas
		■(3)	●(4)	B	③⑤	④⑦	①
0	*Moskva Kaz* **1970** d.	1848	2248	2248	...	...	...
1044	**Samara** . d.	|	1627	1627	...	...	...
2048	Chelyabinsk . d.	▽	1056	1056	...	...	...
	Yekaterinburg . d.	2157*	|	|	1730	1730	1730
2306	Kurgan . d.	0437	1427	△	0011	0011	0011
2573	Petropavl ⊡ KA d.	0925	2005	|	0625	0625	0625
3064	**Astana** KA a.	...	0750	1017	1852	1852	1852
3064	**Astana** KA d.	...	0830	...	1930	1930	1930
3305	Karagandy KA d.	...	1157	...	0024	0024	0024
4407	**Almaty** II KA a.	...	...	...	2356	|	|
4356	Bishkek II KY a.	...	...	...	...	2025	|
4522	Shymkent KA a.	...	...	...	...	...	2241
4755	**Toshkent** UZ a.	...	...	...	...	...	0600

	89UJ	71CJ	83CJ	315FJ	305SZ	303CJ
	Sko	Sko	Sko	Pas	Pas	Pas
	■(1)	C	●	⑥	②⑤	①③
Toshkent UZ d.	...	...	...	0355	...	...
Shymkent KA d.	...	...	...	1325	...	...
Bishkek II KY d.	...	...	...	|	1049	...
Almaty II KA d.	...	...	...	|	|	1445
Karagandy KA d.	...	...	0722	1319	1319*	1319
Astana KA a.	...	...	1045	1722	1722	1722
Astana KA d.	...	0915	1115	1800	1800	1800
Petropavl ⊡ KA d.	1313	|	1745	0246	0246	0246
Kurgan . d.	1904	△	2231	0844	0844	0844
Yekaterinburg . a.	0058	|	|	1515	1515	1515
Chelyabinsk . d.	▽	0232	0232	...	...	...
Samara . a.	|	2100	2100	...	...	...
Moskva Kaz **1970** a.	0457*	1520	1520	...	...	...

km	DUSHANBE *Arrive 5th day*	320EI 330CH
		Pas
		①③⑥
0	**Moskva** Kaz. . d.	1216
198	Ryazan II . d.	1532
409	Michurinsk Vor d.	1834
1073	**Volgograd** . d.	1210
1802	Atyrau KA d.	0820
1932	Makat KA d.	1101
2639	Kungrad UZ d.	0325
3190	Uckuduk II UZ d.	1408
3467	Navoi UZ d.	1921
3712	Karshi UZ d.	2345
4044	Termez UZ d.	|
4269	**Dushanbe** I TA a.	1720

Arrive Moskva on 5th day
Dushanbe I TA d.
Termez UZ d.
Karshi UZ d.
Navoi UZ d.
Uckuduk II. UZ d.
Kungrad UZ d.
Makat KA d.
Atyrau KA d.
Volgograd . d.
Michurinsk Vor d.
Ryazan II . d.
Moskva Kaz . a.

km	VIA AKTOGAY	369NJ	301NJ
		b	●(7)
0	**Novosibirsk** . d.	1410	1410
228	Barnaul . d.	2036	2036
1121	Aktogay KA d.	2015	2015
1678	**Almaty** I KA a.	0817	0817
1687	**Almaty** II KA a.	|	0918
2424	Shymkent KA d.	0022	...
2657	**Toshkent** UZ a.	0725	...

	302CJ
	♥
Toshkent UZ d.	...
Shymkent KA d.	...
Almaty II KA d.	1618
Almaty I KA d.	1710
Aktogay KA d.	0518
Barnaul . d.	2229
Novosibirsk . a.	0244

B – Uneven dates ■(3) May 1 - Oct. 31 ❄.
C – Uneven dates ■(1) May 1 - Oct. 29 ❄.
E – From Moskva ②③⑦ (arrive Toshkent 4th day).
F – From Toshkent ④⑥⑦ (arrive Moskva 4th day).
G – From Moskva ④⑥ (arrive Bishkek on 4th day).
H – From Bishkek ①③ (arrive Moskva on 4th day).
b – Runs approximately every 4 days.
⊙ – Mangyshlak station (12 km from Aktau).
⊡ – Petropavl (KA) times are in Moskva time.
♥ – Even dates [.. *30, 4* ..] (see page 530).
* – More than 24 hours after previous time shown.

▽ – Via Kazan (Table **1990**).
△ – Via Kostanay.
● – Even dates. See page 530.
■ – Uneven dates. See page 530.
❄ – In winter runs every 4 days.
§ – See Table **1965**.
‡ – See Table **1970**.
KA – Kazakhstan (GMT + 6).
KY – Kyrgyzstan (GMT + 6).
TA – Tajikistan (GMT + 5).
UZ – Uzbekistan (GMT + 5).

OTHER SERVICES TO BAKI AND ASTANA 1977

	373*EJ* Pas ●
Tyumen d.	1834
Yekaterinburg a.	0012
Yekaterinburg d.	0052
Chelyabinsk d.	0810
Ufa d.	1752
Samara d.	0324
Saratov I a.	1212
Saratov I d.	1300
Astrakhan I d.	0140
Makhachkala a.	1122
Derbent a.	...
Baki AZ a.	...

	373*SJ* Pas ■(5)
Baki AZ d.	...
Derbent d.	...
Makhachkala d.	1635
Astrakhan I d.	0255
Saratov I a.	1502
Saratov I d.	1557
Samara d.	0130
Ufa d.	1056
Chelyabinsk d.	2045
Yekaterinburg a.	0310
Yekaterinburg d.	0354
Tyumen a.	0940

km		449*OJ* Pas D‡
0	**Kharkiv** UA d.	0034
129	Kupiansk UA a.	0314
368	Liski d.	0906
593	Povorino d.	1405
960	Volgograd a.	2030
960	Volgograd d.	2111
1410	Astrakhan I a.	0448
1410	Astrakhan I d.	0552
1898	Makhachkala a.	1607
1898	Makhachkala d.	1645
2027	Derbent a.	1905
2272	**Baki** AZ a.	0625

	449*SZ* Pas E‡
Baki AZ d.	0215
Derbent d.	0835
Makhachkala a.	1058
Makhachkala d.	1113
Astrakhan I a.	2008
Astrakhan I d.	2054
Volgograd a.	0439
Volgograd d.	0517
Povorino d.	1310
Liski d.	1740
Kupiansk UA a.	2320
Kharkiv UA a.	0214

km		108*KJ* Sko ④B
0	**Kyïv** UA d.	1840
335	Poltava K UA d.	0045
489	**Kharkiv** UA d.	0325
618	Kupiansk UA d.	0604
857	Liski d.	1122
1082	Povorino d.	1508
1462	**Saratov** I d.	2257
1897	Oral / Uralsk d.	1237
2238	Orenburg d.	1820
2569	Orsk d.	0020
3644	**Astana** KA a.	2210
3885	Karagandy KA a.	0220

	107*CJ* Sko ①B
Karagandy KA d.	1350
Astana KA d.	1740
Orsk d.	1014
Orenburg d.	1538
Oral / Uralsk d.	0236
Saratov I d.	1101
Povorino d.	1840
Liski d.	2230
Kupiansk UA d.	0517
Kharkiv UA a.	0738
Poltava K UA a.	1059
Kyiv UA a.	1612

ervice suspended.
②⑤ Apr. 26 - Oct. 18.
②⑥ Apr. 23 - Oct. 15.

● – Even dates (see page 530).
■ – Uneven dates (see page 530).

‡ – A winter service operates every four days via Rostov na Donu (train **369**).

AZ – Azerbaijan (GMT + 4 winter, GMT + 5 summer).
KA – Kazakhstan (GMT + 6).
UA – Ukraine (GMT + 2 winter, GMT + 3 summer).

GEORGIA 1979

+4 *Subject to alteration*

	870	872	852	698	18	684	678	858		602	860 A	
Tbilisi d.	0800	0820	0845	...	0855	...	1540	1815	...	2145	0035	...
Kutaisi a.	|	|	|	1245	1418	1720	2107	|	...	|	|	...
Zugdidi a.	1330	|	|	1620	...	|	...	|	...	0605	|	...
Poti a.	...	1316	|	...	...	|	...	|	...	...	|	...
Batumi a.	...	...	1410	...	...	2112	...	2340	...	...	0615	...

	677	857	697	17	683	871	869	851		601	859 A	
Batumi d.	...	0800	...	...	0825	...	...	1820	...	...	0135	...
Poti d.	...	|	...	...	|	1735	...	|	...	...	|	...
Zugdidi d.	...	|	0755	...	|	|	1750	|	...	2215	|	...
Kutaisi d.	0500	|	1110	1215	1210	|	|	|	...	|	|	...
Tbilisi a.	1045	1325	...	1740	...	2230	2320	2345	...	0630	0705	...

	37 🛏
Tbilisi d.	1630r
Baki AZ a.	0810

	38 🛏
Baki AZ d.	2030
Tbilisi a.	1045

km	🛏	372 W	202 S
	Maxinjauri § d.	...	1535
0	Tbilisi d.	2020	2216
374	Yerevan AR a.	0655	0725

🛏	201 S	371 Y
Yerevan AR d.	1530	2130
Tbilisi a.	0012	0750
Maxinjauri § a.	0710	...

A – Every second day.
S – Every second day mid June - late Sept.
W – ■(3) late Sept to mid June.
Y – ● late Sept. to mid June.

r – One hour later in summer.
AR – Armenia (GMT + 4).
AZ – Azerbaijan (GMT + 4 winter, + 5 summer).
● ■ See page 530.

KAZAKHSTAN and UZBEKISTAN 1980

	4*CJ*	2*TJ*	10*TJ*	87*KH* ■(1)	80*KH* ●
ıa d.	1145	1853	2215	2235	2335
obe a.	|	|	|	1455	|
andy d.	1522	2124	0145	...	0206
ty I a.	0608	|	1716	...	|
ty II a.	0634	0733	...	...	|
kent a.	...	...	...	...	1520

KA	1*TJ*	80*TJ* ■(3)	3*KH*	88*KH* ●	9*TJ*
Shymkent d.	...	1633	...	...	...
Almaty II d.	1931	|	1334	...	...
Almaty I d.	|	|	1400	...	2046
Karagandy d.	0552	0637	0514	...	1228
Aktobe d.	|	|	|	2022	|
Astana a.	0815	0900	0930	1342	1545

KA	37 ■	19 ●
Astana d.	1625	1840
Kandyagash d.	1738*	1046
Atyrau a.	|	1725
Aktau ⊙ a.	1410	...

KA	37 ■(3)	19 ■(3)
Aktau ⊙ d.	1550	...
Atyrau d.	|	2050
Kandyagash d.	1303	0325
Astana a.	1255	1931

UZ	760‡	762‡	10*FJ*	56/58	662
Toshkent d.	0700	0800	0825	2015	2200
Samarkand d.	0908	1008	1159	0008	0238
Bukhara I a.	▽	...	1456	...	0701

UZ	55/57 ⊡	9*FJ*	761‡	759‡	661
Bukhara I d.	...	0745	...	▽	1950
Samarkand d.	0400	1105	1700	1800	0122
Toshkent a.	0806	1423	1910	2010	0536

Mangyshlak station (12 km from Aktau).
To / from Karshi (a. 1020 / d. 1648).
AFROSIYOB – high-speed Talgo train.
More than 24 hours after previous time.

● – Even dates (see page 530).
■ – Uneven dates (see page 530).
⊡ – Subject to alteration.

KA – Kazakhstan (GMT + 6).

UZ – Uzbekistan (GMT + 5).

MOSKVA - ARCHANGELSK, LABYTNANGI and VORKUTA 1985

	16*MJ* Sko	34*JA* Fir F	90*GJ* Sko ●	388*AJ* Pas H	392*AJ* Pas J	10*JA* Sko D	318*MJ* Pas ■	22*JA* Fir B	42*VJ* Fir	653*MJ* Pas
Moskva Yarolslavsk d.	1005	1305	...	...	...	...	1950	2035	2150	...
Yaroslavl d.	1439	1726	...	...	...	...	0020	0048	0156	...
St Peterburg Lad. ▷ d.	|	|	...	1020	1020	1454	|	|	|	...
Vologda I ▷ d.	1843	2133	...	|	|	|	0427	0504	0555	...
Konosha I d.	2205	0100	...	0123	0123	0508	0802	0828	0935	...
Archangelsk a.	0600	|	...	|	|	1351	1821	|	|	...
Velsk d.	...	0306	n	0351	0351	...	...	1025	1135	...
Kotlas Yuzhny d.	...	0725z	0908	0956	0956	...	...	1521	1631	...
Mikun d.	...	1215	1322	1427	1523	...	...	1930	2038	...
Syktyvkar a.	...	1355	|	1747x	1747x	...	...	|	|	...
Sosnogorsk d.	...	...	1810	1948	...	...	...	0001	0129	...
Labytnangi a.	...	...	|	|	...	...	...	1644	|	1045
Vorkuta a.	...	...	0820	0950	...	...	...	...	1435	2048

	317*MJ* Pas ■(2)	34*MJ* Fir F	41*MJ* Fir	15*JA* Sko	9*SJ* Sko E	89*GJ* Sko ●(4)	387*JA* Pas K	391*JA* Pas L	21*NJ* Fir C	653*JA* 655*JA* y
Vorkuta d.	...	...	1635	...	...	1905	2055	...	...	0910
Labytnangi d.	...	...	|	...	...	|	|	...	0750	2211
Sosnogorsk d.	...	...	0551	...	...	0854	1204	...	0051	...
Syktyvkar d.	...	0745	|	...	...	|	0840x	0840x	|	...
Mikun d.	...	1004	1125	...	...	1331	1707	1647	0531	...
Kotlas Yuzhny d.	...	1418z	1551	...	...	1813	2200	2200	0941	...
Velsk d.	...	1854	2056	...	...	u	0350	0350	1459	...
Archangelsk d.	0725	|	|	2010	2043	...	|	|	|	...
Konosha I d.	1810	2142	2305	0427	0554	...	0637	0637	1720	...
Vologda I ▷ d.	2155	0050	0201	0810	|	...	|	|	2023	...
St Peterburg Lad ▷ a.	|	|	|	|	2055	...	2152	2152	|	...
Yaroslavl d.	0221	0522	0603	1221	...	...	...	...	0055	...
Moskva Yarolslavsk a.	0623	0912	0958	1643	...	...	...	...	0446	...

②⑤ (runs 2 - 3 times per week June 3 - Sept. 23).
①⑤ (runs 2 - 3 times per week June 3 - Sept. 24).
①④⑤ (daily Dec. 24 - Jan. 11; June 23 - Sept. 2).
②⑤⑥ (daily Dec. 25 - Jan. 12; June 24 - Aug. 31).
Approx every 3 days (June - Aug also runs as *Sko* **224***CH* and **228***JA*).
Approx every 3 days; uneven dates ■(5) Apr. 23 - Aug. 31.
Approx every 3 days; even dates ●(6) Apr. 26 - Aug. 30.
Approx every 3 days; uneven dates ■(3) Apr. 23 - Aug. 31.
Approx every 3 days; uneven dates ■(3) Apr. 21 - Aug. 31.

n – From Niz. Novgorod (1610), Kirov (2352).
u – To Kirov (0218), Niz. Novgorod (0910).
x – Syktyvkar portion: **305***JA* and **304***JA*.
y – Arrive 2018 on even dates.
z – Kotlas **Uzlovoy**.
▷ – See also Table **1990**.
● – Even dates. See page 530.
■ – Uneven dates. See page 530.
§ – See also Table **1905**.

km		♡
0	**Murmansk** § d.	0830
277	Kandalaksha § d.	1415
665	Belomorsk § d.	2138
1151	**Archangelsk** a.	1000

	♧
Archangelsk d.	1507
Belomorsk § d.	0325
Kandalaksha § d.	1130
Murmansk § a.	1742

♡ – ①⑥ (■ May / Aug; ● June / July / Sept. 2-10). **373***JA* / **371***JA*.
♧ – ④⑥ (■ May / Aug; ● June / July / Sept. 2-10). **371***CH* / **374***JA*.

NOVOSIBIRSK - SEVEROBAIKALSK - TYNDA - NERYUNGRI - TOMMOT 1989

Baikal - Amur Magistrale (BAM)	87*IJ* 348*Y* ●	348*Y* Pas ●	71*IJ* Sko ■(1)		76*EI* Sko ■(7) n	92*IJ* Sko ●(6) n	324*JI* Pas	78*EI* Sko ■ v	
Moskva Yar. **1990** d.	...	...	...	...	1308r	1620	...	...	...
Novosibirsk **1990** d.	...	...	...	...	1504	1652	...	1949	...
Krasnoyarsk **1990** d.	...	1700	...	...	0318	0527	...	0847	...
Ulan Ude **1990** d.	...	|	1110	...	|	|	...	|	...
Irkutsk **1990** d.	1428	|	1849	...	|	|	...	|	...
Tayshet a.	0202	0200	0600	...	1011	1227	...	1531	...
Tayshet d.	0320	0340	0635	...	1051	1257	...	1550	...
Bratsk d.	1308	1308	1308	...	1647	1929	...	|	...
Severobaikalsk d.	0511	0511	0511	...	0720	0905	...	▽	...
Skovorodino d.	...	...	...	...	|	...	...	2321x	...
Tynda a.	...	...	...	...	1023*	...	...	0419	...
Tynda d.	...	...	...	...	1153	...	...	0514	...
Neryungri d.	...	...	...	...	1715	...	0156	1037	...
Tommot a.	...	...	...	...	...	...	0945	...	...
Nizhny Bestyakh ⊕ a.	...	...	...	...	...	...	...	...	...

	323*JI* Pas	75*EI* Sko ■(1) u	91*IJ* Sko ● s	77*EI* Sko ■(3)		71*Y* Sko ■(3)	347*Y* 87*Y* ●(4)	347*Y* Pas ●(4)	
Nizhny Bestyakh ⊕ d.	...	...	...	...	...	...	...	...	...
Tommot d.	1306	...	...	...	...	...	...	...	...
Neryungri d.	2117	2302	...	0210	...	...	...	...	...
Tynda a.	...	0430	...	0716	...	...	...	...	...
Tynda d.	.:.	0650	...	0847	...	...	...	...	...
Skovorodino d.	...	|	...	1341	...	...	...	...	...
Severobaikalsk d.	...	1021*	1200	▽	...	1659	1659	1659	...
Bratsk d.	...	0030	0151	|	...	0736	0819	0819	...
Tayshet a.	...	0630	0835	1907z	...	1337	1824	1849	...
Tayshet d.	...	0725	0905	1912z	...	1415	1944	2014	...
Irkutsk **1990** a.	...	|	|	|	...	0126	0710	|	...
Ulan Ude **1990** a.	...	|	|	|	...	0910	...	|	...
Krasnoyarsk **1990** a.	...	1406	1557	0146	...	...	...	0525	...
Novosibirsk **1990** a.	...	0214	0549	1502	...	...	...	...	...
Moskva Yar. **1990** a.	...	0442r	0552	...	...	...	...	...	...

Novosibirsk on 3rd day, Severobaikalsk on 5th day.
Moskva Kazanskaya.
Novosibirsk 3rd day, Moskva 5th day.
Novosibirsk 5th day, Moskva 7th day.
Uneven dates [.. *31*, *1*, *3*, *7* ..] (see page 530).
4th day.
3rd day.
Via Irkutsk (Table **1990**).

● – Even dates. See page 530.
■ – Uneven dates. See page 530.
Δ – *4182* via Skovorodino.
⊕ – Under construction. In summer a ferry (15 km from station) runs to Yakutsk.
* – Following day (more than 24 hours after previous time shown).

km		364*EI*	667*ZH*
0	**Tynda** d.	1120	...
951	Novy Urgal d.	1100	...
1469	Komsomolsk d.	2350	1400
1857	**Khabarovsk** a.	...	2343

	667*EI*	363*EI*
Khabarovsk d.	1408	...
Komsomolsk d.	2330	1150
Novy Urgal d.	...	0148
Tynda a.	...	0020

1990 MOSKVA - YEKATERINBURG - NOVOSIBIRSK - IRKUTSK - VLADIVOSTOK

km	*TransSiberian Railway*	**14**AJ	**74**EJ	**72**EJ	**140**NJ	**44**EI	**100**EI	**59**AJ	**64**BJ	**702**NJ	**704**NJ	**728**GJ	**706**NJ	**708**NJ	**2**MJ	**8**NJ	**76**EI	**82**IJ	**56**Y	**118**EJ	**12**UJ	**78**EI	**84**MJ
		Fir	*Sko*	*Fir*	*Sko*	*Sko*	*Sko*	*Fir*	*Sko*	♠	♠	≋	♠	♠	*Fir*	*Sko*	*Sko*	*Sko*	*Fir*	*Sko*	*Sko*	*Sko*	*Fir*
		●(4)	■(3)			■(9)	●(9)			①③	②④		④–⑥	①⑤	■(1)	●(4)	■(7)	●(6)	●(6)	■(5)	■(1)	■(6)	♡
					Q		◇	**d**	**D**	④–⑥	⑤⑦			⑥⑦	**R**								
0	**Moskva** Yaroslavskaya ▷ d.	...	...	...	...	0035	0035	...	...	...	...	...	...	...	1320	...	...	...	...	...	...	...	1335
	Moskva Kazanskaya d.	...	...	...	...	|	|	0220**k**	0335**r**	0635**k**	0715**k**	0930**k**	1100**k**	1400**k**	|	...	1308	1308	1318	1318	...	...	|
282	Yaroslavl ▷ d.	...	...	...	...	0431	0431	|	|	|	|	|	|	|	|	...	|	|	|	|	...	...	|
210	Vladimir d.	...	...	...	...	|	|	0454	0653	|	0857	1119	1241	1541	1640	...	|	|	|	|	...	...	1650
461	**Nizhni Novgorod** d.	...	...	...	...	|	|	0755	1120	1010	1110	1351	1448	1748	2017	...	|	|	|	|	...	...	2030
	St Peterburg Ladozhski d.	1530	1530	1709	...	|	|	...	|	...	...	...	...	...	|	...	|	|	|	|	...	...	|
	Vologda I d.	0238	0238	0505	...	|	|	...	|	...	...	...	...	...	|	...	|	|	|	|	...	...	|
917	**Kirov** d.	1243	1243	1448	...	1840	1840	...	1850	...	...	...	...	...	0218	...	|	|	|	|	...	...	0228
1397	Perm II d.	2050	2050	2300	...	0401	0401	...	0341	...	...	...	...	...	0959	...	|	|	|	|	...	...	1033
	Murom I d.	|	|	|	...	|	|	...	|	...	...	...	...	...	|	...	1750	1750	1801	1801	...	...	**y**
	Kazan d.	|	|	|	...	|	|	...	|	...	...	...	...	...	|	...	0200	0200	0210	0210	...	...	...
	Sarapul d.	|	|	|	**a**	|	|	...	|	...	...	...	...	...	|	...	0759	0759	0809	0809	...	...	...
1778	**Yekaterinburg** a.	0213	0213	0432	0559	0928	0928	...	0918	...	...	...	...	...	1510	...	1623	1623	1602	1602	...	...	...
1778	**Yekaterinburg** d.	0252	0252	...	0629	1005	1005	...	1013	...	...	...	...	...	1539	...	1655	1655	1638	1638	...	...	...
2104	Tyumen d.	0747	0726	...	1242	1548	1548	...	1558	...	...	...	...	...	2014	...	2216	2216	2226	2226	**c**	...	...
2676	**Omsk** a.	1628	...	...	2016	2349	2349	...	2359	...	...	...	...	...	0314	...	0538	0538	0616	0616	0948	...	...
2676	**Omsk** d.	1703	...	...	2101	0030	0030	...	0020	...	...	...	...	...	0330	...	0603	0603	0646	0646	1004	...	...
3303	**Novosibirsk** a.	0044	...	...	0545	0833	0833	...	0843	...	...	...	...	...	1101	...	1415	1415	1500	1500	1907	...	...
3303	**Novosibirsk** d.	0134	...	...	...	0930	0930	...	...	...	...	...	...	...	1120	1120	1504	1504	1522	1601	1949	1949	...
3532	Tayga d.	**o**	...	...	...	1324	1324	...	...	...	...	...	...	...	1453	1453	1834	1834	1846	**o**	2354	2354	...
4065	**Krasnoyarsk** d.	...	...	...	...	2207	2207	...	...	...	...	...	...	...	2305	2305	0318	0318	0340	...	0847	0847	...
4483	Tayshet d.	...	...	...	...	0506	0506	...	...	...	...	...	...	...	0541	0541	1051	1014	...	...	1550	1550	...
5152	**Irkutsk** a.	...	...	...	...	1615	1615	...	...	...	...	...	...	...	1559	1559	**u**	2132	...	...	0332	0332	...
5152	**Irkutsk** d.	...	...	...	...	1645	1645	...	...	...	...	...	...	...	1622	1622	...	2212	...	...	0409	0409	...
5608	Ulan Ude d.	...	...	...	...	0055	0055	...	...	...	**6**EI	...	...	...	2317	2317	...	0612	...	...	1255	1255	...
6165	Chita II d.	...	...	...	...	1318	1318	...	...	...	*Fir*	...	...	...	0919	0919	...	...	...	...	0011	0047	...
7274	Skovorodino d.	...	...	...	...	1055	1055	...	...	...		...	...	...	0544	0544	...	...	...	...	...	2321	...
8492	**Khabarovsk** d.	...	...	...	...	0758	0858	...	...	...	1400	...	...	...	0135	0135	...	...	...	...	...	**u**	...
9147	Ussuriysk d.	...	...	...	...	...	2138	...	...	...	2321	...	...	...	1135	1135	...	...	...	...	...	...	...
9258	**Vladivostok** a.	...	...	...	...	...	2357	...	...	...	0115	...	...	...	1330	1330	...	...	...	...	...	...	...

local time ★		**70**CH	**710**NJ	**730**GJ	**41**GJ	**92**IJ	**60**UJ	**16**EJ	**8**EJ	**12**JA	**712**NJ	**90**UJ	**96**NJ	**2**JI	**714**NJ	**32**GJ	**110**EI	**30**NJ	**38**NJ	**68**Y	**4**ZJ	**6**	**20**SZ
		Sko	♠	≋	*Fir*	*Sko*	*Fir*	*Fir*	*Fir*	*Fir*	♠	*Sko*	*Sko*	*Fir*	♠	*Fir*	*Sko*	*Fir*	*Fir*	*Sko*	*Sko*	*Sko*	*Sko*
			F			●(6)	♡	♤	♡	♤		■(3)			Ⓑ			■(3)	●(2)		②	③④	⑥
													▽	☆							**B**	**A**	**P**
	Moskva Yaroslavskaya ▷ d.	1350	...	...	...	1620	...	...	1650	1650	...	...	...	...	...	2005	2235	2250	2250	2305	2345	2345	2345
	Moskva Kazanskaya d.	|	1540**k**	1635**k**	...	|	1638	1638	|	|	1835**k**	1848	1920	1940	2020**k**	|	|	|	|	|	|	|	|
	Yaroslavl ▷ d.	1817	|	|	...	|	|	|	|	|	|	|	|	|	|	|	|	|	|	0320	|	|	|
	Vladimir d.	|	1721	1824	...	1948	|	|	2025	2025	2016	|	|	|	|	2319	0149	0159	0159	|	0252	0252	0252
	Nizhni Novgorod d.	|	1928	2048	2125	2320	|	|	2330	2330	2223	|	|	|	2355	0220	0459	0509	0509	|	0544	0544	0544
	St Peterburg Ladozhski d.	|	...	...	|	|	|	|	|	|	...	|	|	|	...	|	|	|	|	|	|	|	|
	Vologda I d.	|	...	...	|	|	|	|	|	|	...	|	|	|	...	|	|	|	|	|	|	|	|
	Kirov d.	0609	...	...	|	0544	|	|	0555	0555	...	|	|	|	...	0833	1148	1203	1203	1428	1233	1233	1233
+2	Perm II d.	1403	...	...	|	1333	|	|	1323	1343	...	|	|	|	...	...	2030	2010	2010	2220	2020	2020	2020
	Murom I d.	|	...	...	|	|	2112	2112	...	|	...	0006	0021	0034	...	...	|	|	|	|	|	|	|
	Kazan d.	|	...	...	0617	|	0537	0537	...	|	...	0750	0805	0800	...	...	|	|	|	|	|	|	|
	Sarapul d.	|	...	...	...	|	1050	1050	...	|	...	1333	1344	...	...	...	|	|	|	|	|	|	|
+2	**Yekaterinburg** a.	1941	...	...	...	1901	1804	1804	...	1918	...	2127	2235	...	...	...	0157	0129	0129	0336	0138	0138	0138
+2	**Yekaterinburg** d.	2012	...	...	...	1955	1908	...	...	2003	...	2157	2314	...	...	...	0244	0200	0200	0423	0208	0208	0208
+2	Tyumen d.	0320	...	...	...	0042	0226	...	...	0235	...	**p**	0442	...	...	...	0814	0737	0737	1026	0637	0637	0637
+3	**Omsk** a.	1155	...	...	...	0746	**n**	...	...	**t**	...	...	1222	...	...	...	**s**	1544	1544	1837	1337	1337	1337
+3	**Omsk** d.	1211	...	...	...	0808	...	...	...	...	...	...	1252	...	...	...	...	1606	1606	1857	1353	1353	1353
+3	**Novosibirsk** a.	1953	...	...	...	1613	...	...	...	...	...	...	**b**	...	...	...	...	2345	2345	0216	2107	2107	2107
+3	**Novosibirsk** d.	2042	...	...	...	1652	...	...	...	...	...	...	...	...	...	...	...	0034	0034	0305	2126	2126	2126
+	Tayga d.	0020	...	...	...	2031	...	...	...	...	...	...	...	...	...	...	...	**m**	0430	0639	0045	0045	0045
+4	**Krasnoyarsk** d.	0924	...	...	...	0527	...	...	...	...	...	...	...	...	...	...	...	...	**z**	**q**	0914	0914	0914
+5	Tayshet d.	1631	...	...	...	1257	...	...	...	...	...	...	...	...	...	...	...	...	...	...	|	|	|
+5	**Irkutsk** a.	0347	...	...	...	**x**	...	...	...	...	...	...	...	...	...	...	...	...	...	...	0229	0229	0229
+5	**Irkutsk** d.	0422	...	...	...	...	...	...	...	...	...	...	...	...	...	...	...	...	...	...	0314	0314	0314
+5	Ulan Ude d.	1310	...	...	...	...	...	...	...	...	...	...	...	...	...	...	...	...	...	...	1058	1058	1146
+6	Chita II d.	0021	...	...	...	...	...	...	...	...	...	...	...	...	...	...	...	...	...	...	...	...	2252
+6	Skovorodino d.	...	...	...	...	...	...	...	...	...	...	...	...	...	...	...	...	...	...	...	...	...	...
+7	**Khabarovsk** d.	...	...	...	...	...	...	...	...	...	...	...	...	...	...	...	...	...	...	...	...	...	...
+7	Ussuriysk d.	...	...	...	...	...	...	...	...	...	...	...	...	...	...	...	...	...	...	...	...	...	...
+7	**Vladivostok** a.	...	...	...	...	...	...	...	...	...	...	...	...	...	...	...	...	...	...	...	...	...	...

ROSSIYA SUMMARY

km		**2**MJ *Fir* ■(1) **R**	
0	**Moskva** Yar. d.	1320	*1st day*
461	Nizhni Novgorod d.	2017	*1st day*
917	Kirov d.	0218	*2nd day*
1778	Yekaterinburg d.	1539	*2nd day*
2676	Omsk d.	0330	*3rd day*
3303	Novosibirsk d.	1120	*3rd day*
4065	Krasnoyarsk d.	2305	*3rd day*
5152	Irkutsk d.	1622	*4th day*
5608	Ulan Ude d.	2317	*4th day*
8492	Khabarovsk d.	0135	*7th day*
9258	**Vladivostok** a.	1330	*7th day*

MOSKVA - BEIJING via Ulaan Baatar

km	*Trans-Mongolian Railway*	**362**Y *Pas* **e**	**4**ZJ *Sko* ②	**6**ZJ *Sko* § ③**J**	**6**MZ *Sko* ④**K**	**24** *Exp* ④◧
0	*Moskva Yar.* △ d.	...	2345 ②	2345 ③	2345 ④	...
3303	*Novosibirsk* △ d.	...	2126 ④	2126 ⑤	2126 ⑥	...
5152	**Irkutsk** d.	1632	0314 ⑥	0314 ⑦	0314 ①	...
5608	Ulan Ude d.	0136	1058 ⑥	1058 ⑦	1058 ①	...
5863	Naushki 🏛 d.	1220	1656 ⑥	1656 ⑦	1656 ①	...
5886	Suche Bator 🏛 MO d.	*2055	*0014 ⑦	*0014 ①	*0014 ②	...
6265	**Ulaan Baatar** MO a.	*0553	*0650 ⑦	*0650 ①	*0650 ②	...
6265	**Ulaan Baatar** MO d.	...	*0730 ⑦	...	...	*0730 ④
6770	Dzamin Uud 🏛 MO d.	...	*2035 ⑦	...	...	*2035 ④
6780	Erlan 🏛 CH a.	...	2100 ⑦	...	...	2100 ④
7622	**Beijing** CH a.	...	1140 ①	...	...	1140 ⑤

MOSKVA - BEIJING via Harbin

km	*Trans-Manchurian Train name: Vostok*	**20**SZ *Sko* ⑥	6(68
0	*Moskva Yar.* △ d.	2345 ⑥	
1778	*Yekaterinburg* △ d.	0208 ①	
3303	*Novosibirsk* △ d.	2126 ①	
5152	**Irkutsk** d.	0314 ③	
6165	Chita II d.	2252 ③	1
6625	Zabaikalsk 🏛 d.	1305 ④	0
6637	Manzhouli 🏛 CH d.	2359 ④	1
7572	Harbin CH d.	1317 ⑤	
7814	Changchun CH d.	1600 ⑤	
8119	Shenyang CH d.	1934 ⑤	
8961	**Beijing** CH a.	0546 ⑥	

A – To Ulaanbaatar (see below main table).
B – To Ulaanbaatar and Beijing (see below main table).
D – ② from Brest (d. 1109 train **104**BJ), ②⑤⑦ from Minsk (d. 1550), Smolensk (d. 2030), Moskva next day.
F – ②③⑤⑦ (daily Dec. 13 - Jan. 13, Apr. 24 - July 31).
J – Apr. 13, 27, May 11, 25, ③ June 1 - Nov. 2 (also Nov. 16, 30).
K – Apr. 7, 21, May 5, 19, ④ June 2 - Oct. 27 (also Nov. 24, Dec. 8).
P – VOSTOK. To Beijing via Harbin (see below main table).
Q – From Adler on even dates ●(6) (daily June 24 - Sept. 3). Depart Yekaterinburg on 4th day.
R – ROSSIYA (see also summary below main table). Also conveys 🛏 Moskva - Tumangan (North Korea) on 1st, 5th, 17th, 21st of month.
Y – ④⑥ Chita to Manzhouli; daily Chita to Zabaikalsk (arrive 0225).
a – From Adler, Sochi, Rostov (Table **1960**).
b – To Barnaul (a. 0502). On ●(6) to Barnaul (a. 0316), Biisk (0850).
c – From Chelyabinsk ■(1) (Table **1970**), next day from Omsk.
d – From St Peterburg (Table **1900**).
e – Arrives Naushki 0805, Suche Bator 1758. Train number **364**Y from Naushki, **264**IJ from Suche Bator.
k – Moskva **Kurskaya**.
m – To Kemerovo (a. 0516).
n – To Tobolsk (a. 0610), Surgut (a. 1419) and Niznevartovsk (a. 2046).
o – To Novokuznetsk (train **14** a. 0835; train **118** a. 0034).
p – To Petropavl (Table **1975**).

q – To Abakan (a. 0200).
r – Moskva **Belorusskaya**.
s – To Tobolsk (a. 1102), Surgut (a. 2030), Korotchayevo (a. 1043), Novy Urengoy (a. 1250).
t – To Tobolsk (a. 0629), Surgut (a. 1713), Korotchayevo (a. 0552), Novy Urengoy (a. 0752).
u – To Neryungri (Table **1989**).
w – Via Nivhni Tagil (a. 1925).
x – To Severobaikalsk (Table **1989**).
y – To Serov (a. 2310), Priobe (a. 1240).
z – To Tomsk II (a. 0626).
♠ – *Strizh* (Swift) high-speed Talgo train.
≋ – *Lastochka* (Swallow) fast day train.
★ – Shows the number of hours that local time is ahead of Moskva time (all timings within Russia are shown in Moskva time).
◧ – Also ⑥ in summer. Days of running are subject to alteration.
♡ – Even dates Jan., Mar., June, July, Sept. Oct., uneven dates Feb., Apr., May, Aug., Nov., Dec.
♤ – Unven dates Jan., Mar., June, July, Sept. Oct., even dates Feb., Apr., May, Aug., Nov., Dec.
△ – For timings Moskva - Irkutsk see main table.
▽ – Train **96**NJ on uneven dates ■(5), **136**MJ on even dates ●(6).
▷ – Fast day trains run from Moskva Yaroslavskaya to Yaroslavl at 0735, 1445, 1905 (journey 3h 20m).

◇ – Journey 7 days (7 nights) Mos Vladivostok. Conveys 🛏 Mos Ussuriysk - Pyongyang (North Korea) on 12th, 26th of month
☆ – Premium class train; includes sleeping cars with shower/toil
§ – Operated by Mongolian Railw
* – One hour later Mar. 26 - Sept
● – Even dates (see page 530)
●(2) – Even dates [.. *30, 1, 2*..]
●(4) – Even dates [.. *30, 1, 4*..]
●(6) – Even dates [.. *30, 1, 3, 6*..]
●(9) – Even dates [.. *30, 1, 3, 5, 7,*
■ – Uneven dates (see page 53
■(1) – Uneven dates [.. *29, 1*..]
■(3) – Uneven dates [.. *31, 3*..]
■(5) – Uneven dates [.. *31, 2, 5*..]
■(6) – Uneven dates [.. *31, 1, 3, 7*..
■(7) – Uneven dates [.. *31, 2, 4, 7*..
■(9) – Uneven dates [.. *31, 2, 4, 6,*
CH – China (GMT + 8).
MO – Mongolia (GMT + 8 in winter GMT + 9 Mar. 26 - Sept. 24

VLADIVOSTOK - IRKUTSK - NOVOSIBIRSK - YEKATERINBURG - MOSKVA 1990

TransSiberian Railway	67*Y*	77*EI*	11*UJ*	701*NJ*	3*ZJ*	5	41*EI*	703*NJ*	727*GJ*	37*NJ*	29*NJ*	705*NJ*	139*NJ*	19*CH*	707*NJ*	709*NJ*	729*GJ*	69*JA*	71*EJ*	63*BJ*	103*NJ*	73*EJ*	13*NJ*	711*NJ*
	Sko	*Sko*	*Sko*	♠	*Sko*	*Sko*	*Fir*	♠	Lastochka	*Fir*	*Fir*	♠	*Sko*	*Sko*	♠	♠	Lastochka	*Sko*	*Fir*	*Sko*	*Sko*	*Sko*	*Fir*	♠
		■(3)	■(5)	①–⑥	⑤‡	③⑥‡				■(0)	●(2)			①‡	②④⑤⑦	④⑤⑦				①③	⑤	■(1)	■(1)	①⑤⑥⑦
					B	**A**						**F**	**Q**	**P**						**C**	**D**			
ivostok d.	...	...	...	...	...	...	...	...	...	...	...	...	...	...	...	...	...	...	...	...	...	...	...	...
riysk d.	...	...	...	...	...	...	...	...	...	...	...	...	...	...	...	...	...	...	...	...	...	...	...	...
barovsk d.	...	**u**	...	...	...	...	...	...	...	...	...	...	...	...	...	...	...	...	...	...	...	...	...	...
orodino d.	...	1341	...	...	...	...	...	...	...	...	...	...	...	...	...	...	...	...	...	...	...	...	...	...
a II d.	...	1226	1226	...	...	...	...	...	...	...	...	...	...	1843	...	...	...	1727	...	...	...	...	...	...
Ude d.	...	2307	2307	...	0203	0203	...	...	...	...	...	...	...	0538	...	...	...	0443	...	...	...	...	...	...
sk a.	...	0702	0702	...	1006	1006	...	...	...	...	...	...	...	1341	...	...	...	1247	...	...	...	...	...	...
sk d.	...	0730	0730	...	1051	1051	...	...	...	...	...	...	...	1411	...	...	...	1322	...	...	...	...	...	...
het d.	...	1912	1912	...	|	|	...	...	...	...	...	...	...	|	...	...	...	0040	...	...	...	...	...	...
noyarsk d.	**q**	0232	0232	...	0408	0408	...	...	...	**z**	...	...	...	0720	...	...	...	0802	...	...	...	...	...	...
ga d.	0857	1119	1119	...	1217	1217	...	...	...	1015	**m**	...	...	|	...	...	...	1733	...	...	...	...	**o**	...
osibirsk a.	1229	1502	1502	...	1534	1534	...	...	...	1400	1400	...	...	1839	...	...	...	2040	...	...	...	...	2316	...
osibirsk d.	1308	...	1604	...	1553	1553	...	...	...	1450	1450	...	1818	1858	...	...	...	2129	...	2347	2347	...	2356	...
sk a.	2111	...	0018	...	2321	2321	...	...	...	2254	2254	...	0248	0303	...	...	...	0530	...	0708	0708	...	0718	...
sk d.	2128	...	0050	...	2339	2339	...	...	...	2313	2313	...	0318	0328	...	...	...	0557	...	0728	0728	...	0758	...
men d.	0455	...	**c**	...	0642	0642	...	...	...	0613	0613	...	1054	1045	...	...	...	1438	...	1534	1534	1547	1547	...
aterinburg a.	1030	...	...	...	1115	1115	...	...	...	1116	1116	...	1547	1446	...	...	...	2007	...	2048	2048	2056	2056	...
aterinburg d.	1118	...	...	...	1137	1137	...	...	...	1145	1145	...	1618	1517	...	...	...	2102	2052	2122	2122	2132	2132	...
arapul d.	|	...	...	...	|	|	...	...	...	|	|	...	**a**	|	...	...	...	|	|	|	|	|	|	...
azan d.	|	...	...	...	|	|	2207	...	...	|	|	...	...	|	...	...	...	|	|	|	|	|	|	...
urom I d.	|	...	...	...	|	|	|	...	...	|	|	...	...	|	...	...	...	|	|	|	|	|	|	...
n II d.	1730	...	...	...	1740	1740	|	...	...	1830	1830	...	...	2118	...	...	...	0302	0252	0322	0322	0336	0336	...
v d.	0105	...	...	...	0115	0115	|	...	...	0333	0333	...	...	0508	...	...	...	1113	1103	1134	1134	1203	1203	...
ologda I d.	|	...	...	...	|	|	|	...	...	|	|	...	...	|	...	...	...	|	2116	|	|	2232	2232	...
Peterburg Ladozhski a.	|	...	...	...	|	|	|	...	...	|	|	...	...	|	...	...	...	|	0838	|	|	1000	1000	...
ni Novgorod d.	|	...	...	0645	0702	0702	0658	0736	0940	0950	0950	1050	...	1115	1340	1550	1755	|	...	1815	1815	...	...	1900
imir d.	|	...	...	|	1057	1057	...	0943	1157	1330	1330	1257	...	1448	1547	1757	2012	|	...	2224	2224	...	...	|
aroslavl ▷ d.	1304	...	...	|	|	|	...	|	|	|	|	|	...	|	|	|	|	2356	...	|	|	...	...	|
kva Kazanskaya a.	|	...	...	1020**k**	|	|	...	1126**k**	1345**k**	|	|	1440**k**	...	|	1730**k**	1940**k**	2200**k**	|	...	0100**r**	0100**r**	...	...	2235**k**
kva Yaroslavskaya ▷ a.	1658	...	...	...	1358	1358	...	...	...	1630	1630	...	...	1758	...	...	...	0411	...	...	...	...	...	...

	713*NJ*	59*GJ*	75*EI*	81*IJ*	89*UJ*	95*NJ*	55*Y*	117*NJ*	7*EJ*	11*EJ*	91*IJ*	1*MJ*	7*NJ*	35*GJ*	5*EI*	1*GJ*	43*EI*	99*EI*	59*EJ*	15*EJ*	31*GJ*	109*MJ*	49*EJ*	84*EJ*
	♠	*Fir*	*Sko*	*Sko*	*Sko*	*Sko*	*Fir*	*Sko*	*Fir*	*Fir*	*Sko*	*Fir*	*Sko*	*Fir*	*Fir*	*Fir*	*Sko*	*Sko*	*Fir*	*Fir*	*Fir*	*Sko*	*Fir*	*Fir*
			■(1)	●(2)	■(1)		■(3)	●(2)	♤	♡	●(2)	●(8)	■(9)				●(2)	●(2)	♤	♤			♡	♡
		d				▽						**R**				☆		◇						
ivostok d.	...	...	...	...	...	...	...	...	...	...	...	0402	0402	...	1400	...	...	1655	...	...	...	...	...	...
uriysk d.	...	...	...	...	...	...	...	...	...	...	...	0612	0612	...	1602	...	...	1909	...	...	...	...	...	...
barovsk d.	...	...	...	...	...	...	...	...	...	...	...	1632	1632	...	0115	...	0615	0615	...	...	...	...	...	...
vorodino d.	...	...	...	...	...	...	...	...	...	...	...	1134	1134	...	...	...	0321	0321	...	...	...	...	...	...
a II d.	...	...	...	...	...	...	...	...	...	...	...	0841	0841	...	...	...	0147	0147	...	...	...	...	...	...
Ude d.	...	...	...	1050	...	...	...	...	...	...	...	1821	1821	...	...	...	1209	1209	...	...	...	...	...	...
tsk a.	...	...	...	1814	...	...	...	...	...	...	...	0100	0100	...	...	...	2008	2008	...	...	...	...	...	...
tsk d.	...	...	**u**	1902	...	...	...	...	...	...	**x**	0123	0123	...	...	...	2043	2043	...	...	...	...	...	...
shet d.	...	...	0725	0725	...	...	...	...	...	...	0905	1225	1225	...	...	...	0805	0805	...	...	...	...	...	...
snoyarsk d.	...	...	1444	1444	...	...	1454	...	...	...	1630	1915	1915	...	...	...	1524	1524	...	...	...	...	...	...
ga d.	...	...	2303	2303	...	...	2337	**o**	...	...	0211	0339	0339	...	...	...	0023	0023	...	...	...	...	...	...
osibirsk a.	...	...	0214	0214	...	...	0324	0254	...	...	0549	0648	0648	...	...	...	0411	0411	...	...	...	...	...	...
osibirsk d.	...	...	0303	0303	...	**b**	0343	0343	...	...	0638	0707	...	...	...	...	0509	0509	...	...	...	...	...	...
sk a.	...	...	1147	1147	...	1022	1130	1130	...	...	1452	1500	...	...	...	...	1415	1415	...	...	...	...	...	...
sk d.	...	...	1212	1212	...	1100	1200	1200	...	**t**	1509	1518	...	...	...	...	1450	1450	**n**	...	...	**s**	...	...
men d.	...	...	1942	1942	**p**	1921	1931	1931	...	2020	2236	2232	...	...	...	...	2226	2226	0043	...	...	2256	...	...
aterinburg a.	...	...	0049	0049	0058	0113	0121	0121	...	0228	0253	0301	...	...	...	...	0245	0245	0724	...	...	0414	...	...
aterinburg d.	...	...	0120	0120	0128	0203	0211	0211	...	0316	0333	0341	...	...	...	...	0325	0325	0812	0812	...	0448	0219	...
arapul d.	...	...	0952	0952	1009	1029	1019	1019	...	|	|	|	...	...	...	...	|	|	1604	1604	...	|	|	...
azan d.	...	...	1555	1555	1613	1649	1633	1633	...	|	|	|	...	...	...	1945	|	|	2157	2157	...	|	**w**	...
urom I d.	...	...	0008	0008	0020	0115	0105	0105	...	|	|	|	...	...	...	0255	|	|	0454	0454	...	|	|	**y**
m II d.	...	...	|	|	|	|	|	|	0920	0920	0940	0950	...	...	...	|	0930	0930	|	|	...	1240	1250	1250
ov d.	...	...	|	|	|	|	|	|	1654	1654	1724	1734	...	...	...	|	1704	1704	|	|	2030	2114	2124	2124
ologda I d.	...	...	|	|	|	|	|	|	|	|	|	|	...	...	...	|	|	|	|	|	|	|	|	|
Peterburg Ladozhski a.	...	...	|	|	|	|	|	|	|	|	|	|	...	...	...	|	|	|	|	|	|	|	|	|
ni Novgorod d.	2008	1919	|	|	|	|	|	|	2300	2300	2311	2325	...	2335	...	|	|	|	|	|	0301	0319	0329	0329
dimir d.	2215	2300	|	|	|	|	|	|	0211	0211	0248	0258	...	0324	...	|	|	|	|	|	0620	0703	0713	0713
aroslavl ▷ d.	|	|	|	|	|	|	|	|	|	|	|	|	...	|	...	|	0642	0642	|	|	|	|	|	|
skva Kazanskaya a.	2358**k**	0123**k**	0442	0442	0457	0611	0545	0545	|	|	|	|	...	|	...	0710	|	|	0923	0923	|	|	|	|
skva Yaroslavskaya ▷ a.	...	...	...	...	...	...	...	...	0522	0522	0552	0601	...	0629	...	...	1103	1103	...	...	0943	1030	1038	1038

ROSSIYA SUMMARY

km		1*MJ* *Fir* ●(8) **R**	
0	**Vladivostok** d.	0402	*1st day*
66	Khabarovsk d.	1632	*1st day*
50	Ulan Ude d.	1821	*3rd day*
06	Irkutsk d.	0123	*4th day*
93	Krasnoyarsk d.	1915	*4th day*
55	Novosibirsk d.	0707	*5th day*
82	Omsk d.	1518	*5th day*
80	Yekaterinburg d.	0341	*6th day*
41	Kirov d.	1734	*6th day*
97	Nizhni Novgorod d.	2325	*6th day*
58	**Moskva** Yar. a.	0601	*7th day*

BEIJING - MOSKVA via Ulaan Baatar

km	*Trans-Mongolian Railway*	5*VJ* *Sko* ② **J**	3*ZJ* *Sko* ③	5*SZ* *Sko* § ⑤ **K**	23 *Exp* ② ◧	263*IJ* *Pas* **e**
0	**Beijing** CH d.	...	1122 ③	...	1122 ②	...
842	Erlan 🏛 CH d.	...	0059 ④	...	0059 ③	...
852	Dzamin Uud 🏛 MO d.	...	*0240 ④	...	*0240 ③	...
1356	**Ulaan Baatar** MO a.	...	*1435 ④	...	*1435 ③	...
1356	**Ulaan Baatar** MO d.	*1522 ②	*1522 ④	*1522 ⑤	...	2045
1735	Suche Bator 🏛 MO d.	*2310 ②	*2310 ④	*2310 ⑤	...	*1008
1758	Naushki 🏛 d.	2110 ②	2110 ④	2110 ⑤	...	1005
2013	Ulan Ude d.	0203 ③	0203 ⑤	0203 ⑥	...	1720
2469	**Irkutsk** a.	1006 ③	1006 ⑤	1006 ⑥	...	0215
4319	*Novosibirsk* △ a.	1534 ④	1534 ⑥	1534 ⑦	...	...
7622	*Moskva Yar.* △ a.	1358 ⑥	1358 ①	1358 ②	...	...

BEIJING - MOSKVA via Harbin

km	*Trans-Manchurian Train name: Vostok*	19*CH* *Sko* ⑥	653*CH* 683*CH* **Y**
0	**Beijing** CH d.	2300 ⑥	...
841	Shenyang CH d.	0855 ⑦	...
1141	Changchun CH d.	1229 ⑦	...
1388	Harbin CH d.	1540 ⑦	...
2323	Manzhouli 🏛 CH d.	0701 ①	1400
2335	Zabaikalsk 🏛 d.	0812 ①	1345
2795	Chita II d.	1843 ①	0148
3808	**Irkutsk** a.	1341 ②	...
5658	*Novosibirsk* △ a.	1839 ③	...
7183	*Yekaterinburg* △ a.	1446 ④	...
8961	*Moskva Yar.* △ a.	1758 ⑤	...

From Ulaanbaatar (see below main table).
From Beijing and Ulaanbaatar (see below main table).
To Smolensk a. 0702 ④⑥ and Minsk a. 1149 ④⑥.
To Smolensk a. 0702 ①, Minsk a. 1149 ①, Brest a. 1638 ①.
③⑤ (also ①④⑥ Apr. 28 - Sept. 17).
Apr. 12, 26, May 10, 24; ② June 7 - Nov. 1 (also Nov. 29, Dec. 13).
Apr. 8, 22, May 6, 20, ⑤ June 3 - Oct. 28 (also Nov. 11, 25, Dec. 9).
VOSTOK. From Beijing via Harbin (see below main table).
Even dates (daily June 20 - Aug. 30). Arrive Adler on 5th day.
ROSSIYA (see also summary below main table). Also conveys 🛏 Tumangan (North Korea) - Ussuriysk - Moskva four times per month.
⑤⑦ from Manzhouli (Zabaikalsk a. 0925); daily from Zabaikalsk.
To Rostov, Sochi, Adler (Table **1960**).
From Barnaul (d. 1845 on even dates, 2055 on uneven dates).
To Chelyabinsk (Table **1970**).
To St Peterburg (Table **1900**).
Arrives Suche Bator 0440, Naushki 0600. Train number **363***IJ* from Suche Bator, **361***IJ* from Naushki.
Moskva **Kurskaya**.
From Kemerovo (d. 0907).
From Niznevartovsk (d. 0458), Surgut (d. 1008), Tobolsk (1930).
From Novokuznetsk (train **13** d. 1622; train **117** d. 1736).
From Petropavl (Table **1975**).

q – From Abakan (d. 1415 previous day).
r – Moskva **Belorusskaya**.
s – From Novy Urengoy (d. 1450), Korotchayevo (d. 1650), Surgut (d. 0742 2nd day), Tobolsk (d. 1719 2nd day).
t – From Novy Urengoy (d. 1000), Korotchayevo (d. 1225), Surgut (d. 0307 2nd day), Tobolsk (d. 1505 2nd day).
u – From Neryungri (Table **1989**). Train **75** departs Tayshet on 4th day.
w – Via Nivhni Tagil (depart 0455).
x – From Severobaikalsk (Table **1989**), next day from Tayshet.
y – From Priobe (d. 1418), Serov (d. 0149). From Perm 2nd day.
z – From Tomsk II (d. 0719).
♠ – *Strizh* (Swift) high-speed Talgo train.
Lastochka symbol – *Lastochka* (Swallow) fast day train.
◧ – Also ① in summer. Days of running are subject to alteration.
♡ – Even dates Jan., Mar., June, July, Sept. Oct., uneven dates Feb., Apr., May, Aug., Nov., Dec.
♤ – Unven dates Jan., Mar., June, July, Sept. Oct., even dates Feb., Apr., May, Aug., Nov., Dec.
▷ – Fast day trains run from Yaroslavl to Moskva Yaroslavskaya at 0752, 1352, 1932 (journey 3 hours 20 mins).
△ – For timings Irkutsk - Moskva see main table.
▽ – Train **95***NJ* on even dates ●(2), **136***NJ* on uneven dates ■(3).
◇ – Journey 8 days (7 nights) Vladivostok - Moskva. Also conveys 🛏 Pyongyang (North Korea) - Ussuriysk - Moskva twice monthly.

‡ – For day of running from point of origin see below main table.
§ – Operated by Mongolian Railways.
☆ – Premium class train; includes Lux sleeping cars with shower/toilet.
* – One hour later Mar. 26 - Sept. 24.

● – Even dates (see page 530).
●(2) – Even dates [.. *30, 2* ..]
●(8) – Even dates [.. *30, 1, 3, 5, 8* ..]

■ – Uneven dates (see page 530).
■(0) – Uneven dates [.. *31, 1* ..]
■(1) – Uneven dates [.. *29, 1* ..]
■(3) – Uneven dates [.. *31, 3* ..]
■(5) – Uneven dates [.. *31, 2, 5* ..]
■(9) – Uneven dates [.. *31, 2, 4, 6, 9* ..]

CH – China (GMT + 8).
MO – Mongolia (GMT + 8 in winter, GMT + 9 Mar. 26 - Sept. 24).

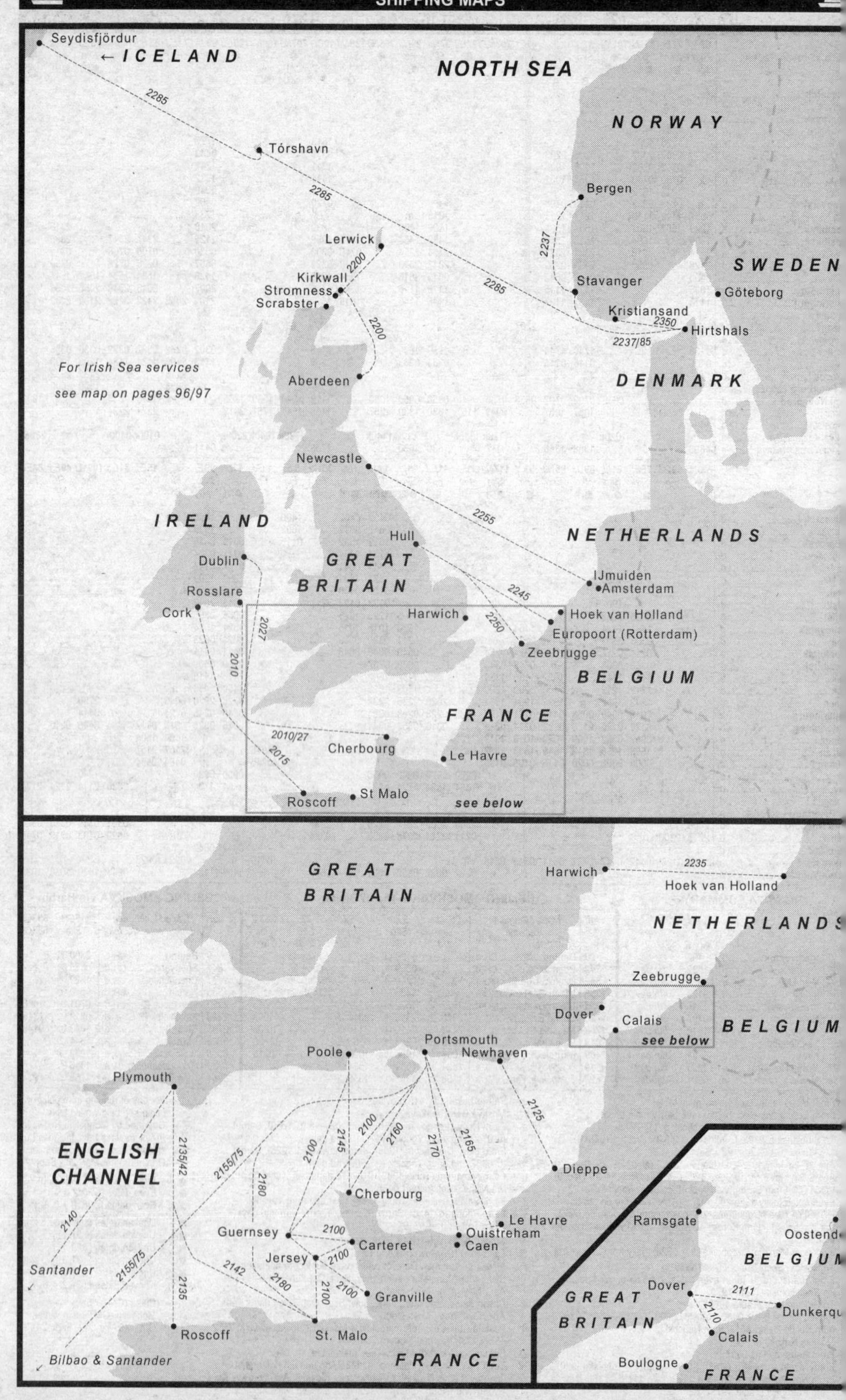

For other shipping routes see relevant country maps

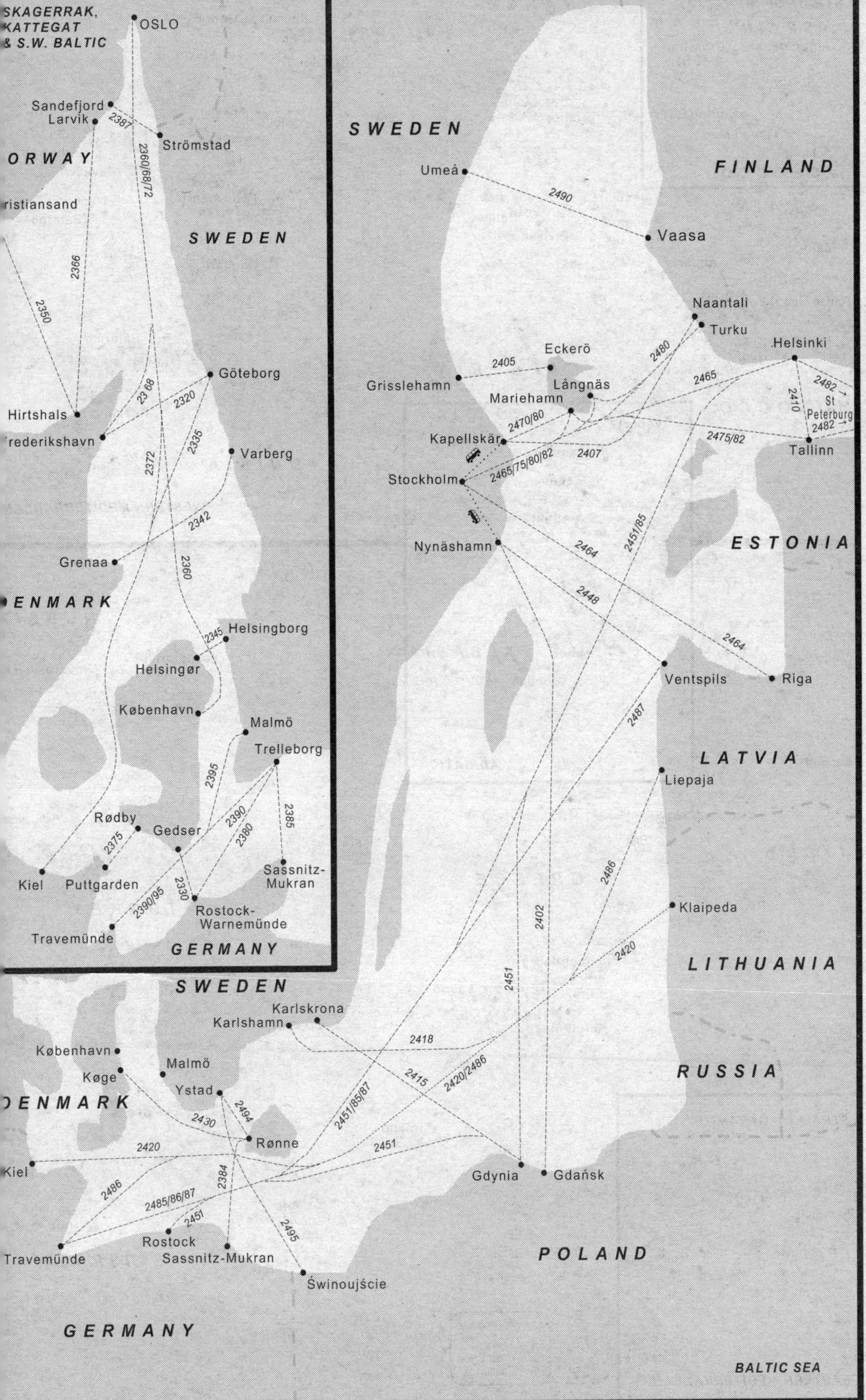
SKAGERRAK, KATTEGAT & S.W. BALTIC
OSLO
Sandefjord
Larvik
2387
Strömstad
2360/68/72
ORWAY
ristiansand
SWEDEN
2366
2350
Göteborg
23 68
2320
Hirtshals
rederikshavn
2335
Varberg
2372
2342
Grenaa
2360
ENMARK
2345
Helsingborg
Helsingør
København
Malmö
Trelleborg
2395
2385
Rødby
Gedser
2390
2380
2375
Kiel
Puttgarden
2330
Sassnitz-Mukran
2390/95
Rostock-Warnemünde
Travemünde
GERMANY
SWEDEN
Umeå
FINLAND
2490
Vaasa
Naantali
Turku
Eckerö
Helsinki
2405
2480
Grisslehamn
Långnäs
2465
2482
St Peterburg
Mariehamn
2410
2470/80
2482
Kapellskär
2475/82
2407
Tallinn
2465/75/80/82
Stockholm
2451/85
ESTONIA
2464
Nynäshamn
2448
2464
Ventspils
Riga
2487
LATVIA
Liepaja
2486
Klaipeda
2402
2420
LITHUANIA
2451
SWEDEN
Karlskrona
Karlshamn
2418
København
Køge
Malmö
2415
RUSSIA
Ystad
2420/2486
2451/85/87
DENMARK
2494
2430
Rønne
2451
2420
Kiel
Gdynia
Gdańsk
2384
2486
2485/86/87
2451
2495
Rostock
Travemünde
Sassnitz-Mukran
POLAND
Świnoujście
GERMANY
BALTIC SEA

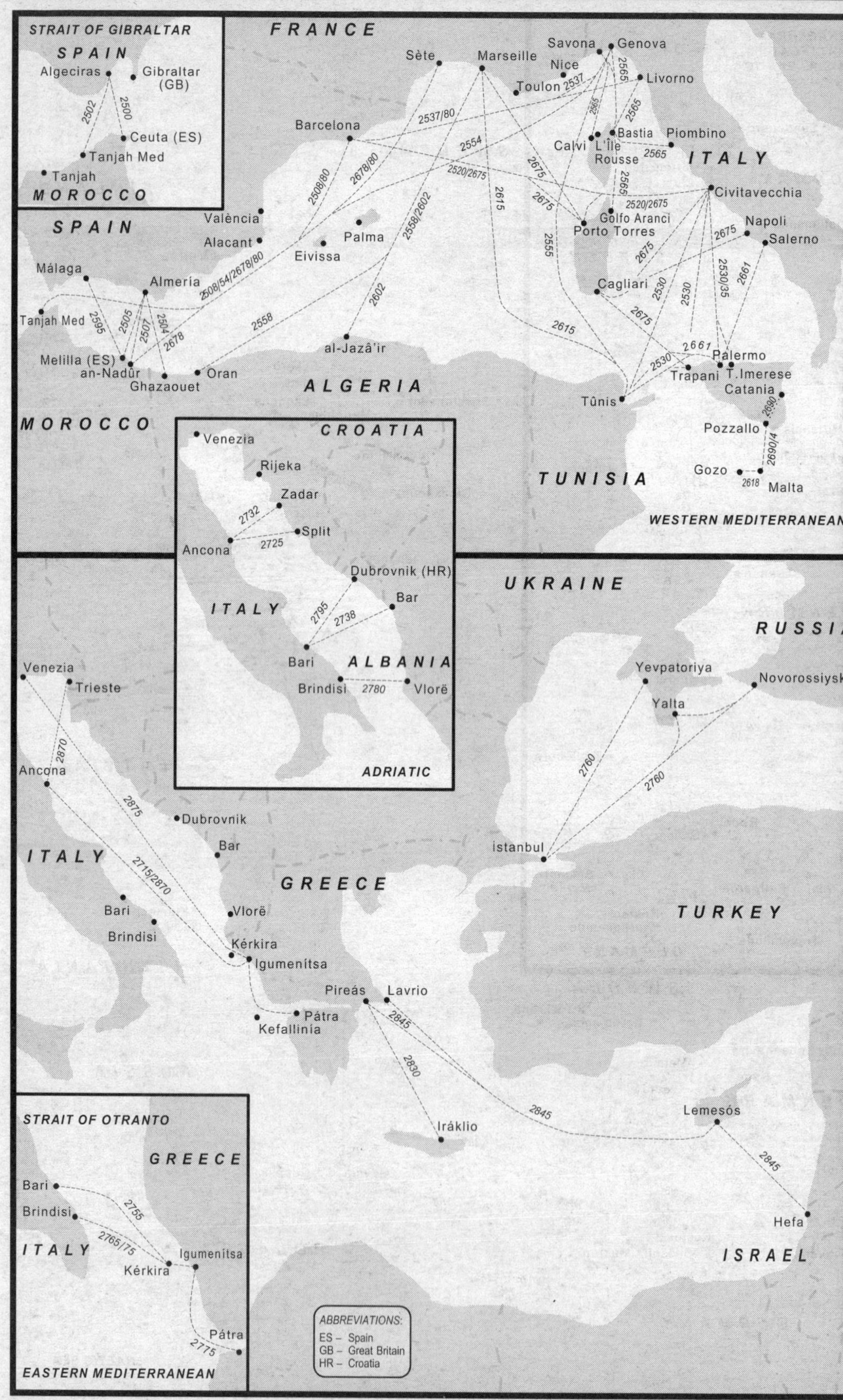
STRAIT OF GIBRALTAR
SPAIN
Algeciras
Gibraltar (GB)
2502
2500
Ceuta (ES)
Tanjah Med
Tanjah
MOROCCO
FRANCE
Sète
Marseille
Savona
Genova
Nice
Toulon
2537
2565
Livorno
Barcelona
2537/80
2554
Calvi
L'Île Rousse
Bastia
Piombino
2565
ITALY
2520/2675
2675
2615
2520/2675
Civitavecchia
València
Alacant
Palma
Eivissa
2508/80
2678/80
2558/2602
2555
Golfo Aranci
Porto Torres
Napoli
Salerno
SPAIN
Málaga
Almería
2508/54/2678/80
Cagliari
2530
2530/35
2661
Tanjah Med
2595
2505
2507
2504
2678
2558
2602
al-Jazâ'ir
2615
Palermo
Trapani
T.Imerese
Catania
Melilla (ES)
an-Nadûr
Ghazaouet
Oran
ALGERIA
Tûnis
2690
Pozzallo
MOROCCO
CROATIA
Venezia
Rijeka
Zadar
2732
Split
2725
Ancona
TUNISIA
Gozo
2618
2690/4
Malta
WESTERN MEDITERRANEAN
Dubrovnik (HR)
Bar
ITALY
2795
2738
UKRAINE
RUSSIA
Bari
ALBANIA
Brindisi
2780
Vlorë
ADRIATIC
Venezia
Trieste
Yevpatoriya
Yalta
Novorossiysk
2870
Ancona
2760
2875
Dubrovnik
Bar
İstanbul
ITALY
2715/2870
GREECE
TURKEY
Bari
Brindisi
Vlorë
Kérkira
Igumenítsa
Pireás
Lavrio
Pátra
Kefallinía
2845
2830
Iráklio
2845
Lemesós
2845
Hefa
ISRAEL
STRAIT OF OTRANTO
GREECE
Bari
Brindisi
2755
2765/75
ITALY
Igumenítsa
Kérkira
Pátra
2775
EASTERN MEDITERRANEAN
ABBREVIATIONS:
ES – Spain
GB – Great Britain
HR – Croatia

SHIPPING CONTENTS

SHIPPING OPERATORS

EMS www.ag-ems.de
fach 11 54, 26691 Emden-Außenhafen: ✆ +49 (0)1805 180 182,
ax +49 21 89 07 405.

.AURO www.alilauro.it
ione Marittima, Piazzale Angioino, 80133 Napoli: ✆ +39 081 497 2222,
ax +39 081 497 2228. Reservations: ✆ +39 (0)81 497 2238.

FÆRGENS www.faergen.dk
gen, Dampskibskajen 3, 3700 Rønne: ✆ +45 70 23 15 15.

K LINES www.anek.gr
kti Kondili Str., 18545 Pireás: ✆ +30 210 4197 420, +30 210 4197 430.
J.K. agent: Viamare Ltd., Suite 3, 447 Kenton Road, Harrow, HA3 0XY:
✆ 020 8206 3420, fax 020 8206 1332.

EÀRIA (EUROLÍNIES MARÍTIMES) www.balearia.com
ció Marítima s/n, 03700 Dénia: ✆ +34 96 642 86 00; call centre: ✆ +34 96 642 87 00.

E LINE www.blueline-ferries.com
1 Vincenti Buildings - Strait Street, Valletta, VLT 1432, Malta
✆ +356 2122 3299
Croatia agent: ✆ +385 21 352 533, fax +385 21 352 482.
taly agent: ✆ +39 071 20 40 41, fax +39 071 20 26 18.

E STAR FERRIES www.bluestarferries.com
- 125 Syngrou Avenue & 3 Torva Street, 117 45 Athína: ✆ +30 210 891 9800,
ax +30 210 891 9829.

FERRIES www.bluferries.it
✆ +39 090 6786 406, fax +39 090 6406 508.

NHOLMERFÆRGEN www.faergen.dk
gen, Dampskibskajen 3, 3700 Rønne: ✆ +45 70 23 15 15.

TTANY FERRIES: www.brittany-ferries.co.uk
ay, Plymouth, PL1 3EW: ✆ 0871 244 1401.
ervations: U.K. ✆ 0871 244 0744; France ✆ +33 825 828 828;
Spain ✆ +34 942 36 06 11.

MERANG SHIPPING COMPANY TOURISM TRAVEL & TRADE S.A.
m Cad. Veli Alemdar Han Kat. 6, 80030 Karaköy - Istanbul: ✆ +90 (0)212 251 7373,
ax +90 (0)212 251 1472.

.EMAR www.caremar.it
See Tirrenia for details.

.OR LINE www.colorline.com
boks 1422 Vika, N-0115 Oslo: ✆ + 47 22 94 44 00, fax +47 22 83 04 30.
Reservations: Norway ✆ +47 22 94 42 00; Denmark ✆ +45 99 56 19 77;
Germany ✆ +49 431 7300 300; Sweden ✆ +46 526 62 000.

MARIT www.comarit.com
ue Mohamed VI, Tanjah: ✆ +212 539 32 00 32, fax +212 539 32 59 00.

MPAGNIE TUNISIENNE DE NAVIGATION www.ctn.com.tn
enue Dag Hammarskjoeld, 1001 Tûnis: ✆ +216 (71) 341 777, fax +216 (71) 345 736.
Reservations: ✆ +33 825 88 80 88.
U.K. agent: Southern Ferries (see Trasmediterranea).

NDOR FERRIES LTD. www.condorferries.co.uk
Harbour Road South, Hamworthy, Poole, BH15 4AJ.
Reservations: ✆ 0845 609 1024.
Information: U.K. ✆ 01202 207 216; Jersey ✆ 01534 872 240; Guernsey 12023 (local calls only); St Malo ✆ (0)825 165 463; Cherbourg ✆ +33 2 33 88 44 88.

RSICA FERRIES www.corsica-ferries.fr
Rue Chanoine Leschi, 20296 Bastia: ✆ +33 4 95 32 95 95, fax +33 4 95 32 14 71.

STINATION GOTLAND www.destinationgotland.se
gatan 2, Box 1234, 621 23 Visby: ✆ +46 (0)498 20 18 00, fax +46 (0)498 20 18 90.
Reservations: ✆ +46 (0)771 22 33 00, fax +46 (0)498 20 13 90.

S SEAWAYS www.dfdsseaways.co.uk
national Port, Parkeston, Harwich CO12 4SR.
International Passenger Terminal, Royal Quays, North Shields, Newcastle, NE29 6EE.
Reservations: U.K. ✆ 0871 522 9955; Denmark ✆ +45 33 42 30 00, +45 7917 7917;
Netherlands ✆ +31 255 54 66 66; Norway ✆ +47 21 62 10 00;
Ostuferhafen 15, 24149 Kiel: ✆ +49 (0)431 20976 420, fax +49 (0)431 20976 102;
Klaipeda: ✆ +370 46 395 051.

.ERÖ LINE www.eckeroline.fi
nerheimintie 10, 00100 Helsinki: ✆ +358 6000 4300, fax +358 9 2288 5547.
Passanger Harbour, Sadama 29, 10111 Tallinn: ✆ +372 664 6000,
fax +372 631 8690.

.ERÖ LINJEN www.eckerolinjen.fi
. Box 158, Torggatan 2, AX-22101 Mariehamn, Åland: ✆ +358 (0)18 28 000,
fax +358 (0)18 28 380.
SE-760 45 Grisslehamn: ✆ +46 (0)175 258 00, fax +46 (0)175 330 54.
Berghamn, AX-22270 Eckerö, Åland: ✆ +358 (0)18 28 300, fax +358 (0)18 38 230.

TMV www.algerieferries.com
Boulevard des Dames, 13002 Marseille: ✆ +33 (0)4 91 90 64 70,
fax +33 (0)4 91 91 59 58. Reservations: ✆ +213 (021) 42 46 50.

EUROPEAN SEAWAYS www.europeanseaways.com
Machis Analatou 111, Neos Kosmos 117 44 Athína: +30 210 9561630,
fax +30 210 9537263.
Customer support: ✆ +30 210 9561630.

FANØFÆRGEN www.faergen.dk
Færgen, Dampskibskajen 3, 3700 Rønne: ✆ +45 70 23 15 15.

FINNLINES www.finnlines.com
Porkkalankatu 20A, FI-00180 Helsinki: ✆ +358 (0)10 343 4500, (0)10 343 4600.

FJORD LINE www.fjordline.com
Skoltegrunnskaien, N-5003, 5003 Bergen: ✆ +47 51 46 40 99, fax +47 55 31 88 00.
Reservations: ✆ +47 51 46 40 99.

FRED. OLSEN S.A. www.fredolsen.es
Polígono Industrial de Añaza s/n, 38109 Santa Cruz de Tenerife: ✆ +34 922 628 200,
fax +34 922 628 232. Reservation: ✆ +34 902 100 107.

FRS www.frs.es
Estación Maritima. P.O. / Apto de correos 13, E-11380 Tarifa - Cádiz: ✆ +34 956 68 18 30,
fax +34 956 62 71 80.

FRS HELGOLINE www.helgoline.de
Norderhofenden 19 - 20, D 24937 Flensburg: ✆ +49 (0)461 864 0, fax +49 (0)461 864 70.

GOZO CHANNEL www.gozochannel.com
Mgarr Harbour, Mgarr Gozo: ✆ +356 2210 9000, fax +356 2155 6743.

GRANDI NAVI VELOCI www.gnv.it
Via Fieschi 17, 16121 Genova: ✆ +39 010 5509 465, fax +39 010 5509 301.
Contact centre: ✆ +39 010 2094 591.
U.K. agent: Viamare (see Anek Lines).

GRIMALDI LINES www.grimaldi-lines.com
Via Marchese Campodisola 13, 80133 Napoli: ✆ +39 081 496 444, fax +39 081 551 7716.
U.K. agent: Viamare (see Anek Lines).

HURTIGRUTEN (NORWEGIAN COASTAL VOYAGE) www.hurtigruten.no
Fredrik Langes gate 14, Postboks 6144, 9008 Tromsø: ✆ +47 970 57 030.
Reservations: ✆ +47 810 30 000.
U.K. reservations: ✆ 0203 603 6213.

INTERNATIONAL MARITIME TRANSPORT CORPORATION (IMTC) www.imtc.co.ma
50 Avenue Paster, 20 300 Casablanca: ✆ +212 (22) 437 620, fax +212 (22) 543 548.
Spain agent: Vapores Suardiaz Andalucia S.A. (VS), Avda. Del Puerto 1 - 6, SP-11006 Cádiz: ✆ +34 956 282 111, fax +34 956 282 846.

IRISH FERRIES www.irishferries.com
P.O. Box 19, Alexandra Road, Dublin 1: ✆ +353 (0)1 855 2222, fax +353 (0)1 855 2272.
Corn Exchange Building, Ground Floor, Brunswick Street, Liverpool L2 7TP:
✆ 08717 300 400, fax 0151 236 0562.
France reservations: ✆ +33 1 70 72 03 26, fax +33 1 70 72 03 27.

ISLE OF MAN STEAM PACKET CO. www.steam-packet.com
Sea Terminal, Douglas, Isle of Man IM1 2RF.
Reservations: ✆ 661 661; U.K. ✆ 08722 992 992; Ireland ✆ +44 8722 992 992.

ISLES OF SCILLY STEAMSHIP CO. www.islesofscilly-travel.co.uk
Travel Centre, Quay Street, Penzance, TR18 4BZ: ✆ 0845 710 5555, fax 01736 334 228.
Overseas reservations: ✆ +44 (0)1736 334 228.

JADROLINIJA www.jadrolinija.hr
Riva 16, 51000 Rijeka: ✆ +385 (51) 666 111, fax +385 (51) 213 116.
U.K. agent: Viamare (see Anek Lines).

LD LINES www.ldlines.co.uk
Continental Ferry Port, Wharf Road, Portsmouth, PO2 8QW: ✆ 0844 576 8836,
fax 01235 84 56 08.
Terminal de la Citadelle, BP 90746, F-76060 Le Havre: ✆ 0825 304 304.
Outside U.K. and France: ✆ +33 (0)2 32 14 52 09.

LINDA LINE OY www.lindaline.fi
Makasiiniterminaali, 00140 Helsinki: ✆ +358 (0)9 668 9700, fax +358 (0)9 668 97070.
Ädala 4a, 10614 Tallinn: ✆ +372 6 999 340, fax +372 6 999 340.
Tallinn port: ✆ +372 6 999 333, fax +372 6 999 330.
Reservations: ✆ +358 (0)600 0668970.

LNP www.lnp.hr
Linijska Nacionalna Plovidba d.d., Boktuljin put b.b., 21000 Split: ✆ +385 (0)21 338 310,
fax +385 (0)21 352 447.

MANCHE ILES EXPRESS www.manche-iles-express.com
Albert Quay, St Helier, Jersey: ✆ 01534 880 756, fax 01534 880 314.
Terminal Building, New Jetty, White Rock, St Peter Port, Guernsey: ✆ 01481 701 316,
fax 01481 701 319.

MARITIMA FERRIES www.maritima-ferries.eu
✆ +33 (0)825 88 80 88.
Information: Bordeaux ✆ 05 56 44 46 07; Le Havre ✆ 02 35 21 53 50;
Marseille ✆ 04 91 56 33 90; Toulon ✆ 04 94 16 66 62.
U.K. agent: Southern Ferries (see Trasmediterranea).

continued on next page

continued from previous page

MEDMAR www.medmargroup.it
Terminal Porta di Massa, Napoli: ✆ +39 (0)81 333 44 11, fax +39 (0)81 333 44 36.

MINOAN LINES www.minoan.gr
17, 25th August Street, 712 02 Heraklion: ✆ +30 2810 399800, fax +30 2810 330308.
Reservations: ✆ +30 210 414 5700.
U.K. agent: Viamare (see Anek Lines).

MOBY LINES www.moby.it
Via Ninci 1, 57037 Portoferraio: ✆ +390 (565) 91 41 33, fax +390 (565) 91 76 52.
Outside Italy: ✆ +49 (0)611 14020, fax +49 (0)611 140 2244.
U.K. agent: Viamare (see Anek Lines).

MOLS-LINIEN www.mols-linien.dk
Færgehavnen, 8400 Ebeltoft: ✆ +45 89 52 52 00, fax +45 89 52 52 90.
Reservations: ✆ +45 70 10 14 18.

MONTENEGRO LINES www.montenegrolines.net
Barska Plovidba, Obala 13 jula bb, 85000 Bar: ✆ +382 30 312 366, fax +382 30 311 652.
Reservations: ✆ +382 30 303 469.

NAVIERA ARMAS www.naviera-armas.com
Juan Rejón 32 - 5 y 6, 35008 Las Palmas de Gran Canaria, España. ✆ +34 (928) 22 72 82, fax +34 (928) 46 99 91.
Call centre: ✆ +34 902 456 500.

NAVIGAZIONE LIBERA del GOLFO www.navlib.it
Molo Beverello, 80133 Napoli: ✆ +39 081 552 07 63, fax +39 081 552 55 89.

NORDIC FERRY SERVICES www.nordic-ferry.com
Damoskibskajen 3, DK-3700 Rønne: ✆ +45 70 23 15 15.

NORDLANDSEKSPRESSEN www.torghatten-nord.no
Postboks 2380, 9271 Tromsø: ✆/fax +47 906 20 700.

NORFOLK LINE www.norfolkline.com
Kranenburgweg 180, 2583 ER The Hague: ✆ + 31 70 35 27 400, fax +31 70 35 27 435.
Reservations: Dover - Dunkerque ✆ 0871 574 7235.
Irish Sea: ✆ 0871 200 0621, 01 800 806 118.

NORTHLINK FERRIES www.northlinkferries.co.uk
Ferry Road, Stromness, KW16 3BH, Orkney: ✆ 01856 88 55 00, fax 01856 85 17 95.
Reservations: ✆ 0845 6000 449.

P & O FERRIES www.poferries.com
Channel House, Channel View Road, Dover, CT17 9TJ: ✆ 08716 645 645; outside U.K.: ✆ +44 1304 863 000.
Belgium ✆ +32 070 70 77 71; France ✆ +33 0825 12 01 56;
Germany ✆ +49 0180 500 9437; Netherlands ✆ +31 020 200 8333;
Spain ✆ +34 902 02 04 61; other countries ✆ +352 34 20 80 82 94.

P & O IRISH SEA www.poirishsea.com
Arran House, 100 Port Ranald Drive, Troon, KA10 6HH.
Larne Harbour, Larne BT40 1AW.
Reservations: U.K. ✆ 0871 66 44 77; Dublin ✆ 01 407 34 34.

POLFERRIES www.polferries.pl
Polish Baltic Shipping Co., ul. Portowa 41, 78 100 Kolobrzeg: ✆ +48 94 35 52 102, fax +48 94 35 52 208.
Reservations: ✆ +48 94 35 52 119, +48 94 35 52 233.

REEDEREI CASSEN EILS www.cassen-eils.de
Bei der Alten Liebe 12, 27472 Cuxhaven: ✆ +49 (0)4721 35082, fax +49 (0)4721 31161.

REGINA LINE www.reginaline.dk
Contact: office@reginaline.dk

ST PETER LINE
1, ul. Karavannaya, St Peterburg: ✆ +7 (812) 702 07 77. www.stpeterline.com

SALAMIS CRUISE LINES www.salamiscruiselines.com
1, G. Katsounotos Str., P.O. Box 50531, 3607 Limassol: ✆ +357 2586 0000, fax +357 2537 4437.

SAMSØFÆRGEN www.faergen.dk
Færgen, Dampskibskajen 3, 3700 Rønne: ✆ +45 70 23 15 15.

SARDINIA FERRIES www.corsica-ferries.fr
5 bis Rue Chanoine Leschi, 20296 Bastia: ✆ +33 4 95 32 95 95, fax +33 4 95 32 14 71.

SCANDLINES GmbH www.scandlines.de
Hochhaus am Fährhafen, 18119 Rostock: ✆ +49 (0)381 5435-0, fax +49 (0)381 5435-678.
Reservations: Germany ✆ +49 (0)1805 11 66 88; Denmark ✆ +45 33 15 15 15, fax +45 3529 02 01; Latvia ✆ +371 6362 07 83, fax +371 6362 06 90; Lithuania ✆/fax +370 46 310561.

SIREMAR
See Tirrenia for details.

SMYRIL LINE www.smyrilline
Yviri Vid Strond 1, Postboks 370, FO-110 Tórshavn: ✆ +298 34 59 00, fax +298 34 59
Reservations: Iceland ✆ +354 570 8600, fax +354 552 9450;
Denmark ✆ +45 96 55 03 60, fax +45 96 55 03 61.
U.K. agent: The Travel Gateway, 2 Morrow Court, Appleford Road, Sutton Courter OX14 4FH: ✆ 0844 576 5503, fax 01235 845108.

SNAV www.s
Stazione Marittima, Molo Angioino, 80133 Napoli: ✆ +39 081 428 55 55, fax +39 081 428 52 59.
U.K. agent: Viamare (see Anek Lines).

STENA LINE www.stenaline
Stena House, Station Approach, Holyhead, LL65 1DQ: ✆ 08447 70 70 70.
Reservations: Denmark ✆ +45 96 200 200; Germany ✆ +49 1805 91 66 66;
Ireland ✆ +353 (0)1204 7777; Netherlands ✆ +31 174 31 58 11;
Northern Ireland ✆ +44 8447 70 70 70; Norway ✆ +47 23 17 91 30;
Poland ✆ +48 58 660 92 00; Sweden ✆ +46 31 704 00 00.

SUPERFAST FERRIES www.superfast
123 - 125 Syngrou Av. & 3 Torva Str., 117 45, Athína: ✆ +30 210 891 9000, fax +30 210 891 9029.
Reservations: ✆ +30 210 891 9800; Germany ✆ +49 451 88 00 61 66, fax +49 451 88 00 61 29.
U.K. agents: The Travel Gateway (see Smyril Line); Viamare (see Anek Lines).

TALLINK SILJA www.tallinksilja
Keilaranta 9, 02151 Espoo: ✆ +358 9 180 41, fax +358 9 180 4402.
Södra Hamnvägen 50A, 10253 Stockholm: ✆ +46 8 666 3330.
Reservations: ✆ +358 600 174 552; rest of Europe ✆ +49 451 58 99 222, fax +49 451 58 99 203; outside Europe ✆ +358 600 15700.

TIRRENIA www.tirre
Rione Sirignano 2, Casella Postale 438, 80121 Napoli: ✆ +39 091 749 31 11, fax +39 091 749 33 66. Call centre: ✆ +39 02 2630 2803.
U.K. agent: The Travel Gateway (see Smyril Line).

TOREMAR www.toren
Via Calafati 6, 57123 Livorno. Call centre: ✆ +39 02 2630 2803.
U.K. agent: S.M.S. Travel & Tourism, 40 /42 Kenway Road, London, SW5 0RA: ✆ 020 7244 8422, fax 020 7244 9829.

TORGHATTEN NORD AS www.torghatten-nor
P.O. Box 2380, 9271 Tromsø: ✆ +47 906 20 700, fax +47 907 20 700.

TRANSMANCHE FERRIES www.transmancheferries.
Ferry Port, Railway Approach, Newhaven, BN9 0DF.
7 Quai Gaston Lalitte, 76200 Dieppe.
Reservations: ✆ 0844 576 8836, fax 01235 84 56 08; outside U.K. and France ✆ +33 (0)2 32 14 52 09.

TRASMEDITERRANEA www.trasmediterrane
Avda. de Europa 10, Parque Empresarial La Moraleja, C.P. 28108 Alcobendas, Madric ✆ +34 (0)91 423 85 00, fax +34 (0)91 423 85 55.
Reservations: ✆ +34(0) 902 45 46 45.
U.K. agent: Southern Ferries, 22 Sussex Street, London SW1V 4RW: ✆ 0844 815 7785, fax 0844 815 7795.

TT-LINE www.ttline.
Zum Hafenplatz 1, 23570 Lübeck-Travemünde: ✆ +49 (0)4502 801-81.
Rostock: ✆ +49 (0)381 67079-0; Trelleborg ✆ +46 (0)410 56-200.

UNITY LINE www.unityli
Plac Rodja 8, 70-419, Szczecin: ✆ +48 (0)91 35 95 795, fax +48 (0)91 35 95 885.
Reservations: ✆ +48 (0)91 35 95 600.
Färjeterminalen, 271 39 Ystad: ✆ +46 (0)411 55 69 00, fax +46 (0)411 55 69 53

USTICA LINES www.usticalin
Via Orlandini 48, 91100 Trapani: ✆ +39 0923 873 813, fax +39 0923 593 200.

VENTOURIS FERRIES www.ventour
17 Gr. Lampraki Str., 185 33 Pireás: ✆ +30 210 482 8001-4, fax +30 210 483 2909.
UK agent: Viamare (see Anek Lines).

VIKING LINE www.vikingli
Lönnrotinkatu 2, FIN-00100 Helsinki: ✆ +358 (0)9 12 351, fax +358 (0)9 647 075.
U.K. agent: Emagine U.K. Ltd, Leigh, WN7 1AZ: ✆ 01942 262 662, fax 01942 606 5

VIRTU FERRIES LTD www.virtuferries.
Sea Passenger Terminal, Pinto Road, Valletta, FRN 1910, Malta: ✆ +356 2206 9022, fax +356 21 235 435.

WASALINE www.wasaline.
Vaasanlaivat, Laivanvarustajankatu 3, FIN - 65170 Vaasa.
Reservations: ✆ +358 (0)207 716 810.

TIME COMPARISON

COMPARAISON DES HEURES   COMPARAZIONE DELLE ORE   ZEITVERGLEICH   COMPARACIÓN DE LAS HORAS

West European Time	*WINTER: GMT* *SUMMER: GMT +1*	Algeria, Morocco, Canaries, Tunisia, Faeroe Islands	East European Time	*WINTER: GMT +2* *SUMMER: GMT +3*	Cyprus
Central European Time	*WINTER: GMT +1* *SUMMER: GMT +2*	Israel			

Daylight Saving Time ('Summer Time') applies between 0100 GMT on March 27 and 0100 GMT on October 30, 2016 *(GMT = Greenwich Mean Time = U*

Time comparison for countries with their own section in the ERT is shown on page 2

BELFAST - CAIRNRYAN 2002

na Line by ship **2016 service**

ngs from Stranraer and Belfast. **(No service Dec. 25)**

lfast		Cairnryan		Cairnryan		Belfast	
30§	→	0550	②③④⑤⑥	0400§	→	0620	②③④⑤⑥
730	→	0950		0500	→	0720	⑦
130	→	1350		0730	→	0950	①②③④⑤⑥
530	→	1750		1130	→	1350	
930	→	2150		1530	→	1750	
00§	→	0120	⑥⑦	1930	→	2150	
30§	→	0150	①②③④⑤	2300§	→	0120	⑥⑦
				2330§	→	0150	①②③④⑤

§ – No foot passengers conveyed.

Subject to alteration during Easter and Xmas/New Year periods

CAIRNRYAN - LARNE 2005

O Irish Sea by ship Journey 2 hours **2016 service**

Until July 2 and August 22 - December 23

art Cairnryan and Larne: 0400①②③④⑤⑥, 0730, 1030①②③④⑤⑥, 1300⑦, 1330①②③④⑤⑥, 1630, 2000, 2300⑦, 2359①②③④⑤.

July 3 - August 21

art Cairnryan and Larne: 0400①②③④⑤⑥, 0730, 1030, 1330, 1630, 2000, 2300⑦, 2359①②③④⑤.

Subject to alteration during Easter and Xmas/New Year periods, and ship's maintenance (Apr. 30 - May 1, May 28, 29).

CHERBOURG - ROSSLARE 2010

n Ferries **2016 service**

rbourg		Rosslare	
800	→	1130	May 9, 11, 17, 23, 25, 31, June 6, 8, 14, 20, 22, 28, July 4, 6, 10, 12, 18, 20, 24, 26, 30, Aug. 1, 3, 7, 9, 11, 15, 17, 21, 23, 25, 29, 31, Sept. 4, 6, 12, 14, 18, 20.
000	→	1400	② Mar. 1 - May 3, Sept. 27 - Dec. 13.
130	→	1430	⑥ Feb. 27 - May 5, Sept. 24 - Dec. 10.
130	→	1530	④ Feb. 25 - Apr. 28, Sept. 22 - Dec. 15.
are		**Cherbourg**	
530	→	1100	May 8, 10, 16, 22, 24, 30, June 5, 7, 13, 19, 21, 27, July 3, 5, 9, 11, 17, 19, 23, 25, 29, 31, Aug. 2, 6, 8, 10, 14, 16, 20, 22, 24, 28, 30, Sept. 3, 5, 11, 13, 17, 19.
800	→	1400	⑦ Feb. 28 - May 1, Sept. 25 - Dec. 11.
130	→	1630	⑤ Feb. 26 - Apr. 29, Sept. 23 - Dec. 9.
130	→	1700	③ Feb. 24 - May 4, Sept. 21 - Dec. 14.

na Line by ship **2016 service**

rbourg		Rosslare	Rosslare		Cherbourg
45⑦	→	0815①	1630⑥	→	1030⑦
30⑤	→	1230⑥	2030④	→	1630⑤
30③	→	1530④	2130②	→	1615③

Subject to alteration during Easter and Xmas/New Year periods

CORK - ROSCOFF 2015

ttany Ferries **2016 service**

ngs from Cork (Ringaskiddy) and Roscoff. **(No winter service)**

ork		Roscoff	
00⑥	→	0700⑦	Apr. 2 - Nov. 5.
oscoff		**Cork**	
30⑤	→	0930⑥	Apr. 1 - May 6; May 20, June 3, 17, July 1, 15, 29, Aug. 12, 26, Sept. 9; Sept. 23 - Nov. 4.
30⑤	→	1000⑥	May 13, 27, June 10, 24, July 8, 22, Aug. 5, 19, Sept. 2, 16.

Times may vary owing to tidal conditions.

DOUGLAS - BELFAST 2020

Of Man Steam Packet Co. by SeaCat **Service to September 30, 2016**

ings from Belfast Albert Quay. **(No winter service)**

uglas		Belfast		Belfast		Douglas	
700	→	0945	See note **A**.	0100	→	0545	See note **D**.
500	→	1745	Mar. 25.	0200	→	0630	June 14.
930	→	0015	See note **C**.	0300	→	0545	June 12.
000	→	0030	June 13.	1045	→	1330	See note **B**.
345	→	0230	June 11.	1115	→	1400	Aug. 24.
				1145	→	1430	Aug. 28.
				1845	→	2130	Mar. 25.

– Mar. 30, Apr. 3, 10, 20, 27, May 4, 8, 11, 22, 25, June 19, 22, 26, 29, July 3, 6, 10, 13, 15, 17, 20, 24, 27, 31, Aug. 3, 10, 17, 24, 28, 30, Sept. 4, 7, 14.

– Mar. 30, Apr. 3, 10, 20, 27, May 4, 8, 11, 22, 25, June 19, 22, 26, 29, July 3, 6, 10, 13, 15, 17, 20, 24, 27, 31, Aug. 3, 10, 17, 30, Sept. 4, 7, 14.

– May 14, Aug. 6, 13, 20, Sept. 10, 17, 24.

– May 15, Aug. 7, 14, 21, Sept. 11, 18, 25.

A special service operates during the TT Race period (May 28 - June 10)

DOUGLAS - DUBLIN 2025

Of Man Steam Packet Co. by SeaCat **2016 service**

ings from Dublin North Wall. **(No regular winter service)**

uglas		Dublin		Dublin		Douglas	
700	→	0955	See note **E**.	0100	→	0545	July 17, 24.
745	→	1040	June 7.	1045	→	1340	See note **F**.
930	→	0015	July 9, 16, 23.	1130	→	1425	May 29.
				1145	→	1440	June 7.

– Mar. 23, 27, May 29, June 15, 21, 28, July 4, 12, 19, 26, Aug. 2, 9, 16, 21, 31.

– Mar. 23, 27, June 15, 21, 28, July 4, 12, 19, 26, Aug. 2, 9, 16, 21, 31.

A special service operates during the TT Race period (May 28 - June 10)

DUBLIN - CHERBOURG 2027

Irish Ferries **2016 service**

Conveys passengers with vehicles only

Dublin		Cherbourg	
1530⑥	→	1330⑦	Jan. 2 - Nov. 5 (not Apr. 9, 16).
Cherbourg		**Dublin**	
1600⑦	→	1000①	July 10, 24, Aug. 7, 21, Sept. 4, 18.
1700⑦	→	1130①	Jan. 3 - Nov. 6 (not Apr. 10, 17, July 10, 24, Aug. 7, 21, Sept. 4, 18).

FISHGUARD - ROSSLARE 2030

Stena Line by ship **2016 service**

(No service Dec. 25, 26)

Fishguard		Rosslare	Rosslare		Fishguard
0230	→	0600	0900	→	1230
1430	→	1800	2115	→	0030

HEYSHAM - DOUGLAS 2035

Isle Of Man Steam Packet Co. **Service to September 30, 2016**

Sailings from Heysham Port and Douglas. **(No service Dec. 25)**

Heysham		Douglas	
0130	→	0500	Apr. 12, May 4.
0145	→	0545	July 1.
0215	→	0545	Daily Feb. 1 - Apr. 11, May 5 - July 9; ①②③④⑤⑥ July 11 - Oct. 31 (also Aug. 28, Sept. 4; not Feb. 28, Mar. 27, May 15, 22, June 14, 26, 30, July 1, Aug. 26).
0315	→	0645	June 30, Aug. 26.
1115	→	1315	June 14.
1200	→	1400	Apr. 12 - 19, 21 - 26, 28 - 30, May 1 - 3.
1330	→	1700	May 4.
1345	→	1715	Sept. 23.
1415	→	1745	①②③④⑤ Feb. 1 - Mar. 11; daily Mar. 14 - Apr. 11, May 5 - Sept. 30 (not June 30, Aug. 25, Sept. 23).
1500	→	1830	Aug. 25.
1530	→	1900	June 30.
Douglas		**Heysham**	
0730	→	0930	June 11, 12, 14.
0800	→	1000	Apr. 12 - 19, 21 - 26, 28 - 30, May 1 - 3.
0800	→	1130	May 4, 25 - 27, Sept. 23.
0815	→	1145	Aug. 26.
0845	→	1215	①②③④⑤ Feb. 1 - Mar. 11; daily Mar. 14 - Apr. 11, May 5 - Sept. 30 (not June 28, July 27, Aug. 26, Sept. 23).
0915	→	1300	July 27.
0930	→	1300	June 28.
1700	→	2130	June 13.
1900	→	2230	Sept. 23.
1945	→	2315	①②③④⑤⑦ Feb. 1 - Apr. 11, May 4 - Sept. 30 (not June 13, 27, 30, July 26, Aug. 24, 25, Sept. 22, 23).
2000	→	2330	Feb. 6, 13, 20, Mar. 5, 12, 19, Apr. 2, 9, May 7, 28, 31, June 4, 10, 11, 18, July 2, Aug. 27, Sept. 3.
2030	→	2359	June 12, Aug. 24, Sept. 22.
2045	→	0015	June 30.
2100	→	0030	July 26.
2130	→	0100	Aug. 25.

A special service operates during the TT Race period (May 28 - June 10)

HOLYHEAD - DUBLIN 2040

Irish Ferries by ship **2016 service**

Sailings from Holyhead and Dublin Ferryport. **(No service Dec. 25, 26)**

Holyhead		Dublin		Dublin		Holyhead	
0240	→	0555	Not Dec. 27.	0155§	→	0525	②③④⑤⑥
0800§	→	1130	②③④⑤⑥	0805	→	1130	
1410	→	1725		1415§	→	1745	②③④⑤
2000§	→	2315	②③④⑤	2055	→	0020	Not Dec. 24.

§ – No foot passengers conveyed.

Sailing times may vary owing to tidal conditions.

Dublin Ferryport - Dublin Busaras (Central Bus Station).

Irish Ferries by fast ferry Journey 2 hours **2016 service**

Sailings from Holyhead and Dublin Ferryport. **(No service Dec. 25, 26)**

Depart Holyhead: 1150, 1715 (not Dec. 24).

Depart Dublin: 0845, 1430 (not Dec. 24).

Dublin Ferryport - Dublin Busaras (Central Bus Station).

Stena Line by ship **2016 service**

Sailings from Holyhead and Dublin Ferryport. **(No service Dec. 25, 26)**

Holyhead		Dublin	Dublin		Holyhead
0230	→	0545	0215	→	0530
0855	→	1210	0820	→	1150
1350	→	1705	1510	→	1825
2030	→	2345	2040	→	2355

Subject to alteration during Easter and Xmas/New Year periods

BIRKENHEAD (LIVERPOOL) - BELFAST 2050

Stena Line **2016 service**

(No service Dec. 24 - 26, 31)

Sailings from Birkenhead Twelve Quays Terminal and Belfast Victoria Terminal.

Birkenhead		Belfast		Belfast		Birkenhead	
1030	→	1830	②③④⑤⑥⑦	1030	→	1830	②③④⑤⑥⑦
2200	→	0600	①⑦	2200	→	0600	①⑦
2230	→	0630	②③④⑤⑥	2230	→	0630	②③④⑤⑥

2052 LIVERPOOL - DUBLIN

P & O Irish Sea **Service to January 2, 2017**

Conveys passengers with vehicles only

Liverpool		Dublin		Dublin		Liverpool	
0300	→	1030	①②③④⑤⑥	0900	→	1700	②③④⑤⑥
0930	→	1730	②③④⑤⑥	1500	→	2330	①②③④⑤
2100	→	0500		1600	→	2359	⑦
				2130	→	0530	

Subject to alteration during holiday periods

2053 LIVERPOOL - DOUGLAS

Isle Of Man Steam Packet Co. **Service to September 30, 2016**
(No winter service)

Sailings from Liverpool Landing Stage and Douglas.

Liverpool		Douglas	
1115	→	1400	Mar. 18, 19, 21, 24, 26, 28, 29, 31, Apr. 1, 2, 4 - 9, 11, May 5 - 7, 9, 12 - 14, 16, 19 - 21, 23, 24, 26 - 28; ①④⑤⑥ June 13 - Sept. 17 (also July 5, Aug. 7, 14, Sept. 6, 19; not July 4, 15, Sept. 8, 15).
1845	→	2130	June 12.
1915	→	2200	Mar. 17 - Sept. 30 (not Mar. 25, Apr. 9, Sept. 4).
1945	→	2230	Apr. 9.
2000	→	2245	June 13 - 15.
2030	→	2315	Sept. 4.
Douglas		**Liverpool**	
0730	→	1015	Mar. 18, 19, 21, 24, 26, 28, 29, 31, Apr. 1, 2, 4 - 9, 11, May 5 - 7, 9, 12 - 14, 16, 19 - 21, 23, 24, 26 - 28; ①④⑤⑥ June 13 - Sept. 17 (also Aug. 7, 14, Sept. 6; not June 30, July 15, Sept. 8, 15, 19).
1000	→	1245	Sept. 24.
1500	→	1745	Mar. 17 - Sept. 30 (not Mar. 25, Sept. 4).
1600	→	1845	June 13 - 15.
1630	→	1915	Sept. 4.
2345	→	0230	June 12.

Sailing times may vary.

Subject to alteration May 28 - June 11, Aug. 21 - Sept. 3

2055 PEMBROKE - ROSSLARE

Irish Ferries **2016 ser**
(No service Dec. 25

Pembroke		Rosslare	Rosslare		Pembroke
0245	→	0645	0845	→	1245
1445	→	1845	2045	→	0045

Sailing times may vary owing to tidal conditions

2065 ROSSLARE - ROSCOFF

Irish Ferries **2016 ser**
(No winter serv

Rosslare		Roscoff		Roscoff		Rosslare	
1600	→	1030	See note **R**.	1830	→	1100	See note **S**.
1730	→	1100	May 6 only.				

R – May 12, 14, 18, 20, 26, 28, June 1, 3, 9, 11, 15, 17, 23, 25, 29, July 1, 7, 13, 15, 21, 2 Aug. 4, 12, 18, 26, Sept. 1, 7, 9, 15.

S – May 7, 13, 15, 19, 21, 27, 29, June 2, 4, 10, 12, 16, 18, 24, 26, 30, July 2, 8, 14, 16, 22, 28, Aug. 5, 13, 19, 27, Sept. 2, 8, 10, 16.

ENGLISH CHANNEL & BAY OF BISCAY

2100 CHANNEL ISLAND SERVICES

POOLE - GUERNSEY / JERSEY by fast ferry

Condor Ferries **2016 service**

Sailings from Poole, St Peter Port and St Helier Elizabeth Terminal.

Jan. 1 - Mar. 23: irregular sailings; Mar. 24 - June 30: daily sailings; July 1 - Oct. 12: 1 – 2 sailings per day; Oct. 14 - Dec. 23: 1 – 3 sailings per week.

Departure times vary owing to tidal conditions.

POOLE - GUERNSEY / JERSEY - ST MALO by fast ferry

Condor Ferries **2016 service**

Sailings by catamaran from Poole, St Peter Port, St Helier Elizabeth Terminal or Albert Quay and St Malo Gare Maritime de la Bourse.

Jan.: occasional sailings; Feb. - Mar.: 1 – 3 sailings per week (no service Feb. 1 - 11, Mar. 1 - 10); Apr. - Oct.: 5 – 7 sailings per week; Nov. - Dec.: 1 – 3 sailings per week. Journey 4½ – 5½ hours.

A change of vessel may be necessary in either Guernsey or Jersey (extended journey time).

Departure times vary owing to tidal conditions.

PORTSMOUTH - GUERNSEY by ship

Condor Ferries **Service to September 18, 2016**

Sailings from Portsmouth Continental Ferry Port and St Peter Port.

Portsmouth		St Peter Port	
0900	→	A	①②③④⑤⑥ until Mar. 31; daily Apr. 1 - May 22; ①②③④⑤⑥ May 23 - Sept. 17 (also Mar. 27, Sept. 18; not May 7).
St Peter Port		**Portsmouth**	
D	→	0630	①②③④⑤⑥ until Mar. 31; daily Apr. 1 - May 22; ①②③④⑤⑥ May 23 - Sept. 17 (also Mar. 27, Sept. 18; not May 7).

A – Most arrivals 1600, but variations possible between 1555 and 2300.
D – Most departures 1720, but variations possible between 1720 and 2359.

Times may vary owing to tidal conditions.

PORTSMOUTH - JERSEY by ship

Condor Ferries **Service to September 18, 2016**

Sailings from Portsmouth Continental Ferry Port and St Helier.

Portsmouth		St Helier	
0900	→	B	①②③④⑤⑥ until Mar. 31; daily Apr. 1 - May 22; ①②③④⑤⑥ May 23 - Sept. 17 (also Mar. 27, Sept. 18; not May 7).
St Helier		**Portsmouth**	
C	→	0630	①②③④⑤⑥ until Mar. 31; daily Apr. 1 - May 22; ①②③④⑤⑥ May 23 - Sept. 17 (also Mar. 27, Sept. 18; not May 7).

B – Most arrivals 1920, but variations possible between 1705 and 2050.
C – Most departures 2120, but variations possible between 1835 and 2220.

Times may vary owing to tidal conditions.

OTHER SERVICES:

Manche îles Express operate catamaran services in summer from Jersey to Carteret, Granville, Sark and Guernsey, and from Guernsey to Alderney and Diélette.

2110 DOVER - CALAIS

DFDS Seaways by ship **2016 serv**

Sailings from Dover Eastern Docks and Calais Maritime. Journey 90 minutes
Conveys passengers with vehicles only.

Depart Dover: 0045, 0240①②③④⑤⑥, 0410①②③④⑤⑥, 0550①②③④⑤⑥, 074
0910①②③④⑤⑥, 1040①②③④⑤⑥, 1215, 1345, 1515, 1650, 1820, 195
2135①②③④⑤⑦, 2305①②③④⑤⑦.

Depart Calais: 0105①②③④⑤⑥, 0230①②③④⑤⑥, 0415①②③④⑤⑥, 0610, 074
0920①②③④⑤⑥, 1055, 1225, 1355, 1530, 1700, 1830, 2010①②③④⑤
2140①②③④⑤⑦, 2315.

P & O Ferries Journey 90 minutes **Service to September 30, 20**

Sailings from Dover Eastern Docks and Calais Maritime. **(No service Dec.**

On night services, conveys passengers with vehicles only (foot passengers may travel 0825 - 19 from Dover, 0645 - 2145 from Calais). Timings subject to variation.

February 1 - 21 and March 13 - September 30

Depart Dover: 0050, 0220①②③④⑤⑥, 0320, 0420①②③④⑤⑥, 0640, 0735, 082
0925, 1015, 1110, 1205, 1255, 1355, 1445, 1540, 1640, 1725, 1835, 1915, 201
2120①②③④⑤⑦, 2205, 2315.

Depart Calais: 0030①②③④⑤⑥, 0120, 0240①②③④⑤⑥, 0435, 0545①②③④⑤
0630⑦, 0645①②③④⑤⑥, 0745, 0840, 0950, 1045, 1135, 1235, 1325, 1420, 152
1605, 1715, 1755, 1850, 1955, 2035, 2145, 2335.

February 22 - March 12

Depart Dover: 0045, 0225①②③④⑤⑥, 0340, 0450①②③④⑤⑥, 0630, 0740, 084
0955, 1100, 1210, 1315, 1425, 1530, 1645, 1745, 1905, 2005, 2125①②③④⑤⑦, 222
2345.

Depart Calais: 0035, 0140, 0310①②③④⑤⑥, 0425, 0550, 0705, 0815, 0940, 1050, 115
1305, 1410, 1525, 1625, 1745, 1840, 2000, 2055, 2215, 2315.

connections:
Calais Port - Calais Ville station 1100 – 1745; Calais Ville station - Calais Port 1030 – 18

2111 DOVER - DUNKERQUE

DFDS Seaways by ship **2016 serv**

Sailings from Dover Eastern Docks and Dunkerque. Journey 2 hours
Conveys passengers with vehicles only

Depart Dover: 0200②③④⑤⑥, 0400①②③④⑤, 0600①②③④⑤⑥, 080
1000①②③④⑤⑥, 1200, 1400, 1600, 1800, 2000①②③④⑤⑦, 220
2359①②③④⑤⑦.

Depart Dunkerque: 0200①②③④⑤, 0400①②③④⑤⑥, 0600, 0800①②③④⑤⑥, 100
1200, 1400, 1600, 1800①②③④⑤⑦, 2000①②③④⑤⑦, 2200①②③④⑤⑦
2359①②③④⑤.

 For international shipping maps – see pages 538 - 540

NEWHAVEN - DIEPPE 2125

DS Seaways — 2016 service
ailings from Newhaven and Dieppe. — (No service Dec. 25)

whaven		Dieppe
000	→	1500
2300	→	0400

Dieppe		Newhaven
0530	→	0830
1800	→	2100

Newhaven ferry terminal is adjacent to Newhaven Town rail station.
For rail services see Table **101**.

Departure times may vary owing to tidal conditions.

PENZANCE - ST. MARY'S 2130

es Of Scilly Steamship Co. — 2016 service
ilings from Penzance Lighthouse Pier (South Pier) and St Mary's. — (No winter service)

m Penzance and St Mary's: sailings on: ①③⑤⑥ Mar. 14 - 19; ①②③④⑤⑥ Mar. 21 - June 25; daily June 27 - Sept. 17; ①②③④⑤⑥ Sept. 19 - Oct. 8; ①③⑤⑥ Oct. 10 - Nov. 5 (also Nov. 6).

Departure times vary owing to tidal conditions
(most sailings Penzance depart 0915, St Mary's depart 1630).

PLYMOUTH - ROSCOFF 2135

ittany Ferries — Departure times vary — Service to October 31, 2016
ailings from Plymouth Millbay and Roscoff.

rom Plymouth: ⑤ Nov. 6 - Dec. 11; daily Dec. 18 - 23, 26 - 30, Jan. 2, 3; ②③④ Mar. 15 - 4; daily Mar. 26 - Oct. 31.

rom Roscoff: ⑤⑥ Nov. 6 - Dec. 12; daily Dec. 19 - 23, 26 - 30, Jan. 2, 3; ③④ Mar. 16 - 24; aily Mar. 25 - Oct. 31.

PLYMOUTH - SANTANDER 2140

ittany Ferries — Service to October 31, 2016
ilings from Plymouth Millbay and Santander. — (No regular winter service)

ymouth		Santander	
1330	→	1000	Jan. 3 only.
1545	→	1215	⑦ Mar. 27 - Oct. 30 (not Aug. 14, 28).
1615	→	1215	Aug. 14, 28.
2030	→	1730	Nov. 6, Mar. 4, Oct. 7.
ntander		**Plymouth**	
1515	→	1030	Nov. 2 only.
1530	→	0930	Mar. 3 only.
2115	→	1615	③ Nov. 11 - Dec. 16, Mar. 30 - Oct. 26.

PLYMOUTH - ST MALO 2142

ittany Ferries — Service to March 31, 2016 — (No summer service)

ilings from Plymouth Millbay and St Malo Terminal Ferry du Naye.

ymouth		St Malo	
2045	→	0815	Nov. 12, 26, Dec. 10, 17.
2045	→	0855	Dec. 3 only.
2045	→	0925	Nov. 19 only.
2200	→	0815	Mar. 8 only.
2300	→	0745	Nov. 7 only.
2300	→	0815	⑥ Nov. 14 - Dec. 12 (also Mar. 17, 24).
St Malo		**Plymouth**	
1050	→	1830	Mar. 8 only.
1110	→	1910	Mar. 22 only.
1230	→	2010	Mar. 15 only.
2030	→	0630	④ Nov. 5 - Dec. 10.

POOLE - CHERBOURG 2145

ittany Ferries — Service to October 31, 2016 — (No service Dec. 25, Jan. 1)

Poole		Cherbourg	
0830	→	1345	See note **R**.

Cherbourg		Poole	
1830	→	2145	See note **P**.
1915	→	2230	July 3 only.
2215	→	0700	See note **Q**.

P – ④⑤⑥⑦ Nov. 1 - Dec. 20; ①④⑤⑥⑦ Jan. 2 - July 4; daily July 7 - Sept. 12; ①④⑤⑥⑦ Sept. 15 - Oct. 31 (also Nov. 2, Dec. 21, 28 - 30, Mar. 29, 30, May 24, 25, 31, June 1; not Dec. 24, July 3).
Q – ①②③ Nov. 3 - Dec. 16; ②③ Jan. 5 - July 6; ②③ Sept. 13 - Oct. 26 (also Dec. 22; not Mar. 29, 30, May 24, 25, 31, June 1).
R – Not Dec. 24, 26, Jan. 2.

🚌 Cherbourg Port - Cherbourg station (operated by Zéphir).

PORTSMOUTH - BILBAO 2155

Brittany Ferries — Service to October 31, 2016
Conveys passengers with vehicles only

Portsmouth		Bilbao	
0830	→	1645§	Dec. 22 only.
0845	→	1415§	② Nov. 3 - Dec. 29; ⑥ Jan. 9 - Mar. 26; ② Mar. 29 - Oct. 25 (not Dec. 22).
1145③	→	1245④	Nov. 4 - Dec. 16, Mar. 30 - Apr. 20, May 18 - Oct. 26.
2230⑦	→	0745②	Nov. 1 - Dec. 13, Jan. 3 - Apr. 24, May 15 - Oct. 30.
Bilbao		**Portsmouth**	
1030②	→	0900③	Nov. 3 - Dec. 15, Jan. 5 - Apr. 26, May 17 - Oct. 25.
1500	→	2130§	Dec. 27, Jan. 2.
1530④	→	1415⑤	Nov. 12 - Dec. 17, Mar. 31 - Apr. 21, May 19 - Oct. 27 (not Oct. 6).
1715	→	2045§	③ Nov. 4 - Dec. 16; ⑦ Jan. 10 - Mar. 27; ③ Mar. 30 - Oct. 26.

§ – One day later.

PORTSMOUTH - CHERBOURG 2160

Brittany Ferries by fast ferry — 2016 service
Sailings from Portsmouth Continental Ferry Port and Cherbourg. **(No regular winter service)**

Portsmouth		Cherbourg	
0715	→	1115	July 3 only.
0730	→	1130	⑤⑥⑦ May 27 - Sept. 4 (not July 3).
0815	→	1500	Jan. 11, Feb. 4, Apr. 25, May 17.
0900	→	1300	Daily Apr. 27 - May 26; ①②③④ May 30 - Sept. 6.
1200	→	1730	Jan. 4 only.
1515	→	1915	⑤⑥⑦ May 27 - Sept. 4 (not July 3).
Cherbourg		**Portsmouth**	
1230	→	1430	⑤⑥⑦ May 27 - Sept. 4 (not July 3).
1630	→	2100	Jan. 11.
1630	→	2115	Feb. 4, Apr. 25, May 17.
1700	→	1900	Daily Apr. 27 - May 26; ①②③④ May 30 - Sept. 5.
2015	→	2215	⑤⑥⑦ May 27 - Sept. 4 (not July 3).
2045	→	2245	July 3 only.

🚌 Cherbourg Port - Cherbourg station (operated by Zéphir).

PORTSMOUTH - LE HAVRE 2165

Brittany Ferries by ship — Service to October 31, 2016
Sailings from Portsmouth Continental Ferry Port and Le Havre Terminal de la Citadelle.

Portsmouth		Le Havre	
0930	→	1600	⑤ Nov. 6 - Mar. 18 (not Dec. 25, Jan. 1).
2145	→	0800	⑤ July 22 - Aug. 26.
2315	→	0800	Nov. 1, 8.
2315	→	0830	Daily Nov. 2 - July 21; ①②③④⑥⑦ July 23 - Aug. 25; daily Aug. 27 - Oct. 31 (not Nov. 8, Dec. 24, 25, 31, Jan. 1, Apr. 29, 30, May 6, 7).
Le Havre		**Portsmouth**	
1200	→	1645	⑤ Nov. 6 - Mar. 18 (not Dec. 25, Jan. 1).
1715	→	2145	①②③④⑥⑦ Nov. 1 - Mar. 17; ①②③⑥⑦ Mar. 19 - Oct. 31 (not Nov. 2, Dec. 24, 31, Apr. 30, May 1, 7, 8).
2200	→	0600	⑤ Nov. 6 - Oct. 28.
2200	→	0715	④ Mar. 24 - Oct. 27.
2230	→	0545	Nov. 2 only.

A shuttle 🚌 service operates between the terminal and railway station

PORTSMOUTH - OUISTREHAM (CAEN) 2170

Brittany Ferries by ship — Service to October 31, 2016 — (No service Dec. 25, Jan. 1)

Sailings from Portsmouth Continental Ferry Port and Ouistreham.

Portsmouth		Ouistreham	
0815	→	1500	Daily Nov. 1 - 9, Nov. 11 - Dec. 17, Dec. 19 - 24, 27 - 31, Jan. 3 - 10, Jan. 12 - Feb. 3, Feb. 5 - Apr. 24, Apr. 26 - May 16, May 18 - Oct. 31.
1445	→	2130	①②③④⑥⑦ Nov. 1 - Mar. 8; ①②④⑤⑥⑦ Mar. 10 - Oct. 31 (not Dec. 24, 31, Jan. 11, Feb. 4, Apr. 25, May 17).
2200	→	0645	⑤ Nov. 6 - Mar. 4; ③ Mar. 9 - Oct. 26.
2245	→	0645	①②③⑥⑦ Nov. 1 - Mar. 2; ①④⑤⑥⑦ Mar. 5 - Oct. 31.
2245	→	0730	④ Nov. 5 - Mar. 3; ② Mar. 8 - Oct. 25 (not Dec. 24, 31).
Ouistreham		**Portsmouth**	
0830	→	1315	①②③④⑥⑦ Nov. 1 - Mar. 3; ①②④⑤⑥⑦ Mar. 5 - Oct. 31 (not Dec. 24, 31, Jan. 11, Feb. 4, Apr. 25, May 17).
1400	→	1915	⑤ Nov. 6 - Dec. 11, Jan. 8 - Mar. 4; ③ Mar. 9 - Oct. 26.
1630	→	2115	①②③④⑥⑦ Nov. 1 - Mar. 3; ①②④⑤⑥⑦ Mar. 5 - Oct. 31 (not Nov. 10, Dec. 24, 31, Jan. 11, Feb. 4, Apr. 25, May 17).
2300	→	0645	Daily (not Dec. 24, 31).

🚌 Ouistreham - Caen station (journey 45 minutes) to connect with most sailings.

2175 PORTSMOUTH - SANTANDER

Brittany Ferries Journey time approx. 24 hours **Service to October 31, 2016**

Sailings from Portsmouth Continental Ferry Port and Santander.

Portsmouth		Santander	
0845	→	1345	⑥ Nov. 7 - Dec. 19; ② Jan. 5 - Mar. 15.
0845	→	1415	⑥ Apr. 2 - Oct. 29 (also Mar. 22).
1000	→	1300	Apr. 29, May 6.
1115	→	1215	⑦ Nov. 8 - Dec. 13.
1145	→	1245	③ Jan. 6 - Mar. 23 (also Apr. 27).
1700	→	1730	⑤ Nov. 13 - Oct. 28 (not Dec. 25, Jan. 1, Mar. 4, Apr. 29, May 6, Oct. 7).
1715	→	1815	② Nov. 10 - Dec. 15, Mar. 29 - Oct. 25.
2230	→	0745	Dec. 20, 27.
Santander		**Portsmouth**	
1415	→	1515	Nov. 1 only.
1515	→	1415	① Nov. 9 - Dec. 14, Mar. 28 - Oct. 31.
1530	→	1415	④ Jan. 7 - Mar. 24 (also May 12; not Mar. 3).
1600	→	1700	Apr. 30, May 7.
1715	→	2045	⑦ Apr. 3 - Oct. 30 (also Mar. 23).
1730	→	1700	Nov. 4 only.
1745	→	2045	⑦ Nov. 8 - Dec. 20; ③ Jan. 6 - Mar. 16.
2030	→	1945	⑥ Nov. 7 - Oct. 29 (not Dec. 26, Jan. 2, Apr. 30, May 7).

2180 PORTSMOUTH - ST MALO

Brittany Ferries **Service to October 31, 2**

Sailings from Portsmouth Continental Ferry Port and St. Malo Terminal Ferry du Naye.

From Portsmouth: ①③⑤⑦ Nov. 1 - Dec. 21, Jan. 1 - Mar. 21; ①③④⑤⑥⑦ Mar. 25 - July 4; daily July 6 - Sept. 5; ①③④⑤⑥⑦ Sept. 7 - Oct. 31 (also Nov. 5, Dec. 22, 2 Jan. 2; not Jan. 3, 4, Mar. 16, July 3).

From St. Malo: ①②⑤⑥⑦ Nov. 1 - Dec. 19; ①②④⑥ Jan. 2 - Mar. 5; ①②④⑤⑥⑦ Mar. 25 - July 5; daily July 7 - Sept. 6; ①②④⑤⑥⑦ Sept. 8 - Oct. 31 (also Dec. 21 - 23, 28, Jan. 3, 6, Mar. 7, 9, 10, 12, 14, 18, 19, 21; not Jan. 5, July 4).

Departure times vary: most sailings Portsmouth d. 2015 (St. Malo a. 0815); St. Malo d. 1 (Portsmouth a. 1820).

NORTH SEA

2200 ABERDEEN - KIRKWALL - LERWICK

NorthLink Ferries **2016 service**

Aberdeen		Kirkwall		Kirkwall		Lerwick
		January 2 - March 31 and November 1 - December 30				
1700④⑥⑦	→	2300④⑥⑦	→	2345④⑥⑦	→	0730⑤⑦①
1900①②③⑤	→	→	→	→	→	0730②③④⑥
		April 1 - October 31				
1700②④⑥⑦	→	2300②④⑥⑦	→	2345②④⑥⑦	→	0730③⑤⑦①
1900①③⑤	→	→	→	→	→	0730②④⑥

Lerwick		Kirkwall		Kirkwall		Aberdeen
		January 2 - March 31 and November 1 - December 30				
1730③⑤	→	2300③⑤	→	2345③⑤	→	0700④⑥
1900①②④⑥⑦	→	→	→	→	→	0700②③⑤⑦①
		April 1 - October 31				
1730①③⑤	→	2300①③⑤	→	2345①③⑤	→	0700②④⑥
1900②④⑥⑦	→	→	→	→	→	0700③⑤⑦①

Subject to alteration during ship maintenance

A 🚐 transfer service is available Kirkwall - Stromness and v.v. in conjunction with evening sailings.

2235 HARWICH - HOEK VAN HOLLAND

Stena Line by ship **2016 service**
(No service Dec. 25, 26)

Sailings from Harwich International Port and Hoek van Holland.

Harwich		Hoek		Hoek		Harwich	
0900	→	1715	①②③④⑤⑥	1345	→	1945	⑥⑦
1000	→	1800	⑦	1415	→	1945	①②③④⑤
2300	→	0800		2200	→	0630	

See Table **15a** for connecting rail services London - Harwich and v.v. and Hoek van Holland - Amsterdam and v.v.

2237 HIRTSHALS - STAVANGER - BERGEN

Fjord Line **2016 service**
(No service Dec. 24)

Hirtshals		Stavanger		Bergen		Stavanger		Hirtshals
				Until May 31				
2000	→	0630	→	1230/1330	→	2000	→	0800
				June 1 - August 31				
2000	→	0630	→	1230/1330	→	2000	→	0730

Variations: no sailings from Hirtshals Jan. 11, 13, Apr. 5, 7; from Bergen Jan. 12, 14, Apr. 6, 8. Operates Hirtshals - Stavanger only Jan. 26, Apr. 26; Stavanger - Hirtshals only Jan. 27, Apr. 27.

Subject to alteration during Xmas/New Year period

2239 LOFOTEN ISLANDS (map page 341)

Torghatten Nord by fast ferry **Service to January 31, 2017**
BODØ - SVOLVÆR (subject to alteration)

Bodø		Svolvær		Svolvær		Bodø	
1715	→	2050	①②③④⑥	0630	→	1000	①②③④⑤⑥
1800	→	2135	⑤	1600	→	1930	⑦
2030	→	2330	⑦				

Torghatten Nord by ship **Service to January 31, 2017**
BODØ - MOSKENES

Bodø		Moskenes		Moskenes		Bodø	
				February 1 June 9 and August 29 - January 31			
0015	→	0330	②④⑤	0700	→	1015	①②③④⑤⑥
0215	→	0630	③	1200	→	1900	⑦
1300	→	1630	⑦	1700	→	2359	⑦
1530	→	1845	③	1900	→	2345	③
1630	→	1945	①②④⑤⑥	2030	→	2345	①②④
2100	→	0015	⑦				
				June 10 - August 28			
0045	→	0415		0600	→	0915	
0430	→	0800	①②③④⑤⑥	1030	→	1430	
0600	→	1000		1400	→	1715	
1015	→	1330		1930	→	2330	
1500	→	1900		2115	→	0030	
1745	→	2100		2359	→	0330	①②③④⑤⑦

2240 NORWEGIAN COASTAL SERVICES (map page 3

Hurtigruten **2016 serv**
BERGEN - TRONDHEIM - TROMSØ - KIRKENES (subject to alterati

NORTHBOUND	WINTER arrive	WINTER depart	SUMMER arrive	SUMMER depart	day	SOUTHBOUND	ALL YEAR arrive	ALL YEAR depart
Bergen ♣	...	2230	...	2000	A	**Kirkenes**	...	1230
Florø	0430	0445	0200	0215	B	Vadsø	|	|
Måløy	0715	0730	0415	0430	B	Vardø	1545	1645
Torvik	1030	1045	0715	0730	B	Båtsfjord	1945	2015
Ålesund	1200	1500	0800	0845	B	Berlevåg	2200	2215
Geiranger ▲	|	|	1325 g	1330 g	B	Mehamn	0045	0100
Urke ▲	|	|	1130 h	1500 h	B	Kjøllefjord	0245	0300
Ålesund	1200	1500	1815¶	1900	B	**Honningsvåg**	0530	0545
Molde	1800	1830	2145	2215	B	Havøysund	0745	0800
Kristiansund	2215	2300	0145	0200	B/C	**Hammerfest**	1045	1245§
Trondheim	0600	1200	0830	1200	C	Øksfjord	1530§	1545§
Rørvik	2045	2115	2045	2115	C	Skjervøy	1915§	1945§
Brønnøysund	0045	0100	0045	0100	D	**Tromsø**	2345	0130
Sandnessjøen	0345	0415	0345	0415	D	Finnsnes	0415	0445
Nesna	0525	0530	0525	0530	D	**Harstad**	0800	0830
Ørnes	0915	0930	0915	0930	D	Risøyhamn	1045	1100
Bodø	1230	1500	1230	1500	D	Sortland	1230	1300
Stamsund	1900	1930	1900	1930	D	Stokmarknes	1415	1515
Svolvaer	2100	2200	2100	2200	D	**Svolvaer**	1830	2030
Stokmarknes	0100	0115	0100	0115	E	Stamsund	2200	2230
Sortland	0245	0300	0245	0300	E	**Bodø**	0230	0415
Risøyhamn	0415	0430	0415	0430	E	Ørnes	0700	0715
Harstad	0645	0800	0645	0800	E	Nesna	1100	1115
Finnsnes	1115	1145	1115	1145	E	Sandnessjøen	1230	1300
Tromsø	1430	1830	1430	1830	E	Brønnøysund	1545	1700
Skjervøy	2230	2245	2230	2245	E	Rørvik	2030	2130
Øksfjord	0200	0215	0200	0215	F	**Trondheim**	0630	1000
Hammerfest	0515	0600	0515	0600	F	Kristiansund	1630	1700
Havøysund	0845	0915	0845	0915	F	Molde	2100	2130
Honningsvåg	1145	1445	1115	1445	F	Ålesund	0030	0100
Kjøllefjord	1700	1715	1700	1715	F	Urke ▲	|	|
Mehamn	1915	1930	1915	1930	F	Geiranger ▲	|	|
Berlevåg	2145	2200	2145	2200	F	Ålesund	0030	0100
Båtsfjord	2345	0015	2345	0015	F/G	Torvik	0215	0230
Vardø	0315	0330	0315	0330	G	Måløy	0515	0545
Vadsø	0645	0715	0645	0715	G	Florø	0745	0815
Kirkenes	0900	...	0900	...	G	**Bergen ♣**	1430	

A – 1st day .... **G** – 7th day.

g – June 1 - Aug. 31.
h – Sept. 1 - Oct. 31.

♣ – Sailings from Bergen Frilenesset.
▲ – Embarkation and disembarkation take place by tender - passengers are required to b at the quay 30 minutes before departure.
¶ – One hour earlier Sept. 1 - Oct. 31.
§ – One hour earlier Apr. 1 - May 31. Sails into Lyngenfjorden after Skjervøy.

2242 HELGOLAND (Germany) services

2016 servic

From:		Operat
BREMERHAVEN	May 4 - Sept. 25	**Reederei Cassen E**
BÜSUM	Apr. 15 - Oct. 9	**Reederei Cassen E**
CUXHAVEN	Mar. 19 - Oct. 30	**FRS Helgoli**
	All year service	**Reederei Cassen E**
HAMBURG	Mar. 19 - Oct. 30	**FRS Helgoli**

HULL - ROTTERDAM 2245

O Ferries — 2016 service (No service Dec. 24, 25, 30, 31)

ilings from Hull King George Dock and Rotterdam Europoort.

Hull		Rotterdam		Rotterdam		Hull	
030	→	0815	①②③④⑤	2030	→	0800	⑥⑦
030	→	0900	⑥⑦	2100	→	0800	①②③④⑤

Subject to alteration during Xmas/New Year period

connections (reservation recommended):
Hull railway station (depart 1715) - King George Dock and v.v.
Rotterdam Centraal Station (depart 1700) - Europoort and v.v.
Amsterdam Centraal Station (depart 1700) - Europoort and v.v.

HULL - ZEEBRUGGE 2250

O Ferries — 2016 service

ilings from Hull King George Dock and Zeebrugge Leopold II Dam.

Hull		Zeebrugge		Zeebrugge		Hull	
830	→	0845	①②③④⑤	1900	→	0830	①②③④⑤
830	→	0930	⑥⑦	1900	→	0900	⑥⑦

Subject to alteration during Xmas/New Year period

connections (reservation recommended):
Hull railway station (depart 1715) - King George Dock and v.v.
Brugge Station (depart 1730) - Zeebrugge and v.v.

NEWCASTLE - IJMUIDEN (AMSTERDAM) 2255

DS Seaways — 2016 service (No service Dec. 24, 25)

ailings from Newcastle International Ferry Terminal, Royal Quays and IJmuiden Felison erminal.

Newcastle		IJmuiden	IJmuiden		Newcastle
1700	→	0930§	1730	→	0900§

– Arrive 30 minutes later on ⑦.

connections:
Newcastle rail station - International Ferry Terminal (North Shields) and v.v.
art Newcastle station 2½ and 1¼ hours before sailing; depart Ferry Terminal following arrival of ship).
Victoria Hotel Amsterdam (near Centraal station) - IJmuiden and v.v.
epart hotel every 10 minutes 1530-1630; depart Ferry Terminal following arrival of ship).

SCRABSTER - STROMNESS 2280

NorthLink Ferries Journey 1 hour 30 minutes — 2016 service

January 3 - May 25 and September 1 - December 31 ♦

From Scrabster: 0845①②③④⑤, 1200⑥⑦, 1900.
From Stromness: 0630①②③④⑤, 0900⑥⑦, 1645.

May 26 - August 31 ♦

From Scrabster: 0845①②③④⑤⑥, 1200⑦, 1315①②③④⑤⑥, 1900.
From Stromness: 0630①②③④⑤⑥, 0900⑦, 1100①②③④⑤⑥, 1645.

♦ – Also Mar. 26, Apr. 9, Sept. 3, 10, 16, 17, 19, 24, Oct. 15, 29.

Subject to alteration during Xmas/New Year period

ICELAND and the FAEROE ISLANDS 2285

Smyril Line — 2016 service (No service Dec. 19 - 31)

	arrive	depart
January 1 - June 10 and August 27 - December 31 ▲		
Hirtshals	1000⑥	1500⑥
Tórshavn	0500①	1400①w
Seydisfjördur	0900②w	2000③w
Tórshavn	1500④w	2100④
June 11 - August 26 ▲		
Hirtshals	1230⑥	1530⑥
Tórshavn	2230⑦	2330⑦
Hirtshals	0930②	1130②
Tórshavn	1730③	1800③
Seydisfjördur	0830④	1030④
Tórshavn	0300⑤	0330⑤

w – Jan. 4 - Mar. 31 and Oct. 31 - Dec. 15 Tórshavn - Seydisfjördur and v.v.: times may be advanced, delayed or cancelled at short notice owing to adverse weather conditions. Contact operator for more details.

▲ – Variations:
Jan. 1 Tórshavn d. 1400; Jan. 3 (not Jan. 2) Hirtshals a. 0600, d. 1100; Jan. 4 Tórshavn a. 2300; June 11 Hirtshals a. 1000; Aug. 27 Hirtshals a. 1230, d. 1630; Dec. 19-31 no sailings.

In poor weather conditions sailings may dock at Klaksvík or Kollafjördur (for Tórshavn), and Frederikshavn or Hanstholm (for Hirtshals).

SKAGERRAK, KATTEGAT & SOUTH WEST BALTIC

BØJDEN - FYNSHAV 2304

sFærgen Journey 50 minutes — Service to September 30, 2016

June 1 - 30

part Bøjden: 0700①②③④⑤⑥, 0900, 1000, 1100, 1200, 1300, 1400, 1500, 1600, 1700, 1900, 2100①④⑤⑥⑦.
part Fynshav: 0600①②③④⑤⑥, 0800, 1000, 1100, 1200, 1300, 1400, 1500, 1600, 1700, 1800, 2000①④⑤⑥⑦.

July 1 - August 7

part Bøjden: 0700①②③④⑤⑥, 0900, 1000, 1100, 1200, 1300, 1400, 1500, 1600, 1700, 1900, 2100.
part Fynshav: 0600①②③④⑤⑥, 0800, 1000, 1100, 1200, 1300, 1400, 1500, 1600, 1700, 1800, 2000.

August 8 - 31

part Bøjden: 0700①②③④⑤⑥, 0900, 1000, 1100, 1200, 1300, 1400, 1500, 1600, 1700, 1900, 2100①④⑤⑥⑦.
part Fynshav: 0600①②③④⑤⑥, 0800, 1000, 1100, 1200, 1300, 1400, 1500, 1600, 1700, 1800, 2000①④⑤⑥⑦.

September 1 - 30

part Bøjden: 0700①②③④⑤⑥, 0900, 1100, 1300, 1500, 1700, 1900, 2100④⑤⑥⑦.
part Fynshav: 0600①②③④⑤⑥, 0800, 1000, 1200, 1400, 1600, 1800, 2000④⑤⑥⑦.

Subject to alteration on and around holidays

EBELTOFT - SJÆLLANDS ODDE 2310

ols-Linien by catamaran — 2016 service

urney 65 minutes

eltoft - Sjællands Odde and v.v.: 6-13 sailings daily in summer; 2-9 in winter.

Subject to alteration during holiday periods

ESBJERG - FANØ 2312

nøFærgen Journey 12 minutes — 2016 service

p to 3 departures hourly: 0530 - 0015 from Esbjerg, 0510 - 0030 from Fanø.

Subject to alteration on and around holidays

FREDERIKSHAVN - GÖTEBORG 2320

Stena Line Journey 2½ - 3½ hours — 2016 service (No service Dec. 25)

Sailings from Frederikshavn Trafikhavn and Göteborg.

From Frederikshavn and Göteborg: June 1-27: 3-4 sailings daily; June 28 - Aug. 14: 5-6 sailings daily; Aug. 15 - Dec. 31: 3-4 sailings daily. Departure times vary.

Subject to alteration on and around holidays

GEDSER - ROSTOCK 2330

Scandlines Journey 2 hours — 2016 service

Sailings from Rostock International Port and Gedser.

Until May 1

Depart Gedser: 0130①②③④⑥, 0330⑤, 0340①, 0700, 0900, 1115, 1330, 1530, 1745, 2000, 2215.
Depart Rostock: 0030⑤, 0130①, 0430①⑥, 0600, 0900, 1115, 1330, 1530, 1745, 2000, 2215.

May 2 - December 18

Depart Gedser: 0230 **A**, 0330①, 0700, 0900, 1100, 1300, 1500, 1700, 1900, 2100, 2345 **H**.
Depart Rostock: 0130①, 0400 **J**, 0600, 0900, 1100, 1300, 1500, 1700, 1900, 2100, 2345 **H**.

G – ②③④⑤⑥ (also ⑦ June 26 - Aug. 14).
H – ①②③④⑤ (also ⑥ June 25 - Aug. 13).
J – ①②③④⑤⑥ (also ⑦ June 26 - Aug. 14).

Subject to alteration on and around holidays

GÖTEBORG - KIEL 2335

Stena Line — 2016 service (No service Dec. 24, 25)

Sailings from Kiel Schwedenkai and Göteborg.

Göteborg		Kiel	Kiel		Göteborg
1845	→	0915	1845	→	0915

Subject to alteration during Easter and Xmas/New Year periods

2342 GRENAA - VARBERG

Stena Line Journey 4-5½ hours **2016 service**

Grenaa		Varberg		Varberg		Grenaa	
			May 7 - June 26				
0100	→	0615	①②③④⑤⑥	0700	→	1125	②③④⑤
1420	→	1845		0850	→	1315	①⑥⑦
				1945	→	0005	①②③④⑤⑦
			June 27 - August 14				
0100	→	0615	June 27 only.	0805	→	1245	
1315	→	1740	Not June 27.	1835	→	2255	
2350	→	0415					
			August 15 - December 22				
0100	→	0615	See note **G**.	0700	→	1125	②③④⑤
1420	→	1845	①②③④⑤⑦	0850	→	1315	①
				1945	→	0005	①②③④⑤⑦

G – ①②③④⑤ (not Aug. 15).

Grenaa port is located approximately 3 km from railway station.

2345 HELSINGØR - HELSINGBORG

Scandlines Journey 20 minutes **2016 service**

From Helsingør and Helsingborg: sailings every 15 minutes (every 30 minutes at night).

Subject to alteration on and around holidays

2350 HIRTSHALS - KRISTIANSAND

Color Line by ship **2016 service** **(No service Dec. 24)**

Hirtshals		Kristiansand		Kristiansand		Hirtshals	
			February 1 - March 28 and April 7 - December 23				
1215	→	1530	See note **M**.	0800	→	1115	See note **M**.
2045	→	2400		1630	→	1945	
			March 29 - April 6				
2130	→	0045	Not Apr. 6.	0800	→	1115	Not Mar 29.

M – Not Apr. 18, May 2, 23, June 6, 20, Aug. 15, 29, Sept. 12, 26, Oct. 10, 24, Nov. 7, 21, Dec. 5, 19.

Fjord Line by catamaran **2016 service** **(No winter service)**

Hirtshals		Kristiansand		Kristiansand		Hirtshals	
			May 4 - June 16 and August 15 - September 4				
1145	→	1400	See note **P**.	0830	→	1045	
1800	→	2015		1500	→	1715	See note **P**.
			June 17 - August 14				
1000	→	1215		0645	→	0900	
1700	→	1915		1330	→	1545	
2330	→	0145	See note **Q**.	2015	→	2230	See note **Q**.

P – Not May 10, 11, 24, 25, 31, June 1, 7, 8, 14, 15, 16, 17, 23, 24, 30, 31.
Q – Not June 21, 22, 28, 29, July 5, 6, 12, 13, Aug. 2, 3, 9, 10.

2355 KALUNDBORG - SAMSØ

SamsøFærgen **2016 service**
Journey 75 – 90 minutes

April 18 - May 1

Depart Kalundborg: 0845, 1215⑥⑦**C**, 1545⑤⑦**C**, 1745①②③④**D**, 1915⑤⑥⑦**C**, 2245**E**.
Depart Ballen (Samsø): 0700, 1030⑥⑦**C**, 1400⑤⑦**C**, 1600①②③④**D**, 1730⑤⑥⑦**C**, 2100**E**.

May 2 - 9

Depart Kalundborg: 0845, 1215③④⑥⑦, 1545③④⑤⑦, 1745①②, 1915③④⑤⑥⑦, 2245⑦.
Depart Ballen (Samsø): 0700, 1030③④⑥⑦, 1400③④⑤⑦, 1600①②, 1730③④⑤⑥⑦, 2100⑦.

May 10 - June 1

Depart Kalundborg: 0845, 1215⑥⑦**F**, 1545⑤⑦**G**, 1745①②③④**H**, 1915⑤⑥⑦**G**, 2245**J**.
Depart Ballen (Samsø): 0700, 1030⑥⑦**F**, 1400⑤⑦**G**, 1600①②③④**H**, 1730⑤⑥⑦**G**, 2100**J**.

June 2 - 30 and August 15 - 28

Depart Kalundborg: 0845, 1215⑥⑦, 1545①②③④⑤⑦ (also June 25), 1915.
Depart Ballen (Samsø): 0700, 1030⑥⑦, 1400①②③④⑤⑦ (also June 25), 1730.

July 1 - 17 and July 26 - August 14

Depart Kalundborg: 0845, 1215⑤⑥⑦, 1545, 1915.
Depart Ballen (Samsø): 0700, 1030⑤⑥⑦, 1400, 1730.

July 18 - 25

Depart Kalundborg: 0215**A**, 0515⑦, 0845, 1215, 1545, 1915, 2245⑥⑦.
Depart Ballen (Samsø): 0030**A**, 0345⑦, 0700, 1030, 1400, 1730, 2100⑥⑦.

August 29 - October 30

Depart Kalundborg: 0845, 1215⑥⑦**B**, 1545⑤⑦, 1745①②③④, 1915⑤⑥⑦.
Depart Ballen (Samsø): 0700, 1030⑥⑦**B**, 1400⑤⑦, 1600①②③④, 1730⑤⑥⑦.

A – July 25 only.
B – Not Oct. 2, 9, 16, 30.
C – Also Apr. 21.
D – Not Apr. 21.
E – Apr. 24 only.
F – Also May 13, 16.
G – Also May 16.
H – Not May 16.
J – May 16 only.

Subject to alteration during holiday periods

2360 KØBENHAVN - OSLO

DFDS Seaways **2016 service**
Sailings from København Dampfærgevej and Oslo Vippetangen (Utstikker 2).

København		Oslo		Oslo		København	
1630	→	0945	Not Dec. 24.	1630	→	0945	Not Dec. 24.

connections:
Movia route 20E operates DFDS terminal - Østerport (Folke Bernadottes Allé) - København (Det Kongelige Teater, Kongens Nytorv) and v.v.
Departs at regular intervals 1000 - 1040 ①–⑥, 1000 - 1025 ⑦ from DFDS terminal; 1345 - 1545 ①–⑥, 1415 - 1545 ⑦ from København. Free to DFDS passengers.

2366 LARVIK - HIRTSHALS

Color Line **2016 se** **(No service Dec**

Larvik		Hirtshals		Hirtshals		Larvik	
			April 6 - June 26 and August 15 - October 31				
0800	→	1145	②③④⑤⑥⑦	1245	→	1630	②③④⑤⑥⑦
1730	→	2115		2215	→	0200	
			June 27 - August 14				
0800	→	1145		1245	→	1630	
1730	→	2115	Not July 13.	2215	→	0200	Not July 13.

2368 OSLO - FREDERIKSHAVN

Stena Line **2016 ser**
Sailings from Oslo Vippetangen and Frederikshavn. **(No service Dec. 24**

Oslo		Frederikshavn		Frederikshavn		Oslo	
1930§	→	0730	See note **F**.	0915‡	→	1845	See note **G**.
				1830	→	0730	See note **H**.

F – ②③④⑤⑥⑦ until June 26; daily June 27 - Aug. 21; ②③④⑤⑥⑦ Aug. 22 - Dec. (also Oct. 3).
G – ③④⑤⑥⑦ until June 26; daily June 27 - Aug. 31; ③④⑤⑥⑦ Aug. 22 - Dec. 31 (also Oct. 3, 4; not June 4, 5).
H – ① until June 20 and from Aug. 22 (also June 4; not Oct. 3).
§ – Depart 1830 on Dec. 31.
‡ – Depart 0830 on Dec. 31.

Subject to alteration on and around holidays

2372 OSLO - KIEL

Color Line **2016 ser** **(No service Dec. 24**

Sailings from Oslo Color Line Terminalen, Hjortnes and Kiel Oslo-Kai.

Oslo		Kiel	Kiel		Oslo
1400	→	1000	1400	→	1000

Oslo Color Line Terminal - Oslo Sentral rail station.
Kiel Oslo-Kai - Hamburg ZOB (Central Bus Station).

2375 PUTTGARDEN - RØDBY

Scandlines Journey 45 minutes **2016 serv**

Departures every 30 minutes (at 15 and 45 minutes past each hour). Sailing times betwe 2215 and 0415 may vary.

Subject to alteration on and around holidays

2380 ROSTOCK - TRELLEBORG

Stena Line Journey 6 - 7½ hours **2016 serv**
Sailings from Rostock Überseehafen and Trelleborg. **(No service Dec. 24, 25**
From Rostock and Trelleborg: June 1 - 19: 5 sailings daily; June 20 - Sept. 4: 5 - 6 sailin daily; Sept. 5 - Dec. 22: 2 - 3 sailings daily; Dec. 23 - 30: 1 sailing per day. Journey tim vary.

Subject to alteration on and around holidays

TT Line Journey 5½ - 6½ hours **2016 serv**
Sailings from Rostock Überseehafen and Trelleborg.
Up to 6 sailings per day.

Subject to alteration during holiday periods

2384 SASSNITZ-MUKRAN - RØNNE

BornholmerFærgen **2016 serv** **(No winter serv**

Sassnitz		Rønne		Rønne		Sassnitz	
			March 19 - April 24 and September 19 - October 29				
1150	→	1510	See note **N**.	0800	→	1120	See note **N**.
1330	→	1730	Sept. 24, Oct. 15, 22.	0900	→	1245	Sept. 24, Oct. 15,
			April 25 - May 16 and September 5 - 18				
1150	→	1510	See note **P**.	0800	→	1120	See note **P**.
1330	→	1730	See note **Q**.	0900	→	1245	See note **Q**.
			May 17 - June 5				
1150	→	1510	④	0800	→	1120	④
1330	→	1730	⑥⑦	0900	→	1245	⑥⑦
			June 6 - 22				
1150	→	1510	④⑥ (also June 20).	0730	→	1100	June 19 only.
1200	→	1530	June 19 only.	0800	→	1120	④⑥ (also June 2
1330	→	1730	⑥⑦ (not June 19).	0900	→	1245	⑥⑦ (not June 19
			June 23 - September 4				
1150	→	1510	See note **R**.	0800	→	1120	See note **R**.
1330	→	1730	⑥⑦ (also Aug. 5, 12).	0900	→	1245	⑥⑦ (also Aug. 5,

N – ④⑥⑦ (also Mar. 28; not Mar. 20, 27, Sept. 24, Oct. 15, 22, 27).
P – ④ (also May 15, 16, Sept. 10; not May 12).
Q – ⑥⑦ (also May 12; not May 15).
R – Not June 26, 27, July 3, 10, Sept. 4.

SASSNITZ-MUKRAN - TRELLEBORG 2385

a Line Journey 4 hours **Service to November 30, 2016**
ings from Fährhafen Sassnitz-Mukran and Trelleborg. **(No service Dec. 24)**

May 9 - June 12 and August 29 - November 30

n Sassnitz: 1345②, 1530①⑦, 1715③④⑤⑥.
n Trelleborg: 0800①②③⑤⑥, 0945⑦, 1130④.

June 13 - August 28

n Sassnitz: 1300, 2300. From Trelleborg: 0745, 1800.

Subject to alteration on and around holidays

STRÖMSTAD - SANDEFJORD 2387

or Line Journey 2½ hours **2016 service**
ngs from Strømstad and Sandefjord: frequent daily departures.

d Line Journey 2½ hours **2016 service**
(No service Jan. 1 - 11)

mstad		Sandefjord	Sandefjord		Strømstad
200	→	1430	0830	→	1100
330	→	2100	1520	→	1750

TRAVEMÜNDE - TRELLEBORG 2390

TT Line **2016 service**
Sailings from Travemünde Skandinavienkai and Trelleborg.
Up to 8 sailings per day.

Subject to alteration during holiday periods

connection available Trelleborg - Malmö railway station and v.v. for certain sailings.

TRAVEMÜNDE - MALMÖ 2395

Finnlines **2016 service** (until further notice)

Travemünde		Malmö		Malmö		Travemünde	
0100	→	1015	⑦	1000	→	1900	②③④⑤⑥
0230	→	1115	②③④⑤	1330	→	2315	⑥
0300	→	1145	①⑥	1600	→	0045	①②③④⑤
1000	→	1900	②③④⑤	1600	→	0100	⑦
1100	→	2000	⑥	2200	→	0700	①②③④⑤⑦
2200	→	0700	Daily.	2300	→	0830	⑥

Subject to alteration during Xmas/New Year period

BALTIC SEA

GDAŃSK - NYNÄSHAMN 2402

ferries **Service to January 31, 2017**

ańsk		Nynäshamn		Nynäshamn		Gdańsk	
800	→	1200	See note A.	1800	→	1200	See note B.

- Feb. 16, 18, 20, 23, 25, 27, Mar. 1, 3, 5, 8, 10, 12, 15, 17, 19, 22, 24, 29, 31, Apr. 2, 5, 7, 9, 12, 14, 16, 19, 21, 23, 26, 28, 30, May 3, 5, 7, 10, 12, 14, 17, 19, 21, 24, 26, 28, 31, June 2, 4, 7, 9, 11, 14, 16, 18, 21, 23, 25, 27, 29, July 1, 3, 5, 7, 9, 11, 13, 15, 17, 19, 21, 23, 25, 27, 29, 31, Aug. 2, 4, 6, 8, 10, 12, 14, 16, 18, 20, 22, 24, 26, 28, 30, Sept. 1, 3, 6, 8, 10, 13, 15, 17, 20, 22, 24, 27, 29, Oct. 1, 4, 6, 8, 11, 13, 15, 18, 20, 22, 25, 27, 29, Nov. 1, 3, 5, 8, 10, 12, 15, 17, 19, 22, 24, 26, 29, Dec. 1, 3, 6, 8, 10, 13, 15, 17, 19, 21, 27, Jan. 2, 4, 6, 8, 10, 12, 14, 17, 19, 21, 24, 26, 28, 31.
- Feb. 1, 17, 19, 22, 24, 26, 29, Mar. 2, 4, 7, 9, 11, 14, 16, 18, 21, 23, 25, 30, Apr. 1, 4, 6, 8, 11, 13, 15, 18, 20, 22, 25, 27, 29, May 2, 4, 6, 9, 11, 13, 16, 18, 20, 23, 25, 27, 30, June 1, 3, 6, 8, 10, 13, 15, 17, 20, 22, 24, 26, 28, 30, July 2, 4, 6, 8, 10, 12, 14, 16, 18, 20, 22, 24, 26, 28, 30, Aug. 1, 3, 5, 7, 9, 11, 13, 15, 17, 19, 21, 23, 25, 27, 29, 31, Sept. 2, 5, 7, 9, 12, 14, 16, 19, 21, 23, 26, 28, 30, Oct. 3, 5, 7, 10, 12, 14, 17, 19, 21, 24, 26, 28, 31, Nov. 2, 4, 7, 9, 11, 14, 16, 18, 21, 23, 25, 28, 30, Dec. 2, 5, 7, 9, 12, 14, 16, 18, 20, 22, 29, Jan. 3, 5, 7, 9, 11, 13, 16, 18, 20, 23, 25, 27, 30.

GRISSLEHAMN - ECKERÖ 2405

kerö Linjen **Service to January 8, 2017**
(No service Dec. 24, 25)

January 11 - June 16 and August 15 - January 8

lehamn		Eckerö		Eckerö		Grisslehamn	
000	→	1300		0830	→	0915	①⑤⑥⑦
500	→	1800		1330	→	1430	
000	→	2245	④⑤⑥⑦	1830	→	1930	

June 17 - August 14

000	→	1300	Not Jan. 1.	0830	→	0915	Not June 25, Jan. 1.
500	→	1800		1330	→	1430	
000	→	2245	Not June 24.	1830	→	1930	
345	→	0245	June 23 only.	2300	→	2400	June 26 only.

NAANTALI - KAPELLSKÄR 2407

nlines **2016 service**
veys passengers with vehicles only **(No service Dec. 24, 25)**

aantali		Kapellskär		Kapellskär		Naantali	
0930	→	1700	May 23 - Sept. 30.	0100	→	1040	See note K.
1100	→	1815	From Oct. 1.	0915	→	1900	
1615	→	2315	See note L.	2145	→	0715	
2245	→	0615					

– ②③④⑤⑥ May 24 - Aug. 31.
– ①②③④⑤ May 23 - Sept. 4.

Subject to alteration on and around holidays

HELSINKI - TALLINN 2410

Eckerö Line by ship **2016 service**
(No service Dec. 24, 25, Jan. 11 - 22)

Sailings from Helsinki Länsiterminaali and Tallinn A-terminal.

Helsinki		Tallinn		Tallinn		Helsinki	
0830	→	1100		0145	→	0645	③④ from Feb. 17.
1530	→	1745		1200	→	1430	
2215	→	0045	②③ from Feb. 16.	1845	→	2115	

Connection: Tram route 9 Helsinki railway sation - Länsiterminaali

Linda Line Oy by hydrofoil **2016 service**
Linda Line Express Journey 1 hour 40 minutes **(No winter service)**
Sailings from Helsinki Makasiiniterminaali and Tallinn Linnahalli.

March 24 - June 26

Depart Helsinki: 0800①②③④⑤⑥, 1000, 1200①②③⑤⑦, 1600, 1800, 2000④⑤⑦.
Depart Tallinn: 0800①②③④⑤⑥, 1000, 1200①②③⑥⑦, 1600, 1800, 2000④⑤⑦.

June 27 - August 14

Depart Helsinki: 0800①②③④⑤⑥, 1000, 1200, 1600, 1800, 2000.
Depart Tallinn: 0800①②③④⑤⑥, 1000, 1200, 1600, 1800, 2000.

August 15 - September 25

Depart Helsinki: 0800①②③④⑤⑥, 1000, 1200①②③⑥⑦, 1600, 1800, 2000④⑤⑦.
Depart Tallinn: 0800①②③④⑤⑥, 1000, 1200①②③⑥⑦, 1600, 1800, 2000④⑤⑦.

Tallink Silja by ship **2016 service**
Sailings from Helsinki Länsiterminaali and Tallinn D-terminal.
Journey 2 hours (§ – 3½ hours, ‡ – 4 hours, ¶ – 4½ hours)

March 28 - April 22

Depart Helsinki: 0730, 1030, 1330, 1630, 1830§, 1930①②③④⑤⑦, 2030⑥, 2130①②③④⑥, 2230①②③④⑤⑦.
Depart Tallinn: 0730, 1030, 1230§, 1330, 1630, 1930①②③④⑤⑦, 2030⑥, 2230①②③④⑤⑦.

April 23 - May 31

Depart Helsinki: 0730, 0900‡, 1030, 1330, 1630, 1830§, 1930①②③④⑤⑦, 2030⑥, 2230①②③④⑤⑦.
Depart Tallinn: 0730, 1030, 1230§, 1330, 1630, 1700⑥‡, 1830①②③④⑤⑦¶, 1930①②③④⑤⑦, 2030⑥, 2230①②③④⑤⑦.

June 1 - December 18

Depart Helsinki: 0730, 1030, 1330, 1630, 1830§, 1930①②③④⑤⑦, 2030⑥, 2230①②③④⑤⑦.
Depart Tallinn: 0730, 1030, 1230§, 1330, 1630, 1930①②③④⑤⑦, 2030⑥, 2230①②③④⑤⑦.

Subject to alteration during Xmas/New Year period

Connection: Tram route 9 Helsinki railway sation - Länsiterminaali

Viking Line by ship Journey 2½ hours **2016 service**
Sailings from Helsinki Katajanokka terminal and Tallinn A-terminal. **(No service Dec. 24, 25)**

Until June 17 and from August 15

Depart Helsinki: 1130, 2000⑦, 2130①②③④⑤⑥.
Depart Tallinn: 0800, 1630⑦, 1800①②③④⑤⑥.

June 18 - August 14

Depart Helsinki: 1030⑦, 1130, 2000⑦, 2130①②③④⑤⑥.
Depart Tallinn: 0800, 1400⑦, 1630⑦, 1800①②③④⑤⑥.

KARLSKRONA - GDYNIA 2415

Stena Line **2016 service (No service Dec. 24, 25)**

Karlskrona		Gdynia		Gdynia		Karlskrona	
0830	→	1900	①	0800	→	1830	⑤
0900	→	1930	②③⑥⑦	0900	→	1930	②③④⑥⑦
1000	→	2030	④	1800	→	0530	③⑦
1800	→	0700	②④	1900	→	0630	①
1900	→	0800	⑤	1930	→	0730	⑤
1930	→	0745	①	2100	→	0900	②③⑥⑦
2030	→	0830	⑥	2130	→	0930	④
2100	→	0900	②③④⑦	2200	→	1000	①
2159	→	0930					

Subject to alteration on and around holidays

2418 KARLSHAMN - KLAIPEDA

DFDS Seaways — **2016 service**

Sailings from Karlshamn Ferry Terminal and Klaipeda International Ferry Port.

Karlshamn		Klaipeda	Klaipeda		Karlsham
1900	→	0900	1900	→	0900

2420 KIEL - KLAIPEDA

DFDS Seaways — **2016 service**

Sailings from Kiel Ostuferhafen and Klaipeda International Ferry Port.

Kiel		Klaipeda	Klaipeda		Kiel
Until April 3					
1400①	→	1230②	1500①	→	1230②
1600②	→	1400③	1730②	→	1400③
1800③	→	1630④	1900③	→	1600④
2000④	→	1800⑤	2100④	→	1800⑤
2200⑤	→	2000⑥	2300⑤	→	1900⑥
2300⑥	→	2200⑦	0100⑦	→	2200⑦
From April 4					
2000	→	1630	2100	→	1600

Departure times may vary owing to tidal conditions.
Subject to alteration during Xmas/New Year period

2430 KØGE - RØNNE

BornholmerFærgen — **2016 service**

Køge		Rønne	Rønne		Køge
0030	→	0600	1700	→	2230

2445 NYNÄSHAMN - VISBY

Destination Gotland — **Service to August 15, 2016**

Nynäshamn		Visby		Visby		Nynäshamn	
May 9 - June 19							
0915	→	1235	① (not June 6)	0700	→	1020	June 6 only.
1120	→	1440	June 6 only.	0730	→	1045	See note **B**.
1125	→	1455	See note **B**.	0805	→	1120	⑦
1200	→	1515	⑦	1245	→	1600	⑤
1635	→	1950	⑤	1535	→	1850	June 6 only.
1935	→	2250	June 6 only.	1600	→	1915	⑤⑥⑦
2005	→	2320	⑤⑥⑦	1630	→	1950	See note **C**.
2100	→	0020	See note **C**.	1730	→	2045	June 5 only.
				1740	→	2055	June 19 only.
				1920	→	2235	⑦ (not June 5, 19).
June 20 - 26							
0700	→	1015	④⑤	0730	→	1045	①②③④⑤⑦
1125	→	1440	③④⑤⑦	0855	→	1210	③⑤⑦
1125	→	1455	①②	1045	→	1400	⑥
1245	→	1600	⑤	1055	→	1410	④
1250	→	1605	③⑦	1245	→	1600	①②④⑥
1445	→	1800	⑥	1355	→	1710	⑦
1500	→	1815	④	1520	→	1835	③④
1635	→	1950	①②④⑥	1535	→	1850	⑦
1745	→	2100	⑦	1630	→	1950	①②③
1910	→	2225	③④	1915	→	2230	④
1945	→	2300	⑦	2340	→	0300	⑦
2100	→	0020	①②③				
2335	→	0250	④				
June 27 - July 3							
0225	→	0540	⑥⑦	0135	→	0450	⑤
0730	→	1045	⑤⑥⑦	0330	→	0645	⑥⑦
0915	→	1235	①	0630	→	0945	⑤⑥⑦
1035	→	1350	⑤⑥⑦	0730	→	1045	①②③④
1125	→	1455	①②③④	0900	→	1215	⑤⑥⑦
1255	→	1610	②③④	0905	→	1220	②③④
1300	→	1615	⑤⑥⑦	1055	→	1410	①
1445	→	1800	①	1135	→	1450	⑤⑥⑦
1540	→	1855	⑤⑥⑦	1430	→	1745	①
1820	→	2135	①	1630	→	1950	①②③④
2100	→	0020		1700	→	2015	⑤⑥⑦
				2225	→	0140	⑤⑥⑦
July 4 - August 15							
0225	→	0540	①②⑥⑦	0135	→	0450	⑤
0625	→	0940	⑦	0330	→	0645	①⑥⑦
0730	→	1045	①⑤⑥⑦	0630	→	0945	①⑤⑥⑦
0915	→	1230	②③④⑤	0705	→	1020	②③④
1035	→	1350	①⑤⑥⑦	0900	→	1215	①⑤⑥⑦
1120	→	1450	②③④	1000	→	1315	②③④
1300	→	1615	①⑤⑥⑦	1135	→	1450	①⑤⑥⑦
1415	→	1730	②③④	1415	→	1730	⑥
1540	→	1855	①⑤⑥⑦	1630	→	1950	②③④
2100	→	0020		1700	→	2015	①⑤⑥⑦
2205	→	0120	②④	1815	→	2130	②③④
2215	→	0130	③	1915	→	2230	①②④ (not Aug. 15).
				1920	→	2235	③
				2225	→	0140	①⑤⑥⑦

B – ①②③④⑤⑥ (not June 6). C – ①②③④ (not June 6).

Additional services operate at peak times;
subject to alteration during Easter and Xmas/New Year periods

🚌 service Stockholm Cityterminalen - Nynäshamn connects with most sailings.

2448 NYNÄSHAMN - VENTSPILS

Stena Line — **2016 service** **(No service Dec. 24, 25)**

Nynäshamn		Ventspils	Ventspils		Nynäshamn
0800⑦	→	1900⑦	0001②	→	1000②
0900①③	→	2000①③	1000③	→	1900③
1900②④	→	0700③⑤	1800⑥	→	0600⑦
2200③⑤	→	1000④⑥	2100④	→	0900⑤
			2200⑦	→	0800①
			2300③⑦	→	0900④①

Subject to alteration on and around holidays

2450 OSKARSHAMN - VISBY

Destination Gotland — **Service to August 15,**

Oskarshamn		Visby		Visby		Oskarshamn	
May 9 - June 19							
1100	→	1400	②	0715	→	1015	②⑥ (also June
1100	→	1400	June 19 only.	1200	→	1455	⑦ (not June 5,
1540	→	1835	⑦ (not June 5, 19).	1620	→	1915	⑤ (also June 5,
2010	→	2305	⑤⑥⑦	1640	→	1935	⑦ (not June 5,
2110	→	0005	①②③④	1700	→	1955	②
				1705	→	2000	①③④
June 20 - 30							
1015	→	1310	⑦	0645	→	0940	⑦
1100	→	1400	①②③④⑤	0715	→	1015	①②③④⑤
1825	→	2120	⑦	1455	→	1750	⑦
2010	→	2305	⑥	1620	→	1915	⑥
2110	→	0005	①②③④⑦	1700	→	2000	①②③④⑦
July 1 - August 15							
1035	→	1330	⑥	0705	→	1000	⑥
1110	→	1405	July 3 only.	0720	→	1015	②③④ (also Jul
1115	→	1410	②③④	1020	→	1315	⑦ (not July 3).
1350	→	1645	⑦ (not July 3).	1440	→	1735	①⑤⑥⑦
1830	→	2125	①⑤⑥⑦	1705	→	2000	②③④
2110	→	0005	②③④	1955	→	2250	See note **Q**.
2350	→	0245	①⑤⑥⑦	2005	→	2300	Aug. 15 only.

Q – ①⑤⑥⑦ (not Aug. 15).

Additional services operate at peak times;
subject to alteration during Easter and Xmas/New Year periods

2451 ROSTOCK - GDYNIA - HELSINKI

Finnlines — **2015 se**

Sailings from Helsinki Vuosaaren satama.

Subject to alteration on and around German and Finnish holidays

SERVICE CURRENTLY SUSPENDED

2464 STOCKHOLM - RIGA

Tallink Silja — **2016 ser**

Sailings from Stockholm Frihamnsterminalen and Riga passenger port.

Stockholm		Riga	
1700	→	1100	Even dates Feb., Apr., May, Aug., Nov., Dec.; uneven dates Jan., Mar., June, July, Sept., Oct.
Riga		**Stockholm**	
1730	→	1030	Even dates Jan., Mar., June, July, Sept., Oct.; uneven dates Feb., Apr., May, Aug., Nov., Dec.

2465 STOCKHOLM - MARIEHAMN - HELSINKI

Tallink Silja — **2016 ser** **(No service Dec.**

Sailings from Stockholm Värtahamnen and Helsinki Olympiaterminaali.

Stockholm		Mariehamn		Helsinki	Helsinki		Mariehamn		Stockholm
Until March 30									
1645	→	2355	→	1030	1700	→	0425	→	0945
March 31 - November 8									
1645	→	2355	→	0955	1700	→	0425	→	0930

🚌 Stockholm Värtahamnen - Ropsten metro station (for Stockholm Centralen).

Viking Line — **2016 ser** **(No service Dec. 24**

Sailings from Stockholm Stadsgården and Helsinki Katajanokka.

Stockholm		Mariehamn		Helsinki	Helsinki		Mariehamn		Stockholm
Until June 16 and August 16 - December 31									
1630	→	2345	→	1010	1730	→	0430	→	1000
June 17 - August 15									
1600	→	2255	→	0915	1800	→	0430	→	0950

Connections:
🚌 Stockholm Cityterminalen (near Central station) - Slussen metro station - Viking Li terminal. Tram no. 4T runs daily from Helsinki city centre to the Viking Line Terminal.

2470 (STOCKHOLM -) KAPELLSKÄR - MARIEHAMN

Viking Line — **2016 serv**

Sailings from Kapellskär and Mariehamn. **(No service Dec. 24, 25, Jan. 7-**

Stockholm (*by* 🚌)		Kapellskär		Mariehamn		Mariehamn		Kapellskär		Stockholm (*by* 🚌)	
January 29 - April 1 and October 2 - December 31											
1000♦	→	1200	→	1530	①②③④	0730	→	0900	→	*1035*♦	①②③④⑤
1230♦	→	1445	→	1800	⑤⑥⑦	1245	→	1400	→	*1540*♦	⑦
1700♦	→	1900	→	2230	①②③④	1600	→	1730	→	*1915*♦	①②③④
1800♦	→	2000	→	2320	⑤⑥⑦	1830	→	1945	→	*2115*♦	⑤⑥⑦
April 2 - 28											
0700♦	→	0900	→	1215	⑥	0730	→	0845	→	*1025*♦	⑥
1000♦	→	1200	→	1530	①②③④	0730	→	0900	→	*1035*♦	①②③④⑤
1230♦	→	1445	→	1800	⑤⑥⑦	1245	→	1400	→	*1540*♦	⑥⑦
1700♦	→	1900	→	2230	①②③④	1600	→	1730	→	*1915*♦	①②③④
1800♦	→	2000	→	2320	⑤⑥⑦	1830	→	1945	→	*2125*♦	⑤⑥⑦
April 29 - June 12 and August 19 - October 1											
0700♦	→	0900	→	1215	⑤⑥	0730	→	0845	→	*1025*♦	⑤⑥
1000♦	→	1200	→	1530	①②③④	0730	→	0900	→	*1035*♦	①②③④
1230♦	→	1445	→	1800	⑤⑥⑦	1245	→	1400	→	*1540*♦	⑤⑥⑦
1700♦	→	1900	→	2230	①②③④	1600	→	1730	→	*1915*♦	①②③④
1800♦	→	2000	→	2320	⑤⑥⑦	1830	→	1945	→	*2115*♦	⑤⑥⑦
June 13 - August 18											
0700♦	→	0900	→	1215		0730	→	0845	→	*1025*♦	
1230♦	→	1445	→	1800		1245	→	1400	→	*1540*♦	
1800♦	→	2000	→	2320		1830	→	1945	→	*2125*♦	

♦ – Connecting 🚌 service from/to Stockholm Cityterminalen (near Central station).

For international shipping maps – see pages 538 - 540

STOCKHOLM - TALLINN via Mariehamn 2475

ink Silja — 2016 service

ngs from Stockholm Värtahamnen and Tallinn D-terminal.

ckholm		Mariehamn		Tallinn	Tallinn		Mariehamn		Stockholm
Until March 30 and November 9 - December 31									
730	→	0100	→	1045	1800	→	0500	→	1015
March 31 - November 8									
730	→	0100	→	1000	1800	→	0500	→	1015

STOCKHOLM - TURKU via Mariehamn / Långnäs 2480

ink Silja — 2016 service

ings from Stockholm Värtahamnen and Turku.

tockholm		Mariehamn		Långnäs §		Turku
0710	→	1345	→	→	→	1915
1930	→	→	→	0255	→	0700

Turku		Långnäs §		Mariehamn		Stockholm
0815	→	→	→	1345	→	1815
2015	→	0045	→	→	→	0610

- Långnäs is 28km from Mariehamn.

learest metro station to Stockholm Värtahamnen is Gärdet (for Stockholm Centralen).

ing Line — 2016 service (No service Dec. 24, 25)

ings from Stockholm Stadsgården and Turku Linnansatama.

ckholm		Mariehamn		Långnäs §		Turku
745	→	1425	→	→	→	1950
000	→	→	→	0320	→	0735

urku		Långnäs §		Mariehamn		Stockholm
845	→	→	→	1425	→	1855
055	→	0110	→	→	→	0630

- Långnäs is 28km from Mariehamn.

connections: Stockholm Cityterminalen (near Central station) - Slussen metro station - Viking Line terminal; Turku city centre - harbour (bus no. 1).

T PETERBURG - HELSINKI - STOCKHOLM - TALLINN 2482

Peter Line — 2016 service

eterburg		Helsinki		Stockholm		Tallinn		St Peterburg
900 **A**	→	0800 **B** / 1600 **B**	→	0800 **C** / 1800 **C**	→	1130 **D** / 1900 **D**	→	0930 **E**

– Sailings from St Peterburg: contact operator for sailing dates and exact times as all timings may vary.

– 1st day; **B** – 2nd day; **C** – 3rd day; **D** – 4th day; **E** – 5th day.

Subject to alteration during Easter and Xmas / New Year periods

TRAVEMÜNDE - HELSINKI 2485

nlines — 2016 service

ailings from Travemünde Skandinavienkai and Helsinki Vuosaaren satama.

Travemünde		Helsinki	Helsinki		Travemünde
0300 ②–⑤	→	0900 ③–⑥	1700 ①–⑥	→	2130 ②–⑦
0300 ⑦	→	0900 ①			
0330 ⑥	→	0930 ⑦			

Subject to alteration on and around German and Finnish holidays

TRAVEMÜNDE - LIEPAJA 2486

ena Line — 2016 service

Travemünde		Liepaja	Liepaja		Travemünde
2100 ③⑦	→	0030 ⑤②	0400 ②	→	0730 ③
			1600 ⑥	→	1800 ⑦

Subject to alteration on and around holidays

TRAVEMÜNDE - VENTSPILS 2487

Stena Line — 2016 service

Travemünde		Ventspils	Ventspils		Travemünde
1730 ⑥	→	1930 ⑦	1000 ⑤	→	1330 ⑥

Subject to alteration on and around holidays

VAASA - UMEÅ (HOLMSUND) 2490

Wasaline — 2016 service (No service Dec. 24, 25)

Vaasa		Umeå		Umeå		Vaasa	
February 1 - June 10 and August 15 - December 22							
0800	→	1130	⑦	0800	→	1330	③
0900	→	1230	④⑤⑥	0900	→	1430	①②
1430	→	1800	③	1300	→	1830	⑦
2000	→	2330	①②⑦	1800	→	2330	④⑤⑥
				1900	→	0030	③
June 11 - August 14							
0800	→	1100	⑥	0800	→	1330	③
0830	→	1200	⑦	0900	→	1430	①②
0900	→	1230	④⑤	1145	→	1645	⑥
1430	→	1800	③	1330	→	1900	⑦
1730	→	2030	⑥	1800	→	2330	④⑤
2000	→	2330	①②	1900	→	0030	③
2030	→	2400	⑦	2100	→	0200	⑥

YSTAD - RØNNE 2494

BornholmerFærgen by fast ferry — 2016 service

3 - 8 sailings daily (less frequent in winter), departure times vary, journey 75 minutes.

See Table **727** for rail connections Ystad - København and v.v.

(KØBENHAVN -) YSTAD - ŚWINOUJŚCIE 2495

Polferries — Service to December 9, 2016

København		Ystad		Świnoujście	
▲	→	1400	→	2000	Daily.
▲	→	2130	→	0530	①②③④⑤ Mar. 25 - June 17; ①②③④⑤⑦ June 18 - Aug. 26; ①②③④⑤ Aug. 27 - Dec. 9 (not May 2 - 6).

Świnoujście		Ystad		København	
1230	→	1900	→	▲	②③④⑤ Mar. 25 - June 17; ①②③④⑤⑦ June 18 - Aug. 26; ②③④⑤ Aug. 27 - Dec. 9 (not May 3 - 6).
1500	→	2200	→	▲	⑦ Mar. 25 - June 17, Aug. 27 - Dec. 9 (not May 1).
2230	→	0615	→	▲	Daily.

▲ – 🚌 operates København railway station - Polferries Terminal and v.v. Times vary - contact operator.

Unity Line — 2016 service (No service Dec. 24, 25, 31)

Ystad		Świnoujście	Świnoujście		Ystad
1330	→	2000	1300	→	2015
2230	→	0645	2300	→	0630

A connecting 🚌 service operates Świnoujście terminal - Szczecin Hotel Radisson SAS and v.v.: Świnoujście depart 0730, Szczecin arrive 0900. Return journey Szczecin depart 1000, Świnoujście arrive 1130.

WESTERN MEDITERRANEAN

ALGECIRAS - CEUTA 2500

aleària (Eurolínies Marítimes) — Service to June 15, 2016

Journey 1½ hours

epart Algeciras: 0600, 0800①②③④⑤⑥, 0930, 1230, 1400, 1600, 1800①②③④⑤⑦, 1900, 2200, 2330.

epart Ceuta: 0600, 0730, 1030①②③④⑤⑥, 1100①②③④⑤⑥, 1130⑦, 1430, 1600, 1730, 2000①②③④⑤⑦, 2030①②③④⑤⑦, 2030⑥, 2330.

asmediterranea by fast ferry — 2016 service

ubject to alteration at Easter and Christmas. Journey 55 minutes

epart Algeciras and Ceuta: 3 – 5 sailings daily, departure times vary.

ALGECIRAS - TANJAH (TANGIERS) MED 2502

asmediterranea Journey 1½ hours — 2016 service

om Algeciras and Tanjah Med: 4 – 6 sailings daily, departure times vary.

Tanjah (Tangiers) Med port is located approximately 45km east of Tanjah. A connecting 🚌 operates between Tanjah Med and Tanjah.

ALMERÍA - GHAZAOUET 2504

asmediterranea — Service to September 16, 2016

lmería		Ghazaouet	
2359	→	0800	②⑤ Feb. 2 - June 28; ③⑤⑥ July 1 - 22; daily July 25, 27, 28, 30, Aug. 2, 3, 10, 11, 15, 17, 18, 20, 24, 26, 29, 31, Sept. 2, 5, 6, 9, 13, 16.

hazaouet		Almería	
1400	→	2200	③⑥ Feb. 3 - June 29; ④⑥⑦ July 2 - 23; daily July 26, 28, 29, 31, Aug. 3, 4, 11, 12, 16, 18, 19, 21, 25, 27, 30, Sept. 1, 3, 6, 7, 10, 14, 17.

ALMERÍA - MELILLA 2505

Trasmediterranea Journey 6 - 8 hours — Service to August 10, 2016

Depart Almería: 1700①, 2359②③④⑤⑥⑦.
Depart Melilla: 0930①, 1400⑤, 1500②③④⑥⑦.

Times may vary (particularly in August).
Additional sailings by fast ferry in summer (journey 3 hours).

Subject to alteration during Easter and Xmas / New Year periods

ALMERÍA - AN-NADÛR (NADOR) 2507

Trasmediterranea Journey 5 - 8 hours — 2016 service

From Almería and an-Nadûr: Feb. - June: daily sailings; July - Aug.: up to 3 sailings daily; Oct. - Dec.: daily sailings.

2508 BARCELONA - TANJAH (TANGIERS) MED

Grandi Navi Veloci Journey 27 - 32 hours **Service to September 30, 2016**

Departure times vary.

From Barcelona: June 3, 7, 10, 12, 14, 15, 17, 19, 21, 23, 24, 26, 28, July 1, 3, 5, 8, 9, 10, 12, 15, 17, 19, 22, 24, 25, 26, 29, 31, Aug. 2, 5, 7, 9, 10, 12, 14, 16, 18, 19, 21, 26, 28, Sept. 2, 4, 9, 11, 16, 18, 23, 25, 30.

From Tanjah Med: June 4, 8, 13, 15, 20, 22, 27, 29, July 4, 6, 11, 13, 18, 20, 25, 27, Aug. 1, 3, 8, 10, 11, 13, 15, 17, 19, 20, 22, 24, 27, 29, 31, Sept. 3, 4, 5, 7, 10, 12, 14, 17, 19, 20, 21, 24, 26, 28.

Tanjah (Tangiers) Med port is located approximately 45 km east of Tanjah. A connecting 🚌 operates between Tanjah Med and Tanjah.

2510 BALEARIC ISLANDS (map page 320)

Baleària (Eurolínies Marítimes)

BARCELONA - CIUTADELLA (MENORCA) — 2016 service

Barcelona		Ciutadella		Ciutadella		Barcelona	
Until May 29							
2230	→	0800	①②③④⑤⑦	1100	→	2030	①②③④⑤⑥
May 30 - October 2							
2355	→	0630	①②③④⑤	1230	→	2200	See note **M**.
2355	→	0630	⑦ July 29 - Sept. 4.	1530	→	2200	See note **N**.
				2355	→	0630	See note **P**.

M – ⑤⑥ July 29 - Aug. 13; ⑥ Aug. 14 - Sept. 4.
N – ②③④⑤ May 30 - July 28; ①②③④ July 29 - Sept. 4; ②③④⑤ Sept. 5 - Oct. 2.
P – ⑦ May 30 - July 28, Sept. 5 - Oct. 2.

BARCELONA - EIVISSA (IBIZA) — Service to October 2, 2016

Barcelona		Eivissa		Eivissa		Barcelona	
2130	→	0600	①②③④⑤	1000	→	1815	②③④⑤
2130	→	0600	⑥⑦ July 2 - Sept. 25.	1000	→	1815	① July 2 - Sept. 25.
				1130	→	1945	⑥⑦ July 2 - Sept. 25.
				2230	→	0700	See note **Q**.

Q – ⑦ May 21 - July 1, Sept. 26 - Oct. 2.

BARCELONA - PALMA — 2016 service

Barcelona		Palma		Palma		Barcelona	
Until May 29							
2230	→	0500	①②③④⑤⑦	1230	→	1945	①②③④⑤
2300	→	0630	①②③④⑤	1230	→	2015	⑥
2300	→	0700	⑦	1400	→	2030	①②③④⑤⑥
May 30 - October 2							
2300	→	0630	①②③④⑤	1230	→	1945	①②③④⑤
2300	→	0700	⑦	1230	→	1945	⑦ July 16 - Sept. 4.
2300	→	0700	⑥ July 16 - Sept. 4.	1230	→	2015	⑥
2355	→	0630	⑥ July 29 - Sept. 4.	1530	→	2200	See note **R**.

R – ⑤⑥⑦ July 29 - Aug. 13; ⑥⑦ Aug. 14 - Sept. 4.

DÉNIA - EIVISSA (IBIZA) - PALMA — Service to May 29, 2016

Dénia		Eivissa		Palma
1730②–⑦	→	2100/2130②–⑦	→	0100③–①
1800①	→	2130/2200①	→	0130②
Palma		**Eivissa**		**Dénia**
0800②–⑦	→	1130/1230②–⑦	→	1600②–⑦
0900①	→	1230/1330①	→	1700①

OTHER SERVICES:

Dénia - Sant Antoni and v.v.:	1–2 sailings daily, journey ±3½ hours.
Formentera - Eivissa and v.v.:	frequent daily services (0700 - 2130), journey 30 - 60 minutes.
València - Palma and v.v.:	6 sailings per week (daily in summer), journey ±7½ hours (some services via Eivissa).

Trasmediterranea **2016 services**

Departure times may vary. All routes subject to alteration on and around holidays.

BARCELONA - EIVISSA (IBIZA) by ship Journey 8 - 14 hours
Depart Barcelona: **Feb. 1 - Apr. 17**: sailings on ②④; **Apr. 18 - June 17**: sailings on ①②③④⑤; **June 20 - Sept. 10**: sailings on ①②③④⑤⑥.
Depart Eivissa: **Feb. 1 - Apr. 17**: sailings on ③⑤; **Apr. 18 - June 12**: sailings on ②③④⑤⑦; **June 14 - Sept. 11**: sailings on ②③④⑤⑥⑦.
Most sailings overnight; additional sailings available.

BARCELONA - MAÓ (MAHÓN) by ship Journey 8 - 9 hours
Depart Barcelona: **Feb. 1 - Apr. 17**: sailings on ①③⑤; **Apr. 18 - June 10**: sailings on ①②③④⑤; **June 13 - Sept. 10**: daily sailings.
Depart Maó: **Feb. 1 - Apr. 17**: sailings on ②④⑥; **Apr. 18 - June 11**: sailings on ②③④⑤⑥; **June 14 - Sept. 11**: daily sailings.
Most sailings overnight; additional sailings available.

BARCELONA - PALMA by ship Journey 6½ - 8½ hours, departure times vary
Depart Barcelona: **Feb. 1 - Apr. 17**: sailings on ①②③④⑤⑦; **Apr. 18 - June 12**: 2230⑦, 2300①②③④⑤; **June 13 - Sept. 9**: 2300.
Depart Palma: **Feb. 1 - Apr. 17**: daily sailings; **Apr. 18 - Sept. 9**: daily sailings.

PALMA - MAÓ (MAHÓN) by ship Journey 5½ hours
Depart Palma: **Feb. 1 - Oct. 30**: 0800⑦.
Depart Maó: **Feb. 1 - Oct. 30**: 1715⑦.

VALÈNCIA - MAÓ (MAHÓN) via Palma by ship Journey 14 - 15 hours
Depart València: **Feb. 1 - Oct. 29**: 2300⑥.
Depart Maó: **Feb. 1 - Oct. 30**: 1715⑦.

VALÈNCIA - PALMA by ship Journey 8 hours
Depart València: **Feb. 1 - Oct. 31**: 2300①②③④⑤⑥.
Depart Palma: **Feb. 1 - Oct. 31**: 1130②③④⑤⑥, 2345⑦.

2512 CANARY ISLANDS

Fred. Olsen **Inter-Island services** **2016 serv**

Playa Blanca (Lanzarote) - Corralejo (Fuerteventura), journey 15 minutes;
Morro del Jable (Fuerteventura) - Las Palmas de Gran Canaria (Gran Canaria), journey 100 minutes;
Agaete (Gran Canaria) - Santa Cruz de Tenerife (Tenerife), journey 60 minutes;
Los Cristianos (Tenerife) - San Sebastián de la Gomera (La Gomera), journey 35 minu
Santa Cruz de La Palma (La Palma) - Los Cristianos (Tenerife).

Naviera Armas **2016 serv**

Huelva - Arrecife (Lanzarote) - Las Palmas (Gran Canaria) - Santa Cruz (Tenerife): 1 sailing per week.

Inter-Island services

Corralejo (Fuerteventura) - Playa Blanca (Lanzarote)	5–6 sailings da
Las Palmas (Gran Canaria) - Arrecife (Lanzarote)	5 sailings per w
Las Palmas (Gran Canaria) - Morro Jable (Fuerteventura)	1 sailing daily.
Las Palmas (Gran Canaria) - Puerto del Rosario (Fuerteventura)	3 sailings per w
Las Palmas (Gran Canaria) - Santa Cruz (Tenerife)	2–3 sailings da
Los Cristianos (Tenerife) - San Sebastián (La Gomera)	1–3 sailings da
Los Cristianos (Tenerife) - Valverde (El Hierro)	3 sailings per w
Santa Cruz (Tenerife) - Arrecife (Lanzarote)	4 sailings per w

Sailing frequencies may change

Trasmediterranea **2016 ser**

CÁDIZ - GRAN CANARIA - TENERIFE - PALMA - LANZAROTE - CÁDIZ

	arrive	*depart*
Cádiz	1230①	1700②
Lanzarote (Arrecife)	2300③	2359③
Gran Canaria (Las Palmas)	0800④	1300④
Tenerife (Santa Cruz)	1700④	2330④
Palma (Santa Cruz)	0800⑤	1600⑤
Tenerife (Santa Cruz)	2130⑤	2330⑤
Gran Canaria (Las Palmas)	0800⑥	1400⑥
Lanzarote (Arrecife)	2330⑥	0100⑦

2520 CIVITAVECCHIA - BARCELONA

Grimaldi Lines **2016 ser**

Civitavecchia		Barcelona		Barcelona		Civitavecchia	
2215	→	1815	①②③④⑤⑥	2215	→	1845	①②③④⑤⑥

2530 CIVITAVECCHIA - SICILY - TÛNIS

Grandi Navi Veloci **Service to September 30, 2**

Civitavecchia		Palermo		Tûnis		Palermo		Civitavecch
Until June 30								
2000⑤	→	0900⑥/1100⑥	→	2100⑥/2300⑥	→	0900⑦/1800⑦‡	→	0900①
July 1 - September 15								
1800⑤	→	0700⑥/1100⑥	→	2100⑥/2300⑥	→	0900⑦/1900⑦	→	1000①
2100①③	→	1000②④		...		2100②④	→	1200③⑤
September 16 - 30								
1800⑤	→	0700⑥/1100⑥	→	2100⑥/2300⑥	→	0900⑦/1900⑦	→	1000①

‡ – Depart 2000 June 19, 26.

Grimaldi Lines **2016 serv**

Civitavecchia		Trapani		Tûnis		Trapani		Civitavecch
1730③	→		→	1400④/1700②	→		→	1430③

2535 CIVITAVECCHIA - TERMINI IMERESE

Grandi Navi Veloci **Service to June 16, 2**

Civitavecchia		Termini Imerese	
2030①③	→	1130②④	Mar. 2 - June 15.
Termini Imerese		**Civitavecchia**	
0200③	→	1700③	Mar. 2 - June 15.
2200④	→	1300⑤	Mar. 3 - June 16.

2537 GENOVA - BARCELONA

Grandi Navi Veloci **Service to September 30, 2**

Genova		Barcelona		Barcelona		Genova	
1300	→	0700	See note **K**.	1300	→	0730	See note **N**.
1800	→	1100	See note **L**.	2300	→	1730	See note **P**.
2000	→	1300	See note **M**.				

K – Mar. 10, 24, Apr. 7, 21, May 5, 19; ④ June 2 - Sept. 29.
L – Mar. 5, 19, Apr. 2, 16, 30, May 14, 28; ⑥ June 11 - Sept. 24.
M – Mar. 14, 28, Apr. 11, 25, May 9, 23, June 6.
N – Mar. 4, 9, 18, 23, 27, Apr. 1, 6, 15, 20, 29, May 4, 13, 18, 27, June 1; ③⑤ June 10 - Sept. 30.
P – Mar. 13, 27 Apr. 10, 24, May 8, 22, June 5.

2547 GENOVA - PALERMO

Grandi Navi Veloci Journey 21 hours **Service to September 30, 2**

From Genova: 2100 **P**, 2300 **Q**. From Palermo: 2100 **P**, 2300 **T**, 2359 **V**.

P – Daily June 13 - Sept. 10 (not June 19, Aug. 15).
Q – ①②③④⑤⑥ Mar. 1 - June 11, Sept. 12 - 30.
T – ①②③④⑤ Mar. 1 - June 10; ①②③④⑤⑥ Sept. 12 - 30.
V – ⑥ Mar. 5 - June 11.

For international shipping maps – see pages 538 - 540

GENOVA - TANJAH (TANGIERS) MED 2554

andi Navi Veloci — Service to October 6, 2016

enova		Tanjah Med		Tanjah Med		Genova	
300	→	1130	④ June 2 - Oct. 6.	2300	→	0730	①③ June 8 - Oct. 5.
800	→	1630	⑥ June 11 - Oct. 1.				

Tanjah (Tangiers) Med port is located approximately 45 km east of Tanjah. A connecting 🚌 operates between Tanjah Med and Tanjah.

All sailings via Barcelona (see Table **2508**)

GENOVA - TÛNIS 2555

andi Navi Veloci Departure times vary. Journey 24 hours — Service to Sept. 30, 2016

m Genova: ③⑥ Mar. 2 - June 11; ①③⑥ June 13 - Aug. 10; ②⑤⑦ Aug. 14 - Sept. 11; ③⑥ Sept. 14 - 28.
m Tûnis: ④⑦ Mar. 3 - June 12; ②④⑦ June 14 - Aug. 11; ①③⑥ Aug. 15 - Sept. 12; ④⑦ Sept. 15 - 29.

MARSEILLE - ORAN 2558

TMV Journey 24 - 25 hours — Service to September 30, 2016

m Marseille: Feb. 10, 24, Mar. 9, 23, Apr. 13, 27, May 10, 20, 31, June 7, 19, 26, July 4, 9, 14, 19, 24, Aug. 1, 5, 12, 18, 25, Sept. 1, 8, 16, 23, 29.
m Oran: Feb. 7, 21, Mar. 5, 20, Apr. 9, 24, May 8, 18, 29, June 9, 21, 28, July 2, 9, 14, 18, 23, 28, Aug. 3, 12, 19, 26, 30, Sept. 6, 9, 17, 24, 30.

Departure times vary.

Other services operate from Marseille to Annâbah and Sakîkdah.

GULF OF NAPOLI (including Gulf of Salerno and Ponziane Islands) 2560

lauro — 2016 services

oli Beverello - Forio: up to 5 sailings daily (summer only). Sailings via Ischia in winter.
oli Beverello or Mergellina - Ischia: up to 15 sailings daily.
oli Beverello - Sorrento: 5 sailings daily.
erno - Capri: daily sailing.
rento - Capri: up to 8 sailings daily (summer only).

Additional infrequent services to Capri operate (summer only) from Ischia, Castellammare di Stábia, Positano and Amalfi.

Sailing frequencies may change

remar — 2016 services

oli - Capri: 3 sailings daily by catamaran, 3 sailings by ship (4/3 in summer).
oli - Ischia: 5 sailings daily by catamaran, 7 sailings by ship (6/8 in summer).
oli - Procida: 7 sailings daily by catamaran, 6 sailings by ship (8/7 in summer).
zuoli - Procida: 1 sailing by catamaran, 5 sailings by ship (1/4 in summer).
cida - Ischia: 5 sailings daily by catamaran, 7 - 10 sailings by ship.
rento - Capri: 4 sailings daily by catamaran.

dmar — 2016 services

oli - Ischia: 3 - 5 sailings daily.
hia - Pozzuoli: up to 8 sailings daily.

Additional infrequent services operate between Pozzuoli, Procida and Ischia.

vigazione Libera del Golfo by *Linea Jet* — 2016 services

oli (Molo Beverello) - Capri: up to 10 sailings daily (more in summer). Journey 40 minutes.
rento - Capri: 6 sailings daily (more in summer). Journey 25 minutes.
dditional services operate (summer only) between Castellammare di Stábia and Capri.

AV Journey 40 minutes — 2016 services

oli (Beverello) - Capri: 0700, 0805, 0930, 1135, 1240, 1440, 1630, 1915.
ri - Napoli (Beverello): 0650, 0805, 0910, 1035, 1240, 1340, 1630, 1810.

rento - Capri: 0715①②③④⑤⑥, 0830, 0950, 1145, 1330, 1550, 1705.
ri - Sorrento: 0800①②③④⑤⑥, 0855, 1120, 1300, 1515, 1635, 1740.

CORSICA 2565

Sailings from mainland FRANCE (map page 171)

RSEILLE - AJACCIO — Service to November 5, 2016

ritima Ferries — Journey 9 - 12 hours

m Marseille:
Uneven dates: Feb., Apr., May, Aug., Nov.; even dates: Mar., June, July, Sept., Oct.
m Ajaccio:
Uneven dates: Mar., June, July, Sept., Oct.; even dates: Feb., Apr., May, Aug., Nov.
lings depart 1900 from Marseille and Ajaccio. Additional departures available in summer.

RSEILLE - BASTIA — Service to November 5, 2016

ritima Ferries — Journey 10 - 13 hours

m Marseille:
Uneven dates: Mar., June, July, Sept., Oct.; even dates: Feb., Apr., May, Aug., Nov.
m Bastia:
Uneven dates: Feb., Apr., May, Aug., Nov.; even dates: Mar., June, July, Sept., Oct.
lings depart 1900 from Marseille, 1830 (1900⑥) from Bastia. Additional departures available in summer.

RSEILLE - L'ÎLE ROUSSE — Service to November 5, 2016

ritima Ferries Departure times vary — Journey 8 - 11½ hours

m Marseille: ①⑤ Feb. 1 - 19; ①③⑤ Feb. 22 - Mar. 4; ①⑤ Mar. 7 - Apr. 8; ①③⑤ Apr. 11 - Nov. 4 (also Mar. 30; not Mar. 28).
m L'Île Rousse: ②⑥ Feb. 2 - 20; ②④⑥ Feb. 23 - Mar. 5; ②⑥ Mar. 8 - Apr. 9; ②④⑥ Apr. 12 - Nov. 5 (also Mar. 31; not Mar. 29).

CORSICA continued 2565

MARSEILLE - PORTO VECCHIO — Service to November 5, 2016

Maritima Ferries Departure times vary — Journey 14 hours

From Marseille: ③⑤ Feb. 3 - 12; ①③⑤ Feb. 15 - Mar. 4; ③ Mar. 9 - 23; ①③⑤ Apr. 6 - Nov. 4 (also Mar. 28).
From Porto Vecchio: ④⑥ Feb. 4 - 13; ②④⑥ Feb. 16 - Mar. 5; ④ Mar. 10 - 24; ②④⑥ Apr. 7 - Nov. 5 (also Mar. 29).

MARSEILLE - PROPRIANO — 2016 service

Maritima Ferries Departure times vary — Journey 9½ - 12½ hours

From Marseille and Propriano: occasional sailings.

NICE - AJACCIO — 2016 service

Corsica Ferries — Journey 4½ - 9 hours

From Nice and Ajaccio: Apr. - June: 5 – 11 sailings per month; July - Aug.: 14 – 19 sailings per month; Sept.: 7 sailings per month.
Most sailings by day, departure times vary.

NICE - BASTIA — 2016 service

Corsica Ferries Journey 5 - 6 hours

From Nice and Bastia: 3 – 5 sailings per week (daily July / Aug.).
Most sailings by day, departure times vary.

Moby Lines

Nice		Bastia	
1100	→	1830	Aug. 16 - Sept. 25.
2230	→	0730	Daily June 1 - Aug. 14; ③⑤ Sept. 28 - Oct. 28; ⑤ Nov. 4 - Dec. 16.
Bastia		**Nice**	
1100	→	1830	June 2 - Aug. 14.
2230	→	0730	Daily Aug. 15 - Sept. 25; ④⑥ Sept. 29 - Oct. 29; ⑥ Nov. 5 - Dec. 17.

NICE - CALVI — 2016 service

Corsica Ferries Journey 4 - 5½ hours

From Nice and Calvi: late-May - early-Sept.: 5 – 7 sailings per week.
Most sailings by day, departure times vary.

NICE - L'ÎLE ROUSSE — 2016 service

Corsica Ferries Journey 5 - 5½ hours

From Nice and L'Île Rousse: May - June: occasional sailings; July - Aug.: 2 - 3 sailings per week; Sept.: occasional sailings.
Most sailings by day, departure times vary.

TOULON - AJACCIO — 2016 service

Corsica Ferries Journey 6 - 10 hours

From Toulon and Ajaccio: Apr. - Sept.: 1 – 2 sailings daily (including daily night sailing).
Departure times vary.

TOULON - BASTIA — 2016 service

Corsica Ferries Journey 9 - 10 hours

From Toulon and Bastia: Apr. - Sept.: 1 – 2 sailings daily.
Most sailings by night. Departure times vary.

TOULON - L'ÎLE ROUSSE — 2016 service

Corsica Ferries Journey 6 - 7 hours

From Toulon and L'Île Rousse: Apr. - May: 1 - 2 sailings per week; June: 2 - 3 sailings per week; July - Aug.: 3 – 6 sailings per week; Sept.: 1 – 3 sailings per week.
All sailings by day, departure times vary.

Other sailings available from Nice and Toulon to Porto Vecchio, and Toulon to Calvi.

Sailings from ITALY

GENOVA - BASTIA — 2016 service

Moby Lines

Genova		Bastia		Bastia		Genova	
2200	→	0800	May 12 - Sept. 29.	1100	→	1730	May 13 - Sept. 30.

LIVORNO - BASTIA — 2016 service

Corsica Ferries Journey 4 hours (night sailings 7½ hours)

From Livorno and Bastia: Apr. - June: 1 – 2 sailings daily; July - Sept: up to 3 sailings daily.
Most sailings by day, departure times vary.

Moby Lines

Livorno		Bastia	
0800	→	1205	May 26 - Sept. 30.
1400	→	1805	June 18 - Sept. 11.
2100	→	0600	④⑤⑥⑦ July 14 - Sept. 4 (not July 21 - 24).
Bastia		**Livorno**	
0800	→	1205	June 19 - Sept. 11.
1400	→	1805	May 26 - Sept. 30.
2100	→	0600	④⑤⑥⑦ July 14 - Sept. 4 (also Sept. 11; not July 21 - 24).

PIOMBINO - BASTIA — 2016 service

Corsica Ferries Journey 2½ hours. Departure times vary.

From Piombino: ③④ June 29 - Sept. 1.
From Bastia: ④⑤ June 30 - Sept. 2.

SAVONA - BASTIA — 2016 service

Corsica Ferries Journey 6 - 10 hours. Departure times vary.

From Savona and Bastia: Apr. - May: 2 – 4 sailings per week; June: 1 – 2 sailings daily; July - Aug.: 2 – 3 sailings daily; Sept.: up to 3 sailings daily.

Other sailings available from Livorno and Savona to L'Île Rousse.

2566 CORSICA - SARDINIA (map page 287)

BONIFACIO - SANTA TERESA DI GALLURA — 2016 service

Moby Lines Journey 60 minutes — **Mar. 24 - Sept. 30 only**
From Bonifacio: 0830, 1200, 1700, 2000.
From Santa Teresa di Gallura: 0700, 1000, 1500, 1830.

Saremar Journey 1 hour
From Bonifacio and Santa Teresa di Gallura: up to 3 sailings per day.

PORTO VECCHIO - GOLFO ARANCI — 2016 service

Corsica Ferries / Sardinia Ferries
From Porto Vecchio and Golfo Aranci: June - Sept.: up to 3 sailings per week.

2570 ITALIAN ISLAND SERVICES (map page 287)
(Egadi, Eolie, Pantelleria, Pelagie and Ustica Islands)

Alilauro — **May 28 - September 11, 2016**
Napoli Mergellina - Stromboli - Panarea - Salina - Vulcano - Lipari and v.v.:
2–3 sailings per week (daily July 1 - Sept. 5).
Sailing frequencies may change

Siremar — 2016 services
NAPOLI - MILAZZO via Stromboli, Ginostra, Panarea, Lipari and Vulcano.

Napoli		Milazzo	Milazzo		Napoli	
2000②⑤	→	1215③⑥	1350①④	→	0800②⑤	Not Apr. 1 - Oct. 31.
			1430①④	→	0800②⑤	Apr. 1 - Oct. 31.

OTHER SERVICES:
Inter-island sailings operate, also from mainland Sicily to the islands. Services operate to differing frequencies (additional sailings in summer).

EOLIE ISLANDS:
Alicudi to Filicudi, Lipari, Milazzo, Rinella, Salina and Vulcano.
Filicudi to Alicudi, Lipari, Milazzo, Rinella, Salina and Vulcano.
Ginostra to Lipari, Milazzo, and Panarea.
Lipari to Alicudi, Filicudi, Ginostra, Milazzo, Panarea, Rinella, Salina, Stromboli and Vulcano.
Milazzo to Alicudi, Filicudi, Ginostra, Lipari, Panarea, Rinella, Salina, Stromboli and Vulcano.
Panarea to Filicudi, Ginostra, Lipari, Milazzo, Rinella, Salina, Stromboli and Vulcano.
Rinella to Alicudi, Filicudi, Lipari, Milazzo, Panarea, Salina, Stromboli and Vulcano.
Salina to Alicudi, Filicudi, Lipari, Milazzo, Panarea, Rinella, Stromboli and Vulcano.
Stromboli to Alicudi, Filicudi, Lipari, Milazzo, Panarea, Rinella, Salina and Vulcano.
Vulcano to Alicudi, Filicudi, Lipari, Milazzo, Panarea, Rinella, Salina and Stromboli.

EGADI ISLANDS:
Favignana to Levanzo, Marettimo and Trapani.
Levanzo to Favignana, Marettimo, and Trapani.
Marettimo to Favignana, Levanzo and Trapani.
Trapani to Favignana, Levanzo and Marettimo.

PANTELLERIA ISLAND:
Trapani - Pantelleria and v.v.

PELAGIE ISLANDS:
Porto Empedocle (Agrigento) - Linosa - Lampedusa and v.v.

USTICA ISLAND:
Palermo - Ustica and v.v.

Ustica Lines by hydrofoil — 2016 services
EGADI & EOLIAN ISLANDS and USTICA
The Sicilian ports of Messina, Milazzo, Palermo and Trapani are linked by island-hopping services serving Alicudi, Favignana, Filicudi, Levanzo, Lipari, Marettimo, Panarea, Rinella, Salina, Stromboli, Ustica and Vulcano.
Services operate to differing frequencies (additional sailings in summer).

MILAZZO - VULCANO by hydrofoil Journey 50 minutes
Until June 19
Depart Milazzo: 0730, 0930, 1500, 1815①②③④⑤⑦, 1910.
Depart Vulcano: 0815, 1225, 1355, 1620, 1750①②③④⑤⑦.
June 20 - September 10
Depart Milazzo: 0630, 0800, 0940, 1230, 1430, 1630, 1930.
Depart Vulcano: 0740, 1035, 1245, 1405, 1755, 1930, 1940.

MILAZZO - PALERMO by hydrofoil
Journey 2½ hours

Milazzo		Palermo		Milazzo	
0630	→	1145/1500	→	2020	Daily June 20 - Sept. 10.

2580 LIVORNO - BARCELONA - TANJAH (TANGIERS) MED

Grimaldi Lines — 2016 service

Livorno		Barcelona		Tanjah Med		Barcelona		Livorno
2330⑥	→	2000/2359⑦	→	1030/1700②	→	2000/2359③	→	2030④

Tanjah (Tangiers) Med port is located approximately 45km east of Tanjah.
A connecting 🚌 operates between Tanjah Med and Tanjah.

2595 MÁLAGA - MELILLA

Trasmediterranea Journey 6-8 hours — 2016 service
From Málaga: 0030②, 1430②③④⑤⑥, 2300⑦.
From Melilla: 0030②③④⑤⑥⑦, 1400①.
Departure times may vary at peak times
Subject to alteration during Easter and Xmas/New Year periods
Also daily sailings by fast ferry in summer (journey 4 hours).

2602 MARSEILLE - AL-JAZÂ'IR (ALGIERS)

ENTMV — Service to September 30, 2

Marseille		al-Jazâ'ir	
1200	→	0800	July 9, 11, 13, 16, 18, 23, 25, 27, 30, Aug. 6, 8, 13, 15, 18, 20, 24, 27, 29, 31, Sept. 3, 5, 19, 22, 24, 28.
1200	→	0900	⑥ Feb. 6 - June 4.
1400	→	0900	Sept. 10.
1500	→	1000	June 30, July 2, 4, 20, Aug. 1, 3, Sept. 8, 17.
1500	→	1100	June 11, 18, 25.
1600	→	1100	June 27.
al-Jazâ'ir		**Marseille**	
1200	→	0800	Feb. 1, 22, May 23, 29, July 8, 10, 12, 16, 17, 19, 24, 26, 30, 31, Aug. 7, 11, 14, 16, 19, 23, 26, 28, 30, Sept. 2, 4, 6, 23.
1200	→	0900	Sept. 20, 26, 29.
1200	→	1000	① Feb. 8 - May 16 (also Sept. 16; not Feb. 22).
1400	→	1000	Sept. 9.
1500	→	1000	June 26, 28.
1500	→	1100	July 1, 3, 21, Aug. 2, 4.
1500	→	1200	June 13, 20.
1500	→	1300	June 6.

Other services operate from Marseille to Annâbah and Sakîkdah.

2615 MARSEILLE - TÛNIS

Compagnie Tunisienne de Navigation — 2016 serv
Departure times vary. Journey 20-24 hours

Until June 9
From Marseille: 1200④. From Tûnis: 1200②.

June 10 - October 1 (departure times vary)
From Marseille: June 12, 16, 18, 21, 23, 25, 28, 30, July 2, 5, 7, 9, 12, 14, 16, 18, 21, 23, 26, 28, 30, Aug. 2, 4, 6, 8, 10, 13, 15, 17, 19, 21, 22, 24, 26, 28, 30, Sept. 2, 4, 7, 9, 11, 13, 16, 18, 22, 25, 29.
From Tûnis: June 11, 14, 17, 20, 22, 24, 27, 29, July 1, 4, 6, 8, 11, 13, 15, 17, 20, 22, 25, 27, 29, Aug. 1, 3, 5, 7, 9, 12, 14, 16, 18, 20, 21, 23, 25, 27, 29, Sept. 1, 3, 6, 8, 10, 1 15, 17, 20, 24, 27, Oct. 1.

October 2 - 31
From Marseille: 1200④. From Tûnis: 1200②.

2618 MGARR (Gozo) - CIRKEWWA (Malta)

Gozo Channel Co. Journey 25 minutes — 2016 serv

October 26 - June 12
From Mgarr: 0130, 0330, 0500, 0600, 0630, 0700, 0730, 0815, 0900, 0945, 1030, 111 1200, 1245, 1330, 1415, 1500, 1545, 1630, 1715, 1800, 1845, 1930, 2015, 2100, 223 2345.
From Cirkewwa: 0200, 0400, 0545, 0630, 0700, 0730, 0815, 1900, 0945, 1030, 1115, 120 1245, 1330, 1415, 1500, 1545, 1630, 1715, 1800, 1845, 1930, 2015, 2100, 2135, 230 0020.

June 13 - October 23 (subject to confirmation)
From Mgarr: 0045, 0200, 0330, 0500, 0600, 0630, 0700, 0730, 0815, 0900, 0945, 103 1115, 1200, 1245, 1330, 1415, 1500, 1545, 1630, 1715, 1800, 1845, 1930, 2015, 210 2145, 2315.
From Cirkewwa: 0120, 0230, 0400, 0545, 0630, 0700, 0730, 0815, 0900, 0945, 1030, 111 1200, 1245, 1330, 1415, 1500, 1545, 1630, 1715, 1800, 1845, 1930, 2015, 2100, 214 2220, 2350.

2625 NAPOLI - PALERMO

Grandi Navi Veloci — Service to September 30, 2

Napoli		Palermo		Palermo		Napoli	
0900	→	1930	See note N.	0900	→	1930	See note N.
2000	→	0630	See note P.	2000	→	0630	See note P.
2100	→	0730	See note N.	2100	→	0730	See note N.

N – July 23, 29-31, Aug. 4-6, 8, 11, 13-15, 19-21, 26-28.
P – Daily Mar. 1 - July 28, Aug. 29 - Sept. 30 (also Aug. 1-3, 7, 9, 10, 12, 16-18, 22-2 not Mar. 6, July 23).

Tirrenia — 2016 serv

Napoli		Palermo	Palermo		Napoli
2015	→	0630	2015	→	0630

2630 NAPOLI - TRAPANI

Ustica Lines by hydrofoil — July 2 - September 3, 2
(No winter servi
⑥: Napoli 1500 → Ustica 1905/1925 → Favignana 2125/2135 → Trapani 2200.
⑥: Trapani 0615 → Favignana 0635/0640 → Ustica 0840/0900 → Napoli 1315.

2661 SALERNO - PALERMO - TÛNIS

Grimaldi Lines — 2016 serv

Salerno		Palermo		Tûnis		Palermo		Salerno
1200①	→	2300①/0100②	→	1430②/1730④	→	0730⑤/1000⑤	→	2000⑤
2330⑤	→	1000⑥/1200⑥	→	2300⑥/0001⑦	→	1530⑦/1900⑦	→	0700①

SARDINIA 2675

Sailings from FRANCE

RSEILLE - PORTO TORRES — 2015 service

aritima Ferries — Journey 16 - 19 hours

om Marseille: 1800 ③ July 1 - Aug. 5.
om Porto Torres: 1430 ④ July 2 - Aug. 6.

E - GOLFO ARANCI — 2016 service

rdinia Ferries — Journey 16 hours

om Nice and Golfo Aranci: up to 3 sailings per week.
Most sailings by night, departure times vary.

Other sailings available from Toulon to Golfo Aranci and Porto Torres.

Sailings from mainland ITALY (map page 287)

ITAVECCHIA - ARBATAX — Service to September 30, 2016

renia

tavecchia		Arbatax	
1900	→	0500	③⑤ May 18 - July 22; ①③ July 25 - Aug. 24; ③⑤ Aug. 31 - Sept. 30.
rbatax		**Civitavecchia**	
2359	→	1030	③⑦ May 18 - July 24; ②④ July 26 - Aug. 25; ③⑦ Aug. 31 - Sept. 28.

ITAVECCHIA - CAGLIARI — Service to September 30, 2016

renia

tavecchia		Cagliari	
1900	→	1030	③⑤ May 25 - July 22; ①③ July 25 - Aug. 24; ③⑤ Aug. 31 - Sept. 30.
2000	→	0845	①②④⑥⑦ May 17 - July 24; ②④⑤⑥ July 26 - Aug. 27; ①②④⑥⑦ Aug. 29 - Sept. 29 (also Aug. 14; not Aug. 6).
2330	→	1215	⑦ July 31 - Aug. 28 (also Aug. 6; not Aug. 14).
agliari		**Civitavecchia**	
1900	→	1030	③⑦ May 18 - July 24; ②④ July 26 - Aug. 25; ③⑦ Aug. 31 - Sept. 28.
2000	→	0845	①②④⑤⑥ May 16 - July 23; ①③⑤⑥⑦ July 25 - Aug. 28; ①②④⑤⑥ Aug. 29 - Sept. 30.

ITAVECCHIA - OLBIA — 2016 service

oby Lines Journey 5 – 5½ hours (night sailings 8 hours). Departure times vary.

om Civitavecchia and Olbia: Jan. - Mar.: 1 sailing daily; Apr.: 1 - 2 sailings daily; May: 1 sailing daily; June - July: up to 3 sailings daily; Aug.: 2 - 4 sailings daily; Sept.: up to 3 sailings daily; Oct. - Dec.: 1 sailing daily.

renia Journey 5 hours (night sailings 8 hours)

om Civitavecchia and Olbia: night sailing every day (d.2230). Additional day sailings in summer.

ITAVECCHIA - PORTO TORRES — 2016 service

rimaldi Lines

tavecchia		P. Torres	
2215	→	0530	②⑥ Feb. 1 - Mar. 22; ②⑤⑥ Mar. 29 - Apr. 30; ①④⑤⑥ May 2 - June 4; ①②④⑤⑥ June 6 - Sept. 17; ②⑥ Sept. 19 - Dec. 27.
. Torres		**Civitavecchia**	
1130	→	1845	③⑦ Feb. 1 - Mar. 20; ③⑥⑦ Mar. 30 - Apr. 24; ②③⑥⑦ Apr. 26 - June 5; ②③⑤ June 7 - Sept. 18; ③⑦ Sept. 20 - Dec. 28.
1230	→	1915	⑥⑦ June 11 - Sept. 18.

NOVA - ARBATAX — 2016 service

renia — No winter service

enova		Arbatax	
2130	→	1300	①⑥ July 18 - Aug. 13; ①⑤ Aug. 15 - Sept. 2.
rbatax		**Genova**	
1400	→	0730	②⑦ July 19 - Aug. 14; ②⑥ Aug. 16 - Sept. 3.

NOVA - OLBIA — 2016 service

oby Lines Journey 9 – 12 hours. Departure times vary.

om Genova and Olbia: Jan. - mid-May: 3 sailings per week; mid-May - end-May: 1 sailing daily; June - July: 2 - 3 sailings daily; Aug: 2 - 4 sailings daily; Sept.: 2 - 3 sailings daily; Oct.: 1 sailing daily; Nov. - Dec.: 3 sailings per week.

renia — Service to September 30, 2016

enova		Olbia	
0900	→	2000	③④⑦ Aug. 17 - Sept. 4.
2030	→	0845	①③⑤ May 23 - July 15, Sept. 5 - 23 (also Sept. 25, 27, 29).
2130	→	0945	①③④⑤⑥ July 18 - Aug. 13; ①⑤ Aug. 15 - Sept. 2.
Olbia		**Genova**	
0900	→	2000	④⑤⑥ July 21 - Aug. 13.
2030	→	0845	②④⑥ May 24 - July 16, Sept. 6 - 24 (also Sept. 26, 28, 30).
2130	→	0945	②⑦ July 19 - Aug. 14; ②③④⑥⑦ Aug. 16 - Sept. 4.

NOVA - PORTO TORRES — 2016 service

randi Navi Veloci Journey 10 – 12 hours

om Genova: depart 2030: ①③⑤ Mar. 23 - May 27; even dates June 2 - July 30; uneven dates Aug. 1 - 31; even dates Sept. 2 - 16 (also May 29, 31, Sept. 19, 21, 23).
om Porto Torres: depart 2030: ②④⑥ Mar. 24 - May 28; uneven dates June 1 - July 31; even dates Aug. 2 - 30; uneven dates Sept. 1 - 17 (also May 30, Sept. 20, 22, 24).

renia — Service to September 30, 2016

Genova		Porto Torres	Porto Torres		Genova
2030	→	0830	2030	→	0830

ORNO - GOLFO ARANCI — 2016 service

ardinia Ferries Journey 6½ – 10 hours. Departure times vary.

om Livorno and Golfo Aranci: Apr. - May: daily sailings; June: 1 - 2 sailings daily; July - Sept.: 2 – 3 sailings daily.

SARDINIA continued 2675

LIVORNO - OLBIA — 2016 service

Moby Lines Journey 6½ hours (night sailings 8 hours).

From Livorno and Olbia: Jan. - May: 1 sailing daily (by night); June - mid-Sept.: day and night sailings; mid-Sept. - Dec.: 1 sailing daily (by night).

Departure times vary (most night sailings d.2100, day sailings d. 0800).

NAPOLI - CAGLIARI — Service to September 30, 2016

Tirrenia

Napoli		Cagliari	
1800	→	0730	② July 19 - Aug. 30.
1900	→	0830	②④ until July 14; ⑤ July 22 - Sept. 2; ②④ Sept. 6 - 29.
Cagliari		**Napoli**	
1900	→	0830	①③ until July 13; ①④ July 18 - Sept. 1; ①③ Sept. 5 - 28.

PIOMBINO - OLBIA — 2016 service

Moby Lines

Piombino		Olbia		Olbia		Piombino	
1430	→	1930	See note **Q**.	0815	→	1330	See note **Q**.

Q – June 1, 4, 5, 11, 12, 16 - 19, 25 - 27, July 2 - 4, 7 - 11, 15 - 18, 22 - 25; ①③④⑥⑦ July 27 - Sept. 11; Sept. 17, 18.

Sailings from SICILY (map page 287)

PALERMO - CAGLIARI — Service to September 30, 2016

Tirrenia

Palermo		Cagliari	
1930	→	0730	⑥ until July 16; ⑦ July 24 - Sept. 4; ⑥ Sept. 10 - 24.
2359	→	1200	③ July 20 - Aug. 31.
Cagliari		**Palermo**	
1030	→	2230	③ July 20 - Aug. 31.
1930	→	0730	⑤ until July 15; ⑥ July 23 - Sept. 3; ⑤ Sept. 9 - 30.

Sailings from SPAIN

BARCELONA - PORTO TORRES — 2016 service

Grimaldi Lines

Barcelona		Porto Torres	Porto Torres		Barcelona
2215①②④⑤⑥	→	1030②③⑤⑥⑦	0630②③⑤⑥⑦	→	1815②③⑤⑥⑦

SÈTE - AN-NADÛR (NADOR) 2678

Grandi Navi Veloci Journey 28 – 30 hours — Service to September 30, 2016

Departure times vary.

From Sète: Mar. 9, 17, 26, Apr. 3, 12, 20, 29, May 7, 16, 25, June 2, 10; ③ June 15 - Sept. 28.
From an-Nadûr: Mar. 2, 11, 19, 28, Apr. 5, 14, 22, May 1, 9, 18, 27, June 4, 12, 20; ⑤ June 24 - Sept. 30.

SÈTE - TANJAH (TANGIERS) MED 2680

Grandi Navi Veloci Journey ±36 hours — Service to September 30, 2016

Departure times vary.

From Sète: Mar. 5, 9, 13, 17, 22, 26, 30, Apr. 3, 8, 12, 16, 20, 25, 29, May 3, 7, 12, 16, 20, 29, June 6, 13, 14, 19, 20, 26, 27, July 3, 4, 10, 11, 17, 18, 24, 25, 31, Aug. 1, 7, 8, 14, 15, 21, 22, 28, 29, Sept. 4, 5, 11, 12, 18, 19, 25, 26.
From Tanjah Med: Mar. 3, 7, 11, 15, 20, 24, 28, Apr. 1, 6, 10, 14, 18, 23, 27, May 1, 5, 10, 14, 18, 22, 31, June 8, 11, 16, 18, 21, 25, 28, July 2, 5, 9, 12, 16, 19, 23, 26, 30, Aug. 2, 6, 9, 13, 16, 20, 22, 27, 29, Sept. 3, 5, 10, 12, 17, 19, 24, 26.

Tanjah (Tangiers) Med port is located approximately 45 km east of Tanjah.
A connecting 🚌 operates between Tanjah Med and Tanjah.

VALLETTA - CATANIA 2690

Virtu Ferries by catamaran Journey 4 hours — 2016 service **(No service Dec. 25)**

From Valletta and Catania: Apr. - May: 4 sailings per week; June - Sept: 5 - 6 sailings per week (daily mid-July - mid-Aug.); Oct. - Dec.: 3 sailings per week.

Departure times vary.

All sailings by catamaran Valletta - Pozzallo and v.v., then by 🚌 to/from Catania (see also Table **2694**).

Subject to alteration during Xmas/New Year period

VALLETTA - POZZALLO 2694

Virtu Ferries by catamaran Journey 1½ hours — 2016 service **(No service Dec. 25)**

From Valletta and Pozzallo: Apr. - Dec.: sailings on ①②③⑤⑥⑦ (daily mid-July - mid-Aug.). 1 – 2 sailings per day, departure times vary.

Subject to alteration during Xmas/New Year period

2695 STRETTO DI MESSINA

MESSINA - REGGIO DI CALABRIA — 2016 service

Ustica Lines **by hydrofoil** Journey 30 minutes *Times may vary*

From Messina:
①-⑤: 0600, 0700, 0730, 0830, 0930, 1025, 1130, 1305, 1340, 1430, 1505, 1600, 1630, 1740, 1905, 2015.
⑥⑦: 0800, 0930, 1100, 1340, 1530, 1700.

From Reggio di Calabria:
①-⑤: 0645, 0745, 0810, 0910, 0940, 1105, 1210, 1345, 1420, 1510, 1545, 1640, 1710, 1820, 1945, 2055.
⑥⑦: 0840, 1010, 1140, 1420, 1610, 1740.

MESSINA - VILLA SAN GIOVANNI — 2016 service

Bluferries **by hydrofoil** Journey 20 minutes

From Messina:
①-⑤: 0615, 0740, 0925, 1120, 1255, 1420, 1650, 1810, 1915.
⑥⑦: 0615, 0925, 1120, 1420, 1810, 1915.

From Villa San Giovanni:
①-⑤: 0710, 0810, 1000, 1210, 1335, 1510, 1735, 1845, 2020.
⑥⑦: 0810, 1000, 1210, 1510, 1845, 2020.

2699 OTHER SERVICES

Corsica Ferries **by fast ferry** — **2016 serv**
(No winter servi

From Piombino and Portoferraio (Elba): June - Sept.: up to 7 sailings daily; journey time 3 minutes.

Moby Lines — **2016 serv**
(No service Dec.

Piombino - Portoferraio (Elba): up to 15 sailings daily in high-summer, less frequent at oth times; journey time 1 hour.

Toremar — **2016 servi**

Services operate from Piombino to Cavo, Pianosa, Portoferraio and Rio Marina; from Livorr to Capraia and Gorgona; from Porto Santo Stefano to Isola del Giglio.

ADRIATIC / EASTERN MEDITERRANEAN / BLACK SEA

2715 ANCONA - PÁTRA via Kérkira and Igumenítsa

Anek Lines / Superfast Ferries — **2016 service**

January 1 - June 30 and September 11 - December 31

Ancona		Igumenítsa		Pátra
1330③④⑤	→	0800④⑤⑥	→	1430④⑤⑥
1630⑥⑦	→	0900⑦①	→	1430⑦①
1900②	→	1430③	→	2100③

Pátra		Igumenítsa		Ancona
1730⑤⑥	→	2300⑤⑥	→	1330⑥⑦
1730①②③④	→	2359①②③④	→	1630②③④⑤

July 1 - September 10

Ancona		Kérkira		Igumenítsa		Pátra
1330	→	→	→	0600	→	1130
1630⑥	→	→	→	0900⑦	→	1430⑦
1630②④	→	0800③⑤	→	0930③⑤	→	1500③⑤

Pátra		Igumenítsa		Kérkira		Ancona
1430	→	2000	→	→	→	1030
1730⑤	→	2300⑤	→	→	→	1330⑥
1730①③	→	2300①③	→	0030②④	→	1400②④

🚌 connection Pátra - Pireás - Athína and v.v. operates most days in summer.

For international journeys only

Minoan Lines — **2016 service**

January 1 - July 31 and August 30 - December 31

Ancona		Igumenítsa		Pátra	Pátra		Igumenítsa		Ancona
1730①	→	1030②	→	1630②	1900①	→	0100②	→	1530②
1400③	→	0700④	→	1300④	1900②	→	0100③	→	1530③
1400④	→	0700⑤	→	1300⑤	1700④	→	2300④	→	1330⑤
1630⑤	→	0930⑥	→	1530⑥	1700⑤	→	2300⑤	→	1330⑥
1630⑥	→	0930⑦	→	1530⑦	1800⑥	→	2359⑥	→	1430⑦
1730⑦	→	1030①	→	1630①	1800⑦	→	2359⑦	→	1430①

August 1 - 29

From Ancona: daily departures (not Aug. 9, 16); sailings on Aug. 23, 24 do not serve Igumenítsa.
From Pátra: daily departures (not Aug. 10, 17); sailings on Aug. 3, 4 do not serve Igumenítsa.

2725 ANCONA - SPLIT

Blue Line / SNAV — **March 21 - November 5, 2016**
(No winter service)

Ancona		Split	
2015	→	0700	①③⑤ Mar. 21 - Apr. 15; ①②③④⑤⑥ Apr. 18 - June 25; daily June 27 - Sept. 17; ①②③④⑤⑥ Sept. 19 - Oct. 22; ①③⑤ Oct. 24 - Nov. 4 (not July 17).

Split		Ancona	
2015	→	0700	②④⑦ Mar. 22 - Apr. 14; ①②③④⑤⑦ Apr. 17 - June 24; daily June 26 - Sept. 16; ①②③④⑤⑦ Sept. 18 - Oct. 21; ②④⑦ Oct. 23 - Nov. 5 (not July 16).

Jadrolinija — **2016 service**
(No service Dec. 25, 26)

Ancona		Split		Split		Ancona	
January 3 - March 21 and November 3 - December 30							
1945	→	0700	①⑤	2000	→	0700	④⑦
March 22 - July 23 and August 29 - November 2							
1945	→	0700	①③⑤	2000	→	0700	②④⑦
July 24 - August 28							
1100	→	1900	⑦ Aug. 21 - 28.	1430	→	2230	⑥ Aug. 6 - 13.
1945	→	0600	⑤	2000	→	0700	②④
1945	→	0700	①③	2030	→	0945	⑦
2359	→	1030	⑥ Aug. 6 - 13.	2200	→	0940	⑥ Aug. 20 - 27.

2732 ANCONA - ZADAR

Jadrolinija — **2016 serv**
(No winter servi

Ancona		Zadar	Zadar		Ancona
June 3 - July 5 and September 9 - 27▲					
2200②⑥	→	0700③⑦	2200①⑤	→	0700②⑥
July 6 - 14 and August 31 - September 8					
2200②④⑥	→	0700③⑤⑦	2200①③⑤	→	0700②④⑥
July 15 - 28 and August 24 - 30					
2200②④⑤⑥	→	0700③⑤⑥⑦	1130⑤⑥	→	1800⑤⑥
			2200①③	→	0700②④
July 29 - August 23					
1230⑦	→	1830⑦	0800⑥	→	1400⑥
1600⑥	→	2200⑥	1130②③④⑤	→	1800②③④⑤
2200⑤	→	0530⑥	2200⑦	→	0700①
2200①②③④	→	0600②③④⑤	2345⑥	→	0700⑦

▲ – June 17, Sept. 9: Zadar depart 1130, Ancona arrive 1800.

2738 BARI - BAR

Montenegro Lines — **2016 servi**

Bari		Bar	
1200	→	0900	Aug. 19 - 23, 26 - 28.
2200	→	0900	②⑤ Feb. 2 - June 3; ①③⑤ June 6 - July 29; July 30, Aug. 1, 3 - 6, 8, 10 - 13, 15, 17, 24, 29, 31; ①③⑤ Sept. 2 - 23 (also May 4, not May 3, 13).

Bar		Bari	
1200	→	0900	July 30, Aug. 4 - 6, 11 - 13.
2200	→	0900	④⑦ Feb. 4 - June 2; ②④⑦ June 5 - July 28; July 31, Aug. 2, 7 9, 14, 16, 18 - 23, 25 - 28, 30; ②④⑦ Sept. 1 - 22 (also Mar. 28, Ma not Mar. 27, May 1).

2755 BARI - PÁTRA via Kérkira and Igumenítsa

Anek Lines / Superfast Ferries — **2016 servi**

Bari		Kérkira		Igumenítsa		Pátra
January 1 - May 1 and October 1 - December 31						
1330⑦	→	→	→	2300⑦	→	0700①
1930①–⑥	→	→	→	0530②–⑦	→	1300②–⑦
May 2 - June 26 and September 12 - 30						
1330⑦	→	→	→	2300⑦	→	0700①
1930①②③⑤⑥	→	→	→	0530②③④⑥⑦	→	1300②③④⑥⑦
1930④	→	0430⑤	→	0600⑤	→	1300⑤
June 27 - July 24 and August 29 - September 11						
1330⑦	→	→	→	2300⑦	→	0700①
1930①②③ →	→	→	0530②③④	→	1300②③④	
1930④⑤⑥	→	0430⑤⑥⑦	→	0600⑤⑥⑦	→	1300⑤⑥⑦
July 25 - August 28						
1300⑤⑥	→	2200⑤⑥	→	2330⑤⑥	...	...
1330⑦	→	→	→	2300⑦	→	0700①
1930①②③⑥	→	→	→	0530②③④⑦	→	1300②③④⑦
1930④	→	0430⑤	→	0600⑤	→	1300⑤

Pátra		Igumenítsa		Kérkira		Bari
January 1 - May 1 and October 1 - December 31						
1800	→	0030	→	→	→	0930
May 2 - June 26 and September 12 - 30						
1800①②④⑤⑥⑦	→	0030②③⑤⑥⑦①	→	→	→	0930②③⑤⑥⑦①
1800③	→	0030④	→	0200④	→	1000④
June 27 - July 24 and August 29 - September 11						
1800①②④⑤	→	0030②③⑤⑥	→	→	→	0930②③⑤⑥
1800③⑥⑦	→	0030④⑦①	→	0200④⑦①	→	1000④⑦①
July 25 - August 28						
1800①②④⑤⑦	→	0030②③⑤⑥①	→	→	→	0930②③⑤⑥①
1800③	→	0030④	→	0200④	→	1000④
...	...	0200⑥⑦	→	0330⑥⑦	→	1030⑥⑦

Subject to alteration during ship maintenance periods

🚌 connection Pátra - Pireás - Athína and v.v.
Tickets available on-board ship and from 30 Amalías av., Síndagma, Athína.

For international shipping maps – see pages 538 - 540

BLACK SEA services 2760

nerang Shipping Company Tourism Travel & Trade S.A.

ANBUL - YALTA - NOVOROSSIYSK — Irregular sailings, journey 30 hours

ANBUL - YEVPATORIYA — Journey 24 hours

BRINDISI - IGUMENÍTSA 2765

naldi Lines — 2016 service

Brindisi		Igumenítsa	Igumenítsa		Brindisi
400①③⑥	→	2300①③⑥	0100①③⑤⑥	→	0830①③⑤⑥
630②⑤⑦	→	0130③⑥①	0300①③⑥	→	1100①③⑥
00①③④⑥	→	0530②④⑤⑦	2359①③⑥	→	0830②④⑦

BRINDISI - PÁTRA 2775

naldi Lines — 2016 service

Brindisi		Pátra	Pátra		Brindisi
00①③④⑥	→	1400②④⑤⑦	1700②④⑤⑦	→	0830③⑤⑥①

BRINDISI - VLORË 2780

opean Seaways — 2016 service

Brindisi		Vlorë	Vlorë		Brindisi
May 20 - July 15 and from September 9					
)①②③④⑤⑥	→	0700②③④⑤⑥⑦	1430①②③④⑤⑥	→	1930①②③④⑤⑥
July 16 - September 8					
2330	→	0700	1430	→	1930

DUBROVNIK - BARI 2795

rolinija — 2016 service (No winter service)

Dubrovnik		Bari	Bari		Dubrovnik
March 23 - May 19 and October 3 - 27					
2200①③	→	0800②④	2200②④	→	0800③⑤
May 20 - June 26 and September 12 - October 2					
2200①③⑤	→	0800②④⑥	2200②④⑥	→	0800③⑤⑦
June 27 - July 18 and August 30 - September 11					
1200⑦	→	1930⑦	2200②④⑥⑦	→	0800③⑤⑦①
2200①③⑤	→	0800②④⑥			
July 19 - August 1					
1200⑤⑥⑦	→	1930⑤⑥⑦	2200②④⑤⑥⑦	→	0800③⑤⑥⑦①
2200①③	→	0800②④			
August 2 - 16					
00③④⑤⑥⑦	→	1930③④⑤⑥⑦	2200②③④⑤⑥⑦	→	0800③④⑤⑥⑦①
2200①	→	0800②			
August 17 - 29					
)①③④⑤⑥⑦	→	0800②④⑤⑥⑦①	1200①④⑤⑥⑦	→	1930①④⑤⑥⑦
			2200②	→	0800③

GREEK ISLANDS 2800

mmary table of regular ⛴ services to the Greek Islands.

Each route is operated by various shipping companies to differing schedules. Additional inter-island routes are operated at less regular intervals.

Pireás to Égina, Póros, Ídra, Spétses, Kíthira, Andikíthira.
Pireás to Sérifos, Sífnos, Mílos, Folégandros.
Pireás to Páros, Íos, Thíra (Santoríni), Iráklio.
Pireás to Náxos, Amorgós, Astipálea.
Pireás to Pátmos, Léros, Kálimnos, Kos, Nísiros, Tílos, Sími, Ródos, Kárpathos, Kásos.
Pireás to Ikaría, Sámos, Híos, Lésvos.
Pireás and **Rafína** to Síros, Dílos, Míkonos, Tínos, Ándros.
Pátra to Zákinthos (Zante), Kefallinía, Itháki, Kérkira (Corfu), Igumenítsa.
Vólos, **Águios Konstantínos** and **Kími** to Skíathos, Skópelos, Alónissos, Skíros.
Kavála to Thásos, Samothráki, Límnos.

PIREÁS - IRÁKLIO 2830

Minoan Lines — 2016 service

Pireás		Iráklio		Iráklio		Pireás	
2100	→	0600	Not July 1 - Aug. 31.	2130	→	0600	Not July 1 - Aug. 31.
2200	→	0630	July 1 - Aug. 31.	2200	→	0630	July 1 - Aug. 31.

Additional sailings on July 2, 9, 16, 23, 24, 29 - 31, Aug. 5 - 7, 12, 13, 19 - 21, 26 - 28, Sept. 3 at 1100 from Pireás and Iráklio.

Anek Lines / Blue Star Ferries — Service to October 31, 2016 (No service Apr. 30, May 1, 14, 21, 28)

Pireás		Iráklio		Iráklio		Pireás	
1400	→	2245	Apr. 29 only.	1400	→	2245	Apr. 29 only.
2100	→	0600	Not Apr. 29.	2100	→	0600	Not Apr. 29.

PIREÁS / LAVRIO - LEMESÓS (LIMASSOL) - HEFA 2845

Grimaldi Lines — 2016 service

Pireás - Lemesós - Hefa: 1 sailing per week – contact operator for details.

Salamis Cruise Lines — 2016 service

Lavrio - Lemesós - Hefa: occasional service – contact operator for details.

TRIESTE - PÁTRA via Igumenítsa 2870

Minoan Lines — 2016 service

Trieste		Ravenna		Ancona		Igumenítsa		Pátra
0430③④	→	→	→	1400③④	→	0700④⑤	→	1300④⑤

Pátra		Igumenítsa		Ancona		Ravenna		Trieste
1900①②	→	0100②③	→	1530②③	→	→	→	2330②③

Variations: no departure from Trieste on Aug. 3, 4, 24, 25; from Pátra on Aug. 1, 2, 22, 23.

For full service Ancona - Igumenítsa - Pátra and v.v. see Table **2715**.

VENEZIA - PÁTRA via Igumenítsa 2875

Anek Lines / Superfast Ferries — 2016 service

Venezia		Igumenítsa		Pátra		Igumenítsa		Venezia
January 1 - June 30 and September 12 - December 31								
1200⑥	→	1430⑦	→	2100⑦ / 2359⑦	→	0630①	→	0700②
1200⑦	→	1430①	→	2100① / 2359⑤	→	0630⑥	→	0700⑦
July 1 - September 11								
1200③	→	1430④	→	2100④ / 2359④	→	0630⑤	→	0700⑥
1200⑥	→	1430⑦	→	2100⑦ / 2359⑦	→	0630①	→	0700②

For international journeys only

OTHER SERVICES 2899

Jadrolinija — 2016 services

Many local services operate to the Islands along the Croatian coast.

LNP — 2016 services

All-year services operate Split - Rogač and Šibenik - Kaprije - Žirje.

Salamis Cruise Lines — 2016 services

Cruises around Greece and the Greek Islands (2 - 9 days, June - Sept.).

Venezia Lines — 2016 services

Services operate Apr. 30 - Oct. 2 from Venezia to Poreč, Pula, Rovinj and Umag.

BEYOND EUROPE
Africa and the Middle East

Introduction

The Beyond Europe section covers principal rail services in a different area of the world each month. There are six areas, each appearing twice yearly as follows:

India:	January and July editions
South East Asia and Australasia:	February and August editions
China:	March and September editions
Japan:	April and October editions
North America:	May and November editions
Africa and the Middle East:	June and December editions

The months have been chosen so that we can bring you up-to-date information for those countries which make seasonal changes.

Details of services in South America can be found in the European Rail Timetable April and October editions and schedules for South Korea in the May and November editions.

Contents

INDEX OF PLACES

by table number

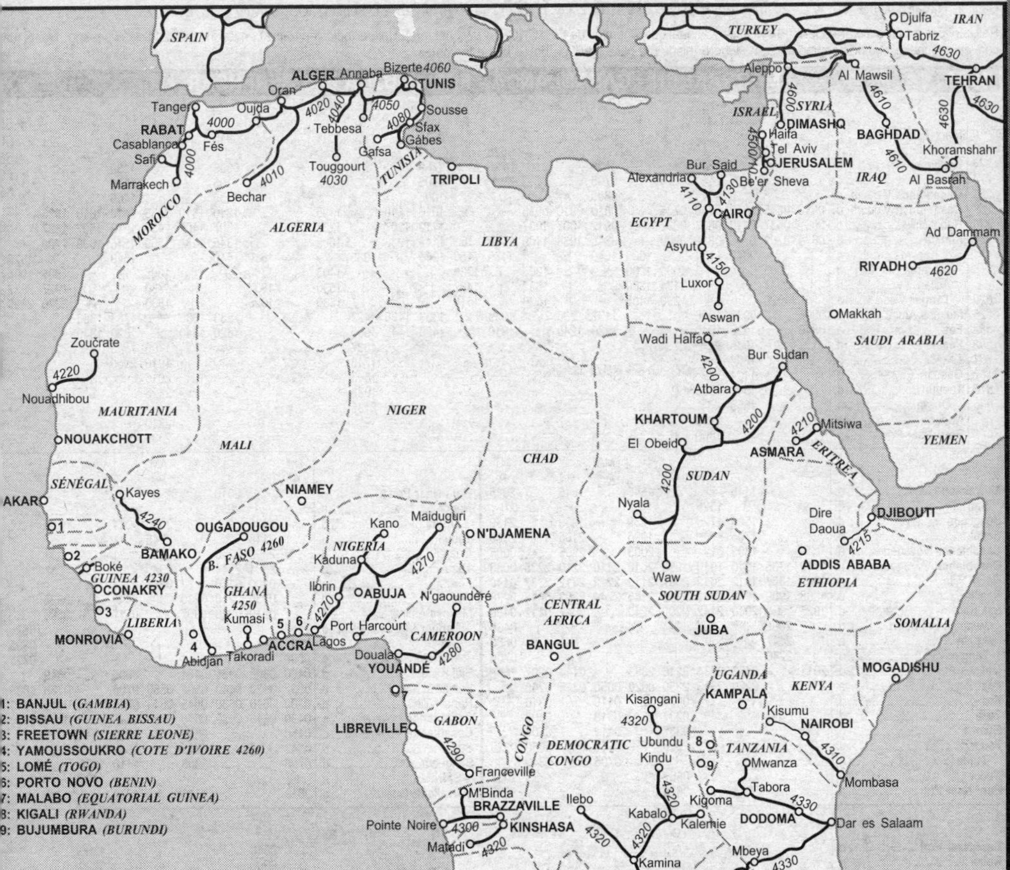

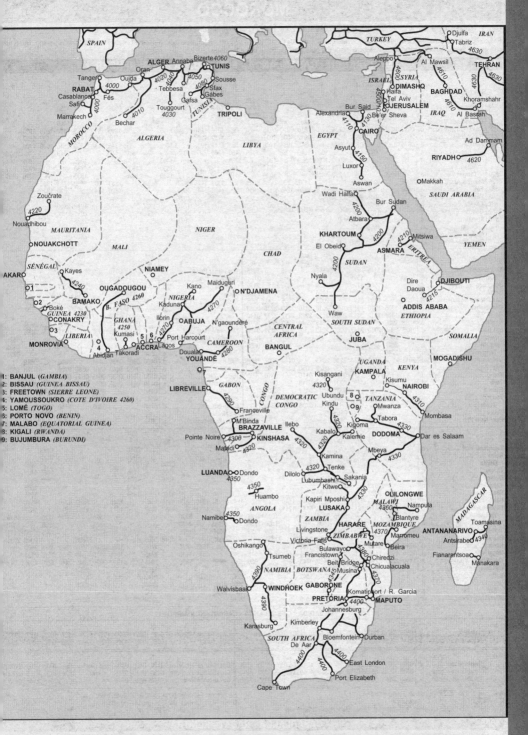

1: **BANJUL** *(GAMBIA)*
2: **BISSAU** *(GUINEA BISSAU)*
3: **FREETOWN** *(SIERRE LEONE)*
4: **YAMOUSSOUKRO** *(COTE D'IVOIRE 4260)*
5: **LOMÉ** *(TOGO)*
6: **PORTO NOVO** *(BENIN)*
7: **MALABO** *(EQUATORIAL GUINEA)*
8: **KIGALI** *(RWANDA)*
9: **BUJUMBURA** *(BURUNDI)*

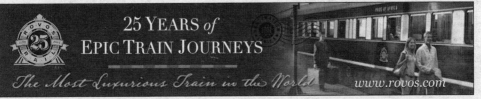

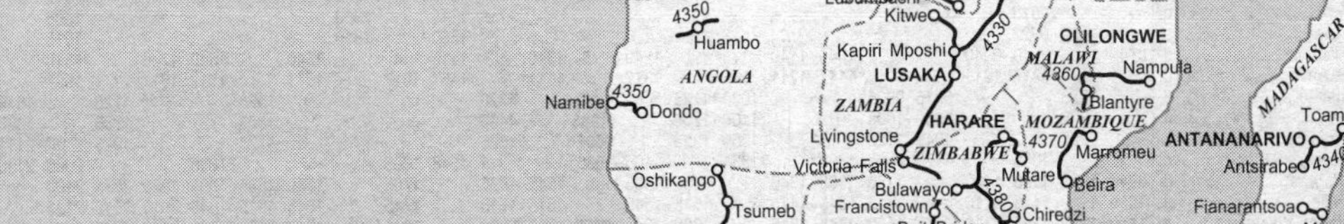

MOROCCO

Capital: **Rabat** (GMT + 0). 2016 Public Holidays: Jan. 1, 11, May 1, July 7, 30, Aug. 14, 20, 21, Sept. 13, Oct. 3, Nov. 6, 18, Dec. 12.

Rail services in Morocco are operated by Office National des Chemins de Fer (ONCF. www.oncf.ma). Unless indicated trains convey 1st and 2nd class seating. Trains ma convey couchette and/or sleeping cars and where this is the case it will be noted in the footnotes.

4000 MARRAKECH - CASABLANCA - FÈS - OUJDA and BENI NSAR

km		⚒			⚒		F					F			B			B							F
0	**Marrakech** Guéliz d.	...	...	...	...	...	...	0445	...	...	...	...	0645	...	...	...	...	...	0845	...	...	1045	...	...	...
*	**Safi** d.	...	...	...	...	...	...	|	...	...	0525	...	|	...	...	...	...	...	|	...	...	|	...	...	...
74	Benguerir d.	...	...	...	...	...	...	0539	...	...	0725	...	0739	...	...	...	...	...	0939	...	...	1139	...	...	...
174	Settat d.	...	...	...	...	...	...	0705	...	...	▬	...	0905	...	...	...	...	...	1105	...	...	1305	...	...	...
257	**Casablanca** V'geurs a.	...	...	...	...	...	...	0805	...	...	...	...	1005	...	...	...	...	...	1205	...	...	1405	...	...	...
257	**Casablanca** V'geurs d.	0510	0535	0610	0710	0735	...	0810	0910	0935	...	...	1010	1110	...	1135	...	...	1210	1310	1335	1410	1510	1535	...
346	Rabat Ville d.	0607	0637	0712	0807	0837	...	0912	1007	1037	...	...	1112	1207	...	1237	...	...	1307	1407	1437	1512	1607	1637	...
386	Kenitra d.	0638	0709	0745	0838	0909	**fa**	0945	1038	1109	...	**fb**	1145	1238	...	1309	...	...	1345	1438	1509	1545	1638	1709	**fc**
471	Sidi Kacem d.	|	|	0840	|	|	1000	1040	|	|	1135	1150	1240	|	1335	|	...	1610	1440	|	|	1640	|	|	1825
	Mechraa Bel Ksiri d.	|	0805	|	|	1005	1100	|	|	1205	|	1233	|	|	|	1405	...	1700	|	|	1605	|	|	1805	1905
	Asilah a.	|	0934	|	|	1134	1300	|	|	1333	|	1437	|	|	|	1530	...	1837	|	|	1730	|	|	1927	2037
620	**Tanger** Ville a.	|	1020	|	|	1230	1405	|	|	1430	|	1515	|	|	|	1630	...	1925	|	|	1830	|	|	2020	2130
526	Meknes Amir d.	0806	...	0933	1006	...	...	1132	1206	...	1229	...	1333	1406	1427	...	...	...	1533	1606	▬	1733	1806	...	...
582	**Fès** a.	0840	...	1020	1040	...	...	1220	1240	...	1310	...	1420	1443	1503	...	...	...	1620	1640	...	1820	1840	...	...
582	**Fès** d.	...	...	1045	▬	...	...	...	...	...	...	...	...	...	1537	...	...	...	...	...	1700	*1845*	...	...	...
701	Taza d.	...	...	1302	...	...	...	...	...	...	...	...	...	...	1748	...	...	...	...	...	1910	*2050*	...	...	...
	Guercif d.	...	...	1404	...	...	...	...	...	...	...	...	...	...	1843	...	...	...	...	...	2015	...	...	...	...
818	Taourirt d.	...	...	1500	1550	...	...	...	...	...	...	...	...	...	1933	...	...	...	...	...	2125	...	...	...	...
935	**Oujda** a.	...	...	1655	|	...	...	...	...	...	...	...	...	...	2135	...	...	...	...	...	|	...	...	...	...
	Nador a.	...	...	...	1735	...	...	...	...	...	...	...	...	...	...	...	...	...	...	...	2310	...	...	...	...
	Beni Nsar Port a.	...	...	...	1800	...	...	...	...	...	...	...	...	...	...	...	...	...	...	...	2335	...	...	...	...

					C		MA 🛏			MT A
Marrakech Guéliz d.	...	...	1445	...	...	1645	...	1845	...	2045
Safi d.	...	...	|	1525	...	|	...	|	...	|
Benguerir d.	...	...	1539	1725	...	1739	...	1939	...	2139
Settat d.	...	...	1705	▬	...	1905	...	2105	...	2305
Casablanca Voyageurs a.	...	...	1805	...	...	2005	...	2205	...	0005
Casablanca Voyageurs d.	1710	1735	1810	1910	1935	2010	2110	2210	2235	0030
Rabat Ville d.	1807	1837	1912	2012	2037	2112	2212	2312	2337	0140
Kenitra d.	1838	1909	1945	2047	2111	2145	2244	2353	0018	0228
Sidi Kacem d.	1925	|	2040	2142	2200	2240	|	0047	0112	0400
Mechraa Bel Ksiri d.	|	2005	|	|	|	|	|	|	|	0438
Asilah a.	|	2147	|	|	|	|	|	|	|	0600
Tanger Ville a.	|	2240	|	|	|	|	|	|	|	0700
Meknes Amir d.	2011	...	2133	2234	2215	2333	|	0144	0207	▬
Fès a.	2045	...	2220	2315	2350	0020	0050	0225	0245	...
Fès d.	...	...	...	...	0020	...	0110	...	0310	...
Taza d.	...	...	...	...	0237	...	0318	...	0509	...
Guercif d.	...	...	...	...	0337	...	0419	...	0607	...
Taourirt d.	...	...	...	...	|	...	0510	...	0650	0820
Oujda a.	...	...	...	...	|	...	0705	...	0840	|
Nador a.	...	...	...	...	0557	...	...	...	...	1003
Beni Nsar Port a.	...	...	...	...	0625	...	...	...	...	1025

	TM A		C		AM 🛏			⚒	
Beni Nsar Port d.	...	...	2010	...	...	...	...	...	...
Nador d.	...	...	2033	...	...	...	...	...	...
Oujda d.	...	1935	|	...	2055	...	...	...	...
Taourirt d.	...	2118	|	...	2245	...	...	...	...
Guercif d.	...	2203	2246	...	2330	...	...	...	...
Taza d.	...	2301	2344	...	0030	...	...	...	...
Fès a.	...	0100	0150	...	0240	...	...	...	...
Fès d.	...	0130	0210	0230	0305	0440	...	0535	...
Meknes Amir d.	...	0210	0246	0307	|	0517	...	0606	...
Tanger Ville d.	2155	|	|	|	|	|	...	|	0525
Asilah d.	2244	|	|	|	|	|	...	|	0605
Mechraa Bel Ksiri d.	0000	|	|	|	|	|	...	|	0725
Sidi Kacem d.	0100	0308	0335	0404	|	0605	...	0649	|
Kenitra d.	0202	0420	0440	0502	0530	0705	...	0738	0835
Rabat Ville d.	0300	0510	0530	0545	0615	0745	...	0815	0915
Casablanca Voyageurs a.	0430	0615	0630	0645	0715	0845	...	0910	1020
Casablanca Voyageurs d.	0450	...	...	0650	...	0850	...	...	...
Settat d.	0542	...	...	0742	...	0942	...	...	...
Benguerir d.	0708	...	...	0908	...	1110	1200	...	...
Safi a.	|	...	...	|	...	|	1402	...	...
Marrakech Guéliz a.	0810	...	...	1010	...	1210	...	...	...

	⚒				G				B			G			B									G
Beni Nsar Port d.	...	...	...	...	...	...	...	...	...	...	...	...	...	...	...	...	0840	...	...	...	...	1200	...	...
Nador d.	...	...	...	...	...	...	...	...	...	...	...	...	...	...	...	...	0906	...	...	...	...	1220	...	...
Oujda d.	...	...	...	...	...	...	...	...	...	...	...	...	...	...	0805	...	|	...	...	...	...	|	1240	...
Taourirt d.	...	...	...	...	...	...	...	...	...	...	...	...	...	...	1005	...	1115	...	...	...	...	1400	1423	...
Guercif d.	...	...	...	...	...	...	...	...	...	...	...	...	...	...	1046	...	1201	...	...	...	...	▬	1507	...
Taza d.	...	...	*0615*	...	...	...	...	...	...	...	...	...	...	...	1145	...	1300	...	...	...	...	...	1606	...
Fès a.	...	...	*0822*	...	...	...	...	...	...	...	...	...	...	...	1350	...	1510	...	...	...	...	...	1815	...
Fès d.	0740	...	0840	0940	...	...	1040	1140	...	...	1240	...	1340	...	1415	1440	...	1540	...	1640	1740	...	1840	...
Meknes Amir d.	0811	...	0917	1011	...	...	1117	1211	...	...	1317	...	1411	...	1457	1517	...	1611	...	1717	1811	...	1917	...
Tanger Ville d.	|	0725	|	|	0815	0925	|	|	1030	1125	|	1250	|	1320	|	|	...	|	1525	|	|	1725	|	1840
Asilah d.	|	0805	|	|	0859	1008	|	|	1106	1206	|	11335	|	1406	|	|	...	|	1605	|	|	1806	|	1930
Mechraa Bel Ksiri d.	|	0925	|	|	1045	1125	|	|	1256	1325	|	1501	|	1525	|	|	...	|	1725	|	|	1925	|	2111
Sidi Kacem d.	|	|	1005	|	1122	|	1205	|	1331	|	1405	1536	|	|	1548	1605	...	|	|	1805	|	|	2005	2150
Kenitra d.	0940	1035	1105	1140	**ga**	1235	1305	1340	...	1435	1505	**gb**	1540	1635	...	1705	...	1740	1835	1905	1940	2035	2105	**gc**
Rabat Ville d.	1015	1115	1145	1215	...	1315	1345	1415	...	1515	1545	...	1615	1715	...	1745	...	1815	1915	1945	2015	2115	2145	...
Casablanca Voyageurs a.	1110	1220	1245	1310	...	1420	1445	1510	...	1620	1645	▬	1710	1820	...	1845	...	1910	2020	2045	2110	2220	2245	...
Casablanca Voyageurs d.	...	...	1250	...	...	...	1450	...	...	...	1650	...	...	...	...	1850	...	...	...	2050	...	...	...	...
Settat d.	...	...	1342	...	...	...	1542	...	...	...	1742	...	...	...	...	1942	...	...	...	2142	...	...	...	...
Benguerir d.	...	...	1508	...	...	...	1708	...	...	...	1908	2000	...	...	...	2108	...	...	...	2308	...	...	...	...
Safi a.	...	...	|	...	...	...	|	...	...	...	|	2202	...	...	...	|	...	...	...	|	...	...	...	...
Marrakech Guéliz a.	...	...	1610	...	...	...	1810	...	...	...	2010	...	...	...	...	2210	...	...	...	0010	...	...	...	...

EL JADIDA - CASABLANCA - CASABLANCA AIRPORT

km		①–⑥									
0	**El Jadida** d.	0630	0830	1030	1130	1230	1430	1730	1830	1930	...
123	**Casablanca** V'geurs a.	0747	0950	1151	1300	1351	1551	1851	1951	2055	...

	①–⑥								
Casablanca V'geurs d.	0627	0827	0920	1027	1227	1427	1627	1727	1932
El Jadida a.	0750	0950	1045	1150	1350	1550	1750	1853	2100

km										
0	**Casablanca** Port d.	0300	0500	0600	0700		1900	2000	2100	2200
	Casablanca V'geurs d.	0313	0513	0613	0713	and hourly	1913	2013	2113	2213
	Casablanca Airport a.	0345	0545	0645	0745	until	1945	2045	2145	2245

Casablanca Airport d.	0400	0600	0700	and hourly	1900	2000	2100	2200
Casablanca V'geurs a.	0430	0630	0730	until	1930	2030	2130	2230
Casablanca Port a.	0445	0645	0745		1945	2045	2145	2245

A – 🛏 1, 2 cl., (12) Marrakech - Tanger and v.v.
B – (12) Tanger - Fés - Oudja and v.v.
C – 🛏 1, 2 cl., (12) Casablanca Voyageurs. - Fès - Beni Nsar Port and v.v.
F – From Fez departs: **fa** 0805, **fb** 0955, **fc** 1655.
G – To Fez arrives: **ga** 1310, **gb** 1710, **gc** 2330.
* – Safi - Benguerir: *142 km*.

4005 CASABLANCA - RABAT - KENITRA

km	↓		⚒	A	⚒	⚒			C																
93	**Casablanca** Port d.	0620	0650	0720	0750	0850	0950	1020	1050	1120	1150	1220	1320	1350	1420	1450	1520	1550	1620	1650	1720	1750	1820	1850	1920
	Ain Seeba d.	0629	0659	0729	0759	0859	0959	1029	1059	1129	1159	1229	1329	1359	1429	1459	1529	1559	1629	1659	1729	1759	1829	1859	1929
0	**Rabat** Ville d.	0732	0752	0832	0855	0952	1052	1132	1155	1222	1252	1332	1422	1452	1532	1552	1622	1652	1732	1752	1832	1852	1932	1952	2032
7	Salé Ville d.	0740	0800	0840	0903	1000	1100	1140	1203	1230	1300	1340	1430	1500	1540	1600	1630	1700	1740	1800	1840	1900	1940	2000	2040
40	**Kenitra** a.	0803	0823	...	0926	1023	1124	...	1227	...	1323	1403	1452	1523	1603	...	1652	1723	1803	1823	1903	1923	2003	2023	2103

↓		⚒	⚒		⚒		⚒	B																	
Kenitra d.	0550	0605	0620	0650	0720	0755	0824	....	0920	1020	...	...	1224	...	1320	1355	1450	1520	1555	...	1650	1720	1755	1824	1850
Salé Ville d.	0617	0632	0647	0717	0746	0820	0849	0919	0947	1047	1117	1216	1249	1317	1347	1420	1517	1547	1620	1646	1717	1747	1820	1849	1917
Rabat Ville d.	0630	0645	0700	0730	0800	0830	0900	0930	1000	1100	1130	1230	1300	1330	1400	1430	1530	1600	1630	1700	1730	1800	1830	1900	1930
Ain Seeba a.	0729	0738	0753	0829	0853	0929	0950	1029	1050	1150	1220	1339	1350	1420	1450	1528	1620	1650	1729	1750	1829	1850	1929	1950	2029
Casablanca Port a.	0740	0750	0803	0840	0903	0940	1000	1040	1100	1200	1230	1340	1400	1430	1500	1540	1630	1700	1740	1800	1840	1900	1940	2000	2040

A – Additional trips: 0820, 0920, 1250. **B** – Additional trips: 1016, 1445. **C** – Additional trips: 2020, 2120, 2150. **D** – Additional trips: 1120, 2024, 2120.

ALGERIA

tal: **Alger** (GMT +1). 2016 Public Holidays: Jan. 1, May 1, June 20, July 5, 7, 8, Sept. 13, 14, Oct. 3, 23, Nov. 1, Dec. 12.

services are operated Société Nationale des Transports Ferroviaires (SNTF. www.sntf.dz). Unless otherwise noted, trains convey first and second class seated mmodation. Long distance overnight trains may convey sleeping cars and/or couchettes and where this is the case it will be shown in the footnotes. Timings are the most nt available and are subject to alteration at any time.

ORAN - GHAZAOUET and BÉCHAR — 4010

TF 2nd class unless indicated

		2✕	2✕	2	2	2		✕A		
Oran	d.	0730	1250	...	1600	1700	...	2330	...	...
Sidi bel Abbès	d.	0835	1355	...	1700	1822	...	0034	...	...
Tlemcen	d.	0956	1512	1700	1851	1942	...	|	...	...
Maghnia	d.	1105	1622	1823	...	...	...	|	...	...
Ghazaouet	d.	...	...	2010	...	...	...	|	...	...
Naâma	a.	...	...	...	...	...	...	0430	...	...
Béchar	a.	...	...	...	...	...	...	0846	...	...

		2	✕A	2	2	2		2	2	
Béchar	d.	...	2300	...	...	...	...	...	...	...
Naâma	d.	...	0309	...	...	...	...	...	...	...
Ghazout	d.	...	|	...	0430	...	...	...	...	...
Maghnia	d.	...	|	0445	0618	0850	...	1405	...	...
Tlemcen	d.	...	|	0550	0740	0955	...	1510	2000	...
Sidi bel Abbès	d.	0540	0649	0706	...	1120	...	1629	2119	...
Oran	a.	0658	0800	0809	...	1222	...	1726	...	...

▬, (12) and ✕ Oran - Béchar and v.v.

ORAN - ALGER — 4020

TF

			2	✕	2B		2	✕	✕	2✕	✕	2
Oran	d.	...	...	0625	...	0800	...	1230	1500	1615	1630	1715
Mohammadia	d.	...	...	0716	0730	0851	1215	1320	|	1700	1728	1813
Mostaganem	a.	...	...	|	0820	|	1305	|	|	|	|	|
Relizane	d.	...	...	0750	...	0923	...	1354	1607	1731	1802	1847
Chlef	d.	...	0530	0846	...	1014	...	1448	1653	1829	1856	...
Khémis Miliana	d.	...	0625	0954	...	1118	...	1554	|	...	...	...
El Affroun ☆	d.	0620	|	1038	...	1204	...	1645	|	...	...	...
Blida ☆	d.	0634	0721	1051	...	1217	...	1658	1829	...	...	...
Alger Agha ☆	a.	0725	0757	1129	...	1256	...	1737	1900	...	...	...

		2	2	2✕	✕	2		✕	2	✕	2	2
Alger Agha ☆	d.	...	...	...	0625	...	0800	1230	...	1500	1658	1800
Blida ☆	d.	...	...	...	0700	...	0829	1305	...	1529	1732	1854
El Affroun ☆	d.	...	...	...	0713	...	0848	1318	...	|	|	1910
Khémis Miliana	d.	...	...	...	0756	...	0931	1401	...	|	1800	...
Chlef	d.	...	...	0650	0854	...	1029	1503	...	1704	1932	...
Relizane	d.	0525	...	0745	1001	...	1132	1604	...	1751	...	...
Mostaganem	d.	|	0540	|	|	1030	|	|	1630	|	...	...
Mohammadia	d.	0600	0630	0823	1034	1120	1205	1642	1720	|	...	...
Oran	a.	0717	...	0911	1130	...	1300	1736	...	1900	...	...

Additional local trains available. **B** – Additional trip: 1740.

TEBESSA, TOUGGOURT and M'SILA — 4030

TF 2nd class only

Constantine	d.	...	...	0515	0545	...	...	...	...	...
Aïn M'Lila	d.	...	...	0601	|	...	...	...	...	...
Oum el Bouaghi	d.	...	...	0658	|	...	...	...	...	...
Sidi Yahia	d.	...	...	0837	|	...	...	...	...	...
Tebessa	a.	...	...	0916	|	...	...	...	...	...
Batna	d.	0430	...	...	0724	...	...	...	...	...
Aïn Touta	d.	|	...	...	|	...	...	...	...	...
Biskra	d.	|	...	...	0921	2000	...	...	...	...
Djamâa	d.	|	...	...	...	2310	...	...	...	...
Touggourt	a.	|	...	...	...	0016	...	...	...	...
Barika	d.	0530	...	...	...	...	...	...	...	...
M'Sila	a.	0649	...	...	...	...	...	...	...	...

M'Sila	d.	...	...	...	...	1644	...	...	...	...
Barika	d.	...	...	...	...	1807	...	...	...	...
Touggourt	d.	...	0100	...	...	|	...	...	...	...
Djamâa	d.	...	0158	...	...	|	...	...	...	...
Biskra	d.	...	0512	...	...	|	...	1500	...	...
Aïn Touta	d.	...	...	...	...	|	...	1631	...	...
Batna	d.	...	...	...	...	1909	...	1656	...	...
Tebessa	d.	...	...	...	...	...	...	|	1510	...
Sidi Yahia	d.	...	...	...	...	...	...	|	1548	...
Oum el Bouaghi	d.	...	...	...	...	...	...	|	1726	...
Aïn M'Lila	d.	...	...	...	...	...	...	|	1821	...
Constantine	a.	...	...	...	...	...	...	1838	1908	...

ALGER - CONSTANTINE - TEBESSA — 4040

TF 2nd class unless indicated

			✕B								✕C
Alger ☆	d.	...	0725	...	...	1230	...	1530	1620	...	2130
Thénia ☆	d.	...	0811	...	...	|	...	|	1705	1736	2214
Bouira	d.	...	0940	...	...	1412	...	1713	1824	1906	2326
Beni Mansour	d.	...	1026	1040	...	1451	...	|	—	...	0011
Béjaïa	a.	...	|	1229	...	|	...	|	...	...	|
Bordj Bou Arreridj	d.	0615	1143	—	...	1553	...	1850	1610	...	0115
M'Sila	a.	0703	|	...	...	1642	...	|	|	...	|
Setif	d.	—	1230	...	...	...	...	1932	1650	...	0204
Constantine	a.	...	1430	...	...	...	...	...	1854	...	0430
Constantine	d.	...	—	1455	...	...	...	...	...	...	0435
El Harrouch	d.	...	...	1541	...	...	...	...	...	...	|
El Milia	d.	...	...	1658	...	...	...	...	...	...	|
Jijel	a.	...	...	1739	...	...	...	...	...	...	|
Ramdane Djamel	d.	...	...	...	...	...	...	...	...	...	0545
Skikda	a.	...	...	...	...	...	...	...	...	...	|
Azzaba	d.	...	...	...	...	...	...	...	...	...	0610
Annaba	a.	...	...	...	...	...	...	...	...	...	0713
Annaba	d.	...	...	...	1640	...	...	...	...	...	...
Bouchegouf	d.	...	...	...	1752	...	...	...	...	...	...
Mechrouha	d.	...	...	...	1848	...	...	...	...	...	...
Souk Ahras	d.	0600	1335	...	1910	...	...	...	...	...	...
Sidi El Hémissi	a.	0709	1444	...	|	...	...	...	...	...	...
Dreá	d.	...	...	...	1957	...	...	...	...	...	...
Oued Kéberit	d.	...	...	...	2036	...	...	...	...	...	...
Tebessa	a.	...	...	...	2149	...	...	...	...	...	...

		✕C						✕B			
Tebessa	d.	...	...	...	...	0430	...	...	...	...	...
Oued Kéberit	d.	...	...	...	...	0541	...	...	...	...	...
Dreá	d.	...	...	...	...	0618	...	...	...	...	...
Sidi El Hémissi	d.	...	...	...	...	|	...	...	...	0719	1602
Souk Ahras	d.	...	...	...	...	0656	...	...	...	0828	1714
Mechrouha	d.	...	...	...	...	0722	...	...	...	—	—
Bouchegouf	d.	...	...	...	...	0810	...	...	...	...	...
Annaba	a.	...	...	...	...	0932	...	...	...	...	...
Annaba	d.	2130	...	...	...	—	...	...	...	...	...
Azzaba	d.	2226	...	...	...	...	...	...	...	...	...
Skikda	d.	|	...	...	...	...	...	...	...	...	...
Ramdane Djamal	d.	2251	...	...	...	...	...	...	...	...	...
Jijel	d.	|	...	...	...	...	...	...	...	0645	...
El Milia	d.	|	...	...	...	...	...	...	...	0725	...
El Harrouch	d.	|	...	...	...	...	...	...	...	0843	...
Constantine	a.	2359	...	...	...	...	...	...	...	0941	...
Constantine	d.	0004	...	...	...	...	...	0640	0741	...	...
Setif	d.	0227	...	0540	...	...	...	0845	1007	—	...
M'Sila	d.	|	...	|	0651	...	...	|	|	...	1700
Bordj Bou Arreridj	d.	0317	...	0620	0740	...	...	0929	1050	...	1748
Béjaïa	d.	|	...	|	|	0800	...	|	...	1650	—
Beni Mansour	d.	0429	...	|	0844	0959	...	1037	...	1850	...
Bouira	d.	0519	0535	0757	0933	...	1015	1121	...	...	1720
Thénia ☆	d.	0636	0700	|	|	...	1133	1230	...	...	1838
Alger ☆	a.	0729	0753	0942	1115	...	...	1315	...	...	...

(1) and ✕ Alger - Constantine and v.v. **C** – ▬ (12) and ✕ Alger - Annaba and v.v. ☆ – Additional local trains available.

TUNISIA

ital: **Tunis** (GMT +1). 2016 Public Holidays: Jan. 1, 14, Mar. 20 Apr. 9, May 1, July 7, 25, Sept. 13, Oct. 3, 15, Dec. 12.

services are operated Société Nationale des Chemins de Fer Tunisiens (SNCFT. www.sncft.com). Unless otherwise noted, trains convey first and second class seated ommodation. Long distance overnight trains may convey sleeping cars and/or couchettes and where this is the case it will be shown in the footnotes. Timings are the most ent available and are subject to alteration at any time.

CFT offers the **Carte Bleue** pass. The pass allows unlimited travel on all scheduled SNCFT services (except the Lézard Rouge tourist train) for a period of 7, 15, or 21 days, are available for each of the three classes of accommodation. Supplements are payable in advance for using certain services. For more information, please visit the website e European agent www.fahrplancenter.com Prices (in Euros): Grand Confort Class 7 days 31.00, 15 days 62.00, 21 days 93.00. First Class 7 days 28.00, 15 days 56.00, 21 s, 84.00. Second Class 7 days 20.00, 15 days 40.00, 21 days 60.00.

GHARDIMAOU - TUNIS — 4050

CFT

		①–⑥	①–⑥					①–⑥		
Ghardimaou	d.	...	...	0500	1020	1245	1530	...	...	...
Jendouba	d.	...	...	0528	1048	1308	1552	...	...	...
Béja	d.	...	0515	0620	1139	1354	1640	...	...	...
Tebourba	d.	0605	|	0740	|	1501	1749	1940	...	...
Tunis Ville	a.	0643	0720	0822	1339	1541	1830	2021	...	...

		①–⑥				⑥		①–⑤		①–⑤
Tunis Ville	d.	0510	0605	1025	1300	1435	1615	1725	...	1755
Tebourba	d.	0550	0648	|	1343	1517	1659	1808	...	1836
Béja	d.	...	0756	1211	1457	1629	1815	...	...	1945
Jendouba	d.	...	0844	1308	1553	...	1908	...	...	...
Ghardimaou	a.	...	0905	1329	1619	...	1934	...	...	...

BIZERTE - TUNIS — 4060

CFT

		①–⑥								
Bizerte	d.	0520	0740	1500	1800	...	...	...	...	...
Mateur	d.	0554	0813	1534	1832	...	...	...	...	...
Tunis Ville	a.	0709	0919	1651	1939	...	...	...	...	...

		①–⑥								
Tunis Ville	d.	0525	1215	...	1545	1825	...	...	...	...
Mateur	d.	0643	1322	...	1652	1944	...	...	...	...
Bizerte	a.	0715	1354	...	1723	2015	...	...	...	...

4070 KALAÂ KASBAH - TUNIS

SNCFT

km		⊡	1	⊡						
	El Kef d.	...	0550	...	...	...	...	...	...	...
0	**Kalaâ Kasbah** d.	...	|	0600a	...	...	1345	...	...	...
44	Dahmani d.	0400	|	0703	...	1420	1449	...	...	...
63	Le Sers d.	0428	0627	0732	...	1438	1428	...	...	...
115	Gaafour d.	0524	0713	0832	...	1524	1618	...	...	...
175	Pont du Fahs d.	0615	|	0922	...	1601	1712	...	...	...
235	**Tunis** Ville a.	0732	0839	1038	...	1654	1829	...	...	...

	⊡			⊡	1	⊡		
Tunis Ville d.	0555	1000	...	1410	1620	1805	...	...
Pont du Fahs d.	0715	1052	...	1528	1711	1922	...	...
Gaafour d.	0806	1129	...	1617	1747	2011	...	...
Le Sers d.	0903	1214	...	1714	1832	2107	...	...
Dahmani d.	0932	1236	...	1742	|	2134	...	...
Kalaâ Kasbah a.	1034	...	...	1844a	|	...	...	...
El Kef a.	...	...	...	...	1908	...	...	...

a – June 5 - Sep. 30.

⊡ – Supplement payable.

4080 TUNIS - SOUSSE - SFAX - TOZEUR

SNCFT

km		1	⊡		1		⊡				⊡	1	⑥	⚒⊡	1	⚒1	1	⊡		⊡	⊡	⊡	🚌
0	**Tunis** Ville d.	0550	0600	...	0820	...	0930	...	...	1235	1305	1405	1420	1535	1620	1735	1720	1800	...	1840	2045	2215	...
59	Bir Bou Rekba ◇ d.	0635	0653	...	0908	...	1023	...	...	1321	1356	1447	1519	1629	|	1831	1802	1853	...	1934	2138	2307	...
64	Hammamet ◇ d.	|	|	...	|	...	|	...	...	|	|	|	1526	|	|	1837	|	|	...	|	|	|	...
76	**Nabeul** ◇ a.	|	|	...	|	...	|	...	...	|	|	|	1545	|	|	1856	|	|	...	|	|	|	...
142	Kalaâ Séghira d.	0723	|	...	1003	...	|	...	...	|	1454	|	...	1735	1802	...	|	|	...	2040	|	|	...
149	**Sousse** d.	0729	0810	...	|	...	1137	...	...	1422	|	1540	...	1742	|	...	|	2011	...	2047	2250	0020	...
174	Monastir d.	...	|	...	|	...	|	...	...	1505	|	...	...	...	|	...	1925	|	...	...	|	|	...
217	**Mahdia** a.	...	|	...	|	...	|	...	...	1603	|	...	...	...	|	...	...	|	...	...	|	|	...
215	El Jem d.	...	0907	...	1050	...	1234	...	...	...	1548	...	...	...	|	...	...	2108	...	...	2347	0117	...
278	**Sfax** d.	...	1000	...	1138	...	1327	...	...	...	1643	...	...	...	1935	...	...	2157	...	...	0040	0215	...
340	Ghraïba d.	...	1052	...	...	...	1418	...	...	...	1735	...	...	...	|	...	...	...	...	...	0134	|	...
422	**Gabès** a.	...	1204	...	...	...	|	...	...	...	1843	...	...	...	2125	...	...	...	...	...	|	0413	0420
	Tataouine a.	...	...	...	...	...	|	...	...	...	...	...	...	...	...	...	...	...	...	...	|	...	0645
482	Gafsa d.	...	...	...	...	...	1634	...	...	...	...	...	...	...	...	...	...	...	...	...	0347	...	...
521	Metlaoui d.	...	...	...	...	...	1711	...	...	...	...	...	...	...	...	...	...	...	...	...	0424	...	...
574	**Tozeur** a.	...	...	...	...	...	1759	...	...	...	...	...	...	...	...	...	...	...	...	...	0512	...	...

		⊡	🚌	⊡	⚒1	⊡	⚒⊡		1	⊡	1	1	⊡			⊡	1	1			⊡		⊡
Tozeur d.	...	2030	...	...	...	...	...	...	...	...	...	...	0630	...	...	...	...	...	...	...	...	...	...
Metlaoui d.	...	2121	...	...	...	...	...	...	...	...	...	...	0721	...	...	...	...	...	...	...	...	...	...
Gafsa d.	...	2200	...	...	...	...	...	...	...	...	...	...	0800	...	...	...	...	...	...	...	...	...	...
Tataouine d.	...	|	2100	...	...	...	...	...	...	...	...	...	|	...	...	...	...	...	...	...	...	...	...
Gàbes d.	...	|	2355	0005	...	...	...	...	...	...	0500	...	|	...	...	1115	...	...	...	...	...	...	1605
Ghraïba d.	...	0011	...	|	...	...	...	...	...	...	|	...	1011	...	...	1229	...	...	...	...	...	...	1717
Sfax d.	...	0115	...	0210	...	...	...	...	...	0530	0653	...	1110	...	...	1330	...	1610	...	...	...	...	1825
El Jem d.	...	0209	...	0258	...	...	...	...	...	0620	|	...	1158	...	...	1420	...	1655	...	...	...	...	1916
Mahdia d.	...	|	...	|	...	...	...	...	...	|	|	...	|	...	...	|	...	|	...	...	1700	...	|
Monastir d.	...	|	...	|	...	...	...	...	0650	|	|	...	|	...	...	|	...	|	...	...	1754	...	|
Sousse d.	...	0315	...	0405	...	0500	0600	...	|	0730	|	0955	1304	...	...	|	1620	|	...	...	1835	...	2025
Kalaâ Seghira d.	...	|	...	|	...	0508	|	...	0721	|	0820	|	|	...	...	1509	|	1740	...	...	|	...	|
Nabeul ◇ d.	...	|	...	|	0530	|	|	...	|	|	|	|	|	...	...	|	|	|	...	...	|	...	|
Hammamet ◇ d.	...	|	...	|	0547	|	|	...	|	|	|	|	|	...	...	|	|	|	...	...	|	...	|
Bir Bou Rekba ◇ d.	...	0418	...	0508	0553	0614	0706	...	0810	0834	|	1047	1407	...	...	1607	1715	1832	...	...	1929	...	2129
Tunis Ville a.	...	0513	...	0601	0655	0712	0805	...	0859	0929	1003	1128	1503	...	...	1703	1805	1921	...	...	2013	...	2223

⊡ – Supplement payable. ◇ – Additional services available with connections from/to Tunis.

4090 SOUSSE - MONASTIR AIRPORT - MAHDIA

SNCFT

km		⚒		⚒				⚒		⚒													
0	**Sousse** Bab El Jedid d.	0550	0630	0710	0750	0830	0910	0950	1030	1110	1150	1230	1310	1350	...	1510	1550	1630	1710	1750	1830	1910	1950
3	**Sousse** Sud d.	0556	0636	0716	0756	0836	0916	0956	1036	1116	1156	1236	1316	1356	...	1516	1556	1636	1716	1756	1836	1916	1956
15	Monastir Airport ✈ d.	0610	0650	0730	0810	0850	0930	1010	1050	1130	1210	1250	1330	1410	...	1530	1610	1650	1730	1810	1850	1930	2010
24	Monastir d.	0625	0705	0745	0825	0900	0945	1025	1105	1145	1225	1305	1345	1425	...	1545	1625	1705	1745	1825	1905	1945	2025
47	Moknine d.	0656	0736	0816	0856	...	1016	1056	1136	1216	1256	1336	1416	1456	...	1616	1656	1736	1816	1856	1936	2016	2056
73	**Mahdia** a.	0730	0810	0850	0930	...	1050	...	1210	1250	1330	1410	1450	1530	...	1650	...	1810	1850	1930	2010	2050	2130

			⚒	⚒	⚒ a		⚒							⚒									
Mahdia d.	...	0520	0555	0620	...	0700	0740	0820	0900	1020	...	1140	1220	1300	1340	1420	...	1540	1620	...	1740	1820	1900
Moknine d.	...	0552	0632	0657	0715	0735	0815	0855	0935	1055	1135	1215	1255	1335	1415	1455	...	1612	1655	1740	1815	1903	1935
Monastir d.	...	0630	0710	0740	0755	0815	0855	0935	1015	1135	1215	1255	1335	1415	1455	1535	...	1655	1735	1820	1855	1940	2015
Monastir Airport ✈ d.	...	0640	0720	0750	0805	0825	0905	0945	1025	1145	1225	1305	1345	1425	1505	1545	...	1705	1745	1830	1905	1950	2025
Sousse Sud d.	...	0656	0735	0805	0820	0840	0920	1000	1040	1200	1240	1320	1400	1440	1520	1600	...	1720	1800	1845	1920	2005	2040
Sousse Bab El Jedid a.	...	0700	0740	0810	0825	0845	0925	1005	1045	1205	1245	1325	1405	1445	1525	1605	...	1725	1805	1850	1925	2010	2045

a – Runs Sept. 14 2015 - May 14 2016 only.

EGYPT

Capital: **Cairo** (GMT +2). 2016 Public Holidays: Jan. 7, 25, Apr. 25, May 1, 2, June 30, July 7, 8, 9, 23, Sept. 13 - 16, Oct. 3, 6, Dec. 12.

Rail services are operated Egyptian National Railways (ENR. www.enr.gov.eg). Unless otherwise noted, trains convey first and second class seated accommodation. L distance overnight trains may convey sleeping cars and/or couchettes and where this is the case it will be shown in the footnotes. Timings are the most recent available and subject to alteration at any time.

4100 MERSA MATRUH - CAIRO and ALEXANDRIA

Egyptian National Railw

km		2	A	2	B					
0	**Mersa Matruh** d.	0705	1335	1545	2300	...	...	...	...	...
84	El Alamein d.	1024	1620	1830	|	...	...	...	...	...
311	**Alexandria** a.	1330	|	2115	|	...	...	...	...	...
509	**Cairo** Main a.	...	2135	...	0600	...	...	...	...	...

	2	A	2	B				
Cairo Main d.	...	0640	...	2300	...	...	...	...
Alexandria d.	0640	|	1330	|	...	...	...	...
El Alamein d.	0924	1145	1717	|	...	...	...	...
Mersa Matruh a.	1205	1415	2020	0600	...	...	...	...

A – June – Sept. only.

B – 🛏 (1, 2 class). June 15 - Sept. 15. From Mersa on ②④⑦, from Cairo on ①③⑥.

4110 CAIRO - ALEXANDRIA

Egyptian National Railw

km		903	965	905	901	909	911	89		913	907	949	917	919	2001	915	923	925	921	927	969	931	935
0	**Cairo** Main d.	0600	0735	0800	0815	0900	1000	1100	...	1200	1250	1315	1400	1410	1500	1515	1600	1715	1800	1900	1935	2015	2230
45	Benha d.	0636	0812	|	0851	|	1036	|	...	1236	1326	1357	|	1500	|	1551	1636	1751	|	|	2017	2050	|
86	Tanta d.	0720	0845	|	0923	|	1108	1205	...	1308	1358	1440	|	1543	|	1623	1720	1832	1903	|	2055	2132	2335
147	Damanhūr d.	0815	...	|	1007	|	1153	|	...	1352	1443	...	|	1635	|	1708	1813	1918	|	|	...	2223	|
208	**Alexandria** a.	0915	...	1030	1100	1130	1250	1340	...	1445	1540	...	1630	1735	1720	1805	1920	2015	2030	2130	...	2320	0105

	936	948	1904	902	906	964	904	900	910	912	914	916	918	966	922		88	994	928	926	2000	930	934
Alexandria d.	...	...	...	0600	0700	...	0800	0815	1000	1200	1300	1400	1500	...	1530	...	1645	...	1800	1900	1930	2000	2200
Damanhūr d.	...	...	...	0700	|	...	|	0920	1100	|	1400	|	|	...	1635	...	|	...	|	|	|	2105	|
Tanta d.	0600	0655	0715	0756	|	0855	|	1008	1145	1330	1500	|	|	1635	1725	...	1825	1900	1930	|	|	2155	2330
Benha d.	0642	0739	0757	0840	|	0932	|	1042	1222	|	1542	|	|	1722	1757	...	|	1942	|	|	|	2227	|
Cairo Main a.	0715	0820	0830	0915	0940	1010	1040	1115	1255	1430	1615	1630	1730	1755	1830	...	1925	2015	2030	2130	2150	2300	0030

ALEXANDRIA and CAIRO - DUMYAT 4120

ptian National Railways 2nd class only

Alexandria d.	...	...	1815	...	...	...	...	...	...
Cairo Main d.	0515	0725	|	1935	...	...	...	...	...
Dumyat a.	1015	1125	2230	2355	...	...	...	...	...

Dumyat d.	0640	0715	1315	1630	...	...	...	...	...
Cairo Main a.	1005	|	1800	2020	...	...	...	...	...
Alexandria a.	...	1210	...	...	...	...	...	...	...

All services are subject to confirmation.

ALEXANDRIA and CAIRO - BÛR SA'ÎD 4130

ptian National Railways 2nd class only

		12	12						
Alexandria d.	...	0430	...	...	1530	...	...	...	...
Cairo Main d.	0615	|	1345	1440	|	1945	...	...	...
Bûr Sa'îd a.	1015	1110	1800	1905	2210	2350	...	...	...

			12			12			
Bûr Sa'îd d.	0530	0725	0930	1300	1730	1825	1815	...	...
Cairo Main a.	0945	|	1335	1710	2135	|	0050	...	...
Alexandria a.	...	1330	...	...	...	0035	...	...	...

All services are subject to confirmation.

CAIRO - EL SUWEIS 4140

ptian National Railways 2nd class only

Cairo Ain Shams d.	0630	0510**n**	0920	1310	1615	1845	2145	...	...
El Suweis a.	0840	0950	1135	1520	1830	2100	2400	...	...

El Suweis d.	0600	1010	1310	1525	1550	1900	2125	...	...
Cairo Ain Shams a.	0815	1215	1525	2005**n**	1805	2110	2335	...	...

All services are subject to confirmation.

n – Cairo Main.

CAIRO - ASWÂN 4150

ptian National Railways

	1902	934	980	982	986	988	88	976	996	886
Cairo Main ◇ d.	0005	0100	0800	1200	1300	1900	2000	2100	2200	2315
El Giza ◇ d.	0030	0130	0825	1225	1325	1925	2025	2125	2230	2340
Béni Suef ◇ d.	|	0250	0940	1350	1443	2045	2147	2243	2348	0100
El Menya ◇ d.	|	0425	1110	1520	1630	2220	2330	0015	0120	0235
Asyût ◇ d.	0455	0620	1300	1715	1830	0010	0125	0215	0310	0430
Sohâg ◇ d.	0625	0740	1430	1850	2000	0125	0250	0340	0435	0545
Qena ◇ d.	0845	1000	1710	2120	2235	0340	0525	0605	0655	0805
Luxor d.	0950	1055	1825	2235	...	0445	0640	0705	0800	0910
Aswân a.	1305	...	2200	0205	...	0800	1015	...	1120	1230

	981	935	983	887	977	1903	997	89	989	987
Aswân d.	0530	...	1000	1500	...	1615	1945	2000	2200	...
Luxor d.	0915	1200	1335	1820	1900	1945	2320	2345	0130	...
Qena ◇ d.	1025	1305	1445	1920	2005	2045	0020	0055	0230	0600
Sohâg ◇ d.	1310	1530	1730	2145	2215	2300	0245	0340	0450	0850
Asyût ◇ d.	1440	1700	1910	2305	2340	0030	0405	0515	0615	1025
El Menya ◇ d.	1630	1845	2110	0055	0130	|	0600	0710	0805	1225
Béni Suef ◇ d.	1805	2025	2242	0230	0305	|	0740	0850	0940	1405
El Giza ◇ d.	1930	|	0010	0355	0425	0525	0900	|	1100	1525
Cairo Main ◇ a.	1950	2205	0030	0415	0455	0545	0920	1035	1120	1545

Additional services available.

OTHER AFRICAN STATES

details of capital cities and public holiday dates please see individual tables.

ess otherwise noted, trains convey first and second class seated accommodation. Some operators also offer third class seating. This will not normally be mentioned in the es, and where it is the only class available will be noted as second class. Long distance overnight trains may convey sleeping cars and/or couchettes. As a general rule, first s sleepers have two berths per cabin, whilst second class has four. The standard of accommodation varies widely with no two countries beng the same. Timings are the latest lable and are valid until further notice, but may change at any time so we suggest you confirm them locally before travelling. In Muslim countries a different timetable may be rated during the festival of Ramadan.

SUDAN and SOUTH SUDAN 4200

dan Railways Corporation

Sudan : **Khartoum** (GMT +3). 2016 Public Holidays : Jan. 1, 8, May 1, June 30, July 7, Sept. 13, Oct. 3, Dec. 12.
South Sudan : **Juba** (GMT +3). 2016 Public Holidays : Jan. 1, 9, Mar. 27, May 1, 16, Jul. 7, 9, 30, Sept. 13, Dec. 25, 28, 31.

	222 ②	101 ④A	212 E	551 B	202 ④C	D01 ④D			
Wadi Halfa d.	1800**b**	...	...	...	0200**d**	...	...	...	...
Abu Hamed d.	0600**c**	...	...	...	0800**e**	...	...	...	...
Dagash d.	...	...	...	...	1030**e**	...	...	...	...
Berber d.	...	...	...	...	2300**e**	...	...	...	...
Bûr Sûdan d.	...	1530**d**	...	...	|	...	...	...	...
Sinkat d.	...	2000**d**	...	...	|	...	...	...	...
Gebeit d.	...	2240**d**	...	...	|	...	...	...	...
Haiya Junction d.	...	0445**e**	...	...	|	...	...	...	...
Atbara a.	...	1255**e**	...	...	2345**e**	...	...	...	...
Atbara d.	...	...	2130	...	0200**f**	...	...	...	...
Ed Dâmer d.	...	...	2300	...	0300**g**	...	...	...	...
Shendî d.	...	...	0300	...	0930**g**	...	...	...	...
Khartoum Bahri a.	...	...	0730	...	1700**g**	...	...	...	...
Khartoum Bahri d.	...	...	...	...	...	2000**d**	...	...	...
Sennâr Junction d.	...	...	...	...	...	0600**e**	...	...	...
Kôsti d.	...	...	...	...	...	1030**e**	...	...	...
Tendelti d.	...	...	...	...	...	1500**e**	...	...	...
Er Rahad d.	...	...	...	⊖	...	2100**e**	...	...	...
El Obeid a.	...	...	...	|	...	2230**e**	...	...	...
Babanusa d.	...	...	...	⊖	...	...	...	...	...
El Daien d.	...	...	...	⊖	...	...	...	...	...
Nyâlâ a.	...	...	...	⊖	...	...	...	...	...

	552 B	221 ④	201 ①C	502 ①D	102 ①A	211 E			
Nyâlâ d.	⊖	...	...	...	...	...	...	...	...
El Daien d.	⊖	...	...	...	...	...	...	...	...
Babanusa d.	⊖	...	...	...	...	...	...	...	...
El Obeid d.	|	...	...	0700**a**	...	...	...	...	...
Er Rahad d.	⊖	...	...	0830**a**	...	...	...	...	...
Tendelti d.	...	...	...	1445**a**	...	...	...	...	...
Kôsti d.	...	...	...	1930**a**	...	...	...	...	...
Sennâr Junction d.	...	...	...	0000**b**	...	...	...	...	...
Khartoum Bahri a.	...	...	...	1030**b**	...	...	...	...	...
Khartoum Bahri d.	...	...	0800**a**	...	...	2130	...	...	...
Shendî d.	...	...	1545**a**	...	...	0200	...	...	...
Ed Dâmer d.	...	...	2200**a**	...	...	0600	...	...	...
Atbara a.	...	...	2300**a**	...	...	0730	...	...	...
Atbara d.	...	...	0100**b**	...	2000**a**	...	...	...	...
Haiya Junction d.	...	...	|	...	0415**b**	...	...	...	...
Gebeit d.	...	...	|	...	1015**b**	...	...	...	...
Sinkat d.	...	...	|	...	1120**b**	...	...	...	...
Bûr Sûdan a.	...	...	|	...	1545**b**	...	...	...	...
Berber d.	...	...	0345**b**	...	...	...	...	...	...
Dagash d.	...	...	1530**b**	...	...	...	...	...	...
Abu Hamed d.	...	1730**d**	1745**b**	...	...	...	...	...	...
Wadi Halfa a.	...	0545**e**	2230**b**	...	...	...	...	...	...

[12] From Bûr Sûdan 1st and 3rd ④ of each month, from Atbara on following ①. Service temporarily withdrawn March 2014.
(couchette) 1 cl., [2]. From El Rahad/ Nyâlâ every two weeks day and time not fixed.
(sleeper) 1 cl., [2]. From Khartoum on 1st and 3rd ① of each month, from Wadi Halfa on following ④. Service temporarily withdrawn March 2014.
(couchette) 1 cl., (sleeper) 2 cl., [3] and (bar). From Khartoum on 2nd ④ of each month, from El Obeid on following ①. Service temporarily withdrawn March 2014. Not operated by SRC.
(couchette) 1 cl., [23].

a – ①.
b – ②.
c – ③.
d – ④.
e – ⑤.
f – ⑥.
g – ⑦.
⊖ – No timings available.

ERITREA 4210

emins de Fer d'Eritrea

	①–⑥ 2	A	⑦ B
Mitsiwa d.	⊖	A	...
Otumlo d.	⊖	|	...
Moncullo d.	...	A	...
Ghinda d.	...	A	...
Nefasit d.	...	A	1000
Asmara a.	...	A	1200

	①–⑥ 2	A	⑦ B
Asmara d.	...	A	0800
Nefasit d.	...	A	0915
Ghinda d.	...	A	...
Moncullo d.	...	A	...
Otumlo d.	⊖	|	...
Mitsiwa a.	⊖	A	...

Capital : **Asmara** (GMT +3).

2016 Public Holidays : Jan. 1, Mar. 8, 25, 27, May 1, 24, July 7, Sep. 1, 13, 27, Dec. 12, 25.

A – No regular service. Charter service available.
B – Minimum 10 passengers required.
⊖ – No information available.

ETHIOPIA 4215

emins de Fer Djibouti Ethiopien

	②⑤	
Diré Daoua d.	0400	...
Dewelé ☎ a.	1400	...
Ali Sabieh ☎ d.	1700	...
Djibouti a.	2200	...

	③⑥	
Djibouti d.	0600	...
Ali Sabieh ☎ d.	1000	...
Dewelé ☎ a.	1300	...
Diré Daoua a.	2200	...

ital : **Addis Abeba** (GMT +3). 2016 Public Holidays : Jan. 7, 19, Mar. 2, Apr. 29, May 1, 3, July 7, Sept. 11, 13, Dec. 12.

outi Tourist Office claims that the train trip to Dire Daoua is amongst the most dangerous in world!

MAURITANIA 4220

SNIM 2nd class only

km			
0	**Nouadhibou** d.	1450	...
652	**Zouèrate** a.	0540	...

Zouèrate d.	1215	...
Nouadhibou a.	0618	...

Capital : **Nouakchott** (GMT +0).

2016 Public Holidays : Jan. 1, May 1, 25, July 5, 6, Sept. 14, 15, Oct. 1, Dec. 12.

SNIM – Société Nationale Industrielle et Minière.

4230 GUINEA

2nd class only   Chemins de Fer Guinea, Chemins de Fer de B

km		①-⑤	①-⑤	①-⑤		①-⑤	①-⑤	①-⑤
0	**Conakry** Portovoya d.	...	0847	1725	**Halte Km 36** d.	0645	...	1916
	Simbaya d.	0600	0940	1829	Simbaya d.	0730	1630	1950
36	**Halte Km 36** a.	0640	...	1906	**Conakry** P'voya a.	0837	1710	...

km		B				B		
0	**Kamsar** d.	0930	...	...	**Sangaredi** d.	1415	...	...
55	Boké d.	1130	...	...	Boké d.	1630	...	...
136	**Sangaredi** a.	1345	...	...	**Kamsar** a.	1830	...	...

Capital: **Conakry** (GMT +0).
2016 Public Holidays: Mar. 28, May 1, 25, Jul. 2, 7, Aug. 15, Sept. 13, Oct. 2, Dec. 1
B – ①④⑤⑦.

4240 MALI

2nd class only   Tran

km		B				A		
0	**Kayes** d.	0715	...	...	**Bamako** d.	0715	...	...
160	Bafoulabé d.	1130	...	...	Kati d.	0815	...	...
308	Kita d.	1805	...	...	Kita d.	1300	...	...
468	Kati d.	2250	...	...	Bafoulabé d.	1935	...	...
493	**Bamako** a.	2345	...	...	Kayes d.	2350	...	...

Capital: **Bamako** (GMT +0).
2016 Public Holidays: Mar. 26, 28, Apr. 6, May 16, 25, Jul. 7, Sep. 13, 22, Dec. 12, 21, 26
A – ①②④⑥.
B – ②③⑤⑦.

4250 GHANA

Ghana Railway Corpora

km		A				A		
0	**Takoradi** d.	2030	...	...	**Kumasi** d.	2030	...	...
276	**Kumasi** a.	0930a	...	...	**Takoradi** a.	0930a	...	...

km		2B	2B	2B		2B	2B	2B
0	**Accra** d.	0740	1000	1400	**Nsawam** d.	0600	1140	1220
40	**Nsawam** a.	0920	1140	1540	**Accra** a.	0740	1320	1400

km		①-⑥	①-⑥	①-⑥		①-⑥	①-⑥
0	**Accra** d.	0500	1215	1700	**Tema** d.	0630	...
	Asoprochona a.	0558	1313	1759	**Asoprochona** d.	0655	1415
	Tema a.	0625	...	1825	**Accra** a.	0755	1515

Capital: **Accra** (GMT +0).
2016 Public Holidays: Jan. 1, Mar. 6, 7, Mar. 25, 28, May, 1, 2, 25, Jul. 1, 7, Sep. 13, 21, De 25, 26.
A – Service operates every second day.   a – Approximate timings.
B – ①-⑥. Additional trains from Accra at 1900, from Nsawam at 1730.

4260 BURKINA FASO - CÔTE D'IVOIRE

Sita

km		②④⑥ 2	⑥ A		①③⑤ 2	④ A
0	**Ouagadougou** d.	...	⊖	**Abidjan** Treichville d.	0900	0700
93	Koudougou d.	...	⊖	**Abidjan** Plateau d.	0920	⊖
349	Bobo Dioulasso d.	...	1400	Anyama d.	1015	⊖
446	Banfora d.	...	⊖	Agboville d.	1240	⊖
495	Niangoloko 🛃 d.	...	⊖	Dimbokro d.	1615	⊖
539	Ouangolodougou d.	...	⊖	Bouaké d.	...	⊖
576	Ferkessédougou d.	...	⊖	Katiola d.	...	⊖
658	Tafiré d.	...	⊖	Tafiré d.	...	⊖
769	Katiola d.	...	⊖	Ferkessédougou d.	...	⊖
820	Bouaké d.	...	⊖	Ouangolodougou d.	...	⊖
958	Dimbokro d.	0900	⊖	Niangoloko 🛃 d.	...	⊖
1064	Agboville d.	1255	⊖	Banfora d.	...	⊖
1115	Anyama d.	1515	⊖	Bobo Dioulasso d.	...	⊖
1141	**Abidjan** Plateau a.	1610	⊖	Koudougou d.	...	⊖
1143	**Abidjan** Treichville a.	1625	⊖	**Ouagadougou** a.	...	⊖

Capitals: **Ouagadougou** (Burkina Faso, GMT +0), **Yamoussoukro** (Côte d'Ivoire, GMT
2016 Public Holidays:
Burkina Faso: Jan. 1, Mar. 28, May 1, 5, Jul. 7, Aug. 15, Sept. 13, Nov. 1, Dec. 12, 25.
Côte d'Ivoire: Jan. 1, Mar. 28, May 1, 5, 16, Jul. 2, 7, Aug. 7, 15, Sept. 13, Nov. 1, 15, Dec 25.
A – [12] and 🍸 Abidjan - Ouagadougou and v.v. Journey time 43 - 48 hours.
⊖ – No timings available.

4270 NIGERIA

Nigerian Railways Corpora

Capital: **Abuja** (GMT +1). 2016 Public Holidays: Jan. 1, Mar. 25, 28, May 1, 29, Jul. 7, Sept. 13, Oct. 1, Dec. 12, 25, 26.

km		⑤A	⑤B	②⑤⑥		①A	⑤B	③⑥⑦
0	**Lagos** Terminal d.	1200	...	0900	**Kano** d.	0900	⊖	...
14	Agege d.	⊖	...	⊖	Zaria d.	⊖	⊖	...
91	Abeokuta d.	⊖	...	⊖	**Kaduna** Junction d.	⊖	⊖	...
193	Ibadan d.	⊖	...	⊖	Minna d.	⊖	...	...
280	Ede d.	⊖	...	⊖	Zungeru d.	⊖	...	...
295	Oshogbo d.	⊖	...	⊖	Jebba d.	⊖	...	...
391	Ilorin d.	⊖	...	1834	Ilorin d.	⊖	...	0900
488	Jebba d.	⊖	...	...	Oshogbo d.	⊖	...	⊖
685	Zungeru d.	⊖	...	...	Ede d.	⊖	...	⊖
744	Minna d.	⊖	...	...	Ibadan d.	⊖	...	⊖
902	**Kaduna** Junction d.	⊖	⊖	...	Abeokuta d.	⊖	...	⊖
986	Zaria d.	⊖	⊖	...	Agege d.	⊖	...	⊖
1126	**Kano** a.	1701a	⊖	...	**Lagos** Terminal a.	1424a	...	2059

km		C	⑤B		C
0	**Port Harcourt** New d.	⊖	⊖	**Maiduguri** d.	⊖
63	Aba d.	⊖	⊖	Buni d.	⊖
113	Umuahia Ibeku d.	⊖	⊖	Gombe d.	⊖
243	Enugu d.	⊖	⊖	Bauchi d.	⊖
375	Oturkpo d.	⊖	⊖	**Kaduna** Junction d.	⊖
463	Makurdi d.	⊖	⊖	Kafanchan d.	⊖
565	Lafia d.	⊖	⊖	Lafia d.	⊖
737	Kafanchan d.	⊖	⊖	Makurdi d.	⊖
916	**Kaduna** Junction d.	⊖	⊖	Oturkpo d.	⊖
1333	Bauchi d.	⊖	...	Enugu d.	⊖
1499	Gombe d.	⊖	...	Umuahia Ibeku d.	⊖
1658	Buni d.	⊖	...	Aba d.	⊖
1801	**Maiduguri** a.	⊖	...	**P Harcourt** New a.	⊖

A – Conveys 🛏 (1 cl.), [2] and ✕.
B – Port Harcourt - Kaduna - Kano and v.v.
C – Port Harcourt - Kaduna - Maiduguri and v.v. Once per week in each direction. Subject to confirmation.
⊖ – No timings available.
a – Next day.

4280 CAMEROON

Cam

Capital: **Youandé** (GMT +1). 2016 Public Holidays: Jan. 1, Feb. 11, Mar. 25, May 5, 20, Jul. 7, Aug. 15, Sept. 13, Dec. 12, 25.

km		151 A	181	103 ①③⑤	191 B	153 A	113 ②④⑥
0	**Douala** Bessengué d.	0600	0730	0900	...	1445	...
72	Edéa d.	|	0910	1210	...	|	...
152	Eséka d.	|	1050	1510	...	|	...
220	Ngoumou d.	|	1230	1720	...	|	...
263	**Yaoundé** d.	0945	1315	1820	1910	1830	...
477	Nanga Eboko d.	...	...	...	2300	...	...
582	Belabo d.	...	...	...	0230	...	0830
686	Mbitom d.	...	...	...	0450	...	1115
910	**N'gaoundéré** a.	...	...	...	1000	...	1800

	184	112 ①③⑤	104 ②④⑥	192 B	152 A	154 A
N'gaoundéré d.	...	0800	...	1915	...	...
Mbitom d.	...	1140	...	0000	...	...
Belabo d.	...	1730	...	0230	...	...
Nanga Eboko d.	...	...	...	0600	...	...
Yaoundé d.	0800	...	0915	1000	1025	1920
Ngoumou d.	0855	...	1030	...	|	|
Eséka d.	1045	...	1250	...	|	|
Edéa d.	1225	...	1600	...	|	|
Douala Bessengué a.	1350	...	1910	...	1410	2305

km		173	175	177		172	174	176
	Douala Bonaberi d.	...	...	...	**Kumba** d.	0750	1130	1530
	Mbanga d.	0920	1300	1730	**Mbanga** d.	0900	1240	1640
	Kumba a.	1030	1410	1840	**Douala** Bonaberi a.	...	...	...

A – Conveys [1] and ✕.   B – Conveys [12] 🛏 2 cl. (2 & 4 berth) 🍸.
☞ – Note: All intermediate and arrival times are approximate.

4290 GABON

Chemins de Fer Trans Gabonn

Capital: **Libreville** (GMT +1). 2016 Public Holidays: Jan.1, Mar. 27, 28, Apr. 17, May 1, 16, July 7, Aug. 15, 16, 17, Sept. 13, Nov. 1, Dec. 25.

km		②	⑤	④	⑦		③	⑦	②	⑤
0	**Owendo** (Libreville) d.	2000	2000	2000	2000	**Franceville** d.	2100	2100	2100	2100
183	Ndjole d.	2310	2305	2330	2330	Moanda d.	2145	2145	2145	2145
340	Booué d.	0245	0240	0255	0255	Lastourville d.	0010	0000	0015	0015
485	Lastourville d.	0510	0510	0535	0535	Booué d.	0250	0250	0250	0250
625	Moanda d.	0715	0720	0805	0805	Ndjole d.	0550	0555	0600	0600
670	**Franceville** a.	0750	0755	0840	0840	**Owendo** (Libreville) a.	0850	0855	0920	0920

CONGO 4300

mins de Fer Congo Océan

	①③⑤ A	① B	①③⑥
Brazzaville d.	0700	1310	1430
Mindouli d.	1000	1715	1730
Loutété d.	1130	|	1850
Nkayi d.	1255	2100	2050
Dolisie d.	1530	0045	...
Pointe Noire a.	1915	0919	...

	②④⑦ A	② B	①③⑥
Pointe Noire d.	0700	1330	...
Dolisie d.	1130	2015	...
Nkayi d.	1335	2300	0750
Loutété d.	1520	2245	0930
Mindouli d.	1650	0030	1100
Brazzaville a.	1950	0500	1350

Capital: **Brazzaville** (GMT +1).
2016 Public Holidays: Jan. 1, Mar. 27, 28, May 1, 5, 16, June 10, Aug. 15, Nov. 1, Dec. 25.

A – GAZELLE – ▬ [12] and ✕.
B – OCEAN – [12] and ✕.

KENYA 4310

a Railways

	②④⑦ A	①③⑤ ⊠	
Mombasa d.	1900	...	...
Voi d.	2320	...	...
Mtito Andei d.	0150	...	...
Makindu d.	0350	...	...
Nairobi a.	1100	...	...
Nairobi d.	...	1830	...
Nakuru d.	...	0105	...
Kisumu a.	...	0920	...

	②④⑦ ⊠	①③⑤ A	
Kisumu d.	1830	...	...
Nakuru d.	0255	...	...
Nairobi a.	0900	...	...
Nairobi d.	...	1900	...
Makindu d.	...	2315	...
Mtito Andei d.	...	0111	...
Voi d.	...	0400	...
Mombasa a.	...	1100	...

Capital: **Nairobi** (GMT +3).
2016 Public Holidays: Jan. 1, Mar. 25, 28, May, 1, 2, June 1, July 18, Oct. 20, Dec. 12, 25, 26.

A – JAMBO KENYA DELUXE – [12] and ✕.
⊠ – Currently suspended.

DEMOCRATIC CONGO 4320

été Nationale des Chemins de Fer du Congo

Capital: **Kinshasa** (GMT +1). 2016 Public Holidays: Jan. 1, 4, 16, 17, Apr. 30, May 1, 17, June 30, Aug. 1, Dec. 24, 25, 31.

	2A	C	B	2D	2④	2			
Sakania d.	...	...	...	...	2000	...	...	...	...
Lubumbashi d.	0300	0700	0700	1300	0822	...	...	...	...
Tenke d.	1500	2000	2000	0200	...	...	...	...	...
Dilolo d.	|	|	|	2200	...	...	...	...	...
Kamina d.	1300	1600	2000	...	...	...	...	...	...
Kabalo d.	2000	|	|	...	...	⊖	...	...	...
Kindu a.	...	|	|	...	...	⊖	...	...	...
Kalemie a.	...	|	|	...	...	...	...	...	...
Mwene Ditu d.	...	1000	2000	...	...	...	...	...	...
Kananga d.	...	...	2200	...	...	...	...	...	...
Ilebo a.	...	...	0900	...	...	...	...	...	...

	2D	C	B	2A	2③	2			
Ilebo d.	...	...	1600	...	...	...	...	...	...
Kananga d.	...	...	0500	...	...	...	...	...	...
Mwene Ditu d.	...	1600	0700	...	...	...	...	...	...
Kalemie d.	...	|	|	...	...	...	...	...	...
Kindu d.	...	|	|	...	...	⊖	...	...	...
Kabalo d.	...	|	|	0600	...	⊖	...	...	...
Kamina d.	...	1100	1100	1400	...	...	...	...	...
Dilolo d.	1500	|	|	|	...	...	...	...	...
Tenke d.	1400	1200	1400	1600	...	...	...	...	...
Lubumbashi a.	0300	1900	2100	2300	0800	...	...	...	...
Sakania a.	...	...	...	...	2000	...	...	...	...

	⑥2		
Kinshasa Est d.	0730	...	...
Matadi a.	1500	...	...

		⑦2	
Matadi d.	...	0715	...
Kinshasa Est a.	...	1445	...

km		2③		
0	**Kisangani** d.	0700	...	...
125	**Ubundu** a.	1700	...	...

	2④		
Ubundu d.	1700	...	...
Kisangani a.	0700	...	...

ll timings are approximate.
From Lubumbashi 2nd and 4th ⑥ of each month. From Kabalo 1st and 3rd ④.
From Lubumbashi 1st ⑥ of each month. From Ilebo on following ①.

C – From Lubumbashi 1st and 3rd ① of each month. From Mwene on following ④.
D – From Lubumbashi 1st and 3rd ④. From Dilolo on following ⑦.
⊖ – No information available.

TANZANIA and ZAMBIA 4330

zania Railways, TAZARA, Zambian Railways

Capitals: **Dodoma** (Tanzania, GMT +3), **Lusaka** (Zambia, GMT +2).
2016 Public Holidays: Tanzania: Jan. 1, 12, Mar. 25, 28, Apr. 7, 26, May 1, July 7, Aug. 8, Sept. 13, Oct. 14, Dec. 9, 12, 25, 26.
2016 Public Holidays: Zambia: Jan. 1, Mar. 8, 12, 25, 28, May 1, 25, July 6, 7, Aug. 3, Oct. 24, Dec. 25.

Tanzania Railways	②⑤ A	③⑥ B	③⑥ B
Dar es Salaam ◧ d.	1700	...	...
Ruvu d.	1931	...	...
Morogoro d.	0015	...	...
Kilosa d.	0235	...	...
Dodoma d.	0810	...	...
Manyoni d.	1214	...	...
Itigi d.	1318	...	...
Tabora a.	1825	...	...
Tabora d.	2010	2100	2130
Kaliua d.	2305	0045	|
Mpanda a.	|	1030	|
Mwanza a.	|	...	0750
Uvinza d.	0330	...	...
Kigoma a.	0725	...	...

	④⑦ B	④⑦ B	④⑦ A
Kigoma d.	...	...	1700
Uvinza d.	...	...	2112
Mwanza d.	...	1800	|
Mpanda d.	1300	|	|
Kaliua d.	2310	|	0136
Tabora a.	0245	0400	0430
Tabora d.	...	...	0725
Itigi d.	...	...	1315
Manyoni d.	...	...	1417
Dodoma d.	...	...	1840
Kilosa d.	...	...	2340
Morogoro d.	...	...	0215
Ruvu d.	...	...	0616
Dar es Salaam ◧ a.	...	...	0850

km	*TAZARA*	② C	⑤ D
0	**Dar es Salaam** ◧ d.	1550	1350
226	Kisaki d.	2013	1910
360	Ifakara d.	2258	2230
496	Mlimba d.	0152	0140
652	Makambako d.	0746	0803
849	Mbeya d.	1323	1440
969	Tunduma d.	1717	1853
970	Nakonde ▦ a.	1622	1758
	Nakonde ▦ d.	1647	1813
1226	Kasama d.	2227	0031
1412	Mpika d.	0148	0445
1652	Serenje d.	0556	0931
1761	Mkushi Boma d.	⊖	1149
1852	**New Kapiri Mposhi** ⊡ a.	0926	1337

	⑤ D	② C
New Kapiri Mposhi ⊡ d.	1400	1600
Mkushi Boma d.	1555	1743
Serenje d.	1817	1947
Mpika d.	2329	0010
Kasama d.	0309	0329
Nakonde ▦ a.	0915	0839
Nakonde ▦ d.	0925	0909
Tunduma d.	1045	1029
Mbeya d.	1500	1428
Makambako d.	2129	2030
Mimba d.	0351	0208
Ifakara d.	0628	0512
Kisaki d.	1035	0757
Dar es Salaam ◧ a.	1546	1210

Zambia Railways	⊗ 2		⑤ E
Kitwe d.	1600	...	...
Ndola d.	1855	...	...
Kapiri Mposhi ⊡ d.	2357	...	...
Kabwe d.	0255	...	...
Chisamba d.	0500	...	...
Lusaka a.	0656	...	...
Lusaka d.	0736	...	1800
Kafue d.	0946	...	1942
Mazabuka d.	1155	...	2104
Monze d.	1417	...	2244
Pemba d.	1558	...	0021
Choma d.	1834	...	0145
Kalomo d.	2108	...	0301
Livingstone a.	0200	...	0627

		⑦ E	①⑤ 2⊗
Livingstone d.	...	1800	2000
Kalomo d.	...	2131	0100
Choma d.	...	2311	0345
Pemba d.	...	0054	0609
Monze d.	...	0153	0749
Mazabuka d.	...	0333	1015
Kafue d.	...	0515	1244
Lusaka a.	...	0627	1424
Lusaka d.	...	...	1454
Chisamba d.	...	...	1648
Kabwe d.	...	...	1946
Kapiri Mposhi ⊡ d.	...	...	2216
Ndola d.	...	...	0336
Kitwe a.	...	...	0600

km	*Zambia Railways*	②⑤ 2	
0	**Mulobezi** d.	0900	...
85	Ngwezi d.	1905	...
163	**Livingstone** a.	0500	...

	③⑥ 2	
Livingstone d.	0500	...
Ngwezi d.	1941	...
Mulobezi a.	0900	...

A – 🛏 1, 2 cl., [2] and ✕ Dar es Salaam - Kigoma and v.v. Subject to confirmation.
B – Subject to confirmation.
C – 🛏 1, 2 cl., ▬ 1, 2 cl., [2] and ✕. Kilimanjaro/Mukuba Express Train.
D – 🛏,1cl. ▬ 1 cl, [12] and ✕. Kilimanjaro/Mukuba Ordinary Train.
E – ▬ (3 and 6 berth), [12] Golden Jubilee Express. Possibly cancelled.
◧ – Stations are approximately 8 km from each other.
⊡ – Stations are approximately 2 km from each other.
⊖ – No information available.
⊗ – Days of running are: From Kitwe 1st week ③, second week ①⑤, From Livingstone 1st week ①⑤, second week ③.

MADAGASCAR 4340

mins de Fer Fianarantsoa-Côte Est / Madarail

Capital: **Antananarivo** (GMT +3). 2016 Public Holidays: Jan. 1, Mar. 28, 29, May 1, 16, June 26, Aug. 15, Nov. 1, Dec, 11, 25.

Madarail	⑤ 2	② 2
Toamasina d.	...	0820
Tampolo d.	...	0951
Ambila-Lemaitso d.	0800	1125
Lohariandava d.	1150	1515
Andasibe ◇ d.	1515	1725
Moramanga a.	1740	1855

	① 2	④ 2
Moramanga d.	0700	1500
Andasibe ◇ d.	0830	1600
Lohariandava d.	1050	1820
Ambila-Lemaitso d.	1340	2200
Tampolo d.	1520	...
Toamasina a.	1650	...

km	*CFFCE*	②④⑥	
0	**Fianarantsoa** d.	0700	...
39	Ranomena d.	0855	...
62	Tolongoina d.	1015	...
79	Manampatrana d.	1110	...
118	Sahasinaka d.	1330	...
163	**Manakara** a.	1600	...

	③⑤⑦ A	
Manakara d.	0645	...
Sahasinaka d.	0900	...
Manampatrana d.	1130	...
Tolongoina d.	1225	...
Ranomena d.	1355	...
Fianarantsoa a.	1600	...

Special tour trains using Michelin railcars run Andasibe - Antananarivo and v.v., For dates contact operator.

BOTSWANA 4345

	502	
Francistown 4380 d.	2100	...
Mahalapye d.	0216	...
Gaborone d.	0605	...
Lobatse a.	0731	...

	501	
Lobatse d.	1910	...
Gaborone d.	2125	...
Mahalapye d.	0056	...
Francistown 4380 a.	0611	...

Capital: **Gaborone** (GMT +2).
2016 Public: Jan. 1, Mar. 25, 28, May 1, 5, July 1, 20, Sept. 30, Dec, 25.

4350 ANGOLA

km		①–⑤	①–⑤	③	⑥	①–⑤	②	⑥	⑥	①–⑤
0	**Luanda** Textang ⊗ d.	0500a	...	...	...	0721	0744	0750	1525	1640
23	Viana ⊗ d.	0528	0700	0700	0745	0803	0930	0834	1610	1732
65	Catete d.	...	0740	0747	0834	0909	|	0927	1704	1827
135	Zenza d.	...	0839	0859	0948	...	1127	...	...	...
190	**Dondo** (Cuanza) a.	...	|	|	1048	...	1220	...	...	...
241	N'dalatando d.	...	1200	1227	...	...	...	...	...	...
424	**Malange** a.	...	1625	1652	...	...	...	...	...	...

	①–⑤	⑥	②	⑥	②⑦	①–⑤	④	⑥
Malange d.	...	...	...	...	0730	...	0730	...
N'dalatando d.	...	...	...	...	1215	...	1215	...
Dondo (Cuanza) d.	...	...	1320	1340	|	...	|	...
Zenza d.	...	...	1418	1450	1516	...	1538	...
Catete d.	1000	1020	|	1600	1615	...	1647	1730
Viana ⊗ d.	1052	1110	1620	1649	1655	1708	1730	1822
Luanda Textang ⊗ a.	1137	114	1701	...	...	1750	...	1855a

km		①–⑤	①–⑤	① g
0	**Lobita** ◧ d.	...	...	0530
33	Benguela ◧ a.	...	...	|
395	**Caála** d.	0630	...	|
408	Dango d.	0730	...	|
423	Huambo d.	0755	1000	1845
453	Cambuio d.	...	1100	|
478	**Katchiungo** a.	...	1155	|
1016	Luena d.	...	...	0300h
1332	Luau a.	...	...	...

	①–⑤	①–⑤	④ g
Luau d.	...	...	...
Luena d.	...	...	2100
Katchiungo d.	1300	...	|
Cambuio d.	1355	...	|
Huambo d.	1455	1600	0700k
Dango d.	...	1622	|
Caála a.	...	1730	|
Benguela ◧ d.	...	...	|
Lobita ◧ a.	...	...	1648k

km		❖		①④
0	**Namibe** d.	...	...	0500
162	Bibala d.	...	...	0845
246	Lubango d.	0600	...	1010
424	Matala d.	1040	...	1320
509	**Dondo** (Lubango) a.	1240	...	|
756	Menongue a.	...	...	1900

	②⑤	
Menongue d.	0500	...
Dondo (Lubango) a.	|	...
Matala d.	1045	...
Lubango d.	1400	...
Bibala d.	1530	...
Namibe a.	1920	...

Capital: **Luanda** (GMT +1). 2016 Public Holidays: Jan. 1, Feb. 4, 17, Mar. 8, 25, Apr. 4, May 1, Sept. 17, Nov. 2, 11, Dec. 25.

⊗ – Additional local trains available. ❖ – Service suspended. **a** – Luanda Muceques. **g** – Timings to be confirmed. **h** – Arrives on ③. **k** – Arrives on ⑥.

◧ – Services dep. Lobita and Benguela at 0600, 1700 journey time 65 mins.

4360 MALAWI

2nd class only Central East African Ra

km		⑥	④	⑤	③
22	Bilila d.	...	0730	...	1625
0	**Balaka** d.	...	0940	0600	1735
16	Nkaya d.	...	1030	0840	...
42	Liwonde d.	...	1115	|	...
114	**Nayuchi** a.	...	1427	|	...
104	Blantyre d.	...	...	1640	...
112	Limbe d.	0900	...	1737	...
233	**Makhanga** a.	1715	...	...	...

	④	③	⑦	④
Makhanga d.	...	...	0700	...
Limbe d.	...	0700	1645	...
Blantyre d.	...	0745	...	...
Nayuchi d.	...	|	...	1500
Liwonde d.	...	|	...	1800
Nkaya d.	...	1315	...	1900
Balaka d.	0600	1453	...	1940
Bilila a.	0710	1605	...	...

Capital: **Lilongwe** (GMT +2).

2016 Public Holidays: Jan. 1, 15, Mar. 3, 25, 28, May 1, June 14, July 6, 7 25.

4370 MOÇAMBIQUE

2nd class only CD do Norte / CF-Moçam

Capital: **Maputo** (GMT +2). 2016 Public Holidays: Jan. 1, Feb. 3, Apr. 7, May 1, June 25, Sep. 7, 25, Oct. 4, Dec. 25.

km		②④⑥	A	
0	**Nampula** d.	0600	...	...
173	Iapala d.	1051	...	...
252	Malema d.	1342	...	...
302	Mutuáli d.	1533	...	...
356	Cuamba d.	1700	⊖	...
464	Mitande d.	...	⊖	...
541	**Nayuci** a.	...	⊖	...

	③⑤⑦	A	
Nayuci d.	...	⊖	...
Mitande d.	...	⊖	...
Cuamba d.	0600	⊖	...
Mutuáli d.	0735	...	...
Malema d.	0933	...	...
Iapala d.	1220	...	...
Nampula a.	1708	...	...

km		⑥⑦	⑥	③
0	**Maputo** d.	0730	0955	1300
208	Chókwe d.	1216	1910	1950
534	**Chicualacuala** a.	...	0349	0342

	④	⑦	⑥⑦
Chicualacuala d.	1300	1015	...
Chókwe d.	2323	2020	1420
Maputo a.	0549	0810	1909

km		⑥	②	①
0	**Beira** d.	0600	1100	2100
28	Dondo d.	0731	1224	2226
120	Muanza d.	1021	1509	0154
187	Inhaminga d.	1208	1656	0415
214	Inhamitanga d.	1259	1742	0505
302	Marromeu a.	1600	|	|
320	**Nhamalabue** a.	...	2125	1024
577	Maotize a.	...	0526	2105

	⑦	③
Moatize d.	...	0600
Nhamalabue d.	...	1618
Marromeu d.	0800	|
Inhamitanga d.	1108	2114
Inhaminga d.	1159	2336
Muanza d.	1346	0204
Dondo d.	1639	0548
Beira a.	1800	0718

km		①–⑤	⑥⑦	⑦–⑤
0	**Maputo** d.	0745	0800	1815
53	Moambe d.	0927	0952	2032
88	**Ressano Garcia** a.	1020	1045	2124

	①–⑥	①–⑤
Ressano Garcia d.	0346	1205
Moambe d.	0506	1317
Maputo a.	0645	1511

A – Once a week. Day of operation varies.

⊖ – No information available.

4380 ZIMBABWE

National Railways of Zimba

Capital: **Harare** (GMT +2). 2016 Public Holidays: Jan. 1, Mar. 25, 28, Apr. 18, May 1, 25, Aug. 8, 9, Dec. 22, 25, 26.

km		①④⑥ A		
0	**Mutare** d.	2100	...	...
77	Nyazura d.	2307	...	...
99	Rusape d.	0010	...	...
166	Macheke d.	0239	...	...
201	Marondera d.	0345	...	...
273	**Harare** a.	0605	...	...

	③⑤⑦ A		
Harare d.	2130	...	...
Marondera d.	2345	...	...
Macheke d.	0100	...	...
Rusape d.	0320	...	...
Nyazura d.	0409	...	...
Mutare a.	0600	...	...

km		B		
0	**Bulawayo** d.	1930	...	...
126	Gwayi d.	2310	...	...
266	Dete d.	0200	...	...
339	Hwange d.	0347	...	...
351	Thomson Junction d.	0455	...	...
472	**Victoria Falls** a.	0800	...	...

	B	
Victoria Falls d.	1900	...
Thomson Jct d.	2230	...
Hwange d.	2303	...
Dete d.	0110	...
Gwayi d.	0340	...
Bulawayo a.	0805	...

km		②⑤⑦ A	①③⑤	
0	**Harare** d.	2000	...	...
44	Norton d.	2120	...	...
127	Chegutu d.	2227	...	...
160	Kadoma d.	2320	...	...
237	Kwekwe d.	0054	...	...
**	Masvingo d.	|	2000	...
302	Gweru d.	0242	0345	...
336	Somabhula d.	|	...	...
369	Shangani d.	|	...	...
486	**Bulawayo** a.	0700	...	...

	①④⑥ A	①③⑤	
Bulawayo d.	2000	...	...
Shangani d.	|	...	...
Somabhula d.	|	...	...
Gweru d.	0030	0245	...
Masvingo a.	|	0955	...
Kwekwe d.	0227	...	...
Kadoma d.	0412	...	...
Chegutu d.	0502	...	...
Norton d.	0620	...	...
Harare a.	0730	...	...

km		③ A	⑦ A	
0	**Bulawayo** d.	1215	1730	...
113	Shangani d.	1513	2045	...
150	Somabhula d.	1607	2140	...
229	Bannockburn d.	1755	2335	...
309	Ngezi d.	1941	0135	...
401	Rutenga d.	2300	0455	...
433	Lundi d.	|	0636	...
500	**Chicualacuala** a.	0251a	|	...
499	Triangle d.	...	0720	...
523	**Chiredzi** a.	...	0758	...

	④ A	① A
Chiredzi d.	...	1530
Triangle d.	...	1620
Chicualacuala d.	1520a	|
Lundi d.	|	1701
Rutenga d.	2000	2000
Ngezi d.	2255	2255
Bannockburn d.	0135	0135
Somabhula d.	0450	0450
Shangani d.	0552	0556
Bulawayo a.	0910	0910

km		④⑦ 2		
0	**Bulawayo** d.	1800	...	...
	Beit Bridge a.	0540	...	...

	①⑤ 2		
Beit Bridge d.	2100	...	...
Bulawayo a.	0845	...	...

km		①⑤ 2	
0	**Bulawayo** ‡ d.	0900	...
196	**Francistown** ‡ **4345** a.	1425	...

	②⑥ 2
Francistown ‡ **4345** d.	1230
Bulawayo ‡ a.	1715

A – 🛏 1, 2 cl. and [2] Ⓡ.
B – 🛏 1 cl., ▬ 2 cl. and [2].

a – Sango Halt.

⊖ – No information available.
** – Masvingo - Gweru *199 km*.

‡ – 🏛 is Plumtree.

4390 NAMIBIA

Sta

Capital: **Windhoek** (GMT +1). 2016 Public Holidays: Jan. 1, Mar. 21, Apr. 3, 6, May 1, 4, 14, 25, Aug. 26, Dec. 10, 25, 26.

km	①–⑤ 12	⑥ A				⑤ A	①–⑤ 12
412	1900	...	↓	d.**Walvisbaai** a.	↑	...	0715
373	2045	1500		d.Swakopmund d.		1000	0530
222	0045	|	↓	d.Usakos d.	↑	|	0150
419	|	|		d. **Otjiwarongo** d.		|	|
282	|	|	↓	d. Omaruru d.	↑	|	|
210	0135	|		d.Kranzberg d.		|	0130
191	0220	|	↓	d.Karibib d.	↑	|	0040
70	0510	|		d.Okahandja d.		|	2205
0	0700	1030	↓	a.**Windhoek** d.	↑	1200a	1915

km	Ⓑ b	③⑥				④⑦	Ⓑ c
0	1940	...	↓	d.**Windhoek** a.	↑	...	0700
97	2210	...		d.Rehobeth d.		...	0425
192	2400	...	↓	d.Kalkrand d.	↑	...	0230
274	0220	...		d.Mariental d.		...	0020
423	0510	...	↓	d.Tses d.	↑	...	2040
505	0700	...		a.**Keetmanshoop** d.		...	1850
505	...	0850	↓	d.**Keetmanshoop** a.	↑	1630	...
681	...	1310		d.Grünau d.		1225	...
732	...	1430	↓	a.**Karasburg** d.	↑	1120	...

km	①–⑥	⑦				①–⑥
0	0850	1120	↓	d.**Oshikango** ♣ a.	↑	1640
60	1010	1235		a.**Ondangwa** ♠ d.		1520
			↓		↑	
	1120	1320		d.**Ondangwa** ♠ a.		1420
	1317	1515	↓	d.Omuthiya ♥ d.	↑	1212
	1443	1631		d.Oshivelo d.		1056
306	1640	1840	↓	a.**Tsumeb** d.	↑	0850

♣ - Rev. Theofelus Hamutumbangela.
♠ - Nehale Lya Mpingana. ♥ - Sam Nujoma.

A – DESERT EXPRESS – 🛏, [1] and ✕. Special service including meals and excursions.

a – departs 1300 in the summer.
b – Also conveys ▬ 2 cl. on ①③⑤. c – Also conveys ▬ 2 cl. on ②④⑦.

SOUTH AFRICA 4400

train / Shosholoza Meyl

tal: **Pretoria** (GMT +2). 2016 Public Holidays: Jan. 1, Mar. 21, 58 Apr. 27, May 1, 2, June 16, Aug. 9, Sep. 24, Dec. 16, 25, 26.

	G	A	③⑤⑦ B	③⑤⑦ C	② 2	⑤ 2	④ E	⑤⑦ D	...	...
Johannesburg d.	1230	1230	1315	1730	...	...	1500	1840	...	...
Germiston d.	1302	|	1350	|	...	...	|	1918	...	...
Standerton d.	|	|	|	|	...	...	|	|	...	...
Newcastle d.	|	|	|	|	...	...	|	0027	...	...
Ladysmith d.	|	|	|	|	...	...	|	0245	...	...
Pietermaritzburg d.	|	|	|	|	...	...	|	0630	...	...
Durban a.	|	|	|	|	...	...	|	0915	...	...
Vereeniging d.	1420	|	1455	1920	...	...	|	...	...	...
Kroonstad d.	1652	|	1725	2150	...	...	|	...	...	...
Bloemfontein a.	1935	|	2020	0032	...	...	|	...	...	...
Bloemfontein d.	...	|	2030	0055	...	...	|	...	...	...
Burgersdorp d.	...	|	|	0634	...	...	|	...	...	...
Queenstown d.	...	|	|	0912	1445	1445	|	...	...	...
East London a.	...	|	|	1325	1000↑	|	|	...	...	...
Cradock d.	...	|	0445	...	|	|	|	...	...	...
Port Elizabeth a.	...	|	0915	...	|	|	|	...	...	...
Klerksdorp d.	...	1625	...	...	|	|	|	...	...	...
Kimberley d.	...	2120	...	...	|	|	2303	...	...	...
De Aar d.	...	0135	...	...	0100	0100	|	...	...	...
Beaufort West d.	...	0600	...	...	0500	0500	0720	...	...	...
Worcester d.	...	1205	...	...	1055	1055	|	...	...	...
Bellville d.	...	1500	...	...	1345	1345	|	...	...	...
Cape Town a.	...	1530	...	...	1410	1410	1616	...	...	...

			⑤⑦ D	③⑤⑦ C	G	② E	③⑤⑦ B	A	⑦ 2	④ 2
Cape Town d.	...	...	...	...	...	0905	...	1000	1025	1025
Belleville d.	...	...	...	...	...	|	...	1035	1105	1105
Worcester d.	...	...	...	...	...	|	...	1330	1355	1355
Beaufort West d.	...	...	...	...	...	1845	...	1950	2005	2005
De Aar d.	...	...	...	...	...	|	...	2345	0010	0010
Kimberley d.	...	...	...	...	...	0300	...	0346	|	|
Klerksdorp d.	...	...	...	...	...	|	...	0826	|	|
Port Elizabeth d.	...	...	...	...	...	|	1500	|	|	|
Cradock d.	...	...	...	...	...	|	1932	|	|	|
East London d.	...	...	...	0900	...	|	|	|	1425↓	|
Queenstown d.	...	...	...	1326	...	|	|	|	1012	1005
Burgersdorp d.	...	...	...	1828	...	|	|	|	...	...
Bloemfontein a.	...	...	...	2136	...	|	0426	|	...	...
Bloemfontein d.	...	...	...	2156	2325	|	0446	|	...	...
Kroonstad d.	...	...	...	0110	0216	|	0752	|	...	...
Vereeniging d.	...	...	...	0325	0500	|	1010	|	...	...
Durban d.	...	...	1915	|	|	|	|	|	...	...
Pietermaritzburg d.	...	...	2153	|	|	|	|	|	...	...
Ladysmith d.	...	...	0145	|	|	|	|	|	...	...
Newcastle d.	...	...	0407	|	|	|	|	|	...	...
Standerton d.	...	...	|	|	|	|	|	|	...	...
Germiston d.	...	...	0917	|	0610	|	1112	|	...	...
Johannesburg a.	...	...	0935	0500	0625	1103	1135	1215	...	...

	③⑤ H		
Johannesburg d.	1800	...	...
Germiston d.	1827	...	...
Pretoria d.	1930	...	...
Witbank d.	2205	...	...
Middelburg d.	2302	...	...
Nelspruit d.	0402	...	...
Kaapmuiden d.	0505	...	...
Komatipoort ▼ a.	0638	...	...
Mokopane d.	...	...	...
Polokwane d.	...	...	...
Makhado d.	...	...	...
Musina ▶ a.	...	...	...

	④⑦ H		
Musina ▶ d.	...	...	...
Makhado d.	...	...	...
Polokwane d.	...	...	...
Mokopane d.	...	...	...
Komatipoort ▼ d.	1800	...	...
Kaapmuiden d.	1926	...	...
Nelspruit d.	2025	...	...
Middelburg d.	0134	...	...
Witbank d.	0215	...	...
Pretoria d.	0500	...	...
Germiston d.	0557	...	...
Johannesburg a.	0616	...	...

Johannesburg - Pretoria and v.v. 56 km. Journey 36 mins. Operator: Gautrain.

From **Johannesburg** Park: Train call at Sandton* 8 mins later.

Ⓐ: 0530, 0550, 0610, 0620, 0630, 0640, 0650, 0700, 0710, 0720, 0730, 0740, 0750, 0800, 0810, 0820, 0830, 0840, 0900, 0920, 0938, 0958, 1018, and every 20mins until 1438, 1538, then every 10 mins until 1828, 1848, 1910, 1930, 1950, 2010, 2030.

Ⓒ: 0530, 0600 and every 30 mins. until 2030.

From **Pretoria**: Trains call at Sandton* 27 mins later.

Ⓐ: 0533, 0553, 0608, 0613, 0623, 0633, 0643, 0653, 0703, 0713, 0723, 0733, 0743, 0753, 0803, 0813, 0823, 0833, 0843, 0853, 0911 and every 20 mins until 1531, 1541, 1551, 1611, then every 10 mins until 1831, 1843, 1903, 1923, 1943, 2003, 2023, 2037.

Ⓒ: 0533, 0603 and every 30 mins until 2003, 2037.

* – Frequent services run throughout the day to/from Sandon and OR Tambo Airport.

TRANS KAROO – [sleeper], [T2] [car] and ✕ Johannesburg - Cape Town and v.v. From Johannesburg ②③⑤⑦ (No [2] on ②). From Cape Town ③⑤⑥⑦ (No [2] on ⑥).
ALGOA – [sleeper], [T2] and ✕ Johannesburg - Port Elizabeth and v.v.
AMATOLA – [sleeper], [T2] and ✕ Johannesburg - East London and v.v.
TRANS NATAL – [sleeper], [T2] [car] and ✕ Durban - Johannesburg and v.v. -PREMIER CLASSE – [sleeper] (1 cl.) [1] and ✕ Johannesburg - Durban and v.v.
PREMIER CLASSE – [sleeper] (1 cl.) [1] and ✕ Johannesburg - Cape Town and v.v.
[2] From Johannesburg on last ⑤ of each month, from Bloemfontein on following ⑦.
KOMATI – [T2] and 🍷 Johannesburg - Komatipoort and v.v.

Musina - Beit Bridge (Zimbabwe): *12 km.* ▼ – Komatipoort - Ressano Garcia (Mozambique): *5 km.*

Classes: [1] Premier Class coaches consist of one or two berth deluxe compartments that convert to sleeper accommodation at night and can accomodate up to 14 passengers.
[T] Tourist Class coaches consist of two or four berth compartments that convert to sleeper accommodation at night and can accomodate up to 28 passengers.
[2] Economy Class consitsts of sitting accommodation only and hold up to 72 passengers.

ISRAEL

ital: **Jerusalem** (GMT +2, add 1 hour in summer). 2016 Public Holidays: Mar. 24, 25, Apr. 23, 29, May 12, June 12, Oct. 3, 4, 12, 17, 24.

services are operated Israel Railways (www.rail.co.il). All services convey a single class of seated accommodation. Timings are the most recent available and are subject to ation at any time, particularly around religious holidays. Tickets and reservations may be purchased up to 7 days in advance of travel at stations or through the website.

NAHARIYYA - TEL AVIV - BEN GURION AIRPORT - MODI'IN 4500

el Railways

	⑦–⑤	⑦–⑤	⑦–⑤	⑦–⑤	⑦–⑤	⑦–④	⑦–④	⑤	⑦–④	⑦–④	⑤		⑦–④	⑦–④	⑤	⑦–④	⑦–④	⑤	⑦–④	⑤a	⑦–④	⑦–④	⑦–④
Nahariyya d.	0013	0113	0213	0313	0357	...	0452	0451	0515	0554	0551		1215	1254	1251	1315	1354	1351	...	1451	1454	1515	...
Akko d.	0021	0121	0221	0321	0405	...	0459	0458	0522	0601	0558		1222	1301	1158	1322	1401	1358	...	1458	1501	1522	...
Qiryat Motzkin d.	0032	0132	0232	0332	0415	...	0509	0508	0532	0611	0608	and at	1232	1311	1308	1332	1411	1408	...	1808	1511	1532	...
Haifa Hof HaKarmel d.	0052	0152	0252	0352	0435	0503	0536	0539	0603	0636	0639	the same	1303	1336	1339	1403	1436	1439	1503	1539	1536	1603	...
Binyamina d.	0112	0212	0312	0412	0455	0526	0556	0602	0626	0656	0702	minutes	1326	1356	1402	1426	1456	1502	1526	1302	1556	1626	...
Tel Aviv Savidor Center a.	0154	0254	0354	0454	0538	0558	0628	0634	0658	0728	0734	past each	1358	1428	1434	1458	1528	1534	1558	1634	1628	1658	...
Tel Aviv Savidor Center d.	0156	0256	0356	0456	0540	0601	0631	0637	0701	0731	0737	hour until	1401	1431	1437	1501	1531	1537	1601	1637	1631	1701	1713
Ben Gurion Airport a.	0210	0310	0410	0510	0558	0619	0649	0655	0719	0749	0755		1419	1449	1455	1533	1549	1555	1619	1655	1649	1719	1731
Modi'in Center a.	...	...	...	...	...	0643	0713	0719	0743	0813	0819		1443	1513	1519	1543	1613	1619	1643	1719	1713	1743	1755

	⑦–④	⑦–④	⑦–④		⑦–④	⑦–④	⑦–④	⑦–④						⑥b		⑥b	⑥a	⑥a	⑥b	⑥ab	⑥ab		
ariyya d.	1554	1615	1654		2015	2054	2148	2313	...		...	...	...	1955	...	2051	2055	2151	2151	2229	2313	...	...
ko d.	1601	1622	1701	and at	2022	2101	2155	2321	...		...	...	...	2002	...	2058	2102	2158	2158	2236	2321	...	...
yat Motzkin d.	1611	1632	1711	the same	2032	2111	2205	2332	...		...	...	...	2012	...	2108	2112	2208	2208	2246	2332	...	...
fa Hof HaKarmel d.	1636	1703	1736	minutes	2103	2136	2236	2352	...		...	...	...	2039	...	2139	2139	2239	2239	2313	2352	...	...
yamina d.	1656	1726	1756	past each	2126	2156	2256	0012	...	⑥	...	...	...	2102	...	2202	2202	2302	2302	2332	0012	...	...
Aviv Savidor Center a.	1728	1758	1828	hour until	2158	2228	2343	0054	...		...	...	...	2134	...	2234	2234	2334	2351	0022	0054	...	...
Aviv Savidor Center d.	1731	1801	1831		2201	2231	2346	0056	...		...	...	...	2137	...	2237	2237	2337	2354	0025	0056	...	...
Gurion Airport a.	1749	1819	1849		2219	2349	0004	0110	...		...	...	...	2155	...	2255	2255	2355	0012	0042	0110	...	...
di'in Center a.	1813	1843	1913		2243	2313	0028	...	...		...	...	...	2219	...	2319	2319	0019	0036	...	...	...	...

	⑦–⑤	⑦–⑤	⑦–⑤	⑦–⑤	⑦–⑤	⑤	⑦–④	⑦–④		⑤	⑦–④	⑦–④	⑤	⑦–④	⑦–④	⑤		⑦–④	⑦–④		⑦–④	⑦–④
di'in Center d.	...	...	...	...		0511	0518	0548		1211	1218	1248	1311	1318	1348	1411	...	1418	1448		1818	1848
Gurion Airport d.	0053	0153	0253	0353	0453	0528	0535	0605		1228	1235	1305	1328	1335	1405	1428	...	1435	1505	and at	1835	1905
Aviv Savidor Center a.	0106	0206	0306	0406	0506	0549	0556	0626	and at	1249	1256	1326	1349	1356	1426	1449	...	1456	1526	the same	1856	1926
Aviv Savidor Center d.	0108	0208	0308	0408	0508	0552	0559	0629	the same	1252	1259	1329	1352	1359	1429	1452	...	1459	1529	minutes	1859	1929
yamina d.	0145	0245	0345	0445	0545	0623	0630	0700	minutes	1323	1330	1400	1423	1430	1500	1523	...	1530	1600	past each	1930	2000
fa Hof HaKarme d.	0205	0305	0405	0505	0610	0647	0649	0724	past each	1347	1349	1424	1447	1449	1524	1542	...	1549	1624	hour until	1949	2024
yat Motzkin d.	0226	0326	0426	0528	0641	0718	0715	0755	hour until	1418	1415	1455	1518	1515	1555	1618	...	1615	1655		2015	2055
ko d.	0236	0336	0436	0838	0652	0727	0724	0804		1427	1424	1504	1527	1524	1604	1627a	...	1624	1704		2024	2104
ariyya a.	0246	0346	0446	0548	0702	0736	0733	0813		1436	1433	1513	1536	1533	1613	1636a	...	1633	1713		2033	2113

	⑦–④	⑦–④	⑦–④	⑦–④	⑦–④	⑦–④	⑦–④					⑥b	⑥ab	⑥a	⑥b	⑥b								
di'in Center d.	1918	1948	2018	2048	2118	2218	2318	...		...	...	2011	2111	2211	2211	2311	...	...	...	...	...	...	...	...
Gurion Airport d.	1935	2005	2035	2105	2135	2235	2335	...		...	...	2028	2128	2228	2228	2328	...	...	...	...	...	...	...	...
Aviv Savidor Center d.	1956	2026	2056	2126	2156	2256	2356	...		...	...	2049	2149	2249	2249	2349	...	...	...	...	...	...	...	...
Aviv Savidor Center d.	1959	2029	2059	2129	2159	2259	2359	...	⑥	...	...	2052	2152	2252	2252	2352	...	...	...	...	...	...	...	...
yamina d.	2030	2100	2130	2200	2230	2330	0044	...		...	...	2123	2223	2323	2337	0037	...	...	...	...	...	...	...	...
fa Hof HaKarme a.	2049	2124	2149	2224	2249	2349	0102	...		...	...	2147	2247	2347	0001	0101	...	...	...	...	...	...	...	...
yat Motzkin d.	2115	...	2219	...	2317	0017	0129	...		...	...	2218	2318	0018	0032	0132	...	...	...	...	...	...	...	...
ko a.	2124	...	2228	...	2326	0026	0138	...		...	...	2228	2328	0027	0041	0141	...	...	...	...	...	...	...	...
ariyya a.	2133	...	2237	...	2335	0035	0147	...		...	...	2236	2336	0036	0050	0150	...	...	...	...	...	...	...	...

Mar. 25, 2016 - Sept. 17, 2016 only. **b** – Sept.18, 2016 - Oct. 28, 2016 only.

4510 NAHARIYYA - TEL AVIV - BE'ER SHEVA — Israel Railw

km		⑦–④	⑦–④	⑤ B	⑤	⑦–④	①–④	⑦	⑤ B	⑤	⑦–④	①–④	⑦	⑤ B	⑤	⑦–④	①–④	⑦	⑤ B	⑤	⑦–④	⑦–④	⑤ B
0	**Nahariyya** d.	...	...	...	0527	0527	...	...	...	0627	0627	...	...	...	0727	0727	...	...	...	0827	0827	...	...
	Akko d.	...	...	...	0534	0534	...	...	...	0634	0634	...	...	...	0734	0734	...	...	...	0834	0834	...	...
20	Qiryat Motzkin d.	...	...	...	0544	0544	...	...	...	0644	0644	...	...	...	0744	0744	...	...	...	0844	0844	...	...
38	Haifa Hof HaKarmel d.	...	...	...	0613	0616	0645	0645	...	0713	0716	0745	0745	...	0813	0816	0846	0846	...	0913	0916	0946	...
71	Binyamina d.	...	...	...	0632	|	|	|	...	0732	|	|	|	...	0832	|	|	|	...	0932	|	|	...
123	**Tel Aviv** Savidor Centre a.	...	...	...	0703	0704	0734	0734	...	0803	0804	0834	0834	...	0903	0904	0934	0934	...	1003	1004	1034	...
123	**Tel Aviv** Savidor Centre d.	0607	0637	0644	0706	0707	0737	0737	0744	0806	0807	0837	0837	0844	0906	0907	0937	0937	0944	1006	1007	1037	1044
143	Lod d.	0627	|	0713	0726	0727	|	0758	0813	0826	0827	|	0858	0913	0926	0927	|	0958	1013	1026	1027	|	1113
186	Kiryat Gat d.	0654	0718	0738	0751	0754	0818	0822	0838	0851	0854	0918	0922	0938	0951	0954	1018	1022	1038	1051	1054	1118	1138
230	**Be'er Sheva** Center a.	0729	0750	0814	0827	0829	0850	0855	0914	0927	0929	0950	0955	1014	1027	1029	1050	1055	1114	1127	1129	1150	1214

	⑤	⑦–④	⑤ B	⑤	⑦–④	⑤ B	⑤	⑦–④	⑤ B	⑤	⑦–④	⑤ B	⑤	⑦–④	⑤ aB	⑤ a	⑦–④	⑦–④	⑦–④	⑦–④	⑦–④	⑦–④
Nahariyya d.	0927	0927	...	1027	...	...	1127	...	...	1227	...	...	1327	...	...	1427	1427	...	1527	...	1627	...
Akko d.	0934	0934	...	1034	...	...	1134	...	...	1234	...	...	1334	...	...	1434	1434	...	1534	...	1634	...
Qiryat Motzkin d.	0944	0944	...	1044	...	...	1144	...	...	1244	...	...	1344	...	...	1444	1444	...	1544	...	1644	...
Haifa Hof HaKarmel d.	1013	1016	...	1113	...	...	1213	...	...	1313	...	...	1413	...	...	1513	1516	1546	1616	1646	1716	1746
Binyamina d.	1032	|	...	1132	...	...	1232	...	...	1332	...	...	1432	...	...	1532	|	|	|	|	|	|
Tel Aviv Savidor Centre a.	1103	1104	...	1203	...	...	1303	...	...	1403	...	...	1503	...	...	1603	1604	1634	1704	1734	1804	1834
Tel Aviv Savidor Centre d.	1106	1107	1144	1206	1207	1244	1306	1307	1344	1406	1407	1444	1506	1507	1544	1606	1607	1637	1707	1737	1807	1837
Lod d.	1126	1127	1213	1226	1227	1313	1326	1327	1413	1426	1427	1513	1526	1527	1613	1626	1627	|	1727	|	1827	|
Kiryat Gat d.	1151	1154	1238	1251	1254	1338	1351	1354	1438	1451	1454	1538	1551	1554	1638	1651	1654	1718	1754	1818	1854	1918
Be'er Sheva Center a.	1227	1229	1314	1327	1329	1414	1427	1429	1514	1527	1529	1614	1627	1629	1714	1727	1729	1750	1829	1850	1929	1950

	⑦–④	⑦–④	⑦–④	⑦–④	⑦–④									⑥ b	⑥ b	⑥ a	⑥ b	⑥ a	⑥ b	⑥ a	⑥ ab		
Nahariyya d.	...	1827	1927	...	...	...		...	...	...	...	...	...	...	...	...	1943	...	2029	2043	2129	...	...
Akko d.	...	1834	1934	...	...	...		...	...	...	...	...	...	...	...	...	1950	...	2036	2050	2136	...	...
Qiryat Motzkin d.	...	1844	1944	...	...	...		...	...	...	...	...	...	...	1947	...	2000	2047	2046	2100	2146	...	...
Haifa Hof HaKarmel d.	1846	1916	2016	...	...	...	⑥	...	...	...	...	...	...	...	2013	...	2031	2113	2113	2131	2213	...	...
Binyamina d.	|	|	|	...	...	...		...	...	...	...	...	...	...	2032	...	2051	2132	2132	2151	2232	...	...
Tel Aviv Savidor Centre a.	1934	2004	2104	...	...	...		...	...	...	...	...	...	...	2104	...	2129	2204	2204	2229	2304	...	...
Tel Aviv Savidor Centre d.	1937	2007	2107	2207	2307	...		...	...	...	...	...	...	2007	2107	2107	2131	2207	2207	2231	2307	...	...
Lod d.	|	2027	2127	2227	2327	...		...	...	...	...	...	...	2027	2127	2127	2152	2227	2227	2252	2327	...	...
Kiryat Gat d.	2018	2054	2154	2254	2354	...		...	...	...	...	...	...	2052	2152	2152	2220	2252	2252	2320	2352	...	...
Be'er Sheva Center a.	2050	2129	2229	2329	0029	...		...	...	...	...	...	...	2128	2228	2228	2256	2328	2328	2356	0028	...	...

	⑦–④	⑤	⑦–④	⑤	⑤ B	⑦–④	⑦–④	⑤	⑤ B	⑦–④	⑦–④	⑤	⑤ B	⑦–④	⑦–④	⑤	⑤ B	⑦–④	⑤	⑤ B	⑦–④	⑤
Be'er Sheva Center d.	0459	0501	0559	0601	0628	0638	0659	0701	0728	0738	0759	0801	0828	0838	0859	0901	0928	0959	1001	1028	1059	1101
Kiryat Gat d.	0532	0535	0632	0635	0702	0708	0732	0735	0801	0808	0832	0835	0902	0908	0932	0935	1002	1032	1035	1102	1132	1135
Lod d.	0559	0559	0659	0659	0726	|	0759	0759	0826	|	0859	0859	0926	|	0959	0959	1026	1059	1059	1126	1159	1159
Tel Aviv Savidor Centre a.	0620	0620	0720	0720	0755	0750	0820	0820	0855	0850	0920	0920	0955	0950	1020	1020	1055	1120	1120	1155	1220	1220
Tel Aviv Savidor Centre d.	0623	0623	0723	0723	...	0753	0823	0823	...	0853	0923	0923	...	0952	...	1023	...	...	1123	...	...	1223
Binyamina d.	|	0653	|	0753	...	|	|	0853	...	|	|	0953	...	|	...	1053	...	...	1153	...	...	1253
Haifa Hof HaKarmel d.	0708	0712	0808	0812	...	0838	0908	0912	...	0938	1008	1012	...	1038	...	1112	...	...	1212	...	...	1312
Qiryat Motzkin d.	0741	0742	0841	0842	...	...	0941	0942	...	...	1041	1042	...	...	...	1143	...	...	1242	...	...	1342
Akko d.	0751	0751	0851	0851	...	...	0951	0951	...	...	1051	1051	...	...	...	1151	...	...	1251	...	...	1351
Nahariyya a.	0800	0800	0900	0900	...	...	1000	1000	...	...	1100	1100	...	...	...	1200	...	...	1300	...	...	1400

	⑦–④	⑤	⑤ B	⑦–④	⑤	⑤ B	⑦–④	⑤ a	⑤ b	⑤ B	⑦–④	⑦–④	⑤ a	⑤ aB	⑦–④	⑦–④	⑦–④	⑦–④	⑦–④	⑦–④	⑦–④	⑦–④
Be'er Sheva Center d.	1159	1201	1228	1259	1301	1328	1359	1401	1401	1428	1438	1459	1501	1528	1538	1559	1638	1659	1738	1759	1838	1859
Kiryat Gat d.	1232	1235	1302	1332	1335	1402	1432	1435	1435	1502	1508	1532	1535	1602	1608	1632	1708	1732	1808	1832	1908	1932
Lod d.	1352	1259	1326	1359	1359	1426	1459	1459	1459	1526	|	1559	1559	1626	|	1659	|	1759	|	1859	|	1959
Tel Aviv Savidor Centre a.	1320	1320	1355	1420	1420	1455	1520	1520	1520	1555	1550	1620	1620	1655	1650	1720	1750	1820	1850	1920	1950	2020
Tel Aviv Savidor Centre d.	...	1323	...	1423	1423	...	1523	1523	1523	...	1553	1623	1623	...	1653	1723	1753	1823	1853	1923	1953	2023
Binyamina d.	...	1353	...	|	1453	...	|	1553	1553	...	|	|	1653	...	|	|	|	|	|	|	|	|
Haifa Hof HaKarmel d.	...	1412	...	1508	1512	...	1608	1612	1612	...	1640	1708	1712	...	1740	1808	1840	1908	1938	2008	2038	2108
Qiryat Motzkin d.	...	1442	...	1541	1542	...	1641	1642	...	...	...	1741	...	...	...	1841	...	1941	...	2041	...	2141
Akko d.	...	1451	...	1551	1551	...	1651	1651	...	...	...	1751	...	...	...	1842	...	1951	...	2051	...	2151
Nahariyya a.	...	1500	...	1600	1600	...	1700	1700	...	...	...	1800	...	...	...	1900	...	2000	...	2100	...	2200

	⑦–④	⑦–④	⑦–④	⑦–④				⑥ b	⑥ b	⑥ a	⑥ b	⑥ a	⑥ b	⑥ ab	⑥ a							
Be'er Sheva Center d.	1959	2059	2159	2259		...	...	1940	2001	2040	2101	2101	2120	2201	2220	...	...	...	...	...	...	...
Kiryat Gat d.	2032	2132	2232	2332		...	...	2014	2035	2114	2135	2135	|	2235	|	...	...	...	...	...	...	...
Lod d.	2059	2159	2259	2359		...	...	2043	2059	2143	2159	2159	|	2259	|	...	...	...	...	...	...	...
Tel Aviv Savidor Centre a.	2120	2220	2320	0020	⑥	...	...	2105	2120	2205	2220	2220	2307	2320	0007	...	...	...	...	...	...	...
Tel Aviv Savidor Centre d.	...	...	...	...		...	...	...	2123	...	2223	2223	...	2323	...	...	...	...	...	...	...	...
Binyamina d.	...	...	...	...		...	...	...	2153	...	2253	2253	...	0010	...	...	...	...	...	...	...	...
Haifa Hof HaKarmel d.	...	...	...	...		...	...	...	2212	...	2312	2312	...	0028	...	...	...	...	...	...	...	...
Qiryat Motzkin d.	...	...	...	...		...	...	...	2241	...	...	2341	...	...	...	...	...	...	...	...	...	...
Akko d.	...	...	...	...		...	...	...	2250	...	...	2350	...	...	...	...	...	...	...	...	...	...
Nahariyya a.	...	...	...	...		...	...	...	2259	...	...	2359	...	...	...	...	...	...	...	...	...	...

B – Also calls at Ben Gurion Airport 18 mins before/after Tel Aviv.

a – Mar. 25, 2016 - Sept. 17, 2016 only.
b – Sept.18, 2016 - Oct. 28, 2016 only.

4515 HERTSLIYYA - TEL AVIV - JERUSALEM — Israel Railw

km		⑦–④	⑤	⑦–④	⑤	⑦–④	⑤	⑦–④	⑤	⑦–④	⑤	⑦–④	⑤	⑦–④	⑤	⑦–④	⑤	⑦–④	⑤	⑦–④	⑤ a	⑦–④	⑦–④	⑦–④
	Hertsliyya d.	...	0602	0629	0702	0729	0802	0829	0902	0929	1002	1029	1102	1129	1202	1229	1302	1329	1402	1429	1502	1529	1629	1729
0	**Tel Aviv** Savidor C d.	0544	0614	0644	0714	0744	0814	0844	0914	0944	1014	1044	1114	1144	1214	1244	1314	1344	1414	1444	1514	1544	1644	1744
20	Lod d.	0604	0634	0704	0734	0804	0834	0904	0934	1004	1034	1104	1134	1204	1234	1304	1334	1404	1434	1504	1534	1604	1704	1804
51	Bet Shemesh d.	0629	0659	0729	0759	0829	0839	0929	0959	1029	1059	1129	1159	1229	1259	1329	1359	1429	1459	1529	1559	1629	1729	1829
82	**Jerusalem** Malha a.	0709	...	0810	0840	0910	0940	1010	1040	...	1140	1210	1239	...	1339	1409	1439a	...	1539a	1609	...	1709	1809	1909

		⑦–④		⑦–④	⑦–④	⑥ ab	⑦–④		
Hertsliyya d.	...	1929	...	2029	2129	...	2229	...	...
Tel Aviv Savidor C d.	...	1944	...	2044	2144	2214	2244	...	...
Lod d.	...	2004	...	2104	2204	2234	2304	...	...
Bet Shemesh d.	...	2029	...	2129	2229	2259	2329	...	...
Jerusalem Malha a.	...	2109	...	...	...	2339	...	...	...

	⑦–④	⑤	⑦–④	⑤	⑦–④	⑤	⑦–④	⑤
Jerusalem Malha d.	...	...	0617	...	0717	0747	0817	0847
Bet Shemesh d.	0559	0629	0659	0729	0759	0829	0859	0929
Lod d.	0623	0653	0723	0853	0823	0853	0923	0953
Tel Aviv Savidor C a.	0644	0714	0744	0814	0844	0914	0944	1014
Hertsliyya a.	0658	0727	0758	0827	0858	0927	0958	1027

	⑤	⑦–④	⑤	⑦–④	⑤	⑦–④	⑤	⑦–④	⑤	⑦–④	⑤ a	⑦–④	⑤ a	⑦–④	⑦–④	⑦–④		⑦–④	⑦–④	⑥ b	⑦–④	⑥ a	
Jerusalem Malha d.	0947	...	1046	1117	1146	...	1246	1316	1346	...	1446	1516	...	1616	1716	1816	...	1916	2017	2050	2117	2150	...
Bet Shemesh d.	1029	1100	1129	1159	1229	1300	1329	1359	1429	1500	1529	1559	1629	1659	1759	1859	...	1959	2059	2128	2159	2228	...
Lod d.	1053	1123	1153	1223	1253	1323	1353	1423	1453	1523	1553	1623	1653	1723	1823	1923	...	2023	2123	2152	2223	2252	...
Tel Aviv Savidor C a.	1114	1144	1214	1244	1314	1344	1414	1444	1514	1544	1614	1644	1714	1744	1844	1944	...	2044	2144	2214	2244	2314	...
Hertsliyya a.	1127	1158	1227	1258	1327	1358	1427	1458	1527	1558	1627	1658	...	1758	1858	1958	...	2058	2158	...	...	...	...

a – Mar. 25, 2016 - Sept. 17, 2016 only. **b** – Sept. 18, 2016 - Oct. 28, 2016 only.

LUXURY and CRUISE TRAINS

. BLUE TRAIN :
xury cruise train running regularly between Pretoria and Cape Town with excursions along the way. Also occasional trips from Pretoria to Durban. ✆ +27 12 334 8459. Fax +27 12 334 8464. /.bluetrain.co.za.

VOS RAIL :
ury cruise train running regularly between: Pretoria and Cape Town, Pretoria and Victoria Falls and Pretoria and Durban. Also occasonial trips to Swakopmund and Dar es Salaam. Most tours ure haulage by the company's preserved steam locomotives. ✆ +27 12 315 8242. Fax +27 12 323 0843. www.rovos.com.

)NGOLOLO EXPRESS :
ous 16 day train journeys throughout Southern Africa with excursions along the way. Tours start from Johannesburg or Cape Town and destinations include Dar es Salaam, Victoria Falls and kopmund. ✆ +27 11 486 4357. Fax +27 11 486 4057. www.shongololo.com.

SYRIA 4600

emins de fer Syriens   Services suspended due to hostilities

Capital: **Dimashq** (GMT +2, add 1 hour in summer). 2016 Public Holidays:

Al Qamishli d.	...	...	...
Al Hasakah d.	...	...	...
Dayr az Zawr d.	...	...	...
Ar Raqqah d.	...	...	...
Aleppo (Halab) a.	...	...	...
Aleppo (Halab) d.	...	...	...
Hamah d.	...	...	...
Hims 2 d.	...	...	...
Dimashq Kadem a.	...	...	...

Dimashq Kadem d.	...	...	...
Hims 2 d.	...	...	...
Hamah d.	...	...	...
Aleppo (Halab) a.	...	...	...
Aleppo (Halab) d.	...	...	...
Ar Raqqah d.	...	...	...
Dayr az Zawr d.	...	...	...
Al Hasakah d.	...	...	...
Al Qamishli a.	...	...	...

km				
0	**Aleppo** (Halab) d.	...	...	...
68	Bismaron d.	...	...	...
95	Jisr ash Shughur d.	...	...	...
199	**Al Ladhiqyah** a.	...	...	...
199	**Al Ladhiqyah** d.	...	...	...
280	Tartus d.	...	...	...
382	Hims 2 d.	...	...	...
526	**Dimashq** Kadem a.	...	...	...

Dimashq Kadem d.	...	...	...
Hims 2 d.	...	...	...
Tartus d.	...	...	...
Al Ladhiqyah a.	...	...	...
Al Ladhiqyah d.	...	...	...
Jisr ash Shughur d.	...	...	...
Bismaron d.	...	...	...
Aleppo (Halab) a.	...	...	...

IRAQ 4610

Railways

n			21
		2C	B
9	Umm Qasr d.	1130	...
1	**Al Basrah** Ma'qil d.	1400	1800
0	An Nasiriyah (for Ur) d.	▬	|
2	Ad Dawanyah d.	...	|
7	Al Hillah (for Babylon) d.	**11**	|
0	**Baghdad** West a.	**A**	0615
0	**Baghdad** West d.	1920	...
7	Samarra d.	2310	...
1	Tikrit d.	|	...
1	Ba'iji d.	|	...
6	**Al Mawsil** a.	0755	...

	20	12
	B	A
Al Mawsil d.	...	1900
Ba'iji d.	...	|
Tikrit d.	...	|
Samarra d.	...	0400
Baghdad West a.	...	0800
Baghdad West d.	1700	▬
Al Hillah (for Babylon) d.	|	...
Ad Dawanyah d.	|	...
An Nasiriyah (for Ur) d.	|	**2C**
Al Basrah Ma'qil a.	0520	0800
Umm Qasr a.	...	1025

Capital: **Baghdad** (GMT +3).

2016 Public Holidays: Jan. 1, 6, May 1, July 7 - 9, 14, Sept. 13 - 16, Oct. 3, 12, Dec. 12, 25

Rail services in Iraq are operated by Iraq Railways. Trains convey second class seating and also sleeping cars where indicated. Information regarding rail services is still very hard to obtain and the schedules shown should be treated as subject to confirmation.

A – 🛏 2 cl. Runs when required.
B – 🛏 2 cl.
C – Runs once per week. Days of operation unknown.

SAUDI ARABIA 4620

udi Railways Organization

ital: **Riyadh** (GMT +3).   2016 Public Holidays: July 7 – 9, 13, Sep. 13 – 16, 23.

services are operated by the Saudi Railways Organization (www.saudirailways.org). There are two types of trains: Modern (shown as **M** in the tables) and Regular (shown as **R**). **M** trains ey first (called Premium and includes refreshments in the waiting rooms) and second class (Standard) seating. **R** trains convey first (called Al-Rihab), second (called Al-Taleaa) and ordinary s (called Al Qafela) seating. Reservations are available from 6 months until 1 hour before departure time

	M	M	R	M	M	R	M	M	M
		⑦–④	⑦–④			⑦–④			⑥–③
Ad Dammam d.	0510	...	0547	0906	1302	1450	1655	1931	2119
Abqaiq d.	0551	...	0630	0947	1343	1534	1739	2012	2200
Al Hufuf d.	0644	0511	0717	1050	1441	1620	1834	2112	2249
Ar Riyad a.	0930	0751	...	1326	1722	...	2115	2351	...

	R	M	R	M	R	M	M	M	
	⑦–④		⑦–④			⑦–④			
Ar Riyad d.	...	0707	...	1103	1338	1455	1732	2125	...
Al Hufuf d.	0546	0948	1055	1345	1616	1734	2011	0009	...
Abqaiq d.	0629	1027	1134	1424	1655	1816	2050	0048	...
Ad Dammam a.	0716	1127	1225	1523	1758	1915	2152	0145	...

IRAN 4630

ia Trains

ital: **Tehran** (GMT +3.5, add 1 hour in summer).
6 Public Holidays: Feb. 11, Mar. 13, 19 - 23, 31, Apr. 1, 21, May 5, 22, June 3, 4, 27, July 7, 31, Sept. 13, 21, Oct. 11, 12, Nov. 21, 30, Dec. 17.
services are operated by Raja Trains, an associate of Islamic Republic of Iran Railways (www.raja.ir). Except where noted as convey 2nd class only, all trains convey sleeping cars which vert to seating for daytime travel. (For services to/from Turkey see Table 1575.)

				●		●		●						●									
Tehran d.	...	...	...	0700	0725	0820	0900	1400	1600	...	...	...	1715	1755	...	...	2025	...	...	...	...	...	...
Mashhad a.	...	...	...	1450	1520	1825	2125	0155	0345	...	...	...	0450	0535	...	...	0800	...	...	...	...	...	...

							●				●			●										
hhad d.	...	...	...	...	...	...	0700	0700	0815	0835	1150	...	...	1830	2000	...	...	...	2050	2205	...	...	...	...
ran a.	...	...	...	...	...	...	1455	1530	1825	2045	0005	...	...	0650	0800	...	...	...	0845	0955	...	...	...	...

Tehran d.	1720	...	1820
Tabriz a.	0545	...	0710

Tabriz d.	1730	...	2015
Tehran a.	0540	...	0850

	A		
Tabriz d.	0630	...	...
Djulfa a.	0910	...	...

	A		
Djulfa d.	1600	...	...
Tabriz a.	1840	...	...

			●
Tehran d.	1310	1400	1400
Bandar e Abbas a.	0640	0755	0845

			●
Bandar e Abbas d.	1310	1400	1500
Tehran a.	0700	0820	0930

Tehran d.	1610	...	1310
Eşfahan d.	|	1400	2220
Shiraz a.	0650	2100	...

Shiraz d.	...	1400	1750
Eşfahan d	2200	2100	|
Tehran a.	0510	...	0840

km			
0	**Tehran** d.	1300	...
924	**Khorramshahr** a.	0755	...

Khorramshahr d.	1100	...
Tehran a.	0530	...

km			
0	**Tehran** d.	1200	...
	Zahedan a.	1040	...

Zahedan d.	1400	...
Tehran a.	1340	...

km			
		ex①	
0	**Mashhad** d.	1025	1915
165	**Sarakhs** a.	1315	2205

		ex①
Sarakhs d.	0510	1500
Mashhad a.	0815	1800

km			
0	**Mashhad** d.	1500	1600
	Eşfahan a.	0935	1115

Eşfahan d.	1500	1600
Mashhad a.	0920	1055

km			
		●	●
0	**Mashhad** d.	1515	2355
	Qom a.	0555	1510

	●	●
Qom d.	1355	2135
Mashhad a.	0400	1150

②④⑤⑦
Even other day.   ▲ – Odd dated days.

ZAHEDAN - QUETTA 4640

m		404	
		A	
0	**Zahedan** d.	1000	...
34	Mirjawa 🏛 a.	1220	...
34	Mirjawa 🏛 d.	1300	...
00	Kuhi Taftan a.	1550	...
00	Kuhi Taftan d.	1700	...
22	Nok Kundi d.	2157	...
39	Dalbandin d.	0540	...
78	Nushki d.	1257	...
39	Wali Khan d.	1740	...
12	Spezand d.	1930	...
37	**Quetta** a.	2025	...

	403	
	B	
Quetta d.	0800	...
Spezand d.	0920	...
Wali Khan d.	1016	...
Nushki d.	1510	...
Dalbandin d.	2240	...
Nok Kundi d.	0557	...
Kuhi Taftan a.	1100	...
Kuhi Taftan d.	1230	...
Mirjawa 🏛 a.	1505	...
Mirjawa 🏛 d.	1515	...
Zahedan a.	1740	...

TE: Pakistan Railways and Raja Trains give different schedules for this train. This table ws the Pakistan Railways version. The Raja version is: Quetta d. 0830 - Zahedan a. 1335 / edan d. 0800 - Quetta a. 1515.
(12) departs on 3rd and 17th of the month.
(12) departs on 1st and 15th of the month.

QUETTA - AMRITSAR 4650

km		23	402	14002
		A	①④	①④
0	**Quetta** d.	0930	...	...
131	Sibi d.	1445	...	...
296	Jacobabad d.	1740	...	...
385	Rohri d.	2010	...	...
840	Khanewal d.	0700	...	...
1127	**Lahore** Junction a.	0930	...	...
1127	**Lahore** Junction d.	...	0800	...
	Wagah a.	...	0835	...
	Wagah d.	...	1130	...
1147	Atari 🏛 a.	...	1150	...
1147	Atari 🏛 d.	...	...	2000
1173	**Amritsar** a.	...	...	2037

	14001	401	24
	①④	①④	A
Amritsar d.	0650	...	...
Atari 🏛 a.	0715	...	...
Atari 🏛 d.	...	1100	...
Wagah a.	...	1410	...
Wagah d.	...	1610	...
Lahore Junction a.	...	1645	...
Lahore Junction d.	...	...	1700
Khanewal d.	...	...	2250
Rohri d.	...	...	0630
Jacobabad d.	...	...	0840
Sibi d.	...	...	1155
Quetta a.	...	...	1700

A – AKBAR EXPRESS
NOTE: Timings are subject to confirmation and connections are not guaranteed.

280 (Summer) PARIS - LE MANS - RENNES and NANTES *TGV Atlant*

Service July 3 - Aug. 28. *For service to July 2/from Aug. 29 see page 182*

TGV trains convey 🍷. Many trains continue to destinations in Tables **281**, **284**, **285**, **288** and **293**. For other trains Massy - Nantes via St Pierre des Corps see Table **335**.

km								*TGV*				*TGV*		*TGV*	*TGV*	*TGV*	*TGV*		*TGV*	*TGV*	*TGV*		*TGV*
								8905			⊖	**8051**		**8807**	**8081**	**8053***	**8911**		**8693**	**8813**	**8715**		**8915**
		①–⑥	Ⓐ	⑥	Ⓐ	Ⓐ	Ⓐ	①–⑥	⑥	Ⓐ	Ⓒ	①–⑥	Ⓐ	①–⑥	Ⓐ								
		k		**h**				**k**	**h**		**b**	**k**		**k**									
0	**Paris** Montparnasse d.	...	...	...	...	...	...	0653	...	...	...	0658	...	0721	0736	0803	0854	...	0908	0954	1008	...	1054
14	Massy TGV d.	...	...	...	...	...	...	0705	...	...	...	|	...	0738	0748	|	|	...	|	|	|	...	|
202	**Le Mans** d.	0612	0620	0637	0620	0650	0700	|	0726	0731	0756	0802	0824	0830	|	0906	|	...	|	1052	|	1105	|
292	Laval d.	|	|	0729	0725	|	|	|	|	|	|	0846	|	|	|	0951	|	...	|	|	|	|	|
327	Vitré d.	|	|	0753	0748	|	|	|	|	|	|	|	|	|	|	|	|	...	|	|	|	|	|
365	**Rennes** a.	|	|	0815	0819	|	|	|	|	|	|	0921	|	|	0952	1025	|	...	1113	|	1213	|	|
251	Sablé d.	0639	0649	...	...	0713	0742	|	0757	0818	0819	...	0846	0853	...	...	|	...	...	|	...	1126	|
299	Angers St Laud **289** d.	0703	0730	...	...	0738	0822	|	0828	0853	0845	...	0911	0917	...	...	1030	...	...	1131	...	1149	|
387	**Nantes 289** a.	0750	...	...	...	0820	...	0908	...	...	0928	...	0950	0956	...	...	1106	...	...	1208	...	1231	1257

	TGV	*TGV*			*TGV*	*TGV*	*TGV*	*TGV*	*TGV*		*TGV*	*TGV*	*TGV*			*TGV*	*TGV*	*TGV*	*TGV*	*TGV*	*TGV*	*TGV*	
	8617	**8975**			**8717**	**8819***	**8621**	**8055**	**8821***		**8059***	**8629**	**8823**			**8825**	**8827***	**8087**	**8729**	**8829**	**8063***	**8633**	
				Ⓐ			⑤	⑥			Ⓐ	Ⓒ	⑤	⑤	⑤	Ⓐ	Ⓒ	⑤	⑥–④	⑤Ⓒ	L	⑤	①–⑥
							g	**h**					**g**	**g**	**g**			**g**	**m**	**g**	**w**	**g**	**k**
Paris Montparnasse d.	1108	1154	...	...	1208	1221	1307	1307	1354	...	1403	1408	1421	...	...	1454	1454	1508	1508	1554	1608	1608	...
Massy TGV d.	|	|	...	...	|	|	|	|	|	...	|	|	|	...	...	|	|	|	|	|	|	|	...
Le Mans d.	1206	|	1223	1301	1306	|	1406	1406	1451	...	|	|	1515	1535	1536	|	1552	|	|	|	|	|	1702
Laval d.	1249	|	|	|	|	|	|	|	|	...	1544	1544	...	|	1624	|	|	|	|	|	|	|	|
Vitré d.	1309	|	|	|	|	|	|	|	|	...	|	|	...	|	1643	|	|	|	|	|	|	|	|
Rennes a.	1328	|	|	|	1418	|	1520	1520	|	...	1620	1619	...	|	1702	|	|	1713	1713	|	1812	1816	|
Sablé d.	...	|	1310	1324	...	1338	...	...	|	...	...	...	...	1557	...	|	|	...	...	|	...	...	1726
Angers St Laud **289** d.	...	1328	1344	1350	...	1402	...	...	1531	...	...	...	...	1621	...	1628	1631	...	...	1729	...	...	1750
Nantes 289 a.	...	1407	...	1432	...	1440	...	...	1607	...	...	...	...	1659	...	1707	1707	...	...	1811	...	...	1829

				TGV			*TGV*	*TGV*	*TGV*	*TGV*	*TGV*			*TGV*	*TGV*	*TGV*		*TGV*	*TGV*			*TGV*	*TGV*
				8737*			**8833**	**8747**	**8643**	**8741***	**8935***		⊖	**8649**	**8839**	**8841**		**8657**	**8943**			**8095**	**8067**
	⑦	Ⓐ	⑥	Ⓐ	①–④	⑦	Ⓐ	⑤	①–④	Ⓒ	Ⓑ	①–④	⑤	⑤	⑤				⑤⑥	⑦	Ⓐ	⑤	①–④
	j		**h**		**x**	**j**		**g**	**x**			**x**	**g**	**g**	**g**				**z**	**j**		**g**	**x**
Paris Montparnasse d.	...	...	...	1641	...	...	1654	1708	1708	1708	1721	...	...	1741	1749	1754	...	1808	1823	...	...	1841	1841
Massy TGV d.	...	...	...	|	...	...	|	|	|	|	|	...	...	|	|	|	...	|	|	...	...	|	|
Le Mans d.	1719	1722	1734	1738	1742	1742	1752	|	|	1806	|	1821	1821	1839	|	1851	...	|	|	1905	1905	|	|
Laval d.	|	|	|	1822	1828	|	|	|	|	1850	|	|	|	1923	|	|	...	|	|	|	|	2017	2018
Vitré d.	|	|	|	|	1846	|	|	|	|	|	|	|	|	|	|	|	...	|	|	|	|	2036	2038
Rennes a.	|	|	|	1858	1910	|	|	1914	1914	1925	|	|	|	1957	|	|	...	2014	|	|	|	2054	2056
Sablé d.	1747	1755	1807	...	...	1805	|	...	...	...	|	1844	1846	...	|	|	...	...	|	1935	1941	...	...
Angers St Laud **289** d.	1816	1826	1837	...	...	1830	1833	...	...	...	|	1910	1911	...	|	1933	...	...	|	2005	2006	...	...
Nantes 289 a.	...	...	...	...	...	1910	1909	...	...	...	1927	1950	1952	...	2000	2009	...	...	2032	...	...	...	...

	TGV	*TGV*	*TGV*	*TGV*	*TGV*			*TGV*	*TGV*	*TGV*	*TGV*		*TGV*	*TGV*	*TGV*	*TGV*	*TGV*	*TGV*	*TGV*	*TGV*	*TGV*	*TGV*	*TGV*
	8945	**8850**	**8979**	**8977**	**8663***			**8761**	**8849**	**8949**	**8851**		**8071**	**8097**	**8853***	**8077**	**8077**	**8679**	**8075**	**8857***	**8857***	**8079**	**8779**
	①–④	⑤	⑥–④	⑤		⑦–④	⑤		⑦	⑤	①–④		⑤Ⓒ	⑤		⑥	①–④	⑤	⑦		⑤⑦	⑦	⑤
	x	**g**	**m**	**g**		**y**	**g**		**j**	**g**	**x**		**g**	**g**		**h**	**x**	**g**	**j**	**J**	**K**	**j**	**g**
Paris Montparnasse d.	1850	1850	1854	1854	1908	...	...	1941	1954	1954	1954	...	2008	2024	2054	2108	2103	2108	2108	2144	2154	2208	2208
Massy TGV d.	|	|	|	|	|	...	...	|	|	|	|	...	|	|	|	|	|	|	|	|	|	|	|
Le Mans d.	|	|	1952	1954	2006	2012	2020	|	|	|	2052	...	2106	2120	|	|	|	|	2206	|	2252	|	2306
Laval d.	|	|	|	|	|	|	|	|	|	|	|	...	2149	|	|	|	2244	|	2250	|	|	2344	2349
Vitré d.	|	|	|	|	|	|	|	|	|	|	|	...	|	|	|	|	|	2259	2311	|	|	|	|
Rennes a.	|	|	|	|	2120	|	|	2145	|	|	|	...	2225	2234	|	2313	2319	2319	2330	|	|	0019	0024
Sablé d.	|	|	2014	2016	...	2035	2042	...	|	|	|	...	...	...	|	...	...	...	...	|	|	...	...
Angers St Laud **289** d.	|	|	2037	2039	...	2059	2104	...	2128	2128	2132	...	...	...	2227a	...	...	...	...	2336	2332	...	...
Nantes 289 a.	2054	2104	2115	2118	...	2141	2144	...	2204	2204	2208	...	...	...	2302a	...	...	...	...	0012	0008	...	...

	TGV	*TGV*	*TGV*	*TGV*	*TGV*		*TGV*	*TGV*	*TGV*		*TGV*	*TGV*			*TGV*				*TGV*	*TGV*	*TGV*		*TGV*
	8800	**8802**	**8052**	**8906**	**8810**		**8702***	**8912**	**8812**		**8914**	**8056***			**8816**				**8818**	**8058**	**8060**		**8062***
	①	Ⓐ	Ⓐ	①	⑥		⚒	②–⑤	①	Ⓐ	①	⚒		Ⓐ		⑥	Ⓐ		Ⓐ	Ⓐ	⑦	Ⓐ	Ⓒ
	u			**k**	**h**			**v**	**u**		**u**	**h**				**h**					**j**		
Nantes 289 d.	0458	0523	...	0630	0630	...	...	0630	...	0634	0701	...	...	...	0730	...	0739	...	0800	...	...	...	...
Angers St Laud **289** d.	0541	0602	...	|	0709	...	...	0713	0714	0718	|	...	...	...	0809	0818	0823	...	0839	...	...	0843	...
Sablé d.	|	0626	...	|	|	...	...	|	|	0740	|	...	...	...	|	0846	0848	...	|	...	...	0908	...
Rennes d.	|	|	0532	|	|	...	0635	|	|	|	|	0704	...	0713	|	|	|	...	|	0805	0805	|	0905
Vitré d.	|	|	0553	|	|	...	|	|	|	|	|	|	...	0732	|	|	|	...	|	|	|	|	|
Laval d.	|	|	0615	|	|	...	0710	|	|	|	|	|	...	0751	|	|	|	...	|	|	0842	|	|
Le Mans d.	0622	0650	0702	|	0750	...	|	0801	0801	0804	|	0821	...	0838	|	0913	0913	...	|	0923	0926	0932	|
Massy TGV a.	|	|	|	|	|	...	|	|	|	...	|	|	...	...	|	...	...	...	|	|	|	...	|
Paris Montparnasse a.	0724	0753	0804	0837	0845	...	0853	0857	0857	...	0906	0917	...	...	0942	...	...	...	1011	1018	1023	...	1117

	TGV	*TGV*	*TGV*	*TGV*	*TGV*	*TGV*	*TGV*	*TGV*			*TGV*	*TGV*		*TGV*			*TGV*	*TGV*	*TGV*	*TGV*		*TGV*	*TGV*
	8618	**8822**	**8064**	**8824**	**8620**	**8926**	**8622***	**8928**			**8974**	**8972**		**8084**			**8932**	**8084**	**8730**	**8834**		**8836**	**8940**
	Ⓐ	Ⓒ			Ⓐ	Ⓐ	Ⓒ	Ⓒ	⑦		⑥	Ⓑ	①–⑥	Ⓐ	①–⑥			Ⓒ				⑤	
									j		**h**	**q**	**k**		**k**							**g**	
Nantes 289 d.	...	0900	...	1000	...	1105	...	1130	1141	...	1200	1200	1204	...	...	...	1301	...	...	1400	...	...	1500
Angers St Laud **289** d.	...	0939	...	1040	...	1145	...	1209	1223	...	1238	1241	1246	...	1250	...	1340	...	...	1439	...	...	|
Sablé d.	...	|	...	|	...	|	...	|	1247	...	|	|	1308	...	1330	...	|	...	...	|	...	...	|
Rennes d.	0905	|	0935	|	1035	|	1105	|	|	...	|	|	|	1235	|	...	|	1305	1405	|	...	...	|
Vitré d.	|	|	|	|	|	|	|	|	|	...	|	|	|	|	|	...	|	|	|	|	...	...	|
Laval d.	|	|	|	|	1112	|	1141	|	|	...	|	|	|	1312	|	...	|	1341	|	|	...	...	|
Le Mans d.	1023	1022	|	|	1157	|	1227	|	1310	...	1321	|	1333	1356r	1402	...	1420	|	|	1520	...	1541	|
Massy TGV a.	|	|	|	|	|	|	|	|	...	...	|	|	...	|	...	...	|	|	|	|	...	|	|
Paris Montparnasse a.	1121	1121	1144	1221	1253	1320	1323	1340	...	...	1418	1420	...	1454r	...	...	1518	1522	1611	1616	...	1638	1708

			TGV				*TGV*	*TGV*			*TGV*		*TGV*	*TGV*			*TGV*	*TGV*		*TGV*	*TGV*	*TGV*	*TGV*
			8646				**8752**	**8944**			**8846**		**8088**	**8088**			**8658**	**8980**		**8848**	**8762**	**8762**	**8762**
	Ⓑ	⑥		⑤		Ⓐ			Ⓐ	⑦			Ⓒ	Ⓐ	⑦	Ⓐ				⑦	Ⓒ	①–④	⑤
	q	**h**		**g**						**j**					**j**					**j**		**x**	**g**
Nantes 289 d.	1519	1539	...	...	...	...	...	1700	...	1705	1729	...	...	...	...	1734	...	1800	...	1830	...	...	...
Angers St Laud **289** d.	1601	1620	...	1648	...	...	...	1740	1744	1746	|	...	...	...	1809	1822	...	1840	...	|	...	...	...
Sablé d.	1625	1645	...	1718	...	...	...	|	1826	1809	|	...	...	...	1838	1843	...	1904	...	|	...	...	...
Rennes d.	|	|	1605	|	...	1637	1705	|	|	|	|	...	1733	1735	|	|	1806	|	...	|	1833	1835	1835
Vitré d.	|	|	|	|	...	1700	|	|	|	|	|	...	|	|	|	|	|	|	...	|	1857	1857	1858
Laval d.	|	|	1642	|	...	1720	|	|	|	|	|	...	1811	1813	|	|	|	|	...	|	|	|	|
Le Mans d.	1648	1714	1726	1747	...	1806	|	1823	1858	1832	|	...	|	1856	1909	1904	|	|	...	|	1955	|	|
Massy TGV a.	...	...	|	...	...	...	|	|	...	...	|	...	|	|	...	...	|	|	...	|	|	|	|
Paris Montparnasse a.	...	...	1822	...	...	...	1911	1920	...	...	1937	...	1945	1953	...	...	2011	2019	...	2037	2052	2048	2054

J – July 8, 13 only.
K – Also Aug. 15; not July 8.
a – 18 - 19 minutes later on July 11, 12.
b – Not July 3.
g – Also July 13.
h – Also July 14.
j – Also Aug. 15.

k – Not Aug. 15.
m – Not July 13.
n – Not Aug. 16.
p – Also July 13, Aug. 15.
q – Not July 14.
r – 10 minutes later on ⑤ (also July 13).
t – Also Aug. 15; not Aug. 14.

u – Also Aug. 16; not Aug. 15.
v – Not July 14, Aug. 16.
w – Not July 13, Aug. 15.
x – Not July 13, 14, Aug. 15.
y – Not July 13, 14.
z – Also July 13, 14.

NOTES CONTINUED ON NEXT PAGE →

NANTES and RENNES - LE MANS - PARIS 280 (Summer)

Service July 3 - Aug. 28. *For service to July 2/from Aug. 29 see page 183*

			TGV 8670*	TGV 8850*			TGV 8982	TGV 8676	TGV 8852*	TGV 8092*	TGV 8780	TGV 8090		TGV 8688	TGV 8682*	TGV 8856	⊖	TGV 8076*		TGV 8958	TGV 8686	TGV 8960	TGV 8796	
	⑤ g	⑤ g			Ⓐ			⑦ j		Ⓒ	① u	②–⑤ v		⑦ j		⑤⑦ p	Ⓒ	⑤⑦ p		⑦ j	⑦ j	⑦ j	⑦ j	
es 289 d.	...	1839	...	1900	1909	...	1930	...	2000	...	...	...	...	...	...	2100	2108	...	...	2200	...	2225	...	...
ers St Laud 289 d.	1844	1927	...	1940	1954	...	|	...	2041	...	...	...	...	...	...	2139	2156	...	...	|	...	2304	...	...
é d.	1928	1950	...	|	2017	...	|	...	|	...	...	...	...	...	...	|	2220	...	...	|	...	|	...	...
ennes d.	|	|	1902	|	|	...	|	1935	|	2005	2005	2005	...	2035	2105	|	|	2135	...	|	2205	|	2235	...
ré d.	|	|	|	|	|	...	|	|	|	|	|	|	...	2056	|	|	|	|	...	|	|	|	|	...
val d.	|	|	|	|	|	...	|	|	|	2043	2043	2043	...	|	|	|	|	2211	...	|	|	|	2312	...
lans d.	2004	2012	|	2022	2039	...	|	2051	|	|	|	|	...	|	|	2220	2243	2255	...	|	|	|	|	...
sy TGV a.	...	...	|	|	...	...	|	|	|	|	|	|	...	|	|	|	...	|	...	|	|	|	|	...
s Montparnasse a.	...	...	2111	2119	...	...	2139	2150	2214	2219	2219	2219	...	2241	2310	2319	...	2353	...	0005	0011	0038	0053	...

ES - CONTINUED FROM PREVIOUS PAGE

To/from Le Croisic (Table **288**).

–🅁, supplement payable, 🍸.

*** – Train number shown is altered as follows:**

8053 runs as 8091 on Ⓒ.
8056 runs as 8080 on Ⓐ.
8059 runs as 8625 on ①–④.
8062 runs as 8618 on ⑥.
8063 runs as 8633 on ⑦.
8076 runs as 8098 on ⑦.
8092 runs as 8094 on ⑥.
8622 runs as 8624 on ⑦.
8640 runs as 8744 on Ⓒ.
8663 runs as 8665 on ⑥–④.
8670 runs as 8672 on ①–④.
8682 runs as 8794 on ⑦.
8702 runs as 8706 on ②–⑥.
8737 runs as 8739 on ⑤.
8741 runs as 8743 on ⑦.
8819 runs as 8919 on ⑤.
8821 runs as 8921 on ⑦–④.
8827 runs as 8927 on ⑥.
8850 runs as 8950 on ⑤⑦.
8852 runs as 8952 on ⑥–④.
8853 runs as 8953 on ⑤.
8857 runs as 8957 on ⑤.
8935 runs as 8937 on ⑦–④.

RENNES - ST MALO 281 (Summer)

Service July 3 - Aug. 28. *For service to July 2/from Aug. 29 see page 183*

n	*TGV trains,* 🅁	TGV 8081	TGV 8091	TGV 8085	TGV 8089	TGV 8087	TGV 8093	TGV 8095	TGV 8099	TGV 8097
		Ⓐ	Ⓒ		A	⑤ g	①–④ x	⑤ g	⑦ j	⑤ g
	Paris Montparnasse **280** d.	0736	0803	1008	1508	1508	1841	1841	1908	2024
0	**Rennes 272** d.	0957	1032	1220	1723	1717	2059	2058	2128	2241
8	Dol **272** d.	1033	1107	1254	|	|	|	2130	|	2312
1	**St Malo** a.	1046	1120	1308	1805	1804	2143	2145	2210	2328

TGV trains, 🅁	TGV 8080	TGV 8084	TGV 8084	TGV 8088	TGV 8088	TGV 8090	TGV 8094	TGV 8092	TGV 8098
	Ⓐ	Ⓐ	Ⓒ	Ⓐ	Ⓒ	Ⓐ	⑥ h	⑦ j	⑦ j
St Malo d.	0605	1144	1215	1637	1638	1908	1908	1910	2048
Dol **272** d.	0620	|	|	1653	1655	|	1924	1925	|
Rennes 272 a.	0654	1229	1259	1729	1727	1955	1955	1959	2130
Paris Montparnasse **280** a.	0917	1454**r**	1522	1953	1945	2219**t**	2219	2219	2353

	Ⓐ	Ⓐ	⑥	⑦ j	Ⓐ	⑥ ⊖h	Ⓐ	⑥	†	†		⚒	⚒	⑤ g	⑥	Ⓐ		⑥	Ⓐ		Ⓐ	⑥	†		①–⑥ k	⑤ g
nes 272 d.	0630	0730	0730	0930	0940	0940	1040	1100	1100	1130	...	1343	1440	1535	1545	1636	...	1730	1800	1831	1931	1940	1945	...	2208	2248
272 d.	0714	0811	0816	1011	1022	1017	1117	1136	1152	1206	...	1426	1519	1611	1621	1717	...	1813	1845	1909	2010	2029	2026	...	2248	2327
lalo a.	0733	0828	0835	1025	1035	1030	1130	1151	1211	1221	...	1445	1533	1625	1635	1733	...	1831	1904	1923	2024	2043	2040	...	2302	2341

	Ⓐ	⑥	Ⓐ P	Ⓐ Q	Ⓐ P			Ⓐ	⑥	†	†	⚒	Z		⑤ g	Ⓐ	⑥	†	Ⓐ	⑥ ⊖	†			⑤ g	Z	
lalo d.	0617	0628	0647	0647	0717	0750	...	0927	0947	0948	1247	1247	1449	...	1647	1718	1720	1748	1816	1818	1827	...	1953	2027	2047	...
272 d.	0635	0648	0704	0705	0735	0804	...	0941	1001	1003	1301	1306	1503	...	1701	1735	1740	1808	1837	1833	1841	...	2008	2041	2102	...
nes 272 a.	0719	0740	0744	0749	0819	0844	...	1019	1039	1043	1341	1349	1537	...	1736	1818	1823	1903	1920	1908	1916	...	2043	2117	2137	...

Daily **except** ⑤ (not July 13).
July 4 - 15, Aug. 16 - 26.
July 18 - Aug. 12.
①②③④⑥ (not July 13, 14, Aug. 15).

g – Also July 13.
h – Also July 14.
j – Also Aug. 15.
k – Not Aug. 15.
r – 10 minutes later on ⑤ (also July 13).
t – ②–⑤ (not July 14, Aug. 16).
x – Not July 13, 14, Aug. 15.

⊖ – To/from Nantes (Table **287**).

DOL - DINAN 282 (Summer)

d class

Service July 3 - Aug. 28. *For service to July 2/from Aug. 29 see page 183*

	Ⓐ		⑥		Ⓐ ⊙	Ⓒ ⊙		⚒	†	⑥		†	Ⓐ		†	⑥	Ⓐ		①–④ x	†	⑤ g		⑤⑥ g	
d.	0701	...	0820	...	1037	1115	...	1305	1428	1525	...	1702	1730	...	1815	1817	1850	...	2016	2030	2136	...	2252	...
an a.	0724	...	0843	...	1100	1138	...	1328	1451	1555	...	1732	1758	...	1838	1845	1920	...	2039	2053	2159	...	2314	...

	Ⓐ	⚒		Ⓒ		Ⓐ P	Q		①–④ x	⑥		⑤ g				†		Ⓐ	Ⓒ		Ⓐ			
an d.	0628	0730	...	0924	...	1215	1227	...	1435	1433	...	1533	...	1622	...	1740	...	1809	1856	...	1934	...	...	...
a.	0656	0757	...	0954	...	1243	1255	...	1458	1456	...	1556	...	1645	...	1803	...	1832	1919	...	1957	...	...	...

Ⓒ July 2 - 10; daily July 14 - Aug. 28.
July 4 - 13.

g – Also July 13.
x – Not July 13, 14, Aug. 15.

⊙ – To/from St Brieuc (Table **299**).

MORLAIX - ROSCOFF 283 (Summer)

d class

Service July 3 - Aug. 28. *For service to July 2/from Aug. 29 see page 183*

m		🚌 Ⓐ	🚌 Ⓐ			🚌 ⑥	⚒		†				🚌 ⑥	🚌 ①–④	🚌 ⑤		🚌 ①–④	🚌 Ⓒ		🚌 ⑤	🚌 †		🚌 ①–④		🚌 ⑤
0	**Morlaix 284** d.	0808	0840	...	1019	1110	1227	...	1255	...	1521	...	1530	1625	1715	...	1810	1820	...	2005	2010	...	2110	...	2140
28	**Roscoff** a.	0840	0915	...	1106	1145	1314	...	1342	...	1608	...	1600	1705	1745	...	1845	1850	...	2037	2040	...	2145	...	2215

	🚌 Ⓐ	🚌 Ⓐ	🚌 ⑥			🚌 †		⚒		🚌 ⚒	🚌 ⑥		①–④ x		†		🚌 ①–④		⑥		⑤ g		🚌 Ⓐ	🚌 †	🚌 ⑤
scoff d.	0630	0755	0820	...	1116	1125	...	1320	...	1330	1630	...	1621	...	1649	...	1710	...	1708	...	1718	...	1830	1935	2040
rlaix 284 a.	0700	0834	0900	...	1203	1200	...	1407	...	1405	1705	...	1708	...	1736	...	1749	...	1755	...	1805	...	1905	2005	2115

Also July 13.
Not July 13, 14, Aug. 15.

All services call at St Pol de Léon (*21 km / 15 mins from Morlaix*).

🚌 call at Roscoff port on days of sailings. *Bus service is subject to alteration.*

284 (Summer) RENNES - ST BRIEUC - MORLAIX - BREST

Service July 3 - Aug. 28. *For service to July 2/from Aug. 29 see page 184*

km	*TGV* trains convey 🍷													*TGV* 8609		*TGV* 8613		*TGV* 8693				*TGV* 8617	
		Ⓐ	Ⓐ	⑥	Ⓐ	⑥	Ⓐ	Ⓐ		⑥	⚒	⚒	†	†	①–⑥		⑤Ⓒ	⚒					
															k		g						
	Paris Montparnasse **280** d.	...	...	...	...	...	...	...	...	...	...	...	...	...	0841	...	0908	...	0908	...	...	...	1108	
0	**Rennes** d.	...	...	...	0620	0640	0700	0720	...	0830	0945	...	0957	...	|	...	1117	...	1120	...	1238	...	1332	
80	Lamballe **299** d.	...	...	...	0723	0745	|	0813	...	0907	1023	...	1035	...	|	...	|	...	1203	...	1316	...	|	
101	**St Brieuc 299** d.	...	...	0651	0737	0800	0746	0828	...	0919	1036	...	1048	...	1134	...	|	...	1216	...	1328	...	1421	
132	Guingamp d.	...	...	0709	...	...	|	...	...	0939	1053	1101	1106	...	1152	...	|	...	1233	...	1346	...	1440	14
158	Plouaret-Trégor d.	...	...	0724	...	...	|	...	...	0953	|	1117	1121	1134	|	...	|	...	1248	...	1404	1410	|	15
175	Lannion a.	...	...	|	...	...	|	...	...	|	|	1134	|	1151	|	...	|	...	1305	...	|	1427	|	15
189	Morlaix d.	0616	0637	0745	...	...	0830	...	...	1012	1123	...	1140	...	1223	...	1242	1259	...	...	1424	...	1509	
215	Landivisiau d.	0631	0700	0801	...	...	|	...	...	1027	|	...	1155	...	|	...	|	1321	...	...	1439	...	|	
230	Landerneau **286** d.	0641	0713	0814	...	...	|	...	...	1037	|	...	1205	...	|	...	1306	1333	...	...	1449	...	|	
248	**Brest 286** a.	0659	0731	0826	...	...	0902	...	...	1049	1158	...	1217	...	1255	...	1317	1353	...	...	1501	...	1542	

		TGV 8639				*TGV* 8621		*TGV* 8625	*TGV* 8629	*TGV* 8641													*TGV* 8633	
		①–④	⑤	Ⓒ		⑤	Ⓐ	①–④	Ⓒ	⑥	⑤		Ⓒ	†	①–④	⚒	⚒		†	Ⓐ	Ⓐ	Ⓐ	⑦	
		x	g			g		x		h	g				x						L	F	j	
Paris Montparnasse **280** d.	...	1208	...	...	...	1307	...	1408	1408	1408	...	...	...	...	...	...	...	...	...	...	...	...	1608	
Rennes d.	1349	1428	1435	1435	...	1524	...	1624	1623	1628	1639	...	...	...	...	...	1700	...	1729	1744	...	...	1817	
Lamballe **299** d.	1447	1508	1514	1513	...	1604	...	|	1703	1711	1716	...	...	...	...	...	1804	...	1807	1823	...	...	|	
St Brieuc 299 d.	1502	1521	1526	1526	...	1617	...	1713	1716	1722	1729	...	...	...	...	1741	1818	...	1820	1835	...	...	1908	
Guingamp d.	...	1539	1544	1543	...	1636	...	1731	1734	...	1746	...	...	1752	...	1806	...	...	1835	1852	...	...	1926	19
Plouaret-Trégor d.	...	|	|	1557	...	|	...	|	1749	...	1800	...	...	1809	...	1823	...	...	1850	1906	1924	1925	|	19
Lannion a.	...	|	|	|	...	|	...	|	|	...	|	...	...	1826	...	1840	...	...	|	|	1941	1942	|	20
Morlaix d.	...	1609	1613	1615	...	1706	1725	1801	1808	...	1818	...	1817	...	1844	...	...	...	1907	1925	...	...	1955	
Landivisiau d.	...	|	|	1630	...	|	1749	|	|	...	1833	...	1838	...	1903	...	...	...	1922	1941	...	...	|	
Landerneau **286** d.	...	|	|	1640	...	|	1801	|	|	...	1843	...	1847	...	1913	...	...	...	1932	1950	...	...	2020	
Brest 286 a.	...	1642	1646	1654	...	1738	1819	1834	1840	...	1855	...	1905	...	1928	...	...	...	1946	2002	...	...	2031	

	TGV 8633					*TGV* 8647	*TGV* 8643					*TGV* 8649	*TGV* 8691		*TGV* 8657		*TGV* 8663	*TGV* 8667	*TGV* 8665				*TGV* 8679	*T* 86
	⑤	⑥	⑥	†	Ⓐ	⑤	①–④		⑤	①–④	†	⑤	⑤				⑤	⑤	⑥–④		†		⑤	(
	g					g	x		g	x		g	g				g	g	m				g	
Paris Montparnasse **280** d.	1608	...	...	...	...	1712	1708	...	...	...	...	1741	1741	...	1808	...	1908	1908	1908	...	...	...	2108	23
Rennes d.	1821	1845	...	1838	1845	|	1922	...	1927	1935	1940	2001	2007	...	2018	...	2123	2128	2124	...	2240	...	2323	
Lamballe **299** d.	|	1924	...	1937	1946	|	2002	...	2006	2027	2018	|	2048	...	|	...	|	2212	2204	...	2317	...	|	
St Brieuc 299 d.	1909	1936	...	1947	1957	2008	2018	...	2019	2038	2031	|	2101	...	2108	...	2213	2223	2219	...	2329	...	0013	04
Guingamp d.	1927	1952	...	...	...	|	2036	...	2037	...	2048	|	2117	...	2126	...	2231	...	2236	...	2349	...	0030	04
Plouaret-Trégor d.	|	2006	2013	...	...	|	2052	...	2051	...	|	|	2133	...	|	...	2246	...	2252	2303	0003	...	|	
Lannion a.	|	|	2030	...	...	|	|	...	|	...	|	|	2150	...	|	...	|	...	|	2320	|	...	|	
Morlaix d.	1956	2024	...	...	...	|	2110	...	2111	...	2119	2129	...	...	2156	...	2304	...	2310	...	0022	...	0059	05
Landivisiau d.	|	2041	...	...	...	|	|	...	|	...	|	|	...	...	|	...	|	...	|	...	0037	...	|	
Landerneau **286** d.	2021	2051	...	...	...	|	|	...	2133	...	|	|	...	...	|	...	2329	...	2334	...	0047	...	|	05
Brest 286 a.	2032	2103	...	...	...	2119	2141	...	2145	...	2150	2200	...	...	2228	...	2340	...	2345	...	0059	...	0130	05

			TGV 8612						*TGV* 8618	*TGV* 8618						*TGV* 8620		*TGV* 8622	*TGV* 8624					*T* 86
	①	②–⑤	①	Ⓐ	①	Ⓐ	Ⓐ	†	⑥	Ⓐ		Ⓐ	Ⓐ	Ⓒ	Ⓐ	Ⓐ	Ⓒ	⑥	⑦		†	⑥		⑤
	u	v	u		u				h									h	j					g
Brest 286 d.	...	...	0446	...	...	0536	...	...	0638	0642	...	0749	...	...	...	0819	...	0842	0842	...	1018	1040	1116	11
Landerneau **286** d.	...	...	|	...	...	0547	...	...	0654	0656	...	0806	...	...	...	|	...	|	|	...	1030	1051	1132	
Landivisiau d.	...	...	|	...	...	0557	...	...	|	|	...	0819	...	...	...	|	...	|	|	...	1040	|	1144	
Morlaix d.	...	...	0520	...	...	0614	...	...	0717	0721	...	0842	...	...	...	0851	...	0916	0916	...	1055	1114	1208	12
Lannion d.	0508	...	|	...	0603	|	...	...	|	|	...	...	...	...	0836	|	0908	|	|	...	|	|	...	
Plouaret-Trégor d.	0524	...	|	...	0620	0632	...	...	|	|	...	...	...	...	0852	|	0925	0935	0935	...	1112	|	...	12
Guingamp d.	0540	0541	0549	...	...	0646	0702	0726	0747	0750	...	...	...	...	0908	0922	...	0950	0950	...	1127	1143	...	12
St Brieuc 299 d.	...	0558	0607	0633	...	0703	0725	0742	0805	0809	...	...	0901	0936	...	0940	...	1009	1009	...	1144	1200	...	13
Lamballe **299** d.	...	0610	0620	0644	...	0715	0740	0754	0818	|	...	...	0916	0951	...	|	...	|	|	...	1156	1212	...	13
Rennes a.	...	0648	0659	0748	...	0754	0840	0850	0855	0859	...	...	1013	1048	...	1025	...	1055	1055	...	1236	1252	...	13
Paris Montparnasse **280** a.	...	...	0917	...	...	...	...	...	1117	1121	...	...	...	...	...	1253	...	1323	1323	...	...	...	...	16

	TGV 8634		*TGV* 8640		*TGV* 8646						*TGV* 8658	*TGV* 8662									*TGV* 8672	*TGV* 8670		
	①–④	⑤	Ⓐ			⑥–④	†		⑤	⑤		⑤Ⓒ	⑤	①–④	†	†	⑤	⑤	†	①–④	①–④	⑤Ⓒ	⑥	①-
	x	g				m			g	g		g	g	x			g	g		x	x	g		x
Brest 286 d.	1146	1208	1247	...	1348	1432	...	...	...	1505	...	1545	...	...	...	1556	...	1606	...	...	1648	1654	...	..
Landerneau **286** d.	|	1220	|	...	|	1443	...	...	...	1516	...	|	...	...	...	1607	...	1617	...	...	|	|	...	..
Landivisiau d.	|	|	|	...	|	1453	...	...	...	1526	...	|	...	...	...	1617	...	1627	...	...	|	|	...	..
Morlaix d.	1219	1243	1321	...	1422	1510	...	...	...	1541	...	1619	...	...	...	1632	...	1643	...	...	1721	|	...	..
Lannion d.	|	|	|	1348	|	|	...	...	1534	|	1600	|	...	...	1625	|	1627	|	1656	1708	|	|	...	17
Plouaret-Trégor d.	1237	|	|	1406	|	1528	...	...	1550	|	1619	|	...	...	1641	|	1644	1700	1712	1724	|	|	...	17
Guingamp d.	1253	1311	1351	1422	1451	1542	...	...	1605	1617	1635	|	...	...	1656	1708	...	1715	1728	1739	1750	1754	...	18
St Brieuc 299 d.	1312	1329	1410	...	1513	1558	1607	...	...	1635	1653	1707	1712	1713	...	1725	...	1732	...	1757	1808	1813	1825	18
Lamballe **299** d.	|	1341	1422	...	|	1610	1621	...	...	1647	1707	|	1723	1726	...	1738	...	1744	...	1810	1821	|	1839	..
Rennes a.	1359	1420	1500	...	1559	1650	1720	...	...	1725	1755	1800	1814	1829	...	1817	...	1821	...	1850	1900	1857	1942	..
Paris Montparnasse **280** a.	1611	...	1718	...	1822	...	...	...	...	...	2011	2011	...	...	...	...	...	...	...	...	2111	2111	...	..

	TGV 8676										*TGV* 8688						*TGV* 8696	*TGV* 8682	*TGV* 8682			*TGV* 8686		
	⑦	Ⓐ	⑤	⑥	⑥	†	Ⓐ	†	†	Ⓐ	⑦	⑥	Ⓐ	⑥	Ⓐ		⑦	⑥	Ⓐ	†	Ⓐ	⑦	⑤	
	j		g							L	j				F		j	h				j	g	
Brest 286 d.	1714	...	...	...	1725	1729	1740	...	...	1800	1815	...	...	1822	1821	...	...	1846	1850	1905	1933	1948	...	..
Landerneau **286** d.	|	...	...	...	1736	1740	1751	...	...	1817	|	...	...	1836	1838	...	...	|	|	1916	1951	2001	...	..
Landivisiau d.	|	...	...	...	1746	1750	|	...	...	1829	|	...	...	1847	1851	...	...	|	|	1926	2003	|	...	..
Morlaix d.	1748	...	...	...	1803	1806	1814	...	...	1852	1848	...	...	1903	1914	...	...	1920	1923	1942	2018	2024	...	..
Lannion d.	|	...	1757	1759	|	|	|	...	1832	|	|	1901	1904	|	...	...	1918	|	|	|	...	|	2028	..
Plouaret-Trégor d.	|	...	1814	|	1821	1824	|	...	1850	1912	|	1917	1920	1924	...	...	|	|	|	2000	...	|	2045	..
Guingamp d.	1819	...	1828	1827	1842	1838	1842	...	1906	...	1918	...	1935	1938	...	...	1947	1950	1952	2014	...	|	...	..
St Brieuc 299 d.	1836	1832	1849	...	1859	1855	1900	1907	...	...	1941	...	...	...	...	...	2005	2008	2011	2031	...	2108	...	..
Lamballe **299** d.	1849	1846	...	...	1911	1907	1912	1922	...	...	|	...	...	...	...	...	2019	2021	|	2043	...	|	...	..
Rennes a.	1925	1940	...	...	1949	1945	1950	2018	...	...	2029	...	...	...	...	...	2059	2059	2059	2121	...	2155	...	..
Paris Montparnasse **280** a.	2150	...	...	...	...	...	...	...	...	...	2241	...	...	...	...	...	2310	2310	2310	...	...	0011	...	..

GUINGAMP - PAIMPOL and v.v.

km		Ⓐ		†	⚒			Ⓐ	Ⓒ		⑤ g
0	Guingamp d.	0640	...	1110	1200	...	1452	1742	1746	...	2135
47	Paimpol a.	0748	...	1218	1308	...	1600	1850	1854	...	2243

	Ⓐ	Ⓒ				Ⓐ	Ⓒ		Ⓐ	†
Paimpol d.	0755	0825	...	1330	...	1627	1632	...	1857	190
Guingamp a.	0903	0933	...	1438	...	1735	1740	...	2005	200

F – July 18 - Aug. 12.
L – July 4 - 15, Aug. 16 - 28.

g – Also July 13.
h – Also July 14.
j – Also Aug. 15.
k – Not Aug. 15.
m – Not July 13.

t – Also Aug. 15; not Aug. 14.
u – Also Aug. 16; not Aug. 15.
v – Not July 14, Aug. 16.
x – Not July 13, 14, Aug. 15.

TGV –®, supplement payable, 🍷.

V trains convey 🍷

RENNES and NANTES - QUIMPER 285 (Summer)

Service July 3 - Aug. 28. *For service to July 2/from Aug. 29 see page 185*

													TGV 8701						TGV 8715			TGV 8719	TGV 8721	
	Ⓐ	Ⓐ	⑥	Ⓐ	Ⓐ	Ⓐ	①	②–⑤		①–⑥	①–⑥	⑦		⑦		Ⓐ	⑥	⑥		⑤		Ⓐ	⑥	⑥
							u	v		k	k	◇j		j				h		g			h	h
Paris Mont **280** d.	...	...	...	...	...	...	...	...	...	...	...	...	0836	...	...	...	...	...	1008	...	...	1108	1108	...
Rennes 287 d.	...	...	...	...	0710	...	...	...	...	0940	...	0936	|	1051	...	...	1133	...	1217	1302	...	1335	1335	...
Nantes ◧ d.	...	...	...	...	|	0651	0730	0738	...	|	0925	|	|	|	...	1118	|	1118	|	|	...	|	|	1312
Savenay ◧ d.	...	...	...	...	|	0714	0752	0802	...	|	0947	|	|	|	...	1141	|	1140	|	|	...	|	|	1336
Redon **287** ◧ d.	...	...	...	0710	0746	0752	0827	0836	...	1018	1023	1019	|	1126	...	1207	1211	1216	1253	1338	...	|	|	1403
Vannes d.	...	0658	0706	0740	...	0821	...	...	...	...	1052	1056	1143	1153	...	1235	...	1245	1319	1407	...	1436	1436	...
Auray d.	...	0712	0721	0751	...	0834	...	...	...	...	1104	1109	1157	1206	...	1248	...	1257	1333	1420	...	1449	1449	...
Lorient d.	0645	0743	0748	0815	...	0854	...	...	...	...	1125	...	1217	1225	...	1307	...	1317	1352	1439	...	1506	1509	...
Quimperlé d.	0659	0758	...	0826	...	0906	...	...	...	...	1137	...	|	1237	...	1319	...	1329	1406	1451	...	...	|	...
Quimper a.	0728	0827	...	0853	...	0933	...	...	...	...	1204	...	1250	1304	...	1346	...	1356	1435	1519	...	...	1542	...

			TGV 8717				TGV 8723														TGV 8729				
	Ⓒ	①–④		Ⓒ			⑤		①–④	⑤	⑤	Ⓐ	⑦		①–④	†	①–④	Ⓒ	⑤		⑥–④	†	①–④	⑤	†
		x					g		x	g	g		j		x		⊖x	⊖	g		m		x	g	
aris Mont **280** d.	...	...	1208	...	...	...	1346	...	...	...	...	...	...	...	...	...	...	...	...	...	1508	...	...	...	...
ıes 287 d.	1350	1400	1422	...	...	...	|	...	...	1610	...	...	...	...	1639	1641	...	...	1700	...	1717	...	...	...	1735
antes ◧ d.	|	|	|	...	...	1520	|	...	...	|	...	1620	1620	...	|	|	1649	1659	|	...	|	1723	1724	1725	|
avenay ◧ d.	|	|	|	...	...	|	|	...	...	|	...	1641	1642	...	|	|	|	|	|	...	|	1745	1747	1747	|
on **287** ◧ d.	1429	1437	|	...	...	1604	|	...	...	1649	...	1710	1710	...	1716	1721	1733	1742	1741	...	|	1811	1821	1821	1830
ıes d.	1459	1507	1522	...	...	1633	1652	...	1700	1720	1731	...	...	...	1743	1751	1801	1809	1811	...	1819	...	...	...	1903
ıy d.	1512	1520	1535	...	...	1646	1706	...	1714	1732	1745	...	...	...	1756	1804	|	|	1824	...	1834	...	...	...	1918
ent d.	1533	1537	1558	1615	...	1707	1724	...	1746	1753	1817	...	...	...	1818	1825	1830	1836	1845	...	1854	...	...	...	1944
ıperlé d.	1544	...	|	1630	...	1719	|	...	1802	1805	1832	...	...	...	1830	1837	|	|	1856	...	|	...	...	...	...
ımper a.	1612	...	1631	1700	...	1747	1758	...	1832	1832	1902	...	...	...	1857	1904	1904	1911	1923	...	1930	...	...	...	...

						TGV 8737	TGV 8739		TGV 8747	TGV 8741	TGV 8743		TGV 8759					TGV 8757		TGV 8761		TGV 5237		TGV 8775	TGV 8779
	Ⓐ	⑥	⑥	Ⓐ	⑤	①–④	⑤		⑤	⑥	⑦		①–④	⑤	①–④	⑦–④	⑦	⑤						⑤	⑤
					⊖g	x	g		g	h	j		x	g	x	m	j	g				♥		g	g
aris Mont **280** d.	...	...	...	...	...	1641	1641	...	1708	1708	1703	...	1808	...	...	...	...	1858	...	1941	...	...	...	2024	2208
ıes 287 d.	1755	1755	...	...	...	1901	1901	...	1918	1929	1929	...	2022	...	...	2030	...	|	...	2149	...	2203	...	2238	0027
antes ◧ d.	|	|	1741	1821	1834	|	|	...	|	|	|	...	|	1950	2000	|	2043	|	...	|	...	|	...	|	|
avenay ◧ d.	|	|	1803	1843	|	|	|	...	|	|	|	...	|	2018	2026	|	2105	|	...	|	...	|	...	|	|
on **287** ◧ d.	1836	1837	1842	1911	1925	1939	1939	...	|	2005	2005	...	|	2045	2054	2110	2131	|	...	2227	...	2240	...	2314	|
ıes d.	1905	...	1912	...	1954	2004	2006	...	2017	2032	2031	...	2123	...	...	2140	...	2201	...	2252	...	2306	...	2341	0129
ıy d.	1918	...	1925	...	2006	...	2020	...	2032	2045	2045	...	|	...	...	2153	...	2214	...	2305	...	2319	...	2355	0142
ent d.	1940	...	1946	...	2028	...	2040	...	2053	2101	2105	...	2150	...	...	2214	...	2233	...	2325	...	2338	...	0014	0159
ıperlé d.	1952	...	1958	...	2039	...	|	...	2107	...	2119	...	|	...	...	2226	...	|	...	2340	...	2351	...	0027	...
ımper a.	2020	...	2025	...	2105	...	2115	...	2135	...	2147	...	2224	...	...	2253	...	2307	...	0009	...	0020	...	0056	...

	TGV 8702	TGV 8706							TGV 8718					TGV 5272			TGV 8720	TGV 8722	TGV 8724						
	①	②–⑥	Ⓐ	Ⓐ	Ⓐ	⑥	Ⓐ	Ⓐ	⚒		Ⓐ	⑥	Ⓐ		Ⓐ		Ⓐ	⑥	⑦		Ⓐ	†	Ⓐ	⑥	Ⓐ
	u	v	S		R	h			h					♥	R			h	j		⊖	⊖		⊖	
ımper d.	0413	...	...	...	0531	...	0600	...	0635	...	...	0705	0717	0739	0754	...	0809	0839	0839	...	0910	0927	0928	0949	1000
ıperlé d.	0443	...	...	...	0559	...	0627	...	0706	...	...	0734	0744	0810	0823	...	0839	0910	0910	...	|	|	0955	|	1027
ent d.	0458	0500	...	...	0610	...	0640	...	0721	...	...	0748	0757	0824	0838	...	0854	0925	0925	...	0945	1002	1008	1023	1039
ıy d.	0516	|	...	...	0631	...	0700	...	0741	...	...	...	0819	0843	0904	...	0914	0945	0945	...	|	|	1029	|	1100
ıes d.	0529	0527	0610	...	0643	...	0712	...	0755	...	...	...	0832	0857	0918	...	0928	0959	0959	...	1013	1029	1041	1050	1113
on **287** d.	0554	0554	0640	0648	0713	0741	0745	0750	0820	...	0851	...	0902	0923	...	...	|	|	|	...	1042	1055	1112	1119	1142
avenay ◧ d.	|	|	|	0724	|	0810	|	0818	|	...	0922	...	|	|	...	...	|	|	|	...	|	|	1140	|	|
antes ◧ a.	|	|	|	0745	|	0831	|	0840	|	...	0945	...	|	|	...	...	|	|	|	...	1124	1141	1201	1200	|
ıes 287 ◧ a.	0629	0629	0744	...	0753	...	0829	...	0859	...	...	...	0937	0959	...	...	1029	1059	1059	...	...	...	...	...	1220
aris Mont **280** a.	0853	0853	...	...	...	...	...	...	1121	...	...	...	...	...	...	...	1253	1323	1323	...	...	...	...	...	...

		TGV 8730						TGV 8744								TGV 8752							TGV 8762	TGV 8762	TGV 8762
	Ⓒ		†	⑥	①–④	⑤	①–④	Ⓒ	Ⓐ	⑤	⑤		⑥	⑥	†		Ⓐ	⑦	†	⑤	①–④	†	Ⓒ	①–④	⑤
					x	g	x			g	g							j		g	x			x	g
ımper d.	1028	1142	1221	...	1232	1238	...	1235	...	1316	...	...	1331	...	...	1429	1512	...	1530	1544	...	1600	1617	1617	1617
ıperlé d.	1055	|	1248	...	1259	1306	...	1305	...	1344	...	...	1358	...	...	1458	1539	...	1557	1611	...	1627	|	|	|
ent d.	1108	1219	1300	1300	1312	1318	...	1324	1332	1356	...	...	1410	...	...	1517	1552	...	1610	1631	...	1640	1656	1656	1656
ıy d.	1129	1240	1320	1328	1331	1337	...	1342	1358	1413	...	...	1432	...	...	1539	1614	...	1632	1653	...	1702	1716	1716	1716
ıes d.	1142	1254	1333	1342	1344	1350	...	1356	1411	1426	...	...	1444	...	...	1553	1626	...	1645	1705	...	1714	1730	1731	1730
on **287** d.	1212	1320	1402	...	1418	1418	1423	1423	...	1459	1505	...	1518	1523	1526	1624	1657	1657	1716	1736	1743	1746	|	|	|
avenay ◧ d.	|	|	|	...	|	|	1449	|	...	|	1528	...	|	1546	1549	|	1722	1729	|	|	1810	1814	|	|	|
antes ◧ a.	|	|	1447	...	|	|	1511	|	...	|	1550	...	|	1608	1611	|	1745	1750	|	|	1833	1834	|	|	|
ıes 287 ◧ a.	1250	1355	...	...	1453	1453	...	1458	...	1534	...	...	1553	...	...	1659	...	...	1752	1815	...	...	1827	1829	1829
aris Mont **280** a.	...	1611	...	...	...	...	...	1725	...	...	...	...	...	...	...	1911	...	...	...	...	...	...	2052	2048	2054

				TGV 8774					TGV 8776	TGV 8780					TGV 8794		TGV 8790				TGV 8798		TGV 8796		
	Ⓐ	Ⓐ	①–④	⑦	⑤	⑦	⑥		⑦	①	†	⑤	①–④		⑦	②–④	D	⑤	Ⓐ		⑦	†	⑦	†	
			x	j	g	j			j	u		g	x		j	q		g	R		j	◇	j	w	
ımper d.	...	...	1706	1715	1722	...	1727	...	1748	1748	1756	1800	1807	...	1834	1846	1845	...	1900	...	1947	...	...	2035	...
ıperlé d.	...	...	1734	|	1750	...	1754	...	|	|	1823	1828	1836	...	1905	|	|	...	1927	...	|	...	...	2103	...
ent d.	1713	...	1746	1751	1805	...	1807	...	1825	1825	1836	1839	1851	...	1920	1921	1922	...	1938	...	2024	...	2059	2117	...
ıy d.	1741	...	1805	1811	1833	...	1831	...	1845	1845	1855	1901	1920	...	1940	1942	1942	...	...	...	2044	2052	2120	2136	...
ıes d.	1755	...	1817	1825	1846	...	1843	...	1859	1859	1908	1913	1934	...	1954	1955	1957	...	...	...	2058	2105	2133	2149	...
on **287** d.	...	1841	1846	1852	...	1857	1914	...	|	|	1937	1940	...	...	2020	|	|	2036	...	...	|	2140	|	2217	...
avenay ◧ d.	...	1908	|	|	...	1926	|	...	|	|	|	|	...	...	|	|	|	2102	...	...	|	|	|	|	...
antes ◧ a.	...	1931	|	|	...	1948	|	...	|	|	|	|	...	...	|	|	|	2125	...	...	|	|	|	|	...
ıes 287 ◧ a.	...	...	1920	1929	...	...	1950	...	|	1959	2012	2015	...	...	2055	2053	2055	...	...	...	2159	2223	2230	2251	...
aris Mont **280** a.	...	...	...	2150	...	...	...	...	2205	2219	...	...	...	...	2310	...	2310	...	...	...	0011	...	0053	...	...

AURAY - QUIBERON and v.v. Service July 2 - Aug. 28 ❦

				⚒	⑦					Ⓑ	
				h	j						
Rennes (above) d.	...	...	...	...	0936	...	...	...	...	...	...
Auray d.	0800	0858	1008	1111	1111	1225	1350	1601	1735	1841	2055
Quiberon a.	0844	0949	1058	1202	1202	1315	1434	1652	1826	1931	2139

									⚒	†	
Quiberon d.	0854	1004	1107	1220	1445	1557	1731	1837	1941	1945	2149
Auray a.	0937	1048	1150	1303	1530	1640	1815	1925	2024	2028	2232
Rennes (above) a.	...	...	...	...	...	...	...	...	...	2223	...

①⑤⑥ (also July 13, 14, Aug. 16; not Aug. 15).
July 4 - 15, Aug. 16 - 26.
July 18 - Aug. 12.

Also July 13.
Also July 14.
Also Aug. 15.
Not Aug. 15.
Not July 13.
Not July 13, 14, Aug. 16.
Also Aug. 16; not Aug. 15.

v – Not July 14, Aug. 16.
w – Not Aug. 14.
x – Not July 13, 14, Aug. 15.
z – Not June 26.

TGV – Ⓡ, supplement payable, 🍷.
⊖ – To/from Brest (Table **286**).
◇ – To/from Quiberon (see below main table).
◧ – See also **287** Nantes - Redon, **287/8** Nantes - Savenay.
♥ – From Lille Europe (Table **11**).

❦ – **June 11 - 19, Sept. 3 - 11:**
From Auray: 1053⑥⑦, 1345⑥⑦, 1545⑥⑦, 1840⑥⑦.
From Quiberon: 1148⑥⑦, 1440⑥⑦, 1740⑥⑦, 1945⑥⑦.

June 25 - July 1:
From Auray: 0800, 1111 **z**, 1350, 1601, 1841, 2055.
From Quiberon: 0854, 1220, 1445, 1740, 1941⚒, 2149.

286 (Summer) BREST - QUIMPER

Service July 3 - Aug. 28. *For service to July 2/from Aug. 29 see page 186*

km		Ⓐ	†	⑥	Ⓐ	Ⓒ		⑥	Ⓑ	⑤ g	Ⓒ	①–④ x		⑤ g	†	①–④ x	⑤ g	⑥	
0	**Brest 284** d.	0730	0747	0813	0945	0954	...	1145	1236	1600	1604	1610	...	1708	1720	1830	1927	2026	...
18	Landerneau **284** d.	0742	|	|	0957	1006	...	1157	1248	1612	1619	1625	...	1723	1732	1843	1939	2042	...
72	Châteaulin d.	0840	|	|	1058	1107	...	1258	1349	1713	1721	1733	...	1833	1838	1941	2037	2143	...
102	**Quimper** a.	0908	0922	0947	1126	1135	...	1326	1417	1741	1750	1801	...	1901	1906	2009	2105	2210	...
	Nantes **285** a.	1124	1141	1200	...	...	...	...	...	...	...	...	...	...	...	...	...	...	...

g – Also July 13.
h – Not Aug. 14.
x – Not July 13, 14, Aug. 15.

	Ⓐ	⑥	†	Ⓐ		Ⓐ	Ⓒ	①–④ x	⑥	⑤ g	†	⑥	†	①–④ x	⑤ g	† h	⑤ g	
Nantes **285** d.	...	...	...	...	...	...	...	...	...	...	...	1659	1659	1649	...	...	1834	...
Quimper d.	0600	0647	0824	1028	...	1440	1444	1703	1757	1803	1808	1912	1913	1911	2006	2030	2114	...
Châteaulin d.	0628	0715	0859	1100	...	1508	1512	1731	1825	1831	1836	|	1942	1943	2039	2058	2142	...
Landerneau **284** d.	0732	0819	1001	1202	...	1608	1614	1834	1927	1935	1938	|	2041	|	2138	2200	2244	...
Brest 284 a.	0745	0832	1014	1215	...	1621	1627	1847	1940	1948	1951	2048	2054	2052	2151	2213	2257	...

CAT 🚌 *31*, journey 90 minutes. *Subject to alteration.*
From Brest : 0700 Ⓐ, 0930 †, 1000 ⚒, 1415 †, 1440 ⚒, 1610 ⑤, 1800 Ⓐ.
From Quimper : 0710 Ⓐ, 1135 ⑤, 1245 1255 ⚒, 1640 ⚒, 1730 Ⓐ, 1740 †.

287 (Summer) RENNES - REDON - NANTES

Service July 3 - Aug. 28. *For service to July 2/from Aug. 29 see page 186*

km		Ⓐ	① u	⑥ h	Ⓐ	Ⓐ	Ⓐ	Ⓐ	Ⓐ B	† B	⑥ B	Ⓐ	⑥ h	†	①–④ x	⑤ g	⑤ g	⑥	⑦ j	①–④ x	⑤ g	Ⓐ	⑦ j	⑤ g	⑥	①–④ x	†
0	**Rennes** § d.	...	...	...	*0629*	0745	*0750*	0850	...	...	...	1208	1229	...	*1245*	1415	*1345*	*1433*	*1433*	1440	1535	...	...	1647	1700	*1644*	...
72	Redon § a.	...	...	...	*0723*	|	*0848*	|	...	...	...	|	|	...	*1347*	|	*1437*	*1518*	*1518*	1515	|	...	...	|	|	*1739*	...
72	Redon ◇ d.	0648	0716	0741	0750	|	0851	|	1042	1055	1119	|	|	1402	1423	|	1505	1523	1526	1523	|	1657	1657	|	|	1743	1746
106	Savenay ◇ d.	0724	0748	0810	0818	|	0922	|	|	|	|	|	|	|	1449	|	1528	1546	1549	|	|	1722	1729	|	|	1810	1814
145	**Nantes** ◇ a.	0745	0812	0831	0840	0859	0945	1005	1124	1141	1200	1323	1349	1447	1511	1529	1550	1608	1611	1607	1650	1745	1750	1805	1815	1833	1834

	†	Ⓐ	Ⓐ	⑦ j	Ⓐ	⑥	Ⓐ	†	⑥ S	①–④ x	⚒	⑤ g	†	⑤ g
Rennes § d.	1729	1745	...	...	1803	1815	1831	1859	1920	1928	1932	...	1948	2029
Redon § a.	|	|	...	...	1905	1855	1917	1938	|	|	2041	...	|	2116
Redon ◇ d.	|	|	1841	1857	...	1901	1926	1945	|	|	...	2036	|	...
Savenay ◇ d.	|	|	1908	1926	...	1928	1954	2013	|	|	...	2102	|	...
Nantes ◇ a.	1845	1900	1931	1948	...	1950	2015	2034	2035	2044	...	2125	2105	...

	Ⓒ	⑥	Ⓐ	Ⓐ	① u	⑥ Sh	⚒ k	⑦ j	⚒	
Nantes ◇ d.	...	...	0651	0724	0730	0820	0925	1007	1118	...
Savenay ◇ d.	...	...	0714	|	0752	|	0947	1029	1140	...
Redon ◇ a.	..	...	0741	|	0827	|	1012	1055	1205	...
Redon § d.	0649	0734	...	|	...	|	*1031*	1101	...	1233
Rennes § a.	0753	0820	...	0842	...	0934	*1108*	1151	...	1338

	⑥ h	⑥ h	Ⓐ	⑥	⑤ g	⑤ g	Ⓑ	⑤ g	①–④ x	Ⓒ	①–④ Bx	Ⓒ B	†	Ⓐ	Ⓐ	⑥	†	Ⓐ	⑥	Ⓐ	⑤ g		⑤ g	①–④ x	⑤ g	⑦ j	①–④ x
Nantes ◇ d.	1256	1312	1440	1503	1535	...	1620	1648	...	...	1649	1659	1723	...	1724	1741	1758	1759	1803	1821	1834	1925	1945	2000	2025	2043	2126
Savenay ◇ d.	|	1336	|	|	|	...	1641	|	...	...	|	|	1745	...	1747	1803	|	|	|	1843	|	|	2018	2026	2047	2105	|
Redon ◇ a.	|	1403	|	|	|	...	1710	|	...	...	1731	1741	1810	...	1821	1831	|	|	|	1911	1923	|	2045	2054	2112	2131	|
Redon § d.	|	...	|	|	|	1701	...	|	1724	1729	...	...	...	1811	...	...	|	|	|	...	...	|	...	...	2119	...	|
Rennes § a.	1410	...	1556	1617	1650	1803	...	1809	1823	1823	...	...	...	1908	...	...	1912	1913	1917	...	...	2044	...	...	2154	...	2240

B – To/from Brest (Table **286**).
S – To/from St Malo (Table **281**).
g – Also July 13.
h – Also July 14.
j – Also Aug. 15.
k – Not Aug. 15.
q – Not July 14.
u – Also Aug. 16; not Aug. 15.
x – Not July 13, 14, Aug. 15.
§ – For other trains Rennes - Redon see Table **285**
◇ – For other trains Redon - Nantes see Table **285**, for Savenay - Nantes see Tables **285** and **288**.

288 (Summer) NANTES - ST NAZAIRE - LE CROISIC

Service July 3 - Aug. 28. *For service to July 2/from Aug. 29 see page 186*

km		Ⓐ	Ⓐ	Ⓐ	⑥ h	Ⓐ	⚒ h	⑦ j	*TGV* **8905** ①–⑥ k	Ⓒ O	*TGV* **8911**	①–⑥ k	Ⓐ	⑦ j	Ⓐ	*TGV* **8915**	Ⓒ	*TGV* **8919** ⑤ g		*TGV* **8921** ⑦–④ y	Ⓐ	*TGV* **8927** ⑥ h	Ⓐ	⑥ h
	Paris Mont. **280** d.	...	...	...	...	...	...	...	0653	...	0854	...	...	...	...	1054	...	1221	...	1354	...	1454	...	...
0	**Nantes 285/7** d.	0616	0642	0656	0719	0753	0800	0903	0913	1002	1110	1150	1202	1223	1234	1303	1433	1444	...	1611	1643	1711	1719	1729
39	Savenay **285/7** d.	0648	0706	0720	0743	0820	0834	0931	|	1027	|	1211	1233	1244	1308	|	1455	|	...	|	1704	|	1741	1753
64	**St Nazaire** d.	0710	0726	0739	0801	0835	0859	0945	0948	1052	1145	1226	1249	1301	1331	1339	1516	1520	...	1648	1728	1747	1757	1808
79	Pornichet d.	...	...	0753	0812	...	0910	0956	1000	1107	|	1239	...	1312	...	1353	1527	|	...	|	1741	|	1809	1819
83	La Baule Escoublac d.	...	...	0800	0822	...	0915	1003	1008	1115	1206	1246	...	1321	...	1404	1534	1537	...	1706	1748	1803	1817	1826
90	**Le Croisic** a.	...	...	0815	0835	...	0926	1016	1021	1133	1215	1259	...	1333	...	1422	1547	1546	...	1715	1802	1813	1832	1839

	Ⓐ T	† T	Ⓐ	⑥ h	⑦ j	①–④ x	*TGV* **8937** ⑦–④ y	*TGV* **8935** ⑤ g	①–④ x	⑤⑥ Og	①–④ x		*TGV* **8943** ⑤⑥ z	⑦ j	*TGV* **8945** ①–④ x	⑥ h	*TGV* **5231** ♥	*TGV* **8949** ⑤ g	①–④ x	⑦ j	*TGV* **8953** ⑤ g	⑦ j	⑤⑥ z
Paris Mont. **280** d.	...	...	...	...	...	...	1721	1721	...	...	...	...	1823	...	1850	...	...	1954	...	...	2054	...	...
Nantes 285/7 d.	1809	1805	1841	1839	1900	1909	1932	1932	...	1945	2006	...	2036	2034	2058	2132	2154	2208	2222	2222	2306	2325	2325
Savenay **285/7** d.	|	1827	1916	1914	1921	1943	|	|	←	2007	2031	...	|	2059	|	2159	|	|	2249	2249	|	2346	2354
St Nazaire d.	1847	1847	1931	1942f	1942	2002	2006	2010	2018	2025	2045	...	2112	2120	2134	2213	2229	2245	2303	2302	2343	0002	0008
Pornichet d.	1858	1858	1942	1952	1952	→	...	2022	2031	2040	...	...	|	2132	|	...	2242	2257	2314	...	|	0013	0019
La Baule Escoublac d.	1907	1907	1949	2002	2002	...	...	2030	2040	2049	...	...	2128	2140	2151	...	2249	2304	2321	...	2359	0020	0026
Le Croisic a.	1920	1920	2002	2015	2015	...	...	2044	2052	2102	...	...	2137	2152	2200	...	2303	2317	2334	...	0008	0033	0037

	Ⓐ	*TGV* **8906** ① k	*TGV* **8912** ②–⑤ v	⑥ h	*TGV* **8914** ① u		Ⓐ	Ⓐ	Ⓐ	Ⓒ	Ⓐ	Ⓒ Ok	Ⓐ	*TGV* **5270** ♥		*TGV* **8926** Ⓐ	*TGV* **8928** Ⓒ	Ⓐ	⑥ h	*TGV* **8932**		Ⓐ	*TGV* **8940**
Le Croisic d.	0512	...	...	0547	0553	...	...	0634	...	0710	0730	0806	0828	0850	...	0957	1024	1036	1035	1143	1219	...	1348
La Baule Escoublac d.	0525	...	...	0557	0604	...	...	0647	...	0722	0744	0820	0841	0904	...	1009	1036	1049	1053	1201	1231	...	1403
Pornichet d.	0532	...	...	0602	|	...	...	0654	...	0729	0751	0825	0846	0911	...	|	|	1057	1103	1207	1238	...	|
St Nazaire d.	0542	0546	0550	0613	0620	...	0626	0705	0742	0741	0807	0837	0858	0924	...	1025	1051	1107	1114	1221	1248	1352	1419
Savenay **285/7** d.	...	0603	|	0626	|	...	0645	0729	0757	0755	0824	0851	0912	|	...	|	|	1122	1129	|	1311	1408	|
Nantes 285/7 a.	...	0624	0624	0648	0655	...	0720	0750	0820	0820	0848	0913	0934	1000	...	1059	1124	1143	1150	1255	1345	1440	1454
Paris Mont. **280** a.	...	0837	0857	...	0906	...	...	...	...	...	...	...	...	...	...	1320	1340	...	...	1518	...	...	1708

	Ⓑ q	*TGV* **8944**	Ⓐ	⑥ h	Ⓐ	⑦ j	Ⓐ O	*TGV* **8950** ⑤⑦ p	①–④ x	⑦ j	Ⓐ		*TGV* **8952** ⑥–④ m	Ⓐ	Ⓒ O	①–④ x	⑤ g	⑦ j	⑥ h	Ⓐ	*TGV* **8958** ⑦ j	*TGV* **8960** ⑦ j	⑤ g
Le Croisic d.	1520	1552	...	1628	...	1651	...	1746	...	1759	1815	...	1854	...	1902	2010	2015	2025	2034	...	2052	2112	...
La Baule Escoublac d.	1536	1603	...	1644	...	1705	...	1801	...	1812	1827	...	1906	...	1921	2023	2030	2037	2047	...	2103	2126	...
Pornichet d.	1542	|	...	1651	...	1712	...	1808	...	1819	1834	...	|	...	1930	2032	2037	2043	2056	...	|	2133	...
St Nazaire d.	1552	1621	1631	1701	1701	1724	1736	1821	1829	1831	1846	...	1921	1926	1945	2042	2052	2055	2106	2116	2121	2146	2214
Savenay **285/7** d.	1609	|	1648	1714	1726	1740	1752	|	1848	1847	1915	...	|	1940	|	2057	2109	2114	2120	2134	|	|	2231
Nantes 285/7 a.	1630	1654	1714	1741	1758	1812	1814	1854	1917	1920	1945	...	1954	2005	2019	2119	2130	2141	2141	2201	2154	2219	2252
Paris Mont. **280** a.	...	1920	...	...	...	...	...	2119	...	...	...	...	2214	...	...	...	...	...	...	...	0005	0038	...

O – To/from Orléans (Table **289**).
T – To/from Tours (Table **289**).
b – 10 minutes **earlier** on July 8, 13.
f – Arrive 1927.
g – Also July 13.
h – Also July 14.
j – Also Aug. 15.
k – Not Aug. 15.
m – Not July 13.
p – Also July 13, Aug. 15.
q – Not July 14.
u – Also Aug. 16; not Aug. 15.
v – Not July 14, Aug. 16.
x – Not July 13, 14, Aug. 15.
y – Not July 13, 14.
z – Also July 13, 14.
TGV –Ⓡ, supplement payable, 🍸.
♥ – From/to Lille Europe (Table **11**); d. 1752, a. 1407 (a. 1423 until July
⊖ – From Le Mans (Table **280**).

InterRail - *for European residents.* website: www.interrail.eu

ERRAIL GLOBAL PASS - valid in 30 European countries:
tria, Belgium, Bosnia-Herzegovina, Bulgaria, Croatia, Czech Republic, mark, Finland, France, Germany, Great Britain, Greece, Hungary, nd (including Northern Ireland), Italy, Luxembourg, FYRO Macedonia, tenegro, Netherlands, Norway, Poland, Portugal, Romania, Serbia, akia, Slovenia, Spain, Sweden, Switzerland and Turkey.
T VALID in the passholder's country of residence (but see below).

CES - GLOBAL PASS

outh is 12-25 years	Youth 1st/2nd cl.	Adult 2nd class	Adult 1st class
ays within 15 days (flexi)	€331/200	€264	€413
ays within 1 month (flexi)	€393/246	€315	€491
days within 1 month (flexi)	€471/292	€374	€588
days within 1 month (flexi)	€579/361	€463	€723
days continuous	€520/338	€414	€650
days continuous	€608/374	€484	€760
onth continuous	€787/479	€626	€983

es correct as at 14/01/16. Accompanied children aged 4-11 travel free a Child Pass; two children can travel with each adult.
bal Pass Senior (60+) gives 10% discount (not for One Country passes).

ERRAIL ONE COUNTRY PASS (O.C.P.) - valid in one country
ers any one of the participating countries above (except Bosnia-zegovina and Montenegro). NOT available for the passholder's country esidence. Note that Benelux (Belgium, Luxembourg, Netherlands) counts one country. *Greece Plus* and *Italy Plus* passes includes Italy - Greece services operated by Attica Group (Superfast Ferries - some routes are jointly with Anek Lines). 1st class Youth passes are also available cept Norway). Prices correct as at 14/01/16.

CES - ONE COUNTRY PASS *3, 4, 6 or 8 days within 1 month*

	Youth	2nd	1st		Youth	2nd	1st
nce, Germany or Great Britain:							
ays	€154	€203	€317	6 days	€208	€283	€445
ays	€164	€223	€349	8 days	€232	€313	€492
tria, Italy Plus, Norway (2nd class only), Spain or Sweden:							
ays	€131	€173	€272	6 days	€187	€256	€401
ays	€154	€197	€308	8 days	€219	€297	€465
elux, Denmark, Finland, Greece Plus, Ireland, Italy or Switzerland:							
ays	€87	€118	€185	6 days	€141	€199	€311
ays	€108	€149	€233	8 days	€176	€239	€376
garia, Croatia, Czech Republic, Greece, Hungary, Poland, Portugal, nania, Slovakia, Slovenia or Turkey:							
ays	€57	€78	€121	6 days	€93	€125	€197
ays	€69	€95	€148	8 days	€107	€148	€231
RO Macedonia or Serbia:							
ays	€42	€56	€89	6 days	€81	€106	€166
ays	€57	€78	€121	8 days	€91	€126	€199

O CAN BUY INTERRAIL PASSES
national of a European country (including Russia) with a valid passport, or one who has lived in Europe for at least six months. Passes can be chased up to three months before travel begins.

PPLEMENTS AND RESERVATION FEES
uired for certain types of high-speed or 'global price' train. International day examples, 2nd class (subject to change): France - Italy *TGV* €33-60 48-80 in 1st class); *Berlin - Warszawa Express* €4; *EC Switzerland - Italy* €11; *Eurostar* passholder fare (e.g. London - Paris from €89); *TGV/ICE* France - Germany €13; *TGV Lyria* (France - Switzerland) from €25; *Thalys* passholder fare from €15; *TGV* Brussels - France €9; *SJ Snabbtåg* Stockholm - København €7. *IC bus* Klagenfurt - Venezia €9 (€13 1st class). Domestic examples: **Croatia** *IC/ICN* €1. **Czech Republic** *SC* €8. **Finland** *Pendolino* €3-7. **France** *TGV* €9 (peak €18), *Intercités* with compulsory reservation €6. **Germany** free on *ICE*. **Greece** *IC* €7-28. **Hungary** *IC* €3. **Italy** *FA*, *FB* and *FR* €10, *IC* €3. **Norway** long-distance trains €6.3. **Poland** *EIP* €10, *EIC/TLK* free. **Portugal** *AP/IC* €5. **Romania** *IC/IR* €1-1.2. **Slovakia** *IC* €5. **Slovenia** *ICS* €3.4 (€5.1 1st class). **Spain** *AVE* €10, most other long-distance trains €6.5, *MD* €4.5. **Sweden** *Snabbtåg* €7.

Night Trains: Passes do not include sleeping accommodation, which is typically €15 to €75 for a couchette, and €35 to €155 for a berth in a sleeping car. Some trains also include reclining seats. Many night trains are globally priced and fares for passholders vary widely. *Thello* (France / Italy) gives 25% discount. Holders of a Global or Sweden One Country Pass can obtain a couchette berth on the *Berlin Night Express* (Berlin - Malmö and v.v.) for €29.

The number of seats allocated to InterRail holders may be limited (e.g. on *TGV* and *Thalys* trains). If sold out, you may have to buy an ordinary ticket. The fold-out Travel Report inside the ticket cover must be filled in. Direct night trains or ferries leaving after 1900 hrs can count as next travel day.

FREE TRAVEL TO THE BORDER, AIRPORT OR SEAPORT
Although it is not possible to purchase an InterRail pass for the holder's own country of residence, from 2016 a Global pass entitles the holder to two free journeys (one outbound, one inbound) between any station in their country of residence and its border, an airport or seaport. Each journey must be completed in one day (no overnight stops allowed), within the overall validity of the pass, or include a travel day if using a flexi pass. Details must be entered in the travel diary.

VALIDITY ON PRIVATE RAILWAYS
InterRail passes are valid on the national railway companies in each country, plus many privately run railways (some give discounts). For details see the InterRail Traveller's Guide or www.interrail.eu. Selected details are as follows (subject to change): **Austria**: free travel on WESTbahn and ROeEE. **Denmark**: free travel on Arriva and DSB-Øresund, 50% discount on Nordjyske Jernbaner (Hjørring - Hirtshals and Frederikshavn - Skagen). **France**: SNCF bus services included. **Germany**: free on most regional services. **Hungary**: GySEV services are included. **Italy**: not valid on NTV's *Italo* trains. **Netherlands**: privately run regional lines are included. **Norway**: Flåmsbana (Myrdal - Flåm) gives 30% discount. **Spain**: FGC gives 50% discount. **Sweden**: most private operators are included. **Switzerland**: free travel on BLS, FART/SSIF, MOB, RhB, SOB, THURBO and ZB. Many others offer 25-50% discount, including AB, ASM, CJ, FB, LEB, MBC, NStCM, RA, RB, RBS, SZU, TMR, TPC, TPF, TRN, WB, WSB. The MGB (Disentis - Brig - Zermatt) offers 50% to under-26s only. Discounted fare on William Tell Express (rail and boat tour). No discounts available on BRB or narrow gauge railways in Jungfrau area (BOB, JB, WAB).

VALIDITY ON FERRY AND BUS SERVICES
The pass includes free deck passage between Italy and Greece on SuperFast Ferries and Minoan Lines (you pay port taxes €7, high-season surcharge €10 June / Sept., €20 July / Aug., and possibly a fuel surcharge); free air-type seats for 1st class pass holders. Many other ferry companies offer discounts (not on cabins), for example: Balearia 20%, Finnlines 30%, Fjord Line 20% (10% high-season), Grimaldi 20%, Irish Ferries 30%, Stena Line 30%, Tallink Silja 20% (high-season), 40% (low-season), Viking Line 50%. Special fares apply on Destination Gotland.

Most Swiss lakes give 50% discount, as does Fjord1 on Norwegian Fjords. Certain bus services in Scandinavia (including Luleå - Haparanda - Tornio - Kemi) and some railway museums are free or discounted. A limited number of tourist attractions, hotels, hostels and cycle hire outlets also offer discounts.

Eurail - *for non-European residents.* website: www.eurail.com www.eurailgroup.org

RAIL GLOBAL PASS - valid in 28 European countries:
stria, Belgium, Bosnia-Herzegovina, Bulgaria, Croatia, Czech Republic, nmark, Finland, France, Germany, Greece, Hungary, Ireland (including thern Ireland), Italy, Luxembourg, Montenegro, the Netherlands, Norway, and, Portugal, Romania, Serbia, Slovakia, Slovenia, Spain, Sweden, tzerland and Turkey.

CES - GLOBAL PASS

outh is 12-25 years	Youth 1st class	Youth 2nd class	Adult 1st class
ays within 1 month	424 USD	345 USD	528 USD
ays within 1 month	516 USD	420 USD	643 USD
days within 2 months	636 USD	518 USD	793 USD
days within 2 months	833 USD	678 USD	1039 USD
days continuous	541 USD	441 USD	673 USD
days continuous	696 USD	566 USD	868 USD
nonth continuous	854 USD	695 USD	1065 USD
nonths continuous	1203 USD	979 USD	1501 USD
nonths continuous	1482 USD	1206 USD	1851 USD

ces correct as at 14/01/16. Accompanied children aged 4-11 travel free a Child Pass; two children can travel with each adult.

WHO CAN BUY EURAIL PASSES
Anyone resident outside Europe (but excluding residents of Russia and CIS or Turkey). Passes are sold through official sales agents and via www.eurail.com.

EURAIL SELECT PASS - 2, 3 or 4 adjoining countries chosen from:
Austria, Benelux (Belgium / Netherlands / Luxembourg), Bulgaria, Croatia / Slovenia, Czech Republic, Denmark, Finland, France, Germany, Greece, Hungary, Ireland (including NIR), Italy, Norway, Poland, Portugal, Romania, Serbia / Montenegro, Slovakia, Spain, Sweden, Switzerland, Turkey.

EURAIL ONE COUNTRY PASS - valid in any one of the following:
Austria, Benelux (Belgium, Luxembourg, the Netherlands), Bulgaria, Croatia, Czech Republic, Denmark, Finland, Greece, Greek Islands, Hungary, Ireland, Italy, Norway, Poland, Portugal, Romania, Scandinavia (Denmark, Finland, Norway, Sweden), Slovakia, Slovenia, Spain, Sweden.

Direct night trains or ferries leaving after 1900 hrs can count as next travel day. Supplements generally not required for *EC, IC, ICE* trains. French *TGV* trains require the reservation fee only. Other supplements are similar to those shown under InterRail above (but may vary). Sleeper/couchette supplements and seat reservations are extra. For One Country Pass and Select Pass prices, and discounts on private railways and ferry companies, see www.eurail.com or www.eurailgroup.org.

546 PONTRESINA / ST MORITZ - SCUOL TARASP

Narrow gauge.

Valid October 17 - December 10. For service May 17 - October 16 see pages 274 and 275.

km		⚒	⚒	⚒	⚒	⑦	⑦			⚒			❖ L				❖ L			L			L	
0	**Pontresina 540/7** ..... d.	...	0535	...	...	0603	...	0702	...	...	0802	...	...		1402	...	...	1502	...	...	1602	...	...	1702
	St Moritz 540/7 ..... d.	0503	|	*0541*	0602	|	0603	|	0702	0723	|	0757	0849**r**	and at	|	1357	1445	|	1457	1538	|	1557	1645	|
5	Samedan **540** .... a.	0510	0542	*0548*	0608	0610	0611**k**	0708	0709**k**	0729	0808	0809**k**	0857	the same	1408	1409**k**	1457	1508	1509**k**	1545	1608	1609**k**	1657	1708
5	Samedan .... d.	0513	...	0600	0609	0613	...	0713	▬	0730	0813	...	0858	minutes	1413	...	1458	1513	...	1545	1613	...	1658	1713
15	Zuoz .... d.	0526	...	0614	0622	0626	...	0727	...	0743	0827	...	0910	past each	1427	...	1510	1527	...	1559	1627	...	1710	1727
32	Zernez .... ⊖ d.	0546	...	0635	▬	0647	...	0747	...	...	0849	...	0929	hour	1449	...	1529	1549	...	1628	1649	...	1729	1749
38	Susch .... d.	0555	...	0641	⚒	0653	...	0753	...	...	0855	...	**s**	until	1455	...	1535	1555	...	1634	1655	...	1735	1755
40	Sagliains **545** ....§ a.	0557	...	0645	0653	0657	...	0756	0758	...	0900	...	|		1500	...	|	1600	...	|	1700	...	|	1800
	Klosters Platz **545**.. a.	|	...	...	|	0723	...	...	|	...	|	...	0955		|	...	1555	|	...	1655	|		1755	|
57	**Scuol-Tarasp 545** .... a.	0626	...	...	0716	...	...	...	0819	...	0923	...	...		1523	...	...	1623	...	...	1723	...	...	1823

Pontresina 540/7........d.	1802	...	1902	...	2002	...	2102	...	2202	...
St Moritz 540/7 ....d.	|	1757	|	1857	|	1957	|	2057	|	2157
Samedan **540**.............a.	1808	1809**k**	1908	1909**k**	2008	2009**k**	2108	2109**k**	2208	2209**k**
Samedan...................d.	1813	...	1913	...	2013	▬	2113	▬	2213	...
Zuoz.........................d.	1827	...	1927	...	2027	...	2127	...	2227	...
Zernez.................. ⊖ d.	1849	...	1949	...	2047	...	2147	...	2247	...
Susch.......................d.	1855	...	1955	...	2053	...	2153	...	2253	...
Sagliains **545** ....§ a.	1900	...	2000	...	2056	2058	2156	2158	2256	...
Klosters Platz **545**....a.	|	...	|	...	...	|	...	|	...	...
Scuol-Tarasp 545 ......a.	1923	...	2023	...	...	2119	...	2219	...	...

	⚒	Ⓐ		⚒					
Scuol-Tarasp 545 ....d.	0541	...	...	0607	0641**j**	...	0741	...	0834
Klosters Platz **545**...........d.	|	0530	...	|	|	...	|	...	|
Sagliains **545** ....§ d.	0601	|	...	|	0703	...	0801	0803	0855
Susch ....d.	...	0553	...	0626	0705	...	▬	0805	0857
Zernez .... ⊖ d.	...	0602	...	0637	0713	...	...	0813	0907
Zuoz ....d.	...	0622	0634**d**	0657	0733	0757**d**	...	0833	0927
Samedan ....a.	...	0633	0646**d**	0711	0747	0811**d**	...	0847**k**	0942
Samedan **540** ....d.	...	0635	0648	0712	0749	0812	0851	0849	0948
St Moritz 540/7 ....a.	...	0643	|	0719	|	0819	0903	|	|
Pontresina 540/7 ....a.	...	...	0655	...	0756	...	...	0856	0955

	L			❖ L				❖ L					L									⑤⑥	
Scuol-Tarasp 545 ......d.	...	0934	...	...	1034	...		...	1634	...	1734	...	...	1834	...	1934	2041	...	...	2141	...	2241	...
Klosters Platz **545**....d.	0901	|	...	1001	|	...	and at	1601	|	...	|	...	1801	|	...	|	|	...	...	|	...	|	...
Sagliains **545** ....§ d.	|	0955	...	|	1055	...	the same	|	1655	...	1755	...	|	1855	...	1955	2101	2103	...	2203	...	2300	2301
Susch.......................d.	0918	0957	...	1017	1057	...	minutes	1617	1657	...	1757	...	1817	1857	...	1957	▬	2105	...	2205	...	...	2303
Zernez.................. ⊖ d.	0929	1007	...	1027	1107	...	past each	1627	1707	...	1807	...	1827	1907	...	2007	...	2113	...	2213	...	...	2310
Zuoz.........................d.	0953	1027	...	1046	1127	...	hour	1646	1727	...	1827	...	1846	1927	...	2027	...	2133	...	2233	...	...	2329
Samedan...................a.	1006	1042	...	1058	1142	...	until	1658	1742	...	1842	...	1858	1942	...	2042	...	2145	...	2245	...	...	2342
Samedan **540**.............d.	1009	1048	1051	1100	1148	1151		1700	1748	1751	1848	1851	1900	1948	1951	2048	2051	2150	2151	2250	2251	...	2343
St Moritz 540/7 ....a.	1016	|	1103	1109	|	1203		1709	|	1803	|	1903	1909	|	2003	|	2103	|	2203	|	2258	...	2350
Pontresina 540/7........a.	...	1055	...	...	1155	...		...	1755	...	1855	...	...	1955	...	2055	...	2156	...	2256	...	...	...

L – [12] St Moritz - Landquart and v.v.

d – ⚒ only.

j – Connection on ⚒.

k – Connects with train in previous column.

r – Subsequent departures at 1045, 1245, 1445.

s – 0849 departure from St Moritz does not call at Susch; subsequent departures at 1135, 1335, 1535.

v – Until Oct. 23.

❖ – Every two hours.

§ – Sagliains station can only be used for changing trains.

⊖ – 🚌 service **Zernez - Malles and v.v.** (journey ± 1 h 35 minu
From **Zernez**: 0715, 0815, 0915, 1015 **v**, 1032, 1115, 1215 **v**
1315, 1415 **v**, 1515, 1615, 1715.
From **Malles / Mals** bahnhof: 0610 **v**, 0657⚒, 0803, 0903, 10
1103, 1203 **v**, 1303, 1403 **v**, 1503, 1545 **v**, 1603, 1703, 1803,

Operator: AutoDaPosta (PA); ✆ +41 (0)81 856 10 90.

As an added extra for readers of this seasonal Summer edition we are including the remaining BEYOND EUROPE sections, in addition to the pages for **Africa and the Middle East** which appear in the preceding pages.

The tables covering **India, South East Asia, Australia and New Zealand**, **China**, **Japan**, **North America**, **South America** and **South Korea** previously appeared in our monthly editions from January to May 2016. Limited updates have been made to these tables for this seasonal edition.

BEYOND EUROPE
India

Introduction

The Beyond Europe section covers principal rail services in a different area of the world each month. There are six areas, each appearing twice yearly as follows:

India:	January and July editions
South East Asia and Australasia:	February and August editions
China:	March and September editions
Japan:	April and October editions
North America:	May and November editions
Africa and the Middle East:	June and December editions

The months have been chosen so that we can bring you up-to-date information for those countries which make seasonal changes.

Details of services in South America can be found in the European Rail Timetable April and October editions and schedules for South Korea in the May and November editions.

Contents

INDEX OF PLACES

by table number

INDIA

Capital: **New Delhi** (GMT +5.5). 2016 Public Holidays: Jan. 26, Mar. 7, 25, Apr. 20, May 21, Aug. 15, 25, Oct. 2, 11, 12, 30, Dec. 13, 25.

Rail services in India are operated by Indian Railways. Most trains convey a selection of first and second class accommodation from the several available. Trains which cor second class only are noted in either the column head or footnotes. Note that Rajdhani and Shatabdi trains convey first class accommodation only. The exact carriage ty available on each train varies. A brief summary of train types and accommodation follows:

Rajdhani (shown as *RDi* in column heads). Air-conditioned first class night trains. Special fares payable. Conveys First Class 2 or 4-berth sleepers (code 1A); two-tier (code or three-tier (code 3A) first class open plan berths. **Shatabdi** (shown as *SDi* in column heads). Air-conditioned first class daytime trains. Special fares payable. Conveys C Class seats (code CC); Executive Chair Class. **Duronto** (shown in column heads as *Duro*). Some non-stop trains, some very limited stop trains. Conveys first class sleep accommodation (codes 1A, 2A, 3A as above); second class non air-conditioned 6-berth (code SL). **Express** (shown in column heads as *Exp*). Most services convey first class conditioned two-tier (code 2A) or three-tier (code 3A) open plan berths; second class 'Sleeper Class' non air-conditioned six-berth (code SL); non air-conditioned second cl seats (code 2S). **Yuva** (shown in column heads as *Yuva*). Low-cost air-conditioned train. Seating accommodation only. During the day, all sleepers and berths convert to sea accommodation. The codes shown are those used by Indian Railways.

Timings are valid until further notice. Short notice changes are possible, especially around religious festivals and during monsoon seasons. Tickets can be purchased f stations or through authorised agents. Reservations are required for travel on all trains shown in this section.

For multiple journies the best value ticket is the Indrail Pass. This is only available to foreign nationals and non-resident Indians. It is personal and non-transferable. Hold should always have their passports ready for inspection. Holders of Indrail Passes are exempted from all reservation fees, sleeping car charges and can travel as they like, f any point in any train in the class it is issued for, within the period of validity. Reservations are essential, particularly on overnight journeys and are allocated on a first come served basis and can be made up to 360 days in advance. There is a maximum luggage allowance of 70Kgs. The exact amount depends upon the type of pass or class of tra Prices for AC CLASS Adult pass: ½ day US$57, 1 day US$95, 2 days US$160, 4 days US$220, 7 days US$270, 15 days US$370, 21 days US$396, 30 days US$495, 60 d US$800, 90 days US$1060. A Child pass is available at half price.

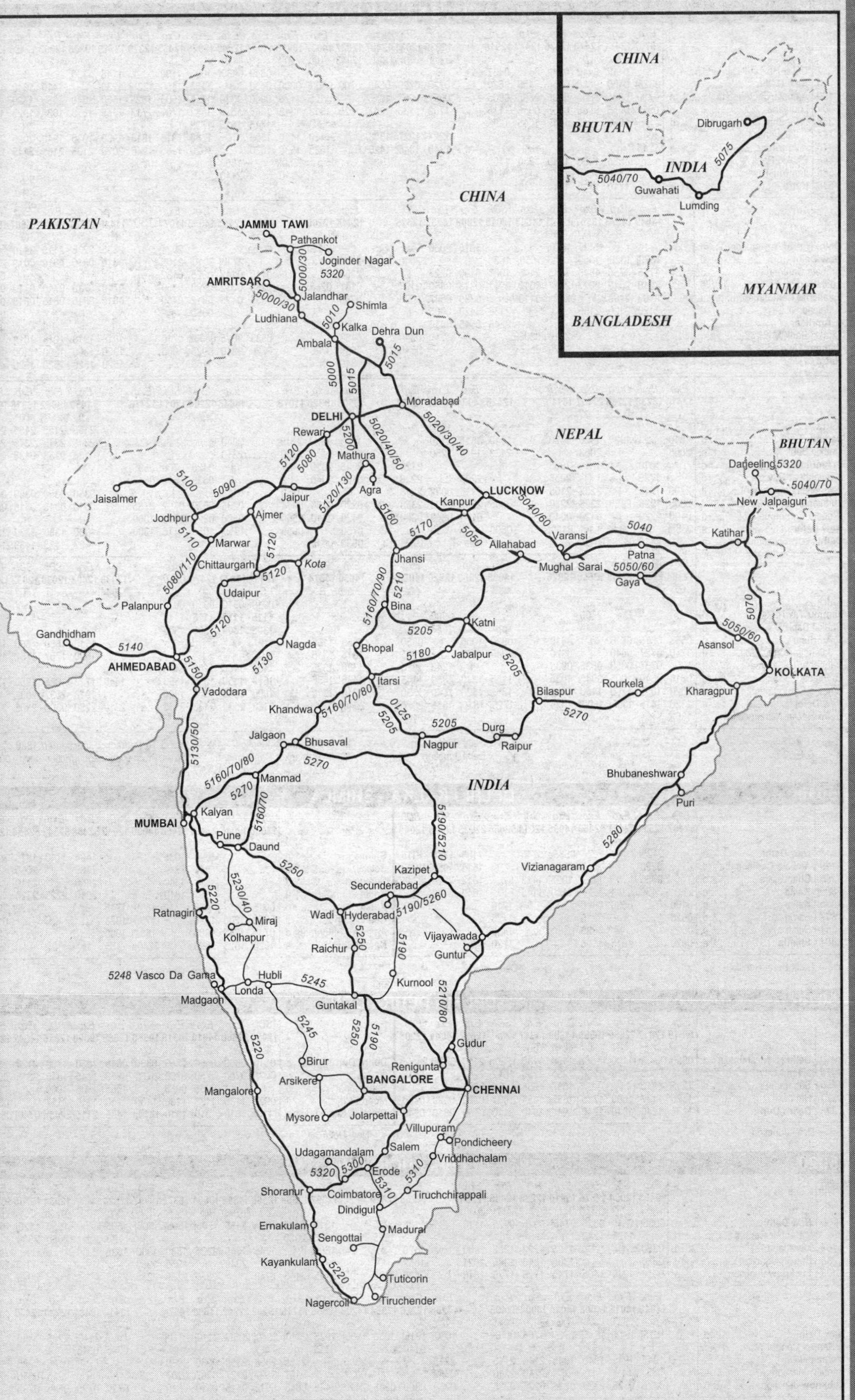
CHINA
BHUTAN
Dibrugarh
INDIA
5075
5040/70
Guwahati
Lumding
MYANMAR
BANGLADESH
PAKISTAN
CHINA
NEPAL
BHUTAN
INDIA
JAMMU TAWI
Pathankot
Joginder Nagar
5320
5000/30
AMRITSAR
Jalandhar
5000/30
Ludhiana
5010
Shimla
Kalka
Dehra Dun
Ambala
5015
5000
5015
Moradabad
DELHI
5200
5020/40/50
5020/30/40
Rewari
Mathura
5120
5080
Jaipur
Agra
5120/130
5100
5090
Jaisalmer
Jodhpur
Ajmer
5110
Marwar
5120
Chittaurgarh
5120
Kota
Udaipur
5080/110
Palanpur
5120
Gandhidham
5140
AHMEDABAD
5150
Nagda
5130
Vadodara
5160
5170
Jhansi
5210
Kanpur
5050
LUCKNOW
5040/60
Allahabad
Varansi
Mughal Sarai
5040
Patna
5050/60
Gaya
Katihar
Dareeling 5320
5040/70
New Jalpaiguri
5070
5050/60
Asansol
KOLKATA
5160/70/90
Bina
Katni
5205
Bhopal
5180
Jabalpur
5205
Itarsi
Bilaspur
Rourkela
Kharagpur
Khandwa
5160/70/80
5210
5205
5270
5205
Durg
Raipur
Jalgaon
Bhusaval
Nagpur
5130/50
5270
5160/70/80
Manmad
5270
5160/70
Kalyan
MUMBAI
Pune
Daund
5190/5210
Bhubaneshwar
Puri
5280
Vizianagaram
5250
Kazipet
Secunderabad
5230/40
5220
Ratnagiri
Miraj
Kolhapur
Wadi
Hyderabad
5190/5260
5250
Raichur
5190
Vijayawada
Guntur
Kurnool
5248 Vasco Da Gama
Hubli
Londa
5245
Madgaon
Guntakal
5210/80
5245
5250
5190
5220
Gudur
Birur
Renigunta
Arsikere
BANGALORE
CHENNAI
Mangalore
Mysore
Jolarpettai
Villupuram
Pondicheery
Salem
Udagamandalam
Vriddhachalam
5320
5300
Erode
5310
5310
Shoranur
Coimbatore
Tiruchchirappalli
Dindigul
Ernakulam
Madurai
Sengottai
Kayankulam
5220
Tuticorin
Nagercoil
Tiruchender

5000 DELHI - AMRITSAR and JAMMU TAWI

Indian Railw

km		Exp 15707	Exp 12471 A	Exp 12473 ⑦	Exp 12475 ④	Exp 12477 ③	Exp 12919		SDi 12029 ex ④	SDi 12031 ④	Exp 12497	SDi 12037 12043	Exp 14037 ex④	Exp 18215 ④	Exp 11057	Exp 12549 ③	Exp 12925	Exp 12483 ⑤	Exp 12379 ⑥	Exp 12715	Exp 19325 ③⑥	Exp 12203 ①②⑤	Exp 12459
7	Delhi Hazrat Nizamuddin d.	...	0412	0412	0412	0412	0437	...	...	...	...	...	...	...	0349	0930f	1005	1100	...	1148	1130	...	...
0	**New Delhi** d.	0325j	0450	0450	0450	0450	0520	...	0720	0720	0640	0700	0800j	0800	0430	|	1105	1150	1225j	1230	|	1410	1340
199	Ambala Cantonment d.	0700	0805	0805	0805	0805	0905	...	0957	0957	1015	|	1125	1125	0940	1310	1455	1505	1525	1550	1640	1655	1720
304	Ludhiana d.	0930	0955	0955	0955	0955	1115	...	1133	1133	1207	1225	1313	1313	1345	1520	1652	1707	1717	1755	1835	1835	1923
356	Jalandhar Cantonment d.	|	1050	1045	1045	1045	1205	...	|	|	|	...	|	|	1445	1615	1739	|	|	|	|	|	|
361	Jalandhar City d.	1040	|	|	|	|	|	...	1227	1227	1303	...	1410	1410	1505	|	1758	1815	1815	1900	1930	1940	2025
440	**Amritsar** a.	1245	|	|	|	|	|	...	1345	1345	1420	...	1535	1535	1630	|	1920	1945	1945	2020	2105	2105	2145
468	Chakki Bank ♥ d.	...	1235	1230	1230	1230	1400	...	...	...	...	...	p	1850k	...	1800	...	...	...	...	...	...	...
568	**Jammu Tawi** a.	...	1440	1440	1440	1440	1610	...	...	...	...	...	...	2110	...	2110	...	...	...	...	...	...	...
646	**Katra** a.	...	1710	1710	1710	1710	...	...	...	...	...	...	...	...	...	...	...	...	...	...	...	...	...

		Exp 14649 ①③⑥	Exp 14673 B	Exp 18507 ③⑥⑦	Exp 22941 ②	Exp 14645	SDi 12013	Exp 12903	Exp 18237	RDi 12425		Exp 12445	Duro 12265 ②⑤⑦		Exp 22401 ①③⑥	Exp 12413	Exp 14033	Exp 11077		Exp 11449 ②	Exp 16031 ①④⑤	Exp 16317 ⑦	Exp 16687 ③
Delhi Hazrat Nizamuddin d.	...	...	...	1417	1420f	...	...	1915	2030	...	...		2215a	...	2215a	...	...	2024	...	2235	2235	2110	2110
New Delhi d.	...	1320j	1320j	1500	|	1550j	1630	|	|	2040	...	2050	|	...	|	2230j	2010j	2105	...	0010	0010	0010	0010
Ambala Cantonment d.	...	1755	1755	1845	1845	2145	1907	0100	0225	|	...	2358	|	...	0110	0142	0025	0132	...	|	|	|	|
Ludhiana d.	...	2010	2010	2027	2027	0010	2043	0313	0450	0107	...	0147	0258	...	0258	0332	0220	0350	...	0710	0710	0710	0710
Jalandhar Cantonment d.	...	2103	2103	|	2123	0110	|	0359	0547	|	...	0238	|	...	0350	0425	0312	0450	...	0815	0815	0815	0815
Jalandhar City d.	...	2120	2120	2155	|	|	2136	0420	0605	|	...	|	|	...	|	|	0350	|	...	|	|	|	|
Amritsar a.	...	2325	2335	2355	|	|	2245	0545	0810	|	...	|	|	...	|	|	|	|	...	|	|	|	|
Chakki Bank ♥ d.	...	...	...	...	2310	0305	...	...	...	0340	...	0430	|	...	0533	0615	0630k	0710	...	1018	1018	1018	1018
Jammu Tawi a.	...	...	...	...	0120	0525	...	...	...	0545	...	0635	0720	...	0720	0810	0925	1005	...	1300	1300	1300	1300
Katra a.	...	...	...	...	...	...	...	...	...	...	...	0840	...		...	...	1150		...	1520	1520	1520	1520

	Exp 12414	Exp 18238	Duro 12266 ①③⑥	Exp 22402 ②④⑦	Exp 18110		RDi 12426	Exp 14034	Exp 12446	Exp 12904		Exp 18508 ③⑥⑦	Exp 19326 ④	Exp 11078		Exp 14646	Exp 12204 ③⑥⑦	SDi 12014	Exp 12716		Exp 11450 ③	Exp 16032 ②⑤⑥	Exp 16318 ①
Katra d.	...	...	...	...	...	...	...	...	1910	...		...	...	...		...	...	...	...	...	2155	2155	2155
Jammu Tawi d.	1810	...	1920	1920	1420	...	1940	1615	2100	...	...	...	...	2145	...	2040	...	...	...	...	2345	2345	2345
Chakki Bank ♥ d.	2005	...	|	2053	|	...	2123	1915	2250	...	...	...	...	2350	...	2310	...	...	...	...	0138	0138	0138
Amritsar d.	|	1610	|	|	1935	...	|	|	|	2125	...	2345	2315	|	...	|	0420	0500	0535	...	|	|	|
Jalandhar City d.	|	1735	|	|	2058	...	|	2205	|	2238	...	0100	0040	|	...	|	0535	0606	0645	...	|	|	|
Jalandhar Cantonment d.	2200	1746	|	2232	2108	...	|	2215	0032	2248	...	|	|	0150	...	0115	|	|	|	...	0350	0350	0350
Ludhiana d.	2305	1925	2325	2325	2220	...	0005	2345	0125	2358	...	0220	0150	0315	...	0235	0630	0702	0755	...	0515	0515	0515
Ambala Cantonment d.	0100	2220	|	0120	0040	...	|	0150	0340	0200	...	0420	0410	0550	...	0500	0820	0838	1000	...	|	|	|
New Delhi a.	0355j	|	|	|	0430j	...	0500	0545j	0650	|	...	0750	|	0955	...	1055j	1055	1115	1300	...	1330	1330	1330
Delhi Hazrat Nizamuddin a.	...	0410	0420a	0420a	...	...	...	...	...	0705	...	0830	0945	...	...	...	...	...	...	...	1433	1433	1433

	Exp 12484 ⑦	Exp 12460	Exp 15708	Exp 12550 ④	Exp 12926		Exp 14038 ex⑤	Exp 12380 ⑦	Exp 12920	Exp 11058		Exp 14650 ①③⑥	Exp 14674 B		Exp 12472 C	Exp 12474 ④	Exp 12476 ①	Exp 12478 ⑦		SDi 12038 12044	Exp 12498	SDi 12030 ex ④	SDi 12032 ④
Katra d.	...	...	...	...	...	...	...	...	...	...	...	...	...	...	0910	0910	0910	0910	...	...	...	...	...
Jammu Tawi d.	...	...	...	0500	...	...	...	...	0900	...	...	...	...	...	1115	1115	1115	1115	...	...	...	...	...
Chakki Bank ♥ d.	...	...	...	0645	...	...	pp	...	1045	...	...	...	...	...	1305	1305	1305	1305	...	...	...	...	...
Amritsar d.	0555	0615	0715	|	0810	...	0930	1055	|	0830	...	1155	1155	...	|	|	|	|	...		1510	1650	1650
Jalandhar City d.	0710	0727	0840	|	0920	...	1045	1210	|	1005	...	1315	1315	...	|	|	|	|	...		1620	1757	1757
Jalandhar Cantonment d.	|	0737	0850	0835	0930	...	|	|	1243	1015	...	1325	1325	...	1450	1450	1450	1450	...	|	|	|	|
Ludhiana d.	0815	0840	1005	0945	1035	...	1155	1310	1350	1145	...	1435	1435	...	1550	1550	1550	1550	...	1640	1723	1855	1855
Ambala Cantonment d.	1020	1055	1200	1150	1305	...	1355	1520	1540	1550	...	1710	1710	...	1800	1800	1800	1800	...	|	1918	2032	2032
New Delhi a.	1320	1415	1505j	1500f	1625	...	1725j	1820j	1855	2020	...	2040j	2040j	...	2130	2130	2130	2130	...	2210	2250	2305	2305
Delhi Hazrat Nizamuddin a.	1353	...	...	...	...	...	...	...	...	2103	...	...	...	...	...	...	...	...	...	...	...	...	...

A – ①②⑤⑥.
B – ②④⑤⑦.
C – ②③⑤⑥.
a – Delhi Sarai Rohilla.
f – Delhi Safdarjang.
j – Delhi Junction.
k – Pathankot Junction.
♥ – Pathankot Cantonment.
p – To Pathankot Junction arr.1830.
pp – From Pathankot Junction dep.0700

5010 DELHI - KALKA - SHIMLA

Indian Railwa

km		Exp 52457	Exp 12311	Exp 52451	Exp 52453	Exp 14095	SDi 12011	Exp 52455	Exp 22925	SDi 12005	SDi 12045 ①–⑥
0	**New Delhi** d.	...	2125j	...	...	0535a	0740	...	1105	1715	1915
199	Ambala Cantonment d.	...	0220	...	...	0950	1030	...	1515	1958	2200
268	Chandigarh d.	...	0350	...	...	1033	1113	...	1612	2048	2245
305	**Kalka** a.	...	0430	...	...	1110	1145	...	1645	2120	...
305	**Kalka** ¶ d.	0400	...	0530	0600	...	...	1210	...	...	...
347	Barog ¶ d.	0625	...	|	0815	...	...	1425	...	...	...
351	Solan ¶ d.	0639	...	|	0829	...	...	1439	...	...	...
401	**Shimla** ¶ a.	0920	...	1015	1105	...	...	1720	...	...	...

	SDi 12006	SDi 12046 ①–⑥	Exp 22926	Exp 52456	Exp 14096	SDi 12012	Exp 52458	Exp 52542	Exp 52454
Shimla ¶ d.	...	...	...	1035	...	...	1425	1740	1815
Solan ¶ d.	...	...	...	1314	...	...	1725	|	2050
Barog ¶ d.	...	...	...	1340	...	...	1750	|	2110
Kalka ¶ a.	...	...	...	1610	...	...	2010	2225	2320
Kalka d.	0615	...	1020	...	1650	1745	...	...	...
Chandigarh d.	0653	1200	1120	...	1730	1823	...	...	...
Ambala Cantonment d.	0738	1242	1305	...	1830	1905	...	...	...
New Delhi a.	1025	1525	1625	...	2240a	2155	...	...	...

a – Delhi Sarai Rohilla.
j – Delhi Junction.
¶ – Narrow gauge railway.

5015 DELHI - DEHRA DUN

Indian Railwa

km		Exp 19019	SDi 12017	Exp 22659 ⑦	Exp 19565 ⑥	Exp 14309 ④⑤	Exp 14317 ①⑦	SDi 12055	Exp 12687 ②⑤	Exp 14041	Exp 12205
0	**Delhi** H. Nizamuddin d.	0550	0645n	1100	1100n	1130	1130	1520n	2110	2215j	2350n
76	Meerut City d.	0845	0805	1230	1230	1255	1255	1642	2251	|	0115
190	Saharanpur d.	1245	1010	|	|	1535	1535	|	0205	|	|
271	Haridwar d.	1525	1127	1600	1715	1655	1655	1937	0320	0623	0400
323	**Dehra Dun** a.	1735	1240	1810	1940	1940	1940	2110	0500	0810	0540

	SDi 12056	Exp 22660 ①	Exp 14310 ②③	Exp 14318 ⑤⑥	Exp 19566 ⑦	Exp 12688 ①⑤	Exp 19020	SDi 12018	Exp 14042
Dehra Dun d.	0510	0550	0550	0550	0550	0645	1030	1700	2120
Haridwar d.	0625	0750	0750	0750	0750	0850	1245	1815	2315
Saharanpur d.	|	|	0955	0955	|	1050	1605	1950	|
Meerut City d.	0927	1136	1136	1136	1136	1230	1910	2117	|
Delhi H. Nizamuddin a.	1115n	1310	1310	1310	1310n	1405	2115	2245n	0740j

j – Delhi Junction.
n – New Delhi.

5020 DELHI - LUCKNOW

Indian Railwa

km		Exp 19403 ③	SDi 12004	Exp 12876 ②⑤⑦	Exp 15910	RDi 12236 ②	RDi 12436 ④⑦	Exp 12204 ③⑥⑦		Exp 14258	Exp 12420		Exp 12392	Exp 12566	Exp 12558	Exp 14312 ①③⑤	Exp 19601 ⑥	Exp 12372 ④	Exp 19407 ⑤	Exp 12524 ③⑦		SDi 12034 ①–⑥	Exp 15708
0	**New Delhi** d.	0035j	0610	0625	0745j	0925	0925	1110	...	1135	1225	...	1310	1415	1450v	1455	1505j	1505j	1505j	1505	...	1550	1520j
	Kanpur Central d.	|	1125	1240	|	|	|	|	...	|	1955	...	|	2020	|	|	|	|	|	|	...	2050	2300
167	Moradabad d.	0350	|	|	1125	1222	1222	1400	...	1520	|	...	1605	|	1745	1845	1825	1830	1830	1825	...	...	|
258	Bareilly Junction d.	0530	|	|	1305	1345	1345	1521	...	1652	|	...	1733	|	|	2040	|	1955	1955	|	...	...	|
493	**Lucknow** Junction a.	0930	1240	1405	1745	1725	1725	1840	...	2135	2125	...	2115	2145	2240	...	2335	2335	2335	2335	...	...	0025

		Exp 14018 ③	Exp 14016 ⑤⑦	Exp 14008 ②④	Exp 14014 ①⑥	Exp 14004 ④⑦	Exp 22408 ①③⑤		Exp 14206	Exp 12226	Exp 12554	Exp 14208	Exp 12556	Exp 15716 ①②④	Exp 19269 ⑤⑥	Exp 12212 ③	Exp 14650 ①③⑥	Exp 14674 A		Exp 13414 ①③⑥	Exp 13484 A	Exp 12230	Exp 12430
New Delhi d.	...	1615j	1615j	1615j	1615j	1755	1815v	...	1830j	1915j	1950	1950j	2025	2040j	2040j	2055v	2110j	2110j	...	2140j	2140j	2205	2325
Kanpur Central d.	...	|	|	|	|	|	|	...	|	0140	0225	|	0315	|	|	|	|	|	...	0545	0545	|	|
Moradabad d.	...	1945	1945	1945	1945	2115	2115	...	2210	|	|	2305	|	2358	2358	2358	0030	0030	...	|	|	0120	0225
Bareilly Junction d.	...	|	|	|	|	2240	2240	...	2352	|	|	0037	|	0127	0127	0127	0207	0207	...	|	|	0255	0345
Lucknow Junction a.	...	0325	0325	0325	0325	0225	0225	...	0350	0300	0345	0420	0445	0515	0515	0515	0610	0610	...	0720	0720	0645	0730

For footnotes and return service see next page ▷ ▷ ▷

LUCKNOW - DELHI 5020

n Railways

	Exp	Exp	Exp	SDi	Exp	Exp	Exp	Exp	Exp	Exp	Exp	Exp		Exp	Exp	Exp	Exp	Exp	RDi	RDi	Exp	Exp	SDi
	14205	**22407**	**12371**	**12033**	**14311**	**14649**	**14673**	**12523**	**19602**	**15279**	**12211**	**19270**		**15715**	**12203**	**12419**	**14003**	**15909**	**12235**	**12435**	**12203**	**12875**	**12003**
		①③⑤	②	①–⑥	④⑤⑦	①③⑥	A	③⑦	②	①⑤	⑥	①②		①③⑥	①②⑤		③⑦		⑥	③⑦	①②⑤	①③⑥	
Lucknow Junction ... d.	0055	0130	0130	...	...	0115	0115	0330	0330	0330	0430	0430	...	0455	0610	0600	0550	0535	0610	0610	0610	1345	1535
Bareilly Junction ... d.	0425	0502	0502	...	0605	0500	0500	|	|	0712	0805	0805	...	0825	0933	|	0958	0920	0933	0933	0933	|	|
Moradabad ... d.	0620	0700	0705	...	0800	0835	0835	0905	0905	0900	0950	0950	...	1005	1107	|	1140	1125	1107	1107	1107	|	|
Kanpur Central ... d.	|	|	|	0600	|	|	|	|	|	|	|	|	...	|	|	0740	|	|	|	|	|	1528	1655
New Delhi ... a.	0950j	1010v	1020j	1120	1130	1230j	1230j	1210	1210	1210j	1235v	1240j	...	1310j	1355	1455	1440	1505j	1355	1355	1355	2145	2215

	Exp	Exp	Exp	Exp	Exp		Exp	Exp	Exp		Exp	Exp	Exp	Exp		Exp	Exp	Exp	Exp		Exp	Exp	Exp	
	15707	**14017**	**14007**	**14015**	**14013**		**13413**	**13483**	**12391**		**14257**	**19408**	**19404**	**12565**		**14207**	**12555**	**12229**	**12553**		**12225**	**12429**	**12557**	
		⑤	④⑥	①③	②⑦		②⑤⑦	B				⑥	③											...
now Junction ... d.	1825	1850	1850	1850	1850	...	1930	1930	2030	...	2045	2130	2130	2120	...	2140	2150	2215	2225	...	2315	2330	2345	...
ly Junction ... d.	|	|	|	|	|	...	|	|	0010	...	0045	0105	0105	|	...	0127	|	0155	|	...	|	0245	|	...
dabad ... d.	|	0120	0120	0120	0120	...	|	|	0155	...	0230	0310	0250	|	...	0325	|	0345	|	...	|	0425	0450	...
npur Central ... d.	2000	|	|	|	|	...	2115	2115	|	...	|	|	|	2258	...	|	2328	|	0005	...	0050	|	|	...
Delhi ... a.	0250j	0450j	0450j	0450j	0450j	...	0440j	0440j	0510	...	0610	0620j	0620j	0535	...	0645j	0550	0715	0640	...	0705j	0725	0750v	...

②④⑤⑦. B – ①③④⑥. j – Delhi Junction. v – Delhi Anand Vihar Terminal.

JAMMU TAWI and AMRITSAR - LUCKNOW 5030

an Railways

	Exp	Exp	Exp	Exp		Exp	Exp	Exp	Exp		Exp		Exp	Exp	Exp	Exp	Exp	Exp	Exp		Exp	Exp	
	15708	**18104**	**14650**	**14674**		**12238**	**15934**	**13050**	**13006**		**12356**		**12588**	**15652**	**15654**	**15098**	**12332**	**13152**	**12204**		**12318**	**12358**	
		③⑤	①③⑥	A			⑤				③⑦		⑥	③	⑤	②	①④⑦		③⑥⑦		②⑤	①④	
Jammu Tawi ... d.	...	...	...	...	...	1400	...	...	...	...	2010	...	2245	2245	2245	2245	2245	1855	...	...	...	...	...
Chakki Bank ♥ ... d.	...	...	...	...	...	1545	...	...	...	...	2150	...	0030	0030	0030	0030	0030	2210	...	...	...	...	...
Amritsar ... d.	0715	1235	1155	1155	...	|	1550	1810	1845	...	|	...	|	|	|	|	|	|	0420	...	0555	0555	...
Jalandhar City ... d.	0840	1350	1315	1315	...	|	1700	1930	1957	...	|	...	|	|	|	|	|	|	0535	...	0710	0710	...
Jalandhar Cantonment ... d.	0850	|	1325	1325	...	1735	|	1940	2007	...	2335	...	0220	0220	0220	0220	0220	0015	|	...	|	|	...
Ludhiana ... d.	1005	1505	1435	1435	...	1835	1800	2050	2115	...	0035	...	0330	0330	0330	0330	0330	0205	0630	...	0815	0815	...
Ambala Cantonment ... d.	1200	1655	1710	1710	...	2100	2030	2310	2330	...	0235	...	0525	0525	0525	0525	0525	0430	0820	...	1015	1015	...
Saharanpur ... d.	|	1830	|	|	...	2225	2200	0055	0115	...	0405	...	0700	0700	0700	0700	0700	0620	|	...	1145	1145	...
Moradabad ... d.	|	2132	0030	0030	...	0135	0105	0420	0445	...	0705	...	1010	1010	1010	1010	1010	1045	1402	...	1450	1455	...
Bareilly Junction ... d.	|	2257	0207	0207	...	|	0240	|	0620	...	0833	...	1142	1142	1142	1142	1142	1230	1521	...	1620	|	...
Lucknow Junction ... a.	0025	0240	0610	0610	...	0710	0800	1145	1025	...	1225	...	1520	1520	1520	1520	1520	1705	1840	...	2005	2005	...

		Exp	Exp	Exp	Exp		Exp	Exp	Exp	Exp		Exp	Exp	Exp	Exp		Exp		Exp	Exp	Exp	Exp	Exp	
		12317	**12357**	**12203**	**15933**		**14649**	**14673**	**13151**	**18103**		**13005**	**13049**	**12355**	**12237**		**15707**		**12331**	**15097**	**15651**	**15563**	**12587**	
		①④	③⑦	①②⑤	④		①③⑥	A		②④				②⑥					③⑥⑦	⑤	②	④	①	
now Junction ... d.	...	0225	0255	0610	0610	...	0115	0115	1040	1525	...	1545	1610	1735	1815	...	1825	...	1950	1950	1950	1950	1950	...
lly Junction ... d.	...	0620	|	0933	0933	...	0500	0500	1515	1917	...	1935	|	2053	|	...	|	...	2330	2330	2330	2330	2330	...
dabad ... d.	...	0815	0815	1107	1110	...	0835	0835	1725	2105	...	2125	2255	2235	2315	...	|	...	0110	0110	0110	0110	0110	...
ranpur ... d.	...	1130	1130	|	1450	...	|	|	2130	0030	...	0125	0305	0145	0230	...	|	...	0425	0425	0425	0425	0425	...
ala Cantonment ... d.	...	1300	1300	1655	1615	...	1755	1755	2310	0210	...	0315	0445	0325	0420	...	0700	...	0548	0548	0548	0548	0548	...
iana ... d.	...	1452	1452	1835	1815	...	2010	2010	0202	0405	...	0556	0723	0543	0640	...	0930	...	0742	0742	0742	0742	0742	...
dhar Cantonment ... d.	...	|	|	|	|	...	2103	2103	0305	|	...	0649	0825	0638	0735	...	|	...	0845	0845	0845	0845	0845	...
andhar City ... d.	...	1548	1548	1940	1940	...	2120	2120	|	0510	...	0707	0845	|	|	...	1040	...	|	|	|	|	|	...
nritsar ... a.	...	1720	1720	2105	2105	...	2335	2325	|	0630	...	0855	1020	|	|	...	1245	...	|	|	|	|	|	...
ki Bank ♥ ... d.	...	...	...	...	...	...	...	...	0505	...	...	...	...	0830	0920	...	...	...	1043	1043	1043	1043	1043	...
nu Tawi ... a.	...	...	...	...	...	...	...	...	0835	...	...	...	...	1030	1125	...	...	...	1235	1235	1235	1235	1235	...

②④⑤⑦.

♥ – Pathankot Cantonment.
** – Amritsar - Jalandhar Cantonment : *84 km*. Jalandhar City - Jalandhar Cantonment : *5 km*.

DELHI - GUWAHATI 5040

an Railways

	km		Exp	Exp	Exp	RDi	RDi	RDi	Exp	Exp	Exp
			12506	**15934**	**15910**	**12436**	**12236**	**12424**	**15708**	**12502**	**12370**
				⑥		④⑦	②			③④⑦	E
)	*0*	**New Delhi** ... d.	0645v	...	0745j	0925	0925	1355	1520j	2345	...
	167	Moradabad ... d.	|	...	1125	1222	1222	|	|	|	0300
	258	Bareilly Junction ... d.	|	...	1305	1345	1345	|	|	|	0430
	493	Lucknow Junction ... d.	|	0810	1810	1735	1735	|	0050	|	0830
	981	Chhapra ... d.	|	2045	0405	0155	0155	|	1005	|	|
)		Kanpur Central ... d.	1300	|	|	|	|	1839	2300↑	0620	|
4		Allahabad ... d.	1552	|	|	|	|	2042	|	0900	|
7		Mughal Sarai ... d.	1825	|	|	|	|	2255	|	|	1425
9		Patna Junction ... d.	2220	|	|	|	|	0210	|	|	1750
9	*1128*	Barauni ... d.	0105	0020	0905	0505	|	0445	1525	|	...
3	*1308*	Katihar ... d.	0455	0410	1350	0845	0845	0750	2010	2050	...
1	*1491*	New Jalpaiguri ... d.	0835	0805	1805	1205	1205	1105	...	0020	...
3	*1742*	New Bongaigaon ... d.	1350	1245	2330	1610	1610	1502	...	0510	...
9	*1899*	**Guwahati** ... a.	1650	1545	0300	1900	1900	1730	...	0845	...

	RDi	RDi	Exp	Exp	RDi	Exp	Exp	Exp	Exp
	12235	**12435**	**12501**	**12369**	**12423**	**12505**	**15933**	**15909**	**15707**
	⑤	②⑥	②③⑥	F			②		
Guwahati ... d.	0540	0540	0615	...	0700	0945	1945	2200	...
New Bongaigaon ... d.	0807	0807	0905	...	0920	1245	2330	0115	...
New Jalpaiguri ... d.	1215	1215	1345	...	1315	1725	0420	0620	...
Katihar ... d.	1525	1525	1705	...	1625	2110	0900	1045	2345
Barauni ... d.	|	1855	|	...	1920	0015	1320	1425	0320
Patna Junction ... d.	|	|	|	2110	2150	0305	|	|	|
Mughal Sarai ... d.	|	|	|	0047	0107	0720	|	|	|
Allahabad ... d.	|	|	0425	|	0256	0945	|	|	|
Kanpur Central ... d.	|	|	0650	|	0508	1255	|	|	2000↓
Chhapra ... d.	2155	2155	|	|	|	|	1710	1940	0845
Lucknow Junction ... d.	0610	0610	|	0730	|	|	0600	0535	1825
Bareilly Junction ... d.	0933	0933	|	1110	|	|	...	0920	|
Moradabad ... d.	1107	1107	|	1240	|	|	...	1125	|
New Delhi ... a.	1355	1355	1300	...	1015	1920v	...	1505j	0250j

①②③⑤⑥.
①③④⑥⑦.

j – Delhi Junction.
v – Delhi Anand Vihar Terminal.

DELHI - PATNA - KOLKATA 5050

an Railways

		Exp	Exp	Duro	Exp	Exp	Exp		Exp	Exp	RDi	Exp	SDi		RDi	RDi	RDi		SDi	Exp	Exp	Exp	Exp	Exp
		12506	**12324**	**12274**	**12312**	**12488**	**15484**		**12332**	**13258**	**12424**	**12368**	**12034**		**12302**	**12314**	**12306**		**12024**	**12570**	**22406**	**12316**	**12318**	**12326**
			④⑦	②⑥					①②⑤				①–⑥		⑥–④		⑤		①–⑥	②⑥	①③⑤	②	③⑥	⑦
)	**New Delhi** ... d.	0645v	0705v	1255	0700j	0730v	0635j	...	...	1330v	1355	1440v	1550	...	1655	1625	1655	...	...	1655v	1655v	...	...	...
)	Kanpur Central ... d.	1300	1340	1753	1430	1355	1520	...	...	|	1839	|	2050	...	2143	2125	2143	...	...	2217	2217	...	...	...
4	Allahabad Junction ... d.	1552	1645	|	1720	1655	1805	...	...	|	2042	|	...	...	2346	|	2346	...	...	0019	0019	...	...	...
7	Muhgal Sarai ... d.	1825	1940	|	2025	2005	2115	...	2215	|	2255	|	...	...	0155	0138	0155	...	...	0232	0232	0255	0238	0238
8	**Patna** Junction ... d.	2155	|	|	|	2325	0035	...	0150	0700f	0200	0645	...	...	|	|	0455	...	0545	0555	0555	0615	0615	0615
2	Gaya ... d.	...	2225	|	2325	...		...	|	...	...	...	...	...	0404	0353	|	...	|	...	...	|	|	
9	Dhanbad ... d.	...	0200	0252	0325	...	...	...	|	...	...	...	...	...	0645	0628	|	...	|	...	...	|	|	|
7	Asansol ... d.	...	0300	|	0436	...	...	...	0820	...	...	...	...	...	|	0719	|	...	1047	...	...	1203	1203	1203
7	**Kolkata** Howrah ... a.	...	0600	0610	0755	...	...	...	1130	...	...	...	...	...	0955	1015e	1240	...	1325	...	...	1510e	1510e	1515k

	Exp	Exp	Exp	Exp	RDI	Exp	Exp	Exp	Yuva	Duro	Exp	Exp	Duro		Exp	Exp	Exp	Exp	Exp	Duro	Exp	Exp	Exp
	13152	**12372**	**12304**	**12382**	**12310**	**12394**	**12330**	**12380**	**12250**	**12260**	**11106**	**12402**	**12276**		**14056**	**12350**	**12370**	**12328**	**12360**	**22214**	**12352**	**13006**	**12334**
		④	A	①②⑤			③	⑦	⑦	C	⑥		③⑤⑦			②	E	④⑦	③⑤⑦	②④⑥			
Delhi ... d.	...	1505j	1615	1615	1715	1725	1905j	1905j	1940	1940	...	2000	2240	...	2340j	2345	...	...	...	...	...	...	...
our Central ... d.	...	|	2345	2345	2203	|	0120	0120	0034	0034	0130	0235	|	...	0600	0620	...	...	...	...	...	...	...
habad Junction ... d.	...	|	0210	0250	0009	|	|	|	0236	|	0400	0513	0610	...	0840	0900	...	...	...	...	...	...	1540a
gal Sarai ... d.	0300	0635	0450	0635	0215	|	|	|	0438	|	0715	0755	...	...	1145	|	1425	1425	...	...	...	1815	1910
a Junction ... d.	|	|	0805	|	0540	0655	|	|	|	|	1055	1130	...	...	1445	1500	1800	1800	2010	2040	2110	2155	2325
aya ... d,	0639	0915	|	0918	...	...	|	0935	|	|	|	...	...	...	...	...	|	|	|	|	|	|	|
nanbad ... d.	1035	1218	|	1228	...	...	1245	1245	0905	0905	|	...	...	...	...	...	|	|	|	|	|	|	|
nsol ... d.	1150	1322	1341	1341	...	...	1357	1357	1001	|	1710	...	...	...	...	...	0006	0006	0207	|	0333	0404	0424
kata Howrah ... a.	1555k	1630	1655	1655	...	...	1725e	1725e	1240	1235e	2145k	...	...	...	...	...	0315	0315	0515k	0540h	0635	0720	0730

③④⑥⑦.
①②⑤⑥.
①②④⑤.

D – ①③④⑦.
E – ①②③⑤⑥.
F – ①③④⑥⑦.

a – Allahabad City
c – Kolkata Chitpur.
e – Kolkata Sealdah.

f – Danapur.
h – Kolkata Shalimar.
j – Delhi Junction.

k – Kolkata.
v – Delhi Anand Vihar Terminal.

For return service see next page ▷ ▷ ▷

5050 KOLKATA - PATNA - DELHI

Indian Railways

km			Duro 12273 ①⑤	Duro 12275 ②④⑥	Exp 14055	Exp 11105 ⑦	Exp 12317 ③⑦	Exp 12325 ④	Exp 12303 B	Exp 12381 ③④⑦	Exp 12371 ①	RDi 12309	Exp 12367	Exp 13257	Exp 12393	Exp 12569 ①⑤	Exp 22405 ②④⑥	Exp 12327 ②⑤	Exp 12315 ④	Exp 12369 F	SDI 12023 ①–⑥	RDI 12305 ⑦	Exp 12301 ①–⑥
0	**Kolkata** Howrah d.	...	1245	....	...	0730k	0740e	0740k	0805	0815	0815	...	...	...	...	...	...	1300	1310e	1300	1405	1405	1655
200	Asansol d.	...	|	....	...	1140	1040	1040	1040	1053	1053	...	...	...	...	...	...	1534	1605	1534	1642	|	|
	Dhanbad d.	...	1558	...	...	|	|	|	|	1205	1205	...	...	...	...	...	...	|	|	|	|	|	2001
	Gaya d.	...	|	...	...	|	|	|	|	1455	1455	...	...	...	...	...	...	|	|	|	|	|	2238
532	**Patna** Junction d.	...	|	...	1315	1820	1615	1615	1615	|	|	1925	1705	1600f	1800	1915	1915	2110	2200	2110	2215	2125	|
744	Mughal Sarai d.	...	|	...	1657	2309	1927	1927	1947	1802	1817	2235	|	|	|	2300	2300	0027	0205	0027	...	0055	0057
896	Allahabad Junction d.	...	|	2240	1925	0115	...	...	2155	2155	|	0028	|	|	|	0055	0055	...	0425	...	...	0246	0243
1091	Kanpur Central d.	...	0055	|	2210	0345	...	...	0030	0013	|	0235	|	|	|	0300	0300	...	0645	...	...	0453	0453
1530	**New Delhi** a.	...	0620	0620	0605j	...	...	...	0735	0735	1015j	0740	0800v	1040v	0750	0820v	0820v	...	...	...	...	1000	1000

			RDi 12313	Yuva 12249 ⑥	Duro 12259 D	SDi 12033 ①–⑥	Exp 12401		Exp 12329 ②	Exp 12379 ⑤	Exp 12349 ①	Exp 12323 ②⑤	Exp 15483	Exp 12505	Exp 13005	Exp 12311	Exp 12333	Exp 12359 ②④⑥	Exp 12487		Exp 12351	Duro 22213 ①③⑤
Kolkata Howrah d.	...	...	1650e	1840	1830e	...	...	...	1310e	1310e	...	1850	...	...	1910	1940	2000	2005	...	...	2035	2205h
Asansol d.	...	...	1920	2052	|	...	...	...	1605	1605	...	2118	...	...	2154	2222	2238	2251	...	...	2322	|
Dhanbad d.	...	...	2025	2156	2156	...	...	...	1715	1715	...	2250	...	...	|	2336	|	|	...	...	|	|
Gaya d.	...	...	2255	|	|	...	...	...	|	2017	...	0210	...	...	|	0300	|	|	...	...	|	|
Patna Junction d.	...	...	|	|	|	...	1810	...	|	|	2235	|	0150	0305	0420	|	0435	0530	0520	...	0605	0640
Mughal Sarai d.	...	...	0117	0232	|	...	2217	...	|	|	|	0520	0545	0720	0807	0638	0842	...	0937	...	...	...
Allahabad Junction d.	...	...	|	0420	|	...	0045	...	|	|	0425	0740	0855	0945	...	0935	1200a	...	1155	...	...	...
Kanpur Central d.	...	...	0518	0628	0625	0600	0325	...	0400	0400	0650	1020	1225	1255	...	1245	...	...	1440	...	...	...
New Delhi a.	...	...	1025	1120	1130	1120	1150	...	1205j	1205j	1300	1700	2240j	1920v	...	2045j	...	...	2100v	...	...	...

For footnotes and return service see previous page.

5060 LUCKNOW - MUGHAL SARAI - PATNA - KOLKATA

Indian Railways

km		Exp 12354 ⑦	Exp 22408 ②④⑦	Exp 18104 ④⑥	Exp 12238	Exp 12328 ④⑦		Exp 12370 A	Exp 13010	Exp 13006	Exp 12876 ②⑤⑦	Exp 12332 ①②⑤		Exp 12358 ①④	Exp 12318 ②⑤		Exp 12326 ⑥	Exp 13050		Exp 13152	Exp 12392	Exp 12372 ④	
493	Haridwar d.	...	...	...	...	2355	...	2355	2230	...	...	...	...	...	...	...	...	...	...	...	...	...	...
0	**Lucknow** Junction d.	0125	0235	0250	0720	0830	...	0830	0845	1050	1430	1530	...	2015	2015	...	2015	1210	...	1720	2130	2345	...
127	Faizabad d.	|	|	0505	|	|	...	|	1105	|	|	|	...	|	|	...	|	|	...	2052	|	|	...
283	Varanasi Junction d.	0720	0805	1004	1240	1305	...	1305	1610	1655	2010	2105	...	0110	0115	...	0115	1915	...	0130	0240	0520	...
300	**Mughal Sarai** d.	0835	...	1135	...	1425	...	1425	1730	1815	2120	2215	...	0220	0238	...	0238	2040	...	0300	0345	0635	...
512	**Patna** Junction d.	|	...	|	...	1800	...	1800	|	2155	|	0150	...	|	0615	...	0615	0230	...	|	0715	|	...
***	Gaya d.	1130	...	1428	...	|	...	|		|	0025	|	...	0445	|	...		|	...	0639	...	0915	...
***	Dhanbad d.	1445	...	...	...	|	...	|	0125	|	...	|	...	0730	|	...	|	|	...	1035	...	1218	...
843	Asansol d.	1550	...	...	...	0006	...	0006	0230	0404	...	0820	...	0825	1203	...	1203	1105	...	1150	...	1322	...
1055	**Kolkata** Howrah a.	1855	...	...	...	0315	...	0315	0655	0720	...	1130	...	1120k	1510e	...	1515k	1545	...	1555k	...	1630	...

		Exp 12353 ⑤	Exp 12371 ①	Exp 22407 ⑦②④	Exp 12317 ③⑦	Exp 12325 ④		Exp 12357 ②⑥	Exp 12327 ②⑤		Exp 12369 B	Exp 13151	Exp 18103 ②④	Exp 13005	Exp 13049		Exp 13009	Exp 12237	Exp 12331 ②⑤⑥				
Kolkata Howrah d.	...	0815	0815	...	0740e	0740k	...	1220k	1300	...	1300	1145k	...	1910	1350	...	2030	...	2355	...	...	...	...
Asansol d.	...	1053	1053	...	1040	1040	...	1457	1534	...	1534	1520	...	2154	1811	...	0016	...	0236	...	...	...	...
Dhanbad d.	...	1205	1205	...	|	|	...	1602	|	...	|	1657	...	|	|	...	0130	...	|	...	...	...	...
Gaya d.	...	1455	1455	...	|	|	...	1843	|	...	|	2115	0408	|	|	...	0500	...	|	...	...	...	...
Patna Junction d.	...	|	|	...	1615	1615	...	|	2110	...	2110	|	|	0420	0215	...	|	...	1015	...	...	...	...
Mughal Sarai d.	...	1817	1817	...	1947	1947	...	2122	0047	...	0047	0152	0722	0827	0737	...	0937	...	1402	...	...	...	...
Varanasi Junction d.	...	1930	1930	1930	2040	2040	...	2205	0155	...	0155	0250	0815	0927	0845	...	1030	1250	1447	...	...	...	...
Faizabad d.	...	|	|	|	|	|	...	|	|	...	|	0620	145	|	|	...	1449	|	|	...	...	...	...
Lucknow Junction a.	...	0120	0120	0120	0210	0210	...	0245	0715	...	0715	1030	1500	1520	1545	...	1820	1805	1940	...	...	...	...
Haridwar a.	...	...	...	...	...	...	...	...	1535	...	1605	...	...	...	...	...	0435	...	...	...	...	...	...

A – ①②③⑤⑥.
B – ①③④⑥⑦.

e – Kolkata Sealdah.
k – Kolkata.

*** – Mughal Sarai - Dhanbad: *402 km*. Gaya - Dhandab: *199 km* Dhanbad - Asansol: *58*

5070 KOLKATA - NEW JALPAIGURI - GUWAHATI

Indian Railways

km		Exp 15657	Exp 12509 A	SDi 12041 ①–⑥	Exp 12507 ④	Exp 15901 ③	Exp 12345	Exp 15959	Exp 12525 ③	Exp 12517 ④⑦	Exp 22511 ④
0	**Kolkata** Howrah d.	0635e	1115	1415	1415	1425	1550	1735	2140k	2140k	2155
213	Rampurhat d.	1050	1428	|	1743	1743	1859	|	|	|	0210
335	Malda Town d.	1355	1730	1910	2015	2015	2145	0210	0410	0410	0520
480	Kishanganj d.	1617	1932	2104	2205	2205	2337	0425	0602	0602	|
567	**New Jalpaiguri** d.	1830	2145	2225	0010	0010	0205	0635	0805	0805	0920
819	New Bongaigaon d.	0040	0225	...	0435	0645	0627	1150	1237	1237	1540
975	**Guwahati** a.	0415	0600	...	0815	1025	0935	1535	1540	1540	1825c

	Exp 15902 ⑥	Exp 12508 ⑤	Exp 12510 B	Exp 15960	Exp 12346	SDi 12042 ①–⑥	Exp 22512 ⑥	Exp 12526 ②	Exp 12518 ③⑥
Guwahati d.	0520	0630	0630	0745	1230	...	1800c	2100	2100
New Bongaigaon d.	0840	0940	0940	1145	1522	...	2120	2355	2355
New Jalpaiguri d.	1425	1425	1425	1655	1925	0530	0320	0355	0355
Kishanganj d.	1530	1530	1530	1810	2032	0635	|	0458	0458
Malda Town d.	1845	1845	1845	2210	2340	0850	0750	0825	0825
Rampurhat d.	2110	2110	2110	|	0158	|	1030	|	|
Kolkata Howrah a.	0045	0045	0045	0545	0510	1335	1415	1500k	1500k

A – ①②⑤⑥⑦. Runs as **12513** on ① and as **12515** on ②.
B – ①②③④⑦. Runs as **12514** on ④ and as **12516** on ③.

c – Kamakhya Junction.
e – Kolkata Sealdah.
k – Kolkata.

5075 GUWAHATI - DIBRUGARH

Indian Railways

km		Exp 15929 ⑦	Exp 15927 ③⑤⑦	Exp 15901 ④	Exp 14056	Exp 15934 ⑦	Exp 15959	RDi 12424	RDi 12236 ③	RDi 12436 ①⑤	Exp 15905 ⑦	Exp 15904 ②⑤
0	**Guwahati** d.	0510	0730	1045	1500	1600	1550	1745	1925	1925	1925	2005
87	Chaparmukh d.	0715	0905	|	1640	1727	1800	|	|	|	|	|
184	Lumding d.	0925	1115	1510	1930	1945	2015	2112	2242	2242	2245	2325
250	Dimapur d.	1045	1237	1657	2050	2106	2140	2230	0015	0015	0015	0050
323	Furkating d.	1232	1430	|	2257	2322	2355	|	|	|	0152	0242
358	Mariani d.	1320	1550	1920	2355	0020	0120	0100	0240	0240	0240	0335
513	New Tinsukia d.	1635	|	|	0310	0410	0435	0345	|	0515	0525	0610
561	**Dibrugarh** a.	1800	1930	2230	0425	0525	0600	0455	0530	0615	0715	0735

	Exp 15928	Exp 15933 ②	Exp 15903 ①⑤	Exp 15902 ⑤	RDi 12435 ①⑤	RDi 12235 ④	RDi 12423	Exp 15960	Exp 15906 ⑥	Exp 14055
Dibrugarh d.	0615	0700	0700	1830	1920	1925	2035	1825	2245	2310
New Tinsukia d.	|	0805	0805	|	2025	|	2140	1940	2350	0020
Mariani d.	0955	1100	1100	2135	2235	2225	0012	2310	0235	0340
Furkating d.	1052	1242	1242	2230	|	|	|	0010	0335	0447
Dimapur d.	1231	1405	1400	2342	0045	0045	0205	0145	0515	0621
Lumding d.	1410	1535	1535	0135	0217	0217	0327	0325	0710	0800
Chaparmukh d.	1543	1720	|	|	|	|	|	0530	|	1020
Guwahati a.	1805	1920	1920	0455	0515	0515	0635	0730	1130	1235

5080 DELHI - JAIPUR - AHMEDABAD

Indian Railways

km		Exp 19708	Exp 12414	SDi 12015	Exp 19264 ①④	Exp 12215 A	Exp 14311 ④⑤⑦	Exp 19270 ①②	Exp 12916	RDi 12958	Exp 19032
0	**Delhi** Junction d.	...	0425	0605n	0820a	0920a	1145	1255	1520	1955n	2230
83	Rewari d.	...	0615	0747	1005	1050	1352	1458	1707	|	0035
157	Alwar d.	...	0716	0842	1110	1145	1452	1557	1806	|	0139
308	**Jaipur** d.	0845	1010	1040	1325	1420	1730	1850	2035	0025	0425
444	Ajmer d.	1115	1220	1245	1600	1640	2015	2140	2250	0229	0650
581	Marwar Junction d.	1315	...	...	1855	|	2226	2359	|	|	0910
749	Abu Road d.	1650	...	...	2205	2120	0125	0245	0350	0605	1200
801	Palanpur d.	1825	...	...	2317	2217	0247	0412	0502	0707	1318
866	Mahesana d.	1951	...	...	0014	|	0416	|	0602	0805	1430
934	**Ahmedabad** a.	2205	...	...	0210	0110	0615	0715	0740	0940	1655

	Exp 19031	RDi 12957	Exp 12915	Exp 12216 B	Exp 14312 ②④⑦	Exp 19263 ③⑦	Exp 19269 ⑤⑥	Exp 12413	SDI 12016
Ahmedabad d.	1005	1740	1830	1940	2020	0050	0050	...	...
Mahesana d.	1202	1850	1949	|	2200	0240	|	...	...
Palanpur d.	13572	2004	2109	2250	2342	0412	0412	...	...
Abu Road d.	1450	2050	2210	2345	0045	0542	0542	...	...
Marwar Junction d.	1740	|	|	|	0327	0830	0830	...	...
Ajmer d.	2050	0055	0230	0500	0610	1105	1105	1405	1545
Jaipur d.	2315	0250	0440	0720	0845	1320	1320	1625	1750
Alwar d.	0141	|	0643	0919	1110	1543	1543	1842	1938
Rewari d.	0320	|	0825	1050	1235	1802	1802	2017	2102
Delhi Junction a.	0505	0730n	1010	1215a	1435	1935a	2000	2200	2240n

A – ①②④⑥.
B – ②③⑤⑦.
a – Delhi Sarai Rohilla.
n – New Delhi.

Indian Railways — DELHI - JODHPUR — 5090

km	Exp 15014	Exp 14659	Exp 12461	Exp 12463 ③⑤⑦		Exp 15013	Exp 12464 ②④⑥	Exp 12462	Exp 14660
0	0440	1735	2115	2225a	d.**Delhi** Junction .... a.	2010	0535a	0645	1115
3	0645	1945	2322	|	d.Rewari .... d.	1855	|	0455	0915
7	0755	2055	0017	0052	d.Alwar .... d.	1703	0233	0310	0717
8	1110	2345	0245	0315	d.Jaipur .... d.	1435	0025	0100	0500
1	|	0241	0514	0550	d.Degana .... d.	|	2120	2208	0127
6	|	0322	0600	0635	d.Merta Road .... d.	|	2035	2132	0043
0	1735	0450	0705	0825	a.**Jodhpur** .... d.	0630	1900	2000	2315

Indian Railways — JODHPUR - JAISALMER — 5100

km	Exp 14659	Exp 22931 ⑥	Exp 15014	Exp 14810		Exp 15013	Exp 14809	Exp 14660	Exp 22932 ⑥
0	0520	0735	1745	2345	d.**Jodhpur** .... a.	0615	1350	2240	2345
65	0634	0835	1903	0058	d.Osian .... d.	0429	1215	2112	2236
137	0744	0940	2007	0207	d.Phalodi .... d.	0327	1117	2001	2138
184	0823	1019	2049	0313	d.Ramdevra .... d.	0223	1012	1913	2052
194	0907	|	|	0400	d.Pokaran .... d.	|	0955	1855	|
198	0915	|	2111	0408	d.Ashapura .... d.	0210	0923	1823	|
301	1130	1250	2315	0600	a.**Jaisalmer** .... d.	0045	0800	1700	1920

Indian Railways — JODHPUR - AHMEDABAD — 5110

km	Exp 16311 ③	Exp 19028 ②	Exp 16507 ④⑥	Exp 16533 ③	Exp 19224	Exp 14707	Exp 12489 ②⑥	Exp 12479	Exp 19066 ⑥	Exp 22473 ①	Exp 17038 D⑤⑦	Exp 22932 ⑥	
0	0300	0330	0540b	0540b	0610	1430	1815	1845	1930b	1920	2115	2355	d.**Jodhpur** .... a.
1	0332	0402	0606	|	0641	1502	1847	1916	|	1956	2147	0027	d.Luni
3	0520	0553	0740	0738	0805	1657	2204c	2032	2138	2138	2315	0202	d.Marwar Junction .. d.
8	0750	0825	1030	1030	1055	1933	|	2345	0040	0040	0213	0450	d.Abu Road .... d.
1	0907	0952	1153	|	1217	2135	0140	0100	|	0155	0327	0557	d.Palanpur .... d.
6	1028	1114	1309	|	1335	2245	|	0155	0305	0308	0435	0702	d.Mahesana .... d.
9	1230	1310	1430	1430	1500	0035	0410	0320	0435	0435	0625	0910	a.**Ahmedabad** .... d.

	Exp 14708	Exp 17037 ④⑤	Exp 16125 ①	Exp 16312 ①	Exp 16508 ③⑤	Exp 16534 ②	Exp 19065 ⑥	Exp 19223	Exp 19027 ⑥	Exp 12480	Exp 12490 ③⑦	Exp 22931 C②⑤
d.**Jodhpur** .... a.	0945	1050	1050	1630	1633b	1633b	1710b	2000	0430	0635	0745	0725
d.Luni	0909	1011	1014	1554	1555	|	|	1916	0358	0546	0709	0651
d.Marwar Junction .. d.	0805	0910	0910	1450	1455	1455	1520	1812	0255	0442	0426c	0550
d.Abu Road .... d.	0443	0608	0608	1155	1155	1155	1237	1530	2345	0132	|	0250
d.Palanpur .... d.	0328	0503	0503	1056	1050	|	|	1428	2250	0033	0155	0155
d.Mahesana .... d.	0154	0308	0240	0912	0920	|	1007	1245	2123	2245	|	2346
a.**Ahmedabad** .... d.	0010	0110	0500	0735	0705	0705	0805	1120	1955	2135	2230	2230

Bhagat Ki Koth. c – Marwar Bhinmal. C – Runs as **22474** on ②. D – Also runs as **16126 on** ①.

Indian Railways — DELHI and JAIPUR - UDAIPUR - AHMEDABAD — 5120

km		Exp 12992	Exp 12315 ⑤	Exp 19602 ②	Exp 15715 ①③⑥	Exp 19665	Exp 12963 A	Exp 12981	52927	Exp 19943	
0	**Delhi** Sarai Rohilla ...... d.	...	...	1230j	1335j	...	1900h	1940	...	...	...
3	Rewari .... d.	...	...	1522	1522	...	|	2107	...	...	...
**	**Jaipur** .... d.	1400	1745	1910	1910	2300	|	|	...	...	...
3	Ajmer .... d.	1610	2030	2140	2130	0125	|	0210	...	...	...
9	Chittaurgarh .... d.	1925	0020	0145	...	0425	0505	0533	...	...	...
3	**Udaipur** City .... d.	2130	0300	0405	...	0645	0720	0750	0810	1745	...
3	Himmatnagar .... d.	...	...	...	...	...	...	...	1810	0155	...
4	**Ahmedabad** .... a.	...	...	...	...	...	...	...	2125	0425	...

	Exp 12316 ①	Exp 19601 ⑥	Exp 15716 ①②④	Exp 12991	Exp 19944	Exp 12982	Exp 12964 B	52928	Exp 19666	
Ahmedabad .... d.	...	...	...	...	2300	...	...	0710	...	...
Himmatnagar .... d.	...	...	...	...	0150	...	...	1030	...	...
Udaipur City .... d.	0020	0020	...	0600	0920	1715	1815	1900	2220	...
Chittaurgarh .... d.	0235	0235	...	0820	...	1930	2050	...	0035	...
Ajmer .... d.	0630	0630	1105	1130	...	2245	|	...	0340	...
Jaipur .... a.	0845	0910	1320	1330	...	|	|	...	0545	...
Rewari .... d.	...	1255	1802	...	...	0345	|	...	...	...
Delhi Sarai Rohilla ... a.	...	1445j	2000j	...	...	0510	0635h	...	...	...

Via Mathura (d. 2110), Sawai Madhopur (d. 2358) and Kota (d. 0125). B – Via Kota (d. 2340), Sawai Madhopur (d. 0055) and Mathura (d. 0430). h – Delhi Hazrat Nizamuddin. j – Delhi Junction. ** – Jaipur - Ajmer: *136 km*.

Indian Railways — DELHI and JAIPUR - MUMBAI and AHMEDABAD — 5130

km		Exp 12904	Exp 19708	Exp 12956	Exp 12215 D	Duro 12264 ①④	Exp 12918 ②④⑥	Exp 12910 ③⑤⑦	RDi 12952	Yuva 12248 ⑥	RDi 12954	Duro 12240 ②④	Exp 12980 ①③⑤	Exp 12926	Duro 22210 ②⑥	Exp 12908 ①④	Exp 12472 A	Exp 12478 ①⑦E	Exp 19024	Exp 19020
0	**Delhi** H Nizamuddin ... d.	0735	...	...	0920h	1055	1355	1535	1625n	1535	1650	...	...	1645n	2325n	2135	2150n	2150n	1325n	2155
4	Mathura .... d.	1000	...	...	|	|	1605	1712	|	1712	1840	...	...	1915	|	|	0010	0010	1705	0135
	Jaipur .... d.	|	0845	1400	1420	|	|	|	|	|	|	1910	2025	|	|	|	|	|	|	|
0	Sawai Madhopur .... d.	1300	|	1610	|	|	|	|	|	|	2038	2105	2245	2205	|	|	0229	0229	2110	0525
8	Kota Junction .... d.	1425	△	1730	△	1540	1955	2010	2105	2010	2150	|	0010	2345	0425	0310	0355	0355	2320	0750
3	Nagda .... d.	1757	|	2105	|	|	|	|	|	|	0024	|	0308	0320	|	|	0727	0727	0445	1315
4	Ratlam .... d.	1910	|	2150	|	1845	2350	2325	0005	2325	0055	0155	0350	0410	0740	|	0820	0820	0600	1435
6	Vadodara .... d.	2320	0030	0144	0313	2236	0430	0307	0324	0307	0423	0600	0805	0821	1121	1107	1215	1230	1053	2005
5	**Ahmedabad** .... a.	|	|	|	|	P	0645	|	|	|	|	|	|	|	|	|	|	1415	|	|
4	Surat .... d.	0120	0222	0335	0451	...	...	0450	0503	0520	0602	|	1013	1025	|	|	1410	...	1335	2238
0	Borivali .... d.	0428	0548	0642	0730	...	...	0730	0731	|	0854	|	1332	1355	|	1554	1723	...	1850	0337
0	**Mumbai** Bandra .... a.	0520c	0635	0740c	0810	...	...	0810	0815c	0920	0945c	1140c	1420	1445	1615c	1635	1805	...	2010c	0420

km		Exp 19019	Exp 19023	Exp 12471 B	Exp 12477 ②③F	Exp 12925	Exp 12216 C	Duro 12263 ②⑤	Exp 12979 ②④⑥	RDi 12951	Exp 12907 ③⑦	Exp 12909 ②④⑥	Yuva 12247 ⑤	Exp 12917 ①③⑤	RDi 12953	Exp 12955	Exp 19707	Exp 12903	Duro 12239 ②⑦	Duro 22209 ①⑤
0	**Mumbai** Bandra .... d.	0005	0725c	0755	...	1135	1245	...	1545	1700c	1635	1635	1635	...	1740c	1850c	2100	2130c	2315c	2315c
9	Borivali .... d.	0045	0810	0831	...	1217	1315	...	1630	1734	1713	1713	|	...	1821	1933	2145	2209	|	|
2	Surat .... d.	0445	1337	1147	...	1547	1600	...	2038	1958	|	2010	2010	...	2055	2245	0102	0115	|	|
	Ahmedabad .... d.	|	|	|	1125	|	|	P	|	|	|	|	|	1720	|	|	|	|	|	|
1	Vadodara .... d.	0655	1607	1345	1343	1743	1738	1849	2242	2128	2305	2146	2146	1935	2231	0039	0254	0305	0405	0405
2	Ratlam .... d.	1240	2055	1805	1805	2200	|	2223	0255	0040	|	0110	0110	2340	0220	0440	|	0720	0750	0740
4	Nagda .... d.	1425	2205	1905	1905	2325	△	|	0355	|	|	|	|	|	0312	0538	△	0815	|	|
9	Kota Junction .... d.	1935	0135	2140	2140	0215	|	0110	0635	0325	0635	0345	0345	0300	0520	0855	|	1105	|	1035
7	Sawai Madhopur .... d.	2130	0315	2257	2257	0350	|	|	0845	|	|	|	|	|	0628	1040	|	1230	1225	|
8	**Jaipur** .... a.	|	|	|	|	|	0705	|	1045	|	|	|	|	|	|	1240	1855	|	1435	|
	Mathura .... d.	0225	0935	0205	0205	0750	|	|	...	|	|	0727	0727	0802	0902	...	...	1620	...	|
	Delhi H Nizamuddin ... a.	0520	1245n	0410	0410	1003	1215h	0655	...	0835n	1345	0940	0940	1040	1055	...	...	1845	...	1630n

A – ②③⑤⑥.
B – ①④⑤⑦.
C – ②③⑤⑦.
D – ①②④⑥.
E – Runs as **12476** on ①. Also as **12474** on ④.
F – Runs as **12475** on ③. Also as **12473** on ⑥.
P – To/from Pune see Table **5160**.

c – Mumbai Central.
h – Delhi Sarai Rohilla.
n – New Delhi.

△ – Via Ahmedabad (Table **5080**).

Indian Railways — GANDHIDHAM - AHMEDABAD — 5140

km		Exp 16335 ⑤	Exp 19452 ④	Exp 16505 ②	Exp 11091 ③	Exp 14312 ②④⑦	Exp 15667 ⑥	Exp 22904 ①④⑥	Exp 19132	Exp 12993 ⑤	Exp 19116
0	**Gandhidham** .... d.	0700	0630	0900	1005	1410	1315	1625	2115	2245	2340
3	Samakhiali .... d.	0800	0732	0956	1105	1510	1420	1718	2215	2345	0041
4	Maliya Miyana .... d.	0838	0814	|	|	1547	1507	|	2252	|	0119
70	Dhrangadhra .... d.	0930	|	1136	1300	1658	|	|	0004	0127	0235
36	Viramgam .... d.	1117	1241	1307	1421	1825	1942	|	0115	|	0345
1	**Ahmedabad** .... a.	1240	1350	1430	1530	1945	2105	2150	0235	0410	0505

	Exp 19131	Exp 14311 ①⑤⑥	Exp 16336 ④	Exp 16506 ①	Exp 12994 ③	Exp 11092 ②	Exp 22093 ①④⑥	Exp 19451 ⑤	Exp 15668 ⑤	Exp 19115
Ahmedabad .... d.	0200	0645	0735	0705	0745	0805	0645	0825	1930	2359
Viramgam .... d.	0304	0800	0841	0822	|	0918	|	0946	2029	0107
Dhrangadhra .... d.	0404	0900	0952	0927	0952	1015	|	|	|	0208
Maliya Miyana .... d.	0515	1022	1056	|	|	|	|	1502	0119	0335
Samakhiali .... d.	0607	1114	1146	1140	1146	1216	1025	1604	0207	0430
Gandhidham .... a.	0715	1215	1300	1300	1300	1320	1130	1720	0320	0530

Indian Railways — AHMEDABAD - MUMBAI — 5150

km		Exp 12972	Exp 12215 A	Exp 22452 ①④	Exp 14707	Exp 19132	Exp 12479	Exp 12489 A B	Exp 12934	Exp 12990 ①④⑥	Exp 19066 ⑦	Exp 22473 ②	Exp 12932 ①–⑥	Exp 19116	Exp 19012	Exp 22932 ⑦	Exp 19216	SDi 12010 ①–⑥	Exp 19028 ②	Exp 19452 ④	Exp 19018	Exp 22928	Duro 12268	Exp 12902	Exp 22904 ①④⑥	Exp 19708	Exp 19006
0	**Ahmedabad** ... d.	0001	0130	0130	0100	0300	0345	0430	0455	0455	0455	0455	0600	0525	0700	0930	0710	1440	1400	1410	2030	2110	2345	2200	2210	2240	2250
4	Anand .... d.	0105	|	0225	0205	0408	0453	0539	0557	0610	|	0610	0658	0634	0819	1035	0839	1534	1515	|	2146	2221	|	2315	|	2341	2353
0	Vadodara .... d.	0152	0313	0317	0252	0455	0540	0626	0644	0700	0700	0700	0745	0721	0908	1130	0947	1616	1603	1603	2245	2308	|	0013	2339	0030	0047
9	Surat .... d.	0350	0451	0515	0442	0705	0735	0820	0840	0855	0855	0855	0927	1000	1125	1350	1240	1758	1835	1835	0055	0108	|	0205	0130	0222	0235
2	Borivali .... d.	0800	0730	0832	0844	1042	1050	1125	1154	1202	1202	1202	1211	1327	1531	1650	1811	2035	2144	2145	0450	0508	|	0526	0416	0548	0612
0	**Mumbai** Bandra a.	0810	0810	0920	0940	1125	1135	1200d	1235c	1240d	1245	1245	1300c	1405	1625c	1735	1915c	2120c	2225	2225	0540	0550	0600c	0625c	0455	0635	0710c

	Exp 12959 ③⑥	SDi 12009 ①–⑥	Exp 19011	Exp 19215	Exp 19027 ⑥	Exp 22451 ①④	Exp 12216 A	Exp 12480	Exp 12933	Exp 12931 ①–⑥	Exp 12490 ③⑦	Exp 12989 ①④⑥	Exp 22931 C②⑤	Exp 19115	Exp 14708	Exp 19131	Exp 19017	Exp 22927	Exp 19005	Exp 19707	Exp 12971	Duro 12267	Exp 12901	Exp 19065 ⑤	Exp 19451 ④	Exp 22903 ③⑤⑦
mbai Bandra .... d.	0005d	0625c	0545c	0820c	1205	1205	1245	1330	1340c	1420c	1435d	1435d	1435	1450	1505	1710	1735	1940	2025c	2100	2130	2325c	2200c	2325	2355	2355
ivali .... d.	0038	0702	0632	0906	1243	1243	1312	1403	1422	1500	1509	1509	1509	1524	1551	1752	1825	2024	2121	2145	2213	|	2258	0005	0030	0030
at .... d.	0420	0936	1033	1415	1600	1600	1600	1727	1740	1800	1827	1827	1827	1906	1925	2142	2202	0027	0042	0102	0140	|	0215	0355	0420	0318
odara .... d.	0610	1107	1242	1705	1748	1748	1738	1915	1928	1940	2018	2018	2018	2135	2151	2340	0006	0226	0235	0254	0322	|	0423	0545	0610	0448
nd .... d.	0642	1136	1313	1750	1819	1819	|	1948	2000	2011	2053	2053	2053	2211	2222	0016	0042	0257	0308	0335	0353	|	0456	|	|	|
medabad .... a.	0805	1245	1500	1945	1930	1930	1920	2115	2125	2140	2210	2210	2210	2340	2350	0140	0210	0420	0435	0505	0515	0550	0635	0745	0805	0625

②③⑤⑦. B – Runs as **12960** on ②⑤. C – Runs as **22474** on ②. c – Mumbai Central. d – Mumbai Dadar.

5160 DELHI - PUNE and MUMBAI

Indian Railways

km		Exp 12172 ③⑥	Exp 12138	Duro 12264 ①④	Exp 12148 ④	Exp 12782 ①	Exp 12630 A	Exp 11078	Exp 12780	Exp 22110 ③	Exp 11058
0	**Delhi** H Nizamuddin .. d.	0010	0515n	1055	0555	0555	0845	1015n	1500	1545	2105
134	Mathura Junction .... d.	|	0740	|	0801	0801	|	1240	1645	|	2343
188	Agra Cantonment....... d.	0300	0835	|	0852	0855	|	1335	1733	1751	0048
306	Gwalior..................... d.	|	1036	|	1104	1104	|	1536	1945	1911	0300
403	Jhansi....................... d.	0610	1235	|	1245	1245	1505	1730	2122	2027	0500
556	Bina.......................... d.	|	1450	|	1505	1505	|	2010	|	|	0900
694	Bhopal....................... d.	1035	1655	|	1710	1710	1925	2220	0115	2345	1115
786	Itarsi .... d.	|	1840	▽	1855	1855	|	0020	0250	|	1325
969	Khandwa .... d.	|	2145	|	2200	2200	|	0325	0535	|	1645
1093	Bhusaval .... d.	1645	2335	|	2355	2355	|	0515	0730	0530	1855
1277	Manmad .... d.	|	0155	|	0215	0215	|	0750	0950	|	2150
1513	Daund .... d.	|	|	|	0755	0755	|	1310	1500	|	|
1589	**Pune**........................ a.	|	|	0710	0915	0915	1105	1510	1620	|	|
1484	Kalyan....................... d.	2255	0625	...	...	...	...	...	...	1050	0245
1521	**Mumbai** LTT .... a.	2345	0735h	...	...	...	...	...	...	1145	0405h

	Exp 11057	Exp 12779	Exp 12171 ①④	Duro 12263 ②⑤	Exp 22109 ②	Exp 12629 B	Exp 12147 ②	Exp 12781 ⑥	Exp 11077
Mumbai LTT............ d.	2330h	...	0755	...	1430	...	...	...	...
Kalyan .... d.	0033	...	0830	...	1507	...	...	...	...
Pune .... d.	|	0410	|	1110	|	0900	1610	1610	1720
Daund .... d.	|	0550	|	|	|	|	1745	1745	1850
Manmad .... d.	0405	1020	|	|	|	|	2155	2155	2330
Bhusaval................... d.	0645	1255	1410	|	2020	|	0025	0025	0215
Khandwa.................... d.	0930	1500	|	|	|	|	0220	0220	0430
Itarsi........................ d.	1250	1735	|	▽	|	|	0445	0445	0715
Bhopal .... d.	1505	1940	2035	|	0210	0045	0630	0630	0910
Bina........................... d.	1745	|	|	|	|	|	0825	0825	1130
Jhansi........................ d.	2040	2358	0038	|	0531	0605	1038	1038	1352
Gwalior .... d.	2218	0115	|	|	0632	|	1157	1157	1520
Agra Cantonment..... d.	0016	0305	0405	|	0757	|	1405	1405	1712
Mathura Junction ..... d.	0117	0402	|	|	|	|	1500	1500	1805
Delhi H Nizamuddin. a.	0347	0620	0655	0655	1025	1300	1710	1710	2022

A – ②③⑤⑥ Runs as **22686** on ②⑥.
B – ③④⑤⑦ Runs as **22685** on ④⑦.
d – Mumbai Dadar.
h – Mumbai CST.
n – New Delhi.
▽ – Via Kota and Vadodara, see Table **5130**.

5170 LUCKNOW - PUNE and MUMBAI

Indian Railways

km		Exp 11016	Exp 12541	Exp 12144 ②	Exp 12174 ②④	Exp 12104 ⑦	Exp 15101 ③	Exp 12597 ②	Exp 12533	Exp 15029 ④	Exp 12108 ②④⑦
0	**Lucknow** Junction..... d.	0040	0355	0235	0550	0630	0630	1335	1945	2240	2245
72	Kanpur Central .... d.	0225	0535	0425	0800	0800	0800	1515	2132	0040	0020
292	Jhansi........................ d.	0715	0942	1020	1200	1200	1155	1905	0142	0437	0345
445	Bina........................... d.	0950	|	1250	|	1410	|	|	|	0710	|
583	Bhopal....................... d.	1200	1345	1445	1635	1635	1630	2320	0605	0935	0820
674	Itarsi .... d.	1355	1525	|	|	1820	1820	0100	0745	1205	|
858	Khandwa .... d.	1720	1810	1850	|	2105	2105	|	1030	1450	|
981	Bhusaval .... d.	1920	1955	2035	2255	2255	2255	0535	1220	1700	1450
1166	Manmad .... d.	2220	|	2245	|	0115	0110	|	1419	1940	|
1402	Daund .... d.	|	|	|	|	0620	|	|	|	|	|
1477	**Pune**......................... a.	|	|	|	|	0805	|	|	|	0405	|
1372	Kalyan........................ d.	0315	|	|	0455	...	|	1100	1845	...	2135
1409	**Mumbai** LTT .... a.	0420	0400	0410	0600	...	0615h	1215h	2005h	...	2235

	Exp 12534	Exp 12542	Exp 15030 ⑥	Exp 12598 ③	Exp 15102 ⑤	Exp 12173 ②⑦	Exp 12107 ①③⑥	Exp 12103 ⑤	Exp 12143 ⑦
Mumbai LTT............ d.	0820h	1110	...	1420	1535h	1625	1625	...	1640
Kalyan .... d.	0913	|	...	1510	1633	1710	1710	...	|
Pune......................... d.	|	|	1045	|	|	|	|	1615	|
Daund .... d.	|	|	|	|	|	|	|	1745	|
Manmad .... d.	1245	|	1725	|	2015	|	|	2155	2145
Bhusaval.................... d.	1510	1750	2020	2055	2230	2240	2240	0025	0025
Khandwa..................... d.	1715	2105	2345	|	0235	|	|	0220	0235
Itarsi .... d.	1930	2335	0225	0135	0515	|	|	0505	|
Bhopal .... d.	2105	0115	0430	0330	0720	0505	0505	0655	0720
Bina........................... d.	|	|	0645	|	|	|	|	0900	0940
Jhansi........................ d.	0210	0527	0855	0735	1225	0925	0925	1112	1225
Kanpur Central.......... d.	0700	0955	1445	1140	1715	1335	1350	1545	1545
Lucknow Junction ... a.	0840	1125	1615	1315	1905	1455	1510	1710	1715

h – Mumbai CST.

5180 MUGHAL SARAI, VARANASI and ALLAHABAD - MUMBAI

Indian Railways

km		Exp 11062 A	Exp 22104 ③	Exp 15267 ⑦	Exp 12545 ⑤	Exp 12361 ①	Exp 19050 ④	Exp 12321	Exp 13201	Exp 18609 ④	Exp 12168	Exp 11094	Duro 12294 ②⑥	Exp 12142	Exp 11060 ①④⑥	Exp 11056 E	Exp 15018	Exp 12335 ②⑤⑦	Exp 15646 ①④	Exp 15648 ③	Exp 11070 ①③Z	Exp 11068 ④⑦	Exp 12166 ②⑤⑥
	Mughal Sarai.................. d.	...	...	...	0532	0532	0307	0827	0422	0700	...	...	...	1450	...	...	...	1755	1755	1755	...	...	...
	Varanasi...................... d.	2320	...	0345	|	|	|	|	|	0800	1025	1120	...	|	...	...	1115	|	|	|	...	...	2020
0	**Allahabad** Junction .... d.	0305	0703	0745	|	|	|	1142	|	1220	|	|	1930	|	1710	1710	1630	|	|	|	1615	2108	2330
103	Manikpur .... d.	0510	0858	|	|	|	|	1335	1050	|	1430	1710	|	|	|	|	1832	|	|	|	1800	2300	|
178	Satna................................ d.	0625	1025	1100	1100	1100	0805	1500	1245	1550	|	1855	2220	2020	2040	2040	2000	2310	2310	2310	|	0025	|
278	Katni................................. d.	0825	1135	1220	1220	1220	0920	1620	1350	1705	1725	1950	|	|	|	|	2115	0030	0030	0030	|	0140	0225
369	Jabalpur .... d.	0950	1305	1400	1400	1400	1110	1755	1520	1930	1855	2120	|	2310	2320	2320	2340	0200	0200	0200	|	0315	0500
614	Itarsi................................. d.	1405	1720	|	1810	1810	|	2225	2045	2345	2320	0130	|	|	0350	0350	0430	0720	0720	0720	0800	0800	0905
791	Khandwa .... d.	1700	|	2045	2045	2045	|	0105	0035	0235	0310	0415	|	|	|	|	0820	1005	1005	1005	1130	1130	|
915	Bhusaval .... d.	1900	|	2230	2230	2230	1930	0300	0235	0420	0455	0615	0905	0740	0810	0810	1020	1155	1155	1155	1335	1335	1345
1099	Manmad .... d.	2115	|	|	0050	0050	|	0535	0455	0640	|	0820	|	0955	|	|	1245	1405	1405	1405	1600	1600	1600
1306	Kalyan............................... d.	0235	0400	0455	0455	0455	|	1015	1023	1100	1125	1255	|	1415	1450	1450	1709	1854	1854	1854	2025	2025	2025
1349	**Mumbai** LTT .... a.	0340	0500	0600	0600	0615h	0735b	1125h	1130	1205	1225	1415h	1450	1515	1555	1555	1805	2000	2000	2000	2130	2130	2130

		Exp 12167	Exp 11093	Exp 11067 ③⑥	Exp 12165 ①④⑤	Exp 15017	Exp 11069 ②⑦Y	Exp 12336 ②④⑦	Exp 15645 ③⑥	Exp 15647 ⑤	Exp 11055 B	Exp 12362 ③	Exp 12546 C①④	Exp 11061 F	Exp 11065 ②④⑦	Exp 22103 ①	Duro 12293 ①⑤	Exp 11071 W	Exp 19049 ①	Exp 15268 ②	Exp 18610 ⑥	Exp 12322	Exp 12141
Mumbai LTT .... d.	...	0035	0010h	0520	0520	0635	0520	0805	0805	0805	1055	1105h	1120	1215	1215	1430	1725	1240	1545b	1550	1550	2130h	2325
Kalyan................................ d.	...	0123	0115	0608	0608	0722	0608	0840	0840	0840	1138	1200	1200	1300	1300	1507	|	1325	|	1633	1633	2235	0021
Manmad.............................. d.	...	|	0455	0940	0940	1105	0940	1215	1215	1215	|	1550	1550	1630	1630	|	|	1650	|	|	2015	0213	0400
Bhusaval............................. d.	...	0730	0720	1200	1200	1335	1200	1440	1440	1440	1740	1815	1815	1905	1905	|	2305	1920	0420	2230	2230	0435	0620
Khandwa .... d.	...	1015	1000	1420	|	1635	1420	1730	1730	1730	|	2050	2040	2130	2130	|	|	2150	|	0235	0235	0655	|
Itarsi .... d.	...	1315	1250	1710	1710	2120	1700	2010	2010	2010	2230	2315	2315	0025	0025	0130	|	0030	|	|	0520	0940	|
Jabalpur .... d.	...	1640	1620	2050	2050	0105	|	2330	2330	2330	0155	0235	0235	0350	0350	0440	|	|	1245	0850	0850	1320	1425
Katni................................... d.	...	1755	1735	2210	|	0225	|	0045	0045	0045	|	0350	0350	0515	0515	0555	|	1010	1408	1030	1030	1435	|
Satna.................................. d.	...	1945	1930	0010	0010	0400	|	0215	0215	0215	0500	0520	0520	0655	0655	0735	0850	1150	1530	1200	1200	1620	1725
Manikpur............................ d.	...	2212	2155	0145	|	0555	0650	|	|	|	|	|	|	0855	0855	0937	|	1330	|	|	|	1812	|
Allahabad Junction .... a.	...	|	|	0350	0350	0810	0850	|	|	|	0950	|	|	1040	1040	1140	1225	1530	|	1550	1558	2025	|
Varanasi........................... a.	...	0345	0440	...	0705	1240	...	|	|	|	...	|	|	1355	1355	...	...	1925	|	1945	1945	|	|
Mughal Sarai...................... a.	...	...	...	...	...	...	...	0855	0855	0855	...	1215	1215	...	...	...	...	...	2210	...	2040	0002	0040

A – Runs as **11066** on ②④⑥.
B – Runs as **11059** on ②④⑥.
E – ②③⑤⑦. D – ①③⑤⑥.
W – Via Bhopal (d. 0235) and Bina (d. 0535).
X – Via Bina (d. 0535) and Bhopal (d. 0740).
Y – Via Bhopal (d. 1845), Bina (d. 2140) and Jhansi (d. 0030).
Z – Via Jhansi (d. 0030), Bina (d. 0245) and Bhopal (d. 0455).
b – Mumbai Bandra
d – Mumbai Dadar.
h – Mumbai CST.

5190 DELHI - SECUNDERABAD - TIRUPATI and BANGALORE

Indian Railways

km		Exp 12650 A	Exp 12708 ③⑤⑦	Exp 12648 ③	Duro 12286 ①⑤	RDi 12438 ⑦	Exp 12724	RDi 22692 C	RDi 22694 ③④⑦	Duro 12214 ①△	Exp 12722
0	**Delhi** H Nizamuddin .. d.	0640	0715	0835	1545	1555	1725n	2045	2045	2300h	2300
134	Mathura Junction .... d.	|	|	1023	|	|	1925	|	|	|	0100
188	Agra Cantonment....... d.	|	|	1115	|	|	2013	|	|	|	0200
306	Gwalior...................... d.	|	|	1305	|	|	2210	|	|	|	0348
403	Jhansi........................ d.	1215	1355	1445	2027	2043	2352	0120	0120	|	0530
556	Bina........................... d.	|	|	1705	|	|	|	|	|	|	0800
694	Bhopal....................... d.	1615	1750	1905	|	0005	0330	0440	0440	|	1015
786	Itarsi .... d.	|	|	2100	|	|	|	|	|	|	1220
1083	Nagpur .... d.	2220	0015	0150	0520	0535	0950	1010	1010	|	1745
1528	Kazipet .... d.	|	0650	0932	|	1127	1647	1607	1607	|	0140
1660	**Secunderabad** .... a.	|	0915	|	1400	1400	1915	1835	1835	2115	0405
***	**Secunderabad** .... d.	|	0930	|	...	...	...	1850	1850	2130	▬
1666	Kacheguda .... d.	0715	0945	1230	...	...	...	|	|	|	...
1772	Mahabubnagar........... d.	|	1124	1400	...	...	...	|	|	|	*Duro*
1902	Kurnool Town .... d.	1107	1338	1610	...	...	...	|	|	|	**12245**
1951	Raichur .... d.	|	|	|	...	...	...	2310	|	|	①③④
1956	Dhone .... d.	|	1515	1745	...	...	...	|	|	|	⑥⑦
2292	Renigunta.................. d.	|	2102	|	...	...	...	|	|	|	1030
2302	**Tirupati** .... a.	|	2135	|	...	...	...	|	|	|	|
2101	Dharmavaram.............. d.	1520	...	2055	...	...	...	0330	|	|	|
2336*	**Bangalore** City.......... a.	1910y	...	0030y	...	...	...	0640	0640	0755y	1600y

	RDI 22691 D	RDi 22693 ②⑤⑥	Duro 12213 ⑥△	Exp 12723	Exp 12649 B	RDi 12437 ③	Duro 12285 ④⑦	Exp 12647 ⑦	Exp 12707 ①③⑤
Bangalore City........ d.	2000	2000	2340y	...	2200y	...	...	2340y	...
Dharmavaram .... d.	2322	|	|	...	0045	...	...	0245	...
Tirupati................. d.	|	|	|	...	|	...	...	|	0545
Renigunta.............. d.	|	|	|	...	|	...	...	|	0605
Dhone......................... d.	|	|	|	...	|	...	...	0545	1210
Raichur .... d,	0245	|	|	...	|	...	...	|	|
Kurnool Town............ d.	|	|	|	...	0427	...	...	0635	1304
Mahabubnagar........... d.	|	|	|	...	|	...	...	0835	1506
Kacheguda .... d.	|	|	|	...	0830	...	...	1040	1650
Secunderabad .... a.	0735	0735	0855	...	|	...	...	|	1735
Secunderabad .... d.	0750	0750	0910	0650	|	1245	1330	|	1755
Kazipet .... d.	0930	0930	|	0842	|	1447	|	1320	1950
Nagpur....................... d.	1530	1530	|	1555	1715	2045	1815	2110	0210
Itarsi .... d.	|	|	|	|	|	|	|	0145	|
Bhopal .... d.	2130	2130	|	2200	2305	0210	|	0330	0815
Bina........................... d.	|	|	|	|	|	|	|	0525	|
Jhansi........................ d.	0056	0056	|	0220	0300	0531	0550	0745	1210
Gwalior .... d.	|	|	|	0332	|	|	|	0925	|
Agra Cantonment..... d.	|	|	|	0523	|	|	|	1124	|
Mathura Junction ..... d.	|	|	|	0608	|	|	|	1215	|
Delhi H Nizamuddin. a.	0555	0555	0700h	0838	0915	1025	1035	1415	1800

A – ①②④⑥⑦.
B – ①③⑤⑥⑦.
C – ①②⑤⑥.
D – ①③④⑦.
h – Delhi Sarai Rohilla.
n – New Delhi.
y – Bangalore Yesvantpur Junction.
△ – Journey 31 - 32 hours.
* – *2415 Kms* via Raichur.
*** – Secunderabad - Kacheguda : *7 km*.

ian Railways

DELHI - AGRA 5200

	Exp	SDi	Exp	Exp	Exp	Exp	Exp	Exp	Exp	Exp	Exp	Exp	Exp	Exp	Exp	Exp	Exp	Exp	Exp	Exp	Exp	Exp	Exp
	12172	**12002**	**18238**	**12138**	**12148**	**12644**	**12646**	**12782**	**12804**	**12280**	**12642**	**12648**	**12808**	**18508**	**13008**	**12618**	**11078**	**12626**	**18478**	**14624**	**19326**	**12716**	**14310**
	③⑥				④	⑤	②	①	③⑦		①⑥	③	A	①④⑦							④		②③
New Delhi d.	...	0600	...	0515	...	...	...	...	...	...	...	...	...	0810	0700	...	1015	1125	...	1220h	...	1320	...
Delhi Hazrat Nizamuddin d.	0010	|	0440	|	0555	0555	0555	0555	0555	0705	0715	0835	0835	0845	|	0915	|	|	1210	|	1005	|	1340
Mathura Junction d.	|	0724	0700	0740	0801	0801	0801	0801	0801	0858	|	1023	1023	1036	1010	1111	1240	1321	1420	1520	1155	1530	1550
Agra Cantonment a.	0255	0757	0812	0830	0850	0850	0850	0850	0850	0947	1010	1110	1110	1125	1145	1205	1330	1405	1515	1605	1250	1620	1640

	Exp	Exp	Exp	Exp	Exp	Exp	Exp	Exp	Exp	RDi	Exp	Exp	Exp	Exp	Exp	Exp	Exp	Exp	Exp	Exp	Exp	Exp	Exp	Exp
	14318	**12191**	**12780**	**11450**	**16032**	**16318**	**12688**	**16688**	**12550**	**12434**	**12612**	**12190**	**12724**	**12616**	**14212**	**12920**	**12448**	**12156**	**12628**	**11058**	**12622**	**12722**	**12422**	**12486**
	⑤⑥			④	③⑥⑦	②	①⑤	⑤	④	③⑤	①												①	②⑤⑥
Delhi d.	...	1405	...	1415	1415	1415	...	1415	1510f	...	...	...	1725	1840	1735	1915	...	...	2115	2050	2230	...	2345	2345
i Hazrat Nizamuddin d.	1340	1421	1500	1435	1435	1435	1435	1445	|	1555	1555	1605	|	|	1757	|	2010	2055	|	2105	|	2300	|	|
ura Junction d.	1550	1620	1645	1708	1708	|	|	|	|	|	|	1815	1925	2047	2031	2140	2217	|	2303	2343	|	0100	|	0151
Cantonment a.	1640	1710	1730	1812	1812	1812	1812	1840	1840	1800	1800	1910	2010	2135	2205	2225	2315	2320	2347	0040	0100	0155	0225	0240

	Exp	Exp	Exp	Exp	Exp	Exp	Exp	Exp	Exp	Exp	Exp	Exp	Exp	Exp	Exp	Exp	Exp	Exp	Exp	Exp	RDi	Exp	Exp	Exp
	11057	**12721**	**12919**	**22181**	**12447**	**12615**	**14623**	**12779**	**12621**	**12171**	**12155**	**12723**	**12549**	**14211**	**12627**	**14309**	**14317**	**19325**	**12192**	**12611**	**12433**	**12189**	**12715**	**12485**
										②⑤			③			④⑤	①⑦	③		⑦	①⑥			①②⑤
Cantonment d.	0016	0050	0125	0209	0225	0250	0155	0305	0353	0405	0450	0523	0536	0600	0645	0708	0623	0623	0735	0757	0757	0818	0840	0915
ura Junction d.	0117	0137	0216	0255	0311	0350	0242	0402	|	|	|	0608	|	0702	0737	0810	0810	0810	0830	|	|	0920	0930	1010
i Hazrat Nizamuddin a.	0347	0405	0435	0515	0525	0600	|	0620	0642	0655	0800	0838	|	0947	0955	1110	1110	1110	1118	1025	1025	1140	1145	|
Delhi a.	0415	...	0500	...	...	0630	0615h	...	0705	...	...	0905	0929f	1020	1030	...	...	...	1150	...	...	...	1210	1300

	Exp	Exp	Exp	Exp	Exp	Exp	Exp	Exp	Exp	Exp	Exp	Exp	Exp	Exp	Exp	Exp	Exp	Exp	Exp	Exp	Exp	Exp	SDi	Exp
	12421	**12617**	**12625**	**18477**	**12647**	**18507**	**12807**	**12781**	**12643**	**12803**	**12147**	**12645**	**12641**	**13007**	**18237**	**11077**	**16787**	**12687**	**12137**	**16031**	**11449**	**12279**	**12001**	**22403**
	④				②	③⑥⑦	B	⑦	④	②⑥	③	①	⑤⑦				③⑦	⑤		①④⑤	②			④
Cantonment d.	0915	1015	1025	1058	1124	1129	1344	1405	1405	1405	1405	1405	1515	1525	1635	1712	1730	1730	1755	1833	1833	1855	2115	2350
ura Junction d.	|	1105	1115	1157	1215	1215	1435	1500	1500	1500	1500	1500	|	1640	1733	1805	|	|	1845	2000	2000	1946	2150	0037
i Hazrat Nizamuddin a.	|	1315	1321	1440	1415	1415	1645	1710	1710	1710	1710	1710	1800	1913	2005	2022	2040	2040	2051	2215	2215	2205	|	|
Delhi a.	1300	...	1345	...	...	1440	...	...	...	...	...	...	...	1940	...	2045	2140	...	2115	2300	2300	...	2330	0320

①②④⑤⑥.
①③④⑤⑦.

f – Delhi Safdarjang.
h – Delhi Sarai Rohilla.

ian Railways

DELHI - BILASPUR 5205

km		SDi	Exp	Exp	Exp	Exp	Exp	Exp	RDi	Exp
		12002	**18508**	**18478**	**18238**	**12410**	**12550**	**12824**	**12442**	**12920**
			①④⑦			A	④	②⑤⑦	②⑥	
0	**Delhi** Hazrat Nizamuddin d.	0600	0845	1210	0440	1520	1510f	1725	1545n	1915n
135	Mathura Junction d.	0724	1036	1420	0700	1730	|	|	|	2140
189	Agra Cantonment d.	0802	1130	1523	0820	1830	1845	|	|	2230
307	Gwalior d.	0933	1323	1736	1050	2030	|	|	|	0035
404	Jhansi d.	1051	1505	1925	1320	2200	2240	2330	2043	0235
557	Bina d.	|	|	|	1640	0015	|	|	|	0515
632	Saugor d.	|	1847	2330	|	|	0210	0240	|	|
819	Katni Murwara d.	|	2205	0410	|	|	0540	0610	|	|
985	Anupper d.	|	0110	0745	|	|	0835	0900	|	|
	Bhopal d.	1400	|	|	1845	0215	|	|	0005	0740
	Itarsi d.	...	|	|	2115	0400	|	|	|	...
	Nagpur d.	...	|	|	0355	0940	|	|	0545	...
	Gondia d.	...	|	|	0556	1128	|	|	0723	...
	Durg d.	...	|	|	0855	1330	1420↓	1510↓	0930	...
	Raipur Junction d.	...	|	|	0955	1415	1320↓	1415↓	1015	...
1136	**Bilaspur** a.	...	0430	1055	1220	1645	1115	1155	1200	...

	Exp	Exp	Exp	RDi	Exp	Exp	Exp	SDi	Exp
	12409	**12823**	**12549**	**12441**	**18477**	**18507**	**18237**	**12001**	**12919**
	B	①④⑥	②	①④		②⑤⑥			
Bilaspur d.	0555	1450	1450	1400	1545	1905	1415	...	...
Raipur Junction d.	0745	1240↑	1240↑	1540	|	|	1620	...	...
Durg d.	0845	1200↑	1200↑	1635	|	|	1715	...	...
Gondia d.	1039	|	|	1824	|	|	1923	...	...
Nagpur d.	1300	|	|	2045	|	|	2205	...	...
Itarsi d.	1750	|	|	|	|	|	0425	...	...
Bhopal d.	1950	|	|	0210	|	|	0635	1515	1735
Anupper d.	|	1725	1725	|	1840	2140	|	|	|
Katni Murwara d.	|	2045	2045	|	2310	0135	|	|	|
Saugor d.	|	2320	2320	|	0200	0420	|	|	|
Bina d.	2205	|	|	|	|	|	0920	|	1940
Jhansi d.	0050	0240	0240	0531	0640	0810	1220	1840	2157
Gwalior d.	0230	|	|	|	0805	0925	1400	1944	2325
Agra Cantonment d.	0418	|	0536	|	1057	1129	1635	2115	0125
Mathura Junction d.	0510	|	|	|	1157	1215	1733	2150	0216
Delhi Hazrat Nizamuddin a.	0720	0905	0929f	1055n	1440	1415	2005	2330	0435

①②③④⑥.
①③④⑤⑥.

f – Delhi Safdarjang.
n – New Delhi.

ian Railways

DELHI - NAGPUR - TIRUPATI and CHENNAI 5210

	Exp	Exp	Exp	Exp	Exp	Exp	Exp	Exp	Exp	RDi	Duro	RDi	RDi	Exp	Exp	Exp	Exp	Exp	RDi	RDi	Exp	Exp	Exp	Exp	Exp
	12650	**12804**	**12644**	**12646**	**12642**	**12652**	**12708**	**18238**	**12626**	**12442**	**12270**	**12438**	**12434**	**12612**	**12688**	**16318**	**16688**	**12724**	**22692**	**22694**	**16032**	**12616**	**12622**	**12722**	**22404**
	C	③⑦	⑤	②	①⑥	②④	③⑤⑦			②⑥	②⑥	⑦	③⑤	①	①⑤	②	⑤		A	③④⑦	③⑥⑦				⑦
Delhi H Nizamuddin d.	0640	0555	0555	0555	0715	0715	0715	0440	1125n	1545n	1545	1555	1555	1555	1435	1435	1445	1725n	2045	2045	1435	1840n	2230n	2300	2345n
Mathura Junction d.	|	0801	0801	0801	|	|	|	0700	1321	|	|	|	|	|	|	|	|	1925	|	|	1708	2047	|	0100	0138
Agra Cantonment d.	|	0852	0852	0852	1015	|	|	0820	1410	|	|	|	1802	1802	1817	1817	1845	2013	|	|	1817	2140	0103	0200	0230
Gwalior d.	|	1104	1104	1104	|	|	|	1050	1610	|	|	|	1925	1925	2015	2015	2055	2210	|	|	2015	2331	0235	0348	|
Jhansi d.	1215	1245	1245	1245	1355	1355	1355	1320	1752	2043	2032	2043	2043	2043	2145	2145	2240	2352	0120	0120	2145	0107	0412	0530	0555
Bina d.	|	1505	1505	1505	|	|	|	1630	1955	|	|	|	|	|	|	|	|	|	|	|	0110	0320	|	0800	|
Bhopal d.	1615	1710	1710	1710	1750	1750	1750	1845	2145	0005	|	0005	0005	0005	0150	0150	0305	0330	0440	0440	0305	0525	0800	1015	1105
Itarsi d.	|	1900	1900	1900	1935	|	|	2115	2355	|	|	|	|	|	|	0335	0530	|	|	|	0530	0725	0945	1220	1305
Nagpur d.	2210	2325	2325	2325	0015	0015	0015	0330	0410	0530	0520	0525	0535	0535	0840	0840	1045	0940	1000	1000	1045	1230	1430	1735	1845
Balharshah d.	...	0305	0305	0305	0340	|	|	▬	0750	...	0810	...	|	0830	1210	1200	1440	▬	...	...	1440	1605	1735	...	2250
Warangal d.	...	0632	0632	0632	|	|	S	*Exp*	1107	...	|	...	1126	|	1533	1533	1843	*Exp*	...	...	1843	1935	2050	...	0302
Vijayawada d.	...	1105	1040	1040	1050	1050	|	**16115**	1500	...	1430	...	1430	1430	1920	1920	2345	**12867**	...	...	0100	2325	0025	...	0730
Gudur d.	...	...	1512	1512	1505	|	|	...	1920	...	|	...	|	1825	|	2343	0430	②	...	...	0740	0400	|	...	1200
Renigunta a.	...	...	1620	1620	|	|	2100	...	2040	...	|	...	|	|	|	0055	0540		...	...	|	|	|	...	|
Tirupati a.	...	...	1650	1650	|	|	2135	...	2052	...	|	...	|	|	|	0120	0605	0122	...	...	|	|	|	...	|
Chennai Central a.	...	...	...	...	1805e	1805e	...	1810e	...	...	2010	...	2015	2015	0215	...	...	|	...	...	1020	0620	0710	...	1425e
Pondicherry a.	...	...	...	...	...	...	...	2230	...	...	...	...	...	...	...	...	...	0850	...	...	...	...	...	...	1845

	Exp	Exp	RDi	RDi	Exp	Exp	Exp	Exp	RDi	RDi	Exp	Duro	RDi	Exp	Exp	Exp	Exp	Exp	Exp	Exp	Exp	Exp	Exp	Exp	Exp	Exp
	22403	**12868**	**22691**	**22693**	**12615**	**12621**	**12723**	**12649**	**12437**	**12433**	**12611**	**12269**	**12441**	**12625**	**12643**	**12645**	**12803**	**12641**	**12651**	**12707**	**18237**	**16687**	**16317**	**16116**	**12687**	**16031**
	③	③	B	③⑥⑦				D	③	⑤⑦	⑥	①⑤	①④		③	⑦	①⑤	④⑥	②⑦	①③⑤		②	⑥		①④	③④⑦
dicherry d.	0905	1230	...	...	...	...	...	...	...	...	...	...	...	...	...	...	...	...	...	...	...	...	...	0535	...	...
nnai Central d.	1300e	|	...	...	1915	2200	...	...	...	0610	0610	0640	...	...	...	...	...	0905e	0905e	...	...	...	...	0930e	0945	0515
rupati d.	|	1945	...	...	|	|	...	...	...	|	|	|	...	0357	0735	0735	...	|	|	0540	...	0935	0935	...	|	|
enigunta d.	|	...	...	...	|	|	...	...	...	|	|	|	...	0420	0800	0800	...	|	|	0605	...	1000	1000	...	|	|
ur d.	1552	▬	...	...	2132	|	...	...	...	|	0801	|	...	0557	0942	0942	...	|	|	|	...	1140	1140	...	|	0817
awada d.	2020	*Exp*	...	...	0205	0420	...	...	...	1200	1200	1240	...	1015	1435	1435	1435	1610	1610	|	...	1625	1625	...	1655	1450
angal d.	2355	**12721**	...	...	0500	0705	...	...	...	1440	|	|	...	1305	1735	1735	1735	|	|	S	...	1945	1945	...	2035	1800
arshah d.	0420		...	...	0855	1110	...	...	...	|	1800	1815	...	1710	2125	2125	2125	2315	|	|	...	2340	2340	...	0040	2250
pur d.	0745	0915	1530	1530	1225	1420	1555	1715	2045	2045	2045	2105	2045	2025	0030	0030	0030	0210	0210	0210	2205	0255	0255	...	0350	0245
d.	1300	1455	|	|	1720	1843	|	|	|	|	|	|	|	0110	0445	0445	0445	0630	|	|	0425	0730	0730	...	|	0810
oal d.	1455	1650	2130	2130	1930	2020	2200	2305	0210	0210	0210	|	0200	0300	0630	0630	0630	0815	0815	0815	0635	0920	0920	...	0950	1000
d.	|	1905	|	|	2130	|	|	|	|	|	|	|	|	0455	0825	0825	0825	|	|	|	0920	|	|	...	|	1235
nsi d.	1930	2130	0056	0056	2340	0028	0220	0300	0531	0531	0531	0550	0531	0707	1038	1036	1036	1210	1210	1210	1205	1405	1425	...	1412	1455
lior d.	|	2252	|	|	0055	0140	0332	|	|	0632	0632	|	|	0825	1157	1157	1157	|	|	|	1358	1530	1530	...	1535	1620
Cantonment d.	2350	0050	|	|	0250	0353	0523	|	|	0757	0757	|	|	1025	1405	1405	1405	1515	|	|	1608	1730	1730	...	1730	1833
nura Junction d.	0036	0139	|	|	0350	|	0608	|	|	|	|	|	|	1115	1500	1500	1500	|	|	|	1710	|	|	...	|	2000
i H Nizamuddin a.	0320n	0405	0555	0555	0600	0642	0838	0915	1025	1025	1025	1035	1045n	1321	1710	1710	1710	1800	1800	1800	1955	2040	2040	...	2040	2215

①②⑤⑥.
①②④⑤.
①②④⑥⑦.
①②④⑥⑦.

S – Via Secunderabad (Table **5190**).
e – Chennai Egmore.
n – New Delhi.

5220 DELHI, AHMEDABAD and MUMBAI - GOA - MANGALORE - TRIVANDRUM

Indian Railw

km		Exp 22150	Exp 12133	Exp 16333	Exp 16335	Exp 16311	Exp 16348	Exp 10111	Exp 16603	Exp 16630	RDi 12432	Exp 12450	SDi 12051	Exp 10103	Exp 12218	Exp 12484	Exp 22660	Exp 16649	Exp 16345	Exp 19578	Exp 16605	Duro 12284	Exp 12619	Exp 12201
		③⑦	A	④	⑤	③					②③⑦	①⑥			③⑤	⑦	①			⑥⑦		⑥		①⑤
0	**Delhi** Hazrat Nizamuddin d.	...	...	...	...	...	...	...	...	...	1055	0725	...	...	1355	1355	1355	...	...	...	...	2135	...	...
458	Kota Junction d.	...	...	...	...	...	...	...	...	...	1540	1320	...	...	1955	1955	1955	...	...	...	...	0310	...	...
****	**Ahmedabad** d.	...	...	1300	1300	1300	...	...	...	...	|	|	...	...	|	|	|	...	...	0327	...	|	...	...
986	Vadodara Junction d.	...	...	1458	1458	1458	...	...	...	...	2238	2146	...	...	0429	0429	0429	...	...	0517	...	1115	...	...
***	**Mumbai** CST d.	...	2200	|	|	|	...	2305	...	...	|	|	0525**d**	0710	|	|	|	...	1140**t**	|	...	|	1520**t**	1655**t**
1397	Panvel d.	2125	2315	2205	2205	2205	...	0030	...	...	0430	0510	0638	0830	1230	1230	1230	...	1255	1315	...	1800	1625	1810
1678	Ratnagiri d.	0200	0345	0255	0255	0255	...	0530	...	...	0915	0945	1045	1315	|	|	|	...	1900	1945	...	2305	2135	2305
1917	**Madgaon** d.	0555	0715	0740	0740	0740	...	1045	...	...	1242	1445	1405	1845	2105	2220	2220	...	2310	2345	...	0225	0135	0225
2166	Udupi d.	0954	1111	1156	1156	1156	...	...	...	...	1620	...	...	...	0052	0112	0112	...	0302	0402	...	|	0540	0622
2234	**Mangalore** Junction d.	1120	1240	1350	1350	1350	1420**c**	...	1745**c**	1815**c**	1800	...	...	...	0225	0310	0310	0500**c**	0440	0605	0720**c**	0810	0730**c**	0810
2365	Cannanore d.	1320	...	1605	1605	1555	1700	...	2015	2110	1955	...	...	...	0420	0515	0515	0715	0655	0815	0935	|	...	1015
2455	Calicut d.	1445	...	1745	1745	1735	1845	...	2200	2305	2120	...	...	...	0550	0640	0640	0900	0835	0950	1125	1135	...	1140
2541	Shoranur d.	1620	...	1950	1950	1950	2105	...	0001	0120	2245	...	...	...	0805	0825	0820	1120	1035	1145	1400	|	...	1320
2574	Trichur d.	1707	...	2038	2038	2038	2150	...	0045	0203	2330	...	...	...	0836	0908	0908	1200	1121	1223	1447	|	...	1415
2645	**Ernakulam** Town d.	1850**j**	...	2200	2200	2200	2335	...	0225**j**	0330	0055**j**	...	...	...	1020**j**	1105**j**	1035	1345	1310**j**	1400**j**	1625**j**	1520**j**	...	1520
2762	Kayankulam d.	...	...	|	0005	0005	0215	...	0432	0555	|	...	...	...	1222	1255	|	1610	1517	1602	1827	...	...	1755
2789	Quilon d.	...	...	0110	0110	0110	0305	...	0535	0705	0315	...	...	...	1320	1355	1355	1715	1615	1710	1930	...	...	1840
2866	**Trivandrum** Central a.	...	...	0250	0240	0250**k**	0445	...	0715	0905	0455	...	...	...	1445**k**	1515**k**	1515**k**	1830	1755	1815	2100	...	...	2025**k**
2937	Nagercoil a.	...	...	...	0415	...	...	...	...	...	...	...	...	...	...	...	...	2050	...	2008	2315	...	...	...

		Duro 12224	Exp 10104	RDi 12431	Exp 12449	Exp 16312	Exp 16336	Exp 16334	Duro 12283	Exp 16604	Exp 16629	Exp 16347	SDi 12052	Exp 10112	Exp 22149	Exp 12134	Exp 12620	Exp 16606	Exp 16650	Exp 12202	Exp 22659	Exp 12217	Exp 12483	Exp 19577
		③⑦		②④⑤	②③	⑥	②	①	②						②⑤ B					④⑦	⑤	⑥	③	①②
Nagercoil d.	...	...	...	...	...	...	1400	...	...	...	...	...	...	...	...	...	...	0200	0420	...	...	...	...	0920
Trivandrum Central d.	...	...	...	1915	...	1535**k**	1535	1535	...	1925	1845	2040	...	...	...	...	...	0340	0620	0845**k**	0845**k**	0920**k**	0920**k**	1055
Quilon d.	...	...	...	2012	...	1630	1630	1630	...	2030	2000	2150	...	...	...	...	...	0445	0723	0940	0940	1015	1015	1155
Kayankulam d.	...	...	...	|	...	1710	1710	|	...	2112	2048	2242	...	...	...	...	...	0526	0810	1015	|	1100	1100	1230
Ernakulam Town d.	...	2330**j**	...	2235**j**	...	2005	2005	2005	2330**j**	2340**j**	2350	0125	...	...	0515**j**	...	...	0745**j**	1100	1250	1250	1250**j**	1250**j**	1435**j**
Trichur d.	...	|	...	2350	...	2120	2120	2120	|	0053	0135	0255	...	...	0610	...	...	0920	1230	1357	1357	1357	1357	1545
Shoranur d.	...	|	...	0050	...	2230	2230	2230	|	0200	0305	0405	...	...	0720	...	...	1035	1400	1505	1505	1505	1505	1700
Calicut d.	...	0100	...	0205	...	0020	0020	0020	0255	0340	0505	0605	...	...	0855	...	...	1230	1555	1635	1635	1635	1635	1830
Cannanore d.	...	|	...	0325	...	0155	0155	0155	|	0525	0655	0755	...	...	1020	...	...	1415	1740	1805	1805	1805	1805	2000
Mangalore Junction d.	...	0425	...	0530	...	0445	0445	0445	0635	0805**c**	1015**c**	1055**c**	...	...	1225	1355	1435**c**	1715**c**	2040**c**	2025	2025	2025	2025	2215
Udupi d.	...	|	...	0650	...	0622	0622	0622	|	...	...	...	...	...	1350	1459	1558	...	...	2146	2146	2146	2146	2340
Madgaon d.	...	0855	0915	1110	1120	1130	1130	1130	1205	...	...	...	1430	1800	1720	1850	2040	...	...	0130	0130	0130	0130	0400
Ratnagiri d.	...	1245	1410	1330	1510	1615	1615	1615	1655	...	...	...	1750	2305	2045	2220	0030	...	...	0505	|	|	|	0810
Panvel d.	...	|	1930	1810	1955	2125	2125	2125	2220	...	...	...	2150	0410	0230	0250	0515	...	...	1020	1100	1100	1100	1340
Mumbai CST a.	...	1815**t**	2140	|	|	|	|	|	|	...	...	...	2305**d**	0550	...	0425	0635**t**	...	...	1155**t**	|	|	|	|
Vadodara Junction d.	...	...	...	0023	0213	0522	0522	0522	0522	...	...	...	...	...	...	...	...	...	...	...	1820	1820	1820	2115
Ahmedabad a.	...	...	...	|	|	0715	0715	0715	|	...	...	...	...	...	...	...	...	...	...	...	|	|	|	2300
Kota Junction d.	...	...	...	0650	1010	...	...	...	1300	...	...	...	...	...	...	...	...	...	...	...	0300	0300	0300	...
Delhi Hazrat Nizamuddin a.	...	...	...	1240	1720	...	...	...	1940	...	...	...	...	...	...	...	...	...	...	...	1040	1040	1040	...

A – From Pune (d. 1845 ③⑦). B – To Pune (a. 0550 ③⑥). c – Mangalore Central. d – Mumbai Dadar. j – Ernakulam Junction. k – Trivandrum Kochuveli. t – Mumbai Lokmaniya Tilak Terminus. z – Journey time 42 - 44 hours. *** – Mumbai CST - Panvel: *68 km*. **** – Ahmedabad - Vadodara: *100*

5230 MUMBAI - PUNE - KOLHAPUR

Indian Railw

km		Exp 11049	Exp 22105	Exp 12148	Exp 12127	Exp 11007	Exp 11301	Exp 11029	Exp 16331	Exp 17031	Exp 11041	Exp 11009	Exp 11019	Exp 16381	Exp 11046	Exp 12125	Exp 12123	Exp 11023	Exp 17411	Exp 22107	Exp 12701	Exp 12115	Exp 11027
		①		⑤					A						③								
0	**Mumbai** CST d.	...	0540	...	0640	0700	0805	0840	1210	1245	1400	1430	1510	1545	...	1625	1710	1750	2023	2100	2150	2245	2345
54	Kalyan d.	0450	0635	...	|	0755	0900	0935	1308	1340	1500	1530	1608	1640	...	|	|	1850	2123	2153	2240	2345	0040
192	**Pune** a.	0750	0908	0930	0957	1105	1140	1240	1545	1630	1800	1840	1900	1915	1930	1950	2025	2155	0010	0030	0120	0210	0325
471	Miraj d.	1400	...	1505	...	...	...	1910	...	...	...	...	...	...	0215	...	...	0440	0552	...	...	...	...
518	**Kolhapur** a.	1525	...	1620	...	...	...	2025	...	...	...	...	...	...	0335	...	...	0605	0720	...	...	...	...

		Exp 16382	Exp 12702	Exp 12116	Exp 17412	Exp 22108	Exp 11010	Exp 12124	Exp 12126	Exp 11024	Exp 11045	Exp 17032	Exp 11042	Exp 11008	Exp 11302	Exp 11030	Exp 12147	Exp 16332	Exp 12128	Exp 22106	Exp 11050	Exp 11039	Exp 11028
											④						②	B			⑥		
Kolhapur d.	...	...	...	...	2030	...	...	...	...	2250	2345	...	...	...	...	0755	0905	...	...	...	1250	1530	...
Miraj d.	...	...	...	...	2138	...	...	...	...	0005	0045	...	...	...	...	0910	1020	...	...	...	1345	1640	...
Pune d.	...	0050	0115	0310	0335	0415	0605	0715	0750	0700	0725	0910	0935	1530	1555	1545	1555	1640	1755	1835	1950	2305	2340
Kalyan d.	...	0325	0343	0540	0610	0645	0847	|	|	1035	...	1150	1220	1823	1835	1850	...	1930	|	2052	2217	...	0230
Mumbai CST a.	...	0440	0455	0650	0725	0805	0953	1025	1115	1150	...	1305	1335	1935	1950	2015	...	2050	2105	2200	...	...	0345

A – Runs as **16339** on ③④⑤⑦ and as **16351** on ②⑥. B – Runs as **16340** on ②③④⑥ and as **16352** on ①⑤.

5240 MUMBAI - PUNE - HUBLI

Indian Railw

km		Exp 16531	Exp 16533	Exp 16209	Exp 16507	Exp 16505	Exp 11005	Exp 11035	Exp 11021	Exp 12782	Exp 12630	Exp 12780
		②	④	①⑥	⑤⑦	③	①⑤⑦	④	②③⑥	②	A	
0	**Mumbai** Dadar d.	...	...	...	...	...	2130	2130	2130	...	...	...
54	Kalyan d.	0105	0105	0105	0105	0105	2213	2213	2213	...	...	...
192	**Pune** d.	0420	0420	0420	0420	0420	0110	0110	0110	0930	1120	1635
338	Satara d.	0713	0713	0713	0713	0713	0400	0400	0400	1208	|	1920
472	Miraj d.	1035	1035	1035	1035	1035	0655	0655	0655	1500	1645	2230
610	Belgaum d.	1330	1330	1330	1330	1330	0905	0905	0905	1710	1850	0050
661	Londa d.	1417	1417	1417	1417	1417	1000	1000	1000	|	|	0205
731	Dharwad d.	1555	1555	1555	1555	1555	1127	1127	1127	1920	2130	...
751	**Hubli** a.	1645	1645	1700	1700	1700	1230	1230	1230	2015	2210	...

	Exp 12781	Exp 16532	Exp 16534	Exp 16210	Exp 16506	Exp 16508	Exp 11006	Exp 11036	Exp 11022	Exp 12779
	⑥	⑥	①	③⑤	⑦	②④	①③④	⑦	②⑤⑥	
Hubli d.	0440	0635	0635	0635	0635	0635	1515	1515	1515	...
Dharwad d.	0505	0700	0700	0700	0700	0700	1540	1540	1540	...
Londa d.	|	0825	0825	0825	0825	0825	1710	1710	1710	1845
Belgaum d.	0720	0940	0940	0940	0940	0940	1805	1805	1805	1950
Miraj d.	1020	1245	1245	1245	1245	1245	2050	2050	2050	2230
Satara d.	1238	1503	1503	1503	1503	1503	2308	2308	2308	0040
Pune d.	1555	1850	1850	1850	1850	1850	0220	0220	0220	0355
Kalyan d.	...	2127	2140	2127	2127	2140	0450	0450	0450	...
Mumbai Dadar a.	...	...	...	...	...	...	0545	0545	0545	...

A – ③④⑥⑦ Runs as **22686** on ③⑦. B – ②③④⑥ Runs as **22685** on ③⑥.

5245 HUBLI - BANGALORE - MYSORE

Indian Railw

km		Exp 17310	Exp 12726	Exp 12777	Exp 11005	Exp 11021	Exp 11035	SDi 12080	Exp 17315	Exp 16507	Exp 16505	Exp 16209	Exp 16531	Exp 16533	Exp 14806	Exp 12782	Exp 17312	Exp 17314	Exp 16591	Exp 17302	Exp 12630	Exp 16590	Exp 16536
		②⑦		③	①②⑥	③④⑦	⑤		①	⑤⑦	③	①⑥	②	④	⑥	②	④	⑥			A		
0	**Hubli** d.	0220	0600	0645	1240	1240	1240	1400	1440	1710	1710	1710	1655	1655	1820	2025	2025	2025	1820	2115	2220	2245	2300
129	Harihar d.	0445	0800	0850	1445	1445	1445	1555	|	1935	1935	1935	|	|	|	2235	2235	2235	|	2335	|	0045	0105
258	Birur d.	0640	1010	1050	1705	1705	1705	1750	1930	2130	2130	2130	|	|	|	0040	0040	0040	|	0145	|	0250	0320
303	Arsikere d.	0740	1100	1200	1810	1810	1810	1840	2020	2255	2255	2255	**G**	**G**	0007	0135	0135	0135	**G**	0305	|	0350	0425
393	Tumkur d.	0940	1230	1327	1930	1930	|	2000	2140	0110	0110	0110	|	|	|	|	0325	0325	|	|	0445	0530	0625
469	**Bangalore** City a.	1125**y**	1405	1500**y**	2130**y**	2130**y**	|	2125	2310**y**	0315	0315	0315	0445	0445	0315**y**	|	0500**y**	0500**y**	0610	|	0620**y**	0700	0810
614	**Mysore** a.	...	...	...	...	...	2140	...	...	...	...	0600	...	...	...	0455	...	...	0920	0700	...	...	1105

			Exp 12778	SDi 12079	Exp 11006	Exp 11022	Exp 11036	Exp 14805	Exp 12629	Exp 12725	Exp 17309	Exp 16535	Exp 12781	Exp 16589	Exp 16532	Exp 16534	Exp 17311	Exp 17313	Exp 16508	Exp 16210	Exp 16506	Exp 17301	Exp 16592
			⑤		①③④	②⑤⑥	⑦	①	B		②⑦		⑤		⑤	⑦	⑤	⑦	①③	②④	⑥		
Mysore d.	...	...	...	...	...	...	0605	...	...	...	...	1600	2010	...	...	...	...	...	...	1815	...	2230	1840
Bangalore City d.	...	...	0440**y**	0600	0630**y**	0630**y**	|	1030**y**	1345**y**	1300	1430**y**	1900	|	2115	1700	1700	2155**y**	2155**y**	2155	2150	2150	|	2200
Tumkur d.	...	...	|	0705	0732	0732	|	|	1450	1405	1535	2020	|	2227	|	|	2305	2305	2305	2305	2305	|	|
Arsikere d.	...	...	0720	0835	0915	0915	0915	1315	|	1545	1700	2205	2320	0010	**G**	**G**	0050	0050	0050	0050	0050	0145	**G**
Birur d.	...	...	0810	0915	1005	1005	1005	|	|	1632	1750	2250	0005	0100	|	|	0135	0135	0140	0135	0135	0225	|
Harihar d.	...	...	1010	1105	1205	1205	1225	|	|	1845	2005	0110	0210	0310	|	|	0330	0330	0350	0330	0330	0450	|
Hubli a.	...	...	1240	1325	1505	1505	1505	1925	2140	2110	2340	0400	0430	0535	0625	0625	0635	0625	0625	0625	0625	0735	1040

A – ③④⑥⑦ Runs as **22686** on ③⑦. B – ②③④⑥ Runs as **22685** on ③⑥. G – Via Guntakal. y – Bangalore Yesvantpur Junction.

an Railways

VASCO DA GAMA - MADGAON - HUBLI 5248

	Exp 18048 A	Exp 17315 ①	Exp 17312 ④	Exp 12779	Exp 12741 ③	Exp 17310 ②
Vasco Da Gama d.	0710	0900	1430	1510	1905	2045
Madgaon d.	0750	0935	1520	1550	1945	2125
Londa d.	1005	1205	1750	1855	...	2340
Hubli a.	1220	1430	2015	...	...	0210

	Exp 17309 ①③	Exp 17316 ④	Exp 12780	Exp 12742 ②	Exp 17311 ⑦	Exp 18047 A
Hubli d.	2350	2350	...	...	0645	0900
Londa d.	0145	0145	0215	...	0840	1040
Madgaon d.	0520	0520	0545	0820	1200	1400
Vasco Da Gama a.	0600	0600	0630	0855	1300	1505

②④⑤⑦.

an Railways

MUMBAI - PUNE - SECUNDERABAD, BANGALORE and CHENNAI 5250

	Exp 11301	Exp 11017 ⑥	Exp 16331 ①	Exp 16339 A	Exp 16351 ②⑥	Exp 17222 ④⑦	Exp 17031	Exp 11073 ①	Exp 11041	Exp 11019	Exp 16381	Exp 19568 ⑤	Exp 16613 ⑦	Exp 17203 ⑥	Exp 17017 ①③④	Exp 19202 ②	Exp 12163	Exp 12701	Exp 11013	Duro 12219 ③⑥	Exp 11043 ⑤	Exp 11027	SDi 12025 ③–①
Mumbai CST d.	0805	1205t	1210	1210	1210	1225t	1245	1320t	1400	1510	1545	...	...	...	...	...	2030d	2150	2235t	2305t	0015t	2345	...
Kalyan d.	0900	1255	1308	1308	1308	|	1340	1408	1500	1608	1640	1945	1945	1945	1945	1945	2110	2240	2318	|	0100	0040	...
Pune d.	1145	1535	1550	1550	1550	1535	1635	1645	1810	1905	1925	2230	2230	2230	2230	2230	0010	0125	0155	0215	0358	0335	0550
Daund d.	1310	|	1705	1705	1705	|	1815	|	1930	2040	2055	|	2355	2355	2355	2355	|	|	|	|	0530	0510	|
Solapur d.	1615	1945	2025	2025	2025	1945	2225	2120	2325	0025	0055	0300	0300	0300	0300	0300	0405	0535	0635	|	0845	0940	0913
Gulbarga d.	1844	2155	2230	2230	2230	2155	0030	2310	0110	0233	0300	0453	0453	0453	0453	0453	0610	0720	0848	|	1055	1148	1042
Wadi d.	1945	2240	2320	2320	2320	2240	0135	0025	0225	0350	0420	0600	0600	0600	0600	0600	0710	0840	1000	|	1205	1255	1130
Vikarabad d.	|	|	|	|	|	|	0359	|	|	|	|	|	|	0820	|	|	|	1032	|	|	|	|	1245
Secunderbad a.	|	|	|	|	|	0150	0555h	|	|	0745	|	|	|	1030	1030	1030	|	1210h	|	1105	|	|	1420
Raichur d.	2135	0010	0050	0050	0050	...	...	0155	0400	...	0610	0720	0720	...	...	...	0835	...	1130	...	1330	1435	...
Adoni d.	2250	|	0230	0230	0230	...	...	0310	0510	...	0725	0840	0840	...	...	...	0950	...	1250	...	1450	1640	...
Guntakal d.	0010	0210	0400	0400	0400	...	...	0405	0630	...	0840	0950	0950	...	...	...	1110	...	1400	...	1630	1800	...
Gooty d.	0055	0240	0435	0435	0435	...	...	0445	0655	...	0910	|	1030	...	...	...	1135	...	1430	...	1702	1830	...
Anantapur d.	0240	|	0540	0540	|	...	...	|	|	...	|	1155	1155	...	...	...	|	...	1535	...	|	|	...
Dharmavaram d.	0415	|	0650	0655	|	...	...	|	|	...	|	1305	1305	...	...	...	|	...	1655	...	|	|	...
Hindupur d.	0550	|	0820	0820	|	...	...	|	|	...	|	1420	1420	...	...	...	|	...	1820	...	|	|	...
Bangalore City a.	0850	|	1028k	1028k	|	...	...	|	|	...	|	1620k	1620k	...	...	...	|	...	2150	...	|	|	...
Cuddapah d.	...	0500	...	...	0720	...	...	0720	1005	...	1145	...	...	...	...	...	1400	...	...	...	1925	2135	...
Renigunta d.	...	0815	...	...	1050	...	...	1015	1300	...	1435	...	...	...	...	...	1650	...	...	...	2230	0100	...
Tirupati a.	...	|	...	...	...	...	...	|	|	...	1510	...	...	...	...	...	|	...	...	...	|	|	...
Arakkonam d.	...	0920	...	...	...	...	...	1135	1430	...	...	...	...	...	...	...	1755	...	...	...	2340	0225	...
Chennai Central a.	...	1100e	...	...	...	...	...	1310	1630	...	...	...	...	...	...	...	1945e	...	...	...	...	0425	...

		Exp 11018 ①	Exp 11028	Exp 11020	SDi 12026 ③–①	Exp 16382	Exp 12702	Exp 19201 ③	Exp 17018 ①②⑥	Exp 17204 ④	Exp 16614 ⑤	Exp 11044 ⑦	Exp 12164	Exp 19567 ①	Exp 17221 ③⑥	Duro 12220 ②⑤	Exp 17032	Exp 11042	Exp 11014	Exp 11074 ②	Exp 11302	Exp 16332 ⑥	Exp 16340 B	Exp 16352 ④⑦
nai Central d.	...	2215e	2250	...	...	...	...	...	...	...	...	...	0650e	...	...	...	...	1155	...	1515	...	...	...	...
konam d.	...	2343	0005	...	...	...	...	...	...	...	...	0430	|	...	...	...	...	1300	...	1620	...	...	...	...
upati d.	...	|	|	...	...	0320	...	...	...	...	...	|	|	...	...	...	...	|	...	|	...	...	...	...
gunta d.	...	0135	0205	...	...	0350	...	...	...	...	...	0720	0925	...	...	...	...	1430	...	1810	...	...	...	2200
apah d.	...	0335	0425	...	...	0600	...	...	...	...	...	0930	1125	...	...	...	...	1640	...	2017	...	...	...	0015
ngalore City d.	...	|	|	...	...	|	...	...	...	...	0720k	|	|	1115k	...	...	...	|	1600	|	2045	2130k	2130k	|
dupur d.	...	|	|	...	...	|	...	...	...	...	0930	|	|	1305	...	...	...	|	1810	|	2235	2330	2330	|
armavaram d.	...	|	|	...	...	|	...	...	...	...	1145	|	|	1435	...	...	...	|	2020	|	0025	0125	0125	|
antapur d.	...	|	|	...	...	|	...	...	...	...	1220	|	|	1500	...	...	...	|	2055	|	0110	0215	0215	|
y d.	...	0615	0800	...	...	0900	...	...	...	...	1320	1215	1355	|	...	...	...	1930	2210	2232	0250	0345	0345	0345
akal d.	...	0735	0850	...	...	1015	...	...	...	...	1420	1315	1500	1715	...	...	...	2025	2245	2305	0320	0420	0420	0420
i d.	...	|	0935	...	...	1120	...	...	...	...	1500	1400	1540	1802	...	...	...	2105	2325	2355	0410	0500	0500	0500
hur d.	...	0930	1105	...	...	1250	...	...	...	...	1610	1505	1650	1915	...	...	...	2220	0030	0105	0540	0630	0630	0630
cunderabad d.	...	|	|	1145	1445	|	1445h	1500	1500	1500	|	|	|	|	2025	2305	2040h	|	|	|	|	|	|	|
arabad d.	...	|	|	|	1541	|	1602	|	|	1619	|	|	|	|	|	|	2205	|	|	|	|	|	|	|
d.	...	1220	1500	1610	1722	1740	1805	1845	1845	1845	1845	1845	1910	2145	0035	|	0050	0145	0305	0405	0800	0905	0905	0905
arga d.	...	1255	1545	1645	1756	1812	1845	1925	1925	1925	1925	1925	1950	2230	0111	|	0130	0225	0343	0440	0845	0943	0943	0943
pur d.	...	1500	1820	1855	1940	2015	2100	2125	2125	2125	2125	2125	2200	0015	0310	|	0350	0440	0600	0650	1120	1150	1150	1150
d d.	...	|	2155	2230	|	2320	|	0030	0030	0030	0030	0030	|	|	|	|	0735	0805	0930	|	1425	1510	1510	1510
e d.	...	1955	2340	2350	2310	0050	0115	0205	0205	0205	0205	0205	0235	0505	0755	0757	0910	0935	1045	1200	1555	1640	1640	1640
an d.	...	2230	0230	0240	...	0325	0343	0437	0437	0437	0437	0440	0500	0747	|	|	1150	1220	1315	1505	1835	1930	1930	1930
bai CST a.	...	2345t	0345	0355	...	0440	0455	...	...	...	...	0545	0600d	...	1105	1105t	1305	1335	1430t	1620	1950	2050	2050	2050

③④⑤⑦.   B – ①②③⑤.   d – Mumbai Dadar.   e – Chennai Egmore.   h – Hyderabad Decan.   k – Bangalore Krishnarajapuram.   t – Mumbai Lokmaniya Tilak Terminus.

an Railways

HYDERABAD - SECUNDERABAD - TIRUPATI and CHENNAI 5260

	Exp 17406	Exp 18646	Exp 17230	Exp 12839	Exp 12704	Exp 12604	Exp 12734	Exp 12764 ④–①	Exp 12760	Exp 12710
Hyderabad Decan d.	...	0950	1125	...	...	1650	...	...	1830	...
Secunderabad d.	0605	1020	1155	...	1555	1715	1805	1830	1855	2255
Guntur d.	|	|	1720	...	2030	2225	2310	|	|	|
Kazipet d.	0820	1240	|	...	|	|	|	2020	2055	0050
Vijayawada d.	1315	1630	|	2040	2125	|	|	0040	0110	0435
Tenali d.	1400	...	1810	2115	...	2312	0002	0108	0138	0502
Gudur d.	1930	...	2225	0125	...	0320	0415	0510	0540	0920
Renigunta d.	2045	...	2355	|	...	|	0532	0632	|	...
Tirupati a.	2125	...	0010	|	...	|	0605	0700	|	...
Chennai Central a.	...	...	...	0345	...	0555	...	...	0815	...

	Exp 12603	Exp 12763 B	Exp 12733	Exp 12759	Exp 12709	Exp 12703	Exp 12840	Exp 17229	Exp 18645	Exp 17405
Chennai Central d.	1645	...	...	1810	...	...	2345	...	...	...
Tirupati d.	|	1700	1825	|	...	...	|	0035	...	0525
Renigunta d.	|	1717	1842	|	...	...	|	0100	...	0542
Gudur d.	1918	1857	2017	2045	2210	...	0152	0247	...	0742
Tenali d.	2317	2208	0010	0015	0137	...	0516	0644	...	1150
Vijayawada d.	|	2335	|	0120	0250	0335	0625	|	1135	1330
Kazipet d.	|	0250	|	0442	0605	|	...	|	1445	1720
Guntur d.	0015	|	0105	|	|	0430	...	0735	|	|
Secunderabad a.	0515	0550	0625	0715	0835	0935	...	1310	1800	2040
Hyderabad Decan a.	0545	...	...	0800	...	...	...	1340	1830	...

①②⑤⑥⑦.   * – *311 km* via Guntur.

an Railways

MUMBAI and PUNE - KOLKATA 5270

	Exp 12859	Exp 12869 ⑦	Duro 12261 C	Duro 12221 ①⑥	Exp 22511 ③	Duro 12289	Exp 12101 A	Exp 12129	Exp 12809	Exp 18029
Mumbai CST d.	0600	1105	1715	...	1130t	2015	2035t	...	2035	2200t
Kalyan d.	0655	1200	|	...	1210	|	2118	...	2134	2250
Pune d.	|	|	|	1515	|	|	|	1825	|	|
Manmad d.	|	|	|	|	1620	|	|	0035	0115	0245
Jalgaon d.	1200	|	|	2033	|	|	|	0235	0310	0440
Bhusaval d.	1250	1815	2305	2255	1845	0205	0300	0330	0350	0515
Akola d.	1445	2010	|	|	2040	|	0450	0525	0610	0745
Badnera d.	1615	2205	|	|	|	|	0645	0700	0745	0945
Wardha d.	1722	|	|	|	|	|	|	0840	0918	1120
Nagpur d.	1905	0145	0415	0415	0145	0720	1000	1020	1125	1330
Gondia d.	2048	0323	|	|	0323	...	1138	1208	1316	1555
Durg d.	2250	0525	|	|	|	...	1343	1410	1530	1835
Raipur Junction d.	2335	0610	|	|	0610	...	1430	1455	1615	1935
Bilaspur d.	0130	0810	1005	1005	0820	...	1625	1650	1815	2225
Jharsuguda d.	0427	1107	|	|	1152	...	|	1947	2140	0200
Raurkela d.	0550	1237	|	|	1325	...	2056	2117	2311	0335
Tatanagar d.	0830	1500	1600	1605	1635	...	2327	2345	0140	0700
Kharagpur d.	1025	1655	|	|	1927	...	0130	0147	0340	0930
Kolkata Howrah a.	1230	1930	1940‡	1940‡	2130	...	0335	0350	0550	1225h

	Duro 12262 D	Duro 12222 ④⑥	Exp 12860	Exp 22512 ⑦	Exp 12870 ⑤	Exp 18030	Exp 12810	Exp 12130	Exp 12102 B	Duro 12290
Kolkata Howrah d.	0820	0820	1350	1435	1435	1500h	2015	2150	2250	...
Kharagpur d.	|	|	1535	1625	1620	1745	2200	2335	0035	...
Tatanagar d.	1145	1145	1732	1815	1815	2005	2352	0132	0230	...
Raurkela d.	|	|	2003	2050	2050	2310	0224	0405	0457	...
Jharsuguda d.	|	|	2143	2220	2220	0055	0400	0552	|	...
Bilaspur d.	1745	1745	0045	0125	0125	0445	0725	0915	0940	...
Raipur Junction d.	|	|	0225	0310	0310	0645	0910	1055	1130	...
Durg d.	|	|	0325	|	0410	0755	1005	1145	1225	...
Gondia d.	|	|	0515	0600	0600	1015	1200	1339	1415	...
Nagpur d.	2325	2325	0730	0830	0830	1340	1420	1550	1630	2040
Wardha d.	|	|	0835	|	|	1505	1533	1646	|	|
Badnera d.	|	|	1015	|	1125	1700	1743	1825	1910	|
Akola d.	|	|	1115	1224	1224	1805	1845	1925	2005	|
Bhusaval d.	0347	0347	1320	1425	1425	2045	2115	2130	2200	0125
Jalgaon d.	|	|	1340	|	|	2110	2140	2155	|	|
Manmad d.	|	0558	|	1630	|	2315	2340	2355	|	|
Pune a.	|	1145‡	|	|	|	|	|	0650	|	|
Kalyan d.	|	...	2005	2205	2205	0350	0410	...	0440	|
Mumbai CST a.	1030‡	...	2120	2315	2315	0450t	0520	...	0545t	0755

①②⑤⑥.   C – ②③④⑦.   h – Kolkata Shalimar.   * – *314 km* from Manmad.

①③④⑦.   D – ①②③⑤.   t – Mumbai Lokmaniya Tilak Terminus.   ‡ – Next day (more than 24 hours after previous time).

5280 KOLKATA - PURI, SECUNDERABAD, TIRUPATI and CHENNAI

Indian Railw

km		Exp	Exp	Exp	Exp	Duro	Exp	Exp	Duro	Exp	Exp	SDi	SDi	Exp	Exp	Duro	Exp	Exp	Exp	Exp	Exp	Exp	Exp	Exp	Exp
		12514	**12508**	**12510**	**12821**	**22203**	**12703**	**11020**	**12245**	**18645**	**22825**	**12073**	**12277**	**12841**	**12663**	**22201**	**18409**	**12863**	**12881**	**12837**	**22642**	**12660**	**15228**	**15644**	**12867**
		⑤	⑥	**A**		②④⑦	**G**		ex①④		②	①–⑥	④–②		**C**	①③⑤			**E**		②⑦	③	①	⑤	⑦
0	**Kolkata** Howrah d.	0105	0105	0105	0600	...	0725	...	1100	1145	1210**h**	1325	1425	1450	1610	2000**d**	1900	2035	2055	2235	2300**h**	2300**h**	2315	2315	2330
116	Kharagpur d.	0300	0300	0300	0745	...	0910	...	|	1352	1405	1515	1615	1635	1800	2220	2055	2230	2250	0025	0145	0145	0145	0115	0115
232	Balasore d.	0427	0427	0427	0930	...	1037	...	|	1550	1540	1644	1743	1805	1927	|	2305	2357	0027	0155	0325	0325	0325	|	0242
409	Cuttack d.	0705	0705	0705	1210	...	1310	...	|	1900	1810	1920	1953	2045	|	|	0159	0235	0320	0435	0600	0600	0600	0515	|
437	Bhubaneswar d.	0755	0755	0755	1250	...	1355	1525	1700	1950	1900	2010	2040	2130	2250	|	0250	0320	0400	0520	0640	0640	0640	0600	0600
456	Khurda Road d.	0840	0840	0840	1325	...	1445	1555	|	2040	1945	...	|	2210	2330	|	0325	0405	0440	0555	0730	0730	0730	0640	0650
500	**Puri** a.	|	|	|	1425	...	|	|	|	|	|	...	2200	|	|	0400	0435	|	0555	0710	|	|	|	0740	|
819	Vizianagram d.	1400	1400	1400	...	...	2005	2115	2205	0240	0120	...	...	|	0435	...	...	0915	...	...	1300	1300	1300	...	1137
879	Visakhapatanam d.	1550	1550	1550	...	1945	2130	2245	|	0415	0245	...	...	0440	0555	...	...	1100	...	...	1430	1430	1430	...	1255
1081	Rajahmundry d.	1852	1855	1855	...	|	0031	0150	|	0812	0554	...	...	0733	0852	...	...	1357	...	...	1750	1750	1750	...	|
1259	Vijayawada d.	2155	2155	2155	...	0044	0335	0525	0435	1135	0850	...	...	1035	1155	...	...	1700	...	...	2055	2055	2055	...	1905
1574	**Secunderabad** a.	0420	|	|	...	0610	0935	1135	|	1800	|	...	...	|	|	...	...	|	...	...	|	|	|	...	|
1637	Renigunta d.	...	|	|	...	...	...	...	1025	...	|	...	...	|	|	...	...	2305	...	...	|	0310	|	...	0105
1647	**Tirupati** a.	...	|	|	...	...	...	...	...	...	|	...	...	|	|	...	...	2320	...	...	|	0325	|	...	0120
1691	**Chennai** Central a.	...	0430	0430	...	...	...	...	...	...	1700	...	...	1720	1955**e**	...	...	...	...	...	0355	...	0355	...	...

	Exp	Duro	Exp	Exp	Exp	Exp	Exp	Exp	Exp	Exp	Exp	Exp	SDi	SDi	Exp	Exp	Exp	Exp	Duro	Exp	Exp	Duro	Exp	Exp
	12664	**22202**	**12840**	**12838**	**12864**	**12882**	**15643**	**18410**	**12509**	**12513**	**11019**	**12842**	**12074**	**12278**	**12659**	**22641**	**12507**	**15227**	**12246**	**18646**	**12704**	**22204**	**12822**	**22826**
	D	②④⑥				**F**	⑥		**B**	⑦			①–⑥	④–②	①	⑤⑦	③	④	ex③⑥		**G**	①③⑥		④
Chennai Central d.	2230**e**	...	2345	...	...	...	...	...	0630	...	...	0845	...	...	...	1000	1000	1000	...	...	...	...	...	1625
Tirupati d.	|	...	|	...	0235	...	...	...	|	...	...	|	...	...	0935	|	|	|	...	...	...	...	...	|
Renigunta d.	|	...	|	...	0300	...	...	...	|	...	...	|	...	...	1000	|	|	|	1655	...	...	...	...	|
Secunderabad d.	|	...	|	...	|	...	...	...	|	0730	0800	|	...	...	|	|	|	|	|	1020	1555	2015	...	|
Vijayawada d.	0540	...	0640	...	0940	...	...	...	1320	1320	1420	1525	...	...	1620	1700	1700	1700	2235	1650	2140	0125	...	2345
Rajahmundry d.	0753	...	0914	...	1205	...	...	...	1529	1527	1641	1737	...	...	1845	1912	1912	1912	|	1927	0003	|	...	0203
Visakhapatanam d.	1205	...	1325	...	1615	...	...	...	1935	1935	2120	2210	...	...	2310	2310	2310	2310	|	2355	0350	0635	...	0635
Vizianagram d.	1304	...	1430	...	1715	...	...	...	2038	2038	2220	|	...	...	0010	0010	0010	0010	0445	0112	0455	...	...	0745
Puri d.	|	1945	|	2000	|	2215	2215	2230	|	|	|	|	...	0600	|	|	|	|	|	|	|	...	1140	|
Khurda Road d.	1825	|	2010	2120	2230	2315	2315	2330	0210	0210	0355	0415	...	|	0540	0540	0540	0540	|	0645	1020	...	1235	1340
Bhubaneswar d.	1850	|	2040	2147	2255	2340	2340	2355	0235	0235	0425	0445	0600	0705	0615	0615	0615	0615	1015	0710	1045	...	1300	1405
Cuttack d.	|	|	2120	2230	2330	0025	0025	0045	0315	0315	...	0525	0632	0730	0650	0650	0650	0650	|	0745	1120	...	1335	1445
Balasore d.	2248	|	0014	0105	0217	0250	|	0337	0622	0622	...	0806	0904	1001	0943	0943	|	0943	|	1143	1352	...	1621	1732
Kharagpur d.	0100	0117	0152	0240	0355	0445	0445	0600	0830	0830	...	0948	1050	1145	1135	1135	1135	1135	|	1347	1530	...	1808	1930
Kolkata Howrah a.	0320	0400**d**	0410	0450	0610	0705	0705	0810	1055	1055	...	1150	1240	1340	1350**h**	1350**h**	1355	1355	1610	1615	1745	...	2015	2130**h**

A – ①②③④. Runs as **12516** on ④. C – ①④⑦. Runs as **12665** on ①. E – ①②④⑤. Runs as **12887** on ①, **12895** on ⑤. G – See Table **5260**. e – Chennai Egm
B – ①④⑤⑥. Runs as **12515** on ①. D – ②⑤⑥. Runs as **12666** on ⑥. F – ①③④⑦. Runs as **12896** on ④, **12888** on ⑦. d – Kolkata Sealdah. h – Kolkata Shalim

5290 CHENNAI - BANGALORE - MYSORE

Indian Railw

km		Exp	Exp	SDi	Exp	Exp	Exp	Exp	Exp	Exp	Exp	Exp	Exp	Exp	SDi	Exp	Exp	Exp	Exp	Exp		Exp	Exp
		15228	**12510**	**12007**	**22625**	**12639**	**12614**	**12552**	**12609**	**12296**	**17311**	**17313**	**12577**	**12607**	**12027**	**16209**	**16021**	**12657**	**12691**	**22682**		**12292**	**16591**
		③	②③④	④–②				⑤			⑤	⑦	④		③–①	②⑦			⑤	④		⑥	
0	**Chennai** Central d.	0415	0455	0600	0725	0750	...	1140	1335	1355	1345	1350	1445	1535	1730	...	2100	2315	2330	2330	...	2330	...
68	Arakkonam d.	0525	0600	|	0830	0855	...	|	1440	1505	1450	1450	1540	1640	|	...	2205	0015	0030	0030	...	0028	...
130	Katpadi d.	0625	0655	|	0920	0955	...	1345	1545	1600	1555	1555	1630	1745	1905	...	2325	0110	0125	0120	...	|	...
214	Jolarpettai d.	0740	0820	|	1035	1107	...	1515	1708	1730	1745	1745	1755	1855	|	...	0042	0225	0245	0240	...	0245	...
350	Krishnarajapuram d.	1000	1040	|	1220	1250	...	|	1915	1935	2010	2010	|	2045	|	...	0240	|	0445	0445	...	0445	...
361	**Bangalore** City a.	1150**y**	1150**z**	1050	1310	1400	1500	1830**y**	2005	2020	2135**y**	2135**y**	2040	2135	2230	0330	0345	0510	0525	0525	...	0600**y**	0630
506	**Mysore** a.	...	...	1300	...	...	1730	...	...	...	...	...	2330	...	...	0600	0650	...	...	0820	...	...	0920

		SDi	Exp	Exp	Exp	Exp	Exp	Exp	Exp	Exp	Exp	Exp	SDi	Exp	Exp	Exp	Exp	Exp	Exp	Exp	Exp	Exp	Exp
		12028	**17312**	**17314**	**12608**	**12610**	**12251**	**12295**	**12578**	**12613**	**22626**	**12640**	**12008**	**16535**	**16210**	**16592**	**12658**	**12291**	**12692**	**22681**	**12509**	**16022**	**15227**
		③–①	⑤	⑦			⑥		⑥				④–②		②④			⑤	⑦	③	③④⑤		③
Mysore d.	...	...	...	...	...	...	...	...	0720	1115	...	...	1415	1600	1815	1840	...	...	...	2010	...	2030	...
Bangalore City d.	...	0600	0530**y**	0530**y**	0630	0800	0830**y**	0900	1010	1345	1430	1500	1625	1850	2130	2150	2240	2245**y**	2300	2300	2330**z**	2345	2355**y**
Krishnarajapuram d.	...	|	0610	0610	0653	0823	|	0923	|	...	1453	1523	|	...	...	...	|	2323	2323	2323	2353	0010	0035
Jolarpettai d.	...	|	0825	0825	0845	1030	1115	1130	1230	...	1645	1715	|	...	...	...	0100	0132	0132	0132	0210	0255	0425
Katpadi d.	...	0900	0930	0930	0950	1150	1235	1240	1340	...	1800	1830	|	...	...	...	0210	|	0245	0245	0320	0410	0710
Arakkonam d.	...	|	1025	1025	1045	1300	|	1335	1430	...	1855	1925	|	...	...	...	0300	0340	0340	0340	0410	0510	0805
Chennai Central a.	...	1100	1155	1155	1215	1430	1535	1505	1555	...	2030	2105	2125	...	...	...	0440	0515	0515	0515	0605	0700	0930

5300 CHENNAI and BANGALORE - TRIVANDRUM

Indian Railw

km		Exp	Exp	SDi	Exp	Exp	Exp	Exp	Exp	Exp	Exp	Exp	Exp	Exp	Exp	Exp	Exp	Exp	Exp	Exp	Exp	Exp	Exp	Exp
		22642	**12516**	**12243**	**22619**	**16331**	**22207**	**15906**	**12697**	**12777**	**12695**	**16315**	**16381**	**12644**	**12646**	**12623**	**12257**	**16526**	**12626**	**22645**	**12511**	**22647**	**17230**	**16318**
		②④	⑤⑦**A**	③–①	③	②	②⑤	②	⑦	③				⑥	③		②④⑦			②	①⑤⑥	④⑦		④
0	**Chennai** Central d.	0415	0445	0715	...	...	1630	...	1515	...	1525	...	...	...	...	1945	...	...	...	2350	2350	2350	...	...
	Tirupati d.	|	|	|	...	...	|	...	|	...	|	...	1515	1655	1655	|	...	...	2054	|	|	|	0015	0122
130	Katpadi d.	0625	0655	|	1135	...	|	1610	1705	...	1720	...	1800	1922	1922	2130	...	...	2320	0150	0150	0150	0235	0350
214	Jolarpettai d.	0730	0830	|	|	...	|	1755	1820	...	1840	...	1930	|	2035	|	...	...	0035	0310	0310	0310	0400	0505
	Bangalore City d.	|	|	|	|	...	|	|	|	1520**y**	|	1700	|	|	|	|	2100**y**	2000	|	|	|	|	|	|
	Krishanrajapuram d.	|	|	|	|	1030	|	|	|	|	|	1725	|	|	|	|	|	2024	|	|	|	|	|	|
	Bangarapet d.	|	|	|	|	1205	|	|	|	1640	|	1810	|	|	|	|	|	2125	|	|	|	|	|	|
335	Salem Junction d.	0905	0955	1125	1420	1540	|	1940	1950	1930	2015	2115	2105	2210	2210	0010	0120	0025	0215	0445	0445	0445	0535	0640
394	Erode Junction d.	1020	1120	1225	1540	1700	|	2040	2050	2030	2125	2230	2210	2320	2320	0110	0220	0130	0320	0610	0610	0610	0705	0815
494	Coimbatore Junction d.	1200	1325	1415	1720	1850	|	2235	|	|	2310	0015	2350	0120	0120	0250	0415	0315	0510	0745	0745	0745	0845	1000
548	Palghat Junction d.	1310	1440	...	1830	2010	|	2355	2330	2330	0030	0135	0115	0235	0235	0405	0535	0435	0625	0900	0900	0900	0950	1110
626	Trichur d.	1430	1607	...	1948	2130	|	0110	0040	0040	0145	0253	0240	0400	0400	0518	0655	0550	0740	1050	1050	1050	1148	1238
697	Ernakulam Town d.	1605**j**	1735	...	2125**j**	2305**j**	0200**j**	0230	0205	0205	0300	0430**j**	0450	0545**j**	0600**j**	0655	0825	0730	0945**j**	1217	1217	1230	1315	1405
814	Kayankulam d.	1820	1950	...	2322	0050	|	|	|	|	0510	0632	0735	0830	...	0905	1037	1000	1217	1445	1445	1445	1550	1622
842	Quilon d.	1920	2045	...	0015	0150	0420	0525	0505	0505	0610	0725	0845	0920	...	1000	1125	1100	1305	1550	1550	1550	1650	1725
919	**Trivandrum** Central a.	2045	2235	...	0120	0320	0545	0705	0635	0630**k**	0735	0900**k**	1005	1100	...	1145	1300**k**	1240	1435	1715	1715	1715	1820	1845
	Nagercoil a.	...	...	...	0243	...	...	0920	...	...	...	...	1101	...	...	...	...	1425	...	...	...	...	...	2040

km		Exp	Exp	Exp	SDi	Exp	Exp	Exp	Exp	Exp	Exp	Exp	Exp	Exp	Exp	Exp	Exp	Exp	Exp	Exp	Exp	Exp	Exp	Exp
		15905	**22620**	**16332**	**12244**	**22646**	**22648**	**17229**	**16382**	**12625**	**12778**	**12515**	**16525**	**12645**	**12643**	**12624**	**16316**	**16317**	**12659**	**22641**	**12258**	**12507**	**12696**	**22208**
		⑥	⑦	⑥	③–①	**B**	①④				④	⑦		⑥	②		②④⑥	⑤	⑦	④⑥	①③⑤	②		③⑥
72	Nagercoil d.	2320	0225	...	...	...	...	...	0715	...	...	...	1050	...	...	...	...	1435	1440	...		...	...	...
0	**Trivandrum** Central d.	0045	0425	0425	...	0610	0610	0715	0855	1115	1250**k**	1240	1245	...	1415	1450	1645**k**	1600	1600	1700	1700**k**	1700	1715	2130
77	Quilon d.	0145	0525	0525	...	0710	0710	0820	1005	1215	1340	1340	1405	...	1500	1550	1740	1705	1705	1758	1758	1758	1815	2225
105	Kayankulam d.	|	0602	0602	...	0745	0745	0900	1044	1257	|	1410	1450	...	1547	1630	1816	1736	1736	1836	1836	1836	1853	|
222	Ernakulam Town d.	0530	0815**j**	0815**j**	...	1015**j**	1020	1155	1325	1545**j**	1655	1705	1805	1900**j**	1850**j**	1930	2030**j**	2040	2040	2055**j**	2110	2110	2135	0040**j**
293	Trichur d.	0640	0940	0940	...	1145	1145	1303	1455	1703	1800	1805	1908	2003	2003	2045	2155	2205	2205	2220	2220	2220	2303	|
371	Palghat Junction d.	0815	1215	1215	...	1405	1405	1520	1650	1845	1945	2005	2120	2145	2145	2225	2330	2355	2355	2355	0015	2355	0045	|
425	Coimbatore Junction d.	0935	1335	1335	1520	1525	1525	1635	1805	2000	|	2130	2255	2320	2320	2350	0100	0125	0125	0125	0140	0125	0210	|
525	Erode Junction d.	1110	1520	1520	1645	1715	1715	1830	2000	2200	2250	2315	0040	0055	0055	0120	0245	0330	0315	0305	0315	0305	0350	|
584	Salem Junction d.	1210	1615	1615	1746	1810	1810	1930	2100	2300	2345	0010	0140	0155	0155	0220	0340	0430	0415	0400	0415	0400	0450	|
	Bangarapet d.	|	|	1950	|	|	|	|	|	|	0235	|	0510	|	|	|	0635	|	|	|	|	|	|	|
	Krishnarajapuram d.	|	|	2125	|	|	|	|	|	|	|	|	0620	|	|	|	0735	|	|	|	|	|	|	|
853	**Bangalore** City a.	|	|	...	|	|	|	|	|	|	0430**y**	|	0720	|	|	|	0835	|	|	|	0930**y**	|	|	|
705	Jolarpettai d.	1355	|	...	|	1950	1950	2120	2320	0045	...	0155	...	|	|	|	...	0610	0605	0550	...	0550	0635	|
789	Katpadi d.	1503	1903	...	|	2055	2055	2240	0050	0202	...	0320	...	0530	0530	0500	...	0725	0725	0710	...	0710	0745	|
912	**Tirupati** a.	...	...	...	|	|	|	0030	0315	0355	...	|	...	0730	0730	|	...	0933	0933	|	...	|	|	|
919	**Chennai** Central a.	...	...	...	2215	2305	2305	...	...	...	...	0605	...	...	...	0730	...	...	...	0930	...	0930	1000	1030

Notes for Tables **5290** and **5300**
A – ⑤⑦ Runs as **12516** on ⑤ and as **12508** on ⑦.
B – ②③⑥⑦ Runs as **12512** on ②③⑦ and as **22646** on ⑥.
j – Ernakulam Junction.
k – Trivandrum Kochuveli.
y – Bangalore Yesvantpur Junction.
z – Bangalore Cantonment.

an Railways — CHENNAI - SENGOTTAI, TUTICORIN, TIRUCHENDER and NAGERCOIL — 5310

	12688	56768	16127	56735	12635	12633	16612	16105	12667	12642	12652	56761
	Exp		*Exp*		*Exp*	*Exp*	*Exp*	*Exp*	*Exp*	*Exp*	*Exp*	
	③⑦	2		2					④	②⑦	③⑤	2
Chennai Egmore ...... d.	0240	...	0740	...	1320	1730	...	1605	1850	1830	1830	...
Chengalpattu .... d.	|	...	0840	...	1420	1830	...	1705	1945	1930	1930	...
Villupuram .... d.	A	...	1035	...	1550	2015	...	1905	2115	2120	2120	...
Vriddhachalam Jct ..... d.	|	...	1112	...	1630	2057	...	|	2207	2207	2207	...
Tiruchchirappalli Jct ... d.	|	...	1310	...	1835	2255	...	1953	0035	0035	0035	...
Dindigul .... d.	1115	...	1445	...	2005	0035	0100	0200	0215	0215	0215	...
Madurai Junction .... d.	1245	...	1615	1715	2125	0155	0205	0300	0325	0325	0345	...
Virudunagar .... d.	▬	...	1655	1800	▬	0240	0250	0342	0412	0412	...	...
Tenkasi .... d.	**56765**	...	|	1957	**56741**	|	|	|	|	|	...	...
Sengottai .... a.	2	...	|	2050	2	|	|	|	|	|	...	...
Vanchi Maniyachchi .. d.	...	1720	1840	...	1905	|	0510	0510	|	0530	...	...
Tuticorin .... a.	...	1845	|	...	|	|	0610	|	|	|	...	...
Tirunelveli Junction ... d.	1840	...	1935	...	2040	0455	...	0620	0630	0630	...	0720
Tiruchender .... a.	2040	...	|	...	...	|	...	0825	|	|	...	0910
Nagercoil Junction ... a.	...	...	2125	...	...	0626	...	...	0805	0810	...	...

	12693	16723	12631	12661	12637	12665	56763	22205	56731	56767	16236	22623	56733
	Exp	*Exp*	*Exp*	*Exp*	*Exp*	*Exp*		*Duro*			*Exp*	*Exp*	
						②	2	①③	2	2		⑤⑦	2
Chennai Egmore ...... d.	1915	1935	2010	2055	2120	2020	...	2230**c**	...	...	...	2245	...
Chengalpattu .... d.	2015	2035	2110	2155	2220	2120	...	|	...	...	...	2340	...
Villupuram .... d.	2205	2225	2240	2330	2345	2255	...	C	...	...	...	0120	...
Vriddhachalam Jct ..... d.	2247	2312	2322	0012	0027	2337	...	|	...	...	...	|	...
Tiruchchirappalli Jct ... d.	0055	0200	0210	0240	0305	0320	...	|	...	...	...	0600	...
Dindigul .... d.	0235	0347	0330	0410	0435	0440	...	|	...	...	0615	0730	...
Madurai Junction .... d.	0345	0500	0435	0530	0615	0635	...	0710	0715	...	0725	0850	1125
Virudunagar .... d.	0430	0540	0515	0617	▬	0717	...	...	0802	...	0807	...	1220
Tenkasi .... d.	|	|	|	0817	**56742**	|	...	...	1010	...	|	...	1430
Sengottai .... a.	|	|	|	0905	2	|	...	...	1045	...	|	...	1500
Vanchi Maniyachchi .. d.	0601	0700	|	...	0820	0846	...	...	...	1000	1000	...	...
Tuticorin .... a.	0710	|	|	...	0930	|	...	...	...	|	1115	...	...
Tirunelveli Junction ... d.	...	0825	0800	...	...	0940	0935	...	...	1115	...	...	...
Tiruchender .... a.	...	|	...	...	...	|	1105	...	...	1310	...	...	...
Nagercoil Junction ... a.	...	1005	...	...	...	1055	...	...	...	...	...	...	...

	56734	56736	56768	16235	56741	56764	12668	12662	12634	12632	22206	56766
				Exp			*Exp*	*Exp*	*Exp*	*Exp*	*Duro*	
	2	2	2		2	2	⑤				②④	
rcoil Junction .... d.	...	...	...	...	...	...	1705	...	1740	...	...	...
uchender .... d.	...	...	1435	...	...	1630	|	...	|	...	...	1755
elveli Junction .... d.	...	...	1620	...	...	1810	1820	...	1905	1925	...	1940
icorin .... d.	...	...	|	1635	1750	...	|	...	|	|	...	▬
i Maniyachchi ... d.	...	...	1719	1713	1850	...	|	...	|	|	...	*Exp*
ngottai .... d.	1200	1550	...	|	▬	...	|	1830	|	|	...	**22624**
nkasi .... d.	1215	1604	...	|	*Exp*	...	|	1845	|	|	...	④⑥
unagar .... d.	1430	1807	...	1835	**12638**	...	2017	2042	2105	2120	...	
rai Junction .... d.	1545	1935	...	1950	2035	...	2115	2130	2150	2210	2245	2115
gul .... d.	...	...	...	2115	2140	...	2212	2235	2252	2315	|	2212
chirappalli Jct ... d.	...	...	...	...	2310	...	2355	0020	0035	0105	|	2350
nachalam Jct ..... d.	...	...	...	...	0104	...	0155	0215	0235	0245	D	|
uram .... d.	...	...	...	...	0220	...	0302	0325	0335	0355	|	0410
galpattu .... d.	...	...	...	...	0355	...	0435	0455	0515	0540	|	0600
nai Egmore .... a.	...	...	...	...	0535	...	0605	0640	0650	0710	0720**c**	0720

	12694	16724	12641	12651	12687	16106	16611	12636	56732	16128	56742	56767	56762	12666
	Exp	*Exp*	*Exp*	*Exp*	*Exp*	*Exp*	*Exp*	*Exp*		*Exp*				*Exp*
			③⑤	②⑦	③⑦				2		2	2	2	⑥
rcoil Junction .... d.	...	1755	1940	...	...	...	...	...	...	0525	...	...	...	0815
uchender .... d.	...	|	|	...	...	1850	...	...	...	|	...	...	0705	|
elveli Junction .... d.	...	1950	2115	...	...	2040	...	...	...	0745	0720	...	0855	0940
icorin .... d.	1950	|	|	...	...	|	2130	...	...	|	|	0845	...	|
i Maniyachchi ... d.	2023	2035	2141	...	...	2105	2230	...	...	0835	0818	0950	...	1015
ngottai .... d.	|	|	|	...	...	|	|	...	0700	|	...	...	...	|
nkasi .... d.	|	|	|	...	...	|	|	...	0713	|	...	...	...	|
unagar .... d.	2145	2200	2307	...	...	2222	0005	...	0925	1000	...	...	...	1135
rai Junction .... d.	2250	2305	0015	0015	2335	2345	0105	0700	1045	1115	...	...	...	1250
gul .... d.	2350	0010	0112	0112	0035	0117	0225	0755	...	1218	...	...	...	1350
chirappalli Jct ... d.	0130	0200	0300	0300	|	0330	...	0900	...	1410	...	...	...	1600
nachalam Jct ..... d.	0320	0350	0450	0450	B	|	...	1045	...	1620	...	...	...	1755
uram .... d.	0425	0510	0550	0550	|	0825	...	1142	...	1720	...	...	...	1855
galpattu .... d.	0610	0710	0730	0730	|	1010	...	1320	...	1910	...	...	...	2040
nai Egmore .... a.	0745	0840	0850	0850	0920**c**	1125	...	1440	...	2115	...	...	...	2210

Via Katpadi (d. 0440), Salem (d. 0730) and Erode (d. 0850).
Via Erode (d.0305), Salem (d. 0400) and Katpadi (d. 0705).

C – Via Salem d. 0305.
D – Via Salem d. 0230.

c – Chennai Central.

an Railways — HILL and MOUNTAIN RAILWAYS — 5320

DARJEELING HIMALAYAN RAILWAY

¶	52541	52587		52574	52573	52575	52571	52572	52559
	A				🚂		🚂	🚂	🚂
					⑦		②④⑦	⑥	
New Jalpaiguri Junction ...... d.	0830	...	...	...	...	...	...	...	...
Siliguri Junction .... d.	0930	...	...	...	...	...	...	...	1030
Sukna .... d.	1002	...	...	...	...	...	...	...	1120
Rangtong .... d.	1036	...	...	...	...	...	...	...	1150
Chunbhati .... d.	|	...	...	...	...	...	...	...	...
Tindharia .... d.	1142	...	...	...	...	...	...	...	...
Mahanadi .... d.	1246	...	...	...	1155	...	...	1540	...
Kurseong .... d.	1330	0700	...	...	1235	...	1400	1920	...
Tung .... d.	1404	0734	...	...	...	...	1445	...	...
Sonada .... d.	1442	0811	...	...	...	...	1550	...	...
Ghum .... d.	1530	0900	...	1220	...	1455	1655	...	...
Darjeeling .... a.	1600	0945	...	1300	...	1535	1745	...	...

¶	52570	52573	52540	52574	52575	52572	52588		52559
	🚂	🚂	B			🚂			🚂
	②④⑥	⑦				⑥			
Darjeeling .... d.	0910	...	1015	1100	1335	...	1530	...	...
Ghum .... d.	1015	...	1050	1150	1425	...	1610	...	...
Sonada .... d.	1105	...	1130	...	...	...	1650	...	...
Tung .... d.	1205	...	1210	...	...	...	1725	...	...
Kurseong .... d.	1245	1015	1300	...	...	1400	1810	...	...
Mahanadi .... d.	...	1125	1336	...	...	1510	...	...	...
Tindharia .... d.	...	...	1442	...	...	...	...	...	...
Chunbhati .... d.	...	...	|	...	...	...	...	...	...
Rangtong .... d.	...	...	1536	...	...	...	...	...	1220
Sukna .... d.	...	...	1613	...	...	...	...	...	1255
Siliguri Junction .... d.	...	...	1640	...	...	...	...	...	1335
New Jalpaiguri Junction .... a.	...	...	1745	...	...	...	...	...	...

KANGRA VALLEY RAILWAY

	52464	52466	18110	52472	14034	52468	52474	14036	52470
	2	2		2		2	2	②④⑥	2
Joginder Nagar .... d.	...	...	...	0720	...	...	1220	...	...
Baijnath Paprola .... d.	0400	0720	...	1050	...	1410	1555	...	1735
Palampur Himachal .... d.	0438	0800	...	1130	...	1451	1641	...	1813
Kangra Mandir .... d.	0550	0946	...	1246	...	1605	1756	...	1946
Pathankot Junction .... a.	1050	1420	...	1730	...	2025	2235	...	2355
Pathankot Junction .... ‡ d.	...	...	1645	...	1905	...	...	2320	...
Delhi Junction .... ‡ a.	...	...	0430	...	0545	...	...	1045	...

	52471	52463	14033	56465	14035	52473	18101	52467	52469
	2	2		2	①③⑤	2		2	2
Delhi Junction .... ‡ d.	...	...	2010	...	2245	...	2200	...	...
Pathankot Junction .... ‡ d.	...	...	0610	...	0820	...	1100	...	...
Pathankot Junction .... d.	0215	0400	...	0645	...	1000	...	1320	1550
Kangra Mandir .... d.	0647	0843	...	1110	...	1503	...	1858	2032
Palampur Himachal .... d.	0806	1001	...	1310	...	1634	...	2014	2139
Baijnath Paprola .... d.	0950	1045	...	1400	...	1805	...	2055	2230
Joginder Nagar .... a.	1125	...	...	...	...	1945	...	...	...

MATHERAN HILL RAILWAY

	96003	52111	52101	11007	52103	11029	95107	92105	95117	52109
	2						2		2	
Mumbai CST ...... ♥ d.	0419	...	...	0700	...	0840	0930	...	1451	...
Neral .... ♥ a.	0623	...	...	0825	...	1003	1109	...	1630	...
Neral .... ♣ d.	...	0640	0750	...	0910	...	...	1040	...	1705
Matheran .... ♣ a.	...	0840	0950	...	1120	...	...	1235	...	1900

	52102	11024	52104	95122	52106	95128	52108	95130	52110	95134
				2		2				
Matheran .... ♣ d.	0720	...	0955	...	1250	...	1515	...	1630	...
Neral .... ♣ a.	0855	...	1140	...	1425	...	1655	...	1810	...
Neral .... ♥ d.	...	1000	...	1223	...	1547	...	1631	...	1857
Mumbai CST ... ♥ a.	...	1150	...	1402	...	1729	...	1810	...	2043

NILGIRI MOUNTAIN RAILWAY

	56141	12671	56136		56143		56138		
Chennai Central .... ‡ d.	...	2115	...	...	...	...	...	...	...
Mettupalaiyam .... ‡ a.	...	0615	...	...	...	...	...	...	...
Mettupalaiyam .... d.	...	...	0710	...	...	...	...	...	...
Coonor .... d.	0745	...	1040	...	1235	...	1630	...	...
Udagamandalam (Ooty) ...... a.	0905	...	1200	...	1350	...	1745	...	...

	56139	56142	56137	12672	56140				
Udagamandalam (Ooty) .... d.	0915	1215	1400	...	1800	...	...	...	...
Coonor .... d.	1025	1320	1515	...	1910	...	...	...	...
Mettupalaiyam .... a.	...	...	1735	...	...	...	...	...	...
Mettupalaiyam .... ‡ d.	...	...	...	1945	...	...	...	...	...
Chennai Central .... ‡ a.	...	...	...	0505	...	...	...	...	...

By main-line train (*Exp*).
Services normally suspended during Monsoon season.
By main-line train. Frequent additional trains (2 cl. only) are available. Journey 1½ – 2 hours.

A – Temporary running ①③⑤. B – Temporary running ②④⑥.
¶ – For up-to-date information see www.dhrs.org

an / Pakistan Rlys — LAHORE - DELHI — 5400

	402	14002
		Exp
	①④	①④
Lahore Jct .... d.	0800	...
Wagah .... a.	0835	...
Wagah .... d.	1130	...
Atari 🛃 .... a.	1150	...
Atari 🛃 .... d.	...	2000
Delhi Junction .... a.	...	0320

	14001	401
	Exp	
	③⑥	①④
Delhi Junction .... d.	2305	...
Atari 🛃 .... a.	0715	...
Atari 🛃 .... d.	...	1100
Wagah .... a.	...	1410
Wagah .... d.	...	1610
Lahore Jct .... a.	...	1645

E: Timings are subject to confirmation and connections are not guaranteed.

Bangladesh / Indian Rlys — KOLKATA - DHAKA — 5450

km		13108	13109
		Exp	*Exp*
		①⑥	②
0	**Kolkata** Chitpur .... d.	0710	0710
122	Gede .... a.	|	|
122	Gede .... d.	|	|
	Darsana 🛃 .... a.	|	|
540	**Dhaka** Cantonment .... a.	1800	1800

	13107	13110
	Exp	*Exp*
	⑤⑦	③
Dhaka Cantonment .... d.	0700	0700
Darsana 🛃 .... d.	|	|
Gede .... a.	|	|
Gede .... d.	|	|
Kolkata Chitpur .... a.	1810	1810

NOTE: Timings are subject to confirmation.

BEYOND EUROPE
South East Asia, Australia and New Zealand

Introduction

The Beyond Europe section covers principal rail services in a different area of the world each month. There are six areas, each appearing twice yearly as follows:

India:	January and July editions
South East Asia and Australasia:	February and August editions
China:	March and September editions
Japan:	April and October editions
North America:	May and November editions
Africa and the Middle East:	June and December editions

The months have been chosen so that we can bring you up-to-date information for those countries which make seasonal changes.

Details of services in South America can be found in the European Rail Timetable April and October editions and schedules for South Korea in the May and November editions.

Contents

INDEX OF PLACES

by table number

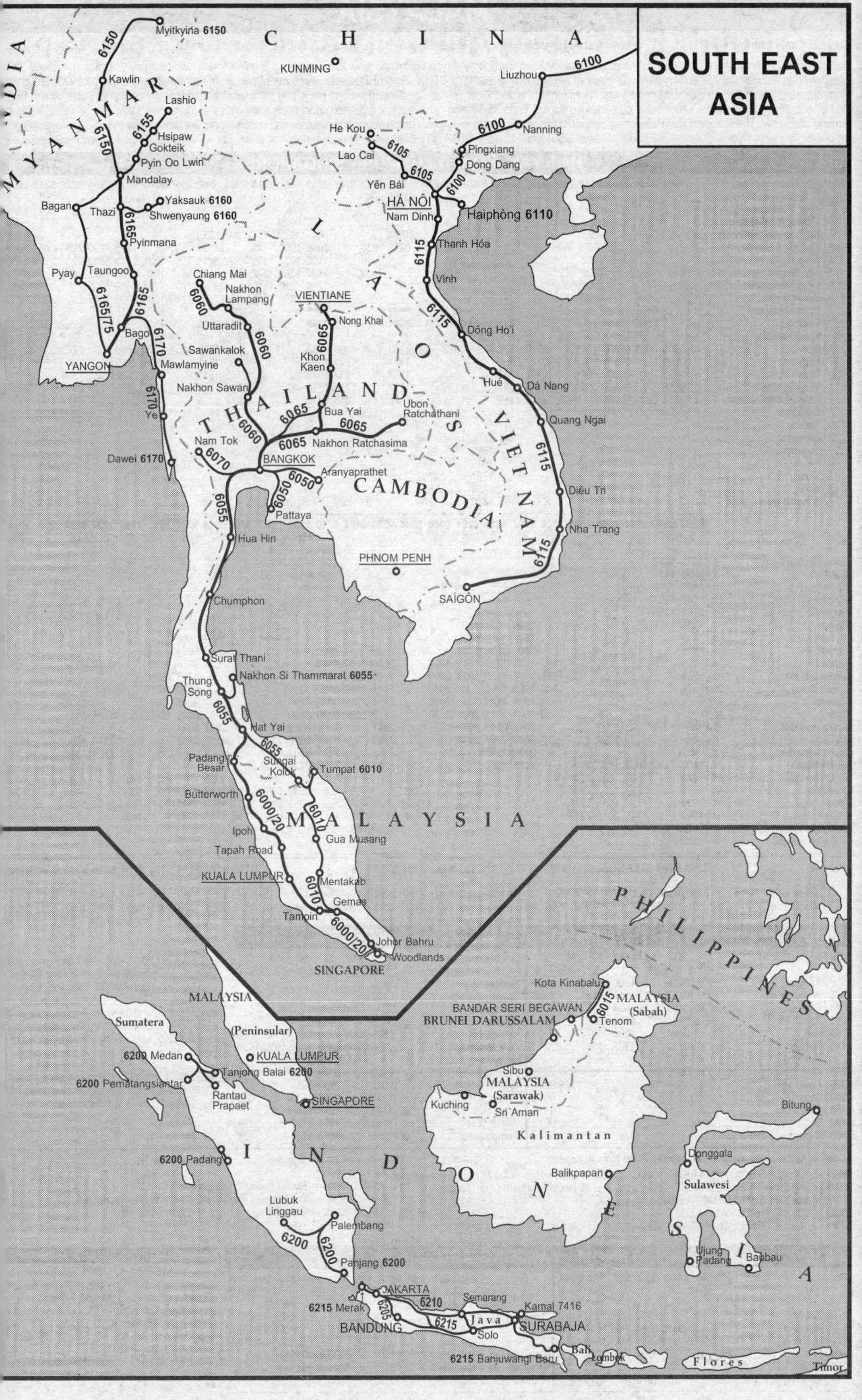
SOUTH EAST ASIA
CHINA
MYANMAR
LAOS
THAILAND
VIETNAM
CAMBODIA
MALAYSIA
PHILIPPINES
INDONESIA
Myitkyina 6150
Kawlin
Lashio
Hsipaw
Gokteik
Pyin Oo Lwin
Mandalay
Bagan
Thazi
Yaksauk 6160
Shwenyaung 6160
Pyinmana
Pyay
Taungoo
Bago
YANGON
Mawlamyine
Ye
Dawei 6170
KUNMING
Liuzhou
Nanning
He Kou
Lao Cai
Yên Bái
Pingxiang
Dong Dang
HÀ NỘI
Nam Dinh
Haiphòng 6110
Thanh Hóa
Vinh
Dông Ho'i
Huê
Dà Nang
Quang Ngai
Diêu Tri
Nha Trang
SAIGÔN
PHNOM PENH
Chiang Mai
Nakhon Lampang
Uttaradit
Sawankalok
Nakhon Sawan
VIENTIANE
Nong Khai
Khon Kaen
Bua Yai
Ubon Ratchathani
Nakhon Ratchasima
Nam Tok
BANGKOK
Aranyaprathet
Pattaya
Hua Hin
Chumphon
Surat Thani
Nakhon Si Thammarat 6055
Thung Song
Hat Yai
Padang Besar
Sungai Kolok
Tumpat 6010
Butterworth
Ipoh
Tapah Road
Gua Musang
KUALA LUMPUR
Mentakab
Gemas
Tampin
Johor Bahru
Woodlands
SINGAPORE
6150
6155
6165
6165/75
6170
6100
6105
6115
6060
6065
6070
6050
6055
6000/20
6010
Sumatera
MALAYSIA
(Peninsular)
6200 Medan
Tanjong Balai 6200
6200 Pematangsiantar
Rantau Prapaet
6200 Padang
Lubuk Linggau
Palembang
Panjang 6200
6200
JAKARTA
6215 Merak
BANDUNG
6205
6210
6215
Semarang
Java
Solo
Kamal 7416
SURABAJA
6215 Banjuwangi Baru
Bali
Lombok
Flores
Timor
Kota Kinabalu
6015
MALAYSIA (Sabah)
Tenom
BANDAR SERI BEGAWAN
BRUNEI DARUSSALAM
Sibu
MALAYSIA (Sarawak)
Kuching
Sri Aman
Kalimantan
Balikpapan
Bitung
Donggala
Sulawesi
Ujung Padang
Baubau

MALAYSIA

Capital: **Kuala Lumpur** (GMT +8). 2016 Public Holidays: Jan. 1, Feb. 8, 9, May 1, 21, June 4, July 6, 7, Aug. 31, Sept. 12, 13, 16, Oct. 2, 29, Dec. 12, 25.

Rail services in Malaysia are operated by Keretapi Tanah Melayu Berhad (Malayan Railways, www.ktmb.com.my), a government owned agency. Trains numbered **9XX** *Electric Train Service – ETS* and convey one class of seating only either ETS Silver, Gold or Platinum and a buffet car, all are air-conditioned. Trains **29XX** are class Commuter service and use air-conditioned EMUs. Overnight trains **26/27** convey air-conditioned second class and thirdclass seating (known locally as Superior and Ecor and air-conditioned couchettes which have 40 curtained bunks. Train **35/36** also convey air conditioned couchettes which have 40 curtained bunks. All non *ETS* trains co second class only. The Malaysia Rail Pass offers unlimited travel on Intercity services. Reservations are required and supplements are payable for the use of sleeping car b on overnight trains. Prices: 5 days US$35.00, 10 days US$55.00, 15 days US$70.00. Child fares approximately half price. For full information go to www.ktmintercity.cor

6000 HAT YAI - KUALA LUMPUR - SINGAPORE

Keretapi Tanah Melayu Be

km		9301	9231	9303	2943	2981	9305	9201	ES43	9203	ES41	947	9213	9307	2951	35	2983	9233	949	2957	9209	9215	2985	9221	9217	2965
			R		2	2		R	2	R	2	2	R		2	R	2	R	2	2	R	R	2	R	R	2
						⑤-⑦										♦	⑤-⑦						⑤-⑦			
	Bangkok **6055** d.	...	...	...	...	...	...	...	...	...	...	...	...	...	...	1445t	...	...	...	...	...	...	...	...	...	...
0	**Hat Yai** Junction d.	...	...	...	...	...	...	...	...	...	...	0730t	...	...	...	0635t	...	...	1305t	...	...	...	...	...	...	...
45	Padang Besar 🏛 d.	...	...	...	0545	0645	...	...	...	0745	...	0925	0930	...	1045	1000	1240	...	1500	1530	1615	1715	1830	2000	...	2040
76	Arau d.	...	...	...	0605	0705	...	...	...	0801	...	...	0946	...	1105	1032	1300	...	—	1550	1631	1733	1850	2016	...	2100
114	Alor Setar d.	...	...	...	0627	0727	...	...	...	0819	...	...	1004	...	1127	1109	1322	...	...	1612	1648	1755	1912	2034	...	2122
205	Bukit Mertajam d.	...	...	...	0720	0820	...	...	...	|	...	...	|	...	1220	1239	1415	...	...	1705	1735	1849	2005	|	...	2215
216	**Butterworth** d.	...	0500	...	0730	0830	...	0745	...	|	...	...	|	...	1230	1300	1425	1455	...	1715	1758	1908	2015	|	2250	2225
227	Bukit Mertajam d.	...	0509	...	...	...	...	0755	...	|	...	—	|	...	—	...	...	1503	...	...	1807	1918	...	|	2259	...
312	Taiping d.	...	0550	...	...	...	...	0841	...	0945	...	**9401**	1129	...	**9309**	...	...	1548	**9311**	...	1852	2005	...	2202	2340	...
344	Kuala Kangsar d.	...	|	...	...	...	...	0857	...	1002	...		|	...		...	...	1605		...	1909	2026	...	2219	2357	...
398	**Ipoh** d.	0500	0633	0730	...	...	0900	0930	...	1032	...	1100	1214	1300	1600	...	...	1634	1800	...	1939	2056	...	2249	0025	...
434	Kampar d.	0521	|	0751	...	...	0921	0951	...	|	...	1121	|	1321	1621	...	...	1653	1821	...	1958	2115	...	2310	—	...
450	Tapah Road d.	0533	|	0803	...	...	0933	1001	...	|	...	1133	|	1333	1633	...	...	1703	1833	...	2008	2124	...	2320	...	...
517	Tanjong Malim d.	0616	|	0846	...	...	1016	1037	...	1135	...	1217	|	1416	1716	...	...	1737	1916	...	2044	2158	...	2358	...	...
604	**Kuala Lumpur** Sentral d.	0716	0835	0946	...	...	1116	1159	...	1254	...	1326	1435	1516	1816	...	...	1847	2016	...	2150	2305	...	0122	...	...
677	Seremban d.	...	...	...	...	...	...	1313	...	1415	...	...	1555	...	...	...	...	...	...	...	...	...	...	0238	**ES45**	...
726	Tampin d.	...	...	...	...	...	...	1347	...	1446	1500	...	...	...	...	...	...	...	...	...	...	...	...	0313		...
779	**Gemas** d.	...	...	...	...	...	...	1401	1450	1510	1540	...	...	...	...	...	...	...	...	...	...	...	...	0340	0410	...
805	Segamat d.	...	...	...	...	...	...	...	1520	...	1613	...	...	...	...	...	...	...	...	...	...	...	...	...	0440	...
864	Paloh d.	...	...	...	...	...	...	...	1629	...	1725	...	...	...	...	...	...	...	...	...	...	...	...	...	0548	...
891	Kluang d.	...	...	...	...	...	...	...	1701	...	1757	...	...	...	...	...	...	...	...	...	...	...	...	...	0622	...
942	Kulai d.	...	...	...	...	...	...	...	1758	...	1858	...	...	...	...	...	...	...	...	...	...	...	...	...	0724	...
974	**Johor Bahru** Sentral a.	...	...	...	...	...	...	...	1840	...	1950	...	...	...	...	...	...	...	...	...	...	...	...	...	0810	...

	ES62	ES42	2984	9304	2986	9306	9202	9216	9204	9308	2966	9234	9404	9310	9500	26	948	ES44	9220	9302	2950	9232	9208	950	9214
	3			R		R	R	R	R			R			R	R	2		R			R	R	2	R
			⑤-⑦		⑤-⑦											♦									
Johor Bahru Sentral d.	0845	1010	...	...	...	...	...	...	...	...	...	...	...	...	...	1900	...	2340	...	...	...	...	...	...	...
Kulai d.	0930	1111	...	...	...	...	...	...	...	...	...	...	...	...	...	1953	...	0025	...	...	...	...	...	...	...
Kluang d.	1106	1209	...	...	...	...	...	...	...	...	...	...	...	...	...	2101	...	0122	...	...	...	...	...	...	...
Paloh d.	1142	1237	...	...	...	...	...	...	...	...	...	...	...	...	...	|	...	0150	...	...	...	...	...	...	...
Segamat d.	1303	1355	...	...	...	...	...	...	...	...	...	...	...	...	...	2257	...	0300	...	...	...	...	...	...	...
Gemas d.	1335	1425	...	...	...	...	1500	...	1600	...	...	...	...	...	...	2356	...	0330	0430	...	...	...	...	...	...
Tampin d.	1415	...	...	...	...	...	1526	...	1628	...	...	...	...	...	...	—	...	—	0500	...	...	...	...	...	...
Seremban d.	—	...	...	...	...	...	1600	1630	1701	...	...	...	...	...	...	...	...	...	0534	...	...	...	...	...	...
Kuala Lumpur Sentral d.	...	...	...	1445	...	1610	1721	1750	1813	1900	...	2000	2100	2340	...	...	...	...	0656	0830	...	0900	0930	...	1100
Tanjong Malim d.	...	...	...	1554	...	1719	1833	1859	1924	2009	...	2102	2214	0049	...	...	...	...	0758	0939	...	|	1033	...	|
Tapah Road d.	...	...	...	1635	...	1800	1909	1940	|	2050	...	2141	2258	0130	...	...	...	...	0836	1020	...	|	1112	...	|
Kampar d.	...	...	...	1644	...	1809	1919	1949	|	2059	...	2151	2310	0139	...	...	...	...	0845	1029	...	|	1122	...	|
Ipoh d.	...	...	...	1705	...	1830	1941	2011	2029	2120	...	2212	2330	0200	0530	...	...		0908	1050	...	1101	1144	...	1306
Kuala Kangsar d.	**36**	...	...	—	...	...	2010	2040	2055	...	...	2241	...	...	0559	...	...	**2982**	0934	...	...	|	1213	...	|
Taiping d.	R	...	...	**2958**	...	...	2028	2057	2144	...	...	2258	...	...	0620	**2944**	...	⑤-⑦	0953	...	...	1144	1230	...	1350
Bukit Mertajam d.	♦	...	...	...	...	...	2116	2142	|	...	...	2343	...	...	0707		...		|	...	...	1227	1315	...	|
Butterworth d.	1400	...	1600	1830	2100	...	2125	2150	|	...	2300	2352	...	...	0728	0800	...	1000	|	...	1250	1335	1338	...	|
Bukit Mertajam d.	1423	...	1609	1839	2109	...	...	...	|	...	2309	...	...	...	0737	0809	...	1009	|	...	1259	...	1348	...	|
Alor Setar d.	1553	...	1702	1932	2202	...	...	...	2243	...	0002	...	...	...	0830	0902	...	1102	1122	...	1352	...	1435	...	1518
Arau d.	1630	...	1726	1956	2226	...	...	...	2302	...	0026	...	...	...	0853	0926	...	1126	1141	...	1616	...	1454	...	1537
Padang Besar 🏛 d.	1840	...	1745	2015	2245	...	...	...	2320	...	0045	...	...	...	0910	0945	0955	1145	1200	...	1435	...	1510	1540	1555
Hat Yai Junction a.	1845t	...	...	...	...	...	...	...	...	...	...	...	...	...	...	...	0950t	...	...	...	...	...	...	1535t	...
Bangkok **6055** a.	1030t	...	...	...	...	...	...	...	...	...	...	...	...	...	...	...	...	...	...	...	...	...	...	...	...

km	◄	ST63	ST65	ST67	ST69	ST71	ST73	ST77	ST81	ST83	ST87	ST91	ST93
0	**Johor Bahru** Sentral d.	0530	0600	0630	0700	0830	0900	1230	1530	1700	1900	2100	2215
4	**Woodlands** ◇ a.	0535	0605	0635	0705	0835	0905	1235	1535	1705	1905	2105	2220

◄	ST70	ST74	ST78	ST82	ST84	ST86	ST88	ST90	ST92
Woodlands ◇ d.	0800	1000	1330	1630	1800	1845	2000	2045	2200
Johor Bahru Sentral d.	0805	1005	1335	1635	1805	1850	2005	2050	2205

6010 TUMPAT - GEMAS

Keretapi Tanah Melayu Berhad

km		51	53	55	57	59	27
		3	3	3	3	3	R ♦
0	**Tumpat** d.	0420	...	1000	1400	...	1930
14	Wakaf Bharu d.	0437	...	1017	1418	...	1948
25	Pasir Mas d.	0455	...	1034	1435	...	2004
53	Tanah Merah d.	0527	...	1123	1511	...	2030
85	Krai d.	0604	...	1200	1607	...	2104
135	Dabong d.	0732	...	1325	1753	...	2217
	Kemubu d.	0745	...	...	1806	...	|
206	**Gua Masang** d.	0935	0940	...	1945	1950	2355
300	Kuala Lipis d.	...	1145	...	...	0325	0212
353	Jerantut d.	...	...	...	...	...	0312
406	Mentakab d.	...	...	...	...	...	0413
492	Bahau d.	...	...	...	...	...	0619
528	**Gemas** a.	...	...	...	...	...	0716

	26	50	52	56	58	60
	R ♦	3	3	3	3	3
Gemas d.	2356	...	...	...	...	...
Bahau d.	0102	...	...	...	...	...
Mentakab d.	0313	...	...	...	...	...
Jerantut d.	0416	...	...	...	...	...
Kuala Lipis d.	0525	0325	...	...	1345	...
Gua Masang d.	0750	0530	0535	...	1550	1555
Kemubu d.	|	...	0716	...	...	1731
Dabong d.	0929	...	0739	1430	...	1744
Krai d.	1043	...	0907	1554	...	1920
Tanah Merah d.	1117	...	0945	1632	...	2035
Pasir Mas d.	1143	...	1038	1706	...	2107
Wakaf Bharu d.	1159	...	1055	1723	...	2124
Tumpat a.	1215	...	1110	1735	...	2135

Since August 2014, work has been taking plac upgrade and rehabilitate the line from Gemas t Gua Musang (**Table 6010**). This work takes pla from 0900 and 2100 and, during this period, nc trains operate and other services may be resch uled. There has been no firm indication as to h long the work will take, but could be for up to t years.

Note: These are the schedules from the latest KTMB timetable but although shown as trains t may well be some bus substitutions.

Notes for Tables **6000**, **6010**. ♦ – Notes, listed by train number.

26/27 – EKSPRES RAKYAT TIMURAN – 🛏 2 cl., (23) Johor Bahru - Gua Musang -Tumpat and v.v.
35/36 – INTERNATIONAL EXPRESS – 🛏 1, 2 cl. and ✕ Bangkok (**49/48**) - Hat Yai and v.v.; 🛏 2 cl. Hat Yai (**35/36**) - Butterworth and v.v.
9XXX – Electric Train Service (2) 🍸.
2XXX – Komuter Electric Train Service (2).

t – Thai time.
◇ – Border point with Singapore.
◄ – Connections with intercity trains are not guaranteed.

6015 TENOM - TANJONG ARU

JKNS

km		201	401	505	502	508	504	504A
			①-⑥	⑦		⑦	①-⑥	①-⑥
							☛	
0	**Tenom** d.	...	...	...	0730	1230	1300	...
	Halogilat d.	...	0600	0810	0854	1353	1444	1740
49	Beaufort a.	...	0658	0911	0951	1455	1545	1839
49	Beaufort d.	0500	...	...	1101	1630	1700	...
101	Papar d.	0611	...	...	1216	1750	1828	...
134	**Tanjong Aru** ◐ a.	0657	...	...	1310	1845	1910	...

	301	303	101A	101	106A	102A	103	104	104
	①-⑥	⑦			⑦	①-⑥		⑦	①-⑥
							☛		
Tanjong Aru ◐ d.	...	...	...	0745	...	...	1340	1706	1736
Papar d.	...	...	...	0829	...	...	1428	1750	1823
Beaufort a.	...	...	...	0940	...	...	1542	1900	1934
Beaufort d.	0500	0700	0750	...	1330	1330	1630a	...	...
Halogilat d.	0556	0758	0853	...	1444	1444	1730a	...	...
Tenom a.	...	...	1013	...	1555	1555	...	...	...

a – ①–⑥ only. ◐ – Kota Kinabalu. ☛ – This service is often cancelled.

Operator: Jabatan Keretapi Negeri Sabah (Sabah State Railways).

6020 BANGKOK - WOODLANDS

The EASTERN AND ORIENTAL EXPRESS Luxury cruise train operating between Bangko Woodlands ◇. 2016 departure dates:
From **Bangkok** depart 1750, journey 3 nights Feb. 7, 16, 25, Mar. 8, 20, 29, Apr. 7, 27, Ma Jun. 1, Jul. 1, 28, Aug. 26, Sep. 20, 29, Oct. 1 Nov. 2, 10, 22, Dec. 1, 25.
From **Woodlands** depart 1500, journey 2 nigl Feb. 3, 12, 21 Mar. 4, 13, 25, Apr. 3, 23, May Jun. 27, Jul. 24, Aug. 22, Sep. 15, 25, Oct. 16 6, 18, 27, Dec. 21.
Operator: Eastern and Oriental Express ✆ U 0845 217 0799. ◇ – Border point with Singa

THAILAND

tal: **Bangkok** (GMT +7).   2016 Public Holidays: Jan. 1, Feb. 22, Apr. 6, 13, 14, 15, May 1, 2, 5, 6, 9, 20, July 18, 19, Aug. 12, Oct. 23, 24, Dec. 5, 10, 12, 31.

services are operated by State Railway of Thailand (www.railway.co.th). Trains may convey any combination of first, second or third class seating as shown in either columns otnotes. Overnight trains may also convey sleeping cars or couchettes. Sleeping cars have lockable two berth compartments which convert into seats during the day. chettes are arranged 'open plan' along the coach and during the day the bottom bunks are used as seats. Dining cars are operated on all important trains. The Thailand Rail s offers twenty days unlimted travel in seated accommodation. Two passes are available. Pass A costs 1550 Baht and does not include supplements for express trains or ning cars. Pass B costs 3000 Baht and includes all supplements.

BANGKOK - BAN PLU TA LUANG and ARANYAPRATHET — 6050

te Railway of Thailand

3rd class only	275	283	281	367	389	279	277	391	371
								A	
Bangkok Hua Lampong .... d.	0555	0655	0800	1010	1210	1305	1525	1635	1740
Makkasan .... d.	0620	0716	0816	1030	1228	1317	1545	1654	1802
Hua Takhe ‡ .... d.	0703	0814	0857	1109	1304	1348	1618	1730	1842
Chachoengsao Junction .... d.	0740	0859	0932	1145	1330	1421	1644	1755	1924
Si Racha Junction .... d.	|	1013a	|	...	...	|	|	...	|
Pattaya .... d.	|	1035a	|	...	...	|	|	...	|
Ban Plu Ta Luang .... a.	|	1120a	|	...	...	|	|	...	|
Prachin Buri .... d.	0858	...	1046	...	...	1522	1741	...	2032
Kabin Buri .... d.	0948	...	1135	...	...	1612	1820	...	...
Aranyaprathet .... a.	1135	...	...	...	...	1735	...	...	...

3rd class only	372	278	280	368	390	282	284	276	386
					B				①–⑤
Aranyaprathet .... d.	...	...	0640	...	...	...	...	1355	...
Kabin Buri .... d.	...	0630	0823	...	...	1325	...	1539	...
Prachin Buri .... d.	0500	0719	0921	...	...	1416	...	1630	...
Ban Plu Ta Luang .... d.	|	|	|	...	...	|	1335a	|	...
Pattaya .... d.	|	|	|	...	...	|	1421a	|	...
Si Racha Junction .... d.	|	|	|	...	...	|	1452a	|	...
Chachoengsao Junction .... d.	0619	0831	1022	1235	1405	1534	1620	1800	2005
Hua Takhe ‡ .... d.	0701	0911	1107	1316	1435	1609	1711	1855	2038
Makkasan .... d.	0751	0958	1148	1354	1512	1655	1807	1940	2116
Bangkok Hua Lampong .... a.	0815	1015	1205	1410	1525	1715	1825	1955	2130

Also at 1700 Ⓐ, 1825.
Also at 0545 Ⓐ, 0705.

a – ①–⑤ only.
‡ – For Suvarnabhumi International Airport.

BANGKOK - HAT YAI - SUNGAI KOLOK — 6055

te Railway of Thailand

	453	175	43	261		171	35	37	463	169	451		83	173	447	167	85	39	41		455	445	457
	3	23	2 🍷	3		C	A	B	3	C	3		B	C	3	C	B	2 🍷	2 🍷		3	3	3
Bangkok Hua Lampong .... d.	...	...	0805	0920	...	1300	1445	1510	...	1535	...	...	1705	1735	...	1830	1930	2250	2250	...	...	...	...
Nakhon Pathom .... d.	...	...	0922	1048	...	1437	1611	1638	...	1715	...	...	1833	1912	...	1958	2059	0009	0009	...	...	...	...
Rachaburi .... d.	...	...	1004	1145	...	1526	1701	1730	...	1820	...	...	1924	2007	...	2050	2150	0052	0052	...	...	...	...
Hua Hin .... d.	...	...	1129	1335	...	1717	1845	1913	...	2010	...	...	2110	2154	...	2234	2336	0224	0224	...	...	...	...
Bang Saphan Yai .... d.	...	...	1321	...	...	1946	2107	2143	...	2249	...	...	2341	0048	...	0111	0232	0433	0433	...	...	...	...
Chumphon .... d.	...	...	1441	...	...	2121	2245	2324	...	0052	...	...	0127	0258	...	0328	0423	0559	0559	...	...	0630	...
Surat Thani ♥ .... d.	...	...	1645	...	...	0027	0126	0203	...	0348	...	...	0427	0603	0613	0628	0716	0805	0815	...	...	0946	...
Thung Song Junction .... d.	...	...	...	...	...	0239	0322	0400	...	0556	...	...	0635	0832	0907	0855	0932	...	0954	...	...	1219	1415
Nakhon Si Thammarat .... a.	...	...	...	...	...	|	|	|	...	|	0600	...	|	0955	|	|	1055	...	|	...	0958	|	|
Trang .... a.	...	...	...	...	...	|	|	|	...	|	|	...	0805	...	|	1036	...	...	|	...	|	|	|
Kantang .... a.	...	...	...	...	...	|	|	|	...	|	|	...	...	...	|	1120	...	...	|	...	|	|	1655
Phatthalung .... d.	...	...	...	...	...	0422	0506	0548	0602	0738	0822	...	...	...	1123	...	...	...	1112	...	1224	1420	...
Hat Yai Junction .... d.	...	0630	...	...	...	0645	0700	0735	0755	0930	1018	...	...	...	1312	...	...	...	1250	...	1433	1650	...
Pattani .... d.	...	0739	...	...	...	0810	...	0858	0919	1050	1145	...	...	...	1448	...	...	...	1404	...	1616	...	...
Yala .... d.	0630	0806	...	...	...	0848	...	0929	0958	1120	1227	...	...	...	1545	...	...	...	1430	...	1710	...	...
Sungai Kolok .... a.	0840	1000	...	...	...	1045	...	1120	1210	...	1450	...	...	...	1800	...	...	...	...	...	...	...	...

	458	262	40	446		174	456	168	448		86	452	170	42	44		84	172	464		38	176	36	454
	3	3	2 🍷	2		C	3	C	3		B	3	C	2 🍷	2 🍷		B	C	3		B	2	A	2
gai Kolok .... d.	...	...	...	...	...	...	...	...	0630	...	...	0855	...	...	...	...	...	1130	1225	...	1420	1455	...	1525
.... d.	...	...	...	...	...	...	0635	...	0828	...	...	1122	1235	1455	...	...	...	1326	1432	...	1609	1637	...	1740
ani .... d.	...	...	...	...	...	...	0716	...	0920	...	...	1206	1306	1519	...	...	...	1405	1528	...	1640	1704	...	...
Yai Junction .... d.	...	...	...	0640	...	...	0918	...	1058	...	...	1350	1445	1623	...	...	...	1539	1705	...	1810	1815	1845	...
thalung .... d.	0600	...	...	0853	...	...	1118	...	1300	...	...	1534	1623	1736	...	...	...	1713	1850	...	1947	...	2019	...
Kantang .... d.	|	...	...	|	...	...	|	1240	|	...	...	|	|	|	...	...	...	|	...	...	|	...	|	...
Trang .... d.	|	...	...	|	...	...	|	1329	|	...	...	|	|	|	...	...	1725	|	...	...	|	...	|	...
akhon Si Thammarat .... d.	0830	...	...	|	...	1300	1355	|	|	...	1500	1805	|	|	...	...	|	|	...	...	|	...	|	...
ng Song Junction .... d.	...	...	...	1058	...	1424	...	1517	1531	...	1620	...	1813	1903	...	...	1912	1927	...	...	2138	...	2207	...
t Thani ♥ .... d.	...	...	1040	1325	...	1647	...	1738	1755	...	1837	...	2014	2041	2041	...	2104	2126	...	...	2328	...	2357	...
mphon .... d.	...	...	1246	1630	...	1936	...	2031	...	...	2122	...	2323	2249	2249	...	2359	0044	...	...	0206	...	0234	...
g Saphan Yai .... d.	...	...	1407	...	...	2128	...	2216	...	...	2308	...	0112	0019	0019	...	0148	0219	...	...	0336	...	0404	...
Hin .... d.	...	1410	1601	...	...	0045	...	0116	...	...	0147	...	0428	0222	0222	...	0415	0456	...	...	0605	...	0629	...
haburi .... d.	...	1600	1741	...	...	0244	...	0306	...	...	0404	...	0625	0350	0350	...	0608	0649	...	...	0749	...	0813	...
hon Pathom .... d.	...	1716	1826	...	...	0340	...	0405	...	...	0500	...	0726	0438	0438	...	0704	0744	...	...	0842	...	0903	...
gkok Hua Lampong .... a.	...	1900	1945	...	...	0510	...	0535	...	...	0630	...	0900	0555	0555	...	0835	0915	...	...	1010	...	1030	...

INTERNATIONAL EXPRESS – See Table **6000**.
🛏 1, 2 cl., (23).

C – 🛏 2 cl., (23).
♥ – Station is at Phun Phin, 13 km away.

BANGKOK - CHIANG MAI — 6060

te Railway of Thailand

	403	407	401	409		111	7	201	3		209	211	109	207		1	13	107	105		51		
	3	3	3	3		23 ✕	2 🍷	23	2 🍷		3	23	B ✕	3		A ✕	A ✕	B ✕	23 🍷		B ✕		
Bangkok Hualampong .... d.	...	...	...	...	...	0700	0830	0925	1050	...	1120	1255	1345	1405	...	1810	1935	2010	2100	...	2200	...	...
Bang Pa In .... d.	...	...	...	...	...	0825	|	1114	|	...	1251	1419	|	1543	...	|	|	|	2211	...	|	...	...
Ayutthaya .... d.	...	...	...	0600	...	0838	0948	1128	1216	...	1305	1432	1519	1558	...	1945	2107	2144	2223	...	2236	...	...
Lop Buri .... d.	...	...	0600	0715	...	0944	1029	1241	1300	...	1423	1538	1623	1727	...	2042	2200	2239	2316	...	0031	...	...
Nakhon Sawan .... d.	...	0500	0811	...	...	1124	1140	1511	1407	...	...	1753	1827	1935	...	2217	2331	0006	0050	...	0224	...	...
Taphan Hin .... d.	...	0617	0936	...	...	1242	1226	1640	1457	...	...	1915	1937	...	...	|	|	0130	0210	...	0337	...	...
Phitsanulok .... d.	0555	0729	1055	...	...	1345	1322	1755	1604	...	...	...	2037	...	...	0018	0149	0238	0309	...	0440	...	...
Uttaradit .... d.	0737	0907	...	...	...	1524	1427	...	1912	...	...	...	2223	...	...	|	0308	0405	0436	...	0606	...	...
Sila At .... d.	0740	0917	...	...	...	1529	1433	...	1915	...	...	...	2237	...	...	0154	0321	0418	0440	...	0620	...	...
Den Chai .... d.	...	1013	...	...	...	1630	1524	...	...	...	...	...	2342	...	...	0251	0419	0515	...	...	0720	...	...
Nakhon Lampang .... d.	...	1236	...	...	...	...	1733	...	...	...	...	...	0204	...	...	0501	0633	...	...	...	1001	...	...
Khun Tan .... d.	...	1330	...	...	...	...	1823	...	...	...	...	...	0258	...	...	0606	0737	...	...	...	1105	...	...
Lamphun .... d.	...	1415	...	...	...	...	1915	...	...	...	...	...	0344	...	...	0651	0821	...	...	...	1150	...	...
Chiang Mai .... a.	...	1435	...	...	...	...	1930	...	...	...	...	...	0405	...	...	0715	0840	...	...	...	1210	...	...

		208	212	202		106	112	210		102	8	402		408	410	4		108	52	14	2		
		3	3	23		23 🍷	23 ✕	3		B ✕	2 🍷	3		3	3	2 🍷		B ✕	B ✕	A ✕	A ✕		
ang Mai .... d.	...	...	...	...	...	...	...	...	...	0630	0850	...	...	0930	...	...	...	...	1530	1700	1800	...	...
phun .... d.	...	...	...	...	...	...	...	...	...	0652	0905	...	...	1000	...	...	...	...	1548	1720	1820	...	...
n Tan .... d.	...	...	...	...	...	...	...	...	...	0736	0947	...	...	1103	...	...	...	...	1650	1824	1921	...	...
hon Lampang .... d.	...	...	...	...	...	...	...	...	...	0837	1041	...	...	1202	...	...	...	...	1804	1927	2017	...	...
Chai .... d.	...	...	...	...	...	...	0730	...	...	1046	1239	...	...	1419	...	...	...	1905	2026	2141	2236	...	...
At .... d.	...	...	...	...	...	0730	0827	...	...	1147	1326	...	...	1533	1630	1950	...	2012	2130	2236	2333	...	...
radit .... d.	...	...	...	...	...	0735	0833	...	...	1153	1332	...	...	1538	1633	2000	...	2019	2137	2242	|	...	...
sanulok .... d.	...	...	...	0605	...	0855	1003	...	...	1318	1444	1345	...	1724	1810	2140	...	2209	2301	0001	0050	...	...
han Hin .... d.	...	...	0530	0718	...	0952	1112	...	...	1428	1532	1458	...	1842	...	2239	...	2320	0007	|	|	...	...
hon Sawan .... d.	...	0500	0701	0835	...	1048	1242	...	...	1556	1622	1630	...	1955	...	0006	...	0048	0114	0159	0241	...	...
Buri .... d.	...	0706	0918	1056	...	1220	1438	1732	...	1806	1728	1845	...	...	...	0130	...	0228	0245	0324	0405	...	...
thaya .... d.	...	0826	1027	1248	...	1311	1559	1848	...	1916	1806	...	...	...	...	0227	...	0321	0339	0424	0459	...	...
g Pa In .... d.	...	0840	1039	1229	...	1323	1616	1903	...	|	|	...	...	...	...	|	...	|	|	|	|	...	...
gkok Hualampong .... a.	...	1020	1210	1405	...	1440	1800	2035	...	2110	1925	...	...	...	...	0400	...	0510	0525	0615	0650	...	...

Conveys 🛏 1, 2 cl.

B – Conveys 🛏 2 cl., (23).

6065 BANGKOK - NONG KHAI and UBON RATCHATHANI

State Railway of Thail

km		425	421	415	431		21	419	135	75	71	427	417	233	145	77	139	69	913	67	133	73	141
		3	3	3	3		2 🍷	3	23 ✕	23 🍷	23 🍷	3	3	3	23 ✕	23 🍷	B ✕	A ✕	3	A ✕	B ✕	23 🍷	23 ✕
0	**Bangkok** Hua Lampong d.	...	...	...	...	...	0545	...	0640	0820	1005	...	...	1140	1520	1835	1855	2000	...	2030	2045	2150	2225
71	Ayutthaya d.	...	...	...	...	...	0659	...	0826	0942	1125	...	...	1307	1657	2002	2026	2141	...	2151	2218	2309	2354
113	Saraburi d.	...	...	...	...	...	0734	...	0910	1018	1204	...	...	1353	1801	2040	2110	2223	...	2232	2302	2345	0036
125	Kaeng Khoi Junction d.	...	...	...	0500	...	0745	...	0923	1030	1216	...	...	1406	1815	2051	2124	2235	...	2246	2315	2355	0053
180	Pak Chong d.	...	...	...	0618	...	0856	...	1056	|	1327	...	...	1524	1949	|	2249	|	...	0017	|	0105	0226
264	Nakhon Ratchasima d.	...	0610	0620	0829	...	1011	1115	1224	|	1443	1420	1600	1705	2125	|	0023	|	...	0153	|	0231	0352
346	Bua Yai Junction d.	...	|	0758	1009	...	|	|	|	1414	|	|	1742	|	|	0048	|	0250	...	|	0357	|	|
450	Khon Kaen d.	...	|	0935	1155	...	|	|	|	1527	|	|	1917	|	|	0206	|	0419	...	|	0535	|	|
569	Udon Thani d.	...	|	1133	...	...	|	|	|	1745	|	|	2140	|	|	0336	|	0558	...	|	0740	|	|
621	**Nong Khai** a.	...	|	1230	...	...	|	|	|	...	|	|	...	|	|	0415	|	0645	0910	|	0835	|	|
627	**Tha Na Laeng** (Laos) a.	...	|	...	...	...	|	|	|	...	|	|	...	|	|	...	|	...	0920	|	...	|	|
376	Buri Ram d.	...	0810	...	...	...	1137	1317	1422	...	1617	1635	...	1916	2341	...	0226	...	...	0344	...	0428	0605
420	Surin d.	0538	0910	...	...	...	1211	1403	1510	...	1711	1723	...	2000	0032	...	0317	...	...	0432	...	0516	0701
515	Si Sa Ket d.	0718	1107	...	...	...	1320	1550	1703	...	1840	1906	...	...	0221	...	0509	...	...	0620	...	...	0900
575	**Ubon Ratchathani** a.	0830	1215	...	...	...	1400	1645	1800	...	...	2015	...	...	0335	...	0615	...	...	0725	...	...	1020

		234	424	72	416	76	428	136	146	432	426	22	914	418	142	74	78	68	420		134	70	140
		3	3	23 🍷	3	23 🍷	3	23 ✕	23 ✕	3	3	2 🍷	3	3	23 ✕	23 ✕	23 ✕	A ✕	3		B ✕	A ✕	B ✕
Ubon Ratchathani d.	...	...	...	...	...	...	0620	0700	0845	...	1235	1450	...	...	1650	...	...	1830	1845	...	...	...	1930
Si Sa Ket d.	...	...	...	...	...	...	0716	0804	0951	...	1344	1531	...	...	1757	1905	...	1930	1948	...	...	...	2028
Surin d.	...	0520	0703	0749	...	...	0905	0939	1130	...	1528	1641	...	...	1931	2025	...	2059	2120	...	...	...	2202
Buri Ram d.	...	0606	0752	0835	...	...	0953	1027	1226	...	1615	1715	...	...	2028	2110	...	2143	...	...	...	...	2250
Tha Na Laeng (Laos) d.	...	|	|	|	...	...	|	|	|	...	|	|	0950	...	|	|	...	|	...	...	...	...	|
Nong Khai d.	...	|	|	|	...	0700	|	|	|	...	|	|	1000	1255	|	|	1815	|	...	...	1830	1910	|
Udon Thani d.	...	|	|	|	0555	0738	|	|	|	...	|	|	...	1340	|	|	1852	|	...	...	1919	1959	|
Khon Kaen d.	...	|	|	|	0757	0912	|	|	|	1355	|	|	...	1536	|	|	2019	|	...	...	2106	2138	|
Bua Yai Junction d.	...	|	|	|	0938	1045	|	|	|	1546	|	|	...	1714	|	|	2136	|	...	...	2246	2317	|
Nakhon Ratchasima d.	...	0822	0950	1018	1125	|	1145	1233	1454	1740	1825	1847	...	1900	2234	2254	|	2337	...	...	|	|	0051
Pak Chong d.	...	1009	...	1127	...	|	...	1400	1635	1914	...	1948	...	...	0003	0024	|	0127	...	...	|	|	0228
Kaeng Khoi Junction d.	...	1136	...	1228	...	1444	...	1530	1750	2030	...	2053	...	...	0132	0158	0222	0246	...	...	0237	0308	0352
Saraburi d.	...	1151	...	1241	...	1455	...	1545	1805	...	...	2106	...	...	0148	0210	0235	0304	...	...	0252	0321	0413
Ayutthaya d.	...	1240	...	1317	...	1535	...	1637	1905	...	...	2142	...	...	0237	0254	0315	0355	...	...	0348	0404	0525
Bangkok Hua Lampong a.	...	1415	...	1455	...	1710	...	1840	2100	...	...	2255	...	...	0425	0435	0500	0550	...	...	0545	0600	0730

A – Conveys 🛏 1, 2 cl., (23).

B – Conveys 🛏 2 cl., (23).

6070 BANGKOK - NAM TOK

State Railway of Thailand

km	485	909	257	259		3rd class only		260	258	910	486
		Ⓒ A								A	
0	...	0630h	0750	1335	↓	**Bangkok** Thon Buri d.	↑	1025	1740	1925h	...
64	...	0820	0902	1503	↓	Nakhon Pathom d.	↑	0921	1631	1809	...
82	0435	0836	0922	1522	↓	Nong Pla Duk Jct d.	↑	0835	1602	1755	1850
133	0607	0927	1035	1626	↓	Kanchanaburi d.	↑	0719	1448	1653	1741
210	0820	...	1235	1830	↓	**Nam Tok** a.	↑	0520	1255	1425	1530

A – Tourist train to River Khwae Bridge (a. 0935) and allied war cemetery at Kanchanaburi. Conveys (23). Ⓡ. Special fare payable. 740 Baht.

h – Bangkok Hua Lampong.

6075 SUVARNABHUMI INTERNATIONAL AIRPORT

Bangkok Makksan - Suvarnabhumi International Airport (jouney 15 minutes non-stop): **Service suspended**.

Suvarnabhumi International Airport - Bangkok Makksan (jouney 15 minutes non-stop): **Service suspended**.

Bangkok Makksan - Suvarnabhumi International Airport (jouney 22 minutes): 0606 and at least 4 journeys a hour until 2351, 0006.

Suvarnabhumi International Airport - Bangkok Makksan (jouney 22 minutes): 0556, 0608 and at least 4 journeys a hour unti 2347, 0002.

VIÊT NAM

Capital: **Há Nôi** (GMT +7). 2016 Public Holidays: Jan. 1, Feb. 7-13, Apr. 16, 30, May 1, 2, Sep. 2.

Rail services are operated by Duóng Sát Viêt Nam (Viêt Nam Railways, www.vr.com.vn). Unless stated trains convey first and second class accommodation. First class has berth compartments, whilst second class has six. Dining facilities (meals brought to your seats) are provided on some trains.

6100 HÁ NOI - BEIJING

Duóng Sát Viêt N

km		5HD1		MR1	T8702	Z6	Z286			DD5
		2		BC	BC	C				
0	**Há Nôi** Gia Lam d.	1130	...	2140	...	...	...	...	...	0730
162	Dong Dang a.	1515	...	0155	...	...	...	...	...	1145
162	Dong Dang 🛃 d.	...	...	0250	...	...	...	...	...	...
207	Pingxiang 🛃 a.	...	...	0431	...	...	...	...	...	...
207	Pingxiang d.	...	...	...	0620	...	...	...	...	...
430	Nanning a.	...	...	...	1010	...	...	...	...	...
430	Nanning d.	...	...	...	...	1100	1400	...	...	...
861	Guilin d.	...	...	...	...	1429	1810	...	...	...
1409	Changsha d.	...	...	...	...	2001	0004	...	...	...
1771	Wuhan Wuchang d.	...	...	...	...	2329	0332	...	...	...
2307	Zhengzhou d.	...	...	...	...	0407	0810	...	...	...
2996	**Beijing** xi a.	...	...	...	...	0955	1349	...	...	...

	Z5	T8701	MR2	Z285		5HD2		DD6
	D	BD	BD			2		
Beijing xi d.	1551	...	...	1750	...	...	...	...
Zhengzhou d.	2201	...	...	2343	...	...	...	...
Wuhan Wuchang d.	0240	...	...	0422	...	...	...	...
Changsha d.	0559	...	...	0747	...	...	...	...
Guilin d.	1136	...	...	1315	...	...	...	...
Nanning a.	1535	...	...	1710	...	...	...	...
Nanning d.	...	1810	...	...	...	...	...	...
Pingxiang a.	...	2201	...	...	...	...	...	...
Pingxiang 🛃 d.	...	...	2241	...	...	...	...	...
Dong Dang 🛃 a.	...	...	2322	...	...	...	...	...
Dong Dang d.	...	...	0022	...	...	0645	...	1540
Há Nôi Gia Lam a.	...	...	0520	...	...	1030	...	1946

B – Conveys 🛏 1 cl. Nanning (**T8701/2**) - Pingxiang (**MR2/1**) - Há Nôi and v.v.

C – Runs daily. On ②⑤ (from Há Nôi) conveys 🛏 1 cl. Há Nôi – Beijing (2 nights).

D – Runs daily. On ④⑦ (from Beijing) conveys 🛏 1 cl. Beijing - Há Nôi (2 nights).

6105 HÁ NOI - LÂO CAÍ

Duóng Sát Viêt N

km		LC3	YB1	SP7	SP1	SP3				
					AB	A				
0	**Há Nôi** d.	0610	1315	2030	2140	2200	...	...	...	...
6	**Há Nôi** Gia Lâm d.	0628	1342	2048	2158	2218	...	...	...	...
155	Yên Bái d.	1150	1810	0040	0140	0223	...	...	...	...
262	Phõ Lu d.	1441	...	0345	0435	0520	...	...	...	...
296	**Lâo Caí** a.	1546	...	0445	0535	0620	...	...	...	...

	LC4			SP8	SP2	SP4	YB2	
				B	AB	A		
Lâo Caí d.	1005	...	...	1940	2035	2110	...	...
Phõ Lu d.	1108	...	...	2036	2134	2209	...	...
Yên Bái d.	1453	...	...	2338	0036	0128	0735	...
Há Nôi Gia Lâm a.	1914	...	...	0405	0430	0507	1203	...
Há Nôi a.	1932	...	...	0420	0445	0522	1235	...

A – 🛏 1, 2 cl., (12) Há Nôi - Lâo Caí and v.v.

B – Conveys private sleeping cars operated by Livitrans: www.livitrans.com

6110 HÁ NOI - HAI PHÒNG

Duóng Sát Viêt N

km		HP1	LP3	LP5	HP3	LP7				
				2						
0	**Há Nôi** Long Bien d.	0600h	0920	1520	1710	1838	...	...	...	...
6	**Há Nôi** Gia Lâm d.	0616	0940	1530	1721	1854	...	...	...	...
57	Hai Duong d.	0716	1055	1652	1817	1958	...	...	...	...
76	Phú Thái d.	0747	1123	1721	|	2026	...	...	...	...
102	**Hai Phòng** a.	0822	1200	1800	1928	2105	...	...	...	...

	LP2	HP4	LP6	LP8	HP2			
			2					
Hai Phòng d.	0605	0800	0905	1500	1845	...	...	...
Phú Thái d.	0641	|	0941	1537	1922	...	...	...
Hai Duong d.	0713	0902	1008	1650	1955	...	...	...
Gia Lâm d.	0828	1007	1119	1726	2056	...	...	...
Há Nôi Long Bien a.	0836	1015	1126	1734	2110h	...	...	...

h – Há Nôi.

HÁ NÔI - SAÍ GÔN 6115

ng Sát Viêt Nam

	SE5 A	SPT1	TN1 B	SNT1		SE1 A	SE19	SE3 A	SE7 A♣
Há Nôi d.	0900	...	1310	...	...	1930	2010	2200	0600
Nam Dinh d.	1046	...	1510	...	...	2114	2149	2340	0747
Ninh Bình d.	1121	...	1548	...	...	2149	2225	0013	0822
Thanh Hóa d.	1237	...	1711	...	...	2258	2339	0116	0933
Vinh d.	1511	...	1950	...	...	0141	0225	0332	1208
Dông Ho'i d.	1940	...	0039	...	...	0550	0639	0740	1636
Hué d.	2250	...	0347	...	...	0856	0950	1035	1955
Dà Nang d.	0143	...	0709	...	...	1141	1220	1315	2247
Quang Ngai d.	0423	...	1010	...	...	1434	...	1535	0121
Diêu Tri d.	0756	...	1338	...	...	1741	...	1836	0423
Nha Trang d.	1144	...	1755	1900	...	2122	...	2212	0835
Phan Thiet d.	|	1310	|	|	...	|	...	|	...
Binh Thuan d.	1619	1332	2253	2339	...	0118	...	0214	...
Saí Gôn (Ho Chi Minh) a.	2121	1834	0341	0328	...	0439	...	0614	...

	SE8 A♣	SPT2	SE6 A	TN2 B		SE2 A	SNT2	SE4 A	SE20 A
Saí Gôn (Ho Chi Minh) d.	...	0640	0800	1210	...	1930	1930	2100	...
Binh Thuan d.	...	1105	1236	1704	...	2255	|	0115	...
Phan Thiet a.	...	1122	|	|	...	|	|	|	...
Nha Trang d.	1326	...	1629	2119	...	0321	0530	0500	...
Diêu Tri d.	1729	...	2117	0150	...	0713	...	0846	...
Quang Ngai d.	2018	...	0011	0521	...	1007	...	1127	...
Dà Nang d.	2259	...	0302	0835	...	1246	...	1413	1840
Hué d.	0136	...	0539	1214	...	1531	...	1647	2133
Dông Ho'i d.	0450	...	0916	1535	...	1845	...	1952	0049
Vinh d.	0926	...	1327	2033	...	2251	...	2353	0553
Thanh Hóa d.	1154	...	1611	2336	...	0119	...	0217	0823
Ninh Binh d.	1314	...	1727	0106	...	0230	...	0321	0956
Nam Dinh d.	1350	...	1803	0143	...	0305	...	0653	1049
Há Nôi a.	1533	...	1958	0330	...	0450	...	0530	1233

Conveys 1, 2 cl., (1) and ✕.   B – Conveys 2 cl., (2).   ♣ – Runs only at peak periods.

MYANMAR

tal: **Yangon** (GMT +6½).   2016 Public Holidays: Jan. 4, 9, Feb. 12, Mar. 2, 22, 27, Apr. 11 - 20, May 1, 20, July 18, 19, Oct. 15, Nov. 13, 23, Dec. 25, 28.

service in Myanmar is provided by Myanmar Railways Corporation (MRC). Unless noted all trains convey first and second class seating (known locallly as upper and ary). All seating is allocated on purchase of tickets. Sleeping cars are operated on overnight trains and bedding is supplied. Sleepers have 6 compartments comprising 4 x 4- ı and 2 x 2-berth.

MYITKYINA - MANDALAY 6150

anmar Railways

	38	56	42	34 B	58				
Myitkyina d.	0430	0745	0910	1350	1510	...	...	...	...
Kawlin d.	1441	1925	0100	0006	0351	...	...	...	...
Shwebo d.	1842	0019	0713	0400	0828	...	...	...	...
Sagaing d.	|	0300	1020	|	1104	...	...	...	...
Mandalay a.	2200	0415	1120	0720	1220	...	...	...	...

	37	33 B	55	57	41				
Mandalay d.	0430	1300	1410	1620	1945	...	...	...	...
Sagaing d.	0510	|	1504	1714	2041	...	...	...	...
Shwebo d.	0713	1533	1724	1934	0020	...	...	...	...
Kawlin d.	1103	1933	2208	0057	0608	...	...	...	...
Myitkyina a.	2200	0630	1045	1330	2105	...	...	...	...

and (12) Myitkyina - Mandalay and v.v.

LASHIO - MANDALAY 6155

anmar Railways

	132	
Lashio d.	0500	...
Hsipaw d.	0940	...
Kyaukme d.	1125	...
Gokteik d.	1325	...
Pyin Oo Lwin a.	1605	...
Pyin Oo Lwin d.	1740	...
Mandalay a.	2240	...

	131	
Mandalay d.	0400	...
Pyin Oo Lwin a.	0752	...
Pyin Oo Lwin d.	0822	...
Gokteik d.	1108	...
Kyaukme d.	1339	...
Hsipaw d.	1515	...
Lashio a.	1935	...

THAZI - YAKSAUK 6160

Myanmar Railways

km		141 z	143
0	**Thazi** d.	0700	0500
197	Kalaw d.	1330	1140
	Aungban d.	⊖	1230
	Heho d.	1540	1345
247	Shwenyaung a.	1700	1450
	Shwenyaung d.	...	1520
	Yaksauk a.	...	1930

	142 z	144
Yaksauk d.	...	0600
Shwenyaung a.	...	0910
Shwenyaung d.	0800	0940
Heho d.	0920	1110
Aungban d.	⊖	1235
Kalaw d.	1145	1325
Thazi a.	1900	2045

z – From / to Naypyitaw (Table **6165**).   ⊖ – Information unavailable at press date.

MANDALAY - BAGAN - YANGON 6165

anmar Railways

	8	6 A	4 A	120	62 B	10/142	32	12	118
Mandalay d.	...	1500	1700	2100	...	z	...	0600	0720
Thazi d.	...	1749	1949	|	...	2200	...	0854	|
Naypyitaw d.	2000	2036	2251	|	...	0209	0800	1154	|
Bagan a.	|	|	|	0450	...	|	|	|	1845
Bagan d.	|	|	|	...	1700	|	|	|	...
Taungoo d.	2235	2318	0127	...	|	0536	1059	1451	...
Bago d.	0258	0316	0549	...	|	1211	1523	1859	...
Yangon a.	0435	0500	0745	...	1030	1440	1700	2100	...

	11	31	9/141	5 A	61 B	3 A	7	119	117
Yangon d.	0600	0800	1100	1500	1600	1700	2030	...	...
Bago d.	0748	0943	1313	1644	|	1848	2213	...	...
Taungoo d.	1231	1410	1937	2059	|	2325	0223	...	...
Bagan a.	|	|	|	|	0931	|	|	...	...
Bagan d.	|	|	|	|	...	|	|	0700	0400
Naypyitaw d.	1522	1700	2255	2332	...	0157	0500	|	|
Thazi d.	1815	...	0330	0211	...	0458	...	|	|
Mandalay a.	2100	...	z	0500	...	0745	...	1430	1555

and (12) Yangon - Mandalay and v.v.
and (12) Runs via Pyay line.

y – From Shwenyaung (Table **6160**).
z – To Shwenyaung (Table **6160**).

*** – Yangon - Bagan: *644 km*. Mandalay - Bagan: *179 km*.

YANGON - MAWLAMYINE - DAWEI 6170

anmar Railways

	¶ ⑥	89	175	35		
Yangon d.	0625	0715	1825	2100	...	...
Bago d.	⊖	0904	2019	2250	...	...
Kyaikto d.	1100	1157	2320	0130	...	...
Mawlamyine a.	...	1650	0400	0600	...	...
Mawlamyine d.	...	...	0430	...	...	...
Ye d.	...	...	1025	...	...	...
Dawei Port a.	...	...	1900	...	...	...

	90	¶ ⑦	36	176		
Dawei Port d.	...	...	...	0540	...	...
Ye d.	...	...	...	1438	...	...
Mawlamyine a.	...	...	...	2025	...	...
Mawlamyine d.	0800	...	1930	2055	...	...
Kyaikto d.	1233	⊖	2355	0130	...	...
Bago d.	1524	⊖	0245	0413	...	...
Yangon a.	1730	⊖	0420	0620	...	...

YANGON - PYAY 6175

MRC

km		63 *	75 *	71			
0	**Yangon** d.	0700	1100	1300	...	...	...
257	**Pyay** a.	1800	2215	2130	...	...	...

			76 *	64 *	72		
Pyay d.	...	...	0200	0615	2330	...	...
Yangoon a.	...	...	1340	1730	0750	...	...

Information unavailable at press date.   * – Trains **63, 64, 75, 76** use Rangoon Kyemyindine station.   ¶ – Service reported as suspended.

INDONESIA

ital: **Jakarta** (GMT +7).   2016 Public Holidays: Jan. 1, Feb. 8, Mar. 9, 25, May 1, 5, 6, Jul. 6, 7, Aug. 17, Sep. 12, Oct. 2, Dec. 12, 25.

services in Indonesia are operated by PT Kereta Api (Indonesian Railways, www.kereta-api.co.id). Trains may convey any of three classes of seated accommodation which known locally as Eksekutif, Bisnis and Ekonomi, shown in the tables as 1, 2 and 3.

SUMATRA 6200

Kereta Api

dan - Pematangsiantar: *127 km* Journey 4 hours
an depart: 1327◐.
atangsiantar depart: 0725◐.

dan - Rantau Prapat: *266 km* Journey 5½ - 6 hours
an depart: 0840, 1037, 1537, 2235.
au Prapat depart: 0840, 1530, 1730, 2310.

dan - Tanjung Balai: *173 km* Journey 4½ hours
an depart: 0735◐, 1232◐, 1755◐.
ung Balai depart: 0855◐, 1435◐, 1940◐.

Padang - Pariaman: Journey 2 hours.
Padang depart: 0600◐, 0910◐, 1400◐, 1640◐.
Pariaman depart: 0545◐, 0850◐, 1415◐, 1620◐.

Palembang - Lubuk Linggau: *305 km* Journey 7 - 8½ hours
Palembang Kertapati depart: 0930◐, 2000.
Lubuk Linggau depart: 0930◐, 2000.

Palembang - Panjang ♠: *401 km* Journey 8 - 8½ hours
Palembang Kertapati depart: 0830◐, 2100.
Panjang depart: 0830◐, 2100.

Conveys 3rd class only.   ♠ – Panjang is also known as Tanjungkarang Telukbetang.

6205 JAKARTA - BANDUNG

PT Kereta

km		20		22	24	32	34	26	28	30
		12		12	12	12	12	12	12	12
0	**Jakarta** Gambir d.	0500	...	0830	1015	1145	1245	1530	1815	2000
12	**Jakarta** Jatinegara d.	|	...	|	|	|	|	|	|	|
173	**Bandung** a.	0834	...	1155	1335	1457	1547	1828	2127	2312

	19	21	31	33		23	25	27
	12	12	12	12		12	12	12
Bandung d.	0500	0630	0735	0835	...	1150	1430	1615
Jakarta Jatinegara a.	0754	0929	1045	1136	...	1447	1736	1920
Jakarta Gambir a.	0804	0940	1056	1148	...	1457	1747	1931

6210 JAKARTA - SEMARANG - SURABAJA

PT Kereta

km		202	62	14	160	16	2	93	64	66	152	68	178	78	56	12		18	206	70	48	158	97	4
		3	12	1	3	1	1	12	12	12	3	12	3	12	1	1		1	3	12	1	3	12	1
	Bandung d.	...	...	...	...	...	...	0955	...	...	...	...	...	...	...	...	...	...	...	...	...	...	1945	...
	Jakarta Kota d.	...	...	...	...	...	...	|	...	...	...	...	...	...	...	...	...	...	...	...	...	...	|	...
	Jakarta Gambir d.	...	0600	0700	...	0910	0930	|	1000	1115	...	1345	...	...	1500	1615	...	1715	...	1845	1915	...	|	2130
	Jakarta Pasar Senen d.	2300	|	|	0715	|	|	|	|	|	1200	|	1400	1545	|	|	...	|	1630	|	|	1945	|	|
0	**Jakarta** Jatinegara d.	|	|	|	|	|	|	|	|	|	|	|	|	|	|	|	...	|	|	|	|	|	|	|
212	Cirebon d.	0212p	0904	0952	1013p	1155	1212	1405	1304	1420	1501	1648	1715p	1847	1752	1907	...	1958	2000p	2153	2212	2247p	2350	0016
288	Tegal d.	0327	...	1052	1122	...	|	...	...	1542	1610	...	1822	2019	1900	2008	...	...	2118	2328	2315	2356	...	|
348	Pekalongan d.	0427	...	1143	1221	...	1350	...	...	...	1707	...	1918	2121	2003	2100	...	...	...	...	0006	0053	...	|
443	**Semarang** Tawang d.	0552n	...	1300	1343	...	1506	...	...	...	1845n	...	2105	2300	2147	2215	...	...	...	...	0135	0216	...	0304
644	Madiun d.	...	...	...	...	...	|	...	...	...	|	...	|	|	0120	...	...	...	...	...	|	...	...	|
737	Kediri d.	...	...	...	...	...	|	...	...	...	|	...	|	|	|	...	...	...	...	...	|	...	...	|
881	**Malang** a.	...	...	...	...	...	|	...	...	...	0117	...	|	|	|	...	...	...	...	...	|	...	...	|
573	Cepu d.	...	...	...	...	...	|	...	...	...	|	...	2218	0109	♣	...	...	...	...	...	0329	...	...	|
610	Bojonegoro d.	...	...	...	...	...	|	...	...	...	|	...	2355	0146	|	...	...	...	...	...	0406	...	...	|
713	**Surabaja** Pasar Turi a.	...	...	...	...	...	1830	...	...	...	2258↑	...	0130	0320	0346b	...	...	...	...	...	0535	...	...	0630

	91	15	61		63	205	11	65	157	17	1	95	67	69	13	201	151	77	159	55	73	47	3
	13	1	12		12	3	1	12	3	1	1	13	12	12	1	3	3	12	3	1	12	1	1
Surabaja Pasar Turi d.	...	...	...	...	...	...	...	...	...	...	0800	...	...	...	...	...	1415↓	1530	...	1600b	1615	1750	2000
Bojonegoro d.	...	...	...	...	...	...	...	...	...	...	|	...	...	...	...	...	|	1710	...	|	1753	1922	|
Cepu d.	...	...	...	...	...	...	...	...	...	...	|	...	...	...	...	...	|	1747	...	♥	1830	1956	|
Malang d.	...	...	...	...	...	...	...	...	...	...	|	...	...	...	...	...	1145	|	...	|	|	|	|
Kediri d.	...	...	...	...	...	...	...	...	...	...	|	...	...	...	...	...	|	|	...	|	|	|	|
Madiun d.	...	...	...	...	...	...	...	...	...	...	|	...	...	...	...	...	|	|	...	1845	|	|	|
Semarang Tawang d.	...	...	...	...	...	...	0600	...	0800	...	1130	...	...	...	1600	1400n	1841n	2005	2100	2230	2043	2205	2331
Pekalongan d.	...	...	...	...	...	...	0718	...	0928	...	1243	...	...	...	1718	1525	2005	2133	2228	2350	2212	2329	|
Tegal d.	...	...	...	...	0600	0630	0810	...	1030	...	|	...	...	1640	1810	1625	2110	2238	2330	0050	2304	0023	|
Cirebon d.	0500	0545	0615	...	0740	0800p	0913	1000	1140p	1400	1422	1500	1515	1830	1913	1738p	2218	2357	0033p	0157	0021	0128	0219
Jakarta Jatinegara a.	|	0825	0914	...	1032	1109	1148	1251	1427	1636	1649	|	1802	2127	2155	2029	0107	0249	0321	0435	|	0405	0447
Jakarta Pasar Senen a.	|	|	|	...	|	1118	|	|	1436	|	|	|	|	|	|	2038	0116	0258	0330	|	|	|	|
Jakarta Gambir a.	|	0836	0925	...	1043	...	1159	1302	...	1648	1700	|	1812	2138	2206	...	...	...	...	0446	|	0415	0457
Jakarta Kota a.	|	...	...	...	...	...	...	...	...	...	...	|	...	...	...	...	...	...	...	...	|	...	...
Bandung a.	0908	...	...	...	...	...	...	...	...	...	...	1908	...	...	...	...	...	...	...	...	0426	...	...

b – Surabaya Gubeng. n – Semerang Poncol. p – Cirebon Prujakan. ♣ – Via Jombang (d. 0245). ♥ – Via Jombang (d. 1704).

6215 JAKARTA - YOGYAKARTA - SURABAJA

PT Kereta

km		192	210	136	164	10	140	52	86	89	174	166	176	44	42	142	8	54	162	138	134	58	87	84
		3	3	2	3	1	12	1	12	12	3	3	3	1	1	12	1	1	3	2	2	12	12	12
	Jakarta Kota d.	...	...	...	...	...	...	...	...	...	...	♠	...	...	...	...	...	...	...	...	...	...	...	...
	Jakarta Gambir d.	...	...	...	...	0800	...	0850	...	...	...	...	...	1645	1745	...	2015	2044	...	...	...	2215	...	...
	Jakarta Pasar Senen d.	0530	...	0615	0645	|	0815	|	...	...	1030	1300	1600	|	|	1800	|	|	2145	1900	2200	|	...	...
0	**Jakarta** Jatinegara d.	|	...	|	|	|	|	|	...	...	|	|	|	|	|	|	|	|	|	|	|	|	...	...
212	Cirebon d.	0851p	...	0927	0950p	1053	1118	1150	...	...	1345p	1630	1930p	1938	2033	2108	2308	2344	0050p	2159	0107	0124	...	...
343	Purwokerto d.	1058	...	1142	1207	1258	1333	1400	...	...	1615	1836	|	2140	2237	2325	0115	0155	0257	0026	0320	0335	...	...
370	Kroya d.	1148	...	1222	1235	1332	1405	|	...	...	|	|	◄	|	|	0000	|	|	0332	|	|	0403	...	...
445	Kutoarjo d.	1318	...	1340	1357	1444	1526	1540	...	...	1819	2054	|	|	0053	0134	0254	0329	0448	|	0502	...	...	...
508	**Yogyakarta** d.	...	...	1440	1505	1542	...	1632	1630	...	|	2206l	|	0105	0200	...	0352	0420	0555l	0316	0605	...	...	0645
568	Solo Balapan d.	...	...	...	...	1635	...	...	1725	...	|	|	0218j	0200	0300	...	0445	...	...	...	0658	...	...	0744
663	Madiun d.	...	...	...	...	...	...	...	1912	...	2255	0050	0450	0325	0433	...	...	...	...	...	...	...	...	0907
756	Kediri d.	...	...	...	...	...	...	...	|	...	|	0235	0636	|	0615	...	...	...	...	...	...	...	...	|
826	Blitar d.	...	...	...	...	...	...	...	|	...	|	...	...	|	0735	...	...	...	...	...	...	...	...	|
900	**Malang** a.	...	1555	...	...	...	...	...	|	...	|	...	...	0810	0920	...	...	...	...	...	...	...	...	|
750	Jombang d.	...	|	...	...	...	...	...	2048	...	0022	...	...	0446↑	...	...	...	...	...	...	...	...	...	1037
831	**Surabaja** Gubeng a.	...	|	...	...	...	...	...	2151	2200	0125	...	...	0620↑	...	...	...	...	...	...	...	...	0900	1140
	Jember d.	...	2040	...	...	...	...	...	...	0155	...	...	...	...	...	...	...	...	...	...	...	...	1300	...
1140	**Banyuwangi Baru** a.	...	2330	...	...	...	...	...	...	0430	...	...	...	...	...	...	...	...	...	...	...	...	1530	...

		139	135	51	208	7	161	90	143	83	165	57	191	173	175	141	133	137	163	53	9	88	85	43
		12	2	1	3	1	3	12	2	12	3	12	3	3	3	12	2	2	3	1	1	12	12	1
Banyuwangi Baru d.	...	...	...	...	0500	...	...	2200	...	...	♦	...	...	...	...	...	...	...	...	...	...	0900	...	...
Jember d.	...	...	...	...	0750	...	...	0037	...	...	...	...	...	...	...	...	...	...	...	...	...	1135	...	...
Surabaja Gubeng d.	...	...	...	...	|	...	...	0426	0935	0730	...	...	...	1200	...	...	...	...	...	...	...	1528	1725	1700
Jombang d.	...	...	...	...	|	...	...	...	1053	0849	...	...	...	1306	...	...	...	...	...	...	...	...	1832	1805
Malang d.	...	...	...	...	1256	...	...	...	|	|	...	...	...	|	...	...	...	...	...	...	...	...	|	1425↑
Blitar d.	...	...	...	...	...	...	...	...	|	|	...	...	...	|	...	...	...	...	...	...	...	...	|	|
Kediri d.	...	...	...	...	...	...	...	...	1237	|	0745	...	...	|	1300	...	...	...	...	...	...	...	|	|
Madiun d.	...	...	...	...	...	...	...	...	...	1028	1000	...	...	1432	1515	...	...	...	...	...	...	...	2016	1938
Solo Balapan d.	...	...	...	...	...	0800	...	...	...	1200	|	...	...	|	1657j	...	1730	...	...	...	2000	...	2142	2058
Yogyakarta d.	...	...	0700	0800	...	0857	0900l	...	...	1255	1243l	...	...	|	|	...	1835	1745	1800l	2000	2057	...	2232	2200
Kutoarjo d.	...	0700	0804	0857	...	0953	1010	...	...	...	1354	...	1700	1817	►	1900	1941	|	1910	2056	2153	...	...	|
Kroya d.	...	0823	|	|	...	|	1128	...	...	...	|	1530	1845	|	|	2034	2103	|	2049	|	|	...	...	|
Purwokerto d.	...	0900	0952	1040	...	1130	1212	...	...	...	1625	1610	1928	2030	|	2110	2151	2050	2136	2245	2333	...	...	0030
Cirebon d.	...	1125	1200	1245	...	1334	1430p	...	...	...	1849	1820	2142p	2240p	2310p	2334	0011	2300	2343p	0050	0140	...	...	0235
Jakarta Jatinegara a.	...	1409	1457	1521	...	1611	1713	...	...	...	2142	2112	0032	0139	0205	0222	0303	0153	0232	0331	0417	...	...	0818
Jakarta Pasar Senen a.	...	1418	1506	|	...	|	1722	...	...	...	2153	|	0041	0148	0214	0231	0312	0202	0241	|	|	...	...	|
Jakarta Gambir a.	...	...	...	1533	...	1622	...	...	...	...	...	2123	...	...	...	...	...	...	...	0342	0428	...	...	0529
Jakarta Kota a.	...	...	...	...	...	...	...	...	...	...	...	...	...	...	...	...	...	...	...	...	...	...	...	...

j – Solo Jebres.
l – Yogyakarta Lempuyangan.
p – Cirebon Prujakan.
♠ – From Merak dep. 0815.
♦ – To Merak arr. 0207.
► – Via Semarang Tawang (d. 1925) and Tegal (d. 2155).
◄ – Via Tegal (d. 2042) and Semarang Twang (d. 2327).

6220 BANDUNG - SURABAYA

PT Kereta

km		80	6	132	100	82	50	180	102	104
		12	1	2	123	12	1		13	13
0	**Bandung** d.	0720	0830	1545	1650	1855	1930	...	...	...
124	Tasikmalaya d.	1016	1119	1853	2002	2153	2224	0825	...	...
156	Banjar d.	1115	1215	1955	2058	2355	2325	0930	...	...
249	Kroya d.	|	1356	2127	2239	0035	0122	|	...	...
324	Kutoarjo d.	1414	1505	2340	0033	0200	0234	1308	...	...
387	**Yogyakarta** d.	1520	1602	0048	0135	0304	0332	1425l	0730	2045
447	Solo Balapan d.	1615	1652	0141	0250	0400	0424	|	0834	2152
542	Madiun d.	...	1810	0305	0408	...	0545	1737	1035	2320
635	Kediri d.	...	|	|	0552	...	|	|	1238	0108
705	Blitar d.	...	|	|	0707	...	|	|	1351	0223
779	**Malang** a.	...	|	|	0901	...	|	|	1537	0400
629	Jombang d.	...	1925	0427	...	...	0706	2032	...	...
710	**Surabaya** Gubeng a.	...	2019	0531	...	...	0812	2136	...	...

	79	5	81	99	49	131	103	179
	12	1	12	123	1	2	13	3
Surabaya Gubeng d.	...	0700	...	...	1830	1900	...	0815
Jombang d.	...	0756	...	...	1735	2011	...	0920
Malang d.	...	|	...	1600	|	|	2015	|
Blitar d.	...	|	...	1746	|	|	2155	|
Kediri d.	...	|	...	1856	|	|	2308	|
Madiun d.	...	0910	...	2055	1915	2146	0115	1112
Solo Balapan d.	0700	1029	1900	2235	2034	2325	0303	|
Yogyakarta d.	0808	1125	2008	2332	2128	0030	0357	1400l
Kutoarjo d.	0910	1225	2109	0031	2223	0141	...	1509
Kroya d.	|	1345	2230	0252	0002	0334	...	|
Banjar d.	1212	1525	0030	0425	0140	0500	...	1845
Tasikmalaya d.	1308	1621	0126	0526	0236	0620	...	2004
Bandung a.	1600	1906	0418	0825	0521	0959	...	...

AUSTRALIA

:al: **Canberra** (GMT +10). 2016 Public Holidays: Jan. 1, 26, Mar. 25, 27, 28, Apr. 25, June 8(not WA), Dec. 25, 26, 27.

state trains are operated by Great Southern Rail (GSR) (www.gsr.com.au). Intrastate services are operated by Government owned agencies NSW Train Link (New South s, www.nswtrainlink.info), Queensland Rail (QR) (Queensland, www.qr.com.au), V/Line (Victoria, www.vline.com.au) and Transwa (Western Australia, www.transwa.wa. au). Unless indicated all trains convey first and second class seated accommodation. On GSR and some overnight trains the first class accommodation is usually a private partment which converts to sleeping berths for night time travel. The exact offering varies by operator and by train. Most longer distance trains also convey a refreshment y. Due to the low frequency of trains reservations are recommended, even if they are not always compulsory. GSR offer the Rail Explorer Pass which gives either 2 or 3 hs unlimited travel in a Red Daynighter Seat on their services. Prices: 2 months AU$545, 3 months AU$655. NSW Train Link offer the Discovery Pass which gives either 14 1 month, 3 months or 6 months unlimited travel on their rail and coach network and are available for travel in either economy or premium. Prices range from AU$ 232 for a 14 economy pass to AU$ 550 for a 6 month premium pass. QR have the Explorer Pass which offers either 1 month (AU$ 299) or 2 months (AU$ 389) unlimited travel on their ces. They also offer the Costal Pass for unlimited travel in one direction between Brisbane and Cairns or vice versa. Prices 1 month AU$ 209, 2 months AU$ 289. ervations are required for all journeys and supplements may also be payable. See www.railaustralia.com.au or www.acprail.com

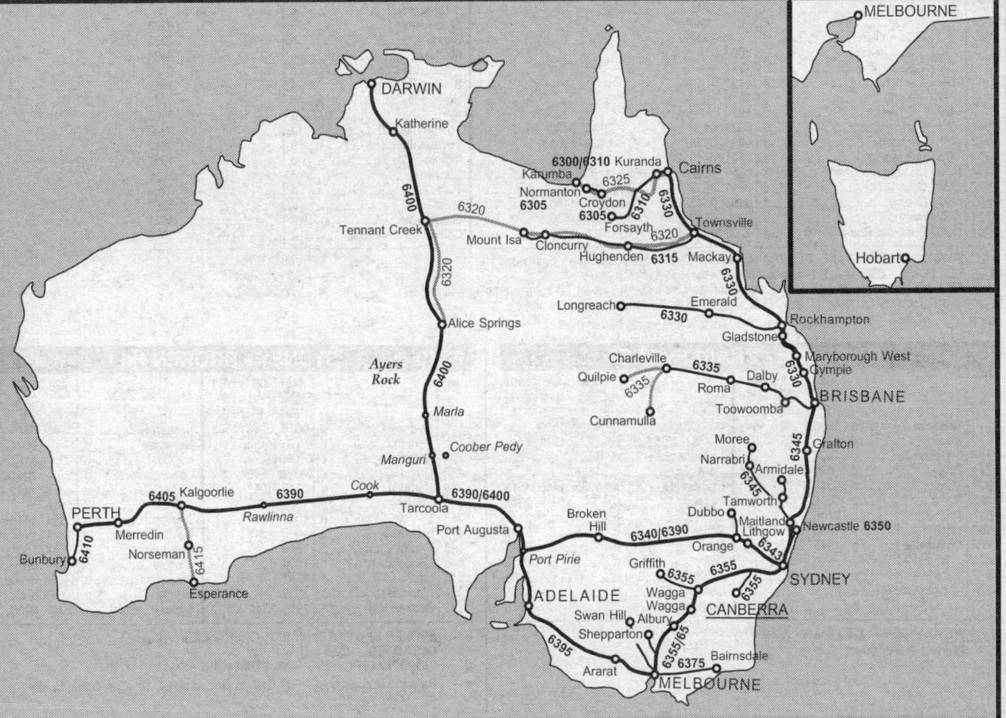

CAIRNS - KURANDA 6300

eensland Rail

n		3K30 2 ab	3K32 2 a		3C61 2 ab	3C65 2 a
0	**Cairns** d.	0830	0930	**Kuranda** d.	1400	1530
	Freshwater d.	0850	0950	Freshwater d.	1532	1702
3	**Kuranda** a.	1025	1125	**Cairns** a.	1555	1725

Not Apr. 30, May 1, 28, 29, Oct. 15, 16, Nov. 12, 13, Dec. 3, 4, 25.
Not May 7, 14, 21, Sept 3,10,17.

CAIRNS - FORSAYTH 6310

ST

n		4 ③B	4 ④B		5 ⑤B	5 ⑥B
0	**Cairns** d.	0630	...	**Forsayth** d.	0830	...
3	Kuranda d.	0810	...	Einasleigh d.	1215	...
4	Mareeba d.	0930	...	Mount Suprise a.	1415	...
4	Almaden a.	1315	...	Mount Suprise d.	...	0815
4	Almaden d.	...	0800	Almaden a.	...	1145
2	Mount Suprise a.	...	1130	Almaden d.	...	1215
2	Mount Suprise d.	...	1215	Mareeba d.	...	|
7	Einasleigh d.	...	1445	Kuranda a.	...	1650
3	**Forsayth** a.	...	1730	**Cairns** a.	...	1830

SAVANNAHLANDER – [2]. Mar. 2 - Dec. 14.
ator: Cairns Kuranda Steam Ltd ✆ +61 7 4053 6848.

TOWNSVILLE - TENNANT CREEK 6320

eyhound

n		489 🚌 D			849 🚌 E	
0	**Townsville** d.	1900	...	**Alice Springs** d.	0900	...
5	Charters Towers d.	2040	...	Barrow Creek d	1235	...
8	Hughenden d.	0010	...	**Tennant Creek** d.	1545	...
0	Richmond d.	0135	...	Barkly Homestead d.	1815	...
4	Julia Creek d.	0315	...	Camooweal d.	2130	...
8	Cloncurry d.	0535	...	**Mount Isa** a.	0010	...
6	**Mount Isa** a.	0655	...	**Mount Isa** d.	0010	...
6	**Mount Isa** d.	0705	...	Cloncurry d.	0135	...
4	Camooweal d.	0915	...	Julia Creek d.	0310	...
3	Barkly Homestead d.	1205	...	Richmond d.	0440	...
7	**Tennant Creek** a.	1415	...	Hughenden d.	0635	...
1	Barrow Creek d.	1650	...	Charters Towers d.	0930	...
2	**Alice Springs** a.	2030	...	**Townsville** a.	1115	...

③⑦. E – ②⑤. Operator: Greyhound Australia ✆ 07 3258 1600.

NORMANTON - CROYDON 6305

Queensland Rail

km		③ A			④ A	
0	**Normanton** d.	0830	...	**Croydon** d.	0830	...
90	Blackbull a.	1115	...	Blackbull a.	1015	...
152	**Croydon** a.	1330	...	**Normanton** a.	1330	...

A – GULFLANDER – [2]. Services usually suspended mid Dec. - mid Feb.

TOWNSVILLE - MOUNT ISA 6315

Queensland Rail

km		3M34 ④⑦C			3231 ①⑤C	
0	**Townsville** d.	1240	...	**Mount Isa** d.	1330	...
138	Charters Towers d.	1540	...	Duchess d.	1515	...
388	Hughenden d.	2020	...	Cl oncurry d.	1745	...
502	Richmond d.	2245	...	Julia Creek d.	2100	...
648	Julia Creek d.	0210	...	Richmond d.	0005	...
780	Cloncurry d.	0520	...	Hughenden d.	0240	...
890	Duchess d.	0745	...	Charters Towers d.	0705	...
977	**Mount Isa** a.	0935	...	**Townsville** a.	1010	...

C – INLANDER – [2] and 🍸 Townsville - Mount Isa and v.v. Ⓡ.

CAIRNS - KARUMBA 6325

Trans North Bus

km		🚌 ①③⑤			🚌 ②④⑥	
0	**Cairns** Central d.	0630	...	**Karumba** d.	0630	...
33	Kuranda d.	0705	...	Normanton d.	0725	...
75	Mareeba d.	0740	...	Croydon d.	0925	...
109	Atherton d.	0820	...	Georgetown d.	1055	...
140	Herberton d.	0835	...	Mount Surprise d.	1240	...
160	Ravenshoe d.	0945	...	Undara d.	1305	...
211	Mount Garnet d.	1015	...	Mount Garnet d.	1355	...
287	Undara d.	1105	...	Ravenshoe d.	1450	...
321	Mount Surprise d.	1130	...	Herberton d.	1520	...
422	Georgetown d.	1325	...	Atherton d.	1540	...
579	Croydon d.	1505	...	Mareeba d.	1615	...
744	Normanton d.	1645	...	Kuranda d.	1640	...
820	**Karumba** a.	1730	...	**Cairns** Central a.	1730	...

Operator: Trans North Bus and Coach ✆ 07 4095 8644.

6330 CAIRNS, TOWNSVILLE and LONGREACH - BRISBANE

Queensland

km	km		A960	V9Q4	Q904	Q904	Q902	Q902		
			①④	◀	②⑤	①④⑥	①④⑥	△		
			C	A	B	B*	B	B*		
0		**Cairns** d.	...	0900	...	...	...	...	...	...
23		Gordonvale d.	...	0931	...	...	...	...	...	...
87		Innisfail d.	...	1050	...	...	...	...	...	...
135		Tully d.	...	1150	...	...	...	...	...	...
178		Cardwell d.	...	1245	...	...	...	...	...	...
232		Ingham d.	...	1338	...	...	...	...	...	...
340		**Townsville** a.	...	1509	...	...	...	...	...	...
340		**Townsville** d.	...	1519	...	...	...	...	...	...
421		Ayr d.	...	1625	...	...	...	...	...	...
432		Home Hill d.	...	1639	...	...	...	...	...	...
531		Bowen d.	...	1745	...	...	...	...	...	...
596		Proserpine d.	...	1830	...	...	...	...	...	...
717		Mackay d.	...	2015	...	...	...	...	...	...
754		Sarina d.	...	2049	...	...	...	...	...	...
869		St Lawrence d.	...	2212	...	...	...	...	...	...
	0	**Longreach** d.	1000	|	...	...	...	...	...	...
	108	Barcaldine d.	1227	|	...	...	...	...	...	...
	194	Jericho d.	1405	|	...	...	...	...	...	...
	249	Alpha d.	1518	|	...	...	...	...	...	...
	422	Emerald d.	1928	|	...	...	...	...	...	...
1042	687	Rockhampton d.	0032	0110	...	...	0710	0730	...	...
1152	797	Gladstone d.	0255	0228	...	...	0828	0904	...	...
1330	975	Bundaberg d.	0501	0410	0515	0515	1009	1127	...	...
1414	1059	Maryborough West d.	0640	0502	0605	0627	1102	1241	...	...
1507	1152	Gympie North d.	0811	0612	0705	0752	1205	1412	...	...
1550	1195	Cooroy d.	0856	0645	0738	0838	1237	1458	...	...
1575	1220	Nambour d.	0928	0710	0800	0918	1257	1530	...	...
1681	1326	**Brisbane** Roma Street a.	1200	0920	0950	1140	1455	1750	...	...

	Q301	Q301	AW57	VCQ5		Q303	Q303	AW57
	②⑤⑦	①④⑥	⑥	▶		△	①④	②
	B	B*	C	A		B*	B	C
Brisbane Roma Street d.	1100	1100	1355	1545	...	1620	1655	1810
Nambour d.	1235	1316	1626	1736	...	1845	1841	2026
Cooroy d.	1258	1340	1649	1757	...	1909	1859	2049
Gympie North d.	1342	1446	1745	1831	...	1957	1932	2145
Maryborough West d.	1443	1611	1910	1933	...	2122	2033	2310
Bundaberg d.	1534	1724	2041	2026	...	2330	2125	0018
Gladstone d.	1713	1946	2309	2210	...	...	...	0246
Rockhampton d.	1845	2125	0103	2341	...	...	...	0440
Emerald d.	...	...	0557	|	...	...	...	0935
Alpha d.	...	...	1007	|	...	...	...	1345
Jericho d.	...	...	1118	|	...	...	...	1456
Barcaldine d.	...	...	1311	|	...	...	...	1650
Longreach a.	...	...	1535	|	...	...	...	1915
St Lawrence d.	...	...	...	0203	...	...	...	...
Sarina d.	...	...	...	0333	...	...	...	...
Mackay d.	...	...	...	0424	...	...	...	...
Prosperine d.	...	...	...	0602	...	...	...	...
Bowen d.	...	...	...	0642	...	...	...	...
Home Hill d.	...	...	...	0748	...	...	...	...
Ayr d.	...	...	...	0802	...	...	...	...
Townsville a.	...	...	...	0902	...	...	...	...
Townsville d.	...	...	...	0912	...	...	...	...
Ingham d.	...	...	...	1052	...	...	...	...
Cardwell d.	...	...	...	1155	...	...	...	...
Tully d.	...	...	...	1254	...	...	...	...
Innisfail d.	...	...	...	1350	...	...	...	...
Gordonvale d.	...	...	...	1521	...	...	...	...
Cairns a.	...	...	...	1605	...	...	...	...

A – SPIRIT OF QUEENSLAND TILT TRAIN – 🛏 R, [2] and 🍷 Brisbane - Cairns and v.v.
B – TILT TRAIN – [12] and 🍷 Brisbane - Bundaberg, Rockhampton and v.v.
B* – [2] and 🍷 Traditional diesel replacement service until mid-2016 whilst Tilt trains are being refurbished.
C – SPIRIT OF THE OUTBACK – 🛏 1cl ✕, [2] and 🍷 Brisbane - Longreach and v.v.
🛏 R – RailBed – This is a seat by day and converts to a lie-flat bed at night.
△ – ②③⑤⑦.
▶ – ①②③⑤⑥.
◀ – ①③④⑤⑦.

6335 BRISBANE - CHARLEVILLE

Queensland Rail

km		3S86	🚌	🚌
		②④	③⑤	③⑤
		D		
0	**Brisbane** ‡ d.	1915	...	...
38	Ipswich d.	2015	...	...
161	Toowoomba d.	2320	...	...
244	Dalby d.	0120	...	...
371	Miles d.	0330	...	...
512	Roma d.	0615	...	...
597	Mitchell d.	0805	...	...
687	Morven d.	1000	...	...
777	**Charleville** a.	1145	1155	1155
875	Wyandra a.	...	1315	|
972	Cunnamulla a.	...	1425	|
876	Cooladdi a.	...	...	1305
998	Quilpie a.	...	...	1430

	🚌	🚌	3907
	③⑤	③⑤	③⑤
			D
Quilpie d.	...	1500	...
Cooladdi d.	...	1640	...
Cunnamulla d.	1500	|	...
Wyandra d.	1625	|	...
Charleville d.	1735	1740	1815
Morven d.	...	...	2000
Mitchell d.	...	...	2150
Roma d.	...	...	2335
Miles d.	...	...	0215
Dalby d.	...	...	0450
Toowoomba d.	...	...	0700
Ipswich d.	...	...	1015
Brisbane ‡ a.	...	...	1125

D – WESTLANDER – [2] and 🍷. [R].
‡ – Brisbane **Roma Street**.

6340 SYDNEY - BROKEN HILL

NSW Train L

km		445	427	WE1
		①		③
		E	F	G
0	**Sydney** Central d.	0618	0718	1503
	Penrith d.	0704u	0806u	|
	Katoomba d.	0759u	0859u	|
155	Lithgow d.	0839u	0940	|
240	Bathurst d.	0947	1052	|
290	Blayney d.	1035	1138	|
323	Orange d.	1059	1202	|
462	**Dubbo** a.	|	1345	|
446	Parkes d.	1248	|	|
546	Condobolin d.	1400	|	|
816	Ivanhoe d.	1631	|	|
1017	Menindee d.	1822	|	|
1125	**Broken Hill** a.	1910	*2245**	0600

	428	446
		②
	F	E
Broken Hill d.	*0345**	0745
Menindee d.	|	0924
Ivanhoe d.	|	1107
Condobolin d.	|	1341
Parkes d.	|	1443
Dubbo d.	1415	|
Orange d.	1554	1644
Blayney d.	1621	1716
Bathurst d.	1707	1801
Lithgow d.	1823	1913s
Katoomba d.	1905s	1954s
Penrith d.	1956s	2045s
Sydney Central a.	2044	2130

E – BROKEN HILL OUTBACK EXPLORER – [2] and 🍷.
F – DUBBO XPT – [12] and 🍷.
G – INDIAN PACIFIC – See Table **6390/6400**.
s – Calls to set down only. **u** – Calls to pick up only. * – Connection by 🚌.

6343 SYDNEY - LITHGOW - BATHURST

Sydney Trains NSW Train L

km		505	507	A	509	529	525	527	503	501	533	4501
		①–⑤	①–⑤		①–⑤	⑥⑦	①–⑤	⑦	⑦	①–⑤	①–⑤	
0	**Sydney** Central d.	0420	0818	1018	1218	1218	1418	1418	1618	1621	1721	1752
55	Penrith **u** d.	0508	0906	1106	1305	1309	1505	1509	1709	1708	1808	1839
110	Katoomba d.	0619	1016	1217	1416	1419	1616	1619	1819	1812	1912	1940
127	Mount Victoria d.	0642	1037	1237	1437	1440	1637	1640	1840	1833	1933	2001
155	**Lithgow** a.	0710	1110	1305	1505	1510	1705	1710	1910	1911	2011	2025
240	**Bathurst** a.	*0815**	*1225**	...	*1625**	*1625**	*1820**	*1820**	*2015**	*2015**	2121	2135

	4502	504	502	506	4506	508	510	534	536	538
	①–⑤	①–⑤	①–⑤	①–⑤	⑥	①–⑤	Ⓒ	①–⑤	⑦	①–⑤
	C		B							
Bathurst d.	0549	*0535**	...	*1005**	*1005**	*1205**	*1205**	*1410**	*1420**	*1820**
Lithgow d.	0657	0724	0925	1125	1137	1325	1337	1525	1537	1934
Mount Victoria d.	0724	0754	0954	1154	1205	1354	1405	1554	1605	2002
Katoomba d.	0740	0814	1013	1213	1225	1413	1425	1613	1625	2021
Penrith **s** d.	0838	0925	1123	1324	1335	1524	1535	1724	1735	2132
Sydney Central a.	0927	1014	1214	1414	1431	1614	1631	1814	1831	2222

A – Additional services: ① – ⑤ 0018, 0621, 1752, 1836, 2018, 2218; ⑥⑦ 0018, 0348, 0548, 0818, 1418, 1618, 1818, 2018, 2218.
B – Additional services: ① – ⑤ 0300, 0415, 0508, 0538, 0608, 1733, 2134; ⑥⑦ 0338, 0438, 0637, 0737, 0937, 1137, 1537, 1737, 1937, 2208.
C – Additional service: ⑥⑦ 0725. **s** – Calls to set down only. **u** – Calls to pick up only. * – Connection by 🚌.

6345 BRISBANE, ARMIDALE and MOREE - SYDNEY

NSW Train L

km	km		036	244	224	032	034			
			H	J	K	L	M			
0		**Brisbane** Roma Street d.	...	...	...	0555	*1510**	...	...	...
182		Casino d.	...	...	...	0820	1930	...	...	...
291		Grafton City d.	0515	...	...	0953	2058	...	...	...
379		Coffs Harbour d.	0626	...	...	1105	2210	...	...	...
		Nambucca Heads d.	0708	...	...	1147	2251r	...	...	...
		Macksville d.	0721	...	...	1200	2305r	...	...	...
483		Kempsey d.	0805	...	...	1243	2347	...	...	...
532		Wauchope d.	0844	...	...	1322	0024	...	...	...
608		Taree d.	0952	...	...	1441	0131	...	...	...
	0	**Armidale** d.	|	...	0840	|	|	...	...	...
	124	Tamworth d.	|	...	1027	|	|	...	...	...
	◐	**Moree** d.	|	0805	|	|	|	...	...	...
	◐	Narrabri d.	|	0910	|	|	|	...	...	...
	◐	Gunnedah d.	|	1014	|	|	|	...	...	...
	168	Werris Creek d.	|	1107	1107	|	|	...	...	...
	264	Scone d.	|	1228	1228	|	|	...	...	...
	290	Muswellbrook d.	|	1248	1248	|	|	...	...	...
794	387	Maitland d.	1253	1355	1355	1732	0410	...	...	...
824	416	Broadmeadow d.	1319	1419	1419	1754	0433	...	...	...
897	499	Gosford d.	1419s	1521s	1521s	1855s	0538s	...	...	...
953	545	Hornsby d.	1459s	1603s	1603s	1936s	0622s	...	...	...
987	579	**Sydney** Central a.	1539	1638	1638	2012	0659	...	...	...

	033	243	223	035	031			
	M	J	K	H	L			
Sydney Central d.	0711	0929	0929	1141	1441	...	...	...
Hornsby d.	0750u	1005u	1005u	1220u	1520u	...	...	...
Gosford d.	0832u	1044u	1044u	1300u	1601u	...	...	...
Broadmeadow d.	0936	1145	1145	1405	1704	...	...	...
Maitland d.	1000	1210	1210	1429	1727	...	...	...
Muswellbrook d.	|	1316	1316	|	|	...	...	...
Scone d.	|	1337	1337	|	|	...	...	...
Werris Creek d.	|	1457	1457	|	|	...	...	...
Gunnedah d.	|	1545	|	|	|	...	...	...
Narrabri a.	|	1652	|	|	|	...	...	...
Moree a.	|	1800	|	|	|	...	...	...
Tamworth a.	|	...	1537	|	|	...	...	...
Armidale a.	|	...	1735	|	|	...	...	...
Taree d.	1241	...	...	1725	2008	...	...	...
Wauchope d.	1348	...	...	1831	2113	...	...	...
Kempsey d.	1426	...	...	1910	2152	...	...	...
Macksville d.	1507	...	...	1955	2234	...	...	...
Nambucca Heads a.	1519	...	...	2009	*2305**	...	...	...
Coffs Harbour d.	1558	...	...	2050	2335	...	...	...
Grafton City d.	1712	...	...	2215	0049	...	...	...
Casino a.	1841	...	...	...	0219	...	...	...
Brisbane Roma Street a.	*2234**	...	...	...	0453	...	...	...

H – GRAFTON XPT – [12] . [R].
J – MOREE EXPLORER – [12] and 🍷. [R].
K – ARMIDALE XPLORER – [12] and 🍷. [R].
L – BRISBANE XPT – [12] Brisbane - Sydney; 🛏 1 cl., [2] Sydney - Brisbane. [R].
M – CASINO XPT – 🛏 1 cl., [2] Casino - Sydney; [12] Sydney - Casino. [R].
r – Calls on request.
s – Calls to set down only.
u – Calls to pick up only.
* – Connection by 🚌.
◐ – Moree - Narrabri: *97 km*. Moree - Gunnedah: *190 km*. Moree - Werris Creek: *255*

NEWCASTLE - SYDNEY 6350

ney Trains

		Ⓐ	Ⓐ	Ⓐ	Ⓐ	Ⓐ	Ⓐ	Ⓐ	Ⓐ	Ⓐ	Ⓐ	Ⓐ		Ⓐ	Ⓐ	Ⓐ	Ⓐ	Ⓐ	Ⓐ	Ⓐ	Ⓐ	Ⓐ	Ⓐ
Newcastle d.	Ⓐ	0210*	0405*	0420*	0503*	0530*	0603*	0623*	0701*	0712*	0801*	0812*	and at the	1301*	1312*	1359*	1413*	1453*	1512*	1601*	1612*	1701*	1803*
Hamilton d.		0231	0425	0440	0525	0552	0625	0645	0725	0736	0825	0836	same minutes	1325	1336	1423	1437	1517	1536	1625	1636	1725	1825
Gosford d.		0357	0536	0606	0635	0705	0735	0806	0835	0900	0936	1000	past each	1436	1500	1533	1601	1638	1700	1736	1800	1836	1936
Sydney Central a.		0527	0656	0726	0756	0826	0855	0926	0955	1025	1056	1126	hour until	1556	1626	1659	1729	1759	1826	1856	1926	1956	2056

	Ⓐ	Ⓐ	Ⓐ	Ⓐ	Ⓐ		Ⓒ	Ⓒ	Ⓒ	Ⓒ	Ⓒ	Ⓒ	Ⓒ	Ⓒ	Ⓒ	Ⓒ	Ⓒ	Ⓒ	Ⓒ	Ⓒ	Ⓒ	Ⓒ	Ⓒ	Ⓒ	Ⓒ
astle d.	1814*	1903*	1914*	2014*	2113*	Ⓒ	0228*	0419*	0508*	0617*	0706*	0816*	0906*	1016*	1106*	1216*	1306*	1416*	1506*	1616*	1705*	1818*	1851*	1952*	2122*
ton d.	1836	1925	1936	2036	2135		0248	0439	0530	0639	0730	0840	0930	1040	1130	1240	1330	1430	1530	1640	1729	1840	1913	2014	2144
ord d.	2000	2036	2101	2200	2302		0414	0551	0651	0751	0851	0951	1051	1151	1251	1351	1451	1551	1651	1751	1851	1951	2039	2140	2304
ey Central a.	2126	2156	2226	2325	0029		0541	0710	0810	0910	1010	1110	1210	1310	1410	1510	1610	1710	1810	1910	2010	2110	2210	2310	0045

		Ⓐ	Ⓐ	Ⓐ	Ⓐ	Ⓐ	Ⓐ	Ⓐ	Ⓐ	Ⓐ	Ⓐ		Ⓐ	Ⓐ	Ⓐ	Ⓐ	Ⓐ	Ⓐ	Ⓐ	Ⓐ	Ⓐ	Ⓐ	Ⓐ	Ⓐ
ey Central d.	Ⓐ	0145	0345	0445	0515	0545	0615	0645	0715	0745	0815	and at the same	1315	1345	1415	1515	1545	1615	1645	1715	1745	1815	1915	2015
ord d.		0311	0512	0612	0635	0712	0735	0812	0841	0912	0935	minutes	1435	1513	1536	1635	1705	1735	1805	1833	1905	1935	2035	2135
lton a.		0441	0637	0737	0746	0837	0858	0937	0956	1038	1047	past each	1558	1641	1704	1746	1819	1848	1920	1943	2020	2046	2158	2258
astle a.		0456*	0654*	0754*	0803*	0854*	0915*	0954*	1013*	1055*	1104*	hour until	1615*	1658*	1721*	1803*	1836*	1905*	1937*	2000*	2037*	2103*	2215*	2315*

	Ⓐ	Ⓐ	Ⓐ	Ⓐ		⑥	Ⓒ	Ⓒ	Ⓒ	Ⓒ	Ⓒ	Ⓒ	Ⓒ	Ⓒ	Ⓒ	Ⓒ	Ⓒ	Ⓒ	Ⓒ	Ⓒ	Ⓒ	Ⓒ	Ⓒ	Ⓒ	Ⓒ
ey Central d.	2115	2145	2245	2345	Ⓒ	0145	0445	0545	0715	0815	0915	1015	1115	1215	1315	1415	1515	1615	1715	1815	1915	2015	2145	2245	2345
ord d.	2235	2313	0015	0115		0311	0615	0717	0841	0936	1036	1136	1236	1336	1436	1536	1636	1736	1836	1936	2036	2142	2315	0015	0115
lton a.	2359	0042	0143	0244		0441	0740	0843	0953	1058	1148	1258	1348	1458	1548	1658	1748	1858	1948	2058	2154	2308	0042	0142	0242
astle a.	0014*	0057*	0158*	0259*		0456*	0757*	0900*	1010*	1115*	1205*	1315*	1405*	1515*	1605*	1715*	1805*	1915*	2005*	2115*	2211*	2325*	0057*	0157*	0257*

By 🚌.

Operator: Sydney Trains ✆ 02 4907 7500.

SYDNEY - CANBERRA, GRIFFITH and MELBOURNE 6355

V Train Link

	631 ⑥⑦A	641 ⑦B	631 ⒶA	623 C	633 A	635 A	621 D			
Sydney Central d.	0657	0657	0704	0732	1208	1812	2032	...	...	...
Moss Vale d.	0839	0839	0854	0921	1354	2004	2218	...	...	...
Goulburn d.	0929	0929	0944	1012	1444	2054	2309	...	...	...
Queanbeyan d.	1051	|	1106	|	1606	2216	|	...	...	...
Canberra a.	1107	|	1122	|	1622	2230	|	...	...	...
Yass Junction d.	...	1053	...	1120	...	...	0017r	...	...	...
Harden d.	...	1144r	...	1211r	...	...	0107r	...	...	...
Cootamundra d.	...	1217	...	1246	...	...	0142	...	...	...
Junee d.	...	1258	...	1327	...	...	0220	...	...	...
Narrandera d.	...	1414	...	|	...	...	|	...	...	...
Griffith a.	...	1520	...	|	...	...	|	...	...	...
Wagga Wagga a.	...	...	...	1354	...	...	0247	...	...	...
The Rock d.	...	...	...	1414r	...	...	0305r	...	...	...
Culcairn d.	...	...	...	1441r	...	...	0332r	...	...	...
Albury 6365 a.	...	...	...	1511	...	...	0403	...	...	...
Wangaratta 6365 d.	...	...	...	1553	...	...	0445	...	...	...
Benalla 6365 d.	...	...	...	1617	...	...	0509	...	...	...
Melbourne S Cross a.	...	...	...	1830	...	...	0725	...	...	...

	632 A	642 ⑦B	634 ⑥⑦A	634 ⒶA	624 C	636 ⑥⑦A	636 ⒶA	622 D		
Melbourne S Cross d.	...	...	...	...	0830	...	...	1950	...	...
Benalla 6365 d.	...	...	...	...	1041	...	...	2154	...	...
Wangaratta 6365 d.	...	...	...	...	1106	...	...	2220	...	...
Albury 6365 d.	...	...	...	...	1149	...	...	2305	...	...
Culcairn d.	...	...	...	...	1221r	...	...	2334r	...	...
The Rock d.	...	...	...	...	1249r	...	...	0002r	...	...
Wagga Wagga d.	...	...	...	...	1307	...	...	0022	...	...
Griffith d.	...	0720	...	...	|	...	...	|	...	...
Narrandera d.	...	0821	...	...	|	...	...	|	...	...
Junee d.	...	0941	...	...	1351	...	...	0048	...	...
Cootamundra d.	...	1032	...	...	1438	...	...	0135	...	...
Harden d.	...	1108r	...	...	1514r	...	...	0241r	...	...
Yass Junction d.	...	1159	...	...	1605	...	...	0305r	...	...
Canberra d.	0650	|	1140	1153	|	1720	1725	|	...	...
Queanbeyan d.	0659	|	1149	1202	|	1729	1734	|	...	...
Goulburn d.	0820	1313	1310	1323	1715	1851	1856	0413	...	...
Moss Vale d.	0913	1413	1413	1415	1804	1944	1950	0502	...	...
Sydney Central a.	1056	1556	1556	1559	1953	2125	2137	0653	...	...

CANBERRA XPLORER – [12] and 🍸.
GRIFFITH XPLORER – [12] and 🍸.
C – MELBOURNE XPT – [12] and 🍸.
D – MELBOURNE XPT – 🛏 1 cl., [12] and ✕.
b – 1432 on ⑥⑦.
r – Calls on request.

MELBOURNE - SHEPPARTON 6360

ne

	①-⑤	⑥	⑦	①-⑤	①-⑤	①-⑤	⑦	①-⑤	①-⑤	⑥⑦
Melbourne S Cross d.	0701	0912	0930	0932	1252	1432	1512	1631	1822	1832
Seymour a.	0833	1027	1052	1053	1410	1554	1632	1808	1945	1951
Seymour d.	0845*	1032	1057	1058	1415	1605*	1640*	1815*	1950	1956
Murchison East d.	|	1107	1132	1133	1450	1650*	|	|	2025	2031
Murchison d.	|	|	|	|	|	1653*	1728*	1903*	|	|
Shepparton a.	0955*	1141	1206	1207	1523	1723*	1800*	1935*	2059	2105

	①-⑤ F	⑥⑦ E	①-⑤	①-⑤	①-⑤	⑦	⑥	①-⑤	⑦	⑤
Shepparton d.	0631	0704	0850*	1040*	1250	1342*	1605	1606	1705	1800*
Murchison d.	|	|	0920*	1107*	|	1407*	|	|	|	1832*
Murchison East d.	0659	0732	|	|	1317	|	1633	1633	1733	|
Seymour a.	0734	0807	1015*	1155*	1352	1457*	1708	1708	1808	1920*
Seymour d.	0736	0809	1034	1214	1354	1512	1710	1710	1810	1955
Melbourne S Cross a.	0910	0928	1154	1335	1515	1635	1829	1835	1929	2122

10 - 12 minutes later on ⑦.
F – Additional service ①-⑤ dep. Shepparton 0515 arr. Melbourne S Cross 0759.
* – By 🚌.

MELBOURNE - ALBURY 6365

ne

		C		①-⑤		D				
Melbourne S Cross d.	0705	0830	1205	1432	1802	1950	...	...	...	...
Seymour a.	0824	|	1319	1554	1930	|	...	...	...	...
Seymour d.	0826	0948u	1321	1605*	1932	2059u	...	...	...	...
Benalla d.	0930	1041	1425	1720*	2036	2154	...	...	...	...
Wangaratta d.	0955	1106	1440	1755*	2101	2220	...	...	...	...
Wodonga d.	1043	|	1538	1840*	2149	|	...	...	...	...
Albury a.	1055	1149	1550	1850*	2200	2305	...	...	...	...

	D		①-⑤		C					
Albury d.	0403	0635	0900*	1245	1511	1720	...	...	...	...
Wodonga d.	|	0645	0910*	1255	|	1730	...	...	...	...
Wangaratta d.	0445	0731	1000*	1341	1553	1816	...	...	...	...
Benalla d.	0509	0758	1035*	1408	1617	1843	...	...	...	...
Seymour a.	|	0900	1200*	1510	|	1945	...	...	...	...
Seymour d.	0605s	0902	1214	1512	1711s	1947	...	...	...	...
Melbourne S Cross a.	0725	1030	1335	1635	1830	2140	...	...	...	...

MELBOURNE XPT – [12] and 🍸 Sydney Central - Melbourne Southern Cross and v.v.
MELBOURNE XPT – 🛏 1 cl., [12] and ✕ Sydney Central - Melbourne Southern Cross and v.v.
s – Calls to set down only.
u – Calls to pick up only.
* – By 🚌.

MELBOURNE - WARRNAMBOOL 6370

ne

	⑥	①-⑤	⑦	⑥	①-⑤	⑦	①-⑤	⑥⑦	①-⑤	
Melbourne S Cross d.	0700	0720	0900	1300	1321	1610	1622	1900	1912	...
Geelong ☛ a.	0810	0828	1008	1408	1426	1708	1732	2008	2020	...
Geelong d.	0813	0833	1013	1413	1431	1720*	1745*	2013	2025	...
Colac d.	0915	0936	1115	1515	1534	1825*	1912*	2115	2128	...
Warrnambool a.	1030	1052	1230	1630	1650	2000*	...	2230	2249	...

	⑥	①-⑤	⑦		⑥	①-⑤	⑦		⑥⑦	①-⑤
Warrnambool d.	0550	0600	0725	...	1130	1208	1210*	...	1730	1750
Colac d.	0708	0719	0843	...	1248	1326	1405*	...	1848	1908
Geelong a.	0810	0825	0945	...	1350	1428	1520*	...	1950	2010
Geelong ☛ d.	0812	0828	0947	...	1352	1430	1552	...	1952	2012
Melbourne S Cross a.	0917	0931	1052	...	1457	1535	1654	...	2057	2117

Additional trains are available Melbourne - Geelong and v.v.
* – By 🚌.

MELBOURNE - TRARALGON - BAIRNSDALE 6375

ne

	①-⑤ Ⓡ	⑥ Ⓡ	⑦ Ⓡ	⑦ Ⓡ C	⑥ Ⓡ	①-⑤ Ⓡ	⑥⑦	①-⑤	⑥⑦ Ⓡ	①-⑤ Ⓡ
Melbourne S Cross d.	0720	0725	0804	1025	1156	1320	1336	1520	1816	1834
Dandenong d.	0805u	0800u	0840u	1100u	1239u	1403u	1419u	1603u	1859u	1916u
Warragul d.	0859	0859	0929	1152	1333	1457	1513	1657	1951	2007
Moe d.	0918	0918	0948	1213	1352	1516	1531	1715	2010	2026
Morwell d.	0932	0932	1001	1223	1404	1528	1541	1728	2023	2039
Traralgon ☛ a.	0942	0942	1011	1235	1414	1538	1553	1740	2033	2049
Sale d.	1019	1020	1049	1400*	1451	1615	1700*	1835*	2111	2126
Bairnsdale a.	1113	1113	1142	1500*	1541	1709	...	...	2204	2218

	①-⑤ Ⓡ	⑥ Ⓡ	①-⑤ B	⑦ Ⓡ	⑥ Ⓡ	①-⑤ Ⓡ	⑦ Ⓡ A	⑥	⑥⑦ Ⓡ	①-⑤ Ⓡ
Bairnsdale d.	0610	0630	...	0750	1222	1245	1255*	...	1637	1820
Sale d.	0659	0720	0755*	0840	1312	1335	1415	1520*	1727	1910
Traralgon ☛ d.	0736	0755	0920	0916	1348	1413	1454	1629	1803	1947
Morwell d.	0747	0806	0929	0927	1359	1424	1503	1638	1814	1958
Moe d.	0759	0817	0939	0938	1413	1436	1512	1647	1825	2009
Warragul d.	0818	0836	0958	0957	1432	1457	1533	1708	1844	2032
Dandenong d.	0909s	0928s	1049s	1046s	1524s	1549s	1626s	1804s	1934s	2138s
Melbourne S Cross a.	0957	1006	1137	1130	1610	1635	1710	1850	2019	2222

Additional trips ①-⑤ 0435, 1515.
Additional trips ①-⑤ 0813, 1658.
Frequent additional trains are available Melbourne - Traralgon and v.v.
B – Additional trip ①-⑤ 0920.
s – Calls to set down only.
u – Calls to pick up only.
* – By 🚌.

6380 MELBOURNE - BENDIGO - SWAN HILL and ECHUCA

km		①-⑤	①-⑤ R	⑥⑦ R	⑥⑦ R	①-⑤	⑥⑦	①-⑤	⑥⑦	①-⑤	①③⑤ 🚌	②④ 🚌	①-⑤ R	⑥⑦ R	①-⑤ R	⑥⑦ R	①-⑥	⑤ 🚌	①-⑤	⑦	⑥	①-⑤	①-⑤	⑥⑦	⑤
0	**Melbourne** S Cross .. d.	0617	0742	0836	0939	1015	1039	1215	1219	1315	...	...	1515	1719	1824	1836	1923	...	2023	2025	2050	2123	2223	2220	2350
38	Sunbury d.	0652	|	|	1011	1048	1109	1248	1251	1351	...	...	1553	1749	|	|	1952	...	2053	2054	2119	2153	2253	2249	0022
78	Woodend d.	0720	0847	0939	1039	1109	1130	1309	1319	1419	...	...	1621	1817	1932	1942	2020	...	2121	2122	2147	2222	2321	2317	0050
92	Kyneton d.	0728	0857	0949	1046	1117	1137	1317	1326	1426	...	...	1628	1824	1942	1952	2027	...	2128	2129	2154	2228	2328	2324	0057
125	Castlemaine d.	0747	0926	1011	1109	1134	1155	1334	1345	1445	...	...	1647	1844	2006	2014	2044	...	2147	2148	2213	2245	2347	2343	0116
162	**Bendigo** ☛ a.	0816	0956	1040	1131	1204	1219	1400	1409	1506	1530	1530	1710	1907	2034	2038	2109**b**	2120	2208	2213	2238	2306	0012	0008	0140
289	Kerang a.	|	1128	1212	|	1356*	1406*	|	|	...	|	1750	|	|	2208	2212	...	2330	...	...	...	...	...	...	...
345	**Swan Hill** a.	|	1210	1254	|	1439*	1448*	|	|	...	1840	1835	|	|	2251	2255	...	0014	...	...	...	...	...	...	...
222	Rochester a.	0940*	...	...	1234	...	...	1510*	1515*	...	...	...	1813	2010	...	...	...	...	...	...	...	...	...	...	...
248	**Echuca** a.	1003*	...	...	1259	...	...	1533*	1538*	...	...	...	1838	2035	...	...	...	...	...	...	...	...	...	...	...

	⑥	①-⑤	⑦	⑥ R	①-⑤ R	①-⑤ R	⑥⑦ R	①-⑤	⑥	⑦ R	①③⑤ 🚌	②④ 🚌	①-⑤	⑥	①-⑤	⑦	①-⑤	①-⑤ R	⑦	⑥ R	⑥⑦ R	⑥	⑦ R	①-⑤	①-⑤
Echuca d.	...	...	...	0703	0716	...	...	0855*	0855*	0903	...	...	...	...	...	1250*	1255*	...	...	...	1608	...	...	...	...
Rochester d.	...	...	...	0726	0739	...	...	0920*	0920*	0926	...	...	...	...	...	1315*	1320*	...	...	...	1631	...	...	...	...
Swan Hill d.	...	...	...	|	|	0710	0710	|	|	|	0900	0900	...	1000*	1050*	|	|	1243	1305*	1330	|	...	1623	1525**a**	...
Kerang d.	...	...	...	|	|	0750	0751	|	|	|	|	0950	...	1046*	1136*	|	|	1323	1351*	1410	|	...	1703	1605**a**	...
Bendigo ☛ d.	0730	0745	0800	0829	0845	0922	0923	1030	1030	1030	1215	1215	1230	1232	1336	1424	1438	1456	1537	1544	1735	1840	1836	1847	2038
Castlemaine d.	0751	0806	0821	0850	0908	0948	0947	1051	1053	1053	...	...	1251	1253	1357	1446	1501	1527	1558	1608	1756	1906	1903	1910	2101
Kyneton d.	0811	0825	0841	0910	0930	1013	1012	1111	1113	1113	...	...	1311	1313	1416	1505	1521	1551	1617	1631	1816	1929	1931	1934	2121
Woodend d.	0819	0833	0849	0918	0939	1024	1023	1120	1121	1121	...	...	1320	1321	1425	1513	1530	1601	1625	1641	1824	1937	1941	1942	2129
Sunbury d.	0850	0858	0919	0950	1011	|	|	1152	1153	1153	...	...	1352	1353	1450	1545	1602	|	1651	|	1856	2002	|	2014	2201
Melbourne S Cross a.	0922	0927	0950	1022	1042	1133	1129	1222	1224	1224	...	...	1422	1424	1521	1618	1632	1704	1722	1743	1927	2032	2041	2043	2230

☛ Additional trains are available Melbourne - Bendigo and v.v. **a** - Connection by 🚌 on ⑤ only. **b** – 2115 on ⑥. * – By 🚌.

6385 MELBOURNE - MARYBOROUGH and ARARAT

km		⑥ R	⑦ R	①-⑤ R	②⑥ A	①-⑤	⑥	⑥ 🚌	①-⑤ R	⑥	①-④	①②④ 🚌	⑦	⑦	①-⑤	①-⑤	⑤ 🚌	①-⑤	⑥⑦ R	①-⑤ R	⑦	①-⑤	⑥⑦	E 🚌
0	**Melbourne** S Cross d.	0815	0815	0817	0805	0917	0915	...	1217	1215	1317	...	1335	1515	1633	1633	...	1751	1815	1826	1915	2025	2055	2125
41	Melton d.	0849	0851	0849	|	0949	0949	...	1249	1249	1349	...	1411	1549	|	|	...	|	1849	1854	1949	2055	2129	|
53	Bacchus Marsh d.	0902	0902	0904	|	1004	1002	...	1304	1302	1404	...	1422	1602	|	|	...	1823	1902	1902	2002	2107	2138	|
82	Ballan d.	0919	0919	0921	|	1021	1019	...	1321	1319	1421	...	1439	1619	|	1722	...	1840	1919	1919	2019	2124	2155	|
122	**Ballarat** ☛ a.	0941	0942	0944	|	1044	1041	1055	1344	1344	1444	1500	1502	1644	1739	1738	1810	1857	1937	1935	2037	2143	2211	2255
180	**Maryborough** a.	|	|	|	|	|	...	1201	|	|	|	1607	|	|	1839	|	1917	|	*2039*	|	|	...	...	2358
210	**Ararat** a.	1043	1040	1044	1139	1216*	...	...	1444	1517*	1616*	...	1642*	1820*	...	1909*	...	2021*	2035	2034	2205*	...	...	...

		①-⑥ 🚌	①-⑤	⑥	⑥	⑥ R	①-⑤	①-⑤ R	①-⑤	⑦	⑥⑦ R	D 🚌	①-⑤	⑥	⑥	①-⑤	⑦	①-⑤ R	⑥⑦	①⑤ A	⑥⑦ R	①-⑤ R	⑦	①-⑤
Ararat d.	...	...	...	...	...	0716	...	0718	...	...	0816a	...	0817*	0825*	0922*	1031*	1131*	1228	1535*	1531	1609	1649	1745*	1730*
Maryborough d.	...	0400	...	...	0710	|	0712	|	...	0810	|	0829	|	|	|	|	|	|	|	|	|	|	|	|
Ballarat ☛ d.	...	0510	0519	0619	0803	0819	0805	0821	0921	0903	0919	0938	1021	1019	1139	1221	1319	1321	1714	|	1714	1802	1914	1912
Ballan d.	...	|	0536	0635	...	0835	...	0837	0937	...	0935	...	1037	1035	1155	1237	1335	1337	1735	|	1735	1825	1935	1935
Bacchus Marsh d.	0500	|	0553	0652	...	0852	...	0854	0954	...	0952	...	1054	1052	1212	1254	1352	1354	1752	|	1752	1845	1952	1952
Melton d.	0508	|	0601	0701	...	0901	...	0903	1003	...	1001	...	1103	1101	1221	1303	1401	1403	1801	|	1801	1854	2001	2003
Melbourne S Cross a.	0542	0640	0631	0739	...	0939	...	0940	1040	...	1039	...	1140	1139	1259	1340	1439	1440	1839	1850	1839	1927	2039	2038

☛ Additional trains are available Melbourne - Ballarat and v.v. **A** – See Table **6395**. **D** – ①②④⑤⑥. **E** – ①②③④⑤⑦. **a** – ⑦ only. * – By 🚌

6390 SYDNEY - PERTH — Great Southern Rail

km		WE1 R ③A			WE2 R ⑦A	
0	**Sydney** Central d.	1503	③	East **Perth** d.	1000	⑦
1125	Broken Hill a.	0600	④	Kalgoorlie a.	2050	:
1125	Broken Hill d.	0820	:	Kalgoorlie d.	0001	①
1688	**Adelaide** Parklands a.	1515	:	**Adelaide** Parklands a.	0720	②
1688	**Adelaide** Parklands d.	2125	:	**Adelaide** Parklands d.	1015	:
	Rawlinna a.	1840	⑤	Broken Hill a.	1725	:
	Rawlinna d.	2110	:	Broken Hill d.	1855	:
4343	East **Perth** a.	1457	⑥	**Sydney** Central a.	1107	③

Note: Train **WE2** has a additional off train excursion at Cook (arr. 1110, dep. 1310).
For footnotes see Table **6400**.

6395 MELBOURNE - ADELAIDE — Great Southern Rail

km		8701 R B ②⑥			8702 R B ①⑤	
0	**Melbourne** S Cross d.	0805	...	**Adelaide** Parklands d.	0745	...
74	Geelong North Shore d.	0942	...	Murray Bridge d.	0949	...
265	Ararat d.	1140	...	Nhill d.	1305	...
381	Horsham d.	1255	...	Dimboola d.	1334	...
416	Dimboola d.	1318	...	Horsham d.	1358	...
454	Nhill d.	1343	...	Ararat d.	1531	...
734	Murray Bridge d.	1605	...	Geelong North Shore d.	1738	...
828	**Adelaide** Parklands a.	1753	...	**Melbourne** S Cross a.	1850	...

B – THE OVERLAND – (12) and 🍸 Melbourne - Adelaide and v.v.
Note: Timetable valid only until June 30, 2017 no published timings beyond this date.

6400 DARWIN - ADELAIDE — Great Southern

km		8506 R ③C			8505 R ⑦C
0	**Darwin** △ d.	1000	③	**Adelaide** Parklands d.	1215
310	Katherine a.	1340	:	Snowtown d.	1446
310	Katherine d.	1820	:	Crystal Brook d.	1520
	Newcastle Waters d.	2220	:	Coonamia ◇ d.	1536
947	Tennant Creek a.	0253	④	Port Augusta a.	1645
947	Tennant Creek d.	0427	:	Port Augusta d.	1700
1414	**Alice Springs** a.	0910	:	**Alice Springs** a.	1345
1414	**Alice Springs** d.	1245	:	**Alice Springs** d.	1800
2661	Port Augusta a.	0648	⑤	Tennant Creek a.	2300
2661	Port Augusta d.	0730	:	Tennant Creek d.	0105
2751	Coonamia ◇ d.	0825	:	Newcastle Waters d.	0445
2775	Crystal Brook d.	0845	:	Katherine a.	0900
2827	Snowtown d.	0925	:	Katherine d.	1300
2973	**Adelaide** Parklands a.	1130	:	**Darwin** △ a.	1730

A – INDIAN PACIFIC – 🛏 1 cl., (12) and ✕ Sydney - Adelaide - Perth and v.v. Fr
Sydney on ③. From Perth on ⑦.
C – THE GHAN – 🛏 1 cl., (2) , ✕ (in 1st class) and 🍸 Darwin - Adelaide and v.v.
Adelaide on ⑦ service will also stop at Maria for an off train excursion. From Darw
③ service will also stop at Manguri for an off train excursion. The Ghan will not op
between Dec. 18, 2016 and Jan. 18, 2017.
Note: There will be a special timetable for the Darwin - Adelaide Ghan between Aug. 3,
and Oct. 26, 2016. Service departs Darwin on ③ at 1000 arriving Adelaide on ⑥ a
and has an extended stop at Coober Pedy on ⑤.
△ – Darwin station is in the suburb of Berrimah. 🚌 connections to and from Darwin
centre are provided by the operator. ◇ – For Port Pirie.

6405 KALGOORLIE - PERTH — All trains 2 cl. and R — Tran

km		AVM2 ①-⑤	AVM8 ⑥	AVM4 d	KPA ①-⑤	KPL ⑥	MEP2 ③	AVM6 d	KPA4 ⑦	KPL2 ①	KPL4 ⑤
0	**Kalgoorlie** d.	...	...	...	0705	0705	...	...	1405	1500	1500
250	Southern Cross d.	...	...	...	0912	0917	...	...	1612	1707	1715
371	Merredin d.	...	...	...	1023	1028	1310	...	1723	1818	1829
427	Kellerberrin d.	...	...	...	1102**c**	1107	1341	...	1802	1857	1908
531	Northam d.	0630	0830	1000	1209	1212	1454	1600	1907	2002	2013
641	Midland d.	0750	0950	1120	1323	1323	1610	1720	2020	2115	2125
653	East **Perth** a.	...	...	...	1345	1345	1630	...	2040	2135	2145

	PKA a	PKL ③	MAV1 d	MEP2 ③	MAV3 d	PKA1 ⑦	PKL1 ①	MAW7 ⑥	PKL3 ⑤
East **Perth** d.	0710	0710	...	0855	...	1410	1515	...	1515
Midland d.	0727	0727	0815	0912	1400	1427	1533	1535	1532
Northam d.	0850	0850	0935	1027	1520	1547	1645	1655	1655
Kellerberrin d.	0956	|	...	1138	...	1653	1750	...	1800
Merredin d.	1027	1027	...	1210	...	1728	1821	...	1831
Southern Cross d.	1144	1144	...	...	...	1845	1938	...	1948
Kalgoorlie a.	1400	1400	...	...	...	2100	2150	...	2205

a – ①②④⑤⑥ only. **c** – ①②④⑤ only. **d** – ①②④⑤ only. NOTE: Trains will only call at intermediate stations if bookings are made in advance.

6410 PERTH - BUNBURY — TransWA

km		103 2 R	105 2 R		102 2 R	108 2 R
0	**Perth** City d.	0930	1755	**Bunbury** d.	0600	1445
30	Armadale d.	0956	1825	Brunswick Junction d.	0617	1502
85	Pinjarra d.	1042	1911	Harvey d.	0632	1517
111	Waroona d.	1100	1929	Waroona d.	0656	1538
136	Harvey d.	1121	1950	Pinjarra d.	0712	1555
157	Brunswick Junction d.	1136	2005	Armadale d.	0755	1639
183	**Bunbury** a.	1155	2025	**Perth** City a.	0830	1715

NOTE: Trains will only call at intermediate stations if bookings are made in advance.

6415 KALGOORLIE - ESPERANCE — Tran

km		671 🚌 ①③	651 🚌 ⑤			700 🚌 ⑦	690 🚌 ③⑤
0	**Kalgoorlie** d.	1430	1430	...	**Esperance** d.	0800	0835
208	Norseman d.	1715	1730	...	Norseman d.	1045	1120
409	**Esperance** a.	1930	1945	...	**Kalgoorlie** a.	1315	1335

NEW ZEALAND

tal: **Wellington** (GMT +12, add one hour in Summer). 2016 public holidays: Jan. 1, 4, Feb. 6, 8, Mar. 25, 28, Apr. 25, June 6, Oct. 24, Dec. 25, 26, 27.

g distance rail services are operated by Tranz Scenic (www.tranzscenic.co.nz). Only one class of accommodation is offered, which is referred to in the tables as second s. All services operated by TranzScenic require compulsory reservation. There are two types of Scenic Rail Passes; the Fixed Pass offers unlimited travel on the TranzScenic vork (not the Capital Connection) and also allows one journey on the Interislander ferry service. Adult prices: 7 days NZ$599, 14 days NZ$699, 21 days NZ$799. The dom Pass offers flexible travel from 3 to 10 days. Adult prices: 3 days NZ$ 417 to 10 days NZ$ 1290. For full information go to www.kiwirailscenic.co.nz.

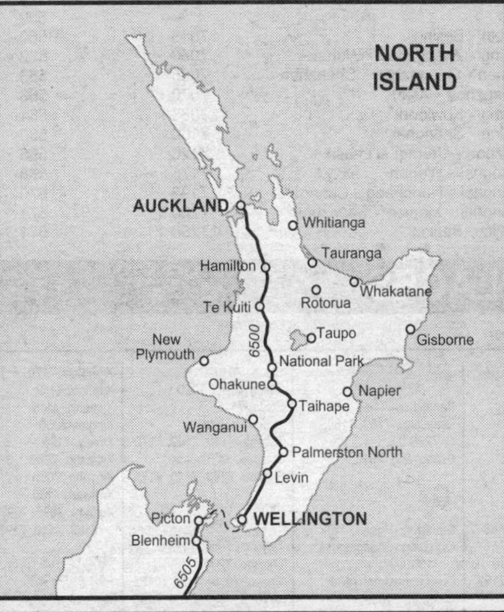

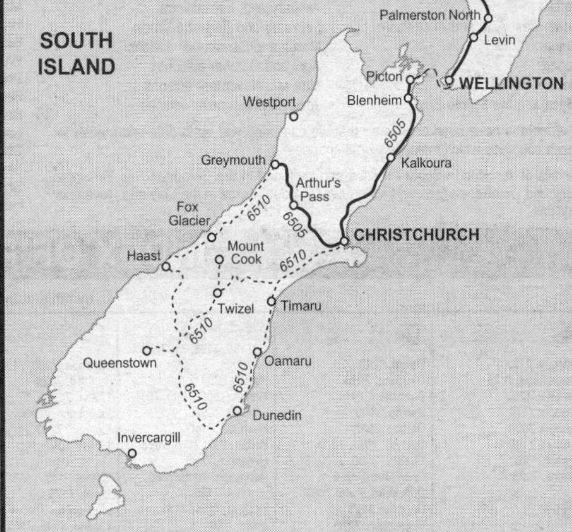

iRail Scenic AUCKLAND - WELLINGTON 6500

1		1203	0201		0200	1205
			R		R	
		①–⑤	①④⑥		②⑤⑦	①–⑤
		B	A		A	B
0	**Auckland** Strand .... d.	...	0745	**Wellington** .... ⊡ d.	0755	1715
4	Papakura .... d.	...	0840	Paraparaumu .... d.	0845	1803
9	Hamilton .... d.	...	1015	Levin .... d.	|	1842
3	Otorohanga .... d.	...	1054	**Palmerston North** .... d.	1000	1920
4	National Park .... d.	...	1315	Ohakune .... d.	1245	...
4	Ohakune .... d.	...	1345	National Park .... d.	1315	...
4	**Palmerston North** .... d.	0615	1620	Otorohanga .... d.	1545	...
0	Levin .... d.	0653	|	Hamilton .... d.	1630	...
2	Paraparaumu .... d.	0732	1730	Papakura .... d.	1755	...
1	**Wellington** .... ⊡ a.	0820	1825	**Auckland** Strand .... a.	1850	...

e: Trains are permitted to depart from intermediate stations earlier than advertised provided that all pre-booked passengers are on board.

NORTHERN EXPLORER – [2] and 🍸. Not Dec. 25, 28. 29.
CAPITAL CONNECTION – [2] and 🍸. Not public holidays or Dec. 25 – Jan 4.

Calls to set down only.
Calls to pick up only.

KiwiRail Scenic PICTON - CHRISTCHURCH 6505

km		803	0701		0700	0804
		R	R		R	R
		D	C		C	D
0	**Picton** .... ⊡ d.	...	1315	**Greymouth** .... d.	...	1345
28	Blenheim .... d.	...	1353	Brunner .... d.	...	1405
157	Kaikoura .... d.	...	1550	Moana .... d.	...	1442
285	Waipara .... d.	...	1740	Otira .... d.	...	1533
318	Rangiora .... d.	...	1809	Arthur's Pass .... d.	...	1557
348	**Christchurch** .... a.	...	1833	Springfield .... d.	...	1712
348	**Christchurch** .... d.	0815	...	**Christchurch** .... a.	...	1805
417	Springfield .... d.	0915	...	**Christchurch** .... d.	0700	...
484	Arthur's Pass .... d.	1042	...	Rangiora .... d.	0732	...
498	Otira .... d.	1103	...	Waipara .... d.	0758	...
	Moana .... d.	1147	...	Kaikoura .... d.	0959	...
565	Brunner .... d.	1221	...	Blenheim .... d.	1153	...
579	**Greymouth** .... a.	1245	...	**Picton** .... ⊡ a.	1220	...

Note: Trains are permitted to depart from intermediate stations earlier than advertised provided that all pre-booked passengers are on board.

C – COASTAL PACIFIC – [2] and 🍸. From Sep. 23 2016 to April 30 2017 only Not Dec. 25.
D – THE TRANZALPINE – [2] and 🍸. Not Dec. 25.

Wellington - Picton ⛴ service ('Interislander'). Journey 3½ hours. Operator: Interislander ✆ +64 4 498 3302.

. 1 - June. 19.
ington – Picton.
), 1445 ②–⑦, 1700 ②–⑥. 2000 ⑦–⑤,
0 ②–⑥
n – Wellington.
5 ②–⑦, 1415, 1845.

June. 20 - Aug. 14.
Wellington – Picton.
0830, 1530 ①–⑥, 1700 ⑦, 2030 ①–⑥, 0400 ②–⑥.
Picton – Wellington.
0930 ②–⑦, 1400, 2230, 0215 ②–⑦.

Aug. 15 - Sept. 4.
Wellington – Picton.
0900, 1445, 2000.
Picton – Wellington.
1045 ②–⑥, 1415, 1845.

Sept 4 - Sept. 30.
Wellington – Picton.
0900, 1445 ②–⑦, 1445 ②-⑦, 1530 ①, 1700 ②–⑥.
2000 ⑦–⑤
Picton – Wellington.
0905 ②–⑥, 1045 ②–⑦, 1415, 1845 ②–⑦, 2215 ①-⑥.

SELECTED SOUTH ISLAND BUS SERVICES 6510

1	Operator	AS	IC	IC	AS	NM	IC	AS	IC	
									⑤⑦	
0	**Christchurch** .... d.	0730	0730	0745	0800	0830	1400	1500	1715	...
2	Ashburton .... d.	0845	0850	0915	0920	0950	1525	1630	1850	...
0	Timaru .... d.	|	|	1030	1025	|	1700	1800	2030	...
0	Oamaru .... d.	|	|	1205	1200	|	1815	1910	2135	...
6	**Dunedin** .... a.	|	|	1340	1350	|	1950	2045	2305	...
4	Geraldine .... d.	0925	1000	...	...	1045	...	...	...	...
1	Fairlie .... d.	1000	1025	...	...	1125	...	...	...	...
1	**Mount Cook** .... a.	|	1300	...	...	|	...	...	...	...
1	**Mount Cook** .... d.	|	1425	...	...	|	...	...	...	...
1	Twizel .... d.	1120	1515	...	...	1330	...	...	...	...
5	Cromwell .... d.	1340	1715	...	...	1530	...	...	...	...
6	**Queenstown** .... a.	1430	1830	...	...	1630	...	...	...	...

Operator	IC	AS	NM	IC	IC	AS	AS	IC	
								⑤⑦	
Queenstown .... d.	...	...	0805	0745	...	...	1500	...	...
Cromwell .... d.	...	...	0910	0920	...	...	1555	...	...
Twizel .... d.	...	...	1110	1130	...	...	1805	...	...
Mount Cook .... a.	...	...	|	1230	...	...	|	...	...
Mount Cook .... d.	...	...	|	1345	...	...	|	...	...
Fairlie .... d.	...	...	1315	1550	...	...	1920	...	...
Geraldine .... d.	...	...	1410	1655	...	...	2000	...	...
Dunedin .... d.	0745	0800	|	|	1250	1430	|	1715	...
Oamaru .... d.	0930	1000	|	|	1500	1635	|	1855	...
Timaru .... d.	1120	1110	|	|	1620	1740	|	2030	...
Ashburton .... d.	1225	1210	1455	1735	1730	1845	2040	2135	...
Christchurch .... a.	1345	1350	1630	1910	1855	2000	2145	2250	...

1	Operator	IC	AS	AS	AS	IC				
0	**Greymouth** .... d.	...	...	...	...	1330	...	...	...	...
1	Hokitika .... d.	...	...	...	...	1455	...	...	...	...
9	Franz Josef .... d.	...	...	...	0800	1705	...	...	...	...
3	**Fox Glacier** .... d.	...	...	...	0845	1740	...	...	...	...
	Paringa .... d.	...	...	...	1005	...	...	...	...	...
1	Haast .... d.	...	...	...	1120	...	...	...	...	...
6	Wanaka .... d.	...	...	...	1435	...	...	...	...	...
3	**Queenstown** .... d.	0745	0915	1500	1615	...	...	...	...	...
4	Cromwell .... d.	0850	1015	1555	...	...	...	...	...	...
5	Alexandra .... d.	0920	1050	1630	...	...	...	...	...	...
7	Roxburgh .... d.	0955	1120	1715	...	...	...	...	...	...
7	Milton .... d.	1130	1240	1830	...	...	...	...	...	...
3	**Dunedin** .... a.	1235	1345	1930	...	...	...	...	...	...

Operator	IC	AS	AS	IC	AS				
Dunedin .... d.	...	...	1000	1355	1530	...	...	...	...
Milton .... d.	...	...	1040	1445	1620	...	...	...	...
Roxburgh .... d.	...	...	1220	1605	1740	...	...	...	...
Alexandra .... d.	...	...	1250	1640	1805	...	...	...	...
Cromwell .... d.	...	...	1340	1705	1830	...	...	...	...
Queenstown .... d.	...	0810	1430	1815	1935	...	...	...	...
Wanaka .... d.	...	0945	...	...	...	...	...	...	...
Haast .... d.	...	1250	...	...	...	...	...	...	...
Paringa .... d.	...	1435	...	...	...	...	...	...	...
Fox Glacier .... d.	0830	1525	...	...	...	...	...	...	...
Franz Josef .... d.	0915	1610	...	...	...	...	...	...	...
Hokitika .... d.	1230	...	...	...	...	...	...	...	...
Greymouth .... a.	1315	...	...	...	...	...	...	...	...

– Atomic Travel. ✆ 03 349 0697. *IC* – Intercity Coachlines. ✆ 09 583 5780. *NM* – Newmans. ✆ 09 583 5780.

BEYOND EUROPE
China

Introduction

The Beyond Europe section covers principal rail services in a different area of the world each month. There are six areas, each appearing twice yearly as follows:

India:	January and July editions
South East Asia and Australasia:	February and August editions
China:	March and September editions
Japan:	April and October editions
North America:	May and November editions
Africa and the Middle East:	June and December editions

The months have been chosen so that we can bring you up-to-date information for those countries which make seasonal changes.

Details of services in South America can be found in the European Rail Timetable April and October editions and schedules for South Korea in the May and November editions.

Contents

INDEX OF PLACES

by table number

China

Capital: Beijing (GMT + 8). 2016 Public Holidays: Jan. 1, Feb. 7, 8, 9, Apr. 4, May 1, June 9, Sept. 15, Oct. 1, 2, 3.

Rail services in the People's Republic are generally operated by Chinese Railways. High-speed services are operated by China Rail High Speed. All times shown are Beijing unless otherwise stated. Schedules in this section are as per the latest information available and are liable to change at any time.

Trains are numbered using a combination of letters and numbers, with the letter indicating the type of train. The fastest trains carry prefixes **C** and **G**. These use the new h speed railways and run at speeds up to 300 km/h on routes such as Wuhan to Guangzhou and Beijing to Tianjin. Other high-speed trains running at speeds of up to 200 km/h prefixed with the letter **D** and **Z**. These trains use both dedicated high-speed railways and normal lines. Ordinary long distance trains are prefixed **T** or **K**. **T** trains make fe stops and thus are considerably quicker than **K** trains. Most **K** trains in this section are only shown to highlight additional connections between major points and may not be sh in their entirety. Also shown are a few trains without prefix letters. These are essentially similar to **K** trains but are slower still and are only shown in this section where there ar higher category trains.

In total seven classes of accommodation are available, but not all will be available on every train. Seated accommodation can be either Hard, Soft, Second or First class. H seats are generally padded plastic seats. This is the cheapest class available and is often very busy. Soft seats are cloth covered and generally can be reclined. Second c seats have five seats per row and are similar to economy class seating on an aeroplane. First class has four seats per row. Sleeping accommodation is available in either H Soft or Deluxe Soft classes. Hard sleepers consist of cabins of six berths (upper, middle and lower), with three beds attached to the wall on either side. The cabin is open and no door. Soft sleepers have four berths and a sliding door. Deluxe Soft cabins have two berths and an en-suite bathroom. Generally **K, T** and **Z** trains convey Soft and H sleepers, and Hard Seats whilst **C, D** and **G** trains convey First and Second class seats. Exact train compositions are **not** shown in the tables.

All travel should be reserved in advance either at stations or through an agent. At many stations you may find it possible to only book for trains calling there, however in m cities such as Beijing, Shanghai and Guangzhou you may be able to purchase all tickets. Some major stations may have English speakers available at ticket desks. Reservat for **Z** and **D** usually open 10 - 21 days in advance. Other classes of train are only usually available 7 - 10 days before departure. In peak seasons such as Spring Festival holic reservations may only open 5 days before departure. Identity documents, such as passports for most foreigners or ID cards for Chinese citizens, are required to buy tickets and to board **C, D** and **G** trains.

More comprehensive train schedules are available (in Chinese!) from Chinese Railways official websites: www.chinamor.cn.net and www.tielu.org. Other unofficial websites s as www.cnvol.com and www.chinatravelguide.com offer timetable search facilities in English. A printed English language timetable is available at www.chinatt.org.

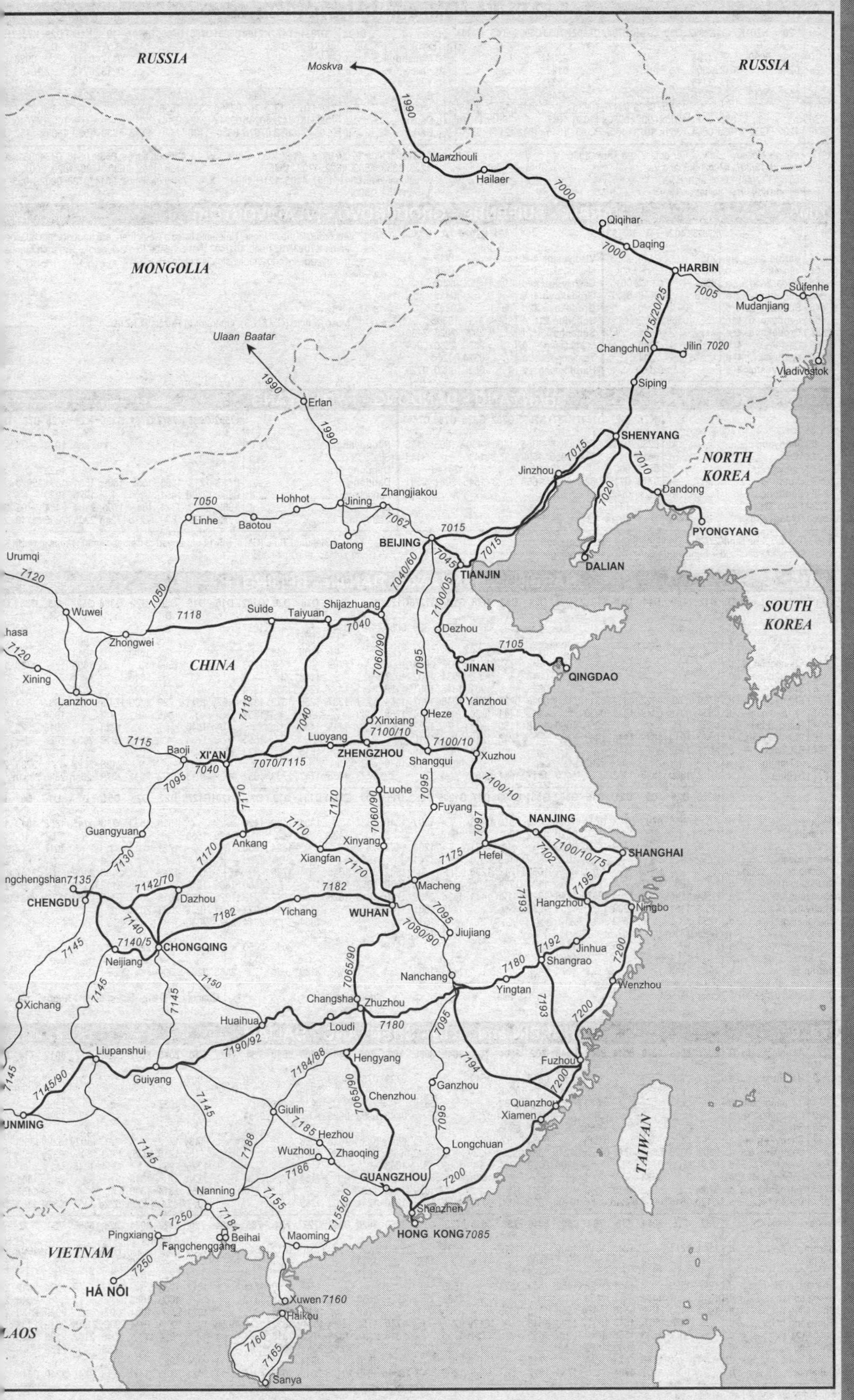
RUSSIA
Moskva
1990
RUSSIA
Manzhouli
Hailaer
7000
Qiqihar
7000
Daqing
HARBIN
7005
Suifenhe
Mudanjiang
MONGOLIA
7015/20/25
Changchun
Jilin 7020
Vladivostok
Ulaan Baatar
1990
Siping
Erlan
SHENYANG
1990
7015
NORTH KOREA
7010
Jinzhou
7020
Dandong
Hohhot
Jining
Zhangjiakou
7050
Linhe
Baotou
7062
Datong
7015
BEIJING
PYONGYANG
7015
DALIAN
Urumqi
7045
TIANJIN
7120
7040/60
7100/05
SOUTH KOREA
7050
Wuwei
7118
Suide
Taiyuan
Shijazhuang
hasa
Zhongwei
7040
Dezhou
7120
CHINA
7060/90
7095
7105
Xining
JINAN
QINGDAO
Lanzhou
7118
7040
Yanzhou
Xinxiang
Heze
7100/10
Luoyang
7100/10
7115
Baoji
XI'AN
ZHENGZHOU
Shangqui
Xuzhou
7070/7115
7040
7095
7100/10
7095
Luohe
7170
7170
7060/90
7095
Fuyang
Guangyuan
7097
NANJING
Ankang
7170
Xinyang
7102
7100/10/75
SHANGHAI
7130
7170
Xiangfan
7175
Hefei
ngchengshan 7135
7142/70
7170
Macheng
7195
7182
CHENGDU
Dazhou
7182
Yichang
WUHAN
7095
7193
Hangzhou
Ningbo
7140
7080/90
Jiujiang
7140/5
CHONGQING
7065/90
7192
Jinhua
7200
7145
Neijiang
7180
Shangrao
7150
Nanchang
Yingtan
Wenzhou
7145
7145
Changsha
Zhuzhou
Xichang
7193
Huaihua
Loudi
7180
7095
7200
7190/92
Liupanshui
Hengyang
7194
Fuzhou
7145
7184/88
7065/90
7200
Guiyang
Ganzhou
7145/90
7145
Chenzhou
Quanzhou
Giulin
Xiamen
UNMING
7095
7185
Hezhou
7188
TAIWAN
7145
Wuzhou
Zhaoqing
Longchuan
7186
GUANGZHOU
7200
Nanning
7155
7250
7184
Shenzhen
7155/60
Pingxiang
Beihai
HONG KONG 7085
Fangchenggang
Maoming
VIETNAM
7250
HÀ NÔI
Xuwen 7160
Haikou
LAOS
7160
7165
Sanya

7000 MANZHOULI and QIQHAR - HARBIN

Chinese Railways, China Rail High Sp

km	20 ⑤A	K20 B	K7193	K7092	D30 D	D7940	D7942 V	D6902 W	K7058	D6906	T48 C	D7904	Read Down / Read Up	D7931 U	T47 C	K7194	D6901 X	D7901	D6905	D6907	19 ⑦A	K19 B	D29 D	K7057
0	0030	0030	...	1736	...	...	...	...	2254	...	...	...	d.**Manzhouli** ... a.	...	...	...	...	...	...	...	0417	0417	...	0928
186	0242	0242	0812	2006	...	...	...	...	0127	...	...	...	d.Hailaer ... d.	...	...	2146	...	...	...	...	0213	0213	...	0703
268	|	|	0943	2115	...	...	...	...	0237	...	...	...	d.Yakeshi ... d.	...	...	2007	...	...	...	...	|	|	...	0522
396	0540	0540	1149	2316	...	...	...	...	0446	...	...	...	d.Boketu ... d.	...	...	1800	...	...	...	...	2251	2251	...	0325
693	|	|	|	|	1222**n**	0829	0917**n**	1028**n**	|	1415	1855	2038	d. Qiqihar ... a.	0711**n**	1013	|	0955**n**	1323	1555	1905	|	|	1639**n**	2247
776	|	|	1803	0411	1255**x**	0902**x**	0950**x**	1108**d**	1047	|	2001**x**	2134**d**	d.Daqing ... d.	0634**d**	0842**x**	1026**d**	0924**x**	1242**x**	1514**x**	|	|	|	1602**d**	2038**x**
935	1232	1232	2133**d**	0644	1351**x**	1013	1052	1153	1345	1543	2144	2226	a.**Harbin** ... d.	0540	0652	0757**d**	0830	1136	1420	1742	1539	1539	1508**x**	1752

A – Beijing - Moscow and v.v. For details see Table **1990**.
B – Beijing(**K19/20**) - Manzhouli and v.v.
C – Beijing(**T47/48**) - Qiqihar and v.v.
D – Beijing(**D29/30**) - Qiqihar and v.v.
d – dong.
n – nan.
x – xi.
U – Additional trips: 0709, 0938, 1008, 1033, 1208, 1258, 1333, 1533, 1612, 1702, 1935.
V– Additional trips: 0547, 1052, 1205, 1216, 1433, 1459, 1754, 1900.
W – Additional trips: 0536, 0648, 0734, 0810, 1136, 1302, 1600, 1738, 1820, 2007.
X – Additional trips: 0614, 0738, 0902, 1055, 1904.

7005 HARBIN - SUIFENHE - GRODEKOVO - (VLADIVOSTOK)

Chinese Railw

km		K7023	402 2	A ③⑥	K7193		401 2	K7024	A ①④	K7194
0	**Harbin** dong ... d.	2126	...	2126	2053	**Vladivostok** ◐ d.	...	...	1215	...
161	Yimianpo ... d.	0019	...	|	|	Ussruiysk ... ◐ a.	...	...	1410	...
355	Mudanjiang ... a.	0335	...	0336**a**	0515	Ussruiysk ... ◐ d.	...	...	0240**c**	...
648	**Suifenhe** ... a.	0618	...	0618	0727	**Grodekovo** ◐ a.	...	...	0415	...
648	**Suifenhe** 🏛 ... d.	...	0930	0930	...	**Grodekovo** ◐ d.	0843	...	0843	...
669	**Grodekovo** .. ◐ a.	...	0559	0559	...	**Suifenhe** 🏛 ... a.	1504	...	1530**c**	...
669	**Grodekovo** .. ◐ a.	...	...	1115	...	**Suifenhe** ... d.	...	2023	2023	2130
766	Ussruiysk ... ◐ a.	...	...	1245	...	Mudanjiang ... d.	...	2330	2330	0044
766	Ussruiysk ... ◐ d.	...	...	2241	...	Yamianpo ... d.	...	0324	0324**d**	|
878	**Vladivostok** . ◐ a.	...	...	0100**b**	...	**Harbin** dong ... a.	...	0620	0620	0729

A– Accordng to the Chinese Timetable twice a week there are through cars attache trains **K7023/7024** and **401/402** that continue to Vladivostok. The train numbe from Grodekovo to Vladivostok is unknown.
a – ④⑦.
b – ①⑤.
c – ②⑤.
d – ③⑥.
◐ – Moscow time (GMT +3). Operator in Russia is **RZhD**.

7010 SHENYANG - DANDONG - PYONGYANG

China Rail High Speed, Chinese Railw

km		K27 A	K27 A	D7647	K7377	K7591	G782	G395	G786	D7641
0	**Shenyang** ... d.	0259	0259	0516	0848	1356	1406	1430**n**	1808	2115
84	Muxi ... d.	0415	0415	|	0956	1509	|	1456	|	2148
217	Fengcheng ... d.	0601	0601	|	1142	1750	|	|	2014**d**	|
277	**Dandong** ... a.	0715	0715	0627	1231	1859	1528	1545	2031	2231
277	**Dandong** ... d.	...	0935	...	...	...	...	...	...	...
282	Sinuiji 🏛 ... ⊗ d.	...	1346	...	...	...	...	...	...	...
506	**Pyongyang** ... ⊗ a.	...	1930	...	...	...	...	...	...	...

	K7592	G785	K7378	G781	G396	K28 A	K28 A	D7648
Pyongyang ... ⊗ d.	...	...	...	...	...	...	1010	...
Sinuiji 🏛 ... ⊗ d.	...	...	...	...	...	...	|	...
Dandong ... a.	...	...	...	...	...	...	1623	...
Dandong ... d.	0712	1212	1353	1552	1609	1831	1831	2023
Fengcheng ... d.	0806	1230**d**	1451	|	|	1920	1920	|
Muxi ... d.	1053	1303	1721	1643	1700	2104	2104	2108
Shenyang ... a.	1322	1339	1839	1727**b**	1724**n**	2205	2205	2140

A – ①③④⑥. Beijing(**K27/28**) - Dandong(**6/5**) - Pyongyang and v.v.
b – Shenyang bei. **d** – Fengcheng dong. **n** – Shenyang nan.
⊗ – Korean Standard Time (GMT +9, 1 hour ahead of Chinese time). Times in North K are subject to confirmation.

7015 HARBIN - SHENYANG - TIANJIN - BEIJING

China Rail High Sp

km	All trains prefix 'D'	D12	D4	D14	D10	G1222	D2	D24	D52	D28	G1206	G1276	G1203	D6	D26	D74	D20	D102	D16	D18	D30 D	D22	G396	G384	D8	G382
0	**Harbin** xi ... d.	...	...	...	...	...	...	...	...	0657	0806	0820	0857	...	0949	...	...	1037	...	...	1353	...	...	...	...	1622
	Jilin ... d.	...	...	...	...	...	...	...	...	|	|	|	|	...	|	1025	...	|	...	...	|	1517	...	1600	...	|
**	Changchun .. d.	...	...	...	...	...	...	0725	...	|	|	|	|	...	|	1108	1115	|	...	...	|	1600	...	1644	...	|
240	Changchun xi .. d.	...	...	...	...	...	...	|	...	0817	0917	0934	1009	...	1109	|	|	1203	...	...	1600	|	...	1656	...	1720
358	Siping dong ... d.	...	...	...	...	...	...	0818	...	|	0954	1002	1037	...	|	1148	|	|	...	...	|	1640	...	|	...	|
538	**Shenyang** bei . a.	...	...	...	...	...	...	0923	...	1001	1045	1051	1129	...	1233	1251	1308	1334	...	...	1726	1737	...	1822	...	1840
538	**Shenyang** bei . d.	0709	07509	0822	0852	0814	0919**y**	0926	0926	1003	1048	1057	1134	1217	1237	1256	1312	1337	1432**y**	1511	1729	1739	1742**n**	1827	1837	1844
761	Jinzhou nan ... d.	0834	0918	0948	1017	0939	|	|	1141	1120	|	1214	1258	1342	|	|	|	1454	1557	|	1846	|	|	|	1956	|
804	Huludao bei ... d.	0852	|	|	|	0956	1050	1058	1159	|	|	1232	|	|	1411	1430	|	|	|	1646	|	|	1925	|	2013	2022
926	Shanhaiguan ... d.	0940	1019	1049	1118	1041	|	|	1243	1218	|	1316	|	|	|	|	|	1553	1659	1734	|	1953	2010	2053	2058	|
964	Beidaihe ... d.	1015	1052	|	1148	|	|	|	|	1248	|	1345	1418	|	|	1515	|	1623	1729	|	|	2027	|	|	2127	|
	Tianjin ... a.	|	|	|	|	1209	|	|	|	|	1456**x**	1450	1530	|	|	|	|	|	|	|	|	|	2138	2223	|	2238
1241	**Beijing** ... a.	1219	1300	1328	1352	...	1406	1417	1531	1451	...	...	...	1723	1728	1747	1753	1831	1937	2013	2222	2231	2229	2256**n**	2330	2331**n**

	G373	D29 D	D5	D21	D15	G383	G381	G395	D17	G1205	D25	D11	D9	G1221	D101	D19	D73	G1201	G1275	D27	D23	D51	D7	D1	D3
Beijing ... d.	...	0658	0703	0713	0731	0730**n**	0753**n**	0910	0915	...	1002	1240	1321	...	1351	1418	1428	...	...	1515	1533	1713	1745	1808	1819
Tianjin ... d.	0737	|	|	|	|	0820	0842	1001	|	1047	|	|	|	1427	|	|	|	1529	1535	|	|	|	|	|	|
Beidaihe ... d.	0904	|	|	0919	0937	0953	|	|	1121	|	1208	1442	|	|	|	1624	1630	1645	|	1721	|	|	|	2017	|
Shanhaiguan ... d.	|	0933	|	|	|	1022	|	1133	|	|	1241	|	1556	|	|	|	1703	|	|	|	|	2006	|	|	|
Huludao bei ... d.	|	|	|	|	1101	|	1050	1217	1233	|	|	1602	|	1645	|	1736	|	|	1759	1842	|	2055	2102	|	2137
Jinzhou nan ... d.	|	1030	1037	|	|	|	1108	1234	|	|	1342	1620	1653	1702	1733	|	1800	1808	1816	|	1908	2112	2119	|	2157
Shenyang bei ... a.	1156**y**	1146	1153	1205	1237**y**	1248	1228	1412**n**	1414	1436	1459	1740	1813	1823	1853	1912	1919	1926	1933	2018	2031	2317	2253	2321**y**	2331
Shenyang bei ... d.	1159**y**	1151	...	1209	...	1251	1230	...	...	1440	1501	1755	...	...	1856	1914	1922	1931	1937	2021	2036	...	...	...	...
Siping dong ... d.	1256	|	...	1322	...	|	|	...	...	|	1614	|	...	...	1954	|	2014	2023	2030	|	|	...	...	...	...
Changchun xi ... d.	1325	1316	...	|	...	|	1346	...	...	1601	1647	|	...	...	2027	|	|	2052	2059	2154	|	...	...	...	...
Changchun ... a.	|	|	...	1405	...	1412	|	...	...	|	|	1918	...	...	|	2043	2050	|	|	|	2209	...	...	...	...
Jilin ... a.	|	|	...	...	...	1455	|	...	...	|	|	...	...	...	|	...	2134	|	|	|	...	...	...	...	...
Harbin xi ... a.	1422	1443	...	...	...	...	1459	...	...	1703	1805	...	...	...	2139	...	...	2153	2203	2300	...	...	...	...	...

D – Beijing(**D29/30**) - Qiqihar and v.v.
n – nan. **x** – Tianjin xi. **y** –Shenyang.
** – Changhcun *0 km* - Siping dong *130 km*.

7020 HARBIN and JILIN - SHENYANG - DALIAN

China Rail High Sp

km	All trains prefix 'G'	8042	8068	8070	8044	8002	8046	702	8004	704	8048	8006	706	708	48	8008	8050	754		710	8010	8052	8054	712	8012	714
0	**Harbin** xi ... d.	...	...	...	...	...	...	0618	...	0649	...	...	0729	0757	0830	...	...	0850	...	0907	...	...	...	1028	...	1128
**	**Jilin** ... d.	...	...	...	...	...	...	|	0648	|	...	...	|	|	|	0849	...	|	...	|	...	...	...	|	...	|
**	Changchun .. d.	...	...	...	...	0623	...	|	0732	|	...	0819	|	|	|	0932	...	|	...	|	1037	...	...	|	1208	|
240	Changchun xi .. d.	...	...	...	...	|	...	0716	|	0757	...	|	0840	0903	0926	|	...	0954	...	1017	|	...	...	1140	1220	1234
358	Siping dong ... d.	...	...	...	...	0659	...	|	0808	|	...	|	|	|	|	|	...	1022	...	|	1120	...	...	1208	|	|
538	**Shenyang** bei . a.	...	...	...	...	0758**y**	...	0834	0902**y**	0920**y**	...	0945	0953**y**	1025**y**	1028	1058	...	1112	...	1143**y**	1212	...	...	1302**y**	1329**y**	1350**y**
538	**Shenyang** bei . d.	0602	0625	0636	0718	0801**y**	0821**y**	0837	0905**y**	0923**y**	0919	0948	0956**y**	1039**y**	1030	1101	1122	...	...	1146**y**	1215	1228**y**	1303	1306**y**	1332**y**	1355**y**
638	Anshan xi ... d.	0638	|	0724	|	|	0900	0920	0944	|	1009	|	1033	|	|	1137	|	...	...	1225	1251	|	1354	1345	1411	|
677	Haicheng xi ... d.	|	|	0738	|	|	|	|	|	1009	|	|	|	|	|	1151	|	...	...	1239	|	1315	|	|	|	1441
715	Yinkou dong ... d.	0700	|	|	0815	0849	|	0941	|	|	|	1039	1055	1132	|	|	|	...	...	1254	1314	1330	|	|	|	1455
921	**Dalian** bei ... a.	0812**d**	0816	0853	0934**d**	0955	1020**d**	1032	1059	1114	1135	1143	1210	1244	1200	1259	1353**d**	...	...	1347	1424**d**	1450**d**	1522**d**	1457	1531**d**	1553

All trains prefix 'G'	782	716	8014	718	764	50	8016	758	8058	720	8018	8060	8020	8062	722	724	786	8064	726	8022	8024	728	8066	730	732
Harbin xi ... d.	1143	1211	...	1246	1317	1400	...	1419	...	1432	...	...	...	...	1544	1612	1645	...	1658	...	...	1749	...	1823	1907
Jilin ... d.	|	|	1238	|	|	|	1409	|	...	|	1458	...	1538	...	|	|	|	...	|	...	1726	|	...	|	|
Changchun ... d.	|	|	1321	|	|	|	1452	|	...	|	1541	...	1621	...	|	|	|	...	|	1723	1810	|	...	|	|
Changchun xi ... d.	1247	1323	|	1357	1425	1456	1504	1523	...	1530	|	...	|	...	1648	1710	1744	...	1811	1734	|	1847	...	1934	2012
Siping dong ... d.	1315	|	1404	|	1453	|	|	|	...	1558	|	...	1658	...	|	1738	1812	...	|	1803	1852	|	...	|	2040
Shenyang bei ... a.	1403	1434	1458**y**	1516	1547**y**	1558	1615	1635	...	1653**y**	1713**y**	...	1749	...	1810**y**	1828	1905	...	1921	1857**y**	1941	2002**y**	...	2046	2130
Shenyang bei ... d.	...	1438	1501**y**	1519	1551**y**	1600	1618	...	1642**y**	1656**y**	1716**y**	1740	1754	1806**y**	1814**y**	1832	...	1924**y**	1926	1902**y**	1944	2006**y**	2110**y**	2049	2133
Anshan xi ... d.	...	|	1533	1555	1640	|	1655	...	1714	1735	|	1816	|	1838	1853	1916	...	|	|	1934	|	2045	2142	2125	|
Haicheng xi ... d.	...	|	|	1609	1652	|	|	...	|	|	1802	|	|	1852	|	1931	...	|	|	|	|	2059	|	2139	|
Yinkou dong ... d.	...	|	1556	1624	...	|	1717	...	|	|	|	|	1846	|	1914	|	...	2011	2024	1957	|	2113	|	|	|
Dalian bei ... a.	...	1633	1707	1724	...	1730	1822	...	1835	1800	1903	1936**d**	1945	2012**d**	2012	2029	...	2111	2121	2103	2147**d**	2218	2247	2240	2314

For footnotes and return service see next page.

DALIAN - SHENYANG - JILIN and HARBIN — 7020

na Rail High Speed

ains prefix 'G'	751	701	8041	8001	703	8043	8003	705	8005	47	8045	707	8007	709	755	8047	8049	8009	8051	711	8011	713	785	8013	715
an bei ... d.	...	0605	0614	0615	0646	0705	0722	0731	0835	0830	0830d	0911	0915d	0943	...	0952d	1038d	1019	1155d	1105	1121	1136	...	1201d	1223
ou dong ... d.	...	|	0711	|	0749	|	|	0833	|	|	0938	1013	|	|	...	1113	|	|	|	|	|	1237	...	1310	|
heng xi ... d.	...	0708	|	|	|	0941	|	|	|	|	0953	|	|	|	...	|	|	|	|	1208	|	|	...	|	|
an xi ... d.	...	|	0732	0753	|	0957	0836	0855	|	|	1007	1035	1039	|	...	1134	1201	1143	1316	|	|	|	...	|	|
yang bei ... a.	...	0756	0802y	0823y	0840y	1034	0913y	0925y	1016	1003	1048	1105y	1127y	1130y	...	1206y	1236	1213y	1352	1252y	1308y	1322	...	1359	1413
yang bei ... d.	0620	0759	...	0826y	0844y	...	0917y	0928y	1019	1005	...	1108y	1130y	1133y	1143	...	...	1217y	...	1256y	1311y	1325	1343	1402	1416
g dong ... d.	0705	|	...	0923	|	...	1013	|	|	|	...	1204	1213	|	|	...	...	|	...	|	1485	|	1443	1454	1509
gchun xi ... d.	0734	0913	...	|	1003	...	1041	1047	|	1111	...	1233	1243	1252	1304	...	...	1334	...	1421	|	1450	1512	|	1537
angchun ... a.	|	|	...	0954	|	...	1051	|	1142	|	...	|	1257	|	|	...	...	1344	...	|	1441	|	|	1530	|
lin ... a.	|	|	...	...	|	...	1134	|	...	|	...	|	1337	|	|	...	...	1427	...	|	1521	|	|	1610	|
bin xi ... a.	0830	1009	...	...	1106	...	...	1156	...	1205	...	1339	...	1348	1400	...	...	...	...	1523	...	1546	1619	...	1640

ains prefix 'G'	717	8015	8053	49	719	781	8017	8055	721	8057	723	8019	8059	725	8021	727	729	8023	8061	761	731	8063	8067	8065	8069
an bei ... d.	1239	1335	1352d	1400	1417	...	1442d	1508d	1532	1541d	1610	1605d	1651d	1650	1740d	1746	1822	1844	1902	...	1912	1954d	2015	2030d	2115
ou dong ... d.	|	|	1459	|	1519	...	|	1631	|	|	1705	|	|	|	|	|	1924	1942	|	...	|	|	2142	|	|
heng xi ... d.	1403	|	|	|	|	...	1559	|	|	1704	|	|	|	1754	|	|	|	|	2012	...	|	|	|	|	|
an xi ... d.	1417	1506	1521	|	1541	...	|	|	1703	|	1727	1742	1815	|	|	1903	1946	2004	|	...	2036	|	2146	2150	|
yang bei ... a.	1447y	1540	1558y	1533	1611y	...	1647y	1720	1733y	1741y	1804y	1820	1852y	1831	1948y	1944	2027	2045	2053	...	2106y	2158	2216y	2220y	2252
yang bei ... d.	1450y	1542	...	1535	1614y	1730	1650y	...	1736y	...	1807y	1824	...	1834	1953y	1951	2030	2048	...	2106	2109y	...	...	...	...
g dong ... d.	|	1634	...	|	|	1816	1744	...	|	...	1901	1922	...	1931	2101	2043	2116	2142	...	2158	|	...	...	...	...
gchun xi ... d.	1609	|	...	1641	1733	1845	|	...	1901	...	1929	|	...	1959	|	2112	2144	|	...	2226	|	...	...	...	...
angchun ... a.	|	1705	...	|	|	|	1827	...	|	...	|	1956	...	|	2134	|	|	2215	...	|	2235	...	...	...	...
lin ... a.	|	...	...	|	|	|	1908	...	|	...	|	2036	...	|	...	|	|	...	...	|	|	...	...	...	...
bin xi ... a.	1712	...	...	1735	1842	1948	...	...	2010	...	2025	...	...	2102	...	2222	2240	...	...	2321	2331	...	...	...	...

Dalian. y – Shenyang. ** – Changhcun *0 km* - Jilin *111 km.* - Siping dong *130 km.*

HARBIN - TIANJIN and BEIJING — 7025

inese Railways

Z188 ♦	K20 ♦	T244	Z62	K28 ♦	Z16	Z2	Z238 ♦	T122 ♦	T48 ♦	Z118	T184	Z158	↓ ↑	T47 ♦	K27 ♦	Z117	Z237 ♦	Z61	Z1	T121 ♦	Z187 ♦	K19 ♦	T243	Z157	T183	Z15
...	1317	1039x	...	...	2125	2141	2141	...	2209	...	0645	1042	d. **Harbin** ... a.	0616	...	...	0725	...	0719	...	...	1449	1551	1652	2000	0704
...	1557	1332	2200	...	|	|	|	2128	|	2355	1029	1248	d. Changchun ... d.	|	...	0435	|	0638	|	0705	...	1214	1330	1455	1725	|
...	1926y	1703	|	...	|	|	0159	0012	0257	0234	1335y	1514	a. **Shenyang** bei .. d.	0124	...	0138	0313	|	|	0356	...	0855y	1039	1227	1408	|
1735	1934y	1711	|	2224y	|	|	0205	0019	0303	0242	1346y	1520	d. **Shenyang** bei .. a.	0116	0239y	0130	0307	|	|	0342	0647	0847y	1026	1217	1400	|
2336	0022	|	|	0304	|	|	|	0418	|	|	1817	|	d. Shanhaiguan ... d.	|	2247	|	|	|	|	2320	0119	0413	|	|	0938	|
|	|	|	|	0338	|	|	|	|	|	|	1907	|	d. Beidaihe ... d.	2124	2159	|	|	|	|	2238	|	|	|	|	|	|
0300	0352	0234	|	0648	|	|	0748	0758	|	|	2138	|	a. **Tianjin** ... d.	|	1906	|	2045	|	|	2010	2130	0041	0356	|	0559	|
...	0546	...	0608	0838	0724	0730	...	...	0914	0952	...	2106	a. **Beijing** ... d.	1857	1727	1655	...	2210	2109	...	...	2300	...	0618	...	2115

BEIJING - BADALING — 7035

inese Railways

m	S201	S203	S205	S207	S209	S211	S213	S215	S217	S219	S221	S227	↓ ↑	S208	S210	S212	S214	S216	S218	S220	S222	S224	S226	S228	S232
0	0612	0758	0834	0902	1057	1242	1314	1335	1524	1711	1741	2128	d. **Beijing** bei ... d.	0947	1212	1240	1312	1500	1643	1725	1739	1854	2111	2143	2303
32	0731	0920	0947	1015	1213	1401	1425	1450	1643	1830	1857	2244	a. **Badaling** △ ... a.	0823	1051	1119	1150	1340	1508	1552	1621	1733	1934	2006	2133

BEIJING - TAIYUAN - XI'AN — 7040

ina Rail High Speed

		D2501 A	D2505	D2531	G603	D2001	G91	G605	D2533	G607	D2513	G609	G611	G613	D2519	D2521	D2003	G615	D2525	G617	D2529	D2005	G619	G621	G623	G625	G627
0	**Beijing** xi ... d.	...	...	...	0723	0752	0840	0917	...	1010	...	1028	1114	1133	...	...	1318	1410	...	1506	...	1529	1657	1802	1807	1904	2005
1	Shijiazhuang ... d.	...	...	...	0854	0933	0949	1039	...	1143	...	1200	1246	1257	...	...	1520	1533	...	1635	...	1724	1820	1924	1936	2026	2115
4	Yangquan bei .. d.	...	...	...	0940	1019	|	1125	...	1229	...	1246	|	1345	...	...	1606	1618	...	1720	...	1810	|	2009	2022	2112	2200
3	**Taiyuan** nan ... a.	...	...	...	1028	1107	1116	1212	...	1316	...	1334	1410	1433	...	...	1654	1707	...	1811	...	1855	1948	2056	2109	2201	2247
3	**Taiyuan** nan ... d.	0700	0825	0925	...	1121	...	...	1212	...	1318	1347	...	...	1510	1605	1700	...	1750	...	1913	1902	...	...	...	...	...
6	Linfen xi ... d.	0829	|	1106	...	1307	...	...	|	...	1454	1537	...	...	1639	1734	1838	...	|	...	|	2053	...	...	...	...	...
9	Yuncheng bei .. d.	0921	1011	|	...	1353	...	...	1433	...	1539	1620	...	...	1717	1819	1932	...	2011	...	2102	...	...	...	...	...	...
2	**Xi'an** bei ... a.	1047	1125	1312	...	...	...	...	1553	...	1705	...	...	...	1837	1945	...	...	2131	...	2240	...	...	...	...	...	...

	G602 B	G604	G92	G606	D2002	G608	D2004	G610	D2502	D2506 C	G614	G616	D2512	G618	G620	D2514	D2006	D2518	G622	D2522	G626	D2532	G628	D2524	D2534	D2530
n bei ... d.	...	...	...	...	...	...	...	...	0810	0938	...	...	1107	...	...	1210	...	1340	...	1458	...	1612	...	1725	1850	1905
cheng bei ... d.	...	...	...	...	...	...	0804	...	|	1044	...	1152	1228	...	...	1338	1425	|	...	|	...	1740	...	1853	|	2025
en xi ... d.	...	...	...	...	0739	...	0851	...	1030	1129	...	1238	1313	...	...	|	1512	1539	...	1645	...	1832	...	1941	|	2110
yuan nan ... a.	...	...	...	...	0916	...	1059	...	1152	1258	...	1414	1449	...	...	1545	1657	1728	...	1800	...	2008	...	2119	2230	2246
yuan nan ... d.	0646	0656	0820	0757	0922	1054	1107	1136	...	...	1341	1425	...	1455	1509	...	1705	...	1753	...	1900	...	2014	...	...	...
gquan bei ... d.	|	0748	|	0848	1012	|	1152	1228	...	...	1432	1519	...	1545	1559	...	1757	...	1844	...	1951	...	2104	...	...	...
azhuang ... d.	0818	0839	0950	0935	1102	1226	1252	1315	...	...	1518	1609	...	1632	1658	...	1844	...	1931	...	2039	...	2152	...	...	...
ing xi ... a.	0940	0958	1100	1054	1255	1344	1503	1435	...	...	1637	1728	...	1745	1816	...	2039	...	2050	...	2158	...	2311	...	...	...

m	All trains prefix 'D'	6801	6803	6805	6807	6809	6811	2531	6813	G671	6815	2533	6817	6819	5091	G673
0	**Xi'an** beii ... d.	0730	0830	0930	1030	1130	1230	1320	1400	1440	1500	1600	1700	1800	1900	2045
7	**Baoji** nan ... d.	0829	0935	1035	1135	1235	1335	1425	1505	1539	1605	1705	1805	1905	2005	2144

trains prefix ''	G672	6802	6804	6806	6808	6810	5096	2532	6812	G674	6814	2534	6816	6818	6820
oji nan ... d.	0800	0900	1000	1100	1200	1300	1400	1500	1530	1600	1630	1730	1730	1930	2030
an bei ... d.	0905	1005	1105	1205	1259	1411	1459	1605	1635	1705	1735	1835	1935	2035	2135

Additional trips: 0904, 1033, 1245, 1333, 1438, 1718, 1830. **B** – Additional trip 1241. **C** – Additional tip: 0905, 0945, 1000, 1250, 1325, 1410, 1748, 1832.

BEIJING - TIANJIN — 7045

ina Rail High Speed

n-speed '**C**' trains (numbers **C20xx**, **C21xx** and **C22xx**). *120 km.* Journey 33 - 38 minutes.

ing nan depart: 0612, 0621, 0632, 0642, 0650, 0700, 0708, 0715, 0724, 0732, 0749, 0808, 0821, 0831, 0849, 0901, 0906, 0911, 0919, 0929, 0939, 0952, 1000, 1008, 1018, 1029, 1042, 1052,
0, 1119, 1129, 1137, 1147, 1205, 1218, 1233, 1241, 1255, 1300, 1307, 1315, 1339, 1344, 1356, 1407, 1423, 1431, 1444, 1454, 1505, 1515, 1525, 1535, 1545, 1551, 1615, 1627, 1635, 1645,
4, 1709, 1718, 1731, 1741, 1749, 1759, 1815, 1825, 1835, 1846, 1851, 1902, 1910, 1925, 1939, 1947, 1957, 2005, 2015, 2027, 2046, 21000, 2119, 2150, 2200, 2227, 2252.

njin depart: 0617, 0634, 0645, 0656, 0702, 0714, 0725, 0738, 0751, 0756, 0805, 0824, 0836, 0841, 0854, 0902, 0917, 0926, 0943, 0954, 0959, 1009, 1017, 1025, 1033, 1038, 1054, 1107,
7, 1135, 1143, 1149, 1201, 1216, 1227, 1242, 1258, 1311, 1319, 1331, 1342, 1355, 1409, 1419, 1428, 1438, 1448, 1511, 1500, 1521, 1529, 1542, 1550, 1600, 1610, 1621, 1631, 1642, 1706,
9, 1724, 1734, 1748, 1800, 1814, 1824, 1832, 1845, 1850, 1901, 1911, 1922, 1927, 1940, 1943, 1950, 2004, 2012, 2035, 2042, 2056, 2107, 2115, 2125, 2139, 2149, 2159, 2210, 2229, 2253.

HOHHOT - LANZHOU — 7050

inese Railways

m	K888 ♦	2635	K43B ♦	K43 ♦	Z179 ♦	↓ ↑	Z180 ♦	K887 ♦	2636	K44 ♦	K44B ♦
0	0835	1535h	2116	2116	2240	d. **Hohhot** dong ... a.	0137	0655	0625	0903	0906
55	1044	1811	2331	2331	0050	d. Baotou ... d.	2349	0500	0432	0703	0703
33	1325	2037	0153	0153	0309	d. Linhe ... d.	2116	0234	0138	0401	0401
76	1802	0045	0546	0546	0707	d. Yinchuan ... d.	1734	2246	1952	0001	0001
88	2215	0335	0914	0914	0941	d. Zhongwei ... d.	1511	1921	1647	2059	2059
95	|	|	1258	|	1315	a. **Wuwei** ... d.	1019	|	|	|	1723
52	|	|	1859	|	1744	a. Jiayuguan ... d.	0553	|	|	|	1136
70	0044	0541	...	1122	...	d. Jingtai ... d.	...	1701	1417	1833	...
57	0234	0710	...	1332	...	d. Beiyin xi ... d.	...	1526	1222	1701	...
44	0425	0915	...	1519	...	a. **Lanzhou** ... d.	...	1321	1036	1526	...

♦ – **NOTES** for Tables **7025** - **7050** (by train number):

- **K19/20** – Beijing(**K19/20**) - Manzhouli and v.v.
- **K27/28** – ①③④⑥. Beijing(**K27/28**) - Dandong(**6/5**) - Pyongyang and v.v.
- **K43/44** – Jiayuggan(**K43B/44B**)& Lanzhou (**K43/44**) - Beijing.
- **T47/48** – Qiqihar(**T48/47**) - Beijing.
- **T121/122** – Changchun(**T122/21**) - Tianjin(**T123/24**) - Guangzhou and v.v.
- **Z179/180** – Beijing(**Z178/180**) - Urümqi and v.v.
- **Z187/188** – Shenyang bei(**Z188/87**) - Tianjin(**Z185/86**) - Shenzhen and v.v.
- **Z237/238** – Harbin(**Z238/37**) - Tianjin(**Z235/36**) - Guangzhou and v.v.
- **K887/88** – Beijing(**K887/88**) - Lanzhou and v.v.
- **b** – Beijing bei. **h** – Hohhot. **t** – Taiyuan.
- **x** – xi. **y** – Shenyang. △ – For Great Wall of China.

7060 BEIJING - WUHAN (- GUANGZHOU)

China Rail High Sp

km	All trains prefix 'G'	93	551	D2201	D295	541	423	507	651	501	529	817	71	531	653	671	307	83	421	95	73	571	511	309	79
0	**Beijing** xi d.	...	...	...	...	...	...	0653	0700	0730	0733	...	0740	...	0821	0815	0830	0900	0907	...	...	0922	0937	0932	1000
281	Shijiazhuang d.	...	...	...	...	...	0800	0816	0821	0852	0857	...	0909	0915	0949	0945	0955	1009	1022	...	...	1051	1059	1055	1109
403	Xingtai dong d.	...	...	...	...	...	|	|	0851	0922	0934	...	0939	0944	|	|	|	|	|	...	...	1121	|	1135	|
456	Handan dong d.	...	...	...	...	...	0847	0858	0916	|	|	...	0957	1002	|	1026	1046	|	1103	...	...	1145	|	1153	|
516	Anyang dong d.	...	...	...	...	...	|	0917	0936	|	1004	...	|	|	1039	|	1105	|	1122	...	...	|	|	1212	|
626	Xinxiang dong d.	...	...	...	...	...	0934	|	|	1012	|	...	|	1049	1117	1124	|	|	1150	...	...	|	1230	|	|
	Xi'an bei **7070** d.	...	...	...	...	...	|	|	|	|	|	0803	|	|	|	|	|	|	|	0948	...	|	|	|	|
693	**Zhengzhou** dong a.	...	...	...	...	...	0956	1007	1022	1033	1046	1022	1058	1111	1138	1146	1154	1130	1211	1150**z**	...	1239	1251	1302	1230
693	**Zhengzhou** dong d.	0800	...	0804**z**	0824**z**	0825	1000	1010	1026	1036	1052	1045	1106	1114	1143	1149	1157	1133	1215	1153**z**	1209	1242	1254	1308	1233
	Xi'an bei **7070** a.	|	...	|	|	|	|	|	1252	|	|	|	|	|	1411	1431	|	|	|	|	|	|	|	|	|
848	Luohe xi d.	|	0800	0909	0923	0902	1037	|	...	|	1129	|	|	|	...	...	|	|	1305	|	1251	|	1329	|	|
1030	Xinyang dong d.	|	0852	1002	1016	0949	1124	|	...	1151	|	1203	|	1247	...	...	|	|	1352	|	1340	1358	|	|	|
1229	**Wuhan** a.	0958	0943	1056**h**	1122**h**	1033	1208	1224**h**	...	1235	1253	1248	1305	1330	...	...	1347**h**	1320	1436	1348	1423	...	1452	1516**h**	1417
	Changsha nan **7065** a.	1116	1127	...	...	1204	1345	...	...	1412	1449	1416	1426	1503	...	...	...	1444	1609	1509	1552	...	...	...	1538
	Guangzhou nan **7065** a.	1339	1419	...	...	1456	...	...	...	...	...	1656	1714	1754	...	...	...	...	...	1730	1831	...	...	...	1759
	Shenzhen bei **7065** a.	...	1458	...	...	...	...	...	...	...	...	1736	1753	1829	...	...	...	...	...	...	1906	...	...	...	...

All trains prefix 'G'	655	831	65	545	429	553	75	835	659	517	839	555	67	69	87	547	519	855	503	673	661	639	521	505	663
Beijing xi d.	0943	...	1033	...	1153	...	...	...	1208	1219	...	1251	1213	1305	1400	...	1405	...	1438	1443	1448	...	1523	1540	1545
Shijiazhuang d.	1120	...	1202	...	1316	...	...	...	1332	1349	...	1406	1342	1428	|	...	1527	...	1600	1605	1618	...	1653	1709	1715
Xingtai dong d.	1152	...	1237	...	1346	...	...	...	1402	|	...	|	1419	|	|	...	|	...	|	1635	1649	...	|	|	|
Handan dong d.	1211	...	|	...	|	...	...	...	1432	1431	...	|	1447	1516	|	...	|	...	1641	1653	|	...	|	1751	1758
Anyang dong d.	|	...	1307	...	1417	...	...	...	|	|	...	|	|	1535	|	...	1627	...	1700	1712	1719	...	1753	|	|
Xinxiang dong d.	|	...	|	...	1445	...	...	...	|	|	...	|	1527	|	|	...	1655	...	1728	1740	|	...	1821	|	|
Xi'an bei **7070** d.	|	1128	|	...	|	...	...	1229	|	|	1305	|	|	|	|	...	|	1517	|	|	|	1527	|	|	|
Zhengzhou dong a.	1316	1342**z**	1349	...	1506	...	...	1449**z**	1514	1525	1533**z**	1534	1548	1617	1624	...	1716	1723**z**	1749	1801	1819	1756	1842	1852	1901
Zhengzhou dong d.	1320	1346**z**	1352	1407	...	...	1435	1452**z**	1521	1528	1536**z**	1537	1551	1620	1627	1643	1720	1726**z**	1752	1803	1824	1811	1845	1855	1904
Xi'an bei **7070** a.	1531	|	|	|	...	...	|	|	1735	|	|	|	|	|	1825	|	|	|	|	2036	2059	|	|	|	2124
Luohe xi d.	...	|	|	1445	...	...	1517	|	...	|	|	|	1633	|	...	1727	|	|	1829	...	...	|	1944	|	...
Xinyang dong d.	...	|	1508	|	...	1530	1604	1613	...	|	|	1645	1715	|	...	|	1844	1857	|	...	...	1928	2039	|	...
Wuhan a.	...	1605	1552	1615	...	1624	1650	1705	...	1737	1742	1734**h**	1759	1812	...	1858	1928	1940	1947	...	...	2012	2138**h**	2055	...
Changsha nan **7065** a.	...	1737	1727	1745	...	1755	1813	1835	...	...	1917	...	1928	1933	...	2026	...	...	2123	...	...	2141	...	2232	...
Guangzhou nan **7065** a.	...	2025	2016	2032	...	2043	2058	2122	...	...	2207	...	2216	2221	...	2308	...	...	...	...	...	...	...	...	...
Shenzhen bei **7065** a.	...	...	...	...	...	...	2139	...	...	...	...	...	...	...	...	...	...	...	...	...	...	...	...	...	...

All trains prefix 'G'	573	523	525	561	669	563	527	565	567	569
Beijing xi d.	1618	1630	1714	1703	1737	1732	1812	1824	1917	2000
Shijiazhuang d.	1741	1753	1836	1841	1859	1905	1942	2000	2033	2109
Xingtai dong d.	|	|	1906	|	|	|	2012	|	2110	|
Handan dong d.	1823	1834	|	1930	1940	1956	|	2041	|	|
Anyang dong d.	|	1853	1936	1949	1959	2015	|	|	2140	|
Xinxiang dong d.	1903	1921	2011	2017	2027	2043	2110	2121	|	2219
Xi'an bei **7070** d.	|	|	|	|	|	|	|	|	|	|
Zhengzhou dong a.	1924	1943	2032	2038	2048	2105	2131	2142	2230	2237
Zhengzhou dong d.	1927	1946	2035	...	2056	...	2134	...	...	...
Xi'an bei **7070** a.	|	|	|	...	2252	...	|	...	...	...
Luohe xi d.	|	2023	2118	...	...	...	2216	...	...	...
Xinyang dong d.	2044	2103	2205	...	...	...	2256	...	...	...
Wuhan a.	2129	2147	2254**h**	...	...	...	2340	...	...	...
Changsha nan **7065** a.	...	...	...	...	...	...	...	...	...	...
Guangzhou nan **7065** a.	...	...	...	...	...	...	...	...	...	...
Shenzhen bei **7065** a.	...	...	...	...	...	...	...	...	...	...

All trains prefix 'G'	90	560	508	564	652	510	502	26	512
Shenzhen bei **7065** d.	...	...	...	...	...	...	...	...	...
Guangzhou nan **7065** d.	...	...	...	...	...	...	...	...	...
Changsha nan **7065** d.	...	...	...	...	...	...	0743	...	...
Wuhan d.	...	...	0708**h**	...	...	0816	0911	...	0924**h**
Xinyang dong d.	...	...	0759	...	...	0901	|	...	1015
Luohe xi d.	...	...	0847	...	...	0949	|	...	|
Xi'an bei **7070** d.	...	...	|	...	0752	|	|	0912	|
Zhengzhou dong a.	...	...	0930	...	1007	1032	1100	1109	1127
Zhengzhou dong d.	0900	0905	0933	0940	1010	1035	1104	1112	1130
Xi'an bei **7070** a.	|	|	|	|	|	|	|	|	|
Xinxiang dong d.	|	|	|	1002	|	1058	1132	|	1154
Anyang dong d.	|	0955	|	1030	|	|	|	|	1222
Handan dong d.	|	|	1035	1051	|	1139	|	|	|
Xingtai dong d.	|	1025	|	|	|	|	1228	|	1252
Shijiazhuang d.	1024	1027	1117	1135	1155	1220	1259	1241	1324
Beijing xi a.	1131	1234	1229	1302	1326	1339	1418	1349	1450

All trains prefix 'G'	640	84	672	656	572	514	566	94	556	832	660	662	96	518	516	88	66	72	430	574	74	568	542	532	822
Shenzhen bei **7065** d.	...	...	...	...	...	...	...	...	...	...	...	...	...	...	...	...	...	0753	...	...	0842	...	...	0940	1000
Guangzhou nan **7065** d.	...	...	...	...	...	...	...	0800	...	0711	...	...	0900	...	...	...	1000	0827	...	...	0922	...	0944	1023	1040
Changsha nan **7065** d.	0820	0900	...	...	...	...	...	1022	...	0957	...	...	1119	...	...	...	1220	1114	...	...	1213	...	1235	1308	1324
Wuhan d.	0951	1020	...	...	1013	1035	...	1143	1035**h**	1133	...	...	1240	1248**h**	1330	...	1341	1246	...	...	1347	...	1411	1440	1453
Xinyang dong d.	1037	|	...	...	1003	1120	...	|	1139	|	...	...	|	1341	|	...	|	|	...	1425	1432	...	1457	1526	1545
Luohe xi d.	|	|	...	...	1150	1207	...	|	|	|	...	...	|	|	|	...	|	1421	...	1507	1519	...	1543	1609	|
Xi'an bei **7070** d.	|	|	0911	1003	|	|	...	|	|	|	1100	1138	|	|	|	1318	|	|	...	|	|	...	|	|	|
Zhengzhou dong a.	1200	1205	1137	1225	1233	1241	...	1328	1327	1344**z**	1340	1404	1435**z**	1452	1516	1517	1526	1456	...	1548	1602	...	1623	1648	1710**z**
Zhengzhou dong d.	1228	1208	1140	1230	1236	1249	1259	...	1332	1355**z**	1343	1410	1438**z**	1455	1519	1524	1529	1459	1545	1553	...	1610	...	1654	1714**z**
Xi'an bei **7070** a.	1446	|	|	|	|	|	|	...	|	1610	|	|	1642	|	|	|	|	|	|	|	...	|	...	|	1944
Xinxiang dong d.	...	|	1202	|	1259	|	1322	...	|	...	1405	|	...	|	|	|	|	|	1607	1615	...	|	...	|	...
Anyang dong d.	...	|	|	|	|	1339	1356	...	1423	...	1434	|	...	|	|	|	|	1543	1635	1650	...	1700	...	1738	...
Handan dong d.	...	|	1257	|	1340	1358	|	...	|	...	1459	|	...	|	|	|	|	1619	|	|	...	1719	...	|	...
Xingtai dong d.	...	|	1315	1345	|	|	1428	...	|	...	|	1523	...	|	|	|	|	|	1705	1723	...	|	...	1811	...
Shijiazhuang d.	...	1332	1345	1416	1425	1449	1500	...	1524	...	1541	1555	...	1626	1642	1648	1653	1703	1736	1754	...	1809	...	1839	...
Beijing xi a.	...	1440	1511	1537	1553	1609	1632	...	1643	...	1711	1716	...	1738	1750	1755	1800	1821	1856	1919	...	1935	...	...	...

All trains prefix 'G'	310	524	68	836	422	308	504	666	570	80	424	506	D2202	70	840	530	826	674	528	670	554	D296	544	546	76
Shenzhen bei **7065** d.	...	...	...	...	...	...	...	...	...	1129	...	...	...	...	...	...	1250	...	...	...	1334	...	...	...	1550
Guangzhou nan **7065** d.	...	...	1115	1135	...	...	...	...	...	1211	...	...	...	1250	1230	...	1329	...	...	...	1414	...	1356	1410	1630
Changsha nan **7065** d.	...	...	1401	1421	1412	...	1433	...	...	1456	1501	1506	...	1538	1517	1554	1617	...	...	...	1714	...	1646	1702	1914
Wuhan d.	1509**h**	1530	1535	1550	1554	1613**h**	1612	...	...	1633	1639	1644	1651**h**	1707	1653	1724	1748	...	1757	...	1900	1830**h**	1827	1833	2041
Xinyang dong d.	|	1615	1620	|	1646	|	1657	...	...	1718	1724	|	1816	1752	1739	1810	1833	...	1843	...	1945	1929	1912	|	2126
Luohe xi d.	|	|	1707	1715	|	|	1737	...	...	|	1804	1809	1908	|	|	1857	1913	...	|	...	2038	2022	2002	|	2223
Xi'an bei **7070** d.	|	|	|	|	|	|	|	1600	...	|	|	|	|	|	|	|	|	1718	|	1805	...	|	|	|	|
Zhengzhou dong a.	1712	1731	1743	1804**z**	1801	1824	1811	1817	...	1832	1842	1850	1956**z**	1906	1906**z**	1932	1957	1942	2002	2009	...	2114**z**	2043	2101**z**	2301
Zhengzhou dong d.	1715	1734	1746	1809**z**	1806	1832	1814	1820	1825	1837	1847	1853	...	1911	1918**z**	1935	2012	1945	2008	2015	...	...	...	...	...
Xi'an bei **7070** a.	|	|	|	2029	|	|	|	|	|	|	|	|	...	|	2139	|	2224	|	|	|	...	...	...	...	...
Xinxiang dong d.	|	|	1808	...	|	1855	|	|	1847	1901	1911	1919	...	|	...	|	...	|	|	2037	...	...	...	...	...
Anyang dong d.	1758	1824	1843	...	1849	|	1857	1903	195	|	1952	|	...	1957	...	2027	...	|	|	2105	...	...	...	...	...
Handan dong d.	|	|	|	...	|	|	1917	1922	|	|	|	2001	...	2018	...	|	...	2100	2114	2124	...	...	...	...	...
Xingtai dong d.	1828	|	|	...	1919	1951	|	|	|	1956	2024	|	...	|	...	|	...	|	|	2142	...	...	...	...	...
Shijiazhuang d.	1859	1918	1945	...	1950	2022	2000	2005	2017	2028	2052	2044	...	2102	...	2130	...	2141	2203	2216	...	...	...	...	...
Beijing xi a.	2020	2044	2057	...	2102	2142	2126	2131	2137	2147	...	2203	...	2220	...	2250	...	2300	2323	2325	...	...	...	...	...

h – Wuhan Hankou.

z – Zhengzhou.

7062 BEIJING - HOHHOT

Chinese Railwa

km	K217	K58	K617	K43 ♦	Z315	Z179 ♦	K263	K573	K597	K89	Z317	K888 ♦			Z180 ♦	Z316	K44 ♦	K618	Z318	K218	K598	K887 ♦	K57	K264	K90
0	0033**x**	0255	1032**x**	1055	1533**x**	1515	1950	2035**x**	2126**x**	2215**x**	2249	2341	↓	d.**Beijing** a. ↑	0936	1426**x**	1942	1935**x**	2139	0405**x**	0458**x**	1355	0427	0715	0720
190	0405	0623	1506	1455	1856	1839	2326	0007	0056	0136	0214	0330	↓	d.Zhangjiakou nan d. ↑	0619	1112	1617	1549	1823	0001	0140	1043	0105	0331	0407
368	0656	|	|	1753	|	|	|	0300	0345	|	|	|		d. Datong d.	|	|	1340	|	|	2053	2304	|	|	|	|
374	0843	0825	1725	1943	2039	2104	0329	0446	0531	0447	|	0647	↓	d.Jining nan d. ↑	0359	0930	1133	1326	|	1854	2109	0841	2221	0037	01103
524*	1006	1016	1848	2106**h**	2148	2227	0507	0609	0652	0603	0506**h**	0810		a.**Hohhot** dong d.	0215	0824	0929	1158	1522**h**	1725	1932	0712	2052	2244	2315
697	1214	1228	...	2304	...	0028	0726	0842	0904	...	0658	1034	↓	a.Baotou d. ↑	2349	...	0703	...	1342	1503	1715	...	1819	2020	...

♦ – NOTES by train number:
K43/44 – Jiayuggan(**K43B/44B**)& Lanzhou (**K43/44**) - Beijing.
Z179/180 – Beijing(**Z179/180**) - Urümqi and v.v.
K887/88 – Beijing(**K887/88**) - Lanzhou and v.v.
h – Hohhot. **x** – Beijing xi.
* – 645km via Datong.

a Rail High Speed — (BEIJING -) WUHAN - GUANGZHOU - SHENZHEN — 7065

All trains prefix 'G'	6011	6101	1103	1001	1105	1107	1111	77	1007	93	551	541	85	1011	1034		501	817	71	531	83	73	95	79	1013
Beijing xi **7060** d.	...	...	...	...	...	...	...	...	...	...	...	...	...	...	...	...	0710	...	0740	...	0900	...	...	1000	...
Xi'an bei **7070** d.	...	...	...	...	...	...	...	...	...	...	...	...	...	...	...	...	|	0803	|	...	|	...	0948	|	...
Zhengzhou dong **7060** d.	...	...	...	...	...	...	...	...	...	0756	...	0825	...	...	...	...	1034	1045	1106	1114	1133	1209	1153**z**	1233	...
Wuhan ♥ d.	...	...	0700	0725	0737	0838	0910	0900	0930	0958	0951	1039	...	1053	1140	...	1238	1251	1308	1338	1323	1427	1351	1420	1444
Yueyang dong d.	...	...	0751	|	0835	0936	|	|	1028	|	1054	|	...	|	|	...	|	1342	|	|	|	|	|	|	1536
Changsha nan a.	...	...	0832	0850	0909	1010	1035	1018	1102	1116	1127	1204	...	1218	1312	...	1412	1416	1426	1503	1440	1552	1509	1538	1610
Changsha nan d.	0700	0706	0835	0854	0912	1014	1038	1021	1105	1119	1131	1207	1227	1221	1316	...	...	1420	1430	1506	...	1556	1512	1541	1614
Zhuzhou xi d.	|	|	|	|	|	1035	1055	|	1122	|	|	1224	|	|	|	...	...	|	|	|	...	|	|	|	|
Hengyang dong d.	|	0745	0921	|	0951	1104	|	|	1151	1159	1218	1246	|	|	1355	...	...	|	1509	1550	...	|	|	|	|
Chenzhou xi d.	0807	0820	|	1008	1026	1139	1159	|	1231	|	1252	1321	|	|	1430	...	...	|	|	1624	...	1703	|	|	|
Shaoguan d.	0840	0853	|	|	|	|	|	|	|	|	|	1359	|	1406	1503	...	...	1600	1617	|	...	|	|	|	1801
Guangzhou nan ♥ a.	0951	0957	1126	1131	1156	1309	1329	1243	1401	1349	1422	1456	1451	1510	1600	...	...	1656	1714	1754	...	1831	1730	1759	1856
Shenzhen bei a.	1032	...	...	1212	...	...	...	1317	1441	...	1458	...	...	1550	1643	...	...	1736	1753	1830	...	1906	...	...	1938

ains prefix 'G'	821	1019	1015	65	831	545	553	75	1021	835	825	1151	839	6027	67	1133	69	1135	1305	547	1139	1141	6121	503	505
ing xi **7060** d.	...	...	...	1028	...	...	...	...	...	...	...	...	...	...	1213	...	1305	...	...	...	...	...	...	1438	1540
i'an bei **7070** d.	1053	...	...	|	1128	...	...	...	...	1229	1235	...	1305	...	|	...	|	...	...	...	...	...	...	|	|
engzhou dong **7060** d.	1315**z**	...	...	1352	1346**z**	1407	...	1435	...	1452**z**	1504**z**	...	1536**z**	...	1551	...	1620	...	...	1643	...	...	...	1752	1855
an ♥ d.	1538	1543	1549	1555	1610	1620	1628	1655	1658	1710	1722	1736	1747	...	1803	1757	1815	1808	...	1901	1925	1932	...	1950	2059
ang dong d.	1629	|	|	1653	|	|	1722	|	1756	1801	|	1834	|	...	1854	1903	|	1911	...	|	2016	2037	...	2048	2158
gsha nan a.	1703	1708	1714	1727	1737	1745	1755	1813	1830	1835	1850	1908	1919	...	1928	1944	1933	1952	...	2026	2057	2111	...	2123	2232
gsha nan d.	1706	1712	1718	1731	1741	1748	1759	1816	1833	1844	1854	1912	1923	1922	1932	1948	1937	1958	2021	2031	2100	2115	2104	...	...
ou xi d.	|	|	|	|	|	|	|	1833	1850	|	|	1929	|	|	|	|	1954	|	|	|	|	|	2121	...	...
yang dong d.	|	|	1757	|	1820	1827	|	1902	|	|	1933	|	|	2001	|	2030	2025	2044	2100	2110	|	2156	|	...	...
zhou xi d.	1820	1826	1832	1846	1855	1902	|	|	1947	|	2008	2026	|	|	2046	2105	|	|	|	2145	2214	2231	2219	...	...
guan d.	1853	1859	|	|	|	|	1947	2003	|	2024	|	2057	2103	|	2119	|	2126	2146	|	|	|	|	2253	...	...
gzhou nan ♥ a.	1950	1956	2000	2016	2025	2032	2043	2058	2117	2122	2138	2156	2207	2211	2217	2234	2222	2243	2254	2308	2344	2354	2350	...	...
zhen bei a.	2030	2036	2040	...	...	...	...	2139	2202	...	2220	...	...	2252	...	...	...	...	...	...	...	...	...	...	...

ains prefix 'G'	502	6102	84	832	1002	94	1104	86	72	1106	96	1004	1108	74	552	542		80	1006	818	532	822	1114	1008	504
zhen bei d.	...	...	...	...	0700	...	...	...	0753	...	...	0830	...	0850	...	...	...	...	0922	0935	0940	1000	...	1025	...
gzhou nan ♥ d.	...	0706	...	0711	0733	0800	0746	0800	0827	0834	0900	0910	0917	0930	0933	0944	...	1000	1006	1016	1023	1040	1102	1106	...
gun d.	...	0759	...	|	0826	|	0839	|	0921	0927	|	1003	1010	1024	1033	1052	...	|	|	|	|	1133	1202	1200	...
zhou xi d.	...	|	...	0838	|	|	|	|	0955	1000	|	|	|	|	1106	|	...	|	1136	1144	1150	1207	|	1233	...
yang dong d.	...	0907	...	0913	|	|	0945	|	1033	1040	|	|	1118	|	|	1153	...	|	1211	|	1225	1242	1303	1308	...
ou xi d.	...	|	...	|	0950	|	|	|	|	|	|	|	|	1149	|	|	...	|	|	|	|	|	|	1337	...
gsha nan a.	...	0948	...	0953	1009	1019	1026	1021	1110	1122	1116	1144	1200	1206	1228	1232	...	1217	1250	1300	1305	1321	1346	1354	...
gsha nan d.	0743	...	0900	0956	1013	1022	1030	...	1114	1131	1119	1148	1205	1210	1232	1235	...	1220	1255	1303	1308	1325	1350	1359	1433
ang dong d.	0818	...	|	1032	|	|	|	...	|	|	|	|	|	1255	1307	|	...	|	|	|	1344	1400	1425	|	1516
an ♥ a.	0908	...	1017	1129	1145	1140	1157	...	1233	1301	1237	1322	1331	1348	1357	1408	...	1338	1422	1429	1434	1452	1522	1526	1607
engzhou dong **7060** a.	1100	...	1205	1344**z**	...	1328	...	...	1456	...	1435**z**	...	...	1557	...	1623	...	1526	...	1649**x**	1648	1714**z**	...	...	1811
i'an bei **7070** a.	|	...	|	1610	...	...	...	...	|	...	1642	...	...	...	...	...	...	|	...	1915	...	1933	...	...	|
jing xi **7060** a.	1418	...	1440	...	...	...	...	...	1821	...	...	...	...	...	...	...	...	1759	...	...	...	...	...	...	2126

ains prefix 'G'	68	836		506	840	70	1032	826	544	546	78	554	1140	1130	1306	1014	1018	548	76	1132	1020	1134	1136	1138	1022
zhen bei d.	...	...	...	...	...	...	1237	1300	...	...	1400	1334	...	...	...	1520	1515	...	1550	...	1624	...	...	...	1736
gzhou nan ♥ d.	1115	1135	...	...	1227	1250	1317	1342	1356	1410	1433	1414	1517	1526	1539	1604	1554	1623	1630	1647	1705	1730	1740	1746	1817
gun d.	1208	1229	...	...	1320	1343	1410	|	|	1503	|	1507	1610	1631	|	|	1647	1729	|	|	|	1823	1840	1846	1910
zhou xi d.	|	1302	...	...	|	1416	1443	1502	1523	1536	|	1540	1650	1704	|	1729	1720	|	1751	1814	1831	1856	|	1919	1943
yang dong d.	|	1337	...	...	|	|	1518	1545	1558	|	|	1620	|	1739	1726	1806	1806	|	1826	1849	1906	1931	|	1954	2018
ou xi d.	|	|	...	...	1454	|	1548	|	|	1640	|	1649	|	|	|	1835	|	|	|	|	|	|	|	2023	2047
gsha nan a.	1352	1416	...	...	1513	1533	1607	1616	1639	1657	1652	1708	1757	1820	1807	1852	1847	1919	1907	1930	1947	2012	2030	2042	2106
gsha nan d.	1355	1421	...	1506	1516	1538	1610	1621	1647	1702	1655	1714	1802	1823	...	1855	1852	1923	1910	1933	1950	2016	2034	2045	2109
ang dong d.	1437	1457	...	1541	1553	1613	1645	1658	1723	1738	|	1750	|	1906	...	1931	1928	1959	|	|	2026	2052	|	2121	2145
an ♥ a.	1529	1547	...	1638	1643	1704	1749	1748	1823	1830	1813	1854	1928	2003	...	2021	2018	2049	2029	2106	2123	2149	2207	2218	2235
engzhou dong **7060** a.	1750	1804**z**	...	1850	1907**z**	1906	...	1957	2043	2101**z**	...	...	...	...	...	...	...	2314	2241	...	...	...	...	...	...
i'an bei **7070** a.	|	2029	...	|	2138	|	...	2235	...	...	...	...	...	...	...	...	...	...	...	...	...	...	...	...	...
jing xi **7060** a.	2104	...	...	2153	...	2220	...	...	...	...	...	...	...	...	...	...	...	...	...	...	...	...	...	...	...

Zhengzhou.

♥ – Additional services operate Wuhan – Guangzhou and v.v.

a Rail High Speed — ZHENGZHOU - XI'AN — 7070

Prefix 'G' unless noted	2002 A	652	817	26	672	98	656	2006	821	831	660	662	835	825	839	88	664	858	666	2012	674	670	D1004	2014	D308 ♦
Xi'an Bei d.	0742	0752	0803	0912	0919	0953	1007	1025	1053	1128	1100	1138	1229	1235	1305	1318	1434	1517	1600	1649	1718	1805	1841	2025	2103
Huashan bei d.	|	|	|	|	0953	|	|	1059	1128	|	1142	1220	1303	|	|	|	1516	|	|	1723	|	1839	1930	2107	2148
Sanmenxia nan d.	0846	0857	0908	|	1023	|	|	1129	|	|	1212	|	1333	1351	1425	|	1546	1614	|	1800	1825	|	2010	2137	2222
Luoyang Longmen d.	0919	|	|	|	1056	|	1145	1209	1231	1306	1245	1323	1406	1425	1458	|	1619	1647	1732	1833	1858	|	2055	2217	2301
Zhengzhou a.	|	|	|	|	|	1150	|	1245	1312	1342	1321	|	1449	1501	1533	|	1655	1723	|	1910	1942	|	2142	2253	2344
Zhengzhou dong a.	1002	1007	1022	1109	1137	|	1225	...	|	|	1340	1404	|	|	|	1517	1718	|	1817	...	2001	2009	...	...	...
Wuhan **7060** a.	...	|	1251	|	|	1348	|	...	1535	1605	|	|	1705	1719	1742	|	|	1940	|	...	|	|	...	...	...
Changsha nan **7065** a.	...	|	1416	|	|	1509	|	...	1706	1737	|	|	1835	1850	1919	|	|	...	|	...	|	|	...	...	...
Gaungzhou nan **7065** a.	...	|	1656	|	|	1735	|	...	1950	2025	|	|	2122	2138	2207	|	|	...	|	...	|	|	...	...	...
Shenzhen bei **7065** a.	...	|	1736	|	|	...	|	...	2030	...	|	|	...	2220	...	|	|	...	|	...	|	|	...	...	...
Beijing xi **7060** a.	...	1326	...	1349	1511	...	1533	...	...	...	1711	1716	...	...	...	1755	2028	...	2131	...	2300	2328	...	...	...

'G' unless noted	D307 ♦	2001 B	2003	651	653	857	671	655	2007	833	96	D1003	659	87	819	823	837	673	661	841	663	665	2013	827	669
Beijing xi **7060** d.	...	...	...	0700	0821	...	0815	1005	...	...	...	...	1207	1400	...	...	...	1443	1448	...	1545	1600	...	...	1737
enzhen bei **7065** d.	...	...	...	|	|	...	|	|	...	...	...	...	|	|	0930	1000	...	|	|	...	|	|	...	1250	|
angzhou nan **7065** d.	...	...	...	|	|	...	|	|	...	0711	0855	...	|	|	1016	1040	1130	|	|	1230	|	|	...	1329	|
angsha nan **7065** d.	...	...	...	|	|	...	|	|	...	0956	1120	...	|	|	1303	1325	1417	|	|	1517	|	|	...	1617	|
han **7060** d.	...	...	...	|	|	0922	|	|	...	1133	1241	...	|	|	1432	1455	1546	|	|	1653	|	|	...	1748	|
gzhou dong d.	...	...	...	1026	1143	|	1149	1320	...	|	|	...	1521	1627	|	|	|	1803	1824	|	1904	1926	...	2012	2056
gzhou d.	0556	0814	0908	|	|	1205	1216	|	1307	1355	1441	1453	|	|	1653	1718	1813	1825	1844	1918	|	|	1940	|	|
ang Longmen d.	0640	0853	0956	1109	1226	1244	1255	1403	1346	1434	|	1542	1604	|	1732	1757	1852	|	1923	1957	1947	2009	2021	|	|
enxia nan d.	0719	0925	1026	|	1303	1317	1328	|	1418	|	|	1635	|	|	1805	1830	|	|	1955	2029	2019	2048	2100	2121	|
han bei d.	0753	0955	1058	1211	|	|	|	1458	1507	1530	|	1715	1659	|	1842	|	1948	2002	|	|	2049	|	|	|	|
Bei a.	0836	1036	1132	1252	1411	1420	1431	1531	1540	1610	1635	1758	1740	1825	1915	1933	2029	2036	2059	2139	2122	2151	2203	2224	2252

/306 – Shanghai(**D306/305**) - Zhengzhou(**D307/308**) - Xi'an bei.

A – Additional trips: 0925, 1203, 1620.

B – Additional trips: 1245, 1657, 1855.

7085 BEIJING, SHANGHAI and GUANGZHOU - SHENZHEN and HONG KONG

GUANGZHOU DONG - SHENZHEN via Dongguan — China Rail High Sp

High-speed '**C**' trains (numbers **C70xx** and **C71xx**). *139 km*. Journey 70 minutes. Trains call at **Dongguan** 34–37 minutes after Guangzhou and 28–32 minutes after Shenzhen.

Guangzhou dong depart: 0616, 0630, 0640, 0648, 0656, 0704, 0712, 0720, 0728, 0748, 0800, 0820, 0830, 0840, 0850, 0900, 0923, 0932, 0942, 0950, 0958, 1006, 1014, 1022, 1036, 1052, 1113, 1122, 1140, 1155, 1206, 1228, 1238, 1246, 1254, 1302, 1310, 1318, 1326, 1348, 1358, 1407, 1415, 1435, 1445, 1457, 1508, 1520, 1534, 1544, 1552, 1600, 1610, 1620, 1630, 1640, 1706, 1715, 1725, 1735, 1747, 1808, 1816, 1832, 1840, 1848, 1900, 1913, 1923, 1934, 1942, 1950, 2010, 2022, 2030, 2040, 2050, 2058, 2106, 2114, 2130, 2146, 2205, 2222, 2237, 22

Shenzhen depart: 0620, 0635, 0651, 0702, 0712, 0726, 0740, 0754, 0804, 0812, 0820, 0828, 0836, 0844, 0852, 0913, 0928, 0947, 0956, 1006, 1016, 1027, 1048, 1100, 1108, 1116, 1124, 1140, 1148, 1200, 1217, 1230, 1239, 1248, 1307, 1320, 1335, 1352, 1402, 1410, 1420, 1436, 1444, 1452, 1512, 1522, 1531, 1539, 1600, 1610, 1621, 1632, 1644, 1700, 1708, 1716, 1724, 1745, 1755, 1805, 1824, 1832, 1840, 1850, 1900, 1910, 1932, 1940, 1956, 2005, 2015, 2025, 2037, 2058, 2106, 2114, 2134, 2147, 2155, 2204, 2214, 2222, 2230, 2238.

GUANGZHOU NAN - SHENZHEN BEI — China Rail High Sp

High-speed '**G**' trains (numbers **G62xx G97XX**)*102 km*. Journey 29 - 44 minutes.

Guangzhou nan depart: 0702, 0717, 0722, 0731, 0820, 0825, 0847, 0908, 0917, 0931, 1018, 1025, 1037, 1044, 1050, 1055, 1100, 1110, 1125, 1145, 1154, 1252, 1312, 1320, 1445, 1457, 1535, 1555, 1620, 1722, 1748, 1814, 1848, 1937, 2013, 2020, 2042, 2207, 2230.

Shenzhen bei depart: 0725, 0758, 0808, 0839, 0945, 0950, 0955, 1008, 1027, 1033, 1134, 1210, 1215, 1221, 1341, 1349, 1420, 1425, 1522, 1600, 1652, 1718, 1747, 1759, 1813, 1826, 1903, 1917, 1923, 1931, 2012, 2040, 2059, 2115, 2125, 2136, 2148, 2226.

Certain trains continue from/to Changsha, Wuhan, Xi'an and Beijing. See Tables **7060**, **7065** and **7070**.

GUANGZHOU - KOWLOON — MTR Corporation

km		Z801	Z807	Z813	Z823	Z817	Z809	Z825	Z815	Z803	Z819	Z827	Z811
0	**Guangzhou** dong d.	0819	0904	0955	1037	1203	1404	1538	1614	1733	1820	2030	2132
82	Dongguan (Changping) d.	0903	0948	1039	1121	|	1448	1622	1658	1817	1904	2114	|
174	**Kowloon** Hung Hom a.	1017	1102	1153	1233	1356	1602	1734	1812	1931	2018	2226	2325

		Z812	Z824	Z820	Z804	Z808	Z814	Z826	Z818	Z810	Z828	Z816	Z802
Kowloon Hung Hom d.	...	0725	0815	0924	1052	1132	1223	1311	1432	1635	1800	1844	2001
Dongguan (Changping) d.	...	0839	0927	1038	1204	|	|	1420	1546	1749	1912	1958	2115
Guangzhou dong a.	...	0924	1012	1123	1251	1326	1417	1508	1631	1834	1957	2043	2200

BEIJING & SHANGHAI - KOWLOON — Chinese Railw

	Z97 A	Z99 B
Beijing xi d.	1300	...
Shanghai d.	|	1802
Kowloon Hung Hom a.	1301	1301

	Z100 A
Kowloon Hung Hom d.	1515
Shanghai a.	1022
Beijing xi a.	...

Note: Trains make no intermediate passenger stops.

A – Odd dates in (2016); Jan., Mar., Jun., Jul., Sep., Oct: Even dates in (2016) Feb., Apr., May, Aug., Nov., Dec.

B – Odd dates in (2016) Feb., Apr., May, Aug., Nov., Dec.; Even dates in (2016) Jan., Mar., Jun., Jul., Sep., Oct.

7090 BEIJING and TIANJIN - WUHAN - NANCHANG and GUANGZHOU — Chinese Railw

km		T126	T95	Z35	Z235	Z189	T123	T145	Z97	Z89	Z161	T167	Z13	T9	Z5	T253	Z77	T1	Z151	Z201	T179	Z121	Z167	Z263	Z137
		♦			♦		♦				♦			♦	♦		♦		♦	♦			♦	♦	♦
0	**Beijing** xi d.	...	...	1140	...	...	...	1209**b**	1300	...	1306	1412	1500**b**	1512	1609	...	1615	1555**b**	1557	1756	...	...	...	...	...
	Tianjin d.	...	...	|	0754	...	0809	|	|	...	|	|	|	|	|	1315	|	|	|	|	...	...	...	...	...
281	Shijiazhuang d.	...	...	|	1207	...	1227	1507	|	1500	1532	1655	1736	1748	1834	1821	1840	1905	1822	2022	...	...	...	...	...
689	Zhengzhou d.	...	...	1733	1551	1643	1651	1937	1847	1859	1909	2124	2101	2220	2201	2236	2207	22491	A	2352	...	...	0150	0335	0449
1225	**Wuhan** Wuchang a.	...	...	2202	2029	2150	2226	0100	2316	2328	2343	0246	0141	...	0234	0331	0240	0348	...	0425	...	...	0653	0812	0935
1225	**Wuhan** Wuchang d.	1544	1735	2210	2050	2217	2239	0120	2322	2346	0003	0305	0156	...	0240	0341	0246	0359	...	0431	0631	0356	0705	0827	0950
1587	Changsha a.	|	2115	0123	0005	0130	0225	0459	0235	0259	0322	|	0514	...	0553	0702	0559	0721	...	0751	0952	1022	1032	1155	1309
1587	Changsha d.	|	2121	0129	0011	0136	0234	0514	0241	0305	...	|	0520	...	...	0708	...	...	...	0752	1000	1028	1038	1201	1315
1639	Zhuzhou d.	|	|	|	0051	|	0327	0558	|	|	...	|	|	...	...	0746	...	...	...	|	1039	|	1117	|	1355
2006	**Nanchang** a.	1922	|	|	|	|	|	1039	|	|	...	0657	|	...	...	|	...	...	...	|	|	|	|	|	|
2297	**Guangzhou** a.	...	0431**f**	0841	0800**d**	0914	1030	...	1001**d**	1023	...	...	1244**d**	...	...	1427	...	...	...	1528	1725	1800	1837	1950	2103

km		Z138	Z202	Z162	T146	Z264	T10	T168	Z6	Z78	Z90	T2	T128	Z190	Z36	Z14	Z286	Z98	T124	Z236	T254	T96	Z152	T180	Z122
		♦	♦	♦		♦	♦		♦	♦			♦						♦	♦			♦		
0	**Guangzhou** d.	0830	0915	...	...	1144	...	...	...	...	1355	...	...	1545	1645	1644**d**	...	1806	1904	2038**d**	1932	1920**g**	...	2120	2210
	Nanchang d.	|	|	...	1310	|	...	1943	...	...	|	...	2135	|	|	|	...	|	|	|	|	|	...	|	|
655	Zhuzhou d.	1526	|	...	1739	|	...	|	...	...	|	...	|	|	|	|	...	|	0138	0354	0234	|	...	0402	|
707	Changsha a.	1604	1637	...	1815	1856	...	|	...	...	2113	...	|	2259	2352	0005	...	0119	0214	0429	0310	0238	...	0449	0525
707	Changsha d.	1610	1643	1649	1825	1918	...	|	1957	2156	2123	2210	|	2305	2358	0011	0004	0125	0224	0438	0321	0244	...	0445	0651
1069	**Wuhan** Wuchang a.	1938	2005	2016	2149	2243	...	2344	2323	0115	0045	0136	0053	0227	0320	0343	0326	0448	0550	0809	0647	0629	...	0808	0902
1069	**Wuhan** Wuchang d.	1956	2016	2022	2157	2302	...	2359	2329	0133	0103	0148	...	0250	0326	0359	0332	0454	0558	0816	0706	...	...	...	...
1605	Zhenghzou d.	0112	0054	0100	0330	0335	0432	0550	0407	0616	0541	0703	...	0812	0804	0845	0810	0934	1127	1324	1228	...	B	...	...
2017	Shijiazhuang d.	...	0415	0421	0747	...	0833	1014	0728	0937	0912	1052	...	...	|	1204	|	|	1540	1706	1712	...	1152	...	...
2436	**Tianjin** a.	...	|	|	|	...	|	|	|	|	...	|	...	...	|	|	|	|	1953	2030	2215	...	|	...	...
2297	**Beijing** xi a.	...	0642	0648	1051**b**	...	1113	1309	0955	1210	...	1355**b**	...	...	1343	1446**b**	1349	1513	...	...	...	...	1426	...	...

♦ – **NOTES** (by train number):
Z5/6 – Beijing(**Z5/6**) - Nanning and v.v. **T9/10** –Beijing(**T9/10**) - Chongqing bei and v.v.
Z77/78 – Beijing xi (**Z77/78**) - Guiyang and v.v.
T123/124 – Changchun (**T122/121**) - Tianjin (**T123/124**) - Guangzhou and v.v.
Z151/152 – Beijing xi (**Z151/152**) - Xining xi and v.v.
T127/28 – Chengdu (**T126/25**) - Wuhan Wuchang (**T127/28**) - Dongguan dong and v.v.
Z137/38 – Urumqi (**Z136/35**) - Zhengzhou (**Z137/38**) - Guangzhou and v.v.
Z168/70 – Guangzhou dong (**Z168/67**) - Jinan (**Z169/70**) - Qingdao and v.v.
Z161/62 – Beijing (**Z161/62**) - Kunming and v.v. **Z201/02** –Beijing(**Z201/02**) - Sanya an
Z235/236 – Harbin (**Z238/237**) - Tianjin (**Z235/36**) - Guangzhou and v.v.
Z263/264 – Lhasa (**Z266/265**) - Zhengzhou (**Z263/64**) - Guangzhou and v.v.
Z285/286 – Beijing (**Z285/286**) - Nanning and v.v.
A – Via Xi'an (Table **7115**. a. 0323). **B** – Via Xi'an (Table **7115**. d. 0226).
b – Beijing. **d** – Guangzhou dong. **f** – To Shenzhen a. 0613. **g** – From Shenzhen d.

7095 BEIJING - NANCHANG - SHENZHEN — Chinese Railw

km		Z167	Z133	Z65	Z107	Z67	K105	Z185	K1619	T127
		♦						♦		♦
0	**Beijing** xi d.	...	1924	1948	1955	2001	2321	...	...	...
* *	**Tianjin** d.	...	|	|	|	|	|	0314	2220	...
147	Renqiu d.	...	|	|	|	|	0103	|	|	...
274	Hengshui d.	...	2130	|	2210	|	0230	0638	|	...
426	Liaocheng d.	...	2252	|	2332	|	0419	0824	|	...
582	Heze d.	...	|	|	0043	|	0553	0946	0506	...
687	Shangqiu nan d.	...	|	|	|	|	0711	1052	0625	...
* * *	**Jinan** d.	1755	|	|	|	|	|	|	|	...
* * *	Xuzhou d.	2202	|	|	|	|	|	|	|	...
855	Fuyang d.	|	|	|	0304	|	0932	1249	0905	...
1091	Macheng d.	|	|	|	|	|	1208	1508	1249	...
1314	Jiujiang d.	|	0616	0623	|	0641	1432	1718	1545	...
1449	**Nanchang** a.	|	0720**x**	0730	0753**x**	0752	1548	1834**x**	1703	...
1449	**Nanchang** d.	|	0737**x**	...	0801**x**	...	1605	1856**x**	1711	1944
1675	Ji'an d.	|	0952	...	1008	...	1835	2059	2026	2158
1861	Ganzhou d.	|	...	...	1217	...	2045	2310	2253	0006
2102	Longchuan d.	|	...	...	|	...	0010	0154	0216	0244
2248	Huizhou d.	|	...	...	1632	...	0224	0342	0408	0434
2310	Dongguan dong d.	|	...	...	|	...	0348	0428	0459	0518
2396	**Guangzhou** dong a.	1837	...	...	|	...	|	|	|	...
2372	**Shenzhen** a.	...	...	...	1751	...	0448	0506	0625**d**	...

	Z66	Z68	Z134	T128	K1620	Z108	K106	Z168
				♦				♦
Shenzhen d.	...	...	...	...	0920**d**	1500	1054	...
Guangzhou dong d.	...	...	...	...	|	|	|	2318
Dongguan dong d.	...	...	...	1148	|	|	|	|
Huizhou d.	...	...	...	1132	1056	1632	1235	|
Longchuan d.	...	...	...	1430	1313	|	1434	|
Ganzhou d.	...	...	...	1723	1641	2051	1803	|
Ji'an d.	...	...	1751	1917	1907	2253	2025	|
Nanchang a.	...	...	1951**x**	2127	2208	0104	2319	|
Nanchang d.	1950	2012	2007**x**	...	2233	0122	2333	|
Jiujiang d.	2058	2106	2114	...	2359	|	0057	|
Macheng d.	|	|	|	...	0236	|	|	|
Fuyang d.	|	|	|	...	0530	0616	0628	|
Xuzhou d.	|	|	|	...	|	|	|	2044
Jinan a.	|	|	|	...	|	|	|	0114
Shangqiu nan d.	|	|	|	...	0739	|	0841	...
Heze d.	|	|	|	...	|	0831	|	...
Liaocheng d.	|	|	|	...	1042	0941	1127	...
Hengshui d.	|	|	0546	...	1243	|	1320	...
Renqiu d.	|	|	|	...	|	|	1439	...
Tianjin a.	|	|	|	...	1606	|	|	...
Beijing xi a.	0738	0746	0803	...	...	1315	1618	...

♦ – **NOTES** (by train number):
T127/28 – Chengdu(**T126/25**) - Wuhan Wuchang(**T127/28**) - Dongguan dong and v.v.
Z168/67 – Guangzhou dong(**Z168/57**) - Jinan(**Z169/70**) - Qingdao and v.v.
Z185/86 – Shenyang bei(**Z188/87**) - Tianjin(**Z185/86**) - Shenzhen and v.v.
d – Shenzhen dong. **x** – Nanchang xi.
* * – Tianjin *0 km* - Renqiu *142 km*. * * * – Jinan *0 km* - Xuzhou *319 km* - Fuyang *54*

7097 BEIJING - BENGBU - HEFEI — China Rail High Sp

All trains prefix '**G**'

km	1673 C	345 C	433	261	321 C	241 C	323 C	7405	325 C	29	7433	271	↓
0	...	...	...	0715	0840	...	1010	...	1205	1335	...	1850	d.**Beijing** nan
406	...	0657	0851	0903	1031	1112**j**	1159	...	1325	1517	...	2032	d.Jinan xi
692	0658	0823	1018	|	1200	1253	1317	...	1459	|	...	2145	d.Xuzhou dong
848	0743	0909	1104	1050	|	|	1356	1401	|	|	2045	2224	d.**Bengbu** nan
911	|	0927	1123	1108	|	1351	1414	1423	1558	|	2130	|	d.Huainan dong
980	0840**n**	1006**n**	1149	1142	1340**n**	1430**n**	1500**n**	1509**n**	1638**n**	1737	2142	2314	a.**Hefei**

↑	7432	246	262	326 C	322 C	7402	7406	30	242 C	324 C	434
Beijing nan a.	...	...	1146	2219	1823	...	...	1742	...	2013	...
Jinan xi d.	...	0947**j**	1008	2026	1638	...	...	1602	1731**j**	1833	2032
Xuzhou dong d.	...	0826	0850	1857	1518	...	...	|	1544	1704	1915
Bengbu nan d.	0704	0748	0805	1817	|	1019	1323	|	1503	1614	1830
Huainan dong d.	0647	0728	0746	1752	|	|	1306	|	1444	|	|
Hefei d.	0607	0648	0706**n**	1705**n**	1345**n**	0915**n**	1226**n**	1340	1404	1515**n**	1750

j – Jinan. **n** – Hefei nan. **C** – To/from Table **7193**.

ina Rail High Speed — BEIJING, ZHENGZHOU and NANJING - SHANGHAI and HANGZHOU — 7100

	G7505	G7349	D2281	G7197	D3135	G7589	G7291	D5431	G297	G101	G103	G105	G11	G221	G107	G109	G111	G1	G113	G211	G41	G115	G117	G13	D291
			A			a		A						Q											
Beijing nan d.	...	...	...	...	...	...	...	...	...	0700	0705	0736	0800	...	0805	0815	0835	0900	0905	0931T	0917	0932	0943	1000	...
Dezhou dong d.	...	...	...	...	...	...	...	...	...	|	|	|	|	...	0921	0931	|	|	1020	1025	1036	|	|	|	...
Jinan xi d.	...	...	...	...	...	...	...	...	0720	0841	0846	0924	0934	0936j	0949	1008	1017	|	1046	1052	1102	1123	1138	1134	...
Zhengzhou d.	...	...	...	...	...	...	...	...	|	|	|	|	|	|	|	|	|	|	|	|	|	|	|	|	0855
Shangqiu d.	...	...	...	...	...	...	...	...	|	|	|	|	|	|	|	|	|	|	|	|	|	|	|	|	1034
Xuzhou dong d.	...	...	...	...	...	0708	0755	0721	0845	0959	1006	1029	|	1108	1100	1119	|	|	1153	|	|	1243	1256	|	1236
Bengbu nan d.	...	...	...	...	...	0753	0840	0815	0924	|	1045	|	|	|	|	|	|	|	|	|	1247	|	|	|	1341
Nanjing nan d.	0720	0730	0745f	0750	0810f	0847	0939	0916	1008	1116	1126	1151	1156	1224	1216	1246	1300	1241	1309	1314	1331	1400	1414	1348	1431
Zhenjiang nan d.	0741	0751	0821	|	0835	0909	|	0937	1029	1137	|	|	|	1245	|	|	|	|	|	1335	|	|	|	|	|
Changzhou bei d.	0800	0810	0853	0830	0910	0928	1013	1004	1049	|	|	|	|	|	|	|	1334	|	1342	|	|	|	|	|	|
Wuxi dong d.	0819	0829	0910	0849	0927	0947	1032	1024	|	|	1214	|	|	1316	|	1332	|	|	|	1406	1417	|	|	|	|
Suzhou bei d.	0832	0842	0929	0902	0945	0959	1044	1037	1113	1214	|	1258	|	|	|	|	1358	|	1406	|	|	|	1514	|	|
Shanghai Hongqiao a.	0855	0907	1015	0932	1037	1030	1111h	1113	1136	1237	1242	1321	1309	1344	1326	1400	1421	1348	1429	1434	1446	1514	1541	1455	1549
Hangzhou dong a.	0957	1005	1132	...	1205	1141	...	1217	...	...	...	...	...	...	...	...	...	...	...	...	1544	...	...	...	...

	G229	G213	G121	G15	G123	G125	G127	G129	G133	G7293	G135	G137	G3	G43	G141	G143	G215	D281	G17	G225	G145	G1202	G19	G147	D285
	Q																			Q					
ing nan d.	...	1044T	1028	1100	1105	1110	1135	1215	1252	...	1302	1345	1400	1405	1425	1436	1438T	...	1500	...	1510	1533T	1600	1605	...
hou dong d.	...	1144	1157	|	1227	1232	1258	1331	1414	...	1424	1512	|	1519	1547	1552	1531	...	|	...	|	|	1715	1726	...
n xi d.	1207j	1210	1224	1234	1253	1258	1324	1358	1440	...	1450	1538	|	1545	1616	1624	1600	...	1634	1630j	1658	1713	1741	1752	...
hengzhou d.	|	|	|	|	|	|	|	|	|	...	|	|	|	|	|	|	|	1420	|	|	|	|	|	|	1510
hangqiu d.	|	|	|	|	|	|	|	|	|	...	|	|	|	|	|	|	|	1555	|	|	|	|	|	|	1640
hou dong d.	1336	1322	1343	|	|	|	1438	1505	1545	1551	1602	1650	|	1657	1725	|	1714	1746	|	1806	1822	1837	1847	|	1902
gbu nan d.	|	|	|	|	|	1444	|	|	|	1633	|	|	|	|	|	|	|	1830	|	|	1901	|	|	|	|
jing nan d.	1453	1439	1459	1448	1521	1529	1601	1626	1701	1724	1732	1811	1741	1816	1841	1905	1831	2013	1848	1924	1946	1954	2005	2020	2035
njiang nan d.	|	|	|	|	|	|	|	1649	1722	|	|	|	|	|	|	1926	|	|	|	|	|	2016	|	2045	2108
ngzhou bei d.	1527	|	1533	|	1555	|	|	|	|	1758	|	|	|	1850	1923	|	|	2059	|	1958	2033	2039	|	|	2137
i dong d.	|	1532	1552	|	|	|	1648	1721	1801	|	|	1857	|	|	|	1958	1919	2123	|	|	|	2058	|	|	2220
hou bei d.	1550	1544	1604	|	|	1634	|	|	|	1822	1836	|	|	1915	1950	2010	1938	2136	|	2022	|	2110	|	2130	2232
nghai Hongqiao a.	1612	1607	1627	1555	1642	1659	1916	1749	1836	1850h	1859	1927	1848	1938	2013	2033	2002	2213	1956	2045	2107	2134	2116	2154	2258
angzhou dong a.	...	...	...	...	...	...	...	...	...	...	...	...	...	2046	...	...	...	...	...	...	...	...	...	...	...

	G149	G151	G21	G153	G157	G233	G201	G203	D321	D305
						Q				♦
ing nan d.	1625	1635	1700	1715	1744	...	1755	1900	2123	...
hou dong d.	1749	1759	|	|	|	...	|	|	|	...
n xi d.	1820	1830	1841	1858	1926	1909j	1943	2041	|	...
hengzhou d.	|	|	|	|	|	|	|	|	|	2348
hangqiu d.	|	|	|	|	|	|	|	|	|	|
hou dong d.	1933	1947	2000	2011	2045	2027	2105	2153	|	0222d
gbu nan d.	|	|	|	2049	|	|	2142	2232	|	|
jing nan d.	2054	2113	2118	2134	2202	2151	...	2310	0637f	0518f
njiang nan d.	2116	|	2139	|	|	|	...	...	|	|
ngzhou bei d.	|	2147	|	|	2236	|	...	...	|	0626
i dong d.	2148	|	|	|	2255	2238	...	...	0804	|
hou bei d.	|	2211	2216	2227	|	2250	...	...	|	0712g
nghai Hongqiao a.	2224	2235	2239	2251	2323	2313	...	...	0912h	0801h
angzhou dong a.	...	...	...	...	...	...	...	...	...	...

	G202	G204	D282	G102	G222	G104	G106	G108	D286	G110
					Q					
Hangzhou dong d.	...	...	...	...	...	...	...	...	...	...
Shanghai Hongqiao d.	...	...	0625	0643	0705	0659	0710	0720	0734	0730
Suzhou bei d.	...	...	|	0709	|	|	0734	|	0807	0756
Wuxi dong d.	...	...	0658	0720	0734	|	|	0757	|	|
Changzhou bei d.	...	...	0723	|	|	0742	|	|	|	0820
Zhenjiang nan d.	...	...	|	|	0805	|	0811	|	0908	0841
Nanjing nan d.	...	0732	0800	0809	0826	0816	0832	0851	0930	0903
Bengbu nan d.	0735	0829	|	|	|	|	|	0937	|	|
Xuzhou dong d.	0821	0909	1030	|	0944	0939	0950	1019	1151	1037
Shangqiu d.	|	|	1159	|	|	|	|	|	1257	|
Zhengzhou d.	|	|	1336	|	|	|	|	|	1429	|
Jinan xi d.	0940	1028	...	1039	1053j	1044	1103	1132	...	1149
Dezhou dong d.	|	|	...	1105	...	1110	|	1158	...	|
Beijing nan a.	1133	1213	...	1218	...	1223	1242	1311	...	1333

	G12	G2	G112	G114	G212	G230	G116	G1204	G14	G118	G42	G122	G7292	G16	G124	G128	G130	G412	G134	G136	G138	G140	G4	G226	G214
						Q																		Q	
Hangzhou dong d.	...	...	...	...	...	...	...	...	...	...	0925	...	...	...	...	...	...	...	...	...	...	...	...	...	...
nghai Hongqiao d.	0800	0900	0805	0818	0853	0908	0934	0939	1000	0954	1028	1046	1155h	1100	1105	1115	1126	1223	1302	1317	1329	1341	1400	1405	1454
hou bei d.	|	|	0830	|	|	0933	|	1004	|	1023	|	1112	1225	|	|	1140	1151	|	|	|	1354	1405	|	1430	1522
i dong d.	|	|	|	0855	0931	|	1006	1016	|	1035	1058	|	|	|	1135	|	1203	|	1339	|	|	1417	|	1442	|
ngzhou bei d.	0842	|	|	|	|	0957	1025	1040	|	|	|	1140	1249	|	|	|	1222	|	|	1405	1418	|	|	|	|
njiang nan d.	|	|	|	0927	1004	1017	|	1100	|	|	1130	|	1308	|	|	1217	|	|	|	1425	|	1453	|	|	|
jing nan d.	0916	1009	0921	0949	1026	1038	1101	1122	1109	1128	1151	1216	1330	1209	1221	1238	1256	1349	1427	1446	1452	1514	1509	1528	1624
gbu nan d.	|	|	|	1040	|	1122	1151	|	|	|	|	|	|	|	1305	|	|	|	1511	|	|	|	|	|	|
hou dong d.	1032	|	1056	1122	1148	1203	1230	1246	|	1254	1311	1334	1524	|	1345	1407	1420	1513	1557	1602	|	|	|	1652	1750
hangqiu d.	|	|	|	|	|	|	|	|	|	|	|	|	...	|	|	|	|	|	|	|	|	|	|	|	|
hengzhou d.	|	|	|	|	|	|	|	|	|	|	|	|	...	|	|	|	|	|	|	|	|	|	|	|	|
n xi d.	1144	|	1209	1233	1302	1318j	1342	1403	1323	1412	1427	1452	...	1423	1502	1524	1544	1643	1702	1720	1735	1745	|	1823j	1905
hou dong d.	|	|	|	|	|	...	1410	|	|	|	|	1519	...	|	1528	1550	1610	1709	1728	|	|	1811	|	...	|
ing nan a.	1316	1348	1408	1412	1418T	...	1523	1526T	1458	1544	1606	1633	...	1555	1655	1713	1723	1840	1853	1906	1923	1931	1848	...	2022T

	G142	G18	G146	G148	G20	G150	G152	D292	G234	G216	G22	G154	G44	G158	G7294	G206	G298	D3136	G7391	D5432	D3126	D322	G7590	D2282	D306
									Q											A			b	A	♦
Hangzhou dong d.	...	...	...	...	...	...	...	...	...	...	...	...	1615	...	...	...	...	1638	...	1705	2009	...	1747	1731	...
nghai Hongqiao d.	1421	1500	1505	1534	1600	1605	1620	1610	1632	1638	1700	1714	1724	1734	1744	...	1808	1802	1805	1832	2123	1953h	1904	1908	2200h
hou bei d.	|	|	1530	1559	|	1630	|	1637	|	1703	|	1739	1755	|	1816	...	1832	1849g	|	1905	2153g	|	1936	1944	2244g
i dong d.	1458	|	1542	|	1630	|	|	1659	|	|	1730	|	|	|	1828	...	1844	1906	|	1917	2212	2056	1948	2001	|
ngzhou bei d.	|	|	|	1623	|	|	|	|	|	1727	|	|	|	1822	1847	...	1903	1933	|	1938	2228	|	2007	2018	|
njiang nan d.	|	|	1614	|	|	|	|	|	1726	|	|	1816	1834	|	|	...	|	2005	|	1959	|	|	|	2053	|
jing nan d.	1544	1609	1637	1657	1716	1727	1735	1752	1747	1801	1816	1837	1856	1905	1924	2000	1947	2028f	2119	2021	2312f	2230f	2042	2116	0035f
gbu nan d.	1628	|	|	|	|	|	|	1857	|	|	|	|	|	1950	2019	|	|	...	...	2123	...	|	2134	...	|
hou dong d.	1710	|	1755	1821	|	|	1853	1952	1903	1926	1934	|	2011	|	2103	2115	2127	...	...	2212	...	|	2218	...	0323d
hangqiu d.	|	|	|	|	|	|	|	2121	|	|	|	|	|	|	...	|	|	...	...	...	...	|	...	...	|
hengzhou d.	|	|	|	|	|	|	|	2255	|	|	|	|	|	|	...	|	|	...	...	...	...	|	...	...	0553
n xi d.	1838	1823	1911	1933	1937	2001	2008	...	2019j	2038	2052	2108	2118	2140	...	2221	2246	...	...	...	...	|	...	...	...
hou dong d.	...	|	|	1959	2004	2027	2032	...	...	|	|	|	|	|	...	|	...	...	...	...	...	|	...	...	...
ing nan a.	2018	1955	2050	2112	2117	2147	2152	...	...	2156T	2224	2240	2301	2319	...	2352	...	...	...	...	...	0739	...	...	...

ina Rail High Speed — BEIJING and NANJING - HANGZHOU and NINGBO — 7102

All trains prefix 'G'	1671	1503	7615	7609	7607	61	63	51	1481	57	31	55	7639	7611	1483	1222	167	D658	59	35	7605	53	45	D2224	37	39
	C	B				B	A		B			A			B		A						B			
Beijing nan d.	...	...	...	...	...	...	...	0700T	...	0720	0830	0810	...	...	...	1212T	1257	...	1340	1505	...	1535T	1541	...	1610	1647
Dezhou dong d.	...	...	...	...	...	...	...	0800	...	0847	|	0926	...	...	...	1316	1419	...	1502	|	...	|	1720	...	1738	|
Jinan xi d.	...	...	...	...	...	0708	0726j	0826	...	0913	1004	0957	...	...	...	1343	1445	...	1531	1653	...	1656	1747	...	1804	1835
Xuzhou dong d.	...	...	...	...	...	0834	0859	0939	...	1024	|	1114	...	...	...	1455	1556	...	1643	1811	...	1814	1852	...	1909	1955
Nanjing nan d.	0654	0832	0081	0938	0953	1002	1029	1056	1128	1149	1222	1238	1338	1357	1518	1616	1719	1805	1809	1928	1848	1933	2008	2026	2039	2116
Yixing d.	0736	0914	0934	1027	1035	1045	1106	1141	1217	1225	|	|	1434	1439	1600	1659	|	1924	1854	|	1937	2020	2044	2112	2122	|
Huzhou d.	0801	0932	0959	1045	1109	1103	1127	1200	1248	|	1310	1333	1452	1504	1625	1718	1821	1949	1913	2030	2002	|	2103	2149	2141	2218
Hangzhou dong a.	0829	1000	1021	1113	1131	1125	1156	1221	1309	1304	1331	1355	1513	1525	1646	1739	1842	2030	1934	2052	2023	2059	2131	2221	2202	2239
Ningbo a.	...	...	1134	...	...	...	1252	1328	...	1408	...	1454	...	1621	...	1838	1941	2150	2036	...	...	...	...	...	...	...

	34	D2223	D656	32	1221	58	36	54	46	7640	1492	168	7604	7606	56	1482	7612	52	40	60	1484	7636	62	64	1504
									B		A	A			A	B					B		B	A	B
gbo d.	...	...	0638	...	0739	0745	...	...	...	...	...	1035	...	...	1200	...	1300	1351	...	1436	...	1732	...	1706	...
gzhou dong d.	0720	0733	0800	0830	0836	0852	0905	0927	0952	0958	1103	1138	1209	1220	1249	1330	1413	1447	1518	1545	1623	1837	1737	1808	2044
hou d.	0743	0806	0841	0853	0900	|	0935	0958	1015	1028	1126	1213	1232	1250	1312	|	1436	1510	1541	|	1653	1900	1807	|	2107
ng d.	0802	0836	0910	|	0919	|	|	1017	1041	1047	1152	1232	1258	1309	|	|	1502	1536	1607	|	1713	1926	1835	|	2126
jing nan d.	0845	0949	1006	0942	1002	1019	1031	1055	1117	1119	1238	1324	1337	1348	1421	1458	1548	1619	1643	1703	1753	2012	1919	1937	2205
hou dong d.	1012	...	...	|	1133	1141	1153	1222	1234	...	...	1500	...	...	1539	...	...	1741	1759	1830	...	...	2055	2120	...
n xi d.	1124	...	...	1156	1251	1257	1308	1334	1348	...	...	1616	...	...	1657	...	...	1849	1917	1950	...	...	2213	2242	...
hou dong d.	|	...	...	|	1318	1323	1335	|	1414	...	...	1642	...	...	|	...	...	1916	1943	|	...	...	...	...	...
jing nan a.	1302	...	...	1328	1408T	1436	1449	1451T	1533	...	...	1803	...	...	1836	...	...	2006T	2056	2129	...	...	...	...	...

To/from Table **7200**. **B** – To/from Table **7192**. **C** – To/from Table **7193**. **Q** – To/from Qingdao (Table **7105**). **T** – Time at Tianjin xi not Beijing. **a** – To Ningbo arr. 1239.
From Ningbo dep.1645. **d** – Xuzhou. **f** – Nanjing. **g** – Suzhou. **h** – Shanghai. **j** – Jinan. **k** – Hangzhou. **D305/306** – Shanghai(**D306/305**) - Zhengzhou(**D307/308**) - Xi'an bei and v.v.

7105 BEIJING - JINAN - QINGDAO

Chinese Railways, China Rail High Sp

km	All unmarked trains prefix 'D'	Z169 A	6019	6001	6003	6005	G177	G247	G221 S	G179	G171	G181	6007	G231 S	G183	G185	G187	6009	G189	6011	G173	G1207	G191	G
0	**Beijing** nan d.	...	...	...	...	...	0725	...	...	0927	...	1045	...	...	1149	1242	1247	...	1318	...	...	...	1420	1
122	**Tianjin** nan d.	...	...	...	...	...	0803	...	...	1003	1051x	1121	...	...	|	|	|	...	|	...	1352x	1505x	|	1
314	Dezhou dong d.	...	...	...	...	...	0852	...	...	1049	1151	1213	...	...	1312	1404	1409	...	1440	...	|	|	1540	
426	**Jinan** d.	0140	0609	0710	0817	0957	0939	0949	1055	1135	1241	1259	1316	1322	1404	1445	1458	1452	1524	1531	1547	1647	1630	1
536	Zibo d.	0248	0653	0753	0902	1046	1022	1034	1139	1218	1332	1344	1400	1406	1447	1529	1541	1535	1608	1615	1631	1730	1713	1
636	Weifang d.	0349	0737	0830	0946	1124	1059	1112	1221	1255	1418	1426	1438	1444	1530	1606	1619	1612	1644	1653	1715	1812	1751	1
819	**Qingdao** a.	0528	0841b	0948	1100	1248	1212	1226	1334	1408	1532	1539	1535	1602	1650	1720	1732	1739	1803	1812	1828	1909b	1910	1

	6013	G243	G195	G227 S	G197	6015	G199	6017	G235 S
Beijing nan d.	...	...	1546	...	1642	...	1725	...	...
Tianjin nan d.	...	...	1638	...	1718	...	|	...	...
Dezhou dong d.	...	...	1732	...	1804	...	1848	...	...
Jinan d.	1712	1743	1819	1825	1849	1906	1936	1951	2021
Zibo d.	1759	1826	1906	1954	1933	1955	2019	2035	2104
Weifang d.	1837	1903	1945	1954	2017	2038	2102	2113	2147
Qingdao a.	1951	2022	2058	2112	2131	2151	2216	2238	2300

	6002	G1208		6004	G224 S	G178	G180	G182	G
Qingdao d.	0546	0621b	...	0643	0655	0702	0710	0753	0
Weifang d.	0701	0723	...	0759	0804	0816	0826	0907	0
Zibo d.	0745	0800	...	0839	0846	0859	0909	0949	1
Jinan d.	0833	0855	...	0929	0934	0954	1004	1039	1
Dezhou dong d.	...	0943	...	...	...	|	1042	1117	
Tianjin nan a.	...	1033x	...	...	...	1115	1126	|	
Beijing nan a.	...	...	...	...	...	1158	1202	1237	1

	G244	G172	G232 S	6006	G186	6008	G188	G190	G192	6010	G194	Z170 A	G248	6012	G228 S	G196	G198	6014	G174		G236 S	G200	6016	6
Qingdao d.	0813	0902	0917	0910	0929	1009	1022	1127	1213	1221	1232	1310	1324	1337	1354	1429	1600	1601	1610	...	1623	1710	1845	1
Weifang d.	0927	1017	1032	1024	1045	1121	1138	1242	1323	1331	1341	1522	1444	1451	1503	1539	1715	1658	1726	...	1737	1826	2001	2
Zibo d.	1017	1055	1115	1102	1128	1202	1221	1321	1401	1425	1419	1609	1522	1528	1540	1622	1752	1735	1804	...	1814	1912	2047	2
Jinan d.	1110	1145	1203	1150	1218	1250	1311	1411	1452	1513	1513	1734	1610	1616	1630	1712	1842	1841	1856	...	1909	2002	2201	2
Dezhou dong d.	...	|	...	...	|	...	|	1507	1538	...	|	...	...	...	...	|	|	...	1948	...	...	|	...	
Tianjin nan a.	...	1321x	...	...	|	...	1434	|	1631	...	|	...	...	...	...	1834	|	...	2039x	...	...	|	...	
Beijing nan a.	...	...	...	...	1418	...	1514	1622	1706	...	1717	...	...	...	...	1917	2040	...	...	...	...	2201	...	

A – Guangzhou dong(**Z168/57**) - Jinan(**Z169/70**) - Qingdao and v.v. S – To/from Shanghai Hongqiao (Table **7100**). b – Qingdao bei. **x** –Tianjin xi.

7110 SHANGHAI - NANJING - ZHENGZHOU

Chinese Railwa

km		K290 ♦	T112 ♦	Z167 ♦	T116 ♦	T138 ♦	K152	Z164 ♦	Z40 ♦		K282 ♦
0	**Shanghai** d.	0843	A	...	1542	1552	1647	1916	1945	...	2040
84	Suzhou d.	0955	1316	...	1635	1644	1753	|	2039	...	2204
126	Wuxi d.	1027	1352	...	1705	1713	1825	2030	2105	...	2236
165	Changzhou d.	1058	1421	...	1734	1740	1856	|	2134	...	2307
237	Zhenjiang d.	1146	1505	...	1816	|	|	|	|	...	|
301	**Nanjing** d.	1249	1555	...	1903	1909	2042	2203	2259	...	0058
485	Bengbu d.	1511	1737	...	2048	2054	0017	2342	0033	...	0300
649	Xuzhou d.	1733	1926	2202	2224	2230	|	0108	0209	...	0506
795	Shangqiu d.	1923	|	|	2343	2351	0508	|	|	...	0653
998	**Zhengzhou** a.	2139	2248	0130	0138	0201	0740	0352	0451	...	0902

	T137 ♦	Z163 ♦	T115 ♦	Z39 ♦	T111 ♦	Z168 ♦	K289 ♦	K151	K284 ♦
Zhengzhou d.	0214	0256	0316	0310	0612	1643	1748	1821	1938
Shangqiu d.	|	|	0507	|	|	|	|	2051	|
Xuzhou d.	0521	0547	0645	0604	0925	2044	2201	|	2342
Bengbu d.	0655	0710	0826	0736	1101	...	|	0039	|
Nanjing d.	0839	0850	1023	0916	1246	...	0153	0243	0334
Zhenjiang d.	0928	|	|	0953	1331	...	0238	0325	|
Changzhou d.	1011	|	|	1032	1414	...	0326	0413	|
Wuxi d.	1040	1017	1206	1057	1443	...	0357	0444	0541
Suzhou d.	1112	|	1236	1136	1517	...	0429	0516	|
Shanghai a.	1233	1128	1333	1224	B	...	0534	0630	0721

For footnotes see Table **7120**.

7115 ZHENGZHOU - XI'AN - LANZHOU

Chinese Railwa

km	Z135 ♦	T117 ♦	T139 ♦	Z265 ♦	Z165 ♦	Z41 ♦		T197 ♦	T193 ♦	T113 ♦	Z151 ♦	T23 ♦	T223 ♦		Read Down / Read Up		T140 ♦	Z136 ♦	T118 ♦	T24 ♦	T224 ♦	Z166 ♦	Z266 ♦	Z42 ♦	T114 ♦	T194 ♦	T198 ♦	Z152 ♦
0	0128	0152	0210	0352	0411	0500	...	2118	2250	2301	...	...	...	↓	d. **Zhengzhou** a.	↑	0208	0439	0258	...	...	0250	0313	0304	0604	0554	0640	...
124	0254	0317	|	|	|	0620	...	2303	0020	0034	...	...	...		d. Luoyang d.		|	0319	|	...	...	|	|	|	0441	0433	0517	0700
512	0726	0749	0821	0941	1000	1051	...	0341	0455	0501	0323	...	...	↓	a. **Xi'an** d.	↑	2002	2241	2024	...	...	2101	2115	2108	0005	2353	0040	0226
512	0738	0759	...	1000	1008	1101	...	0349	0505	0513	0333	...	0558		d. **Xi'an** a.		...	2233	2014	...	2146	2053	2107	2100	2344	2334	0025	0213
685	0918	0945	...	|	|	1241	...	0535	0654	0702	0517	0822	0822	↓	d. Baoji d.	↑	...	2056	1836	1958	1958	|	|	1931	2200	2153	2248	|
840	1100	1132	...	|	|	1418	...	0712	0831	0839	0653	|	|		d. Tianshui d.		...	1818	1556	|	|	|	|	1645	1920	1911	2004	2215
1188	1511	1536	...	1647	1710	1807	...	1114	1219	1235	1057	1352	1352	↓	a. **Lanzhou** d.	↑	...	1357	1136	1157	1157	1229	1305	1237	1440	1457	1540	1744

For footnotes see Table **7120**.

7118 BEIJING - LANZHOU

Chinese Railwa

km		Z69 ♦	T175 ♦	T41	Z55		T7 ♦	Z21 ♦		
0	**Beijing** xi d.	1000	1312	1422	1500	...	1632	2010	...	...
291	Shijiazhuang bei d.	1307	1626	1732	1759	...	1952	2255	...	...
395	Yangquan bei d.	1404	|	|	1915	...	2054	|	...	...
516	**Taiyuan** d.	1510n	1836	2000	2025n	...	2215	0044	...	...
701	Lvliang d.	1640	2047	2210	|	...	2359	|	...	...
790	Suide d.	1736	2143	2338	|	...	|	|	...	...
1283	**Xi'an** a.	|	|	0507	|	...	0620	|	...	...
1267	Zhongwei d.	2253	0242	...	0301	...	...	0725	...	...
1524	**Wuwei** a.	0216	|	...	|	...	...	|	...	...
1573	**Lanzhou** a.	...	0744	...	0800	...	...	1226	...	...

	Z22 ♦	T42	T176 ♦	T8 ♦		Z56	Z70 ♦	
Lanzhou d.	1617	...	150/	...	...	2040	...	...
Wuwei d.	|	...	|	...	...	|	0505	...
Zhongwei d.	2131	...	2038	...	...	0217	0837	...
Xi'an d.	|	1936	|	2247	...	|	|	...
Suide d.	|	0141	0200	|	...	|	1253	...
Lvliang d.	|	0238	0259	0542	...	|	1351	...
Taiyuan d.	0351	0427	0448	0734	...	0847n	1533n	...
Yangquan bei d.	|	|	0542	|	...	|	1641	...
Shijiazhuang bei d.	0548	0631	0643	0924	...	1107	1744	...
Beijing xi a.	0820	0922	0929	1228	...	1336	2020	...

7120 LANZHOU - ÜRÜMQI and LHASA

Chinese Railways, China Rail High Spe

km		D2701	D2703	D2711 C	Z151 ♦	Z179 ♦	T197 ♦	T193 ♦	Z135 ♦	T295	Z41 ♦	Z69 ♦
	Zhongwei d.	...	...	...	...	0941	...	...	...	...	...	2253
0	**Lanzhou** d.	0812x	0830x	1050x	1112	|	1130	1234	1527	1638	1830	|
188	Xining d.	0921	0956	1201	1348	|	|	|	1717	|	2017	0222
303	Wuwei d.	|	|	|	...	1323	1438	1544	|	1954	|	
770	Jiayuguan d.	1243n	1310n	1527n	...	1800	1930	2039	2137	0057	0026	0654
1067	Liuyuan d.	1434n	1454n	1719n	...	2057	2233	2339	0048	0402	0317	1004
1339	Hami d.	1619	1635	1856	...	0004	0139	0245	0401	0718	0623	1310
1749	Turpan d.	1838b	1854b	2115b	...	0438	0549	0640	0742	1112	0927b	1651
1892	**Ürümqi** nan a.	1937	1953	2214	...	0620	0718	0809	0908	1241	1044	1835

	Z70 ♦	T296	T194 ♦	Z180 ♦	Z42 ♦	T198 ♦	Z136 ♦	Z152 ♦	D2704	D2706	D2
Ürümqi nan d.	1302	1430	1732	1758	1926	1908	1917	...	0921	0946	1(
Turpan d.	1434	1605	1920	1935	2048b	2104	2056	...	1022b	1047b	12
Hami d.	1820	2003	2357	2347	0016	0109	0051	...	1249	1312	14
Liuyuan d.	2128	2308	0345	0259	0321	0430	0406	...	1431n	1452n	16
Jiayuguan d.	0032	0216	0652	0553	0612	0736	0719	...	1626n	1640n	17
Wuwei d.	0505	0716	1138	1019	|	1217	|	...	|	|	
Xining d.	|	|	|	|	1042	|	|	1500	1958	2009	21
Lanzhou a.	|	1022	1440	|	1222	1521	1342	1729	2114x	2122x	22
Zhongwei a.	0822	...	...	1456	...	...	...	...	...	...	

km		D2741	D2747	D2745	D2749	D2743	Z21 ♦	T175 ♦	T23 ♦	T223 ♦	Z265 ♦	Z165 ♦
0	**Zhongwei** d.	...	...	...	...	...	0725	0242	...	...	...	...
306	**Lanzhou** d.	0740x	0755	1345x	1710	1745x	1241	0802	1407	1407	1702	1725
534	Xining d.	0849	0914	1454	1828	1900	1530	1031	1702	1702	1939	2050
	Jiayuguan nan a.	1153	1202	1822	2124	2214	|	...	|	|	|	|
1352	Golmud d.	...	...	...	...	...	2250	...	0007	0007	0245	0401
2172	Naqu d.	...	...	...	...	...	0841	...	0954	0954	1201	1323
2449	**Lhasa** a.	...	...	...	...	...	1355	...	1420	1420	1625	1755

	T24 ♦	T224 ♦	Z166 ♦	Z266 ♦	Z22 ♦	T176 ♦	D2750	D2744	D2748	D2742	D2
Lhasa d.	1105	1105	1135	1300	1530	...	...	...	...	...	
Naqu d.	1515	1513	1543	1625	1900	...	...	...	...	...	
Golmud d.	0117	0117	0159	0306	0600	...	...	...	...	...	
Jiayuguan nan a.		|	|	|	|	...	0717	0825	1240	1255	18
Xining d.	0822	0822	0907	1030	1333	1215	1023	1157	1530	1607	2
Lanzhou a.	1137	1137	1211	1249	1557	1452	1136x	1304x	1649	1720x	23
Zhongwei a.	...	...	...	...	2121	2025	...	...	...	...	

♦ – **NOTES** for Tables **7110**, **7115 7118** and **7120** (by train number):

T7/8 – Beijing xi(**T7/8**) - Chengdu and v.v.
Z21/22 – Beijing xi(**Z21/22**) - Lhasa and v.v.
T23/24 – Chengdu(**T22/21**) - Lanzhou(**T23/24**) - Lhasa and v.v.
Z39/41 – Urumqi(**Z42/41**) - Zhengzhou(**Z39/40**) - Shanghai and v.v.
Z69/70 – Beijing xi(**Z69/70**) - Urumqi and v.v.
T111/114 – Lanzhou(**T114/13**) - Zhengzhou(**T111/12**) - Hangzhou and v.v.
T115/118 – Lanzhou(**T118/17**) - Zhengzhou(**T115/16**) - Shanghai and v.v.
Z135/36 – Urumqi(**Z136/35**) - Zhengzhou(**Z137/38**) - Guangzhou and v.v.
T137/140 – Xian(**T140/139**) - Zhengzhou(**T137/138**) - Shanghai and v.v.
Z151/152 – Beijing xi(**Z151/152**) - Xining and v.v.
Z163/166 – Lhasa(**Z166/165**) - Zhengzhou(**Z163/164**) - Shanghai and v.v.
Z168/70 – Guangzhou dong(**Z168/67**) - Jinan(**Z169/70**) - Qingdao and v.v.
T175/176 – Beijing xi(**T175/176**) - Xining xi and v.v. **Z179/180** –Beijing(**Z179/80**) - Urumqi and v.v.
T193/194 – Zhengzhou(**T193/194**) - Urumqi and v.v. **T197/198** –Zhengzhou(**T197/198**) - Urumqi and v
T223/224 – Lhasa(**T224/223**) - Xian(**T221/222**) - Chongqing and v.v.
Z265/266 – Lhasa(**Z266/265**) - Zhengzhou(**Z263/64**) - Guangzhou and v.v.
K282/284 – Shanghai(**K282/284**) - Zhengzhou(**K283/281**) - - Chengdu and v.v.
K289/290 – Shanghai(**K290/289**) - Zhengzhou(**K291/292**) - - Chengdu and v.v.
A – From Hangzhou dep. 1020. **B** – To Hangzhou arr. 1851.
C – Additional trip: 0938. **D** – Additional trip: 1027.
b – bei. **n** –nan. **x** – xi.

ÜRÜMQI - ALMATY - ASTANA 7125

	5801	13 *CJ* ①⑥n	13/53 ①
Ürümqi d.	2358	2341	2341
Shihezi d.	0258	|	|
Kuitun d.	0456	|	|
Alashankou a.	0950	0802	0802
Alashankou 🏛 d.	...	1100	1100
Druzhba 🏛 a.	...	0920	0920
Druzhba d.	...	1240	1240
Beskol' d.	...	1612	1612
Aktogay a.	...	1812	1812
Aktogay d.	...	1852	1912
Ush Tobe d.	...	2322	|
Kapchagay d.	...	0352	|
Almaty I a.	...	0504	|
Almaty II a.	...	0550	|
Karagandy a.	...	...	0820
Astana a.	...	...	1216

	5802	54/14 ⑥	14 *TJ* ②⑦u
Astana d.	...	1620	...
Karagandy d.	...	2142	...
Almaty II d.	...	|	0015
Almaty I d.	...	|	0102
Kapchagay d.	...	|	0215
Ush Tobe d.	...	|	0643
Aktogay a.	...	1033	1059
Aktogay d.	...	1139	1139
Beskol' d.	...	1400	1400
Druzhba a.	...	1635	1635
Druzhba 🏛 d.	...	1950	1950
Alashankou 🏛 a.	...	2210	2210
Alashankou d.	2308	2350	2350
Kuitun d.	0511	|	|
Shihezi d.	0716	|	|
Ürümqi a.	1043	0950	0950

Numbered 13 *KH* on ⑥.
Numbered 14 *CJ* on ②.

For connections to Moscow see Table **1975**.
Operators: Chinese Railways and Kazakstan Temir Zholy.

Chinese Railways XI'AN - CHENGDU 7130

km		K291 C	K245	T7 A	K5	T24 B	K879	K385	K869	K165 D
	Zhengzhou d.	2149	2317	...	...	...	...	...	1337	...
0	**Xi'an** d.	0451	0619	0641	1320	...	1950	2038	2121	2212
173	Baoji d.	0716	0855	0842	1548	2012	2207	2253	2332	0038
523	Guangyuan nan d.	|	|	|	0029	|	|	0734	0828	|
727	Mianyang d.	1957	2056	1913	0353	|	1014	1106	1142	|
842	**Chengdu** a.	2133	2228	2040	0516	0816	1144	1239	1336	1426

		T8 A	K880	K166 D	K870	K292 C	K386	T22 B	K6	K246
Chengdu d.	...	0900	1255	1326	1442	1635	1747	2045	2114	2138
Mianyang d.	...	1047	1432	1510	1625	1821	1937	|	2250	2314
Guangyuan nan d.	...	1418	|	|	2108	2159	2312	0126	|	0244
Baoji d.	...	2049	0345	0411	0629	0703	0718	0758	1014	1046
Xi'an a.	...	2226	0544	0612	0840	0907	0917	...	1215	1243
Zhengzhou a.	...	...	...	...	1636	1733	...	...	...	1934

A – Bejing xi(**T7/8**) - Chengdu and v.v.
B – Chengdu(**T22/21**) - Lanzhou(**T23/24**) - Lhasa and v.v.
C – Shanghai(**K290/289**) - Zhengzhou(**K291/292**) - - Chengdu and v.v.
D – Xi'an(**K165/66**) - Kunming and v.v.

CHENGDU - QINGCHENGSHAN 7135

6101	6103	6105	6107	6109	6111	6113	6115	6117	6121	6123		All unmarked trains prefix 'C'		6102	6104	6106	6108	6110	6112	6114	6116	6120	6122	6124
0648	0854p	0922p	1035p	1301p	1619	1620	1808p	1916	2107p	2125p	↓	d. **Chengdu** a.	↑	0823p	1027p	1059p	1228p	1413p	1738p	1850	1911p	2055p	2239	2258
0725	0826	0955	1110	1328	1650	1716	1827	1957	|	2157	↓	d. Dujiangyan d.	↑	0802	1003	1029	1149	|	1703	1753	1840	2031	2210	2229
0733	0934	1003	1118	1336	...	1724	...	2005	2140	2205	↓	a. **Qingchengshan** d.	↑	0750	0952	1018	1139	1349	...	1742	...	2020	2153	2218

Xipu.

na Rail High Speed CHENGDU - CHONGQING 7140

All trains prefix 'D'	G308	2202	2244	638	G8501	2224	2208	G8581	2264	2238	2256	G311	G8509	2260	G8511	365	G8517	G8519	634	G8525	5132	G8527	G8529
Chengdu dong d.	0702	0717	0709	0729	0750	0802	0822	0822	0909	0915	0921	0927	1009	1023	1032	1055	1200	1218	1333	1335	1331	1407	1427
Suining d.	|	|	0814	|	|	|	0921	|	|	|	1021	|	|	|	|	|	|	|	1436	|	|	|	|
Tongnan d.	0820	|	0845	0855	|	|	|	|	|	1032	1058	1045	|	|	|	|	|	|	1506	|	1448	|	|
Hechuan d.	0845	|	|	|	|	0939	|	|	|	1100	1124	1111	|	1201	|	1239	|	|	1532	|	1515	|	|
Chongqing bei **7182** a.	0910	0921	0929	0939	0932	1004	1029	1004	1113	1125	1149	1136	1137	1226	1214	1304	1328	1401	1557	1517	1540	1535	1602

rains prefix 'D'	G8531	G8535	5102	G8547	5134	G8549	G8551	G8555	G8557
ngdu dong d.	1445	1549	1750	1819	1855	1919	1942	2101	2148
ing d.	|	|	1857	|	|	|	|	|	|
gnan d.	|	|	1927	|	|	|	|	|	|
huan d.	|	|	1952	|	|	|	|	|	|
ngqing bei **7182** a.	1628	1731	2017	2001	2050	2102	2117	2243	2330

All trains prefix 'D'	G8502	G8504 A	5105	G8506	G8508	G8510	G8512	G8514	5131
Chongqing bei 7182 d.	0730	0800	0808	0820	0847	0907	1008	1030	1104
Hechuan d.	|	|	|	|	|	|	|	|	1136
Tongnan d.	|	|	|	|	|	|	|	|	|
Suining d.	|	|	0918	|	|	|	|	|	|
Chengdu dong a.	0913	0943	1015	0954	1030	1050	1137	1213	1311

ains prefix 'D'	G8516	G8518	633	G8530	366	G8534	5133	2259	G8544	2201	G312	G846	2255	2237	637	2207	G8552	2223	G8554	2242	G307	2262	G8558
ngqing bei **7182** d.	1122	1145	1349	1422	1510	1538	1618	1724	1734	1736	1743	1823	1842	1858	1913	1923	1951	1958	2021	2009	2055	2108	2159
uan d.	|	|	|	|	1537	|	1645	|	|	|	1810	|	1911	|	1940	1951	|	2026	|	2036	2122	2136	|
nan d.	|	|	|	|	|	|	1711	|	|	1821	|	|	|	|	2005	2017	|	|	|	|	2147	2202	|
ing d.	|	|	1458	|	|	|	|	1834	|	|	|	|	|	|	|	2044	|	|	|	|	|	|	|
ngdu dong a.	1305	1326	1559h	1605	1726	1707	1826	1930	1917	1937	1945	2006	2046	2101	2128	2150	2127	2202	2204	2217	2302	2317	2335

Additional trips: 1217, 1238, 1308, 1341, 1404, 1501, 1552, 1607, 1631, 1711, 1901, 1930, 2122.
Additional trips: 0916, 0933, 1106, 1123, 1250, 1316, 1519, 1613, 1638, 1657, 1730, 1752, 2032.

na Rail High Speed CHENGDU - DAZHOU 7142

All trains prefix 'D'	5182	5184	5186	5162	5188	5164	5192	5174	5156 A	5194
Chengdu dong d.	0813h	0930h	1017	1219h	1429	1602	1648	1703	1846	2038
Suining d.	|	|	1116	|	|	|	|	1804	1945	2137
Nanchong d.	|	1106	1153	1351	|	1730	1818	1840	2019	2213
Dazhou a.	1104	1224	1311	...	1703	...	1948	...	...	2325

All trains prefix 'D'	5181	5179	5185	5161 C	5189	5163 B	6195	5191	5193	5195
Dazhou d.	0659	...	1119	...	1332	...	...	1718	1912	2015
Nanchong d.	0834	1024	1247	1407	1459	1753	1642	1847	2040	213/
Suining d.	|	1058	|	|	1531	1826	|	1921	2113	2212
Chengdu dong a.	0957	1159h	1411	1532	1628	1923	1859h	2018	2214	2313h

Chengdu. **A** – Additional trips: 0750, 1141, 1953. **B** – Additional trips: 1149, 2204. **C** – Additional trips: 1516, 2058.

nese Railways CHENGDU - NANNING and KUNMING 7145

	K1273	K853	K829 B	K1139	K485	K1223	K144	T8897	K482 B
Chengdu dong d.	0831h	0852	1011h	1041	1359	1300h	1451	1908	...
Neijiang d.	1230	1257	1412	1441	|	1644	|	|	...
Yibin d.	1446	1513	1628	1659	|	1854	|	|	...
Liupanshui d.	2316	0124	0037	0140	|	0421	|	|	...
Chongqing d.	|	|	|	|	1931	|	2033	|	...
Zunyi d.	|	|	|	|	0234	|	0336	0418	...
Guiyang d.	0237	|	0530	|	0545	0924	0705	0736	...
Jinchengjiang d.	...	|	1220	|	...	1658	1254	▬	...
Liuqiao a.	...	|	1530	|	...	1942	1524	**K364**	...
Litang d.	...	|	...	|	...	...	|	**B**	...
Nanning a.	...	|	...	|	...	...	1908	0055	1010
Qujing d.	...	0519	...	0656	...	...	...	|	|
Kunming a.	...	0722	...	0846	...	...	...	1305	2256

	K854	K1224	K830 B	K486	K1140	K363 B	K1274	K143	K481 B
Kunming d.	0850	...	...	...	0952	1005	...	...	1715
Qujing d.	1046	...	...	...	1137	|	...	...	|
Nanning d.	|	...	...	...	|	2202	...	0940	0549
Litang d.	|	...	...	...	|	▬	...	1114	...
Liuqiao d.	|	0211	0637	...	|	**T8898**	...	1326	...
Jinchengjiang d.	|	0431	0856	...	|		...	1530	...
Guiyang d.	|	1123	1349	1438	|	2002	1808	2033	...
Zunyi d.	|	|	|	1909	|	2237	|	0005	...
Chongqing d.	|	|	|	0241	0241	|	|	0738	...
Liupanshui d.	1513	1610	1745	|	|	|	2309	|	...
Yibin d.	2304	2327	0034	|	0007	|	0916	|	...
Neijiang d.	0131	0151	0252	|	0242	|	1224	|	...
Chengdu dong a.	0545h	0529h	0633h	0727	0829h	0739	1740h	1258	...

	K113	K165 D	K145	K1501	K117	T8869			
Chengdu d.	1300	1457	1430	1655	1728	1755	...	...	...
Xichang d.	2311	0051	0017	0148	0210	0455	...	...	...
Panzhihua d.	0215	0422	0402	0548	0453	0756	...	...	...
Kunming a.	0731	0947	0923	1038	...	...	...	...	...

	K114		T8870		K146	K1502	K166 D	K118	
Kunming d.	0848	...	...	...	1815	1905	1932	...	...
Panzhihua d.	1403	...	1649	...	2313	2346	0035	1153	...
Xichang d.	1645	...	1936	...	0417	0254	0343	1439	...
Chengdu a.	0405	...	0926	...	1324	1222	1252	2332	...

To / from Guangzhou (Table **7155**). **D** – Xi'an(**K165/66**) - Kunming and v.v. **b** – Chongqing bei. **h** –Chengdu. * – *993 km* via Yibin.

nese Railways CHONGQING - ZHUZHOU - GUANGZHOU 7150

		K72 F	K204	K334	K578	K194	K686	K778	
Chongqing bei d.	...	0800	1225	1320	1350	1419	1520	1550	...
Fuling d.	...	0914	1339	1434	1511	1530	1639	1710	...
Qianjiang (Chongqing) d.	...	1141	1648	1732	1805	|	1906	2006	...
Huaihua d.	...	1557	2058	2252	2220	2311	2331	0026	...
Loudi d.	...	1948	|	0311	0216	|	0331	|	...
Zhuzhou a.	...	2202	0248	0525	0426	0512	0518	0608	...
Chenzhou d.	...	...	0615	...	...	0907	0851	0929	...
Guangzhou a.	...	...	1045	...	...	1342	1257	1400	...

	K777	K71 F	K577	K333	K193		K685	K203	
Guangzhou d.	1603	...	...	...	1449	...	1621	1951	...
Chenzhou d.	2013	...	...	...	1915	...	2029	2351	...
Zhuzhou d.	0004	0359	1538	1202	2346	...	2358	0305	...
Loudi d.	|	0538	1726	1412	0122	...	0131	|	...
Huaihua d.	0553	1016	2207	1858	0625	...	0537	0916	...
Qianjiang (Chongqing) d.	1028	1523	0235	0323	1209	...	0946	1352	...
Fuling d.	1313	1802	0453	0600	1435	...	1228	1638	...
Chongqing bei a.	1434	1926	0602	0721	1558	...	1345	1805	...

Shanghai nan (**K71/2**) - Chongqing and v.v.

7155 NANNING - GUANGZHOU — Chinese Railways

km		K829 A	K363 B	K481 B
0	**Nanning** d.	...	2225	0605
**	**Liuqiao** d.	1547	|	|
120	Litang d.	|	|	|
263	Yuli d.	1930	0216	0942
438	Maoming dong d.	2304	0516	1259
700	Zhaoqing d.	0249	0817	1638
787	Fuoshan d.	0423	1008	1855
809	**Guangzhou** a.	0451	1107	2020

	K364 B	K830 A	K482 B
Guangzhou d.	1210	1700	2115
Fuoshan d.	1240	1730	2152
Zhaoqing d.	1410	1858	2313
Maoming dong d.	1816	|	|
Yuli d.	2100	0145	0606
Litang d.	|	|	|
Liuqiao a.	|	0615	|
Nanning a.	0040	...	0954

A – To/from Chendgu (Table **7145**).
B – To/from Kunming (Table **7145**).
** – Liuqiao - Litang: *135 km.*

7160 GUANGZHOU - SANYA — Chinese Railw

km		K511 C	Z201 B	K1167
0	**Guangzhou** d.	1732	1551	1908
22	Fuoshan d.	1803	1633	1939
109	Zhaoqing d.	1948	1840	2132
361	Maoming dong d.	2335	2158	0042
488	Zhanjiang xi d.	0114	2314	|
601	Xunwen d.	|	0103	0426
794	Haikou a.	0621	0440	0757
1157	**Sanya** a.	...	0855	...

	K512 C	K1168	Z
Sanya d.	...	...	1
Haikou d.	2320	2008	2
Xunwen d.	0314	|	
Zhanjiang xi d.	0433	0040	0
Maoming dong d.	0545	0201	0
Zhaoqing d.	0850	0510	0
Fuoshan d.	1017	0712	0
Guangzhou a.	1045	0749	0

B – Beijing(**Z201/02**) - Sanya and v.v.
C – Shanghai(**K511/12**) - Haikou and v.v.

7165 HAIKOU - SANYA — China Rail High Spe

High-speed '**D**' trains (numbers **D73xx**). *289 km 284km from Haikou dong.* Journey 2 - 2¼ hours. * – To/from Haikou.

Haikou dong depart : 0700, 0724, 0800, 0840*, 0843, 0900, 0915, 0935, 1000*, 1025, 1038, 1050, 1120, 1200 1228, 1300, 1330, 1355, 1430*, 1440, 1450, 1508, 1510, 1550, 1600, 1610, 164 1710, 1735*, 1755, 1812, 1830, 1900, 1930, 2029, 2045, 2045*, 2100, 2120*, 2120, 2205.

Sanya depart : 0700*, 0700, 0715, 0730, 0740, 0750*, 0815, 0820, 0930*, 1015, 1050, 1115, 1137, 1205, 1225, 1245, 1250, 1305, 1330, 1410, 1430*, 1435, 1500, 1515*, 1545, 1625, 16 1720, 1755*, 1820*, 1830, 1900, 2000, 2020, 2050, 2105*, 2125, 2200.

7170 ZHENGZHOU and WUHAN - CHENGDU and CHONGQING — Chinese Railw

km		K389	K257	K1269	K507	K205	K351	Z122	K283 D	T221 A	K805	K909	T247	K819	K15	K817		T125 C	K1063	K117		K357		T9 B	K
	Zhengzhou d.	...	0358	...	0612	0638	...	...	0920	...	...	1355	...	1610	1617	1725	...	...	2000	2055	...	...	...	2235	
0	**Wuhan** Wuchang d.	0648	|	2107	|	|	0911	0923	|	...	1134	|	1926	|	|	|	...	0113	|	|	...	2341	...	|	1
165	Suizhou d.	0929	|	|	|	|	|	|	|	...	1423	|	2118	|	|	|	...	0307	|	|	...	|	...	|	
334	Xiangfan d.	1100y	1114	|	1317	1340	1348y	1230y	|	...	1642y	2245	2319	|	2309	|	...	|	0256	0424	...	|	...	0510	
500	Shiyan d.	1258	1310	|	1528	1544	1556	|	1922	...	1855	0051	0118	|	0130	|	...	0646	0517	0625	...	|	...	0700	
*	**Xi'an** d.	|	|	|	|	|	|	|	|	2210	|	|	|	|	|	|	...	|	|	|	...	|	...	|	
702	Ankang d.	1541	1555	|	1803	1815	1825	1613	2151	|	2222	0322	0332	0218	0352	0358	...	0900	0753	0850	...	|	...	0921	
978	Dazhou d.	|	|	0827	2151	|	2233	1939	|	0537	0245	0707	0716	0620	0734	0742	...	1238	1156	1226	...	1232	...	1303	0
1137	Nanchong d.	|	|	|	|	|	0050	|	|	|	|	|	0858	|	|	0951	...	1446	|	1421	...	|	...	|	0
1204	Suining d.	|	|	|	|	|	0309	2144	|	|	|	|	0944	|	|	1042	...	1600	|	1504	...	|	...	|	0
1375	**Chengdu** a.	0441	0558	|	|	0830	0450	2302	1130	|	|	|	1112d	|	|	1234	...	1750	|	1702	...	|	...	|	0
1233	**Chongqing** bei a.	...	...	1133	0219a	...	...	...	...	0813	0535	0948	...	0917	1018	...	...	...	1452	...	...	1527	...	1549	

			K508	K806	K910	T10 B	K1258	K16		T248	K390	K1270	T222 A	K818	K820	K258	Z124	K1064	K206		K281 D	T126 C	K358	K352	K
Chongqing bei d.	...	...	0804a	0807	1054	1112	...	1223	...	...	...	1808	2028	...	2140	...	...	2300	...	...	...	...	2320	...	
Chengdu d.	...	...	|	|	|	|	1005d	|	...	1238	1010	|	|	1918	|	1353	1729	|	1735	...	1837	2235	|	2350	2
Suining d.	...	...	|	|	|	|	|	|	...	1413	|	|	|	2124	|	|	|	|	|	...	|	0034	|	0129	0
Nanchong d.	...	...	|	|	|	|	1257	|	...	1502	|	|	|	2226	|	|	|	|	|	...	|	0128	|	0221	0
Dazhou d.	...	...	1221	1124	1357	1413	1441	1510	...	1741	|	2106	2311	0023	0033	|	2041	0157	|	...	|	0330	0208	0438	0
Ankang d.	...	...	1547	1505	1713	1723	|	1822	...	2049	2242	|	|	0333	0341	0318	2337	0511	0559	...	0611	0644	|	0756	0
Xi'an a.	...	...	|	|	|	|	|	|	...	|	|	|	0538	|	|	|	|	|	|	...	|	|	|	|	
Shiyan d.	...	...	1842	1750	2011	1959	|	2056	...	2326	0115	|	...	|	|	0555	|	0757	0901	...	0852	0938	|	1056	1
Xiangfan d.	...	...	2130	2027y	2300	2210	|	2339	...	0154	0323y	|	...	|	|	0825	0349y	1041	1156	...	|	|	|	1415y	
Suizhou d.	...	...	|	2201	|	|	|	|	...	0319	|	|	...	|	|	|	|	|	|	...	|	1305	|	|	
Wuhan Wuchang a.	...	...	|	0108	|	|	0525	|	...	0507	0820	0846	...	|	|	|	0637	|	|	...	|	1528	1703	1958	
Zhengzhou a.	...	...	0539	...	0745	0417	...	0628	...	...	...	...	...	1253	1330	1543	...	1822	1856	...	1917	...	...	...	2

A – Lhasa(**T224/23**) - Xian(**T221/22**) - Chongqing.
B – Beijing(**T9/10**) - Chongqing.
C – Chengdu(**T126/25**) - Wuhan Wuchang(**T127/28**) - Dongguan dong and v.v.
D – Shanghai(**K282/284**) - Zhengzhou(**K283/281**) - Chengdu and v.v.
a – Chongqing.
d – Chengdu dong.
y – Xiangfan dong.
* – Xian *0 km* - Dazhou *53*

7175 SHANGHAI - NANJING - WUHAN — China Rail High Sp

km	All trains prefix '**D**'	3077	637	3003	2207	3073	G599	3057	2213	3065	G577	2216	G677	3022	3091	3061	3069	3081	3027	3094	3007	3011	3033	3015	3043	3087	3
0	**Shanghai** ♣ d.	...	0609	0630	0639	0650	0715	0715	0730	0820	0834	0839	0840	0915	1015	0942	1018	...	1330	1427	1353	1452	1507	1607	1647	1652	1
84	Suzhou d.	...	0643	0710	0718	0736	0740b	0752	0810	0857	0859b	0919	0905b	0946	1055b	1018	1054	...	1406	|	1434	1532	1543	1643	1739	1730b	1
126	Wuxi d.	...	0702	0734	0749	0755	|	0809	0830	0920	0911d	0938	0917d	1004	1112d	1100	1111	...	1423	1514d	1451	1549	1600	1700	1806	|	1
165	Changzhou d.	...	0721	0753	0808	0814	0806b	0832	0849	0937	0930b	|	0940b	1022	|	1119	1128	...	1440	1549b	1509	1606	1617	1717	|	1800b	1
237	Zhenjiang d.	...	0750	0836	0842	0849	0834n	0859	0923	1004	|	|	|	1054	|	1152	1200	...	1508	|	1536	1633	1653	1749	1843	1826n	
311	**Nanjing** nan d.	0738	0830	0910	0916	0922	0905	0932	0957	1037	1005	1110	1015	1126	1211	1228	1232	1510	1539	1629	1608	1703	1724	1821	1915	1853	1
468	Hefei nan d.	0846	0945	1012	1017	1031	1007	1042	1105	1156	1115	1217	1121	1241	1319	1330	1341	1614	1641	1737	1710	1805	1826	1923	2021	1955	2
555	Liuan d.	0916	1015	1042	1047	1101	1037	1112	1136	1226	1146	1247	1151	1311	1349	1400	1411	1644	1711	|	1740	1835	1856	1953	2051	2025	2
827	**Wuhan** Hankou a.	1106	1207	1224h	1236	1246	1217	1300	1323	1407	1325h	1426	1336h	1522g	1529	1602	1625	1833	1858	2001	1921	2022	2048	2144	2232	2211	2
1119	*Yichang dong* **7182** a.	1304	1415	...	1439	1455	...	...	1547	...	...	1646	...	...	...	...	...	2042	...	...	2132	...	...	...	...	...	

All trains prefix '**D**'	3028	3016	3093	3012	3034	3008	3044	3082	3088	3048	3004	3058	G678	2214	3066	G600	G578	2218	3092	3074	3024	3062	638	3070	3078	2
Yichang dong **7182** d.	...	...	...	...	...	0640	...	0830	...	...	...	...	...	1144	...	...		1301	...	1333	...	...	1417	...	1518	1
Wuhan Hankou d.	0720	0735	0805	0820	0838	0908	0947	1050	1019	1121g	1251h	1334	1335h	1401	1435	1501	1511h	1517	1556	1547	1546g	1630	1636	1700	1739	1
Liuan d.	0914	0926	0955	1013	1039	1102	1142	1250	1203	1342	1500	1530	|	1558	1641	1635	1647	1720	1753	1739	1758	1819	1835	1904	1937	1
Hefei nan d.	0950	1001	1031	1048	1114	1140	1218	1328	1242	1417	1531	1608	1547	1636	1717	1707	1723	1758	1829	1815	1833	1856	1909	1943	2013	1
Nanjing nan d.	1057	1113	1137	1159	1215	1246	1328	1430	1340	1538	1629	1724	1645	1755	1820	1805	1834	1856	1931	1914	1946	2009	2029	2051	2113	2
Zhenjiang d.	|	1145	1200n	|	1247	1321	1358	...	1407n	|	1701	1753	1712n	1829	1850	|	|	1929	1953n	1946	2021	|	|	2129	...	2
Changzhou d.	1154	1217	1221b	1315	1328	1353	1434	...	1433b	1628	1730	1825	|	1858	1927	|	1909b	2015	2017b	2021	2059	|	|	2156	...	2
Wuxi d.	1213	1234	1301d	1332	1344	1410	1513	...	1505d	1645	1750	1842	1750d	1917	2003	1852d	1932d	2034	2051d	2040	2116	2123	2143	2213	...	2
Suzhou d.	1232	1252	1313b	1351	1407	1428	1531	...	1537b	1702	1809	1900	1802b	1936	2022	1909b	1945b	2053	2104b	2059	2133	2142	2202	2231	...	2
Shanghai Hongqiao a.	1307	1325	1353	1426	1447	1502	1605	...	1619	1730	1857	1934	1826	2015	2058	1944	2008	2132	2139	2140	2208	2220	2235	2259	...	2

♣ – **Shanghai** Hongqiao. **b** – Changzhou/Shuzhou bei. **d** – Wuxi dong. **g** – Wuhan Wuchang. **h** – Wuhan. **n** – Zhenjiang nan.

7180 SHANGHAI - NANCHANG and ZHUZHOU - GUANGZHOU — Chinese Railw

km		K1185	T169	K71 F	T81 A	T77 B	Z99	K79 D	K11	K527	K739 E	K511 C
0	**Shanghai** nan d.	0907	1113	1412	1434	1606	1802a	1835	1851	1914	1934	2017
80	Jiaxing d.	1016	1158	1508	1525	1656	|	1931	1940	2004	2036	2106
188	Hangzhou nan d.	1132	1307	1620	1633	1810	|	2049	2114	2140	2153	2216
312	Yiwu d.	|	1416	1743	1753	|	|	2217	2259	|	2331	0007
360	Jinhua d.	1337	1500	1830	1836	2006	2108	2316	2345	2358	0047	0059
446	Quzhou d.	1434	1550	1925	1931	2058	|	0012	0042	0056	0142	0154
557	Shangrao d.	1614	1711	2051	2112	2216	|	0133	|	0249	|	0326
673	Yingtan d.	1804	1825	2211	2230	2353	|	0322	0345	0407	0428	0442
813	**Nanchang** a.	2007	|	|	|	|	|	|	|	|	|	|
1128	Wuchang a.	...	|	|	|	|	|	|	1120	|	|	|
1044	Pingxiang d.	...	|	|	|	|	|	0718	...	0850	0915	|
1125	**Zhuzhou** a.	...	|	0345	0335	0435	0305	0828	...	0954	1048	|
1125	**Zhuzhou** d.	...	|	...	0403	0450	0321	0846	...	1024	1108	|
1259	Hengyang d.	...	|	...	0540	0614	|	...	...	1153	...	|
1406	Chenzhou d.	...	|	...	...	...	|	...	...	1339	...	|
1559	Shaoguan dong d.	...	0245	...	...	...	|	...	...	1529	...	1452
1780	**Guangzhou** a.	...	0530	...	...	...	1008d	...	...	1808	...	1714

	K528	K1186	K80 D	K12	K512 C	T170	K740 E	Z100	T82 A	K72 F	T
Guangzhou d.	0749	...	...	...	1103	1455	...	1812d	...	...	
Shaogun dong d.	1009	...	...	...	1336	1713	...	|	...	...	
Chenzhou d.	1154	...	...	...	1538	|	...	|	...	...	
Hengyang d.	1350	...	...	...	1730	|	...	|	2027	...	0
Zhuzhou a.	1515	...	1530	...	1855	|	2307	0051	2143	...	0
Zhuzhou d.	1533	...	1546	...	1913	|	2330	0111	2202	2222	0
Pingxiang d.	1629	...	1643	...	|	|	|	|	2254	|	
Wuchang d.	|	...	|	1620	|	|	|	|	|	|	
Nanchang d.	|	1800	|	|	|	|	|	|	|	|	
Yingtan d.	2058	2011	2108	2335	0002	0107	0518	|	0302	|	0
Shangrao d.	2211	2148	2222	|	0130	|	0706	|	|	|	0
Quzhou d.	2323	2333	2345	0200	|	0424	0856	|	0518	0624	0
Jinhua d.	0025	0042	0049	0307	0408	0526	1005	0706	0630	0726	1
Yiwu d.	0102	0120	|	0344	0446	0603	1042	|	0704	0826	1
Hangzhou nan d.	0226	0247	0253	0516	0629	0728	1210	|	0835	0955	1
Jiaxing d.	|	0346	0356	0616	0732	0829	1317	|	0933	1058	1
Shanghai nan a.	0413	0504	0516	0746	0855	0955	1504	1022a	1034	1200	1

A – Shanghai nan(**T81/82**) - Nanning and v.v.
B – Shanghai nan(**T77/78**) - Guilin and v.v.
C – Shanghai(**K511/12**) - Haikou and v.v.
D – Shanghai nan(**K79/80**) - Kunming and v.v.
E – Shanghai nan(**K739/40**) - Kunming and v.v.
F – Shanghai nan (**K71/2**) - Chongqing and v.v.
a – Shanghai.
d – Guangzhou dor

WUHAN - YICHANG - CHONGQING 7182

ina Rail High Speed

km	All unmarked trains prefix 'D'	633	2251	2277	366	2259	2201	3077	2255	2237	637	2207	3073	2213	2223	2242	G307	657	2216	G309	2226	2271	2232	3257	3081	3007
	Shanghai **7175** ..... d.	...	...	...	...	...	...	...	...	...	0609	0639	0650	0730	...	...	...	...	0829	...	...	...	...	...	...	1353
	Nanjing nan **7175** .. d.	...	...	...	...	...	...	0738	0825	...	0830	0916	0923	0957	0952	...	...	1020	1110	...	...	...	...	...	1510	|
	Nanchang **7194** .... d.	...	...	...	...	...	...	|	|	0840	|	|	|	|	|	1029**x**	...	|	|	...	1232**x**	...	1159**x**	1508	|	|
0	**Wuhan** Hankou......... d.	0705	0755	0844	0805	1043	1100	1109	1200	1210	1215	1244	1255	1335	1320	1325	1354	1400	1435	1530	1546	1522	1536	1817	1836	1925
3	Tianmen nan............. d.	0747	|	0920	0847	1119	|	|	|	|	1258	|	|	|	1356	1407	1446	1436	1518	|	1622	1612	1633	|	|	2002
4	Xiantao xi................. d.	|	0841	|	|	|	|	1156	|	1256	|	|	|	1430	|	|	1502	1452	1534	|	1638	|	|	|	1929	2018
4	Qianjiang (Hubei)...... d.	0809	|	|	0909	1142	1152	|	1253	|	|	1336	1354	|	1418	1429	1514	1504	1546	1624	|	1634	1655	1910	|	2030
4	Jingzhou .... d.	0837	0916	1010	0937	1211	1221	1231	1321	1331	1343	1404	1422	1507	1446	1457	1542	1532	1614	1652	1712	1702	1723	1939	2003	2058
2	**Yichang** dong........... d.	0921	1006	1050	1025	1250	1301	1304	1407	1415	1434	1447	1455	1557	1526	1536	1621	1613	1650	1731	1750	1741	1812	2013	2042	2132
7	Lichuan.................... d.	1150	1245	1329	1307	1523	1541	...	1640	1653	1704	1721	...	|	1753	1810	1854	1846	1922	2005	|	2024	2043	...	...	...
5	**Chongqing** bei **7140** a.	1337	1443	1523	1458	1715	1728	...	1832	1851	1903	1913	...	2020	1947	1956	2044	2033	2117	2201	2213	2220	2235	...	...	...

nmarked trains ix 'D'	3008	3082	3258	2214	658	2234	G310	2272	2218	2228	3074	G308	2202	2244	638	2224	2208	3078	2238	2256	2260	365	2278	2252	634
ngqing bei **7140** .... d.	...	...	...	0726	0735	0741	0810	0828	0842	0905	...	0923	0933	0940	0950	1012	1037	...	1136	1156	1239	1316	1327	1536	1605
uan................................. d.	...	...	...	|	|	0934	|	1020	1033	|	...	1113	1124	|	1149	|	1229	..	|	1351	1430	1510	1524	1727	1802
ang dong......................... d.	0640	0830	0900	1144	1152	1202	1239	1253	1301	1324	1333	1352	1359	1407	1417	1426	1500	1518	1554	1625	1655	1743	1803	1955	2043
zhou................................. d.	0720	0911	0940	1220	1233	1245	1319	1329	1342	1401	1408	1431	1437	1443	1453	1508	1541	1553	1631	1703	1731	1817	1839	2038	2119
jiang (Hubei)................... d.	0748	|	1008	1249	1302	1314	1347	1357	1410	|	1437	|	1510	|	1522	|	|	|	1659	1732	1759	1845	1907	2107	|
tao xi .... d.	0800	|	1020	|	1315	|	|	|	|	|	|	|	1533	|	|	1545	1616	1627	|	1745	1811	|	|	|	|
men nan .... d.	0816	0959	|	|	|	|	1409	1421	1431	|	|	1518	1549	1527	|	|	1632	1643	1721	1802	1827	1908	1929	|	2205
an Hankou .... a.	0900	1042	1111	1350	1402	1420	1453	1502	1507	1520	1535	1555	1643	1603	1623	1636	1712	1718	1807	1843	1901	1951	2012	2156	2241
Nanchang **7194**............. a.	|	|	1443	|	|	1804	...	...	|	1843**x**	|	...	...	|	|	|	|	|	2159	|	...	...	...	...	...
anjing nan **7175** .... a.	1241	1430	...	1751	1758	...	...	...	1852	...	1910	...	...	1930	2027	2020	2057	2113	...	2218	...	...	...	...	...
hanghai Hongqiao **7175** . a.	1502	...	...	2015	...	...	...	...	2132	...	2140	...	...	...	2235	...	2315	...	...	...	...	...	...	...	...

km	All unmarked trains prefix 'D'	5921	5931	5927	5815	5923	5817	5712	5906	5819	5936	5953	5853	5993	5702	5801	5857	5716	5955	5877	5863	5722	G555	G1032	5867	5726
0	**Wuhan** Hankou......... d.	0601	0612	0619	0635	0640	0700	0730**c**	0736	0800	0823	0905	0944	0958	1020**c**	1115	1238	1233**c**	1347	1456	1609	1620**c**	1739	1823	1852	2059**c**
3	Tianmen nan............ d.	|	|	|	|	0716	0736	0818	|	0836	|	0941	1021	1040	1108	1151	|	|	1424	1533	1651	1711	1816	1900	1939	|
4	Xiantao xi................. d.	|	|	|	|	|	0752	|	|	|	0910	|	1037	|	1123	|	|	1337	|	|	|	|	|	|	1957	|
4	Qianjiang (Hubei)...... d.	|	|	|	0727	0738	|	0840	0829	0858	|	1003	|	1102	|	|	|	|	1449	1555	1713	1733	1838	1921	2011	|
4	Jingzhou .... d.	0715	0727	0736	0755	0806	0826	0907	0858	0928	0946	1031	1113	1130	1158	1240	1355	1413	1518	1623	1741	1800	1906	1949	2041	2225
2	**Yichang** dong........... a.	0754	0800	0808	0828	0839	0905	0940	0930	1001	1020	1105	1147	1209	1231	1312	1428	1448	1558	1656	1816	1839	1945	2023	2122	2259

nmarked trains ix 'D'	5854	5711	5896	G556	G1034	5816	5858	5701	5878	5956	5864	5715	5868	5820	5998	994	5725	5954	5826	5721	5848	5932	5924	5928	5922
ang dong......................... d.	0617	0730	0800	0820	0840	0855	0919	1000	1024	1125	1225	1343	1523	1612	1639	1704	1752	1810	1833	1856	2010	2017	2030	2038	2130
zhou................................. d.	0657	0810	0834	0900	0922	0932	0954	1034	1104	1200	1309	1419	1605	1653	1719	1746	1828	1850	1908	1931	2048	2057	2106	2112	2204
njiang (Hubei)................... d.	0725	0838	|	0928	|	|	1022	1102	|	|	1337	1448	|	1722	1749	1815	1857	1918	|	1959	|	|	|	|	|
tao xi .... d.	0737	0850	|	|	|	1006	|	|	|	1234	|	|	|	1734	|	|	|	|	|	|	|	|	|	|	|
men nan .... d.	0754	0907	0918	0950	1010	1022	1044	1124	1148	|	1359	|	1652	1751	1813	1837	1920	1940	1952	2021	|	|	|	|	|
han Hankou .... a.	0837	1002**c**	0959	1027	1051	1058	1119	1213**c**	1223	1325	1444	1557**c**	1757	1832	1852	1913	2009**c**	2021	2028	2117**c**	2202	2210	2220	2226	2317

Wuchang. **h** – Wuhan. **x** – Nanchang xi.

CHANGSHA - GUILIN - NANNING - BEIHAI and FANGCHENGGANG 7184

ina Rail High Speed

km	D8232	431	D8236	423	1505	1503	529	1501	D8242	421	433	All unmarked trains prefix 'G'	434	422	424	1502	530	D8231	1504	1506	D8235	432	D8241
				A	E	E	A	E		A	D		D	A	A	E	A		E	E			
62	...	0706	...	1216	...	...	1301	...	...	1444	1449	d.Wuhan ....a.	1457	1548	1633	...	1720	...	...	...	...	2333	...
0	...	0841	...	1350	1406	1440	1449	1529	...	1617	1632	d.**Changsha** nan........a.	1316	1408	1458	1523	1548	...	1602	1703	...	2155	...
77	...	0927	...	1436	1453	1522	1529	1609	...	1704	1715	d.Hengyang dong.......a.	1235	1313	1414	1435	1503	...	1513	1609	...	2113	...
*	0814	|	1358	|	|	|	|	|	1735	|	|	d. Hezhou ....d.	|	|	|	|	|	1335	|	|	1702	|	2223
19	0957	1228	1514**b**	1721	1727	1819	1831	1908	1938	1952	2002	d.**Guilin** ....d.	0956	1035	1121	1144	1207	1217**b**	1228	1325	1526	1826	2041
75	1108	1333	1631	1827	1833	1936	1950	2021	2045	2059	2110	d.Liuqiao ....d.	0850	0927	1007	1031	1048	1055	1112	1216	1416	1712	1934
87	1224	1455	1753	1955	1949	2058	2106	2137	2201	2227	2233	a.**Nanning** dong.........d.	0730	0800	0845	0905	0920	0930	0940	1050**n**	1245	1545	1815

km	8323	8293	8203	8265	8263	8295	G1505	8209	8267	8269	3523	All trains prefix 'D'	8202	3522	G1506	8262	8274	8264	8294	8268	8222	8296	8272
								X			V		Z	W									
0	0800	0820	1024	0950	1155	1320	1727	1350	1455	1605	1639**b**	d.**Guilin** ....a.	1005	1037**b**	1318	1312	1429	1537	1710	1857	2224	2239	2300
56	0905	0937	1130	1056	1301	1431	1833	1502	1610	1716	1805	d.Liuqiao ....d.	0903	0909	1216	1210	1320	1428	1605	1743	2122	2135	2158
68	1021	1105	1352	1212	1429	1559	1949	1624	1733	1839	1927	a.**Nanning** dong.........d.	0744	0750	1050**n**	1042**n**	1200	1218	1434	1555**n**	1957	2004	2032**n**
68	...	1125	...	1232	1450	1620	2010	...	1753	1900	...	d.**Nanning** dong.........a.	...	...	1028**n**	1021**n**	1157	1214	1431	1533**n**	...	1956	2012**n**
96	...	|	...	1319	1537	|	2058	...	1840	1947	...	d.Qinzhou dong.........d.	...	...	0935	0928	1033	1129	|	1440	...	|	1919
87	...	|	...	1400	1624	|	2139	...	1927	2034	...	a.Beihai......................d.	...	...	0852	0845	0950	1040	|	1350	...	|	1830
39	...	1227	...	...	...	1722	...	...	...	...	...	a.Fangchenggang bei d.	...	...	...	...	...	...	1250	...	...	1810	...

To/from Table **7060**. **D** – To/from Table **7097**. **E** – To/from Table **7192**. **V** – Additional trips: 1752, 1912.
- Additional trips: 0930, 1015. **X** – additional trips: 0720, 0957, 1813, 1938, 1944, 2010, 2055. **Z** – Additional trips: 0704, 0855, 1025, 1245, 1715, 1815, 1859.
Guilin bei. **n** – Nanning. ** 185 km from Guilin.*

GUIYANG - GUILIN - GUANGZHOU 7185

ina Rail High Speed

km	3551	211	2861	2827	2809	2813	3523	G2917	2815	2825	2819	2823	All trains prefix 'D'	3552	2804	3522	2822	G2918	2824	212	2814	2828	2816	2818	2820
	A		B												E	D									
0	0645	0800	0811	1023	1207	1327	1347	1425	1529	1546	1742	1812	d.**Guiyang** bei........a.	1149	1258	1320	1414	1400	1725	1814	2039	2151	2225	2251	2311
08	0907**x**	|	1034	1253	1424	1603	1631**x**	|	1805	1816	2024	2044	d.**Guilin** xi..............d.	0927**x**	1028	1041**x**	1156	|	1453	|	1809	1905	1954	2040	2100
93	...	|	1150	1406	1545	1714	...	|	1925	1935	2141	2157	d.Hezhou ....d.	...	0915	...	1033	|	1340	|	1640	1751	1835	1934	1954
78	...	|	1253	|	1649	1823	...	|	2024	2054	2237	2254	d.Zhaoqing dong .....d.	...	0806	...	0930	|	|	|	1547	1648	1737	|	1857
54	...	1210	1330	1546	1731	1905	...	1852	2102	2136	2313	2335	a.**Guangzhou** nan .d.	...	0730	...	0847	0932	1200	1400	1510	1605	1654	1802	1820

Additional trips: 1631, 1900. **B** – Additional trips: 0855, 0908, 0918, 0939, 1044, 1126, 1218, 1451, 1508, 1641, 1812. **D** – Additional trip: 1305.
Additional trips: 0926, 0943, 1037, 1135, 1235, 1450, 1521, 1548, 1713. **x** –Guilin bei.

BEIHAI - NANNING - GUANGZHOU 7186

ina Rail High Speed

km	All unmarked trains prefix 'D'	3601	3625	3693	G2913	3605	201	3695	3634	3701	3638	G2911	3661	3611	3613	3617	203	3619	3689	3642	3621	G2915	3623	3648	3705	3685
		A																								
	Fangchenggang bei... d.	...	...	...	...	...	...	...	...	0900	...	...	...	...	...	...	...	...	...	...	...	...	...	...	1740	...
0	**Beihai** ▶ .... d.	...	...	...	...	...	...	...	0806	|	0920	...	1014	...	...	...	...	...	...	1505	...	...	...	1700	|	...
1	Qinzhou dong .... d.	...	...	...	...	...	...	...	0849	|	0958	...	1057	...	...	...	...	...	...	1554	...	...	...	1749	|	...
7	**Nanning** dong ▶ ...... d.	0700	0730	0750	0800	0810	0830	0900	0955	1025	1105	1135	1202	1300	1330**n**	1450	1500	1600	1630	1700	1715	1800	1830	1855	1905	1920
7	Guigang .... d.	0753	0822	0742	0852	0902	|	0952	1047	1123	1157	1227	1254	1352	1429	1542	|	1652	1722	1752	1813	1852	1922	1953	2003	2013
4	Wuzhou nan .... d.	0913	0941	0956	1007	1024	|	1103	1212	1242	1316	1347	1407	1518	1555	1701	|	1818	1847	1909	1933	2013	2043	2112	2122	2134
4	Zhaoqing dong .... d.	1028	1050	1105	1124	1133	|	1207	1327	1351	1431	1456	1516	1627	1703	1810	|	1927	|	2017	2041	2124	2152	2222	2237	2243
0	**Guangzhou** nan .... a.	1105	1133	1142	1200	1216	1149	1244	1405	1435	1508	1538	1553	1710	1740	1846	1819	2004	2035	2056	2118	2203	2230	2306	2319	2326
2	Shenzhen bei .... a.	...	...	...	1240	...	...	...	...	...	...	1619	...	...	...	...	...	...	...	...	...	2244	...	...	...	...

unmarked trains efix 'D'	3602	G2916	2372	3632	2362	2364	3604	3636	204	3608	3610	3706	3612	3690	3614	G2914	3616	202	3662	3640	3702	3646	G2912	3620	3624	3684
			B																							
Shenzhen bei .... d.	...	0652	...	...	...	...	...	...	...	...	...	...	...	...	...	1300	...	...	...	...	...	...	1645	...	...	...
angzhou nan........ d.	0742	0740	0753	0735	0808	0821	0832	0906	1005	1030	1125	1153	1215	1207	1315	1340	1349	1430	1456	1528	1615	1645	1727	1740	1915	1945
aoqing dong.......... a.	|	0819	0837	|	0845	0905	0911	|	|	1114	1203	|	1259	1245	1353	1418	1433	|	1534	1606	1653	|	1805	1818	1959	2023
zhou nan .... d.	0939	0930	0945	0924	0957	1013	1023	1055	|	1221	1314	1342	1410	1356	1504	1529	1544	|	1650	1723	1804	1842	1922	1935	2110	2140
igang.................... d.	1056	1035	1102	1041	1120	1130	1140	1207	|	1338	1438	1459	1527	1519	1621	1646	1716	|	1802	1846	1921	1953	2033	2046	2221	2251
nning dong ▶...... a.	1146	1125	1158	1131	1211	1220	1230	1257	1324	1428	1528	1549	1617	1609	1711	1736	1820**n**	1749	1853	1942	2017	2043	2121	2136	2311	2341
nzhou dong .... d.	...	...	...	1242	...	...	...	1404	...	...	...	|	...	...	...	...	...	...	1959	2053	|	2152	...	...	...	...
ihai ▶ .... a.	...	...	...	1323	...	...	...	1445	...	...	...	|	...	...	...	...	...	...	2046	2133	|	2239	...	...	...	...
ngchenggang bei .. a.	...	...	...	...	...	...	...	...	...	...	...	1716	...	...	...	...	...	...	...	...	2142	...	...	...	...	...

- Additional trips. 0818, 0910, 0920, 0940, 1210, 1225, 1235, 1250, 1315, 1350, 1420, 1446, 1520. **n** – Nanning.
- Additional trips. 0840, 0855, 0938, 0950, 1055, 1415, 1625, 1750, 1810, 1840, 1850, 1900. ▶ – Additional trains are available Nanning dong – Beihai and v.v.

7188 CHANGSHA/ZHUZHOU - NANNING Chinese Railways

km	T81 A	T77 B	Z5 C	Z285 D				T82 A	Z6 C	Z286 D	T78 B
0	...	...	...	...	↓	d.**Nanchang** .... d.		...	...	...	...
231	...	...	...	...		d.Pingxiang .... a.	↑	2249	...	...	...
* *	...	...	0559	0747	↓	d. **Changsha** .... d.		|	1949	2358	...
312	0335	0435	|	|		a.**Zhuzhou** .... d.	↑	2202	|	|	0258
312	0403	0450	|	|		d.**Zhuzhou** .... a.		2143	|	|	0243
437	|	|	|	|	↓	d.Loudi .... d.	↑	|	|	|	|
446	0558	0630	0800	0955		d. Hengyang .... d.		2027	1757	2207	0127
808	|	1040	1130	1315b	↓	d.Guilin .... d.	↑	|	1428	1755b	2105
989	|	...	1320	1514		d.Liuqiao .... d.		|	1302	1617	...
1124	1704	...	|	|		d.Litang .... d.		0946	|	|	...
1244	1846	...	1535	1710	↓	a.**Nanning** .... a.	↑	0805	1100	1400	...

A – Shanghai nan(**T81/82**) - Nanning and v.v. **B** – Shanghai nan(**T77/78**) - Guilin and v.v.
C – Beijing(**Z5/6**) - Nanning and v.v. **D** – Beijing(**Z285/6**) - Nanning and v.v.
* * – Changsha *0 km* - Zhuzhou *52 km*. **b** – Guilin bei.

7190 CHANGSHA/ZHUZHOU - KUNMING Chinese Railwa

km	Z161 G	Z77 F	K79 H	K739 E				K80 H	Z162 G	Z78 F	K7
* *	0328	0605	...	...	↓	d.**Changsha** .... a.		...	1643	2141	.
0	|	|	0846	1105		d. **Zhuzhou** .... a.	↑	1530	|	|	23
145	0529	|	|	1248	↓	d.Loudi .... d.		1344	0433	1941	20
440	0933	1202	1457	1712		d.Huaihua .... d.	↑	0948	1036	1550	16
709	1311	1544	1906	2107		d.Kaili .... d.		0558	0647	1157	11
917	1530	1801	2136	2324	↓	a.**Guiyang** .... d.	↑	0333	0423	0934	08
917	1542	...	2200	2343		d.**Guiyang** .... a.		0319	0403	...	08
948	|	...	2323	|	↓	d.Anshun .... d.	↑	0203	|	...	07
1146	1905	...	0154	0319		d.Liupanshui .... d.		0007	0107	...	05
1378	2124	...	0507	0623		d.Qujing .... d.		2118	2239	...	00
1525	2241	...	0653	0813	↓	a.**Kunming** .... a.	↑	1935	2111	...	22

E – Shanghai nan(**K739/40**) - Kunming and v.v. **F** – Beijing xi(**Z77/78**) - Guiyang and
G – Beijing(**Z161/62**) - Kunming and v.v. **H** – Shanghai nan(**K79/80**) - Kunming and
* * – Changsha *0 km* - Loudi *177 km*.

7192 SHANGHAI - HANGZHOU - NANCHANG - CHANGSHA – GUIYANG China Rail High Spe

km	All trains prefix 'G'	1321	1383	1371	1341	85 C	1505 B	1323	1343	1503 AB	1325	1347	1501 B	61 A	1349	1327	1481 A	1387	1373	1355	1357	1305 C	1483 A	1361	1365	45 A
0	**Shanghai** ♥ ... d.	0625	0645	0723	0733	0800	...	0822	0900	...	0930	0950	1003	...	1049	1147	...	1220	1240	1348	1501	1525	...	1643	1740	...
84	Jiaxing nan ..... d.	|	0715	0754	0810	|	...	0854	|	...	|	1020	1032	...	1118	1225	...	1249	|	|	1530	|	...	1719	1810	...
159	**Hangzhou** ♣ .. d.	0721	0749	0828	0838	0848	0919	0930	0949	1003	1033	1053	1103	1134	1152	1252	1313	1325	1342	1452	1557	1614	1652	1746	1842	2144
268	Yiwu .... d.	0755	0830	0902	|	|	0954	|	|	1036	1107	1134	|	|	1226	1333	|	1359	1423	1526	|	|	1727	1820	|	2226
320	Jinhua .... d.	0813	|	0920	0937	|	1012	1022	1035	1056	|	|	1155	1221	1244	|	1359	|	|	1544	|	1700	1737	1838	1927	2244
398	Quzhou .... d.	|	|	0946	|	|	1037	1045	|	|	|	|	|	1244	|	|	1422	|	|	|	|	|	1808	1901	|	2305
500	Shangrao .... d.	0909	0935	|	1027	|	1107	1124	|	1149	1219	|	1247	1313	|	|	1452	1502	1519	1629	|	1749	1837	1930	2019	...
604	Yingtan bei ...... d.	0937	1012	1046	|	|	1135	1152	1142	1217	|	|	|	1341	1353	1457	1520	1530	1548	1958	1742	|	1905	1959	|	...
744	**Nanchang** xi ... a.	1016	1111	1121	1135	1105	1211	1227	1217	1252	1316	1341	1343	1417	1440	1532	1602	1613	1623	1740	1817	1845	1947	2034	2111	...
1086	**Changsha** nan a.	1151	...	1253	1311	1224	1402	1408	1343	1434	1454	1517	1525	...	1615	1711	1749	...	1808	1924	1942	2013	2141	2213	2254	...
1211	Loudi nan .... d.	1246	...	1343	...	...	...	1458	...	...	1544	...	...	...	...	1802	1842	...	1900	...	...	...	...	...	...	...
1418	Huaihua nan ... a.	1343	...	1440	...	...	...	1558	...	...	1641	...	...	...	...	1858	1935	...	1957	...	...	...	...	...	...	...
1586	**Guiyang** bei ... a.	1537	...	...	...	...	...	1750	...	...	1829	...	...	...	...	2053	2126	...	...	...	...	...	...	...	...	...

All trains prefix 'G'	46 A	1492 A	1382	1384	1342	1346	1482 A	1348	1350	86 C	1352	1374	1354	1322	62 A	1484 A	1686	1356	1324	1358	1502 B	1328	1504 AB	1506 B	1330	13
Guiyang bei .... d.	...	...	...	...	...	...	......	...	...	...	...	...	...	0909	...	0806	0936	...	1008	...	...	1159	...	...	1401	.
Huaihua nan .... d.	...	...	...	...	...	...	...	...	...	...	...	0923	...	1102	...	0953	1123	...	1155	...	...	1352	...	...	1555	.
Loudi nan .... d.	...	...	...	...	...	...	...	...	...	...	...	1023	...	1203	...	1053	1223	...	1255	...	...	1453	...	...	1648	.
Changsha nan .... d.	...	...	...	...	0700	0800	0840	0900	0927	1024	1040	1108	1142	1245	...	1132	1318	1340	1348	1500	1527	1532	1607	1708	1727	18
Nanchang xi .... d.	...	0806	0732	0811	0846	0943	1034	1026	1113	1147	1216	1244	1318	1428	1437	1324	1520	1533	1527	1622	1707	1712	1746	1848	1917	19
Yingtan bei .... d.	...	0845	0815	0838	|	1024	|	1102	1150	|	1253	1321	|	1507	1520	1401	1557	|	1615	1701	1743	|	1822	1924	1954	
Shangrao .... d.	...	0914	0843	0929	|	|	1140	|	|	|	1322	1350	1417	1535	1548	1430	1634	|	1643	|	1811	1835	1851	1952	2022	
Quzhou .... d.	0827	|	0913	|	1006	1110	|	|	|	|	|	1420	|	1605	1618	1500	...	|	|	|	|	1912	|	2022	|	21
Jinhua .... d.	0850	1000	0936	1034	|	|	1226	1208	1304	|	1415	1443	1511	|	1641	1524	...	1724	1743	1808	1905	1942	1947	2045	2117	21
Yiwu .... d.	0908	1018	|	1052	|	1144	1244	|	|	|	1433	1501	1529	1639	1659	1542	...	1743	|	|	1923	2000	2005	2105	2136	21
Hangzhou dong .... d.	0948	1059	1030	1127	1114	1220	1325	1255	1350	1402	1515	1536	1603	1715	1733	1615	...	1821	1832	1856	2011	2048	2039	2150	2210	22
Jiaxing nan .... d.	...	...	1055	1152	1147	|	...	|	|	|	|	|	1635	|	...	...	...	1854	1859	|	2040	2120	...	...	|	
Shanghai Hongqiao . a.	...	...	1129	1219	1214	1319	...	1340	1454	1450	1607	1638	1703	1822	...	...	...	1921	1926	1942	2114	2148	...	...	2302	23

A – To/from Table **7102**. **B** To/from Table **7184**. **C** – To/from Table **7065**. ♥ – Shanghai Hongqiao. ♣ – Hangzhou dong.

7193 BEIJING - HEFEI - SHANGHAI - HANGZHOU - FUZHOU - XIAMEN China Rail High Spe

km	All trains prefix 'G'	1651	1611	1671	1631	1621	1653	1673	1655	1601	345 A	1657	1633	1659	321 A	1686	241 A	1635	323 A	301	1637	325 A	303	1639	7371	7381	73
	Beijing nan ... d.	...	...	...	...	...	...	...	...	...	...	...	...	...	0840	...	...	...	1010	1040	...	1205	1230	...	...	...	.
	Xuzhou dong . d.	...	...	...	...	...		0658	...	...	0823	...	...	...	1200	...	1253	...	1317	1350	...	1459	1538	...	...	...	.
	Hefei nan .... d.	...	0733	...	...	0758	...	0846	...	0923	1010	...	...	...	1348	...	1438	...	1506	1531	...	1644	1720	...	1454	...	.
0	**Shanghai** ♥ ... d.	0658	|	...	0754	|	0816	|	0925	|	|	1018	1228	1258	|	...	|	1435	|	|	1519	|	|	1724	1814	1917	20
84	Jiaxing nan ..... d.	|	|	...	0826	|	|	|	0955	|	|	1048		1335	|	...	|	1506	|	|	1558	|	|	1800	|	1956	21
159	**Hangzhou** ♣ .. d.	0805	|	0832	0853	|	0905	|	1028	|	|	1120	1330	1400	|	...	|	1538	|	|	1625	|	|	1828	1930	2029	21
304	Yiwu .... d.	0846	|	0907	|	|	|	|	|	|	|	1155		1434	|	...	|	1612	|	|	1659	|	|	|	2015	2110	22
352	Jinhua .... d.	0904	|	0930	0945	|	0957	|	1114	|	|	|	1422	|	|	...	|		|	|	1717	|	|	|	2034	2128	22
438	Quzhou .... d.	|	|	1006	|	|	|	|		|	|	|		|	|	...	|	1646	|	|	|	|	|	|	2055	2150	23
549	Shangrao .... d.	0958	1009	1042	1033	1049	1116	1121	1206	1218	1245	1305	1512	1547	1627	1639	1715	1722	1748	1813	1827	1912	1955	2018	...	...	.
768	Nanping bei .... d.	1108	1113	1152	1138	1159	1219	1231	1316	|	|	1408	1632	1650	|	1750	1819	1832	1851	1923	|	|	2105	2128	...	...	.
889	**Fuzhou** .... d.	1147	1159	1246	1222	1234	1258	1317	1407	1413	1430	1502	1715	1750	1816	1843	1900	1908	1937	1958	2020	2101	2140	2211	...	...	.
	Quanzhou .... d.	1305	1316	1403	...	...	1414	1430	1518	1524	...	|	...	1910	1940	2002	2026	...	|	...	...	2217	...	...	...	...	.
1134	**Xiamen** bei ..... a.	1331	1343	1429	...	...	1440	1501	1544	1550	...	1645	...	1943	2007	2034	2058	...	2127	...	...	2244	...	...	...	...	.

All trains prefix 'G'	7382	7372	302	1632	1634	322 A	242 A	1652	1672	324 A	1688	7380	304	1636	1638	326 A	1624	1602	348	1654	1656	1676	1612	1640	1658	16
Xiamen bei .... d.	...	...	...	...	...	0720	0747	0757	...	0901	0929	...	...	...	...	1059	...	1254	...	1336	1409	1454	1503	...	1615	17
Quanzhou .... d.	...	...	...	...	...	|	0820	0830	...	0929	0957	...	...	...	...	1127	...	1321	...	1403	1436	1526	1531	...	1648	17
Fuzhou .... d.	...	...	0700	0800	0855	0912	0933	0959	1030	1049	1122	...	1213	1225	1245	1252	1300	1435	1450	1529	1555	1644	1651	1752	1807	18
Nanping bei .... d.	...	...	0736	0836	|	|	1010	1043	1113	|	1206	...	1250	1302	1321	|	1343	1512	|	1612	1632	1721	1743	|		19
Shangrao .... d.	...	...	0846	0952	1049	1059	1113	1155	1227	1236	1314	...	1402	1408	1441	1432	1500	1615	1637	1728	1748	1838	1849	1943	1956	20
Quzhou .... d.	0624	0647	|	1025	|	|	|	|	|	|	...	1343	|	|	1513	|	|	|	|	1809	1827	|	|	2015	2032	
Jinhua .... d.	0654	0717	|	|	|	|	|	1241	1320	|	...	1420	|	1506	|	|	|	|	|	1839	1850	|	|	2039	2102	21
Yiwu .... d.	0712	0735	|	1106	1203	|	|	1310	1338	|	...	1442	|	|	1548	|	|	|	|	|	1908	|	|	2057	2121	21
Hangzhou dong .... d.	0753	0817	|	1142	1244	|	|	1345	1412	|	...	1523	|	1555	1627	|	|	|	|	1935	1945	|	|	2140	2157	22
Jiaxing nan .... d.	|	0849	|	1209	|	|	|	1410	...	|	...	...	|	1620	|	|	|	|	|	|	|	|	|	|	|	|
Shanghai Hongqiao . a.	0859	0924	|	1237	1336	|	|	1438	...	|	...	...	|	1655	1723	|	|	|	|	2029	2047	|	|	2233	2243	23
Hefei nan .... a.	...	1234	1124	...	...	1336	1357	...	...	1509	...	...	1640	...	...	1658	1734	1841	1917	...	...	2111	2122	...	...	.
Xuzhou dong .... d.	...	...	1303	...	...	1518	1541	...	...	1704	...	...	1837	...	...	1857	...	...	2057	...	...	2310	...	...	...	.
Beijing nan .... a.	...	...	1618	...	...	1823	...	...	...	2013	...	...	2141	...	...	2219	...	...	...	...	...	...	...	...	...	.

A – To/from Table **7097**. ♥ – Shanghai Hongqiao. ♣ – Hangzhou dong.

7194 WUHAN - NANCHANG - FUZHOU and XIAMEN China Rail High Spe

km	All trains prefix 'D'	6501	6521	6503	6523	6525	6527	6505	3262	3241	3276	6529	6507	3223	3258	6509	295	3272	6531	6533	2234	3245	2228	6511	2244	3227	22
0	**Wuhan** Hankou d.	...	...	...	...	...	...	...	0810	0825	0830	...	...	1110c	1116	...	1145	1232	...	...	1447	1525	1526	...	1609	1749c	18
118	Huangshi .... d.	...	...	...	...	...	...	...	0929	0941	|	...	...	1205	1234	...	|	1354	...	...	1607	1622	1638	...	|	1843	19
368	**Nanchang** xi... d.	0648x	0725x	0751x	0855	0909	0953	1026x	1133	1141	1203	1250x	1345x	1407	1443	1450	1510	1601	1720x	1758	1808	1850	1849	1915	1937	2042	215
732	Sanming bei.... d.	0915	1005	1025	1119	1139	1215	1301	1349	...	1420	1531	1600	...	...	1711	1732	1824	1956	2015	2033	...	2111	2149	2158	...	.
927	**Fuzhou** .... a.	1030	|	1148	|	|	|	1415	1504	...	|	|	1709	...	...	1826	1847	|	|	|	|	...	2233	2258	2307	...	...
1068	**Xiamen** bei ..... a.	...	1220	...	1321	1357	1418	...	...	...	1628	1745	...	...	...	...	...	2047	2233z	2229	2236	...	...	...	...	...	.

All trains prefix 'D'	3222	2237	2242	2232	3247	6502	2226	6522	3274	6524	3226	296	3257	6504	6506	6508	6526	3278	3242	3261	6528	6510	6530	6512	6532	65
Xiamen bei .... d.	...	...	...	0715	...	...	...	0850	0918	0910	...	...	...	...	...	...	1421	1445	...	...	1548	...	1653	...	1814z	18
Fuzhou .... d.	...	...	0655	|	...	0827	0839	|	|	|	...	1054	...	1314	1407	1440	|	|	...	1535	|	1724	|	1910	|	
Sanming bei .... d.	...	...	0813	0932	...	0946	0956	1108	1138	1124	...	1211	...	1431	1524	1558	1627	1709	...	1652	1827	1842	1858	2021	2054	21
Nanchang xi .... d.	0802	0840x	1029	1159	1209x	1218x	1232	1327x	1403	1340	1428x	1436	1508	1655x	1739	1819	1859x	1940	1910	1919	2042	2111x	2113	2245	2318x	23
Huangshi .... d.	|	1054	|	1359	1411	...	1422	...	|	...	1625	1640	1705	...	...	...	...	2132	2059	|	...	...	...	...	...	..
Wuhan Hankou .... a.	1040c	1204	1318	1525	1518	...	1540	...	1706	...	1719c	1756	1813	...	...	...	...	2301	2210	2227	...	...	...	...	...	..

c – Wuchang. x – Nanchang. z – Xiamen.

SHANGHAI - HANGZHOU - FUZHOU - XIAMEN - SHENZHEN and LONGYAN — 7200

...na Rail High Speed

All trains prefix D	3111	3145	3131	2287	2285	3125	3107	2281	3135	2283	2293
								B			
Nanjing nan ......d.	...	...	...	...	...	0625n	...	0745	0810	...	...
Shanghai ♥.....d.	...	0640	0738	0747	0843	0851	0940	1028	1042	1121	...
Jiaxing nan ....d.	...	0710	0815	0842	0926	0944	1027	1105	1133	|	...
Hangzhou ♣ ...d.	0733	0743	0843	0910	1004	1014	1125	1135	1210	1231	...
Ningbo..............d.	0850	0908	0954	1017	1125	1131	1225	1236	1325	1339	...
Taizhou ....d.	0951	1009	|	|	1226	1232	1326	1343	1426	1434	...
Wenzhou nan ...d.	1043	1101	1153	1210	1318	1330	1424	1441	1518	1534	1553
Fuzhou nan .....d.	1254	1316	1357	1415	1529	1536	1620	1639	1729	1746	1757
Quanzhou.........d.	1358	1420	1501	1513	1628	1633	1725	1745	1834	1839	|
Xiamen bei.......d.	1428	1453	1528	1542	1657	1702	1755	1816	1913	1908	1925
Zhangzhou ....d.	1449	|	1549	1605	1719	1725	1816	|	1934	1930	1945
Longyan.......a.	|	1557	1640	|	|	|	|	|	2018	|	|
Chaoshan.........d.	1603	...	...	1705	1818	1843	1927	1936	...	2039	2050
Huizhou nan .....d.	1747	...	...	1854	2006	2018	2115	2131	...	|	2233
Shenzhen bei...a.	1821	...	...	1925	2037	2051	2149	2211	...	2253	2306

All trains prefix D	3136	2282	2294	3108	3132	2284	3126	3146	2286	2288	3112
		B									
Shenzhen bei d.	...	0700	0756	0811	...	0847	0907	...	0955	1045	1117
Huizhou nan ..d.	...	0735	0825	0840	...	|	0942	...	1024	1114	1146
Chaoshan ......d,	...	0921	1014	1029	...	1106	1132	...	1221	1311	1350
Longyan ....d.	0822	|	|	|	1058	|	|	1244	|	|	|
Zhangzhou.....d.	0913	|	|	|	1149	1219	1247	1329	1334	|	1451
Xiamen bei ....d.	0937	1046	1147	1158	1212	1244	1312	1351	1359	1439	1516
Quanzhou ......d.	|	1113	|	1226	1245	|	1339	1418	1425	1512	1545
Fuzhou nan....d.	1120	1214	1321	1336	1351	1428	1442	1529	1547	1619	1647
Wenzhou nan.d.	1327	1427	1533	1542	1558	1624	1649	1738	1748	1831	1900
Taizhou..........d.	1424	|	...	1633	1655	1720	1739	1828	1844	|	|
Ningbo ....d.	1532	1624	...	1742	1759	1831	1855	1934	1954	2021	2050
Hangzhou ♣.d.	1638	1731	...	1910	1930	1950	2016	2053	2115	2145	2201
Jiaxing nan ....d.	1711	|	...	1942	|	2025	|	2140	2203	2223	...
Shanghai ♥..a.	1755	1900	...	2011	2034	2055	2119	2210	2238	2253	...
Nanjing nan ...a.	2028k	2116k	...	...	...	...	2312k	...	...	...	...

All unmarked trains prefix 'D'	6201	3231	G7541	G7501	379	G7543	377	G7505	3201	3213	3205	G63	5431	3215	3207	G7511	3209	G55	3217	3101	381	G7545	3103	G7521	G167
	R		P									A	B					A							A
Nanjing nan .... d.	...	...	...	...	...	...	...	0720	...	0752	...	1029	0916	...	...	...	...	1238	...	...	...	...	...	...	1719
Shanghai Hongqiao.. d.	...	...	0614	0650	0703	0708	...	0905	0810	|	0920	|	1116	...	1135	1153	1208	|	...	1509	1445	1552	1602	1648	|
Jiaxing nan .... d.	...	...	|	0728	0744	0739	...	0934	|	|	1010	|	1146	...	1220	|	1244	|	...	1536	1535	|	|	1724	|
Hangzhou dong........ d.	...	0718	0708	0800	0815	0810	0824	0959	0925	0945	1038	1200	1220	...	1257	1302	1320	1409	1556	1630	1620	1657	1721	1757	1848
Ningbo .... d.	...	0834	0817	0856	0922	0915	0948	1059	1047	1103	1200	1255	1353	1414	1426	1404	1440	1459	1726	1751	1740	1809	1829	1909	1953
Taizhou...................... d.	...	0929	0918	0958	1023	1016	1049	...	|	1204	1301	1356	1454	|	1527	1506	|	1554	1827	1852	|	1910	1925	2010	2054
Wenzhou nan............ d.	...	1028	1015	1048	1121	1107	1141	...	1236	1257	1359	1447	1602	1613	1619	1557	1634	1647	1919	1944	1933	2007	2025	2100	2145
Fuzhou nan............. d.	0640	1238	...	...	1324	...	1351	...	1451	1502	1601	...	...	1822	1840	...	1846	1859f	2136	2151f	2139	...	2225	...	...
Quanzhou .... d.	0745	1335	...	...	1425	...	1449	...	1549	1613	1654	...	...	1934	1946	...	1951	...	2243	...	...	...	...	...	...
Xiamen bei .... a.	0816	1402	...	...	1452	...	1515	...	1615	1640	1721	...	...	2000	2012	...	2017	...	2310	...	...	...	...	...	...

...nmarked trains ...ix 'D'	G7504	G7506	G168	G7540	3102	G56	382	3104	G7542	6202	G7546	3216	G7516	3218	3208	3214	5432	3210	G64	3206	3202	3146	378	380	3232
	T		A			A				Q							B		A						
...men bei......................... d.	...	...	...	...	...	...	...	...	...	0829	...	0817	...	0844	0954	1014		...	...	1300	1324	1351	1426	1535	1558
...anzhou........................... d.	...	...	...	...	...	...	...	...	...	0902	...	0849	...	0917	1026	1041	..	1040	...	1327	1351	1418	1459	1602	1630
...hou nan........................ d.	...	...	...	...	0740f	0800f	0737	0830	...	1030f	...	0956	...	1022	1130	1142	...	1107	...	1436	1459	1529	1606	1706	1743
...nzhou nan .... d.	0631	0729	0836	0827	0958	1007	0943	1038	1052	...	1122	1200	1212	1225	1339	1356	1402	1208	1512	1637	1707	1738	1819	1915	1944
...zhou .... d.	0721	0825	0926	1001	1043	1058	1034	|	1142	...	1218	1250	1308	1319	1429	1446	1452	1415	1602	|	|	1828	|	2005	2040
...gbo.............................. d.	0825	0929	1035	1106	1146	1154	1132	1235	1254	...	1316	1352	1418	1425	1537	1547	1558	1505	1706	1838	1905	1934	2013	2110	2140
...gzhou dong .... d.	0920	1035	1138	1202	1300	1249	1237	1340	1409	...	1419	...	1523	1533	1653	1704	1705	1604	1808	2000	2033	2053	2135	2230	2237
...ing nan .... d.	0945	1107	|	1234	|	|	1303	1425	1441	...	1452	...	1556	...	1729	|	1738	1751	|	2035	2103	2140	2210	...	...
...nghai Hongqiao .... a.	1019	1134	|	1308	1414	|	1355	1536	1516	...	1520	...	1624	...	1805	|	1813	1838	|	2105	2144	2210	2249	...	...
...jing nan .... a.	...	...	1320	...	...	1419	...	...	...	...	...	...	...	...	...	1855	2019	|	1933	...	...	...	...	...	...

All trains prefix 'D'	681	6571	2327	6403	2311	2295	6405	2297	2301	6407	2323	6409	2303	6451	2311	6381	G1601	6575	2307	685	2309	6415	671	6417	6419
Fuzhou .... d.	...	0658	...	0732	...	...	0818		...	0924	...	0943	...	...	1226	...	1413	1425	...	...	...	1634	...	1829	2006
Fuzhou nan.............. d.	...	|	0722	0749	0759	0813	0835	...	0919	0942	0936	|	1020	1004	1243	1342	|	|	1457	...	1548	1652	1816	1852	2023
Quanzhou .... d.	0724	0818	|	0851	0857	0914	|	...	1017	1040	1034	|	|	1112	1345	1455	1524	1542	|	...	|	1757	1929	1956	2128
Xiamen bei .... d.	0800	|	0908	0920	0932	0949	1016	1034	1055	1108	1115	1129	1154	1203	1419	|	1556	1616	1624	1712	1717	1827	2000	2024	2202
Zhangzhou.................. d.	|	0902	0933	0947	0953	1010	1037	1055	|	1129	|	1150	1215	|	|	1537	1618	1637	1645	1743	1738	|	2021	2051	2223
Longyan .... a.	|	0950	|	1037	|	|	1121	|	|	1219	|	1234	|	1302	|	1617	|	1733	|	|	|	1938	|	2141	2307
Chaoshan .... d.	0926	...	1040	...	1100	1121	...	1200	1214	...	1241	...	1320	...	1547	...	1729	...	1757	1850	1856	...	2129	...	...
Huizhou nan................ d.	1120	...	1228	...	1242	|	...	1348	1356	...	1423	...	|	...	|	...	1905	...	1945	2040	|	...	|	...	...
Shenzhen bei .... a.	1153	...	1259	...	1321	1349	...	1422	1432	...	1501	...	1534	...	1809	...	1936	...	2016	2112	2117	...	2338	...	...

...rains prefix 'D'	6382	6576	2308	G1602	6434	682	2310	3146	6436	6438	6440	684	2324	6442	2304	6444	6460	2296	2328	2306	672	2298	2312	6448	686
...enzhen bei.................... d.	...	...	0831	0852	...	0916	0945	...	...	...	...	1249	1405	...	1455	...	...	1520	1535	1605	1620	1639	1653	...	1805
...zhou nan .... d.	...	...	0901	0927	...	0947	|	...	...	...	...	|	1440	...	|	...	...	1555	1604	1634	1649	1714	1724	...	1834
...aoshan......................... d.	...	...	1039	1115	...	1137	1208	...	...	...	...	1504	1625	...	1715	...	...	1746	1801	1826	1847	1907	1914	...	2031
...ongyan......................... d.	0715	1026	|	|	1141	|	|	1244	1250	1344	1510	|	|	1727	|	1745	1810	|	|	|	|	|	|	1959	|
...angzhou .... d.	0800	1111	1200	1230	1237	1242	|	1329	1351	1435	1604	|	1745	1818	|	1837	1905	1859	1915	1936	|	2009	|	2044	|
...men bei........................ d.	0824	1136	1237	1254	1305	1315	1345	1351	1414	1509	1630	1649	1809	1839	1848	1902	1929	1723	1938	2000	2031	2036	2043	2114	2210
...anzhou......................... d.	0857	1203	1304	1321	1334	...	1412	1418	1454	1538	1657	...	|	1907	1915	1931	1956	1948	2005	2028	2058	2103	2110	2141	2241
...hou nan........................ a.	1000	1300	1405	|	|	...	1519	1525	|	1641	1802	...	1945	|	2019	2034	2059	...	2104	2132	2156	2202	2208	2248	...
...hou .... a.	...	1319	...	1430	1437	...	...	...	1609	1658	1818	...	...	2022	...	2050	...	...	...	...	...	...	...	2307	...

SHANGHAI - HANGZHOU - NINGBO — 7202

...ina Rail High Speed

All trains prefix 'G'	7331	7301	7361	7351	7309	7313	7315	7319	7321	7553	7329
	U										
Shanghai ♥.....d.	0620	0635	0837	1008	1130	1328	1430	1633	1729	1930	2137
Jiaxing nan ....d.	|	0704	0914	1038	|	|	1501	1709	1805	2006	2206
Hangzhou.........d.	0712	0740	0950	1107	1244	1434	1537	1745	1841	2036	2235.

All trains 'G'	7554	7552	7304	7330	7312	7314	7318	7364	7320	7336	7324
			V								
Hangzhou .....d.	0725d	0706d	0800	0858d	1129	1306	1450	1538	1553	1658d	1800
Jiaxing nan ....d.	0757	0738	0838	0930	1214	|	|	|	1625	1724	1831
Shanghai ♥..d.	0831	0812	0912	0957	1241	1404	1549	1718	1659	1759	1905

All trains prefix 'G'	7503	7505	7507	7509	7511	7595	7515	7517	7519	7525	7527
	W										
Shanghai ♥.....d.	0805	0905	1013	1100	1153	1305	1400	1456	1547	1800	2021
Jiaxing nan ....d.	0834	0934	1043	1128	|	1341	1429	1525	1613	1830	2052
Hangzhou dong.d.	0859	0959	1109	1204	1302	1418	1501	1551	1652	1903	2124
Ningbo............a.	0952	1059	1209	1257	1356	1511	1554	1644	1752	2003	2231

	7502	7504	7572	7506	7510	7512	7514	7518	7520	7522	7524
	X										
Ningbo..........d.	0711	0825	0857	0929	1124	1228	1321	1527	1619	1727	1820
Hangzhou dong d.	0822	0920	1000	1038	1226	1330	1424	1632	1725	1826	1920
Jiaxing nan ....d.	0854	0946	1032	1110	1258	1355	|	1704	1757	1904	1952
Shanghai ♥..a.	0928	1012	1108	1138	1325	1433	1530	1732	1832	1931	2020

...es for Tables **7200** and **7202**.

To/from Beijing Table **7102**. **B** – To/from Table **7100**.

Additional trip: 1800. **Q** – Additional trips: 0651**x**, 0923, 1005, 1003**x**, 1053, 1204, 1227, 1318, 1329, 1524, 1529, 1534**x**, 1629**x**, 1718**x**, 1723, 1808**x**, 1945, 2019, 2024, 2049, 2102, 2108.
Additional trips: 0640**n**, 0700, 0741, 0824, 0848**n**, 0856, 0912**n**, 0913, 0950, 1027, 1119, 1211**n**, 1305, 1406, 1419**n**, 1509, 1611, 1529**n**, 1720, 1810, 1852**n**.
Additional trips: 1837, 1928. **U** – Additional trips: 1230, 1823. **V** – Additional trips: 1900, 1959. **W** – Additional trips: 0832, 1030, 1440. **X** – Additional trips: 0732, 1023, 1700, 1737.
Hangzhou dong. **f** – Fuzhou. **h** – Hangzhou. **k** – Nanjing. **n** – Fuzhou nan. **x** –Xiamen. ♥ – Shanghai Hongqiao.

HÁ NÔI - BEIJING — 7250

...inese Railways, Duóng Sát Viêt Nam

	DD3		MR1	T8702	Z6	Z286			
	2		BC	BC	C				
Há Nôi Gia Lam ....d.	0600	...	2140	...	...	...	...	...	...
Dong Dang ....a.	1135	...	0155	...	...	...	...	...	...
Dong Dang 🛃........................d.	...	...	0250	...	...	...	...	...	...
Pingxiang 🛃 ....a.	...	...	0431	...	...	...	...	...	...
Pingxiang...........................d.	...	...	...	0620	...	...	...	...	...
Nanning.............................a.	...	...	...	1010	...	...	...	...	...
Nanning.............................d.	...	...	...	...	1100	1400	...	...	...
Guilin..................................d.	...	...	...	...	1429	1810	...	...	...
Changsha.............................d.	...	...	...	...	2001	0004	...	...	...
Wuhan Wuchang...................d.	...	...	...	...	2329	0332	...	...	...
Zhengzhou...........................d.	...	...	...	...	0407	0810	...	...	...
Beijing xi...............................a.	...	...	...	...	0955	1349	...	...	...

	Z5	T8701	MR2		Z285	DD4			
	D	BD	BD			2			
Beijing xi ....d.	1551	...	...	...	1750	...	...	...	...
Zhengzhou ....d.	2201	...	...	...	2343	...	...	...	...
Wuhan Wuchang...................d.	0240	...	...	...	0422	...	...	...	...
Changsha.............................d.	0559	...	...	...	0747	...	...	...	...
Guilin..................................d.	1136	...	...	...	1315	...	...	...	...
Nanning.............................a.	1535	...	...	...	1710	...	...	...	...
Nanning.............................d.	...	1810	...	...	...	...	...	...	...
Pingxiang ....a.	...	2201	...	...	...	...	...	...	...
Pingxiang 🛃.........................d.	...	...	2241	...	...	...	...	...	...
Dong Dang 🛃 ....a.	...	...	2322	...	...	...	...	...	...
Dong Dang............................d.	...	...	0022	...	...	1305	...	...	...
Há Nôi Gia Lam ....a.	...	...	0520	...	...	1902	...	...	...

Conveys 🛏 1 cl. Nanning (**T8701/2**) - Pingxiang (**MR2/1**) - Há Nôi and v.v.
Runs daily. On ②⑤ (from Há Nôi) conveys 🛏 1 cl. Há Nôi – Beijing (2 nights).

D – Runs daily. On ④⑦ (from Beijing) conveys 🛏 1 cl. Beijing - Há Nôi (2 nights).

BEYOND EUROPE
Japan

Introduction

The Beyond Europe section covers principal rail services in a different area of the world each month. There are six areas, each appearing twice yearly as follows:

India:	January and July editions
South East Asia and Australasia:	February and August editions
China:	March and September editions
Japan:	April and October editions
North America:	May and November editions
Africa and the Middle East:	June and December editions

The months have been chosen so that we can bring you up-to-date information for those countries which make seasonal changes.

Details of services in South America can be found in the European Rail Timetable April and October editions and schedules for South Korea in the May and November editions.

Contents

INDEX OF PLACES

by table number

JAPAN

Capital: Tokyo (GMT+ 9). 2016 Public Holidays: Jan. 1, 11, Feb. 11, Mar, 20, 21, Apr. 29, May 3 - 5, July 18, Aug. 11Sep. 19, 22, Oct. 10, Nov. 3, 23, Dec.

Operators: Most rail services in Japan are operated by the six private regional railway companies which are marketed as a whole as Japan Railways (JR); there a[illegible] also a number of private railways, some quite large, which are not shown in this section. The six regional operators are JR Central (jr-central.co.jp), JR E[illegible] (www.jreast.co.jp), JR Hokkaido (www.jrhokkaido.co.jp), JR Kyushu (www.jrkyushu.co.jp), JR Shikoku (www.jr-shikoku.co.jp) and JR West (www.westjr.co[illegible]

Services: Except where noted, all trains convey first and second class seated accommodation (known locally as "Green" and "Standard" respectively). Seat reserva[illegible] is obligatory in first class and a supplement must be paid. No trains convey restaurant cars, but nearly all main-line services have some kind of refreshm[illegible] service available, often in the form of box-meals or in vending machines. The few remaining overnight trains have one or two berths in first class and 2 [illegible] berths in second. Trains are very punctual and delays are rare.

Timings: The latest available timings are shown. The availability of english language timetable information varies by operator. An english language booklet of timeta[illegible] for high-speed and principal long distance trains is available on application from the Japan National Tourism Organization in London (✆ 020 7398 567[illegible] www.seejapan.co.uk), however it does not list all stations. Much more detailed information can be obtained using the Hyperdia Timetable and Route Sea[illegible] website, which is also available in english (www.hyperdia.com/en).

Tickets: Tickets can be purchased from windows or machines at stations. A basic one-class fare structure applies according to the distance travelled. Rural lines hav[illegible] slightly higher fare. Supplements are payable for travel on high-speed and express services, for the use of first class, and in some cases where a JR group t[illegible] uses the line of a private operator.

Passes: The Japanese Railways Group offers the Japan Rail Pass (www.japanrailpass.net). To qualify for a pass you must enter the country under the status o[illegible] "temporary visitor" and your passport must be endorsed with this stamp. When you purchase your pass, which cannot be done in Japan, you will receive [illegible] Exchange Order which must be exchanged, within 3 months, for an actual pass. This is done at any of 43 JR stations most of which do not open until 1000. [illegible] JR Pass is not valid on Nozomi and Mizuho trains and a supplement is payable for any sleeping berths, but it is valid for all other JR Group Railways, some [illegible] buses and the JR ferry from Miyajima to Miyajimaguchi. You can travel in a higher class by paying the relevant supplements. The pass is valid from the date [illegible] first used. Ages for the child pass are from 6 to 11.

Prices: Adult first (Green) class 7 Day ¥38800/14 Day ¥ 62950/21 Day ¥84870, Adult second (Ordinary) class 7 Day ¥29110/14 Day ¥46390/21 Day ¥59[illegible] Child first (Green) class 7 Day ¥19440/14 Day ¥31470/21 Day ¥40930, Child second (Ordinary) class 7 Day ¥14550/14 Day ¥23190/21 Day ¥29670. A variety of more region specific passes are also available.

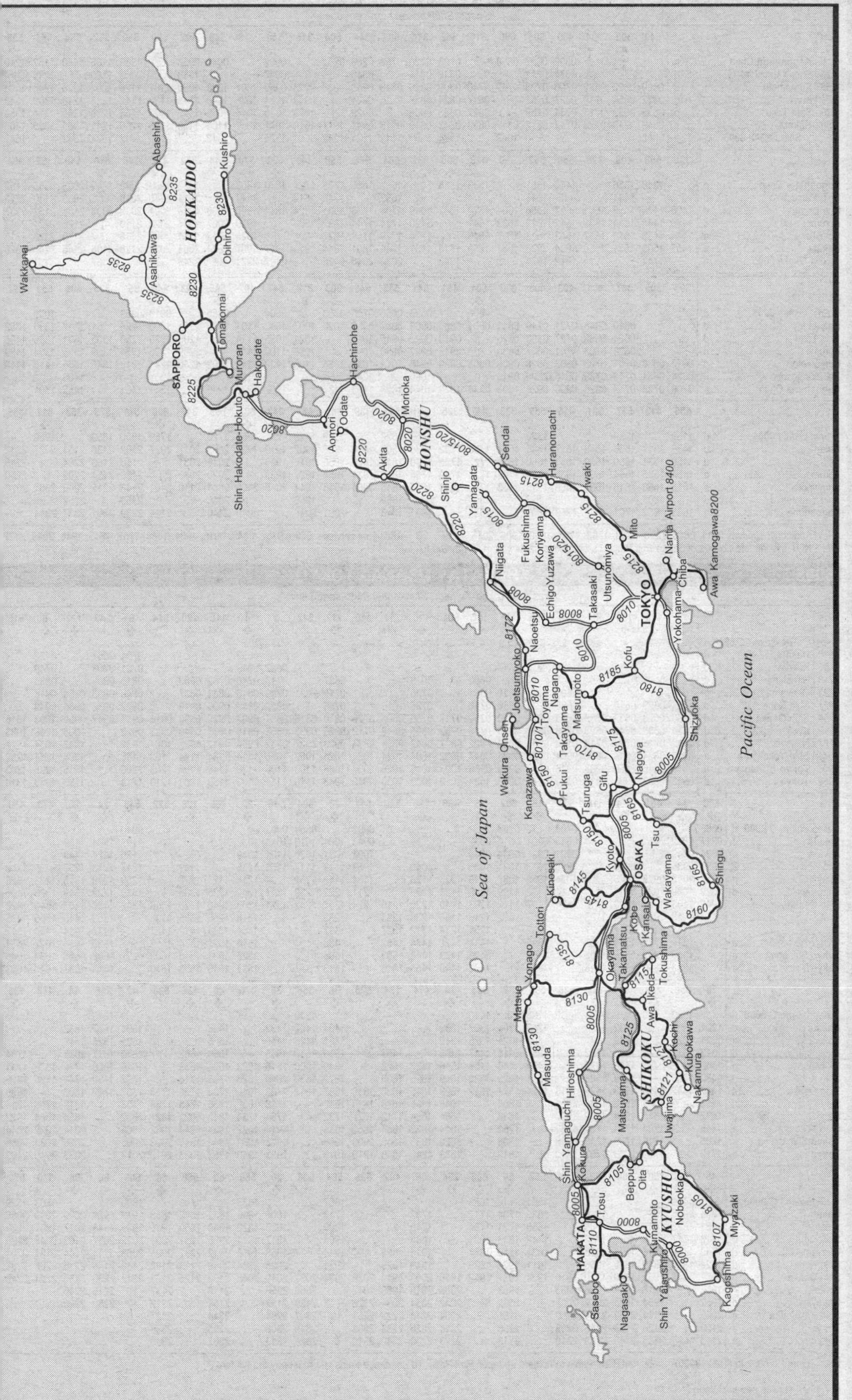

HOKKAIDO
HONSHU
SHIKOKU
KYUSHU
Sea of Japan
Pacific Ocean
Wakkanai
Abashiri
Asahikawa
Kushiro
Obihiro
SAPPORO
Tomakomai
Muroran
Hakodate
Shin Hakodate-Hokuto
Aomori
Hachinohe
Odate
Morioka
Akita
Shinjo
Yamagata
Sendai
Haranomachi
Fukushima
Koriyama
Iwaki
Mito
Niigata
Utsunomiya
Takasaki
EchigoYuzawa
Naoetsu
Joetsumyoko
Nagano
TOKYO
Narita Airport 8400
Chiba
Awa Kamogawa 8200
Yokohama
Kofu
Matsumoto
Toyama
Wakura Onsen
Kanazawa
Takayama
Fukui
Tsuruga
Gifu
Nagoya
Shizuoka
Kyoto
OSAKA
Tsu
Wakayama
Shingu
Kinosaki
Kobe
Kansai
Tottori
Yonago
Matsue
Okayama
Takamatsu
Tokushima
Awa Ikeda
Kochi
Kubokawa
Nakamura
Matsuyama
Uwajima
Masuda
Hiroshima
Shin Yamaguchi
Kokura
HAKATA
Tosu
Beppu
Oita
Nobeoka
Miyazaki
Kumamoto
Shin Yatsushiro
Kagoshima
Sasebo
Nagasaki
8235
8230
8225
8020
8220
8015/20
8215
8015
8008
8010
8172
8010/1
8150
8170
8175
8185
8180
8005
8165
8160
8145
8135
8130
8115
8125
8121
8105
8110
8107
8000

8000 KAGOSHIMA - HAKATA JR Ky

Kyushu Shinkansen high-speed line

km		540	302 A	304	400	308	600 ✣	310	542	314	602 ✣	544	604 ✣	316	546	318	548	402	320	550	552	554	404	556
0	**Kagoshima** Chuo d.	...	...	...	0608	0627	0658	...	0703	0729	0758	0803	0854	...	0902	...	0940	0953	...	1039	1105	1140	1152	1240
126	Shin Yatsushiro d.	...	...	...	0654	0711	|	...	0748	0814	|	0848	|	...	0947	...	|	1038	...	|	1150	|	1236	|
158	Kumamoto d.	0600	0623	0639	0706	0723	0742	0746	0800	0826	0842	0900	0938	0923	0959	1007	1028	1050	1107	1128	1202	1228	1248	1328
224	Kurume d.	0632	0654	0710	0727	0755	|	0817	0824	0858	|	0924	|	0954	1024	1039	1048	1111	1138	1149	1223	1248	1309	1348
230	Shin Tosu d.	0635	0659	0715	0731	0759	|	0822	0828	0906	|	0929	|	1003	1029	1044	1053	1115	1143	1153	1228	1253	1314	1353
256	**Hakata** a.	0649	0712	0728	0744	0812	0817	0836	0842	0919	0915	0941	1011	1018	1041	1057	1105	1128	1155	1206	1241	1305	1326	1405
	Shin Osaka **8005** a.	0942	...	...	...	...	1042	...	1124	...	1142	1224	1242	...	1324	...	1342	...	...	1442	1524	1542	...	1642

	326	558	408	328	560	562	330	410	606 ✣	332	564	566	568	340	608 ✣	570	344	572	412	348	610 ✣	458	352	354
Kagoshima Chuo d.	...	1340	1356	...	1440	1501	...	1533	1558	...	1607	1636	1705	1727	1800	1803	...	1829	1903	1929	1949	2008	2055	2139
Shin Yatsushiro d.	...	|	1441	...	|	1546	...	|	|	...	1652	|	1749	1812	|	1848	...	1914	1948	2015	|	2053	2140	2225
Kumamoto d.	1408	1428	1453	1501	1527	1558	1601	1620	1642	1649	1704	1723	1801	1824	1844	1900	1936	1926	2001	2039	2033	2105	2152	2237
Kurume d.	1439	1448	1514	1533	1547	1619	1633	1641	|	1720	1724	1744	1822	1856	|	1920	2007	1947	2022	2110	|	2126	2224	2308
Shin Tosu d.	1444	1453	1518	1537	1552	1623	1637	1646	|	1724	1729	1748	1827	1901	|	1925	2012	1951	2027	2115	|	2130	2228	2313
Hakata a.	1457	1505	1531	1550	1604	1636	1651	1659	1715	1737	1741	1801	1840	1913	1917	1937	2024	2004	2039	2128	2106	2145	2243	2325
Shin Osaka **8005** a.	...	1742	...	...	1842	1924	...	...	1942	...	2034	2048	2125	...	2142	2221	...	2249	...	...	2337	...	...	...

	303	305	307	401	403	405	313	601 ✣	451	541	543	545	603 ✣	319 B	547	407	605 ✣	323	549	551	325	409	553	327
Shin Osaka **8005** d.	...	...	...	...	...	...	...	0600	...	0625	0650	0715	0753	...	0804	...	0859	...	0918	0959	...	...	1059	...
Hakata d.	...	...	0610	0645	0721	0749	0811	0831	0857	0909	0932	0958	1020	1007	1042	1101	1128	1151	1206	1236	1251	1317	1336	1352
Shin Tosu d.	...	...	0624	0658	0737	0803	0826	|	0910	0922	0946	1012	|	1021	1055	1114	|	1205	1220	1250	1305	1331	1350	1405
Kurume d.	...	...	0628	0703	0741	0807	0830	|	0915	0927	0950	1016	|	1026	1100	1119	|	1209	1225	1254	1309	1335	1354	1409
Kumamoto d.	0612	0638	0701	0723	0803	0828	0908	0905	0936	0948	1011	1037	1054	1103	1120	1140	1202	1240	1245	1315	1345	1356	1415	1440
Shin Yatsushiro d.	0624	0651	0713	0735	0816	00840	0919	|	|	1000	|	1049	|	...	|	1153	|	...	1257	|	...	1408	|	...
Kagoshima Chuo a.	0709	0735	0757	0820	0900	0925	1003	0948	1022	1044	1058	1133	1137	...	1207	1237	1245	...	1341	1401	...	1452	1501	...

	555	413	557	331	415	559	333	417	335	561	563	339	565	567	343	607 ✣	569	347	609 ✣	571	573	353	611 ✣	355
Shin Osaka **8005** d.	1159	...	1259	...	...	1359	...	...	...	1459	1520	...	1559	1620	...	1659	1720	...	1759	1820	1859	...	1959	...
Hakata d.	1436	1517	1536	1546	1617	1636	1644	1708	1722	1736	1802	1816	1836	1902	1919	1932	2002	2017	2027	2102	2136	2151	2227	2232
Shin Tosu d.	1450	1531	1550	1559	1631	1650	1658	1722	1735	1750	1818	1829	1850	1916	1933	|	2016	2031	|	2116	2150	2204	|	2245
Kurume d.	1454	1535	1554	1604	1635	1654	1702	1726	1740	1754	1822	1834	1854	1920	1938	|	2020	2035	|	2120	2154	2209	|	2250
Kumamoto d.	1515	1556	1615	1634	1656	1715	1733	1748	1811	1815	1848	1904	1915	1944	2015	2006	2044	2110	2101	2143	2215	2240	2301	2320
Shin Yatsushiro d.	|	1608	|	...	1708	|	...	1800	...	|	1859	...	|	1956	...	|	2056	...	|	2155	|	2252	|	...
Kagoshima Chuo a.	1603	1652	1701	...	1752	1801	...	1844	...	1901	1943	...	2001	2040	...	2049	2140	...	2144	2239	2301	2337	2344	...

A – Additional services 0711, 0810, 1208, 1308, 1708, 1735, 1806, 1906, 2015, 2119. **B** – Additional services: 0700, 0732, 0842, 0916, 1054, 1448, 1752, 1845, 1946, 2045, 2122.
✣ – NOT available to holders of Japan Rail Pass. To use these trains you must pay the full fare.

8005 HAKATA - OSAKA - TOKYO JR Central, JR

Sanyo and *Tokaido Shinkansen* high-speed lines

km		200 ✣	100 ✣	102 ✣	504	104 ✣	506	106 ✣	108 ✣	508	110 ✣	214 ✣	510	112 ✣	512	2 ✣	4 ✣	118 ✣	120 ✣	514	6 ✣	540 k	122 ✣	8 ✣	516
	Kagoshima C **8000** d.	...	...	...	...	...	...	...	...	...	...	...	...	...	...	...	...	...	...	...	...	...	...	...	...
0	**Hakata** d.	...	...	...	...	...	...	...	...	...	...	...	...	...	...	0605	0632	...	...	...	0704	0651	...	0732	...
56	Kokura d.	...	...	...	...	...	...	...	...	...	...	...	...	...	...	0622	0649	...	...	...	0721	0708	...	0749	...
248	Hiroshima d.	...	...	...	...	...	...	...	0600	...	0619	...	...	0637	...	0713	0740	0752	0800	...	0813	0806	...	0835	...
393	Okayama d.	...	...	...	...	0600	...	0620	0641	...	0700	...	...	0718	...	0749	0816	0833	0837	...	0849	0853	0858	0916	...
521	Shin Kobe d.	...	0609	0619	...	0636	...	0656	0716	...	0736	...	...	0756	...	0822	0849	0906	0916	...	0922	0930	0936	0949	...
554	Shin **Osaka** d.	0600	0623	0633	0608	0650	0627	0710	0730	0717	0750	0803	0726	0810	0816	0837	0903	0920	0930	0916	0937	0942	0950	1003	1016
593	Kyoto d.	0614	0638	0648	0623	0706	0642	0726	0745	0732	0805	0818	0742	0826	0833	0853	0918	0936	0945	0933	0953	...	1005	1018	1033
727	Nagoya d.	0649	0715	0724	0718	0742	0734	0803	0822	0827	0842	0854	0834	0903	0927	0932	0954	1012	1022	1027	1032	...	1042	1054	1127
1044	Shin Yokohama a.	0806	0834	0844	0852	0904	0922	0924	0944	0952	1004	1014	1022	1024	1052	1055	1114	1134	1144	1152	1155	...	1204	1214	1252
1063	**Tokyo** Shinagawa a.	0817	0846	0856	0903	0916	0933	0936	0956	1003	1016	1026	1033	1036	1103	1106	1126	1146	1156	1203	1206	...	1216	1226	1303
1069	**Tokyo** a.	0823	0853	0903	0910	0923	0940	0943	1003	1010	1023	1033	1040	1043	1110	1113	1133	1153	1203	1210	1213	...	1223	1233	1310

	600 ✣	14 ✣	464	124 ✣	518	542	16 ✣	602 ✣	18 ✣	466	126 ✣	520	544	20 ✣	604 ✣	546	22 ✣	468	128 ✣	522	548	24 ✣	26 ✣	470	130 ✣
Kagoshima C **8000** d.	0658	...	...	...	...	0703	...	0758	...	...	...	...	0803	...	0854	0902	...	...	...	...	0940	...	...	...	...
Hakata d.	0817	0832	...	...	...	0843	0904	0917	0932	...	...	...	0943	1004	1013	1043	1032	...	...	...	1107	1104	1132	...	...
Kokura d.	0834	0849	...	...	...	0901	0921	0934	0949	...	...	...	1001	1021	1030	1101	1049	...	...	...	1125	1121	1149	...	...
Hiroshima d.	0921	0935	...	0949	...	0953	1013	1021	1035	...	1049	...	1053	1113	1117	1153	1135	...	1149	...	1217	1213	1235	...	1252
Okayama d.	0957	1016	0928	1028	...	1034	1050	1057	1116	1023	1128	...	1134	1149	1153	1234	1216	1123	1228	...	1258	1249	1316	1223	1328
Shin Kobe d.	1029	1049	1025	1106	...	1111	1122	1129	1149	1125	1206	...	1211	1222	1230	1311	1249	1225	1306	...	1330	1322	1349	1325	1406
Shin **Osaka** d.	1042	1103	1040	1120	1116	1124	1137	1142	1203	1140	1220	1216	1224	1237	1242	1324	1303	1240	1320	1316	1342	1337	1403	1340	1420
Kyoto d.	...	1118	1056	1136	1133	...	1153	...	1218	1156	1236	1233	...	1253	...	...	1318	1256	1335	1333	...	1353	1418	1356	1435
Nagoya d.	...	1154	1134	1212	1227	...	1232	...	1254	1234	1312	1327	...	1332	...	...	1354	1334	1412	1427	...	1432	1454	1434	1512
Shin Yokohama a.	...	1314	1322	1334	1352	...	1355	...	1414	1422	1434	1452	...	1455	...	...	1514	1522	1534	1552	...	1555	1614	1622	1634
Tokyo Shinagawa a.	...	1326	1333	1346	1403	...	1406	...	1426	1433	1446	1503	...	1506	...	...	1526	1533	1546	1603	...	1606	1626	1633	1646
Tokyo a.	...	1333	1340	1353	1410	...	1413	...	1433	1440	1453	1510	...	1513	...	...	1533	1540	1553	1610	...	1613	1633	1640	1653

	28 ✣	550	232 ✣	30 ✣	132 ✣	526	552	32 ✣	554	34 ✣	474	134 ✣	528	36 ✣	556	38 ✣	476	40 ✣	136 ✣	530	42 ✣	558	44 ✣	478	138 ✣
Kagoshima C **8000** d.	...	1039	...	...	...	...	1105	...	1140	...	...	...	...	...	1240	...	...	...	...	...	...	1340	...	...	...
Hakata d.	1204	1208	...	1232	...	...	1243	1304	1307	1332	...	...	...	1404	1407	1432	...	1448	...	...	1504	1507	1532	...	...
Kokura d.	1221	1225	...	1249	...	...	1301	1321	1325	1349	...	...	...	1421	1425	1449	...	1505	...	...	1521	1525	1549	...	...
Hiroshima d.	1313	1317	...	1335	1352	...	1356	1413	1417	1435	...	1452	...	1513	1517	1535	...	1556	1602	...	1613	1617	1635	...	1704
Okayama d.	1349	1358	...	1416	1428	...	1434	1449	1458	1516	1423	1528	...	1549	1558	1616	1523	1632	1638	...	1649	1658	1716	1622	1741
Shin Kobe d.	1422	1430	...	1449	1506	...	1511	1522	1530	1549	1525	1606	...	1622	1630	1649	1625	1705	1716	...	1722	1730	1749	1725	1816
Shin **Osaka** d.	1437	1442	1450	1503	1520	1516	1524	1537	1542	1603	1540	1620	1616	1637	1642	1703	1640	1720	1730	1716	1737	1742	1803	1740	1830
Kyoto d.	1453	...	1505	1518	1536	1533	...	1553	...	1618	1556	1636	1633	1653	...	1718	1656	1736	1745	1733	1753	...	1818	1756	1845
Nagoya d.	1532	...	1542	1554	1612	1627	...	1632	...	1654	1634	1712	1727	1732	...	1754	1734	1812	1822	1827	1832	...	1854	1834	1922
Shin Yokohama a.	1655	...	1704	1714	1734	1752	...	1755	...	1814	1822	1834	1852	1855	...	1914	1922	1934	1944	1952	1955	...	2014	2022	2044
Tokyo Shinagawa a.	1706	...	1716	1726	1746	1803	...	1806	...	1826	1833	1846	1903	1906	...	1926	1933	1946	1956	2003	2006	...	2026	2033	2056
Tokyo a.	1713	...	1723	1733	1753	1810	...	1813	...	1833	1840	1853	1910	1913	...	1933	1940	1953	2003	2010	2013	...	2033	2040	2103

	48 ✣	560	50 ✣	480	52 ✣	534	562	54 ✣	606 ✣	254 ✣	56 ✣	482	536	564	538	60 ✣	566	62 ✣	568	64 ✣	608 ✣	96 ✣	98 ✣	570	572
Kagoshima C **8000** d.	...	1440	...	...	...	...	1501	...	1558	...	...	...	...	1607	...	...	1636	...	1705	...	1800	...	...	1803	1829
Hakata d.	1604	1606	1632	...	1648	...	1638	1704	1717	...	1732	...	...	1743	...	1806	1803	1832	1842	1858	1919	1928	2000	1939	2006
Kokura d.	1621	1625	1649	...	1705	...	1655	1721	1734	...	1749	...	...	1800	...	1825	1820	1849	1859	1915	1935	1945	2017	1957	2023
Hiroshima d.	1713	1717	1735	...	1752	...	1747	1813	1821	...	1835	...	...	1903	...	1917	1911	1935	1951	2001	2022	2037	2103	2048	2120
Okayama d.	1749	1758	1816	1723	1828	...	1834	1849	1857	...	1916	1823	...	1944	...	1953	1958	2012	2032	2036	2058	2114	2144	2131	2201
Shin Kobe d.	1822	1830	1849	1825	1906	...	1911	1922	1929	...	1949	1925	...	2021	...	2025	2034	2049	2113	2108	2130	2146	2216	2208	2237
Shin **Osaka** d.	1837	1842	1903	1840	1920	1916	1924	1937	1942	1950	2003	1940	2026	2034	2037	2040	2048	2103	2125	2123	2142	2200	2230	2221	2249
Kyoto d.	1853	...	1918	1856	1936	1933	...	1953	...	2005	2018	1956	2042	...	2053	2056	...	2118	...	2137	...	2215	2246	...	...
Nagoya d.	1932	...	1954	1934	2012	2027	...	2032	...	2042	2054	2034	2125	...	2129	2132	...	2154	...	2212	...	2250	2320	...	...
Shin Yokohama a.	2055	...	2114	2122	2134	2152	...	2155	...	2204	2214	2222	2251	...	2307	2254	...	2314	...	2327	...	...	...	...	...
Tokyo Shinagawa a.	2106	...	2126	2133	2146	2203	...	2206	...	2216	2226	2233	2303	...	2319	2306	...	2325	...	2338	...	...	...	...	...
Tokyo a.	2113	...	2133	2140	2153	2210	...	2213	...	2223	2233	2240	2310	...	2326	2313	...	2332	...	2345	...	...	...	...	...

k – From Kumamoto (Table **8000**). ✣ – NOT available to holders of Japan Rail Pass. To use these trains you must pay the full fare.

For return service see next page ▷ ▷ ▷

entral, JR West

HAKATA - OSAKA - TOKYO 8005

Sanyo and *Tokaido Shinkansen* high-speed lines

	601 ✣	541	543	95 ✣	545	603 ✣	97 ✣	547	99 ✣	1 ✣	3 ✣	605 ✣	501	5 ✣	549	7 ✣	461	9 ✣	551	11 ✣	503	13 ✣	463	15 ✣	553	17 ✣
........d.	...	...	...	...	...	...	...	...	...	0600	0616	...	0626	0630	...	0650	0703	0710	...	0730	0733	0750	0803	0810	...	0830
Shinagawa......d.	...	...	...	...	...	...	...	...	0600	0607	0623	...	0634	0637	...	0657	0710	0717	...	0737	0740	0757	0810	0817	...	0837
'okohama ....d.	...	...	...	...	...	...	...	...	0611	0618	0634	...	0646	0649	...	0709	0722	0729	...	0749	0752	0809	0822	0829	...	0849
a..............d.	...	...	...	0620	...	...	0706	...	0729	0735	0754	...	0821	0812	...	0835	0911	0851	...	0914	0919	0933	1011	0951	...	1014
..............d.	...	...	...	0656	...	...	0743	...	0803	0809	0830	...	0916	0849	...	0913	0949	0927	...	0952	1013	1010	1049	1027	...	1052
saka ....d.	0600	0625	0650	0712	0715	0753	0759	0804	0818	0824	0845	0859	0930	0905	0918	0929	1005	0942	0959	1009	1026	1025	1105	1042	1059	1109
obe..............d.	0613	0638	0703	0725	0729	0806	0812	0817	0832	0838	0859	0913	...	0919	0932	0942	1019	0956	1012	1023	...	1039	1119	1056	1112	1123
ma...............d.	0651	0716	0741	0757	0807	0839	0844	0855	0904	0910	0931	0946	...	0951	1011	1020	1123	1028	1046	1056	...	1111	1220	1128	1146	1156
ima...............d.	0727	0757	0822	0838	0848	0915	0920	0936	0940	0951	1007	1023	...	1032	1052	1056	...	1109	1127	1132	...	1147	...	1209	1227	1232
...............d.	0813	0851	0913	0925	0940	1002	1012	1023	1032	1037	1059	1110	...	1119	1147	1143	...	1156	1218	1223	...	1239	...	1256	1318	1323
a ....a.	0829	0907	0930	0941	0956	1018	1028	1040	1048	1053	1115	1126	...	1135	1204	1159	...	1211	1234	1240	...	1255	...	1311	1334	1339
oshima C **8000**. a.	0948	1044	1058	...	1133	1137	...	1207	...	...	...	1245	...	...	1341	...	...	...	1401	...	...	...	...	...	1501	...

	505	103 ✣	465	19 ✣	555	21 ✣	507	105 ✣	467	23 ✣	557	25 ✣	509	225 ✣	469	27 ✣	559	29 ✣	511	109 ✣	471	31 ✣	561	33 ✣	563	513
........d.	0833	0850	0903	0910	...	0930	0933	0950	1003	1010	...	1030	1033	1100	1103	1110	...	1130	1133	1150	1203	1210	...	1230	...	1233
Shinagawa......d.	0840	0857	0910	0917	...	0937	0940	0957	1010	1017	...	1037	1040	1107	1110	1117	...	1137	1140	1157	1210	1217	...	1237	...	1240
'okohama ....d.	0852	0909	0922	0929	...	0949	0952	1009	1022	1029	...	1049	1052	1119	1122	1129	...	1149	1152	1209	1222	1229	...	1249	...	1252
a..............d.	1019	1033	1111	1051	...	1114	1119	1133	1211	1151	...	1214	1219	1242	1311	1251	...	1314	1319	1333	1411	1351	...	1414	...	1419
..............d.	1113	1110	1148	1127	...	1152	1213	1210	1248	1227	...	1252	1313	1319	1349	1327	...	1352	1413	1410	1449	1427	...	1452	...	1513
saka ....d.	1126	1125	1205	1142	1159	1209	1226	1225	1305	1242	1259	1309	1326	1333	1405	1342	1359	1409	1426	1425	1505	1442	1459	1509	1520	1526
obe..............d.	...	1139	1219	1156	1212	1223	...	1239	1319	1256	1312	1323	...	...	1419	1356	1412	1423	...	1439	1519	1456	1512	1523	1534	...
ma...............d.	...	1216	1320	1228	1246	1256	...	1316	1420	1328	1346	1356	...	...	1520	1428	1446	1456	...	1516	1620	1528	1546	1556	1612	...
ima...............d.	...	1252	...	1309	1327	1332	...	1352	...	1409	1427	1432	...	...	...	1509	1526	1532	...	1553	...	1609	1627	1632	1653	...
...............d.	...	...	...	1356	1418	1423	...	...	...	1456	1518	1523	...	...	...	1556	1618	1623	...	...	...	1656	1718	1723	1744	...
a ....a.	...	...	...	1411	1434	1439	...	...	...	1511	1534	1539	...	...	...	1611	1634	1639	...	...	...	1711	1734	1739	1800	...
oshima C **8000**. a.	...	...	...	...	1603	...	...	...	...	...	1701	...	...	...	...	...	1801	...	...	...	...	...	1901	...	1943	...

	111 ✣	473	35 ✣	565	37 ✣	567	515	113 ✣	475	39 ✣	607 ✣	41 ✣	569	517	115 ✣	477	43 ✣	609 ✣	45 ✣	519	571	117 ✣	479	47 ✣	573	49 ✣
........d.	1250	1303	1310	...	1330	...	1333	1350	1403	1410	...	1430	...	1433	1450	1503	1510	...	1530	1533	...	1550	1603	1610	...	1630
Shinagawa......d.	1257	1310	1317	...	1337	...	1340	1357	1410	1417	...	1437	...	1440	1457	1510	1517	...	1537	1540	...	1557	1610	1617	...	1637
'okohama ....d.	1309	1322	1329	...	1349	...	1352	1409	1422	1429	...	1449	...	1452	1509	1522	1529	...	1549	1552	...	1609	1622	1629	...	1649
a..............d.	1433	1511	1451	...	1514	...	1519	1533	1611	1551	...	1614	...	1619	1633	1711	1651	...	1714	1719	...	1733	1811	1751	...	1814
..............d.	1510	1548	1527	...	1552	...	1613	1610	1648	1627	...	1652	...	1713	1710	1749	1727	...	1752	1813	...	1810	1849	1827	...	1852
saka ....d.	1525	1605	1542	1559	1609	1620	1626	1625	1705	1642	1659	1709	1720	1726	1725	1805	1742	1759	1809	1826	1820	1825	1905	1842	1859	1909
obe..............d.	1539	1619	1556	1612	1623	1634	...	1639	1719	1656	1712	1723	1734	...	1739	1819	1756	1813	1823	...	1834	1839	1919	1856	1912	1923
ma...............d.	1616	1720	1628	1646	1656	1712	...	1716	1820	1728	1750	1756	1812	...	1816	1920	1828	1846	1856	...	1912	1916	2020	1928	1946	1956
ima...............d.	1656	...	1709	1726	1732	1753	...	1756	...	1809	1826	1832	1853	...	1856	...	1904	1922	1932	...	1953	1956	...	2004	2027	2032
...............d.	...	...	1756	1818	1823	1844	...	...	...	1856	1913	1923	1944	...	...	...	1956	2009	2023	...	2044	...	...	2056	2118	2123
a ....a.	...	...	1811	1834	1839	1900	...	...	...	1911	1930	1939	2000	...	...	...	2011	2025	2039	...	2100	...	...	2111	2134	2139
oshima C **8000**. a.	...	...	...	2001	...	2040	...	...	...	...	2049	...	2140	...	...	...	...	2144	...	...	2239	...	...	...	2301	...

	521	51 ✣	481	53 ✣	611 ✣	55 ✣	523	119 ✣	765	121 ✣	57 ✣	123 ✣	527	59 ✣	529	125 ✣	127 ✣	531	129 ✣	257 ✣	533	131 ✣	133 ✣	135 ✣	263 ✣	265 ✣
........d.	1633	1650	1703	1710	...	1730	1733	1750	...	1800	1810	1830	1833	1850	1903	1910	1930	1933	1950	2000	2003	2010	2030	2050	2110	2123
Shinagawa......d.	1640	1657	1710	1717	...	1737	1740	1757	...	1807	1817	1837	1840	1857	1910	1917	1937	1940	1957	2007	2010	2017	2037	2057	2117	2130
'okohama ....d.	1652	1709	1722	1729	...	1749	1752	1809	...	1819	1829	1849	1852	1909	1922	1929	1949	1952	2009	2019	2022	2029	2049	2109	2129	2142
a..............d.	1819	1833	1911	1851	...	1914	1919	1933	...	1942	1951	2014	2019	2033	2111	2051	2114	2119	2133	2142	2210	2151	2212	2233	2250	2258
..............d.	1913	1910	1949	1927	...	1952	2013	2010	...	2019	2027	2052	2113	2110	2203	2127	2152	2213	2210	2219	2302	2227	2250	2309	2326	2332
saka ....d.	1926	1925	2005	1942	1959	2009	2026	2026	2052	2035	2042	2109	2126	2126	2216	2142	2209	2226	2226	2233	2316	2242	2306	2325	2339	2345
obe..............d.	...	1939	2019	1956	2013	2023	...	2039	2105	2048	2056	2122	...	2139	...	2156	2222	...	2239	...	...	2256	2320	2339	...	...
ma...............d.	...	2016	2111	2028	2046	2056	...	2116	2152	2124	2129	2200	...	2213	...	2232	2259	...	2313	...	...	2332	2357	...	...	...
ima...............d.	...	2052	...	2109	2122	2132	...	2156	...	...	2205	2240	...	2250	...	2312	...	...	2354	...	...	...	...	...	...	...
...............d.	...	2140	...	2156	2209	2223	...	...	...	...	2256	...	...	2341	...	...	...	...	...	...	...	...	...	...	...	...
a ....a.	...	2155	...	2211	2225	2239	...	...	...	...	2311	...	...	2356	...	...	...	...	...	...	...	...	...	...	...	...
oshima C **8000**. a.	...	...	...	...	2344	...	...	...	...	...	...	...	...	...	...	...	...	...	...	...	...	...	...	...	...	...

NOT available to holders of Japan Rail Pass. To use these trains you must pay the full fare.

ast JR West

TOKYO - ECHIGO YUZAWA - NIIGATA 8008

Joetsu Shinkansen high-speed line

	481	301	401	303	305	403	307	309	311	313	315	317	319	321	323	325	327	329	331	333	405	335	337
Tokyo ....**8010/15/20** d.	...	0608	0636	0700	0748	0804	0824	0852	0912	0928	1016	1040	1140	1240	1340	1440	1516	1540	1616	1640	1708	1716	1740
Tokyo Ueno ....**8010/15/20** d.	...	0614	0642	0706	0754	0810	0830	0858	|	0934	1022	1046	1146	1246	1346	1446	1522	1546	1622	1646	1714	1722	1746
Omiya...................**8010/15/20** d.	...	0634	0702	0726	0814	0830	0850	0918	0935	0954	1042	1105	1206	1306	1406	1506	1542	1606	1642	1706	1734	1742	1806
Takasaki.....................................d.	...	0659	0737	0811	0839	0906	0919	0950	|	1027	1105	1134	1231	1331	1431	1531	|	1631	1713	1731	1806	1816	1834
Echigo Yuzawa ....d.	0700	0724	0806	0836	0909	0935	0945	1025	|	1053	1136	1200	1301	1401	1501	1601	|	1701	|	1801	1835	1842	1904
Nagaoka.......................................d.	0726	0750	...	0846	0935	...	1008	1052	|	1114	1201	1221	1326	1427	1526	1626	1645	1726	1754	1828	...	1903	1931
Tsubame Sanjo ....d.	0737	0800	...	0859	0946	...	1018	1102	|	1124	1211	1231	1336	1437	1536	1636	|	1736	1804	1839	...	1913	1941
Niigata......................................a.	0750	0813	...	...	0959	...	1031	1115	1049	1136	1223	1243	1348	1450	1548	1648	1704	1747	1816	1852	...	1925	1954

	407	339	409	411	341	413	343	415	345	347	349	473	351	417	475								
o ....**8010/15/20** d.	1752	1812	1816	1832	1852	1912	1936	1952	2004	2024	2052	2112	2140	2228	2300	...	...	...	...	...	...	...	...
o Ueno ....**8010/15/20** d.	1758	1818	1822	1838	1858	1918	1942	1958	2010	2030	2058	2118	2146	2234	2306	...	...	...	...	...	...	...	...
a...............................**8010/15/20** d.	1818	1838	1842	1858	1918	1938	2002	2018	2030	2050	2118	2138	2206	2254	2326	...	...	...	...	...	...	...	...
saki..d.	1850	1902	1916	1931	1950	2011	2031	2057	|	2123	2153	2210	2239	2326	2358	...	...	...	...	...	...	...	...
go Yuzawa ....d.	1920	1929	1945	2000	2016	2040	2058	2126	|	2153	2223	...	2309	2355	...	...	...	...	...	...	...	...	...
oka...d.	...	1950	...	...	2042	...	2119	...	2134	2219	2244	...	2333	...	...	...	...	...	...	...	...	...	...
ame Sanjo ....d.	...	2000	...	...	2052	...	2129	...	2144	2230	2254	...	2343	...	...	...	...	...	...	...	...	...	...
ta..a.	...	2012	...	...	2105	...	2141	...	2156	2243	2306	...	2356	...	...	...	...	...	...	...	...	...	...

	470	400	472	300	402	302	304	404	306	308	310	312	406	314	408	316	410	318	320	322	324	326	
ta..d.	...	...	...	0605	...	0631	0656	...	0719	0751	0825	0904	...	0920	...	1015	...	1119	1218	1319	1413	1419	...
ame Sanjo ....d.	...	...	...	0617	...	0644	0709	...	0731	0804	0837	|	...	0932	...	1028	...	1131	1231	1331	|	1431	...
oka...d.	...	...	...	0628	...	0655	0720	...	0742	0815	0848	|	...	0943	...	1039	...	1142	1242	1342	1432	1442	...
go Yuzawa ....d.	...	0607	...	|	0708	0722	|	0748	0808	0842	0909	|	0928	1009	1030	1105	1130	1208	1308	1408	|	1508	...
saki..d.	0617	0637	0653	0713	0738	0748	0802	0817	0838	0912	0934	|	1003	1034	1102	1135	1202	1238	1338	1438	|	1538	...
a...............................**8010/15/20** d.	0651	0710	0727	0747	0815	0823	0835	0851	0915	0939	1003	1020	1035	1103	1135	1203	1235	1303	1403	1503	1535	1603	...
o Ueno ....**8010/15/20** d.	0711	0731	0747	0807	0835	0843	0855	0911	0935	0959	1023	|	1055	1123	1155	1223	1255	1323	1423	1523	1555	1623	...
o ....**8010/15/20** a.	0716	0736	0752	0812	0840	0848	0900	0916	0940	1004	1028	1043	1100	1128	1200	1228	1300	1328	1428	1528	1600	1628	...

	328	330	332	334	336	338	340	342	412	344	346	414	348	416	350								
ta..d.	1504	1513	1609	1623	1649	1723	1744	1812	...	1856	1916	...	2018	...	2134	...	...	...	...	...	...	...	...
ame Sanjo ....d.	1516	1525	1622	1635	1701	1735	1756	1824	...	1908	1929	...	2031	...	2147	...	...	...	...	...	...	...	...
oka...d.	1527	1536	1633	1646	1712	1746	1807	1835	...	1919	1940	...	2042	...	2158	...	...	...	...	...	...	...	...
go Yuzawa ....d.	1548	1602	|	1712	1733	1812	1828	1901	1913	1940	2006	2036	2109	2140	2224	...	...	...	...	...	...	...	...
saki..d.	|	1631	|	1742	1803	1842	1858	|	1942	2010	2035	2107	2138	2210	2250	...	...	...	...	...	...	...	...
a...............................**8010/15/20** d.	1635	1703	1725	1815	1835	1915	1927	1947	2015	2035	2103	2143	2203	2243	2315	...	...	...	...	...	...	...	...
o Ueno ....**8010/15/20** d.	1655	1723	1755	1835	1855	1935	1947	2007	2035	2055	2123	2203	2223	2303	2335	...	...	...	...	...	...	...	...
o ....**8010/15/20** a.	1700	1728	1800	1840	1900	1940	1952	2012	2040	2100	2128	2208	2228	2308	2340	...	...	...	...	...	...	...	...

8010 TOKYO - NAGANO - TOYAMA - KANAZAWA

JR East JR

Hokuriku Shinkansen high-speed line

km		591	501	551	601	503	603	553	521	505	555	507	557	605	509	559	607	561	609	563	611	565	613
			R			R				R		R		A	R								
0	**Tokyo** 8008/15/20 d.	...	0616	0628	0652	0720	0724	0752	0812	0836	0844	0920	0932	0944	1024	1032	1104	1124	1204	1224	1304	1324	1404
4	**Tokyo** Ueno 8008/15/20 d.	...	0622	0634	0658	0726	0730	0758	0818	0842	0850	0926	0938	0950	|	1038	1110	1130	1210	1230	1310	1330	1410
31	Omiya 8008/15/20 d.	...	0642	0654	0718	0746	0750	0818	0838	0902	0909	0946	0958	1010	1048	1058	1130	1150	1230	1250	1330	1350	1430
109	Takasaki d.	...	|	0719	0749	|	0823	0843	|	|	0934	|	|	1042	|	1123	1202	1216	1302	1316	1402	1416	1502
151	Karuizawa d.	...	|	0735	0810	|	0844	0900	|	|	0950	|	1035	1103	|	1140	1218	|	1323	|	1418	|	1523
194	Ueda d.	...	|	0754	0828	|	0902	0918	|	|	1009	|	1054	1121	|	1155	1237	|	1341	|	1437	|	1541
226	**Nagano** d.	0611	0740	0808	0840	0845	0914	0932	0941	1002	1021	1047	1107	1133	1146	1209	1248	1254	1353	1358	1448	1454	1553
	Joetsumyoko d.	0635	|	0931	...	|	...	0958	|	|	1048	|	1130	...	|	1235	...	1312	...	1421	...	1512	...
392	**Toyama** d.	0716	0827	0912	...	0932	...	1039	1028	1049	1129	1135	1212	...	1233	1317	...	1353	...	1502	...	1553	...
	Shin Takaoka d.	0725	|	0921	...	|	...	1048	|	|	1138	|	1221	...	|	1326	...	1402	...	1511	...	1602	...
454	**Kanazawa** a.	0738	0846	0935	...	0951	...	1102	1047	1108	1152	1154	1235	...	1252	1339	...	1416	...	1525	...	1616	...

		615	569	617	511	571	619	513	621	573	515	623	575	517	625	539	577	627	519	629	631	
					R			R			R			R					R			
Tokyo 8008/15/020 d.	...	1504	1524	1552	1624	1632	1652	1724	1732	1804	1824	1840	1904	1924	1932	1956	2012	2036	2104	2132	2208	...
Tokyo Ueno 8008/15/20 d.	...	1510	1530	1558	1630	1638	1658	1730	1738	1810	1830	1846	1910	1930	1938	2002	2018	2042	2110	2138	2214	...
Omiya 8008/15/20 d.	...	1530	1550	1618	1650	1658	1718	1750	1758	1830	1850	1906	1930	1950	1958	2022	2038	2102	2130	2158	2234	...
Takasaki d.	...	1602	1616	1650	|	1723	1750	|	1827	|	|	1934	1956	|	2023	|	2104	2127	|	2227	2302	...
Karuizawa d.	...	1618	1632	1711	|	1739	1806	|	1848	1911	|	1955	2013	|	2044	|	2121	2149	|	2248	2323	...
Ueda d.	...	1637	|	1730	|	1758	1825	|	1906	1931	|	2014	2032	|	2103	|	2140	2206	|	2307	2342	...
Nagano d.	...	1649	1657	1742	1748	1812	1837	1851	1918	1955	1951	2026	2055	2051	2114	2121	2154	2218	2228	2319	2353	...
Joetsumyoko d.	...	...	1716	...	|	1835	...	|	...	2018	|	...	2118	|	...	|	2217	...	|	...	...	...
Toyama d.	...	...	1757	...	1835	1916	...	1938	...	2059	2038	...	2159	2138	...	2208	2258	...	2316	...	...	...
Shin Takaoka d.	...	...	1806	...	|	1925	...	|	...	2108	|	...	2208	|	...	2216	2307	...	|	...	...	...
Kanazawa a.	...	...	1820	...	1854	1938	...	1958	...	2122	2058	...	2222	2158	...	2230	2321	...	2335	...	...	...

	600	602	604	500	606	608	552	502	536	610	504	554	612	506	556	508	558	560	614	616	562	618
			B	R				R			R			R		R						
Kanazawa d.	...	...	...	0600	...	...	0612	0700	0708	...	0748	0723	...	0848	0823	0946	0921	1056	...	...	1156	...
Shin Takaoka d.	...	...	...	|	...	...	0628	|	0722	...	|	0737	...	|	0837	|	0939	1110	...	...	1210	...
Toyama d.	...	...	...	0619	...	...	0637	0719	0732	...	0807	0747	...	0907	0847	1005	0945	1119	...	...	1219	...
Joetsumyoko d.	...	...	...	|	...	...	0717	|	|	...	|	0827	...	|	0927	|	1028	1159	...	...	1259	...
Nagano d.	0602	0618	0642	0707	0711	0722	0742	0807	0820	0824	0855	0900	0926	0955	1000	1053	1100	1224	1126	1227	1320	1323
Ueda d.	0614	|	0654	|	0723	0734	0754	|	|	0836	|	0912	0939	|	1012	|	1112	|	1138	1239	|	1336
Karuizawa d.	0634	0642	0714	|	0742	0754	0814	|	|	0856	|	0932	0959	|	1032	|	1132	|	1158	1259	|	1355
Takasaki d.	0650	0702	0734	|	0758	0814	0830	|	|	0916	|	0948	1019	|	|	|	1148	1301	1218	1315	1401	1415
Omiya 8008/15/20 d.	0715	0735	0759	0807	0827	0843	0855	0907	0919	0947	0955	1015	1047	1055	1115	1155	1215	1327	1247	1347	1427	1447
Tokyo Ueno 8008/15/20 d.	0735	0755	0819	0827	0847	0903	0915	0927	0939	1007	1015	1035	1107	1115	1135	1215	1235	1347	1307	1407	1447	1507
Tokyo 8008/15/20 a.	0740	0800	0824	0832	0852	0908	0920	0932	0944	1012	1020	1040	1112	1120	1140	1220	1240	1352	1312	1412	1452	1512

	620	566	622	568	624	530	626	570	510	572	512	574	514	576	516		630	578	518	590		
									R		R		R		R				R			
Kanazawa d.	...	1356	...	1450	...	1552	...	1609	1647	1650	1751	1809	1851	1902	1947	...	...	2017	2100	2135	...	...
Shin Takaoka d.	...	1410	...	1504	...	|	...	1623	|	1704	|	1823	|	1916	|	...	...	2031	|	2149	...	...
Toyama d.	...	1419	...	1513	...	1612	...	1632	1706	1713	1811	1832	1911	1925	2006	...	...	2041	2120	2158	...	...
Joetsumyoko d.	...	1459	...	1553	...	|	...	1713	|	1757	|	1913	|	2009	|	...	...	2121	|	2238	...	...
Nagano d.	1427	1520	1523	1618	1623	1700	1709	1734	1755	1822	1859	1938	1959	2034	2055	...	2115	2146	2208	2302	...	...
Ueda d.	1439	|	1536	1630	1636	|	1721	1746	|	1834	|	1950	|	2046	|	...	2127	2158	|	...	...	...
Karuizawa d.	1459	|	1555	1646	1655	|	1740	1806	|	1854	|	2009	|	2105	|	...	2147	2218	|	...	...	...
Takasaki d.	1515	1601	1615	1715	1715	|	1800	1822	|	1910	|	2026	|	2121	|	...	2207	2234	|	...	...	...
Omiya 8008/15/20 d.	1547	1627	1647	1727	1747	1803	1827	1847	1855	1935	1959	2051	2057	2147	2155	...	2235	2259	2307	...	...	...
Tokyo Ueno 8008/15/20 d.	1607	1647	1707	1747	1807	1823	1847	1907	1915	1955	2019	2111	|	2207	2215	...	2255	2319	2327	...	...	...
Tokyo 8008/15/20 a.	1612	1652	1712	1752	1812	1828	1852	1912	1920	2000	2024	2116	2119	2212	2220	...	2300	2324	2332	...	...	...

8011 TOYAMA - KANAZAWA

JR East JR

Tsurugi Shinkansen high-speed lines

km		701	703	705	707	709	711	713	715	717	719		721	723	725	727	729	731	733	735			
0	**Toyama** d.	0612	0642	0725	0751	0831	1022	1113	1253	1417	1517	...	1542	1617	1711	1811	1959	2016	2127	2333	...	...	...
19	Shin Takaoka d.	0621	0651	0734	0800	0840	1031	1121	1302	1426	1526	...	1551	1626	1720	1820	2008	2025	2136	2342	...	...	...
59	**Kanazawa** a.	0635	0705	0748	0813	0853	1045	1135	1317	1439	1540	...	1604	1639	1734	1833	2022	2038	2150	2356	...	...	...

		700	702	704	706	708	710	712	714 •	716	718	720	722	724	726	728	730	732	734			
Kanazawa d.	...	0647	0758	0949	1034	1128	1228	1328	1428	1509	1709	1738	1838	1923	2025	2106	2219	2306	2337	...	...	...
Shin Takaoka d.	...	0701	0812	1003	1048	1142	1242	1342	1442	1523	1723	1752	1852	1937	2039	2120	2233	2320	2351	...	...	...
Toyama d.	...	0710	0821	1012	1057	1151	1251	1351	1451	1532	1732	1801	1901	1946	2048	2129	2242	2329	2359	...	...	...

8015 TOKYO - SHINJO and MORIOKA

JR

Yamagata and *Tohoku Shinkansen* high-speed line

km		41	121	201	203	123	123	125	205	127	127	43	129	129	131	131	45	133	133	47	135	135	49	137	137
									B																
0	**Tokyo** 8010/20 d.	0604	0612	0620	0640	0712	0712	0732	0744	0808	0808	0848	0856	0856	0924	0924	0940	1000	1000	1036	1100	1100	1136	1200	1200
4	**Tokyo** Ueno 8010/20 d.	0610	0618	0626	0646	0718	0718	0738	0750	0814	0814	0854	0902	0902	|	|	0946	1006	1006	1042	1106	1106	1142	1206	1206
31	Omiya 8010/20 d.	0630	0638	0646	0706	0738	0738	0758	0810	0834	0834	0914	0922	0922	0948	0948	1006	1026	1026	1102	1126	1126	1202	1226	1226
109	Utsunomiya d.	0654	0702	0719	0737	0806	0806	0824	0844	0905	0905	0939	0946	0946	|	|	1031	1050	1050	1131	1150	1150	1229	1250	1250
214	Koriyama d.	0725	0731	0757	0822	0834	0834	0856	0926	0933	0933	1007	1017	1017	|	|	1059	1119	1119	1200	1219	1219	1257	1319	1319
255	Fukushima d.	0740	0747	0815	0841	0850	0853	0915	0940	0949	0950	1025	1033	1034	1048	1051	1114	1135	1138	1217	1235	1238	1317	1335	1338
295	Yonezawa d.	|	0820	|	|	0926	|	|	|	1025	|	|	1105	|	1121	|	|	1210	|	|	1307	|	|	1409	|
342	Yamagata d.	|	0859	|	|	1008	|	|	|	1104	|	|	1137	|	1152	|	|	1246	|	|	1344	|	|	1444	|
369	Murayama d.	|	0927	|	|	1031	|	|	|	...	|	|	...	|	1212	|	|	1308	|	|	...	|	|	1507	|
404	**Shinjo** a.	|	0955	|	|	1054	|	|	|	...	|	|	...	|	1235	|	|	1331	|	|	...	|	|	1530	|
325	Sendai (Honshu) d.	0802	...	0841	0902	...	0919	0938	1006	...	1011	1049	...	1100	...	1114	1136	...	1204	1239	...	1304	1339	...	1404
497	**Morioka** a.	0919	...	...	...	...	...	...	...	...	...	1207	...	...	...	...	1254	...	...	1354	...	...	1454	...	...

	139	139	53	141	141	55	143	143	57	145	145	147	149	149	151	153	153	157	157	219	59	159	159	221
																	A							
Tokyo 8010 8020 d.	1300	1300	1336	1400	1400	1436	1500	1500	1536	1600	1600	1636	1700	1700	1728	1800	1800	1916	1916	1928	2020	2044	2044	2056
Tokyo Ueno 8010 8020 d.	1306	1306	1342	1406	1406	1442	1506	1506	1542	1606	1606	1642	1706	1706	1734	1806	1806	1922	1922	1934	2026	2050	2050	2102
Omiya 8010 8020 d.	1326	1326	1402	1426	1426	1502	1526	1526	1602	1626	1626	1702	1726	1726	1754	1826	1826	1942	1942	1954	2046	2110	2110	2122
Utsunomiya d.	1350	1350	1431	1450	1450	1531	1550	1550	1631	1650	1650	1731	1750	1750	1818	1850	1850	2008	2008	2026	2110	2134	2134	2150
Koriyama d.	1419	1419	1502	1519	1519	1602	1619	1619	1702	1719	1719	1800	1819	1819	1855	1919	1919	2038	2038	2103	2138	2203	2203	2228
Fukushima d.	1435	1438	1517	1535	1538	1617	1635	1638	1717	1735	1738	1818	1836	1838	1910	1936	1937	2056	2057	2117	2156	2219	2220	2243
Yonezawa d.	1512	|	|	1611	|	|	1707	|	|	1808	|	|	1909	|	|	2012	|	2128	|	|	|	2251	|	|
Yamagata d.	1550	|	|	1650	|	|	1746	|	|	1844	|	|	1945	|	|	2047	|	2159	|	|	|	2326	|	|
Murayama d.	...	|	|	1714	|	|	...	|	|	1906	|	|	...	|	|	...	|	2221	|	|	|	...	|	|
Shinjo a.	...	|	|	1740	|	|	...	|	|	1929	|	|	...	|	|	...	|	2245	|	|	|	...	|	|
Sendai (Honshu) d.	...	1504	1539	...	1604	1639	...	1704	1739	...	1804	1842	...	1904	1930	...	1958	...	2123	2143	2220	...	2246	2303
Morioka a.	...	...	1654	...	...	1754	...	...	1854	...	...	...	...	...	...	...	...	...	...	...	2331	...	...	...

A - Additional trip: 1828. B - Additional trips: 1012, 1212, 1412, 1612, 1736, 1836. For return service see next page ▷ ▷ ▷

TOKYO - SHINJO and MORIOKA 8015

Yamagata and *Tohoku Shinkansen* high-speed line

	202	204	206 C	120	120	122	122	124	126	128	128	210	130	132	132	134	136	136	42	138	138	212	44	140	140	46
ka d.	...	...	...	...	...	...	0631	...	...	...	...	...	...	...	...	...	...	...	1007	...	...	...	1107	...	...	1207
(Honshu) d.	0606	0624	0650	...	0712	...	0743	0805	0824	...	0844	0900	0924	...	0941	1024	...	1041	1124	...	1144	1200	1224	...	1244	1324
njo d.	|	|	|	0540	|	...	|	|	|	0716	|	|	|	...	|	|	0916	|	|	...	|	|	|	1117	|	|
ayama d.	|	|	|	0603	|	...	|	|	|	0740	|	|	|	...	|	|	0940	|	|	...	|	|	|	1140	|	|
agata d.	|	|	|	0625	|	0708	|	|	|	0802	|	|	|	0903	|	|	1002	|	|	1057	|	|	|	1208	|	|
ezawa d.	|	|	|	0703	|	0738	|	|	|	0840	|	|	|	0937	|	|	1037	|	|	1136	|	|	|	1238	|	|
nima d.	0633	0646	0716	0739	0739	0814	0814	0835	0846	0916	0916	0922	0951	1013	1013	1049	1116	1116	1150	1216	1216	1223	1250	1316	1316	1350
ma d.	0647	0704	0730	0753	0753	|	|	0849	0902	0930	0930	0936	1006	1027	1027	1104	1130	1130	1205	1230	1230	1239	1305	1330	1330	1405
miya d.	0723	0742	0810	0822	0822	|	|	0918	0934	0958	0958	1020	1038	1058	1058	1134	1158	1158	1234	1258	1258	1320	1334	1358	1358	1434
8010/20 d.	0751	0811	0839	0847	0847	0913	0913	0943	0959	1023	1023	1051	1103	1123	1123	1159	1223	1223	1259	1323	1323	1351	1359	1423	1423	1459
Ueno 8010/20 d.	0811	0831	0859	0907	0907	|	|	1003	1019	1043	1043	1111	1123	1143	1143	1219	1243	1243	1319	1343	1343	1411	1419	1443	1443	1519
8010/20 a.	0816	0836	0904	0912	0912	0935	0935	1008	1024	1048	1048	1116	1128	1148	1148	1224	1248	1248	1324	1348	1348	1416	1424	1448	1448	1524

	142	142	214	48	144	144	50	146	146	52	148	148	150	150	152	154	154	156	156	54	56	158	158	58	160	60
ka d.	...	...	...	1307	...	...	1407	...	...	1507	...	...	...	...	...	...	...	...	...	1754	1840	...	...	1940	...	2029
i (Honshu) d.	...	1344	1400	1424	...	1444	1524	...	1544	1624	...	1634	...	1644	1725	...	1744	...	1844	1910	2000	...	2017	2054	...	2147
njo d.	...	|	|	|	1318	|	|	...	|	|	...	|	1517	|	|	...	|	1711	|	|	|	1843	|	|	1957	|
ayama d.	...	|	|	|	1342	|	|	...	|	|	...	|	1542	|	|	...	|	1737	|	|	|	1906	|	|	2021	|
agata d.	1304	|	|	|	1404	|	|	1504	|	|	1546	|	1607	|	|	1705	|	1803	|	|	|	1931	|	|	2043	|
ezawa d.	1340	|	|	|	1438	|	|	1540	|	|	1623	|	1638	|	|	1741	|	1838	|	|	|	2012	|	|	2117	|
nima d.	1416	1416	1423	1450	1516	1516	1550	1616	1616	1650	1701	1701	1716	1716	1750	1816	1816	1916	1916	1933	2023	2049	2049	2124	2155	2209
ma d.	1430	1430	1439	1505	1530	1530	1605	1630	1630	1705	1715	1715	1730	1730	1805	1830	1830	1930	1930	1947	2042	2104	2104	2138	2209	2224
miya d.	1458	1458	1520	1534	1558	1558	1631	1658	1658	1734	1746	1716	1758	1758	1836	1859	1859	1959	1959	2022	2110	2134	2134	2206	2238	2253
8010/20 d.	1523	1523	1551	1559	1623	1623	1659	1723	1723	1759	1811	1811	1823	1823	1903	1923	1923	2023	2023	2047	2135	2159	2159	2231	2303	2319
Ueno 8010/20 d.	1543	1543	1611	1619	1643	1643	1719	1743	1743	1819	1831	1831	1843	1843	1923	1943	1943	2043	2043	2107	2155	2219	2219	2251	2323	2339
8010/20 a.	1548	1548	1616	1624	1648	1648	1724	1748	1748	1824	1836	1836	1848	1848	1928	1948	1948	2048	2048	2112	2200	2224	2224	2256	2328	2344

Additional trips: 0734, 1600, 1808, 1920, 2037. For return service see previous page ▷ ▷ ▷

TOKYO - AKITA and AOMORI - HAKODATE 8020

Akita, Tohoku and Hokkaido Shinkansen high-speed lines

		91 Ⓡ		93 Ⓡ	95 Ⓡ	95 Ⓡ	1 Ⓡ	1 Ⓡ	111 Ⓡ	3 Ⓡ	3 Ⓡ	101 Ⓡ	5 Ⓡ	7 Ⓡ	7 Ⓡ	9 Ⓡ	9 Ⓡ	11 Ⓡ	13 Ⓡ	13 Ⓡ	15 Ⓡ	17 Ⓡ	17 Ⓡ
Tokyo 8010 8015 d.	...	...	...	...	...	...	0632	0632	0716	0736	0736	0756	0820	0840	0840	0908	0908	0936	1020	1020	1044	1120	1120
Tokyo Ueno 8010 8015 d.	...	...	...	...	...	...	0638	0638	0722	0742	0742	0802	|	0846	0846	0914	0914	|	1026	1026	1050	1126	1126
Omiya 8010 8015 d.	...	...	...	...	...	...	0658	0658	0742	0802	0802	0822	0844	0906	0906	0933	0933	1000	1046	1046	1110	1146	1146
Sendai (Honshu) d.	...	...	...	...	0640	0640	0806	0806	0858	0912	0912	0936	0952	1016	1016	1042	1042	1108	1154	1154	1217	1254	1254
Morioka d.	...	...	...	0654	0758	0800	0849	0848	1011	0954	0956	1049	1032	1057	1059	1123	1125	1148	1235	1237	1301	1335	1337
Tazawako d.	...	...	...	|	0831	|	|	0921	...	1025	|	...	|	1128	|	1158	|	|	1311	|	...	1407	|
Kakunodate d.	...	...	...	|	0845	|	|	0935	...	1039	|	...	|	1142	|	1217	|	|	1325	|	...	1421	|
Omagari d.	...	...	...	|	0859	|	|	0947	...	1051	|	...	|	1154	|	1229	|	|	1337	|	...	1433	|
Akita a.	...	...	...	|	0932	|	|	1024	...	1124	|	...	|	1230	|	1301	|	|	1408	|	...	1504	|
Hachinohe d.	...	...	...	0727	...	0836	0922	...	...	...	1032	...	|	...	1127	...	1202	|	...	1305	...	...	1414
Shin **Aomori** a.	...	0632	...	0755	...	0904	0950	...	...	...	1100	...	1119	...	1151	...	1229	1235	...	1329	...	...	1443
Shin **Hakodate Hokuto** ♥ a.	0654	0738	0814	0903	...	1007	1058	...	...	...	...	...	1222	...	...	...	...	1338	...	1437	...	...	...
Hakodate ♥ a.	0713	*0809*	0833	*0934*	...	*1046*	*1125*	...	...	...	...	...	*1249*	...	...	...	...	*1406*	...	*1502*	...	...	...

	19 Ⓡ	19 Ⓡ		21 Ⓡ	21 Ⓡ	23 Ⓡ	23 Ⓡ	25 Ⓡ	25 Ⓡ	27 Ⓡ	27 Ⓡ	113 Ⓡ	29 Ⓡ	29 Ⓡ	115 Ⓡ	31 Ⓡ	31 Ⓡ	103 Ⓡ	33 Ⓡ	33 Ⓡ	105 Ⓡ	35 Ⓡ	35 Ⓡ	37 Ⓡ
8010 8015 d.	1220	1220	...	1320	1320	1420	1420	1520	1520	1620	1620	1656	1720	1720	1756	1820	1820	1856	1920	1920	1940	2016	2016	2136
Ueno 8010 8015 d.	1226	1226	...	1326	1326	1426	1426	1526	1526	1626	1626	1702	1726	1726	1802	1826	1826	1902	1926	1926	1946	|	|	|
8010 8015 d.	1246	1246	...	1346	1346	1446	1446	1546	1546	1646	1646	1722	1746	1746	1822	1846	1846	1922	1946	1946	2006	2040	2040	2200
ai (Honshu) d.	1354	1354	...	1454	1454	1554	1554	1654	1654	1754	1754	1839	1854	1854	1939	1954	1954	2030	2055	2055	2115	2148	2148	2307
ka d.	1435	1437	...	1535	1537	1635	1637	1735	1737	1835	1837	1954	1935	1937	2054	2035	2037	2143	2136	2138	2223	2230	2231	...
awako d.	1511	|	...	1607	|	1712	|	1809	|	1913	|	...	2008	|	...	2112	|	...	2207	|	...	|	|	...
unodate d.	1525	|	...	1621	|	1728	|	1823	|	1928	|	...	2022	|	...	2125	|	...	2220	|	...	|	|	...
agari d.	1537	|	...	1633	|	1741	|	1835	|	1942	|	...	2034	|	...	2138	|	...	2232	|	...	2323	|	...
ta a.	1608	|	...	1708	|	1812	|	1906	|	2013	|	...	2105	|	...	2208	|	...	2303	|	...	2353	|	...
nohe d.	...	1505	...	...	1614	...	1705	...	1814	...	1909	...	...	2013	...	...	2109	...	...	2206	...	...	2308	...
Aomori a.	...	1529	...	...	1643	...	1729	...	1843	...	1937	...	...	2040	...	...	2137	...	...	2230	...	...	2336	...
Hakodate Hokuto ♥ a.	...	1634	1730	...	1751	...	1832	...	1950	...	...	...	...	2148	...	...	...	...	...	2333	...	...	...	...
date ♥ a.	...	*1705*	1749	...	*1820*	...	*1859*	...	*2015*	...	...	...	...	*2229*	...	...	...	...	...	*0005*	...	...	...	...

	2 Ⓡ	102 Ⓡ	4 Ⓡ	112 Ⓡ	6 Ⓡ		8 Ⓡ	104 Ⓡ	10 Ⓡ	10 Ⓡ	114 Ⓡ	12 Ⓡ	12 Ⓡ		14 Ⓡ	14 Ⓡ	16 Ⓡ	16 Ⓡ	18 Ⓡ	18 Ⓡ	20 Ⓡ	20 Ⓡ	22 Ⓡ	22 Ⓡ
date ♥ d.	...	...	...	...	...	...	...	...	...	*0601*	...	...	*0657*	0746	...	...	...	*0848*	...	*0956*	...	...	...	*1153*
Hakodate Hokuto ♥ d.	...	...	...	...	...	...	...	...	...	0635	...	...	0734	0808	...	...	...	0931	...	1049	...	...	...	1244
Aomori d.	...	...	0617	...	...	...	0649	...	...	0743	...	...	0837	...	...	0952	...	1039	...	1152	...	1239	...	1352
nohe d.	...	...	0641	...	...	...	0717	...	...	0811	...	...	0905	...	...	1016	...	1107	...	1216	...	1307	...	1416
ta d.	...	...	|	...	0608	...	|	...	0715	|	...	0810	|	...	0912	|	1006	|	1106	|	1213	|	1306	|
agari d.	...	...	|	...	0640	...	|	...	0747	|	...	0842	|	...	0949	|	1038	|	1140	|	1246	|	1339	|
unodate d.	...	...	|	...	|	...	|	...	0757	|	...	0855	|	...	0959	|	1054	|	1156	|	1257	|	1350	|
awako d.	...	...	|	...	|	...	|	...	0811	|	...	0908	|	...	1013	|	1108	|	1210	|	1311	|	1408	|
ka d.	...	0610	0711	0716	0736	...	0800	0810	0850	0850	0857	0950	0950	...	1050	1050	1150	1150	1250	1250	1350	1350	1450	1450
ai (Honshu) d.	0636	0721	0752	0833	0816	...	0855	0921	0930	0930	1013	1030	1030	...	1130	1130	1230	1230	1330	1330	1430	1430	1530	1530
8010 8015 a.	0743	0830	0859	0950	0925	...	1006	1030	1038	1038	1130	1138	1138	...	1238	1238	1338	1338	1438	1438	1538	1538	1638	1638
Ueno 8010 8015 a.	|	0851	|	1011	|	...	1026	1050	1058	1058	1150	1158	1158	...	1258	1258	1358	1358	1458	1458	1558	1558	1658	1658
8010 8015 a.	0807	0856	0923	1016	0947	...	1032	1056	1104	1104	1156	1204	1204	...	1304	1304	1404	1404	1504	1504	1604	1604	1704	1704

		24 Ⓡ	24 Ⓡ	106 Ⓡ	26 Ⓡ	26 Ⓡ	108 Ⓡ	28 Ⓡ	28 Ⓡ	30 Ⓡ	30 Ⓡ	32 Ⓡ	32 Ⓡ	34 Ⓡ		36 Ⓡ	36 Ⓡ	38 Ⓡ	38 Ⓡ	96 Ⓡ	96 Ⓡ	98 Ⓡ	100 Ⓡ	
date ♥ 8225 d.	...	...	*1302*	...	...	*1414*	...	...	...	...	*1545*	...	...	*1651*	1727	...	...	...	*1801*	...	*1906*	*2000*	*2116*	2213
Hakodate Hokuto ♥ d.	...	...	1335	...	...	1444	...	...	...	...	1617	...	...	1721	1749	...	...	...	1836	...	1937	2039	2159	2235
Aomori d.	...	...	1438	...	...	1552	...	...	1638	...	1722	...	1744	1824	...	...	1838	...	1944	...	2040	2147	2305	...
nohe d.	...	...	1506	...	...	1616	...	...	1706	...	|	...	1812	|	...	...	1906	...	2012	...	2108	2215	...	...
ta d.	...	1413	|	...	1506	|	...	1612	|	1634	|	1710	|	|	...	1817	|	1911	|	2015	|	|	...	...
agari d.	...	1447	|	...	1539	|	...	1647	|	1708	|	1743	|	|	...	1849	|	1944	|	2048	|	|	...	...
unodate d.	...	1458	|	...	1551	|	...	1658	|	1718	|	1754	|	|	...	1859	|	1954	|	2058	|	|	...	...
awako d.	...	1512	|	...	1608	|	...	1712	|	1734	|	1810	|	|	...	1913	|	2010	|	2112	|	|	...	...
ka d.	...	1550	1550	1607	1650	1650	1707	1750	1750	1815	1815	1850	1850	1913	...	1950	1950	2050	2050	2151	2151	2247	...	...
ai (Honshu) d.	...	1630	1630	1721	1730	1730	1821	1830	1830	1857	1857	1930	1930	1953	...	2030	2030	2130	2130	2301	2301	...	...	...
8010 8015 a.	...	1738	1738	1830	1838	1838	1930	1938	1938	2006	2006	2038	2038	2100	...	2138	2138	2238	2238	...	...	...	...	...
Ueno 8010 8015 a.	...	1758	1758	1850	1858	1858	1950	1958	1958	2025	2026	2058	2058	|	...	2158	2158	2258	2258	...	...	...	...	...
8010 8015 a.	...	1804	1804	1856	1904	1904	1956	2004	2004	2032	2032	2104	2104	2123	...	2204	2204	2304	2304	...	...	...	...	...

Services to/from Hakodate change at Shin Hakodate Hokuto. NOT Ⓡ.

trains run on a different schedule on ©.

8105 HAKATA - MIYAZAKI JR Ky

km																									
0	**Hakata** d.	...	...	...	...	...	...	...	0622	...	0700	0731	0802	0823	0902	...	0921	0957	...	1019	1057	...	1119	1157	...
67	Kokura d.	...	...	...	...	...	...	0639	0715	...	0800	0833	0857	0917	0948	...	1009	1040	...	1109	1139	...	1209	1239	...
186	Beppu d.	...	...	...	...	...	0739	0804	0833	...	0922	0951	1014	1034	1057	...	1128	1150	...	1225	1249	...	1327	1349	...
198	Oita d.	...	...	...	...	0700	0750	0815	0844	0909	0932	1006	1024	1044	1106	1111	1138	1200	1207	1235	1258	1304	1336	1359	1406
322	Nobeoka d.	0515	0645	0712	0806	0911	...	1028	...	1104	...	1208	...	...	...	1309	...	...	1408	...	...	1512	...	...	1613
405	**Miyazaki** a.	0624	0800	0832	0916	1019	...	1136	...	1210	...	1309	...	...	...	1413	...	...	1516	...	...	1624	...	...	1723
412	**Miyazaki** Airport a.	0634	0814	0842	0930	1029	...	1147	...	1220	...	1317	...	...	...	1422	...	...	1524	...	...	1632	...	...	1732

Hakata d.	1257	...	1319	1357	...	1419	1457	...	1519	1557	...	1619	1657	...	1719	1757	...	1819	1857	1920	1959	2020	2103	2205
Kokura d.	1339	...	1409	1439	...	1509	1541	...	1609	1641	...	1709	1741	...	1808	1841	...	1911	1941	2012	2047	2115	2153	2304
Beppu d.	1449	...	1525	1550	...	1627	1650	...	1726	1752	...	1827	1852	...	1925	1953	...	2035	2052	2136	2205	2238	2314	0027
Oita d.	1459	1504	1535	1600	1605	1636	1700	1706	1736	1802	1805	1837	1906	...	1935	2002	2018	2045	2102	2149	2216	2248	2325	0036
Nobeoka d.	...	1730	...	...	1814	...	...	1910	...	...	2017	...	...	2127	...	...	2227	...	...	...	...	...	...	...
Miyazaki a.	...	1837	...	...	1925	...	...	2016	...	...	2122	...	...	2236	...	...	2330	...	...	...	...	...	...	...
Miyazaki Airport a.	...	1846	...	...	1937	...	...	...	...	...	...	...	...	...	...	...	...	...	...	...	...	...	...	...

Miyazaki Airport d.	...	...	...	...	...	...	...	...	...	...	...	...	...	...	...	...	...	...	0925	...	...	1020	...	...	1126
Miyazaki d.	...	...	...	...	...	...	...	...	0558	...	...	0700	...	...	0806	...	...	...	0936	...	...	1030	...	...	1136
Nobeoka d.	...	...	...	...	...	...	...	...	0706	...	...	0806	...	...	0911	...	...	...	1036	...	...	1141	...	...	1242
Oita d.	0445	0521	0558	0640	0713	0746	0810	0842	0908	0910	0939	1006	1011	1045	1108	1111	1145	1210	1238	1245	1311	1340	1345	1411	1440
Beppu d.	0453	0530	0606	0648	0722	0755	0818	0851	...	0919	0947	...	1020	1053	...	1120	1153	1218	...	1253	1320	...	1353	1420	...
Kokura d.	0613	0650	0731	0810	0844	0919	0939	1005	...	1041	1105	...	1141	1205	...	1241	1305	1341	...	1405	1441	...	1505	1539	...
Hakata a.	0716**a**	0749**a**	0830**b**	0855**a**	0940**a**	1003	1022**c**	1047**e**	...	1128	1148	...	1228	1247	...	1328	1346	1428	...	1446	1528	...	1547	1628	...

Miyazaki Airport d.	...	1215	...	...	1321	...	...	1422	...	...	1525	...	1626	...	...	1719	1753	...	1825	1930	2023	...	...	2119	...
Miyazaki d.	...	1229	...	...	1331	...	...	1433	...	...	1535	...	1639	...	...	1731	1803	...	1841	1943	2040	...	...	2130	2235
Nobeoka d.	...	1338	...	...	1437	...	...	1539	...	...	1641	...	1745	...	...	1840	1918	...	1949	2053	2143	...	...	2235	2346
Oita d.	1511	1540	1545	1610	1640	1645	1710	1740	1745	1811	1842	1911	1939	1941	2012	2055	...	2143	2148	...	...	2255	...	...	...
Beppu d.	1520	...	1553	1618	...	1653	1718	...	1753	1820	1851	1919	...	1950	2020	2104	...	2151	...	...	...	2304	...	...	...
Kokura d.	1639	...	1705	1739	...	1805	1840	...	1905	1943	2009	2041	...	2112	2139	2229	...	2311	...	...	...	...	...	...	...
Hakata a.	1728	...	1748	1830	...	1848	1930	...	1947	2030	2057	2128	...	2201	2227	2323	...	2359	...	...	...	...	...	...	...

a – arrival time 2/3 minutes earlier on Ⓒ. **b** – arrival time 0819 on Ⓒ. **c** – arrival time 1023 on Ⓒ. **e** –arrival time 1050 on Ⓒ.

8107 MIYAZAKI - KAGOSHIMA JR Ky

km											
0	**Miyazaki** d.	0557	0716	0815	0919	1015	1225	1416	1621	1736	1855
79	Kirishima-Jingu d.	0717	0836	0938	1038	1137	1342	1537	1739	1855	2022
95	Hayato d.	0733	0852	0954	1057	1154	1359	1553	1756	1912	2041
123	**Kagoshima** d.	0803	0922	1021	1123	1222	1424	1619	1827	1937	2110
126	**Kagoshima** Chuo a.	0807	0926	1025	1127	1226	1428	1623	1831	1941	2114

Kagoshima Chuo d.	0559	0737	0849	0959	1150	1419	1618	1716	1828
Kagoshima d.	0603	0741	0854	1004	1154	1424	1623	1721	1833
Hayato d.	0634	0819	0921	1032	1220	1448	1649	1748	1904
Kirishima-Jingu d.	0652	0836	0938	1050	1238	1504	1706	1805	1921
Miyazaki a.	0823	1002	1057	1209	1402	1620	1826	1934	2038

8110 HAKATA - SASEBO and NAGASAKI JR Ky

km																								
						Ⓐ	Ⓒ																	
0	**Hakata** d.	0558	0633	0717	0729	0753	0754	0814	0834	0856	0915	0931	0955	1015	1032	1055	1115	1132	1155	1232	1255	1332	1355	1432
29	Tosu d.	0619	0655	0740	0758	0816	0816	0838	0857	0916	0938	0956	1016	1038	1058	1115	1138	1158	1215	1258	1315	1358	1415	1458
	Shin Tosu d.	0623	0659	0744	0801	0820	0820	0843	0901	0920	0942	1000	1020	1042	1102	1121	1142	1202	1219	1302	1320	1402	1419	1502
54	Saga d.	0636	0712	0801	0815	0833	0833	0857	0915	0933	0956	1016	1033	1056	1117	1134	1156	1216	1233	1316	1333	1416	1433	1516
117	**Sasebo** a.	|	|	|	0925	|	|	...	1024	|	|	1125	|	|	1227	|	|	1324	|	1425	|	1524	|	1625
154	**Nagasaki** a.	0801	0835	0926	...	0950	0950	...	...	1049	1123	...	1149	1222	...	1250	1322	...	1349	...	1450	...	1550	...

Hakata d.	...	1455	1515	1532	1555	1615	1632	...	1655	1715	1732	1755	1815	1833	1900	1915	1933	2000	2033	2100	2133	2211	2233	2256	2335
Tosu d.	...	1515	1538	1558	1615	1638	1658	...	1716	1739	1758	1815	1837	1858	1920	1942	1957	2021	2058	2120	2158	2230	2256	2317	2358
Shin Tosu d.	...	1519	1542	1602	1619	1642	1702	...	1720	1743	1802	1820	1842	1902	1924	1946	2001	2025	2103	2124	2202	2234	2300	2321	0002
Saga d.	...	1533	1556	1616	1633	1656	1716	...	1733	1756	1816	1833	1857	1916	1938	2002	2016	2038	2117	2138	2217	2247	2313	2335	0016
Sasebo a.	...	|	|	1724	|	|	1826	...	|	|	1925	|	|	2023	|	...	2128	|	2229	|	2321	|	...	0038	...
Nagasaki a.	...	1650	1724	...	1755	1823	...	...	1853	1926	...	1953	2026	...	2056	...	...	2158	...	2257	...	2359	...	...	...

		Ⓒ	Ⓐ	Ⓒ	Ⓐ	Ⓒ	Ⓐ	Ⓒ	Ⓐ			Ⓒ	Ⓐ	Ⓒ	Ⓐ	Ⓒ									
Nagasaki d.	...	...	...	0558	0600	...	...	0625	0625	...	0728	...	...	...	...	...	0829	...	0846	0920	...	0946	1020	...	1046
Sasebo d.	...	...	...	|	|	0621	0621	|	|	0708	|	...	0806	0806	...	...	|	0847	|	|	0944	|	|	1043	|
Saga d.	0626	0705	0705	0718	0718	0731	0731	0756	0756	0819	0845	0859	0912	0912	0926	0926	0945	0953	1013	1034	1053	1113	1135	1153	1213
Shin Tosu d.	0640	0717	0717	0730	0730	0745	0745	0809	0809	0834	0858	0914	0925	0925	0940	0940	0958	1006	1026	1047	1107	1126	1148	1207	1226
Tosu d.	0645	0722	0722	0735	0735	0749	0749	0813	0813	0839	0902	0918	0932	0932	0944	0944	1002	1012	1031	1052	1112	1130	1152	1212	1230
Hakata a.	0707	0743	0747	0756	0759	0809	0815	0830	0835	0905	0920	0938	0953	0954	1005	1006	1021	1034	1053	1112	1134	1152	1213	1234	1253

Nagasaki d.	...	1220	...	1320	...	1420	...	1446	1520	...	1546	1620	...	1647	1720	...	1751	1820	...	1854	1919	...	2023	...	2131
Sasebo d.	1143	|	1243	|	1342	|	1443	|	|	1541	|	|	1642	|	|	1743	|	|	1845	|	|	1952	|	2100	|
Saga d.	1252	1334	1353	1434	1453	1535	1552	1612	1635	1653	1713	1736	1753	1814	1836	1853	1914	1936	1954	2018	2039	2057	2142	2210	2246
Shin Tosu d.	1306	1347	1407	1447	1507	1547	1607	1626	1647	1707	1426	1749	1807	1827	1848	1907	1927	1949	2007	2031	2051	2107	2156	2223	2258
Tosu d.	1312	1351	1412	1452	1512	1552	1613	1630	1652	1712	1730	1753	1812	1831	1852	1912	1931	1953	2013	2035	2055	2113	2200	2227	2302
Hakata a.	1334	1412	1434	1513	1534	1613	1636	1651	1713	1734	1753	1814	1835	1852	1914	1935	1951	2013	2038	2055	2115	2135	2222	2250	2321

8115 TAKAMATSU - TOKUSHIMA JR Shi

km																							
									a											a			
0	**Takamatsu** d.	...	0705	0823	0910	1011	...	1107	1206	1312	...	1412	1512	1612	...	1715	1813	...	1917	2005	2120	...	2223
10	Yashima d.	...	0714	0833	0920	1022	...	1117	|	1323	...	1423	1522	1622	...	1725	1822	...	1927	2016	2131	...	2234
64	Ikenotani d.	...	0804	0924	1009	1115	...	1205	|	1407	...	|	1612	|	...	1814	|	...	2017	2106	2225	...	|
75	**Tokushima** a.	...	0814	0936	1018	1125	...	1213	1304	1415	...	1520	1620	1716	...	1823	1924	...	2027	2115	2234	...	2334

				b											b							
Tokushima d.	0543	0701	...	0823	0922	...	1028	1131	1224	...	1325	1426	...	1528	1646	1728	...	1830	1932	2034	...	2202
Ikenotani d.	0554	0712	...	0834	0932	...	|	1140	1233	...	|	1436	...	1537	|	1737	...	1838	|	|	...	2211
Yashima d.	0644	0804	...	0920	1022	...	|	|	1322	...	1423	1522	...	1622	|	1822	...	1926	2028	2130	...	2308
Takamatsu a.	0654	0813	...	0931	1032	...	1137	1234	1331	...	1433	1532	...	1632	1744	1832	...	1937	2038	2140	...	2318

a – From Okayama (dep. 1 hour earlier). b – To Okayama (arr. 1 hour later).

8118 TOKUSHIMA - AWA IKEDA JR Shi

km		*LEX*	*LEX*	**A**	*LEX*		*LEX*		*LEX*			*LEX*	
0	**Tokushima** d.	0648	0903	0950	1201	1317	1501	1532	1757	1800	1927	2017	2106
74	**Awa Ikeda** a.	0810	1014	1151	1315	1515	1616	1730	1916	2005	2117	2134	2253

	LEX	**B**	*LEX*		*LEX*		*LEX*		*LEX*	*LEX*	
Awa Ikeda d.	0648	0652	0834	0943	1125	1237	1333	1539	1637	1950	2007
Tokushima a.	0803	0855	0947	1128	1236	1422	1445	1720	1746	2104	2157

A – Additional trips: 0540, 0609, 0721, 1145, 1446, 1905. B – Additional trips: 0622, 0753, 1032, 1429, 1654, 1809. 1841Ⓐ.

8121 UWAJIMA - KUBOKAWA JR Shi

km											
0	**Uwajima** ‡ d.	...	0604	0939	1136	1535	1730	1830	...	...	...
82	**Kubokawa** ‡ a.	...	0828	1145	1347	1750	1937	2040	...	...	...

Kubokawa ‡ d.	0622	0940	1324	1517	1658	1843	...	...	...
Uwajima ‡ d.	0828	1215	1534	1721	1915	2044	...	...	...

‡ – Japan Rail Pass holders must pay a supplement to travel between these stations.

hikoku — UWAJIMA - KUBOKAWA — 8121

Uwajima ‡ d.	...	0604	0939	1136	1535	1730	1830	...	...	...
Kubokawa ‡ a.	...	0809	1145	1347	1750	1937	2040	...	...	...

Kubokawa ‡ d.	0622	0940	1324	1517	1658	1843	...	...	...	...
Uwajima ‡ d.	0828	1215	1534	1721	1915	2044	...	...	...	...

Japan Rail Pass holders must pay a supplement to travel between these stations.

hikoku — OKAYAMA and TAKAMATSU - MATSYUAMA and UWAJIMA — 8125

Okayama d.	...	...	...	...	...	...	...	0723	...	...	0832	...	...	0925	...	...	1035	...	...	1135	...	...	1235	...
Takamatsu d.	...	...	...	0517	...	0600	...	|	0737	...	|	0845	...	|	0940	...	|	1047	...	|	1150	...	|	1250
Utazu d.	...	...	...	|	...	|	...	0802	0802	...	0913	0913	...	1006	1006	...	1116	1113	...	1214	1214	...	1314	1314
Imabari d.	...	...	0629	0711	...	0756	...	0930	0930	...	1041	1041	...	1135	1135	...	1241	1241	...	1339	1339	...	1443	1443
Matsuyama a.	0548	0648	0710	0758	0808	0836	0903	1005	1005	1014	1115	1115	1125	1210	1210	1227	1315	1315	1324	1413	1413	1428	1517	1517
Uwajima a.	0713	0813	...	...	0930	...	1024	...	...	1131	...	...	1244	...	...	1350	...	...	1446	...	...	1551	...	...

ama d.	...	1335	...	...	1435	...	...	1535	...	...	1635	...	...	1735	...	1835	...	...	1935	...	...	2039	...	...	2200
amatsu d.	...	|	1350	...	|	1450	...	|	1550	...	|	1650	...	|	1750	|	1858	...	|	1952	...	|	2059	2220	|
d.	...	1414	1414	...	1515	1515	...	1615	1615	...	1715	1715	...	1814	1814	1912	1917	...	2009	2012	...	2114	2117	2239	2235
ri d.	...	1541	1541	...	1645	1645	...	1745	1745	...	1847	1847	...	1947	1947	2052	2052	...	2156	2156	...	2255	2255	0019	0019
yama a.	1527	1616	1616	1632	1724	1724	1730	1827	1827	1842	1924	1924	1935	2028	2028	2132	2132	2148	2236	2236	2246	2331	2331	0055	0055
ma a.	1650	...	...	1749	...	...	1857	...	...	2009	...	...	2057	2204	...	...	...	2306	...	...	0005	...	...	...	...

ma d.	...	...	...	...	...	...	0533	...	...	0635	0635	0738	...	...	0840	...	...	0949	...	...	1042	...	...	1155	...
yama d.	...	0505	0505	...	0613	0613	0658	0720	0720	0810	0810	0903	0915	0915	1007	1021	1021	1118	1123	1123	1213	1220	1220	1317	...
ri d.	0437	0541	0541	...	0650	0650	...	0756	0756	0847	0847	...	0957	0957	...	1059	1059	...	1202	1202	...	1259	1259	...	...
d.	0606	0715	0714	0753	0827	0826	...	0926	0925	1020	1021	...	1133	1132	...	1234	1233	...	1335	1334	...	1435	1434	...	...
amatsu a.	|	|	0737	0811	|	0844	...	|	0944	1038	|	...	|	1154	...	|	1254	...	|	1355	...	|	1455	...	...
ama a.	0643	0751	...	...	0900	...	...	0959	...	...	1058	...	1210	...	...	1310	...	...	1410	...	...	1511	...	...	...

ma d.	...	...	1256	...	...	1358	...	...	1456	...	...	1603	...	...	1708	...	...	1809	...	1907	...	2018	...	2116	...
yama d.	1326	1326	1413	1423	1423	1520	1528	1528	1618	1628	1628	1726	1737	1737	1834	1841	1841	1927	1932	2030	2036	2135	2140	2238	2304
ri d.	1405	1405	...	1501	1501	...	1606	1606	...	1704	1704	...	1813	1813	...	1919	1919	...	2009	...	2111	...	2215	...	2343
d.	1535	1534	...	1635	1636	...	1735	1736	...	1835	1836	...	1938	1939	...	2052	2051	...	|	...	|	...	|	...	...
amatsu a.	|	1555	...	1655	|	...	1754	|	...	1854	|	...	1956	|	...	|	2109	...	2155	...	2258	...	0004	...	...
ama a.	1611	...	...	...	1711	...	...	1811	...	...	1911	...	...	2011	...	2129	...	...	...	...	...	...	...	...	...

hikoku — OKAYAMA and TAKAMATSU - KOCHI - NAKAMURA — 8127

Okayama d.	...	...	0708	...	...	0851	1005	1105	...	1205	*1305*	1405	1505	1605	...	1705	...	...	1805	1905	...	2005	...	2139
Takamatsu d.	0604	0720	|	...	0825	|	|	|	...	|	|	|	|	|	...	|	...	1826	|	|	...	|	2027	|
Awa Ikeda d.	0706	0829	0829	...	0924	1020	1122	1234	...	1332	*1425*	1523	1630	1734	...	1834	...	1935	1935	2029	...	2138	2138	2257
Kochi a.	0817	0939	0939	0953	1037	1130	1229	1341	1349	1442	1543	1639	1741	1848	1855	1945	1953	2050	2050	2146	2153	2250	2250	0004
Kubokawa ‡ d.	0927	...	...	1057	...	1249	...	...	1454	...	1651	1806	...	...	2010	...	2104	...	...	...	2300	...	...	...
Nakamura ‡ a.	1004	...	...	1132	...	1324	...	...	1531	...	1727	1846	...	...	2049	...	2139	...	...	...	2336	...	...	...

Nakamura ‡ d.	...	...	...	...	0608	0700	...	...	0924	...	1111	...	...	1324	...	...	1510	...	1647	...	...	*1745*	1934	...
Kubokawa ‡ d.	...	...	...	...	0648	0741	...	...	1004	...	1157	...	...	1402	...	...	1551	...	1728	...	...	*1824*	2012	...
Kochi d.	0451	0600	0700	0700	0801	0904	0913	1013	1113	1213	1302	1313	1413	1504	1513	1613	1713	1713	1834	1837	1934	1934	2115	2120
Awa Ikeda d.	0600	0709	0813	0813	0907	...	1020	1122	1223	1322	...	1424	1523	...	1620	1719	1823	1823	...	1946	2040	2040	...	2228
Takamatsu a.	0702	|	0921	|	|	...	|	|	|	|	...	|	|	...	|	|	|	1925	...	|	2142	|	...	2325
Okayama a.	...	0838	...	0938	1033	...	1140	1240	1340	1441	...	1541	1641	...	1741	1847	1941	...	...	2111	...	2157	...	...

Vest — TOTTORI and OKAYAMA - IZUMOSHI - YAMAGUCHI — 8130

												5													
Tottori d.	...	0704	...	0824	...	0944	...	...	1140	...	...	1338	...	...	1508	...	...	1742	...	1843	...	...	2049	...	...
Kurayoshi d.	...	0733	...	0858	...	1012	...	...	1209	...	...	1409	...	...	1539	...	...	1811	...	1914	...	...	2122	...	...
Okayama d.	...	|	0705	|	0804	|	0904	1004	|	1104	1204	|	1304	1404	|	1504	1604	|	1704	|	1804	1904	|	2005	2140
Niimi d.	...	|	0810	|	0908	|	1011	1107	|	1207	1312	|	1413	1508	|	1610	1707	|	1807	|	1907	2008	|	2111	2243
Yonago d.	0552	0808	0917	0930	1016	1047	1118	1219	1241	1318	1418	1441	1520	1620	1613	1723	1823	1846	1921	1948	2027	2123	2156	2219	2351
Matsue d.	0615	0836	0942	...	1040	1111	1141	1242	1303	1340	1443	1504	1544	1644	1637	1746	1847	1912	1946	...	2050	2146	...	2242	0013
Izumoshi d.	0640	0906	1010	...	1104	1136	1209	1307	1326	1408	1509	1527	1609	1716	1707	1813	1919	1941	2017	...	2115	2210	...	2307	0037
Hamada d.	0806	1014	...	...	...	1250	...	...	1438	▬	...	1641	...	...	1824	...	...	2050	...	...	...	...	...	...	...
Masuda d.	0840	1051	...	...	...	1325	...	...	1514	1616	...	1718	...	...	1903	...	...	2122	...	...	...	...	...	...	...
Tsuwano a.	0910	*1205*	...	...	...	1355	...	...	...	1656	...	1749	...	...	...	...	...	...	...	...	...	...	...	...	...
Yamaguchi a.	1000	*1316*	...	...	...	1443	...	...	...	1816	...	1837	...	...	...	...	...	...	...	...	...	...	...	...	...
Shin **Yamaguchi** a.	1014	*1354*	...	...	...	1457	...	...	...	1841	...	1851	...	...	...	...	...	...	...	...	...	...	...	...	...

Shin **Yamaguchi** d.	...	...	...	...	...	...	...	...	...	...	...	...	0852	...	*0912*	...	...	...	1253	...	*1329*	...	...	1712	...
Yamaguchi d.	...	...	...	...	...	...	...	...	...	...	...	...	0907	...	0946	...	...	...	1307	...	1358	...	...	1727	...
Tsuwano d.	...	...	...	...	...	...	...	...	...	...	...	...	0958	...	1110	...	...	...	1355	...	1519	...	...	1815	...
Masuda d.	...	...	...	...	...	0552	...	0702	...	...	...	...	1031	...	1150	1217	...	...	1430	...	1600	1607	...	1851	...
Hamada d.	...	...	...	...	...	0624	...	0738	...	...	...	...	1103	...	▬	1250	...	...	1503	...	▬	1640	...	1924	...
Izumoshi d.	0443	0531	...	0627	0723	0736	0831	0854	0934	1032	...	1134	1210	1234	1331	1359	1433	1530	1614	1630	1717	1748	1827	2035	...
Matsue d.	0508	0556	...	0658	0751	0800	0857	0924	1001	1057	...	1201	1235	1301	1400	1424	1459	1600	1645	1659	1743	1815	1907	2104	...
Yonago d.	0533	0622	0700	0724	0819	0825	0922	0950	1026	1125	1217	1226	1303	1325	1428	1450	1527	1628	1711	1726	1815	1841	1923	2127	2040
Niimi d.	0640	0729	|	0834	0934	|	1036	|	1136	1235	|	1337	...	1438	1537	|	1637	1737	|	1837	1925	|	2033	...	|
Okayama a.	0741	0834	|	0938	1035	|	1138	|	1238	1338	|	1438	...	1539	1638	|	1738	1838	|	1938	2024	|	2136	...	|
Kurayoshi d.	...	...	0733	...	...	0858	...	1027	...	...	1258	...	...	...	...	1521	...	...	1743	...	...	1914	...	...	2112
Tottori a.	...	...	0804	...	...	0927	...	1058	...	...	1327	...	...	...	...	1552	...	...	1816	...	...	1942	...	...	2140

Vest — KYOTO - KURAYOSHI — 8135

	1	3	5	7		9	11	13	
Kyoto d.	0706	0850	1052	1252	...	1452	1656	1935	...
Shin Osaka d.	0730	0916	1116	1316	...	1516	1719	2000	...
Osaka d.	0737	0924	1124	1324	...	1524	1726	2006	...
Himeji d.	0836	1022	1220	1420	...	1620	1822	2108	...
Kamigori ‡ d.	0902	1048	1243	1444	...	1644	1845	2131	...
Chizu ‡ d.	0944	1130	1323	1524	...	1725	1931	2214	...
Tottori d.	1014	1159	1353	1556	...	1753	2001	2242	...
Kurayoshi a.	1044	1229	1422	1623	...	...	2032	...	...

	2	4	6	8	10		12	14	
Kurayoshi d.	0608	0812	1014	1218	1425	...	1624	*1743*	...
Tottori d.	0639	0853	1046	1254	1454	...	1654	1840	...
Chizu ‡ d.	0708	0921	1115	1322	1522	...	1725	1908	...
Kamigori ‡ d.	0751	1003	1202	1401	1600	...	1804	1947	...
Himeji d.	0814	1025	1225	1424	1624	...	1828	2009	...
Osaka d.	0924	1120	1321	1521	1719	...	1936	2106	...
Shin Osaka d.	0929	1124	1326	1526	1724	...	1942	2112	...
Kyoto a.	0953	1147	1348	1548	1748	...	2006	2138	...

Vest — OKAYAMA - TOTTORI — 8140

Okayama d.	0647	0914	1105	1343	1724	1946	...	...	...
Kamigori ‡ d.	0725	0950	1142	1419	1803	2022	...	...	...
Chizu ‡ d.	0811	1036	1226	1501	1845	2104	...	...	...
Tottori a.	0838	1104	1253	1533	1917	2131	...	...	...

Tottori d.	0705	1002	1400	1621	1858	2035	...	...	...
Chizu ‡ d.	0734	1033	1427	1652	1932	2103	...	...	...
Kamigori ‡ d.	0820	1115	1510	1733	2014	2148	...	...	...
Okayama a.	0857	1148	1545	1811	2048	2222	...	...	...

Japan Rail Pass holders must pay a supplement to travel between these stations.

8145 KYOTO and OSAKA - KINOSAKI

JR

km																							
0	**Kyoto** d.	0732	0836	0925	1025	1125	...	1225	1325	...	1425	1525	...	1625	1728	...	1828	1928	...	2037	...	2137	...
76	Ayabe d.	0839	0945	1032	1135	1231	...	1340	1431	...	1535	1631	...	1735	1841	...	1945	2045	...	2149	...	2243	...
89	Fukuchiyama d.	0849	0953	1041	1144	1245	...	1349	1444	...	1544	1640	...	1743	1854	...	1954	2054	...	2158	...	2252	...
148	Toyooka d.	0943	...	...	...	1340	...	...	1541	...	...	...	...	...	1950	...	...	...	...	...	...	...	...
158	**Kinosaki** Onsen a.	0952	...	...	...	1349	...	...	1549	...	...	...	...	...	...	...	...	...	...	...	...	...	...

Kinosaki Onsen d.	...	...	...	...	...	...	...	...	...	...	1039	...	...	1232	...	...	...	...	...	1612	...	...	...
Toyooka d.	...	...	...	...	...	0742	...	...	...	...	1049	...	...	1242	...	...	...	...	...	1622	...	...	...
Fukuchiyama d.	...	0602	0657	...	0743	0838	...	0947	1044	...	1145	1244	...	1346	1444	...	1543	1644	...	1728	1825	...	1929
Ayabe d.	...	0612	0712	...	0753	0855	...	0958	1059	...	1156	1300	...	1356	1459	...	1556	1659	...	1740	1842	...	1942
Kyoto a.	...	0719	0821	...	0903	1007	...	1107	1207	...	1307	1407	...	1507	1607	...	1707	1808	...	1849	1953	...	2048

km																							
0	Shin **Osaka** d.	0806	...	0904	1005	...	1105	...	1205	1305	...	1405	...	1505	1705	...	1801	...	1906	2006	...	2107	...
4	**Osaka** d.	0812	...	0910	1012	...	1111	...	1211	1311	...	1411	...	1511	1711	...	1811	...	1912	2012	...	2110	...
118	Fukuchiyama d.	0955	...	1046	1146	...	1243	...	1350	1442	...	1546	...	1647	1853	...	2002	...	2055	2155	...	2255	...
178	Toyooka d.	1049	...	1143	1242	...	...	...	1445	...	...	1641	...	1747	...	...	2056	...	...	...	...	...	...
188	**Kinosaki** Onsen a.	1058	...	1152	1250	...	...	...	1454	...	...	1650	...	1756	...	...	...	...	...	...	...	...	...

Kinosaki Onsen d.	...	...	...	...	...	...	...	...	...	...	0933	...	1133	...	1330	...	1435	...	1530	...	...	1702	1818
Toyooka d.	...	...	...	...	...	...	...	...	...	...	0943	...	1143	...	1339	...	1445	...	1540	...	...	1712	1828
Fukuchiyama d.	...	0550	0652	...	0745	...	0840	...	0949	...	1046	...	1246	...	1442	...	1545	...	1646	...	1722	1817	1927
Osaka a.	...	0733	0839	...	0926	...	1019	...	1123	...	1223	...	1423	...	1621	...	1720	...	1820	...	1855	1949	2101
Shin **Osaka** a.	...	0739	0846	...	0932	...	1025	...	1129	...	1229	...	1429	...	1628	...	1726	...	1828	...	1901	1955	2106

8150 KANAZAWA - NAGOYA and OSAKA

IR, JR

km																								
0	**Osaka** d.	...	...	...	...	0710	...	0740	...	0758	0810	0840	0857	...	0912	0942	...	1012	1042	...	1112	1142	...	1212
4	Shin **Osaka** d.	...	...	...	...	0714	...	0744	...	0803	0814	0844	0901	...	0917	0946	...	1016	1046	...	1116	1146	...	1216
43	Kyoto d.	...	...	...	...	0738	...	0810	...	0831	0841	0909	0925	...	0942	1010	...	1040	1110	...	1140	1210	...	1240
	Nagoya 8175 d.	...	...	...	...	|	...	|	0750	|	|	|	1058	0850	|	|	0948	|	|	...	|	|	1148	|
	Gifu 8170 d.	...	...	...	...	|	...	|	0810	0955	|	|	1037↑	0911	|	|	1012	|	|	...	|	|	1212	|
	Maibara d.	...	...	...	...	|	0809	|	0859	0921↑	|	|	1005↑	0956	|	|	1056	|	|	1156	|	|	1256	|
137	Tsuruga d.	...	...	...	...	0830	0840	0902	0927	...	0938	|	...	1026	1035	|	1126	1134	|	1226	1234	|	1326	1334
191	Fukui d.	0600	0650	0720	0745	0902	0915	0937	1002	...	1012	1031	...	1101	1110	1133	1201	1208	1232	1301	1308	1335	1401	1408
268	**Kanazawa** 8155 a.	0650	0737	0810	0832	0946	1003	1023	1049	...	1102	1113	...	1148	1156	1217	1248	1256	1317	1348	1356	1420	1448	1456
334	Nanao d.	...	...	...	*0948*	...	...	...	...	...	...	*1216*	...	...	...	...	*1401*	1401	...	...	...	...	*1552*	*1552*
339	Wakura Onsen a.	...	...	...	*0954*	...	...	...	...	...	...	*1221*	...	...	...	...	*1407*	1407	...	...	...	...	*1557*	*1557*

km																								
	Osaka d.	1312	...	1412	...	1512	...	...	1612	1642	...	1712	1742	...	1812	1842	...	...	1927	...	2007	...	2054	...
	Shin **Osaka** d.	1316	...	1416	...	1516	...	...	1616	1646	...	1716	1746	...	1816	1846	...	...	1931	...	2012	...	2058	...
	Kyoto d.	1340	...	1440	...	1540	...	...	1640	1709	...	1740	1809	...	1840	1909	...	...	1954	...	2037	...	2121	...
0	**Nagoya** 8175 d.	|	1348	|	...	|	...	1548	|	|	...	|	|	1748	|	|	...	...	|	1948	|	...	|	...
30	Gifu 8170 d.	|	1410	|	...	|	...	1611	|	|	...	|	|	1811	|	|	...	...	|	2012	|	...	|	...
80	Maibara d.	|	1456	|	1556	|	...	1656	|	|	1756	|	|	1856	|	|	1956	...	|	2056	|	...	|	2156
126	Tsuruga d.	1434	1526	1534	1626	1634	...	1724	1732	|	1826	1834	|	1926	1933	2006	2026	...	2050	2126	2133	...	2218	2226
180	Fukui d.	1508	1601	1607	1701	1708	...	1759	1805	1830	1900	1908	1930	2001	2007	2038	2101	...	2124	2201	2208	...	2247	2301
257	**Kanazawa** 8155 a.	1556	1648	1653	1750	1756	...	1847	1852	1913	1950	1956	2015	2050	2056	2121	2148	...	2209	2250	2256	...	2329	2348
323	Nanao d.	...	...	...	...	*1932*	...	...	...	...	...	*2059*	...	...	...	...	...	...	...	...	...	...	...	...
328	Wakura Onsen a.	...	...	...	...	*1938*	...	...	...	...	...	*2105*	...	...	...	...	...	...	...	...	...	...	...	...

Wakura Onsen d.	...	...	...	...	...	...	...	...	*0630*	*0630*	...	...	...	...	...	*0841*	*0841*	...	...	1014	*1014*	...	...
Nanao d.	...	...	...	...	...	...	...	...	*0636*	*0636*	...	...	...	...	...	*0848*	*0848*	...	...	1020	*1020*	...	...
Kanazawa 8155 d.	0500	0535	0548	0607	0648	...	0645	0715	0748	0805	...	0815	0848	0903	...	0948	0953	1048	1056	1124	1148	1156	1248
Fukui d.	0548	0620	0639	0658	0739	...	0729	0803	0838	0848	...	0905	0936	0946	...	1036	1042	1136	1143	1209	1236	1244	1336
Tsuruga d.	0622	0653	0712	0736	0812	...	0801	0837	0912	|	...	0939	1010	|	...	1110	1116	1209	1216	|	1310	1316	1410
Maibara d.	0656	|	0752	|	0844	...	|	|	0950	|	...	|	1044	|	...	1150	|	1244	|	|	1350	|	1444
Gifu 8170 d.	...	|	0829	|	...	...	|	|	1026	|	...	|	...	|	...	1227	|	...	|	|	1427	|	...
Nagoya 8175 a.	...	|	0851	|	...	...	|	|	1048	|	...	|	...	|	...	1248	|	...	|	|	1448	|	...
Kyoto a.	...	0751	...	0837	...	...	0855	0934	...	1011	...	1037	...	1109	...	...	1209	...	1309	1337	...	1409	...
Shin **Osaka** a.	...	0817	...	0901	...	...	0919	0958	...	1035	...	1101	...	1132	...	...	1232	...	1332	1401	...	1432	...
Osaka a.	...	0822	...	0906	...	...	0925	1003	...	1039	...	1106	...	1137	...	...	1237	...	1337	1406	...	1437	...

Wakura Onsen d.	...	...	*1300*	*1300*	...	...	...	...	...	...	*1520*	*1520*	...	...	...	*1741*	*1741*	...	...	...	...	...	...
Nanao d.	...	...	*1306*	*1306*	...	...	...	...	...	...	*1527*	*1527*	...	...	...	*1747*	*1747*	...	...	...	...	...	...
Kanazawa 8155 d.	1348	1356	1417	1448	1457	1519	1548	1601	1613	...	1648	1656	...	1748	1756	1842	1853	1943	2006	2035	2108	2135	2206
Fukui d.	1436	1443	1507	1536	1544	1607	1636	1644	1706	...	1736	1744	...	1837	1842	1928	1942	2031	2056	2120	2155	2224	2253
Tsuruga d.	1510	1515	1541	1610	|	1642	1710	|	1741	...	1810	1815	...	1910	1915	2001	2015	2106	2129	2150	...	...	...
Maibara d.	1550	|	|	1650	|	|	1744	|	|	1802↓	1850	|	1825↓	1944	|	|	2055	|	2201	|	...	...	...
Gifu 8170 d.	1626	|	|	1726	|	|	...	|	|	1725↓	1925	|	1743	...	|	|	2129	|	...	|	...	...	...
Nagoya 8175 a.	1649	|	|	1749	|	|	...	|	|	1703	1946	|	|	...	|	|	2150	|	...	|	...	...	...
Kyoto a.	...	1609	1637	...	1707	1739	...	1809	1838	1850	...	1908	1922	...	2009	2054	...	2202	...	2244	...	...	...
Shin **Osaka** a.	...	1632	1701	...	1730	1803	...	1832	1902	1914	...	1932	1946	...	2032	2117	...	2225	...	2307	...	...	...
Osaka a.	...	1637	1706	...	1735	1809	...	1837	1907	1918	...	1937	1951	...	2037	2122	...	2230	...	2312	...	...	...

8160 OSAKA - SHINGU

JR W

km		1	3	5		7	9	11		13	15	17		19	21	23		25	27	29		31	
39	Kyoto d.	...	0836	...	...	*0936*	*1039*	...	...	...	...	...	...	...	...	1747	...	...	...	...	...	...	...
0	Shin **Osaka** d.	0733	0903	0932	...	1015	1115	1215	...	1315	1415	1515	...	1615	1715	1815	...	1915	2015	2115	...	2146	...
14	**Osaka** Tennoji d.	0759	0921	0949	...	1033	1132	1232	...	1332	1432	1532	...	1632	1736	1836	...	1936	2036	2136	...	2206	...
75	Wakayama d.	0853	1005	1036	...	1117	1214	1317	...	1417	1518	1618	...	1717	1822	1936	...	2025	2125	2224	...	2253	...
181	Shirahama d.	1012	1130	1203	...	1245	1327	1449	...	1538	1646	1747	...	1845	1946	2055	...	2156	2253	...	...	...	...
234	Kushimoto d.	1103	1224	...	...	...	1431	...	...	1631	...	1843	...	...	2036	...	...	2259	...	...	...	...	...
261	**Kii Katsuura** d.	1134	1257	...	...	...	1503	...	...	1703	...	1916	...	...	2109	...	...	2335	...	...	...	...	...
276	**Shingu** a.	1149	1313	...	...	...	1520	...	...	1719	...	1932	...	...	2134	...	...	2352	...	...	...	...	...

		2	4Ⓐ	4Ⓒ	6	8	10	12	14		16	18	20		22	24			26	28	30	32	34
Shingu d.	...	...	...	...	...	...	0630	...	0838	...	...	1028	...	...	1243	...	...	...	1418	...	1541	...	1755
Kii Katsuura d.	...	...	...	...	...	...	0648	...	0853	...	...	1045	...	...	1258	...	...	...	1435	...	1557	...	1810
Kushimoto d.	...	...	...	...	...	...	0721	...	0926	...	...	1120	...	...	1330	...	...	...	1512	...	1630	...	1843
Shirahama d.	...	...	...	...	0640	0712	0821	0920	1029	...	1118	1227	1317	...	1433	1518	...	...	1621	...	1728	1819	1945
Wakayama d.	...	0604	0626	0638	0809	0843	0950	1049	1150	...	1249	1350	1450	...	1553	1649	...	...	1748	1818	1850	1949	2106
Osaka Tennoji d.	...	0701	0725	0731	0900	0934	1034	1134	1235	...	1335	1435	1535	...	1635	1734	...	...	1834	1904	1934	2034	2149
Shin **Osaka** a.	...	0720	0751	0751	0922	0951	1051	1150	1250	...	1350	1450	1550	...	1650	1750	...	...	1851	1920	1950	2050	2206
Kyoto a.	...	...	...	...	...	...	1117	...	...	...	...	...	...	...	...	*1834*	...	...	...	...	2019	...	...

NAGOYA - SHINGU 8165

Central

	1	3	5	7						
Nagoya d.	0805	1001	1258	1947	...	...	...	...	...	...
Yokkaichi ‡ d.	0837	1037	1337	2019	...	...	...	...	...	...
Suzuka ‡ d.	0845	1046	1345	2027	...	...	...	...	...	...
Tsu ‡ d.	0901	1101	1400	2042	...	...	...	...	...	...
Matsusaka d.	0916	1116	1416	2057	...	...	...	...	...	...
Taki d.	0924	1129	1424	2104	...	...	...	...	...	...
Kumano Shi d.	1114	1318	1605	2253	...	...	...	...	...	...
Shingu a.	1134	1337	1624	2314	...	...	...	...	...	...
Kii Katsuura a.	1156	1356	1642	...	...	...	...	...	...	...

	2	4	6	8						
Kii Katsuura d.	...	0855	1224	1711	...	...	...	...	...	...
Shingu d.	0620	0913	1244	1730	...	...	...	...	...	...
Kumano Shi d.	0640	0933	1305	1750	...	...	...	...	...	...
Taki d.	0819	1118	1449	1931	...	...	...	...	...	...
Matsusaka d.	0826	1126	1456	1938	...	...	...	...	...	...
Tsu ‡ d.	0841	1142	1512	1954	...	...	...	...	...	...
Suzuka ‡ d.	0854	1154	1525	2006	...	...	...	...	...	...
Yokkaichi ‡ d.	0904	1204	1534	2015	...	...	...	...	...	...
Nagoya a.	0941	1241	1610	2049	...	...	...	...	...	...

Japan Rail Pass holders must pay a supplement to travel between these stations.

NAGOYA - TOYAMA 8170

Central, JR West

Nagoya d.	0745	0843	0939	1048	1143	1248	1448	1543	1743	1943
Gifu 8150 d.	0805	0903	1010	1108	1206	1308	1508	1606	1805	2006
Mino Ota d.	0826	0923	1032	1129	1226	1328	1529	1629	1829	2030
Gero d.	0919	1014	1131	1227	1324	1423	1626	1733	1933	2130
Takayama d.	1002	1100	1220	1315	1408	1510	1716	1817	2018	2215
Hida Furukawa d.	...	1113	1233	1328	...	1524	1731	...	...	...
Toyama a.	...	1229	...	1445	...	1636	1852	...	...	...

Toyama d.	...	...	0800	0952	...	...	1302	...	...	1713
Hida Furukawa d.	...	...	0918	1106	...	1306	1419	...	...	1826
Takayama d.	0646	0800	0938	1124	1233	1330	1439	1536	1644	1846
Gero d.	0732	0845	1026	1211	1318	1418	1525	1621	1727	1928
Mino Ota d.	0827	0948	1119	1316	1420	1519	1619	1715	1818	2020
Gifu 8150 d.	0852	1012	1141	1341	1441	1541	1641	1741	1841	2043
Nagoya a.	0913	1033	1202	1402	1502	1602	1702	1802	1903	2102

NIIGATA - NAOETSU - JOETSUMYOKO 8172

East

	LEX	*LEX*	*LEX*			*LEX*		*LEX*	[R]	
Niigata d.	0737	1021	1304	1522	1702	1624	1758	2002	2100	...
Nagaoka d.	0828	1117	1355	1626	1804	1715	1901	2054	2203	...
Naoetsu d.	0925	1212	1449	1739	1910	1809	2006	2149	2303	...
Joetsumyoko ‡ a.	0939	1225	1504	1754	1927	1822		2203	...	

	[R]	*LEX*			*LEX*	*LEX*	*LEX*		*LEX*	
Joetsumyoko ‡ d.	...	0725	...	0900	1033	1307	1726	1807	2128	...
Naoetsu d.	0615	0741	0831	0921	1047	1322	1740	1840	2142	...
Nagaoka d.	0722	0834	0935	1027	1140	1415	1834	1952	2233	...
Niigata a.	0831	0925	1033	1127	1230	1507	1925	2053	2225	...

Japan Rail Pass holders must pay a supplement to travel to / from this station.

NAGOYA - NAGANO 8175

Central

Nagoya 8150 d.	0700	0800	...	0900	1000	...	1100	1200	...	1300	1400	...	1500	1600	...	1740	1840	...	1940	...	...	...	...
Nakatsugawa d.	0750	0850	...	0950	1050	...	1150	1250	...	1350	1450	...	1550	1650	...	1830	1930	...	2032	...	...	...	...
Kiso Fukushima d.	0829	0925	...	1025	1126	...	1226	1325	...	1425	1525	...	1626	1726	...	1907	2007	...	2110	...	...	...	...
Shiojiri d.	0859	0956	...	1055	1155	...	1255	1354	...	1454	1554	...	1655	1755	...	1936	2035	...	2138	...	...	...	...
Matsumoto d.	0909	1007	...	1105	1205	...	1305	1404	...	1504	1604	...	1705	1806	...	1946	2046	...	2149	...	...	...	...
Nagano a.	1001	1058	...	1157	1254	...	1353	1456	...	1555	1655	...	1753	1858	...	2039	2134	...	2239	...	...	...	...

no d.	...	0609	0744	...	0900	1000	...	1100	1201	...	1300	1404	...	1500	1600	...	1700	1811	...	1940	...	...	...
umoto d.	...	0704	0836	...	0951	1050	...	1153	1253	...	1352	1453	...	1553	1653	...	1751	1906	...	2031	...	...	...
iri d.	...	0714	0846	...	1003	1103	...	1203	1303	...	1403	1503	...	1603	1703	...	1803	1919	...	2041	...	...	...
Fukushima d.	...	0743	0913	...	1030	1130	...	1230	1330	...	1430	1530	...	1630	1730	...	1830	1948	...	2108	...	...	...
tsugawa d.	...	0822	0950	...	1106	1206	...	1306	1406	...	1507	1607	...	1709	1809	...	1909	2026	...	2144	...	...	...
ya 8150 a.	...	0917	1045	...	1201	1301	...	1401	1501	...	1601	1701	...	1805	1905	...	2005	2121	...	2234	...	...	...

SHIZUOKA - KOFU 8180

Central

Shizuoka d.	0816	0940	1140	1340	1540	1740	1940	...	...	...
Fuji d.	0844	1014	1211	1411	1611	1811	2011	...	...	...
Kofu a.	1028	1208	1402	1602	1802	1959	2204	...	...	...

Kofu d.	0624	0844	1043	1237	1435	1636	1836	...	...	...
Fuji d.	0811	1037	1234	1429	1629	1828	2032	...	...	...
Shizuoka a.	0837	1102	1301	1456	1656	1855	2059	...	...	...

TOKYO - KOFU - MATSUMOTO 8185

East

		B																						
Tokyo Shinjuku d.	0700	0730	0800	0830	0900	1000	1100	1200	1300	1400	1500	...	1600	...	1700	1730	1800	...	1900	...	2000	2100	...	...
Hachioji d.	0729	0803	0833	0908	0939	1034	1130	1231	1331	1430	1531	...	1631	...	1734	1808	1837	...	1935	...	2034	2133	...	...
Kofu d.	0829	0908	0929	1016	1039	1129	1232	1329	1431	1524	1632	...	1728	...	1834	1915	1936	...	2036	...	2131	2240	...	...
Chino d.	0908	0952	1007	1059	1124	1204	1314	1407	1515	1600	1716	...	1804	...	1916	1958	2012	...	2121	...	2208	2324	...	...
Kami Suwa d.	0915	0957	1012	1104	1130	1209	1319	1412	1521	1605	1722	...	1809	...	1922	2004	2017	...	2126	...	2214	2329	...	...
Shiojiri d.	0931	1015	1029	1119	1146	|	1336	1426	1537	|	1738	...	1825	...	1940	2021	2033	...	2143	...	2229	2346	...	...
Matsumoto a.	0939	1023	1038	1128	1156	1231	1346	1435	1546	1626	1748	...	1834	...	1950	2031	2042	...	2152	...	2238	2355	...	...

																A								
umoto d.	...	0608	0651	0800	0851	...	0914	0954	1108	1200	...	1302	1347	...	1449	1519	1547	1658	...	1718	1835	1921	2000	...
iri d.	...	0617	0659	0809	0900	...	0924	1003	|	1208	...	1311	1356	...	1458	1527	1555	1707	...	1727	1843	1930	2008	...
Suwa d.	...	0634	0713	0825	0915	...	0941	1021	1130	1225	...	1328	1413	...	1512	1544	1615	1722	...	1744	1859	1946	2025	...
) d.	...	0639	0719	0831	0921	...	0946	1026	1135	1230	...	1333	1419	...	1518	1550	1620	1728	...	1750	1905	1951	2031	...
d.	...	0724	0756	0910	1003	...	1031	1106	1211	1312	...	1409	1503	...	1555	1632	1702	1805	...	1833	1942	2030	2109	...
ioji d.	...	0831	0851	1005	1104	...	1133	1204	1305	1410	...	1504	1601	...	1650	1732	1801	1902	...	1934	2036	2135	2206	...
o Shinjuku a.	...	0914	0926	1040	1136	...	1204	1233	1333	1441	...	1533	1634	...	1726	1807	1836	1935	...	2009	2106	2207	2236	...

	C										
Tokyo Shinjuku d.	1030	1130	1230	1330	1430	1530	1630	1830	1930	2200	2300
Hachioji d.	1103	1202	1302	1402	1502	1602	1704	1906	2008	2234	2336
Kofu d.	1208	1310	1408	1509	1608	1709	1809	2012	2113	2341	0040

	D										
Kofu d.	0708	0812	0929	1129	1229	1329	1425	1527	1610	1727	1856
Hachioji d.	0821	0919	1033	1233	1333	1433	1531	1630	1714	1832	2003
Tokyo Shinjuku a.	0904	0956	1104	1305	1405	1504	1603	1707	1751	1909	2037

Some trains run on a slightly different schedule on Ⓒ. **A** - From Minami Otari dep. 1422. **B** - To Minami Otari arr. 1142. **C** - Aditional trip 0930. **D** - Additional trip 2002.

TOKYO - IZUKYU SHIMODA and SHUZENJI 8195

East

			[R]		ⒸB	ⒸD	[R]			[R]
Tokyo d.	0900	0900	0925j	1000	1030	1030	1100	1200	1200	1300
Yokohama d.	0924	0924	0959	1024	1054	1054	1124	1224	1224	1324
Odawara d.	1002	1002	|	1102	1132	1132	|	1301	1301	|
Atami d.	1023	1025	1056	1122	1154	1156	1219	1323	1325	1419
Ito ‡ d.	1047	|	1118	1146	1216	|	1237	1346	|	1442
Izukyu Shimoda ‡ a.	1136	|	1215	1236	1324	|	1329	1448	|	1541
Mishima ‡ d.	...	1040	...	...	...	1211	...	...	1340	...
Shuzenji ‡ a.	...	1108	...	...	...	1239	...	...	1406	...

	Ⓖ	[R]				[R]		C	[R]	Ⓒ
Shuzenji ‡ d.	...	...	...	1235	...	...	...	1539	...	A
Mishima ‡ d.	...	...	...	1305	...	...	...	1606	...	...
Izukyu Shimoda ‡ d.	...	1006	1208	|	1302	1413	1504	|	1605	1649
Ito ‡ d.	1004	1105	1305	|	1406	1510	1602	|	1700	1805
Atami d.	1032	1128	1332	1332	1429	1533	1629	1629	1726	1830
Odawara d.	1050	1146	1349	1349	1449	|	1646	1646	|	1848
Yokohama d.	1129	1222	1426	1426	1526	1627	1723	1723	1824	1934
Tokyo a.	1154	1241	1449	1449	1549	1649	1746	1746	1859j	1958

Additional trips on Ⓒ at 1135[R], 1342.
Additional trip on Ⓒ at 1330.
C – Additional trip on Ⓒ at 1418.
D – Additional trip on ⑥ at 1330.
j – Tokyo **Shinjuku**.
‡ – Japan Rail Pass holders must pay a supplement to travel between these stations.

TOKYO - AWA KAMOGAWA 8200

East

Tokyo d.	0715	0900	1000	1100	1300	1500	1700	1800	1900	2100	2200
Soga d.	0753	0935	1033	1134	1334	1534	1733	1834	1935	2134	2232
Oami d.	0805	0947	1046	1146	1346	1546	1745	1848	1949	2148	2246
Mobara d.	0813	0955	1054	1154	1353	1553	1753	1856	1957	2158	2254
Kazusa Ichinomiya d.	0820	1002	1105	1202	1401	1601	1800	1908	2008	2206	2301
Katsuura a.	0846	1030	1130	1227	1426	1625	1832	...	2033	2230	2326
Awa Kamogawa a.	...	1054	1155	1252	1453	...	...	...	...	...	...

Awa Kamogawa d.	...	0738	0838	...	1137	1407	1534	1638	...	...	...
Katsuura d.	0726	0808	0905	1009	1206	1436	1559	1704	1811	...	2007
Kazusa Ichinomiya d.	0753	0833	0930	1034	1234	1502	1631	1738	1836	1929	2039
Mobara d.	0759	0839	0937	1041	1241	1508	1638	1744	1842	1936	2045
Oami d.	0810	0847	0945	1049	1249	1516	1646	1752	1850	1948	2053
Soga d.	0824	0902	1002	1102	1302	1531	1700	1805	1903	2001	2106
Tokyo a.	0859	0934	1036	1135	1335	1603	1734	1840	1936	2034	2139

8205 TOKYO - MANZA KAZAWAGUCHI and MAEBASHI

JR

km		Ⓒ			[R]	[R]	Ⓐ[R]	Ⓒ	Ⓐ	Ⓐ[R]	Ⓐ[R]
0	**Tokyo** Ueno ... d.	0900	1000	1212	1900	2000	2100	2129**j**	2129**j**	2200	2250
27	Omiya ... d.	0926	1026	1237	1925	2025	2124	2201	2201	2227	2316
62	Kumagaya ... d.	0952	1052	1302	1951	2053	2151	2228	2228	2254	2342
102	**Takasaki** ... d.	1021	1123	1335	2022	2126	2221	2301	2301	2326	0012
164	**Naganohara Kusatsuguchi** . a.	1126	1231	1441	|	|	|	|	|	|	...
112	**Maebashi** ... a.	...	...	...	*2046*	2136	*2247*	2313	2313	2337	...

	Ⓐ[R]	Ⓐ[R]	Ⓒ		Ⓒ		Ⓒ		Ⓐ
Maebashi ... d.	0726	*0748***k**	*0748***k**	0835	0908	...	...	...	1734**k**
Naganohara Kusatsuguchi d.	|	|	|	|	|	1102	1356	1543	|
Takasaki ... d.	0739	0810	0810	0848	0922	1206	1503	1646	1741
Kumagaya ... d.	0810	0842	0842	0920	0953	1238	1530	1716	1810
Omiya ... d.	0841	0912	0912	0951	1022	1306	1600	1744	1837
Tokyo Ueno ... a.	0911**j**	0939	0939	1014	1054**j**	1331	1624	1809	1900

j – Tokyo **Shinjuku**. **k** –Shim-Maebashi.

8210 TOKYO - NIKKO

JR

km		[R]	[R]	[R]	[R]						
0	**Tokyo** Shinjuku ... d.	0730	1031	1301	1732	...	...	...	...	...	...
27	Omiya ... d.	0802	1102	1332	1802	...	...	...	...	...	...
135	Tobu **Nikko** ... ‡ d.	0929	|	|	|	...	...	...	...	...	...
140	**Kinugawa** Onsen ... ‡ a.	...	1238	1512	1940	...	...	...	...	...	...

	[R]	[R]	[R]	[R]						
Kinugawa Onsen . ‡ d.	0813	1038	1505	...	...	...	...	...	...	...
Tobu **Nikko** ... ‡ d.	|	|	|	1639	...	...	...	...	...	...
Omiya ... d.	0949	1217	1646	1804	...	...	...	...	...	...
Tokyo Shinjuku ... a.	1018	1248	1719	1836	...	...	...	...	...	...

‡ – Japan Rail Pass holders must pay a supplement to travel to/from this station.

8215 TOKYO - SENDAI

JR

km	All trains [R]																								
	Tokyo Shinagawa ... d.	0644	...	...	...	...	...	...	0944	...	1014	1044	1114	...	1144	1214	1244	1314	...	1344	1414	1444	...
0	**Tokyo** Ueno ... d.	0700	0730	0800	...	0830	0900	0930	1000	...	1030	1100	1130	...	1200	1230	1300	1330	...	1400	1430	1500	...
67	Tsuchiura ... d.	0742	0818	0850	...	0916	|	1016	|	...	1115	|	1215	...	|	1313	|	1413	...	|	1513	|	...
118	Mito ... d.	0811	0850	0919	...	0950	1016	1048	1106	...	1148	1207	1248	...	1307	1345	1407	1445	...	1507	1546	1607	...
124	Katsuta ... d.	0817	0855	0925	...	0955	1021	1053	1111	...	1153	1212	1252	...	1312	1350	1412	1450	...	1512	1551	1612	...
150	Hitachi ... d.	0834	0915	0941	...	...	1040	...	1126	...	...	1232	...	...	1327	...	1430	1511	...	1527	...	1630	...
212	Iwaki ... △ a.	0918	...	1023	...	...	1124	...	1207	...	...	1315	...	...	1409	...	1514	...	...	1609	...	1714	...
290	Haranomachi ... △ d.	...	...	...	...	...	...	...	...	...	...	...	...	...	...	...	...	...	...	...	...	...	...
361	**Sendai** (Honshu) ... △ a.	...	...	...	...	...	...	...	...	...	...	...	...	...	...	...	...	...	...	...	...	...	...

All trains [R]																							
Tokyo Shinagawa ... d.	...	1544	1614	1644	...	...	1744	...	...	1844	...	...	...	1944	...	...	2044	...	...	...	2144	...	...
Tokyo Ueno ... d.	...	1600	1630	1700	1730	...	1800	1815	1830	1900	...	1915	1930	2000	2015	2030	2100	2115	2130	...	2200	2215	2230
Tsuchiura ... d.	...	|	1711	|	1816	...	1839	1905	1915	1939	...	2008	2015	2040	2107	2117	2142	2208	2216	...	2239	2310	2321
Mito ... d.	...	1706	1744	1808	1848	...	1909	...	1947	2009	...	...	2051	2110	2142	2150	2211	...	2250	...	2312	2342	2355
Katsuta ... d.	...	1712	1749	1813	1853	...	1914	...	1952	2014	...	...	2056	2118	2147	2156	2217	...	2256	...	2317	2347	2359
Hitachi ... d.	...	1730	...	1831	...	...	1932	...	2012	2032	...	...	...	2135	...	2214	2235	...	2316	...	...	...	...
Iwaki ... △ a.	...	1811	...	1915	...	...	2015	...	...	2116	...	...	...	2217	...	2256	2319	...	...	...	...	...	...
Haranomachi ... △ d.	...	...	...	...	...	...	...	...	...	...	...	...	...	...	...	...	...	...	...	...	...	...	...
Sendai (Honshu) ... △ a.	...	...	...	...	...	...	...	...	...	...	...	...	...	...	...	...	...	...	...	...	...	...	...

All trains [R]				Ⓐ									Ⓒ										
Sendai (Honshu) ... △ d.	...	...	...	...	...	...	...	...	...	...	...	...	...	...	...	...	...	...	...	...	...	...	...
Haranomachi ... △ d.	...	...	...	...	...	...	...	...	...	...	...	...	...	...	...	...	...	...	...	...	...	...	...
Iwaki ... △ d.	...	...	...	...	...	...	...	0613	...	...	0703	0739	...	0818	...	0920	...	1017	...	...	1120	...	...
Hitachi ... d.	...	...	...	...	0542	...	...	0701	0719	...	0745	0822	...	0901	...	1002	1027	1102	...	...	1202	...	...
Katsuta ... d.	...	...	0539	0553	0602	0620	0700	0720	0739	...	0804	0841	0904	0921	0947	1021	1047	1121	...	1147	1221	1247	...
Mito ... d.	...	...	0545	0559	0608	0626	0706	0726	0745	...	0810	0848	0911	0927	0953	1027	1053	1127	...	1153	1227	1253	...
Tsuchiura ... d.	...	0606	0620	0631	0640	0700	0739	0758	0819	...	0839	0920	0942	|	1025	|	1125	|	...	1225	|	1325	...
Tokyo Ueno ... a.	...	0705	0723	0734	0746	0804	0843	0858	0910	...	0935	1006	1023	1037	1108	1137	1208	1237	...	1308	1337	1408	...
Tokyo Shinagawa ... a.	...	...	...	...	...	...	...	0913	...	...	0952	1021	...	1051	1122	1151	1222	1251	...	1322	1351	1422	...

All trains [R]																							
Sendai (Honshu) ... △ d.	...	...	...	...	...	...	...	...	...	...	...	...	...	...	...	...	...	...	...	...	...	...	...
Haranomachi ... △ d.	...	...	...	...	...	...	...	...	...	...	...	...	...	...	...	...	...	...	...	...	...	...	...
Iwaki ... △ d.	...	...	1323	...	...	1418	...	1518	...	...	...	1618	...	1721	...	...	...	1816	...	1918	...	...	2016
Hitachi ... d.	...	...	1405	...	...	1502	...	1602	...	1626	...	1702	...	1803	...	...	...	1900	...	2000	...	...	2100
Katsuta ... d.	...	1347	1421	1447	...	1521	1547	1621	...	1647	...	1721	1747	1821	...	1847	...	1921	1947	2021	...	2047	2121
Mito ... d.	...	1353	1427	1453	...	1527	1553	1627	...	1653	...	1727	1753	1827	...	1853	...	1927	1953	2027	...	2053	2127
Tsuchiura ... d.	...	1425	|	1525	...	|	1625	|	...	1725	...	|	1824	|	...	1924	...	|	2024	|	...	2124	2156
Tokyo Ueno ... a.	...	1509	1537	1609	...	1639	1706	1738	...	1807	...	1839	1907	1938	...	2006	...	2037	2106	2139	...	2205	2238
Tokyo Shinagawa ... a.	...	1522	1551	1623	...	1653	...	1752	...	...	...	1852	...	1952	...	...	...	2052	...	2154	...	...	2253

△ – Limited Express services Iwaki - Sendai and v.v. are suspended due to earthquake damage. Some local services may be available.

8220 NIIGATA - AOMORI - HAKODATE

JR E

km				LEX	LEX	LEX	LEX	LEX	LEX	LEX	LEX	LEX
0	**Niigata** ... d.	...	...	...	0827	...	1058	1233	1501	...	1717	2120
168	Sakata ... d.	0535	0634	...	1039	...	1305	1441	1731	...	1931	2329
273	Akita ... d.	0725	0828	0834	1204	1241	...	1604	1841	1932	...	...
377	Odate ... d.	...	...	1004	...	1414	...	...	...	2103	...	...
421	Hirosaki ... d.	...	...	1042	...	1452	...	...	...	2142	...	...
455	Shin Aomori ... d.	...	...	1111	...	1523	...	...	...	2211	...	...
459	**Aomori** ... d.	...	...	1117	...	1529	...	...	...	2216	...	...

	LEX	LEX	LEX	LEX	LEX	LEX	LEX	LEX	LEX	LEX
Aomori ... d.	...	...	...	...	0908	...	...	1242	...	1601
Shin Aomori ... d.	...	...	...	...	0912	...	...	1248	...	1607
Hirosaki ... d.	...	...	...	...	0939	...	...	1321	...	1634
Odate ... d.	...	...	...	...	1016	...	...	1400	...	1711
Akita ... d.	...	...	...	0915	1143	1258	...	1527	1635	1841
Sakata ... d.	0528	0646	0901	1047	...	1426	1557	...	1804	...
Niigata ... a.	0731	0851	1104	1257	...	1632	1801	...	2007	...

8225 HAKODATE and MURORAN - SAPPORO

JR Hokka

km				1		3		5	7	9		11	13			15			17	19	21	23
0	**Hakodate** ... d.	...	...	0610	...	0728	...	0854	1005	1048	...	1216	1351	...	...	1456	...	...	1635	1751	1849	1955
18	Shin **Hakodate Hokuto** ... **8020** d.	...	...	0628	...	0748	...	0913	1024	1109	...	1234	1411	...	...	1515	...	...	1655	1811	1909	2014
112	Oshamambe ... d.	...	...	0734	...	0901	...	1021	1132	1220	...	1343	1522	...	...	1625	...	...	1808	1923	2016	2122
154	Toya ... d.	...	...	0758	...	0928	...	1047	1156	1246	...	1409	1548	...	...	1649	...	...	1833	1950	2042	2147
	Muroran ... d.	0527	0656	|	...	|	...	|	|	|	1348	|	|	1626	...	|	...	1812	|	|	|	|
190	Higashi-Muroran ... d.	0541	0710	0825	0923	0956	...	1115	1223	1315	1400	1437	1615	1638	...	1717	...	1824	1905	2019	2110	2214
207	Noboribetsu ... d.	0556	0724	0837	0937	1009	...	1128	1235	1328	1415	1450	1628	1653	...	1730	...	1839	1918	2032	2122	2227
248	Tomakomai ... d.	0622	0749	0900	1002	1035	...	1153	1259	1353	1441	1514	1652	1719	...	1755	...	1904	1943	2057	2146	2251
275	Minami Chitose ... d.	0641	0807	0916	1022	1052	...	1211	1316	1410	1459	1530	1708	1737	...	1811	...	1923	2000	2114	2203	2307
319	**Sapporo** ... a.	0714	0838	0948	1101	1127	...	1241	1348	1441	1534	1604	1741	1811	...	1841	...	1955	2034	2148	2233	2340

km		2	4		6	8	10		12			14	16	18		20	22			24		
0	**Sapporo** ... d.	0600	0652	0730	0839	0930	1044	1124	1215	...	1355	1332	1444	1539	1602	1632	1810	1854	...	2000	2200	...
44	Minami Chitose ... d.	0628	0702	0759	0911	1000	1115	1158	1245	...	1427	1401	1515	1611	1632	1705	1841	1927	...	2028	2234	...
71	Tomakomai ... d.	0644	0739	0818	0929	1018	1132	1219	1302	...	1445	1419	1533	1627	1651	1725	1858	1945	...	2044	2253	...
112	Noboribetsu ... d.	|	0804	0845	0955	1043	1156	1245	1327	...	1509	1443	1557	1654	1721	1750	1923	2011	...	2108	2309	...
129	Higashi-Muroran ... d.	0718	0817	0859	1008	1057	1210	1300	1340	...	1524	1456	1610	1708	1737	1803	1936	2026	...	2120	2334	...
136	**Muroran** ... a.	|	|	...	|	|	|	1311	|	...	1536	|	|	|	1748	|	|	2037	...	|	2346	...
	Toya ... d.	|	0844	...	1036	1124	1235	...	1408	...	...	1525	1636	1734	...	1831	2004	...	...	2146	...	...
	Oshamambe ... d.	0806	0944	...	1104	1152	1302	...	1436	...	...	1549	1701	1802	...	1857	2031	...	...	2211	...	...
	Shin **Hakodate Hokuto** ... **8020** d.	0912	1024	...	1219	1308	1411	...	1552	...	...	1655	1810	1909	...	2005	2140	...	...	2317	...	...
	Hakodate ... a.	0927	1038	...	1234	1324	1425	...	1608	...	...	1709	1825	1924	...	2020	2155	...	...	2331	...	...

SAPPORO - KUSHIRO — 8230

Hokkaido

Sapporo d.	0700	0754	0854	1024	1153	1416	1608	1724	1832	1940	2104
Minami Chitose d.	0730	0826	0926	1056	1226	1448	1641	1756	1905	2011	2132
Obihiro d.	0926	1032	1140	1310	1422	1700	1900	2018	2121	2220	2341
Kushiro a.	1100	...	1320	...	1556	1839	...	2159	...	2355	...

Kushiro d.	...	0626	...	0823	...	1124	...	1339	1614	...	1900
Obihiro d.	0645	0802	0847	0957	1101	1257	1330	1520	1747	1922	2034
Minami Chitose d.	0900	1014	1108	1153	1324	1507	1544	1722	1944	2143	2228
Sapporo a.	0933	1045	1140	1226	1356	1541	1619	1756	2015	2215	2258

SAPPORO - WAKKANAI and ABASHIRI — 8235

Hokkaido

Sapporo d.	0721	0748	0941	1230	1508	1730	1748	...	...	...
Takikawa d.	0820	0842	1039	1331	1603	1829	1839	...	...	...
Asahikawa d.	0900	0917	1118	1411	1642	1908	1917	...	...	...
Wakkanai a.	|	1253	|	1822	|	|	2258	...	...	...
Kamikawa d.	0940	...	1201	...	1728	1953	...	...	...	...
Abashiri a.	1240	...	1506	...	2037	2301	...	...	...	...

Abashiri d.	0620	...	0923	1326	...	...	1718	...	...	...
Kamikawa d.	0924	...	1229	1629	...	...	2021	...	...	...
Wakkanai d.	|	0700	|	|	1344	1700	|	...	...	...
Asahikawa d.	1011	1041	1311	1713	1734	2045	2105	...	...	...
Takikawa d.	1047	1114	1347	1749	1810	2118	2140	...	...	...
Sapporo a.	1146	1206	1446	1847	1914	2209	2240	...	...	...

SHIN CHITOSE AIRPORT - SAPPORO - ASAHIKAWA — 8240

Hokkaido

Shin Chitose Airport d.	...	...	...	...	...	...	...	...	...	...	...	...	...	...	...	...	...	...	...	...	...	...	...	...
Minami Chitose d.	...	...	...	...	...	...	...	...	...	...	...	...	...	...	...	...	...	...	...	...	...	...	...	...
Sapporo d.	0635	0800	0825	0900	0930	...	1000	1100	1200	1300	1400	1430	1500	1600	1630	1700	1800	1830	1900	1930	2000	2100	2200	2305
Takikawa d.	0727	0852	0917	0952	1022	...	1052	1152	1252	1352	1452	1522	1552	1652	1722	1752	1852	1922	1952	2022	2052	2152	2252	2357
Asahikawa a.	0800	0925	0950	1025	1055	...	1125	1225	1325	1425	1525	1555	1625	1725	1754	1825	1925	1955	2025	2055	2125	2225	2325	0030

kawa d.	...	0518	0600	0645	0719	0755	0830	0900	...	1000	1100	1200	1300	1400	1430	1500	1530	16000	1630	1700	1800	1830	1900	2000	2200
awa d.	...	0550	0632	0717	0750	0827	0902	0932	...	1032	1132	1232	1332	1432	1502	1532	1602	1632	1702	1732	1832	1902	1932	2032	2232
oro a.	...	0643	0733	0826	0845	0920	0955	1025	...	1125	1224	1325	1425	1525	1555	1625	1655	1725	1755	1825	1925	1955	2025	2125	2325
ni Chitose a.	...	...	...	...	...	...	...	...	...	...	...	...	...	...	...	...	...	...	...	...	...	...	...	...	...
Chitose Airport a.	...	...	...	...	...	...	...	...	...	...	...	...	...	...	...	...	...	...	...	...	...	...	...	...	...

SUMMARY OF OVERNIGHT TRAINS — 8300

km			A [R]	B [R]						
	Takamatsu d.	...	...	2126	...	...	...	...	...	...
	Kojima d.	...	...	2201	...	...	...	...	...	...
0	**Izumoshi** d.	...	1855	|	...	...	...	...	...	...
33	Matsue d.	...	1927	|	...	...	...	...	...	...
62	Yonago d.	...	1956	|	...	...	...	...	...	...
140	Niimi d.	...	2120	|	...	...	...	...	...	...
221	**Okayama** a.	...	2230	2222	...	...	...	...	...	...
	Okayama d.	...	2234	2234	...	...	...	...	...	...
397	Osaka d.	...	0034	0034	...	...	...	...	...	...
773	Shizuoka d.	...	0440	0440	...	...	...	...	...	...
925	Yokohama d.	...	0645	0645	...	...	...	...	...	...
954	**Tokyo** a.	...	0708	0708	...	...	...	...	...	...

					B [R]	A [R]			
Tokyo d.	...	...	...	...	2200	2200	...	...	...
Yokohama d.	...	...	...	...	2224	2224	...	...	...
Shiuoka a.	...	...	...	...	0020	0020	...	...	...
Osaka d.	...	...	...	...	|	|	...	...	...
Okayama a.	...	...	...	...	0627	0627	...	...	...
Okayama d.	...	...	...	...	0631	0634	...	...	...
Niimi d.	...	...	...	...	|	0744	...	...	...
Yonago d.	...	...	...	...	|	0905	...	...	...
Matsue d.	...	...	...	...	|	0931	...	...	...
Izumoshi a.	...	...	...	...	|	0958	...	...	...
Kojima d.	...	...	...	...	0653	...	...	...	...
Takamatsu a.	...	...	...	...	0727	...	...	...	...

SUNRISE IZUMO 🛏 1, 2 cl., (2) Izumoshi - Tokyo and v.v. B – SUNRISE SETO 🛏 1, 2 cl., (2) Takamatsu - Tokyo and v.v.
As well as De-lux, single and twin berth compartments both trains have *Nobinobi* – open-plan sleeping areas categorised as seats.

AIRPORT RAIL LINKS — 8400

3U CENTRAL JAPAN INTERNATIONAL AIRPORT

Limited Express [R] service Meitetsu Nagoya - Central Japan International Airport and v.v. *44 km.* Journey 30 minutes. (Frequent additional slower trains are available, not [R]). Operator: tsu.

Meitetsu Nagoya at 0600Ⓐ, 0602Ⓒ, 0628Ⓐ, 0630Ⓒ, 0648Ⓐ, 0653Ⓒ, 0720, 0750Ⓒ, 0751Ⓐ, 0820Ⓒ, 0823Ⓐ, 0850, 0920, 0950, 1020, 1050, 1120, 1150, 1220, 1250, 1320, 1350, 1420, 1520, 1550, 1620, 1650, 1719Ⓐ, 1720Ⓒ, 1749Ⓐ, 1750Ⓒ, 1819Ⓐ, 1820Ⓒ, 1849Ⓐ, 1850Ⓒ, 1919Ⓐ, 1920Ⓒ, 1949Ⓐ, 1950Ⓒ, 2019Ⓐ, 2020Ⓒ, 2049Ⓐ, 2050Ⓒ, 2119Ⓐ, 2120Ⓒ.

Central Japan International Airport at 0703Ⓐ, 0713Ⓒ, 0726Ⓐ, 0729Ⓒ, 0759Ⓒ, 0800Ⓐ, 0829Ⓒ, 0834Ⓐ, 0907, 0937, 1007, 1037, 1107, 1137, 1207, 1237, 1307, 1337, 1407, 1437, 1507, 1607, 1637, 1706Ⓐ, 1707Ⓒ, 1736Ⓐ, 1737Ⓒ, 1806Ⓐ, 1807Ⓒ, 1836Ⓐ, 1837Ⓒ, 1906Ⓐ, 1907Ⓒ, 1936Ⓐ, 1937Ⓒ, 2007, 2037, 2107, 2137, 2207.

SAI AIRPORT

UKA' Limited Express service Kyoto - Shin Osaka ■ - Kansai Airport and v.v. *100 km.* Journey 80 - 90 minutes. Operator: JR West.

Kyoto at 0545, 0621, 0644, 0714, 0745, 0817, 0848, 0930, 1000, 1030, 1100, 1130, 1200, 1230, 1300, 1330, 1400, 1430, 1500, 1530, 1600, 1630, 1700, 1730, 1800, 1830, 1900, 1930, 2000,

Kansai Airport at 0630, 0727, 0755, 0845, 0916, 0946, 1016, 1046, 1114, 1144 and ½ hourly until 1614, 1644, 1716, 1746, 1816, 1846, 1916, 1946, 2016, 2046, 2125, 2216.

Trains call at Shin Osaka 28 - 33 minutes after Kyoto and 45 - 50 minutes after Kansai Airport.

YO HANEDA AIRPORT

ed Express service Tokyo Shinagawa - Haneda Airport International Terminal △ and v.v. *14 km.* Journey 20 minutes. Operator: Keikyu Railway.

Tokyo Shinagawa at 0552 and every 10 - 15 minutes until 2300.

Haneda Airport International Terminal at 0530 and every 10 - 15 minutes until 2330.

Most trains continue to/from Haneda Aiport Domestic Terminal, journey 3 minutes.

ORAIL service Tokyo Hamamatsucho – Haneda Airport International Terminal□ and v.v. (JR pass valid) *14 km.* Journey 13 minutes(Haneda Express), 15 minutes, (rapid) 24 minutes (stopping). Operator: Tokyo Monorail Co Ltd.

Tokyo Hamamatsucho at 0458 and every 3 - 10 minutes until 0001.

Haneda Airport International Terminal at 0517 and every 3 - 10 minutes until 0010.

All trains continue to/from Haneda Aiport Domestic Terminal 1, journey 3 - 5 minutes and Aiport Domestic Terminal 2, journey 5 - 7 minutes.

YO NARITA AIRPORT

ITA EXPRESS' Limited Express [R] service Tokyo - Narita Airport Terminal 1 ▽ and v.v. *79 km.* Journey 55 minutes. Operator: JR East.

Tokyo at 0618, 0700, 0715, 0731, 0800, 0830, 0900, 1003, 1033, 1103, 1134, 1203, 1233, 1303, 1333, 1403, 1433, 1503, 1533, 1603, 1633, 1703, 1733, 1803, 1833, 1903, 2003.

Narita T1 at 0744, 0813, 0850, 0915, 0945, 1015, 1045, 1114, 1145, 1220, 1245, 1314, 1345, 1418, 1444, 1514, 1544, 1619, 1644, 1716, 1744, 1815, 1848, 1912, 1946, 2044, 2144.

Trains also call at Narita Airport Terminal two, 2/3 minutes before/after Terminal one. Additional slower trains(not [R]) are available about hourly each direction.

LINER' Limited Express [R] service Tokyo Ueno Keisei - Narita Airport Terminal one ▷ and v.v. *69 km.* Journey 45 minutes. Operator: Keisei Electric Railway.

Tokyo Ueno Keisei at 0558, 0630, 0650Ⓐ, 0654Ⓒ, 0710Ⓐ, 0716Ⓒ, 0732Ⓐ, 0736Ⓒ, 0752Ⓐ, 0756Ⓒ, 0817Ⓐ, 0819Ⓒ, 0843Ⓐ, 0846Ⓒ, 0920, 1000, 1040, 1100, 1140, 1220, 1300, 1400, 1440, 1500, 1520, 1540, 1600, 1620, 1640, 1700, 1740Ⓒ, 1745Ⓐ, 1820.

Narita Airport Terminal 1 at 0728Ⓐ, 0734Ⓒ, 0817Ⓐ, 0822Ⓒ, 0915Ⓒ, 0924Ⓐ, 0958, 1038, 1118, 1158, 1258, 1338, 1358, 1418, 1438, 1458, 1518, 1538, 1558, 1618, 1638, 1658, 1718Ⓒ, Ⓐ, 1738Ⓒ, 1740Ⓐ, 1810Ⓐ, 1818Ⓒ, 1848Ⓐ, 1858Ⓒ, 1930Ⓐ, 1938Ⓒ, 2010Ⓒ, 2011Ⓐ, 2038Ⓒ, 2043Ⓐ, 2109, 2149Ⓐ, 2150Ⓒ, 2230.

Trains also call at Narita Airport Terminal two, 3/5 minutes before/after Terminal one. Additional slower trains are available.

PORO SHIN CHITOSE AIRPORT

and Rapid service Sapporo - Shin Chitose Airport and v.v. *47 km* Journey 48minutes (local *) 38 minutes (rapid). All services call at Minami-Chitose 3/4 minutes before/after Shin Chitose rt. Operator: JR Hokkaido.

Sapporo at 0602*, 0616, 0631, 0643, 0703, 0716, 0733, 0748, 0805, 0820, 0835, 0850, 0905, 0920, 0935, 0950, 1005, 1020, 1035, 1050 and at the same minutes past the hour until 1805, , 1835, 1850, 1905, 1920, 1935, 1950, 2005*, 2015*, 2025, 2045, 2055*, 2110*, 2138*, 2151.

Shin Chitose Airport at 0656*, 0704*, 0723*, 0734*, 0748*, 0815, 0830, 0845, 0900, 0915, 0930, 0945, 1000, 1015, 1030, 1045 and at the same minutes past the hour until 2000, 2015, 2030, , 2104, 2116, 2130, 2150, 2205, 2215, 2235, 2253.

BEYOND EUROPE
North America

Introduction

The Beyond Europe section covers principal rail services in a different area of the world each month. There are six areas, each appearing twice yearly as follows:

India:	January and July editions
South East Asia and Australasia:	February and August editions
China:	March and September editions
Japan:	April and October editions
North America:	May and November editions
Africa and the Middle East:	June and December editions

The months have been chosen so that we can bring you up-to-date information for those countries which make seasonal changes.

Details of services in South America can be found in the European Rail Timetable April and October editions and schedules for South Korea in the May and November editions.

Contents

INDEX OF PLACES

by table number

CANADA

;al: **Ottawa** (GMT -5). 2016 Public Holidays: Jan. 1, Mar. 25, July 1, Sep. 5, Oct. 10, Nov. 11, Dec. 25.

›rincipal operator in Canada is Via Rail (Via Rail ✆ 1 888 842 7245. www.viarail.ca). Timings shown are the most recently available and are subject to alteration at any time, ›specially around public holidays. Details of other operators can be found in relevant tables. Unless otherwise noted all trains carry first and second class seated ›nodation. In Canada first class is called 'Via1' and second class is called 'Economy'. Most very long distance trains convey sleeping cars, and where this is the case it is ›ed in the footnotes. Almost all sleeping car accommodation in North America has two berths per compartment, some of which are en-suite, although the exact product ›ng varies by operator and route. Most trains also convey some form of catering, but again the actual service offered varies considerably. Tickets are available from staffed ›ns, websites and through authorised ticketing agents. A reservation is neccessary for travel on very long distance Via Rail trains, but generally not for corridor services such ›ontréal - Ottawa/Toronto and Toronto - Windsor/London/Sarnia.

›ail does not have any form of rail pass but it does offer discounts to Youths (12 - 25), Children, and Seniors (60+).

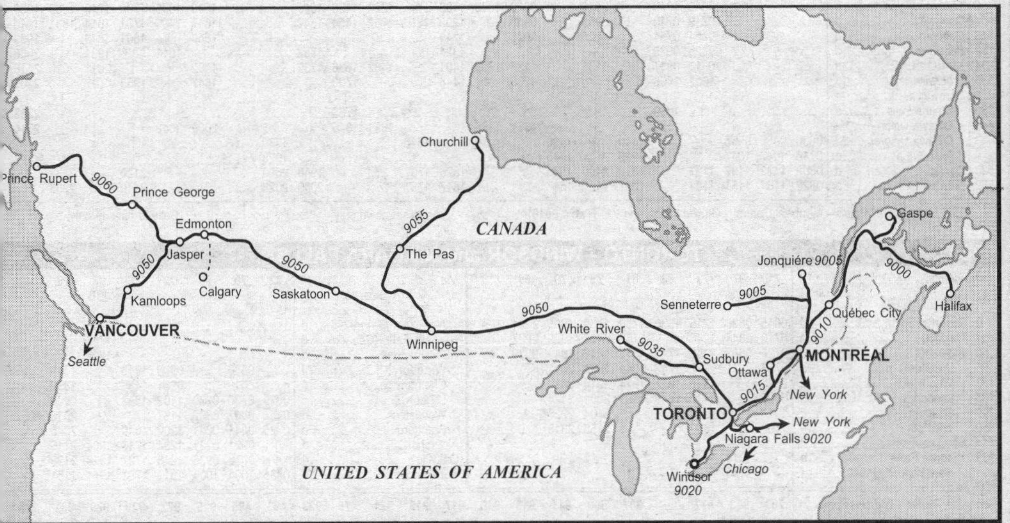

Rail — GASPÉ and HALIFAX — 9000

		15	17
		[R]	[R]
		③⑤⑦	③⑤⑦
		A	Z B
9	**Halifax** d.	1300	...
6	Truro d.	1431	...
2	Amherst d.	1608	...
5	**Moncton** d.	1717	...
5	**Moncton** d.	1732	...
6	Miramichi d.	1937	...
4	Campbellton d.	2318	...
0	**Gaspé** d.	|	1520
7	Percé d.	|	1639
8	Bonaventure d.	|	1930
5	Matapédia d.	2252	2252
5	Mont Joli d.	0126	0126
6	Rimouski d.	0201	0201
2	Rivière du Loup d.	0352	0352
0	**Sainte Foy 9010** a.	0613	0613
	Montréal Central **9010** a.	1003	1003

	16	14
	[R]	[R]
	③⑤⑦	③⑤⑦
	Z B	A
Montréal Central **9010** d.	1900	1900
Sainte Foy 9010 d.	2249	2249
Rivière du Loup d.	0113	0113
Rimouski d.	0301	0301
Mont Joli d.	0339	0339
Matapédia d.	0610	0610
Bonaventure d.	0909	|
Percé d.	1158	|
Gaspé a.	1317	|
Campbellton d.	...	0748
Miramichi d.	...	1123
Moncton a.	...	1323
Moncton d.	...	1338
Amherst d.	...	1442
Truro d.	...	1622
Halifax a.	...	1751

OCEAN – [2] Montréal - Halifax and v.v.
[2] Montréal - Gaspé and v.v.
During infrastructure work currently in progress, trains 16 and 17 will not be operating and train services between Matapédia and Gaspé will be suspended. As an alternative you can travel on trains 14 and 15 between Montréal and Matapédia.

Via Rail — JONQUIÈRE and SENNETERRE — 9005

km		604	606	600	602		
		[R] 2	[R] 2	[R] 2	[R] 2		
		②④	⑦	②④	⑦		
717	**Senneterre** d.	0545	0845	...	...	...	...
561	Clova d.	0750	1050	...	...	...	...
495	Parent d.	0850	1150	...	...	...	...
297	La Tuque d.	1153	1453	...	...	...	...
510	**Jonquière** d.	|	|	0810	1110	...	...
444	Chambord d.	|	|	0911	1211	...	...
341	Lac Édouard d.	|	|	1105	1405	...	...
251	Rivière à Pierre d.	|	|	1240	1540	...	...
217	**Hervey** a.	1325	1625	1350	1650	...	...
217	**Hervey** d.	1400	1700	1400	1700	...	...
170	Shawinigan d.	1448	1748	1448	1748	...	...
0	**Montréal** Central a.	1715	2015	1715	2015	...	...

		601	605	603	607		
		[R] 2	[R] 2	[R] 2	[R] 2		
		①③	⑤	①③	⑤		
Montréal Central d.	...	0815	0910	0815	0910	...	...
Shawinigan d.	...	1043	1138	1043	1138	...	...
Hervey a.	...	1130	1225	1130	1225	...	...
Hervey d.	...	1140	1235	1200	1255	...	...
Rivière à Pierre d.	...	1234	1329	|	|	...	...
Lac Édouard d.	...	1408	1503	|	|	...	...
Chambord d.	...	1605	1700	|	|	...	...
Jonquière a.	...	1710	1805	|	|	...	...
La Tuque d.	...	...	...	1318	1413	...	...
Parent d.	...	...	...	1625	1720	...	...
Clova d.	...	...	...	1721	1816	...	...
Senneterre a.	...	...	...	1940	2035	...	...

Rail — QUÉBEC CITY - MONTRÉAL — 9010

	15	17	33	35	37	637	39	29	
	2	2							
	①④⑥	①④⑥	①–⑤		①–⑤	⑦	①–⑤		
	A *	Z B *	C		C	C	C		
Québec City Palais ▽ d.	...	...	0527	0805	1300	1300	1500	1745	...
Ste. Foy ▽ d.	0628	0628	0553	0830	1326	1326	1526	1811	...
Charny ▽ d.	|	|	|	0838**u**	|	|	|	|	...
Drummondville d.	0836	0836	0711	1014	1507	1507	1652	1949	...
St. Hyacinthe d.	0915	0915	|	1043	|	|	|	2020	...
St. Lambert ▽ d.	0950	0950	0814	1111	1601	1601	1757**s**	2047	...
Montréal Central ▽ a.	1003	1003	0825	1122	1612	1612	1808	2058	...

	20	622	22	24	26	28		16	14
						C		2	2
	①–⑤	⑥⑦	①–⑤		①–⑥	ex⑥		③⑤⑦	③⑤⑦
			C		C	C		Z B *	A *
Montréal Central ▽ d.	0605	0853	0843	1245	1610	1815	...	1900	1900
St. Lambert ▽ d.	0618	0905	0905	1308	1632	1838	...	1925	1925
St. Hyacinthe d.	0645	0930	0945**f**	|	|	1905	...	1958	1958
Drummondville d.	0709	0958	0958	1401	1740	1942	...	2047	2047
Charny ▽ d.	|	|	|	1555	|	|	...	|	|
Ste. Foy ▽ d.	0911	1143	1143	1603	1919	2111	...	2204**a**	2234**a**
Québec City Palais ▽ a.	0934	1206	1206	1626	1941	2133	...	...	...

OCEAN – [2] Montréal Central - Halifax and v.v. (Table **9000**).
[2] Montréal Central - Gaspé and v.v. (Table **9000**).
[12] Québec City Palais - Montréal Central - Ottawa Union and v.v. (Table **9015**).
During infrastructure work currently in progress, trains 16 and 17 will not be operating and train services between Matapédia and Gaspé will be suspended.

a – Arrival time. f – ⑥⑦ only.
u – Request stop. Calls to pick up only. s – Calls to set down only.
* – A shuttle operates between Sainte-Foy and Québec City Palais [R] required.
▽ – Local traffic not carried Montréal Cenrtal - St Lambert and v.v., or Québec City Palais - Charny and v.v.

9015 MONTRÉAL - OTTAWA - TORONTO Via

km		651	655	41	641	43	51	61	643	33	633	63	45	65	47	35	55	67	647	69	59	37	637	669
		2	2							A												A	A	
		①–⑤	⑥	①–⑤	⑥	①–⑤	①–⑤	①–⑥	⑥⑦	①–⑤	⑥⑦						⑦–⑤		⑦–⑤			①–⑤	⑦	
0	**Montréal** Central d.	...	...	...	...	...	0610	0635	...	0840	0840	0855	...	1055	...	1137	...	1545	...	1640	...	1650	1650	1840
19	Dorval d.	...	...	...	...	...	0634	0703	...	0912	0905	0920	...	1119	...	1210	...	1608	...	1704	...	1724	1824	1904
100	Alexandria d.	...	...	...	...	...	0718	|	...	0956	0952	|	...	|	...	1259	...	|	...	|	...	1807	1807	|
187	**Ottawa** Union a.	...	...	...	...	...	0810	|	...	1046	1045	|	...	|	...	1345	...	|	...	|	...	1856	1856	|
187	**Ottawa** Union d.	...	...	0530	0640	0720	0825	|	0910	...	...	|	1030	|	1230	1345	1530	|	1700	|	1817	...	...	|
253	Smiths Falls d.	...	...	0622	0726	|	0913	|	0959	...	...	|	|	|	|	|	|	|	|	|	1916	...	...	|
	Cornwall d.	...	...	|	|	|	|	0755	|	...	...	1013	|	1211	|	|	|	1659	|	|	|	...	...	1955
298	Brockville d.	...	...	0651	0755	|	0942	|	1033	...	...	|	|	1257	1357	1625	1654	|	|	1834	1951	...	...	|
378	**Kingston** d.	0532	0645	0734	0838	0914	1026	0924	1116	...	...	1143	1233	1341	1446	1709	1738	1826	1856	1917	2035	...	...	2120
451	Belleville d.	0614	0725	0816	0919	|	|	1002	1200	...	...	|	|	1422	1529	1749	1818	|	|	|	2117	...	...	|
520	Cobourg d.	0656	0806	0850	0951	|	1137	|	1234	...	...	|	|	1459	|	1823	1852	|	|	|	2157	...	...	|
581	Oshawa d.	0739	0842	0927	1029	|	|	1111	1314	...	...	1355	|	1532	1638	1856	1925	2010	|	2101	2232	...	...	2304
633	**Toronto** Union a.	0825	0914	1002	1102	1125	1242	1141	1347	...	...	1407	1448	1603	1715	1928	1957	2039	2116	2130	2307	...	...	2333

km		22	32	632	60	50	34	62	26	52	40	64	28	42	44	66	38		46	646	68	650	668	48
		A					2		A				A											
		①–⑤	①–⑤	⑥⑦	①–⑥	①–⑥			①–⑥				⑦–⑤	①–⑤					⑦–⑤	⑦–⑤	⑦–⑤	①–⑤		①–⑥
0	**Toronto** Union d.	...	...	...	0640	0640	...	0920	...	0920	1045	1130	...	1220	1420	1515	...	...	1540	1635	1700	1740	1800	1835
51	Oshawa d.	...	...	...	0719	0719	...	0953	...	0953	|	1208	...	1252	1454	1547	...	...	1617	1706	1731	1814	1833	1916
113	Cobourg d.	...	...	...	0754	0754	...	1025	...	1025	|	1243	...	|	|	|	...	...	1650	|	1801	1849	|	1953
182	Belleville d.	...	...	...	0829	0829	...	|	...	|	|	1321	...	|	|	1652	...	...	|	1811	|	1931	|	2036
254	**Kingston** d.	...	...	...	0911	0911	...	1138	...	1138	1252	1401	...	1432	1636	1732	...	...	1802	|	|	2011	2016	2116
335	Brockville d.	...	...	...	1002	1008	...	|	...	1235	|	1448	...	|	1720	|	...	...	1847	|	1953	...	|	2203
428	Cornwall d.	...	...	...	|	|	...	|	...	|	|	|	...	|	|	|	...	...	|	|	|	...	|	|
380	Smiths Falls d.	...	...	...	|	1039	...	|	...	|	|	|	...	|	1750	|	...	...	|	|	|	...	|	2233
446	**Ottawa** Union a.	...	...	...	|	1129	...	|	...	1351	1455	|	...	1631	1846	|	...	...	2009	2042	|	...	|	2316
	Ottawa Union d.	0630	0955	0955	|	...	1140	|	1400		...	|	1610	...	...	|	1830	...	...	...	|	...	|	...
	Alexandria d.	0716	1047	1047	|	...	1229	|	1445		...	|	|	...	...	|	1925	...	...	...	|	...	|	...
520	Dorval d.	0809	1132	1132	1137	...	1318	1400	1529		...	1626	1737	...	...	1948	2009	...	...	...	2129	...	2234	...
539	**Montréal** Central a.	0828	1151	1151	1157	...	1337	1420	1547		...	1647	1757	...	...	2009	2028	...	...	...	2149	...	2255	...

A – 12 Québec City Palais - Montréal Central - Ottawa Union and v.v. (Table **9010**). s – Calls to set down only. u – Calls to pick up only.

9020 TORONTO - WINDSOR and NIAGARA FALLS GO Transit, Via

km	*Via Rail*	71	97	73	83	81	75	79	69	
			Ⓡ B							
					①–⑤	⑥	⑦–⑤			
0	**Toronto** Union d.	0645	0820	1215	1635	1730	1730	1905	2204	...
34	Oakville d.	0710	0844	1240	|	1756	1756	1929	2227	...
56	Aldershot d.	0725	0857	1258	1713	1812	1812	1943	2239	...
96	Brantford d.	0753	|	1327	1743	1844	1844	2011	...	...
139	Woodstock d.	0825	|	1355	1812	1914	1914	2039	...	...
185	London d.	0905	|	1430	1849	1955	2001	2124	...	...
290	Chatham d.	1013	|	1539	...	...	2104	2227	...	...
360	**Windsor** a.	1102	|	1630	...	...	2156	2318	...	...
114	St. Catharines d.	...	0954	...	...	...	...	...	...	...
133	**Niagara Falls** (Canada) a.	...	1016	...	...	...	...	...	...	...
	New York Penn **9205** a.	...	2150	...	...	...	...	...	...	...

Via Rail	82	70	80	72	76	98	78	
						Ⓡ B		
	①–⑤	①–⑥	⑦					
New York Penn **9205** d.	...	...	...	...	...	0715	...	...
Niagara Falls (Canada) d.	...	...	...	...	...	1745	...	...
St. Catharines d.	...	...	...	...	...	1808	...	...
Windsor d.	...	0530	...	0905	1345	|	1745	...
Chatham d.	...	0618	...	0951	1430	|	1832	...
London d.	0625	0730	0730	1102	1543	|	1942	...
Woodstock d.	0654	0807	0807	1131	|	|	2014	...
Brantford d.	0725	0841	0841	1202	1640	|	2045	...
Aldershot d.	|	0921	0921	1234	1713	1904	2115	...
Oakville d.	|	0938	0938	1248	1727	1918	2129	...
Toronto Union a.	0835	1004	1004	1311	1752	1941	2151	...

km	*GO Transit - 2nd class only*	703	903	477		907	909	911	913	915	917	919	921	479	923	493	495	925	927	929	929	931	933
		①–⑤	①–⑤			①–⑤							⑥⑦	①–⑤	⑥⑦	①–⑤	①–⑤	⑥⑦		①–⑤	⑥⑦		
0	**Toronto** Union d.	0613	0655	0743	...	0843	0943	1043	1143	1243	1343	1443	1543	1610	1643	1700	1737	1743	1843	1943	1943	2043	2143
34	Oakville d.	0651	0733	0824	...	0924	1024	1124	1224	1324	1424	1524	1624	1639	1724	1732	1809	1824	1924	2024	2024	2124	2224
51	Burlington a.	0710	0752	0844	...	0944	1044	1144	1244	1344	1444	1544	1644	1658	1744	1752	1829	1844	1944	2044	2044	2144	2244
114	St. Catharines a.	*0815**	*0857**	*0949**	...	*1049**	*1149**	*1249**	*1349**	*1449**	*1549**	*1649**	*1754**	*1816**	*1854**	*1907**	*1939**	*1954**	*2054**	*2149**	*2154**	*2249**	*2349**
133	**Niagara Falls** (Canada) a.	*0840**	*0922**	*1014**	...	*1114**	*1214**	*1314**	*1414**	*1519**	*1619**	*1719**	*1819**	*1841**	*1919**	*1932**	*2004**	*2019**	*2119**	*2214**	*2219**	*2314**	*0014**

GO Transit - 2nd class only	704	490	492	496	908	710	910	912	914	916	918	920	922	922	924	726	926	928	730	930	932	934	936
		①–⑤	①–⑤	①–⑤	⑥⑦	①–⑤	⑥⑦						⑥⑦	①–⑤	⑥⑦	①–⑤	⑥⑦		⑤				
Niagara Falls (Canada) d.	...	*0451**	*0521**	*0556**	*0632**	*0652**	*0727**	*0827**	*0927**	*1022**	*1122**	*1222**	*1322**	*1331**	*1422**	*1452**	*1522**	*1622**	...	*1722**	*1822**	*1922**	*2022**
St. Catharines d.	...	*0511**	*0541**	*0621**	*0657**	*0717**	*0752**	*0852**	*0952**	*1052**	*1147**	*1247**	*1347**	*1356**	*1447**	*1517**	*1547**	*1647**	*1742**	*1747**	*1847**	*1947**	*2047**
Burlington d.	0537	0621	0651	0736	0814	0837	0907	1007	1107	1207	1307	1407	1507	1516	1607	1637	1707	1807	1842	1907	2007	2107	2207
Oakville d.	0555	0644	0714	0758	0832	0856	0926	1026	1126	1226	1326	1426	1526	1535	1626	1656	1726	1826	1901	1926	2026	2126	2226
Toronto Union a.	0638	0714	0742	0832	0915	0941	1010	1111	1211	1311	1411	1511	1610	1620	1710	1741	1810	1911	1946	2011	2111	2211	2311

B – THE MAPLE LEAF – 12 and 🍸 Toronto (**97/98**) - Niagara Falls (**64/63**) - New York and v.v. (Table **9210**). * – Connection by 🚌 (Route 12).

9025 TORONTO - COCHRANE Ontario Northland

km		421	🚌
		①–⑤	
		C	
0	**Toronto** Bay Street d.	...	0915
143	Washago d.	...	1145
164	Gravenhurst d.	...	1220
219	Huntsville d.	...	1315
351	**North Bay** a.	...	1450
351	**North Bay** d.	...	1615*
513	Cobalt d.	...	1755
529	New Liskeard d.	...	1825
571	Engleheart d.	...	1920
643	Swastika d.	...	r
677	Matheson d.	...	2115*
754	**Cochrane** a.	...	2230
754	**Cochrane** d.	0900	...
	Fraserdale d.	1045r	...
	Moose River d.	1235r	...
1053	**Moosonee** a.	1350	...

	🚌	422
		①–⑤
		C
Moosonee d.	...	1700
Moose River d.	...	1807r
Fraserdale d.	...	1957r
Cochrane a.	...	2145
Cochrane d.	0830	...
Matheson d.	1000*	...
Swastika d.	r	...
Engleheart d.	1145	...
New Liskeard d.	1245	...
Cobalt d.	1310	...
North Bay a.	1500	...
North Bay d.	1600*	...
Huntsville d.	1740	...
Gravenhurst d.	1850	...
Washago d.	1910	...
Toronto Union a.	2145	...

C – POLAR BEAR EXPRESS – 2 and 🍸 Cochrane - Moosonee and v.v. Ⓡ also ⑦ in summer. r – Calls on request. * – Change buses.

9030 TORONTO - SARNIA 2nd class Via

km		85	87
0	**Toronto** Union d.	1055	1740
34	Brampton d.	1129	1814
47	Georgetown d.	1140	1826
79	Guelph d.	1206	1851
101	Kitchener d.	1232	1918
143	Stratford d.	1309	1955
195	London d.	1417	2114
290	**Sarnia** a.	...	2220

	84
Sarnia d.	0610
London d.	0732
Stratford d.	0840
Kitchener d.	0918
Guelph d.	0944
Georgetown d.	1010
Brampton d.	1020
Toronto Union a.	1053

9035 WHITE RIVER - SUDBURY Via

km		186	
		2	
		③⑤⑦	
0	**White River** d.	0700	...
79	Franz d.	0820	...
209	Chapleau d.	1045	...
341	Biscotasing d.	1245	...
484	**Sudbury** § a.	1550	...

	185
	2
	②④⑥
Sudbury § d.	0900
Biscotasing d.	1130
Chapleau d.	1415
Franz d.	1630
White River a.	1745

§ – Sudbury is 10 km from Sudbury Junction (Table **9050**).

9040 HEARST - SAULT STE MARIE

km		632	632
		2 D	2 D
		②⑤⑦	②⑤⑦
0	**Hearst** d.	0800	0830
82	Oba d.	0915	0945
126	Mosher d.	0955	1030
162	Franz d.	1045	1115
211	Hawk Junction d.	1150	1225
282	Eton d.	1310	1340
292	Agawa Canyon d.	1325	1355
475	**Sault Ste. Marie** a.	1740	1810

	631	631
	2 D	2 D
	①④⑥	①④⑥
Sault Ste. Marie d.	0900	0920
Agawa Canyon d.	1305	1325
Eton d.	1320	1340
Hawk Junction d.	1500	1520
Franz d.	1545	1605
Mosher d.	1630	1650
Oba d.	1710	1730
Hearst a.	1840	1900

D – Service suspended until further notice.

9045 THE PAS - PUKATAWAGAN Keewatin Railw

km		291	
		F	
		①④	
0	**The Pas 9055** d.	1115	...
88	Cranberry Portage d.	1355	...
251	**Pukatawagan** a.	1845	...

	290
	F
	②⑤
Pukatawagan d.	1000
Cranberry Portage d.	1515
The Pas 9055 a.	1730

F – Operated by Keewatin Railway Company. To book ✆ 204 623 5255.

Rail TORONTO - VANCOUVER 9050

	1 🅁 A			2 🅁 A	
Toronto Union .... d.	2200	②⑥	**Vancouver** Pacific .... a.	2030	②⑤
Washago .... d.	0040	③⑦	Agassiz .... d.	2233	:
Parry Sound .... d.	0242	:	**Kamloops** North .... a.	0600	③⑥
Sudbury Junction .... § d.	0513	:	**Kamloops** North .... d.	0635	:
Capreol .... a.	0538	:	Valemount .... d.	1250	:
Capreol .... d.	0608	:	**Jasper** .... a.	1600	:
Foleyet .... d.	1059	:	**Jasper** .... d.	1730	:
Oba .... d.	1351	:	Edson .... d.	2020	:
Homepayne .... d.	1520	:	**Edmonton** .... a.	2300	:
Longlac .... d.	1749	:	**Edmonton** .... d.	2359	:
Sioux Lookout .... d.	0009	①④	Wainwright .... d.	0315	④⑦
Red Lake Road .... d.	0209	:	Biggar .... d.	0645	:
Winnipeg .... a.	0800	:	**Saskatoon** .... a.	0800	:
Winnipeg .... d.	1145	:	**Saskatoon** .... d.	0825	:
Portage la Prairie .... d.	1309	:	Melville .... d.	1240	:
Rivers .... d.	1458	:	Rivers .... d.	1645	:
Melville .... d.	1727	:	Portage la Prairie .... d.	1930	:
Saskatoon .... a.	2207	:	**Winnipeg** .... a.	2045	:
Saskatoon .... d.	2232	:	**Winnipeg** .... d.	2230	:
Biggar .... d.	2359	:	Red Lake Road .... d.	0251	①⑤
Wainwright .... d.	0300	②⑤	Sioux Lookout .... d.	0542	:
Edmonton .... a.	0622	:	Longlac .... d.	1303	:
Edmonton .... d.	0737	:	Hornepayne .... d.	1610	:
Edson .... d.	1013	:	Oba .... d.	1710	:
Jasper .... a.	1300	:	Foleyet .... d.	1958	:
Jasper .... d.	1430	:	**Capreol** .... a.	0018	②⑥
Valemount .... d.	1607	:	**Capreol** .... d.	0048	:
Kamloops North .... a.	2309	:	Sudbury Junction ...... § d.	0117	:
Kamloops North .... d.	2344	:	Parry Sound .... d.	0433	:
Agassiz .... d.	|	:	Washago .... d.	0649	:
Vancouver Pacific .... a.	0942	③⑥	**Toronto** Union .... a.	0930	②⑥

THE CANADIAN – 🛏 1 cl., (2) and ✕ Toronto - Vancouver and v.v. From Toronto on ②⑥ (also ④ May. 5 - Oct. 13). From Vancouver on ②⑤ (also ⑦ May 1 - Oct. 9).
Request stop.
Sudbury Junction is 10 km from Sudbury (Table **9035**).

R ROCKY MOUNTAINEER TOURS 9065

	D	E	G	H		H	E	D	G
tle .... d.	...	...	...	1510	**Calgary** .... d.	...	...	...	...
couver ‡ .... a.	...	...	...	2045	Banff .... d.	...	...	0740	...
couver ‡ .... d.	0730	0730	...	...	Lake Louise .... d.	...	...	0900	...
Vancouver ... d.	|	|	0740	...	**Jasper** .... d.	...	0810	|	0655
histler .... ♥ a.	|	|	1130	...	Kamloops .... ♥ a.	...	1700	1815	|
histler .... ♥ d.	|	|	0710	...	Kamloops .... ♥ d.	...	0735	0735	|
uesnel .... ♥ a.	|	|	1930	...	Quesnel .... ♥ a.	...	|	|	1930
uesnel .... ♥ d.	|	|	0710	...	Quesnel .... ♥ d.	...	|	|	0710
loops .... ♥ a.	1730	1730	|	...	Whistler .... ♥ a.	...	|	|	1930
loops .... ♥ d.	0625	0745	|	...	Whistler .... ♥ d.	...	|	|	1510
asper .... a.	|	1800	2030	...	**N. Vancouver** .... a.	...	|	|	1900
e Louise .... a.	1830	...	...	...	**Vancover** ‡ .... a.	...	1730	1730	...
f .... a.	1930	...	...	...	**Vancouver** ‡ .... d.	0810	...	...	...
gary .... a.	...	...	...	...	Seattle .... a.	1315	...	...	...

FIRST PASSAGE TO THE WEST – For 2016 dates contact operator. ◀
JOURNEY THROUGH THE CLOUDS – For 2016 dates contact operator. ◀
RAINFOREST TO GOLD RUSH – For 2016 dates contact operator. ★
COASTAL PASSAGE – For 2016 dates contact operator. ★
Services operate on selected dates from late April to early October.
Services opeate on selected dates from mid May to early October.
Vancouver Cottrell Street.
Compulsory overnight stop, arrival time are flexible.
ator: Rocky Mountaineer Railtours (www.rockymountaineer.com)

Via Rail WINNIPEG - CHURCHILL 9055

km		693 🅁 B			692 🅁 B	
0	**Winnipeg** .... d.	1205	②⑦	**Churchill** .... d.	1930	②④⑥
88	Portage la Prairie .... d.	1315r	:	Herchmer .... d.	0003	③⑤⑦
283	Dauphin .... d.	1706r	:	Giliam (Nelson River)... d.	0530	:
484	Canora **a** .... d.	1946	:	**Thompson** .... a.	1130	:
549	Endeavour **a** .... d.	2054r	:	**Thompson** .... d.	1400	:
635	Hudson Bay **a** .... d.	2232r	:	Thicket Potage .... d.	1622	:
777	**The Pas 9045** .... a.	0145	①③	Wabowden .... d.	1811	:
777	**The Pas 9045** .... d.	0230	①③⑤	Cormorant .... d.	2147	:
843	Cormorant .... d.	0412	:	**The Pas 9045** .... a.	2330	③⑤⑦
996	Wabowden .... d.	0748	:	**The Pas 9045** .... d.	0315	①⑥
1073	Thicket Potage .... d.	0937	:	Hudson Bay **a** .... d.	0427r	:
1149	**Thompson** .... a.	1200	:	Endeavour **a** .... d.	0555r	:
1149	**Thompson** .... d.	1700	:	Canora **a** .... d.	0718	:
1401	Giliam (Nelson River) ..... d.	2330	:	Dauphin .... d.	1206	:
1540	Herchmer .... d.	0426	②④⑥	Portage la Prairie .... d.	1537r	:
1697	**Churchill** .... a.	0900	②④⑥	**Winnipeg** .... a.	1645	①⑥

B – 🛏 1 cl., (2) and ✕ Churchill - Winnipeg and v.v Note only runs on days shown.
a – Sasakatchewan, always standard time. r – Request stop.

Via Rail PRINCE RUPERT - JASPER 9060

km		5 🅁 C ③⑤⑦			6 🅁 C ③⑤⑦	
0	**Jasper** .... d.	1245	③⑤⑦	**Prince Rupert** .... d.	0800	③⑤⑦
174	McBride .... d.	1444	:	Terrace (Kitimat) .... d.	1025	:
409	**Prince George** .... a.	1908	:	New Hazelton .... d.	1230r	:
409	**Prince George** .... d.	0800	①④⑥	Smithers .... d.	1424	:
560	Fort Fraser .... d.	1032r	:	Fort Fraser .... d.	1757r	:
795	Smithers .... d.	1420	:	**Prince George** .... a.	2029	:
869	New Hazelton .... d.	1537r	:	**Prince George** .... d.	0945	①④⑥
1007	Terrace (Kitimat) .... d.	1805	:	McBride .... d.	1348	:
1160	**Prince Rupert** .... a.	2025	:	**Jasper** .... a.	1830	:

C – (2) and 🍸 (also (1) and ✕, from Jasper on June 15, 19, 24, 29, July 3, 8, 13, 17, 22, 27, 31, Aug. 5, 10, 14, 19, 24, 28, Sept. 2, 7, 11, 16, 21, 25; from Prince Rupert on June 17, 22, 26, July 1, 6, 10, 15, 20, 24, 29, Aug. 3, 7, 12, 17, 21, 26, 31, Sept. 4, 9, 14, 18, 23, 28). Compulsory overnight stop in **Prince George**. Passengers must arrange their own accommodation.
r – Request stop.

West Coast VANCOUVER - MISSION CITY 9070

km			①-⑤	①-⑤		①-⑤	①-⑤		①-⑤	
0	**Vancouver** Waterfront .... d.		1550	1620	...	1650	1730	...	1820	...
26	Coquitlam .... d.		1619	1649	...	1719	1759	...	1849	...
68	**Mission City** .... a.		1705	1735	...	1805	1845	...	1935	...
			①-⑤	①-⑤		①-⑤	①-⑤		①-⑤	
	Mission City .... d.	...	0525	0555	...	0625	0655	...	0725	...
	Coquitlam .... d.	...	0610	0640	...	0710	0740	...	0810	...
	Vancouver Waterfront .... a.	...	0640	0710	...	0740	0810	...	0840	...

Operator: West Coast Express ✆ 604 488 8906.

Greyhound 🚌 CALGARY - EDMONTON 🚌 9090

km		5200 ex⑦	5204 ①⑤⑥	5206	5208	5210 a	5214	5216 ⑤⑦	5218 ex②	5222 ⑤⑦	5224
0	**Calgary** .... d.	0030	0700	0800	1201	1300	1600	1700	1800	1900	2000
303	**Edmonton** .... a.	0605	1030	1150	1550	1720	1930	2050	2150	2230	2350
		5201	**5205** ①⑤⑥	**5207**	**5211** ex⑥	**5209**	**5215** ex②③	**5217** ex⑥	**5219** ⑤⑦	**5223** ex②	**5225** ⑤⑦
	Edmonton .... d.	0045	0700	0800	1300	1400	1600	1700	1800	1900	2000
	Calgary .... a.	0610	1050	1150	1720	1750	1930	2050	2150	2250	2330

a – ①④⑤⑦

UNITED STATES OF AMERICA

ital: **Washington DC** (GMT -5, add one hour in summer). 2016 Public Holidays: Jan. 1, 18, Feb. 15, May 30, July 4, Sep. 5, Oct. 10, Nov. 11, 24, Dec. 25, 26.

principal operator in the USA is Amtrak (✆ 1 800 872 7245. www.amtrak.com). Details of other operators can be found in relevant tables. Unless otherwise noted all trains y first and second class seated accomodation known as 'Business' and 'Coach' class respectively. Acela Express trains running between Boston, New York and Washington vey business class and an enhanced seated accommodation, confusingly called 'First Class'. Most very long distance trains convey sleeping cars, and where this is the case detailed in the footnotes. Almost all sleeping car accommodation in North America has two berths per compartment, some of which are en-suite, although the exact product ing varies by operator and route. Most trains also convey some form of catering, but again the actual service offered varies considerably. Timings shown are the latest able and are subject to alteration around public holidays and it is recommended that you confirm all timings locally as short notice changes are possible. Tickets are available staffed stations, websites and through authorised ticketing agents. Amtrak requires reservations on practically all of its services, and also requires that you have identity uments available for inspection.

rak offers the 'USA Rail Pass' It is available to both US citizens and foreign nationals and has the option of three validity periods: 15 day/8 segments of travel, 30 day/12 ments of travel and 45 day/18 segments of travel. The pass is valid in coach class on the entire Amtrak system. Be warned though: this program is now revenue/capacity aged and may not be available on all trains all the time. The pass is not valid on the Autotrain, Acela Express trains, Thruway buses numbered 7000 – 7999 and the adian portion of trains operated jointly by Amtrak and VIA Rail Canada. The pass alone is not valid for travel; tickets and where neccessary reservations, must be obtained for segment of travel. Upgrades to higher levels of accommodation may be possible subject to capacity and the payment of relevant supplements. Travel is limited to no more four one-way journeys over any given route segment. A segment is any time you get on and then get off a train or bus, regardless of the length of that journey. For full details the Amtrak website (www.amtrak.com).

ite Pass and Yukon Railroad SKAGWAY - WHITEHORSE 9100

m		1 A	Ba	Bb	🚌		🚌	Ba	Bb	2 C
0	**Skagway** Shops .... d.	0730	0740	1210	1400	**Whitehorse** .... d.	0730	...	...	...
22	White Pass ▶ .... 🚉 d.	|	|	|	|	Carcross .... a.	0845	...	...	...
41	Fraser .... a.	0900	0925	1415	1445	Carcross .... d.	0845	...	...	1300
41	Fraser .... d.	0900	...	...	1500	Bennett .... a.	|	...	...	1430
65	Bennett .... a.	1015	...	...	|	Bennett .... d.	|	...	...	1515
65	Bennett .... d.	1130	...	...	|	Fraser .... a.	1000	...	...	1600
08	Carcross .... a.	1300	...	...	1600	Fraser .... d.	1000	1020	1445	1600
08	Carcross .... d.	...	...	...	1600	White Pass ▶ .... 🚉 d.	|	|	|	|
77	**Whitehorse** .... a.	...	...	...	1730	**Skagway** Shops .... a.	1100	1205	1630	1745

May 31 - Sept. 3. From Skagway ②③④⑤.
May 3 - Sep 27. Not May 5, 6, 13, 16. Sep. 11, 18, 19, 23, 25, 26. **a** - Not Sep. 22, 27. **b** - Not May 3, 4, 7, 14. Sep.4, 17, 24.
May 31 - Sept. 3. From Carcross ②③④ Also from Carcross ⑥ departing 1200.

☛ For services crossing the US/Canadian border passengers must provide proof of citizenship. All services 🅁. All times shown are Alaska time.

▶ – Between May 3 and Sept. 27 a White Pass Summit round trip excursion operates. Departs Skagway 0815 **c** and 1245 **e** daily. Additional trips 1630 on ②③ between May 24 and Aug. 31.

c – Not May 5, 6, 13, 16, 22, Aug. 28, Sept. 11, 18, 19, 23, 25, 26.

e – Not May 5, 6, 13, 16, 22, June 5, 19, July 3, 17, Aug. 14, 28, Sept. 11, 18, 19, 23, 25, 26.

Operator: White Pass & Yukon Railroad ✆ Skagway 907 983 2217. www.wpyr.com

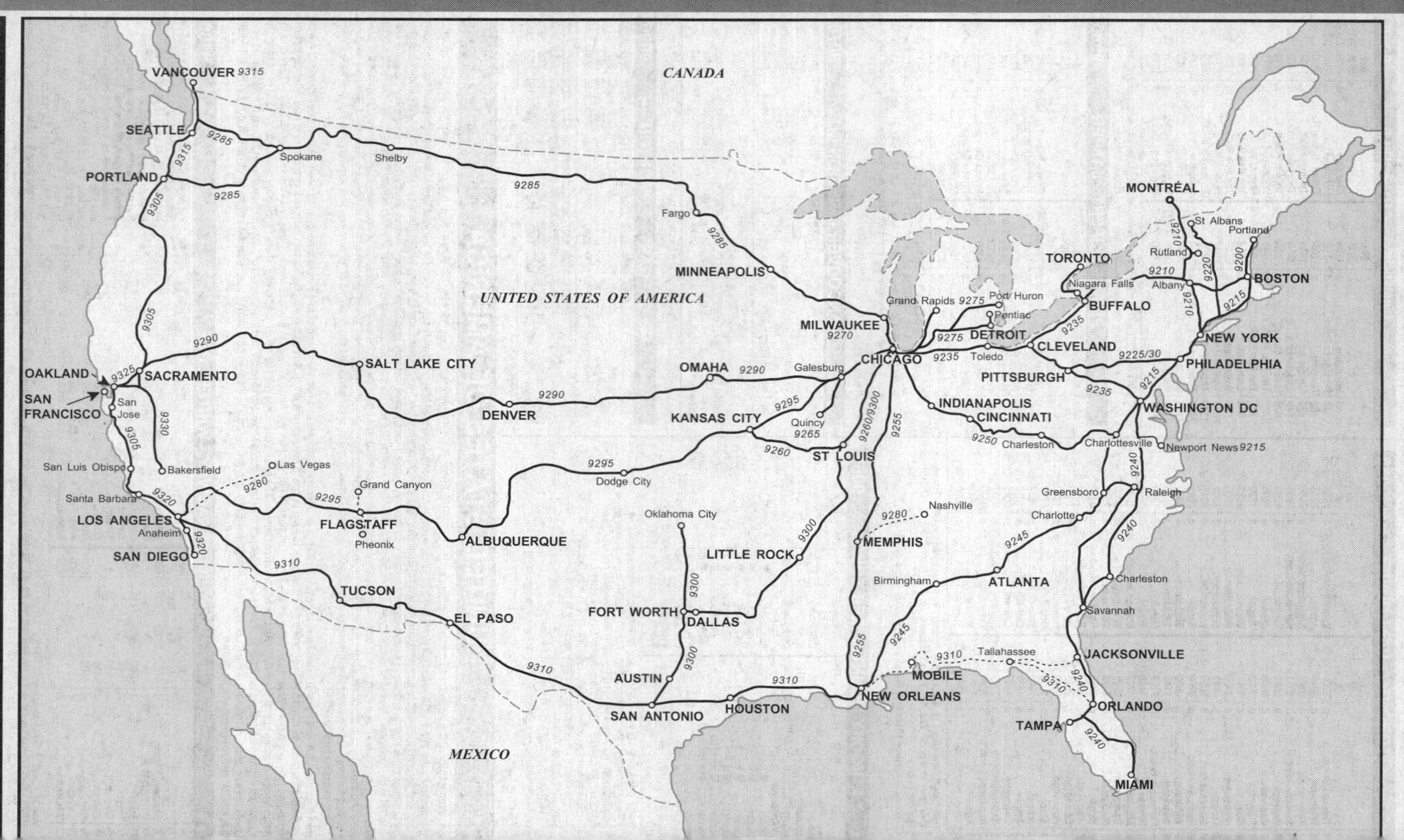
CANADA
UNITED STATES OF AMERICA
MEXICO
VANCOUVER 9315
SEATTLE
PORTLAND
Spokane
Shelby
Fargo
MINNEAPOLIS
MILWAUKEE
9270
CHICAGO
Grand Rapids 9275
Port Huron
Pontiac
DETROIT
Toledo
TORONTO
Niagara Falls
BUFFALO
CLEVELAND
PITTSBURGH
MONTRÉAL
St Albans
Portland
Rutland
Albany
BOSTON
NEW YORK
PHILADELPHIA
WASHINGTON DC
Newport News 9215
INDIANAPOLIS
CINCINNATI
Charleston
Charlottesville
Greensboro
Raleigh
Charlotte
Charleston
Savannah
JACKSONVILLE
ORLANDO
TAMPA
MIAMI
Tallahassee
MOBILE
NEW ORLEANS
ATLANTA
Birmingham
MEMPHIS
Nashville
ST LOUIS
Galesburg
Quincy
9265
KANSAS CITY
OMAHA
LITTLE ROCK
Oklahoma City
FORT WORTH
DALLAS
AUSTIN
SAN ANTONIO
HOUSTON
Dodge City
ALBUQUERQUE
DENVER
SALT LAKE CITY
EL PASO
TUCSON
FLAGSTAFF
Grand Canyon
Pheonix
Las Vegas
SACRAMENTO
OAKLAND
SAN FRANCISCO
San Jose
Bakersfield
San Luis Obispo
Santa Barbara
LOS ANGELES
Anaheim
SAN DIEGO
9200
9210
9215
9220
9225/30
9235
9240
9245
9250
9255
9260
9260/9300
9280
9285
9290
9295
9300
9305
9310
9315
9320
9325
9330

ALASKA — 9105

ska Railroad

km			D	E	Ab	Bc	B	C
						④	⑦	④–①
)	**Fairbanks**	d.	...	...	0815	...	0830	...
5	Denali	d.	...	...	1230	...	1230	...
5	Hurricane	d.	...	...	|	1445	1445	1600
2	Talkeetna	d.	...	...	1655	1650	1650	1915
3	Wasilla	d.	...	...	1815	1825	1825	...
2	**Anchorage**	a.	...	...	2000	2000	2000	...
2	**Anchorage**	d.	0645	0945	...	...	...	...
5	Girdwood	d.	0800	1100	...	...	...	...
2	**Portage**	a.	|	1130	...	...	...	...
a	Whittier	d.	|	1245	...	...	...	...
2	**Portage**	d.	|	1325	...	...	...	...
5	Spencer	a.	|	1345	...	...	...	...
5	Spencer	d.	|	1355	...	...	...	...
3	Grandview	a.	|	1520	...	...	...	...
)	**Seward**	a.	1105	...	...	...	...	...

		Aa	B	Bc	C	E	D
			⑥	④	④–①		
Seward	d.	...	...	...	...	...	1800
Grandview	d.	...	...	...	...	1530	|
Spencer	a.	...	...	...	...	1630	|
Spencer	d.	...	...	...	...	1640	|
Portage	a.	...	...	...	...	1715	|
Whittier	d.	...	...	...	...	1845	|
Portage	d.	...	...	...	...	1920	|
Girdwood	d.	...	...	...	...	1940	2055
Anchorage	a.	...	...	...	...	2115	2215
Anchorage	d.	0815	0830	0830	...	...	...
Wasilla	d.	0935	0950	0950	...	...	...
Talkeetna	d.	1120	1125	1125	1245	...	...
Hurricane	a.	|	1340	1340	1500	...	...
Denali	d.	1600	1555	...	...	...	...
Fairbanks	a.	2000	2000	...	...	...	...

DENALI STAR – [2] and ✕ (**Aa** May 11 – Sept. 17. **Ab** May 12 – Sept. 18)
[2] Sept. 19 2015 – May 8 2016.
\- 1st ④ of every month Oct. 1 2015 – May 5 2016.
HURRICANE TURN – [2] May 12 – Sept. 19.

D – COASTAL CLASSIC – [2] and ✕ May 7 – Sept. 18.
E – GLACIER DISCOVERY – [2] and ✕ May 28 – Sept. 19.
a – Kms from Portage.
Operator : Alaska Railroad ✆ Anchorage 907 265 2620. Fax 907 265 2323.

BRUNSWICK - PORTLAND - BOSTON — 9200

ntrak

m			680	690	682	692	684	694	686	696	688	698
			①–⑤	⑥⑦	①–⑤	⑥⑦	①–⑤	⑥⑦	①–⑤	⑥⑦	①-⑤	⑥⑦
0	**Brunswick**	d.	...	...	0705	0725	...	...	...	...	1825	1825
4	Freeport	d.	...	...	0720	0740	...	...	...	...	1840	1840
7	**Portland**	d.	0520	0600	0800	0820	1240	1305	1435	1505	1920	1920
6	Old Orchard Beach ≪≪	d.	0535	0613	0813	0835	1255	1320	1450	|	1933	1935
2	Saco	d.	0542	0622	0822	0842	1300	1327	1457	1527	1942	1942
8	Wells	d.	0559	0639	0839	0859	1317	1345	1514	1544	1959	1959
4	Dover	d.	0617	0657	0857	0917	1335	1402	1532	1602	2017	2017
3	Durham	d.	0625	0704	0905	0925	1343	1510	1540	1610	2025	2025
1	Exeter	d.	0639	0717	0918	0938	1356	1423	1553	1623	2038	2038
8	Haverhill	d.	0700	0737	0939	0959	1419	1444	1614	1644	2104	2058
2	**Boston** North	a.	0750	0825	1030	1050	1510	1535	1705	1735	2200	2150

		681	691	683	693	685	695	687	697	689	699
		①–⑤	⑥⑦	①–⑤	⑥⑦	①–⑤	⑥⑦	①–⑤	⑥⑦	①–⑤	⑥⑦
ston North	d.	0905	0925	1125	1155	1700	1700	1805	2000	2325	2325
erhill	d.	0953	1013	1212	1243	1748	1748	1852	2048	0013r	0013r
ter	d.	1014	1034	1232	1304	1809	1809	1912	2114	0034r	0034r
ham	d.	1027	1047	1245	1317	1822	1822	1925	2127	0047r	0047r
er	d.	1035	1055	1252	1324	1830	1830	1932	2134	0055r	0055r
ls	d.	1053	1113	1310	1341	1848	1848	1950	2151	0113r	0113r
o	d.	1110	1130	1328	1358	1905	1905	2006	2208	0127r	0127r
Orchard Beach ≪≪	d.	1115	1137	1335	1403	1910	1910	2013	2213	0132r	0132r
tland	a.	1135	1125	1355	1420	1925	1920	2035	2320	0150	0150
eport	d.	1215	1230	...	...	2005	2005	...	...	...	...
nswick	a.	1230	1245	...	...	2020	2020	...	...	...	...

Calls on request. ≪≪ – Seasonal stop. Station open mid-June to mid-October only.

NEW YORK - ALBANY - RUTLAND, MONTREÁL and NIAGARA FALLS — 9210

ntrak

m			63	69	281	281	233	283	235	291	255	49	237	253	239	293	241	243	259	245	261
					⑦–③	④–⑥			①–⑤	⑥–④	⑤		①–⑤	⑥⑦	①–④	⑤		①–⑤	⑥⑦	①–⑤	⑥⑦
			F	2H	J	J		J		K		G				K					
0	**New York** Penn ▼	d.	0715	0815	1020	1020	1120	1320	1420	1515	1515	1540	1640	1715	1747	1747	1915	2055	2115	2245	2335
4	Yonkers ▼	d.	0744	0844	|	|	1144	1344	1444	1539	1539	|	|	1739	|	|	1939	2119	2139	|	|
54	Croton Harmon ▼	d.	0803	0903	1101	1101	1203	1403	1503	1558	1558	1626u	|	1758	1832	1832	1958	2138	2158	2326	0016
8	Poughkeepsie ▼	d.	0845	0945	1143	1143	1245	1445	1545	1640	1640	1710u	|	1840	1922	1922	2040	2220	2240	0008	0058
42	Rhinecliff Kingston	d.	0900	1000	1158	1158	1300	1500	1600	1655	1655	|	1813	1855	1937e	1937e	2055e	2236e	2255e	0023e	0113e
34	Hudson	d.	0920	1020	1218	1218	1320	1520	1620	1715	1715	|	1833	1915	1957e	1957e	2115e	2256e	2315e	0043e	0134e
29	**Albany** Rensselaer	a.	0950	1050	1245	1245	1350	1545	1650	1745	1745	1820u	1900	1945	2020	2020	2145	2325	2345	0115	0205
29	**Albany** Rensselaer	d.	1000	1110	...	1300	...	1600	...	1800	...	1905u	...	...	...	2030	...	...	...	...	...
58	Schenectady	d.	1024	1134	...	1323	...	1623	...	1824	...	1932	...	...	...	2054	...	...	...	...	...
38	Saratoga Springs	d.	|	1202	...	|	...	|	...	1850	...	|	...	...	...	2123	...	...	...	...	...
91	**Rutland**	a.	|	|	...	|	...	|	...	2048	...	|	...	...	...	2318	...	...	...	...	...
36	Westport	d.	|	1404	...	|	...	|	...	...	...	|	...	...	...	...	...	...	...	...	...
00	Plattsburgh	d.	|	1517	...	|	...	|	...	...	...	|	...	...	...	...	...	...	...	...	...
7	**Montréal** Central	a.	|	1911	...	|	...	|	...	...	...	|	...	...	...	...	...	...	...	...	...
32	Utica	d.	1141	...	...	1440	...	1740	...	...	...	2048	...	...	...	...	...	...	...	...	...
59	Syracuse	d.	1243	...	...	1544	...	1844	...	...	...	2149	...	...	...	...	...	...	...	...	...
97	Rochester	d.	1402	...	...	1708	...	2006	...	...	...	2309	...	...	...	...	...	...	...	...	...
06	Buffalo Exchange St.	a.	1524	...	...	1833e	...	2133e	...	...	...	2355d	...	...	...	...	...	...	...	...	...
45	**Niagara Falls** USA	a.	1646	...	...	1945	...	2245	...	...	...	...	...	...	...	...	...	...	...	...	...
	Toronto Union **9020**	a.	1942	...	...	...	...	...	...	...	...	...	...	...	...	...	...	...	...	...	...

		230	232	250	234	252	260	236	280	240	254	290	238	282	284	292	256	242	48	244	68	64	296	288
		①–⑤	①–⑤	⑥⑦	①–⑤	⑥	⑥⑦	①–⑤	④–⑥	①–③	⑦	①–⑤	④–⑦	①–③	⑦–③	⑥	⑦	①–⑤					⑦	⑦
									J			K		J	J	K			G		2H	F	K	J
oronto Union **9020**	d.	...	...	...	...	...	...	...	...	...	...	...	...	...	...	...	...	...	...	...	...	0820	...	...
gara Falls USA	d.	...	...	...	...	...	...	...	0330	...	...	...	...	0540	...	...	...	...	...	...	...	1210	...	1440
falo Exchange St	d.	...	...	...	...	...	...	...	0405	...	...	...	...	0615	...	...	...	...	0851d	...	...	1245	...	1515
chester	d.	...	...	...	...	...	...	...	0516	...	...	...	...	0726	...	...	...	...	0950	...	...	1353	...	1626
acuse	d.	...	...	...	...	...	...	...	0636	...	...	...	...	0846	...	...	...	...	1118	...	...	1508	...	1746
ca	d.	...	...	...	...	...	...	...	0731	...	...	...	...	0943	...	...	...	...	1215	...	...	1609	...	1841
ontréal Central	d.	...	...	...	...	...	...	...	|	...	...	...	...	|	...	...	...	...	|	...	1020	|	...	|
lattsburgh	d.	...	...	...	...	...	...	...	|	...	...	...	...	|	...	...	...	...	|	...	1325	|	...	|
Vestport	d.	...	...	...	...	...	...	...	|	...	...	...	...	|	...	...	...	...	|	...	1429	|	...	|
Rutland	d.	...	...	...	...	...	...	...	|	...	...	0800	...	|	...	1100	...	...	|	...	|	|	1705	|
aratoga Springs	d.	...	...	...	...	...	...	...	|	...	...	0937	...	|	...	1246	...	...	|	...	1645	|	1847	|
nenectady	d.	...	...	...	...	...	...	...	0923	...	...	1017	...	1133	...	1328	...	...	1358	...	1727	1827	1923	2033
any Rensselaer	a.	...	...	...	...	...	...	...	0950	...	...	1050	...	1155	...	1355	...	...	1455	...	1757	1855	1955	2100
any Rensselaer	d.	0505	0555	0610	0655	0710	0810	0820	1005	1005	1005	1110	1205	1205	1305	1410	1410	1510	1545	1605	1815	1915	2015	2115
dson	d.	0530	0620	0635	0720	0735	0835	0845	1030	1030	1030	1135	1231	1231	1330	1435	1435	1536	|	1630	1840	1940	2040	2140
ncliff Kingston	d.	0550	0640	0656	0742	0756	0856	0906	1051	1051	1051	1156	1252	1252	1350	1455	1455	1558	1631s	1652	1901	2001	2101	2200
ughkeepsie ▼	d.	|	|	0710	|	0810	0910	0920	1110	1110	1110	1210	1310	1310	1410	1510	1510	1615	1648s	1710	1915	2015	2115	2217
ton Harmon ▼	d.	0643	0731	0750	|	0850	0950	1959	1150	1150	1150	1250	1350	1350	1450	1550	1550	1655	1728s	1750	1956	2055	2155	2257
nkers ▼	d.	|	|	0811	|	0911	1011	1021	|	1211	|	1311	1411	|	1511	1611	1611	1716	|	|	2017	2116	2216	|
w York Penn ▼	a.	0730	0815	0845	0920	0945	1040	1050	1245	1245	1245	1345	1445	1445	1545	1645	1645	1748	1823	1845	2050	2150	2250	2345

THE MAPLE LEAF – [12] and 🍸 Toronto (**97/98**) - Niagara Falls (**64/63**) - New York and v.v. (Table **9020**).
LAKE SHORE LIMITED – 🛏 1, 2 cl., [2] and ✕ New York - Albany - Chicago and v.v.
ADIRONDACK – [2] and 🍸 New York - Montréal and v.v.
EMPIRE SERVICE – [12] and 🍸 New York - Niagara Falls and v.v.
ETHAN ALLEN EXPRESS – [12] and 🍸 New York - Rutland and v.v.

d – Buffalo **Depew**. e – Train may leave before time shown.
s – Calls to set down only. u – Calls to pick up only.
▼ – Local traffic not carried. Frequent services are operated by Metro North Railroad.
NOTE: Some schedules will change after July 13.

9215 BOSTON - NEW YORK - WASHINGTON - NEWPORT NEWS

Most trains 🍷 Am

km		65	67	151	111		Acela 2103		89	131	51		Acela 2107	79	183	Acela 2109	Acela 2203	153	185	Acela 2151	Acela 2205	155	141	Acela 2153
		⑤⑥	⑦–④	①–⑤	①–⑤		①–⑤			⑥	③⑤⑦		①–⑤		①–⑤	①–⑤	⑥	⑥⑦	①–⑤	①–⑤	⑦	⑥⑦	①–⑤	①–⑤
									♦		♦			♦										
0	**Boston** South d.	2130	2130	...	...	...	...	...	...	...	...	...	...	...	...	...	...	...	...	0505	...	...	...	0605
69	Providence d.	2222	2222	...	...	...	...	...	...	...	...	...	...	...	...	...	...	...	...	0540	...	...	...	0643
169	New London d.	2331	2331	...	...	...	...	...	...	...	...	...	...	...	...	...	...	...	...	0624	...	...	...	|
	Springfield MA d.	|	|	...	...	...	...	...	...	...	...	...	...	...	...	...	...	...	...	|	...	...	0555	|
	Hartford d.	|	|	...	...	...	...	...	...	...	...	...	...	...	...	...	...	...	...	|	...	...	0635	|
251	New Haven d.	0035	0035	...	...	...	...	...	...	...	...	...	...	...	...	...	...	...	...	0706	...	...	0737	0814
301	Stamford d.	0121	0121	...	...	...	...	...	...	...	...	...	...	...	...	...	...	...	...	0752	...	...	0827	0900
373	**New York** Penn a.	0215	0215	...	...	...	...	...	...	...	...	...	...	...	...	...	...	...	...	0844	...	...	0921	0945
373	**New York** Penn d.	0300	0325	0440	0530	...	0600	...	0605	0645	0645	...	0700	0705	0717	0800	0800	0805	0810	0900	0900	0905	0935	1000
389	Newark NJ d.	0320	0345	0457u	0546u	...	0615u	...	0622u	0702	0705u	...	0715u	0724u	0734	0815u	0814	0822u	0827	0915	0914u	0922	0952	1015
519	**Philadelphia** 30th St. d.	0432	0500	0607	0657	...	0718	...	0732u	0815	0815u	...	0816	0835	0844	0916	0916	0935	0939	1013	1016	1032	1113	1113
670	Baltimore Penn d.	0543	0610	0732	0800	...	0821	...	0842u	0930	0930u	...	0919	0945	0950	1019	1019	1044	1046	1113	1119	1145	1220	1216
687	BWI Airport d.	0556	0625	0745	0815	...	|	...	|	0944	|	...	|	|	1004	|	1032	1057	1059	1129	1132	1201	1233	1229
735	**Washington** Union a.	0630	0700	0820	0850	...	0855	...	1000u	1020	1100u	...	0953	1025	1040	1054	1057	1135	1136	1155	1157	1235	1306	1254
735	**Washington** Union d.	0700	0730	...	...	...	...	...	1000u	...	1100u	...	...	1053	...	...	...	...	...	...	...	...	...	...
822	Fredricksburg d.	0805	0836	...	...	...	...	...	|	...	|	...	...	1156	...	...	...	...	...	...	...	...	...	...
911	Richmond d.	0908	0944	...	...	...	...	...	1207	...	|	...	...	1259	...	...	...	...	...	...	...	...	...	...
1042	**Newport News** a.	1115	1145	...	...	...	...	...	...	...	|	...	...	...	...	...	...	...	...	...	...	...	...	...
1092	Norfolk a.	*1215**	*1250**	...	...	...	...	...	...	...	|	...	...	...	...	...	...	...	...	...	...	...	...	...
	Virgina Beach a.	*1255**	*1330**	...	...	...	...	...	...	...	|	...	...	...	...	...	...	...	...	...	...	...	...	...
915	Charlottesville d.	...	...	...	...	...	...	...	...	...	1352	...	...	...	...	...	...	...	...	...	...	...	...	...
1012	**Lynchburg** a.	...	...	...	...	...	...	...	...	...	...	...	...	...	...	...	...	...	...	...	...	...	...	...

	143	X 2495	95	Acela 2155	Acela 2211	91	405	195	Acela 2295	125	Acela 2117	Acela 2251	Acela 2213	157	147	145	171	99	Acela 2159	133	Acela 2121	X 2493	93
	⑥⑦	①–⑤	①–⑤	①–⑤	⑦		⑥⑦	⑥⑦	⑥	①–⑤	①–⑤	⑥	⑦	⑦	⑥	⑦	①–⑤	⑥⑦	①–⑤	⑤	①–⑤	①–⑤	①–④
		🚌				♦	2															🚌	
Boston South d.	...	...	0610	0715	...	...	...	0640	0735	...	...	0805	...	...	...	...	0815	0840	0910	...	...	...	0930
Providence d.	...	...	0650	0750	...	...	...	0720	0813	...	...	0840	...	...	...	...	0855	0919	0946	...	...	...	1011
New London d.	...	...	0745	|	...	...	...	0817	|	...	...	|	...	...	...	...	0948	1019	|	...	...	...	1112
Springfield MA d.	0630	0640	|	|	...	...	0730	|	|	...	...	|	...	0800	0835	...	|	|	|	...	...	1000	|
Hartford d.	0708	0715	|	|	...	...	0805	|	|	...	...	|	...	0837	0909	...	|	|	|	...	...	1033	|
New Haven d.	0809	0835	0843	|	...	...	0855	0909	0943	...	...	1013	...	0939	1018	...	1040	1109	1113	...	...	1150	1209
Stamford d.	0858	...	0930	0959	...	...	...	0958	|	...	...	1058	...	1028	1111	...	1129	1158	1158	...	...	...	1258
New York Penn a.	0950	...	1021	1045	...	...	...	1050	1115	...	...	1145	...	1125	1213	...	1220	1253	1245	...	...	...	1348
New York Penn d.	1005	...	1035	1100	1100	1102	...	1105	...	1135	1200	1200	1200	1205	1250	1255	1235	1317	1300	1309	1400	...	1402
Newark NJ d.	1022	...	1053	1115	1114u	1122u	...	1123	...	1152	1215u	1214	1214u	1222	1307	1312	1252	1335	1315	1325u	1415u	...	1419
Philadelphia 30th Street d.	1135	...	1202	1216	1216	1235u	...	1234	...	1303	1316	1316	1316	1333	1418	1417	1414	1448	1413	1430	1513	...	1527
Baltimore Penn d.	1247	...	1320	1320	1319	1355u	...	1340	...	1420	1419	1419	1419	1443	1525	1525	1527	1553	1516	1541	1616	...	1633
BWI Airport d.	1300	...	1333	|	1332	|	...	1353	...	1434	|	1432	1432	1456	1538	1535	1544	1606	1529	1556	1629	...	1646
Washington Union a.	1336	...	1403	1354	1357	1505u	...	1425	...	1506	1453	1459	1457	1530	1610	1612	1620	1635	1554	1630	1653	...	1715
Washington Union d.	...	...	1430	...	...	1505u	...	1450	...	1555	...	...	...	1600	1635	1650	1650	1700	...	...	...	...	1750
Fredricksburg d.	...	...	1540	...	...	|	...	1601	...	1712	...	...	...	1710	|	|	|	1808	...	...	...	...	1901
Richmond d.	...	...	1648	...	...	1707	...	1704	...	1824	..	...	...	1822	|	|	|	1911	...	...	...	...	2006
Newport News a.	...	...	1852	...	...	...	...	...	...	|	...	...	...	|	|	|	|	2106	...	...	...	...	...
Norfolk a.	...	...	*1950**	...	...	...	...	...	...	2038	...	...	...	2036	|	|	|	*2155**	...	...	...	...	...
Virgina Beach a.	...	...	*2030**	...	...	...	...	...	...	...	...	...	...	...	|	|	|	*2225**	...	...	...	...	...
Charlottesville d.	...	...	...	...	...	...	...	...	...	...	...	...	...	...	1901	1916	1923	...	...	...	...	...	...
Lynchburg a.	...	...	...	...	...	...	...	...	...	...	...	...	...	...	2014	2029	2036	...	...	...	...	...	...

	401	161	19	Acela 2253	Acela 2163	85	87	71	97	173	463	Acela 2165	Acela 2221	127	163	129	Acela 2167	Acela 2255	159	193	Acela 2119	Acela 2225	135
	⑥⑦	⑥⑦		⑥⑦	①–⑤	①–⑤	⑦	⑥		①–⑤	⑥⑦	①–⑤	⑦	①–⑤	⑥⑦	①–⑤	①–⑤	⑦	⑥⑦	①–⑤	①–⑤	⑦	⑥⑦
	2		♦						♦		2												
Boston South d.	...	0940	...	1100	1105	...	...	...	...	1115	...	1210	...	...	1140	...	1305	1300	...	...	...	...	1340
Providence d.	...	1020	...	1135	1143	...	...	...	...	1156	...	1246	...	...	1220	...	1341	1335	...	...	...	...	1419
New London d.	...	1115	...	|	|	...	...	...	...	1248	...	|	...	...	1318	...	|	|	...	...	...	...	1513
Springfield MA d.	1040	|	...	|	|	...	...	...	...	|	1240	|	...	...	|	...	|	|	...	...	...	...	|
Hartford d.	1114	|	...	|	|	...	...	...	...	|	1316	|	...	...	|	...	|	|	...	...	...	...	|
New Haven d.	1200	1209	...	1308	1313	...	...	...	...	1340	1405	1413	...	...	1409	...	1513	1508	...	...	...	...	1609
Stamford d.	...	1258	...	1353	1358	...	...	...	...	1429	...	1458	...	...	1458	...	1558	1553	...	...	...	...	1658
New York Penn a.	...	1352	...	1442	1445	...	...	...	...	1520	...	1545	...	...	1550	...	1645	1643	...	...	...	...	1750
New York Penn d.	...	1405	1415	1500	1500	1505	1504	1504	1515	1535	...	1600	1600	1605	1605	1642	1700	1700	1705	1739	1800	1800	1805
Newark NJ d.	...	1422	1437u	1514	1515	1522	1521	1521	1538u	1553	...	1615	1614u	1622	1622	1658u	1715	1714	1722	1756	1815u	1814u	1822
Philadelphia 30th Street d.	...	1535	1555u	1616	1613	1630	1635	1635	1658u	1657	...	1713	1716	1735	1737	1814	1813	1816	1835	1914	1913	1916	1935
Baltimore Penn d.	...	1647	1712u	1719	1716	1742	1748	1748	1817u	1802	...	1814	1819	1842	1849	1924	1915	1919	1946	2025	2016	2019	2049
BWI Airport d.	...	1700	|	1732	1729	1756	1800	1800	|	1815	...	1827	1832	1855	1903	1937	1929	1932	1959	2038	2029	2032	2102
Washington Union a.	...	1736	1830u	1758	1754	1825	1835	1835	1925u	1851	...	1853	1857	1930	1941	2010	1955	1957	2035	2113	2053	2059	2140
Washington Union d.	...	...	1830u	...	...	1905	1900	1900	1925u	...	...	...	...	...	...	...	...	...	...	...	...	...	...
Fredricksburg d.	...	...	|	...	...	2017	2012	2010	|	...	...	...	...	...	...	...	...	...	...	...	...	...	...
Richmond d.	...	...	|	...	...	2116	2113	2122	2134	...	...	...	...	...	...	...	...	...	...	...	...	...	...
Newport News a.	...	...	|	...	...	...	...	|	...	...	...	...	...	...	...	...	...	...	...	...	...	...	...
Norfolk a.	...	...	|	...	...	...	...	2336	...	...	...	...	...	...	...	...	...	...	...	...	...	...	...
Virgina Beach a.	...	...	|	...	...	...	...	...	...	...	...	...	...	...	...	...	...	...	...	...	...	...	...
Charlottesville d.	...	...	2052	...	...	...	...	...	...	...	...	...	...	...	...	...	...	...	...	...	...	...	...
Lynchburg a.	...	...	2200	...	...	...	...	...	...	...	...	...	...	...	...	...	...	...	...	...	...	...	...

	55	Acela 2171	Acela 2257	57	475	465	165	175	Acela 2259	Acela 2173	467	167	Acela 2297	123	Acela 2175	187	177		139	497	169	3479	179
	①–⑤	①–⑤	⑦	⑥⑦	①–⑤	⑦	⑥⑦	①–⑤	⑦	①–⑤	⑥	⑥	⑦	⑦	①–⑤	①–⑤	①–⑤		⑦	⑦	⑥⑦	①–⑤	①–⑤
	♦			♦	2	2					2									2		🚌	
Boston South d.	...	1510	1505	...	...	...	1510	1520	1605	1615	...	1635	1710	...	1720	...	1735	...	1740	...	1840	...	1845
Providence d.	...	1545	1543	...	...	...	1550	1601	1640	1650	...	1714	1748	...	1755	...	1814	...	1820	...	1920	...	1925
New London d.	...	|	|	...	...	...	1649	1657	|	|	...	1813	|	...	|	...	1915	...	1915	...	2016	...	2017
Springfield MA d.	1450	|	|	1450	1605	1610	|	|	|	|	1727	|	|	...	|	...	|	...	|	1940	|	1855	|
Hartford d.	1532	|	|	1526	1642	1647	|	|	|	|	1806	|	|	...	|	...	|	...	|	2015	|	1931	|
New Haven d.	1639	1713	1713	1639	1735	1731	1739	1745	1813	1826	1900	1909	1913	...	1920	...	2013	...	2009	2100	2109	2050	2110
Stamford d.	1728	1759	1758	1728	...	...	1828	1833	1858	1911	...	1958	1958	...	2005	...	2103	...	2058	...	2158	...	2159
New York Penn a.	1825	1845	1845	1825	...	...	1927	1926	1945	1958	...	2050	2045	...	2050	...	2151	...	2150	...	2250	...	2250
New York Penn d.	1845	1900	1900	1901	...	...	2001	1940	2000	2013	...	2105	...	2105	2105	2110	2205	...	2205	...	2305	...	...
Newark NJ d.	1903	1915	1914	1918	...	...	2018	1958	2014	2028	...	2122	...	2122u	2120	2127	2222	...	2222	...	2322	...	...
Philadelphia 30th Street d.	2014	2013	2016	2028	...	...	2132	2114	2116	2125	...	2235	...	2233	2218	2237	2332	...	2335	...	0032	...	...
Baltimore Penn d.	2121	2114	2119	2136	...	...	2241	2228	2219	2227	...	2344	...	2342	2321	2343	0042	...	0044	...	0142	...	...
BWI Airport d.	|	2128	2132	2149	...	...	2255	2242	2232	2240	...	2357	...	2355	|	2356	0055	...	0057	...	0155	...	...
Washington Union a.	2201	2155	2159	2225	...	...	2334	2312	2258	2304	...	0035	...	0035	2357	0031	0132	...	0135	...	0232	...	...
Washington Union d.	...	...	...	...	...	...	...	...	...	...	...	...	...	...	...	...	...	...	...	...	...	...	...
Fredricksburg d.	...	...	...	...	...	...	...	...	...	...	...	...	...	...	...	...	...	...	...	...	...	...	...
Richmond d.	...	...	...	...	...	...	...	...	...	...	...	...	...	...	...	...	...	...	...	...	...	...	...
Newport News a.	...	...	...	...	...	...	...	...	...	...	...	...	...	...	...	...	...	...	...	...	...	...	...
Norfolk a.	...	...	...	...	...	...	...	...	...	...	...	...	...	...	...	...	...	...	...	...	...	...	...
Virgina Beach a.	...	...	...	...	...	...	...	...	...	...	...	...	...	...	...	...	...	...	...	...	...	...	...
Charlottesville d.	...	...	...	...	...	...	...	...	...	...	...	...	...	...	...	...	...	...	...	...	...	...	...
Lynchburg a.	...	...	...	...	...	...	...	...	...	...	...	...	...	...	...	...	...	...	...	...	...	...	...

♦ – NOTES, LISTED BY TRAIN NUMBER:

19/20 – CRESCENT – 🛏 1, 2 cl., 🚃 2 and ✕ New York - Washington - New Orleans and v.v.
50/51 – CARDINAL – 🛏 1, 2 cl., 🚃 2 and 🍷 Chicago - Washington - New York and v.v.
54/55 – VERMONTER – 🚃 12 and 🍷 Washington - New York - New Haven - St Albans and v.v.
56/57 – VERMONTER – 🚃 12 and 🍷 Washington - New York - New Haven - St Albans and
79/80 – CAROLINIAN – 🚃 12 and 🍷 New York - Washington - Charlotte and v.v.
89/90 – PALMETTO – 🚃 12 and 🍷 New York - Washington - Savannah and v.v.

trak Most trains 🍸

NEWPORT NEWS - WASHINGTON - NEW YORK - BOSTON 9215

		Acela		X					Acela	Acela		X					Acela			Acela			
	66	2190	190	3490	150	450		110	2150	2290	170	3470		160	460	180	2100	162	130	2154	98	172	54
		①–⑤	①–⑤	①–⑤	⑥⑦	⑥⑦		①–⑤	①–⑤	⑥	①–⑤	①–⑤		⑥⑦	⑥⑦	①–⑤	①–⑤	⑥⑦	①–⑤	①–⑤		①–⑤	⑥⑦
				🚌		2						🚌									♦		♦
Lynchburg d.	...	...	...	...	...	...	...	...	...	...	...	...	...	...	...	...	...	...	...	...	...	...	...
Charlottesville d.	...	...	...	...	...	...	...	...	...	...	...	...	...	...	...	...	...	...	...	...	...	...	...
Virginia Beach d.	*1430**	...	...	...	...	...	...	...	...	...	...	...	...	...	...	...	...	...	...	...	...	...	...
Norfolk d.	*1515**	...	...	...	...	...	...	...	...	...	...	...	...	...	...	...	...	...	...	...	...	...	...
Newport News d.	1720	...	...	...	...	...	...	...	...	...	...	...	...	...	...	...	...	...	...	...	...	...	...
Richmond d.	1900	...	...	...	...	...	...	...	...	...	...	...	...	...	...	...	...	...	...	...	0432	...	...
Fredericksburg d.	1957	...	...	...	...	...	...	...	...	...	...	...	...	...	...	...	...	...	...	...	|	...	...
Washington Union a.	2120	...	...	...	...	...	...	...	...	...	...	...	...	...	...	...	...	...	...	...	0707s	...	...
Washington Union d.	2210	...	0312	...	0312	...	...	0357	0455	...	0448	...	...	0522	...	0527	0555	0617	0625	0655	0707s	0722	0727
BWI Airport d.	2238	...	0337	...	0337	...	...	0422	|	...	0516	...	...	0550	...	0554	0616	0645	0652	0716	|	0750	0754
Baltimore Penn d.	2254	...	0352	...	0352	...	...	0438	0525	...	0531	...	...	0605	...	0610	0629	0700	0709	0729	0812s	0806	0809
Philadelphia 30th Street d.	0010	...	0512	...	0512	...	...	0547	0627	...	0642	...	...	0716	...	0724	0731	0817	0826	0831	0930s	0917	0917
Newark NJ d.	0122	...	0622	...	0622	...	...	0702	0728	...	0757	...	...	0827	...	0825s	0832s	0926	0942	0930	1040s	1026	1027
New York Penn a.	0140	...	0641	...	0642	...	...	0724	0745	...	0816	...	...	0846	...	0849	0854	0946	1003	0948	1100	1046	1047
New York Penn d.	0240	0620	0655	...	0700	...	...	...	0800	0803	0830	...	...	0900	...	...	...	1000	...	1003	...	1100	1130
Stamford d.	0324	0706	0747	...	0748	...	...	...	0847	0848	0919	...	...	0948	...	...	...	1048	...	1048	...	1148	1218
New Haven d.	0440	0758	0837	0840	0840	0842	...	...	0936	0937	1013	1030	...	1044	1046	...	...	1144	...	1137	...	1244	1323
Hartford d.	|	|	|	0929	|	0923	...	...	|	|	|	1115	...	|	1128	...	...	|	...	|	...	|	1411
Springfield MA a.	|	|	|	1010	|	1003	...	...	|	|	|	1155	...	|	1205	...	...	|	...	|	...	|	1458
New London d.	0534	0837	0926	...	0929	...	...	...	|	|	1100	...	...	1129	...	...	...	1232	...	|	...	1332	...
Providence d.	0656	0918	1017	...	1025	...	...	...	1053	1057	1155	...	...	1225	...	...	...	1328	...	1256	...	1423	...
Boston South a.	0758	1005	1105	...	1115	...	...	...	1140	1145	1245	...	...	1315	...	...	...	1420	...	1345	...	1515	...

	Acela					Acela	Acela					Acela	Acela				Acela	Acela					Acela	Acela
	2104	56	152		86	2158	2250	184	164	464	20	2160	2208	174	82	154	2110	2252	84	88	488		2164	2212
	①–⑤	①–⑤	⑥⑦		①–⑤	①–⑤	⑥⑦	①–⑤	⑥⑦	⑥⑦		①–⑤	⑦	①–⑤	⑥	⑦	①–⑤	⑦	①–⑤	⑥⑦	⑥⑦		①–⑤	⑥⑦
		♦									♦													
nchburg d.	...	...	...	...	...	...	...	...	...	...	0556	...	...	...	...	...	...	...	...	...	...	...	...	...
harlottesville d.	...	...	...	...	...	...	...	...	...	...	0709	...	...	...	...	...	...	...	...	...	...	...	...	...
nia Beach d.	...	...	...	...	...	...	...	...	...	...	|	...	...	...	...	...	...	...	...	...	...	...	...	...
olk d.	...	...	...	...	...	...	...	...	...	...	|	...	...	...	...	...	...	...	0610	0615	...	...	...	...
port News d.	...	...	...	...	...	...	...	...	...	...	|	...	...	...	...	...	...	...	|	|	...	...	...	...
mond d.	...	...	...	...	0600	...	...	...	0635	...	|	...	...	0700	0735	...	...	...	0818	0825	...	...	...	...
ericksburg d.	...	...	...	...	0656	...	...	...	0733	...	|	...	...	0800	0832	...	...	...	0919	0925	...	...	...	...
hington Union a.	...	...	...	...	0815	...	...	...	0900	...	0953s	...	...	0933	0944	...	...	...	1039	1056	...	...	...	...
hington Union d.	0755	0807	0807	...	0840	0855	0855	0917	0925	...	0953s	0955	0955	1010	1020	1017	1055	1055	1110	1125	...	...	1155	1155
Airport d.	0816	0832	0835	...	0908	0916	0916	0945	0953	...	|	1016	1016	1037	1048	1045	1116	1116	1138	1153	...	...	|	1216
more Penn d.	0829	0849	0851	...	0923	0929	0929	1001	1008	...	1055s	1029	1029	1053	1104	1101	1129	1129	1154	1208	...	...	1225	1229
adelphia 30th Street d.	0933	0958	1009	...	1040	1032	1034	1112	1120	...	1208s	1131	1134	1205	1218	1215	1231	1234	1305	1319	...	...	1327	1334
ark NJ d.	1030s	1103	1125s	...	1147	1130	1136	1222	1229	...	1325s	1230	1235s	1315	1328	1328	1330s	1336	1411	1428	...	...	1430	1435s
York Penn a.	1051	1121	1147	...	1205	1148	1153	1242	1247	...	1346	1248	1258	1335	1346	1348	1353	1353	1430	1446	...	...	1446	1457
York Penn d.	...	1133	...	...	1230	1203	1203	...	1300	...	...	1303	...	1400	1400	...	...	1403	...	1500	...	...	1500	...
nford d.	...	1218	...	...	1318	1248	1248	...	1348	...	...	1348	...	1448	1448	...	...	1448	...	1548	...	...	1545	...
Haven d.	...	1325	...	...	1410	1337	1337	...	1444	1450	...	1437	...	1544	1544	...	...	1537	...	1644	1650	...	|	...
artford d.	...	1413	...	...	|	|	|	...	|	1541	...	|	...	|	|	...	...	|	...	|	1736	...	|	...
pringfield MA a.	...	1500	...	...	|	|	|	...	|	1616	...	|	...	|	|	...	...	|	...	|	1815	...	|	...
London d.	...	...	...	...	1452	|	|	...	1532	...	...	|	...	1635	1634	...	...	|	...	1733	...	...	|	...
idence d.	...	...	...	...	1547	1454	1458	...	1630	...	...	1556	...	1730	1726	...	...	1657	...	1827	...	...	1751	...
ton South a.	...	...	...	...	1635	1545	1547	...	1720	...	...	1645	...	1830	1816	...	...	1746	...	1920	...	...	1845	...

				Acela	Acela				Acela	Acela				Acela	Acela							Acela	Acela	Acela
	176	3476	140	2166	2254	186	194	96	2168	2260	94	494	156	2170	2256	148	92	168	132	432	134	2172	2220	2258
	①–⑤	①–⑤	⑥⑦	①–⑤	⑦	①–⑤	⑦	⑥	①–⑤	⑥	①–⑤	①–⑤	⑥⑦	①–⑤	⑦	①–⑤		⑥	⑦	⑦	④⑤	①–⑤	⑥	⑦
		🚌															♦							
ynchburg d.	0738	...	...	...	...	...	...	...	...	...	...	...	0959	...	...	...	...	...	...	...	...	...	...	...
harlottesville d.	0852	...	...	...	...	...	...	...	...	...	...	...	1113	...	...	...	...	...	...	...	...	...	...	...
nia Beach d.	|	...	...	...	...	...	*0610**	*0610**	...	...	*0700**	...	|	...	...	...	...	...	...	...	...	...	...	...
olk d.	|	...	...	...	...	...	*0650**	*0650**	...	...	*0740**	...	|	...	...	...	...	...	...	...	...	...	...	...
port News d.	|	...	...	...	...	...	0830	0830	...	...	0915	...	|	...	...	...	...	...	...	...	...	...	...	...
mond d.	|	...	...	...	...	...	1019	1019	...	...	1109	...	|	...	...	...	1216	...	...	...	...	...	...	...
ericksburg d.	|	...	...	...	...	...	1117	1117	...	...	1208	...	|	...	...	...	|	...	...	...	...	...	...	...
shington Union a.	1120	...	...	...	...	...	1235	1235	...	...	1335	...	1335	...	...	...	1438s	...	...	...	...	...	...	...
shington Union d.	1205	...	1222	1255	1255	1302	1305	1325	1355	1355	1405	...	1420	1455	1455	1502	1438s	1522	1522	...	1527	1555	1555	1555
Airport d.	1232	...	1249	|	1316	1329	1332	1352	|	1416	1433	...	1447	1516	1516	1529	|	1549	1549	...	1551	|	1616	1616
more Penn d.	1247	...	1305	1330	1329	1344	1351	1411	1425	1429	1449	...	1504	1529	1529	1545	1547s	1605	1605	...	1606	1625	1629	1629
adelphia 30th Street d.	1358	...	1415	1432	1434	1458	1505	1523	1527	1534	1559	...	1619	1631	1634	1657	1705s	1715	1715	...	1731	1727	1734	1734
ark NJ d.	1502	...	1528	1530	1536	1612	1615	1632	1630	1636	1705	...	1727	1730	1736	1810	1823s	1828	1828	...	1837s	1830	1836s	1837
York Penn a.	1520	...	1548	1546	1553	1632	1635	1650	1646	1653	1722	...	1746	1746	1753	1831	1850	1846	1848	...	1855	1846	1857	1853
York Penn d.	1530	...	1630	1600	1603	...	1700	1725	1703	1703	1742	...	...	1802	1803	1845	...	1900	1930	...	...	1900	...	1903
nford d.	1618	...	1718	|	1648	...	1748	1812	1748	1748	1831	...	...	1847	1848	1935	...	1948	2018	...	...	1945	...	1948
Haven d.	1734a	1720	1826	1733	1737	...	1840	1901	1837	1837	1932b	1930	...	1936	1937	2044	...	2044	2114	2120	...	2034	...	2037
artford d.	|	1810	1919	|	|	...	|	|	|	|	|	2016	...	|	|	2131	...	|	|	2210	...	|	...	|
pringfield MA a.	|	1850	2000	|	|	...	|	|	|	|	|	2055	...	|	|	2220	...	|	|	2250	...	|	...	|
London d.	1824	...	...	|	|	...	1932	1951	|	|	2024	...	...	|	|	...	...	2135	2207	...	...	2113e	...	|
idence d.	1919	...	...	1854	1856	...	2025	2044	1956	1959	2116	...	...	2054	2055	...	...	2235	2302	...	...	2154	...	2154
ton South a.	2012	...	...	1940	1946	...	2115	2135	2045	2048	2210	...	...	2145	2145	...	...	2326	2355	...	...	2245	...	2246

							Acela	Acela						Acela				Acela				Acela	Acela	
		178	126	146		80	2122	2222	136	196	192		166	2124	138	50	158	2126	188	182	90	2128	2228	
		①–⑤	⑦	⑥			①–⑤	⑦	⑤	①–④	⑥		⑦	①–⑤	①–⑤	③⑤⑦	⑥⑦	①–⑤	①–⑤	⑥⑦		①–⑤	⑦	
						♦										♦					♦			
ynchburg d.	...	...	...	...	...	...	...	...	...	...	...	...	...	...	...	...	...	...	...	...	...	...	...	...
harlottesville d.	...	...	...	...	...	...	...	...	...	...	...	...	...	...	...	1519	...	...	...	...	...	...	...	...
nia Beach d.	...	...	...	...	...	...	...	...	...	...	...	...	...	...	...	|	...	...	...	...	...	...	...	...
olk d.	...	...	...	...	...	...	...	...	...	...	...	...	...	...	...	|	...	...	...	...	...	...	...	...
port News d.	...	...	...	...	...	...	...	...	...	...	...	...	...	...	...	|	...	...	...	...	...	...	...	...
mond d.	...	...	...	...	...	1412	...	...	...	...	...	...	...	...	...	|	...	...	...	...	1714	...	...	...
ericksburg d.	...	...	...	...	...	1506	...	...	...	...	...	...	...	...	...	|	...	...	...	...	|	...	...	...
shington Union a.	...	...	...	...	...	1629s	...	...	...	...	...	...	...	...	...	1819s	...	...	...	...	1942s	...	...	...
shington Union d.	...	1602	1622	1622	...	1629s	1655	1655	1702	1702	1717	...	1717	1755	1802	1819s	1817	1855	1907	1917	1942s	1955	1955	...
Airport d.	...	1629	1648	1649	...	|	|	1716	1729	1729	1744	...	1744	|	1830	|	1844	|	1934	1944	|	|	2016	...
more Penn d.	...	1645	1704	1705	...	1747s	1725	1729	1745	1745	1801	...	1801	1825	1846	1916s	1901	1925	1951	2001	2115s	2025	2029	...
adelphia 30th Street d.	...	1755	1815	1816	...	1900s	1827	1834	1859	1859	1916	...	1916	1927	1958	2026s	2012	2031	2107	2117	2224s	2130	2134	...
ark NJ d.	...	1903	1923s	1926	...	2013s	1930s	1935s	2022	2021s	2027	...	2027	2030s	2112	2138s	2124s	2133s	2214s	2226	2336s	2231s	2235s	...
York Penn a.	...	1925	1947	1946	...	2035	1952	1958	2043	2042	2046	...	2046	2051	2133	2158	2147	2154	2236	2251	2356	2252	2257	...
York Penn d.	...	1950	...	2000	...	...	...	...	2057	...	...	...	2100	...	...	...	...	...	...	...	...	...	...	...
nford d.	...	2045	...	2048	...	...	...	...	2149	...	...	...	2148	...	...	...	...	...	...	...	...	...	...	...
Haven d.	...	2142	...	2154	...	...	...	...	2259	...	...	...	2241	...	...	...	...	...	...	...	...	...	...	...
artford d.	...	|	...	2250e	...	...	...	...	2356e	...	...	...	|	...	...	...	...	...	...	...	...	...	...	...
pringfield MA a.	...	|	...	2320	...	...	...	...	0030	...	...	...	|	...	...	...	...	...	...	...	...	...	...	...
London d.	...	2232	...	...	...	...	...	...	...	...	...	...	2331	...	...	...	...	...	...	...	...	...	...	...
idence d.	...	2329	...	...	...	...	...	...	...	...	...	...	0020	...	...	...	...	...	...	...	...	...	...	...
ton South a.	...	0020	...	...	...	...	...	...	...	...	...	...	0110	...	...	...	...	...	...	...	...	...	...	...

2 – SILVER STAR – 🛏 1, 2 cl., 2 and ✕ New York - Washington - Tampa - Miami and v.v.

8 – SILVER METEOR – 🛏 1, 2 cl., 2 and ✕ New York - Washington - Orlando - Miami and v.v.

Arrives at 1712. **b** – Arrives 1921. **e** – May leave earlier than time shown.

Calls to set down only. **u** – Calls to pick up only. * – Connection by 🚌.

X – Due to track work replacement 🚌 services will operate until July 2016.

NOTE: Due to track work replacements all services are subject to alterations throughout the summer.

9220 ST ALBANS - SPRINGFIELD — Amtrak

km		55 ①–⑤ A	57 ⑥⑦ A
0	**St. Albans** d.	0925	0925
38	Burlington Essex Jct. d.	0954	0954
70	Waterbury d.	1019	1019
90	Montpelier d.	1032	1032
133	Randolph d.	1105	1105
189	White River Jct. d.	1142	1142
205	Windsor VT d.	1159	1159
225	Claremont d.	1209	1209
252	Bellows Falls d.	1230	1230
291	Brattleboro d.	1301	1301
360	Northampton d.	1401	1401
397	**Springfield** MA a.	1435	1435
609	*New York Penn* **9215** a.	1825	1825
974	*Washington U* **9215** a.	2159	2225

	54 ⑥⑦ A	56 ①–⑤ A
Washington U **9215** d.	0730	0810
New York P **9215** d.	1130	1133
Springfield MA d.	1515	1515
Northampton d.	1557	1557
Brattleboro d.	1656	1656
Bellows Falls d.	1726	1726
Claremont d.	1745	1745
Windsor VT d.	1754	1754
White River Jct. d.	1815	1815
Randolph d.	1852	1852
Montpelier d.	1927	1927
Waterbury d.	1939	1939
Burlington Essex Jct. d.	2008	2008
St. Albans a.	2040	2040

A – VERMONTER – 🚃12 and 🍸 Washington - New York - New Haven - St Albans and v.v.

9225 HARRISBURG - PITTSBURGH — Amt

km		43 B	
	New York Penn **9230** d.	1052	...
	Philadelphia **9230** d.	1242	...
0	**Harrisburg** d.	1436	...
95	Lewistown d.	1546	...
154	Huntingdon d.	1622	...
186	Tyrone d.	1648r	...
213	Altoona d.	1706	...
275	Johnstown d.	1800	...
334	Latrobe d.	1841r	...
346	Greensburg d.	1852	...
401	**Pittsburgh 9235** a.	2005	...

	42 B
Pittsburgh 9235 d.	0730
Greensburg d.	0811
Latrobe d.	0821r
Johnstown d.	0904
Altoona d.	1001
Tyrone d.	1017r
Huntingdon d.	1044
Lewistown d.	1121
Harrisburg a.	1255
Philadelphia **9230** a.	1455
New York Penn **9230** a.	1650

B – PENNSYLVANIAN – 🚃12 and 🍸 Pittsburgh - Harrisburg - New York and v.v.
r – Calls on request.

9230 NEW YORK - PHILADELPHIA - HARRISBURG — Amt

KEYSTONE SERVICE

km		601	605	607	611	661	641	1663	643	43	645	615	609	665	647	649	667	651	653	669	655	671		619
		①–⑤	①–⑤	①–⑤	⑥	⑥⑦	①–⑤	⑥⑦	①–⑤	B	①–⑤	⑦	①–⑤	⑥⑦	①–⑤	①–⑤	⑥⑦	①–⑤	①–⑤	⑥⑦	①–⑤	⑥⑦		①–⑤
0	**New York** Penn **9215** d.	0325	0440	0530	0300	0700	0725	0909	0930	1052	1205	1205	1255	1305	1411	1444	1513	1603	1710	1717	1835	1953	...	2110
16	Newark NJ **9215** d.	0345	0457u	0546u	0320	0717u	0742u	0927u	0946u	1109u	1222u	1222	1310u	1323u	1428	1459	1532u	1620u	1727u	1734u	1852u	2009u	...	2127
146	**Philadelphia** 30th St a.	0452	0602	0653	0427	0820	0850	1035	1050	1215	1325	1330	1417	1426	1533	1612	1638	1723	1830	1836	2000	2015	...	2252
146	**Philadelphia** 30th St d.	0520	0625	0725	0725	0835	0900	1055	1100	1242	1335	1355	1445	1445	1545	1645	1655	1735	1842	1855	2015	2145	...	2259
178	Paoli d.	0546	0651	0751	0750	0900	0923	1120	1123	1312	1359	1420	1510	1510	1610	1711	1721	1802	1907	1921	2040	2210	...	2324f
255	Lancaster d.	0630	0735	0830	0834	0945	1007	1203	1207	1352	1443	1504	1555	1555	1650	1758	1805	1847	1953	2005	2125	2255	...	0009f
300	Elizabethtown d.	0647	0752	0845	0850	1001	1024	1220	1224	1406	1500	1521	1611	1611	1704	1814	1821	1903	2009	2021	2141	2311	...	0025f
315	**Harrisburg** a.	0715	0815	0905	0915	1025	1050	1245	1250	1426	1525	1540	1635	1635	1730	1840	1845	1930	2035	2045	2205	2330	...	0050

	640	642	600	660	644	662	646	664	648	666	650	42	670	652	654	672	656	618	658	674	610	612	620	6
	①–⑤	①–⑤	①–⑤	⑥⑦	①–⑤	⑥	①–⑤	⑥⑦	①–⑤	⑥⑦	①–⑤	B	⑥⑦	①–⑤	①–⑤	⑥⑦	①–⑤	①–④	⑤	⑦	⑥	⑦	①–⑤	①
Harrisburg d.	0500	0555	0645	0720	0800	0820	0900	0930	1000	1120	1200	1305	1405	1520	1630	1705	1735	1840	1840	1905	1905	2020	2030	2
Elizabethtown d.	0517	0612	0702	0737	0816	0837	0917	0947	1015	1137	1217	1323	1422	1537	1647	1722	1752	1857	1857	1922	1922	2037	2047	2
Lancaster d.	0535	0630	0721	0755	0832	0855	0933	1005	1032	1155	1235	1340	1440	1554	1705	1740	1810	1912	1912	1940	1940	2055	2102	2
Paoli d.	0619	0723	0809	0841	0910	0941	1018	1049	1110	1241	1316	1424	1528	1637	1750	1825	1855	1955	1955	2025	2025	2140	2144	2
Philadelphia 30th St a.	0645	0750	0835	0905	0935	1005	1040	1110	1135	1305	1345	1455	1555	1705	1825	1850	1923	2020	2020	2050	2050	2210	2210	2
Philadelphia 30th St d.	0700	0805	0850	0823	0945	1030	1055	1125	1145	1330	1405	1525	1610	1718	1850	1910	1940	2110	2036	2110	2120	0010	...	0
Newark NJ a.	0812f	0906f	0953s	1031	1047f	1142f	1157f	1231f	1252f	1440f	1508f	1630s	1713f	1833f	1954f	2014f	2045f	2214	2142f	2214f	2226s	0122s	...	0
New York Penn a.	0830	0926	1015	1049	1105	1159	1215	1249	1310	1457	1526	1650	1732	1853	2012	2034	2103	2234	2200	2234	2249	0140	...	0

B – PENNSYLVANIAN – see Table **9225**. f – May leave before time shown. s – Calls to set down only. u – Calls to pick up only.

9235 BOSTON - CHICAGO — Amtrak

km		29 E	449 C	49 D
0	**Boston** South d.	...	1250	...
70	Worcester d.	...	1403	...
157	Springfield MA d.	...	1523	...
242	Pittsfield d.	...	1639	...
	New York **9205** d.	...	|	1540
320	**Albany** R'laer d.	...	1800	1905
349	Schenectady d.	...	...	1932
558	Syracuse d.	...	...	2149
686	Rochester d.	...	...	2309
784	Buffalo Depew d.	...	...	2359
931	Erie d.	...	...	0148
◇	**Washington** U d.	1605	...	|
◇	Harper's Ferry d.	1716	...	|
◇	Martinsburg d.	1745	...	|
◇	Cumberland d.	1924	...	|
◇	Pittsburgh **9225** d.	2359	...	|
◇	Alliance d.	0139	...	|
1083	**Cleveland** d.	0259	...	0345
1179	Sandusky d.	0402	...	0455
1254	Toledo d.	0522	...	0615
1379	Waterloo d.	0636	...	0733
1467	Elkhart d.	0729	...	0825
1494	South Bend d.	0751	...	0849
1629	**Chicago** Union a.	0845	...	0945

	30 E	48 D	448 C
Chicago Union d.	1840	2130	...
South Bend d.	2109	2359	...
Elkhart d.	2129	0022	...
Waterloo d.	2023	0115	...
Toledo d.	2349	0320	...
Sandusky d.	0040	0412	...
Cleveland d.	0154	0550	...
Alliance d.	0305	|	...
Pittsburgh **9225** d.	0520	|	...
Cumberland d.	0932	|	...
Martinsburg d.	1101	|	...
Harper's Ferry d.	1131	|	...
Washington U a.	1305	|	...
Erie d.	...	0720	...
Buffalo Depew d.	...	0851	...
Rochester d.	...	0950	...
Syracuse d.	...	1118	...
Schenectady d.	...	1358	...
Albany R'laer a.	...	1455	1505
New York **9205** a.	...	1823	|
Pittsfield d.	...	...	1609
Springfield MA d.	...	...	1733
Worcester d.	...	...	1844s
Boston South a.	...	...	2001

9240 WASHINGTON - MIAMI — Amtr

km		89 F	91 G	97 H
0	**New York** Penn d.	0605	1102	1515
16	Newark NJ d.	0622u	1122u	1538u
146	Philadelphia 30th St d.	0732u	1235u	1658u
297	Baltimore Penn d.	0842u	1355u	1817u
362	**Washington** Union d.	1000u	1505u	1925u
536	Richmond d.	1219	1717	2144
581	Petersburg d.	1254	1751	2218
738	Rocky Mount d.	1429	1921	2350
852	**Raleigh** d.	|	2101	|
882	Fayetteville d.	1605	|	0122
1015	Florence d.	1744	|	0313
1167	Charleston SC d.	1919	|	0451
1328	Savannah d.	2104	0418	0640
1565	**Jacksonville** a.	...	0639	0909
1565	**Jacksonville** a.	...	0659	0934
1792	Winter Park d.	...	0943	1226
1800	Orlando d.	...	1020	1304
1829	Kissimmee d.	...	1044	1326
1959	**Tampa** d.	...	1237	|
	Winter Haven d.	...	1335	1413
1955	Sebring d.	...	1416	1454
2120	West Palm Beach a.	...	1617s	1647s
2189	Fort Lauderdale a.	...	1717s	1743s
2224	**Miami** Amtrak a.	...	1758	1839

	98 H	92 G	9
Miami Amtrak d.	0810	1150	
Fort Lauderdale d.	0850u	1230u	
West Palm Beach d.	0947u	1327u	
Sebring d.	1123	1502	
Winter Haven d.	1207	1548	
Tampa d.	|	1727	
Kissimmee d.	1256	1848	
Orlando d.	1335	1932	
Winter Park d.	1352	1949	
Jacksonville a.	1647	2225	
Jacksonville d.	1707	2303	
Savannah d.	1931	0122	0
Charleston SC d.	2117	|	1
Florence d.	2312	|	1
Fayetteville d.	0037	|	1
Raleigh d.	|	0845	
Rocky Mount d.	0209	1003	1
Petersburg d.	0333	1128	1
Richmond d.	0432	1216	1
Washington Union a.	0707s	1438s	19
Baltimore Penn a.	0812s	1547s	21
Philadelphia 30th St a.	0930s	1705s	22
Newark NJ a.	1040s	1823s	23
New York Penn a.	1100	1850	2

Notes for Table **9235** and **9240**.

C – 🛏 1, 2 cl., 🚃 and 🍸 Boston(**449/448**) - Albany(**48/49**) - Chicago and v.v.
D – LAKE SHORE LIMITED – 🛏 1, 2 cl., 🚃 and ✕ New York(**49/48**) - Albany(**49/48**) - Chicago and v.v.; conveys 🛏 1, 2 cl., 🚃 and 🍸 Boston(**449/448**) - Albany(**48/49**) - Chicago and v.v.
E – CAPITOL LIMITED – 🛏 1, 2 cl., 🚃 and ✕ Washington - Chicago and v.v.
F – PALMETTO – 🚃12 and 🍸 New York - Washington - Savannah and v.v.
G – SILVER STAR – 🛏 1, 2 cl., 🚃 and ✕ New York - Washington - Tampa - Miami and v.v.
H – SILVER METEOR – 🛏 1, 2 cl., 🚃 and ✕ New York - Washington - Orlando - Miami and v.v.

s – Calls to set down only.
u – Calls to pick up only.
◇ – Washington - Cleveland distances: Washing *0 km*, Harper's Ferry *88 km*, Martinsburg *118* Cumberland *234 km*, Pittsburgh *478 km*, Allia *613 km*, Cleveland *702 km*.

9245 WASHINGTON - CHARLOTTE - NEW ORLEANS — Amtr

km		73 2	75 2	79 A	19 B
	New York Penn **9215** d.	...	...	0705	1415
0	**Washington** Union d.	...	...	1053	1830
174	Richmond d.	...	...	1308	|
219	Petersburg d.	...	...	1341	|
376	Rocky Mount d.	...	...	1511	|
490	**Raleigh** d.	0645	1145	1650	|
619	Greensboro d.	0821	1321	1832	0022
645	High Point d.	0838	1338	1848	0039
699	Salisbury d.	0914	1414	1924	0117
766	**Charlotte** a.	1004	1504	2012	0245
890	Spartanburg d.	...	...	...	0414
940	Greenville d.	...	...	...	0501
1102	Gainesville d.	...	...	...	0658
1179	**Atlanta** d.	...	...	...	0838
1344	Anniston d.	...	...	...	1000
1447	Birmingham d.	...	...	...	1208
1536	Tuscaloosa d.	...	...	...	1307
1692	Meridian d.	...	...	...	1504
1829	Hattiesburg d.	...	...	...	1638
2018	**New Orleans** a.	...	...	...	1932

	20 B	80 A	74 2	76 2
New Orleans d.	0700	...	...	...
Hattiesburg d.	0930	...	...	...
Meridian d.	1107	...	...	...
Tuscaloosa d.	1244	...	...	...
Birmingham d.	1424	...	...	...
Anniston d.	1559	...	...	...
Atlanta d.	2004	...	...	...
Gainesville d.	2059	...	...	...
Greenville d.	2258	...	...	...
Spartanburg d.	2339	...	...	...
Charlotte d.	0146	0700	1200	1715
Salisbury d.	0232	0743	1244	1759
High Point d.	0316	0817	1320	1835
Greensboro d.	0344	0839	1342	1857
Raleigh d.	|	1025	1521	2036
Rocky Mount d.	|	1152	...	...
Petersburg d.	|	1317	...	...
Richmond d.	|	1412	...	...
Washington Union a.	0953	1629	...	...
New York Penn **9215** a.	1346	2035	...	...

A – CAROLINIAN – 🚃12 and 🍸 New York - Washington - Charlotte and v.v.
B – CRESCENT – 🛏 1, 2 cl., 🚃 and ✕ New York - Washington - New Orleans and

WASHINGTON - CHICAGO 9250

Amtrak

km		51 ③⑤⑦ A	851 B		50 ②④⑥ A	851 B
	New York P **9215** ...... d.	0645	...	**Chicago** Union .... d.	1745	1745
0	**Washington** Union .... d.	1100	...	Lafayette .... d.	2157	2157
9	Culpeper .... d.	1225	...	Crawfordsville .... d.	2231r	2231r
1	Charlottesville .... d.	1352	...	**Indianapolis** .... a.	2350	2350
8	Clifton Forge .... d.	1613	...	**Indianapolis** .... d.	2359	...
3	White Sulpher Springs .. d.	1705	...	Cincinnati .... d.	0327	...
8	Charleston WV .... d.	2029	...	South Portsmouth .... d.	0545	...
6	Huntington .... d.	2151	...	Huntington .... d.	0716	...
8	South Portsmouth .... d.	2257	...	Charleston WV .... d.	0821	...
2	Cincinnati .... d.	0141	...	White Sulpher Spings ...... d.	1139	...
9	**Indianapolis** .... a.	0515	...	Clifton Forge .... d.	1244	...
9	**Indianapolis** .... d.	0600	0600	Charlottesville .... d.	1549	...
4	Crawfordsville .... d.	0658r	0658r	Culpepper .... d.	1635	...
7	Lafayette .... d.	0736	0736	**Washington** Union ...... a.	1819	...
3	**Chicago** Union .... a.	1005	1005	*New York P* **9215** ...... a.	2158	...

CARDINAL – 🛏 1, 2 cl., [2] and 🍸 Chicago - New York and v.v.
HOOSIER STATE – [2] Chicago - Indianapolis and v.v. Runs on days Trains **50/51** do not operate.
Request stop.

CHICAGO - NEW ORLEANS 9255

Amtrak

km		391 D	393 E	59 C		58 C	390 D	392 E
0	**Chicago** Union ..... d.	0815	1605	2005	**New Orleans** .... d.	1345	...	...
92	Kankakee .... d.	0922	1712	2123r	Hammond .... d.	1445	...	...
208	Champaign ‡ .... d.	1025	1815	2234	McComb .... d.	1532r	...	...
323	Effingham .... d.	1129	1919	2337r	Jackson .... d.	1744	...	...
408	Centralia .... d.	1216	2006	0025r	Yazoo City .... d.	1842r	...	...
498	Carbondale .... d.	1345	2135	0126	Greenwood .... d.	1937	...	...
725	Newbern .... d.	...	...	0356r	Memphis .... d.	2240	...	...
850	Memphis .... d.	...	...	0650	Newbern .... d.	0022r	...	...
1051	Greenwood .... d.	...	...	0900	Carbondale .... d.	0316	0730	1615
1136	Yazoo City .... d.	...	...	0951r	Centralia .... d.	0410r	0823	1708
1207	Jackson .... d.	...	...	1120	Effingham .... d.	0457r	0907	1752
1334	McComb .... d.	...	...	1240r	Champaign ‡ .... d.	0610	1014	1859
1419	Hammond .... d.	...	...	1328	Kankakee .... d.	0713r	1115	2000
1503	**New Orleans** .... a.	...	...	1532	**Chicago** Union ..... a.	0900	1300	2145

C – CITY OF NEW ORLEANS – 🛏 1, 2 cl., [2] and ✕ Chicago - New Orleans and v.v.
D – SALUKI – [12] and 🍸 Chicago - Carbondale and v.v.
E – ILLINI – [12] and 🍸 Chicago - Carbondale and v.v.
r – Request stop.
‡ – Champaign Urbana.

CHICAGO - ST. LOUIS - KANSAS CITY 9260

Amtrak

km		311 F	301 G	303 G	313 F	21 H	3 J	305 G	307 G	
0	**Chicago** Union .... d.	...	0700	0925	...	1345	1500	1715	1900	...
0	Joliet Union .... d.	...	0757	1015	...	1440u	|	1805	1950	...
8	Pontiac .... d.	...	|	1106	...	1527	|	1856	2041	...
4	Bloomington .... d.	...	0914	1139	...	1604	|	1929	2114	...
2	Lincoln .... d.	...	|	1210	...	1637	|	2002	2147	...
8	Springfield IL .... d.	...	1015	1250	...	1714	|	2039	2224	...
0	Carlinville .... d.	...	|	1328	...	1749r	|	2119	2304	...
4	Alton .... d.	...	1122	1359	...	1822	|	2150	2335	...
7	**St. Louis** .... d.	0915	1220	1500	1600	1921	|	2245	0030	...
0	Kirkwood .... d.	0944	...	...	1629	...	|	...	...	...
8	Jefferson City .... d.	1136	...	...	1822	...	|	...	...	...
0	Sedalia .... d.	1246	...	...	1939	...	|	...	...	...
6	Lee's Summit .... d.	1404	...	...	2050	...	|	...	...	...
2	**Kansas City** .... a.	1455	...	...	2140	...	2211	...	...	...

	300 G	302 G	22 H	4 J	314 F	304 G	306 G	316 F	
Kansas City .... d.	...	...	...	0743	0815	...	...	1600	...
Lee's Summit .... d.	...	...	...	|	0851	...	...	1636	...
Sedalia .... d.	...	...	...	|	1004	...	...	1749	...
Jefferson City .... d.	...	...	...	|	1118	...	...	1903	...
Kirkwood .... d.	...	...	...	|	1313	...	...	2058	...
St. Louis .... d.	0435	0640	0755	|	1355	1500	1730	2140	...
Alton .... d.	0520	0725	0843	|	...	1545	1815	...	...
Carlinville .... d.	0550	0755	0915r	|	...	1614	1845	...	...
Springfield IL .... d.	0632	0837	0955	|	...	1656	1932	...	...
Lincoln .... d.	0700	0905	1025	|	...	1724	2000	...	...
Bloomington .... d.	0731	0946	1108	|	...	1756	2036	...	...
Pontiac .... d.	0759	1014	1139	|	...	1823	2104	...	...
Joliet Union .... d.	0859	1119	1256s	|	...	1926	2202	...	...
Chicgo Union .... a.	1000	1220	1352	1515	...	2040	2310	...	...

RIVER RUNNER – [12] and 🍸 St Louis - Kansas City and v.v.
LINCOLN SERVICE – [12] and 🍸 Chicago - St. Louis and v.v.
H – TEXAS EAGLE. See Table **9300**.
J – SOUTHWEST CHIEF. See Table **9295**.
r – Request stop.
s – Calls to set down only.
u – Calls to pick up only.

CHICAGO - QUINCY 9265

Amtrak

km		381 A	5 C	3 D	383 B						380 B	4 D	382 A						
0	**Chicago** Union .... d.	0735	1400	1500	1755	...	...	...	...	**Quincy** .... d.	0612	...	1730	...	...	...	...	...	...
6	Princeton .... d.	0921	1544	1646	1941	...	...	...	...	Galesburg .... d.	0738	1208	1856	...	...	...	...	...	...
9	Galesburg .... d.	1018	1638	1738	2038	...	...	...	...	Princeton .... d.	0831	1258	1949	...	...	...	...	...	...
3	**Quincy** .... a.	1158	...	...	2218	...	...	...	...	**Chicago** Union .... a.	1035	1515	2153	...	...	...	...	...	...

CARL SANDBURG – [12] and 🍸 Chicago Union - Quincy and v.v.
ILLINOIS ZEPHYR – [12] and 🍸 Chicago Union - Quincy and v.v.
C – CALIFONIA ZEPHYR – See Table **9290**.
D – SOUTHWEST CHIEF – See Table **9295**.

CHICAGO - MILWAUKEE 9270

Amtrak 2nd class

km		329 ①–⑤ a	331	333	335	337	339	341	343 ⑥ b	
0	**Chicago** Union .... d.	0610	0825	1020	1305	1515	1708	2005	2310	...
0	Sturtevant .... d.	0710	0925	1120	1405	1615	1814	2105	0010	...
5	**Milwaukee** Airport .... a.	0724	0939	1134	1419	1629	1828	2119	0024	...
8	**Milwaukee** .... a.	0739	0954	1149	1434	1644	1845	2134	0039	...

	330 ①–⑤	332	334	336	338	340	342	344 ⑥ b	
Milwaukee .... d.	0615	0805	1100	1300	1500	1745	1935	2340	...
Milwaukee Airport .... d.	0626	0815	1110	1310	1510	1755	1945	2350	...
Sturtevant .... d.	0643	0828	1123	1323	1523	1808	1958	2303	...
Chicago Union .... a.	0757	0934	1229	1429	1629	1914	2104	0009	...

From Sept. 3 operates ①–⑥.
To Sept. 3 only.

CHICAGO - GRAND RAPIDS, PORT HURON, DETROIT and PONTIAC 9275

Amtrak

km		8465 🚌	350 K	8150 🚌	352 ⑦ K	8365 🚌 P	364 L	358 ①–⑥ K	354 K	370 M	8354 🚌
0	**Chicago** Union ..... CT d.	...	0710	...	1250	...	1600	1630	1800	1830	...
0	Benton Harbour . ET d.	...	|	...	|	...	|	|	|	2115	...
2	**Grand Rapids** .. ET a.	0818	|	...	|	1643	|	|	|	2339	...
4	Michigan City .... CT d.	|	|	...	1358	|	|	1738	1901	...	...
1	Niles .... ET d.	|	0953	...	1533	|	1833	1913	2035	...	...
1	Kalamazoo .... a.	0915	1052	...	1608	1740	1912	1948	2110	...	2200d
8	Battle Creek .... a.	...	1120	1201d	1640	...	1945	2020	2142	...	|
5	East Lansing .... d.	...	|	1335	|	...	2054	|	|	...	0022
2	Durand .... d.	...	|	|	|	...	2131	|	|	...	|
9	Flint .... d.	...	|	1540	|	...	2202	|	|	...	0125
3	**Port Huron** .... a.	...	|	...	|	...	2338	|	|	...	...
1	Jackson .... d.	...	1218a	...	1733	...	...	2125	2247	...	...
0	Ann Arbor .... d.	...	1305a	...	1916	...	...	2216	2330	...	...
9	Dearborn .... d.	...	1343a	...	1844e	...	...	2244e	0008e	...	...
0	**Detroit** .... d.	...	1410a	...	1912e	...	...	2311e	0035e	...	...
4	**Pontiac** .... a.	...	1510a	...	2011	...	...	0011	0137	...	...

	371 M	351 K	365 L	8351 🚌	8353 🚌	8364 🚌	357 ①–⑥ K	353 ⑦ K	8555 🚌	355 K
Pontiac .... d.	...	0515	...	...	...	...	...	1035	...	1850
Detroit .... d.	...	0558	...	...	...	...	...	1120	...	1933
Dearborn .... d.	...	0622	...	...	...	...	...	1142	...	1954
Ann Arbor .... d.	...	0657	...	...	...	...	...	1216	...	2030
Jackson .... d.	...	0739	...	...	...	...	...	1257	...	2110
Port Huron .... d.	...	|	0620	...	...	...	...	|	...	|
Flint .... d.	...	|	0732	...	0845	...	...	|	1620	|
Durand .... d.	...	|	0804	...	|	...	...	|	|	|
East Lansing .... d.	...	|	0845	...	0950	...	...	|	1720	|
Battle Creek .... d.	...	0834	0952	...	1115	...	1225	1354	|	2205
Kalamazoo .... d.	...	0917	1025	1030	...	1415	1256	1435	2020	2246
Niles .... ET d.	...	|	1103	|	...	|	1329	1506	...	2323
Michigan City ...... CT d.	...	|	|	|	...	|	|	|	...	2254
Grand Rapids ET d.	0600	|	|	1122	...	1512	|	|	...	|
Benton Harbour ET d.	0816	|	|	...	...	...	|	|	...	|
Chicago Union .. CT a.	0911	1039	1155	...	...	...	1439	1618	...	0027

WOLVERINE – [12] and 🍸 Chicago - Pontiac and v.v.
BLUE WATER – [12] and 🍸 Chicago - Port Huron and v.v.
PERE MARQUETTE – [2] Chicago - Grand Rapids and v.v.
P – Additional trip 1923.
a – ⑦ only.
d – Departure time.
e – Can leave before time shown.
CT – Central Time.
ET – Eastern Time.

NOTE:
Summer track work schedules valid to September 23.

SELECTED BUS ROUTES 9280

Greyhound

km	*Greyhound* 🚌 *service*	1529	1535	1539	1537	1511					*Greyhound* 🚌 *service*	1502	1510	1514	1508	1504				
0	**Nashville** .... d.	0315	0645	1125	1700	2235	...	...	...	...	**Memphis** .... d.	0510	0920	1340	2030	2300	...	...	...	...
7	**Memphis** .... a.	0700	1045	1525	2055	0220	...	...	...	...	**Nashville** .... a.	0905	1315	1740	0015	0255	...	...	...	...

km	*Greyhound* 🚌 *service*	6001	1683	6021	6023	6005	6009	6029	6013	6017 ⑦	6025
0	**Las Vegas** NV .... d.	0135	0345	0700	0800	0915	1201	1515	1715	1930	2330
1	**Los Angeles** .... a.	0825	0900	1440	1325	1600	1715	2215	2230	0105	0430

Greyhound 🚌 *service*	6034	6002	1682	6006	6012	6010	6014	6044 ⑤	1302	6048
Los Angeles .... d.	0030	0615	0815	1000	1215	1415	1500	1815	1830	2300
Las Vegas NV .... a.	0530	1410	1325	1655	1730	2140	2020	2330	0020	0430

9285 CHICAGO - SEATTLE — Amtrak

km		7 A	27 B	🚌 8948		🚌 8909	28 B	8 A
0	Chicago Union d.	1415	...	...	Vancouver BC d.	1130	...	...
137	Milwaukee d.	1552u	...	...	Portland d.	|	1645	...
241	Columbus d.	1702	...	...	Vancouver WA d.	|	1707	...
314	Wisconsin Dells d.	1749	...	...	Pasco d.	|	2057	...
386	Tomah d.	1827	...	...	Seattle King St. d.	1530	|	1640
452	La Crosse d.	1911	...	...	Everett d.	...	|	1739
673	Minneapolis / St Paul a.	2203	...	...	Wenatchee d.	...	|	2042
673	Minneapolis / St Paul d.	2220	...	...	Spokane a.	...	0013	0040
773	St. Cloud d.	0024	...	...	Spokane d.	...	...	0125
1058	Fargo d.	0324	...	...	Sandpoint d.	...	...	0230
1194	Grand Forks d.	0441	...	...	Whitefish d.	...	...	0741
1332	Devils Lake d.	0602	...	...	Essex d.	...	...	0850r
1522	Minot d.	0906	...	...	Shelby d.	...	...	1133
1958	Glasgow d.	1226	...	...	Havre d.	...	...	1322
2072	Malta d.	1325	...	...	Malta d.	...	...	1442
2212	Havre d.	1504	...	...	Glasgow d.	...	...	1537
2381	Shelby d.	1722	...	...	Minot d.	...	...	2147
2537	Essex d.	1941r	...	...	Devils Lake d.	...	...	2337
2624	Whitefish d.	2116	...	...	Grand Forks d.	...	...	0102
2924	Sandpoint d.	1349	...	...	Fargo d.	...	...	0218
3030	Spokane a.	0140	...	...	St. Cloud d.	...	...	0519
3030	Spokane d.	0215	0245	...	Minneapolis / St Paul a.	...	...	0743
3306	Wenatchee d.	0535	|	...	Minneapolis / St Paul d.	...	...	0800
3501	Everett d.	0838	|	...	La Crosse d.	...	...	1047
3554	Seattle King St. a.	1025	|	1045	Tomah d.	...	...	1126
3265	Pasco d.	...	0535	|	Wisconsin Dells d.	...	...	1208
3621	Vancouver WA d.	...	0918	|	Columbus d.	...	...	1257
3638	Portland a.	...	1010	|	Milwaukee d.	...	...	1407s
	Vancouver BC a	...	...	1415	Chicago Union a.	...	...	1555

A – EMPIRE BUILDER – 🛏 1, 2 cl., 🚃 and 🍷 Chicago - Spokane - Seattle and v.v.
B – EMPIRE BUILDER – 🛏 1, 2 cl., 🚃 Chicago - Spokane - Portland and v.v.
s – Calls to set down only. u – Calls to pick up only.

9290 CHICAGO - SAN FRANCISCO — Am

km		5 C	🚌		🚌	
0	Chicago Union d.	1400	...	San Francisco ‡ d.	0750	
261	Galesburg d.	1638	...	Emeryville d.	0825	0
330	Burlington d.	1725	...	Martinez d.	...	0
450	Ottumwa d.	1853	...	Sacramento d.	...	1
806	Omaha a.	2255	...	Truckee d.	...	1
806	Omaha d.	2305	...	Reno d.	...	1
892	Lincoln d.	0014	...	Winnemucca d.	...	1
1049	Hastings d.	0147	...	Elko d.	...	2
1261	McCook d.	0343	...	Salt Lake City a.	...	0
1668	Denver Union a.	0715	...	Salt Lake City d.	...	0
1668	Denver Union d.	0805	...	Provo d.	...	0
1770	Winter Park d.	1007	...	Green River d.	...	0
1791	Granby d.	1037	...	Grand Junction d.	...	1
1966	Glenwood Springs d.	1353	...	Glenwood Springs d.	...	1
2109	Grand Junction d.	1610	...	Granby d.	...	1
2279	Green River d.	1758	...	Winter Park d.	...	1
2516	Provo d.	2126	...	Denver Union a.	...	1
2587	Salt Lake City a.	2305	...	Denver Union d.	...	1
2587	Salt Lake City d.	2330	...	McCook d.	...	2
3010	Elko d.	0303	...	Hastings d.	...	0
3232	Winnemucca d.	0540	...	Lincoln d.	...	0
3514	Reno d.	0836	...	Omaha a.	...	0
3569	Truckee d.	0937	...	Omaha d.	...	0
3785	Sacramento d.	1413s	...	Ottumwa d.	...	0
3879	Martinez d.	1526s	...	Burlington d.	...	1
3922	Emeryville a.	1610	1625	Galesburg d.	...	1
3936	San Francisco ‡ a.	...	1700	Chicago Union a.	...	1

C – CALIFORNIA ZEPHYR – 🛏 1, 2 cl., 🚃 and 🍷 Chicago - Emeryville and v.v.
s – Calls to set down only.
‡ – San Francisco Transbay Temporary Terminal.

9295 CHICAGO - LOS ANGELES — Amtrak

km		3 D			4 D	
0	Chicago Union d.	1500	...	Los Angeles Union d.	1810	...
261	Galesburg d.	1738	...	San Bernardino d.	1954	...
329	Fort Madison d.	1842	...	Victorville d.	2105	...
677	Kansas City a.	2211	...	Barstow d.	2151	...
677	Kansas City d.	2245	...	Needles d.	0018	...
783	Topeka d.	0029	...	Kingman * d.	0128*	...
1001	Newton d.	0245	...	Williams Junction * d.	0345*	...
1247	Dodge City d.	0525	...	Flagstaff * a d.	0437*	...
1488	Lamar d.	0659	...	Winslow * d.	0535*	...
1572	La Junta d.	0830	...	Gallup d.	0821	...
1704	Trinidad d.	0950	...	Abuquerque a.	1142	...
1741	Raton d.	1056	...	Abuquerque d.	1210	...
1918	Las Vegas NM d.	1238	...	Lamy d.	1317	...
2022	Lamy d.	1424	...	Las Vegas NM d.	1503	...
2132	Abuquerque a.	1555	...	Raton d.	1650	...
2132	Abuquerque d.	1645	...	Trinidad d.	1749	...
2391	Gallup d.	1908	...	La Junta d.	1941	...
2595	Winslow * d.	1950*	...	Lamar d.	2240	...
2690	Flagstaff * a d.	2057*	...	Dodge City d.	0027	...
2768	Williams Junction * d.	2133*	...	Newton d.	0259	...
2967	Kingman * d.	2346*	...	Topeka d.	0518	...
3067	Needles d.	0049	...	Kansas City a.	0724	...
3337	Barstow d.	0339	...	Kansas City d.	0743	...
3398	Victorville d.	0418	...	Fort Madison d.	1109	...
3472	San Bernardino d.	0532	...	Galesburg d.	1208	...
3588	Los Angeles Union a.	0815	...	Chicago Union a.	1515	...

D – SOUTHWEST CHIEF – 🛏 1, 2 cl., 🚃 and 🍷 Chicago - Los Angeles and v.v.
a – Thruway buses operate to/from the Grand Canyon and Pheonix.
* – Do not observe DST, schedule times will be one hour later from November 1 2016.

9300 CHICAGO - SAN ANTONIO — Amtr

km		821 2 E	21 F		22 F	8 2
0	Chicago Union d.	...	1345	Los Angeles Union d.	2200b	
148	Pontiac d.	...	1527	San Antonio a.	0450b	
298	Springfield IL d.	...	1714	San Antonio d.	0700	
457	St. Louis a.	...	1921	San Marcos d.	0832	
457	St. Louis d.	...	2000	Austin d.	0931	
717	Poplar Bluff d.	...	2342	Taylor d.	1022	
813	Walnut Ridge d.	...	0037	Temple d.	1125	
1007	Little Rock d.	...	0310	Fort Worth a.	1358	
1127	Arkadelphia d.	...	0420r	Fort Worth d.	1420	17
1240	Texarkana d.	...	0558	Gainesville d.	|	18
1384	Longview d.	...	0828	Ardmore d.	|	19
1588	Dallas a.	...	1130	Oklahoma City d.	|	21
1588	Dallas d.	...	1150	Dallas a.	1520	
336c	Oklahoma City d.	0825	|	Dallas d.	1540	
172c	Ardmore d.	1023	|	Longview d.	1815	
109c	Gainesville d.	1105	|	Texarkana d.	2043	
1638	Fort Worth a.	1223	1325	Arkadelphia d.	2202r	
1638	Fort Worth d.	...	1410	Little Rock d.	2339	
1844	Temple d.	...	1643	Walnut Ridge d.	0141	
1906	Taylor d.	...	1736	Poplar Bluff d.	0244	
1962	Austin d.	...	1830	St. Louis a.	0719	
2011	San Marcos d.	...	1912	St. Louis d.	0755	
2060	San Antonio a.	...	2155	Springfield IL d.	0955	
2060	San Antonio d.	...	0245a	Pontiac d.	1139	
4389	Los Angeles Union a.	...	0535a	Chicago Union a.	1352	

E – HEARTLAND FLYER – 🚃 🍷
F – TEXAS EAGLE – 🛏 1, 2 cl., 🚃 and 🍴🍷 Chicago (21/22) - San Antonio (421/42
Los Angeles and v.v.
a – San Antonio - Los Angeles ②④⑦ only. Arrives Los Angeles ①③⑤. See Table 931
b – Los Angeles - San Antonio ③⑤⑦ only. Arrives San Antonio ①④⑥. See Table 931
c – km from Fort Worth. r – Stops on request.

9305 SEATTLE - LOS ANGELES — Amtrak

km		🚌	11 G	5011		5014 🚌	14 G	6014 🚌
	Vancouver BC d.	0530	...	...	Los Angeles ◐ d.	...	1010	...
0	Seattle King St. d.	0900	0935	...	Santa Barbara d.	...	1240	...
64	Tacoma d.	▬	1021	...	San Luis Obispo d.	...	1535	...
114	Olympia d.	...	1111	...	Paso Robles d.	...	1637	...
151	Centralia d.	...	1135	...	Salinas d.	...	1828	...
219	Kelso Longview d.	...	1219	...	San Jose d.	...	2023	...
282	Vancouver WA d.	...	1258	...	Oakland a.	...	2124	...
298	Portland a.	...	1350	...	Oakland d.	...	2139	2135
298	Portland d.	...	1425	...	San Francisco ‡ d.	2110	|	2205
382	Salem d.	...	1537	...	Emeryville a.	2145	2154	▬
496	Eugene d.	...	1710	...	Emeryville d.	...	2204	...
691	Chemult d.	...	2008	...	Martinez d.	...	2246	...
808	Klamath Falls d.	...	2200	...	Sacramento d.	...	2359	...
976	Dunsmuir d.	...	0035	...	Chico d.	...	0147	...
1067	Redding d.	...	0221	...	Redding d.	...	0306	...
1186	Chico d.	...	0350	...	Dunsmuir d.	...	0456	...
1320	Sacramento d.	...	0635	...	Klamath Falls d.	...	0817	...
1397	Martinez d.	...	0734	...	Chemult d.	...	0932	...
1441	Emeryville a.	🚌	0810	...	Eugene d.	...	1236	...
1441	Emeryville d.	6011	0820	0825	Salem d.	...	1355	...
	San Francisco ‡ a.	0745	|	0855	Portland a.	...	1532	...
1449	Oakland a.	0825	0835		Portland d.	...	1602	...
1449	Oakland d.	...	0850	...	Vancouver WA d.	...	1621	...
1573	San Jose d.	...	1007	...	Kelso Longview d.	...	1654	...
1624	Salinas d.	...	1148	...	Centralia d.	...	1739	...
1780	Paso Robles d.	...	1338	...	Olympia d.	...	1804	...
1835	San Luis Obispo d.	...	1520	...	Tacoma d.	...	1853	🚌
2025	Santa Barbara d.	...	1802	...	Seattle King St. a.	...	2012	2100
2190	Los Angeles ◐ a.	...	2100	...	Vancouver BC a.	...	...	0015

G – COAST STARLIGHT – 🛏 1, 2 cl., 🚃 and 🍷 Seattle - Los Angeles and v.v.
‡ – San Francisco Transbay Temporary Terminal.
◐ – Los Angeles Union.
NOTE: Due to extensive trackwork schedules are subject to change.

9310 NEW ORLEANS - LOS ANGELES — Amtr

km		1257 🚌 J	1 ①③⑥ H		2 ③⑤⑦ H	15 🚌
0	Orlando d.	1855	...	Los Angeles Union d.	2200	
235	Jacksonville d.	2145	...	Pomona d.	2241	
509	Tallahasse d.	0115	...	Palm Springs d.	0036	
998	Mobile d.	0535	...	Yuma * d.	0247	
1230	New Orleans a.	0755	...	Maricopa * d.	0540	
1230	New Orleans d.	...	0900	Tucson * d.	0815	
1434	New Iberia d.	...	1156r	Benson * d.	0915r	
1462	Lafeyette d.	...	1224	Lordsburg d.	1215r	
1581	Lake Charles d.	...	1355	El Paso a.	1510	
1678	Beaumont d.	...	1548	El Paso d.	1535	
1810	Houston d.	...	1855	Alpine d.	2045	
2146	San Antonio a.	...	0005	Del Rio d.	0102	
2146	San Antonio d.	...	0245	San Antonio a.	0450	
2418	Del Rio d.	...	0549	San Antonio d.	0625	
2765	Alpine d.	...	1038	Houston d.	1210	
3114	El Paso a.	...	1322	Beaumont d.	1405	
3114	El Paso d.	...	1347	Lake Charles d.	1529	
3350	Lordsburg d.	...	1613r	Lafeyette d.	1715	
3539	Benson* d.	...	1718r	New Iberia d.	1741r	
3619	Tucson* d.	...	1935	New Orleans a.	2140	
3757	Maricopa* d.	...	2102	New Orleans d.	...	10
4021	Yuma* d.	...	2349	Mobile a.	...	13
4253	Palm Springs d.	...	0202	Tallahasse a.	...	23
4371	Pomona d.	...	0404s	Jacksonville a.	...	02
4422	Los Angeles Union a.	...	0535	Orlando a.	...	04

H – SUNSET LIMITED – 🛏 1, 2 cl., 🚃 and 🍴🍷; Conveys TEXAS EAGLE (421/2) S
Antonio - Los Angeles and v.v.
J – Operated by Greyhound USA. Change at Mobile.
r – Calls on request.
s – Calls to set down only.
* – Do not observe DST, schedule times will be one hour later from November 1 2016.

VANCOUVER - SEATTLE - PORTLAND - EUGENE 9315

trak Most trains 🍷

	503 ①-⑤ A	Bus D	505 ⑥⑦ A	501 A	11 B	513 A	507 A	Bus	509 A	Bus	517 A
Vancouver (Canada) d.	...	...	...	...	*0530**	0630	*0900**	...	*1130**	1600	1735
Bellingham d.	...	...	...	...	|	0832	|	1510	|	|	1937
Mount Vernon d.	...	...	...	...	|	0902	|	1545	|	|	2007
Everett d.	...	...	...	...	|	0952	|	1630	|	|	2059
Seattle King Street a.	...	...	...	...	*0900**	1055	*1245**	1730	*1530**	1945	2200
Seattle King Street d.	...	...	...	0725	0935	1115	1410	▬	1805	▬	...
Tukwila ✈ d.	...	...	...	0739	|	1129	1424	...	1819	...	...
Tacoma d.	...	...	...	0808	1021	1158	1453	...	1848	...	...
Olympia d.	...	...	...	0845	1111	1235	1530	...	1925	...	...
Centralia d.	...	...	...	0906	1135	1256	1551	...	1945	...	...
Kelso Longview d.	...	...	...	0947	1219	1337	1632	...	2027	...	...
Vancouver WA d.	...	...	...	1025	1258	1415	1710	...	2105	...	...
Portland a.	...	...	...	1105	1350	1505	1750	Bus	2145	Bus	...
Portland d.	0600	0700	0935	*1125**	1425	*1525**	1805	1900	...	2155	...
Salem d.	0707	0820	1140	*1225**	1537	*1645*c	1911	2005t	...	2320t	...
Albany d.	0736	0855	1110	*1300**	1610	*1720*c	1940	2040t	...	2359t	...
Eugene a.	0835	0945	1210	*1350**	1703	*1810*c	2040	2130	...	0050	...

	510 A	Bus	500 ①-⑤ A	502 ⑥⑦ A	Bus	504/6 A	516 A	14 B	Bus C	508 A
Eugene d.	...	...	0530	*0530**	0720	0900a	*1140**	1236	1315	1600
Albany d.	...	...	0611	*0620**	0810	0943a	*1235**	1322	1405	1643
Salem d.	...	...	0641	*0655**	0850	1012a	*1305**	1355	1440	1712
Portland a.	...	...	0805	*0805**	1010	1135a	*1415**	1532	1545	1835
Portland d.	...	...	0820	0820	▬	1200	1450	1602	...	1850
Vancouver WA d.	...	...	0835	0835	...	1215	1505	1621	...	1905
Kelso Longview d.	...	...	0910	0910	...	1250	1540	1654	...	1940
Centralia d.	...	...	0951	0951	...	1331	1621	1739	...	2021
Olympia d.	...	...	1012	1012	...	1352	1642	1804	...	2042
Tacoma d.	...	...	1054	1054	...	1434	1724	1853	...	2124
Tukwila ✈ d.	...	...	1122	1122		1502	1752	|	...	2152
Seattle King Street a.	...	...	1200	1200	Bus	1550	1830	2012	...	2230
Seattle King Street d.	0745	1045	*1225**	...	1345	*1645*b	1850	*2100**	...	...
Everett d.	0836	|	*1310**	...	|	|	1942	|	...	...
Mount Vernon d.	0926	|	*1355**	...	|	|	2027	|	...	...
Bellingham d.	0957	|	*1425**	...	|	|	2100	|	...	...
Vancouver (Canada) a.	1145	1415	...	...	1715	*2015*b	2250	*0015**	...	....

CASCADES – 🅁 and 🍷.
COAST STARLIGHT – Table **9305**.
Additional trips 1445, 1730.
Additional trip 1040.

a – By Bus on ①-⑤ timings Eugene 0825, Albany 0920, Salem 1000 arrive Portland 1130.
b – Connection by Bus ⑥⑦ only.
c – Connection by Bus on ⑥⑦ runs 10 mins. earlier.

t – Paid ticket required to board.
✈ – Sea Tac Airport.
* – Connection by Bus.

SAN LUIS OBISPO - LOS ANGELES - SAN DIEGO 9320

trak Most trains 🍷

PACIFIC SURFLINER

		Bus	562	564	566		Bus	768			572		774	580	Bus	582	Bus	784		790 ①-⑤	1790 ⑥⑦	Bus	796
San Luis Obispo d.	...	...	...	...	...	...	0350	....	...	....	...	...	0650	...	...	...	1030	...	...	1335	1400	1540	...
Santa Maria d.	...	...	...	...	...	...	0440	...	...	...	...	...	0726a	...	...	...	1120u	...	...	1411a	1436a	1635	...
Santa Barbara d.	...	...	...	...	...	...	0630	0649	...	...	...	...	0922	...	1255	...	1345	1404	...	1612	1640	1840	1859
Oxnard d.	...	...	...	...	...	...	...	0743	...	...	...	...	1013	...	1350	...	...	1457	...	1707	1735	...	1951
Los Angeles Union a.	...	...	...	...	...	...	...	0935	...	...	...	...	1210	...	1535	...	...	1650	...	1910	1920	...	2145
Los Angeles Union d.	...	0230	0615	0725	0830	...	...	0955	...	...	1115	...	1230	1500	...	1610	...	1710	...	1930	1940	...	2210
Anaheim d.	...	|	0652	0803	0909	...	...	1036	...	...	1154	...	1309	1538	...	1648	...	1749	...	2011	2021	...	2249
San Juan Capistrano d.	...	0355s	0725	0842	0949	...	...	1113	...	...	1234	...	1344	1612	...	1723	...	1823	...	2048	2055	...	2321
Oceanside d.	...	0430s	0805	0914	1025	...	...	1147	...	...	1309	...	1419	1645	...	1756	...	1903	...	2120	2128	...	2357
San Diego a.	...	0515	0900	1010	1122	...	...	1240	...	...	1403	...	1515	1750	...	1903	...	2009	...	2230	2239	...	0106

		761 ①-⑤	1761 ⑥⑦	763	Bus	565	1567 ⑥⑦	567	769	Bus	573	777	579	583			785	Bus	591	Bus			595	Bus
Diego d.	...	...	...	0600	...	0705	0805	0823	0925	...	1041	1200	1340	1440	...	...	1600	...	1845	...	...	...	2059	2210
anside d.	...	...	...	0658	...	0757	0911	0928	1018	...	1146	1253	1431	1541	...	...	1700	...	1938	...	...	...	2201	2310
Juan Capistrano d.	...	...	...	0730	...	0830	0945	0957	1048	...	1218	1325	1505	1620	...	...	1733	...	2008	...	...	...	2231	2345
neim d.	...	...	...	0804	...	0903	1021	1042	1124	...	1253	1400	1538	1655	...	...	1808	...	2048	...	...	...	2306	|
Angeles Union a.	...	...	...	0846	...	0946	1104	1125	1210	...	1340	1445	1625	1740	...	...	1855	...	2135	...	...	...	2352	0125
Angeles Union d.	...	0735	0750	0910	...	...	...	...	1230	...	...	1505	...	...	...	...	1915	...	...	2150	...	...	...	...
ard d.	...	0921	0921	1043	...	...	...	...	1405	...	...	1638	...	...	...	...	2046	...	...	2345	...	...	...	...
ta Barbara d.	...	1022	1022	1145	1150	...	...	...	1505	1510	...	1743	...	...	...	...	2150	2155	...	0035	...	...	...	...
ta Maria d.	...	1216a	1216a	...	1320	...	...	...	...	1635	...	1937a	...	...	...	...	...	2325	...	...	...	...	...	...
Luis Obispo a.	...	1300	1300	...	1415	...	...	...	...	1715	...	2035	...	...	...	...	...	0015	...	...	...	...	...	...

Guadalupe - Santa Maria.

s – Calls to set down only.

SAN JOSE and SAN FRANCISCO - SACRAMENTO 9325

trak 2nd class Most trains 🍷

CAPITOL CORRIDOR

	520 ①-⑤	522 ①-⑤	720 ⑥⑦	524 ①-⑤	724 ⑥⑦	526 ①-⑤	528 ①-⑤	728 ⑥⑦	530 ①-⑤	732 ⑥⑦	532 ①-⑤	734 ⑥⑦	534 ①-⑤	736 ⑥⑦	536 ①-⑤	538 ①-⑤	540 ①-⑤	738 ⑥⑦	542 ①-⑤	742 ⑥⑦	544*	746 ⑥⑦	546 ①-⑤	548 ①-⑤	748 ⑥⑦
San Jose d.	...	...	...	0640	0750	...	0905	1010	...	...	1220	1250	...	...	...	1510	...	1610	1620	1710	1750	...	1915	...	2110
Oakland JLS ¶ d.	0525	0625	0750	0745	0855	0915	1015	1115	1215	1225	1325	1355	1450	1525	1530	1620	1650	1717	1730	1820	1855	1955	2020	2205	2215
San Francisco ‡ d.	*0505*e	*0605*e	*0730*e	*0720*e	*0825*e	*0845*e	*0945*e	*1045*e	*1145*e	*1155*e	*1250*e	*1325*e	*1420*e	*1455*e	*1500*e	*1550*e	*1620*e	*1645*e	*1655*e	*1745*e	*1815*e	*1925*e	*1955*e	*2135*e	*2145*e
Emeryville d.	0535	0635	0800	0755	0905	0925	1025	1125	1225	1235	1335	1405	1500	1535	1540	1630	1700	1727	1745	1830	1905	2005	2030	2215	2225
Martinez d.	0614	0714	0839	0834	0944	1004	1104	1204	1304	1314	1414	1444	1539	1614	1619	1709	1739	1806	1824	1909	1944	2044	2109	2254	2304
Sacramento a.	0723	0823	0948	0948	1058	1113	1218	1318	1413	1423	1528	1558	1648	1723	1722	1823	1848	1918	1938	2012	2058	2153	2228	0003	0018

	521 ①-⑤	523 ①-⑤	723 ⑥⑦	525 ①-⑤	527 ①-⑤	529 ①-⑤	727 ⑥⑦	531 ①-⑤	729 ⑥⑦	533 ①-⑤	535 ①-⑤	733 ⑥⑦	537 ①-⑤	737 ⑥⑦	541 ①-⑤	741 ⑥⑦	543 ①-⑤	743 ⑥⑦	545 ①-⑤	745 ⑥⑦	747 ⑥⑦	547 ①-⑤	549 ①-⑤	749 ⑥⑦	551 ①-⑤	751 ⑥⑦
ramento d.	0430	0530	0550	0620	0700	0740	0810	0820	0915	0920	1010	1040	1210	1210	1410	1410	1535	1555	1640	1640	1740	1740	1850	1910	2110	2110
tinez d.	0529	0629	0649	0719	0759	0839	0909	0920	1014	1019	1109	1139	1309	1309	1509	1509	1634	1654	1739	1739	1839	1839	1949	2009	2209	2210
eryville d.	0610	0710	0730	0800	0840	0920	0950	1000	1055	1100	1150	1220	1350	1350	1550	1550	1715	1735	1820	1820	1920	1920	2030	2050	2250	2250
an Francisco ‡ a.	*0640*e	*0750*e	*0800*e	*0835*e	*0915*e	*0950*e	*1020*e	*1030*e	*1125*e	*1130*e	*1220*e	*1250*e	*1420*e	*1420*e	*1620*e	*1620*e	*1745*e	*1805*e	*1850*e	*1850*e	*1950*e	*1950*e	*2055*e	*2115*e	*2315*e	*2315*e
land JLS ¶ a.	0621	0721	0741	0816	0851	0938	1001	1016	1106	1116	1201	1236	1401	1401	1608	1601	1726	1746	1838	1838	1931	1931	2046	2108	2308	2308
Jose a.	0738	0838	0858	...	1013	...	1118	...	1223	...	1318	...	1518	1518	...	1718	1848	1908	...	...	2048	2058	2355b	2355b	...	...

Connection by Bus, change at **Emeryville**.
Connection by Bus San Francisco - Emeryville and v.v.

‡ – San Francisco Transbay Temporary Terminal.
¶ – Oakland Jack London Square.
* – Train **744** on ⑥⑦ runs 15mins later throughout.

OAKLAND and SAN FRANCISCO - BAKERSFIELD 9330

trak 2nd class Most trains 🍷

SAN JOAQUIN

	Bus ◧	702	712	714	716	Bus ◧	704	718		
Oakland JLS ¶ d.	0530	...	0730	1005	1315	1515	...	1755	...	...
San Francisco ‡ d.	0450	...	*0705*e	*0935*e	*1245*e	1435	...	*1655*e	...	...
Emeryville d.	0515	...	0740	1015	1325	1500	...	1805	...	...
Martinez d.	|	...	0819	1054	1404	|	...	1904	...	...
Sacramento d.	|	0640	|	|	|	|	1655	|	...	...
Lodi d.	|	0718	|	|	|	|	1733	|	...	...
Stockton San Joaquin d.	0715d	0736d	0917	1149	1503	1720d	1751d	1939	...	...
Modesto d.	...	0809	0945	1217	1531	...	1824	2012	...	...
Merced d.	...	0853	1033	1301	1615	...	1908	2055	...	...
Madera d.	...	0921	1101	1335	1648	...	1936	2128	...	...
Fresno d.	...	0958	1138	1413	1723	...	2009	2203	...	...
Hanford d.	...	1032	1213	1448	1758	...	2043	2237	...	...
Bakersfield a.	...	1205	1344	1614	1929	...	2210	2358	...	...
Los Angeles a.	...	*1430**	*1610**	*1840**	*2155**	...	*0035**	*0220**	...	...

	711	701	Bus ◧	713	715	717	703	Bus ◧		
Los Angeles d.	*0135**	*0410**	...	*0735**	*1045**	*1305**	*1510**	...	...	...
Bakersfield d.	0445	0715	...	1005	1325	1545	1820	...	...	...
Hanford d.	0603	0833	...	1127	1448	1707	1941	...	...	...
Fresno d.	0642	0910	...	1207	1527	1747	2020	...	...	...
Madera d.	0707	0940	...	1232	1552	1812	2045	...	...	...
Merced d.	0741	1011	...	1311	1630	1845	2118	...	...	...
Modesto d.	0820	1053	...	1346	1706	1925	2156	...	...	...
Stockton S.Joaquin d.	0854	1124d	1135d	1423	1743	2006	2229d	2240d	...	...
Lodi d.	|	1139	|	|	|	|	2244	|	...	...
Sacramento a.	|	1235	|	|	|	|	2335	|	...	...
Martinez d.	0958	...	|	1524	1834	2059	...	|	...	...
Emeryville d.	1043s	...	1305	1608s	1919s	2146s	...	0015	...	...
San Francisco ‡ a.	*1120*e	...	1325	*1640*e	*1955*e	*2215*e	...	0040	...	...
Oakland JLS ¶ a.	1055	...	1255	1620	1933	2158	...	2359	...	...

Stockton **Downtown**. Also known as ACE station.
Connection by Bus San Francisco - Emeryville and v.v.
Calls to set down only.

* – Connection by Bus.
◧ – Calling order is San Francisco - Emeryville - Oakland – Stockton and v.v.
‡ – San Francisco Transbay Temporary Terminal.
¶ – Oakland Jack London Square.

CALIFORNIA

This section is intended to give a brief overview of rail services in California that are not operated by Amtrak. All services in this section are operated using modern air-conditi rolling stock and convey a single class of accommodation, known locally as coach class, equivelant to european 2nd class. Timings are the latests available and may chang any time. Tickets must be purchased seperately for each network and are generally not valid on parallel Amtrak services.

9350 SAN FRANCISCO - SAN JOSE

Caltr

km			ex①	Ⓐ	Ⓐ	Ⓐ	Ⓐ	Ⓐ	Ⓐ	Ⓐ	Ⓐ	Ⓐ	Ⓐ	Ⓐ	Ⓐ	Ⓐ	Ⓐ	Ⓐ	Ⓐ	Ⓐ		Ⓐ	Ⓐ	Ⓐ	
0	**San Francisco** △ d.	Ⓐ	0001	0455	0525	0606	0624	0644	0656	0712	0719	0724	0744	0756	0812	0819	0824	0844	0856	0900	and	1500	1537	1610	1
22	Millbrae d.		0025	0519	0549	0624	0649	0702	0717	0732	|	0749	0802	0817	0832	|	0849	0902	0917	0922	at the	1525	1556	1626	
44	Redwood City d.		0051	0545	0615	0645	0715	0722	0732	|	|	0815	0822	0832	|	|	0915	0922	0932	0948	same	1551	1620	|	
47	Menlo Park d.		0056	0550	0620	0650	|	0728	0738	|	0806	|	0828	0838	|	0906	|	0928	0938	0953	minutes	1556	1626		
55	Palo Alto d.		0059	0553	0623	0653	0722	0732	0741	0754	0809	0822	0832	0841	0854	0909	0922	0932	0941	0958	past each	1601	1630	1647	1
58	Mountain View d.		0110	0605	0635	0703	|	0744	0749	0801	0817	|	0844	0849	0901	0917	|	0944	0949	1010	hour	1613	1643	1654	1
	Sunnyvale d.		0116	0610	0640	|	|	0749	|	|	|	|	0849	|	|	|	|	0949	|	1015	until	1618	1648	|	
71	Santa Clara d.		0125	0619	0649	|	0736	0802	|	|	|	0836	0902	|	|	|	0936	1002	|	1025		1628	1657	|	
75	**San Jose** Diridon a.		0134	0628	0658	0720	0745	0811	0803	0816	0834	0845	0910	0903	0916	0934	0945	1010	1003	1034		1638	1704	1709	1

	Ⓐ	Ⓐ	Ⓐ	Ⓐ	Ⓐ	Ⓐ	Ⓐ	Ⓐ	Ⓐ	Ⓐ	Ⓐ	Ⓐ	Ⓐ	Ⓐ	Ⓐ	Ⓐ	Ⓐ		Ⓒ		Ⓒ	⑥		Ⓒ	
San Francisco △ d.	1633	1628	1655	1712	1720	1733	1728	1755	1812	1820	1833	1828	1855	1933	2040	2140	2240	Ⓒ	0815	and	2115	2215		1159	1
Millbrae d.	1650	1657	1714	1730	|	1750	1757	1814	1830	|	1850	1857	1914	1957	2105	2205	2305		0839	at the	2139	2239		1215	1
Redwood City d.	1708	1724	1730	|	|	1808	1824	1830	|	|	1908	1924	1930	2023	2131	2231	2331		0909	same	2209	2309	A	1235	1
Menlo Park d.	|	1730	1736	|	|	|	1830	1836	|	|	|	1930	1936	2028	2136	2236	2336		0916	minutes	2216	2316	L	|	
Palo Alto d.	1716	|	1740	1752	1804	1816	|	1840	1852	1904	1916	|	1940	2031	2140	2240	2340		0919	past each	2219	2319	S	1241	1
Mountain View d.	|	1738	1752	1759	1814	|	1838	1852	1859	1914	|	1938	1952	2043	2152	2252	2352		0931	hour	2231	2331	O	1249	1
Sunnyvale d.	1726	1743	1757	|	1820	1826	1843	1857	|	1920	1926	1943	1957	2048	2157	2257	2357		0936	until	2236	2336		1954	1
Santa Clara d.	|	1752	1810	|	|	|	1852	1910	|	|	|	1952	2010	2057	2206	2306	0006		0945		2245	2345		|	
San Jose Diridon a.	1736	1800	1820	1814	1830	1835	1900	1920	1914	1930	1935	2000	2018	2106	2213	2313	0013		0953		2253	2353		2005	2

		Ⓐ	Ⓐ	Ⓐ	Ⓐ	Ⓐ	Ⓐ	Ⓐ	Ⓐ	Ⓐ	Ⓐ	Ⓐ	Ⓐ	Ⓐ	Ⓐ	Ⓐ		Ⓐ	Ⓐ	Ⓐ	Ⓐ	Ⓐ	Ⓐ	Ⓐ
San Jose Diridon d.	Ⓐ	0505	0545	0557	0603	0645	0650	0657	0703	0718	0745	0750	0757	0803	0822	0915	and	1415	1440	1505	1545	1608	1622	1631
Santa Clara d.		0511	|	0604	|	|	|	0704	|	0724	|	|	0806	|	0828	0921	at the	1421	1446	1512	1551	1614	|	|
Sunnyvale d.		0520	|	0621	0616	|	0702	0721	0716	0734	|	0802	0823	0816	0836	0931	same	1431	1455	1522	1600	|	|	|
Mountain View d.		0525	0600	0626	|	0700	0707	0726	|	0740	0800	0807	0829	|	0842	0937	minutes	1437	1459	1527	1605	|	1635	1648
Palo Alto d.		0537	0608	0639	0626	0708	0719	0739	0726	|	0808	0819	0842	0827	|	0949	past each	1449	1511	1540	1618	1629	1644	1656
Menlo Park d.		0540	|	0642	|	|	|	0742	|	0748	|	|	0845	|	0851	0942	hour	1452	1514	1543	1621	|	1648	1659
Redwood City d.		0545	|	0648	0633	|	|	0748	0733	0754	|	|	0851	0835	0857	0958	until	1458	1519	1548	1627	1637	1654	|
Millbrae d.		0610	0629	0703	0650	0729	|	0803	0750	0821	0829	|	0908	0852	0924	1023	⊠	1523	1543	1613	1646	1704	1709	|
San Francisco △ a.		0638	0647	0722	0707	0747	0803	0822	0807	0851	0847	0903	0927	0909	0950	1050		1550	1604	1640	1706	1732	1727	1743

	①–⑤	Ⓐ	Ⓐ	Ⓐ	Ⓐ	Ⓐ	Ⓐ	Ⓐ	Ⓐ	Ⓐ	Ⓐ	Ⓐ	Ⓐ	Ⓐ	Ⓐ	Ⓐ		⑥	Ⓒ		Ⓒ	⑥		Ⓒ	
San Jose Diridon d.	1640	1645	1708	1722	1731	1740	1745	1808	1822	1831	1845	1850	1930	2030	2130	2230	Ⓒ	0700	0800	and	2100	2230		1035	1
Santa Clara d.	1646	|	1714	|	|	1746	|	1814	|	|	|	1856	1936	2036	2136	2236		0705	0805	at the	2105	2235		|	
Sunnyvale d.	1700	|	|	|	|	1800	|	|	|	|	|	1905	1946	2046	2146	2246		0714	0814	same	2114	2244	A	1045	1
Mountain View d.	1705	1700	|	1735	1748	1805	1800	|	1835	1848	1901	1910	1951	2051	2151	2251		0719	0819	minutes	2119	2249	L	1050	1
Palo Alto d.	1720	1708	1729	1744	1756	1820	1808	1829	1844	1856	1911	1922	2004	2104	2204	2304		0731	0831	past each	2131	2301	S	1058	1
Menlo Park d.	1723	|	|	1748	1759	1923	|	|	1848	1859	1914	1925	2007	2107	2207	2307		0734	0834	hour	2134	2304	O	|	
Redwood City d.	1729	|	1737	1754	|	1829	|	1837	1854	|	1920	1930	2012	2112	2212	2312		0741	0841	until	2141	2311		1104	1
Millbrae d.	1748	1729	1804	1809	|	1848	1829	1904	1909	|	1943	1955	2038	2138	2238	2338		0810	0910		2210	2340		1123	1
San Francisco △ a.	1806	1749	1833	1827	1843	1906	1849	1932	1927	1943	2002	2023	2104	2204	2304	0004		0838	0938		2238	0008		1141	1

⊠ – On Ⓐ, the 11xx, 12xx and 13xx trains depart 1110, 1210 and 1310 and run 5 minutes earlier throughout.

△ – San Francisco 4th and King Street.

9352 SAN JOSE - STOCKTON

Altamont Corridor Expre

km		①–⑤	①–⑤	①–⑤	①–⑤						
0	**San Jose** Diridon d.	1535	1635	1735	1838	...	...	...	...	...	...
	Santa Clara d.	1540	1640	1740	1843	...	...	...	...	...	...
	Great America d.	1549	1649	1749	1852	...	...	...	...	...	...
	Fremont d.	1605	1705	1805	1908	...	...	...	...	...	...
	Pleasanton d.	1628	1728	1828	1931	...	...	...	...	...	...
	Livermore d.	1637	1737	1837	1940	...	...	...	...	...	...
	Tracy d.	1711	1811	1911	2014	...	...	...	...	...	...
125	**Stockton** Downtown a.	1747	1847	1947	2050	...	...	...	...	...	...

	①–⑤	①–⑤	①–⑤	①–⑤					
Stockton Downtown d.	0420	0535	0640	0705	...	...	...	...	...
Tracy d.	0451	0606	0711	0736	...	...	...	...	...
Livermore d.	0525	0640	0745	0810	...	...	...	...	...
Pleasanton d.	0533	0648	0753	0818	...	...	...	...	...
Fremont d.	0555	0710	0815	0840	...	...	...	...	...
Great America d.	0613	0728	0833	0858	...	...	...	...	...
Santa Clara d.	0620	0735	0840	0905	...	...	...	...	...
Stockton a.	0632	0747	0852	0917	...	...	...	...	...

9354 OXNARD - LOS ANGELES

Metrol

km		①–⑤	①–⑤	①–⑤	①–⑤	①–⑤		①–⑤	①–⑤	①–⑤ A	⑥⑦ B	①–⑤	①–⑤		B	①–⑤	①–⑤	①–⑤	B		①–⑤	①–⑤	①–⑤ B	⑥⑦ B	①–⑤	
0	**Oxnard** d.	...	...	0539	0617	0656	...	...	...	0743	0743	...	...	...	1018	...	...	...	1457	...	...	...	1707	1735	...	1
32	Moorpark d.	0504	...	0600	0638	0717	...	...	...	0808	0808	0825	...	...	|	1418	...	...	1520	...	...	1657	1736	1804	...	
62	Chatsworth d.	0528	...	0624	0702	0741	...	...	0825	0840	0840	0849	1050	...	1114	1442	...	...	1552	...	1640	1727	1812	1833	...	2
77	Van Nuys d.	0541	...	0637	0715	0754	...	...	0838	0856	0856	0902	1103	...	1128	1455	...	...	1614	...	1653	1745	1831	1845	...	2
86	Burbank Airport ✈ d.	0549	0613	0645	0723	0802	...	0835	0846	0904	0904	0910	1111	...	1135	1503	1537	1615	1622	...	1705	1753	1839	1853	2030	2
92	Downtown Burbank d.	0555a	0617a	0652a	0730a	0808a	...	0839a	0852a	0909	|	0916a	1117a	...	|	1509a	1541a	1619a	|	...	1710a	1759a	|	|	2035	
107	**Los Angeles** Union a.	0615	0638	0714	0750	0830	...	0902	0917	0935	0935	0942	1140	...	1215	1533	1600	1640	1650	...	1730	1820	1910	1920	2055	2

	①–⑤	①–⑤	①–⑤	①–⑤ A	⑥⑦ B	①–⑤		①–⑤	①–⑤	B	①–⑤	B		①–⑤	①–⑤	B	①–⑤	①–⑤		①–⑤	①–⑤	①–⑤	①–⑤	B	①
Los Angeles Union d.	0538	0652	0715	0735	0750	0800	...	0830	0855	0920	0950	1230	...	1243	1450	1500	1515	1535	...	1633	1710	1755	1840	1915	1
Downtown Burbank d.	0554a	0707	0731	|	|	0816a	...	0846a	0911a	|	1006	|	...	1259	1506a	|	1531	1551	...	1649a	1726	1811	1856	|	20
Burbank Airport ✈ d.	0601	0712	0736	0800	0812	0825	...	0855	0920	0942	1011	1252	...	1304	1515	1522	1536	1556	...	1654	1731	1816	1901	1937	2
Van Nuys d.	...	0723	0743	0810	0821	...	...	...	...	0952	1019	1302	...	1311	...	1532	1543	1603	...	1701	1738	1823	1908	1947	
Chatsworth d.	...	0738	0810	0832	0833	...	...	...	...	1004	1035	1314	...	1326	...	1544	1605	1618	...	1716	1753	1838	1923	1959	
Moorpark d.	...	0810	...	0857	0857	...	...	...	...	|	...	1339	...	1358	...	|	...	1647	...	1740a	1817a	1908	1947a	|	
Oxnard a.	...	...	...	0921	0921	...	...	...	...	1053	...	1405	...	...	...	1633	...	...	...	1801	1838	...	2014	2046	

9356 LANCASTER - LOS ANGELES

Metrol

km		①–⑤	①–⑤	①–⑤	①–⑤		①–⑤	⑥⑦	①–⑤	①–⑤		⑥⑦	①–⑤	①–⑤	⑥⑦		①–⑤	⑥⑦	①–⑤	①–⑤		①–⑤	⑥⑦	①–⑤	⑥⑦	①
0	**Lancaster** d.	0358	0455	0520	...	...	0610	0625	0652	...	...	0855	0900	...	1110	...	1135	1240	...	1340	...	...	1425	...	1815	1
	Via Princessa d.	0450	0549	0614	...	...	0704	0719	0746	0903	...	0953	0954	1125	1204	...	1229	1332	1345	1434	...	1515	1519	...	1912	1
82	Santa Clarita d.	0456	0555	0620	0653	...	0710	0725	0752	0909	...	1000	1000	1131	1210	...	1235	1338	1351	1440	...	1521	1525	1705	1918	1
106	Downtown Burbank d.	0530	0631	0703	0725	...	0748	0800	0827	0945	...	1035	1038	1211	1248	...	1317	1413	1428	1522	...	1556	1559	1741	1953	1
121	**Los Angeles** Union a.	0553	0655	0726	0742	...	0815	0825	0855	1011	...	1100	1105	1240	1315	...	1345	1440	1450	1550	...	1620	1630	1810	2020	2

	①–⑤	①–⑤	①–⑤	⑥⑦		①–⑤	①–⑤	⑥⑦	①–⑤		①–⑤	⑥⑦	①–⑤	⑥⑦		①–⑤	①–⑤	⑥⑦	①–⑤		①–⑤	①–⑤	①–⑤	⑥⑦	①
Los Angeles Union d.	0630	0730	0825	0845	...	0940	1115	1140	1200	...	1355	1415	1540	1550	...	1600	1645	1725	1735	...	1750	1830	1940	2055	2
Downtown Burbank d.	0647	0746	0842	0902	...	0956	1131	1157	1217	...	1411	1432	1556	1607	...	1616	1701	1742	1749	...	1806	1846	1956	2112	2
Santa Clarita d.	0725	0824	0918	0938	...	1031	1217	1233	1252	...	1445	1508	1631	1643	...	1655	1741	1818	1822	...	1841	1920	2031	2148	2
Via Princessa d.	0731	0843	0924	0944	...	1050	1214	1239	1306	...	1500	1513	1637	1649	...	...	1748	1824	...	...	1847	1926	2037	2154	2
Lancaster a.	0840	...	1045	1055	...	...	1320	1350	...	...	...	1620	1750	1755	...	...	1855	1925	...	...	2000	2032	2140	2300	2

A – Operated by Amtrak. Metrolink tickets valid on this service.
B – Operated by Amtrak. Metrolink tickets not valid on this service.
a – Trains can leave up to 5 minutes ahead of schedule.

LOS ANGELES - SAN BERNARDINO 9358

trolink

	⑥	①–⑤	①–⑤	⑥⑦	①–⑤	⑦	⑥	①–⑤	⑥⑦	①–⑤	⑥⑦	①–⑤	①–⑤	⑥⑦	①–⑤	①–⑤	⑥⑦	①–⑤	①–⑤	⑥	①–⑤	①–⑤	⑥⑦	①–⑤	⑥
		A																							
Los Angeles Union ... d.	0615	0734	0905	0900	1017	1010	1035	1105	1210	1241	1345	1355	1501	1600	1555	1658	1735	1735	1824	1910	1928	2039	2100	2146	2330
El Monte ... d.	0635	0807	0935	0920	1041	1031	1057	1136	1232	1311	1407	1420	1526	1621	1620	1722	1757	1803	1848	1932	1952	2104	2121	2211	2350
Covina ... d.	0651	0826	0953	0938	1059	1050	1115	1153	1250	1329	1425	1437	1543	1638	1637	1740	1815	1822	1906	1950	2010	2121	2139	2228	0005
Pomona North ... d.	0702	0840	1006	0950	1112	1059	1127	1206	1302	1342	1436	1450	1556	1649	1650	1753	1827	1835	1919	2001	2023	2134	2150	2242	0016
San Bernardino ... a.	0754	0932	1054	1045	1200	1152	1222	1254	1400	1430	1540	1538	1651	1745	1743	1841	1922	1923	2014	2054	2111	2222	2240	2329	0105

	①–⑤	①–⑤	①–⑤	⑥⑦	①–⑤	⑥	①–⑤	⑥⑦	①–⑤	⑥⑦	①–⑤	⑦	①–⑤	⑥	①–⑤	⑥⑦	①–⑤	⑥⑦	①–⑤	⑥	①–⑤	①–⑤	⑥⑦	①–⑤	⑥
	B																								
Bernardino ... d.	0600	0628	0653	0700	0759	0825	0849	0950	0959	1130	1133	1230	1228	1305	1335	1407	1512	1535	1600	1655	1716	1814	1830	1949	2115
ona North ... d.	0648	0715	0741	0741	0847	0906	0939	1034	1047	1213	1223	1308	1317	1349	1423	1449	1601	1618	1649	1739	1811	1917	1914	1037	2200
ina ... d.	0659	0727	0752	0751	0858	0916	0949	1044	1058	1223	1234	1317	1329	1359	1435	1459	1612	1628	1700	1749	1823	1928	1924	2048	2210
lonte ... d.	0716	0743	0809	0807	0915	0935	1006	1101	1115	1243	1251	1332	1345	1419	1451	1514	1632	1647	1722	1809	1848	1952	1944	2105	2230
Angeles Union ... a.	0738	0807	0831	0835	0939	1005	1028	1130	1139	1315	1315	1400	1407	1450	1513	1540	1655	1715	1747	1840	1910	2014	2015	2127	2255

Also from Los Angeles Union on ①–⑤ at 0546, 1533, 1622, 1805.

B – Also from San Bernardino on ①–⑤ at 0348, 0421, 0440, 0512, 0538, 0600.

LOS ANGELES - RIVERSIDE 9360

trolink

n		①–⑤	①–⑤	①–⑤	①–⑤	①–⑤	①–⑤				
0	**Los Angeles** Union ... d.	1320	1615	1700	1730	1800	1830	...	...	...	...
	Industry ... d.	1355	1650	1735	1805	1835	1905	...	...	...	...
0	Downtown Pomona ... d.	1404	1659	1744	1814	1844	1914	...	...	...	...
1	**Riverside** Downtown .. a.	1448	1742	1827	1858	1925	1957	...	...	...	...

	①–⑤	①–⑤	①–⑤	①–⑤	①–⑤	①–⑤				
Riverside Downtown d.	0447	0542	0615	0650	0810	1507	...	...	...	...
Downtown Pomona . d.	0520	0615	0648	0723	0843	1540	...	...	...	...
Industry ... d.	0529	0624	0657	0732	0852	1549	...	...	...	...
Los Angeles Union . a.	0610	0707	0735	0815	0935	1635	...	...	...	...

n		①–⑤	①–⑤	①–⑤	①–⑤	⑥⑦	①–⑤	①–⑤	①–⑤	①–⑤	⑥⑦
0	**Los Angeles** Union ... d.	0545	...	...	...	1515	1535	1620	1730	1850	1915
	Fullerton ... d.	0619	...	...	...	1549	1609	1654	1804	1924	1949
	West Corona ... d.	0643	...	...	...	1613	1635	1718	1828	1948	2013
9	**Riverside** Downtown .. a.	0715	0910	1300	1630	1652	1703	1745	1855	2025	2055
	Perris Downtown ... a.	...	0955	1345	1716	...	1748	1830	1935	...	...

	①–⑤	①–⑤	①–⑤	⑥⑦	①–⑤	⑥⑦	①–⑤	①–⑤	①–⑤	
Perris Downtown ... d.	0445	0513	0550	...	0751	...	1136	1451		...
Riverside Downown d.	0527	0556	0632	0750	0835	0900	1220	1535	1807	...
West Corona ... d.	0551	0618	0656	0814	...	0924	...	...	1831	...
Fullerton ... d.	0616	0643	0721	0839	...	0949	...	...	1854	...
Los Angeles Union . a.	0705	0732	0810	0930	...	1040	...	...	1945	...

RIVERSIDE - OCEANSIDE 9362

trolink

m		①–⑤	①–⑤	①–⑤	①–⑤	⑥⑦	①–⑤	⑥⑦	①–⑤	①–⑤	①–⑤
0	**San Bernardino** ... d.	0441	0520	0557	...	0705	...	0900	...	1222	...
	Riverside Downtown .. d.	0500	0539	0616	0659	0725	0728	0920	1018	1240	1501
25	West Corona ... d.	0523	0604	0639	0722	0849	0752	0944	1041	1304	1526
	Anaheim Canyon ... d.	0541	0625	0658	0742	0811	0812	1007	1059	1325	1545
	Orange ... d.	0548	0633	0707	0753	0822	0822	1017	1106	1334	1554
78	Santa Ana ... d.	0553	0638	0712	0758	0827	0828	1023	1111	1340	1600
94	Irvine ... d.	0607	0655	0726	0813	0842	0842	1039	1127	1354	1615
13	San Juan Capistrano .. d.	0626	...	...	...	0903	...	1100	...	1409	...
26	San Clemente ... d.	0636	...	...	...	0913	...	1110	...	1418	...
60	**Oceanside** ... a.	0703	...	...	...	0955	...	1150	...	1453	...

	①–⑤	①–⑤	①–⑤	①–⑤	⑥⑦	①–⑤	①–⑤	⑥⑦	①–⑤	①–⑤
Oceanside ... d.	0739	...	...	...	1451	...	...	1628	1625	...
San Clemente ... d.	0802	...	...	...	1514	...	...	1650	1646	...
San Juan C'strano ... d.	0811	...	...	...	1529	...	...	1700	1657	...
Irvine ... d.	0827	0923	1250	1537	1548	1606	1655	1718	1728	1845
Santa Ana ... d.	0839	0935	1303	1550	1601	1619	1707	1730	1741	1857
Orange ... d.	0844	0940	1308	1557	1607	1624	1712	1735	1746	1902
Anaheim Canyon ... d.	0851	0946	1314	1603	1616	1631	1719	1742	1753	1909
West Corona ... d.	0909	1004	1334	1622	1638	1652	1738	1804	1811	1930
Riverside D'town ... a.	0944	1029	1410	1657	1708	1717	1806	1833	1837	2005
San Bernardino ... a.	...	1058	...	...	1738	1741	1830	1913	1905	...

LOS ANGELES - OCEANSIDE 9364

trolink

	①–⑤	①–⑤	⑥⑦		①–⑤	⑥⑦	①–⑤		⑥⑦	①–⑤	①–⑤		①–⑤	①–⑤	①–⑤		⑥⑦	①–⑤	①–⑤		①–⑤	①–⑤		①–⑤	
Los Angeles Union ... d.	0650	0758	0840	...	...	1050	...	...	1400	1411	1519	...	1547	...	1630	...	1640	1650	1746	...	1840	*1850*	...	...	...
Fullerton ... d.	0725	0833	0915	...	1000	1125	1340	...	1435	1446	1556	...	1625	1655	1710	...	1715	1725	1823	...	1916	1935	...	2210	...
Anaheim ... d.	0732	0840	0922	...	1007	1132	1347	...	1442	1454	1603	...	1633	1702	1717	...	1722	1733	1831	...	1923	1943	...	2218	...
Orange ... d.	0738	0845	0927	...	1012	1137	1352	...	1447	1459	1608	...	1638	1707	1722	...	1727	1739	1837	...	1928	1947	...	2223	...
Santa Ana ... d.	0744	0850	0932	...	1017	1142	1357	...	1452	1505	1613	...	1643	1712	1727	...	1732	1745	1842	...	1933	1952	...	2227	...
Irvine ... d.	0800	0904	0946	...	1031	1206	1411	...	1506	1521	1627	...	1659	1718	1741	...	1746	1801	1856	...	1947	2005	...	2241	...
San Juan Capistrano .. d.	...	0920	1001	...	...	1213	...	...	1521	...	1646	...	...	...	1757	...	1801	...	1912	...	2004	...	...	2258	...
San Clemente ... d.	...	0930	1012	...	...	1225	...	...	1534	...	1659	...	...	...	1806	...	1815	...	1922	...	2017	...	...	2307	...
Oceanside ... a.	...	1001	1052	...	...	1300	...	...	1615	...	1728	...	...	...	1837	...	1855	...	1954	...	2046	...	...	2335	...

	①–⑤	①–⑤	①–⑤		①–⑤	①–⑤	①–⑤		①–⑤	①–⑤	⑥⑦		①–⑤	①–⑤	⑥⑦		⑥⑦	①–⑤	①–⑤		①–⑤	①–⑤	⑥⑦		①–⑤
eanside ... d.	...	0443	0516	...	0542	...	0634	...	...	...	0815	...	...	...	1124	...	1324	1459	1526	...	...	...	1736	...	...
Clemente ... d.	...	0506	0539	...	0604	...	0656	...	...	...	0838	...	...	...	1150	...	1346	1521	1548	...	...	...	1758	...	...
Juan Capistrano ... d.	...	0515	0548	...	0613	...	0705	...	...	...	0850	...	...	...	1200	...	1400	1531	1557	...	...	...	1811	...	...
ne ... d.	0415	0532	0603	...	0629	0710	0722	...	0813	0854	0908	...	0908	1140	1219	...	1417	1550	1615	...	1717	1805	1829	...	2100
nta Ana ... d.	0427	0544	0616	...	0643	0722	0734	...	0825	0906	0920	...	0920	1152	1231	...	1429	1604	1629	...	1729	1817	1841	...	2112
ange ... d.	0432	0552	0621	...	0649	0727	0739	...	0830	0911	0925	...	0925	1157	1236	...	1434	1609	1634	...	1734	1822	1846	...	2117
aheim ... d.	0436	0557	0626	...	0655	0732	0744	...	0835	0916	0930	...	0929	1201	1241	...	1439	1614	1639	...	1739	1827	1851	...	2122
erton ... d.	0443	0604	0635	...	0702	0741	0751	...	0842	0925	0937	...	0941	1215	1248	...	1446	1624	1646	...	1746	1840	1858	...	2135
s **Angeles** Union ... a.	0525	0645	0720	...	0745	0819	0840	...	0926	1004	1030	...	...	...	1337	...	1539	...	1726	...	1827	*1945*	1956	...	...

OCEANSIDE - SAN DIEGO 9366

oaster

n		①–⑤	①–⑤	①–⑤	①–⑤	①–⑤	⑥⑦		①–⑤	①–⑤	⑥⑦		⑥⑦	①–⑤	①–⑤	⑥	①–⑤	⑥⑦	①–⑤	⑥	⑤		①–⑤	⑥⑦	⑤	
																						C	C	C		C
0	**Oceanside** ... d.	0512	0601	0649	0713	0742	0823	...	0943	1108	1109	...	1356	1442	1532	1533	1712	1721	1741	1825	1842	1903	2120	2127	2151	2357
	Carlsbad Village ... d.	0516	0605	0654	0717	0746	0828	...	0948	1113	1113	...	1401	1447	1536	1538	1717	1726	1746	1830	1848	1908	2125	2132	2156	0003
	Encinitas ... d.	0527	0615	0705	0728	0757	0839	...	0959	1124	1124	...	1412	1500	1549	1550	1728	1737	1756	1841	1859	1923	2132	2139	2207	0012
7	Solana Beach ... d.	0532	0620	0713	0736	0802	0845	...	1007	1132	1131	...	1420	1505	1554	1556	1735	1744	1801	1847	1905	1929	2140	2148	2213	0019
	Sorrento Valley ... d.	0541	0629	0722	0746	0814	0854	...	1016	1141	1140	...	1429	1514	1603	1605	1744	1753	1811	1856	1915	1939	2157	2155	2222	0026
	San Diego Old Town. a.	0601	0655	0746	0810	0837	0916	...	1038	1207	1206	...	1450	1536	1628	1629	1808	1814	1837	1924	1942	2002s	2220s	2228s	2243	0059s
8	**San Diego** SF Depot . a.	0610	0702	0753	0817	0845	0924	...	1047	1214	1214	...	1458	1544	1635	1636	1816	1823	1845	1930	1950	2009	2230	2239	2251	0106

	①–⑤	①–⑤	⑥⑦	①–⑤	⑥⑦	①–⑤				⑥⑦	①–⑤	①–⑤	⑥⑦	①–⑤	①–⑤	①–⑤	⑥	①–⑤	①–⑤	⑥⑦	①–⑤	⑤		⑥	⑤
			C	C				C															C		
Diego SF Depot ... d.	0625	0741	0805	0823	0939	0940	...	1041	...	1229	1251	1405	1517	1538	1623	1655	1656	1740	1826	1911	1915	2012	2059	2314	2315
Dlego Old Town ... d.	0631	0747	0812	0830u	0945	0946	...	1048u	...	1236	1257	1411	1524	1544	1629	1701	1703	1746	1832	1918	1921	2018	2106u	2321	2321
rrento Valley ... d.	0653	0809	0834	0854	1008	1010	...	1111	...	1300	1319	1433	1545	1606	1651	1724	1725	1808	1854	1943	1943	2040	2128	2342	2343
ana Beach ... d.	0703	0822	0843	0903	1017	1024	...	1122	...	1309	1330	1443	1554	1617	1700	1734	1735	1820	1904	1953	1953	2050	2139	2352	2353
cinitas ... d.	0710	0829	0850	0909	1022	1030	...	1130	...	1314	1336	1449	1600	1623	1708	1740	1742	1826	1910	1958	1959	2056	2145	2358	2359
lsbad Village ... d.	0723	0841	0904	0923	1040	1044	...	1142	...	1329	1347	1501	1612	1635	1721	1752	1754	1838	1922	2010	2011	2108	2157	0011	0011
eanside ... a.	0728	0846	0910	0928	1045	1053	...	1149	...	1335	1354	1507	1620	1641	1728	1758	1800	1845	1930	2016	2018	2115	2202	0019	0020

- Operated by Amtrak. Coaster tickets generally valid on this service.

s – Calls to set down only.

u – Calls to pick up only.

OCEANSIDE - ESCONDIDO 9368

printer

m		D	D	D	D		D	D	D	D
0	**Oceanside** ... d.	0533	0633	0733	0833	and at	1733	1833	1933	2033
	Vista Transit Center ... d.	0556	0656	0756	0856	the same	1756	1856	1956	2056
	San Marcos Civic Ctr .. d.	0613	0713	0813	0913	minutes past each	1813	1913	2013	2113
34	**Escondido** ... a.	0626	0726	0826	0926	hour until	1826	1926	2026	2126

	D	D	D	D		D	D	D	D
Escondido ... d.	0533	0633	0733	0833	and at	1733	1833	1933	2033
S. Marcos Civic Ctr .. d.	0544	0644	0744	0844	the same	1744	1844	1944	2044
Vista Transit Center . d.	0557	0657	0757	0857	minutes past each	1757	1857	1957	2057
Oceanside ... a.	0626	0726	0826	0926	hour until	1826	1926	2026	2126

- Additional services: from **Oceanside** at 0403 ①–⑤ and hourly until 1003 ①–⑤, 1103 and hourly until 1803, 1903 ①–⑤, 2003 ①–⑤; from **Escondido** at 0403 ①–⑤ and hourly until 0903 ①–⑤, 1003 and hourly until 1703, 1803 ①–⑤, 1903 ①–⑤, 2003 ①–⑤. Additional later evening services are available on ⑤⑥.

BEYOND EUROPE - SOUTH AMERICA

9900 MEXICO — Ferromex

km		▶ A	①④⑥ B		⊕ A	②⑤⑦ B
0	**Chihuahua** d.	0600	0600	**Los Mochis** d.	0600	0600
132	Cuauhtémoc d.	0825	0825	El Fuerte d.	0816	0819
295	Creel d.	1120	1147	Témoris d.	1120	1124
355	Divisadero d.	1304	1341	Bahuichivo d.	1220	1224
	Posada Barrancas d.	1311	1352	San Rafael d.	1325	1328
370	San Rafael d.	1337	1416	Posada Barrancas d.	1343	1346
	Bahuichivo d.	1428	1512	Divisadero d.	1422	1414
440	Témoris d.	1525	1612	Creel d.	1544	1539
570	El Fuerte d.	1823	1919	Cuauhtémoc d.	1837	1907
655	**Los Mochis** a.	2022	2128	**Chihuahua** a.	2054	2134

km		⑥ C			⑥ C	
0	**Guadalajara** d.	1045	...	**Amatitán** d.	1700	...
	Amatitán a.	1145	...	**Guadalajara** a.	1800	...

A – EL CHEPE – 1 and ✕. B – EL TARAHUMARA – 2 and 🍸.
C – TEQUILA EXPRESS – 1 Currently trip by 🚌 as train is being refurbished.
▶ – ②③⑤⑦. ⊕ – ①③④⑥.

9905 HONDURAS — FC de Hondu

km		①–⑤	①–⑤	①–⑤	①–⑤	①–⑤	①–⑤	①–⑤	①–⑤	①
0	**S Pedro Sula** Est d.	0730	0830	0930	1030	1130	1230	1330	1430	1
3	**S Pedro Sula** Central a.	0750	0850	0950	1050	1150	1250	1350	1450	1

		①–⑤	①–⑤	①–⑤	①–⑤	①–⑤	①–⑤	①–⑤	①–⑤	①
S Pedro Sula Central d.	...	0800	0900	1000	1100	1200	1300	1400	1500	1
S Pedro Sula Est a.	...	0820	0920	1020	1120	1220	1320	1420	1520	1

9910 PANAMA — Panama Canal

km		①–⑤			①–⑤
0	**Ciudad Panama** d.	0715	...	**Colon** d.	1715
77	**Colon** a.	0815	...	**Ciudad Panama** a.	1815

9915 COSTA RICA — INCOF

km		①–⑤	①–⑤	①–⑤	①–⑤	①–⑤	①–⑤	①–⑤	①–⑤	①–⑤	①–⑤	①–⑤	①–⑤	
0	**San José** Pacifico d.	0500	0612	0617	0635	0728	0805	1612	1611	1707	1738	1737	1842	...
8	Pavas Metropolis III d.	0535	|	0648	|	|	|	|	1651	|	|	1816	|	...
10	**S Antonio de Belén** a.	...	0640	...	0710	0803	0841	1643	...	1742	1814	...	1919	...

	①–⑤	①–⑤	①–⑤	①–⑤	①–⑤	①–⑤	①–⑤	①–⑤	①–⑤	①–⑤	①–⑤	①–⑤	①–⑤	①–⑤
S Antonio de Belén d.	...	0557	0642	...	0715	0815	0845	1621	1645	...	1800	...	1830	1920
Pavas Metropolis III d.	0537	|	|	0649	|	|	|	|	|	1655	|	1818	|	|
San José Pacifico a.	0615	0631	0715	0726	0755	0840	0917	1655	1720	1737	1830	1900	1905	2000

km		①–⑤	①–⑤	①–⑤	①–⑤	①
0	**Freses de Curidabat** d.	0651	0801	1705	1811	1
4	Universidad Costa Rica d.	0700	0808	1714	1819	1
15	**San José** Pacifico a.	0728	0832	1739	1841	1

		①–⑤	①–⑤	①–⑤	①–⑤	①
San José Pacifico d.	...	0617	0728	1628	1739	1
Universidad Costa Rica d.	...	0641	0750	1654	1800	1
Freses de Curidabat a.	...	0650	0759	1701	1807	1

km		①–⑤	①–⑤	①–⑤	①–⑤	①–⑤	①–⑤	①–⑤	①–⑤	①–⑤	①–⑤	△
0	**San José** Atlantico d.	0530	0600	0630	0700	0730	0800	1530	1600	1630	1700	1730
10	**Heredia** a.	0600	0630	0700	0730	0800	0830	1600	1630	1700	1730	1800

	①–⑤	①–⑤	①–⑤	①–⑤	①–⑤	①–⑤	①–⑤	①–⑤	①–⑤	①–⑤	
Heredia d.	0600	0630	0700	0730	0800	0830	1600	1630	1700	1730	1
San José Atlantico a.	0630	0700	0730	0800	0830	0900	1630	1700	1730	1800	1

△ – ①–⑤. Also at 1800①–⑤, 1830①–⑤, 1900①–⑤, 1930①–⑤.
▽ – ①–⑤. Also at 1830①–⑤, 1900①–⑤, 1930①–⑤, 2000①–⑤.

9920 CUBA — Unión de los Ferrocarriles Cuban

km					9		11	15	7		73
			2	2		2	D	2	2		
		◧	◧	◧	◧	◧	◧	◧	◧	◧	◧
0	**Habana** La Coubre d.	...	0740	0840	...	1600	1813	1853	2121	...	0715a
90	Matanzas d.	...	|	|	...	|	|	|	2354	...	|
	Varadero d.	...	|	|	...	|	|	|	|	0815	|
286	Santa Clara d.	...	1200	1325	1425	2045	|	0220	0540	|	|
	Cienfuegos d.	...	|	|	|	|	|	|	|	1325	1335
	Trinidad d.	0800	|	|	|	|	|	|	|	1500	1745
	Sancti Spiritus d.	0925	1320	|	1550	2205	|	|	0833	...	▬
436	Ciego de Avila d.	1045	1525	|	1710	2330	|	0300	...	...	...
538	Camagüey d.	1240	1720	1735	2126	0120	0407	0450	...	...	...
714	Bayamo d.	|	|	|	|	|	|	|	...	...	...
770	**Manzanillo** a.	|	|	|	|	|	|	|	...	...	...
652	Las Tunas d.	1440	2000	|	0110	0330	|	|	...	...	...
729	Cacocúm d.	|	|	|	|	|	|	1017	...	...	...
806	Combinado d.	|	|	|	|	|	|	|	...	...	...
	Holguim d.	1555	|	2035	0235	0435	|	|	...	...	◧
	Baracoa d.	|	|	...	|	|	|	|	...	...	1330
884	**Guantanamo** a.	|	|	...	|	|	|	1238	...	...	1640
854	**Santiago de Cuba** a.	1925	2340	...	0605	0805	1005	...	...	...	1820

				16	8		12		10	
	2	2	2		2	◧	D	2		
	◧	◧	◧	◧	◧		◧	◧	◧	
Santiago de Cuba d.	0735	...	0800	...	...	1930	2345	2315	0720	
Guantanamo d.	0930	...	|	0850	...	|	|	|	|	
Baracoa a.	1235	...	|	|	...	|	|	|	|	
Holguim d.	▬	0840	1135	|	...	2035	|	|	1105	
Combinado d.	...	|	|	|	...	|	|	|	|	
Cacocúm d.	...	|	|	1300	...	|	0300	|	|	
Las Tunas d.	...	0955	1330	|	...	0020	|	0335	1305	
Manzanillo d.	...	|	|	|	...	|	|	|	|	
Bayamo d.	...	|	|	|	...	|	|	|	|	
Camagüey d.	...	1150	1530	1655	...	0220	0600	0515	1552	
Ciego de Avila d.	**74**	1425	1725	1916	...	0415	0830	0700	1725	
Sancti Spiritus d.	◧	1545	1845	|	2045	0535	|	0825	1910	
Trinidad a.	0530	|	|	|	|	0655	|	|	|	15
Cienfuegos d.	0700		|	|	|	...	|	|	|	16
Santa Clara d.	|	1705	|	2130	0015	...	1115	1005	2243	
Valadero a.	|	|	|	|	|	...	|	|	...	2
Matanzas d.	|	|	|	0100	0526	...	1400	|	...	
Habana La Coubre a.	1730a	2050	0030	0233	0755	...	1532	1541	...	

D – 1 Habana Central - Santiago de Cuba and v.v. a – Havana Tulipan. ◧ – Services run about every second or third day and **ALL are subject to confirmation, please check loca**

9925 VENEZUELA

km		①–⑤	①–⑤	①–⑤		①–⑥	①–⑥	①–⑥	①–⑥	①–⑥	①–⑥		①–⑥	①–⑥	①–⑥	①–⑤	①–⑤	①–⑤		①–⑤	①–⑤	①
0	**Caracas** d.	0500	0520	0540	and every	0900	1000	1100	1200	1300	1400	...	1500	1600	1700	1720	1740	1800	and every	2020	2040	2
24	Charallave Norte d.	0517	0537	0557	20 minutes	0917	1017	1117	1217	1317	1417	...	1517	1617	1717	1737	1757	1817	20 minutes	2037	2057	2
32	Charallave Sur d.	0522	0542	0602	until	0922	1022	1122	1222	1322	1422	...	1522	1622	1722	1742	1802	1822	until	2042	2002	2
41	**Cúa** a.	0531	0551	0611		0931	1031	1131	1231	1331	1431	...	1531	1631	1731	1751	1811	1831		2051	2011	2

		①–⑤	①–⑤	①–⑤		①–⑥	①–⑥	①–⑥	①–⑥	①–⑥	①–⑥		①–⑥	①–⑥	①–⑥	①–⑤	①–⑤	①–⑤		①–⑤	①–⑤	①
Cúa d.	...	0500	0520	0540	and every	0900	1000	1100	1200	1300	1400	...	1500	1600	1700	1720	1740	1800	and every	2020	2040	21
Charallave Sur d.	...	0509	0529	0549	20 minutes	0909	1009	1109	1209	1309	1409	...	1509	1609	1709	1729	1749	1809	20 minutes	2029	2049	21
Charallave Norte d.	...	0514	0534	0554	until	0914	1014	1114	1214	1314	1414	...	1514	1614	1714	1734	1754	1814	until	2034	2054	21
Caracas a.	...	0531	0551	0611		0931	1031	1131	1231	1331	1431	...	1531	1631	1731	1751	1811	1831		2054	2011	21

9930 COLOMBIA

BARRANCABERMEJA — Coopsercol Ltda

km										
0	**Puerto Parra** d.	...	...	0510	...	...	...	...	...	...
65	Barrancabermeja d.	0600	...	0725	...	1130	...	1430	1700	...
95	**García Cardena** a.	0700	...	...	...	1230	...	1530	1800	...

García Cardena d.	...	0700	...		...	1230	...	1530	...	1800
Barrancabermeja d.	...	0800	...	1300	...	1330	...	1630	...	1900
Puerto Parra a.	...	...	...	1515	...	...	...	...	...	...

All services subject to confirmation, please check locally.

BOGOTÁ - ZAPAQUIRÁ — Turistr

km		⑥⑦			⑥⑦	⑥
0	**Bogotá Sabana** d.	0815	...	**Zapaquirá** d.	1235	.
15	Usaquen d.	0915	...	Cajicá d.	1305	15
34	La Caro d.	1015	...	La Caro d.	...	15
40	Cajicá d.	|	...	Usaquen d.	...	16
53	**Zapaquirá** a.	1105	...	**Bogotá** Sabana a.	...	17

9935 ECUADOR — FC del Ecuad

km	All trains 🅁		32 ②⑥⑦		All trains 🅁		31 ⑥⑦	③
0	**Quito** d.	...	0800	...	**Latacunga** d.	...	...	...
45	Machachi d.	...	1010	...	Lasso d.	...	...	...
62	Cotopaxi d.	...	1100	...	Cotopaxi d.	...	1330	1500
80	Lasso d.	...	...	...	Machachi d.	...	1435	1550
110	**Latacunga** a.	...	...	...	**Quito** a.	...	1640	1756

km	All trains 🅁	31 ⑥⑦	③-⑦		All trains 🅁	36 ③-⑦	⑥⑦	
0	**Otavalo** a.	0800	...	...	**Salinas** d.	1345	1345	...
30	**Ibarra** d.	1040	1040	...	**Ibarra** a.	1630	1630	...
61	**Salinas** a.	1230	1230	...	**Otavalo** d.	...	1830	...

km	All trains 🅁	A ②–⑦	②–⑦	④–⑦
0	**Riobamba** d.	...	...	1200
41	Colta d.	...	...	1300
98	Alausi d.	0800	1100	...
111	Sibambe d.	0900	1200	...
154	**Bucay** a.	...	...	...
				④–⑦
87	**Bucay** d.	...	...	1430
21	Yaguachi d.	...	...	1745
0	**Duran** a.	...	...	1845

All trains 🅁	④–⑦		
Duran d.	0800	...	..
Yaguachi d.	0920	...	..
Bucay a.	1145	...	.
	B ②–⑦	②–⑦	④-
Bucay d.	...	...	
Sibambe d.	1000	1300	..
Alausi d.	1030	1330	..
Colta d.	...	...	15
Riobamba a.	...	...	16

A – Additional trip 1500. B – Additional trip 1700.

PERU 9940

POROY - MACHU PICCHU — Inca Rail / Perurail

	71	81	41	301	61	601	31	501	33	203	11	43			73	303	603	45	75	51
	B	B a	I 1	A	I 2	B	A	A	B	A	C	I 1			B	A	A	I 1	B	B
Poroy △ ....d.	...	...	...	...	...	U	...	...	...		0810	...	...	...	...	...	...	...	...	...
Ollantaytambo....d.	0505	0610	0640	0705	0720	0800	0808*	0853	0850*	1005*	|	1115	...	...	1258	1327	1537	1636	1900	2100
Machu Picchu ..a.	0634	0740	0801	0827	0848	0924	0954	1029	1052	1211	1224	1245	...	...	1425	1450	1702	1809	2045	2245

	50	72	42		302	204	44	74	32	304	64	504	34	604	12	606	84	46		76
	B	B	I 1		A	A	I 1	B	A	A	I 2	A	B	A	C	A	B	I 1		B
ıu Picchu ....d.	0535	0853	0830	...	1056	1337	1430	1455	1520	1548	1612	1622	1643	1723	1750	1810	1820	1900	...	2150
taytambo..........d.	0744	1052	1010	...	1232	1504	1556	1631	1730*	1729	1750	1810	1853*	1919*	|	1951	2005	2032	...	2335
y △ ....a.	...	...	...	...	...	...	...	...	...	U	...	...	...	...	2200	...	...	...	...	...

A – VISTADOME – [1] and 🍸.
B – EXPEDITION – [2] and 🍸.
C – HIRAM BINGHAM – [1] and ✕.
D – 2016 Mar. 24, Apr. 15, May 27, Jun. 26, Jul. 28, Aug. 27, Sep, 16, Oct. 7, 29.
E – 2016 Mar. 27, Apr. 17, May 29, Jun. 29, Jul. 31, Aug.30, Sep. 18, Oct. 9, Nov. 1.
I – Inca Rail. www.incarail.com
U – To/ From Urubamba dep. 0650 arr.1843
a – Additional trip 0745.

Poroy is *13 km* from **Cusco**, connection by bus. * Until April 30 will arrive/leave from Pachar 1hr 50 mins from Cusco. Bus journey to/from Pachar is NOT included in the fare.

CUSCO - PUNO

EAN EXPLORER. *385 km. Journey 10 hours.*
Cusco at 0800 ①③⑥ (also ⑤ Apr. - Oct.).
Puno at 0800 ①③⑥ (also ⑤ Apr. - Oct.).
s convey [12] and ✕. Operator: Perurail.

LIMA - HUANCAYO

TREN DE LA SIERRA. *332 km. Journey 12 hours.*
From Lima at 0700 on dates in note **D** but may vary.
From Huancayo at 0700 on dates in note **E** but may vary.
Trains convey [12] and ✕. Operator: FC Central Andino.

TACNA - ARICA

62 km. Journey 1½ hours. 2nd class.
From Tacna. 0600, 1700
From Arica. 0800, 1900
Operator: FC Tacna Arica.

HUANCAYO - HUANCAVELICA

127 km. Journey 5¼ hours.
From Huancayo. ①③⑤ 0630.
From Huancavelica. ②④⑥ 0630
Operator: FC HH.

BOLIVIA 9945

rroviária Andina / Ferroviária Oriental

PUERTO QUIJARRO - SANTA CRUZ DA LA SIERRA — FO

ı			13	7
			②④⑦	①③⑤
)	**Puerto Quijarro** .... d.	...	1300	1800
5	Rivero Torrez......... d.	...	1540	2010
)	Roboré .... d.	...	1914	2248
4	San José Chiquitos d.	...	2323	0152
	Pozo del Tigre .... d.	...	0229	|
)	**SC da la Sierra**..... a.	...	0540	0700

		14	8
		①③⑤	②④⑦
SC da la Sierra .. d.	...	1320	1800
Pozo del Tigre .... d.	...	1626	|
San José Chiquitos d.	...	1945	2308
Roboré .... d.	...	2357	0212
Rivero Torrez...... d.	...	0312	0448
Puerto Quijarro . a.	...	0602	0700

SANTA CRUZ DE LA SIERRA - YACUIBA — FO

km		2		
		④		
0	**SC de la Sierra**..... a.	1530	...	...
115	Cabezas................ d.	1945	...	...
239	Charaguá .... d.	2322	...	...
360	Boyuibe .... d.	0229	...	...
434	Villa Montes........... d.	0513	...	...
533	**Yacuíba** .... a.	0805	...	...

	1		
	⑤		
Yacuíba............. d.	1700	...	...
Villa Montes....... d.	1948	...	...
Boyuibe .... d.	2235	...	...
Charaguá........... d.	0135	...	...
Cabezas .... d.	0535	...	...
SC de la Sierra .. a.	0955	...	...

OURO - VILLAZÓN — FA

ı		2	16	68
		②⑤	③⑦	①④
)	**Oruro**.................. d.	1430	1900	...
3	Uyuni.................... d.	2140	0250	0330
1	**Avaroa** .... a.	|	|	0930
4	Atocha.................. d.	2355	0520	...
1	Tupiza .... d.	0310	0905	...
2	**Villazón** .... a.	0605	1205	...

	1	15	67
	③⑥	①④	①④
Villazón............ d.	1530	1530	...
Tupiza .... d.	1825	1905	...
Atocha .... d.	2145	2300	...
Avaroa........... d.	|	|	1200
Uyuni................. d.	2359	0145	1810
Oruro .... a.	0705	0930	...

OTHER SERVICES IN BOLIVIA — FA

km	②④⑥			③⑤⑦
0	0800	↓	d.**Cochabamba**...... d.	1645
216	1645	↓	a.**Aiquille**........... a. ↑	0800

km	①④			②⑤
0	0800	↓	d.**Viacha** .... d.	1410
208	1420	↓	a.**Charaña** .... a. ↑	0800

km	②④⑥			①③⑤
0	0800	↓	d.**Potosí** .... d.	1400
171	1400	↓	a.**Sucre** El Tejar .... a. ↑	0800

km	A			A
0	0800	↓	d.**El Alto** .... d.	1820
77	1320	↓	a.**Guaqui** .... a. ↑	1600

A – 2nd Sunday of every month.

BRAZIL 9950

trada de Ferro do Carajás / Estrada de Ferro Vitória a Minas

SÃO LUIS - PARAUAPEBAS — EFC

m		⑥ 12			⑦ 12	
0	...	0800	↓	d.**São Luis**.............. a. ↑	2200	...
6	...	1016		d.Arari .... d.	1941	...
5	...	1040	↓	d.Vitória do Mearim .. d. ↑	1913	...
3	...	1156		d.Santa Inês............. d.	1804	...
4	...	1256	↓	d.Alto Alegre .... d. ↑	1659	...
1	...	1319		d.Mineirinho.............. d.	1634	...
9	...	1340	↓	d.Auzilândia.............. d. ↑	1613	...
5	...	1402		d.Altamira................. d.	1551	...
4	...	1430	↓	d.Presa de Porco ..... d. ↑	1525	...
34	...	1526		d.Nova Vida .... d.	1429	...
3	...	1741	↓	d.Acailandia.............. d. ↑	1219	...
50	...	1957		d.São Pedro .... d.	0956	...
38	...	2131	↓	d.Marabá.................. d. ↑	0829	...
35	...	2222		d.Itainopolis .... d.	0731	...
51	...	2350	↓	a.**Parauapebas** .... d. ↑	0600	...

BELO HORIZONTE - VITÓRIA — EFVM

km		2			2	
0	...	0730	↓	d.**Belo Horizonte** .... a. ↑	2010	...
71	...	0903		d.Dois Irmãos .... d.	1830	...
97	...	1002	↓	d.Rio Piracicaba ...... d. ↑	1732	...
149	...	1048		d.Drumond................ d.	1639	...
173	...	1116	↓	d.Antonio Dias .... d. ↑	1605	...
	...	1152		d.Mario Carvalho ..... d.	1532	...
286	...	1315	↓	d.Periquito .... d. ↑	1405	...
339	...	1420		d.G Valadares .... d.	1314	...
415	...	1547	↓	d.Conselheiro Pena . d. ↑	1125	...
484	...	1704		d.Aimorés .... d.	1026	...
532	...	1804	↓	d.Colatina .... d. ↑	0927	...
588	...	1859		d.Piraqueacú .... d.	0829	...
612	...	1926	↓	d.Fundão .... d. ↑	0802	...
657	...	2012		d.Flexal...................... d.	0715	...
664	...	2030	↓	a.**Vitória** .... d. ↑	0700	...

DRUMOND - ITABIRA — EFVM

km		2			2	
0	...	1645		d.**Drumond** .... a.	1026	...
35	...	1741	↓	a.**Itabira** .... d. ↑	0930	...

PORTO SANTANA - SERRA DO NÁVIO

km		②④⑦ 2		Temporarily suspended.	①③⑥ 2	...
0	...	1000	↓	d.**Porto Santana** .... a. ↑	1205	...
	...	1320		d.Porto Grande .... d.	0847	...
130	...	1403	↓	d.Dona Maria............ d. ↑	0807	...
150	...	1445		d.Cupixi...................... d.	0725	...
162	...	1505	↓	d.Munquba .... d. ↑	0705	...
179	...	1540		d.Pedra Branca do Amapari . d.	0630	...
194	...	1610	↓	a.**Serra do Návio** ..... d. ↑	0600	...

URUGUAY 9955

rrocarriles del Estado

m																						
			①–⑤			①–⑤	⑥	⑥	①–⑤		①–⑤		①–⑤	⑥	①–⑤	①–⑤		⑥	①–⑤	①–⑤			
0	**Montevideo** Nueva Terminal ....d.	...	0655	...	...	1015	1035	1320	1330	...	1500	...	1545	1550	1730	1750	...	1810	1845	2010	...	...	...
8	Sayago.........d.	...	0709	...	...	1029	1048	1333	1344	...	1514	...	1600	1604	1744	1804	...	1824	1900	2024	...	...	...
9	Las Piedras ....d.	...	0730	...	...	1050	1111	1356	1405	...	1535	...	1627	1629	1807	1825	...	1847	1922	2045	...	...	...
6	Progreso.........d.	...	0743	...	...	1103	1124	1409	...	...	1548	...	1641	1643	1824	1838	...	1901	1936	2058	...	...	...
2	Canalones ....d.	...	...	...	...	...	...	...	...	...	...	...	...	1707	1844	...	...	1924	1959	...	...	...	...
3	**25 de Augosto**.........a.	...	...	...	...	...	...	...	...	...	...	...	...	1737	1914	...	...	1954	2029	...	...	...	...

		①–⑤		⑥	①–⑤	①-⑤	⑥	①–⑤			①–⑤	⑥		①–⑤		①–⑤	⑥	①–⑤	①–⑤				
de Augosto.........d.	...	0435	...	0530	0530	...	0635	...	...	...	...	...	...	...	...	...	...	...	...	...	...	...	...
ıalones ....d.	...	0504	...	0600	0559	...	0705	...	...	...	...	...	...	...	...	...	...	...	...	...	...	...	...
ogreso.........d.	...	0529	...	0623	0623	0715	0728	0755	...	...	1120	1135	...	...	...	1555	1555	1700	1850	...	...	...	...
s Piedras ....d.	...	0544	...	0638	0638	0731	0743	0807	...	...	1132	1147	...	1415	...	1607	1609	1714	1901	...	...	...	...
yago.........d.	...	0607	...	0701	0702	0754	0806	0829	...	...	1154	1209	...	1436	...	1628	1631	1738	1926	...	...	...	...
ntevideo N Terminal.........a.	...	0622	...	0716	0717	0809	0821	0843	...	...	1208	1223	...	1450	...	1642	1645	1753	1940	...	...	...	...

ARGENTINA 9960

rrobaires — BUENOS AIRES - MAR DEL PLATA — 9960A

km		6701	6701	305	307	315	319	6073	
		①–⑤	⑥⑦		⑤	①③⑤	⑤	Ⓐ	
0	**Buenos Aires** ‡.........d.	0355	0824	1345	1510	1640	1640	1648	...
14	Chascomús.........d.	0551	1018	|	|	1830	1830	1847	...
04	Dolores.........d.	...	...	1658	1832	2002	2002	...	...
71	Maipú ....d.	...	...	|	|	2107	|	...	...
46	**Pinamar**.........a.	...	...	|	|	|	2258	...	...
99	**Mar del Plata** ....a.	...	...	2018	2147	2323	...	...	...

		6702	308	6704	306	320	316	
		①–⑤	⑦			⑦	②④⑦	
r del Plata.........d.	...	...	1155	...	1420	...	1630	...
Pinamar.........d.	...	...	|	...	|	1630	|	...
ipú ....d.	...	...	|	...	|	|	1846	...
lores.........d.	...	...	1536	...	1736	1911	1957	...
ascomús.........d.	...	1104	|	1919	|	2040	2136	...
enos Aires ‡ ....a.	...	1305	1837	2044	2103	2230	2330	...

Buenos Aires Plaza Constitución.
e: Because of flooding these services may not operate.

Ferrobaires — BUENOS AIRES - BAHÍA BLANCA / TANDIL — 9960C

km	317		1351	351					318	352	1352
	②⑤	⑥	①③⑤	②④				⑥	③⑦	③⑤	②④⑦
0	1705	...	1952	1952	↓	d.**Buenos Aires** ‡...... a.	↑	...	0555	1020	1020
64	1825	...	2015	2015		d.Cañuelas................ d.		...	0436	0850	0850
107	1911	...	2159	2159	↓	d.Monte .... d.	↑	...	0346	0756	0746
179	2041	...	2327	2327		d.Las Flores............... d.		...	0126	0614	0614
269	2241	...	|	|	↓	d. Rauch .... d.	↑	...	0020	|	|
330	2359	0945	|	|		a. **Tandil** .... d.		1715	2240	|	|
374	...	1200	|	|	↓	a. Vela............. d.	↑	1445	...	|	|
289	...	...	0121	0121		d.Azul .... d.		...	...	0412	0412
332	...	...	0246	0246	↓	d.Olavarria .... d.	↑	...	...	0300	0300
420	...	...	|	0424		d. Laprida .... d.		...	...	0102	|
490	...	...	|	0539	↓	d. Pringles .... d.	↑	...	...	2349	|
488	...	...	0555	|		d.Coronel Suárez .... d.		...	...	|	2340
538	...	...	0655	|	↓	d.Pigüé .... d.	↑	...	...	|	2234
	...	...	0756	|		d.Tornquist................. d.		...	...	|	2128
680*	...	...	0941	0950	↓	a.**Bahía Blanca** Sud .. d.	↑	...	...	1935	1940

‡ – Buenos Aires Plaza Constitución.

9960 ARGENTINA

9960D BUENOS AIRES - LINCOLN / REALICÓ / PEHUAJO — Ferrobaires / SOF

km		1331 ①–⑤	115 ①②⑥	115 ③	115 ④	153 ⑤	101 ⑥	103 ⑥	111 ⑤	
0	**Buenos Aires** Once d.	1730	1835	1835	1835	1953	...	...	2105	...
98	Mercedes DFS d.	2003	2103	2103	2103	2220	...	...	2332	...
158	Chivilcoy Sud d.	...	2231	2231	2231	2349	...	...	0101	...
209	Bragado d.	...	0013	0013	2349	0125	0130	...	0240	...
261	9 de Julio d.	...	0111	0111	...	0214	|	...	0338	...
310	Carlos Casares a.	...	0155	0155	...	0250	|	...	0422	...
363	**Pehuajo** a.	...	...	...	...	0402	|	...	...	...
523	Catriló a.	...	...	...	...	0847	|	0943	...	...
606	Santa Rosa a.	...	...	...	...	|	|	1225	...	...
263	Los Toldos d.	...	...	...	...	|	0348	...	...	...
313	**Lincoln** d.	...	...	...	...	|	0536	...	...	...
336	General Pinto d.	...	...	...	...	|	0641	...	...	...
390	Ameghino d.	...	...	...	...	|	0841	...	...	...
446	General Villegas d.	...	...	...	...	|	1005	...	...	...
559	**Realicó** a.	...	...	...	...	|	1302	...	...	...
644	General Pico a.	...	...	...	...	1053	1534	...	...	...

	102 ⑦	104 ⑦	154 ⑦	1332 ①–⑤	1112 ①②③	112 ⑤	116 ④	1112 ⑥
General Pico d.	1116	...	1521	...	...	...	...	...
Realicó d.	1351	...	|	...	...	...	...	...
General Villegas d.	1648	...	|	...	...	...	...	...
Ameghino d.	1810	...	|	...	...	...	...	...
General Pinto d.	2010	...	|	...	...	...	...	...
Lincoln d.	2115	...	|	...	...	...	...	...
Los Toldos d.	2303	...	|	...	...	...	...	...
Santa Rosa d.	|	1429	|	...	...	...	...	...
Catriló a.	|	1720	1725	...	...	...	...	...
Pehuajo d.	|	...	2232	...	...	...	...	...
Carlos Casares d.	|	...	0007	...	0502	0502	...	0713
9 de Julio d.	|	...	0056	...	0546	0546	...	0757
Bragado d.	0300	...	0200	...	0701	0701	0701	0912
Chivilcoy Sud d.	...	...	0314	...	0821	0821	0821	1032
Mercedes DFS d.	...	...	0443	0610	0949	0949	0949	1200
Buenos Aires Once a.	...	...	0709	0849	1210	1210	1210	1421

9960E BUENOS AIRES - GENERAL ALVEAR — Ferrobaires

km	357 ②⑤	383 ⑦		381 ⑤			378 ①③		384 ①	382 ⑥
0	1730	...	...	...	↓	d.**B. Aires** P Constitución a.	0931	...	...	...
17	|	1830	...	2002		d.Temperley a.	|	...	1015	1344
98	1953	2020	...	2140	↓	d.Empalme Lobos d.	0721	...	0937	1159
136	|	2153	...	2312		d.Roque Pérez d.	|	...	0703	1025
185	|	2330	...	0050	↓	a.Saladillo d.	|	...	0525	0847
233	|	0143	...	0303		a.**General Alvear** d.	|	...	0313	0635
205	2222	...	...	...	↓	a. **25 de Mayo** d.	0450	...	...	...

9960F BASAVILBASO - CONCORDIA — SOFSE

km		613 ①–⑤					614 ①–⑤	
0	**Basavilbaso** d.	0700	...	...	**Concordia** d.	...	...	...
56	Villaguay Este d.	0828	...	...	Villaguay Este d.	...	...	...
61	Villaguay Central d.	...	...	...	Villaguay Central d.	...	...	...
56	Villaguay Este d.	...	...	...	Villaguay Este d.	...	1643	...
171	**Concordia** a.	...	...	...	**Basavilbaso** a.	...	1812	...

9960G BUENOS AIRES - TUCUMÁN — SOFSE

km		265 ①⑤	277			266 ③	266 ⑥	278
0	**B. Aires** Retiro d.	0847	1607	...	**Tucumán** d.	1616	2101	...
294	Rosario Sur d.	|	2235	...	La Banda d.	2005	0050	...
314	Rosario Norte d.	1614	...	...	Colonia Dora d.	2303	0348	...
523	Rafaela d.	2128	...	...	Pinto d.	0023	0508	...
684	Ceres d.	0057	...	...	Ceres d.	0242	0727	...
791	Pinto d.	0304	...	...	Rafaela d.	0603	1048	...
858	Colonia Dora d.	0431	...	...	Rosario Norte d.	1130	1615	...
1020	La Banda d.	0729	...	...	Rosario Sur d.	|	|	0026
1170	**Tucumán** a.	1108	...		**B. Aires** Retiro a.	1915	0045	0654

9960H BUENOS AIRES - CÓRDOBA — SOFSE

km		215 ①②	215 ⑥	269 ①④		268 ③⑦		216 ①⑤⑦
0	**B. Aires** Retiro d.	*	**	2048	**Córdoba** Mitre d.	1406	...	1700
314	Rosario Norte d.	...	...	0501	Villa Maria d.	1807	...	2108
384	Cañada de Gómez d.	...	...	0819	C de Gómez d.	2139	...	...
566	Villa Maria d.	0545	0700	1032	Rosario Norte d.	2329	...	...
708	**Córdoba** Mitre a.	0953	1108	1433	**B. Aires** Retiro a.	0722	...	...

*– Not on holiday ①. **– Runs on holiday ①.

9960J VILLA BALLESTER - ZÁRATE — SOFSE

km		2051	2503	2505		2500	2502	2504
0	**Villa Ballester** d.	0210	0952	1907	**Zárate** d.	0529	1202	2143
119	Escobar d.	0318	1100	2019	Escobar d.	0619	1255	2237
187	**Zárate** a.	0408	1150	2109	**Villa Ballester** a.	0727	1403	2345

9960K SÁENZ PEÑA - CHOROTOS — SOFSE

km		102			101	
0	**Sáenz Peña** d.	1700	...	**Chorotis** d.	0326	...
119	General Pinedo d.	2046	...	General Pinedo d.	0524	...
187	**Chorotis** a.	2244	...	**Sáenz Peña** a.	0912	...

9960L VIEDMA - BARILOCHE — SEFE

km		361 ①③⑤		363 ⑤			362 ①③⑤	3
0	**Viedma** ◧ d.	...	...	1800	**Bariloche** d.	...	1700	1
189	San Antonio Oeste d.	...	...	2200	Ing Jacobacci d.	...	2145	2
625	Ing Jacobacci d.	0530	...	0655	S Antonio Oeste d.	...	...	0
819	**Bariloche** a.	1010	...	1135	**Viedma** ◧ a.	...	...	1

◧ – 🚌 connections available to / from B. Blanca and Buenos Aires (operator El Pinguin

9960M PARANÁ - CONCEPCIÓN DEL URUGUAY — SOFS

km		①③⑤	2302 ⑤			①③⑤	2303 ⑦
0	**Paraná** d.	...	1300	...	**C del Uruguay** d.	1230	1300
46	Crespo d.	...	1415	...	Basavilbaso d.	1400	1430
120	Nogoyá d.	...	1600	...	Nogoyá d.	...	1710
216	Basavilbaso d.	0600	1830	...	Crespo d.	...	1900
280	**C del Uruguay** a.	0735	2010	...	**Paraná** a.	...	2010

9960N BUENOS AIRES - ALBERDI - RUFINO — Ferrobair

km		565 ⑤	513 ①–④	1513 ⑤		566 ⑦	514 ②–⑤	1
0	**B. Aires** Retiro d.	1615	1800	1800	**Rufino** d.	2228	...	
111	Mercedes d.	|	2030	2031	**Alberdi** d.	2359	...	0
209	Chacabuco d.	1954	2216	2217	Junin d.	0139	0450	0
255	Junin a.	2040	2304	2304	Chacabuco d.	0227	0545	0
336	**Alberdi** a.	2217	...	0205	Mercedes d.	|	0749	0
421	**Rufino** a.	2351	...	...	**B. Aires** Retiro a.	0605	1024	1

9960P SALTA - SOCOMPA — Tren a las Nub

km		809 ✕a			810 ✕a
0	**Salta** d.	0705**b**	...	**Socompa** d.	...
53	El Alisal d.	0909	...	Viaducto La Polvorilla d.	1530
68	Chorillos d.	0943	...	Chorillos d.	2121
218	Viaducto La Polvorilla a.	1510	...	El Alisal d.	2156
570	**Socompa** a.	...	...	**Salta** a.	2348

a – Operates ②⑥ till Dec. 5. also Dec. 6. **b** - Passengers should arrive at 0615.

9960Q SALTA - GÜEMES — SOFS

km		2802 ①–⑥	2804 ①–⑤		2801 ①–⑥	28 ①
0	**Salta** d.	1230	1930	**Güemes** d.	0630	15
46	**Güemes** a.	1407	2107	**Salta** a.	0807	16

9960R RESISTENCIA - LOS AMORES — SOFS

km		①–⑤	⑥⑦			①–⑤	⑥⑦
	Resistencia d.	1255	...	...	**Los Amores** d.	0053	0053
0	Cacui d.	1346	1346	...	La Sabana d.	0210	0210
120	La Sabana d.	1812	1812	...	Cacui a.	0635	0635
147	**Los Amores** a.	1928	1928	...	**Villa Ballester** a.	0717	...

9960S EL TREN DEL FIN DEL MUNDO

km	a	b	c					a	b	c	
0	0930	1000	1200	1500	↓	d.**Fin Del Mundo** a.	↑	1140	1155	1410	17
8	1030	1050	1300	1600	↓	a.**Parque Nacional** d.	↑	1040	1115	1310	16

a - Sept. 1 - Apr. 30. **b** - May 1 - Aug. 31. **c** – departs 30mins later during **b**.

9965 CHILE

Empresa de los Ferrocarriles del Estad

SANTIAGO - CHILLÁN — EFE

km	22001	22017 ⑦	22011 ①-⑤	22013 ⑥				22022 ⑦	22202 ①-⑥	22012 ⑦ C	22014
0	0820	1940	2000	2030		d.**Santiago** Alameda a.		1511	1940	2225	2305
	0846	2006	2026	2069	↓	d.San Bernardo d.	↑	1447	1916	2201	2241
85	0938	2058	2118	2148		d.Rancagua d.		1356	1825	2110	2150
138	1012	2132	2152	2222	↓	d.San Fernando d.	↑	1322	1751	2036	2116
191	1041	2201	2221	2251		d.Curicó d.		1250	1719	2004	2044
	1054	2214	2234	2304	↓	d.Molina d.	↑	1239	1708	1953	2033
258	1129	2249	2309	2339		**d.Talca** d.		1204	1633	1918	1958
278	1147	2307	2327	2357	↓	d.San Javier d.	↑	1147	1616	1901	1941
308	1206	2326	2346	0016		d.Linares d.		1125	1558	1843	1923
348	1231	2351	0011	0041	↓	d.Parral d.	↑	1055	1530	1815	1855
382	1253	0013	0033	0103		d.San Carlos d.		1033	1508	1753	1833
400	1310	0030	0050	0120	↓	a.**Chillán** d.	↑	1015	1450	1735	1815

VICTORIA - TEMUCO

km		22931 ①–⑤	22933	22935		22932 ①–⑤	22934	229
0	**Victoria** d.	0630	1140	1820	**Temuco** d.	0930	1645	20
44	Lautaro d.	0718	1228	1908	Lautaro d.	1010	1725	20
73	**Temuco** a.	0757	1307	1947	**Victoria** a.	1057	1812	21

TALCA - CONSTITUCIÓN

km		20701		20703		20702		207
0	**Talca** d.	0730	...	1645	**Constitución** d.	0715	...	16
	Gonzalez Bastias d.	0907	...	1822	Gonzalez Bastias d.	0907	...	18
89	**Constitución** a.	1054	...	2009	**Talca** a.	1039	...	19

SANTIAGO - SAN FERNANDO — Ferrobaire

km		601	607 ⑦	609 ⑦	611 ⑦	615 ⑦	617 Ⓐ	519 ⑦	521 Ⓐ	621 ⑥	523 Ⓐ
0	**Santiago** Alameda d.	0845	1030	1130	1230	2010	2030	2040	2100	2100	2125
	San Bernardo d.	0916	1101	1201	1301	2041	2101	2111	2131	2131	2156
85	Rancagua d.	1026	1211	1311	1411	2151	2211	2220	2240	2241	2305
138	**San Fernando** a.	1112	1257	1357	1457	2237	2257	...	...	2327	...

	500 Ⓐ	502 Ⓐ	610		614 ⑦	618 ⑦	620 ⑦	526 ⑦		62
San Fernando d.	...	...	0543	...	1433	1513	1553	...	...	21
Rancagua d.	0530	0600	0630	...	1520	1600	1640	1740	...	22
San Bernardo d.	0640	0710	0740	...	1630	1710	1750	1850	...	23
Santiago Alameda a.	0710	0740	0810	...	1700	1740	1820	1920	...	23

C – Additional trip ⑦ 1350.

South Korea

Rail services in South Korea are operated by Korea National Railways under the brand names 'Korail' and 'AREX'. All services convey at least Economy class seating (show the tables as '2nd class') with many trains (and all KTX high-speed services) also conveying 1st class accommodation. Timings shown are the latest available.

9970 SEOUL - BUSAN Ko

km	KTX high-speed	101	103	107	109	111	113	115	117	351	119	121	123	301	125	353	127	129	131	133	135	303	137	139	141
0	**Seoul** Main .... **9971** d.	0515	0530	0625	0640	0700	0730	0745	0800	0822	0830	0900	0930	0955	1000	1020	1030	1050	1100	1200	1230	1240	1300	1310	1330
96	Cheonan Asan .. **9971** d.	|	0609	0704	0720	0740	|	|	0839	|	0905	|	1009	1030	|	|	1105	|	1139	1235	|	1314	|	|	1405
160	Daejeon .... **9971** d.	0615	0635	0730	0751	0811	0836	0846	0911	1004	0931	1000	1035	1057	1102	1157	1132	1151	1206	1301	1336	1341	1405	1417	1432
293	Dongdaegu .... **9971** d.	0659	0719	0820	0841	0856	0920	0936	0955	1054	1021	1044	1119	1141	1146	1241	1216	1235	1250	1351	1420	1425	1458	1509	1517
348	Miryang .... **9971** d.	|	|	|	|	|	|	|	|	|	|	|	|	1213	|	|	|	|	|	|	|	1456	|	|	|
409	**Busan** .... a.	0752	0813	0909	0925	0945	1004	1029	1044	1143	1110	1137	1208	1252	1235	1330	1305	1324	1339	1440	1509	1535	1553	1559	1607

KTX high-speed	145	147	149	151	305	153	155	355	157	307	159	161	163	309	165	167	357	169	171	173	311	175	177	179	181
Seoul Main .... **9971** d.	1415	1430	1455	1530	1540	1555	1630	1640	1700	1720	1725	1800	1830	1840	1850	1900	1905	1930	2000	2030	2040	2100	2130	2200	2230
Cheonan Asan ... **9971** d.	|	1505	|	1604	|	|	1705	|	|	1755	1805	|	1905	|	1929	|	|	|	2035	|	2115	2140	|	2239	2309
Daejeon .... **9971** d.	1516	1530	1551	1631	1640	1655	1731	1817	1806	1822	1831	1900	1931	1942	1956	2008	2054	2030	2107	2126	2141	2206	2235	2304	2335
Dongdaegu .... **9971** d.	1600	1614	1642	1715	1731	1739	1821	1901	1850	1911	1921	1950	2015	2026	2040	2058	2140	2114	2157	2210	2231	2250	2319	2348	0019
Miryang .... **9971** d.	|	|	|	|	1802	|	|	|	|	1944	|	|	|	2101	|	|	|	|	|	|	2302	|	|	|	|
Busan .... a.	1649	1703	1732	1759	1841	1828	1914	1950	1939	2023	2010	2039	2108	2141	2129	2141	2233	2208	2246	2259	2341	2344	0008	0042	0108

KTX high-speed	102	104	106 ①–⑤	108	302	110	112	114	116	304	118	120	122	124	126	128	352	130	132	134	306	136	138	354	140
Busan .... d.	0500	0515	0530	0600	0610	0630	0655	0730	0755	0820	0830	0900	0920	0930	0950	1000	1015	1030	1100	1200	1210	1220	1225	1240	1300
Miryang .... **9971** d.	|	|	|	|	0649	|	|	|	|	0858	|	|	|	|	|	|	|	|	|	|	1249	|	|	|	|
Dongdaegu .... **9971** d.	0550	0610	0620	0650	0726	0720	0745	0820	0850	0933	0920	0950	1010	1020	1040	1050	1105	1125	1151	1251	1324	1310	1320	1330	1350
Daejeon .... **9971** d.	0642	0656	0707	0742	0818	0806	0831	0906	0942	1019	1006	1042	1056	1106	1132	1136	1151	1217	1243	1337	1416	1356	1407	1422	1437
Cheonan Asan ... **9971** d.	0705	|	|	0805	0841	|	0854	|	1005	|	1035	1105	|	|	|	1200	|	|	1307	1400	1439	|	|	|	|
Seoul Main .... **9971** a.	0745	0755	0812	0845	0917	0910	0934	1005	1045	1118	1112	1141	1154	1158	1231	1236	1334	1317	1342	1440	1514	1455	1506	1601	1530

KTX high-speed	144	146	148	150	308	152	154	156	158	160	162	164	356	166	310	168	170	172	174	358	176	178	312	180	182
Busan .... d.	1400	1410	1430	1440	1445	1510	1540	1600	1630	1640	1700	1725	1750	1800	1820	1825	1900	1925	2000	2020	2030	2050	2055	2125	2200
Miryang .... **9971** d.	|	|	|	|	1523	|	|	|	|	|	|	|	|	|	1900	|	|	|	|	|	|	|	2135	|	|
Dongdaegu .... **9971** d.	1450	1500	1520	1530	1557	1605	1630	1651	1720	1730	1756	1811	1845	1855	1938	1920	1950	2021	2050	2110	2120	2141	2209	2220	2255
Daejeon .... **9971** d.	1542	1546	1606	1623	1643	1652	1722	1743	1806	1816	1842	1903	1931	1947	2024	2006	2042	2107	2142	2156	2206	2233	2255	2312	2341
Cheonan Asan ... **9971** d.	1605	|	|	|	|	|	1745	|	|	1840	|	1927	|	|	2053	2029	2105	|	2205	|	2235	|	2324	|	0010
Seoul Main .... **9971** a.	1640	1649	1710	1720	1742	1747	1820	1837	1910	1916	1946	2007	2115	2046	2133	2109	2145	2212	2241	2340	2315	2337	0004	0010	0051

9971 SEOUL - MASAN Kor

km	KTX high-speed	401	403	405	407	409	411	413	415	417	419
0	**Seoul** Main .... **9970** d.	0515	0545	0840	0910	1040	1345	1610	1705	1910	2210
96	Cheonan Asan ... **9970** d.	|	0624	|	|	|	|	|	|	1950	|
160	Daejeon .... **9970** d.	0615	0656	0947	1011	1140	1442	1716	1811	2017	2310
293	Dongdaegu .... **9970** d.	0702	0743	1034	1101	1230	1526	1802	1855	2109	0002
348	Miryang .... **9970** d.	|	0819	1107	1131	1303	1558	|	1927	|	0034
387	Changwon Jungang .... d.	0801	0845	1132	|	1329	1624	1902	1953	2207	|
397	Changwon .... d.	0809	|	|	1206	1338	|	|	2003	2215	0105
401	**Masan** .... a.	0814	0855	1143	1211	1343	1634	1912	2008	2220	0110
	Jinju .... a.	...	0922	...	1236	1409	1701	...	...	2247	...

KTX high-speed	402	404	406	408	410	412	414	416	418
Jinju .... d.	...	0615	...	0958	...	1305	1500	1733	...
Masan .... d.	0513	0641	0915	1024	1230	1331	1526	1800	1950
Changwon .... d.	0519	0647	|	1030	1236	|	1532	|	1956
Changwon Jungang . d.	0527	|	0928	1039	|	1342	|	1811	|
Miryang .... **9970** d.	0555	0719	|	1103	1304	|	1604	|	2028
Dongdaegu ..... **9970** d.	0629	0759	1033	1138	1343	1436	1638	1905	2103
Daejeon .... **9970** d.	0715	0851	1119	1225	1429	1522	1730	1951	2150
Cheonan Asan **9970** d.	|	0915	|	|	|	|	|	2014	|
Seoul Main ..... **9970** a.	0820	0955	1223	1325	1526	1620	1834	2054	2249

9972 SEOUL - GWANGJU - MOKPO Kor

km	KTX high-speed	501	503	505	507	551	509	511	513	553	515	555	517	519	557	521	559	523	525	561	527		563	529	565
0	**Seoul** Yongsan . **9973** d.	0520	0610	0637	0755	0815	0853	0950	1037	1055	1205	1250	1305	1320	1405	1420	1510	1550	1650	1733	1857	...	1920	2010	2115
93	Cheonan Asan .. **9973** d.	|	0648	|	0833	0854	|	1024	|	1133	|	|	|	1358	|	1454	|	|	|	1811	|	...	|	2048	|
121	Osong .... d.	0609	0703	0726	|	|	0941	|	|	1148	1252	|	1353	|	|	1509	|	|	1737	|	1945	...	2008	2103	|
240	Iksan .... **9973** d.	0638	0731	0801	0919	0934	1010	1110	1154	1216	1326	1356	1421	1443	1519	1543	1623	1656	1812	1856	2020	...	2042	2132	2233
287	Jeongeup .... d.	0654	|	0817	0935	|	|	1126	1210	|	1342	|	|	1459	1535	1559	1640	|	1828	1912	2036	...	2058	2148	|
337	**Gwangju** Songjeong .. d.	0713	0801	0836	0954	1002	1039	1145	1228	1243	1400	1423	1450	1517	1552	1617	1657	1736	1846	1929	2054	...	2115	2206	2300
405	**Mokpo** .... a.	0746	0838	0913	1030	...	1116	1218	1305	...	1437	...	1523	1554	...	1654	...	1802	1923	...	2131	...	...	2243	...

KTX high-speed		552	502	554	504	506	508	510	556	512	514	558	516	560	518	520	562	522	564	524		526	528	566	530
Mokpo .... d.	...	...	0525	...	0715	0820	0930	1015	...	1100	1205	...	1340	...	1500	1600	...	1705	...	1805	...	1850	2000	...	2105
Gwangju Songjeong .. d.	...	0530	0603	0715	0754	0859	1009	1050	1115	1138	1244	1340	1419	1505	1539	1639	1655	1744	1815	1844	...	1926	2039	2125	2140
Jeongeup .... d.	...	0548	0621	|	0812	0917	|	1108	1133	1156	1302	|	1437	1523	1558	1657	1713	|	1834	1902	...	1944	2057	|	2188
Iksan .... **9973** d.	...	0605	0642	0744	0829	0934	1038	1130	1150	1217	1319	1409	1454	1545	1614	1715	1729	1812	1850	1919	...	2000	2114	2154	2215
Osong .... d.	...	0632	0716	0817	0856	|	|	1203	1218	1250	1353	|	1529	|	1642	|	1803	|	1924	1953	...	2027	2149	|	|
Cheonan Asan ... **9973** d.	...	|	0728	|	0909	1020	|	1215	|	|	1405	1444	|	1626	1654	1750	|	1847	1936	|	...	2039	|	|	2250
Seoul Yongsan .. **9973** a.	...	0716	0804	0902	0947	1058	1145	1248	1303	1334	1442	1518	1614	1704	1731	1825	1847	1924	2010	2038	...	2117	2233	2258	2327

9973 SEOUL - YEOSU Kor

km	KTX high-speed	701	703	705	707	709	711	713	715	717	719
0	**Seoul** Yongsan .. **9972** d.	0520	0705	0853	1055	1420	1520	1650	1820	2050	2140
93	Cheonan Asan ... **9972** d.	|	0745	|	1133	1454	|	|	1858	2128	|
	Osong .... d.	0609	0759	0941	1148	1509	1608	1737	1912	|	|
240	Iksan .... **9972** d.	0640	0834	1012	1218	1545	1636	1814	1948	2207	2252
266	Jeonju .... d.	0656	0850	1028	1234	1601	1653	1830	2004	2223	2308
326	Namwon .... d.	0722	0916	1054	1300	1627	1719	1856	2031	2249	2334
394	Suncheon .... d.	0755	0947	1132	1331	1706	1751	1932	2103	2323	0005
434	**Yeosu** Expo .... a.	0816	1009	1154	1352	1725	1812	1953	2124	2344	0024

KTX high-speed	702	704	706	708	710	712	714	716	718
Yeosu Expo .... d.	0500	0740	0945	1030	1250	1400	1610	1755	1915
Suncheon .... d.	0521	0802	1004	1052	1312	1422	1632	1816	1937
Namwon .... d.	0554	0836	1038	1126	1343	1455	1706	1853	2007
Jeonju .... d.	0620	0903	1106	1153	1410	1522	1733	1920	2034
Iksan .... **9972** d.	0642	0919	1130	1217	1426	1545	1750	1937	2050
Osong .... d.	0716	|	1203	1250	1454	|	|	2011	|
Cheonan Asan **9972** d.	0728	|	1215	|	1507	1626	1825	|	|
Seoul Yongsan **9972** a.	0804	1027	1248	1334	1544	1704	1903	2057	2158

9974 INCHEON AIRPORT ✈ - SEOUL ARE

Incheon Airport ✈ - **Seoul** Main and v.v. 2nd class only. Journey 45 minutes.

From **Incheon Airport** ✈ at 0520, 0600, 0630, 0722, 0800, 0835, 0920, 0952, 1030, 1100, 1127, 1151, 1230, 1300, 1330, 1356, 1426, 1454, 1530, 1602, 1640, 1713, 1800, 1846, 1920, 19 2020, 2100, 2140. Frequent additional slower services (calling at Gimpo Airport ✈) run 5 – 6 times per hour 0523 – 2342 (journey 55 – 60 minutes Incheon - Seoul).

From **Seoul** Main at 0600, 0625, 0657, 0736, 0822, 0900, 0935, 1025, 1049, 1135, 1200, 1228, 1300, 1330, 1403, 1429, 1457, 1531, 1600, 1634, 1706, 1750, 1822, 1900, 1943, 2022, 2050, 21 2200. Frequent additional slower services (calling at Gimpo Airport ✈) run 5 – 6 times per hour 0520 – 2338 (journey 55 – 60 minutes Seoul - Incheon).

d class Korail SEOUL - CHUNCHEON 9975

l Yongsan - **Namchuncheon** and v.v. *93 km*. Journey 69 – 78 minutes.

Seoul Yongsan. Most trains call at **Gapyeong** 56 – 64 minutes later: On ①–⑤ at 0600, 0700, 0800, 0830, 0900, 1000, 1100, 1200, 1300, 1400, 1500, 1600, 1700, 1800, 1830, 1900, 2000, , 2115, 2200; on ⑥⑦ at 0600, 0700, 0800, 0830, 0900, 0930, 1000, 1030, 1100, 1130, 1200, 1230⑥, 1300, 1330⑥, 1400, 1430, 1500, 1530, 1600, 1630, 1700, 1730, 1800, 1830, 1900, 1930, , 2030, 2100, 2130⑥, 2200.

Namchuncheon. Most trains call at **Gapyeong** 15 – 19 minutes later: On ①–⑤ at 0611, 0643, 0711, 0743, 0813, 0913, 1013, 1113, 1213, 1313, 1413, 1513, 1613, 1710, 1813, 1913, 1941, , 2113, 2213; on ⑥⑦ at 0613, 0713, 0803⑥, 0829, 0858, 0929, 1003, 1031, 1103⑥, 1129, 1203⑥, 1229, 1303, 1329, 1403, 1503, 1529, 1603, 1629, 1655, 1729, 1803, 1829, 1900, 1929, , 2029, 2103, 2133, 2213.

ail SEOUL - ANDONG and DAEGU - BUSAN 9976

	1771	1773	1775	1777	1601	1779	1781		1621	1783	1603	1785	1605	1787	1789		1681	1607	1791	1793	1795	1609	1623
	2	2	2	2		2	2		2	2		2		2	2		2 A		2	2	2		2
Seoul Cheongnyangni .. **9977** d.	...	...	...	...	0640	...	...	...	0825	...	1040	...	1305	...	...	...	...	1510	...	...	...	1907	2113
Wonju **9977** d.	...	...	...	...	0746	...	...	...	0934	...	1148	...	1413	...	...	...	...	1619	...	...	...	2029	2219
Jecheon **9977** d.	...	...	...	...	0829	...	...	...	1016	...	1229	...	1453	...	...	...	...	1700	...	...	...	2110	2300
Yeongju **9978** d.	...	...	...	...	0932	...	...	...	1117	...	1330	...	1552	...	...	...	...	1759	...	...	...	2209	0000
Andong **9978** d.	...	...	...	...	1000	...	...	...	1147	...	1401	...	1621	...	...	...	1736	1833	...	...	...	2239	0032
Dongdaegu **9978** d.	0700	0730	0830	0930	...	1030	1135	...	|	1400	...	1600	...	1700	1730	...	|	...	1905	2000	2120	...	|
Gyeongju d.	0813	0842	0948	1041	...	1148	1248	...	1408	1510	...	1709	...	1809	1843	...	1933	...	2023	2115	2236	...	0229
Taehwagang (Ulsan) d.	0853	0918	1023	1121	...	1226	1328	...	1453	1551	...	1748	...	1848	1922	...	2008	...	2106	2155	2312	...	0306
Haeundu d.	0951	1006	1119	1209	...	1322	1427	...	1553	1647	...	1845	...	1934	2017	...	2102	...	2206	2248	0004	...	0353
Busan Bujeon a.	1010	1022	1138	1225	...	1342	1443	...	1612	1707	...	1907	...	1952	2036	...	2121	...	2226	2306	0022	...	0409

		1602	1772	1774	1622	1776	1682	1604		1778	1780	1606	1782	1784	1608	1786		1788	1610	1796	1792	1794	1790	1624
			2	2	2	2	2 A			2	2		2	2		2		2		2	2	2	2	2
an Bujeon d.	...	...	0547	0603	0720	0745	0912	...	...	0925	1152	...	1305	1357	...	1500	...	1535	...	1645	1736	1957	2105	2245
ındu d.	...	...	0602	0621	0738	0803	0930	...	...	0942	1210	...	1321	1416	...	1515	...	1554	...	1701	1754	2016	2124	2301
ıwagang (Ulsan) d.	...	...	0646	0717	0832	0855	1024	...	...	1040	1305	...	1405	1509	...	1608	...	1649	...	1749	1849	2108	2215	2350
ɔngju d.	...	...	0721	0757	0916	0936	1106	...	...	1119	1342	...	1444	1549	...	1653	...	1732	...	1826	1932	2149	2255	0026
ɔngdaegu **9978** a.	...	...	0841	0911	|	1050	|	...	...	1228	1454	...	1556	1711	...	1804	...	1851	...	1942	2047	2255	0002	|
ong **9978** d.	...	0715	...	...	1119	...	1258	1325	...	...	...	1520	...	...	1720	...	...	...	1920	...	...	...	...	0220
ıgju **9978** d.	...	0750	...	...	1159	...	...	1402	...	...	...	1557	...	...	1758	...	...	...	1957	...	...	...	...	0253
eon **9977** d.	...	0843	...	...	1253	...	...	1455	...	...	...	1653	...	...	1857	...	...	...	2053	...	...	...	...	0350
ju **9977** d.	...	0934	...	...	1342	...	...	1534	...	...	...	1735	...	...	1944	...	...	...	2135	...	...	...	...	0429
ıl Cheongnyangni .. **9977** a.	...	1043	...	...	1452	...	...	1642	...	...	...	1857	...	...	2049	...	...	...	2241	...	...	...	...	0538

To/from Donghae (Table **9978**).

rail SEOUL - DONGHAE 9977

n		1631	1633	1635	1637	1639	1661	1641		
							⑥⑦			
0	**Seoul** Cheongnyangni . **9976** d.	0705	0910	1210	1413	1613	2210	2325	...	...
5	Wonju **9976** d.	0828	1017	1328	1515	1720	2312	0032	...	...
5	Jecheon **9976** d.	0921	1106	1410	1558	1800	2351	0112	...	...
	Yemi d.	1016	1201	1508	1649	1854	|	0202	...	...
	Mindungsan d.	1037	1221	1529	1710	1915	0058	0222	...	...
	Taebaek d.	1109	1251	1601	1744	1948	0132	0254	...	...
	Dogye d.	1139	1321	1629	1813	2016	0200	0322	...	...
	Donghae a.	1220	1358	1709	1855	2054	0238	0400	...	...
	Jeongdongjin a.	1248	1427	1736	1924	2123	0307	0428	...	...

	1662	1632	1634	1636	1638	1640	1642		
	⑥⑦								
Jeongdongjin d.	2355	0500	0715	0815	1040	1500	1640	...	...
Donghae d.	0024	0528	0743	0843	1109	1528	1710	...	...
Dogye d.	0103	0609	0824	0922	1151	1611	1753	...	...
Taebaek d.	0131	0634	0852	0949	1219	1639	1824	...	...
Mindungsan d.	0205	0706	0926	1021	1251	1711	1856	...	...
Yemi d.	0228	0727	0949	1042	1311	1732	1921	...	...
Jecheon **9976** d.	0321	0822	1049	1142	1403	1829	2017	...	...
Wonju **9976** d.	0403	0906	1129	1229	1447	1918	2104	...	...
Seoul C'yangni **9976** a.	0505	1016	1243	1336	1554	2029	2216	...	...

rail 2nd class DAEGU - DONGHAE 9978

n		1672	1682	1674						
			A							
0	**Dongdaegu** **9976** d.	0615	...	1630	...	...	...	...	...	...
7	Andong **9976** d.	0802	1259	1820	...	...	...	...	...	...
4	Yeongju **9976** d.	0839	1331	1859	...	...	...	...	...	...
	Cheoram d.	1022	1516	2044	...	...	...	...	...	...
	Dogye d.	1052	1547	2114	...	...	...	...	...	...
	Donghae a.	1132	1628	2151	...	...	...	...	...	...
	Jeongdongjin a.	1200	1702	2220	...	...	...	...	...	...

	1671	1681	1673						
		A							
Jeongdongjin d.	0630	1335	1738	...	...	...	...	...	...
Donghae d.	0658	1402	1807	...	...	...	...	...	...
Dogye d.	0738	1444	1853	...	...	...	...	...	...
Cheoram d.	0804	1514	1923	...	...	...	...	...	...
Yeongju **9976** d.	0954	1702	2114	...	...	...	...	...	...
Andong **9976** d.	1025	1734	2145	...	...	...	...	...	...
Dongdaegu **9976** a.	1239	...	2330	...	...	...	...	...	...

To/from Busan Bujeon (Table **9976**).

rail 2nd class DAEGU - POHANG 9979

n		1751	1753	1755	1757					
0	**Dongdaegu** d.	0600	0900	1500	1830	...	...	...	...	...
	Yeongcheon d.	0634	0935	1535	1906	...	...	...	...	...
3	**Pohang** a.	0751	1052	1653	2025	...	...	...	...	...

	1752	1754	1756	1758					
Pohang d.	0620	1125	1425	1915	...	...	...	...	...
Yeongcheon d.	0735	1246	1553	2035	...	...	...	...	...
Dongdaegu a.	0808	1318	1629	2107	...	...	...	...	...

rail 2nd class DAEGU - MASAN 9980

n		1901	1903	1905	1907	1909	1911	1913	1915	1031
0	**Dongdaegu** d.	0640	0920	1145	1405	1630	1700	1840	2125	2257
7	Miryang d.	0722	1007	1229	1451	1714	1746	1931	2211	2329
	Changwon Jungang d.	0755	1039	1300	1527	1748	1825	2009	2246	0000
	Changwon d.	0803	1048	1308	1536	1756	1835	2018	2255	0009
5	**Masan** a.	0808	1053	1313	1541	1801	1840	2023	2300	0014

	1902	1904	1032	1906	1908	1910	1912	1914	1916
Masan d.	0540	0835	0924	1157	1355	1600	1730	1843	2057
Changwon d.	0546	0841	0930	1203	1401	1606	1736	1849	2103
Changwon Jungang d.	0556	0850	0939	1213	1410	1616	1746	1858	2113
Miryang d.	0633	0920	1005	1250	1445	1651	1821	1929	2144
Dongdaegu a.	0729	1006	1037	1342	1531	1745	1916	2016	2238

rail 2nd class MOKPO - BUSAN 9981

n		1944	1972	1952	1954	1441	1942	1974		
0	**Mokpo** d.	...	...	...	0923	...	...	...	...	...
	Gwangju Songjeong d.	...	0640	...	1025	...	...	1931	...	...
5	Seogwangju d.	...	0649	...	1034	1351	...	1941	...	...
	Boseong d.	...	0804	...	1142	1500	...	2048	...	...
6	**Suncheon** d.	0600	0905	1000	1241	1556	1715	2143	...	...
4	Jinju d.	0727	...	1129	1415	...	1841	...	...	...
0	Masan d.	0815	...	1217	1502	...	1928	...	...	...
4	Changwon d.	0821	...	1223	1508	...	1934	...	...	...
	Changwon Jungang d.	0830	...	1233	1517	...	1944	...	...	...
5	Samnangjin d.	0857	...	1303	1543	...	2008	...	...	...
3	**Busan** Bujeon a.	0940	...	1352	1627	...	2052	...	...	...

	1971	1442	1951	1941	1953	1973	1943		
Busan Bujeon d.	...	...	0625	1035	1305	...	1854	...	...
Samnangjin d.	...	...	0715	1121	1350	...	1947	...	...
Changwon Jungang d.	...	...	0743	1148	1417	...	2018	...	...
Changwon d.	...	...	0752	1157	1426	...	2027	...	...
Masan d.	...	...	0800	1204	1433	...	2034	...	...
Jinju d.	...	...	0847	1251	1519	...	2118	...	...
Suncheon d.	0555	0725	1020	1413	1645	1735	2239	...	...
Boseong d.	0650	0826	1120	...	...	1831	...	...	...
Seogwangju d.	0803	0935	1231	...	...	1941	...	...	...
Gwangju Songjeong a.	0812	...	1241	...	...	1953	...	...	...
Mokpo a.	...	...	1336	...	...	...	...	...	...

Robert Foster's Column

Robert Foster is a long-standing customer and supporter of the European Rail Timetable who played a key role in its rebirth in 2014. In an occasional column Robert shares some of his own thoughts based on his recent travel experiences.

The most recent high-speed line opening in France was the cross-border route from Perpignan to Barcelona, mostly situated within Spain, which began operation in December 2013. The new line has been a disappointment and only carries four all-year round trains in each direction, two serving Paris and one each Lyon and Marseille, the Toulouse - Barcelona train having now been relegated to summer only operation. Low occupancy of the latter is hardly surprising given that it leaves Toulouse at 0806 and does not return until 2142. This means that in either direction it is inaccessible from or to most of the six routes that feed into Toulouse and, even for those stations with which connection is possible, the times are very unsociable for what will usually be a leisure journey. If the Toulouse train was to leave two hours later and return three hours earlier, not only would this reduce the long layover in Barcelona and connect with all lines at Toulouse, but would also enable extension of the train from and to Bordeaux (departing approximately 0750, arriving 2055). If this suggestion gives rise to complaint that the earliest train from Perpignan to Barcelona was too late – currently the Toulouse train leaves there at 1000 – then there is an easy solution. That is to extend the 0755 Figueras - Barcelona - Madrid back from Perpignan at 0730 where it would connect perfectly with the 2139 Paris to Portbou overnight train, so delivering passengers to Barcelona at 0845 and Madrid at 1145. This would compensate to some extent for the withdrawal of the Paris - Barcelona overnight train which, together with the Paris - Madrid overnight train, succumbed when the new line opened.

The opening of the final stretch of the TGV Est high-speed line to Strasbourg, scheduled for July 3, has caused the demise of the Brussels - Basel trains via Luxembourg and Strasbourg. Latterly the two trains in each direction took over seven hours, a far cry from the TEE units which from 1976 onwards – displaced from the *Cisalpin* and *Lemano* Paris/Genève to Milano by hauled TEE stock – did two return journeys in under six hours, and Zürich in seven. From July there will be two Brussels - Strasbourg TGVs calling at Lille with unusually good connections to and from London St Pancras. It is a huge pity that one of these trains does not continue another 75 minutes to and from Basel, the gateway to central and eastern Switzerland. The 1517 from Brussels, which connects with the 1258 departure from St Pancras and arrives Strasbourg 1901, could reach Basel by 2020 so giving Bern and Zürich arrivals by 2130. The 0717 from Brussels would have ample time to continue to Basel with a layover of 90 minutes before returning as the 1510 from Strasbourg. That would produce a Basel departure at 1345, St Pancras arrival at 1903, so enabling a rail passenger to have lunch in Basel, dinner in London, or get home to anywhere in England between South Devon, South Wales and Newcastle by 2300.

The night trains on this route to Brig, Chur, Milano and Roma – which until the 1990s ran from Oostende – continued for ten years after the opening of the Channel Tunnel before succumbing to the combined effects of the autoroute and the low-cost airlines. In February 1998 I took the overnight train from Brussels to Switzerland which ran as 33 vehicles in trains of 18 and 15. Five years later the train disappeared.

For some years now no overnight train has served Brussels. Given the expected withdrawal of the Köln - Warsaw/Praha *Jan Kiepura* overnight train, it would seem beneficial to restore operation of the Paris - Moscow train via Brussels (instead of Strasbourg) which additionally would allow far better connections from / to London.

As can be seen from what is written here, there is a strong case for more international cooperation between Europe's railway administrations.